MARK TWAIN'S
LITERARY RESOURCES

Volume Two

Mark Twain's Literary Resources

A Reconstruction of His Library and Reading

VOLUME TWO

Author-Title Annotated Catalog and Reader's Guide

ALAN GRIBBEN

FOREWORD BY THOMAS A. TENNEY

NewSouth Books

Montgomery

NewSouth Books
105 S. Court Street
Montgomery, AL 36104

PUBLISHER'S CATALOGING-IN-PUBLICATION DATA

Names: Gribben, Alan, author.
Title: Mark Twain's literary resources : a reconstruction of his library and reading, vol. two / Alan Gribben; foreword by Thomas A. Tenney.
Other titles: Mark Twain's library
Description: Montgomery : NewSouth Books, [2022] | Includes bibliographical references and index.
Identifiers: LCCN 2022937407 (print) | ISBN 9781588383952
Subjects: LCSH: Twain, Mark, 1835–1910—Library—Catalogs. | Twain, Mark, 1835–1910—Books and reading. | Private libraries—United States—Catalogs.
LC record available at https://lccn.loc.gov/2022937407

Design and composition by Randall Williams

Additional typesetting by Mikia Holloway and Sarah G. Williams

Printed in the United States of America by Lightning Source

Cover image: "Mark Twain and Friend (Danbury)." Courtesy of Susan Durkee, artist, www.susandurkee.com.

For Suzanne La Rosa and Randall Williams,

innovative editors, fearless publishers

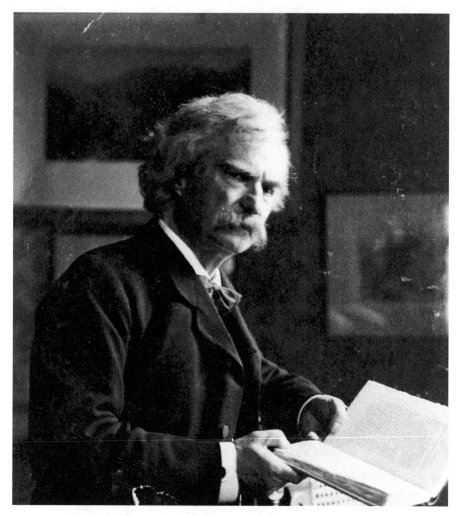

Mark Twain, 1901 (Library of Congress, USZ62-2877).

Contents

A Note about the Foreword

In 2004 Thomas A. Tenney (1931–2012) composed a Foreword for this present book that he hoped soon to publish under the auspices of his *Mark Twain Journal*. That edition never materialized, mainly because I could not find sufficient free time while I was a department administrator and classroom instructor (and parent) to make the multitudinous revisions and additions required by new information that had come to light since my original effort to catalog Twain's library and reading in 1980.

Now it seems fitting to publish Dr. Tenney's much-delayed Foreword (with a few modifications in his phrasing owing to the lapsed time) and thereby honor his encouragement of the book now titled *Mark Twain's Literary Resources*. — A.G.

Foreword

THOMAS A. TENNEY

Forty-two years out of print and nearly impossible to find at any price, the most important single reference book on Mark Twain is now available in a new and enlarged edition.

Mark Twain's Library: A Reconstruction, first published in 1980, dispelled at once any notion of the greatest of our national authors as an untaught vernacular genius, ignorant of any world of letters beyond the river towns and mining camps.

Over more than five decades' work, much of it initially in the Mark Twain Papers in the Bancroft Library at the University of California at Berkeley, Alan Gribben gathered records of thousands of books, plays, poems, songs, and other published items with which Mark Twain was familiar. That record, citing notebooks, letters, and annotated books, sold out almost immediately after it was issued in 1980. The reception by Mark Twain scholars was overwhelming, as may be seen in the reviews that soon appeared.

In addition to the inevitable corrections, this new edition adds nearly a thousand new Catalog entries, including books from the once-inaccessible Mark Twain Research Foundation and the superb Nick Karanovich collection. Scholars and general readers also assisted Alan Gribben by calling his attention to a variety of items that had escaped his wide and close-meshed net.

The Mark Twain who emerges from Gribben's pages is far more interesting and complex than one might imagine from the speculation of most who have written about him. This history of a mind reveals a wide-ranging interest in the thinking of others, from the classics to his own day and in more than his own language.

Mark Twain's reading and his responses in the margins of his books also reveal his warm human sympathy and his disgust with the cruelty and stupidity of which man is capable. His contempt for slavery and racism is well documented in his writings, its sources emanating from both direct observation and his reading. Some cruel incidents in *A Connecticut Yankee* are drawn from the slave narratives of Charles Ball and others, while his annotation in William Still's *The Underground Rail Road* (1883) shows his continuing interest during and after publication of *Adventures of Huckleberry Finn* in the actual route an escaping enslaved person could follow to safety in Canada.

Surrounded by an intelligent wife, three lively daughters, and their circle of well-read friends, Mark Twain was not entirely given over to the sexism of his day. His Connecticut Yankee satirically recommended extending the franchise to any woman of forty who could be shown to know as much as her son aged twenty-one. His unpublished "Comment on Woman & a Certain Book" is a scathing denunciation of Thomas A. Janvier's satire of the suffrage movement, *The Women's Conquest of New York*; Twain blames the mothers of America for not teaching their sons greater respect for women's minds and fortitude.

No study of this sort is ever complete. Publication of *Mark Twain's Library: A Reconstruction* in 1980 brought forward such a flood of new material that Gribben's file drawers were soon replenished. There will no doubt be supplementary discoveries resulting from this present Catalog. The story of Mark Twain's intellectual growth as revealed in his reading and in his response to his reading is of continuing significance, and many will find Gribben's book useful not only as a reference tool but also as a reading experience of their own.

Introduction to the Annotated Catalog

Alan Gribben

Volume One of *Mark Twain's Literary Resources* recounted my efforts to reconstruct Twain's library and reading and summarized my discoveries. Volume Two submits the tangible results from more than fifty years of research. Part I of this Introduction to Volume Two briefly reviews my search and its conclusions. Part II is a manual for consulting the Annotated Catalog. Part III provides the abbreviations for the editions, inventories, collections, catalogs, individuals, and scholarly studies cited in the Catalog entries.

PART I: SUMMARY

Volume Two of *Mark Twain's Literary Resources* lists and describes the library and reading of Samuel Clemens and his family that I began inventorying in 1969. At times this project served as a hobby of sorts for evenings and weekends; too often, I am afraid, it became an obsession that consumed my summers and transformed me into the scholarly equivalent of Melville's relentless Ahab. The documenting materials took over the second-largest room in my family's house—and then the accumulating book shelves, file cabinets, and card boxes eventually spilled out of that crowded room into an adjoining space the previous owners had used as a recreation room.

Reasons Behind Such a Project

Justifications for this time-consuming inquiry begin with the fact that for writers active in the second half of the nineteenth century the print media entirely dominated the dissemination of ideas, opinions, and templates. The influence of films and television remained decades away, with the Internet a distant and unimagined prospect. Thus a knowledge of Clemens's reading enables us to trace many threads of thought that prompted or affected his literary productions. We can identify the prominent fields of his interest as well as his venturesome explorations.

The number and the caliber of the authors and titles I turned up effectively answer the recurrent charges by elitist literary critics and historians that Twain was more or less an intellectual lightweight whose writings merely survive on the fading strength of their comical qualities. I demonstrate that he read challenging works of philosophy, history, comparative religions, science, and astronomy, and that he was familiar with most of the respected literary

Alan Gribben's home office, 2020.

of more than a third of the books owned by Clemens and his family. This problem was compounded by two auctions in 1911 and 1951 of nearly all of the remaining library volumes. Only sketchy listings indicate what was sold at these auctions, and additional books were liquidated at the sales that did not appear in their inadequate catalogs. The majority of the auctioned items—especially those knocked down at the first sale—have never resurfaced.

artists who wrote in English in addition to European authors whose works he read in French, German, and Italian.

Furthermore, during our current non-reading era in which a large percentage of students seem less and less interested in the subjects that literature instructors teach, it is edifying and inspiring to realize that this perfect example of an autodidact—a boy withdrawn from school at the age of eleven who had no formal instruction in the subjects his contemporaries mastered in high school and college—nevertheless trained himself as a reader to the point where he assembled a family library of more than three thousand volumes, not counting the many hundreds of vanished books that went unrecorded.

Difficulties Impeding the Project

Despite these reasons for looking at Samuel Clemens's library and reading, investigations were hampered by the donations and losses

The Quarry Farm Books

Clemens could have sampled any of the books in the Langdons's and Cranes' family libraries during the twenty-plus summers he spent in Elmira, New York. Knowing their titles helps us grasp how intellectual and stimulating Clemens must have found the atmosphere into which he had been admitted by his marriage. These volumes still remain where they ultimately coalesced on the shelves at Quarry Farm, though the ones containing Clemens's marginalia have been transferred to the Mark Twain Archive at Elmira College.

In compiling my Annotated Catalog I naturally included the books that belonged to Theodore W. Crane (1831–1889) and his spouse Susan Langdon Crane (1836–1924), the owners of Quarry Farm. What to do about the Langdon family's library presented me with something of a problem. I elected to list and describe all of the earlier titles in this collection that bear the numbered bookplates of the "J. Langdon Family Library," since these were unquestionably accessible to Clemens and their subject matter might well have caught Clemens's eye. The other Langdon volumes in the Quarry Farm library, mostly unmarked, represent a commingling of the collections of various members of the extended family; they can be theoretically viewed as possibly available to Clemens if one wants to speculate further about which of these could have tempted him to open their covers.

Quite a few of these books originated from an avid reader, Ida Clark Langdon (1849–1934), the wife of Charles Jervis Langdon (1849–1916). She and her husband continued to paste the "J. Langdon Family Library" bookplates in books they acquired long after the death of the family patriarch Jervis Langdon (1809–1870); those volumes, shelved in their Elmira home, would presumably have been seen by Clemens only when he visited them. This fact gives one pause about including every single one of those titles, despite their Langdon family bookplates; I have chosen to list the works that strike me as most likely to have snagged his attention whenever he called on the Langdons.

Especially I tried to steer clear of the large number of books that belonged to the couple's daughter Ida Langdon (1880–1964), who taught English literature classes at Elmira College. She annotated her own library volumes in handwriting that looks somewhat like a blend of Samuel Clemens's and Olivia Clemens's, and visitors to Quarry Farm have frequently mistaken her notes and markings for the marginalia of Clemens or his wife.

Twain's Book Donations to the Mark Twain Library

A little more than a year after beginning this reconstruction project I arrived at the Mark Twain Library in Redding, Connecticut. Peggy Sanford (1941–2013), the librarian there from

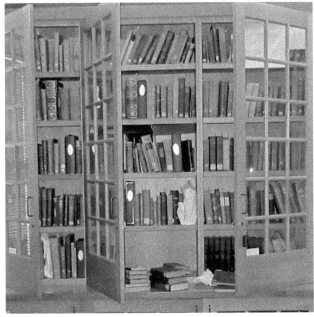

Top: 1911 interior of the Mark Twain Library in Redding, Connecticut (Courtesy of the Mark Twain Library). Bottom: Clemens's and Clara's book donations to the Mark Twain Library.

A bookshelf of Mark Twain association copies in the collection of Kevin Mac Donnell (Photograph by Kevin Mac Donnell).

of my study—and indeed, until the Mark Twain House and Museum at Hartford spent more than $200,000 to acquire nearly 300 books from the 1951 auction that were being re-auctioned in San Francisco in 1997; and until the world's largest private collector of Twainiana, the rare book dealer Kevin Mac Donnell of Austin, Texas, succeeded in assembling hundreds of volumes from Twain's library—the books in Redding constituted the largest collection of Twain association copies.

That was because, of course, Samuel Clemens liked Redding so much, and believed in the benefits of public libraries to such a degree, that he and his daughter Clara donated more than half of their family's library collection, amounting to at least several thousand titles, to help found the fledging Mark Twain Library in Redding. His secretary Isabel V. Lyon delivered many of these books to the Library at his request, but it is unclear how the rest of the volumes were transported from Stormfield. A week before Clemens's death in April 1910 he wrote a check to the evolving Library for $6,000—a very large amount in that century—to build and furnish a structure to house its books. His donation far surpassed those of other individuals, even the most affluent ones. For Clemens the proliferation of public libraries ranked among the greatest achievements that had occurred during his lifetime. Everywhere he went he had rated town and cities, and even hotels and ships,

1962 until 1979, and several library volunteers, especially Marge Webb (1905–1992), made me feel at home in that tight-knit rural community. This hospitality continued under the next librarian, Anne Cushman, who served as librarian between 1979 and 1984, and it never wavered up to and including the decade (2011–2021) that Beth Dominianni was the Library's director. Gradually, and understandably, I began to think of the Mark Twain Library at Redding as sort of the spiritual center

by the presence or absence of a library and the quality of its reading materials.

Clemens's donations to the Redding library were generous and wide-ranging—highlights of these gifts included family Bibles; Biblical studies; fiction by Harriet Beecher Stowe, Hamlin Garland, Jules Verne, William Makepeace Thackeray, and Daniel Defoe; poetry by John Milton, Robert Browning, Rudyard Kipling, and Alfred Lord Tennyson; North American histories by Francis Parkman; volumes on birds, animals, and natural history; an account of balloon ascents; literary works in the German language; histories of Europe and the United States; essays by Charles Dudley Warner and Henry David Thoreau; a work about human psychology; lectures by Bret Harte; letters between John Adams and his wife Abigail; and the correspondence of Thomas Carlyle and Ralph Waldo Emerson.

When I first visited the Mark Twain Library on September 9, 1970 it had suffered understandable criticism among Twain scholars and editors owing to the fact that its immense collection of his library books had dwindled to barely more than 200 volumes. Peggy Sanford seemed embarrassed about this fact and urged me to peruse the Library's bookshelves to see if, with my experience in seeing Twain's habits of annotating his library books, I could recognize any additional volumes containing Twain's handwriting, and I was glad to do this. I pulled more than thirty books out of general circulation, and we finally counted a total of approximately 240 that seemed likely to have been donated by the Clemenses, father and daughter.

What happened to the other several thousand or more? Well, their fate was what happens to all books loaned to borrowers by libraries. Many were checked out so often that they started to fall apart and were discarded. Large numbers, like ordinary library volumes, were misplaced and never returned by patrons. These losses were compounded in the early 1950s when a librarian returned from a regional librarians' conference where the attendees were urged to discard older books from their collections to make room for newer titles. She contacted a used book dealer who hauled away a pickup truckload of books bearing nineteenth-century imprints. Going through the winnowed volumes, the purchaser began to wonder if a few might have an unappreciated value. As a result a rare book dealer in New

Twain in 1873, the year **The Gilded Age** *was published (National Portrait Gallery, Smithsonian Institution; photograph by Jeremiah Gurney, NPG 80.283).*

*Above: First page, 1908 Accession Book.
Right: Mark Twain Library stamp in
Brewer's* **Dictionary of Miracles.**

York City, Howard S. Mott, soon listed more than sixty signed Clemens association copies in his 1952 catalog. Fortunately those few got recorded in this manner. One wonders how many others simply floated away in that Mark Twain Library transaction because they were unsigned with that famous name even though they contained Clemens's marginalia.

I had difficulty obtaining a publisher for my initial study of Mark Twain's reading because it was so lengthy, but I finally signed a contract in 1977. At that point I went back to Redding one last time to check my accuracy about certain titles before I submitted my final manuscript. It was then that the Mark Twain Library more than redeemed itself when two library volunteers, Marge Webb and Dorothy Munro, notified me that they had found the long-lost 152-page accession book that registered, in incredible detail, the authors, titles, publishers, dates, and number of pages for 1,751 of the books that Clemens, his daughter Clara, and Isabel Lyon had presented to the library. Stop the presses! My publisher waited patiently for three long years while I laboriously inserted these new additions into my Catalog, making it even longer than before. (Part of my sense of urgency stemmed from the fact that I was an assistant professor seeking tenure at the University of Texas at Austin, and proof of scholarly publication was required.)

Samuel Clemens gave hundreds of books to at least one other library in the last years of his life, but the library in Redding was the only institution that kept a meticulous record of what he donated. So although less than one tenth of Clemens and his daughter's gifts to Redding survived the various losses, we nonetheless have a far better idea of the exact books and their editions that he deposited there than we do of the many, many hundreds that were either donated elsewhere or were auctioned off later.

As I delved deeper into Clemens's correspondence, interviews, autobiography, and legal documents, I became convinced that in fact the Mark Twain Library at Redding had employed his donations precisely as he had intended. He hardly gave those books to this fledgling collection as a lasting memorial to his literature; he bequeathed them instead as a founding collection to jump-start a circulating library, an institution he had supported in every town and city where he resided or visited. He would have been elated that so many of his books were literally read to pieces, and probably have been sardonically amused by that well-meaning librarian's lapse in judgment by tossing out titles he inscribed or annotated. After all, he couldn't take those books with him when he went aloft with Halley's Comet, and his recently married daughter was destined to move away soon with her new conductor husband, Ossip Gabrilowitsch. Moreover, inasmuch as Mark Twain's contemporary reputation was principally that of a travel writer and literary humorist, any books he had owned scarcely had the value in the first decade of the twentieth century as the supposedly far more precious volumes handled and read by "serious" writers such as Emerson, Holmes, Lowell, Whittier, Hawthorne, or Longfellow.

Sometimes on sleepless nights I have fallen to wondering whether the *subsequent* accession book might someday be found in the attic, basement, or file cabinets of the Mark Twain Library at Redding. The log those library volunteers located in 1977 ended at the bottom of its last page with the number 2,315 (because it also listed books from donors other than Clemens and his daughter Clara), but I have run across books now held in other collections that were donated by the Clemenses to the Mark Twain Library (they display its characteristic purple oval stamp) and bear Mark Twain Library accession numbers into the 3000s and even the 4000s. Clearly that conscientious early library assistant ran out of space in the first accession book and started filling out a second one. The first number in it would be 2,316. It has been a fantasy of mine that this record might turn up during my lifetime, even though I am no longer an eager assistant professor but instead a retired professor emeritus. We would then have a much better idea about the variety of books that made up the Clemens family's library in Hartford. My disturbing nocturnal nightmares, on the other hand, imagine that this incredible bonanza is finally located on the very day I transmit the Annotated Catalog to my publisher. I am reminded of the chagrin the renowned Twain scholar Walter Blair (1900–1992) felt when, having edited with Victor Fischer the variorum edition of *Adventures of Huckleberry Finn* in 1988, he learned in 1990 that the first half of the manuscript, supposedly lost forever, had been discovered in a long-unopened trunk in Southern California.

Reconstructing Clemens's Library and Reading in Catalog Form

Samuel L. Clemens's reading tastes prove to be as varied, shifting, and inquisitive as one might anticipate from what we know of this restless man's personality and career. By locating

Clemens with an unidentified book, Quarry Farm, c. 1903 (Library of Congress, Prints and Photographs Online Catalog, digital id: cph 3b08272).

mentioned or to which he had direct access. The contents of the Catalog thus encompass a wide range of potential literary resources that Mark Twain could draw upon.

The Clemenses Shared Their Reading

Where possible the Annotated Catalog incorporates the reading of members of Clemens's immediate family, since they often exchanged their books and magazines. Given his creation of various child heroes, Clemens's knowledge of children's literature was presumably crucial to his development as a writer. He often read to his daughters from their own books until they reached their teens and he undoubtedly looked into their libraries out of curiosity as to what the younger audience (book consumers for whom, after all, he himself partially wrote) was reading. His wife Olivia's reading may have had a similar importance for his work; the biographer Albert Bigelow Paine claimed that Clemens and Charles Dudley Warner were spurred to attempt *The Gilded Age* (1873) as the result of a dinner-table argument with their wives about the inferior novels "in which their wives were finding entertainment" (*MTB* [1912], p. 476). Whether or not Clemens agreed with Olivia's preferences in reading, he was constantly aware of her current favorites. That his entire family was conversant with the writings

and inspecting more than 1,000 surviving volumes from his family library; reviewing rare book auction catalogs; examining his published and unpublished letters, notebooks, and manuscripts; exploring newspaper and magazine interviews with Twain, memoirs of his associates, family correspondence, and records of his household expenditures; and looking over scholarly books and articles that demonstrate literary connections in his writings, I have been able to establish that the Clemenses' library contained well over 3,000 volumes. In addition he read several thousand books, articles, and other materials he obtained or came across elsewhere. These findings are presented under author or title headings in the following Annotated Catalog that lists and describes nearly 6,000 books, short stories, essays, articles, poems, plays, operas, songs, newspapers, and magazines that Clemens

of authors venerated in the latter nineteenth century—Shakespeare, Longfellow, Tennyson, Eliot, Meredith, Browning—is confirmed by the Annotated Catalog, but it also lists the tremendous number of lesser-known writers with which they were likewise familiar.

Clemens's Reading in His Later Years

Mark Twain's unpublished and often unfinished stories, novels, plays, and essays furnished significant testimony for this study; frequently they contained literary allusions more explicit than the works published in his lifetime. But scholars who seek only information concerning his reading prior to 1890 may be dismayed at the relative scarcity of facts in this Catalog about the periods when he was composing his best-known novels, *The Adventures of Tom Sawyer*, *Adventures of Huckleberry Finn*, and *A Connecticut Yankee in King Arthur's Court*, as compared to the larger percentage of Catalog entries that chart his post-1900 reading interests. The disproportionately greater amount of information about Clemens's later years, following the repayment of his financial debts and his return to the United States, is attributable to several factors. First of all, his immense popularity at that time brought him a deluge of presentation and gift copies, many of which are recorded here. Most of the letters that accompanied these volumes still survive in the Mark Twain Papers in the Bancroft Library at the University of California at Berkeley, since Clemens traveled less during his final decade and so retained more of his correspondence and

reading materials than was previously possible. Moreover, by then he was such a celebrity that newspaper and magazine interviewers regularly inquired into his literary opinions. Isabel V. Lyon's meticulous journals chronicled his daily activities after 1902, a resource available to us from no other period of his life. Albert Bigelow Paine's biography emphasized the reading in which Clemens engaged during his four final years, merely sketching an impression of previous periods. Finally, Clemens's (putative) retirement from business affairs left him greater leisure to explore the writings of other authors. In the last few years of his life, in fact, he found opportunities to sign the flyleaves of numerous volumes that (to judge from his marginalia and other signs of usage) he had purchased and read or reread many years before. He signed the first volume of W. E. H. Lecky's *History of European Morals* "S L. Clemens/1906," even though he had read and annotated the book for many years. His

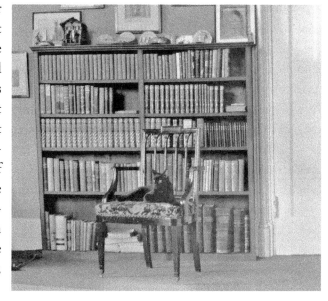

Clara's cat Bambino and Jean's bookshelf, New York (Collection of Kevin Mac Donnell).

In 1895, Twain returned to the lecture platform as a way to pay off his debts. From left, Olivia, Twain, Clara, Major Pond, and Mrs. Pond traveled together. Major Pond organized, promoted, and kept a journal of Twain's North American Lecture Tour. (Collection of Kevin Mac Donnell)

copy of George Combe's *Notes on the United States of America* (1841), one of the books he consulted for *Life on the Mississippi*, bears an anachronistic signature in the first volume, "S L. Clemens/1909." Students of his earlier major works can only remind themselves that his final library additions shed light on his long-term intellectual preoccupations and illuminate the preparation behind his *Mysterious Stranger* manuscripts; even the titles of books he read in 1909 and 1910 tell us something about the mind of *Huckleberry Finn's* creator.

The notably large number of Harper & Brothers titles that Clemens and his daughter Clara donated to the Mark Twain Library in Redding suggests that he cajoled his publisher into contributing volumes to the community library he was founding. Should these, in that case, be listed in this Annotated Catalog? I concluded that they do qualify as his literary resources for three reasons: (1) he signed and annotated quite a number of them, (2) from the outset of his career he had felt entitled to gratis copies of all books brought out by his publishers, and (3) given his innate curiosity he probably leafed through or read parts of a sizable proportion of these works.

Clemens's Accomplishments as a Reader

Even with the considerable number of unknown losses and donations, the magnitude of Clemens's reading as documented in the

Catalog will astonish many people. His curiosity about books and his recorded responses to his reading reflect an intellect more receptive to new influences and more critically mature than we have sometimes given him credit for possessing. Anxious to maintain his identity with the relatively unread audience for whom he profitably wrote subscription books, he was always self-conscious about his extensive literary knowledge. Unable in certain instances to share the opinions of acclaimed critics like William Dean Howells and Brander Matthews, he disguised his own abilities as a critic, jocularly creating his private "Library of Literary Hogwash" and donning cap and bells for the Boston and New York literary establishments, just as he would eventually act the role of jester for Henry H. Rogers's financial and political circle. Sufficient evidence survives, however, for us to gauge the hours of amusement and edification that Clemens privately gained from books—in armchairs and beds, at home and in hotels, on ships and trains, anytime he could indulge a vice he ranked with the pleasures of cigars and billiards and whiskey. Admirers of Mark Twain venerate the photographs of him at work writing; we should equally value the rarer photographs that show him engaged in a complementary activity of the creative mind, reading.

Losses and Gains

As I completed this scholarly undertaking I thought about Clemens and his wife Olivia and the elaborate library room they built in Hartford, Connecticut, and I pondered how their family library collection energized his imagination but then drifted piecemeal into the winds. Much in human life ends with losses, attrition, dispersal. So there was something satisfying about bringing *Mark Twain's Literary Resources* into print in the twenty-first century. This book will likely endure in print or electronic form; the depth of Twain's library collection and the impact of his reading will not be lost again.

Yet I must also confess to feeling a personal sense of loss. The moment that readers of *Mark Twain's Literary Resources* open the Annotated Catalog and the detailed Reader's Guide, they will instantly absorb as much as I have ever known about these subjects. I will no longer be privileged to answer telephone and email inquiries such as those that arrived for decades.

But then I remind myself that this act of letting go, of sharing everything one has learned, is, after all, what investigative scholarship must always have as its ultimate and unselfish goal.

PART II: HOW TO USE THE ANNOTATED CATALOG

Information in the Annotated Catalog is arranged alphabetically under authors' names. Whenever feasible the authors' birth and death dates, along with the birth and death dates of illustrators, editors, and translators, were determined by consulting more than one reputable source. Anonymous works are listed by title. Catalog entries for books give the basic bibliographic data—titles, places of publication, publishers' names, and dates of publication—for editions Clemens owned, borrowed, knew of, or, shall we say, brushed against. These facts were often obtained from auction catalogs when the books themselves could not be studied. Some of this information necessarily amounts to conjecture on my part and is accordingly placed within square

One side of the large library, Mark Twain House, Hartford, Connecticut (Courtesy of the Mark Twain House and Museum; photograph by Frank Grace).

brackets. If the volumes themselves could be inspected, their titles and publishers are rendered in the form that appeared on the title pages; this means that the Annotated Catalog's versions will occasionally differ from the titles on the covers and spines, in online listings, or in booksellers' or auction catalogs. The reader is informed of signatures or inscriptions on endpapers or flyleaves; marginalia in the text by Clemens or his family; descriptions of the volumes in bookdealers' catalogs; provenance of the books, if determined; current locations of the volumes, if known; and whether the original association copies, photocopies, or other sources were consulted for this study. Every effort was made to reproduce the inscriptions and annotations with accuracy, including their punctuation, where the actual association copies could be examined; however, these reports must often derive from less reliable catalog descriptions.

Ink and pencil colors of signatures and marginalia are noted when they can be verified; this even extends to describing as "brown" or "brown-black" ink that was no doubt initially black in hue before a process of oxidation took place over the decades. Book auction prices derive from records in the Mark Twain Papers in the Bancroft Library at the University of California at Berkeley, the Mark Twain House and Museum in Hannibal, Missouri, or from book collectors' auction notes that were shared with me.

A Note On Names

Where possible this book follows the prevailing scholarly custom of distinguishing between Samuel L. Clemens the private citizen and Mark Twain the author, lecturer, and public celebrity. The line between these two identities is sometimes difficult to distinguish, as numerous commentators have pointed out.

Per the suggestion of Louis J. Budd, whose interest in my research continued unabated until his death in 2010, *Mark Twain's Literary Resources* uses the names Olivia Langdon and (later) Olivia Clemens rather than "Livy" to refer to the woman Clemens married. In his later years Professor Budd held the belief that "Livy" was a privileged term of personal endearment reserved for her husband, family, and their circle of close friends; he recommended that twenty-first-century scholars avoid a tone of undue familiarity by employing her given name "Olivia" in order to confer more dignity and status to her as an individual meriting attention in her own right.

Reasons for Being Precise about Dating and Documenting

At first glance it might seem that the Annotated Catalog is overly scrupulous about recording the date when a book was seen and authenticated by me or by another person. This effort at exactitude reflects an intention to leave behind as full a record as possible of the association copies that could be conclusively verified during my research. A great many of Clemens's reading materials have already disappeared forever, and history teaches us that theft, fire, vandalism, recorded or unrecorded sales, careless heirs, and other sources of loss will inevitably winnow the surviving remnants of his library. It seemed advisable to specify the date they were definitely present at a given location, and to identify who looked at them.

Scholarship Cited in the Annotated Catalog

A tremendous amount of research regarding Mark Twain's reading preceded and accompanied mine, of course. A Critical Bibliography in Volume One and a Supplemental Critical Bibliography in Volume Two supply citations to the abundant books and articles that are mentioned. Discussions by scholars that focus on a specific author or title are incorporated within or listed after the most relevant Catalog entry. One important goal of *Mark Twain's Literary Resources* is to organize the mounting scholarship on Mark Twain's literary knowledge into a conveniently usable format—collating the known facts about Clemens's library and reading with the scholarly publications that treat the uses he made of them. This should reduce duplication and uncredited borrowing.

A Note on Citation Forms in the Annotated Catalog

The process of collecting and assembling so many disparate pieces of information—in whatever time I could spare from my responsibilities as (at first, a graduate student, and then) a husband, father, department head (for twenty years) and an English professor (for forty-five years)—required a total of five decades of effort between 1969, when I chose the topic as a doctoral dissertation, and 2019, when Volume One issued from NewSouth Books. During that substantial period of time the style manuals sponsored by the Modern Language Association (MLA) introduced bewilderingly rapid alterations in their specifications for citing sources. At various points the MLA guides even seemed to reverse themselves on stylistic procedures within a relatively short span. I

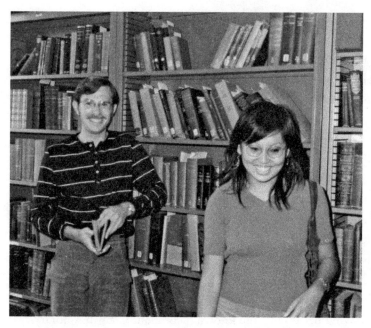

Alan Gribben and Irene Wong, Mark Twain Project, Berkeley, California, 1971 (Photograph by J. S. Gribben).

excluded from this Catalog, despite the urgings of various scholars and book collectors that these be listed. This worthwhile endeavor of cataloging all of the copies of his works that he autographed or annotated should become a special project for someone else. Not only are there are a great number of inscribed titles extant, which would further delay the publication of this Catalog, but Clemens's autographs and notes are quite different in those volumes from the signatures and marginalia he placed in books published by other writers. It is better not to intermix these two types of notations and markings in a single study. (In this connection, see Ronald Wesley Hoag—"All That Glitters Is Not Mark Twain: The Strange Case of the Riverdale '3,'" *Mark Twain Journal* 29 (Fall 1991): 2–9—for an account of an elaborate forgery of purported Twain annotations within a set of his published works. The present writer played a role in detecting this fraud, owing to my familiarity with subtle characteristics of Clemens's handwriting in the cramped space of book margins.)

finally concluded that the best solution for constructing reliable, enduring citations in my Annotated Catalog would be to provide the fullest possible information about books and articles, spelling out all words and including all numerals. Of course this means that the Catalog will inevitably seem out of synch with the MLA guides' latest stipulations about abbreviating the names of journals and publishers, omitting cities, or formulaically citing volume numbers, issues, and pages, but the user will nevertheless have the advantage of viewing every reference in its most inclusive form.

Omissions

While the Catalog and its commentaries attempt to be comprehensive, they cannot be truly exhaustive in every respect. A few boundaries had to be established. All copies of Mark Twain's own writings, signed or unsigned, are

Besides omitting Mark Twain's own writings, no attempt is made here to include his purely business associations. This Catalog stops at the time of Clemens's death in April 1910 and therefore omits the numerous books that Clara Clemens Gabrilowitsch (later Clara Samossoud) subsequently acquired and the many authors with whom she eventually became acquainted. Perhaps it ought to be noted that the chapter headings for *A Gilded Age* (1873) are not contained in the Catalog; Clemens probably never knew—or cared to know—the esoteric sources from which J. Hammond Trumbull culled them. With certain exceptions, music compositions are generally included only if they possess lyrics; they are nearly always listed by the lyricist rather than the composer of the melody. Traditional ballads, folk songs, minstrel songs, and spirituals usually appear under their titles.

Scope of the Annotated Catalog

It has been impossible to duplicate the lifetime reading of someone as voraciously curious about books as Samuel Clemens, even over the course of fifty-plus years of effort. All the same, this endeavor to follow Clemens's forays into bookshops and publishers' lists enabled me to sample broadly the wealth of what was available in print to readers of that era in the United States, England, France, Germany, and Italy. Clemens led me up many weed-choked alleyways of nineteenth- and early twentieth-century literature and thought, introducing me to unorthodox subjects and obscure authors I never would have encountered otherwise, and likewise renewed my acquaintance with literary classics. Whenever time allowed I returned to this Catalog and commented on perceived relationships between his reading and his writings. Countless topics remain unexplored, however, and the facts presented in the Annotated Catalog offer future scholars and general readers tantalizing connections to investigate.

Anyone who might wish to extend the scope of this Catalog can pursue the infinite by surveying Mark Twain's "professional" reading. In this category are the multitudinous stories and articles in magazine issues that contain a piece by Twain. Indeed, the most committed student should probably consider all issues of those newspapers and magazines to which he subscribed or for which he wrote with some regularity—especially the *Atlantic*, *Century*, and *Harper's*—as conceivably part of his reading. He must have read many issues of newspapers and magazines that contained interviews with him or accounts of his activities. Any of the selections in anthologies that reprinted one of his sketches might have attracted his interest. He undoubtedly read other titles issued by his publishers, particularly those in Tauchnitz's *Collection of British and American Authors* series, which he is known to have admired. All of these possibilities are left out of the Catalog in favor of more tangible evidence. The books issued by Clemens's own publishing firm, Charles L. Webster & Company, are included, however, since Clemens oversaw its operations so closely for nearly a decade.

PART III: CATALOG CITATIONS

A Note on Editions of Mark Twain's Works

Authors of Mark Twain studies still confront a dilemma in referring to literary texts. No authentic "complete edition" of Mark Twain's writings yet exists, and the numerous collections of his works—few with identical pagination—contain textual errors, omissions, and alterations. The solution to these problems is forthcoming: the editorial team of the Mark Twain Project in the Bancroft Library at the

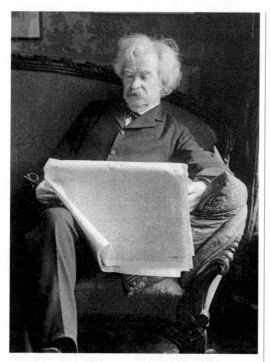

Clemens reading the New York Sun, *May 7, 1901 (Library of Congress, Prints and Photographs Online Catalog, digital id: ds 05448).*

University of California at Berkeley is preparing a reliable edition of both his previously published and his unpublished works, returning if feasible to the original manuscripts for textual authority. Wherever possible *Mark Twain's Literary Resources* refers the reader to volumes in this University of California Press series.

However, because of the prevailing state of transition toward a truly "complete" edition, I cite literary passages by the one uniform phenomenon observable among the various editions commonly owned by individuals and libraries—chapter numbers. Chapters in Mark Twain's books are usually short enough to make citation by chapter numbers more convenient than citation by

pages in one among many editions. Thus, the designation "(*AC*, Ch. 4)" refers the reader to Chapter four of *The American Claimant.* A table explaining the abbreviations of book titles and other citations follows. The Annotated Catalog, the Critical Bibliography (in Volume One), and the Supplement to the Critical Bibliography (in Volume Two) supply the full imprint information for these and many additional books and articles.

Book Catalogs Listing Volumes from Clemens's Library

A1911. "The Library and Manuscripts of Samuel L. Clemens," Anderson Auction Company, Catalogue No. 892. To be sold 7–8 February 1911 at the Anderson Auction Company, 12 East 46th Street, New York City.

> Items #1–500 were mostly books from Clemens's library, with the exception of approximately twenty manuscripts and books written by Clemens interspersed throughout. The 483 volumes generally contained manuscript fragments added by Albert Bigelow Paine to enhance their value as collectors' items.

American Art Association, Anderson Galleries, "The Mark Twain Collection of Irving S. Underhill," Sale No. 3911 (29 April 1931).

> Item #116 was Clemens's copy of Anatole France's *The Crime of Sylvestre Bonnard;* the other items were letters and first editions.

The Bookman, "A Mark Twain Collection," Catalogue No. 25 (1970), 2243 San Felipe Road, Houston, Texas.

> Items #328–331 were books from Clemens's library. The collection was formerly owned by William Hill of Houston. Its purchaser was Mrs. Nancy Susan Reynolds of Greenwich, Connecticut; she presented the collection to Wake Forest University in 1970.

C1951. "Mark Twain Library Auction," 10 April 1951, 2005 North LaBrea Avenue, Hollywood, California. E. F. Whitman, auction manager; Frank O'Connor, auctioneer.

> The sale took place in two sessions—at 1 p.m. and 7:30 p.m.—at the home of Clara (Clemens) Samossoud. Newspaper articles at the time referred to "the sale of 3,000 volumes from Twain's library," but the auction sheet listed only 310 books. Jacob Blanck described the unorthodox sale in the *Antiquarian Bookman* (5 May 1951; also 26 May 1951). Another account of the auction appeared in *American Book-Prices Current, 1950–51* (New York: R. R. Bowker, 1951), pp. 105–106, largely supplied by Glen Dawson of Dawson's Bookshop in Los Angeles.

Chicago Book and Art Auctions, Inc., Sale No. 30 (25 January 1933), 410 South Michigan Avenue.

> Items #64 and #65 were books from Clemens's library. Franklin J. Meine was listed as the secretary and manager of this auction firm.

Christie's 1991, sale of Mark Twain Research Foundation items, including association copies, owned by Chester L. Davis, 17 May 1991.

Chester L. Davis (1903–1987) allowed Alan Gribben to view certain volumes in this collection when Gribben visited Perry, Missouri in 1970. The 1991 sale following Davis's death scattered this collection widely.

"Deficiencies of Lincoln Warehouse Inventory," 3 April 1947, prepared by the Henry E. Huntington Library and Art Gallery.

A list of items missing from the Mark Twain Papers when Clemens's daughter Clara sent that collection to the Huntington Library. Among the absent items were two books from Clemens's library.

Fleming 1972. "List and Descriptive Material from the Personal Library of S. L. Clemens," John F. Fleming, Inc. (March 1972), 322 East 57th Street, New York City.

Included fifteen volumes from Clemens's library, most of them originally sold at the 1951 auction in Hollywood.

Hunley 1958. "Mark Twain: A Collection of First Editions, Association Copies, Biographies and Books from His Library," Maxwell Hunley Rare Books (June 1958), 9533 Santa Monica Boulevard, Beverly Hills, California.

Items #20–153 were books from Clemens's library.

Lew David Feldman, "House of El Dieff" Catalogue (1954), New York City.

Listings #229r and #248 offered a total of four books from Clemens's library.

Lew David Feldman, "House of El Dieff" Catalogue, "American Books" (1955), New York City.

Listed three books from Clemens's library originally sold at the 1951 auction in Hollywood.

Lew David Feldman, "House of El Dieff" Catalogue (1957), New York City.

Listed two books owned by Clemens.

L1912. Lexington Book Shop, Catalogue No. 19 (1912), 120 East 59th Street, New York City. Christian Gerhardt and Maximillian Harzof, proprietors.

Items #1–29 were books purchased at the 1911 auction of Clemens's library.

Mott 1952. "A Mark Twain Catalogue" (1952), Howard S. Mott, 8 West 40th Street, New York City.

Items #21 and #35–97 were volumes from Clemens's library. The catalog carried no date; in an interview in the 1970s Mr. Mott, by then the proprietor of an antiquarian bookshop in Sheffield, Massachusetts, told Alan Gribben that he believed he had issued that list in 1952.

Parke-Bernet Galleries, Inc., "The Splendid Collection of Books, Autographs, Manuscripts of Samuel L. Clemens Formed by the Late Alan N. Mendleson, New York," Sale No. 1719 (11–12 December 1956), New York City.

Items #95 and #130 were from Clemens's library.

Parke-Bernet Galleries, Inc., "Mark Twain Items and Other Americana" (21–22 May 1957), New York City.

Included three Clemens library books (items #122–124) from the Harnsberger collection.

Also auctioned was a book (item #121) presented by Clemens to Elsie Leslie Milliken.

"Retz Appraisal" (1944). "Inventory and Appraisal of the Estate of the Late Samuel L. Clemens (Mark Twain) Contained in the Lincoln Warehouse Corp., 1195 Third Avenue, New York, New York," 17 January 1944. Charles Retz, Inc. of New York City. 14 pp.

Pages 4–12 listed and estimated the value of the books in the Mark Twain Papers in 1944. Page 10 simply referred to one group of books as "a collection of 19 volumes, miscellaneous in character," valued at $7.

Seven Gables Bookshop, Inc., "First and Other Editions of Samuel L. Clemens," List No. 3 (August 1972), 3 West 46th Street, New York City.

Items #139 and #140 were from Clemens's library.

Sotheby's 2003. "The Mark Twain Collection of Nick Karanovich." Sotheby's, 1334 York Avenue, New York City. Auction held on 19 June 2003. Catalog production overseen by Selby Kiffer. Introductory essay, "Books from the Library of Samuel L. Clemens," written by Alan Gribben (pp. 154–155).

Lots 182–248 (pp. 156–221) consisted of association copies, many accompanied by photographs of Clemens's inscriptions or marginalia. Nick Karanovich (1938–2003), a resident of Fort Wayne, Indiana, had been recognized for several decades as one of the foremost collectors of Twainiana.

Zeitlin 1951. "Books from the Library of Mark Twain . . . Purchased at the Sale of the Library of His Daughter Clara Clemens Samossoud, April 10–14, 1951," Zeitlin & Ver Brugge, Booksellers, List No. 132 (May 1951), 815 North La Cienega Boulevard, Los Angeles, California.

The six-page catalog contained forty-seven books from Clemens's library (items #7–53). The proprietors explained: "We were fortunate enough to attend this sale and obtain a number of hooks . . . which should be of great interest to the future students of the mind and work of this great American."

Clemens at his desk, New York, 1903 (Library of Congress, Prints and Photographs Online Catalog, digital id: cph 3a29488).

Abbreviations

Collections, Correspondents, Documents, and Terms

ABP — Albert Bigelow Paine (1861–1937), Clemens's designated biographer

AD — Samuel L. Clemens's Autobiographical Dictations (typed manuscripts in the Mark Twain Papers, Bancroft Library, University of California at Berkeley)

adapt. — adaptor

ASSSCL — Albert and Shirley Small Special Collections Library, University of Virginia, Charlottesville

ALS — Autograph letter, signed

Ball 2016 — Inventory of books in or from the Quarry Farm library prepared on 21 June 2016 by Nathaniel Ball, (then) Archivist, Mark Twain Archive, Gannett-Tripp Learning Center, Elmira College, Elmira, New York. The list contained the titles of books still at Quarry Farm as well as those that were transferred to the Mark Twain Archive at Elmira College. It also included volumes that could not be located in 2016.

Berg — Henry W. and Albert A. Berg Collection, New York Public Library, Astor, Lenox and Tilden Foundations

Clara — Clara Langdon Clemens (1874–1962), daughter of Samuel and Olivia Clemens

Ch. — Chapter

Columbia — Columbia University Library, New York City

comp. — compiler

contr. — contributor

cop. — copyright date

CU-MARK — Mark Twain Papers, Bancroft Library, University of California at Berkeley

CWB — Clifton Waller Barrett Collection, Albert and Shirley Small Special Collections Library, University of Virginia, Charlottesville (ASSSCL)

DV — Prefix designating certain literary manuscripts in the Mark Twain Papers

ed. — editor

eds. — editors

HHR — Henry Huttleston Rogers (1840–1909), a vice-president of the Standard Oil Company who became Samuel L. Clemens' financial savior in the latter 1890s

Huntington — Henry E. Huntington Library, San Marino, California

Illus. — Illustrated.

illus. — illustrator

inscr. — inscribed by

Intro. — Introduction

IVL — Isabel V. Lyon (1863–1958), Clemens's private secretary

Jean — Jane Lampton Clemens (1880–1909), daughter of Samuel and Olivia Clemens

JHT — The Reverend Joseph H. Twichell (1838–1918), Clemens's Hartford minister friend

ListABP — "List of Books, Etc. Left with A. B. Paine," a nineteen-page typescript titled "LIST OF BOOKS, ETC./ Left with A. B. Paine/'Markland' Redding,/Conn." The checklist contains more than 350 titles of books, newspapers, and magazines that were in the possession of Clemens's designated biographer Albert Bigelow Paine when Clemens died in 1910. This document later came into the possession of Jervis Langdon Jr., who gave it to the Mark Twain House and Museum in Hartford, Connecticut. In 1979 the list was located among miscellaneous records that Langdon had donated. Paine returned the majority of the items to Clara Clemens Gabrilowitsch, but he retained a few in his own collection. A large number of the listed books have disappeared altogether.

ms. — manuscript

MT — Mark Twain, the pen name of Samuel L. Clemens (1835–1910)

MTHM — Mark Twain House and Museum, Hartford, Connecticut

MTLAcc — Accession records, Mark Twain Library, Redding, Connecticut, a list of book donations 1908–1910 (a bound volume of handwritten entries that was discovered in 1977). The last entry was assigned the accession number 2315. A subsequent volume that continued this list of the many hundreds of books donated by Clemens and his daughter Clara Clemens Samossoud has never been found.

MTM — Mark Twain Memorial, Hartford, Connecticut (later renamed the Mark Twain House and Museum), which formerly housed its book collection in the adjacent Stowe-Day Library.

MTP — Mark Twain Papers, Bancroft Library, University of California at Berkeley

NB — Holograph notebook in the Mark Twain Papers, Berkeley

NYPL — New York Public Library

OLC — Olivia Langdon Clemens (1845–1904), the wife of Samuel L. Clemens

Olivia — Olivia Langdon Clemens (1845–1904), the wife of Samuel L. Clemens

p. — page

Paine — Prefix designating certain literary manuscripts in the Mark Twain Papers

PH — Photocopy

pp. — pages

Pref. — Preface

Princeton — Princeton University Library

prod. — producer

pseud. — pseudonym

QF Martinez — Appraisal of the Langdon family's Quarry Farm library books by Emily Schweizer Martinez Out-of-Print Books, 313 Westinghouse Road, Horseheads, New York. The document is undated, but presumably it was prepared for tax purposes at the time of the Langdons' gift of Quarry Farm to Elmira College in 1982. (The appraiser made a memorandum on the document indicating that on 31 May she received a check in the amount of $300 for her services.) Both portions of this collection — the books originally in the residences of the Langdon family members and those belonging to Theodore and Susan Crane in their hillside home, Quarry Farm — were accessible to Samuel Clemens during his many summer sojourns in Elmira. Many of the volumes listed by Martinez were published after the date of Clemens's last visit to Elmira in 1907 and are therefore omitted from *Mark Twain's Literary Resources*.

Repr. — Reprinted

SLC — Samuel L. Clemens (1835–1910)

Susy — Olivia Susan Clemens, known as "Susy" (1872–1896), daughter of Samuel and Olivia Clemens

trans. — translator

TS — Typescript

WDH — William Dean Howells (1837–1920), the author and editor who was one of Clemens's closest friends

Yale — American Literature Collections, Beinecke Rare Book and Manuscript Library, Yale University, New Haven, Connecticut

PUBLISHED WORKS CITED

AC — *The American Claimant* (novel, published in 1892)

AL — *American Literature* (scholarly journal)

AMT — Henry W. Fisher, *Abroad with Mark Twain and Eugene Field*. New York: Nicholas L. Brown, 1922

AutoMT 1–3 — *Autobiography of Mark Twain*, ed. Harriet Elinor Smith *et al.* 3 vols. Berkeley: University of California Press, 2010–2015

CG — *Contributions to "The Galaxy" 1868–1871 by Mark Twain*, ed. Bruce R. McElderry, Jr. Gainesville, Florida: Scholars' Facsimiles & Reprints, 1961

CofC — *Clemens of the "Call": Mark Twain in San Francisco*, ed. Edgar M. Branch. Berkeley: University of California Press, 1969

Complete Interviews — *Mark Twain: The Complete Interviews*, ed. Gary Scharnhorst. Tuscaloosa: University of Alabama Press, 2006

Courtship — Susan K. Harris, *The Courtship of Olivia Langdon and Mark Twain*. Cambridge: Cambridge University Press, 1996.

CTMT — Daniel Morley McKeithan, *Court Trials in Mark Twain and Other Essays*. The Hague: Martinus Nijhoff, 1958

CTSS&E 1–2 — *Mark Twain: Collected Tales, Sketches, Speeches, & Essays*, ed. Louis J. Budd. 2 vols. New York: Library of America, 1992

CY — *A Connecticut Yankee in King Arthur's Court*, ed. Bernard L. Stein. Berkeley: University of California Press, 1979

Day by Day — David H. Fears, *Mark Twain Day by Day: An Annotated Chronology of the Life of Samuel L. Clemens*. 4 vols. Banks, Oregon: Horizon Micro Publishers, 2008–2013 (Volume One was reissued in an enlarged second edition in 2014)

DE — *The Writings of Mark Twain,* Definitive Edition. New York: Gabriel Wells, 1922

DearMT — *Dear Mark Twain: Letters from His Readers*, ed. R. Kent Rasmussen. Berkeley: University of California Press, 2013

ET&S 1–2 — *Early Tales & Sketches*, ed. Edgar Marquess Branch and Robert H. Hirst. 2 vols. Berkeley: University of California Press, 1979, 1981

Family Sketch — *A Family Sketch and Other Private Writings by Mark Twain, Livy Clemens, and Susy Clemens*, ed. Benjamin Griffin. Oakland: University of California Press, 2014

FE — *Following the Equator* (travel narrative, 1897)

FM — *Mark Twain's Fables of Man*, ed. John S. Tuckey. Berkeley: University of California Press, 1972

GA — *The Gilded Age* (novel, 1873)

HF — *Adventures of Huckleberry Finn*, ed. Victor Fischer and Lin Salamo. Berkeley: University of California Press, 2003

HH&T — *Hannibal, Huck & Tom*, ed. Walter Blair. Berkeley: University of California Press, 1969

IA — *The Innocents Abroad* (travel narrative, 1869)

IE — Albert E. Stone, *The Innocent Eye*. New Haven: Yale University Press, 1961

LAMT — Edgar M. Branch, *The Literary Apprenticeship of Mark Twain*. Urbana: University of Illinois Press, 1950

LE — *Letters from the Earth*, ed. Bernard DeVoto. New York: Harper & Row, 1962

LH — *Letters from Honolulu*, ed. John W. Vandercook. Honolulu: Thomas Nickerson, 1939

LLMT — *The Love Letters of Mark Twain*, ed. Dixon Wecter. New York: Harper & Brothers, 1949

LMT — Mary Lawton, *A Lifetime with Mark Twain: The Memoirs of Katy Leary*. New York: Harcourt, Brace and Co., 1925

LMTJHT — *The Letters of Mark Twain and Joseph Hopkins Twichell*, ed. Harold K. Bush, Steve Courtney, and Peter Messent. Athens: University of Georgia Press, 2017

LonMiss — *Life on the Mississippi* (travel narrative, 1883)

LSI — *Letters from the Sandwich Islands*, ed. G. Ezra Dane. Stanford: Stanford University Press, 1938

Man in White — Michael Shelden, *Mark Twain, Man in White: The Grand Adventures of His Final Years*. New York: Random House, 2010.

MFMT — Clara Clemens, *My Father, Mark Twain*. New York: Harper & Brothers, 1931

MMT — William Dean Howells, *My Mark Twain: Reminiscences and Criticisms*, ed. Marilyn Austin Baldwin. Baton Rouge: Louisiana State University Press, 1967

MS — *The Mysterious Stranger* (collective manuscripts, first accurately published in 1969)

MSM — *Mark Twain's Mysterious Stranger Manuscripts*, ed. William M. Gibson. Berkeley: University of California Press, 1969

MTA — *Mark Twain's Autobiography*, ed. Albert Bigelow Paine. 2 vols. New York: Harper & Brothers, 1924

MTAb — Dewey Ganzel, *Mark Twain Abroad.* Chicago: University of Chicago Press, 1968

MTAL — Arthur L. Scott, *Mark Twain at Large.* Chicago: Henry Regnery Co., 1969

MTAm — Bernard DeVoto, *Mark Twain's America.* Boston: Little, Brown, and Co., 1932

MTB — Albert Bigelow Paine, *Mark Twain: A Biography.* New York: Harper & Brothers, 1912

MTBE — *Mark Twain at the Buffalo Express: Articles and Sketches by America's Favorite Humorist,* ed. Joseph B. McCullough and Janice McIntire-Strasburg. DeKalb: Northern Illinois Press, 2000

MTBP — Franklin R. Rogers, *Mark Twain's Burlesque Patterns.* Dallas: Southern Methodist University Press, 1960

MTBus — *Mark Twain, Business Man,* ed. Samuel C. Webster. Boston: Little, Brown, and Co., 1946

MTC — Sydney J. Krause, *Mark Twain as Critic.* Baltimore: Johns Hopkins Press, 1967

MTCor — *Mark Twain: San Francisco Correspondent,* ed. Henry Nash Smith and Frederick Anderson. San Francisco: Book Club of California, 1957

MTDW — Henry Nash Smith, *Mark Twain: The Development of a Writer.* Cambridge: Harvard University Press, Belknap Press, 1962

MTE — *Mark Twain in Eruption,* ed. Bernard DeVoto. New York: Harper & Brothers, 1940

MT&EB — Hamlin Hill, *Mark Twain and Elisha Bliss.* Columbia: University of Missouri Press, 1964

MTEnt — *Mark Twain of the "Enterprise,"* ed. Henry Nash Smith. Berkeley: University of California Press, 1957.

MTFP — Henry Nash Smith, *Mark Twain's Fable of Progress.* New Brunswick: Rutgers University Press, 1964

MTG — Edgar H. Hemminghaus, *Mark Twain's Germany.* New York: Columbia University Press, 1939

MT&GA — Bryant Morey French, *Mark Twain and The Gilded Age.* Dallas: Southern Methodist University Press, 1965

MTGF — Hamlin Hill, *Mark Twain: God's Fool.* New York: Harper & Row, 1973

MT&GWC — Arlin Turner, *Mark Twain and G. W. Cable.* East Lansing: Michigan State University Press, 1960

MTH — Walter Francis Frear, *Mark Twain and Hawaii.* Chicago: Lakeside Press, 1947

MT&HF — Walter Blair, *Mark Twain & Huck Finn.* Berkeley: University of California Press, 1960

MTHHR — *Mark Twain's Correspondence with Henry Huttleston Rogers,* ed. Lewis Leary. Berkeley: University of California Press, 1969

MT&HI — Elizabeth Wallace, *Mark Twain and the Happy Island.* Chicago: A. C. McClurg & Co., 1913

MTHL — *Mark Twain-Howells Letters,* ed. Henry Nash Smith and William M. Gibson. Cambridge: Harvard University Press, Belknap Press, 1960

MT in Elmira — *Mark Twain in Elmira,* ed. Robert D. Jerome, Herbert A. Wisbey, Jr., and Barbara E. Snedecor. Second edition. Elmira: Elmira College Center for Mark Twain Studies, 2013.

MT&JB — Howard G. Baetzhold, *Mark Twain and John Bull.* Bloomington: Indiana University Press. 1970

MTL — *Mark Twain's Letters,* ed. Albert Bigelow Paine. New York: Harper & Brothers, 1917

MTLA — Gladys C. Bellamy, *Mark Twain as a Literary Artist.* Norman: University of Oklahoma Press, 1950

MTLBowen — *Mark Twain's Letters to Will Bowen,* ed. Theodore Hornberger. Austin: University of Texas, 1941

MTLC — Paul Fatout, *Mark Twain on the Lecture Circuit.* Bloomington: Indiana University Press, 1960

MTLet 1–6 — *Mark Twain's Letters,* ed. Edgar M. Branch, Michael B. Frank, Kenneth M. Sanderson *et al.* 6 vols. Berkeley: University of California Press, 1988–2002

MTLM — *Mark Twain's Letters to Mary,* ed. Lewis Leary. New York: Columbia University Press, 1961

MTLMusc — *Mark Twain's Letters in the Muscatine Journal,* ed. Edgar M. Branch. Chicago: Mark Twain Association of America, 1942

MTLP — *Mark Twain's Letters to His Publishers,* ed. Hamlin Hill. Berkeley: University of California Press, 1967

MTLW — *Mark Twain the Letter Writer,* ed. Cyril Clemens. Boston: Meador Publishing Co., 1932

MTMF — *Mark Twain to Mrs. Fairbanks,* ed. Dixon Wecter. San Marino, California: Huntington Library, 1949

MTM&L — DeLancey Ferguson, *Mark Twain: Man and Legend.* Indianapolis: Bobbs-Merrill, 1943

MTMW — Edward P. Wagenknecht, *Mark Twain: The Man and His Work,* 3rd ed. Norman: University of Oklahoma Press, 1967

MTN — *Mark Twain's Notebook,* ed. Albert Bigelow Paine. New York: Harper & Brothers, 1935

MTPP — *Mark Twain on Potholes and Politics: Letters to the Editors,* ed. Gary Scharnhorst. Columbia: University of Missouri Press, 2014

MTS (1910) — *Mark Twain's Speeches,* ed. Albert Bigelow Paine. New York: Harper & Brothers, 1910

MTS (1923) — *Mark Twain's Speeches,* ed. Albert Bigelow Paine. New York: Harper & Brothers, 1923

MTSatan — John S. Tuckey, *Mark Twain and Little Satan.* West Lafayette: Purdue University Studies, 1963

MTSF — *Mark Twain's San Francisco,* ed. Bernard Taper. New York: McGraw-Hill Co., 1963

MT&SH — Kenneth S. Lynn, *Mark Twain and Southwestern Humor.* Boston: Little, Brown, 1960

MTSM — Minnie M. Brashear, *Mark Twain: Son of Missouri.* Chapel Hill: University of North Carolina Press, 1934

MTSP — Louis J. Budd, *Mark Twain: Social Philosopher.* Bloomington: Indiana University Press, 1962

MTSpk — *Mark Twain Speaking,* ed. Paul Fatout. Iowa City: University of Iowa Press, 1976

MTTMB — *Mark Twain's Travels with Mr. Brown,* ed. Franklin Walker and O. Ezra Dane. New York: Alfred A. Knopf, 1940

MTW — Bernard DeVoto, *Mark Twain at Work.* Cambridge: Harvard University Press, 1942

MTWY — Ivan Benson, *Mark Twain's Western Years.* Stanford: Stanford University Press, 1938

NAH — Walter Blair, *Native American Humor.* New York: American Book Co., 1937; San Francisco: Chandler Publishing Co., 1960

NF — Kenneth R. Andrews, *Nook Farm. Mark Twain's Hartford Circle.* Cambridge: Harvard University Press, 1950

N&J 1–3 — *Mark Twain's Notebooks & Journals,* eds. Frederick Anderson, Michael B. Frank, Kenneth M. Sanderson, *et al.* 3 vols. Berkeley: University of California Press, 1975–1979

OMT (1920) — Van Wyck Brooks, *The Ordeal of Mark Twain.* New York: E. P. Dutton & Co., 1920

OMT (1933) — Van Wyck Brooks, *The Ordeal of Mark Twain,* rev. ed. New York: E. P. Dutton & Co., 1933

OPMT — Arthur L. Scott, *On the Poetry of Mark Twain.* Urbana: University of Illinois Press, 1966

Pen — *A Pen Warmed-up in Hell: Mark Twain in Protest,* ed. Frederick Anderson. New York: Harper & Row, 1972

P&P — *The Prince and the Pauper,* ed. Victor Fischer and Lin Salamo. Berkeley: University of California Press, 1979

PRI — *The Pattern for Mark Twain's "Roughing It,"* ed. Franklin R. Rogers. Berkeley: University of California Press, 1961

PW — *Pudd'nhead Wilson* (novel, 1894)

RI — *Roughing It,* ed. Harriet Elinor Smith and Edgar Marquess Branch. Berkeley: University of California Press, 1993

RL — *Republican Letters,* ed. Cyril Clemens. Webster Groves, Missouri: International Mark Twain Society, 1941

RP — *Report from Paradise,* ed. Dixon Wecter. New York: Harper & Brothers, 1952

S&B — *Mark Twain's Satires & Burlesques,* ed. Franklin R. Rogers. Berkeley: University of California Press, 1967

SCH — Dixon Wecter, *Sam Clemens of Hannibal.* Boston: Houghton Mifflin Co., 1952

SL — Thomas J. Reigstad, *Scribblin' for a Livin': Mark Twain's Pivotal Period in Buffalo.* Amherst, New York: Prometheus Books, 2013

S&MT — Edith Colgate Salsbury, *Susy and Mark Twain.* New York: Harper & Row, 1965

SN&O — *Sketches New and Old* (collection of stories, 1875)

SSix — *Sketches of the Sixties.* Second ed. San Francisco: John Howell, 1927

TA — *A Tramp Abroad* (travel narrative, 1880)

TG — Guy A. Cardwell, *Twins of Genius.* East Lansing: Michigan State College Press, 1953

TIA — *Traveling with the Innocents Abroad: Mark Twain's Original Reports from Europe and the Holy Land,* ed. Daniel Morley McKeithan. Norman: University of Oklahoma Press, 1958

TIH — Roger B. Salomon, *Twain and the Image of History.* New Haven: Yale University Press, 1961

TJS — *The Adventures of Thomas Jefferson Snodgrass,* ed. Charles Honce. Chicago: Pascal Covici, 1928

TS — *The Adventures of Tom Sawyer* (1876), as published in *The Adventures of Tom Sawyer, Tom Sawyer Abroad, Tom Sawyer, Detective,* ed. John C. Gerber, Paul Baender, and Terry Firkins. Berkeley: University of California Press, 1980

TSA — *Tom Sawyer Abroad* (novel, 1894)

UCLC — Paul Machlis, *Union Catalog of Letters to Clemens.* Berkeley: University of California Press, 1992

UH — Robert Regan, *Unpromising Heroes.* Berkeley: University of California Press, 1966

W1868 — *Washington in 1868,* ed. Cyril Clemens. Webster Groves, Missouri: International Mark Twain Society, 1943

WG — *The Washoe Giant in San Francisco,* ed. Franklin Walker. San Francisco: George Fields, 1938

WIM? — *What Is Man? and Other Philosophical Writings,* ed. Paul Baender. Berkeley: University of California Press, 1973

WWD? — *Mark Twain's Which Was the Dream? and Other Symbolic Writings of the Later Years,* ed. John S. Tuckey. Berkeley: University of California Press, 1968

Clemens, New York, 1901 (National Portrait Gallery, Smithsonian Institution, gift of Katie Loucheim. Photograph by Alfred J. Meyer, NPG_76_71).

this is that same "agreeable" young woman heretofore referred to.

And when she died, and Stella heard that Swift had written beautifully regarding her, " that does not surprise me," said Mrs. Stella, " for we all know the Dean could write beautifully about a broomstick." A woman—a true woman ! Would you have had one of them forgive the other ? — *Yes.*

In a note in his biography, Scott says that his friend Dr. Tuke, of Dublin, has a lock of Stella's hair, enclosed in a paper by Swift, on which are written in the Dean's hand, the words: " *Only a woman's hair.*" An instance,

---

of her affections—to the hope of which she had clung amid every vicissitude of his conduct towards her. The most probable bar was his undefined connection with Mrs. Johnson, which, as it must have been perfectly known to her, had, doubtless, long elicited her secret jealousy, although only a single hint to that purpose is to be found in their correspondence, and that so early as 1713, when she writes to him —then in Ireland—' If you are very happy, it is ill-natured of you not to tell me so, *except 'tis what is inconsistent with mine.*' Her silence and patience under this state of uncertainty for no less than eight years, must have been partly owing to her awe for Swift, and partly, perhaps, to the weak state of her rival's health, which, from year to year, seemed to announce speedy dissolution. At length, however, Vanessa's impatience prevailed, and she ventured on the decisive step of writing to Mrs. Johnson herself, requesting to know the nature of that connection. Stella, in reply, informed her of her marriage with the Dean ; and full of the highest resentment against Swift for having given another female such a right in him as Miss Vanhomrigh's inquiries implied, she sent to him her rival's letter of interrogatories, and, without seeing him, or awaiting his reply, retired to the house of Mr. Ford, near Dublin. Every reader knows the consequence. Swift, in one of those paroxysms of fury to which he was liable, both from temper and disease, rode instantly to Marley Abbey. As he entered the apartment, the sternness of his countenance, which was peculiarly formed to express the fiercer passions, struck the unfortunate Vanessa with such terror that she could scarce ask whether he would not sit down. He answered by flinging a letter on the table, and, instantly leaving the house, remounted his horse, and returned to Dublin. When Vanessa opened the packet, she only found her own letter to Stella. It was her death warrant. She sunk at once under the disappointment of the delayed, yet cherished hopes which had so long sickened her heart, and beneath the unrestrained wrath of him for whose sake she had indulged them. How long she survived the last interview is uncertain but the time does not seem to have exceeded a few weeks."—SCOTT.

Writing 5 years for a rival journal was an instance of "patience" as unique as it was merciful & considerate.

Swift was sea-sick. He hurt the people where the sweetest was in some way off.

Clemens was hardly a passive reader. His repeated perusals of Thackeray's Lectures *produced opiniated marginalia in both ink and pencil.*

*Annotated Catalog of the Library
and Reading of Samuel L. Clemens*

First Pages of Alphabetical Sections

A

ABBEY, EDWIN AUSTIN (1852–1911) and **ALFRED PARSONS** (1847–1920), illustrators and compilers. *Old Songs, with Drawings by Edwin A. Abbey and Alfred Parsons.* New York: Harper & Brothers, 1889. 121 pp.

    Catalogs: *A1911,* "folio, art cloth, gilt top, uncut, N.Y. 1889," with a sheet of Clemens's notes laid in, lot 368, sold for $2; *L1912,* "small folio," lot 22, sold for $6.50. More than a hundred woodcuts by Abbey and Parsons accompany a dozen English ballads and songs, including "With Jockey to the Fair," "The Leather Bottell," "Barbara Allen," "Sally in Our Alley," "Kitty of Coleraine," and "Sweet Nelly."

ABBEY, HENRY (1842–1911), comp. *Bright Things from Everywhere: A Galaxy of Good Stories, Poems, Paragraphs, Wit, and Wisdom, Selected by Henry Abbey.* Albany, New York: J. B. Lyon Company, Printers, 1888. 167 pp.

    Source: MTLAcc, entry #366, volume donated by Clemens.

———. *The City of Success, and Other Poems.* First edition. Original maroon pictorial cloth, gilt. New York: D. Appleton and Co., 1884. 142 pp.

    Inscription: inscribed "To Samuel L. Clemens, from Henry Abbey."

    Marginalia: Clemens's pencil markings occur on nine pages in the title poem.

    Provenance: inscribed by Dan Beard as "Vice-President" of the Mark Twain Library in Redding, Connecticut, stating that this volume was sold by the Library as a duplicate at a fair. It contains the purple stamps of the Mark Twain Library. Victor Jacobs owned the book in 1986 (Jacobs to Alan Gribben, 15 October 1986). Jacobs sold his collection before he died in 1996. Eventually it was obtained by Nick Karanovich (1938–2003), Fort Wayne, Indiana.

    Catalogs: Swann Auction Galleries (New York City), Catalogue 285 (4–5 April 1951), "8vo, gilt-pictorial cloth; top edge gilt, inscribed copy—'To Samuel L. Clemens, from Henry Abbey.', with authenticating rubber stamp, signed by Dan Beard, backstrip spotted," item #566, $3.50; "Victor and Irene Murr Jacobs Collection," Sotheby's, New York City, 29 October 1996, lot 313, sold with four other books for a total of $9,312; *Sotheby's 2003,* #216, $3,500 (sold with five other inscribed books).

    Location: collection of Kevin Mac Donnell, Austin, Texas.

    Copy examined: Clemens's copy, in July 2004 in Austin, Texas.

———. *Poems, by Henry Abbey.* New York: D. Appleton and Co., 1879. 149 pp.

    Source: MTLAcc, entry #2130, volume donated from Clemens's library by Clara Clemens Gabrilowitsch in 1910.

———. *The Poems of Henry Abbey.* New, enlarged edition. Kingston, New York: Henry Abbey, 1885. 256 pp.

    Source: MTLAcc, entry #2016, volume donated from Clemens's library by Clara Clemens Gabrilowitsch in 1910.

ABBOTT, CHARLES CONRAD (1843–1919). *In Nature's Realm.* Illustrated by Oliver Kemp (1887–1934). Trenton, N.J.: A. Brandt, 1900. 309 pp.

    Source: MTLAcc, entry #1938, volume donated from Clemens's library by Clara Clemens Gabrilowitsch in 1910. Outdoor walks and keen observations of the natural world around us.

ABBOTT, JACOB (1803–1879). *Agnes.* Franconia Stories Series. Illus. New York: Harper & Brothers, 1904. 224 pp.

    Source: MTLAcc, entry #1203, volume donated by Clemens.

———. *Ellen Linn.* Franconia Stories, Volume 7. New York: Harper & Brothers, [cop. 1852]. 215 pp.

    Source: MTLAcc, entry #1862, volume donated from Clemens's library by Clara Clemens Gabrilowitsch in 1910. Olivia Clemens read to her daughters from the stories about Beechnut, Rodolphus, Ellen Linn, and other children in March and April 1880 (*S&MT* [1965], p. 118). In "A Cat Tale" (written in 1880), Mark Twain's Cattaraugus "had not failed to observe how harmoniously gigantic language and a microscopic topic go together" when he read "the able 'Franconia Series'" (*Concerning Cats,* ed. Frederick Anderson [San Francisco: Book Club of California, 1959], pp. xii, 15; Budd, *CTSS&E,* 1: 770).

    Stone, *IE* (1961), pp. 25–27.

———. *Ellen Linn.* Franconia Stories Series. Illus. New York: Harper & Brothers, 1904. 215 pp.

    Source: MTLAcc, entry #503, volume donated by Clemens.

———. *History of Mary, Queen of Scots.* Illus. New York: Harper & Brothers, 1904. 286 pp.

    Source: MTLAcc, entry #1204, volume donated by Clemens.

———. *History of Pyrrhus.* Illus. New York: Harper & Brothers, 1899. 304 pp.

    Source: MTLAcc, entry #1696, volume donated by Clemens.

———. *History of Queen Elizabeth.* Illus. New York: Harper & Brothers, 1876. 281 pp. [Publisher and pages conjectured.]

    Inscription: "S. L. Clemens, Hartford, 1877" on the endpaper.

    Catalog: *A1911,* "12mo, cloth, N.Y. 1876," quotes the signature, lot 1, sold for $1.25.

———. *Jonas's Stories; Related to Rollo and Lucy* (1839). Original stories issued separately in six volumes.

    No copies owned by Clemens have been discovered, but he obviously (see *The Rollo Books* entry) read these often-reprinted stories that included "Jonas a Judge," "Jonas on a Farm in Winter," "Jonas on a Farm in Summer," and others. He considered introducing Jonas and Rollo into *Tom Sawyer Abroad* in 1892 (NB 32, TS p. 19, MTP).

———. *Learning to Think.* The Little Learner Series. New York: Harper & Brothers, 1856. 192 pp.

    Source: MTLAcc, entry #1913, volume donated from Clemens's library by Clara Clemens Gabrilowitsch in 1910. In November 1877 James R. Osgood & Company of Boston billed Clemens for "1 set Learning to Think" (Scrapbook #10, p. 69, MTP). There were four other titles in this series, which had been published in 1856–1857: *Learning to Talk, Learning to Read, Learning about Common Things,* and *Learning about Right and Wrong.*

———. *Malleville.* Franconia Stories Series. Illus. New York: Harper & Brothers, 1904. 219 pp.

    Source: MTLAcc, entry #436, volume donated by Clemens.

———. *Mary Erskine.* Franconia Stories Series. Illus. New York: Harper & Brothers, 1904. 202 pp.

    Source: MTLAcc, entry #435, volume donated by Clemens.

———. *Mary, Queen of Scots.* Illus. New York: Harper & Brothers, 1900. 286 pp.

    Source: MTLAcc, entry #1912, volume donated from

Clemens's library by Clara Clemens Gabrilowitsch in 1910.

———. *Richard the Second of England*. Makers of History Series. Illus. New York: Harper & Brothers, 1904. 347 pp.
    Source: MTLAcc, entry #429, volume donated by Clemens.

———. *Rodolphus*. Franconia Stories Series. Illus. New York: Harper & Brothers, 1904. 227 pp.
    Source: MTLAcc, entry #1196, volume donated by Clemens.

———. *The Rollo Books: Work; Talk; Read; Play; Water; Air; Fire; Sky; School; Travels; Correspondence; Vacation; Museum; and Experiments*. 14 volumes. Original green cloth, gilt stamped, some wear to edges and corners. New York: Sheldon & Co., n.d. [The title page of Volume 2 is dated 1880.]
    Inscriptions: The *Work* volume is inscribed by Olivia Clemens on the front free endpaper: "Susie/19th March 1876/4th Birthday/Mamma." The front free endpaper of the *Talk* volume is inscribed by Olivia Clemens: "Susie Clemens/1876/Mamma Hartford." Below that inscription Olivia Clemens later added in a different ink a reference to the first story in the book: "'Little-girl-left-the-gate-open book'/Jean 1883–84." The *Vacation* volume is inscribed by Olivia Clemens in brown ink on the front free endpaper: "Susie Clemens/from Mamma/March 19th/Hartford CT." The *Play* volume is inscribed by Olivia Clemens in dark purple ink on the front free endpaper, "Susie Clemens/Hartford/1876." Olivia Clemens inscribed the *School* volume in light purple ink on the front free endpaper, "Susie Clemens/March 19th 1877." The *Work* volume is not inscribed, nor are the *Correspondence, Travels, Museum, Experiments, Sky, Fire, Air,* and *Water* volumes inscribed. On the front free endpapers of two volumes Olivia Clemens drew intricate pen-and-ink sketches. In the *Read* volume she sketched entwined branches around her inscription to Susy: "Susie/19th March 1876/4th Birthday/Mamma." In the *Play* volume on the right side of the endpaper she drew a vertical tree trunk with a large branch curving downward to the left, explaining in pencil on the next flyleaf: "(View of a branch of a beech tree seen from the study window in winter.)"
    Catalogs: *C1951*, 24 volumes belonging to Jean and Clara Clemens, no edition specified, J37; "Property from the Library of Mark Twain," Butterfield & Butterfield, San Francisco, Sale 6613 (16 July 1997), "14 vols.," lot 2701.
    Location: Mark Twain House and Museum, Hartford, Connecticut.
    Copies examined: Susy Clemens's copies of fourteen volumes, subsequently in the possession of Clara Clemens. Viewed in Hartford in 1997.
    The Clemens girls owned all of the books in the Rollo series, published initially between 1839 and 1855. Abbot assured parents about the "instructive" purposes of his books by their subtitles, such as *Rollo at Play; or, Safe Amusements* (1838). The virtuous little Rollo was well known to the Clemens family. On 29 July 1877 Olivia Clemens wrote to Clemens about reading to Susy "that ever interesting story in Rollo, 'Little Girl, *little girl,* you have left the gate open,' etc" (*LLMT*, pp. 202–204). This and other comments in her letter seem to take for granted Clemens's familiarity with the outline of the story; probably he had read it to Susy previously. He mentions Rollo's mother

in "A Cat Tale" (written in 1880). In December 1881 he jotted down an idea for burlesquing Rollo's tour of Paris, Rome, Naples, and other cities and countries with his uncle in *Rollo's Travels*: "Rollo & his Uncle Visit the Hotels. Make a sketch of it," he wrote in Notebook 19 (*N&J* 2: 415). He had another inspiration in May 1887: "Write a Rollo with a Jonas in it who is sodden with piety & self-righteousness" (NB 26, *N&J* 3: 293). His references to Abbott's characters thereafter were less caustic: in August 1892 he thought of arranging for Tom and Huck to meet Rollo and Jonas in Africa in *Tom Sawyer Abroad* (NB 32, TS p. 19); in June 1893 he had the idea of portraying Rollo's visit to heaven (NB 33, TS p. 20); in June 1898 he wanted to assemble Rollo and Jonas among other young heroes of fiction (NB 40, TS p. 27); and he listed the *Rollo Books* under a notebook heading "For Cheap Books" (NB 40, TS p. 58) in July 1899, possibly contemplating another publishing venture. He alluded to Jonas and Rollo once again in 1900 (NB 43, TS p. 3).
    Richard S. Lowry, *"Littery Man": Mark Twain and Modern Authorship* (New York: Oxford University Press, 1996), pp. 92–94, 98, 99.

———. *Rollo's Tour in Europe: In Geneva; In Scotland; In Naples; In Paris; In Switzerland; In Rome; In Holland; In London; On the Atlantic; On the Rhine*. 10 volumes. Original green cloth, gilt stamped, light wear to edges and corners. New York: Sheldon & Co., 1880.
    Inscriptions: Volumes 1–6 and 8–10 were inscribed by Olivia Clemens, "Jean Clemens/Hartford/1891/Mamma." Volume 7 was inscribed "Jean Clemens/from Clara L. Clemens/&/from Mamma."
    Catalogs: *C1951*, 24 volumes belonging to Jean and Clara Clemens, no edition specified, #J37; "Property from the Library of Mark Twain," Butterfield & Butterfield, San Francisco, Sale 6613 (16 July 1997), "10 vols.," lot 2701.
    Location: Mark Twain House and Museum, Hartford, Connecticut.
    Copies examined: Jean Clemens's unmarked copies of ten volumes. Viewed in Hartford in 1997.

———. *Stories of Rainbow and Lucky: Selling Lucky*. First edition. Original red cloth, gilt. Worn condition, with ink stains. New York: Harper, 1860. 183 pp.
    Inscription: signed by Julie Langdon in a childish hand, "Julie Langdon/1888./From Mama & P". [The last line was crossed out in the same ink of the inscription.]
    Presumably this copy was part of the Langdon family library before being given to Julie, the daughter of Charlie and Ida Clark Langdon. It is the fourth volume of a five-volume set recounting the adventures of a free fourteen-year-old African American named Rainbow who lives in the North but nevertheless suffers racial discrimination. In this volume he travels to Boston to sell a horse named Lucky. Very likely the volume would have been available at some point to Clara, Susy, and Jean Clemens (and their parents) during their sojourns in Elmira, New York.
    Location: collection of Kevin Mac Donnell, Austin, Texas (Mac Donnell to Alan Gribben, 11 March 2015).

———. *Stuyvesant*. Franconia Stories Series. Illus. New York: Harper & Brothers, 1904. 203 pp.
    Source: MTLAcc, entry #1169, volume donated by Clemens.

———. *Wallace; A Franconia Story.* Franconia Stories, No. 2. Illus. New York: Harper & Brothers, [cop. 1878]. 203 pp.

> Source: MTLAcc, entry #1861, volume donated from Clemens's library by Clara Clemens Gabrilowitsch in 1910.

———. *Wallace; A Franconia Story.* Illus. New York: Harper & Brothers, 1904. 203 pp.

> Source: MTLAcc, entry #1582, volume donated by Clemens.

———. *The Way to Do Good; or, The Christian Character Mature.* Tattered brown cloth, corner flaking, half of the spine missing. Boston: William Pierce, 1836. 348 pp.

> Provenance: bookplate #569 of the "J. Langdon Family Library" on the front pastedown endpaper.
>
> Catalog: Ball 2016 inventory, signature illegible, brown cloth, spine half missing, Jervis Langdon's Family Library #569.
>
> Location: Mark Twain Archive, Elmira College, Elmira, New York.
>
> Copy examined: unmarked copy available to Clemens whenever he visited the Langdons in Elmira. Examined on 27 May 2015.

ABBOTT, JOHN STEVENS CABOT (1805–1877). *Daniel Boone, The Pioneer of Kentucky.* American Pioneers and Patriots Series. Illus. New York: Dodd & Mead, 1872. 331 pp.

> Source: MTLAcc, entry #543, volume donated by Clemens. Subsequently sold to Dan Beard the artist, who lived in Redding, Connecticut.

The brother of Rollo's creator devoted himself to histories and biographies for adult readers, and the Clemenses' library contained a good many of these titles. Clemens was not always pleased with Abbott's writing, however. On 8 June 1883 Clemens was amused by nine-year-old Clara's efforts to comprehend her father's penciled comment on the flyleaf of Abbott's *Daniel Boone*: "A poor slovenly book; a mess of sappy drivel & bad grammar" ("A Record of the Small Foolishnesses of Susie & 'Bay' Clemens [Infants]," MS p. 101, ASSSCL; Griffin, *Family Sketch*, p. 88).

———. "Heroic Deeds of Heroic Men," *Harper's Magazine* 30.175 (December 1864): 3–20; (January 1865): 150–166; (March 1865): 425–439; and other installments through Volume 34.203 (April 1867): 559–571.

Mark Twain intended to quote from these seventeen installments for historical details in *Life on the Mississippi* (1883), but he eventually deleted the sections of the manuscript that relied on Abbott's accounts. At one time he had particularly wanted to use a clipping from the chapter that appeared in *Harper's Magazine* 32.189 (February 1866): 302, for an Appendix that would describe the Battle of Memphis, but this portion also was dropped from the final version of *Life on the Mississippi*. Abbott's essays were based on Union war records; each of them described events in a different theater of conflict, ranging from Arkansas to Texas to Virginia to Florida. They displayed a pro-Union bias (Abbott requested that participants of the battles address corrections to him in New Haven, Connecticut), and tended to imbue the episodes of the recent war with glorification befitting the title of his series. If Clemens did not read all of the installments, he probably studied those that pertained to the Mississippi Valley engagements.

———. *History of Cyrus the Great.* Illus. New York Harper & Brothers, 1904. 289 pp.

> Source: MTLAcc, entry #1152, volume donated by Clemens.

Cyrus the Great (550–529 BCE) founded the Persian Empire.

———. *History of Darius the Great.* Illus. New York: Harper & Brothers, 1899. 286 pp.

Darius the Great (558?-486 BCE) was an early king in Asia Minor.

> Source: MTLAcc, entry #1156, volume donated by Clemens.

———. *History of Genghis Khan.* Illus. New York: Harper & Brothers, 1904. 335 pp.

> Source: MTLAcc, entry #1155, volume donated by Clemens.

———. *History of Henry the Fourth, King of France and Navarre.* Illus. New York: Harper & Brothers, 1904. 335 pp.

> Source: MTLAcc, entry #1158, volume donated by Clemens

———. *History of Hernando Cortez.* Illus. New York: Harper & Brothers, 1900. 348 pp.

> Source: MTLAcc, entry #1157, volume donated by Clemens.

———. *The History of Hortense, the Daughter of Josephine, Queen of Holland, Mother of Napoleon III.* Illus. New York: Harper & Brothers, 1900. 379 pp.

> Source: MTLAcc, entry #1160, volume donated by Clemens.

———. *History of Joseph Bonaparte, King of Naples and of Italy.* Illus. New York: Harper & Brothers, 1904. 391 pp.

> Source: MTLAcc, entry #1161, volume donated by Clemens.

———. *History of Julius Caesar.* Illus. New York: Harper & Brothers, 1904. 278 pp.

> Source: MTLAcc, #1153, volume donated by Clemens.

———. *History of King Philip, Sovereign Chief of the Wampanoags.* Illus. New York: Harper & Brothers, 1904. 410 pp.

> Source: MTLAcc, entry #1151, volume donated by Clemens.

———. *History of Louis Philippe, King of the French.* Illus. New York: Harper & Brothers, [cop. 1871]. 405 pp.

> Source: MTLAcc, entry #1164, volume donated by Clemens.

———. *History of Madame Roland.* Illus. New York: Harper & Brothers, 1904. 304 pp.

> Source: MTLAcc, entry #1162, volume donated by Clemens.

———. *History of Margaret of Anjou [1430–1482].* Illus. New York: Harper & Brothers, 1904. 316 pp.

> Source: MTLAcc, entry #1159, volume donated by Clemens.

———. *History of Marie Antoinette [1755–1793].* Illus. New York: Harper & Brothers, 1904. 322 pp.

> Source: MTLAcc, entry #1163, volume donated by Clemens.

———. *The History of Napoleon Bonaparte [1769–1821].* 2 vols. New York: Harper & Brothers, [cop. 1883].

> Source: *MTLAcc,* entries #1497 and #1498, volumes donated by Clemens.

———. *History of Richard the Third.* Illus. New York: Harper

& Brothers, 1904. 337 pp.

> Source: MTLAcc, entry #1166, volume donated by Clemens.

———. *History of Romulus*. Illus. New York: Harper & Brothers, 1904. 310 pp.

> Source: MTLAcc, entry #1154, volume donated by Clemens.

———. *The History of the Civil War in America; Comprising a Full and Impartial Account of the Origin and Progress of the Rebellion, of the various Naval and Military Engagements, of the Heroic Deeds Performed by Armies and Individuals, and of Touching Scenes in the Field, the Camp, the Hospital, and the Cabin*. 2 vols. Illus. Marbled endpapers. New York: Henry Bill, 1863–1866.

> Inscription: a yellow "ORION CLEMENS" bookplate is at the top of the front marbled pastedown endpaper of Volume I.
>
> Location: Mark Twain Library, Redding, Connecticut (Volume I only, 507 pp.).
>
> Copy examined: Orion Clemens's copy of Volume I. Has the red ink accession number "2869". Viewed in 1970, on 15 June 1982, and again on 8 November 2019.

———. *History of William the Conqueror*. New York: Harper & Brothers, 1904. 291 pp.

> Source: MTLAcc, entry #1165, volume donated by Clemens.

ABERIGH-MACKAY, GEORGE ROBERT (1848–1881). *Serious Reflections and Other Contributions, Etc.* Bombay: Bombay Gazette Press, 1881.

> In March 1896 Clemens consulted this "brilliant little book called 'Serious Reflections' by the late George Aberigh-Mackay—the best & delightfulest work in its line that I have seen in many a day" (NB 36, TS p. 55) for information concerning the rank and prerogatives of Indian royalty. Clemens was visiting Jeypore at the time.

ABT, FRANZ (1819–1885). "Fly away birdling" (song, published in 1868).

> On 31 May 1876 Mark Twain gave a reading at the Asylum Hill Congregational Church. The audience was also entertained by vocalists who sang "Fly Away Birdling" (Andrews, *Nook Farm* [1950], p. 50). Abt was a prolific German composer of popular music.

ACKLOM, GEORGE MOREBY (1870–1959). *Margaret, An Idyll.* Portland, Maine: Smith & Sale, 1898. 106 pp.

> Source: MTLAcc, entry #2133, volume donated from Clemens's library by Clara Clemens Gabrilowitsch in 1910.
>
> Acklom, born in India to English parents, was educated at Cambridge before emigrating to Canada. In 1907 he would move to New York City and become a prolific editor, translator, literary critic, and writer.

ADAMS, CHARLES ABEL (1854–1921). *Pete's Devils.* Illus. Chicago: Scroll Publishing Co., 1902. 239 pp.

> Source: MTLAcc, entry #1914, volume donated from Clemens's library by Clara Clemens Gabrilowitsch in 1910.
>
> Fictionalized adventures of hunting bear, moose, and other game while gold prospecting on the Shushetna River in the Alaskan wilderness. Pete is a Native American guide who subscribes to local lore about devils who hold sway over the vicinity. The white hunters begin to believe him.

ADAMS, CHARLES FOLLEN (1842–1918). *Leedle Yawcob Strauss, and Other Poems.* Illustrated by Morgan J. Sweeney ("Boz").

Boston: Lee and Shepard, 1878. 147 pp.

> Source: MTLAcc, entry #2131, volume donated from Clemens's library by Clara Clemens Gabrilowitsch in 1910.
>
> Clemens and Adams corresponded in 1877 (MTP). In Mark Twain's Autobiographical Dictation of 31 July 1906 he named "Yawcob Strauss" as one of the American humorists who "are now heard of no more, and are no longer mentioned" (*MTE*, p. 201; *AutoMT* 2: 153). Adams employed a Pennsylvania Dutch dialect in writing humorous verses.

ADAMS, CHARLES FRANCIS, JR. (1835–1915). "Of Some Railroad Accidents," *Atlantic Monthly* 36 (November 1875): 571–582.

> In 1875 Charles Francis Adams, the brother of author and historian Henry Adams (1838–1918), was becoming something of a railroad expert; he would publish *Railroads: Their Origin and Problems* (1878), would serve as a state and federal railroad commissioner, and in 1884 would be named president of the Union Pacific Railroad. Soon after Clemens read Adams's essay in the November 1875 *Atlantic Monthly* he facetiously remarked to Howells that he was worried about "how awkwardly I do jumble words together; & how often I do use three words where one would answer." Alluding to Adams's recent article, he predicted: "I shall become as slovenly a writer as Charles Francis Adams if I don't look out," but then he added that he wrote this "in jest" because he would never "drop so far toward his & Bret Harte's level." He gave Howells an invented example of their type of verbose, cluttered sentence (23 November 1875, *MTHL*, p. 112).
>
> Clemens probably felt that Adams's article did not merit its appearance in the same issue in which installments of Howells's *Private Theatricals* and Henry James' *Roderick Hudson* were published. Adams's piece related the details of six well-known rail accidents that resulted in deaths. His very first sentence would have prompted Clemens to reach for a pencil to mark revisions: "The assertion has a strange, at first, indeed, almost a harsh and brutal sound, and yet it is unquestionably true, that, so far as the general welfare, the common good of mankind is concerned, few lives are so profitably expended as those of the unfortunate victims of railroad accidents" (p. 571). Adams's optimism sprang from his belief that each accident and its resultant investigation brought about new precautions and safety inventions. Clemens—who rode railways regularly—might have shared Adams's appreciation for this progress, but he was invariably offended by periphrastic sentences.

ADAMS, EDWARD PAYSON (1833–1897). *Story Sermons from Les Misérables.* Illustrated by Sarah Taylor Adams (1869–1894). Preface by Mabel Gardiner (Hubbard) Bell (1857–1923). Rochester, New York: Western New York Institution for Deaf Mutes, 1895. 152 pp.

> Source: MTLAcc, entry #1863, volume donated from Clemens's library by Clara Clemens Gabrilowitsch in 1910.
>
> The Reverend Edward Payson Adams was a Universalist minister in Dunkirk, New York. His daughter Sarah Taylor Adams attended the Rochester School for the Deaf before moving to New York City and becoming an art teacher. Mabel Bell, the wife of the inventor Alexander Graham Bell, was herself deaf and had become a benefactor to

causes assisting the deaf.

ADAMS, HENRY [BROOKS] (1838–1918). *Democracy, An American Novel*. Leisure Hour Series. New York: Henry Holt and Co., 1880. 374 pp. Reissued by the same firm in 1883. [Clemens's edition has not been determined.]

Clemens entered the title and publisher of this work in Notebook 22 (*N&J* 3: 50) in 1884, presumably unaware of the identity of its author. *Democracy* had been published anonymously, and was mistakenly assumed by many to be the work of either John Hay or Clarence King.

Critics have been baffled and displeased by the lack of evidence indicating that the historian, novelist, editor, and Harvard professor Adams and Clemens were acquainted, or at least that they knew each other very well. An illuminating study of thematic parallels in the two men's writings is available in Tony Tanner's "The Lost America—The Despair of Henry Adams and Mark Twain," *Modern Age* 5.3 (Summer 1961): 299–310; reprinted in *Mark Twain: A Collection of Critical Essays*, ed. Henry Nash Smith. Twentieth Century Views Series (Englewood Cliffs, New Jersey: Prentice-Hall, 1963), pp. 159–174, which summarized their strangely similar personal tragedies and astutely analyzed the identical intellectual questions they explored in their writings. Tanner did not suggest direct mutual influence, but thought it "strange that Adams and Clemens never seem to have met," especially since they are "two of the most notable alienated figures of their age" (p. 309). Tanner speculated that Mark Twain's selecting the name Henry Adams to use in Section 6 of "What Is Man?" (written in 1905) resulted from his knowledge of the real Henry Adams. But Paul Baender—*What is Man? and Other Philosophical Writings* (1973), p. 553—effectively refuted this hypothesis, showing that "Adams" and another name that Twain employed in "What Is Man?" had been invented and utilized in Twain's previous fiction.

Charles Vandersee—"The Mutual Awareness of Mark Twain and Henry Adams," *English Language Notes* 5.4 (June 1968): 285–292—discovered that, contrary to a widely shared supposition, Mark Twain and Henry Adams did meet at least once—on 28 January 1886, when Twain was visiting Washington, D. C. for a Senate committee hearing on copyright legislation. Vandersee relied on an article by Joseph B. Gilder, "Glimpses of John Hay," *The Critic* 47.3 (September 1905): 248–252, in which Gilder reported an evening he spent at the home of Henry Adams in the company of Adams, Twain, John Hay, and "the editor of the *Century Magazine*" (Richard Watson Gilder). "Mark Twain was droll as usual" and Henry Adams "lived up to his reputation as a graceful and pregnant talker" (p. 248).

Unfortunately Vandersee then went on to depict that evening's conversation as the basis for Twain's using the name Henry Adams to represent a fictional unhappy man in "What Is Man?" Vandersee also found significance in Mark Twain's naming a character Henry Adams in "The £1,000,000 *Bank*-Note (1892)," though he conceded that this Adams was unlike the real man in every respect. The fact is that Twain had a lifelong affinity for the name "Adam," and the name of Henry Adams probably occurred to him simply as a convenient designation for an Anglo-American. Twain's reliance on the name in 1892 most likely proves nothing except that the actual Adams was only an ephemeral acquaintance: Twain typically displayed a delicate reluctance to allude in print to people he knew well—especially in regard to using their names for literary characters. While Vandersee's conclusions about Twain's employment of the name "Henry Adams" are questionable, his collection of facts about Adams's interest in Mark Twain's work is illuminating.

Paul L. Kegel, "Henry Adams and Mark Twain: Two Views of Medievalism," *Mark Twain Journal* 15.3 (Winter 1970–1971): 11–21; Jeanne M. Schinto, "The Autobiographies of Mark Twain and Henry Adams: Life Studies in Despair," *Mark Twain Journal* 17.4 (Summer 1975): 5–7; Warren L. Chernaik, "The Ever-Receding Dream: Henry Adams and Mark Twain as Autobiographers," *First-Person Singular: Studies in American Autobiography*, ed. A. Robert Lee (London: Vision; New York: St. Martin's, 1988), pp. 72–1903.

ADAMS, JOHN (1735–1826). *Familiar Letters of John Adams and His Wife Abigail Adams [1744–1818], During the Revolution. With a Memoir of Mrs. Adams*. Ed. by Charles Francis Adams (1807–1886). Green cloth, gilt lettering and design. New York: Hurd and Houghton, 1876. 424 pp.

Inscription: inscribed by Olivia Clemens on the front flyleaf in black ink, "S. L. Clemens/Hartford". Someone jotted "OLC" hastily in pencil on the upper right hand corner of the front free endpaper.

Marginalia: a few pencil markings. On page 9 Clemens drew a heavy vertical pencil bracket around the portion of a paragraph in John Adams' letter of 2 July 1774 in which Adams advised his wife to keep his letters in a safe and "preserve" them, since "they may exhibit to our posterity a kind of picture of the manners, opinions, and principles of these times of perplexity, danger, and distress."

Location: Mark Twain Library, Redding, Connecticut. Displays the Library's purple oval stamps.

Copy examined: Clemens's copy. Displays the original Mark Twain Library accession number in red ink ("2832"). Examined in 1970, on 15 June 1982, and again on 10 November 2019.

Mark Twain joked about John Quincy Adams's reported last words ("This is the last of earth. I am content.") in a sketch titled "Earthquake Almanac" (17 October 1865), writing, "This is the last of earth-quakes" (*Early Tales & Sketches* 2: 299). He referred to these sentences again in "The Last Words of Great Men" (Buffalo *Express*, 11 September 1869). Clemens held the editor of the Adamses' correspondence, Charles Francis Adams (1807–1886), in high regard; during a newspaper interview in 1876 he spoke of him as "a pure man, a proved statesman" ("Political Views of a Humorist," New York *Herald*, 28 August 1876; Scharnhorst, *Complete Interviews*, p. 6).

ADAMS, (SIR) JOHN (1857–1934). *The Herbartian Psychology Applied to Education, Being a Series of Essays Applying the Psychology of Johann Friedrich Herbart*. Boston: D. C. Heath & Co., 1897. 284 pp. English edition: London: Isbister, 1897. 284 pp. [Clemens's edition has not been identified.]

Catalog: ListABP (1910), "Psychology, Adams", no other information supplied.

Adams sent Clemens a copy of his book in 1897 but Clemens did not respond until Adams inquired about his opinion. On 5 December 1898 Clemens wrote from the Hotel

Krantz in Vienna to praise *The Herbartian Psychology* and express agreement with its principles. Adams was then on the faculty of the Free Church Training College in Glasgow. Clemens's letter was published in part by Adams in his *Everyman's Psychology* (Garden City, New York: Doubleday, Doran & Co., 1929), pp. 202–203. Lawrence Clark Powell published its entire text in "An Unpublished Mark Twain Letter," *American Literature* 13.4 (January 1942): 405–407. Clemens apologized for reading the volume so slowly: "I cannot take things in swiftly if I wish to understand them—and also make marginal notes" (p. 406). He informed Adams that he had taken the book to bed with him "between 10 yesterday morning and 12 at night" and thus "was able to read to page 232 without a break—an uninterrupted view" (Powell, pp. 405–406). Although Clemens mentioned a "mind-scheme" of his own that he had written the previous summer, he claimed that "(shall I confess it?) I have never read Locke nor any other of the many philosophers quoted by you" (p. 406). Clemens seemed to assume that Adams would concur with his own theory that "man's proudest possession—his mind—is a mere machine."

John S. Tuckey traced the effect of Adams's book on Mark Twain's "The Great Dark" (written 1898), which treats the dream psychology of the mind (*WWD?*, p. 17). Subsequently Clemens met Adams in London, on 2 June 1900 (NB 43, TS p. 14). Clemens's copy of *Herbartian Psychology*, which contained his "marginal notes," has never been found. Despite Clemens's enthusiasm for Adams's treatise, in 1911 Adams would publish an extremely unsympathetic criticism of Twain's "What Is Man?" (published anonymously in 1906, it had appeared in England after the author's death with his name on the title page). Adams dismissed Twain's entire Socratic dialogue in "Mark Twain as Psychologist," *The Bookman* (London) 39 (March 1911): 270–27, stating that Twain's style was unsuited for "this class of composition" and that he was obviously "working in an unfamiliar medium." Twain's basic assumption of man's dual mental nature Adams rejected outright. He concluded by advising readers to avoid this "discouraging" book; "we can well believe that many temperaments will be greatly depressed by Twain's ingenious pages."

Gregg Camfield, "Transcendental Hedonism? Sex, Song, Food, and Drink in *No. 44, The Mysterious Stranger* and 'My Platonic Sweetheart,'" *Centenary Reflections on Mark Twain's* No. 44, The Mysterious Stranger, ed. Joseph Csicsila and Chad Rohman (Columbia: University of Missouri Press, 2009), pp. 127–143.

ADAMS, JOSEPH HENRY (1867–1941). *Harper's Machinery Book for Boys.* Half-title: Harper's Practical Books for Boys. Illus. New York: Harper & Bothers, 1909. 373 pp.
Source: MTLAcc, entry #1181, volume donated by Clemens.

ADAMS, MYRON (1841–1895). *The Continuous Creation; An Application of the Evolutionary Philosophy to the Christian Religion.* Boston: Houghton, Mifflin and Co., 1889. 259 pp.
Source: MTLAcc, entry #795, volume donated by Clemens.

ADAMS, SAMUEL HOPKINS (1871–1958). "The Great American Fraud: The Scavengers," *Collier's* 37.26 (22 September 1906):

16–18, 24–25.
K. Patrick Ober, *Mark Twain and Medicine: "Any Mummery Will Cure"* (Columbia: University of Missouri Press, 2003), 68–71, 306–307 documented Mark Twain's involvement in questioning the truthfulness of Dr. Isaac Oppenheimer in connection with Adams's muckraking exposé of those claiming to cure addictions.

ADAMS, SARAH (FLOWER) (1805–1848). "Nearer, my God, to Thee" (hymn, published in 1841). Lowell Mason (1792–1872), composer.
Either Clemens or his wife Olivia marked this hymn in their copy of *Laudes Domini: A Selection of Spiritual Songs, Ancient and Modern* (1884), compiled by C. S. Robinson. (See that Catalog entry.) The dying Helen in Mark Twain's "Was It Heaven? or Hell?" (1902) hears the organ music from her daughter's funeral downstairs: "Why—it is a hymn! and the sacredest of all, the most touching, the most consoling. . . . 'Nearer, my God, to Thee,/Nearer to Thee,/E'en though it be a cross/That raiseth me.'" Twain could count on this passage, occurring near the end of his story, to wring his readers' emotions. The hymn had gained enduring popularity in 1859, when Lowell Mason set it to music. The solemn melody of the hymn's first stanza evoked the pathos of bereavement.

ADAMS, WILLIAM TAYLOR (1822–1897), pseud. "Oliver Optic."
In a letter to William Dean Howells written on 4 July 1877 Clemens alluded to "Oliver Optic," the pseudonym of the prolific Massachusetts author of stories and novels for boys (*MTHL*, p. 187).

ADDISON, JOSEPH (1672–1719).
Minnie M. Brashear saw traces of the "character" essays from Joseph Addison and Richard Steele's *Spectator*, a periodical of social satire and literary criticism, in Mark Twain's earliest sketches, including his portrayal of Jim Smiley (*MTSM*, p. 228). Whatever the case, Twain seldom alluded to either writer. In "A Memorable Midnight Experience" (1874) he mentioned seeing Addison's monument in Westminster Abbey—a complimentary reference, but in Chapter 36 of *A Tramp Abroad* (1880) he comically attributed the phrase "up a stump" to the English essayist. Carlyle Smythe believed he was translating Mark Twain's genuine sentiments in 1898 when he observed that "Addison and Goldsmith are thrown away upon him" ("The Real 'Mark Twain,'" p. 31). This may be another instance where Clemens's early veneration gave way to a hostile re-estimate at a later period, but Addison hardly seems to have been a vital part of his literary development.

An Address to the Presbyterians of Kentucky: Proposing a Plan for the Instruction and Emancipation of Their Slaves by a Committee of the Synod of Kentucky. Newburyport, Kentucky: Charles Whipple, 1836. 36 pp.
Bound with six other anti-slavery pamphlets; see the Catalog entry for William E. Channing, *Letter to J. G. Birney.*

ADE, GEORGE (1866–1944). *Fables in Slang* (comic sketches, published in 1899).
Olivia Clemens noted on 19 June 1902 that "Mr. George Ade (author of Fables in Slang)" joined Dr. Clarence Rice and Rodman Gilder for luncheon with the Clemenses at their Riverdale home (OLC's Diary, DV 161, MTP). The opening sketch in *Fables*, "The Fable of the Visitor Who Got a Lot for Three Dollars," describes a phrenologist

who delivered invariably favorable opinions of his clients' skulls; Ade drew the characteristic moral that "A good Jolly is worth Whatever you Pay for it" (*Fables in Slang* [Chicago: Herbert S. Stone,1900], p. 7). Mark Twain depicted a strikingly similar phrenological charlatan in Book II (Chapter 2) of his travesty of history textbooks, "The Secret History of Eddypus, the World-Empire," written in 1901 and 1902 (*FM* [1972], pp. 349–353).

Gribben, "Mark Twain, Phrenology and the 'Temperaments': A Study of Pseudoscientific Influence" (1972). (A revised version of this essay appears in Volume One of the present work.)

———. *Forty Modern Fables*. New York: R. H. Russell, [cop. 1900]. 303 pp.

Source: MTLAcc, entry # 1508, volume donated by Clemens.

———. *More Fables*. Illustrated by Clyde J[ames]. Newman (1873–1959). New York: Duffield & Co., 1906. 218 pp.

Inscription: the front free endpaper is signed in pencil: "Gerald R. Maloney."

Marginalia: a pencil sketch on the front pastedown endpaper depicts a rakish young man wearing a Panama hat and smoking a cigarette. Someone has printed the name "Mr. Knight Byrd" beneath the picture.

Provenance: Antenne-Dorrance Collection, Rice Lake, Wisconsin.

Location: Mark Twain Archive, Gannett-Tripp Learning Center, Elmira College, Elmira, New York.

Copy examined: Clemens's copy. Page 11 is folded down. Examined on 28 May 2015. This copy was temporarily lost in 1970 when I visited Rice Lake, but subsequently the book was discovered in a school library in Eau Claire, Wisconsin and was restored to the Antenne-Dorrance Collection in 1971. Ann Cameron Harvey's checklist of the collection in 1966 stated that this volume contained no markings, so the now-present penciled signature and drawing were evidently added while the book was missing.

———. *People You Know*. Illustrated by John T[inney]. Mc-Cutcheon (1870–1949) and others. New York: R. H. Russell, 1903. 224 pp.

Source: MTLAcc, entry #1352, volume donated by Clemens.

———. *Pink Marsh. A Story of the Streets and Town*. Illustrated by John T[inney]. McCutcheon (1870–1949). New York: Grosset & Dunlap, [cop. 1897]. 196 pp.

Inscription: signed "S. L. Clemens, 1905, Dec. 29. From Wm. Dean Howells" on the front pastedown endpaper.

Catalogs: ListABP (1910), "Pink Marsh, Ade"; *C1951*, #47c, sold for $12.50. Listed among books signed by Mark Twain.

Location: Franklin Meine Collection, University of Illinois at Urbana-Champaign.

Clemens may not have encountered this book until Howells sent him this copy in 1905. On 22 July 1908 he wrote to Howells from Redding: "Thank you once more for introducing me to the incomparable Pink Marsh. I have been reading him again after this long interval, & my admiration of the book has overflowed all limits, all frontiers. I have personally known each of the characters in the book & can testify that they are all true to the facts, & as exact as if they had been drawn to scale" (*MTHL*, p.

832). He also praised the illustrator, whom he declared to be "the peer of the writer." Ade based his novel about a bootblack who becomes a railroad porter on a series of sketches he had written for the Chicago *Record*, and Clemens obviously welcomed a book in dialect that dealt with an African American of the urban North. "Pink—oh, the shiftless, worthless, lovable black darling! Howells, he deserves to live forever," he declared (*MTHL*, p. 832). In his Autobiographical Dictation of 31 July 1906 Mark Twain mentioned Ade as a currently notable American humorist (*AutoMT* 2: 152).

Henry B. Wonham, "'I Want a Real Coon': Mark Twain and Late-Nineteenth-Century Ethnic Caricature," *American Literature* 72.1 (March 2000): 117–152.

———. *True Bills*. Illus. New York: Harper & Brothers, 1904. 154 pp.

Source: MTLAcc, entry #1351, volume donated by Clemens.

Adventures at Sea, by F[rank]. H. Converse, John R. Coryell, Rear-Admiral T. H. Stevens, Maria Louise Pool, and Others. Illus. New York: Harper & Brothers, 1908. 198 pp.

Source: MTLAcc, entry #519, volume donated by Clemens. Accounts of whale-hunts, storms, wrecks, castaways, rescues, and other sea experiences.

Adventures in Field and Forest, by Frank H[amilton]. Spearman [1859–1937], Harold Martin, F. S. Palmer, William Drysdale, and Others. Illus. New York: Harper & Brothers, 1909. 212 pp.

Source: MTLAcc, entry #1200, volume donated by Clemens.

Adventures of Famous Travellers in Many Lands, with Descriptions of Manners, Customs, and Places. Thrilling Adventures on Land and Sea. Illus. New York: W. L. Allison Co., [189–]. 299 pp.

Source: MTLAcc, entry #1867, volume donated from Clemens's library by Clara Clemens Gabrilowitsch in 1910. Jean Clemens's copy.

Adventures with Indians, by Philip V[errell]. Mighels, W[illiam]. O[sborn]. Stoddard, Major G. B. Davis, U.S.A., Frances McElrath, and Others. Harper's Adventures Series. Illus. New York: Harper & Brothers, 1908. 234 pp.

Source: MTLAcc, entry #417, volume donated by Clemens.

AESOP (c. 620–c. 560 BCE). *Aesop's Fables. A New Edition, with Proverbs and Applications. With Over One-Hundred Illustrations*. London: Bliss, Sands & Co., 1897. [Aesop's identity is so ancient and obscure that some authorities believe a collective authorship was eventually attributed to "Aesop."]

Source: checklist of books in the possession of Mr. and Mrs. James Dorrance, Rice Lake, Wisconsin, compiled in 1966 by Ann Cameron Harvey: "*Aesop's Fables*, London: Bliss, Sands & Co., 1897. No markings. Uncut pages."

Provenance: formerly part of the Antenne-Dorrance Collection, Rice Lake, Wisconsin, but now missing. The book was present when Ann Cameron Harvey compiled a checklist of the Antenne-Dorrance Collection in 1966; it was missing when I visited Rice Lake in 1970 and it did not accompany the other association copies that Robert and Katharine Antenne donated to the Mark Twain Archive at Elmira College. Harvey's notes furnished the information for this entry.

Location: currently unknown.

Clemens requested a copy of *Aesop's Fables* in a letter Olivia Clemens wrote on his behalf to Chatto & Windus on 13 September 1898 (Welland, *Mark Twain in England*, p. 189; MTP).

————. *Bewick's Select Fables of Aesop and Others. . . . I. Fables Extracted from Dodsley's (Select Fables of Aesop). II. Fables with Reflections [selected from S. Croxall's translation of Aesop]. . . . III. Fables in Verse. To Which Are Prefixed, the Life of Aesop, and an Essay upon Fable by Oliver Goldsmith [1730–1774]. . . . Faithfully Reprinted from the Rare Newcastle Edition Published by T. Saint in 1784. With the Original Wood Engravings by Thomas Bewick [1753–1828], and an Illustrated Preface by Edwin Pearson.* London: Bickers & Son, [1871]. 312 pp. [The publisher and date are conjectured, since this edition was reprinted in 1878 by Longman & Company of London.]

Catalog: *A1911*, "4to, half roan (binding broken), Lond., n.d.," lot 39, sold for $2.50.

————. *The Fables of Aesop.* New York: Hurd & Houghton, [cop. 1865]. 311 pp.

Source: MTLAcc, entry #2160, volume donated from Clemens's library by Clara Clemens Gabrilowitsch in 1910. On 14 July 1880 Estes & Lauriat of Boston billed Clemens the amount of $1.35 for "1 Aesop," very likely this book. Clemens paid for it on 20 July 1880 (MTP Receipts File). Olivia Clemens mentioned in a letter of February 1885 that "the children have been reading to me from their private books tonight, . . . Clara from Aesop's Fables" (*Twainian* 39.5 [September-October 1980]: 3).

Minnie M. Brashear commented on a puzzling incongruity: despite Mark Twain's experiments with fables such as "The Five Boons of Life" (and in spite of his ability to fashion anecdotes about animals, one might add), "no reference to Aesop or La Fontaine is to be found in his [literary] writings" *(MTSM* [1934], p. 233). However, Twain did mention Aesop in an 1895 interview: "They [the temperance reformers] remind me of one of *Aesop's Fables*, where the fox lost his tail in a trap, and then called all the other foxes together, . . . and urged them all to dispense with their caudal appendages" ("Mark Twain on Prohibition," *Licensing Guardian*, New South Wales, 1895; Scharnhorst, *Complete Interviews*, p. 219).

AFLALO, FREDERICK GEORGE (1870–1918). *A Sketch of the Natural History of Australia, with Some Notes on Sport.* Illustrated by F. Seth. London: Macmillan and Co., 1896. 307 pp.

Mark Twain requested a copy of this book from Chatto & Windus on 13 November 1896, supplying the name of its author, title, and publisher (Berg, NYPL). He was engaged in writing *Following the Equator* (1897) at a London address.

AGASSIZ, ELIZABETH CABOT (CARY) (1822–1907), ed. *Louis Agassiz, His Life and Correspondence.* 2 vols. Boston: Houghton, Mifflin and Co., 1885. Reprinted in 1886, 1887, 1888, 1890, and in other years. [Clemens's edition is undetermined.]

This book probably helped alter Mark Twain's attitude toward Louis Agassiz (1807–1873), the famous naturalist. In Twain's early writings he employed Agassiz's name for comic effect. In a letter to the *Alta California* on 6 June 1867 he claimed that he had mistaken Bladder-nose Jake in Harry Hill's saloon for Professor Agassiz of Harvard

(MTTMB [1940], pp. 270–274). He had similar fun with Agassiz's serious-minded pursuits in "Concerning a Rumor," a piece published in the January 1871 issue of *The Galaxy*; pretending to refute a rumor that Agassiz was losing his sanity, he explained that Agassiz's eccentric behavior merely resulted from his efforts to catch and identify the thousand varieties of flies. But after Twain read the biographical work edited by Agassiz' wife, his tone became more respectful. He referred to the book in January 1898 while he was living in London: "You have an instance of this [X-ray vision] in the biography of Agassiz. In a dream he *saw through* the stone that contained a fossil shell, & woke up & drew a picture of that shell; & when he broke open the stone, his picture was correct" (NB40, *MTN*, p. 350). Olivia Clemens wrote to Clara on 10 July 1903 about her admiration for Agassiz's fortitude in facing the prospect of blindness when he was a young man; he practiced the study of fossils by touch alone so that he would not be forced to give up his career (TS in MTP). In Notebook 48, probably in 1906, Clemens wrote regretfully, "I heard Phillips & Agassiz only once" (TS p. 10). Possibly Clemens was referring to a lecture Agassiz gave in Elmira, New York on 21 November 1868; Clemens arrived in Elmira from Pittsburgh that very day (Fears, *Day by Day* 1.2: 324). The Elmira *Daily Advertiser* reported on Agassiz's lecture on 14, 23, and 28 November 1868 (Mary Boewe to Alan Gribben, 19 November 1987).

AGUILAR, GRACE (1816–1847). *The Days of Bruce; A Story from Scottish History* (novel, posthumously published in 1852). Often reprinted in the 1870s and 1880s.

This tale of the Scottish struggle for independence in the fourteenth century had great appeal for the Clemens girls, perhaps because its central characters included three dauntless women. Olivia Clemens recorded in her diary on 12 July 1885 that she and her children "are reading together" this book at Quarry Farm, and are enjoying it "very much" (DV 161, MTP). According to Albert Bigelow Paine, the Clemens children named their Quarry Farm playhouse "Ellerslie" from "Grace Aguilar's *The Days of Robert* [*sic*] *Bruce*" (Paine, *MTB* [1912], p. 824; Salsbury, *S&MT* [1965], p. 204). But see the Catalog entry for Jane Porter's *The Scottish Chiefs* (1810), which describes a more probable source for the girls' fascination with Ellerslie and merely alludes to Robert the Bruce. Aguilar's novel, on the other hand, was centered on Robert the Bruce (1274–1329)—his intrigues, alliances, battles, negotiations, and victories—rather than on the sad story of the guerrilla chieftain William Wallace (c. 1272–1305), associated in legend with a vicinity supposedly called Ellerslie. Many years later Clara recalled *The Days of Bruce* as one of the girls' favorite books, and implied that her father sometimes read it to them *(MFMT* [1931], p. 25).

AHN, JOHANN FRANZ (1796–1865). *Ahn's First German Book, Being the First Division of Ahn's Rudiments of the German Language.* Ed. by Peter Henn. New York: E. Steiger & Co., [cop. 1873].

Inscription: signed on the front pastedown endpaper, "S. L. Clemens, Hartford, Feb. 2, '76".

Marginalia: numerous notes by Clemens. On page 63 beside "Here they are" Clemens wrote "I say Hier sind sie."

Catalogs: ListABP (1910), "First German Reader, Ahn",

two listings; *A1911*, "12mo, boards, N.Y. 1873, . . . with numerous additions and emendations in Clemens' autograph," quotes signature, lot 233, sold for $1.50; George D. Smith, New York City, "Catalogue of Books, No. 165" (1911), quotes the signature and one marginal note, item #164, $4.50.

Brandi Besalke, "'Ein sehr glueklicher Kind, you bet': Mark Twain and the German Language," *Mark Twain Annual* 5 (2007): 109–122.

———. *Ahn's First German Book*. Ed. by Peter Henn. New York: E. Steiger, 1873. 64 pp.

Catalog: ListABP (1910), "German Primer", no other information provided.

Source: MTLAcc, entry #368, volume donated by Clemens.

———. *Ahn's Second German Book*. Ed. by Peter Henn. New York: E. Steiger, 1873. 194 pp.

Source: MTLAcc, entry #369, volume donated by Clemens.

———. *First French Course* [unidentified edition].

Catalog: ListABP (1910), "First French Course", no other information supplied.

———. *Udvalgte Skitzer [Selected Skits]*. [An unidentified Danish translation of Mark Twain's *Sketches, New and Old*].

Catalog: ListABP (1910), "Udvalgte Skitzer, Ahn", no other information supplied.

AIKEN, GEORGE L. (1830–1876). *Uncle Tom's Cabin; or, Life Among the Lowly* (play, produced in New York, 1853).

Clemens probably was introduced to Harriet Beecher Stowe's novel through this crude adaptation for the stage written by Aiken, a dime-novelist. In his letter of 2 February 1867 to the *Alta California* Clemens recalled his first sojourn in New York City: "When I was here in '53, . . . 'Uncle Tom's Cabin' was in full blast and had already run one hundred and fifty nights. Everybody went there in elegant toilettes and cried over Tom's griefs. But now. . . . Uncle Tom draws critical, self-possessed groups of negroes and children at Barnum's Museum" (*MTTMB* [1940], p. 84).

AIKIN, LUCY (1781–1864). *Memoirs of the Court of King James the First*. 2 vols. Boston: Wells & Lilly, 1822. [Publisher conjectured.]

Catalog: *A1911*, "2 vols., 8vo, calf (somewhat rubbed), Bost. 1822," lot 3, sold for $4.50.

———. *Memoirs of the Court of Queen Elizabeth*. Philadelphia: Abraham Small, 1823.

Roger B. Salomon's introduction to a never-published edition of Mark Twain's *The Prince and the Pauper* identified this edition as one of the background books to which Twain referred in his working notes for the novel (DV115; Salomon's TS in MTP). Salomon pointed out that Twain ultimately mentioned the young Elizabeth in the novel far less frequently than he originally intended. The Iowa-California Edition of *The Prince and the Pauper*, ed. Victor Fischer and Lin Salamo (Berkeley: University of California Press, 1979), did not cite Aikin's book as one of Twain's sources.

AINSWORTH, WILLIAM HARRISON (1805–1882). *Jack Sheppard; A Romance*. Illustrated by George Cruikshank (1792–1878). London, n. d. [First edition published in London in 1839; reprinted thereafter by various publishers in England and the United States. Clemens's edition has not been established.]

Inscription: the flyleaf is signed "S. L. Clemens, London, 1874."

Catalog: *A 1911*, "8vo, cloth (loose), Lond., n.d.," lot 4, sold for $5.

Clemens was familiar with this lurid if idealized story of criminal life in eighteenth-century England long before he purchased a copy in London. In an early character sketch entitled "Jul'us Caesar" (1856?) he ridiculed a possibly fictional boardinghouse lodger who "was decidedly literary, after a fashion of his own, and . . . such instructive and entertaining books as . . . 'Jack Sheppard,' &c., &c., were food and drink to his soul" (TS in MTP, DV400). Ainsworth's 1839 novel was based on the life of a famous London robber, thief, and escape artist, born in 1702, who was finally caught and hanged in 1724.

———. *The Lord Mayor of London; or, City Life in the Last Century*. Copyright Edition. 2 vols. Collection of British Authors Series. Leipzig: B. Tauchnitz, 1862. 314 pp.

Source: MTLAcc, entries #1830 and #1831, both volumes donated from Clemens's library by Clara Clemens Gabrilowitsch in 1910.

ALCOTT, LOUISA MAY (1832–1888). *Little Men: Life at Plumfield with Jo's Boys* (novel, published in 1871).

In Alcott's sequel to *Little Women* an orphan boy arrives at an unconventional school conducted by the former Jo March and her new husband. Coleman O. Parsons conceded that his basis for supposing that Clemens read *Little Men* to his daughters must be "purely conjectural." Parsons did produce a convincing demonstration of similarities between the burning of a toy village by the Plumfield children in Chapter 8 of *Little Men* and the fire episode in "The Chronicle of Young Satan" (written 1897–1900), during which Philip Traum callously brushes the fleeing victims back into the flames ("Background of *The Mysterious Stranger* [1960], p. 66).

Gibson, ed., *MSM* (1969), p. 22 n. 49; Linda Black, "Louisa May Alcott's *Huckleberry Finn*," *Mark Twain Journal* 21.2 (Summer 1982): 15–17.

———. *Little Women; or, Meg, Jo, Beth and Amy* (novel, published in two parts in 1868 and 1869).

"Some of the Little Women" was how Mark Twain signed a poem entitled "The Last Word" that appeared in the 25 September 1869 issue of the Buffalo *Express* (*OPMT* [1966], p. 70). A letter from Olivia and Samuel Clemens to Susan L. Crane written on 16 April 1870 begins, "My darling Little Woman" (*MTLet* 4: 107). On 1 January 1881 Clemens received a bill from Brown & Gross, Hartford booksellers, for the purchase of *Little Women* on 16 December 1880, probably as a Christmas gift (MTP). The book would have been almost a mandatory acquisition for any late-nineteenth-century household containing young girls.

Alcott is sometimes cited as one of those who condemned Twain's *Adventures of Huckleberry Finn* (1885); she allegedly denounced the novel as unfit for "our pure-minded lads and lasses" and suggested that Twain "had best stop writing" such stories (for example, Justin Kaplan, *Mr. Clemens and Mark Twain* [1966], p. 268, quoting A. L. Vogelback, "The Publication and Reception of *Huckleberry Finn*," *American Literature* 11.3 [November 1939]: 260–272). Alcott's purported reaction fits nicely with the censure of the novel by the Library Committee of Concord, Massachusetts. The problem is that the *only* source for her supposed castigation of Twain's book appeared in the first chapter ("The Titaness") of the not-always-reliable *The Mauve Decade: American Life at the End of the Nineteenth Century* (1926) by Thomas Beer (1889–1940). Beer's "Appendix" to *The Mauve Decade* cites "an unprinted letter [from Alcott] to Frances Hedges Butler" as his text for her remark. Unless this long-missing letter ever turns up, we should be cautious about placing too much credibility in Beer's quotation.

Two very rewarding studies have looked at *Little Women* in connection with Mark Twain: Roberta Seelinger Trites, *Twain, Alcott, and the Birth of the Adolescent Reform Novel* (Iowa City: University of Iowa Press, 2007); and Beverly Lyon Clark, *The Afterlife of* Little Women (Baltimore: Johns Hopkins University Press, 2014).

———. *Little Women; or, Meg, Jo, Beth, and Amy.* Illustrated by Frank T[hayer]. Merrill (1848–1923). Boston: Little, Brown & Co., [cop. 1896]. 586 pp.
   Source: MTLAcc, entry #462, volume donated by Clemens.
———. *Little Women; or, Meg, Jo, Beth, and Amy.* Illustrated by Frank T[hayer]. Merrill (1848–1923). New York: Harper & Brothers, [cop. 1896]. 586 pp.
   Source: MTLAcc, entry #1182, volume donated by Clemens.
———. *Moods.* Boston: Loring, Publisher, 1864. 297 pp.
   Assembling evidence of coincidental phenomena in "Mental Telegraphy" (1891), Mark Twain quotes from a Boston *Post* article that notes striking parallels between *Emily Chester. A Novel* (1864) and Louisa May Alcott's novel, *Moods* (1864). These similarities occurred even though "Miss Anna M. Crane, of Baltimore" and Alcott were strangers who lived hundreds of miles apart. Twain does not indicate that he has read either work. Alcott's *Moods* is centered around a failed marriage resulting from a young woman's emotionally impetuous decisions.
———. *An Old-Fashioned Girl.* Boston: Roberts Brothers, 1870. 376 pp.
   Inscription: "For Ida, May 14th, 1870," possibly in Clemens's hand. [Ida B. Clark, 1849–1934, would marry Charles Jervis Langdon, Olivia Clemens's brother, on 12 October 1870.]
   Catalogs: list of books transferred by Mark Woodhouse on 9 July 1987 from the Quarry Farm library to the Mark Twain Archive, Elmira College, Elmira, New York; Ball 2016 inventory, inscribed "For Ida, May 14th,1870," poor condition.
   Location: Mark Twain Archive, Gannett-Tripp Learning Center, Elmira College, Elmira, New York.
ALDEN, ISABELLA (1841–1930). *Pansy's Picture Book.* Illus. First edition. Boston: Lothrop Publishing Co., 1876. 374 pp. [Edition conjectured; various reprintings followed.]
   Source: ListABP (1910) ("Pansy's Picture Book").
   A volume of children's stories and poems.
ALDEN, HENRY MILLS (1836–1919). *God in His World: An Interpretation.* New York: Harper & Brothers, 1890. 270 pp. [Publisher and pages conjectured.]
   Catalog: *A1911,* "12mo, cloth, N.Y. 1890," quotes a laid in sheet of manuscript notes, lot 187, sold for $2.50.
   Clemens presumably received this theological treatise, an affirmative and sweeping survey of history and Christian

Realism written by the editor of *Harper's Weekly*, as a presentation copy. It has not reappeared since the 1911 auction. Alden would attend Clemens's Seventieth Birthday Dinner at Delmonico's in New York City on 5 December 1905.
ALDEN, WILLIAM LIVINGSTON (1837–1908). *The Adventures of Jimmy Brown, Written by Himself and Edited by W. L. Alden.* New York: Harper & Brothers, 1905. 236 pp.
   Source: MTLAcc, entry #1583, volume donated by Clemens.
   Clemens was generally not pleased to receive examples of Boy Books emulating Tom Sawyer's adventures, so he probably did not welcome Jimmy Brown's mischievous pranks in chapters titled "Playing Circus," "Bee-Hunting," "My Pig," "Going to Be a Pirate," "Our Balloon," and so forth.
———. *The Cruise of the "Ghost."* Illus. New York: Harper & Brothers, 1904. 210 pp.
   Source: MTLAcc, entry #432, volume donated by Clemens.
———. *Jimmy Brown Trying to Find Europe, Written by Himself and Edited by W. L. Alden.* Illus. New York: Harper & Brothers, 1905. 164 pp.
   Source: MTLAcc, entry #600, volume donated by Clemens.
———. *Shooting Stars as Observed from the "Sixth Column" of the Times.* New York: G. P. Putnam's Sons, 1878. 224 pp.
   "N. Y. Times funy Man—little girl who got up drama of Robinson Crusoe," noted Mark Twain in 1880 while compiling a list of potential material for his projected anthology of American humor (NB 19, *N&J* 2:366). Three sketches from Alden's collected columns from the New York *Times* eventually appeared in *Mark Twain's Library of Humor* (1888)—"Carrie's Comedy," a nonsensical dramatization of Defoe's *Robinson Crusoe* purportedly written by a young girl; "The Belle of Vallejo"; and "Mr. Simpkin's Downfall."
ALDRICH, THOMAS BAILEY (1836–1907). "The Ballad of Babie Bell, also known as "Baby Bell" (poem, published in 1855; collected in *The Ballad of Babie Bell and Other Poems* [1859]).
   The Mark Twain-Thomas Bailey Aldrich relationship got off to a rough start late in 1870, when Aldrich mistakenly accused Twain of plagiarizing Bret Harte; Clemens objected on 15 January 1871 (*MTLet* 4: 304). Aldrich withdrew the charge and apologized to Clemens on 22 January 1871 and again in February 1871 (see *MTLet* 4: 305; Reigstad, *SL*, pp. 182–183). Things improved rapidly after that. On 27 January 1871 Twain wrote a conciliatory letter to Aldrich that recalled a night of revelry in Virginia City, Nevada in December 1863 when Artemus Ward entertained a crowded room in Barnum's Restaurant by "thickly reciting a poem about a certain infant you wot of, & interrupting himself & *being* interrupted every few lines by poundings of the table & shouts of 'Splennid, by Shorzhe!' Finally, a long, vociferous, poundiferous & vitreous jingling of applause announces the conclusion," followed by Ward's demand that everyone "stan' up & drink health & long life to Thomas Bailey Aldrich!" (*MTLet* 4: 317). In an era when infant deaths bereaved countless families, this consolatory poem described in flowery language how "the gates of Heaven were left ajar," enabling "dainty Baby Bell" to descend to earth briefly, only to grow feverish and be summoned back by "the messenger from unseen lands." See also the Catalog entry below.

———. *Cloth of Gold and Other Poems*. Boston: James R. Osgood and Company, 1874. 183pp.

Inscription: presentation inscription by Aldrich on the verso of the front flyleaf, "Unalterably, T. B. A./Boston/ Dec. 1874."

Catalog: *C1951*, #77c, $25; mistakenly listed in the category of books signed by Clemens.

Location: Albert and Shirley Small Special Collections Library, University of Virginia, Charlottesville. Donated by Clifton Waller Barrett.

Copy examined: Clemens's copy, in 1970.

On 20 November 1874 Clemens jokingly predicted a day when "the old-time fire" would have "mostly gone out" of Aldrich's poetry in his old age (SLC to William Dean Howells, *MTLet* 6: 292; *AutoMT* 3: 262). Clemens complimented the author regarding his recent book from Hartford on 18 December 1874: "I read the 'Cloth of Gold' through, coming down in the cars, & it is just *lightning* poetry. . . . 'Baby Bell' always seemed perfection, before, but now that I have children it has got even beyond *that*" (*MTL*, pp. 239–240; *MTLet* 6: 321). Modern readers must assume that Clemens made the latter declaration on the basis of friendship rather than literary criticism. To the modern taste the poem Clemens admired would seem to define the term "bathos." This was the first volume of poetry Aldrich gave Clemens, though several volumes of Aldrich's fiction already formed part of Clemens's library. It is important to note how much Aldrich's conversational abilities impressed Clemens throughout his life. On 10 June 1879 Clemens wrote to Joseph H. Twichell from Paris: "Aldrich was here a week or so, & what a rattling time we did have. That fellow is blindingly bright" (*LMTJHT*, p. 92). During an interview published in the New York *World* on 31 May 1891, Twain declared, "I hold that T. B. Aldrich is the wittiest man I ever met. I don't believe his match ever existed on this earth" (*Complete Interviews*, p. 135). In a letter to Susy Clemens written on 11 May 1893 Clemens lavished praise on Aldrich's character; he is "fine in heart, fine in mind, fine in every conceivable way, sincere, genuine, & lovable beyond all men save only Joe Jefferson" (quoted in Christie's catalogue, New York City, 11 May 1987, item #23). In the course of a newspaper interview in 1895 Twain remarked, "When it comes to brilliancy, why I've heard Tom Bailey Aldrich keep up a running fire of the most inimitable repartee. Talk about wit, why, Tom Bailey Aldrich has said 1,500 if not 15,000 things as brilliant as the things Talleyrand [Charles Maurice de Talleyrand-Périgord, 1754–1838] said" (New York *Sun*, 27 January 1895, *Complete Interviews*, p. 146). Even after Aldrich's literary reputation had begun to decline, Clemens would still defend his poetry in an Autobiographical Dictation of 3 July 1908: "Aldrich was never widely known; his books never attained to a wide circulation; his prose was diffuse, self-conscious, and barren of distinction in the matter of style; his fame as a writer of prose is not considerable; his fame as a writer of verse is also very limited, but such as it is it is a matter to be proud of. It is based not upon his output of poetry as a whole but upon half a dozen small poems which are not surpassed in our language for exquisite grace and beauty and finish. These gems are known and admired and loved by the one person in ten thousand who is capable of appreciating them at their just value" (*MTE*, p. 293; *AutoMT* 3: 241). The numerous books by Aldrich in Clemens's library constituted one of his largest collections of writings by a single author.

Caroline Ticknor supplied a moving account of Clemens's speech in Portsmouth, New Hampshire on the occasion of the posthumous opening to the public of the former home of Aldrich's grandfather, which was to serve as a museum. Clemens, the principal speaker, "was jocose and merry, and all his reminiscences of Aldrich were set forth in such a vein as he might have indulged in had the subject been seated side him on the platform. I can remember his reiterating forcibly: 'This isn't Aldrich's funeral!'" (*Glimpses of Authors* [Boston: Houghton Mifflin, 1922], p. 150). Charles Hammond Gibson likewise remembered hearing Clemens speak at the Portsmouth Music Hall on 30 June 1908 at the dedication of the Thomas Bailey Aldrich Memorial Museum and left a vivid account of how Clemens revived the heat-stricken crowd: "He drew a smile and laughter. . . . He had really said something that none of the other distinguished speakers had been able to describe. He was the outstanding feature of the occasion. . . . He was the projectionist who projected the soul of Aldrich once more into our midst" ("My Last Impression of Mark Twain," *Mark Twain Journal* 7.2 [Winter-Spring 1945–1946]: 6). Clemens privately doubted that the Aldrich Memorial Museum would attract many visitors, and wished that "Aldrich the brilliant, Aldrich the sarcastic, Aldrich the ironical, Aldrich the merciless" could have been on hand at the museum opening ceremony in Portsmouth "to make fun of it" (3 July 1908 AD, *AutoMT* 3: 241). Susan Goodman and Carl Dawson's *William Dean Howells: A Writer's Life* (Berkeley: University of California Press, 2005), pp. 393–395 provided a mordant account of this lugubrious and protracted ceremony.

———. *Flower and Thorn, Later Poems*. Boston: J. R. Osgood and Co., 1877. 148 pp.

Inscription: inscribed by Aldrich to Clemens and also signed by Clemens.

Catalogs: ListABP (1910), "Flower & Thorn, Aldrich"; *C1951*, D78.

———. "The Friend of My Youth," *Atlantic Monthly* 27.160 (February 1871): 169–177.

Mark Twain included this prose character sketch in *Mark Twain's Library of Humor* (1888). It recounted the career of a gifted sharper and gambler called Governor Dorr who periodically touched Aldrich for funds, always reminding him that he was "the friend of my youth."

———. *From Ponkapog to Pesth*. Boston: Houghton, Mifflin and Co., 1883. [The fourth edition appeared in 1884, the seventh edition in 1890. The edition of Clemens's copy has not been established.]

Catalogs: ListABP (1910), "From Ponkapog to Pesth, Aldrich"; *C1951*, #46c, $30, "given to Mark Twain by the author," edition unspecified. Listed among the books signed by Clemens.

Aldrich narrated here a journey that started from a little New England village (Ponkapog) and stretched to include the Hungarian capital (Pesth), with a side-excursion to

Morocco.

———. *Judith of Bethulia, A Tragedy*. Boston: Houghton, Mifflin and Co., 1904. 98 pp. Reprinted in 1905.

Catalogs: ListABP (1910), "Judith of Bethulia, Aldrich"; *C1951*, #54c, $20, "given to Mark Twain by the author," edition unspecified. Listed among books signed by Clemens.

Judith of Bethulia was Aldrich's dramatization of his earlier narrative poem, *Judith and Holofernes* (1896). The play was produced in Boston in 1904. On 7 December 1904 Isabel Lyon made a pertinent entry in her journal: "And then Mr. Thomas Bailey Aldrich came in to ask Mr. Clemens and Jean to go tonight to see a tragedy that he has recently written" (1903–1906 Diary, TS p. 31, MTP).

———. "The Little Violinist," *St. Nicholas Magazine* 1.6 (April 1874): 358–361.

"The Little Violinist's prayer struck water in my lower level, as the silver miner says when he is affected. Pretty sketch—good sketch," wrote Clemens to Aldrich on 24 March 1874 (*MTLet* 6: 91). Aldrich's story amounted to an appeal to curtail the exploitation of young children in show business. It related the life of London-born James Speaight (1866–1874), the so-called "Young Americus," an actual child prodigy who learned the violin at an early age and by the time he was five was playing in *The Black Crook* at Niblo's Garden in New York. He had complained of a pain in his heart after a Boston concert in January 1874 and died that night of an undiagnosed cardiac condition. Aldrich quoted the boy's dying prayer as published in an obituary at the time, "*Gracious God, make room for another child in Heaven.*"

———. *Marjorie Daw and Other People*. Boston: J. R. Osgood and Co., 1873. 272 pp. Reprinted in 1874, 1875, and 1878; reissued by Houghton, Mifflin and Co. in 1882, 1884, 1885, etc. [Clemens's edition is undetermined.]

Catalogs: ListABP (1910), "Marjorie Daw, Aldrich"; *C1951*, #45c, $30, "given to Mark Twain by the author," edition unspecified. Listed among the books signed by Clemens.

In a letter to Howells written on 14 September 1876 Clemens alluded to the "genius" possessed by "the man that wrote Marjorie Daw" (*MTHL*, p. 153). On 28 January 1876 Clemens had sent a very friendly postcard to Aldrich: "I am perfectly delighted! I would rather have captured you than any man I know" (*Sotheby's 2003*, #38). *SCH* [1952], p. 232.

———. *Mercedes, and Later Lyrics*. Boston: Houghton, Mifflin and Co., 1884. 111 pp. [Edition conjectured.]

Catalog: ListABP (1910), "Mercedes, Aldrich", no other information provided.

———. "An Old Town by the Sea," *Harper's Monthly* 49.293 (October 1874): 632–650.

Clemens expressed pleasure in a letter to William Dean Howells on 20 September 1874 that Aldrich had made Olivia Clemens "the happiest & proudest woman in the land" by mentioning one of her forbearers in his description of Portsmouth, New Hampshire (*MTLet* 6: 234).

———. *An Old Town by the Sea*. Boston: Houghton, Mifflin and Co., 1893. 123 pp.

At a time when Clemens was being driven nearly to desperation by his financial plight, he wrote to Aldrich from New York City on 6 December 1893 to report that he

had stayed up until 3 o'clock in the morning reading *An Old Town by the Sea*. "Portsmouth [, New Hampshire] was become the town of my boyhood—with all which that implies & compels. . . . I enjoyed it all—every line of it; & I wish there had been more" (Houghton Library, Harvard University).

———. *Poems* [unidentified edition].

Catalog: ListABP (1910), "Poems, Aldrich", no other information provided.

———. *Ponkapog Papers*. Boston: Houghton, Mifflin and Co., 1903.

Clemens informed Howells from Florence on 17 January 1904 that he had stayed up late to read this book "night before last," and then relied on whiskey to help him sleep (*MTHL*, p. 779). Clemens presumably referred to *Ponkapog Papers* when he wrote to Aldrich from Florence on 14 February 1904: "The publishers sent me your book three or four weeks ago, & it gave me a most stimulating & delicious time—& did also patly and timely justify & reinforce some laudations of you which I had dictated the day before (in my Autobiography)" (Houghton Library, Harvard University). Isabel Lyon related in her journal entry for 28 July 1904 that "this evening" Richard Watson Gilder "sauntered in" while she was playing euchre with Clemens and Jean in Lee, Massachusetts. "We kept on with our game, and Mr. Gilder read bits of 'Ponkapog Papers' and Kipling's 'Five Seas'. Mr. Clemens told of the day in Florence that he read Mr. Aldrich's comment upon Mark Twain's humor in the 'Ponkapog Papers', speaking of it as being deep rooted" (1903–1906 Journal, TS p. 25, MTP). Aldrich's miscellaneous essays opened with "Leaves from a Notebook"; there he observed, "Mark Twain's humor is not be classed with the fragile plants; it has a serious root striking deep down into rich earth, and I think it will go on flowering indefinitely" (p. 17).

———. *Prudence Palfrey. A Novel*. Frontispiece. First edition, original green cloth, gilt, spine and corners worn, shaken, with a cloth folding box. Boston: James R. Osgood & Co., 1874. 311 pp.

Inscription: inscribed in ink on the front free endpaper, "Mark/from his friend/T. B. A."

Marginalia: numerical computations in Clemens's hand in black ink on the rear flyleaf.

Catalogs: ListABP (1910), "Prudence Palfrey, Aldrich"; *C1951*, #38c, presentation copy, mistakenly listed with books containing Clemens's signature; Christie's, New York City, 1–2 February 1988 auction, lot 451, sold for $1,045; Rulon-Miller Books, Minneapolis, Minnesota, List 23 (Spring 1988), "presentation copy to Mark Twain," item 22, priced at $2,500 (catalog sent by Thomas A. Tenney to Alan Gribben on 15 November 1988); Buddenbrooks, Newburyport, Massachusetts, offered on 21 June 2012, has the bookplate of Carrie Estelle Doheny, "neatly restored at some time in the distant past," item #24273, priced at $8,950.

Provenance: Carrie Estelle Doheny Collection, St. John's Seminary, Camarillo, California. Purchased by Mrs. Doheny from Maxwell Hunley, Beverly Hills rare book dealer, in 1951 for $39.50; she donated it to St. John's Seminary in 1952. Auctioned for $1,045 by Christie's in New York City in 1988 on behalf of St. John's Seminary and the Archdiocese of Los Angeles. See Nick Karanovich, "Sixty Books from Mark Twain's Library," *Mark Twain Journal* 25.2 (Fall 1987): 9–20.

Location: currently unknown.

Copy examined: Clemens's copy, at St. John's Seminary. Has the bookplate of "Estelle Doheny."

Clemens urged Aldrich to publish an unnamed forthcoming book—probably *Prudence Palfrey*—by subscription, even offering to negotiate personally with Elisha Bliss of the American Publishing Company (ALS, SLC to Aldrich, 24 March 1874, Houghton Library, Harvard University; *MTLet* 6: 89). Aldrich evidently neglected this offer, but he did ask Clemens for assistance in depicting the western mining scenes in the novel and mailed Clemens proofs of the novel. Clemens sent a lengthy list of proposed revisions concerning mining terminology and lore, together with suggestions about miners' living habits; in an accompanying undated letter he diplomatically added: "I think it is ma[r]velous that you have made so few mistakes about mining, & that what you have written about it sounds so easy-going & natural" (ALS, Washington University, St. Louis, Missouri). The portion of Aldrich's novel that involves mining begins with Chapter 5, in which the hero John Dent resolves to earn a fortune in the California mines: "I mean to come back independent, or not at all" (p. 77). But the California regions with which Mark Twain was familiar are not Dent's ultimate destination; in Chapter 6 he winds up in "the new gold regions" in Montana (p. 97). Nevertheless, Clemens's participation in the planning and writing of *Prudence Palfrey* insures that he knew this novel more thoroughly than through casual reading.

———. *The Queen of Sheba*. Original cloth, light spotting on covers, minor wear. Boston: James R. Osgood and Co., 1877. 270 pp.

Inscription: inscribed by Aldrich in ink on the half-title page, "Samuel L. Clemens/from his friend/T. B. Aldrich."

Marginalia: Clemens marked numerous passages in pencil. He made one long vertical line down the margin of page 55, and drew other vertical lines on pages 56, 57, 60, 65, 67, 69 (the first line here is underlined), 70, 78, 96, 98, 119, 139, 141, 151, 154, 164, 170, 178, 181, 185, 195, 201 (on this page he made double vertical marks beside a sentence: "At home, if you love a girl you tell her so; over here, you go and tell her grandmother."), 232, and 247 (on which he drew double vertical marks at this sentence: "They have got what our French friends call a fixed idea, which is generally an idea that requires a great deal of fixing.").

Catalogs: *C1951*, #67c, $50, "given to Mark Twain by the author," erroneously listed among the books signed by Clemens; "Property from the Library of Mark Twain," Butterfield & Butterfield, San Francisco, Sale 6613 (16 July 1997), item #2666.

Location: Mark Twain House and Museum, Hartford, Connecticut.

Copy examined: Clemens's copy. Viewed in 1997 in Hartford, Connecticut.

Clemens wrote a letter to Aldrich on 17 November 1877 in which he praised *The Queen of Sheba*: "Your book came at 10 this morning. . . . So I ordered breakfast & a pipe

to be brought up to the bed—which would give me a chance to glance at the book. Result: I have read every line of the bewitching thing & have lost my day's work & am not in the least sorry. . . . It is a delicious situation where that young fellow gets into the asylum" (ALS, Middlebury College, Middlebury, Vermont). In Chapter 4 of the novel, Edward Lynde inadvertently wanders into an asylum for the insane in northern New Hampshire, attempts to converse with the inmates (whom he believes to be local villagers), and is himself mistaken for a lunatic by the guards and incarcerated in a padded cell. One of the inmates of the asylum is a girl who believes herself to be the Queen of Sheba.

———. *The Sisters' Tragedy, with Other Poems, Lyrical and Dramatic*. Boston: Houghton, Mifflin and Co., 1891. 108 pp.

Inscription: in black ink, tipped in on the verso of the half-title page: "S. L. Clemens, from/his young/friend,/T. B. Aldrich/Feb'y 1891."

Location: Mark Twain Library, Redding, Connecticut. Donated from Clemens's library by Clara Clemens Gabrilowitsch in 1910 (MTLAcc, entry #2132).

Copy examined: Clemens's copy, examined in 1970 and again on 15 June 1982. It has the accession number "2132".

On 21 February 1891 Clemens wrote to Aldrich from Hartford: "I thank you ever so much for the poems." He jokingly alluded to the stanzas headed "Tennyson," in which (he claimed) he expected to find himself cited (Houghton Library, Harvard). The opening lines of Aldrich's poem titled "Tennyson" pose a question: "Shakespeare and Milton—what third blazoned name/ Shall lips of after-ages link to these?"

———. *The Stillwater Tragedy*. First edition. Original brown decorated cloth, gilt. Boston: Houghton, Mifflin and Co., 1880. 324 pp.

Inscriptions: inscribed by Aldrich on the flyleaf opposite the title page: "Mark, from his friend, T. B. Aldrich." A 1951 auction label is pasted below that inscription on the same leaf, with "70c" written in pencil below the label. Clara Clemens Gabrilowitsch's library shelf number ("F/Ls13") appears on the front pastedown endpaper.

Marginalia: The chapter numbers for Chapters 23 and 25 are heavily underlined.

Catalogs: ListABP (1910), "Stillwater Tragedy, Aldrich"; *C1951*, #70c, $27.50, presentation copy, listed erroneously among the books signed by Clemens.

Location: collection of Kevin Mac Donnell, Austin, Texas.

Source: description sent by Mac Donnell to Alan Gribben, 28 August 2017.

On 15 September 1880 Clemens wrote to Aldrich from Elmira: "Thank you ever so much for the book—I had already finished it, & prodigiously enjoyed it, in the periodical of the notorious Howells, but it hits Mrs. Clemens just right" (Middlebury College; Paine, *MTL* [1917], pp. 385–386). *The Stillwater Tragedy* had been serialized in the *Atlantic Monthly* 45.270–275 (April-September 1880). Aldrich here uncharacteristically produced a murder mystery that he set in a New England manufacturing town. A young man becomes the chief suspect. Aldrich would succeed William Dean Howells as editor of the *Atlantic Monthly* in 1881.

————. *The Story of a Bad Boy*. Boston: Fields, Osgood & Co., 1869. [Edition conjectured.]

Critical interpretations of the Thomas Bailey Aldrich-Mark Twain literary relationship have largely centered on this quasi-autobiographical novel that Aldrich set in his boyhood home town of Portsmouth, New Hampshire. Strangely enough, however, Clemens's copy of this book—like so many others that might offer significant revelations about his reading—has utterly disappeared. The only opinion about it that be expressed in writing was unfavorable; shortly before his marriage he wrote to Olivia Langdon from New Haven, where he was lecturing: "I have read several books, lately, but none worth marking, & so I have not marked any. I started to mark the Story of a Bad Boy, but for the life of me I could not admire the volume much" (27 December 1869, *LLMT*, p. 132; *MTLet* 3: 440). Perhaps he later altered this estimation; at any rate he extracted "How We Astonished the Rivermouthians" for inclusion in *Mark Twain's Library of Humor* (1888). In June 1898 Mark Twain scheduled Tom Bailey to be among the children he wanted to assemble in his projected "Creatures of Fiction" tale (NB 40, TS p. 26).

Quite late in his life Twain told Paine that Aldrich was writing *The Story of a Bad Boy* at the same time he himself was beginning *The Adventures of Tom Sawyer*, and that the two of them compared their works in progress (*MTB* [1912], p. 1456)—which may or may not have been a mistaken recollection. In 1985 I wrote an essay, "'I Did Wish Tom Sawyer Was There': Boy-Book Elements in *Tom Sawyer* and *Huckleberry Finn*," which in part noted the coincidence of Aldrich's 1869 novel and Twain's abortive attempt to utilize some Hannibal childhood memories, "Boy's Manuscript." The latter fragment had (then) long been dated as composed in 1870. Subsequent to my 1985 article, however, Twain's "Boy's Manuscript" was more accurately placed in the period of 1868 or very early in 1869. Aldrich's *The Story of a Bad Boy* started running serially in the January 1869 issue of *Our Young Folks*, so there is still an intriguingly close connection of dates. See also Alan Gribben, "Manipulating a Genre: *Huckleberry Finn* as a Boy Book" (1988) and Alan Gribben, "Tom Sawyer, Tom Canty, and Huckleberry Finn: The Boy Book and Mark Twain" (2017) (revised versions of both essays appear as chapters in Volume One of this present work). Walter Blair, "On the Structure of *Tom Sawyer*" (1939), p. 78; Blair, *MT&HF* (1960), p. 64; Blair, ed., *HH&T* (1969), p. 158 n. 12; Albert B. Stone, *IE* (1961), pp. 27–31, 65; Jim Hunter, "Mark Twain and the Boy-Book" (1963), p. 433; Robert L. Coard, "Tom Sawyer, Sturdy Centenarian," *Midwest Quarterly* 17 (July 1976): 329–349; Evelyn Geller, "Tom Sawyer, Tom Bailey, and the Bad-Boy Genre," *Wilson Library Bulletin* 51.3 (November 1976): 245–250; Everett Carter, "The Modernist Ordeal of Huckleberry Finn," *Studies in American Fiction* 13.2 (Autumn 1985): 175–176; Marcia Jacobson, *Being a Boy Again: Autobiography and the American Boy Book* (1994); Richard S. Lowry, *"Littery Man": Mark Twain and Modern Authorship* (New York: Oxford University Press, 1996), pp. 88–89; Tim Prchal, "The Bad Boys and the New Man: The Role of Tom Sawyer and Similar Characters in the Reconstruction of Masculinity," *American Literary*

Realism 36.3 (Spring 2004): 187–205; and Alan Gribben, "Boy Books, Bad Boy Books, and *The Adventures of Tom Sawyer*," in *The Adventures of Tom Sawyer*, ed. Beverly Lyon Clark. Norton Critical Edition Series (New York: W. W. Norton, 2007), pp. 290–306.

————. *The Story of a Bad Boy*. Boston: James R. Osgood and Co., 1877. 261 pp.

Provenance: bookplate #441 of the "J. Langdon Family Library" on the front pastedown endpaper.

Catalog: Ball 2016 inventory, red cloth, gilt lettering and design, Jervis Langdon Family Library #441.

Location: Mark Twain Archive, Elmira College, Elmira, New York.

Copy examined: unmarked copy available to Clemens whenever he visited the Langdons in Elmira. Examined on 27 May 2015.

————. *The Story of a Cat*. Translated from the French of Émile de Bédollière. Illustrated by L. [ivingston York Yourtee ("Hop")] Hopkins (1846–1927). Boston: Houghton, Mifflin and Co., 1879. [Edition conjectured.]

Catalog: ListABP (1910), "Story of a Cat, Aldrich", no other information provided.

————. *Wyndham Towers*. Boston: Houghton, Mifflin and Co., 1890. 80 pp. [Edition conjectured.]

Catalogs: ListABP (1910), "Wyndham Towers, Aldrich"; *C1951*, #72c, $25, presentation copy, listed among books signed by Clemens.

Clemens must have received an advance copy of the lengthy, serio-comic poem titled *Wyndham Towers*, for he wrote to Aldrich from Hartford on 19 November 1889: "It's a lovely book, & I thank you ever so much," and promised to send him a copy of *A Connecticut Yankee in King Arthur's Court* (Houghton Library, Harvard University). Aldrich published no other volumes during this period.

ALEXANDER, CECIL FRANCES (HUMPHREYS) (1818–1895). "The Burial of Moses" (poem, published in 1856).

Cecil Frances Alexander was the wife of an Irish Anglican prelate; she wrote tracts in the Oxford Movement as well as hymns and verses whose subject was generally the Old Testament. Van Wyck Brooks may have been overstating the case when he asserted that "The Burial of Moses" became for Clemens a literary touchstone (*The Ordeal of Mark Twain*, rev. ed. [New York: B. P. Dutton & Co., 1933], p. 191), but he was only echoing Albert Bigelow Paine, who had cited this "noble and simple poem" as "a sort of literary touchstone" for Clemens (*MTB* [1912], pp. 217, 338). There can be no doubt that Clemens was impressed with Alexander's poem about the unrevealed site of Moses' tomb, particularly its first stanza, in the 1860s and 1870s. Paine reported that he "often" recited its "stately lines" during his sojourn in Virginia City, Nevada (*MTB*, pp. 216–217). "The Burial of Moses" opens with four compressed lines: "By Nebo's lonely mountain,/On this side Jordan's wave,/In a vale in the land of Moab,/There lies a lonely grave." In 1867 Clemens copied the entire poem onto the first four pages of Notebook 9 (*N&J* 1:380–382), seemingly from memory (to judge from discrepancies), and also noted its title farther on in the same notebook (p. 438). He quoted part of the poem in his *Alta California* letter of 12 September 1867, and he employed four lines from the first stanza in Chapter

42 of *Innocents Abroad* (1869). Chapter 6 of *Roughing It* (1872) alludes to "The Mysterious Grave of Moses." A sentence in Chapter 36 of *A Tramp Abroad* (1880)—"The secret of his sepulture, like that of Moses, must remain a mystery always"—originated from the last lines of the poem: "God hath his mysteries of grace,/Ways that we cannot tell,/He hides them deep, like the secret sleep/Of him he loved so well." Whether these five references qualify "The Burial of Moses" as one of Clemens's "touchstones" is a question for each reader to decide.

———. "Once in royal David's city" (Christmas carol, first published as a poem in 1848; set to music in 1849 by Henry John Gauntlett [1805–1876]).

Either Clemens or his wife Olivia marked this hymn in their copy of *Laudes Domini: A Selection of Spiritual Songs, Ancient and Modern* (1884), compiled by C. S. Robinson. (See that Catalog entry.) Its first lines provide the setting of a divine birth: "Once in royal David's city/Stood a lowly cattle shed."

ALEXANDER, WILLIAM (1824–1911). *Primary Convictions; Being Discussions Delivered on Subjects Connected with the Evidences of Christianity [at] Columbia College.* New York: Harper & Brothers, 1893. 322 pp.

Source: MTLAcc, entry #1392, volume donated by Clemens.

Alexander, Lord Bishop of Derry and Raphoe, was the husband of Cecil Frances Alexander (1818–1895), the hymnist and poet (see her Catalog entry above) who wrote the well-known hymn "All things bright and beautiful." Alexander himself was also a poet as well as a Church of Ireland prelate.

ALEXANDER, WILLIAM DEWITT (1833–1913). *A Review of a Pastoral Address by the Right Rev. T. N. Staley, D.D., Reformed Catholic Bishop of Honolulu, Containing a Reply to Some of His Charges Against the American Protestant Mission to the Hawaiian Islands.* Honolulu: Printed by H. M. Whitney, 1865. 87 pp.

Mark Twain quoted from this book, citing its author and title, in his letter of 1 July 1866 published in the Sacramento *Weekly Union* issue for 4 August 1866 (Dane, *LSI*, p. 123). He sought to demonstrate the heartless attitude of Established Church clergymen toward funerals conducted by Dissenting ministers. See also the Catalog entry for Henry Mayhew's *London Labour and the London Poor*. William De Witt Alexander was a respected Hawaiian historian, linguist, and map-maker. The Reverend Thomas Nettleship Staley (1823–1898) had delivered his pastoral address, later published in the *Pacific Commercial Advertiser* and subsequently as a book, in his church on New Year's Day in 1865.

ALFORD, HENRY (1810–1871). "Say, Wilt Thou Think of Me When I'm Away" (poem, more properly titled "Filioae Dulcissimae. Easter Offering").

Alford, an English clergyman, poet, and scholar, was Dean of Canterbury from 1857 until 1871. On 9 March 1871 Olivia Clemens copied this poem into her commonplace book (DV161, MTP). A reflection on human mortality, it muses about the difficulty of remembering everything about those we love, relating that struggle to the challenge of maintaining faith in Christ.

ALGER, HORATIO, JR. (1832–1899).

Yes, it does seem rather odd that not a single surviving book or remark indicates Clemens's awareness of the phenomenon in juvenile literature that Alger achieved. His didactic formulas for boyhood success surely must have caught Clemens's attention, but no evidence of this fact has yet surfaced.

ALGER, RUSSELL ALEXANDER (1836–1907). *The Spanish-American War.* Portrait and maps. New York: Harper & Brothers, 1901. 466 pp.

Inscription: signed on a front flyleaf, "S. L. Clemens, Riverdale-on-Hudson, Oct. 13, 1901."

Catalog: *A1911*, "8vo, cloth, gilt top, uncut, N.Y. 1901," quotes the autograph, lot 7, sold for $4.

Alger was President William McKinley's Secretary of War from 5 March 1897 until 1 August 1899, when he resigned at McKinley's request.

———. [Identical copy.]

Source: MTLAcc, entry #1708, volume donated by Clemens.

ALLEN, ALEXANDER VIETS GRISWOLD (1841–1908). *Life and Letters of Phillips Brooks.* 2 vols. Illus. New York: E. P. Dutton and Co., 1900. [Allen's book was reprinted in 1901 in 3 volumes. The edition Clemens read is conjectured.]

That Clemens's reading tastes could differ markedly from those of his friend the Reverend Joseph H. Twichell is apparent from their responses to this biography of the prominent American Episcopal bishop Phillips Brooks (1835–1893), who held the pastorate of Trinity Church in Boston for more than twenty years. Writing to Twichell from Saranac Lake, New York on 28 August 1901, Clemens jokingly rebuked Twichell: "Just a word, to scoff at you, with your extravagant suggestion that I read the biography of Phillips Brooks—the very dullest book that has been printed for a century. Joe, ten pages of Mrs. Cheney's masterly biography of her father—no, *five* pages of it—contain more meat, more sense, more literature, more brilliancy, than that whole basketful of drowsy rubbish put together" Indeed, "in that dead atmosphere" even Brooks himself "wearied me; *oh* how he wearied me!" (SLC to Joseph H. Twichell, 28 August 1901, *MTL*, p. 712; *LMTJHT*, p. 284). It is conceivable that Clemens was referring to Arthur Brooks' brief biography, *Phillips Brooks* (1893), but Allen's lengthier and more recent work seems the far more probable object of Clemens's derision. Mary (Bushnell) Cheney's *Life and Letters of Horace Bushnell* had appeared in 1880. In 1902 Mark Twain would name Horace Bushnell as the "greatest clergyman that the last century produced" (speech to the Art Students' Association, St. Louis, Missouri, 7 June 1902, *MTLW* (1932); *MTSpk* (1976), p. 444).

ALLEN, CHILION BROWN (1836–1922) and **MARY AUGUSTA (WOOD) ALLEN** (1841–1908). *The Man Wonderful in the House Beautiful: An Allegory Teaching the Principles of Physiology and Hygiene, and the Effects of Stimulants and Narcotics.* New York: Fowler & Wells Co., [cop. 1883; authors' preface dated 6 August 1884]. 366 pp.

Clemens informed Charles L. Webster on 16 June 1887 from Hartford that "I shall keep 'The Man Wonderful' and read it" (*MTLP*, p. 218). Mary Augustus Allen was a physician and social reformer who would write a series of books on the subject of women's sexual health, including *What a Young Girl Ought to Know* (1897) and *What a Young*

Woman Ought to Know (1899). Dr. Allen was an officer in the Women's Christian Temperance Union and several chapters of *The Man Wonderful and the House Beautiful* warn against the dangers of alcohol and smoking. Clemens might not have enjoyed the chapter inveighing against any "dandy" who smokes cigars (p. 266).

ALLEN, ELIZABETH ANN (CHASE) AKERS (1832–1911). "Rock Me to Sleep, Mother" (poem, published 1860; song, cop. 1860, melody by several composers, including J. Max Mueller (b. 1842), Ernest Leslie, and John Hill Hewitt).

Historians almost unanimously agree that Allen wrote this poem in May 1860 and published it under the pen name "Florence Percy" in the 9 June 1860 issue of the *Saturday Evening Post*. In the wake of its immediate and continued popularity its authorship was claimed by various writers, especially Alexander M. W. Ball of Elizabeth, New Jersey. The first stanza contains the most famous lines: "Backward, turn backward, O Time, in your flight,/Make me a child again just for to-night"; the refrain echoes the poem's title: "Rock me to sleep, mother—rock me to sleep!" The speaker in the poem expresses weariness with "toil" and "tears" and longs to relive her carefree childhood again. The poem was soon set to music by several composers, which only heightened its immense appeal.

In "Letter from Carson City," a sketch published in the *Territorial Enterprise* on 3 February 1863, Clemens included "Rock me to sleep, mother" in a list of songs he had listened to at the Governor's house (*ET&S* 1: 197). Mark Twain alluded to the poem in his letter to the *Alta California* from Capernaum in September 1867; he urged his readers to come to Galilee if they sought solitude. "If these things are not food for rock me to sleep mother, none exist, I think," he wrote (*TIA*, p. 226). In 1868 he burlesqued the dispute over its authorship by using its diction and meter in a satiric poem that ridiculed Ball, one of the chief claimants; Twain's poem appeared in the Cincinnati *Evening Chronicle* for 4 March 1868 (see the *Twainian* 2 [February 1943]: 2–3 and 2 [March 1943]: 6; and Scott, *OPMT* [1966], pp. 10, 65). Twain alluded to the controversial status of this poem in Chapter 31 of *Innocents Abroad* (1869); he also used his earlier allusion to the Sea of Galilee region as "food for rock me to sleep, mother" in Chapter 48. References to the heated dispute over the poem's authorship recurred throughout his lifetime. In "Mental Telegraphy" (published in 1891, but written previously) he recalled that "there was a war of this kind over . . . 'Rock Me to Sleep, Mother.'" In 1901 the poet Allen wrote Twain to dispute his views about the Shelley matter, and she received in reply two strongly worded attacks on Shelley and his biographer Edward Dowden in letters Twain wrote to her on 17 and 30 July 1901 (Richard Cary, "In Further Defence of Harriet Shelley: Two Unpublished Letters by Mark Twain," *Mark Twain Journal* 16.4 [Summer 1973]: 13–15). No. 44 quotes several lines from Allen's poem—"Backward, turn backward, O Time, in thy flight—/Make me a child again, just for to-night!"—while he parades an Assembly of the Dead to show the world's history in Chapter 32 of "No. 44, The Mysterious Stranger," written between 1902 and 1908 (*MSM* [1969], pp. 395, 397). To show his disdain for human endeavors, No. 44 misquotes the lines in minor

ways and ascribes them to "Beautiful Snow," another poem that had numerous claimants. Clemens informed Howells on 14 April 1903 that he refused to "regard as frauds the several claimants" to "Rock Me to Sleep, Mother"; he interpreted them instead as additional manifestations of "mental telegraphy" (*MTHL*, p. 767). In Clemens's copy of Samuel G. Bayne's *The Pith of Astronomy*, which Clemens signed in 1909, he alluded to "Rock me to sleep, rock me to sleep" in a marginal comment on page 6. He quoted the poem once again in Part 9 of *Is Shakespeare Dead?* (1909) to remind his readers about the phenomenal talents evinced in Shakespeare's canon: "Ordinarily when an unsigned poem sweeps across the continent like a tidal wave whose roar and boom and thunder are made up of admiration, delight, and applause, a dozen obscure people rise up and claim the authorship. . . . Do you remember 'Rock Me to Sleep, Mother, Rock Me to Sleep'? Do you remember 'Backward, turn backward, O Time, in thy flight! Make me a child again just for to-night'? I remember them very well. Their authorship was claimed by most of the grown-up people who were alive at the time." He also wrote "Rock me to sleep" in a set of undated notes (*A1911*, lot 202). David E. E. Sloane looked at how Twain introduced the poem into his last major work of fiction ("*No. 44, The Mysterious Stranger* as Literary Comedy," *Centenary Reflections on Mark Twain's No. 44, The Mysterious Stranger*, ed. Joseph Csicsila and Chad Rohman [Columbia: University of Missouri Press, 2009], pp. 184–185). Joe B. Fulton concluded that "the poem seems to have been powerfully evocative for Clemens" and that for him it became "a symbol of the desire to escape from history" (*The Reconstruction of Mark Twain: How a Confederate Bushwhacker Became the Lincoln of Our Literature* [Baton Rouge: Louisiana State University Press, 2010], p. 131).

———. *The Triangular Society. Leaves from the Life of a Portland Family.* Portland, Maine: Hoyt, Fogg & Donham, 1886. 381 pp.

Source: MTLAcc, entry #461, volume donated by Clemens.

ALLEN, HORACE NEWTON (1858–1932). *Things Korean; A Collection of Sketches and Anecdotes, Missionary and Diplomatic.* New York: Fleming H. Revell Co., [cop. 1908]. 256 pp.

Inscription: "To 'Mark Twain' with the profound respect of the author, Horace N. Allen."

Location: Mark Twain Library, Redding, Connecticut.

Copy examined: Clemens's copy, with the red ink accession number "3275". Examined in 1970 and again on 15 June 1982.

Allen wrote other books on Korean literature, missions, and politics; most were published by the Methodist Publishing House in Seoul, Korea.

ALLEN, JAMES LANE (1849–1925). *Aftermath; Part Second of "A Kentucky Cardinal."* Illustrated by Hugh Thomson (1860–1920). New York: Macmillan Co., 1906. 138 pp.

Source: MTLAcc, entry #1860, volume donated from Clemens's library by Clara Clemens Gabrilowitsch in 1910.

Nature provides a balm for the wounded spirit of a man whose wife dies in childbirth.

———. *The Choir Invisible.* First edition. Original cloth, gilt top, uncut. New York: Macmillan Co., 1897. 361 pp.

Inscription: the front pastedown endpaper is inscribed

"Sincerely Yours, James Lane Allen."

Marginalia: A rare book catalog issued by City Bookshop (24 April 1948), #409 (PH in MTP) quoted a lengthy quotation that Clemens copied onto a front flyleaf: "There is a heritage of heroic example and noble obligation, not reckoned in the Wealth of Nations, but essential to a nation's life; the contempt of which, in any people, may not slowly, mean even its commercial fall. Very sweet are the uses of prosperity, the harvests of peace and progress, the fostering sunshine of health and happiness and length of days in the land. But there be things 'the good of' which and 'the use of' which are beyond all calculation of worldly goods and earthly uses, things such as Love, Honour, and the Soul of Man, which cannot be bought with a price, and which do not die with death. And they who would fain live happily 'ever after' should not leave these things out of the lesson of their lives. M.T./December 1900." These sentences were not taken from *The Choir Invisible*, but came from Chapter 6 of Juliana Horatia Ewing's *Jackanapes* (1884). It is odd that he used the initials "M.T." in signing the quoted matter; this might indicate he was giving the book to someone outside the family (assuming the handwriting is not a forgery).

A poignant ending concludes this novel, which begins in 1795 in the wilderness of Kentucky.

———. *The Choir Invisible*. New York: Macmillan Co., 1898. 361 pp.

Source: MTLAcc, entry #1833, volume donated from Clemens's library by Clara Clemens Gabrilowitsch in 1910.

———. *A Kentucky Cardinal; A Story*. New York: Macmillan Co., 1905. 138 pp.

Source: MTLAcc, entry #1835, volume donated from Clemens's library by Clara Clemens Gabrilowitsch in 1910.

A reclusive lover of nature reluctantly cages a bird in a bid to win the love of his neighbor.

———. *Summer in Arcady; A Tale of Nature*. New York: Macmillan Co., 1897. 170 pp.

Source: MTLAcc, entry #1834, volume donated from Clemens's library by Clara Clemens Gabrilowitsch in 1910.

A novel in which romance blossoms amid the exquisite beauties of nature in rural Kentucky.

ALLEN, THOMAS G. *Letter from an Ex-Sailor and Ex-Tramp to Hon. Geo. S. Boutwell, Ex-Governor and Ex-Secretary of Treasury*. St. Louis, 5 October 1900. 15 pp.

Marginalia: a small amount on pages 11–12.

Location: Mark Twain Papers, Bancroft Library, University of California at Berkeley (Paine 89aa).

Copy examined: Clemens's copy.

George Sewall Boutwell (1818–1905) had served as governor of Massachusetts and as Secretary of the U. S. Treasury (1869–1873). He had led the impeachment of President Andrew Johnson. Allen's paperbound political campaign pamphlet excoriated President William McKinley for "the prosecution of a death-dealing destructive war, in order to subjugate the Liberty-loving Filipinos" (pp. 10–11). Clemens annotated only the two pages that directly assailed McKinley's conduct. Since McKinley had originally decried the annexation of Cuba as "criminal aggression," Clemens wrote "Mr. Criminal Aggression McKinley" in pencil at the bottom of page 11. On page 12 he noted: "By their fruits ye shall know *Xnity*".

ALLEN, WILLIAM FRANCIS (1830–1889), **CHARLES PICKARD WARE** (1840–1921), and **LUCY McKIM GARRISON** (1842–1877), comp. *Slave Songs of the United States*. New York: A. Simpson & Co., 1867. 155 pp. [Edition conjectured.]

Clemens very likely meant this volume, believed to be the earliest published collection of African American spirituals, when he wrote "The Slave Songs of the South—advertised in the South" in Notebook 19 (*N&J* 2:394) in 1881. *Slave Songs* contained "Roll, Jordan, roll" and many of his other favorite spirituals, but no evidence confirms that he acquired the book. See also the Catalog entry for Spirituals.

ALLESTREE, RICHARD (1619–1681). *The Whole Duty of Man, Laid Down in a Plain Familiar Way for the Use of All* (London, published in 1658).

A devotional work that was extremely popular for two centuries, *The Whole Duty of Man* was published anonymously but is generally attributed to the English clergyman and scholar Richard Allestree, Canon of Christ Church and Professor of Divinity at Oxford. It may have been one of Jane Lampton Clemens's reference books while rearing her family; at least Clemens teased his mother about her dependence on "that useful and highly entertaining volume" in a letter from Carson City written on 20 March 1862 (*PRI*, p. 35; *MTLet* 1: 175). In that same letter he joked that he had become a greater "Fund of useful information" about the Native American than "the whole duty of man" (*MTLet*: 176). He mentioned the book facetiously as "light reading" in Notebook 4 (*N&J* 1:83) in 1865, and later recalled the ubiquity of *The Whole Duty of Man* on the parlor tables in Honolulu when he had been there in 1866 (*FE*, Chapter 3, 1897). Mark Twain's *Alta California* readers were informed in his 5 April 1868 letter that the *Quaker City* passengers had brought this work along on the voyage (*TIA*, p. 303). An unfinished play he wrote about the trip in 1867 ("The Quaker City Holy Land Excursion," *MTLet* 2: 404–414) mentioned this title in the ship library (Act II, scene 1). A stubborn Kanaka horse the narrator rides on the island of Hawaii in Chapter 76 of *Roughing It* (1872) believes that stopping at every "house or a hut" is "an essential part of the whole duty of man, and his salvation not to be compassed without it." In Chapter 1 of "Those Extraordinary Twins" (1894) Twain contrasted the natures of his Siamese twins by specifying their choices in reading matter: Luigi sat down with Paine's *Age of Reason*, whereas Angelo chose Allestree's devotional tract.

ALLIBONE, SAMUEL AUSTIN (1816–1889). *A Critical Dictionary of English Literature and British and American Authors, Living and Deceased*. 3 vols. Philadelphia: J. B. Lippincott & Co., 1858–1871. [Reprinted in 1874 and other years.]

On 5 November 1879 Mark Twain referred an unidentified correspondent who sought his biography to "Allibone's Dictionary of Authors; (although I am not sure, . . . as I have not seen the work, but only *heard* it was in it)" (PH in MTP; Sotheby's sale, 29 October 1996, lot 215). There *was* a "Twain, Mark" entry in Allibone's work. Making preparations in 1880 to edit *Mark Twain's Library of Humor*, Twain intended to "examine Drake's & Allibone's Dictionaries of Authors to see who *have* been humorists" (NB 19, *N&J* 2:364).

ALLINGHAM, WILLIAM (1824–1889). *William Allingham, A Diary.* Ed. Helen (Paterson) Allingham (1848–1926) and Dollie (Caroline Maitland) Radford (1858–1920). 8vo, original cloth. London: Macmillan and Co., 1907. 404 pp.

> **Inscription:** the front free endpaper is inscribed "S. L. Clemens from Clara, Xmas, 1907".
>
> **Marginalia:** notes, underlinings, and marginal marks throughout. On page 98, regarding men supporting ideas in which they do not believe, Clemens commented, "All America is doing it, in these days of the insane Roosevelt." Where Clemens accidentally made several ink blots on page 150, he wrote at the bottom of the page, "Oh, damn!" On page 162 he noted: "Suicide silly! Damnation, they are the only sane people in this crazy world."
>
> **Catalogs:** ListABP (1910), "William Allingham, Allingham"; *C1951, #7a,* $22.50, listed among books containing marginalia by Clemens, no edition specified; Swann Galleries, 14 November 2002, quotes inscription and a few marginalia, "annotated throughout," described as "worn along front joint and at edges," lot 288, sold for $6,500; Exhibition, "The Mark Twain Collection of Susan Jaffe Tane," Division of Rare Book and Manuscript Collections, Cornell University, April 2010 (the catalog reproduced pages 150–151).
>
> Irish poet Allingham's book contains correspondence from and reminiscences of various authors, including Tennyson, Carlyle, and Rossetti.

———. *Sixteen Poems by William Allingham. Selected by William Butler Yeats.* Dundrum, Ireland: Dun Emer Press, 1905. 34 pp.

> **Inscription:** "S. L. Clemens/1908."
>
> **Marginalia:** no markings. Page 27 is turned down at the poem titled "Twilight Voices."
>
> **Catalog:** *A1911,* "8vo, boards, linen back, uncut, Dundrum (Ireland), 1905,. . . Limited edition," quotes the signature, lot 144, $4.50.
>
> **Provenance:** W Van R. Whitall bookplate is partially pasted over a W. T. H. Howe bookplate dated 1920.
>
> **Location:** Henry W and Albert A. Berg Collection, New York Public Library, in 1970.
>
> **Copy examined:** Clemens's copy.

ALLMOND, MARCUS BLAKEY (1851–1909). *Estelle and Other Poems.* Louisville, Kentucky: J. P. Morton & Co., [cop. 1884]. 79 pp.

> **Source:** MTLAcc, entry #2005, volume donated from Clemens's library by Clara Clemens Gabrilowitsch in 1910.

ALLYN, EUNICE GIBBS (1847–1916). *The Cats' Convention.* Illustrated by the author. New York: Cochrane Publishing Co., 1909. 255 pp.

> **Inscription:** "For Samuel Clemmens [*sic*] (Mark Twain)/'He prayeth best who loveth best/All things both great and small;/For the dear God who loveth us/He made and loveth all.' (Col.)/Eunice Gibbs Allyn." Her quotation came from a poem Clemens knew well, Samuel Taylor Coleridge's *The Rime of the Ancient Mariner.*
>
> **Location:** Mark Twain Library, Redding. Donated in 1910 by Clara Clemens Gabrilowitsch (MTLAcc, entry #2159).
>
> **Copy examined:** Clemens's copy, containing the red ink accession number "2159". Examined in 1970 and again on 15 June 1982. The illustrations are endearing, provided that one likes cats. (Clemens did.)
>
> Allyn was a writer, poet, illustrator, and social reformer in

Dubuque, Iowa. In earlier days she had been a national newspaper correspondent.

ALTROCCHI, JULIA (COOLEY) (1893–1972). *The Poems of a Child; Being Poems Written Between the Ages of Six and Ten.* Introduction by Richard Le Gallienne (1866–1947). Blue cloth. New York: R. H. Russell, 1904. 151 pp.

> **Source:** MTLAcc, entry #1692, volume donated by Clemens.

———. [An identical copy. Green cloth.]

> **Inscription:** Clemens inscribed the front pastedown endpaper in black ink: "SL. Clemens/1905/A remarkable book."
>
> **Provenance:** Antenne-Dorrance Collection, Rice Lake, Wisconsin.
>
> **Location:** Mark Twain Archive, Gannett-Tripp Learning Center, Elmira College, Elmira, New York. Gift received from Robert and Katharine Antenne in 1994.
>
> **Copy examined:** Clemens's copy. Examined on 27 May 2015.

ALTSHELER, JOSEPH ALEXANDER (1862–1919). *The Candidate; A Political Romance.* New York: Harper & Brothers, 1905. 429 pp.

> **Source:** MTLAcc, entry #1836, volume donated from Clemens's library by Clara Clemens Gabrilowitsch in 1910.

AM. COL. N. E. SOCIETY, DEC. 22, 1886. N.p., [1886]. 93 pp. Paperbound.

> **Source:** MTLAcc, entry #341, volume donated by Clemens. Unidentified. Presumably this report was issued by the American Colonization Society, which had continued to support the nation of Liberia even after the American Civil War rendered pointless the Society's earlier efforts to transport African Americans freed from enslavement to that region of Africa.

The American Architect and Building News (weekly periodical, Boston). [First issue published on 1 January 1876.]

> Osgood & Co. billed Clemens $6.00 for the back numbers of 1876, purchased on 13 March 1877 (Scrapbook #10, p. 69, MTP).

American Art Review. Boston: Dana Estes and Charles E. Lauriat, 1880.

> **Catalog:** Ball 2016 inventory, black leather, gilt lettering, oversized volume, good condition.
>
> **Location:** Quarry Farm library shelves, under the supervision of the Mark Twain Archive, Elmira College, Elmira, New York.
>
> One of the many books available to Clemens whenever he was browsing in the Cranes' library shelves during his visits to Elmira.

The American Bookmaker (monthly periodical). Bristol, Connecticut: Moore Publishing Co. [The first issue was published in July 1885.]

> On 21 October 1889 Clemens mentioned in a letter that he had read the current issue of this printers' journal because of his interest in the Paige typesetter (SLC to Mr. Taylor, ALS in Mrs. Robin Craven Collection, PH in MTP).

The American Church Missionary Register (monthly periodical). New York: American Missionary Society of the Protestant Episcopal Church.

> In his 20 May 1867 letter to the *Alta California* Mark Twain reported on this journal: "Mr. Rising edits her, and she is a credit to him" (*MTTMB* [1940], p. 210). The Reverend Franklin Samuel Rising (c. 1833–1868)

served as a domestic missionary to the Nevada Territory and rector of St. Paul's Church in Virginia City. He soon became the Secretary of the American Missionary Society of the Protestant Episcopal Church. Upon learning that Rising had perished in a steamboat collision on the Ohio River on 4 December 1868, Clemens wrote to Olivia Langdon, calling Rising "a steadfast friend" and "a noble young fellow" and reminiscing about Rising's efforts "to get at the better natures of the rough population around him" (*MTLet* 2: 333).

Andrew Forest Muir, "Note on Twain and Rising," *California Historical Society Quarterly* 34.4 (December 1955): 317–322.

The American Cyclopaedia: A Popular Dictionary of General Knowledge. Ed. by George Ripley (1802–1880) and Charles A[nderson]. Dana (1819–1897). 16 vols. New York: D. Appleton and Co., 1873–1876.

Source: MTLAcc, entries #694–709. Complete set donated by Clemens.

In Chapter 55 of *Roughing It* (1872) Mark Twain acknowledged that he "fell back" on "the 'American Cyclopedia,'" which he called "that steadfast friend of the editor, all over this land," when he was pressed by newspaper deadlines in Virginia City. Twain referred to this resource numerous times thereafter. In 1882 he expressed pleasure that Whitelaw Reid's biography had not been sketched in the *Cyclopaedia* published by Appleton (NB 19, *N&J* 2:423). In 1884 he received a statement for his "Amer. Encyclopedia" in the amount of $92.25 and another charge of $35 "for Annuals to Encyclopedia" (Charles L. Webster to SLC, 2 September 1884, MTP). Twain gave this reference work as his source for his knowledge about early Irish history and the Pope's deceptive policies in an entry made in July 1885 in Notebook 24 (*N&J* 3: 167). He resolved to "look in supplements to Appleton" in July 1888 for information about the Franco-Prussian War (NB 28, *N&J* 3: 405). Twain intended to credit *The American Cyclopaedia* in a projected Appendix to *A Connecticut Yankee in King Arthur's Court* as his source of knowledge about the process of excommunication and interdiction (NB 29 [1889], *N&J* 3: 502, 506). His allusions to *The American Cyclopaedia* are implicitly complimentary, and the series should be considered one of his central reference sources for American history and biography. As a general reference tool he ranked it second only to the *Encyclopaedia Britannica*. The last edition of *The American Cyclopaedia* was issued in 1883–1884. See also the Catalog entry for *Appletons' Annual Cyclopaedia and Register of Important Events*.

American Miscellany. A Magazine of Complete Stories (periodical). Boston: James H. Brigham. [Published 1865–1874].

In Chapter 36 of Mark Twain and Charles Dudley Warner's *The Gilded Age* (1873), Laura Hawkins refers to this magazine as "literary fatty degeneration of the heart." Its editor and publisher James H. Brigham (c. 1833–1915) never recovered financially from the great Boston fire of 1872 and suspended the magazine within a few years.

The American Nation: A History from Original Sources by Associated Scholars. Ed. by Albert Bushnell Hart (1854–1943). 28 vols. American Nation Series. New York: Harper & Brothers, 1906–1918.

Inscriptions: *A1911* listed Vols. and 16 and 17 as being signed "S. L. Clemens, 1907"; however, the Lexington Book Shop Catalogue Number 19 [1912] reported that Volume 16, Hart's *Slavery and Abolition, 1831–1841*, was signed "S. L. Clemens, 1906" on the front pastedown endpaper.)

Catalogs: ListABP (1910), "American Nation 2 v., Hart", no other information supplied; *A1911*, "3 vols. 12mo, cloth, . . . autograph, 'S. L. Clemens, 1907,' in first two volumes," lot 8, sold for $4.50; *Lexington 1912*, 3 vols. only, lots #13 (Hart, $3.50), #14 (Matteson, $2.00), and #17 (Hosmer, $3.50).

Clemens quite possibly owned more volumes in the set, but only three were offered at the 1911 auction: Volume 16 (published in 1906), *Slavery and Abolition, 1831–1841*, by Albert Bushnell Hart (1854–1943), signed "S. L. Clemens, 1906"; Volume 21 (published in 1907), *The Outcome of the Civil War, 1863–1865*, by J[ames]. K[endall]. Hosmer (1834–1927), signed "S. L. Clemens, 1907"; and Volume 28 (published in 1908), *Analytic Index*, compiled by David Maydole Matteson (1871–1949).

American Ornithology for the Home and School. Ed. by Chester Albert Reed (1876–1912). Dark green cloth, gilt lettering, photograph of a bluebird on the front cover. Worcester, Massachusetts: Charles K. Reed, 1901. 246 pp. [Bound issues of only the first year of publication, Volume 1.1–12 (January-December 1901): 1–246. The periodical would continue publishing issues until 1906.

Source: MTLAcc, entry #1974, Volume 1 only (1901, 246 pp.) donated from Clemens's library by Clara Clemens Gabrilowitsch in 1910.

Inscription: the front free endpaper is signed "Jean Lampton Clemens/Riverdale on the Hudson./November 19th 1902".

Location: Mark Twain Library, Redding, Connecticut. Displays the Library's purple oval stamps.

Copy examined: Jean Clemens's unmarked copy. Has the red ink Mark Twain Library accession number "1974". Examined in 1970, in June 1982, and again on 8 November 2019.

AMIEL, HENRI FRÉDÉRIC (1821–1881). *Amiel's Journal: The Journal Intime of Henri-Frédéric Amiel.* Translated with an introduction and notes by Mrs. Humphry Ward [Mary Augustus (Arnold) Ward (1851–1920)]. London: Macmillan and Co., 1894. 318 pp.

Inscription: signed on the front flyleaf, "Olivia L. Clemens/London/<1896>1897".

Marginalia: notes and markings in pencil throughout. A loose note is enclosed; its handwriting resembles Clara Clemens's: "Equality (the era of)/means the triumph of/mediocrity./Il Penseroso—Poésies Maximes/Amiel".

Provenance: stamp, charge-card pocket, and call number of the Mark Twain Library, Redding. Donated to that collection by Clemens (MTLAcc, entry #1785).

Catalog: *Mott 1952*, #35, $15.

Location: Mark Twain House and Museum, Hartford. Anonymous gift received in 1963.

Copy examined: Olivia Clemens's copy. Examined in August 1987. The notes appear to be in her hand. An unknown authority has erroneously identified these comments and a loose note in the book as Susy Clemens's writing, though Susy did not accompany her parents to London and died on 18 August 1896.

Mark Twain attested that he found an edition of "Amiel's Journal" among "35 cloth-bound books" on a shelf in Kaltenleutgeben in 1898 ("The Great Republic's Peanut Stand," unpublished manuscript, MTP).

Among the Daisies. Poems Old and New. Edited by E[mma]. B[each]. Illus. Sold by Subscription Only. Hartford: American Publishing Co., 1884. 194 pp.

Catalog: *A1911,* "4to, cloth, Hartford, 1884," lot 11, sold for $2.50.

The publisher advertised this anthology of American and English poetry as "a book of rare beauty and merit; being a collection of all the poems that have ever been written about the daisy" (Hill, *MT&EB*, p. 183).

ANICET-BOURGEOIS, AUGUSTE (1806–1871). *Le Bossu [The Hunchback]* (play, performed in Paris in 1862).

Adapted from *Le Petite Parisien,* a novel written by Paul Féval (1816–1887), the drama *Le Bossu* received an English translation by Charles Fechter (1824–1879) and was performed in the United States as *The Duke's Motto* (1864). (It also was produced under another title, *The Duke's Daughter; or, the Hunchback of Paris. A Drama in Three Acts.*) Mark Twain was familiar with the play, since a column he wrote for *The Golden Era,* "More Spiritual Investigations" (11 March 1866), quoted a line the play had made famous. Attending "a private fireside séance" held by a pair of mediums, Twain calls forth one of the many spirits in the other world named Smith. "I am here," the spirit announces. "Staunch and true," answers Twain, echoing a character in *Le Bossu,* the Duke De Nevers.

ANDERSEN, HANS CHRISTIAN (1805–1875). *Bilderbuch ohne Bilder [Picture Book without Pictures].* Nach der fünsten dänischen Ausgabe, Deutsch von Edmund Lobedanz. Red cloth. Berlin: Grote'sche Verlagsbuchhandlung, 1874. 80 pp.

Location: Mark Twain Library, Redding, Connecticut.

Copy examined: Clemens's unmarked copy. Examined in 1970 and again on 15 June 1982. Contains the red ink accession number "4096".

Colonel Sellers mistakenly refers to Andersen as a great painter in Chapter 19 of Mark Twain's *The American Claimant* (1892). In Twain's "Is He Living or Is He Dead?" (1893) the character named Smith relates "one of Hans Andersen's beautiful little stories."

———. *The White Swans and Other Tales.* Illus. by Alice Havers (1850–1890) with chromolithographs. Original quarter cloth and white lithographic pictorial boards, gilt. New York: E. P. Dutton, n. d.

Inscription: card with silk ribbon laid in, with inscription from Susan Crane: "Merry Christmas/To Miss Ida Langdon/From/Aunt Susie." Ida Langdon (1880–1964) was the daughter of Charles Jervis and Ida Clark Langdon, and a playmate of her cousins Jean, Susy, and Clara Clemens.

Location: collection of Kevin Mac Donnell, Austin, Texas. Purchased from the Langdon family.

Source: description by Mac Donnell sent to Alan Gribben, 28 August 2017.

The Langdons' library was accessible to Clemens whenever he visited their home in Elmira, and Ida Langdon may have shared her girlhood reading with the Clemens daughters.

ANDERSON, RASMUS BJÖRN (1846–1936) and **JÓN BJARNASON** (1845–1914), trans. *Viking Tales of the North. The Sagas of Thornstein, Viking's Son, and Fridthjof the Bold. Trans. from the Icelandic by R. B. Anderson and J. Bjarnason. Also [Esaias] Tegnér's [1782–1846] Fridthjof's Saga, Trans. into English [in Verse] by G[eorge]. Stephens [1813–1895].* Chicago: S. C. Griggs & Son, 1877. 370 pp.

Clemens purchased this book on 20 March 1877, according to a receipt from Osgood and Company (Scrapbook #10, p. 69, MTP).

See also the Catalog entries for Esaias Tegnér.

ANDERSON, RUFUS (1796–1880). *The Hawaiian Islands: Their Progress and Condition Under Missionary Labors.* Boston: Gould and Lincoln, 1864. 450 pp. [A third edition was issued in 1865; the edition Clemens consulted is unknown.]

Mark Twain noted the author and title of this book on his copy of James Jackson Jarves' *History of the Hawaiian or Sandwich islands* (*N&J* 1:105). The impolite character called Mr. Brown, referring to Anderson by name, castigates such "books shoemakered up by them pious bushwhackers in America" in a letter Twain wrote for the 25 August 1866 issue of the Sacramento *Weekly Union* (Dane, *LSI* [1938], pp. 151–152).

ANDREWS, LORRIN (1795–1868). *A Dictionary of the Hawaiian Language, to Which is Appended an English-Hawaiian Vocabulary and a Chronological Table of Remarkable Events.* Honolulu: Printed by H. M. Whitney, 1865. 559 pp.

Clemens mentioned this resource in Notebook 6 (1866, *N&J* 1:206).

ANDREWS, LOUIS ROBINS (1877–1911). *The White Peril; or, How I Cured Myself of Consumption at Home.* Revised edition. Original purple cloth, lettered in white. Danbury, Connecticut: White Peril Co., 1909. 277 pp.

Inscription: the front free endpaper is inscribed in black ink, "Dr. Samuel L. Clemens,/With compliments of/The Author,/Louis R. Andrews."

Marginalia: Clemens noted at the top of page 133: "We come into life to represent a crime committed against us by our parents—a repetition of the crime that brought man into the world." He is cynically rebutting Andrews's high-minded explanation of "Life's Purpose" that quotes the newspaper poet Ella Wheeler Wilcox (1850–1919) and appears directly below Clemens's annotation: "We Come Into This World to Better It, and to Perfect Ourselves. These Are Life's Highest Aims." This is the only note Clemens made in the book.

Provenance: MTLAcc, entry #1494, volume donated by Clemens. In 1984 a West Coast collector sold the volume to John Jenkins of the Jenkins Company Rare Books and Manuscripts, Austin, Texas. Jenkins soon sold it to an acquaintance in Las Vegas, Nevada.

Source: photocopies of the endpapers, title page, pages 132–133, and the spine, all provided on 17 December 1984 by Kevin Mac Donnell, then an employee of the Jenkins Company.

Location: collection of Kevin Mac Donnell, Austin, Texas.

Copy examined: photocopies of Clemens's copy. Contains the purple stamps of the Mark Twain Library in Redding, Connecticut as well as a library charge slip pasted on the rear free endpaper. Displays the red ink library accession number "1494". Acquired by Kevin Mac Donnell in 2019

(Mac Donnell to Alan Gribben, 22 November 2019). Andrews listed himself as a professional piano tuner in the Danbury, Connecticut city directories of the 1900s. He would die on 1 September 1911.

Anecdote Library. Portraits and Views.
Inscription: signed "S. L. Clemens" on the front pastedown endpaper.
Catalog: *A1911*, "16mo, calf (loose), imperfect," no publisher or date provided, quotes the signature, lot 12, sold for $1.75.
Books with this title were published in London throughout the 1820s, 1830s, and 1840s, and variant titles appeared in the United States in subsequent decades, making it impossible to identify any particular candidate for this cryptic listing.

ANÍCHKOVA, ANNA MITROFANOVNA AVINOVA, PSEUD. "IVAN STRANNIK" (1868–1935). *The Shadow of the House.* Translated from the French by Emma A. Clinton. Green cloth. New York: McClure, Phillips & Co., 1906. 307 pp.
Inscription: the front pastedown endpaper is signed in black ink, "S. L. Clemens/1906."
Marginalia: grammatical correction on page 27 in black ink; at the bottom of the page Clemens comments: "It is a clumsy translation,—this book. (Sometimes.)" On page 85 Clemens wrote "armoué" beside the word "armoury." There are no other markings.
Provenance: Antenne-Dorrance Collection, Rice Lake, Wisconsin.
Location: Mark Twain Archive, Gannett-Tripp Learning Center, Elmira College, Elmira, New York.
Copy examined: Clemens's copy. Examined on 28 May 2015.
Anichkova often wrote fiction in French that depicted Russians living abroad. She and her husband maintained a literary salon in Paris for several decades, becoming acquainted with writers such as Anatole France. In *L'ombre de la maison* (1904) the protagonist Helene Tourgorine tolerates a marriage of incompatibility for the sake of her child and the respectability of her family's name.

"ANNIE LAURIE" (old Scottish song).
Mentioned by Clemens as "that sweet thing" in Notebook 5 (1866, *N&J* 1:121). William Douglas (c. 1672–1748) is generally credited as the author of the poem on which the song was based. See also the Catalog entry for Bayard Taylor's "The Song of the Camp" (poem).

ANTHON, CHARLES (1797–1867). *A Classical Dictionary, Containing an Account of the Principal Proper Names Mentioned in Ancient Authors.* New York: Harper & Brothers, 1880. 1,451 pp. [Publisher and pages conjectured.]
Inscription: "S. L. Clemens, Hartford, June, 1881" on flyleaf.
Catalogs: *A1911*, "8vo, sheep (torn and broken)," quotes the autograph, lot 14, sold for $1; *L1912*, lot 3, sold for $5.
Anthon compiled names occurring in classical Greek and Roman literature and history.

Appletons' Annual Cyclopaedia and Register of Important Events of the Year. 10 vols. New York: D. Appleton and Co., 1877, 1879, 1880, 1881, 1883, 1884 (three copies), 1885, and 1886.
Source: MTLAcc, entries #711 through #720, volumes donated by Clemens.
See also the Catalog entry for *The American Cyclopaedia.*

[*Appletons' Annual Cyclopaedia and Register of Important Events.*] *A General and Analytical Index to Appletons' Annual Cyclopaedia.* Comp. by Thomas Jefferson Conant (1802–1891). New York: D. Appleton & Co., 1878. 810 pp.
Source: MTLAcc, entry #710, volume donated by Clemens.
[*The Arabian Nights.*] *Far-Famed Tales from the Arabian Nights' Entertainments . . . with Notes from Lane's Edition.* Two volumes in one. Original green cloth, gilt. New York: David G. Francis, Formerly C. S. Francis & Co., n. d. [Evidently dating from the 1860s, since David G. Francis took over from C. S. Francis in 1860 and Jervis Langdon died in 1870.]
Inscription: an ink inscription by Clemens on the front flyleaf has been almost entirely erased except for the name "Langdon."
Provenance: has the bookplate of Jervis Langdon on the front pastedown endpaper: "J. LANGDON'S FAMILY LIBRARY, No. 313." A note on the front free endpaper promises "with critical notes by M.T.", but none is to be found.
Marginalia: Faint ink markings appear to have been erased in Part I on pages 25 ("The Merchant and the Genie"), 33 ("The Third Man and the Mule"), 299 ("Ali Babba and the Forty Robbers"). In Part II a leaf was laid in long ago as a marker at pages 326–327 ("About Hassan the Wag").
Location: collection of Kevin Mac Donnell, Austin, Texas. Acquired from the Langdon family in May 2016 (email, Mac Donnell to Alan Gribben, 16 May 2016).
Source: detailed descriptions of the "well-worn" volume sent on 9 June 2016 and 12 July 2016 by Mac Donnell to Gribben. Mac Donnell notes that the publisher completely deleted an unnamed story in Part II from page 263 to page 318; the story was also removed from the book's table of contents.

[*The Arabian Nights.*] *The Thousand and One Nights, Commonly Called, in England, The Arabian Nights' Entertainments. A New Translation from the Arabic, with Copious Notes. By Edward William Lane [1801–1876]. Illustrated by . . . William Harvey [1796–1866].* 3 vols. London: Charles Knight & Co., 1839–1841.
Inscription: in pencil on a front flyleaf: "S. L. Clemens, Hartford, 1877. A rare and valuable copy."
Marginalia: pencil note by Clemens on the endpaper.
Catalogs: *C1951*, #11c, "3 vols.," listed among books signed by Clemens; item #29 in Zeitlin & Ver Brugge Booksellers List No. 132 (May 1951), price $37.50.
Location: undetermined at present.
Lane's bowdlerized translation would become available in a revised edition in 1859. Richard Burton's more exotic version of *The Book of Thousand Nights and a Night* would not be published until 1885–1888. In July 1877 Clemens made a memorandum to go to a secondhand bookstore in New York City and "get 2d hand Arabian Nights" along with other miscellaneous books (NB 13, *N&J* 2:38). Apparently he required help in completing his set of volumes, for on 10 December 1877 he thanked Andrew Chatto of London "for the other half of the Arabian Nights" (Berg, NYPL). It may also be relevant that Olivia Clemens's ledger of expenses while the Clemenses visited Munich included a charge of "2.25" for "Arabian Nights" (NB 13a, 1878). A childhood friend of Clemens in Hannibal, Charley Curtis, recalled that young Sam Clemens "used to get a lot of the boys—Ed Pierce, Bill Nash, Ben Coontz, 'Gene Freeman,

Ruel Gridley, Tom Blankenship, and John Meredith—and tell the Arabian Nights stories to us. His father, John M. Clemens, owned the only copy of the book in town, and after Sam had digested it thoroughly he related the whole thing to us, decorated in his own way" (Homer Bassford, "The Friends of Mark Twain's Boyhood," *Saturday Evening Post* 173.12 [22 September 1900]: 15). Clara Clemens recalled that her father occasionally related stories from *The Arabian Nights* while his family was dining (*MFMT*, p. 56). In 1924 Henry Pochmann logically included the work among those dozen books he selected in "The Mind of Mark Twain" as Clemens's lifetime library classics. Harold Aspiz found "at least eight references to the *Arabian Nights*, establishing it as one of his favorite books" ("Mark Twain's Reading" [1949], p. 187). The following instances of Twain's references to the work's title or characters signify the extent of his lifelong fondness for the collection. Next to the Bible and Shakespeare plays, it was the literary source from which he consciously and recurrently drew the most allusions.

Mark Twain alluded to *The Arabian Nights* in his 10 September 1866 letter to the Sacramento *Weekly Union* (*LH*, p. 57) and in 2 February and 2 March 1867 letters to the *Alta California* (*MTTMB* [1940], pp. 86, 119; *TIA*, p. 26). *The Innocents Abroad* (1869) contains references in Chapters 8 ("it can never be found in any book save the Arabian Nights"), 12 ("perfumes of Araby"), 13 ("the tame achievements of Aladdin and the Magii of Arabia"), 18 ("Aladdin's palace"), 33 ("all the wild tales in the Arabian Nights"), 34 ("in the mysterious land where the giants and genii of the Arabian Nights once dwelt . . . where Princes and Princesses flew through the air on carpets"), and 44 ("when heroes and heroines of the Arabian Nights walked the streets . . . or flew away toward Bagdad on enchanted carpets"). *The Arabian Nights* often occurred to Clemens during his courtship of Olivia Langdon and their subsequent sojourn in Buffalo. On 12 December 1867 he lamented to Mary Mason Fairbanks about his prospects with Olivia: "I can't turn an inkstand into Aladdin's lamp" (*MTLet* 2: 134). On 4 December 1868 he referred to "the fabled copper vessel of Arabian story" in a letter to Olivia (*MTLet* 2, p. 305). A letter from Clemens to Schuyler Cofax, 10 or 11 December 1869 (*MTLet* 3: 421) alluded to "Open Sesame"; another from Clemens to Joel Benton, 20 February 1870, compared his new Buffalo house to "our Aladdin's Palace" (*MTLet* 4: 74). "As the Persians say—on your head be it!" Clemens quipped to a correspondent on 1 December 1874 (*MTLet* 6: 300), a likely reference to *The Arabian Nights*. He repeated this phrase—"then, (as the Arabs say,) 'On my head be it!'"—in a letter to Pamela A. Moffett on 23 July 1875 (*MTLet* 6: 515). There is an allusion in Chapter 49 of *A Tramp Abroad* (1880) to a "curious robbery" in St. Mark's Cathedral in Venice that "might be smuggled into the 'Arabian Nights,' and not seem out of place there." In Notebook 19 in 1880 Clemens fantasized about "Arabian Nights Supernaturals" (*N&J* 2: 359). He alluded to "The Old Man of the Sea," a figure in the tale of Sindbad the Sailor, in a letter to William Dean Howells written on 8 January 1880 (*MTHL*, p. 287), A comical reference came to Clemens's mind in 1881 in Notebook 19 (*N&J* 2: 428):

"The Talkative barber in Arabian Nights." In "The Walt Whitman Controversy" (DV36, MTP), probably written around 1882, Mark Twain mentions it as one of the "old bad books" that he owns. He spoke of Aladdin and his lamp in "On Adam," a speech delivered on 23 May 1883 (*MTSpk*, p. 178). Twain gleefully wrote a ten-chapter burlesque of Scherezade's tales told to "King Shahriyar" in 1883, titling it "1,002d Arabian Night," but Howells was unimpressed and the piece would not be published until 1967 (Rogers, *S&B*, pp. 91–133). Howells liked the opening passages but complained that much of the rest made him feel like "a fellow-sufferer with the Sultan from Sheherazade's [sic] prolixity" and found the tone to be "a little too broad, as well as exquisitely ludicrous" (*MTHL*, pp. 441–442). Twain alludes to Aladdin's lamp in Chapter 55 of *Life on the Mississippi* (1883). *The Arabian Nights* as well as *Don Quixote* inspire Tom Sawyer's raid on the Sunday-school picnickers in Chapter 3 of *Adventures of Huckleberry Finn* (1885); Huck also refers to "a thousand and one tales" in Chapter 23 of *Huckleberry Finn*, but confusedly associates them with King Henry VIII's tendency to execute his wives. On 20 January 1887 Twain named *The Arabian Nights* as one of his favorite books in a letter to the Reverend Charles D. Crane (ALS, Shapell Manuscript Library, Beverly Hills, California). In that same letter Twain also selected it as one of the best works for young people to read. Twain referred to *The Arabian Nights* in a letter to Howells written on 15 February 1887 (*MTHL*, p. 586); in "At the Shrine of St. Wagner" (1891); in Notebook 30 (1891; *N&J* 3: 605); in "Marienbad—A Health Factory" (1891); and in "The £1,000,000 Bank-Note" (1893). Tom Sawyer relies on *The Arabian Nights* in Chapters 7 (the missing camel), 9 ("he begun to tell about it out of the Arabian Nights"), 10 (the dervish and the camel-driver), 12 (the prince and the flying bronze horse), and 13 of *Tom Sawyer Abroad* (1894). Twain cited *The Arabian Nights* in Notebook 37 (1896), TS p. 37. In *Following the Equator* (1897), Twain used *The Arabian Nights* metaphorically as he had previously in *The Innocents Abroad* to describe marvelous sights in Chapters 38 (three allusions: "*Bombay!*. . . —the Arabian Nights come again!," "genii and giants and Aladdin lamps," and "dressed for a part in the Arabian Nights"), 39 ("this was the land of the Arabian Nights"), and 43 ("a terribly realistic chapter out of the 'Arabian Nights'"). Chapter 42 of *Following the Equator* declares of a Hindu wedding: "It was another Aladdin show." There are additional references in NB 40 (July 1899), TS p. 58; Clemens's letter to Henry H. Rogers on 9 April 1900—"As the genii say in the Arabian Nights, 'I hear and I obey'" (*MTHHR*, p. 442); "To My Missionary Critics" (1901); "It's the Arabian Nights come again!" in Chapter 4 of Twain's "No. 44, The Mysterious Stranger," written 1902–1908 (*MSM*, p. 211); "Yes— . . . like the Arabian tales of the Thousand Nights" in "What Is Man?" (1906), Part 5 *WIM?*, p. 179; the 13 August 1906 Autobiographical Dictation, which alludes to Susy Clemens's concept of India as "a land made out of poetry and moonlight for the Arabian Nights to do their gorgeous miracles in" (*MTE*, p. 310; *AutoMT* 2: 176); an Autobiographical Dictation of 30 July 1907 describing the Oxford pageant ("it was the Arabian Nights come again") (*AutoMT* 3: 93); and in a letter from Clemens to Dorothy Sturgis written on 27 October 1908 that contains an allusion (Columbia University). Asked to nominate two stories for inclusion in *Favorite Fairy Tales: The Childhood Choice of Representative Men and Women* (1907; see that Catalog entry), Twain chose "Aladdin and the Wonderful Lamp" and "Ali Baba and the Forty Thieves." The magic carpet is mentioned in Chapter 2 of Twain's *Extract from Captain Stormfield's Visit to Heaven* (1909).

[*The Arabian Nights*.] *The Thousand and One Nights; or, The Arabian Nights' Entertainments. A New Edition.* "Alta Edition" lettered on cover. Philadelphia: Porter & Coates, [1881]. 543 pp.

Inscription: signed "S. L. Clemens" in brown ink on the front pastedown endpaper.

Catalog: *C1951*, D62, listed with books signed by Clemens.

Provenance: formerly in the collection of Chester L. Davis (1903–1987), Executive-Secretary, Mark Twain Research Foundation, Perry, Missouri.

Location: currently undetermined.

Copy examined: Clemens's copy, in 1970 in Perry, Missouri.

ARCHER, WILLIAM (1856–1924). *America To-Day: Observations and Reflections.* New York: Charles Scribner's Sons, 1899. 260 pp. [Edition conjectured.]

Catalog: ListABP (1910), "America Today, Archer", no other information supplied.

Born in Scotland, Archer became a leading drama critic in London. His observations of American government, history, and literature, based partly on his travels in the United States, attempted to be judgmental yet balanced.

ARGYLL, JOHN GEORGE EDWARD HENRY DOUGLAS SUTHERLAND CAMPBELL, NINTH DUKE OF (1845–1914). *Viscount Palmerston, K. G. By the Marquis of Lorne, K. T.* The Prime Ministers of Queen Victoria Series. General Ed. Stuart Johnson Reid (1848–1927). New York: Harper & Brothers, 1892. 235 pp. [Publisher and pages conjectured.]

Catalog: *A1911*, "12mo, cloth, N.Y. 1892," a portion of a sheet of Clemens's notes laid in, lot 299, sold for $1.

Henry John Temple Palmerston (1784–1865) was prime minister of England from 1855 until 1865.

ARISTOTLE (384–322 BCE).

Aristotle was a student of Plato in ancient Athens who gained lasting fame and influence of his own. In the course of annotating Oliver Wendell Holmes' *Autocrat of the Breakfast-Table* in 1869 Clemens paused in Chapter 11 where Holmes mentions Aristotle (p. 302) and asked, "Did you ever read a single paragraph of Aristotle, Livy—I never did" (Bradford A. Booth, "Mark Twain's Comments on Holmes' *Autocrat*" [1950], p. 463). Twain would refer to Aristotle's extraordinary mind in Chapter 21 of *The American Claimant* (1892) and would allude to Aristotle as a self-appointed naturalist "authority" in an Autobiographical Dictation of 30 May 1907 (*MTE*, pp. 22–23, 24; *AutoMT* 3: 68).

Philip C. Kolin, "Mark Twain, Aristotle, and *Pudd'nhead Wilson*," *Mark Twain Journal* 15.2 (Summer 1970): 1–4.

The Armies of To-day; A Description of the Armies of the Leading Nations. Illus. New York: Harper & Brothers, [cop. 1892]. 438 pp.

Source: MTLAcc, entry # 1369, volume donated by Clemens.

Eight separate essays by different military authorities described the states of equipment, standing armies, and preparedness of the United States, Great Britain, France, Germany, Russia, Austro-Hungary, Italy, and Mexico, with a concluding essay devoted to "The Military Situation in Europe." Brigadier General Wesley Merritt (1834–1910) summarized the wartime readiness of United States military forces; Viscount Garnet Wolseley (1833–1913) did the same for Great Britain; and Thomas A. Janvier (1849–1913) surveyed the Mexican troops.

ARNDT, ERNST MORITZ (1769–1860). "Das Lied vom Feldmarschall" (song, published in 1813).

Clemens copied (in German) the six stanzas of this war song into Notebook 23 in late October 1884 (*N&J* 3: 76–77). Arndt was a German patriotic poet; this song paid tribute to the military feats of Gebhard Lebrecht von Blücher.

ARNIM, MARY ANNETTE (BEAUCHAMP) VON (1866–1941), pseud. "Elizabeth." (In 1916 she would become Mary Annette Russell, Countess Russell.) *The Solitary Summer.* New York: Macmillan Co.; London: Macmillan Co., 1899. 190 pp. [Edition conjectured.]

The Australian-born Arnim came to Clemens's attention in 1900, when he wrote, "A Solitary Summer by author of Elizabeth & her German Garden" (NB 43, TS p. 2a). Arnim's immensely popular, semibiographical novel titled *Elizabeth and Her German Garden* had appeared in 1898. It drew upon her pleasant existence at her husband's country estate at Nassenheide in Prussia, where she had moved from Berlin in 1896. A follow-up novel in 1899, *The Solitary Summer*, portrayed her exasperated search for a space and identity apart from family and marital responsibilities. Gradually she finds peace in the garden she superintends at her husband's extensive estate. Following her husband's death in 1910, in 1916 Arnim would marry the older brother of the philosopher and mathematician Bertrand Russell, thereby becoming the Countess Russell.

Horst Kruse made a case for Twain's having borrowed a version of this author's name ("Elisabeth von Arnim") for Marget Regen's Dream-Self ("The Old Mamsell and the Mysterious Stranger: Mark Twain's Encounter with German Literature and the Writing of 'No. 44, The Mysterious Stranger,'" *American Literary Realism* 39.1 [Fall 2006]: 64–73, especially pages 70–73).

ARNOLD, (SIR) EDWIN (1832–1904). *India Revisited.* "Author's Edition." Red cloth. Boston: Roberts Brothers, 1886. 324 pp.

Inscription: inscribed in black ink on the front flyleaf, in Olivia Clemens's handwriting: "Saml. L. Clemens/Nov. 30th 1886/ Hartford/ Livy".

Provenance: Antenne-Dorrance Collection, Rice Lake, Wisconsin.

Location: Mark Twain Archive, Gannett-Tripp Learning Center, Elmira College, Elmira, New York.

Copy examined: Clemens's copy. Examined on 28 May 2015.

————. *The Light of Asia; or, The Great Renunciation (Mahâbhinishkramana), Being the Life and Teachings of Gautama, Prince of India and Founder of Buddhism (As told in Verse by an Indian Buddhist).* [First published in 1879; reprinted in 1880, 1881, and other years by Roberts Brothers of Boston as well as other firms. The edition in the Clemenses' library is undetermined.]

Catalog: *C1951*, J7, listed among the books owned by Jean and Clara Clemens.

Gautama Buddha, originally Siddhartha Gautama, renounced worldly luxuries and in the sixth and fifth centuries BCE founded the faith known as Buddhism. Arnold's book-length poem combined numerous legends surrounding the Buddha and received much acclaim.

————. *Pearls of the Faith; or, Islam's Rosary. Being the Ninety-nine Beautiful Names of Allah (Asmâ-el-husnâ). With Comments in Verse by Various Oriental Sources (as Made by an Indian Musulman).* Boston: Roberts Brothers, 1883. 319 pp. [Publisher and pages conjectured.]

Inscription: the front flyleaf is signed, "S. L. Clemens, 1883".

Catalog: *A1911*, "12mo, cloth, Bost. 1883," quotes the autograph, lot 15, sold for $3.

ARNOLD, GEORGE (1834–1865). *Drift: A Sea-Shore Idyl and Other Poems.* Ed. and memoir by William Winter (1836–1917). Brown cloth, calf spine and half cover, marbled endpapers, gilt edges. Boston: Ticknor and Fields, 1866. 177 pp.

Inscription: signed by the author, George Arnold.

Provenance: bookplate #47 of the "J. Langdon Family Library" on the front pastedown endpaper.

Catalog: Ball 2016 inventory, brown cloth, gilt lettering, blind design, gilt edge pages, signed by the author and by C. J. Langdon, Jervis Langdon Family Library #47.

Location: Mark Twain Archive, Elmira College, Elmira, New York.

Copy examined: unmarked copy available to Clemens whenever he visited the Langdons in Elmira. Examined on 27 May 2015.

ARNOLD, MATTHEW (1822–1888). *Civilization in the United States: First and Last Impressions of America.* [Excerpted in the pages of *Nineteenth Century* 23.134 (April 1888): 481–496; issued that same year in book form.]

"Matthew Arnold's civilization is *superficial polish*," Mark Twain observed in April 1888 (NB 27, *N&J* 3: 383). Yet in a letter written to Robert Louis Stevenson on 15–17 April 1888 Clemens blamed the "heedless" American press for misconstruing Arnold's "kind intent" (ALS in John Howell Papers, Silverado Museum, St. Helena, California). A few months later he castigated Arnold for preferring "that worm-eaten & dilapidated social structure in England" (NB 28, *N&J* 3: 406). D. M. McKeithan deduced that Mark Twain intended his speech titled "On Foreign Critics" (27 April 1890, *MTS* [1923], pp. 150–153; Fatout, *MTSpk* [1976], pp. 257–260) as a retort to Arnold's criticisms, but Arnold's unexpected death in April 1888 compelled him to omit all personal references. McKeithan also demonstrated that Mark Twain's speech included a quotation from Sir Lepel Henry Griffin (1840–1908) by way of Matthew Arnold's *Civilization in the United States* (1888—published in magazine form under another title); Arnold had modified it slightly in *Civilization* from Griffin's *The Great Republic* (1884) (McKeithan, "The Occasion of Mark Twain's Speech 'On Foreign Critics,'" *Philological Quarterly* 27.3 (July 1948): 276–279; this essay was collected in McKeithan's *Court Trials in Mark Twain* [1958], pp. 144–147). Twain's indignation still showed plainly in Chapter 10 of *The American Claimant*

(1892), in which Lord Berkeley listens to the assistant editor of the *Daily Democrat* read two passages from Arnold's book—both critical of the Americans' lack of awe and respect—and argue that Arnold overlooked the chief virtue of American journalism: "its frank and cheerful irreverence."

D. M. McKeithan's "More About Mark Twain's War With English Critics of America," *Modern Language Notes* 63.4 (April 1948): 221–228 (collected in *Court Trials in Mark Twain*, pages 148–155) disagreed in a few respects with John B. Hoben's "Mark Twain's *A Connecticut Yankee*: A Genetic Study" (1946). Leland Krauth, *Mark Twain & Company: Six Literary Relations* (Athens: University of Georgia Press, 2003), took a look at the entire Twain-Arnold relationship and detected certain values they held in common.

————. *Essays in Criticism. Second Series.* (London, published in 1888).

Arnold's essay on Shelley in this volume probably was the source of Arnold's opinions to which Mark Twain alluded in his "In Defence of Harriet Shelley" (1894).

Alex Brink Effgen, "Mark Twain's Defense of Virtue from the Offense of English Literature: Matthew Arnold and Percy Shelley," *Mark Twain Annual 11* (2013): 77–95.

————. *Poems.*

Catalog: *C1951*, O14, listed among the books that contained Olivia Clemens's signature.

ARNOT, ROBERT (b. 1860), ed. *The Earl of Beaconsfield, K. G. [Benjamin Disraeli, 1804–1881]. Keys to the Famous Characters Delineated in His Historical Romances, with Portraits and Biographies.* Critical appreciation by Henry Pereira Mendes (1852–1937). New York and London: M. Walter Dunne, [cop. 1904].

Inscription: presentation inscription in black ink: "Herbert S. Burt, Esq./Compliments of the Publisher/January, Nineteen hundred and five". Bookplate of Herbert Seymour Barnes on the front pastedown endpaper.

Location: Mark Twain Library, Redding, Connecticut.

Copy examined: almost certainly a spurious addition to Clemens's library. Though Albert E. Stone, Jr. included this title in his catalog of Clemens's books in 1955, and though it was shelved with Clemens's library when I visited Redding in 1970, I could see no reason to presume that this unmarked volume belonged to him. It has no accession number or Mark Twain Library stamps. Examined in 1970 and again in June 1982.

Clemens did know of Benjamin Disraeli's writings; see the Catalog entry for Disraeli.

ARNOULD, (SIR) JOSEPH (1814–1886). *Life of Thomas, First Lord Denman [1779–1854], Formerly Lord Chief Justice of England.* 2 vols. Boston: Estes & Lauriat, 1874.

Inscriptions: Clemens signed both Volumes I and II in pencil on their front flyleaf: "Saml L. Clemens/Hartford 1874."

Marginalia: some annotations in Volume I; there are no markings in Volume II.

Catalogs: *A1911*, #64, Volume I only, sold with fourteen other volumes by various authors for $8.50 total; Stan. V. Henkels (Philadelphia), Catalogue 1057 (14 May 1912), "Vol. 1," item #121; Volume I only offered for sale in 1963 by John Swingle of Alta California Rare Books,

Berkeley, California.

Location: Volume I was given to the Mark Twain House and Museum in Hartford by an anonymous donor in 1965; Volume II is in the Mark Twain Library, Redding, Connecticut.

Copy examined: Clemens's copy of Volume I was inspected by Diana Royce, former Librarian of the Stowe-Day Memorial Library in Hartford, who corresponded with me. Subsequently I inspected that volume in Hartford in August 1987. Volume I has an *A1911* sale label. Clemens's copy of Volume II has the red ink Mark Twain Library accession number "3010". I examined Volume II in 1970 and again on 15 June 1982.

Arrhenius, Svante [August] (1859–1927). *The Life of the Universe as Conceived by Man from the Earliest Ages to the Present Time.* Harper's Library of Living Thought Series. Translated from the Swedish by Dr. H[arold]. [W.] Borns. Illus. 2 vols. London and New York: Harper & Brothers, 1909.

Catalog: *C1951*, D16, listed among the books signed by Clemens.

Arrhenius was a Swedish physicist and physical chemist who won the Nobel Prize for Chemistry in 1903. His *The Life of the Universe* opens with this sentence: "The human races on the lowest grade of evolution live merely for the day" (p. 1).

——————. *Worlds in the Making; The Evolution of the Universe.* Translated from the Swedish by H[arold]. [W.] Borns. Illus. New York: Harper & Brothers, 1908. 230 pp.

Source: *MTLAcc*, entry #538, volume donated by Clemens. *Worlds in the Making* takes up the effects of volcanoes, earthquakes, solar heat, gravity, the collisions of "celestial bodies," and other questions about dynamic activity that were intriguing scientists at the beginning of the twentieth century.

Art and Letters. An Illustrated Review. Ed. by Frédéric Masson (1847–1923). (Monthly periodical, published January 1888–December 1889.) New York: Charles Scribner's Sons; London: Boussod, Valadon & Co. [English edition of *Les lettres et les arts.*]

Catalogs: *A1911*, "January to December, 1888 (not consecutive), 11 parts, small folio, original wrappers, uncut (some pages soiled)," lot 16, sold for $2.50; George D. Smith, New York City, "Catalogue of Books" (1911), accompanied by three sheets of desk blotting paper, one piece signed by Clemens, item #15, $18.

Arthur, Timothy Shay (1809–1885).

The little do-gooder heroine of "The Story of Mamie Grant, the Child-Missionary" (1868) hopes that she "may yet see my poor little name in a beautiful Sunday School book, & maybe T. S. Arthur may write it. Oh, joy!" (*S&B*, pp. 33–39). Twain again mentioned Arthur as an extremely popular writer, but implied that the quality of his work was questionable in "A General Reply," *Galaxy* 10.5 (November 1870): 733 (reprinted in *CTSS&E* 1: 486–487). Laura Hawkins complains in Chapter 36 of *The Gilded Age* (1873) that the peanut boys in railway cars always try to sell one a "Tupper or a dictionary or T. S. Arthur if you are fond of poetry." Arthur's most popular book had been the temperance novel *Ten Nights in a Bar-Room, and What 1 Saw There* (1854).

Artistic Houses; Being a Series of Interior Views of a Number of the Most Beautiful and Celebrated Homes in the United States; with a Description of the Art Treasures Contained Therein. [Ed. by George William Sheldon (1843–1914).] Illus. 2 vols. in 4. Limited edition of 500 copies. New York: Printed for subscribers by D. Appleton and Co., 1883–1884.

Catalog: *A1911*, "over 200 plates, proofs on India paper, in 10 sections, wrappers, . . . velvet-covered board portfolio, brass-tipped corners, . . . N.Y. 1883–4," lot 17, sold for $8.

Clemens was furious when he received a bill for $300 for these books. Calling it "a humiliating swindle," he vowed to order a like amount of other books from D. Appleton & Company and then make them repossess *Artistic Houses* as payment (Clemens to Charles L. Webster, 8 February 1885, *MTBus*, pp. 298–299). There is no evidence that he carried out this threat. Among the New York City mansions depicted in *Artistic Houses* were those of Louis C. Tiffany, Alexander T. Stewart, J. Pierpont Morgan, and William H. Vanderbilt. Opulent homes in other American cities were also included.

The Art Journal (London periodical, published 1839–1912. Between 1875 and 1881 an American edition was published by D. Appleton and Company with similar but not identical contents).

On 12 May 1875 Clemens announced a choice of three prizes for the winning contestant in a fund-raising spelling bee at the Asylum Hill Congregational Church of Hartford. The 13 May 1875 issue of the Hartford *Courant* published Clemens's preliminary remarks and described one of the prizes as a fine arts magazine: "The *London Art Journal*, Appleton, American publisher, in monthly parts."

Leah A. Strong, "Mark Twain on Spelling," *American Literature* 23.3 (November 1951): 357–359; Fatout, *MTSpk* (1976), pp. 94–96.

Artman, Adelia (Cobb), "Mrs. S. R. Artman" (1869–1936). *Glimpses of the Sunny South.* Illus. New York: F. T. Neely & Co., 1903. 176 pp.

Source: *MTLAcc*, entry #802, volume donated by Clemens. This Indiana writer was prominent in the founding of the International Travel Study Club and wrote these poems after a lengthy tour of the American South. She had married Samuel R. Artman (1866–1930) in 1889.

Ralph W. Stark, "The Artmans—Sam and Addie," *Boone: Your County Magazine* 5.25 (February 1978): 8–11.

Asher, Georg Michael (1827–1905), ed. *Henry Hudson the Navigator. The Original Documents in Which His Career Is Recorded. Collected, Partly Translated, and Annotated.* London: Printed for the Hakluyt Society, 1860. 292 pp.

In "Official Report to the I.I.A.S." (written in 1909) Mark Twain cited Asher's opinion that the mermaid Henry Hudson claimed to have seen was "probably a seal" (*LE*, p. 150). Asher wrote only this one book on Hudson's exploits.

Ashton, John (1834–1911). *English Caricature and Satire on Napoleon I.* A New Edition. 115 illustrations. London: Chatto & Windus, 1888. 454 pp. [A two-volume edition in 1884 preceded this one-volume work. Clemens's edition is unknown.]

Source: Maxwell Hunley and John Valentine's "Mark Twain Autograph Sale" (1951) reported that a book titled "Napoleon in Caricature" sold for $20 at the Hollywood auction of Clemens's library.

Napoleon I (1769–1821), Emperor of the French, had

been detested by the English. Ashton's work collected the venomous attacks of satirists as well as cartoonists.

ASSOLLANT, ALFRED (1827–1886). *The Fantastic History of the Celebrated Pierrot. Written by the Magician Alcofribas and Translated from the Sogdian by Alfred Assollant. Rendered into English by A. G. Munro.* Illustrated by Yan' Dargent (1824–1899). London: Sampson Low & Co., 1875. 262 pp.

　Source: MTLAcc, entry #1864, volume donated from Clemens's library by Clara Clemens Gabrilowitsch in 1910. Despite its elaborate title, this was a work of fiction by Alfred Assollant.

ASTOR, WILLIAM WALDORF, 1ST VISCOUNT ASTOR (1848–1919). *Sforza, A Story of Milan.* New York: Charles Scribner's Sons, 1889. 282 pp.

　Source: MTLAcc, entry #11, volume donated by Clemens. Ludovico Sforza (1452–1508) held the title of the Duke of Milan.

————. *Valentino. An Historical Romance of the Sixteenth Century in Italy.* New York: Charles Scribner's Sons, 1885. 325 pp.

　"Valentino. Ch Scribner Sons" wrote Clemens in December 1885 (NB 25, *N&J* 3: 216).

　Cesare Borgia (c. 1476–1507) was the Duke of Valentinois.

ATHENAEUS OF NAUCRATIS (fl. 2nd-3rd centuries CE). *The Deipnosophists; or, Banquet of the Learned, of Athenaeus.* Translated from the Latin by C[harles]. D[uke]. Yonge (1812–1891). Classical Library Series. 3 vols. Original green cloth, stamped gold, gold on spine. Volume III worn, rebacked with original spine laid down, hinges reinforced. London: Henry G. Bohn, 1853–1854. [Volumes 13–15 in Bohn's Classical Library series.]

　Inscription: each volume is signed "Saml L. Clemens,/ Hartford, 1875". Volume III has this signature, place, and date on the half-title page.

　Marginalia: none in Volume III; Volumes I and II have not been inspected.

　Catalogs: *A1911*, "2 vols. [presumably Volumes I and II], 12mo, cloth (one cover loose), quotes the signatures, lot 19, sold for $2.50; Christie's, New York City, 1–2 February 1988 auction, lot 466, Volume III only, sold with two other books for $2,200; "The James S. Copley Library, Sotheby's auction, New York City, 17 June 2010, Volume III only, lot 556, reproduces Clemens's inscription in facsimile, sold with five other titles for $4,250.

　Provenance: shelfmark ("L/H46") of Clara Clemens Gabrilowitsch's private library in Detroit is visible on the front pastedown endpaper in Volume III. Volume III only was purchased by Carrie Estelle Doheny from Maxwell Hunley in 1940 for $12.20 and donated to St. John's Seminary, Camarillo, California. Volume III only was sold by Christie's in 1988 (lot 466) on behalf of St. John's Seminary and the Archdiocese of Los Angeles. Acquired then by J. L. Feldman.

　Locations: Volumes I and II have not been located. Volume III is in the collection of Kevin Mac Donnell, Austin, Texas. Acquired in 2010 (Mac Donnell to Alan Gribben, 29 June 2010). It has the leather book label of Estelle Doheny on the verso of the half-title page.

　Copy examined: Clemens's copy of Volume III, when it belonged to St. John's Seminary.

　Athenaeus, a Greek scholar who wrote in Naucratis, Egypt, recorded much information about the contemporary life and culture around him. *The Deipnosophists; or, Banquet of the Learned* is his only surviving work.

ATHERTON, GERTRUDE FRANKLIN (HORN) (1857–1948). *Ancestors; A Novel.* New York: Harper & Brothers, 1907. 709 pp.

　Source: MTLAcc, entry #1837, volume donated from Clemens's library by Clara Clemens Gabrilowitsch in 1910. Once widely known, the American author Grace Atherton produced a long list of novels, short stories, biographies, and histories.

————. *The Bell in the Fog, and Other Stories.* New York: Harper & Brothers, 1905. 301 pp.

　Source: MTLAcc, entry #1249, volume donated by Isabel V. Lyon, Clemens's secretary.

————. [Another identical copy.]

　Source: MTLAcc, entry #1250, volume donated by Clemens.

————. *Rulers of Kings; A Novel.* New York: Harper & Brothers, 1903. 413 pp.

　Source: MTLAcc, entry #954, volume donated by Clemens.

　Louis J. Budd—"Gertrude Atherton on Mark Twain," *Mark Twain Journal* 21.3 (Spring 1983): 18—located and reprinted an extraordinarily appreciative summary of Twain's literary talents that Atherton published in 1903 and then repeated in 1904. "Any one of his gifts makes the success of the average author. The least he does is powerfully imagined and perfectly executed. But the world takes him as a matter of course." In a long paragraph she went on to specify his various achievements.

————. *The Traveling Thirds.* New York: Harper & Brothers, 1905. 295 pp.

　Source: MTLAcc, entry #1100, volume donated by Clemens.

ATKINSON, EDWARD (1827–1905).

　In Chapter 28 of *Life on the Mississippi* (1883), Mark Twain concludes his discussion of the Mississippi River Commission by deferring to Atkinson's view: "One thing will be easily granted by the reader: that an opinion from Mr. Edward Atkinson, upon any vast national commercial matter, comes as near ranking as authority as can the opinion of any individual in the Union." Appendix B to *Life on the Mississippi* publishes Atkinson's optimistic assessment of the river-control project, signed and dated in Boston on 14 April 1882. Twain does not identify the source for Atkinson's brief essay. Atkinson specialized in economic subjects and predictions.

ATKINSON, WILLIAM WALKER (1862–1932), pseud. "Yogi Ramacharaka." *Advanced Course in Yogi Philosophy and Oriental Occultism.* Chicago: The Yogi Publication Society, 1905. 337 pp.

　Inscription: the front free endpaper is signed in pencil "Clara Clemens".

　Marginalia: pencil markings in the table of contents and pencil markings and deletions on pages 289, 291, 297, 298, 303, 315, 317, 323 (crossing out the word "student"), and 337 (deleting two stilted, condescending sentences addressed to "our students").

　Location: Mark Twain Library, Redding, Connecticut.

　Copy examined: Clara Clemens's copy. Contains the red ink accession number "3186" and the oval purple stamps of the Mark Twain Library. Examined in 1970 and again on 15 June 1982.

Atlantic Monthly Magazine (Boston periodical, began publication in 1857).

R. J. Ellis—"'No Authority at All': Harriet Prescott Spofford's 'Down the River' and Mark Twain's *Huckleberry Finn*," *Mark Twain Annual 4* (2006): 33–53—made a case for concluding that Twain saw Spofford's short story in the October 1865 issue of the *Atlantic Monthly*. Clemens read the *Atlantic* so steadily during William Dean Howells's tenure as its editor that virtually no issue between 1871 and 1881 should be ruled out of any list of his probable reading material. On 6 January 1875 he expressed his pleasure upon learning that his "Old Times on the Mississippi" sketches would earn him a subscription to the magazine in addition to his fee (*MTLet* 6: 339). "I read the entire Atlantic this time. Wonderful number," he wrote to Howells on 4 July 1877 (*MTHL*, p. 187). The arrival of the journal at his hotel was a cheery event when he was abroad. In Heidelberg, he wrote to Howells on 26 May 1878, he spent one evening "tilted back . . . with a pipe & the last Atlantic" (*MTHL*, p. 230). In Baden-Baden he "went to bed early" on 10 August 1878, "with the new home magazines [*Harper's* and *Atlantic*], which I had saved all day & wouldn't cut a leaf" (NB 15, *N&J* 2:134). On 21 January 1879 Clemens praised a review of Bayard Taylor's final work that had appeared in the January issue (*MTHL*, p. 246).

It seems likely that Clemens continued to read the journal with some regularity between 1881 and 1890, the period when his friend Thomas Bailey Aldrich succeeded Howells to the editorship. Mark Twain mentioned the *Atlantic* in February 1879 (NB 17, *N&J* 2:269–271); in "Mental Telegraphy," quoting an article in the June 1882 issue; in a letter to Charles L. Webster, 27 January 1885 (*MTBus*, p. 298); and in his tentative 1889 appendix for *A Connecticut Yankee in King Arthur's Court* (NB 28 and NB 29, *N&J* 3: 412, 503), which cited Edward Jarvis's statistics in 1869 issues of the magazine. Roger Salomon (*TIH*, p. 111 n. 9) traced an 1889 reference by Twain to an article by H. T. Tuckerman titled "The Old Bankers of Florence," *Atlantic Monthly* 24.145 (1869): 629–637. In October 1891 Clemens copied a description of Emily Dickinson's residence from an article by Thomas W. Higginson that had appeared the same month in the *Atlantic Monthly* (NB 31, TS pp. 8–9). In an Autobiographical Dictation of 29 April 1908 Clemens reported, "Last night I read in the *Atlantic* a passage from one of Rev. Dr. Van Dyke's books"; he was referring to an article by Henry Bradford Washburn in the May 1908 *Atlantic* issue that had quoted from Van Dyke (*AutoMT* 3: 226).

Auber, Daniel François Esprit (1782–1871). *The Crown Diamonds [Les Diamants de la Couronne]* (romantic comic opera, written in 1841).

Mark Twain reviewed a performance of this opera—"put upon the stage in creditable shape on Monday evening"—in the 15 October 1864 issue of *The Californian*. His review, titled "Still Further Concerning That Conundrum," concentrated upon a prop-man who moved furniture between scenes (*SSix*, pp. 131–135; *ET&S* 2 [1981]: 81–85).

Krause, *MTC* (1967), pp. 52–56; Randall Knoper, *Acting Naturally: Mark Twain in the Culture of Performance* (Berkeley: University of California Press, 1995), p. 40.

Audubon, John James (1785–1851). *The Birds of America, from Drawings Made in the United States and Their Territories.* Reissued by John Woodhouse Audubon (1812–1862). Plates engraved by J[ulius]. Bien (1826–1909). 5 vols. New York: Roe, Lockwood & Son; also George R. Lockwood, 1860, 1870.

Catalog: *A1911*, "4 vols., royal 8vo of text . . . and an elephant folio vol. of 106 plates (1860 edition). . . . The text (8 vols. in 4) describes many more birds than are illustrated in the folio, and is not the text that should accompany these plates," catalog specifies the publishers and years of publication, lot 20, sold for $85.

Location: Special Collections, McFarlin Library, University of Tulsa (Volumes 3–4, 5–6, and 7–8, dated 1870).

Source: email notification from Jennifer Donner, Special Collections Librarian, McFarlin Library, to Alan Gribben, 16 April 2018. She reported that each of the volumes contains the *A1911* sale label. "One of the books has three unidentified and detached book covers" laid in, she added.

Audubon's original folio was published in London between 1827 and 1838; the text was first issued in Edinburgh in 1831–1839. The chromolithographic plates made by Julius Bien in 1858–1859 for a reissue of the folio are not faithful reproductions, particularly in regard to the background in the pictures, and are considered vastly inferior to the original hand-colored engravings. But Audubon had charged $1,000 per set for his four volumes of engraved prints (of which 2,000 sets were issued), and these treasured books were unattainable for most buyers in the nineteenth century.

Clemens may never have fully understood that the reissue he purchased was merely valuable and not truly rare. Audubon's *Birds of America* was one of the very few antiquarian items that he showed a keen interest in possessing simply as a printed artifact. He noticed an advertisement for the set in an Estes & Lauriat catalog, and promptly (on 1 August 1880) requested Howells to investigate the offer for him in Boston. "I think the price is $150," he wrote. "It can't be in very good condition, I suppose, at that figure; but if it is, & is complete, & of Audubon's own issue . . . won't you please ask them to ship it" (*MTHL*, pp. 318–319). Surely Howells informed him that it was merely a reissue. On 25 August 1880 Estes & Lauriat of Boston billed Clemens for "Audubon's Birds of America. Plates in 1 vol folio. Text in 4 vols 8vo" that cost $150 and was sent by express to Hartford (MTP). On at least one occasion he put the illustrations to practical use; George Washington Cable reported from Hartford on 13 February 1884 about a day he passed with Clemens in Hartford: "Part of the time—I forgot to say—was spent in consulting Audubon to identify a strange & beautiful bird that we had seen at breakfast time from the window of the library" (*MT&GWC*, p. 32). The costly first folio continued to fascinate Mark Twain; his Autobiographical Dictation of 30 January 1907 contained an anecdote about one of Audubon's relatives who "possessed a copy, in perfect condition, of Audubon's great book," but was hoodwinked by a cunning university professor into selling it to him for one-tenth its true value (*MTE*, p. 96; *AutoMT* 2: 413).

AUERBACH, BERTHOLD (1812–1882). *Black Forest Village Stories*. Translated from the German by Charles Goepp (1827–1907). Illus. New York: Leypolt & Holt, 1869. 377 pp. Repr. by H. Holt and Co., 1874. [Clemens's edition has not been determined.]

Mark Twain seems to have read Auerbach's *Schwarzwälder Dorfgeschichten* (1843), which became available to American audiences in 1869, translated as *Black Forest Village Stories*. The English translation contained tales entitled "The Gawk," "The Pipe of War," "Manor-House Farmer's Vefela," "Nip-Cheeked Toney," "Ivo the Gentleman," "Florian and Crescence," and others. Its accessibility in an English translation argues against his using a German-language edition. In Chapter 22 of *A Tramp Abroad* (1880) Twain described a typical "heroine of one of Auerbach's novels," with her "Black Forest clothes, and her burned complexion, her plump figure, . . . and the plaited tails of hemp-colored hair hanging down her back." In the same chapter he also remarked that he "found the Black Forest houses and villages all that the Black Forest stories have pictured them."

———. *On the Heights; A Novel*. 3 vols. Authorized Edition. Trans. from the German by Fanny E. Bunnett (1832–1875). Leipzig: B. Tauchnitz, 1867.

Source: MTLAcc, entry #1838, Volume 3 only donated from Clemens's library by Clara Clemens Gabrilowitsch in 1910. All the pages after page 432 are missing in Volume 3.

Auerbach's *Auf der Höhe.[On the Heights.] Roman in acht büchern* had been published in Stuttgart, Germany in 1865, with later reprintings. Clemens jotted down the author and the German title of this book in May 1885 (NB 24, N&J 3: 147).

L' Aurore. Littéraire, artistique, social (French periodical). Published 18 October 1897–29 May 1900[?].

In January 1898 Clemens "wrote Percy Mitchell (Paris) & asked him to try & get a copy of 'Aurore' for me (containing Zola's grand letter)" (NB40, TS p. 8). Mitchell sent the requested copy to Clemens in London. Presumably Zola's letter concerned the Dreyfus case.

AUSTEN, JANE (1775–1817). *Mansfield Park. A Novel*. Collection of British Authors Series. Leipzig: Bernhard Tauchnitz, 1867. 442 pp.

Source: MTLAcc, entry #1839, volume donated from Clemens's library by Clara Clemens Gabrilowitsch in 1910.

———. *Northanger Abbey and Persuasion*. London: George Routledge and Sons, n.d. 448 pp.

Location: Mark Twain Library, Redding, Connecticut. Donated from Clemens's library by Clara Clemens Gabrilowitsch in 1910 (MTLAcc, entry #1840).

Copy examined: Clemens's unmarked copy, in 1970 and 1982. Contains the red ink accession number "1840". The rear pastedown endpaper displays the sticker of "Brown & Gross Booksellers, Hartford, CT."

———. *Pride and Prejudice* (novel, published in 1813).

Mark Twain did not mention Jane Austen in his correspondence, literary works, or notebooks before 1895, but during the last fifteen years of his life he displayed an unrelenting contempt for her novels that astonished and amused his friends. So great was his hatred for her mode of writing that the mere mention of her name could provoke him into a seething denunciation of Austen and her idolaters. His hostility toward Austen seems especially strange because her critical champions in the United States, William Dean Howells and Brander Matthews, were men with whom Mark Twain generally tried to agree.

The first indication of the irritation she caused him is an entry he made in Notebook 36 while on Board the *Mararoa* in December 1895: "In past year have read Vicar of Wakefield & some of Jane Austin [*sic*]. Thoroughly artificial" (TS p. 3). In January 1896, still in the Indian Ocean, he perused the ship library and then resolved, "I must read that devilish Vicar of Wakefield again. Also Jane Austin [*sic*]" (NB 37, TS p. 3). This intention gave rise to his famous dismissal of her literary merit in Chapter 62 of *Following the Equator* (1897), where he claimed that on the afternoon of 10 April 1896 he wrote in his diary: "Jane Austen's books, too, are absent from this [ship] library. Just that one omission alone would make a fairly good library out of a library that hadn't a book in it."

Austen would remain linked in his mind with Oliver Goldsmith, Sir Walter Scott, James Fenimore Cooper, and other writers whose mannered fiction was vastly over-praised. When Brander Matthews defended these authors against Twain's cavils in "New Trials for Old Favorites," *Forum* 25 (August 1898): 749–760, Joseph H. Twichell let Twain know that he sided with Matthews in gently chastising Twain for ridiculing Goldsmith and Cooper. Twain replied in a letter written to Twichell on 13 September 1898 that he knew he must lack Matthews's qualifications as a critic. Matthews could always distinguish the good points in any work he read, Twain explained. Consequently "I haven't any right to criticise books, & I don't do it except when I hate them. I often want to criticise Jane Austen, but her books madden me so that I can't conceal my frenzy from the reader, & therefore I have to stop every time I begin" (*MTL* [1917], 2: 667; *LMTJHT* [2017], p. 220). Paine's edition of *Mark Twain's Letters* indicated no ellipsis here, but in 1920 Brander Matthews added the full text of Mark Twains' remarks to Twichell about Austen: "Every time I read that mangy book, 'Pride and Prejudice,' I want to dig her up & beat her over the skull with her own shin-bone" (Matthews, "Mark Twain and the Art of Writing," *Harper's Magazine* 141.845 [October 1920]: 635–643, collected in *Essays on English* [1921], p. 264; reprinted by Arthur L. Scott, *Mark Twain: Selected Criticism* [Dallas: Southern Methodist University Press, 1955], pp. 148–162; revised edition in 1967, pp. 159–173; corrected version of Twain's letter published in *LMTJHT* [2017], p. 220). Matthews hastened to assure his readers that Mark Twain "expressed his desire to desecrate her grave only in a letter to an intimate familiar with his imaginative exaggeration" (p. 265). (In 1875 Clemens had used a similarly bizarre image of violence directed at the gravesite of François Rabelais.) In a copy of George Trevelyan's *The Life and Letters of Lord Macaulay* (1904) that Clemens inscribed to Isabel V. Lyon in September 1905, Clemens objected to Thomas Macaulay's view of Jane Austen: "He is praising those odious books again" (II: 394). On the following page, where Macaulay attempted to correct an instance of punctuation in Austen's *Persuasion* to elucidate the passage, Clemens scoffed, "You could not confuse the meaning if you removed *all* of the punctuation-marks;

or even if you rearranged them at random."

One of the abortive attempts to comment on Austen's novels that Mark Twain found he had "to stop every time" resides in the Mark Twain Papers (DV201), an undated and unfinished manuscript of seven and a half pages titled "Jane Austen." Twain began this piece by remarking: "Whenever I take up 'Pride & Prejudice' or 'Sense & Sensibility,' I feel like a barkeeper entering the Kingdom of Heaven" (quoted in *MTB*, p 1500; though quoting directly from the manuscript, Paine reported that Twain uttered these remarks in June 1909 during a train ride from Baltimore to Redding—an obvious misrepresentation of facts). Twain's meaning becomes apparent in his succeeding comments in the essay: a barkeeper from the Bowery would probably try at first to hobnob with the "ultra-good Presbyterians" he would encounter in Heaven, but he simply would not enjoy their company. He himself feels a similar discouragement, Twain explains, after repeated efforts to recognize the "high art" acclaimed by respected critics. He has seldom been able to read through "to the other end" of Austen's books because of their common fault—"She makes me detest all her people, without reserve." Twain avoids any further disparagement of Austen's artistry; he merely confesses that he is not to be classed among the Elect who can enjoy her novels and appreciate their elusive virtues.

Clemens was less reserved in his discussions with friends. Howells needled him about their friendly dispute in a letter written on 1 May 1903 when Clemens was ailing in Riverdale: "Now you're sick, I've a great mind to have it out with [you] about Jane Austen. If you say much more I'll come out and read 'Pride and Prejudice' to you" (*MTHL*, p. 769). Clemens did not restrict his arguments to Howells, Twichell, or Matthews, however; on 7 November 1906 Isabel Lyon noted that during dinner he and Kate Douglas (Wiggin) Riggs "had a friendly battle over Jane Austen, whose books the King abhors and Mrs. Riggs delights in" (IVL Journal, TS p. 201, MTP). Clemens obviously savored the set-to; the next day he wrote to Jean about the dinner party of the preceding evening at 21 Fifth Avenue: "A very pleasant party, & good talk. Some of it violent. Because Mrs. Riggs & I do not agree about Jane Austin [*sic*]. She respects Jane Austin [*sic*], whilst it is the one desire of my heart to dig her up" (Berg, NYPL). Jean, like Twichell, could probably finish that sentence for herself.

The vehemence of Mark Twain's outbursts against Austen's fiction is phenomenal. He never slackened his fire on Howells's position, writing on 18 January 1909: "To me his [Edgar Allan Poe's] prose is unreadable—like Jane Austin's [*sic*]. No, there is a difference. I could read his prose on salary, but not Jane's. Jane is entirely impossible. It seems a great pity to me that they allowed her to die a natural death" (*MTHL*, p 841). Howells would recall sadly in *My Mark Twain* (1910): "His prime abhorrence was my dear and honored prime favorite, Jane Austen. He once said to me . . . , 'You seem to think that woman could write,' and he forebore withering me with his scorn, apparently because we had been friends so long, and he more pitied than hated me for my bad taste" (p. 16). We may assume that this lapse in Twain's critical judgment weighed heavily with Howells when he characterized his

friend for posterity in *My Mark Twain* (1910) as "the most unliterary" of his author acquaintances.

Various interpreters have attempted to account for the animadversions Twain insistently lodged against Austen. Van Wyck Brooks oversimplified the matter in 1920 by stating that "when he roars and rages against the novels of Jane Austen we can see that buried self taking vengeance upon Mr. Howells, with whom Jane Austen was a prime passion, who had even taken Jane Austen as a model" (*The Ordeal of Mark Twain* [New York: E. P. Dutton & Co., 1920, p. 183). But there is no question that Clemens's diatribes were directed at least in part against a nexus of literary standards with which he found himself in sharp disagreement. It is intriguing, in this regard, to remember Clara Clemens's testimony that Austen was one of the authors—along with George Meredith—from whose works Olivia Clemens often read to the family at Quarry Farm, with Clemens sniping in the background (*MFMT* [1931], p. 61).

Brander Matthews opened up a profitable line of inquiry in his *Essays on English* (1921), speculating that Austen's artistic vision may have seemed restricted to Mark Twain; possibly "her little miracles of observation seemed to him only the carving of cherry-stones" (p. 264). Conceivably Twain felt a distaste for her "placid and complacent acceptance of a semi-feudal social organization, stratified like a chocolate layer-cake, with petty human fossils in its lower formations" (p. 265). Richard Poirier developed an explanation along somewhat similar lines in *A World Elsewhere: The Place of Style in American Literature* (New York: Oxford Press, 1966). According to Poirier, Twain represented "a significant American dissatisfaction with the kind of social ordering of existence that takes place in her novels" (p. 145). Austen was confident that her audience "can be satisfied by social unions, especially by marriage" (p. 147); by contrast, Twain, like Huck Finn, entertained "some larger distrust of social structures themselves" (p. 148). Twain and other American writers lacked "her positive vision of social experience" and "the capacity to imagine society as including the threat of conformity and artificiality and [yet] as offering, nevertheless, beneficial opportunities for self-discovery" (p. 153). Poirier suggested that "Jane Austen's satire has behind it a confidence that English society gives everyone a chance, as the society in *Huckleberry Finn* does not, to find a place that can be called 'natural'" (p. 163).

Although Clemens was capable of inflating the literary merits of his friends like Thomas Bailey Aldrich and Charles Dudley Warner, in general he was discerning and sometimes quite illuminating in assessing the books he read. Nevertheless, he clearly displayed a critical blind spot in misjudging Austen's worth so badly. The abusive vitriol behind his pronouncements against her far exceeds the usual license he granted himself as a public humorist. In this instance (and several others) he was basically incapable of making allowances for previous literary fashions; he tended to evaluate Romantic-era works (those by Scott, Cooper, and Poe, for instance) against the standards of the new realistic style of fiction he was practicing. Yet Howells, who himself championed the precepts of realism, had the capacity to appreciate the virtues of superior writing that had been produced in historical periods that applauded nearly opposite goals from the straight-on prose of realism. For Clemens, however, every deviation from late nineteenth-century subject matter and narrative forms presented an opportunity for ridicule and dismissal. The more that respected authorities like Howells and Matthews, commentators who reviewed literature professionally, attempted to reason with Clemens, the more defensive he became and the more he despaired of ever comprehending their veneration for Nathaniel Hawthorne, George Meredith, Henry James, George Eliot, and other subtle and gradual story-tellers who tried his patience as a reader. He felt permanently locked out of the refined class of readers who savored as delectable these masters of precisely drawn social canvasses and slowly unraveling episodes. It seems ironic that Clemens, who himself had written a complex picaresque novel set on a meandering river, had so little appetite for intertwined plot complications and expanding character development in earlier works. But even the staunchest champions of the authors whom Clemens lambasted must concede that his diatribes, however unwarranted, often reach a level of hilarious humor in the exaggerated tenor of their unjustifiable indignation.

———. *Sense and Sensibility* (novel, published in 1811). In an undated manuscript titled "Jane Austen" (DV201, MTP) Mark Twain specified some of his objections to this novel. These remarks, which offer a key to understanding the grounds for his disagreement with her novelistic techniques, are important because his other statements about Austen's writings are so general. He claims to be rereading the first third of *Sense and Sensibility* at the moment, and he closes the essay with a catalogue of the characters and his criticisms of their portrayals. Elinor is a "harmless waxwork," Edward "an unpleasant shadow," Willoughby "criminal & filthy," and the others strike him as being similarly offensive in various ways. His comments end abruptly at the top of a page after he has noted these cavils. Evidently his critical standards required the creation of at least one character with whom he might identify and sympathize; finding none, he lost patience with Austen's novel of manners and its emphasis on dialogues from an earlier English society. Emily Auerbach made a lighthearted effort to excuse Twain's animus in "'A Barkeeper Entering the Kingdom of Heaven': Did Mark Twain Really Hate Jane Austen?," *Virginia Quarterly Review* 75.1 (Winter 1999): 109–120, reprinted in Auerbach's *Searching for Jane Austen* (Madison: University of Wisconsin, 2004). See also the Catalog entry for William Lyon Phelps's "Introduction" to the Chawton Edition of *The Novels and Letters of Jane Austen* (1906).

AUSTIN, ALFRED (1835–1913). *Flodden Field; A Tragedy*. New York: Harper & Brothers, 1903. 137 pp.
Source: MTLAcc, entry #1456, volume donated by Clemens.
The Battle of Flodden Field in 1513 was a significant victory for the English troops. The Scottish forces lost more than 10,000 men.

———. *A Tale of True Love, and Other Poems*. New York: Harper and Brothers, 1902. 139 pp.
Source: MTLAcc, entry #643, volume donated by Clemens.
Mark Twain asked Chatto & Windus in 1896 to locate the poem written by Alfred Austin on the Jameson raid in South Africa (Welland, *Mark Twain in England*, p. 171). Twain poked fun at Tennyson's successor as poet laureate on several occasions. In 1896, the year that Victoria appointed Austin to the laureateship, Twain read a silly poem of his own invention about an egg-laying mammal to a lecture audience in Benares, India, and then commented that "the present Laureate is just the same kind of poet as I am" (quoted in Coleman O. Parsons, "Mark Twain: Sightseer in India," *Mississippi Quarterly* 16.2 [Spring 1963]: 88). For Chapter 36 of *Following the Equator* (1897) Twain constructed a poem using sixty-six colorful names of Australian towns and then conceded, "Perhaps a poet laureate could do better, but a poet laureate gets wages, and that is different." He was more direct in belittling Austin in Chapter 66, blaming him for over-hastiness in glorifying the actions of South Africans whose motives were not clear: "The new poet laureate lost no time. He came out with a rousing poem lauding Jameson's prompt and splendid heroism in flying to the rescue of the women and children." Disregarding the possible facts of the case, Austin "produced a poet-laureatic explosion of colored fireworks which filled the world's sky with giddy splendors."
But Clemens eventually became more receptive to the poems and verse dramas of Austin, who so often wrote of loneliness and death. Albert Bigelow Paine was present when Clemens, grieving over Jean's death in December 1909, "read aloud some lines by Alfred Austin, which Mrs. Crane had sent him—lines which he had remembered in the sorrow for Susy" (*MTB*, p. 1551). Paine quoted the lines: "When last came sorrow, around barn and byre/ Wind-carven snow, the year's white sepulchre, lay./'Come in,' I said, 'and warm you by the fire':/And there she sits and never goes away."

AUSTIN, JANE (GOODWIN) (1831–1894). *The Desmond Hundred*. Round-Robin Series. Boston: James R. Osgood and Co., 1882. 330 pp. [One of the Round-Robin Series of anonymous novels written by "the best writers" that the Osgood firm began publishing and promoting in 1881. Subsequently Austin acknowledged her authorship of this novel.]
Catalog: Ball 2016 inventory, green cloth, red and black lettering, signed by Charles Jervis Langdon [1849–1916, Olivia Langdon Clemens's brother], Jervis Langdon Family Library bookplate #617.
Location: Quarry Farm library shelves, under the supervision of the Mark Twain Archive, Elmira College, Elmira, New York.
In Austin's novel, The Desmond Hundred referred to a large stretch of New England woods and the mysterious house they surrounded. These 100 acres of forest were once the park on an early estate. Austin was an American novelist and short story author who lived in Boston and belonged to the American Antiquarian Society.

———. *Mrs. Beauchamp Brown*. No Name Series. Boston: Roberts Brothers, 1880. 319 pp.
Source: MTLAcc, entry #13, volume donated by Clemens.
In July 1880 J. R. Barlow, Hartford booksellers, billed

Clemens for "1 Mrs. Brown (No Name Series) $1.00," a volume purchased on 10 May 1880; Clemens paid the bill on 5 July 1880 (receipt in MTP).

———. *Standish of Standish: A Story of the Pilgrims.* Illus. Boston: Houghton Mifflin, The Riverside Press, 1895.

Inscription: inscribed "Susan L. Crane, Quarry Farm Jan. 1, 1896, Julie, Jervis, & Ida Langdon."

Catalog: Ball 2016 inventory, green cloth, gilt lettering, gilt top page edges, "very good" condition.

Location: Quarry Farm library shelves, under the supervision of the Mark Twain Archive, Elmira College, Elmira, New York.

This was one of the many volumes accessible to Clemens in his final visits to Quarry Farm in Elmira.

AUSTIN, MARY (HUNTER) (1868–1934). *Lost Borders.* Illus. New York: Harper & Brothers, 1909. 209 pp.

Source: MTLAcc, entry #1841, volume donated from Clemens's library by Clara Clemens Gabrilowitsch in 1910.

The Illinois-born Austin moved to the San Joaquin Valley in California in 1888. *Lost Borders* mediated the tensions between the California desert and its animals and people. Her writings often examined that formidable land as well as women's prescribed roles in contrast with the prerogatives enjoyed by men of that era.

———. *Santa Lucia, A Common Story.* New York: Harper & Brothers, 1908. 345 pp.

Source: MTLAcc, entry #10, volume donated by Clemens.

Austin's novel takes a harsh look at the institution of marriage and its effects on the lives of three women in a small California town.

AUSTIN, MAUDE MASON (1861–1939). *'Cension. A Sketch from Paso Del Norte.* Illus. New York: Harper & Brothers, 1896. 159 pp.

Ranch life brings together Mexican and American characters in this romantic novel.

AUTHORS CLUB. *Manual of the Authors Club.* Quarter vegetable vellum paper label, uncut. New York: De Vinne Press, [1894]. [250 copies printed.]

As a member of the Authors Club, Clemens would presumably have received a copy of the *Manual*, which contained its constitution, committees, articles of incorporation, and list of members. See also the Catalog entry for *First Book of the Authors Club*.

▍B

BABCOCK, MALTBIE DAVENPORT (1858–1901). *Thoughts for Every-Day Living from the Spoken and Written Words of Maltbie Davenport Babcock.* New York: Charles Scribner's Sons, 1901. 192 pp.

Catalogs: QF Martinez, good condition; Ball 2016 inventory, green cloth, gilt lettering, inscribed on a laid in card (possibly by Susan Crane) "Dear Jervis, Jan. 26, 1903," erasures on the card indicate a $5 price for the book but are otherwise illegible.

Location: Quarry Farm library shelves, under the supervision of the Mark Twain Archive, Elmira College, Elmira, New York.

Babcock was a prominent Presbyterian pastor and hymnwriter. This book was available to Clemens during his final visits to Elmira.

Baby Days; A Selection of Songs, Stories and Pictures, for

Very Little Folks. With an Introduction by the Editor of "St. Nicholas" [Mary Mapes Dodge, 1831–1905]. New York: Scribner & Co., [cop. 1877]. 192 pp.

An undated letter from Clemens to Theodore Langdon's family, "Xmas Morning" [1877?], thanks the Langdons for *Baby Days* and other books given to Olivia and the Clemens girls (MTP). A cryptic entry by Clemens in Notebook 24 (1885) perhaps recalls a remark by one of the children: "Katy give me Baby Days with cover torn off" (*N&J* 3: 164). *Baby Days* contained children's pieces selected from Dodge's *St. Nicholas Magazine*, which had begun publication in 1873.

BACHELLER, IRVING (1859–1950). *Darrel of the Blessed Isles.* Illustrated by Arthur I[gnatius]. Keller (1866–1924). Boston: Lothrop Publishing Co., [cop. 1903]. 410 pp.

Source: MTLAcc, entry #1511, volume donated by Clemens.

———. *Eben Holden; A Tale of the North Country.* Fourth edition. Original red cloth, gilt. Extremities rubbed, rear hinge cracked. Boston: Lothrop Publishing Co., [cop. 1900]. 432 pp.

Inscription: (in black ink) on the front free endpaper: "My dear Mark Twain: Let me introduce my old friend Uncle Eb and credit me what you will on the great debt I owe you. Irving Bacheller/320 St. Nicholas Ave N.Y./Dec. 5, 1900."

Provenance: shelfmark of Clara Clemens Gabrilowitsch's library collection in Detroit. Purchased by Mrs. Doheny from Maxwell Hunley of Beverly Hills in 1940 for $12.20. Belonged to the Carrie Estelle Doheny Collection, St. John's Seminary, Camarillo, California, for more than four decades. Sold at auction by Christie's on behalf of St. John's Seminary on 17 October 1988 (lot 1174) for $1,320.

Catalog: *Sotheby's 2003*, #183, $800.

Location: collection of Kevin Mac Donnell, Austin, Texas.

Copy examined: Clemens's unmarked copy, in July 2004.

Bacheller's best-known novel was first published on 2 July 1900; it sold so rapidly that copies issued in March 1901 were imprinted "250,000th." The homespun sayings and generous deeds of Eben Holden, a hired man on a farm in upper New York state, soon became familiar to a generation of American readers. On 14 December 1900 Clemens wrote to Bacheller: "The book has this moment arrived. . . . A thousand thanks; have longed for the book. . . . I will . . . stretch out with a pipe and have a good time" (Irving Bacheller, *From Stores of Memory* [New York: Farrar & Rinehart, 1938], p. 62; date of the letter supplied from the ALS in ASSSCL).

Bacheller later recalled that he once tried to interest Clemens in writing syndicated material for newspapers but was turned down (Irving Bacheller, "Writing for the Fireplace," *Mark Twain Quarterly* 2.1 (Fall 1937): 23). In another reminiscence, Bacheller told of an entire afternoon Clemens once spent with him at Bacheller's club, drinking hot Scotch and telling stories; after four hours Clemens left to have dinner with Henry H. Rogers and his wife. Clemens acknowledged that he had dominated the conversation, merely saying, "I have enjoyed every damned word of it" (*Coming Up the Road: Memories of a North Country Boyhood* [Indianapolis: Bobbs-Merrill, 1928], p. 283–288).

———. *Eben Holden; A Tale of the North Country.* Illus. Boston:

Lothrop Publishing Co., [cop. 1900]. 432 pp.

> **Source:** MTLAcc, entry #885, volume donated by Clemens.

———. *Eben Holden's Last Day A-Fishing*. New York: Harper & Brothers, 1907. 60 pp.

> **Source:** MTLAcc, entry #16, volume donated by Clemens.

———. [Another identical copy.]

> **Source:** MTLAcc, entry #1510, volume donated by Clemens.

———. *The Hand-Made Gentleman; A Tale of the Battles of Peace*. New York: Harper & Brothers, 1909. 332 pp.

> **Source:** MTLAcc, entry #1034, volume donated by Clemens.

———. [Another identical copy.]

> **Source:** MTLAcc, entry #2180, volume donated by Clara Clemens Gabrilowitsch in 1910.

———. *The Master, Being in Part Copied from the Minutes of the School for Novelists, a Round Table of Good Fellows Who, Long Since, Dined Every Saturday at the Sign o'the Lanthorne, on Golden Hill in New York City*. New York: Doubleday, Page & Co., 1909. 302 pp.

> **Inscription:** inscribed on the front free endpaper: "Yours for peace/Irving Bacheller/Riverside Ct./Dec. 3 '09"; signed on the front pastedown endpaper: "Catherine Leary/Reading/Conn."
> **Provenance:** formerly in the Antenne-Dorrance Collection, Rice Lake, Wisconsin.
> **Location:** Mark Twain Archive, Gannett-Tripp Library, Elmira College, Elmira, New York.
> **Copy examined:** Clemens's copy, presumably. It seems improbable that Bacheller inscribed this presentation copy to Clemens's housekeeper rather than to Clemens.

———. *The Master of Silence. A Romance*. Fiction, Fact, and Fancy Series, ed. Arthur Stedman (1859–1908). New York: Charles L. Webster & Co., 1892. 176 pp.

> Advertised in the *Publishers' Trade List Annual 1893* as "the first novel of Mr. Irving Bacheller, the head of the Bacheller newspaper syndicate. . . . A striking study of a mind-reader's experiences." Issued by Clemens's publishing firm in the "Fiction, Fact and Fancy" series edited by Arthur Stedman.

———. *Silas Strong, Emperor of the Woods*. Original red cloth. New York: Harper & Brothers, 1906. 339 pp.

> **Inscription:** "To Mark Twain/who, I hope, for/this little book/will credit me/something on my/great debt to him./Irving Bacheller/Riverside Conn./April 2 1906"; signed on the front pastedown endpaper: "S L Clemens/1906/Apl./21 Fifth avenue."
> **Catalogs:** ListABP (1910), "Silas Strong, Bacheller"; *C1951*, #25c, listed among books signed by Clemens; Parke-Bernet Galleries, "English and American First Editions . . . Collected by Jean Hersholt, Beverly Hills, California," Sale No. 1503 (New York City), March 1954, item #175, p. 31; Lew David Feldman, "American Books" (1955), Catalogue of House of El Dieff, item #41, price $46.75.
> **Provenance:** Bookplate of Jean Hersholt on the rear pastedown endpaper.
> **Location:** Albert and Shirley Small Special Collections Library, University of Virginia, Charlottesville. Donated by Clifton Waller Barrett.
> **Copy examined:** Clemens's copy, in 1970.

———. [Another identical copy.]

> **Source:** MTLAcc, entry #1449, volume donated by Clemens.

———. *Vergilius; A Tale of the Coming of Christ*. New York: Harper & Brothers. 1904. 279 pp.

> **Source:** MTLAcc, entry #1512, volume donated by Clemens.

BACON, DELIA SALTER (1811–1859). *The Philosophy of the Plays of Shakspere Unfolded*. Preface by Nathaniel Hawthorne (1804–1864). Boston: Ticknor and Fields, 1857. 582 pp. [Edition conjectured.]

> Bacon was an American writer who lived in England. She became violently insane soon after publishing this book, which originated the theory that the Shakespearean plays were written by a group directed by Francis Bacon. In the first part of Mark Twain's *Is Shakespeare Dead?* (1909), Twain recalled the sensation Delia Bacon's book aroused, tracing his curiosity about the Baconian heresy back to his piloting days on the Mississippi River: "My fifty years' interest in that matter—asleep for the last three years—is excited once more. It is an interest which was born of Delia Bacon's book—away back in that ancient day—1857, or maybe 1856." According to these recollections, Clemens "discussed, and discussed, and discussed, and disputed and disputed and disputed" her book with a pilot named George Ealer, who "bought the literature of the dispute as fast as it appeared." Looking around a gold miner's cabin in Jackass Hill, California, Clemens noted in January 1865 that the dwelling had no planking on its floor, yet he could see "Byron Shakspeare, Bacon Dickens, & every kinds of only first class Literature" (Notebook 4, *N&J* 1: 70). Was Clemens linking Delia Bacon's book with Shakespeare's name here, or (more unlikely) did he mean Francis Bacon?

BACON, FRANCIS (1561–1626). *Novum Organum by Lord Bacon*. Ed. Joseph Devey (1825–1897). Library of Universal Literature. Vol. 22. [St. Louis, Missouri:] St. Louis Publishing Co., 1901. 290 pp.

> **Catalog:** Ball 2016 inventory, formerly among the library books at Quarry Farm.
> **Location:** location undetermined in 2016.
> Bacon's philosophical treatise was originally published in 1620. The editorial team at the Mark Twain Project in the Bancroft Library at the University of California at Berkeley has identified a passage in Mark Twain's Autobiographical Dictation of 4 September 1907 as deriving from Bacon's treatise. Concerning philosophical progress, Twain said, "As pointed out by Lord Bacon some centuries ago, those prejudices, predilections, and inheritances shall have been swept away" (*AutoMT* 3: 127). Did Twain possibly acquire this copy during his visit to Missouri in late May and early June of 1902?

———. *The Promus of Formularies and Elegancies (Being Private Notes, Circ. 1594, Hitherto Unpublished) by Francis Bacon. Illustrated and Elucidated by Passages from Shakespeare by Mrs. Henry Pott [Constance Mary (Fearon) Pott, 1833–1915], with Preface by E[dwin]. A[bbott]. Abbott [1838–1926]*. Boston: Houghton, Mifflin & Co., 1883. 628 pp.

> **Catalog:** *A1911*, "Facsimile, thick 8vo, cloth, uncut, Bost. 1883," lot 24, sold for $5.50. Pott attempted to demonstrate parallels of expression in Bacon's commonplace book

and the works attributed to William Shakespeare. In an Autobiographical Dictation on 11 January 1909 Mark Twain admitted that "from away back towards the very beginning of the Shakspeare-Bacon controversy I have been on the Bacon side" (*AutoMT* 3: 298).

Bacon, George Washington & Company, Ltd. *Bacon's "Midget" Map. Central and West London.* Blue cloth cover. London: G. W. Bacon and Co., n. d. 63 pp., plus fold-out map and index of streets.

Source: listed by Albert E. Stone in his catalog of Clemens's books in the Mark Twain Library at Redding in 1955.

Copy examined: when I looked over this small map booklet on 15 June 1982, I was unable to find any justification for thinking that Clemens ever owned it. There was no marginalia, no signature, no markings, and no library accession number. Since page 4 lists the rates for "Motor Cab Fares," the booklet would likely have been a post-1910 item. Robert Regan made a careful study of this same item and pointed out that the Central London Railway mentioned on page 3 only reached Liverpool Street in 1912; Regan concluded that this edition of *Bacon's "Midget" Map* was published between 1912 and 1915 (Robert Regan to Alan Gribben, 18 June 1982). Conceivably Stone saw another, earlier Bacon edition in the Mark Twain Library, but if so I could not find it in 1970 or 1982 or during my later visits.

Bacon, Josephine Dodge (Daskam) (1876–1961). *The Madness of Philip and Other Tales of Childhood.* Illustrated by F[anny]. Y[oung]. Cory (1877–1972). New York: McClure, Phillips, & Co., 1902. 223 pp.

Source: MTLAcc, entry #459, volume donated by Clemens. The gifted illustrator Fanny Young Cory would go on to produce delightful drawings for various other books as well as two syndicated cartoons, "Sonnysayings" and "Little Miss Muffett."

———. *The Memoirs of a Baby.* Illustrated by F[anny]. Y[oung]. Cory (1877–1972). New York: Harper & Brothers, 1905. 272 pp.

Source: MTLAcc, entry #1455, volume donated by Clemens.

———. [Another identical copy].

Source: MTLAcc, entry #1695, volume donated by Clemens.

———. *Ten to Seventeen; A Boarding-School Diary.* Illus. New York: Harper & Brothers, 1908. 261 pp.

Source: MTLAcc, entry #1584, volume donated by Clemens.

Bacon, Mary Schell (Hoke) (1870–1934), pseud. "Dolores M. Bacon," ed. *Songs Every Child Should Know: A Selection of the Best Songs of All Nations for Young People.* New York: Doubleday, Page, & Co., 1907. 221 pp.

Source: MTLAcc, entry #479, volume donated by Clemens. Bacon compiled over 100 songs, categorized by theme and going back as far as William Shakespeare. Pages xiii-xiv of Bacon's Foreword quote a parody that Mark Twain wrote in 1868 ridiculing Alexander M. W. Ball, a man who falsely claimed the authorship of the once-popular poem and song "Rock Me to Sleep, Mother." I am grateful to Jo Dee Benussi for calling Bacon's Foreword to my attention.

Badeau, Adam (1831–1895). *Grant in Peace. From Appomattox to Mount McGregor. A Personal Memoir.* Hartford,

Connecticut: S. S. Scranton & Co., 1887. 591 pp.

Clemens instructed Charles L. Webster on 6 June 1886 to offer Badeau a ten-percent royalty because "it promises to be an interesting book—gossipy & entertaining to all kinds of readers" (*MTLP*, p. 198). On 6 December 1886 Clemens wrote to Webster: "I have read 'Grant in Peace' up to the present time, and there hasn't been a dull chapter thus far. It is mighty well written" (*MTLP*, p. 209). In 1889, after a Hartford firm had published the book, Badeau attempted to sue Webster & Company for not bringing out *Grant in Peace* (*MTLP*, p. 210 n. 2).

Badlam, Alexander (1809–1894). *The Wonders of Alaska.* Illustrated, maps. San Francisco: Bancroft Co., 1890. 152 pp.

Inscription: inscribed on the front flyleaf in black ink: "Samuel L. Clemens, Esq.,/Compliments of/Alex. Badlam."

Location: Mark Twain Library, Redding, Connecticut.

Copy examined: Clemens's copy. Has a red ink accession number: "3407". Examined in 1970 and again in June 1982.

Badlam wrote to Clemens on 13 June 1890 (CU-MARK).

Baedeker, Karl [Ludwig Johannes] (1801–1859). *Austria, Including Hungary, Transylvania, Dalmatia, and Bosnia. Handbook for Travellers.* [Edition not established.]

In an undated note to Chatto & Windus, Clemens requested a copy of Baedeker's *Austria* (ALS in Berg, NYPL). Karl Baedeker's sons succeeded him in operating the family firm—first Ernest Baedeker (1833–1861), next Karl Baedeker, Jr. (1837–1911), and then, in 1878, Fritz Baedeker (1844–1925). An avid traveler like Clemens naturally depended on guidebooks, and he relied on those of Baedeker and John Murray interchangeably. However, in September 1878 Clemens praised "the curious & useful details Baedeker goes into for the protection of the tourist. He has run Murray out of Europe" (Notebook 16, *N&J* 2: 193).

———. *Italy. Handbook for Travellers.* Part 1, Northern Italy, 4th rev. ed. (1877); Part 2, Central Italy and Rome, 5th rev. ed. (1877); Part 3, Southern Italy and Sicily, 6th rev. ed. (1876). 3 vols. Leipsic: Karl Baedeker, 1876–1877. [The first edition had been published in 1867.]

Clemens praised Baedeker's *Italy* for "curious & useful details" about Lake Como on 24 September 1878 (NB 16, *N&J* 2: 193). He mentioned the guidebook in May 1892 (NB 32, TS p. 5). Later he disparaged its praise of the architecture and decorations of the Villa di Quarto near Florence in a January 1904 Autobiographical Dictation (*AutoMT* 1: 230).

———. *London and Its Environs. Handbook for Travellers.* 10th rev. ed. Leipsic: Karl Baedeker, 1896. 424 pp. [Includes "Index of Streets."]

In 1896 Clemens could not find Tedworth Square listed in Baedeker's *London* (NB 39, TS p. 17).

———. *Paris and Its Environs. Handbook for Travellers.* 6th rev. ed. Leipsic: Karl Baedeker, 1878.

Clemens referred to this guide in June 1879 (NB 18, *N&J* 2: 314). In 1878 the Baedekers had moved their publishing from Coblence to Leipzig.

———. *The Rhine from Rotterdam to Constance. Handbook for Travellers.* 6th ed. Leipsic: Karl Baedeker, 1878. 341 pp.

Clemens presumably used this guidebook in July 1878; see Notebook 15 (*N&J* 2: 116).

———. *Switzerland and the Adjacent Portions of Italy, Savoy, and the Tyrol. Handbook for Travellers.* 7th ed. Leipsic: Karl Baedeker, 1877. 470 pp.

Mark Twain made references to this guidebook in Notebook 15 (1878, *N&J* 2: 77), Notebook 16 (1878, *N&J* 2: 161), and Chapter 35 of *A Tramp Abroad* (1880). Twain questioned Baedeker's estimates of distances on a few occasions, but the majority of his references to Baedeker's *Switzerland* were complimentary and a few were exceedingly favorable. In one of his notebooks in 1878, for instance, he praised "the iron integrity of Baedeker, who tells the petrified truth about hotels & everything. A wonderful guide book—a marvelous faithful & painstaking work—you can go anywhere without a human guide, almost. And this book is absolutely correct & reliable" (NB 16, *N&J* 2: 161). He repeated a version of these remarks in Chapter 46 of *A Tramp Abroad* (1880): "Baedeker knows all about hotels, railway and diligence companies, and speaks his mind freely. He is a trustworthy friend of the traveler." Chapters 22, 28, 35, 36, 38, and 39 of *A Tramp Abroad* contain other generalized references to Baedeker's series of guidebooks.

———. *Traveller's Manual of Conversation, in Four Languages: English, French, German, Italian, with Vocabulary, Short Questions, Etc.* Nineteenth edition. Coblenz: K. Baedeker, 1869.

Inscription: "D. R. Ford/New York".

Catalogs: QF Martinez, "Good Condition"; Ball 2016 inventory, red cloth, gilt lettering.

Location: Mark Twain Archive, Gannett-Tripp Learning Center, Elmira College, Elmira, New York.

This foreign language resource was available to Clemens whenever he visited Quarry Farm in Elmira.

BAGBY, GEORGE WILLIAM (1828–1883). *A Week in Hepsidam; Being the First and Only True Account of the Mountains, Men, Manners and Morals Thereof; Also, a Description of the Lion That Roareth, the Whangdoodle That Mourneth, and the Guyascutus That Sendeth the Whangdoodle Whithersoever He Willeth, by G[e]o. Wash. Meekins (Political Voyageur).* Richmond, Virginia: George W. Gary, 1879. 66 pp.

This political satire by Bagby, a Virginia humorist, is one possible source of Clemens's cryptic notation in 1880 in Notebook 19, "Gnaw a file & flee to the mountains of Hepsidam" (see *N&J* 2: 362).

BAGEHOT, WALTER (1826–1877). *Biographical Studies.* New edition. Ed. by Richard Holt Hutton (1826–1897). 12mo, cloth. London: Longmans, Green and Co., 1895. 398 pp. [Publisher and pages conjectured.]

Inscription: inscribed in Clemens's hand, "S. L. Clemens from Mr. Skrine, Calcutta, April, 1896". (He refers to Francis Henry Bennett Skrine, 1847–1933.)

Marginalia: several corrections and a few passages marked in pencil.

Catalogs: *A1911*, "12mo, cloth, Lond. 1895," quotes the autograph and mentions the marginalia, lot 25, sold for $3.50; *L1912*, #5, $7.50; American Art Association (New York City), sale catalogue for the collection of the late William F. Gable of Altoona, Pennsylvania (8 January 1925), "New Edition, London, 1895," lot 123, sold for $15 (with one other book).

Bagehot sketches the lives of a number of British statesmen, including Robert Peel (1788–1850), William Ewart Gladstone (1809–1898), Henry John Temple, 3rd Viscount Palmerston (1784–1865), and Benjamin Disraeli (1804–1881).

BAGOT, RICHARD (1860–1921). *The Passport.* New York: Harper & Brothers, 1905. 417 pp.

Source: MTLAcc, entry #1432, volume donated by Clemens.

BAHADUR RANA, MINA. *Balabodhini.* Benares: Light Press, 1895.

Inscription: illegible letters on the front free endpaper, below which Clemens has written in pencil: "The above is the autograph of the celebrated recluse & deity. (author of this book)—whose name is—Sri 108 Matparahmahansa-parivra-jakacharyaswamibhaskara-nandaraswati.) He gave us the book Feb. 5/96, in his garden, where his enshrined image is, & where both he & his image are worshiped. The devotee does not presume to pronounce his name without preceding it by saying, 'Sri' (a honorific title) 108 times. He then adds the name—& it will be observed that the name is a tidy little thing itself. S L C. Benares, Feb. 5/96". On the pastedown endpaper Clemens added, also in pencil, "By the rule of his anchorriteship he goes naked except when ladies are admitted to his presence; he then wears a strip of linen about his loins. Temples are built in his honor. His marble image is in them & is worshiped as a deity. Mark Twain". It was extremely unusual for Clemens to use his pen name in inscribing his library books, but in this case he was preparing a literary source for a forthcoming book; Chapter 53 of *Following the Equator* (1897) would rely on these notes and would reproduce the title page of this book in facsimile.

Location: Detroit Public Library. A bookplate on the front pastedown endpaper reads: "Presented by Mrs. Ossip Gabrilowitsch" (i.e., Clemens's daughter Clara, who resided for a period in Detroit with her orchestra conductor husband).

Copy examined: photocopy of Clemens's inscriptions in the Mark Twain Papers in 2001.

———. [Identical copy, apparently.]

Provenance: Willard S. Morse Collection.

Catalog: "A Check List of the Mark Twain Collection Assembled by the Late Willard S. Morse . . . [compiled by] Ellen K. Shaffer and Lucille S. J. Hall. Los Angeles: Dawson's Book Shop, June 1942, p. 3 [the catalog had no entry numbers]. "The Bahadur's Book from which illustrations are taken. Contains several autograph notations by Twain." This entry lists fourteen illustrations removed from the Bahadur volume, ten of them with notes by Twain, of which eight were used in *Following the Equator*.

Location: Dawson's Book Shop sold the Willard S. Morse Collection en bloc to Yale University.

Source: Dawson's Book Shop catalog and notes in the collection of Kevin Mac Donnell, Austin, Texas (Mac Donnell to Alan Gribben, email, 1 September 2013).

BAILEY, ALICE WARD (1857–1922). *Mark Heffron. A Novel.* New York: Harper & Brothers, 1896. 354 pp.

Source: MTLAcc, entry #1513, volume donated by Clemens.

Two women are attracted to a man who has returned to their town after deeply studying various schools of philosophy.

BAILEY, HENRY CHRISTOPHER (1878–1961). *Colonel*

Greatheart. Illustrated by Lester Ralph (1877–1927). Indianapolis, Indiana: Bobbs-Merrill Co., [cop. 1908]. 472 pp.

Source: MTLAcc, entry #876, volume donated by Mrs. Ralph W. Ashcroft (formerly Isabel V. Lyon), Clemens's secretary.

Bailey's novel was set in the era of the Civil War in England, 1642–1649. The illustrator of this book, Lester Ralph, had drawn the pictures for Mark Twain's *Eve's Diary* (1906).

———. [Another identical copy.]

Source: MTLAcc, entry #964, volume donated by Mrs. Ralph W. Ashcroft (formerly Isabel V. Lyon), Clemens's secretary.

BAILEY, JAMES MONTGOMERY (1841–1894), pseud. "Danbury News Man." *Life in Danbury: Being a Brief but Comprehensive Record of the Doings of a Remarkable People, Under More Remarkable Circumstances, and Chronicled in a Most Remarkable Manner, by the Author, James M. Bailey, "The Danbury News Man;" and Carefully Compiled with a Pair of Eight-Dollar Shears, by the Compiler.* Boston: Shepard and Gill, 1873. 303 pp.

Mark Twain's Library of Humor (1888) contained four sketches from this volume—"The Female Baseball Nine," "An Italian's View of a New England Writer," "After the Funeral," and "What He Wanted It For." Twain alluded to "the Danbury News' happy remarks" in Notebook 18 (1879, *N&J* 2: 300). Another favorable reference occurred in Notebook 19 (1880, *N&J* 2: 362, 429). But in an Autobiographical Dictation on 31 July 1906 (*MTE*, p. 201; *AutoMT* 1: 153) Twain listed "the 'Danbury News Man'" among the writers he found in a "mortuary volume" of humorists who "are no longer mentioned."

Blair, "On the Structure of *Tom Sawyer*" (1939), pp. 78–79.

BAILEY, PHILIP JAMES (1816–1902). *Festus: A Poem.* New York: James Miller, n.d. 391 pp.

Source: MTLAcc, entry #656, volume donated by Clemens.

BAIN, FRANCIS WILLIAM (1863–1940). *A Digit of the Moon; A Hindoo Love Story. Translated from the Original Manuscript.* Second edition. London: James Parker and Co., 1901. 118 pp. [The first edition was published in 1899.]

Inscription: (originally) on the front pastedown endpaper: "S. L. Clemens, 1903".

Catalogs: *A1911*, "12mo, boards, vellum back, uncut, Lond. 1901," quotes the signature, lot 26; offered for sale in an Internet auction, 23 March 2012, http://historical.ha.com/c/item.zx?saleNo=629&lotNo=25670, asking $2,600. Oddly, the book has now been rebound with "Mark Twain" stamped in gilt on the spine; the inscription and the *A1911* sale label has now been moved to a "page inserted just before the half-title."

Bain was suspected of writing this story himself. It concerns a king who must ask a princess a question she cannot answer in order to win her hand in marriage.

———. *An Incarnation of the Snow.* New York: Putnam's Sons, 1908.

Provenance: sold at the 1951 auction in Hollywood but not listed in the sale sheet for that event.

Catalog: "Property from the Library of Mark Twain," Butterfield & Butterfield, San Francisco, Sale 6613 (16 July 1997), lot 2712.

Location: Mark Twain House and Museum, Hartford, Connecticut.

Copy examined: copy from Clemens's (or Jean Clemens's) library. Viewed in Hartford in 1997.

BAINBRIDGE, OLIVER (1877–1922). *The Devil's Note Book.* Illustrated by [Jesse Sylvester] "Vet" Anderson (1875–1966). New York: Cochrane Publishing Co., 1908. 154 pp.

"I have sent you a copy of the 'Devil's Note Book' with hearty congratulations on your seventy-third birthday" (Bainbridge to Clemens, 1 December 1908, ALS in MTP). Bainbridge's *Devil's Note Book* was a darkly humorous novel. Its author became a prominent explorer, writer, and lecturer; the illustrator, "Vet" Anderson (a veteran of the Spanish-American War), would go on to draw cartoons, comic strips, and early animated short films.

BAINTON, GEORGE (1847–1925), comp. and ed. *The Art of Authorship. Literary Reminiscences, Methods of Work, and Advice to Young Beginners, Personally Contributed by Leading Authors of the Day.* New York: D. Appleton and Co.; London: J. Clarke & Co., 1890. 355 pp. [The first edition was published in London.]

Mark Twain contributed a brief letter on his "methods of composition" that Bainton published on pages 85–88, so Twain presumably received a copy of this book. Twain's letter is the source of his widely quoted "lightning" and lightning-bug" comparison; he advocated that writers take pains to choose "that exceedingly important brick, the *exact* word" (p. 88; ALS in MTHM). Bainton was a Congregationalist minister who lived in Coventry, England and corresponded widely with prominent authors and composers.

BAKER, CHARLES HINCKLEY (1864–1924). *Life and Character of William Taylor Baker [1841–1903], President of the World's Columbian Exposition and of the Chicago Board of Trade, by His Son.* Illus. New York: The Premier Press, 1908. 293 pp.

Inscription: on the front free endpaper: "To Mr. Samuel L. Clemens/'Mark Twain'/with the compliments and good/wishes of the author/Chas. H. Baker/June 12th 1908".

Marginalia: inscribed in Clemens's hand in black ink on the front pastedown endpaper: "A valuable book, & capably constructed. A tribute from a son to his father which does honor to both. SL C./June/08." No other annotations or markings.

Provenance: Contains the stamps, charge-slip jacket, and call number of the Mark Twain Library, Redding, Connecticut. Donated by Clemens (MTLAcc, entry #1380).

Catalog: *Mott 1952*, item #36, $22.50.

Location: donated to the Mark Twain House in Hartford, Connecticut as an anonymous gift in 1963.

Copy examined: Clemens's copy. Examined in August 1987.

William Taylor Baker was a Chicago business executive who constructed electric power plants in Seattle, Washington. All three hundred copies of this book were published for free distribution. The author of this biography, his son, was an engineer who moved to Florida but remained a loyal donor to Cornell University in Ithaca.

BAKER, GEORGE AUGUSTUS, JR. (1849–1906). *Point-Lace and Diamonds. Poems by George A. Baker, Jr.* Illustrated by Addie Ledyard. New York: F. B. Patterson, 1875. 153 pp.

Source: MTLAcc, entry #616, volume donated by Clemens. Baker's verse affected a colloquial tone. A number of the poems depict young men's romances that end ironically;

for example, in "A Legend of St. Valentine" a suitor is caught sending an identical love poem to two women who (unknown to him) are cousins and who mock his clumsy ploy. Subsequent editions of *Point-Lace and Diamonds* removed the hyphen from its title. Addie Ledyard was a prolific artist who often illustrated her sister Laura W. Ledyard's books.

BAKER, (SIR) RICHARD (1568–1645). *A Chronicle of the Kings of England, from the Time of the Romans Government, unto the Death of King James the First . . . with a Continuation to the Year 1660 by E[dward]. Phillips [1630–c. 1696].* [Editions containing Phillips's "Continuation" were first published in London in 1660.

Mark Twain quotes from this "voluminous and very musty old book" (about the commission that tried Charles I) in a newspaper sketch for the San Francisco *Morning Call* issue of 16 September 1864 (*CofC*, pp. 111–112). Mark Andre Singer of the Mechanics' Institute Library in San Francisco examined the 1660, 1665, 1670, 1674, and 1684 editions of *Chronicle of the English Kings* and concluded that Clemens must have consulted the 1665 edition. This was the only edition containing the passage that Clemens quoted and it was exhibited at the 1864 Mechanics' Fair in San Francisco, 201 years after its printing (Email from Singer to Alan Gribben, 7 October 2003).

BAKER, (SIR) SAMUEL WHITE (1821–1893). *Cast Up by the Sea*. Illus. New York: Harper & Brothers, [n. d.]. 419 pp. [Harper & Brothers issued this novel in 1869, the year it was first published.]

Source: MTLAcc, entry #1585, volume donated by Clemens.

The story opens in 1784 on the coast of Cornwall when a shipwreck mysteriously casts up a live baby and a small treasure. Every possible nautical adventure seems to follow, including smugglers, a kidnapping, life among natives in a foreign land, slave-hunters, a romance, and a marriage. There is even a conveniently staged prediction of an eclipse.

BALDWIN, JAMES (1841–1925). *The Horse Fair*. New York: Century Co., 1895. 418 pp.

Source: MTLAcc, entry #1873, volume donated from Clemens's library by Clara Clemens Gabrilowitsch in 1910.

———. *A Story of the Golden Age*. Illustrated by Howard Pyle (1853–1911). New York: Charles Scribner's Sons, 1887. 268 pp.

Inscription: inscribed in Olivia Clemens's hand on the front flyleaf: "Clara L. Clemens/Christmas 1887/Aunt Ida". The front free endpaper is missing.

Marginalia: Clemens listed and added up in pencil a column of figures on the last page of Scribner's catalog of juvenile books at the back of the volume, quite possibly a computation for books he wished to order.

Catalog: ListABP (1910) ("Story of the Golden Age, Baldwin").

Location: Mark Twain Papers, Bancroft Library, University of California at Berkeley.

Copy examined: Clara Clemens's copy of Baldwin's popularized rendition of Greek myths.

BALDWIN, JAMES MARK (1861–1934). *The Story of the Mind*. Library of Useful Stories Series. Illus. New York: D. Appleton and Co., 1899. 236 pp.

Inscription: on the half-title page in black ink: "Mark II/

(Mr. Clemens)/ from Mark I/(Mr. Baldwin)".

Marginalia: Clemens made a few pencil underlings on page 7 in Chapter I, "The Science of the Mind—Psychology." There are profuse pencil markings and annotations throughout Chapter II ("Introspective Psychology") and Chapter III ("Comparative Psychology"). No notes or marks occurred beyond page 38 in Chapter III—not even in Chapter X, provocatively titled "The Genius and His Environment" (which mentioned Thomas Carlyle).

The Story of the Mind was a basic textbook designed to inform laymen about prevailing theories of psychology. In Chapter II Baldwin described how the mind *acts*, explaining the differences between the new concept of mental processes and the earlier view held by the Scottish School of "faculty" psychology. On page 8, at the beginning of Chapter II, Clemens wrote vertically in pencil in the margin: "Who is *we*? & who is Mind? Two independent entities. Able to reason together & dispute?" On page 13, writing in pencil: "fried down too much?" Clemens made several other notes in pencil, including (p. 18) "'Low bridge!' becomes instinct" and (p. 21) "it is"—the latter in opposition to Baldwin's assertion that "the mind is not a mere machine doing what the laws of its action prescribe."

Chapter III elicited the largest share of Clemens's marginalia in the book; there Baldwin described "animal instinct" (using the housecat as an example) and gave theories of animal-play. On page 24 Clemens reflected, in pencil: "There is no mental *growth*. There is extension of mental *action*, but not of capacity." A little farther on, where Baldwin discussed the view that "there is no absolute break between man and the higher animals," Clemens noted, "no frontier." The following comments are representative samples of Clemens's penciled annotations, many of them written vertically in the margins:

p. 24: Clemens noted, emphatically: "He [i.e., man] is wholly a machine."

p. 25: Regarding animal instinct: "It *was* thought—now it is instinct. Petrified thought."

p. 25: Of the statement that a cat abhors water and is incapable of swimming: "She *can* swim".

p. 27: Written vertically in margin: "copulation—instinct, in man."

p. 28: "Elephant builds a timber-pile."

p. 28: Of different bird calls that resulted by isolating baby birds from hearing the notes of their species: "Xn & Mahometan".

p. 29: Concerning instinct operating in various situations: "Bee butts head against window all day—an ant would seek another way out. Or a dog."

p. 29: Regarding the origin of instinct: "Bird that became a meat-eater."

p. 30: In reference to Reflex Theory: "Horse shies at the same old place after the thing has been removed—memory & imagination. Putting on pants."

p. 32: "At first, *thought*—later, instinct—reflex action".

p. 33: Of Lapsed Intelligence: "Dog making his bed?" (written vertically in the margin).

p. 36: Concerning the difficulty a chicken has in learning how to drink water: "Sandwich mountain mule afraid of water—then tried to bite it. Has no inherited instinct to drink it."

Location: Mark Twain Library, Redding, Connecticut. Displays the Library's purple oval stamps.

Copy examined: Clemens's copy. Examined in 1970, in June 1982, and again on 8 November 2019. Has the red ink original accession number "3891" that is crossed out and replaced by "3172" in black ink.

Baldwin visited Clemens on 2 June 1900 in London, accompanied by Sir John Adams. Clemens made a memo that "Prof. J. Mark Baldwin of Princeton" would arrive and that he "writes books on psychology" (NB 43, TS p. 14). Either then or shortly thereafter Baldwin presented Clemens with *The Story of the Mind*, which was first published in 1898. Clemens wrote to Baldwin on 5 June 1900: "Thank you very much for the book. So far—up to the middle—I find no attempts to deceive, and am gaining confidence" (quoted in Baldwin's *Between Two Wars 1861–1921* [Boston: Stratford, 1926], p. 111). Baldwin invited him to visit Oxford, but Clemens reluctantly declined for family reasons on 7 June 1900 (NB 43, TS p. 16; TS in MTP).

Stone, *IE* (1961), pp. 237, 239–241; Randall Knoper, "'Silly creations of an imagination that is not conscious of its freaks': Multiple Selves, Wordless Communication, and the Psychology of Mark Twain's *No. 44, The Mysterious Stranger*," *Centenary Reflections on Mark Twain's* No. 44, The Mysterious Stranger, ed. Joseph Csicsila and Chad Rohman (Columbia: University of Missouri Press, 2009), pp. 144–156.

BALDWIN, JOSEPH GLOVER (1815–1864). *The Flush Times of Alabama and Mississippi. A Series of Sketches.* New York: D. Appleton and Co., 1853. 330 pp. Reprinted in 1872; also issued by other firms in various years. [Edition undetermined.]

In a piece for the Buffalo *Express* (27 November 1869), Mark Twain lamented the death of "a fortunate and distinguished son of a distinguished father, (Hon. Joseph G. Baldwin, once a Supreme Judge of California, and the author of a formerly exceedingly popular book, 'The Flush Times of Alabama and Mississippi.')" (*MTBE*, p. 97). Twain used quotation marks in alluding to "our 'flush times'" in Virginia City in Chapter 47 of *Roughing It* (1872), a possible echo. He included Baldwin's book title in his list of potential material for an anthology of humor in 1880 (NB 19, *N&J* 2:361, 363), in 1882 (NB 20, *N&J* 2:461), and in 1887 (NB 27, *N&J* 3: 328), but *Mark Twain's Library of Humor* (1888) failed to include any humorous sketches by Baldwin.

Kenneth S. Lynn, *MT&SH* (1960), p. 117.

BALDWIN, SAMUEL DAVIES, D. D. (1818–1866). *Armageddon; or, the Overthrow of Romanism and Monarchy; the Existence of the United States Foretold in the Bible, Its Future Greatness; Invasion by Allied Europe; Annihilation of Monarchy; Expansion into the Millennial Republic, and its Dominion Over the Whole World.* Cincinnati, Ohio: Applegate & Co., 1854. 480 pp. [Copyrighted in 1845; initially published by the Nashville Methodist Publishing House. The edition owned by Clemens is undetermined.]

Catalog: ListABP (1910), "Armageddon, Baldwin", no other information provided.

Clemens wrote to his brother Orion on 26 April [1861]: 'Orion, bring down 'Armageddon' with you if you have it.

If not, *buy* it" (*MTBus*, p. 61; *MTLet* 1: 120). This book of prophecy, written by a minister in Nashville, Tennessee, foretold the end of the world between 1860 and 1875, with Armageddon centering in the Mississippi Valley.

BALFE, MICHAEL WILLIAM (1808–1870). *The Bohemian Girl* (opera, performed in 1843). Libretto by Alfred Bunn (1796–1860).

In 1865 Mark Twain claimed that he had "cultivated" his taste to the point where he could "close one eye in an opera and tell 'Norma' from the 'Bohemian Girl'" (Virginia City *Territorial Enterprise*, 3–5 June 1865; reprinted by Gary Scharnhorst, "Additional Mark Twain Contributions to the Virginia City *Territorial Enterprise*, 1863–66," *American Literary Realism* 47.1 [Fall 2014]: 90). *The Bohemian Girl* included the popular song "I dreamt I dwelt in marble halls."

BALFOUR, ARTHUR JAMES BALFOUR (1848–1930), First Earl. *A Defense of Philosophic Doubt; Being an Essay on the Foundation of Belief.* London: Macmillan and Co., 1879. 355 pp.

Inscription: presentation copy from George Wyndham to Knox Little, an English divine. Wyndham was the private secretary of its author, Balfour. Someone, possibly Canon Little, added a maxim by Mark Twain on the flyleaf: "'There is something fascinating about Science,—one gets such wholesale returns of conjecture out of such a trifling investment of fact.'—Mark Twain."

Catalog: *L1912*, lot 6, sold for $12.50, listed as belonging to Clemens's library, yet (unlike the other items) not specified as originating from the 1911 Anderson Auction. This is especially puzzling inasmuch as the book apparently does not contain Clemens's signature. Very likely this copy of *A Defense of Philosophic Doubt* was included in the 1912 catalog merely because it contained a maxim attributed to Mark Twain. The volume is a highly dubious association copy unless it can be found to contain additional evidence of a Clemens connection.

BALL, CHARLES (b. 1780 or 1781). *Slavery in the United States: A Narrative of the Life and Adventures of Charles Ball, A Black Man, Who Lived Forty Years in Maryland, South Carolina, and Georgia, as a Slave Under Various Masters, and Was One Year in the Navy with Commodore [Joshua] Barney [1759–1818] During the Late War [i.e., the War of 1812].* New York: John S. Taylor, 1837. 517 pp. [Publisher and pages conjectured. Ball's slave narrative was later published under another title, *Fifty Years in Chains; or, the Life of an American Slave* (New York: H. Dayton, 1858), but this was not the version listed in the *A1911* auction catalog (see below).]

Inscription: on the front flyleaf: "S. L. Clemens, 1902".

Catalog: *A1911*, "12mo, cloth (imperfect), foxed and loose in binding, N.Y. 1837," quotes the signature, lot 435, sold for $1.25.

Ball's story was transcribed from his oral narrative in Philadelphia by an editor identified only as "Fisher." It is suspected that Ball later changed his name to avoid detection as someone who had escaped enslavement, which has made his date of death virtually impossible to learn. Ball's life while enslaved was horrific. He endured and witnessed terrible whippings, contemplated suicide repeatedly, and eventually was permanently parted from his wife and children.

In 1889 Twain noted Ball's name as one of the sources for

A Connecticut Yankee in King Arthur's Court (1889) that he intended to acknowledge in an appendix to the novel (NB 29; see *N&J* 3: 501, 503, 506). He relied on Ball's narrative for various details regarding slavery in *A Connecticut Yankee*, especially in Chapters 21 and 34, including (in the latter chapter) the public demand that the King and the Yankee produce "proofs that ye are freemen." Howard G. Baetzhold's "The Course of the Composition of A Connecticut Yankee" (1961) revealed that Twain wrote "Autobiography of Charles Ball" in the margin of a manuscript page ("Course," p. 211, n. 36). This and other obligations to Ball's book are documented in the explanatory and textual notes for *A Connecticut Yankee in King Arthur's Court*, ed. Bernard L. Stein (Berkeley: University of California Press, 1979). Clemens wrote to Sue Crane on 29 August 1901: "You have a small book by a negro named Ball, which tells of terrible things in the Dismal Swamp in slavery times. Won't you send it to me—for use?" (MTP). Presumably he intended to employ it in writing his projected piece on lynchings in the American South.

Roger B. Salomon, *TIH* (1961), p. 109 n. 8; James D. Williams, "The Use of History" (1965), pp. 109–110; Baetzhold, *MT&JB* (1970), pp. 151, 350 n. 33, 352 n. 39; Lucinda H. MacKeithan, "Huck Finn and the Slave Narratives: Lighting Out as Design," *Southern Review* 20.2 (April 1984): 247–264.

BALL, OONA HOWARD (BUTLIN) (1867–1941), pseud. "Barbara Burke." *Barbara Goes to Oxford*. London: Methuen & Co., 1907. 294 pp.
  Source: MTLAcc, entry #2171, volume donated from Clemens's library by Clara Clemens Gabrilowitsch in 1910.

BALLANTYNE, ROBERT MICHAEL (1825–1894). *Erling the Bold; A Tale of the Norse Sea-Kings*. Illustrated by the author. Philadelphia: J. B. Lippincott & Co., 1870. 437 pp.
  Source: MTLAcc, entry #24, volume donated by Clemens. "I have read & sent home . . . Erling the Bold" (Clemens to Olivia Clemens, Steubenville, Ohio, 10 January [1872], *LLMT*, pp. 172–173; *MTLet* 5: 15, 16). Erling the Bold was based on *The Heimskringla*, or *Chronicles of the Kings of Norway*, a poetic chronicle of Norse history and myth by Snorri Sturluson (1178–1241).

———. *Erling the Bold*. New York: J. W. Lovell Co., [cop. 1883]. 437 pp.
  Source: MTLAcc, entry #2165, volume donated from Clemens's library by Clara Clemens Gabrilowitsch in 1910.

BALLOU, MATURIN MURRAY (1820–1895). *Under the Southern Cross; or, Travels in Australia, Tasmania, New Zealand, Samoa, and Other Pacific Islands*. Boston: Ticknor and Co., [1888]. 405 pp. [Edition conjectured.]
  On 3 September 1895 Clemens noted: "'Under the Southern Cross.' Get this mess of self-complacent twaddle" (NB 35, TS p. 41). At the time he was on board the *Warrimoo*, having left Hawaii and approaching the equator.

BALZAC, HONORÉ DE (1799–1850). *Balzac's Contes Drolatiques; Droll Stories Collected from the Abbeys of Touraine, Translated into English [by George Robert Sims (1847–1922)], Complete and Unabridged*. Illustrated by [Paul] Gustave Doré (1832–1883). London: Chatto & Windus, 1874. 650 pp. [This is most likely the edition owned by Clemens, but other firms

published similar Balzac volumes in 1874.]
  In an undated manuscript entitled, "The Walt Whitman Controversy" (DV36, MTP), probably written around 1882, Mark Twain cites two tales and a picture by Doré on page 211 to support his contention that Whitman's offending lines are surpassed in vulgarity by the so-called classics found in many Victorian homes. Henry Fisher remembered hearing Mark Twain advise Bram Stoker that "the only satisfactory way to do a witchcraft story is to filch it bodily from Balzac. The Frenchman got the thing down to perfection in one of his Droll yarns" (*AMT*, p. 181).

———. *The Comedy of Human Life*. Translated from the French by Katharine Prescott Wormeley (1830–1908). Introductions by George Frederic Parsons (1840–1893). 17 vols. Boston: Roberts Brothers, 1885–1893. [Edition conjectured—a surmise based on the fact that Roberts Brothers brought out the major American edition of Balzac's works in the latter-nineteenth century.]
  Catalog: *C1951*, #025, six volumes only, no edition indicated, listed with books signed by Olivia Clemens: *Louis Lambert, The Magic Skin, Seraphita, Cousin Pons, Bureaucracy*, and *Ursula*.
  Clara Clemens summarized the plot of *The Magic Skin* in her commonplace book (Paine 150, MTP), probably around 1888. Clemens mentioned Balzac favorably in 1867 (NB 8, *N&J* 1:326), 1886 (NB 26, *N&J* 3: 239), and 1891 ("Aix, the Paradise of the Rheumatics"). Katy Leary, the family's housekeeper, believed that the French novel she found in the billiard room and enjoyed until Olivia took it away from her was "maybe" an English translation of Balzac. "I used to hear Mr. Clemens talk about his [Balzac's] books," she recalled. "He thought they was wonderful" (*LMT* [1925], p. 56). It seems likely that the Clemenses owned other novels in Balzac's grand series that have not survived.

———. *The Country Doctor* [*Le médecin de campagne*]. Translated from the French by Katharine Prescott Wormeley (1830–1908). Boston: Roberts Brothers, 1887. 304 pp. [Edition conjectured; this was the first English-language edition published in the United States.]
  One of five book titles Clemens listed in September 1887 was "County Doctor—Balzac" (NB 27, *N&J* 3: 317).

———. *Une Fille d'Eve*. Paris, 1840.
  Inscription: signed on the front flyleaf, "S. L. Clemens."
  Catalog: *A1911*, "Vol. 1, 8vo, unbound, poor copy, Paris, 1840," signature quoted, lot 27, sold for $1.25.

———. *Oeuvres complètes illustrées*. 48 volumes. An early illustrated edition. One of 100 sets. Contemporary three-quarter black and dark brown morocco and marbled boards, original printed wrappers preserved in nearly every volume, untrimmed. Paris: Paul Ollendorff, 1900–1912. The bindings are not uniform in materials and patterns.
  Inscriptions: two volumes (*D'enfant Maudit* (issued in 1901) and *La Peau de Chagrin* (issued in 1900) have Clara Clemens Gabrilowitsch's signature on the front flyleaf, using her married name.
  Marginalia: Nearly half of the volumes are annotated with marginal lines, underlinings, and a few words. Most of the heavier-looking markings are characteristic of Clara, but other, more lightly written, marginal lines and spelling corrections in the texts resemble those made by Clemens in

his books. There are annotations in three of the six volumes published in 1900, in two of the three 1901 volumes, in the single 1902 volume, in all three of the 1906 volumes, in four of the eight 1907 volumes, in six of the fourteen 1908 volumes, none in the 1912 volume, and in five of the twelve undated volumes. In all, twenty-three of the forty-eight volumes contain annotations. Clemens seemingly perused the pre-1909 volumes of this set of Balzac.

Provenance: Clara Clemens Samossoud withheld this set of books from the 1951 auction. In 1966 her husband Jacques A. Samossoud bequeathed them to Henry and Mary Shisler of Cardiff by the Sea, California, who sold them in 1981. Each volume contains the signed bookplate of Nick Karanovich of Fort Wayne, Indiana, stating that he obtained this set in 1983 from Maurice Neville, a rare book dealer who acquired them from Clara Clemens Samossoud's residual estate.

Location: collection of Kevin Mac Donnell, Austin, Texas

Sources: Mac Donnell to Alan Gribben, 27 February 2012; email, Mac Donnell to Gribben, 28 July 2004.

————. *Le Père Goriot* (1834).

"Description of the boarding house in 'Pere Goriot,'" wrote Clemens in 1888 (NB 27, *N&J* 3: 385).

BANCROFT, FREDERIC (1860–1945). *The Life of William H. Seward.* 2 vols. New York: Harper & Brothers, 1900.

Source: MTLAcc, entries #861 and #862, volumes donated by Clemens.

William Henry Seward (1801–1872) was a United States Senator from New York whose radical anti-slavery views kept him from being nominated for president. Abraham Lincoln appointed him Secretary of State and he served in that office from 1861 until 1869. It was Seward who negotiated the purchase of Alaska in 1867.

BANCROFT, HUBERT HOWE (1832–1918). *Literary Industries. A Memoir.* New York: Harper & Brothers, 1891. 446 pp.

Source: MTLAcc, entry #1792, volume donated by Clemens.

This book was originally published as Volume 39 of *The Works of Hubert Howe Bancroft* (San Francisco: History Co., 1890). On page 363 Bancroft quoted from an 1876 letter he received from Charles Dudley Warner, reporting Clemens's enthusiastic response to the first volume of Bancroft's *Native Races.* John Walton Caughey's *Hubert Howe Bancroft, Historian of the West* (Berkeley: University of California Press, 1946) also related Mark Twain's opinion of *Native Races* as passed along by Charles Dudley Warner (pp. 150–151), quoting from Bancroft's *Literary Industries,* p. 363.

————. *The Native Races of the Pacific States of North America.* 5 vols. New York: D. Appleton and Co.; San Francisco: A. L. Bancroft & Co., 1874–1876.

Mark Twain was one of many notables who in 1876 received a presentation copy of *Native Races* during Bancroft's campaign for national recognition and endorsements. In *Literary Industries. A Memoir* (1890) Bancroft quoted a letter from his files that Charles Dudley Warner had written to him on 11 October 1876: "Mr Clemens was just in and was in an unusual state of enthusiasm over the first volume, especially its fine style. You may have a picture of his getting up at two o'clock this morning and, encased in a fur overcoat, reading it till daylight" (p.

363). Clemens remembered what he found in Bancroft's volumes. At the top of a page in Thomas Wright's *Early Travels in Palestine,* a volume Clemens signed in 1877, he wrote of the disfiguration of lips by enlargement: "This can be done by some Indians on our Northwest Coast. (See Bancroft.)" (p. 229). Twain drew upon *Native Races* for a chapter of *A Tramp Abroad* (1880) that compared courtship and marriage customs of primitive tribes with those of contemporary French society (Box 6, #7, MTP), but he eventually discarded the essay (*N&J* 2: 314 n. 46).

BANGS, JOHN KENDRICK (1862–1922). *Bikey the Skicycle & Other Tales of Jimmieboy.* Illustrated by Peter Newell (1862–1924). New York: Riggs Publishing Co., 1902. 321 pp.

Source: MTLAcc, entry #1586, volume donated by Clemens.

————. *The Booming of Acre Hill, and Other Reminiscences of Urban and Suburban Life.* Illustrated by C[harles]. Dana Gibson (1867–1944). New York: Harper & Brothers, 1900. 266 pp.

Source: MTLAcc, entry #17, volume donated by Clemens.

————. *Cobwebs from a Library Corner.* New York: Harper & Brothers, 1899. 101 pp.

Source: MTLAcc, entry #1340, volume donated by Clemens.

————. *Coffee and Repartee.* Illus. New York: Harper & Brothers, 1901. 123 pp.

Source: MTLAcc, entry #1209, volume donated by Clemens.

————. *The Genial Idiot, His Views and Reviews.* New York: Harper & Brothers, 1908. 215 pp.

Source: MTLAcc, entry #960, volume donated by Clemens.

————. *Ghosts I Have Met and Some Others.* Illustrated by Peter Newell (1862–1924), A[rthur]. B[urdett]. Frost (1851–1928), and F[rederick]. T[hompson]. Richards (1864–1921). New York: Harper & Brothers, 1899. 191 pp.

Source: MTLAcc, entry #20, volume donated by Clemens.

————. *A House-Boat on the Styx.* Illus. New York: Harper & Brothers, 1902. 171 pp.

Source: MTLAcc, entry #1514, volume donated by Clemens.

————. *The Inventions of the Idiot.* New York: Harper & Brothers, 1904. 185 pp.

Source: MTLAcc, entry #959, volume donated by Clemens. Bangs married his secretary the year that this book was published. Laura Skandera Trombley described Isabel Lyon's disappointment at this development (*Mark Twain's Other Woman: The Hidden Story of His Final Years* [New York: Alfred A. Knopf, 2010], pp. 26–27).

————. *Mrs. Raffles; Being the Adventures of an Amateur Crackswoman.* Illustrated by Albert Levering (1869–1929). New York: Harper & Brothers, 1905. 180 pp.

Source: MTLAcc, entry #961, volume donated by Clemens. These short stories chronicle the exploits of the invented widow of E. W. Hornung's fictional jewel thief Arthur J. Raffles.

————. *Olympian Nights.* Illus. New York: Harper & Brothers, 1902. 224 pp.

Source: MTLAcc, entry #962, volume donated by Clemens.

————. [Another identical copy.]

Source: MTLAcc, entry #1274, volume donated by Clemens.

————. *Over the Plum-Pudding.* Illus. New York: Harper &

Brothers, 1901. 244 pp. [Edition and pages conjectured.]
Inscription: "S. L. Clemens, Riverdale, Oct. 1901."
Catalog: *A1911*, "First edition. . . . 12mo, half cloth, N.Y. 1901," quotes the signature, lot 28, sold for $8.
This was a collection of Bangs' short stories.
———. *Peeps at People; Being Certain Papers from the Writings of Anne Warrington Witherup [pseud.]*. Illustrated by Edward Penfield (1866–1925). New York: Harper & Brothers, 1899. 185 pp.
Source: MTLAcc, entry #19, volume donated by Clemens.
———. *A Proposal Under Difficulties*. Blue cloth. New York: Harper & Brothers, 1905.
Provenance: has the shelfmarks of Clara Clemens Gabrilowitsch's numbering system for her library books during her Detroit years. Sold at the 1951 auction in Hollywood but not listed in the sale sheet.
Catalog: "Property from the Library of Mark Twain," Butterfield & Butterfield, San Francisco, Sale 6613 (16 July 1997), lot 2712.
Location: Mark Twain House and Museum, Hartford, Connecticut.
Copy examined: unmarked copy belonging to the Clemens family library. Viewed in Hartford in 1997.
———. *The Pursuit of the House-Boat*. Illustrated by Peter Newell (1862–1924). New York: Harper & Brothers, 1900. 204 pp.
Location: Mark Twain Library, Redding, Connecticut. Donated by Clemens (MTLAcc, entry #1105*)*.
Copy examined: Clemens's copy, unmarked.
———. *R. Holmes & Co.; Being the Remarkable Adventures of Raffles Holmes, Esq., Detective and Amateur Cracksman by Birth*. Illustrated by Sydney Adamson (fl. 1892–1914). New York: Harper & Brothers, 1906. 231 pp.
Source: MTLAcc, entry #18, volume donated by Clemens. Bangs creates in these short stories a parody of (and a moral tug-of-war between) two famous crime figures. Raffles Holmes is supposedly the son of Sherlock Holmes and the grandson of the gentleman jewel thief Arthur J. Raffles.
———. [Another identical copy.]
Source: MTLAcc, entry #25, volume donated by Clemens.
———. [Another identical copy.]
Source: MTLAcc, entry # 1248, volume donated by Clemens.
———. *A Rebellious Heroine: A Story*. Illustrated by W.[illiam] T.[homas] Smedley (1858–1920). Original tan pictorial cloth, gilt. New York: Harper & Brothers, 1896. 225 pp.
Inscription: the front endpaper is inscribed in ink to Ida Clark Langdon: "To Mrs. Charles J. Langdon with many thanks for her charming hospitality from John Kendrick Bangs, April 20, 1897." The whimsical humorist visited Elmira, New York in 1897 and signed Ida Clark Langdon's guestbook during his visit.
Provenance: Langdon family library. Charles J. Langdon and his wife Ida Clark Langdon lived in the family mansion in Elmira. (It was Charles who had introduced Clemens to his sister Olivia Langdon.) There is no direct evidence that Clemens saw this volume.
Location: collection of Kevin Mac Donnell, Austin, Texas (Mac Donnell to Alan Gribben, 29 November 2011).
———. *Toppleton's Client; or, A Spirit in Exile*. New York:

Charles L. Webster & Co., 1893. 269 pp.
Advertised by Clemens's publishing firm as a semi-humorous story of the supernatural about a barrister and his soul (*Publishers' Trade List Annual 1893*), this seems to have been Bangs' earliest publication of which Clemens had any direct knowledge. However, Bangs' farcical *The Tiddledywink Tales* (1891) had been such a success with the public that it is hard to believe Clemens would not have been aware of Bangs as an offbeat, rising writer. Clemens possessed copies of most of Bangs' subsequent books. One hardly thinks of Clemens and Bangs as particularly close associates, but these nearly twenty titles (many with multiple copies) represent a significant part of Clemens's surviving library.
———. *The Worsted Man; A Musical Play for Amateurs*. Illus. New York: Harper & Brothers, 1905. 86 pp.
Source: MTLAcc, entry #654, volume donated by Clemens.
———. [Another identical copy.]
Source: MTLAcc, entry #655, volume donated by Clemens.
BANIM, JOHN (1798–1842). *Damon and Pythias, A Tragedy, in Five Acts* (play, first performed in London in 1821).
In 1853, having seen the celebrated actor Edwin Forrest play the leading role of Spartacus in Robert Montgomery Bird's *The Gladiator*, Clemens lamented, "I am sorry I did not see him play 'Damon and Pythias'—the former character being his greatest" (Clemens to Pamela Moffett, New York City, October 1853, *MTL*, p. 24; *MTLet* 1: 16). Edwin Forrest (1806–1872) was nearing the end of his acting career.
BARBER, JOSEPH (active 1862–1871). *War Letters of a Disbanded Volunteer, Embracing His Experiences as Honest Old Abe's Bosom Friend and Unofficial Adviser* (published in 1864).
Mark Twain's autobiographical dictation of 31 July 1906 cited "the 'Disbanded Volunteer'" as an example of an outmoded type of cacographic humor that merely depended on "an odd trick of speech and spelling" for its transitory popularlity (*AutoMT* 2: 153). Barber published a few other books, including *Crumbs from the Round Table: A Feast for Epicures* (1866). His *War Letters of a Disbanded Volunteer* received by far the most notice.
BARCLAY, JAMES TURNER (1807–1874). *The City of the Great King; or, Jerusalem As It Was, As It Is, and As It Is To Be*. Philadelphia: J. Challen and Sons, 1858. 627 pp.
Mark Twain reported that this book was one of those recommended for *Quaker City* passengers to bring with them (*Daily Alta California*, 5 April 1868; *TIA*, p. 303).
BARDSLEY, CHARLES WAREING ENDELL (1843–1898). *Curiosities of Puritan Nomenclature*. London: Chatto & Windus, 1880; New York: R. Worthington, 1880.
Bardsley's book did more than its title implied, tracing English names from the time of the Norman Conquest but most fully treating the era of Puritan belief. In a brief, eleven-page chapter titled "The Influence of Puritanism on American Nomenclature" Bardsley demonstrated the impact of English Puritan thought on the naming of children among the leading families of New England. See the following Bardsley entry.
———. *Our English Surnames: Their Sources and Significances*. London: Chatto &. Windus, 1873. The second edition (1875) was retitled as *English Surnames*.
In the same purple ink in which Clemens made his

declaration of reading preferences on a discarded envelope in 1909, he also listed among other titles "2 books by Rev. C. W. Bardsley" (MTP, Notebook fragments file). Bardsley's *Curiosities* and his *English Surnames* seem the most likely references, since they were the best known of his works on English nomenclature. He also produced *The Romance of the London Directory* (London, 1879).

Gribben, "'I Detest Novels, Poetry & Theology'" (1977). A revised version of this essay appears in Volume One of the present work.

Baring-Gould, Sabine (1834–1924). *In Exitu Israel; An Historical Novel.* New York: Macmillan & Co., 1870. 385 pp.

Source: MTLAcc, entry #2166, volume donated by Mrs. Gabrilowitsch in 1910.

The Reverend Joseph H. Twichell wrote to Clemens on 25 June 1877: "I send you by mail to-day Baring-Gould's novel 'In Exitu Israel,' which it has taken me longer than I thought to procure" (MTP). Clemens replied on 27 June from Elmira: "Exitu-Israel has just come—many thanks, Joe—I'll give you an opinion. Been reading a lot of French rot here & am glad to get this" (*LMTJHT*, p. 62). The opinion he may have delivered to Twichell is unknown, but his comments to Mary Mason Fairbanks on 6 August 1877 were complimentary. He mentioned to her that he had read "'In Exitu Israel,' a very able novel by Baring-Gould, the purpose of which is to show the effect of some of the most odious of the privileges of the French nobles under *l'ancien regème* [*sic*], & of the dischurching of the Catholic Church by the National Assembly in '92" (*MTMF*, p. 208). Among many other accomplishments, Baring-Gould was the author of the lyrics for the hymn "Onward, Christian Soldiers." Its melody was composed by Arthur S. Sullivan (1842–1900).

Blair, "French Revolution" (1957), p. 23; Blair, *MT&HF* (1960), p. 310; Baetzhold, *MT&JB* (1970), pp. 350 n. 34, 347–348 n. 21.

———. *Legends of Old Testament Characters, from the Talmud and Other Sources.* London: Macmillan and Co., 1871. [Edition conjectured.]

Source: ListABP (1910), "Legends of Old Testament Characters, Baring-Gould".

Kelly Anspaugh, "Huck Finn Meets an Old Master," *Mark Twain Journal* 27.1 (Spring 1989):10, pointed out a possible connection between Baring-Gould and Twain's fondness for the story of Moses.

Barker, Edmund Henry (1788–1839). *Literary Anecdotes and Contemporary Reminiscences of Professor Porson and Others. From the Manuscript Papers of the Late E. H. Barker.* Two vols. in one. London: J. R. Smith, 1852. [Edition conjectured.]

Philip H. Highfill, Jr. noticed that Anecdote No. CCCXXX-IV ("The Two Thieves") on page 282 relates the same method of testing for gender (tossing something between a seated person's legs) that a woman employs in Chapter 11 of *Adventures of Huckleberry Finn* (1885) to detect Huck's subterfuge ("Incident in *Huckleberry Finn*," *Mark Twain Journal* 11.3 [Fall 1961]: 6). Richard Porson (1759–1808) was a professor of Greek at Cambridge University.

Barker, Mary Anne (Stewart), afterwards Lady Broome (1831–1911). *Station Amusements in New Zealand, by Lady Barker.* Copyright Edition. British Authors Series. Leipzig: Bernhard Tauchnitz, 1874. 288 pp.

Catalog: *C1951*, Dl, $8, listed among the books signed by Clemens, Tauchnitz Edition specified.

———. *Station Life in New Zealand, by Lady Barker.* Copyright Edition. British Authors Series. Leipzig: Bernhard Tauchnitz, 1874. 279 pp.

Catalog: *C1951*, D1, $8, listed among the books signed by Clemens, Tauchnitz Edition specified.

In connection with New Zealand, Clemens mentioned Barker's book in Notebook 34 (TS p. 36, MTP) and wrote in December 1895: "At great intervals they have much snow & very hard winters in the Middle Island; Lady Barker tells of one" (NB36, TS p. 3, MTP).

Barnes, Albert (1798–1870). *Notes, Explanatory and Practical, on the New Testament. First Epistle of Paul to the Corinthians.* New York: Harper & Brothers, 1848. 357 pp.

Source: MTLAcc, entry #944, volume donated by Clemens. Mulling over the kinds of books that endure, Clemens mentioned, in a note dating from 1896 or later, "Barnes' Notes" as a representative "Religious" work. See the Catalog entry for É. Zola, *Rome.*

———. *Notes, Explanatory and Practical, on the New Testament. Epistles of Paul to the Ephesians, Philippians, and Colossians.* Illus. New York: Harper & Brothers, 1850. 331 pp.

Source: MTLAcc, entry #945, volume donated by Clemens.

———. *Notes, Explanatory and Practical, on the New Testament. Epistle to the Hebrews.* Illus. New York: Harper & Brothers, 1851. 335 pp.

Source: MTLAcc, entry #946, volume donated by Clemens.

———. *Notes, Explanatory and Practical, on the New Testament. Book of Revelation.* Illus. New York: Harper & Brothers, 1852. 506 pp.

Source: MTLAcc, entry #947, volume donated by Clemens.

———. *Notes, Explanatory and Practical, on the New Testament. General Epistles of James, Peter, John and Jude.* New York: Harper & Brothers, 1852. 459 pp.

Source: MTLAcc, entry #948, volume donated by Clemens.

———. *Notes, Explanatory and Practical, on the New Testament. Second Epistle to the Corinthians and the Epistle to the Galatians.* New York: Harper & Brothers, 1852. 398 pp.

Source: MTLAcc, entry #949, volume donated by Clemens.

———. *Notes, Explanatory and Practical, on the New Testament. Acts of the Apostles.* Map. New York: Harper & Brothers, 1853. 356 pp.

Source: MTLAcc, entry #950, volume donated by Clemens.

———. *Notes, Explanatory and Practical, on the New Testament. Epistles of Paul to the Thessalonians, to Timothy, to Titus, and to Philemon.* New York: Harper & Brothers, 1853. 355 pp.

Source: MTLAcc, entry #951, volume donated by Clemens.

———. *Notes, Explanatory and Practical, on the New Testament. Epistle to the Romans.* New York: Harper & Brothers, 1853. 328 pp.

Source: MTLAcc, entry #952, volume donated by Clemens.

———. *Notes, Explanatory and Practical, on the New Testament. The Gospels.* Illus. New York: Harper & Brothers, 1854. 413 pp.

Source: MTLAcc, entry #953, volume donated by Clemens.

Barnes, James (1866–1936). *The Blockaders, and Other Stories.* New York: Harper & Brothers, 1905. 203 pp.

Source: MTLAcc, entry #421, volume donated by Clemens.

———. *For King or Country. A Story of the American Revolution.*

Illus. New York: Harper & Brothers, 1905. 269 pp.

  Source: MTLAcc, entry #1311, volume donated by Clemens.

———. *A Loyal Traitor; A Story of the War of 1812*. Illustrated by A. J. Keller (1866–1924). New York: Harper & Brothers, 1905. 306 pp.

  Source: MTLAcc, entry #1305, volume donated by Clemens.

  The illustrator's name, A. J. Keller, was likely a variant employed by the prolific Arthur Ignatius Keller; their birth and death dates are identical.

———. *The Son of Light Horse Harry*. Illustrated by W[illiam]. E[llis]. Mears (1868–1945). New York: Harper & Brothers, 1904. 242 pp.

  Barnes' novel about the Confederate General Robert E. Lee (1807–1870) was one of four "Harper's books" for which Clemens's business agent in Florence took receipt in 1904 (Sebastiano V. Cecchi to Clemens, 30 July 1904, MTP); later the business agent mentioned that Clemens left this book behind in Florence (Sebastiano V. Cecchi to Clemens, 4 November 1904, MTP).

BARNEY, BILL (b. 1855). *The Bright Side of Country Life*. Dallas, Texas: Farmers' Printing Co., 1906. 227 pp.

  Source: MTLAcc, entry #570, volume donated by Clemens.

BARNUM, PHINEAS TAYLOR (1810–1891). *Dollars and Sense; or, How to Get On. The Whole Secret in a Nutshell*. Illustrated by W[illiam]. W[allace]. Denslow (1856–1915). New York: H. S. Allen, 1890. 488 pp. [Edition and pages conjectured.]

  Inscription: inscribed "To Saml. L. Clemens, Esq. (Mark Twain) with kind regards of P. T. Barnum, Bridgeport, Conn., Oct. 16, 1890."

  Catalog: *A1911*, "Square 8vo, full stamped roan, gilt top and edges, N.Y. 1890," quotes the inscription, lot 29, sold for $9.50.

———. *Struggles and Triumphs; or, Forty Years' Recollections of P. T. Barnum. Written by Himself. Author's Edition. Revised, Enlarged, Newly Illustrated and Written Up to March, 1874, by the Author*. Original deluxe half green polished calf, gilt spine, red leather label, deluxe presentation binding. Joints and spine extremities repaired. Cloth clamshell case. Buffalo, New York: Warren, Johnson & Co., 1874. 780 pp. [The copyright notice is dated 1871, but page 780 prints a letter dated 6 April 1875 that is signed "Publishers" and notes that Barnum has just been elected mayor of Bridgeport, Connecticut; it also includes a letter by Barnum dated 23 April 1875. (These details and the description of the volume were supplied by Thomas L. Edsall, 19th Century Shop, Baltimore, Maryland to Alan Gribben, 19 July 1994.)]

  Inscriptions: the front free flyleaf is signed in black ink: "To/ Saml L Clemens Esq/With kind regards of the author/P. T. Barnum/Waldemere June 21st 1875". (Waldemere, built in 1869, was Barnum's huge gingerbread mansion facing Long Island Sound.) Notations about the sale of this volume ("D-77") for $37.50 at the Hollywood auction in 1951 are visible on the front pastedown endpaper, where Clara Clemens Gabrilowitsch's shelfmark ("Bb/ Ls33") from her Detroit private library system of classification also appears.

  Catalogs: *C1951*, D77, "signed by author to S. L. C.," edition unspecified, erroneously listed with books autographed by Clemens, $37.50; "Twain's Copy of One

of His Favorite Books," 19th Century Shop, Baltimore, Maryland, "one of the most wonderful 19th-century American association copies we have ever handled," July 1994, unpriced.

  Catalog: ListABP (1910) ("Life of P. T. Barnum").

  Source: description provided to Alan Gribben on 19 July 1994 by Thomas L. Edsall of the 19th Century Shop, Baltimore, Maryland.

  Location: currently unknown.

  Copy examined: photocopies of the title page and flyleaves supplied by the 19th Century Shop in 1994.

  It would seem inevitable that Barnum's extravagant claims, revolving menageries, incessant self-promotions, grandiose residences, and periodic political forays attracted and held Clemens's attention. Moreover, both men used the same lecture bureaus, lived only fifty miles apart in Connecticut, and shared an affection for the former minstrel dancer-turned-journalist-and author Ralph Keeler. Early on, though, Twain's references to Barnum were as unflattering as his gibes at Horace Greeley. In 1867 Twain ridiculed the showman in "Barnum's First Speech in Congress" and several other sketches. One of these in the San Francisco *Alta California* (March 1867) complained that "there is little or nothing . . . worth seeing" in Barnum's Museum. Twain's "Some Learned Fables for Good Old Boys and Girls" (1875) has an illiterate manager of the Waterside Museum named "Varnum" who employs a man to manufacture bone ornaments and primitive flint weapons. However, after Barnum took no public offense and the two men exchanged correspondence beginning in January-February 1875 (*MTLet* 6: 368–369), personal visits, and complimentary copies of their works, Twain's attitude softened. A letter from Barnum to Clemens written on 2 November 1876 refers to his upcoming stay at Clemens's house and their mutual support for Rutherford B. Hayes in the election ("Mark Twain and Related Material," Robert T. Slotta [1998], item 29). Albert Bigelow Paine recorded Clemens's recollection that "when the *Life of P. T. Barnum, Written by Himself*, appeared, . . . he [Clemens] sat up nights to absorb it, and woke early and lighted the lamp to follow the career of the great showman" (*MTB*, p. 410).

The men remained friendly correspondents and over the years Barnum sought to exploit Mark Twain to publicize his shows and circuses, while Twain used Barnum and some of his escapades as literary material. Commentators have surmised that Barnum's opulent home, Iranistan, was what a bewildered Hank Morgan has in mind when guessing that the "towers and turrets" of Camelot must be "Bridgeport" in Chapter 1 of *A Connecticut Yankee in King Arthur's Court* (1889). Harold Aspiz pointed out similarities between an anecdote in P. T. Barnum's autobiography and the remark by Pudd'nhead Wilson about killing his half of a dog that brands Wilson as the town fool in Chapter 1 of *Pudd'nhead Wilson* (1894) ("The Other Half of Pudd'nhead Wilson's Dog" *Mark Twain Journal* 17.4 [Summer 1975]: 10–11). In Chapter 53 of *Following the Equator* (1897), Twain speculates about the sensation Barnum might have made by acquiring one of the living gods worshiped by Hindus in India ("or found a substitute that would answer"). "I knew Mr. Barnum well," states Twain in Chapter 64 of *Following the Equator*, recounting Barnum's controversial efforts to purchase British national treasures such as Nelson's Column, Shakespeare's birthplace house, and Jumbo the elephant (the latter with tragic results). Their mutual fascination with showmanship, image-creation, and duplicity obviously gave them a lasting connection. Assessing Clemens's lifelong reading habits, Paine included Barnum's *Life* among Clemens's favorite books that "showed usage" (*MTB*, p. 1540). Barnum biographer Neil Harris identifies similarities in both men's lives, including the facts that each fathered three girls, of whom one died early, lost a wife, suffered financial bankruptcy, dissented from religious orthodoxy, and admired gadgetry (p. 284).

Hamlin Hill, "Barnum, Bridgeport and *The Connecticut Yankee*," *American Quarterly* 16.4 (Winter 1964): 615–616; Neil Harris deftly explored parallels between Twain and Barnum in *Humbug: The Art of P. T. Barnum* (Chicago: University of Chicago Press, 1973, repr. 1981), pp. 157, 190–191, 194, 282–287; Howard G. Baetzhold, "Mark Twain on Scientific Investigation: Contemporary Allusions in 'Some Learned Fables for Good Old Boys and Girls,'" in *Literature and ideas in America: Essays in Memory of Harry Hayden Clark*, ed. Robert Falk (Athens: Ohio University Press, 1975), pp. 128–154; David E. E. Sloane, "A Note on Barnum and Twain," *Mark Twain Review* (Mark Twain Society of Korea) 5 (December 2000): 5–20; and Christine Benner Dixon, "This Way to the Egress: The Humbug of Barnum and Twain," *Mark Twain Annual 16* (2018): 47–63.

BARR, ROBERT (1850–1912). "How to Write a Short Story," *The Bookman* 5 (March 1897): 42–44. [Contribution to a symposium.]

"I like your article ever so much," Clemens wrote from Vienna on 29 September 1897 (PH in MTP). On 23 October 1897 Clemens requested that his British publisher send "an early copy" of *More Tramps Abroad* (1897) to "Robert Barr" (*Sotheby's 2003*, #90). A note Twain apparently wrote in 1898 on the verso of a leaf in a copy of his *The Man That Corrupted Hadleyburg* refers to Robert Barr (*A1911*, lot 312). Shortly after Clemens died Barr published a series of three reminiscences about his conversations with Clemens in a monthly magazine he edited, *The Idler* (London) 39.93 (June 1910): 1013–1019; 39.94 (July 1910): 1120–1125; and 39.95 (August 1910): 1231–1236.

———. *A Prince of Good Fellows.* Illustrated by Edmund J[oseph]. Sullivan (1869–1933). New York: McClure, Phillips & Co., 1902. 340 pp.

Source: MTLAcc, entry #2170, volume donated from Clemens's library by Clara Clemens Gabrilowitsch in 1910. Barr's historical novel is based on the life of James V, King of Scotland.

———. *A Woman Intervenes; or, the Mistress of the Mine.* Illustrated by Hal [Henry William Lowe] Hurst (1865–1938). New York: F. A. Stokes Co., [cop. 1896]. 375 pp. [Edition conjectured.]

Writing to the Scottish-born author and editor Robert Barr on 19 June 1897 from Weggis, Switzerland (dating the letter the "next day" following a visit by Barr), Clemens lavished rare praise on Barr's recent novel. Clemens began

by withdrawing some earlier comments he had made the previous day: "If I have seemed to offer you any advice in the literary trade, I take it back." That was because, he explained, "when I got back from the pier I took up A Woman Intervenes, to read until the family should be ready to go boating. . . . If engagements are to be kept, they must be kept before Chapter 8; for after that point they will be violated. One is in the rush of the story, then, & cannot get ashore any more until the end. He is helpless. . . . I read through to the end without stopping (& without skipping a line). And yet my custom is to skip liberally." Clemens had particular praise for Barr's "style," which he found to be "honest, simple, straightforward, unostentatious, unruffled; barren of impertinences & familiarities; dignified, refined, self-respectful, & respectful toward the reader; bright, snappy, humorous, moving; & the story flows from the sources to the mouth without a break—& stays between the banks all the way, too." Moreover, "the characters are alive, & are distinctly discriminated." In sum, he wrote, "I have had great pleasure in this book" (quoted in *Sotheby's 2003*, #89; also quoted in The 19th Century Rare Book and Photograph Shop, Catalog 127, June 2010). This salvo of compliments should not be overlooked by those seeking to comprehend Clemens's literary criteria for fiction. This is also the only place I have found where Clemens admits to a reading habit that accounts for the numerous unopened leaves in his library books: "my custom is to skip liberally."

Chapter 8 of Barr's novel opened by introducing a politician named Fleming. "He was immensely popular with a certain class in the smoking-room. He was lavishly free with his invitations to drink, and always had a case of good cigars in his pocket, which he bestowed with great liberality. He had the habit of slapping a man boisterously on the back, and saying, 'Well, old fellow, how are you? How's things?' He usually confided to his listeners that he was a self-made man; had landed at New York without a cent in his pocket, and look at him now!" But at this point Fleming promptly blurts out a secret.

Jo Dee Benussi pointed out to me that Barr's artist Hal Hurst (along with Dan Beard) had illustrated the Chatto & Windus edition of Twain's *The American Claimant* (1892).

BARRAS, CHARLES M. (1826–1873). *The Black Crook; An Original, Magical and Spectacular Drama in Four Acts* (first produced in New York City on 12 September 1866).

When Mark Twain gazed upon the chorus girls in the dazzling production of *The Black Crook* at Niblo's Garden on Broadway, he knew that he had encountered at last the evil allurements so often associated with the stage. For his California readers he criticized the extravaganza as "the wickedest show you can think of. . . . A shrewd invention of the devil" that displayed "all possible compromises between nakedness and decency" (2 February 1867 letter to *Alta California*, MTTMB, pp. 84–85). Twain referred to *The Black Crook* again in a 23 February 1867 letter to the *Alta California* (MTTMB, p. 110) and in a 31 August 1867 letter published in the New York *Tribune* (25 October 1867 issue, TIA, p. 132). "Think of this insect [the Reverend Sabine] condemning the whole theatrical service as a disseminator of bad morals because it has Black Crooks in it," he wrote in "The Indignity Put Upon

the Remains of George Holland by the Rev. Mr. Sabine"
(1871). On 31 March 1873 he addressed the Monday
Evening Club in Hartford on "License of the Press" and
reminded the audience how "our newspapers—all of them,
without exception—glorify the 'Black Crook' and make
it an opulent success— they could have killed it dead
with one broadside of contemptuous silence if they had
wanted to" (*MTS* [1923], p. 48).
Krause, *MTC* (1967), pp. 38–43.

BARRAS, PAUL FRANÇOIS JEAN NICHOLAS (1755–1829).
Memoirs of Barras, Member of the Directorate. Ed. by George
Duruy (1853–1918). Translated from the French by Charles
É[mile]. Roche (1847–1935). 4 vols. New York: Harper &
Brothers, 1895–1896.
  Inscriptions: Volume I is signed on the front flyleaf "S. L.
  Clemens/1895"; Volume II is signed on the front flyleaf
  "S. L. Clemens./l895/From J. Henry Harper."
  Marginalia: Clemens wrote the word "French" in the
  margins of pages 6 and 12 of Volume I, indicating his
  opinion of excitable Gallic behavior.
  Catalogs: *C1951*, #18c, $14, 2 vols. only; *Fleming 1972*,
  2 vols. only; Sotheby Parke Bernet, New York City, Sale
  number 3482 (25 February 1976), 2 vols. only, "original
  cloth in quarter morocco cases," "Property of a New York
  City Collector" (John F. Fleming), lot 10, sold for $300
  (*American Book Prices Current, 1976*, p. 207).
  Provenance: Frederick Anderson, then Editor of the Mark
  Twain Papers in the Bancroft Library at the University of
  California, Berkeley, examined these two volumes at the
  New York City office of John F. Fleming in April 1972
  (Anderson to James D. Hart, 17 April 1972; photocopies
  sent to Alan Gribben).
  Barras witnessed the French Revolution and its aftermath.

BARRETT, JOHN (1866–1938). *Admiral George Dewey; A Sketch
of the Man.* Illus. New York: Harper & Brothers, 1899. 280 pp.
  Source: MTLAcc, entry #1202, volume donated by
  Clemens.

BARRIE, (SIR) JAMES MATTHEW (1860–1937). *The Little
Minister* (London, published in 1891).
  Clemens spent the afternoon and evening of 3 July 1892
  "absorbed in" *The Little Minister* in his bed at the Union
  League Club in New York City (NB 31, TS pp. 57–58.
———. *The Little White Bird; or, Adventures in Kensington
Gardens.* New York: Charles Scribner's Sons, 1902. 349 pp.
  Inscription: "Susan L. Crane/Quarry Farm/April 1903."
  Catalog: Ball 2016 inventory, green cloth with gilt lettering
  and design, good condition.
  Location: Quarry Farm library shelves, under the supervi-
  sion of the Mark Twain Archive, Elmira College, Elmira,
  New York.
  Clemens had access to the Quarry Farm library books during
  his final visits to Elmira.
———. *Margaret Ogilvy, by Her Son* (1896).
  Clara Clemens sent an undated note to Clemens's publisher,
  Chatto & Windus, in 1896: "My Father would be very
  much obliged to you if you could send to him as soon as
  possible a copy of Barrie's last book "Margaret Ogilvie
  [*sic*]" (PH in MTP). Hodder & Stoughton of London
  published Barrie's poignant biography of his mother in
  1896. In a letter to the London *Daily Chronicle* published
  on 18 November 1896 and titled "An American Pirate,"

Mark Twain blamed Barrie for not taking the proper legal
steps to protect his own books against copyright piracy
(*MTPP*, p. 162).
———. *Neither Dorking Nor the Abbey* (one-page tribute, first
published in 1909).
  Catalog: ListABP (1910), "Neither Dorking Nor the Abbey,
  Barrie", no other information provided.
  A controversy arose when the ashes of the author George
  Meredith (1828–1909) were scheduled to be buried near
  the village of Dorking rather than in Westminster Abbey.
  Objecting to that decision, Barrie wrote a brief but moving tribute to Meredith, calling him "one of the greatest
  since Shakespeare" and assuring readers that Meredith's
  place was among "the immortals" rather than in any grave,
  wherever it might be located. Barrie's polemic appeared
  in the London *Westminster Gazette* (26 May 1909), but
  was later reprinted both with and without wrappers by
  various printers.
———. *Peter Pan, or the Boy Who Wouldn't Grow Up* (play,
produced in 1904).
  Ten days after Maude Adams opened in *Peter Pan*, Mark
  Twain informed Charles Frohman, the New York City
  theatrical manager, on 16 November 1905 that he had
  delivered "outspoken praises" of the play in a newspaper
  interview because "it hadn't a defect," and he thanked
  Frohman for the tickets (MTP). As an author prominently
  identified with the joys, hazards, and brevity of youth
  and innocence, Twain was bound to be entertained by
  the concept behind *Peter Pan*.
———. *A Window in Thrums.* London: Hodder and Stoughton, 1889. 217 pp.
  On 4 July 1892—directly after finishing Barrie's *The Little
  Minister*—Clemens rose at the Union League Club in
  New York City, breakfasted, read the newspaper, "wrote
  a letter or two," and then "began 'A Window in Thrums'"
  (NB 31, TS p. 58).

BARRILI, ANTONIO GIULIO (1836–1908). *The Eleventh Com-
mandment; A Romance.* Translated from the Italian by Clara
Bell (1834–1927). Rev. and corrected. New York: W. S.
Gottsberger, 1882. 377 pp.
  Source: MTLAcc, entry #2184, volume donated from Cle-
  mens's library by Clara Clemens Gabrilowitsch in 1910.

BARRITT, LEON. *How to Draw; A Practical Book of Instruction
in the Art of Illustration.* Illus. New York: Harper & Brothers,
1904. 107 pp.
  Source: MTLAcc, entry #1225, volume donated by
  Clemens.

BARTHÉLEMY, JEAN-JACQUES (1716–1795). *Travels of Anacharsis
the Younger in Greece, During the Middle of the Fourth Century
Before the Christian Era. By the Abbé Barthelemi.* Translated
from the French [by William Beaumont]. [Contributions by Jean
Dennis Barbié du Bocage, 1760–1825.] 4 vols. London: G.
G. and J. Robinson, 1796. [The title page promised a "Fifth
Volume" that would contain "Maps Plans, Views, and Coins,"
but that volume was not included in the set.]
  Catalog: *A1911*, "4 vols., 8vo, sheep, . . . Lond. 1796," lot
  30, sold for $1.50.
  Provenance: An inscription indicates that three volumes
  were given to Eudocia F. Dewey "from Father, 1915."
  These books were later signed by a Professor Poisson,
  who retired in Victoria, British Columbia; his signature

is dated "'46." In the mid-1950s Professor Poisson gave the three volumes to L. G. Crossman, then a professor of English at the University of Regina in Canada. On 2 December 1980 Professor Emeritus Crossman wrote to Alan Gribben, offering to sell the volumes, since "they ought to be in a collection somewhere." Gribben made arrangements with Dechend Turner, then Director of the Humanities Research Center at the University of Texas at Austin, for the purchase of the set of three volumes for $250. The sale took place on 20 January 1981, and on 26 January 1981 Crossman wrote to Gribben that "I sent the books today—registered airmail. I addressed them to Dechend Turner since his name appears on the order form."

Location: Volumes I, II, and III belong to the Harry Ransom Center, University of Texas at Austin.

Copy examined: Clemens's copy of Volumes I, II, and III, unmarked but with the *A1911* sale label in each volume. The covers are worn and brittle. The front cover of Volume 1 is loose; the other two front covers have been taped to the volumes.

The antiquarian Abbé Barthélemy's fictional journal, first published in 1788, described the imaginary travels of an actual sixth-century Scythian philosopher who visited Athens in the sixth century BCE. Little is known about Anacharsis and most of the writings attributed to him are suspect.

BARTLETT, JOHN (1820–1905), comp. *The Shakespeare Phrase Book.* Boston: Little, Brown & Co., 1881. 1,034 pp. [Edition conjectured.]

Clemens noted the title and publisher in February 1882 (NB 20, *N&J* 2: 446).

BARTLETT, WILLIAM HENRY (1809–1854). *Walks About the City and Environs of Jerusalem* (London, 1844).

Bartlett's was among the "assortment of books" recommended to *Quaker City* passengers before they departed (*Daily Alta California*, 5 April 1868; McKeithan, *TIA*, p. 303).

BARZINI, LUIGI, SR. (1874–1947). *Pekin to Paris; An Account of Prince Borghese's Journey Across Two Continents in a Motor-Car.* Translated from the Italian by L. P. de Castelvecchio. Intro. by Prince [Scipione] Borghese (1871–1927). Illus. New York: M. Kennerley, 1908. 645 pp.

Source: MTLAcc, entry #585, volume donated by Clemens.
Journalist Barzini accompanied Prince Borghese in the automobile that won this no-rules-apply motor car race in 1907.

BASHKIRTSEVA, MARRIÂ KONSTANTINOVNA (1860–1884; some sources accept 1858–1884 instead). *Marie Bashkirtseff; The Journal of a Young Artist, 1860–1884.* Translated from the Russian by Mary J[ane]. Serrano (d. 1923). New York: Cassell & Co., [1889]. 434 pp.

Catalog: *C1951*, #75c, $10, listed among books signed by Clemens.

In December 1889 Clemens jotted down the subtitle and publisher in Notebook 29: "The Journal of a Young Artist. Cassell" (*N&J* 3: 536). On 14 January 1906 Isabel Lyon noted that Mark Twain spoke of "Marie Bashkirtseff's enchanting and naively frank journal" as being "a perfect delight" (IVL Journal, TS p. 123, MTP). Bashkirtseva's journal shocked some readers because of its frank acknowledgement of a woman's sexual allure as

a means of advancement.

BASKERVILLE, ALFRED, ed. and trans. *The Poetry of Germany; Consisting of Selections from Upwards of Seventy of the Most Celebrated Poets, Translated into English Verse, with the Original Text on the Opposite Page.* Fourth edition. Baden-Baden: Haendcke & Lehmkuhl, 1876. 332 pp.

Source: MTLAcc, entry #624, volume donated by Clemens.
Edgar H. Hemminghaus reported seeing Clemens's copy of this book on the shelves of the Mark Twain Library, Redding, Connecticut in 1945 ("Mark Twain's German Provenience," pp. 467–468), but it had vanished by the time Albert E. Stone compiled a catalog of the Clemens holdings in 1955 and I was similarly unable to locate at in 1970. Hemminghaus supplied the publisher and date in his article, but he did not mention inscriptions or marginalia.

BATCHELLER, TRYPHOSA BATES (1876–1952). *Glimpses of Italian Court Life; Happy Days in Italia Adorata.* Third edition. Frontispiece, illus. Green cloth, gilt. New York: Doubleday, Page & Co., 1906. 469 pp.

Inscriptions: the front free endpaper is inscribed in black ink: "To/Mr. Samuel Clemens/'Mark Twain'/The wonderful, the great,/the genuine American of/whom we are all so proud./From his admiring/friend/Tryphosa Bates Batcheller/Nov. 9, 1907." There is a typed label above the inscription: "Purchased by A. J. Krechel/at Mark Twain Library Auction/April, 1951, Hollywood, Calif." The front pastedown endpaper bears a penciled notation, "87D". (The *C1951* auction sheet, highly incomplete, did not include this number.)

Catalog: offered on eBay on 16 August 2003. The description stated that the volume came from the 1951 auction in Hollywood; Batcheller's presentation note was reproduced in a miniature facsimile.

Location: Mark Twain Archive, Gannett-Tripp Learning Center, Elmira College, Elmira, New York. Donated by Martin Zehr on 23 August 2006.

Copy examined: Clemens's copy, on 25 May 2016 at Elmira College.
Batcheller was a socially prominent American singer who wrote travel and historical books about the European countries she resided in or visited.

BATES, CHARLOTTE FISKE (1838–1916).
The Cambridge, Massachusetts schoolteacher and poet Bates sent Mark Twain a poem addressed to Twain on 17 December 1884 (*DearMT*, pp. 107–109).

BATES, GEORGE WASHINGTON (pseud. of William G. Baker). *Sandwich Island Notes. By a Haölé.* Illus. New York: Harper & Brothers, 1854. 493 pp.

Harriet Elinor Smith and Edgar Marquess Branch identified *Sandwich Island Notes* as one of Mark Twain's literary resources in describing the Sandwich Islands in Chapters 64, 66, 76, and elsewhere in *Roughing It* (1872); see their 1993 edition, pp. 709–710, 714, and 739. William G. Baker (Bates' real name) apparently led a rather sordid life in the United States. According to the 16 March 1854 issue of Brooklyn *Daily Eagle*, after swindling several women of money with promises of, or actually committing to, matrimony, Baker went to Mobile, Alabama, where he was certified as a Presbyterian missionary. He then left for California "under the name of Washington Bates."

The same year that his *Sandwich Island Notes* appeared in print he was arrested on the charge of bigamy following another matrimonial misdeed. The only clue to the Reverend Baker/Bates' age appears in W. O. Smith's "Reminiscences" (*The Friend* [Honolulu] 64.10 [October 1907]: 9–11): "I remember particularly one visitor, a middle aged man, calling himself Washington Bates, who spent a considerable time at different places on the island [Kauai], making prolonged visits at missionary homes and who afterwards busied himself in proclaiming about the luxurious table which the missionaries set" (p. 11).

BATT, JOHN HERRIDGE (1845–1905). *Dr. Barnardo, the Foster-Father of "Nobody's Children."* Illus. London: S. W. Partridge & Co., 1904. 196 pp.

    Source: MTLAcc, entry #835, volume donated by Albert Bigelow Paine, Clemens's designated biographer. Possibly Clemens saw this book, since the men exchanged reading materials.

    Thomas John Barnardo set up missions for homeless and destitute children of London's East End. His charitable work was periodically controversial (for its religious overtones and its clashes with governmental and nonprofit agencies) but undeniably effective. He was often short of funding for his efforts, and the Reverend Batt's book offered welcome publicity. Unfortunately Dr. Barnardo (the "Dr." title was honorary since he did not complete his medical training) would die the next year.

BATTLE ABBEY. *The Roll of Battle Abbey, Annotated. By [Sir] John Bernard Burke [1814–1892].* Illus. London: Edward Churton, 1848. [Edition conjectured.]

    Clemens wrote to Mary Mason Fairbanks on 2 November 1872: "Now years ago it used to be a curious study to me, to follow the variations of a family name down through a Peerage or a biography from the Roll of Battle-Abbey to the present day—& manifold & queer were the changes, too" (*MTMF*, p. 167; *MTLet* 5: 206).

The Battle for the Pacific, and Other Adventures at Sea, by Rowan Stevens, Yates Sterling, Jr., William J. Henderson, G. E. Walsh, Kirk Munroe, F.H. Spearman, and Others. Illus. New York: Harper & Brothers, 1908. 238 pp.

    Source: MTLAcc, entry #452, volume donated by Clemens.

    ———. [Another identical copy.]

    Source: MTLAcc, entry #521, volume donated by Clemens.

    ———. [Another identical copy.]

    Source: MTLAcc, entry #1071, volume donated by Clemens.

BAUM, LYMAN FRANK (1856–1919). *Father Goose; His Book.* Illustrated by William W[allace]. Denslow (1856–1915). Chicago: Geo. M. Hill Co., [cop. 1899]. 104 pp.

    Source: MTLAcc, entry #1874, volume donated from Clemens's library by Clara Clemens Gabrilowitsch in 1910.

    Baum's book was published on 25 September 1899. On 3 November 1899 Charles Warren Stoddard urged Clemens to obtain a copy of this book and then praise it in print (Fears, *Day by Day*, p. 306). On 18 November 1899 Clemens thanked Ann W. Denslow, the illustrator's wife, for sending a copy of *Father Goose* (Fears, *Day by Day*, p. 313), and added encomiums ("it marks a new era in nursery literature") that promptly went into the Chicago *Tribune*. One wishes for some evidence that Clemens went on to read Baum's *The Wonderful Wizard of Oz* (1900),

but none has been forthcoming.

    See also the Catalog entry for Denslow's *Mother Goose.*

BAUSCH, PIETER, pseud. "Peet Boetser."

    Mark Twain was initially amused by the letters he received from this Dutch writer, and even published part of their correspondence in "A Capable Humorist," *Harper's Weekly* 53.2722 (20 February 1909): 13. Subsequently Twain stopped replying to the persistent would-be author residing in Amsterdam (*AutoMT* 3: 290–295; 599–600).

BAUSMAN, FREDERICK (1861–1931), pseud. "Aix." *Adventures of a Nice Young Man; A Novel, by Aix.* New York: Duffield, 1908. 407 pp. [Publisher conjectured.]

    Inscription: inscribed on the front flyleaf, "S. C. I've been reading your books long enough. Suppose you read the first chapter of mine. Aix."

    Catalogs: *A1911*, "12mo, buckram, gilt top, uncut, N.Y. 1908," quotes the inscription, lot 5, sold for $3.50; *L1912*, quotes the inscription, lot 1, sold for $6.50.

BAXTER, RICHARD (1615–1691). *The Saints' Everlasting Rest; or, A Treatise on the Blessed State of the Saints, in Their Enjoyment of God in Heaven.* Abridged by Benjamin Fawcett (1715–1780). Flaking, loose leather cover, loose flyleaves. Philadelphia: Jonathan Pounder, 1817. 310 pp.

    Inscription: on the front free endpaper in black ink: "Betsey Chichester's Book/Presented by a friend".

    Location: Mark Twain Library, Redding, Connecticut.

    Copy examined: not a copy belonging to Clemens or his family, though for some reason—presumably his documented familiarity with the work (see below)—this unmarked book has been shelved with the books that Clemens and Clara Gabrilowitsch donated to the Redding library. The volume displays the purple Mark Twain Library stamps but does not contain an accession number. Chichester may have been the married name of Betsey Hill, whose descendants donated various other books to the Mark Twain Library.

    Although this was not Clemens's copy of *The Saints' Everlasting Rest*, he was more than passingly familiar with that devotional tract first published in 1650. Mark Twain urged young people to read only "good" books such as *Saints' Rest* and *Innocents Abroad* in "Advice to Youth," a speech delivered on 15 April 1882 (*MTSpk*, p. 171). He also cited Baxter's faith in a dismal hell in Notebook 22 (1883, *N&J* 3: 32) and listed *Saints' Rest* among the books on the parlor tables of Honolulu homes when he visited the Sandwich Islands in 1866 (Chapter 3 of *Following the Equator* [1897]). Twain's working notes for one version of *The Mysterious Stranger* referred to "Baxter looking over the balusters of heaven" at those writhing in agony below in hell (NB 40 [1898], TS p. 51). In a section of "What Is Man?" written in 1898 but eventually discarded, the Young Man concedes that the sight of their children burning in hell will not discountenance the parents but rather "will increase the joys of heaven for them—as Baxter of the 'Saint's [*sic*] Rest' has painted" (*WIM?*, p. 482).

    Joe B. Fulton, "'Jonathan Edwards, Calvin, Baxter & Co.': Mark Twain and the Comedy of Calvinism," *John Calvin's American Legacy*, ed. Thomas J. Davis (New York: Oxford University Press, 2010), pp. 239–255.

BAYLIS, THOMAS HENRY (1817–1908). *The Temple Church and Chapel of St. Ann, Etc.: An Historical Record and Guide.* Second ed. Illus. London: George Philip and Son, 1895. 152 pp.

Inscription: "CLEMENS" written in pencil on the front flyleaf; on the half-title page in black ink (not Clemens's hand) appears: "The Middle Temple Library/Author's Copy/13 May 1895/T. Henry Baylis." The book is also stamped on several pages: "MIDDLE TEMPLE".

Marginalia: no notes, but Clemens's pencil markings begin on page 56 at discussion of the two societies of inner and middle Temple and continue on nearly every page thereafter (especially in the chapter concerning "The Knights Templar, Their History") up to page 113. He made only one subsequent mark (p. 145), beside a reference to the sword with which Thomas of Canterbury was killed.

Catalogs: *A1911*, "12mo, half cloth, Lond. 1895," describes the inscription, lot 31, sold for $3.25; *The Bookman* (Houston, Texas), Catalog no. 25 (1970), Hill Collection, item #328.

Location: Wake Forest University, Winston-Salem, NC. Donated by Nancy Susan Reynolds.

Copy examined: Clemens's copy, in 1970.

BAYLOR, FRANCES COURTENAY (1848–1920), later Barnum. *Juan and Juanita.* Illustrated by Henry Sandham (1842–1910). Boston: Ticknor and Co., 1888. 288 pp.

Source: MTLAcc, entry #1875, volume donated from Clemens's library by Clara Clemens Gabrilowitsch in 1910. Baylor married in 1896 and changed her surname to Barnum (which apparently causes problems for bibliographers and others seeking information about her). She wrote mostly juvenile fiction. After escaping from their Native American captors the young Juan and Juanita in this novel try to find their way back to Mexico on their own.

Copy examined: Clemens's copy.

———. *Juan and Juanita.* Illustrated by Henry Sandham (1842–1910). First edition. Original turquoise pictorial cloth, gilt. Boston: Ticknor and Co., 1888. 276 pp.

Inscription: inscribed in pencil on the front flyleaf, "Ida Langdon/From Aunt Livy." A card on the front flyleaf is inscribed by Olivia Clemens on her daughter's behalf: "Merry Christmas/to/Dear Ida/from her loving cousin/Jean." Ida Langdon (1880–1964) was the daughter of Charles Jervis and Ida Clark Langdon, and a playmate of her cousins Jean, Susy, and Clara Clemens. No marginalia are visible.

Provenance: originally in the Langdon family library.

Location: collection of Kevin Mac Donnell, Austin, Texas (Mac Donnell to Alan Gribben, 29 November 2011).

BAYLY, THOMAS HAYNES (1797–1839). "Fly away, pretty moth" (ballad, words and music by Bayly).

Albert Bigelow Paine relates how Clemens picked up a guitar and sang "Fly Away, Pretty Moth" to mollify the indignant mother of the "Chapparal Quails" at Jackass Hill (*MTB*, p. 269).

———. "Gaily the troubadour" (poem, song).

In 1881 Mark Twain constructed an atrocious doggerel parody of this song to commemorate James R. Osgood's departure for England in June 1881 (NB 19, *N&J* 2: 386–387). In 1897 he recalled hearing the song in his youth in "Villagers of 1840–3" (*HH&T*, p. 34).

———. "The long ago." Better known as "Long, long ago" (song, published in 1843).

Mark Twain favorably mentioned "Long, Long Ago" in

Notebook 16 (1878, *N&J* 2: 212) and included the song among the music on the piano in "The House Beautiful" as depicted in Chapter 38 of *Life on the Mississippi* (1883). Brought to mind by Susy's death, its lines were quoted in Notebook 39 (January 1897), TS p. 57, and its title was mentioned in the same notebook (TS p. 58). The song's opening lyrics evoke past joys: "Tell me the tales that to me were so dear,/Long, long ago, long, long ago,/Sing me the songs I delighted to hear,/Long, long ago, long ago."

———. "The Mistletoe Bough" (poem).

Mark Twain reflected on Bayly's ballad while musing over plot possibilities for a manuscript he would never complete, "The Mysterious Chamber" (DV56, MTP), probably written in 1875. "We have a noble situation in the 'Mistletoe Bough,'" Twain reminded himself in his working notes, "where the bride accidentally shuts herself into a chest and her fate is a mystery for 60 years. But the situation is too brief."

———. "The Pilot" (poem, song).

Two lines are quoted in "About All Kinds of Ships" (1893): "O pilot, 'tis a fearful night;/There's danger on the deep." Mark Twain's burlesque poem "The Aged Pilot Man" in Chapter 51 of *Roughing It* (1872) very likely owes something to Bayly's "The Pilot" though other models have also been suggested.

———. "Shed not a tear." Also known as "When I am gone" (poem, song, published in the 1840s). Arranged by several composers, including Rosa V. Johnson.

This seems like the best candidate for a song titled "When I Am Gone" that occurred to Clemens's mind several times. Thoughts of Susy Clemens's death brought "When I Am Gone" to Clemens's mind in London in January 1897 (NB 39, TS p. 58). On 6 June 1902, rehearsing memories of Hannibal, Clemens made a note to use the same song in his next story about Tom Sawyer and Huck Finn (NB 45, TS p. 16). Bayly's lyrics are resigned; the first lines begin, "Shed not a tear o'er your friend's early bier,/When I am gone, when I am gone." The second verse is philosophical about human mortality: "Plant ye a tree that may wave over me,/When I am gone, when I am gone;/Sing ye a song if my grave you should see,/When I am gone, I am gone./Come at the close of the bright summer's day,/Come when the sun sheds his last ling'ring ray,/Come and rejoice that I thus passed away,/When I am gone, I am gone." The version quoted here appeared in a volume in Clemens's family library, J. P. McCaskey's *Franklin Square Song Collection: Two Hundred Favorite Songs* (1892).

———. "She wore a wreath of roses" (song).

This piece was among the music on the piano in "The House Beautiful" in Chapter 38 of *Life on the Mississippi* (1883).

BAYNE, SAMUEL GAMBLE (1844–1924). *A Fantasy of Mediterranean Travel.* Illus. New York: Harper & Brothers, 1909. 104 pp.

Inscription: the front free endpaper is inscribed by the author: "To Sam'l. L. Clemens/With the author's compliments/New York/1909."

Provenance: donated by Clemens to the Mark Twain Library, Redding, Connecticut (MTLAcc, entry #1488). Contains the oval bookstamps of the Redding library.

Location: Special Collections, Elihu Burritt Library, Central

Connecticut State University, New Britain, Connecticut.
Copy examined: photocopies of the inscription and title
page in 1979. The book is unmarked.

———. *On a Jaunting-Car Through Donegal and Connemara*.
Illus. Cloth, gilt top, uncut. New York, 1902.

Inscription: signed "S. L. Clemens/1902" on the front
pastedown endpaper. Inscribed to Mark Twain "with the
compliments of a new recruit in the hope that some day
he may visit Ireland. . . ."

Catalog: Anderson Galleries, No. 1704, 24–26 January
1923, #245.

———. *The Pith of Astronomy (Without Mathematics): The
Latest Facts and Figures as Developed by the Giant Telescopes*.
Illus. New York: Harper & Brothers, 1907. 122 pp.

Inscription: signed in brown ink on the front pastedown
endpaper: "S L. Clemens/1909."

Marginalia: numerous notations in brown ink, black ink,
and pencil between pages 12 and 92; none thereafter. A
few of Clemens's comments ridicule Bayne's efforts to
simplify his subject matter. On page 40, where Bayne
mentions that "a web of cloth as long as from the earth
to the moon" would still be insufficient to encircle Jupiter,
Clemens penciled some advice: "A rope of the same length
would serve just as well & would be cheaper, also easier
to manage in windy weather. I recommend the rope."
To Bayne's description of certain asteroids as being "no
larger than rocks" (p. 66), Clemens objects in pencil:
"This is inexact, because we do not know the precise size
of a rock." Clemens asks whether Bayne means "the Rock
of Gibraltar" or the "small kind" desired by the child in
"Rock me to sleep, rock me to sleep." Other marginalia
are serious, such as the note in black ink above Bayne's
reference to the persecution of Bruno and Galileo (p. 83):
"The Church has burned many other men besides Bruno
for denying lies which it got out of the great central source
of lies, the Bible." Frequently Clemens uses Bayne's figures
to speculate about distances in the galaxy. An unidentified
person has added a few notes in pencil (on pp. 24–25,
for instance). Clemens made computations in brown ink
on the back flyleaf and rear pastedown endpaper. Three
newspaper clippings are inserted: an address by Professor
Percival Lowell, "How the World Dies," Boston *Evening
Transcript*, 2 April 1909, is pinned to the front free endpaper; an article about Jupiter from the New York *Sun*,
21 January [1910?], is pinned to page 39; and an article
about Neptune clipped from the New York *Herald*, 20
November 1909, is pinned to page 55.

Catalogs: *C1951*, #32a, $20; *Bennett & Marshall Catalogue
No. 9* (1970), Los Angeles, item #10, $200.

Location: Mark Twain Papers, Bancroft Library, University
of California at Berkeley. Purchased from John Howell
Books of San Francisco in 1970 for $250.

Copy examined: Clemens's copy. Contains a *C1951* label.
Albert Bigelow Paine reported that when Clemens moved
into the Hamilton Hotel in Bermuda in November
1909 he "brought along a small book called *The Pith
of Astronomy*—a fascinating little volume—and he read
from it about the great tempest of fire in the sun" (*MTB*,
p. 1542).

*The Bazar Book of Health: The Dwelling, the Nursery, the
Bed-room, the Dining-room, the Parlor, the Library, the*

Kitchen, and the Sick-room. New York: Harper & Brothers,
1873. 280 pp.

Source: MTLAcc, entry #1353, volume donated by
Clemens.

The weekly magazine *Harper's Bazar* (a spelling retained into
the 1920s) spun off books on women, health, and fashion.

BEACH, REX ELLINGWOOD (1877–1949). *The Barrier*. Illustrated by Denman Fink (1880–1956). New York: Harper &
Brothers, 1908. 310 pp.

Source: MTLAcc, entry #2161, volume donated from Clemens's library by Clara Clemens Gabrilowitsch in 1910.

The Barrier was the second-best-selling novel in 1908.

———. *The Silver Horde; A Novel*. Illustrated by Harvey
T[homas]. Dunn (1884–1952). New York: Harper & Brothers, 1909. 390 pp.

Source: MTLAcc, entry #1820, volume donated by
Clemens.

Beach's novel became the third-best-selling work of fiction
in 1909.

BEALL, EDGAR CHARLES (1853–1930).

Samuel Clemens occasionally experimented with phrenological readings, and one of these took place in Cincinnati, Ohio in January 1884. The examiner was Dr. Edgar
Charles Beal, editor of *The Phrenological Journal* and a
prolific author whose *The Brain and the Bible; or, The
Conflict Between Mental Science and Theology* (1881) had
contained a preface by the prominent atheist Robert G.
Ingersoll. Dr. Beall lost no time in reporting his famous
client's attributes; on 4 January 1885 the Cincinnati *Commercial Gazette* carried an article titled "Mark Twain's Head
Analyzed." (I am grateful to Victor Fischer and Robert H.
Hirst for drawing my attention to this newspaper item
that appeared on page 8, column 5.) Beall found that
Twain's head "measures 22 ½ inches, which is half an
inch less than the average intellectual giant. . . . He has
very ardent affections, strong love of approbation, sense
of justice, firmness, kindness and ability to read character;
with small self-esteem, love of gain, or inclination to
the supernatural." The phrenologist also detected that
he was "excellent in wit, but super-excellent in humor.
Secretiveness is very marked in . . . the nearly closed eyes,
compressed lips, slow, guarded manner of speech, etc."
Beall praised "the temperament of our great humorist,
which is . . . the spare, angular mental, or mental-motive,
which is favorable to hard sense, logic, general intelligence
and insight into human nature."

There is no direct evidence that Clemens grew familiar with
the various writings of Dr. Beall, who became recognized
as the leading authority in phrenology and the field of
what he termed "physiology." By 1905 he had relocated to
Manhattan, New York, where he continued to be listed in
cities directories as a practicing "Phrenologist" and his *The
Life Sexual: A Study of the Philosophy, Physiology, Science,
Art, and Hygiene of Love* (1905) caused a national stir.
In 1927 he would again be in the news when he issued
a character reading of Ruth Snyder, a woman facing the
death penalty for a sensational crime, helping murder her
husband Albert to collect life insurance money. Beall died
in Manhattan on 24 January 1930.

BEARD, DANIEL CARTER (1850–1941). *Moonblight and Six
Feet of Romance*. Illustrated by the author. New York: Charles

L. Webster & Co., 1892. 221 pp.
Advertised in *Publishers' Trade List Annual 1893* by Clemens's publishing firm.

———. *Moonblight and Six Feet of Romance*. Intro. by Louis F[reeland]. Post (1849–1928). Trenton, N.J.: Albert Brandt, 1904. 238 pp.

Inscription: autographed "Mark Twain" in black ink on the front pastedown endpaper, which is also inscribed by the author: "To My Dear Friend/and hero/Mark Twain,/A man who dares to say what he believes,/May he live a thousand years!/Dan Beard/1904". It was highly unusual for Clemens to sign his pen name in a book written by another author. This must have been done as a special favor.

Catalog: ListABP (1910), "Moonblight, Beard", no other information provided.

Location: Mark Twain Library, Redding, Connecticut.

Copy examined: Clemens's copy. It has no accession number. Examined in 1970 and again in June 1982.

Although Beard's inscription in this presentation copy is dated 1904, it was not until 9 August 1905 that its publisher Albert Brandt wrote to Clemens in Dublin, New Hampshire: "It affords me great pleasure to be able to unite with our mutual friend, Mr. Daniel Carter Beard, in sending you by to-day's mail, a special autographed copy of the new edition of 'Moonblight and Six Feet of Romance'" (MTP). The death of Olivia Clemens in June 1904 may account for Brandt's delay in mailing the book. Beard's novel concerned the labor movement, and its introduction was written by the assistant secretary of labor, Louis F. Post.

William V. Kahler, "Mark Twain: Adult Hero of Daniel Carter Beard," *Mark Twain Journal* 18.3 (Winter 1976–1977): 1–4.

BEATTIE, WILLIAM (1793–1875). *Life and Letters of Thomas Campbell [1777–1844].* 2 vols. New York: Harper & Brothers, 1850.

Source: MTLAcc, entry #1748, Volume II only (521 pp.), donated by Clemens.

Mark Twain was familiar with this British poet whose *The Pleasures of Hope* (1799) had produced an immense sensation at the beginning of the nineteenth century.

BEATTY, DANIEL F[ISHER]. (1848–1914). *In Foreign Lands, from Original Notes.* Washington, New Jersey: Daniel F. Beatty, Publisher, 1878. 97 pp.

Inscription: "Compliments of Daniel F. Beatty/Jany 8th 1878" written in ink on flyleaf.

Marginalia: a few penciled notes by Clemens; numerous notes in pencil and ink by another hand, possibly Joseph H. Twichell's. One of the latter notes (on page 97), mocking Beatty's blatant plug for his "Piano and Organ Establishment" in Washington, New Jersey, is dated 5 January 1884.

Catalogs: ListABP (1910), "Foreign Lands (comment in M. T.'s handwriting), Beatty"; "Retz Appraisal" (1944), p. 4, valued at $20.

Location: Mark Twain Papers, Bancroft Library, University of California at Berkeley.

Copy examined: Clemens's copy.

Here is another unlabeled addition to Mark Twain's hypothetical Library of Literary Hogwash. Beatty issued this account of his European trip partly to publicize the pianos

and organs manufactured by his firm in Washington, New Jersey. Clemens shared the book with a friend, who also indulged in sarcastic commentary along its margins. The handwriting suggests that the Reverend Joseph H. Twichell might have been the unidentified fellow reader. In response to Beatty's glowing description of the "bright and glorious day" on which he departed (p. 1), Clemens quipped: "If *I* had been Nature, no matter how glad I was to see him go, I would have acted exactly as usual." Beatty claimed that his family, his employees, and his fellow townsmen all turned out at the railroad depot to watch his departure; Clemens noted, "Why *everybody's* glad" (p. 2). During Beatty's account of his sojourn in Paris Clemens remarked: "Fact is, his English needs interpreting as well as his French" (p. 20). "The pious liar," Clemens wrote above Beatty's description of his "narrow escape" from Italian bandits (p. 43). "Gosh!" Clemens exclaimed of Beatty's less-than-breath-taking account of a glacier. "When this fellow isn't praying he is always lying," Clemens observed of Beatty's conduct while at sea en route home (p. 87). Concerning the absurdly elevated language Beatty attributed to the sailors on his ship ("this is a noble vessel, the best that ever rode the waves"), Clemens simply commented: "How like a sailor!" (p. 87). Arthur L. Scott erred in attributing two comments and a dated note to Clemens (*MTAL* [1969], pp. 130, 319 n. 17); all three were written by the unidentified reader.

BEAUMONT, FRANCIS (1584–1616) and JOHN FLETCHER (1579–1625). *A King and No King* (play, performed in 1611).

Dr. James Ross Clemens remembered that "in one of [John] Ford's [*sic*] plays a Roman general named Bessus [actually the Bessus character is an Iberian captain] specialized in making strategic movements to rear. (This type of braggadocio behavior was in the tradition of the Ben Jonson's cowardly braggart Captain Bobadil in *Every Man in His Humour* [1598].) At this cautious gentleman Mark never tired of poking fun and likened him to several of our generals in the Civil War" ("Some Reminiscences of Mark Twain" [1929], p. 125).

BECKE, LOUIS (1855–1913). *By Reef and Palm.* Intro. by the Earl of Pembroke [George Robert Charles Herbert, 1850–1895]. Third ed. London: T. Fisher Unwin, 1895. 220 pp.

Inscription: the title page was autographed by Louis Becke, who also inscribed the front free endleaf: "To S. L. Clemens/from Louis Becke/Sydney Sept. 1895".

Marginalia: no markings. Pages 43–54 have been removed.

Catalogs: *C1951*, #55c, erroneously listed with books containing Clemens's signature; Maxwell Hunley Rare Books Catalogue (June 1958), item #20, $5.

Provenance: collection of Frank C. Willson (1889–1960), Melrose, Massachusetts.

Location: Harry Ransom Center, University of Texas, Austin. Purchased from Margarete Willson in 1962.

Copy examined: Clemens's copy.

Mark Twain was at first uncertain about Becke's name. Reaching the Fiji Islands in September 1895, Twain resolved to "quote from X's (Beake?) two books about island life" (NB 35, TS p. 48). Soon thereafter he reminded himself to "read Philip Beake's delightful stories 'Palm'—forget the name" (NB 35, TS p. 49). After receiving a copy of *By Reef and Palm*, Twain praised it as "one of the best books that has been produced in recent years" (Melbourne, Australia *Herald Standard*, 27 September 1895; Scharnhorst, *Complete Interviews* [2006], p. 231; Shillingsburg, *At Home Abroad: Mark Twain in Australasia* [1988], p. 71, had quoted the same words, but attributed them to an interview published in the Sydney *Bulletin*, 5 October 1895; perhaps the newspapers shared the content of that interview). Twain wrote to Becke from Sydney on 24 September 1895 "to thank you again for your book, which I find stands the sharp test of a third reading, whereas few are the books that can do that. Don't stop; search out *all* the Island tales & print them" (Mitchell Library, State Library of New South Wales, Sydney, Australia). He elaborated in an interview published in the Sydney, Australia *Bulletin* of 4 January 1896: "The chief charm of Louis Becke's stories for me is that the author seems to be chronicling facts and incidents he's seen—things he's lived amongst and knows all about" (Scharnhorst, *Complete Interviews*, p. 266). In these short stories Becke, an Australian trader in the South Pacific islands, wrote unsentimentally about white men's behavior toward island women and other subjects that he treated with equal frankness.

Francis V. Madigan, Jr., "Mark Twain's Passage to India" (1974).

BECKER, KARL FRIEDRICH (1777–1806). *Erzählungen aus der alten Welt für die Jugend [Old World Stories for the Young]* (published in 1810).

Clemens wrote the title of this book about Greek myths in Notebook 24 (May 1885, *N&J* 3: 148).

BEECHER, CATHERINE ESTHER (1800–1878). *An Appeal to the People in Behalf of Their Rights as Authorized Interpreters of the Bible.* New York: Harper & Brothers, 1860. 380 pp.
  Source: MTLAcc, entry #1815, volume donated by Clemens.

————— and **HARRIET ELIZABETH (BEECHER) STOWE** (1811–1896). *Principles of Domestic Science; As Applied to the Duties and Pleasures of Home. A Text-Book for the Use of Young Ladies in Schools, Seminaries, and Colleges.* New York: J. B. Ford and Co., 1870. 390 pp. [Publisher and pages conjectured.]
  Catalog: *A1911*, "12mo, cloth, N.Y. 1870, with numerous annotations by a former owner," a small sheet of notes by Clemens laid in, lot 440, sold for $1.

—————. *Religious Training of Children in the School, the Family, and the Church.* New York: Harper & Brothers, 1864. 413 pp.
  Source: MTLAcc, entry #943, volume donated by Clemens.

BEECHER, EDWARD (1803–1895). *The Conflict of the Ages; or, The Great Debate on the Moral Relations of God and Man.* Fifth edition. Original black cloth, gilt. Boston: Phillips, Sampson & Co., 1854.
  Inscription: the front free endpaper is inscribed in ink: "Susie L. Crane/Elmira Sept 6th, 1867." On the flyleaf she added in pencil: "Bought at Harrisburg about 16 Aug 1867." (It appears she changed "25th Aug" to "16th Aug" in that latter inscription.)
  Marginalia: a few pages have faint marginal brackets, likely by Susan Crane. In pencil on the rear free endpaper in Crane's hand are page references to "16/25/31/42". To the right of Crane's page references is a single page reference ("218?") that is possibly in Clemens's hand. On that page there is a different style of marginal bracket with

two question marks beside it, marking a passage that reads: "Indeed, a large proportion of the human race, if not the majority, have always believed in some form of the doctrine of the pre-existence of man." Beecher's text discusses points of theological doctrine concerning God, pre-existence, and atonement.
  Location: collection of Kevin Mac Donnell, Austin, Texas. Acquired in May 2016 from the Langdon family (email, Mac Donnell to Alan Gribben, 16 May 2016).
  Source: detailed description of the "worn and well-read" volume sent on 9 June 2016 by Mac Donnell to Gribben. This book would have been available to Clemens in the Quarry Farm library.

BEECHER, HENRY WARD (1813–1887). *The Life of Jesus, The Christ.* [One volume only. 510 pp.] Illus. New York: J. B. Ford and Co., 1871. 387 pp. [Part I only; no other parts of this edition were published in 1871.]
  Catalog: *A1911*, "Imp. 8vo, stamped morocco (rubbed), gilt edges , one vol. only, N.Y. 1871," lot 33, sold for $1.
  As Clemens acidly remembered the events leading to the fall of his publishing house, Charles L. Webster "agreed to resurrect Henry Ward Beecher's *Life of Christ.* I suggested that he ought to have tried for Lazarus" (2 June 1906 Autobiographical Dictation, *MTE*, pp. 188–189; *AutoMT* 2: 77). Beecher's *The Life of Jesus* was brought out in two volumes by Bromfield and Co. of New York in 1891.

[—————.] *Memorial of Henry Ward Beecher* (published in 1887).
  In 1985 a bookdealer sold a letter in which Clemens informed a man who sent him a *Memorial of Henry Ward Beecher* published in 1887 that he already owned a copy of it (Kevin Mac Donnell to Alan Gribben, 1985). There were two formal tributes to Beecher published at that time: *Henry Ward Beecher: A Memorial* (Brooklyn, New York: Plymouth Church, 1887), 167 pp. and *Memorial of Henry Ward Beecher* (New York: J. H. Knight, 1887), 192 pp.

—————, comp. *Plymouth Collection of Hymns and Tunes, for the Use of Christian Congregations.* New York: A. S. Barnes & Co., 1855. 484 pp. [Reprinted in 1856, 1857, 1858, 1859, 1860, and other years until 1872. The edition to which Clemens referred has not been determined.]
  Twain had the impression that "the tunes are a shade too complicated for the [*Quaker City*] excursionists" (Mark Twain's letter published in the New York *Herald*, 20 November 1867, *TIA*, pp. 315–316; *MTLet* 2: 402). The library on the *Quaker City* contained fifteen copies of the *Plymouth Collection of Hymns* (reported by Dr. Abraham R. Jackson, New York *Herald*, 21 November 1867). As soon as the passengers "get a settled stomach in them they get out their Plymouth Collections and start another storm" (unfinished play, "The Quaker City Holy Land Excursion," Act 2, Sc. 1, written in 1867). A character in a play fragment dating from 1867 expresses exasperation: "Plymouth Collection—*ain't* they never going to let up!" (*N&J* 1: 487). Twain praised Beecher's "felicity of expression" to Emma Beach and planned "to send Mr. Beecher my book as soon as I recover from this rush of business (ALS, 8 January 1868, Christie's auction catalog, 17 October 1981). Twain mentioned that the *Quaker City* passengers were expected to bring copies of *Plymouth Collection* along on the voyage (5 April 1868 *Daily Alta California; TIA*, p. 303). Twain cited Beecher's

hymn collection for the hymns sung aboard the *Quaker City* in Chapters 1, 4, and 55 of *The Innocents Abroad* (1869). He credited it as the source of a hymn by Phoebe Hinsdale Brown in a letter Twain wrote to William Dean Howells on 8 November 1876 (*MTHL*, p. 162). Detective Bullet of New York City theorizes in Twain's "Cap'n Simon Wheeler, The Amateur Detective" (written in 1877) that Millicent Griswold killed her sweetheart with a copy of the *Plymouth Collection* (*S&B* [1967], pp. 252, 257).

———. *Plymouth Pulpit: A Weekly Publication of Sermons Preached by Henry Ward Beecher in Plymouth Church, Brooklyn.* New York: Fords, Howard, Hulbert, 1868–1884.

Clemens wrote to Olivia Langdon from Davenport, Iowa on 14 January 1869 during a lecture tour: "Yes I lay abed till 1 P.M[.], . . . & re-read Beecher's sermon on the love of riches being the root of evil" (*MTLet* 3: 39)—thus accounting for his activities on 3 January 1869 in Fort Wayne, Indiana. (Olivia had mailed Clemens an issue of this new magazine; see *MTLet* 2: 353–356). When James Redpath tried to recruit Clemens to return to the lecture circuit, Clemens reported the extent of his resistance: "I have just declined to lecture in Boston next season at a higher figure than Redpath says he is to pay Mr. Beecher" (Clemens to Philadelphia lecturer manager Thomas Burnett Pugh [1829–1884], Elmira, New York, 17 July [year uncertain], *Sotheby's 2003*, #21). A letter from Clemens to Joseph H. Twichell written in July 1874 suggests that Clemens had become convinced that Beecher was guilty to some degree for the sexual scandal damaging his reputation (*LMTJHT*, p. 47).

Susan K. Harris, "'Hadleyburg': Mark Twain's Dual Attack on Banal Theology and Banal Literature," *American Literary Realism* 16.2 (Autumn 1983): 240–252, especially p. 247.

———. *Royal Truths.* Green cloth. Boston: Ticknor and Fields, 1868. 324 pp.

Inscription: "Ida Clark." (Ida B. Clark would marry Olivia Langdon's brother Charles Jervis Langdon in 1870.)

Provenance: bookplate #552 of the "J. Langdon Family Library" on the front pastedown endpaper.

Catalog: Ball 2016 inventory, green cloth, gilt lettering and design, signed by Ida Clark, Jervis Langdon's Family Library #552.

Location: Mark Twain Archive, Elmira College, Elmira, New York.

Copy examined: unmarked copy that might have been available to Clemens whenever he visited Charles and Ida Langdon's home in Elmira. Examined on 27 May 2015.

———. *Star Paper; or, Experiences of Art and Nature.* New York: J. C. Derby, 1855. 359 pp.

There is no record that Clemens owned or read this book of essays, but given his fascination with medieval England, its contents would have appealed to him. Beecher recounted a series of Hank Morgan-like musings as he visited the sites of Kenilworth and Warwick Castle. "I would, if I could," wrote Beecher, "come and sit in this [Kenilworth] court at evening—after sunset, or by moonlight. Then should I not see flitting shadows and forms, and hear low airy voices? . . . At last I awoke. Three hours had passed like a dream" (p. 16). At Warwick Castle, Beecher recalled, "Never had I seen any pile around which were

historic associations, blended not only with heroic men and deeds, but savoring of my own childhood. And now, too, am I to see, and understand by inspection, the things which [Sir Walter] Scott has made so familiar to all as mere words—moats, portcullises, battlements, keeps or mounds, arrow-slit windows, watch-towers. They had a strange effect upon me; they were perfectly new, and yet familiar old friends" (p. 18). Farther on, Beecher added, "It was a historic dream breaking forth into a waking reality" (p. 19). Then he related how he "ascended to the roof of the tower, and looked over the wide glory of the scene. . . . Here where warriors looked out, or ladies watched for their knight's return. How did I long to stand for one hour, really, in their position and in their consciousness, who lived in those days; and then to come back, with the new experience, to my modern self!" (p. 21).

BEECHER, LYMAN (1775–1863). *Autobiography, Correspondence, Etc., of Lyman Beecher, D.D.* Edited by Charles Beecher [1815–1900]. Illus. 2 vols. New York: Harper & Brothers, 1864–1865.

Mark Twain quoted from page 245 of the first volume of Beecher's *Autobiography, Correspondence, Etc.* for a footnote to his manuscript of *Life on the Mississippi* (1883), illustrating the coarse behavior that prevailed in early-day America. Eventually he decided to delete this note from the final version of his book. Beecher described an ordination at Plymouth, Connecticut which he attended as a young pastor around 1810; he was embarrassed and angered to find that all of his fellow preachers at the assemblage drank liquor heavily, smoked pipes, and roared noisily at their stories. Beecher found the scene as offensive as "a very active grog-shop" and closed the description by assuring his readers that he attended no more ordinations "of that kind. . . . My heart kindles up at the thoughts of it now" (1: 245, 246).

BEECHER, THOMAS KINNICUT (1824–1900). *In Time with the Stars; Stories for Children.* Elmira, New York: H. H. Billings, 1901. 165 pp.

Source: MTLAcc, entry #1876, volume donated from Clemens's library by Clara Clemens Gabrilowitsch in 1910.

There is a division of opinion as to whether his middle name was spelled "Kinnicut" or "Kinnicutt." I lean toward the former.

———. *Jervis Langdon, 1809–1870.* Original three-quarter brown morocco, gilt, with mounted photographic frontispiece. [Elmira, New York:] Printed for Use of Friends, and Not for Sale [, 1870]. [Contains the text of Thomas K. Beecher's eulogy for Olivia Clemens's father that was delivered on 21 August 1870 in the Elmira Opera House.]

Provenance: this copy originally belonged to Hosmer H. Billings, an Elmira bookseller; his initials are written faintly on the front pastedown endpaper. At some point the book was acquired by Susan Crane, Clemens's sister-in-law and the owner of Quarry Farm.

Location: collection of Kevin Mac Donnell, Austin, Texas. Acquired in May 2016 from the Langdon family (email, Mac Donnell to Alan Gribben, 16 May 2016).

Source: detailed description of this "quite scarce" volume sent on 9 June 2016 by Mac Donnell to Gribben.

This book would have been available to Clemens in the Langdon family library.

————. *Our Seven Churches*. Blue cloth, gilt. New York: J. B. Ford & Co., 1870. 167 pp.

Inscription: the front flyleaf is inscribed in brown ink, "Susie L. Crane—/from T. K. B./Oct 17, 1870."

Catalog: Ball 2016 inventory, good to fair condition.

Provenance: found on the bookshelves of the library at Quarry Farm in 1987. No bookplate.

Location: Mark Twain Archive, Elmira, College. Elmira, New York. Transferred to that collection from Quarry Farm by Mark Woodhouse on 9 July 1987.

Copy examined: an unmarked religious work available to Clemens for perusal during his many summer visits to the Cranes' Quarry Farm. Examined on 27 May 2015.

Our Seven Churches was dedicated to Horace Bushnell (1802–1876). Beecher's eight lectures in the volume describe the seven churches in Elmira, New York, endeavoring to say positive things about the Baptists, Presbyterians, Congregationalists, Methodists, Catholics, and other denominations.

————. *Our Seven Churches*. Terra cotta cloth, gilt. New York: J. B. Ford & Co., 1871. 167 pp.

Inscription: the front flyleaf is inscribed by Charles Jervis Langdon (1849–1916), Clemens's brother-in-law, to his wife, Ida (Clark) Langdon (1849–1934): "To my dear Ida/April 13th 1874/CJL." Tipped in above the inscription is a calling card signed by Thomas K. Beecher. Laid in is a cabinet portrait of Beecher, also signed.

Location: collection of Kevin Mac Donnell, Austin, Texas. Purchased from the Langdon family.

Source: description provided by Mac Donnell to Alan Gribben, 28 August 2017. The book has no markings.

This volume would have been available to Clemens whenever he visited the Langdon residence in Elmira, New York.

————. *Our Seven Churches*. Terra cotta cloth, gilt. New York: J. B. Ford & Co., 1871. 167 pp.

Catalog: Ball 2016 inventory, good condition, no bookplate noted.

Location: Quarry Farm library shelves, under the supervision of the Mark Twain Archive, Elmira College, Elmira, New York.

Clemens had access to the Quarry Farm library books during his visits to Elmira.

————. *Our Seven Churches*. Blue cloth. New York: J. B. Ford & Co., 1871. 167 pp.

Provenance: noticed by Alan Gribben on the bookshelves of the library at Quarry Farm in 2015. Does not display the usual "J. Langdon Family Library" bookplate.

Location: Quarry Farm library shelves, under the supervision of the Mark Twain Archive, Elmira College, Elmira, New York.

Copy examined: an unmarked religious work available to Clemens for perusal during his many summer visits to the Cranes' Quarry Farm. Examined on 27 May 2015.

————. *Our Work as a Church*. Original buff printed wrappers. N. p., n. d. [Elmira, 1872.]

Inscriptions: signed at the end of the text (in type): "Thomas K. Beecher, Elmira, July, 1872." Inscribed on the front wrapper in ink by Clemens's brother-in-law Charles Langdon: "April 1872 . . . by the pastor . . . Charles J. Langdon, Elmira, N. Y."

Marginalia: pencil brackets and quotation marks in the text,

probably in the hand of Charles Langdon.

Location: collection of Kevin Mac Donnell, Austin, Texas. Purchased in May 2016 from the Langdon family (email, Mac Donnell to Alan Gribben, 16 May 2016).

Source: detailed descriptions of the volume sent on 9 June 2016 and on 28 August 2017 by Mac Donnell to Gribben.

Thomas K. Beecher was pastor of the Park Street Church. When a new building was planned he wrote this booklet to promote the idea and explain the funding. Mark Twain had published a piece, "The New Beecher Church," in the New York *Times* on 23 July 1871. The new church held its first service in 1875. Beecher became a close friend to Samuel and Olivia Clemens, officiating at their wedding and conducting the funeral for Susy Clemens.

MT in Elmira (2013), pp. 113–119.

The Beecher Trial: A Review of the Evidence. Reprinted from the New York "Times" of July 3, 1875. With Some Revisions and Additions. Fourth edition. New York: n.p., 1875. 34 pp. 25¢ pamphlet.

Marginalia: none except for Clemens's penciled arithmetical computations on the back cover.

Catalog: ListABP (1910), "Beecher Trial", no other information provided.

Location: Mark Twain Papers, Bancroft Library, University of California at Berkeley.

Copy examined: Clemens's copy.

In 1874 Henry Ward Beecher was accused of adultery with Elizabeth Tilton but was acquitted after a sensational trial.

BEECHER, WILLIAM CONSTANTINE (1849–1928) and SAMUEL SCOVILLE (1834–1902), assisted by Mrs. Henry Ward [Eunice White Bullard] Beecher (1813–1897). *A Biography of Rev. Henry Ward Beecher [1813–1887]*. New York: C. L. Webster & Co., 1888. 713 pp.

Clemens's publishing firm brought out this memorial biography that encompassed the minister and social reformer Beecher's entire life.

BEERBOHM, JULIUS (1854–1906). *Wanderings in Patagonia; or, Life Among the Ostrich-Hunters*. Illus. New York: Henry Holt & Co., 1879. 294 pp. [Another edition: London: Chatto & Windus, 1879. 278 pp. Clemens's edition is unknown.]

Wanderings in Patagonia was one of the book titles Clemens listed in 1909 in connection with his declaration that he preferred to read "history, biography, travels, curious facts & strange happenings, & science" (MTP, Notebook fragments file). See my essay, "'I Detest Novels, Poetry & Theology': Origin of a Fiction Concerning Mark Twain's Reading" (1977); a revised version of this article appears in Volume One of the current work. Beerbohm's narrative recounted his journey through a virtually unexplored region of South America in 1877.

BEERS, CLIFFORD WHITTINGHAM (1876–1943). *A Mind That Found Itself; An Autobiography*. London: Longmans, Green, and Co., 1908. 363 pp.

Inscription: signed on the front pastedown endpaper, "S. L. Clemens, 1908."

Catalogs: *A1911*, "8vo, cloth, Lond. 1908," quotes signature, lot 34, sold for $4; Parke-Bernet Galleries (New York City), Sale number 1013 (29 November 1948), quotes the signature on the front pastedown endpaper, has the *A1911* sale label, lot 89, sold for $35 (according to *Book*

Auction Records 1948–49 [London, 1950] 46: 45).

Beers offers a rare first-person account of grappling with mental illness.

BEERS, ETHEL LYNN (1827–1879). "The Picket-Guard" (poem), better known as "All Quiet on the Potomac Tonight" (1861).

Writing to the Virginia City *Territorial Enterprise* on 4 December 1867 about the vagaries of the winter weather in Washington, D.C., Mark Twain joked: "If Grant expresses an opinion between two whiffs of smoke, it spits a little sleet uneasily; if all is quiet on the Potomac of politics, one sees only the soft haze of Indian summer." Beers' poem was set to music in 1863 by John Hill Hewitt (1801–1890) and proved to be so popular as both a poem and a song that a number of writers besides Beers claimed credit for its authorship.

BEETON, SAMUEL ORCHART (1831–1877). *Beeton's Complete Letter-Writer for Ladies and Gentlemen; A Useful Compendium of Epistolary Materials Gathered from the Best Sources, and Adapted to Suit an Indefinite Number of Cases.* London: Ward, Locke & Co., [1873]. [Another edition was published in 1895. Clemens's edition is unidentified.]

During Clemens's sojourn in Bermuda in January 1908 he presented Elizabeth Wallace "with a precious volume which he had discovered in the island book store, entitled *Beeton's Complete Letter-Writer for Gentlemen.* . . . He had written this inscription on the blank page, 'To Young Lady desirous of perfecting Herself in the Epistolary Art [date in full]. Dear Miss _____: Try Beeton, Trust Beeton, Beeton is your friend. Have no fear. Sincerely yours, S. L. Clemens.'" Wallace remembered that "this choice book we carried with us and regaled ourselves, from time to time, with particularly rare specimens of the epistolary art" (*MT&HI* [1913], p. 35).

Clemens had long been familiar with the formulas of *Beeton's Complete Letter-Writer* and its several dozen counterparts by other authors. Brown & Gross, Hartford booksellers, billed him on 1 January 1881 for "1 Letter Writer" purchased on 11 October 1880 (receipt in MTP). In Chapter 4 of "Simon Wheeler, Detective," a novel Mark Twain worked on between 1877 and 1898, the enslaved Toby ludicrously misapplies model letters from *The People's Ready Letter-Writer* (*S&B* [1967], pp. 354, 355–356, 385–386).

BEHN, APHRA (AMIS) (1640–1689). *Love-Letters Between a Nobleman and His Sister; With the History of Their Adventures.* Sixth edition. 3 vols. London: Printed for D. Brown, J. Tonson, B. Tookes, G. Strahan, S. Ballard, W. Mears, and F. Clay, 1721. [Publisher's name supplied.]

Catalogs: *A1911*, "Part II, . . . 12mo, old calf (rubbed and cracked), some pages stained, Lond. 1721," a sheet of notes by Clemens laid in, lot 301, sold for .75¢, "Part II" only; H. A. Levinson, 141 E. 47th Street, Catalogue 28 (1947), contains the *A1911* label, sixth edition, Part II only.

Behn's epistolary novel explored a recent scandal. Ford Grey, First Earl of Tankerville, had run off with his sister-in-law, Lady Henrietta Berkeley. Because the novel was published anonymously its authorship has sometimes been in dispute.

BELASCO, DAVID (1853–1931).

About this playwright, theater owner, and stage producer, Clemens once remarked to Albert Bigelow Paine: "The literary man should have a collaborator with a genius for stage mechanism. . . . Belasco cannot write a play himself, but in the matter of acting construction his genius is supreme." Belasco had staged Twain's *The Prince and the Pauper*, which Twain called "a collection of literary garbage before he got hold of it" (*MTB*, p. 1414).

BELCHER, (LADY) DIANA (JOLLIFFE) (c. 1805–1890). *The Mutineers of the "Bounty" and Their Descendants in Pitcairn and Norfolk Islands.* Illus. New York: Harper & Brothers, 1871. 377 pp.

Inscription: inscribed by Olivia Clemens, "S. L. Clemens/ Buffalo/N.Y." (The Clemenses would move from Buffalo to Hartford in November 1871, so this book entered their library sometime earlier that year.)

Catalogs: ListABP (1910), "Mutineers of the Bounty, Lady Belcher"; *C1951*, D60, listed (erroneously) with books signed by Clemens.

Marginalia: one word written by Clemens on page 229.

Provenance: once owned by the American aviator E. Hamilton Lee; subsequently in the possession of Paul Melzer of Paul Melzer Fine Books, Redlands, California (Melzer to the Mark Twain Papers, 25 October 1994).

Albert Bigelow Paine was told that *Mutineers of the "Bounty"* was one of the books Clemens and Theodore Crane favored during their leisure-hours reading in the summer of 1874 (*MTB*, p. 510).

BELL, JOHN JOY (1871–1934). *Ethel.* Brown cloth. New York: Harper & Brothers, 1903. 197 pp.

Inscription: signed in black ink on the front free endpaper, "SL. Clemens/1903."

Provenance: Antenne-Dorrance Collection, Rice Lake, Wisconsin.

Location: Mark Twain Archive, Gannett-Tripp Learning Center, Elmira College, Elmira, New York.

Copy examined: Clemens's copy. Examined on 28 May 2015.

———. *Jess & Co.* Original gray-green pictorial cloth. Title page printed in red and black. New York: Harper & Brothers, 1904. 297 pp.

Inscriptions: inscribed in black ink by Clemens to his daughter Clara: "A nice book for a good child,/which is Clara,/from her Father/1904." Clara later inscribed the front free endpaper to the purchaser of her Hollywood home: "To Vivien Wescoatt/on her birthday June 10th/ from/'a good child which is'/Clara."

Marginalia: the leaves have been opened throughout the volume. A note on a half-sheet of paper in pencil by Clara Clemens is laid in at pages 210–211: "'She clings to her paddle' (the rest-cure.)"

Provenance: shelfmark of Clara Clemens Gabrilowitsch's library in Detroit. Alan Gribben discovered this volume among Clemens family materials in the Wescoatt house in Hollywood in 1987 while inspecting the bookshelves, at the request of the Wescoatt heirs, in the house formerly owned by Clara Clemens Samossoud. Nick Karanovich of Fort Wayne, Indiana acquired the volume in 1987.

Catalog: *Sotheby's 2003*, #184, $2,500.

Location: collection of Kevin Mac Donnell, Austin, Texas.

Copy examined: Clara Clemens's copy, seen in 1987 and viewed again in Austin in July 2004.

This is a more serious novel about village life than some of

Bell's other fiction.

———. *Later Adventures of Wee Macgreegor*. New York: Harper & Brothers, 1904. 214 pp.

Source: MTLAcc, entry #1587, volume donated by Clemens.

———. [Another identical copy.]

Source: MTLAcc, entry #1877, volume donated from Clemens's library by Clara Clemens Gabrilowitsch in 1910.

———. *Mr. Pennycook's Boy*. New York: Harper & Brothers, 1905. 272 pp.

Source: MTLAcc, entry #1588, volume donated by Clemens.

———. *Oh! Christina!* New York: F. H. Revell Co., [cop. 1909]. 159 pp.

Source: MTLAcc, entry #1916, volume donated from Clemens's library by Clara Clemens Gabrilowitsch in 1910.

BELL, LILIAN LIDA (1867–1929). *The Expatriates; A Novel*. New York: Harper & Brothers, 1902. 432 pp.

Source: MTLAcc, entry #1435, volume donated by Clemens.

———. *The Instinct of Step-fatherhood*. New York: Harper & Brothers, 1898. 228 pp.

Source: MTLAcc, entry #21, volume donated by Clemens. The title story is one of Bell's seven short stories collected here.

———. *A Little Sister to the Wilderness; A Novel*. New York: Harper & Brothers, 1901. 267 pp.

Source: MTLAcc, entry #1515, volume donated by Clemens.

———. *The Love Affairs of an Old Maid*. New York: Harper & Brothers, 1899. 188 pp.

Source: MTLAcc, entry #673, volume donated by Clemens.

BELLAMY, EDWARD (1850–1898). *Looking Backward, 2000–1887*. Boston: Ticknor and Co., 1888. 470 pp. [Edition conjectured; Clemens's copy has not been located.]

In Edward Bellamy's *Looking Backward* (1888), Julian West awakens in a twentieth-century utopia, whereas Hank Morgan in Twain's *A Connecticut Yankee in King Arthur's Court* (1889) attempts to reform a medieval dystopia. Despite obvious time-travel similarities between the novels, no one has disputed the apparent order of occurrence emerging from Mark Twain's notebooks and letters—that "when *A Connecticut Yankee* was ready for the printers, Twain found time to read Edward Bellamy's *Looking Backward*," as Louis J. Budd stated (*MTSP*, p. 145). Twain finished revising his novel early in November 1889; his publishing firm issued the book on 10 December 1889. Almost as though determined to frustrate later scholars who might naturally speculate about an influence, Twain made a precise entry in Notebook 29: "Began 'Looking Backward' Nov. 5, 1889, on the train. A fascinating book" (*N&J* 3: 526).

From Hartford on 1 December 1889 Mark Twain declined with regret an invitation from Sylvester Baxter of the Boston *Herald* to meet Bellamy, whom Twain called "the man who has made the accepted heaven paltry by inventing a better one on earth" (Berg, quoted in *MTHL*, p. 622). Twain wrote Baxter on 19 December 1889 about his anticipation "to get acquainted with the maker of the latest & best of all the Bibles" (Berg, NYPL, quoted in *MTHL*, p. 622). Howells recalled correctly that Twain

"was fascinated with *Looking Backward* and had Bellamy to visit him" (*MMT* [1910], p. 38). He entertained Bellamy and Baxter at his Hartford house on 3 January 1890 (*MTHL*, p. 622 n. 2), and later that year he listed Bellamy in Notebook 29 as the designated recipient of a complimentary copy of *A Connecticut Yankee* (*N&J* 3: 569). In an undated letter Susy Clemens mentioned to Grace King that "Mr. Bellamy was here [in Hartford] the other day for a few hours. He is a very sweet [two words illegible] in appearance with a pleasant eye, and gentle smile. He and Papa had some very interesting talk upon the subjects which he discusses in 'Looking Backward.' Papa's admiration for the book and it's [*sic*] views and purpose is very great. We like Mr. Bellamy exceedingly" (Laura Skandera to Alan Gribben, 21 January 1990, quoting a New Orleans source for the letter, John M. Coxe). In a South Africa interview in 1896 Twain talked about "the Bellamy 'boom.' He knows Bellamy well." Twain said that "hundreds of thousands of people in the United States had accepted that book as a new Gospel." At this point *Looking Backward* was selling "two thousand copies a day," whereas its first edition "was about as scrofulous-looking and mangy a volume as I have set eyes on." Only the sales of *Trilby* and *Ben-Hur* were comparable, Twain noted (Johannesburg *Star*, 18 May 1896; *Complete Interviews* [2006], pp. 302–303).

Salomon, *TIH* (1961), p. 39; Henry Nash Smith, *Mark Twain's Fable of Progress* (1964).

———. *Looking Backward, 2000–1887*. Boston: Houghton, Mifflin & Co., 1889. 470 pp.

Catalog: Ball 2016 inventory, green-blue cloth, black and gilt lettering, poor condition, erasures, bookmark laid in is inscribed "Jervis, Easter 1892".

Location: Quarry Farm library shelves, under the supervision of the Mark Twain Archive, Elmira College, Elmira, New York.

Clemens had access to the Langdon library books during his visits to Elmira.

BELLINI, VINCENZO (1801–1835). *Norma* (opera, performed in 1831). Libretto by Felice Romani (1788–1865).

In 1865 Mark Twain asserted that he had "cultivated" his taste to the point where "I could close one eye in an opera and tell 'Norma' from the 'Bohemian Girl'" (Virginia City *Territorial Enterprise*, 3–5 June 1865; reprinted by Gary Scharnhorst, "Additional Mark Twain Contributions to the Virginia City *Territorial Enterprise*, 1863–66," *American Literary Realism* 47.1 [Fall 2014]: 90).

BELLOWS, JOHN (1831–1902). *Dictionary for the Pocket: French and English, English and French*. Rev. by Alexandre Beljame (1843–1906). Second ed. London: Trübner & Co., 1877. 605 pp. [The first edition appeared in 1873].

Catalog: ListABP (1910), "Fr.-Eng. Dict.", no other information provided. Bellows's dictionary might possibly be this book.

Mark Twain mentioned this book three times in his notebooks—its author and title (1878, *N&J* 2: 158), its appearance resembles a pocket New Testament, and it is an "admirable dictionary" (*N&J* 2: 314, 316). In "Paris Notes" (1882) Twain claimed that the Protestant worshipers at a church in Paris actually hold "Mr. Bellows' admirable and exhaustive little French-English dictionary" instead of a "morocco-bound Testament" and surreptitiously study its lexicon. Bellows wrote to Twain on 5 March, 24 April, and 6 June 1883 to thank him for this "kind and humorous notice" (MTP), and on the verso of Bellows's first letter Mark Twain wrote, "John Bellows author of the admirable little French-English Dictionary."

Bell's Life in London and Sporting Chronicle (periodical, published 1822–1886).

Mark Twain alluded to this magazine as his source for euphemistic boxing terminology in a column for the San Francisco *Golden Era*, 11 October 1863 (*WG*, p. 28; *CTSS&E* 1: 49–56).

BENHAM, WILLIAM GEORGE. *The Laws of Scientific Hand Reading; A Practical Treatise on the Art Commonly Called Palmistry.* Illus. New York: G. P. Putnam's Sons, 1903. 635 pp.

Inscription: signed in ink, "Clara Clemens."

Marginalia: pencil marks and notes, apparently Clara Clemens'.

Catalogs: *C1951*, J33, listed among the books belonging to Jean and Clara Clemens; "Property from the Library of Mark Twain," Butterfield & Butterfield, San Francisco, Sale 6613 (16 July 1997), lot 2712.

Location: Mark Twain House and Museum, Hartford, Connecticut.

Copy examined: Clara Clemens's copy. Viewed in Hartford in 1997.

BENJAMIN BEN JONAH, OF TUDELA (1130–1173). *The Itinerary of Rabbi Benjamin of Tudela.* [Published under several titles and in various languages since the sixteenth century.]

Clemens read and marked passages (pp. 63–126) in the version included in Thomas Wright's *Early Travels in Palestine* (1848), a volume he signed in 1877. He also mentioned the travels of this twelfth-century Jewish merchant in Notebook 28 (1888–1889), in the context of his *A Connecticut Yankee* sources (*N&J* 3: 475).

BENKARD, JOHANN PHILIPP (1763–1852). *Geschichte der Deutschen Kaiser und Könige. [History of the German Emperors and Kings.] Zu den Bildern des Kaisersaals. 4e aufl.* Illus. Frankfort-a-M: H. Keller, 1869, 155 pp.

Inscription: signed on the front flyleaf: "S. L. Clemens, Frankfort-a-M./May 4, 1878."

Catalog: *A1911*, "12mo, cloth, Frankford-a-M 1869," quotes the signature, lot 35, sold for $1.

BENNETT, EMERSON (1822–1905).

William Baker discovered that while Clemens was working for Wrightson's printing shop in Cincinnati in 1856 and 1857 the firm published four titles by this novelist, who had earlier lived in Cincinnati—*The Forest Rose, The Prairie Flower, Mike Fink,* and *Leni Lecti* ("Mark Twain in Cincinnati: A Mystery Most Compelling," *American Literary Realism* 12.2 [Autumn 1979]: 312 n. 30). In Chapter 19 of *Roughing It* (1872) Mark Twain scoffed at the frontier adventure stories Bennett wrote for the dime-novel trade.

Franklin R. Rogers, *MTBP* (1960), p. 68; French, *MT&GA* (1965), p. 36; Baetzhold, *MT&JB* (1970), pp. 346–347 n. 10; Rogers, ed., *RI* (Iowa-California Edition, 1972), p. 568; Smith and Branch, eds., *RI* (University of California Press, 1993), pp. 129, 607; Jarrod Roark, "Beneath Mark Twain: Detecting Sensational Residues in Twain's Early Writing," *Mark Twain Annual* 12 (2014): 14–29.

BENNETT, SANFORD FILLMORE (1836–1898). "The sweet by and by" (hymn, cop. 1868). Melody by Joseph Philbrick Webster (1819–1875).

Mark Twain first joked about the enduring popularity of this piece in a letter to D. F. Appleton on 5 December 1877: "There is a new song here [in Hartford] which you may not have heard, and if you care for music we shall be very glad indeed to sing it for you, by telephone. . . . I think it is called 'In the Sweet By-and- Bye'" (*The New England Society of the City of New York, Seventy-second Anniversary Celebration* [New York, 1877], p. 84). In the notebook Twain kept for 1878 he groused that this was a pretty and moving song—"at first" (NB 17, *N&J* 2: 240). The idea of this tired tune's being sung over the telephone appealed to him so much that Rosannah Ethelton sings its "exquisitely soft and remote strains" several times on that instrument (flatting many notes in the effort) in "The Loves of Alonzo Fitz Clarence and Rosannah Ethelton" (1878). (Twain had sketched this antic in Notebook 14 [*N&J* 2: 49] in 1877.) Hank Morgan hears a band salute the Queen in Chapter 17 of *A Connecticut Yankee in King Arthur's Court* (1889) "with what seemed to be the crude first-draft or original agony of the wail known to later centuries as 'In the Sweet Bye and Bye.' . . . For some reason the queen had the composer hanged, after dinner." A few pages farther on Hank himself gives the Queen permission to hang the entire band for their painful rendition of this song. Twain referred to the piece again in Notebook 33 (October 1893), TS p. 35. The Young Man in *What Is Man?* (written 1898–1906) alluded to it as an example of "the new popular song with the taking melody [that] sings thro' one's head day and night, asleep and awake, till one is a wreck" (*WIM?*, p. 178). Again in *Christian Science* (1907) Twain used it as an illustration of "how wearisome the sweetest and touchingest things can become, through rep-rep-repetition" (Book 2, Chapter 7, *WIM?* [1973], p. 323). Yet in spite of numerous gibes at the song, Clemens claimed in a letter to his sister-in-law following Olivia's death that he had always associated the song with his wife, a surprising fact if true. He wrote to Susan Crane on 9 September 1904 that a street-organist playing "The Sweet By and By" outside his hotel reminded him that he initially heard the tune played in December 1867 at the time he first saw Olivia, and that during the period of their engagement they often sang it in the evenings (MTP). The first two lines of the chorus are reassuring: "In the sweet by and by,/We shall meet on that beautiful shore." Perhaps it *was* merely the repetitiveness to which Clemens objected, but the public and the private man seem strikingly at odds concerning this Christian hymn.

BENNETT, WILLIAM COX (1820–1895). "Baby May" (poem).

Clemens wrote to Mary Mason Fairbanks on 6 July 1873 about his meeting the English poet in London: "W. C. Bennett (you remember his poem 'Baby May' in the Bryant Selections)" (*MTMF*, p. 173; *MTLet* 5: 402). The poem in Bryant's *Library of Poetry and Song* (1870) consists of a long catalogue of praises for his infant daughter (her "slumbers" are "sweet angel-seemings"), concluding, "Beauty all that beauty may be;—/That's May Bennett; that's my baby" (p. 76).

BENSON, EDWARD FREDERIC (1867–1940). *The Book of Months.*

New York: Harper & Brothers, 1903. 299 pp.

Source: MTLAcc, entry #847, volume donated by Clemens.

———. *Dodo: A Detail of the Day.* New York: F. M. Lupton Publishing Co., n.d. 213 pp. Paperbound. [First published in 1893.]

Marginalia: on page 1 Clemens wrote, "Did you ever read it? It came out about 1897 I think. Very clever it was conceded and made him famous. He has written others since, but in a more serious vein."

Source: Information for this entry derives from a letter of 13 November 1963 from Whitlock's, Inc. (New Haven, Connecticut) to the Mark Twain House in Hartford, Connecticut, offering the book for sale. There is no indication as to how the volume was identified as part of Clemens's personal library. Whitlock's reported that "the pages are chipped and the title page torn." Although the price was only $10, the Mark Twain House declined to purchase this volume because of their (since altered) policy of acquiring only those books which Clemens had in his library prior to 1891.

The English novelist Benson modeled his controversial title figure on a music composer and women's rights advocate, Ethel Smyth. (She was flattered.)

———. *The Judgment Books.* New York: Harper & Brothers, 1895. 176 pp.

Source: MTLAcc, entry #1321, volume donated by Clemens.

In this supernatural thriller an artist experiences eerie sensations as he paints a portrait; personality traits seem to be transferring between himself and his sitter.

BENT, JAMES THEODORE (1852–1897). *A Freak of Freedom; or, the Republic of San Marino.* Map of San Marino. Illus. First edition. Original brown pictorial cloth, gilt. London: Longmans, Green, and Co., 1879. 271 pp.

Inscription: signed in pencil in large, hastily scrawled letters on the half-title page: "S L Clemens/London '79."

Marginalia: brief notations totaling thirteen words on three pages—27 (a question mark beside the word "professes," and "animal" altered to "bear"), 36, and 38 ("A marvelous sentence" written vertically next to a convoluted periodic sentence that Clemens marked with a vertical line). On page 36 Clemens criticized the author's syntax in stating, "A small hamlet belonging to the Republic has grown up round a well, where the saint used to baptize his converts, springing from underneath a cliff." Clemens queried: "Did the converts spring, or was it the saint?" Clemens marked fourteen other pages—39, 43, 58, 59, 238, 239, 242, 243, 245, 248, 249, 258, 261, and 268—with marginal rules, underlinings, and other marks, most of them either calling attention to careless grammatical usages or highlighting the absurdities of such a tiny government.

Catalogs: *A1911*, "12mo, cloth, Lond. 1879," quotes inscription and some marginalia, lot 36, sold for $9; offered from the Samuel Freedman collection, September 1983, item 179; Second Life Books, Lanesborough, Massachusetts, Catalog 47 (November 1984), item D, has the *A1911* auction label, $950; *Sotheby's 2003*, #185, $2,250.

Provenance: acquired by Nick Karanovich of Fort Wayne, Indiana in 1984 from Second Life Books. Mr. Karanovich sent me a photocopy of the front cover, inscription, and

marginalia on 10 December 1984.

Location: collection of Kevin Mac Donnell, Austin, Texas.

Copy examined: Clemens's copy, viewed in July 2004. Displays the purple stamp of the Mark Twain Library of Redding, Connecticut on the front pastedown endpaper; the library charge sheet and pocket have been torn off the rear endpapers. Also has an *A1911* auction label on the front pastedown endpaper, so it was evidently retrieved from the Mark Twain Library in Redding sometime after it was donated in order to be sold at the 1911 sale.

San Marino, believed to be the world's oldest republic, is surrounded by Italy.

BENT, SAMUEL ARTHUR (1841–1912). *Short Sayings of Great Men. With Historical and Explanatory Notes.* Boston: J. R. Osgood & Co., 1882. 610 pp.

Inscription: signed carelessly in pencil on the front free endpaper: "S L Clemens/Harford 1885".

Marginalia: "some notations" by Clemens, according to the 1911 auction catalog. On page 289 Clemens, next to an entry for the London humorist, editor, and playwright Douglas Jerrold (1803–1857), recorded one of that writer's witticisms vertically in pencil in the margin: "To a borous [*sic*, apparently] poet who asked, 'Have you seen my Descent into Hell'? Jerrold said, 'No, but I'd like to.'"

Catalog: *A1911*, "12mo, cloth, Bost. 1882, with some autograph notations," lot 37, sold for $1.75.

Provenance: in 1986 the volume was in the possession of Professor Frank L. Byrne of Kent State University (Byrne to the Mark Twain Papers, 3 June 1986).

Copy examined: photocopy of the front endpapers and page 289 of a volume that belonged to Clemens. The front pastedown endpaper bears an *A1911* auction label.

Clemens requested a copy of this book in a postscript to a letter he wrote to James R. Osgood & Company on 6 January 1883 (*MTLP*, p. 162).

BENTON, KATE ARNOLD (BRADLEY) (1867–1899). *Geber; A Tale of the Reign of Harun al Raschid, Khalif of Baghdad.* New York: Frederick A. Stokes Co., [1900]. 487 pp.

Source: MTLAcc, entry #880, volume donated by Mrs. Ralph W. Ashcroft (formerly Isabel Lyon), Clemens's secretary.

A historical romance set in the ancient Arab world, the Khalif summons a physician and astrologer to Damascus to treat the Khalif's ailing wife. The author Benton died while the book was in press.

———. [Another identical copy.] Fourth edition. [cop. 1900]. 487 pp.

Inscription: "title page signed in black ink: "Clara Clemens/1907".

Marginalia: pencil marks at pages 3, 216, 235, 282, and 427.

Provenance: Brentano's Booksellers, New York City sticker on the rear pastedown endpaper.

Location: Mark Twain Library, Redding, Connecticut. Donated from Clemens's library by Clara Clemens Gabrilowitsch in 1910 (MTLAcc, entry #2162).

Copy examined: Clara Clemens's copy. Has the red ink accession number "2162". Examined in June 1982.

BENTON, JOEL (1832–1911). *The Truth about "Protection."* New York: C. L. Webster & Co., 1892. 35 pp.

Clemens's firm issued this publication about United States tariffs.

BENTZON, THÉRÈSE (1840–1907), pseud. "Madame Marie-Thérèse Blanc."

Mark Twain had fun with the review and translation of his "Jumping Frog" story that this French author and critic published in the 15 July 1872 issue of *Revue des deux mondes*. He re-translated her translation as "The Jumping Frog in English, Then in French, Then Clawed Back into a Civilized Language Once More by Patient, Unremunerated Toil" and included it in *Sketches, New and Old* (1875).

Beowulf (Old English poem, 10th century).

Clemens jokingly alluded to this famous literary work in a letter of 10 January 1870 to Olivia Langdon (*MTLet* 4: 16).

BÉRANGER, PIERRE JEAN DE (1780–1857).

Discussing French humorists in a letter of 8 January 1875 to Louise Chandler Moulton, Clemens alluded to "my very distant acquaintance, Beranger" (*MTLet* 6: 343).

BERARD, AUGUSTA BLANCHE (1824–1901). *Berard's History of the United States*. Rev. by Celeste E. Bush. Illus. Philadelphia: Cowperthwait & Co., [cop. 1878]. 352 pp.

Source: MTLAcc, entry #813, volume donated by Clemens. The title page was missing.

BERGER, ALFRED, FREIHERR VON (1853–1912). *Habsburg. Märchenspiel in drei Acten [Habsburg. Fairy Tale Play in Three Acts]*. Wien: Carl Konegen, 1898. 120 pp.

Clemens mentioned Berger in Notebook 42 while in Vienna in December 1897 (TS p. 52). He referred to Berger's verses in September 1898 (NB 40, TS p. 40), and he translated fourteen lines of verse from *Habsburg* into English for Joseph H. Twichell on 25 September 1898 so that Twichell could sample Berger's "recent fairy-drama" (*LMTJHT*, pp. 223–224). Mark Twain's "The Memorable Assassination" (written in 1898) closes with nine of these lines "to convey the spirit of the verses."

BERGER, FRANÇOIS. *New Method of Learning the French Language*. New York: D. Appleton and Co., 1882. 138 pp. [Edition conjectured.]

Catalog: ListABP (1910), "New Method (French), Berger", no other information supplied.

BERKELEY, GEORGE (1685–1753). "On the Prospect of Planting Arts and Learning in America" (published in 1752).

Mark Twain parodies stanza 6 of Berkeley's poem ("Westward the course of empire takes its way/The four first acts already past") in Chapter 60 of *Life on the Mississippi* (1883), where Twain reminds readers that "the missionary comes after the whiskey"—or in other words, "Westward the Jug of Empire takes its way." Admittedly Twain might also have had in mind the observation of John Quincy Adams (1767–1848), "Westward the star of empire takes its way" ("Oration at Plymouth," 1802).

BERLICHINGEN, GÖTZ VON (1480–1562).

The autobiography of this German feudal knight was published posthumously in 1731. It was used by Goethe as a source for the drama *Götz von Berlichingen* (1773), which Sir Walter Scott translated in 1799. Mark Twain seems to have seen a version of this work, or at least to have known of its existence. Twain alludes to Berlichingen as "the famous old robber knight and rough fighter" and refers to him in Chapters 11, 12, 14, and 15 of *A Tramp Abroad* (1880). Berlichingen's memoirs are specifically

mentioned in Chapter 12, and Twain says that he purchased "a facsimile" of a letter that Berlichingen wrote in Heibronn in 1519.

Beverly R. David, "What's in a Name? Twain's Goethe Hero in *A Tramp Abroad*," *Mark Twain Journal* 26.1 (Spring 1988): 30–32, explored how Twain relied on Goethe's *Götz von Berlichingen*. See also the Catalog entry for Goethe's play.

Bermuda [unidentified book].

Catalog: ListABP (1910), "Bermuda", listed twice, no other information supplied.

BERNAND, WILLIAM BAYLE (1807–1875).

In "Concerning the American Language" (1882) Mark Twain alludes to the satires of "your Mr. Bernand" about American's pronunciations. Louis J. Budd deduced that Twain was referring to the English playwright William Bayle Bernand (*CTSS&E* 1: 832, 1066).

BERNARD, A. HERMANN. *Legends of the Rhine*. Translated from the German by Fr. Arnold. Mayence: Joseph Halenza, 187?. 316 pp. [First English edition published in 1862.]

Edgar H. Hemminghaus saw Clemens's copy on the shelves of the Mark Twain Library, Redding, Connecticut in 1945 ("Mark Twain's German Provenience" [1945], p. 473), but the volume has since disappeared. The potential relevance of *Legends of the Rhine* to Twain's *A Tramp Abroad* (1880) merits investigation. Bernard retold fifty-three stories, including "The Mermaid," "Heidelberg," "The Maiden's Leap," "The Mouse-tower," "Lorelay [sic]," "The Lion-slayer," "The Heads of Stone," and "St. Clemens Church."

BERNARD, FRÉDÉRIC (1820–1868), pseud. "Théodore Pelloquet." *Wonderful Escapes*. Translated from the French and edited by Richard Whiteing (1840–1928). Illus. New York: Scribner, Armstrong & Co., 1872. 308 pp. [Uncredited illustrations by Émile Antoine Bayard (1837–1891) from the French edition.]

Source: MTLAcc, entry #2001, volume donated from Clemens's library by Clara Clemens Gabrilowitsch in 1910.

This qualifies as one of the most important previously overlooked literary resources in Mark Twain studies. Originally published as *Les évasions célèbres* in Paris in 1869, Frédéric Bernard's book related in chronological order more than forty supposedly true tales of escape from imprisonment in dungeons and towers. Many of the wily prisoners manufactured useful implements in their cells, just as Tom Sawyer exhorts Jim to do in the later chapters of *Adventures of Huckleberry Finn* (1885). The fortunate escapees included Benvenuto Cellini, Baron Trenck, and Casanova de Seingalt. The French journalist, writer, art critic, and caricaturist Bernard, born in Seurre cote-d'or, died of alcoholism in Nice at the age of only forty-eight on 28 December 1868. In addition to his early and relatively unnoticed death, his later obscurity also resulted from his frequent use of a pseudonym, Pelloquet.

BERNARD, JOHN (1756–1828). *Retrospections of America, 1797–1811. . . Edited from the Manuscript by Mrs. [William] Bayle Bernard*. Intro., notes, and index by Laurence Hutton (1843–1904) and Brander Matthews (1852–1929). Illus. New York: Harper & Brothers, 1887. 380 pp.

Source: MTLAcc, entry #1711, volume donated by Clemens.

Clemens made an entry in Notebook 23 in 1885 relevant

to Bernard's account of the early American stage: "Get Brander Matthews after the diary of the Boston Comedian's father" (*N&J* 3: 115). The book's editor, Mrs. Bernard, was the widow of John Bernard' son, William Bayle Bernard (1807–1875). Bernard traveled widely throughout the newly created United States, and *Retrospections of America* contains his impressions of slavery (he traveled as far south as Charleston), the ubiquity of tobacco chewing and smoking, the American author Charles Brockden Brown, and many other recollections.

BERNARD, VICTOR FERDINAND (b. 1845). *L'art d'intéresser en classe; Nouveau manuel de lecture et de conversation. 3 éd.* Boston: Carl Schoenhof, 1885. 224 pp.

 Inscription: unknown (the front flyleaf has been torn out).
 Marginalia: some markings in pencil throughout and pencil notes (not in Clemens's hand) on pages 20, 30, and 31.
 Location: Mark Twain Library, Redding, Connecticut.
 Copy examined: presumably Clemens's copy. Has the accession number "3676" written in pencil. Examined in 1970 and again in June 1982.
 L'art d'intéresser en classe consisted of stories, anecdotes, and fables chosen for students. In 1876 Bernard moved to the United States, where he taught in various schools in the Northeast.

BERNER, ERNST (1853–1905). *Geschichte des Brandenburgisch-Preussischen* Staates *[History of the Brandenburg-Prussian States]*. Heiligenstadt: Franz W. Cordier, [cop. 1891]. 154 pp.
 Source: MTLAcc, entry #376, volume donated by Clemens.

BERRIAT-SAINT-PRIX, JACQUES (1769–1845). *Jeanne d'Arc [1412–1431], ou Coup-d'oeil sur les révolutions de France au temps de Charles VI et de Charles VII, et surtout de la Pucelle d'Orléans.* Paris: Pillet, 1817. 368 pp.
 Mark Twain listed Berriat-Saint-Prix among the "authorities examined" for Twain's *Joan of Arc* (1896) on the page preceding the "Translator's Preface," but he erred regarding the book title; see Ronald Jenn and Linda A. Morris, "The Sources of Mark Twain's *Personal Recollections of Joan of Arc*," *Mark Twain Journal* 55.1–2 (Spring/Fall 2017): 55–74.

BERTHOLET, ALFRED (1868–1951). *The Transmigration of Souls.* Translated from the German by Henry John Chaytor (1871–1954). New York: Harper & Brothers, 1909. 133 pp.
 Source: MTLAcc, entry #1489, volume donated by Clemens.
 As the title suggests, Alfred Bertholet, a professor of theology at the University of Basle, mounted an argument on behalf of the concept of reincarnation. The Reverend Chaytor was the headmaster of Plymouth College in England.

BESANT, (SIR) WALTER (1836–1901). *All in a Garden Fair.* New York: J. W. Lowell Co., [cop. 1883]. 353 pp.
 Source: MTLAcc, entry #26, volume donated by Clemens.

———. *All Sorts and Conditions of Men; An Impossible Story.* A New Edition. London: Chatto & Windus, 1894. 331 pp.
 Source: MTLAcc, entry #2163, volume donated from Clemens's library by Clara Clemens Gabrilowitsch in 1910.
 In November 1897 Olivia Clemens wrote to Chatto & Windus with a request: "Will you also please send Besant's 'All Sorts and Conditions of Men' and his 'Dorothy Forster'" (Berg, NYPL).

———. *All Sorts and Conditions of Men; An Impossible Story.*

New York: Harper & Brothers, n.d. 412 pp.
 Source: MTLAcc, entry #2177, volume donated from Clemens's library by Clara Clemens Gabrilowitsch in 1910.

——— and **JAMES RICE** (1843–1882). *The Chaplain of the Fleet.* New York: Dodd, Mead & Co., n.d. 447 pp.
 Source: MTLAcc, entry #2167, volume donated from Clemens's library by Clara Clemens Gabrilowitsch in 1910.

——— and **JAMES RICE**. *The Chaplain of the Fleet.* London: Chatto & Windus, 1888. 447 pp.
 Source: MTLAcc, entry #2179, volume donated from Clemens's library by Clara Clemens Gabrilowitsch in 1910.

———. *Dorothy Forster; A Novel.* London: Chatto & Windus, 1895. 312 pp.
 Source: MTLAcc, entry #2172, volume donated from Clemens's library by Clara Clemens Gabrilowitsch in 1910.
 In November 1897 Olivia Clemens requested a copy of this book from Chatto & Windus (Berg, NYPL).

———. *For Faith and Freedom.* London: Chatto & Windus, 1890. 334 pp.
 Source: MTLAcc, entry #2174, volume donated from Clemens's library by Clara Clemens Gabrilowitsch in 1910.

———. *The French Humorists, from the Twelfth to the Nineteenth Centuries.* Boston: Roberts Brothers, 1874. 455 pp. [Edition conjectured; the book had a previous London edition in 1873.]
 On 8 January 1875 Clemens wrote to Louise Chandler Moulton, who had reviewed Besant's book, "I think I must get the book you are writing about, for it doubtless separates & points out some excellencies in Rabelais which even I might see" (*MTLet* 6: 343).

———. *London. A New Edition.* Illus. London: Chatto & Windus, 1894. 343 pp.
 Catalog: *A1911*, "8vo, cloth, uncut, Lond. 1894," lot 38, sold for $1.25.
 Clemens wrote to Andrew Chatto on 3 January 1895: "Many thousand thanks! The books arrived yesterday, & Besant's 'London' kept me most pleasantly awake the whole night, & lost me my day's work to-day" (ALS, Mark Twain Boyhood Home and Museum, Hannibal, Missouri).

———. *The Pen and the Book.* With a chapter on "Copyright and Literary Property" contributed by G[eorge]. H[erbert]. Thring (1859–1941), Secretary of the Society of Authors. London: Thomas Burleigh, 1899. 347 pp.
 Marginalia: extensive underscorings and marginal notes by Clemens on approximately thirty pages. His penciled marginalia occur mainly in passages discussing the costs and methods of book publishing and the financial relationships among authors, publishers, and booksellers. Clemens paused to compute Mary Baker Eddy's profits for *Science and Health* on pages 155–156. He liked Besant's attitude toward royalties: "His main point that those who hold that lit. men should not endeavor to make as much money as they can, talk nonsense. Those who say it 'are chiefly the unsuccessful writers'" (p. 134). Clemens also commented: "In our day it seems *indecent* to confess hunger for money—& yet if you have that you can add all other things to yourself" (p. 146). On page 177 he figured up his receipts for *Life on the Mississippi* (1883), concluding that they amounted to "robbery" and noting that he only "cleared about 65¢ on 40,000 copies." Commiserating with authors whom Besant describes as having been victimized by publishers, Clemens exclaimed

on page 180: "Why, there are more fools than I." Farther on he used the top margin of the page titled "Chapter VII. The Method of the Future" to advocate a system for book sales that would use the postal system to "offer the book *directly* to the man himself"; "selling books through booksellers is infinitely stupid," he asserted (p. 207). At the bottom of the same page he added: "I published Huck Finn—success. Pub'd 3 & paid pub a royalty—poor job." On page 265 he elaborated on his proposal "to abolish the *bookseller* & use the P.O.—make *it* the middleman & reduce the prices." (Clemens's fantasy was a century before Internet online book distribution!)

Catalogs: ListABP (1910), "The Pen and the Book, Besant"; *C1951*, #27a, $20.

Provenance: in the collection of Justin G. Turner (1898–1976), a Los Angeles real estate investor and noted collector of books and manuscripts, in 1970.

Location: currently undetermined.

Copy examined: photocopy of marginalia provided in 1979 by Howard G. Baetzhold of Butler University. Justin G. Turner of Turner Investments in Los Angeles had permitted Baetzhold to make this copy. On 4 February 1999 Baetzhold sent his original photocopy of the marginalia to the Mark Twain Papers, Bancroft Library, University of California.

Mark Twain referred to Besant's review of *Joan of Arc* in a letter to Chatto & Windus written on 29 October 1896 (ASSSCL). On 22 February 1898 Twain wrote from Vienna (ALS in Berg, NYPL) to thank Besant for his kind words about *Adventures of Huckleberry Finn* ("My Favorite Author and His Best Book," *Munsey's Magazine* 18.5 [February 1898]: 659–664). Besant's flattering essay was probably responsible for Mark Twain's withdrawing from an agreement to review *The Pen and the Book* for *Harper's Monthly*. Twain explained to John Kendrick Bangs on 2 March 1899 that he had to give up the attempt soon after the book arrived: "Besant is a friend of mine, and there was no way of doing a review that wouldn't cut into his feelings and wound his enthusiastic pride in his insane performance. . . . There isn't a rational page in it. Why, a person might as well undertake to review a lunatic asylum" (Francis Hyde Bangs, *John Kendrick Bangs* [New York: A. A. Knopf, 1941], p. 203). The preface to Besant's *The Pen and the Book* stated that it was "written for the guidance and the instruction of those young persons who are thinking of the literary life."

_____ and **James Rice**. *The Seamy Side, A Story*. London: Chatto & Windus, 1880. [Published in the United States as: *The Seamy Side; A Novel*. New York: Dodd, Mead & Co., 1880.]

Lane Cooper, in "Mark Twain's Lilacs and Laburnums," *Modern Language Notes* 47.2 (February 1932): 85–87, recognized several striking resemblances between the weather and scenery in Chapters 15 and 26 of *The Seamy Side* and Chapter 4 of Mark Twain's "A Double-Barrelled Detective Story" (1902), in which Twain introduces a "solitary œsophagus" into a purple passage describing October scenery.

Paine, *MTB* (1912), pp. 1136–39; and K. Patrick Ober, M.D., "The Pre-Flexnerian Reports: Mark Twain's Criticism of Medicine in the United States," *Annals of Internal Medicine* 126.2 (15 January 1997): 158 (I am grateful to JoDee Benussi for spotting this latter article online in 2006).

Bethune, George Washington (1805–1862). *Memoirs of Mrs. Joanna Bethune [1770–1849], by Her Son*. New York: Harper & Brothers, 1863. 250 pp.

Source: MTLAcc, entry #1749, volume donated by Clemens.

Bettersworth, Alexander Pitts (1830–1903). *John Smith, Democrat: His Two Days' Canvass (Sunday Included) for the Office of Mayor of the City of Bunkumville*. Springfield, Illinois: H. W. Rokker, 1877. 249 pp.

John Smith conducts an unorthodox campaign for the office of mayor of a small Illinois town. Bettersworth subsequently wrote a science fiction novel, *The Strange Ms., by ____, M.D.* (1883), about the few survivors after a comet strikes the earth.

Source: MTLAcc, entry #27, volume donated by Clemens.

Beveridge, Albert Jeremiah (1862–1927). *The Russian Advance*. New York: Harper & Brothers, 1904. 486 pp.

Source: MTLAcc, entry #1360, volume donated by Clemens.

Biart, Lucien (1828–1897). *Adventures of a Young Naturalist*. Ed. and adapted by Parker Gillmore (1835–1900). Illus. New York: Harper & Brothers, n.d. 491 pp. [Biart's book was first published in 1870.]

Source: MTLAcc, entry # 1589, volume donated by Clemens.

Biart described his travels in Mexico. The book's editor, Parker Gillmore, was an intrepid travel writer in his own right.

Bible.

Clemens and members of his family acquired more than thirty copies of the Bible. In the course of reading Clemens's literary works, letters, and notebooks, and making an unsystematic and *very* incomplete record, I noticed more than 400 instances in which he alluded to specific biblical passages—excluding his references to Adam, Eve, Noah, or other familiar figures. He adverted to thirty-eight of the sixty-six books in the Bible. Twenty-four of the thirty-nine Old Testament books and fourteen of the twenty-seven New Testament books figured in his writings. The majority of his allusions (more than seventy-six) referred to the Book of Genesis; he alluded to passages in other books in the following descending order: Matthew (sixty-two); Luke (forty-five), John, especially the raising of Lazarus (thirty-one); Exodus (thirty references, especially "a stranger in a strange land," 2:22); Judges (eighteen); Isaiah (thirteen); Numbers (thirteen, including " a voice like Balaam's ass" in Chapter 69 of *Roughing It*); I Samuel (twelve); I Kings (twelve); Mark (twelve); the others ten or fewer. But these were only the most obvious usages that I thought to jot down as I went along in my research. The number of such allusions is far greater than the time I could afford for documentation of their multitudinous forms. His relationship with this key religious work requires (and has received) specialized studies devoted solely to his varied interpretations. The Annotated Catalog therefore lists only representative examples of his manifold Biblical references.

My computations and those of other scholars suggest the

breadth of his familiarity with the book as well as his emphasis on the narratives in Genesis and also those in the New Testament books describing the life of Christ. Explicit evidence of his admiration for the majestic sweep of Old Testament verses is easy to find. Recounting the story of Joseph in Chapter 47 of *The Innocents Abroad* (1869), Twain referred to the Bible as a "book. . . gemmed with beautiful passages." He mused, "Who taught those ancient writers their simplicity of language, the felicity of expression, their pathos, and above all, their faculty of sinking themselves entirely out of sight of the reader and making the narrative stand out alone and seem to tell itself?" George Wharton James quoted an anecdote that Charles Warren Stoddard told about Mark Twain's affection for certain books of the Old Testament. One night in 1873 Stoddard "lay as one entranced" listening to Clemens read from the Bible in a hotel room in Liverpool, England. "Never in my life," Stoddard said, "did I hear anyone read so perfectly, so beautifully, so thrillingly as Mark read that night. He gave me the whole of the book of Ruth, and half the time never looked at the page; and then some of the most exquisite passages of the book of Isaiah. Few people knew it, but he was more familiar with the Bible, and loved it better, than many of the professional religionists" (p. 13) ("How Mark Twain Was Made" in the February 1911 issue of *National Magazine* [Boston], reprinted on pages 1–13 of George Wharton James' *California Scrapbook: A Collection of Articles* [Limited edition. Los Angeles: N. A. Kovach, 1945]).

While in general Twain's references tended to be respectful and even reverential, his comedic side of course was always apt to break through. For instance, his report from Carson City of "Another Bloody Massacre" (17 November 1863 Virginia City *Territorial Enterprise*) made slangy use of Samson's feats in the Book of Judges (*ET&S* 1: 329). A letter of 4 October 1872 to George H. Fitzgibbon complained of a delayed photographer: "If the world had had to wait on that man to build the Ark, we wouldn't have had the flood yet!" (*MTLet* 5: 194). A female stagecoach passenger in Chapter 2 of *Roughing It* (1872), initially quiet, suddenly became talkative and gossipy: "The fountains of her great deep were broken up, and she rained the nine parts of speech forty days and forty nights, metaphorically speaking" (Cf. the Book of Genesis, 7:11–12). He alluded to the Prodigal Son in Chapter 55 of *Roughing It* (1872). To Mary Mason Fairbanks on 2 November 1872 he compared his reception in England to that of "a Prodigal Son getting back home again" (*MTLet* 5: 205). In 1881 he wrote a humorous fourteen-page manuscript titled "Adam's Expulsion" (originally titled "Adam's Expulsion from Paradise") (ms. sold by Christie's, New York City, 1–2 February 1988 auction, lot 476). "O stultification, where is thy sting," Clemens wrote facetiously in a letter of 31 August 1884 to William Dean Howells, echoing 1 Corinthians 15 (*MTHL*, p. 501). On 14 March1887 he marveled in a letter to the Reverend Joseph H. Twichell that "so insignificant a matter as the chastity or unchastity of an Elizabeth Tilton could clip the locks of this Samson & make him as other men" (*LMTJHT*, p. 141). In a newspaper interview he gave on 16 October 1900 he averred that he had "wrestled, like Jacob, day

and night," with French grammar (*Complete Interviews*, p. 356). In his personal copy of W. W. Jacobs's *Salthaven* (1908) he excoriated the useless phrases in some writers' narratives, concluding facetiously, "Damn such rubbish! As St. Paul said to the Corinthians." Denouncing the publisher Charles L. Webster's attitude toward the company's subscription agents (in a 29 May 1906 Autobiographical Dictation), Clemens recalled how "Webster delivered the law to them as from Mount Sinai" (*MTE*, p. 181; *MTAuto* 2: 66). In a spoofing letter addressed to "Miss Marjory" on 30 October 1908 Clemens pretended to confuse Pontius Pilate, John Milton, and Moses, writing, "I never cared for him, although an ancestor. He ought to have known he was in no condition to carry things down a mountain" (ALS sold by Alan Fox Rare Books, Catalog 1, December 1980, item #10). In an undated manuscript note he listed "Joseph's Harmless Deceits" (such as pretending "he had to talk through interpreter") in the Book of Genesis, concluding that "Joseph's deceits are literary and they justify our novels, romances, histories and other like fictions" (*A1911* catalog, lot 149).

Echoes of biblical passages are more prevalent in Mark Twain's earlier works, as when he alluded to how "in old times Pharaoh's gentle daughter took Moses out of the bulrushes and warmed him, kind soul!" (San Francisco *Examiner* 8 November 1865, quoted by Gary Scharnhorst in "'Also Some Gin': More Excerpts from Mark Twain's 'San Francisco Letters' of 1865–66," *Mark Twain Journal* 26.1 [Spring 1988]: 22–23). Twain paraphrased and abbreviated Psalms 107: 23–24 in Notebook 7 (January 1867): "They that go down to the sea in ships see the wonders of the great deep" (*N&J* 1:291). He would repeat this paraphrase in a 9 March 1870 Buffalo *Express* column (*MTBE*, p. 159) and in a letter of 1 April 1870 (*MTLet* 4: 544). To the Reverend H. Twichell he bragged that his lecture in Toledo, Ohio in January 1869 had been so successful that he "swept down . . . like a Besom of Destruction—don't know what a Besom of Destruction is, but it is a noble sort of expression"; in Isaiah 14:23 (as Twain certainly recalled) the promise is made that "I will sweep it with the besom of destruction, saith the Lord of hosts" (*MTLet* 3: 68; *LMTJHT*, p. 21). In an unsent letter written to Whitelaw Reid on 7 March 1873 Twain quipped: "To my mind Judas Iscariot was nothing but a low, mean, premature Congressman" (*MTLet* 5: 311). Jeremiah 31:15 may have suggested the name Rachel for the enslaved woman in "A True Story" (1874) who grieved over her lost children (Susan K. Harris, "Mark Twain's Bad Women," *Studies in American Fiction* 13.2 [Autumn 1985]: 168 n. 12). Attempting to define "good art" in Notebook 17 in 1879, Clemens speculated that it "shall be farthest from resembling anything in heaven or on earth or in the waters up the earth"—consciously echoing Exodus 4 as well as Deuteronomy 20:4 (*N&J* 2: 241). The gospels of Matthew, Mark, and Luke were invoked when he quoted a mayor's encouraging advice about a sickly mulberry tree: "she will generally seem to be dead; but not so; she only sleepeth" (unsent letter to the New York *Evening Post*, 23 November 1880, *MTPP*, p. 132). The largest concentration of allusions is to be found in *The Innocents Abroad* (1869). In the section of that book devoted to his travels through the Holy Land he is unfailingly worshipful in all mentions of Christ's teachings and acts. These findings can be augmented by more thorough studies in the future, but as they stand they bear out Henry A. Pochmann's first study of the Bible as a source for Mark Twain's works (1924): "Of the one hundred and twenty-four Biblical allusions which I have found in Mark Twain's books, eighty-nine are in *Innocents Abroad*" ("Mind of Mark Twain," p. 7). From puns and simple allusions in Twain's early writings he moved to affectionate joshing about the Bible at mid-career, ending, in his last decade, with broadside blasts at the stories it related and the religion it propounded. His respect for the literary achievement of the book as a collection of writings central to European and American history and culture never varied, but he came to feel, as he wrote in 1890, that "the Christian's Bible is a drug-store. Its contents remain the same; but the medical practice changes" ("Bible Teaching and Religious Practice," *WIM?* [1973], p. 71). Even in his final years, however, he evinced an intricate knowledge of the Bible as he wrote "fables" based on its characters and events. His title for "To the Person Sitting in Darkness" (1901) came from Matthew 4: 16 in the King James Version. Biblical names and incidents permeated his last writings. Robert Rowlette—"Mark Twain's Barren Trees in *The Mysterious Stranger*: Two Biblical Parallels," *Mark Twain Journal* 16.1 (Winter 1971): 19–20—pointed out how Twain blended two of Christ's miracles in Matthew (21: 18–22) and Mark (11: -1–14, 20–24) in portraying acts by Satan in *The Mysterious Stranger*. In an Autobiographical Dictation of 30 May 1907 Twain alluded to the account in 1 Kings 17 of how "the ravens fed Elijah" (*AutoMT* 3: 67). A famous phrase from Matthew—"Strait is the way and narrow is the gate"—figured in his recollection on 2 December 1907 of an earlier conversation with Andrew Carnegie (*AutoMT* 3: 188). In 1909, angry at Ralph Ashcroft, Clemens likened him to Ananias, struck dead for telling a lie under oath in Acts 5: 1–10 (*AutoMT* 3: 331). (A few years earlier Mark Twain had similarly compared Mary Baker Eddy to "the lamented Ananias" in "Mrs. Eddy in Error," *North American Review* 176.557 [April 1903]: 517.) A letter he wrote on 30 June 1909 kiddingly mentioned the "raising of Lazarus, b'Jesus" (ALS, Special Collections, Washington University Libraries).

Mark Twain's attitude toward the Bible is complex enough to have led a number of scholars to treat the topic in greater detail than is possible here. Alexander Jones paid attention to Mark Twain's use of the Bible in "Mark Twain and Religion" (Doctoral dissertation, University of Minnesota, 1950). Allison Ensor published a brief but quite helpful study, *Mark Twain and the Bible*, in 1969. Ensor concluded that "there is not much evidence that he read the Bible systematically; his citations of the Bible could more often than not have come from sermons, conversations, or memories of Sunday school teaching" (*MT&B*, p. 99). However, various copies of the Bible that Clemens read have gradually become available, and there is now evidence of his rather thorough study in his heavily annotated Bible in the Harry Ransom Center at the University of Texas in Austin, as well as in other surviving copies. Ensor's succinct volume is worth reading

nonetheless for its valuable section on Mark Twain's three major biblical images: the Prodigal Son, the Fall of Man (Adam and Eve), and Noah and the Flood (pp. 29–72). Robert A. Rees produced a helpful doctoral dissertation, "Mark Twain and the Bible: Characters Who Use the Bible and Biblical Characters" (University of Wisconsin, 1966), that was far more detailed than most studies of Twain's familiarity with the Christian Bible. Earl Reimer followed in 1970 with "Mark Twain and the Bible: An Inductive Study" (Doctoral dissertation, Michigan State University, 1970), which included a useful concordance to Mark Twain's biblical references in his published writings. Reimer was interested in tone, purpose, and technique, and placed Twain's biblical allusions "nearer 3000 than 1000" (p. 7). This became the first effort to catalogue these allusions, though it was admittedly incomplete because it lacked access to materials in the Mark Twain Papers at Berkeley. Other studies—especially those by Stanley Brodwin and Louis J. Budd—commented on Mark Twain's use of individual books of the Bible. Brodwin's "The Humor of the Absurd: Mark Twain's Adamic Diaries," *Criticism* 14.1 (Winter 1972): 49–64, which examined Mark Twain's efforts to transmogrify the Adamic biblical myth, along with Brodwin's "The Theology of Mark Twain: Banished Adam and the Bible," *Mississippi Quarterly* 29 (Spring 1976): 167–189, demonstrating Twain's familiarity with Biblical characters and topics in its powerful first story, showed what can be done in following a fertile theme in Twain's works. A significant number of studies have focused on the Book of Exodus, since there are multiple echoes of the Moses story in *Adventures of Huckleberry Finn*. Louis J. Budd's highly informative "Mark Twain on Joseph the Patriarch," *American Quarterly* 16.4 (Winter 1964): 577–586 followed Twain's fascination with that Old Testament story throughout his writings, and incidentally treated contemporary American sentiments about the biblical figure Joseph.

The Bible According to Mark Twain, ed. Howard G. Baetzhold and Joseph McCullough (Athens: University of Georgia Press, 1995) demonstrated Twain's highly creative uses of the Bible and traced dozens of his allusions. Many other secondary sources are available: Helen C. Van Grundy, "The Influence of the Bible on the Major Works of Mark Twain," Master's thesis, Southwest Texas State University, 1953; Kenneth S. Lynn, *Mark Twain and Southwestern Humor* (Boston: Little, Brown and Co., 1959), pp. 208, 211, 213, 243 (on Moses and the Pharoah); Betty L. Sloan, "Biblical Allusions in Mark Twain's Long Narratives," Master's thesis, Oklahoma State University, 1963 (115 pp.); Allison Ensor, "Twain's *Adventures of Huckleberry Finn*, Chapter 37," *Explicator* 27 (1967): item 20; Thomas Werge, "Mark Twain and the Fall of Adam," *Mark Twain Journal* 15.2 (Summer 1970): 5–13; Robert D. Arner, "Acts Seventeen and *Huckleberry Finn*: A Note on Silas Phelps' Sermon," *Mark Twain Journal* 16.2 (1972): 12; Billy G. Collins, "Huckleberry Finn: A Mississippi Moses," *Journal of Narrative Technique* 5.2 (May 1975): 86–104; Kenneth Seib, "Moses and the Bulrushers: A Note on *Huckleberry Finn*," *Mark Twain Journal* 18.4 (Summer 1977): 13–15 (focusing on Exodus 2:1–15); William R. Macnaughton, *Mark Twain's Last Years as a Writer*

(Columbia: University of Missouri Press, 1979), 152–153 (concerning Matthew 4–5); Joseph B. McCullough, "Uses of the Bible in *Huckleberry Finn*," *Mark Twain Journal* 19.3 (Winter 1978–1979): 2–3; Allison R. Ensor, "Mark Twain's Yankee and the Prophets of Baal," *American Literary Realism* 14.1 (Spring 1981): 38–42, citing parallels in 1 Kings 18 involving "Elijah's contest with the prophets of Baal, carried out on Mount Carmel" following King Ahab's accusations (p. 38); Tom Quirk, "The Legend of Noah and the Voyage of Huckleberry Finn," *Mark Twain Journal* 21.2 (Summer 1982): 21–23; Earl F. Briden, "Huck's Great Escape: Magic and Ritual," *Mark Twain Journal* 21.3 (Spring 1983): 17–18 (on the Mosaic dimension of the novel); Stanley Brodwin, "Mark Twain in the Pulpit: The Theological Comedy of *Huckleberry Finn*," *One Hundred Years of Huckleberry Finn: The Boy, His Book, and American Culture*, ed. Robert Sattelmeyer and J. Donald Crowley [Columbia: University of Missouri Press, 1985], pp. 371–385; Robert Sattelmeyer, "'Interesting, but Tough': *Huckleberry Finn* and the Problem of Tradition," *One Hundred Years of Huckleberry Finn*, pp. 357–363, 368–370; Jon Powell, "Trouble and Joy from 'A True Story' to *Adventures of Huckleberry Finn*: Mark Twain and the Book of Jeremiah," *Studies in American Fiction* 20.2 (Autumn 1992): 145–154; Kelly Anspaugh, "'I Been There Before': Biblical Typology and *Adventures of Huckleberry Finn*," *American Notes & Queries* 7 (October 1994): 219–223; Anthony J. Berret, "Huck Finn's Library: Reading, Writing, and Intertextuality," *Making Mark Twain Work in the Classroom*, ed. James S. Leonard (Durham: Duke University Press, 1999), pp. 207–208; John S. Bergsma and Scott Hahn, "Noah's Nakedness and the Curse of Canaan," *Journal of Biblical Literature* 124.1 (Spring 2005): 25–40)—regarding the Book of Genesis; Joe B. Fulton, *The Reverend Mark Twain: Theological Burlesque, Form, and Content* (Athens: Ohio State University Press, 2006); Harold K. Bush, Jr., *Mark Twain and the Spiritual Crisis of His Age* (Tuscaloosa: University of Alabama Press, 2007); Lawrence I. Berkove and Joseph Csicsila, *Heretical Fictions: Religion in the Literature of Mark Twain* (Iowa City: University of Iowa Press, 2010); Jenifer Elmore and C. Dale Girardi, "Reversing the Curse: Slavery, Child Abuse, and *Huckleberry Finn*," *American Literary Realism* 49.1 (Fall 2016): 1–20 (concerning the Books of Genesis and I Kings, particularly). See also the Catalog entry for "The Lord's Prayer."

BIBLE. ENGLISH. N.D. *The Holy Bible, Containing the Old and New Testaments*. King James Version. Brown leather, gilt lettering. Loose spine. Oxford: University of Oxford Press, n.d. Sold by Thomas Nelson and Sons, New York, n. d. No page numbers.

Inscription: "O. L. S. Clemens" is embossed in gold lettering on front cover.

Location: Mark Twain Library, Redding, Connecticut.

Copy examined: Most likely Olivia Clemens's copy (Olivia Louise Clemens), although it might have been Susy Clemens's confirmation Bible (Olivia Susan Clemens). In either case, the extra initial in the embossed name is puzzling. A Library accession number "4520" was written in pencil and in red ink. The Book of Genesis is loose in the binding. Examined in 1970, in June 1982, and again

on 8 November 2019.

BIBLE. ENGLISH. N.D. *The Holy Bible*. Illus. Springfield, Mass.: W. J. Holland, n.d. 1494 pp.

Source: MTLAcc, entry #1, volume donated by Clemens.

BIBLE. ENGLISH. N.D. *Holy Bible*. N.p., n.d. 1061 pp. Lacks title page.

Source: MTLAcc, entry #2309, volume donated from Clemens's library by Clara Clemens Gabrilowitsch in 1910.

BIBLE. ENGLISH. 1817. *The Holy Bible: Containing the Old and New Testaments, Together with the Apocrypha*. King James Version. Philadelphia: M. Carey, 1817. 1080 pp. Bound in at the rear is *A Brief Concordance to the Holy Scriptures of the Old and New Testaments . . . by John Brown* (1722–1787), 72 pages, with a publication date of 1818.

Marginalia: contains handwritten Clemens-Lampton "Family Records" at pages 834–835. Loose fragmentary notes by Jane Lampton Clemens scattered throughout volume.

Catalogs: ListABP (1910), "Bible", no other information provided; 17 January 1944 Charles Retz, Inc. appraisal (p. 5). Valued at $10.

Location: Mark Twain Papers, Bancroft Library, University of California at Berkeley.

Copy examined: Jane Lampton Clemens's copy. When Mollie Clemens died in 1904 (Orion had died in 1897), Clemens requested only two specific books from her executor: John Marshall Clemens's encyclopedia "& my mother's old illustrated family Bible, if it still exists" (Clemens to Mr. Carpenter, Florence, 14 Feb. 1904, MTP).

BIBLE. ENGLISH. 1827. *The Holy Bible*. Oxford: Clarendon Press by Samuel Collingwood and Co., 1827.

Provenance: an explanatory card in the book reported: "Mark Twain's Bible, found at the American Publishing Company, when the company went out of business." Donated to the Mark Twain House and Museum in Hartford by Mrs. John Helmer Johnson in 1957.

Location: belonged to the Mark Twain House and Museum in Hartford, Connecticut for several decades. Reported as "missing" from the Mark Twain Collection in the Stowe-Day Library, where it was being kept, in August 1987.

Copy examined: conceivably a copy Clemens once had an opportunity to see or use. I inspected it in 1970, concluding that the book represented a dubious addition to Clemens's personal library.

BIBLE. ENGLISH. [1841]. *The Comprehensive Bible, Containing the Old and New Testaments*. Original full black morocco, elaborately gilt, raised bands, gilt compartments, all edges gilt. London: Printed for Samuel Bagster. Hartford: Republished by H. Huntington, Jun., 1841.

Inscription: a letter affixed at the center of the cover reads "Mr. & Mrs. J. Langdon/Presented by/T. S. Berry."

Marginalia: the three genealogy leaves preceding the New Testament are filled with Langdon family births, deaths, and marriages from 1804 to 1873. No births are recorded after 1817, no deaths after 1873, and no marriages after 1814. A large hand-embroidered silk page-marker is laid in at the New Testament.

Location: collection of Kevin Mac Donnell, Austin, Texas. Acquired from the Langdon family in May 2016 (email, Mac Donnell to Alan Gribben, 16 May 2016).

Source: detailed description of the volume, with "no markings in text," sent on 9 June 2016 by Mac Donnell to Gribben.

This book would have been available to Clemens in the Langdon family library.

BIBLE. ENGLISH. [1846]. *The Holy Bible: Containing the Old and New Testaments According to the Authorized Version, with Introductory and Concluding Remarks to Each Book.* The half-title page reads *The Miniature Quarto Bible.* Brown leather, gilt lettering. London: Samuel Bagster and Sons, n.d. [The editor's preface is dated 1846.] 1,338 pp. plus index. [Despite the descriptive term "miniature," this is a very large, oversize volume.]

Location: Mark Twain Library, Redding, Connecticut. It shows a red ink accession number ("4518") as well as a later black ink accession number ("2205").

Copy examined: an unmarked copy believed by Peggy Sanford, a former librarian of the Mark Twain Library, Redding, Connecticut, to have once formed part of Clemens's personal library. She showed this copy to me in 1970, and I examined it again in June 1982 and once more on 10 November 2019. One wishes that the second accession list would turn up to confirm the actual donor, but it does seem quite likely that this was among the books that Clara Clemens Gabrilowitsch gave to the Mark Twain Library.

In a letter of 13 May 1869 Clemens urged Olivia Langdon: "You must take the Bagster Bible once more, & transcribe the next section of sequences in the life of Christ & send to me. . . . I must ask you to follow the old plan again" (*MTLet* 3: 225). The prominent London publisher Samuel Bagster (1772–1851) gained fame for his elaborately annotated editions of the Christian Bible.

BIBLE. ENGLISH. 1855. *Holy Bible.* New York: American Bible Society, 1855. 768 pp.

Source: MTLAcc, entry #2311, volume donated from Clemens's library by Clara Clemens Gabrilowitsch in 1910.

BIBLE. ENGLISH. 1860. *The Holy Bible, Containing the Old and New Testaments, Translated Out of the Original Tongues; and with the Former Translations Diligently Compared and Revised.* Philadelphia: J. B. Lippincott & Co., 1860.

Inscriptions: inscribed on the front pastedown endpaper: "Mark Twain for Joe Ed. Weller, 11/28/76". Another inscription in very light pencil reads, "Elisabeth M Miller/A gift from my Aunt[?] Miller". A bookplate has been removed.

Catalog: Ball 2016 inventory, black boards, gilt design and lettering, gilt edge pages, good condition.

Location: Quarry Farm library shelves, under the supervision of the Mark Twain Archive, Elmira College, Elmira, New York.

Clemens had access to this copy of the Bible whenever he visited Quarry Farm in Elmira.

BIBLE. ENGLISH. 1862. *The Holy Bible, Containing the Old and New Testaments, Translated Out of the Original Tongues; and with the Former Translations Diligently Compared and Revised.* New York: American Bible Society, 1862.

Inscription: "Mary E. Clemens,/Carson City,/December 25, 1863."

Marginalia: contains detailed Clemens family records compiled by Mary (Mollie) Clemens, Samuel Clemens's sister-in-law. On the flyleaf Mollie noted sadly: "Jennie commenced to read this through, and read as far as page

16 or 17." Mollie's daughter died in 1864.

Provenance: given by Mollie Clemens to Mrs. Joseph Montgomery Casey of Fort Madison, Iowa, shortly before Mollie passed away in 1904. It was never actually in Samuel L. Clemens's possession. A description of the book and photocopies of Mollie's genealogy were sent to the Mark Twain Papers in 1968 by Rachel M. Varble, Fort Mitchell, Kentucky.

Location: currently unknown.

BIBLE. ENGLISH. 1863. *The Holy Bible, Containing the Old and New Testaments.* King James Version. Oxford: Oxford University Press for the British and Foreign Bible Society, 1863. [Unpaged.]

Inscription: the flyleaf is inscribed in purple ink by Clemens: "Mrs. Jane Clemens/From Her Son—/Jerusalem, Sept. 24, 1867." Below that is an illegible inscription in faded ink ending "by O. C." Wooden covers; front cover stamped: "Mrs. Jane Clemens from her son."

Catalogs: ListABP (1910), "Bible (Clemens family)"; 17 January 1944 Charles Retz, Inc. appraisal, p. 4, valued at $50.

Location: Mark Twain Papers, Bancroft Library, University of California at Berkeley.

Copy examined: Jane Lampton Clemens's copy.

BIBLE. ENGLISH. 1866. *The Holy Bible, Containing the Old and New Testaments: Translated Out of the Original Tongues; and with the Former Translations Diligently Compared and Revised.* King James Version. London: George E. Eyre and William Spottiswoode for the British and Foreign Bible Society, 1866.

Inscription: signed in pencil on the flyleaf opposite the title page: "Saml. Clemens./Constantinople,/Sept. 2, 1867./ Please return this book to stateroom No. 10, in case you happen to borrow it."

Marginalia: pervasive penciled markings, brackets, and underlinings (with a few additions in brown ink) are concentrated most thickly in the New Testament—especially the Book of Matthew. Further annotations in pencil and brown ink occur on the rear flyleaves. Examples: "At 27 goes to C— after temptation & begins his 4 yrs preaching. . . . Fame went abroad in Gal—touched the eyes of the blind—went healing & preaching through Gal. . . . Went to Naz—admired but suspected—They knew his family & his low estate. He wrought few miracles." Clemens chronicled other events in the life of Christ on these rear flyleaves. They bear directly on Chapters 46–56 of *The Innocents Abroad* (1869), where Mark Twain describes Gennesaret, Palestine, Galilee, Capernaum, Nazareth, Jerusalem, and the Garden of Gethsemane.

Catalog: 17 January 1944 Charles Retz, Inc. appraisal (p. 5); valued at $30.

Reported as missing in "Deficiencies of Lincoln Warehouse Inventory," 3 April 1947, in a checklist prepared by the Henry E. Huntington Library and Art Gallery, San Marino, California, p. 3, TS copy in MTP. Thus the Bible was originally part of the Mark Twain Papers, which Clara Clemens Samossoud eventually bequeathed to the University of California at Berkeley.

Location: Harry Ransom Center, University of Texas, Austin. Purchased in 1962 from Margarete Willson as part of the Mark Twain Collection assembled by her husband

Frank C. Willson (1889–1960) of Melrose, Massachusetts.

Copy examined: Clemens's copy, used during his tour of the Holy Land in 1867. The volume is leather-bound, with a metal clasp.

Gribben, "Mark Twain's Library Books in the Humanities Research Center" (1979): 13.

BIBLE. ENGLISH. 1867. *Holy Bible.* Glasgow: W. Collins, S. & Co., 1867. 977 pp.

Source: MTLAcc, entry #2312, volume donated from Clemens's library by Clara Clemens Gabrilowitsch in 1910.

BIBLE. ENGLISH. 1869. *The Holy Bible, Containing the Old and New Testaments.* King James Version. Illustrated with chromolithographs. Original full brown morocco, elaborately embossed, gilt, raised bands, brass clasp. Oxford: Oxford University Press, 1869. The front cover is lettered in gilt: "Mother's Gift" in Gothic type.

Inscriptions: the genealogy leaves before the New Testament record the wedding on 12 October 1870 of Charles and Ida Langdon and the births of their three children: Julia (1871), Jervis (1875), and Ida (1880). No other markings.

Location: collection of Kevin Mac Donnell, Austin, Texas. Acquired from the Langdon family in 2016 (Mac Donnell to Alan Gribben, 30 August 2017).

Here was another Bible accessible to Clemens whenever he visited the Langdon residence in Elmira, New York.

BIBLE. ENGLISH. 1872. *The Holy Bible Containing the Old and New Testaments According to the Authorized Version.* Illustrated by [Paul] Gustave Doré (1832–1883). 2 vols. London, New York: Cassell, Petter, and Galpin, [1872–1876]. [This edition is conjectured, based on the reference below.]

Chief Inspector Blunt refers to the Bible illustrated by Doré ("the Doré costs a hundred dollars a copy, Russian leather, beveled") during an interrogation he conducts in Chapter 1 of Mark Twain's "The Stolen White Elephant" (1882).

BIBLE. ENGLISH. 1872. *The Holy Bible Containing the Old and New Testaments Translated Out of the Original Tongues; and with the Former Translations Diligently Compared and Revised.* Royal 8vo., leatherbound. New York: American Bible Society, 1872.

Inscriptions: "MR. & MRS. CLEMENS" is stamped in gold on the cover. A laid in bookmark has the name "Clara Clemens" written several times in ink in a young hand, together with a name that appears to be "Miss Lulu Bowman". Two locks of hair are also laid in the volume, as is the October page from a Catholic 1903 calendar and some other items that appear to be of a later date.

Provenance: unknown.

Source: Christopher Martin of San Francisco brought this volume to the Mark Twain Papers on 7 January 1999 seeking assistance for authenticating it as an association item. The book had recently been given to his family by an unidentified elderly man.

Copy examined: photocopies of the front page and the bookmark. This qualifies as a possible but very mysterious addition to the Clemens family library.

BIBLE. ENGLISH. 1874. *New Illustrated Bible for the Young; With a Brief History of Each Book Prefixed to the Same, . . . The Whole Designed to Make Plain, and Quicken the Interest of Youthful Readers in, the Word of God.* Ed. by George Maclean. 150 illustrations. Philadelphia: American Family Bible Publishing Co., cop. 1874. 500 pp.

Inscription: gilt-stamped on the front cover: "Susie and Clara". Gold lettering also reads: "Honor Thy Father and Thy Mother."

Source: MTLAcc, entry #1216, volume donated by Clemens.

Provenance: listed in the card catalog of the Mark Twain Library, Redding, Connecticut, but missing in 1970 and thereafter.

Catalog: *Mott 1952*, #72, $12.50.

The Philadelphia subscription book publisher George Maclean issued numerous titles on varied subjects in the 1860s and 1870s. In addition to permitting the edition of *New Illustrated Bible for the Young* sponsored by the American Family Bible Publishing Company, Maclean's firm also released and promoted this work under its own imprint in 1874. Maclean drew on the research of more than a dozen Biblical commentators and the drawings of various illustrators in compiling this work.

BIBLE. ENGLISH. [1875]. *The English Version of the Polyglot Bible, Containing the Old and New Testaments* [bound with] *Cruden's Concordance.* "Facsimile Large Edition." Original full maroon morocco, gilt, all edges gilt. London: Samuel Bagster, n.d. [Also contains a separate imprint of the Apocrypha, following the New Testament.]

Inscription: none, but the Bible seems to be missing a half title page or a blank leaf before the title page.

Marginalia: Three ink notes written by Olivia Clemens in the margins relate Susy Clemens's progress in learning the scriptures in 1877 and 1878. In Exodus XX Olivia made a note in purple ink: "Susie began to learn the com[mandments] March 18th, 1877—finished July 1877." Another note in purple ink appears at Psalms XXIII: "Susie finished learning Jan. 1878." At Matthew V, Olivia made another note in purple ink: "Susie finished learning the beatitudes March 11th, 1877." Olivia Clemens made a pencil note on the rear flyleaf: "Lessons begin in Aix les Bains, June 28th '91/Luke IX 23rd-26th." There are numerous purple ink and pencil notes by Olivia Clemens and probably another family member throughout the Books of Genesis, Exodus, Esther, Psalms, Proverbs, Jeremiah, Matthew, Luke, John, Ephesians, Colossians, Revelation, and Romans. A number of marked passages pertain to the subject of lying. A calling card with Olivia Langdon Clemens's maiden name is laid in the volume.

Provenance: black ink accession number ("3134") and twenty-one purple stamps of the Mark Twain Library in Redding, Connecticut. A library pocket and a library charge slip have been removed from the rear free and pastedown endpapers.

Catalog: *Mott 1952*, #51, $45.

Location: collection of Kevin Mac Donnell, Austin, Texas.

Copy examined: Susy and Olivia Clemens's copy, in July 2004.

This could conceivably be the Bible to which Clemens refers in a letter written to William Dean Howells from Florence on 6 June 1904 following Olivia Clemens's death: "To-day, treasured in her worn old Testament, I found a dear & gentle letter from you . . . about our poor Susy's death. I am tired & old; I wish I were with Livy" (*MTHL*, p. 785). Clemens owned another Samuel Bagster copy of *The Apocrypha* (see the Catalog entry below among the New Testament editions).

BIBLE. ENGLISH. 1885. *Holy Bible*. Revised Edition. New York: Harper & Brothers, 1885. 514 pp.

> Source: MTLAcc, entry #1364, volume donated by Clemens.

BIBLE. GERMAN. 1874. *Die Bibel nach der deutschen uebersetzung von d. Martin Luthers*. Portrait. Leipzig, 1874.

> Catalog: *A1911*, "12mo, stamped roan, Leipzig, 1874," lot 41, sold for $1.

BIBLE. NEW TESTAMENT. ENGLISH. [Edition unknown].

> John Marshall Clemens owned a copy of the New Testament, according to the appraisal of his personal property at the time of his death in 1847 as reported by John Francis McDermott ("Mark Twain and the Bible," *Papers on Language and Literature* 4.2 [Spring 1968]: 195–198). McDermott's brief note reprints a comic letter by Mark Twain joking about his knowledge of Bible passages; at its conclusion, however, McDermott appends the contents of John Marshall Clemens's small personal library that was revealed by the appraisal of his property filed after his death in 1847 in the Marion County Probate Court, Palmyra, Missouri (p. 198). McDermott consulted these files to "show that Clemens could have read the Bible as a boy" (p. 198). The elder Clemens owned only twenty-five or thirty books, mostly volumes of Missouri law cases (p. 198). One large Bible and two small ones also appear in the list of his estate.

BIBLE. NEW TESTAMENT. ENGLISH. 1859. *The New Testament of Our Lord and Saviour Jesus Christ*. "159th edition." Original black cloth. New York: American Bible Society, 1859. 306 pp.

> Inscription: two front flyleaves are missing. The front pastedown endpaper is signed in a round, youthful hand: "Sam./Samuel/Clemens."
>
> Marginalia: a few markings in ink in the Book of Matthew.
>
> Provenance: contains a red-ink accession number of the Mark Twain Library, Redding, Connecticut. Donated from Clemens's library by Clara Clemens Gabrilowitsch in 1910 (MTLAcc, entry #2313).
>
> Catalog: *Mott 1952*, #73, $85.
>
> Location: Albert and Shirley Small Special Collections Library, University of Virginia, Charlottesville. Donated by Clifton Waller Barrett.
>
> Copy examined: Clemens's copy, in 1970. He probably had this book with him during his piloting days on the Mississippi River. That would make it one of the earliest books we know him to have owned and kept.
>
> Clemens's allusions to the New Testament were numerous and sometimes subtle. Interviewed in Australia in 1895 he remarked, "What is humor? It is as difficult almost to answer as the more important question put by Pilate," referring to John 18.38, "What is truth?" (Gary Scharnhorst, *Complete Interviews*, p. 204).

BIBLE. NEW TESTAMENT. ENGLISH. 1863. *The New Testament and Psalms, Translated Out of the Original Greek*. Brown morocco, blind-tooled. New York, 1863.

> Marginalia: numerous pencil and ink notes on the front and rear flyleaves.
>
> Catalogs: *A1911*, "24mo, morocco (worn), with numerous notes on the fly-leaves, N. Y. 1863," a card containing Clemens's notes (on the verso of a 1905 note about his seventieth birthday) laid in, lot 362; Anderson Auction Galleries (New York City), Catalog number 1027 (28–29

April 1914), "18mo, brown morocco, blind-tooled, New York, 1863, "Mark Twain's copy of the New Testament. . . . Pencil and ink notations at the front and back of the book," contains the *A1911* sale label, lot 148.

BIBLE. NEW TESTAMENT. ENGLISH. 1865. *New Testament*. New York: American Bible Union, 1865. 979 pp.

> Source: MTLAcc, entry #2310, volume donated from Clemens's library by Clara Clemens Gabrilowitsch in 1910.

BIBLE: NEW TESTAMENT. ENGLISH. 1867. *Holy Bible. The New Testament*. Original black leather spine, raised bands, gilt, with inlaid cedar, ebony, and olive wood boards, front cover titled in Hebrew. London: Printed by George E. Eyre & William Spottiswoode, 1867.

> Inscription: Charley Langdon's penciled initials are visible at the rear. [Evidently he acquired this book during the *Quaker City* excursion. The foot of the spine is lettered "Jerusalem" and the front pastedown endpaper consists of a view of the ancient city.]
>
> Location: collection of Kevin Mac Donnell, Austin, Texas. Acquired from the Langdon family in May 2016 (email, Mac Donnell to Alan Gribben, 16 May 2016).
>
> Source: detailed description of the volume sent on 9 June 2016 by Mac Donnell to Gribben.

BIBLE. NEW TESTAMENT. ENGLISH. 1869. *The New Testament of Our Lord and Saviour Jesus Christ*. Original full morocco, spine and front board stamped in gilt, front joint repaired. London: Strahan & Co., 1869.

> Inscription: the title page is inscribed by Olivia Clemens in ink: "The Clemens's/S. L. & O. L./Feby 2d 1870". This was the day that Clemens and Olivia Langdon were married.
>
> Marginalia: two passages marked for reading in the Epistle of Paul the Apostle to the Ephesians, "Feb. 2, 1870—12 p.m./ also [p.] 388 (13)." (The latter notation is in another hand.)
>
> Catalogs: *A1911*, "12mo, morocco, gilt edges, Lond. 1869," quotes the signature, lot 361, sold for $5 (sold to the "Mark Twain Company"); *C1951*, 39C, $105, listed among books signed by Clemens; "Property from the Library of Mark Twain," Butterfield & Butterfield, San Francisco, Sale 6613 (16 July 1997), lot 2667.
>
> Provenance: in 1970 this volume was reportedly owned by Dr. Max Lewis Busch, Pasadena, California.
>
> Location: Mark Twain House and Museum, Hartford, Connecticut. Purchased in 1997.
>
> Copy examined: Clemens's copy, shared with Olivia. Viewed in Hartford in 1997.

BIBLE. NEW TESTAMENT. ENGLISH. 1881. *New Testament*. Oxford, England: University Press, 1881. 332 pp.

> Source: MTLAcc entry #910, volume donated by Clemens.

BIBLE. NEW TESTAMENT. ENGLISH. 1881. *New Testament*. Revised Version. New York: Harper & Brothers, 1881. 442 pp.

> Source: MTLAcc, entry #1471, volume donated by Clemens.

BIBLE. NEW TESTAMENT. ENGLISH. 1881. *New Testament*. Revised Version. American Edition. New York: Harper & Brothers, 1881. 652 pp.

> Source: MTLAcc, entry #1813, volume donated by Clemens.

BIBLE. NEW TESTAMENT. ENGLISH. 1881. *The New Testament of Our Lord and Saviour Jesus Christ: Translated Out of the Original Greek and with the Former Translations Diligently

Compared and Revised. Philadelphia: Porter & Coates, 1881.

Inscription: signed Olivia L. Langdon, Dec. 1881" [Olivia Lewis Langdon, 1810–1890, widow of Jervis Langdon].

Catalog: Ball 2016, black leather, spine missing, signed by Olivia L. Langdon.

Location: Mark Twain Archive, Elmira College, Elmira, New York.

This Bible was accessible to Clemens whenever he visited the Langdon residence in Elmira.

BIBLE. NEW TESTAMENT. ENGLISH. N.D. *New Testament.* Lacks the title page. Only a fragment of the dedication leaf remains. Rebound in green morocco. Gray folding-case.

Provenance: found in the library of the former Hollywood, California residence of Clara Clemens Samossoud. Letter laid in from Alan Gribben to Nick Karanovich, 29 June 1987, explaining the reasons for believing the book might have once belonged to the Clemens family library. Subsequently in the collection of Nick Karanovich, Fort Wayne, Indiana.

Catalog: *Sotheby's 2003,* #220, $900 (sold with four other miscellaneous titles).

Copy examined: copy possibly from the Clemenses' library. The inscriptions, if any, might have been removed for souvenirs by visitors to the Hollywood home. The property was not well maintained or supervised after a certain point.

BIBLE. NEW TESTAMENT. ARABIC. 1867. *Arabic New Testament, Printed at the American Mission Press.* Presented by the American Mission to [Arabic words] Passenger [*sic*] of the Steamer Quaker City. Beirut, Syria, September 1867. [This explanation appears as a printed English-language label affixed to the front pastedown endpaper.]

Inscription: on the front free endpaper Clemens wrote in ink: "At Sea, October, 1867./To Sammy Moffett—/From his Uncle Sam'l./Read this book carefully, Sammy, & study its precepts well. In urging this, I am inspired by the hope that you will derive as much satisfaction from its perusal as I have done. No words can express the comfort this little book has been to me. Often, in lonely nights at sea, I have taken her down & tackled her, first at one end & then at the other, & finally sailed in at the middle & waltzed out at both ends, while tears of gratitude suffused my eyes for the blessed missionary brick that. . . ." On the recto of the front free endpaper, in a much younger hand, someone (presumably Samuel E. Moffett) has written, rather faintly, "To Sammy Moffett/From his uncle". A price of "$100" appears in the upper corner above this latter inscription.

Marginalia: on the verso of the front free endpaper Clemens noted in ink, "This rose has a history."

Provenance: has the sticker of "F. Rosenzweig/Bookbinder. Beirut" on the rear pastedown endpaper.

Catalog: City Book Auction, Sale number 305 (14 April 1945), "12mo, full 19th century purpose sheep-skin, gilt spine (rubbed), gilt sides, metal corners, gilt edges," quotes the entire "incomplete" inscription, lot 88.

Location: Mark Twain House and Museum, Hartford, Connecticut.

Copy examined: photocopies of the front pastedown endpaper, front free endpaper, and verso of the front free endpaper of a book inscribed by Clemens. These photocopies were made in July 1984. I examined the

book itself in August 1987.

BIBLE. NEW TESTAMENT. GERMAN. 1877. *Das Neue Testament unsers Herrn und Heilandes Jesu Christi.* Small, with black cloth cover. New York: Amerikanische Bibel-Gesellschaft, 1877.

Inscription: a bookplate on the front pastedown endpaper contains an inscription to Susy Clemens dated 22 April 1878 indicating that this book was a shipboard gift from a passenger (the name is not legible) on Captain C. L. Brandt's *Holsatia.* Clemens and his family boarded that ship in New York City on 11 April 1878 for a voyage to Hamburg, where they arrived on 25 April 1878 (Fears, *Day by Day* 1.2: 809–810).

Location: Mark Twain Library, Redding, Connecticut.

Copy examined: Susy Clemens's copy. I did not see this volume in 1970 but when I revisited the collection in Redding in June 1982 it had been added to the shelves containing Clemens's library books. It has a red ink Mark Twain Library accession number, "4097".

BIBLE. NEW TESTAMENT. NATIVE AMERICAN. 1661. See the Catalog entry for *Two—and an Indian* (unidentified book).

BIBLE. NEW TESTAMENT. *The Apocrypha.* London: S. Bagster & Sons, n.d. 155 pp.

Source: MTLAcc, entry #911, volume donated by Clemens.

BIBLE. NEW TESTAMENT. *The Apocryphal New Testament; Being All the Gospels, Epistles, and Other Pieces Now Extant . . . Not Included in the New Testament, by Its Compilers in the Authorized New Testament. Translated from the Original Tongues* [by Jeremiah Jones (1693–1724) and William Wake (1657–1737)]. Illus. London: Printed for W[illiam]. Hone, 1821. 251 pp.

Mark Twain made various references to the Apocrypha. An entry in Notebook 8 ("Apochraphal [*sic*] Bible") in 1867 (*N&J* 1: 321) has a clear relationship to the letter Twain wrote from New York City to the San Francisco *Alta California* on 2 June 1867: "In one of the libraries here I have found an edition of 1621 of the Apocryphal New Testament. It is rather a curious book." Twain then quotes numerous miracles attributed to Christ, adding that "one is inclined to wonder why the conclave of 318 Bishops . . . in the fourth century . . . rejected" these particular "ancient manuscripts" (*Alta California,* 4 August 1867). He again referred to the Apocrypha in a letter of 2 June 1867 (*MTTMB,* pp. 251–254). Notebook 9 (1867) alludes to "Christ's 30 years of life in the slow village of Nazareth," perhaps referencing the Apocrypha (*N&J* 1: 426). Chapter 51 of Twain's *The Innocents Abroad* (1869) recounts extraordinary miracles allegedly performed by the infant Christ, citing "an edition of 1621 of the Apocryphal New Testament"; these and other beliefs "have been ruled out of our modern Bible," Twain remarks, even though "they were accepted gospel twelve or fifteen centuries ago." Barbara Schmidt deduced that Clemens had actually consulted an 1821 (NOT 1621) edition of *The Apocryphal New Testament* edited by William Hone; she points out that the text of Hone's edition matches the text that Twain twice quoted (Email, Schmidt to Kevin Mac Donnell and Alan Gribben, 8 September 2015). Benjamin Griffin, a member of the Mark Twain Project editorial team, concurred with Schmidt's conclusion (Email, Griffin to Schmidt, 8 September but 2015). Publisher, bookseller, and political pamphleteer William Hone (1780–1842) first brought out his *Apocryphal New Testament* in 1820; it had various reprintings in England and the United States, including an 1821 edition by Hone.

William M. Gibson noted the influence of the apocryphal books of the New Testament on Twain's "The Chronicle of Young Satan" (written 1897–1900; see especially *MSM*, pp. 46–50). As Gibson observed, "The resemblance of the boy Jesus to Philip Traum is unmistakable" (p. 16). Donald Malcolm—"Mark Twain's Gnostic Old Age: Annihilation and Transcendence in 'No. 44, The Mysterious Stranger,'" *American Literary Realism* 28.2 (Winter 1996): 41–58—referenced Twain's familiarity with "apocryphal Biblical materials" (56.n. 12). See also the Catalog entry for Henry Copley Greene (trans.), *The Gospel of the Childhood of Our Lord Jesus Christ* (1904), a later translation of the boyhood portions of the Apocrypha.

Gladys Bellamy (*MTLA* [1950], pp. 352–353); Coleman O. Parsons ("Background" [1960], pp. 60–61); Albert E. Stone (*IE* [1961], pp. 233–235, 241); William M. Gibson (*MSM* [1969], p. 16 n. 31); David Shapiro-Zysk, "The Separation of Church and Twain: Deist Philosophy in *The Innocents Abroad*," *Mark Twain Annual 4* (2006): 25–32.

BIBLE. NEW TESTAMENT. *Apocryphal New Testament*. Boston: Colby & Rich, 1882. 291 pp.
Source: MTLAcc, entry #925, volume donated by Clemens.

BIBLE. OLD TESTAMENT. ENGLISH. *Old Testament. Revised Version*. 4 vols. Cambridge: University Press, 1885.
Source: MTLAcc, entries #1809–#1812, volumes donated by Clemens.

BIBLE. OLD TESTAMENT. ENGLISH. *The Book of Psalms*. Large type edition. Original flexible black morocco, gilt, all edges gilt. New York: American Bible Society, 1868.
Inscription: signed on the front flyleaf by Olivia Clemens's mother, Olivia Lewis Langdon (1810–1890): "Mrs. Jervis Langdon." The volume does not contain the usual Jervis Langdon "Family Library" bookplate, perhaps because his wife kept the book for her exclusive use.
Location: collection of Kevin Mac Donnell, Austin, Texas. Acquired from the Langdon family in May 2016 (email, Mac Donnell to Alan Gribben, 16 May 2016).
Source: detailed description of the volume, "no markings in the text," sent on 9 June 2016 by Mac Donnell to Gribben.
This book would have been available to Clemens in the Langdon family library.

Bible Stories in Bible Language. New York: D. Appleton & Co., 1869. 197 pp.
Source: MTLAcc, entry #918, volume donated by Clemens.

Bibliothèque Morale de La Jeunesse (1858).
This vague title appeared in Albert E. Stone, Jr.'s catalog of Clemens's books that he found in the Mark Twain Library, Redding, Connecticut in 1955, but in 1970 I was unable to locate any volume bearing an imprint of that French juvenile fiction series. Stone was not certain that the book had belonged to Clemens or his family; it contained a "French schoolboy's bookmark."

BICKERSTETK, EDWARD HENRY (1825–1906). *Yesterday, To-day, and Forever; A Poem, in Twelve Books*. New York: R. Carter & Brothers, 1870. 441 pp.
Source: MTLAcc, entry #634, volume donated by Clemens.

BIERCE, AMBROSE GWINETT (1842–1914?). *Cobwebs from an Empty Skull* (published in 1874).

Bierce and Clemens dined together at the Whitefriars Club in the fall of 1872 during Bierce's stay in England. Seven fables in Bierce's *Cobwebs from an Empty Skull* would be included in *Mark Twain's Library of Humor* (1888), including "The Dog and the Bees." Clemens declared that Bierce's "exquisite things" for *Fun* [a Victorian weekly] in 1874 were "just delicious" (SLC to C. W. Stoddard, 1 February 1875, *MTLet* 6: 364). "Bierce is in San Francisco, Clemens noted (Clemens to Millet, 7 August 1877, Harvard). "Bierce's Fables," Clemens jotted (NB 19, [July 1880], *N&J* 2: 366); a similar entry was repeated in 1881 (p. 429). Clemens mentioned Bierce as a West Coast ally in a letter to J. B. Pond, 24 May 1895 (Berg). On 6 May 1906 Bierce recalled that he had met Clemens "two or three times. . . . I think pretty well of him, but doubt if he cared for me and can't, at the moment, think of any reason why he *should* have cared for me" (Grenander, pp. 474–475). "Ambrose Bierce, who is still writing acceptably for the magazines to-day," is how Clemens referred to Bierce in 1906 (13 June 1906 Autobiographical Dictation, *MTE*, p. 262; *AutoMT* 2: 118).

M. E. Grenander—"California's Albion: Mark Twain, Ambrose Bierce, Tom Hood, John Camden Hotten, and Andrew Chatto," *Papers of the Bibliographical Society of America* 72.4 (1978): 455–475—provided a judicious overview of their acquaintance. Lawrence I. Berkove discussed the impact of the West on Twain and Bierce in "The Sagebrush School Revived," *A Companion to the Regional Literatures of America*, ed. Charles Crow (Malden, Massachusetts: Blackwell, 2003), pp. 324–343. Berkove subsequently dissected the sometimes respectful, sometimes tense Twain-Bierce relationship in "Kindred Rivals: Mark Twain and Ambrose Bierce," *Critical Insights: Mark Twain*, ed. R. Kent Rasmussen (Pasadena, California: Salem Press, 2011), pp. 110–135. See also Ben Tarnoff, *The Bohemians: Mark Twain and the San Francisco Writers Who Reinvented American Literature* (New York: Penguin Press, 2014), pp. 184–185 *passim*.

——— [pseud. "Dod Grile"]. *Nuggets and Dust Panned Out in California by Dod Grile*. London: Chatto & Windus, 1873.
Clemens's references to Bierce were generally favorable, but on 8 April 1874 he wrote from Hartford to Chatto & Windus with a condemnatory verdict. Although "'Dod Grile' (Mr. Bierce) is a personal friend of mine, & I like him exceedingly," Clemens began, *Nuggets and Dust* "is the vilest book that exists in print—or very nearly so. . . . Bierce has written some admirable things—fugitive pieces—but none of them are among the 'Nuggets.'. . . For every laugh . . . there are five blushes, ten shudders & a vomit. The laugh is too expensive" (*MTLet* 6: 101–102).

M. E. Grenander, "'Five Blushes, Ten Shudders and a Vomit': Mark Twain on Ambrose Bierce's *Nuggets and Dust*," *American Literary Realism* 17.2 (Autumn 1984): 169–179, quoted Clemens's letter, thoughtfully analyzed Bierce's volume of essays, sketches, and speculated about what circumstances might have aroused Clemens's ire.

BIGELOW, EDITH EVELYN (JAIFRAY) (1861–1939). *Diplomatic Disenchantments, A Novel*. New York: Harper & Brothers, 1895. 235 pp.
Source: MTLAcc, entry #1676, volume donated by

Clemens.

Bigelow based this novel on her travel experiences with her husband Poultney Bigelow.

BIGELOW, JOHN (1817–1911). *The Mystery of Sleep.* New York: Harper & Brothers, 1905. 226 pp.

Source: MTLAcc, entry #1386, volume donated by Clemens.

Citing authorities as diverse as Pliny, Ovid, the Bible, Mohammed, Dante, Voltaire, and Swedenborg, Bigelow sets out to prove "that we are developed spiritually during our sleeping hours" (p. iv) and that dreams are important and usually valid.

———. *The Principles of Strategy, Illustrated Mainly from American Campaigns.* First edition. Large 4to. Original red cloth, gilt, 32 folding maps. London: T. Fisher Unwin, 1891. 200 pp.

Inscription: (by the author's son) "To S. L. Clemens—a very interesting book from a friend to both book and S. L. C., Poultney Bigelow, June 1, [19]00." Evidently Clemens received this book in London, where he and Poultney Bigelow often socialized.

Provenance: several marks and numbers indicate preparation for processing and shelving this volume in the Mark Twain Library in Redding, Connecticut, but there are none of the usual purple library stamps.

Catalog: Howard S. Mott Rare Books and Autographs, Sheffield, Massachusetts, September 1989, $300. "We know nothing about the provenance of the Bigelow book. It came to us in a collection of military books formed by a collector" (Howard S. Mott to Alan Gribben, 9 September 1989).

Location: collection of Kevin Mac Donnell, Austin, Texas.

Copy examined: Clemens's copy, unmarked, in July 2004.

Pages 161–200 and twenty of the maps in *The Principles of Strategy* focus on the Vicksburg campaign of 1863. John Bigelow, an attorney, newspaper editor, and statesman, had been an important diplomat during the American Civil War, persuading the French that their best interests lay with the Union. While in Paris he discovered the manuscript of Benjamin Franklin's autobiography and published it, also writing a biography of Franklin. He was instrumental in founding the New York Public Library, among other achievements. On 26 October 1875 Clemens had written from Hartford to John Bigelow's wife Jane Tunis Poultney Bigelow: "I ask a thousand pardons, but I spent a week in New York, & business drove the matter clear out of my otherwise empty head, where it was reposing companionless in the midst of a vast & howling solitude." She had requested an autograph (*Sotheby's 2003*, #30).

BIGELOW, POULTNEY (1855–1954). *The Children of the Nations; A Study of Colonization and Its Problems.* Original cloth, cracked front hinge, slight rubbing on edges and corners. New York: McClure, Phillips & Co., 1901. 365 pp.

Inscriptions: inscribed by the author, "To Clara Clemens at/a moment when no one/appreciates the hand/of a friend more than/Poultney Bigelow/Feb. 2, '01." A note that may be in Clara Clemens Samossoud's hand (or that of its purchaser) on the front pastedown endpaper reads: "Purchased from Mark Twain's/Library—April 10 1951/Clara Clemens his/daughter."

Catalogs: ListABP (1910), "Children of the Nations, Bigelow"; *C1951*, J4, listed among books owned by Clara

and Jean Clemens; "Property from the Library of Mark Twain," Butterfield & Butterfield, San Francisco, Sale 6613 (16 July 1997), lot 2711.

Location: Mark Twain House and Museum, Hartford, Connecticut.

Copy examined: Clara Clemens's copy. Viewed in Hartford in 1997.

Almost certainly Bigelow, son of the eminent John Bigelow, would also have sent Clemens himself a complimentary copy of this book, given its fulsome dedication: "To/ Mark Twain/The most philosophic of Travellers,/the most travelled of Philosophers/—who loves his country yet speaks ill of/no other—these pages are dedicated in/sign of affectionate regard by the author." Bigelow's topic, "mother countries" and their colonies, unquestionably would have interested Clemens. Bigelow had been among those who generously tried to give Clemens money after the failure of his publishing business.

———. *The German Emperor and His Eastern Neighbors.* Fiction, Fact, and Fancy Series, ed. Arthur Stedman (1859–1908). New York: Charles L. Webster & Co., 1892. 179 pp.

It seems highly probable that Clemens read this book issued by his own publishing firm. He mentioned Bigelow's name in NB 31 (April 1892), TS p. 38; also in NB 38 (May 1896), TS p. 20. He received a letter of condolence from Bigelow about Susy Clemens's death (Bigelow to Clemens, 24 August 1896, MTP); sent Bigelow a complimentary copy of *Following the Equator* (NB 42, TS p. 74); referred to Bigelow as "that old American friend of the German Emperor's & mine" (Clemens to Andrew Chatto, 24 September 1899, PH in MTP); and spoke at Bigelow's London house-opening on 11 May 1900 (London *Daily Express*, 17 May 1900, p. 2).

———. *History of the German Struggle for Liberty.* 4 vols. Illus. New York: Harper & Brothers, 1899–1905.

Inscription: Volume I is signed in pencil on the front pastedown endpaper: "S L Clemens/steamship 'Irene'/'03" [Clemens added the word "steamship" in black ink]; Volume III is signed in black ink on the front pastedown endpaper: "S. L. Clemens/1903".

Marginalia: a few pencil marks throughout Volume I only.

Catalogs: *C1951*, D30, $12; *Zeitlin 1951*, #7, $20.

Location: Mark Twain Papers, Bancroft Library, University of California at Berkeley. Gift of Jake Zeitlin.

Copies examined: Clemens's copies.

Before sailing for Italy in 1903 Clemens wrote to Frederick A. Duneka of Harper & Brothers: "Won't you send vols. I & II of Poultney Bigelow's History on board the ship?" (21 October 1903, TS in MTP). He gave Duneka the location, stateroom, and sailing hour.

———. *History of the German Struggle for Liberty.* 3 vols. Illustrated by R[ichard]. Caton Woodville (1856–1927). New York: Harper & Brothers, 1903.

Source: MTLAcc, entries #1709 and #1710, volumes donated by Clemens. The set lacks Volume III.

Edgar Hemminghaus noticed Clemens's copy of this set in the Mark Twain Library at Redding in 1945 ("Mark Twain's German Provenience" [1945], p. 475 n. 109), but neither Albert E. Stone (in 1955) nor I (in 1970) could find these volumes.

———. *Paddles and Politics: Down the Danube.* Illus. Original cloth, mild wear. New York: Charles L. Webster & Co., 1892. 253 pp.

Inscription: the front flyleaf, which likely bore an inscription, has been removed. The very light offsetting of an inscription in ink is visible on the pastedown endpaper but cannot be read.

Provenance: sold (but not listed) at the 1951 auction in Hollywood, a not-uncommon slip-up in that hastily compiled sheet.

Catalog: "Property from the Library of Mark Twain," Butterfield & Butterfield, San Francisco, Sale 6613 (16 July 1997) lot 2668.

Location: Mark Twain House and Museum, Hartford, Connecticut.

Copy examined: Clemens's copy, in Hartford in 1997.

How could Clemens have resisted reading this account of a canoe voyage down the "Mississippi of Europe" to the Black Sea, especially one published by his own firm?

BIRCH, SAMUEL.

In Chapter 58 of *Following the Equator* (1897) Mark Twain quotes Captain Birch's account of military action during the Indian mutineers' siege of Lucknow, and his description of the rescue and evacuation of Inglis' forces inside the garrison. Francis Madigan ("Mark Twain's Passage to India," p. 360) discovered that Mark Twain quoted Birch's narrative from Lady Julia Inglis' *The Siege of Lucknow, A Diary.*

BIRD, ROBERT MONTGOMERY (1806–1854). *The Gladiator* (play, performed in 1831).

"I did not like parts of it much, but other portions were really splendid," Clemens wrote of a production that starred the famed actor Edwin Forrest as Spartacus (Clemens to Pamela Moffett, New York City, October 1853, *MTL,* p. 24; *MTLet* 1: 16). Forrest (1806–1872) was not without his detractors, as history shows. Clemens and Olivia later saw Bird's play on 1 February 1884 (Clemens to Howells, Hartford, 2 February 1884, *MTHL,* p. 467).

———. *Nick of the Woods; or The Jibbenainosay* (novel, published in 1837).

In Clemens's "The Mysterious Murders in Risse," a manuscript dated 1 August 1859, the narrator remarks that young Count Ritter von Muller would have been "a genial companion to our own 'Nick of the Woods,'" from whom "he probably borrowed an idea or so" (Jean Webster McKinney Family Papers, Randolph Rare Book Room, Vassar College Library). I am grateful to Robert H. Hirst for noticing this allusion. The fictional "Jibbenainosay" was a ruthless killer of Native Americans. Chapter 55 of Mark Twain's *Life on the Mississippi* (1883) contains the story of a Hannibal carpenter who claimed to be "the Mysterious Avenger" (a sobriquet interestingly similar to the Mysterious Stranger) and supposedly terrorized young Sam Clemens by vowing to murder and mutilate all human beings named Lynch. "This ass had been reading the 'Jibbenainosay,' no doubt, . . . but as I had not yet seen the book then, I took his inventions for truth," explains Twain. Louisa H. Medina (c. 1813–1838) adapted Bird's *Nick of the Woods; or, The Jibbenainosay* for a stage production performed in New York City in 1839. Her tremendously popular melodrama portrayed Native Americans even more unsympathetically than Bird's novel

had. The term "Jibbenainosay" signified an avenging devil. Walter Blair, "French Revolution" (1957), p. 23; Blair, *MT&HF* (1960), p. 117 n. 15; and Blair, *HH&T* (1969), pp. 139, 336–337.

"BIRD WALTZ" (song).

"Bird waltz" was among the music adorning the piano in "The House Beautiful," Chapter 38 of Mark Twain's *Life on the Mississippi* (1883).

BIRKELAND, KNUT BERGESEN (1857–1925). *Light in the Darkness; or, Christianity and Paganism. Reminiscences of a Journey Around the Globe.* Illus. Minneapolis, Minnesota.: Minnehaha Publishing Co., 1900. 669 pp.

Source: MTLAcc entry #577, volume donated by Clemens.

BIRNEY, JAMES G[ILLESPIE] (1792–1857). *Letter to Ministers and Elders, on the Sin of Holding Slaves, and the Duty of Immediate Emancipation.* New York: S. W. Benedict, [1834?]. 18 pp.

Bound with six other pamphlets; see the Catalog entry for William E. Channing, *Letter to J. G. Birney.*

Birney was initially a slave owner in Alabama and then Kentucky, but freed these enslaved people and became an outspoken abolitionist. He relocated to Ohio, where his anti-slavery newspaper proved to be so unpopular that his presses were twice destroyed by pro-slavery mobs. He would run for President on the Liberty Party platform in 1840 and 1844, although he received little national support.

BIRRELL, AUGUSTINE (1850–1933). *Obiter Dicta.* Nineteenth edition. Original green coth, gilt, uncut. London: Eliot Stock, 1896. [Birrell's title can be translated as "incidental remarks" or "unofficial expressions."]

Inscription: signed in black ink, "S L. Clemens/1907/London. June 21." (This was a week before Clemens received his honorary degree from Oxford University.)

Marginalia: Clemens corrected a verb tense in black ink in a sentence on page 172. Not all of the leaves have been opened in the book's seven essays.

Catalog: *A1911,* "12mo, cloth, Lond. 1896," quotes the signature, lot 43, sold for $4.75.

Provenance: bears the bookplate of William Harris Arnold (1854–1923), the author of *Ventures in Book Collecting* (1923). That book did not mention Mark Twain.

Location: collection of Kevin Mac Donnell, Austin, Texas.

Copy examined: Clemens's copy. Examined in Austin in July 2004. Contains the *A1911* sale label.

English politician and barrister Birrell was known for his offbeat humor and his love of books. This was the first collection of his opinionated essays about literary figures and other subjects. On 25 June 1907 Birrell introduced Mark Twain as "a true consolidator of nations" at a Pilgrims Club luncheon held in his honor at the Savoy (Paine, *MTB,* pp. 1389–91; Fears, *Day by Day,* p. 690).

BISHOP, ARTEMAS (1795–1872). *Na Huaolelo a me na olelo kikeke ma ka Beritania a me ka olelo Hawaii, no na Haumana e ao ana i kela a me keia. A Manual of Conversations, Hawaiian and English. Hawaiian Phrase Book.* Honolulu: Henry M. Whitney, 1854.

Clemens referred to it as a "small phrase-book" (Notebook 6 [1866], *N&J* 1: 196, 234–236).

BISHOP, EMILY MONTAGUE (MULKIN) (1858–1916). *Seventy Years Young; or, The Unhabitual Way.* New York: B. W.

Huebsch, 1907. 205 pp.

Source: MTLAcc, entry #843, volume donated by Isabel V. Lyon, Clemens's secretary.

Was this book purchase an effort on Isabel V. Lyon's part to make her employer feel better about his advanced age? Bishop gives health advice and suggests—as inspirational speakers and writers still do—that an aging person is only as old as he thinks he is. Years are "the mere arbitrary measurement of time!" (p. 4). Bishop, alas, only lived to be fifty-eight.

BISHOP, LEVI (1815–1881). *The Poetical Works of Levi Bishop. Third Edition. With a Sketch of the Life of the Author.* Detroit: E. B. Smith & Co., 1876. 547 pp.

Inscription: inscribed on the front flyleaf: "This book belongs to/S. L. Clemens's/Library of Hogwash./Hartford, 1876."

Marginalia: Clemens underlined sentences in the biographical sketch of Bishop, and at its conclusion he wrote: "The record of a respect-worthy & very valuable citizen, whose humble little distinctions & inconsequential achievements have been a great satisfaction to him & a hurt to no one; a nice well-meaning old man, whose only blemish was a penchant for constructing jingling twaddle & regarding it as poetry' (p. xvii). Other marginal notes include "Rot" scrawled at the head of a poem titled "The Oyster" (p. 490). In the margin beside Bishop's definition of poetry (a prose essay, p. 504), Clemens wrote: "This is the ignoramus teaching the ignoramus."

Catalogs: ListABP (1910), "Bishop's Poetical Works"; *C1951*, #49a, $27.50.

Location: The Newberry Library, Chicago, Illinois. Incorrectly cited by Arthur L. Scott (*OPMT* [1966], p. 20) as the property of the Mark Twain Papers in the Bancroft Library at the University of California at Berkeley.

Copy examined: I am grateful to Richard Colles Johnson, then (1978) Bibliographer of the Newberry Library, for providing a photocopy of Clemens's notations for my use.

Levi Bishop was a prominent attorney, politician, and historian in Detroit, Michigan. The final stanza of the poem that Clemens scorned, "The Oyster," is worth quoting: "Away with salad, gobbler, quail,/In quiet, or in royster;/Nor can the ortolan avail;/They all must soon ignobly fail,/Beside the luscious oyster" (p. 490). Another sample, "The Train Whistle" (p. 94) likewise illustrates Bishop's poetic limitations: "While thus from home we travel far,/For pleasure or for gain;/We take, at night, the 'sleeping car;'/Then howls, our slumbers to debar,/The whistle of the train."

BISHOP, WILLIAM HENRY (1847–1928). *Detmold: A Romance* (novel, serialized in the *Atlantic Monthly* from December 1877 through June 1878; published as a book in Boston by Houghton, Osgood & Co., 1879).

Jerome Loving identified Bishop as the "now forgotten" author "with a most acceptable novel" whom Mark Twain remembered in an Autobiographical Dictation of 11 January 1906 (*MTAuto* 2: 266) as having had the bad luck to follow his controversial speech at the Whittier Birthday banquet on 17 December 1877 (Loving, "Twain's Whittier Birthday Speech and Howells," *Howellsian* 8.2 [Fall 2005]: 6; *Mark Twain: The Adventures of Samuel L. Clemens* [Berkeley: University of California Press,

2010], pp. 225–226). *Detmold*, a love story set in Italy, had presumably qualified Bishop to obtain this honored position in the list of speakers.

BISMARCK, OTTO EDUARD LEOPOLD VON (1815–1898). *Bismarck, The Man and the Statesman; Being the Reflections and Reminiscences of Otto, Prince von Bismarck, Written and Dictated by Himself after His Retirement from Office.* Translated from the German by Arthur John Butler (1844–1910). Portraits. 2 vols. New York: Harper & Brothers, 1899. [Edition conjectured.]

When W. B. Northrop interviewed Clemens at Lake Saranac, New York in 1901, Northrop noted, "On the floor near the chair were some books, one of which, 'Bismarck's Memoirs,' is a favourite work with the author" (W. B. Northrop, "Mark Twain in the Woods," New York *World Sunday Magazine*, 21 July 1901, pp. 1–2; *With Pen and Camera: Interviews with Celebrities* [London: R. A. Everertt & Co., 1904], p. 40). Bismarck's *Gedanken und Errinerungen* had been published in Germany in 1898 and the former German Chancellor's autobiography was subsequently translated and published in London in 1898 by Smith and Elder. It seems most likely that in 1901 Clemens would have been in possession of the New York edition of that work.

Rebecca Hooker, "Additions to the Mark Twain Library," *American Literary Realism* 38.3 (Spring 2006): 277.

———. [An identical two-volume copy.]

Catalog: Ball 2016 inventory, 2 vols., no inscriptions noted, blue cloth, gilt lettering, gilt and silver design, good condition.

Location: Quarry Farm library shelves, under the supervision of the Mark Twain Archive, Elmira College, Elmira, New York.

Clemens had access to this book whenever he visited Quarry Farm in Elmira.

———. *The Love Letters of Bismarck; Being Letters to His Fiancée and Wife, 1846–1889.* Translated from the German by Charlton Thomas Lewis (1834–1904). Illus. Black cloth. New York: Harper & Brothers, 1901. 428 pp.

Marginalia: beside some verse quoted by Bismarck (p. 25) Clemens noted in pencil: "I have never seen lines of poetry all of one length before." No other notes or markings.

Provenance: Antenne-Dorrance Collection, Rice Lake, Wisconsin.

Location: Mark Twain Archive, Gannett-Tripp Learning Center, Elmira College, Elmira, New York.

Copy examined: the volume was temporarily on loan when I visited Rice Lake in 1970, but I was eventually able to examine it at Elmira College on 28 May 2015.

BIZET, ALEXANDRE CÉSAR LEOPOLD, CALLED GEORGES (1838–1875). *Carmen* (opera, performed in 1875).

Olivia Clemens wrote to her husband from Paris on 26 April 1894: "On Sunday I saw by the paper that on Monday there would be a representation of 'Carmen' at greatly reduced rates. I thought that was a good time for Susy and me to go" (ALS, quoted in the *Twainian* 37 [May-June 1978]: 4).

BJØRNSON, BJØRNSTJERNE (1832–1910). *A Happy Boy. A Tale of Norwegian Peasant Life.* Translated from the Norwegian by Helen R. A. Gade. Boston: Sever, Francis & Co., 1870. 120 pp.

Source: MTLAcc, entry #1923, volume donated from

Clemens's library by Clara Clemens Gabrilowitsch in 1910.

"Bjornsen's books—Houghton," Clemens wrote in Notebook 22 (1883), *N&J* 3: 41.

BLACK, CLEMENTINA MARIA (1853–1922). *An Agitator; A Novel*. New York: Harper & Brothers, 1895. 177 pp.

> Source: MTLAcc, entry #1320, volume donated by Clemens.
>
> Black was primarily an activist for women's rights who also wrote fiction reflecting her passionate advocacy of the suffragist and trade union movements.

BLACK, WILLIAM (1841–1898). *A Daughter of Heth. A Novel*. New York: Harper & Brothers, n.d. 323 pp.

> Source: MTLAcc, entry #1430, volume donated by Clemens.

———. *Donald Ross of Heimra*. New York: Harper & Brothers, n.d. 355 pp.

> Source: MTLAcc, entry #1517, volume donated by Clemens.

———. *In Far Lochaber; A Novel*. New York: Harper & Brothers, n.d. 299 pp.

> Source: MTLAcc, entry #1516, volume donated by Clemens.
>
> The Scottish-born novelist Black moved to England to enter journalism, but he and his popular fiction often returned to Scotland.

———. *Judith Shakespeare; Her Love Affairs and Other Adventures*. Illustrated by E[dwin]. A[ustin]. Abbey (1852–1911). New York: Harper & Brothers, n.d. 391 pp.

> Source: MTLAcc, entry #1519, volume donated by Clemens.
>
> A historical novel about the venerated playwright's daughter.

———. *Kilmeny*. New York: Harper & Brothers, 1870. 136 pp.

> Source: MTLAcc, entry #967, volume donated by Clemens.

———. *Madcap Violet* (novel, published in 1876).

> Clemens mentioned this novel by Black in Notebook 19 in January 1882 *(N&J* 2: 422).

———. *The Maid of Killeena*. New York: Harper & Brothers, 1875. 151 pp.

> Source: MTLAcc, entry #968, volume donated by Clemens.

———. *Prince Fortunatus. A Novel*. Illus. New York: Harper & Brothers, 1905. 432 pp.

> Source: MTLAcc, entry #1520, volume donated by Clemens.

———. *Stand Fast, Craig-Royston!* Illus. New York: Harper & Brothers, n.d. 429 pp.

> Source: MTLAcc, entry #1145, volume donated by Clemens.

———. *The Strange Adventures of a House-Boat. A Novel*. Illus. New York: Harper & Brothers, 1892. 258 pp.

> Source: MTLAcc, entry #1412, volume donated by Clemens.

———. *That Beautiful Wretch; A Brighton Story*. New York: Harper & Brothers, n.d. 240 pp.

> Source: MTLAcc, entry #1518, volume donated by Clemens.

———. *White Wings; A Yachting Novel* (published in 1880).

> On 29 August 1880 Clemens remarked in a letter to Joseph H. Twichell, "The papers say that Harte & William Black are bumming around together in the [Scottish] Highlands. I suspect at bottom these two are kindred spirits" (*LMTJHT*, p. 101). Clemens subsequently became aware that Black's rather despicable character named Frederick Smethurst in *White Wings* was modeled on George W. Smalley, a friend of Whitelaw Reid (Notebook 19 [January 1882], *N&J* 2: 422).

———. *Wild Eelin: Her Escapades*. New York: Harper & Brothers, 1899. 512 pp.

> Source: MTLAcc, entry #1522, volume donated by Clemens.

———. *Yolande. A Novel*. New York: Harper & Brothers, 1905. Illus. 462 pp.

> Source: MTLAcc, entry #1521, volume donated by Clemens.

BLACKMORE, RICHARD DODDRIDGE (1825–1899). *Lorna Doone: A Romance of Exmoor*. Illus. New York: Harper Brothers, n.d. 576 pp.

> Source: MTLAcc, entry #1327, volume donated by Clemens.

———. *Lorna Doone: A Romance of Exmoor* (novel, published in 1869).

> Catalog: *C1951*, D4, $17.50, no edition specified.
>
> One wishes that both copies of this novel had not dropped into the void; at least one of them might have contained Clemens's reactions to this supernatural story.

———. *Perlycross; A Novel*. New York: Harper & Brothers, 1901. 493 pp.

> Source: MTLAcc, entry #1523, volume donated by Clemens.

BLACKWOOD, HELEN SELINA (SHERIDAN), BARONESS DUFFERIN AND CLANEBOYE (1807–1867). "The lament of the Irish emigrant" (song, published in 1843). Melody by William Richardson Dempster (1808–1871).

> In "Letter from Carson City," a sketch published in Virginia City on 3 February 1863, Clemens quoted the first line from this tragic ballad, "I'm sitting on the stile, Mary" (*ET&S* 1: 197). He mentioned the song favorably in October 1878 (NB 16, *N&J* 2: 212).

Blackstone's Commentaries.

> William Blackstone (1723–1780) originally published his famous treatises on the English system of law between 1765 and 1769. These were revised and supplemented thereafter. John Marshall Clemens's personal property included "4 vols Blackstone's Commentaries," according to the appraisal of his personal property filed on 21 May 1847 in the Marion County Probate Court, Palmyra, Missouri (reported by John Francis McDermott in "Mark Twain and the Bible," *Papers on Language and Literature* 4.2 [Spring 1968]: 195–198). The elder Clemens owned only twenty-five or thirty books at the time of his death, mostly volumes of Missouri law cases. In September 1888 Samuel Clemens referred to Chapter 27 of Book 4 about the history of methods used to judge guilt or innocence as summarized in *Blackstone's Commentaries* (Notebook 28, *N&J* 3:423).

Blackwood's Magazine (monthly periodical founded in 1817, published in Edinburgh until 1905).

> References: Chapter 43 of *A Tramp Abroad* (1880); the January 1883 issue was used in an unpublished MS (Paine 91, MTP); Clemens mentioned an 1871 bound issue (Clemens to Howells, Florence, 4 Dec. 1903, *MTHL*, p. 775); and Clemens disgustedly found "fifty-four bound

volumes . . . running backward from about 1870" in a bookcase at Villa di Quarto in January 1904 (Autobiographical Dictation, *AutoMT* 1: 235).

BLAIKIE, WILLIAM (1843–1904). *How to Get Strong and How to Stay So.* Rev. edition. New York: Harper & Brothers, 1902. 293 pp.

Source: MTLAcc, entry #398, volume donated by Clemens.

BLAINE, HARRIET BAILEY (STANWOOD) (1828–1903). *Letters of Mrs. James G. Blaine.* Ed. by Harriet S[tanwood]. (Blaine) Beale (1872–1958). 2 vols. 8vo, original cloth, quarter morocco case. New York: Duffield and Co., 1908.

Inscriptions: both volumes inscribed by Clemens: "S L. Clemens/Xmas, 1908/From Clara".

Catalogs: *C1951*, #52c, $12; *Fleming 1972*, 2 vols.; Sotheby Parke Bernet, New York, Sale number 3482 (25 February 1976), "2 vols.," from a New York City collector (John F. Fleming), lot 11, sold for $250 (*American Book Prices Current, 1976*, p. 207).

Provenance: Frederick Anderson, then Editor of the Mark Twain Papers in the Bancroft Library at the University of California, Berkeley, examined this volume at the New York City office of John F. Fleming in April 1972 (Anderson to James D. Hart, 17 April 1972, photocopy sent to Alan Gribben).

BLANC, CHARLES (1813–1882). *The Grammar of Painting and Engraving. Translated from the French of Blanc's Grammaire des Arts du Dessin.* Translated from the French by Kate (Newell) Doggett (1828–1884). Illus. New York: Hurd and Houghton; Cambridge: Riverside Press, 1874. 330 pp.

Inscriptions: inscribed by Clemens in pencil on the front flyleaf: "Livy Clemens/1874." Clemens also wrote on the front pastedown endpaper: "Howells/37 Concord avenue/Cambridge".

Marginalia: a few pencil markings throughout, not Clemens's, on pages 9, 17, 22, and 23.

Location: Mark Twain Library, Redding, Connecticut.

Copy examined: Olivia Clemens's copy. Accession number "3510" recorded in pencil in the volume. Examined in 1970 and again in June 1982.

BLAND, EDITH (NESBIT) (1858–1924). *The Book of Dragons.* Illustrated by H[arold]. R[obert]. Millar (1869–1942). New York: Harper & Brothers, 1901. 190 pp.

Source: MTLAcc, entry #510, volume donated by Clemens.

———. *The Red House; A Novel.* Illustrated by A[rthur]. I[gnatius]. Keller (1866–1924). New York: Harper & Brothers, 1903. 274 pp.

Source: MTLAcc, entry #1038, volume donated by Clemens.

———. *The Wouldbegoods.* Illustrated by Reginald B[athurst]. Birch (1856–1943). New York: Harper & Brothers, [cop. 1900]. 313 pp.

Source: MTLAcc, entry #1195, volume donated by Clemens.

BLAND, HENRY MEADE (1863–1931). *A Song of Autumn, and Other Poems.* San Jose, California: Pacific Short Story Club, [cop. 1907]. 96 pp.

Source: MTLAcc, entry #2012, volume donated from Clemens's library by Clara Clemens Gabrilowitsch in 1910.

BLAND, JAMES ALLEN (1854–1911). "Oh! Dem golden slippers" (minstrel song imitating a plantation spiritual, copyrighted

by Bland in 1879).

Bland was an African American composer and banjo entertainer. Clemens heard two cabin hands sing Bland's popular song to a banjo accompaniment on Horace Bixby's *City of Baton Rouge* in 1882 (NB 21, *N&J* 2: 562). While visiting Hartford in June 1888, the Finnish author and reformer Baroness Alexandra Gripenberg heard Clemens sing "a comical song about a certain African American called Moses 'who wanted to have golden slippers but couldn't get them.' That was the refrain and was sung with real American, Mark Twain humor" (Ernest J. Moyne, "Mark Twain Meets a Lady from Finland," *Mark Twain Journal* 11.2 [Summer 1960]: 25). In August 1889 Clemens listed "Golden Slippers" among his favorite spirituals and other songs (NB 29, *N&J* 3: 513).

BLATCHFORD, ROBERT (1851–1943), pseud. "Nunquam." *Merrie England* (published in 1893).

On 5 August 1898 Clemens, residing near Vienna, responded to Kate Littlewood, who had written to him from California about Theosophy and other philosophies: "Yes, I should *very* much like to have a 'volume or two' of Blatchford's, since you allow me to suggest it, & I hope your gift will include 'Merrie England' & the Essay on the humorists" (James S. Copley Library, LaJolla, California, photocopy of ALS sent to Alan Gribben by Nick Karanovich on 2 August 1984). British journalist, author, and prominent socialist and atheist Blatchford had founded a laborite newspaper, *The Clarion*, in 1891 and wrote articles in it under the name "Nunquam." He collected his Fabian-inspired socialist articles into a book titled *Merrie England*. Blatchford's *Impressionist Sketches* (London: Clarion, 1897) had surveyed a range of subjects, including humor. Blatchford, incidentally, would later castigate Clemens's literary tastes in *The Clarion*; see "A Scotch Tilt Against Mark Twain," *Literary Digest* (New York City) 68.2 (8 January 1921): 35.

"BLAU IST DAS BLÜMELEIN [LITTLE BLUE FLOWERS]" (song). Clemens listed this title among his favorite songs (NB 29 [August 1889], *N&J* 3: 513). A number of song titles and folk songs made use of the words "blau blümelein." A song with that name, for example, was published by the pianist and composer Emil Evers (1861–1934) in 1882. It is difficult to determine which composer and song Clemens had in mind.

BLICHER, STEEN STEENSON (1782–1848). *The Minister of Veilby* (novel, published in 1829).

Mark Twain's footnote at the beginning of *Tom Sawyer, Detective* (1896), cites "an old-time Swedish [*sic*] criminal trial" as the source for his story. J. Christian Bay's concise and authoritative essay—"*Tom Sawyer, Detective*: Origin of the Plot," in *Essays Offered to Herbert Putnam*, eds. William Warner Bishop and Andrew Keogh (New Haven: Yale University Press, 1929), pp. 80–88—first explained how Twain borrowed from a Danish (not Swedish) murder mystery novel in constructing *Tom Sawyer, Detective*. Although *The Minister of Veilby* was apparently a literary starting-point, Twain never read the book himself; he apparently learned about its plot from the wife of the Ambassador of Denmark to the United States. Bay became interested in the origins of Twain's story at the time of its publication in 1896, corresponded about the problem with Albert Bigelow Paine while Twain was still living, finally located its apparent source in Blicher's novel, *The Minister of Veilby*, and then worked out the manner in which Twain heard the tale. Blicher had based his novel on a seventeenth-century murder trial in Denmark. The fullest explication of this theory about the germ of *Tom Sawyer, Detective* appears in John C. Gerber's introduction in *The Adventures of Tom Sawyer, Tom Sawyer Abroad, Tom Sawyer, Detective*, ed. John C. Gerber, Paul Baender, and Terry Firkins (Berkeley: University of California Press, 1980), pp. 345–355. (However, the knowledge that Mark Twain ordered a copy of Samuel M. Phillipps's *Famous Cases of Circumstantial Evidence*, which contains the "Case of Sören Qvist," perhaps offers another, equally compelling explanation.) Adolf B. Benson, "Mark Twain's Contacts with Scandinavia," *Scandinavian Studies and Notes* (University of Kansas) 14 (August 1937): 159–167, relied on Paine's biography and Twain's (then) published letters and Autobiographical Dictations to establish Twain's relations with Scandinavia. Benson's central topic was Twain's use of a Danish source for *Tom Sawyer, Detective* (1896), which Benson admitted that J. Christian Bay had already discovered and explained in print in 1929. Benson recapitulated this story because "I do not believe [Bay's] essay] to be generally known" (p. 165). D. M. McKeithan, *CTMT* (1958) likewise summarized the information that Bay had provided, explaining that the 1929 collection of essays was out of print.

Yasuhiro Takeuchi, "Tracking Twain: The Unfulfilled Pursuit in Mark Twain's Detective Fiction," *American Literary Realism* 48.2 (Winter 2016): 166–182.

BLISS, EDGAR JANES (1842–1906). *The Peril of Oliver Sargent*. New York: Charles L. Webster & Company, 1891. 177 pp.

Clemens's publishing firm advertised Bliss' book as being reminiscent of *Dr. Jekyll and Mr. Hyde*, a study of "the dual character of man" (*Publishers' Trade List Annual 1893*). Bliss substituted alcohol for the transforming drug and added an optimistic ending.

BLISS, PHILIP PAUL (1838–1876). "Only an armour-bearer" (hymn).

A calm Sabbath in Bermuda was "profaned" by Mark Twain's neighbors' singing this hymn to the accompaniment of a metallic piano (NB 13 [May 1877], *N&J* 2: 19).

_____, IRA DAVID SANKEY (1840–1908), JAMES McGRANAHAN (1840–1907), and GEORGE COLES STEBBINS (1846–1945), joint eds. *Gospel Hymns Consolidated, Embracing Volumes No. 1, 2, 3, and 4, without Duplicates, for Use in Gospel Meetings and Other Religious Services*. New York, Chicago: Biglow & Main; Cincinnati, New York: J. Church & Co., 1883. 400 pp. [Publisher, date, and pages conjectured.]

Inscription: signed "S. L. Clemens, 1887" on the front flyleaf.

Catalog: *A1911*, "Embracing Nos. 1, 2, 3 and 4, For Use in Gospel Meetings, etc., 12mo, boards, N.Y. n.d.," quotes the signature, lot 194, sold for $1.

BLISS, WILLIAM ROOT (1825–1906). *Paradise in the Pacific; A Book of Travel, Adventure, and Facts in the Sandwich Islands*. New York: Sheldon and Co., 1873. 207 pp.

Clemens noted the title of Bliss' book on the rear cover of his copy of James Jackson Jarves's *History of the Hawaiian or Sandwich Islands* (*N&J* 1: 104–105).

BLIX, RAGNVALD (1882–1958). *Le Voile Tombe: Caricatures par Blix*. Paris: Librairie Nilsson [imprimerie Bröderna Lagerström, Stockholm], 1908. [A collection of twenty-four color prints.]

Inscription: inscribed "Mark Twain/le maître des hautes-oeuvres/de Blix/le traître [?] des chefs-d'oeuvres."

Catalogs: ListABP (1910), "Le voile tombe"; 17 January 1944 Charles Retz Appraisal (p. 5). Valued at $10.

Location: Mark Twain Papers, Bancroft Library, University of California at Berkeley.

Copy examined: Clemens's copy.

An accompanying letter from Blix, 8 December 1908, thanks Clemens for a letter of praise and offers to send him the original of any caricature he especially liked. Blix's prints mimicked the master painters of Western Europe. On 28 December 1908 Clemens thanked him with a postcard for "the Mona Lisa. . . my never-ending delight" (Kobenhavns Auktioner, #12496). From Stormfield on 12 August 1909 Clemens praised "the holy smirk" on his Mona Lisa caricature, which reminded him of "our own Mother Eddy" (ALS, MTP). Blix' drawings often appeared in a magazine Clemens enjoyed, *Simplicissimus* (see that Catalog entry).

BLOOMFIELD-MOORE, CLARA SOPHIA (JESSUP) (1824–1899), pseud. "Mrs. Harrietta Oxnard Ward." *Sensible Etiquette of the Best Society, Customs, Manners, Morals, and Home Culture. Compiled from the Best Authorities*. Philadelphia: Porter & Coates, 1878. 567 pp.

Source: MTLAcc, entry #2144, volume donated from Clemens's library by Clara Clemens Gabrilowitsch in 1910.

Intent on writing a burlesque book of etiquette, Clemens wrote to James R. Osgood on 7 March 1881: "Yes, send me a collection of etiquette books" (Harvard University, TS in MTP).

BLOSS, CELESTIA ANGENETTE [LATER BREWSTER] (1812–1855). *Bloss' Ancient History, for the Use of Families and Schools*. [First published in Rochester, New York in 1845, 427 pp.; various other editions followed. John Jacob Anderson (1821–1906) revised an 1867 edition. The Clemens family's edition has not been identified.]

Catalog: ListABP (1910), "Bloss' Ancient Hist.", no other information provided.

BLOUET, [LÉON] PAUL (1847 or 1848–1903), pseud. "Max O'Rell." *A Frenchman in America: Recollections of Men and Things*. New York: Cassell Publishing Co., 1891. 365 pp. [Edition conjectured. Published originally as *Un Français en Amérique*.]

Catalog: *C1951*, #57a, $22.50, listed among the books containing Clemens's marginal notes.

The French humorist and novelist Blouet provided a generally good-natured account of his 1889–1890 lecture tour in the United States and Canada, a journey that encompassed New York City, Buffalo, Chicago, Detroit, St. Paul, Cincinnati, Boston, and Washington, D. C., as well as cities in Virginia, Wisconsin, and Maine, and performances in Montreal, Quebec, and Toronto. His lecture agent Major James B. Pond would later arrange the United States portion of Mark Twain's global tour. In a few chapters Blouet ventured opinions—for instance, in "Notes on American Women" (XII), "Reflections on the Typical American" (XV), and "American Humor"

(XLII). He did not disguise the hardships involved in a tour with so much grueling travel, and complained of the sameness in appearance of the American towns through which he passed.

———. *John Bull & Co.; The Great Colonial Branches of the Firm: Canada, Australia, New Zealand, and South Africa.* Illus. London: Frederick Warne, 1894. 322 pp. [Edition conjectured. Clemens's publishing firm Charles L. Webster & Company also published this title in 1894.]

In August 1896 Andrew Chatto reported that he had sent Clemens several books that he requested, including *John Bull & Co.* (Welland, *Mark Twain in England*, p. 168).

———. "Mark Twain and Paul Bourget," *North American Review* 160.460 (March 1895): 302–310.

Blouet contended that by reading a wretched translation in a New York City paper, Mark Twain missed the nuances of Paul Bourget's *Outre-Mer*. Twain's ridicule of *Outre-Mer* was "unkind, unfair, bitter, hasty." Blouet charged that morals in America are actually lower than those in Paris. Bourget's book "has passed over Mark Twain's head." From *Outre-Mer* Twain might at least have learned "a lesson in politeness and good manners" (p. 310). In response to Blouet's defense, Twain published "What Paul Bourget Thinks of Us" (1895); referred to O'Rell unfavorably in a letter to General Lloyd Stephens Bryce, 9 March [1895] (ASSSCL); and brought up his literary quarrel with O'Rell in an interview published in the Melbourne, Australia *Argus*, 16 September 1895, remarking that "it was he who did all the talking" (Scharnhorst, *Complete Interviews*, p. 198). The Sydney *Evening News* reported that O'Rell had challenged Twain to a duel during the flap, but that Twain treated this gesture as a publicity stunt and called it "twaddle." Twain added, "Bourget . . . is a man of great literary reputation and capacity. . . . I said nothing offensive about him. He is an entirely respectable person." Regarding Max O'Rell, on the other hand, "as a literary person I conceive he had no rank whatever" (Sydney, Australia *Evening News*, 16 September 1895; *Complete Interviews*, p. 200–201). Seeking the last word, Twain included another essay, "A Little Note to M. Paul Bourget," in *How to Tell a Story and Other Essays* (1897).

———. *Woman and Artist.* New York: Harper & Brothers, 1900. 228 pp.

Source: MTLAcc, entry #1638, volume donated by Clemens.

Dora Grantham, wife of the artist Philip Grantham, conceived of herself as "her husband's comrade in art" (p. 6). However, complications ensued in the succeeding chapters of this novel, which Blouet dedicated to his own wife.

BLOWITZ, HENRI GEORGES STEPHANE ADOLPHE OPPER DE (1825–1903). *Memoirs of M. de Blowitz.* First edition. Frontispiece portrait of Blowitz. Original dark green pictorial cloth, gilt, uncut. New York: Doubleday, Page and Co., 1903. 321 pp.

Inscription: inscribed by Clemens in ink, "S L. Clemens/N. Y. City, Oct., 1903./From Frank Doubleday." (See the Catalog entry for Frank N. Doubleday for a possibly relevant anecdote.)

Catalogs: ListABP (1910), "Memoirs of De Blowitz"; *C1951*, #99c, $7.50, listed among books signed by

Clemens.

Clemens passingly mentioned the French journalist and author Blowitz in 1888 in Notebook 28 (*N&J* 3: 427). On 12 October 1903 Clemens thanked Frank N. Doubleday for sending some books, then added in a postscript: "I've dipped into Blowitz and find him quaintly & curiously interesting. I think he tells the straight truth, too. I knew him a little, 23 years ago" (*MTL*, p. 746; ALS in MTP).

Location: collection of Kevin Mac Donnell, Austin, Texas.

Copy examined: Clemens's unmarked copy, in July 2004.

BOCCACCIO, GIOVANNI (1313–1375). *The Decameron or Ten Days' Entertainment of Boccaccio. A Revised Translation by* W[alter]. K[eating]. Kelly [d. 1867]. Bohn's Standard Library Series. London: H. G. Bohn, 1869. 545 pp.

Inscription: signed twice ("S. L Clemens") on the first pages of advertisements, and also signed on the verso of the frontispiece portrait: "S. L. Clemens, 1872".

Catalogs: *C1951*, #73c, $25; *Zeitlin 1951*, #8, $35.

In Clemens's copy of George Trevelyan's *The Life and Letters of Lord Macaulay*, where Macaulay praised the *Decameron* as "elegant, amusing, and . . . strikingly delicate," Clemens remarked, "This Boccaccio business is a perfect enigma. He must have read an expurgated edition." However, Clemens envied Boccaccio's freedom in expressing things "unprintable (in our day)" (NB 14 [May 1878], *N&J* 2: 87). In "The Walt Whitman Controversy" (DV36, MTP), written about 1882, Mark Twain states that he owns "an English copy, but [I] have mislaid it" and has borrowed a French edition from a neighboring clergyman—a joke intended to emphasize the ubiquity of the book. In 1888 he mentioned the *Decameron* (F. Hopkinson Smith "probably does not know that the story is in the Decameron; and I didn't, until your letter came") in a letter to Baroness Alexandra Gripenberg (27 December 1888, PH in MTP). He also alluded to the *Decameron* in Notebook 32 (May 1892), TS p. 8; in a letter to Susan Crane, 30 September 1892 from Florence (*MTL*, p. 571); and in Twain's "Private History of the 'Jumping Frog' Story" (1894). Boccaccio is identified as a great Italian writer in "Three Thousand Years Among the Microbes" (written in 1905, *WWD?*, p. 529).

———. *Stories of Boccaccio (The Decameron) Translated from the Italian into English with Eleven Original Etchings by Léopold Flameng [1831–1911].* Translated by Walter Keating Kelly (d. 1867). Philadelphia: G. Barrie, [1881]. 493 pp.

Inscription: inscribed in an uncharacteristic signature on the flyleaf: "This is authorized/Mark Twain".

Location: Albert and Shirley Small Special Collections Library, University of Virginia, Charlottesville. Donated by Clifton Waller Barrett, who obtained the volume from a Virginia collector, Jennings Wise.

Copy examined: conceivably Clemens's copy, though its provenance is not traceable to Clemens's library and the signature is dubious. Several illustrations in the book daringly (for the time) portray nude women.

BÔCHER, FERDINAND (1832–1902), ed. *College Series of French Plays; With English Notes, by Ferdinand Bôcher.* Complete in one volume. Fifth edition. New York: Leypoldt & Holt Co., 1870. [Each play is numbered separately.]

Inscription: signed "Livy L. Clemens/1873" in pencil on

the title page.

Marginalia: several penciled underlinings and notes occur throughout. A hand other than Clemens's made a note about pronouncing "voilà" on page 6. A penciled underlining appears on page 8, along with a note defining "pour que." Clemens wrote "George Dolby's phrase." in pencil on page 41 in *La Bataille de Dames*, a play by Eugène Scribe and Ernest Legouvé, underlining the words "mais ce n'est là qu'un détail." George Dolby (1831–1900) was the English theatrical agent who managed the reading tours of both Charles Dickens and Mark Twain. Twain would praise Dolby as a man "full of life and strength and spirits, a tireless and energetic talker, and always overflowing with good nature and bursting with jollity" (*AutoMT* 1: 162).

Location: Mark Twain Library, Redding, Connecticut.

Copy examined: Olivia Clemens's copy that Clemens also read. Examined in June 1982 and on 10 November 2019. Contains a red ink accession number: "3663".

Its contents include works by Eugène Scribe (1791–1861), Ernest Legouvé (1807–1903), Émile De Girardin (1802–1881), Jules Sandeau (1811–1883), Eugène Marin Labiche (1815–1888), and August Vacquerie (1819–1895).

BOGGS, SARA ELIZABETH (SIEGRIST) (1843–1904). *Sandpeep*. Illustrated by May Bartlett (1872–1959, later known as Mrs. May [Bartlett] Fairchild). Boston: Little, Brown, and Co., 1906. 421 pp.

Source: MTLAcc, entry #2178, volume donated from Clemens's library by Clara Clemens Gabrilowitsch in 1910.

Boggs wrote fiction about crime and trials. In *Sandpeep* an orphan girl, living with her aunt on the rugged coast of Maine, becomes the governess for a summer cottager. Gradually she is pulled into a dangerous family mystery.

BOHNY, NIKLAUS (1815–1856). *Neues Bilderbuch. Anleitung zum Anschauen. Denken, Rechnen, und Sprechen fur Kinder. [New Picture Book. Instructions for Watching, Thinking, Calculating, and Speaking for Children.]* Esslingen: I. F. Schreiber, 187?. [The first edition of the book was published in 1845. A new edition appeared in the latter 1870s.]

Clemens noted the title, author, and publisher of this picture book for children in Notebook 22 in 1883 (*N&J* 3: 41).

BOIELDIEU, FRANÇOIS ADRIEN (1775–1834). *Le Calife de Bagdad* (comic opera, performed in 1800).

Clemens listed "Ouverture—Caliph of Bagdad" among his possible choices for a music box in 1878 (NB 16, *N&J* 2: 212).

———. *La Dame Blanche [The White Lady]* (light opera, performed in 1825).

"Not noise, but music," Clemens noted after attending a performance in Munich on 14 January 1879 (*N&J* 2: 261).

BOILEAU-DESPRÉAUX, NICOLAS (1636–1711). *Épîtres*.

Clemens quoted (and altered slightly) a sardonic couplet on materialism from Épître V (lines 85–86) in Notebook 1 (1855), *N&J* 1: 38. He may have copied it from a French grammar book.

BOLTON, SARAH KNOWLES (1841–1916). *Famous American Authors*. New York: Thomas Y. Crowell, 1887. 398 pp. [Edition conjectured.]

Source: ListABP (1910), "Famous American Authors, Bolton".

Clemens was among the seventeen writers described in this volume, which included biographical sketches of such early luminaries as Irving, Emerson, Longfellow, Holmes, and Lowell, as well as of Clemens's contemporaries Howells, Warner, Gilder, Aldrich, and Cable. Clemens was allowed to edit the essay about him that appeared on pages 365–386, and in a letter of 7 July 1887 he congratulated Bolton on "a happy success" and declared that she had "done it well" (American Antiquarian Society). An interesting anecdote on page 271 records that as a youth Clemens was beaten up by a fireman while living in Philadelphia. A smaller edition of 197 pages, lacking the essay on Mark Twain, was published by the same firm in 1905.

BONAR, HORATIUS (1808–1889). "Beyond the smiling and the weeping" (hymn, published in 1849).

Either Clemens or his wife Olivia wrote part of the title of this hymn in their copy of *Laudes Domini: A Selection of Spiritual Songs, Ancient and Modern* (1884), compiled by C. S. Robinson. (See that Catalog entry.) Its first line is comforting: "Beyond the smiling and the weeping/I shall be soon."

———. "The Church has waited long" (hymn, published in 1845). Its melody was most notably composed by William Howard Doane (1832–1915); however, others also set the hymn to music.

In the second installment of Mark Twain's "Extract from Captain Stormfield's Visit to Heaven" (*Harper's Monthly Magazine* CXVI.DCXCII [January 1908: 275—Part II in this version, but titled Chapter 4 in subsequent editions), "The prodigious choir struck up—'We long to hear thy voice,/To see thee face to face.'" Stormfield calls it "noble music, but the uneducated chipped in and spoilt it, just as the congregations used to do on earth." Shortly thereafter the celestial choir moved on to sing "The whole wide heaven groans,/And waits to hear that voice."

Frustrated researchers sometimes concluded that Twain invented these verses of a contrived hymn, but the lyrics did come from an actual—and once well-known—sacred poem written by a prominent Scottish clergyman and hymn-writer, Horatius Bonar, D. D., minister of the Free Church at Kelso. The hymn somewhat daringly laments the passing of so many centuries as generations of worshippers awaited the promised Second Coming. Its first four stanzas (each a quatrain) recalled the patience required of believers: "The Church has waited long/Her absent Lord to see;/And still in loneliness she waits,/A friendless stranger she." Second verse: "Age after age has gone,/Sun after sun has set,/And still, in weeds of widowhood,/She weeps, a mourner yet." Third verse: "Saint after saint on earth/Has lived, and loved, and died;/And as they left us one by one,/We laid them side by side." Fourth verse: "We laid them down to sleep,/But not in hope forlorn;/We laid them but to ripen there/Till the last glorious morn." Twain chose to quote the first two lines from each of two stanzas near the hymn's end (but not from the concluding stanza) to celebrate the ironically triumphant entry of a sainted barkeeper into Stormfield's Heaven: "We long to hear Thy voice,/To see Thee face to face,/To share Thy crown and glory then,/As now we share Thy grace." Finally, "The whole creation groans,/And waits to hear that voice/That shall her beauteousness restore,/And make her wastes rejoice." In quoting from the latter stanza, Twain altered "The whole creation groans," to read instead "The whole wide heaven groans," better befitting the expansive heavenly space that Stormfield was exploring. See a related Catalog entry, *Old Abe's Jokes; Fresh from Abraham's Bosom*.

BOND, ALVAN (1793–1882), ed. *Young People's Illustrated Bible History*. Intro. by Alvan Bond, D. D. Spine loose. Norwich, Connecticut: Henry Bill Publishing Co., 1878. 584 pp.

   Inscription: "Olivia Susan Clemens/From her Grandmother/Olivia Langdon/ Dec. 25th 1879."

   Location: Mark Twain Library, Redding, Connecticut.

   Copy examined: Susy Clemens's copy. Examined in 1970 and again in June 1982.

   Bond adapted a work by John Kitto (1804–1854), *An Illustrated History of the Holy Bible*, issued by the same Norwich publishing house in 1866 and repeatedly reprinted.

_____, ed. *Young People's Illustrated Bible History*. Illus. Norwich, Connecticut: Henry Bill Publishing Co., 1908. 584 pp.

   Source: MTLAcc, entry #1215, volume donated by Isabel V. Lyon, Clemens's secretary.

BONNER, JOHN (1828–1899). *A Child's History of the United States*. 3 vols. New York: Harper & Brothers, 1899.

   Source: MTLAcc, entries #1148–#1150, volumes donated by Clemens.

BONSAL, STEPHEN (1865–1951). *Morocco As It Is*. New York: Harper & Brothers, 1893. Illus. 349 pp.

   Source: MTLAcc, entry #1712, volume donated by Clemens.

BONWICK, JAMES (1817–1906). *The Lost Tasmanian Race*. London: Sampson Low, Marston, Searle and Rivington, 1884. 216 pp. [Edition conjectured but almost certain.]

   Twain made references to the author and title in Notebook 35 (September 1895, TS p. 53, MTP), passages deleted from the final version of *Following the Equator* (MS in Berg, NYPL), and Chapter 27 of *Following the Equator* (1897), where he quotes Bonwick.

   Dennis Welland, "Mark Twain's Last Travel Book" (1965), p. 46; Howard G. Baetzhold, *MT&JB* (1970), pp. 183, 357 n. 10; Francis Madigan, "Mark Twain's Passage to India" (1974), p. 355; Dennis Welland, *Mark Twain in England* (1978), pp. 179–180.

Book for an Hour. First edition. New York: Benjamin J. Such, 1873.

   Mark Twain sued the publisher to stop the publication of this volume, which included several unauthorized sketches by Twain. In the second, revised edition (1873), the publisher Such included only one Twain sketch and quoted snidely from Twain's testimony (Kevin Mac Donnell to Alan Gribben, 2 August 2004).

BOOK OF COMMON PRAYER. *The Book of Common Prayer, and Administration of the Sacraments; and Other Rites and Ceremonies of the Church, According to the Use of the Protestant Episcopal Church in the United States of America. Together with the Psalter, or Psalms of David*. New York: D. Appleton & Co., 1870. 564 pp.

   Source: MTLAcc, entry #2314, volume donated from Clemens's library by Clara Clemens Gabrilowitsch in 1910.

   Catalog: ListABP (1910), "Common Prayer", no other

information provided.

   On 13 February 1870 Clemens praised a minister's "kindness to the stranger within his gates," one of the commandments in the *Book of Common Prayer* (*MTLet* 4: 72).

   See also the Catalog entry for *The Order for Daily Evening Prayer*.

The Book of Mormon (a sacred text of the Church of Jesus Christ of the Latter-day Saints). [Written by Joseph Smith, 1805–1844.]

   Mark Twain tended to be highly skeptical of newly founded denominations that deviated from the general beliefs of Protestant Christianity, as his disparagements of Mary Baker Eddy's writings about Christian Science thoroughly illustrate. In Chapters 12–17 of *Roughing It* (1872) he gave a mixed review of the then-unpopular Mormon settlements in Utah. Chapter 16 in *Roughing It* takes up *The Book of Mormon*. "All men have heard of the Mormon Bible, but few except the 'elect' have seen it, or, at least, taken the trouble to read it. I brought away a copy from Salt Lake. The book is a curiosity to me, it is such a pretentious affair, and yet so 'slow,' so sleepy; such an insipid mess of inspiration. It is chloroform in print. If Joseph Smith composed this book, the act was a miracle—keeping awake while he did it was, at any rate." Twain delivers a detailed analysis of its sources and prose style, writing in part that *The Book of Mormon* "seems to be merely a prosy detail of imaginary history, with the Old Testament for a model; followed by a tedious plagiarism of the New Testament. The author labored to give his words and phrases the quaint, old-fashioned sound and structure of our King James's translation of the Scriptures; and the result is a mongrel—half modern glibness, and half ancient simplicity and gravity." Twain's appraisal concludes that "the Mormon Bible is rather stupid and tiresome to read, but there is nothing vicious in its teachings. Its code of morals is unobjectionable—it is 'smouched' from the New Testament and no credit given."

   In 1972 Franklin R. Rogers compared various texts with the one Mark Twain quoted, and deduced that he used *The Book of Mormon*, Third European Edition (Liverpool: F. D. Richards, 1852) (*RI*, Iowa-California edition (1972), p. 564), but the 1993 revised edition of *Roughing It* in The Works of Mark Twain Series published by the Mark Twain Project in Berkeley and edited by Harriet Elinor Smith and Edgar Marquess Branch instead cited the Sixth European Edition published in Liverpool in 1866 (*RI*, p. 1026).

The Book of Pleasures. 1. The Pleasures of Hope, by Thomas Campbell. 2. The Pleasures of Memory, by Samuel Rogers. 3. The Pleasures of Imagination, by Mark Akenside. Philadelphia: Key & Biddle, 1836. 187 pp.

   Source: MTLAcc, entry #2048, volume donated from Clemens's library by Clara Clemens Gabrilowitsch.

   See also the Catalog entries for Thomas Campbell and for Samuel Rogers.

BOONE, HENRY BURNHAM (1872–1932) and **KENNETH BROWN** (1868–1958). *The Redfields Succession, A Novel*. New York: Harper & Brothers, 1903. 318 pp.

   Source: MTLAcc, entry #1524, volume donated by Clemens.

   Henry Burnham Boone was an attorney who collaborated

on several novels with his brother-in-law Kenneth Brown, a newspaper reporter and editorial writer.

Booth, Edwin [Thomas] (1833–1893).

At a Clover Club dinner in New York City in 1885, this New York actor, famous for his Shakespearean roles, arrived late and seated himself next to Mark Twain, who remarked, "This is the most surprising set of fellows I ever saw in my life. . . . I heard witticisms and repartee which would have done credit to a collection of noted wits. And the strangest part of it is, Booth, this jollification has been going on for five hours and I am evidently the only fellow here who feels his liquor" (Louis N[anna]. Megargee [1855–1905], "The Clover Club Has Been and Is a Teacher," in *Bohemia: A Symposium of Literary and Artistic Expression by Men and Women*, ed. Alexander K[elly]. McClure [1828–1909]. Limited edition. Philadelphia: International League of Press Clubs, 1904], p. 337). Percy MacKaye, in *Epoch: The Life of Steele MacKaye, Genius of the Theater in Relation to His Times & His Contemporaries; A Memoir by His Son*. 2 vols. (New York: Boni & Liveright, 1927), 1: 117], repeated this anecdote, citing as his source the New York *World*. MacKaye placed the incident in Philadelphia, where the Clover Club had another chapter that convened regularly, but it seems more likely that Booth and Twain would have been in New York City.

Booth, Josiah (1852–1930). *Everybody's Guide to Music, with Illustrated Chapters on Singing and Cultivation of the Voice*. New York: Harper & Brothers, [cop. 1893]. 176 pp.

Source: MTLAcc, entry #1684, volume donated by Clemens.

Booth, William Stone (1864–1926). *Some Acrostic Signatures of Francis Bacon, Baron Verulam of Verulam, Viscount St. Alban, Together with Some Others, All of Which Are Now for the First Time Deciphered and Published*. Boston: Houghton Mifflin Co., 1909. 631 pp. [Edition conjectured.]

Catalog: ListABP (1910), "Acrostic Signatures—Bacon, Booth", no other information provided.

Isabel Lyon's records indicate that John [Albert] Macy (1877–1932) brought galley proofs of Booth's book to show Clemens when Macy visited Stormfield on 8 January 1909 (Berg, NYPL, TS in MTP). Clemens talked excitedly of the forthcoming book in an Autobiographical Dictation of 11 January 1909, expressing hope that this could prove to be the "bombshell" that could "unhorse Shakspeare permanently and put Bacon in the saddle" (*AutoMT* 3: 299). He thereupon produced the first pages of *Is Shakespeare Dead?* (1909). Macy subsequently sent a published copy of Booth's book to Clemens; the volume arrived on 5 February 1909 (IVL notes, Berg, NYPL, TS in MTP). Albert Bigelow Paine reported that Booth's *Acrostic Signatures* established Bacon's authorship of the Shakespeare canon as far as Clemens was concerned (*MTB*, pp. 1479, 1485–86).

Shelden, *Man in White* (2010), pp. 316–317.

Boothby, Guy Newell (1867–1905). *My Strangest Case*. Illus. Boston: L. C. Page & Co., 1901. 300 pp.

Source: MTLAcc, entry #30, volume donated by Clemens. London detective George Fairfax becomes involved in an international hunt for a jewel thief.

Borrowings; A Compilation of Helpful Thoughts from Great

Authors. San Francisco, CA: C. A. Murdock & Co., 1889. 78 pp.

Source: MTLAcc, entry #647, volume donated by Isabel V. Lyon, Clemens's secretary.

Boscawen, William St. Chad (1854–1913). *The First of Empires, "Babylon of the Bible" in the Light of Latest Research*. New York: Harper & Brothers, 1903. 356 pp.

Source: MTLAcc, entry #1294, volume donated by Clemens.

Bosguérard, Marie de (1844–19—). *Scènes Enfantines [Children's Scenes.]* Illus. Paris: May et Motteroz, Directeurs, n.d. 118 pp. [Advertised in French publications in 1891.]

Provenance: unknown; possibly not from the Clemenses' library. It was shelved with their books in 1970, however.

Location: Mark Twain Library, Redding, Connecticut.

Copy examined: unknown owner's book, examined in 1970, June 1982, and on 10 November 2019. No accession number, no library stamp, no inscription, no markings. Albert E. Stone did not include it in the list of Clemens association copies he compiled in 1955.

Boston *Evening Transcript* (newspaper).

Mark Twain refers to a February 1903 issue in *Christian Science*, Book 2, Chapter 7 (1907). A clipping from the 2 April 1909 issue—"How the World Dies," a lecture by Professor Percival Lowell—is pinned to the front free endpaper of Clemens's copy of Bayne's *Pith of Astronomy*.

Boston *True Flag* (weekly newspaper, published 1851–1890).

Mentioned in Clemens's "Jul'us Caesar," an unpublished manuscript written around 1856 (DV400, MTP).

Boswell, James (1740–1795). *The Life of Samuel Johnson, LL.D. New Edition, with Notes and Additions by J. W. Croker [1780–1857]*. 2 vols. New York: Harper & Brothers, 1875. [Edition conjectured.]

Edition: One of the twenty-one books for which Estes & Lauriat of Boston billed Clemens on 14 July 1880 was "1 Johnson $2.50"; since many of the books were listed by title rather than author, Boswell's *Johnson* may have recently joined Clemens's library (MTP). With the standard cloth binding this Harper & Brothers edition sold for $4 at retail prices; but Clemens generally received a substantial author's discount from bookdealers. In "English As She Is Taught" (1887) Mark Twain begins by quoting an anecdote from "Croker's Boswell's Johnson."

Sam and Orion Clemens occasionally turned to Boswell's biography when they required filler for columns in the Hannibal *Journal* in 1852–1853 (Brashear, *MTSM*, p. 143). "Every great man ^ personage ^ must be shadowed by a parasite who is infinitely little—Johnson had his Boswell," Clemens wrote on the flyleaf of A. S. Evans' *Our Sister Republic*, which was published in 1870 (*A1911*, #159). Clemens mentioned Boswell in Notebook 12 (July 1873, *N&J* 1: 563). In a biography that Clemens signed in 1879 (Moritz Busch's *Bismarck in the Franco-German War*), Clemens made a note on its page 98: "A perfect Boswell for/honesty." Writing facetious captions for menu items for a Hartford banquet in June 1881, Clemens attributed a pompous bit of nonsense to "Doctor Samuel Johnson" (Beinecke Rare Book and Manuscript Library, Yale University; Everett Emerson to Alan Gribben, 29 October 1982). On 20 January 1887

Clemens named Boswell's *Life of Samuel Johnson* as one of his favorite books in a letter to the Reverend Charles D. Crane (ALS, Shapell Manuscript Library, Beverly Hills, California). He alluded to Boswell's *Johnson* in "Mental Telegraphy" (published in 1891); referred to Johnson as "that great man and his imposing diction" ("Which Was It?" written 1899–1903, *WWD?*, p. 278); and mentioned Johnson in a letter to Howells, 14 April 1903 (*MTHL*, p. 767). Henry Fisher recalled Clemens's saying that he had never read Johnson's writings, but from Boswell had gained the impression that Johnson was anti-American in the Revolution, anti-Catholic, pro-monarchy, and a zealous Protestant (*AMT*, pp. 71, 150–153).

———. *The Life of Samuel Johnson, LL.D.* 5 vols. London: George Bell and Sons, 1884.

Catalog: Ball 2016 inventory, tan boards, marbled edges of pages, 5 volumes.

Location: Quarry Farm library shelves, under the supervision of the Mark Twain Archive, Elmira College, Elmira, New York.

Clemens had access to these books whenever he visited Quarry Farm in Elmira.

BOTHMER, (COUNTESS) MARIE, GRÄFIN VON (1845–1921). *German Home Life.* New edition. London: Longmans, Green & Co., 1878. 312 pp.

Inscription: signed in pencil on the front free endpaper: "Olivia L. Clemens/Paris 1879."

Marginalia: notes and markings in pencil by Clemens. On page 216, where Bothmer tells how Prussian princes often join their peasants on the battlefields, Clemens notes: "You never saw Victoria's tribe at it."

Catalog: *Mott 1952*, #57, $15.

Location: Mark Twain Papers, Bancroft Library, University of California at Berkeley.

Copy examined: copy shared by Samuel and Olivia Clemens. Contains the bookstamps of the Mark Twain Library at Redding.

BOUCICAULT, DION (1820–1890) *Arrah-na-Pogue; or, The Wicklow Wedding* (play, performed in 1864).

Twain made references to this romantic melodrama set during the Irish rebellion of 1798 in "'Mark Twain' on the Ballad Infliction" in the San Francisco *Californian* of 4 November 1865 (*MTWY*, p. 195). The play incorporated a traditional Irish ballad, "The wearing of the green." "It was [Edward H.] House & Dion Boucicault that wrote Arrah-na-Pogue in partnership," Clemens informed Elisha Bliss on 9 June 1870 (*MTLet* 4: 148–149). Later, however, Clemens changed his mind about this authorship. In a letter of 5 February 1890 to Dean Sage castigating House, Clemens corrected the record: "It turns out, now, that he didn't write Arrah-na-Pogue (as he always claimed). I thought he was a dramatist" ("Literary Miscellany," Catalog 280, William Reese Company, New Haven, Connecticut, ALS, item #85). "House didn't write Arrah na Pogue," Clemens averred in Notebook 29 in March 1890 (*N&J* 3: 545). In 1907 Clemens still was seething about this misrepresentation when he dictated a portion of his autobiography on 28 August 1907 that referred to "Boucicault's great play" (*AutoMT* 3: 115). See also the Catalog entry for "Wearing of the green."

———. *The Octoroon; or, Life in Louisiana* (play, produced in 1859).

Clemens alluded to a San Francisco production of this play in a sketch ("City Marshall Perry") apparently published in the Virginia City *Territorial Enterprise* on 4 March 1863; it specifically referred to "the character of 'Old Pete' in Dion Boucicault's 'Octoroon'" (*ET&S* 1: 237–238, 473). The enslaved Pete was kind and elderly in this melodrama about miscegenation that highlighted slavery's cruel contradictions. The tragic octoroon figure appeared in American literature numerous times before Mark Twain's Roxy in *Pudd'head Wilson* (1894), as Michael Orth reminded readers. One "widely advertised" version of her plight was the focus of Boucicault's melodrama, and "we know that Mark Twain the writer later knew Boucicault" ("*Pudd'nhead Wilson* Reconsidered, or the Octoroon in the Villa Viviani," *Mark Twain Journal* 14.4 [Summer 1969]: 13). Adrienne Bond similarly pointed out that "tragic Octoroon" stereotypes proliferated in the wake of Boucicault's *The Octoroon* ("Disorder and the Sentimental Model: A Look at *Pudd'nhead Wilson*," *Southern Literary Journal* 13.2 [1981]: 59–71).

———, adaptor. *Rip Van Winkle* (play, dramatized from Washington Irving's tale, produced in 1865).

Olivia Clemens (and presumably Clemens, too) attended a performance of this "one-character" play featuring Joseph Jefferson "last night" (SLC to Charles Dudley Warner, Elmira, 5 May 1874; *MTLet* 6: 126–127). Clemens hoped that *Colonel Sellers* might "run twenty years . . . like Jo Jefferson's 'Rip Van Winkle'" (SLC to Robert Watt, 26 January 1875; *MTLet* 6: 359). On 27 November 1885 the Clemenses played host to Jefferson for an early dinner in their home; afterwards Olivia Clemens took Susy and Clara to see Jefferson in *Rip Van Winkle* and "they enjoyed it all immensely" (OLC's Diary, DV161, MTP; Fears, *Day by Day* 1.2: 1394).

———. *The Shaughraun* (play, produced in 1874).

Twain alluded to "when the 'Shaughran'[*sic*] was played at Wallack's" in Chapter 10 of *A Tramp Abroad* [1880]). He also referred to "Con [Conn] the Shaughran" [*sic*] (Clemens to Howells, 18 February 1884, *MTHL*, p. 474). Boucicault's popular melodrama was set in the Fenian uprising in 1866. The play's title signified "wanderer."

BOULGER, DOROTHY HENRIETTA (HAVERS) (1847–1923), pseud. "Theo. Gift." [Boulger's birth name was sometimes listed as "Dora."] *Maid Ellice, A Novel.* Leisure Hour Series, No. 95. New York: Henry Holt and Co., 1878. 463 pp.

Source: MTLAcc, entry #140, volume donated by Clemens. This novel is mistakenly attributed to Eleanor Frances Poynter (1840–1929).

———. *A Matter-of-Fact Girl, A Novel.* Leisure Hour Series, No. 126. New York: Henry Holt and Co., 1881. 351 pp.

Catalog: Ball 2016 inventory, yellow cloth, gilt, black lettering and design, J. Langdon Family bookplate #612, fair condition.

Location: Quarry Farm library shelves, under the supervision of the Mark Twain Archive, Elmira College, Elmira, New York.

Clemens had access to these books whenever he visited the Langdons in Elmira.

The novels of this English author often had latent feminist themes. She married in 1867, resulting in a name change that complicated the record of her publications.

BOURDILLON, FRANCIS WILLIAM (1852–1921). "Light" (poem, published in 1878). Better known as "The Night Has a Thousand Eyes."

Olivia Clemens copied and sent this brief (two-stanza) love poem to Clemens on 31 July 1894 while she was waiting for him in Paris (TS in MTP). Its second verse is dramatic: "The mind has a thousand eyes,/And the heart but one;/ Yet the light of a whole life dies/When love is done."

BOURGET, CHARLES JOSEPH PAUL (1852–1935), known as "Paul Bourget." *Cosmopolis.* New York: Amblard & Meyer, 1893. [Edition conjectured.]

"To call together several thousand nice people & dissect & ransack a putrid body before them—what business has one to do that? Where is the *raison d'être* of Cosmopolis?" (NB 34 [1895], TS p. 2). Set in nineteenth-century Rome, *Cosmopolis* intertwined the lives of individuals of differing national backgrounds. Clemens may have been startled by unmistakable elements of French Naturalism in the novel.

———. *Outre-Mer: Impressions of America* (published in 1895). The travels of the French writer and critic Bourget within the United States introduced him to a number of things he liked but much to deplore. His observations covered New York City, Newport, Rhode Island (where he spent the summer), Georgia, and Florida. He wrote separate chapters on "The Lower Orders" (workingmen, farmers, and cowboys) and "Education." His comment about Newport captured much of his attitude: "The American spirit seems not to understand moderation" (p. 47). A serialized version of *Outre-Mer* provoked two rebuttals by Mark Twain, "What Paul Bourget Thinks of Us" (1895) and "A Little Note to M. Paul Bourget" (1897). Twain's correspondence echoed his dislike of the book: "I am translating a French article which I wish to abuse" (SLC to HHR, Entretat, 30 September 1894, *MTHHR*, p. 79); "M. Paul Bourget and his idiotic 'Outre Mer'" (SLC to HHR, Rouen, 11 October 1894, *MTHHR*, p. 85); "he is too small game to go after elaborately" (SLC to HHR, Rouen, 13 October 1894, *MTHHR*, p. 85); he is "wretchedly small game, . . . but I kind of love small game" (SLC to Gen. Lloyd Stephens Bryce, Rouen, 13 October 1894, Yale University). Paul Blouet defended Bourget against Twain's attacks ("Mark Twain and Paul Bourget," *North American Review* 160.460 [March 1895]: 302–310). A memorandum in Twain's Notebook 37 mentioned Bourget in a derogatory fashion on (8 April 1896, TS p. 29). It is interesting that Clara Clemens attributed one of the quotations in her commonplace book to Bourget (undated, Paine 150, MTP). See also the Catalog entry for Paul Blouet.

Louis J. Budd, *MTSP* (1962), p. 160; Sydney J. Krause, *MTC* (1967), p. 282 n. 19; Arthur L. Scott, *MTAL* (1969), pp. 183–184.

BOURKE, (CAPTAIN) JOHN GREGORY (1846–1896). *On the Border with [General George] Crook [1829–1890].* New York: Scribner, 1891. 491 pp.

Clemens made efforts to obtain this book for his publishing firm (Clemens to Howells, 10 February 1891, *MTHL*, pp. 634–635). Colonel Sellers's scheme for materializing cavalry seems to satirize Crook's plan for pacifying the American Indians, as William M. Gibson and Henry Nash

Smith pointed out (*MTHL*, p. 635 n. 1).

BOURRIENNE, LOUIS ANTOINE FAUVELET DE (1769–1834). *Memoirs of Napoleon Bonaparte. By . . . His Private Secretary.* London: Lockwood, 1888. [First published in 1829 in Paris.]

The title, place of publication, and date of this edition were listed in Clara Clemens's commonplace book, probably around 1888 (Paine 150, MTP). Napoleon I (1769–1821) ruled as Emperor of France.

BOUTET DE MONVEL, LOUIS MAURICE (1851–1913). *Joan of Arc.* First edition in English. Illus. Original lavender cloth, gilt. New York: The Century Co., 1907. [Oblong volume of large color illustrations, accompanied by a brief narrative.] First published in French in 1896.

Inscription: "To Dorothy Quick/with the love of/S L. Clemens/ 1907./21 Fifth Ave."

Location: Mark Twain Papers, Bancroft Library, University of California at Berkeley.

Copy examined: copy intended for Dorothy Quick, but retained by Clemens.

"The pictures he liked best were one of Joan in her prison talking to her 'Saints,' and the one of the battle scenes," recalled Dorothy Quick (Mrs. James Adams Mayer) in *Enchantment: A Little Girl's Friendship with Mark Twain* (Norman: University of Oklahoma Press, 1961), p. 145.

———. [An identical copy.]

Inscription: inscribed by Clemens in ink, "Margaret Illington, M. A. [i. e., Member of the Aquarium," Clemens's group of youthful "angelfish"]/with the love of/S L. Clemens/Xmas, 1908." Illington (1879–1934) was the wife of theatrical producer Daniel Frohman and the only adult member of Twain's cherished "Aquarium."

Location: collection of Kevin Mac Donnell, Austin, Texas. Obtained in 1985.

Copy examined: gift copy presented by Clemens. Examined in July 2004.

BOWMAN, ELMER. "Go way back and sit down" (song, 1901). Melody by Al Johns (1878–1928).

In a book that Clemens signed and annotated in 1902, he referred to the song "Go way back & sit down"; see the Catalog entry for Andrew D. White's *A History of the Warfare of Science with Theology in Christendom.* Mark Twain later referred to the song in Book II, Chapter 8 of *Christian Science* (1907, published in *WIM?*, pp. 341, 574). Bowman and Johns were pioneering African American music composers.

BOYESEN, HJALMAR HJORTH (1848–1895). *Essays on German Literature.* New York: Charles Scribner's Sons, 1892.

Catalog: Ball 2016 inventory, blue cloth with gilt lettering, good condition.

Location: Quarry Farm library shelves, under the supervision of the Mark Twain Archive, Elmira College, Elmira, New York.

Another book available to Clemens whenever he visited Quarry Farm in Elmira.

———. *Goethe and Schiller: Their Lives and Works, Including a Commentary on Goethe's Faust.* New York: Charles Scribner's Sons, 1879. 424 pp.

Catalog: Ball 2016 inventory, brown cloth, gilt lettering, Jervis Langdon's Family Library #496, Mark Twain Archive.

Location: Mark Twain Archive, Elmira College, Elmira,

New York.

Copy examined: an unmarked copy accessible to Clemens whenever he visited the Langdons in Elmira. Examined on 27 May 2015. Bookplate #496 of the "J. Langdon Family Library" on the front pastedown endpaper.

————. *Gunnar; A Tale of Norse Life.* Boston: James R. Osgood and Co., 1874. 292 pp.

Source: MTLAcc, entry #1917, volume donated from Clemens's library by Clara Clemens Gabrilowitsch in 1910.

Boyesen's romantic novel about Gunnar Thorson and his love for the socially unattainable Ragnhild was interwoven with descriptions of Norse mythology, folk beliefs (in fairies, for example), and peasant customs. On 17 January 1877 Clemens wrote from Hartford to the Norwegian author, scholar, and college professor Boyesen, who had immigrated to the United States in 1869: "You can't imagine how much pleasure your visit gave us, & how sorry we were to let you go—nor how the whole household missed you when you were gone, nor how sincerely we all wished you back again. Whenever you get a holiday, mind you we are to have the biggest share of it that you can spare" (*Sotheby's 2003*, #32). Very likely Boyesen had been a guest speaker at the Saturday Morning Club there in Hartford. On 20 November 1878 Clemens reported to Joseph H. Twichell from Munich that "yesterday afternoon" he had tried to connect with the Boyesens but had failed (*LMTJHT*, p. 82). He had better luck in Paris in June 1879 (*LMTJHT*, p. 91). Clemens wrote to Boyesen on 23 April 1880 to thank him for complimenting "the *new* book" (Marc L. Ratner, "Two Letters of Mark Twain," *Mark Twain Journal* 12.2 [Spring 1964]: 9).

Louis J. Budd, *MTSP* (1962), p. 115.

————. *Gunnar; A Tale of Norse Life.* Boston: James R. Osgood and Co., 1875. 292 pp.

Inscription: signed by Ida C. Langdon (1849–1934), who had married Charles Jervis Langdon in 1870. Clemens periodically visited their residence in Elmira, New York.

Catalog: Ball 2016 inventory, green cloth, gilt lettering, J. Langdon Family bookplate #524, fair condition.

Location: Quarry Farm library shelves, under the supervision of the Mark Twain Archive, Elmira College, Elmira, New York.

————. *Ilka on the Hill-top, and Other Stories.* New York: C. Scribner's Sons, 1881. 240 pp.

Source: MTLAcc, entry #1918, volume donated from Clemens's library by Clara Clemens Gabrilowitsch in 1910.

————. *Literary and Social Silhouettes.* New York: Harper & Brothers, 1894. 218 pp.

Catalog: C1951, J29, listed among books belonging to Jean and Clara Clemens.

————. *Queen Titania.* New York: Charles Scribner's Sons, 1881. 254 pp.

Source: MTLAcc, entry #1921, volume donated from Clemens's library by Clara Clemens Gabrilowitsch in 1910.

A letter from Clemens to Boyesen, 26 October 1881, thanked Boyesen for a copy of *Queen Titania* and in return promised to send the next book he would publish (Anderson Galleries, Sale No. 411 [10 May 1934], item #133). Clemens wrote on 11 January 1882 to express how "mightily delighted" he was with Boyesen's "review of my book" and urged Boyesen to "stop with us a day or two

on your way to Boston" (Marc L. Ratner, "Two Letters of Mark Twain," *Mark Twain Journal* 12.2 [Spring 1964]: 9, 17). Per Seyersted, "The Drooping Lily: H. H. Boyesen as an Early American Misogynist," *Americana Norvegica* 3 (1971): 74–87, traced Clemens's relationship with Boyesen and suggested that they did not see eye to eye during the later phases of Boyesen's developing hostility toward American women.

BOYLAN, GRACE (DUFFIE) (c. 1861–1935). *The Kiss of Glory*. Illustrated by J[oseph]. C[hristian]. Leyendecker (1874–1951). New York: G. W. Dillingham, [cop. 1902]. 298 pp.

Source: MTLAcc, entry #1103, volume donated by Clemens.

BOYLE, VIRGINIA (FRAZER) (1863–1938). *Devil Tales*. Illustrated by A[rthur]. B[urdett]. Frost (1851–1928). New York: Harper & Brothers, 1900. 211 pp.

Source: MTLAcc, entry #29, volume donated by Clemens.

————. [Another identical copy.]

Source: MTLAcc, entry #1509, volume donated by Clemens.

Clemens wrote familiarly to the Tennessee writer Virginia Frazer Boyle, author of *Brokenburne: A Southern Auntie's War Tale* (1897) and *Devil Tales* (1900), on 14 February 1901 (16 November 1935 Memphis newspaper clipping in MTP). Later she sent him her book of ten short stories, *Devil Tales*. On 16 September 1901 Clemens notified Boyle from Ampersand, New York: "They have arrived last night, & I have drunk to them & from them 'with my heart,' & to the holy & pathetic things which they stand for & symbolize, the golden days of a vanished youth" ("Literary Miscellany," Catalog 280, William Reese Company, New Haven, Connecticut, ALS, item #93). The stories were based on supernatural tales related to her as a girl by African American house servants. Boyle would quote from Clemens's letter in her memoir *Songs from the South* (Memphis: S. C. Toof & Co., 1939), adding that Clemens also thanked her for "the darling poem" that was "eloquent with the spirit of those same lost and lamented days" (p. 16).

Olivia Clemens extended an invitation to "Mrs. Virginia Boyle" on 26 May 1902 from her Riverdale address: "I have been sorry not to send for you and Mr. Boyle to come here; but in these days we have had very little time to ourselves. . . . If you and Mr. Boyle cared to come up some afternoon & take a cup of tea with *me* without my good man, I should be glad to see you" (*Sotheby's 2003*, #10). "Few will know, better than you, the weight of the blow which has fallen upon us," Clemens wrote to Boyle upon Olivia Clemens's death in June 1904 (*Sotheby's 2003*, #110). To a newspaper reporter in 1935 Boyle recalled Clemens's praise for her *Devil Tales*: "Say, I liked all those stories pretty well. There is one I wished I had written. It was 'Kingdom of the Micajah'" (Marshall Smith, "Friends of Mark Twain Recall Writer's Love for Memphis—Scene of His Sorrow," Memphis *Press-Scimitar*, November 1935).

————. *Serena, A Novel.* New York: A. S. Barnes & Co., 1905. 378 pp.

Source: MTLAcc, entry #4, volume donated by Clemens.

Inscription: inscribed to Mark Twain by the author.

From Dublin, New Hampshire, Clemens wrote to Boyle on 18 July 1905: "I shall find your book there [at my home] if it doesn't come here--& there is the right place, for I do not read anything that is interesting when I am at work, because it breaks my thread, & summer is my work time" ("Literary Miscellany," Catalog 280, William Reese Company, New Haven, Connecticut, ALS, item #99).

Boys on the Railroad, by Molly Elliot Seawell [1860–1916], James Barnes [1866–1936], Ellen Douglas Deland [1860–1923], John R. Coryell, E. Carruth, and Others. Harper's Athletic Series. Illus. New York: Harper & Brothers, 1909. 213 pp.

> Source: MTLAcc, entry #1452, volume donated by Clemens.
>
> Short stories by various authors with the dangers of railroading as a theme.

BOYTON, PAUL (1848–1924). *The Story of Paul Boyton. Voyages on All the Great Rivers of the World. . . . A Rare Tale of Travel and Adventure. . . . A Book for Boys, Old and Young.* Milwaukee: Riverside Printing Co., 1892. 358 pp.

> "No terms till we see the MS," Clemens noted (NB 27 [October 1887], *N&J* 3: 341). On 7 May 1888 Clemens referred to "Captain Boyton's ten-cent adventures" for a "juvenile level" (SLC to Fred J. Hall, Hartford, *MTLP*, p. 245).

BRACE, CHARLES LORING (1826–1890). *Gesta Christi; or, A History of Humane Progress Under Christianity* (London, 1880).

> Howells recommended this book to Mark Twain on 17 October 1889 to help him appreciate the medieval monastic life Twain satirized in *A Connecticut Yankee in King Arthur's Court* (1889) (*MTHL*, p. 614).

BRACHET, AUGUSTE (1844–1898) and J. DUSSOUCHET (1843–1910). *Petite Grammaire Française.* Green cloth, black spine and lettering. Paris: Librairie Hachette et Cie, 1884. 139 pp.

> Inscription: "Clemens" written in ink on the front cover by Olivia Clemens.
>
> Location: Mark Twain Library, Redding, Connecticut. Displays a red ink accession number ("3621") and a subsequent black ink accession number ("3674").
>
> Copy examined: copy belonging to the Clemens family. Examined in 1970, in June 1982, and again on 10 November 2019. No markings. No endpapers in the front or rear of the volume; apparently this was as published.

BRADDON, MARY ELIZABETH (1835–1915). *An Ishmaelite.* New York: George Munro, [1884]. 338 pp.

> Source: MTLAcc, entry #2182, volume donated from Clemens's library by Clara Clemens Gabrilowitsch in 1910.
>
> The English author Braddon set this sensation novel in France. Her most notorious novel had been *Lady Audley's Secret* (1862). Braddon herself had an open secret; she and the publisher John Maxwell began living together outside of marriage in 1861 because his wife had become insane and was institutionalized. Braddon and Maxwell were not able to marry until 1876 when his first wife passed away. Even after that marriage Braddon continued to write her novels under her maiden name.

———. *Phantom Fortune.* Chicago: Belford, Clarke & Co., [188–?]. 408 pp.

> Source: MTLAcc, entry #31, volume donated by Clemens.
>
> A novel of London society that reflects the vagaries of wealth and status. The lives of two sisters are followed as they make their way in an uncertain world that depends on investments in India, family favors, and other factors.

Racial and ethnic slurs are tossed around.

———. *The Trail of the Serpent* (novel, first published in 1861).

> Mark Twain concluded "Lucretia Smith's Soldier" (San Francisco *Californian*, 3 December 1864) with a paragraph beginning, "Such is life, and the trail of the serpent is over us all." As Edgar M. Branch and Robert H. Hirst noticed, Braddon's sensation novel had been serialized in *The Golden Era* in 1863 and 1864 and its distinctive title derived from Part II of Thomas Moore's narrative poem *Lalla Rookh* (1817): "Some flow'rets of Eden ye still inherit,/But the trail of the Serpent is over them all." Twain would later evince familiarity with Moore's long work, but he had almost certainly encountered Braddon's book, especially since it had been dramatized in San Francisco in September 1864 (*ET&S* 2: 531). Braddon would become best known for *Lady Audley's Secret* (1862), in which the wife of a wealthy man plots murders in order to keep a secret that would threaten her status in English society.

———. *The Venetians; A Novel.* New York: Harper & Brothers, 1892. 442 pp.

> Source: MTLAcc, entry #1090, volume donated by Clemens.

BRADLEY, EDWARD (1827–1889), pseud. "Cuthbert Bede." *The Adventures of Mr. Verdant Green.* Three volumes in one. Illustrated by the author. Ninetieth thousand. New York: Carleton, 1878. [Publisher conjectured.]

> Inscription: "S. L. Clemens, Hartford, 1878."
>
> Catalog: *A1911*, "12mo, cloth, N.Y.1878," quotes the signature, lot 32, sold for $4.50.
>
> Verdant Green is portrayed as a freshman at Oxford University.

BRADLEY, (WILLIAM M.) AND CO., PHILADELPHIA. *Atlas of the World for Commercial and Library Reference.* Philadelphia: L. D. Maltby & Co., William M. Bradley & Bros., 1886. 139 pp. 75 color maps.

> Source: MTLAcc, entry #2, volume donated by Clemens.

BRADY, CYRUS TOWNSEND (1861–1920). *The Bishop; Being Some Account of His Strange Adventures on the Plains.* Illus. New York: Harper & Brothers, 1903. 304 pp.

> Source: MTLAcc, entry #984, volume donated by Clemens.

———. *For Love of Country: A Story of Land and Sea in the Days of the Revolution.* Illus. New York: Charles Scribner's Sons, 1904. 354 pp.

> Source: MTLAcc, entry #36, volume donated by Clemens.

———. *The Grip of Honor: A Story of Paul Jones and the American Revolution.* Illus. New York: Charles Scribner's Sons, 1904. 246 pp.

> Source: MTLAcc, entry #32, volume donated by Clemens.

BRASSEY, (LADY) ANNA (ANNIE) ALLNUTT (1839–1887). *A Voyage in the Sunbeam, Our Home in the Ocean for Eleven Months.* Copyright Edition. 2 vols. Leipzig: Bernhard Tauchnitz, 1879.

> Catalog: *C1951*, D1, $8, 2 vols.
>
> The wealthy Lady Brassey kept a meticulous record of her trip around the world in a large schooner with both sails and a steam engine. The lengthy journey took her to South America, Tahiti, Hawaii, Japan, China, and the Middle East. She provides meticulous details of the sights she saw and the natives she encountered, but little interpretation of indigenous customs or the effects of colonialism.

BRAY, ANNA ELIZA (KEMPE) STOTHARD (1790–1883). *Joan of Arc, and the Times of Charles the Seventh, King of France.*

London: Griffith and Farran, 1874. 360 pp.

This title headed a list of six books about Joan of Arc that Chatto & Windus prepared for Clemens at his request in 1892 (Clemens to Chatto & Windus, Florence, 13 October 1892; Welland, *Mark Twain in England*, p. 158; PH of the list and letter in MTP).

BRECK, SAMUEL (1771–1862). *Recollections of Samuel Breck, with Passages from His Notebooks*. Ed. by Horace Elisha Scudder (1838–1902). Philadelphia: Porter & Coates, 1877. 310 pp.

Catalog: ListABP (1910), "Recollections of Samuel Breck, Scudder".

In November 1877 James R. Osgood & Company of Boston billed Clemens for a book purchased on 4 June 1877: "Recollections of Saml Breck." The price of $2 was discounted to $1.60 (Scrapbook #10, p. 69, MTP). Breck described his life in Boston and Philadelphia.

BRÉE, MALVINE (b. 1861). *The Groundwork of the Leschetizky Method; Issued with His Approval by His Assistant, Malvine Brée, with Forty-Seven Illustrative Cuts of Leschetizky's Hand. Translated from the German by Dr. Th[eodor] Baker [1851–1934]*. New York: G. Schirmer, 1902. [Publisher conjectured.]

Catalog: *A1911*, "folio, flexible cloth, N.Y. 1902," with a four-line note by Clemens laid in, lot 386, sold for $1.

Includes both elementary and advanced exercises employed by Theodor Leschetizky (1830–1915).

BREEN, HENRY H. (1805–1882). *Modern English Literature: Its Blemishes & Defects*. London: Longman, Brown, Green, & Longmans, 1857. 307 pp.

Inscription: inscribed across the title page by Clemens in pencil: "Saml. L. Clemens/Hartford 1876/Use with care, for it is a scarce book—England had to be ransacked in order to get this copy—or the bookseller speaketh falsely."

Marginalia: marked and annotated by Clemens in blue-black ink, particularly in the lengthy chapter titled "Plagiarism" (pp. 209–296). Breen amassed many dozens of cases in which textual evidence demonstrates either conscious or unconscious borrowing of memorable thoughts and phrases. On that topic Clemens defended Alexandre Dumas's assertion that "the man of genius does not steal; he conquers: and what he conquers, he annexes to his empire," noting in the margin of page 218: "A good deal of truth in it. Shakespeare took other people's quartz and extracted gold from it—it was a nearly valueless commodity before" (quoted by Walter Blair, *MT&HF* [1960], p. 60).

Catalogs: ListABP (1910), "Modern English Literature (note), Breen"; "Retz Appraisal," p. 5, valued at $40.

Location: Mark Twain Papers, Bancroft Library, University of California at Berkeley.

Copy examined: Clemens's copy.

In a manuscript probably written soon after he obtained Breen's *Modern English Literature*, "Comments on English Diction," Mark Twain observed that "one is sleepily unconscious of the blemishes that disfigure our best literature until he inspects a page of it through Mr. Breen's disenchanting magnifier" (quoted by Jervis Langdon in *Some Reminiscences* [1938], p. 20; repr. in *Mark Twain in Elmira* [2013], pp. 212–216). Twain favored books that exposed fallacies in common assumptions, so the thesis that supposedly impeccable "masterpieces" of English literature are in reality riddled with grammatical flaws

and uncredited borrowings predictably had an irresistible appeal for him. He must have especially enjoyed Breen's final chapter, "Literary Impostors" (pp. 297–307) with its accounts of one-celebrated works such as James Macpherson's *Poems of Ossian* that completely duped the public. In 1887 he turned to Breen's book for the names of twenty-four luminaries, including Thomas Carlyle, Thomas Macaulay, and Walter Scott, who employed "bad grammar and slovenly English" sufficiently to exonerate General Grant from Matthew Arnold's strictures on his ungrammatical constructions (speech to the Army and Navy Club of Connecticut, 27 April 1887, *MTSpk*, pp. 225–227). Paine considered *Modern English Literature* to have been among Mark Twain's favorite books, and he reported that on one occasion Twain used the volume as a text for a paper on slipshod English that he prepared for the Saturday Morning Club in Hartford (*MTB*, p. 1539). *MT&HF* (1960), pp. 59–60; *MTC* (1967), p. 113.

BRENNAN, GEORGE HUGH (1865–1918). *Bill Truetell, A Story of Theatrical Life*. Illustrated by James Montgomery Flagg (1877–1960). Chicago: A. C. McClurg & Co., 1909. 282 pp.

Source: MTLAcc, entry #2175, volume donated from Clemens's library by Clara Clemens Gabrilowitsch in 1910.

Brennan listed himself in the Fall River, Massachusetts city directories as a theatrical manager (though sometimes as a newspaper editor). His novel tells the story of the American theater through the life of one actor.

BREWER, EBENEZER COBHAM (1810–1897). *A Dictionary of Miracles: Imitative, Realistic, and Dogmatic, with Illustrations*. Spine cracked. London: Chatto and Windus, 1884. 582 pp.

Inscription: on the half-title page, in purple ink, by Olivia Clemens: "S L. Clemens/Rue de L'Universite 169/Paris 1895".

Marginalia: Clemens made vertical pencil marks on page xxxiii at the account of miracles associated with the body of William of Norwich, who was supposedly murdered by Jews. Clemens marked with black ink the entry for "Imposture: Richard Mainy"—a man supposedly possessed by the Devil (pp. 190–191), drawing a series of vertical marginal brackets. Under the entry for "Celibacy" he used black ink to insert a question mark beside the word "celibacy." On page 496 Clemens underlined the word "consummated" in the sentence "when the marriage was consummated, Marie [Jeanne Marie de Maillé] told her young husband she had made a vow to Christ of perpetual virginity."

Location: Mark Twain Library, Redding, Connecticut.

Copy examined: Clemens's copy, viewed in 1970 and again in June 1982. Has the pencil accession number of "1234".

———. *A Dictionary of Phrase and Fable, Giving the Derivation, Source, or Origin of Common Phrases, Allusions, and Words That Have a Tale to Tell*. Third edition [according to the Preface, p. viii]. Reddish-orange cloth, gilt lettering on spine. London: Cassell, Petter, & Galpin & Co., [1872]. 983 pp. [Publication date supplied.]

Provenance: Beth Steinhardt Dominianni, Library Director of the Mark Twain Library at Redding, reported that a family with "long ties to Redding" had donated this book to her institution (email to Alan Gribben, 17 April 2017). It seems probable that Clara Clemens Gabrilowitsch donated this volume to the Mark Twain Library and that it was subsequently sold at one of the periodic book sales to benefit the Library.

Location: Mark Twain Library, Redding Connecticut. Displays the purple oval stamps of the Mark Twain Library.

Copy examined: Clemens's copy. Viewed on 8 November 2019. The title page has been removed and the spine is loose. On the rear pastedown endpaper the original accession number in pencil ("2533") was crossed out in black ink and a new number assigned in the same ink: "4002". The volume shows a price of $1.50

On 14 July 1880 Estes & Lauriat of Boston billed Clemens for "1 Phrase & Fable $2.50"; Clemens paid on 20 July 1880 (receipt in MTP).

——. *Guide to the Scientific Knowledge of Things Familiar.* New York: C. S. Francis & Co., 1855. 490 pp.

Inscription: the front free endpaper is signed in pencil, "Lydia A. Hill/Redding Ridge/Conn."

Location: Mark Twain Library, Redding, Connecticut.

Copy examined: someone shelved this volume with the books donated to the Mark Twain Library by Clemens and his daughter Clara Clemens Gabrilowitsch, but it does not belong there. Descendants of the Hill family donated various books with early imprints to the Redding community library that usually (like this one) contain the purple Mark Twain Library oval stamps but no accession number. I examined the unmarked volume in June 1982 and recommended that it be removed from the Clemens collection.

——. *The Reader's Handbook of Allusions, References, Plots and Stories. Thirteenth thousand.* London: Chatto & Windus, 1892. 1,399 pp.

Inscription: "S. L. Clemens. 1895 Paris."

Provenance: formerly in the Mark Twain Library at Redding, Connecticut.

Catalog: *Mott 1952*, #37, $12.50.

Brewster, (Sir) David (1781–1868). *The Martyrs of Science; or, The Lives of Galileo, Tycho Brahe, and Kepler* (first published in London in 1841).

In the same purple ink with which he made his well-known declaration of his predilections as a reader in 1909, Clemens listed at the top of the same discarded envelope: "The Agony Column./2 books by Rev. C. W. Bardsley/ Wanderings in Patagonia./ The Martyrs of Science (Brewster)" (MTP). The first title refers to a novel published in 1909. See Gribben, "'I Detest Novels, Poetry & Theology'" (1977); a revision of this essay appears as a chapter in Volume One of the present work.

Bridgman, L[ewis]. J[esse]. (1857–1931). "To Mark Twain" (poem).

A prolific illustrator of children's books and history scenes, Bridgman also wrote light verse. Inspired by what appeared to be the ghost of a little girl whispering in Mark Twain's ear in a photograph of the author reading in bed, Bridgman produced a two-stanza poem speculating that she was Twain's secret muse (*Harper's Weekly* 50.2607 [8 December 1906]: 1748). Clemens was a regular reader of the Harper magazines.

Briggs, Charles Augustus (1841–1913). "Criticism and Dogma," *North American Review* 182.595 (June 1906): 861–874.

Mark Twain scoffed at this article by (in his words) "the most

daringly broad-minded religious person now occupying an American pulpit" in his 20 June 1906 Autobiographical Dictation, *AutoMT* 2: 131). Owing to Briggs' liberal views on scriptural interpretation he had left the Presbyterian Church in 1898 and become an Episcopalian priest.

Brine, Mary Dow (Northam) (1816–1913). *Grandma's Attic Treasures. A Story of Old-Time Memories.* Illus. New York: E. P. Dutton and Co., [1881]. 94 pp. [Poetry.]

In a long, rhyming poem a grandmother relates the story of her happy marriage. She returns again and again to thoughts of some furniture formerly in her attic that unscrupulous antique dealers got from her at a bargain price. (A family table is eventually recovered.) Annie Moffett Webster wrote to her brother Samuel E. Moffett on 19 December 1881 about her Christmas gift-buying excursion in downtown New York City: "We meant to go to Leggat's but I was thankful to stop at Dutton's on Broadway and buy all the books we wanted there. We bought 'Grandma's Attic Treasures' for Aunt Livy" (MTP).

——. *My Boy and I; or, On the Road to Slumberland.* Illustrated by Doris Wheeler (1856–1940). Designed by Louis C. Tiffany & Co. Oblong, leather-bound. New York: George W. Harlan & Co., 1881. 60 leaves. [Illustrator, publisher, binding, and pages supplied.]

Catalog: *A1911*, "oblong, 8vo, leather covers, N.Y. 1881," lot 48, sold for $2.

Twelve poems and lullabies express tender motherly love for an infant.

Brinkley, Frank (1841–1912), ed. *Japan; Described and Illustrated by the Japanese; Written by Eminent Japanese Authorities and Scholars.* Illustrated with photographs, some of them hand-colored. Original ¾ brown morocco. 5 vols. Boston: J. B. Millet Co., [cop. 1904]. Bound at the Monastery Hill Bindery.

Inscription: signed in Volume I only, on the first flyleaf: "S L Clemens/(Mark Twain)".

Location: Albert and Shirley Small Special Collections Library, University of Virginia, Charlottesville. Donated by Clifton Waller Barrett.

Copy examined: a copy purportedly belonging to Clemens, examined in 1970. The uncharacteristic signature makes one extremely cautious about certifying this as a genuine association item. A number of other forged association copies were identically inscribed by Eugene Field II. This was not Clemens's habitual signature for his library books.

Brisbin, James Sanks (1837–1892). *Trees and Tree-Planting.* New York: Harper & Brothers, 1888. 258 pp.

Source: MTLAcc, entry #1802, volume donated by Clemens.

Bristed, Charles Astor (1820–1874). *Five Years in an English University.* Third edition, revised. Original russet cloth, gilt, brown-coated endpapers. New York: G. P. Putnam & Sons, 1873. 572 pp.

Inscription: in pencil on the front free endpaper: "S. L. Clemens/1873".

Marginalia: Clemens's penciled brackets or marks on pages 59, 61, 62, 65, and 77; page 95 was folded down.

Catalogs: *A1911*, "12mo, cloth, N.Y. 1873," quotes signature, lot 49, sold for $2.25; *L1912*, lot 7, sold for $5; Christie's, New York City, 1–2 February 1988 auction, lot 465, sold for $$2,750 (with three other books) to

Randall House, Los Angeles.

Provenance: purchased for $35 from Maxwell Hunley Rare Books of Beverly Hills by Estelle Doheny and donated in 1945 to St. John's Seminary, Camarillo, California, where it became part of the Carrie Estelle Doheny Collection for more than four decades. Sold by Christie's on behalf of St. John's Seminary and the Archdiocese of Los Angeles in 1988. Contains the bookmark of Frederick W. Skiff, West Haven, Connecticut. Subsequently in the collection of Nick Karanovich, Fort Wayne, Indiana.

Location: collection of Kevin Mac Donnell, Austin, Texas.

Copy examined: Clemens's copy, in 1970. Has an original Putnam advertising bookmark laid in. Displays the *A1911* sale label on the front pastedown endpaper. Also has the bookplate of "Estelle Doheny."

Bristed's book contrasted the American system of higher education with that of Cambridge University.

BRODHEAD, EVA WILDER (MCGLASSON) (1870–1915). *Bound in Shallows; A Novel.* Illus. New York: Harper & Brothers, 1897. 271 pp.

Source: MTLAcc, entry #1526, volume donated by Clemens.

The Kentucky-born fiction writer Brodhead resided frequently in Colorado after her marriage in 1894.

———. *Diana's Livery.* New York: Harper & Brothers, 1891. 286 pp.

Source: MTLAcc, entry #1439, volume donated by Clemens.

Set in a fictional Shaker community in Kentucky, the romance novel *Diana's Livery* raised issues of utopian possibilities and gender prerogatives.

———. *An Earthly Paragon; A Novel.* Illustrated by Frank V[incent]. DuMond (1865–1951). New York: Harper & Brothers, 1892. 207 pp.

Source: MTLAcc, entry #1624, volume donated by Clemens.

BRONTË, CHARLOTTE (1816–1855), pseud. "Currer Bell." *Jane Eyre.* Illus. New York: T. Y. Crowell & Co., [cop. 1890]. 313 pp.

Source: MTLAcc, entry #1044, volume donated by Isabel V. Lyon, Clemens's secretary. Title page loose.

———. *Jane Eyre* (novel, published in 1847).

Catalog: Olivia Clemens owned a copy bound with Brontë's *Villette* (1862 ed.), according to *Mott 1952*, #38.

In a newspaper interview conducted in Pittsburgh and published on 29 December 1884 Mark Twain referred to *Jane Eyre* as an often-read novel "which in many households finds a place between a Bible and the prayer book" (Scharnhorst, ed., *Complete Interviews*, p. 64). Olivia Clemens gave a copy of *Jane Eyre* to Katy Leary as part of her attempt to advance her housekeeper's meager education (*LMT*, p. 59). Clemens mentioned Brontë's manuscript humorously in some ruminations in June 1891 about changes introduced into the publishing field by the typewriter: "If Jane Eyre was written in that woman's customary hand—500 words to the square inch & a microscope required—no wonder no publisher accepted it" (NB 30, *N&J* 3: 639).

———. *Life and Works of Charlotte Brontë and Her Sisters.* Illus. 7 vols. London: Elder & Co., 1872–1873. [Edition conjectured. The set was reprinted at least seven times between 1872 and 1903. It contained all of the novels written by the Brontës.]

Catalog: *C1951*, #76c, $13, edition unspecified, listed among the books signed by Clemens.

Clemens alluded to "gigantic geniuses like those Brontë sisters" in a letter of 21 October 1881 sent to an aspiring Canadian writer, Bruce Weston Munro. "And yet even they were enabled to do it only because they had a capital of experience to draw from that was nearly as prodigious as their genius" (*Sotheby's 2003*, #48).

———. *Shirley. A Tale.* New York: Derby & Jackson, 1856. 572 pp.

Source: MTLAcc, entry #966, volume donated by Clemens.

———. *Shirley.* Illus. Philadelphia: Porter & Coates, n.d. 587 pp.

Source: MTLAcc, entry #2173, volume donated from Clemens's library by Clara Clemens Gabrilowitsch in 1910.

———. *Shirley* (novel, originally published in 1849).

Olivia Clemens owned a copy bound with Brontë's *Villette* (1862 edition), according to *Mott 1952*, item #38.

———. *Villette.* New York, 1862.

Inscription: "Olivia L. Langdon. Spuyten Duyvil. June 1863."

Catalog: *Mott 1952*, #38, $5, bound with Brontë's *Shirley* and *Jane Eyre*.

Clara Clemens listed the title of this novel in her commonplace book (1888?-1904, Paine 150, MTP).

BRONTË, EMILY (1818–1848), pseud. "Ellis Bell" and ANNE BRONTË (1820–1849), pseud. "Acton Bell." *Wuthering Heights and Agnes Grey, by Ellis and Acton Bell.* New edition, rev. Preface by Charlotte Brontë (1816–1855). 2 vols. Leipzig: B. Tauchnitz, 1851.

Source: MTLAcc, entry #2183, Volume I only (336 pp.), donated from Clemens's library by Clara Clemens Gabrilowitsch in 1910.

While summering at Kaltenleutgeben, Austria in 1898 Mark Twain wrote a fragmentary sketch about a maid whom he called "Wuthering Heights" (DV236, MTP). He never makes clear how she reminds him of the novel, but since she "talks all the time" perhaps he thought she resembled the major narrator in *Wuthering Heights*, the housekeeper Nelly Dean. The fragment is not successfully humorous. Clemens wrote to Jean in July 1906 from Henry H. Rogers' sumptuous home in Fairhaven, Massachusetts: "I got up at 5 in the morning yesterday at Wuthering Heights" (MTP).

BROOKS, ARTHUR (1845–1895). *Phillips Brooks.* New York: Harper & Brothers, 1893. 50 pp.

Source: MTLAcc, entry #1205, volume donated by Clemens.

"Just a word to scoff at you, with your extravagant suggestion that I read the biography of Phillips Brooks—the very dullest book that has been printed for a century. Joe, ten pages of Mrs. Cheney's masterly biography of her father—no, *five* pages of it—contain more meat, more sense, more literature, more brilliancy, than that whole basketful of drowsy rubbish put together" (SLC to Joseph H. Twichell, 28 August 1901, *MTL*, p. 712; *LMTJHT*, p. 284). It is most probable that Clemens was referring to Alexander V. G. Allen's *Life and Letters of Phillips Brooks* (1900), but Arthur Brooks' brief biography remains a remote possibility. Mary (Bushnell) Cheney's *Life and*

Letters of Horace Bushnell had appeared in 1880. Clemens felt that Horace Bushnell was the "greatest clergyman that the last century produced" (speech to the Art Students' Association, St. Louis, Missouri, 7 June 1902, *MTLW*, TS in MTP).

BROOKS, ELBRIDGE STREETER (1846–1902). *Chivalric Days, and the Boys and Girls Who Helped to Make Them.* Illus. New York: G. P. Putnam's Sons, 1886. 308 pp.

Source: MTLAcc, entry # 1924, volume donated from Clemens's library by Clara Clemens Gabrilowitsch in 1910. A dozen stories written for children and spanning twenty centuries of historical events.

BROOKS, HENRY S[PONG]. (1831–1910). *A Catastrophe in Bohemia, and Other Stories.* New York: Charles L. Webster & Co., 1893. 372 pp.

Clemens's publishing firm advertised this volume of twelve short stories set in mining towns in localities of Lower California and Mexico (*Publishers' Trade List Annual 1893*). Many of them had previously appeared in *Overland Monthly*. The London-born Brooks came to California in 1849 and became an authority on mining. In the 1890s he moved to the East Coast and eventually settled in Dobbs Ferry, New York.

BROOKS, JOHN GRAHAM (1846–1938). *The Social Unrest: Studies in Labor and Socialist Movements.* New York: Macmillan Co., 1903. 394 pp.

Source: MTLAcc, entry #548, volume donated by Clemens.

BROOKS, NOAH (1830–1903). "Personal Reminiscences of Lincoln," *Scribner's Monthly* 15.5 (March 1878): 673–681.

In "About Magnanimous-Incident Literature" (1878) Mark Twain quotes Brooks' anecdote about Abraham Lincoln's praising the acting of J. H. Hackett, who afterward became an annoying office-seeker. The story appears on page 675 of Brooks' essay.

————— and ISAAC BROMLEY (1833–1898). "Punch, Brothers, Punch" (newspaper jingle, published in 1875).

The jingle served as a source for Mark Twain's sketch, "Punch, Brothers, Punch!" (1876), initially titled "A Literary Nightmare." Twain included the "author of Punch Brothers Punch (now on Tribune)" in his lengthy list of humorists compiled in 1881 (NB 19, *N&J* 2: 429). Brooks is also mentioned in Notebook 22 (1884, *N&J* 3: 58).

R. Kent Rasmussen, *Critical Companion to Mark Twain: A Literary Reference to His Life and Work*, 2 vols. (New York: Facts on File, 2007), 1: 420.

BROOKS, WALTER (1856–1933), trans. *Stories from Four Languages Retold in English.* New York: Brentano's, [cop. 1905]. 335 pp.

Source: MTLAcc, entry #2168, volume donated from Clemens's library by Clara Clemens Gabrilowitsch in 1910.

BROUGH, WILLIAM (1826–1870). *The Field of the Cloth of Gold* (stage extravaganza, produced in 1868).

Hawley, Goodrich & Company of Hartford charged Clemens on 24 May 1880 for "one ticket to 'The Field of the Cloth of Gold' $1.00" (receipt in MTP).

BROUGHAM, JOHN (1810–1880). *The Christian Martyrs under Constantine and Maxentius* (spectacle, produced in 1867).

Mark Twain poked fun at the production performed at Barnum's Museum, in which a menagerie of wild animals was marched across the stage (2 March 1867 letter to the *Alta California*; *MTTMB*, pp. 118–119).

————— (adapt.). *David Copperfield. A Drama in Two Acts. Adapted from Dickens' Popular Work of the Same Name.* New York: S. French & Son, n.d. 24 pp.

Source: MTLAcc, entry #2126a, volume donated from Clemens's library by Clara Clemens Gabrilowitsch in 1910. Brougham first produced this adaptation in New York City in 1851.

————— (adapt.). *Dombey and Son* (dramatization of Dickens' novel).

Mark Twain lauded Dan Setchell's characterization of Captain Cuttle in "A Voice for Setchell" (*Californian* 3 [27 May 1865]: 9; *ET&S* 2 [1981]: 172–173). Subsequently in Notebook 6 (1866) he used "Sea Monster" and "Captain Cuttle" as nicknames for passengers he met aboard the *Ajax* (*N&J* 1: 188). He alluded to Setchell's role as Captain Cuttle as late as 15 January 1903 (NB 46, TS pp. 5, 6). Brougham had first produced this adaptation in New York City in 1848.

Edgar M. Branch, "'My Voice is Still for Setchell': A Background Study of 'Jim Smiley and His Jumping Frog,'" *PMLA* 82.7 (December 1967): 598.

—————. *The Lottery of Life: A Story of New York* (play, produced in 1868).

Grace King attended Augustin Daly's production of this crime melodrama with the Clemenses on 20 November 1888. "We had Daly's own stage box—and Daly's company, most of the time," she reported. "Oh, it was all great fun!" (King to May King McDowell, 22 November 1888; quoted by Robert Bush, "Grace King and Mark Twain," *American Literature* 44.1 [March 1972]: 44; Fears, *Day by Day* 2: 324).

BROWN, ALEXANDER (1843–1906). *The Genesis of the United States.* Portraits. Illus. Maps. 2 vols. Boston: Houghton, Mifflin and Co., 1890.

Inscription: on the flyleaves of both volumes: "S. L. Clemens, Hartford, December, ["Dec." in Volume II] 1890".

Catalogs: *A1911*, "Royal 8vo, cloth, Bost. 1890," quotes the signature, lot 50, sold for $1.50, Volume 2 only; *C1951*, D28, sold for $2.50, presumably Volume I only; *Zeitlin 1951*, item #9, sold for $25, Volume I only.

Clemens must have objected initially to receiving Brown's book, for on 10 December 1890 Houghton, Mifflin and Company wrote: "We beg to enclose herewith the slip of paper which seemed to warrant us in sending you a copy of Alexander Brown's work on the 'Genesis of the United States.'" On the envelope of their letter Clemens wrote in pencil: "Pay it. SLC" (MTP).

BROWN, ALICE (1857–1948). *Judgment, A Novel.* Illustrated by W[illiam]. T[homas]. Smedley (1858–1920). New York: Harper & Brothers, 1903. 195 pp.

Source: MTLAcc, entry #2169, volume donated from Clemens's library by Clara Clemens Gabrilowitsch in 1910. W. T. Smedley illustrated Mark Twain's "A Dog's Tale" (1903).

BROWN, EMMA ELIZABETH (b. 1847). *Life of Oliver Wendell Holmes [1809–1894].* Boston: D. Lothrop and Co., 1884. 304 pp.

Inscription: signed "SL. Clemens" in ink.

Catalog: *C1951*, D19, $15, listed among books signed by Clemens.

Location: acquired on eBay on 11 June 2021 by Stacy

Mosher, Brooklyn, New York. The volume is unmarked.

BROWN, HORATIO ROBERT FORBES (1854–1926). *Studies in the History of Venice*. 2 vols. Original green cloth, extremities slightly rubbed. New York: E. P. Dutton and Company, 1907.

Inscriptions: the front pastedown endpaper of Volume I is signed in ink: "Feb. 1908./S L. Clemens"; the front pastedown endpaper of Volume II is signed in ink: "S L. Clemens/Feb. 1908."

Marginalia: a lengthy (182-word) note written in ink on the front free endpaper of Volume I describes Clemens's (purported) meeting with Brown in Venice thirty years earlier, signed "S. L. C." and dated 21 February 1908. In this account Clemens claims that Brown lost twelve years of his life when his book manuscript was burned in a fire and he had to begin his research all over again. "The tragedy had made his *head* (& upper face) suddenly & quite visibly old, but his body hadn't had time, yet, to catch up" (quoted in Christie's auction catalog). The dates do not jibe with Brown's birth date, Brown does not mention any such fire in his preface, and ten of the twenty essays had appeared in print long before this book was published, so the story must have been invented. Clemens made one correction in black ink in the preface of Volume I, p. ix. Pages 35 and 179 were folded over in Volume I; page 177 (at the subject of Othello) was folded over in Volume II.

Catalogs: ListABP (1910), "Venetian History, Brown"; *C1951*, #37a, $60.

Provenance: Carrie Estelle Doheny Collection, St. John's Seminary, Camarillo, California. Donated by Mrs. Doheny in 1951 after she purchased the volumes for $95 from Zeitlin & Ver Brugge, Booksellers, Los Angeles. Sold at auction by Christie's on behalf of St. John's Seminary on 17 October 1988 (lot 1175) for $4,380.

Copies examined: Clemens's copies.

BROWN, JAMES BALDWIN (1820–1884). *The Home Life, in the Light of Its Divine Idea*. New York: D. Appleton & Co., 1866. 327 pp. [Edition conjectured.]

In a letter written to Olivia Langdon on 5 December 1868 from New York City, Clemens alluded to her forbidding him "to read the 'Home Life'" (*MTLet* 2: 314). He seems to refer to this Christian domestic guide by Brown, an English Congregational minister with generally liberal theological leanings.

Harris, *Courtship* (1996), pp. 96–97.

BROWN, JAMES MOORE (1799–1862). *The Captives of Abb's Valley; A Legend of Frontier Life*. Philadelphia: Presbyterian Board of Publication, [cop. 1854]. 168 pp.

Source: MTLAcc, entry #546, volume donated by Clemens. Describes an eighteenth-century massacre in Virginia, after which two children were carried into captivity by raiding Shawnees.

BROWN, JOHN, M.D. (1810–1882). *Letters of Dr. John Brown, with Letters from Ruskin, Thackeray, and Others. Edited by His Son [John Brown, Jr., 1846–1926] and D[avid]. W[illiam]. Forrest. D. D. [d. 1918] with Biographical Introductions by Elizabeth T. McLaren*. London: Adam and Charles Black, 1907. 367 pp.

Catalogs: ListABP (1910), "Letters of Dr. John Brown"; *C1951*, #45a, $85, listed among the books containing

Clemens's marginal notes.

Dr. Brown's son John Brown, Jr. wrote to Clemens on 22 December 1907 (PH in MTP). Clemens replied to him on 20 June 1908 to report that he had "economized the 'Letters,' tasting them at intervals & making them last." He especially singled out Dr. Brown's description of Olivia Clemens, "just as she was" (PH in MTP). In an August 1873 letter Dr. Brown had referred to Mrs. Clemens as "a startlingly pretty little creature, with eyes like a Peregrine's" (p. 224). In a letter dated only 1879 Olivia Clemens expressed concern about Dr. Brown's admitting that he felt profound depression: "I receive good every time I even *think* of you. Can a life that produces that effect on others be a wasted life?" (p. 358).

———. *Marjorie Fleming, A Sketch; Being the Paper Entitled "Pet Marjorie": A Story of Child-Life Fifty Years Ago* (first published in 1863). [Edition unidentified.]

Location: unknown.

Marjorie Fleming (1803–1811), a Scottish child prodigy, poet, and diarist who died at the age of eight, was one of the child figures whom Clemens came to adore. In 1904 Clemens inscribed a note to Clara Clemens on the front pastedown endpaper of his copy of L. Macbean's *The Story of Pet Marjorie* (1904): "This enlargement will properly go with the first 'Marjorie Fleming' which Dr. John Brown gave to your mother in Edinburgh in 1873. S. L. C." (Carrie Estelle Doheny Collection, St. John's Seminary). He repeated this reference when he came to write "Marjorie Fleming, the Wonder Child" (1909): Dr. Brown "gave my wife his little biography of Marjorie, and I have it yet." But in composing this sketch Mark Twain actually relied on Macbean's book, which contained a reprint of Brown's sketch; Twain heavily annotated this portion of the Macbean volume.

On 14 February 1906 Clemens wrote to Gertrude Natkins (whom he often called "Marjorie") from New York City to explain that he had purchased a copy of Dr. John Brown's *Marjorie Fleming* for her, but "fell to reading it, & became fascinated as always before"; he promised to send it along soon (PH in MTP). He wrote to Natkins again on 24 March 1906 about Brown's "little comrade of his musings & his dreams" in terms that invite comparisons with Twain's "My Platonic Sweetheart" (written in 1898). On 2 February 1906 Twain dictated a tribute to "Dr. John Brown, that noble and beautiful soul—rescuer of marvelous Marjorie from oblivion" (*AutoMT* 1: 328). Clemens wrote to Dr. Brown's son on 5 August 1909 to recall how Dr. John Brown had given Olivia Clemens a copy of *Marjorie Fleming* "& read passages to us. . . . I remember it so clearly, so vividly!" (PH in MTP).

———. "Rab and His Friends" (short story, first published in 1859).

Clemens complimented Brown on 27 April 1874 for the many friends "Rab" had made since its first publication, assuring him that "Rab's friends are your friends" (*MTL*, p. 218; *MTLet* 6: 122). Mark Twain pointedly specified that an edition of "Rab" was visible in the "richly furnished apartment" of Aunt Susan, "a refined and sensible lady, if signs and symbols may go for anything," in "The Loves of Alonzo Fitz Clarence and Rosannah Ethelton" (1878). Clemens adopted a dog named "Rab" in 1885 ("a noble dog") but soon had to send him back because he ran into the street to greet every passing horse and wagon and street car (ALS, 22 September 1882, Hartford, published in "Mark Twain on Rab," *Mark Twain Quarterly* 5.3 [Fall-Winter 1942–1943]: 19). Twain drew on autobiographical recollections when he caused Alice Edwards to remind Henry in "The Great Dark" (written 1898) that "Doctor John Brown, of *Rab and His Friends*," had visited them in Edinburgh (*WWD?*, p. 128). In December 1903 Twain alluded to Dr. Brown at a lunch; George Gregory Smith implied that Twain identified him as the author of "Rab and His Friends" (Ralph H. Orth, "George Gregory Smith and Mark Twain: Florence, 1903–1904," *Mark Twain Journal* 41.2 [Fall 2003]: 31). Twain mentioned Brown's "Rab" story again in an Autobiographical Dictation on 2 February 1906 (*AutoMT* 1: 328) and referred to it as "that pathetic and beautiful masterpiece" in another dictation on 5 February 1906 (*AutoMT* 1: 329). Brown's story is sentimental and depressing by turns.

K. Patrick Ober, *Mark Twain and Medicine: "Any Mummery Will Cure"* (Columbia: University of Missouri Press, 2003), pp. 10–11.

———. *Spare Hours*. Boston: Ticknor and Fields, 1862. 458 pp. [Contains "Rab and His Friends" on pp. 21–40.]

Inscription: none, but one front flyleaf seems to be missing.

Marginalia: a stray pencil mark, apparently not intentional, on page 149 (which is turned down) at the story entitled "My Father's Memoir."

Location: Mark Twain Library, Redding, Connecticut.

Copy examined: Clemens's copy. Examined in 1970 and again in June 1982. Has a black (not red) ink accession number: "2913". The binding is loose.

Eighteen philosophical essays ponder a wide variety to subjects ranging from courageous dogs to the lamented Arthur H. Hallam to theories of art to a valiant victim of dwarfism.

Brown, Katharine Holland (1874–1931). *Diane; A Romance of the Icarian Settlement on the Mississippi River.* Illustrated by S. J. Dudley. New York: Doubleday, Page & Co., 1904. 440 pp.

Source: MTLAcc, entry #957, volume donated by Isabel V. Lyon, Clemens's secretary.

Brown's subject was a socialist utopian community founded in Nauvoo, Illinois in 1849. Its residents dispersed in 1860.

Brown, Mary Irene (1872–1895). *Poems*. Cambridge, Massachusetts: Riverside Press, 1906. 82 pp.

Source: MTLAcc, entry #2014, volume donated from Clemens's library by Clara Clemens Gabrilowitsch in 1910.

Brown, Phoebe (Hinsdale) (1783–1861). ["Autobiography." Unpublished MS.]

On 16 December 1881 Clemens wrote to Howells from Hartford about Joseph H. Twichell's bringing over Brown's "MS autobiography (written in 1848,)" with the result that "by George I came near not getting to bed at all, last night, on account of the lurid fascinations of it. Why in the nation it has never got into print, I can't understand" (*MTHL*, p. 381).

———. "I love to steal a while away" (hymn).

Clemens burlesqued this hymn in an 8 November 1876 letter to William Dean Howells (*MTHL*, p. 162), and mentioned it again in a 16 December 1881 letter to Howells (*MTHL*, p. 381).

Brown, William Hubbard (1796–1867). *An Historical Sketch of the Early Movement in Illinois for the Legalization of Slavery, Read at the Annual Meeting of the Chicago Historical Society, December 5th, 1864.* Fergus's Historical Series, Number Four. Chicago: Fergus Printing Co., 1876. 30 pp.

Inscription: "Mark Twain" written in ink at the top of the front cover, with a flourish added underneath the name.

Location: unknown.

Copy examined: a photocopy of the front cover bearing a purported "Mark Twain" signature.

This pamphlet was offered to rare book seller Kevin Mac Donnell of Austin, Texas in 2012 (Mac Donnell to Alan Gribben, email, 4 February 2012), who declined to purchase it. The "autograph," rather crudely written, appears to have been copied from one of the volumes bearing a facsimile of Mark Twain's signature in the "Authorized Edition" of his works. Clemens hardly ever used his pen name when inscribing volumes in his personal library. Mac Donnell conjectured that this was another of the books and pamphlets in which Eugene Fields II and/or Harry Sickles forged Twain's autograph during the 1920s and 1930s. That surmise seems warranted, and in any event this is definitely not a Mark Twain association item.

Brown, William Wells (1814–1884). *Clotel; or, The President's Daughter: A Narrative of Slave Life in the United States* (1853); *Clotelle: A Tale of the Southern States* (1864); *Clotelle; or, The Colored Heroine* (1867).

No surviving copies of any variant version of Brown's powerful novel about life for those enslaved have been connected with Clemens, but see William H. Andrews, "Mark Twain, William Wells Brown, and the Problem of Authority in New Southern Writing," *Southern Literature and Literary Theory*, ed. Jefferson Humphries (Athens: University of Georgia Press, 1990), pp. 1–21.

Lucinda H. MacKeithan, "Huck Finn and the Slave Narratives: Lighting Out as Design," *Southern Review* 20.2 (April 1984): 247–264.

Browne, Charles Farrar (1834–1867), pseud. "Artemus Ward." *Artemus Ward, His Book.* Illus. New York: Carleton, 1867. 224 pp.

On the verso of a letter to James Redpath written on 24 October 1871 Mark Twain made several lecture notes that the editorial staff at the Mark Twain Project in Berkeley have identified (from the page numbers assigned by Twain) as deriving from this edition of Ward's writings (collection of Kevin Mac Donnell, Austin, Texas; *MTLet* 4: 478).

Clemens became friends with Browne in Virginia City in 1863, but not before he wrote a newspaper piece that mimicked Artemus Ward's cacography (Branch, *LAMT*, pp. 103–104). Browne died of consumption in England on 6 March 1867, much mourned as a comedic genius. "The New York *World* is not generally regarded as a humorous paper, but . . . one of its heaviest editorials would make Artemus Ward turn in his grave," Twain wrote in 1869 (Buffalo *Express*, 19 August 1869; *MTBE*, p. 9). A letter from Twain to James Redpath written on 24 October 1871 made clear his determination to take "*Artemus Ward, Humorist*, for my subject" in a series of upcoming lectures (*MTLet* 4: 478). Twain gave a lecture on "Artemus Ward, Humorist" on 16 December 1871, receiving $125 from the Boston Lyceum Bureau for his talk (*Sotheby's 2003*, lot 19). Twain quoted a commemorative poem about Browne in 1871; see the Catalog entry for the English writer James Rhoades, "On the Death of Artemus Ward." Browne was the subject of Twain's "First Interview with Artemus Ward," published in 1871. Marginalia Clemens wrote in M. de L. Landon's *Saratoga in 1901* (1872) charged Landon with using Ward's material "(& poorly stolen at that").

In 1879 Twain made an entry in his notebook, "2 or 3 yarns of Artemus Ward" (NB 18, *N&J* 2: 303). Artemus Ward was included in two lists of humorists to be considered for an anthology of American humor (NB 19 [1880], *N&J* 2: 363 and [1881], *N&J* 2: 429). Twain wrote "Art. Ward—306" in pencil at the top of the front cover of a copy of Twain's *Sketches, New and Old* (Leipzig: Bernhard Tauchnitz, 1883); extensive pencil notes on that book's front and back wrappers outline programs for Twain's lectures (collection of Kevin Mac Donnell, Austin, Texas; Gribben examined them in July 2004). Nine pieces by Artemus Ward—"A Visit to Brigham Young," "Women's Rights," "One of Mr. Ward's Business Letters," "On 'Forts,'" "Fourth of July Oration," "High-Handed Outrage at Utica," "Artemus Ward and the Prince of Wales," "Interview with Lincoln," and "Letters to His Wife"—appeared in *Mark Twain's Library of Humor* (1888), which had Twain's personal approval of its contents. Artemus Ward is mentioned as an eminent American humorist in Chapter 9 of *A Connecticut Yankee in King Arthur's Court* (1889). Twain praised Ward in a newspaper interview (Winnepeg, Canada *Nor'-Wester*, 27 July 1895, p. 1; *Complete Interviews*, pp. 163–164). Twain noted in 1903 that Ward was "beloved in England" (NB 46 [15 January 1903], TS p. 6), and Ward's name appeared in Twain's Notebook 48 (1906?), TS p. 10. However, in a 31 July 1906 Autobiographical Dictation (*MTE*, p. 202; *Auto* 2: 153), Twain included "Artemus Ward" among a list of American humorists "whose writings and sayings were once in everybody's mouth but are now heard of no more." He somewhat disparagingly attributed Ward's quondam popularity to "an odd trick of speech and spelling," comparing him to Josh Billings and Petroleum V. Nasby.

In 1932 Bernard DeVoto listed a mere "fifty words" that represented Mark Twain's verbal indebtedness to Artemus Ward, including the "Is He Dead?" joke from *Innocents Abroad* (1869). "Their minds were disparate, their intentions antagonistic, their methods incommensurable," DeVoto declared. "They were humorists and in the production of humor Artemus Ward was chronologically the first. That is all" (*MTAm*, pp. 219–221). Edgar M. Branch noted other similarities, however: affectations of naiveté, logical confusions, comic lists of words, anti-climax, understatement" (*LAMT* [1950], p. 104). Yet Branch concluded that Twain learned far more from Ward about the art of lecturing (i.e., performing in public, telling stories) than the writing of literature—a valid point. Walter Blair in *Native American Humor* (1937) also noted a few parallels, but followed DeVoto's lead in stating that "it is probable . . . that neither author particularly influenced the writings of the other. Both were following a well-established

tradition in American humor" (p. 150).

Dissenting opinions have been expressed vigorously. Harold Aspiz protested DeVoto's slighting of Ward as a model for Mark Twain's literary style and mounted a counter-argument that was full-scale but necessarily (at that time) based on circumstantial evidence ("Mark Twain's Reading" [1949], pp. 99–104). Aspiz incidentally nominated Ward's "The Loss of the Good Ship Polly Anne: A Pathetical Nautical Ballad" as a possible precursor of Twain's "The Aged Pilot Man" in *Roughing It* (1872). The Norton Critical Edition of *Huckleberry Finn* (1961), edited by Bradley, Beatty, and Long, reprinted Ward's "Artemus Ward and the Prince of Wales" sketch and recommended its comparison with Huck's discourse on kings and royal pretensions. A dissent from DeVoto's opinion was raised by Robert Rowlette in "'Mark Ward on Artemus Twain': Twain's Literary Debt to Ward," *American Literary Realism* 6.1 (Winter 1973): 12–25, which disputed Bernard DeVoto's "pontifical" opinion that Mark Twain owed almost nothing to Charles Farrar Browne. Rowlette's article helpfully summarized nearly all commentators' opinions on the issue of Twain's indebtedness to Ward. Rowlette convincingly lined up parallel treatments of the Mormons in Ward's writings and in Twain's *Roughing It* (1872) and located other striking examples of borrowing in Mark Twain's *The Innocents Abroad* (1869) and *Sketches, New and Old* (1875). Rowlette illustrated how often Twain used Ward's jokes, anecdotes, catch-phrases, snappers, and one-liners. Twain seemingly ceased that practice around 1872, though a few more correspondences are recognizable in *Life on the Mississippi* (1883). Presumably Twain disliked the growing public recognition that he was imitating Ward. Paul C. Rodgers, Jr., in "Artemus Ward and Mark Twain's 'Jumping Frog,'" *Nineteenth-Century Fiction* 28.3 (December 1973): 273–286, traced Ward's influence on the deadpan narration of, and his role as audience for, Twain's famous story. It was from Ward that Twain learned his "famous pose of comic innocence" (p. 279). Originally Twain intended for Ward to include the "Jumping Frog" story in *Artemus Ward, His Travels*; this explains why Twain's epistolary frame was addressed to "Mr. A. Ward." Readers err, Rodgers insisted, if they ignore Ward's function as Twain's putative audience for the tale. David E. E. Sloane, who had written "Mark Twain as a Literary Comedian: The Heritage of Artemus Ward in the 1860's" (Doctoral dissertation, Duke University, 1971), followed up with his *Mark Twain as a Literary Comedian* (Baton Rouge: Louisiana State University Press, 1979), adeptly investigating the Twain-Ward relationship. James Edward Caron, *Mark Twain: Unsanctified Newspaper Reporter* (Columbia: University of Missouri Press, 2008) relied on and extended Sloane's observations. John R. Pascal's *Artemus Ward: The Gentle Humorist* (Saarbrücken, Germany: VDM Verlag Dr. Müller Aktiengesellschaft & Co., 2009) analyzed *Artemus Ward's Panorama* and its illustrations and pondered what changes might have taken place in American literary history if Browne had lived to rival Mark Twain instead of dying of tuberculosis at the age of thirty-two. Kevin Mac Donnell, "How Samuel Clemens Found 'Mark Twain' in Carson City," *Mark Twain Journal* 50.1–2 (Spring/Fall 2012): 9–47, especially pages 26–32, documented Twain's gradual decision to abandon some of Artemus Ward's techniques of humor. Robert Rowlette, "Mark Twain's Indebtedness to Artemus Ward" (Master's thesis, University of Colorado, 1957); James C. Austin, *Artemus Ward* (New York: Twayne Publishers, 1964); John J. Pullen, "Mark Twain and Artemus Ward: A Bittersweet Friendship Is Born in Nevada," *Nevada Historical Society Quarterly* 22.3 (Fall 1979): 163–185; Judith Yaross Lee, "The Sociable Sam Clemens: Mark Twain Among Friends," *American Literary Realism* 50.3 (Spring 2018): 245–246; and David E. E. Sloane, "Literary Comedians," *Mark Twain in Context*, ed. John Bird (Cambridge, England: Cambridge University Press, 2020), pp. 58–66. See also the Catalog entry for *Vanity Fair*, a humor journal with which Ward was associated.

———. *Artemus Ward, His Travels*. Illustrated by [Edward F.] Mullen (active 1859–1879). Original green cloth, gilt. New York: Carleton; London: S. Low, Son & Co., 1870. 231 pp.

Inscription: the front flyleaf is inscribed by Dan Beard in black ink: "This book is from/Mark Twain's private/library. Stormfield./Redding, Conn./Dan Beard/Vice President/Mark Twain Library." Beard's note of authentication was likely intended to enhance the volume's value at a book fair held to raise funds for the Mark Twain Library in Redding, Connecticut. Beard was a resident of Redding during the years Clemens lived there, and the artist donated several books from his own library collection to the community library.

Marginalia: Clemens made the following pencil notes on the front free endpaper, writing sideways: "Wendell P[hillips] 95/sewing s[oc]iety 95/Built fire 99/Onions do/flap jax 101." These notations refer to passages and page numbers in the text. Clemens drew marginal brackets on pages 14, 17, 18, 19, 21, 22, 24, 26, 36, 37. 38, 39, 63, 67, 70, 72, 95, 99, 100, and 101, and also made marks on ten other pages.

Provenance: red ink accession number ("3097") of the Mark Twain Library, Redding, Connecticut on the rear endpaper, upper center. On the lower inner corner of the rear pastedown endpaper is the ticket of Maxwell Hunley, rare book dealer, Beverly Hills, California.

Location: collection of Kevin Mac Donnell, Austin, Texas. Purchased from Maxwell Hunley in January 1973 for $80.

Copy examined: Clemens's copy, in July 2004.

Artemus Ward, His Travels (first published in 1865) was the volume to which Ward invited Mark Twain to contribute a comic piece. Snafus involving the mails and the date of receipt instead sent Twain's classic "Jim Smiley and His Jumping Frog" into the pages of the doomed New York *Saturday Press* (see *ET&S* 2: 262–272).

This is the book in which Artemus Ward related (in Part II, Chapter VII, pp. 156–162) the most famous version of Horace Greeley's wild ride to Placerville, California with the daredevil stagecoach driver Hank Monk, during which Greeley, imploring Monk to slow down, bounced around so much that his bald head went through the canvas roof. Monk's only reaction was an admonition that storytellers would often repeat, "*Keep your seat, Horace!*" (p. 159). In Chapter 20 of *Roughing It* (1872) Twain would make fun of how frequently Western travelers encountered

variations of this tale.

A piece included in Ward's book, "Affairs Around the Village Green," drew significant praise from Clemens's cherished friend William Dean Howells in an introduction Howells would write for *Artemus Ward's Best Stories*, ed. Clifton Johnson (New York: Harper & Brothers, 1912). Conceding that Browne had "no such inventive gift as Clemens" (p. xiii), Howells nonetheless acknowledged that "in some of his beginnings Mark Twain formed himself from, if not on, Artemus Ward. The imitation could not last long; the great master was so immensely the master . . . and it by no means impeaches his superiority. I think him incomparably the greater talent, and yet not always. In such a sketch as 'Affairs Around the Village Green,' where Browne consents to be most himself, there is a sweetness, a gentleness, a fineness in the humor and the quaint unexpectedness of its turns, which is not surpassed by anything that Clemens did" (pp. xiv-xv). Ward's brief "Village Green" narrative relates his move from unsatisfactory lodgings in New York City to the tranquility of his former home of "some years past"—a village of forty elm-shaded houses and a general store. "To the right of us is a mountain—to the left a lake. The village nestles between. Of course it does. I never read a novel in my life in which the villages didn't nestle. Villages invariably nestle. It is a kind of way they have." Ward is pleased that there is a village green, "although I have not as yet danced on my village green, as the melodramatic peasant usually does his." At the general store Ward often encounters "an old Revolutionary soldier" who "distinctly remembers Washington; they all do." After a series of amusing gags and puns, Ward ends by reviewing the various fates of his former school friends.

Kevin Mac Donnell, "Was Huck Quaker? The Inner Light in *Adventures of Huckleberry Finn*," *Mark Twain Journal: The Author and His Era* 56. 2 (Fall 2018): 49–50.

———. *Artemus Ward in London, and Other Papers*. Illustrated by J. H. Howard. New York: Carleton, Publisher, 1867. 229 pp.

As both Bernard DeVoto in 1932 and (more fully, in *Mark Twain as a Literary Comedian* [1979]) David E. E. Sloane pointed out, Ward preceded Twain in developing the "Is he dead?" gag, although Twain's version in *the Innocents Abroad* (1869) was much more elaborate and far funnier. In "The Greenlion and Oliver Cromwell," the landlord of the Greenlion asks Ward, "And this Mr. Cromwell—is he dead?" (p. 32).

———. *Artemus Ward's Panorama (As Exhibited at the Egyptian Hall, London.) Edited by His Executors*, T[homas]. W[illiam]. Robertson [1829–1871] and E[dward]. P[eron]. Hingston [1823–1876]. First edition. Illus. New York: G. W. Carleton & Co.; London: John Camden Hotten; 1869. 213 pp.

Catalog: ListABP (1910), "My Panorama, Ward", no other information provided. [The spine of *Artemus Ward's Panorama*" bore that wording in gilt lettering: "My Panorama/Yours truly/A. Ward."]

The editorial staff at the Mark Twain Project in Berkeley identified lines in Mark Twain's lecture notes that come from Thomas William Robertson's introduction to this book (*MTLet* 4: 479–481). Twain made these jottings on the verso of a letter of 24 October 1871 he sent to James

Redpath (collection of Kevin Mac Donnell, Austin, Texas).
———. "Babes in the Woods" (Ward's most famous lecture, first performed in 1861).

The Virginia City *Evening Bulletin* of 19 December 1863 reported that "Mark Twain, of the [Virginia City] *Enterprise* in commenting on the lecture of Artemus Ward says: 'There are perhaps fifty subjects treated in it, and there is a passable point in every one of them, and a healthy laugh, also, for any of God's creatures who hath committed no crime the ghastly memory of which debars him from smiling again while he lives. The man who is capable of listening to the Babes in the Wood from beginning to end without laughing either inwardly or outwardly must have done murder, or at least meditated it, at some time during his life.' This accounts for the fact of Mark's solemnity of appearance while listening to the lecture," kidded this writer for the rival *Evening Bulletin* (*Mark Twain in the Virginia Evening Bulletin and the Gold Hill Daily News*, ed. Clarence D. Basso [Reno, Nevada: Clarence D. Basso, 2013], p. 26). Clemens lauded Browne ("one of the kindest & gentlest men in the world") in a letter of 18 December 1879 to Frank B. Earnest, adding, "I think his lecture on the 'Babes in the Wood' was the funniest thing I ever listened to" (New York *Times*, 2 January 1880; PH in MTP). Clemens wrote "Babes in the Wood" in Notebook 40 (June 1898), TS p. 27.

Ward's "Babes in the Wood" was put forward by James C. Austin as Mark Twain's source for "The Invalid's Tale" ("Artemus Ward, Mark Twain, and the Limburger Cheese," *Midcontinent American Studies Journal* 4.2 [Fall 1963]: 70–73). In an especially illuminating study, Edgar M. Branch—"'The Babes in the Wood': Artemus Ward's 'Double Health' to Mark Twain," *PMLA* 93.5 (October 1978): 955–972—published a text from 1863 of Browne's famous lecture and pointed out numerous techniques and topics that Twain incorporated into his own speeches and published sketches.

BROWNE, IRVING (1835–1899). *Our Best Society* (play, first performed in 1868).

Browne adapted George William Curtis's satiric essays on New York City society, *Potiphar Papers* (1853), for a four-act "parlor comedy" staged by the Hartford Dramatic Society in 1875. Clemens made a curtain-raiser speech preceding its 12 November 1875 performance (*MTLet* 6: 589–591). See also the Catalog entry for G. W. Curtis, *Potiphar Papers*.

BROWNE, JOHN ROSS (1821–1875). *Adventures in Apache Country: A Tour Through Arizona and Sonora with Notes on the Silver Regions of Nevada*. Illus. New York Harper & Brothers, 1869. 535 pp. [First edition; no copy of this title belonging to Clemens has been reported.]

On 16 October 1872 Browne wrote to his wife about encountering Clemens at Judge George Turner's lodging in London. "He is just the same dry, quaint old Twain we knew in Washington. I believe he is writing a book over here. He made plenty of money on his other books—some of it mine" (*MTLet*, 5: 170 n. 2).

———. *Crusoe's Island: A Ramble in the Steps of Alexander Selkirk. With Sketches of Adventure in California and Washoe.* New York: Harper & Brothers, 1864.

Harold Aspiz speculated that Mark Twain used this book in preparing *Roughing It* (1872) ("Mark Twain's Reading" [1949], p. 311). Franklin R. Rogers concentrated on the portion of *Crusoe's Island* composed of "A Dangerous Journey" (first published as two articles in *Harper's Monthly* for May and June 1862); Rogers could not prove that Twain read this section, but "he was personally acquainted with Browne and, therefore, probably knew of his narrative" (*MTBP* [1960], pp. 69–70). Twain stayed overnight with Browne and his family in Oakland, California in 1866 during Twain's lecture tour. In the *Alta California* issue of 1 February 1868 Twain referred to Browne as "a good man and a talented one; a literary man and consequently entitled to high honors" (*MTLet*, 2: 230 n. 7). Browne eventually arranged for Twain to receive a remunerative government appointment, but Twain declined it.

———. "A Peep at Washoe," *Harper's New Monthly Magazine* 22 (December 1860–February 1861).

Clemens repeatedly recommended this series about Browne's adventures in southern Nevada to his family as a forthright introduction to the Far West region in which he was then living. "Take, for a winter view, J. Ross Browne's picture, in Harper's Monthly," he urged Jane Lampton Clemens and Pamela A. Moffett on 8 February 1862 (*MTLet*, 1: 157). On 10 May 1862 he mentioned the series in a letter he wrote jointly with Orion to the Keokuk *Gate City* (Rogers, *PRI*, p. 45; see also *MTL*, p. 65). Actually Browne's articles are broad burlesques, not factual—so Clemens was jesting (Rogers, *PRI* (1961), p. 41).

Blair, *NAH* (1937, 1960), pp. 158–159; Diane R. De-Nyse, "J. Ross Browne and Mark Twain: The Question of Literary Influence" (Master's thesis, University of Wyoming, 1965).

———. *Yusef; or the Journey of the Frangi: A Crusade in the East.* Illus. New York: Harper & Brothers, 1853. 421 pp. [First edition; no copy of this title belonging to Clemens appears to have survived.]

Browne seems warranted in claiming (privately) that Mark Twain benefited significantly from the precedents that Browne had set in travel writings that preceded Twain's. Joaquin Miller thought that "if there had been no *Yusef* there would have been no *Innocents Abroad* (*MTLet*, 5: 170 n. 2). Perhaps Browne should have given his book a more descriptive title, since it described his travels in Italy and Greece as well as Turkey and the Holy Land. Instead he named it after his colorful dragoman and guide in the desert regions, Yusef Badra, whose battle cry was "Badra, Badra forever!"

Franklin Walker, *Irreverent Pilgrims: Melville, Browne, and Mark Twain in the Holy Land* (Seattle: University of Washington Press, 1974).

BROWNE, JUNIUS HENRY (1833–1902). *The Great Metropolis; A Mirror of New York. A Complete History of Metropolitan Life and Society, with Sketches of Prominent Places, Persons and Things in the City, As They Actually Exist.* Hartford, Connecticut: American Publishing Co., 1869. 700 pp.

Expressing impatience with Elisha Bliss' delays in bringing out *The Innocents Abroad*, Mark Twain reminded his publisher on 22 July 1869 that "the delay for the 'Metropolis' damaged my interests" (*MTLP*, p. 23).

———. *Sights and Sensations in Europe: Sketches of Travel and Adventure.* Illus. Hartford, Connecticut: American Publishing

Co., 1871. 591 pp.

On 22 July 1869 Clemens, resentful about Elisha Bliss' slowness in issuing *The Innocents Abroad*, demanded of the publisher: "Are you going to publish it *before* Junius Henri Brown's [*sic*] Travels in Italy and Germany, or after?" (*MTLP*, p. 23). Jane Lampton Clemens wrote to her son and Olivia on 11 April 1874, asking if Clemens and Charles Dudley Warner would donate books to the reading room opened by the Women's Christian Temperance Union in Fredonia, New York. According to the 9 December 1874 issue of the Fredonia *Censor*, Clemens gave his mother sixteen volumes to present to the newly opened reading room. Accession records in the Darwin R. Barker Library, which succeeded the WCTU reading room and acquired its book collection, indicate that a copy of Browne's *Sights and Sensations in Europe* was one of Clemens's gifts. Most of the books were publications of the American Publishing Company.

BROWNE, (SIR) THOMAS (1605–1682).

In a humorous caption for a banquet menu item in June of 1881, Clemens pretended to be quoting from Sir Thomas Browne, though that reference to "the difference between a salmon and morality is wide" is facetious (Beinecke Rare Book and Manuscript Library, Yale University; letter from Everett Emerson to Alan Gribben, 29 October 1982). Twain made several additional references to Browne: one of the "world's master-minds" ("Which Was It?" written 1898–1903, *WWD?*, p. 306); "that wise old philosopher" (SLC to William Lyon Phelps, 24 April 1901, *MTL*, p. 707–708); "old Sir Thomas Browne" could account for a supposed miracle (SLC to Joseph H. Twichell, 24 April 1901, *LMTJHT*, p. 280).

BROWNE, THOMAS ALEXANDER (1826–1915), pseud. "Rolf Boldrewood." *Old Melbourne Memories*. London: Macmillan and Co., 1896.

Ralph [*sic*] Boldrewood" and other Australian writers have built out of their native materials "a brilliant and vigorous literature, and one which must endure," Mark Twain predicted (Chapter 22 of *FE* [1897]).

Francis Madigan, "Mark Twain's Passage to India" (1974), p. 355.

BROWNELL, CHARLES DE WOLF (1822–1909). *The Indian Races of North and South America, Comprising an Account of the Principal Aboriginal Races: A Description of Their National Customs, Mythology, and Religious Ceremonies; The History of Their Most Powerful Tribes, and of Their Most Celebrated Chiefs and Warriors: Their Intercourse and Wars with the European Settlers; and a Great Variety of Anecdote and Description, Illustrative of Personal and National Character.* Illus. Hartford: American Publishing Co., 1865. 760 pp. [Contains a concluding essay, "The Sioux Massacre" (in Minnesota), written by J[oel]. T[yler]. Headley (1813–1897).]

Clemens wrote to Elisha Bliss, Jr. from Buffalo on 29 October 1870 to say that he was "suffering" for a copy of "the 'Indian Races'" and three other titles published by Bliss's firm (*MTLet* 4: 217).

BROWNELL, EDWARD F. (1840–1905). [Unidentified poem.]

Samuel Clemens knew Brownell in Keokuk, Iowa while Clemens was assisting Orion Clemens at his printing office in the mid-1850s. Albert Bigelow Paine refers to "a young man named Edward Brownell, who clerked in the book-store on the ground floor" (*MTB*, p. 104), and as the "young Brownell" who predicted that Clemens was "too lazy ever to write a book" (*MTB*, pp. 106, 107). On 29 July 1874 Clemens wrote to Orion from Elmira about having had "a delightful visit with Ed Brownell, who was one of the best boys in Keokuk in my day, & one of the smartest" (*MTLet* 6: 196). Orion then sent Clemens a poem (presumably) by Brownell, and Clemens replied on 21 September from Hartford: "Tell Ed the poem is the finest thing I ever read--& I would not lie about a small matter" (*MTLet* 6: 238). Brownell would serve as the cashier of the Keokuk National Bank until his death in February 1905.

BROWNELL, HENRY HOWARD (1820–1872).

"Brownell (funny poems.)," Mark Twain noted in his jottings for an anthology of humorists in July 1880 (NB 19, *N&J* 2: 361). Brownell published light newspaper verse in addition to the serious Civil War poetry upon which his reputation rests.

BROWNING, ELIZABETH BARRETT (1806–1861). *Aurora Leigh* (blank verse romance, published in 1856).

In June 1868 Olivia Langdon recorded in her commonplace book that she was reading *Aurora Leigh* (Paine 150, MTP). Clemens found *Aurora Leigh* to be impenetrably obscure and turned to Olivia Langdon for explanations in letters of 18 October and 30 October 1868 (Wecter, *LLMT*, p. 34; *MTLet* 2: 268, 274) and 12 January 1869 (*MTLet* 3: 26). In a letter postmarked in Ouchy, Switzerland on 2 October 1891 Susy Clemens informed her college friend Louise Brownell: "I have been rereading Aurora Leigh. . . . It seems to me the woman was greater than almost any one else that ever lived" (Hamilton College Archives). On 30 September 1896 Samuel Clemens wished to obtain the works of Mrs. Browning—but *"not Aurora Leigh"* (NB 39, TS p. 6).

Harris, *Courtship* (1996), pp. 26, 35, 94, 97–99, 108, 130.

——. *Aurora Leigh, and Other Poems by Elizabeth Barrett Browning*. New York: James Miller, 1865. 400 pp.

Inscription: "Susie L. Crane/Theodore/June 11, 1867.

Marginalia: written in pencil on the rear endpaper: "This went out with Lizzie & Susie to the woods on Oct. 19, 1864, a day of unusual richness & beauty."

Catalog: Ball 2016 inventory, leather, gilt lettering and design, good to fair condition, inscribed by Theodore Crane to Susie L. Crane, June 11, 1867.

Location: found by Alan Gribben and David E. E. Sloane in the Langdon family library at Quarry Farm on 13 August 1989; transferred to the Mark Twain Archive, Elmira College.

Copy examined: an unmarked volume to which Clemens had access at Quarry Farm.

——. *Casa Guidi Windows* (published in 1851).

Listed in Clara Clemens's commonplace book sometime between 1888 and 1904 (Paine 150, MTP).

——. *The Poems of Elizabeth Barrett Browning*.

Inscription: Olivia Clemens's signature.

Catalog: *C1951*, O16, edition not supplied.

In a courting letter of 14 February 1869 Clemens alluded to Olivia Langdon's capacity to "unravel the marvelous ravings of Old Mother Browning. . . . You assault one of her impenetrable sentences & tear off its shell & bring its sense to light" (*MTLet* 3: 95). A few months later he lightheartedly referred to "some dark & bloody mystery out of the Widow Browning" (Clemens to Olivia Langdon, 17 May 1869, *LLMT*, p. 96; *MTLet* 3: 241). In the second week of their marriage Olivia appended a teasing note to a letter Clemens wrote to Mary Mason Fairbanks on 13 February 1870: "We [Olivia, Pamela Moffett, and Annie Moffett] will make Mr Clemens read aloud to us in Mrs Browning—Felicity to us—but what to him?" (*MTLet* 4: 72). There is a complimentary reference to Mrs. Browning (about how much she valued a sincere compliment) in a letter from Clemens to Charles F. Wingate written on 31 March 1870 (*MTLet* 4: 102). "If they were to set *me* to review Mrs. Browning," Clemens wrote to Olivia on 2 February 1873, "it would be like asking you to deliver judgment upon the merits of a box of cigars" (*MFMT*, p. 47; *MTLet* 5: 293). Elizabeth Barrett Browning's *Collected Poems* are mentioned in a letter written by Olivia and Clara Clemens to Chatto & Windus on 20 August 1899.

———. "A Rhapsody of Life's Progress" (poem, published in 1844).

In a letter postmarked in Ouchy, Switzerland on 2 October 1891 Susy Clemens informed her college friend Louise Brownell: "I have been rereading Aurora Leigh and that poem of Mrs. B's entitled 'A Rhapsodie [*sic*] of Life's Progress'.... She saw everything between earth and sky to be seen by microscope or telescope.... The beautiful, exquisite thing!" (Hamilton College Archives).

——————— and **ROBERT BROWNING** (1812–1889). *Sonnets from the Portuguese and Other Poems; One Word More and Other Poems.* Intro. by Richard Watson Gilder (1844–1909). Limp leather covers, joints shattered, marbled endpapers, edges and corners rubbed. New York: Century Co., 1905.

Inscription: the half-title page is inscribed in black ink by Richard Watson Gilder, "This book belongs to/one (there is but one) Clara Clemens/&the Introduction therein-/to was written by/one (one is enough)/R W Gilder/1905–6."

Marginalia: a few passages are marked in pencil. These do not appear to be Clemens's markings, except for a vertical mark on page 62 that might possibly be his. Gilder also corrects "daughter of the poet" (p. xxxviii) to read "wife of the poet."

Provenance: sold at the 1951 auction in Hollywood but not listed in the hastily compiled sale sheet.

Catalog: "Property from the Library of Mark Twain," Butterfield & Butterfield, San Francisco, Sale 6613 (16 July 1997), lot 2711.

Location: Mark Twain House and Museum, Hartford, Connecticut.

Copy examined: Clara Clemens's copy. Viewed in Hartford in 1997.

BROWNING, ROBERT (1812–1889).

I outlined Clemens's infatuation with Browning's poetry in "'It Is Unsatisfactory to Read to One's Self': Mark Twain's Informal Readings," *Quarterly Journal of Speech* 62 (February 1976): 49–56 and discussed the topic more fully in "'A Splendor of Stars & Suns': Twain as a Reader of Robert Browning's Poems," *Browning Institute Studies* 6 (1978): 87–103. (Revised versions of these essays appear in Volume One of this present work.) Those essays explained that Clemens's reverence for Browning's verse

represented one of his few convergences with the tastes of the elite, most discerning literary critics of his day, a fact that made Browning a doubly important figure for him. He acquired and annotated an extensive collection of the poet's works. When one examines Clemens's favorite poems by Rudyard Kipling, William Morris, and others, his fondness for Browning's poetry is explained; he preferred dramatic situations, self-revealing speakers, and implied actions. He chose poems that would have an emotional effect on his audience; he read Browning mainly to select material for the oral interpretations at which he excelled. Browning very likely helped Clemens appreciate Italy and the city of Florence, and Browning's monologues influenced Twain's later experiments with monologues.

Clemens made other comments about Browning in addition to the remarks quoted in those two articles. An initial reference to Browning was facetious rather than complimentary. In a humorous Buffalo *Express* column published on 2 October 1869 in which Twain pretended to answer the questions posed in a book titled *Mental Photographs: An Album for Confessions of Tastes, Habits, and Convictions* (see the Catalog entry for its editor, Robert Saxton), he answered "Robert Browning, when he has a lucid interval" to the query about his favorite poet (*Mark Twain at the Buffalo Express: Articles and Sketches by America's Favorite Humorist*, ed. Joseph b. McCullough and Janice McIntire-Strasburg [DeKalb: Northern Illinois Press, 2000], p. 63). Later his tone changed. Katy Leary told Mary Lawton that on a typical evening "Mr. Clemens would have Browning or Dickens and would read aloud to his family" before the fireplace (*LMT*, p. 8). On 20 January 1887 Clemens named Browning as one of his favorite authors in a letter to the Reverend Charles D. Crane (ALS, Shapell Manuscript Library, Beverly Hills, California). Clemens assured William Dean Howells on 22 August 1887 that he had succeeded in getting Browning "in focus" (*MTHL*, p. 848). Clemens wrote with delight to Mary Hallock Foote on 2 December 1887 to report that "I've been Browning-reader forty-two weeks, now, & my class has never lost a member by desertion." Indeed, he vowed to Foote, "Put me in the right condition & give me room according to my strength" (echoing one of his bragging raftsmen in Chapter 3 of *Life on the Mississippi* [1883]), "& I can read Browning so Browning himself can understand it. It sounds like stretching, but it's the cold truth. Moral: don't explain your author; read him right & he explains himself" (quoted by William Lyon Phelps, *Autobiography*, p. 66). He read Browning to a group on 12 September 1888, but the women's "unresponsiveness" made it a "failure" (Notebook 28, *N&J* 3: 420–422). He planned to quote Browning in *A Connecticut Yankee in King Arthur's Court* (NB 28, *N&J* 3: 420), and listed several Browning poems in December 1888 (NB 28, *N&J* 3: 435).

Olivia Clemens wrote to her mother on 15 September 1890 about Clemens entertaining fellow vacationers in the Catskill Mountains with Browning readings (ALS in MTHM). He also beguiled some visitors to Venice with a Browning reading at the Hotel Danieli in May 1892 (Fears, *Day by Day* 2: 709). In January 1897 Clemens recalled wistfully that Susy "was fond of Browning" (NB 39, TS p. 48). Arthur L. Scott found Mark Twain's elegies to Susy—"Broken Idols," (written 1898) and "In Dim & Fitful Visions They Flit Across the Distances" (written 1902) to be "perhaps influenced by Browning" in their dramatic monologue form (*OPMT* [1966], p. 31). Howard G. Baetzhold correctly concluded that "Clemens knew Browning's works better than those of any other poet except Kipling" (*MT&JB* [1970], p. 289). William Lyon Phelps, a Yale professor of English and a respected critic and speaker who had a lengthy friendship with Clemens, described Clemens's oral readings of Robert Browning's verse in "Mark Twain," *Yale Review* 25 (1936): 291–310. Three years later, Phelps' *Autobiography, with Letters* (New York: Oxford University Press, 1939) again discussed Clemens's passion for Robert Browning's poetry (pp. 64–66) and quoted a comment that Clemens jotted down in one of the Browning volumes that Clara Clemens Samossoud had allowed Phelps to examine (see the Catalog entry for Browning's *Dramatis Personae* [1886]).

Benjamin DeCasseres—*When Huck Finn Went Highbrow*. Limited edition of 125 copies. New York: Thomas F. Madigan, 1934—reproduced in facsimile Clemens's letter to Mary Hallock Foote of 2 December 1887, to which DeCasseres added a printed transcription and nearly five pages of comments about Clemens's elaborate Browning classes. See also Harold K. Bush, Jr., "'Broken Idols,': Mark Twain's Elegies for Susy and a Critique of Freudian Grief Theory," *Nineteenth Century Literature* 57.2 (September 2002): 237–268; Bush subsequently reprinted the "In Memoriam" and "Broken Idols" poems in *Mark Twain and the Spiritual Crisis of His Age* (Tuscaloosa: University of Alabama Press, 2007), pp. 241–250.

———. "After" (poem).
See the Catalog entry for Browning's poetic prequel, "Before."

———. *Agamemnon, La Saisiaz, Dramatic Idyls, and Jocoseria*. Boston: Houghton, Mifflin and Co., 1885. 547 pp.
Inscription: the front flyleaf is inscribed by Clemens in black ink, "Livy L. Clemens/ 1886".
Marginalia: profusely annotated by Clemens in pencil. Several poems are marked with especial thoroughness, including "Muléykeh" (pp. 377–386), in which Clemens wrote the instruction "'sh!" beside the stanza describing the theft of Hóseyn's steed (p. 383). Clemens marked "Ivàn Ivànovitch" extensively. In another poem that reflects Clemens's careful attention, "Clive," he jotted "I said," "he said," "he retorted," and other explanatory insertions that could assist listeners at an oral reading.
Catalog: *C1951*, #48a, one of "8 vols." of Browning, $72 total.
Location: Mark Twain Papers, Bancroft Library, University of California at Berkeley. Donated in July 1978 by Robert Dawson Wallace of Ft. Myers, Florida. Wallace purchased this and six other Browning volumes in 1952 from Dawson's Bookshop in Los Angeles.
Copy examined: Olivia Clemens's copy, annotated by Clemens.

———. *The Agamemnon of Aeschylus; La Saisiaz; The Two Poets of Croisic; Dramatic Idyls; Jocoseria; Ferishtah's Fancies; and Parleyings*. Volume VI, *The Poetic and Dramatic Works of*

Robert Browning. Boston: Houghton, Mifflin and Co., 1887.
Inscription: the front free endpaper of Volume VI is signed in black ink, "Livy L. Clemens/1888."
Marginalia: four poems are marked in the table of contents: "Martin Relph," "Ivàn Ivànovitch," "Muléykeh," and "Helen's Tower." "Tray" (pages 142–143) from *Dramatic Idyls* is marked profusely for reading aloud. This poem about a dog that saves a little girl from drowning and then plunges back into the stream to rescue her doll concludes with a threat of cruel vivisection for the animal. Clemens timed the reading of "Tray" at "3" minutes. "Muléykeh," he estimated on page 163, would take him "about 15 m." He underlined words or made emphasis marks in nearly every line of that poem (pages 163–167). On page 164 he reminded himself to reflect "SCORN" when reading the line "But I love Muléykeh's face." Similarly on page 166 he noted that he should read certain lines "*NOT* loud" and other lines "LOUD". No other poems contain markings.
Provenance: discovered on the shelves of the Langdon library at Quarry Farm, to which Clemens had access during his many summers in Elmira, New York. Transferred to the Mark Twain Archive on 9 July 1987 by Mark Woodhouse.
Catalog: Ball 2016 inventory, Volume VI, green cloth, gilt lettering, Mark Twain Archive.
Location: Mark Twain Archive, Elmira College, Elmira, New York.
Copy examined: photocopies of Olivia Clemens's inscription and Clemens's marginalia supplied on 5 March 1985 by Herbert A. Wisbey, then director of the Center for Mark Twain Studies at Elmira College.

In 1990 Gretchen Sharlow published an informative essay arguing for a connection between Mary Mason Fairbanks and Clemens's interest in Robert Browning. According to Sharlow, Professor Hiram Corson of Cornell University mentioned in the Boston *Literary World* on 2 April 1883 that Mary Mason Fairbanks was conducting a Browning Circle in Cleveland, Ohio. Sharlow's article also deciphered the various markings that Clemens invented to guide his oral performances of Robert Browning's poetry. For example, a small rectangle drawn horizontally meant a long enough pause to give the readers time to imagine the scene or emotion, whereas an "X" designated a brief pause. An upward slanting line instructed Clemens to inflect his voice upward; a downward slanting line was the opposite. He devised other visual cues as well (Gretchen Sharlow, "Mark Twain Reads Browning Again: A Discovery in the Langdon-Crane Family Library at Quarry Farm," *Mark Twain Journal* 28.2 [Fall 1990]: 24–29).

———. "Andrea del Sarto" (dramatic monologue, published in 1855).
Mark Twain read this meditative, self-revealing monologue at Smith College on 21 January 1889 (NB 28, *N&J* 3: 436). Robert Underwood Johnson particularly recalled Clemens's "remarkably sympathetic" rendition of "Andrea del Sarto" during readings he performed at the Hotel Danieli in Venice in May 1892 (*Remembered Yesterdays* [Boston: Little, Brown, and Co., 1923], pp. 320–321). Fears, *Day by Day* 2: 709.

———. *Asolando; Fancies and Facts*. Eighth edition. London: Smith, Elder & Co, 1890. 157 pp.
Inscription: inscribed on the half-title page, in pencil, "For

Mr. Clemens/with Mrs. Bronson's/affectionate regards/ Venice 1892." On 25 May 1892 Clemens wrote to thank Katherine C. Bronson "ever so much for those books" (MTP; Fears, 2: 709).

Location: Mark Twain Library, Redding, Connecticut. Donated from Clemens's library by Clara Clemens Gabrilowitsch in 1910 (MTLAcc, entry #2018).

Copy examined: Clemens's unmarked copy. Examined in 1970 and again in June 1982. Has an accession number in pencil, "2018".

————. *Asolando; Fancies and Facts.* Author's Edition. Boston: Houghton, Mifflin & Co., 1890. 114 pp.

Source: MTLAcc, entry #2013, volume donated from Clemens's library by Clara Clemens Gabrilowitsch in 1910.

————. *Balaustion's Adventure, Aristophanes' Apology, Pacchiarotto and Other Poems.* Boston: Houghton, Mifflin and Co., 1885. 644 pp.

Inscription: the front flyleaf is inscribed by Clemens in black ink, "Livy L. Clemens/1886."

Marginalia: a few pencil markings in the table of contents. Clemens also marked one poem for reading aloud—"A Forgiveness," the confession of a Spanish nobleman guilty of murder.

Location: Mark Twain Papers, Bancroft Library, University of California at Berkeley. Donated in July 1978 by Robert Dawson Wallace of Ft. Myers, Florida. Wallace purchased this and six other Browning volumes in 1952 from Dawson's Bookshop in Los Angeles.

Catalog: *C1951*, #48a, one of "8 vols." of Browning, $72 total.

Copy examined: Olivia Clemens's copy, annotated by Clemens.

————. "Before" (poem).

The first of Browning's two poems about a vengeful duel, "Before," begins, "Let them fight it out, friend. Things have gone too far"; that poem ends, "Let them go then! Both the fighters to their places!/While I count three, step you back as many paces!" The follow-up poem, "After," concludes, "I stand here now, he lies in his place:/Cover the face!" Clara Clemens mixed up two of Clemens's favorite pieces to read aloud when she wrote of her father's rendition of "After": "Never shall I forget the ring of awe in his voice as he read the last words of Clive [*sic*], 'Cover the face'" (*MFMT*, p. 66).

————. *Christmas-Eve and Easter Day; Men and Women; In a Balcony; Dramatis Personae; Balaustion's Adventure; Prince Hohenstiel-Schwangau; Fifine at the Fair.* Volume IV, *The Poetic and Dramatic Works of Robert Browning.* Boston: Houghton, Mifflin and Co., 1887.

Marginalia: Clemens marked seven poems in the table of contents: "Christmas-Eve," "Fra Lippo Lippi," "Andrea del Sarto," "Gold Hair: A Story of Pornic," "Rabbi Ben Ezra," "Confessions," and "Prospice." His profuse pencil markings occur throughout "Christmas-Eve" and "Andrea del Sarto." On page 1 Clemens estimated the time it would take to read "Christmas-Eve" at "10 min" and reminded himself to start out "Conversational & lazy." He apparently only intended to read aloud Parts I and II of that poem; his underlinings and emphasis marks stop where he drew two diagonal lines at the end of Part II on page 4. He estimated the reading time for "Andrea del

Sarto" at "24 min." on page 83 and proceeded to mark nearly every line of that poem. "See over" he noted at line 6 on page 85. At line 29 on page 85 he placed three exclamation marks on either side of this line: "But all the play, the insight and the stretch—/Out of me, out of me!" Clemens reminded himself that the poem's narrator was "pointing to 2 pictures" when he declared, "Rafael did this, Andrea painted that" on page 86. Page 87 is absolutely covered with emphatic pencil markings. No other marginalia appear in the volume.

Catalogs: Ball 2016, Volume IV, green cloth, gilt lettering, Mark Twain Archive.

Location: Mark Twain Archive, Elmira College, Elmira, New York. Transferred to that collection from Quarry Farm on 9 July 1987 by Mark Woodhouse.

Copy examined: photocopies of the marginalia in a copy marked by Clemens that were sent by to Alan Gribben by Herbert A. Wisbey, then Director of the Center for Mark Twain Studies, on 5 March 1985. The volume had just been discovered in the Langdon family library, to which Clemens had access during his many summer visits to Quarry Farm.

An 1888 Elmira newspaper item seems relevant; it describes the "delightful entertainments" furnished by Samuel Clemens's readings at the Main Street home of Mr. and Mrs. J. B. Stanchfield "last Tuesday evening." (The reporter noted that Clemens's daughter Clara "is named for Mrs. Stanchfield who has been, since girlhood, the intimate friend of Mrs. Clemens.") "Words fail to describe the delight of hearing him read in a parlor. His interpretation of Browning . . . would have thoroughly discouraged the poet, for Mr. Clemens demonstrated the fact that Browning could be understood without Prof. Corson's aid" (*Saturday Tidings* [weekly], Elmira, New York, 15 September 1888, TS sent to Alan Gribben by Gretchen Sharlow in February 1987).

Gretchen Sharlow, "Mark Twain Reads Browning Again: A Discovery in the Langdon-Crane Family Library at Quarry Farm," *Mark Twain Journal* 28.2 (Fall 1990): 24–29; Greg Sevik, "Poetry, Prosody, Parody: Mark Twain's Rhythmic Thought," *Mark Twain Annual 13* (2015): 130–148.

————. "Clive" (poem, published in 1880).

Mark Twain included "Clive" in his program of readings for Bryn Mawr in 1891 (NB 30 [February 1891], *N&J* 3: 605, 609); mentioned the poem in June 1891 (NB 30, *N&J* 3: 639); and planned to quote the entire poem in *Following the Equator* (1897), according to a note he made at sea on 11 April 1896 (NB 37, TS p. 36). The poem, an old man's reminiscences about Robert Clive's words, deeds, and suicide, has the dramatic monologue form that Clemens favored. See also the Catalog entry for Browning's *Agamemnon* (1885).

————. *The Complete Works of Robert Browning.* Edited by John H. Finley. New Century Library Series. 6 vols. Brown calf. London: Thomas Nelson & Sons, n. d. [Quite likely the 1899 edition, though Finley's edition had been available in several formats as early as 1868].

Provenance: Clara Clemens Samossoud's second husband, Jacques A. Samossoud, bequeathed this set from Clara's personal library to their friends Henry and Mary Shisler of Cardiff by the Sea, California in 1966 (Mary Shisler to Alan Gribben, 17 September 1980).

Location: currently unknown. The Shislers sold many of the books they inherited from Samossoud to Maurice Neville in 1981; this set might have been among them.

———. *Dramas by Robert Browning.* Two vols. in one. Half-calf binding with marbled paper boards. Illus. Boston: Houghton, Mifflin and Co., 1885. [Contains *Paracelsus, Pippa Passes, King Victor and King Charles, Colombe's Birthday, A Blot in the 'Scutcheon, The Return of the Druses,* and *A Soul's Tragedy.*]

Inscription: the front flyleaf is inscribed by Clemens in black ink, "Livy L. Clemens/1886."

Marginalia: Clemens used pencil in marking *King Victor and King Charles* for reading aloud.

Catalog: *C1951,* #48a, one of "8 vols." of Browning, $72 total.

Location: Mark Twain Papers, Bancroft Library, University of California at Berkeley. Donated in July 1978 by Robert Dawson Wallace of Ft. Myers, Florida. Wallace purchased this and six other identically bound Browning volumes in 1952 from Dawson's Bookshop in Los Angeles.

Copy examined: Olivia Clemens's copy, annotated by Clemens.

———. *Dramatic Lyrics, Romances, Etc.* Volume 2 of *The Poetic and Dramatic Works of Robert Browning.* Riverside Edition. 6 vols. Boston: Houghton, Mifflin and Co., 1887.

Catalog: *A1911,* "3 vols., 12mo, cloth, gilt tops, uncut (several fly-leaves missing), Bost.: Riverside Press, 1887, numerous underscorings in pencil in one volume," lot 52, sold with two other Browning volumes, $2.25 total price.

It seems a special pity that this (presumably annotated) volume remains missing since the 1911 auction, since it contained the types of dramatic poems that Clemens relished and that his audiences often requested him to read aloud: "Soliloquy of the Spanish Cloister," "My Last Duchess," "How They Brought the Good News from Ghent to Aix," "After," and "Up at a Villa—Down in the City," among others.

———. *Dramatis Personae, Dramatic Romances and Lyrics, Strafford, Etc.* Boston: Houghton, Mifflin and Co., 1884. 612 pp.

Marginalia: on the second flyleaf of this worn and much-marked volume, Clemens explained: "The pencilings in this book are inexplicable, except by this explanation, which is the true one: they were made in order to give the eye instant help in placing & shading emphases—a very necessary precaution when one reads Browning aloud. SLC". Robert Dawson Wallace transcribed this comment and other marginalia in "An Analytical-Historical Study of the Factors Contributing to the Success of Mark Twain as an Oral Interpreter," (1962), pp. 291–346. Among the poems that Clemens marked most meticulously were "Easter-Day," "Abt Vogler," and "Rabbi Ben Ezra."

Catalog: *C1951,* #48a, one of "8 vols." of Browning, $72 total.

Location: Mark Twain Papers, Bancroft Library, University of California at Berkeley. Donated in July 1978 by Robert Dawson Wallace of Ft. Myers, Florida. Wallace purchased this and six other identically bound Browning volumes in 1952 from Dawson's Bookshop in Los Angeles.

Copy examined: Clemens's copy.

Robert Dawson Wallace, "An Analytical-Historical Study of the Factors Contributing to the Success of Mark Twain as an Oral Interpreter" (Doctoral dissertation, University of Southern California, 1962), studied Twain's use of published writings in his professional platform appearances. In Chapters 4 and 5 Wallace expertly investigated Twain's speech patterns, lecture revisions and stage techniques. On pages 291–346 Wallace transcribed and discussed Twain's notes and markings in seven volumes of Robert Browning's poetry that were sold at the 1951 auction in Hollywood. Twain devised his system of penciled notations, as he wrote in his copy of *Dramatis Personae*, "in order to give the eye instant help in placing & shading emphases—a very necessary precaution when one reads Browning aloud" (quoted by Wallace, p. 291). In 1978 Wallace donated Twain's set of Robert Browning's works to the Mark Twain Papers in the Bancroft Library, University of California at Berkeley.

———. *Dramatis Personae, Dramatic Romances and Lyrics, Strafford, Etc.* Riverside Edition. Boston: Houghton, Mifflin and Co., 1886.

Marginalia: on the flyleaf Clemens wrote in pencil: "Remark dropped after finishing 'Easter Day'—& requested by the class to 'write it down': One's glimpses & confusions, as one reads Browning, remind me of looking through a telescope (the small sort which you must move with your hand, not clock-work): You toil across dark spaces which are (to *your* lens) empty; but every now & then a splendor of stars & suns bursts upon you & fills the whole field with flame. Feb. 23, 1887." (quoted almost entirely in Paine's *MTB* [1912], p. 847; also quoted in William Lyon Phelps' *Autobiography, with Letters* [1939], p. 65). Phelps, who examined the volume independently, reported that Clemens was making this observation on 23 February 1887. Albert Bigelow Paine wrote that "in another note he speaks of the 'vague dim flash of splendid humming-birds through a fog'" (*MTB*, p. 847). Paine recorded the fact that Clemens "indicated with pencil every shade of emphasis which would help to reveal the poet's purpose" (*MTB*, p. 846). Clemens marked words for emphasis in three poems in particular—"Rabbi Ben Ezra" (pp. 89–99), "Mr. Sludge, 'The Medium'" (pp. 183–197), and "Rudel to the Lady of Tripoli" (pp. 295–296). He also made a few brief notes, such as (at the bottom of page 194 in "Mr. Sludge, 'The Medium'"): "& here is the *true* tale—without embellishments."

Catalog: ListABP (1910), "Dramatis Personae, Browning", no other information provided.

Provenance: the front pastedown endpaper has a label from the 1951 Hollywood auction. The bookplate of the Pacific Coast Browning Foundation, 18 April 1951, presenting the volume to "Waldo H. Dunn, with sincere appreciation of your interest and co-operation during these years that the Browning Foundation Collection has had a home in the Scripps College Library," is partially pasted over that auction label. On the front free endpaper is the bookplate of the Ohio State University Libraries.

Location: Special Collections, University Libraries, Ohio State University, Columbus, Ohio.

Copy examined: photocopies of the front pastedown and free endpaper, the front free endpaper, and sample marginalia on 192–195 in "Mr. Sludge, 'The Medium,'" sent to Alan Gribben by Robert A. Tibbetts, then Curator of

Special Collections, 17 February 1982.

"I suppose I have read Rabbi Ben Ezra [to the Browning class] . . . a couple of dozen times" (SLC to Mary Mason Fairbanks, 22 March 1887, *MTMF*, pp. 260–261). Mark Twain planned to include that poem in his program for a reading on 2 April 1889 (NB 28, *N&J* 3: 462). After luncheon on 8 March 1907 "Mrs. Whitmore asked him to read Rabbi Ben Ezra to us—which he did" (IVL Journal, TS p. 229, MTP).

———. *Ferishtah's Fancies*. Boston: Houghton, Mifflin and Co., 1886. 91 pp.

Inscription: inscribed by Clemens in black ink on the front flyleaf: "Livy L. Clemens/1887."

Location: Mark Twain Library, Redding, Connecticut.

Copy examined: Olivia Clemens's unmarked copy. The volume has a penciled accession number—"3139". Examined in 1970 and again in June 1982.

Clara Clemens described this poem and "Caliban Upon Setebos" in her commonplace book (c. 1888, Paine 150, MTP).

———. *Fifine at the Fair, Red Cotton Night-Cap Country, and the Inn Album*. Boston: Houghton, Mifflin and Co., 1883. 663 pp. [Contains *Fifine at the Fair*, *Prince Hohenstiel- Schwangau, Saviour of Society*, *Herve Riel*, *Red Cotton Night-Cap Country*, *The Inn Album*.]

Inscription: the front flyleaf is inscribed by Clemens in black ink, "Livy L. Clemens/1886."

Catalog: *C1951*, #48a, one of "8 vols." of Browning, $72 total.

Location: Mark Twain Papers, Bancroft Library, University of California at Berkeley. Donated in July 1978 by Robert Dawson Wallace of Ft. Myers, Florida. Wallace purchased this and other Browning volumes in 1952 from Dawson's Bookshop in Los Angeles.

Copy examined: Olivia Clemens's copy, unmarked.

———. "How They Brought the Good News from Ghent to Aix" (poem, published in 1845).

Jervis Langdon (1875–1952) recalled that Clemens's listeners in Hartford "invariably demanded at the end of his Hartford readings three favorites, 'How They Brought the Good News from Ghent to Aix,' 'Up at a Villa, Down in the City,' and, for climax, 'The Battle of Naseby'" ("Some Reminiscences," collected in *MT in Elmira* [2013], p. 208). In Browning's thundering poem three horsemen set out to carry a fateful message, but two of the animals collapse from exhaustion, "And there was [only] my Roland to bear the whole weight/Of the news which alone could save Aix from her fate."

———. *Illustrations to Browning's Poems*. [See the Catalog entry for the Browning Society.]

———. *The Letters of Robert Browning and Elizabeth Barrett Browning 1845–1846*. Third impression. 2 vols. London: Smith, Elder & Co., 1899.

Marginalia: a few pencil markings in both volumes, apparently not by Clemens. Post-1910 pencil sketches of unknown persons are laid in between pages 542 and 543.

Location: Mark Twain Library, Redding, Connecticut.

Copies examined: most likely Clemens's copies. I found these volumes on the circulating shelves in 1970 and I examined them again in June 1982 and on 10 November 2019. They have a red ink accession number—"3068",

plus the standard Mark Twain Library oval purple stamps. These are in line with other donations from the Clemens household.

———. *The Letters of Robert Browning and Elizabeth Barrett Browning 1845–1846*. 2 vols. New York: Harper & Brothers, 1899.

Catalog: Ball 2016 inventory, green cloth with gilt lettering and design, some pages are uncut in Volume II, good condition.

Location: Quarry Farm library shelves, under the supervision of the Mark Twain Archive, Elmira College, Elmira, New York.

Clemens had access to the Quarry Farm library books during his final visits to Elmira.

———. "Memorabilia" (poem, published in 1855).

Mark Twain read "Memorabilia" and Shelley's "Skylark" at a Shelley-Keats memorial program on 14 February 1907 (IVL Journal, TS p. 225). Browning's awestruck speaker begins, "Ah, did you once see Shelley plain,/And did he stop and speak to you?"

———. *Men and Women*. Boston: Ticknor and Fields, 1856.

Inscription: in brown ink on the flyleaf: "Livie L. Langdon/1864/New York."

Marginalia: on the front free endpaper Clemens noted in pencil the name of a dramatic monologue inside, "Saul." Clemens marked most of the poems for reading aloud, indicating stresses, connecting stanzas, and glossing terms. He also penciled a number of marginal notes, of which those surrounding "Old Pictures in Florence" (pp. 206–216) are the most extensive and significant.

Catalogs: ListABP (1910), "Men and Women, Browning"; "Retz Appraisal," p. 5, valued at $15.

Location: Mark Twain Papers, Bancroft Library, University of California at Berkeley.

Copy examined: Clemens's copy, originally belonging to Olivia Clemens.

———. *Men and Women and Sordello*. Two vols. in one. Boston: Houghton, Mifflin and Co., 1884.

Inscription: the front flyleaf is inscribed by Clemens in black ink, "Livy L. Clemens/1886."

Marginalia: a few pencil marks.

Catalog: *C1951*, #48a, one of "8 vols." of Browning, $72 total.

Location: Mark Twain Papers, Bancroft Library, University of California at Berkeley. Donated in July 1978 by Robert Dawson Wallace of Ft. Myers, Florida. Wallace purchased this and six other Browning volumes in 1952 from Dawson's Bookshop in Los Angeles.

Copy examined: Olivia Clemens's copy, marked by Clemens.

———. "Muléykeh" (poem, published in 1880).

Mark Twain planned to read Browning's "Horse-race" (i.e., "Muléykeh") to a Smith College audience on 26 November 1888, along with another Browning poem, Uncle Remus' tales, and some of Twain's own stories (NB 28, *N&J* 3: 435). He would return to Smith College for a reading on 21 January 1889; in Notebook 28 he jotted, "Muléykeh (Dram. Idyls)" (*N&J* 3: 436). In "Muléykeh," included in *Dramatic Idyls*, Hóseyn races against a thief riding Hóseyn's own horse, Muléykeh the Pearl. Twain used this poem in a reading he gave in New York City on 13

April 1889 (NB 28, *N&J* 3: 469). See also the Catalog entries for Browning's *Agamemnon* (1885) and for C. E. S. S. Norton's "The King of Denmark's Ride."

———. *Parleyings with Certain People of Importance in Their Day*. Boston: Houghton, Mifflin and Co., 1887.

Marginalia: seven of the nine narrative poems have been annotated or densely marked in pencil by Clemens. All in all, 105 of the 187 pages in the volume are either annotated or marked. His notes in the book amount to seventy-three separate annotations totaling some 260 words. Only two poems are entirely ignored—"With Gerard de Lairesse" (pp. 115–133) and "Fust and His Friends: An Epilogue" (the final poem in the volume). There are extremely profuse markings in "With Bernard de Mandeville" (pp. 23–36). "With Daniel Bartoli" (pp. 39–53) contains numerous speculations about possible interpretations; some were canceled as new meanings emerged and were recorded. At the bottom of page 49, for example, Clemens wondered: "(Is this to say our girl found a lion (a King) about to <destroy> diminish a dukedom, using the duke's love for *her* as a means, & she nobly checkmated his little game by renouncing her big chance & backing out from the marriage?)" On page 51, where the Duke is called a fool, Clemens queried, "'Fool' because he *allowed* her to renounce the marriage?" At the conclusion of "George Bubb Dodington," Clemens attempted a summary: "Let him speak sincerely from his heart, & this is what he would have to confess. When the people recognized that he was telling the bold clear *truth*, they would fall down, overawed by the splendid sincerity." Writing sideways in the margin in pencil on page 151, Clemens noted, "Religions, for instance." Clemens's penciled markings underscore lines, add stress marks to denote intonations, and offer explanatory notes—all no doubt in preparation for public readings. In many places, as on pages 94–95 of the poem "Francis Furini," virtually every line contains underlinings and metrical accent marks to denote oral stresses.

Catalogs: *C1951*, #56a, $75; *Sotheby's 2003*, #186, $10,000.

Provenance: Carrie Estelle Doheny Collection, St. John's Seminary, Camarillo, California. Donated by Mrs. Doheny in 1951 after she purchased it from Maxwell Hunley Rare Books for $82. Auctioned by Christie's on 21 February 1989, lot #1757, on behalf of St. John's Seminary for $7,700.

Copy examined: Clemens's copy, at St. John's Seminary in Camarillo in 1970 and again prior to the Sotheby's auction on 19 June 2003. Oddly, there is no signature or inscription. The number "56a" appears in pencil on the verso of the front free flyleaf, indicating that this volume derived from the *C1951* sale in Hollywood.

Albert Bigelow Paine reported that during the winter of 1886–1887 Mark Twain entertained his Browning class with "rich, sympathetic and luminous" readings from *Parleyings with Certain People* (*MTB* [1912], p. 846). Gribben, "'A Splendor of Stars & Suns'" (1978), p. 98.

———. *Parleyings with Certain People of Importance in Their Day*. London: Smith, Elder & Co., 1887. 268 pp.

Inscription: the front free flyleaf is missing.

Marginalia: someone other than Clemens (possibly Olivia Clemens; see the next Catalog entry for Browning's

Parleyings) copied notes from the New York *Tribune* onto the verso of the half-title page and throughout the book in black ink. Some pages remain unopened.

Location: Mark Twain Library, Redding, Connecticut. Donated from Clemens's library by Clara Clemens Gabrilowitsch in 1910 (MTLAcc, entry #2019).

Copy examined: a Browning volume belonging either to Clemens or to Olivia Clemens. It shows the red ink accession number "2019". Examined in June 1982 and on 10 November 2019.

———. *Parleyings with Certain People of Importance in Their Day*. Boston: Houghton, Mifflin and Co., 1887.

Inscription: signed in black ink, "Livy L. Clemens/1887." A bookseller mistakenly wrote "Mss. notes by Mark Twain" at the top of the front pastedown endpaper.

Marginalia: in Olivia Clemens's hand on the verso of the front free endpaper: "The notes in this work are/taken from a critique of the book that appeared in the/N. Y. Tribune. The key note of the work is/the relation of evil to good,/the duty of man to/'Accept good with bad.'" On the page introducing the fifth personality, Francis Furini, Olivia wrote in ink: "A Tuscan painter of the/last century, and priest/as well." On the page introducing Charles Avison, she wrote in ink: "A musical composer/ of the last century".

Provenance: ListABP (1910), "Parleyings, Browning"; a *C1951* auction label is affixed to the front pastedown endpaper. Accompanying the photocopy (see below) in the Mark Twain Papers is a photocopy of an unidentified rare bookseller's listing of the volume as having been sold in 1951 and "signed on flyleaf 'Livy L. Clemens 1887'. Manuscript notes by Mark Twain [*sic*]. Two full pages plus numerous chapter interpolations."

Location: the volume belonged to Mrs. Walter O. Thompson of Turlock, California in 1982 (letter from Robert H. Hirst to Alan Gribben, 27 August 1982). In 1983 the volume was owned by a resident of Palo Alto, California who did not wish to be identified.

Copy examined: photocopies of Olivia Clemens's inscription and marginalia sent to the Mark Twain Papers on 5 August 1982 and relayed to Alan Gribben on 27 August 1982. I subsequently examined another photocopy dated 3 May 1983 in the Mark Twain Papers at Berkeley.

———. *Pauline; Paracelsus; Strafford;Sordello; Pippa Passes; King Victor and King Charles. The Poetic and Dramatic Works of Robert Browning*. Riverside Edition. 6 vols. Boston: Houghton, Mifflin and Co., 1887. 412 pp. [Volume I only.]

Inscription: the front free endpaper is missing in Volume I.

Marginalia: Clemens heavily marked and annotated Volume I in pencil; the marginalia are confined to "Paracelsus" and "Sordello" (pp. 65–261). Several of his notes are dated between March and May 1889. He made extremely intense underscorings and emphasis marks for oral readings between pages 65 and 88 (especially in 82–83) in "Paracelsus" and on pages 200–201 in "Sordello." Clemens recorded his progress in reading along the margins: "Finished here March 20/89. I *declare!* What *time* it is!" (p. 81); "stopped here Mch 27" (p. 101); "Stopped here Apl. 4/89" (p. 196); "Begin *here* Apl. 24/89" (p. 207); "Begin here May 1/89" (p. 225); "Begin here May 15 '89" (p. 249); "Begin here May 22/89" (p. 261). A plethora of notes edit the material for reading aloud, adding underlinings for emphasis, marks for syllable stress, and notes for comprehension. On page 66 Clemens wondered, "Sarcasm?" and then answered himself on page 68, "Sarcasm." On that latter page Clemens added, "Festus should show these signs, this being a rehearsal." On page 82 he glossed Browning's reference to "the marvelous art," adding "of printing". Toward the bottom of that page Clemens crossed out seven names of "the gods of Israel" in Browning's poem. No pages are marked between pages 109 and 193. On page 195 Clemens attached the name "Shelley" to a reference to "spirit." On page 196 Clemens noted, "(hill-cat?)". He pondered on page 197, "The Emperor? Ostensibly on the Ghib side?—really against Pope & Italy?" On page 198 Clemens asked, "Emperor Charlemagne? Or Barbarossa?" Clemens summed up as "ambushes" the situation in the bottom half of page 200. Vertically on page 201 Clemens explained: "He will separate Sordello from the Dante-Sordello amalgam." At the bottom of page 201 Clemens jotted, "Vaporize & release the quicksilver." "Day-dreams," Clemens noted on page 212. He wrote "All Greek" beside the last ten lines on page 215. No markings appear between page 226 and 248.

Provenance: bookseller's sticker on rear pastedown endpaper, "Fitch & Billings/Booksellers/Elmira, N. Y."

Location: Mark Twain Library, Redding, Connecticut. Donated from Clemens's library by Clara Clemens Gabrilowitsch in 1910.

Copy examined: Clemens's copy, viewed in 1970 and again in June 1982. Has a red ink accession number, "3137".

——. *The Poetical Works of Robert Browning.* Copyright Edition. 2 vols. 12mo, original gift binding of crimson morocco, elaborate gilt, decorated silk endpapers, wear at corners and spines. Leipzig: Bernhard Tauchnitz, 1872.

Inscription: the front flyleaf of Volume I is inscribed in black ink: "To Susie Clemens,/These volumes,(in place/of a promised mud turtle,)/are presented, with the/love of/Papa./May 25, 1882./N.B. The turtle was to have been/brought from New Orleans, but I gave/up the idea because it seemed cruel./S.L.C." The front flyleaf of Volume II is also inscribed in black ink: "To Susie Clemens, from Papa." (Clemens revisited the Mississippi River in 1882 to gather material for his book of reminiscences, *Life on the Mississippi* (1883). Susy Clemens was then ten years old.)

Marginalia: Volume II has pencil marks by two poems on friendship; there is also a sketch of a girl's beautiful face possibly drawn by Clemens. Other pencil markings in both volumes do not look like they were made by Clemens.

Catalog: did not appear in *C1951*. Sold by Christie's, New York City, at the 1–2 February 1988 auction, 2 volumes, lot 452, for $4,500.

Provenance: for more than three decades the books were in the Carrie Estelle Doheny Collection, St. John's Seminary, Camarillo, California. Mrs. Doheny donated them in 1951 after she purchased the volumes from Maxwell Hunley Rare Books (Beverly Hills) for $100. Christie's sold the volumes on behalf of St. John's Seminary and the Los Angeles Archdiocese in February 1988.

Location: Volumes I and II are both in the collection of Kevin Mac Donnell, Austin, Texas.

Copies examined: Susy Clemens's copies of Volumes I and

II, at St. John's Seminary in 1970 and again in Austin, Texas in July 2004. Both volumes bear the bookplate of "Estelle Doheny."

These two volumes have the earliest date of the Browning books Clemens acquired for his family's library.

——. *Rabbi Ben Ezra.* Second edition. Limited edition of 475 copies. Portland, Maine: Thomas B. Mosher, MDCCCCXX. 22 pp. [Although this edition was first published in 1909, these Roman numerals register a much later year.]

Provenance: Antenne-Dorrance Collection, Rice Lake, Wisconsin. The book was temporarily on loan when I catalogued the collection in 1970.

Location: Mark Twain Archive, Gannett-Tripp Learning Center, Elmira College, Elmira, New York.

Copy examined: Clemens's copy, purportedly. However, the Roman numerals and a printed date at the rear indicate that this edition appeared in 1920, ten years after Clemens's death. This same craft press sent Clemens a 1900 limited edition of Dante Gabriel Rossetti's *Hand and Soul* (see that Catalog entry). Examined on 28 May 2015.

——. *Red Cotton Night-Cap Country; Aristophanes' Apology; The Inn Album; Pacchiarotto and How He Worked in Distemper; and Other Poems.* Volume V of *The Poetic and Dramatic Works of Robert Browning.* Riverside Edition. 6 vols. Boston: Houghton, Mifflin and Co., 1887.

Catalog: A1911, "3 vols., 12mo, cloth, gilt tops, uncut (several fly-leaves missing), Bost.: Riverside Press, 1887, numerous underscorings in one volume," lot 52, sold with two other Browning volumes; total price $2.25.

——. *The Ring and the Book.* Two volumes in one. Boston: Houghton, Mifflin and Co., 1885.

Inscription: The front flyleaf is inscribed by Clemens in black ink, "Livy L. Clemens/1886."

Marginalia: a few notes and markings in pencil, including (at the top of page 265) the reminder "Next (Nov. 16)" written above Giuseppe Caponsacchi's speech.

Catalog: *C1951*, #48a, one of "8 vols." of Browning, $72 total.

Location: Mark Twain Papers, Bancroft Library, University of California, Berkeley. Donated in July 1978 by Robert Dawson Wallace of Ft. Myers, Florida. Wallace purchased this and six other Browning volumes in 1952 from Dawson's Bookshop in Los Angeles.

Copy examined: Olivia Clemens's copy, annotated by Clemens.

——. *The Ring and the Book.* Volume III of the 6-volume Riverside Press Edition of *The Poetic and Dramatic Works of Robert Browning.* Two volumes in one (329 pp. and 332 pp.). Original brown cloth, gilt. Boston: Houghton, Mifflin and Co., 1887.

Inscription: the front flyleaf is signed in brown ink: "S. L. Clemens/1887."

Marginalia: heavily annotated in pencil for oral readings with one or more words underlined in virtually every line of the text in the first volume from page 8 to page 121 (a total of 3,700 lines). There are also numerous accent marks, marginal lines, and question marks. Clemens wrote forty-three words in the margins, mostly cues for reading the text aloud. At page 81, he jotted, "Begin in the fall." On page 211 he wrote "June 17, '87." At page 304 he noted, "Read next time Nov. 23." In the second volume, at page 21 Clemens reminded himself, "Begin here Dec 6,/87." At page 64 he wrote, "Begin here Dec. 21/87." On pages 71–72 he underlined one or more words in thirty-two lines of text, and added a word in the margin. Page 102 has the notation, "Begin here Dec. 21 /87." At page 132 he wrote, "Begin here Jan. 11/88 & quote first description on page 71 of 'Hyacinthus'". On pages 132–134 he underlined one or more words in eighty-one lines of text. He did not make any further markings after page 134 in the second volume. In summary, then, this book offers evidence that between June 1887 and January 1888 he prepared for oral performances by underlining between 4,000 and 5,000 words in more than 3,800 lines of text on more than 120 pages, along with inserting other markings and writing more than seventy-five words in the margins.

Catalog: *A1911*, "3 vols., 12mo, cloth, gilt tops, uncut (several fly-leaves missing), Bost.: Riverside Press, 1887, numerous underscorings in pencil in one volume," lot 52, sold with two other Browning volumes; total price $2.25.

Location: collection of Kevin Mac Donnell, Austin, Texas. Acquired in 2016 (Mac Donnell to Alan Gribben, email, 6 April 2016.

Source: descriptive letter from Mac Donnell to Alan Gribben, 22 April 2016.

Mary Bushnell Cheney attended one of the Browning study sessions at Clemens's Hartford home and heard him resume reading *The Ring and the Book* where he left off previously ("Mark Twain as a Reader" [1911], p. 6). Grace King, too, happened to visit the Clemenses during the summer of 1887 when Clemens was reading *The Ring and the Book* to his class: "To him there were no obscure passages to be argued over, no guesses at meaning. . . . He understood Browning as did no one else I ever knew" (*Memories* [1932], p. 84).

———. *Sordello* (poem, published in 1840).

When Mary Bushnell Cheney visited Clemens's Browning class in 1887 she observed that "in *Sordello* only we saw him confused and perplexed, and after two readings the book was abandoned" ("Mark Twain as a Reader" [1911], p. 6). Clemens joked about the obscurity of *Sordello* in Notebook 38 [June 1896], TS p. 32, doubting whether Browning himself knew the meaning of certain passages. (Clemens attributed the joke to his lecture agent Carlyle Smythe.)

———. *Strafford* (poem, published in 1837).

Sir Thomas Wentworth Strafford (1593–1641), the chief advisor to King Charles I, was accused by Parliament of despotic actions, tried, and beheaded. As Mary Bushnell Cheney listened to Clemens's reading of *Strafford*, "the grand character of that man and the nation-wide canvas of the drama were brought out conspicuously and to our intense delight" ("Mark Twain as a Reader," *Harper's Weekly* 55 [7 January 1911]: 6). Cheney had attended one of his Browning Society readings, which she describes rapturously in this letter to the editor. Brief but sharply etched, it is one of our most vivid glimpses of Clemens's techniques in reading poetry.

———. "Up at a Villa—Down in the City" (poem, published in 1855).

"I suppose I have read [to the Browning class] . . . Up in the Villa a couple of dozen times & Abt Vogler, Caliban in Setebos, & some others nearly as often. Ben Ezra & Abt Vogler are called for the oftenest—yes, & Up in a Villa. We should read Easter Day just as often, but for its length" (SLC to Mary Mason Fairbanks, 22 March 1887, *MTMF*, pp. 260–261). The title "Up at a Villa" was entered in Notebook 28 twice (November 1888, *N&J* 3: 433, 435). Jervis Langdon (1875–1952) recalled that Clemens's listeners "invariably demanded at the end three favorites, 'How They Brought the Good News from Ghent to Aix,' 'Up at a Villa, Down in the City,' and, for climax, 'The Battle of Naseby'" ("Some Reminiscences," collected in *MT in Elmira* [2013], p. 208). The Reverend Joseph H. Twichell declared in an essay on Mark Twain in 1896 that "whoever may have had the good fortune to hear his rendering of anything from Browning—for instance, 'Up at a Villa—Down in the City,' which is one of his favorites—will not be likely to forget the pleasure of it" (p. 822).

BROWNING SOCIETY. London. *Illustrations to Browning's Poems. . . . With a Notice of the Artists and the Pictures by E[rnest]. W[illiam]. Radford [1857–1919]*. London: Published for the Browning Society by N. Trübner & Co., Part I, 1882; Part II, 1883.

On a blank front flyleaf in a copy of Edgar Watson Howe's *The Story of a County Town* (1883) that Howe inscribed to Clemens in March 1884, Clemens penciled a bibliographic note: "Illustrations/to/Browning's Poems/(With a notice of the/Artists and Pictures)/by/Ernest Radford,/published for/The Browning Society/by N. Trubner & Co., 57 & 59 Ludgate Hill/London E. C." (quoted in *The Twainian* 27 [March-April 1968]: 1 and also in Christie's Catalogue 7286, 17 May 1991 sale, Lot 79, p. 41).

BRUCE, ROBERT (OF WALLELBERDINA, SOUTH AUSTRALIA) (c. 1836–1908). *Re-Echoes from Coondambo*. Adelaide, Australia: W. K. Thomas & Co., 1902. 437 pp.

Source: MTLAcc, entry #1691, volume donated by Clemens.

BRÜCKE, ERNST WILHELM RITTER VON (1819–1892). *Vorlesungen über Physiologie [Lectures on Physiology]*. [Published in 1873–1874.]

Mark Twain specifically referred to this work in a letter from Vienna in which he condemned the practice of vivisection, dated 26 May 1899 and addressed to Sidney G. Trist, Secretary of the London Anti-Vivisection Society (Hemminghaus, "Mark Twain's German Provenience," p. 476; Fears, *Day by Day* 3: 254). Brücke was a professor of physiology and microscopic anatomy in Vienna.

BRUEYS, DAVID AUGUSTIN DE (1640–1723). *L'Avocat Patelin: A Comedy in Three Acts. Adapted by the Abbé Brueys from the Famous Farce of the Fifteenth Century and First Performed at the Théâtre Français in 1705. Translated by Samuel F. G. Whitaker*. 12mo, original decorated wrappers over flexible boards with printed dust-jacket. Half maroon morocco slipcase. London: T. Fisher Unwin, 1905. 95 pp.

Inscription: the front free endpaper is inscribed, "To Mark Twain, this slight attempt at a presentment of 15th-18th century humour, with the Translator's profound yet affectionate respect. Independence Day, 1907." [This volume was presented to Clemens while he was in England to receive an honorary doctorate from Oxford University.]

Marginalia: Clemens mainly used this volume as an

impromptu notebook for ideas he would use for a dinner speech to the Savage Club in London on 6 July 1907. On the rear free endpaper he wrote a brief essay of about 150 words in brown ink concerning, among other things, "interviewer vulgarities—insists upon first person—their phrasing necessarily becoming his, not mine. He puts humor in my mouth—thinks humor necessary, which I don't" (New York *Times*, 9 February 1911, www.twain-quotes.com). He also condemned the "detestable, not to say idiotic" practice of using the third-person form in British Parliamentary debate; "it does [not?] save a single word of space. Very often you must translate it back to 1st person before you can find out what it means." Clemens cited the Duke of Oxford's effort to allude to Tennyson's "The Splendor Falls" in *The Princess, A Medley* (1847) as an example of what an absurdity this third-person convention can produce. Another sixty-five words appear on the rear pastedown endpaper in the same brown ink; these relate to the "Oxford pageants," the antiquity of England, the paleontologist Othniel Charles Marsh ("we had the first horse—O. C. Marsh"), international copyright laws ("You give us silly copyright law & criminal—which rob the author to fatten the publisher"), and other matters. No notes or markings are visible in the text.

Catalogs: *A1911*, "12mo, wrapppers, uncut, Lond. 1905," quotes the inscription and notes by Clemens, lot 481, $8; Christie's, (1989), #1758; Glenn Horowitz, Bookseller, 141 East 44th Street, Suite 808, New York City, Catalog 19 (1989), item #39, priced at $6,500; *Sotheby's 2003*, #187, $4,000.

Provenance: Carrie Estelle Doheny Collection, St. John's Seminary, Camarillo, California. Mrs. Doheny donated the volume in 1953 after obtaining it from Maxwell Hunley Rare Books, Beverly Hills. Auctioned on 21 February 1989 by Christie's (lot #1758) on behalf of St. John's Seminary for $2,420. Subsequently it became part of the Nick Karanovich collection in Fort Wayne, Indiana.

Location: Mark Twain Papers, Bancroft Library, University of California at Berkeley. Purchased at the 2003 Sotheby's auction.

Copy examined: Clemens's copy, when it was at St. John's Seminary in 1970. Has the bookplate of "Estelle Doheny." Fatout, ed., *Mark Twain Speaking* (1976), p. 574.

BRUNER, JANE W. (1845–1909). *Free Prisoners: A Story of California Life*. Philadelphia: Claxton, Remsen & Haffelfinger, 1877. 258 pp.

James R. Osgood & Company of Boston billed Clemens for Bruner's *Free Prisoners* in 1877 (Scrapbook #10, p. 69, MTP). He made the purchase on 19 July 1877.

Clemens knew Mrs. Bruner in California before she divorced her husband and became a San Francisco author, painter, and aspiring playwright. He mentions Bruner and her "book?" in late 1882 (NB 20, *N&J* 2: 508), presumably alluding to *Free Prisoners*, a romantic novel about the Gold Rush set in San Francisco and the Sierra Nevada foothills.

———. *A Mad World* (play, produced in 1882).

Bruner levied on her prior acquaintanceship with Mark Twain in California to obtain from him a reading of her play. After he missed its New Haven preview she sent a copy to him on 7 April 1882, seeking his opinion "even if it is unfavorable—I want to know my fate" (MTP). In Notebook 20 (April 1882) Mark Twain noted: "[William] Gillette ask Chas W Butler [an actor] about Mrs. Bruner's play—'A Mad World'" (*N&J* 2: 461).

BRUSH, CHRISTINE (CHAPLIN) (1842–1892). *The Colonel's Opera Cloak*. No Name Series. Boston: Roberts Brothers, 1879. 228 pp.

Clemens noted this book title in Notebook 19 early in the summer of 1881 (*N&J* 2: 397). The novel's events have at their center an ornate, scarlet-lined blue coat belonging to a ruined Southerner, Colonel St. John. Certain children's scenes remind one of *The Adventures of Tom Sawyer*, and the author endeavors to render the dialect of African American speech in the South.

BRYANT, H. T. "Balm of Gilead" (minstrel song, arranged by H. T. Bryant).

A case could be made that the song Clemens's liked to play on the piano and sing, "I had an old horse whose name was Methusalem," derived from the Bryant's Minstrels' popular "Balm of Gilead." One verse of the Bryant tune goes "My old grey horse, he came from Jerusalem,/Came from Jerusalem;/My old grey horse he came from Jerusalem/He kick so high they put him the museum/Down in Alabam." Portions of the song may have plantation roots. This particular verse about the horse has been preserved in print with a number of variants in phrasing. See Albert Bigelow Paine's *Mark Twain: A Biography* (1912), pp. 295–296 and *Mark Twain of the "Enterprise"* (ed. Henry Nash Smith, 1957), pp. 52, 219 n. 5 for two accounts of Clemens singing this song that had many versions.

BRYANT, WILLIAM CULLEN (1794–1878). "The Battle-Field" (poem, published in 1839).

Mark Twain attributes "the lie of virtuous ecstasy" to Bryant for writing that "truth crushed to earth will [*sic*] rise again" ("My First Lie, and How I Got Out of It" [1899]).

———, comp. *The Family Library of Poetry and Song. Being Choice Selections from the Best Poets, English, Scottish, Irish, and American*. New York: J. B. Ford and Co., 1870. 950 pp. [Edition conjectured.]

When Mark Twain met William Cox Bennett in London in 1873, he reminded Mary Mason Fairbanks: "You remember his poem 'Baby May' in the <Whittier> Bryant Selections" (6 July 1873, *MTMF*, p. 173; *MTLet* 5: 402); Bennett's rhapsodic tribute to his infant daughter appeared on page 4 of Bryant's anthology. To a correspondent seeking Bryant's autograph, Clemens explained on 31 July 1873: "There is a volume (issued by Scribner I think, some 3 or 4 years ago) of selections from the whole world's poets which contains Bryant's autograph—the collection *is compiled by* <Wh> Bryant but I forget its title" (SLC to "Dear Sir," ALS, Massachusetts Historical Society; *MTLet* 5: 423). Clemens recalled correctly: below the frontispiece portrait of Bryant in *The Family Library* appears his autograph; facsimile autographs of other poets are scattered through the volume.

Clemens's familiarity with this anthology opens up the possibility that he knew pieces by many poets whose books he never owned or mentioned, for Bryant's *Family Library* remains one of the most (perhaps *the* most) comprehensive one-volume collections of poetry published in the United States. His selections ran the gamut from established masterpieces by Coleridge and Wordsworth to the near-doggerel of contemporary versifiers for American newspapers and magazines. All periods are represented, commencing with that of Chaucer.

———. *Poems of William Cullen Bryant*. Illustrations engraved by the Brothers Dalziel. New York: D. Appleton & Co., [cop. 1854].

Provenance: bookplate of the "J. Langdon Family Library, No. 57."

Catalogs: QF Martinez; Ball 2016 inventory, gilt edges, brown leather, embossed lettering, J. Langdon Family Library, No. 57.

Location: Quarry Farm library shelves, under the supervision of the Mark Twain Archive, Gannett-Tripp Learning Center, Elmira College, Elmira, New York.

Copy examined: an unmarked copy to which Clemens had access whenever he visited the Langdons in Elmira. Examined on 26 May 2015.

—————— and SYDNEY HOWARD GAY (1814–1888). *A Popular History of the United States, from the First Discovery of the Western Hemisphere by the Northmen, to the End of the Civil War*. 4 vols. Three-quarter deep purple morocco, raised bands, cloth sides, all edges gilt, marbled endpapers. New York: Charles Scribner's Sons, 1883.

Inscriptions: the first three volumes are identically inscribed in ink on their front flyleaves by Clemens to Clara Clemens on her tenth birthday: "Clara Langdon Clemens/ from Mama & Papa/June 8, 1884." Volume IV is more simply inscribed "Clara Langdon Clemens/from Mama & Papa/1884." (Clemens accidentally inscribed the rear flyleaf of Volume II upside down and then re-inscribed the book at the front.) Clara Clemens Gabrilowitsch's library shelfmark from her Detroit years appears in pencil on the endpaper of each volume. Three of the volumes have the 1951 Hollywood sale label on their front endpaper.

Location: collection of Kevin Mac Donnell, Austin, Texas.

Source: letter from Mac Donnell to Alan Gribben, 10 December 2014.

Clemens notified Charles L. Webster on 20 March 1884 that "the Bryant History has arrived" (*MTBus*, p. 242); on 2 September 1884 Webster sent Clemens a statement of his personal expenses charged against Charles L. Webster & Company that included a charge of $31.80 for the purchase on 22 March 1884 of "1 Set of Bryants U.S. Histy" (MTP).

———. "Thanatopsis" (poem, published in 1817, revised in 1821).

In a public letter written in 1872 Mark Twain ranked Bryant with Longfellow and Holmes as celebrated poets (Hartford *Evening Post*, 6 December 1872, *MTPP*, p. 47). A character calling himself "Holmes" claimed the authorship of Bryant's Thanatopsis" in Mark Twain's ill-fated Whittier Birthday Dinner speech on 17 December 1877 (*MTB*, p. 1646).

Smith, "'That Hideous Mistake of Poor Clemens's'" (1955).

BRYCE, LLOYD STEPHENS (1851–1917). *Friends in Exile. A Tale of Diplomacy, Coronets, and Hearts*. New York: Harper & Brothers, 1900. 270 pp.

Source: MTLAcc, entry #1438, volume donated by Clemens.

Bryce had been the owner and editor of the *North American Review* from 1889 until 1896. *Friends in Exile* was a work of fiction.

BUCHANAN, THOMPSON (1877–1937). *The Castle Comedy*. Illustrated by Elizabeth Shippen Green (1871–1954). New York: Harper & Brothers, 1904. 236 pp.

Source: MTLAcc, entry #986, volume donated by Clemens. A romance novel involving one of Napoleon's soldiers.

———. *Judith Triumphant*. New York: Harper & Brothers, 1905. 255 pp.

Source: MTLAcc, entry #33, volume donated by Clemens. Buchanan set this romance during the siege of the Assyrians under Holofernes against the Jews of Bethulia.

BUCHHEIM, KARL ADOLF (1828–1900). *Materials for German Prose Composition; or, Selections from Modern English Writers*. Ninth edition. New York: G. P. Putnam's Sons, 1885. 252 pp.

Source: MTLAcc, entry #382, volume donated by Clemens.

BUCK, CHARLES (1771–1815), comp. *Anecdotes; Religious, Moral, and Entertaining, by the Late Rev. Charles Buck, Author of Theological Dictionary. Alphabetically Arranged, and Interspersed with a Variety of Useful Observations. With a Preface by Ashbel Green* [1762–1848]. Two vols. in one. New York: J. C. Riker, 1831. [202 pp. + 190 pp.]

Inscription: "J. Langdon [Clemens's father-in-law], Salina, June 1, 1833."

Marginalia: Clemens marked a few passages in the margin.

Catalogs: *A1911*, "8vo, cloth (loose), N.Y. 1831," quotes the signature and describes the marginalia, lot 53, sold for $6; Ball 2016 inventory, "Langdon, June 1st, 1833," red cloth, lacks the binding and back cover.

Location: Mark Twain Archive, Elmira College, Elmira, New York.

Somehow this volume found its way back into the Langdon family library at Quarry Farm. Possibly the Mark Twain Company bought it at the auction and returned it to Susan Crane or the Langdon family. This happened in a several instances.

The Reverend Buck assembled witty quotations by figures ranging from Julius Caesar to Sir Walter Raleigh to Lord Chesterfield.

[BUCK, SIR EDWARD (1838–1916).] *Indo-Anglian Literature*. Second Issue. For Private Circulation Only. Calcutta: Thacker, Spink and Co., 1887. [The first edition was published in 1883. The preface is merely signed merely "B. A." and no author's name appears on the title page. However, the book has been certified to be the work of Sir Edward Buck (James Kennedy, W. A. Smith, and A. F. Johnson, *Dictionary of Anonymous and Pseudonymous English Literature* [Edinburgh: Oliver and Boyd: 1928–1932], 3: 149; 6: 282).]

Inscription: on the front cover of this paperbound volume Clemens wrote in pencil, "Lt Gov of Bengal".

Marginalia: Clemens made notes in pencil throughout the book and cut out certain sections for use in *Following the Equator* (1897). Keshav Mutalik quoted various annotations (including Clemens's quip on page 67, "A very heavy day for a child") in *Mark Twain in India* (1978).

Catalog: ListABP (1910), "Indo-Anglican Literature; "Retz Appraisal" (1944), p. 9, valued at $15.

Location: Mark Twain Papers, Bancroft Library, University of California at Berkeley.

Copy examined: Clemens's copy.

The book consists of supposedly humorous examples of English prose culled from letters and essays written by

Indians. In Chapter 61 of *Following the Equator* (1897) Mark Twain mentions his receiving *Indo-Anglican Literature* in the mail; he finds it "well stocked with 'baboo' English—clerky English, booky English, acquired in the schools," but adds that "strange as some of these wailing and supplicating letters are, humble and even groveling as some of them are, and quaintly funny and confused as a goodly number of them are, there is still a pathos about them, as a rule, that checks the rising laugh and reproaches it." Nevertheless he proceeds to quote a number of extracts that he finds amusing. Sir Edward Buck held several prominent posts, including Secretary of the Revenue and Agricultural Department and Secretary to the Government of India.

Mutalik, *MT in India* (1978), pp. 112–113.

BUCKINGHAM, JAMES SILK (1786–1855). *America, Historical, Statistic, and Descriptive.* 2 vols. New York: Harper & Brothers, 1841. [No edition established; other firms varied the number of volumes.]

Dewey Ganzel concedes that "Buckingham is not mentioned by Twain in his list of travelers [cited in *Life on the Mississippi*] . . . , but Twain wrote that there were other authorities which he consulted but did not list" ("Twain, Travel Books, and *Life on the Mississippi*" [1962], p. 47 n. 14). Ganzel suspects that Twain used Buckingham's *America* as a source in referring to anti-abolitionist mobs in Philadelphia, a passage he later dropped from the final version of *Life on the Mississippi* (1883).

If Twain did procure a copy of Buckingham's travel book, he found a treasure trove of information about early-day North America along the Eastern seaboard. Buckingham visited Washington, D. C., Baltimore, Providence, Philadelphia, Boston, and New York City. He went throughout New York State, visiting Albany, Rochester, Buffalo, Niagara Falls, and numerous other towns and sites. He delivered reports on poverty and crime, slavery and abolitionism, prison reform, mental asylums, Native Americans, Shaker communities, national manners, and a host of other topics. His work has to be one of the most detailed and informative records set down in print by any of the nineteenth-century English travelers to the United States.

Ganzel, "Twain, Travel Books, and *Life on the Mississippi*" (1962), pp. 43–44.

BUCKLAND, FRANCIS TREVELYAN (1826–1880). *Curiosities of Natural History.* Third Series. Second edition. 2 vols. London: Richard Bentley, 1868.

Inscription: on the verso of the front free endpaper in Volume II: "To Saml L. Clemens/ with the sincere regard of his friend/the Editor/Henry Lee [1826–1888]/Sept. 17th 1872".

Location: Mark Twain Library, Redding, Connecticut (Volume II only).

Copy examined: Clemens's copy of Volume II, unmarked. 365 pp. Has a penciled accession number—"2972". Examined in 1970 and again in June 1982.

Clemens mentioned Buckland several times in his English journals of 1872, once about Buckland's strong reputation as a natural historian and again in connection with a controversy about Ben Jonson's burial place in Westminster Abbey (*MTLet* 5: 586, 604).

It is difficult to describe the swirling potpourri of facts and anecdotes that Buckland lays before the reader. Volume I explores domestic and foreign species of frogs, tadpoles, lizards, toads, rats, snakes, cobras, fish, monkeys, elephants, porpoises, lobsters, whales, and other animal life as well as fossils and museum collections. The contents of Volume II vary according to the series number, but the copy that Clemens owned contains accounts of giantism, dwarfism, mummies, fire-eaters, Maori songs and wrestling, P. T. Barnum's collection, talking fish, Blondin the tightrope walker, ancient English crypts, Ben Jonson's grave, cruelty to animals, migrating salmon patterns, human remains found in a glacier, fairy sightings, and many, many other subjects.

BUCKLE, HENRY THOMAS (1821–1862). *History of Civilization in England.* 2 vols. [Volume I was published in 1857; Volume II appeared in 1861. Clemens's edition has not been established.]

One of Mark Twain's sources for *A Connecticut Yankee in King Arthur's Court* (1889) was listed in a version of his projected appendix: "King's evil. Hist Civilization" (NB 29 [1889], *N&J* 3: 506).

Buckle's somewhat modest title is misleading; his two-volume work also chronicled the histories of France, Spain, and Scotland as well as England. Moreover, Buckle's book formed a treatise against superstition in all forms and in favor of ideas that liberate the intellect of nations. He paused to discuss the eminent philosophers and historians of each of the four countries, weighing their contributions and their faults. In a word, *History of Civilization in England* has the same philosophical cast as W. E. H. Lecky's histories, and it should rank much higher in our thinking about Twain's intellectual background.

On 4 January 1896 Twain noted that "Buckle says the bulk of population of India is the Sudras—the workers, the farmers, the creators of wealth. Their name—laborer—is a term of contempt" (NB 36, TS p. 16). Comparing Australasia with India, he reminded himself on 5 January 1896 to "see previous quotation from Buckle" (NB 36, TS p. 18). In Chapter 39 of *Following the Equator* (1897) Twain quotes from Buckle's description of the *Sudra* laborer caste and its humble station in Indian society. This definition comes from Chapter 2 of Volume I of Buckle's *History of Civilization in England*. Buckle termed the condition of *Sudras* "slavery, abject, eternal slavery" (*History of Civilization in England*, 2 vols. [New York: D. Appleton and Co., 1866] 2: 56–58). Buckle's premature death prevented his completing the far larger scope of his planned history of civilization.

BUCKLEY, ARABELLA BURTON (LATER MRS. FISHER) (1840–1929). *The Fairy-Land of Science.* New York: H. M. Caldwell Co., n.d. 266 pp. [*Fairy-Land of Science* was first published in 1879].

Source: MTLAcc, entry #1590, volume donated by Clemens.

Elementary lectures for children about the wonders of nature to be observed all around them.

———. *Life and Her Children: Glimpses of Animal Life from the Amoeba to the Insects.* Illus. New York: D. Appleton & Co., 1885. 312 pp.

Source: MTLAcc, entry #1939, volume donated from

Clemens's library by Clara Clemens Gabrilowitsch in 1910.

At Quarry Farm on 2 July 1885 Olivia Clemens noted: "Tonight I was reading to Susy and Clara from a book 'Life and her Children' a very interesting book on the lower forms of Animal Life" (OLC Diary, DV161, MTP; *Family Sketch*, p. 100). She also recorded on 12 July that "we are reading together 'Life and her Children'" (OLC Diary).

BUCKLEY, JAMES MONROE (1836–1920). *A History of Methodism in the United States*. 2 vols. New York: Harper & Brothers, 1898.

Source: MTLAcc, entries #1817 and #1818, volumes donated by Clemens.

BUCKNER, ALICE MORRIS (1841–1918). *Towards the Gulf; A Romance of Louisiana*. New York: Harper & Brothers, [cop. 1886]. 315 pp.

Source: MTLAcc, entry #239, volume donated by Clemens. The now-forgotten Buckner's novel courageously addressed the prejudice against racial miscegenation. In depicting the nagging suspicions of a Louisiana husband about the racial pedigree of his wife, the novel foreshadowed Kate Chopin's later short story, "Desirée's Baby" (1893). Lafcadio Hearn praised Buckner's book to no avail, as did William Dean Howells.

Sarah Wadsworth and Wayne A. Wiegand, *Right Here I See My Own Books: The Woman's Building Library at the World's Columbian Exposition* (Amherst: University of Massachusetts Press, 2012), pp. 151–152.

BUÉ, HENRI. *Early French Lessons*. Twenty-first edition. London: Dulau & Co., Hachette & Co., 1900. 57 pp.

Marginalia: none by Clemens. Heavy pencil markings—possibly by Jean or Clara Clemens—on pages 1, 32–33.

Provenance: sticker on the rear pastedown endpaper: Brentano's Booksellers & Stationers, Union Square, New York.

Location: Mark Twain Papers, Bancroft Library, University of California at Berkeley.

Copy examined: copy belonging to a member of Clemens's family.

"BUFFALO GALS" (minstrel song, published in 1848).

Mark Twain complained in the Buffalo *Morning Express* issue of 23 August 1869 about an organ grinder who had stuck with this tune: "'Buffalo gals' is fresh and exciting, but one notices after several days that it lacks variety" (Reigstad, *SL*, p. 73). Twain later recalled that while navigating dangerous snags the river pilot named Stephen calmly whistled "Buffalo gals, can't you come out to-night, can't you come out to-night, can't you come out to-night" (Ch. 14, *LonMiss* [1883], published previously in "Old Times on the Mississippi" [1875]). In Chapter 2 of *The Adventures of Tom Sawyer* (1876) "Jim came skipping out at the gate with a tin pail, and singing "Buffalo gals." The same tune, "Buffalo Gals," was one of the songs sung by a South Carolina African American for the boys in Chapter 26 of "No. 44, The Mysterious Stranger" (written 1902–1908, *MSM*, pp. 354–355). Since "microbes like sentimental music best," the cholera germ sang "Buffalo Gals Can't You Come Out To-night" and "Bonny Doon" for ten years in "Three Thousand Years Among the Microbes" (written in 1905, *WWD?*, p. 462). Twain remembered it as one of the "rudely comic" songs introduced by minstrel troupes of the 1840s (30

November 1906 AD, *MTE*, p. 114; *AutoMT* 2: 296).

Sharon D. McCoy, "'I ain' no dread being': The Minstrel Mask as Alter Ego," *Centenary Reflections on Mark Twain's No. 44, The Mysterious Stranger*, ed. Joseph Csicsila and Chad Rohman (Columbia: University of Missouri Press, 2009), pp. 31–32; and Henry B. Wonham, "Mark Twain's Last Cakewalk: Racialized Performance in *No. 44, The Mysterious Stranger*," *Centenary Reflections on Mark Twain's No. 44, The Mysterious Stranger* (2009), pp. 46–47

BUFFUM, EDWARD GOULD (1820–1867). *Sights and Sensations in France, Germany, and Switzerland*. New York: Harper & Brothers, 1869. 310 pp.

Source: MTLAcc, entry #1713, volume donated by Clemens.

BULFINCH, THOMAS (1796–1867). *The Age of Chivalry; or, Legends of King Arthur*. Brown cloth. Rebound, with parts of the original spine incorporated in the new spine. The title page is missing. The preface is not dated. A printed dedication honors Mrs. Joseph Coolidge. 414 pp. [The 414-page edition was copyrighted in 1858 with many subsequent English and American reprintings.]

Catalog: ListABP (1910), "Age of Chivalry, Bulfinch", no other information provided.

Provenance: described as having been Clara Clemens's book. Donated to the Mark Twain House and Museum in the spring of 1987 by Yvonne Rogow of Los Angeles. Rogow's father was a friend of Clara Clemens's Samossoud's secretary Phyllis Harrington. Yvonne Rogow served as the executor of Harrington's estate.

Location: Mark Twain House and Museum, Hartford, Connecticut.

Copy examined: a copy very likely owned by Clara Clemens, unmarked, that would have been available to her father. Viewed in August 1987 in Hartford.

Bulfinch included *The Mabinogion*, a collection of Welsh tales based on Celtic legends, in this volume. (Bulfinch spelled it *Mabinogeon*.)

———. *The Age of Fable; or, Beauties of Mythology*. Boston: J. E. Tilton and Co., 1863. 488 pp.

Inscription: inscribed on the flyleaf: "Livia L. Langdon, Jan. 1864," to which Clemens added: "Her father's hand. Noe [?] Livy was 19 then. She would be 63 now. S. L. C. (1908, Nov. 1)" (*Zeitlin 1951*, p. 2).

Catalogs: *C1951*, D79, erroneously listed as part of a two-volume set; *Zeitlin 1951*, #10, $25, "worn, spine torn, loose."

Most of the stories derive from ancient Greece and Rome (Bullfinch especially credits Ovid and Virgil), but a few are drawn from other cultures.

———. *The Age of Fable; or, Beauties of Mythology*. Boston: J. E. Tilton and Co., 1865. 488 pp.

Marginalia: Clemens noted on the flyleaf: "The feet of the avenging deities are shod with wood. Justice is lame—slow but sure" (*Zeitlin 1951*, p. 6).

Catalogs: *C1951*, D79, erroneously listed as part of a two-volume set; *Zeitlin 1951*, #53, $10, "worn, spine torn."

On 3 January 1869, (Clemens reported later to Olivia Langdon), "I lay abed [in Fort Wayne, Indiana] till 1 P.M[.], & read . . . a most entertaining volume containing the Grecian & other Mythologies in a condensed form—& smoked thousands of cigars, & was excessively happy" (14 January 1869, *MTLet* 3: 39). Most of the stories derive from ancient Greece and Rome (Bullfinch especially credits Ovid and Virgil), but a few are drawn from other cultures.

BULLEN, FRANK THOMAS (1857–1915). *The Cruise of the Cachalot Round the World after Sperm Whales* (published in London, 1898).

WWD?, p. 100.

———. *The Log of a Sea-Waif: Being Recollections of the First Four Years of My Sea Life*. Second Impression. Illus. London: Smith, Elder & Co., 1899. 349 pp.

Inscription: Bullen used black ink on the recto of the frontispiece to inscribe a presentation: "To Mark Twain/as the tiniest mark of/grateful recognition of sorrow/lightened, care driven away,/and even health restored by/the sweet and genial influences/of his incomparable books/with the undying love/and gratitude of the/Author/F T Bullen/London March 30/1900".

Location: Mark Twain Library, Redding, Connecticut.

Copy examined: presentation copy to Clemens. Has a red ink accession number: "2828". Examined in 1970 and again June 1982.

Mark Twain was aware that he was to meet "Bullen, author of the 'Cruise of the Cachelot'" [*sic*] at a dinner in London on 29 March 1900 (NB 43, TS p. 6a). Bullen wrote to Mark Twain on 5 April 1900 (MTP).

BUNNER, HENRY CUYLER (1855–1896). *The Midge*. New York: Charles Scribner's Sons, 1886. 235 pp.

"Get 'The Midge' by H C Bunner," Clemens reminded himself about Bunner's first novel (NB 26 [June? 1886], *N&J* 3: 240). Set in the French Quarter of New York City, *The Midge* relates an odd adoption by a bachelor. In December 1893 Clemens wished to "write Bunner" (NB 33, TS p. 42). Novelist, poet, playwright, and editor Bunner would die of tuberculosis in his early forties.

———. *Three Operettas. Music by Oscar Weil [c. 1839–1921]*. Illustrations by C[harles]. D[ater]. Weldon (1855–1935) and Charles Jay Taylor (1855–1929). Gray pictorial cloth depicting three black cats sporting gold crowns and orange ruffs. New York: Harper & Brothers, 1897. 163 pp.

Catalogs: *A1911*, "Oblong 4to, cloth, N.Y. 1897," lot 55, sold for $5; *Sotheby's 2003*, lot 220, sold for $900 (sold with four other miscellaneous titles).

Provenance: collection of Nick Karanovich, Fort Wayne, Indiana.

Copy examined: Clemens's copy. Viewed at the 2003 Sotheby's sale.

———— and **EDWARD A. DITHMAR** (1854–1917). *A Portfolio of Players*. Illus. 110 numbered copies. New York: Privately printed by J. W. Bouton, 1888.

Portraits of Augustin Daly, Laurence Hutton, William Winter, Brander Matthews, and other figures associated with Augustin Daly's theatrical company.

BUNYAN, JOHN (1628–1688) *The Complete Works of John Bunyan*. Intro. by the Reverend John P[utnam]. Gulliver (1819–1894). Philadelphia: Bradley, Garretson & Co., 1874.

Provenance: bookplate of "Langdon Family Library No. 519".

Catalog: Ball 2016 inventory, brown cloth, gilt lettering, design, and page edges, J. Langdon Family Library bookplate #519.

Location: Quarry Farm library shelves, under the supervision of the Mark Twain Archive, Elmira College, Elmira, New York.

Clemens had access to these books whenever he visited the Langdons in Elmira.

Liam Purdon, "John Bunyan's *The Pilgrim's Progress* and Mark Twain's *Adventures of Huckleberry Finn*," *Mark Twain Journal: The Author and His Era* 56.2 (Fall 2018): 69–84, saw possible connections between this edition and Twain's famous novel.

———. *The Pilgrim's Progress*. London, 1862.

Marginalia: contains a marginal note reportedly in Samuel Clemens's hand: "The natural argument of the sinner" (*Mott 1952*).

Provenance: Orion Clemens's bookplate, affixed while he was Territorial Secretary of Nevada.

Catalog: *Mott 1952*, #39, $30.

———. *The Pilgrim's Progress as Originally Published by John Bunyan, Being a Fac-Simile Reproduction of the First Edition*. London: Elliot Stock, 1875. [Reproduces the 1678 edition (Part 1) and the 1684 edition (Part 2).]

Inscription: inscribed in brown ink on the front free endpaper: "Saml. L. Clemens/Hartford, 1875." The hand resembles Olivia Clemens's more than her husband's.

Marginalia: double vertical pencil mark on page 2; another double vertical pencil mark on page 64; single vertical pencil marks on pages 70, 71, 72, and 73; blue ink marks on pages 260–265; no marks in the second part (the 1684 edition). On page 6 of the 1678 text Clemens wrote: "Correct picture of selfishness & baseness." Howard G. Baetzhold explained that in this passage Pliable leaves Christian alone in the Slough of Despond (*MT&JB* [1970], p. 374). See Chester L. Davis, "Mark Twain's Personal Marked Copy of John Bunyan's 'Pilgrim's Progress,'" *The Twainian* 18 (May-June 1959): 1–2.

Catalogs: *C1951*, #42c; *Hunley 1958*, #24, $15.

Provenance: formerly in the collection of Chester L. Davis (1903–1987), Executive-Secretary, Mark Twain Research Foundation, Perry, Missouri.

Location: currently unknown.

Copy examined: Clemens's copy, briefly, in 1970 in Perry, Missouri. Thomas A. Tenney later sent me photocopies of the inscription, title page, and marginalia that Chester L. Davis had had allowed him to make on 2 September 1980.

Mark Twain often referred to *Pilgrim's Progress*, which had first been published in 1678. For example, he alluded to it in Act II, Scene i of "The *Quaker City* Holy Land Excursion" (a play he wrote in 1867). *Pilgrim's Progress* was among the books that the *Quaker City* passengers were advised to bring on their journey (*Daily Alta California*, 5 April 1868; *TIA*, p. 303). Twain eventually gave his first book—*Innocents Abroad, or The New Pilgrim's Progress* (1869)—the subtitle he originally considered (in variant form) as his main title. In the text of *Innocents Abroad*, however, he merely alludes to the Slough of Despond in the first part of the book and only makes subtle efforts to construct parallels between the two books. Chapter 44 of *The Gilded Age* (1873) contains a possible reference: "This was by contrast the maddest Vanity Fair one could conceive." (But see also the Catalog entry for

William Makepeace Thackeray's novel titled *Vanity Fair*.) In Chapter 2 of *The Adventures of Tom Sawyer* (1876), Cardiff Hill seemed "a Delectable Land, dreamy, reposeful and inviting" (evoking the Delectable Mountains seen by Bunyan's Christian) on the Saturday morning that Tom is sentenced to whitewash Aunt Polly's fence. Twain mentioned that he envied Bunyan because "solitary imprisonment" offered him "the *best* of opportunities" for writing (SLC to Mary Mason Fairbanks, 6 August 1877, *MTMF*, pp. 206–207).

In handwriting that closely resembles his script of the 1880s, Twain copied passages from *Pilgrim's Progress* onto eight manuscript pages, which he headed "From The Pilgrim's Progress, by John Bunyan" (DV 117, MTP). All of these excerpts describe heaven according to the narrator's vision, replete with white robes, wings, crowns of gold, golden harps, reunions with departed friends, ringing bells, and streets of gold. At the end of these extracts Twain resolved to write an account depicting "Mr. J. G. Elliott's Visit to the New Jerusalem," which presumably evolved into Twain's *Extract from Captain Stormfield's Visit to Heaven* (1909).

Huckleberry Finn's thumbnail summary of *Pilgrim's Progress* has become celebrated: on the Grangerfords' parlor table he discovered the story of "a man that left his family it didn't say why. . . . The statements was interesting, but tough" (Ch. 17, *HF* [1885]). Twain told Howells he "would rather be damned to John Bunyan's heaven" than read Henry James' *The Bostonians* (21 July 1885, *MTHL*, p. 534). A close knowledge of Bunyan's work and familiarity with his life (Twain cites Southey's biography of Bunyan) is evident in Twain's burlesque "cipher" argument that John Milton must have written *Pilgrim's Progress*; in the course of the deliberately specious reasoning Twain suggests an interpretation that seems serious—"The Dream must be read between the lines—then it becomes a grisly & almost Hudibrastic Satyre" (NB 27 [September 1887], *N&J* 3: 328, 327). Twain had a brainstorm early in October 1887 about promoting a "stereopticon panorama of Bunyan's Pilgrim's Progress" that would provide a travelogue of "twenty interesting cities" and "would clear a fortune in a year" (NB 27, *N&J* 3: 334). He listed the title in March 1888 (NB 27, *N&J* 3: 379); halfheartedly tried to make a joke about Bunyan in 1892 (NB 32, TS p. 47); and alluded to *Pilgrim's Progress* in an entry in Notebook 41: "Nobody would go to Bunyan's heaven now" (TS p. 40, MTP). Chapter 51 of Twain's *Following the Equator* (1897) compares the Brahmin faith to Bunyan's journey as suggested by the capitalized landmarks ("Well of Long Life") and its progressive "Great Pilgrimage." Two chapters farther on Twain noted that one of the Hindu living gods, "like John Bunyan's Christian[,] . . . bade perpetual good-bye to his family, as required, and went wandering away" (Ch. 53, *FE*). Speaking to political prisoners in South Africa in 1896, Twain pretended to offer words of comfort: "Look at Bunyan. . . . 'The Pilgrim's Progress' would never have been written if Bunyan hadn't been in gaol! . . . . Bunyan was enjoying the company of devils and angels and other scarecrows, leading his hosts through all the perils of battles and sieges and enjoying all the intoxicating delight of glorious war without its dangers. He simply superintended!" ("Mark Twain in Gaol," Pretoria

Press, 25 May 1896; reprinted in the *Mark Twain Journal* 40.1 [Spring 2002]: 39). In working notes about 44 for "Schoolhouse Hill," probably written in 1898, Twain's character revealed that Bunyan was mistaken in details about heaven ("not so small; & Presbyterians are not so plenty") (*MSM*, p. 440). Twain recalled that, addressing political prisoners in Pretoria, he had joked about Bunyan's advantages as a writer who had been shut up "in a cell" and therefore produced *Pilgrim's Progress* ("Mark Twain Home, an Anti-Imperialist," New York *Herald*, 16 October 1900; *Complete Interviews*, p. 355). Twain seemed briefly sincere in an undated review of a book by George Woodward Warder, "About Cities in the Sun" (written in 1901 [?], DV357, MTP), where he acknowledges what a "wonderful experience" it would be to stand in the New Jerusalem "& hear Shakspeare & Milton & Bunyan read from their noble works" (MS p. 19).

Howard G. Baetzhold, *MT&JB* (1970), pp. 264–265; Harold T. McCarthy, "Mark Twain's Pilgrim's Progress: *The Innocents Abroad*," *Arizona Quarterly* 26.3 (Autumn 1970): 249–258; Alfred Bendixen, "Huck Finn and *Pilgrim's Progress*," *Mark Twain Journal* 18.3 (Winter 1976–1977): 21; Robert Sattelmeyer, "'Interesting, but Tough': *Huckleberry Finn* and the Problem of Tradition," *One Hundred Years of Huckleberry Finn: The Boy, His Book, and American Culture*, ed. Robert Sattelmeyer and J. Donald Crowley (Columbia: University of Missouri, 1985), pp. 354–355; Joe B. Fulton, "Mark Twain's New Jerusalem: Prophecy in the Unpublished Essay 'About Cities in the Sun,'" *Christianity and Literature* 55.2 (Winter 2006): 173–194; Eleftheria Arapoglou, "Mark Twain's 'Spatial Play': Venice and the Holy Land in *The Innocents Abroad*," *Mark Twain Annual* 6 (2008): 101–117; and Liam Purdon, "John Bunyan's *The Pilgrim's Progress* and Mark Twain's *Adventures of Huckleberry Finn*," *Mark Twain Journal: The Author and His Era* 56.2 (Fall 2018): 69–84.

———. *The Pilgrim's Progress. With a Life of the Author and Bibliographical Notes by Robert Southey [1774–1843]*. Illustrated by William Harvey (1796–1866). London: John Hogg, 1881. 402 pp. [Edition conjectured; there were earlier editions by Southey.]

Clemens cited "*Southey's Bunyan*" as a source in September 1887 (NB 27, *N&J* 3: 328).

———. [*The Pilgrim's Progress*. Chinese.] *The Pilgrim's Progress (in the Canton Vernacular)*. Illus. 2 vols. Pink title pages. Fifty-eight woodcuts. Original tan boards, wrappers bound in, tan suede spine. Canton, China, 1870–1871. [Bound as two volumes in one.]

Inscriptions: on the wrapper of Volume I in Clemens's hand: "Bunyan's/Pilgrim's/Progress,/Part I./Sent from Bangkok/Siam by H. R. H. the/Rajah of Ambong and Morocco/in the Island of Borneo. The/prince is a full-blooded Yank[ee], and was born in Boston./Hartford, March, 1882." On the wrapper of Volume II Clemens wrote in black ink, "Part II."

Provenance: G. W. Torrey wrote to Clemens about sending this book on 1 January and 17 July 1882 (Machlis, *UCLC*, p. 307).

Catalogs: *A1911*, "2 vols. 8vo, wrappers, as issued, Canton, China, 1870–71," quotes the inscription, lot 56; George D. Smith, New York City, "Catalogue of Books,

No. 165" (1911), quotes the signature, "2 vols.," item #45. $15; Philip M. Neufeld sale, Christie's, New York City, 25 April 1995, "fore-corners a bit worn, horizontal tear across the title page of vol. 1 and a text leaf, some browning to leaves," lot #100, sold for $1,150; *Sotheby's 2003*, #188, $2,250.

Copy examined: Clemens's copy, at the 2003 Sotheby's auction.

———. [*The Pilgrim's Progress*. French and English.]
In November 1877 James R. Osgood & Company billed Clemens $1.08 for "1 Fr. & Eng. Pilgrim's Progress" purchased on 12 February 1877 (receipt in Scrapbook #10, p. 69, MTP).

———. [*The Pilgrim's Progress*. Hawaiian.] *Ka Hele Malihini Ana mai Keia Ao Aku a Hiki i kela Ao: He Olelonane I Hoo- halikeia Me He Moeuhane la* [Translated from the English by Artemus Bishop (1795–1872).] Honolulu: Mea Paipalapala A Na Misionari, 1842. 418 pp.

Inscription: in pencil by Clemens on the flyleaf: "Sam. L. Clemens/From Rev. S. C. Damon/Honolulu, Hawaii,/ March 22/1866." Opposite, on the verso of the front free endpaper, Clemens wrote in pencil: "Bunyan's Pilgrim's/ Progress./To Sammy Moffett,/St Louis,/From his aged Uncle/Sam Clemens".

Location: Albert and Shirley Small Special Collections Library, University of Virginia, Charlottesville. Donated by Clifton Waller Barrett.

Copy examined: Clemens's copy, in 1970. Has the bookplate of Clifton Waller Barrett.

BURDER, GEORGE (1752–1832). *Village Sermons; or, One Hundred and One Plain and Short Discourses, on the Principal Doctrines of the Gospel.* 4 vols. Philadelphia: W. W. Woodward, 1821. [Volume IV only, 288 pp.]

Location: Mark Twain Library, Redding, Connecticut. Volume IV only.

Copy examined: inexplicably shelved in June 1982 with the volumes donated to the Mark Twain Library by Clemens and his daughter Clara Gabrilowitsch, but this was definitely not a book belonging to him or his family. It has the purple oval Mark Twain Library stamps, but no inscription, markings, or accession number. Presumably someone mistakenly grouped it with the Clemens donations simply because it bore an old imprint.

BURDETTE, ROBERT JONES (1844–1914). *The Rise and Fall of the Mustache and Other "Hawk-Eyetems."* Burlington, Iowa: Burlington Publishing Co., 1877. 328 pp.

In Notebook 20 (March 1882) Mark Twain noted "Teach-ing boy about Wash (Reader)—an allusion to a sketch by Burdette entitled "The Artless Prattle of Childhood" (*N&J* 2: 450). Twain took Burdette's story from pages 102–107 of *The Rise and Fall of the Mustache and Other "Hawk-Eyetems,"* shortened it, changed the title to "The Simple Story of G. Washington," and included it in *Mark Twain's Library of Humor* (1888). The narrator of the sketch attempts unsuccessfully to instruct a five-year-old boy about George Washington's tree-chopping incident, but each detail supplied by the adult only adds to the boy's confusion.

Burdette's skill with "happy remarks" is mentioned in Notebook 18 (1879, *N&J* 2: 300). His name appeared in 1880 in Mark Twain's list of humorists to be considered for an anthology (NB 19); in 1881 Twain included his name again in a long list of humorists (NB 19, *N&J* 2: 362, 429). Twain made a note to send a complimentary copy of *The Prince and the Pauper* (1881) to "'Hawkeye' R. J. Burdette" (NB 19, *N&J* 2: 384); he inscribed and sent a copy of his book to Burdette from Hartford on 20 December 1881 (the book is now in MTHM). Burdette wrote to Clemens humorously on 29 July 1882 (*DearMT*, pp. 93–94). Clemens planned to "refer to & quote from" Burdette in a projected "Essay on Humor" (NB 24 [Au-gust 1885], *N&J* 3: 172). He decreed that *Mark Twain's Library of Humor* "must have . . . Burdette's very latest & best. Lots of Burdette," and reminded himself to "get a book fm B'dette" (NB 27 [September 1887], *N&J* 3: 321). He sketched a brief compliment to Burdette for inclusion in the proposed preface to *Library of Humor* (NB 27 [1887], *N&J* 3: 314). The published version of *Mark Twain's Library of Humor* (1888) contained eleven pieces by Burdette—surpassed only by Mark Twain's twenty.

Burdette was designated to receive a complimentary copy of *A Connecticut Yankee in King Arthur's Court* (1889) (NB 29 [1889], *N&J* 3: 500, 501). Twain mentioned Burdette among the "seventy-eight other American humorists" whose vogue passed within forty years (31 July 1906 AD, *MTE*, p. 201; *AutoMT* 2: 152). A biography that quoted extensively from Burdette's letters, journals, and profes-sional writings, *Robert J. Burdette: His Message. Edited from His Writings by His Wife Clara B. Burdette* (Philadelphia: John C. Winston Co., [cop. 1922]), contained Burdette's impression of Clemens's Hartford house (pp. 135–136) and quoted an undated letter from Clemens concerning plagiarism and unconscious borrowing (p. 136).

Walter Blair, "On the Structure of *Tom Sawyer*" (1939), p. 79.

BURGESS, GELETT (1866–1951). *Are You a Bromide? or, The Sulphitic Theory Expounded and Exemplified According to the Most Recent Researches into the Psychology of Boredom, Includ-ing Many Well-Known Bromidioms Now in Use.* New York: B. W. Huebsch, 1906. 63 pp. [Edition conjectured; repr. in 1907, 1908, and 1910.]

Catalog: *C1951*, J8, edition unspecified, "presented by the author to Jean," listed among the books of Jean and Clara Clemens.

"Nearly forty years ago," Burgess would later recall, he "saw Mark Twain seated smoking on a bench in Washington Square" and spoke to him about wanting to write novels. The problem was, Burgess explained to Twain, "my Nem-esis, the Purple Cow, has become so widely known and quoted that I was afraid I would never be taken seriously. I couldn't get rid of the beast, I said." Twain "laid a hand upon my knee and said, 'I wouldn't worry about that son. There's a lot of writers trying to be humorous who are so poor they can't even keep a cow'" (Gelett Burgess, "A Famous Author Tells About His Meeting with Mark Twain," *Mark Twain Quarterly* 1.1 [Fall 1936]: 13).

BURGESS, W[ILLIAM]. STARLING (1878–1947). *The Eternal Laughter and Other Poems.* Intro. by Julian Hawthorne (1846–1934). Illustrated by Edward Lyne and Edmund H. Garrett (1853–1929). Boston: W. B. Clarke Co., 1903. 60 pp.

Source: MTLAcc, entry #632, volume donated by Clemens. Later an aviation pioneer, Burgess would also become a noted designer of yachts and automobiles. Despite the book's title, Burgess's poems are anything but humorous; in the inflated language popular in that era he ponders life, dreams, separations, the forces of nature, and the mysteries of death.

BURGIN, GEORGE BROWN (1856–1944). *Tomalyn's Quest, A Novel*. New York: Harper & Brothers, 1897. 279 pp.

Source: MTLAcc, entry #1527, volume donated by Clemens.

BURKE, EDMUND (1729–1797). *Articles of Charge of High Crimes and Misdemeanors Against Warren Hastings* (published in 1786).

Burke, "regarded by many as the greatest orator of all times," is quoted in Mark Twain's "Edmund Burke on Croker and Tammany," a speech to the Order of the Acorns, 17 October 1901, later published in *Harper's Weekly*, 19 October 1901 (Box 3, No. 1, MTP). In the speech (reprinted in a shortened version in *MTS* [1910] and more fully in *MTSpk* [1976, pp. 404–413]), Twain refers to "the unsmirched great name of Edmund Burke" and "the mighty shade of Edmund Burke." See also *MTB*, p. 1145. In an entirely different connection, Barbara Ladd discussed affinities between Burke's concept of the sublime and certain descriptions of the grandeur of the majesty of natural scenery ("'Night after Night and Day after Day': Mark Twain and the Natural World," *Mark Twain Annual 17* [2019]: 11–27).

———. "Letter to Hercules Langrishe on the Subject of the Roman Catholics of Ireland" (1792).

"Why don't the temperance agitators remember Edmund Burke's words? 'Lawful indulgence is the only check on illicit gratification'" ("Mark Twain on Prohibition," *Licensing Guardian*, New South Wales, 1895; Scharnhorst, *Complete Interviews*, p. 220).

Burke's Peerage. A Genealogical and Heraldic History of the Peerage and Baronetage of the United King. [First compiled in 1826 by John Burke (1787–1848), Irish genealogist.]

"See legend in the Peerage," Clemens wrote beside an account of some repartee between Lord Darnley and Lord Henry in Peter Cunningham's edition of *The Letters of Horace Walpole* (Volume IX, page 401, 1866 ed.). "I've been glancing through Burke," says Colonel Sellers (Ch. 5, *AC* [1892]).

BURNAND, (SIR) FRANCIS COWLEY (1836–1917), better known as "F. C. Burnand." *Happy Thoughts* (comic sketches of social life published in London in 1868, after being serialized earlier in *Punch*; reprinted in Boston by Roberts Brothers in 1869 and subsequently). [Clemens's edition is undetermined.]

Clemens reported to Olivia Clemens from London on 23 December 1873 that "we all went last night to hear Burnand read his Happy Thoughts" (*MTLet* 5: 532). In 1881 or early 1882 Clemens slightly erred in writing the title and the author's name ("Happy Thought Burnham" [*sic*]) in Notebook 19 (*N&J* 2: 428). Burnand wrote for, illustrated, and edited (beginning in 1880) the humor magazine *Punch*; he also turned out many burlesques and farces for English audiences, including the libretto for Arthur Sullivan's popular comic opera, *Cox and Box* (produced in 1866), based on John Maddison Morton's one-act farce *Box and Cox*.

BURNETT, FRANCES (HODGSON) (1849–1924). *A Fair Barbarian*. Boston: James R. Osgood and Co., 1881. 258 pp.

Inscription: signed in pencil on the front free endpaper, "Ida C. Langdon". Ida Clark Langdon (1849–1934) was married to Charles Jervis Langdon (1849–1916).

Provenance: bookplate #511 of the "J. Langdon Family Library" on the front pastedown endpaper.

Catalog: Ball 2016, orange cover with black lettering and design, Jervis Langdon's Family Library #511.

Location: Mark Twain Archive, Elmira College, Elmira, New York.

Copy examined: unmarked copy, orange-yellow cloth, available to Clemens whenever he visited the Langdons' home in Elmira. Examined on 27 May 2015.

James R. Osgood reported sending a copy of this book to Clemens on 2 April 1881, after receiving Clemens's request of 30 March: "Please send me the enclosed dam book. Got the others. Much obliged" (*MTLP*, p. 136).

———. *Little Lord Fauntleroy*. Illustrated by Reginald B[athurst]. Birch (1856–1943). New York: Charles Scribner's Sons, 1886. 209 pp.

Inscription: the front flyleaf is inscribed in black ink in Clemens's hand: "Clara Clemens/Christmas, 1886./ From Papa."

Location: Mark Twain Library, Redding, Connecticut.

Copy examined: Clara Clemens's unmarked copy, which perhaps also served as the household copy. Has a black ink Mark Twain Library accession number—"2822". Examined in 1970 and again in June 1982.

Early in 1881 Mark Twain made a memorandum to send Mrs. Burnett a complimentary copy of *The Prince and the Pauper* (NB 19, *N&J* 2: 385). In a letter to the Reverend Fred V. Christ written on 28 August 1908 he claimed credit for thus providing her with the model for *Little Lord Fauntleroy*, which had been published serially in *St. Nicholas* in 1885–1886 (Mark Twain Papers; *MTL*, p. 814; Fears, *Day by Day*, 4: 1025). He also alluded to Burnett in Notebook 27 (January 1888) as an author enjoying a fortunate arrangement with her publisher (*N&J* 3: 363), and repeated this point in "Concerning the British Pirates (1888), referring to "Mrs. Burnett" as being among the authors of "choice and valuable literature" whose English royalties had been protected by the Century Company (Heritage Book Shop, Catalog 176 [1989], item #232). Burnett was among the literary luminaries present at Clemens's Seventieth Birthday Dinner at Delmonico's in New York City on 5 December 1905. Scharnhorst, ed., *DearMT*, pp. 262–263.

———. [Another identical copy.]

Source: Donated from Clemens's library by Clara Clemens Gabrilowitsch in 1910 (MTLAcc, entry #1925).

———. *Louisiana*. First edition. Original brown cloth, gilt. New York: Charles Scribner's Sons, 1880. 163 pp.

Inscription: signed on the front flyleaf in pencil: "S. L. Clemens, Hartford, 1880."

Catalog: *A1911*, "first edition,, frontispiece, 12mo, cloth, N.Y. 1880," quotes the signature, lot 57, sold for $3.75.

Location: collection of Kevin Mac Donnell, Austin, Texas.

Source: letter to Alan Gribben from Kevin Mac Donnell, 15 July 2014.

In the novel a Southern girl named Louisiana attends a girls' school where she is befriended by a fellow student named Olivia from upstate New York who shows her how to fit in. Olivia's brother then falls for Louisiana, but complications ensue.

———. [Another identical copy.]

Source: MTLAcc, entry #2181, volume donated from Clemens's library by Clara Clemens Gabrilowitsch in 1910.

———. *That Lass O'Lowries*. New York: Scribner, Armstrong & Co., 1877. 269 pp.

Provenance: bookplate #486 of the "J. Langdon Family Library" on the front pastedown endpaper.

Catalog: Ball 2016, black cloth, red and gold lettering and design, inscribed "City of Richmond" at sea, [?] 11th 1897.

Location: Mark Twain Archive, Elmira College, Elmira, New York.

Copy examined: an unmarked copy accessible to Clemens whenever he visited the Langdons in Elmira. Examined on 27 May 2015.

———. *That Lass O'Lowrie's*. New York: C. Scribner's Sons, 1888. 269 pp.

Source: MTLAcc, entry #2164, volume donated from Clemens's library by Clara Clemens Gabrilowitsch in 1910.

BURNEY, FRANCES (FANNY) (1752–1840), later Frances d'Arblay. *Evelina; or, The History of a Young Lady's Entrance into the World*. Collection of British Authors Series. Leipzig: Bernhard Tauchnitz, 1850. 444 pp. [Edition conjectured. This novel of manners was first published in 1778.]

Catalog: *C1951*, D1, $8, "Miss Burney—Evalina" [sic] listed among volumes signed by Clemens, no edition identified.

The English novelist Fanny Burney would have been quoted ("where printable") in Mark Twain's proposed appendix to *A Connecticut Yankee in King Arthur's Court* in 1889 (Howard G. Baetzhold, "Course of Composition" [1961], p. 200). Twain later desired to review her works and other "old-time literary mud idols" (NB 33 [1894], TS p. 61).

BURNHAM, AVIS A., LATER STANWOOD (b. 1827). *Fostina Woodman: The Wonderful Adventurer*. [The first edition of this sixty-page novel was published in Boston in 1850.]

Catalog: ListABP (1910), "Fostina Woodman, Burnham", no other information provided.

A tale of the California Gold Rush.

BURNHAM, CLARA LOUISE (ROOT) (1854–1927). *Next Door*. Boston: Houghton Mifflin Co., 1886. 371 pp.

Clemens noted the title and author of this novel in September 1887 (*N&J* 3: 316). Burnham was the daughter of the composer George F. Root (1820–1895), whose "The Battle Cry of Freedom" became an anthem during the Civil War.

BURNS, ROBERT (1759–1796).

A literary critic is a person who assumes "all the genial, warm-hearted jolly Scotch poetry" to be by Burns, quipped Mark Twain (17 June 1865 *Californian*; quoted in *LAMT*, p. 141; *ET&S* 2: 195). In Chapter 36 of *The Innocents Abroad* (1869) Twain, viewing a stone staircase built by the (later impoverished) Duc de Richelieu in Odessa, quotes a bitter remark attributed to Burns' mother upon seeing monument to her son: "Ah, Robbie, ye asked them for bread and they hae gi'en ye a stane." In a paragraph intended for a letter to U. S. Representative Samuel S. Cox (but possibly not included), Clemens on 8 February 1875 alluded to "the heirs of one Scott or Burns or Milton in a hundred years" as the targets of lawmakers

who severely restricted literary copyrights" (*MTLet* 6: 377). Twain listed Burns' poetry as one of the "old bad books" on his library bookshelves ("The Walt Whitman Controversy," DV36, MTP, written around 1882). He amused himself in 1895 by inventing rhyming couplets in Burns' Scottish dialect (NB 35, TS pp. 49, 63). In Chapter 5 of *Following the Equator* (1897) Twain told of fooling some ship passengers with an invented "Burns" quotation: "There were nae bairns but only three—/Ane at the breast, twa at the knee."

Baetzhold, *MT&JB* (1970), p. 275.

———. "Auld lang syne" (poem, published in 1796; song, published in 1799).

Clemens mentioned the song in Thomas Jefferson Snodgrass's letter of 18 October 1856 that was published in the Keokuk *Post* (*TJS*, p. 6). Writing under the pseudonym "Soleather" in the New Orleans *Crescent* of 21 July 1859 he claimed that he could now play "Old Lang Syne" on a fiddle (Branch, "A New Clemens Footprint," p. 499). Then, as "Mark Twain" in a sketch published in the *Californian* on 29 October 1864, he asserted that "Auld Lang Syne" with certain "variations" was the only piece he could play on an accordion (*ET&S* 2: 95–99; *CTSS&E* 2: 97–101). He practiced writing burlesque verses set to "Air—Auld Lang Syne" in Notebook 7 in January 1867 (*N&J* 1: 274). Twain subsequently composed two burlesque songs—"Miss Slimmens" (*MTTMB*, pp. 63–64) in 1867 and "Ye Equinoctial Storm" (*OPMT*, pp. 8–9) in 1868—that were to be sung to the tune of "Auld Lang Syne." He mentioned the song as a candidate for his music box in 1878 (NB 16, *N&J* 2: 212) and included it among a list of his (presumably) favorite songs in August 1889 (NB 29, *N&J* 3: 513).

Edgar M. Branch, "A New Clemens Footprint: Soleather Steps Forward," *American Literature* 54.1 (December 1982): 497–510.

———. "Ye banks and braes o' Bonnie Doon" (poem, written in 1791; song, published in 1792).

"Tunes are good remembrancers," Clemens explained to Olivia Langdon on 19 December 1868. "Almost every one I am familiar with, summons instantly a face when I hear it. It is so with the Marseillaise, with Bonny Doon and a score of others" (*MFMT*, p. 23; *MTLet* 2: 334). He mentioned "Bonny Doon" favorably in 1878 (NB 16, *N&J* 2: 212). Clemens remembered this as one of the songs that "tended to regrets for bygone days and vanished joys" ("Villagers of 1840–3," written in 1897, *HH&T*, p. 34). Forty-four repeats the song title in Chapter 1 of "Schoolhouse Hill" (written in 1898, *MSM*, p. 179). In "Three Thousand Years Among the Microbes" (written in 1905) the cholera germ amused the microbes by singing "Bonny Doon" and "Buffalo Gals" for ten years (*WWD?*, p. 462); after he was married, however, the narrator became sentimental about the song: "Always in the dream I hear distant music—distant and faint, but always sweet, always moving: 'Bonny Doon.' It was Margaret's favorite, therefore it was mine too" (*WWD?*, p, 464). "Bonnie Doon" was one of the airs Clemens requested Isabel Lyon to play on the orchestrelle on 6 and 14 February 1906 (IVL Journal, TS p. 135, MTP; IVL Journal, Harry Ransom Center, University of Texas at Austin). Undoubtedly it was one of the "three little Scotch songs" Clemens requested Clara to sing to him on his death bed (*MFMT*, p. 290). Albert Bigelow Paine listed it among the songs Clemens liked especially well (*MTB*, p. 1555).

———. "The Campbells are comin'" (Scottish national song, written in 1790).

One of the tunes Clemens requested Isabel Lyon to play for him on 6 and 14 February 1906 was this one (IVL Journal, TS pp. 132, 135, MTP). He enjoyed that Scotch air in December 1909, Albert Bigelow Paine reported (*MTB*, p. 1555).

———. "Comin' thro' the rye" (poem, song, written in 1782).

"Just as the soprano was in the midst of that touching ballad" (Ch. 31, *GA* [1873]—a chapter written by Charles Dudley Warner).

———. "Flow gently, sweet Afton" (Scottish air, written in 1791).

Clara sang this to Clemens as he lay dying (Ralph Holmes, "Mark Twain and Music" [1922]).

———. "Man Was Made to Mourn" (poem, written in 1784).

Mark Twain informed A. H. H. Dawson on 24 January 1880: "I have the highest appreciation of Burns's genius, & the greatest respect for his memory," even though Twain himself feels that "Man was *not* made to Mourn" (MTP). In Letter #7 Satan quotes two lines (*"Man's* inhumanity to man/Makes countless thousands mourn!") ("Letters to the Earth," written October-November 1909, *LE*, p. 36; also *WIM?*, p. 434). In 1898 and again in 1904 Clemens mused: "God's inhumanity to man/Makes countless thousands mourn" (NB 42, TS p. 61; NB 47, TS p. 18).

———. *Merry Muses of Caledonia* (a collection of bawdy Scottish songs privately printed around 1800 and afterwards in facsimile editions).

Clemens noted the author and title in 1879 (NB 18, *N&J* 2: 335). Burns both contributed to and collected the erotic verses in this collection.

———. "My heart is in the highlands" (poem, song written in 1789).

"That passenger's heart is in the highlands, so to speak," when his mule trods a mountain path (Chapter 35 of *A Tramp Abroad* [1880]).

———. "Scots wha hae' wi' Wallace bled" (song, written in 1793, published in 1794).

No. 44 mentions this song title in Chapter 1 of Mark Twain "Schoolhouse Hill" (written in 1898, *MSM*, p. 179). Twain disparaged Mary Baker Eddy's remarks about her descendant's relationship to this Scottish air (*Christian Science* [1907], Book II, Chapter 1, *WIM?*, p. 268).

———. "Tam O'Shanter's Ride" (poem, written in 1790).

"The dance that Tam O'Shanter witnessed was slow in comparison to it" (letter from Carson City, 3 February 1863, *MTEnt*, p. 56). "Nothing like it [the French *can-can*] had ever been seen on earth since trembling Tam O'Shanter saw the devil and the witches at their orgies that stormy night in 'Alloways auld haunted kirk'" (Ch. 14, *IA* [1869]).

———. "To a Louse, on Seeing One on a Lady's Bonnet at Church" (poem, published in 1786).

William M. Gibson, *The Art of Mark Twain* (New York: Oxford University Press, 1980), pp. 145–148, and Jim Zwick, "Who Wrote the Couplet? Textual Variants in Mark Twain's 'Salutation to the Twentieth Century,'" *Mark Twain Journal* 27.1 (Spring 1989): 38 n. 4, gave credit to Burns' poem for the final lines added to the condemnatory greeting Twain issued in 1900—"Give her the glass: it may from error free her/When she shall see herself as others see her."

———. "To a Mouse" (poem, published in 1786).

Clemens humorously misquoted this Burns' poem ("the best laid gangs of mice & men are often frustratified") in a letter to Thomas Bailey Aldrich, 24 March 1874 (*MTLet* 6: 90).

———. *The Works of Robert Burns*. Edited by the Ettrick Shepherd [pseud. of James Hogg] (1770–1835) and William Motherwell (1797–1835). Engraved title pages and plates. 5 volumes. 12mo, cloth, uncut. Slightly foxed. Glasgow, 1836.

Inscription: the front endpaper of Volume I is inscribed by Clemens: "'No more these simple flowers belong/To Scottish maid & lover;/Sown in the common soil of song,/They bloom the wide world over.'/Whittier./Truly yours/S. L. Clemens/Hartford, 1889." The tone of the formal inscription, quoting the first stanza of John Greenleaf Whittier's poetic tribute, "Burns. On Receiving a Sprig of Heather in Blossom" (1854), suggests that this set was a gift to someone other than a family member. See the Catalog entry for a similarly inscribed book, Allan Cunningham's *The Life of Robert Burns*. Both of these seem to have been given as presents (or prizes?) at the same time.

Catalog: Parke-Bernet, Catalog 27 (16–17 April 1941), lot #371 (PH in MTP).

———. *The Works of Robert Burns*. Biographical essay by John Gibson Lockhart (1794–1854). New York: Leavitt & Allen, n.d. 438 pp. [Most likely this Leavitt & Allen edition was published in 1856.]

Source: MTLAcc, entry #2122, volume donated from Clemens's library by Clara Clemens Gabrilowitsch in 1910. Could this be another of the very few volumes from his youthful days that Clemens kept with him for a lifetime?

Burnz, Eliza Boardman (1832–1903). *Burnz' Phonic Shorthand for Schools, Business Writing and Reporting, Arranged on the Basis of Isaac Pitman's "Phonography."* Fourteenth Edition, Revised and Improved. New York: Burnz & Co., 1901. [Edition conjectured.]

In "A Simplified Alphabet," a brief essay written in 1899 and first published posthumously in *What Is Man? and Other Essays* (1917), Mark Twain called for a more logical-sounding alphabet: "I will insert the alphabet here as I find it in Burnz's *Phonic Shorthand*. It is arranged on the basis of Isaac Pitman's *Phonography*. . . . the originator and father of scientific phonography. He made it public seventy-three years ago" (*The Complete Essays of Mark Twain*, ed. Charles Neider [Garden City, NY: Doubleday & Co., 1963], p. 545). The English-born Mrs. Burnz believed in spelling reform so much that she changed her own name from Burns to Burnz and named her daughter Foneta. She came to be known as "The Mother of Women Stenographers," but also worked with Elizabeth Cady Stanton on behalf of the women's suffrage movement (*New York Times*, 23 June 1903, p. 7).

Burr, Enoch Fitch (1818–1907). *Ecce Coelum; or, Parish Astronomy. In Six Lectures. By a Connecticut Pastor*. Boston:

Noyes, Holmes & Co., [cop. 1867]. 198 pp.
   Source: MTLAcc, entry #540, volume donated by Clemens.
BURROUGHS, JOHN (1837–1921). *Bird and Bough.* Boston:
Houghton, Mifflin & Co., 1906. 70 pp.
   Source: MTLAcc, entry #2011, volume donated from Cle-
   mens's library by Clara Clemens Gabrilowitsch in 1910.
———. *Birds and Bees: Essays.* Intro. by Mary Elizabeth Burt
(1850–1918). Boston: Houghton, Mifflin & Co., 1887. 88 pp.
   Source: MTLAcc, entry #1940, volume donated from Cle-
   mens's library by Clara Clemens Gabrilowitsch in 1910.
Clemens mentioned "Burroughs" among the authors of
"choice and valuable literature" whose English royalties
were being protected ("Concerning the British Pirates,"
1888, quoted in Heritage Book Shop, Catalog 176
[1989], item #232).
———. [Another identical copy.]
   Source: MTLAcc, entry #1941, volume donated from Clemens's library by Clara Clemens Gabrilowitsch in 1910.
———. "Hard Fare," essay collected in *Signs and Seasons*
(published in 1886).
This was identified by Sherwood P. Cummings in "Science and Mark Twain's Theory of Fiction" (1958) as the
article by Burroughs to which Mark Twain alluded in
his 19 August 1907 Autobiographical Dictation (*MTE,*
pp. 336–337; *AutoMT* 3: 105). Burroughs, speaking at
a dinner for Sidney Lee in New York City, was reminded
by Clemens of a piece Burroughs had published about
the ecological cycles of forest growth.
_____, ed. *Songs of Nature.* New York: McClure, Phillips
& Co., 1901. 359 pp. [Publisher conjectured.]
   Inscription: on front pastedown endpaper: "S. L. Clemens,
   Riverdale, Jan. 1902."
   Catalog: *A1911,* "12mo, cloth, gilt top, uncut, N.Y. 1901,"
   quotes the signature, lot 58, sold for $3.50.
Burroughs attended Mark Twain's Seventieth Birthday
Dinner on 5 December 1905 at Delmonico's in New
York City. Clemens would say that Burroughs was "a
heavyweight" who intimates that "he knows more about
an animal than the animal knows about itself" (29 May
1907 AD, *MTE,* p. 19; *AutoMT* 3: 62); moreover, Bur-
roughs backs up his assertions merely by his "say-so" (30
May 1907 AD, *MTE,* p. 24; *AutoMT* 3: 68).
———. *Winter Sunshine.* New York: Hurd and Houghton,
1876. 234 pp.
   Provenance: bookplate #416 of the "J. Langdon Family
   Library" on the front pastedown endpaper.
   Catalog: Ball 2016, red cloth, gilt and black lettering and
   design, Jervis Langdon Family Library #416, worn edges.
   Location: Mark Twain Archive, Elmira College, Elmira,
   New York.
   Copy examined: an unmarked copy available to Clemens
   whenever he visited the Langdons in Elmira. Examined
   on 27 May 2015.
BURROWS, S[TEPHEN]. M[ONTAGU]. (1856–1935). *The Buried
Cities of Ceylon: A Guide Book to Anuradhapura and Polon-
naruwa. With Chapters on Dambulla, Kalawewa, Mihintale,
and Sigiri.* Second edition. Colombo[, Ceylon]: A. M. & J.
Ferguson, 1894. 106 pp.
   Marginalia: annotation scattered throughout. On page
   59 Mark Twain noted in pencil along the margin: "This
   guide-book is about as mouldy an antiquity as the temples

it treats of." On page 62 he adds: "A nobly-padded guide-
book. Puts in all the *a & b & c,* with nothing to refer to."
   Catalogs: ListABP (1910), "Buried Cities of Ceylong,
   Burrows"; "Retz Appraisal" (1944), p. 5, valued at $10.
   Location: Mark Twain Papers, Bancroft Library, University
   of California at Berkeley.
   Copy examined: Clemens's copy.
BÜRSTENBINDER, ELISABETH (1838–1918), pseud. "E. Wer-
ner." *Glück auf! [i.e., Good luck!] Roman von E. Werner.* Zweite
Auflage. 2 vols. Leipzig: Ernst Keil, 1877.
   Catalog: *Zeitlin 1951,* #49, $3.
   Location: Mark Twain Papers, Bancroft Library, University
   of California at Berkeley. Gift of Jake Zeitlin.
   Copy examined: Clemens's unmarked copies.
———. *Vineta. Roman von E. Werner.* 1. Band. Zweite Auflage.
Leipzig: Ernst Keil, 1877. [Two volumes in one.]
   Catalog: *Zeitlin 1951,* #50, $2.
   Location: Mark Twain Papers, Bancroft Library, University
   of California at Berkeley. Gift of Jake Zeitlin.
   Copy examined: Clemens's unmarked copy.
BURT, MARY ELIZABETH (1850–1918). *Literary Landmarks: A
Guide to Good Reading for Young People, and Teachers' Assistant.*
Illus. Boston: Houghton, Mifflin & Co., 1889. 152 pp.
   Source: MTLAcc, entry #449a, volume donated by
   Clemens.
Burt recommended 700 titles on various topics that were
suitable for young people.
_____, ed. *Poems That Every Child Should Know; A Selec-
tion of the Best Poems of All Times for Young People.* Illustrated
by Blanche [Adele] Ostertag (b. 1872). New York: Doubleday,
Page, & Co., 1907. 355 pp.
   Source: MTLAcc, entry #481, volume donated by Clemens.
BURTON, NATHANIEL JUDSON (1822–1887), co-comp. *The
Christian Hymnal. A Selection of Psalms and Hymns, with
Music, for Use in Public Worship.* Hartford, Connecticut:
Hamersley & Co., 1877 [Jointly compiled by Burton, Joseph
Hopkins Twichell (1838–1918), and Edwin Pond Parker
(1836–1920).]
   Inscription: "S. L. Clemens. From Rev. J. H. Twichell,
   Munich, Bavaria, Feb. 1879."
   Catalog: *A1911,* #78, $1.25.
———. *Yale Lectures on Preaching and Other Writings.* Ed. by
Richard E[ugene]. Burton (1861–1940). New York: Charles
L. Webster & Company, 1888. 639 pp. [Includes a memorial
address about Burton prepared by the Reverend Joseph H.
Twichell (1838–1918).]
Clemens voted "yes," Charles L. Webster "no" on the idea
of publishing Burton's sermons "at half-profits" (SLC to
Webster, 30 October 1887, TS in MTP). The book figured
prominently in Clemens's notebook of the period (NB
27, *N&J* 3: 339 *passim*).
Richard E. Burton recalled Clemens's good deed in publish-
ing his father's Yale lectures: "The royalty to my mother
was ten times better than if it had been brought out in the
usual ten percent trade way" ("Mark Twain in the Hartford
Days," *Mark Twain Quarterly* 1.4 (Summer 1937): 5).
BURTON, RICHARD EUGENE (1861–1940). *Message and Melody;
A Book of Verse.* First edition. Original sage cloth, gilt. Boston:
Lothrop Publishing Co., [cop. 1903]. 186 pp.
   Inscription: inscription in black ink on the front free
   endpaper: "To Mark Twain/from his gratefully/Richard

Burton/April 1903".

Provenance: Mark Twain Library, Redding, Connecticut. Donated from Clemens's personal library by Clara Clemens Gabrilowitsch in 1910 (MTLAcc, entry #2020).

Catalog: *Mott 1952*, #40, $4.

Location: collection of Kevin Mac Donnell, Austin, Texas.

Copy examined: Clemens's copy, with no marginalia, in July 2004.

According to Richard Burton's later account, Clemens critiqued his Hartford neighbor Burton's admittedly "immature writing" and got his first poem published in *Century Magazine.* Clemens also arranged for Charles L. Webster & Company to publish the lectures and sermons of Burton's father, who had died in 1887 (see the Catalog entry above). "We'll make a big, portly volume of it," Clemens promised, "and we'll make it a religious classic!" Things went as promised; Richard Burton's mother received a munificent royalty and her husband's book, "known to thousands of clergymen," remained "still alive after exactly fifty years" (Richard E. Burton, "Mark Twain in the Hartford Days," *Mark Twain Quarterly* 1.4 (Summer 1937): 5). Richard Burton praised Mark Twain as an "indisputable genius" in *Literary Leaders of America* (Chautauqua, New York: Chautauqua Press, 1903), pp. 311–312.

BURTON, (SIR) RICHARD FRANCIS (1821–1890). *Personal Narrative of a Pilgrimage to El-Medinah and Meccah.* 2 vols. Tauchnitz edition. [No date supplied.]

Catalog: *C1951*, D1, $8 ea., listed among the books signed by Clemens.

Burton accomplished this early (1855–1856) and famous description of these holy sites by disguising himself and risking his liberty (if not his life) to visit areas closed to Europeans.

BURTON, WILLIAM EVANS (1802–1860), comp. *The Cyclopaedia of Wit and Humor; Containing Choice and Characteristic Selections from the Writings of the Most Eminent Humorists of America, Ireland, Scotland, and England.* 2 vols. New York: D. Appleton and Co., 1858. [Repr. in the 1850s, 1860s, and 1870s. Clemens's edition has not been identified.]

Catalog: ListABP (1910), "Cyclopedia of Wit and Humor, Burton", no other information supplied.

This became Mark Twain's model for his own *Library of Humor* (1888) after George Gebbie, a Philadelphia subscription publisher, proposed that he assemble an anthology of humorists "similar to Burtons Encyclopaedia" (Gebbie to SLC, 14 July 1880, MTP). Twain wrote "Burton's Cyclopédia D. Appleton, 1858" in Notebook 19 *(N&J* 2: 361, 364) and followed the entry with a series of suggestions for possible writers who might be included. Eventually he would bring out the volume through his own publishing firm. It should be noted that in 1874 Clemens had donated a volume titled *Wit and Humor* to the reading room sponsored by the Women's Christian Temperance Union in Fredonia, New York; however, no record of its author or publisher survives (Jane L. Clemens to SLC, 11 April 1874, ALS in MTP; Fredonia *Censor,* 9 December 1874; records of Darwin R. Barker Library, Fredonia, New York).

BURY, JOHN BAGNELL (1861–1927). *The Student's Roman Empire. A History of the Roman Empire from Its Foundation to the Death of Marcus Aurelius (27 B.C.-180 A.D.).* Illustrations and two maps. Original black cloth, gilt. New York: American Book Co., [190?]. 638 pp.

Inscription: the front pastedown endpaper is signed in black ink "S L. Clemens/1908".

Catalogs: *A1911*, "12mo, cloth, N.Y., n.d.," quotes the signature, lot 59, sold for $2; Christie's South Kensington, 13 May 1994, lot 94; *Sotheby's 2003*, #232, $3,250 (sold with two other titles).

Provenance: the signature of Tilghman H. Sharp is visible on the rear free endpaper. Subsequently the volume was owned by Connie Gibbes, Westport, Connecticut. The book came into her possession "after the death of a neighbor in Baltimore, Tilghman H. Sharp, a Virginian in his eighties" (Gibbes to Gribben, 25 May 1978). Eventually *The Student's Roman Empire* joined the collection of Nick Karanovich, Fort Wayne, Indiana.

Location: collection of Kevin Mac Donnell, Austin, Texas.

Copy examined: Clemens's copy, in July 2004. It displays the *A1911* auction label.

BUSBECQ, OGIER GHISLAIN DE (1522–1592). *The Life and Letters of Ogier Ghiselin de Busbecq, Seigneur of Bousbecque, Knight, Imperial Ambassador.* Ed. by Charles Thornton Forster (1836–1891) and Francis Henry Blackburne Daniell (1845–1921). 2 vols. London: C. Kegan Paul & Co., 1881.

Inscription: Volume II is signed on the front free flyleaf, "S. L. Clemens/1888."

Catalogs: *A1911*, "2 vols., 8vo, half calf, Lond. 1881, "quotes the signature, lot 170, $3.50; Anderson Auction Galleries (New York City), Sale number 1113 (8 December 1913), "2 vols., 8vo, half calf, London, 1881, "Clemens copy, with his signature in Vol. 2," has the *A911* sale label, lot 80, 2 vols., $3.00; Swann Galleries, Sale number 56 (16 September 1943), has the *A1911* sale label, lot 340, $6.00 (PH of Swann catalog in MTP).

Provenance: formerly in the collection of Cyril Clemens, Kirkwood, Missouri.

Location: currently uncertain.

Copy examined: photocopies of the title pages of both volumes and the flyleaf bearing Clemens's inscription. Both volumes have the *A1911* sale label affixed to the front pastedown endpaper. Above these sale labels are the large signatures of "Cyril Clemens". (The photocopies were provided in 1982 by Thomas A. Tenney, who visited Cyril Clemens in Kirkwood, Missouri and was allowed to make copies of his collection.)

Busbecq was an ambassador for Emperor Ferdinand I to the sultan at Constantinople and later served as the Paris ambassador for Emperor Rudolph II. A volume of his letters first appeared in 1589.

BUSCH, MORITZ (1821–1899). *Bismarck in the Franco-German War 1870–1871.* "Authorized Edition." Two vols. in one. Red cloth. New York: Charles Scribner's Sons, n.d.

Inscription: pencil inscription in Clemens's hand on the front flyleaf: "SL. Clemens/Dec. Xmas, 1879./From S. <L.> E. Moffett."

Marginalia: approximately twenty-five penciled vertical lines and brackets in Volume I, beginning on page 25; only five markings in Volume II between pages 21 and 31. No markings thereafter. Clemens made a few penciled comments in the margins. Writing vertically on page 98,

Clemens noted: "A perfect Boswell for/honesty." Below that, on the same page, he added in pencil: "Pepys." On page 325 of Volume I, where Bismarck complained of ill-treatment by the French press and asked, "What can the public be, on whose belief in such stories people can confidently reckon?", Clemens drew a bracket and wrote: "This is a good point."

Provenance: Antenne-Dorrance Collection, Rice Lake, Wisconsin.

Location: Mark Twain Archive, Gannett-Tripp Learning Center, Elmira College, Elmira, New York.

Copy examined: Clemens's copy. Examined on 28 May 2015.

The book is mentioned in a letter from Samuel E. Moffett to Pamela Moffett, 24 December 1879 (MTP). "It is funny that you should happen to hit upon the very book I have been wanting," Clemens wrote (SLC to Samuel E. Moffett, 26 December 1879 (MTP). Mark Twain referred to Bismarck in Chapter 7 and "Appendix C" of *A Tramp Abroad* (1880).

The Prussian statesman Otto von Bismarck (Otto Eduard Leopold) (1815–1898) became the first chancellor of the German empire.

———. *Unser Reichskanzler: Studien zu einem Charakterbilde.* *[Our Reich Chancellor: Studies on a Character Image.]* 2 vols. Leipzig: F. W. Grunow, 1884. [Publisher conjectured.]

Catalog: *A1911*, "2 vols., 12mo, half morocco, Leipzig, 1884," lot 60, sold for $1.50.

BUSCH, WILHELM (1832–1908). *Max und Moritz; eine bubengeschichte in sieben streichen.* Sechsundfunfzigste Auflage. München: Verlag von Braun und Schneider, n.d. 53 pp.

Inscription: inscribed in black ink on the front pastedown endpaper: "Jean L. Clemens/Berlin/January 2, 1909".

Location: Mark Twain Library, Redding, Connecticut.

Copy examined: Jean Clemens's copy. Has a red ink Mark Twain Library accession number: "3972".

Rhymed poetry depicts the misbehavior of two boys.

———. *Schnurrdiburr oder Die Bienen* [*Schnurrdiburr or The Bees*].

Catalog: *C1951*, J13, listed among books of Jean and Clara Clemens.

An intricate picture story for children containing actual facts about bees and beehives.

BUSH, HENRY (HEINRICH BUSCH) (b. c. 1830). *The Harp of the Day; or, The Adventures and Travels of a Photographic Artist; With Other Poems.* Second ed. (San Francisco, California: Published by the author, 1865).

In an uncredited newspaper report published in the Virginia City *Territorial Enterprise* on 22 February 1866 Mark Twain humorously mentioned "the fine epic—his famed 'Harp of the Day' written by "Mr. Henry Bush, the daguerrean artist" (Robert H. Hirst, "New (Old) Mark Twain Found in Bancroft Scraps," *Bancroftiana* Number 115 [Fall 1999]: 1). Born in Prussia, Bush had been a California gold miner before turning to photography to earn a living. His *The Harp of the Day* was written in the form of a lengthy poem.

BUSHNELL, FRANCES LOUISA (1834–1899). *Poems.* New York: Privately printed [at the De Vinne Press], 1900. 81 pp.

Source: MTLAcc, entry #2015, volume donated from

Clemens's library by Clara Clemens Gabrilowitsch in 1910.

The Connecticut poet Frances Bushnell was the daughter of Horace Bushnell (1802–1876) and Mary Apthorp Bushnell (1805–1905). *Poems* was a posthumous collection of selections from her poetry.

BUSHNELL, HORACE (1802–1876). *Christian Nurture.* [Partially published in 1847 as *Views of Christian Nurture*; enlarged and retitled in 1860, it was reprinted often in New York by Charles Scribner and Company].

Writing from Elmira, New York on 25 June 1870 Clemens requested Charles Scribner and Company: "Please send me Dr. Bushnell's volume entitled 'Christian Nurture'" (*MTLet* 4: 158). A pregnant Olivia Clemens and her husband were likely interested in books about religious education for children; Langdon Clemens would be born on 2 November 1870. Clemens came to feel that Horace Bushnell was the "greatest clergyman that the last century produced" (speech to the Art Students' Association, St. Louis, Missouri, 7 June 1902, *MTSpk*, p. 444). In Bushnell's numerous writings the longtime Hartford Congregational clergyman would help move New England theology away from the sternness of Old Testament Calvinism and toward an appreciation of the divinity in nature and the potential goodness in mankind. R. W. Lewis's *The American Adam: Innocence, Tragedy, and Tradition in the Nineteenth Century* (Chicago: University of Chicago Press, 1955) described how Bushnell "worried the theologians, won an impressive following among his [North Church] congregation and became the city's first citizen" (p. 67).

BUTLER, ELLIS PARKER (1869–1937). *Pigs Is Pigs.* Illustrated by Will Crawford (1869–1944). Brown decorated cloth. New York: McClure, Phillips & Co., 1906. 37 pp.

Inscription: presentation inscription to "Mark Twain" in black ink on the front free endpaper by Butler, dated April 1906 in Flushing, New York.

Provenance: Antenne-Dorrance Collection, Rice Lake, Wisconsin.

Location: Mark Twain Archive, Gannett-Tripp Learning Center, Elmira College, Elmira, New York.

Copy examined: Clemens's unmarked copy. Examined on 28 May 2015.

Butler's humorous little story about a disagreement between an express agent and a man taking receipt of a shipment of two guinea pigs enjoyed immense if fleeting popularity.

———. *Pigs Is Pigs.* [Another copy.]

Catalog: *C1951*, #78c, presentation copy to Mark Twain from the author, listed among books signed by Mark Twain.

———. "The Reformation of Uncle Billy," *Century Magazine* 57.4 (February 1899): 538–541.

In January 1889 Butler wrote Clemens a humorously semi-literate letter from Muscatine, Iowa asking if "it wd pay me to quit farmin an go to book makin" (*DearMT*, pp. 138–140). "Say—that fish-liar tale in the Century which arrived this morning is *mighty* well done," Clemens wrote to Richard Watson Gilder from Vienna on 2 February 1899 (PH in MTP). In Butler's story the members of the First Church of a small village who gather in front of a grocery store every day resolve to break seventy-eight-year-old

Billy Matison's habit of lying about the fish he never catches. Led by the "deacon," they confront Billy when he returns from fishing and gradually compel him to reduce the weight of the fish he allegedly hooked until he finally agrees that he didn't catch one at all. But (little did they know!) he really did have a bass that weighed "four pound, two ounces" (p. 541). He doesn't tell them about it since they seem intent on "reforming" him, but simply weighs it after they leave. Today Butler's dialect sketch of rural characters strikes one as both clumsy and silly.

BUTLER, NICOLAS MURRAY (1862–1947).
Educator, writer, and Columbia University president Butler would call Clemens "a warm friend of many years and for whose personality and genius I had the warmest admiration." He termed Clemens "a figure and a personality never to be forgotten. I could tell anecdotes of him by the hour" ("Nicolas Murray Butler Receives Mark Twain Medal," *Mark Twain Quarterly* 2.2 [Winter 1937–1938]: 14).

BUTLER, SAMUEL (1612–1680). *Hudibras. With Notes by Rev. Treadway Russell Nash [1725–1811]*. Illus. 2 vols. London: Henry Washbourne, 1847. [Publisher conjectured.]
    Catalog: *A1911*, "2 vols., 8vo, full polished calf, gilt backs and tops (backs slightly split), Lond. 1847," lot 61, sold for $1.50.
    Mark Twain noted in his 1872 English journal that "Butler who wrote 'Hudibras'" is buried in Westminster Abbey (*MTLet* 5: 603), a fact he also mentioned in "A Memorable Midnight Experience" (written in 1872, *MTB*, p. 469). "Ida—Hudibras," Clemens wrote and then canceled in Notebook 28 (December 1888, *N&J* 3: 439), referring to his sister-in-law Ida Clark Langdon (1849–1934). Twain slightly misquoted the mock heroic poem *Hudibras* in an 1895 interview: "Compound the sins they feel inclined for/By damning those they've got no mind for" ("Mark Twain on Prohibition," *Licensing Guardian*, New South Wales, 1895; Scharnhorst, *Complete Interviews*, p. 221).

BUTLER, SAMUEL (1835–1902). *Life and Habit* (London, published in 1877).
    Clemens noted the title and author ("'Life & Habit' by Butler") of this rebuttal of the Darwinian theory (NB 17 [November 1878], *N&J* 2: 247). Butler attempted (from a scientific point of view, not a religious one) to refute a major element in Darwin's findings.

BUTLER, WILLIAM ALLEN (1825–1902). *Nothing to Wear: An Episode of City Life*. Boston: Houghton, Mifflin & Company.
    Mark Twain included "*Nothing to Wear*" in *Mark Twain's Library of Humor* (1888), and credited an unspecified Houghton, Mifflin edition. In "Mental Telegraphy" (1891) Twain mentioned the vigorous dispute over the authorship of *Nothing to Wear*, which had been published anonymously *Harper's Weekly* in 1857. Butler's humorous poem was written in rhyming couplets. David E. E. Sloane looked at how Twain introduced the poem into his last major work of fiction ("*No. 44, The Mysterious Stranger* as Literary Comedy," *Centenary Reflections on Mark Twain's No. 44, The Mysterious Stranger*, ed. Joseph Csicsila and Chad Rohman [Columbia: University of Missouri Press, 2009], pp. 174, 184).

BYERS, SAMUEL HAWKINS MARSHALL (1838–1933). *The Happy Isles, and Other Poems*. New York: Charles L. Webster & Co., 1891. 162 pp.
    Clemens's publishing firm issued this volume. It included five poems such as "The Tramp of Sherman's Army" (pp. 72–76), which commemorated Union victories and generals or paid tribute to fallen soldiers. Byers' elegy to "The Nation's Dead" (pp. 152–155) praised those who lost their lives for the Northern cause: "They sleep to-day in silent lines,—/Heroic men, whom Fame hath lent/The glory that forever shines,/To be their lasting monument" (p. 155). The other thirty-three poems are highly miscellaneous but consistently inflated in tone.

BYNNER, [HAROLD] WITTER (1881–1968). *An Ode to Harvard and Other Poems*. Boston: Small, Maynard & Co., 1907. 119 pp.
    On 25 February 1906 Bynner visited Clemens and "recited a little poem of his own which is to appear shortly in McClure's" (IVL Journal, TS p. 138, MTP). Clemens wrote to Bynner on 5 October 1906 from Dublin, New Hampshire to support Bynner's decision to devote himself to poetry: "With your reputation you can have your freedom and yet earn your living" (*MTL*, p. 798). After Isabel Lyon read *An Ode to Harvard and Other Poems*, Clemens "chatted for a few minutes with me about Walter [*sic*] Bynner's verses" on 25 August 1907 (IVL Journal, TS p. 272, MTP). When Bynner addressed a poem to Clara Clemens, her father affected indignation that he was not the first subject in the household to inspire Bynner's poetic impulse (*MTL*, p. 798). Bynner "sent Clara [Clemens] a copy of my first book, 'An Ode to Harvard,'" and then was kiddingly chided by Clemens for not addressing it to him (Bynner to Rodman Gilder, December 1938, MTP). The fifty-six-page-long title poem in Bynner's *An Ode to Harvard and Other Poems* (1907) concluded: "O mean to all those others whom you'll see/The thousand things in one you mean to me!/O lift forever on the shield of truth,/Before the armies of mortality,/The sounding challenge of the spear of youth!"

BYRON, GEORGE GORDON [NOEL] (1788–1824). *Childe Harold's Pilgrimage; A Romaunt*. London: John Murray, 1860. 192 pp.
    Source: MTLAcc, entry #2047, volume donated from Clemens's library by Clara Clemens Gabrilowitsch in 1910.
——. *Childe Harold's Pilgrimage; A Romaunt*. New York: Cassell & Co., 1886. 192 pp.
    Source: MTLAcc, entry #973, volume donated by Clemens. The photographer on the *Quaker City* excursion, William Evans James, recorded in his diary that among the evening entertainments on 27 June 1867, "Mark Twain read this evening . . . Byron's Coliseum by Moonlight" ("The Diary of W. E. James," edited by Randolph I. James, http://www.twainquotes.com/wejames.html). In Canto IV of *Childe Harold's Pilgrimage*, the speaker gazes upon the Coliseum "when the rising moon begins to climb" and reflects on the dying vision of a gladiator who was "butchered, to make a Roman holiday!" In Chapter 27 of *The Innocents Abroad* (1869), Twain called attention to the fact that he was "the only free white man of mature age" who had written about the Coliseum and its gladiators without alluding to Byron's famous line, "butchered to make a Roman holyday." (Byron's Canto IV, stanza 141 had spelled it "Roman Holiday.") "All went merry

as a marriage bell," Twain wrote in 1870 ("The Facts in the Case of the Great Beef Contract" [May 1870], *CG*, p. 39), borrowing from the poem. Twain again joked about Byron's celebrated phrase regarding the Coliseum in March 1892 (NB 31, TS p. 35). In Chapter 2 of *The American Claimant* (1892), Twain writes, "But banish care, it's no time for it now—on with the dance, let joy be unconfined is my motto, whether there's any dance to dance, or any joy to unconfine." This seems to echo Byron's line, "On with the dance, let joy be unconfined," in *Childe Harold's Pilgrimage* (Barbara Schmidt to Alan Gribben, email, 27 January 2001).

————. "The Destruction of Sennacherib" (poem, published in 1815).

This was one of Mark Twain's favorite poems. However, he jokingly attributed it to Melton Mowbray of Dutch Flat in a column published in the 10 June 1865 *Californian* (*ET&S* 2: 186). Subsequently he protested mightily in the columns of the *Californian* when he was accused of not knowing the piece (Branch, *LAMT*, p. 142; *ET&S* 2: 193–195, 206–207). The misunderstanding arose over his spoof in "Answers to Correspondents" (collected in *SN&O*). In a letter published in the Sacramento *Weekly Union* (27 October 1866) Twain alternated lines from "Destruction" and Wolfe's "Burial of Sir John Moore" to create a composite that burlesques both (*LSI*, pp. 199–200; repr. in *OPMT*, p. 54). Twain quoted from "Destruction" and listed its title in Notebook 9 (1867, *N&J* 1: 424, 438). In an *Alta California* letter (26 January 1868) he wrote that this was the only poem he ever memorized: "I never knew but one poem by heart in my life—it was impressed upon my mind at school by the usual process, a trifle emphasized" (*TIA*, p. 235). Still, he omitted the reflections of stars shining on the Sea of Galilee when he revised his *Alta* letters for *Innocents Abroad* (1869); that imagery occurs in lines 3 and 4 of the first stanza: "The Assyrian came down like the wolf on the fold,/And his cohorts were gleaming in purple and gold;/And the sheen of their spears was like stars on the sea,/When the blue wave rolls nightly on deep Galilee." In Chapter 21 of *Tom Sawyer* (1876) the Examination Evening recitations at the schoolhouse include the poem beginning "The Assyrian came down like the wolf on the fold,/And his cohorts were gleaming in purple and gold"; schoolmaster Dobbins listens distractedly to this same declamatory gem in Act III of "Tom Sawyer: A Play" (written 1875–1884, mainly in 1884, *HH&T*, p. 303). In November or December 1895 Twain burlesqued the poem by substituting New Zealand names for various words (NB 35, TS p. 63). A chestnut of Hannibal school exhibitions was "The Assyrian came down like a wolf on the fold,/And his cohorts were gleaming with purple and gold," Twain recalled in a speech he delivered at the Hannibal High School graduation exercises on 30 May 1902. Twain used the first verse of "The Destruction of Sennacherib" for a shorthand exercise that interrupts "Advice to Paine," written in April 1910 (George N. Meissner Collection, Washington University, St. Louis, Missouri; PH in MTP). The phrase "Assyrian came down" also appears in an undated set of notes he made (*A1911*, lot 202).

————. *Don Juan* (narrative poem, published 1819–1824). "Get Don Juan," Clemens noted in Germany in November 1891 (NB 31, TS p. 13).

————. "Elegy on Thyrza" (poem).

See the Catalog entry for Francis Turner Palgrave's compilation, *The Golden Treasury of the Best Songs and Lyrical Poems in the English Language* (1894), in which Clemens marked this poem quite notably.

————. *Mazeppa* (narrative poem, published in 1819).

In a column published in the *Californian* on 1 July 1865 Mark Twain imitated some lines from Byron's *Mazeppa* (*ET&S* 2: 216), concluding with the colloquial exclamation: "GEE-WHILLIKINS!"

————. *Poems of Lord Byron, Tastefully Selected.* 2 vols. London, n.d.

Inscription: "Susy Clemens with the love of her Papa. Florence, Xmas, 1892."

Catalogs: ListABP (1910), "Byron's Poems"; Lew David Feldman, "American Books" (1955), #173, $50, described as a tiny pocket reprint, Volume I only.

See also the Catalog entry for Francis Turner Palgrave's compilation, *The Golden Treasury of the Best Songs and Lyrical Poems in the English Language* (1894), in which Clemens marked a number of Byron's poems.

————. "The Prisoner of Chillon" (poem, published in 1816). "Whose story Byron has told in such moving verse" (Ch. 42, *A Tramp Abroad* [1880]).

————. *The Select Poetical Works of Lord Byron . . . with a Memoir of the Author.* Boston: Phillips, Sampson, & Co., 1851. 406 pp.

Inscription: in pencil: "A Gift from Henry Clemens/To his Sister M. E. C./ March 1855." Also contains the bookplate of Orion Clemens on the front pastedown endpaper.

Provenance: Clemens's older brother Orion married Mollie Eleanor Stotts on 19 December 1854. Henry Clemens (1838–1858) was the youngest of the three brothers. Presumably this was one of the "175 or 200 books" that Samuel Clemens "selected from Orion's library" upon the death of Mollie Clemens in 1904, since Orion had died in 1897 (Samuel Clemens to Susan Crane, Florence, 15 February 1904, ALS in MTP).

Location: Harry Ransom Center, University of Texas at Austin. Obtained from the Frank C. Willson Collection in 1962. Willson (1889–1960) was a prominent Mark Twain collector in Melrose, Massachusetts; his widow Margarete sold his collection in 1962.

Copy examined: a volume belonging to Mollie Clemens.

Byron's verse contributed to "sentimentality and romance among young folk" during Clemens's childhood in Hannibal, he would recall in 1897 ("Villagers of 1840–3," *HH&T*, pp. 34–35). In a letter from Philadelphia dated 3 February 1854 that was published in Orion Clemens's newspaper, Samuel Clemens quoted doggerel verse that appeared in the Philadelphia *Ledger* and remarked mockingly, "What do you think of that? Will not Byron lose some of his popularity now?" (Edgar M. Branch, "Three New Letters by Samuel Clemens in the Muscatine *Journal*," *Mark Twain Journal* 22.1 [Spring 1984]: 2). Entering a gold miner's cabin in Jackass Hill, California in January 1865, Clemens observed in Notebook 4 that the dwelling had no planking on its floor, yet he could

see "Byron Shakspeare, Bacon Dickens, & every kinds of only first class Literature" (*N&J* 1: 70). That same year, Twain alluded to Byron's "ardent love poetry, tricked out in affluent imagery" (*Californian*, 17 June 1865; quoted in *LAMT*, p. 141; *ET&S* 2: 195). Paul Baender's detailed study, "Mark Twain and the Byron Scandal" (1959), established that in 1869 Twain wrote six unsigned Buffalo *Express* editorials commenting on Harriet Beecher Stowe's article, "The True Story of Lady Byron's Life," *Atlantic Monthly* 24.143 (September 1869). Twain alluded to "the loose but gifted Byron" and his "misspent life" with its "lucid and unintoxicated intervals" ("Political Economy," published in *The Galaxy* in 1870, collected in *SN&O* in 1875). Twain referred to "the Byron-scandal case" in October 1871 in the second installment of his "Brace of Brief Lectures on Science" that appeared in the *American Publisher*, a Hartford magazine. The crew on the boat in "The Aged Pilot Man" threw overboard "A box of books, a cow,/A violin, Lord Byron's works,/A rip-saw and a sow" in an effort to save the vessel (Ch. 51, *Roughing It* [1872]). In "The Walt Whitman Controversy" (perhaps written in 1882) Twain noted that Byron's works might well be considered indecent, yet he owns them (DV36, MTP). Byron's was one of the spirits conjured up at the Hotchkiss house in Chapter 4 of the "Schoolhouse Hill" version of *The Mysterious Stranger* (written in 1898), but his poetry was "rhymy and jingly. . . for his mind had decayed since he died" (*MSM*, p. 206).
Paul Baender, "Mark Twain and the Byron Scandal," *American Literature* 30.4 (January 1959): 467–485; Howard G. Baetzhold, *MT&JB* (1970), pp. 280–283.
———. "To Thomas Moore" (poem, written in 1817).
Twain quoted this poetic tribute in "About All Kinds of Ships" (1893). His letter to Andrew Carnegie of 28 April 1908 ("here's a health to Carnegie") echoed lines that occur in the first and last stanzas of Byron's poem (*CTSS&E* 2: 95).
———. *The Two Foscari: An Historical Tragedy* (published in 1821).
An allusion occurs in Chapter 23 of Mark Twain's *The Innocents Abroad* (1869).
———. "The Vision of Judgment" (satirical poem, published in 1822).
Described in an unpublished burlesque letter purportedly written by Byron in the Under-World and addressed to Mark Twain (Paine 260, MTP).
———. *The Works of Lord Byron, in Verse and Prose. Including His Letters, Journals, Etc.* New York: Leavitt & Allen, 1863. 627 pp.
Source: MTLAcc, entry #2123, volume donated from Clemens's library by Clara Clemens Gabrilowitsch in 1910.
An early publication date like this one raises the possibility that the book was among the few titles Clemens retained during his river piloting years and the succeeding decades.
———. "Written After Swimming from Sestos to Abydos" (poem, published in 1812).
Mark Twain alludes to this poem in Chapter 33 of *The Innocents Abroad* (1869).
BYRON, HENRY JAMES (1834–1884). *Jack the Giant Killer; or, Harlequin King Arthur and Ye Knights of Ye Round Table* (extravaganza, produced in London in 1859).
Clemens probably saw R. G. Marsh's Juvenile Comedians

perform this nursery-tale burlesque in Carson City in January 1864 (Franklin R. Rogers, *MTBP*, p. 105). No one seems to have speculated about this drama's eventual connection with Mark Twain's *A Connecticut Yankee in King Arthur's Court* (1889).

C

CABELL, ISA CARRINGTON (1860–1923). *Seen from the Saddle.* Intro. by Charles Dudley Warner. Harper's Black and White Series. New York: Harper & Brothers, 1893. 161 pp.
Clemens wrote from Florence on 12 March 1893 to his daughter Clara, catching her up on recent family news and mentioning that "Mrs. Cabell has sent Susy [Clemens] a copy of her miniature book, 'A Summer on Horseback' is the title I think. It is dedicated to Susy Warner, & Charley Warner writes the introduction" (*Sotheby's 2003*, #71). Widowed in 1883, Cabell had been the literary editor of the Hartford *Courant* from 1889 until 1892. Her book described sights and conversations while exploring the New England roads around Hartford.
CABELL, JAMES BRANCH (1879–1958) *Chivalry*. Illus. by Elizabeth Shippen Green (1871–1954), William Hurd Lawrence (1866–1938), and Howard Pyle (1853–1911). New York: Harper & Brothers, 1909. 223 pp. [Nine of the ten short stories in this collection were previously published in *Harper's Monthly* between 1905 and 1909.]
Cabell set these tales in medieval France, England, and Spain, imbuing the fictional events and antiquated diction with a dreamlike, fantasy quality. Albert Bigelow Paine noted that Clemens read *Chivalry* in November 1909 "with great enjoyment"; he admired "the subtle poetic art with which Cabell has flung the light of romance about dark and sordid chapters of history" (*MTB*, p. 1535). Cabell would write to Paine on 1 November 1911: "That which you tell me of Mr. Clemens has awakened—and I don't care who knows it—a defiant joy. As far back as I can remember I have loved him, as one among innumerable millions. For twenty years—to be exact—I have revered and understood that Mark Twain was only incidentally a maker of jokes" (*Between Friends: Letters of James Branch Cabell and Others*, ed. Padraic Colum and Margaret Freeman Cabell [New York: Harcourt, Brace & World, 1962], p. 193). Eugene Saxton of the George H. Doran Company informed Cabell on 16 September 1920: "A manuscript went through my hands the other day by Mrs. W. H. Allen dealing with some intimate pages in the life of Mark Twain. He was a great friend of the Allen family and stopped for quite a while at their place in Bermuda. What caught my eye in the course of the manuscript was this paragraph about a volume of yours entitled *Chivalry*. It ran: 'He told us that just before he came to us he had read *Chivalry* by James Branch Cabell. He gave the book to Helen, inscribing it: TO HELEN SCHUYLER ALLEN, THESE MASTERPIECES WITH THE LOVE OF S. L. C. The period of the book fascinated Mr. Clemens. He also thought it wonderfully well written. He said the mere language was wonderfully beautiful, so strong and direct as to be almost Biblical in its beauty. "The Story of the Housewife" was his favorite.' This may be old stuff to you but on the chance that it was news, I thought I would send it along to you" (*Between Friends: Letters of*

James Branch Cabell and Others, pp. 192–193). See also Marion Schuyler Allen, "Some New Anecdotes of Mark Twain," *Strand Magazine* [London] 46.272 [August 1913]: 166–173. In an introduction to an edition of *Chivalry* published by Robert M. McBride & Company of New York in 1921, author and editor Burton Rascoe (1892–1957) recalled "the esteem in which Mark Twain held the genius of Mr. Cabell as it was manifested as early as a dozen years ago. Mr. Cabell wrote *The Soul of Melicent* [1913], or, as it was rechristened on revision, *Domnei*[: *A Comedy of Woman-Worship*, 1921], at the great humorist's request, and during the long days and nights of his last illness it was Mr. Cabell's books which gave Mark Twain his greatest joy" (p. xiii). See also "Chronicle and Comment," *The Bookman* 38.1 (September 1913): 5 for a fuller explanation of Twain's involvement with Cabell's story about the fictional French locale of Poictesme.

———. *Gallantry*. Green decorated cloth. New York: Harper & Brothers, 1907. 334 pp.

> **Provenance:** Antenne-Dorrance Collection, Rice Lake, Wisconsin.
>
> **Location:** Mark Twain Archive, Gannett-Tripp Learning Center, Elmira College, Elmira, New York.
>
> **Copy examined:** almost certainly Clemens's copy, unmarked. Examined on 28 May 2015.
>
> One of Cabell's novels in the saga of Poictesme series, set in a vaguely medieval French province and mixing parody with admiration.

———. *The Line of Love*. Illustrated by Howard Pyle (1853–1911). New York: Harper & Brothers, 1905. 291 pp.

> **Inscription:** on the front pastedown endpaper in black ink, within the decorated borders: "S L. Clemens/Oct. 1905."
>
> **Provenance:** formerly in the possession of Albert Bigelow Paine. Subsequently in the personal collection of Bigelow Paine Cushman (1928–2003), then Professor of English, Western Connecticut State College, Danbury, Connecticut.
>
> **Location:** currently unknown.
>
> **Copy examined:** Clemens's copy, unmarked. Viewed in August 1987 at the residence of Professor Cushman and his wife Anne in Deer Isle, Maine.
>
> Clemens praised *The Line of Love*, a collection of short stories, in a letter to Frederick A. Duneka of Harper & Brothers on 9 October 1905. It was "the charmingest book I have read in a long time"; even the archaic speech, to which he often objected, "allures & bewitches, the art of it is so perfect" (Harper & Row).

CABLE, GEORGE WASHINGTON (1844–1925). *The Cavalier* (novel, published in 1901).

> "Your book came three days ago. . . . I finished reading the story night before last. From start to finish it kept me electrically a-tingle with its rush & go, & charmed with its brilliances of phrasing & its other manifold fascinations" (SLC to Cable, Riverdale, 15 October 1901, Cardwell, *TG*, p. 111). Cable made a humorous speech at Mark Twain's Seventieth Birthday Dinner on 5 December 1905 at Delmonico's in New York City (New York *Times*, 6 December 1905). In 1907 Cable would write to various friends and authors suggesting that on April 1st they simultaneously address autograph requests to Twain as an April Fool's prank (ALS, Cable to Miss

Violet Beach, collection of Kevin Mac Donnell, Austin, Texas). Cable was one of the members of the American Academy and National Institute of Arts and Letters who spoke at a memorial meeting in Carnegie Hall honoring Twain on 30 November 1910.

———. *Dr. Sevier* (novel, published in 1884).

> In promoting Cable's upcoming appearance in Hartford in 1883, Clemens indicated a familiarity with the "passages of nicely-shaded German dialect, from a novel which is still in manuscript" (Hartford *Courant*, 30 March 1883, *MTPP*, p. 139). He heard Cable read selections from this book—generally "Mary's Night Ride"—on their 1884–1885 lecture tour (NB 23, *N&J* 3: 82, 118). Cable also read the parts called "Kate and Ristofolo," "Narcisse in Mourning," and "Richling's Visit to Kate." In Chapter 46 of *Life on the Mississippi* (1883) Mark Twain singled out Cable as one of the authors who had abandoned the "old, inflated style" of Southern writers and instead adopted "modern English." In the next chapter (47), he praised Cable's oral readings of French dialects. Guy A. Cardwell's *Twins of Genius* (East Lansing: Michigan State College Press, 1953) published letters exchanged by Clemens and Cable and referred to *Dr. Sevier* (p. 12). See also Arlin Turner's *Mark Twain and George Washington Cable: The Record of a Literary Friendship* (East Lansing: Michigan State University Press, 1960), which included valuable correspondence and biographical information about the entire Twain-Cable friendship. Louis D. Rubin, Jr.'s *George W. Cable: The Life and Times of a Southern Heretic* (New York: Pegasus, 1969) described the Twain-Cable tour of 1884–1885 and praised Cable's bold efforts to champion the rights of African Americans.
>
> Frederick Trautman, "The Twins of Genius: Public Readings by George Washington Cable and Mark Twain in Pennsylvania," *Pennsylvania History* 43.3 (July 1976): 214–225.

———. *The Grandissimes. A Story of Creole Life*. New York: Charles Scribner's Sons, 1882.

> **Inscription:** on half-title page: "To S. L. Clemens. Yours truly, G. W. Cable. Hartford, Apl 4, 1883." On this date Clemens introduced Cable at a public reading in Unity Hall in Hartford (Fears, *Day by Day* 1: 887). Cable's novel had first appeared in 1880.
>
> **Marginalia:** on page 111 in the margin, written in black ink: "Same old device." The Christie's catalog (1988) indicated that this remark was "apparently not in Clemens's hand." No other annotations.
>
> **Provenance:** Carrie Estelle Doheny Collection, St. John's Seminary, Camarillo. Donated by Mrs. Doheny in 1940 after its purchase from Maxwell Hunley in 1940 for $12.20. Auctioned by Christie's in 1988 on behalf of St. John's Seminary and the Archdiocese of Los Angeles.
>
> **Catalog:** Christie's, New York City, 1–2 February 1988 auction, lot 454, sold for $ 770 to Heritage Book Shop, Los Angeles.
>
> **Location:** currently undetermined.
>
> **Copy examined:** Clemens's copy, when it was at St. John's Seminary.

———. *The Grandissimes. A Story of Creole Life*. Original cloth, spine faded and ends lightly rubbed. New York: Charles Scribner's Sons, 1883.

> **Inscription:** inscribed by the author in ink, "To/Saml L.

Clemens/from/G. W. Cable/Hartford, Nov. 20, 1883."
This was the day Cable arrived to visit the Clemenses
(Fears, *Day by Day* 1: 1188).

Provenance: has the shelfmarks of Clara Clemens Gabrilowitsch's library system that she employed during
her Detroit years.

Catalogs: *C1951*, 98c, edition not supplied, listed among
books signed by Clemens, $40; "Property from the Library
of Mark Twain," Butterfield & Butterfield, San Francisco,
Sale 6613 (16 July 1997), lot 2669.

Location: Mark Twain House and Museum, Hartford,
Connecticut.

Copy examined: Clemens's copy. Viewed in Hartford in
1997.

Howells wrote to Cable that he and Clemens were so
impressed with *The Grandissimes* that they "went about
talking Creole all day" (Kjell Ekström, "The Cable-
Howells Correspondence," *Studia Neophilologica* 22
[1949–1950]: 53, cited by Guy A. Cardwell in *Twins
of Genius*, p. 123 n. 125). On 2 May 1882 Clemens
informed Olivia from New Orleans that Cable had read
to neighborhood children "from the Grandissimes &
sketches" (*LLMT*, p. 212). Clemens published a letter in
the Hartford *Courant* on 30 March 1883 urging that "a
full house" greet Cable's upcoming platform appearance
in that city. Clemens's letter mentioned episodes from
The Grandissimes, including "[Raoul] Innerarity and his
famous 'pigshoe' representing 'Louisihanna rif-fusing
to hanter the union'" as well as "those charming Creole
women" (*MTPP*, p. 139). In Chapter 44 of *Life on the
Mississippi* (1883) Mark Twain referred to "the South's
finest literary genius, the author of 'The Grandissimes.'"
As proof of Twain's esteem for Cable's novel, *Mark Twain's
Library of Humor* (1888) contained "Frowenfeld's Clerk"
(i.e., Chapter 23, "Frowenfeld Keeps His Appointment")
from *The Grandissimes*. (In that episode Joseph Frowenfeld,
a New Orleans apothecary, interviews a Creole artist who
applies for a job as a clerk, with comical misunderstandings and diverging expectations.) Twain's "Concerning
the British Pirates" (1888) alluded to "Cable" among
those authors of "choice and valuable literature" whose
English royalties were being adequately protected (quoted
in Heritage Book Shop, Catalog 176 [1989], item #232).
James B. Pond, *Eccentricities of Genius: Memories of Famous
Men and Women of the Platform and Stage* (New York: G.
W. Dillingham Co., 1900), pp. 231, 370. Albert Bigelow
Paine, *MTB* (1912), p. 784; Fred Lorch, "Cable and His
Reading Tour with Mark Twain in 1884–85," *American
Literature* 23.4 (January 1952): 471–486; *The Love Letters
of Mark Twain*, ed. Dixon Wecter (New York: Harper &
Brothers, 1949), pp. 218–240; Guy Cardwell, "Mark
Twain's 'Row' with George Cable," *Modern Language
Quarterly* 13.4 (December 1952): 363–371; Abe C. Ravitz
and Norris Yates, "Mark Twain, Cable, and the Philistine,"
Mark Twain Journal 10.1 (Summer 1955): 14, 23.

———. *Madame Delphine*. New York: Charles Scribner's
Sons, 1881.

Inscription: on half-title page: "To S. L. Clemens/Yours
truly G. W. Cable, Hartford, April 4, 1883." On this date
Clemens introduced Cable at a public reading at Unity

Hall in Hartford (Fears 1: 887).

Catalogs: "The Fine Library of the Late Ingle Barr," Parke-
Bernet, Los Angeles, Sale No. 68, 18–19 February 1973,
item #82; purchased by Seven Gables Bookshop, New
York City, for $190. (Warren Howell of San Francisco
described the volume in a written report to the Mark Twain
Papers in Berkeley at the time the book was sold in 1973.)

Location: Mark Twain House and Museum, Hartford,
Connecticut. Given by an anonymous donor in 1973
(*Mark Twain Memorial Newsletter* 7 [August 1973]: 5).

Copy examined: Clemens's copy, unmarked. Examined
in August 1987.

Clemens may have received another copy of *Madame Delphine* from Cable in 1881, or Cable may have autographed
a volume he had sent earlier when he visited the Clemens
household in April 1883. At any rate, Clemens already
seems to refer to *Madame Delphine* in a letter of 17 July
1881 to Cable: "The book has come; I read it last night,
& the charm of it, & the pain of it, & the deep music
of it are still pulsing through me" (Cardwell, *TG*, p. 81).

———. *Old Creole Days*. 12mo, original pictorial green cloth,
extremities rubbed. New York: Charles Scribner's Sons, n.
d. [cop. 1879].

Inscription: in ink on half-title page: "To/S. L. Clemens/
from/G. W. Cable/Apl 4, 1883—Hartford." On this date
Clemens introduced Cable at a public reading at Unity
Hall in Hartford (Fears, *Day by Day* 1: 887).

Catalogs: ListABP (1910), "Old Creole Days, Cable", no
other information provided; Christie's, New York City,
1–2 February 1988 auction, lot 453, sold for $1,100 to
Heritage Book Shop, Los Angeles.

Provenance: Carrie Estelle Doheny Collection, St. John's
Seminary, Camarillo, California. Donated by Mrs.
Doheny in 1940 following its purchase from Maxwell
Hunley Rare Books of Beverly Hills for $12.20. Sold
on behalf of St. John's Seminary and the Los Angeles
Archdiocese at a Christie's auction in 1988.

Location: currently undetermined.

Copy examined: Clemens's copy, when it was at St. John's
Seminary.

William Dean Howells recalled Clemens's skillful oral rendition: "I remember especially his raptures with Mr. Cable's
Old Creole Days, and the thrilling force with which he
gave the forbidding of the leper's brother . . . 'Strit must
not pass!'" (*MMT* [1910], pp. 99–100). In a letter to the
Hartford *Courant* (30 March 1883) promoting Cable's
upcoming visit to Hartford, Clemens praised "Jean-ah
Poquelin," which had appeared in *Old Creole Days* in
1879 (*MTPP*, p. 139). Clemens referred to "'Posson
Jone,'" one of the stories collected in *Old Creole Days*,
when he wrote about that Hartford lecture-reading by
Cable: "He got out his Parson Jones, & by George he
just simply carried the house by storm" (ALS, SLC to
"My Dear Waring," 6 April 1883, ASSSCL); Clemens
repeated the same compliment in another letter of the
same date to Frances A. Cox (TS in MTP).

———. *Old Creole Days*. Original maroon cloth, gilt, floral
endpapers. New York: Charles Scribner's Sons, 1883.

Inscriptions: half-title page inscribed by Cable in ink,
"To Saml. L. Clemens/from/G W. Cable/Hartford,
Nov. 20, 1883." This was the day Cable arrived to visit

the Clemenses (Fears, *Day by Day* 1: 1188). An added inscription by Julia Langdon Loomis on the verso of the frontispiece states, "Clara gave this to me in May 1910."

Marginalia: the story "'Posson Jone'" has passages amounting to approximately six pages canceled in pencil, as though to abbreviate the text for reading aloud.

Provenance: collection of Nick Karanovich of Fort Wayne, Indiana.

Catalog: *Sotheby's 2003*, lot #189, $3,500.

Copy examined: Clemens's copy, at the Sotheby's auction in 2003.

———. *Old Creole Days. Part I. Madame Delphine. Café des Exiles. Belles Demoiselles Plantation.* 2 vols. Original blue cloth, gilt, light wear. New York: Charles Scribner's Sons, 1883. [Only Part I.]

Inscription: inscribed on the half-title page: "To Mrs. Saml. L. Clemens/from G. W. Cable/Hartford, Nov. 20, 1883." This was the day Cable arrived to visit the Clemenses (Fears, *Day by Day* 1: 1188).

Provenance: the front pastedown endpaper displays the shelfmarks of the library numbering system Clara Clemens Gabrilowitsch employed during her years in Detroit. Subsequently the book became part of Carrie Estelle Doheny Collection, St. John's Seminary, Camarillo, California. Donated in 1940 after its purchase from Maxwell Hunley Rare Books of Beverly Hills for $12.20. Later sold for $960 by Christie's in New York City (lot 1176) on 17 October 1988 on behalf of St. John's Seminary.

Catalogs: *Sotheby's 2003*, lot #190, $700; James Cummins, Bookseller, 23 September 2005, "a tremendous association copy. . . . morocco ex-libris of Estelle Doheny," $3,000.

Location: collection of Kevin Mac Donnell, Austin, Texas. "I recently bought it" (email, Mac Donnell to Alan Gribben, 5 December 2018).

Copy examined: Olivia Clemens's unmarked copy, when it belonged to St. John's Seminary. Has the leather book label of "Estelle Doheny." Supplemented by a description sent by Mac Donnell to Alan Gribben, 31 December 2018.

———. *Old Creole Days, Part. II.* New York: C. Scribner's Sons, 1883. 155 pp.

Source: MTLAcc, entry #2192, volume donated by Clara Clemens Gabrilowitsch in 1910. This volume was subsequently lost or discarded.

———. *Strange True Stories of Louisiana* (published in 1889). Cable wrote to Clemens from Northampton, Massachusetts on 6 January 1890: "I have asked my publishers . . . to send you a copy of my *Strange True Stories of Louisiana*" (Cardwell, *TG*, p. 110).

CABOT, JAMES ELLIOT (1821–1903). *A Memoir of Ralph Waldo Emerson [1803–1882].* 2 vols. Boston: Houghton, Mifflin & Co., 1887.

Olivia Clemens informed Grace King on 7 August 1888: "I am just now reading the new Life of Emerson by Cabot. . . . I enjoy it exceedingly, but I don't think I like Emerson as well as I did before reading it. He seems so very cold, so removed from the passions and struggles of other men" (ALS, Louisiana State University, Baton Rouge).

CADDY, FLORENCE (1837–1923). *Footsteps of Jeanne d'Arc; A Pilgrimage.* London: Hurst and Blackett, 1886. 375 pp.

Included in a six-book list of books about Joan of Arc prepared for Mark Twain by Chatto & Windus in 1892

(Box 36, no. 6, PH in MTP).

Dennis Welland, *Mark Twain in England*, p. 158; Ronald Jenn and Linda A. Morris, "The Sources of Mark Twain's *Personal Recollections of Joan of Arc*," *Mark Twain Journal: The Author and His Era* 55.1–2 (Spring/Fall 2017): 55–74.

CAESAR, GAIUS JULIUS (100–44 BCE). *Caesar's Commentaries on the Gallic and Civil Wars. Literally Translated. With the Supplementary Books Attributed to [Aulus] Hirtius [c. 90–43 BCE]; Including the Alexandrian, African, and Spanish Wars.* Trans. by W[illiam]. A[lexander]. McDevitte (1834–1909) with W. S. Bohn. Original embossed purple cloth, gilt. Half brown morocco folding-case. New York: Harper & Brothers, 1885. 572 pp.

Inscription: signed by Clemens on the front flyleaf in pencil: "S. L. Clemens/Hartford, 1885./Presented by President Smith of Trinity College." The Reverend George Williamson Smith was president of Trinity College, according to *Geer's Hartford City Directory, 1886*.

Marginalia: pencil mark on page 35 (underlining the word "crushing") and a stray pencil mark at the bottom of page 97. The top corners of pages 43, 65, 75, 79, 83, 119, and 299 have been folded down.

Catalogs: *A1911*, "12mo, cloth, N.Y. 1885," quotes the inscription, lot 62, sold for $6; *Sotheby's 2003*, #232, sold for $3,250 (with two other titles about ancient Rome).

Provenance: collection of Nick Karanovich, Fort Wayne, Indiana.

Location: collection of Kevin Mac Donnell, Austin, Texas.

Copy examined: Clemens's copy, inspected at the 2003 Sotheby's sale and again at Kevin Mac Donnell's residence in July 2004.

In Paris in the spring of 1879 Mark Twain joshingly invented some thoughts about masturbation that he attributed to Caesar's *Commentaries* in a sketch written for the Stomach Club, "Some Thoughts on the Science of Onanism" (DV200, MTP; *MTSpk*, p. 125). U. S. Grant's *Memoirs* had only one equal, in Twain's opinion: "Caesar's Commentaries (on the Gallic War & the Civil War)" (NB 24 [June 1885], *N&J* 3: 160). In Chapter 41 of *Following the Equator* (1897) an Indian prince "strode to his throne with the port and majesty—and the sternness—of a Julius Caesar coming to receive and receipt for a back-country kingdom." In 1906 Twain would recall, "By chance, I had been comparing the [Grant] memoirs with Caesar's 'Commentaries.' . . . The same high merits distinguished both books—clarity of statement, directness, simplicity, unpretentiousness, manifest truthfulness, fairness and justice toward friend and foe alike, soldierly candor and frankness, and soldierly avoidance of flowery speech" (1 June 1906 AD, *MTE*, p. 183; *AutoMT* 2: 71).

———. *Commentarii d C. Iulio Cesare, tradotti per Agostino Urtica della Porta, Genovese. Et postillati delli nomi moderni.* Illustrated with woodcuts. Italian dark brown morocco cover, rebacked with the spine largely preserved. Venice: Bernardinus de Vitalibus, 1517.

Provenance: Italian ownership notation on the title page: "Questo libro è di Michele Dati" along with a twentieth-century name: "M. Cardigan." Has the bookplate of the collector Charles Butler on the front pastedown endpaper, which also bears a printed label from the 1951 Hollywood auction of the Clemens family's library books.

Location: Bancroft Library, University of California at Berkeley (*not* placed in the Mark Twain Papers, and the volume did *not* originate from the books belonging to Clara Clemens Samossoud). Gift from Frank Naisbitt of San Francisco in April 1990.

Copy examined: photocopies of the endpapers and photocopies of a copy that was *not* part of the Clemens family's library, since the contents of Charles Butler's library were not sold until 1911–1914 (Clemens had died in 1910). The source of the 1951 auction label is a mystery. In deciding that this book should not be considered a Clemens association copy I also consulted photocopies of an evaluation made in 1990 by Bernard M. Rosenthal, Booksellers, Berkeley, California, as well as memoranda in the Mark Twain Papers at Berkeley written on 20 April 1990 by a member of the editorial staff.

CAINE, [THOMAS HENRY] HALL (1853–1931). *The Eternal City*. Maroon cloth, gilt lettering and decorations. New York: D. Appleton and Co., 1901. 638 pp.

Inscription: on the front free endpaper, vertically in black ink: "George Melville Lincoln/January 28th 1902". [George Melville Lincoln (1846–1914) was a resident of Manhattan in 1902; Clemens was living in nearby Riverdale, New York. One is left to imagine the methods by which this volume might have changed hands.]

Marginalia: small hatch mark ("#") at the top of page 35.

Location: Mark Twain Library, Redding, Connecticut.

Copy examined: very possibly Clemens's copy, inspected in 1970 and again on 10 November 2019. In 1970 this copy of *The Eternal City* was shelved with the Clemens books in the Mark Twain Library. It has the Mark Twain Library purple oval stamps and the red ink accession number "2319". Most, but not all, of the books donated to that community library up to the number "2315" were the gifts of Clemens and his daughter Clara Clemens Samossoud, so this does seem like a good possibility, in spite of its inscription.

Caine's novel depicts a Christian revolution in science fiction terms. It was a best-seller.

———. *The Manxman, A Novel*. Tenth edition. New York: D. Appleton and Co., 1895. 529 pp.

Inscriptions: library bookplate of the lecture agent James B. Pond (1838–1903) on the front pastedown endpaper; inscribed on the flyleaf: "To/Major James B. Pond,/ With the author's/v[er]y cordial greetings,/Hall Caine/New York/7 Nov/95." Pond explained on the second flyleaf: "This volume was the traveling companion of The Mark Twain Troup which left Cleveland July 16, 1895—& sailed on board the S. S. Warrimoo, at Victoria, B.C. Aug. 23, 1895 where the party separated. . . . This book was read on that journey by Mr. & Mrs. Clemens, Miss Clara Clemens, & Mrs. J. B. Pond,—& later by Major Pond himself—about the time it was submitted for the author's signature. J. B. Pond."

Marginalia: on the rear flyleaf Olivia Clemens penciled memoranda about food expenses on the trip; these are dated 17–23 July 1895.

Location: Mark Twain House and Museum, Hartford, Connecticut. Gift of Professor Norman Holmes Pearson

(1909–1975) of Yale University in 1965.

Copy examined: James B. Pond's copy, read by Clemens. Examined in August 1987.

The plot of this romantic novel set on the Isle of Man revolves around a woman loved by two men who like and admire each other.

CAIRNES, JOHN ELLIOTT (1823–1875). *The Character and Logical Method of Political Economy*. [Second ed.] New York: Harper & Brothers, n.d. 235 pp. [Preface dated 1875.]

Source: MTLAcc, entry #669, volume donated by Clemens.

CALDWELL, GEORGE WALTER, M.D. (1866–1946). *Oriental Rambles*. Illus. Poughkeepsie, New York: George W. Caldwell, [cop. 1906]. 251 pp.

Inscription: on the front free endpaper: "To the Genial philosopher/'Mark Twain'/with the compliments of the constructor/George W. Caldwell/Nov. 20, 1906".

Marginalia: a few words were written in pencil (in a feeble-looking hand) in the table of contents next to certain geographical locations: "Japan," "China" (p. 5), "India" (p. 6), a pencil line was drawn between XXXVI and XXXVII separating "The Indian Ocean" and "Egypt" (p. 7).

Location: Mark Twain Library, Redding, Connecticut.

Copy examined: Clemens's copy. Some leaves are unopened. Has the Mark Twain Library accession number in red ink—"3253". Examined in 1970 and again June 1982.

CALVERT, GEORGE HENRY (1803–1889. *Wordsworth: A Biographical Aesthetic Study*. Boston: Lee and Shepard, 1878. 232 pp.

Inscription: "Ida C. Langdon/1878". Ida Clark Langdon (1849–1934) was married to Charles Jervis Langdon (1849–1916).

Provenance: bookplate of J. Langdon Family Library #646.

Catalog: Ball 2016 inventory, green cloth with gilt lettering, good condition.

Location: Quarry Farm library shelves, under the supervision of the Mark Twain Archive, Elmira College, Elmira, New York.

This book was available to Clemens whenever he visited the Langdons' home during his numerous trips to Elmira.

CALVIN, JOHN (1509–1564). [Originally Jean Chauvin or Caulvin, the French theologian active as a Protestant religious reformer in Geneva, Switzerland.]

Joe B. Fulton discussed Twain's references to Calvinism in *The Reverend Mark Twain: Theological Burlesque, Form, and Content* (Columbus: Ohio State University Press, 2006), pp. 11, 16, 17, *passim*; "The French Barber: Calvin as a Source of Burlesque in Mark Twain," *Sober, Strict, and Scriptural: Collective Memories of John Calvin, 1800–2000*, ed. Johan de Niet, Herman Paul, and Bart Wallet (Leiden, Netherlands: Brill, 2009), pp. 337–356; and also in "'Jonathan Edwards, Calvin, Baxter & Co.': Mark Twain and the Comedy of Calvinism," *John Calvin's American Legacy*, ed. Thomas J. Davis (New York: Oxford University Press, 2010), pp. 239–255.

CAMERON, MARGARET (1867–1947). *The Cat and the Canary*. Illustrated by W[illiam]. D[odge]. Stevens (1870–1942). New York: Harper & Brothers, 1908. 62 pp.

Source: MTLAcc, entry #454, volume donated by Clemens.

———. *The Involuntary Chaperon*. Illus. New York: Harper & Brothers, 1909. 348 pp.

Source: MTLAcc, entry #1480, volume donated by

Clemens.

CAMERON, VERNEY LOVETT (1844–1894). *Across Africa*. 2 vols. Tauchnitz Edition. [Editions of Cameron's book by several publishers, including that of Bernhard Tauchnitz, first appeared in 1877.]

Catalog: *C1951*, D1, listed among books signed by Clemens, Tauchnitz Edition, red leather, $8 each volume.

CAMPAN, JEANNE LOUISE HENRIETTE (GENET) (1752–1822). *Mémoires sur la Vie Privée de Marie Antoinette [1755–1793]*. [Published in 1822.]

Mark Twain intended to mention this book (or the English translation) in his proposed appendix to *A Connecticut Yankee in King Arthur's Court* (1889) "in support of the assertion that there were not real ladies and gentlemen before our century" (Howard G. Baetzhold, "Course of Composition" [1961], p. 200). The one-page manuscript of Mark Twain's appendix is now in the Berg Collection, New York Public Library.

CAMPBELL, ALEXANDER (1788–1866). [Co-founder of the evangelical Campbellite religious sect.]

Without citing specific readings on Clemens's part, Gary Scharnhorst demonstrated Samuel Clemens's close familiarity with Missourians who subscribed to the Campbellite movement of the 1840s and 1850s ("Clemens and the Campbellites," *Mark Twain Annual 12* [2014]: 136–142). See also Ernest Lee Tuveson, "A Connecticut Yankee in the Mystical Babylon," in *Redeemer Nation: The Idea of America's Millennial Role* (Chicago: University of Chicago Press, 1968), Appendix, which traced "the fatalistic feeling throughout that Hank Morgan's model reforms are somehow doomed from the start" partly to Clemens's early exposure to the Campbellites.

CAMPBELL, GERTRUDE ELIZABETH (BLOOD) (1857–1911), LADY COLIN CAMPBELL and MARY (FRENCH) SHELDON (1847–1936). *Everybody's Book of Correct Conduct; Being Hints for Everyday Life*. New York: Harper & Brothers, 1893. 182 pp.

Source: MTLAcc, entry #1332, volume donated by Clemens.

CAMPBELL, JOHN (1779–1861), First Baron Campbell. *Lives of the Chief Justices of England*. 4 vols. Illus. Boston: Estes & Lauriat, 1873.

Inscription: Volume 1 is signed in black ink on the front flyleaf: "S. L. Clemens/1874." Volume 2 is signed and inscribed in black ink/on the front flyleaf, "S. L. Clemens/Hartford/Conn./ Apparently the proof-reader/was drunk, all the way/through."

Marginalia: typographical corrections and grammatical notes in Clemens's hand, in black ink, particularly on page 143 of Volume 1 but also elsewhere throughout the four volumes.

Catalogs: *A1911*, "15 vols., 8vo, cloth, Bost.: Estes & Lauriat, 1874," quotes the signatures and characterizes and quotes the marginalia, lot 64, sold with eleven other volumes for a total of $8.50; Stan. V. Henkels (Philadelphia), Catalogue 1057 (14 May 1912), "4 vols.," item #121; offered for sale in 1964 by John Swingle of Alta California Rare Books, Catalog 22, Berkeley, California, for $350 (PH in MTP).

Location: Mark Twain House and Museum, Hartford, Connecticut. Gift of an anonymous donor in 1965.

Copies examined: Clemens's copies were not available for inspection when I visited Hartford in 1970. Information in this entry was thus initially compiled from *A1911*, photocopies of Clemens's inscription and marginalia on file in the Mark Twain Papers in the Bancroft Library at the University of California at Berkeley, and a report prepared by Diana Royce, then (in 1984) Librarian of the Stowe-Day Memorial Library in Hartford. However, in August 1987 I was able to examine the volumes in Hartford.

———. *Lives of the Lord Chancellors and Keepers of the Great Seal of England, from the Earliest Times Till the Reign of Queen Victoria. By Lord Campbell. New Edition, Edited by John Allan Mallory, of the New York Bar.* 10 vols. Boston: Estes & Lauriat, 1874–1875.

Inscription: the front flyleaf of Volume 1 is signed and dated in pencil, "Saml L. Clemens/Hartford, Oct. 1874." The flyleaves or half-title pages of Volumes 2–10 are signed in pencil, "Saml L. Clemens/Hartford 1874."

Marginalia: annotation on pages 148, 163, 165, 183, 200, and 232 of Volume 1, and on various pages of the other volumes. Mainly these brief notes in pencil and black ink criticize the grammar and overall prose style. "Sad grammar," Clemens penciled on p. 232 of Volume 1, the most extensively corrected volume.

Catalogs: *A1911*, "15 vols., 8vo, cloth, Bost.: Estes & Lauriat, 1874," quotes the signatures and characterizes and quotes the marginalia, lot 64, nine vols. (lacking Vol. 6) sold with six other vols. for $8.50 total; Stan. V. Henkels (Philadelphia), Catalogue 1057 (14 May 1912), "10 vols., lacking vol. 6," item #121; nine vols. offered for sale in 1963 by John Swingle of Alta California Rare Books, Berkeley, California. *Mott 1952*, #41 listed Volume 6 only, priced at $10.

Provenance: Volume 6 contains the book stamps of the Mark Twain Library, Redding, Connecticut.

Location: all ten volumes are now in Mark Twain House and Museum, Hartford, Connecticut. Volume 6 was the gift of an anonymous donor in 1963; the other nine volumes were donated anonymously in 1965.

Copies examined: Clemens's copies were not available for inspection when I visited Hartford in 1970; preliminary information for this entry was compiled from *A1911*, *Mott 1952*, a card catalog in the Mark Twain House, photocopies of marginalia in the Mark Twain Papers in the Bancroft Library at the University of California at Berkeley, and a report prepared by Diana Royce, Librarian of the Stowe-Day Memorial Library in Hartford in 1984. However, in August 1987 I was able to examine the volumes in Hartford.

CAMPBELL, (SIR) JOHN LOGAN (1817–1912). *Poenamo: Sketches of the Early Days of New Zealand. Romance and Reality of Antipodean Life in the Infancy of a New Colony*. London: Williams and Norgate, 1881. ["Poenamo" was the Maori name for New Zealand.]

Inscription: on the half-title page, "To Mrs Clemens/ POENAMO is presented by the author/Eugene [*sic*] Campbell./Kilbeyee, Auckland 25-11-95".

Marginalia: on the copyright page is an undated ("Saturday morning") note by Campbell requesting Olivia Clemens to invite Clemens to visit his verandah for a smoke. On the last page of Campbell's memoir *Poenamo* is a brief note, presumably by Olivia Clemens, about Rangitoto, a mountain near Auckland (p. 360). A lengthy and sad note by Campbell in pencil ("the blow fell upon me that I was not to see my darling child alive. . . . And so we are alone in our old age") is tipped in horizontally across page 359. Campbell's beloved daughter Ida, born in 1859, had died in 1880.

Catalog: *C1951*, O11, erroneously listed with books containing Olivia Clemens's signature.

Location: Mark Twain House and Museum, Hartford, Connecticut. Obtained from Maxwell Hunley Rare Books of Beverly Hills at the recommendation of Alan Gribben in 1970; Hunley had purchased it at the 1951 auction and was offering it for sale at $87.50.

Copy examined: Olivia Clemens's copy. Examined in Beverly Hills in 1970 and again in Hartford in August 1987. Francis Madigan, "Mark Twain's Passage to India" (1974), pp. 355–356.

CAMPBELL, THOMAS (1777–1844). "Battle of Hohenlinden" (poem, published in 1802, became song lyrics).

Four men attempt to recite this heroic war poem while drinking aboard a Sacramento steamboat in Mark Twain's "On Linden, Etc." (*The Californian*, 7 April 1866; *SSix*, pp. 208–209). In his 1872 English journal Twain made note of the stone in Westminster Abbey that "covers Campbell the poet" (*MTLet* 5: 603).

———. *Gertrude of Wyoming; or, the Pennsylvanian Cottage.* Illus. New York: D. Appleton & Co., 1858. 94 pp.

Provenance: bookplate #59 of "J. Langdon Family Library."

Catalog: Ball 2016 inventory, wood with green textured leather covering, gilt lettering and design, poor condition.

Location: Quarry Farm library shelves, under the supervision of the Mark Twain Archive, Elmira College, Elmira, New York.

Copy examined: an unmarked copy available to Clemens whenever he visited the Langdons' home during his numerous trips to Elmira. Examined on 26 May 2015.

Scottish poet Campbell's romantic epic recounts the slaughter of hundreds of American colonists that took place in 1778 when British troops and their Native American allies invaded the Wyoming Valley in Pennsylvania during the American Revolution.

———. "The Last Man" (poem, published in 1823).

Viewing the vast crater of Haleakala, surrounded by banks of clouds below him, Mark Twain wrote that he "felt like the Last Man, neglected of the judgment, and left pinnacled in mid-heaven, a forgotten relic of a vanished world" (*Roughing It* [1872], Chapter 76). Campbell's poem of that name depicts "the last of human mould,/That shall Creation's death behold,/As Adam saw her prime!"

———. "Lochiel's Warning" (poem, published in 1801).

Mark Twain recalled in a speech he delivered at the Hannibal High School graduation exercises on 30 May 1902 that the school exhibitions during his boyhood invariably included lines from Campbell's poem: "Lochiel, Lochiel, beware of the day/When the lowlands shall meet you in battle array,/For a field of the dead rushes red on my sight,/And the clans of Culloden were scattered in flight." The Battle of Culloden in 1746 was disastrous for the Highlanders and essentially ended the Jacobite Rising.

———. "Ye Mariners of England" (battle poem, published in 1801).

Mark Twain quotes from the third stanza in "About All Kinds of Ships" (1893); these booming verses are "the stateliest lines in the literature of the sea." Three of Campbell's four stanzas have the same refrain: "While the stormy winds do blow;/While the battle rages loud and long,/And the stormy winds do blow." On 4 February [1903] Clemens wrote to Olivia: "And now the stormy winds do blow, as the sailor-ballad says" (MTP). But there was another potential source for Clemens's allusion; see the Catalog entry for a sea shanty titled "The Mermaid."

———. *The Pleasures of Hope* (poem, published in 1799).

In Chapter 6 of *Following the Equator* (1897) Mark Twain quotes "an invocation from Thomson [*sic*]" that he found in a book [titled *Polynesia*] by the Reverend Michael Russell: "Come, bright Improvement! on the car of Time,/And rule the spacious world from clime to clime." Twain comments: "Very well, Bright Improvement has arrived, you see, with her civilization, and her Waterbury, and her umbrella, and her third-quality profanity, and her humanizing-not-destroying machinery, and her hundred-and-eighty-death-rate, and everything is going along just as handsome!" Midway through Part I of Thomas Campbell's "The Pleasures of Hope" occur these rhyming couplets: "I watch the wheels of Nature's mazy plan,/And learn the future by the past of man./Come, bright Improvement! On the car of Time,/And rule the spacious world from clime to clime." Twain's mistaken attribution of these lines was corrected from "Thomson" to "Campbell" in subsequent editions of *Following the Equator*. See also the Catalog entry for *The Book of Pleasures*.

CAMPBELL, WILLIAM WILFRED (1861–1918). "Love" (poem, published in 1891, better known by the first words of its opening line, "Love Came at Dawn"). Collected in Campbell's *Beyond the Hills of Dream* (1899).

Mark Twain reported that "the authorship has now been traced" when he identified, in the *North American Review* 185.612 (5 April 1907): 677, this somber, two-stanza poem as the source of "some verses . . . found among Susy's papers after her death" (22 January 1907 AD, *AutoMT* 2: 376). It begins, "Love came at dawn when all the world was fair," but concludes grimly.

CAMPBELL-COPELAND, THOMAS, ed. and comp. *Cleveland and Stevenson: Their Lives and Record. The Democratic Campaign Book for 1892, with a Handbook of American Politics Up to Date, and a Cyclopedia of Presidential Biography.* Illus. Three volumes in one. New York: C. L. Webster & Co., 1892. 438 pp.

This voters' guide to the primary contest between Grover Cleveland (1837–1908) and Adlai Ewing Stevenson (1835–1914) was issued by Clemens's publishing firm, whose operations he often supervised.

———. *Harrison and Reid: Their Lives and Record. The Republican Campaign Book for 1892, with a Handbook of American Politics Up to Date, and a Cyclopedia of Presidential Biography.* Illus. Three volumes in one. New York: C. L. Webster & Co., 1892. 438 pp.

Clemens's publishing firm, whose operations he often supervised, issued this voters' guide to the primary contest between Benjamin Harrison (1833–1901) and Whitelaw Reid (1837–1912).

CANFIELD, DOROTHY (1879–1958).

Canfield, who had recently earned her Ph.D. degree at Columbia University and had not yet begun her creative writing career, was one of the guests at Mark Twain's Seventieth Birthday celebration held at Delmonico's in New York City on 5 December 1905.

CANFIELD, FLAVIA A. (CAMP) (1844–1930). *The Kidnapped Campers; A Story of Out-of-Doors.* Illus. New York: Harper & Brothers, 1908. 312 pp.

Source: MTLAcc, entry #1409, volume donated by Clemens.

The mother of writer Dorothy Canfield, Flavia Canfield was a painter and young adult author. Married to the fourth president of Ohio State University, she became a social reformer and women's rights advocate.

CAPE TOWN, SOUTH AFRICA. *Photographic Views of Cape Town, South Africa.* Cape Town, 1896.

Inscription: presented to Mark Twain by the Members of the Owl Club as a memento of his visit to South Africa, July 13, 1896.

Catalog: *A1911*, "folio, padded morocco, gilt edges, Cape Town, 1896, signed by members of the Owl Club," quotes inscription, lot 18, sold for $6.

"CAPTAIN KIDD" (English ballad).

Mark Twain included "The Captive Pirate's Lament" [*sic*] among the songs that display "soft sentimentality about the sea" in "About All Kinds of Ships" (1893). Louis J. Budd concluded that Twain was alluding to "the traditional English ballad 'Captain Kidd'" (*CTSS&E* 2: 1021 n. 96). William Kidd (born c. 1645) was hanged in 1701, and several ballads purported to reveal his thoughts as he awaited his execution. In 1907 Twain recalled a line from the ballad, alluding to "Captain Kydd . . . 'when he sailed, when he sailed'" (*Christian Science*, Book II, Chapter 15, *WIM?*, pp. 356, 574).

CARDELLI, CESARE. *Nouvelle Methode Pratique de Langue Italienne.* Paris, 1882.

Inscription: (according to a paraphrase in *Mott 1952* catalog) "Jean Clemens, 169 rue de l'université, Paris, 16 November 1894."

Catalog: *Mott 1952*, #42, $2.50.

CAREY, HENRY (1687–1743). "Sally in our alley" (song, 1715?). Words and melody by Carey. Also known as "Of all the girls that are so smart."

Twain's cholera germ-narrator sang "Sally in Our Alley" in "Three Thousand Years Among the Microbes" (written in 1905, published in *WWD?*, p. 462). Four lines convey the song's essence: "Of all the girls that are so smart/There's none like pretty Sally;/She is the darling of my heart,/And she lives in our alley." See also the Catalog entry for E. A. Abbey, *Old Songs* (1889).

CARLETON, WILL (1845–1912). *City-Ballads.* New ed. Illus. New York: Harper & Brothers, 1906. 164 pp.

Source: MTLAcc, entry #652, volume donated by Clemens.

In 1885 Clemens and Julian Hawthorne corresponded about the fact that certain members of the Authors' Club in New York City, founded in 1882, were voting to exclude Carleton from membership; however, at the next meeting the poet was duly welcomed into the organization (Gary Scharnhorst, "Mark Twain and Julian Hawthorne," *Mark Twain Annual 10* [2012]: 47–54). In a letter composed on 15 April [no year given] from Hartford, Clemens advised "Mr. Carleton" that he had "got the wrong idea" about an unidentified book Carleton had written. "I have read it through, with great care & interest, & am convinced that it is something much better than a humorous work, in that it is a fine & stately & beautiful tragedy" (ALS, Chapin Library, Williams College, Williamstown, Massachusetts). Clemens's handwriting (in pencil) seems to belong to the 1880s. Clemens included "Will Carleton" in an undated list of authors (*A1911*, lot 343).

———. *City Festivals.* Illus. New York: Harper & Brothers, 1893. 161 pp.

Source: MTLAcc, entry #1686, volume donated by Clemens.

———. *Songs of Two Centuries.* Illus. New York: Harper & Brothers, 1902. 157 pp.

Source: MTLAcc, entry #801, volume donated by Clemens. Despite the broad implications of the title, this is not a compendium of songs but rather a book of poems about home, rural life, and patriotism.

———. [Another identical copy.]

Source: MTLAcc, entry #1687, volume donated by Clemens.

CARLISLE, GEORGE LISTER (1852–1930). *Around the World in a Year.* Illus. New York: R. G. Cooke, 1908. 310 pp.

Source: MTLAcc, entry #582, volume donated by Clemens. Carlisle recounts his travels with his wife and daughter through Europe, Egypt, India, China, Japan, and Hawaii until their safe return to Grand Central Station in New York City.

CARLYLE, JANE BAILLIE (WELSH) (1801–1866). *Letters and Memorials of Jane Welsh Carlyle, Prepared for Publication by Thomas Carlyle [1795–1881].* Ed. by James Anthony Froude (1818–1894). 3 vols. London, 1883. [Edition conjectured.]

Clemens's letter of 3 November 1884 to a cousin of William Dean Howells (PH in MTP) indicates that he read Jane Carlyle's *Letters* when they were issued in 1883.

CARLYLE, THOMAS (1795–1881). *Carlyle's Complete Works.* The Sterling Edition. 20 vols. Boston: Estes and Lauriat, 1885.

Catalog: Ball 2016 inventory, 20 vols., conditions range from good to fair, the front covers are broken on six volumes.

Location: Quarry Farm library shelves, under the supervision of the Mark Twain Archive, Elmira College, Elmira, New York.

This set was available to Clemens at Quarry Farm in Elmira, New York.

———. *The Correspondence of Thomas Carlyle and Ralph Waldo Emerson 1834–1872.* Ed. by Charles Eliot Norton (1827–1908). 2 vols. Brown cloth, gilt lettering. Boston: James R. Osgood and Co., 1883.

Inscription: the flyleaves of both volumes are torn out.

Marginalia: a note in pencil at the top of page 61 in Volume 1 resembles Clemens's hand; a line was drawn on that page to the name of Andrews Norton (1786–1853) in the text and the query posed: "Father of the editor of this book?" (He was.) Pencil marks characteristic of Clemens's marginalia occur on pages 207, 217–218, and 222 of the first volume, which contains 368 pages. No marks are evident in the second volume, which has 383 pages.

Location: Mark Twain Library, Redding, Connecticut.

Copy examined: I discovered these volumes on the shelves of the circulating collection on 11 September 1970. The marginalia, the publisher, the date of publication, and the fact that their flyleaves have been ripped out convince me that these volumes originally belonged to Clemens. I examined them again in June 1982 and on 10 November 2019. Volume 1 has the red ink Mark Twain Library accession number "2843"; Volume 2 is similarly designated as "2844".

————. *Critical and Miscellaneous Essays* (published in 1838). "Get Carlyle's 'Essays'" (NB 24 [June 1885], *N&J* 3: 160).

————. *The French Revolution: A History*. 2 vols. New York: Harper & Brothers, 1856.

Inscriptions: the front free endpaper of Volume I is inscribed in pencil: "Livy Langdon/ Elmira, N. Y." Half-title page of Volume I inscribed in black ink "Mrs. S L. Clemens/ 1870." Both inscriptions are in Clemens's hand; the latter one resembles his signature of the post-1900 period (he added "Mrs." after signing the book).

Marginalia: annotated by Clemens throughout Volume I in purple pencil, blue ink, and black ink. On page 13, at "Ye are heard in Heaven," Clemens rejoined: "Yes, after a thousand years. Let us sing praises, for wonderful promptness, O Providential Show-Coach!"

Catalogs: ListABP (1910), "French Revolution 2 vols., Carlyle"; *C1951*, #22a, $25, edition not specified, listed among the books containing notations by Clemens.

Location: Volume I only, Mark Twain House and Museum, Hartford, Connecticut. Donated by Mrs. John L. Martin of Darien, Connecticut.

Copy examined: Olivia Clemens's copy of Volume I, read by Clemens. Examined in August 1987. Volume II has not been located.

Albert Bigelow Paine reported that Clemens's copy of *The French Revolution* was "among the volumes he read oftenest," although "there were not many notes" in his copy. Mark Twain attacked Carlyle for his anti-democratic sympathies in a 27 August 1869 Buffalo *Express* column (Baetzhold, *MT&JB*, p. 327 n. 33). Clemens believed that he first began reading *The French Revolution* in 1871 and observed that his view of the Girondin and Sansculotte factions had reversed over the years, according to a letter he wrote to William Dean Howells on 22 August 1887 (*MTL*, 2:490; *MTHL*, p. 595). He called Carlyle's work "one of the greatest creations that ever flowed from a pen" (SLC to Mary Mason Fairbanks, 6 August 1877, *MTMF*, p. 207), catalogued French barbarities from it in Paris in 1879 (NB 18, *N&J* 2: 321–322), and read the book in Paris in 1879 because "The Reign of Terror interested him," Paine explained (*MTB*, p. 644). For a Hartford banquet held in June 1881 Clemens ascribed one of his humorous menu captions to "Thomas Carlyle" (Beinecke Rare Book and Manuscript Library, Yale University; Everett Emerson to Alan Gribben, 29 October 1982).

On 20 January 1887 Clemens named Carlyle's *The French Revolution* as one of his favorite books in a letter to the Reverend Charles D. Crane (ALS, Shapell Manuscript Library, Beverly Hills, California). Mark Twain intended for the book to comprise part of his projected "Royalty

& Nobility Exposed" series (NB 26 [May 1887], *N&J* 3: 295). "Every time I have read it since [1871], I have read it differently—being influenced . . . by Taine & St. Simon," Clemens wrote in that (previously cited) letter to Howells on 22 August 1887 (*MTHL*, p. 595). The Revolution itself was "that immortal benefaction. . . . It was the noblest & the holiest thing & the most precious that ever happened in this earth," he announced to Howells (22 September 1889, *MTHL*, p. 613).

Mark Twain mentioned the book title in July 1893 (NB 33, TS p. 22), visited Carlyle's home in November 1896 and saw the "one small scrap of the 1st vol of French Revolution left" (NB 39, TS p. 21), and mentioned the French Revolution, depicted mobs, and employed passwords, secret grips, and oaths in "Tom Sawyer's Conspiracy" (written 1897–1900) that suggest Carlyle's book (Walter Blair, *HH&T*, pp. 158, 167). "I have a reverent affection for Carlyle's books, and have read his *Revolution* eight times," Twain wrote seriously in "My First Lie, and How I Got Out of It" (1899). Charlotte Teller recalled that when she was writing her play entitled *Mirabeau* Clemens lent her his own copy of *French Revolution* (Teller's preface to a privately printed pamphlet of Twain's letters to her, Berg, NYPL, TS in MTP). On 3 November 1909 Clemens "finished the evening by reading . . . a fine pyrotechnic passage—the gathering at Versailles," Paine reported (*MTB*, p. 1535). During Clemens's final stay in Bermuda, which commenced in November 1909 and ended in April 1910, his hostess observed that Carlyle's *French Revolution* was one of the books that entertained Clemens in the mornings (Marion Schuyler Allen, "Some New Anecdotes of Mark Twain," *Strand Magazine* [London] 46.272 [August 1913]: 168). Shortly before Clemens died, he reportedly turned again to his copy of *The French Revolution* (Hartford *Courant*, 22 April 1910, cited by Baetzhold, *MT&JB*, p. 87). Henry M. Alden repeated the story that when Clemens "was about to die, [he] turned to Carlyle's *French Revolution*" (*Bookman* [1910], p. 366).

Walter Blair, "French Revolution" (1957), pp. 21–35; Blair, *MT&HF* (1960), pp. 117, 310–311; Hamlin Hill and Walter Blair, eds., *The Art of Huckleberry Finn* (1962), pp. 429–444; James D. Williams, "Use of History" (1965), p. 106; Howard G. Baetzhold, *MT&JB* (1970), pp. 28–31, 42, 128–160 (esp. pp. 143–148), 329, 343 n. 39; Wesley Britton, "Carlyle, Clemens, and Dickens: Mark Twain's Francophobia, the French Revolution, and Determinism," *Studies in American Fiction* 20.2 (Autumn 1992): 197–204; Baetzhold, "'Well, My Book Is Written'" (1996), pp. 41–77; and especially Joe B. Fulton, *Mark Twain in the Margins: Quarry Farm Marginalia and* A *Connecticut Yankee in King Arthur's Court* (Tuscaloosa: University of Alabama Press, (2000), pp. 21, 81–100, 175–179; Delphine Louis-Dimitrov, "The Democratic Reconfiguration of History in Mark Twain's *Personal Recollections of Joan of Arc*," *American Literary Realism* 51.2 (Winter 2018): 162–179.

————. *The French Revolution: A History*. 3 vols. Original reddish-brown cloth. New York: Scribner, Welford and Co., 1871 (Volumes I and II); London: Chapman and Hall, 1871

(Volume III).

Marginalia: Clemens made long vertical lines on page 160 of Volume I starting at "O poor mortals" and ending at "Where ye are is no abiding." He marked with emphatic small brackets the statement about "how ye make this Earth bitter for each other" and underlined the following sentence in the next paragraph regarding the longing for freedom: "it is the deep commandment, dimmer or clearer, of our whole being, to be *free*." Nonetheless, Clemens wrote on an undated envelope, presumably in 1881 upon Carlyle's passing, "Carlyle is gone. Let us adore/Like castigated spaniels round his bier/He loathed theYankee all his day/The loather of the Yankee name. . . ." (American Art Association [New York City], Sale catalogue [8 January 1925], "autograph notes," lot 121).

Provenance: Volume I discovered in the Langdon family library shelves at Quarry Farm in 1984 by Charles and Mary Boewe.

Catalogs: QF Martinez, 3 vols., Scribner, Welford & Co., 1871, good condition; Ball 2016 inventory, 3 vols., Vols. I and II issued by Scribner, Welford and Co., Vol. III published by Chapman and Hall, brownish red cloth, gilt and black lettering and designs.

Locations: Volume I contains marginalia and is in the Mark Twain Archive, Gannett-Tripp Learning Center, Elmira College, Elmira, New York. Volumes II and III lack marginalia and are still on the shelves in the Quarry Farm library under the supervision of the Mark Twain Archive.

Copy examined: copy of Volume I belonging to the Cranes. Clemens had access to this three-volume work during his many summer visits to Quarry Farm in Elmira, New York. Viewed in May 2002, but this entry was also assisted by photocopies of title pages and Clemens's annotations supplied on 7 November 1984 by Herbert A. Wisbey, then director of the Center for Mark Twain Studies at Quarry Farm. Mark Woodhouse answered queries about the Carlyle volumes in the Mark Twain Archive in an email of 9 August 2012.

————. *The French Revolution: A History*. 2 vols. Brown cloth. New York: Harper & Brothers, n. d.

Inscription: the front free endpaper of Volume II is signed in ink, "Susan L. Crane/Quarry Farm 1888".

Marginalia: Joe B. Fulton meticulously reported and discussed Clemens's annotations in *Mark Twain in the Margins: Quarry Farm Marginalia and A Connecticut Yankee in King Arthur's Court* (Tuscaloosa: University of Alabama Press, 2000), pp. 81–100 and 175–179. Of special importance is the lengthy response to Carlyle's book that Clemens began on the last page of Volume 2 (page 429) and then continued on the blank verso of that page preceding the Index; it reads in part: "Finish, Sept. 10th, '88." This is a *picture* of the French Revolution, but in only a limited way a History of it. . . . The Revolution had a *result*—a superb, a stupendous, a most noble & sublime result—to-wit, *French Liberty*, & in a degree, *Human* Liberty--& was worth a million times what it cost, of blood, & terror, & various suffering, & titanic labor. And this fair & shapely creation was not worth Carlyle's pains to paint. . . . He should have given a chapter showing what the French laws were before the Revolution, & what they were when the Revolution's

work was finished."

Catalog: QF Martinez, p.122, *The French Revolution: A History*, 2 vols., Harper & Brothers, 1888 [*sic*], good condition; Ball 2016 inventory, 2 vols., Harper & Brothers, undated edition, Mark Twain Archive.

Location: Mark Twain Archive, Gannett-Tripp Learning Center, Elmira College, Elmira, New York. Volumes 1 and 2 were transferred from the Quarry Farm library shelves to the Mark Twain Archive by Mark Woodhouse on 9 July 1987.

Copy examined: Susan Crane's copy, which Clemens read and annotated during one of his many summer visits to Quarry Farm. Joe B. Fulton guessed that he made these notes in July 1903 (*Mark Twain in the Margins* [2000], p. 104). Viewed on 17 May 2002.

————. *History of Friedrich II. of Prussia, Called Frederick the Great*. Illus. 10 vols. London: Chapman and Hall, [1871]. [Date of publication conjectured.]

Inscription: in Volume 1: "S. L. Clemens, Hartford, Conn."

Catalog: *A1911*, "10 vols., 8vo, cloth, Lond.: Chapman & Hall, n.d.," quotes the signature, lot 65, sold for $26. The *A1911* catalog does not supply the date of publication for Clemens's copies, but one citation in Notebook 20 (1882) is correct for the thirty-volume Chapman and Hall "Library Edition" of *Thomas Carlyle's Collected Works* (1871), of which *History of Friedrich II. Of Prussia* was a part (*N&J* 2: 503).

Clemens requested *Frederick the Great* from his own publisher in 1882; W. Rowlands of James R. Osgood & Co. replied on 22 July 1882, describing three available editions—The Library Edition and The People's Edition issued by Chapman & Hall, or the Harper & Brother's edition (MTP). In the early autumn of 1882 Clemens noted that "Fred the Great was a bad speller—& Carlyle can't account for it!" (NB 20, *N&J* 2: 503). While sojourning in the Swiss Alps, Clemens fumed at "Frederick the Great Scoundrel" (NB 31 [September 1891], TS p. 4). In Chapter 21 of *The American Claimant* (1892) Lord Berkeley reflects that once he himself "was a very Frederick the Great for resolution and staying capacity."

————. *Letters*. [Full title and edition unknown.]

Isabel Lyon noted that in assisting with Clemens's packing for his departure from Dublin, New Hampshire on 17 October 1905, she "sent back to Library" a one-volume edition of Carlyle's *Letters* Clemens had borrowed (IVL Daily Reminder, Mark Twain Archive, Gannett-Tripp Learning Center, Elmira College, Elmira, New York).

————. *Life of John Sterling* (originally published in 1851). Sterling (1806–1844) was a Scottish clergyman and author. Clemens requested this book from James R. Osgood & Company in 1882; on 22 July 1882 W. Rowlands replied in behalf of the firm, describing editions of Carlyle's works then available (MTP).

————, ed. *Oliver Cromwell's Letters and Speeches: With Elucidations*. Illus. 5 vols. London: Chapman and Hall, 1871 (Volumes IV and V, n.d.).

Catalog: Ball 2016 inventory, Volumes I, II, and III published in New York by Scribner, Welford, and Co.; Volumes IV and V issued in London by Chapman and Hall; reddish-brown cloth, gilt lettering and black lettering and design.

Location: Quarry Farm library shelves, under the supervision of the Mark Twain Archive, Elmira College, Elmira, New York.

This set was available to Clemens at Quarry Farm in Elmira, New York.

———, ed. *Oliver Cromwell's Letters and Speeches: With Elucidations.* Illus. 5 vols. London: Chapman and Hall, n.d.

Inscription: in Volume 2: "S. L. Clemens, Hartford, 1883."

Catalog: *A1911*, "5 vols., 8vo, cloth, Lond.: Chapman & Hall, n.d.," quotes the signature in Volume 2, lot 66, sold for $7.50.

On 22 July 1882 an employee of James R. Osgood & Company, responding to Clemens's request, described three editions of Carlyle's works that included *Cromwell's Letters and Speeches* (W. Rowlands to SLC, MTP). Mark Twain set down the germ for "The Death Disk" (1901) in Notebook 22 (*N&J* 3: 14, 1883) after reading Carlyle's commentary on Letter 90, dated 8 March 1648 (1870 Chapman and Hall ed., 2: 106, 122–123). He also sent a dramatic scene based on the episode to Howells on 20 December 1883, suggesting that they collaborate in writing "a tragedy" (*MTHL*, p. 459 n. 1; the precise source was originally discovered by Howard G. Baetzhold). Cromwell's career is recalled by Tom Sawyer in "Tom Sawyer's Conspiracy," written 1897–1900 (*HH&T*, p. 168). Twain affixed an introductory footnote to "The Death Disk" (1901), acknowledging his source as Carlyle's edition of *Cromwell's Letters and Speeches.* "It takes a Cromwell . . . ten years to raise the standards of English official and commercial morals to a respect-worthy altitude," Twain later asserted (30 January 1907 AD, *MTE*, p. 81; *AutoMT* 2: 409).

———. *On Heroes, Hero-Worship, and the Heroic in History.* [Collected in Clemens's copy of *Sartor Resartus.*]

A passage in Lecture I, "The Hero as Divinity," proposes a "life is a dream" explanation similar to the one that 44 delivers in "No. 44, The Mysterious Stranger," written 1902–1908 (*MSM*, pp. 403–405): "This World is after all but a show,—a phenomenon or appearance, no real thing. All deep souls see into that,—the Hindoo Mythologist, the German Philosopher,—the Shakespeare, the earnest Thinker wherever he may be: 'We are such stuff as Dreams are made of.'" In a 1909 Autobiographical Dictation Mark Twain spoke of Henry H. Rogers in terms also evoking Carlyle's book: "Hero worship consists in just that. Our heroes are the men who do things which we recognize with regret and sometimes with a secret shame that we cannot do" (*MTA*, 1: 263–264).

Robert Regan, *UH* (1966), pp. 66–67.

———. *Past and Present.* New York: Scribner, Welford, and Co., 1872.

Catalog: Ball 2016 inventory, reddish-brown cloth, gilt lettering on spine, black lettering on cover design.

Location: Quarry Farm library shelves, under the supervision of the Mark Twain Archive, Elmira College, Elmira, New York.

Copy examined: unmarked copy to which Clemens had access whenever he visited Quarry Farm in Elmira.

———. *Past and Present.* [Another copy. Collected in Clemens's copy of *Sartor Resartus.*]

———. *Reminiscences,* ed. James Anthony Froude (1818–1894).

Authorized Edition. New York: Charles Scribner's Sons, 1881. 536 pp.

Inscription: the front free endpaper is signed in pencil, "Ida C. Langdon." Ida Clark Langdon (1849–1934) was married to Charles Jervis Langdon (1849–1916).

Provenance: has the bookplate (#546) of the "J. Langdon Family Library."

Catalog: Ball 2016 inventory, brown cloth, gilt lettering, top edge of spine worn, otherwise in good condition.

Location: Quarry Farm, under the protection of the Mark Twain Archive, Elmira College, Elmira, New York.

Copy examined: unmarked copy to which Clemens had access whenever he visited the Langdons' home in Elmira. Examined on 26 May 2015. Page 464 is turned down.

———. *Sartor Resartus, Heroes and Hero-Worship, and Past and Present. Complete in One Volume.* London: Ward, Lock, and Co., n.d.

Inscription: in light black ink on the front free endpaper: "S L Clemens/1888".

Catalogs: *A1911*, "12mo, boards, cloth back, N.Y., n.d.," place of publication erroneously reported as New York, quotes the signature, lot 6, sold for $4.50; Lew David Feldman, "House of El Dieff, Inc." (1957), item #987, $17.50.

Provenance: collection of Frank C. Willson (1889–1960), Melrose, Massachusetts.

Location: Harry Ransom Center, University of Texas at Austin. Purchased in 1962 from Mrs. Margarete Willson, the widow of Frank C. Willson.

Copy examined: Clemens's copy. Contains the *A1911* sale label on the front pastedown endpaper.

More than a few chapters of Mark Twain's *A Connecticut Yankee in King Arthur's Court* (1889) dwell on the social advantages conveyed by elaborate clothes, beginning with the Yankee's introduction to the Round Table in Chapter 2: "Around it sat a great company of men dressed in such various and splendid colors that it hurt one's eyes to look at them." In the Queen's dungeon in Chapter 18 languishes a prisoner whose crime it was to have remarked "that men were about all alike, and one man as good as another, barring clothes." The King and the Yankee easily disguise themselves in Chapter 27 by shedding their costly raiment and adopting a "costume being in effect universal among the poor, because of its strength and cheapness." Henry W. Fisher recorded that, while living in London, Clemens once made up a doggerel poem that went in part: "Life's . . ./ A Drama by Teufelsdroeckh [*sic*] (*AMT*, p. 160). Fisher added that Twain coined the imaginary name "Castle Teufelsdröckh" for a noble's residence in Berlin in 1891 (*AMT*, p. 202). In Chapter 37 of *Following the Equator* (1897) Twain inveighs against European clothes—"a sign of insecurity," he called them, adding that "our clothes are a lie"; later he declared that "the skin of every human being contains a slave. It is the clothes that make the man" (NB 47 [1904], TS pp. 18–19).

Despite the fact that he had signed his own copy of *Sartor Resartus* in 1888 and had marked other copies, on 8 February 1905 Mark Twain assured David A. Munro, associate editor of the *North American Review*, "I have never read Sartor Resartus," though he then consented to make certain changes in the clothes-philosophy expressed in "The Czar's Soliloquy" (1905) (Berg Collection). Howard

G. Baetzhold properly termed Clemens's assertion as "inconceivable" *(MT&JB* [1970], p. 234). When "The Czar's Soliloquy" appeared in the March 1905 issue of *North American Review*, Twain acknowledged the precedent of Teufelsdröckh near its beginning.

D. S. Bertolotti, Jr., "Mark Twain Revisits the Tailor," *Mark Twain Journal* 13.4 (Summer 1967): 18–19; Howard G. Baetzhold, "Course of Composition" (1961), p. 202; James D. Williams, "Use of History" (1965), p. 106; Lawrence I. Berkove and Joseph Csicsila, *Heretical Fictions: Religion in the Literature of Mark Twain* (Iowa City: University of Iowa Press, 2010), p. 167.

————. *Sartor Resartus & Lectures on Heroes*. London: Chapman and Hall, 1858.

Inscription: on the half-title page, in pencil: "Clara Langdon Clemens/Sydney, Australia/Sept. 1895."

Marginalia: Clemens made penciled vertical marks and vertical brackets up to page 207. He also jotted figures and notes in pencil on the rear pastedown endpaper (the rear free endpaper has been removed). Most of these notes have been brushed over and are now illegible, but one of them reads "327" and another refers to a place on page 359 (in "The Hero as King") where Clemens recorded that he stopped reading here.

Location: Mark Twain Library, Redding, Connecticut.

Copy examined: Clara Clemens's copy with Clemens's annotations. Examined in 1970 and again in June 1982 and on 10 November 2019. Displays the red ink Mark Twain Library accession number "2848" and the Library's purple oval stamps. The front pastedown endpaper carries the bookseller sticker of Angus & Robertson, Sydney. The rear pastedown endpaper has a bookseller sticker of Bone & Son, London.

————. *Sartor Resartus: The Life and Opinions of Herr Teufelsdröckh. In Three Books*. Frontispiece portrait of Carlyle. Original reddish-brown cloth, gilt, spine broken, certain pages loose. New York: Scribner, Welford & Co., 1871. [The *"Three Books"* are included in this single volume.]

Marginalia: Clemens's characteristic pencil markings are scattered throughout. There is a long vertical line on page 9 in the first two paragraphs of Chapter 3, "Reminiscences"; brackets and a vertical line on page 10; underlining on page 15 at "'But I . . . am alone with the Stars'"; underlining on page 18; a long, looping bracket around the discussion of "The World in Clothes" in Chapter 5 (page 25); brackets, an underlining, and "X's" on pages 34–35; an "X," an underline, and a vertical line on page 40; brackets around "The beginning of all Wisdom is to look fixedly on Clothes, or even with eyesight, till they become *transparent*" (page 45); a vertical line and underlining on page 47; underlining beneath "Man is properly the *only* object that interests man" and brackets around the paragraph (page 51); a bracket and underlining on page 54; an "X" and long underlinings in Chapter 9, "The Everlasting Yea" (page 127); "X's," underlinings, and vertical lines on pages 130–131; heavy underlining, a bracket, and a double vertical line on page 135; vertical lines on pages 144–145; underlining on page 146; underlining in the comment about religion "wearing for herself new Vestures" (page 149); brackets and underlining on page 155; vertical lines on page 158; triple vertical lines made into large

exclamation marks (!!!) at Carlyle's statement, "Perhaps in the most thickly-peopled country, some three days annually might suffice to shoot all the able-bodied Paupers that had accumulated within the year. Let Governments think of this" (page 159); vertical lines and brackets on page 170; and a vertical line and underlining on page 204.

Provenance: found among the books in the Langdon family library at Quarry Farm in the mid-1980s.

Catalog: Ball 2016 inventory, reddish-brown cloth, gilt lettering on spine, black lettering on cover design, "binding and some pages loose."

Location: Mark Twain Archive, Gannett-Tripp Learning Center, Elmira College, Elmira, New York.

Copy examined: a volume belonging to the Cranes (with no inscription) that Clemens read and marked heavily. Viewed in May 2002. These extensive markings further serve to render as preposterous Clemens's claim in 1905 that he had never read *Sartor Resartus*.

————. *Wilhelm Meister's Apprenticeship and Travels*. 3 vols. London: Chapman and Hall (Volume I); New York: Scribner, Welford, and Co. (Volumes II and III), 1874.

Catalog: Ball 2016 inventory, reddish-brown cloth, gilt lettering on spine, black lettering on cover design.

Location: Quarry Farm library shelves, under the supervision of the Mark Twain Archive, Elmira College, Elmira, New York.

Copy examined: unmarked copy to which Clemens had access whenever he visited Quarry Farm in Elmira.

Carlyle translated Johann Wolfgang Goethe's *bildungsroman* (1795–1796, rev. 1829) from the German.

CARMAN, BLISS (1861–1929). *Low Tide on Grand Pré: A Book of Lyrics*. New York: C. L. Webster & Co., 1893. 120 pp.

Clemens's publishing firm, which he often supervised, issued this volume of poetry by the Canadian poet Carman, who resided in the United States. Carman would be among those who attended Clemens's Seventieth Birthday Dinner at Delmonico's in New York City on 5 December 1905. The scenic Grand-Pré area of Nova Scotia is a tidal marshland.

CARNAN D'ACHE, pseud. of EMMANUEL POIRÉ (1858–1909). *Bric à Brac; Album par Carnan d'Ache*. Paris: E. Plon, n.d. 52 pp.

Caricatures and cartoons by the French wit and comic artist Carnan d'Ache. Clemens noted the title, author, and publisher in December 1893 when he was in New York City (NB 33, TS p. 40).

CARNEGIE, ANDREW (1835–1919). *James Watt*. New York: Doubleday, Page & Co., 1905. 241 pp.

Inscription: inscribed in pencil on the half-title page: "To one I am proud to/call friend/ Mr. Clemen<t>s/Andrew Carnegie/Dec 16th 1905".

Marginalia: no markings, but page 37 is folded down.

Location: Mark Twain Library, Redding, Connecticut.

Copy examined: Clemens's copy.

Clemens and Carnegie would facetiously refer to each other as "St. Mark" and "St. Andrew." Carnegie was one of the guests at the Seventieth Birthday celebration for Mark Twain held at Delmonico's on 5 December 1905. See also the Catalog entry for Henry Dircks, *The Life, Times and Scientific Labours of the Second Marquis of Worcester*, for related information about Clemens's view of James

Watt (1736–1819).

———. *Round the World*. Original red cloth, gilt, yellow-coated endpapers. New York: Charles Scribner's Sons, 1888. 360 pp. [First published in 1884.]

Catalogs: *A1911*, "12mo, cloth, N.Y., 1888," lot 69; 19th Century Shop, Catalog 36, September 1994, item #107, contains the *A1911* sale label, $850; *Sotheby's 2003*, #212, $6,000 (sold with five other history and travel titles).

Provenance: collection of Nick Karanovich, Fort Wayne, Indiana.

Location: collection of Kevin Mac Donnell, Austin, Texas.

Copy examined: Clemens's copy, unmarked, in July 2004. Has an *A1911* sale label.

This might have been one of the books that Clemens acknowledged receiving from Carnegie on 17 March 1890 (NYPL). Carnegie's travel log of his voyage around the world with his friend William W. Vandervort featured his impressions of Japan, China, India, Egypt, and Italy.

———. *Triumphant Democracy; or Fifty Years' March of the Republic*. New York: Charles Scribner's Sons, 1888. 519 pp.

Inscription: on the dedicatory page, in Carnegie's hand: "S. L. Clemens, Esq. with regards of his fellow Republican/ Andrew Carnegie."

Catalog: *A1911*, "12mo, cloth, N.Y. 1888," quotes the inscription, lot 68, sold for $11.

Provenance: collection of Frank C. Willson (1889–1960), Melrose, Massachusetts.

Location: Harry Ransom Center, University of Texas at Austin. Purchased in 1962 from Margarete Willson, the widow of Frank C. Willson.

Copy examined: Clemens's copy.

On 17 March 1890 Clemens thanked Carnegie for "the books," and added that *Triumphant Democracy* was a "favorite" volume that "helped to fire me up" for writing *A Connecticut Yankee in King Arthur's Court* (1889). Clemens was rereading the anti-monarchical *Triumphant Democracy* again just then, he said (NYPL). Carnegie dedicated his book "To the BELOVED REPUBLIC under whose equal laws I am made the peer of any man, although denied political equality by my native land." *Triumphant Democracy* set out to vindicate the American republic against its English critics. It endeavored to show that America has more of everything—art, music, literature, products, and institutions. The Scottish-born Carnegie concluded, "So, my fellow Republicans, the world is coming rapidly to your feet, the American Constitution is being more and more generally regarded as the model for all new nations to adopt and for all old nations to strive for" (p. 506). In a 1903 Italian interview (if it was reported correctly), Mark Twain seemed ambivalent about his friend: "Andrew Carnegie, the Jesus Christ of riches, the evangelist of the Omnipotent Dollar, is sometimes amusing; at others, he is tiresome. When he throws out his great theories of high social economics, his extraordinary meditations on capitalistic-aerostatic socialism, you would rather move the stone of Sisyphus or fill the well of Saint Patrick, two examples which are very well suited to his reformist eccentricities. Carnegie, however, is . . . consecrating great sums on behalf of charities. Penance fitting for a sinner!" In an unidentified article headlined "Mark Twain Says It's All Rubbish," Twain defended Andrew Carnegie's "kindly,

courteous nature" (clipping in James D. Hart's scholarship file; sent to Alan Gribben in 1980).

James D. Williams, "Use of History" (1965), pp. 106–107; Howard G. Baetzhold, *MT&JB* (1970), pp. 341 n. 19, 342, n. 17; Michael Shelden, *Man in White* (2010), pp. 155–162.

CARTER, JOHN HENTON (1832–1910), pseud. "Commodore Rollingpin." *Commodore Rollingpin's Almanac* [Sometimes appearing as *Commodore Rollingpin's Annual*, it was published for numerous years beginning in 1872].

John Henton Carter was a St. Louis reporter for the *St. Louis Post-Dispatch* as well as being a humorous writer and a river historian of sorts. Mark Twain was in touch with Carter during Twain's brief stay in St. Louis in 1882 and the men corresponded before and after that visit. Carter occasionally reprinted, with permission, some of Twain's material. Chapter 16 of *Mark Twain's Life on the Mississippi* (1883) credits "Commodore Rollingpin's Almanac" for detailed records of the fastest steamboat trips made on the Mississippi River.

Blair, MT&HF (1960), pp. 286–287; Hill, *MTLP* (1967), pp. 156–157.

———. *The Log of Commodore Rollingpin: His Adventures Afloat and Ashore*. New York: G. W. Carleton, 1874. 258 pp.

It seems highly likely that Mark Twain knew of Carter's compilation of these largely humorous sketches and poems about river life, since Carter's book first appeared around the time when Twain resolved to write an *Atlantic Monthly* series about his days as steamboat pilot.

Lee Ann Sandweiss, *Seeking St. Louis: Voices from a River City, 1670–2000* (St. Louis: Missouri Historical Society Press, 2000), p. 277; Thomas Ruys Smith, "'The Mississippi Was a Virgin Field': Reconstructing the River Before Mark Twain, 1865–1875," *Mark Twain Journal* 53.2 (Fall 2015): 55–56.

Cartoons from "Punch." Illus. 4 vols. London: Bradbury, Agnew & Co., 1906.

Inscriptions: the front pastedown endpaper of each volume is signed "S. L. Clemens/ 1906". The bookplate of William Harris Arnold is affixed to the front pastedown endpaper.

Catalogs: *A1911*, "Vols. I-IV. Illustrated. 4 vols., 4to, cloth, London. 1906," quotes the signatures, lot 393, sold for $5.50; *Literature List No. 126*, Pt. 2 (1971), Strand Book Store, New York City, item #4611, $200.

Location: Mark Twain House and Museum, Hartford, Connecticut. Four volumes, donated anonymously in 1975 through Black Sun Books, New York City. Valued at $400 (Polly Peck, then an administrator of the Mark Twain House, supplied this information.)

Copies examined: Clemens's copies. Examined in August 1987. The *A1911* sale label is present.

CARTWRIGHT, JULIE (1851–1924), also known as Mrs. Henry Ady. *Jean François Millet: His Life and Letters*. London: Swan Sonnenschein & Co., 1896. 396 pp.

Catalog: Ball 2016 inventory, green cloth, gilt lettering, gilt top edges, good condition.

Location: Quarry Farm library shelves, under the supervision of the Mark Twain Archive, Elmira College, Elmira, New York.

This biography was available to Clemens at Quarry Farm in Elmira.

CARTWRIGHT, PETER (1785–1872). *Autobiography of Peter Cartwright, the Backwoods Preacher.* Ed. by William Peter Strickland (1809–1884). New York: Carlton & Porter, 1857. 525 pp. [Publisher and pages conjectured.]

> **Catalog:** *A1911*, "12mo, cloth (worn), N.Y. 1857," lot 70, sold for $1.50.

Cartwright was a frontier Methodist circuit rider and revival preacher.

CASANOVA DE SEINGALT, GIACOMO (1725–1798). *Mémoires de Jacques Casanova de Seingalt, Écrits par lui-même.* 10 vols. Paris: Paulin, Librari-Éditeur, 1833–37. [Rebound.]

> **Inscriptions:** Volume I is signed in pencil on the front free endpaper: "S. L. Clemens/Paris, July 1879"; Volume II is signed: "S. L. Clemens/Paris, 1879." The other volumes are not inscribed.
>
> **Marginalia:** pencil markings are scattered throughout the volumes: Volume I contains vertical lines on pages 98, 282, 284, 380, heavy underlining in the first paragraph of page 107, and notes and markings on pages 255 and 358; Volume II has no markings except for Clemens's signature; Volume III contains neither a signature nor any marks; Volume IV has vertical pencil lines on pages 307, 308, 315, 316, 355, 363, 364, 365, 427, 445, and (at the conclusion of the first paragraph on page 200) a note, "Horrible!" Penciled diagrams are on the recto and verso of the front free endpaper in Volume V, together with vertical marks on pages 8 and 15. No markings are visible in Volumes VI, VII, or VIII. Pencil marks occur on pages 32 and 42 of Volume IX. No markings are visible in Volume X, but the front free endpaper contains small holes where Clemens once pinned his pamphlet copy of *The Case of C. O. Godfrey* (now in MTP).

Catalog: *C1951*, D5, $40.

Location: University Research Library, University of California at Los Angeles.

Copies examined: Clemens's copies, in 1970.

On 26 February 1880 Clemens explained to his brother Orion that Casanova's Mémoires "are not printed in English. . . . He frankly, flowingly, & felicitously tells the dirtiest & vilest & most contemptible things on himself, without ever suspecting that they are other than things which the reader will admire & applaud" (*MTBus*, pp. 143–144). In "The Walt Whitman Controversy" (written in 1882?) Mark Twain listed Casanova's Mémoires among the "old bad books" he owns, and quoted a comically expurgated passage from Chapter 5 of "that richest of all rich mines" of obscenity (DV36, MTP). Clemens mentioned "the fifth volume of Casanova" in French among his recent reading in a letter to Edward H. House on 14 January 1884 (ASSSCL). In Chapter 35 of *Adventures of Huckleberry Finn* (1885) Tom Sawyer models himself on the "heroes" of this and other books. Hank Morgan referred to the torture of "Louis XV.'s poor awkward enemy" in Chapter 18 of *A Connecticut Yankee in King Arthur's Court* (1889), and cited "the pleasant Casanova" as his source for the horrific ordeal of the French fanatic Robert François Damiens, who attempted to assassinate the king in 1757 (see also *CY*, p. 563).

Henry Pochmann, "The Mind of Mark Twain" (1924), pp. 16, 151.

CASE, FRANCES POWELL (1855–1936), pseud. "FRANCES

POWELL. *The Prisoner of Ornith Farm.* New York: Charles Scribner's Sons, 1906. 315 pp. [Portrait of the author tipped in on the front pastedown endpaper.]

> **Inscription:** inscribed in black ink on the front free endpaper: "'He didn't ever have to tell anybody to mind their manners—everybody was always good-mannered where he was. Everybody loved to have him around, too; he was sunshine—'/Mr. Samuel Langhorne Clemens/with sincere admiration—and respect./ Frances Powell Case/Flotsam,/ Wainscott, Long Island./August, 1906."
>
> **Location:** Mark Twain Library, Redding, Connecticut.
>
> **Copy examined:** Clemens's copy, unmarked. Examined in 1970 and again in June 1982. Has a red ink Mark Twain Library accession number—"2569".

CASEMENT, (SIR) ROGER DAVID (1864–1916). *Treatment of Women and Children in the Congo State; What Mr. Casement Saw in 1903.*

> King Leopold quotes extensively from a pamphlet about Casement's observations, excoriating "that spy, that busy-body" in "King Leopold's Soliloquy" (1905). In 1904 Casement had delivered an official report to Parliament on the human rights abuses he witnessed in the Belgian Congo. During World War I Casement, an Irish nationalist, would be stripped of his title and hanged for treason in 1916.

The Case of C. O. Godfrey. [Hannibal, Missouri? 1880?]. 11 pp. Tiny, unbound pamphlet.

> **Inscription:** in pencil on front of first leaf: "Both of these 'ladies' are wealthy, & move in the first society of their city. I knew them as little girls. SLC." Below this he added: "The guilt of neither of them is doubted" (*HH&T*, p. 26 n. 4).
>
> **Location:** Mark Twain Papers, Bancroft Library, University of California at Berkeley. Pinholes penetrate all of the leaves where the pamphlet was once attached to the first flyleaf of Volume 10 of *Mémoires de Jacques Casanova de Seingalt.*
>
> **Copy examined:** Clemens's copy.

The pamphlet presents the proceedings of a trial held by the Congregational church of Hannibal to judge the personal morals of a parishioner, C. O. Godfrey, charged with adultery. His admissions are extremely detailed, though he denied actually having sexual intercourse with the woman, Mrs. M. E. Cruikshank. Mrs. Cruikshank's husband, John, was suspected of an adulterous affair with Mrs. C. P. Heywood.

Cassell's Dictionary of Cookery, with about 9,000 Recipes. Illus. London: Cassell and Co. [Exact edition unknown; there were many].

> The Clemenses requested a copy of this book in 1896 (Clemens via Olivia Clemens to Chatto & Windus, December 1896, Berg Collection, New York Public Library).

CASTER, ANDREW. *Pearl Island.* Illustrated by Florence Scovel Shinn (1871–1940). New York: Harper & Brothers, 1903. 267 pp.

> **Marginalia:** Clemens had a low opinion of this novel about two youths shipwrecked in the Indian Ocean. He penciled a total of 263 derogatory comments and markings throughout the book. On the front free endpaper, he wrote, vertically: "The conversations in this book are incomparably idiotic." Across the top of the title page: "Containing many interesting facts plundered from

the cyclopedia." There are numerous similarly sneering comments in the margins, for example (bottom of page 63): "Son of a bitch, why don't you pray—& *say* you are thankful?" On the verso of an illustration opposite page 259, written vertically: "This person has even stolen material from the French fraud who was exposed in London in 1900." Beside a hint in the concluding paragraph (p. 267) that Caster might relate additional adventures in another volume: "If you do, you ought to be flayed & then hanged."

Catalog: ListABP (1910), "Pearl Island, Ros".

Provenance: Antenne-Dorrance Collection, Rice Lake, Wisconsin.

Location: Mark Twain Archive, Gannett-Tripp Learning Center, Elmira College, Elmira, New York. Donated in 1994.

Copy examined: Clemens's copy.

Mark Woodhouse, "'Flayed and Then Hanged': Samuel Clemens Reads Pearl Island," *American Literary Realism* 42.1 (Fall 2009): 72–78. (Woodhouse was the curator of the Mark Twain Archive when the Antennes donated this annotated volume.)

———. *Pearl Island*. Illustrated by Florence Scovel Shinn (1871–1940). New York: Harper & Brothers, 1903. 267 pp.

Source: MTLAcc, entry #448, volume donated by Clemens.

Catalogue of Oil Paintings. Illus. Melbourne: Ferguson & Mitchell, 1904. 37 pp. (36 illustrations).

Source: MTLAcc, entry #402, volume donated by Isabel V. Lyon, Clemens's secretary.

Cat and Dog Stories (unidentified book title).

Catalog: ListABP (1910), "Cat and Dog Stories", no other information supplied.

CATELIN, CAMILLE DE (PSEUD. "STÉPHEN D'ARVE") (1820–1909). *Histoire du Mont Blanc et de la vallée de Chamonix. Ascensions catastrophes célèbres, depuis les prémières explorations*. Preface by Francis Wey (1812–1882). 2 vols. in one. Paris: Delagrave, [1878].

In Chapter 40 of *A Tramp Abroad* (1880) Mark Twain quotes from D'Arve's grisly account of the discovery in 1861 of the remains of three mountaineers lost in 1820; they had been frozen in a glacier. Twain mentions Stéphen d'Arve's book by its title in Chapter 44, and quotes directly from it in Chapter 45 concerning eleven mountain climbers frozen to death in 1870 while descending Mont Blanc.

CATHER, WILLA SIBERT (1873–1947). "The Palatine" (poem), *New York Times Review* 14 (May 22, 1909): 317; reprinted in *McClure's Magazine* 33.2 (June 1909): 158–159.

Clemens praised the initial publication of "The Palatine" in a conversation with Albert Bigelow Paine: "Here is a fine poem, a great poem, I think" (*MTB*, p. 1501).

———. *The Troll Garden*. New York: McClure, Phillips & Co., 1905. [Collection of short stories.]

"We sent you a little while ago a copy of 'The Troll Garden' by Miss Willa Sibert Cather. . . . We are venturing to call it to the attention of a few people, like yourself, of discernment and appreciation of the better sort of thing" (John S. Phillips, McClure, Phillips & Co., to SLC, 14 April 1905, MTP). Cather would attend the Seventieth Birthday celebration dinner for Mark Twain held at Delmonico's in December 1905.

CATLIN, GEORGE (1796–1872).

Mark Twain's quotes from Catlin's *Indian Tribes*, Volume 1, p. 86 in a discarded chapter of *A Tramp Abroad* (1880) that describes courtship and marriage practices among primitive tribes (verso of MS p. 70, Box 6, no. 7, MTP). Caitlin's observations of North American Indian customs appeared under several titles and in various editions; none of them is specifically titled *Indian Tribes*.

CATULLUS, GAIUS VALERIUS (c. 84–54 BCE). *The Works of Catullus and* [Albius] *Tibullus [c. 60–90 BCE], and the Vigil of Venus. A Literal Prose Translation, with Notes, by Walter K[eating]. Kelly [1810–1870]. Metrical Versions by [George] Lamb [1784–1834] and [James] Grainger [c. 1721–1766] Appended*. Bohn's Classical Library Series. Frontispiece. Original dark green cloth, gilt. London: Henry G. Bohn, 1854. 400 pp.

Inscription: inscribed by Clemens in ink on the title page: "Saml. L. Clemens/Hartford, 1875."

Catalogs: A1911, "12mo, cloth, uncut, Lond.: Bohn, 1854," quotes signature, lot 71, sold for $4.50; *Selections from the Library of William E. Boeing, Part II* (2011), comp. Joseph C. Baillargeon, Restoration Books, Seattle, Washington, p. 64.

Copy examined: a facsimile of Clemens's inscription was reproduced in the Boeing catalog.

Location: collection of Kevin Mac Donnell, Austin, Texas. He reported that the *A1911* auction label is present on the front pastedown and that page 49 (only) is folded down (Mac Donnell to Alan Gribben, 29 November 2011). No marginalia are visible.

"Catullus" is the playful name of a cat in Twain's "A Cat Tale" (written in 1880).

CAWOOD, JOHN (1775–1852). "Hark! what mean those holy voices" (hymn).

See the Catalog entry for George Jarvis Geer, composer.

CAZIN, ACHILLE AUGUSTE (1832–1877). *The Phenomena and Laws of Heat*. Trans. and ed. by Elihu Rich (1819–1875). Illus. New York: Scribner, Armstrong & Co., 1872. 265 pp.

Source: MTLAcc, entry #1987, volume donated from Clemens's library by Clara Clemens Gabrilowitsch in 1910.

CELLINI, BENVENUTO (1500–1571). *The Life of Benvenuto Cellini, Newly Translated into English*. Trans. from the Italian by John Addington Symonds (1840–1893). Illustrated by F[rederic]. [Auguste] Laguillermie (1841–1907). 2 vols. London: J. C. Nimmo, 1888.

Cellini would have been cited in Mark Twain's proposed appendix to *A Connecticut Yankee in King Arthur's Court* (Howard G. Baetzhold, "Course of Composition" [1961], p. 200). In Chapter 17 of that novel (1889), Hank Morgan alludes to "Benvenuto Cellini, that rough-hewn saint, ten centuries later." In July 1892, aboard the S. S. *Lahn*, Clemens noted: "Symod's [sic] Life of Cellini. Nimmo" (NB 32, TS p. 11). (See also the Catalog entry for Kingsley's *Heroes*.) Cellini's account of Florentine Renaissance life influenced "A Whisper to the Reader," the preface to *Pudd'nhead Wilson* (1894), which mentions Giotto's campanile, Dante's awaiting Beatrice, and a Ghibelline outbreak. Cellini was to appear in Mark Twain's projected "Back Number" magazine (NB 33 [January 1894], TS p. 46). In an essay often known as "Memories of a Missouri Farm" (DV274[2], MTP), an early section of Mark Twain's autobiography probably written in the winter of 1897–1898, he remarked: "The incident of Benvenuto Cellini and the salamander must be accepted as authentic and trustworthy" (*MTA*, 1: 95; *AutoMT* 1: 209). Subsequently he would say: "If Benvenuto Cellini's salamander had been in that place [the Whittier Birthday dinner] he would not have survived to be put into Cellini's autobiography" (11 January 1906 AD, *AutoMT* 1: 266). The salamander incident occurs in Chapter 1 of Cellini's Autobiography: when Cellini was five years old, his father, spying a rarely seen salamander emerge from logs in the hearth and seem to enjoy the warmth of the flames, boxed his son's ear so that he would remember the incident. Twain remarked in an Autobiographical Dictation on 23 February 1906 that "Benvenuto tells a number of things that any other human being would be ashamed of" (*AutoMT* 1 378).

Olin Harris Moore, "Mark Twain and Don Quixote" (1922), pp. 333–335; Henry Pochmann, "Mind of MT" (1924), p. 15.

————. *Memoirs of Benvenuto Cellini, A Florentine Artist; Written by Himself: Containing a Variety of Information Respecting the Arts, and the History of the Sixteenth Century. Now first Collated with the New Text of Guiseppe Molini [1772–1856]; and Corrected and Enlarged from the Last Milan Edition, with Notes and Observations by G[iovanni]. P[alamede]. Carpani [1775–1857]. Translated by Thomas Roscoe [1791–1871].*

"Autobiog's? I didn't know there were any but old Franklin's & Benvenuto Cellini's," Clemens remarked to William Dean Howells on 6 June 1877 (*MTHL*, p. 180). A series of notes show that Cellini's *Memoirs* were much on Clemens's mind in 1878 and 1879. "Benvenuto Cellini (what an interesting autobiography is his!)," he jotted in October 1878 (NB 17, *N&J* 2: 227). In that same month he made a memorandum to "send to Chatto for . . . Benvenuto" (NB 17, *N&J* 2: 234). He alluded to "that most entertaining of books, Benvenuto's. It will last as long as his beautiful Perseus" (NB 17 [October 1878], *N&J* 2: 229). References in Notebook 17 (1878, *N&J* 2: 234) duplicate language from the explanatory notes in *Memoirs of Benvenuto Cellini*, trans. Thomas Roscoe (London: Henry G. Bohn, 1850). Cellini is mentioned jokingly in Notebook 18 (1879, *N&J* 2: 298). The royal furniture in Tom Canty's new room "is beautiful by designs which wellnigh made it priceless, since they were the work of Benvenuto" (Chapter 7 of *P&P* [1881]). Tom Sawyer is astounded that Huck Finn has never read "Benvenuto Chelleeny . . . nor none of them heroes" (Chapter 35 of *HF* [1885]). "One believes St. S[imon] & Benvenuto," Clemens observed (NB 26 [1886], *N&J* 3: 239).

Centennial Ode. Illus. [Unidentified poem].

James R. Osgood & Company of Boston billed Clemens $3.20 ($4.20 before his author's discount) for "Centennial Ode Ill[d]," purchased on 21 January 1877; Clemens paid the bill on 13 November 1877 (Scrapbook #10, p. 69, MTP). Evidently this was not Rebecca S. Pollard's *Centennial and Other Poems* (1876), since Clemens signed his copy of her book in 1876. See the Catalog entry for Bayard Taylor's *The National Ode* (1877), a more likely candidate.

Les Cent Nouvelles Nouvelles (collection of French tales, first published in 1462).

In "The Walt Whitman Controversy" (1882?) Mark Twain states that he owns a copy of these tales, although their licentiousness surpasses that allowed modern works (DV36, MTP).

The Century Cyclopedia of Names. A Pronouncing and Etymological Dictionary of Names in Geography, Biography, Mythology, History, Etc. Ed. by Benjamin Eli Smith (1857–1913) et al. New York: Century Co., 1900. 1085 pp.

Catalog: *A1911*, "4to, cloth, uncut, N.Y. 1900, &c.," lot 128, sold for $8.

Century Magazine (published 1881–1930; previously titled *Scribner's Monthly*).

On 18 March 1885 Clemens wrote to Robert Underwood Johnson in response to an invitation to contribute an essay: "I would like mighty well to be in the Century War Series. . . . The fact is, the War Series is the greatest thing of these modern times" ("Three Mark Twain Letters," *Mark Twain Quarterly* 7.1 [Summer-Fall 1945]: 24). In a subsequent letter to Underwood on 15 August 1885 Clemens called Century Magazine "the best magazine that was ever printed," noting that this was "not intemperate language" ("Twain to R. U. Johnson," *Mark Twain Quarterly* 6.4 [Winter-Spring 1945]: 23). Clemens wished to "scrapbook" a story from the April 1891 issue—"Notes by T. Cole on the 'Adoration'" (NB 30 [April 1891], *N&J* 3: 617). Issues were supposed to be mailed to him in Europe in May 1891 (NB 30, *N&J* 3: 628). He was disgruntled with an article about a portrait of Columbus (SLC to Mr. Hogue, 14 October 1892, ASSSCL); mentioned an article about Nikola Tesla "in Jan. or Feb. Century" (SLC to OLC, 7 February 1894, partially published in *MTL*, p. 609); recommended to Susy and Clara Clemens an article in the February 1894 issue (SLC to OLC, 9 February 1894, *LLMT*, p. 294); complained to F. G. Whitmore that it has been "many months" since a Century issue had arrived (7 October 1894, CWB); complained to F. G. Whitmore on 6 November 1894 from Paris that the last three numbers of Century arrived all at once (MTP); received a subscription by mail while residing in Kaltenleutgeben, Austria (SLC to JHT, 13 Sept. 1898, *MTL*, p. 666; *LMTJHT*, p. 220); praised several pieces "in the Century which arrived this morning" in 1899 (SLC to Richard Watson Gilder, Vienna, 2 Feb. 1899, PH in MTP); and consulted "the bound Century" at the offices of the Century Company in 1901 (SLC to R. U. Johnson, postcard, 31 March 1901?, ASSSCL).

CERVANTES SAAVEDRA, MIGUEL DE (1547–1616). *Don Quixote.* Illus.

Catalog: *C1951*, #4c, "with illustrations," $25, edition not indicated, listed among books signed by Clemens.

Location: unknown. This is one of the most tantalizing items still missing from the Hollywood auction.

On 18 March 1861, in St. Louis, Clemens called *Don Quixote* one of his "beau ideals of fine writing" (SLC to Orion Clemens, *MTL*, p. 45; *MTLet* 1: 117). The countryside in the southern provinces of Spain seemed "precisely as it was when Don Quixote & Sancho Panza were possible characters," he observed on 24 October 1867 (SLC to Jane Lampton Clemens and family, *MTL*, p. 138; *MTLet* 2: 99). From Rochester, New York he seriously advised

Olivia Langdon on 2 March 1869 not to finish the book until he could censor it for her: "Don Quixote is one of the most exquisite books that was ever written, & to lose it from the world's literature would be as the wresting of a constellation from the symmetry & perfection of the firmament," but "neither it nor Shakespeare are proper books for virgins to read until some hand has culled them of their grossness" (*LLMT*, p. 76; *MTLet* 3: 132–133). On 6 January 1870 Clemens informed Olivia from New York City that he would entrust his copy of *Don Quixote* to Susan Crane's safekeeping until his return: "I hold her strictly responsible for it. And she might as well abuse Livy as abuse that book" (*MTLet* 4: 1). Mark Twain mentioned Don Quixote in "A Royal Compliment" (September 1870 *Galaxy*, *CG*, p. 73). Cervantes's writings formed one of the topics of discourse in Twain's innuendo-laden *1601* (written in 1876).

Cervantes, Clemens noted, had the *"best* of opportunities" for writing a masterpiece—"solitary imprisonment, by compulsion" (SLC to Mollie Fairbanks, 6 August 1877, *MTMF*, pp. 206–207). Simon Wheeler "was another Don Quixotte [*sic*], and his library of illustrious shams [was] as honored, as valued, and as faithfully studied and believed in as was the Don's" ("Simon Wheeler, Detective," written 1877–1898?, *S&B*, p. 439). Clemens made a note about Don Quixote in 1880 (NB 19, *N&J* 2: 359). "When DeSoto stood on the banks of the Mississippi . . . 'Don Quixote' was not yet written" (Chapter 1, *LonMiss* [1883]); later, *Don Quixote* "swept the world's admiration for the mediaeval chivalry-silliness out of existence," but Scott's *Ivanhoe* restored it (Chapter 46, *LonMiss*). Twain resolved in November 1893 to "speak to Howells" about dramatizing *Don Quixote* (NB 33, TS p. 38). Addressing political prisoners in South Africa in 1896, Twain reminded the men that "Cervantes, too, was likewise privileged to suffer durance vile and was thus enabled to write 'Don Quixote,' a romance which would exist as long as language endured. . . . Cervantes was roaming about on the wings of imagination in company with such delightful spirits as Don Juan [*sic*] and Sancho Panza" ("Mark Twain in Gaol," Pretoria *Press*, 25 May 1896; reprinted in the *Mark Twain Journal* 40.1 [Spring 2002]: 39). The devil in "Conversation with Satan" (fragment, written in 1898) bears the "features of 'Don Quixotte[*sic*]'" (Paine 255, MTP, quoted in *MSM* [1969], p. 17). "We should not have had the pleasure of reading *Don Quixote* if Cervantes had not spent several years in prison," Twain recalled telling the Jameson raiders incarcerated at Pretoria ("Mark Twain Home, an Anti-Imperialist," New York *Herald*, 16 October 1900; *Complete Interviews*, p. 355). The cholera germ in "Three Thousand Years among the Microbes" (written in 1905) names two of the microbes "Don Quixotte [*sic*]" and "Sancho Panza" (*WWD?*, p. 472). In working notes for "No. 44, The Mysterious Stranger" (written 1902–1908), the character known as 44 was supposed to summon "St George from the past, Don Quixotte [*sic*] from the future & *try* to interest a tournament" (*MSM*, p. 464). Soon after Clemens's death, Henry Watterson shared vivid reminiscences of his relationship with the author; they included a reference Clemens made to Cervantes ("Mark Twain—An Intimate Memory," *American Magazine* 70 (July 1910): 372–375.

Olin Harris Moore, "Mark Twain and Don Quixote" (1922), pp. 337–339 especially, initiated the discussion of Cervantes's importance to Mark Twain; many other scholars followed his lead: Henry Pochmann, "The Mind of Mark Twain" (1924), pp. 17 n. 3, 152; Mary Teresa Roades, "*Don Quixote* and *A Connecticut Yankee in King Arthur's Court*," *Mark Twain Quarterly* 2.4 (Summer-Fall 1938): 8–9; Ferguson, *MTM&L* (1943), p. 26; Lois M. Sutton, "The Influence of Don Quixote in the Works of Mark Twain," Master's thesis, Baylor University, 1946; Stephen Gilman, "Cervantes en la obra de Mark Twain," *Cuadernos de Insula* 1 (Madrid, 1947): 204–222; Gladys Bellamy, *MTLA* (1950), p. 46; George Santayana, "Tom Sawyer and Don Quixote," *Mark Twain Quarterly* 9.2 [Winter 1952]: 1–3; Mary Teresa Roades, "Was Mark Twain Influenced by the Prolog to *Don Quixote*?," *Mark Twain Quarterly* 9.2 [Winter 1952]: 4–6, 24; Walter Blair, *MT&HF* (1960), p. 349; Robert Regan, *UH* (1966), p. 133; Edward Wagenknecht, *MTMW* (1967), p. 62; Sydney Krause, *MTC* (1967), p. 118 n. 7; Walter Blair, ed., *HH&T* (1969), p. 109; Jeanne Bugliari, "The Picaresque as a Flaw in Mark Twain's Novels," *Mark Twain Journal* 15.4 (Summer 1971): 10–12; Edward L. Galligan, "True Comedians and False: *Don Quixote* and *Huckleberry Finn*," *Sewanee Review* 86.1 (Winter 1978): 66–83 (argued that Tom Sawyer was a "false comedian"); Joseph H. Harkey, "Mark Twain's Knights and Squires," *Mark Twain Journal* 20.3 (Winter 1980–1981): 6–13 (quite comprehensive); Walter L. Reed, *An Exemplary History of the Novel: The Quixote Versus the Picaresque* (Chicago: University of Chicago Press, 1981), pp. 197–231, argued that in *A Connecticut Yankee in King Arthur's Court* Twain recognized some darker, less alluring aspects of Quixotic visions; and Everett Carter, "The Modernist Ordeal of Huckleberry Finn," *Studies in American Fiction* 13.2 (Autumn 1985): 178–179. Arturo Serrano-Plaja, *"Magic" Realism in Cervantes: Don Quixote as Seen Through Tom Sawyer and The Idiot*. Trans. by Robert S. Rudder (Berkeley: University of California Press, 1970) merits special notice. He credited Twain for recognizing the "magic" in *Don Quixote* and substituting a child, Tom Sawyer, for the knight—thus heightening the perplexity between real life (Hannibal) and games (chivalresque). "Mark Twain helps us see something essential which mere literary criticism has not seen: the highly childish character of Don Quixote and Sancho" (p. 25). Seranno-Plaja treated *Tom Sawyer* and *Huckleberry Finn* in detail, primarily because they illuminate the achievements of Cervantes's masterpiece. Twain's work is discussed most significantly on pages 20–27, 81–95, 100–101, 114–115, 117–118, 130–213 passim of this book, which contains no index. In 2016 Michael David MacBride challenged the assumptions of Olin H. Moore and other commentators who insisted that Tom Sawyer was modeled on Don Quixote; MacBride argued that Jim is more logically "the real embodiment of Quixote himself" ("The Quixotic Dream of Mark Twain's Jim," *Mark Twain Annual* 14 (2016): 93–103.

———. *The Exemplary Novels of Miguel de Cervantes Saavedra: To Which Are Added El Buscapié, or, The Serpent; and La Tia Fingida, or, The Pretended Aunt*. Trans. from the Spanish by

Walter K[eating]. Kelly (1810–1870). Engraved frontispiece of the author. Original embossed brown cloth, gilt. Front cover loosening, ends of spine and corners worn. First edition. London: Henry G. Bohn, 1855. 484 pp.

Inscription: half-title page signed in brown ink: "Saml. L. Clemens/Hartford, 1875."

Provenance: shelfmark of Clara Clemens Gabrilowitsch's private library in Detroit. Donated to the Carrie Estelle Doheny Collection, St. John's Seminary, Camarillo, California by Mrs. Doheny in 1940 after its purchase from Maxwell Hunley Rare Books, Beverly Hills, for $12.20. Sold by Christie's in 1988 at the behest of St. John's Seminary and the Archdiocese of Los Angeles. Subsequently in the collection of Nick Karanovich, Fort Wayne, Indiana.

Catalogs: Christie's, New York City, 1–2 February 1988 auction, lot 465, sold (with three other books) for $2,750 to Randall House, Los Angeles; *Sotheby's 2003*, #221, sold with four other literature titles for $9,500.

Location: collection of Kevin Mac Donnell, Austin, Texas.

Copy examined: Clemens's unmarked copy, in July 2004. Has the bookplate of "Estelle Doheny."

———. *Galatea, A Pastoral Romance by Miguel de Cervantes Saavedra. Literally Translated by G[ordon]. W[illoughby]. J[ames]. Gyll [1818–1878].* London, 1867.

Inscription: on title page: "Saml. L. Clemens, Hartford, 1875."

Catalog: *A1911*, "12mo, cloth, Lond. 1867," quotes the signature, lot 74, sold for $3.

CHABANNES, CLÉMENTINE (DE LA MORRE) COMTESSE AR-MAND DE (1813–1901). *La Vierge Lorraine, Jeanne d' Arc: son histoire au point de vue de l'héroïsme, de la sainteté et du martyre.* Nouvelle Edition. Paris: E. Plon, Nourrit et Cie, 1890. Paperbound volume.

Marginalia: heavily annotated by Clemens in pencil and brown ink. Excerpts quoted in Salomon, *TIH* (1961), pp. 175, 178, 178 n. 4 and Stone, *IE* (1961), pp. 216–217, 224 n. 2.

Catalog: "Retz Appraisal" (1944), p. 8, valued at $20.

Location: Mark Twain Papers, Bancroft Library, University of California at Berkeley.

Copy examined: Clemens's copy.

Mark Twain listed this book among his "authorities examined" in writing *Joan of Arc* (1896) on the page preceding the "Translator's Preface."

Ronald Jenn and Linda A. Morris, "The Sources of Mark Twain's *Personal Recollections of Joan of Arc*," *Mark Twain Journal* 55.1–2 (Spring/Fall 2017): 55–74.

CHADWICK, JOHN WHITE (1840–1904). *George William Curtis, An Address.* Illus. New York: Harper & Brothers, 1893. 76 pp.

Source: MTLAcc, entry #1208, volume donated by Clemens.

The preface indicates that this eulogy was delivered on 22 February 1893 at the Brooklyn Institute of Arts and Sciences. Clemens was living in Florence, Italy at the time (Fears, *Day by Day* 2: 768). George William Curtis (1824–1892) had been an editor, essayist, and public speaker with strong ties to the Unitarian Church and the Republican Party. He was prominent in the national movement to reform the civil service system.

———. *Old and New Unitarian Belief.* Boston: G. H. Ellis,

1894. 246 pp. [Edition conjectured.]

Clemens wrote from London to his sister Pamela A. Moffett on 28 March 1897 to say that "Livy will be glad to read 'Beliefs of Unitarians.' [*sic*], & she will get value out of it; I am quite likely to read it myself, but my appetite is not over-strong" (Vassar College, Poughkeepsie, New York).

CHAFFERS, WILLIAM (1811–1892). *Handbook of Marks and Monograms on Pottery and Porcelain.* London: Bickers & Son, 1874. [Edition conjectured.]

Catalog: *C1951*, O12, listed among books containing Olivia Clemens's signature.

CHAILLÉ-LONG, CHARLES (1842–1917). *Central Africa: Naked Truths of Naked People. An Account of Expeditions.* Illustrated from sketches by the author. New York: Harper & Brothers, 1877. 330 pp.

Source: MTLAcc, entry #1724, volume donated by Clemens.

Mark Twain quotes from *A Summer in Africa* (no author's name supplied) and "Syme's" *Central Africa* in a discarded chapter from *A Tramp Abroad* (1880) that compares French courtship and marriage practices with the rituals of African tribes (MS p. 99, Box 6, no. 7, MTP). In both cases he seems to have been disguising the name of Chaillé-Long, who had published his provocatively titled *Central Africa: Naked Truths of Naked People* in 1877.

CHALMERS, JAMES (1841–1901). *Pioneer Life and Work in New Guinea, 1877–1894.* Map. Illus. London: The Religious Tract Society, 1895. 255 pp. [Edition conjectured.]

In March 1896, as Clemens was leaving India, he took down a passage from "New Guinea in '77–85' [*sic*] written by a missionary" (NB 36, TS p. 63).

CHALMERS, THOMAS (1780–1847). *The Works of Thomas Chalmers.* 3 vols. Bridgeport: M. Sherman, 1829.

Inscription: the front free endpaper of Volume I is signed in pencil, "J. Langdon".

Provenance: bookplates #337 and #338 of the "J. Langdon Family Library."

Catalog: Ball 2016 inventory, two volumes only, brown leather, poor condition.

Location: Quarry Farm library shelves, under the supervision of the Mark Twain Archive, Elmira College, Elmira, New York.

Copy examined: unmarked volumes available to Clemens whenever he visited Elmira. Only two volumes survive. Examined on 26 May 2016.

CHAMBERLIN, WILBUR J. (1866–1901).

Mark Twain cited Chamberlin as "the head of the Laffan news service in China" in an indignant letter to the New York *Tribune*, "Mark Twain's Answer," concerning the repercussions of the Boxer Rebellion (*MTPP*, p. 164).

Chambers's Cyclopaedia of English Literature: A History, Critical and Biographical, of British and American Authors, with Specimens of Their Writings. Originally Edited by Robert Chambers [1802–1871]. Revised by Robert Carruthers (1799–1878). [Edition not established; a Third edition of eight volumes appeared in 1880.]

Complaining about international copyright policy to William Dean Howells on 30 October 1880, Clemens mentioned, "I can buy ... Chambers's Cycopedia, 15 vols., cloth, for $7.25 (we paid $60)" (*MTHL*, p. 334). The number of volumes expanded as the original work added entries, but there is no record of a fifteen-volume format published by 1880.

Chambers's Journal of Popular Literature, Science, and Arts (periodical, Edinburgh, published under this title 1854–1897).

Hamlin Hill, "Mark Twain's 'Brace of Brief Lectures on Science,'" *New England Quarterly* 34.2 (June 1961): 228–239, pinpointed this journal as the source of paleontological information in Mark Twain's "A Brace of Brief Lectures on Science" (published in September and October 1871). Hill's article reprinted these two articles by Twain that appeared in the *American Publisher*, a monthly Hartford magazine edited by Orion Clemens. Twain's articles, Hill notes, reveal a dual awareness of (1) the comic potentiality of scientific imprecision and guesswork, and (2) unmistakable sympathy for the inductive methods used to proceed toward elusive truths. They satirized the tendency of scientists to hypothesize from meager evidence about the dates, conditions, and customs of prehistoric man. Twain was relying on an anonymous review article of Louis Figuier's *Primitive Man* (1870) entitled "Our Earliest Ancestors" that appeared in *Chambers's Journal* 47 (13 August 1870): 521–524. On 7 July 1871 Clemens wrote to Orion Clemens from Elmira to suggest corroboration for his points: "Look in the library—any late work on paleontology will furnish the facts. I got mine from an article in Chamber's [*sic*] Edinburgh Journal (have lost it since)" (*MTLet* 4: 429).

CHAMBERS, JULIUS (1850–1920). *The Destiny of Doris; A Travel-Story of Three Continents.* Illus. New York: Continental Publishing Co., 1901. 336 pp.

Source: MTLAcc, entry #2193, volume donated from Clemens's library by Clara Clemens Gabrilowitsch in 1910.

A fictionalized love story—the narrator resolves to marry Doris's mother—barely interrupts his description of foreign sights and a multitude of realistic photographs. The Mediterranean Coast, Egypt, and Italy are the principal destinations.

CHAMBERS, ROBERT (1802–1871), comp. *Domestic Annals of Scotland from the Reformation to the Revolution* [edition unknown; possibly the three-volume Third edition published by W. & R. Chambers of Edinburgh in 1874].

A letter from Clemens and his wife to Frederick J. Hall written in London on 27 September 1900 refers to an anecdote he had recently read in *Domestic Annals of Scotland* (Sotheby's catalog, 21 July 1992, item #47). I am grateful to JoDee Benussi for noticing this addition to Clemens's reading.

———. *Vestiges of the Natural History of Creation.* Intro. by Henry Morley (1822–1894). Morley's Universal Library Series. London: George Routledge and Sons, 1887. 286 pp.

Location: Special Collections, Elihu Burritt Library, Central Connecticut State University, New Britain, Connecticut.

Copy examined: photocopy of the title page in 1979. A card laid in the volume attests: "This is from M.T.'s Lib—flyleaf (probably inscribed) torn out. Some markings & underlining by S.L.C. No marginal notations. HLM". An accession notation on the title page accords with those found in other books that Clemens donated to the Mark Twain Library in Redding, Connecticut.

Mark Twain joshingly alludes to "Vestiges of Creation" as the work of T. H. Huxley (1825–1895) in his satirical "review"

of a non-existent book ("A Book Review," *Galaxy* 11.2 [February 1871]: 314; *CG*, pp. 122, 156). Huxley strenuously opposed the ideas inherent in Chambers's book, which had first been published anonymously in 1844.

CHAMBERS, ROBERT WILLIAM (1865–1933). *Cardigan; A Novel.* Illus. New York: Harper & Brothers, 1902. 513 pp.

Source: MTLAcc, entry #1312, volume donated by Clemens.

Chambers's literary reputation has not worn well, but he was both prolific and financially successful. Oddly, Clemens did not seem to own the *The King in Yellow* (1895), a collection of short stories that has maintained a following among science fiction buffs and is the only work by Chambers still discussed today.

———. *The Conspirators, A Romance.* Illus. New York: Harper & Brothers, 1905. 226 pp. Damaged copy.

Source: MTLAcc, entry # 1495, volume donated by Clemens.

———. *The Makers of Moons.* New York: G. P. Putnam's Sons, 1896. 401 pp.

Source: MTLAcc, entry #1046, volume donated by Clemens.

———. *River-Land, A Story for Children.* Illustrated by Elizabeth Shippen Green (1871–1954). New York: Harper & Brothers, 1904. 92 pp.

Source: MTLAcc, entry #507, volume donated by Clemens.

———. *A Young Man in a Hurry, and Other Short Stories.* Illus. New York: Harper & Brothers, 1904. 284 pp.

Source: MTLAcc, entry #81, volume donated by Clemens.

———. [Another identical copy.]

Source: MTLAcc, entry #1272, volume donated by Clemens.

CHAMISSO, ADELBERT VON (1781–1838). *Peter Schlemihl's wundersame Geschichte.* Nürnberg: J. L. Schrag, 1835.

Marginalia: underlinings and translations in Clemens's hand.

Location: unknown. Edgar H. Hemminghaus saw Clemens's copy in the Mark Twain Library at Redding in 1945 ("MT's German Provenience," p. 470), and Albert E. Stone included it in his catalog of Clemens's books still at the Mark Twain Library, Redding in 1955. However, the Mark Twain Library has since listed the volume as "not found," and I was unable to locate it on the premises in 1970 or thereafter. Information for this entry is taken from records in the Mark Twain Library, Redding.

———. *Peter Schlemihl's wundersame Geschichte.* Leipzig: Philipp Reclam, n.d. 72 pp.

Source: MTLAcc, entry #379, volume donated by Clemens.

———. *Peter Schlemihl's wundersame Geschichte. Nach des Dichters Tode neu hrsg. von Julius Eduard Hitzig [1780–1849]. Mit Anmerkungen und Vocabulair zum Uebersetzen ins Englische von F. Schröer.* Elfte Auflage. Hamburg: J. F. Richter, 1879. 93 pp.

Inscription: signed in pencil on the front free endpaper: "S. L. Clemens/Hartford, Conn."

Provenance: *C1951* auction label on the front pastedown endpaper.

Catalog: *Zeitlin 1951,* item #44, $35.

Location: Mark Twain Papers, Bancroft Library, University of California at Berkeley.

Copy examined: Clemens's copy, bound with Karl Gustav Nieritz' *Die Wunderpfeife.*

———. *The Shadowless Man; or, The Wonderful History of Peter Schlemihl*. Illus. London, n.d.

Inscriptions: "S. L. Clemens, Venice, Oct. 1878." Also signed "Olivia L. Clemens."

Catalog: *A1911*, "12mo, wrappers (one cover missing), Lond., n.d.," signatures quoted, lot 75, sold for $4.75.

In Chamisso's novella, first published in 1814, Peter Schlemihl sells his shadow to a strange man for an unending supply of gold, but finds that this lack of a natural appearance renders him a social outcast. Refusing to purchase his shadow back for the price of his soul, he becomes a wanderer who seeks scientific discoveries in the field of natural history.

Horst Kruse, "Chamisso's Peter Schlemihl and Mark Twain's Mysterious Stranger: German Literature and the Composition of the Mysterious Stranger Manuscripts," *Centenary Reflections on Mark Twain's* No. 44, *The Mysterious Stranger*, ed. Joseph Csicsila and Chad Rohman (Columbia: University of Missouri Press, 2009), pp. 71–87—an illuminating study.

CHAMPLIN, JOHN D[ENISON]., JR. (1834–1915). *Young Folks' Cyclopaedia of Common Things*. Illus. New York: Henry Holt & Co., 1879. 690 pp.

Clemens purchased "1 Cyclo. Common Things" at author's discount on 20 December 1880, according to a bill from Brown & Gross, Hartford booksellers (receipt dated 1 January 1881, MTP).

———, ed. *Cyclopedia of Painters and Paintings*. Charles C[allahan]. Perkins (1823–1886), "Critical Editor." 4 volumes. "More Than Two Thousand Illustrations." Burgandy cloth, some wear to edges and corners, rear hinge cracked in Volume 4, many leaves uncut in all four volumes. New York: Charles Scribner's Sons, 1887.

Inscriptions: all four volumes are inscribed "Livy L. Clemens/1889" in large ink lettering, presumably by Clemens but in an unusual hand.

Provenance: sold at the 1951 Hollywood auction but not listed in the hastily compiled sale sheet.

Catalog: "Property from the Library of Mark Twain," Butterfield & Butterfield, San Francisco, Sale 6613 (16 July 1997), lot 6700.

Location: Mark Twain House and Museum, Hartford, Connecticut.

Copy examined: Olivia Clemens's copy, with no notable markings. Viewed in Hartford in 1997.

———. *Young Folks' Cyclopaedia of Persons and Places*. Illus. New York: Henry Holt & Co., [1880].

A bill from Brown & Gross, Hartford booksellers, records Clemens's purchase at author's discount of "1 Cyclo. Persons & Places" on 20 December 1880 (receipt dated 1 January 1881, MTP).

CHAMPNEY, ELIZABETH (WILLIAMS) (1850–1922). *All Around a Palette*. Illustrated by J[ames]. Wells Champney (1843–1903). Boston: Lockwood, Brooks, and Co., 1878. 314 pp.

Source: MTLAcc, entry #449b, volume donated by Clemens.

Short stories for young adults arranged thematically by an artist's palette of colors.

———. *In the Sky-Garden*. Illustrated by J[ames]. Wells Champney (1843–1903)]. Boston: Lockwood, Brooks, &

Co., 1887. 211 pp.

Source: MTLAcc, entry #1919, volume donated from Clemens's library by Clara Clemens Gabrilowitsch in 1910.

An introduction to astronomy and constellations for young people.

———. *Rosemary and Rue*. Round-Robin Series, No. VII. Boston: James R. Osgood and Co., 1881. [One of the Round-Robin Series of anonymous novels written by "the best writers" that the Osgood firm began publishing and promoting in 1881.]

Catalog: Ball 2016 inventory, green cloth, red and black lettering, signed by Charles Jervis Langdon [Olivia Langdon Clemens's brother, 1849–1916], Jervis Langdon Family Library bookplate #619.

Location: Quarry Farm library shelves, under the supervision of the Mark Twain Archive, Elmira College, Elmira, New York.

This book was available to Clemens whenever he visited the Langdons' home. Its settings, characters, and subplots beggar description: New England, the American Revolution, a staunch Quaker family, a proud Jewish family, Yorktown, the destructive French Revolution—even the Wandering Jew turns up at the conclusion.

CHANDLER, IZORA CECILIA (SWARTZ) (1850–1906). *A Dog of Constantinople*. Illustrated by the author. New York: Dodd, Mead & Co., 1896. 215 pp.

Inscription: "Susan L. Crane/July 1899/Miss St. John".

Catalogs: QF Martinez, top edge gilt, good condition; Ball 2016 inventory, gray cloth, gilt lettering.

Location: Quarry Farm library shelves, under the supervision of the Mark Twain Archive, Elmira College, Elmira, New York.

This volume was available to Clemens at Quarry Farm in Elmira, New York.

CHANEY, GEORGE LEONARD (1836–1922). *"Alo'ha!": A Hawaiian Salutation*. Boston: Roberts Brothers, 1880 [cop. 1879]. 299 pp.

Clemens listed the author, title, publisher, and (illegible) publication date on the back of his copy of J. J. Jarves' *History of the Hawaiian or Sandwich Islands* (*N&J* 1: 105). In this travel book a pastor visits Hawaii and describes its history and customs.

CHANNING, W[ILLIAM]. E[LLERY] (1780–1842). *Letter of William E. Channing to J. G. Birney*. Boston: James Munroe and Co., 1837.

Marginalia: "writing on title [page]" (*A1911*). See below.

Catalog: *A1911*, "12mo, marbled calf, writing on title, Bost. 1837"; "Bound with other antislavery pamphlets: Narrative of Amos Dresser, N. Y. 1836; Declaration of Sentiment[s] and Constitution of the American Anti-Slavery Society, N. Y. 1835; Antislavery Catechism, by Mrs. Child, first edition, Newburyport, 1836; and three others." Lot 76, sold for $2 total.

Provenance: this same volume, inaccurately referred to as "*Anti Slavery* . . . written by William E. Channing" and "published by James Monroe [*sic*] and Company, 1837," was offered on eBay on 15–22 February 2003 with a starting bid of $199. "I am selling this book for a friend who had acquired it some years ago. . . . Book cover has completely separated from binding and pages have some faint staining." An accompanying photograph shows that the volume has an *A1911* sale label on the front endpaper. The words "Anti-Slavery" are embossed in gold on the spine. Someone (not Clemens) has written "Farmington Anti-Slavery Society No. 9" in ink at the top of the title page. A page of Clemens's holograph manuscript is laid in. (Barbara Schmidt notified Alan Gribben about this eBay listing.) In 2006 Robert Slotta of Admirable Books had possession of this group, describing it as "a series of seven various pamphlets bound together in full marbled calf," and offering it for sale in his *Twainucopia* catalog, item #3, pp. 6–7, with an accompanying illustration.

Channing wrote his supportive pamphlet for the reformer James Gillespie Birney (1792–1857) after a pro-slavery mob burned the presses of Birney's abolitionist newspaper in Cincinnati. For the additional three pamphlets not listed in the *A1911* catalog, see the Catalog entries for *An Address to the Presbyterians of Kentucky*, James G. Birney's *Letter to Ministers and Elders, on the Sin of Holding Slaves, and the Duty of Immediate Emancipation*, and David Ruggles's *The Abrogation of the Seventh Commandment by the American Churches*.

———. *The Works of William E. Channing, D. D.* Tenth Complete Edition. Six volumes. Boston: George G. Channing, 1849.

> **Inscription:** bookplate of "J. Langdon Family Library" (Numbers 164 through 169) on the front pastedown endpaper.
>
> **Sources**: email from Mark Woodhouse, Archivist, Elmira College, Elmira, New York to Alan Gribben, 5 January 2015, reporting no marginalia in the volumes; Ball 2016 inventory, 6 volumes, navy cloth, gilt lettering, embossed design on cover, good condition, "My Dearest Ella" inscribed in Volume I.
>
> **Location:** Quarry Farm library shelves, under the supervision of the Mark Twain Archive, Elmira College, Elmira, New York.
>
> This set was available to Clemens whenever he visited the Langdons in Elmira, New York.
>
> Dwayne Eutsey, "God's *Real* Message: *No. 44, The Mysterious Stranger* and the Influence of Liberal Religion on Mark Twain," *Mark Twain Annual 3* (2005): 53–66.

CHAPIN, ANNA ALICE (1880–1920). *Wotan, Siegfried, and Brünnhilde*. New York: Harper & Brothers, 1899. 133 pp.

> **Source:** MTLAcc, entry #1683, volume donated by Clemens.
>
> A guide to *Der Ring des Nibelungen* (The Ring Cycle) by Richard Wagner (1813–1883).

CHAPIN, WILLIS O[RMEL] (1860–1917). *The Masters and Masterpieces of Engraving*. Sixty engravings and heliogravures. New York: Harper & Brothers, 1894. 266 pp. [Publisher and pages conjectured.]

> **Catalog:** *A1911*, "60 engravings and heliogravures, royal 8vo, full stamped and gilt morocco, gilt top, uncut, N.Y. 1894," lot 157, sold for $8.
>
> In the next two centuries this book became a collectible item owing to its craftsmanship and scope.

CHAPMAN, EDWIN O. (1844–1926), ed. *Home Book of Poetry*. New York: Worthington Co., 1890. 399 pp.

> **Source:** MTLAcc, entry #617, volume donated by Albert Bigelow Paine, Clemens's designated biographer. Possibly Clemens saw this book, since the men exchanged reading materials.

CHAPMAN, FRANK MICHLER (1864–1945). *Handbook of Birds of Eastern North America*. Illus. New York: D. Appleton & Co., 1903. 431 pp.

> **Inscription:** in Clemens's hand in black ink on the front pastedown endpaper: "To/Jean Clemens/with her Father's love/Sept. 1903." Someone (possibly Clemens himself) traced a photograph presenting a side view of Clemens's head onto onionskin paper with black ink and glued it to the first flyleaf of the book.
>
> **Location:** Mark Twain Library, Redding, Connecticut. Donated from Clemens's library by Clara Clemens Gabrilowitsch in 1910 (MTLAcc, entry #1943).
>
> **Copy examined:** Jean Clemens's unmarked copy. Has the red ink accession number of the Mark Twain Library, "1943".

———. *The Warblers of North America*. Illus. New York: D. Appleton & Co., 1907. 306 pp.

> **Inscription:** on the front free endpaper in Jean Clemens's hand: "Jean L. Clemens/August 1907."
>
> **Location:** Mark Twain Library, Redding, Connecticut. Donated from Clemens's library by Clara Clemens Gabrilowitsch in 1910 (MTLAcc, entry #1942).
>
> **Copy examined:** Jean Clemens's copy. Examined in 1970 and again in June 1982. Has the red ink Mark Twain Library accession number, "1942".

CHAPPLE, JOSEPH MITCHELL (1867–1950), comp. *Heart Throbs in Prose and Verse Dear to the American People*. Boston: Chapple Publishing Co., 1905. 436 pp.

> **Source:** MTLAcc, entry #630, 416 [*sic*] pages, donated by Clemens.
>
> This anthology resulted from a contest in 1904 and 1905 sponsored by the *National Magazine* of Boston that awarded 840 prizes for submitted poems and prose extracts. (Mark Twain was quoted or alluded to four times.) Another volume of *Heart Throbs* would be published in 1911. The editors mentioned that Henry Wadsworth Longfellow's "A Psalm of Life" was one of the most popular nominations.

CHARLES, ELIZABETH (RUNDLE) (1828–1896). *Diary of Mrs. Kitty Trevylyan; A Story of the Times of Whitefield and the Wesleys*. New York: M. W. Dodd, 1864. 436 pp.

> **Source:** MTLAcc, entry #1851, volume donated from Clemens's library by Clara Clemens Gabrilowitsch in 1910.
>
> George Whitefield (1714–1770) was the charismatic English evangelist who founded the Calvinistic Methodists and toured North America seven times. John Wesley (1703–1791) founded Methodism and was sometimes assisted by his brother Charles Wesley (1707–1788).

———. *Chronicles of the Schönberg-Cotta Family*. New York: M. W. Dodd, 1864. 552 pp.

> **Source:** MTLAcc, entry #1857, volume donated from Clemens's library by Clara Clemens Gabrilowitsch in 1910.
>
> A fictionalized account of the Protestant Reformation inspired in Germany by Martin Luther (1483–1546) as told by two siblings, Else and Fritz Schönberg.

CHARLESWORTH, MARIA LOUISA (1819–1880). *Ministering Children: A Tale Dedicated to Childhood*. Boston: American Tract Society, 1862.

> **Inscription:** "Ida Clark from Trinity Sunday School/Christmas 1862". [Ida B. Clark, 1849–1934, would marry Charles Jervis Langdon in 1870 and thereby become

Olivia Clemens's sister-in-law.]

Source: among the books transferred by Mark Woodhouse from the Quarry Farm library to the Mark Twain Archive on 9 July 1987.

Location: Mark Twain Archive, Elmira College, Elmira, New York.

Clemens could have seen this book during his visits to the Langdons' house.

CHAUCER, GEOFFREY (c. 1343–1400). *The Canterbury Tales by Geoffrey Chaucer from the Text and with Notes and Glossary of Thomas Tyrwhitt [1730–1786].* New edition. Illustrated by Edward Corbould (1815–1905). Boston: Lee and Shepard, 1874. 586 pp. [Obsolete letters are modernized in this edition (the "thorn" is rendered as "th," for example), but the archaic diction and syntax are not altered.]

Inscription: Clemens wrote in black ink on the front flyleaf: "For/Livy Clemens/Dec. 1874,/S.L.C."

Marginalia: pencil marks and a few notes. Page 33 in "The Knight's Tale" is turned down; pencil notes in "The Wife of Bath's Prologue" at page 166, with notes on word meanings; a line in the "Frere's Tale" ("But if it be to hevy or to hote") on page 193 underlined in pencil and a note added by Clemens: "500 yrs old"; line drawn in pencil on page 282 to the word *"heronçeaux"* in a textual note, with "I can tell a hawk from a heronshaw—(heronceaux?)—Hamlet" added in margin; penciled bracket around lines 916–917 of "The Squire's Tale" on p. 296 ("Therefore behoveth him . . . herd I say"); a few other pencil markings and notes.

Catalog: *C1951*, #44c, $25.

Provenance: collection of Frank C. Willson (1889–1960), Melrose, Massachusetts.

Location: Harry Ransom Center, University of Texas at Austin. Purchased in 1962 from Willson's widow, Margarete.

Copy examined: Olivia Clemens's copy, annotated by Clemens, in 1979.

Chaucer is mainly distinguished by his "broken-English poetry" (*Californian*, 17 June 1865, *LAMT*, p. 142; *ET&S* 2: 195). "Tabard Inn in Southwark" was one of Mark Twain's entries in "Middle Age phrases for a historical story" (DV1 14, MTP). In Chapter 21 of *A Connecticut Yankee in King Arthur's Court* (1889) Hank Morgan and Sandy join a "company of pilgrims [which] resembled Chaucer's in this: that it had in it a sample of about all the upper occupations and professions the country could show, and a corresponding variety of costume"; en route to the Valley of Holiness these pilgrims told merry tales that would have embarrassed "the best English society twelve centuries later." On 6 and 7 January 1897 Twain amused himself with working notes "for a farce or sketch" (or perhaps "an Operetta") that would employ "pilgrims to Canterbury" accompanied by Chaucer himself (NB 39, TS p. 43; NB 40, TS p. 1). Twain alluded to "Chaucer's rotten spelling" in "A Simplified Alphabet" (written in 1899). "Chaucer and a lot of other people who did not know how to spell anyway," he quipped in a speech at the Associated Press dinner (19 September 1906, *MTSpk*, p. 526). Sandy McWilliams attempts unsuccessfully to communicate "with one Langland and a man by the name of Chaucer" in *Extract from Captain Stormfield's Visit to*

Heaven (1909) (Wecter, *RP* [1952], p. 78).

Gribben, "Mark Twain's Library Books in the Humanities Research Center" (1979): 15–16.

———. *Chaucer for Children: A Golden Key.* Ed. by Mary Eliza (Joy) Haweis (1852–1898), "Mrs. H[ugh]. R[eginald]. Haweis." Illustrated by the editor. London: Chatto & Windus, 1877. 112 pp.

Source: MTLAcc, entry #1219, volume donated by Clemens.

"Chaucer for Children/Chatto & Windus," Olivia Clemens wrote in her notebook for 1878 (MTP). Clemens entered the same title in Notebook 18 (1879, *N&J* 2: 335). Haweis's adaptation presented selections from the original text and a modernized poetical version in parallel columns.

CHEEVER, HENRY THEODORE (1814–1897). *The Island World of the Pacific; Being the Personal Narrative and Results of Travel Through the Sandwich or Hawaiian Islands, and Other Parts of Polynesia.* New York: Harper & Brothers, 1851. [Edition undetermined; the book was reissued in 1855, 1856, and 1871.]

Twain's Mr. Brown persona excoriates "these mush-and-milk preacher travels," naming "Mr. Cheever's book" (Sacramento *Weekly Union*, 25 August 1866; Dane, *LSI* (1938), pp. 151–152).

CHENEY, MARY (BUSHNELL) (1840–1917), ed. *Life and Letters of Horace Bushnell.* New York: Harper & Brothers, 1880. 579 pp. [Edition conjectured.]

Writing to the Reverend Joseph H. Twichell from Saranac Lake, New York on 28 August 1901, Clemens lightheartedly scolded Twichell: "Just a word, to scoff at you, with your extravagant suggestion that I read the biography of Phillips Brooks—the very dullest book that has been printed for a century. Joe, ten pages of Mrs. Cheney's masterly biography of her father—no, *five* pages of it—contain more meat, more sense, more literature, more brilliancy, than that whole basketful of dull drowsy rubbish put together." (*MTL*, p. 712; *LMTJHT*, p. 284). Clemens seems to be disparaging Alexander Viets Griswold Allen's *Life and Letters of Phillips Brooks* (1900). In 1902 Mark Twain would refer to Horace Bushnell (1801–1876) as the "greatest clergyman that the last century produced" (speech to the Art Students Association, St. Louis, Missouri, 7 June 1902, Cyril Clemens, *MTLW* [1932], pp. 113; Fatout, *MTSpk* [1976], pp. 444).

CHERRY, ANDREW (1762–1812). "The Bay of Biscay" (song). Composer, John Davy (1763–1824).

Mark Twain's humorous sketch in the 9 April 1868 issue of the Chicago *Republican*, "My Trip on the *Henry Chauncey*," concluded with a tribute to his roommate on the ship, Captain Cox of San Francisco. "I recall his honest attempts to help the choir out on Sunday mornings with his stormy 'Bay of Biscay,' which he sang with strict impartiality to all the church tunes which were ever started" (reprinted in the *Mark Twain Quarterly* 4.2 [Fall-Winter 1940–1941]:5). "The Bay of Biscay" (c. 1805) begins "Loud roar'd the dreadful thunder,/The rain a deluge show'rs,/The clouds were rent asunder/By lightning's vivid pow'rs." Its concluding fourth stanza ends with these lines: "A sail in sight appears,/We hail her with three cheers,/Now we sail, with the gale,/From the Bay of Biscay, O!" The Bay of Biscay was a dangerous gulf in the North Atlantic Ocean.

Chesebrough, Robert Augustus (1837–1933). *A Reverie and Other Poems.* New York: J. J. Little & Co., 1889. 83 pp. [Edition conjectured.]

"I reckon even Cheseborough's [*sic*] poetry failed to kill him" (SLC to Henry H. Rogers, Paris, 11 November 1894, *MTHHR*, p. 94). Chesebrough, the inventor of Vaseline, lived on to be ninety-six years old; he ate a spoonful of his petroleum jelly every day, and used it to cure scrapes, burns, and all of his other bodily ailments. Chesebrough concluded his preface to *A Reverie and Other Poems* with the promise that "if . . . you like my style, I may assail you again" (p. 4). The last poem in the volume, "Epitaph," ends with a pun that Clemens might have enjoyed: "He lived in falsehood year by year,/At last in *truth*, he does *lie* here."

Chesterton, G[ilbert]. K[eith]. (1874–1936). *The Club of Queer Trades.* Illus. New York: Harper & Brothers, 1905. 270 pp.

Marginalia: a deletion and grammar correction in ink on page 95.

Location: Mark Twain Library, Redding, Connecticut. (MTLAcc, entry #2194, volume donated from Clemens's library by Clara Clemens Gabrilowitsch in 1910.)

Source: I could not locate this volume in 1970 or when I revisited Redding in June 1982, but the New York *Times* reported on 19 April 2010 that Heather C. Morgan, then the director of the Mark Twain Library, had found the book in the fiction section. Beth Dominianni, the next library director of the Mark Twain Library, subsequently verified that *The Club of Queer Trades* is now housed with Clemens's other former library volumes. (At some point it had been rebound and barcoded as a regular library book.) There is no signature or inscription, Dominianni reported (email to Alan Gribben, 19 September 2014). This collection of six detective stories recounts the investigations of Basil and Rupert Grant. Each short story features someone who earns a livelihood in an odd manner (i. e., a "queer trade"). Chesterton provided a prefatory "Appreciation" for *Pudd'nhead Wilson* in the so-called Definitive Edition of Twain's works (New York, Gabriel Wells, 1922–1925)

———. *Orthodoxy.* New York: John Lane Co., 1909. 299 pp.

Source: MTLAcc, entry #2195, volume donated from Clemens's library by Clara Clemens Gabrilowitsch in 1910. Chesterton mounts a wide-ranging defense of certain ethical virtues of the Christian religion.

Kevin Belmonte, *Defiant Joy: The Remarkable Life and Impact of G. K. Chesterton* (New York: Thomas Nelson/HarperCollins, 2011).

Child, Lydia Maria (1802–1880). *Anti-slavery Catechism.* Newburyport, Kentucky, 1836. [Bound as a volume with W. E. Channing's *Letter to J. G. Birney,* along with six other pamphlets. See the W. E. Channing entry for more information.]

Catalog: *A1911*, "Antislavery Catechism, by Mrs. Child, First edition, Newburyport, 1836," lot 76, sold for $2 total.

Child, Theodore (1846–1892). *Delicate Feasting.* New York: Harper & Brothers, n.d. 214 pp. [First published in 1890.]

Source: MTLAcc, entry #1801, volume donated by Clemens.

According to *Publishers' Weekly* (12 April 1890), *Delicate Feasting* was far from being another compilation of recipes. Instead, it sought to "elevate" cooking, eating, and table-service to the dignity of a delicate feast. The book presented "what good eating is and how to get it."

———. *Wimples and Crisping-Pins; Being Studies in the Coiffure and Ornaments of Women.* Illus. New York: Harper & Brothers, 1895. 209 pp.

Source: MTLAcc, entry #1358, volume donated by Clemens.

Declaring that "coiffure is an art, and a great art, the chiefest of the decorative arts, inasmuch as its function is to adorn the most perfect of nature's works, the beauty of woman," Child examines "the dressing of hair and the adornment of beauty" (p. x) as portrayed in "the painting and sculpture of past ages" (p. xi). He describes in detail the fashions that prevailed in Egypt, Asia, Athens, Rome, Florence, Venice, the eighteenth century, and the Romantic Period.

Childs, George William (1829–1894). *Recollections.* First edition. Original quarter green cloth, blue cloth boards, gilt. Philadelphia: J. B. Lippincott Co., 1890. 404 pp.

Inscriptions: the front flyleaf has been neatly excised and probably contained either Clemens's signature and/or Childs' presentation inscription to Clemens.

Marginalia: the penciled number "10," possibly in Clemens's hand appears on the second flyleaf. The oval purple stamp of the Mark Twain Library at Redding occurs at several points in the text, and the red ink Mark Twain Library accession number "829" appears on the rear pastedown endpaper.

Provenance: MTLAcc, entry #829, volume donated by Clemens.

Location: collection of Kevin Mac Donnell, Austin, Texas (Mac Donnell to Alan Gribben, 3 June 2014).

Page 10 tells how Childs began working at a bookstore at age twelve, developing good habits by rising early, washing the pavement, making the fire, and sweeping the store. Pages 70–139 recount his friendship with President Ulysses S. Grant. Childs publishes excerpts from letters from Poe, Hawthorne, Whittier, Holmes, Lowell, and Longfellow. Though Clemens and Childs were acquainted, Childs does not mention Clemens in the book.

L. W. Michaelson, "Four Emmeline Grangerfords," *Mark Twain Journal* 11.3 [Fall 1961]: 10–12.

"Child's Keepsake" (unidentified possible book).

Source: ListABP (1910), "Child's Keepsake". This might or might not refer to a book title.

Chittenden, Hiram Martin (1858–1917). *History of Early Steamboat Navigation on the Missouri River: Life and Adventures of Joseph LaBarge [1815–1899], Pioneer Navigator and Indian Trader, for Fifty Years Identified with the Commerce of the Missouri Valley.* 2 vols. New York: Francis P. Harper, 1903.

Inscription: inscribed "To Saml L. Clemens/from/Frederic Remington/ 1906" by Remington on the front free endpapers of both volumes.

Location: Mark Twain Library, Redding, Connecticut.

Copies examined: Clemens's copies, unmarked. The red ink Mark Twain Library accession number "3122" appears in Volume 1; "3123" appears in Volume 2. The first volume has 248 pages and the second volume contains 461 pages. Examined in 1970 and again in June 1982 and on 10 November 2019.

Chittenden, L[ucius]. E[ugene]. (1824–1900). *Recollections* *of President Lincoln and His Administration.* New York: Harper & Brothers, 1891. 470 pp.

> **Catalog:** Ball 2016 inventory, blue cloth, gilt lettering, gilt top edge pages, good condition.
>
> **Location:** Quarry Farm library shelves, under the supervision of the Mark Twain Archive, Elmira College, Elmira, New York.
>
> This volume was available to Clemens at Quarry Farm in Elmira, New York.

CHOPIN, FREDERIC (1810–1849). *Pianoforte Werke.* 3 vols. Leipzig: C. F. Peters, n. d. [One volume is in the original red cloth with gilt; another is in the original flexible maroon leather with gilt; the third volume has been rebound in later buckram.]

> **Inscription:** Clara Clemens wrote "Clemens" in pencil on the title page of the first volume.
>
> **Marginalia:** Leschetizky made pencil notations in some of the pieces showing fingering and pedal intervals, as well as his German instructions about dynamics and expression. Clara added a few notes in English in the cloth-bound volume.
>
> **Location:** collection of Kevin Mac Donnell, Austin, Texas.
>
> **Source:** supplementary inventory sent by Mac Donnell to Alan Gribben, 28 August 2017.
>
> Leaving Quarry Farm in June 1889, Clemens made a memorandum about retrieving some piano books for Clara Clemens in Hartford: "Bring Chopin & Beethoven—in drawing-room—⊠ square, red-bound" (*N&J* 3: 494). Theodor Leschetizky (1830–1915) was an eminent Polish pianist.

CHOPIN, KATE (BORN CATHERINE O'FLAHERTY) (1850–1904). A great many of Clemens's library books were either lost or donated without any record made of their titles, so we cannot be certain whether he owned copies of Chopin's short stories or her acclaimed novel, *The Awakening* (1899). We do know that he had a special fondness for stories and novels set in the Deep South; see, for example, the Catalog entries for Virginia Boyle and Grace King.

Whether or not he knew of her writings, Kate Chopin certainly held Mark Twain's works in high esteem. In an essay she published in 1900, "Development of the Literary West: A Review," she declared that people in the American West would "have enough to be proud of" if all they had was "only Mark Twain" (*Critical Insights: The Awakening,* ed. Robert C. Evans [Ipswich, Massachusetts: Salem Press, 2014], p. 75). Interviewed in 1902 about which literary classics she might recommend that the school board purchase for children to read, Chopin listed various works and then added, "I don't know how they would keep Mark Twain's books out. The children would read them anyhow, whether they were given to them or not. I have a daughter who has read 'Tom Sawyer' and 'Huckleberry Finn' to tatters" (St. Louis *Post-Dispatch,* 9 September 1902, p. 2, quoted by Robert C. Evans in *Critical Insights: The Awakening,* p. 106).

Kate Chopin's Private Papers, ed. Emily Toth and Per Seyersted (Bloomington: Indiana University Press, 1998), pp. 223–225.

CHORLEY, HENRY FOTHERGILL (1808–1872). "God, the all-terrible" (hymn, published in 1842). Also known as "God, the omnipotent." Melody, "Russian Hymn" [1833] by F.

Lvov. [The third and fourth stanzas were added in 1870 by John Ellerton (1826–1893).]

Mark Twain's "The War Prayer" (written in 1904 or 1905) quotes and slightly paraphrases the opening lines of the first stanza: "An organ-burst . . . shook the building, and . . . the house rose, with glowing eyes and beating hearts and poured out that tremendous invocation—God the all-terrible! Thou who ordainest,/Thunder thy clarion and lightning thy sword!" Twain does not include the refrain, "Give to us peace in our time, O Lord."

CHRĒSTOMANOS, KŌNSTANTINOS (1867–1911), alternate name of Constantin Christomanos. *Tagebuchblätter [Diary Leaves]. I. Folge. II. Auflage, etc.* Wien: Verlag von Moritz Perles, 1889. 285 pp.

> **Inscription:** by Jean Clemens on front free endpaper, in black ink: "To the/Black Spider/with the wishes for as peaceful/a Christmas as is possible under/the existing circumstances; of/her most affectionate/Jean Clemens/ Vienna 1898."
>
> **Location:** Mark Twain Library, Redding, Connecticut.
>
> **Copy examined:** Clara Clemens's gift copy. The front free endpaper is loose. Has the red ink Mark Twain Library accession number "4005".
>
> Chrēstomanos's diaries described his stay in Austria-Hungary and his friendship with Empress Elisabeth of Austria (1837–1898), who was later stabbed to death by an Italian anarchist. That assassination on 10 September 1898 perhaps partly accounts for Jean Clemens's somber inscription in the book.

CHRISTIAN, EUGENE (1860–1930) and MOLLIE (GRISWOLD) CHRISTIAN. *Uncooked Foods & How to Use Them: A Treatise on How to Get the Highest Form of Human Energy from Food. With Recipes for Preparation, Healthful Combinations and Menus.* Illus. New York: Health-Culture Co., [cop. 1904]. 246 pp.

> **Source:** MTLAcc, entry #400a, volume donated by Clemens.

The Christian Hymnal: A Selection of Psalms and Hymns, with Music, for Use in Public Worship, ed. Nathaniel J. Burton (1824–1887), Edwin Pond Parker (1836–1920), and Joseph H. Twichell (1838–1918).

> **Inscription:** "S. L. Clemens. From Rev. J. H. Twichell, Munich, Bavaria, Feb. 1879."
>
> **Catalog:** *A1911,* "Square 12mo, cloth, Hartford, 1877," quotes the signature, lot 78.

[CHRISTIAN SCIENCE]. [Unidentified Christian Science tracts.] London: George Morrish, n.d.

> **Source:** MTLAcc, entry #926, "'C. S.' Tracts, London, Geo. Morrish, n.d., 206 pp.," volume donated by Clemens.
>
> George Morrish (1814–1911) was a Christian publisher in London.

Christian Science Hymnal.

> Discussed in Book 2, Chapter 7 of *Christian Science* (1907).

The Christian Science Journal 13.2–12 (April 1895–March 1896). Septimus J[ames]. Hanna (1845–1921), ed. Boston: J. Armstrong. 542 pp. [Bound volume.]

> **Inscriptions:** on the front pastedown endpaper in black ink: "SL. Clemens/1903"; on the paper cover of the first issue, in Isabel Lyon's hand: "Isabel Lyon/from/Mr. Clemens."
>
> **Marginalia:** profusely annotated in black ink and (predominantly) pencil. Several notes on pages 428–429 establish the fact that Clemens read the volume in 1902

as well as 1903. The front pastedown endpaper is filled with Clemens's record of the approximately sixty pages he annotated. There are numerous computations of the sales for Eddy's *Science and Health* and the growth of her churches and their membership. Clemens's comments on Eddy are as caustic as one might expect. A few notes touch upon other topics: above the assertion that while Christian Science occasionally is fatal to its practitioners, "medicine also fails," Clemens penciled: "What Dr. Rice [Clarence C. Rice, Clemens's physician-friend] says/A concession at last—doctors kill, too" (p. 254). At the top of the following page, where Emerson is quoted concerning the "severe morality" of women, Clemens notes: "It may achieve woman's rights".

Catalog: AAA-Anderson Galleries, Sale Number 4158, 28 February-1 March 1935, item #97, bound copy of Vol. XII of *Christian Science Journal*, 1895, "with marginal notes by Clemens on 43 different pages, totaling about 425 words," including this note: "If ever I have puerperal fever I shall not go osteo nor C S but fill up with formalin" (PH of catalog entry in MTP).

Location: Henry W. and Albert A. Berg Collection, New York Public Library.

Copy examined: Clemens's copy.

Mark Twain alludes to later issues of *The Christian Science Journal* in *Christian Science* (1907): in Book 1, Chapter 6 he quotes from the October 1898 issue as a chapter epigraph; in Chapter 7 he mentions the *Journal*; in Book 2, Chapter 2 he quotes from the January 1899 issue (*WIM?*, p. 272); in Chapter 5 of Book 2 he quotes from the January 1901 issue (*WIM?*, p. 286); in Chapter 7 he quotes from an article in the February 1898 issue (*WIM?*, p. 328); and he quotes a paragraph from the "Editor's Table" of the March 1902 number in Chapter 8 of Book 2 (*WIM?*, p. 341).

Robert Peel, *Mary Baker Eddy*, pp. 194–206.

CHRISTIAN SCIENCE. *List of Members of the Mother Church* [of Boston]. 10 February 1903. Boston. [Paperbound volume.]

Inscription: signed on the cover: "S. L. Clemens, March 1903."

Catalog: *A1911*, "12mo, wrappers," quotes the signature, lot 79, sold for $1.50.

———. *Official Report of the National Christian Science Association*. Boston: National Christian Science Association, 1890.

Mark Twain quotes from the *Official Report*—citing page numbers—in *Christian Science* (1907), Book 2, "Mrs. Eddy in Error."

Christian Union (magazine, published 1870–1893; subsequently became *The Outlook*).

Mark Twain joked about the propriety of this religious weekly, sending William Dean Howells in September or October 1879 a ribald manuscript (*1601*) that he purportedly contemplated submitting to this journal edited by Henry Ward Beecher and Lyman Abbott (*MTHL*, p. 271). The Clemenses subscribed to the publication (*MTB*, p. 820); in the 11 June 1885 issue Twain read a letter republished from *Babyhood* entitled "What Ought He to Have Done?" and replied with a letter about disciplining children that was published in the 16 July 1885 issue of *Christian Union*. See *MTB*, pp. 819–820, 1409; on the latter page Albert Bigelow Paine recounts an amazing

coincidence about Clemens wanting some items from the *Christian Union* and a stranger stopping him on the street and giving him the clippings he sought. See also *The Twainian* (May 1944), 1–4 and *Dear Mark Twain* (2013), ed. R. Kent Rasmussen, pp. 115–119.

Chronicles of the Crusades; Contemporary Narratives of the Crusade of Richard, Coeur de Lion [1157–1199], by Richard of Devizes [c. 1150–c. 1200] [trans. by Dr. John Allen Giles (1808–1884)] and Geoffrey de Vinsauf [fl. c. 1208–1213], and of the Crusade of Saint Louis, by Lord John de Joinville. [Trans. by Thomas Johnes (1748–1816)]. London: G. Bell and Sons, 1876. 562 pp. [Publisher and date conjectured; the work was originally published in 1848 in Bohn's Antiquarian Library series.]

Inscription: on the verso of the frontispiece: "S. L. Clemens, Hartford, 1877."

Catalogs: *A1911*, "12mo, cloth, Lond. 1876," quotes the signature, lot 80, lot for $2; *L1912*, lot 8, sold for $5.

James R. Osgood & Company of Boston billed Clemens in November 1877 for "1 Chronicles of Crusaders" [*sic*] purchased on 24 October 1877 (Scrapbook #10, p. 69, MTP). In December 1884 Mark Twain thought of describing a battle between "Prince de Joinville's Middle Age Crusaders" and "a modern army" equipped with new weaponry (NB 23, *N&J* 3: 86). Twain requested de Joinville's *Memoirs of the Crusades* from Chatto & Windus in 1891 while he was in France (NB 31, TS p. 6, MTP). The French chronicler Jean de Joinville (1224?-1317?) accompanied Louis IX to Egypt on the Sixth Crusade.

CHURCH, ALFRED JOHN (1829–1912). *Two Thousand Years Ago; or, The Adventures of a Roman Boy*. Illustrated by Adrien Marie (1848–1891). London: Blackie & Son, 1886. 384 pp.

Source: MTLAcc, entry #1920, volume donated from Clemens's library by Clara Clemens Gabrilowitsch in 1910.

———. *With the King at Oxford; A Tale of the Great Rebellion*. Illus. New York: Dodd, Mead & Co., n.d. 298 pp.

Source: MTLAcc, entry #2198, volume donated from Clemens's library by Clara Clemens Gabrilowitsch in 1910.

In this historical novel set in the seventeenth century the narrator follows Charles I up to his trial and execution in the English Civil War.

CHURCH, DANIEL WEBSTER (1852–1926). *The Enigma of Life; A Solution of the Great Mystery* (published in 1892).

See the following entry.

———. *The Records of a Journey. A Prologue*. Greenfield, Iowa: Berlin Carey Co., [cop. 1888]. 80 pp.

Source: MTLAcc, entry #641, volume donated by Clemens.

Church, an attorney in Greenfield, Iowa, wrote to Clemens on 7 May 1892: "When my former book 'The Records of a Journey' was published I sent you a copy of it. And although it probably did not attract your attention I have concluded to try again, and hence send you the succeeding volume 'The Enigma of Life'" (MTP). Church's bizarre *Records of a Journey*, written in free verse, is the account (supposedly, according to the book's "Introduction," sent from an unknown correspondent) of a man's search for his inheritance. Inasmuch as it concludes that "we are now of princely lineage/And have come into our kingdom" and that all highways "lead to the Eternal City," John Bunyan's *Pilgrim's Progress* would seem to have been Church's inspiration. If this volume had survived, it might have offered another example s of Clemens's habit of decorating additions to his "Library of Literary Hogwash" with excoriating marginalia.

Church, Frederick Edwin (1826–1900).

Although there is no evidence that Clemens read anything this renowned, Hartford-born landscape painter ever wrote, Frederick Church deserves a brief mention as a cultural force of the era. Clemens was awestruck by Church's "Heart of the Andes" painting when he viewed it in St. Louis in March 1861; it was "the most wonderfully beautiful painting which this city has ever seen. . . . I have seen it several times, but it is always a new picture—*totally new*. . . . You will never get tired of looking at the picture" (*MTLet* 1: 116). In June 1887 Clemens visited Church's "Olana" estate on the Hudson River with the Warners and Grace King, and Clemens read aloud to the group from Rudyard Kipling's poetry (Bush, "Grace King and Mark Twain [1972], pp. 34, 35).

Katherine E. Bishop, "'A Wilderness of Oil Pictures': Reframing Nature in *A Tramp Abroad*," *Mark Twain Annual* 17 (2019): 72–87.

Church, Richard William (1815–1890). *Bacon.* English Men of Letters Series. New York: Harper & Brothers, 1902. 214 pp.

Source: MTLAcc, entry #1750, volume donated by Clemens.

Church, Samuel Harden (1858–1943). *Horatio Plodgers; A Story of To-Day.* New York: W. B. Smith & Co., [cop. 1881]. 136 pp. [First edition.]

Source: MTLAcc, entry #73, volume donated by Clemens.

Horatio Plodgers was the first novel attempted by this Pittsburgh, Pennsylvania railroad superintendent. In an undated letter Church asked Twain to provide a preface for the book, but Twain declined (R. Kent Rasmussen to Gribben, email, 8 December 2010, citing correspondence in the Mark Twain Papers, Bancroft Library, University of California at Berkeley; see also *MTLet* 6: 551 for corroboration that Church and Clemens knew each other). Church's extravagant novel follows the campaign strategies of a politician who cynically considers latching onto women's rights as a winning issue. Church would go on to write respected works of history as well as other publications.

———. [Another identical copy.]

Source: MTLAcc, entry #987, volume donated by Clemens.

Churchill, Winston (1871–1947). *Mr. Crewe's Career.* Illus. by Arthur I[gnatius]. Keller (1866–1924), Margaret West Kinney (d. 1872), and Troy Kinney (1871–1938). New York: Macmillan Co., 1908. 498 pp.

Source: MTLAcc, entry #2199, volume donated from Clemens's library by Clara Clemens Gabrilowitsch in 1910.

Mr. Crewe's Career was the best-selling novel of 1908. Indeed, the St. Louis-born Winston Churchill, who came to resent the inevitable confusion of his name with that of the rising British politician (whom he met in Boston in 1900), had been a best-selling author for two decades beginning in 1898. His most popular novel was *Richard Carvel* (1901), which sold over two million copies. He began by writing historical novels, including *The Crisis*, the best-selling work of fiction in 1901, and *The Crossing* (1904); thereafter he turned to fiction with political,

social reform, religious, and moral themes. He moved to New Hampshire in 1899, entered state politics, stopped writing in 1919, and became a noted painter of watercolors. It seems almost impossible that Clemens did not own more than two of this prominent author's novels; this must be another of those cases where his association copies were either lost or donated without any record being made of their titles.

———. *A Modern Chronicle.* Illustrated by J[ames]. H[amlin]. Gardner Soper (1877–1939). New York: Macmillan Co., 1910. 524 pp.

Source: MTLAcc, entry #2200, volume donated from Clemens's library by Clara Clemens Gabrilowitsch in 1910.

———. *Richard Carvel.* Illustrated by Carlton [Theodore] Chapman (1860–1925) and [Charles] Malcolm Fraser (1868–1949). New York: Macmillan Co., 1899. 538 pp.

Catalog: Ball 2016 inventory, red cloth, gilt lettering, gilt page tops, fair condition.

Location: Quarry Farm library shelves, under the supervision of the Mark Twain Archive, Elmira College, Elmira, New York.

This volume was available to Clemens at Quarry Farm in Elmira, New York.

Churchill, Winston Spencer (1874–1965).

Mark Twain first met Winston Churchill in March 1900 at a dinner at Sir Gilbert Parker's home (17 August 1907 Autobiographical Dictation, *AutoMT* 3: 102, 491). A few months later Twain introduced Churchill, recently a correspondent in South Africa during the Anglo-Boer War, at Churchill's lecture at the Waldorf-Astoria in New York City on 12 December 1900 (*AutoMT* 3: 102, 491). In his remarks Twain made it clear that he had not agreed with certain British actions during this conflict. Much later Churchill recalled that in addition to introducing the young reporter Twain gave him autographed copies of his works and "showed me much kindness": "It is 55 years since I saw Mark Twain but he is still vivid in my memory—the most interesting man I ever knew" (Lee Meriwether, "Me and Mark Twain," *Mark Twain Journal* 10.3 [Fall-Winter 1957]: 19).

Cicero, Marcus Tullius (106–43 BCE). *Select Orations.* Translated from the Latin by C[harles]. D[uke]. Yonge (1812–1891). New York: Harper & Brothers, 1888. 580 pp. [Publisher and page numbers conjectured.]

Inscription: signed by Clemens.

Marginalia: a few markings and notes, including: "8:15 'till bedtime read German."

Catalogs: *A1911*, "12mo, cloth (back weak; a few pages loose and defective), N.Y. 1888," quotes the signature, describes the notes, and quotes one note, lot 81, sold for $1.75; George D. Smith, New York City, "Catalogue of Books" (1911), has Clemens's signature, item #67, $5.50.

De Legibus, 3:15; *Philippics*, 4:4; and *Paradoxa*, 6:3, 49 are literary sources for Mark Twain's "Political Economy" (1870), according to a research paper prepared for Professor Henry Pochmann by Lewis Lawson. In the early 1900s Twain listed Cicero among the "intellectual giants" in "Proposal for Renewal of the Adam Monument Petition" (Tuckey, *FM*, p. 452). Finley Peter Dunne ("Mr. Dooley") asserted that Twain offered to "collaborate on an essay 'De Amicitia' that would be better than Cicero's"

(*Mr. Dooley Remembers: The Informal Memoirs of Finley Peter Dunne*, ed. Philip Dunne [Boston: Little, Brown, 1963], p. 267). An early commentator, Herbert Edward Mierow, "Cicero and Mark Twain," *Classical Journal* 20 (December 1924): 167–169, making no claim that Twain was familiar with Cicero, scoffed at Twain's late sarcasm in comparison with Cicero's more stoic outlook. When we face death "we shall not turn to the great American writer whose humor at the last turned to ashes and whose hilarity was lost in the depths of pessimism"; instead we will find "solace in the calm words of the great Roman Republican" (p 169).

[THE CID *(c. 1043–1099)]. The Chronicle of the Cid*. Edited with an introduction and appendix by Richard Markham. Translated from the Spanish by Robert Southey (1774–1843). Illustrated by H[arry]. W[hitney]. McVickar (1860–1905) and Alfred [Laurens] Brennan (1853–1921). Original red, black, and gold pictorial cloth, cloth split at joints, spine-ends rubbed, cloth rubbed and soiled. New York: Dodd, Mead & Co., 1883. 313 pp.

Inscription: the front flyleaf is inscribed by Clemens to his daughter in ink, "Merry Christmas/to/Clara Clemens/1884./From Papa."

Provenance: the books left with Clemens's biographer Albert Bigelow Paine following Clemens's death in 1910 included an unspecified edition of *The Chronicle of the Cid* (ListAPB). Presumably the book that Paine initially retained was the same book later sold at the 1951 Hollywood auction. (See below.)

Catalogs: *C1951*, 84c, specifies Richard Markham's edition, listed among volumes signed by Clemens, $16; "Property from the Library of Mark Twain," Butterfield & Butterfield, San Francisco, Sale 6613 (16 July 1997), lot 2684.

Location: Mark Twain House and Museum, Hartford, Connecticut. Acquired in 1997.

Copy examined: Clara Clemens's unmarked copy. It has the library shelfmarks of the numbering system that Clara Clemens Gabrilowitsch used during her Detroit years. Viewed in Hartford in 1997.

Chapters 5, 10, and 13 of Twain's "A Horse's Tale" allude to *The Cid* (JoDee Benussi to Alan Gribben, email, 1 October 2006).

City and State (political weekly).
See the Catalog entry for Herbert Welsh.

CLARK, CHARLES HEBER (1841–1915), pseud. "Max Adeler." *Elbow-Room; A Novel without a Plot*. Illustrated by Arthur B[urdett]. Frost. New York: John W. Lovell Co., 1876. 384 pp. [Edition conjectured; the first edition appeared in 1876 but there were other publishers and reprintings.]

Clark's meandering *Elbow-Room*, more like a collection of comic sketches than a novel, is set "in a village wherein there is elbow-room for the physical and intellectual man that the characters in this book may be supposed to be, to do and to suffer" (p. 17). At the outset of Chapter 19, titled "An Unruly Meter," a character named Mr. Butterwick disputes an outrageous natural gas bill for $350,000, but the officious clerk at the gas office stubbornly refuses to second-guess the gas meter. Returning to his house, Mr. Butterwick "beat the meter into a shapeless mass, tossed it into the street, and turned off the gas" (p. 238). In July 1880 Mark Twain listed "Max Adler" [*sic*] among the

humorists being considered for inclusion in a projected anthology (NB 19, *N&J* 2: 361). Twain, who had his own beefs with the Hartford City Gas Light Company (see for example, his furious letter of 12 February 1891, published in *Mark Twain's Helpful Hints for Good Living: A Handbook for the Damned Human Race*, ed. Lin Salamo, Victor Fischer, and Michael B. Frank [Berkeley: University of California Press, 2004], pp. 41–42), used this snippet of *Elbow-Room's* Chapter 19 in *Mark Twain's Library of Humor* (1888), titling it "Butterwick's Little Gas Bill" (pp. 664–665). Strangely, Twain listed its authorship as "Anonymous" and supplied no publisher or book title in the credits at the rear of volume. Had Twain or his editorial collaborator Charles H. Clark perhaps lost the notes for this item, was the piece unattributed in a periodical where they found it, or did Twain suppose that Clark would never notice this bit of borrowing?

———. *The Fortunate Island and Other Stories*. Illus. Boston: Lee & Shepard, 1882. 333 pp.

Source: MTLAcc, entry #3, volume donated by Clemens.
Mark Twain and Adeler (writing then as "John Quill" in the Philadelphia *Evening Bulletin*) engaged in a squabble in 1870 over the literary ownership of several fictional plot devices. Twain referred to him as "a literary sneak thief" (SLC to Frank Fuller, 26 April 1870, *MTLet* 4: 120) and as "John Quill, a literary thief" (SLC to James Redpath, 10 May 1870, *MTLet* 4: 128). On 19 November 1870 Clemens , writing to Mary Mason Fairbanks, renewed his charge that "a Philadelphia imbecile by the name of 'John Quill'" had plagiarized him, but reported with satisfaction that the offender had now "passed out of the literary world" (*MTLet* 4: 240). Twenty years later Twain discussed (New York *World*, 12 January 1890) whether *A Connecticut Yankee in King Arthur's Court* (1889) had borrowed from Max Adeler's "The Fortunate Island," as Clark had charged in the New York *World* on 4 November 1889. David Ketterer investigated this plagiarism charge and traced the first publication of Clark's story to his *An Old Fogey and Other Stories* (1881), where it appeared as "Professor Baffin's Adventures" (Ketterer, "'Professor Baffin's Adventures' by Max Adeler: The Inspiration for *A Connecticut Yankee in King Arthur's Court*," *Mark Twain Journal* 24.1 [Spring 1986]: 24–34). That issue aside, given Clemens's inquisitive tendencies to collect (or at least cursorily read) virtually every example of American humor, it is hard to believe that Clemens was not familiar as well with Max Adeler's wildly comical *Out of the Hurly-Burly; or Life in an Odd Corner* (1874), though no evidence of that likelihood has yet surfaced.

Walter Blair, "On the Structure of *Tom Sawyer*" (1939), pp. 77–78 (a mention of Clark); Edward S. Foster, "*A Connecticut Yankee* Anticipated: Max Adeler's *Fortunate Island*," *Ball State University Forum* 9.4 (Autumn 1968): 78–76; David Ketterer, "'The Fortunate Island' by Max Adeler: Its Publication History and *A Connecticut Yankee*," *Mark Twain Journal* 29.2 (1991): 28–32; Horst Kruse, "Literary Old Offenders: Mark Twain, John Quill, Max Adeler, and Their Plagiarism Duels," *Mark Twain Journal* 29.2 (Fall 1991): 10–27—an excellent introduction to the loose notions of literary plagiarism at the time; *Charles Heber Clark: A Family Memoir: The Autobiography of the*

American Humorist "Max Adeler," ed. David Ketterer (New York: Peter Lang Publishing, 1995); Horst H. Kruse, "The Motif of the Flattened Corpse: Mark Twain, Max Adeler, and the Tall Tale Tradition," *Studies in American Humor* n.s. 3.4 (1997): 47–53; *Critical Companion to Mark Twain,* ed. R. Kent Rasmussen (New York: Facts On File, 2007), 2: 634.

CLARK, FRANCIS EDWARD (1851–1927). *The Mossback Correspondence, Together with Mr. Mossback's Views on Certain Practical Subjects, with a Short Account of His Visit to Utopia.* Boston: D. Lothrop & Co., [cop. 1889]. 194 pp.
Source: MTLAcc, entry #798, volume donated by Clemens. Christian sketches in the form of letters from a religious curmudgeon.

———. *A New Way Around an Old World.* Illus. New York: Harper & Brothers, 1902. 213 pp.
Source: MTLAcc, entry #512, volume donated by Clemens. The book describes Clark's missionary travel to Russia and Siberia. Clark was a prominent Congregational minister in Boston, editor of *Christian Endeavor World,* and president of World's Christian Endeavor Union.

CLARK, FREDERICK THICKSTUN (b. 1858). *The Mistress of the Ranch; A Novel.* New York: Harper & Brothers, 1897. 357 pp.
Source: MTLAcc, entry #1528, volume donated by Clemens.
A young heiress arrives to take possession of a ranch she has inherited near Eden City in the Rocky Mountains.

CLARK, [EDWARD HEWES] GORDON. *The Church of St. Bunco; A Drastic Treatment of a Copyrighted Religion—Un-Christian Non-Science.* New York: The Abbey Press, [1901]. 251 pp.
Inscription: on flyleaf in pencil by Clemens: "Xn Science/—formerly Quimby Science."
Marginalia: numerous penciled notes in the first hundred pages, concentrated especially in the passages detailing Mary Baker Eddy's unacknowledged indebtedness to Phineas Parkhurst Quimby (1802–1866). Clemens wrote vertically in the margin of page 96 concerning the genesis of Christian Science religion: "1866 is the date of the theft, not the publication of it. That seems to have happened in 1875."
Catalogs: ListABP (1910), "Church of Saint Bunco, Clark"; *C1951,* #62a, $25.
Location: Mark Twain Papers, Bancroft Library, University of California at Berkeley. Purchased from Maxwell Hunley Rare Books of Beverly Hills for $35 in 1956.
Copy examined: Clemens's copy.
In Book II, Chapter 15 of *Christian Science* (1907) Mark Twain tried to link Eddy's doctrines of mental healing to those advanced earlier by the American healer Phineas Parkhurst Quimby: "If she borrowed the Great Idea, did she carry it away in her head, or in manuscript?" Later he boldly wrote to J. Wylie Smith that Eddy's getting hold of Quimby's healing principle "was a tramp stealing a ride on the lightning express" (7 August 1909, MTP). Twain asserted in "The International Lightning Trust" (written in 1909) that Eddy had merely devised a new name and religion for Quimby's ideas (*FM,* p. 99). Edward Hewes Gordon Clark wrote a series of book-length exposés on various subjects.

CLARK, IMOGEN. *We Four and Two More.* Illus. New York: T.

Y. Crowell & Co., [cop. 1909]. 274 pp.
Source: MTLAcc, entry #1487, volume donated by Clemens.

CLARKE, ADAM (1762–1832). *Discourses on Various Subjects Relative to the Being and Attributes of God, and His Works in Creation, Providence, and Grace.* Third edition. 3 vols. New York: M'Elrath & Bangs, 1831.
Inscription: title page of Volume I signed in black ink: "Morris Hills Book".
Location: Mark Twain Library, Redding, Connecticut.
Copy examined: in June 1982 these volumes had been mistakenly shelved with the books donated to the Mark Twain Library by Clemens and his daughter Clara Gabrilowitsch. The Clarke volumes have no markings and no accession number and obviously originated from the numerous book donations made by the descendants of the Hill family of Redding Ridge. They should not be included in any list of Clemens's library collection.

CLARKE, ALBERT GALLATIN, JR. (1861–1904). *The Arickaree Treasure, and Other Brief Tales of Adventurous Montanians.* New York: Abbey Press, [cop. 1901]. 232 pp.
Source: MTLAcc, entry #74, volume donated by Clemens.

CLARKE, EDWARD H[AMMOND]. (1820–1877). *Sex in Education; or, A Fair Chance for Girls.* Boston: J. R. Osgood and Co., 1873. 181 pp. [Publisher and pages conjectured.]
Catalog: *A1911,* "12mo, cloth, Bost. 1873," lot 83, sold for $1.
Clarke's controversial book prompted book-length responses in 1874 by Eliza Bisbee Duffey and Julia Ward Howe.

CLARKE, JAMES FREEMAN (1810–1888). *Memorial and Biographical Sketches.* Boston: Houghton, Osgood and Co., 1878. 434 pp.
Estes & Lauriat of Boston charged Clemens on 14 July 1880 for "1 Memo Sketches $1.25" (receipt in MTP). The book sold for $2 in retail bookstores, but Clemens generally received an author's discount. Clarke's subjects in *Memorial and Biographical Sketches* included John Albion Andrew, James Freeman, Charles Sumner, Theodore Parker, Samuel Gridley Howe, William Ellery Channing, Walter Channing, Ezra Stiles Gannett, Samuel Joseph May, Susan Dimock, George Keats, Robert J. Breckinridge, George Denison Prentice, Junius Brutus Booth the elder, George Washington, Shakespeare, Jean Jacques Rousseau, and William Hull.
James Freeman Clarke was an early abolitionist who became associated with the Transcendental school of thought (he purchased Brook Farm after its utopian experiment failed) and advocated for the expansion of women's rights. The author of books on theology and other topics, he long served as a Unitarian minister and was an influential editor.

———. *Selections from Sermons Preached to the Church of the Disciples.* Boston: J. A. Lowell, n.d. [Small unbound pamphlet of twenty leaves, tied together with purple ribbon. Arranged by seasons, such as "Spring: Seed Time—Resurrection—Immortality."]
Location: Mark Twain Papers, Bancroft Library, University of California at Berkeley. It is gathered with other Olivia Clemens association items in DV162.
Copy examined: Olivia Clemens's copy.

CLARKE, MARCUS ANDREW HISLOP (1846–1881). *The Austral Edition of the Selected Works of Marcus Clarke, Together with a Biography and Monograph of the Deceased Author, Compiled and Edited by Hamilton [Nisbet Crawford] Mackinnon [1847–1897]*. Melbourne: Fergusson & Mitchell, 1890. 504 pp.

Marginalia: notes and editorial revisions by Clemens in black ink and pencil throughout Part I, "Australia of the Past." No markings occur beyond page 169. Clemens edited "The Seizure of the 'Cyprus'" (pp. 112–117) for inclusion in a projected "APPENDIX" to *Following the Equator* (1897). "Reads like romance," he observed on page 16 about some details of the story. He also marked for quotation certain passages in "Buckley, the Escaped Convict" (pp. 131–140), and heavily annotated "The South Australian Land Bubble" (pp. 141–148).

Catalog: ListABP (1910), "Works of Marcus Clarke", no other information supplied.

Provenance: sold at the *C1951* sale, but not listed in its auction sheet.

Location: Mark Twain Papers, Bancroft Library, University of California at Berkeley. Gift of the U. C. L. A. General Library.

Copy examined: Clemens's annotated copy.

In September 1895 Clemens noted "Collected Works of Marcus Clark" [*sic*] (NB 35, TS p. 53). Regarding the penal colonies in early Australia, Clemens wrote on 2 November 1895: "Gentleman said Marcus Clark exaggerated. . . . But that won't do" (NB 34, TS p. 25). On 11 January 1896 Clemens apparently referred to an edition of Clarke's *Works*: "See that trial in Vol III 300 lashes one day, *500* the next. The man died" (NB 37, TS p. 8). Dennis Welland, "Mark Twain's Last Travel Book" (1965), pp. 45–46.

————. *For the Term of His Natural Life*. Black cloth, embossed design. London: Richard Bentley and Son, 1893. 472 pp.

Inscription: by Clara Clemens in black ink at top of "Preface" (page iii): "To/ Kathleen with love/from/Clara L. Clemens/July 1896."

Provenance: Antenne-Dorrance Collection, Rice Lake, Wisconsin.

Location: Mark Twain Archive, Gannett-Tripp Learning Center, Elmira College, Elmira, New York.

Copy examined: gift volume from Clara Clemens, presumably to Katy Leary, the Clemenses' housekeeper. Examined on 28 May 2015.

Clara Clemens recalled attending a play based on Clarke's novel in Melbourne; she and her parents found it "gruesome," but "did not . . . regret" having seen it (*MFMT*, p. 145). Clemens's own notes reveal that they saw the performance in Sydney: "Even when the chain-gang were humorous they were still a most pathetic sight. . . . That old convict life . . . [was] invented in hell & carried out by Xtian devils" (NB 36 [December 1895], TS p. 5). Mark Twain mentioned Clarke's works about the penal colony repeatedly in newspaper interviews during his global tour. The Melbourne *Evening News* quoted his recollection that "Marcus Clarke, who is not read as much as he should be in America, but whose works cannot be kept back in the future, . . . described the Tasmanian coast as being like molten lead poured into water" (26 September 1895; *Complete Interviews*, p. 224). A reporter for the Melbourne *Age* (27 September 1895) noted that Twain "rested for the day with the aid of a pipe and a book, which was no other

than *For the Term of His Natural Life*." Twain stated that he was "charmed with Marcus Clarke's best read book . . . which he would gladly linger over" (*Complete Interviews*, p. 233). On that same day, speaking to a reporter for the Melbourne *Herald Standard*, Twain alluded to Clarke's description of Sydney Harbor in "that masterly work, *For the Term of His Natural Life*. The figure I refer to I regard as one of the most striking in the whole of literature" (*Complete Interviews*, p. 228). During a newspaper interview published on 4 January 1896, Twain opined that "*For the Term of His Natural Life* is the finest Australian novel, and Gabbett, the cannibal, as strongly-drawn a character as I ever met. But what gave me the greatest pleasure in reading that book was that all the time I felt that I was reading history" (Sydney, Australia *Bulletin*; Scharnhorst, *Complete Interviews*, p.264).

In the original manuscript of *Following the Equator* (1897) Mark Twain called *For the Term of His Natural Life* "the book that stands at the head of Australian literature. . . . It reads like a dream of hell," and he quoted at length the scene in which Troke and Burgess, prison officers, flog young Kirkland to death and flog Rus Dawes, another convict, into insane ravings. But the final text of *Following the Equator* (1897) omitted these passages (Francis Madigan, "MT's Passage to India" [1974], pp. 349–351, 356). Twain did mention Clarke passingly but approvingly in a list of Australian writers that appears in Chapter 22 of the published version of *Following the Equator*.

————. "Introduction" in Adam Lindsay Gordon's *Poems* (published in 1894).

Mark Twain originally quoted a lengthy portion from Clarke's introduction for Chapter 9 of *Following the Equator* (1897), but later canceled the passage. See the Catalog entry for Adam Lindsay Gordon.

Madigan, "Mark Twain's Passage to India" (1974), pp. 351–353, 358.

CLARKE, MARY VICTORIA COWDEN (1809–1898). *The Complete Concordance to Shakespeare, Being a Verbal Index to All the Passages in the Dramatic Works of the Poet*. New and revised edition. Boston: Little, Brown and Co., 1875.

Inscription: on the front free endpaper in pencil: "S. L. Clemens/Hartford 1876".

Marginalia: markings at certain Shakespearean references to "Child" (five horizontal pencil lines) and "Twain" (six horizontal pencil lines).

Provenance: identical handwritten numbers in ink at the top of the title page ("1653") and the copyright page ("1653") link this volume to the Mark Twain Library at Redding, which received many hundreds of donations from Clemens and his daughter Clara.

Catalog: *Mott 1952*, #43, $12.50.

Location: Fontbonne College Library, Fontbonne College, St. Louis, Missouri.

Copy examined: photocopies of the front free endpaper, title page, copyright page, and two unnumbered pages of the text. I am grateful to Sister Jane Behlmann, then Audiovisual Librarian of the Fontbonne College Library, for providing information and photocopies.

CLARKE, REBECCA SOPHIA (1833–1906) (pseud. "Sophie May"). *Janet, a Poor Heiress*. Boston: Lee and Shepard, 1882.

[Publisher is conjectured.]

Inscription: "From Mamma. Xmas 1890."

Catalog: *Mott 1952*, #44, $2.50.

The author, a native of Maine, wrote novels for young people.

———. *Quinnebasset Girls.* Illus. Boston: Lee and Shepard, 1877. 336 pp.

Inscription: (on front free endpaper, in pencil) "From/Aunt Carrie/Xmas 1889."

Location: Mark Twain Library, Redding, Connecticut.

Copy examined: unmarked copy belonging to one of Clemens's daughters. Contains an accession number written in black ink: "2729."

CLARKE, SAMUEL (1599–1683). *A Mirror or Looking-Glass Both for Saints & Sinners Wherein is Recorded as Gods Great Goodness to the one , so his Seveare Judgment Against the other, wherevnto is added a Geographicall Description of all the knowne world and allso of the Chiefest Citys Both Ancient and modern &c.* Large folio, original leather-covered boards, chipped on the edges, re-backed with a dark brown morocco spine with gilt lettering. London: R. Gaywood, 1671. 702 pp. plus index.

Inscriptions: *A1911* sale label is affixed to front pastedown endpaper. Above that is affixed a canceled check from D. M. McKeithan to Scribner's Book Store for $85. Above that check someone listed in pencil the page numbers on which Clemens made notes. At the bottom of the page is the bookplate of Alan Gribben recording his receipt of this book as a gift from D. M. McKeithan in September 1980. Clemens did not sign this book, but then it was his usual habit not to place his signature in the truly antique volumes in his library collection.

Marginalia: Clarke was a Puritan clergyman in England during the tumultuous period of mounting religious dissent leading up to the execution of King Charles I. *A Mirror or Looking-Glass Both for Saints & Sinners* avoids political topics by drawing theological lessons from the actions of historical figures. Clemens made notes on eighteen pages; the first appears on page 40 and the last ("A case of delirium tremens.") on page 511. He also marked many other passages starting on page 30. He used pencil up to page 79 but began employing blue ink on page 82 where, in reference to Saturus, who resolved to forsake wife, children, house, and possessions for the love of Christ, Clemens wrote "Atrocious Scoundrel." He agreed with the opinion of Laelius Socinus that a man may be saved without the knowledge of the Scriptures: "Sensible, again" (p. 276). "Now what a stately lie is this," Clemens wrote in ink on page 307 beside an account of the devastation that befell some Jews after Julian the Apostate gave them permission to rebuild their temple at Jerusalem. At a description of the power in prayer demonstrated by Fulgentius, who was able to keep his own city in safety when the rest of the province was captured by the Moors, Clemens commented: "They ought to have hired him to travel around" (p. 462). Farther down the same page, to an assertion concerning the ability of the Church, by fervent and frequent prayer, to restore a prominent person to health, Clemens noted: "It failed in Gen. Garfield's case." (President' Garfield, shot by an assassin on July 2, 1881, lingered in pain for more than eleven weeks before dying on 19 September 1881.)

Catalogs: *A 1911*, "folio, unbound, title damaged, Lond.

1671, some passages marked by Mr. Clemens and some notes in his handwriting," quotes selected marginalia, lot 84, sold for $10; Scribner's Book Store, New York City (1956), $85.

Provenance: formerly in the collection of the Mark Twain scholar Daniel Morley McKeithan, Austin, Texas. He purchased it from Scribner's Book Store in New York City in April 1956 for $85.

Location: collection of Alan Gribben, Montgomery, Alabama. A generous gift from Daniel Morley McKeithan (1902–1985), who said that the compiler of *Mark Twain's Library: A Reconstruction* (1980) "deserved to own a memento from Clemens's personal library."

Copy examined: Clemens's copy. Examined in 1980 and 2017.

Paul Baender, *WIM?* (1973), p. 3 n. 7.

CLARKE, SAMUEL (1684–1750). *Promises of Scripture.* New York: American Tract Society, n.d. 348 pp.

Source: MTLAcc, entry #2315, volume donated from Clemens's library by Clara Clemens Gabrilowitsch in 1910.

Clarke, a nonconformist clergyman and theological writer at St. Albans, was the nephew of Samuel Clarke (1599–1683); see the preceding Catalog entry. Clarke first published his influential and often-reprinted *Promises of Scripture* in 1720.

CLAY, HENRY (1777–1852). *Speeches.*

Huckleberry Finn noted that Henry Clay's *Speeches* was one of the volumes on the parlor table at the Grangerford house (*HF* [1885], Chapter 17). The Kentucky politician Clay served as senator, Speaker of the House of Representatives, and Secretary of State. He promoted the Missouri Compromise of 1820 and twice nearly became President of the United States.

CLELAND, JOHN (1709–1789). *Fanny Hill: Memoirs of a Woman of Pleasure* (erotic novel; published in two volumes, 1748–1749). [Edition unidentified.]

"I have labored hard to get a copy of 'Fannie Hill' [*sic*] for him [an unidentified "old man"] to read, but I have failed sadly" (SLC to William H. Clagget, Carson City, 8 March 1862, *MTLet* 1: 171). Two decades later Clemens wrote to his then-publisher about a ludicrous manuscript he had read: "The Earl's [Jesse Leathers'] literary excrement charmed me like Fanny Hill. I just wallowed in it" (SLC to James R. Osgood, Hartford, 30 March 1881, *MTLP*, p. 136). This was one of Clemens's most explicit acknowledgments of his appetite for erotic literature.

CLEMENS, OLIVIA SUSAN ("SUSY") (1872–1896). *The Love Chase* (play, privately performed in 1889).

Mary Bushnell Cheney and her family along with other friends were invited to the Clemens home for a social visit on the evening of Thanksgiving Day in 1889. In the drawing-room seventeen-year-old Susy, her sisters, and several other girls performed a play Susy had written. They wore ancient Greek costumes. Susy had the largest role, "Music." Albert Bigelow Paine thought the play's title was "The Triumph of Music" (*MTB*, p. 883), but other sources refer to it as *The Love Chase* (a shepherd boy was one of the characters). See Fears, *Day by Day*, pp. 442–443; also Kym Soper, *Hartford Courant*, 18 February 1999, quoting David Bush, then director of public information for the Mark Twain House and Museum).

CLEMENS, ORION (1825–1897). "Autobiography of a Coward." "Confessions of a Life That Was a Failure," "The Autobiography of an Ass" (variant titles of an unpublished manuscript that Orion began in 1879).

Philip A. Fanning's *Mark Twain and Orion Clemens: Brothers, Partners, Strangers* (Tuscaloosa: University of Alabama Press, 2003) describes how Clemens coerced Orion into producing what Fanning terms "a grotesque parody of an autobiography, an "exercise in self-abuse" (p. 183), which amounted to a "degrading project" (p. 185). Clemens described and shared sections of Orion's manuscript with William Dean Howells in 1880 (SLC to WDH, 1 April 1880; SLC to WDH, 9 June 1880; WDH to SLC, 14 June 1880; *MTHL*, pp. 296, 312–313, 315). Purportedly Clemens destroyed part of Orion's manuscript (Dixon-Wecter, *SCH*, p. 286 n. 33). Perhaps fortunately for all involved, the remainder of this humiliating autobiography was later lost in Grand Central Station by Clemens's designated biographer Albert Bigelow Paine (Dixon Wecter, *SCH*, p. 282 n. 31; Barbara Schmidt, "Paine in the Lost and Found," *Mark Twain Journal* 31.2 [Fall 1993]: 32).

CLEMENS, WILL MONTGOMERY (1860–1931). *Mark Twain, His Life and Work: A Biographical Sketch*. San Francisco: The Clemens Publishing Co., 1892. 211 pp. [Reprinted as *Mark Twain, His Life and Work: A Biographical Sketch*. New York and Chicago: F. Tennyson Neely, 1894. 213 pp. This later edition added two pages chronicling the collapse of Charles L. Webster & Company, blaming it on "incompetent and inexperienced men" who made blunders while Mark Twain was occupied elsewhere.]

Will M. Clemens sent more than a dozen letters to Mark Twain beginning on 26 November 1877 and continuing over the next decades that sought favors and permissions. His *Famous Funny Fellows: Brief Biographical Sketches of American Humorists* (Cleveland, Ohio: W. W. Williams, 1882) quoted two letters in which Twain responded to Will M. Clemens's inquiries. It may not have helped Twain's attitude toward Will M. Clemens that his sketch of Twain referred to him as "the prince of funny men" but awarded the title of "king of American humorists" to Artemus Ward (Charles Farrar Browne). The younger Clemens did not discourage, and of course benefited from, persistent rumors that he was either a nephew or cousin of the famous Mark Twain (*DearMT*, pp. 50–52). However, no record has ever been found of Will M. Clemens's attempting to substantiate a lineal relationship with the prominent author.

Samuel Clemens wrote to Will Clemens on 1 January 1900 to forbid the publishing of any quotations "from those letters, nor from any other letters of mine. I hope you will destroy the letters—it is what [James] Redpath ought to have done. . . . Such letters should not even be published after a man is dead, let alone while he is alive. They are gross exposures of the vanities & trivialities of their writers. . . . Consider them blue-penciled straight through. . . . Don't re-read them to see how unimaginably silly & infantile & nauseating they are, but put them in the fire, where they belong" (*Sotheby's 2003*, lot #99). On 11 June 1900 Clemens warned the Bowen-Merrill Company not to issue another volume by Will M. Clemens, which was to be titled *The Mark Twain Story Book* (NB 43, TS p.

16). Clemens grumbled to Henry H. Rogers from London on 13 June 1900: "Here is this troublesome cuss, Will M. Clemens, turning up again. . . . Clemens can't write books—he is a mere maggot who tries to feed on people while they are still alive" (*MTHHR*, p. 447). Finley Peter Dunne testified how much Samuel L. Clemens detested "a bad poet of the same name as his, who traded, or so he thought, on a wholly fictitious relationship. He described this poetaster to George Harvey in language that George, who was himself a free-spoken man, could only repeat in a whisper (*Mr. Dooley Remembers: The Informal Memoirs of Finley Peter Dunne*, ed. Philip Dunne [Boston: Little, Brown, 1963], p. 244). Almost certainly Dunne's reference was to Will M. Clemens, who under the pseudonym "Rodney Blake" had compiled and edited *Hasty Pudding Poems: A Collection of Impulsive and Impromptu Verses* in 1901 (a work reprinted in 1905 as *After Dinner Verse*), to which Will M. Clemens contributed a prefatory poem, a comical German dialect poem titled "Hoch der Kaiser," and perhaps other pieces. Although Will M. Clemens was primarily known (if at all) as a minor biographer of well-known Americans of his day, he also tried to establish his own literary credentials, publishing, for example, *Sixty and Six: Chips from Literary Workshops* (1897) and *Mistakes of Authors: A Manual for Writers and Others* (1900). See also the Catalog entry for Charlotte (Perkins) Gilman.

CLEMENT, CLARA ERSKINE (1834–1916). *Painters, Sculptors, Architects, Engravers, and Their Works: A Handbook*. Illus. [Published in 1874 and thereafter reissued frequently by several publishers; James R. Osgood & Company of Boston published the seventh edition in 1882].

Catalog: *C1951*, O6, listed with books signed by Olivia Clemens, edition not supplied.

Clement is often listed in bibliographies as Clara Erskine (Clement) Waters.

CLEVELAND, CECILIA (b. 1850). *The Story of a Summer; or, Journal Leaves from Chappaqua*. New York: G. W. Carleton & Co., 1874. 273 pp.

Inscription: a large, careless signature in pencil on the front free endpaper, "S. L. Clemens."

Marginalia: profuse pencil brackets, vertical lines, and underlinings throughout, starting on page 14 and ending on page 273. In addition Clemens made notes, most of them acerbic, on fifteen pages. One pencil note on page 15 changes Cleveland's "at Chappaqua." to read "at dismal Chappaqua." There are several notes written in the top and side margins of page 51. Another note on page 52 beside a put-down of Saratoga simply reads, "Specimen". On page 56 Clemens wrote two notes. He jotted a question mark next to Cleveland's reference to "a Dissenting church for a next-door neighbor" (page 59). "Old farmer" Clemens wrote on page 88 about a grandparent who is mentioned. Sarcastic notes appear on pages 90, 91, 92, 93, and 97. Another note mocks a poem on page 188. On page 219 Clemens scoffs at a description of "Uncle Barnes." Page 221 has a note by Clemens, as does page 268.

Provenance: in 1988 the volume was in the possession of Bob Seymour, Colebrook, Connecticut.

Location: Mark Twain House and Museum, Hartford, Connecticut. The book had joined this collection by at least 2006, when it was listed among the volumes needing repair ("Support the Book Conservation Fund," Mark Twain House and Museum, internet membership report, 1 October 2006).

Copy examined: photocopy of Clemens's annotations sent to Alan Gribben by Marianne J. Curling, then curator of the Mark Twain Memorial (later renamed the Mark Twain House and Museum), on 29 December 1988. The majority of the notes by Clemens are not clearly legible in the photocopy.

"I have written a rather lengthy review of that unfortunate & sadly ridiculous book of Miss Cleveland's about Chappaqua. . . . I aim my moral, not at the poor girl herself, but at her injudicious friends (for permitting the publication)" (SLC to Jerome B. Stillson of the New York *World*, 23 March 1874, ASSSCL; *MTMF*, pp. 185–186 n. 2; *MTLet* 6: 86). If Clemens ever published this piece it has gone undetected, and no manuscript of the review has turned up. Dixon Wecter mistakenly thought that this was the book to which Clemens referred in informing Mary Mason Fairbanks, "I ain't going to write that lady, because it isn't pleasant to say no to a stranger" (*MTMF*, p. 185), but the editors at the Mark Twain Project in Berkeley established that Wecter misdated Clemens's letter, which was actually written two years later, on 24 March 1876 (*MTLet* 6: 87 n. 5). The Mark Twain Project editors pointed out that the author of *The Story of a Summer* was a niece of Horace Greeley (she employed his country home and farm as her settings), a national figure about whom Clemens held ambivalent views, and the publisher was George W. Carleton, for whom Clemens had a lifelong antipathy.

————. [Identical copy.]
Catalog: Ball 2016 inventory, blue cloth, gilt lettering, bookplate of J. Langdon's Family Library #476, good condition.
Location: Quarry Farm library shelves, under the supervision of the Mark Twain Archive, Elmira College, Elmira, New York.
This volume was available to Clemens whenever he visited the Langdon residence in Elmira, New York.

CLEVELAND, GROVER (1837–1908), JAMES G[ILLESPIE]. BLAINE (1830–1893), HENRY WATTERSON (1840–1921), and GEORGE F[RANKLIN]. EDMUNDS (1828–1919). *What Shall We Do With It? (Meaning the Surplus). Taxation and Revenue Discussed.* New York: Harper & Brothers, 1888. 68 pp.
Source: MTLAcc, entry #1736, volume donated by Clemens.
A collection of previously published strategies about tariff measures.

CLEVELAND, OHIO *Herald* (newspaper).
Clemens had various reasons for being familiar with the *Herald*, including the fact that the husband of his friend Mary Mason Fairbanks was one of the paper's chief shareholders. See, among other confirming sources, Jeffrey Steinbrink's *Getting to Be Mark Twain* (Berkeley: University of California Press, 1991), pp. 9, 10, 17, 29–38 *passim*.

CLEVENGER, SHOBAL VAIL (1843–1920). *The Evolution of Man and His Mind. A History and Discussion of the Evolution and Relation of the Mind and Body of Man and Animals.* Chicago: Evolution Publishing Co., 1903. 615 pp.
Inscription: in black ink on front pastedown endpaper:

"SL. Clemens/1903".
Marginalia: numerous markings and notes in pencil up to page 113; none thereafter. Clemens's comments indicate mild divergences with the physician, neurologist, and pathologist Clevenger's views. On page 26 Clevenger states that, though mankind "has still his brutish instincts," nonetheless "Evolution shows that he advances." Clemens extended this sentence to read "—toward altar & halter." At the bottom of page 49 Clemens's inclinations toward cynicism again came to the fore; he noted: "But then the modern human race is frankly devoted to the game of grab, just as the race was earlier devoted to piety & hypocrisy" (quoted in Roger B. Salomon's *TIH* [1961], p. 132).
Catalog: ListABP (1910), "Evolution of Man and His Mind, Clevenger".
Location: Mark Twain Papers, Bancroft Library, University of California at Berkeley. Purchased from Maxwell Hunley Rare Books of Beverly Hills in 1953 for $20.
Copy examined: Clemens's copy.
In "Was the World Made for Man? (probably written in 1903), Mark Twain relied on Clevenger's estimate about the age of humankind—though he misidentified his source.
LE (1962), p. 212; *WIM*? (1973), pp. 102, 545 n. 102.
————. *Fun in a Doctor's Life, Being the Adventures of an American Don Quixote in Helping to Make the World Better.* Atlantic City, N.J.: Evolution Publishing Co., 1909. 293 pp.
Inscription: on the front free endpaper: "To Sam L. Clemens/from his old townsman/of Louis in the 50's/S. V. Clevenger/Park Ridge, Ill/Christmas 1909".
Marginalia: notes and markings in ink and pencil up to page 93. Beside a reference to Lord Bacon's many activities, Clemens added in black ink, "And writing Shakspeare, which he certainly did" (p. 13). Heavy black ink markings alongside a quoted Wells Fargo express receipt that stated: "This company will not be responsible for the acts of God, Indians or other public enemies of the government" (p. 18). Page 20 is also marked in black ink. There are pencil notes and/or markings on pages 50 ("Kerosene is better"), 51, 52, and 82. Clemens did not mark the passage about river boats on page 90 that mentions his name.
Location: Mark Twain Library, Redding, Connecticut.
Copy examined: Clemens's copy. Viewed in 1970 and again in June 1982. Oddly, no accession number is visible.

CLEWS, HENRY (1836–1923). *Twenty-Eight Years in Wall Street.* Illus. New York: J. S. Ogilvie, 1887. 724 pp. Simultaneously: New York: Irving Publishing Co., 1887. 687 pp. [The Irving Publishing Company issued an expanded edition of 717 pages in 1888 that attached dozens of book reviews ("Opinions of the Press") praising the first edition.]
In November 1886 Clemens instructed Charles L. Webster to obtain Clews' book for their firm, but not be generous in his contract terms (NB 26, *N&J* 3: 271–272). New York banker Henry Clews' meandering compilation of financial history and investment advice was partly an advertisement for his banking house, Henry Clews & Company. In sixty-three chapters he told the stories of Commodore Vanderbilt, Daniel Drew, the Rothschilds, and other financial titans; explained the Wall Street stock exchange; reviewed the financial panics that had afflicted the banking system; discouraged women from speculating

in the stock market (supposedly "they lack the mental equipment"); rehearsed the manipulations of the Tweed political machine; and predicted future investment trends. For an analysis of Clemens's successes and failures as a businessman, see the Catalog entry for Moses Smith, *Plain Truths about Stock Speculation*.

CLIFFORD, LUCY (LANE) (1846–1929), "Mrs. W. K. Clifford." *Margaret Vincent, A Novel*. New York: Harper & Brothers, 1902, 356 pp.

Source: MTLAcc, entry #75, volume donated by Clemens. Clifford chose to publish under her married name as a tribute to her husband, an eminent mathematician and philosopher who had died in 1879 at the age of thirty-three. Her fictional protagonists tend to be women struggling against overwhelming odds.

———. [Another identical copy.]

Source: MTLAcc, entry #1270, volume donated by Clemens.

———. *Mrs. Keith's Crime; A Record*. New York: Harper & Brothers, 1901. 234 pp.

Source: MTLAcc, entry #1529, volume donated by Clemens.

This was Clifford's first and best-known novel, which came out in 1885. A dying widow resolves to kill her dying daughter as an act of mercy.

CLIFFORD, WILLIAM KINGDON (1845–1879). *Lectures and Essays by the Late William Kingdon Clifford*. Ed. by Leslie Stephen (1832–1904) and Frederick Pollock (1845–1937), with an intro. by Pollock. 2 vols. London: Macmillan and Co., 1879.

Marginalia: one volume contains a handwritten note by Clemens.

Catalogs: *A1911*, "8vo, cloth, Lond. 1879," laid in is a "small sheet" of notes made by Clemens, lot 101, sold for $1.50, Volume 1 only; *L1912*, lot 9, sold for $3, Volume 1 only.

Location: Franklin Meine Collection, University of Illinois at Urbana-Champaign (both volumes, according to the library card).

Copy examined: none. Information compiled from photocopies of library card supplied by a respondent, Mrs. Mary Ceibert.

Clifford, often credited for introducing the concept of geometric algebra, was the husband of author Lucy Clifford (see the preceding entry). He passed away half a century before her death occurred.

CLODD, EDWARD (1840–1930). *The Story of Creation: A Plain Account of Evolution*. New and revised edition. Illus. Original maroon cloth, spine stamped in silver. London: Longmans, Green, and Co., 1894. 242 pp. Bookseller's sticker on rear endpaper: Wildman & Lyell, Auckland, New Zealand.

Inscription: in black ink, "To Miss Clara Clemens,/with every good wish/from Carlyle Smythe". (Smythe was Mark Twain's lecture agent during portions of his world tour in 1895–96.)

Provenance: Contains the shelfmark from Clara Clemens Gabrilowitsch's private library collection when she resided in Detroit. Became part of the Carrie Estelle Doheny Collection, St. John's Seminary, Camarillo, California. Auctioned for $1,320 with one other title by Christie's in New York City on 17 October 1988 (lot 1185) on behalf of St. John's Seminary. Subsequently owned by

Nick Karanovich of Fort Wayne, Indiana.

Catalog: *Sotheby's 2003*, #193, $3,000 (sold with four other titles from the Clemens family's library).

Location: collection of Kevin Mac Donnell, Austin, Texas.

Copy examined: Clara Clemens's unmarked copy, in July 2004. Has the bookplate of "Estelle Doheny."

Clodd evinces a pro-Darwinian thesis as he describes, among other examples, the duck-billed platypus (pages 126–127). This animal species amused Mark Twain immensely in his notebooks and in *Following the Equator* (1897).

CLOUSTON, JOSEPH STORER (1870–1944). *The Adventures of M. D'Haricot*. Illustrated by Albert Levering (1869–1929). New York: Harper & Brothers, 1902. 365 pp.

Source: MTLAcc, entry #76, volume donated by Clemens. A diehard French Royalist flees to England and, having given up on a French monarchy ever being reestablished, narrates his life among the English and how he eventually fell in love.

———. *The Lunatic at Large; A Novel*. Illustrated by Latimer J. Wilson. New York: F. M. Buckles & Co., [cop. 1905]. 312 pp.

Source: MTLAcc, entry #1095, volume donated by Clemens.

This was Clouston's most popular novel, and even resulted in sequels.

———. *Our Lady's Inn; A Novel*. New York: Harper & Brothers, 1903. 324 pp.

Source: MTLAcc, entry #989, volume donated by Clemens.

COAN, TITUS MUNSON (1836–1921). *Ounces of Prevention*. New York: Harper & Brothers, 1888. 188 pp.

Source: MTLAcc, entry# 1383, volume donated by Clemens.

The son of Hawaiian missionaries, Titus Munson Coan, M.D., was educated at Williams College and received his medical training at the New York College of Physicians and Surgeons. He served as a surgeon in the Civil War, and for a time was assigned to Admiral David Farragut's squadron. Afterward a longtime New York City physician, he produced a manual of household medicine, *Ounces of Prevention*, that included topics such as Colds, and How to Check Them; Winter Clothing; Ventilation; Country-House Drainage; Wells and Well-Water; Food for Children; and The Care of the Eyes. As parents who had lost a young son to disease, the Clemenses were very concerned with the prevention of illnesses; see K. Patrick Ober, M.D., "Mark Twain and Family Health in Nook Farm," *Mark Twain Journal: The Author and His Era* 56.1 (Spring 2018): 23–71. Coan was additionally interested in the concept of human "temperaments," an idea that always intrigued Clemens; see the Catalog entry for *Galaxy. An Illustrated Magazine of Entertaining Reading*.

COBB, AUGUSTUS G[ARDINER]. (1850–1930). "Earth-Burial and Cremation," *North American Review* 135.310 (September 1882): 266–282.

Mark Twain introduced information from this article into his discussion of cremation in Chapter 42 of *Life on the Mississippi* (1883). He contemplated adding other material from Cobb's essay (*N&J* 2: 502), but deleted that section before publication. Cobb was the President of the United States Cremation Company and Vice-President of the New York Cremation Society. He would subsequently expound his arguments in *Earth-Burial and Cremation:*

The History of Earth-Burial and Its Attendant Evils, and the Advantages Offered by Cremation (1892).

COBB, SYLVANUS, JR. (1823–1887).

Mark Twain mentioned Cobb as a highly popular writer, but implied that the quality of his work was questionable in a column for the 12 November 1870 Buffalo *Express* (*MTBE*, p. 252) and in "A General Reply," *Galaxy* 10.5 (November 1870): 733 (reprinted in *CTSS&E* 1, pp. 486–487). Cobb specialized in sensation fiction that appeared in *The Flag of Our Union*, the New York *Ledger*, and various other journals. He published hundreds of short stories and more than one hundred novels.

COBBE, FRANCES POWER (1822–1904). *Life of Frances Power Cobbe as Told by Herself, with Additions by the Author, and Introduction by Blanche Atkinson [b. 1846]*. Illus. Red cloth. London: S. Sonnenschein & Co., 1904. 722 pp.

Inscription: "S. L. Clemens, London July 1907."

Marginalia: many marked paragraphs and notes, according to the *A1911* catalog description, which also reports that Clemens observed on a flyleaf: "To the pure all things are impure. S.L.C." Where the text refers to Charles Kingsley's salutation to Miss Cobbe as "At *last*, Miss Cobbe, at *last* we meet," Clemens quipped: "What he really said was 'at l–l–ast we m-m-meet'—for he was a delightful stammerer."

Catalogs: *A1911*, "12mo, cloth, Lond. 1904, quotes signature and notes, lot 102, sold for $9.50; Parke-Bernet Galleries, New York City, Sale Number 672 (7–8 May 1945), lot 132, "12mo, cloth, London, 1904, the front pastedown endpaper inscribed, 'To the pure all things are impure. S. L. C.,'" with marginal notes by Clemens "on a few pages," contains the *A1911* auction label, sold for $16.

Location: Mark Twain Papers, Bancroft Library, University of California at Berkeley. Contains the *A1911* sale label.

Source: UCB Library Catalog, 12 June 2006.

Emily E. Vandette, "Animals and Animal Rights," *Mark Twain in Context*, ed. John Bird (Cambridge, England: Cambridge University Press, 2020), pp. 271–273.

———. *The Peak in Darien, with Some Other Inquiries Touching Concerns of the Soul and the Body. An Octave of Essays*. Boston: Geo. H. Ellis, 1882. 266 pp.

Source: MTLAcc, entry #914, volume donated by Clemens. The essays in Cobbe's collection weigh the merits of believing in Christianity versus subscribing to atheism, severely criticize the scientific practice of vivisection, argue for the fitness of women to serve as Christian ministers, scoff at medicinal nostrums, and ponder the possibility of an afterlife.

COBBETT, WILLIAM (1763–1835). *A Year's Residence in the United States of America, Treating of the Face of the Country, The Climate, the Soil, . . . and of the Usual Manner of Living; of the Manners and Customs of the People; and, of the Institutions of the Country, Civil, Political, and Religious. . . . In Three Parts*. Illus. New York: Clayton and Kingsland, Printers, 1819. [Publisher conjectured.] Paged continuously.

Marginalia: a few notations in pencil by Clemens.

Catalog: *A1911*, "Part III, 12mo, boards, foxed, N.Y. 1819, with a few notations in pencil in the handwriting of Mr. Clemens," lot 103, sold for $1. [Part III of Cobbett's work incorporated (and credited) a journal kept by Thomas Hulme during his travels through Ohio and Illinois.

Hulme's impressions of the United States were favorable.] Gary Scharnhorst's *Mark Twain: The Complete Interviews* (p. 90 n. 2) and Rebecca Hooker's "Additions to the Mark Twain Library" (*American Literary Realism* 38.3 [Spring 2006]: 276) suggested that Twain was referring to Griffith Owen Corbett's *Notes on Rupert's America: Its History and Resources* (1868), in an interview published in the Chicago *Tribune* on 9 July 1886 that quotes Clemens as saying, "It is strange . . . how little has been written about the Upper Mississippi. . . . Along the Upper Mississippi every hour brings something new. . . . Few people ever think of going there, however. Dickens, Corbett, Mother Trollope, and the other discriminating English people who 'wrote up' the country before 1842 had hardly an idea that such a stretch of river scenery existed. Their successors have followed in their footsteps, and . . . of course we ignore the finest part of the Mississippi." However, Griffith Owen Corbett's book was little known and was only eighty-eight pages in length. It seems more plausible that the newspaper reporter misunderstood Clemens and that he said "Cobbett" rather than "Corbett." Cobbett's three-volume account of his impressions during the early days of the United States was likely among the books by British authors that James R. Osgood sent to Clemens in July 1882 for research as he was writing *Life on the Mississippi* (1883). The boisterous and opinionated William Cobbett had visited the United States between 1792 and 1800 and again between 1817 and 1819. He liked most of what he saw. Indeed, an angry "Postscript" to Volume III, "Fearon's Falsehoods," vigorously defends the United States and its citizens against Henry Bradshaw Fearon's criticisms and Fearon's implication that Cobbett shared these views. (See the Catalog entry for Fearon.)

Dewey Ganzel, "Twain, Travel Books" (1962), p. 41 n. 4.

COBDEN, RICHARD. See the Catalog entry for John Morley.

CODNER, ELIZABETH (HARRIS) (1824–1919). 'Even me" (hymn, 1860, melody added in 1862 by William B[atchelder]. Bradbury (1816–1868).

On 31 March 1869 Clemens wrote to Susan Crane from Hartford: "We play euchre every night, & sing 'Geer' [John Cawood's 'Hark! What mean those holy voices, melody composed by George Jarvis Geer], which is Livy's favorite, & 'Even Me,' which is mine, & a dozen other hymns" (*MTLet* 3: 181). This explains why Clemens had made a note for Olivia Langdon's eyes—dated midnight, 25 March 1869—in the margin of his copy of Oliver Wendell Holmes's *Autocrat of the Breakfast-Table* (at page 251): "I wish 'Even Me' to be sung at my funeral" (quoted by Bradford A. Booth, "Mark Twain's Comments on Holmes's *Autocrat*," *American Literature* 21.4 [January 1950]: 461). Codner's hymn could be seen as an extension of Clemens's efforts in courting Olivia to adopt the pose of a reformed one-time Western carouser; it stresses the unworthiness of sinners to receive God's grace, as the first two stanzas make clear: "Lord, I hear of showers of blessing,/Thou art scattering, full and free!/Showers the thirsty land refreshing/Let some portion fall on me,/Even me,/Let some portion fall on me. [Second stanza:] Pass me not, O God my Father,/Sinful though my heart may be;/Thou might'st leave me, but the rather/Let Thy mercy light on me,/Even me, even me!/Let Thy mercy light on me." A subsequent stanza reads, in part: "Have I long in sin been sleeping?/. . . . /Oh, forgive and rescue me,/ Even me, even me!/Oh, forgive and rescue me." Allison R. Ensor, "The Favorite Hymns of Sam and Livy Clemens," *Mark Twain Journal* 25.2 (Fall 1987): 21–22, points out variants in the lyrics in different hymnals.

CODY, WILLIAM FREDERICK (1846–1917). *The Adventures of Buffalo Bill, by Col. William F. Cody (Buffalo Bill). To Which Is Appended a Short Sketch of His Life.* New York: Harper & Brothers, [cop. 1904]. 156 pp.
   Source: MTLAcc, entry #438, volume donated by Clemens.
———. [Another identical copy.]
   Source: MTLAcc, entry #1172, volume donated by Clemens.
———. *The Adventures of Buffalo Bill, by Col. William F. Cody (Buffalo Bill). To Which Is Appended a Short Sketch of His Life.* Red cloth. New York: Harper & Brothers, 1905. 156 pp.
   Inscription: on front pastedown endpaper: "SL. Clemens/ Sept. 1905".
   Marginalia: pencil line on page 126 next to figures for pony-express riders' speed. No other markings.
   Provenance: Antenne-Dorrance Collection, Rice Lake, Wisconsin.
   Location: Mark Twain Archive, Gannett-Tripp Learning Center, Elmira College, Elmira, New York.
   Copy examined: Clemens's copy. Examined on 28 May 2015.
   The horse named "Soldier Boy" in "A Horse's Tale" (1906) was once Buffalo Bill's "favorite horse, out of dozens." The description of Cody in Chapter 1 is specific enough to have been influenced by Cody's *The Adventures of Buffalo Bill.*
———. *The Life of the Hon. William F. Cody, Known as Buffalo Bill, the Famous Hunter, Scout and Guide. An Autobiography.* Illus. Hartford, Connecticut: F. B. Bliss, [1879]. 365 pp.
   At the time that Mark Twain was collecting Far West materials to use in "Huck Finn and Tom Sawyer among the Indians" (written in 1884), Charles L. Webster wrote him from New York City on 9 July 1884: "1 sent you Buffalo Bill's, also an old frontier book" (MTP). Clemens replied on 10 July: "Package has arrived—Buffalo Bill's book, I hope" (*MTBus*, p. 267). When Cody's Wild West show came to Elmira in 1884, Clemens attended it on September 9th and 10th, declaring in a letter to Cody written on 10 September that the extravaganza "stirred me like a war song." He praised the genuineness of the show and urged Cody to take it to England (David Fears, *Day by Day* 1 [2]: 1244). Neither Clemens nor Cody ever mentioned meeting each other.
   HH&T (1969), pp. 85–86, 336; Charles C. Bradshaw, "Animal Welfare and the Democratic Frontier: Mark Twain's Condemnation of Bullfighting in *A Horse's Tale*," *Mark Twain Annual 17* (2019): 140–158.

COFFIN, CHARLES CARLETON (1823–1896). *Abraham Lincoln.* Illus. New York: Harper & Brothers, [cop. 1892]. 542 pp.
   Source: MTLAcc, entry #867, volume donated by Clemens.
   Although Coffin's biographies and histories were primarily written for young adults, they included dates and details that evinced careful research.
———. *The Boys of '76. A History of the Battles of the Revolution.* Illus. New York: Harper & Brothers, 1904. 398 pp.
   Source: MTLAcc, entry #1183, volume donated by Clemens.

———. *Drum-Beat of the Nation: The First Period of the War of the Rebellion from Its Outbreak to the Close of 1862.* Illus. New York: Harper & Brothers, [cop. 1887]. 478 pp.
   Source: MTLAcc, entry #864, volume donated by Clemens.
———. *Marching to Victory: The Second Period of the War of Rebellion.* Illus. New York: Harper & Brothers, [cop. 1888]. 491 pp.
   Source: MTLAcc, entry #865, volume donated by Clemens.
———. *Old Times in the Colonies.*
   Catalog: *C1951*, #13c, $27.50, listed with books signed by Clemens.
   According to a bill from Brown & Gross, Hartford booksellers, Clemens purchased "1 Old Times Colonies $2.40" on 22 November 1880, but the same statement also credits him for $2.40 on 7 December 1880 for "1 Old Times Colonies" (MTP). Perhaps the bookkeeper made an error in the latter entry, meaning to charge Clemens for a second copy.
———. *Old Times in the Colonies.* New York: Harper & Brothers, [cop. 1880]. 460 pp.
   Source: MTLAcc, entry #863, volume donated by Clemens.
———. *Redeeming the Republic: The Third Period of the War of the Rebellion.* Illus. New York: Harper & Brothers, [1889]. 478 pp.
   Source: MTLAcc, entry #866, volume donated by Clemens.
———. *The Story of Liberty.* Illus. New York: Harper & Brothers, [cop. 1878].
   Inscription: in Clemens's hand on the front flyleaf in blue ink: "Merry Christmas/to/Margaret Warner/from/Susie & Clara Clemens/1883."
   Location: Mark Twain House and Museum, Hartford, Connecticut. Given by an anonymous donor in 1963.
   Copy examined: a gift copy from Clemens's children. Examined in August 1987.
   Probably Clemens meant this children's book about European history when he noted in May 1888: "Get Jean a 'Liberty'" (NB 27, *N&J* 3: 390).

COFFIN, ROBERT BARRY (1826–1886), pseud. "Barry Gray."
   In a letter of 9 February 1871 Thomas Bailey Aldrich kiddingly threatened, if Clemens failed to look up Aldrich "when you come to Boston," to reveal that Clemens's real nom de plume is "Barry Gray" (*AutoMT* 4: 319). New York literary bohemian, journalist, and humorous author Coffin had written several books, including *My Married Life at Hillside* (1865) and *Cakes and Ale at Woodbine; From Twelfth Night to New Year's Day* (1868). Coffin had succeeded Aldrich as editor of the *Home Journal* in 1858.

COGGINS, PASCHAL H[ESTON] (1852–1917). "Old Sile's Clem," *Harper's Monthly* 96.576 (May 1898): 922–928.
   Coggins's sentimental dialect sketch describes the experiences of a homeless, wandering boy, Clement Smedley, who seeks a home for himself and his horse Nap in a backwoods region after his employer Sile Farley dies. Young Clem is eventually adopted by a kindly farmer, Uncle Billy Churchman.
   Clemens wrote to Joseph H. Twichell on 26 May 1898 from Austria: "Have you read 'Old Sile's Clem?' (May 'Harper.') I feel sure that it must be the best back-settlement study that was ever printed. O, the art of it! How well Coggins knows his ground, and what a sure and reserved and delicate touch he has. . . . There are things which the

finest genius cannot counterfeit with exactness, cannot perfectly imitate, & back-settlement wit is one of these, I think. . . . Watch out for Paschal H. Coggins; he is valuable and entitled to a grateful welcome" (*LMTJHT*, pp. 215–216). Attorney and author Coggins did not fulfill Clemens's expectations, though he did produce several mystery novels under the pseudonym "Sidney Marlow" as well as two legal advice books, *Law and How to Keep Out of It* (1901) and *Parliamentary Law* (cop. 1909). Clemens would pay similar tribute to a sketch by Ellis Parker Butler in the February 1899 *Century Magazine* that also combined pathos, American humor, and regional dialect.

COKE, E[DWARD]. T[HOMAS] (1807–1888). *A Subaltern's Furlough: Descriptive of Scenes in Various Parts of the United States, Upper and Lower Canada, New-Brunswick, and Nova Scotia, During the Summer and Autumn of 1832*. 2 vols. First edition. Original faded tan pebbled cloth, paper spine label. Front hinge parted, rebacked with original spine and label laid down. New York: J. & J. Harper, 1833. [Only Volume I of Clemens's copy has been found.]

Inscriptions: Beverly Hills bookseller Maxwell Hunley made pencil notes on the front endpapers of Volume I.

Marginalia: Volume I marked and annotated in pencil by Clemens on pages 78, 101, 148, 153, 154, 155, and 164. Clemens's notes amount to seventy-three words scattered over six pages. On page 78 Clemens turned down the page corner and commented about the fact that English carriages customarily pass each other on the left, whereas in the United States it is just the opposite: "So we even changed that. How did that ever happen? It is odd." In the margin of page 101, beside the passage in which Coke casually mentions spending "several agreeable hours" with Andrew Jackson, Clemens penciled: "Any foreign scrub can familiarly visit the President—whereas with us it is held a high honor." At the top of that same page Clemens scoffed at "That barn, the White house," and at the bottom of the page he noted about the White House: "These people usually strain their politeness, & try to compliment it, as they do the steamboats." (Clemens folded down the top corner of this page.) Pages 148, 153, and 154 contain notes and marks. Along the bottom margin of page 155 Clemens penciled: "English efforts to write as Americans talk—I guess, calc'late, reckon & c". At the top of page 164, which contains a description of the untidy appearance of rutted, dank East Hartford, Clemens noted, "*Old* Hartford." There are a few other notes and several more page corners are turned down.

Catalogs: ListABP (1910), "A Subaltern's Furlough, Coke", no other information supplied; Christie's, New York City, 1–2 February 1988, lot 466, Volume I only, sold with two other books for $2,200. J. L. Feldman listed Volume I in his Catalog 41; "The James S. Copley Library," Sotheby's auction, New York City, 17 June 2010, lot 556, sold with five other titles for $4,250.

Provenance: the front pastedown endpaper of Volume I has the shelfmark ("T/H27") of Clara Clemens Samossoud's private library numbering system from her Detroit years. Donated to the Carrie Estelle Doheny Collection, St. John's Seminary, Camarillo, California, by Mrs. Doheny in November 1940 after its purchase from Maxwell Hunley Rare Books of Beverly Hills. Sold by Christie's of New York City in 1988 on behalf of St. John's Seminary and the Archdiocese of Los Angeles.

Location: Volume I only in the collection of Kevin Mac Donnell of Austin, Texas. Acquired in 2010 (Mac Donnell to Alan Gribben, 29 June 2010).

Copy examined: Clemens's copy of Volume I, when it was at St. John's Seminary. It had the leather bookplate of "Estelle Doheny" on the front pastedown endpaper.

COLBY, FRANK MOORE (1865–1925). *Imaginary Obligations*. New York: Dodd, Mead & Co., 1906. 335 pp.

Marginalia: notes in black ink by Clemens on pages 62, 63, and 110; passages marked on pages 120 and 121. Clemens's note on page 62 concerns Colby's reference to "a schoolboy mind" that edits a paper; Clemens observed: "It fits another living public man—also Mr. McKinley." A note on page 63 makes the same assertion about those who display a "taint of commonness." Regarding a discussion of hazing practices at West Point, Clemens wrote: "They made the place unsatisfactory to Whistler & to Edgar A. Poe."

Provenance: sticker of Brentano's Booksellers of New York City on the rear pastedown endpaper.

Catalogs: A1911, "12mo, cloth, N.Y. 1905," quotes one of three notes by Clemens, "also letter of presentation of the book by Edgar Jay Chapman to Mr. Clemens," lot 105, sold for $4.50; George D. Smith, New York City, "Catalogue of Books" (1911), quotes several notes by Clemens, item #74, $15; Dawson's Bookshop Catalog number 70 (1930), p. 8, "laid in . . . Autographed Letter Signed, from Eleanor Jay Chapman to Mr. Clemens, 4 pp. l2mo, no place or date, relative to sending the above work to Clemens"; Chicago Book & Art Auction, Inc., Sale number 30 (25 January 1933), E. W. Evans Collection, p. 12, with "an ALS laid in from Eleanor Jay Chapman to Clemens."

Location: Henry W. and Albert A. Berg Collection, New York Public Library.

Copy examined: Clemens's copy, containing the *A1911* sale label.

The witty if somewhat elitist Frank Moore Colby was an American educator, editor, and essayist. *Imaginary Obligations*, much of which could be classified as literary and dramatic criticism, would prove to be his most popular book.

COLE, T[IMOTHY] (1852–1931). "Notes by T. Cole on the 'Adoration,'" *Century Magazine* 41.6 (April 1891): 842–843. Cole's brief note describes Leonardo da Vinci's unfinished painting, "The Adoration of the Magi." Page 843 reproduces Cole's engraving of a detail from the painting, which he copied in the Uffizi Gallery in Florence. Cole depicts the work meticulously, gives its measurements, and specifies exactly where it hangs. He even records the colors of each section. He concludes by asserting that "Adoration" in his opinion "far surpasses anything else of its kind" (p. 842). Cole's brief note and his wood engraving accompany W. J. Stillman's "Leonardo da Vinci, 1452–1519" (pp. 838–842), an essay that was part of the Italian Old Masters series in the *Century*.

Clemens wished to "scrap-book the 'Adoration' 842–3 April Century, 1891," he reminded himself in April (NB 30, *N&J* 3: 617). The *Century* had dispatched the artist Cole to Europe to prepare wood engravings from paintings by the Old Masters.

COLEMAN, F[RANK]. M[ORRIS] (1860–1915). *Typical Pictures of Indian Natives, Being Reproductions from Photographs*. Illus. Bombay: "The Times of India" Office, 1898. 50 pp.

Source: MTLAcc, entry #1221, volume donated by Clemens.

In 1892 Morris had acquired *The Times of India* in partnership with Thomas Bennett. Morris would perish on the *S. S. Persia* when it was torpedoed by Germany in 1915.

COLERIDGE, SAMUEL TAYLOR (1772–1834). *The Complete Works of Samuel Taylor Coleridge*. 7 volumes. New York: Harper & Brothers, 1871–1875. [Only four volumes are present.]

Provenance: the surviving volumes have the shelfmarks of Clara Clemens Gabrilowitsch's library numbering system during her Detroit years. Sold at the 1951 auction in Hollywood but not listed in the sale sheet.

Catalog: "Property from the Library of Mark Twain," Butterfield & Butterfield, San Francisco, Sale 6613 (16 July 1997), "4 vols. (of 7)," lot 2712.

Location: Mark Twain House and Museum, Hartford, Connecticut (Volumes 1, 2, 3, and 6 only).

Copies examined: copies of four volumes (of the original seven) belonging to the Clemens family library. Viewed in Hartford in 1997.

———. *The Complete Works of Samuel Taylor Coleridge*. Ed. by William Greenough Thayer Sledd (1820–1894). 7 vols. New York: Harper & Brothers, 1884.

Source: MTLAcc, entries #1751–1756, 2771, complete set donated by Clemens.

———. *The Poems of Samuel Taylor Coleridge*. Ed. by Derwent Coleridge (1800–1883) and Sara Coleridge (1802–1852). Copyright Edition. Collection of British Authors Series. Leipzig: B. Tauchnitz, 1860. 344 pp.

Source: MTLAcc, entry #2050, volume donated from Clemens's library by Clara Clemens Gabrilowitsch in 1910.

———. *The Rime of the Ancient Mariner*. Illus. by Joseph Noël Paton (1821–1901). New York: 1875.

Inscription: on flyleaf: "Saml. L. Clemens, Hartford. 1875."

Catalog: *A1911*, "oblong 4to, decorative cloth, gilt top and edges, N.Y. 1875," quotes the signature, lot 106, $4.

Location: undetermined.

In 1866 Clemens referred to Captain James Smith of the *Ajax* as "Ye Ancient Mariner" (NB 6, *N&J* 1: 188). He jocularly addressed Emma B. Beach as "Ancient Mariner" in a letter from Washington, D.C. on 10 February 1868 (Bradford A. Booth, "Mark Twain's Friendship with Emma Beach," *Mark Twain Journal* 8.1 [Winter 1947]: 8; *MTLet* 2: 183). The "waiter . . . kept his ancient-mariner eye steadily & accusingly on us while our breakfast cooked" (NB 13 [May 1877], *N&J* 2: 15). During a snow-storm Riley backed his hapless victim "against an iron fence, buttonholed him, fastened him with his eye, like the ancient mariner, and proceeded to unfold his narrative" in Chapter 26 of *A Tramp Abroad* (1880), a miniature burlesque of Coleridge's mariner lecturing the Wedding Guest. "A visiting pilot" on a steamboat named the *Skylark*, "a poor old broken-down, superannuated fellow," is referred to as "the ancient mariner" in Chapter 30 of *Life on the Mississippi* (1883). Farther on, in Chapter 50, whenever a group of pilots was gossiping and bragging,

the sudden appearance of Captain Isaiah Sellers, a true "ancient mariner" and "Son of Antiquity," would bring instant silence to their conversation. The hero and heroine of Mark Twain's abortive "Burlesque Sea Story" (written in 1895) hear "a burst of mocking laughter" that sounds like "ship-wrecked mariners gone mad with hunger and thirst and misery," and discover that "the hush of death lay upon ship and sea" (DV331, MTP). Twain's "The Enchanted Sea-Wilderness" (written in 1896) also resembles the dismal shipboard scenes in Coleridge's fantastic poem (*WWD?*, pp. 76–86). Twain told a reporter in 1900 that when he finally repaid his enormous business debts he "felt like the Ancient Mariner when the dead albatross fell into the sea. I became a new man" ("Mark Twain Home, An Anti-Imperialist," New York *Herald*, 16 October 1900; Scharnhorst, ed., *Complete Interviews*, p. 355). Andrew Carnegie, declared Mark Twain, has "the deadliest affliction I know of. He is the Ancient Mariner over again; it is not possible to divert him from his subject" (2 December 1907 AD, *MTE*, pp. 37–38; *AutoMT* 3: 182).

In "A Second Possible Source for Mark Twain's 'The Aged Pilot Man,'" *Revue de littárature comparée* 36 (July-September 1962): 451–453, Roger L. Brooks proposed that "the poetic form and certain lines" of Twain's comical poem in Chapter 51 of *Roughing It* (1872) "evince a remarkable similarity to Coleridge's 'The Ancient Mariner'" ballad (pp. 451–452). (Twain had credited an old song called "The Raging Canal.")

S. B. Liljegren, "Revolt" (1945), p. 24; Scott, *OPMT* (1960), p. 5; Baetzhold, *MT&JB* (1970), p. 277.

———. *The Rime of the Ancient Mariner*. Illustrated by [Paul] Gustave Doré (1832–1883). New York: Harper & Brothers, 1876. [Folio-size book.]

Inscription: the front flyleaf is inscribed by Clemens in violet ink, "To Livy L. Clemens/Nov. 27, 1876./From S. L. Clemens".

Catalogs: *A1911*, "folio, cloth, gilt edges, N.Y. 1876," quotes inscription, lot 135, purchased by the Mark Twain Company for $37; offered again at the *C1951* auction, lot D74, "autographed by S. L. Clemens," sold for $225.

Location: Mark Twain House and Museum, Hartford, Connecticut. Donated by Mrs. John L. Martin of Darien, Connecticut.

Copy examined: Olivia Clemens's copy. Examined in August 1987. There is an *A1911* sale label on the front endpaper.

———. *Selections from Coleridge: The Rime of the Ancient Mariner, Christabel, and Kubla Khan*. Ed. Lincoln R. Gibbs. Boston: Ginn and Co., 1898. 90 pp.

Catalog: Ball 2016 inventory, green cloth with black lettering, good condition.

Location: Quarry Farm library shelves, under the supervision of the Mark Twain Archive, Elmira College, Elmira, New York.

This volume was available to Clemens at Quarry Farm in Elmira, New York.

COLERIDGE, SARA (COLERIDGE) (1802–1852). *Memoir and Letters of Sara Coleridge*. Ed. by Edith Coleridge (1832–1911). New York: Harper & Brothers, 1874. 528 pp. [Edition is conjectured. The first edition was published in London in 1873].

On 29 June 1874 Olivia Clemens wrote to Clemens: "Sara Coleridge says in writing to her husband of one of their children 'Don't fancy that children will listen to lectures either in learning or morality,'" adding that there is "more that I would like to quote but will wait and read it to you" (*The Twainian* 37 [November-December 1978]: 3–4; *MTLet* 6: 174–175). In a letter of 1 July 1874 Olivia Clemens referred to the book again, "How I do love our babies and how I do desire to have wisdom given me for their guidance—There is much in this life of Sara Coleridge that is suggestive on this subject" (*MTLet* 6: 176).

———. *Phantasmion, A Fairy Tale. By Sara Coleridge. With an Introductory Preface by Lord [John Duke] Coleridge [1820–1894, First Baron Coleridge].* Boston: Roberts Brothers, 1874. 348 pp. [Originally published in London in 1837 as *Phantasmion: Prince of Palmland*.]

Estes & Lauriat of Boston billed Clemens on 14 July 1880 for "1 Phantasmion .75¢" and he paid the bill on 20 July (receipt in MTP). No other titles in this period are sufficiently similar to cause doubt that Clemens or Olivia Clemens bought a copy of Coleridge's book.

Lord Coleridge's Preface explains that *Phantasmion*, "the product of the enforced leisure on a sick bed[,] . . . was first given to the world in 1837" (p. iii).

COLLIER, ROBERT JOSEPH (1876–1918).

Robert Collier was the son of Peter F. Collier, who founded *Collier's Weekly* in 1888; Robert worked at the magazine and would succeed to its editorship in 1909. Finley Peter Dunne called Robert Collier "a much loved friend" of Clemens, though the older author "always treated Collier and me as if we were still in our adolescence. . . . He would say, 'I like you young fellows. I like to have you around me. But you mustn't expect me to listen to your opinions.'" On one occasion he joshingly said to Dunne, "Collier is all right. He is not strictly speaking a man of culture. He is only a publisher. But he has literary associations. So far as a man in his ignorant trade can be, he's a man of letters." Collier was on the committee with Clemens and Howells to receive Maxim Gorki when the Russian revolutionary visited the United States in 1906 (*Mr. Dooley Remembers: Finley Peter Dunne*, ed. Philip Dunne [Boston: Little, Brown, 1963], pp. 249–250, 254).

[COLLIER, WILLIAM FRANCIS. *History of the British Empire.*] Originally published in London in 1867. Revised editions were published in Nelson's School Series issued by T. Nelson and Sons of London in the succeeding decades. [This edition is unknown, since the title page is missing.]

Inscription: in pencil at the top of the table of contents: "Clara Langdon Clemens/Ballarat October 1895,/ Australia."

Marginalia: a few notes in pencil, seemingly by either Clara or Olivia Clemens.

Provenance: contains book stamps of the Mark Twain Library, Redding, Connecticut.

Catalog: *Mott 1952*, #45, $2.50.

Location: Mark Twain House and Museum, Hartford, Connecticut. Anonymous gift in 1963.

Copy examined: presumably Clara Clemens's book, but it lacks all leaves up to the table of contents. Merely the author's last name—Collier—is recoverable; since the book narrates English history from its beginnings, the author and title can be supplied with some certainty.

Examined in August 1987.

Collier, a professor at Trinity College in Dublin, wrote many history books for schools and young readers.

Collier's Weekly (periodical, published 1888–1957).

A photograph of Clemens that Albert Bigelow Paine took in 1906 (now in MTP) shows him reading an unidentifiable issue of *Collier's Weekly* in bed. To the editors of *Collier's* Clemens expressed approval on 6 July 1908 about the installments of Wallace Irwin's *Letters of a Japanese Schoolboy* that were appearing in the magazine (Yale). Clemens ridiculed Norman Hapgood's editorial praise of Theodore Roosevelt that appeared in the 11 July 1908 issue (14 July 1908 AD, *MTE*, pp. 24–32; *AutoMT*: 3: 254). Clemens's nephew Samuel E. Moffett joined the staff of *Collier's* in 1908; when Moffett died that year Clemens quoted from Moffett's obituary published by the magazine in a piece Clemens titled "Samuel Erasmus Moffett" written on 16 August 1908 (MTP).

COLLIN, GRACE LATHROP (1874–1913). *Putnam Place.* New York: Harper & Brothers, 1903. 262 pp.

Source: MTLAcc, entry #1440, volume donated by Clemens.

William Dean Howells favorably reviewed *Putnam Place* in *Harper's Weekly*, but Clemens dissented in a letter to Howells. "Putnam Place did not much interest me; so I knew it was high literature. I have never been able to get up high enough to be at home with high literature" (SLC to WDH, Riverdale, 29 April 1903, *MTHL*, p. 769). Howells continued the argument in a jesting spirit from New York City on 1 May 1903: "But you'd better take a brace, and try to get up as high as 'Putnam Place'" (*MTHL*, p. 769). Such remarks by Clemens tended to encourage his friend to think of him as essentially "unliterary." *Putnam Place* collected Collins's short stories about the declining influence of older values in New England.

COLLINS, [WILLIAM] WILKIE (1824–1889). *Armadale; A Novel.* New York: Harper & Brothers, 1905. 658 pp.

Source: MTLAcc, entry #1675, volume donated by Clemens.

———. *Basil.* Illus. New York: Harper & Brothers, 1904. 336 pp.

Source: MTLAcc, entry #1142, volume donated by Clemens.

———. *The Lady in White* (novel, published in 1860).

If Clemens decided to acquire *any* works of fiction by Collins, one would think he would have obtained *The Lady in White*, an early and notable crime detection novel. When a researcher encounters odd gaps in his library like this one it is well to recall the great number (hundreds, perhaps even a thousand or more) of his book donations that went unrecorded.

———. *The New Magdalen. A Novel.* Illus. New York: Harper & Brothers, [cop. 1873]. 325 pp.

Source: MTLAcc, entry #1141, volume donated by Clemens.

Clemens met Wilkie Collins at a dinner in London, as he informed Mrs. Fairbanks on 6 July 1873 (*MTLet* 5: 402). He received complimentary tickets to Collins's dramatized version of *The New Magnalen* in London but was unable to go (*MTLet* 5: 405 n. 7). Clemens did attend a dinner for Collins in Boston on 16 February 1874 (Fears, 1.2, p.

574; SLC to James Redpath, 13 February 1874, *MTLet* 6: 34). In 1897 he recalled the prominent authors who attended a "Longfellow-Whittier-Trowbridge-Wilkie Collins dinner" (NB 42, TS p. 22). Mark Twain quoted Collins's statement that "Cooper is the greatest artist in the domain of romantic fiction yet produced by America" as an epigraph to "Fenimore Cooper's Literary Offences" (1895), citing no specific source.

———. *The Two Destinies; A Novel*. Illus. New York: Harper & Brothers, 1905. 312 pp.
> Source: MTLAcc, entry #1530, volume donated by Clemens.

COLLINS, WILLIAM (1721–1759). "Ode Written in the Beginning of the Year 1746" (published in 1747). Better recognized as "How Sleep the Brave."
> Clemens started a letter of 30 January 1862 sent to his mother from Carson City with lines from this poem intermixed with lines from other poets' works. "Bully, isn't it?" he asked (*PRI*, p. 29; *MTLet* 1: 146). The English poet Collins's tribute to soldiers who die for their nation, then well known, opens, "How sleep the brave, who sink to rest,/By all their country's wishes blest!" Clemens had borrowed the first line.

COLLYER, ROBERT (1823–1912). *Nature and Life: Sermons.* Boston: Horace B. Fuller, 1867. 313 pp.
> Source: MTLAcc, entry #904, volume donated by Clemens.
> On 17 January 1869 Clemens wrote to Olivia Langdon from Chicago: "In the cars, the other day I bought a volume of remarkable sermons—they are from the pen & pulpit of Rev. Geo. [*sic*] Collyer, of Chicago: I like them very much. . . . They are more polished, more poetical, more elegant, more rhetorical, & more dainty & felicitous in wording" than Henry Ward Beecher's sermons (*LLMT*, p. 53; *MTLet* 3: 46). Unitarian minister Robert Collyer was pastor of the First Unity Church on the North Side of Chicago.

COLQUHOUN, ARCHIBALD ROSS (1848–1914). *Greater America*. Maps. New York: Harper & Brothers, 1904. 436 pp.
> Source: MTLAcc, entry #1714, volume donated by Clemens.
> Collquhoun undertakes a (too often equivocal) discussion of race relations in the United States, the nation's evolving policies of colonialization, the future of the Philippines and Cuba, and American foreign relations in general.

COLTON, ARTHUR WILLIS (1868–1943). *"The Debatable Land." A Novel*. New York: Harper & Brothers, 1901. 312 pp. [Publisher conjectured.]
> Inscription: "S. L. Clemens, Riverdale, Dec. 1901."
> Catalog: *A1911*, "12mo, cloth, N.Y. 1901," quotes the signature, lot 108, sold for $2.75.
> A romance that begins and ends in New England, but deeply involving the Civil War and Antietam.

COLTON, C. WOOLWORTH. *Colton's New Sectional Map of the State of Arkansas*. New York: G. W. & C. B. Colton, 1874.
> Inscriptions: the verso of the folded map is signed boldly in the center in black ink, "Mark Twain". The autograph seems patently forged. At the top of the opposite folded section appears the stamped ink signature of "Rev. W. G. Manley." Two prices written in different hands appear below the latter signature: "5.00" and "3,500."
> Provenance: offered for sale online in 2005 by the Heritage

Book Shop, Los Angeles, California. "Hand colored. Signed by Mark Twain on verso map. Folding pocket in embossed brown cloth folder with gilt title on cover. Light soiling."
> Copy examined: photocopies of the "Mark Twain" autograph and the bookseller's catalog entry sent to Alan Gribben by Kevin Mac Donnell of Austin, Texas on 18 August 2005. This is almost certainly a forgery, probably perpetrated in the twentieth century.

———. *County & Township Map of Ohio, Indiana & Michigan*. Large hand-colored folding map in original cloth folding case, gilt, some minor edge-tears. New York: Colton, 1865.
> Inscription: signed on the verso of the map in brown ink, "Mark Twain."
> Source: laid in is a letter to the Mark Twain collector Nick Karanovich of Fort Wayne, Indiana from a prominent bookseller attesting the authenticity of the item and asking a price of $300. A second letter, dated a week later after Karanovich had determined that the signature was a forgery, offered to let Karanovich keep the map as an example of a fake (notes in the collection of Kevin Mac Donnell, Austin, Texas). Possibly this spurious autograph was created by the Utah forger Mark Hofmann (b. 1954), who was sentenced to life imprisonment in 1987 for murders related to his forgeries.
> Location: currently part of the forgery collection of a prominent expert in historical documents, Kenneth W. Rendell, in Somerville, Massachusetts.

COLUMBUS, CHRISOPHER (1451–1506). *Writings of Christopher Columbus, Descriptive of the Discovery and Occupation of the New World*. Ed. and intro. by Paul Leicester Ford (1865–1902). Fiction, Fact, and Fancy Series, ed. Arthur Stedman (1859–1908).New York: Charles L. Webster & Co., 1892. 255 pp.
> Clemens's publishing firm issued this book, so he may have examined it in manuscript or book form. Columbus's reputation has risen and fallen over the centuries. In Clemens's era the admiration for the explorer's feats was at its zenith.
> Mark Twain's writings evoked the name of Columbus and the date of his great discovery, 1492, numerous times, usually to convey a sense of historical momentousness. See the Catalog entry for Frederick Ober's *Columbus the Discoverer* for a sampling of these many allusions. Laurence Bergreen's *Columbus: The Four Voyages, 1492–1504* describes Columbus's ingenious use of a lunar eclipse to terrify a tribe of recalcitrant Native Americans, a device that Hank Morgan would employ in Chapter 6 of *A Connecticut Yankee in King Arthur's Court* (1889).

COLVIN, VERPLANCK (1847–1920). *The Adirondack Region*. Illus. Albany, N. Y.: Weed, Parsons & Co., 1880. 536 pp.
> Source: MTLAcc, entry #578, volume donated by Clemens.
> Author, illustrator, and topographical engineer Colvin advocated the preservation of unspoiled areas of the Adirondacks. He explored and mapped the wilderness and was instrumental in 1885 in establishing the Adirondack Forest Preserve to halt the clear-cutting of timber lands. A peak in the region was named Mount Colvin in his honor.

COMBE, GEORGE (1788–1858). *Notes on the United States of North America, During a Phrenological Visit in 1838–9–40*. 2 vols. Philadelphia: Carey & Hart, 1841. [Only Volume I of Clemens's copy has been located.]

Inscription: in black ink on the front pastedown endpaper of Volume I: "SL. Clemens/1909."

Marginalia: Volume I contains a few markings and notes in brown ink and pencil. The fullest comment appears on page 94, where Combe quotes a "highly intelligent friend" who prophesied the fall of the Church of England within five years; Combe himself predicts that this will occur in fifty years. Clemens wrote vertically in brown ink along the margin: "The one highly intelligent prophet missed it by 5 years, & the other by 70—& still no prospect."

Catalogs: ListABP (1910), "Combe's Tour of the U. S. 2 v."; *A1911*, "Vol. I, 12mo, cloth (torn), Phila. 1841," quotes the signature, lot 109, sold for $1.

Location: Volume I only in the Mark Twain Papers, Bancroft Library, University of California at Berkeley. Acquired from the University of California at Los Angeles in 1971 after I discovered that it was shelved in the Circulation Department of the U.C.L.A. general library, where it had accidentally been cataloged. (I had ordered a copy of Combe's book through the Interlibrary Loan Service at the University of California at Berkeley because I wanted to determine why Clemens had been interested in this title. Imagine my astonishment when Clemens's own signed copy arrived at the Interlibrary Loan desk! I initially thought I was hallucinating when I opened the volume and saw his signature as I was walking down the Doe Library hallway.)

Copy examined: Clemens's copy of Volume I, in 1971.

George Combe founded the Phrenological Society in 1820 and established the *Phrenological Journal* in 1823. In 1838 he embarked on a lecture tour to the United States and Canada during which he met numerous Americans of importance and described their phrenological features. Mark Twain himself had an interest in phrenology from an early age. He would refer to Combe's book in the manuscript of *Life on the Mississippi* (1883) as his authority for the severity of laws regulating morality in early-day Hartford. He added in his footnote that "this Scot always praised us when he could; and found fault with us reluctantly"—but that entire passage was dropped from the final version of *Life on the Mississippi*. Twain's other extracts would have quoted Combe's descriptions in Volume II, Chapter 5 about the barbaric treatment of insane poor people in Pennsylvania. Twain was also struck by Combe's account of how pedestrians in Philadelphia were obliged to give way to wheel-barrows. Here is another clear instance of Clemens's signing a volume many years after he originally purchased and read it.

Dewey Ganzel, "Twain, Travel Books" (1962), p. 41 n. 4; Alan Gribben, "Mark Twain, Phrenology, and the 'Temperaments': A Study of Pseudoscientific Influence," *American Quarterly* 24.1 (March 1972): 45–68 (a revised version of this essay appears as a chapter in Volume One of the present work).

COMBE, WILLIAM (1742–1823). *The History and Antiquities of the City of York, from Its Origin to the Present Times*. Illus. 3 vols. York, England, 1785.

Inscription: each volume is signed: "Saml. L. Clemens, York, July 19, 1873."

Marginalia: numerous notes in Volume 1. For example,

Clemens made a note about "Jane Hodson, wife of the Chancellor of the Cathedral, died in 1638, giving birth to her 24th child, she being in her 38th year." Clemens wondered about an eight-year-old son of Edward III who was buried in 1344 with money paid every year for prayers for his soul. Clemens queried: "Question—if the prayers are still said." He noted that the "man that made the big window in the Minster, 1430, got 4 shillings a day for it and was not to be over 3 years at it." Regarding the expulsion of Jews in the time of Edward I, Clemens commented: "The question is, when did savagery cease in England?" He also observed: "Edward's son was the first nobleman that was ever beheaded in England—started the fashion." The *A1911* and 1920 auction catalogs quote a few other minor notes.

Catalogs: *A 1911*, "3 vols., 12mo, half cloth, not returnable, York, 1785," quotes signature and marginalia, lot 242, sold for $10 for 3 vols; Anderson Auction Galleries (New York City), Sale number 1525 (4 November 1920), "12mo, boards, cloth backs, "autograph ... in each volume" (quoted), "numerous marginal notes by Mr. Clemens" in Volume 1 (four examples are quoted), lot 10, for sale $45.

Clemens and Olivia visited York in July 1873. He wrote to Olivia Lewis Langdon on 20 July 1873 about "this queer old walled town, with its crooked, narrow lanes" and described York Cathedral and many historical events connected with the city (*MTLet* 5: 419). Combe's book is now considered to be merely a compilation derived from an earlier history.

Baender, ed, *WIM?* (1973), pp. 83, 543.

Comet (newspaper, published in 1871).

On 5 May 1871 Clemens wrote to praise an amateur newspaper edited and published by a youth named Henri Gerard in Newburgh, Orange County, New York: "The 'Comet' is a neat paper & a readable one" (*MTLet* 4: 390). Clemens subscribed for three copies, with one of them to be sent to his eleven-year-old nephew Samuel E. Moffett. The newspaper lapsed after 1871.

COMMYNES, PHILIPPE DE (c. 1447–1511). *The Memoirs of Philip de Commines, Lord of Argenton: Containing the Histories of Louis XI. and Charles VIII., Kings of France, and of Charles the Bold, Duke of Burgundy. To Which is Added, the Scandalous Chronicle, or Secret History of Louis XI., by Jean de Troyes [pseud. of Jean de Roye, fl. 1460–1483]*. Ed. by Andrew R[ichard]. Scoble (1831–1916). Original dark green cloth, spine lettered in gilt, Volume II shaken, hinges weak. 2 vols. London: Henry G. Bohn, 1856. [Only Volume II of Clemens's copy has been located.]

Inscription: Beverly Hills bookseller Maxwell Hunley made pencil notes on the front free endpaper.

Marginalia: Volume II contains Clemens's pencil markings on six pages and one comment at the top of page 35 in black ink (near the underscored word "nobility"): "Nowhere in this book, as far as I can remember, are the common people ever thought of." Clemens made marginal lines or exclamation marks in pencil on pages 37, 40, 94, 145, and 152–153. Pages 34 and 168 were turned down. The leaves were not cut between pages 177 and 296 and from 397 to the end. The leaves were opened beginning with the "Scandalous Chronicles" of Louis of Valois. Page

352 was folded down. The index leaves remain uncut.

Provenance: the front pastedown endpaper of Volume II displays the shelfmarks ("Bc/LS34") of Clara Clemens Samossoud's private library numbering system during her Detroit years. Subsequently Volume II was purchased in 1940 for $5 by Estelle Doheny from Maxwell Hunley Rare Books of Beverly Hills. She donated it to the Carrie Estelle Doheny Collection, St. John's Seminary, Camarillo, California. Sold by Christie's in New York City in 1988 (lot 466) at the request of St. John's Seminary and the Archdiocese of Los Angeles.

Catalogs: Christie's, New York City, 1–2 February 1988 auction, Volume II only, sold with two other books for $2,200; subsequently listed by J. L. Feldman in Catalog 63; "The James S. Copley Library," Sotheby's auction, New York City, 17 June 2010, Volume II only, lot 556, sold with five other titles for $4,250.

Location: Volume II only in the collection of Kevin Mac Donnell, Austin, Texas. Acquired in 2010 (Mac Donnell to Alan Gribben, 29 June 2010).

Copy examined: Clemens's copy of Volume II, when it was at St. John's Seminary.

The *Mémoires* of the shrewd, instinctive French courtier and diplomat Philippe de Commynes chronicled the history of his period and captured unsparing character sketches of Charles the Bold, Louis XI, Charles VIII, and other prominent figures.

COMSTOCK, J[OHN]. L[EE]. (1789–1858). *Elements of Geology; Including Fossil Botany and Palæontology. A Popular Treatise on the Most Interesting Parts of the Science. Designed for the Use of Schools and General Readers.* New York: Pratt, Woodford, and Co., 1851. 432 pp.

Inscription: signed on the front free endpaper in pencil with a youthful flourish below the name: "Samuel L. Clemens/1856./June 25th, 1856." On the first flyleaf, vertically, in pencil: "Jennie N. Curtis/1915." Clemens was living in Keokuk, Iowa in the summer of 1856.

Marginalia: pencil mark around Charles Lyell's works in the list of "Authorities" at the front of book. A few money figures on the rear pastedown endpaper do not appear to be Clemens's. Several stray pencil marks are visible on the first pages of the volume.

Provenance: bookplate on the front pastedown endpaper identifies the volume as #583 from the library of Charles L. Webster, New York City. Priced at $15 in the corner of the front free endpaper. A Yale University bookplate dated 1946 is affixed to the rear pastedown endpaper.

Location: Beinecke Library, Yale University.

Copy examined: Clemens's copy, very possibly the earliest-acquired book from his library to have survived. Presumably Clemens's mother or sister brought the volume East when they moved to Fredonia, New York to live with Annie (Moffett) Webster and her husband; the Charles L. Websters later moved to New York City in 1882, when Jane Lampton Clemens returned to Keokuk, Iowa, and Pamela (Clemens) Moffett left for California to live with her son Samuel. Evidently this book remained in Webster's library.

J. Michael Pratt, "A Fossil Guide to Mark Twain's Essay 'Was the World Made for Man?,'" *Mark Twain Annual* 3 (2005): 81–89.

CONANT, CHARLES ARTHUR (1861–1915). *The Principles of Banking.* New York: Harper & Brothers, 1908. 487 pp.

Source: MTLAcc, entry #536, volume donated by Clemens.

———. *The Principles of Money and Banking.* 2 vols. New York: Harper & Brothers, 1905.

Source: MTLAcc, entries #534 and #535, volumes donated by Clemens.

———. *The Principles of Money and Banking.* 2 vols. New York: Harper & Brothers, [cop. 1905].

Source: MTLAcc, entries #1698 and #1699b, volumes donated by Clemens.

Confession of Faith (unidentified book).

Source: ListABP (1910), "Confession of Faith (notes on the cover)."

Several religious denominations have published such titles, and it is difficult to guess the book to which Albert Bigelow Paine so cryptically referred. Jo Dee Benussi noticed that Henry Ward Beecher's Plymouth Church in Brooklyn issued a booklet titled *The Confession of Faith, Covenant, Ecclesiastical Principles, Forms of Admission, Etc.* (*MTLet* 2: 356), and suggested to me that Olivia Clemens might have sent a copy of it to Clemens in 1868. This seems to be the most plausible possibility of those I have turned up.

CONGREVE, WILLIAM (1670–1729). *The Mourning Bride* (tragedy, performed in 1697).

By the mid-1860s Clemens was apparently familiar with at least the famous first line of this play: "Music hath charms to soothe the savage breast." William Gillis testified that he reminded Clemens how "upon the occasion of our visit to the young ladies of French Flat you told me that 'music had charms to sooth the savage' and advised me to cultivate—if I had any—my talent for it" (William Robert Gillis [1849–1929], *Memories of Mark Twain and Steve Gillis [1838–1918]: Personal Recollections of the Famous Humorist* [Sonora, California: Printed by the Banner, 1924], p. 39).

CONKLING, ALFRED RONALD (1850–1917). *The Life and Letters of Roscoe Conkling [1829–1888], Orator, Statesman, Advocate.* New York: Charles L. Webster & Company, 1889. 709 pp.

Clemens's publishing firm issued this biography of the United States Senator from New York who vigorously opposed the policies of several presidents.

CONN, HERBERT WILLIAM (1859–1917). *The Story of Germ Life: Bacteria.* [The first edition was published in New York and London in 1897; the edition that Mark Twain consulted has not been established.]

Henry J. Lindborg—"A Cosmic Tramp: Samuel Clemens' *Three Thousand Years Among the Microbes,*" *American Literature* 44.4 (January 1973): 652–657—looked at Twain's concepts of microscopic life in the context of the "materials which would have been available to him from popular sources" (p. 652). Mainly Twain relied on C. W. Saleeby's *The Cycle of Life,* but Lindborg also identified (p. 654 n. 9) the title of another book Twain employed in "Three Thousand Years Among the Microbes" (written in 1905). H. W. Conn's book was apparently the source for Twain's point that most bacteria are harmless and often actually beneficial. (In one place Lindborg accidentally referred to the author as "R. D. Conn" and confusingly called the book "*Life of the Germ.*") Twain's narrator alludes to a prior existence "when I was studying micrology under Prof. H. W. Conn. . . . We knew that . . . the microbe was the protector and preserver. . . . We also knew that the human race . . . charged *all* microbes with being disease-germs" (*WWD?*, p. 523–524). According to Twain's narrator, Conn had grasped the vital part played by microbes in the life cycle on earth.

Connecticut Magazine: An Illustrated Monthly 9.2 (April-May-June 1905).

> Source: ListABP (1910), "Conn. Magazine, Apl 1905".

> Clemens might have been interested in several items in this issue of the Hartford periodical, including articles titled "Is the World Growing Better?" and "The Last of the Beechers."

CONRAD, JOSEPH (1857–1924). *The Mirror of the Sea.* New York: Harper & Brothers, 1906. 329 pp.

> Source: MTLAcc, entry #1175, volume donated by Clemens.

> Frederick R. Karl, "Joseph Conrad and Huckleberry Finn," *Mark Twain Journal* 11.2 (Summer 1960): 21–23 (mostly about Conrad's *Heart of Darkness*); George P. Clark, "Joseph Conrad and Mark Twain," *Mark Twain Journal* 19.2 (Summer 1978): 12–15 (mostly about Conrad's *Heart of Darkness* but also discusses "The Secret Sharer").

———. *Nostromo; A Tale of the Seaboard.* New York: Harper & Brothers, 1904. 631 pp.

> Location: Mark Twain Library, Redding, Connecticut. Donated by Clemens (MTLAcc, entry #1326).

> Copy examined: Clemens's copy, unmarked. Examined in 1970 and again in June 1982.

> In a New York *Morning Telegraph* interview published on 6 August 1924, Conrad recalled beginning to read Mark Twain in the 1880s, starting with *The Innocents Abroad.* Although the English prefer *Adventures of Huckleberry Finn,* Conrad said, he thought *Life on the Mississippi* was Twain's "nicest" work, adding, "Many a time, when I was down in the Congo Free State, I thought of him looking for snags" (Dale B. J. Randall, "Conrad Interviews, No. 5: Tracy Hammond Lewis," *Conradiana* 3.2 (1971–1972): 67–73).

———. *The Secret Agent; A Simple Tale.* New York: Harper & Brothers, 1907. 373 pp.

> Source: MTLAcc, entry #77, volume donated by Clemens.

———. [Another identical copy.]

> Source: MTLAcc, entry #1423, volume donated by Clemens.

CONWAY, MONCURE DANIEL (1832–1907). *Autobiography: Memories and Experiences of Moncure Daniel Conway.* 2 vols. Original blue cloth, gilt-lettered spine, top edges gilt. Frontispiece portrait of Conway, 11 plates, 9 facsimiles of letters. Boston: Houghton Mifflin and Co., 1904.

> Inscription: on the front pastedown endpapers of both volumes in black ink: "S L. Clemens/Oct. 1905."

> Marginalia: profuse markings and notes, chiefly in pencil, throughout both volumes, including forty-five annotations on thirty pages amounting to 530 words and marginal rules, underlinings, and other markings on fifty-eight additional pages. At Thomas Carlyle's description of his marriage (quoted by Conway in the first volume, page 108), Clemens wrote, "It is as if he were speaking of Livy, & of me." Conway's recollections repeatedly stirred Clemens's autobiographical tendencies. After a list of his

childhood acquaintances in Hannibal at the top of page 147 ("Ed Buchanan the blacksmith, Little Joe and Big Joe, Mrs. Holliday, aunt Betsy Smith, Becky Pavey, Neil Moss") and at the bottom of the same page ("Clay Moss, John Briggs, Will, Bart, Sam & Mary Bowen (Mrs. Green) [,] John & Charley Meredith (Orion's adventure), John Garth, Helen Kercheval, Mary Miller, Artemissa Briggs, Sam Honeyman, Nash"), Clemens wrote sideways in the margin: "They are all gone; why were they created?" (He had earlier listed and identified most of these same names in his fragmentary "Villagers of 1840–3," probably written in 1897.) Horizontally in the margin of the same page he added two names not connected with Hannibal, "Joe Jefferson" and "Chas. L. Webster" (The famous melodrama actor Joseph Jefferson, whom Conway referred to on this page as "our beloved," died on 17 May 1905. Clemens's nephew and sometime business manager Charles L. Webster had passed away in 1891.) On page 277 of the first volume Clemens noted in pencil, "I seem to have met the most of the people mentioned in this book." Where Conway praises Edward Everett (1: 286), Clemens queries, "Is this the idiot I talk about in 'A Tramp Abroad' on the steamboat on a Swiss lake? But *that* ass seemed to be a son or grandson." Running across the name of Ford Madox Ford, Clemens recalled him as "a fine & lovable person, & yet did not believe in hell & its inventor" (2: 135) Where Conway discusses the Savage Club, Clemens recalls: "The Prince of Wales (Ed. VII), Nansen, Stanley & I were the (in 1898) then only honorary members of the Savage Club" (2: 137). Certain names (including Anthony Trollope and Charles Darwin) occurred to Clemens on page 138 of the second volume even though Conway did not introduce them there: "Sir Thomas Hardy . . . Charles Kingsley. [Robert] Browning. George Dolby & Ch. Warren Stoddard, Ambrose Bierce, Joaquin Miller & imitator Harte's Condensed Novels—perished in a canoe. Now I recall his name—Prentice Mulford." In that second volume Conway alludes to an 1867 dinner given "to Charles Dickens, about to visit America," drawing this remark from Clemens: "(a memorable visit for me!) I met Livy at the St. Nicholas [Hotel, in New York City], & took her to the reading (toward end of December) on Mrs. Hooker's ticket" (p. 140). He corrects Conway's impression (2: 144) that Clemens devised a scheme of frustrating autograph hounds by having Olivia Clemens forge his signature: "No. She never dealt in deception." (Clemens started reading these volumes in November 1904 while he was still deeply mourning Olivia's death.) Many other reminiscences occupy the margins of various pages, including the passage (2:146) in which Conway recalls showing the Clemenses around Paris in 1879. *The Twainian* published Clemens's marginalia (42.2 [March-April 1983]: 1–4; 42.3 [May-June 1983]: 1–4; 42.4 [July-August 1983]: 1–3).

Catalogs: ListABP (1910), Autobiography of M. D. Conway 2 vols."; *C1951*, #35a, $50, 2 vols.; *Christie's 1991*, 17 May 1991, lot 77; *Sotheby's 2003*, lot 195, $16,000; The 19th Century Rare Book and Photograph Shop, Catalog 127, June 2010, priced at $27,000.

Provenance: contains the shelfmark of Clara Clemens Gabrilowitsch's private library collection when she resided in Detroit. Purchased by the Mark Twain Research Foundation, Perry, Missouri (and kept in Chester L. Davis's home in Perry, Missouri). Subsequently in the collection of Nick Karanovich, Fort Wayne, Indiana.

Location: currently unknown.

Copy examined: Clemens's copy, one of the most autobiographically revealing of all Clemens's annotated books, at the home of Chester L. Davis (1903–1987) in Perry, Missouri, and again at the Sotheby's auction in 2003.

American clergyman, author, and social reformer Moncure Conway was born in Virginia and graduated from Harvard Divinity School. A dedicated abolitionist before the Civil War, he moved to England in 1864 and became a pastor at the Unitarian South Place Chapel in London. He and Clemens met in London in 1872. On 15 December 1873, acting on Conway's advice, Clemens sent Alfred Lord Tennyson complimentary tickets to his lecture ("Mark Twain," Heritage Bookshop, Los Angeles, 1997, item #125). Clemens succeeded in getting Conway to visit him in Hartford for three days in December 1875 (*MTLet* 5: 599–600). Conway acted as Clemens's London agent from 1876 until 1881, even carrying the manuscript of *The Adventures of Tom Sawyer* to England for publication, and they maintained their friendship thereafter. In November 1885 Conway and his daughter visited the Clemenses in Hartford (OLC Diary, 28 November 1885, MTP; Fears, *Day by Day* 1.2: 1384).

Conway sent Clemens a heartfelt condolence letter upon Olivia Clemens's death, calling him an "old comrade of happy years, comrade now in bereavement" (Dennis Welland, *Mark Twain in England* [1978], p. 226). Clemens made a note in the autumn of 1904 about a favorable review of Conway's newly published *Autobiography*: "This is a good notice. Dr. Conway ought to see it. I have ordered the book, & I know I shall enjoy it" (Welland, *Mark Twain in England*, p. 227). Isabel Lyon noted on 30 November 1904 at 21 Fifth Avenue in New York City: "Tonight at dinner Mr. Clemens was talking of Moncure D. Conway. He is reading Conway's autobiography just published, and it made him hark back to the days in London 25 years ago" (1903–1906 Journals, TS p. 28, MTP). Albert Bigelow Paine reported that Conway's autobiography "gave him [Clemens] enjoyment" (*MTB*, p. 1540). Conway's book of reminiscences, along with Thomas W. S. Higginson's *Cheerful Yesterdays* and *Contemporaries*, almost certainly influenced Mark Twain's eventual choice of a narrative mode for his own autobiography, which he would launch in earnest (following earlier, sporadic attempts) in 1906. Conway soon discarded the strictly chronological organization of his first chapters in favor of a thematic approach that allowed him to discuss more fully the individuals, literary groups, and social sets with which he had become acquainted at various phases of his life.

Mark Twain's Hannibal, Huck & Tom (1969), pp. 28–40; Dennis Welland, *Mark Twain in England* (1978), pp. p. 226–227; Dwayne Eutsey, "Waking from This Dream of Separateness: Hinduism and the Ending of *No. 44, The Mysterious Stranger*," *Mark Twain Annual* 7 (2009): 66–77.

———. *Demonology and Devil-Lore* (published in London in 1879).

Clemens was well aware of Conway's labors in compiling this work (see *MTLet* 6: 600–601). On 19 January [1880] Clemens wrote to Conway from Elmira upon receiving an unspecified book: "If I enjoy it as much as I have enjoyed your devil-lore I shall know it is a happy success" (ALS, Columbia University).

Coleman O. Parsons, "Background," p. 60; Dwayne Eutsey, "Devil-Lore and Avatars: Moncure Conway's Likely Influence on *No. 44, The Mysterious Stranger*," *Mark Twain Journal* 54.1 (2016): 95–115.

———. "Laureate Despair, A Discourse Given at South Place Chapel, December 11th 1881, by Moncure D. Conway." London: 11, South Place, 1881. [Nineteen-page pamphlet bound in a paper cover.]

Location: current location undetermined.

In 1882 Clemens thanked Conway for this study of Tennyson that was "as beautiful as music" (Welland, *Mark Twain in England*, p. 225).

———. *A Necklace of Stories*. Illustrated by W[illiam]. J[ohn]. Hennessy (1839–1917). London: Chatto & Windus, 1880. 206 pp.

On 19 January [1880] Clemens wrote to Conway from Elmira upon receiving an unspecified book: "We received your beautiful book . . . but . . . the children laid hands on it as a sort of right, & walked it off to the nursery. If I enjoy it as much as I have enjoyed your devil-lore I shall know it is a happy success" (ALS, Columbia University). JoDee Benussi suggested that Clemens might be referring to Conway's *A Necklace of Stories* (letter, Benussi to Alan Gribben, 4 November 2007). Her speculation seems logical, given that the names of Conway's dozen stories would have intrigued Clemens's daughters: "The Invisible Queen," "Bernard and Robin Redbreast," "The Naturalist, the Child, and the Humming-bird," "The Bucket and the Acorn," "The Unfinished Island," and similar titles.

———. *The Sacred Anthology: A Book of Ethnical Scriptures, Collected and Edited by Moncure Daniel Conway.* [The first edition was published in 1874, but the edition owned by Clemens has not been established.]

Marginalia: Albert Bigelow Paine quoted from Clemens's annotation written on a flyleaf: "RELIGION/The easy confidence with which I know another man's religion is folly teaches me to suspect that my own is also. MARK TWAIN, 19th Cent. A. D." In another note Clemens observed: "I would not interfere with any one's religion, either to strengthen it or to weaken it. I am not able to believe one's religion can affect his hereafter one way or the other, no matter what that religion may be. But it may easily be a great comfort to him in this life—hence it is a valuable possession to him" (*MTB*, p. 1584).

Catalogs: ListABP (1910), "Sacred Anthology, Conway"; *C1951*, #38a, $47.50, listed among books annotated by Clemens.

Location: currently unknown.

Conway wrote to Clemens on 10 December 1873, when they were both in London, promising that they could get together soon: "My big book will be out this week; the dumb demon will be exorcised; I shall be a freeman." Clemens replied the same day, suggesting that he and Conway each exchange their most recent book (*MTLet* 5: 502).

Dwayne Eutsey, "Waking from This Dream of Separateness: Hinduism and the Ending of *No. 44, The Mysterious*

Stranger," *Mark Twain Annual 7* (2009): 66–77.

———. *The Wandering Jew*. First edition. Original maroon cloth, spine lettered gilt, brown coated endpapers, rebacked with original spine laid down, worn, upper cover stained and faded along bottom, water damage to front cover, hinges shaken. New York: Henry Holt and Co., 1881. 292 pp.

Marginalia: Clemens annotated Conway's opening passage on page 4 in which an Armenian bishop, visiting Christian monks in England in 1228, reported that he had recently dined with the "the famous Joseph" who witnessed the crucifixion of Christ. According to the prelate, a man calling himself Joseph was living frugally and penitently among Armenian Christians, refusing all gifts and hoping for eventual forgiveness. Whenever he reached the age of 100 he fainted and became "as young as when his doom was pronounced" (p. 4). Writing vertically in ink, Clemens remarked: "There! My idea is not new. It has often seemed to me that one living & un-killable witness would be worth a billion hearsay miracles & such-like nonsense." Conway's narrative rehearses the legend that Cartaphilus, Pontius Pilate's door-keeper, struck Christ on the neck and said, "Go, Jesus; go on faster: why dost thou linger?" Consequently he found himself doomed to await Christ's second coming. Cartaphilus was later "baptized by Ananias (who had baptized Paul) under the name Joseph" (p. 5). On page 5 Clemens corrected a date in pencil, altering "1682" to read "1282." Where the eternally cursed traveler is said to have "washed himself in the two head-springs of the river Nile, which arise in the southern part of Aethiopia" (page 18), Clemens queried in ink, "Stanley, is it so?" On page 19 at the assertion "that there was no corner of the earth where he had not been present," Clemens asked skeptically, "Forgot to visit America?" The verso of the front flyleaf displays pencil notations: "1698 #102 6<u>00</u>."

Catalogs: ListABP (1910), "Wandering Jew, Conway", no other information provided; "The James S. Copley Library," Sotheby's auction, New York City, 17 June 2010, "upper cover stained and faded along bottom, Clemens's marginal notes on p. 4 and elsewhere," lot 556, sold with five other titles for $4,250.

Provenance: Clara Clemens Samossoud's private library shelfmark ("H/H7") appears in pencil on the verso of a front free endpaper. A small slip pasted in the book records its purchase by A. J. Krechel at the 1951 sale in Hollywood, though the title was not listed in the hastily prepared auction catalog. By 1982 the book belonged to John Feldman of Aurora, Colorado. He temporarily placed it on deposit in the Special Collections, Rare Books Room, University of Colorado at Boulder (Nora J. Quinlan, then Head, Special Collections, Rare Books Room, to Alan Gribben, 10 December 1985). It was auctioned in New York City on 17 June 2010, when it was purchased by Kevin Mac Donnell.

Location: collection of Kevin Mac Donnell, Austin, Texas (Mac Donnell to Alan Gribben, 29 June 2010).

Copy examined: photocopies of title page and annotations sent to Alan Gribben by John Feldman on 7 February 1982. The handwriting is unmistakably that of Clemens. He did not sign the volume.

Conway's study began with chapters titled "The Legend,"

"The Undying Ones," and "Sources of the Myth," and included chapters called "The Weird of the Wanderer" and "The Wandering Jew in Folk-Lore."

COOK, CLARENCE CHATHAM (1828–1900). *The House Beautiful: Essays on Beds and Tables, Stools and Candlesticks*. Illustrated by Henry Marsh (1826–1912) and others. New York: Scribner, Armstrong and Co., 1878. 336 pp. [Originally published serially in *Scribner's Monthly*.]

In an undated letter to Theodore and Susan Crane written on "Xmas Morning," Clemens wisecracked: "I have taken Ida's House Beautiful & Baby Days & Ik Marvel's book & shall give Livy & the children copies of my works in place of them" (MTP). Walter Blair speculated that Mark Twain "borrowed the ironic name" for Chapter 38 of *Life on the Mississippi* (1883), "The House Beautiful," from Cook's title (*MT&HF*, p. 291).

Lucille M. Schultz, "Parlor Talk in Mark Twain: The Grangerford Parlor and the House Beautiful," *Mark Twain Journal* 19.4 (Summer 1979): 14–19, especially 18 n. 5.

COOK, THEODORE ANDREA (1867–1928). *Old Touraine: The Life and History of the Famous Chateâux of France*. 2 vols. New York: J. Pott & Co., 1900.

Clemens noted the title and number of volumes on a flyleaf of Notebook 44 in 1901 (MTP).

COOKE, EDMUND VANCE (1866–1932). *Chronicles of the Little Tot*. Illustrated by Clyde O[smer]. De Land (1872–1947). New York: Dodge Publishing Co., [1905]. 118 pp.

Inscription: on the front free endpaper Cooke inscribed a poem of two stanzas headed "Samuel Langhorne Clemens at Seventy/To/Mark Twain at the same age" and dated at "Cleveland, Nov. 30th, 1905."

Provenance: curiously, the volume contains the book stamps and red-ink accession number of the Mark Twain Library at Redding, Connecticut, yet it was also catalogued in the "Retz Appraisal" of items belonging to the Mark Twain Estate in 1944 (p. 7), when it was valued at $5. Presumably Clemens or Clara had a change of heart about donating the volume to the Redding library.

Location: Mark Twain Papers, Bancroft Library, University of California at Berkeley.

Copy examined: Clemens's copy.

"Under another cover I send you a memento, with inscription," wrote Cooke from Cleveland, Ohio on 26 November 1905. He signed his letter "with my warmest esteem and deepest admiration" (MTP). *Chronicles of the Little Tot* consists of verses charting the growth phases of infants into older children. The poems resemble those of James Whitcomb Riley; some are saccharine and adoring, some are written in comical dialect, some are purportedly written by the children themselves. Cooke had already published in 1903 his most famous poem, the inspirational "How Did You Die?

Dear Mark Twain: Letters from His Readers, ed. R. Kent Rasmussen (Berkeley: University of California Press, 2013), pp. 222–223.

COOKE, GRACE (MacGOWAN) (1863–1944). *Their First Formal Call*. Illustrated by Peter Newell (1862–1924). New York: Harper & Brothers, 1906. 55 pp.

Source: MTLAcc, entry #453, volume donated by Clemens.

Two boys, trying to practice exactly prescribed etiquette, call on the Claiborne sisters with humorous results.

COOKE, ROSE (TERRY) (1827–1892). "Freedom Wheeler's Controversy with Providence: A Story of Old New England" (short story), *Atlantic Monthly* 40 (July 1877): 65–84.

"I read the entire Atlantic this time," Clemens informed Howells on 4 July 1877 from Elmira. "Mrs. Rose Terry Cooke's story was a ten-strike. I wish she would write 12 old-time New England tales a year" (*MTHL*, p. 187). Cooke wrote Clemens on 18 August 1880 to praise his "Mrs. McWilliams and the Lightning" (*DearMT*, p. 74). Early in 1881 Clemens reminded himself to send a complimentary copy of *The Prince and the Pauper* to this local-colorist who was born in West Hartford and lived then in Winsted, Connecticut. In February 1889 he noted, "Rose Terry Cooke,/Pittsfield, Mass./Read there March 6" (NB 28, *N&J* 3:448). This was the same date that Cooke inscribed a presentation copy of her *Steadfast: The Story of a Saint and a Sinner* to him (see the Catalog entry below). Cooke's fiction was notable for its ironic humor.

———. *Somebody's Neighbors*. Boston: J. R. Osgood and Co., 1881. 421 pp.

Source: MTLAcc, entry #2201, volume donated from Clemens's library by Clara Clemens Gabrilowitsch in 1910. This collection of New England character studies includes "Freedom Wheeler's Controversy with Providence," "Mrs. Flint's Married Experience," "Miss Lucinda," and nine other short stories.

———. *Steadfast: The Story of a Saint and a Sinner*. First edition. Original green cloth, gilt. Boston: Ticknor and Co., 1889. 426 pp.

Inscription: inscribed to Clemens by the author in black ink on the front free endpaper: "S. L. Clemens/With cordial gratitude/from one of the/Pittsfield 'Old Women'/R. T. C./March 6th/1889." This was the same day Clemens visited Pittsfield, Massachusetts at her request to read to the Wednesday Morning Club, a young women's literary society, at the Academy of Music for the benefit of the Old Ladies' Home and Union (*N&J* 3: 448–449 n. 137). Presumably Clemens had made a humorous reference to "old women" in his remarks at the meeting, to which Cooke's inscription was a good-natured response. (She was now in her sixties.) A faintly penciled number, "783," is visible on the lower outside corner of the front pastedown endpaper. Cooke had written to Clemens on 26 January 1889 to ask if he would speak at this benefit event.

Provenance: offered for sale in June 1976 by Seven Gables Bookshop, New York City. Priced at $125.

Location: collection of Kevin Mac Donnell, Austin, Texas. Acquired in 1982 for $280 from "an East Coast book dealer" (Mac Donnell to Alan Gribben, 7 June 1982).

Copy examined: Clemens's unmarked copy, in July 2004 in Austin, Texas.

Steadfast: The Story of a Saint and a Sinner was one of Cooke's efforts to move beyond the confines of short fiction and treat the New England region and its characters in greater depth.

COOLBRITH, INA D[ONNA] (1841–1928).

The degree of Clemens's friendship with this San Francisco Bay Area poet, journalist, and (later) librarian is debated. He contributed to a fund when her house was destroyed in the 1906 earthquake, but no evidence has yet surfaced that he owned copies of her books, *A Perfect Day and Other Poems* (1881) and *Songs from the Golden Gate* (1895). Will M. Clemens, a would-be biographer of Mark Twain, called on Coolbrith in 1893 (see the Catalog entry for Charlotte Perkins Gilman). Two studies sympathetic to Coolbrith's lifetime dilemmas are Ben Tarnoff's *The Bohemians: Mark Twain and the San Francisco Writers Who Reinvented American Literature* (New York: Penguine Press, 2014) and Nicole Amare and Alan Manning, "The Mormon Entombed in Mark Twain's Heart: Ina Coolbrith and Samuel Clemens," *Mark Twain Journal: The Author and His Era* 55.1–2 (Spring/Fall 2017): 159–192.

COOPER, JAMES FENIMORE (1789–1851). *Leather-Stocking Tales: The Pathfinder; The Deerslayer; The Last of the Mohicans*.
Edition: unknown.
Catalog: *C1951*, O23, listed among books belonging to Olivia Clemens.

Cooper became synonymous for Clemens with wholly unwarranted sentimental and idealized notions of American Indian tribes. Clemens's experiences in the Far West disabused him of his youthful literature-induced fantasies about the inherent nobility of every Native American, and the poverty and squalor he found endemic among the Nevada and California aborigines made him disgusted with the "romances" he had once enjoyed. In 1897 he recalled that Cooper was one of the Hannibal idols during his childhood, when "any young person would have been proud of a 'strain' of Indian blood" ("Villagers of 1840–3," *HH&T*, p. 34). He wrote to Jane Lampton Clemens from Carson City on 20 March 1862 to ridicule Cooper's "lordly sons of the forest" and to provide instead "a full and correct account of these lovely Indians—not gleaned from Cooper's novels, Madam" (*MTLet* 1: 175–176). In his letter of 5 June 1867 to the *Alta California* he wrote about marauding natives: "I suppose the humanitarians want somebody to fight the Indians that J. Fenimore Cooper made. There is just where the mistake is. The Cooper Indians are dead—died with their creator" (*MTTMB*, p. 266).

"Recall their mighty deeds! Remember Uncas!" Mark Twain admonished the putative "Indians" he encountered in "A Day at Niagara" (1869, later reprinted as "Niagara" in *Sketches, New and Old* in 1875). Cooper's Indians "are an extinct tribe that never existed," he argued in Chapter 20 of *The Innocents Abroad* (1869), and in Chapter 50 he quipped: "Commend me to Fenimore Cooper to find beauty in the Indians, and to Grimes [William C. Prime] to find it in the Arabs." In Chapter 19 of *Roughing It* (1872) Twain maintained that he had formerly been "a disciple of Cooper and a worshipper of the Red Man—even of the scholarly savages in the 'Last of the Mohicans,'" but the Goshoot tribe caused him to see how he had been "viewing him through the mellow moonshine of romance." A chastened Tom Sawyer admits in Chapter 4 of the fragmentary "Huck Finn and Tom Sawyer among the Indians," written in 1884, that his erroneous ideas about Native Americans came from "Cooper's novels" (*HH&T*, p. 109). Huckleberry Finn in Chapter 9 of that same work is relieved that Tom "had about got it through his noodle, by this time, that book Injuns and real Injuns is different" (p. 138).

Later, in 1894, Twain planned to make "a vicious and

entertaining book" by reviewing Cooper and other novelists whom "the last two generations of Englishmen and Americans admired" (SLC to Henry H. Rogers, 16 May 1894, *MTHHR*, pp. 53–54). To Olivia Clemens he revealed, "I am writing a review of Fenimore Cooper's *Deerslayer*—the most idiotic book I ever saw" (London, 16 May 1894, quoted in *The Twainian* 37 [July-Aug. 1978]: 1). He published "Fenimore Cooper's Literary Offences" in July 1895, concentrating on *The Deerslayer* and *The Pathfinder* and scoffing at the Leather-Stocking books as the "Broken Twig Series"; he took issue in that essay with Brander Matthews and other critics, and facetiously sought to prove that Cooper violated eighteen of the nineteen "rules governing literary art in the domain of romantic fiction." In another sally against Cooper's over-estimators, "Fenimore Cooper's Further Literary Offences" (published by Bernard DeVoto as "Cooper's Prose Style" in *Letters from the Earth* [1962], pp. 137–145), written in 1894 or 1895, Twain berated *The Last of the Mohicans*. Brander Matthews gently rebuked Twain in an introduction to an edition of the *Leather-Stocking Tales* published by G. P. Putnam's Sons in 1896. More vigorous was D. L. Maulsby's defense of Cooper's *Leather-Stocking Tales* against Mark Twain's attempts "to judge him by the newly-set-up criterion of realism" ("Fenimore Cooper and Mark Twain," *Dial* [Chicago] 22.256 [16 February 1897]: 107–109). Maulsby urged Twain and others to develop "a catholic taste" that can appreciate 'the American romance of adventure" (p. 109). Twain countered in Chapter 22 of *Following the Equator* (1897), remarking that "Fenimore Cooper lost his chance. . . . He wouldn't have traded the dullest of them [the Australian aborigines] for the brightest Mohawk he ever invented." When Joseph H. Twichell indicated that he sided with Matthews's defense of Cooper against Twain's cavils in "New Trials for Old Favorites," *Forum* 25 (August 1898): 749–760, Twain replied to Twichell on 13 September 1898: "I like Brander Matthews. . . . When you say he earned your gratitude for cuffing me for my crimes against the Leatherstockings & the Vicar, I ain't making any objection" (*LMTJHT* [2017], p. 220).

Sydney J. Krause—"Cooper's Literary Offences: Mark Twain in Wonderland," *New England Quarterly* 38.3 (September 1965): 291–311—explored the "literary mayhem pure and simple" committed by Mark Twain's sophistical persona." Chapter 8 of Krause's *Mark Twain as Critic* (pp. 128–147) presented a slightly revised version of Twain's essay mocking Cooper. Larzer Ziff argued that Clemens's firm belief in craftsmanship and precision accounted for his antipathy toward Cooper's fiction ("Authorship and Craft: The Example of Mark Twain," *Southern Review* 12 [Spring 1976]: 246–260). In 1983 Craig Cotora amusingly set out to prove that in *A Connecticut Yankee in King Arthur's Court* (1889) Twain himself violated the same nineteen rules that "govern the domain of romantic fiction," according to Twain's 1895 critique of Cooper's writing ("Mark Twain's Literary Offenses, or the Revenge of Fenimore Cooper," *Mark Twain Journal* 21.3 [Spring 1983]: 19–20).

S. B. Liljegren, "Revolt" (1945), pp. 35, 43–49; Krause, *MTC* (1967), p. 134; W. R. Moses, "Mark Twain's Best

Satire of Cooper," *Mark Twain Journal* 21.4 (Fall 1983): 25–27; Carter Revard, "Why Mark Twain Murdered Injun Joe—and Will Never Be Indicted," *Massachusetts Review* 40.4 (Winter 1999): 643–670; and Kerry Driscoll, *Mark Twain among the Indians and Other Indigenous People* (Oakland: University of California Press, 2018), pp. 5, 12, 28 *passim*.

———. *Pages and Pictures, from the Writings of James Fenimore Cooper, with Notes*. Ed. Susan Fenimore Cooper (1813–1894). Illus. New York: W. A. Townsend and Co., 1861. 400 pp.

Inscription: "Susie E. Crane/Livia/Decr. 25th 1864" (in calligraphy).

Catalog: Ball 2016 inventory, brown cloth, gilt lettering, black cloth design, gilt top page edges, good/fair condition.

Location: Quarry Farm library shelves, under the supervision of the Mark Twain Archive, Elmira College, Elmira, New York.

Susan Cooper provides a narrative description of, and extracts from, her father's novels and other writings. The book, available to Clemens at Quarry Farm in Elmira, New York, contains numerous steel and wood engravings of scenes from Cooper's fiction.

———. *The Pioneers; or, The Sources of the Susquehanna: A Descriptive Tale*. Leather Stocking Tales Series. Original cloth, hinges cracked, light wear. New York: Hurd and Houghton, 1876.

Inscription: inscribed by Olivia Clemens, "Susy Clemens/Hartford Dec. 25th 1881/Merry Christmas/from/Mamma."

Provenance: has the shelfmark numbering system employed by Clara Clemens Gabrilowitsch during her Detroit years.

Catalogs: *C1951*, J32, listed among books belonging to Jean and Clara Clemens; "Property from the Library of Mark Twain," Butterfield & Butterfield, San Francisco, Sale 6613 (16 July 1997), lot 2702.

Location: Mark Twain House and Museum, Hartford, Connecticut.

Copy examined: Susy Clemens's copy, which was later in the possession of Clara Clemens. Examined in Hartford in 1997.

Sacvan Bercovitch, "Huckleberry Bumppo: A Comparison of *Tom Sawyer* and *The Pioneers*," *Mark Twain Journal* 14.2 (Summer 1968): 1–4.

———. *The Spy: A Tale of the Neutral Ground* (novel, published in 1821).

Wesley Britton noted that Chapter 11 of Cooper's *The Spy* contains a comedic exchange between an uneducated housekeeper and a physician who try to discuss arrangements for a deceased neighbor but have difficulty understanding each other. Britton suggested that this might have contributed an idea for Twain's famous "Buck Fanshaw's Funeral" episode in *Roughing It* (1872) (Wesley Britton to the Mark Twain Forum, 17 February 2003).

COOPER, SUSAN FENIMORE (1813–1894). *Rural Hours, by a Lady*. New York: George P. Putnam, 1851.

Catalogs: Ball 2016 inventory, green cloth, fair condition, signed by Mrs. Jervis Langdon, bookplate of Jervis Langdon's Family Library #159.

Location: Quarry Farm library shelves, under the supervision of the Mark Twain Archive, Elmira College, Elmira,

New York.

Clemens had access to this book whenever he visited the Langdon home in Elmira.

The daughter of the novelist James Fenimore Cooper was one of the earliest amateur naturalists and the first woman to write a book, *Rural Hours* (1850), about the advantages of preserving and appreciating wilderness areas against the encroachment of industrial and agricultural uses. She kept diary-like records of her walks around Cooperstown, New York and the trees, plants, and animal life she observed.

COPPÉE, FRANÇOIS [EDOUARD JOACHIM] (1842–1908). *The Rivals*. Illus. New York: Harper & Brothers, 1893. 99 pp.

Source: MTLAcc, entry #2202, volume donated from Clemens's library by Clara Clemens Gabrilowitsch in 1910.

A sentimental novella about the French theater, passionate young love, and the rise from poverty (and eventual return to those circumstances) of two once-glamorous women.

COPPÉE, HENRY (1821–1895). *Grant and His Campaigns: A Military Biography*. Illus. Marbled covers and endpapers, calf spine. New York: Charles B. Richardson, 1866. 521 pp.

Provenance: bookplate #66 of the "J. Langdon Family Library" on the front pastedown endpaper.

Location: Mark Twain Archive, Elmira College, Elmira, New York.

Copy examined: unmarked copy available to Clemens whenever he visited the Langdons in Elmira. Examined on 27 May 2015.

CORBETT, GRIFFITH OWEN: see the Catalog entry for W. Cobbett.

CORELLI, MARIE (1855–1924). *The Greatest Queen in the World. A Tribute to the Majesty of England. 1837–1900*. First edition. 16mo. Fine contemporary Reviere & Son three-quarter morocco binding, raised bands, gilt, original wrappers bound in. London: Skeffington & Son, 1900. 37 pp.

Inscription: the verso of the front free endpaper is signed in brown ink, "S. L. Clemens/(Mark Twain)". This was not Clemens's usual form for signing his library books. The bookplate of Alice K. Berg is affixed to the front pastedown endpaper.

Provenance: purchased from a Chicago, Illinois book dealer in the late 1970s by Nick Karanovich, a Fort Wayne collector of Twainiana.

Copy examined: viewed at a Mark Twain conference in Tuscaloosa, Alabama on 15 October 1981 when it was owned by Nick Karanovich. Examined again in July 2004 in Austin, Texas when it was offered for sale (as a detected forgery) by the prominent collector and rare bookseller Kevin Mac Donnell, who also sent Alan Gribben a photocopy of the signature on 18 August 2005. (Even identified and labeled forgeries of Mark Twain association items have a monetary value today; in 2004 Mac Donnell priced this copy of *The Greatest Queen in the World* for sale at $250.) On the same endpaper where the purported autograph appears Mac Donnell explicitly labeled (in ink) the Clemens/Twain signature as fraudulent. This is one of the more carefully executed forgeries, but the odds are greatly stacked against any possibility the signature is genuine. In Mac Donnell's opinion it was the work of the infamous dealer in forged materials Harry Sickles. Many of Eugene Field II's spurious signings of Twain's name originated in Illinois, but during one decade

(approximately 1927 to 1937) the two men, Sickles and Field, seem to have operated in partnership. This small monograph was Corelli's tribute to Queen Victoria.

Mark Twain had much to say about Marie Corelli, none of it good, in a portion of his autobiography dictated in 1907 after he had spent a day with her in England. He recounted how he had previously met her at a dinner party in Germany in the 1890s and "took a dislike to her at once." Upon encountering her again in Stratford he concluded that "she is the most offensive sham, inside and out, that misrepresents and satirizes the human race to-day" (*Mark Twain in Eruption*, pp. 323, 325–326; Charles Neider, ed., *The Autobiography of Mark Twain*, pp. 380, 382; *AutoMT* 3: 98–99).

CORNARO, LUIGI (1475–1566). *The Art of Living Long. A New and Improved English Version of the Treatise by the Celebrated Venetian Centenarian, with Essays by Joseph Addison [1672–1719], Lord [Francis] Bacon [1561–1626], and Sir William Temple [1628–1699]*. Illus. Milwaukee: William F. Butler, 1903. 214 pp. [A translation of *Discorsi della vita sobria*.] [Publisher and pages conjectured.]

Catalog: *A1911*, "royal 8vo, cloth, gilt top, Milwaukee, 1903," lot 112, sold for $2.50.

Despite the birthdates of 1464 or 1467 proposed for the author by several sources, the generally accepted date of 1475 deprives the publisher of the claim that Cornaro became a true centenarian. However, he did live a long life after adopting (around the age of forty) a physician-prescribed regimen of small, easily digestible meals. To that habit Cornaro added moderation in all other things and an easygoing, temperate approach to life's vicissitudes. A eulogy at the end of the volume describes his equitable, cheerful attitude toward friends and acquaintances. Bacon's essay was titled "History of Life and Death"; Temple's was titled "Health and Long Life"; Addison's brief commentary on Conaro came from an issue of *The Spectator* published in 1711.

Cornhill Magazine (1860–1975).

Early in 1879 Clemens annotated a clipping from the January 1879 issue of this London magazine. See the Catalog entry for George Barnett Smith.

CORSON, HIRAM (1828–1911). *An Introduction to the Study of Robert Browning's Poetry* (published in 1886).

Clemens's study group on Browning heard a lecture by this Cornell professor. "Prof. Corson is coming to give us a reading," Clemens wrote proudly to Mary Mason Fairbanks on 22 March 1887 (*MTMF*, p. 261). Clemens quite likely had read Corson's recently published book.

CORY, ANNIE SOPHIE (1868–1952), PSEUD. "VICTORIA CROSS." *Life's Shop Window*. New York: M. Kennerley, [cop. 1907]. 371 pp.

Source: MTLAcc, entry #2207, volume donated from Clemens's library by Clara Clemens Gabrilowitsch in 1910. Subsequently withdrawn from circulation by the librarian, according to a record in the Mark Twain Library.

Under several pseudonyms, Cory furnished what were considered rather daring novels for their time. They typically combined unconventional women in exotic settings with sexual passion and a search for true romantic love.

Cosmopolitan (periodical, published 1886–).

Clemens disliked David Ker's travel essay but praised "that

charming Chinese story" by another author in an issue he read in March 1889 (NB 28, *N&J* 3: 457); see the Catalog entry for Wong Chin Foo. In December 1893 he reminded himself to send Olivia a copy of the "story by Miss [Ida M.] Van Etten" in the March 1893 issue of *Cosmopolitan* (NB 33, TS p. 42); see the Van Etten entry. Mark Twain published essays and stories in the *Cosmopolitan* beginning in 1893.

COTES, SARA JEANNETTE (DUNCAN) (1861–1922). *An American Girl in London.* Illustrated by F[rederick]. H[enry]. Townsend (1868–1920). London: Chatto & Windus, 1891. 321 pp.
Source: MTLAcc, entry #995, volume donated by Clemens.

COTTIN, SOPHIE (1770–1807). *Elizabeth; or, The Exiles of Siberia. A Tale, Founded upon Facts.* Trans. from the French. [The first English translation of this fictional work was published in 1795; various editions were published subsequently. Clemens's edition has not been determined.]
On 21 October 1881 Clemens sent a request to James R. Osgood and Company: "Please send me Elizabeth, or the Exile[s] of Siberia" (MTP). I am grateful to JoDee Benussi for noticing this reference in David H. Fears' *Mark Twain Day by Day* 1.2: 1021.

COTTLER, G[UILLAUME] (1832–1903). *Cours Complet de Langue Allemande.* Paris: Berlin Frères. Librairie Classique Eugène Belin, 1893. 168 pp.
Inscription: signed by Jean Clemens in purple ink on the half-title page: "Jean Clemens/le 2 Février 1894/Paris/École Monceau." The front free endpaper is missing. Bookplates were torn off the front and rear pastedown endpapers.
Location: Mark Twain Library, Redding, Connecticut.
Copy examined: Jean Clemens's copy. Has a red ink Mark Twain Library accession number—"3624". Examined in 1970 and again in June 1982 and on 10 November 2019.

COTTON, A[LFRED]. J[OHNSON] (1800–1875). *Cotton's Sketch-Book. Auto-Biographical Sketches of the Life, Labors and Extensive Home Travels of Rev. A. J. Cotton, An Early Pioneer in the Wilds of the Once "Far West,"* . . . *in Short, Convenient Chapters.* Portland, Maine: B. Thurston & Co., 1874. 216 pp.
Location: Mark Twain Library, Redding, Connecticut.
Copy examined: quite possibly Clemens's unmarked copy, since it was grouped with Clemens's personal books when Albert E. Stone visited Redding in 1955 (and also when I saw it in 1970 and again in June 1982). Has the oval purple "Mark Twain Library" stamps in it and a red ink Mark Twain Library accession number, "3893". Only the second accession record book (still missing) could settle the question of whether it definitely came from Clemens's personal library.
Cotton described, with some humor, his experiences as a Methodist Episcopal preacher in early-day Dearborn County, Indiana.

COULTON, GEORGE GORDON (1858–1947). *From St. Francis to Dante: Translations from the Chronicle of the Franciscan Salimbene (1221–1288); with Notes and Illustrations from Other Medieval Sources.* Second revised edition. Frontispiece of the Baptistery of Parma. Original green cloth, gilt. Half maroon morocco slipcase. London: David Nutt, 1907. 446 pp.
Inscription: signed on the front pastedown endpaper: "S L. Clemens/June, 1909./Stormfield. From James M. Beck." Inscribed by Beck in June 1909 on the half-title page: "To

Samuel L. Clemens with kind regards."
Marginalia: markings and notes in pencil and black ink throughout; his notes total 136 words on eleven pages, and six other pages have vertical lines. A number of additional pages were folded down at the upper corners. Above a passage on page 81 that attributed earthquakes to wind trapped in cavernous mountains, Clemens wrote in ink: "Theological 'science,' you see, was as 'ansome a product 600 years ago as it is in Gladstone's & Canon Lightfoot's day." On page 144 Clemens made an observation in ink, writing vertically, "In that Golden Age of Idiots a man was not only able to believe God loved him, but actually to *feel* it. We cannot imagine such a condition. We cannot imagine the President of the United States in love with a louse." Where a man named Albergio is destroyed for making a "foul and boorish . . . gesture at the heaven," Clemens scoffed, "Yes, making that offensive gesture is what brought him sorrow and disaster. God could stand his crimes, but not his manners" (p. 250). "This is extraordinary," Clemens wrote on page 283 beside the assertion that the Bishop of Liège counted two abbesses and a nun among his concubines and had fourteen children in twenty-two months. "More than half a child every month," marveled Clemens. "In fact it is almost exactly 5/8 of a child per month." At page 318, in reference to St. Dominic's pulling apart a shrieking sparrow which had interrupted his studies and therefore seemed to him the Devil incarnate, Clemens noted in ink: "Another heroic hunter, like Roosevelt."
Catalogs: ListABP (1910), "From St. Frances to Dante, Coulton"; Christie's (1989), lot 1759; *Sotheby's 2003,* #196, $2,750.
Provenance: formerly in the Carrie Estelle Doheny Collection, St. John's Seminary, Camarillo, California. Donated by Mrs. Doheny in 1940 after its purchase from Maxwell Hunley Rare Books of Beverly Hills for $12.20. Christie's sold the volume for an amount between $1,000 and $1,500 on 21 February 1989 on behalf of St. John's Seminary. Subsequently belonged to Nick Karanovich's collection in Fort Wayne, Indiana.
Location: undetermined at present.
Copy examined: Clemens's copy, when it was at St. John's Seminary. Has the bookplate of "Estelle Doheny."

COURTHOPE, WILLIAM JOHN (1842–1917). *Addison.* English Men of Letters Series. New York: Harper & Brothers, 1902. 182 pp.
Source: MTLAcc, entry #1287, volume donated by Clemens.

Cow-Boys Ballads. N.p., n.d. 81 pp.
Source: MTLAcc, entry #2008, volume donated from Clemens's library by Clara Clemens Gabrilowitsch in 1910.

COWIE, WILLIAM (1846–1913). *Latter-Day Poems.* Syracuse, New York: Wolcott's Bookshop, 1904. 251 pp.
Source: MTLAcc, entry #646, volume donated by Clemens. Born in Scotland, Cowie had held the posts of county clerk and mayor in Syracuse. In 1908 he would be appointed postmaster. Above all, however, he was known locally for his love of literature and his collection of books.

COWLEY, ABRAHAM (1618–1667). *Essays.* Ed. and intro. by Henry Morley (1822–1894). New York: Cassell & Co.,

1886. 192 pp.

Source: MTLAcc, entry #975, volume donated by Clemens. Collected here are some of Cowley's most pithy and perspicacious essays, including "Of Liberty," "Of Greatness," "Of Solitude," and "Dangers of an Honest Man."

COWPER, WILLIAM (1731–1800). "Verses Supposed to be Written by Alexander Selkirk, During His Solitary Abode in the Island of Juan Fernandez" (poem, published in 1782).

Cowper, Dryden, and Shelley produced "all the poetry that everybody admires and appreciates, but nobody ever reads or quotes from," Mark Twain quipped (*Californian*, 17 June 1865; *LAMT*, p. 142; *ET&S* 2: 195). "Oh, Solitude, where are the charms which sages have seen in thy face?" quotes Twain in Chapter 9 of *Innocents Abroad* (1869). Clemens declared that Olivia Clemens "is lord of all she surveys," paraphrasing a line in the first stanza, "I am monarch of all I survey" (Clemens to Mary Mason Fairbanks, 13 February 1870, *MTLet* 4: 71). Earl F. Briden hazarded a guess that in depicting Huck's initial loneliness and the tameness of animals on Jackson's Island (Chapters 8 and 9, *Adventures of Huckleberry Finn* [1885]), Twain "may have adopted a handful of details from Cowper's memorable reworking" of Alexander Selkirk's story about being marooned on an uninhabited island ("Huck's Island Adventure and the Selkirk Legend," *Mark Twain Journal* 18.3 [Winter 1976–1977]: 12–14). See also the entries for Alexander Selkirk as well as Daniel Defoe's *Robinson Crusoe* (1719).

COX, GEORGE W[ILLIAM]. (1827–1902). *The Mythology of the Aryan Nations*. 2 vols. Covers and spines nearly detached. London: Longmans, Green, and Co., 1870.

Inscriptions: Volume 1 inscribed, "F. E. Chambers/—?ham/ New Jersey. Volume 2 is inscribed, "J. Henry Wescott Aug. 1, 1870."

Marginalia: The number "88" is written at the bottom of page 460 in Volume 1.

Provenance: both volumes have the shelfmarks of Clara Clemens Gabrilowitsch's library numbering system during her Detroit years. Both volumes were sold at the 1951 auction in Hollywood but not listed in the hastily prepared sale sheet.

Catalogs: ListABP (1910), "Mythology of the Aryan Nations, Cox"; "Property from the Library of Mark Twain," Butterfield & Butterfield, San Francisco, Sale 6613 (16 July 1997), "2 vols.," lot 2712.

Location: Mark Twain House and Museum, Hartford, Connecticut (two volumes).

Copies examined: Clemens's copies of both volumes. Viewed in Hartford in 1997.

Cox amassed an encompassing appraisal of Indo-European myths ranging from the death scene of King Arthur to Norse sagas to ancient Greek gods to Vishnu and Krishna of India.

COX, SAMUEL SULLIVAN (1824–1889), known as "Sunset Cox." *The Diversions of a Diplomat in Turkey*. New York: Charles L. Webster & Co., 1887. 685 pp.

Cox praised Mark Twain's humor in an often-delivered speech that Cox eventually expanded and placed in print in 1876 as *Why We Laugh* (*MTLet* 6: 29). Clemens discussed the manuscript of Cox's *Diversions of a Diplomat* (but stated that he had not read it) in a letter to the

Ohio lawyer on 9 July 1887 (PH in MTP). Clemens's publishing firm issued Cox's *Diversions of a Diplomat in Turkey* in 1887 and 1893, and four sketches from the book appeared in *Mark Twain's Library of Humor* (1888).

———. *The Isles of the Princes; or, The Pleasures of Prinkipo*. Illus. New York: G. P. Putnam's Sons, 1887. 381 pp.

Source: MTLAcc, entry #573, volume donated by Clemens. Cox recounts sights and experiences from his travel in Turkey.

COZZENS, FREDERICK SWARTWOUT (1818–1869). *Acadia; or, A Month with the Blue Noses*. Engraved frontispiece and illustration. Original brown cloth. Spine chipped at top and bottom. New York: Derby & Jackson, 1859. 329 pp. [Cozzens sometimes spelled his first name as "Frederic."]

Marginalia: unmarked, but page corners are folded down (as Clemens often did) at pages 48 (a large fold), 62, 81, 83, and 93.

Catalogs: Union Galleries (New York City), Sale number 41 (7–8 May 1935), "12mo, original cloth, New York, 1859," card autographed "Sincerely yours, Mark Twain" laid in, has the *A1911* sale label, lot 113; In Our Time Bookshop, Cambridge, Massachusetts, Catalogue 75 (January 1977), "8vo, cloth, . . . a few nicks to the spinal extremity," contains the *A1911* sale label, no markings, item #65, priced at $100. (For whatever reason, the Anderson Auction Company did not list this book for the auction in 1911, but there were other instances where this omission happened.) Listed in *Sotheby's 2003*, #220, sold with four other miscellaneous titles for a total of $900. Listed by James Cummins, Bookseller, New York City, on 22 February 2006, "with the monogrammed bookplate of William Inglis Morse and his blind stamp on flyleaf," $1,000.

Provenance: *A1911* auction item, but not listed in its catalog. The front flyleaf has a monogrammed bookplate of William Inglis Morse dated 1929. An inscription by G. A. Van Nosdall above a bookdealer's catalog entry is dated December 1936 in New York City. Sold to Jenkins Rare Books, Austin, Texas and offered for $225 in August 1980; acquired on 9 September 1980 by Alan Gribben, who passed it along to Nick Karanovich of Fort Wayne, Indiana. A signed bookplate on the front pastedown endpaper, prepared at Karanovich's request, attests to the book's authenticity: "From Samuel L. Clemens' personal library/Alan Gribben/Austin, Texas/1980."

Copy examined: Clemens's copy. Viewed in 1980 and again at the 2003 Sotheby's sale. Contains the *A1911* auction label on the front pastedown endpaper.

Cozzens employs dashes of sarcasm in describing his travels through the province of Novia Scotia and his encounters with its Acadian residents. His chronicle of early-day explorations of the Nouvelle France region in Chapter 2 (where a page is turned down) strongly resembles Mark Twain's historical summary in the opening pages of *Life on the Mississippi* (1883).

———. *The Sparrowgrass Papers; or, Living in the Country*. Philadelphia: T. B. Peterson & Brothers, n.d. (originally published in 1856).

Mark Twain's Library of Humor (1888) credited two pieces to this volume: "A Family Horse" and "Getting a Glass of Water."

somehow

CRAIK, DINAH MARIA (MULOCK) (1826–1887). *Christian's Mistake.* New York: Harper & Brothers, 1871. 260 pp.

Source: MTLAcc, entry #1634, volume donated by Clemens.

This was quite likely the book to which Clemens referred on 10 January 1872 when he notified Olivia Clemens from Steubenville, Ohio that he was sending home "a novel by the author of John Halifax—forgotten the name of it" (*MTLet* 5: 15). Eventually the Clemenses' family library would contain two dozen volumes by this author, one of their larger collections of any single writer.

———. *The Cousin from India.* New York: Harper & Brothers, 1904. 229 pp.

Source: MTLAcc, entry #414, volume donated by Clemens.

———. *Hannah.* New York: Harper & Brothers, 1904. 310 pp.

Source: MTLAcc, entry #1139, volume donated by Clemens.

———. *The Head of the Family; A Novel.* Illus. New York: Harper & Brothers, 1905. 528 pp.

Source: MTLAcc, entry #1328, volume donated by Clemens.

———. *A Hero, Bread Upon the Waters, Alice Learmont.* New York: Harper & Brothers, n.d. 269 pp.

Source: MTLAcc, entry #1138, volume donated by Clemens.

———. *His Little Mother, and Other Tales and Sketches.* New York: Harper & Brothers, 1881. 269 pp.

Source: MTLAcc, entry #1635, volume donated by Clemens.

———. *Is It True? Tales, Curious and Wonderful.* New York: Harper & Brothers, 1904. 208 pp.

Source: MTLAcc, entry #1611, volume donated by Clemens.

———. *John Halifax, Gentleman. A Novel.* Green cloth. New York: Carleton, Publisher, 1870. 485 pp.

Inscription: the front flyleaf is signed in pencil, "Ida C. Langdon." Ida Clark Langdon (1849–1934) was married to Charles Jervis Langdon (1849–1916).

Provenance: bookplate #468 of the "J. Langdon Family Library" on the front pastedown endpaper.

Catalog: Ball 2016 inventory, green cloth, gilt lettering, signed by Ida C. Langdon, from Jervis Langdon's Family Library #468, Mark Twain Archive.

Location: Mark Twain Archive, Elmira College, Elmira, New York.

Copy examined: unmarked copy available to Clemens whenever he visited the Langdon residence in Elmira. Examined on 27 May 2015.

In a sketch written on 20 August 1863 Mark Twain alluded to "reading that high-flown batch of contradictions and inconsistencies, 'John Halifax, Gentleman'" (San Francisco *Daily Morning Call*, 30 August 1863; *ET&S* 1: 283). When Olivia Langdon recommended that he read Craik's *A Life for a Life*, Clemens promised dutifully on 5 December 1868 to do so only because she had liked it, since "otherwise I should take it up with a prejudice against the author of 'Halifax'" (*MTLet* 2: 314). On 10 January 1872 Clemens notified Olivia Clemens from Steubenville, Ohio that he was sending home "a novel by the author of John Halifax—forgotten the name of it" (*MTLet* 5: 15). Katy Leary recalled that Olivia Clemens was forever trying

to upgrade the reading tastes of her housekeeper by giving her copies of "Dickens or John Halifax, or something dull and good like that" (*LMT*, p. 56).

———. *John Halifax, Gentleman.* New York: Thomas Y. Crowell Co., 1897. 504 pp.

Catalog: Ball 2016 inventory, gray cloth, gold lettering, gilt page edges, poor condition.

Location: Quarry Farm Library shelves, under the supervision of the Mark Twain Archive, Elmira College, Elmira, New York.

Clemens had access to this book during his later visits to Quarry Farm in Elmira.

———. *John Halifax, Gentleman.* New York: Harper & Brothers, 1903. 485 pp.

Source: MTLAcc, entry #1632, volume donated by Clemens.

———. *A Life for a Life, A Novel.* New York: Harper & Brothers, n.d. 396 pp.

Source: MTLAcc, entry #1630, volume donated by Clemens.

Clemens's letter to Olivia Langdon on 5 December 1868 from New York City mentions his intention to read "*A Life for a Life* . . . & shall like it, no doubt, because you do" (*LLMT*, p. 356; *MTLet* 2: 314). On 17 February 1869 Clemens wrote to her from Titusville, Pennsylvania: "I read & marked 'A Life for a Life' in the cars yesterday—I like it right well" (MTP; *MTLet* 3: 104).

———. *The Little Lame Prince.* Illus. New York: Harper & Brothers, n.d. 194 pp.

Source: MTLAcc, entry #1188, volume donated by Clemens.

———. *Little Sunshine's Holiday: A Picture from Life.* New York: Harper & Brothers, 1904. 210 pp.

Source: MTLAcc, entry #422, volume donated by Clemens.

———. *Miss Moore.* Illus. New York: Harper & Brothers, 1904. 235 pp.

Source: MTLAcc, entry #418, volume donated by Clemens.

———. *Mistress and Maid, A Household Story.* New York: Harper & Brothers, 1904. 327 pp.

Source: MTLAcc, entry #1629, volume donated by Clemens.

———. *A Noble Life.* New York: Harper & Brothers, n.d. 302 pp.

Source: MTLAcc, entry #1631, volume donated by Clemens.

———. *The Ogilvies. A Novel.* New York: Harper & Brothers, n.d. 421 pp.

Source: MTLAcc, entry #1633, volume donated by Clemens.

———. *Olive. A Novel.* Illus. New York, 1905.

Catalog: *A1911*, "post 8vo, cloth, N.Y. 1905," with a sheet of notes by Clemens about literary figures laid in, lot 349, sold for $1.

———. *Plain Speaking.* New York: Harper & Brothers, 1882. 249 pp.

Source: MTLAcc, entry #1329, volume donated by Clemens.

———. *Poems.* Boston: Ticknor and Fields, 1866. [Publisher and date are conjectured.]

Around 1865 Olivia Langdon copied a poem, "Philip, My King," into her commonplace book; sometime thereabouts she also inserted a handwritten copy of "Outward Bound" in the same commonplace book, crediting it to Miss Mulock (DV161, MTP). Clemens employed the refrain from "Too Late," a poem collected in this *Poems* volume— "Douglas, Douglas, tender and true"—to satirize the advertising techniques employed by Harper & Brothers to promote Charles Dudley Warner's *Library of the World's Best Literature* (SLC to WDH, Kaltenleutgeben, 16 August 1898, *MTHL*, p. 676).

———. *Songs of Our Youth. Set to Music by Various Composers.* New York: Harper & Brothers, 1875. 93 pp.

Marginalia: a penciled musical notation at the top of page 89 indicates a B flat note for the song "Douglas, Douglas, tender and true." It appears to be most likely in the hand of Clara Clemens.

Catalogs: *A1911*, "4to, cloth, N.Y. 1875," with a sheet of notes by Clemens laid in, lot 348, sold for $1.50; Chicago Book and Art Auctions (Chicago), Catalogue number 7 (14–15 April 1931), "small 4to, original cloth, enclosed in half green morocco slipcase, red lettering pieces, inner cloth wrapper, New York, 1875," has the *A1911* sale label and a sheet of Clemens's notations laid in, lot 92.

Location: Morris L. Parrish Collection, Department of Rare Books and Special Collections, Firestone Library, Princeton University, Princeton, New Jersey.

Copy examined: photocopies of the front endpapers (showing that the sheet of Clemens's miscellaneous notes is still laid in) sent to Alan Gribben by Gabriel Swift, Reference Librarian, on 26 April 2017, and photocopies of the *1911* sale label and the notation on page 89 sent by Brianna Cregle, Special Collections Assistant, on 1 May 2017.

———. *Studies from Life.* New York: Harper & Brothers, 1861. 290 pp.

Source: MTLAcc, entry #1140, volume donated by Clemens.

In this underrated collection of reflective essays Craik hunted out English literary and historical sites such as Stonehenge, Old Sarum, and Salisbury Plain ("Old Stones"), puzzled over the vagaries of publishing ("Silence for a Generation"), explored the evolution of literature written for young people ("'Want Something to Read'"), expressed concern about the obstacles immigrants must confront ("Brother Jonathan's Pet"), lamented the illusions regarding armed conflict ("War-Sparkles"), protested the over-analyzation of the lives of deceased authors ("Literary Ghouls"), sympathetically followed the lives of a nest of cuckoos in her garden ("My Babes in the Wood"), and addressed nine other topics.

———. *Twenty Years Ago. From the Journal of a Girl in Her Teens.* New York: Harper & Brothers, 1904. 354 pp.

Source: MTLAcc, entry #1167, volume donated by Clemens.

———. *A Woman's Thoughts about Women, by the Author of "John Halifax, Gentleman."* New York: Rudd & Carleton, 1858.

Inscription: "Livi L. Langdon/June 1864".

Source: library card in the Mark Twain Library at Redding, Connecticut. I could not locate any copy with this publisher and date of publication when I visited Redding in 1970 and in June 1982. (See a similar but different entry below.)

———. *A Woman's Thoughts about Women.* New York: Follett,

Foster & Co., 1864. 309 pp.

Inscription: the front free flyleaf is signed in black ink, with a flourish: "Livie L. Langdon/June 1864".

Location: Mark Twain Library, Redding, Connecticut.

Copy examined: Olivia (Langdon) Clemens's unmarked copy. Has a red ink accession number of the Mark Twain Library—"2881". Examined in June 1982.

Craik described the opportunities and duties, social and moral, for women who are young or old.

CRAIK, GEORGE LILLIE (1798–1866). *A Manual of English Literature and of the History of the English Language, with Numerous Specimens.* Tenth edition. London: Charles Griffin and Co., n.d. [Preface signed by "H. C." in April 1883.] 560 pp.

Inscription: signed by Olivia Clemens in black ink on the front flyleaf: "Olivia L. Clemens/Hartford/1888".

Marginalia: a vertical pencil mark characteristic of Clemens is visible on page 131 where Chaucer is ranked with Spenser, Shakespeare, and Milton.

Location: Mark Twain Library, Redding, Connecticut.

Copy examined: Olivia Clemens's copy. Examined in 1970 and again in June 1982.

CRAMER, ZADOK (1773–1814). *The Navigator; Containing Directions for Navigating the Monongahela, Allegheny, Ohio, and Mississippi Rivers; with an Ample Account of These Much Admired Waters . . . and a Concise Description of Their Towns, Villages, Harbours, Settlements, etc., with Accurate Maps of the Ohio and Mississippi.* Seventh edition, "Improved and Enlarged." 12mo. 28 woodcut maps. Sheep-backed marbled paper-covered boards. Pittsburgh: Cramer, Spear & Eichbaum, 1811.

Inscription: signed by Clemens in ink on the front pastedown endpaper, "S L. Clemens/1909/from Col. A. G. Paine." Presumably this presenter was Augustus Gibson Paine, Sr. (1839–1915), a wealthy New York City financier.

Catalogs: ListABP (1910), "The Navigator"; Zadok Cramer, *The Navigator*, Pittsburgh, 1811, signed in 1909, catalog of Heritage Rare Books, Los Angeles, California, 2009; Donald Heald Rare Books, 124 East 74th Street, New York, NY 10021, "Americana & Canadiana including American Cartography," Spring 2010 catalog, item #25, "given to Clemens in 1909 by friend and New York businessman Augustus G. Paine," offered for $12,500.

Location: currently unknown.

CRANDALL, CHARLES HENRY (1858–1923). *Representative Sonnets by American Poets, with an Essay on the Sonnet, Its Nature and History.* Boston: Houghton, Mifflin and Co.; Cambridge, The Riverside Press, 1890. 361 pp. [Water marks on top.]

Marginalia: stained by a red ribbon on page 51.

Location: Mark Twain Library, Redding, Connecticut.

Copy examined: when I visited the Mark Twain Library in June 1982 this volume had been added to the shelves holding the book donations made by Clemens and his daughter Clara Gabrilowitsch. (It had not been included there when I first cataloged the collection in 1970.) There is no justification for viewing the Crandall volume as deriving from the Clemens family library. It has no Mark Twain Library stamps, no accession number, and no indications whatever that the Clemenses ever owned the book. I recommended that it be discarded.

CRANE, STEPHEN (1871–1900). *The Monster and Other Stories.*

Illus. New York: Harper & Brothers, 1899. 189 pp.

Source: MTLAcc, entry #1531, volume donated by Clemens.

It is somehow gratifying to know that Clemens had in his possession this volume containing three of Crane's finest short works—"The Monster," a moving study of irony and prejudice in a small town; "The Blue Hotel," arguably Crane's best Western tale; and "His New Mittens," a poignant glimpse of boyhood pride and resolve.

CRANE, THOMAS (1843–1903) and ELLEN B. HOUGHTON (1853–1922). *Abroad*. Illus. London: Marcus Ward & Co., [1882]. 56 pp.

Source: MTLAcc, entry #1879, volume donated from Clemens's library by Clara Clemens Gabrilowitsch in 1910.

Poems about European cities by various writers accompany Crane's large, evocative illustrations with color plates created by Houghton. Thomas Crane was the elder brother of Walter Crane and Ellen Houghton was Walter Crane's cousin. A companion volume, *London Town* would appear in 1883.

CRANE, WALTER (1845–1915). *The Baby's Opera: A Book of Old Rhymes with New Dresses. The Music by the Earliest Masters.* Illustrated by Walter Crane. Engraved by Edmund Evans (1826–1905). First edition. Oblong volume. London: George Routledge and Sons, 1877. 62 pp. [Edition conjectured; another edition was published in London by Frederick Warne and Co, 1900.]

Catalog: ListABP (1910), "Baby's Opera, Crane".

A lavishly illustrated volume of children's songs and nursery rhymes.

———. "Ye Frog He Would A'Wooing Go" (story, textile).

The Clemenses decorated their children's nursery in wallpaper designed by this decorative artist and storyteller who belonged to the Aesthetic Movement in England. Crane created tiles, ceramics, textiles, and wallpapers copied from illustrations in his more than fifty books, which included *The Baby's Own Aesop*. "Ye Frog He Would A'Wooing Go" tells of the courtship of the Frog and the Mouse that was interrupted by two cats. See Eleanor Mancusi, "Walter Crane & Victorian Children's Literature," *Victorian Homes* (Winter 1994): 32–35.

CRAWFORD, EMILY (c. 1831–1915). "Notes from Paris," *Truth: A Weekly Journal*, 5 April 1894 issue.

When Clemens wrote to Olivia Clemens on 15 April 1894 he mentioned that Poultney Bigelow had sent Clemens "a copy of 'Truth' for April 5 with the article 'Notes from Paris' marked. It is by Mrs. Crawford, & talks about that luncheon and about Bigelow and me" (ALS in MTP). I am indebted to JoDee Benussi for noticing this reference. See also the Catalog entries for the editor, Henry DuPré Labouchère, and for *Truth: A Weekly Journal*.

CRAWFORD, FRANCIS MARION (1854–1909). *Corleone; A Tale of Sicily*. 2 vols. New York: Macmillan Co., 1897.

Catalog: Ball 2016 inventory, Volume 1 only, green cloth, gilt lettering, good condition.

Location: Quarry Farm Library shelves (Volume 1 only), under the supervision of the Mark Twain Archive, Elmira College, Elmira, New York.

Clemens had access to this book during his later visits to Quarry Farm in Elmira.

———. *Love in Idleness: A Tale of Bar Harbor* (novel, published in 1894).

A reporter for the Sydney, Australia *Bulletin* (12 October 1895) noticed that Clara Clemens "took no interest in pap's talk." Instead, she "read 'Love in Idleness'—a shilling's-worth of fiction in blue covers. Perhaps it is rather trying to spend a lifetime with a professional humorist, who is expected to be funny all the time" (quoted by Miriam Jones Shillingsburg, *At Home Abroad: Mark Twain in Australasia*, p. 71). Crawford took his title, *Love in Idleness*, from a common wildflower, a type of pansy, which Shakespeare mentioned in several plays.

———. *A Roman Singer*. Boston: Houghton, Mifflin & Co., 1884. 378 pp.

Source: MTLAcc, entry #78, volume donated by Clemens.

Clemens nominated Crawford for membership in the American Academy of Arts and Letters in 1905 (SLC to Robert Underwood Johnson, 28 April 1905, American Academy of Arts and Letters).

CRAWFORD, LOUISA (MACARTNEY) (1790–1858). "Kathleen Mavourneen" (song, published in 1837 or 1840). Melody by Frederick Nicholls Crouch [1808–1896]. [The lyrics are sometimes ascribed to Crouch or to others.]

Annie (Moffett) Webster recalled that Clemens sang a parody of this plaintive ballad during the period when he resided in St. Louis (1857–1861), substituting "Samuel Clemens" throughout for "Kathleen Mavourneen" (*MT-Bus*, pp. 39–40). The song became immensely popular during the Civil War.

CRAWFORD, SAMUEL WYLIE (1827–1892). *The Genesis of the Civil War: The Story of Sumter, 1860–1861*. New York: Charles L. Webster & Co., 1887. 486 pp.

Catalog: *A1911*, "thick 8vo, full dark brown morocco, blind tooled covers, gilt edges, N.Y. 1887," lot 113, sold for $4.25.

Clemens mentioned the author of this eye-witness account early in 1887—"General Crawford's book" (NB 26, *N&J* 3: 276); his publishing firm had accepted the manuscript in 1886 (*MTB*, p. 831).

CREMONY, JOHN C[AREY]. (1815–1879). *Life Among the Apaches*. San Francisco: A. Roman & Co., 1868. 322 pp.

Nina Baym noted—but did not press the case—that Cremony awed tribes of Apaches and Maricopas with his predictions about eclipses of the moon and a display of gunpowder fireworks that somewhat anticipated a couple of Hank Morgan's miraculous deeds in *A Connecticut Yankee in King Arthur's Court* (1889). See especially pages 98–102 and 147–152 of Cremony's book. However, Baym cautioned that although there seem to be plot and verbal parallels, Cremony's depiction of Native American psychology is entirely the opposite of the medieval psychology presented in *A Connecticut Yankee* (Baym to Alan Gribben, emails exchanged on 17 July, 8 August, 10 August, 20 August, and 21 August 2003). Still, it is worth remembering that in 1884 Clemens was seeking books about Native Americans in order to "take Huck Finn out there" to the plains and mountains of the Far West, as he informed his business manager Charles L. Webster. Cremony, incidentally, had scorn for those humanitarians who thought that gestures of accommodation would easily placate and educate the tribes with which he was familiar.

CRIM, MARTHA JANE (1864–1909), pseud. "Matt Crim."

Adventures of a Fair Rebel. Frontispiece by Dan[iel Carter] Beard (1850–1941). New York: Charles L. Webster & Co., 1891. 323 pp.

A young girl travels from North Carolina to Georgia during the Civil War. Issued by Clemens's publishing firm.

———. *Elizabeth, Christian Scientist*. New York: Charles L. Webster & Co., 1893. 350 pp.

Clemens's publishing firm advertised this as "a novel of a girl who leaves her Georgia mountain home to convert the world to Christian Science." Her destiny, however, "is to be loved and wedded" (*Publishers' Trade List Annual 1893*).

———. *In Beaver Cove and Elsewhere*. Illustrated by E[dward]. W[indsor]. Kemble (1861–1933). New York: Charles L. Webster & Co., 1892. 346 pp.

Clemens's firm published these short stories about life in the Georgia mountains.

The Crisis in China, by George B. Smyth, Rev. Gilbert Reid, Charles Johnston [and Others], Reprinted by Permission from the North American Review. Maps. New York: Harper & Brothers, 1900. 271 pp.

Source: MTLAcc, entry #1742, volume donated by Clemens.

The Critic (New York City periodical, published 1881–1906).

Jeannette L. Gilder and her brother Joseph Benson Gilder founded this review of literature, drama, and art in 1881. It was a weekly publication until 1898 when it became a monthly. (In 1906 it would be absorbed into *Putnam's Magazine*.) "Please have 'The Critic' sent regularly and permanently to Mrs. Clemens, Care Drexel Harjes & Co." (SLC to Frank G. Whitmore, n.d. [1893?], MTP). On 26 April 1894 Olivia Clemens cited this magazine in asking her husband to obtain a copy of "Prof. C. Fontaine's 'Livre de Lecture et de Conversation.' It is spoken very well of by the Critic & I should like it if you could get it & bring it to me when you come" (ALS, formerly in the Mark Twain Research Foundation, Perry, Mo.; quoted in *The Twainian* 37 [May-June 1978]: 4).

CROCKETT, SAMUEL RUTHERFORD (1859–1914). *Bog-Myrtle and Peat: Tales, Chiefly of Galloway, Gathered from the Years 1889 to 1895*. London: Bliss, Sands and Foster, 1895. 426 pp.

Source: MTLAcc, entry #2205, volume donated from Clemens's library by Clara Clemens Gabrilowitsch in 1910.

Crocket's collection of poems and short stories pays tribute to the Galloway region in southwestern Scotland.

———. *Cleg Kelley, Arab of the City: His Progress and Adventures* (published in 1895).

The Scottish novelist wrote Clemens on 23 August 1897: "I've got some boys I'd like to send you, if I might. I think Tom and Huck would like to know them. One of them is called 'Cleg Kelly.' Hully Gee, what a scrap there'd a been if Tom and Cleg had met" (MTP). Crockett had become a prominent member of the sentimental "Kailyard" school of rural Scottish writing. Clemens replied to Crockett on 17 September 1897, "I know Cleg & am fond of him" (MTP). On 23 October 1897 Clemens asked his British publisher to send "an early copy" of *More Tramps Abroad* to "S. R. Crockett" (*Sotheby's 2003*, #90). Surveying English literature in an 1897 newspaper interview in Vienna, Clemens said he considered Crockett to be one of the "good and splendid" contemporary authors (Odessa *News* [Odesskie *Novosti*], 8 October 1897; translated and

reprinted by M. Thomas Inge and George Munro, "Ten Minutes with Mark Twain," *American Literary Realism* 15.2 [Autumn 1982]: 262).

———. *The Dark o' the Moon. A Novel*. Illus. Original dark green pictorial cloth, gilt lettering. New York: Harper & Brothers, 1902. 453 pp.

Inscription: signed in ink on the front free endpaper: "S. L. Clemens, 1902."

Marginalia: there is a small pencil mark in the margin of page 395.

Catalog: *A1911*, "12mo, cloth, N.Y. 1902," quotes signature, lot 114, sold for $2.25.

Location: collection of Kevin Mac Donnell, Austin, Texas. Acquired in 2019 (Mac Donnell to Alan Gribben, 22 November 2019).

———. *The Men of the Mountain*. Illus. New York: Harper & Brothers, 1909. 316 pp.

Source: MTLAcc, entry #1446, volume donated by Clemens.

———. *The Play-Actress*. New York: G. P. Putnam's Sons, 1894. 194 pp.

Source: MTLAcc, entry #2185, volume donated from Clemens's library by Clara Clemens Gabrilowitsch in 1910. A Presbyterian minister learns a lesson from an unlikely source.

———. *The Raiders; Being Some Passages in the Life of John Faa, Lord and Earl of Little Egypt*. 2 vols. Collection of British Authors Series. Leipzig: B. Tauchnitz, 1894.

Source: MTLAcc, entries #2186 and #2206, volumes donated from Clemens's library by Clara Clemens Gabrilowitsch in 1910.

John Faa is a gypsy (today more politely known as Roma) chieftain in this romance.

———. *The Red Axe*. Illustrated by Frank Richards (1863–1935). New York: Harper & Brothers, 1902. 370 pp.

Source: MTLAcc, entry #1532, volume donated by Clemens.

———. *The Stickit Minister*. [Edition undetermined.]

Catalogs: ListABP (1910), "Stickit Minister, Crockett"; *C1951*, D65, listed with books signed by Clemens.

The title story, first published in 1893, recounted the struggles of a self-sacrificing minister who appears to be a stickit (stuck fast) ne'er-do-well failure. This volume also included other short stories and in several editions was more fully titled *The Stickit Minister & Some Uncommon Men*.

———. *Tales of Our Coast*. Illustrated by Frank Brangwyn (1867–1956). London: Chatto & Windus, 1896. 171 pp.

Source: MTLAcc, entry #2204, volume donated from Clemens's library by Clara Clemens Gabrilowitsch in 1910.

Tales of Our Coast collects five sea stories by Crockett ("Smugglers of the Clone"), Harold Frederic (1856–1898, "The Path of Murtogh"), Gilbert Parker (1862–1932, "'There Is Sorrow on the Sea'"), W. Clark Russell (1844–1911, "'That There Mason'"), and "The Roll-Call of the Reef" by a writer identified only as "Q."

CROKER, BITHIA MARY (SHEPPARD) (1847–1920). *The Cat's-Paw*. Lippincott's Select Novels Series. Philadelphia: J. B. Lippincott Co., 1903. 374 pp. Paperbound.

Source: MTLAcc, entry #71, volume donated by Clemens.

The Irish-born novelist and short story author Croker

followed her husband to India and set much of her fiction, as with *The Cat's Paw*, in India.

——. *Mr. Jervis*. Lippincott's Select Novels Series. Philadelphia: J. B. Lippincott Co., 1903. 397 pp. Paperbound.

Source: MTLAcc, entry #70, volume donated by Clemens. Originally published in 1897, this was another of Croker's novels set in India.

CROLY, GEORGE (1780–1860). *Tarry Thou Till I Come; or, Salathiel, the Wandering Jew*. Edited and intro. by Isaac K. Funk (1839–1912). Introductory letter by Lewis Wallace (1827–1905). Illustrated by [Bror] T[hure] de Thulstrup (1848–1930). New York: Funk & Wagnalls Co., 1901. 588 pp.

Source: MTLAcc, entry #1277, volume donated by Clemens.

CRONISE, TITUS FEY (1830–1910). *The Natural Wealth of California; Comprising Early History; Geography, Topography, and Scenery; Climate; Agriculture and Commercial Products; Geology, Zoology, and Botany; Mineralogy, Mines, and Mining Processes; Manufactures; Steamship Lines, Railroads, and Commerce; Immigration, Population and Society; Educational Institutions and Literature; Together with a Detailed Description of Each County; Its Topography, Scenery, Cities and Towns, Agricultural Advantages, Mineral Resources, and Varied Productions*. Illus. San Francisco: H. H. Bancroft & Co., 1868. 696 pp.

Source: MTLAcc, entry #747, volume donated by Clemens. This would seem to be the earliest surviving book in Clemens's library about the state where he spent those crucial years in the 1860s. It seems likely that he obtained this volume when he returned to San Francisco in 1868. Chapter 12 is entirely devoted to "City and County of San Francisco." A list of prominent literary authors and their works on page 684 includes Bret Harte and Charles Warren Stoddard but not Mark Twain.

CROOKES, WILLIAM (1832–1919). *Diamonds*. Illus. Red cloth. London: Harper & Brothers, 1909. 146 pp.

Inscription: signed on the front pastedown endpaper in black ink: "SL. Clemens/1909".

Provenance: Antenne-Dorrance Collection, Rice Lake, Wisconsin.

Location: Mark Twain Archive, Gannett-Tripp Learning Center, Elmira College, Elmira, New York.

Copy examined: Clemens's copy.

Crookes describes the geology of the diamond, "the hardest substance found in nature or fashioned by art" (p. 2). He reports in detail about his visits to the Kimberley diamond mines in South Africa, especially the De Beers Consolidated Mines. It seems relevant that in the years 1870–1871 Mark Twain had concocted a scheme to send John Henry Riley to Kimberley to report on these mines so that Twain could produce a book on the subject. In 1907 Twain said that he was skeptical of Crookes' scientific renown because of his credulity about Archdeacon Wilberforce's Holy Grail (12 September 1907 AD; *MTE*, p. 345; *AutoMT* 3: 133). Archdeacon [Albert] Basil Orme Wilberforce (1841–1916), Canon of Westminster Abbey and Chaplain of the House of Commons, initially seemed willing to believe in the authenticity of an artifact supposedly found in Glastonbury in 1906.

CROOKS, GEORGE RICHARD (1822–1897). *The Life of Bishop Matthew Simpson [1822–1885], of the Methodist Episcopal Church*. Illus. New York: Harper & Brothers, 1891. 524 pp.

Source: MTLAcc, entry #1757, volume donated by Clemens.

CROSBY, ERNEST HOWARD (1856–1907). *Captain Jinks, Hero*. Illustrated by Dan[iel Carter] Beard (1850–1941). New York: Funk & Wagnalls Co., 1902. 393 pp.

Clemens wrote to Dan Beard on 18 January 1902 to praise Beard's pictures for an unnamed book, probably this one (PH in MTP). In February 1902 he wrote to an unidentified recipient, most likely Crosby, to testify that "Chapter X. of 'Captain Jinks' is a successful satire on General Funston" (PH in MTP); this praise was later published in the Springfield, Massachusetts *Republican* on 12 April 1902. Crosby was president of the Anti-Imperialist League of New York; see Jim Zwick, *Mark Twain's Weapons of Satire: Anti-Imperialist Writings on the Philippine-American War* (Syracuse, New York: Syracuse University Press, 1992), pp. 109–111.

——. *Swords and Ploughshares*. New York: Funk & Wagnalls Co., 1902. 126 pp.

Source: MTLAcc, entry #613, volume donated by Clemens. A collection of poems by Crosby, many of which have virulently anti-war and anti-imperialist themes.

CROSS, ROSETTA OTWELL (1849–1902). *The Suffering Millions*. "Edited by a graduate of the University of Michigan." Brown cloth. Ann Arbor, Michigan: The Courier Office, Printers, 1890. 283 pp.

Inscriptions: signed "Edward Bacon" on the front and rear endpapers.

Marginalia: the front pastedown endpaper has an assessment by Clemens written in ink: "The trouble about this book/is, that it isn't bad enough/to be good. Every now &/then it drops into something/resembling English./ SLC". Clemens read the volume in the summer of 1902 while staying at the Sewalls's home in York Harbor, Maine.

Location: owned in 2012 by Grace Croft of Orlando, Florida. The book passed to her through her mother's side of the family.

Peter Salwen, "Be Sure and Save the Gentians!," *Mark Twain Journal* 48.1–2 (Spring/Fall 2010): 105–116, related the circumstances under which Clemens came to read Rosetta Otwell Cross' *The Suffering Millions*. Cross' melodramatic novel, interspersed with Biblical verses and warnings about the destruction of families by alcohol, depicts the pain inflicted on a wife and children by her husband's drinking habits and his devotion to a mistress. In the closing pages the erring husband and his mistress are shot by her jealous lover; the husband asks his wife and God to forgive him as he dies.

CROTHERS, SAMUEL McCHORD (1857–1927). *The Gentle Reader*. Boston: Houghton, Mifflin and Co., 1904. 321 pp.

Source: MTLAcc, entry #797, volume donated by Clemens. Crothers provides interesting essays on miscellaneous topics related to the author's reading interests and the reflections they engender. He discusses at length Charles Ellms' *The Pirates Own Book: Authentic Narratives of the Most Celebrated Sea Robbers* (see the Ellms entry in the Catalog).

CROUCH, ARCHER PHILIP (1858–1934). *Señorita Montenar*. Illus. New York: Harper & Brothers, 1898. 300 pp.

Source: MTLAcc, entry #1533, volume donated by

Clemens.
Crouch set this historical romance along the coast of Chile.

Crowe, Catherine (1790–1876). *Susan Hoply; or, The Trials and Vicissitudes of a Servant Girl: A Tale of Great Interest.* Illus. London: E[dward]. Lloyd, [1842]. 444 pp. Bound with Thomas Peckett Prest (1810–1859), *The Death Grasp; or, A Father's Curse: A Romance of Startling Interest.* London: E[dward] Lloyd, [18--]. 222 pp. [Note: Other editions of Crowe's novel spell the title as *Susan Hopley.* Prest was the author of numerous penny dreadfuls.]

Inscriptions: signed "S. L. Clemens (Mark Twain)" on the front free endpaper, with a notation that Clemens gave the book to Eugene Field in 1889. Tipped to the front free endpaper is a 1935 notarized statement by Eugene Field II stating that the book came from his father's estate. This statement is repeated on the rear free endpaper. Eugene Field II (1880–1947) is known to have forged the signatures of Clemens, Lincoln, and other prominent figures in numerous books that he passed off as originating from his poet father's library.

Catalog: offered for sale and explicitly identified as a forgery in a 1986 bookseller's catalog, item #51, priced at $80 (photocopy of the page from an unidentified rare book catalog sent to Alan Gribben by Kevin Mac Donnell on 27 June 1986).

Cruikshank, Robert (1789–1856). *Cruikshank at Home: A New Family Album of Endless Entertainment.* Illus. Four volumes in two. Red leather. London: H. G. Bohn, 1845.

Inscriptions: the front flyleaf is signed, "Yr Truly/S. L. Clemens (Mark Twain)". Also (ostensibly) signed on the half title by the poet Eugene Field (1850–1895). The Clemens signature was a highly uncharacteristic form for his book inscriptions. On the rear free flyleaf, in ink, appears: "This book came/from the library/of my father Eugene/Field./Eugene Field II./Oct. 20, 1920". There is no question that Field, Jr. has committed one of his early forgeries here with the Clemens autograph, and probably he signed his father's name as well.

Location: Special Collections, Michigan State University Library. Donated on 29 September 1952 by Charles G. Munn of Jackson, Michigan. Appraised then at $100.

Sources: "Found in the Vault: A Presentation Inscription by Mark Twain—Or Is It?," *Adversaria: Special Collections Provenance at MSU,* 21 March 2014; "Update: Mark Twain, Eugene Field, and a Skeptical Odyssey in the Stacks," *Adversaria: Special Collections Provenance at MSU,* 23 September 2014. These two articles provide facsimiles of the purported signatures.

Cumming, John (1807–1881). *The Great Consummation. The Millennial Rest; or, The World As It Will Be.* New York: G. W. Carleton, 1863. [Edition conjectured.]

Mark Twain wrote to the *Alta California* on 19 April 1867 to report that the porter at the Heming House in Keokuk (actually he stayed at the Deming House) had brought him a copy of *The Great Consummation* for his reading pleasure (*MTTMB,* p. 153). In Chapter 57 of *The Innocents Abroad* (1869) he told the same story, altering the hotel name to "Benton House." Cumming was a minister of the Scottish National Church who wrote evangelistic sermons.

Cundall, Joseph (1818–1895), pseud. "Stephen Percy." *Robin Hood and His Merry Foresters* (London, 1841; New York and Boston, 1842).

Alan Gribben—"How Tom Sawyer Played Robin Hood 'by the Book,'" *English Language Notes* 13.3 (March 1976): 201–204—described Mark Twain's use of this literary source (a revised version of this essay appears as a chapter in Volume One of the present work). I found that Tom Sawyer quotes directly from this children's book in Chapters 8 and 26 of *The Adventures of Tom Sawyer* (1876). Inasmuch as the illustrator True Williams obviously copied the cover illustration of Cundall's *Robin Hood and His Merry Foresters* when producing a sketch of Robin Hood for page 200 of *Tom Sawyer,* Twain must have obtained a copy of Cundall's book while writing his novel or soon thereafter. Twain's familiarity with Cundall's version of the Robin Hood legend indicates that he associated it with his Hannibal childhood, which is important because so little is known about his earliest reading. In an undated set of notes apparently connected with *The Adventures of Tom Sawyer,* Twain wrote: "89—Robin Hood—after cat & warts . . . 92—Sits down on a nettle after shooting his last arrow—close R H with that" (*A1911,* lot 454). On 19 December 1883 Clemens wrote to his nephew Jervis Langdon about "the fascination" that the story of Robin Hood held "when I was your age—a fascination so great that it paled the interest of all other books & made them tame & colorless. . . . I have always regretted that I did not belong to Robin Hood's gang" (ALS, formerly in the collection of Jervis Langdon, Jr.; PH in MTP). See also the Catalog entries for Howard Pyle's *The Merry Adventures of Robin Hood of Great Renown* (1883).

Cunliffe-Owen, Marguerite (de Godart) (1859–1927). *The Cradle of the Rose.* Illustrated by the author. New York: Harper & Brothers, 1908. 320 pp.

Source: MTLAcc, entry #1853, volume donated from Clemens's library by Clara Clemens Gabrilowitsch in 1910. The Clemens family obviously enjoyed this author, accumulating more than a dozen volumes of her works. The titled Cunliffe-Owen and her aristocrat husband had moved from France to the United States in 1885. Her familiarity with the royal courts of Europe served her well in writing biographies and historical novels. She also was a popular (and cynical) newspaper columnist.

———. *A Doffed Coronet, A True Story.* Illus. New York: Harper & Brothers, 1902. 545 pp.

Source: MTLAcc, entry #7, volume donated by Clemens.

———. [Another identical copy.]

Source: MTLAcc, entry #1346, volume donated by Clemens.

———. *Emerald and Ermine; A Tale of the Argoät.* Illustrated by the author. New York: Harper & Brothers, 1907. 329 pp.

Inscription: "To Doctor Clemens/With the compliments/of the Author./25th May 08."

Marginalia: nine pages are turned down, but there are no marks or notes.

Catalog: "Retz Appraisal" (1944), p. 4, valued at $5.

Location: Mark Twain Papers, Bancroft Library, University of California at Berkeley.

Copy examined: Clemens's copy.

———. [Another identical copy.]

Source: MTLAcc, entry #1856, volume donated from Clemens's library by Clara Clemens Gabrilowitsch in 1910.

———. *Gray Mist; A Novel.* Illustrated by the author. New York: Harper & Brothers, 1906. 282 pp.
  Source: MTLAcc, entry #1507, volume donated by Clemens.
———. [Another identical copy.]
  Source: MTLAcc, entry #1854, volume donated from Clemens's library by Clara Clemens Gabrilowitsch in 1910.
———. *Imperator et Rex, William II of Germany.* Illus. New York: Harper & Brothers, 1905. 282 pp.
  Source: MTLAcc, entry #1298, volume donated by Clemens.
———. *A Keystone of Empire, Francis Joseph of Austria.* Illus. New York: Harper & Brothers, 1903. 322 pp.
  Source: MTLAcc, entry #1297, volume donated by Clemens.
———. [Another identical copy.]
  Catalog: *A1911,* "8vo, cloth, gilt top, uncut, N.Y. 1903," lot 21, $2.
———. *The Martyrdom of an Empress.* Illustrated with sixteen halftone plates. Original mustard cloth, gilt. Brown cloth folding case. New York: Harper & Brothers, 1902. 287 pp.
  Inscription: the front flyleaf is inscribed in ink by Clemens's daughter: "Jean L. Clemens/Glencote/Tyringham/Mass./From Father,/October, 1904." (The Clemenses stayed with the Gilders at their home in Tyringham in the Berkshires as they adjusted to life without Olivia Clemens.)
  Catalogs: *C1951,* #68c, $10, listed among the books signed by Clemens; *Sotheby's 2003,* #194, $1,300 (sold with two other titles from the Clemens family's library).
  Provenance: contains the shelfmarks of Clara Clemens Gabrilowitsch's private library when she resided in Detroit. Offered for sale in 1990 by Charles Agvent Books, Mertztown, Pennsylvania, "Item 68c in the 1951 Hollywood Mark Twain Library Fiasco," initially priced at $5,000 (Charles Agvent to Nick Karanovich, 9 June, 13 June 1990; copies of this correspondence sent to Alan Gribben by Nick Karanovich on 4 July 1990). Subsequently belonged to the collection of Nick Karanovich in Fort Wayne, Indiana.
  Location: collection of Kevin Mac Donnell, Austin, Texas. Obtained in 2003.
  Copy examined: Jean Clemens's unmarked copy, in July 2004. Kevin Mac Donnell discovered that this book appears in a photograph Jean Clemens took of her cat sitting in a chair. The title is visible in the bookcase behind the chair, on the second shelf from the bottom.
———. *The Tribulations of a Princess.* Portraits from photographs. New York: Harper & Brothers, [cop. 1901]. 378 pp.
  Source: MTLAcc, entry #1506, volume donated by Clemens.
———. *The Tribulations of a Princess.* Portraits from photographs. New York: Harper & Brothers, 1901. 379 pp.
  Source: MTLAcc, entry #1855, volume donated from Clemens's library by Clara Clemens Gabrilowitsch in 1910.
———. *The Trident and the Net; A Novel.* Illustrated by the author. New York: Harper & Brothers, 1905. 550 pp.
  Source: MTLAcc, entry #1317, volume donated by Clemens.
———. [Another identical copy.]
  Inscription: on the front pastedown endpaper: "S. L.

Clemens, 1906."
  Catalog: *A 1911,* "8vo, cloth, N.Y. 1905," quotes the signature, lot 460, sold for $2.25.
CUNNINGHAM, ALLAN (1784–1842). *The Life of Robert Burns.* Second edition. Frontispiece portrait of Burns. 12mo, original boards, spine loose, several pages repaired. London: James Cochrane & Co., 1835. 380 pp.
  Inscriptions: in Clemens's hand on the front flyleaf, quoting the nineteenth stanza from John Greenleaf Whittier's twenty-nine-stanza poem titled "Burns. On Receiving a Sprig of Heather in Blossom" (1854): "'O'er rank & pomp, as he had seen,/I saw the Man uprising;/No longer common or unclean,/The child of God's baptizing!'/(Whittier.[)]/Truly Yours,/S L Clemens/Hartford, 1889." (text from a photocopy that corrects the 1912 sale catalog). The formal tone of this inscription suggests that this was intended as a gift volume to someone outside the Clemens family. See the Catalog entry for a similarly inscribed set of volumes, *The Works of Robert Burns.* Very likely Clemens inscribed these presents (or prizes?) at the same time. On the rear pastedown endpaper a bookseller noted a price: "$150.00 net."
  Catalogs: Anderson Auction Company (New York City), Sale number 378 (11–12 April 1905), "12mo, original boards, cloth back, uncut, London, 1835, flyleaf inscription" (quoted), lot 166, sold for $20.50 (PH in MTP); Anderson Auction Galleries (New York City), Sale number 941 (27–29 February 1912), the library of the late Captain J. F. Hinckley of St. Louis, "12mo, original boards, cloth back (loose, and several leaves repaired), in silk slip cover, enclosed in maroon levant morocco case, by Sangorski and Sutcliffe, London, 1835," quotes the four-line inscription from Whittier on the flyleaf, lot 223.
  Location: Special Collections, Washington University Libraries, St. Louis, Missouri. Ms. Kelly Brown of Special Collections notified me about this association copy on 12 May 2015 and sent me a photocopy of Clemens's flyleaf inscription. Their library catalog traces it to the George N. Meissner collection.
  Copy examined: Clemens's copy. I examined it in St. Louis on 10 August 2015.
———. "A Wet Sheet and a Flowing Sea" (poem, British sea song, published in 1825).
  In February 1882 Mark Twain declared that the title of this poem and song "has always been meaningless to me," owing to his ignorance of nautical terminology (NB 20, *N&J* 2: 448). He quoted from the song in "About All Kinds of Ships" (1893). Cunningham's poem depicts the life of robust sailors whose ship "like the eagle free/. . . leaves/Old England on the lee."
CUPPLES, GEORGE (1822–1891). *The "Green Hand." A "Short" Yarn.* No. 68, Franklin Square Library Series. New York: Harper & Brothers, 1879. 83 pp.
  Clemens wrote "Green Hand 68 (No.)" in Notebook 19 (1881, *N&J* 2: 395). On 23 May 1881 he requested of James R. Osgood: "Please send me No's 68 and 142 of Harper's Franklin Square Library (Green Hand and Sailor's Sweetheart.)" (*MTLP,* p. 136). See the Catalog entry for W. C. Russell.
  Stone, *IE* (1961), p. 161; Blair, *HH&T* (1969), p. 145.
CURIE, MARIE (1867–1934). "Radium and Radioactivity,"

Century Magazine 67.3 (January 1904): 461–466.

Satan quotes from this article ("what Madame Curie says about radium") in "Sold to Satan" (written in 1904). See also the Catalog entry for Ernest George Merritt.

Sherwood P. Cummings, "Mark Twain and Science" (doctoral dissertation, 1950).

Current Literature: A Magazine of Record and Review (New York): 6.4 (April 1891): 481–640. [A single issue, paper covers.]

Inscription: Clemens penciled across the top of the front cover: "Contains Copyright bill." (Pages 484–489 reprinted the full text of the International Copyright Bill.)

Marginalia: Clemens annotated the main points of the Copyright Bill in pencil, for example (p. 485): "2 copies to Lib. Cong." He also made corrections to "The Demon and the Fury" by the American humorist "M. Quad" (Charles Bertrand Lewis) of the Detroit *Free Press* on pages 544 and 545 and cut out two paragraphs of that sketch to use in the whimsical "Weather for Use in This Book" appendix to *The American Claimant* (1892). Pages 630–631 of this same issue of *Current Literature* contained an account of a dust-storm in Australia taken from E. W. Hornung's novel, *A Bride from the Bush* (1890); Twain cut out several sections of those pages for the same purpose.

Catalogs: ListABP (1910), "Current Literature Apl, 1891 (note)"; "Retz Appraisal" (1944), p. 7, valued at $20.

Location: Mark Twain Papers, Bancroft Library, University of California at Berkeley.

Copy examined: Clemens's copy.

Current Literature (1888–1925) began as a monthly digest publishing poems and excerpts from literary works and essays; in 1913 it altered its title and focus to *Current Opinion*.

CURTIS, CHARLES ALBERT (1835–1907). *Captured by the Navajos*. Illus. New York:

Harper & Brothers, 1904. 291 pp.

Source: MTLAcc, entry #1591, volume donated by Clemens.

Two young boys fight off Navajos and Apaches in this novel about a United States cavalry desert outpost.

CURTIS, DAVID A. (1846–1923). *Stand Pat; or, Poker Stories from the Mississippi*. Illustrated by Henry Roth. New York: L. C. Page & Co., 1906. 269 pp.

Source: MTLAcc, entry #2208, volume donated from Clemens's library by Clara Clemens Gabrilowitsch in 1910.

Twenty stories about poker games played by Stumpy, Gallagher, Kenney, and others in 1881 in the town of Brownsville, Arkansas. Gunplay was always a possibility.

CURTIS, GEORGE WILLIAM (1824–1892). *Early Letters of George Wm. Curtis to John S[ullivan]. Dwight [1813–1893]; Brook Farm and Concord*. Ed. by George Willis Cooke (1848–1923). New York: Harper & Brothers, 1898. 294 pp.

Source: MTLAcc, entry #1463, volume donated by Clemens.

Cooke provides a lengthy biographical sketch of this phase of Curtis's life before presenting Curtis's letters to Dwight. John W. Chadwick's earlier tribute, "Recollections of George William Curtis" (*Harper's Monthly* 86.513 [February 1893]: 469–476, had noted that Clemens, unlike many other literati, never got around to visiting Curtis's summer home in Ashfield, Massachusetts: "There did *not*

come Mark Twain, one year because he was 'getting old and rheumatic,' and another year because 'all that was past, and he *was* old and rheumatic'" (p. 474).

———. *The Howadji in Syria*. New York: Harper & Brothers, 1867. 350 pp. [Edition conjectured. Initially published by Harper & Brothers in 1852. The edition that Clemens read has not been established.]

Curtis recounted his travels in Syria, dividing his book into three sections: "The Desert," "Jerusalem," and "Damascus." "Howadji" was the term he heard everywhere applied to a foreign tourist like himself. Clemens wrote to Emeline Beach on 10 February 1868 from Washington, D.C.: "You know very well that I am particularly fond of a happy expression, & that I never tired of reading that Howadji in Syria, simply because it could furnish that charm in such profusion" (quoted in Bradford A. Booth's "Mark Twain's Friendship with Emeline Beach," *American Literature* 19.3 [November 1947]: 219–230). Leon Dickinson's preliminary draft of explanatory notes for a never-published Iowa-California Edition of *The Innocents Abroad* (1869) deduced that Twain's drew on Curtis's book for Twain's account of a Turkish bath in Chapter 34. Curtis's description of the various steps of the bathing process is even more detailed than Twain's, but Curtis was far more satisfied than Twain with the final result: "You exist in exquisite sensation, but are no longer conscious of a body. . . . The cool, fragrant dimness permeates your frame. You fall softly into sleep as into an abyss of clouds," Curtis wrote in Chapter 7 of the "Damascus" section of *The Howadji in Syria*.

———. *Potiphar Papers* (published in 1853).

On 12 November 1875 Clemens made a brief speech before the curtain was raised at an amateur production in Hartford of a comedy by Irving Browne (1835–1899)—*Our Best Society*—adapted from Curtis's *Potiphar Papers*. Clemens's remarks indicated, though jokingly, a familiarity with the chief characters in Curtis's satire of New York City society (*MTLet* 6: 589–590). One piece from Curtis's collection of essays—"Rev. Cream Cheese and the New Livery"—would appear in *Mark Twain's Library of Humor* (1888).

———. *Prue and I*. Illus. New York: Harper & Brothers, 1899. 223 pp.

Source: MTLAcc, entry #1534, volume donated by Clemens.

Mark Twain's Library of Humor (1888) described Curtis's *Prue and I* as "a book of romantic essays" that was "one of the loveliest books in the language" (p. 35). In these sketches an elderly bookkeeper meditates philosophically about a lost love ("Prue") and places himself in the imaginary company of the wealthy and the famous, past and present.

CURTIS, LILLIAN E. (1852–1900). *Forget-Me-Not. Poems*. Albany, New York: Weed, Parsons and Co., 1872. 112 pp.

Inscription: "To Mark Twain/from his sincere friend/and admirer/Edwin F. Schirely." At the top of the title page is his signature: "E. F. Schirely/7/ 12/89." Presumably this donor had heard of Twain's appetite for "Hogwash Literature."

Marginalia: Clemens read the volume thoroughly in search of humorous passages, commenting in pencil, correcting syntax and rhymes, and occasionally making outright gibes such as the one on page 56 ("Letter to My Cousin, J. W. H., On His Birthday"): "Did he have to stand this every year?" Her poem begins, "It is thy birthday, cousin dear;/ Twelve ere this one thou hast seen,/And I wish I could be near,/On this that numbers thee thirteen." On page 58, at the penultimate stanza of the same poem, Clemens urged: "Hit him again next year." The volume concludes on page 112 with a quatrain titled "A Question": "Dear friends, all who've been kind enough,/This little volume, to peruse with care,/Tell me candidly, do you think it/ Another castle in the air?"

> **Provenance:** Antenne-Dorrance Collection, Rice Lake, Wisconsin.
>
> **Location:** Mark Twain Archive, Gannett-Tripp Learning Center, Elmira College, Elmira, New York.
>
> **Copy examined:** Clemens's copy.

CURTIS, NATALIE, LATER (FROM 1917) NATALIE CURTIS BURLIN (1875–1921), ed. *The Indians' Book; An Offering by the American Indians of Indian Lore, Musical and Narrative, to Form a Record of the Songs and Legends of Their Race, Recorded and Edited by Natalie Curtis; Illustrations from Photographs and from Original Drawings by Indians.* Original tan buckram with color pictorial design, stamped in orange, white, and green, paper label, uncut and largely unopened. New York: Harper and Brothers, 1907. 573 pp.

> **Inscription:** the front pastedown endpaper is inscribed by Clemens in black ink, "A book made & illustrated by Indians. S L. Clemens, 1907. November, 21 Fifth Ave." Clara Clemens Gabrilowitsch's shelf mark ("HU/H11") also appears on the front pastedown endpaper.
>
> **Marginalia:** in the upper margin above the portrait of a Pawnee man named Letakots-Lesa, opposite page 98, Clemens noted, "My, but he is wickedly handsome!" The following pages have been opened: i–x, 32–45, 99–114, and 243–246, plus a few individual pairs of leaves. The opened sections included the foreword and part of the contents (to page 278) as well as texts depicting the Plains Indians, Dakotas (Sioux), Pawnees, and Winnebagos.
>
> **Catalogs:** *C1951*, #10c, $20, signed by Clemens, merely listed as *The Indians Book—made and illustrated by Indians* [*sic*]; *Sotheby's 2003*, #198, $2,500; afterwards offered by Heritage Book Shop, Los Angeles ("Largely unopened. . . . Some edge wear, but a very attractive and clean copy"); sold for $3,200 by Bloomsbury Auctions, New York City, in an eBay auction on 28 November 2007.
>
> **Provenance:** California Book Auction, 11 December 1997, lot 4035. Subsequently in the collection of Nick Karanovich, Fort Wayne, Indiana.
>
> **Location:** collection of Kevin Mac Donnell, Austin, Texas. Mac Donnell notified Alan Gribben and described this book on 28 August 2017.
>
> **Copy examined:** Clemens's copy, at the Sotheby's auction in 2003.

CURTIS, WILLIAM ELROY (1850–1911). *The Capitals of Spanish America.* Illus. New York: Harper & Brothers, [cop. 1888]. 715 pp.

> **Source:** MTLAcc, entry #1378, volume donated by Clemens.

A former United States diplomat to Latin America, Curtis described his travels to virtually every nation in Central and South America, commencing with chapters on Mexico, Guatemala, Honduras, and Nicaragua, and concluding with his impressions of Chile, Peru, and Patagonia. Many other countries were included.

CUSACK, [MARGARET ANNA] KNOWN AS MARY FRANCIS (her birth date is variously reported as 1829, 1830, or 1832; she died in 1899) (pen name, "Sister Mary Francis Clare"). *Three Visits to Knock. With the Medical Certificates of Cures and Authentic Accounts of Different Apparitions.* Green cloth, gilt. The cover reads "Irish Fireside Library." New York: P. J. Kennedy, 1898. 135 pp. [Bound with John MacPhilpin's *The Apparitions and Miracles at Knock.* New York: P. J. Kennedy, 1898.]

> **Inscription:** signed on the verso of the front flyleaf in black ink: "Clemens."
>
> **Marginalia:** Clemens marked the volume in pencil up to page 86; he also commented on page 98 about the eviction of Irish tenants around Knock because of poor harvests.
>
> **Provenance:** Antenne-Dorrance Collection, Rice Lake, Wisconsin.
>
> **Location:** Mark Twain Archive, Gannett-Tripp Learning Center, Elmira College, Elmira, New York.
>
> **Copy examined:** Clemens's copy. Examined on 27 May 2015.

Three visions—of the Virgin Mary and Saints Joseph and John—were allegedly seen in 1879 and 1880 in the parish chapel at Knock, a tiny village in County Mayo, Ireland. Pilgrims to the site soon reported miraculous cures. While heading northward from New Orleans on a steamboat in 1882 Clemens noted the title of MacPhilpin's book and resolved to "compare one of these with a miracle from the Bible" (*N&J* 2: 475–476). He may have been aware then of Cusack's writings on the visions, since she was the chief proponent of their authenticity. Cusack's *Three Visits to Knock* was first published in London and Dublin in 1882; an earlier version, *An Apparition at Knock*, had appeared in 1880.

CUSTER, ELIZABETH (BACON). (1842–1933). *"Boots and Saddles"; or, Life in Dakota with General Custer.* Original pictorial cloth, minor wear and soiling. New York: Harper & Brothers, [1885]. 312 pp.

> **Inscription:** the front free flyleaf, which probably bore an inscription, has been removed. (An offset of Clemens's inked signature seems to be slightly visible on the opposite page.)
>
> **Provenance:** sold in 1951 at the Hollywood auction, but not included in the checklist of the sale (a not-uncommon occurrence at that hasty disposition of books by a furniture auctioneer).
>
> **Catalog:** "Property from the Library of Mark Twain," Butterfield & Butterfield, San Francisco, Sale 6613 (16 July 1997), lot 2670.
>
> **Location:** Mark Twain House and Museum, Hartford, Connecticut.
>
> **Copy examined:** Clemens's copy. Viewed in 1997.

General George Armstrong Custer lived from 1839 until his nationally publicized death in 1876. Clemens noted "Boots & Saddles E. B. Custer" in Notebook 24 (May 1885), *N&J* 3: 148.

Elizabeth Custer's lectures and books helped shaped her late husband's popular image as a fallen American hero.

———. *Tenting on the Plains; or, General Custer in Kansas and*

Texas. New York: Charles L. Webster & Co., 1887. 403 pp.

Inscription: the front flyleaf is signed in black ink, "Clara L. Clemens/Elmira/July 1888".

Location: Mark Twain Library, Redding, Connecticut.

Copy examined: Clara's Clemens's copy, published by her father's firm. Examined in 1970 and again in June 1982. Has a red ink Mark Twain Library accession number, "2430". Clemens met Elizabeth Custer in Onteora, New York, and she wrote him half a dozen letters (Louise Barnett, "Libbie Custer & Mark Twain," *Research Review: The Journal of the Little Big Horn Association* 11.2 [Summer 1997]: 17–19).

CUSTER, GEORGE ARMSTRONG (1839–1876). *My Life on the Plains*. [First published in 1874; the 1881 edition that was published in New York by Sheldon and Company contained 256 pages.]

On the verso of Clemens's letter of 10 July 1884 to Charles L. Webster (containing a request for Col. Richard I. Dodge's book), Webster wrote: "My Life on the Plains/Gen. G. A. Custer USA/Sheldon & Co" (PH in MTP). Webster presumably would have acquired an 1881 edition for Clemens. General Custer had died in the famous battle of Little Big Horn on 25 June 1876.

Blair, *HH&T* (1969), p. 86.

CUTTER, BLOODGOOD H[AVILAND]. (1817–1906). *Lines on the Egyptian Obelisk: "Cleopatra's Needle."* Flushing, New York: W. R. Burling, Printer, 1881. 8 pp.

Catalog: ListABP (1910), "Lines to an [*sic*] Egyptian Obelisk, Cutter", no other information provided.

———. *The Long Island Farmer's Poems. Lines Written on the "Quaker City" Excursion to Palestine, and Other Poems. By Bloodgood H. Cutter, Mark Twain's "Lariat" in "Innocents Abroad."* New York: N. Tibbals & Sons. Published for the Author, 1886. 499 pp.

Source: purportedly Mark Twain's copy, offered for sale by I. K. Brussell, Brooklyn, New York, 9 July 1966, $15 (note on file in MTP).

Mark Twain preserved this poetaster's place in American letters by calling him the "Poet Lariat" and chuckling over his verse in *The Innocents Abroad* (1869), beginning in Chapter 7 where he is introduced as "a good-natured enterprising idiot" whose poems represent "a grievous infliction." Thereafter Twain took pleasure in encouraging Cutter's publication of his effusions. Notebooks 8 (1867, *N&J* 1: 334–335, 340), 9 (1867, *N&J* 1: 448, 450), and 46 (1903) contain references to Cutter. Bradley, Beatty, and Long's edition of *Huckleberry Finn* (1962) reprinted an example of Cutter's "lugubrious, sentimental, and semi-literate verse" (p. 252).

Mildred H. Smith, "Bloodgood Cutter and Mark Twain," *Long Island Forum* 32 (December 1969): 226–230, examined the odd relationship between Twain and the amateur poet. Richard Conway, "Mark Twain and the 'Poet Lariat,'" *Mark Twain Journal* 19.1 (Winter 1977–1978): 18, took note of Cutter's verse. John Lockwood's "The Poet Lariat's Home," *Mark Twain Journal* 47.1–2 (Spring/Fall 2009): 96–125 reprinted a newspaper reporter's lengthy interview with Bloodgood Cutter published in 1890 and provided samples of Cutter's verse. See also L. W. Michaelson, "Four Emmeline Grangerfords," *Mark Twain Journal* 11.3 (Fall 1961): 10–12.

CUTTER, CALVIN (1807–1873?). *Anatomy and Physiology*. Illus. Boston: Benjamin B. Mussey and Co., 1848. 342 pp.

Inscriptions: the front endpapers are signed in pencil "Hawley" and (separately) "Lydia" (presumably Lydia Hill, whose signature is found in various other books of early imprint donated to the Mark Twain Library at Redding).

Location: Mark Twain Library, Redding, Connecticut.

Copy examined: an unmarked copy of uncertain provenance. Someone made a note in the 1950s or early 1960s that a copy of the 1848 edition of Calvin Cutter's *Anatomy and Physiology*, a book that had possibly belonged to Clemens, was part of the Mark Twain Library collection in Redding, Connecticut. It reportedly had the inscription "Lydia" in it. However, by the time I inventoried the holdings of the Mark Twain Library in 1970, there was no sign of this volume except for that brief and cryptic notecard on which someone had written its title, inscription, and the notation "(?MT Library)". Although I could not find this book in 1970, I finally located it during a return visit to Redding in June 1982. It does not have the customary Mark Twain Library accession number and the inscription "Lydia" gives one pause, as does the early date of publication. Numerous other books lacking accession numbers and formerly owned by early-day Redding Ridge residents Lydia and Betsey Hill were donated to the Mark Twain Library, and Cutter's *Anatomy and Physiology* was almost certainly among these Hill family contributions. I do not believe that this volume belonged to the Clemens family library.

Under variant titles Cutter's book was published repeatedly in the 1870s following its first edition in 1845, which had been followed by editions throughout the 1840s and 1850s such as *First Book of Anatomy, Physiology, and Hygiene. For Grammar Schools and Families* (Philadelphia: J. B. Lippincott & Co. 1854). Cutter's seems to be the most likely candidate for the volume that Becky Thatcher accidentally tore in Chapter 20 of *The Adventures of Tom Sawyer* (1876), an act for which the angry schoolmaster gave Tom "the most merciless flaying that even Mr. Dobbins had ever administered." The University of California Press edition of *The Adventures of Tom Sawyer* (ed. John C. Gerber, Paul Baender, and Terry Firkins, 1980) stated that Clemens owned an 1850 edition of Cutter's *A Treatise on Anatomy, Physiology, & Hygiene* published in Boston by Benjamin B. Mussey and Co. (*The Adventures of Tom Sawyer, Tom Sawyer Abroad, Tom Sawyer, Detective*, p. 487), though the editors do not cite a source for this information. It would seem logical that Twain might have consulted Cutter's *New Analytic Anatomy, Physiology and Hygiene, Human and Comparative* (Philadelphia: J. B. Lippincott, 1874), but no evidence of that fact has turned up. Beverly Lyon Clark's Norton Critical Edition of Twain's novel (W. W. Norton, 2007, p. 208) reprinted the frontispiece diagram of the human body from Cutter's 1855 edition; in the picture Cutter chastely omitted all sexual organs.

Cyclopædia of American Literature, Embracing Personal and Critical Notices of Authors, and Selections from Their Writings, From the Earliest Period to the Present Day. Ed. by Evert A[ugustus]. Duyckinck (1816–1878) and George L[ong]. Duyckinck (1823–1863). Additions by Michael Laird Simons (1843–1880). 2 vols. Philadelphia: T. E. Zell, 1875.

[Edition conjectured.]

Clemens wrote to Michael Laird Simons on 27 and 28 January 1873 with information and suggestions about his forthcoming biographical entry in this work (*MTLet* 5: 283–287).

Horst H. Kruse, "A Matter of Style: How Olivia Langdon Clemens and Charles Dudley Warner Tried to Team and to Tame the Genius of Mark Twain," *New England Quarterly* 72.2 (June 1999): 232–250.

▌ D

DAGLESS, THOMAS. *The Light in Dends Wood, and Other Stories.* London: Greening & Co., 1903. 116 pp.

Source: MTLAcc, entry #112, volume donated by Clemens. Inasmuch as this copy is missing, there can never be any certainty that Clemens decided it qualified for his cherished "Library of Literary Hogwash" (see the relevant chapter in Volume One of this present work). JoDee Benussi (Benussi to Alan Gribben, 28 February 2007) noticed that a work written by Thomas Dagless was selected by a wag named Harry J. Graham for inclusion in his privately printed *The Fifty Worst Books* (1907?) where it was compared to the pathetic *Irene Iddesleigh*, a novel by Margaret Ann Ross ("Emanda M'Kittrick Ros") that would draw Clemens's ridicule in 1906. One rare book dealer described Dagless's four tales in *The Light in Dends Wood, and Other Stories* as "bizarre," "sensationalist," "exotic," "weird," and possessing "a ridiculously high body count but almost nothing in the way of narrative" (J and M Books, Limited, Towcester, United Kingdom, 2017). One can only speculate about the hilarious marginalia Clemens perhaps wrote in his now-vanished copy.

DAHLGREN, MADELEINE VINTON (1825–1898). *Chim: His Washington Winter.* New York: C. L. Webster & Co., 1892. 344 pp.

These adventures of a terrier dog named Chim were brought out by Clemens's publishing firm, which he often supervised.

———. *Memoir of John A[dolphus]. Dahlgren [1809–1870], Rear-Admiral United States Navy, by His Widow.* New York: Charles L. Webster & Co., 1891. 660 pp.

Dahlgren's biography was issued by Clemens's publishing firm, which Clemens often supervised. It had been published earlier (in 1882) by James R. Osgood and Company. Among other feats in his career, Dahlgren, in his capacity as a Navy ordnance officer, had invented a new, more effective type of cannon to mount in ships.

DAILEY. *War Pictures.* [Unidentified book.]

Catalog: ListABP (1910), "War Pictures, Dailey", no other information provided.

DALLAS, JACOB A. (1825–1857). "Up the Mississippi," *Emerson's Magazine and Putnam's Monthly* 40.5 (October 1857): 433–456.

W. Rowlands of James R. Osgood & Company responded on 22 July 1882 to an undated request from Mark Twain for books relating to the Mississippi River. Rowlands informed him that they were sending "a number of 'Emerson's Magazine,' with 'Up the Miss.' by J. A. Dallas in it" (MTP). Twain was doing research for his projected *Life on the Mississippi* (1883). Painter, panoramist, and illustrator Jacob A. Dallas had visited New Orleans in 1852 and illustrated this article about steamboat travel with more than two dozen evocative drawings of scenery, architecture, steamboats, crew members, and enslaved people. He made so many critical comments about the whisky-drinking, tobacco-smoking inhabitants of the river wharves that this should be considered one of Twain's major inspirations for portions of his travel narrative. The title of the article would seem to promise many sights upriver, but the majority of Dallas's article describes the exotic character of New Orleans and the agricultural processes of the surrounding sugar plantations. The final paragraph concludes, "In a future number we shall probably resume the subject, . . . giving picturesque views of the Upper Mississippi"; however, in this same magazine issue the editor announced the untimely death of Dallas at the age of thirty-two from dysentery in New York City.

DALTON, JAMES (1785–1862). *The Gentleman in Black, and Tales of Other Days.* Illustrated by George Cruikshank (1792–1878) and others. Red cloth cover. London: C. Daly, 1845. 392 pp.

Inscriptions: the front free endpaper was amateurishly autographed in ink, "S. L. Clemens/(Mark Twain)". The pen name is underscored with a flourish. Above that is the signature in ink of "Mr. C. Reeve". A bookplate affixed to the front pastedown endpaper reads, "Mr. Charles Reeve./ London & Westminster". The large signature of "Cyril Clemens" is written in ink above this bookplate. A book dealer made a note on the rear pastedown endpaper in an attempt to add authentication: "[$]25.00/1st Edition/ MARK TWAIN'S COPY".

Provenance: photocopies of the endpapers, flyleaves, and title page, sent to Alan Gribben in September 1980 by Thomas A. Tenney (1931–2012), who was examining the collection of Cyril Clemens (1902–1999) in Kirkwood, Missouri.

Location: Harry Ransom Center, University of Texas at Austin. Acquired from Cyril Clemens along with six other books on 28 March 1986, for payments of $5,000 to Cyril Clemens and $5,000 to his *Mark Twain Journal*. Thomas A. Tenney, Cyril Clemens, and Alan Gribben (then an English professor at the University of Texas at Austin) negotiated this agreement in an exchange of letters written between 20 August 1985 and 27 April 1986. *The Gentleman in Black* had already been identified as a spurious association copy and was obtained by the Harry Ransom Center merely as a literary curiosity.

Copy examined: photocopies of the endpapers, flyleaves, and title page provided by Thomas A. Tenney in 1980. The signature is assuredly a forgery. This clumsily copied Mark Twain "autograph" resembles others perpetrated by Eugene Field II. Confirmed by examination of the volume in Austin in 1986.

The Gentleman in Black was first published anonymously in London in 1831. Although the book is usually attributed to the British author James Dalton, who wrote occult fiction, it has occasionally been ascribed to John Yonge Akerman (1806–1873), who produced a work titled *Tales of Other Days* and who sometimes wrote under the pseudonym "Paul Pindar." The plot of "The Gentleman in Black" is a wry variant of the man-sells-his-soul-to-the-devil story. In a labored conclusion to this tale, Comte Louis Desonges retains the legal services of a wily attorney named Bagsby, who cleverly extricates him from the terms of the infernal contract. "'Fool that I was!' exclaimed the gentleman in black, rising and stamping violently on the floor, 'to think of signing any paper without bringing my own lawyer'" (p. 114). The volume also contains twenty-five shorter stories. Several of these purport to be German legends—including "The Castle of Stauffenburg, A Legend of the Rhine" and "Waldeck, A Tale from the German"—that resemble in mood and effect those Twain relates with relish in *A Tramp Abroad* (1880). Twain might well have enjoyed *The Gentleman in Black, and Tales of Other Days* if he ever read it, but this was not the copy he owned.

DALY, AUGUSTIN (1838–1899). *Divorce* (play, performed in 1871).

Grace King remembered seeing this play with the Clemenses at Daly's Fifth Avenue Theatre, probably in 1887 when she visited Hartford and took a side-trip to New York City to meet William Dean Howells. Ada Rehan and Mrs. John Drew had the leading female roles in *Divorce*; Daly provided the Clemenses and King with a proscenium box (King, *Memoirs*, p. 87). Joseph Francis Daly's *The Life of Augustin Daly* (New York: Macmillan Co., 1917) included a few letters from Mark Twain to Daly, as well as several references to Twain's endeavors as a playwright. John Drew's *My Years on the Stage* (New York: E. P. Dutton and Company, 1922) described Clemens's keen interest in Daly's Theatre during the 1880s, unfortunately without providing much specific information about the plays he attended or praised. But it confirms Clemens's infatuation with the dramatic arts.

——————— (adapt.). *The Lottery of Love* (play, performed in 1888). [An adaptation of *Les surprises du divorce* by Alexandre Charles Auguste Bisson (1848–1912) and Antony Mars (1862–1915).]

In the autumn of 1888 Clemens promised to take his family to see the one-act curtain-raiser that preceded this adaptation by Daly, Justin Huntly McCarthy's *The Wife of Socrates* (SLC to Daly, undated ALS, Houghton Library, Harvard University).

DALY, THOMAS AUGUSTINE (1871–1948). *Canzoni*. Illustrated by John [French] Sloan (1871–1951). Philadelphia: Catholic Standard and Times Publishing Co., 1906. 172 pp.

Inscription: on the front free endpaper in black ink: "To/Samuel L. Clemens,/Master Craftsman,/with the admiring regards/of his/humble servant,/T. A. Daly/Oct. 13/'06".

Location: Mark Twain Library, Redding, Connecticut. Donated from Clemens's library by Clara Clemens Gabrilowitsch in 1910 (MTLAcc, entry #2023).

Copy examined: Clemens's unmarked copy of a collection of brief poems, often in Italian dialect. It has the red ink Mark Twain Library accession number "2023".

DALZIEL, GEORGE (1815–1902). *The Little Flower Girl, and Other Stories in Verse, by "Robin."* London: W. S. Sonnenscheim, 1884. 111 pp.

Source: MTLAcc, entry #626, volume donated by Clemens. Far better known as a master engraver in London, Dalziel also wrote a number of books of various types.

DANA, CHARLES ANDERSON (1819–1897), comp. *The Household Book of Poetry. Collected and Edited by Charles A.*

Dana. Eleventh edition. Revised and enlarged. New York: D. Appleton and Co., 1869. 816 pp.

Inscription: on a flyleaf: "Merry Christmas to Livie L. Langdon from her Brother Dec. 25th 1868".

Catalog: *C1951*, O27; *Zeitlin 1951*, #13, $6.50.

Location: Mark Twain Papers, Bancroft Library, University of California at Berkeley.

Copy examined: Olivia Clemens's copy.

DANA, JAMES DWIGHT (1813–1895). *Manual of Mineralogy, including Observations on Mines.* New ed., rev. and enl. Philadelphia: T. Bliss & Co., 1864. 456 pp.

Source: MTLAcc, entry #816, volume donated by Clemens.

DANA, RICHARD HENRY (1815–1882). *To Cuba and Back. A Vacation Voyage.* Boston: James R. Osgood & Company, 1875. 288 pp.

Inscription: signed in pencil on a flyleaf: "Saml L. Clemens/Hartford 1876".

Provenance: collection of Frank C. Willson (1889–1960), Melrose, Massachusetts.

Location: Harry Ransom Center, University of Texas at Austin. Purchased in 1962 from Mrs. Margarete Willson.

Copy examined: Clemens's copy, unmarked. Page 170 is folded down.

———. *Two Years Before the Mast: A Personal Narrative. New Edition, with Subsequent Matter by the Author.* Original green cloth replaced; bound in early-twentieth-century polished blue calf, raised bands, gilt. Boston: James R. Osgood, 1876. [A reprint of the 1869 revised edition with an added chapter, "Twenty-Four Years After."]

Inscription: the front flyleaf is signed vertically in pencil, S. L. Clemens/Hartford, 1876."

Marginalia: a number of passages were marked with pencil and ink. In the first line of page 262 Clemens wrote the word "Consul" in brown ink above the line to correct broken type. In the same ink he made two marginal marks on page 327 (at lines 20 and 23), and he made one or more pencil lines in the margins of pages 250, 252 (3), 254, 255, 256, 258 (3), 260 (2), and 328. At pages 116 and 285 there is an erasure in the margin. Marginal pencil lines on page 7 and 55 have also been erased. Additional markings may have been lost in the rebinding process (probably performed between 1911 and 1915), when the text was washed, resewn, and slightly trimmed. All but two of the surviving pencil lines in the margins are therefore very faint, and it is possible that some pencil markings were eradicated altogether. Despite this rebinding, the paper gives evidence that the book was heavily worn and much-used by Clemens; some page gatherings are loose or out of alignment, the text is soiled in places, and the sewing is loose. Under UV light inspection it becomes apparent that the upper corners of the following pages were deliberately folded down: 15, 17, 45, 53, 122, 174, 175, 252, 253, 255, 258, 325, and 327.

Catalogs: *A1911*, "12mo, original cloth, Bost. 1876," quotes the signature and mentions "passages marked," lot 116, sold for $6; *Sotheby's 2003*, #221 (sold with four other literature titles), $9,500; offered on eBay in February-March 2010.

Provenance: formerly in the collection of Nick Karanovich of Fort Wayne, Indiana.

Location: collection of Kevin Mac Donnell, Austin, Texas.

Acquired in March 2010 for $3,900.

Copy examined: Clemens's copy. Viewed at the 2003 Sotheby's sale. Has the *A1911* auction label remounted on a front flyleaf. Kevin Mac Donnell reported details about the book in a letter to Alan Gribben, 2 April 2010, noting that it was "heavily worn and well-read."

Albert Bigelow Paine remarked that Dana's *Two Years before the Mast* (first published in 1840) was one of the "reliable favorites" enjoyed by Clemens and Theodore Crane on the lawn of Quarry Farm during the summer of 1874 (*MTB*, p. 511). Mrs. James T. Fields recorded in her diary that on 27 April 1876 Clemens, her host in Hartford, had awakened early and "had been re-reading Dana's *Two Years before the Mast* in bed and revolving subjects for his Autobiography," an interesting linking ("Bret Harte and Mark Twain in the 'Seventies': Passages from the Diaries of Mrs. James T. Fields," *Atlantic Monthly* 130.3 [September 1922]: 346). In April 1878 Clemens expressed his preference for the narratives of Dana or Franchère, which show "that a common sailor's life is often a hell," over the "lying story-books which make boys fall in love with the sea" (NB 14, *N&J* 2: 69). Paine emphasized that *Two Years* was a book "he loved, and never tired of," during his adult lifetime (*MTB*, p. 1540); this assertion is borne out by Mark Twain's quoting from the work in Part 7 of *Is Shakespeare Dead?* (1909) to show that "Richard H. Dana served two years before the mast, and had every experience that falls to the lot of the sailor. . . . His sailor-talk flows from his pen with the sure touch and the ease and confidence of a person who has *lived* what he is talking about, not gathered it from books and random listenings."

A brief vignette that Dana relates in Chapter 35 of the 1869 edition (an incident omitted from most subsequent editions) became Clemens's favorite passage in the book and served him as a reliable literary source on several occasions. In Dana's version, the narrator, on board the *Alert*, recounts at second-hand how "a man named Sam, on board the Pilgrim, used to tell a story of a mean little captain in a mean little brig, in which he sailed from Liverpool to New York." This captain "insisted on speaking a great, homeward-bound Indiaman, with her studding-sails out on both sides, sunburnt men in wide-brimmed hats on her decks, and a monkey and paroquet in her rigging. . . . There was no need of his stopping her to speak her, but his vanity led him to do it and then his meanness made him so awestruck that he seemed to quail. He called out, in a small, lisping voice, 'What ship is that, pray?' A deep-toned voice roared through the trumpet, 'The Bashaw, from Canton, bound to Boston. Hundred and ten days out! Where are you from?' '*Only* from Liverpool, *sir*,' he lisped, in the most apologetic and subservient voice" (pp. 413–414). Dana very nearly spoils the story by explaining it: "But the humor will be felt by those only who know the ritual of hailing at sea. No one says 'sir,' and the 'only' was wonderfully expressive."

Mark Twain's repetitious notebook entries reveal that he was practicing its delivery for many years. In March 1888 he copied into Notebook 27 the key lines he would later use to great effect: "The Bashaw of Bengal [Dana's *Bashaw* from Canton lacked this alliteration], 260 days out [Dana's ship was only 110 days away from port] from Calcutta [another addition by Twain],—homeward bound!—the Mary Ann, 3 days out from Boston—only goin to Liverpool" (*N&J* 3: 378). Two years later Twain entered another variation of the same elements in Notebook 30: "'The <Bashaw> Begum of Bengal 116 days out from <Hong *Kong*> Canton, homeward *bound*. What vessel's that?'" (*N&J* 3: 580). Again in 1904 Twain jotted down a mental rehearsal of the sketch: "'The Begum of Bengal!'" (NB 46, TS p. 34). Finally on 10 July 1907 Twain introduced the story into his address at the Town Hall banquet in Liverpool, the occasion of what Hamlin Hill called "the most poignant speech of his entire career" (*MTGF*, p. 175). In this ultimate recital of the borrowed anecdote, Twain credited Dana's book but altered the details: "Came the answer back through a speaking trumpet, 'The *Begum of Bengal*, a hundred and twenty-three days out from Canton—homeward bound! What ship is that?' The little captain's vanity was all crushed out of him, and most humbly he squeaked back: 'Only the *Mary Ann*, fourteen hours out from Boston, bound for Kittery Point with—with nothing to speak of!'" (*MTSpk*, p. 582). Twain recounted this moment, with slightly altered phrasing, in an Autobiographical Dictation of 2 October 1907 (*AutoMT* 3: 149–150). Shortly thereafter Twain retold the story as the climax to his final Lotos Club speech on 11 January 1908, crediting the *Begum* with 148 days out from Canton and saying it was an incident he gathered "many, many years ago . . . from Mr. Dana's *Two Years Before the Mast*" (*MTSpk*, p. 609).

Mark Twain Speaking, ed. Paul Fatout (1976), pp. 577–583; David E. E. Sloane, "Some Twain Sources and How They Affected His Sense of Self," *American Literary Realism* 45.1 (Fall 2012): 49–59. Sloane's "Additional Information and a Correction," *American Literary Realism* 45.3 (Spring 2013): 283, citing Barbara Schmidt's research on Dana's *Bashaw* from Canton anecdote, explained that this story "was taken out" of various editions. See also the Catalog entry for S. A. Hammett, *The Wonderful Adventures of Captain Priest*.

DANTE ALIGHIERI (1265–1321). *The Divine Comedy of Dante Alighieri*. Translated from the Italian by Henry Wadsworth Longfellow (1807–1882). Authorized Edition. 3 vols. Leipzig: Bernhard Tauchnitz, 1867.

Source: MTLAcc, entries #2043–2045, volumes donated from Clemens's library by Clara Clemens Gabrilowitsch in 1910.

Chapter 24 of *The Innocents Abroad* (1869) refers to visiting Dante's grave in Florence. Dante was one of the "names familiar to every school-boy in the Christian world," Clemens noted in 1878 (NB 17, *N&J* 2: 227). Chapter 27 of *Life on the Mississippi* (1883) quotes Frances Trollope's depiction of the desolate-looking mouth of the Mississippi River: "Had Dante seen it, he might have drawn images of another Bolgia [as depicted in *Inferno*, the first part of *The Divine Comedy*] from its horrors." In May 1892 Clemens alluded to "Dante's Francesca di Rimina [*sic*] & that romantic tragedy" (NB 32 [May 1892], TS p. 8), and also mentioned it twice in a letter to Susan Crane from Florence on 30 September 1892 (*MTL*, pp. 570–571). (Dante consigned to the Circle of the Lustful in Hell a contemporary of his, Francesca di Rimini, who, finding herself trapped in an unhappy marriage, fell in love with her brother-in-law. She was murdered by her jealous husband.) In June 1893 Clemens passed the "window in Monastery where Dante wrote part of the Divine Comedy" (NB 33, TS p. 18). Dante is mentioned in the preface to *Pudd'nhead Wilson* (1894), "A Whisper to the Reader." Dante's name also occurs in Twain's "Instructions in Art" (1903) and the narrator mentions him rather reverently in Chapter XVI of "Three Thousand Years Among the Microbes" (written in 1905, *WWD?*, p. 529).

———. *The Divine Comedy of Dante Alighieri.* Translated from the Italian by Charles Eliot Norton (1827–1908). 3 vols. Boston: Houghton, Mifflin and Co., 1891–1892.

Catalog: Ball 2016 inventory, Volumes 1 and 3 only, green cloth, gilt lettering and top edges, good condition.

Location: Quarry Farm library shelves, under the supervision of the Mark Twain Archive, Elmira College, Elmira, New York.

This work was available to Clemens during his later visits to Quarry Farm in Elmira.

———. *The Divine Comedy of Dante Alighieri.* Translated from the Italian by Henry Wadsworth Longfellow (1807–1882). 3 vols. Boston: Houghton, Mifflin and Co., 1895.

Source: MTLAcc, entries #1768 and #1769, Volumes 2 (*Purgatorio*) and 3 (*Paradiso*) only, donated by Clemens.

———. *The Vision; or, Hell, Purgatory and Paradise of Dante Alighieri.* Translated from the Italian by Henry Francis Cary (1772–1844). With biography, notes and index. Illustrated by John Flaxman (1755–1826). New York: D. Appleton & Co., 1864. 587 pp.

Source: MTLAcc, entry #2022, volume donated from Clemens's library by Clara Clemens Gabrilowitsch in 1910. W. R. Moses, "The Pattern of Evil in *Adventures of Huckleberry Finn*," *Georgia Review* 13.2 (1959): 161–166; Thomas Werge, "The Sin of Hypocrisy in "The Man That Corrupted Hadleyburg" and *Inferno XXIII*," *Mark Twain Journal* 18.1 (Winter 1975–1976): 17–18; W. Gerald Marshall, "Twain's 'A Curious Dream' and *The Inferno*," *Mark Twain Journal* 21.3 (Spring 1983): 41–43; Lawrence I. Berkove, "The Reality of the Dream: Structural and Thematic Unity in *A Connecticut Yankee*," *Mark Twain Journal* 22.1 (Spring 1984): 11.

DARBY, SARAH. *That Affair in Philadelphia.* New York: Broadway Publishing Co., 1909. 75 pp.

Source: MTLAcc, entry #2209, volume donated from Clemens's library by Clara Clemens Gabrilowitsch in 1910.

DARLEY, FELIX OCTAVIUS CARR (1822–1888). *Compositions in Outline by Felix O. C. Darley, from Hawthorne's Scarlet Letter* [novel, published in 1850]. 12 plates. Boston: Houghton, Mifflin & Co., [cop. 1879]. [Publisher conjectured.]

Catalogs: *A1911*, "oblong folio, wrappers, Bost., n.d.," with "two lines of original manuscript by Mr. Clemens (notes) as follows: 'How I did not get my bill through,' and 'Biography of Garrett Davis,'" lot 118, sold for $2.25; George D. Smith, New York City, "Catalogue of Books" (1911), notes by Clemens laid in (one refers to "Biography of Garrett Davies [*sic*]"), item #91, $7.50. [See the Catalog entry for Garrett Davis.]

———. *Compositions in Outline by Felix O. C. Darley, from [Sylvester] Judd's Margaret* [novel, published in 1845]. Engraved

by Konrad Huber. Large folio, red leather cover loose and in poor condition. Spine broken and missing. New York: Middleton, [cop. 1856]. Only 8 unnumbered pages remain.

Catalogs: *A1911*, "oblong folio, morocco (rubbed), Middleton, N.Y. [1856]," lot 117, sold for $2.50; Ball 2016 inventory, oversize volume, cover in poor condition.

Provenance: discovered by Herbert A. Wisbey in 1985 in the Quarry Farm library in Elmira, New York. Oddly, it bears the *A1911* sale label. There are no markings in the volume (Wisbey, then director of the Center for Mark Twain Studies at Elmira College, to Alan Gribben, 5 March 1985). Gretchen Sharlow transferred the book to the Mark Twain Archive in 1988.

Location: Mark Twain Archive, Gannett-Tripp Learning Center, Elmira College, Elmira, New York.

Copy examined: an unmarked copy from Clemens's personal library, inspected in Elmira on 11 August 1988. The volume contains an *A1911* label on the front pastedown endpaper. All of the sheets have been removed between "The Master" and "The Widow Wright," presumably to frame and hang or else paste in scrapbooks.

Clemens notified Dr. John Brown on 28 February 1874 that he had shipped him a copy of this American illustrator's book of drawings inspired by *Margaret. A Tale of the Real and the Ideal, Blight and Bloom.* "We in America think a deal of Darley's work," Clemens wrote (*MTL*, p. 215; *MTLet* 6: 53). Brown replied that it "is the best bit of American art I have seen—it is constantly out & greatly admired" (*MTL* 6: 57). See also the Catalog entry for Sylvester Judd.

———. *The People of America.* Franklin Pictorial Library Series. Illus. New York: Philip J. Cozans, 1857. 128 pp.

Inscription: inscribed on the recto of the frontispiece, "Jennie Clemens".

Location: Mark Twain Library, Redding, Connecticut. Donated by Clemens (MTLAcc, entry #526).

Copy examined: unmarked copy belonging to Clemens's niece, Orion Clemens's daughter, who died in 1864. Spine and binding are loose; leaves may be missing. Examined in 1970 and again in June 1982.

———. *The Poets of the West: A Selection of Favourite American Poems with Memoirs of Their Authors.* Illustrated by F. O. C. Darley, J[ohn]. H[enry]. Hill (1839–1922), [Myles] Birket Foster (1825–1899), and others. 8vo. Brown gold-tooled morocco, custom slipcase. London: Sampson Low, Son & Co., 1859. 127 pp.

Inscriptions: the front flyleaf is signed, "S. L. Clemens/ (Mark Twain)" and "Eugene Field,/Chicago, Sept. 14, 1895". [This was a highly uncharacteristic signature form for Clemens in books.]

Catalog: Jeffrey H. Marks, Rare Books, Rochester, New York (2014), explicitly described by the bookseller as yet another forgery by Eugene Field II, priced at $750.

DARROW, ALLEN R. (1826–1906). *Iphigenia: A Legend of the Iliad, and Other Poems.* Buffalo, NY: C. L. Sherrill Co., 1888. 98 pp. Paperbound, ribbon-tied.

Source: MTLAcc, entry #2009, volume donated from Clemens's library by Clara Clemens Gabrilowitsch in 1910.

Darrow was born in Connecticut, served in the Union Army, and worked as an agent for the Star Oil Company in Buffalo, New York city, where he belonged to the Prospect

Avenue Baptist Church. He would publish another book of poems in 1897, *Poems of the Gospel*, which a New York religious weekly newspaper, *The Outlook* (57.13 [27 November 1897], p. 773), dismissed as "commonplace descriptions of Scriptural incidents, far more poetical as well as real in the original prose."

DARWIN, CHARLES ROBERT (1809–1882). *The Descent of Man, and Selection in Relation to Sex.* 2 vols. New York: D. Appleton and Co., 1871. [Only Clemens's copy of Volume 1 has been located.]

Inscription: the front flyleaf is missing in Volume 1.

Marginalia: plentiful annotation in Volume 1, of which samples are quoted by Sherwood Cummings in "Mark Twain's Acceptance of Science" (1962).

Provenance: "ListABP" (1910), "Descent of Man v 1", no other information provided.

Location: Volume 1 only in Mark Twain Papers, Bancroft Library, University of California at Berkeley.

Copy examined: Clemens's copy of Volume 1.

On 2 July 1871 Clemens wrote to Jim [James N.] Gillis from Elmira ("would you like to read Darwin?"), offering to buy any of Darwin's books and forward them to Gillis (*MTLet* 4: 428). Albert Bigelow Paine reported that *The Descent of Man* belonged to Clemens's "earlier reading, . . . a book whose influence was always present, though I believe he did not read it any more in later years" (*MTB*, p. 1540). Chapter 19 of *Roughing It* (1872) alludes to "Darwinians" in denouncing the Goshoot tribe of American Indians. Clemens "talked with the great Darwin" at Grasmere in the English Lake District in August 1879 (NB 18, *N&J* 2: 339). He referred jokingly to Darwin's concept of "rudimentary" forms in Notebook 18 (1879, *N&J* 2: 349) and in Chapter 35 of *A Tramp Abroad* (1880). "Mr. Darwin was grieved to feel obliged to give up his theory that the monkey was the connecting link between man and the lower animals" ("Some Thoughts on the Science of Onanism," written in 1879, DV200, no. 3, MTP; *MTSpk*, p. 126). "Mr. Darwin's *Descent of Man* had been in print five or six years, and the storm of indignation raised by it was still raging in pulpits and periodicals," recalled Mark Twain in "A Monument to Adam" (1905), describing an aborted, half-serious proposal he had ventured in 1879. Clemens's invectives against Whitelaw Reid recorded in Notebook 20 (1882) included the allegation that Reid was "<the Remote Darwinian> The Missing link" (*N&J* 2: 442). In a passage eventually deleted at James R. Osgood's suggestion from Chapter 24 of *Life on the Mississippi* (1883), the yarn-spinning Rob Styles joked about "a nervous, sedentary, student-sort of a man, trying to cipher out the Development business, and Survival of the Fittest, and one thing or another" (quoted by Everett Emerson, *Mark Twain: A Literary Life* [Philadelphia: University of Pennsylvania Press, 2000], p. 136).

Much later, probably in 1897, Twain wrote, "It obliges me to renounce my allegiance to the Darwinian theory of the Ascent [*sic*] of Man from the Lower Animals" ("The Lowest Animal," *LE*, p. 223). Clemens referred to "the Missing Link" in a letter of 20 November 1905 that excoriated a patent medicine salesman (http://www.lettersofnote.com/2010/01/youre-idiot-of-33rd-degree.html?m=3D1).

On 25 June 1907 Mark Twain related at the Society of the Pilgrims Luncheon held in his honor in London the report of "Professor [Charles Eliot] Norton, of Harvard" that Darwin had instructed his chambermaid never to touch certain volumes by his bedside, since "with those books I read myself to sleep every night." These included works by Twain (Fatout, *MTSpk*, p. 559; Sir Harry Brittain, "My Friend Mark Twain," *Mark Twain Journal* 11.3 [Fall 1961]: 2. Twain quoted this speech in an Autobiographical Dictation of 25 July 1907 (*AutoMT* 3: 79).

Waggoner, "Science in the Thought of Mark Twain" (1937), pp. 365–366; Cummings, "Mark Twain's Social Darwinism," *Huntington Library Quarterly* 20 (1957): 163–175; Cummings, "Mark Twain's Acceptance of Science," *Centennial Review* 6 (1962): 245–261; Cummings, "*What Is Man?*: The Scientific Sources," in *Essays on Determinism in American Literature*, ed. Sydney J. Krause (Kent: Kent State University Press, 1964), pp. 108–116; Philip Williams, "Mark Twain and Social Darwinism," *Essays and Studies in English Language and Literature* 49–50 (1966): 143–172; Baetzhold, *MT&JB* (1970), pp. 56–59; *What Is Man? and Other Philosophical Writings*, ed. Paul Baender (Berkeley: University of California Press, 1973), pp. 61, 83, 542; James D. Wilson, "'The Monumental Sarcasm of the Ages': Science and Pseudoscience in the Thought of Mark Twain," *South Atlantic Bulletin* 40 (May 1975): 72–82; Stan Poole, "In Search of the Missing Link: Mark Twain and Darwinism," *Studies in American Fiction* 13.2 (Autumn 1985): 201–215; Sherwood Cummings, *Mark Twain and Science: Adventures of a Mind* (Baton Rouge: Louisiana State University, 1988), pp. 7, 33–34, *passim*. Aaron Derosa considered some Dawinian implications in Twain's literature, especially *Adventures of Huckleberry Finn*, in "Europe, Darwin, and the Escape from *Huckleberry Finn*," *American Literary Realism* 44.2 (Winter 2013): 157–173. See also Gregg Camfield, "The Art of Judicious Lying," *Mark Twain Annual* 16 (2018): 112–113.

——. *The Descent of Man, and Selection in Relation to Sex.* New edition, revised. New York: D. Appleton and Co., 1887. 688 pp. [Part of Clemens's 12-volume set of Darwin's writings.]

Catalog: "Mark Twain Collection," *The Bookman*, No. 25 (1970), #329.

Location: Wake Forest University, Winston-Salem, North Carolina. Donated by Nancy Susan Reynolds.

Copy examined: Clemens's unmarked copy, in 1970.

——. *The Different Forms of Flowers on Plants of the Same Species.* Illus. New York: D. Appleton and Co., 1884. [Part of Clemens's 12-volume set of Darwin's writings.]

Catalog: "Mark Twain Collection," *The Bookman*, No. 25 (1970), #329.

Location: Wake Forest University, Winston-Salem, North Carolina. Donated by Nancy Susan Reynolds.

Copy examined: Clemens's unmarked copy, in 1970.

——. *The Effects of Cross and Self-Fertilisation in the Vegetable Kingdom.* New York: D. Appleton and Co., 1883. [Part of Clemens's 12-volume set of Darwin's writings.]

Catalog: "Mark Twain Collection," *The Bookman*, No. 25 (1970), #329.

Location: Wake Forest University, Winston-Salem, North

Carolina. Donated by Nancy Susan Reynolds.

Copy examined: Clemens's unmarked copy, in 1970.

———. *The Expression of the Emotions in Man and Animals.* New York: D. Appleton and Co., 1886. [Part of Clemens's 12-volume set of Darwin's writings.]

Inscription: signed on the second flyleaf in black ink: "SL. Clemens/Hartford, 1887."

Marginalia: numerous pencil marks by Clemens on page 31 (the powerful force of habit—caterpillars will die rather than eat the leaves of an unfamiliar tree), pp. 36, 38 (reflex actions), pp. 76–77 (joy and terror indicated in animals), p. 87 (an ape known to sing), 91 (dog barking), 94 (bird courtship sounds), 135, 138–139, 145, 167, and others.

Catalog: "Mark Twain Collection," *The Bookman,* No. 25 (1970), #329.

Location: Wake Forest University, Winston-Salem, North Carolina. Donated by Nancy Susan Reynolds.

Copy examined: Clemens's copy, in 1970.

Clemens noted in February or March 1891 that he wished to "examine Darwin again" to see what he stated about the correlation of a lunatic's hair condition and his prognosis; Clemens thought that Darwin found that dry, harsh hair means "not curable" (NB 30, *N&J* 3: 606). In Chapter 12 of *The Expression of the Emotions in Man and Animals* Darwin does claim that correlations exist between hair condition and mental states, and he specifically alludes to the "dryness and harshness" of hair that accompanies insanity. One mental institution, Darwin reports, has noticed that its patients show marked improvement "whenever their hair ceases to be rough and unmanageable" (p. 296).

In Notebook 30 Clemens also wrote in connection with Darwin's research: "Monkeys emit a low chuckling laugh when you tickle them under the armpits" (*N&J* 3: 607). In Chapter 5 of *Expression of the Emotions* Darwin notes, regarding expressions of pleasure by monkeys: "If a young chimpanzee be tickled—and the armpits are particularly sensitive to tickling, as in the case of our children,—a more decided chuckling or laughing sound is uttered" (p. 131). Clemens memorized the fact, for in Paris during April or May 1895, devising his attacks on man's supposed superiority among living creatures, he noted: "Man has been called the laughing animal to distinguish him from the others—but the monkey laughs" (NB 34, TS p. 9). Later he observed that monkeys, like man, are capable of laughter, "as Mr. Darwin pointed out" ("The Lowest Animal," written about 1897, *LE*, p. 225). Mark Twain also probably owes to Darwin the inspiration for one of his most celebrated maxims—"Man is the Only Animal that Blushes. Or needs to" (Chapter 27, *FE* [1897]). Chapter 13 of Darwin's *Expression of the Emotions* begins: "Blushing is the most peculiar and the most human of all expressions. Monkeys redden from passion, but it would require an overwhelming amount of evidence to make us believe that any animal could blush" (p. 309).

———. *The Formation of Vegetable Mould, Through the Action of Worms, with Observations on Their Habits.* Illus. New York: D. Appleton and Co., 1885. [Part of Clemens's 12-volume set of Darwin's writings.]

Marginalia: no annotation except for a brown ink mark at the top of page 17 (concerning the structure of worms).

Catalog: "Mark Twain Collection," *The Bookman,* No. 25 (1970), #329.

Location: Wake Forest University, Winston-Salem, North Carolina. Gift of Nancy Susan Reynolds.

Copy examined: Clemens's copy, in 1970.

———. *Insectivorous Plants.* New York: D. Appleton and Co., 1886. [Part of Clemens's 12- volume set of Darwin's writings.]

Catalog: "Mark Twain Collection," *The Bookman,* No. 25 (1970), #329.

Location: Wake Forest University, Winston-Salem, North Carolina. Gift of Nancy Susan Reynolds.

Copy examined: Clemens's unmarked copy, in 1970.

———. *Journal of Researches into the Natural History and Geology of the Countries Visited During the Voyage of H.M.S. Beagle Round the World.* New ed. New York: D. Appleton and Co., 1887. [Part of Clemens's 12-volume set of Darwin's writings.]

Inscription: signed on the second flyleaf in black ink: "S L. Clemens/Hartford, 1887."

Catalog: "Mark Twain Collection," *The Bookman,* No. 25 (1970), #329.

Location: Wake Forest University, Winston-Salem, North Carolina. Given by Nancy Susan Reynolds.

Copy examined: Clemens's copy, in 1970.

WIM? (1973), p. 181.

———. *Journal of Researches into the Natural History and Geology of the Countries Visited During the Voyage of the H.M.S. Beagle Round the World.* Illus. Original cloth. Light wear, hinges cracked but firm, light wear and soiling to extremities. London: T. Nelson and Sons, 1890. 615 pp.

Inscription: the front free flyleaf is signed by Clemens in pencil: "S L Clemens/Hartford, Oct. 28/90."

Marginalia: annotations by Clemens totaling approximately sixty-three words on twenty pages, either commenting on contents in the margins or correcting the text. On page 49, Clemens insultingly compared his departed private secretary and her husband to a fungus: "The Ashcrofts are of this breed." Regarding the Fuegians, Clemens wrote in black ink (in a late hand) on page 261: Surely they *must* believe in a kind & just & compassionate God who loves his dear children & strains himself to make them happy." On page 263 Clemens groused, writing vertically in the margin in black ink, "Can any plausible excuse be furnished for the crime/of creating the human race?" Notes on pages 442–443, written vertically in black ink, compare the "Christian civilization" and the "Pagan civilization." Clemens made long vertical pencil marks on pages 264, 265, 317, 324, and 335. Pages 136–137, 275, 311, 312, and 317 contain Clemens's corrections of grammar written in black ink in the text.

Catalogs: *C1951,* #56c, $25, listed among books signed by Clemens; "Property from the Library of Mark Twain," Butterfield & Butterfield, San Francisco, Sale 6613 (16 July 1997), lot 2671.

Location: Mark Twain House and Museum, Hartford, Connecticut.

Copy examined: Clemens's copy, viewed in 1997 in Hartford.

———. *The Life and Letters of Charles Darwin.* Ed. by Francis Darwin (1848–1925). 2 vols. New York: D. Appleton and

Co., 1888.

Inscriptions: Volumes I and II are both inscribed identically: "Susan L. Crane/Quarry Farm/July 30, 1890" on the front free endpaper (Volume I) and the first flyleaf (Volume II).

Marginalia: pencil marks occur on page 238 of Volume II around a passage relating Darwin's sense of awe when in the rain forests of Brazil. Out of all his travels, he declared, "I felt most sublime in the forests."

Catalog: Ball 2016 inventory, brown cloth, gilt lettering on the spine, black decoration on the front cover, blind decoration on the rear cover.

Location: Mark Twain Archive, Gannett-Tripp Learning Center, Elmira College, Elmira, New York.

Isabel V. Lyon noted in her Daily Reminder on 17 October 1905—while preparing to leave Dublin, New Hampshire—that she "sent back to Library" two volumes of Darwin's letters, presumably borrowed by Clemens (MTP). This important biographical work assembled by Darwin's son was also available to Clemens whenever he visited Quarry Farm in Elmira.

————. *The Movements and Habits of Climbing Plants*. Second edition, revised. Illus. New York: D. Appleton and Co., 1884. [Part of Clemens's 12-volume set of Darwin's writings.]

Catalog: "Mark Twain Collection," *The Bookman*, No. 25 (1970), #329.

Location: Wake Forest University, Winston-Salem, North Carolina. Gift of Nancy Susan Reynolds.

Copy examined: Clemens's unmarked copy, in 1970.

————. *On the Origin of Species by Means of Natural Selection, or the Preservation of Favored Races in the Struggle for Life*. New York: D. Appleton and Co., 1884. [Part of Clemens's 12-volume set of Darwin's writings.]

Marginalia: small ink dot in margin of page 106 at summary of Chapter 5. No other markings.

Catalog: "Mark Twain Collection," *The Bookman*, No. 25 (1970), #329.

Location: Wake Forest University, Winston-Salem, North Carolina. Donated by Nancy Susan Reynolds.

Copy examined: Clemens's copy, 1970.

In September 1872 Clemens visited London, and his account of the trip mentioned Darwin facetiously: "We entered the great Zoological Gardens with Mr. Henry Lee. . . . I wanted to find Mr. Darwin's baboon that plays mother to a cat, but did not succeed. So Darwin invented that. In the House of Monkeys there was one long, lean, active fellow that made me a convert to the theory of Natural Selection. He made a natural selection of monkeys smaller than himself to sling around by the tail" (*The Twainian* 36 [March-April 1977]: 3; *MTLet* 5: 587). "This is what Mr. Darwin might call a 'rudimentary' sign," Mark Twain joked in 1882 ("Concerning the American Language"). Twain's concept of natural law as he articulated it on 6 November 1895 appears to have been influenced by Darwin's *Origin of Species* (1859): "There is nothing kindly, nothing benificent, nothing friendly in Nature toward *any* creature, except by capricious fits & starts; that Nature's attitude toward all life is profoundly vicious, treacherous & malignant" (NB 34, TS p. 31). In Chapter 8 of *Following the Equator* (1897) Twain called the duck-billed platypus "a survival—a survival of the fittest. Mr. Darwin invented the theory that goes by that name,"

attributing this remark to an English naturalist in New Zealand. In Twain's "Three Thousand Years Among the Microbes" (written in 1905) a man-turned-cholera germ observes that "evolution is the law of policies: Darwin said it," but erroneously recalls that "Socrates endorsed it, Cuvier proved it and established it for all time in his paper on 'The Survival of the Fittest,'" another of Twain's late attempts to achieve humor through mangled "histories" (*WWD?*, p. 467).

Sherwood Cummings, "Mark Twain's Social Darwinism" (1957), p. 165; Howard G. Baetzhold, *MT&JB* (1970), p. 56; Harold K. Bush, "'Nature Shrieking' and Parasitic Wasps: Mark Twain, Theodicy, and the War of Nature," *Mark Twain Annual 17* (2019): 112–113.

————, assisted by Francis Darwin (1848–1925). *The Power of Movement in Plants*. Illus. New York: D. Appleton and Co., 1885. [Part of Clemens's 12-volume set of Darwin's writings.]

Catalog: "Mark Twain Collection," *The Bookman*, No. 25 (1970), #329.

Location: Wake Forest University, Winston-Salem, North Carolina. Donated by Nancy Susan Reynolds, in 1970.

Copy examined: Clemens's unmarked copy.

————. *The Variation of Animals and Plants Under Domestication*. Second ed., rev. 2 vols. New York: D. Appleton and Co., 1884. [Part of Clemens's 12-volume set of Darwin's writings.]

Catalog: "Mark Twain Collection," *The Bookman*, No. 25 (1970), #329.

Location: Wake Forest University, Winston-Salem, North Carolina. Gift of Nancy Susan Reynolds.

Copy examined: Clemens's copy, in 1970.

Sherwood Cummings, "Mark Twain's Social Darwinism" (1957), p. 165.

————. *The Various Contrivances by Which Orchids Are Fertilised by Insects*. Second edition, revised. Illus. New York: D. Appleton and Co., 1886. [Part of Clemens's 12-volume set of Darwin's writings.]

Catalog: "Mark Twain Collection," *The Bookman*, No. 25 (1970), #329.

Location: Wake Forest University, Winston-Salem, North Carolina. Gift of Nancy Susan Reynolds.

Copy examined: Clemens's unmarked copy, in 1970.

————. *What Mr. Darwin Saw in His Voyage Round the World in the Ship "Beagle."* Compiled by Wendell Phillips Garrison (1840–1907). Illus. New York: Harper & Brothers, 1904. 228 pp.

Marginalia: no markings, but pages 85 and 125 are folded down.

Location: Mark Twain Library, Redding, Connecticut. Donated by Clemens (MTLAcc, entry #1179).

Copy examined: Clemens's copy, unmarked. Has the red ink Mark Twain Library accession number "1179". Crudely rebound with modern tape. Has early Mark Twain Library purple stamps. Examined briefly in 1970 and more thoroughly in June 1982.

Garrison compiled this adaptation for younger readers from Darwin's notebooks.

DASENT, GEORGE WEBBE (1817–1896), ed. and trans. *The Story of Burnt Njal; or, Life in Iceland at the End of the Tenth Century*. 2 vols. Edinburgh, 1861.

Catalog: *Mott 1952*, #47, $2.50, Vol. 2 only, inscribed to

Jean Clemens from "G. D."

DAUDET, ALPHONSE (1840–1897). *Sidonie. (Fromont jeune et Risler aîné.)* Trans. from the French by Mary (Neal) Sherwood (1840–1897). Boston: Estes and Lauriat, 1877. [Translator and publisher conjectured.]

  Inscription: signed on a flyleaf: "S. L. Clemens, Hartford, 1877."

  Marginalia: a few notes.

  Catalog: *A1911*, "12mo, cloth, Bost. 1877, . . . a few marginal notes," quotes the signature, lot 119, sold for $2; George D. Smith, New York City, "Catalogue of Books" (1911), quotes the signature, item #92, $5.

———. *The Immortal; or, One of the "Forty."* Trans. from the French by Arthur Woollgar Verrall (1851–1912) and Margaret de G[audrion]. (Merrifield) Verrall (1859–1916). Illus. Chicago: Rand, McNally & Co., 1889. 307 pp.

  Source: MTLAcc, entry #2210, volume donated from Clemens's library by Clara Clemens Gabrilowitsch in 1910.

———. *Le siège de Berlin, et d'autres contes, par Alphonse Daudet.* New York: W. R. Jenkins, 1885. 73 pp. [Reissued repeatedly by the same firm in the 1880s. Edition conjectured. No English edition was published until 1903.]

  "Examine 'The Siege of Berlin,' & perhaps publish it in the Century," wrote Mark Twain in March 1889 (NB 28, *N&J* 3: 461).

DAVIE, OLIVER (1857–1911). *Nests and Eggs of North American Birds.* Fifth edition, revised. Illus. Columbus, Ohio: Landon Press, 1898. 545 pp.

  Inscription: signed on the front flyleaf in black ink: "Jean Lampton Clemens,/Riverdale on the Hudson/New York/1903."

  Provenance: bookseller's sticker of G. P. Putnam's Sons of New York City on the front pastedown endpaper.

  Location: Mark Twain Library, Redding, Connecticut. Donated from Clemens's library by Clara Clemens Gabrilowitsch in 1910 (MTLAcc, entry #1944).

  Copy examined: Jean Clemens's copy. Has the red ink Mark Twain accession number "1944."

DAVIES, ACTON (1870–1916). *Maude Adams.* Illus. New York: Frederic A. Stokes Co., cop. 1901. 110 pp. [Edition conjectured.]

  Catalog: ListABP (1910), "Maude Adams, Davies", no other information supplied.

  The prominent actress Maude Adams (1872–1953) starred in James Barrie's *The Little Minister* in 1897 and would become a sensation in his 1905 play *Peter Pan; or, The Boy Who Wouldn't Grow Up.* Davies was a noted drama critic who later became a press agent.

DAVIES, HUBERT HENRY (1876–1917). *Cousin Kate* (play, produced in 1903).

  On 12 February 1904 Mark Twain gave a curtain-raiser speech for a benefit performance of *Cousin Kate* in Florence, Italy (Hamlin Hill, *MTGF*, p. 82; Fears, *Day by Day* 3: 951–952).

DAVIS, GARRETT (1801–1872).

  A brief note by Samuel Clemens was laid in Felix Octavius Carr Darley's *Compositions in Outline by Felix O. C. Darley, from Hawthorne's Scarlet Letter* to enhance the book's sale price at the 1911 auction; it read: "How I did not get my bill through," and "Biography of Garrett Davis." (See the Catalog entry for F. O. C. Darley.) The context

for Clemens's memorandum is not explained. Davis was a Kentucky attorney and state politician who opposed secession before and during the Civil War. He served in the United States Senate from 1861 until his death in 1872.

DAVIS, GEORGE BRECKENRIDGE (1847–1914). *The Elements of International Law.* New York: Harper & Brothers, [cop. 1900]. 612 pp.

  Source: MTLAcc, entry #1363, volume donated by Clemens.

  Quite likely Clemens consulted this book for information about international copyright, an issue in which he invested much time and energy.

DAVIS, L[EMUEL]. CLARKE (1835–1904), ed. The *Story of the Memorial Fountain to Shakespeare at Stratford-upon-Avon.* Red cloth, gilt lettering and decoration. Cambridge: Riverside Press, 1890. 261 pp.

  Inscription: inscribed on the front pastedown endpaper, in black ink: "Mrs. Samuel L. Clemens/with cordial regards of/L. Clarke Davis/June 3, 1890". The frontispiece was signed in black ink "George W. Childs" and inscribed in the same ink: "To his friend/Mrs. S. L. Clemens/1890". (Childs was the donor of the Shakespeare fountain.)

  Location: Mark Twain Library, Redding, Connecticut.

  Copy examined: Olivia Clemens's unmarked copy. Has the red ink Mark Twain Library accession number "3282". Examined in 1970 and again in June 1982 and on 8 November 2019.

  Newspaper journalist and editor Clarke Davis was married to author Rebecca Harding Davis (1831–1910), an early Realist novelist.

DAVIS, MOLLIE EVELYN (BORN MARY EVELINA MOORE) (1852–1909). *An Elephant's Track and Other Stories.* Illus. New York: Harper & Brothers, 1897. 276 pp.

  Source: MTLAcc, entry #1535, volume donated by Clemens.

  The Texas poet, short story writer, novelist, and editor Davis was best known for her dialect regional stories of the American South.

DAVIS, NORAH (1861–1936). *Wallace Rhodes, A Novel.* New York: Harper & Brothers, 1909. 335 pp.

  Source: MTLAcc, entry #1109, volume donated by Clemens.

  In *Wallace Rhodes* a widower living in the Mississippi Delta marries his son's fiancée. This was the third novel of a Huntsville, Alabama author who wrote unflinchingly about the financial hardships and social stresses of early-twentieth-century white Southerners (Eleanor Newman Hutchens, "Norah Davis 1861–1936," *Huntsville Historical Review* (Huntsville-Madison County Historical Society) 13.3–4 [July-October 1983]: 21–29).

DAVIS, RICHARD HARDING (1864–1916). *The Bar Sinister.* Illustrated by E[dmund]. M[arion]. Ashe (1867–1941). New York: C. Scribner's Sons, 1903. 108 pp.

  Source: MTLAcc, entry #1880, volume donated from Clemens's library by Clara Clemens Gabrilowitsch in 1910.

  The first-person autobiography of a tough bull-terrier dog, *The Bar Sinister* appeared in the same year (1903) as Mark Twain's pathetic short story, "A Dog's Tale"

———. *Gallegher and Other Stories.* Illustrated by Charles Dana Gibson (1867–1944). New York: Charles Scribner's

Sons, 1903. 236 pp.
Source: MTLAcc, entry #113, volume donated by Clemens.
————. *Her First Appearance.* Illustrated by Charles Dana Gibson (1867–1944) and E[dmund]. M[arion]. Ashe (1867–1941). New York: Harper & Brothers, 1901. [Publisher conjectured.]
Inscription: signed "S. L. Clemens, Riverdale-on-Hudson, Nov. 1901."
Catalogs: *A1911*, "12mo, cloth, gilt top, uncut, N.Y. 1901," quotes signature, lot 120, sold for $5; item #208 sold from Library of Charles B. Feinberg, 21 May 1968, $130 (*American Book-Prices Current* [New York: Columbia Univ. Press, 1971], p. 214).
————. *Soldiers of Fortune.* Illustrated by Charles Dana Gibson (1867–1944). London: W. Heinemann. 1897. 288 pp.
Source: MTLAcc, entry #2211, volume donated from Clemens's library by Clara Clemens Gabrilowitsch in 1910. Davis's romantic novel, set in a fictional Latin American country, employs mining operations as the impetus for a coup and counter-coup.
————. *Vera, the Medium.* Illustrated by Frederic Dorr Steele (1873–1944). New York: Charles Scribner's Sons, 1908. 216 pp.
Source: MTLAcc, entry #121, volume donated by Clemens. During a supper and ball given by Robert Collier at Sherry's Restaurant in New York City on 13 February 1908, Clemens would no doubt have been introduced to another celebrity, Richard Harding Davis (Fears, *Day by Day* 4: 890).
DAVIS, ROBERT G[RIMES] (1819–1872). *Reports of a Portion of the Decisions Rendered by the Supreme Court of the Hawaiian Islands, in Law, Equity, Admiralty and Probate, 1857–1865.* Honolulu: Government Press, 1866.
Clemens examined this volume with the critical eye of a former typesetter in 1866, pronouncing it "elegantly printed & bound—800 pages—in a shape [to] do honor to any printers" (NB 6, *N&J* 1: 204).
DAVIS, SAMUEL POST (1850–1918). *Short Stories.* San Francisco: Golden Era Co., 1886. 189 pp.
Davis moved to Nevada in 1875 and in 1879 became the editor of the Carson City *Morning Appeal.* "The First Piano in a Mining Camp," a tale from Davis's *Short Stories* about an expensive hoax played on some miners on Christmas Eve, appeared in *Mark Twain's Library of Humor* (1888). Davis's fiction was well represented in *The Sagebrush Anthology: Literature from the Silver Age of the Old West*, ed. Lawrence I. Berkove (Columbia: University of Missouri Press, 2006).
DAVIS, VARINA ANNE JEFFERSON (1864–1898). *A Romance of Summer Seas; A Novel.* New York: Harper & Brothers, 1898. 278 pp.
Source: MTLAcc, entry #1099, volume donated by Clemens.
DAVITT, MICHAEL (1846–1906). *The Fall of Feudalism in Ireland; or, the Story of the Land League Revolution.* New York: Harper & Brothers, 1904. 751 pp.
Source: MTLAcc, entry #593, volume donated by Clemens. On 13 December 1896, in London, Clemens noted: "Met Michael Davitt to-day" (NB 39, TS p. 33). A passionate advocate of home rule for Ireland, Davitt went on global lecture tours that included New Zealand. In Chapter 30

of *Following the Equator* (1897) Mark Twain observed of Dunedin, New Zealand: "This town justifies Michael Davitt's praises." Clemens's business agent listed Davitt's *Fall of Feudalism* as one of "four Harper's books" from Messrs. French, Lemon & Co. that arrived in Florence after Clemens departed following Olivia's death in June 1904 (S. V. Cecchi to SLC, 30 July 1904, Haskard & Co., Bankers, Florence). On 4 November 1904 the parcel still had not been forwarded from Florence (Cecchi to SLC, Haskard & Co., Bankers).
DAWSON, A[LEC]. J[OHN]. (1872–1951). *The Genteel A. B.* Illustrated by W[illiam]. Ralston (1848–1911). Blue cloth. London, 1907. 319 pp.
Inscription: on the front flyleaf Dawson quoted three stanzas from Mark Twain's doggerel poem, "The Aged Pilot Man" (see Chapter 51 of *Roughing It* [1872]), attributing them to "Gems of Classic Thought, c.f. The World's Poetical Masterpieces, Twain's Reliques." An ALS from Dawson is pasted on the front pastedown endpaper, dated 3 May 1908 from Tigh-Na-Rosan, Nairn, N. B., Scotland, inviting Clemens to return: When will you come back again? The U. S. shouldn't be selfish; we too have rights. . . Yours so affectionately."
Catalogs: *A1911*, "12mo, cloth (covers loose), Lond. 1907," quotes the inscription, lot 121, sold for $10; George D. Smith, New York City, "Catalogue of Books" (1911), quotes the inscription, item #94, $20; American Art Association (New York City), sale catalogue for the collection of the late William F. Gable of Altoona, Pennsylvania (8 January 1925), letter from Dawson pasted on the front pastedown endpaper, a poem of fourteen lines copied on the front flyleaf, has the *A1911* sale label, lot 125, sold for $9.00 (with one other book).
Location: Mark Twain Papers, Bancroft Library, University of California at Berkeley.
Source: University of California at Berkeley Library Online Catalog, 2018.
DAWSON, WILLIAM JAMES (1854–1928) and **CONINGSBY WILLIAM DAWSON** (1883–1959), eds. *The Great English Essayists. Introductions and Notes.* Lights of Literature Series. New York, 1909.
Inscription: signed on the front pastedown endpaper: "S. L. Clemens, 1909. See de Quincy [*sic*]."
Catalog: *A1911*, "12mo, cloth, N.Y. 1909," quotes the signature, lot 158, sold for $2.50.
Clemens's inscription refers to Thomas De Quincey's powerful "Joan of Arc," an essay the Dawsons reprinted on pages 186–195.
————, eds. *The Great English Letter-Writers, with Introductory Essays and Notes.* The Reader's Library Series. 2 vols. New York: Harper & Brothers, 1909. [Only Volume 1 has been located.]
Inscription: signed in brown ink on the front pastedown endpaper of Vol. 1: "SL. Clemens/1909."
Marginalia: lengthy comment in brown ink at bottom of page 93, where Robert Louis Stevenson explains his religion of kindness; Clemens wrote in part: "To him, all his listeners are alike, & the same sermon will fit them all. He is evidently as ignorant as a priest or a Bible—or a god." Another note in brown ink in the margin of page 114 expresses disgust at a paean to Shakespeare's

Stratford birthplace written by Benjamin Robert Haydon (1786–1846): "you hear the very breezing of the trees he himself heard, and listen to the humming watery ripple of the river he must often have enjoyed. Clemens objected: "Now where *is* the use in spewing up all these raptures over that third-rate actor, who never wrote a line in his life?" Clemens made grammatical corrections in a letter from David Hume (p. 138) and a letter from John Keats (p. 266), eliminating wordy constructions. On page 143, at Coleridge's describing his employment as that of "writing MS. sermons for lazy clergymen," Clemens underlined four lines and wrote above them: "Oh, grotesque trade!" To Southey's assertion that "literature cannot be the business of a woman's life, and it ought not to be" (p. 197), Clemens noted at the bottom of the page: "That settles it!" No additional markings or notes.

Provenance: Volume 1 formerly in the Antenne-Dorrance Collection, Rice Lake, Wisconsin.

Location: Volume 1 only in the Mark Twain Archive, Gannett-Tripp Learning Center, Elmira College, Elmira, New York.

Copy examined: Clemens's copy, in 1970 and again in 2015.

DAY, HOLMAN FRANCIS (1865–1935). *The Eagle Badge; or, The Skokums of the Allagash*. Illus. New York: Harper & Brothers, 1908. 290 pp.

Source: MTLAcc, entry #1319, volume donated by Clemens.

A city boy encounters the challenge of log-rolling in Maine.

———. *King Spruce; A Novel*. Illustrated by E[dwin]. Roscoe Shrader (1878–1960). New York: Harper & Brothers, 1908. 372 pp.

Source: MTLAcc, entry #415, volume donated by Clemens.

In this romantic novel a college man pits himself against a timber baron in the great Maine woods.

DAY, THOMAS (1748–1789). *History of Sandford and Merton* (juvenile story, published 1783–1789).

Mark Twain thought of introducing the good farmboy Harry Sandford and the badly spoiled Tommy Merton into *Tom Sawyer Abroad* (1894). In June 1898 he considered having "Sanford & Merton" [*sic*] join other child "Creatures of Fiction" in a projected but never realized tale (NB 40, TS p. 27), and he jotted down and then canceled "<Sandford & Merton>" in January 1910 (NB 49, TS p. 1). The English author Thomas Day had introduced a long-lasting pair of characters into this early novel written for children.

DE AMICIS, EDMONDO (1846–1908). *Holland and Its People*. [Translated from the Italian by Caroline Town (Stebbins) Tilton (1824–1903).] The Zuyder-Zee Edition. Only 600 numbered copies printed. Illustrated by Samuel Colman (1832–1920), R[obert]. Swain Gifford (1849–1905), Joseph Pennell (1857–1926), Charles A[dams]. Platt (1861–1933), and Charles A. Vanderhoof (1853–1918). New York: G. P. Putnam's Sons, The Knickerbocker Press, 1885. 397 pp.

Marginalia: no signature or marginalia, but a tipped in manuscript note written in ink by Clemens reads: "The Secret Removal of Plymouth Rock. We stand utterly amazed & confounded in the contemplation of such a crime as this."

Catalogs: *A1911*, "royal 8vo, decorative cloth, uncut, N.Y. 1885, The Zuyder-Zee Edition, limited and numbered," lot 10, sold for $5.75; Catalogue 174 (1989),

Heritage Book Shop, Los Angeles, California, "4to, full green crushed morocco, elaborately gilt, . . . green cloth open-ended slipcase," one of 325 copies on linen paper, contains the *A1911* sale label and a tipped-in note about "The Secret Removal of Plymouth/Rock," item #204, priced at $1,500.

Location: Rare Book and Manuscript Library, University of Illinois at Urbana-Champaign, Urbana, Illinois.

Source: Email from Julie Christenson, Velde Fellow, Rare Book and Manuscript Library, University of Illinois, to Alan Gribben, 30 September 2015, in reply to Gribben's inquiry. The book bears the *A1911* sale label. The cover is bound in morocco with tooled and gilt floral decorations and red and green morocco inlays. The book is in good condition.

———. *Spain and the Spaniards*. [Translated from the Italian by Wilhelmina W. Cady (b. 1851), later Mrs. Wilhelmina Cady Rocco-Scotti.] The Guadalquiver Edition. No. 329 of 600 limited edition numbered copies. Illustrated by R[obert]. Swain Gifford (1840–1905), W. St. John Harper (1851–1910), Samuel Colman (1832–1920), and others. Small folio. Original dark green cloth with gilt, handmade paper, uncut edges, initial letters in red, plates inserted. New York: G. P. Putnam's Sons, Knickerbocker Press, 1885. 463 pp.

Catalog: *A1911*, "Japanese tissue paper, small folio, gilt tooled cover design, edges uncut, N.Y. 1885, The Guadalquiver Edition, limited and numbered," lot 9, $12.

Provenance: bookseller's label of Hitch, Billings & Co., Elmira, New York on the rear pastedown endpaper. Has the *A1911* sale label. The volume also contains the bookplate of Christine Alexander Graham, the bibliophile wife of Maryland lawyer and politician Samuel Miller Breckinridge Long (1881–1958).

Location: collection of Kevin Mac Donnell, Austin, Texas. Obtained in 2008 from Robert Slotta.

Source: letter from Kevin Mac Donnell to Alan Gribben, 24 June 2008. Mac Donnell reported that the volume contains no markings.

Spain and the Spaniards was first published as *Spagna* (Firenze, 1873); G. P. Putnam's Sons copyrighted the English translation in 1880. At first Clemens was unsure of its title: "An Italian in Spain—Putnam's Sons" he jotted in Notebook 25 in November or December 1885 (*N&J* 3: 215). He soon received the volume as a Christmas gift; he wrote to Jervis, Julie, and Ida Langdon from Hartford on 28 December 1885: "I thank you with enthusiasm; for that 'Spain' was a book which I more wanted than any other book that could be named. It gives me nightly peace, now, & I think of you when I read it" (MTP). The typography and paper pleased him especially, for he later proposed to Charles L. Webster that their publishing firm print a copy of Grant's *Memoirs* "on paper like that in De Amici's 'Spain'—ragged edges & 2 or 3-inch margins" for presentation to Pope Leo XIII (17 June 1886, *MTBus*, p. 361).

———. *Studies of Paris*. [Translated from the Italian by Wilhelmina W. Cady (b. 1851), later Mrs. Wilhelmina Cady Rocco-Scotti.] New York: G. P. Putnam's Sons, 1879.

Estes & Lauriat of Boston billed Clemens on 14 July 1880 for "1 Studies of Paris .65¢" (receipt in MTP). *Studies of Paris* contained descriptions of Paris and the Exposition as well as essays on Victor Hugo and Zola.

DEAN, HENRY CLAY (1822–1877). *Crimes of the Civil War, and Curse of the Funding System* (published in 1868).

Mark Twain praised Dean, "an erratic genius," for his skills as a political orator in Chapter 57 of *Life on the Mississippi* (1883). Twain mentioned seeing him once in Keokuk, Iowa. Brook Thomas pointed out that by the time Twain wrote his book Dean was most famous for *Crimes of the Civil War, and Curse of the Funding System*, "a lost-cause screed" that scathingly condemned Reconstruction policies and their consequences for the South ("*Adventures of Huckleberry Finn* and Reconstruction," *American Literary Realism* 50.1 (Fall 2017): 18.

DE BURY, (BARONESS) MARIE [PAULINE ROSE] BLAZE (STEWART) (1813–1894). "The Spiritualization of Thought in France," *The Contemporary Review* (London) 60.311 (November 1891): 642–743.

Someone other than Clemens wrote this author and title on the rear endpaper of Clemens's copy of Robert Louis Stevenson's *The Pocket R. S. S.* (1904), citing the *Review of Reviews*. De Bury wrote a series of investigatory articles about France that were listed in *Review of Reviews*. In 1893 she reported on "The Problem of Crime in France" in *The Contemporary Review*.

The Declaration of Sentiments and Constitution of the Anti-Slavery Society. New York: American Anti-Slavery Society, 1835. 16 pp. [Publisher and pages conjectured.] [One of seven anti-slavery pamphlets bound with William Ellery Channing's *Letter J. G. Birney* (1837).]

Catalog: *A1911*, "Declaration of Sentiment [*sic*] and Constitution of the American Anti-Slavery Society, N.Y. 1835," bound with other anti-slavery pamphlets, lot 76, sold for $2 total.

DE COLANGE, LEO [AUGUSTE] (1819–1889), ed. *The Picturesque World; or, Scenes in Many Lands: With One Thousand Illustrations on Wood and Steel of Picturesque Views from All Parts of the World*. 2 vols. Boston: Estes & Lauriat, 1878.

Catalog: Ball 2016 inventory, brown leather, gilt lettering, gilt edge pages, Volume II only.

Location: Quarry Farm library shelves, under the supervision of the Mark Twain Archive, Elmira College, Elmira, New York.

This picture book was available to Clemens whenever he visited Quarry Farm in Elmira.

DEEPING, [GEORGE] WARWICK (1877–1950). *Bertrand of Brittany*. New York: Harper & Brothers, 1908. 369 pp. [Publisher and pages conjectured.]

Inscription: signed on the front pastedown endpaper: "S. L. Clemens."

Catalog: *A1911*, "12mo, cloth, N.Y. 1908," quotes the signature, lot 123, sold for $1.25.

This historical romance by the English physician-author Deeping, set in fourteenth-century France, had castles, drawbridges, armor, and cross-bows.

———. *Bess of the Woods*. New York: Harper & Brothers, 1906. 406 pp.

Source: MTLAcc, entry #1538, volume donated by Clemens.

The Sussex physician Deeping set this romantic novel on a large estate in eighteenth-century England. It centers around a mysterious woman who lives in the forest.

———. *The Slanderers*. New York: Harper & Brothers, 1905. 384 pp.

Source: MTLAcc, entry #1539, volume donated by Clemens.

In this romantic novel an unhappy marriage leads to rumors.

———. *A Woman's War; A Novel*. New York: Harper & Brothers, 1907. 354 pp.

Source: MTLAcc, entry #1540, volume donated by Clemens.

A physician in a small village, Dr. James Murchison, struggles to control his alcoholism. His wife and family suffer along with him as his reputation is impugned.

DE FLERS, ROBERT (1872–1927) and **GASTON-ARMAN DE CAILLAYET** (1869–1915). *Love Watches*. [Comedy in four acts, adapted by Gladys Unger. Produced by Charles Frohman at the Lyceum Theatre in New York City on 27 August 1908, with Billie Burke as Jacqueline.]

Isabel Lyon recorded on 26 September 1908, a Saturday: "In the afternoon the King had a box at the Lyceum to see Billie Burke in her new play 'Love Watches'" (IVL Journal, TS p. 332, MTP). Dorothy Sturgis Harding recalled that during her visit to Stormfield in 1908, "one day Mr. Clemens took us all into New York to see Billie Burke in *Love Watches*. He took us back stage to meet her in the 'green room'" ("MT Lands an Angel-fish," *Columbia Library Columns* 16 [February 1967]: 9).

DEFOE, DANIEL (1661–1731). *The Journal of the Plague Year* (historical fiction, published in 1722).

In remarks to an interviewing reporter in New Zealand in 1895, Mark Twain indicated that he was quite familiar with this book and pointed out Defoe's advantage in writing the account: "He knew London . . . , every spot and corner of it." Consequently "Defoe described what he saw, and added the equivalents which he had observed, and so he got his wonderful study" (Wellington, New Zealand *Mail*, 12 December 1895; Scharnhorst, *Complete Interviews*, p. 261).

Coleman O. Parsons, "Mark Twain in New Zealand," *South Atlantic Quarterly* 61 (Winter 1962): 74.

———. *The Life and Strange Surprising Adventures of Robinson Crusoe, of York, Mariner, Who Lived Eight-and-Twenty Years All Alone in an Uninhabited Island on the Coast of America. . . . Written by Himself*. Ninth edition. [Volume 1]. *The Further Adventures of Robinson Crusoe, Being the Second and Last Part of His Life*. Seventh edition. [Volume 2]. 2 vols. Plates and map. London: Printed for T. Woodward, 1747. [The first edition of the novel had been published in 1719.]

Inscriptions: Volume 1 inscribed in ink (not in Clemens's hand): "S. L. Clemens from Edward J. Eveleigh/Wyndham/Aug. 1879." [The *A1911* catalog read the presenter's name as "Edward S. Gudeisk.] Volume 2 has an identical inscription without the date. Above these inscriptions, in another, older hand, appears: "Letitia Parker her Book/March 9th 1755". An *A1911* sale label is affixed to the front pastedown endpaper.

Catalog: *A1911*, "2 vols., 12mo, old calf (rubbed and broken), Lond. 1747," quotes the inscriptions, lot 124, sold for $7.50.

Location: Department of Rare Books and Special Collections, University Library, University of Michigan, Ann Arbor (Karla M. Vandersypen, then Assistant Rare Book

Librarian, to Alan Gribben, 3 June 1987). Donated to the University Library by a former University regent, Lucius Lee Hubbard, on 27 October 1924. Hubbard collected books about imaginary voyages.

Copy examined: photocopies of the library catalog card and the book's inscriptions, sent by Karla M. Vandersypen on 3 June 1987. This book appears in every respect to have belonged to Clemens's library.

Clemens's fascination with Defoe's fictional castaway and his eventual companion Friday began early in his writing career and continued unabated throughout his lifetime. During his visit to the Sandwich Islands in 1866 Clemens imagined how "dark savages come from some mysterious locality as they did with Crusoe, & have great battles & then eat up the prisoners" (NB 6, *N&J* 1: 184). Clemens wrote to Olivia Langdon on 6 January 1870 from New York City about his frustrating experiences in a railroad car: "I read 3 pages of Robinson Crusoe, lost & found the book some twelve or fifteen times, & finally lost it for good a couple of hours ago" (*MTLet* 4: 1). In a letter to James Henry Riley written on 2 December 1870, Clemens enthusiastically compared his idea of dispatching Riley to investigate the South African diamond fields to Defoe's sending "the ingenious Robinson W. Crusoe" to test life on a deserted island (*MTLet* 4: 261). Mark Twain began a never- actualized fragment in 1875, "The Mysterious Chamber," for which his working notes (DV56, MTP) specified a number of parallels between his bridegroom's confinement in a dungeon and Robinson Crusoe's artful uses of his time and materials at hand.

In 1879 Twain joked about Robinson Crusoe's reliance on masturbation in "Some Thoughts on the Science of Onanism" (DV200, no. 3, MTP; *MTSpk*, p. 125; Budd, *CTSS&E* 1: 722). Clara Clemens listed *Robinson Crusoe* among the favorite books from which Clemens often read to his daughters (*MFMT*, p. 25). Joliet and Marquette "one day came upon the footprints of men in the mud of the western bank [of the Mississippi River]—a Robinson Crusoe experience which carries an electric shiver with it yet, when one stumbles on it in print" (Chapter 2, *LonMiss* [1883]). "Robinson Crusoe leaves the bag of doubloons in the wreck, a fine literary point, but untrue," wrote Clemens in August 1885. "No man would have done that" (NB 24, *N&J* 3: 173). On 20 January 1887 Clemens recommended Defoe's *Robinson Crusoe* as among the best reading for young boys in a letter to the Reverend Charles D. Crane (ALS, Shapell Manuscript Library, Beverly Hills, California).

When Clemens inventoried the chief characteristics of various authors in March 1888, he approvingly set down "tone" beside Defoe's name (NB 27, *N&J* 3: 379). On 16 March 1888 Clemens wrote to Olivia from the Murray Hill Hotel in New York City, lamenting: "Here I have been, Crusoing on a desert hotel—out of wife, out of children, out of linen, out of cigars" (*LLMT*, p. 250). Hank Morgan recognizes the similarities of his situation in Chapter 7 of *A Connecticut Yankee* (1889): "I saw that I was just another Robinson Crusoe cast away on an uninhabited island, with no society but some more or less tame animals, and if I wanted to make life bearable I must do as he did—invent, contrive, create, reorganize

things; set brain and hand to work, and keep them busy."

Beset by financial difficulties, Clemens fell back on a favorite book in February 1891, planning for his publishing house to issue *Robinson Crusoe* in twenty-five-cent installments (NB 30, *N&J* 3: 605). Clemens thought of "Buckley" (William Buckley, 1780–1856) as the "first Crusoe" of Australia and "Murrell" as the "second Crusoe" (NB 35 [September 1895], TS p. 53). James Murell (or Murrells, or Morrill), 1824–1865, a sailor on the *Peruvian* who was shipwrecked in Queensland in 1846, lived among the natives for seventeen years After his eventual rescue he expressed opposition to the killing off of the natives. The island of Port Louis has "no good hotel or club, no company, no society, no comrade after 4, a Robinson Crusoe loneliness & isolation," or so Clemens had heard (Notebook 38 [1896], TS p. 7). "Like Crusoe upon the footprint & is aghast," noted Mark Twain on 1 June 1896 (NB 38, TS p. 28). "Breed a new [William] Buckley-Crusoe," he wrote to Chatto & Windus from Kaltenleutgeben on 26 September 1898, in reference to the Australian explorer William Buckley (Berg, NYPL). Clemens listed Defoe's book title in Notebook 40 (July 1899), TS p. 58, under a heading, "*For Cheap Books*". On 9 September 1905 Isabel Lyon heard Clemens, in speaking about journal-keeping, allude to "the splendid Robinson Crusoe narrative and how interested you are in everything he took away from the ship" (IVL Journal, TS p. 96, MTP). See also the Catalog entries for William Cowper and for Alexander Selkirk.

———. *The Life and Surprising Adventures of Robinson Crusoe of York, Mariner*. Illustrated by Gordon [Frederick] Browne (1858–1932) and Ernest Griset (1844–1907). New York: A. L. Burt Co., n.d. [1902]. 452 pp. [Voyageur Book Shop in Milwaukee, Wisconsin performed research concerning this edition and learned that A. L. Burt did not incorporate until 1902 and began by issuing literary classics.]

Source: MTLAcc, entry #599, volume donated by Clemens.

———. *Moll Flanders and The History of the Devil. The Novels and Miscellaneous Works of Daniel Defoe*. Original red cloth, spine lost, front board present but detached, corners rubbed. London: Bell & Daldy, 1871. 580 pp. [The first edition of the novel had been published in 1721.]

Marginalia: Clemens made annotations consisting of fifty words and also marked a few passages. On the verso of the half-title page, Clemens quoted in pencil several passages that he had found and marked in pencil on pages 44 and 31: "44/Fame & fools make an assembly./They that yield when they are asked, are one step before them that were never asked to yield, & two steps before them that yield before they are asked./31". On page 50 Clemens quibbled: "These are ornaments, not capital, madam," referring to a woman's attributes of beauty, wit, manners, education, virtue, and so forth, a list that Clemens marked vertically. On page 52, writing vertically in pencil, Clemens rejoiced, regarding an account of how Moll helped blacken the reputation of a "debauched" man who had spurned her female friend, "This is delicious—the innocent gusto of it." The leaves of pages 289–296 remain uncut; these begin *The History of the Devil*. There are no markings beyond that point.

Provenance: has the shelfmarks of Clara Clemens

Gabrilowitsch's library system during her Detroit years; sold at the 1951 Hollywood auction but not listed in the rapidly compiled sale sheet, a lamentably common occurrence at that strange event.

Catalog: "Property from the Library of Mark Twain," Butterfield & Butterfield, Sale 6613 (16 July 1997), lot 2672.

Location: Mark Twain House and Museum, Hartford, Connecticut.

Copy examined: Clemens's copy. Viewed in Hartford in 1997.

In "The Walt Whitman Controversy," possibly written in 1882, Mark Twain testified that his personal library contained this book despite its coarseness and obscenity (DV36, MTP).

———. *Robinson Crusoe in Words of One Syllable*. Ed. by Lucy Aikin (1781–1864), pseud. "Mary Godolphin." New York: McLoughlin Brothers, 1869. 93 pp.

Source: MTLAcc, entry #1934, volume donated from Clemens's library by Clara Clemens Gabrilowitsch in 1910.

———. *Roxana, or The Fortunate Mistress* (novel, published in 1724).

William Dean Howells urged Clemens to read this novel for "the deepest insights" into the human soul and "the best and most natural English that a book was ever written in. You will find it in the Bohn library" (9 August 1885, *MTHL*, p. 536). Henry Nash Smith and William M. Gibson reported that "there is no conclusive evidence that Mark Twain read *Roxana,*" but pointed out the likelihood that the enslaved Roxana in *Pudd'nhead Wilson* (1894) may owe her name to Defoe's novel (*MTHL*, p. 537 n. 2).

De Forest, John William (1826–1906). "The Hungry Heart," *Lippincott's Magazine* 6.1 (July 1870): 189–245.

A correspondent wrote Mark Twain on 30 August 1870 to compare De Forest's story to Twain's description in the *Galaxy* of literary "hogwash" (*DearMT*, p. 23). The letter partially quoted a passage from the first page of De Forest's story in *Lippincott's Magazine*, which reads in its entirety: "Every woman in these days needs two husbands—one to fill her purse, and one to fill her heart; one to dress her, and one to love her. It is not easy to be the two in one" (p. 189).

———. *Kate Beaumont* (novel, published in 1872).

When De Forest wrote to Clemens on 31 July 1874 suggesting work on a joint volume of sketches, Clemens noted on the envelope of his letter: "J. W. De Forest, Novelist" MTP). On 5 January 1875 De Forest, writing to William Dean Howells, praised Twain's "A True Story" (1874) as "a really great thing, amazingly natural & humorous, & touching even to the drawing of tears"; Howells sent De Forest's letter to Clemens (*MTLet* 6: 349). Clemens jotted down the title of De Forest's *Kate Beaumont* in March 1882, shortly before departing for New Orleans (NB 20, *N&J* 2: 452). *Kate Beaumont* depicted two slaveholding families in antebellum South Carolina engaged in a feud resembling medieval territorial disputes.

Blair, *MT&HF* (1960), pp. 218–219, 318. Frank Bergmann, "Mark Twain and the Literary Misfortunes of John William De Forest," *Jahrbuch für Amerikastudien* 13 (1968): 249–252, pondered why a friendship between De Forest and Mark Twain failed to develop and published the letter from De Forest to Mark Twain of 31 July 1874.

De Forest, Julia Brasher (1853–1910). *A Short History of Art*. Illus. New York: Dodd, Mead, and Co., [cop. 1881]. 365 pp.

Inscription: an erased inscription in brown ink on the third flyleaf is still partly legible: "Mrs. Orion Clemens/ Keokuk—/1887," it appears to read. Orion and Mollie Clemens were living in Keokuk, Iowa in 1887 (Fanning, *Mark Twain and Orion Clemens*, p. 206). A later inscription in black ink at the top of the title page reads: "Dec. 15, 1892 [*sic*]/I. V. Lyon from —.—.—. [three illegible initials]. Isabel V. Lyon was not yet affiliated with Clemens's family in 1892, so the latter inscription, which appears to be in her handwriting, is puzzling.

Marginalia: a penciled note by Isabel Lyon at the top of page 13 refers to an article in the August 1916 issue of the *Century Magazine*.

Location: Mark Twain House and Museum, Hartford, Connecticut. Purchased in 1962 for $15.

Copy examined: volume once belonging to Mollie Clemens (1834–1904), later acquired by Clemens, and afterward in the possession of Isabel V. Lyon (1868–1958). Examined in August 1987.

De Forest, Lockwood (1850–1932), ed. *Indian Domestic Architecture*. Boston: Heliotype Printing Co., [cop. 1885]. [Twenty-five photographic plates; no text.]

Inscription: flyleaf inscribed by Clemens: "Livy L. Clemens/ Christmas/ 1885./From SLC".

Catalogs: ListABP (1910), "Indian Domestic Architecture (signature)"; "Retz Appraisal" (1944), p. 9, valued at $15.

Location: Mark Twain Papers, Bancroft Library, University of California at Berkeley.

Copy examined: gift copy from Clemens to his wife.

The photographs in this large volume record impressive examples of Hindu and Muslim houses in India. De Forest states in his brief introduction that such artistry in wood and stone carving, "with all the advantages of the caste system," is currently in danger of expiring unless European and American patronage is increased. In the early 1880s Lockwood had been consulted about interior decoration details for the Clemenses' Hartford house. Inserted in the volume is a photographic copy of the "Lotto Portrait of Columbus" by Lorenzo Lotto (1476–1554), accompanied by a description written by Frank H. Mason of Frankfort, Germany. (See the Catalog entry for John C. Van Dyke, "The Lotto Portrait.")

De Graff, Esmond Vedder (1835–1885). *The School-Room Guide, Embodying the Instruction Given the Author at Teachers' Institutes, in New York and Other States, and Especially Intended to Assist Public School Teachers in the Practical Work of the School-Room*. Syracuse, New York: C. W. Bardeen, 1882. 444 pp.

Source: MTLAcc, entry #814, volume donated by Clemens.

"De Hurst, C." (pseud.). *How Women Should Ride*. Illus. New York: Harper & Brothers, 1892. 248 pp.

Source: MTLAcc, entry #844, volume donated by Clemens. There were few other manuals published about female horsemanship. Quite likely this book was purchased for Jean Clemens, who loved riding and admired animals.

De Kroyft, [Susan] Helen (Aldrich) (1818–1915). *The Story of Little Jakey*. Illus. Brown cloth, gilt, gilt edges. New York: Hurd and Houghton; Cambridge: Riverside Press,

1876. 132 pp.

Provenance: blank bookplate (no number) of the "J. Langdon Family Library."

Catalogs: Mark Woodhouse's 2013 inventory list of the Langdon family library; Ball 2016 inventory, brown cloth, gilt lettering, gilt edge pages, from the J. Langdon Family Library, fair condition.

Location: Quarry Farm library shelves, under the supervision of the Mark Twain Archive, Elmira College, Elmira, New York.

Copy examined: unmarked copy to which Clemens had access whenever he visited the Langdon residence in Elmira. Examined on 26 May 2015.

Helen De Kroyft published other types of books besides this venture into juvenile fiction. She had been blinded by an eye infection in 1845, and her ability to write literature was considered so remarkable that to encourage her many notable individuals and families subscribed in advance of the publication of her works.

DE LANCEY, MAGDALENE (HALL) (1793–1822). *A Week at Waterloo in 1815. Lady De Lancey's Narrative; Being an Account of How She Nursed Her Husband, Colonel Sir William Howe De Lancey, Quartermaster-General of the Army, Mortally Wounded in the Great Battle.* Ed. by Major B[ernard]. R[owland]. Ward (1863–1933). Illus. London: J. Murray, 1906. 136 pp. [Publisher conjectured.]

Inscription: presentation copy inscribed: "Mark Twain, with the compliments of the editor, August, 1906." Signed on the front pastedown endpaper: "Mark Twain, December, 1906." [This was a rare ownership inscription for a volume destined for Clemens's library; its unusual form presumably reflected the author's presentation of the book to "Mark Twain."]

Catalog: *A1911*, "square 12mo, cloth, gilt top, uncut, Lond. 1906," quotes the signature and inscription, lot 280, sold for $6.

DE LAND, ELLEN DOUGLAS (1860–1923). *Alan Ransford, A Story.* Illustrated by Harry C. Edwards (1868–1922). New York: Harper & Brothers, [cop. 1897]. 281 pp.

Source: MTLAcc, entry #1413, volume donated by Clemens.

Born in New York state, Deland wrote primarily for the young adult book market.

———. *In the Old Herrick House, and Other Stories.* Illus. New York: Harper & Brothers, [cop. 1896]. 282 pp.

Source: MTLAcc, entry #1304, volume donated by Clemens.

———. *Josephine.* Illustrated by W[illiam]. E[llis]. Mears (1868–1945). New York: Harper & Brothers, 1904. 273 pp.

Source: MTLAcc, entry #446, volume donated by Clemens.

———. *A Little Son of Sunshine; A Story for Boys and Girls.* Illustrated by W[illiam]. E[llis]. Mears (1868–1945). New York: Harper & Brothers, 1906. 284 pp.

Source: MTLAcc, entry #1592, volume donated by Clemens.

———. *Miss Betty of New York.* Illustrated by Rachael Robinson (1878–1919). New York: Harper & Brothers, 1908. 285 pp.

Source: MTLAcc, entry #1102, volume donated by Clemens.

———. *Oakleigh.* Illus. New York: Harper & Brothers, [cop.

1895]. 233 pp.

Source: MTLAcc, entry #1536, volume donated by Clemens.

Deland set this romantic novel in Massachusetts.

DELAND, MARGARET WADE (CAMPBELL) (1857–1945). *The Awakening of Helena Richie.* Illustrated by Walter Appleton Clark (1876–1906). New York: Harper & Brothers, [1906]. 357 pp. [Date of publication and the illustrator are conjectured.]

Source: MTLAcc, entry #1821, volume donated by Clemens.

———. *Dr. Lavendar's People.* Illustrated by Lucius W[alcott]. Hitchcock (1868–1942). New York: Harper & Brothers, 1903. 370 pp.

Source: MTLAcc, entry #1537, volume donated by Clemens.

Hitchcock would be tapped to illustrate Twain's "The Death Disk" (1901) and *A Horse's Tale* (1907).

———. *Good for the Soul.* New York: Harper & Brothers, 1899. 86 pp.

Source: MTLAcc, entry #116, volume donated by Clemens.

———. [Another identical copy.]

Source: MTLAcc, entry #660, volume donated by Clemens.

———. *John Ward, Preacher* (novel, published in 1888).

Deland's best-selling novel depicts a religious conflict between a Calvinist minister and his wife who holds more liberal religious views. "Surely the test of a novel's characters is that you feel a strong interest in them & their affairs—the good to be successful, the bad to suffer failure," reasoned Clemens in February 1889. "Well in John Ward, you feel *no* divided interest, no discriminating interest—you want them all to land in hell together, & right away" (NB 28, *N&J* 3: 446).

———. *Where the Laborers Are Few.* Illustrated by Alice Barber Stephens (1858–1932). New York: Harper & Brothers, 1909. 85 pp.

Source: MTLAcc, entry #2212, volume donated from Clemens's library by Clara Clemens Gabrilowitsch in 1910.

DE LA PASTURE, ELIZABETH (BONHAM) (1866–1945). *The Man from America, A Sentimental Comedy.* New York: E. P. Dutton & Co., 1907. 417 pp.

Source: MTLAcc, entry #1313, volume donated by Clemens.

———. *Peter's Mother.* New York: E. P. Dutton & Co., 1905. 354 pp. [A new edition, with an introduction, was published in 1906. 354 pp. Clemens's edition is undetermined.]

Isabel V. Lyon wrote to Mrs. Franklin G. Whitmore on 17 August 1908, thanking her for some books and reporting that Clemens "found Peter's Mother a 'perfect Godsend'" (MTHM). In *Peter's Mother,* set in England, a recent widow exercises her sense of selfhood against the wishes of her son and several relatives.

DE LA RAMÉE, MARIE LOUISE (1839–1908), pseud. "Ouida." *Bimbi: Stories for Children.* Original cloth, rubbing on edges and corners. Philadelphia: J. B. Lippincott & Co., 1882.

Inscription: the front flyleaf is inscribed, "Jean Clemens/ December 25th, 1889/Hartford/Mamma." [This was Jean Clemens's ninth Christmas.]

Catalogs: *C1951*, J12, no information about edition supplied, listed with the books belonging to Jean and Clara Clemens; "Property from the Library of Mark Twain,"

Butterfield & Butterfield, San Francisco, Sale 6613 (16 July 1997), lot 2708.

Location: Mark Twain House and Museum, Hartford, Connecticut.

Copy examined: Jean Clemens's unmarked copy. Viewed in Hartford in 1997.

Mark Twain mentioned "Miss De La Ramé (Ouida)" in "A Petition to the Queen of England" (1887) concerning international copyright. The opinionated De la Ramée was hardly charitable in a 4 April 1901 letter to Sydney C. Cockerell, remarking that Twain "usually bores me with his ceaseless strain after jokes; and he is very obtuse about many matters, being uneducated"; however, she conceded that she "enjoyed. . . immensely" Twain's 1901 essay, "To the Person Sitting in Darkness" (Elizabeth Lee, *Ouida: A Memoir* [London: T. Fisher Unwin, 1914], pp. 185–186).

———. *Under Two Flags.* Philadelphia: J. B. Lippincott Co., 1887. 652 pp.

Source: MTLAcc, entry #983, volume donated by Albert Bigelow Paine, Clemens's designated biographer. Possibly Clemens saw this book, since the men exchanged reading materials. The pages after 448 are missing.

An English aristocrat joins a fictional equivalent of the French Foreign Legion in Algeria.

DEL MAR, ALEXANDER (1836–1926). *The Worship of Augustus Caesar [63 BCE-14 CE], Derived from a Study of Coins, Monuments, Calendars, Aeras, and Astronomical and Astrological Cycles, the Whole Establishing a New Chronology and Survey of History and Religion.* New York: Cambridge Encyclopedia Co., 1900. 346 pp. [Publisher and pages conjectured.]

Inscription: signed "S. L. Clemens, 1909."

Catalog: *A1911*, "thick 8vo, buckram, uncut, N.Y. 1900," quotes the signature, lot 125, sold for $2.

Clemens received a bill from The Truth Seeker Company, Publishers, Booksellers, and Importers of Freethought Works, New York City, on 20 April 1909 for "1 Worship of Caesar $3.00" (MTP). Clemens paid the bill on 3 May 1909. See also the Catalog entry for *The Truth Seeker.*

DEMAREST, MARY AUGUSTA (LEE) (1838–1888). "My ain countrie" (poem, hymn, published in 1861and set to music in 1864). Melody by Ione T. Hanna (1837–1924); adapted by Hubert P[latt]. Main (1839–1925).

Clemens listed this hymn—also known as "I am far frae my home"—among his favorite songs in August 1889 (NB 29, *N&J* 3: 513). The first stanza provides a sample of its Scottish dialect: "I am far frae my home, an' I'm weary aftenwhiles,/For the langed for hame bringin', an' my Father's welcome smiles;/An' I'll ne'er be fu' content, until mine een do see/The gowden gates o' Heav'n an' my ain countrie."

DE MILLE, JAMES (1833–1880). *Cord and Creese; A Novel.* Harper's Franklin Square Library Series, No. 746. New York: Harper & Brothers, [cop. 1897]. 305 pp.

Source: MTLAcc, entry #1035, volume donated by Clemens.

A professor at Dalhousie University in Nova Scotia, De Mille set the adventures in this novel on the high seas. Two chapter titles can convey the flavor: Chapter V ("The Mystery of Coffin Island") and Chapter VII ("Manuscript Found in a Bottle").

———. *A Strange Manuscript Found in a Copper Cylinder.*

Illustrated by Gilbert Gaul (1855–1919). New York: Harper & Brothers, [cop. 1888]. 291 pp.

Source: MTLAcc, entry #1843, volume donated from Clemens's library by Clara Clemens Gabrilowitsch in 1910. This was one of the popular Canadian author's most inventive and enduring novels, though published posthumously. Four Englishmen find and discuss a floating manuscript that details the adventures of a sailor named Adam More, who encounters a dystopian society in the Antarctic.

———. [Another identical copy.]

Source: MTLAcc, entry #1859, volume donated from Clemens's library by Clara Clemens Gabrilowitsch in 1910.

DEMING, P[HILANDER] (1829–1915). *Adirondack Stories.* Boston: Houghton, Osgood and Co., 1880. 192 pp.

Clemens informed Joseph H. Twichell on 29 August 1880 from Elmira, New York: "I have read 'John's Trial,' & like it very much indeed. It has the advantage of Bret Harte's rot, that it is sincere. I mean to read the rest, to-day" (*LMTJHT*, p. 101). I am grateful to JoDee Benussi for noticing this reference (Benussi to Alan Gribben, email, 25 April 2008). "John's Trial" was the third of eight short stories in *Adirondack Stories.* The narrator recounts how a charge of murder against the captain of a sloop on Lake Champlain, John Wilson, shortened his life and killed his mother because their community shunned them after he was twice released from jail owing to a lack of evidence. At the end of the story the supposed victim, Wilson's cousin William, returns after a long absence at sea and belatedly exonerates the accused man. See also the Catalog entry for Bret Harte, *The Twins of Table Mountain, and Other Stories.*

DE MORGAN, WILLIAM [FREND] (1839–1917). *Alice-for-Short: A Dichronism.* New York: H. Holt & Co., 1907. 563 pp.

Source: MTLAcc, entry #2213, volume donated from Clemens's library by Clara Clemens Gabrilowitsch in 1910. Alice Kavanagh's impoverished life is transformed by a kindly artist whom she eventually, after many plot developments, decides to marry. A haunted house figures in the story.

DEMOSTHENES (384–322 BCE). *Several Orations of Demosthenes, Exciting the Athenians to Oppose the Exorbitant Power of Philip King of Macedon. Translated in the Years 1702 and 1744 from the Original Greek.* London: J. and R. Tonson and S. Draper in the Strand, 1744. 342 pp.

Catalog: Ball 2016 inventory, leather, poor condition.

Location: Quarry Farm library shelves, under the supervision of the Mark Twain Archive, Elmira College, Elmira, New York.

This work would have been available to Clemens whenever he visited Quarry Farm in Elmira.

DENNY, W. H. [WILLIAM HENRY LEIGH DUGMORE] (1853–1915). Singer, actor, playwright, music composer.

Denny (his adopted stage name) worked with Mark Twain on the script for *The Death-Wafer,* a play performed in 1902 at the Carnegie Lyceum in New York City that was based on Twain's story "The Death Disk" (1901) (*Sothbey's 2003,* #102). Denny had once been a member of the Gilbert and Sullivan Opera Company and had a distinguished career on the British stage. In 1882 he had toured with Lillie Langtry.

DENSLOW, WILLIAM WALLACE (1856–1915), editor and illustrator. *Denslow's Mother Goose; Being the Old Familiar Rhymes and Jingles of Mother Goose.* Hand-lettered by Frederic

W. Goudy (1865–1947). New York: McClure, Phillips & Co., 1901. 96 pp.

Inscription: autographed presentation copy from Denslow. Also signed: "S. L. Clemens, Riverdale, Nov. 1901."

Catalog: *A1911*, "4to, boards, N.Y. 1901," mentions the inscription and quotes the signature, lot 126, sold for $4.25. See also the Catalog entry for F. L. Baum's *Father Goose; His Book*.

DEPEW, CHAUNCEY M[ITCHELL]. (1834–1928). *Orations and After-Dinner Speeches of Chauncey M. Depew*. New York: Cassell Publishing Co., 1889. 537 pp.

Depew was a railroad executive, prominent Republican politician, and a noted public speaker. Clemens apparently intended to obtain his first collection of addresses for the Charles L. Webster & Company publishing firm, writing "Depew's 'Ready Speaker'—*now* is the time" in Notebook 27 in 1888 (*N&J* 3: 376). A letter Clemens wrote on 11 May 1904 to Joseph H. Twichell jokingly likened Depew's profile to a marble statue of the Florentine political figure Cosimo I (1519–1574) (*LMTJHT*, p. 335). Depew's later book, *Memories of Eighty Years* (New York: Scribner's 1923) recounted several occasions when he dined with Clemens in the company of others, including at social gatherings in Homburg and a dinner given by Sir Henry Irving in London. Depew made it clear that "as a give-and-take story teller Mark Twain was not a success"; Depew declared that he had known various story-tellers such as Irwin S. Cobb who were superior. Rather, it was Twain's drawl, gestures, mannerisms, and acting ability that got his audiences to laugh ("Presidents and Others," *American Legion Monthly* 2.1 [January 1927]: 12).

DEPPING, GUILLAUME (1829–1901). *Wonders of Bodily Strength and Skill, in All Ages and All Countries*. Trans. from the French by Charles Russell. Illus. New York: Scribner, Armstrong & Co., 1873. 338 pp.

Source: MTLAcc, entry #1998, volume donated from Clemens's library by Clara Clemens Gabrilowitsch in 1910.

DE QUINCEY, THOMAS (1785–1859). *Miscellanies: Chiefly Narrative* (essays, first published in 1854).

Chatto & Windus in 1892 recommended "De Quincey's Joan of Arc in his 'Miscellanies'" among the historical sources that Mark Twain might wish to consult as he contemplated his projected book (Welland, *Mark Twain in England*, p. 158). In 1909 Clemens signed his name and wrote "See de Quincy" [*sic*] on the front pastedown endpaper of his copy of *The Great Essayists* (1909), edited by William James Dawson and Coningsby William Dawson. He was referring to De Quincey's admiring and impassioned essay, "Joan of Arc," which the Dawsons reprinted on pages 186–195 of their book.

———. *The Works of Thomas de Quincey*. 12 vols. Boston: Houghton, Mifflin and Co., 1876–1877. [Includes *Confessions of an English Opium-Eater* (Volume I), *Autobiographic Sketches* (Volume II), *Literary Reminiscences* (Volume III), *Literary Criticism* (Volume IV), *The Eighteenth Century in Scholarship and Literature* (Volume V), *Biographical and Historical Essays* (Volume VI), *Essays in Ancient History and Antiquities* (Volume VII), *Essays on Christianity, Paganism, and Superstition* (Volume VIII), *Essays in Philosophy* (Volume IX), *Politics and Political Economy* (Volume X), *Romances and Extravaganzas* (Volume XI), and *Narrative and Miscellaneous Papers* (Volume XII).

Catalog: Ball 2016 inventory, brown marble boards, 12 volumes, no recorded inscriptions or marginalia.

Location: Quarry Farm library shelves, under the supervision of the Mark Twain Archive, Elmira College, Elmira, New York.

These volumes would have been available to Clemens whenever he visited Quarry Farm in Elmira.

DERBY, GEORGE HORATIO (1823–1861), pseud. "John Phoenix." *Phoenixiana; or, Sketches and Burlesques* (collection of sketches, published in 1856).

Derby died at the age of only thirty-eight. One of the first fan letters that Mark Twain received compared him flatteringly to John Phoenix, "the great humorist who is now in heaven" (*DearMT*, p. 19). Seven years before Mark Twain's invented statue gave a raspberry to the world ("The Petrified Man," 1862) Phoenix had employed the same offensive gesture in a ship's figurehead, as Walter Blair pointed out ("The Petrified Man and His French Ancestor," p. 2). "They made *me* feel like John Phenix [*sic*] in Boston," Twain wrote in Notebook 5 (1866, *N&J* 1: 153). He hinted at a feeling of rivalry in a letter of 14 December 1866 to the Clemens family from San Francisco: "I sail tomorrow . . . leaving more friends behind me than any newspaper man that ever sailed out of the Golden Gate, Phoenix not excepted" (*MTBus*, p. 89; *MTLet* 1: 373). Twain borrowed phrases from Derby's "The Death of Squibob" for a sketch titled "The Last Words of Great Men" that appeared in the 11 September 1869 issue of the Buffalo *Express* (Bellamy, pp. 23–24; *MTBE*, pp. 44–47). Describing Fort Yuma in California, Twain remarked in a column for the Buffalo *Express*, "There is a tradition (attributed to John Phoenix) that a very, very wicked soldier died there, once" (13 November 1869, *MTBE*, p. 91). Twain alluded to this same anecdote about Fort Yuma in Chapter 56 of *Roughing It* (1872) and in Notebook 18 (1879, *N&J* 2: 347), again connecting John Phoenix with it.

Twain repeatedly included Phoenix in the lists of American humorists he compiled for a planned anthology—Notebook 19 (1880), *N&J* 2: 363; Notebook 19 (1881), *N&J* 2: 429; Notebook 24 (August 1885), *N&J* 3: 172; and Notebook 27 (March 1888), *N&J* 3: 379). When *Mark Twain's Library of Humor* appeared in 1888 it contained eight sketches from *Phoenixiana*. This fact quite possibly explains why no copies of Derby's book are among the extant remnants of Twain's library collection. As I explained in "Mark Twain Reads Longstreet's *Georgia Scenes*" (*Gyascutus: Studies in Antebellum Southern Humorous and Sporting Writing*, New Series 5–6 [1978]: 101–111), an essay reprinted in Volume One of this present study, Twain tore apart certain volumes from which he chose selections for his humor anthology and gave the printer these pages for typesetting copy. Twain included "Derby" in a 31 July 1906 Autobiographical Dictation (*MTE*, p. 201; *AutoMT* 2: 153) that listed the many American humorists whose vogue had passed. However, in an interview Twain granted on 8 June 1907, he quoted John Phoenix's quip that his own autobiography "may be relied upon as authentic, as it is written exclusively by me" (Scharnhorst, ed., *Complete* Interviews, p. 555). Twain alluded to John

Phoenix in "Dress Reform and Copyright" (1908), and he mentioned "Phoenix—didn't understand precisely" in some unidentified notes on a sheet sold at the *A1911* auction (lot 399).

George R. Stewart's *John Phoenix, Esq., The Veritable Squibob: A Life of Captain George H. Derby, U.S.A.* (New York: H. Holt and Co., 1937) briefly outlined textual evidence of Mark Twain's having employed John Phoenix's literary devices (pp. 77–78 and 235 n. 198). Gladys Carmen Bellamy's "Mark Twain's Indebtedness to John Phoenix," *American Literature* 13.1 (March 1941): 29–43 (reprinted in *On Mark Twain: The Best from American Literature*, ed. Louis J. Budd and Edwin J. Cady [Durham: Duke University Press, 1987]: 23–24), sought to disprove Bernard DeVoto's casual dismissal of George Horatio Derby as an influence on Mark Twain. One of her points concerned Twain's reliance on Derby for material in his ill-fated 1877 Whittier Birthday Dinner speech. She was also convincing in demonstrating the effects of *Phoenixiana* (1855) on Twain's "Some Learned Fables for Good Old Boys and Girls" and "The Petrified Man."

Bernard DeVoto, *MTAm* (1932), pp. 165–166; Walter Blair, "The Petrified Man and His French Ancestor," *Mark Twain Journal* 19.1 (Winter 1977–1978): 1–3; *Roughing It* (1993), ed. Harriet Elinor Smith and Edgar Marquess Branch, p. 695; and James E. Caron, "Why 'Literary Comedians' Mislabels Two Comic Writers, George Derby ("John Phoenix") and Sam Clemens ("Mark Twain")," *Studies in America Humor*, New series 3, No. 22 (2010): 43–67.

DESPARD, CHARLOTTE (FRENCH) (1844–1939). *The Rajah's Heir; A Novel*. No. 109, Series of Selected Novels. Philadelphia: J. B. Lippincott Co., 1890. 454 pp.

Source: MTLAcc, entry #1858, volume donated from Clemens's library by Clara Clemens Gabrilowitsch in 1910.

In *The Rajah's Heir* a young man living in England inherits an Indian Rajah's wealth and status. Despard was an Anglo-Irish social reformer and novelist. Her husband with whom she had traveled in India and Europe died in the year this novel was published.

DE VINNE, THEODORE LOW (1828–1914). *The Invention of Printing* (published in 1876).

"Get Devinney's [*sic*] History of Printing," Clemens jotted in October 1887 (NB 27, *N&J* 3: 338).

See Bruce Michelson's *Printer's Devil: Mark Twain and the American Publishing Revolution* (Berkeley: University of California Press, 2006) for related information on this general topic.

Devotional Hymns. Selected from Various Authors [, ed. Anson Davies Fitz Randolph, 1820–1896]. New York: Anson D. F. Randolph, 1866. 116 pp. plus six-page index. [Words only, 76 hymns.]

Source: MTLAcc, entry #661, volume donated by Clemens.

DE VOE, WALTER (1874–1959). *Healing Currents from the Battery of Life, Teaching the Doctrine of the Positive and Negative Mind of God, and of the Lord Jesus Christ as the Mediator Between the Two States of Being*. Woodlawn, Illinois; Chicago, Illinois: College of Freedom, 1904. 182 pp. [Edition conjectured; second edition copyrighted in 1905 with 229 pp.]

Catalog: ListABP (1910), "Healing Currents, De Voe", no edition specified.

Healing Currents espouses faith cures, mind cures, and health culture. De Voe (often spelled "Devoe" in his publications) was initially attracted to Christian Science but became associated with the New Thought movement. He eventually founded a mystical religious order, the Eloist Ministry of Brookline, Massachusetts, which offered spiritual healing and developed the believers' psychic sensitivity.

DEWING, MARIA RICHARDS (OAKEY) (1855–1927), "Mrs. T. W. Dewing." *Beauty in Dress*. New York: Harper & Brothers, 1881. 196 pp.

Source: MTLAcc, entry #400, volume donated by Clemens.
———. *Beauty in the Household*. Illus. New York: Harper & Brothers, 1882. 183 pp.

Source: MTLAcc, entry #796, volume donated by Clemens.

DIAZ, ABBY (MORTON) (1821–1904). *The Jimmyjohns, and Other Stories*. Illus. Boston: J. R. Osgood and Co., 1878. 262 pp.

Source: MTLAcc, entry #490, volume donated by Clemens.

The title story concerns twin boys, Jimmy and Johnny Plummer, who were called "the Jimmyjohns" in their neighborhood.

See also the Catalog entry for *Simple Stories* for another probable library book written by Diaz.

DICK, THOMAS (1774–1857). *The Practical Astronomer, Comprising . . . Practical Descriptions of All Kinds of Telescopes . . . A Particular Account of the Earl of Rosse's Large Telescopes, and Other Topics Associated with Astronomy*. New York: Harper & Brothers, 1846. 437 pp.

Inscription: signed in pencil on first flyleaf: "Henry Clemens/Hannibal/Mo." Two bookplates are affixed to the front pastedown endpaper, somewhat crudely printed by letterpress. The top one reads: "The Property of/Henry Clemens/No. 2." The other bookplate reads "THE PROPERTY OF/HENRY CLEMENS/HANNIBAL MO." [the latter bookplate is partially effaced].

Provenance: formerly in the collection of Ralph Gregory (1909–2015), a former curator of the Mark Twain Birthplace Memorial Shrine in Florida, Missouri (now called the Mark Twain Birthplace State Historic Site). Gregory received the volume in 1965 from Mrs. Gertrude Shotwell of Greybull, Wyoming. Mrs. Shotwell was born Mary Gertrude Stotts in 1882, the daughter of Joseph Patterson Stotts (d. 1893). She lived with Orion and Mollie (Stotts) Clemens in Keokuk from the age of nine onward.

Location: in August 2017 the volume belonged to Ralph Gregory's daughter, Nancy Gregory Kimball, Marthasville, Missouri, who had inherited his book collection.

Copy examined: a volume owned by Clemens's younger brother Henry, who was killed in a steamboat explosion in 1858.

DICKENS, CHARLES [John Huffam] (1812–1870).

Clemens's attitudes toward Dickens resemble the pattern noticeable in his opinions about Scott, Cooper, and Poe: early admiration, even emulation, followed by increasing disenchantment until finally, in his late years, Clemens completely disavows any interest in, or influence by, the great English novelist's works. Clemens recalled in "Villagers of 1840–3" that Scott, Cooper, Dickens, Byron, and Marryat were the favorite writers in Hannibal during his boyhood (*HH&T*, p. 34). He also remembered with gratitude that one of his fellow lodgers at a St. Louis boarding house in 1853 "was fond of Dickens, Thackeray, Scott & Disraeli, & was the only reading-man in the establishment . . . equipped with fine literary apprecia-tions" (SLC to Frank E. Burrough, 15 December 1900, Southeast Missouri State College, Cape Girardeau). Albert Bigelow Paine reported that Keokuk residents recalled young Clemens's carrying "a volume of Dickens" under his arm in 1856 and 1857 (*MTB*, p. 106).

Entering a gold miner's cabin in Jackass Hill, California in January 1865, Clemens observed in Notebook 4 that the dwelling had no planking on its floor, yet he could see "Byron Shakspeare, Bacon Dickens, & every kinds of only first class Literature" (*N&J* 1: 70). During his days as a newspaper writer in California in the 1860s, however, Clemens decided that certain fellow authors were unfairly seeking immediate literary renown by "ambitiously and undisguisedly imitating Dickens," particularly Bret Harte, whose "pathetics" came straight out of Dickens's novels (14 June 1906 AD, *MTE*, p. 265; *AutoMT* 2: 119). Thereafter Harte and Dickens and issues of originality seemed inextricably linked in Clemens's mind, and his professed aversion for Dickens's writings grew more pro-nounced decade by decade. Conceivably this disaffection was furthered initially by envy of Dickens as an artist on the lecture platform, for at the time that Mark Twain was entering the lecture circuit Dickens was carrying the nation by storm with readings from his novels. Amanda Adams—"Performing Ownership: Dickens, Twain, and Copyright on the Transatlantic Stage," *American Literary Realism* 43.3 (Spring 2011): 223–241—tellingly com-pared Dickens's and Twain's approaches to their public readings. Shortly before Clemens saw Dickens perform in New York City, Clemens wrote to his family on 19 November 1867: "You bet you when Charles Dickens sleeps in this room next week, it will be a gratification to him to know that I have slept in it also" (*MTBus*, p. 94; *MTLet* 2: 104; their texts differ). Following Dickens's death, Twain published a sketch in the September 1870 issue of the *Galaxy*, "The Approaching Epidemic," pre-dicting that lecturers exploiting Dickens's fame would soon sweep through the nation. Chapter 55 of *Roughing It* (1872) refers to Dickens's notable productivity as an author. In his 1873 English journal Clemens noted with awe that "to this day people come & put flowers on the slab" beneath which Dickens was buried in Westminster Abbey (*MTLet* 5:601). In a letter to Olivia written from London on 22 December 1873 Clemens promised to look for "the Thackeray & Dickens" (*MTLet* 5: 529).

With a few exceptions, Clemens thereafter began to express reservations about Dickens's style. In 1876 Clemens complained in "Comments on English Diction" that "Sir Walter Scott and Mr. Dickens were distressingly given to using too many words" (quoted by Jervis Langdon in *Some Reminiscences* [1938], *MT in Elmira*, p. 213). Still, surveying English literature in an 1897 newspaper interview in Vienna, Clemens said he "places Dickens very high" (Odessa *News* [*Odesskie Novosti*], 8 October 1897; translated and reprinted by M. Thomas Inge and George Munro, "Ten Minutes with Mark Twain," *American Liter-ary Realism* 15.2 [Autumn 1982]: 262). William Dean

Howells's admiration for Dickens's characters (Howells would devote three chapters to Dickens in *Heroines of Fiction* [1902]) seemed not to have much effect on his friend Clemens. Joseph H. Twichell observed in 1896 that "his literary tastes are in instances surprising; e.g., he does not relish Dickens" ("Mark Twain," p. 822). An artist who painted a portrait of Clemens in London, probably around 1900, testified: "I was a little surprised to find that he had no good word to say for the works of Charles Dickens. He seemed to be quite blind to his qualities, and for the life of him he failed to see where the humour came in" (Edwin A. Ward, *Recollections of a Savage* [New York: Frederick A. Stokes Co., 1923], p. 250). During a newspaper interview published on 10 April 1904 in the New York *Times*, Twain observed, "Every generation has its own authors. Look at Dickens. At one time nothing went down that was not a little tinted with the Dickens style; now who would allow that?" (Scharnhorst, *Complete Interviews*, p. 495). And in June 1909 Clemens affected the pose of unlettered genius by claiming: "I don't know anything about anything, and never did. My brother used to try to get me to read Dickens, long ago. I couldn't do it—I was ashamed; but I couldn't do it" (*MTB*, pp. 1500–01). An apothegm by Jean de La Bruyère comes to mind from his witty *Les "Caractères" de Théophraste* (1688), a work Clemens may have known: "A man feeds on the ancients and intelligent moderns; he squeezes and drains them as much as possible; he stuffs his works with them; and when at last he becomes an author and thinks he can walk alone, he lifts up his voice against them, and ill-treats them, like those lusty children, grown strong through the healthy milk on which they have been fed, who thereupon beat their nurses."

Clemens's strenuous avowals of unfamiliarity with Dickens are contradicted by his multitudinous references to the novelist's writings, leading scholars to speculate about his motives. Minnie M. Brashear thought that Clemens's disclaimer of an early knowledge of Dickens either resulted from a lapse of memory or (which seems more likely) "boredom at the critics' insistence upon a Dickens influ-ence and his own belief that his knowledge of Dickens was too slight to justify any such critical assumption" (*MTSM* [1934], p. 212). Stephen Leacock's "Two Humor-ists: Charles Dickens and Mark Twain," *Yale Review* 24 (Autumn 1934): 118–129 commented on the "singular dissimilarity" of the two authors; Dickens's starting point was of a different kind. Edgar H. Hemminghaus, *Mark Twain in Germany* [1939], quoted Friedrich Schönemann's appraisal of the various similarities and dissimilarities shared by Dickens and Twain (p. 104). Albert E. Stone, Jr. observed that "what put Twain off was the very aspect of Dickens's fiction that made him so successful and invited imitation—his pathos" (*IE* [1961], pp. 15, 17). Harold Aspiz concluded that "most of Mark Twain's reading of Dickens took place during the years before 1870" ("Mark Twain's Reading" [1949], p. 209), but this assumption can now be modified by evidence introduced in the following entries. Howard G. Baetzhold presumed that Clemens "was merely giving way to his mood of the moment," but added that such a rejection of Dickens probably stemmed from his unconscious efforts to diminish his literary models, to appear to be an "original" (*MT&JB* [1970], pp. 304, 317). Baetzhold provided a convenient review of Mark Twain's allusions to Dickens's characters (*MT&JB*, pp. 304–317) and amplified these findings in "Mark Twain and Dickens: Why the Denial?" (*Dickens Studies Annual* 16 [1987]: 189–219), deducing that "Mark Twain's enthusiasm did cool over the years. But evidence shows that Dickens continued to occupy an important place in the reading of the whole Clemens family" (p. 215). The most comprehensive treatment of Clemens's knowledge of Dickens's novels is Joseph H. Gardner's "Mark Twain and Dickens," *PMLA* 84.1 (January 1969): 90–101, which helpfully categorized Charles Dickens's works into three groups: those Twain certainly knew, those he probably had read, and those he is not believed to have known. Gardner surveyed Clemens's lifelong references to Dickens and observed that "for over fifty years Clemens was a constant and careful reader of Dickens. . . . But his distaste for anything that suggested Dickens idolatry remained constant and unambiguous" (p. 101).

Perhaps the best gauge of the extent of this distaste is obvious in the catalog entries below: despite Clemens's lifelong preoccupation with Dickens's characters and narrative mode, relatively few books by Dickens have been identified as part of the library belonging to Clemens himself. All the same, Clemens had ready access to, and even annotated, the Dickens volumes on the Quarry Farm library shelves when he and his family spent their frequent summer sojourns there. (See the Catalog entry below for *Works of Charles Dickens*.)

———. *The Battle of Life; A Love Story*. London: G. Routledge & Sons, 1889. 255 pp.

Source: MTLAcc, entry #2216, volume donated from Clemens's library by Clara Clemens Gabrilowitsch in 1910.

———. *A Child's History of England* (first edition published 1852–1854).

Catalog: ListABP (1910), "Child's Hist. of England, Dickens", no other information supplied.

Olivia Clemens wrote to her husband on 28 November 1871 to relate that she was reading this book but finding it "almost too condensed" (ALS in MTP; quoted by Joseph H. Gardner, "Mark Twain and Dickens" (1969), p. 91; *MTLet* 4: 505 n. 7).

———. *A Christmas Carol in Prose*. Illustrated by Sol[omon] Eytinge, Jr. (1833–1905) and engravings by A[ndrew]. V[arick] S[tout]. Anthony (1835–1906). Original green cloth. Boston: Fields, Osgood & Co., 1869.

Inscription: Clemens used purple ink to write on the recto of the frontispiece: "Merry Christmas to/Our Sister/signed—Both/Buffalo, 1870."

Marginalia: Page 15 is marked, quite possibly by Susan Crane, at the point in the story where Scrooge proclaims that "every idiot who goes about with 'Merry Christmas' on his lips should be boiled with his own pudding, and buried with a stake of holly through his heart."

Provenance: Clemens and Olivia gave this book to her sister Susan Crane ten months after their marriage. Susan and Theodore Crane had just taken possession of Quarry Farm on a hillside overlooking Elmira, New York, following the death of Susan and Olivia's father Jervis Langdon in August 1870. Clemens would take his family to Quarry

Farm every summer for more than two decades and would often browse in the Cranes' library for books to read.

Location: collection of Kevin Mac Donnell in Austin, Texas (Mac Donnell to Alan Gribben, 29 November 2011).

Clemens closed a letter of 17 December 1870 to Mrs. Fairbanks with the story's famous concluding words (which Clemens placed in quotation marks), "'God bless us, every one'" (*MTMF*, p. 144; *MTLet* 4: 274). Dickens's story had first appeared in 1843.

———. *Great Expectations*. London: Chapman & Hall, n.d. 462 pp. [Novel, first published in book form in 1861.]

Source: MTLAcc, entry #2217, volume donated from Clemens's library by Clara Clemens Gabrilowitsch in 1910.

———. *The Life and Adventures of Martin Chuzzlewit*. London: Chapman and Hall, n. d. [Dickens's novel had first appeared in 1843–1844.]

Provenance: bookplate of J. Langdon Family Library #616. Clemens had access to these books whenever he visited Elmira.

Location: Mark Twain Archive, Elmira College, Elmira, New York.

Source: Mark Woodhouse's inventory list of Langdon family library books (Mark Twain Archive, Elmira College). This copy was accessible to Clemens whenever he visited the Langdon residence in Elmira.

———. *Little Dorrit*. Copyright Edition. Illustrated by H[ablot]. K[night]. Browne (1815–1882), "Phiz." Collection of British Authors Series. 4 vols. Leipzig: B. Tauchnitz, 1856–1857.

Source: MTLAcc, entries #979, #2222–2224. Volume 1 donated by Clemens; Volumes 2, 3, and 4 donated from Clemens's library by Clara Clemens Gabrilowitsch in 1910. Possibly Clemens signed Volume 1 in 1892, since the accession book erroneously listed this as the publication date for the 240-page book.

———. *Little Dorrit*. 2 vols. New York: J. W. Lovell Co., 1883.

Source: MTLAcc, entry #2221, Volume 1 only, donated from Clemens's library by Clara Clemens Gabrilowitsch in 1910.

———. *Master Humphrey's Clock*. Copyright Edition. Collection of British Authors Series. 3 vols. Leipzig: B. Tauchnitz, 1846.

Source: MTLAcc, entries #2219 and #2220, Volumes 2 and 3 only, donated from Clemens's library by Clara Clemens Gabrilowitsch in 1910.

———. *The Old Curiosity Shop*. 2 vols. London: Chapman & Hall, 1858.

Source: MTLAcc, entry #2214, Volume I only (435 pp.), donated from Clemens's library by Clara Clemens Gabrilowitsch in 1910.

———. *The Old Curiosity Shop*. 2 vols. Boston: Ticknor & Fields, 1858.

Source: MTLAcc, entry #1267, Volume II only (435 pp.), donated by Clemens.

———. *Our Mutual Friend*. London: Chapman & Hall, n.d. 523 pp.

Source: MTLAcc, entry #2215, volume donated from Clemens's library by Clara Clemens Gabrilowitsch in 1910.

———. *Our Mutual Friend*. New York: D. Appleton & Co., 1878. 340 pp.

Source: MTLAcc, entry #1266, volume donated by

Clemens.

———. *The Poems and Verses of Charles Dickens*. Ed. by Frederick George Kitton (1856–1904). New York: Harper & Brothers, 1903. 206 pp.

Source: MTLAcc, entry #1147, volume donated by Clemens.

———. *A Tale of Two Cities*. New York: J. W. Lovell Co., 1882. 352 pp.

Source: MTLAcc, entry #2218, volume donated from Clemens's library by Clara Clemens Gabrilowitsch in 1910.

———. *A Tale of Two Cities*. London: Chapman and Hall, n. d.

Provenance: bookplate of J. Langdon Family Library #96.

Location: Mark Twain Archive, Elmira College, Elmira, New York.

Source: Mark Woodhouse's inventory list of Langdon family library books (Mark Twain Archive, Elmira College). This copy of the novel was accessible to Clemens anytime he visited the Langdons' home in Elmira.

———. *Works of Charles Dickens*. Household Edition. Illustrated by F[elix]. O[ctavius]. C[arr]. Darley (1822–1888) and John Gilbert (1817–1897). 55 vols. Three-quarters bound morocco, aqua-colored marbled covers, endpapers, and edges. New York: Hurd and Houghton, 1866–1871. [The set is in very worn condition.]

Inscriptions: the front flyleaves of most volumes are inscribed in black ink "Theodore W. Crane/Dec. 25, 1870/Susie" and others have "Theodore W. Crane/Dec. 25, '70/Susie" or "Theodore W. Crane/Elmira N. Y./Dec. 25, 1870/Susie". Some inscriptions lack the name "Susie". Various volumes are additionally signed "T. W. Crane" in ink, and others similarly in pencil. In a few volumes Theodore Crane added the date, "Dec. 25, 1870."

Location: Mark Twain Archive, Gannett-Tripp Learning Center, Elmira College, Elmira, New York. Mr. and Mrs. Jervis Langdon donated the forty-two volumes in 1977. The surfacing of this large set placed virtually all of Dickens's works within Clemens's reach during his many summer visits to Quarry Farm. Clemens and his brother-in-law Theodore Crane (1831–1889) often shared reading materials. See, for another example, the Catalog entry for the Cranes' set of Shakespeare's *Works*.

Copies examined: forty-two volumes of Theodore Cranes' set of Dickens to which Clemens had access—and obviously read a number of the volumes—during his visits to Elmira. Examined in November 1986 and again on 11 August 1988. The following entries provide information about individual volumes in this set that were available to Clemens over the years whenever he stayed at Quarry Farm in Elmira, New York. Time constraints did not allow me to make note of every pencil marking that seemed to be Clemens's in each of the surviving volumes; I concentrated on comments and markings that scholars might deem most significant.

———. *American Notes for General Circulation* (travel narrative, published in 1842).

See the Catalog entry below for *Pictures from Italy and American Notes*.

———. *Barnaby Rudge*. Household Edition. 2 vols. New York: Hurd and Houghton, 1869. [Historical novel, originally published in 1841.]

Inscription: "Theodore W. Crane/Dec. 25, 1870".

Marginalia: Clemens annotated both volumes. In Volume I (1869) of *Barnaby Rudge* Clemens made small, horizontal or diagonal black pencil ticks on pages 60, 97, 105, 173, 198, 209, and 257. On page 208, beside the final paragraph containing the widow's flowery plea to God on behalf of her son's safety, Clemens made a long, wavering vertical pencil line in the margin. Someone, apparently Clemens, has listed the pages with these penciled tick marks on the rear free endpaper; evidently the purpose was to remind him where he stopped reading each time. One of the recorded page numbers, 151, begins Chapter 13 and thus did not need a tick mark in the margin at that point. In Volume II (1869) of *Barnaby Rudge* Clemens made horizontal or diagonal pencil ticks on pages 42, 134, 159, 169, 211, 255, 290, 296, 302, 308, and 312, presumably marking where he stopped reading at various times. On the rear endpaper he listed in pencil these same pages, plus 94 and 146.

Catalog: Ball 2016 inventory, green marbled cover, leather binding with gilt lettering, 2 vols.

Location: Mark Twain Archive, Elmira College, Elmira, New York.

Presumably it was Clemens himself who extracted a paragraph from a magazine article about the unavailing efforts by some American tourists to visit the Maypole Inn and pinned the clipping to a leaf in Notebook 14 (1878, *N&J* 2: 91). The essay was James Payn's "An Adventure in a Forest; or, Dickens's Maypole Inn," *Harper's Magazine* (July 1878): 298–302. Clara Clemens once recorded in her commonplace book the opinion that "'Barnaby Rudge' has no less power to interest me today than it had when I was thirteen years old" (Clara would have been thirteen in 1887), and she set down a long synopsis of, and commentary on, the novel (Paine 150, MTP). In a newspaper interview Mark Twain gave in 1895 he implied that he had read *Barnaby Rudge* as a young man: "How I used to laugh at Simon Tappertit," he remarked (Sydney [Australia] *Morning Herald*, 17 September 1895, *Complete Interviews*, p 206).

Joseph H. Gardner, "Mark Twain and Dickens" (1969), p. 91.

———. *Bleak House*. Household Edition. 4 vols. New York: Hurd and Houghton, 1870. [Novel, originally published in 1852–1853.]

Inscription: "Theodore W. Crane/Elmira, N. Y./Dec. 25, 1870".

Marginalia: Clemens made annotations in Volumes I, II, and III. Volume I contains numbers in pencil on the rear free endpaper, seemingly where Clemens stopped reading temporarily: 187, 191, 210, 222, 230, 242, 250, 277, and 292. All of those pages except 187, 242, 250, and 292 contain Clemens's horizontal or vertical tick marks to designate the precise place where his reading should resume.

Catalog: Ball 2016 inventory, green marbled cover, gilt lettering on spine, 4 vols.

Location: Mark Twain Archive, Elmira College, Elmira, New York.

Dixon Wecter anachronistically reported that Orion

Clemens published excerpts from *Bleak House* (published in 1852–1853) in his Hannibal *Journal* in 1851–1852 (*SCH*, p. 240). Joseph H. Gardner cites Wecter's biography in conjecturing that these installments "may have been the first Dickens [Sam] Clemens read" ("MT and Dickens" [1969], p. 92). Gardner misconstrued an entry in Clemens's notebook for January 1882, hypothesizing that Clemens shopped in Montreal bookstores to buy a copy of *Bleak House* for Anna Dickinson when in actuality Clemens wrote "Courting Anna Dickinson—going to educate her—buy Bleak House" (NB 19, *N&J* 2: 420) among a long list of Whitelaw Reid's supposed foibles. Clara Clemens set down lengthy character analyses and discussions of *Bleak House* in her commonplace book (Paine 150, MTP), so at least one copy of the novel entered the Clemens household.

———. *Christmas Books*. Household Edition. 2 vols. New York: Hurd and Houghton, 1866.
Inscription: "Theodore W. Crane/Elmira, New York/Dec. 25 1870".
Catalog: Ball 2016 inventory, green marbled cover, leather binding with gilt lettering, 2 vols.
Location: Mark Twain Archive, Elmira College, Elmira, New York.

———. *David Copperfield*. Household Edition. 4 vols., New York: Hurd and Houghton, 1867. [Originally published in 1849–1850 as *The Personal History of David Copperfield*.]
Inscription: "Theodore W. Crane/ Dec. 25, 1870".
Catalog: Ball 2016 inventory, green cloth with gilt lettering, rough cut pages, only Volumes III and IV are present.
Location: Mark Twain Archive, Elmira College, Elmira, New York.

Edgar M. Branch and Robert H. Hirst note that the subject of Clemens's "Jul'us Caesar" sketch (written in 1855 or 1856) "is similar to Tommy Traddles in *David Copperfield*" (*ET&S* 1: 110). One definite reference occurs in a letter Clemens wrote on 30 June 1866: "that long native word means—well, it means Uriah Heep boiled down—it means the soul and spirit of obsequiousness" Sacramento *Weekly Union*, 4 August 1866; *LSI*, p. 111). On 31 December 1867 Clemens heard Dickens read from *David Copperfield* at Steinway Hall in New York (the date established by Howard G. Baetzhold, "Mark Twain's 'First Date' with Olivia Langdon," *Bulletin of the Missouri Historical Society* 11 [1955]: 155–157); Clemens later recalled that Dickens "did not merely read, but also acted. His reading of the storm scene in which Steerforth lost his life was so vivid, and so full of energetic action, that the house was carried off its feet, so to speak" (11 October 1907 AD, *MTE*, p. 213; *AutoMT* 3: 165). Mark Twain wrote a review of the Steinway Hall reading for the *Alta California* (reprinted in *The Twainian* 6 [March-April 1948]: 3–4). Franklin R. Rogers advanced the theory that Billy's courtship of Amy in "The Boy's Manuscript," written around 1870, began as a literary burlesque of David Copperfield's doting courtship of Dora (*MTBP* [1960], pp. 102–104), a suggestion with which Howard G. Baetzhold concurred; Baetzhold contributed additional parallel details (*MT&JB* [1970], pp. 312–314). In 1875 Willie Gill accused Twain of modeling his Colonel Sellers character on Dickens's Wilkins Micawber (*MTLet* 6: 375). Clemens notified

Henry H. Rogers on 17 November 1898 that he had been approached by several London dramatists with offers to adapt one of his recent stories for the stage; "Barkis is willing," quipped Clemens, quoting Peggotty's suitor (*MTHHR*, p. 378). Mark Twain's most explicit tribute to the novel occurs in his fragmentary "Three Thousand Years Among the Microbes" (written in 1905); in Chapter 10 "Huck," a cholera germ, renames his microbe chums after his favorite literary characters—Don Quixote, Gulliver, Rip Van Winkle, and David Copperfield (*WWD?*, p. 472).
Alan Gribben, "Manipulating a Genre: *Huckleberry Finn* as Boy Book," *South Central Review* 5.4 (Winter 1988): 15–21. (A revised version of this essay appears as a chapter in Volume One of this present work.)

———. *Dombey and Son*. Household Edition. 4 vols. New York: Hurd and Houghton, 1869. [Novel, first published 1846–1848.]
Inscription: "Theodore W. Crane/Dec. 25, 1870".
Catalog: Ball 2016 inventory, 3 vols. only (I, II, and IV), green marbled cover, leather binding, gilt lettering.
Location: Mark Twain Archive, Elmira College, Elmira, New York.

Clemens wrote to his mother from Carson City, Nevada on 30 January 1862 to describe a wagon-ride to Humbolt; he and his three companions took along a few luxuries, he reported—"two dogs, Watt's Hyms [*sic*], fourteen decks of cards, 'Dombey and Son'" (quoted in *PRI*, p. 30; *MTLet* 1: 147). In a letter to William H. Clagget from Carson City on 28 February 1862 he rehearsed the tag-lines and characteristics associated with the major characters of the novel: Susan Nipper, Captain Cuttle, Mr. Toots, Biler, Florence, Major Bagstock, and Captain Jack Bunsby; then (to make sure that Clagget knew he was quoting from memory) he ended by wishing that he had the book at hand so he could continue the list (CWB; *MTLet* 1: 166–167). "As Captain Cuttle would say," Mark Twain remarked in a piece on spirit mediums that appeared in the 11 February 1866 issue of the *Golden Era* (*WG*, p. 126); aboard the *Ajax* in 1866 Clemens was amused by a boy "leaning to roll of ship like Capt. Cuttle," the name Clemens gave Captain James Smith of the *Ajax* (NB 6, *N&J* 2: 181). Meanwhile in 1865 or 1866 Olivia Langdon copied two purple passages from *Dombey and Son* into her commonplace book (DV161, MTP). In August 1885 Clemens jotted down his opinion that as a humorous character "Captain Cuttle is good anywhere," whether on the stage or in a novel (NB 24, *N&J* 3: 172). Clemens was fond of John Brougham's dramatization of *Dombey and Son* (see the Brougham entry). On 15 January 1903 Clemens mentioned Captain Cuttle in his appointment book (NB 46, TS pp. 5, 6).
Harris, *Courtship* (1996), pp. 108–112, 122–123.

———. *Great Expectations*. Household Edition. 2 vols. New York: Hurd and Houghton, 1866.
Inscription: "Theodore W. Crane/Dec. 25, 1870".
Catalog: Ball 2016 inventory, Volume I only, green marbled cover, leather binding, gilt lettering.
Location: Mark Twain Archive, Elmira College, Elmira, New York.

Dennis S. R. Welland's "Mark Twain and the Victorians," *Chicago Review* 9 (Fall 1955): 101–109 provided a starting-point for discussing the correspondences between Dickens's and Twain's masterpieces. J. M. Ridland—"Huck, Pip, and Plot," *Nineteenth-Century Fiction* 20 (December 1965): 286–290—conceded that he "cannot prove" that Mark Twain read *Great Expectations*, but argued convincingly that the "conscience" episode in Chapter 21 of *Huckleberry Finn* (1885) owes something to Pip's helping the convict Magwitch, all the time believing that he is only showing cowardice. Ridland also pointed out that a German steamer on the Thames runs over a rowboat and a galley at the conclusion of *Great Expectations*, frustrating Pip's efforts to help Magwitch escape, much as the collision of the steamboat and the raft in Chapter 16 of *Huckleberry Finn* sets back Jim's plans for obtaining his freedom. Nicolaus C. Mills, first in "Social and Moral Vision in *Great Expectations* and *Huckleberry Finn*," *Journal of American Studies* 4.1 (July 1970): 61–72, and then in *American and English Fiction in the Nineteenth Century: An Antigenre Critique and Comparison* (Bloomington: Indiana University Press, 1973), pp. 92–109, also argued for a recognition of parallels between the novels. In an Autobiographical Dictation of 30 May 1907 Mark Twain quoted Joe Gargery's optimistic phrase: "Do you know that expression, 'what larks!' It describes what I was feeling" (*AutoMT* 3: 69).

Jerome Meckier, "'What Noble Horseshoes the Man Might Have Made': Mark Twain Comments on Dickens in *Life on the Mississippi*," *Dickens Quarterly* 18.3 (September 2001): 121–128.

———. *Hard Times.* Household Edition. 2 vols. New York: Hurd and Houghton, 1870.

Inscription: "Theodore W. Crane/Dec. 25, 1870". [Novel, first published in book form in 1854.]

Marginalia: Clemens annotated these volumes.

Catalog: Ball 2016 inventory, green marbled cover, leather binding with gilt lettering, 2 vols.

Location: Mark Twain Archive, Elmira College, Elmira, New York.

Dickens's *Hard Times* implicitly criticized the social conditions in England's industrial cities.

———. *Life and Adventures of Martin Chuzzlewit.* Household Edition. 4 vols. New York: Hurd and Houghton, 1866.

Inscription: "Theodore W. Crane/Dec. 25, 1870".

Catalog: Ball 2016 inventory, green marbled cover, leather binding with gilt letter, only Volumes I, II, and IV are present.

Location: Mark Twain Archive, Elmira College, Elmira, New York.

Clemens had read the novel closely by 20 November 1860, when he wrote to his brother Orion from St. Louis, comparing the nurse who was attending Pamela Moffett after the birth of her child with Sarah Gamp and quoting Sairey's lenient views on alcoholic refreshments (*MTLet* 1: 104–105). Clemens again referred to *Martin Chuzzlewit* in a letter of 6 February 1861 to Orion, predicting a day in the future when Laura Wright "and I (like one of Dickens's characters,) are Another's" (*MTBus*, p. 57; *MTLet* 1: 112). His allusion (as Howard G. Baetzhold explained in *MT&JB* [1970], p. 305) was to Augustus Moddle's hyperbolic letter to Charity Pecksniff—"I love another. She is Another's"—in the final, fifty-fourth chapter of the

novel (obviously, therefore, Clemens had found time to read *Martin Chuzzlewit* during his stint as a Mississippi River pilot). He alluded to Mark Tapley in a letter to William Claggett written on 18 April 1862 (*MTLet* 1: 193). He may have meant *Martin Chuzzlewit* in criticizing Dickens's attempt "to produce a Yankee dialect. . . . He made his Yankee talk as no Yankee" (NB 12 [1873]), *N&J* 1: 552–553). In a speech about "The Ladies" at the Scottish Corporation of London" (1873) he included the nurse "Sairey Gamp" among a list of "sublime women" (*MTSpk*, p. 80; *MTLet* 5: 490). In an article published in the 16 July 1885 issue of the *Christian Union*, "What Ought He to Have Done? Mark Twain's Opinion," Twain referred to "Mrs. Pecksniff Twain." There are notable parallels between Martin Chuzzlewit's hopeful trip to America and Lord Berkeley's idealistic pilgrimage to the home of his plebian kin in Chapter 1 of *The American Claimant* (1892). In an interview published in the 26 September 1895 Melbourne *Evening News*, Twain recalled how "Dickens, in *Martin Chuzzlewit* and his *American Notes*, told us a great many unpleasant truths, but they were truths undoubtedly" (*Complete Interviews* [2006], p. 224). Cairo, Illinois had been a particular target in *American Notes for General Circulation* for Dickens's disillusionment with conditions along the Mississippi River, and in *Martin Chuzzlewit* Dickens portrayed Cairo as the hellish City of Eden.

Abigail Ann Hamblen, "The American Scene: Dickens and Mark Twain," *Mark Twain Journal* 12.3 (Winter 1964–1965): 9–11, 16.

———. *Little Dorrit.* Household Edition. New York: Hurd and Houghton, 1869.

Inscription: "Theodore W. Crane/Dec. 25, 1870".

Catalog: Ball 2016 inventory, green marbled cover, leather binding with gilt lettering, only Volume 3 is present.

Location: Mark Twain Archive, Elmira College, Elmira, New York.

On 18 October 1856 Clemens quoted "Mr. Clennam at the Circumlocution Office" in his third letter from Thomas Jefferson Snodgrass to the Keokuk *Saturday Post* (*TJS*, p. 12). Joseph H. Gardner ("MT and Dickens" [1969], p. 92) cited another allusion in "The Mint Defalcation," *Territorial Enterprise*, 8 January 1866. In his May 1870 *Galaxy* column Mark Twain declared: "I only know that if a man lives long enough, he can trace a thing through the Circumlocution Office of Washington" ("The Facts in the Case of the Great Beef Contract" [1870], *CG*, pp. 40–41).

———. *Martin Chuzzlewit.* (See the Catalog entry above for *Life and Adventures of Martin Chuzzlewit.*)

———. *Master Humphrey's Clock, New Christmas Stories.* Household Edition. New York: Hurd and Houghton, 1869.

Inscription: "Theodore W. Crane/Dec. 25, 1870".

Marginalia: Clemens's annotations are present. The volume displays six short remarks by Clemens in pencil; several of these object to Dickens's sense of humor. For example, on page 24, Clemens drew three parenthetical brackets in the margin and observed, "Descriptive enough but not funny—though it purports to be." This is the passage where Dickens writes: "He was a very substantial citizen indeed. His face was like the full moon in a fog, with two little holes punched out for his eyes, a very ripe pear stuck on for his nose, and a wide gash to serve for a mouth." Another Clemens comment on page 32, also in pencil, takes note of a typographical error: "Printers & proof-readers let odd blunders occur sometimes. Evidently, when this story appeared in numbers, the colon (:) closed a number. The 2 marked lines began the next number & here they've heedlessly put them in again—an awkward repetition, but a mistake easily made." (Clemens made three parenthetical brackets in the margin to mark this problem in a sentence at mid-page.) On page 50 he noted in pencil: "This must have been a pretty flat periodical, in some of its minor features." In pencil he jotted, at the end of page 77, "Pretty flat." On page 100 he inserted a vertical line and wrote, regarding the appearance of two women, "daylight must have come again." On page 113 he added a brief compliment: "good".

Catalog: Ball 2016 inventory, green marbled cover, leather binding with gilt lettering.

Location: Mark Twain Archive, Elmira College, Elmira, New York.

———. *The Mystery of Edwin Drood.* Household Edition. New York: Hurd and Houghton, 1871.

Inscription: "Theodore W. Crane/Dec. 25, 1870". [Dickens's unfinished novel was first published in 1870.]

Catalog: Ball 2016 inventory, green marbled cover, leather binding with gilt lettering.

Location: Mark Twain Archive, Elmira College, Elmira, New York.

———. *Nicholas Nickleby.* Household Edition. 4 vols. New York: Hurd and Houghton, 1867. [Originally published 1838–1839.]

Inscription: "Theodore W. Crane/Dec. 25, 1870, Elmira, NY".

Marginalia: Clemens's marginalia in Volumes II, III, and IV. Volume II has half a dozen vertical pencil marks and six notes, mostly favorable, including a comment on page 39: "We can forgive/the American Notes./Martin Chuzzlewit." On page 46 of that volume Clemens wrote, "Curious old oyster—& very natural." A vertical line in pencil at mid-page designates Mrs. Nickleby's optimistic speech to Kate. "These are the ways of good society in Montana," Clemens wrote on page 53. In Volume III Clemens drew a vertical line on page 70. On page 117 he wrote, "What *is* that everlasting whitey-brown paper?"

Catalog: Ball 2016 inventory, green marbled covers, leather binding with gilt lettering, 4 vols.

Location: Mark Twain Archive, Elmira College, Elmira, New York.

In assigning names of his favorite literary characters to his twelve microbe friends, "Huck" the cholera germ of "Three Thousand Years Among the Microbes" (written in 1905) at first calls one of them Nicholas Nickleby. But Mark Twain—probably realizing that he already had included David Copperfield and had not yet listed Don Quixote, dropped this penultimate name from the list (*WWD?*, p. 472).

———. *The Old Curiosity Shop; and Reprinted Pieces.* Household Edition. 3 vols. New York: Hurd and Houghton, 1870.

Inscription: "Theodore W. Crane/Dec. 25, 1870".

Marginalia: Clemens annotated all three volumes. There are four marginal notes in Volume I (1870), including (on

page 10): "This is that *luxury* of life, that dreamy, undefined longing that comes with the early spring—a yearning after tranquil islands in lonely seas; balmy air; the lullaby wash of wavelets upon some far-away shore—a yearning whose desire is *Heaven,* really, though the soul does not know it." On page 12 Clemens wrote "habit." as well as "*do* they *thou* people there?" On page 22 he noted, "I suppose the old miscreant is going out to gamble, now." In the same volume Clemens made a bracket on page 67 at the top two lines and (on page 72) a vertical parenthetical line just past midway down the page. In Volume III, on page 194, Clemens made a long, wavering vertical pencil line beside a paragraph describing grief as "The blank that follows death—the weary void—the sense of desolation that will come upon the strongest minds, when something familiar and beloved is missed at every turn."

Catalog: Ball 2016 inventory, green marbled cover, leather binding with gilt lettering, 3 vols.

Location: Mark Twain Archive, Elmira College, Elmira, New York.

Both Joseph H. Gardner ("Mark Twain and Dickens" [1969], p. 91) and Howard G. Baetzhold (*MT&JB* [1970], p. 307) speculated plausibly that a newspaper sketch titled "Mark Twain Overpowered" in the 2 December 1865 *Californian* (*SSix*, pp. 191–193) may be a literary burlesque of Nelly's devotion to her grandfather. Twain's piece concerns eight-year-old "Addie" and her drunken Uncle Lige.

———. *Oliver Twist.* Household Edition. 2 vols. New York: Hurd and Houghton, 1866. [Novel, originally published 1837–1839.]

Inscription: "Theodore W. Crane/Dec. 25, 1870".

Marginalia: Clemens made annotations in both volumes. In Chapter 43, Clemens made a penciled bracket in the margin on page 175 beside Fagin's remark to the effect that no one looks out for anyone's interests but his own: "Some conjurers say that number three is the magic number, and some say number seven. It's neither, my friend, neither. It's number one."

Catalog: Ball 2016 inventory, green marbled cover, leather binding with gilt lettering, 2 vols.

Location: Mark Twain Archive, Elmira College, Elmira, New York.

In February 1868 Mark Twain declared in the Washington *Intelligencer,* while criticizing the successes of Vinnie Ream in obtaining government contracts for her sculpture, that "it would take but little to turn my sympathies in favor of the Artful Dodger" (reprinted in the *Mark Twain Quarterly* 5.2 [Summer 1942]: 11; and in Cyril Clemens, *W1868,* p. 36). To William Bowen, in a letter of 23 July 1871 written in Elmira, Clemens quipped that "any such By-Law as the one you mention, was an ass," paraphrasing Mr. Bumble's ejaculation—"the law is a ass"—from Chapter 51 of *Oliver Twist* (*MTLet* 4: 438).

———. *Our Mutual Friend.* Household Edition. 4 vols. New York: Hurd and Houghton, 1866.

Inscription: "Theodore W. Crane/Dec. 25, 1870".

Marginalia: Clemens annotated all four volumes. Volume I has no markings except for a number written on the rear free endpaper: "148". Volume II of the same novel has a pencil mark on page 60, and this page is recorded on the rear free endpaper.

Catalog: Ball 2016 inventory, green marbled cover, leather binding with gilt lettering, 4 vols.

Location: Mark Twain Archive, Elmira College, Elmira, New York.

In a letter to Mrs. Fairbanks from Chicago on 7 January 1869 Clemens claimed that the odor of cigars "makes you 'drop into poetry' like Silas Wegg" in *Our Mutual Friend* (*MTMF* [1949], p. 65; *MTLet* 3: 16); Howard G. Baetzhold (*MT&JB* [1970], p. 306) discovered two other instances where Clemens employed this locution—in *W1868* [1943], p. 11 and *MTH* [1947], p. 367. In a perceptive note ("Gaffer Hexam and Pap Finn," *Modern Philology* 66.2 (November 1968): 155–156, Joseph H. Gardner corrected one of Walter Blair's source attributions. Gardner showed that Pap Finn's angry rebukes and threats upon learning that his son has been taught to read actually derived from Chapter 6 of Book One of Dickens's *Our Mutual Friend*, not from Jerry Cruncher in *A Tale of Two Cities*. The unsavory Hexam assaults his son Charley for learning how to read and write. Gardner also spotted other similar elements, including a description of drunkenness and threats with a knife.

———. *Pickwick Papers.* Household Edition. New York: Hurd and Houghton, 1866. [Originally published 1836–1837.]

Inscription: "Theodore W. Crane/Dec. 25, 1870".

Catalog: Ball 2016 inventory, green marbled cover, leather binding with gilt lettering.

Location: Mark Twain Archive, Elmira College, Elmira, New York.

In a letter of 5 December 1863 from Carson City, Mark Twain knowledgeably reviewed and praised James Stark's "recital of the speech of Sergeant Buzfuz, in the great breach of promise case of Bardell vs. Pickwick. . . . Heretofore I had looked upon that as the tamest of Mr. Dickens's performances" (*MTEnt*, p. 92). Twain presumably had Mr. Pickwick's sumptuous feasts in mind when he complained, in a mock review of Homer's *Odyssey*, that Homer "exhibits as animal a relish in describing" food, "& its preparation & annihilation, as does Mr. Dickens" (Paine 8, MTP). In a series of notes to himself set down in June, July, and August 1885 for an essay on humor, Clemens stated that he detected no humor in *Pickwick Papers* "except the kind the clown makes in the circus. . . . Every line in the book says: 'Look at me—ain't I funny!'"; "if there is a humorous passage in the Pickwick Papers, I have never been able to find it"; only the characters "in Pickw Papers, & the body-snatcher in Tale of 2 Cities" did not strike Clemens as amusing (NB 24, *N&J* 3: 163, 168, 172). In an interview published in the New York *World* on 31 May 1891, Twain remarked, "I can't read *Pickwick* as a whole, only parts of it" (*Compete Interviews*, p. 135). During an interview he gave in September 1895 in Australia he confessed that he "used to laugh" at Samuel Weller and his father, "but I can't do it now somehow" (Sydney *Morning Herald*, 17 September 1895, *Complete Interviews*, p 206).

Joseph H. Gardner, "Mark Twain and Dickens" (1969), p. 100.

———. *Pictures from Italy and American Notes.* Household Edition. 2 vols., New York: Hurd and Houghton, 1869.

[Travel sketches, originally published in 1846.]

Inscription: "Theodore W. Crane/Dec. 25, 1870".

Catalog: Ball 2016 inventory, green marbled cover, leather binding with gilt lettering, 2 vols.

Location: Mark Twain Archive, Elmira College, Elmira, New York.

Joseph H. Gardner ("MT and Dickens" [1969], p. 91) suggested that Mark Twain's description of the tomb of St. Carlo Borromeo in Chapter 18 of *The Innocents Abroad* (1869) may owe something to Dickens's account. Howard G. Baetzhold demonstrated that Twain's description of Leonardo's "The Last Supper" in Chapter 19 of *The Innocents Abroad* bears a strong resemblance to Dickens's reactions. (Dickens criticizes those who praise excellences which are no longer present) (*MT&JB* [1970], pp. 310–312). However, Robert Regan—in "Mark Twain, 'The Doctor' and a Guidebook by Dickens," *American Studies* 22.1 (Spring 1981): 35–55—urged scholars to recall how vehemently Twain objected to "borrowing from other professional, well-known writers" (p. 45). Similarities in certain passages between Dickens's and Twain's accounts of the same scenes did not occur because Twain was reading Dickens's book, Regan maintained, but resulted from the fact that Twain was relying on travel letters written by one of his favorite companions on the *Quaker City* voyage, Dr. Abraham Reeves Jackson—and it was Jackson who was relying on Dickens's narrative. "I am convinced that when they wrote their descriptions of *The Last Supper*, Jackson and not Clemens had a copy of *Pictures from Italy* open before him" (p. 40), Regan contended. Like most travelers to Italy, Dickens recorded his impressions of Vesuvius and Pompeii—two sites that always intrigued Clemens.

Indicating a familiarity with *American Notes for General Circulation*, Clemens resolved to "see Dickens for a note on Cairo" while he was returning from his Mississippi River excursion in May 1882 (NB 20, *N&J* 2: 482). Obviously he was aware that in Chapter 12 of that travel narrative Dickens had dismissed Cairo, Illinois as "a hotbed of disease, an ugly sepulchre, a grave uncheered by any gleam of promise: a place without one single quality, in earth or air or water, to commend it." But in Chapter 25 of *Life on the Mississippi* (1883) Twain prudently forbore quoting Dickens's horrific description, merely noting that "Cairo is a brisk town now; and is substantially built, and has a city look about it which is in noticeable contrast to its former estate, as per Mr. Dickens's portrait of it." In Chapter 38 of *Life on the Mississippi* Twain referred to Dickens's disapproval of the habit of Mississippi Valley residents to refer to their river steamboats as "floating palaces." Dickens's derogatory view of Twain's beloved river may have played a role in altering his attitude toward the English author. In an interview published in the 26 September 1895 Melbourne *Evening News*, Twain recalled how "Dickens, in *Martin Chuzzlewit* and his *American Notes*, told us a great many unpleasant truths, but they were truths undoubtedly" (*Complete Interviews*, p. 224).

Dewey Ganzel, "Twain, Travel Books" (1962), p. 41 n. 4.

———. *Sketches by Boz.* Household Edition. 2 vols. New York:

Hurd and Houghton, 1866. [Originally published in 1836.]

Inscription: "Theodore W. Crane/Dec. 25, 1870".

Catalog: Ball 2016 inventory, green marbled cover, leather binding with gilt lettering, 2 vols.

Location: Mark Twain Archive, Elmira College, Elmira, New York.

Mark Twain listed "Boz" among the authors esteemed by residents of ante-bellum Hannibal, Missouri. Along with Scott, Cooper, and other such writers, this literary diet induced "sentimentality and romance among young folk" which was "soft, sappy, melancholy" ("Villagers of 1840–3" [1897], Blair, *HH&T* [1969], p. 35). In an interview published in the New York *Times* on 26 November 1905 Twain spoke about the feat of switching from comic sketches to more serious writing: "Dickens had his troubles when he tried to stop jesting. The *Sketches by Boz* introduced him as a funny man. . . . But Boz and his creator kept right on being in earnest, and they listened after a time" (*Complete Interviews*, p. 518).

———. *A Tale of Two Cities*. Household Edition. 2 vols. New York: Hurd and Houghton, 1866.

Inscription: "Theodore W. Crane/Dec. 25, 1870".

Marginalia: Clemens's marginalia in both volumes. In Volume I, Clemens jotted a disparaging comment about Dickens's sense of humor (p. 76): "Dickens deliberately meant this poor stuff to be funny—& as he did not expunge it, it stands to reason that he thought it *was* funny." A criticism by Clemens of the character Jerry Cruncher appears on page 216 of Volume I: "It is a noble book; it is a pity it is degraded & disfigured by this Jerry's silly presence." In Volume II, Clemens made a vertical pencil mark on page 162.

Catalog: Ball 2016 inventory, green marbled cover, leather binding with gilt lettering, 2 vols.

Location: Mark Twain Archive, Elmira College, Elmira, New York.

"It is uncertain when Clemens first read *A Tale of Two Cities*, but it was by far his favorite" among Dickens's novels, stated Joseph H. Gardner in "Mark Twain and Dickens" (1969), p. 92. Howard G. Baetzhold (*MT&JB* [1970], p. 349 n. 29) believed that Mark Twain must have read the novel before he wrote "Open Letter to Commodore Vanderbilt" (1869), which describes Vanderbilt's careless mode of driving his carriage past pedestrians. Walter Blair developed the idea that Mark Twain might have gained an inspiration for the graveyard scene in Chapter 9 of *The Adventures of Tom Sawyer* (1876) from Book 2, Chapter 14 of *A Tale of Two Cities*, in which a frightened boy watches three body-snatchers at work in a graveyard ("French Revolution" [1957], p. 22; *MT&HF* [1960], p. 61). Howard G. Baetzhold agreed that the scene in which the junior Jerry Cruncher observes his father and two companions robbing graves must have contributed to the episode at Hoss Williams' grave in *Tom Sawyer*, especially since Clemens evidently had no personal recollection of grave robbers in Hannibal, Missouri (*MT&JB* [1970], pp. 315–316). However, Albert E. Stone, Jr. argued that "the superior skill with which Twain mixes humor and the atmosphere of terror cannot simply be attributed to . . . an unconscious debt to *A Tale of Two Cities*. . . . Any specific literary source has been kept firmly in the

background" (*IE* [1961], p. 67).

All members of Clemens's family read this novel while they sojourned in Paris in 1879 *(MTB*, p. 644); even Katy Leary, who had resisted Olivia Clemens's urging to read *A Tale of Two Cities*, finally read the book along with Mrs. Susan Crane when the family visited France (*LMT*, pp. 56–57). Walter Blair focused on the probable influence of the novel on *Adventures of Huckleberry Finn* (1885) in "French Revolution" (1957), pp. 21–35 and *Mark Twain & Huck Finn* (1960), pp. 128, 311–312; some of the passages from Dickens's novel that Blair cited were reproduced in facsimile in Hill and Blair's *The Art of Huckleberry Finn* (1962), pp. 417–427. Howard G. Baetzhold supplied additional intricate parallels in *MT&JB* [1970], pp. 149–151. Clemens cited "the body-snatcher [Jerry Cruncher] in Tale of 2 Cities" as one of Dickens's humorous creations that failed to amuse (NB 24 [August 1885], *N&J* 3: 172). Mark Twain complained about the same character, Jerry Cruncher, in an interview published in the New York *World* on 31 May 1891: "*Tale of Two Cities* . . . is a beautiful work spoilt for me by that ostensibly humorous character, Jerry" (*Complete Interviews*, p. 135). In Vienna in the late 1890s Clemens told Henry W. Fisher that on his last visit to Paris, Dickens's *A Tale of Two Cities* was one of the guides his family used in visiting "the places of horror" (*AMT*, p. 59). On another unspecified later occasion Clemens supposedly said: "I have always been a great admirer of Dickens, and his 'Tale of Two Cities' I read at least every two years. . . . I have finished 'The Two Cities' for the 'steenth time" (*AMT*, p. 60). In June 1909 Clemens reportedly told Albert Bigelow Paine: "Yes, I have read *The Tale of Two Cities*, and could do it again. I have read it a good many times" (*MTB*, pp. 1500–01). On 16 September 1909, writing from Stormfield to the Democratic politician Champ Clark of Missouri about the need for further copyright reform, Clemens brought up Dickens's name: "Last week the cablegrams said a public subscription was being taken up to save a grand-niece of Dickens's from starving. She would be sharing a vast income with Dickens's publisher if Parliament had not robbed one citizen to fatten another one" (*Sotheby's 2003*, #132).

Wesley Britton, "Carlyle, Clemens, and Dickens: Mark Twain's Francophobia, the French Revolution, and Determinism," *Studies in American Fiction* 20.2 (Autumn 1992): 197–204.

———. *The Uncommercial Traveller*. Household Edition. New York: Hurd and Houghton, 1869.

Inscription: "Theodore W. Crane/Dec. 25, 1870".

Catalog: Ball 2016 inventory, green marbled cover, leather binding with gilt lettering.

Location: Mark Twain Archive, Elmira College, Elmira, New York.

DICKERSON, MARY CYNTHIA (1866–1923). *The Frog Book: North American Toads and Frogs*. Illustrated with photographs by the author. New York: Doubleday, Page & Co., 1906. 253 pp.

Source: MTLAcc, entry #745, volume donated by Clemens.

DICKINSON, ANNA ELIZABETH (1842–1932). *A Crown of Thorns, or Ann Boleyn* (play, produced in 1876).

Clemens saw Anna Dickinson's performance in the Boston

production of this play she wrote and in which she played the title role, on 8 May 1876; the play had opened on 4 April 1876 (*MTHL*, pp. 117, 133–134). "Poor Anna Dickinson, she was high up in the popular sky then," Clemens noted in April 1909 in his copy of James Russell Lowell's *Letters* (Volume Two, page 14).

———. *A Ragged Register (Of People Places and Opinions)*. New York: Harper & Brothers, 1879.

Inscription: "Mrs. Olivia Langdon with the faithful love of Anna E. Dickinson 8/11/79". (Jervis Langdon's widow Olivia Langdon [1810–1890] was Olivia Clemens's mother.)

Catalogs: cataloged in the Quarry Farm library in the 1980s; Ball 2016 inventory, fair to good condition, inscribed by Anna E. Dickinson to Mrs. Olivia Langdon.

Location: Mark Twain Archive, Elmira College, Elmira, New York. Transferred from the Quarry Farm library to the Mark Twain Archive by Mark Woodhouse on 9 July 1987.

Copy examined: a volume belonging to Clemens's mother-in-law. Clemens had access to these volumes during his summer visits to Elmira.

In 1874 Clemens endeavored to assist Dickinson in negotiations with Elisha Bliss of the American Publishing Company, but these efforts bore no fruit (Clemens to Dickinson, 8–10 July 1874, *MTLet* 6: 180). It is not clear which of her book manuscripts Clemens sought to promote. *A Ragged Register (Of People Places and Opinions)* opens with the narrator deciding, "I want to go somewhere away from city walls and sewer smells and 'L' abominations. Of that I am sure—but *where*?" (p. 5). This intention leads to a book-length recollection (and rejection) of many cities and scenes already visited. After reviewing these memories the narrator still remains stuck in New York City, irresolute.

DICKINSON, EMILY ELIZABETH (1830–1886).

Clemens at least knew of the reclusive poet, for he quoted Thomas W. Higginson's description of her father's house in Notebook 31 (October 1891), TS pp. 8–9. That verbal picture derived from Higginson's recent article, "Emily Dickinson's Letters," which also quoted a number of her individual poems (*Atlantic Monthly* 67.4 [October 1891]: 444–456). In a letter to Clemens on 23 October 1898 William Dean Howells quoted the second stanza from Dickinson's poem about death, "The bustle in a house," identifying its source and asking Clemens rhetorically whether he was familiar with the lines (*MTHL*, p. 681).

DICKINSON, FRANCES MINTO (1820–1898). *Diary of an Idle Woman in Italy*. 2 vols. Collection of British Authors Series. Leipzig: Bernhard Tauchnitz, 1872.

Catalog: *C1951*, D1, $8, listed among books signed by Clemens.

Dickinson set a series of these *Diary of an Idle Woman* books in Italy, Sicily, Spain, and Constantinople. Libraries and biographical guides sometimes refer to her as "Frances Elliot" because she was briefly married to Gilbert Elliot (1800–1891), Dean of Bristol. Dickinson was a close friend of Charles Dickens, Anthony Trollope, and Wilkie Collins, and it is said that portions of Collins's sensation novel *Woman in White* (1860) were based on her life.

DICKINSON, GOLDSWORTHY LOWES (1862–1932). *Letters from a Chinese Official; Being an Eastern View of Western Civilization*. Brown paper boards. New York: McClure, Phillips &

Co., 1904 [cop. 1903]. 75 pp.

Marginalia: many penciled notes and markings in Clemens's hand; the comments are favorable toward Dickinson's point of view, but criticize the American government, newspapers, and missionaries (particularly William Scott Ament, 1851–1909). In pencil on the front pastedown endpaper Clemens wrote: "The first & foremost—shall we say the only?—function & mission of our civilization is to hunt up ways to multiply wants. And—consequently—to propagate hardship & worry." Clemens's annotations are characterized by his sarcastic remark on page 23: "Brother Ament, D.D., missionary pirate, is out there ameliorating this barbarism the best he can." A newspaper clipping of Lionel Strachey's satirical poem, "Progressional" (a parody of "Onward, Christian Soldiers") is pinned to the front free endpaper. Sabine Baring-Gould (1834–1924) was the author of the lyrics for the original hymn; its melody was composed by Arthur S. Sullivan (1842–1900). Arthur L. Scott quoted from Clemens's marginal notes in *Mark Twain at Large* (1969), p. 265.

Catalogs: ListABP (1910), "Letters of a Chinese Official"; "Retz Appraisal" (1944), p. 9, date of publication erroneously listed as 1914, valued at $15.

Location: Mark Twain Papers, Bancroft Library, University of California at Berkeley.

Copy examined: Clemens's copy; possibly he was initially curious about *Letters from a Chinese Official* because of the similarities to his own early pieces, "Goldsmith's Friend Abroad Again" (1870–1871).

DILKE, CHARLES WENTWORTH (1843–1911). *Greater Britain: A Record of Travel in English-Speaking Countries During 1866 and 1867* (published in 1868).

Clemens attended Dilke's dinner parties in London in the summer of 1873 and dictated "Sir Chas Wentworth Dilke's Greater Britain" into his stenographic journal (NB 12, *N&J* 1: 529). See also a note that Clemens wrote to the Dilkes in June 1873 (*MTLet* 5: 386 n. 1). Dilke's *Greater Britain* provided a sweeping panorama of the nations in which English was the predominant language, relying on his travels in the United States, Canada, Australia, New Zealand, India, and islands in Polynesia. He seemed especially concerned with the struggle between races, viewing non-English-speaking peoples as a threat. In the United States he explored the residual effects of the enslavement of African Americans in Virginia, the exclusionary nature of the Mormons in Utah, and the sound of alien languages in San Francisco's Chinatown.

Stephen Gwynn and Gertrude M. Tuckwell, *The Life of the Rt. Hon. Sir Charles W. Dilke, Bart., M. P.* 2 vols. (London: John Murray, 1918) 1: 160.

—————, ed. *Old English Plays; Being a Selection from the Early Dramatic Writers*. 6 vols. Black leather, marble boards, gilt. Extensive mold in pages. London: Whittingham and Rowland, Printed for John Martin, Bookseller, 1815.

Catalog: Ball 2016 inventory, Vols. V and VI only.

Location: Quarry Farm library shelves, under the supervision of the Mark Twain Archive, Elmira College, Elmira, New York.

These volumes would have been available to Clemens whenever he visited Elmira. When the set was complete (only the last two volumes are now present), Volume I contained

Christopher Marlowe's *The Tragedy of Dr. Faustus*. Volume V included Thomas Middleton's *Women Beware Women*. Many lesser-known playwrights were represented.

DILL, (SIR) SAMUEL (1844–1924). *Roman Society from Nero [37–68 CE] to Marcus Aurelius [121–180 CE].* London: Macmillan and Co., 1905. 639 pp. [Publisher and pages conjectured.]

Catalog: *A1911,* "thick 8vo, cloth, uncut, Lond. 1905," lot 129, sold for $1.75.

——. *Roman Society in the Last Century of the Western Empire.* Second edition, revised. Original blue cloth, gilt. Lightly stained, spine frayed, inner hinges repaired. London: Macmillan and Co., 1905. 459 pp.

Inscription: the front pastedown endpaper is signed in black ink, "S L. Clemens/Oct. 1905."

Marginalia: inked notations by Clemens on six pages totaling 105 words. In addition there are ink corrections or marks on three other pages. The corners of a dozen additional pages have been folded down. Where Dill insisted that "an age should be judged by its ideals, not by the mediocrity of conventional religion masking worldly self-indulgence" (p. 136), Clemens underlined "ideals" and wrote vertically in ink in the margin: "But evidently there were 2 sets of ideals, & apparently the per[s]ons by whom the age is to be judged were very few in number as compared with the others. See p. 141." On page 141 Dill stated, "If Salvianus be accurate, the Church must have utterly failed in raising the mass of Gallic people to a higher life," contrasting "the small class who renounced fortune and family ties at the call of Christ, and the monsters of cruel rapacity and unbridled lust described by Salvianus." Clemens noted, "That looks like good sense" on page 137, underlining in ink Dill's statement that the "unbelieving" Epicureans interpreted "the calamities of Gaul" as proving "the indifference of the Deity to the fortunes of men." On page 138 in a vertical note in the margin Clemens speculated, regarding an opinion by the ancient theologian Salvianus (ordained c. 428 CE): "Suppose Rockefeller had a thousand children & never did anything/for them, but sat at home in comfort & expected the poor to take care/of them for him? Would he find a preacher like this one to excuse him?/We couldn't ever get along without the pulpit's brilliances, I reckon." (In that passage Dill had recounted the selfish greediness of many Christian ascetics in Rome who emulated "the richest class.") On page 139 Dill describes fifth-century Rome as a period when "the churches are emptied, the holy mysteries of the altar are contemptuously deserted for the feverish excitement of the circus," next to which Clemens placed two vertical marks and wrote vertically in the margin, "Christian Spain & the bull-fight to-day." On page 223, where Dill recounts how the Roman governor Apollinaris Sidonius (430?–487) concluded his life as "a devoted Christian pastor" who "had learned to believe in the grander mission of the Christian Church," Clemens mockingly defined that institution as "the powerful Civilization-Obstructor."

Catalogs: ListABP (1910), "Roman Society, Dill" (this could possibly refer instead to the now-vanished volume listed in the previous entry above); *C1951,* #9a, $30; *Sotheby's 2003,* #199, $4,250; Robert Slotta, Admirable

Books, Hilliard, Ohio, *Twainucopia* catalog (2006), item #17, $9,500.

Provenance: in 1970 this volume was in the collection of film producer Robert Daley, Burbank, California. Subsequently it belonged to Nick Karanovich of Fort Wayne, Indiana before being auctioned by Sotheby's in 2003.

Location: currently unknown.

Copy examined: Clemens's copy, at the Sotheby's sale in 2003. Photocopies of the title page and marginalia, sent by Robert Daley in 1976 to the Mark Twain Papers in the Bancroft Library at the University of California at Berkeley, were examined on 29 August 1985. Robert Slotta's Admirable Books catalog reproduced the marginalia on pages 138, 223, and elsewhere in the Dill volume.

DILLINGHAM, CHARLES (1868–1934).

Dillingham, a Hartford-born theater critic-turned-Broadway producer, worked with Clemens throughout 1902 on a stage production titled *Huckleberry Finn,* which premiered in Hartford. A series of letters from Clemens to Dillingham indicates a friendly relationship, such as the letter Clemens sent him on 22 August 1902: "The play came, but before I could snatch a look at it Mrs. Clemens was prostrated with a so serious illness that I have been a sick-nurse ever since" (*Sotheby's 2003,* #107).

DIMSDALE, THOMAS JOSIAH (1831–1866). *The Vigilantes of Montana; or, Popular Justice in the Rocky Mountains. Being a Correct and Impartial Narrative of the Chase, Trial, Capture, and Execution of Henry Plummer's Road Agent Band, Together with Accounts of the Lives and Crimes of Many of the Robbers and Desperadoes, the Whole Being Interspersed with Sketches of Life in the Mining Camps of the "Far West"; Forming the Only Reliable Work on the Subject Ever Offered the Public.* Virginia City, Montana Territory: Montana Post Press, D. W. Tilton & Co., 1866. 269 pp. [Edition conjectured.]

On 15 September 1870 Clemens wrote to the postmaster of Virginia City, Nevada, Hezekiah L. Hosmer, asking for information about the desperado Joseph Alfred Slade (Mark Twain, *Roughing It,* ed. Harriet Elinor Smith and Edgar Marquess Branch [Berkeley: University of California Press, 1993], pp. 585–588, 811, 1034). It seems likely that the postmaster either sent him a copy of Thomas J. Dimsdale's book or at least recommended it. In any event, Twain provides the author and title in a footnote to quotations from Dimsdale's "bloodthirstily interesting little Montana book" in Chapter 10 of *Roughing It* (1872) and in Chapter 11 recommends its account of the hanging of the outlaw Slade in "the thrilling little book" as being "well worth reading." Twain quotes from Dimsdale's book far more lengthily than was his usual practice in using sources in the 1870s. His copy of *The Vigilantes of Montana* has so far not been located. Dimsdale, born in Yorkshire, England, was editor of the Montana *Post.* He would die of tuberculosis at the age of thirty-five shortly after publishing his defense of vigilante actions in the Territory of Montana.

DIRCKS, HENRY (1806–1873). *The Life, Times and Scientific Labours of the Second Marquis of Worcester. To Which is Added, A Reprint of His Century of Inventions, 1663, with a Commentary Thereon.* First edition. Contemporary three-quarter tan calf, raised bands, gilt compartments, marbled sides and end papers, top edges gilt. London: Bernard Quaritch, 1865.

Inscription: signed on the front blank flyleaf in pencil: "S. L. Clemens/Hartford, 1886."

Marginalia: two marginal lines at page 27 (near references to the introduction of coaches and hacks in London between 1625 and 1635, and an allusion to the prosecution of Galileo). Page 56 has a corner folded down. At page 164 there is a marginal line near Edward Somerset's heartfelt concern for the safety of "the lowest person of this nation."

Provenance: Clara Clemens Gabrilowitsch's library numbering shelf marks are visible on the verso of the front free endpaper: "Bw/LS 1/2".

Catalogs: *C1951*, D39; *Zeitlin 1951*, #14, $35.

Location: collection of Kevin Mac Donnell, Austin, Texas.

Source: description sent by Mac Donnell to Alan Gribben, 28 August 2017.

Paul Baender deduced that Mark Twain got from this book the idea that Edward Somerset (1601–1667), the Second Marquis of Worcester, had preceded James Watt (1736–1819) in developing a steam engine. In a footnote to Part 5 of "What Is Man?" (1906), Twain states that "the Marquess of Worcester had done all of this more than a century earlier" (*WIM?*, p. 183). Dircks was a civil engineer and inventor. He reproduced in facsimile Edward Somerset's *Century of Inventions* (1663) at the rear of this biography of Somerset, paged continuously with Dircks' text. (See also the Catalog entry for Andrew Carnegie, *James Watt*.)

DISRAELI, BENJAMIN (1804–1881), First Earl of Beaconsfield. *Alroy. A Romance.* Copyright Edition. Collection of British Authors Series. Leipzig: B. Tauchnitz, 1846. 286 pp.

Source: MTLAcc, entry #2225, volume donated from Clemens's library by Clara Clemens Gabrilowitsch in 1910. Clemens once recalled that a friend he made in 1853 while living in a St. Louis boarding house "was fond of Dickens, Thackeray, Scott, & Disraeli, & was the only reading-man in the establishment" (SLC to Frank E. Burrough, 15 December 1900, ALS, Southeast Missouri State College, Cape Girardeau). Twain's humorous speech in London about "The Ladies" (1873) joshingly referred to "our great new Scotchman, Ben Disraeli" (*MTSpk*, p. 80; *MTLet* 5: 490). In 1879 Clemens noted the name "Disraeli" in Notebook 17 (*N&J* 2: 270). The British statesman and novelist Disraeli twice served as prime minister.

———. *Coningsby; or, The New Generation.* Collection of British Authors Series. Leipzig: B. Tauchnitz, 1844. 442 pp.

Source: MTLAcc, entry #2226, volume donated from Clemens's library by Clara Clemens Gabrilowitsch in 1910.

———. *Lothair.* Loose signature of front pages. Green cloth, gilt lettering. New York: D. Appleton and Co., 1870. 371 pp.

Inscription: gilt-edged library bookplate on front pastedown endpaper: "J. LANGDON'S FAMILY LIBRARY. No. 433". The right half of the front free endpaper has been torn off vertically, as though to remove a signature or notes. This is an odd defacement unlike that in any other book Clemens is known to have handled.

Marginalia: Page 29 is folded down at the upper corner, and Clemens underlined in pencil two words in its last line, "Lord St. Jerome *loved conversation*." Clemens made a vertical pencil mark on page 30 beside the first paragraph, in which Lord St. Jerome states that he himself

sits silent during the witty conversations at his dinners because "there must be an audience." Clemens corrected the text on page 62 in pencil by crossing out the word "An" and adding the phrase "Duke of York was the" in order to complete his identification: "Duke of York was the heir-apparent to the throne". On page 63 Clemens underlined "CRECY HOUSE" in pencil and added in the margin: "now Stafford House." The top corners of pages 76, 81, 95, 103, and 110 are folded down. Some pencil marks on page 156 do not appear to be Clemens's. On page 169 Clemens made a long vertical mark from the first paragraph down to the Chapter 43 heading. There is also a vertical pencil mark on page 180 at the first paragraph. Clemens made a vertical pencil mark on page 182 at the two paragraphs beginning, "The dancing had ceased." Pages 185–192 were opened rather roughly. Clemens made a vertical pencil mark on page 188 at the paragraph beginning, "I never know." He made another vertical pencil mark on page 190 down to the Chapter 47 heading. There is a vertical pencil mark on page 196 beside its first paragraph. Page 201 is folded over at the top. There are no further markings in the volume.

Catalog: Ball 2016 inventory, green cloth, gilt lettering, J. Langdon's Family Library #433.

Location: Mark Twain Archive, Elmira College, Elmira, New York.

Copy examined: a book belonging to the Langdon family that Clemens annotated. Susan K. Harris found this volume while she was perusing the Langdon family library shelves at Quarry Farm on 15 September 1999. Clemens's handwriting and markings were verified by Alan Gribben and the volume was immediately transferred to the Mark Twain Archive at Elmira College. Examined again in the Mark Twain Archive on 17 May 2002.

———. *Tancred; or, The New Crusade* (novel, published in 1847).

Clara Clemens listed the title of Disraeli's *Tancred* in her commonplace book (Paine 150, MTP).

DISRAELI, ISAAC (1766–1848). *Curiosities of Literature: Consisting of Anecdotes, Characters, Sketches, and Observations, Literary, Critical, and Historical. With a View of the Life and Writings of the Author by His Son, the Right Hon. B. Disraeli.* Ed. by Benjamin Disraeli, First Earl of Beaconsfield (1804–1881). 4 vols. New York: A. C. Armstrong and Son, 1880. [Edition conjectured. Originally published 1791–1834, this work was available throughout Clemens's lifetime in various editions.]

Catalog: *C1951*, D31, $16, 4 vols. only, no edition supplied, listed among books signed by Clemens.

Clemens would assuredly have relished the miscellaneous nature of this collection and Disraeli's implicit insistence on the connections between literature and history. His topics included Literary Blunders, Literary Controversy, Literary Impostures, Destruction of Books, Poverty of the Learned, and Imprisonment of the Learned. We must lament the apparent loss of this set of volumes. Isaac Disraeli was Benjamin Disraeli's father.

DISTURNELL, JOHN (1801–1877). *Sailing on the Great Lakes and Rivers of America.* Philadelphia: J. Disturnell, 1874. 266 pp. [Place, publisher, date, and pages conjectured].

Franklin R. Rogers discovered that Mark Twain used this guidebook in constructing the section of *Life on* the Mississippi (1883) that describes the Upper Mississippi River. For Chapter 59 of Life on the Mississippi he "borrowed with only four minor changes the passage concerning the 'sublime Maiden's Rock'" and inserted parodies of Disturnell's phrases into the old panoramist's long-winded speech (Rogers, *MTBP*, pp. 91–93, 171 n. 63). Disturnell wrote nearly a dozen travel guides that emphasized geographical features of the United States.

Ditmars, Raymond Lee (1876–1942). *The Reptile Book: A Comprehensive Popularized Work*. Illustrated with photographs. New York: Doubleday, Page, & Co., 1907. 472 pp.
> Source: MTLAcc, entry #744, volume donated by Clemens.

Dix, Beulah Marie (1876–1970), later Beulah Marie Dix Flebbe, and **Carrie A[nna]. Harper** (1872–1919). *The Beau's Comedy*. New York: Harper & Brothers, 1902. 320 pp.
> Source: MTLAcc, entry #1541, volume donated by Clemens.
>
> Dix was a playwright, novelist, and children's author. Harper was an associate professor of English at Mount Holyoke College.

Dix, Morgan (1827–1908), comp. *Memoirs of John Adams Dix [1798–1879], Compiled by His Son*. 2 vols. New York: Harper & Brothers, 1883.
> Source: MTLAcc, entries #1760 and #1761, volumes donated by Clemens.
>
> John Adams Dix was a Major General in the Civil War who later served as a United States Senator and Governor of New York state.

Dixon, Thomas, Jr. (1864–1946). *The Leopard's Spots: A Romance of the White Man's Burden—1865–1900*. Illustrated by C[harles]. D[avid]. Williams (1875–1954). New York: Doubleday, Page & Co., 1902. 465 pp.
> Inscription: signed on the first flyleaf in black ink: "SL. Clemens/Riverdale, March 1902". No markings.
>
> Catalogs: *C1951*, D49; "Mark Twain Collection," *The Bookman*, No. 25 (1970), #330.
>
> Location: Wake Forest University, Winston-Salem, North Carolina. Donated by Nancy Susan Reynolds.
>
> Copy examined: Clemens's copy, in 1970.
>
> *The Leopard's Spots*, set in North Carolina, Boston, and New York, was the first of Dixon's trilogy of novels about the rise of the Ku Klux Klan. (*The Clansman* would be a best-seller in 1905.) Five years after Clemens died *The Leopard's Spots* would heavily influence D. W. Griffith's famous but controversial film, *The Birth of a Nation* (1915).

Dixon, William Hepworth (1821–1879). *History of Two Queens: Catherine of Aragon and Anne Boleyn*. London: Hurst & Blackett, 1873.
> Clemens entered the author, title, and publisher in Notebook 12 (July 1873, *N&J* 1: 559), presumably intending to purchase the book.

Doane, T[homas]. W[illiam] (1852–1885). *Bible Myths and Their Parallels in Other Religions: Being a Comparison of the Old and New Testament Myths and Miracles with Those of Heathen Nations of Antiquity, Considering Also Their Origin and Meaning*. Fourth ed. Illus. Front pastedown endpaper is loose. New York: The Commonwealth Co., [cop. 1882]. 589 pp.
> Inscription: signed on the front pastedown endpaper in black ink: "SL. Clemens/Innocence at Home/1908."
>
> Marginalia: profuse pencil markings and some notes begin on page 7, where "women" is altered to "woman" in a marginal note. Next to the first paragraph of page 17 Clemens made a vertical pencil mark at Doane's discussion of myths and "the historical inaccuracy" of the Biblical account of the Fall of Man. Doane explained on page 61 that Mohammed . . . declared that he had received every page of the Koran from the hand of the angel Gabriel," to which Clemens added, in black ink: "And Mrs. Eddy & her 'Science & Health.'" In the margin of page 125 Clemens inserted a comment vertically in black ink: "Apparently Jupiter was a formidably active co-respondent." In Chapter 12, "The Miraculous Birth of Christ Jesus," Clemens's pencil markings become numerous in pages 128–135. There are pencil marks on pages 128, 129, 130, 133, 134, 135, and 147. Where Doane mentioned, on page 197, that "priests, robbers, peasants, and others" bore the name "Jesus" in Biblical times, Clemens marked the passage with a pencil and in the left margin wrote in pencil, "The modern form of/the name is John Smith." Clemens crossed out "nor" on page 198 and wrote "and" in the left-hand margin in pencil. On page 223 he crossed out "mostly" and underlined "on the 25th of December." In the left margin of page 235 he wrote in pencil: "How could he refer to John only/when he said 'some?'" On page 249 Clemens changed "Narduk" to "Marduk" with black ink. (Marduk was the foremost god of ancient Babylonia.) Clemens penciled a grammatical correction on page 251 in a quotation from an ancient medal. In pencil Clemens wrote vertically in pencil in the left margin of page 267: "The human spirit of superiority—/inherited from the monkey"; on the opposite side of the same page he noted in pencil: "The Cheneys often saw Home [presumably Daniel Dunglas Home (1833–1886), the Scottish spiritualist medium who grew up in the United States from the age of nine] rise & fly at his ease/when they were all boys together. Later, [Charles] Dickens, [Thomas Henry] Huxley/& others saw Home do this." Clemens was reminded of Home's feats by a quotation Doane took from Lucian, who averred that he saw a foreigner "carried through the air in daylight, and walking on the water, and passing leisurely and slowly through the fire". At page 269 Clemens altered "earlier" to "later" with a pencil; on page 271 he wrote the German language equivalent of "well said" ("gut gesazt") in pencil beside a quotation from Celsus; on page 272, where Doane summarized dogmatic thought as "Do not examine. *Only believe*," Clemens wrote in pencil at the top of that quotation: "They still say it"; also in pencil he noted: "An early 'seance.'" Two religious leaflets were inserted at pages 278–279, a chapter where Crishna and Jesus were compared: "Creation's Story. Redemption's Glory" (four pages) and "The Bible v. Neo-Science, by Iconoclast" (a six-page pamphlet by the Universal Zetetic Society."
>
> Location: Mark Twain Library, Redding, Connecticut.
>
> Copy examined: Clemens's copy, viewed in 1970 and again in June 1982 and on 8 November 2019. Has the red ink Mark Twain Library accession number "2641".
>
> It seems significant that Clemens noted the author, title, and publisher of Doane's book on page 389 of his copy of Harry V. M. Phelips's *The Churches and Modern Thought* (1907), which Clemens signed in London in July 1907. Doane was an early advocate of the Free Thought movement

that sought to subject Biblical beliefs to tests of science and logic. This was one of the most thoroughly annotated books that Clemens's signed in his final years, though he might have acquired and read it earlier than 1908.

DOBSON, [HENRY] AUSTIN (1840–1921), ed. *The Quiet Life. Verses by Various Hands.* Prologue and Epilogue by the editor. Illustrated by Edwin Austin Abbey (1852–1911) and Alfred Parsons (1847–1920). New York, 1899.

    Catalog: *A1911*, "4to, cloth (slightly stained), gilt top, uncut, N.Y. 1899," lot 130, sold for $2.25.

    E. W. Kemble recalled that Clemens praised Edwin Austin Abbey's drawings for *The Quiet Life* (Kemble, "Illustrating *Huckleberry Finn*" [1930]).

———. *Vignettes in Rhyme and Vers de Société (Now First Collected).* [Published in London in 1873.]

    Ida Langdon (1880–1964) related how the Langdon family celebrated her grandmother's birthday one August when the Clemens girls were young: "My sister had written a little romantic comedy, really no more than a dramatic dialogue in the manner of Austin Dobson's *Vignettes in Rhyme.* Jean Clemens and I were to play its two parts, she as a fairy-tale prince, I as a milkmaid. My uncle [Clemens], who was very fond of amateur theatricals, was to coach us!" (*MT in Elmira* 2013], p. 52).

Doctrines and Disciplines of the Methodist Episcopal Church. Leather cover, flaking. New York: B. Waugh and T. Mason, for the Methodist Episcopal Church, 1833. 164 pp.

    Location: Mark Twain Library, Redding, Connecticut.

    Copy examined: when I visited the Mark Twain Library in June 1982 this volume, presumably because of its early imprint, had been shelved with books donated by Clemens and his daughter Clara Gabrilowitsch. It has the purple oval Mark Twain Library stamps but no accession number. I recommended that this unmarked volume be separated from the books that once belonged to the Clemens family. There is no reason to believe that it had any connection with them.

DODD, ANNA BOWMAN (1855–1929). *Cathedral Days: A Tour in Southern England.* Illus. Boston: Little, Brown, and Co., 1901. 390 pp.

    Inscription: inscribed in black ink on the front free endpaper: "Mrs. Clemens/Happy/New Year!/Marie Van Vorst/1902."

    Location: Mark Twain Library, Redding, Connecticut.

    Copy examined: Olivia Clemens's copy, unmarked. Has the red ink Mark Twain Library accession number "3287".

DODD, LEE WILSON (1879–1933). *A Modern Alchemist, and Other Poems.* Boston: R. G. Badger, 1906. 135 pp.

    Source: MTLAcc, entry #640, volume donated by Isabel V. Lyon, Clemens's secretary. She and Clemens often shared their reading.

DODGE, MARY ABIGAIL (1833–1896), pseud. "Gail Hamilton." *A New Atmosphere.* Boston: Ticknor and Fields, 1865. 310 pp. [Edition conjectured.]

    Dodge, a protégé of the prominent Washington politician James G. Blaine, frequently urged in her publications that American women become more independent and self-sufficient. Laura Skandera-Trombley speculated that "it is likely that Clemens was aware" of this novel about women's rights ("'The Mysterious Stranger': Absence of the Female in Mark Twain Biography," *Mark Twain's*

Humor: Critical Essays, ed. David E. E. Sloane [New York: Garland Publishing, 1993], p. 589 n. 2).

———. *Skirmishes and Sketches.* Boston: Ticknor and Fields, 1865. 447 pp.

    Source: MTLAcc, entry #912, volume donated by Clemens. A collection of widely varying essays, some amounting to literary criticism and others to brief biographies, while still others addressed myriad subjects. There is even a plea to Civil War soldiers and commanders to rein in their drunken sprees.

———. *Stumbling-Blocks.* Boston: Ticknor and Fields, 1864. 435 pp.

    Source: MTLAcc, entry #913, volume donated by Clemens. Dodge analyzes church membership, religious instruction, marital relations, and other topics in the light of Christian teachings and the perspective of real-world experience.

DODGE, MARY ELIZABETH (MAPES) (1831–1905). *Hans Brinker; or, the Silver Skates. A Story of Life in Holland.* Illus. New York: Scribner, Armstrong & Co., 1874. 347 pp.

    Source: MTLAcc, entry #1881, volume donated from Clemens's library by Clara Clemens Gabrilowitsch in 1910. Hans Brinker was one of the child figures Mark Twain wished to put into a story with many other "Creatures of Fiction" (NB 40 [June 1898], TS p. 26), but the nearest he came to employing that name was the paralyzed, deaf and dumb Johann Brinker of "No. 44, The Mysterious Stranger." Clemens wrote a letter on 18 December 1903 to Dodge, a friend of the Clemenses and the editor of *St. Nicholas Magazine*, recounting Olivia's health problems and her grueling voyage to Italy with inconsiderate passengers, adding, "I hope to meet some of them in hell yet" ("Mark Twain and Related Material," Robert T. Slotta [1998], item #93).

———. *Hans Brinker; or, The Silver Skates.* New preface by Mary Mapes Dodge. Illustrated by Allen B. Doggett (1860–1926). Mauve decorated cloth, gilt, binding designed by Maragrate Armstrong. New York: Scribner's Sons, 1897.

    Inscription: inscribed by Dodge in ink, "Albert Bigelow Paine/With the sincere compliments/of Hans & Gretel Brinker/and Mary Mapes Dodge/March 26, 1900."

    Location: collection of Kevin Mac Donnell, Austin, Texas (Mac Donnell to Alan Gribben, 14 April 2015). Mac Donnell reported that the copy is unmarked.

    Clemens had access to Paine's library books during Paine's preparations for writing his biography.

———. "Miss Malony on the Chinese Question" (sketch).

    Mark Twain's Library of Humor contained this Irish dialect piece, which had appeared in *St. Nicholas Magazine* and *Scribner's* before it was collected in Dodge's *Theophilus and Others* (1876). The sketch contains surprisingly explicit racial references.

———. *Rhymes and Jingles.* Illus. New York: Scribner, Armstrong & Co., 1875. 271 pp. The last page is missing.

    Source: MTLAcc, entry #1694, volume donated by Clemens.

DODGE, RICHARD IRVING. (1827–1895). *Our Wild Indians: Thirty-Three Years' Personal Experience among the Red Men of the Great West. A Popular Account of Their Social Life, Religion, Habits, Traits, Customs, Exploits, Etc., with Thrilling Adventures and Experiences on the Great Plains and in the Mountains of Our Wide Frontier.* Intro. by General William Tecumseh

Sherman (1820–1891). Portrait of the author. Illus. 8vo, cloth. Hartford, Connecticut: A. D. Worthington and Co., 1883. 653 pp.

Marginalia: the volume contains 375 notes by Clemens. On page 62 Clemens referred to the American Indian as being "volatile as a Frenchman, and yet patient." On page 75, Clemens wrote, "Success succeeds." He noted on page 81, "killing a husband and child (among the Indians) is no impairment of respectability." At the top of page 108 Clemens quipped, "So these fellows are always making medicine." At the bottom of the same page he wrote, also in pencil: "We have to keep our God placated with prayers, & even then we are never sure of him—how much higher & finer is the Indian's God." He again compared the Native Americans' Great Spirit with the Christian Deity on page 112: "Our illogical God is all-powerful in name, but impotent in fact; the Great Spirit is not all-powerful, but does the very best he can for his injun, and does it free of charge." Albert E. Stone quoted from these annotations in *Innocent Eye* (1961), p. 177.

Catalogs: *A1911*, "thick 8vo, cloth, Hartford, Conn., 1883, quotes representative marginalia, lot 132, sold for $25; George D. Smith, New York City, "Catalogue of Books" (1911), quotes representative marginalia, item #192, $50; "Mark Twain and Related Material," Robert T. Slotta, Admirable Books, Hilliard, Ohio (1998), item # 44, "over 350 handwritten notes," five marginalia are quoted and page 108 is reproduced in facsimile. (Slotta had notified Alan Gribben on 14 August 1997 that he possessed this volume.)

Location: currently unknown.

"Send to me, right away, a book by *Lieut. Col. Dodge, USA*, called '25 Years on the Frontier'—or some such title—I don't remember just what. . . . I think he has written only the one book; & so any librarian can tell you the title of it," Clemens wrote to his business agent Charles L. Webster on 6 July 1884. He went on to explain that he planned to "take Huck Finn out there" to the plains and mountains (*MTBus*, pp. 264–265). "I sent you Dodge's book yesterday," Webster notified Clemens on 9 July 1884 from New York (MTP). But on 10 July 1884 Clemens wrote to Webster impatiently after receiving what Webster assumed to be the volume he desired: "'Our Wild Indians' is Col. Dodge's *second* book. The title of his *first* one contains the words 'twenty-five-years,' & you will find it in the catalogue of any big library, no doubt. The present one is useful to me, but I want *that* one also" (PH in MTP). The bill for personal expenses that Webster eventually sent to Clemens on 2 September 1884 (items charged against Charles L. Webster & Co. in Clemens's name) included two of Dodge's books—*Our Wild Indians* and *Life on the Plains* [sic]—at a total cost of $3.84; both volumes were listed as having been purchased on 14 July 1884 (MTP). Walter Blair synopsized Mark Twain's acquisition, use, and disposal of these books in *Hannibal, Huck & Tom* (1969), p. 85; Twain "chiefly depended upon Dodge's books" for information about Native American depravity in writing "Huck Finn and Tom Sawyer among the Indians" in 1884 (p. 87). He also borrowed information about American Indian religious beliefs, the Germaine massacre, prairie fog, the waterspout phenomenon, and

the Native Americans' custom of not harming travelers believed to be insane (*HH&T*, pp. 87, 329–337). (In 1870 five members of the Germain family were killed by members of a raiding Cheyenne tribe and four of their daughters were taken as captives. The attack occurred near Fort Wallace, Kansas.) On page 536 Dodge graphically discussed the Native Americans' abilities to invent "new devices of torture" and to discover "how to prolong to the utmost those already known." They experimented with "the amount of whipping, cutting, flaying, and burning that he will make a human body undergo, without seriously affecting the vital power." Albert E. Stone, Jr. presumed that Twain approved of Dodge's comment on page 529 about the Native Americans' barbarity toward white female captives: "Cooper, and some other novelists, knew nothing of Indian character and customs when they placed their heroines prisoners in their hands" (Stone, *IE*, p. 179). Dodge claimed that gang-rape generally followed such captures. See also the Catalog entry for Jacob P. Dunn, *Massacres of the Mountains*.

Kerry Driscoll, *Mark Twain among the Indians and Other Indigenous People* (Oakland: University of California Press, 2018), pp. 11, 195–199, 208, 223, 227, 336, 389.

———. *The Plains of the Great West and Their Inhabitants, Being a Description of the Plains, Game, Indians, &c. of the Great North American Desert*. Intro. by William [Henry] Blackmore (1827–1878). Illus., maps. New York: G. P. Putnam's Sons, 1877. 448 pp.

Inscription: signed "S. L. Clemens, Hartford, 1877."

Catalogs: *A1911*, "thick 8vo, cloth, N.Y. 1877," quotes the signature and mentions that there are "passages marked," lot 131, sold for $14; George D. Smith, New York City, "Catalogue of Books" (1911), quotes the signature, item #100, $30.

Clemens purchased a copy of Dodge's *The Plains of the Great West and Their Inhabitants* on 21 January 1877, according to a bill he received from James R. Osgood & Co. in November 1877 (Scrapbook #10, p. 69, MTP). On 22 February 1877, when Rutherford Hayes' election seemed confirmed, Clemens wrote to Howells from Hartford that he hoped the new president "will put Lt. Col. Richard Irwin [sic] Dodge (Author of 'The Great Plains & their Inhabitants') at the head of the Indian Department. There's a man who knows all about Indians, & yet has some humanity in him" (*MTHL*, p. 172). Dodge, for whom Dodge City, Kansas was named, would go on to a military career of distinction. William Blackmore, author of the introduction to Dodge's book, was an English attorney and investor who had traveled throughout the American West and commissioned photographers to make a record of Native Americans and their culture. Financially pressed and emotionally distraught, Backmore would commit suicide a year later, on 12 April 1878.

———. *The Plains of the Great West and Their Inhabitants, Being a Description of the Plains, Game, Indians, &c. of the Great North American Desert*. Intro. by William [Henry] Blackmore (1827–1878). Illus., maps. Spine and binding are loose. New York: G. P. Putnam's Sons, 1877. 448 pp.

Marginalia: Penciled dates on the front free endpaper are not in Clemens's or Olivia's hand: "Saturday June 30, 1877./Monday December 7, 1877". Contains a pencil mark at the description of a flood on page 84. On page 431 someone other than Clemens noted, "Harlan Colfax Co." At the bottom of page 432 Clemens wrote in pencil, regarding the weakness of human nature, "This sentiment is easily understood but badly expressed." There are other penciled annotations between pages 432 and 434. A summarizing remark at the end of Dodge's Chapter 44, "Conclusion" (written at the bottom of page 440), raises the possibility that someone was recording Clemens's dictation, since it is not in Clemens's handwriting but resembles his sentiments: "Very well put forth. Such a man's relation of his experiences is worth a whole winter's talk in Congress."

Location: Mark Twain Library, Redding, Connecticut.

Copy examined: one of Clemens's copies, though it is unsigned. Has the purple oval stamps of the Mark Twain Library and the red ink Mark Twain Library accession number "2485". Examined in 1970 and again in June 1982 and also on 8 November 2019. For whatever reason, the library stamp of the Mercantile Library/New York" appears in purple ink on four pages—XIV, XV, 3, and 247. On the verso of Clemens's letter of 10 July 1884 urging Charles L. Webster to send him a copy of Dodge's "first" book, Webster wrote: "The Plains of the Great West, and Their Inhabitants/G P Putnam & Son" (PH in MTP). A statement of account that Webster sent Clemens on 2 September 1884 included charges for two "Indian Books" purchased on 14 July 1884, one of them Dodge's "Life on the Plains" (sic) (MTP). Wayne R. Kime's "Huck Among the Indians: Mark Twain and Richard Irving Dodge's The Plains of the Great West and Their Inhabitants," Western American Literature 24.4 (February 1990): 321–333 mulled over Walter Blair's opinion that Dodge might have given Mark Twain more information than he wanted about the fate of women captured by certain Native American tribes.

Blair, HH&T (1969), pp. 329–337; Baender, WIM? (1973), pp. 452, 580; James C. McNutt, "Mark Twain and the American Indian" (1978); Kerry Driscoll, Mark Twain among the Indians and Other Indigenous People (Oakland: University of California Press, 2018), pp. 195–196, 201, 212, 215, 224, 357, 389.

DODGE, THEODORE AYRAULT (1842–1909). Great Captains: A Course of Six Lectures . . . on the Art of War of the Campaigns of Alexander, Hannibal, Caesar, Gustavus Adolphus, Frederick, and Napoleon. Boston: Ticknor and Co., 1889. 219 pp.

In Notebook 18 (1889) Clemens made an entry: "Great Captains—Dodge—Ticknor" (N&J 3: 450).

DODGSON, CHARLES LUTWIDGE (1832–1898), pseud. "Lewis Carroll." Alice's Adventures in Wonderland. Illustrated by Peter Newell (1862–1924). New York: Harper & Brothers, [cop. 1901]. 187 pp.

Source: MTLAcc, entry #439, volume donated by Clemens. On an undated photograph of Clemens that he autographed in Hartford to Messrs. Pemberton-Hinks, Clemens inscribed a sentiment—"Quarrels begun with roses breed no bloodshed!"—that conceivably alluded to Chapter 8, "The Queen's Croquet-Grounds," in which three playing-card gardeners fall to quarreling while painting white roses red. Clemens recalled that in 1879 he found Dodgson, whom he met in England, to be "the stillest and shyest full-grown

man I have ever met except 'Uncle Remus'" (AutoMT 2: 232). Olivia Clemens wrote to Clemens in March 1880 that she and the children "are almost half through 'Alice in Wonderland'" (ALS in MTHM, quoted in S&MT, p. 118). In 1895 Mark Twain told an Australian reporter that he had always regarded Lewis Carroll as "a true and subtle humorist" (Sydney Morning Herald, 17 September 1895, quoted in MT&JB, p. 36; Scharnhorst, Complete Interviews, pp. 205–206). In October 1908 Twain referred to "the immortal Alice"—a phrase that he had also used in an Autobiographical Dictation on 22 March 1906 (AutoMT 1: 433)—in a letter to Francis Wilson praising L. M. Montgomery's Anne of Green Gables (quoted in advertising for the Montgomery book in the back pages of its later editions). Twain enjoyed the Cheshire Cat, but (like many of us) had difficulty remembering which of Dodgson's books this character appeared in; he saw a young woman pianist in London in November 1896 who, following her performance, mustered "a machine-made smile, & it could have sat for the portrait of the Cheshire Cat in Alice in the Looking Glass. Wonderland?" (NB 39, TS p. 20). He alludes again to the grinning feline from Chapter 6 of Alice in Wonderland in Chapter 30 of "No. 44, The Mysterious Stranger" (written 1902–1908): "she smiled quite Cheshirely (my dream-brother's word, he knew it was foreign and thought it was future, he couldn't be sure)" (MSM, p. 381).

———. Alice's Adventures in Wonderland. Illustrated by W[illiam]. H[enry]. Walker (1865–1940). Color pictorial boards. London: John Lane/The Bodley Head; New York: John Lane Co., [1907]. [First edition with these illustrations.]

Inscriptions: inscribed on the front free endpaper, "From Mark Twain's Library sale/bought by Prof. John Ward Stimson/& presented to his/dear little niece/Miss Helen Edith Nightingale/on Christmas/1911." (Dan Beard conducted book sales in August 1910 and August 1911 to benefit the Mark Twain Library in Redding, Connecticut.) Artist, author, and lecturer Stimson (1850–1930) was a summer resident of Redding during those years. Stimson's niece Helen Edith Nightingale (1904–1991) was seven years old when she received this book; she made pencil notations in a childish hand on the rear free endpaper: "E/E--/Edith N." On the front pastedown endpaper is pasted an original photograph of Clemens and Albert Bigelow Paine playing billiards with an inscription to its right: "Mark Twain/at Redding/Conn./playing/billiards/with his/secty." Below Stimson's inscription to his niece on the front free endpaper is the later bookplate of Stan Marx (1920–1994), a resident of Darien, Connecticut and a founder of the Lewis Carroll Society. Marx's son would recall in 2017 that his father purchased the volume at a Darien, Connecticut library sale in the 1950s or 1960s.

Location: collection of Kevin Mac Donnell, Austin, Texas. All information derives from a letter from Mac Donnell to Alan Gribben, 6 April 2017. Mac Donnell reported that there are no markings in the volume and also no stamps or markings of the Mark Twain Library in Redding; nonetheless the book clearly has connections with Clemens, Stormfield, and Redding.

Though the illustrations for this edition found a permanent place in the Alice's Adventures in Wonderland parade of famous artworks, W. H. Walker became better known as the London architect William Henry Romain-Walker.

———. *The Hunting of the Snark, and Other Poems and Verses.* Illustrated by Peter Newell (1862–1924). New York: Harper & Brothers, [cop. 1903]. 248 pp.

Source: MTLAcc, entry #412, volume donated by Clemens.

———. [Another identical copy.]

Source: MTLAcc, entry #2051, volume donated from Clemens's library by Clara Clemens Gabrilowitsch in 1910.

———. *Rhyme? And Reason?* Illus. Original red pictorial cloth, gilt. New York: MacMillan, 1884. 214 pp. Sixty-five illustrations by A[rthur]. B[urdett]. Frost (1851–1928) and nine by Henry Holiday (1839–1927). [Fantasy and humorous poems, six of them "published for the first time."]

Inscription: the front flyleaf is inscribed in ink, "Ida Langdon/From S. L. C." The initials could either refer to Samuel L. Clemens or Susan Langdon Crane, but Crane seems the more likely presenter because it was Olivia Clemens who usually inscribed the books they gave to the Langdon children. (Ida Langdon was the daughter of Charles Jervis Langdon and Ida Clark Langdon, and was a playmate of the Clemens daughters.) Clemens made free use of the Langdon family library when he was in town.

Provenance: this volume belonged to the Langdon family library.

Location: collection of Kevin Mac Donnell, Austin, Texas (Mac Donnell to Alan Gribben, 29 November 2011).

———. *Through the Looking-Glass, and What Alice Found There.* By Lewis Carroll. Illustrated by John Tenniel (1820–1914). Thirty-ninth thousand. New York: Macmillan & Co., 1875. 224 pp. [The novel was first published in 1871.]

Inscription: the front pastedown endpaper is inscribed in Olivia Clemens's handwriting: "Daisy Warner—/from Mrs. Clemens/Christmas, 1876."

Location: Mark Twain House and Museum, Hartford, Connecticut.

Copy examined: an unmarked gift volume from Olivia Clemens, indicative of the esteem in which Lewis Carroll's books were held by the Clemenses. Examined in August 1987.

A nonsense poem in Carroll's *Through the Looking-Glass,* "Jabberwocky," stuck in Clemens's mind. The Hartford *Courant* reported on 14 December 1876 that Clemens was scheduled to auction off, for the benefit of a charity, a collection of whimsical tree stump and root sculptures created by Julia Jones Beecher; Clemens playfully called them "Jabberwocks" (Barbara Schmidt, www.twainquotes.com). In a letter to their sculptor on 30 May 1880 about an assortment of these figures assembled in his drawing-room, Clemens remarked: "They are real creatures out of Wonderland," he declared, "secretly alive, natural, proper, and ungrotesque to eyes used to them in the world they came from—and so they take the fiction all out of the Jabberwock and I recognize and accept him as a fact" (*S&MT,* p. 119; date corrected by the Mark Twain Project editors; "Jabberwock Letter," *Mark Twain Society Bulletin* 1 [February 1978]: 1, 3). Clemens auctioned these items on Saturday, 5 June 1880 (Fears, *Day by Day* 1.2: 1880). Susy Clemens longed for *Through the Looking-Glass* while passing idle hours (*"read, sew, read, sew"*) in Florence, she wrote to Clara on 29

April 1893 (TS in Harnsberger Collection; *S&MT,* p. 331; PH in MTP). See also the Catalog entry for Annis Ford Eastman, *A Flower of Puritanism (Julia Jones Beecher) 1826–1905,* which reprinted Clemens's letter to Beecher on pages 61–62.

———. *Through the Looking-Glass and What Alice Found There.* Illustrated by Peter Newell (1862–1924). Ivory white cover, gilt. New York: Harper & Brothers, 1902. 211 pp.

Inscription: signed on the front pastedown endpaper in black ink: "SL Clemens/1902".

Provenance: Antenne-Dorrance Collection, Rice Lake, Wisconsin.

Location: Mark Twain Archive, Gannett-Tripp Learning Center, Elmira College, Elmira, New York.

Copy examined: Clemens's copy, unmarked. Examined on 28 May 2015.

———. *Through the Looking-Glass and What Alice Found There.* Illustrated by Peter Newell (1862–1924). New York: Harper & Brothers, [cop. 1902]. 211 pp.

Source: MTLAcc, entry #419, volume donated by Clemens.

DODS, JOHN BOVEE (1795–1872). *Spirit Manifestations Examined and Explained. Judge [John Worth] Edmonds [1816–1874] Refuted; or, An Exposition of the Involuntary Powers and Instincts of the Human Mind.* New York: De Witt & Davenport, [cop. 1854].

Inscription: signed in pencil on the front pastedown endpaper: "Orion Clemens."

Provenance: formerly in the collection of Ralph Gregory (1909–2015), a curator of the Mark Twain Birthplace Memorial Shrine, Florida, Missouri (now named the Mark Twain Birthplace State Historic Site). Mr. Gregory was given the book by Mrs. Mary Gertrude (Stotts) Shotwell of Greybull, Wyoming in 1965. (See the Catalog entry for Thomas Dick's *The Practical Astronomer* for an explanation of the provenance.)

Location: in August 2017 the volume belonged to Ralph Gregory's daughter, Nancy Gregory Kimball, Marthasville, Missouri.

Copy examined: Orion Clemens's copy, presumably read by his brother but never actually in Samuel Clemens's library. The American spiritualist Judge John Worth Edmonds was an early supporter of the Fox sisters and the Rochester rappings; he subsequently practiced as a medium himself.

DOLE, NATHAN HASKELL (1852–1935). *Peace and Progress, Two Symphonic Poems: The Building of the Organ; Onward.* Limited and numbered edition. Boston: Privately printed [by The Plimpton Press], 1904.

Inscription: "S. L. Clemens, 1905."

Catalog: *A1911,* "thin 8vo, vellum, uncut, Bost. 1904, Japan paper, limited and numbered edition," quotes the signature, lot 133, sold for $3.25.

[DÖLLINGER, JOHANN JOSEPH IGNAZ VON (1799–1890) and JOHANNES N. HUBER (1830–1879), pseud. "Janus."] *The Pope and the Council. By Janus. Authorized Translation from the German.* Boston: Roberts Brothers, 1870.

Catalog: *A1911,* "12mo, cloth, Bost. 1870," with a sheet of Clemens's notes that listed authors ("Prescott, Parkman, Moore,' etc.") laid in, lot 252, sold for .50¢.

Döllinger and Huber attacked the doctrine of papal infallibility in the Catholic Church.

DONNELL, ANNIE HAMILTON (1862–1943). *Rebecca Mary.*

Illustrated by Elizabeth Shippen Green (1871–1954). New York: Harper & Brothers, 1905. 193 pp. [Publisher and pages conjectured.]

Inscription: signed on the front pastedown endpaper: "S. L. Clemens, 1905."

Catalog: *A1911*, "12mo, cloth, N.Y. 1905," quotes the signature, lot 134, sold for $3.

———. *The Very Small Person*. Illustrated by Elizabeth Shippen Green (1871–1954). New York: Harper & Brothers, 1906. 193 pp.

Source: MTLAcc, entry #1593, volume donated by Clemens.

DONNELLY, IGNATIUS (1831–1901). *Atlantis: The Antediluvian World*. New York: Harper & Brothers, [cop. 1882]. 490 pp.

Source: MTLAcc, entry #1715, volume donated by Clemens.

Drawing on various ancient sources, Donnelly launched the myth that a lost, now-submerged continent with a superior civilization engendered all subsequent civilizations.

———. *Caesar's Column. A Story of the Twentieth Century*. Chicago: F. J. Schulte & Co., [cop. 1890]. 367 pp.

Source: MTLAcc, entry #122, volume donated by Clemens.

In a prophetic view of New York City in 1988, Donnelly imagined a technologically advanced but dehumanized and nightmarish society that deserved to be overthrown.

———. *The Great Cryptogram: Francis Bacon's Cipher in the So-Called Shakespeare Plays*. Chicago: R. S. Peale & Co., 1888. 998 pp.

In a letter written to Fred J. Hall on 9 July 1887 from Elmira, Clemens deleted a sentence that mentioned a forthcoming book: "<Couldn't we get Ignatius Donelly's [sic] Shakspeare-cipher book? . . .> No—we don't want it" (*MTBus*, p. 384). But later Clemens insisted that he had very much wanted to publish *The Great Cryptogram*, and in a letter to Orion Clemens on 7 September 1887 he blamed Charles L. Webster ("probably never heard of Bacon & didn't know there was a controversy") for losing this opportunity (MTP; *AutoMT* 3: 604). Susy Clemens wrote to Edward H. House on that day about "a great discussion in our family at the present time, upon . . . the authority of Shakespeares plays. . . . Mama revolts at the mere idea, but papa favors Bacon, & so do I" (*AutoMT* 3: 604). An entry in Clemens's Notebook 27 in November 1887 reiterates Webster's alleged failure in this regard (*N&J* 3: 347).

Clemens was interested in Donnelly's theories even apart from their publishing prospects, however; he had probably read *The Great Cryptogram* by the time he jotted down Donnelly's name and the phrase "Bacon-Shakspere" in Notebook 27 in September 1887 (*N&J* 3: 309), since he soon began to make notes for a burlesque that would prove Milton actually wrote *Pilgrim's Progress* (*N&J* 3: 325–328). Alex Beringer saw evidence of Twain's familiarity with Donnelly's *Great Cryptogram* in *Tom Sawyer's Conspiracy*, which Twain wrote sometime between 1894 and 1898 ("The Politics of Puffery in *Tom Sawyer's Conspiracy*," *Mark Twain Annual 14* (2016): 114–126). In 1909 Clemens testified that he both "published" and "read" Donnelly's book when it first appeared in 1888; he found it then "an ingenious piece of work," but nearly everyone scoffed at it. Though Donnelly's acrostics did not entirely convince

Clemens, he was enormously impressed by the point Donnelly made about Shakespeare's never having used any Stratford scenes in his plays and poems (11 January 1909 AD, MTP; *AutoMT* 3: 299).

DONWORTH, GRACE (1857–1945), pseud. "Jennie Allen." *The Letters of Jennie Allen to Her Friend Miss Musgrove*. Illustrated by Frederic R[odrigo]. Gruger (1871–1953). Boston: Small, Maynard and Co., 1908. 291 pp.

Source: MTLAcc, entry #2227, volume donated from Clemens's library by Clara Clemens Gabrilowitsch in 1910.

Donworth, an artist living in Machias, Maine, deliberately misspelled many words in this clever but fictional correspondence. According to documents in the Maine State Library, it was Donworth's brother, a Boston attorney, who called the letters to Twain's attention. In an Autobiographical Dictation of 5 October 1906 Mark Twain termed these letters "an innocent fraud, . . . since they make pleasant reading and can harm no one. They are to be multiplied and a book is to be made of them" (*AutoMT* 2: 247). In a letter written a day earlier Twain had offered his assistance in locating a publisher for the amusing jest (*AutoMT* 2: 569–570). An advertising flyer for Donworth's book in 1908 quoted praise by Mark Twain: "Here is a letter written by a woman right out of her heart of hearts. There's no spelling that can begin with it [sic] on this planet outside of the White House." Twain's words in the flyer were extracted from a speech he made to the Associated Press on 19 September 1907 advocating Andrew Carnegie's Simplified Spelling system. Twain quoted an example of Jennie Allen's cacography to demonstrate that her thoughts were perfectly understandable even though they were grossly misspelled. Albert Bigelow Paine's biography summarized the minor hoax and Twain's amused reaction to it (*MTB*, pp. 1318–1319).

DORÉ, [PAUL] GUSTAVE (1832–1883) and BLANCHARD JERROLD (1826–1884). *London: A Pilgrimage*. Illus. London: Grant & Co., 1872. [Edition conjectured; the *C1951* sale merely listed "London, by Gustave Dore and Blanchard, Jerrold (Ill.)."]

Catalog: *C1951*, D73, signed by Clemens.

Doré's drawings captured with notable realism both the metropolitan glory and the wretched poverty of the English capital. Jerrold supplied the prose text. In Clemens's English journals of 1872 he marvels over the paintings and prints he viewed in the Gustave Doré Gallery in London (*MTLet* 5: 614–621). He mentions Doré's illustrations in Chapters 34 and 50 of *A Tramp Abroad* (1880), Chapter 1 of "The Stolen White Elephant" (1882), and in Notebook 39 (26 September 1896), TS p. 3.

DOUBLEDAY, FRANK NELSON (1862–1934). [A publisher's anecdote about Mark Twain.]

Frank N. Doubleday recalled that when his New York City office was still at Sixteenth Street and Union Square, "Mark Twain drifted in, smoking a cigar that could be smelled a mile. . . . He began to look around among the volumes on the shelves. . . . Mark went around and found a book he wanted, took out a pencil and wrote on the flyleaf, *To my friend, Samuel L. Clemens, with the kind regards of F. N. Doubleday*, put it under his arm, and disappeared" (*The Memoirs of a Publisher* [Garden City, New York: Doubleday & Co., 1972], p. 88). One candidate for what Doubleday regarded as this "good joke" might be the copy of *Memoirs of M. de Blowitz*, published by Doubleday, Page & Co., that Clemens inscribed in1903 (see the Blowitz entry), even though Clemens wrote its inscription in ink rather than pencil.

DOUBLEDAY, NELLIE BLANCHAN (DE GRAFF), PSEUD. "NELTJE BLANCHAN" (1865–1918). *Bird Neighbors: An Introductory Acquaintance with One Hundred and Fifty Birds Commonly Found in the Gardens, Meadows, and Woods about Our Homes.* Intro. by John Burroughs (1837–1921). Illus. New York: Doubleday, Page & Co., 1898. 234 pp.

> Inscription: "Susan L. Crane/Quarry Farm/Dec. 25, 1899". [Obviously a Christmas gift.]
> Catalog: Ball 2016 inventory, brown cloth, gray lettering, good condition.
> Location: Quarry Farm library shelves, under the supervision of the Mark Twain Archive, Elmira College, Elmira, New York.

Nellie Blanchan De Graff married the prominent American publisher Frank N. Doubleday in 1886 but elected to write her nature books under the pseudonym of Neltje Blanchan. Clemens had access to this work during his last visits to Quarry Farm in Elmira.

———. *Bird Neighbors: An Introductory Acquaintance with One Hundred and Fifty Birds Commonly Found in the Gardens, Meadows, and Woods about Our Homes.* Intro. by John Burroughs (1837–1921). Illus. New York: Doubleday, Page & Co., 1904. 234 pp.

> Catalog: Ball 2016 inventory, brown cloth, gray lettering, good condition.
> Location: Quarry Farm library shelves, under the supervision of the Mark Twain Archive, Elmira College, Elmira, New York.

Clemens had access to this work during his last visits to Quarry Farm in Elmira.

———. *Bird Neighbors. An Introductory Acquaintance with One Hundred and Fifty Birds Commonly Found in the Gardens, Meadows, and Woods about Our Homes.* Intro. by John Burroughs (1837–1921). New York: Doubleday, Page & Co., 1908. 234 pp.

> Source: MTLAcc, entry #746, volume donated by Clemens.

———. *Birds That Every Child Should Know.* Illustrated with photographs. New York: Doubleday, Page & Co., 1907. 281 pp.

> Source: MTLAcc, entry #480, volume donated by Clemens.

———. *Nature's Garden: An Aid to Knowledge of Our Wild Flowers and Their Insect Visitors.* Illustrated with photographs by Henry Troth (1860–1945) and A[rthur]. R[adclyffe]. Dugmore (1870–1955). New York: Doubleday, Page, & Co., 1907. 415 pp.

> Source: MTLAcc, entry #739, volume donated by Clemens.

———. *Wild Flowers: An Aid to Knowledge of Our Wild Flowers and Their Insect Visitors.* Illus. New York: Doubleday, Page & Co., 1904. 415 pp.

> Catalog: Ball 2016 inventory, Nature Library, Vol. IX.
> Location: Quarry Farm library shelves, under the supervision of the Mark Twain Archive, Elmira College, Elmira, New York.

Clemens had access to this work during his last visits to Quarry Farm in Elmira.

DOUGLASS, FREDERICK (c. 1818–1895).

It would be hard to believe that Clemens did not encounter one of the versions of Douglass's famous slave narrative—see quite possibly *Life and Times of Frederick Douglass, Written by Himself* (1881). In any event, on 12 January 1881 Clemens wrote to President James A. Garfield on Douglass's behalf, asking that Douglass be reappointed Marshall of the District of Columbia, a post he had held since 1877. "I so honor this man's high and blemishless character," Clemens wrote, "and so admire his brave, long crusade for the liberties and elevation of his race. He is a personal friend of mine" (*MTL* [1917] 1: 393–394). Douglass instead received the office of Recorder of Deeds, which he filled until 1886.

Lucinda H. MacKeithan, "Huck Finn and the Slave Narratives: Lighting Out as Design," *Southern Review* 20.2 (April 1984): 247–264.

DOWDEN, EDWARD (1843–1913). *The Life of Percy Bysshe Shelley* (published in 1886).

In a letter postmarked on 3 April 1893 Susy Clemens wrote to her college friend Louise Brownell that she was reading "Life of Shelley at present and find it the most interesting of biographies. . . . I am especially drawn toward Harriet, who seems to me a gracious and pathetic figure," she reported. "Shelley I am sure wasn't quite sane but he *is* adorable!" (Hamilton College Archives). A subsequent letter to Brownell, postmarked in Venice, Italy on 10 April 1893, added that the biography "leaves a sad, sad impression behind it. How cruel that poets cannot learn to adjust the requirements of their dreams and ideals to the real actual life they must live" (Hamilton College Archives). Mark Twain's "In Defence of Harriet Shelley" (1894) castigated Dowden's biography as "a literary cake-walk" and a "fat diet spread for the righteous." He again criticized Dowden's book in a letter of 17 July 1901 (Richard Cary, "In Further Defence of Harriet Shelley: Two Unpublished Letters by Mark Twain," *Mark Twain Journal* 16.4 [Summer 1973]: 13).

Paul Baender, "Mark Twain and the Byron Scandal" (1959), p. 478; Sydney J. Krause (*MTC* [1967], pp. 99–105); Alex Brink Effgen, "Mark Twain's Defense of Virtue from the Offense of English Literature: Matthew Arnold and Percy Shelley," *Mark Twain Annual 11* (2013): 77–95.

———. *Shakspere: A Critical Study of His Mind and Art.* New York: Harper & Brothers, n. d. 386 pp.

> Source: MTLAcc, entry #1396, volume donated by Clemens.

Dowden first published this book in London in 1875. Harper & Brothers (the publisher of the copy Clemens owned) brought out editions of *Shakspere: A Critical Study of His Mind and Art* in 1880 and 1906. Both had 386 pages, so it is unclear which one of these Clemens possessed.

DOWNES, ALFRED MICHAEL (1862–1907). *Fire Fighters and their Pets.* Illus. New York: Harper & Brothers, 1907. 185 pp.

> Source: MTLAcc, entry #517, volume donated by Clemens.

———. *Fire Fighters and Their Pets.* Illus. New York: Harper & Brothers, 1908. 185 pp.

> Source: MTLAcc, entry #1184, volume donated by Clemens.

"DOWN IN TENNESSEE" (minstrel song). Lyrics sometimes

credited to T. H. Tooker. Tune: "Down on the Farm."

Clemens recalled "Way down in Tennessee" when making a list of older song titles in 1878 (NB 16, *N&J* 2: 212). There are several songs containing that phrase, but only "Down in Tennessee" employs the exact words "'way down in Tennessee" as a conclusion to each of its four stanzas as well as the chorus. "Down in Tennessee" is a sentimental lament by a formerly enslaved man, emancipated upon his master's death, who "left dat good ole home 'mid other scenes to roam." Formerly he had a good life: "It was in dat happy clime whar' its sunny all the time,/And de mocking birds in de trees, sing merrily." He remembers those bygone days fondly: "Den no thought ob sorrow ebber troubled me;/In de fields I'd sing all day for my heart was light and gay/On de ole plantation, 'way down in Tennessee."

DOWTY, A[GLEN]. A. (1847–1902?) [and **SAMUEL ORCHART BEETON** (1830–1877), **GEORGE ROSE EMERSON**, and **EUSTACE CLARE GRENVILLE** (1824–1881)]. *The Coming K--: A Set of Idyll Lays.* London: S. O. Beeton, 1873. 245 pp.

Michael Claxton observed that this parody of Tennyson's *Idylls of the King*, like Mark Twain's *A Connecticut Yankee in King Arthur's Court* (1889), connects Merlin "with the world of Victorian conjuring" and criticizes "magic that exploits superstition" ("*A Connecticut Yankee* and Victorian Magic," *Philological Review* 30.1 [Spring 2004]: 1–14). However, apparently no record survives of Clemens's ownership of or contact with this book.

DOYLE, (SIR) ARTHUR CONAN (1859–1930).

That Mark Twain derived satisfaction from burlesquing Doyle's Sherlock Holmes detective stories is well known. Walter Blair believed that Twain "had an ambivalent attitude toward detectives and detective stories. He admired brilliant deductions," yet "he was irked by pretentious and arrogant detectives in life and in books" (*HH&T* [1969], p. 155). Howard G. Baetzhold agreed that "what especially irked him . . . was Doyle's insistence on the almost supernatural intellectuality of his detective" (*MT&JB* [1970], p. 299). As true as these observations may be, however, it cannot be denied that Twain mainly objected to other people's detectives—those of Pinkerton and Doyle, particularly—and gave indications in *Pudd'nhead Wilson* (1894) and other stories that he wished for his own characters to master the complex art of reasoning by deductions. Moreover, Twain was always on the lookout for materials to burlesque (a holdover habit from his days as a West Coast journalist), and for him literary burlesque did not necessarily signify intense disrespect; often it was merely his instinctive method of paying literary homage to a famous work.

Though Clemens donated a now-lost 1904 edition of *A Study in Scarlet, and the Sign of the Four* to the community library he helped found in Redding, apparently not a single copy of Doyle's detective books has survived from Clemens's personal library. Consequently Howard G. Baetzhold (*MT&JB*, pp. 299, 300–304, 381 n. 15) and other scholars have performed a fair amount of their own detective-sleuthing in efforts to determine which of Sherlock Holmes' feats has parallels in each of Mark Twain's burlesques. Cases have been made for adding Doyle's principal earlier books to Clemens's reading log:

A Study in Scarlet (1887), *The Sign of the Four* (1890), *The Adventures of Sherlock Holmes* (1892), *The Memoirs of Sherlock Holmes* (1894), and *The Hound of the Baskervilles* (1902). Jeanne Ritunnano, "Mark Twain vs. Arthur Conan Doyle on Detective Fiction," *Mark Twain Journal* 16.1 (Winter 1971–1972): 10–14 observed that the plot of *A Study in Scarlet* "imposes order on human events," whereas Twain's "A Double-Barrelled Detective Story" "chooses life-like disorder over artificial unity" (p. 13). W. Keith Kraus, "Mark Twain's 'A Double-Barrelled Detective Story': A Source for the Solitary Oesophagus," *Mark Twain Journal* 16.2 (Summer 1972): 10–12, likewise focused on Doyle's *A Study in Scarlet*. Kraus blamed "part of the failure" of Twain's "Double-Barrelled" story on his decision to imitate "Doyle's intricate structure."

However, most of Twain's references to Holmes are too general in nature to allow exact identification of parallel passages. Certainly he seemed to have Holmes in mind when he described "Simon Wheeler, Detective" (written 1877–1898?) as "a born detective," unlike "the 'booky' one, that brilliant, sagacious, all-seeing, all-divining creation of the great modern novelists" (*S&B*, p. 438). Perhaps Twain got from Sherlock Holmes his notion to have the wise man deduce from the camel's footprints that it is lame in Chapter 7 of *Tom Sawyer Abroad* (1893–1894). The sleuthing procedures in *Pudd'nhead Wilson* (1894) probably owe something to Holmes' exploits. In *Tom Sawyer, Detective* (1894) Huck Finn is the Dr. Watson-chronicler of the mystery's solution. The Australian aborigine, Twain insists in Chapter 17 of *Following the Equator* (1897), can detect minute differences "not detectible by you or me, or by the late Sherlock Holmes." (In the December 1893 issue of *Strand Magazine* Doyle had temporarily killed Holmes in the "The Adventure of the Final Problem.")

Walter Blair traced influences of Doyle's "Silver Blaze" (collected in *The Memoirs of Sherlock Holmes*) and "The Boscombe Valley Mystery," as well as *The Sign of the Four*, that are evident in "Tom Sawyer's Conspiracy," written 1897–1900 (*HH&T*, pp. 158–159). Twain wrote to Henry H. Rogers about his inspiration for writing "A Double-Barrelled Detective Story": "I happened upon a text for a story. . . . It is a burlesque of Sherlock Holmes" (6 September 1901, *MTHHR*, p. 469). Howard G. Baetzhold presumed that Clemens was referring to the first installment of *The Hound of the Baskervilles*, which had appeared in the August 1901 issue of *Strand Magazine* (*MT&JB*, p. 299); this conjecture seems likely, for on 8 September 1901 Clemens alluded to "the recent resurrection" of Sherlock Holmes in a letter to Joseph H. Twichell, telling Twichell that "the seed" for "A Double-Barrelled Detective Story" (published in 1902) "was planted in your house, many years ago, when you sent me to bed with the book of a new author, not heard of by me until then—Sherlock Holmes. I planned to make fun of that pompous sentimental 'extraordinary man' with his cheap & ineffectual ingenuities—but the plan wouldn't sprout. . . . But this time I've pulled it off" (*MTB*, p. 1139; *LMTJHT*, p. 288). Howard G. Baetzhold argued that the "seed-book" Twichell pressed upon Twain was Doyle's *A Study in Scarlet* (1887), which has much of its setting in Utah, concerns a "human bloodhound," and is also somewhat "double-barrelled" in its structure, like Twain's story (*MT&JB*, pp. 300–304). Sherlock Holmes is introduced as a character in Chapter 6 of "A Double-Barrelled Detective Story" (1902), yet his nephew Fetlock Jones asserts that Holmes "can't detect a crime except where he plans it all out beforehand and arranges the clews"; the miners in Hope Canyon yearn for a look at "the great scientific detective," but Holmes proves adept only in arranging theatrical effects and he is thoroughly humiliated in Chapter 8. Twain evidently intended to mention Sherlock Holmes in "The Secret History of Eddypus" (written 1901–1902), because he wrote his name among his B-2 working notes (*FM*, p. 469). In 1905 he entered A. Conan Doyle's name in Notebook 48 (TS p. 1), and in 1905 or 1906 he recalled hearing a joke about Sherlock Holmes' reaching heaven and identifying Adam and Eve, because they had no navels (NB 48, TS p. 11). James S. Leonard saw possible links with Doyle's detective in Twain's last major literary effort ("*No. 44, The Mysterious Stranger*: The Final Soliloquy of a 'Littery Man,'" *Centenary Reflections on Mark Twain's No. 44, The Mysterious Stranger*, ed. Joseph Csicsila and Chad Rohman [Columbia: University of Missouri Press, 2009], pp. 172–173).

———. *The Crime of the Congo* (polemical exposé, published in 1909).

Doyle mentioned sending a copy of this book in a letter to Clemens on 9 October 1909, and Clemens began a reply on [15] October 1909 ("I have received your book, 'The Crime of the Congo'"), but only half-completed his letter assailing King Leopold's atrocities (MTP). On 29 October 1909 Albert Bigelow Paine wrote to Doyle to explain that because of Clemens's heart disease he "does not permit himself to read any matter pertaining to the cruelties practiced there. . . . Mr. Clemens thanks you most sincerely for the booklet you sent, and for your cordial letter" (*Sir Arthur Conan Doyle: Centenary 1859–1959* [London: John Murray, 1959], p. 73).

———. *The Great Shadow; A Novel*. New York: Harper & Brothers, 1893. 218 pp.
Source: MTLAcc, entry #2228, volume donated from Clemens's library by Clara Clemens Gabrilowitsch in 1910.
Doyle set this historical novel on the English-Scottish border during the Napoleonic wars.

———. *Rodney Stone*. New York: D. Appleton and Co., 1896.
Inscription: C. J. Langdon/The Waldorf/Nov. 25/96" [Charles Jervis Langdon, 1849–1916].
Catalog: Ball 2016 inventory, red cloth, silver lettering, good condition, signed by C. J. Langdon.
Location: Quarry Farm library shelves, under the supervision of the Mark Twain Archive, Elmira College, Elmira, New York.
This historical novel was accessible to Clemens when he visited the Langdons in Elmira, *Rodney Stone* is set in the Regency era and largely concerns prize fighting. There is also a gothic mystery involved.

———. *Round the Red Lamp; Being Facts and Fancies of Medical Life*. New York: D. Appleton and Co., 1894.
Inscription: C. J. Langdon [Charles Jervis Langdon, 1849–1916].
Catalog: Ball 2016 inventory, red cloth, gold and silver lettering, fair condition, signed by C. J. Langdon.
Location: Quarry Farm library shelves, under the supervision of the Mark Twain Archive, Elmira College, Elmira, New York.
A collection of fifteen short stories that was accessible to Clemens when he visited the Langdons in Elmira. A red lamp signified the office of a general practitioner in England. The contents range from graphic medical procedures, including amputations and the treatment of sexual diseases, to outright fantasy tales.

———. *The Stark Munro Letters; Being a Series of Twelve Letters Written by J. Stark Munro, M. B., To His Friend and Former Fellow-Student, Herbert Swanborough, of Lowell, Massachusetts, During the Years 1881–1884. Edited and Arranged by A. Conan Doyle*. Illus. Red cloth, gold and silver lettering. New York: D. Appleton and Co., 1895.
Inscription: C. J. Langdon/The Waldorf/Nov. 25/96" [Charles Jervis Langdon, 1849–1916].
Catalog: Ball 2016 inventory, good condition.
Location: Quarry Farm library shelves, under the supervision of the Mark Twain Archive, Elmira College, Elmira, New York.
A novel, partially based on Doyle's early days in medical practice, that was accessible to Clemens when he visited the Langdons in Elmira.

———. *A Study in Scarlet, and the Sign of the Four*. New York: Harper & Brothers, 1904. 287 pp.
Source: MTLAcc, entry #1543, volume donated by Clemens.

———. *The War in South Africa: Its Cause and Conduct*. New York, 1902.
Inscription: signed on cover: "S. L. Clemens."
Catalog: *A1911*, "12mo, original wrappers, N.Y. 1902," quotes the signature, lot 137, sold for $1.

DRAKE, FRANCIS SAMUEL (1828–1885). *Dictionary of American Biography* (published in 1872).
"Examine Drake's & Allibone's Dictionaries of Authors to see who *have* been humorists," Mark Twain reminded himself in 1880 when he began contemplating an anthology of humor (NB 19, *N&J* 2: 364).

———. *Indian History for Young Folks*. Illus. New York: Harper & Brothers, [cop. 1884]. 479 pp.
Source: MTLAcc, entry #1186, volume donated by Clemens.
Drake recounts the "heroic, but hopeless, struggle for self-preservation" (p. 5) of the Native Americans from their first contact with Europeans up to what he terms the "Recent Indian Wars." Although he concludes by urging his readers to read Richard Irving Dodge's *Our Wild Indians* (1883), Drake shows a surprising amount of empathy (for that day) for the defeated people who are his subject. "We cannot help sympathizing in some degree with the Indian in his patriotic effort to preserve his country" (p. 5), he concedes, though he goes on to deplore the depredations carried out by tribal raids against white settlers. Since Drake sketches the Native Americans' customs as well as the major battles and massacres, this book should be added to Mark Twain's potential resources for the fragmentary "Huck and Tom among the Indians" manuscript he began in 1884.

DRAKE, JOSEPH RODMAN (1795–1820). "The American Flag"

(poem, published in 1836).

Mark Twain copied the last four lines from this poem, beginning, "Forever float that standard sheet," into Notebook 5 (*N&J* 1: 146). See also the Catalog entry for *Ocean Scenes; or, The Perils and Beauties of the Deep*, which contained this patriotic poem by a young American poet who died early of tuberculosis.

DRAKE, SAMUEL ADAMS (1833–1905). *The Heart of the White Mountains, Their Legend and Scenery.* Illustrated by W[illiam]. Hamilton Gibson (1850–1896). New York: Harper & Brothers, 1882. 318 pp.

Source: MTLAcc, entry #1227, volume donated by Clemens.

Dramatists of the Restoration. [Ed. by James Maidment (1793–1879) and William Hugh Logan.] 14 vols. Limited edition of 450 copies. Edinburgh: W. Paterson, 1872–1879. [Contains dramatic works by Aston Cokain (1608–1684), John Crowne (1641–1712), William D'Avenant (1606–1668), John Lacy (1615?-1681), Shackerley Marmion (1603–1639), John Tatham (fl. 1632–1664), and John Wilson (1626–1696).]

Catalogs: *A1911*, "13 vols., 12mo, cloth, uncut, Edinb. 1875, Paterson's fine edition with historical notes," lot 138, sold for $10 total; *Lexington 1912*, 13 vols., lot 10, sold for $20 total.

DRAPER, JOHN WILLIAM (1811–1882). *History of the Intellectual Development of Europe.* Revised Edition, in Two Volumes. New York: Harper & Brothers, [cop. 1876].

Inscriptions: title pages of Volume I and Volume II signed in pencil at the top: "Ida C. Langdon". Ida Clark Langdon (1849–1934) was married to Charles Jervis Langdon (1849–1916).

Provenance: bookplates #560 (Volume I) and #561 (Volume II) of the "J. Langdon Family Library" on the front pastedown endpapers.

Catalog: Ball 2016 inventory, J. Langdon's Family Library #560, 2 vols, red cloth with gilt lettering.

Location: Mark Twain Archive, Elmira College, Elmira, New York.

Copy examined: unmarked copies accessible to Clemens whenever he visited the Langdons in Elmira. Examined on 27 May 2015.

———. *Human Physiology, Statistical and Dynamical; or, The Conditions and Course of the Life of Man.* Illus. New York: Harper & Brothers, 1856. 649 pp. [Place, publisher, date, and pages are conjectured.]

Catalog: *C1951*, D3, $7.50, listed as signed by Clemens. Clemens's early life was so peripatetic that it is difficult to imagine him taking this book along on his travels; it might have been a later acquisition. Still, its early date of publication should be taken into account in reconstructing Clemens's possible early reading. Born in England, the American physician, research scientist, and historian John William Draper sought corroboration of various then-current theories. *Human Physiology* contained many curious "facts," such as the assertion that the "total weight" of all Americans is "two thousand six hundred and thirteen millions of pounds" (p. 541). His remarks on women must have seemed old-fashioned even by the 1880s: their personalities, he wrote, illustrate "phrenological predominance of the moral over the intellectual regions of the brain" (p. 546). But Clemens found a flattering

description to send to the ill Olivia on 31 March (1903?): "Hear Dr. Draper writing about you prophetically, thirty years ago [*sic*], in his great work on 'physiology,' chapter on Woman." Clemens then quotes a passage about the "beautiful qualities" of women, who remain devoted to their husbands until, "at the close of a long life checkered with pleasures and misfortunes," the aged man finds that "her affection alone is unchanged, true to him in sickness as in health, in adversity as in prosperity, true to the hour of death" (ALS in MTP).

DREISER, THEODORE (1873–1943). *Sister Carrie.* First edition. Original red cloth, lettered in black. New York: Doubleday, Page & Co., 1900.

Inscription: inscribed by Albert Bigelow Paine, "This is a copy of the first edition of Dreiser's first book. It is now quite valuable, I believe. A. B. P. 1930." (Paine was essentially correct; only 456 copies of this first Doubleday, Page edition were sold.)

Location: collection of Kevin Mac Donnell, Austin, Texas.

Source: letters from Kevin Mac Donnell to Alan Gribben, 20 March 2014 and 3 June 2015. Mac Donnell explained that this unmarked volume was "probably acquired by Paine by the time he moved in with Twain to become his official biographer in 1906 . . . and like other books in Paine's library, [was] available to Twain for reading. It is also possible that Frank Doubleday sent this copy directly to Twain just as he did with other Doubleday publications at that time, or that Frank Norris (who was then employed by Doubleday as a reader and had urged publication of the novel) included Twain among the 129 to whom he sent publicity copies, hoping for an endorsement." Mac Donnell noted that Frank Doubleday helped Clemens obtain a New York City apartment in October 1900 when he returned to the United States after five years abroad, indicating the closeness of their relationship at that time.

In "Mark Twain: Three Contacts," *Esquire* 4 (October 1935): 22, 162, 162A-162B, Dreiser claimed to have had three meetings with Twain (or "three direct contacts," as Dreiser refers to them) in New York City in 1894, 1900, and 1907–1908. Dreiser was supposedly seeking to confirm his suspicions that Twain was more at odds with the genteel literary establishment than generally appeared. He also allegedly saw him on two other occasions in public settings, making a total of five encounters—once briefly on a New York City street, a few years later when he called at Twain's house on Tenth Street but failed to get the interview he was seeking, then sometime between 1905 and 1907 in the back room of a New York City saloon (when Twain was supposedly drunk and garrulous), and subsequently at two different public dinners at which Twain was sober. Bernard DeVoto and other Mark Twain scholars have expressed skepticism about whether several (or perhaps any) of these meetings actually took place. One reason for doubt is Dreiser's assertion that during his third talk with Clemens (the one in the saloon) the famous humorist supposedly complained about his marital misery (Dreiser to H. L. Mencken, 2 December 1920, *Letters of Theodore Dreiser: A Selection* [Philadelphia: University of Pennsylvania Press, 1959], pp. 305–306).

See also Thomas P. Riggio, "Mark Twain and Theodore Dreiser: Two Boys Lost in a Cave," *Mark Twain Journal*

19.2 (Summer 1978): 20–25, an examination of parallels in the authors' lives and writings; and "From 'Mark Twain: Three Contacts,'" *Mark Twain Journal* 42.2 (Fall 2004): 30–31, which reprinted Dreiser's reminiscences about Clemens that appeared in the October 1935 issue of *Esquire*.

DRESSEL, C[ONSTANTINE]. M. F. *The Cuban Spanish American War, Sketched by C. M. F. Dressel*. New York: Dressel Co., 1898. 12 pp.

> **Inscription:** on the title page: "To Mark Twain (S. L. Clemens)/C. M. F. Dressel. Nov. 16/98."
>
> **Marginalia:** Clemens scrawled on the cover in pencil: "Keep it," and underlined in pencil several lines in the footnotes.
>
> **Location:** Mark Twain Papers, Bancroft Library, University of California at Berkeley.
>
> **Copy examined:** Clemens's copy.

DRESSER, AMOS (1812–1904). *Narrative of Amos Dresser; with Stone's [Asa A. Stone, 1810–1835] Letters from Natchez, an Obituary Notice of the Writer, and Two Letters from Tallahassee, Relating to the Treatment of Slaves*. New York: American Anti-slavery Society, 1836. 42 pp. [One of seven pamphlets bound as a volume with W. E. Channing's *Letter to J. G. Birney* (1837).]

> **Catalog:** *A1911*, "Narrative of Amos Dresser, N.Y., 1836," lot 76, sold for $2 total.

DRESSER, HORATIO WILLIS (1866–1954). *The Heart of It. A Series of Extracts from "The Power of Silence" and "The Perfect Whole."* Ed. by Helen Campbell (1839–1918) and Katharine Westendorf. New York: G. P. Putnam's Sons, 1901. 145 pp.

> **Source:** MTLAcc, entry #670, volume donated by Clemens.
>
> Dresser espoused the principles of spiritual healing and eventually joined the New Thought movement. His father had quarreled with Mary Baker Eddy over her reliance on Phineas P. Quimby's ideas.

DREYFUS, ALFRED (1859–1935). *Lettres d'un Innocent; The Letters of Captain Dreyfus to His Wife*. Trans. from the French by L. G. Moreau. Portraits. Dark blue cloth, gray lettering, red design. New York: Harper & Brothers, 1899. 234 pp.

> **Catalog:** Ball 2016 inventory, dark blue cloth, gray lettering and red design, fair condition, "material removed."
>
> **Location:** Quarry Farm library shelves, under the supervision of the Mark Twain Archive, Elmira College, Elmira, New York.
>
> This book was accessible to Clemens when he visited Quarry Farm in Elmira.

DREYFUS, LILIAN GERTRUDE (SHUMAN) (b. 1876). *From Me to You*. Boston: Lee and Shepard, 1898. 92 pp.

> **Source:** MTLAcc, entry #873, volume of poems donated by Mrs. Ralph W. Ashcroft (formerly Isabel V. Lyon), Clemens's secretary. She and Clemens often shared reading materials.

DRUMMOND, HAMILTON (1857–1935). *A Man of His Age*. Illustrated by J[ohn]. Ambrose [De] Walton (1874–1963). New York: Harper & Brothers, 1900. 303 pp.

> **Source:** MTLAcc, entry #1544, volume donated by Clemens.
>
> Advertised as a historical romance set in the Huguenot wars of the sixteenth century.

DRUMMOND, HENRY (1851–1897). *"Beautiful Thoughts" from Henry Drummond*. Comp. by Elizabeth Cureton. New York: James Pott & Co., 1892. 280 pp.

> **Source:** MTLAcc, entry #930, volume donated by Clemens. Selections from Drummond's writings arranged in a calendar form.

———. *The Greatest Thing in the World. An Address*. London: Hodder and Stoughton, 1890. [Edition conjectured.]

> Albert Bigelow Paine reported that the Scottish evangelical writer and lecturer Drummond called on Clemens in Hartford (*MTB*, p. 661). This visit took place on 30 September 1887, when Drummond found the humorist to be highly amusing, "droll," respected, aesthetic, and altruistic (George Adam Smith, *The Life of Henry Drummond* [New York: Doubleday & McClure Co., 1898]; Fears, *Day by Day 2*: 213–214). Perhaps the newspaper publicity attendant upon Drummond's death on 11 March 1897 aroused Clemens's interest in the efforts of Drummond to reconcile science and theology; in London in April 1897 Clemens listed four of Drummond's books in his notebook: "Natural Law in the Sp. ⊠/Ascent of Man/ Pax Vobiscum/ Greatest Thing in the World" (NB 41, TS p. 21). Clemens requested copies of these same books in an undated postcard sent to Andrew Chatto of Chatto & Windus on 16 or 18 April 1897 (Berg).

———. *The Lowell Lectures on the Ascent of Man*. London: Hodder and Stoughton, 1894. [Edition conjectured.]

> **Catalog:** *C1951*, O3, listed as containing Olivia Clemens's signature. Clemens noted the title in Notebook 41 (April 1897) and requested a copy of the book in an undated postcard to Andrew Chatto of Chatto & Windus in London (Berg).

———. *Natural Law in the Spiritual World*. London: Hodder and Stoughton, 1883. [Edition conjectured.]

> Clemens recorded the title in his notebook in April 1897 (NB 41, TS p. 21) and requested the work in an undated postcard to Andrew Chatto (Berg). In 1898 Clemens had access in Kaltenleutgeben, Austria to an edition of "419 pages" ("The Great Republic's Peanut Stand," unpublished manuscript, MTP).

———. *Pax Vobiscum. An Address*. London: Hodder and Stoughton, 1890. [Edition conjectured.]

> Clemens made note of the title in April 1897 (NB 41, TS p. 21) and requested Andrew Chatto to send him a copy of the book (undated postcard, Berg). *Pax vobiscum* is a Latin salutation in the Catholic Mass, "Peace be with you."

DRUMMOND, WILLIAM HENRY (1854–1907). *The Great Fight. Poems and Sketches*. Ed. by May Isobel (Harvey) Drummond (1869–1939). Illustrated by Frederick Simpson Coburn (1871–1960). Green cloth, gilt. New York: G. P. Putnam's Sons, [cop. 1908]. 158 pp.

> **Inscription:** in pencil on the front flyleaf: "Clara Clemens/ from J. B. Learmont."
>
> **Provenance:** Antenne-Dorrance Collection, Rice Lake, Wisconsin.
>
> **Location:** Mark Twain Archive, Gannett-Tripp Learning Center, Elmira College, Elmira, New York.
>
> **Copy examined:** Clara Clemens's copy, unmarked. Examined on 28 May 2015.
>
> The dialect verses of this Irish-born Canadian poet were greatly enjoyed in his day.

———. *The Habitant, and Other French-Canadian Poems*. Intro. by Louis Fréchette (1839–1908). Illustrated by Frederick

Simpson Coburn (1871–1960). New York: G. P. Putnam's Sons, 1902. 137 pp. [Publisher 's name supplied.]

Inscription: signed "S. L. Clemens, Riverdale, Jan. 1903."

Catalogs: *A1911*, "thin 8vo, cloth, N.Y. 1902," quotes the signature, lot 139, sold for $7.50; George D. Smith, New York City, "Catalogue of Books" (1911), quotes the signature, item #103, $12.

Dryden, John (1631–1700).

Mark Twain named John Dryden in 1865 as one of those responsible for "all the poetry that everybody admires and appreciates, but nobody ever reads or quotes from" (*Californian*, 17 June 1865, quoted in *LAMT*, p. 142; *ET&S* 2 [1981], p. 195).

Drysdale, William (1852–1901). *The Mystery of Abel Forefinger*. Harper's Young People Series. Illus. New York: Harper & Brothers, 1894. 208 pp.

Source: MTLAcc, entry #1451, volume donated by Clemens.

This work of young adult fiction takes two boys on adventures in Mexico and the West Indies. The "mystery" of the character named Abel Forefinger turns out to be his invention of a way to manufacture and preserve flour made from bananas.

DuBarry, Marie Jeanne Bécu (1743–1793). *Memoirs of Madame DuBarri*. Translated from the French [of Baron Étienne Léon de Lamothe-Langon] by the translator of "Vidocq" [Henry Thomas Riley (1816–1878)]. 4 vols. New York: Merrill and Baker, n.d. [Edition conjectured.]

The Comtesse DuBarry was the last mistress of King Louis XV, who lived from 1721 until 1764. Pleading for mercy, DuBarry was beheaded during the French Revolution. William Dean Howells sent Clemens the first three volumes of an unspecified DuBarry edition on 21 December 1877, promising to send the fourth as soon as he regained it from a borrower (*MTHL*, p. 211). The Mark Twain Papers in the Bancroft Library at the University of California at Berkeley contain thirteen pages of extracts from DuBarry's *Memoirs* (DV416), formerly inserted in a family scrapbook dated 1878–1879 (Scrapbook #21, MTP) and written in purple ink by Orion Clemens on the Crystal-Lake Mills writing paper that Twain used between 1876 and 1880. Presumably Orion copied the passages at his brother's direction. One quotation from Volume 1 tells of the discovery of the putrefied bodies of Madame de Mellamière's lovers; the second passage from the same volume describes more commonplace events in the French court. The citations (except for one mistake by the copyist in citing page 43 instead of page 41 for the first-named passage) accord with the pagination of the edition listed for this entry. DuBarry's *Memoirs* may be the book Clemens meant when he wrote Edward H. House on 14 January 1884 that he had recently diverted himself by reading "in English, . . the second volume of The Autobiography of a Whore" (CWB). Mark Twain planned to credit DuBarry in his projected appendix to *A Connecticut Yankee in King Arthur's Court* for "Lettres de cachet" forms and "Castle d'If" (NB 29 [1889], *N&J* 3: 505). Henry W. Fisher mentioned hearing Clemens refer at least once to DuBarry's *Memoirs* (*AMT*, p. 64).

Du Chaillu, Paul Belloni (1835–1903). *The Country of the Dwarfs* (published in 1872).

Catalogs: ListABP (1910), "Country of Dwarfs, Du Chaillu"; *C1951*, #50a, $40, listed among books containing marginalia by Clemens, edition unspecified.

An account of African explorations.

———. *Wild Life Under the Equator. Narrated for Young People.* Illus. New York: Harper & Brothers, [cop. 1866]. 363 pp.

Source: MTLAcc, entry #1174, volume donated by Clemens.

Duff-Gordon, Lucie (Austin) Lady (1821–1869). *Letters from Egypt*. Edited by Janet Ann Duff-Gordon Ross (1842–1927). Intro. by George Meredith (1828–1909). New York: McClure, Phillips & Co., 1904.

Marginalia: two pencils marks on page 23 and two more pencil marks on page 25.

Catalog: ListABP (1910), "Letters from Egypt, Gordon," no other information provided.

Provenance: has the shelf marks of Clara Clemens Gabrilowitsch's library numbering system that she employed during her Detroit years. It was sold at the 1951 auction in Hollywood but not listed in the hastily prepared sale sheet.

Catalog: "Property from the Library of Mark Twain," Butterfield & Butterfield, San Francisco, Sale 6613 (16 July 1997), lot 2712.

Location: Mark Twain House and Museum, Hartford, Connecticut.

Copy examined: Clemens's copy. Viewed in Hartford in 1997.

Lady Duff-Gordon traveled to a warm climate hoping to mitigate the effects of a fatal disease and sent back memorable letters. On 14 October 1892 Susy Clemens wrote to her college friend Louise Brownell from Florence, Italy about meeting "Miss Duff Gordon granddaughter of the Lady Duff Gordon who wrote those interesting *Travels in India* [*sic*]" (Hamilton College Archives). Witter Bynner testified that Janet Duff-Gordon Ross's American publisher, McClure, Phillips & Company, sent her Clemens's "enthusiastic comment" about her edition of Lady Duff-Gordon's *Letters from Egypt*, which Clemens had called "a literature in themselves." She replied, "I am expecting Mr. Clemens here next month" (Bynner, *Prose Pieces*, ed. James Kraft [New York: Farrar Straus Giroux, 1979], p. 39).

Dugmore, Arthur Radclyffe (1870–1955). *Bird Homes. The Nests, Eggs, and Breeding Habits of the Land Birds*. Illus. New York: Doubleday, Page & Co., 1902. 183 pp.

Inscription: signed in black ink on the front free endpaper, "Jean Lampton Clemens/Riverdale on the Hudson/November 18th 1902."

Location: Mark Twain Library, Redding, Connecticut. Donated from Clemens's library by Clara Clemens Gabrilowitsch in 1910 (MTLAcc, entry #1946).

Copy examined: Jean Clemens's copy, unmarked. Has the red ink Mark Twain Library accession number "3836"—evidently an error.

———. *Bird Homes. The Nests, Eggs, and Breeding Habits of the Land Birds*. Nature Library. Illus. New York: Doubleday, Page & Co., 1904.

Catalog: Ball 2016 inventory, Quarry Farm library, current location undetermined.

Available during Clemens's final visits to Quarry Farm

in Elmira.

———. *Nature and the Camera. How to Photograph Live Birds and Their Nests, Animals, Wild Game.* Illus. New York: Doubleday, Page & Co., 1902. 126 pp.

Inscription: inscribed on the front pastedown endpaper in black ink: "To Jean Clemens/from me,/her Father,/ Sept. '03."

Location: Mark Twain Library, Redding, Connecticut. Donated from Clemens's library by Clara Clemens Gabrilowitsch in 1910 (MTLAcc. entry #1945).

Copy examined: Jean Clemens's copy, unmarked. No accession number is visible.

DUMAS, ALEXANDRE (1802–1870), known as Dumas *père*. *Celebrated Crimes* (published in Paris in 1839–1840).

Dumas's *Celebrated Crimes* collects the details of eighteen famous cases, including two crimes that would have especially intrigued Clemens—"Martin Guerre" and "The Man in the Iron Mask." Walter Blair pointed out that in Chapter 35 of *Adventures of Huckleberry Finn* (1885) Tom Sawyer seems to know how a prisoner could write on a shirt, something that happened in Dumas's *The Man in the Iron Mask* as well as in *The Count of Monte Cristo* ("The French Revolution and *Huckleberry Finn*" [1957], p. 26 n. 31). Kevin Michael Scott, in "'There's More Honor': Reinterpreting Tom and the Evasion in *Huckleberry Finn*,'" *Studies in the Novel* 37.2 (Summer 2005): 187–207, observed that Tom Sawyer's casting "Jim as the prisoner in *The Man in the Iron Mask*, a man imprisoned because of his face," created "a powerful metaphor for the place of African Americans after the Civil War" (p. 194). The 2003 Mark Twain Project edition of *Adventures of Huckleberry Finn* (pp. 446–447) traced other parallels between *The Man in the Iron Mask* and Twain's novel.

———. *The Count of Monte-Cristo.* 2 vols. London: G. Routledge and Sons, n.d. 754 pp.

Source: MTLAcc, entry #2229, Volume 2 only, donated from Clemens's library by Clara Clemens Gabrilowitsch in 1910.

Before leaving on the *Quaker City* in 1867 Mark Twain reminded himself to purchase an unspecified book by Dumas (NB 8, *N&J* 1: 326). In Chapter 11 of *The Innocents Abroad* (1869) he mentions visiting the Castle d'If in which the "heroes of 'Monte Cristo'" whiled away their confinement in "damp, dismal cells"; there he also catalogues some of the prisoner's implements—pen, lamp, chisel, blood-ink—that would plague the hapless Jim in *Huckleberry Finn* (1885). Robert E. Morsberger, "Pap Finn and the Bishop's Candlesticks: Victor Hugo in Hannibal," *CEA Critic* 31 (April 1969): 17, summarized various elements that Mark Twain's *Adventures of Huckleberry Finn* apparently borrowed from *The Man in the Iron Mask*, *The Count of Monte Cristo*, and *Twenty Years After*. Kevin Michael Scott, in "'There's More Honor': Reinterpreting Tom and the Evasion in *Huckleberry Finn*,'" *Studies in the Novel* 37.2 (Summer 2005): 187–207, argued that Twain's use of the "unjustly imprisoned nobleman . . . problematizes any reading of the ending as being necessarily or only a condemnation of Tom [Sawyer] and what he represents" (p. 195).

Olin H. Moore, "Mark Twain and Don Quixote" (1922), pp. 333–335; Henry Pochmann, "The Mind of Mark

Twain" (1924), pp. 15, 158–159; Walter Blair, "French Revolution" (1957), p. 25; Franklin Rogers, *MTBP* (1960), p. 149.

———. *Novels.* New Edition. Illus. 14 vols. London: George Routledge & Sons, 1880. Includes *The Count of Monte Cristo; The Three Musketeers; Twenty Years After; The Vicomte of Bragelonne: Ten Years After* (2 vols.); *Marguerite de Valois; Chicot the Jester; The Forty-five Guardsmen; The Conspirators; The Regent's Daughter; Memoirs of a Physician; The Queen's Necklace; The Taking of the Bastille;* and *The Countess de Charny.* [Edition conjectured. According to an advertisement in the 1880 edition of *Routledge's Guide to London and Its Suburbs*, George Routledge & Sons of London had just issued in 1880 a fourteen-volume set of Dumas's novels—"A New Edition"—whose titles exactly match the *A1911* description of Clemens's set.]

Catalog: *A1911*, "14 vols. 12mo, cloth. Lond.: Routledge, n.d.," names the thirteen titles in the set (*The Vicomte de Bragelonne: Ten Years After* consists of two volumes), lot 140, sold for $4 total.

Dumas's works furnished Clemens with escapist reading on numerous occasions. In a letter playfully addressed to his infant daughter Susy on 9 May 1872, Clemens informed her that "many's the night I've lain awake till 2 oclock in the morning reading Dumas & drinking beer, listening for the slightest sound you might make" (*LLMT*, p. 174; *MTLet* 5: 85). Chapter 55 of *Roughing It* (1872) mentions the acclaimed productivity of Dumas. On 23 April 1877 Clemens wrote to Olivia Clemens from the St. James Hotel in New York City: "I had a delightful afternoon. I left behind me those 2 men who have not been absent from my thoughts (& my hate) for months—[John T.] Raymond & [Bret] Harte—so I read Dumas & was serene & content" (*LLMT*, p. 194). That reading seems reflected in a fragmentary novel Mark Twain possibly began in 1875, "The Mysterious Chamber" (DV56, MTP). Although set in eighteenth-century Italy rather than France, this tale of "jealousy and revenge" with its haunted castle, ancient sword, dark corridors, dusty cobwebs, iron doors, treasure chests, interrupted betrothal, and a prisoner confined in dungeon conditions who writes with home-made ink, is reminiscent of Dumas as well as various Gothic novels. Clemens continued to show an interest in Dumas's writings beyond the 1870s. "Get the rest of Dumas at the German Buchhandlung," he reminded himself in 1885 (NB 24, *N&J* 3: 143). Henry W. Fisher remembered that in the late 1890's Clemens told him Dumas was one of the guides the Clemenses used to look up "the places of horror" in Paris (*AMT*, p. 59). Robert E. Morsberger—"Pap Finn and the Bishop's Candlesticks: Victor Hugo in Hannibal," *CEA Critic* 31 (April 1969): 17—listed elements that Mark Twain's *Adventures of Huckleberry Finn* seemingly took from *The Man in the Iron Mask*, *The Count of Monte Cristo*, and *Twenty Years After*.

———. *Taking the Bastille, or Six Years Later.* Red cloth, gilt. London: George Routledge and Sons, n.d. 283 pp.

Inscription: signed in pencil on the front free endpaper: "SL Clemens/Hartford 1877."

Provenance: Antenne-Dorrance Collection, Rice Lake, Wisconsin.

Location: Mark Twain Archive, Gannett-Tripp Learning

Center, Elmira College, Elmira, New York.

Copy examined: Clemens's copy, unmarked. Examined on 28 May 2015. This volume might have been part of the *Novels* set listed in the Catalog entry above that was sold at the *A1911* auction, lot 140, or conceivably Clemens could have owned two copies of the same edition of this book. On 6 August 1877 Clemens mentioned reading "one of Dumas' novels, 'The Taking of the Bastille,'" in a letter to Mary Mason Fairbanks (*MTMF*, p. 208).

————. *Les Trois Mousquetaires* (novel, published 1844).

Catalog: ListABP (1910), "Les Trois Mousquetaires, Dumas", no other information supplied.

————. *The Vicomte of Bragelonne: Ten Years After* (parts of which are often published separately as *Louise de la Vaillière* and *The Man in the Iron Mask*).

Mark Twain called Dumas "the great Mulatto in the Iron Mask" in 1867 (*Alta California*, 17 May 1867; *MTTMB*, p. 170). Twain's Wild Man in "The Wild Man Interviewed" (1869) claims that he "moped in a French dungeon for fifteen years, and wore a ridiculous Iron Mask." In Chapter 11 of *The Innocents Abroad* (1869) Twain mentions seeing "the noisome cell where the celebrated 'Iron Mask'—that ill-starred brother of a hard-hearted king of France—was confined. . . . These dank walls had known the man whose dolorous story is a sealed book forever!" Walter Blair warned that this reference "does not prove that he was familiar with the book" by 1869 ("French Revolution," p. 27 n. 31). On 14 July 1880 Estes & Lauriat of Boston sent Clemens a bill for twenty-one books, including "1 Iron Mask $1"; Clemens paid the bill on 20 July 1880 (receipt in MTP). Blair proposed that the *Iron Mask* taught Twain about its legendary figure and suggested the ideas of scratching messages on tin plates (Chapter 36 of *Huckleberry Finn* [1885]) and smuggling notes in a loaf of bread (the witch pie) (Blair, "French Revolution," p. 27 n. 31). Clemens noted "Villeneuve (Iron Mask 8 days)" in Notebook 31 (TS p. 8) in October 1891. Tom Sawyer and Huck Finn "hunted out the old chain and padlock and two keys that we used to play out the Prisoner of the Basteel with" in Chapter 3 of "Tom Sawyer's Conspiracy," written 1897–1900 (*HH&T*, p. 178).

Dumas, Alexandre (1824–1895), known as Dumas *fils*. *Camille* (play, performed in 1852 as *La Dame aux camélias*).

On 20 December 1905 Isabel Lyon recorded: "Ah, we saw [Sarah] Bernhardt in Camille today. . . . She goes beyond [Eleonora] Duse's art in that play, in all but the gambling scene" (IVL Journal, TS p. 115, MTP).

————. *Le Demi-Monde* (play, performed in 1855).

Clemens received a bill from James R. Osgood & Company of Boston in November 1877 for "1 Les Demi Monde [sic], 2 v.," purchased on 9 August 1877 (Scrapbook #10, p. 69, MTP).

Du Maurier, George Louis Palmella Busson (1834–1896). *A Legend of Camelot, Pictures and Poems, Etc.* Illus. First edition. Original quarter green decorated cloth and decorated boards, gilt. Oblong quarto. New York: Harper & Brothers, 1898. 95 pp.

Catalogs: *A1911*, "oblong 4to, boards, cloth back, gilt edges, N.Y. 1898," lot 141, sold for $3; *Sotheby's 2003*, #200, $3,000 (sold with two other titles about English

history and lore).

Provenance: formerly in the collection of Nick Karanovich, Fort Wayne, Indiana. Karanovich acquired it from Doug Price Photographs, Ann Arbor, Michigan, for $600 (Doug Price to Karanovich, 2 October 1985, PH of this letter sent to Alan Gribben by Nick Karanovich).

Location: collection of Kevin Mac Donnell, Austin, Texas.

Copy examined: Clemens's unmarked copy, in July 2004, as well as a photocopy of the title page and representative samples provided by Nick Karanovich (Karanovich to Alan Gribben, 4 October 1985). Most of the material, some of it mere doggerel but with amusing caricatures, had appeared previously in *Punch*. The volume contains the *A1911* sale label and a description of the volume clipped from the *A1911* catalog (lot 141), together with a page of a Twain manuscript (possibly one of the pages from his 1905 notebook) affixed to the front pastedown endpaper.

————. *The Martian* (novel, published in 1896, illustrated by the author).

In October 1907 Clemens told Isabel Lyon to make a note of the fact that "Harper paid Du Maurier 50 000 for the Martian" (Isabel Lyon Notebook #3, MTP).

————. *Peter Ibbetson*. Illustrated by the author. New York: Harper & Brothers, 1904. 418 pp.

Source: MTLAcc, entry #1545, volume donated by Clemens.

A lengthy conversation with Polly Peck of the Mark Twain House in Hartford in July 1984 persuaded me to view Du Maurier's *Peter Ibbetson* as a work that possibly gave Mark Twain the courage, in 1898, to write "My Platonic Sweetheart." Du Maurier's novel purported to be the journal of an imprisoned murderer who has "dream" meetings, conversations, and travels with his beloved Mary, Duchess of Towers. He speaks of these encounters as "my inner life" (p. 273). The woman appeared to him again and again, taking him here and there, teaching him about the nature of life and human love. "Wonderful scenes passed before my mental vision" (p. 33). He had known Mary as a young girl, Mimsey Seraskier, and they later found that they were capable of "a double dream, a dream common to us both" (p. 247), and therefore found "privileges . . . probably no human beings could have ever enjoyed before" (p. 335). She sustained him in this manner through twenty-eight years as an inmate of prison and subsequently of a criminal lunatic asylum. He was convicted of killing a man who had blighted both their lives. Eventually the narrator dies in the midst of recording her philosophy and messages.

————. *Peter Ibbetson*. Illustrated by the author. New York: Harper & Brothers, 1904. 418 pp.

Source: MTLAcc, entry #1545, volume donated by Clemens.

————. *Social Pictorial Satire; Reminiscences and Appreciations of English Illustrators of the Past Generation*. Illus. New York: Harper & Brothers, 1893. 100 pp.

Source: MTLAcc, entry #1357, volume donated by Clemens.

Du Maurier primarily describes his association with the English humor magazine *Punch* and its artists, particularly Charles Keene (1823–1891) and John Leech (1817–1864).

———. *Trilby* (novel, published in 1894).

The Sydney, Australia *Sunday Times* (15 September 1895) reported Mark Twain's claim that he had not read Du Maurier's *Trilby* (note from Miriam J. Shillingsburg to Alan Gribben, April 1987). Later, however, Twain referred to *Trilby* in a newspaper interview published in the Durban [South Africa] *Natal Mercury Weekly*, 8 May 1896 (reprinted in the *Natal Witness*, 9 May 1896, and the Pretoria *Press*, 15 May 1896): "I think the reason of its great popularity is merely that it gives a felicitous view of a sort of artistic Parisian life which was fresh to the world, and taking. It was most happily done, and out of the common of what people were reading" (Scharnhorst, *Complete Interviews*, p. 299). A few days later Twain referred to its huge sales, comparing it in that respect to *Ben-Hur* and *Looking Backward* (Johnnesburg *Star*, 18 May 1896; *Complete Interviews*, p. 303). In an undated statement Clemens mentioned the lucrative publishing terms that Harper & Brothers voluntarily gave Du Maurier when *Trilby* turned out to be a gigantic success (*MTHHR*, pp. 533–534). Du Mauier's fictional Trilby O'Ferrall is a model in Bohemian Paris who falls in love with an artist, Little Billee. However, Trilby succumbs to a musician-hypnotist named Svengali, who manipulates her abilities to the point where she makes a sensational tour as a gifted vocalist. After Svengali dies Trilby can recall little of her life with him, and soon she, too, dies.

DU MAURIER, GUY LOUIS BUSSON (1865–1915). *An Englishman's Home; A Play in Three Acts.* New York: Harper & Brothers, 1909. 131 pp.
Source: MTLAcc, entry #1101, volume donated by Clemens.

DUNBAR, PAUL LAURENCE (1872–1906). *Majors and Minors: Poems.* Toledo, Ohio: Hadley & Hadley, [cop. 1895]. 148 pp.
Inscription: inscribed on the verso of the frontispiece, in pencil: "To S. L. C./fm/J. B. Pond/Sept. 10 '96." [James B. Pond (1838–1903) was Mark Twain's lecture agent during the North American segment of his 1895–1896 tour.]
Marginalia: Clemens changed "led" to "let" in the left margin of page 29, in pencil. On page 47 he altered "foot" to "span" in pencil in the second poem.
Location: Mark Twain Library, Redding, Connecticut. Donated from Clemens's library by Clara Clemens Gabrilowitsch in 1910 (MTLAcc, entry #2054).
Copy examined: Clemens's copy, a gift from James B. Pond after Clemens's lecture tour around the world. Examined in 1970 and again in June 1982. Has the red ink Mark Twain Library accession number "2054".

Dunbar is considered the first truly influential African American poet. William Dean Howells praised his *Majors and Minors* in the 27 June 1896 issue of *Harper's Weekly*. Dunbar's "Majors" were written in Standard English; the "Minors" were his dialect poems.
Shelley Fisher Fishkin, "Race and the Politics of Memory: Mark Twain and Paul Laurence Dunbar," *Journal of American Studies* 40.2 (August 2006): 283–309.

DUNCAN, NORMAN (1871–1916). *The Cruise of the Shining Light.* New York: Harper & Brothers, 1907. 344 pp.
Source: MTLAcc, entry #120, volume donated by Clemens.
The Canadian author Duncan sets this novel along the Newfoundland coast.

———. *Every Man for Himself.* Illus. New York, 1908.
Inscription: signed on the front pastedown endpaper, "S. L. Clemens, 1909."
Catalog: *A1911*, "12mo, cloth, N.Y. 1908," quotes the signature, lot 142, sold for $2.25.
Ten short stories depict the rugged lives of fishermen who take their chances on the Newfoundland coast.

DUNCAN, ROBERT KENNEDY (1868–1914). *The Chemistry of Commerce: A Simple Interpretation of Some New Chemistry.* Illus. New York: Harper & Brothers, 1907. 263 pp.
Source: MTLAcc, entry #1799, volume donated by Clemens.
Twelve chapters explain the promising ways that chemistry can aid manufacturing. The topics include catalysis, nitrogen, rare earths, high temperature, glass-making, industrial alcohol, microbe inoculation, and cellulose.

DUNCKLEY, HENRY (1823–1896). *Lord Melbourne.* New York: Harper & Brothers, 1890. 248 pp.
Source: MTLAcc, entry #1759, volume donated by Clemens.
William Lamb (1779–1848), 2nd Viscount Melbourne, served as Queen Victoria's first Prime Minister.

DUNN, JACOB PIATT (1855–1924). *Massacres of the Mountains: A History of the Indian Wars of the Far West.* Illus. New York: Harper & Brothers, 1886. 784 pp.
Source: MTLAcc, entry #1716, volume donated by Clemens.
Dunn graphically documents more than twenty slaughters perpetrated by American Indians, white settlers, and the U. S. Cavalry, including the Mountain Meadows massacre and the Little Big Horn. His narratives teem with bloody details of Native Americans' raids and tortures; on pages 489–490, for example, he describes how the Sioux tribes would torture a prisoner by building a fire on the man's stomach while he was outstretched and staked to the ground. Dunn's preface urges a standard nineteenth-century solution to the "Indian problem": Christian conversion and "civilization."
Walter Blair demonstrated that in "Huck Finn and Tom Sawyer among the Indians," apparently written in 1884, Mark Twain borrowed the majority of his details about American Indian customs from several books written by Richard Dodge (*HH&T* [1969], pp. 84–88, 328–337). If Twain by any chance sought corroboration of Dodge's reports, or if he wrote part of the uncompleted manuscript later than the date Blair conjectured for its composition, then Dunn's book—copyrighted and published in 1886—reinforced the authority of Dodge's assertions about Native American depravity. For instance, Dunn states that "the treatment of women, by any Indians, is usually bad, but by the plains Indians especially so. When a woman is captured by a war-party she is the common property of all of them, each night, till they reach their village, when she becomes the special property of her individual captor. . . . If she resists she is 'staked out,' that is to say, four pegs are driven into the ground and a hand or foot tied to each, to prevent struggling. She is also beaten, mutilated, or even killed, for resistance" (p. 427). In fact, there is an entry in Dunn's index for "Women, white, treatment by Plains Indians." In Twain's "Huck and Tom among the Indians," the discovery of four stakes

signaling the gang-rape of Peggy Mills (at the site where Huck secretly notices a torn and bloody piece of her dress) sickened Brace Johnson and apparently prevented Twain from taking the story beyond this grisly development. But Blair pointed out that Dodge's *Plains of the Great West* (1877) likewise mentions the use of stakes in the rape of women prisoners (*HH&T*, p. 336).

Dunne, Finley Peter (1867–1936), pseud. "Mr. Dooley." *Dissertations by Mr. Dooley.* New York: Harper & Brothers, 1906. 313 pp.

   Inscriptions: signed in black ink on the front pastedown endpaper, "S. L. Clemens/1906." There is also a 1951 auction designation—"D51"—in pencil on the front pastedown endpaper. Jake Zeitlin's bookshop price ($30) is noted in pencil on the front free endpaper.

   Catalogs: *C1951*, D51; *Zeitlin 1951*, #15, $30.

   Provenance: formerly part of Cyril Clemens's collection in Kirkwood, Missouri in 1985.

   Location: Harry Ransom Center, University of Texas at Austin. Acquired from Cyril Clemens along with six other books on 28 March 1986, for payments of $5,000 to Cyril Clemens and $5,000 to his *Mark Twain Journal*. Thomas A. Tenney, Cyril Clemens, and Alan Gribben (then an English professor at the University of Texas at Austin) negotiated this agreement in an exchange of letters written between 20 August 1985 and 27 April 1986.

   Copy examined: Clemens's unmarked copy in Austin in 1986. A copy of the *C1951* Hollywood sale catalog is laid inside with a check mark next to item D51.

   A typical exchange in *Dissertations* is this one in "Short Marriage Contracts": "'Who is George Meredith?' asked Mr. Hennessy. 'Ye can search me,' said Mr. Dooley. 'What is th' charge again' him?'" Norman Hapgood recalled Dunne as the only younger person "whom I ever heard address Mr. Clemens as Mark to his face. . . . It was a pleasant relation between these two humorists, and many an hour spent in billiards" (*Changing Years* [1930], p. 211). Isabel Lyon's journal contains an entry for 7 December 1904: "This has been a day of events—for this morning Mr. Dunne (Mr. Dooley) came for a closeting with Mr. Clemens" (1903–1906 Diary, TS p. 31, MTP). Lyon also recorded on 20 October 1905 Clemens's analysis of a sentence by Dunne in which "one or two non-essential words are left out: 'Why do people marry Lillian Russell?'" (IVL Journal, TS p. 109, MTP). Elmer Ellis's biography *Mr. Dooley's America: A Life of Finley Peter Dunne* (New York: Alfred A. Knopf, 1941) reported that Dunne and Clemens first met at a London dinner (pp. 126–127) and that when Thomas W. Lawson was writing a muckraking exposé of Clemens's financial savior Henry H. Rogers in 1904–1905, Clemens asked Dunne to make fun of Lawson (pp. 212–213). Dunne was one of the guests at the Seventieth Birthday celebration held for Mark Twain at Delmonico's on 5 December 1905.

   Clemens wanted Dunne in the literary group that Clemens tried to organize in New York City in 1906 for the purpose of entertaining visiting foreign authors (SLC to WDH, 10 April 1906, *MTHL*, p. 804). Clemens mentioned Dunne as a currently familiar name in American humor in his 31 July 1906 Autobiographical Dictation (*MTE*, p. 201; *AutoMT 2*: 152). In a subsequent dictation, Clemens

said that Dunne "is brilliant; he is an expert with his pen, and he easily stands at the head of all the satirists of this generation" (22 January 1907 AD, *AutoMT 2*: 377). He joked in *Christian Science* (1907) that "style" at least would differentiate "Mr. Dooley's books" from those by "the late Jonathan Edwards" (Book 1, Chapter 3). Clemens wrote to Jean Clemens from Fifth Avenue on 26 January 1906: "Dooley came & played billiards yesterday & won a dollar" (TS in MTP); the next month he chatted with Dunne when leaving a party in New York City shortly after midnight (19 February 1908 AD, *AutoMT 3*: 211). On 18 February 1909 Clemens wrote to Dunne from Redding, Connecticut to urge a reconvening of their "G. D. A." (God Damned Association) "The Association has been separate & wandering & voiceless too long—let's not fail to get together this time & make a noise. . . . Adieu, good-bye, aufwiedersehen, O only righteous one!" (*Sotheby's 2003*, #130). Letters from Dunne were among the only sort of mail ("friendly letters & letters from friends, of an unirritating sort") that Clemens allowed Jean to send him in Bermuda in 1909 (SLC to Jean Clemens, 6 December 1909, MTP). Dunne would recount amusing anecdotes about Clemens in 1936 (reprinted in *Mr. Dooley Remembers: The Informal Memoirs of Finley Peter Dunne*, ed. Philip Dunne [Boston: Little, Brown and Co., 1963], pp. 239–268). There Dunne recalled that he met Clemens through Robert Collier. "He always treated Collier and me as if were still in our adolescence. . . . He would say, 'I like you young fellows. I like to have you around me. But you mustn't expect me to listen to your opinions. They are too immature. Wait till you and Collier have made a reputation. Then you can talk to me and I will stay awake.'"

   Walter Blair and Hamlin Hill, *America's Humor: From Poor Richard to Doonesbury* (New York: Oxford University Press, 1978), pp. 384–387; Holger Kersten, "Mark Twain's 'Assault of Laughter': Reflections on the Perplexing History of an Appealing Idea," *Mark Twain Annual 16* (2018): 69.

Dunphy, Thomas and **Thomas J. Cummins.** *Remarkable Trials of All Countries, Particularly of the United States, Great Britain, Ireland, and France.* New York, 1878. [Publisher uncertain. Several brought out editions. One had 464 pp.]

   Inscription: signed on front pastedown endpaper, "S. L. Clemens, 21 5th Avenue, 1907."

   Catalog: *A1911*, "8vo, cloth, N.Y. 1878," quotes the signature, lot 145, sold for $3.25.

   Clemens signed a number of books that he had read earlier with a much later date of inscription (he seemed to have more leisure for recording ownership and dates as he perused his library collection during his final decade). This copy of *Remarkable Trials of All Countries* brings to mind William Dean Howells's observation that Clemens "was always reading some vital book. It might be some out-of-the-way book, but it had the root of the human matter in it: a volume of great trials" (*My Mark Twain* [1910], p. 15).

Dunster, H[enry]. P[eter] (1814–1904). *Historical Tales of Lancastrian Times.* Illustrated by John Franklin. Blue cloth. London: Griffith and Farran, 1864. 376 pp.

   Inscription: Olivia Clemens wrote on the flyleaf in pencil:

"S. L. Clemens/ 1873".

Location: Mark Twain Library, Redding, Connecticut.

Copy examined: Clemens's unmarked copy. Has the accession number of the Mark Twain Library—"3105". Examined in 1970 and again in June 1982.

The Reverend Dunster specialized in the historical period of Richard II.

Duoir, Paul. "My Kingdom" (poem, published in 1865).

Mark Twain quotes, parodies, and berates this poem in an early sketch, "Real Estate versus Imaginary Possessions, Poetically Considered," San Francisco *Californian*, 28 October 1865 (*SSix* [1927], pp. 188–190; Scott, *OPMT* [1966], pp. 55). Twain makes fun of the fact that Duoir's "Kingdom" turned out to be "One True Woman's Heart" rather than something more tangible. Sydney J. Krause traced "My Kingdom" to the 20 October 1865 issue of the San Francisco *Evening Bulletin* (*MTC* [1967], pp. 84–86). Duoir was still living in San Francisco as late as 1884, but other information about him is hazy.

Louis J. Budd, *CTSS&E* (1981) 1: 1037). Scharnhorst, *The Life of Mark Twain* (2018) 1: 205–206.

Duplessis, Georges (1834–1899). *The Wonders of Engraving.* Illus. New York: Charles Scribner & Co., 1871. 338 pp.

Source: MTLAcc, entry #2000, volume donated from Clemens's library by Clara Clemens Gabrilowitsch in 1910.

Dussouchet, Jean Jacques (1843–1909). *Petite Grammaire Française.* Paris: Librairie Hachette et Cie, 1883. 152 pp.

Inscription: signed on the front free endpaper, "Clara L. Clemens/Jan. 4th 1887." There is a bookseller's sticker on the front pastedown endpaper: "F. W. Christern/37 West 23d Street/New York".

Marginalia: penciled annotations by a young student on pages 1, 2, 3, 7, 14, 15, 17. Some pages are missing from the front section.

Location: Mark Twain Library, Redding, Connecticut.

Copy examined: Clara Clemens's copy. Has the red ink Mark Twain Library accession number "3622".

Dwight, James (1852–1917). *Practical Lawn Tennis.* Illus. New York: Harper & Brothers, 1893. 168 pp.

Source: MTLAcc, entry #808, volume donated by Clemens.

Dyar, Muriel Campbell (1875–1963). *Davie and Elisabeth, Wonderful Adventures.* New York: Harper & Brothers, 1908. 131 pp.

Source: MTLAcc, entry #1198, volume donated by Clemens.

Usually classified as early science fiction.

Dyer, Louis (1851–1908). *Machiavelli and the Modern State: Chapters on His "Prince," His Use of History and His Idea of Morals, Being Three Lectures Delivered in 1899 at the Royal Institution.* Boston: Ginn and Co., 1904. 163 pp.

In a laudatory essay, "William Dean Howells" (1906), Mark Twain selected an excerpt from Howells's "Easy Chair" column, a paragraph reviewing Louis Dyer's *Machiavelli and the Modern State*, to illustrate "how clear, how limpid, how understandable" Howells's prose always is. See also the Catalog entry for P. Villari, *Life and Times of Niccolò Machiavelli.*

Dziewicki, Michael Henry (1851–1928). *Entombed in Flesh.* London: W. Blackwood & Sons, 1897. 282 pp.

Source: MTLAcc, entry #996, volume donated by Clemens.

Clemens mentioned the title of this novel when computing costs of book publishing on the front free endpaper of an 1896 edition of Emile Zola's *Rome.* In an unpublished manuscript titled "The Great Republic's Peanut Stand," Clemens listed "Entombed in the Flesh; 66,000 words, 282 pages" among the "shelf of 35 cloth-bound books—English and American" available to him in "this little Austrian village" [Kaltenleutgeben] in 1898 (MS in MTP).

E

Eadie, John (1810–1876), ed. *A New and Complete Concordance to the Holy Scriptures, on the Basis of [Alexander] Cruden [1699–1770].* Intro. by David King (1806–1883). New York: American Tract Society, n.d. [Eadie's "Note to the Fourteenth Edition" is dated 1850.] 561 pp.

Inscription: in purple ink on the front free endpaper, possibly Clemens's hand: "Livie L. Langdon/Feb 2d 1870" (the date of her wedding). [He usually spelled her name as "Livy." Was he deferring to her family's spelling on this special day?]

Marginalia: pencil marks throughout at the following entries: Ass (every entry); Blind, Adjective; Error and Errors; Fowl and Fowls; Low (Deuteronomy 28:43, "shalt come down very low"); Run, Runnest, Runneth, Running (one penciled word in Clemens's hand beside Lev. 15:2, 22:4: "dispute"); Safe; Second; Seventh Month, Seventh Year; Stole and Stolen; Stop; Struck; Swift; Third; Threw, Throw, Throwing, Thrown.

Provenance: contains the bookstamps and traces of a charge-slip jacket from the Mark Twain Library, Redding, Connecticut.

Catalog: *Mott 1952*, #48, $3.

Location: Mark Twain House and Museum, Hartford, Connecticut. Gift of an anonymous donor in 1963.

Copy examined: Olivia Clemens's copy, apparently consulted by her husband. Examined in August 1987.

Earle, Maria Theresa (Villiers) (1836–1925), "Mrs. C. W. Earle." *Pot-pourri from a Surrey Garden.* Appendix by Lady Constance Lytton [Constance Georgina, Lady Lytton, 1869–1923]. London: Smith, Elder, & Co., 1897.

Clemens jotted down the title (erroneously writing "Summer Garden") and the author's name in 1900 (NB 43, TS p. 2a). The contents of *Pot-pourri* fit its name, ranging from observations on gardening, weather, suburbs, recipes, and reading to advice on families, schools, and dress. Lady Lytton's Appendix describes the Japanese art of arranging cut flowers.

Eastlake, Charles L[ocke]. (1833–1906). *Hints on Household Taste in Furniture, Upholstery, and Other Details.* Edited, with notes, by Charles C[allahan]. Perkins (1823–1886). First American edition, from the revised London edition. Boston: James R. Osgood and Co., 1872.

Inscription: signed on the second flyleaf, "Livy L. Clemens/1872".

Catalogs: *A1911*, "8vo, cloth, Bost. 1872," quotes the signature, lot 147, sold for $2.75 (sold to the Mark Twain Company); *C1951*, O15; *Hunley 1958*, #38, $6.50, contains an *A1911* auction label.

Location: Mark Twain House and Museum, Hartford, Connecticut. Gift of Professor Norman Holmes Pearson (1909–1975) of Yale University.

Copy examined: Olivia Clemens's copy, unmarked but it

appears well-used. The volume contains colored samples of wallpaper design and colored plates of parquetry floor patterns. Examined in August 1987. Has the *A1911* auction label on the front pastedown endpaper.

Eastman, Annis [Bertha] Ford (1852–1910). "A Dose of Paradise" (short short story, published in *The Independent* [New York City], 24 June 1897).

Olivia Clemens clipped and preserved this story in her diary (MTP). Evidently she showed it to Clemens, for several markings and corrections in brown ink appear to be his ("she felt sick" is changed to "she fell ill"). Eastman and her husband Samuel E. Eastman were assistant pastors of Park Church in Elmira, New York, and knew the Clemenses well. Her tale concerns an ill and exhausted woman who imagines a visit to heaven during her sickness. Returning to "her dingy rooms, homely table, troublesome children, monotonous work," she decides that "Paradise is good, but home is better." A final paragraph urges women to recognize their own paradises here on earth.

———. *A Flower of Puritanism (Julia Jones Beecher) 1826–1905.* Elmira, New York: Press of Snyder Brothers, [1905]. 73 pp.

Catalog: AAA-A (New York City), Sale number 4400 (25 May 1938), "Clemens' copy, with 'Mrs. X' on p. 65 crossed out and 'Susy Crane,' the real name of the lady, written by him on the margin; a portion of two leaves has also been torn out, presumably by him," lot 138.

Eastman and her husband had become the joint pastors of Park Church in 1900 upon the death of the Reverend Thomas K. Beecher. She wrote this memorial pamphlet to commemorate the passing of Julia Jones Beecher, Beecher's widow, in 1905. Pages 61–62 reprint a letter of 30 May 1880 from Clemens to Julia Beecher about a hobby she enjoyed—collecting tree stumps and roots in the countryside, decorating them in the shapes of fantastic animals, and donating them to charity sales. Clemens temporarily stored a few of these in his house and complimented the artistry of what he termed her "Jabberwocks"; "They grow so in grotesque grace hour by hour," he wrote. "Don't leave a root unutilized in Chemung County" (p. 61), he urged.

———. [Another identical copy.] First edition. Original brown printed wrappers.

Provenance: from the library of Susan Crane, Clemens's sister-in-law and the owner of Quarry Farm.

Location: collection of Kevin Mac Donnell, Austin, Texas. Purchased from the Langdon family in May 2016 (email, Mac Donnell to Alan Gribben, 16 May 2016).

Source: detailed description of the volume with "no markings" sent on 9 June 2016 by Mac Donnell to Gribben. This book would have been available to Clemens in the Langdon family library.

———. [Another identical copy.]

Marginalia: one vertical pencil mark in the righthand margin at the top of page 63.

Provenance: gift of Professor Benjamin H. Lehman.

Location: The General Library at the University of California at Berkeley, which lists it as "Mark Twain's copy with his marginal annotations."

Copy examined: an online digital reproduction of the pages was available through Hathitrust on 18 December 2017. I was unable to detect any reasons to believe that this copy

belonged to Clemens. A cataloging librarian most likely jumped to conclusions.

Easton, Matthew George (1823–1894). *Illustrated Bible Dictionary.* (First published in 1897.)

Catalog: ListABP (1910), "Ill. Bible Dict., Easton", no other information provided.

Eaton, Winnifred (1875–1954), pseud. "Onoto Watanna" (also known privately, 1901–1917, as Mrs. Bertrand W. Babcock). *A Japanese Blossom.* Illustrated by L[ee]. W[oodward]. Ziegler (1868–1952). New York: Harper & Brothers, 1906. 264 pp.

Source: MTLAcc, entry #1314, volume donated by Clemens.

Winnifred Eaton, born half-Chinese and half-English in Canada, adopted a Japanese-sounding pen name and wrote quaintly delicate novels about a land she had never seen. It is believed that Winnifred Eaton's *Miss Numè: A Japanese-American Romance* (1899) was the first novel written by an Asian American. She is sometimes confused with her sister Edith Maude Eaton (1865–1914), who wrote under the name Sui Sin Far.

Diana Birchall, *Onoto Watanna: The Story of Winnifred Eaton* (Urbana: University of Illinois Press, 2001); Dominika Ferens, *Edith and Winnifred Easton: Chinatown Missions and Japanese Romances* (Urbana: University of Illinois Press, 2002); and Jean Lee Cole, *The Literary Voices of Winnifred Eaton: Redefining Ethnicity and Authenticity* (New Brunswick, New Jersey: Rutgers University Press, 2002).

———. *A Japanese Nightingale.* Illustrated by Genjiro Yeto [born Genjiro Kataoka, 1867–1924]. Original cloth, some rubbing on edges and corners. New York: Harper & Brothers, 1901. 225 pp.

This was one of Eaton's most successful novels in terms of sales.

Inscription: signed "Olivia Clemens/Riverdale/1901."

Catalogs: ListABP (1910), "Japanese Nightingale, Watanna"; *C1951*, O7, listed among volumes signed by Olivia Clemens, edition unspecified; "Property from the Library of Mark Twain," Butterfield & Butterfield, San Francisco, Sale 6613 (16 July 1997), lot 2700.

Location: Mark Twain House and Museum, Hartford, Connecticut.

Copy examined: Olivia Clemens's unmarked copy. Viewed in Hartford in 1997.

———. *The Wooing of Wistaria, by Onoto Watanna.* New York: Harper & Brothers, 1902. 388 pp. [Publisher and pages conjectured.]

Inscription: the front pastedown endpaper is signed "S. L. Clemens, 1902."

Catalog: *A1911*, "12mo, cloth, N.Y. 1902," quotes the signature, lot 477, sold for $1.50.

Eayrs, M[arshall]. P. (1844–1897). "When I am far away" (song, published in 1876).

This song best fits the lyrics that Clemens recorded on his trip down the Mississippi River in the spring of 1882: "Piano playing and singing aboard the 'Gold Dust.' Song 'When I am far away, Oh then you'll love me still.' Deep pathos" (Notebook 21, *N&J* 2: 532). The words to M. P. Eayrs' song are sufficiently similar: "The signal from the ocean strand,/Floats o'er the waters blue;/It bids me press thy parting hand,/And breathe my last adieu:/But oft on mem'ry's glowing wing,/My heart will fondly stray,/And still to thee with rapture cling,/When I am far away,/And still to thee with rapture cling,/When I am far away." Eayrs, a Boston music teacher and church organist, wrote other sentimental ballads for the Oliver Ditson Company in Boston, including "Song of the Sea" and "The Parting."

EBBARD, RICHARD J. *How to Acquire and Strengthen Will-Power. Modern Psycho-Therapy. A Specific Remedy for Neurasthenia and Nervous Diseases.* [First edition in 1902 published in London by the Modern Medical Publishing Company; many editions followed, some of them published by Fowler & Wells Company in New York City.]

> Catalog: ListABP (1910), "Will Power, Ebbard", no edition specified.
>
> Clemens cast a wide net in seeking relief for Jean Clemens's health problems. Ebbard, who identified himself as a professor at the "Sanum Institute" in London, advocated a version of self-hypnotism to gain control of one's mental tendencies. Certain later editions discussed Christian Science, which would also have interested Clemens.

EBERS, GEORG MORITZ (1837–1898). *Eine Aegyptische König-stochter. Historischer Roman [An Egyptian Royal Daughter. Historical Novel].* 3 vols. Leipzig: Carl Reigner, 1885.

> Source: MTLAcc, entry #387, Volume 3 only, donated by Clemens.

EBNER VON ESCHENBACH, MARIE FREIFRAU (1830–1916). *Margarete.* Stuttgart: J. G. Cotta, 1895. 144 pp.

> Source: MTLAcc, entry #373, volume donated by Clemens.

EBSWORTH, J[OSEPH]. WOODFALL (1824–1908), ed. *Choyce Drollery: Songs and Sonnets. Being a Collection of Divers Excellent Pieces of Poetry, of Several Eminent Authors. Now First Reprinted from the Edition of 1656. To Which Are added the Extra Songs of MERRY DROLLERY, 1661, and an Antidote Against Melancholy, 1661.* Boston, Lincolnshire: Robert Roberts, Strait Bar-Gate, 1876. 426 pp.

> Inscriptions: signed in pencil on the front free endpaper, "S. L. Clemens/Hartford, 1876". Cyril Clemens signed the facing pastedown endpaper at the top. On the verso of the front free endpaper appears a note in ink: "Only 400 this size/No 109/RR". Two penciled prices appear above Clemens's signature: "$5.25" and "30⁰⁰".
>
> Catalogs: *C1951*, #28c; *Zeitlin 1951*, #16, $30.
>
> Provenance: Thomas A. Tenney photocopied pages from this volume when it was in the collection of Cyril Clemens of Kirkwood, Missouri in April 1985.
>
> Location: Harry Ransom Center, University of Texas at Austin. Acquired from Cyril Clemens along with six other books on 28 March 1986, for payments of $5,000 to Cyril Clemens and $5,000 to his *Mark Twain Journal.* Thomas A. Tenney, Cyril Clemens, and Alan Gribben (then an English professor at the University of Texas at Austin) negotiated this agreement in an exchange of letters written between 20 August 1985 and 27 April 1986.
>
> Copy examined: photocopies of the title page and inscriptions sent to Alan Gribben by Thomas A. Tenney in April 1985. Confirmed by examination of the volume in Austin in 1986.
>
> Some of these lyrics are bawdy tributes to maids of easy virtue, prostitutes, and the pleasures of fornication. Other poems plead for kisses, toast the joys of true love, celebrate English heroes and historical events, and extol

wine and ale. The archaic diction, of course, resembles Mark Twain's phrasing in *1601* (1880), which Twain wrote in 1876. A few examples can illustrate these matters, such as "The Maid of Tottenham" (pp. 45–47): "As I went to Tottenham/Upon a Market-day,/There met I with a faire maid/Cloathed all in gray,/Her journey was to London/With buttermilk and Whay." Fifth stanza: "And when they came upon the plain/Upon a pleasant green,/The fair maid spread her l...s abroad,/The young man fell between,/Such typing of a Garter/I think was never seen." From "The Highway Man's Song" (p. 60): "I keep my Horse, I keep my Whore,/I take no Rents, yet am not poore./. . . And all this comes of, *Deliver your purse, sir.*" From "The Force of Opportunity" (p. 235): "Then give your Ladies leave to prove/The things the which your selves do love;/For any woman, what ere she be,/Will yield to Opportunity."

_____, ed. *Westminster Drolleries, Both Parts, of 1671, 1672; Being a Choice Collection of Songs and Poems, Sung at Court and Theatres. . . . Now First Reprinted from the Original Editions.* Illus. Boston, Lincolnshire: R[obert]. Roberts, 1875. 125, 132 pp.

> Inscriptions: signed in black ink on the front free endpaper, "Saml. L. Clemens/Hartford 1875." Cyril Clemens signed the front pastedown endpaper in blue ink: "Cyril Clemens". The printer made a note in ink on the verso of the front free endpaper: "400 copies only, of which/this is No 124./RR". Could this controlled and numbered printing be what gave Mark Twain the later idea for carefully circulating his *1601* (1880) among a select group of trusted friends? A later bookseller priced *Westminster Drolleries* in pencil on the rear pastedown endpaper: "$150⁰⁰ net."
>
> Catalogs: *C1951*, D58; *Zeitlin 1951*, #17, $20.
>
> Provenance: Clara Clemens Gabrilowitsch's penciled shelfmark from her Detroit library is visible on the front pastedown endpaper. The number "D58" from the 1951 Hollywood auction can be seen at the bottom of the front pastedown endpaper.
>
> Location: Special Collections, Washington University Libraries, St. Louis, Missouri. Ms. Kelly Brown of Special Collections notified Alan Gribben about this book in an e-mail message on 12 May 2015 and sent photocopies of the title page and the inscription. The volume was a gift from the collection of Cyril Clemens (1902–1999), Kirkwood, Missouri.
>
> Copy examined: Clemens's copy. Examined on 10 August 2015 in St. Louis. Page iv has been torn open, indicating that someone read the volume.
>
> This is a facsimile edition of songs and poems that treat romantic love in a Metaphysical manner. Ebsworth supplies a lengthy and defensive introduction (preparing the reader for "a touch of coarseness") as well as notes.

ECKSTORM, FANNIE (HARDY) (1865–1946). *The Penobscot Man.* Boston: Houghton, Mifflin and Co., Riverside Press, 1904. 326 pp.

> Catalog: *A1911*, "12mo, cloth, Bost.: Riverside Press, 1904," lot 148, sold for $1.
>
> Houghton, Mifflin and Company wrote to Clemens on 8 August 1904: "At the suggestion of the author, we take pleasure in sending you . . . a complimentary copy of 'The Penobscot Man' by Fannie Hardy Eckstorm. We believe

that years ago you took a trip up Katahdin and down the West Branch with the same Lewey Ketchum who figures in two of the stories." Isabel Lyon recorded a reply at the bottom of the letter: "Away indefinitely or would send thanks himself" (MTP). Eckstorm based her book on her knowledge of the fur traders and lumbermen along the Penobscot River in Maine.

————. *The Woodpeckers*. Illus. First edition. Original green cloth, gilt. Boston: Houghton, Mifflin and Co., 1901. 131 pp.

Inscription: inscribed by Clemens, "To/Jean Clemens/from her Father/Sept. '03."

Catalog: *Mott 1952*, #49, $30.

Location: collection of Kevin Mac Donnell, Austin, Texas.

Copy examined: Jean Clemens's copy, with no marginalia, in July 2004. Contains the purple ownership stamps of the Mark Twain Library, Redding, Connecticut.

Eckstorm describes the appearance, capabilities, and habits of North American species of woodpeckers. Jean Clemens was an avid bird-watcher. Isabel V. Lyon's journal in 1907 recorded that Jean had identified twenty-seven different species of birds in one day at the Katonah sanitarium where she was staying. Twain would note Jean's interest in birds in his "The Death of Jean" (1909).

————. [An identical copy.]

Source: MTLAcc, entry #1947, volume donated from Clemens's library by Clara Clemens Gabrilowitsch in 1910.

The Eclectic Magazine of Foreign Literature, Science, and Art (New York periodical, published 1844–1898).

Catalogs: *A1911*, "Eclectic Magazine. For 1860. Portraits. 3 vols., small 4to, half morocco, N.Y. 1860," lot 149, sold for $2; Walpole Galleries (New York City), Catalogue 112, 21 February 1919, "3 vols., tall 8vo, half morocco," item #122.

On 8 January 1870 Clemens instructed Olivia Langdon about the huge number of stars and the vast space beyond earth, as well as earth's ancient pedigree; his sources of information were two anonymous articles: "The Early History of Man," *Eclectic Magazine* 11 (January 1870): 1–16, and "Solar Wonders," *Eclectic Magazine* 11 (January 1870): 112–114; see *MTLet* 4: 12). In January 1888 Clemens wrote "The Eclectic—annually" in Notebook 27 (*N&J* 3: 371). There is also evidence that Clemens acquired the November 1869 issue of *The Eclectic*; see *MTLet* 3: 394.

Sherwood Cummings, *Mark Twain and Science* (1988), p. 11.

Eddy, Mary (Baker) G. (1821–1910). *Manual of the Mother Church, the First Church of Christ, Scientist, in Boston, Massachusetts*. Eleventh edition. 12mo, original red cloth. Boston: Christian Science Publishing Society, 1899. 95 pp.

Inscription: the title page is signed in ink, diagonally, "Frederick W. Peabody/Notations by Mark Twain."

Marginalia: penciled underlinings and other pencil and ink markings, with numerous, mostly caustic comments by Clemens (predominantly in ink but a few in pencil) totaling about 215 words on thirty-two pages. On page 50, for example, he quipped, "Out you go!" beside a passage stipulating that letters from the Pastor Emeritus must be read in their entirety in an open meeting or else "the offender shall be dropped from the Church." At the bottom of that page Clemens observed, "For a pastor

emeritus she/seems to have a good deal/of authority!" On the same page Clemens wondered "How will she find out?" at the prohibition against "a mental malpractitioner or a hypnotizer." The five notes and other markings on this page are reproduced in facsimile in both the Christie's catalog and the Heritage Book Shop catalog in 1981.

Provenance: formerly owned by Frederick W. Peabody, Eddy's biographer. Subsequently the volume gained the bookplate of John Gribbel.

Catalogs: Parke-Bernet Galleries, Sale 223, 31 October 1940, lot 186; Christie's, New York City, "The Prescott Collection . . . of the Estate of Marjorie Wiggin Prescott," 6 February 1981 sale, lot 56, sold with five letters from Clemens to Frederick W. Peabody written in 1902 and 1903. (Marjorie Wiggin Prescott was the daughter of banker Albert Wiggin.) Purchased by the Heritage Book Shop, Beverly Hills, California, for $8,500 (this price included letters laid in the volume). Offered on eBay in April 2006 and February 2013 by History for Sale, the internet service of Gallery of History. "Signed by its owner, Peabody, with handwritten notes by Mark Twain, who used it in preparing his famous 1907 polemic against Mary Baker Eddy." One page is reproduced that shows long pencil brackets down both sides of the text of an unnumbered page. The asking price was $65,000. Offered again by History for Sale on eBay in June 2016, "signature page lightly soiled, glue stains at blank left margin, cover stained at upper edge, worn at upper and lower edges of spine, overall fine condition," ten pages of Clemens's dense marginalia are reproduced (25, 29, 32, 33, 36, 37, 38, 40, 41, 42), priced at $65,000.

Copy examined: photocopy of page 50 reproduced in the Christie's 1981 catalog entry for lot 56, sent by Nick Karanovich to Alan Gribben in January 1981. Also viewed the online reproductions of Clemens's marginal notes. They are clearly authentic.

On 15 December 1902 Clemens, writing from Riverdale, New York, promised Frederick W[illiam]. Peabody (1862–1938): "I shall take good care of the Church Manual & return it to you. I never knew until now, who sent it to me. I do not remember asking for it. . . . But I find it useful. I thought it was my own, so I have marginal-noted it, & am very sorry" (ALS, quoted in Parke-Bernet Galleries Catalogue, Sale No. 223, 31 October, 1940, lot 186). The next year Clemens wrote Peabody again on 4 April 1903: "I am most cussedly sorry I made marginal notes in your Church Manual, & I apologize. . . I had forgotten it was a borrowed book until you convicted me with my own post-card" (Heritage Book Shop, Beverly Hills, California, 1981 catalog, item #56; PH in MTP). Paul Baender correctly determined that Mark Twain largely relied on a copy of the eleventh (1899) edition in writing *Christian Science* (1907) (*WIM?*, p. 561). In the section of *Christian Science* titled "Mrs. Eddy in Error," Twain roundly assailed her *Manual*: "Her governance is all there; all in that deceptively innocent-looking little book, that cunning little devilish book, that slumbering little brown volcano, with hell in its bowels. In that book she has planned out her system, and classified and defined its purposes and powers."

————. *Manual of the Mother Church, The First Church of*

Christ, Scientist, in Boston, Massachusetts. Twenty-eighth Edition. 12mo, original brown cloth, morocco-backed case. Boston: Christian Science Publishing Society, 1903. 111 pp.

Inscription: signed on the front pastedown endpaper in pencil, "S L. Clemens/March 1903." Above this signature and date Clemens wrote in pencil: "The lead pencil alterations/in this book indicate/the wording in the issue of/1902.—25th edition". On the title page Clemens crossed out the word "eighth" in pencil and made it read "Twenty-fifth Edition." He also (in pencil) altered the publication date from "1903" to "1902".

Marginalia: profusely annotated in pencil throughout by Clemens. Few of the notes express opinions; apparently he was merely making a working comparison of editions. His extensive revisions and notations run throughout the book, from the Table of Contents to page 104. Page 15 alone contains at least twenty individual penciled revisions, for instance. In the last line on page 34, regarding the duty of members to subscribe to Church periodicals, Clemens noted, "This is new. (not in the '99 edition[).] He found a passage about "The Title of Mother" to be "Vastly modified." Clemens tipped in a half-page of penciled revisions on page 72 to replace a deleted section titled "Students of the Books." On page 84, at the stipulation that the all-male Publication Committee "shall accept the candidates proposed by its Pastor Emeritus," Clemens wrote, vertically, "Boss". All in all, this must be regarded as one of the most thoroughly annotated volumes in Clemens's library, and though most comments do not reflect any of his own thinking, the various markings do signify a substantial investment of his time.

Catalogs: ListABP (1910), "Church Manual (Chr. Sci)". Sold at the *C1951* sale, though not listed in its catalog (which was not unusual); purchased by Jean Hersholt; listed by Parke-Bernet Galleries, Sale Number 1503, New York City, 23 March 1954, item 309, "many alterations by Clemens, in some instances whole paragraphs rewritten, one section of seventeen lines written out and tipped in at p. 72. Corrections and notes on about sixty pages," sold for $130 (PH of catalog page in MTP); listed in "American Books," Lew David Feldman Catalogue (1955), #243, $143.

Provenance: A copy of the (same) twentieth-eighth edition of *Manual of the Mother Church,* signed identically by Clemens in 1903 and also containing his dense pencil annotations, formerly belonged to the Mark Twain Papers, Bancroft Library, University of California at Berkeley. In 1970 it was recorded as having been missing since around 1964 and presumed stolen.

Location: Mark Twain House and Museum, Hartford, Connecticut. The volume had been part of that collection "since at least 1955," according to Joseph S. Van Why, then Director of the Stowe-Day Foundation, who recalled its acquisition in an interview with Alan Gribben in July 1984. From all indications, this would seem to be the same volume that once belonged to the Mark Twain Papers in Berkeley.

Copy examined: Clemens's copy, in July 1984. A *C1951* label is pasted below Clemens's dated signature on the front pastedown endpaper. The bookplate of Hollywood actor and book collector Jean Hersholt (1886–1956) is affixed to the rear endpaper. A green cloth box holds the book; the box bears a sticker reading "From the Library of/Jean Hersholt/No. T.34." I examined the book again in August 1987 in Hartford.

Clemens vigorously disputed some of Eddy's claims and fretted about the rising popularity of what he saw as her cult (an undue alarm on his part which in the course of time conceivably contributed to his own daughter's adoption of that very religion during the California phase of her life). Clemens wrote to Frank Bliss on 4 March 1903, requesting a copy of the 1902 edition of Eddy's *Manual* ("I have an *old* copy," he added). He wanted Bliss to borrow the book from his Hartford or Boston friends (PH in MTP).

———. *Miscellaneous Writings 1883–1896.* Boston: J. Armstrong, 1897.

Catalog: ListABP (1910), "Miscellaneous Writings, Eddy", no other information provided.

Mark Twain criticized "the divinity-circuit style" of *Miscellaneous Writings* in Chapter 7 of Book 1, *Christian Science* (1907). In Chapter 3 of Book II he quoted from the preface of this "fat volume."

———. "O'er waiting harp strings of the mind" (hymn, published in 1887). Melody by William Lyman Johnson (1869–1948).

"Pretty good, quite fair to middling" (*Christian Science* [1907], Book 1, Chapter 7).

———. *Retrospection and Introspection.* Twentieth thousand. Boston: Joseph Armstrong, 1902. 130 pp.

Marginalia: annotated by Clemens in both pencil and ink. Most of the notes are sarcastic, such as "Christ before the doctors" (p. 24); "awkward English", and "Quote the Bible & any other works" (p. 26). Clemens sneered, "She's inspired. Maybe I am, too, but uninspired I could beat that." (p. 28, referring to Eddy's poem titled "The Country Seat," which reminds Clemens of "Tom Moore").

Catalogs: ListABP (1910), "Retrospection and Introspection, Eddy"; "Retz Appraisal" (1944), p. 8, valued at $40.

Location: Mark Twain Papers, Bancroft Library, University of California at Berkeley.

Copy examined: Clemens's copy, in 2001.

Clemens wrote to W. D. McCrackan from Riverdale on 5 December 1902 to request a copy of Eddy's autobiography, *Retrospection and Introspection* (MTP). When the book had not arrived by 1 January 1903 he wrote again, asking McCrackan to "inquire why" (PH in MTP), and made a memorandum in Notebook 46 on 2 January 1903 about reminding McCrackan (TS p. 4). He treated Eddy's autobiography extensively in Book II of *Christian Science* (1907), ridiculing her supposed statements of fact and her mode of writing.

———. "Saw ye my Saviour?" (hymn, published in 1888). Melody composed by Lyman F[oster]. Brackett (1852–1937). Mark Twain mentions this hymn in *Christian Science* (1907), Book 1, Chapter 7.

———. *Science and Health; A Key to the Scriptures.* Tenth ed. 2 vols. Boston: published by the author, 1884. [Only Clemens's copy of Volume 2 is known to exist.]

Inscription: Volume 2 is signed in black ink on the front pastedown endpaper, "SL. Clemens/Riverdale, New York

City, 1902."

Marginalia: Volume 2 contains annotation by Clemens.

Catalogs: ListABP (1910), "Science and Health 2 vols., Eddy", also "Science and Health v. 1, Eddy", also "Science and Health, Eddy"; subsequently in the "Retz Appraisal" (1944), "p. 8, "Science and Health," Volume 2 only, valued at $25.

Location: Volume 2 only in Mark Twain Papers, Bancroft Library, University of California at Berkeley.

Copy examined: Clemens's copy of Volume 2.

Clemens talked to the dentist he regularly consulted in Elmira, New York on the subject of Mary Baker Eddy. "All occult things attracted him," recalled Franklin B. Darby after Clemens's death. "He was interested in spiritualism and Christian Science, but believed in neither. He told me that he had read Mrs. Eddy's book from beginning to end and from end to beginning and found it equally interesting read either way" ("Mark Twain's Carbuncle," ms. reproduced by Kevin Mac Donnell, 2005). In a letter to Frederick W. Peabody that Clemens wrote from Riverdale on 15 December 1902 he insisted that he was "not combating" Christian Science and indeed "I haven't a thing against it. Making fun of that shameless old swindler, Mother Eddy, is the only thing about it I take any interest in" (ALS, Christie's, 6 February 1981 sale, lot 56). In any event, *Science and Health* (initially published in 1875) antagonized Mark Twain far more than any of Eddy's other writings, and became, it may be said, a true obsession for him during his final decade. He objected to the immense power that it seemed to wield over large numbers of people, he insisted that Eddy had purloined its chief ideas from Phineas Parkhurst Quimby, and he was convinced that because she had hired ghost-writers to produce or at least edit much of the text, she deserved no credit for the book that bore her name.

Mark Twain included (but then canceled) a paragraph from *Science and Health* in the working notes for "The Chronicle of Young Satan," written 1897–1900 (*MSM*, p. 417). On 4 February 1899 he expressed curiosity in a letter to Joseph H. Twichell as to "who collars the cash that comes in from 'The Christian Science Journal' and from Eddy's book, 'Science & Health with Key to the Scriptures'?" (*LMTJHT*, p. 230). In 1901 and 1902 Twain labored doggedly at a manuscript he never could finish—"The Secret History of Eddypus, the World-Empire"—that was largely prompted by growing public faith in Eddy's *Science and Health*. John S. Tuckey viewed Twain's "Eddypus" as a fictional presentation of Mark Twain's anxieties about her doctrines, "a nightmare vision of a future in which the religion of Mrs. Eddy has become all-powerful as a world empire whose leader is both pope and monarch" (*FM*, p. 316). On 21 July 1903, commenting on an address by Eddy to her followers, Clemens admitted to Joseph H. Twichell that "everything the old sow does, interests me" (*LMTJHT*, p. 322) In an interview, "Mark Twain on the Law of Copyright," *Sketch* (London), 30 (March 1904): 376, he joked about his rheumatism, saying that "Mother Eddy has not taught me yet how to suppress my imaginings" (*Complete Interviews*, p. 494). He cast aspersions on Eddy's "cloudy & complacent romance" which purported to be "a Substitute for the Scriptures"

in an undated, unpublished criticism of G. W. Warder's *The Cities of the Sun* (DV357, MTP). In Chapter 13 of "Three Thousand Years among the Microbes" (written 1905) Twain launched into a punning onslaught against the "Giddyites" sect whose chief text is "Science and Wealth, with Key to the Fixtures" *(WWD?,* pp. 491–494). The fad-prone Stanchfield Garvey in "The Refuge of the Derelicts" (written 1905–1906) is infatuated with principles "drawn from 'Science and Health'" (*FM*, p. 240).

In 1906 Mark Twain marveled at the multitude of Americans prepared to believe in *Science and Health* "although they can't understand a line of it" who also "worship the sordid and ignorant old purloiner of that gospel—Mrs. Mary Baker G. Eddy" (22 June 1906 AD, MTP). He again leveled an attack on the book in another Autobiographical Dictation of 5 October 1906, claiming that Quimby was its true author and ruminating upon how easy, "today, it is to humbug the human race" (MTP). In "Papers of the Adam Family" Twain predicted by the Law of Periodical Repetition that Mrs. Eddy's book, "its orgies of style and construction tamed by an educated disciple," would be inflicted upon the human race again and again (*LE*, p. 101). At the beginning of *Is Shakespeare Dead?* (1909) Twain remarked upon Eddy's "flimsy" claim "that she wrote *Science and Health* from the direct dictation of the Deity."

Mark Twain's full-length review of *Science and Health*, however, occurs in his scathing but heavy-handed assault upon Eddy's fictional empire, *Christian Science*, published in 1907. Paul Baender's annotated edition of this lengthy diatribe turned up the somewhat surprising fact that at various junctures in the work Mark Twain used no fewer than *five* different editions of *Science and Health*—those of 1881 (*WIM?*, p. 575); 1883 (*WIM?*, p. 271); 1884 (Vol. 2 of which survives in MTP; *WIM?*, p. 293); 1898 (*WIM?*, pp. 554–555); and 1899 (*WIM?*, p. 339). Among the insults that he levels in Book II, Chapter 2 of *Christian Science* is the charge that portions here are "not English—I mean, grown-up English. But it is fifteen-year-old English," and he points out an "immense contrast between the legitimate English of *Science and Health* and the bastard English of Mrs. Eddy's miscellaneous work, and between the maturity of one diction and the juvenility of the other" (*WIM?*, pp. 272–273). See also the Catalog entries for James Henry Wiggin and Livingston Wright.

Robert Peel—*Mary Baker Eddy: The Years of Authority* (New York: Holt, Rinehart and Winston, 1977), pp. 198–209, 447–452—unsympathetically reviewed Mark Twain's opposition to Eddy and her doctrines in Chapter 6 of the third volume of this three-volume biography of Mary Baker Eddy. See Randall Knoper, *Acting Naturally: Mark Twain in the Culture of Performance* (Berkeley: University of California Press, 1995), pp. 185–187 for an intriguing explanation for Twain's antipathy to Eddy's views. K. Patrick Ober, *Mark Twain and Medicine: "Any Mummery Will Cure"* (Columbia: University of Missouri Press, 2003), pp. 219, 221, briefly commented. Gregg Camfield, "Transcendental Hedonism? Sex, Song, Food, and Drink in *No. 44, The Mysterious Stranger* and 'My Platonic Sweetheart,'" *Centenary Reflections on Mark Twain's No. 44, The Mysterious Stranger*, ed. Joseph Csicsila and

Chad Rohman (Columbia: University of Missouri Press, 2009), pp. 127–143, perceived some ironies. Michael Sheldon vividly summarized Twain's feelings about Eddy (*Man in White* [2010], pp. 67–76).

Hamlin Hill, "Afterword," *Christian Science* (New York: Oxford University Press, 1996), pp. 1–12.

EDEN, HORATIA KATHARINE FRANCES (GATTY) (1846–1945). *Juliana Horatia Ewing and Her Works*. New York: E. & J. B. Young & Co., 1885. 88 pp.

Catalog: Ball 2016 inventory, tan boards, poor condition.

Location: Quarry Farm library shelves, under the supervision of the Mark Twain Archive, Elmira College, Elmira, New York.

Mark Twain had access to this biography whenever he visited Quarry Farm in Elmira. In a speech Twain made in 1907 he referred to "an English authoress, well known in her day, who wrote beautiful child tales, touching and lovely in every way. In a little biographical sketch of her I found that her last hours were spent partly in reading a book of mine, until she was no longer able to read. That has always remained in my mind, and I have always cherished it as one of the good things of my life. I had read what she had written, and had loved her for what she had done" ("The Savage Club Dinner," 6 July 1907, *MTSpk* [1976], pp. 572–573). Twain did not name the writer, but Jo Dee Benussi noticed that the memoir by Juliana Ewing's sister Horatia Katharine Frances (Gatty) Eden—*Juliana Horatia Ewing and Her Books* (1896)—related this story (Benussi to Alan Gribben, email, 13 February 2006). As Juliana Ewing lay dying of incurable "blood poisoning" in 1885, testified her sister Horatia, "one of the very few books which she liked to have read aloud was Mark Twain's 'Adventures of Huckleberry Finn'; the dry humour of it,—the natural way in which everything is told from a boy's point of view,—and the vivid and beautiful descriptions of river scenery—all charmed her." Horatia reported that Juliana Ewing also enjoyed listening to Twain's account of the bizarre disfigurement of "Aurelia's Unfortunate Young Man" (1864), a sketch that "made her laugh so much" (pp. 78–79).

EDGEWORTH, MARIA (1767–1849). *Classic Tales by Maria Edgeworth. With a Biographical Sketch by Grace A[tkinson] Oliver [1844–1899]*. Boston: Roberts Bros., 1883. 332 pp.

Source: MTLAcc, entry #1926, volume donated from Clemens's library by Clara Clemens Gabrilowitsch in 1910.

——— and RICHARD LOVELL EDGEWORTH (1744–1817). *Essay on Irish Bulls* (originally published in 1802). [Edition uncertain.]

Catalog: ListABP (1910), "Essay on Irish Bulls, Edgeworth", no other information provided.

The Anglo-Irish writer Maria Edgeworth and her father sought in this publication to counter what they considered a distorted English view of the Irishman. The title referred to a colloquialism for supposed Irish linguistic blunders.

———. *The Parent's Assistant; or, Stories for Children*. Illus. Philadelphia: J. B. Lippincott & Co., 1883. 535 pp.

Source: MTLAcc, entry #807, volume donated by Clemens.

EDLER, KARL ERDMANN (1844–1931). *Der Kampf um die Kunst. Drei Novellen. [The Battle for Art: Three Novels]*. Wien: Wilhelm Frick, 1895. 196 pp.

Source: MTLAcc, entry #375, volume donated by Clemens.

EDMUNDSON, SARAH EMMA EVELYN (1841–1898), pseud. "S. Emma E. Edmonds." (Later, after 1867, known as Mrs. Sarah Emma Seelye.) *Nurse and Spy in the Union Army: Comprising the Adventures and Experiences of a Woman in Hospitals, Camps and Battle-Fields*. Illus. Hartford: W. S. Williams & Co., 1865. 384 pp.

Clemens recollected that "Nurse & Spy" sold 200,000 copies when he computed the possibilities for U. S. Grant's *Memoirs* in June 1885 (NB 24, *N&J* 3: 159).

EDWARDS, AMELIA ANN BLANFORD (1831–1892). *Barbara's History* (published in 1864).

Susy Clemens praised this novel involving bigamy to her sister Clara from Venice on 10 April 1893: "It resembles 'Jane Eyre' a good deal . . . and it isn't grand and stunning like 'Wages'" (*S&MT*, p. 329). *Barbara's History* helped establish the literary reputation of this English writer.

———. "Give Me Three Grains of Corn, Mother" (poem, song). Sometimes subtitled: "The Irish Famine." [Sheet music for the song version was in print by 1848.]

This seven-stanza exercise in pathos was the third title listed in the program of the "Country School Exhibition," a shipboard program of amateur talent that Clemens helped organize on the *Montana* on 10 July 1868 (*Alta California*, 6 September 1868; reprinted in *The Twainian* 7 [November-December 1948]: 5). It was to be a "Duett" performed by "Messrs. L. & H." Perhaps the sentiment in the piece was too strong for its inclusion in the similar schoolhouse declamations executed in Chapter 21 of *Tom Sawyer*; the poem's fifth stanza began: "What has poor Ireland done, mother,—/What has poor Ireland done,/That the world looks on, and sees us starve,/Perishing one by one?" Clemens wrote "Give me 3 grains of corn" on the cover of his copy of F. B. Ogilvie's *Two Hundred Old-Time Songs* (1896).

———. *A Thousand Miles Up the Nile*. Illustrated by the author. London: Longmans, Green & Co., 1877. 732 pp. [Edition conjectured; a second, often-reprinted edition was issued in 1888, and a London edition by George Routledge and Sons appeared in 1890.]

Catalog: ListABP (1910), "1000 Miles up the Nile, Edwards", no other information provided.

———. *Untrodden Peaks and Unfrequented Valleys. A Midsummer Ramble in the Dolomites*. Illus. Second edition. Original multicolored pictorial cloth, gilt, corners and spine ends frayed and worn, front hinge cracked. London: George Routledge and Sons, 1890. 389 pp.

Inscription: by the author in black ink on the half-title page: "I wish that Mr. & Mrs. Clemens had been with L. & the writer on this journey,—but if so, Mr. Clemens would have written a book so much better than 'Untrodden Peaks and Unfrequented Valleys' that the present volume would never have been committed by Amelia B. Edwards,/Jan. 27/90." (The inscription incorporated the printed title of the book on this half-title page.)

Marginalia: a number (possibly "95"), not in Clemens's hand, was written at the bottom of page 41.

Catalogs: *A1911*, "square 8vo, pictured cloth, Lond. 1890," quotes the inscription, lot 150, sold for $5.25; California Book Auction Galleries, San Francisco, June 1988, "with Mark Twain's autograph card laid in," $450 plus 10% (TS record in MTP, citing *Manuscripts* 41.1 [Winter 1989]:

45); Phillip J. Pirages Fine Books and Manuscripts, McMinnville, Oregon, Catalogue 14, December 1988, book contains the *A1911* sale label, catalog quotes the inscription, $850; *Sotheby's 2003*, #217, $4,000 (sold with four other inscribed books).

Provenance: obtained from Phillip J. Pirages Fine Books and Manuscripts for $850 on 7 December 1988 by Nick Karanovich, Fort Wayne, Indiana (Karanovich to Alan Gribben, 12 December 1988).

Location: collection of Kevin Mac Donnell, Austin, Texas.

Copy examined: Clemens's unmarked copy, in July 2004. Contains an *A1911* sale label at the bottom of the front pastedown endpaper.

EDWARDS, ANNIE (1830–1896). *Ought We To Visit Her? A Novel.* New York: Sheldon and Co., [cop. 1871]. 194 pp.

Source: MTLAcc, entry #2230, volume donated from Clemens's library by Clara Clemens Gabrilowitsch in 1910. A tale of unfair social ostracism in the English provinces.

EDWARDS, JONATHAN (1703–1758). *Freedom of the Will* (published in 1754).

Early in 1902 the Reverend Joseph H. Twichell loaned Clemens a copy of *Freedom of the Will* for perusal on his way back from Hartford to Riverdale (*MTL*, pp. 719–720). Clemens wrote a lengthy analysis of the book, which he read "from Bridgeport to N.Y. thence to home; & continuously until near midnight." The reading experience was searing, he informed Twichell: "I wallowed & reeled with Jonathan in his insane debauch"; it left him with "a strange & haunting sense of having been on a 3-days' tear with a drunken lunatic" (*MTB*, pp. 1156–57; *LMTJHT*, p. 299). The work is lit, he wrote, by "the glare of a resplendent intellect gone mad—a marvelous spectacle." Clemens found himself agreeing with Edwards's assumptions that man never creates an impulse by his own will, and that "in his natural state" he is universally dominated by selfish motives. These views concurred with Clemens's notions of Necessity and Motive. But "then he suddenly flies the logical track & (to all seeming) makes the *man* & not those exterior forces responsible to God for the man's thoughts, words[,] & acts. It is frank insanity," All this comes about, unfortunately, when Edwards "was pointed straight for the only rational & possible next station on *that* piece of road: the irresponsibility of man to God" (*MTB*, p. 1157; *LMTJHT*, p. 300).

The copy of *Freedom of the Will* that Twichell loaned Clemens in 1902 was not his first introduction to Edwards's doctrines. In June 1882 Clemens had noted the title of an early biographical sketch of Edwards that he subsequently obtained (see the Catalog entry for Samuel Hopkins), and this book included excerpts from Edwards's diary and sermons. The following year Clemens alluded to Edwards's faith in a tormenting Hell (NB 22 [1883], *N&J* 3: 32). In 1889 or 1890 he reminded Andrew Lang that the Salvation Army is more effective than Jonathan Edwards in converting the poor to Christianity (*MTL*, p. 527). A passage Clemens read in Meredith Townsend's *Asia and Europe* (1901) reminded him of Edwards's thought, and he wrote Edwards's name in the margin of page 14 at Townsend's explanation of the Mohammedan philosophy "that God acts because He wills, and not because He is bound by His own nature. 'These to hell and I care not,

these to heaven and I reck not.' It seems to the European an abominable explanation," wrote Townsend. Mark Twain thought of joking about Edwards in a speech at Princeton University for which he made notes on 14 October 1902 (NB 45, TS p. 31). (Presumably Twain was aware that Edwards had been appointed president of the College of New Jersey—later renamed Princeton—shortly before he died in March 1758.) After Olivia's death Clemens wrote to Twichell on 28 July 1904 to vent his opinion that the human race can muster no more evidence of its intelligence regarding the limits of human responsibility than can "Jonathan Edwards in his wildest moments" (*LMTJHT*, p. 347). He mentioned Edwards once again in Book II, Chapter 3 of *Christian Science* (1907): "If the late Jonathan Edwards should rise up and tell me he wrote Mr. Dooley's books, I should answer and say that the marked difference between his style and Dooley's is argument against the soundness of his statement."

Hill, *MTGF* (1973), p. 48; William H. Shurr, *Rappaccini's Children: American Writers in a Calvinist World* (Lexington: University Press of Kentucky, 1981), pp. 19–35; Joe B. Fulton, *The Reverend Mark Twain: Theological Burlesque, Form, and Content* (Columbus: Ohio State University Press, 2006), pp. 57, 153; Joe B. Fulton, "'Jonathan Edwards, Calvin, Baxter & Co.': Mark Twain and the Comedy of Calvinism," *John Calvin's American Legacy*, ed. Thomas J. Davis (New York: Oxford University Press, 2010), pp. 239–255.

EGGLESTON, EDWARD (1837–1902). *The End of the World: A Love Story* (novel, published in 1872).

Clemens scoffed at ranking Edward Eggleston "on the same level" with James Russell Lowell's first *Biglow Papers* (as did a laudatory piece appearing in the *Christian Union*) on the basis of *The Hoosier Schoolmaster* and *The End of the World* (Clemens's comment on a clipping enclosed with a letter of 20 April 1873 to Whitelaw Reid; *MTLet* 5: 348). Perhaps Clemens did not care for the German dialect in the novel, or conceivably he already felt proprietary about descriptions of river steamboating and resented Eggleston's efforts in that direction. William Dean Howells, however, had applauded the book's realism in the December 1872 issue of *Atlantic Monthly*.

Thomas Ruys Smith, "'The Mississippi Was a Virgin Field': Reconstructing the River Before Mark Twain, 1865–1865," *Mark Twain Journal* 53.2 (Fall 2015): 50–52.

———. *A First Book in American History.* New York: D. Appleton & Co., 1889. 203 pp.

Source: MTLAcc, entry #1594, volume donated by Clemens.

———. *The Hoosier Schoolmaster: A Story of Backwoods Life in Indiana* (novel, published in 1871).

See the entry above for Eggleston's *The End of the World*.

George W. Crandall, "Emperors and Little Empires: The Schoolmaster in Nineteenth-Century American Literature," *Studies in American Humor*, n.s. 2, 5.1 (Spring 1986): 51–61.

———. *The Mystery of Metropolisville.* Illus. New York: Orange Judd and Co., 1873. 320 pp. [Edition conjectured.]

In a letter of 20 April 1873 to Whitelaw Reid, Mark Twain referred to this forthcoming work as "an absolutely worthless book" in arguing that his and Charles Dudley

Warner's *The Gilded Age* (1873) was "worth ten such messes of ill-digested stuff as this Metropolisville thing." He enclosed with his letter a clipping from the *Christian Union* that heralded Eggleston as "the coming American novelist" and predicted large sales for his soon-to-be-released novel, *The Mystery of Metropolisville* (*MTLet* 5: 347–348). But Clemens later defended Eggleston's novel (which he mistakenly called "Mystery of Mechanicsville") somewhat lefthandedly in a notebook that he kept in Paris during 1879. Comparing the book to those by Rabelais, Fielding, and Smollett, he argues that evidently "it depends on who writes a thing whether it is coarse or not" (NB 18, *N&J* 2: 303). Actually, though, Eggleston's novel is highly moralistic, sentimental, and professedly Christian in outlook. Perhaps Clemens meant the rude, unrefined prairie-town society that Eggleston depicted during the period of rampant land speculation in Minnesota in 1856. In this respect, with its emphasis on colorful local characters and the motive of revenge, *The Mystery of Metropolisville* prefigured another novel set in a similarly bleak, indifferent landscape—Edgar Watson Howe's *The Story of a Country Town* (1883), of which Twain would heartily approve. Bryant Morey French discerned similarities between Eggleston's novel and *The Gilded Age* (1873); see French's *Mark Twain and "The Gilded Age"* (1965), pp. 229, 231–232. Twain mentioned Eggleston twice in his notebooks—in January 1888 (NB 27, *N&J* 3: 363) and December 1889 (NB 29, *N&J* 3: 536). He also included "Eggleston" among the authors of "choice and valuable literature" whose English royalties were being efficaciously protected by his publisher ("Concerning the British Pirates, written in 1888, quoted in "Holiday Miscellany," Heritage Book Shop, Catalog 176 [1989], item #232). In a letter of 1888, incidentally, Eggleston expressed an unfavorable opinion of Twain, whom he ranked as "only a good clown" (William Randel, *Edward Eggleston*. Twayne United States Authors Series, No. 405 [New York: Twayne Publishers, 1963], pp. 81–82).

EICKEMEYER, RUDOLF, JR. (1862–1932). *Winter, Pictured by Rudolf Eickemeyer, Jr.* Intro. by Sadakichi Hartmann (1867–1944). Illus. New York: R. H. Russell, 1903. 55 pp.
  Source: MTLAcc, entry #1366, volume donated by Clemens.
  Eickemeyer was a noted photographer.

ELDER, SAMUEL J[AMES]. (1850–1918). "Duration of Copyright," *Yale Law Journal* 14.8 (1 June 1905): 417–423.
  On 12 June 1905 Elder, a Boston attorney, wrote to Clemens: "I have taken the liberty to have the publishers send you a copy of the Yale Law Journal containing my article on 'Duration of Copyright.'" He added: "You will notice that my article . . . takes up your suggestion in the North American" (MTP). A letter by Clemens on copyright legislation had appeared in the January 1905 issue of the *North American Review*. On 21 June 1905 Clemens replied to Elder: "I have read your article with great interest—& also with great profit. I am glad to have it & I thank you" (TS in MTP).

ELDERKIN, JOHN (1841–1926). *A Brief History of the Lotos Club.* New York: [Press of Macgowan & Slipper, 1895]. 166 pp.
  Inscription: presentation copy inscribed by Elderkin, dated

15 April 1895.
  Catalog: *Hunley 1958.*
  The volume contains an account of the 1893 dinner in Clemens's honor, along with a transcript of his speech. Clemens was an active member of the Lotos Club in New York City.

ELDRIDGE, GEORGE DYRE (1848–1926). *In the Potter's House.* New York: Doubleday, Page & Co., 1908. 338 pp.
  Source: MTLAcc, entry #125, volume donated by Clemens. Eldridge was an insurance executive and actuary. His novel took its title from lines in the *Rubáiyát*: "Once more within the Potter's house alone/I stood, surrounded by the Shapes of clay."

ELGIN, JAMES BRUCE (1811–1863). *Letters and Journals of James, Eighth Earl of Elgin, Governor of Jamaica, Governor-General of Canada, Envoy to China, Viceroy of India.* Ed. by Theodore Walrond (1824–1887). Preface by Arthur Penrhyn Stanley (1815–1881). London: J. Murray, 1872. 467 pp.
  "Lord Elgin's Diary & Letters," Clemens noted late in April 1888 (NB 27, *N&J* 3: 383).

ELIOT, CHARLES WILLIAM (1834–1926). *John Gilley, Maine Farmer and Fisherman.* True American Types Series. Boston: American Unitarian Association, 1905. 72 pp.
  John Gilley (1822–1896) had been a resident of Sutton's Island, Maine. C. L. Stebbins of the American Unitarian Association wrote to Clemens on 6 April 1905 to inform him that he would soon receive the first volume in the "True American Types" series, written by the president of Harvard. (Eliot was president of Harvard from 1869 until 1909.) Stebbins asked Clemens to contribute a volume to these sketches of "sterling American manhood." They sought a biography of "some plodder in some quiet walk of life," an obscure individual. "We wish to have represented a typical character of the middle West and we can think of no better one than a Mississippi deck-hand." On the back of the second page of Stebbins' letter Isabel V. Lyon noted Clemens's refusal (MTP).

ELIOT, GEORGE, PSEUD. OF MARIAN (EVANS) CROSS (1819–1880). *Adam Bede.* 2 vols. New York: J. W. Lovell Co., 1883. 484 pp.
  Source: MTLAcc, entries #980 and #1261, volumes donated by Clemens.
  Susy Clemens wrote from Bryn Mawr in 1890 to report, "I am reading 'Daniel Deronda' and enjoying it, endlessly; much more than I did Adam Bede" (*S&MT*, p. 279; ALS in MTHM).

———. *Adam Bede.* New York: Worthington Co., 1887. 377 pp.
  Source: MTLAcc, entry #1260, volume donated by Clemens.

———. *Adam Bede.* Handy Volume Edition. Boston: Estes and Lauriat, 1887.
  Catalog: Ball 2016 inventory, brown boards with marbling.
  Location: Quarry Farm library shelves, under the supervision of the Mark Twain Archive, Elmira College, Elmira, New York.
  This book was available to Clemens whenever he visited Quarry Farm in Elmira.

———. *Adam Bede.* 2 vols. Illus. New York: Harper & Brothers, 1899.
  Source: MTLAcc, entries #1132 and #1262, volumes

donated by Clemens.

———. *Complete Poems.* Intro. by Matthew Browne (pseud. of W[illiam]. B[righty]. Rands (1823–1882). Handy Volume Edition. Boston: Estes and Lauriat, 1887.

    Catalog: Ball 2016 inventory, reddish brown cloth, marbled covers, gilt lettering on the spine, no marginalia reported.

    Location: Quarry Farm library shelves, under the supervision of the Mark Twain Archive, Elmira College, Elmira, New York.

This book was available to Clemens whenever he visited Quarry Farm in Elmira.

———. *Daniel Deronda.* 2 vols. New York: Harper & Brothers, [cop. 1876].

    Source: MTLAcc, entries #2232 and #2233, volumes donated from Clemens's library by Clara Clemens Gabrilowitsch in 1910.

Clemens told Howells in a letter from Elmira on 21 July 1885 that he had recently attempted to read this novel: "I dragged through three chapters, losing flesh all the time, & then was honest enough to quit, & confess to myself that I haven't *any* romance-literature appetite, as far as I can see" (*MTHL*, p. 533). Clemens's opinion obviously was not shared by members of his household: Clara Clemens's commonplace book (1888?) quotes and discusses *Daniel Deronda* and refers frequently to Eliot's life and her writing in general (Paine 150, MTP); indeed, George Eliot seems to have provided Clara's major reading experiences during her adolescence. Susy mentioned "reading 'Daniel Deronda' and enjoying it, endlessly" at Bryn Mawr in 1890 (*S&MT*, p. 279; ALS in MTHM). On 2 January 1908 Isabel V. Lyon, a brevet member of Clemens's family, noted that she herself was "reading 'Daniel Deronda' with greater delight than ever" (IVL Journal, TS p. 290, MTP). This novel was one of Eliot's most complex works of fiction, and somewhat daring (for its time) in the introduction of Jewish characters and their subculture in England.

———. *Daniel Deronda.* 4 vols. Copyright Edition. Collection of British Authors Series. Leipzig: Bernhard Tauchnitz, 1876.

    Source: MTLAcc, entry #2234, Volume I only (296 pp.), donated from Clemens's library by Clara Clemens Gabrilowitsch in 1910.

———. *Daniel Deronda.* New York: Geo. Munro, [1883?]. 553 pp.

    Source: MTLAcc, entry #1265, volume donated by Clemens.

———. *Daniel Deronda.* 2 vols. New York: Harper & Brothers, 1905. 427 pp.

    Source: MTLAcc, entry #1134, Volume II only (427 pp.), donated by Clemens.

———. [Another identical edition, Volume II only].

    Source: MTLAcc, entry #1264, volume donated by Clemens.

———. *Daniel Deronda.* Handy Volume Edition. 2 vols. Boston: Estes and Lauriat, 1887.

    Catalog: Ball 2016 inventory, reddish-brown cloth, marbled covers, gilt lettering on the spine.

    Location: Quarry Farm library shelves, under the supervision of the Mark Twain Archive, Elmira College, Elmira, New York.

This book was available to Clemens whenever he visited Quarry Farm in Elmira.

———. *Felix Holt, the Radical.* Illus. New York: Harper & Brothers, 1906. 529 pp.

    Source: MTLAcc, entry #1548, volume donated by Clemens.

———. *The George Eliot Birthday Book.* Portrait. Boston, 1882.

    Inscriptions: signed by members of the Clemens family.

    Catalog: *A1911,* "Oblong 16mo, cloth, with autographs of many of the Clemens family, Bost. 1882," lot 6, sold for $3.25.

———. *George Eliot's Life as Related in Her Letters and Journals. Arranged and Edited by Her Husband, J[ohn]. W[alter]. Cross [1840–1924].* 3 vols. Volume I has contemporary half calf, morocco spine labels, top of spine snagged, rubbed edges and corners, marbled endpapers. New York: Harper & Brothers, 1885. Volume I has 348 pp. [Volumes II and III are not present.]

    Marginalia: pencil markings throughout do not appear to be Clemens's. A holograph note, possibly in Olivia Clemens's hand, appears on page 317 of Volume I near an account of the death of a child: "Calm about it."

    Provenance: Volume I has the shelfmarks of Clara Clemens Gabrilowitsch's library numbering system during her Detroit years. Sold at the 1951 Hollywood auction, but not listed in its very incomplete sale catalog sheet.

    Catalog: "Property from the Library of Mark Twain," Butterfield & Butterfield, San Francisco, Sale 6613 (16 July 1997), "Vol. I only," lot 2703.

    Location: Mark Twain House and Museum, Hartford, Connecticut, Volume I only.

    Copy examined: Olivia Clemens's copy of Volume I, presumably shared with Clemens and Clara Clemens. Viewed in Hartford in 1997.

On 7 June 1885 Olivia Clemens began a new diary by noting: "I am reading with great interest 'George Elliott's Life' [sic] by her husband J. W. Cross. It is most delightful. . . . The only thing in the book that annoys me is her constant mentions of her ill health" (DV161, MTP). Very probably Clemens read or at least discussed this work with Olivia, for in late October 1885 he thought of writing an article about "Carlyle's whines & complaints," especially regarding his chronic stomach trouble, and "George Elliott's [sic] ditto" (NB 25, *N&J* 3: 206). Clara Clemens expressed fervent admiration for George Eliot in her commonplace book (1888?) and quoted devotedly from Cross' biography in its pages (Paine 150, MTP).

Harris, *Courtship* (1996), pp. 114–115.

———. [Identical copy.]

    Inscription: "Ida C. Langdon/May 15th 1885" in Volume I. Ida Clark Langdon (1849–1934) was married to Charles Jervis Langdon (1849–1916).

    Catalog: Ball 2016 inventory, 3 vols., green boards with gilt lettering, little paper men inserted in Volume II at the Chapter Index page.

    Location: Quarry Farm library shelves, under the supervision of the Mark Twain Archive, Elmira College, Elmira, New York.

Another book available to Clemens whenever he visited the Langdon residence in Elmira.

———. *George Eliot's Life as Related in Her Letters and Journals. Arranged and Edited by Her Husband, J[ohn]. W[alter]. Cross*

[1840–1924]. 3 vols. New York: Harper & Brothers, 1899.
Source: MTLAcc, entries #1135, #1136, and #1758, three volumes donated by Clemens.

———. *George Eliot's Works*. 12 vols. New York: Harper & Brothers, 1885.
Catalog: Ball 2016 inventory, lacks Volumes XI and XII, also is missing the first half of Volume VI (*Middlemarch*).
Location: Quarry Farm library shelves, under the supervision of the Mark Twain Archive, Elmira College, Elmira, New York.
This set was available to Clemens whenever he visited Quarry Farm in Elmira.

———. *Impressions of Theophrastus Such*. New York: Harper & Brothers, [188–].
234 pp.
Source: MTLAcc, entry #1546, volume donated by Clemens.

———. *Middlemarch: A Study of Provincial Life*. 2 vols. Harper's Library Edition of the Novels of George Eliot. Red marbled covers and endpapers, leather spine, worn. New York: Harper & Brothers, n.d. [Only the second volume has been discovered.]
Inscription: inscribed in pencil on the verso of the front free endpaper, "Clemens". The hand appears to be that of Olivia Clemens.
Marginalia: pencil marks in the second volume on pages 15, 99, 156, 185, 209, 269, 387, 395, 396, 403. No other markings.
Provenance: Antenne-Dorrance Collection, Rice Lake, Wisconsin.
Location: Mark Twain Archive, Gannett-Tripp Learning Center, Elmira College, Elmira, New York (the second volume only).
Copy examined: copy of the second volume belonging to a member of Clemens's family, very possibly Olivia. Examined on 28 May 2015.
Clemens praised Howells' *Indian Summer* by relating how he himself "bored through Middlemarch during the past week, with its labored & tedious analyses of feelings & motives, its paltry & tiresome people, its unexciting & uninteresting story, & its frequent blinding flashes of single-sentence poetry, philosophy, wit, & what-not, & nearly died from the over-work. I wouldn't read another of those books for a farm." Clemens concluded with a compliment to his friend Howells: "You make all the motives & feelings perfectly clear without analyzing the guts out of them, the way George Eliot does. I can't stand George Eliot, & Hawthorne & those people; I see what they are at, a hundred years before they get to it, & they just tire me to death" (*MTHL*, pp. 533–534). Nevertheless Clemens could not tolerate utter ignorance of Eliot's identity or stature: he castigated Charles L. Webster's ignorance because "once in a drawing-room company some talk sprang up about George Eliot and her literature. I saw Webster getting ready to contribute. . . . He filled that vacancy with this remark, uttered with tranquil complacency: 'I've never read any of his books, on account of prejudice'" (29 May 1906 AD, *MTE*, pp. 180–181; *AutoMT* 2: 65). Webster's son, Samuel C. Webster, doubted the veracity of this anecdote and noted in his own copy of *Mark Twain in Eruption* that his father

"had a set of G. E." (marginalia on p. 180, book in MTP).

———. *Middlemarch*. Handy Volume Edition. 2 vols. Boston: Estes and Lauriat, 1887.
Inscription: "Ida Langdon". Ida Langdon (1880–1964), the daughter of Charles Jervis and Ida Clark Langdon, presumably added her signature long after her mother acquired these volumes.
Catalog: Ball 2016 inventory, reddish-brown cloth, marbled covers, gilt lettering on the spine.
Location: Quarry Farm library shelves, under the supervision of the Mark Twain Archive, Elmira College, Elmira, New York.
This book was available to Clemens whenever he visited the Langdons in Elmira.

———. *Middlemarch: A Study of Provincial Life*. New York: T. Y. Crowell & Co., n.d. 776 pp.
Source: MTLAcc, entry #2231, volume donated from Clemens's library by Clara Clemens Gabrilowitsch in 1910.

———. *The Mill on the Floss*. Boston: Estes and Lauriat, 1885.
Inscription: "Ida C. Langdon/May 15th/1885". Ida Clark Langdon (1849–1934) was married to Charles Jervis Langdon (1849–1916).
Catalog: Ball 2016 inventory, no marginalia reported.
Location: Quarry Farm library shelves, under the supervision of the Mark Twain Archive, Elmira College, Elmira, New York.
This book was available to Clemens whenever he visited the Langdons in Elmira.

———. *The Mill on the Floss*. Handy Volume Edition. Boston: Estes and Lauriat, 1887.
Catalog: Ball 2016 inventory, reddish brown cloth, marbled covers, gilt lettering on the spine, no marginalia reported.
Location: Quarry Farm library shelves, under the supervision of the Mark Twain Archive, Elmira College, Elmira, New York.
This book was available to Clemens whenever he visited Quarry Farm in Elmira.

———. *The Mill on the Floss*. Illus. New York: Harper & Brothers, 1902. 464 pp.
Catalogs: MTLAcc, entry #1547, volume donated by Clemens.

———. [Another copy. Edition unknown.]
Catalog: ListABP (1910), "Mill on the Floss, Eliot", no other information provided.

———. *Miscellaneous Essays*. Handy Volume Edition. Boston: Estes and Lauriat, 1887.
Catalog: Ball 2016 inventory, reddish brown cloth, marbled covers, gilt lettering on the spine, no marginalia reported.
Location: Quarry Farm library shelves, under the supervision of the Mark Twain Archive, Elmira College, Elmira, New York.
This book was available to Clemens whenever he visited Quarry Farm in Elmira.

———. [Identical copy.]
Inscription: "Ida C. Langdon/May 15th/1885". Ida Clark Langdon (1849–1934) was married to Charles Jervis Langdon (1849–1916).
Catalog: Ball 2016 inventory, no marginalia reported.
Location: Quarry Farm library shelves, under the supervision of the Mark Twain Archive, Elmira College, Elmira,

New York.

This book was available to Clemens whenever he visited the Langdons in Elmira.

———. *Poems, Together with Brother Jacob and The Lifted Veil.* New York: Harper & Brothers, 1885. 380 pp.

Source: MTLAcc, entry #1133, volume donated by Clemens.

———. [Another identical copy.]

Source: MTLAcc, entry #1263, volume donated by Clemens.

———. *Romola.* 2 vols. Copyright Edition. Collection of British Authors Series. Leipzig: B. Tauchnitz, 1863.

Source: MTLAcc, entries #2235 and #2236, volumes donated from Clemens's library by Clara Clemens Gabrilowitsch in 1910.

On Sunday, 11 August 1878, Clemens recorded in Notebook 15: "Been reading Romola yesterday afternoon, last night & this morning; at last I came upon the only passage which has thus far *hit me with force*—Tito compromising with his conscience & resolving to do, not a bad thing, but not the *best* thing." Clemens had purchased the volume "24 hours ago in Heidelberg," yet "nothing in the book had taken hold of me till I came to that one passage on page 112 Tauchnitz edition" (*N&J* 2: 135).

Perhaps this historical novel set in fifteenth-century Florence gave Mark Twain his interest in the celebrated monk of Ferrara, Girolamo Savonarola (1452–1498). He mentioned Savonarola among historical personages and events in "How to Make History Dates Stick" (unpublished until 1914). "George, old Savvanarola [*sic*]—gee! they only just *burnt* him," wisecracks Dug Hapgood upon taking some medicine in Chapter 12 of "Which Was It?" (written 1899–1903, *WWD?*, p. 291). In 1901 Twain declared that "a Savonarola can quell and scatter a mob of lynchers with a mere glance of his eye" ("The United States of Lyncherdom," *Pen*, p. 156). Another source from which Clemens might have learned about Savonarola is Margaret Oliphant's *The Makers of Florence* (1888), Chapters 9 through 13.

———. *Romola.* New York, 1869.

Catalog: *A1911*, "8vo, unbound, N.Y. 1869," lot 151, sold for $1.

———. *Romola.* Handy Volume Edition. 2 vols. Boston: Estes and Lauriat, 1887.

Catalog: Ball 2016 inventory, reddish brown cloth, marbled covers, gilt lettering on the spine, no marginalia reported.

Location: Quarry Farm library shelves, under the supervision of the Mark Twain Archive, Elmira College, Elmira, New York.

This book was available to Clemens whenever he visited Quarry Farm in Elmira.

———. *Romola.* The Florentine Edition. Illus. 2 vols. Philadelphia, 1890.

Catalog: *A1911*, "2 vols., 12mo, cloth, vellum backs, gilt escutcheons on covers, gilt tops (back of one vol. and several pages stained), Phila. 1890, The Florentine Edition, fine copy, with the exception noted," lot 152, sold for $3.25.

———. *Scenes of Clerical Life.* Handy Volume Edition. Boston: Estes and Lauriat, 1887.

Catalog: Ball 2016 inventory, reddish brown cloth, marbled

covers, gilt lettering on the spine, no marginalia reported.

Location: Quarry Farm library shelves, under the supervision of the Mark Twain Archive, Elmira College, Elmira, New York.

This book was available to Clemens whenever he visited Quarry Farm in Elmira.

———. *The Spanish Gypsy. A Poem.* Boston: Ticknor & Fields, 1868. 287 pp.

Source: MTLAcc, entry #2024, volume donated from Clemens's library by Clara Clemens Gabrilowitsch in 1910.

ELIZABETH, QUEEN OF RUMANIA (1843–1916), pseud. "Carmen Sylva." *A Real Queen's Fairy Tales. By Carmen Sylva.* Trans. by Edith Hopkirk. Illustrated by H[arold]. [Edward Hughes] Nelson (1871–1948) and A[lfred]. G[arth]. Jones (1872–1955). Chicago, 1901.

Inscription: signed, "S. L. Clemens, Riverdale-on-Hudson, Feb. 22, 1902."

Catalog: *A 1911*, "8vo, decorative cloth, Chicago, 1901," quotes the signature, lot 445, $4.25.

In "Does the Race of Man Love a Lord?" (1902) Mark Twain referred to "that charming and lovable German princess and poet, Carmen Sylva, Queen of Roumania," who "remembers yet that the flowers of the woods and fields 'talked to her' when she was a girl, and she sets it down in her latest book." Twain quotes passages from her account of the homage shown to her by squirrels, birds, wasps, bees, and dogs. Arthur Sherburne Hardy (1847–1930) testified that on a visit he and wife made to the Queen of Rumania, "One of Mark Twain's books was in her hand. She was much interested to learn that we knew him, asking a thousand questions about him and begging us to assure him of the many good laughs he had given her" (*Things Remembered* [Boston: Houghton Mifflin Co., 1923], p. 160).

ELLIOT, CHARLES S. (1846–1910), ed. *Songs of Yale: A New Collection of College Songs.* Ed. by Charles S. Elliot. Rev. and enl. by Elmer P. Howe (1851–1918). Fifth edition. New York: Taintor Brothers, Merrill & Co., 1880. 172 pp.

Catalog: *A1911*, "12mo, cloth, N.Y. 1880," with a small sheet of notes by Clemens, lot 497, withdrawn from sale.

Location: Mark Twain House and Museum, Hartford, Connecticut. Donated in 1965 by Olivia Loomis Lada-Mocarski.

Copy examined: Clemens's copy, containing the *A1911* sale label on the front pastedown endpaper. No inscription or markings, but the book appears used. Examined in August 1987.

ELLIOTT, CHARLES WYLLYS (1817–1883). *The Book of American Interiors. Prepared by Charles Wyllys Elliott from Existing Houses.* Illus. First edition. Small folio. Original cloth. Boston: James R. Osgood and Co., 1876. 135 pp.

Inscription: in Olivia Clemens's hand on the front free endpaper, "To/The Cranes/Merry Christmas!/From the Clemenses./Hartford, Dec. 25, 1875."

Catalog: M & S Rare Books, Weston, Massachusetts, Catalog 19, Part 1, p. 7, item #77, priced at $75. Both the edition and inscription were reported. "The book was obtained in the Elmira, N.Y. area."

Location: Mark Twain House and Museum, Hartford, Connecticut.

Copy examined: photocopies of the inscription and title

page provided by Diana Royce, then Librarian of the Stowe-Day Memorial Library, Hartford, on 3 October 1984. She found no marginalia. I also examined a photocopy of the M & S Rare Books catalog entry. In August 1987 I saw the book itself in Hartford.

Elliott's book included interior views of the homes of such literary figures as William Cullen Bryant, Donald G. Mitchell, and Henry Wadsworth Longfellow, as well as various other non-literary personages.

———. *Remarkable Characters and Places of the Holy Land*. Hartford, Connecticut: J. B. Burr & Co., 1867. 640 pp.

Dewey Ganzel established the identity of this work, which Mark Twain referred to only as "C. W. B.'s 'Life in the Holy Land'" in Chapter 48 of *The Innocents Abroad* (1869), where he quotes with scorn its description of the Sea of Gallilee ("Guidebooks" [1965], p. 88 n. 18). Leon T. Dickinson's explanatory notes for a projected but never-published Iowa-California Edition of *The Innocents Abroad* pointed out that "Life in the Holy Land" was the short title stamped on the cover of Elliott's volume and that Mark Twain quoted Elliott more approvingly in Chapter 56 (MTP).

Hirst, "Making of *The Innocents Abroad*" (doctoral dissertation, 1975).

ELLIOTT, CHARLOTTE (1789–1871). "Just as I am, without one plea" (hymn, published in 1835). William B[atchelder]. Bradbury (1816–1868), composer.

"You hear him [Mark Twain's character named Robert Wicklow] sing 'Just as I am—poor, wretched, blind'—just you hear him sing that, once, and see if you don't melt all up and the water come into your eyes!" ("A Curious Experience" [1881]). This was the first line in the fourth stanza of Elliott's hymn.

ELLIOT, DANIEL GIRAUD (1835–1915). *The Life and Habits of Wild Animals*. Illustrated by Joseph Wolf (1820–1899). Engraved by J[osiah]. W[ood]. Whymper (1813–1903) and Edward Whymper (1840–1911). London: Alexander Macmillan & Co., 1874. 72 pp. [Publisher and pages conjectured.]

Inscription: signed on the front endpaper: "Saml. L. Clemens. London, Dec. 21, 1873."

Catalog: *Mott 1952*, #50, $12.50.

ELLIOTT, GEORGE W. (1830–1898). "Bonny Eloise (The Belle of the Mohawk Vale)" (song, published in 1858). Lyrics by George W. Elliott; music composed by John Rogers Thomas (1830–1896).

Initially Clemens was impressed on his lecture tour in 1868 when "my poet-friend Mr. Elliott" gave him a hospitable welcome in Fort Plain, New York and introduced him to his wife, "a good, genuine little woman" who had been "the original of the 'Bonnie Eloise' of the old song so popular ten years ago" (SLC to Olivia Langdon, 20 December 1868, *MTLet* 2: 335).

———. "The Blush Rose" and "The Dead Canary" (poems).

Elliott besieged Clemens with sentimental poems. In the 26 August 1869 issue of the Buffalo *Express* Clemens acknowledged having received a copy of "The Blush Rose." On 6 September 1869 Clemens referred to Elliott as "the Dead Canary," dismissed "that long-metre wail about a Blush Rose," and ridiculed this journalist-poetaster's efforts in a letter to Olivia Langdon. "I meant it for a solemn *truth* when I said his poetry was bad. . . I do so long to drop

him a line that would give him exquisite anguish—but I can't waste powder on such small game as that. . . . That creature is oozing his poetical drivel from his system all the time. No subject, however trivial, escapes him. And he dotes upon—he worships—he passionately admires, every sick rhyme his putrid brain throws up in its convulsions of literary nausea." Clemens went on to denounce "this awful bosh, this accumulation of inspired imbecility, this chaos of jibbering idiocy tortured into rhyme. He is the funniest ass that brays in metre this year of our Lord 1869" (*MTLet* 3: 336). Clearly Elliott's verse qualified for the collection of wretched literary efforts that Clemens would later call his "Library of Literary Hogwash." Elliott was the associate editor of the Fort Plain, New York *Mohawk Valley Register*, in which he published his poetry. Several of his pieces had been set to music by others, including "The Banks of the Genesee" (1858). In the 1870s and 1880s Elliott would be employed as a newspaper editor and journalist in Rochester, New York.

ELLIOTT, JAMES W[ILLIAM] (1833–1915). *Mother Goose's Nursery Rhymes and Nursery Songs. Set to Music* (published in 1870).

Clemens seems to refer to Elliott's musical collection in Notebook 19 (1881), though the author's name did not match: "Mother Goose—W A Elliott" (*N&J* 2: 394). In June 1898 Mark Twain decided to "introduce Mother Goose & her people" into his planned piece on childhood "Creatures of Fiction" (NB 40, TS p. 27).

ELLIS, WILLIAM (1794–1872). *Three Visits to Madagascar During the Years 1853–1854–1856*. Illus. New York: Harper & Brothers, 1859. 514 pp.

Source: MTLAcc, entry #1717, volume donated by Clemens.

ELLMS, CHARLES (1805–1851). *The Pirates Own Book; or, Authentic Narratives of the Lives, Exploits, and Executions of the Most Celebrated Sea Robbers*. [The first edition, published in Boston in 1837, was followed by several other editions in the 1840s and 1850s. The edition owned by Clemens has not been established. A Boston printer, Samuel N. Dickinson (1801–1848), is sometimes erroneously credited as this book's compiler.]

Catalog: ListABP (1910), "Pirate's [sic] Own Book", no other information provided.

Ellms, a one-time Boston stationer, became an author and compiler of popular literature and almanacs. His *The Pirates Own Book* collected the stories of Blackbeard, Captain Kidd, and numerous other buccaneers. The volume concluded with the bloodthirsty lyrics of the "Pirate's Song" (p. 432). See also the Catalog entry for S. M. Crothers's *The Gentle Reader*.

ELMORE, JAMES B[UCHANAN]. (1857–1942). *Love Among the Mistletoe and Poems*. Alamo, Indiana: Published by the author, 1899. 233 pp.

Inscription: in brown ink on the front pastedown endpaper: "S. L. Clemens/1902/Hogwash, but not atrocious enough to be first-rate."

Marginalia: ink markings on pages 48, 69, 70, 72, 213, 214.

Provenance: Antenne-Dorrance Collection, Rice Lake, Wisconsin.

Location: Mark Twain Archive, Gannett-Tripp Learning Center, Elmira College, Elmira, New York.

Copy examined: Clemens's copy, another addition to his

hypothetical "Library of Literary Hogwash."

The title piece, "Love Among the Mistletoe," was a forty-seven-page, highly overwrought novella. Elmore's lackluster poems resembled this one, "Over the Hills to the School House": "Over the hills to the school house/The teacher is plodding his way,/To instruct those frolicsome urchins/Who, like snowbirds, are busy at play."

ELY, RICHARD THEODORE (1854–1943). *French and German Socialism in Modern Times.* New York: Harper & Brothers, [cop. 1883]. 274 pp.

Source: MTLAcc, entry #691, volume donated by Clemens.

EMANUEL, WALTER LEWIS (1869–1915). *A Dog Day; or, The Angel in the House.* Illustrated by Cecil Charles Windsor Aldin (1870–1935). New York: E. P. Dutton, [cop. 1902]. 60 pp.

Inscription: on the front free endpaper, "The Major/with much love/from Annie an [*sic*] Louise". Second flyleaf inscribed: "To/S. L. Clemens,/BECAUSE HE LIKED IT?/Personally &/with great affection to/the Major:—"

Marginalia: someone has laboriously printed captions in ink for all of the illustrations, naming members of Clemens's Stormfield circle—Isabel Lyon, Clemens, "the Major," and cats called Sinbad, Omar Kayam [*sic*], and Tammany.

Location: Mark Twain House and Museum, Hartford, Connecticut. Donated by Eugene Grummond in 1958.

Copy examined: Clemens's copy, a gift from Dorothy Sturgis (see the Catalog entry for Rudyard Kipling's *The Brushwood Boy*, which explains the nickname "the Major"). Examined in August 1987.

A dog keeps a diary of his day in the house. Canine humor.

———. *The Dogs of War.* Illustrated by Cecil Charles Windsor Aldin (1870–1935). First edition. Original tan pictorial cloth, gilt. London: Bradbury, Agnew, & Co., [cop. 1906]. 243 pp.

Inscription: presentation copy to Clemens inscribed by Emanuel at 17 Holland Park Avenue, London.

Provenance: Mark Twain Library, Redding, Connecticut. Donated by Clemens (MTLAcc, entry #506). Eventually acquired by Nick Karaovich, Fort Wayne, Indiana.

Catalogs: *Mott 1952*, #52, $12.50; *Sotheby's 2003*, #216, $3,500 (sold with five other inscribed books).

Location: collection of Kevin Mac Donnell, Austin, Texas.

Copy examined: Clemens's unmarked copy, in July 2004.

EMERSON, RALPH WALDO (1803–1882). "Brahma" (poem, published in 1857).

Mark Twain burlesqued this poem ("I pass and deal *again!*") in his controversial 17 December 1877 Whittier Birthday dinner speech (quoted in *MTB*, p. 1645; *MTSpk*, p. 133). Henry Pochmann, "The Mind of MT" (1924), p. 42; Henry Nash Smith, "'That Hideous Mistake'" (1955).

———. "Domestic Life" (essay, published in 1858).

Clemens had a quotation from this essay—"The ornament of a house is the friends who frequent it"—engraved in brass over the fireplace in his library of the Hartford house in 1874. "Mind you, it is from Emerson," he wrote to an unidentified correspondent on 19 September 1881 (Yale University). William Dean Howells reported this fact in *My Mark Twain* (1910), p. 32.

———. *Emerson's Essays.* New York: Worthington Co., 1886. 320 pp.

Source: MTLAcc, entry #682, volume donated by Clemens.

———. *Emerson's Essays. First and Second Series.* Riverside Paper Series. Pale green cover. Paperbound, fragile and tattered.

Boston: Houghton, Mifflin & Co., n.d. [An advertisement on the rear cover refers to the *Atlantic Monthly* of 1890.]

Inscriptions: signed in ink on the cover, "S. L. Clemens/Hartford/Conn." An *A1911* sale label is affixed to the verso of the front cover. A bookseller's note on the half-title page priced the volume at $22.50.

Marginalia: Clemens drew penciled brackets and vertical lines in the margins of "Self-Reliance," the only essay he marked. On the first page of Emerson's "Self-Reliance" a note at the top of the page by Cyril Clemens explains: "My markings are underlines./The others apparently are Mark Twain's./C. C." Clemens made a pencil mark on page 52 and used a slanted pencil line on page 56 to mark Emerson's criticism: "We come to wear one cut of face and figure, and acquire by degrees the gentlest asinine expression." Clemens bracketed the last two lines of page 57 with pencil where Emerson disparages "the other terror" of our "reverence for our past act or word". A fainter vertical line above that calls attention to "a pariah minister." Brackets enclose the last nine lines of page 59 about character and overt actions. Double brackets on page 60 call attention to a cardinal quality: "Honor is venerable to us because it is no ephemera. It is always ancient virtue." A vertical line on page 63 pays homage to Emerson's remark about "Alfred [the English king] and Scanderbeg [an Albanian national hero] and Gustavus [the Swedish king]. . . . As great a stake depends on your private act to-day as followed their public and renowned steps." Clemens made a heavy pencil bracket at Emerson's question, "Whence then this worship of the past?"

Catalogs: *A1911*, "12mo, wrappers, Bost., n.d.," quotes the signature, lot 154, sold for $1.25; Swann Auction Galleries (New York City), Catalogue 386 (30 September 1954), "thick 12mo, printed wrappers, defective; in buckram slipcase, Boston, n.d. . . . Inscribed on wrapper—'S. L. Clemens, Hartford, Conn.'", item #323 (PH in MTP).

Provenance: in 1985 this volume belonged to the collection of Cyril Clemens, Kirkwood, Missouri.

Location: Harry Ransom Center, University of Texas at Austin. Acquired from Cyril Clemens along with six other books on 28 March 1986, for payments of $5,000 to Cyril Clemens and $5,000 to his *Mark Twain Journal*. Thomas A. Tenney, Cyril Clemens, and Alan Gribben (then an English professor at the University of Texas at Austin) negotiated this agreement in an exchange of letters written between 20 August 1985 and 27 April 1986.

Copy examined: photocopies of the cover, the verso of the cover, and assorted pages of a book belonging to Clemens (photocopies sent by Thomas A. Tenney to Alan Gribben in April 1985). Confirmed by examination of the volume in Austin in 1986.

Clemens's acquaintance with Emerson's writings may have begun in Hannibal; in 1906 Clemens recalled with amusement that Emerson turned down Orion Clemens's offer for publication of one of his works in the Hannibal *Journal* in 1853 (10 September 1906 AD, *MTE*, p. 236; *AutoMT* 2: 233). Mark Twain defined a literary "connoisseur" in 1865 as one who is secure if he attributes "all the poetry that you can't understand, to Emerson" (*California*, 17 June 1865; *LAMT* [1950], p. 142). In November 1872 Emerson described in a letter to his sister Ellen his impression of Clemens when they crossed the Atlantic on the *Batavia* (Edward D. Forbes, "Ralph Waldo Emerson," *The Saturday Club: A Century Completed*, ed. Edward D. Forbes and John H. Finley, Jr. [Boston: Houghton Mifflin Co., 1958], pp. 27–41); Emerson found "his conversation amusing." On 22 December 1875 Joseph H. Twichell wrote to Clemens excitedly about extracts from FitzGerald's *Omar Khayyám* that had appeared in the Hartford *Courant*: "Read it, and we'll talk it over. There is something in it very like the passage of Emerson you read me last night, in fact identical with it in thought" (quoted in Paine's *MTB* [1912], p. 615 n. 1; date corrected from Paine's implied but erroneous guess of 1878; *AutoMT* 3: 159).

A rapscallion calling himself "Mr. Emerson" was one of the literary "imposters" who imposed on a lonely California miner in Twain's dinner speech at the celebration of John Greenleaf Whittier's seventieth birthday in Boston on 17 December 1877 (*MTB* [1912], pp. 1643–1647; *MTSpk* [1976], pp. 110–114). Clemens visited Emerson in Concord with Howells in April 1882; Emerson died shortly thereafter on 27 April, while Clemens was on the Mississippi River. "So glad I visited him," Clemens wrote in June 1882 (NB 20, *N&J* 2: 486). He intended to "say a word about that visit" in *Life on the Mississippi* (1883), but wanted mainly to describe "our going in the evening to reverently look at his *house*" (*N&J* 2: 486). Henry W. Fisher remembered that around 1891 Clemens called Emerson a man "who valued impressions and ideas above everything—in his way as great a man as Virchow and certainly a great benefactor of his countrymen," but also spoke of Emerson's losing his memory in the late 1870s (*AMT* [1922], p. 103). In "The German Chicago" (1892) Mark Twain described Theodor Mommsen, the German classical scholar and historian, as possessing an "Emersonian face." Having a bit of fun with hallowed names, Twain in "The Secret History of Eddypus" (written in 1901 and 1902) preposterously credited "Ralph Waldo Edison" as the inventor of yellow journalism (*FM*, p. 327). Late in 1902 or early in 1903 Clemens wrote to the ill Olivia Clemens about two books he had been reading—Adelaide Sartoris's *A Week in a French Country House* and Alice Hegan Rice's *Mrs. Wiggs of the Cabbage Patch*. "My! what a contrast between the richness & brilliancy & finish of the one & the poverty & crudeness & vulgarity of the other! It's an experience!" Here, he asserted, was "the difference" between Emerson and a minstrel show (MTP). Twain alluded to Emerson in a speech on copyright reform on 7 December 1906 (*MTS* [1923], p. 327; Fatout, *MTSpk* [1976], p. 535).

Hemminghaus, *MTG* (1939), pp. 115–117; Stone, *IE* (1961), pp. 11–12; Bruce Michelson, *Mark Twain on the Loose: A Comic Writer and the American Self* (Amherst: University of Massachusetts Press, 1995), p. 42; Dwayne Eutsey, "'An Immense Revelation': The Correct Date and Significance of the Article That Prompted Joseph Twichell's *Rubaiyát* Note to Mark Twain," *Mark Twain Journal* 53.1 (Spring 2015): 106–111.

———. *Essays by Ralph Waldo Emerson. First Series*. New and revised edition. Boston: Houghton, Mifflin and Co., The Riverside Press, 1884. 343 pp.

Catalogs: QF Martinez, "Good Condition"; Ball 2016 inventory, blue cloth, gilt lettering, gilt top edge pages. This collection of essays, which includes Emerson's influential "Self-Reliance" essay, was available to Clemens whenever he visited Quarry Farm in Elmira.

———. "Hymn Sung at the Completion of the Concord Monument, April 19, 1836 (poem, published in 1837).

Douglas Anderson—"*Huckleberry Finn* and Emerson's 'Concord Hymn,'" *Nineteenth Century Literature* 40.1 (June 1985): 43–60—asserted that Emerson's poem inspired themes and passages in Mark Twain's novel, though "heavily veiled and perhaps unconscious," and even prompted one of E. W. Kemble's drawings for the book. Twain alluded to the famous last line from the first stanza in "To the Person Sitting in Darkness" (1901): "in that utterance he [President McKinley] fired another 'shot heard round the world.'"

———. *Letters and Social Aims*. Brown cloth, fair condition. Boston: James R. Osgood and Co., 1876. 314 pp.

Inscriptions: Clemens inscribed the front flyleaf in black pencil: "Livy Clemens/1876/Hartford". A pink bookplate on the front pastedown endpaper reads "General Library/of/THE PARK CHURCH/in/Elmira, N. Y./No. 841". The title page has a bookstamp: "The Park Church/Elmira, N. Y./1877". Either Olivia Clemens or a church librarian noted the donor on the title page in black ink: "Mrs. Clemens."

Marginalia: Clemens made vertical pencil marks on page 154 at the final paragraph in Emerson's essay titled "The Comic," where a physician in Naples advises a patient suffering from melancholy to attend a performance of the comedian Carlini [*sic*], who was "convulsing Naples with laughter." The patient replied, "I am Carlini [*sic*]." (This was the last sentence of Emerson's essay.) Carlo Antonio Bertinazzi (1710–1783), known as "Carlino," was a celebrated Harlequin in the old Italian comedy; he was reputed to have suffered depression in his later years. Clemens also made three vertical pencil marks on page 205 of the essay titled "Progress of Culture" beside Emerson's discussion of the will, the wit, and the talent. On the rear flyleaf and the rear pastedown endpaper someone noted, in pencil and black ink, a list of days and months, perhaps as reading assignments for a book club?

Location: Park Church Library, Elmira, New York. Discovered in the fall of 1987 by Gretchen Sharlow, then chair of the Historical Committee at Park Church.

Copy examined: a book given to Olivia Clemens by Clemens and also read and annotated by him. Examined on 12 August 1988.

———. *Miscellanies; Embracing Nature, Addresses, and Lectures*. Boston, 1858.

Marginalia: the front pastedown endpaper bears a lengthy biographical note: "Ralph Waldo Emerson, born in Boston, May 25, 1803. Son of Rev. Wm. Emerson, pastor of the 1st church in that city. Graduated at Harvard in August, 1821. After leaving college taught school 5 years. In 1826 was approbated to preach but on account of failing health spent the winter in S. Carolina and Florida. In March 1829, was ordained as colleague of Henry Ware at 2nd Unitarian Church of Boston; was of a clerical race-line of ministers on father's or mother's side; he was the eighth in this line. Married in 1830, Sept. Feb. 1831 wife died; in 1832 asked to be dismissed from his charge because of differences of opinion. Never a pastor afterwards. A lecturer and writer. In 1835 began to live at Concord and married again. MARK TWAIN." (quoted in the Union Galleries catalog).

Catalog: Union Galleries (New York City), Sale number 50 (19 September 1935), the collection of Nicholas Orlando, with additions, "12mo, original cloth, slightly worn, Boston, 1858, Mark Twain's copy," quotes the lengthy signed note on the front pastedown endpaper, lot 76.

Neither the date of the book's publication nor the phrasing of Clemens's alleged biographical sketch of Emerson (which seems more like a schoolbook exercise than the notes of an author who, significantly, very seldom signed his library books with his pen name) makes a convincing case for the authenticity of this association item. The volume must be classified as a highly dubious addition to Clemens's personal library until it can be examined. It was first auctioned in 1935 along with another item quite likely spurious; see the Catalog entry for Isaac Taylor, *Fanaticism, By the Author of Natural History of Enthusiasm* (1834).

———. "Mithridates" (poem, first published in 1847).

Henry Pochmann identified this poem as the source for Mark Twain's allusion in the 17 December 1877 Whittier Birthday dinner speech (quoted in *MTB* [1912], p. 1644; *MTSpk* [1976], p. 111): "Give me agates for my meat" (Pochmann, "The Mind of MT" [1924], pp. 41, 161).

Henry Nash Smith, "'That Hideous Mistake'" (1955).

———. "Monadnoc" (poem, first published in 1847).

Henry Pochmann cited this poem as the source for Mark Twain's quoted lines— "Is yonder squalid peasant all/ That this proud nursery could breed?" (quoted in *MTB* [1912], p. l646)—in Twain's Whittier Birthday dinner speech on 17 December 1877 ("The Mind of MT" [1924], pp. 41, 161; *MTSpk* [1976], p. 113). In Dublin, New Hampshire on 16 May 1906 Isabel Lyon reported in her journal: "Just before dinner I went onto the porch and Mr. Clemens sat there with Emerson's poems. He read Monadnock [sic]. There we sat under its mighty shadows and he read the stately poem as no one else in the world can read. After dinner he read much more of Emerson" (TS p. 159, MTP).

Henry Nash Smith, "'That Hideous Mistake'" (1955).

———. "The Over-Soul" (essay, first published in 1841).

The last entry in Olivia Clemens's commonplace book, probably written about 1871, is a quotation from Emerson's essay: "In sickness, in languor, give us a strain of poetry or a profound sentence, and we are refreshed; or produce a volume of Plato or Shakespeare or remind us of their names and instantly we come into a feeling of longevity" (MS p. 108, MTP).

———, ed. *Parnassus*. Boston: Houghton, Mifflin & Co., 1882. 534 pp.

Source: MTLAcc, entry #2025, volume donated from Clemens's library by Clara Clemens Gabrilowitsch in 1910. *Parnassus*, first copyrighted in 1874, was a major poetry anthology in its day. Organized thematically, the volume sampled English and American poets from Chaucer to Longfellow. Five of Bret Harte's verses were included.

———. *Selections from the Writings of Ralph Waldo Emerson, Arranged Under the Days of the Year*. Boston: Houghton, Mifflin & Co., 1889.

Source: MTLAcc, entry #2128, volume donated from Clemens's library by Clara Clemens Gabrilowitsch in 1910.

———. "Song of Nature" (poem, published in 1859).

Mark Twain burlesqued several lines from this poem—"I tire of globes and aces!/Too long the game is played!" (quoted in *MTB* [1912], p. 1645; *MTSpk* [1976], p. 113)—in his risky speech at the 17 December 1877 Whittier Birthday dinner in Boston, as Henry Pochmann pointed out in "The Mind of Mark Twain" (1924), pp. 41, 161.

Henry Nash Smith, "'That Hideous Mistake'" (1955); Bruce Michelson, *Mark Twain on the Loose: A Comic Writer and the American Self* (Amherst: University of Massachusetts Press, 1995), pp. 18–25; Richard S. Lowry, *"Littery Man": Mark Twain and Modern Authorship* (New York: Oxford University Press, 1996), pp. 24–33.

EMMET, ROSINA (LATER SHERWOOD) (1854–1948). *Pretty Peggy Painting Book*. New York: Dodd, Mead & Co., 1880. 64 pp. [Edition conjectured. This was one of a "Pretty Peggy" series of children's books.]

Catalog: ListABP (1910), "Pretty Peggy's [sic] Painting Book", no other information provided.

EMMETT, DANIEL DECATUR (1815–1904). "Dixie's land (I wish I was in Dixie's land)" (minstrel song, 1860).

"If a Democrat were elected, Hereford was to carry the flour to the tune of 'Dixie,'" Mark Twain wrote in a 16 May 1864 letter from Virginia City (*MTEnt* [1957], p. 187). Clemens mentioned it in 1885 as a song sung by Confederate troops that antagonized nearby Federal soldiers (NB 25, *N&J* 3: 201). He repeated this reference to the Civil War episode in an undated note (*A1911*, lot 439). Twain praised "Dixie" as "that antidote for melancholy, merriest and gladdest of all military music on any side of the ocean" (Chapter 13 of "A Horse's Tale" [1906]).

———. "The jolly raftsman" (minstrel song, c. 1844, popularized by—and often attributed to—Daniel Decatur Emmett, who composed the music. The lyrics, though, seem to have been written by Andrew Evans).

In Chapter 3 of *Life on the Mississippi* (1883) Huckleberry Finn relates how he swam to a large raft and listened to its crew amuse themselves: "They sung 'jolly, jolly raftsman's the life for me,' with a rousing chorus." Twain also included this passage in Chapter 16 of *Adventures of Huckleberry Finn* (1885), but it was eventually omitted. The lyrics for the song's chorus are indeed suggestive of a way of life : "My raft's by the shore, she's light and free,/ To be a jolly raftsman is the life for me;/And as we glide along, our song shall be,/Dearest Dinah, I love but thee."

———. "Jordan am a hard road to trabbel [or] trabel [or] travel" (minstrel banjo song, published in 1853). Banjo melody by Thomas F. Briggs (1824–1854). [Some sources attribute the words of the song to Briggs, but the majority favor Emmett as the lyricist.]

Clemens noted the title twice in Notebook 9 (*N&J* 1: 421, 437) during his own arduous journey through the Holy Land in 1867.

———. "Old Dan Tucker" (minstrel song, published in 1843).

In 1864 Mark Twain recalled hearing an amateur violinist

practice playing "Old Dan Tucker"; "he performed that so badly that he could throw me into fits" (*ET&S* 2: 95–99; *CTSS&E* 1: 97–101). This was one of the "rudely comic" songs of the early minstrel shows, Twain recalled (30 November 1906 AD, *MTE*, p. 114; *AutoMT* 2: 296).

Encyclopaedia Britannica. *A Dictionary of Arts, Sciences, and General Literature.* Ninth ed. Illus. 24 vols. With 4 vols. of the American Supplement [1883–1889] and the one-volume Index. Together, 29 vols. Boston, 1875–1889.

> **Catalog:** *A1911*, "24 vols., with 4 vols. of the American Supplement and 1 vol. Index. Together, 29 vols., 4to, half Russia (several broken), Bost. 1875–89," lot 155, sold for $5.50 total.

Clemens wrote to his mother-in-law, Mrs. Jervis Langdon, on 22 December [1875?] "to tell you how thoroughly delighted I am with the Cyclopedia & how much the book transcends even *its* splendid reputation. You could not have given me a thing I should prize more highly" (MTHM; *MTLet* 6: 602); very likely he had received the first volumes of the new ninth edition, with the rest promised as they were issued. In 1876 he solemnly assured Mrs. James T. Fields that his early deprivation of reading materials left him able to read only the encyclopedia. ("Which is not true—he reads everything," added Mrs. Fields in her diary, later published as *Memories of a Hostess*, p. 245.) Clemens referred to "Cyclo. Britan." [*sic*] in July 1885 as his source for a bit of English history (NB 24, *N&J* 3: 167). On 6 December 1888 he paid tribute to this reference work in a letter (once again) to Mrs. Jervis Langdon: "Yes, indeed, mother dear, the Supplementary volumes & Index will be a vastly valuable addition to what is already the most valuable book in the house. The Brittanica [*sic*] grows upon one, all the time; & I have long ago arrived at the opinion that the other Cyclopedias are of small consequence as compared to it. Livy & I couldn't choose a better Christmas present than these additional volumes" (MTHM).

He would never bother to learn the proper spelling of its title, but there is evidence to corroborate his dependence on "the most valuable book in the house." Intending to sketch the absurdities of Prussian monarchies and wars, Clemens first noted in July 1888: "Look in Cyclo. Britain—for Franco-Prus'n war" (NB 28, *N&J* 3: 405). When Rudyard Kipling dropped in upon Clemens at his brother-in-law's home in Elmira in August of 1889, Clemens promptly assumed the pose of untutored genius that he had tried out previously on Mrs. Fields—and even gave the same example of his reading habits. "Personally I never care for fiction or story-books," he told Kipling. "'What I like to read about are facts and statistics of any kind. Just now, for instance, before you came in'—he pointed to an encyclopaedia on the shelves—'I was reading an article about "Mathematics"'" ("Rudyard Kipling on Mark Twain," New York *Herald*, 17 August 1890, collected in *From Sea to Sea* [1899]). Whether or not Clemens truly preferred facts over fiction, the *Britannica* was often his initial source of information when he tackled a new project. On 13 October 1892, for example, he wrote to Chatto & Windus from the Villa Viviani at Florence, where he lacked reference books: "Won't you please look at the bottom of the article on Joan of Arc in

the Encyclopedia Brittanica [*sic*] & send me a list of the books one is referred to for information on the subject?" (PH in MTP). Chatto & Windus sent Twain a copy of the sources listed in the *Encyclopedia Britannica* and offered "to take any amount of trouble to take further particulars" (Welland, *Mark Twain in England*, p. 158). Henry W. Fisher reported that in Paris in May 1894 Clemens looked up the entry for Queen Elizabeth of England to search for any hints that perhaps she was really a man (*AMT* [1922], pp. 52–53). In "Concerning the Jews" (1899) Mark Twain quotes population figures, and then modestly avows: "I take them from memory; I read them in the Encyclopaedia Britannica about ten years ago." Scharnhorst, *Complete Interviews*, p. 125; Fears, *Day by Day* 2: 402–405.

Encyclopaedia Britannica. *A Dictionary of Arts, Sciences, and General Literature.* Ninth ed. Illus. 24 vols. New York, 1878.

> **Inscriptions:** each volume is signed by Orion Clemens.
> **Catalog:** *A1911*, "Ninth Edition, . . . 24 vols. 4to, cloth, N.Y. 1878, all the volumes have the autograph of Orion Clemens," lot 156, sold for $2.50 total.

English and Swedish Dictionary (unidentified book).

> **Source:** ListABP (1910), "English and Swedish Dictionary".

The English Cyclopædia, Conducted by Charles Knight [1791–1873]. *A New Dictionary of Universal Knowledge.* 23 vols. Illus. London: Bradbury, Evans & Co., 1866–1873. Each of the volumes had a focus within four "Divisions": Geography, Natural History, Biography, and Arts and Sciences. Numerous volumes added "Supplements."

> **Catalog:** Ball 2016 inventory, 23 vols, bookplates ranging from #294–313 and 407–410 of the "J. Langdon Family Library," green cloth boards, gilt lettering, fair to good condition.
> **Location:** Quarry Farm library shelves, under the supervision of the Mark Twain Archive, Elmira College, Elmira, New York.
> **Copy examined:** unmarked volumes, examined on 26 May 2015.

This set was available to Clemens whenever he visited Quarry Farm in Elmira.

ENGLISH, THOMAS DUNN (1819–1902). "Ben Bolt; or, oh! don't you remember" (song, 1848). Melody composed by Nelson Kneass (1823–1868).

Clemens mentioned this sentimental ballad in a letter of 25 November 1867 to Charles Webb (*MTLet* 2: 115). He told Albert Bigelow Paine that he was "thrilled" when he met the author, a New Jersey physician, in the 1890s, for he had sung "Ben Bolt" in his childhood (*MTB*, p. 1555). The meeting between Twain and English almost certainly took place at the Authors Club of New York, where both men held memberships. This latter club erected a monument to English after his death in 1902. Under a 1 June 1903 heading in his appointment book Clemens remarked: "Sweet Alice, Ben Bolt. I met the author once at the Authors' Club in his age. He looked it" Then Clemens added: "Alice was a poor thing, & Ben was a cad" (NB 46, TS p. 18). (A line in the song asks, "Don't you remember sweet Alice, Ben Bolt?")

———. *The Boy's Book of Battle-Lyrics: A Collection of Verses Illustrating Some Notable Events in the History of the United States of America, from the Colonial Period to the Outbreak of the Sectional War.* Illus. New York: Harper & Brothers, 1885. 168 pp.

> **Source:** MTLAcc, entry #1190, volume donated by Clemens.
>
> English wrote twenty-three poems and one song about historical battles in North America, prefacing each with a prose description of the scenario. He elected to avoid "the battles of the late sectional war," owing to "the nearness of the conflict" (viii).

EPICTETUS (c. 55–135 CE). *A Selection from the Discourses of Epictetus, with the Encheiridion.* Trans. from the Greek by George Long (1800–1879). New York and London: G. P. Putnam's Sons, [cop. 1892]. 260 pp.

> **Inscription:** pencil inscription on the front free endpaper in Clara Clemens's hand, "Samuel L. Clemens/&/Clara Clemens/Paris, 1894."
>
> **Marginalia:** pencil marks resembling Clemens's characteristic ones occur on pages 167, 168, 169, 170, 171, 226, and 245. Clara Clemens wrote in pencil on page 227: "Anybody knows that." She made other notes and markings on pages 220, 223, 225, 228, 229, 235, 243, 245, and 246.
>
> **Location:** Mark Twain Library, Redding, Connecticut.
>
> **Copy examined:** Clemens's copy, shared with his daughter Clara. Has the red ink Mark Twain Library accession number "4100" and the Library's purple oval stamps. Examined in 1970 and again in June 1982.
>
> The Greek Stoic philosopher Epictetus, once a Roman slave, reflected on the possibilities and the limitations of the human will.

———. *Epictetus: Selections from His Discourses as Reported by Arrian* [of Nocomeia, 92–175 CE] *and from the Fragments of Stobæus and Others, with the Enchiridion.* Edited and translated from the Greek by Benjamin E[li]. Smith (1857–1913). Leather cover, spine stamped. New York: Century Co., 1900. 245 pp.

> **Marginalia:** one vertical pencil mark, apparently by Clara, on page 49.
>
> **Provenance:** has the shelfmarks of the library numbering system that Clara Clemens Gabrilowitsch employed during her Detroit years. Sold at the 1951 auction in Hollywood but not listed in the sale sheet provided for that chaotic event.
>
> **Catalog:** "Property from the Library of Mark Twain," Butterfield & Butterfield, San Francisco, Sale 6613 (16 July 1997), lot 2712.
>
> **Location:** Mark Twain House and Museum, Hartford, Connecticut.
>
> **Copy examined:** copy from the Clemens family library. Viewed in Hartford in 1997.

ERCKMANN, ÉMILE (1822–1899) and **ALEXANDRE CHATRIAN** (1826–1890). *Madame Thérèse; or, The Volunteers of '92.* Translated from the Thirteenth Edition by Charlotte L[ottie]. Forten [Grimke] (1837–1914). Preface by Thomas W[entworth]. Higginson (1823–1911). New York: Charles Scribner and Co., 1869. 289 pp. [Edition conjectured. Many American editions appeared, but this was perhaps the most often-reprinted one.]

> **Catalog:** "ListABP," "Madame Therese, Erckmann-Chatrian",

no edition specified.

> **Location:** currently unknown.
>
> The novel *Madame Thérèse* (1863) was set amid the events of the French Revolution.

———. *The Polish Jew* (novel, published in 1871).

> A newspaper interview published on 8 October 1897 reported that "on his table" Clemens had a copy of *The Polish Jew* by Erckmann-Chatrian (M. Thomas Inge, "Ten Minutes with Mark Twain: An Interview," *American Literary Realism* 15.2 [Autumn 1982]: 262).

———. *Waterloo; A Sequel to the Conscript of 1813.* Trans. from the French. New York: Charles Scribner and Co., 1869. 368 pp. [Edition conjectured.]

> From Geneva, New York on 4 December 1871 Clemens wrote to Olivia Clemens about meeting an Episcopal minister from Syracuse named "Rev. Mr. Foster" who was "a noble, splendid fellow—a Twichell." Foster so impressed Clemens with his "whole-hearted cordiality" that upon parting from him "I gave him 'Waterloo,' & told him to read it & then mail it to you, as I had marked it somewhat" (*MTLet* 4: 506–507). Olivia's letter of 7 January 1872 indicates apprehension that Foster had neglected his promise to send the historical novel along to her (*MTLet* 4: 508 n. 3; *MTLet* 5: 17 n. 4). In Chapter 64 of *Roughing It* (1872) Mark Twain referred to Kamehameha the Great of the Sandwich Islands as "a sort of a Napoleon in military genius and uniform success."

The Ethical World (London periodical, published 1898–1900).

> In Notebook 43 Clemens wrote in 1900: "The Ethical World for '99. Cloth, 12.6/17 Johnson Court/Fleet St (Pub. Co.)" (TS p. 2).

ERSKINE, RALPH (1685–1752). *Gospel Sonnets; or, Spiritual Songs. In Six Parts.* Leather cover, spine torn, hinges loose. Lansingburgh[, New York:] Penniman & Bliss, 1806. 324 pp.

> **Inscription:** the front flyleaf is signed, "Polly Betts's Book./ Reading 1808." [Redding, Connecticut was originally known as Reading.]
>
> **Location:** Mark Twain Library, Redding, Connecticut.
>
> **Copy examined:** when I revisited the Mark Twain Library in June 1982 someone had added this volume of religious poems to the shelves holding books donated by Clemens and his daughter Clara Gabrilowitsch. The unmarked volume has no purple Mark Twain Library stamps, no accession number, and no indication that it had any connection with the Clemens family. I recommended that it be removed from the Clemens collection.

EUCKEN, RUDOLF CHRISTOF (1846–1926). *Christianity and the New Idealism: A Study in the Religious Philosophy of Today.* Trans. from German by Lucy Judge (Peacock) Gibson (1872–1953) and William Ralph Boyce Gibson (1869–1935). New York: Harper & Brothers, 1909. 163 pp.

> **Source:** MTLAcc, entry #1490, volume donated by Clemens.

EURIPIDES (c. 485–406 BCE). *The Plays of Euripides.* Translated and with an introduction by Edward P[hilip]. Coleridge (1863–1936). 2 vols. London: George Bell & Sons, 1891.

> **Catalog:** Ball 2016 inventory, Volume II only, red cloth and boards, gilt top edges of pages, good condition.
>
> **Location:** Quarry Farm library shelves (Volume II only), under the supervision of the Mark Twain Archive, Elmira

College, Elmira, New York.

Copy examined: unmarked copy available to Clemens during his many visits to Quarry Farm in Elmira.

EVANS, (COL.) ALBERT S[TEVENS]. (1831–1872). *Our Sister Republic: A Gala Trip Through Tropical Mexico in 1869–70.* Illus. Published by Subscription Only. Hartford, Connecticut: Columbian Book Co., 1870. 518 pp.

Marginalia: in pencil Clemens wrote on the third flyleaf: "Every great man ^ personage ^ must be shadowed by a parasite who is infinitely little.—Johnson had his Boswell, Seward his Evans, Victoria her 'John'" (quoted in *A1911*). William Henry Seward (1801–1872) was the U. S. Secretary of State from 1861 until 1869. On page 192 Clemens vertically penciled the word "delicious" beside Evans's account of haggling with a Mexican vendor over the price of a pair of boots, even though (by Evans's own admission) "they were cheap at twice or three times the money, according to our American ideas." Clemens penciled the word "coarse" on page 225 at Evans's story about an American who bought a rancho and unsuccessfully tried to breed mules. Clemens drew a pencil mark on page 378 alongside a paragraph about Emperor Norton of San Francisco; another pencil mark on page 385 at a description of the pity felt by Mexicans, especially women, for prisoners convicted of being revolutionaries; and two pencil marks on page 386 by the story of Evans's conversation in Spanish about a foreigner, in his presence. Clemens also commented unfavorably on Evans's mentioning that "I wore a [military] uniform which I felt bound to honor while in a foreign land" (p. 387).

Catalogs: *A1911*, "8vo, half morocco, Hartford, 1870," quotes inscription, lot 159, sold for $10; George D. Smith, New York City, "Catalogue of Books" (1911), quotes the inscription, item #265, $22.50.

Location: Henry W. and Albert A. Berg Collection, New York Public Library.

Copy examined: Clemens's copy, containing the *A1911* auction label and the bookplate of William F. Gable, both on the front pastedown endpaper.

Asked about Evans, Clemens wrote to Elisha Bliss, Jr. on 28 January 1870 that "fools are so cheap & so plenty that I had placed him in that category, for charity's sake" (*MTLet* 4: 40). Clemens and Evans had engaged in an acrimonious feud in California in the mid-1860s when both were newspaper reporters (Smith and Anderson, *MTCor; MTLet* 4: 41 n. 1). On 29 October 1870 Clemens wrote to Elisha Bliss, Jr. again about Evans, ridiculing his military title ("who made him a *Colonel?*"), belittling his writing abilities ("a one-horse newspaper reporter, who has been trying all his life to make a joke"), alleging that "he would run from a sheep," assuring Bliss that "*I* know him like a book," and requesting a copy of Evans's *Our Sister Republic*, which he is "suffering" to read (*MTLet* 4: 216–217). Evans was among many casualties when the steamer *Missouri*, sailing from New York City to Havana, burned at sea on 22 October 1872.

EVANS, ELIZABETH EDSON (GIBSON) (1832–1911). *The Story of Kaspar Hauser from Authentic Records.* London: Swan Sonnenschein & Co., 1892. 188 pp.

Clemens developed a friendship with the American-born expatriate author Elizabeth E. Evans and her scholar-linguist husband Edward Payson Evans (1831–1917) after meeting them in Munich in June 1892. Horst H. Kruse—"Mark Twain's *Pudd'nhead Wilson*: From Farce to Satire: The Unrecorded Contributions of Elizabeth E. and Edward P. Evans," *American Literary Realism* 50.3 (Spring 2018): 224–240—took note of the similar motif of exchanged infants in both *The Story of Kaspar Hauser* and Twain's novel that appeared in 1894. Kruse quoted a postscript to a letter Clemens wrote to the Evanses on 13 July 1893 in which Clemens reports that he had sent *The Story of Kaspar Hauser* to Krankenheil "for the others to read" (227).

EVANS, HOWARD (1839–1915), pseud. "Noblesse Oblige." *Our Old Nobility.* London: Political Tract Society, 1879. [Originally appeared as a series of articles in the *Echo*, a London newspaper published between 1868 and 1905.]

Clemens jotted "'Our Old Nobility' (from Echo)" in Notebook 18 while he was in England in August 1879 (*N&J* 2: 339). Evidently he had learned that Evans's book attacked the hereditary aristocracy and traced the genealogy of various noble families; it also contained a chapter criticizing the Church of England. A decade later Clemens would gain ammunition for *A Connecticut Yankee in King Arthur's Court* (1889) from a similar work by George Standring (see the Catalog entry for Standring).

EVELYN, JOHN (1620–1706). *Diary and Correspondence of John Evelyn.* Ed. by William Bray (1736–1832). Portraits, illus. 4 vols. London, 1872. [Publisher undetermined.]

Marginalia: numerous marked paragraphs and marginal notes by Clemens.

Catalog: *A1911*, "4 vols. 12mo, cloth, Lond. 1872, with numerous marked paragraphs and marginal notes by Mr. Clemens," lot 160, sold for $10.

At a time when Clemens was rereading Pepys' *Diary*, he mentioned to Edward H. House on 14 January 1884 that he had also just finished reading "the fourth volume of Evelyn" (ASSSCL).

———. *Diary and Correspondence of John Evelyn.* Ed. by William Bray (1736–1832). New edition. Portraits, illus. 4 vols. London: Bickers and Son, 1879.

Catalog: Ball 2016 inventory, brown leather, gilt lettering and edges.

Location: Quarry Farm, under the supervision of the Mark Twain Archive, Elmira College, Elmira, New York.

Copy examined: unmarked copy available to Clemens during his many visits to Quarry Farm in Elmira. Examined on 26 May 2015.

EVERETT, DAVID (1770–1813). "You'd Scarce Expect One of My Age" (poem for declamation by children). Also called "The Boy Reciter" and "My First Speech."

Everett wrote this juvenile recitation of thirteen rhyming couplets in 1791; it found its way into print by at least 1797. It seems likely that Mark Twain organized the "Country School Exhibition" presented on 10 July 1868 aboard the *Montana* that he described in a letter to the *Alta California* (published on 6 September 1868; reprinted in *The Twainian* [November-December 1948]: 5). The first selection on the program was "Oration—You'd scarce expect one of my age—Mr. G. W." In Chapter 21 of *The Adventures of Tom Sawyer* (1876), at the Examination Evening in the village schoolhouse, "a very little boy stood up and sheepishly recited, 'You'd scarce expect one of my age to speak in public on the stage, etc'—accompanying himself with the painfully exact and spasmodic gestures which a machine might have used—supposing the machine to be a trifle out of order." This is also one of the pieces dutifully recited "with stilted elocution and cast-iron gestures" by Old Dobbins's pupils in Act 3 of "Tom Sawyer: A Play," written 1875–1884 (*HH&T*, p. 303).

EVERETT, HENRIETTA DOROTHY (HUSKISSON) (MRS. H. D. EVERETT) (1851–1923), pseud. "Theo. Douglas." *Iras: A Mystery*. New York: Harper & Brothers, 1896. 251 pp.

> Source: MTLAcc, entry # 1542, volume donated by Clemens.

An Egyptologist falls in love with a mummy who had been placed under a supernatural spell.

EWING, JULIANA HORATIA (GATTY) (1841–1885). *Daddy Darwin's Dovecot: A Country Tale*. Illustrated by Randolph Caldecott (1846–1886). Original pictorial boards, spine missing, corners worn. London: Society for Promoting Christian Knowledge, [c. 1884].

> Inscription: the front flyleaf is inscribed, "Clara L. Clemens/June 8th, 1886/(From Mamma.)" This was Clara Clemens's twelfth birthday.
>
> Catalogs: *C1951*, J15, erroneously listed as "2 vols.," listed among the books of Jean and Clara Clemens; "Property from the Library of Mark Twain," Butterfield & Butterfield, San Francisco, Sale 6613 (16 July 1997), lot 2709.
>
> Location: Mark Twain House and Museum, Hartford, Connecticut.
>
> Copy examined: Clara Clemens's unmarked copy. Viewed in Hartford in 1997.

Ewing, the daughter of a Yorkshire clergyman and the wife of British Army officer, wrote a number of highly popular children's books. See the Catalog entry for her sister Horatia Katharine Frances (Gatty) Eden's *Juliana Horatia Ewing and Her Works* regarding a compliment Mark Twain paid to Juliana Horatia Ewing in a speech Twain delivered in 1907.

———. *The Dolls' Wash*. Illustrated by R[ichard]. André (1834–1907). London: Society for Promoting Christian Knowledge; New York: E. & J. B. Young & Co., 1883. 32 pp. [Edition conjectured.]

> Source: MTLAcc, entry #1882, volume donated from Clemens's library by Clara Clemens Gabrilowitsch in 1910.

A picture book relating in verse how three girls discover that washing clothes is a difficult chore, and thus they realize how hard their laundress Sally works.

———. *Jackanapes*. Illustrated by Randolph Caldecott (1846–1886). Reprint ("Eightieth Thousand"). London: Society for Promoting Christian Knowledge, n. d. [c. 1884]. 47 pp.

> Inscription: the front free endpaper is inscribed in ink by Olivia Clemens's mother, Olivia Lewis Langdon, to her grandson, the son of Charles Jervis Langdon, on his twelfth birthday: "Jervis Langdon/from/Grandma/Jany 26th 1875–1887."
>
> Location: collection of Kevin Mac Donnell, Austin, Texas (Mac Donnell to Alan Gribben, 29 November 2011). Purchased from the Langdon family.

Clemens would copy a lengthy, high-flown sentiment from Chapter 6 of *Jackanapes* (published in 1884) onto a flyleaf of James Lane Allen's *The Choir Invisible* (1897). See that entry. This would indicate that Clemens somewhere had access to a copy of *Jackanapes*, assuming that his handwritten note is authentic.

———. *Lob Lie-by-the-Fire; or, The Luck of Lingborough*. Illustrated by Randolph Caldecott (1846–1886). Original pictorial color boards. Spine perished. London: Society for Promoting Christian Knowledge; New York: E. & J. B. Young, n. d. [c. 1886]. 72 pp.

> Inscription: on the front free flyleaf, in black ink in Olivia Clemens's handwriting, "Clara L. Clemens/June 8th, 1886/(From Mamma.)" (This was a present for Clara's twelfth birthday.)
>
> Provenance: Carrie Estelle Doheny Collection, St. John's Seminary, Camarillo, California. Donated by Mrs. Doheny in 1940 after its purchase from Maxwell Hunley Rare Books of Beverly Hills. Auctioned by Christie's for $275 on 21 February 1989 at the behest of St. John's Seminary. Subsequently it joined the collection of Nick Karanovich of Fort Wayne, Indiana.
>
> Catalog: *Sotheby's 2003*, #193, $3,000 (sold with four other titles from the Clemens family library).
>
> Location: collection of Kevin Mac Donnell, Austin, Texas.
>
> Copy examined: Clara Clemens's unmarked copy, in July 2004. Has the bookplate of "Estelle Doheny."

———. *Lob Lie-by-the-Fire; or, the Luck of Lingborough*. Illustrated by Randolph Caldecott (1846–1886). Original pictorial color boards. London: Society for Promoting Christian Knowledge, n. d. [c. 1886]. 72 pp.

> Inscription: the half-title page is signed in ink "Isabel V. Lyon/November, 1894." Presumably Lyon had this volume in her possession when she went to work for the Clemenses in 1902.
>
> Location: collection of Kevin Mac Donnell, Austin, Texas (Mac Donnell to Alan Gribben, 29 November 2011).

———. *Lob Lie-by-the-Fire; or, the Luck of Lingborough*. Illustrated by Randolph Caldecott (1846–1886). Original pictorial color boards. London: Society for Promoting Christian Knowledge, n. d. [c. 1886]. 72 pp.

> Inscription: the front free endpaper is inscribed in ink by Olivia Clemens's mother to her grandson, the son of Charles Jervis and Ida Clark Langdon, on his fourteenth birthday: "Jervis Langdon/from/Olivia Lewis Langdon/Jany 26th 1875–1880."
>
> Location: collection of Kevin Mac Donnell, Austin, Texas (Mac Donnell to Alan Gribben, 29 November 2011). Purchased from the Langdon family.

EYRE, EDWARD JOHN (1815–1901). *Journals of Expeditions of Discovery into Central Australia, and Overland from Adelaide to King George's Sound, in 1840–1, Including an Account of the Manners and Customs of the Aborigines, and the State of Their Relations with Europeans*. 2 vols. London, 1845.

> "Sir George Grey and Mr. Eyre testify that the natives dug wells fourteen or fifteen feet deep" (Chapter 22 of *Following the Equator* [1897]).

▌F

FABBRI, CORA RANDALL (1871–1892). *Lyrics*. New York: Harper & Brothers, [cop. 1892]. 162 pp.

> Source: MTLAcc, entry #1689, volume donated by Clemens.

FABRE, JOSEPH-AMANT (1842–1916). *Procès de condamnation de Jeanne d'Arc, d'apres les textes authentiques, . . . traduction avec éclaircissements, par Joseph Fabre.* Paris: C. Delagrave, 1884. [Reprinted in 1895.]

Mark Twain listed this book among his "authorities examined" for *Joan of Arc* (page preceding the "Translator's Preface").

Ronald Jenn and Linda A. Morris, "The Sources of Mark Twain's *Personal Recollections of Joan of Arc*," *Mark Twain Journal* 55.1–2 (Spring/Fall 2017): 55–74.

"FADING, STILL FADING, THE LAST BEAM IS SHINING" (HYMN). Also known as "The last beam."

In a postscript to a letter Clemens wrote to Olivia Langdon on 30 October 1868 he asked, "What was the name of that hymn we fancied so much in church one day? 'Fading, Still Fading' is beautiful,—old, but beautiful" (*MTLet* 2: 274). Clemens considered this hymn for one of the ten tunes he selected for the four-hundred-dollar music box he purchased in Geneva in 1878 (NB 16, *N&J* 2: 211)—though he referred to it by its second line: "Father in Heaven, the day is declining." In Chapter 6 of *Life on the Mississippi* (1883), a chapter first published in "Old Times" (1875), he wrote about one of his hair-raising experiences as a cub pilot: On a dark night "Mr. Bixby made for the shore and soon was scraping it, just the same as if it had been daylight. And not only that, but singing: 'Father in heaven, the day is declining,' etc." Clemens may have learned the anonymous hymn from Henry Ward Beecher's *Plymouth Collection of Hymns* (1855), where it appeared as No. 1353; he owned a copy of this hymnal. The first stanza is: "Fading, still fading, the last beam is shining,/Father in heaven! the day is declining,/Safety and innocence fly with the light,/Temptation and danger walk forth with the night;/ From the fall of the shade till the morning bells chime,/ Shield me from danger, save me from crime./Father, have mercy, through Jesus Christ our Lord, Amen." Arthur M. Kompass—"Twain's Use of Music: A Note on *Life on the Mississippi*" (*American Quarterly* 16.4 [Winter 1964]: 616–619)—reprinted the lyrics of "The Last Beam" and showed how aptly its lyrics, placing faith in God as a shield against the dangers of darkness, suited the situation Horace Bixby faced as a pilot.

FALKENER, EDWARD (1814–1896). *Ephesus and the Temple of Diana.* Illus. London: Day & Son, 1862. 346 pp.

David Roessel—"Mark Twain at Ephesus," *Mark Twain Journal* 27.1 (Spring 1989): 27–31—established the fact that Falkener's book was the "most comprehensive account of Ephesus" at the time Twain visited the ancient site in 1867, and that, directly or indirectly, Twain presumably relied on Falkener's descriptions of the archeological excavations in writing his travel letters and *The Innocents Abroad* (1869). See also the Catalog entry for John Turtle Wood, *Discoveries at Ephesus.*

FARGUS, FREDERICK JOHN (1847–1885), pseud. "Hugh Conway." *Circumstantial Evidence, and Other Stories.* New York: N. L. Munro, 1884. 123 pp.

Source: MTLAcc, entry #1847, volume donated from Clemens's library by Clara Clemens Gabrilowitsch in 1910.

Following the premature death of the English author Frederick John Fargus, several American publishers, including N. L. Munro, pirated (and retitled) stories from his recent collection *Bound Together* (1884), publishing them under the invented title *Circumstantial Evidence, and Other*

Stories. Fargus had displayed considerable talent in crime fiction, mysteries, and tales of the supernatural.

FARRAR, CHARLES SAMUEL (1826–1903). *History of Sculpture, Painting, and Architecture. Topical Lessons, with Specific References to Valuable Books.* Chicago: Townsend MacCoun, 1881. 142 pp.

Clemens entered the author and title of this book in Notebook 22 while he was thinking up suitable prizes in 1883 for a children's contest about memorizing historical dates (*N&J* 3: 26.).

FARRAR, FREDERIC WILLIAM (1831–1903). *Truths to Live By, A Companion to Everyday Christian Life.* First edition. Original brown cloth, gilt. New York: Thomas Whittaker, 1890.

Inscription: "Mrs. S. L. Clemens/With the kindest regards/ of her husband's old friend/Geo. W. Childs/June 3, 1890." Childs was the co-owner of the Philadelphia *Public Ledger* along with Anthony Drexel, and also a friend of President Ulysses S. Grant.

Marginalia: Olivia Clemens made frequent underlinings and marginal lines in blue ink in Chapter 14, "The Results of the Sense of Sonship" (pp. 197–213), where Farrar takes I John iii.3 as his text and explains how mankind, by obedience to God and imitation of Christ, can achieve "salvation." The chapter argues that Hope leads to Effort, and Effort then leads to Purification.

Provenance: Numerous pages bear the purple-blue stamp of the Mark Twain Library in Redding, Connecticut. The end papers have been replaced; they may have shown traces of that same library's charge slip as well as the library's accession number.

Location: collection of Kevin Mac Donnell, Austin, Texas (Mac Donnell to Alan Gribben, 21 July 2011).

———. *Westminster Abbey.* Illustrated by Herbert Railton (1857–1910). London: Isbister & Co., 1897. 82 pp.

Inscription: "Clara Clemens/A souvenir of a visit to the loveliest/and most loveable thing in Christendom./KE)/ London 11th: III: 97".

Marginalia: there are vertical pencil markings such as Clemens typically made on pages 49, 50, 57, 63, 72, 73, 74, 77, and 82.

Location: Mark Twain Library, Redding, Connecticut.

Copy examined: Clara Clemens's copy. Displays the red ink Mark Twain Library accession number "3852". Examined in 1970 and again in June 1982.

In 1883 Farrar became the archdeacon of Westminster Abbey. Subsequently (in 1895) he was named the Dean of Canterbury.

FARRINGTON, MARGARET VERE (later Mrs. Margaret Vere Livingston) (1863–1914). *Tales of King Arthur and His Knights of the Round Table.* Illustrated by Alfred Fredericks (1835–1926) and others. Cover loose. New York: G. P. Putnam's Sons, 1888. 276 pp. [Dedicated by the author to "Mr. George W. Cable."]

Inscription: inscribed by Olivia Clemens in black ink on the second flyleaf, "Jean Clemens".

Source: MTLAcc, entry #1883, Jean Clemens's copy, volume donated by Clara Clemens Gabrilowitsch in 1910.

Location: Mark Twain Library, Redding, Connecticut.

Copy examined: Jean Clemens's unmarked copy, acquired long after Mark Twain conceived the plot for *A Connecticut Yankee in King Arthur's Court* (1889), but this is still an interesting coincidence. It displays the red ink Mark

Twain Library accession number "1883". Examined in 1970 and again in June 1982.

Faux, William. *Memorable Days in America; Being a Journal of a Tour to the United States, Principally Undertaken to Ascertain, by Positive Evidence, the Condition and Probable Prospects of British Emigrants; Including Accounts of Mr. Birbeck's Settlement in the Illinois; And Intended to Shew Men and Things as They Are in America.* London, 1823.

Peter G. Beidler, "'Fawkes' Identified: A New Source for *Huckleberry Finn*?," *English Language Notes* 29.3 (1992): 54–60, made a convincing case for supposing that this was the "Fawkes" book that Clemens asked his publisher James R. Osgood to send him. (Osgood replied positively to the request on 31 July 1882). Clemens was reading a variety of titles by early British travelers to America in the course of writing *Life on the Mississippi* (1883). Faux's account of the mistreatment of enslaved African Americans is unsparing, and Beidler noted several suggestive parallels between what Faux observed and incidents in *Adventures of Huckleberry Finn* (1885). The whereabouts of Clemens's copy, if he did receive and read it, has never been recorded. Faux described himself as merely "an English farmer," but he was a shrewd observer.

Faversham, Julie (Opp) (1871–1921). *The Squaw Man. A Novel.* Adapted from the play by Edwin M[ilton]. Royle (1862–1942). Illus. New York, 1906. 293 pp. [Faversham's birthdate is sometimes published as 1873, but this seems to have been an actor's preference.]

Inscription: signed on the front pastedown endpaper, "S. L. Clemens, 1906".

Catalogs: *A1911*, "8vo, cloth, N.Y. 1907," quotes the signature, lot 162, sold for $3.25; George D. Smith, New York City, "Catalogue of Books" (1911), quotes the signature, item #115, $8.50.

Faversham was a prominent actress. Utah playwright Edwin Milton Royle had several notable successes. His *The Squaw Man* was produced in 1905.

Favorite Album of Fun and Fancy. Illustrated by Ernest Griset (1844–1907) and others. London, Paris, and New York: Cassell, Petter, Galpin & Co., [1880]. 192 pp.

Source: MTLAcc, entry #1871, volume donated from Clemens's library by Clara Clemens Gabrilowitsch in 1910. This book of absurd drawings and silly stories was first advertised in 1880.

Favorite Fairy Tales: The Childhood Choice of Representative Men and Women. Illustrated by Peter Newell (1862–1924). First edition. Ivory paper-covered boards, gilt lettering on the cover and spine and gilt on the top edges. New York: Harper & Brothers, 1907. 355 pp.

Inscription: the front pastedown endpaper is signed in black ink: "S L. Clemens/ 21 Fifth Ave., Dec./07." Below that is an *A1911* auction label.

Catalog: *A1911*, "8vo, boards, gilt top, uncut, N.Y. 1907," quotes the signature, lot 169, sold for $3.50.

Provenance: The volume bears the bookplate of William F. Gable (1856–1921), who married Mary (Gable) Norton. Thomas W. Norton, a professor of sociology who taught at Lafayette College from 1967 to 2004, inherited the book. When Professor Norton passed away in 2005 his family donated *Favorite Fairy Tales* and other items from the William F. Gable Collection to the Skillman Library

at Lafayette College.

Location: Special Collections and College Archives, Skillman Library, Lafayette College, Easton, Pennsylvania. I am grateful to the director of that collection, Diane Windham Shaw, for calling my attention to this acquisition in 2012.

Copy examined: Clemens's copy, on 4 October 2012. Several leaves are uncut in the "Ali Baba and the Forty Thieves" story, as are also pages 354–355 at the end of the book.

Mark Twain was one of the prominent authors, literary critics, and personalities (including Henry James, Jane Addams, Grover Cleland, Julia Ward Howe, Nicholas Murray Butler, Howard Pyle, and William Dean Howells) invited to nominate these stories, which included "Jack the Giant-Killer" and "The Ugly Duckling." Two tales from *The Arabian Nights* were credited to Twain as his favorites: "Aladdin and the Wonderful Lamp" and "Ali Baba and the Forty Thieves." Both of their texts in this collection were reprinted from *The Blue Fairy Book* edited by Andrew Lang (London: Longmans, Green and Co., [1899]).

Fawcett, John (1739–1817). "Lord, dismiss us with Thy blessing" (hymn, published in 1773).

On 19 December 1868 Clemens wrote to Olivia Langdon that "the melody of an old familiar hymn is sounding in my ear. It comes like a remembered voice—like the phantom of a form that is gone, a face that is no more. You know the hymn—it is 'Oh, refresh us.'" He remembered the hymn, he explained, because he sang it frequently during the return voyage from the Sandwich Islands in 1866, since it was the "only *one* hymn that I knew." He refers to it as "that simple old hymn . . . freighted with *infinite* pathos!" (*MFMT*, p. 23; *MTLet* 2: 333). The phrase "O refresh us" occurs in the first stanza of the hymn: "Lord, dismiss us with thy blessing,/Fill our hearts with joy and peace,/Let us each thy love possessing/Triumph in redeeming grace./O refresh us,/Traveling through this wilderness."

Fawcett, William Lyman (d. 1901). "History of the Two Pillars," *Atlantic Monthly* 33.195 (January 1874); 85–91; "Old-Time Oriental Trade," *Atlantic Monthly* 36.216 (October 1875): 468–475.

Fawcett was a Chicago financial editor. In April 1875 William Dean Howells sent Clemens a letter Fawcett had written to Howells; in an accompanying letter Howells referred to Fawcett's piece in the January 1874 *Atlantic Monthly*. Clemens replied on 25 or 26 April 1875 from Hartford: "Good for Fawcett!" and alluded to Fawcett's "Ancient Oriental Trade" article, praising this former "Mississippi pilot" for showing "brains" (*MTLet* 6: 463). Fawcett would follow up his "History of the Two Pillars" essay by publishing *Gold and Debt; An American Hand-Book of Finance* (Chicago, 1877).

Fearon, Henry Bradshaw (1793–1842). *Sketches of America. A Narrative of a Journey of Five Thousand Miles Through the Eastern and Western States of America.* Third edition. London: Printed by Straham and Spottiswoode, Printers, for Longman, Hurst, Rees, Orme, and Brown, 1819. 454 pp.

Marginalia: pencil marks throughout, including several underscorings and 114 vertical lines and brackets. Notes in pencil amounting to seventy-eight words occur between pages 251 and 358. Examples: "River scenery," "opp St. Louis?," and "alas." On page 251, beside an allusion to swearing heard in Kentucky, Clemens wrote "yet." Next to Fearon's observation on page 269 that some Native American Indians own enslaved African Americans and allow their own women to be hired to pick cotton, Clemens noted, "Whites, Negroes & Indians about on a par—all savages." At the top of page 295 he jotted, "Today, Jap indemnity." At the top of page 324 he alluded to Thomas Moore's visit to the United States in 1803, writing, "Tom Moore heads the list." At the top of page 325 he characterized Englishmen. Beside the first paragraph on page 358 he again noted Moore's name.

Catalogs: *A1911*, "8vo, cloth back, uncut (worn, library stamp on title; library label on cover), Lond. 1819, a few marginal notes and passages marked in Mr. Clemens' autograph," lot 163, sold for $1.25; *Alta California*, List No. 15 (1963), item #34, "Rebacked. Some foxing. A very good copy. In half morocco slipcase," reproduces in facsimile the marginalia on page 269, asking price $500; its sale for $200 on 27 October 1965 was recorded in *American Book-Prices Current Index 1960–1965* (New York, 1968), p. 368.

Provenance: bookplate on the front pastedown endpaper reads "PRESENTED BY/ Mr. John Mayle/Librarian".

Location: Mark Twain House and Museum, Hartford, Connecticut. Donated anonymously in 1965.

Copy examined: Clemens's copy. Examined in August 1987. Displays the *A1911* sale label.

Henry Bradshaw Fearon (whose name is sometimes confused with that of a London surgeon of that era) was a London wine merchant and traveler. In July 1882 Mark Twain requested his publisher to send "books relating to the river"; on 22 July 1882 W. Rowlands replied for James R. Osgood that he was sending "a lot of books relating to travel in the U. S. by English people in the first half of the century; twenty-five volumes in all" (*MTLP* [1967], p. 158 n. 2). Twain cited Fearon's book in a passage he eventually deleted from the *Life on the Mississippi* manuscript; those observations (taken from page 167) emphasized the necessity of joining a church in early-day America. See also the Catalog entry for William Cobbett, who took issue with Fearon's attitude.

Dewey Ganzel, "Twain, Travel Books" (1962), p. 41 n. 4.

"DER FELDMARSCHALL" ["Song of the Fieldmarshal"]. (German folk song.)

Clemens included this title among a list of his favorite songs in August 1889 (NB 29, *N&J* 3: 513).

FELSEN, H. V. *Geträumt und Erlebt [Dreams and Experiences].* Wien: J. N. Vernay, 1891. 126 pp. Paperbound.

Source: MTLAcc, entry #385, volume donated by Clemens.

FÉNELON, FRANÇOIS DE SALIGNAC DE LA MOTHE- (1651–1715). *Les aventures de Télémaque, fils d'Ulysse.* Ed. by Louis Fasquelle (1808–1862). New York: Ivison, Phinney, Blakeman, 1867.

Presumably Clemens referred to this edition when he made a memorandum in Notebook 8 in 1867 to "get Telemaque" (*N&J* 1: 326).

FENN, FREDERICK (1868–1924) and **RICHARD PRYCE** (1864–1942). *'Op-o'-Me-Thumb. A Play in One Act* (cop. 1904).

Clemens spoke at a performance of this play on behalf of the Educational Alliance on 23 April 1908 (IVL Journal, TS p. 319, MTP; *MTSpk*, pp. 620–621).

FENN, GEORGE MANVILLE (1831–1909). *The Chaplain's Craze;*

Being the Mystery of Findon Friars. New York: Harper & Brothers, 1886. 206 pp.

Inscription: signed on the title page, "Clemens."

Catalog: *A1911*, "12mo, cloth, N.Y., n.d.," quotes signature, lot 164, sold for $1.25.

The English author Fenn wrote more than a hundred novels, many of them intended for a young adult audience.

FENOLLOSA, MARY (McNEILL) (1865–1954), pseud. "Sidney McCall." *The Breath of the Gods.* Boston: Little, Brown and Co., 1905. 431 pp. [A novel.]

Source: MTLAcc, entry #1021, volume donated by Clemens.

The Alabama-born Mary Fenollosa married the eminent expert on Asian art and culture Ernest Fenollosa (1853–1908) in 1895. Her novel *The Breath of the Gods* was largely set in Japan amid American diplomatic maneuverings. It later became both a play and an opera.

———. [Another identical copy.]

Source: MTLAcc, entry #1051, volume donated by Clemens.

FERGUSSON, JAMES (1808–1886). *A History of Architecture in All Countries from the Earliest Times.* Illus. 2 vols. Boston: S. E. Cassino, 1883. [Publisher supplied.]

Catalog: *A1911*, "2 vols., royal 8vo, cloth, uncut, Bost. 1883," lot 165, sold for $4.

The Scottish architectural historian Fergusson specialized in the architecture of ancient India, but he was also highly competent in describing the buildings of ancient Greece, Rome, and other civilizations.

FERRERO, GUGLIELMO (1871–1942). *The Greatness and Decline of Rome.* 5 vols. Volumes I and II translated by Alfred Eckhard Zimmern (1879–1957); Volumes III-V translated by Henry John Chaytor (1871–1954). New York: G. P. Putnam's Sons, 1907–1909.

Inscription: each volume is signed "S. L. Clemens, 1909."

Catalogs: *A1911*, "portrait on Japan paper, 5 vols., 8vo, cloth, uncut, N.Y. 1909," quotes the inscriptions, lot 166, sold for $14.50; Stan. V. Henkels (Philadelphia), Catalogue 1057 (14 May 1912), "5 vols., 8vo, cloth, uncut, New York, 1909, "autograph in each volume, 'S. L. Clemens, 1909.'", item #120.

Jervis Langdon (1875–1952) recalled that Clemens praised the Italian journalist, historian, and novelist Ferrero as "the greatest historian that ever lived—he has succeeded in making Julius Caesar uninteresting!" ("Some Reminiscences," collected in *MT in Elmira* [2013], p. 208). Ferrero would eventually be arrested (in 1925) and exiled from Italy (in 1929) for his opposition to the rise of Fascism.

FERRIS, GEORGE TITUS (1840–1920). *Gems of the Centennial Exhibition; Consisting of Illustrated Descriptions of Objects of an Artistic Order . . . at the Philadelphia International Exhibition of 1876.* Illus. New York: D. Appleton & Co., 1877. 164 pp.

Source: MTLAcc, entry #1228, volume donated by Clemens.

The Yale-educated Ferris was employed as a newspaper journalist and editor for a series of newspapers in New Jersey.

FETRIDGE, WILLIAM PEMBROKE (1827–1896). *Harper's Handbook for Travelers in Europe and the East.* New York: Harper and Brothers, 1862. 459 pp. [An expanded, 599-page edition with the same title was issued in 1865; it added descriptions of cities and sites in Canada and the United States.]

In an unpublished essay, Leon Dickinson revealed that in Chapter 44 Mark Twain used a quotation from page 347 of Fetridge's book: "Though old as history itself, thou art fresh as the breath of spring, blooming as thine own rose-bud, and fragrant as thine own orange-flower, O Damascus, pearl of the East!" (TS in MTP). Fetridge, who resided in both Boston and Paris, wrote travel guides and also published and sold books.

FIELD, EUGENE (1850–1895). *Culture's Garland: Being Memoranda of the Gradual Rise of Literature, Art, Music and Society in Chicago, and Other Western Ganglia*. Intro. by Julian Hawthorne (1846–1934). Boston: Ticknor and Co., 1887. 325 pp.

Clemens included two pieces by the Chicago newspaper columnist and poet Field—"His First Day at Editing" and "Oon Criteek De Bernhardt"—in *Mark Twain's Library of Humor* (1888), naming this book as their source. When Clemens visited St. Louis in June 1902 he participated in dedication ceremonies for a memorial tablet at Field's birthplace. In a brief speech Clemens paid tribute to "a man who, by his life, made bright the lives of all who knew him, and by his literary efforts cheered the thoughts of thousands who never knew him" (*MTB* [1912], pp. 1174–75; also reported in "The Mark Twain Memorial," *Mark Twain Quarterly* 1.1 [Fall 1936]: 8).

———. *The Holy Cross and Other Tales*. Blue cloth. Cambridge, Massachusetts and Chicago: Stone & Kimball, 1893. 191 pp.

Marginalia: On page 31 the word "me" was deleted in pencil and corrected in the margin to read "I" in the phrase "you and me". This type of grammatical revision was habitual for Clemens, but despite the brevity of this notation it does not quite look like his alteration.

Provenance: this volume was found in a bookcase in the Mark Twain Library in Redding in 1981 by a library volunteer, Charles Shipman, and was then added to the shelves holding books donated by Clemens and his daughter Clara Gabrilowitsch.

Location: Mark Twain Library, Redding, Connecticut.

Copy examined: I looked at this book closely in June 1982. It bears no accession number, no purple Mark Twain Library stamps, no other markings besides the small revision on page 31, and no convincing indications that it belonged to Clemens or a member of his family. I do not believe that the book should be part of the Clemens collection.

———. *A Little Book of Profitable Tales*. New York: Charles Scribner's Sons, 1890. 286 pp. [Edition conjectured.]

In a letter of 11 January 1891 to the Hartford author Annie E. Trumbull (1857–1949), Clemens thanked her for "Field's book. . . . I read the Cyclopeedy aloud & the Frau & I greatly enjoyed it" (TS in MTP). Field's dialect story "The Cyclopeedy" told how a book agent named Lemuel Higgins sold Leander Hobart a subscription to a serially published encyclopedia, but the volumes arrived so slowly that whichever volume Hobart needed at the moment invariably had yet to arrive. Just as Hobart lay dying the Z volume finally made it to his door. He did not live to see the Index delivered.

FIELD, JOSEPH M. (1810–1856), pseud. "Everpoint." *The Drama in Pokerville, the Bench and Bar of Jurytown, and Other Stories* (the first edition appeared in 1847 with illustrations by

F[exlix]. O[ctavius]. C[arr]. Darley (1822–1888).

Field's varied life as an actor, dramatist, theater manager, newspaper columnist, and editor made him a prominent if somewhat unfocused figure in Southern frontier humor. His best-known work, *The Drama in Pokerville, the Bench and Bar of Jurytown, and Other Stories*, included title sketches believed to have been based on his daunting theatrical experiences in the village of Wetumpka, Alabama. Bernard DeVoto proposed the last sketch in this collection of Field's newspaper pieces—"A Resurrectionist and His Freight"—as the model for Mark Twain's "grotesquely awful story about smells, 'The Invalid's Story,'" written in 1879 but held back until its inclusion in "Some Rambling Notes of an Idle Excursion" (1882) (DeVoto, *MTAm*, pp. 252–254). Walter Blair found other parallels in Field's volume (*NAH*, pp. 177–183). For example, Twain might have been familiar with Field's version of "The Death of Mike Fink," to which Twain seems to refer in working notes for *Adventures of Huckleberry Finn* ("about Carpenter & Mike Fink") and in Notebook 20 in April 1882: "Mike Fink shooting tin cup off Carpenter's head" (*N&J* 2: 459). Blair also pointed out parallels between the Duke's playbills for Bricksville in *Huckleberry Finn* (1885) and those posted by Mr. T. Fitzgerald in the initial title story of Field's *Drama in Pokerville* (Blair, *MT&HF* [1960], pp. 303–304). In addition, Blair noted (*NAH*, p. 154) that Field's "Kicking a Yankee," a sketch not included in Field's *The Drama in Pokerville*, developed the same theme that Clemens employed in his first-published tale, "Dandy Frightening the Squatter" (1852). The actress and celebrity journalist and lecturer Kate Field (1838–1896) was Joseph M. Field's daughter.

FIELD, KATE (1838–1896).

It seems quite odd, given the prominence she attained in a whirlwind career as a journalist, actress, lecturer, author, and social reformer, that no publications by Kate Field appear to have survived from Clemens's library. Perhaps a volume or two will turn up yet. Clemens met her in 1871, 1873, and 1875 (*MTLet* 6: 355 n. 2). He wrote to her on 9 June 1873 blaming "Providence" for the fact that they had not become acquainted; her latest book at that point was *Hap-Hazard* (Boston: James R. Osgood and Co., 1873), a collection of her experiences as a lecturer in the United States and abroad (*MTLet* 5: 375). Clemens objected strongly, in a letter to Jerome B. Stillson written on 19 January 1875, to the implication that he had seen and applauded her performance as Laura Hawkins in the Hartford performance of Twain's *Colonel Sellers* play. In an accompanying letter Clemens denounced Field as "the most inveterate sham & fraud & manipulator of newspapers I know of" (*MTLet*, 6: 354; *MTPP*, p. 86). Somewhat more charitably, in 1898, Clemens recalled her as "a good creature" for whom "a perishable and fleeting notoriety was the disaster of her life." She had died "forgotten of the world" (*AutoMT* 3: 151–152). Someone in Clemens's household owned a copy of Lilian Whiting's heartfelt tribute to Kate Field; see the Catalog entry for Whiting's *After Her Death*.

Karl Kiralis, "Two Recently Discovered Letters by Mark Twain," *Mark Twain Journal* 15.3 (Winter 1970–1971): 1–5; reprinted as "Two Recently Discovered Letters:

Mark Twain on Kate Field," *Mark Twain Journal* 20.2 (Summer 1980): 1–4; Gary Scharnhorst, "He Is Amusing But Not Inherently a Gentleman,': The Vexed Relations of Kate Field and Samuel Clemens," *Legacy* 18 (Spring 2002): 193–204; and Gary Scharnhorst, *Kate Field: The Many Lives of a Nineteenth-Century American Journalist* (Syracuse: Syracuse University Press, 2008).

FIELDING, HENRY (1707–1754). *The History of the Adventures of Joseph Andrews and His Friend, Mr. Abraham Adams* (novel, published in 1742).

Around 1882 Clemens mentioned that he owned a copy of this book ("The Walt Whitman Controversy," DV36, MTP). In 1894 he laid down plans to write honest reviews of "Joseph Adams" [*sic*], and other literary classics (NB 33, TS p. 61).

———. *Tom Jones, A Foundling* (novel, published in 1749). Clemens's attitude toward Fielding's works was simultaneously negative and envious. He was repelled by the social mores he found reflected in the pages of *Tom Jones*, yet he professed an admiration for the fidelity with which Fielding's books mirrored his society and for the prevailing moral tolerance that allowed their publication. Clemens expressed his feelings about *Tom Jones* and his creator in the late winter (possibly in March) of 1879, while he was living in Paris. Evidently the licentiousness he thought he saw rampant there left him in no mood for encountering hedonism in an eighteenth-century English novel. "Been reading that disgusting Tom Jones," he wrote in Notebook 18. "The same old paltry stuff & poverty of invention— . . . gambling & whoring & beggary & enlisting & fighting, & finally his magnificent father turns up—[Smollett's] Roderick Random over again." Squire Western alone suited Clemens's notions of characterization: "he is the only man whose violent death one does not hunger for" (*N&J* 2: 294). Clemens made additional comments about *Tom Jones* in the succeeding pages of Notebook 18: "no drearier reading," he declared in defiance of the usual critical opinions (p. 298). He was indignant that "people praise Tom Jones & Rod. Random" (p. 303).

These cavils were curiously altered, however, when Mark Twain first alluded to *Tom Jones* in print in Chapter 50 of *A Tramp Abroad* (1880). There he commented that "Fielding and Smollett could portray the beastliness of their day in the beastliest language; we have plenty of foul subjects to deal with in our day, but we are not allowed to approach them very near, even with nice and guarded forms of speech." In "The Walt Whitman Controversy," perhaps written in 1882, Twain hinted similarly that he found the parlor-table standard of decorum both hypocritical and inconsistent, and that he chafed under its strictures; *Tom Jones* was one of the "old bad books" on his and everyone's library shelves, he pointed out (DV 36, MTP). Twain seemed to accept Fielding's novel as a sociological survey of English society during a prior period. He intended to quote from Fielding ("where printable") in a proposed appendix to *A Connecticut Yankee in King Arthur's Court* (see Howard G. Baetzhold, "Course of Composition" [1961], p. 200), and in Chapter 4 of *A Connecticut Yankee* (1889) Hank Morgan reports that "many of the terms used . . . by this great assemblage of the first ladies and gentlemen in the land would have

made a Comanche blush. . . . However, I had read 'Tom Jones,' and 'Roderick Random,' and other books of that kind, and I knew that the highest and first ladies and gentlemen in England had remained little or no cleaner in their talk, and in the morals and conduct which such talk implies, clear up to a hundred years ago." On 27 April 1890 Twain made a speech, "On Foreign Critics," in which he reminded his audience sarcastically that when the American Revolution took place, "Tom Jones and Squire Western were gentlemen" in England (*MTSpk* [1976], p. 259). As late as 1894 Clemens listed *Tom Jones* among the English classics for which he planned to "write a really honest review" (NB 33, TS p. 61).

FIELDING-HALL, HAROLD (1859–1917), pseud. "H. Fielding." *Thibaw's Queen*. Illus. New York: Harper & Brothers, 1899. 294 pp.

Source: MTLAcc, entry #1042, volume donated by Clemens.

Suphayalat (c. 1859–1925), the wife of Prince Thibaw and thus the last queen of Burma, acquired a reputation for ruthlessness. British colonial forces sent the couple into exile in 1885. Fielding-Hall's unsparing book cemented her cruel image.

FIELDS, ANNIE (ADAMS) (1834–1915). *Charles Dudley Warner*. New York: McClure, Phillips & Co., 1904.

Fields quoted Clemens's favorable comments about Warner in several places (see pages 38–40), which makes it highly likely that Clemens acquired or at least glanced through a copy of her biography.

———. *Whittier; Notes of His Life and of His Friendships*. New York: Harper & Brothers, [cop. 1893]. 103 pp.

Source: MTLAcc, entry #653, volume donated by Clemens.

Annie Fields had been the wife of the *Atlantic Monthly* editor James T. Fields, who died in 1881. After his death she began to write biographies and edit memoirs. She became a very close friend of Sarah Orne Jewett. In 1922 M. A. DeWolfe Howe would edit a volume based on Annie Fields' diaries, *Memories of a Hostess*, which included some observations about Clemens's reading preferences (see the Critical Bibliography).

———. [Another identical copy.]

Source: MTLAcc, entry #838, volume donated by Clemens.

FIELDS, JAMES THOMAS (1817–1881). *Ballads and Other Verses*. Boston: Houghton, Mifflin and Co., 1881. 133 pp. [Edition conjectured.]

Fields edited the *Atlantic Monthly* between 1861 and 1870, but he was also a writer and publisher. In July 1880 Clemens wrote "The Alarmed Skipper, by James T. Fields" in a list of humorists and their works to be considered for an anthology (NB 19, *N&J* 2: 361). When *Mark Twain's Library of Humor* appeared in 1888 it contained two poems by Fields—"The Alarmed Skipper" (sometimes called "The Nantucket Skipper") and "The Owl-Critic," both taken from Fields' *Ballads and Other Verses*.

——— and EDWIN P[ERCY]. WHIPPLE (1819–1886), eds. *The Family Library of British Poetry from Chaucer to the Present Time (1350–1878)*. Boston: Houghton, Osgood and Co., 1878.

Inscription: "For Theodore/From Mother/Dec 25th, 1878."

Catalog: Ball 2016 inventory, brown leather, marble edges

and pastedowns.

Location: Quarry Farm library shelves, under the supervision of the Mark Twain Archive, Elmira College, Elmira, New York.

Copy examined: an unmarked copy available to Clemens during his many visits to Quarry Farm in Elmira. Examined on 26 May 2015.

———. *Hawthorne*. Boston: James R. Osgood and Co., 1876. 128 pp.

Inscription: inscribed at the top of the title page in black ink: "With the author's regards."

Provenance: Antenne-Dorrance Collection, Rice Lake, Wisconsin.

Location: Mark Twain Archive, Gannett-Tripp Learning Center, Elmira College, Elmira, New York.

Copy examined: an unmarked copy belonging to a member of the Clemens family, most probably Clemens. Examined on 28 May 2015.

———. *Old Acquaintance. Barry Cornwall and Some of His Friends*. Boston: James R. Osgood and Co., 1876. 121 pp.

Inscription: on the front free endpaper in black ink: "For Mrs. Clemens/with the cordial regards of/James T. Fields/May 1876."

Provenance: Antenne-Dorrance Collection, Rice Lake, Wisconsin.

Location: Mark Twain Archive, Gannett-Tripp Learning Center, Elmira College, Elmira, New York.

Copy examined: an unmarked gift copy belonging to Olivia Clemens. Examined on 28 May 2015.

"Barry Cornwall" was the pseudonym of Bryan Waller Procter (1787–1874), an English poet, biographer, and man of letters.

FIGUIER, LOUIS (1819–1894). *Primitive Man*. Revised translation. Illus. Original rust brown cloth, gilt, corners worn, inner hinges broken, dampstain on front cover and some leaves. New York: D. Appleton & Co., 1871. 348 pp.

Inscriptions: signed in pencil on the front free flyleaf, "Saml. L. Clemens/July, 1871." As a small joke the half-title page is also inscribed in pencil so as to incorporate the title and read: "Saml. L. Clemens,/The *Primitive Man*".

Marginalia: numerous notations in pencil, beginning on page 1 and ending on page 133. They only total sixty words. Pages 154–158 have been cut open, however, so Clemens probably read the entire book. Brief notes occur on pages 14, 15, 45, 46, 65, 71, 91, 94, 95, and 108. Clemens's comment on page 71 resembles the skeptical view he would express about archeology in "A Brace of Brief Lectures" (published in September and October 1871): at Figuier's identification of bones "gnawed by hyaenas" Clemens objected, "(?—or merely *supposed*? can any man classify the teeth-marks on a bone 50,000 years old?[)]" Similarly he labeled as "absurd" the assertions on page 91 that human teeth marks were detected on various bones.

Provenance: There is a Mark Twain Library accession number ("2020") written in black ink on the front pastedown endpaper, so one must assume that Clara Clemens Gabrilowitsch retrieved this volume from the books that she and her father donated to that community library. Subsequently it belonged to the Carrie Estelle Doheny Collection at St. John's Seminary, Camarillo, California. Mrs. Doheny had donated it in 1940 following its purchase from Maxwell Hunley Rare Books of Beverly Hills. It became one of the books auctioned by Christie's in New York City (lot 1177), selling for $960 on 17 October 1988 at the behest of St. John's Seminary.

Location: collection of Kevin Mac Donnell, Austin, Texas (Mac Donnell to Alan Gribben, 28 August 2017).

Copy examined: Clemens's copy, which contains a bookseller's sticker from Hall Brothers, Elmira, New York on the rear endpaper. It also has an Estelle Doheny bookplate. I examined this volume in 1970 when it was at St. John's Seminary.

In a letter to Orion Clemens of 7 July 1871 from Elmira, Clemens informed Orion that he got his scientific information about "paleontology" used in his "Brace of Brief Lectures on Science" from "an article in Chamber's [*sic*] Edinburgh Journal" (*MTLet* 4: 429, 430). Hamlin Hill explained (in "Mark Twain's 'Brace of Brief Lectures on Science,'" *New England Quarterly* 34.2 [June 1961]: 228–239) that Twain had based his essays on an anonymous review of Figuier's *Primitive Man* from the 13 August 1870 issue of *Chambers's Journal of Popular Literature, Science, and Art*. Although Twain's first installment of "Lectures" in *The American Publisher* (September 1871), a monthly Hartford magazine, was accompanied by an extended passage from *Primitive Man*, Hill was then (in 1961) not certain that Twain actually possessed first-hand knowledge of Figuier's book, a fact now established. As Hill made clear, Twain's articles display both scorn for the far-fetched theories of scientists and a sympathy for their trial-and-error inductive procedures and for archeological and paleontological efforts as a whole.

FILIPPINI, ALEXANDER [ORIGINALLY ALESSANDRO] (1849–1917). *Handy Volume Culinary Series*. 7 vols. New York: Charles L. Webster & Co., 1892.

Clemens's publishing firm advertised this series as the recipes of Delmonico's chef of twenty-five years. There are one hundred recipes for each of seven categories of dishes—soups, fish, eggs, poultry and game, salads and entrees, sauces, and desserts. The Swiss-born Filippini had retired from Delmonico's in 1888 and turned to cookbook-writing.

———. *The Table: How to Buy Food, How to Cook It, and How to Serve It*. New York: Charles L. Webster & Co., 1889. 507 pp. Repr. in 1890 and 1891, with supplements.

Clemens's publishing firm boasted that this volume contained 1,550 recipes. Some of its dishes evidently pleased the Clemenses' palates; on 7 October 1891 Clemens wrote from Germany to ask that Chatto & Windus send a copy of *The Table* "(cookbook issued by Webster & Co., New York)" to his next address in Berlin (ASSSCL). In a note dated 13 December 1890 on letterhead stationery of The Players Club, Clemens requested of his publisher Fred J. Hall: "Please send Mrs. Clemens 2 copies of the cook book—new edition" (Berg, NYPL). In 1900 he made a cryptic memorandum in Notebook 43: "Delmonico (?) Cookbook" (TS p. 32).

FILLEBROWN, REBEKAH HUDDELL (MILLER) (1842–1917). *Rhymes of Happy Childhood*. Illustrated by Edwin John Prittie (1879–1963). Philadelphia: J. C. Winston Co., 1908. 119 pp.

Source: MTLAcc, entry #2028, volume donated from

Clemens's library by Clara Clemens Gabrilowitsch in 1910.

Brief, humorous, rhyming poems about children's thinking. The color illustrations are cleverly drawn.

FILLMORE, JOHN COMFORT (1843–1898). "A Study of Indian Music," *Century Magazine* 47.4 (February 1894): 616–623.

Clemens recommended this article to his daughters ("I think it will interest them") in a letter written to Olivia Clemens on [9] February 1894 (*LLMT*, p. 294). Fillmore's essay described Native American songs in technical terms. The final paragraph concludes: "Those whom we are accustomed to despise as an inferior and barbarous race reveal, in the glimpse this music affords into their inner life, a noble religious feeling" (p. 623). Fillmore emphasized the powerful spirituality discernible in the tribal music he studied on a Nebraska reservation. One can surmise that Clemens's reading, as evidenced here, gradually mitigated some of his prejudice against the defeated remnants of a race he had encountered much earlier in the American West.

James C. McNutt, "Mark Twain and the American Indian" (1978); and Kerry Driscoll, *Mark Twain among the Indians and Other Indigenous People* (Oakland: University of California Press, 2018), pp. 225–226.

FINCH, FRANCIS MILES (1827–1907). "Smoking Song" (poem).

Clemens borrowed passages from this piece in constructing a limerick, "Sparkling & Bright," in 1866 (NB 5, *N&J* 1: 157). See also the Catalog entry for C. F. Hoffman.

FINLEY, MARTHA FARQUHARSON (1828–1909), pseud. "Martha Farquharson." *Elsie Dinsmore* (children's book, published in 1867).

Finley was the American author of a well-known juvenile series, the Elsie Books (twenty-six volumes), whose virtuous heroine was Elsie Dinsmore.

See Harold H. Kolb, Jr., "Mark Twain, Huckleberry Finn, and Jacob Blivens" (1979).

First Book of the Authors Club, Liber Scriptorum, ed. Arthur [Griffin] Stedman (1859–1908). Limited edition of 251 copies. New York: Authors Club, 1893.

Catalog: Catalogue 174 (1989), Heritage Book Shop, Los Angeles, California, "signed by Twain, . . . 4to, full straight-grained morocco, decorated in gilt and blind, . . . in a cloth, open-ended slipcase," item #244, priced at $2,000.

Mark Twain contributed a short story, "The Californian's Tale," to this volume, which was conceived as a fund-raiser to build a home for the Authors Club. Each copy sold for $100 and each author signed 251 copies of his own contribution. Dozens of authors participated, including William Dean Howells and Edward Eggleston. See the New York *Times* (21 January 1894), p. 23. See also the Catalog entry for *Authors Club*.

A First German Course, Containing Grammar, Delectus, and Exercise-Book, with Vocabularies, and Materials for German Conversation. On the Plan of Dr. William Smith's [1813–1893] "Principia Latina." Third ed., revised. New York: Harper, 1856. 237 pp. Repr. by Harper & Brothers in 1876. 158 pp. [At the head of the title: "The German Principia, Part I."]

In March 1878 Clemens noted "The First German Principia—A First [German] Course. Harper" in Notebook 14 (*N&J* 2: 54). Somewhat later he considered using it in *A Tramp Abroad*: "Begin chapter with Ollendorff & First German Reader" (NB 14, *N&J* 2: 60).

FISCHER, HENRY WILLIAM HUBERT (1856–1932), pseud. "Ursula, Countess von Eppinghoven." *Private Lives of William II [1859–1941] and His Consort [Empress Auguste Viktoria, 1858–1921] and Secret History of the Court of Berlin, from the Papers and Diaries Extending Over a Period, Beginning June, 1888, to the Spring of 1898, of Ursula, Countess von Eppinghoven.* 2 vols. Original gray cloth, boards soiled and rubbed, spine label stained. New York: Fischer's Foreign Letters, [1898].

Marginalia: approximately seventeen pages in Volume II contain Clemens's markings or annotations that total around forty-five words. On the front free endpaper he wrote vertically, in large script, in pencil, "In more than one place in her book the authoress tries hard to make us believe that the stock of imperial linen is very slender, but before she gets done washing it in public we perceive that she has been deceiving us." Clemens made vertical pencil marks in Volume II on pages 99, 100, 103, 120, 122, 126, 140, 182, 183, 185, 191, 203, 310, 323, 327, and 329. On page 124 he penciled "Good!" in the margin and underlined the word "Innocent." He corrected in pencil "as the Germans to say" to read "as Shakespeare says" on page 330.

Catalogs: ListABP (1910), "William II 2 v., Fischer"; *C1951*, #57c, listed among the books signed by Clemens, sold for $5; "Property from the Library of Mark Twain," Butterfield & Butterfield, San Francisco, Sale 6613, 16 July 1997, lot 2673, Volume II only.

Location: Mark Twain House and Museum, Hartford, Connecticut (Volume II only).

Copy examined: Clemens's copy of Volume II only, in 1997 in Hartford.

Fischer, identifying himself as president of Fischer's Foreign Letters and News, wrote Clemens on 12 April 1904: "Will you do me the honor to accept, with my best wishes, the set of 'PRIVATE LIVES OF WILLIAM II' coming herewith. You once told me of your great and lasting fondness for the Margravine of Bayreuth; well, here is a continuation of the story of Voltaire's friend" (MTP). (Fischer, it should be noted, more often spelled his name Fisher.)

FISH, WILLISTON (1858–1939). *Short Rations.* Illustrated by C[harles]. J[ay]. Taylor (1855–1929). New York: Harper & Brothers, 1899. 189 pp.

Source: MTLAcc, entry #1550, volume donated by Clemens.

Williston's inter-connected, often humorous short stories depicted the tedium of Army life in garrisons.

FISHER, GEORGE PARK (1827–1909). *Essays on the Supernatural Origin of Christianity, with Special Reference to the Theories of Renan, Strauss, and the Tübingen School.* New edition. Original blue cloth, brown-coated endpapers, gilt, wear at the bottom of the spine. New York: Charles Scribner's Sons, 1887. 627 pp.

Inscription: signed in black ink on the front free flyleaf, "S L. Clemens/1887."

Catalogs: *A1911*, "8vo, cloth, N.Y. 1887," quotes the signature, lot 167, sold for $3; Christie's, New York City, 1–2 February 1988 auction, lot 465, sold with three other books for $2, 750 to Randall House, Los Angeles;

Sotheby's 2003, #231, $2,500 (sold with three other titles).

Provenance: Donated to the Carrie Estelle Doheny Collection, St. John's Seminary, Camarillo, California, by Mrs. Doheny in 1945 following its acquisition from Maxwell Hunley Rare Books of Beverly Hills for $35. Auctioned by Christie's in 1988 at the behest of St. John's Seminary and the Archdiocese of Los Angeles. Has the bookplate of Frederick W. Skiff.

Location: collection of Kevin Mac Donnell, Austin, Texas.

Copy examined: Clemens's unmarked copy, at St. John's Seminary in 1970. Displays the *A1911* sale label on the front pastedown endpaper. Also has the bookplate of "Estelle Doheny."

Fisher's *Essays on the Supernatural Origin of Christianity* mounts a detailed apologetic on behalf of the Christian faith against the inroads made by skepticism and unbelief.

FISHER, LAURA HOPE (1848–1925). *Figures and Flowers for Serious Souls*. Buffalo, N.Y.: Moulton, Wenborne & Co., [cop. 1888]. 160 pp.

Source: MTLAcc, entry #642, a volume of poetry donated by Isabel V. Lyon, Clemens's secretary. This may have been her own copy (in which case it should be remembered that she and Clemens often shared their reading materials), or she may have taken Clemens's copy to the Library at his request.

The poet and composer Fisher lived in Walpole, Massachusetts. *Figures and Flowers for Serious Souls* contains forty-six poems, many of them written in vernacular dialect, most of them cynical in tone.

FISK, MAY ISABEL (TAYLOR) (b. 22 May 1887). *Monologues*. New York: Harper & Brothers, 1903. 190 pp.

Source: MTLAcc, entry #360, volume donated by Clemens. Fisk was a talented actor, drama coach, and pioneering female literary humorist. On 23 January 1903 she married Clinton Bowen Fisk, Jr. (1871–1909), a Columbia University graduate (1892) and newspaperman connected with the New York *Evening Journal* and the New York *American*, and the couple became socially prominent in New York City. However, his health began to decline in 1906 and he died of influenza at the age of thirty-eight in a hotel in San Antonio, Texas on 29 November 1909. Oddly, she was not mentioned in his obituary or on his grave marker in Coldwater, Michigan. (He was a son of the Civil War General Clinton Bowen Fish [1828–1890], who had grown up and married in Coldwater. Fisk University was named for the senior Fisk.) It might be significant that several of May Isabel Fisk's dramatic monologues joke about the desirability of divorce.

In the first decades of the twentieth century she performed her comic monologues on stage. However, by 1922 she had moved to England and in that year she married Malcolm Campbell-Johnston (1871–1938), a London political figure who had studied law in California. She published a new monologue (*The Silent Sex*) with Harper & Brothers in 1923, and copyrighted additional ones in 1931, 1932, and 1933. In 1940 she was a widow living in Los Angeles and on 21 August 1941, at the age of fifty-four, she was granted repatriation to the United States. For several years she lived in Los Angeles, and she may have hoped for a break in Hollywood; on 29 December 1945 she wrote to producer Harvey Taylor, enclosing a copy of her *Monologues* (1903) (ALS, Arundel Books, Seattle, Washington, offered for sale on 8 April 2020). After moving to Redondo Beach, California she acquired a large tract of land, and this resulted in a series of court cases with decisions rendered in 1946, 1947, and 1953. She was by then known as May Isabel Campbell-Johnston. Her death date has not been established, but a Trust in her name was dissolved in 1946.

Julia Hans, "'Landy Goshen! Here comes a whole troop o' them city boarders': May Isabel Fisk's Dialect Monologues," *Studies in American Humor* New Series 3, No. 22 (2010): 129–145; Ed Piacentino, "Mark Twain and May Isabel Fisk: Parallels in Comic Monologues," *Mark Twain Journal* 49.1–2 (Spring/Fall 2011): 92–108.

———. [Another identical copy.]

Source: MTLAcc, entry #1551, volume donated by Clemens.

———. *The Talking Woman (Monologues)*. Illus. New York: Harper & Brothers, 1907. 169 pp.

Source: MTLAcc, entry #359, volume donated by Clemens. Fisk had attended Mark Twain's Seventieth Birthday celebration at Delmonico's in 1905.

FISKE, D[ANIEL]. WILLARD (1831–1904).

Willard Fiske, professor of Icelandic studies and languages at Cornell University and also its first librarian, was a longtime friend of the Clemenses after being introduced to them by the Reverend Joseph H. Twichell. He knew them in Italy in 1892, too, since Fiske had moved there by then and was residing at the Villa Forini and later the Villa Landor in Florence. Fiske, in fact, made the arrangements for the Clemenses to rent the Villa Viviani. It therefore seems somewhat likely that Clemens might have encountered one of Fiske's writings on Iceland or (Fiske's other great interest) chess. This probability was raised by Jules Hojnowski and endorsed by R. Kent Rasmussen (Rasmussen to Alan Gribben, email, 29 June 2002). Fiske had less of a role in the Clemenses' renting the large Villa di Quarto, but he followed the negotiations and was sympathetic to their dissatisfaction with the place. (Fiske would die in Frankfurt, Germany on 17 September 1904, three months after Olivia Clemens passed away.) Mary Leah Christmas speculated that Clemens probably donated volumes from his personal library to one or more of Fiske's periodic appeals for books that he could send to Icelandic libraries ("'Youth' and the 'Old Icelandic Scholar': The Friendship of Mark Twain and Willard Fiske," a paper presented at the 2001 State of Mark Twain Studies conference at Elmira College; summarized in an email posting by Christmas to the Mark Twain Forum on 14 February 2005).

Tsuyoshi Ishihara, "Mark Twain's Italian Villas," *Mark Twain Journal* 52.1 (Spring 2014): 18–39.

FISKE, JOHN (1842–1901). *The Beginnings of New England; or, The Puritan Theocracy in Its Relations to Civil and Religious Liberty*. Boston: Houghton, Mifflin and Co., 1889. 296 pp.

Inscription: "OLC" hastily written in pencil on the upper right corner of the front free endpaper.

Marginalia: Clemens's vertical pencil marks appear on pages 47, 54, and 122 (at the mention of the first Dutch settlement at Hartford). Page 56 is turned down. The rear pastedown endpaper bears the sticker of "Brown &

Gross, Booksellers, Hartford, Ct."

Location: Mark Twain Library, Redding, Connecticut.

Copy examined: copy belonging to Olivia Clemens and read by Clemens. Displays the red ink Mark Twain Library accession number "3128" and the Library's purple oval stamps. I could not locate this volume in 1970 but on my return visit to Redding in June 1982 it had been found and placed with Clemens's other library books.

In preparing for his departure for Elmira in June 1889 Clemens noted "'Beginnings of New England.' Fisk" [*sic*], apparently intending to bring along or obtain the book (NB 29, TS p. 9).

———. *A Century of Science and Other Essays.* Boston: Houghton, Mifflin and Co., 1900. 466 pp.

Inscription: on the front flyleaf, "S L. Clemens/Riverdale-on-Hudson/ Feb. 1902."

Marginalia: Clemens made numerous pencil markings (underlinings and vertical lines) and marginal notes (primarily jotting down scientists' names such as Lyell, Pasteur, Koch, Linnaeus, Lamarck, Faraday, Darwin, Wallace, and Spencer) throughout the first essay, "A Century of Science" (pp. 1–38). Page 55 is turned down in the essay on "Sir Harry Vane." Pencil markings and ink notes occur in the chapter titled "The Arbitration Treaty" (pp. 166–193). On page 179, where Fiske mentions the *Trent* affair [a diplomatic crisis between the United States and Great Britain that occurred during the Civil War in 1861], Clemens wrote vertically, "The 'Maine' is a case in point." Fisk argues on page 180 that a "growing moral sentiment . . . condemns most warfare as wicked," which caused Clemens to observe in the margin: "It could have prevented the foolish war with Spain." No markings are visible in other parts of the book.

Catalog: *C1951*, #69c, $12.50.

Location: Mark Twain Papers, Bancroft Library, University of California at Berkeley. Donated in 1973 by Professor Blake Nevius of the Department of English, University of California at Los Angeles. Professor Nevius purchased the volume at the 1951 auction.

Copy examined: Clemens's copy, in 2001.

———. "Charles Darwin," *Atlantic Monthly* 49.296 (June 1882): 835–845.

Mark Twain quotes extensively from Fiske's obituary essay about Darwin's death in the postscript section of "Mental Telegraphy" (published in 1891), which discusses the Darwin-Wallace coincidence of theories in 1858.

———. *The Discovery of America, with Some Account of Ancient America and the Spanish Conquest.* 2 vols. Boston: Houghton, Mifflin and Co., 1892.

At Riverdale on 13 April 1902 Mark Twain made notes for a love story set in the "Quaternary Epoch," two million years ago. He immediately thought of the solution to one problem: "For the early scenery & animals, see John Fiske's Discovery of America, vol. I" (NB 45, TS p. 10). In a speech at Carnegie Hall on 22 January 1906, Twain joked: "The historian, John Fiske, whom I knew well and loved, was a spotless and most noble and upright Christian gentleman, and yet he swore once" (*MTSpk* [1976], p. 481).

FITCHETT, WILLIAM HENRY (1845–1928). *The Tale of the Great Mutiny.* Illus. First edition. Original blue-green cloth, gilt.

New York: Charles Scribner's Sons, 1901. 384 pp.

Inscription: the front free endpaper is signed and dated in pencil, "S L. Clemens/Riverdale-on-Hudson/Feb. 1901."

Catalogs: *C1951*, #50c, $10, listed among books signed by Clemens; *Sotheby's 2003*, #212, $6,000 (sold with five other titles on history and travel).

Provenance: collection of Nick Karanovich, Fort Wayne, Indiana.

Location: collection of Kevin Mac Donnell, Austin, Texas.

Copy examined: Clemens's unmarked copy, at the Sotheby's auction in 2003. Contains the *C1951* sale label.

Fitchett provides another account of the Sepoy rebellion in India between 1857 and 1859.

FITZBALL, EDWARD (1792–1873). *Maritana* (opera, produced in 1845). Libretto by Fitzball; William Vincent Wallace (1812–1865), composer. Based on the play *Don César de Bazan* by Adolphe Philippe D'Ennery (1811–1899) and Philippe François Pinel, known as "Dumanoir" (1806–1865).

Clemens made a favorable reference to "Maritana. Alas those chimes so sweetly singing" in 1878 (NB 16, *N&J* 2: 213). Act II of *Maritana* opens with an aria by Lazarillo, beginning: "Alas! those chimes, so sweetly pealing,/Gently dulcet to the ear,/Sound like Pity's voice, revealing,/To the dying, 'death is near!'" See also the Catalog entry for Victor Hugo, *Ruy Blas* (play).

FITZGERALD, PERCY HETHERINGTON (1834–1925). *The Life of George the Fourth, Including His Letters and Opinions.* New York: Harper & Brothers, 1881. 921 pp.

Source: MTLAcc, entry #1765, volume donated by Clemens.

King George IV (1762–1830) ruled Great Britain after 1820.

———. *The Romance of the English Stage.* 2 vols. London: Richard Bentley & Son, 1874.

Inscriptions: the title page of Volume I is signed in black ink, "George Augustus Sala/25 Victoria St./S.W./April 1891". The title page of Volume II is signed in black ink, "G. A. Sala/1891."

Marginalia: below the inscription on the title page of Volume I Sala wrote in black ink: "A wearisome farrago of bald, bad, bookmaking scissorism."

Location: Mark Twain Library, Redding, Connecticut.

Copy examined: two volumes signed by the English journalist and travel writer George Augustus Sala (1828–1895). After a highly successful writing career Sala tried to launch *Sala's Journal*, fell heavily into debt, and in 1895 obliged to sell the contents of his huge personal library collection. Thereafter these books became widely scattered, and this one ended up in the Mark Twain Library at Redding. It has no markings, no Mark Twain Library stamps, and no accession number, yet for some reason it had been added to the shelves holding the Clemens family's library books when I visited Redding in June 1982. I saw no basis for leaving it there.

FLAGG, JOHN HENRY (1843–1911). *Lyrics of New England, and Other Poems.* Cedar Rapids, Iowa: Torch Press, 1909. 142 pp.

Inscription: inscribed by Flagg on the front free endpaper, "Saml L. Clemens,/with affectionate/Regards of/The Author."

Location: Mark Twain Library, Redding, Connecticut. Donated from Clemens's library by Clara Clemens

Gabrilowitsch in 1910 (MTLAcc, entry #2026).

Copy examined: Clemens's unmarked copy, with many leaves still unopened. Examined in 1970 and again in June 1982. It has the red ink Mark Twain Library accession number "2026".

———. *The Monarch and Other Poems.* New York: Privately printed, 1902. 102 pp.

Inscription: inscribed by Flagg on the front free flyleaf, "To S. L. Clemens,/with unfailing Regards of/The Author/Oct 18, 1904."

Location: Mark Twain Library, Redding, Connecticut.

Copy examined: Clemens's unmarked copy. Examined in 1970 and again in June 1982. It displays the red ink accession number of the Mark Twain Library, "3144".

———. [An identical copy.]

Marginalia: Clemens marked pages 5–6 and 8 with a pencil, and commented at the bottom of page 5: "Those two [stanzas]—never mind about details—successfully give you the atmosphere." The pages he marked contain "The Brook," a poem of eleven quatrains that begins "I am the brook, the nimble brook,/Born in my tranquil, shaded nook" (p. 5) and then follows the brook's downhill flow until it fatalistically allows itself to be absorbed by the sea: "To Nature's law I bow content,/That law which none can circumvent" (p. 8).

Provenance: Antenne-Dorrance Collection, Rice Lake, Wisconsin.

Location: Mark Twain Archive, Gannett-Tripp Learning Center, Elmira College, Elmira, New York.

Copy examined: Clemens's copy. Examined on 28 May 2015.

Flagg became associate counsel for Standard Oil in 1882 and therefore had an office in New York City, so Clemens's friendship with Henry H. Rogers might have brought him into contact with this corporate attorney. Flagg also belonged to the Authors Club in New York City, another place where he and Clemens might have met. In 1900 Flagg became afflicted with an incurable illness and, bedridden in Brattleboro, Vermont, he began writing poetry.

FLAMINI, FRANCESCO (1868–1922), ed. *Compendio di storia della letteratura Italiana ad uso delle scuole secondarie.* Quarta edizione, reveduta e corretta. Livorno: Raffaello Giusti, Editore. Libraio-Tipografo, 1904. 297 pp.

Inscription: signed in black ink on the front free endpaper: "Jean L. Clemens/Villa di Quarto/Firenze./Febbraio 1904."

Marginalia: unmarked except for the name "Flamini" written in brown ink on the verso of the title page.

Catalog: *Mott 1952,* #53, $2.

Location: Mark Twain House and Museum, Hartford, Connecticut. Gift of an anonymous donor in 1963.

Copy examined: Jean Clemens's copy. Examined in August 1987.

Included are excerpts from Machiavelli, Ariosto, Petrarch, Tasso, and other Italian authors.

FLAMMA, ARIO (1882–1961). *Dramas.* New York: Ario Flamma, 1909.

Location: formerly in the Mark Twain Library, Redding, Connecticut. Recorded by Albert F. Stone in 1955, but listed as missing in 1963. I was unable to find the

volume in 1970.

The first play by this Italian-American dramatist was dedicated to Mark Twain.

FLAMMARION, [NICOLAS] CAMILLE (1842–1925), pseud. "Fulgence Marion." *L'inconnu. The Unknown.* New York: Harper & Brothers, 1905. 488 pp.

Source: MTLAcc, entry #1806, volume donated by Clemens.

Here is another book whose loss one laments, in case it contained marginal comments by Clemens. Flammarion cited case histories of telepathic communications from the dying, psychic recognition by animals, survival after death, apparitions, premonitory dreams, and other phenomena of parapsychology.

———. *Stories of Infinity: Lumen—History of a Comet—In Infinity.* Translated from the French by S. R. Crocker. Boston: Roberts Brothers, 1873. 287 pp. [Edition and publisher conjectured.]

The French astronomer Flammarion would found the French Astronomical Society in 1887. Flammarion's *Stories of Infinity* endeavored to give the reader a concept of the vastness of time and the immensity of space in relationship to the relatively recent history of humans. In Notebook 22 (1884), Clemens made a cryptic note about "Rambouillon's [*sic*] 'Stories of Infinity,'" then added parenthetically: "(ask Holt *himself*)" (*N&J* 3: 50). Henry Holt (1840–1926) had founded his publishing company in 1873; was Clemens going to ask him why he let Roberts Brothers instead of Holt & Company bring out *Stories of Infinity*?

———. *Wonderful Balloon Ascents; or, the Conquest of the Skies. A History of Balloons and Balloon Voyages. From the French of F. Marion.* Illus. New York: Charles Scribner & Co., 1871. 218 pp.

Location: Mark Twain Library, Redding, Connecticut. Donated by Clemens (MTLAcc, entry #575).

Copy examined: Clemens's copy, unmarked.

Flammarion's enthusiasm for this airborne experience was so great that he would make a balloon ascent on his honeymoon in 1874. Mark Twain was repeatedly drawn to the idea of writing about balloon voyages; see the Catalog entry for Jules Verne, *Five Weeks in a Balloon.*

———. *The Wonders of Optics.* Translated from the French and edited by Charles William Quin. Illus. The Illustrated Wonder Library Series. New York: Scribner, Armstrong & Co., 1872. 276 pp.

Source: MTLAcc, entry #1986, volume donated from Clemens's library by Clara Clemens Gabrilowitsch in 1910.

FLAUBERT, GUSTAVE (1821–1880). *Madame Bovary: Provincial Manners.* Trans. by Eleanor Marx Aveling (1855–1898). London: Vizetelly & Co., 1886. 383 pp.

In March 1888 Clemens made note of "Mme. Bovary—Translated by Mrs. Marx Aveling—English Edition" (NB 27, *N&J* 3: 378). Here is Twain's closest recorded brush with Karl Marx, since this edition of the novel was translated by Marx's daughter Eleanor Marx Aveling. When Clemens was preparing to board the *Princess Irene* for a voyage to Italy in 1903, he requested Frederick A. Duneka of Harper & Brothers to send a copy of *Madame Bovary* to his stateroom (21 October 1903, TS in MTP). His reaction to this portrayal of the unsatisfied emotional cravings of a village doctor's wife went unrecorded. Flaubert's novel, celebrated for its quiet power and realistic details, was originally published in 1857.

———. *Salammbô* (published in 1862).

On 5 August 1909 Albert Bigelow Paine noticed that Clemens had been reading a copy of *Salammbô*, which Paine had loaned him. When Paine asked Clemens his opinion of the book, Clemens told him that he "read every line of it," but found only "a continuous procession of blood and slaughter and stench. . . . It has great art—I can see that. That scene of the crucified lions and the death cañon and the tent scene are marvelous, but I wouldn't read that book again without a salary" (*MTB*, p. 1516). Flaubert's historical novel is set during a siege of ancient Carthage by mercenaries in the third century BCE. Salammbô is a priestess of the moon goddess.

FLEMING, GEORGE (1858–1938). *Kismet.* "No Name Series." Illus. Boston: Roberts Brothers, 1877. 338 pp.
  Provenance: bookplate #487 of the J. Langdon Family Library."
  Catalog: Ball 2016 inventory, black cloth, orange lettering and design, piece of spine loose, poor condition.
  Location: Quarry Farm library shelves, under the supervision of the Mark Twain Archive, Elmira College, Elmira, New York.
  Copy examined: unmarked copy that was available to Clemens whenever he visited the Langdons' home in Elmira.
FLEMING, THOMAS (1853–1931). *Around the "Pan" with Uncle Hank. His Trip Through the Pan-American Exposition.* New York: Nut Shell Publishing Co., 1901. 262 pp.
  Source: MTLAcc, entry #365, volume donated by Clemens. The Pan-American Exposition, a World's Fair, displayed the achievements of the Western Hemisphere. It took place in Buffalo, New York in the summer and fall of 1901.
FLETCHER, CHARLES ROBERT LESLIE (1857–1934). *An Introductory History of England, from the Earliest Times to the Close of the Middle Ages.* Maps. New York: E. P. Dutton & Co., 1904. 397 pp. [Publisher conjectured.]
  Inscription: signed on the front pastedown endpaper, "S. L. Clemens, 21 Fifth Avenue, 1905."
  Catalog: *A1911*, "8vo, cloth, N.Y. 1904," quotes the signature, lot 168, sold for $2.
FLETCHER, ELLA ADELIA (1846–1934). *The Woman Beautiful: A Practical Treatise on the Development and Preservation of Woman's Health and Beauty, and the Principles of Taste in Dress.* Green cloth, green and red decorations and lettering. New York: Brentano's Publishers, 1901. 535 pp.
  Inscription: the front free endpaper is missing.
  Marginalia: there are large penciled check marks (seemingly Clara Clemens's) on pages 186 and 187 and a broad pencil mark (such as Clara Clemens often made) on page 259 at the topic of "Shampoo for moist hair." Two consecutive vertical penciled brackets resembling Clemens's habitual ones appear at passages discussing the uses of perfumes and incenses as purifying agents and moth-preventives. On page 448 someone drew a pencil line under the "therapeutic use of cinnamon" and in the margin penciled the word "Curative"; the hand resembles Clemens's.
  Copy examined: Albert E. Stone recorded this book in his checklist of Clemens's donations to the Mark Twain Library at Redding, Connecticut in 1955. Stone reported

that the flyleaf was missing. I was unable to locate the book in 1970, but on a return visit in June 1982 I found it. I inspected it again on 10 November 2019. It would appear that both Clemens and his daughter Clara looked into the volume.
  Fletcher's book idealized the turn-of-the-century Gibson girl image and endeavored to prescribe every aspect of female fashion and beauty, along with hints about health. In subsequent years Fletcher became an adherent of the New Thought movement and her publications delved into yoga as well as occult interpretations of astrology, palmreading, and spiritualism (see Kurt Leland, *Rainbow Body: A History of the Western Chakra System from Blavatsky to Brennan* [Lake Worth, Florida: Ibis Press/Nicolas-Hays, 2016], pp. 159–161).

Fliegende Blätter [Flying Pages] (German weekly periodical).
  On 1 March 1883 Clemens notified Christian B. Tauchnitz: "I should like to become a permanent subscriber to the *Fliegende Blätter*; and I would also like to buy ten or twelve of the back numbers" (TS in MTP). This richly illustrated humor and satire magazine (its name translates in English as *Flying Leaves*) was published in Munich for nearly a century, 1845–1944.

FLOTOW, (BARON) FRIEDRICH VON (1812–1883). *Martha, or the Market at Richmond (Martha, oder Der Market zu Richmond)* (opera, performed 1847). Libretto by Friedrich Wilhelm Riese (1805–1879).
  In 1865 Mark Twain reviewed a Virginia City performance of *Martha* and praised "that enchanting old song, 'The Last Rose of Summer'" (Virginia City *Territorial Enterprise*, 3–5 June 1865; reprinted by Gary Scharnhorst in "Additional Mark Twain Contributions to the Virginia City *Territorial Enterprise*, 1863–66," *American Literary Realism* 47.1 [Fall 2014]: 90). See also the Catalog entry for Thomas Moore's "The Last Rose of Summer."

FOGAZZARO, ANTONIO (1842–1911). *Il Mistero del Poeta: Romanzo [The Poet's Mystery].* Milano: Baldini, Castoldi & Co., 1900. 409 pp. [Publisher and pages conjectured but virtually certain.]
  Inscription: "To Jean Clemens on a Birthday, July 26th 1903."
  Catalog: *Mott 1952*, #54, $3.50.
  Fogazzaro lived in Vicenza, Italy and wrote novels (including *Il Mistero del Poeta*), short stories, and poetry. He urged reforms in the Catholic Church and thereby drew its enmity.

FONSECA, JOSÉ DA (c. 1792–1866) and PEDRO CAROLINO. *The New Guide of the Conversation in Portuguese and English in Two Parts.* Intro. by Mark Twain. Boston: James R. Osgood & Co., 1883. 182 pp. [Twain's introduction appears on pages viii–xi.]
  Sources: ListABP (1910), "New Guide of the Conversation, Carolino", listed twice; MTLAcc, entry #817, volume donated by Clemens.
  Mark Twain's introduction to this unauthorized edition of a badly botched phrasebook ridiculed its principal writer, who was evidently Carolino, as "an honest and upright idiot who believed he knew something of the English language." These overly literal translations of English idioms have amused many other readers besides Twain.

FONTAINE, CAMILLE (1855–1923). *Livre de lecture et de*

conversation. Boston: D. C. Heath & Co., [cop. 1893]. 249 pp. "I want to bother you once more about a French book," Olivia Clemens wrote to her husband from Paris on 26 April 1894. "There was a new book come out in New York pub. by D. C. Heath & Co. called Prof. C. Fontaine's 'Livre de Lecture et de Conversation.' It is spoken very well of by the Critic & I should like it if you could get it & bring it to me when you come" (ALS, formerly in the Mark Twain Research Foundation, Perry, Mo.; quoted in *The Twainian* 37 [May-June 1978]: 4). *The Critic* was a New York City magazine of literary criticism.

FONVIELLE, WILFRID DE (1824–1914). *Thunder and Lightning*. Translated from the French and edited by Thomas Lamb Phipson (1833–1908). Illus. N. Y.: Scribner, Armstrong & Co., 1872. 285 pp.

> Source: MTLAcc, entry #1985, volume donated from Clemens's library by Clara Clemens Gabrilowitsch in 1910.
>
> Inasmuch as imagery of thunder and lightning permeate Mark Twain's writings, this popularized study of lightning and its victims should be looked at closely. A sketch of Benjamin Franklin's experiment with a kite serves as the frontispiece, and thirty-nine other wood engravings illustrate the text. Fonvielle's sixty-one chapters explore every conceivable manifestation of what the Translator's Preface calls "the electric phenomena of our atmosphere" that are "Nature's most energetic forces" (p. 7). St. Elmo's Fire is treated in Chapter 6, "Sheet Lightning" in Chapter 8, "Peculiar Cases of Death by Lightning" in Chapter 53, and "The History of Lightning-Conductors" in Chapter 61. Besides being a prolific science writer Fonvielle was an avid balloonist, another subject that fascinated Twain. It would be surprising if Clemens did not own *Travels in the Air* (1871) by James Glaisher (1809–1903), a work to which Fonvielle contributed, but no association copy survived or was recorded.

FOOTE, MARY (HALLOCK) (1847–1938). *John Bodewin's Testimony*. Boston: Ticknor and Co., 1886. 344 pp.

> In addition to becoming an acclaimed magazine illustrator, Mary Foote gained a notable reputation for her "Local Color" stories of mining life in the American West, a region where she had accompanied her engineer husband to various railroad and mining sites. In September 1886 Clemens noted the author and title of this novel, along with some instructions: "(if they've *got* it.)—Don't send for it" (NB 26, *N&J* 3: 253). Clemens wrote admiringly to Mary Foote on 2 December 1887: "Ten years ago I was a platform-humorist & you a singer of plaintive Scotch ballads that were full of heart-break & tears. And now we have changed places. You are a platform-humorist (among other things), & I am reader to a Browning class!" (ALS sold by Christie's, New York City, 1–2 February 1988 auction, lot 470). Three decades later he referred to Clara Clemens's "dear & valued & level-headed friend & mine, Mary Foote," who is "a fine human being, of full age" (29[?] August 1906, *MTHL*, p. 819). It seems highly likely that Clemens owned more than one title of Foote's writings, but no others seem to be extant.

FORBES, ARTHUR LITTON ARMITAGE (1845–1926). *Two Years in Fiji*. London: Longmans, Green and Co., 1875. 340 pp. [Edition conjectured.]

> At the end of a list of books that Clemens read in London in November 1896 appears "2 Years in F.—Lytton Forbes" (NB 39, TS p. 26). Subsequently he quoted from Forbes' book (merely citing "Forbes's 'Two Years in Fiji'") in Chapter 8 of *Following the Equator* (1897), where he presented Forbes' account of two foreigners who mysteriously appeared in Fiji and whose homeland could never be determined.

FORBES, FRANK. *How to Be Happy Through Living*. London: Neville & Co., [1902]. 112 pp.

> Source: MTLAcc, entry #396, volume donated by Clemens.

FORBES-MITCHELL, WILLIAM (1836–1905) (earlier known as William Mitchell). *Reminiscences of the Great Mutiny, 1857–59, Including the Relief, Siege, and Capture of Lucknow, and the Campaigns in Rohilcund and Oude*. London: Macmillan and Co., 1893. 295 pp. [Publisher and pages conjectured.]

> Catalog: *C1951*, # 29c, presentation copy, $10.
>
> This work could arouse strong emotions. For example, on 21 May 1894 Robert Louis Stevenson wrote to Forbes-Mitchell, formerly a Sergeant in the 93rd Sutherland Highlanders, to relate how he read *Reminiscences of the Great Mutiny* aloud to his wife and her daughter, "choking upon sobs," adding, "You have made me proud and glad to be a Scotsman" (Argyll and Sutherland Highlanders Regimental Museum). Mark Twain entered the name of the author and the title in Notebook 35 while he was visiting New Zealand in October-November 1895 (TS p. 64). In Chapter 54 of *Following the Equator* (1897) Twain stated that he had read about military marches with the temperatures at 138 degrees "in Sergeant-Major Forbes-Mitchell's account of his military experiences in the Mutiny . . . and in Calcutta I asked him if it was true, and he said it was." Born on 19 January 1836 in Tough, Aberdeenshire, Forbes-Mitchell would die in Calcutta on 11 February 1905, having published *The Gospel of Regeneration of the Anglo-Indian and Eurasian Poor* (1900).

FORBUSH, EDWARD HOWE (1858–1929). *Useful Birds and Their Protection*. Published under direction of the Massachusetts State Board of Agriculture. Boston: Wright & Potter Printing Co., n.d. 437 pp.

> Inscription: presentation copy from the author, inscribed on the front free flyleaf:
>
> "Mr. Samuel L. Clemens/with the compliments/and kind regards/of E. H. Forbush/Boston/May 24, 1909."
>
> Location: Mark Twain Library, Redding, Connecticut. Donated from Clemens's library by Clara Clemens Gabrilowitsch in 1910 (MTLAcc, entry #1948).
>
> Copy examined: Clemens's copy, unmarked. Examined in 1970 and again in June 1982. Displays the red ink Mark Twain Library accession number "1948".

FORD, HARRIET (1868–1949). *A Gentleman of France* (play, produced in 1901).

> Clemens and his wife attended a matinée performance on 1 February 1902 in New York City (SLC to Elisabeth Marbury, 10 February 1902, ASSSCL). The historical romance starred Eleanor Robson (1879–1979), the long-lived actress (and, later, author and playwright). Set in Renaissance France and featuring swordplay scenes, *A Gentleman of France* had opened at Wallach's Theatre on 30 December 1901.

FORD, PAUL LEICESTER (1865–1902), ed. *A House Party: An Account of the Stories Told at a Gathering of Famous American*

Authors, The Story Tellers Being Introduced by Paul Leicester Ford. Intro. by Paul Leicester Ford. Boston: Small, Maynard & Co., 1901. 418 pp.

On 7 March 1901 Ford attended a meeting of the Thursday Evening Club in the home of William M. Sloane; Mark Twain was there to read an unpublished story, so they presumably met. The advertising for Ford's book later infuriated Twain, since he felt it implied that he and other prominent American authors had contributed pieces to *A House Party.* (The book explained that a large number of "distinguished authors" had been invited to contribute short fictional pieces; readers were to participate in a contest by guessing who had written the twelve anonymous stories.) On 9 January 1902 Twain mailed form letters to some of the twenty-three listed authors, seeking to determine whether twelve of them actually *had* written stories for *A House Party,* or whether the publishers had perpetrated a fraud. Evidently the responses he received from Thomas Bailey Aldrich, George Washington Cable, Winston Churchill, F. Marion Crawford, and others satisfied him that no further action was warranted. Cable, Sarah Orne Jewett, Owen Wister, and Frank Stockton were among the dozen writers whose stories did appear in the volume. Paul Leicester Ford, who edited and contributed a story to the collection, would be murdered by his brother on 8 May 1902.

Cardwell, *Twins of Genius* (1953), pp. 111–112.

"FOR HE'S A JOLLY GOOD FELLOW" (college song, sung to a very old tune).

Clemens referred to this song in "*A Champagne Cocktail and a Catastrophe': Two Acting Charades*" (privately printed, 1930); in Chapter 11 of *Pudd'nhead Wilson* (1894); and again in a 28 January 1907 Autobiographical Dictation (*MTE,* p. 76; *AutoMT* 2: 389). The second verse of this popular song lingered in Twain's memory. The narrator in Twain's "Three Thousand Years Among the Microbes (written in 1905) leads his group in singing "'We won't go home till mor-or-ning—/Till daylight doth appear!'" (*WWD?*, p. 488). See also the Catalog entry for Stephen Foster's "We won't go home till morning."

FORMAN, JUSTUS MILES (1875–1915). *Buchanan's Wife; A Novel.* Illustrated by Will Grefé (1875–1957). New York: Harper & Brothers, 1906. 262 pp.

Source: MTLAcc, entry #131, volume donated by Clemens.

————. *The Island of Enchantment.* Illustrated by Howard Pyle (1853–1911). Purple cloth, decorated. New York: Harper & Brothers, 1905. 106 pp.

Inscription: signed in black ink on the front pastedown endpaper, "SL. Clemens/1905".

Provenance: Antenne-Dorrance Collection, Rice Lake, Wisconsin.

Location: Mark Twain Archive, Gannett-Tripp Learning Center, Elmira College, Elmira, New York. The matching cardboard box for this volume is in the Mark Twain Papers, Bancroft Library, University of California at Berkeley; it bears Clemens's note: "Family miniatures (early)". Katy Leary left the box behind when she chose Forman's volume as a keepsake after Clemens's death in 1910, since he apparently kept photographs in that box.

Copy examined: Clemens's copy, unmarked. Examined on 28 May 2015.

————. [An identical copy.]

Source: MTLAcc, entry #1048, volume donated by Clemens.

————. *Jason, A Romance.* Illustrated by W[illiam]. Hatherell (1855–1928). New York: Harper & Brothers, 1909. 357 pp.

Source: MTLAcc, entry #2238, volume donated from Clemens's library by Clara Clemens Gabrilowitsch in 1910.

————. *A Stumbling Block.* New York: Harper & Brothers, 1907. 310 pp.

Source: MTLAcc, entry #1552, volume donated by Clemens.

FORNERON, HENRI (1834–1886). *Louise de KerToualle, Duchess of Portsmouth, 1649–1734; or, How the Duke of Richmond Gained His Pension. Compiled from State Papers Preserved in the Archives of the French Foreign Office by H. Forneron. With Portraits, Facsimile Letter, etc., and a Preface by Mrs. G. M. Crawford.* Third edition. New York: Scribner & Welford, 1888. 346 pp. [Initially published in 1887 in London by Swan Sonnenschein.]

Perhaps Clemens was looking for more racy narratives of court affairs and intrigues like those of Saint-Simon when he wrote a reminder about the American edition of this work in November 1887: "Book about Chas II & Kerouaille, translated by Mrs. M. G. Crawford, pub by Scribner & Welford" (NB 27, *N&J* 3: 351). Another entry in the same notebook adds: "Louise de Kerouaille./Scribner & Welford" (December 1887, *N&J* 3: 358). Louise-Renée de Kérouaille was a French mistress of Charles II (1630–1685); the Duke of Richmond (1672–1723) was their son. Forneron's book provided (for its time) a surprisingly frank account of the days "when Louise de Kerouaille was above the crowned Queen at Whitehall" (p. xi), describing her stratagems as an agent of Louis XIV while "consciously trying to bring England into subjection to France" (p. xiv). In 1907 Clemens would mention Charles II disparagingly as one who pulled down English standards of "official and commercial morals" that were raised by Oliver Cromwell (30 January 1907 AD, *MTE,* p. 81; *AutoMT* 2: 409).

FORNEY, JOHN W[IEN]. (1817–1881). *Anecdotes of Public Men.* Volume 1. New York: Harper & Brothers, [cop. 1873]. 444 pp. [A continuation would appear in 1881 as Volume 2.]

Source: MTLAcc, entry #1464, Volume 1 only, donated by Clemens.

Forney's stories recounting actions and remarks of well-known men, which had appeared earlier in Philadelphia and Washington newspapers, are arranged without any discernible principle of organization. There is an index, however, that lists figures such as Daniel Webster, P. T. Barnum, Edwin Forrest, Charles Dickens, Frederick Douglass, and General Ulysses S. Grant.

FORSTER, JOHN (1812–1876). *The Life of Jonathan Swift. Volume the First, 1667–1711.* New York: Harper & Brothers, 1876. 487 pp.

Source: MTLAcc, entry #1766, volume donated by Clemens.

Here is another lost book that almost certainly contained marginalia. Clemens held strong opinions about Swift; see, for example, the Catalog entry for W. M. Thackeray, *Thackeray's Lectures. The English Humourists.*

FORSYTH, GEORGE ALEXANDER (1837–1915). *Thrilling*

Days in Army Life. Illustrated by Rufus Fairchild Zogbaum (1849–1925). New York: Harper & Brothers, 1902. 197 pp.

Source: MTLAcc, entry #501, volume donated by Clemens.

FORSYTH, WILLIAM (1812–1899). *The Novels and Novelists of the Eighteenth Century, in Illustration of the Manners and Morals of the Age*. New York: D. Appleton and Co., 1871. 339 pp. [Edition conjectured.]

On 14 July 1880 Estes & Lauriat of Boston billed Clemens for "1 Novels & Novelists," and Clemens paid on 20 July (receipt in MTP). Forsyth's book was the only one published with this title between 1870 and 1880.

FOSTER, MARY LOUISE (1873–1910), pseud. "Louise Forsslund." *The Ship of Dreams; A Novel*. New York: Harper & Brothers, 1902. 307 pp.

Source: MTLAcc, entry #130, volume donated by Clemens.

FOSTER, STEPHEN COLLINS (1826–1864). "De camptown races (Gwine to run all night)" (minstrel song, published in 1850).

Nicodemus Dodge plays "Camptown Races" with a comb and paper in Chapter 23 of *A Tramp Abroad* (1880). Jasper and Martha, enslaved workers in the kitchen, sing this "gay song" to banjo accompaniment in "Which Was It?," written 1899–1903 (*WWD?*, p. 420). Clemens recalled "Camptown Races" as one of the "rudely comic" songs in early minstrel shows (30 November 1906 AD, *MTE*, p. 114; *AutoMT* 2: 296).

———. "Ellen Bayne" (minstrel song, published in 1854).

Outside the ice cream parlor in Indiantown, prior to the Civil War, young people were "plaintively singing 'Sweet Ellen Bayne'" in "Which Was It?," written 1899–1903 (*WWD?*, p. 302). Clemens remembered it as one of the "sentimental songs" worked into the later minstrel shows (30 November 1906 AD, *MTE*, p. 114; *AutoMT* 2: 296).

———. "Hard times come again no more" (song, published in 1854).

A character named Louis in Mark Twain's "Three Thousand Years Among the Microbes" (written in 1905) shouts a drinking toast, "'To Old Times Come Again—to stay!'" (*WWD?*, p. 488). This boisterous usage seems incongruous with the sad, plaintive tone of Foster's song.

———. "Massa's in de cold, cold ground" (minstrel song, published in 1852).

Clemens recalled that early-day residents of Hannibal enjoyed this and other "Negro Melodies" that tended toward "regrets for bygone days and vanished joys" ("Villagers of 1840–3," written in 1897, *HH&T* [1969], p. 34). Evidently Clemens was remembering the final years of his residence in Hannibal.

———. "My old Kentucky home, good night" (minstrel song, published in 1853).

Hannibal residents liked this song when he was a youth, Clemens recalled in 1897 ("Villagers of 1840–3," *HH&T*, p. 34).

———. "Nelly Bly" (minstrel song, published in 1849).

This was one of the "sentimental songs" that Clemens remembered from the later minstrel shows (30 November 1906 AD, *MTE*, p. 114; *AutoMT* 2: 296).

———. "Old Black Joe" (minstrel song, published in 1860).

In 1882 Clemens heard two African American cabin hands sing this song to banjo accompaniment on Horace Bixby's *City of Baton Rouge* (NB 21, *N&J* 2: 562). It is often classified as the last song Foster composed for minstrel shows.

———. "Old Dog Tray" (minstrel song, published in 1853).

In "On Linden, Etc." (*The Californian*, 7 April 1866; *SSix* [1926], pp. 208–209) Mark Twain comically blunders in recalling a line from "Old Dog Tray," mistakenly believing that he is quoting Thomas Campbell's "Hohenlinden." In 1866 Twain heard the ship's choir on the *America* sing this and other "d-dest, oldest, vilest songs"; "D—n Dog Tray," he groused in Notebook 7 (*N&J* 1: 262–263). He reported to his *Alta California* audience on 23 December 1866 that the ship's choir sang this and other "venerable melodies" (*MTTMB* [1940], p. 28); in his 1 January 1867 letter he lost patience at continually hearing these "wretchedest old songs in the world" while amidst natural scenic beauty at sea. "Confound Dog Tray!" he snapped (*MTTMB*, p. 59). Much later, in 1897, he recollected hearing the song in ante-bellum Hannibal, one of those whose lyrics "tended to regrets for bygone days and vanished joys" ("Villagers of 1840–3," *HH&T*, p. 34).

———. "Old folks at home" (minstrel song, published in 1851). Also called "Swanee River."

Clemens included this among his favorite songs in August 1889 (NB 29, *N&J* 3; 513). In 1897 he listed "Swanee River" among the "Negro Melodies" favored by Hannibal townspeople during his boyhood ("Villagers of 1840–3," *HH&T*, p. 34). The enslaved South Carolina man in Chapter 26 of Mark Twain's "No. 44, The Mysterious Stranger" (written 1902–1908) sings this minstrel song, "and there was never anything so beautiful, never anything so heart-breaking, oh, never any music like it below the skies!" (*MSM* [1969], pp. 355–356).

Sharon D. McCoy, "'I ain' no dread being': The Minstrel Mask as Alter Ego," *Centenary Reflections on Mark Twain's No. 44, The Mysterious Stranger*, ed. Joseph Csicsila and Chad Rohman (Columbia: University of Missouri Press, 2009), pp. 29–33; and Henry B. Wonham, "Mark Twain's Last Cakewalk: Racialized Performance in *No. 44, The Mysterious Stranger*," *Centenary Reflections on Mark Twain's No. 44* (2009), pp. 46–47.

———. "We won't go home till morning" (song, published c. 1842).

The narrator in Mark Twain's "Three Thousand Years Among the Microbes" (written in 1905) leads his group in singing "'We won't go home till mor-or-ning—/Till daylight doth appear!'" (*WWD?*, p. 488). These are the last two lines of the chorus of Foster's song (though usually Foster's lyrics are reprinted as "does appear" rather than "doth appear"). By the 1870s these lines had somehow become the second stanza of a vastly popular song, "For He's a Jolly Good Fellow"; see that Catalog entry.

———. "Willie we have missed you" (song, published in 1854).

Clemens mentioned this as a song (about a son returning home) generally seen on music stands in parlors in Honolulu when he visited the port in 1866 (Chapter 3, *FE* [1897]).

FOTHERGILL, JESSIE (1851–1891). *The First Violin; A Novel*. Leisure Hour Series, No. 101. New York: Henry Holt and Co., 1878. 432 pp.

Inscription: "Ida C. Langdon". Ida Clark Langdon (1849–1934) was married to Charles Jervis Langdon (1849–1916).

Catalog: Ball 2016 inventory, dark yellow cloth, gilt and

black lettering and design, signed by Ida C. Langdon, fair condition.

Location: Quarry Farm library shelves, under the supervision of the Mark Twain Archive, Elmira College, Elmira, New York.

This book was available to Clemens whenever he visited the Langdons in Elmira.

————. *Healey*. New York: George Munro, [cop. 1885]. 233 pp.

Source: MTLAcc, entry #2237, volume donated from Clemens's library by Clara Clemens Gabrilowitsch in 1910.

English author Fothergill's first novel in 1875 was *Healey: A Romance*, set amid the cotton-mills in Lancashire. She published a new edition of it in London in 1884.

FOUQUIER, ARMAND (b. 1817). *Causes célèbres de tous les peoples*. Folio, 28 parts bound in one volume. Three-quarter black calf, red morocco label, gilt. Paris: Lebrun et cie, [1874.] [The date of publication is conjectured.]

Marginalia: a table of contents appears to be written in Olivia Clemens's hand. "C[harles?] Clark/Temple" is written in another hand with some page numbers.

Catalogs: *A1911*, "4to, half calf, no title, . . . Paris, n.d., with ms. list of contents in Mr. Clemens' autograph," lot 72, sold for $1.25 (no author provided); Parke-Bernet Galleries, New York City, Sale number 272 (7–8 May 1945), lot 139, half calf, title page lacking, the front flyleaf "bears a manuscript list of the contents in Mark Twain's autograph, about sixty words, also twenty-nine numerals in his hand," contains the *A1911* auction label; Rare Books and Documents Auction, World Trade Center, Boston, 14 October 2000, Lot 95, Mark Twain's copy, "*Causes célèbres de tous les peoples*. 4to, half calf, manuscript table of contents in his hand, has the *A1911* sale label, fair condition," gavel price $534.38."

Location: collection of Kevin Mac Donnell, Austin, Texas.

Copy examined: Clemens's copy, in July 2004. Contains the *A1911* auction label. Bookseller George Goodspeed's price and description slip (in 1964) is laid in, along with a postcard from Jacob Blanck to Goodspeed attesting that the volume came from the 1911 sale.

This collection of forty-five stories of infamous crimes, murders, imposters, and trials (of which this is an incomplete gathering of twenty-nine), was issued in parts between 1858 and 1874. The entire text is in French. One tale in this volume concerning an imposter would have especially interested Clemens. Here is one of the books that corroborate William Dean Howells's point about Clemens always "reading some vital book" such as "a volume of great trials" (*My Mark Twain* [1910], p. 15).

D. M. McKeithan, *Court Trials in Mark Twain* (1958); Edwin Briden, "Law," *Mark Twain Encyclopedia*, pp. 445–448.

FOWLER, (SIR) MONTAGUE (1858–1933), Fourth Baronet. *Some Notable Archbishops of Canterbury*. London: Society for Promoting Christian Knowledge, 1895. 222 pp.

Inscription: inscribed on the verso of the front free endpaper, in black ink: "To 'Mark Twain'/from the author/Montague Fowler/a tribute to a giant from a pigmy/June 22, 1899." Part of the second flyleaf has been torn out. Something was once tipped in at the recto of the frontispiece, but this tipped-in piece of paper is now missing except for

its top fragment.

Marginalia: pencil marks, very likely Clemens's, on page 101 at the sentence, "His father died when he [Matthew Parker] was only twelve years of age." Matthew Parker (1504–1575) was Queen Elizabeth's Archbishop from 1559 until 1575.

Location: Mark Twain Library, Redding, Connecticut.

Copy examined: Clemens's copy, unmarked. Examined in 1970 and again in June 1982. It has the Mark Twain Library accession number "3028".

Fowler was an eminent figure in the Church of England.

FOWLER, ORSON SQUIRE (1809–1887). *Love and Parentage, Applied to the Improvement of Offspring, Including Important Directions and Suggestions to Lovers and the Married Concerning the Strongest Ties and the Most Momentous Relations of Life*. Fortieth ed. New York: Fowler & Wells, [cop. 1844].

Inscription: contains the bookplate and signature of "J. H. Hatch/August 26/1861".

Marginalia: markings on pages 53 and 54.

Provenance: owned in 1970 by Ralph Gregory (1909–2015), then curator of the Mark Twain Birthplace Memorial Shrine, Florida, Missouri (now called the Mark Twain Birthplace State Historic Site). Mr. Gregory resided in Marthasville, Missouri.

Location: in August 2017 the volume belonged to Ralph Gregory's daughter, Nancy Gregory Kimball, Marthasville, Missouri.

Copy examined: a copy that plausibly belonged to Orion Clemens. Given to Mr. Gregory in 1965 by Mrs. Mary Gertrude (Stotts) Shotwell, who lived in Orion and Mollie Clemens's home. See the Catalog entry for Thomas Dick's *Practical Astronomer* for an explanation of this provenance.

——————— and LORENZO NILES FOWLER (1811–1896). *New Illustrated Self-Instructor in Phrenology and Physiology*. New York: Fowler & Wells, n.d. [Revised edition cop. 1859; reprinted in 1877, 1890, and presumably in other years as well.]

Inscription: signed on the front endpaper, "Clemens, 1901," a date that corresponds with Clemens's appointment with Jessie Allen Fowler (1856–1932) of the Fowler & Wells firm for a phrenological character reading on 7 March 1901; she probably presented him with this volume when he underwent an analysis at her office in New York City (Notebook 44, TS p. 7).

Marginalia: in the chart of phrenological faculties at the front of the book, marks are placed beside "Self-Esteem," "Veneration," and "Calculation." These are three of the organs found to be predominant in "Bishop" Mark Twain in Book 2 (Chapter 2) of "The Secret History of Eddypus, the World-Empire," written 1901–1902.

Catalog: *A1911*, "12mo, cloth, N.Y. n.d.," quotes the signature and describes the markings, lot 385, sold for $3.50.

I explained in "Mark Twain, Phrenology and the 'Temperaments'" (1972) how Mark Twain inserted a satire on the Fowler & Wells method of examination into "The Secret History of Eddypus" (*FM* [1972], pp. 348–353). He took a portion of a phrenologist's "lecture" there practically verbatim from the preface (p. viii) of the Fowler brothers' *Self-Instructor in Phrenology and Physiology*.

Madeline B. Stern, "Mark Twain Had His Head Examined," *American Literature* 41.2 (May 1969): 207–218; Madeline B. Stern, *Heads and Headlines: The Phrenological Fowlers*

(Norman: University of Oklahoma Press, 1971); Alan Gribben, "Mark Twain, Phrenology and the 'Temperaments': A Study of Pseudoscientific Influence," *American Quarterly* 24.1 (March 1972): 45–68 (a revised version of this essay appears as a chapter in Volume One of the present work.) Stanley Finger's "Mark Twain's Phrenological Experiment: Three Renditions of His 'Small Test,'" *Journal of the History of the Neurosciences* 29.1 (2020): 101–118 was largely based on, but extended, Gribben's findings.

FOWLER, SAMUEL PAGE (1800–1888), ed. *Salem Witchcraft: Comprising More Wonders of the Invisible World, Collected by Robert Calef [1648–1719]; and Wonders of the Invisible World, by Cotton Mather [1663–1728]; Together with Notes and Explanations by Samuel P. Fowler.* Boston: W. Veazie, 1865. 450 pp.

  Marginalia: Clemens rollicks through Mather's *Wonders of the Invisible World* (1693), adding sarcastic notes to many of the putative "proofs" of witchcraft and occasionally suggesting that the accusers were drunk when they imagined their visions. His knowledge of European history restrains him from wholly denouncing the Puritan government in the American colonies, however. He notes on page 341: "Well, their infamies covered but one year, & were heartily confessed & repented of; whereas Europe's iniquities in the same line covered eight centuries. Nothing so fantastic, & ignorant, & barbarous, as these Salem Witch-trials can be found, outside of the Scriptures." On the last page of the book Clemens wrote: "Calef really deserves a monument." Robert Calef's *More Wonders of the Invisible World* (1700) exposed the shoddy evidence and subsequent apologies of the Salem, Massachusetts persecutors whom Cotton Mather had applauded in his *Wonders of the Invisible World.* Mather's credulity about the Salem episode cast a permanent shadow over his previous reputation as a towering intellectual figure in the New World colonies. All of Clemens's marginalia are in bluish-black ink.

  Catalogs: ListABP (1910), "Salem Witchcraft, Fowler"; *C1951*, #3a, $35; *Zeitlin 1951*, #11, $75.

  Location: Mark Twain Papers, Bancroft Library, University of California at Berkeley.

  Copy examined: Clemens's heavily underlined and annotated copy.

FOWLER, THOMAS (1832–1904). *Locke.* English Men of Letters Series. New York: Harper & Brothers, 1899. 200 pp.

  Source: MTLAcc, entry #1283, volume donated by Clemens.

  The English philosopher John Locke, notable particularly for *An Essay Concerning Human Understanding* (1690), lived from 1632 to 1704.

FOX, CAROLINE (1819–1871). *Memories of Old Friends, Being Extracts from the Journals and Letters of Caroline Fox, of Penjerrick, Cornwall, from 1835–1871.* Ed. by Horace Noble Pym (1844–1896). Philadelphia: J. B. Lippincott & Co., 1882. [Edition conjectured.]

  In April 1882 Clemens wrote "Caroline Fox's Memories" in Notebook 20 (*N&J* 2: 460) shortly before he made trips to Boston and New York City. He might have been interested in her vivid portraits of the prominent English authors—Carlyle, Wordsworth, Mill, Coleridge, Macaulay, and others—with whom she had associated.

FOX, JOHN, JR. (1863–1919). *The Little Shepherd of Kingdom Come.* Illustrated by F[rederick]. C[offay]. Yohn (1875–1933). New York: C. Scribner's Sons, 1903. 404 pp.

  Source: MTLAcc, entry #998, volume donated by Clemens. Fox's novel was a best-seller in 1903.

———. *A Mountain Europa.* New York: Harper & Brothers, 1899. 192 pp.

  Source: MTLAcc, entry #1553, volume donated by Clemens.

———. *The Trail of the Lonesome Pine.* Illustrated by F[rederick]. C[offay]. Yohn (1875–1933). New York: C. Scribner's Sons, 1909. 422 pp.

  Source: MTLAcc, entry #999, volume donated by Clemens. *The Trail of the Lonesome Pine* was fifth on the list of best-sellers in 1909.

———. [Another identical copy.] Leaves loose.

  Source: MTLAcc, entry #878, volume donated by Mrs. Ralph W. Ashcroft (formerly Isabel V. Lyon), Clemens's secretary.

FOXALL, EDWARD WILLIAM (1857–1926), pseud. Gizen-no-Teki. *Colorphobia. An Exposure of the "White Australia" Fallacy.* Sydney: R. T. Kelley, 1903. 236 pp.

  Inscription: inscribed on the verso of the front free endpaper in black ink: "To Samuel L. Clemens/Mark Twain)/with compliments/of/"Gizen-no-Teki"/(E. W. Foxall)/Sydney/Australia/14 July 1903."

  Location: Mark Twain Library, Redding, Connecticut.

  Copy examined: Clemens's unmarked copy. Has the red ink Mark Twain Library accession number "2525". Examined in 1970 and again in June 1982.

  Foxall's Japanese pseudonym could be loosely translated as "The Enemy of Hypocrisy."

  Diana H. Wyndham, *Striving for National Fitness: Eugenics in Australia* (London: Glaton Institute, 2003).

FOXE, JOHN (1516–1587). *The Book of Martyrs* (English edition published in 1563).

  The English Protestant historian Foxe related the persecutions of John Wycliffe, William Tyndale, and other victims of efforts to suppress the Protestant movement. Mark Twain recalled that a copy of "Fox's [sic] Martyrs" generally could be seen on the parlor tables of the wooden cottages he visited in Honolulu in 1866 (*FE* [1897], Ch. 3).

FRAIPONT, GUSTAVE (1849–1923). *The Art of Sketching.* Trans. from the French by Clara Bell (1834–1927). Preface by Edwin Bale (1842–1923). Fifty illustrations by the author. New York: Charles L. Webster & Co., 1893. 100 pp.

  Published by Clemens's firm, in whose decisions he usually participated.

FRANCE, ANATOLE, pseud. of Jacques Anatole François Thibault (1844–1924). *The Crime of Sylvestre Bonnard (Member of the Institute).* Translation and introduction by Lafcadio Hearn (1850–1904). 12mo, cloth. New York: Harper & Brothers, 1906. 281 pp.

  Inscription: Clemens wrote in black ink on the front pastedown endpaper: "The world has said that the French have wit, but not humor: (meaning humor 'on the American plan,' no doubt.) The humor in this book is either that, or it is better than that./S L. Clemens/1906."

  Marginalia: numerous markings, grammatical corrections, and notes—generally charitable.

  Catalogs: *A1911*, "12mo, cloth, N.Y. 1906," quotes the principal note by Clemens, lot 229, sold for $21;

Anderson Auction Galleries, Sale number 1873 (10–11 November 1924), has the *A1911* sale label, item #220, $40; "Irving S. Underhill Collection," American Art Association, Anderson Galleries, Sale No. 3911 (29 April 1936), #116, $100.

Location: Henry W. and Albert A. Berg Collection, New York Public Library.

Copy examined: Clemens's copy, in 1970. Contains the *A1911* sale label.

Clemens wrote enthusiastically to Olivia Clemens from Washington, D. C. on 13 January 1891: "I've got a charming book for you to read—'The Crimes [*sic*] of Sylvester Bonnard'" (ALS, MTP). Alan Gribben, "Anatole France and Mark Twain's Satan," *American Literature* 47.4 (January 1976): 634–635, suggested the possibility that Twain absorbed an idea for ending "No. 44, The Mysterious Stranger" from an episode in Anatole France's *Le Crime de Sylvestre Bonnard* (1881). (A revised version of this essay appears as a chapter in Volume One of the present work.)

———. [Another identical copy.]

Source: MTLAcc, entry #1554, volume donated by Clemens.

———. *L'Île des Pingouins [Penguin Island]* (published in 1908). Elizabeth Wallace wrote Clemens about this witty satire in 1909 and ordered a copy to be sent to him. On 13 November 1909 Clemens reported from Redding: "No, I haven't read it, but you make me *want* to read it—hungry to read it, in fact. I am all ready for it" (*MT&HI*, p. 134).

———. *Vie de Jeanne d'Arc* (published in 1908).

Quite probably this is the work that Clemens wrote to Andrew Lang about on 25 April 1908 from 21 Fifth Avenue in New York City: "I haven't seen the book nor any review of it. . . . I don't want to have to read it in French—I should lose the nice shades. . . . But there'll be a translation soon, nicht wahr? I'll wait for it" (MTP). Lang alluded to France's book in his own *The Maid of France, Being the Story of the Life and Death of Jeanne D'Arc* (London: Longmans, Green and Co., 1908). A two-volume English translation of France's biography did soon appear—*The Life of Joan of Arc* (London: J. Lane, 1909).

FRANCIS, PHILIP W. *The Remarkable Adventures of Little Boy Pip.* Illustrated by Merle Johnson (1874–1935). San Francisco and New York: Paul Elder & Co., [cop. 1907]. 60 pp.

Source: MTLAcc, entry #497, volume donated by Isabel V. Lyon, Clemens's secretary. This may have been her own copy (in which case it should be remembered that she and Clemens often shared their reading materials), or (more likely in this instance) she may have taken Clemens's copy to the Library at his request.

In this children's book a young boy journeys with the Welsh Rabbit into an enchanted swamp.

FRANÇOIS, LOUISE VON (1817–1893). *Die Letzte Reckenburgerin. [The Last Reckenbergerin].* Berlin: Janke, 1888.

Catalog: *C1951*, #64c, $5, listed among books signed by Clemens.

François's historical novel, initially rejected by publishers, made her a celebrity in 1871.

FRÄNKEL, RANUDO. *Erstes Lesebuch. Leichte Erzählungen für ganz Kleine artige Kinder von drei bis sechs Jahren [First Reader: A German Reader for Beginners].* Illus. Leipzig: Verlag von Emil

Berndt, 1877. 18 pp.

Inscription: Jean Clemens traced over Olivia Clemens's brown ink inscription with a heavy lead pencil: "Jean Clemens, from Mamma/April 26th 1888./Hartford, Conn."

Catalog: ListABP (1910), "Erstes Lesebuch, Fraenkel", no other information provided.

Location: Mark Twain Papers, Bancroft Library, University of California at Berkeley.

Copy examined: Jean Clemens's copy, unmarked, with the bookstore sticker of "F. W. Christern/37 West 23d Street/New York" on the front pastedown endpaper.

FRANKLIN, BENJAMIN (1706–1790). *The Life of Benjamin Franklin, Written by Himself. Now First Edited from Original Manuscripts and From His Printed Correspondence and Other Writings, by John Bigelow [1817–1911].* 3 vols. First edition thus. Engraved portrait. Original rust cloth, gilt. Philadelphia: J. B. Lippincott & Co., 1875.

Inscription: signed in pencil in each volume, "Saml. L. Clemens/Hartford 1875". Bookplate of Frank A. Vanderlip (which has the appearance of dating from the 1920s) on the front pastedown endpaper in all three volumes.

Marginalia: On page 109 of Volume I, Clemens made a small pencil slash in the margin beside a passage where Franklin's father complimented his grammar and punctuation but faulted his writing style. The number "300" or "309" is written in pencil in Clemens's hand on the final rear flyleaf. Uncut pages 375, 418–419, 422–423, 430–431, 434–435, 526–527, 538–439, 550–551, 554–555, and 578–579 were unopened in Volume I and therefore remained unreadable. In Volume II Clemens made a marginal pencil line on page 10 where Franklin described "sawyers destroying sawmills" during London riots. He drew a marginal pencil line on page 11 and added a note, "Wilkes is another Kenealy, apparently." (Robert Wilkes [1665–1732] was an actor and London theatre manager who discouraged Franklin's friend James Ralph from attempting a stage career. Edward Vaughan Hyde Kenealy [1818–1880] behaved outrageously when acting as a counsel for Orton, the Tichborne claimant, and was also charged with other scandals.) Clemens underlined with pencil a passage on page 18 about Franklin serving his country; made a marginal pencil line on page 22 at advice on an early marriage; underlined the text on that page reading, "Be in general virtuous, and you will be happy"; and on page 27 inserted a marginal line where Franklin described his interest in experiments with electricity. There are no pencil markings in Volume III.

Catalogs: *A1911*, "3 vols., 12mo, cloth, Phila. 1875," quotes the signatures and describes the marginalia as "a few ms. annotations in the margins," lot 172, sold for $11.50; Swann Galleries, New York City, Sale 1363 (28 February 1985), 3 volumes, "slightly worn," lot 309, pre-sale estimate $500–$750, sold for $1,540 (according to a note of 1 March 1985 to Alan Gribben from Nick Karanovich, who had made a losing bid of $1,325).

Location: collection of Kevin Mac Donnell, Austin, Texas.

Copy examined: Clemens's copy, in July 2004. Top edges are uncut, with many pages still unopened.

Clemens forever associated Franklin with Orion Clemens's short-lived regimens for exercise, diet, and sleep, but occasionally Clemens showed that he himself venerated

Franklin's achievements. Dixon Wecter learned that Orion scattered Franklin's maxims through the Hannibal newspapers he edited in the early 1850s (*SCH* [1952], p. 235). When Sam Clemens reached Philadelphia in 1853 he lost little time before informing Orion that he had viewed Franklin's grave (26 October 1853, *MTL*, p. 27; *MTLet* 1: 20). Later (in 1856 and 1857) Sam Clemens worked in Orion's printing shop in Keokuk, Iowa, which Orion chose to name the Ben Franklin Book and Job Office.

Mark Twain would remember Franklin's maxims, but always remained skeptical about their universal applicability. He headed his column in the 3 July 1864 issue of the San Francisco *Golden Era* with Franklin's "early to bed and early to rise" maxim, urging (with tongue in cheek) his readers to heed such advice (*WG* [1938], p. 83; *ET&S* 2: 24–25). He ironically characterized Franklin's optimistic philosophy in a letter from San Francisco on 23 December 1865: when the newspaperman gets up in the morning he can do as old Franklin did, and say, "This day, and all days, shall be unselfishly devoted to the good of my fellow-creatures—to the amelioration of their condition" (quoted in *LAMT* [1950], p. 154; *ET&S* 2: 417). In the comic sketch, "Private Habits of Horace Greeley" (1868), Twain reported that Greeley arises at 3 o'clock in the morning and quotes Franklin's lines to his assembled family: "Early to bed and early to rise/Makes a man healthy, wealthy, and wise"—another gibe at the maxim that had appeared in *Poor Richard's Almanack*. Twain discussed Franklin's maxims in "The Last Words of Great Men" (Buffalo *Express*, 11 September 1869), where he asserted that Josh Billings's "proverbial originality" transcended the efforts of "Franklin, the author of Poor Richard's quaint sayings; Franklin, the immortal axiom-builder, who used to sit up nights reducing the rankest old threadbare platitudes to crisp and snappy maxims that had a nice, varnished, original look in their new regimentals" (*MTBE*, p. 46). Twain joked in another Buffalo *Express* sketch in 1869, "The Latest Novelty": "Be virtuous and you will be eccentric." He continued this bantering in "The Late Benjamin Franklin" (*Galaxy* 10.1 [July 1870]: 138–140), in which he quoted maxims by Franklin and claimed they are "full of animosity toward boys." Yet he had mentioned Franklin approvingly as a historical figure ("a Benjamin Franklin or other laboring man") in "About Smells" (*Galaxy* 9.5 [May 1870]: 721–722). On 9 May 1872 he playfully paraphrased Franklin again by advising his infant daughter Susy to "be virtuous & you will be happy" (*MTLet* 5: 85).

The origins of Clemens's malice became clear when he began to write a humorous biography of his brother in 1877, "Autobiography of a Damned Fool." In Chapter 3 of "Autobiography of a Damned Fool" the hapless narrator relates: "I presently got hold of a copy of Benjamin Franklin's autobiography, and was charmed with it. I saw that here was a man after my own heart" (*S&B* [1967], p. 144). (Some fragmentary notes that Twain made after reading Franklin's work [Box 37, MTP] could date from this period and might derive from John Bigelow's edition of 1875.) Franklin's *Autobiography* figures prominently in this "Damned Fool" piece. The tributes to Franklin seem sincere on Twain's part as well as the Fool's: "Franklin had

the welfare of his fellow beings far more at heart than his own" (p. 144); "Franklin was broad, liberal, catholic" (p. 145); "The moving impulse of Franklin's every act was a principle," except that "Franklin had a disposition to accumulate money for his own selfish uses" (p. 145). The problem is the Fool's ludicrous attempts to emulate him. "I read Franklin with avidity, and took him for a model," the fool explains (p. 145). These efforts include self-education at the hearthside, noondays without lunch to work overtime, private practice in oratory, and cold baths. But the Fool's idolatry abates after he falls ill from a chilly plunge in an ice-covered creek, his interpretation of Franklin's advice about cold baths. Twain reveals a considerable knowledge of Franklin's *Autobiography* in writing "Autobiography of a Damned Fool" (perhaps he read or reread the work at this time in order to discover his brother Orion's motives for behavior that had seemed puzzling to him in the 1850s), but he is intent upon poking fun at those who, like the Fool, idealize human existence and only strive after "noble," altruistic ends.

In any event, when William Dean Howells queried him about suitable autobiographies for a forthcoming series of "Choice Autobiographies," Clemens replied without hesitation on 6 June 1877: "Autobiog's? I didn't know there *were* any but old Franklin's & Benvenuto Cellini's" (*MTHL*, p. 180)—linking Franklin's work with one of Clemens's favorite books. (A complete edition of Franklin's *Autobiography* had finally become available in English in 1867.) Franklin remained a constant presence in Mark Twain's writings: he referred to him in 1878 while criticizing a manuscript by Orion (DV415, MTP); he playfully claimed that "the immortal Franklin" endorsed masturbation in "Some Thoughts on the Science of Onanism" in 1879 (DV200, no. 3, MTP; *MTSpk* [1976], p. 125); and he gently burlesqued the adages espoused by Franklin ("Go to bed, get up early") in "Advice to Youth," a speech he made on 15 April 1882 (*MTSpk*, p. 169). In "Affeland (Snivelization)," which exists only as a fragment probably written in 1892, Twain again created in young Albert a character who resembles Orion: "At twelve he read the life of Franklin, and at once set about making a Franklin of himself. For a month he lived scantly [*sic*] on bread and vegetables, did his studying at night by the light of a single candle, rose before dawn, bathed in deadly cold water, practiced gymnastic exercises in his room, took stated walks, framed a set of austere rules of conduct, listened sharply to the sermon, Sundays, and from memory bored the family with it at dinner. . . . Then at the end of the month he retired . . . and plunged into some new ambition or other" (*S&B*, pp. 170–171). Here again the onus is placed upon a silly imitator, and not on Franklin's original principles. Indeed, "Franklin's Autobiography" promptly occurred to Clemens in January 1894 as ideal material for his projected "Back Number" magazine (NB 33, TS p. 46).

Always, however, Clemens was drawn back to Orion's preoccupation with Franklin. The caption under a frontispiece photograph of Mark Twain in *Following the Equator* ruefully advises, "Be good & you will be lonesome." In "Villagers of 1840–3," sketches of early Hannibal residents that Clemens wrote in 1897, Orion

Clemens is thinly disguised as Oscar Carpenter, who, "at 18, wrote home to his mother, that he was studying the life of Franklin and closely imitating him; that in his boarding house he was confining himself to bread and water" (*HH&T* [1969], p. 40). Likewise in the third chapter of Twain's uncompleted "Hellfire Hotchkiss," also written in 1897, a character called Oscar Carpenter models himself on Franklin, arising at four in the morning "because that was Franklin's way," and dividing his day "on the Franklin plan—eight hours for labor, eight for sleep, eight for study, meditation and exercise" (*S&B*, p. 202). (Orion Clemens would die on 11 December 1897.) In 1898 Clemens thought up an addition to Franklin's "healthy, wealthy, and wise" maxim: "too wise to do it again," Clemens appended (NB 42, TS p. 68).

Mark Twain's "What Is Man?" (Part 6, 1906) relates an experiment with ants and sugar that Sir John Lubbock credited Franklin with performing, but Paul Baender noted that Twain apparently altered the details in order to endow the ants with even more intelligence than Franklin reported (*WIM?* [1973], pp. 196–197). In "Which Was It?" (written 1899–1903) Twain described General Landry of Indiantown as "the very image of Benjamin Franklin, broad benignant face and all" (*WWD?* [1969], p. 275). Twain mentioned Franklin's ambassadorial duties in "Diplomatic Pay and Clothes" (1899), and Franklin's name is mixed up among the "wonderful men" of the nineteenth century in "The Secret History of Eddypus," written 1901–1902—where the reference is complimentary (*FM* [1972], p. 357). The cholera germ in "Three Thousand Years among the Microbes" (written in 1905) names his yellow-fever-germ friend "Benjamin Franklin," and he respects this "renowned specialist" who instructs him about the true nature of life forces (*WWD?*, p. 449). In a speech delivered in 1906, "Introducing Doctor Van Dyke," Twain linked himself with Franklin, Edison, and others who, like Adam, lacked a college education (*MTSpk*, p. 488). Twain's "The Refuge of the Derelicts" (written 1905–1906), returned a final time to Orion's follies: Stanchfield Garvey, like Orion (and Sam Clemens), began working as a printer's apprentice; "he had a burning ambition to be a Franklin; so he lived strictly on bread and water, studied by the firelight instead of using candles, and practised [*sic*] swimming on the floor. Then he discarded Franklin, and imitated somebody else a while" (*FM*, p. 240).

Allison Ensor, "The Downfall of Poor Richard: Benjamin Franklin as Seen by Hawthorne, Melville, and Mark Twain," *Mark Twain Journal* 17.3 (Winter 1974–1975): 14–18; Philip Fanning, *Mark Twain and Orion Clemens: Brothers, Partners, Strangers* (Tuscaloosa: University of Alabama Press, 2003), pp. 33–34.

———. *Poor Richard's Almanack: Selections from the Prefaces, Apothegms, and Rimes with a Facsimile in Reduction of the Almanack for 1733.* Full leather, tooled design, all edges gilt. New York: Century Co., 1899. 221 pp.

Provenance: from the library of Clemens's sister-in-law, Susan Crane, Elmira, New York. This volume would have been accessible to Clemens whenever he visited Quarry Farm after 1899.

Location: collection of Kevin Mac Donnell, Austin, Texas.

No signature or markings. Acquired from the Langdon family in June 2016 (Mac Donnell to Alan Gribben, 14 June 2016).

FRANKLIN, SAMUEL RHOADES (1825–1909). *Memories of a Rear-Admiral Who Has Served for More than Half a Century in the Navy of the United States.* New York: Harper & Brothers, 1898. 398 pp.

Source: MTLAcc, entry #1764, volume donated by Clemens.

FRANZOS, KARL EMIL (1848–1904). *The Jews of Barnow. Stories.* Trans. from the German by [Ms.] M. W. Macdowall [of Garthland]. Preface by Barnet Phillips (1828–1905). New York: D. Appleton and Co., 1883. 334 pp.

Source: MTLAcc, entry #554, volume donated by Clemens. *The Jews of Barnow*, set in a Polish ghetto and published when Franzos was living in Vienna before he moved to Berlin, constituted his first collection of short stories. The first of these eight stories was titled "The Shylock of Barnow." Another story was named "Two Saviours of the People."

———. [Identical copy.]

Provenance: bookplate #626 of the "J. Langdon Family Library."

Catalog: Ball 2016 inventory, brown cloth, gilt lettering on the spine, red lettering on the cover.

Location: Quarry Farm, under the supervision of the Mark Twain Archive, Elmira College, Elmira, New York.

Copy examined: unmarked copy available to Clemens during his many visits to Elmira. Examined on 26 May 2015.

———. "Namensstudien" ["Name Studies"] (essay, published in 1880, later collected in Franzos's *Aus der grossen Ebene; neue Bilder aus Halb-Asien.* [*From the Great Plain; New Cultural Images from Half-Asia.*] Stuttgart: Adolph Bonz & Comp., 1888. [The edition Mark Twain consulted is conjectured.]

In describing the systems by which Jews were renamed ("in a way to make the angels weep"), Mark Twain culls ridiculous examples such as "Abraham Bellyache" from Franzos's book, citing the author and title in a footnote ("Concerning the Jews" [1899]).

Budd, *CTSS&E* 2: 1028–1029.

FRASER, WILLIAM ALEXANDER (1859–1933). *The Lone Furrow.* New York: D. Appleton and Co., 1907. 354 pp.

Source: MTLAcc, entry #133, volume donated by Isabel V. Lyon, Clemens's secretary.

This may have been her own copy (in which case it should be remembered that she and Clemens often shared their reading materials), or (more likely in this instance) she may have taken Clemens's copy to the Library at his request.

FRAZER, JAMES GEORGE (1854–1941), comp. *Passages of the Bible, Chosen for Their Literary Beauty and Interest.* London: Adam and Charles Black, 1895. 467 pp. [Publisher conjectured.]

Catalog: *A1911*, "post 8vo, art cloth, gilt top, uncut, Lond. 1895," lot 40, sold for $5.50.

FRÉCHETTE, LOUIS HONORÉ (1839–1908).

Mark Twain complimented this Canadian journalist and poet (and brother-in-law of William Dean Howells) in a speech at the Windsor Hotel in Montreal on 8 December, 1881, referring to him as "a fellow craftsman . . . who has created an epoch in this continent's literary history" (Fatout, ed., *MTSpk* [1976], pp. 158, 160).

FREDERIC, HAROLD (1856–1898).

It would be illuminating to find proof that Clemens encountered Frederic's best novel, *The Damnation of Theron Ware* (1896), or any of his other novels, but solid evidence has thus far been lacking. One would think that Frederic's poignant collection, *Marsena and Other Stories of the Wartime* (1894), about boys' emotional experiences on the home front during the Civil War—"The Eve of the Fourth" and "My Aunt Susan," for instance—would have especially appealed to Clemens. He did own a book, S. R. Crockett's *Tales of Our Coast* (see its Catalog entry) that contained a sea story by Frederic, "The Path of Murtogh."

In any event, Mark Twain delicately defended Frederic's moral reputation in a speech at the Savage Club Dinner on 6 July 1907; informed by a previous speaker that Frederic listened to readings from Twain's books during his fatal illness, Twain told the audience: "I did not know Harold Frederic personally, but I have heard a great deal about him, and nothing that was not pleasant, and nothing except such things as lead a man to honor another man and to love him. I consider that it is a misfortune of mine that I have never had the luck to meet him, and if any book of mine read to him in his last hours made those hours easier for him and more comfortable, I am very glad and proud of that" (*MTSpk* [1976], p. 572). As many in Twain's audience must have known, after the married Frederic moved to England he had established a second household with his mistress.

FREELAND, ISABELLE (MCMURRAY) (1848–1930). *Thoughts in Verse*. Columbus, Ohio: New Franklin Printing Co., [cop. 1909]. 45 pp. Paperbound.

Source: MTLAcc, entry #2027, volume donated from Clemens's library by Clara Clemens Gabrilowitsch in 1910.

Freeland, who died on 12 October 1930, became a leader in the women's suffrage movement and served as president of the Ohio Newspaper Women's Association.

FREEMAN, EDWARD AUGUSTUS (1823–1892). *The Historical Geography of Europe*. Second ed. 2 vols. London: Longmans, Green, and Co., 1882.

Inscription: Volume I was inscribed by Clemens in black ink on the half-title page: "Livy L. Clemens/1886."

Catalog: *Mott 1952*, #55, $3, Vol. I only.

Location: Volume I only in Mark Twain House and Museum, Hartford, Connecticut.

Copy examined: Olivia Clemens's unmarked copy of Volume I. Contains the stamps, traces of a charge-slip jacket, and call number of the Mark Twain Library, Redding, Connecticut. Examined only Volume I in in August 1987.

FREEMAN, MARY ELEANOR (WILKINS) (1852–1930). *By the Light of the Soul; A Novel*. Illustrated by Harold Matthews Brett (1880–1955). New York: Harper & Brothers, 1907. 497 pp.

Source: MTLAcc, entry #1000, volume donated by Clemens.

Clemens is known to have owned or been familiar with nearly twenty short stories, short story collections, and novels by Freeman, the regional writer known for her portraits of rural New England who changed her name from Mary E. Wilkins when she married in 1902. Given that he acquired so many of her books, one would expect him to have possessed a copy of *The Wind in the Rose Bush* (1903), tales hinting at the supernatural, but we must

always keep in mind the significant percentage of his library's contents that were lost, donated, or sold without any record of their titles. In any event, this substantial collection of Freeman's works indicates how extremely receptive Clemens could be to fiction written by talented women. Photographs show that Freeman was seated next to the honored author during the dinner at Delmonico's on 5 December 1905 celebrating Mark Twain's seventieth birthday, an indication of her stature in Twain's estimation. Freeman provided a prefatory "Appreciation" for *The Gilded Age* in the so-called Definite Edition of Twain's works (New York: Gabriel Well, 1922–1925).

———. *Evelina's Garden*. New York: Harper & Brothers, 1904. 120 pp.

Source: MTLAcc, entry #1339, volume donated by Clemens.

———. *The Fair Lavinia, and Others*. Illus. New York: Harper & Brothers, 1907. 308 pp.

Source: MTLAcc, entry #1555, volume donated by Clemens.

———. [An apparently identical copy.]

Inscription: signed on the front pastedown endpaper, "S. L. Clemens, 1907".

Catalog: *A1911*, "12mo, cloth, N.Y. 1907," quotes the signature, lot 173, sold for $1.50.

———. *Giles Corey, Yeoman; A Play*. Illus. New York: Harper & Brothers, 1893. 108 pp.

Source: MTLAcc, entry #1201, volume donated by Clemens.

———. *The Givers; Short Stories*. Illus. New York: Harper & Brothers, 1904. 296 pp.

Source: MTLAcc, entry #1001, volume donated by Clemens.

———. *A Humble Romance, and Other Stories*. New York: Harper & Brothers, 1887. 436 pp.

Inscriptions: the front free endpaper is signed (crudely) in black ink, "Olivia L. Clemens"; the ink did not adhere to the paper and the signature is barely legible. On the front pastedown endpaper Clemens noted in black ink: "Dec. 4, 1905. She has been in her grave a year & a half to-morrow. She probably made that attempt with that annoying pen eighteen years ago when she was 42 & looked ten years younger. I know she did not lose her temper, but kept it & her sweet dignity unimpaired. If I was present I probably laughed, for we had no cares then—I could easier cry, now. It is many years since I have seen this book. Susy was 15 then; she is gone, these nine years & more. I have just closed my seventieth year." The day after Clemens wrote this note he attended his Seventieth Birthday Dinner at Delmonico's in New York City, an event at which he personally escorted Mary Wilkins Freeman to her seat, which was to the right of his own chair (New York *Times*, 6 December 1905).

Catalog: "Retz Appraisal" (1944), p. 12. Valued at $50.

Location: Mark Twain Papers, Bancroft Library, University of California at Berkeley.

Copy examined: Olivia Clemens's unmarked copy. The sticker of Brown & Gross, Hartford booksellers, is affixed to the rear pastedown endpaper.

———. *Jane Field; A Novel*. Illus. New York: Harper &

Brothers, 1905. 267 pp.

> **Source:** MTLAcc, entry #1080, volume donated by Clemens.

———. *The Love of Parson Lord, and Other Stories.* Illus. New York: Harper & Brothers, 1901. 233 pp.

> **Source:** MTLAcc, entry #232, volume donated by Clemens.

———. *Madelon; A Novel.* New York: Harper & Brothers, 1904. 376 pp.

> **Source:** MTLAcc, entry #1079, volume donated by Clemens.

———. *A New England Nun, and Other Stories.* New York: Harper & Brothers, [cop. 1891]. 468 pp.

> **Source:** MTLAcc, entry #1107, volume donated by Clemens.

———. "The Old-Maid Aunt," Chapter 2 of *The Whole Family* (a composite novel by twelve authors), *Harper's Bazar* 42.1 (January 1908): 16–26.

Invited to contribute to *The Whole Family*, a novel narrated by a dozen different characters who would be created by twelve eminent authors, Mark Twain read the first two chapters sent by the editor of *Harper's Bazar*. He liked William Dean Howells's depiction of the father ("well done"), but he had reservations about the second chapter, written by Mary Wilkins Freeman. Explaining in an autobiographical dictation of 29 August 1906 why he declined to supply the boy's chapter ("the imagined boy would have to tell his story *himself*, and let me act merely as his amanuensis"), Twain commented on Freeman's writings without naming her. "A lady followed Howells, and furnished the old-maid sister's chapter. This lady is of high literary distinction; she is nobly gifted; she has the ear of the nation, and her novels and stories are among the best that the country has produced; but *she* did not tell those tales, she merely held the pen and they told themselves. . . . [However, she] wrote the old-maid sister's chapter out of her own head, without any help from the old maid. The result is a failure. It is a piece of pure literary manufacture, and has the shop-marks all over it" (*MTE*, p. 244; *AutoMT* 2: 190). Faithful readers of *Harper's Bazar* would likely not have concurred with Twain's assessment, and even today his appraisal seems to ignore the amusing ironies Freeman achieved in taking on the assignment. In her chapter, spinster aunt Elizabeth Talbert returns to visit her brother and his family in Eastridge, where she once had several beaus. Her relatives underestimate Aunt Elizabeth's sophistication and attractiveness; they are astonished when Ned Temple's wife storms into their house to complain that Elizabeth took a stroll with her husband, who had once courted Elizabeth. "'If you can't get a husband for yourself,' said she, 'you might at least let other women's husbands alone!'" The aunt calms the irate wife ("I cannot imagine myself making such a spectacle over any mortal man," Elizabeth muses), and assures her of Ned Temple's faithfulness. "It was all highly ridiculous, but it actually ended up in my going into the Temple house and showing Ned's wife how to do up her hair like mine. . . . Then I taught her how to put on her corset and pin her shirt-waist taut in front and her skirt behind. It ended in her fairly purring around me" (pp. 24–25). The Talbert family is flabbergasted by the effects produced by "old" aunt Elizabeth. Ned Temple

avers that she "had not changed at all." Twain may have been annoyed by the arch tone of Elizabeth's monologue. See also an Catalog entry for *The Whole Family* (1908).

———. *Pembroke; A Novel.* Illus. New York: Harper & Brothers, [cop. 1894]. 330 pp.

> **Source:** MTLAcc, entry #1082, volume donated by Clemens.

———. *Pembroke.* New York: Harper & Brothers, 1903. 330 pp.

> **Source:** MTLAcc, entry #1670, volume donated by Clemens.

———. *The Portion of Labor.* Illus. First edition. Original blue cloth, gilt. Half blue morocco folding-case. New York: Harper & Brothers, 1901. 563 pp.

> **Inscriptions:** the front free flyleaf is signed in black ink, "S L. Clemens/Riverdale, Nov. 1901." Contains the bookplate of Eudoria Dewey, who wrote on the front pastedown endpaper, "Father bought these books of Mark Twain's for Lonnie—when he was in the Phila. Hospital 1911."
> **Catalogs:** A1911, "12mo, cloth, N.Y. 1901," quotes the signature, lot 485, sold for $2.75; *Sotheby's 2003*, #221, $9,500 (sold with four other literature titles).
> **Provenance:** a gift inscription and bookplate of Eudoria Dewey; a signature on the front free flyleaf of Docia D. Jones. This copy belonged to the collection of Robert Daley, Burbank, California, in the 1970s. Subsequently it was in the collection of Nick Karanovich, Fort Wayne, Indiana.
> **Location:** collection of Kevin Mac Donnell, Austin, Texas.
> **Copy examined:** Clemens' unmarked copy, in July 2004. Has the *A1911* sale label.

The subject matter here is unusual for Freeman—a labor strike at a large shoe factory in an industrial town—but she still managed to depict in Ellen Brewster another strong and resolute New England woman such as often appeared in Freeman's fiction.

———. *The Shoulders of Atlas; A Novel.* New York: Harper & Brothers, 1908. 294 pp.

> **Source:** MTLAcc, entry #879, volume donated by Mrs. Ralph W. Ashcroft (formerly Isabel Lyon), Clemens's secretary.

———. [Another identical copy.]

> **Source:** MTLAcc, entry #1003, volume donated by Mrs. Ralph W. Ashcroft (formerly Isabel Lyon), Clemens's secretary.

———. *Six Trees; Short Stories.* Illus. New York: Harper & Brothers, 1903. 207 pp.

> **Source:** MTLAcc, entry #1002, volume donated by Clemens.

———. *Young Lucretia, and Other Stories.* Illus. New York: Harper & Brothers, 1905. 258 pp.

> **Source:** MTLAcc, entry #1081, volume donated by Clemens.

FRENCH, ALICE (1850–1934), pseud. "Octave Thanet." *The Missionary Sheriff; Being Incidents in the Life of a Plain Man Who Tried to Do His Duty.* Illustrated by A[rthur]. B[urdett]. Frost (1851–1928) and Clifford Carleton (1867–1946). New York: Harper & Brothers, 1897. 248 pp.

> **Source:** MTLAcc, entry #303, volume donated by Clemens.

French set these short stories about an ordinary man, Amos Wickliff, in Davenport, Iowa. Although the author's social and racial views were entirely conventional for the time, she is sometimes given credit (perhaps partly because of her lifelong relationship with a woman in Arkansas named Jane Crawford) for inserting coded lesbian messages into her fiction, though this is not particularly evident in *The Missionary Sheriff*. Alice French was one of the authors who contributed a story to the collection titled *A House Party* (1901), edited by Paul Leicester Ford (see that Catalog entry).

———. [Another identical copy.]

Source: MTLAcc, entry #1078, volume donated by Clemens.

Free Russia: The Organ of the English Society of Friends of Russian Freedom (London journal, 1890–1915).

In an unpublished letter to *Free Russia* written in the summer of 1890, Mark Twain quoted from an article titled "Our Plan of Action" that had appeared in the first issue of the journal in June 1890 (Scharnhorst, *MTPP* [2014], p. 156).

French-English Dictionary. [Unidentified book.]

Catalog: ListABP (1910), "Fr.-Eng. Dict.", no other information provided.

See the Catalog entry for John Bellows, *Dictionary for the Pocket: French and English, English and French*, which might have been this book that Albert Bigelow Paine kept to consult in writing Mark Twain's biography.

FRENCH, HARRY [HENRY] W[ILLARD] (1854–1915). *Our Boys in India: The Wanderings of Two Young Americans in Hindustan, with Their Adventures on the Sacred Rivers and Wild Mountains, Etc.* Illus. Boston: Lee and Shepard, 1883. 484 pp.

Inscription: inscribed "December 25th 1882/Jervis Langdon/from Grandma". Jervis Langdon (1875–1952) was the son of Charles Jervis Langdon (1849–1916) and Ida B. Clark Langdon (1849–1934). His grandmother was Olivia Lewis Langdon (1810–1890).

Catalog: Ball 2016 inventory, glossy boards, heavily illustrated, color pictures on the cover.

Location: Quarry Farm library shelves, under the supervision of the Mark Twain Archive, Elmira College, Elmira, New York.

This book might have been available to Clemens whenever he visited the Langdons in Elmira.

FRÉNILLY, AUGUSTE FRANÇOIS FAUVEAU DE (1768–1848). *Recollections of Baron de Frénilly, Peer of France (1768–1828).* Ed. with introduction and notes by Arthur Chuquet (1853–1925). Trans. by [George] Frederic [William] Lees (b. 1872). Frontispiece portrait of the Baron de Frénilly. Original blue cloth, gilt. Tear at the head and foot of spine. New York: G. P. Putnam's Sons, 1909. 382 pp.

Inscription: the front pastedown endpaper is signed "S L Clemens, 1909."

Marginalia: Clemens seemed to focus on the shortcomings of the translator Lees, an Englishman from Hartlepool, Durham. Clemens made pen or pencil corrections of vocabulary or syntax on ten pages—30, 32, 49, 54, 60, 74, 97, 133, 165, and 216—emending "may" for "should," "Bréjole and me" for "Bréjole and I," "afraid" for "frightened," "under which I should have liked to have passed it" for "under which I should have liked to have passed it," and similar revisions. On page 54 Clemens made a slightly more complex alteration, changing "Alas! the King was the last sort of man to succeed Louis XV. He was a

good man and a good husband—pious, chaste, virtuous, just and humane" to read instead ,"Alas! the King was the last sort of man to succeed Louis XV; for the King was a good man and a good husband—pious, chaste, virtuous, just and humane." Clemens then commented in ink in the bottom margin: "It is very bad workmanship to save words at the expense of clarity. This translator could quite fairly be charged with paying compliments to Louis XV. How would he defend himself?" The corner of page 216 is folded down.

Catalogs: *C1951*, # 16c, listed among books signed by Clemens; *Sotheby's 2003*, #201, $1,900. Offered for sale in 2012 by Charles Parkhurst Rare Books, Prescott, Arizona, first American edition, "housed in a custom slipcase," for $7,200. The book was sold in December 2015 to an unidentified purchaser (telephone call by Alan Gribben to Charles Parkhurst).

Provenance: contains the shelfmark of Clara Clemens Gabrilowitsch's private library system in Detroit. Subsequent to the 1951 Hollywood auction the volume belonged to Nick Karanovich of Fort Wayne, Indiana.

Copy examined: Clemens's copy, at the 2003 Sotheby's auction. Previously the place of publication and the publisher had been erroneously conjectured as a London edition published by William Heinemann in Gribben, *Mark Twain's Library: A Reconstruction* [1980], p. 246.

Leah Dobrinksa, "In Defense of Marginalia," *The New Antiquarian*, 8 June 2015, blog of the Antiquarian Booksellers Association of America, reported Clemens's revisions.

FREUD, SIGMUND (1856–1939).

In view of Clemens's sojourn in Vienna between 1897 and 1899, his wide range of social connections in that city, and Freud's enjoyment of Twain's writings and lecture style, it has been tempting (but apparently erroneous) to assume that the two men met during those years. It has likewise been difficult to accept the lack of evidence connecting Clemens with any publications by the founder of psychoanalysis. (It must always be remembered, however, that many hundreds of book titles from Clemens's library shelves went unrecorded because volumes were lost, donated, or sold without any record kept of their titles.)

Carl Dolmetsch, "Twain and Freud: Vienna's Odd Couple?" *William and Mary: The Alumni Magazine* 54.1 (July-August 1986): 8–12; Dolmetsch, *"Our Famous Guest": Mark Twain in Vienna* (Athens: University of Georgia Press, 1992).

FREYTAG, GUSTAV (1816–1895). *Soll und Haben: Roman in Sechs büchern [Debit and Credit: A Novel in Six Books].* 2 vols. Leipzig: Verlag von G. Hirzel, 1890.

Inscriptions: inscribed "Jervis Langdon" and also (presumably later) by Jervis Langdon (1875–1952) and Eleanor Sayles Langdon (1878–1971).

Catalogs: QF Martinez, "Good Condition"; Ball 2016 inventory, 2 vols., red cloth, black and gold design.

Location: Quarry Farm library shelves, under the supervision of the Mark Twain Archive, Elmira College, Elmira, New York.

Conceivably Clemens might have seen this book before or after Jervis Langdon married Eleanor Sayles in 1902. *Soll und Haben* depicts nineteenth-century bourgeois Polish life. In the latter half of the twentieth century this merchant novel became controversial owing to its portrayal of the moneylender Veitel Itzig, which seemed implicitly anti-Semitic to many readers.

Friendship's Offering; A Christmas, New Year, and Birthday Present for MDCCCLII. Illus. 12mo. Philadelphia: E. H. Butler & Co., 1852. 330 pp. [This title was issued yearly in Philadelphia with varying publishers' names between 1841 and 1855.]

    Inscription: inscribed "Susan A. Langdon from her father J. Langdon." [Susan Langdon (1836–1924) later married Theodore W. Crane in 1858.]

    Catalog: Ball 2016 inventory, black cloth, gilt design, inscribed to Susan Langdon from her father, fair condition.

    Location: Mark Twain Archive, Elmira College, Elmira, New York. Transferred from the Quarry Farm library to the Mark Twain Archive by Mark Woodhouse on 9 July 1987.

    Copy examined: a copy accessible to Clemens during his many summer visits to Elmira, New York.

Mark Twain's catalog of books typically found in "The House Beautiful" along the Mississippi before the Civil War includes "'Friendship's Offering,' and 'Affection's Wreath,' with their sappy inanities illustrated in die-away mezzotints" (Chapter 38, *Life on the Mississippi* [1883]). These recalled book titles illustrated Twain's familiarity with parlor-table fixtures in American homes. His main objection to them was his conviction that nobody ever really read through these gift-book concoctions. Among the books stacked on the corners of the Grangerfords' parlor table, Huckleberry Finn finds "*Friendship's Offering*, full of beautiful stuff and poetry; but I didn't read the poetry" (Chapter 17, *HF* [1885]).

Twain also associated these volumes with excessively elegant phrasing, one of the literary rules he claimed that James Fenimore Cooper habitually violated: "When a personage talks like an illustrated gilt-edged, tree-calf, hand-tooled, seven- dollar Friendship's Offering" at one point, he ought not to "sound like a negro minstrel" farther on ("Fenimore Cooper's Literary Offences" [1895]). As late as 1907 Twain derided Eddy's reference to "the heart of a moonbeam" as "a pretty enough Friendship's-Album expression—let it pass, though I do think the figure a little strained" (*Christian Science* [1907], Book 2, Chapter 2).

FRISBIE, ALVAH LILLIE (1830–1917). *The Siege of Calais and Other Poems.* Des Moines, Iowa: Mills & Co., 1880. 166 pp.

    Source: MTLAcc, entry #625, volume donated by Clemens.

The English siege of Calais, France took place in 1346 and 1347; the Reverend Frisbie's title poem about that event and its ultimate resolution occupies the first forty-eight pages of this volume. Frisbie served as a chaplain in the Civil War and then was the pastor of Plymouth Congregational Church in Des Moines, Iowa from 1871 until his retirement in 1899. It is easy in the twenty-first century to disparage the stilted diction that characterized so much nineteenth-century American poetry, but even allowing for the immense shifts in taste the verse of this earnest clergyman is so labored that one suspects Clemens sought it out for his hypothetical "Library of Literary Hogwash." Frisbie's volumes were not among the books that survived from Clemens's library, so his marginalia, if any, is lost to us. Here is a sample of what he might have read and annotated, the opening lines of "My Friends": "I sit in

silence in my room;/Through open windows floating come/The mingling sounds of voices near,/But none is spoken for my ear./I sit alone—no welcome face/Lights up the still and cloistered place;/No sprightly word of treasured friends/Its charm to my seclusion lends" (p. 105).

————. *Songs of Sorrow and Miscellaneous Poems.* Des Moines, Iowa: Mills & Co., 1873. 63 pp.

    Source: MTLAcc, entry #638, volume donated by Clemens.

FRISWELL, JAMES HAIN (1825–1878). "The Story of Adam and Eve, by One of Their Descendants." "Written by J. H. F. for the *Boston Courier*." A six-page stapled pamphlet made from pasted-up galley proofs.

    Inscription: on a presentation label affixed to the verso of the front wrapper Friswell wrote in black ink: "'Mark Twain'—/With Author's Compliments." An embossed cover label reads: "D.U.S."[?]MISCELLANY/10E/1908".

    Location: Mark Twain Library, Redding, Connecticut.

    Copy examined: Clemens's copy, unmarked. I did not see this pamphlet in 1970 but it had been added to the Clemens holdings when I revisited the collection in June 1982.

FRITH, WILLIAM POWELL (1819–1909). *My Autobiography and Reminiscences.* 2 vols. New York: Harper & Brothers, 1888.

    Source: MTLAcc, entries #1762 and #1763, volumes donated by Clemens.

Elected to the Royal Academy in 1853, Frith specialized in painting everyday English crowd scenes.

FROISSART, JEAN (c. 1338–c. 1410). *Chronicles of England, France, Spain, and the Adjoining Countries, from the Latter Part of the Reign of Edward II. To the Coronation of Henry IV.* Trans. from the French by Thomas Johnes (1748–1816). Intro. by John Lord (1810–1894). Illus. New York: Leavitt & Allen, 1853. 634 pp. [Edition conjectured.]

    Catalog: *A1911*, "illustrated, imp. 8vo, cloth, N.Y. 1853," lot 174, sold for $1.50.

Mark Twain alluded to "old dead Froissart's poor witticism" (about a family tree that "had but one limb to it") in "A Burlesque Autobiography" (1871, DV409, MTP). "Quote Shaks & Froissart," Twain reminded himself in working notes for *The Prince and the Pauper* jotted down in 1879 (DV115, MTP).

FROST, ARTHUR BURDETT (1851–1928).

Frost is perhaps best known for illustrating Joel Chandler Harris's *Uncle Remus* books, but he also wrote humorous sketches, including *Stuff and Nonsense* (1884) and *The Bull Calf and Other Tales* (1892). E. W. Kemble remembered that Clemens expressed admiration for the "humor" of Arthur Burdett Frost (Kemble, "Illustrating *Huckleberry Finn*" [1930]).

FROUDE, JAMES ANTHONY (1818–1894). *Caesar; A Sketch* (first published in London, 1879).

Intent upon comparing the dying U. S. Grant with Julius Caesar in June 1885, Clemens wrote "Froude's Caesar" in Notebook 24 (*N&J* 3: 160).

————. *History of England from the Fall of Wolsey to the Defeat of the Spanish Armada.* 12 vols. New York: Scribner, Armstrong, and Co., 1866–1973. [Edition conjectured. Some volumes in this edition have the imprint of Charles Scribner and Co.]

    Catalog: *C1951*, D76, incomplete, 10 vols. only, signed by Clemens.

Clemens was already making plans in July 1877 to assemble material from his home library to study for writing *The*

Prince and the Pauper (1881). On his way home to Hartford from New York City he made a memorandum to "get Froude & notes" (NB 13, *N&J* 2: 39). In his working notes for *The Prince and the Pauper* he referred to "Froude, iv" and also cited incidents in Chapters 17 and 18 of Volume V (DV115, MTP).

———. *Oceana, or England and Her Colonies*. London: Longmans, Green and Co., 1886. [Edition conjectured.]

In August 1896 Andrew Chatto notified Clemens that he had sent him a copy of Froude's *Oceana* as requested (Welland, *Mark Twain in England*, p. 168).

———. *Short Studies on Great Subjects*. New York: Charles Scribner and Co., 1868. 534 pp.

> Inscriptions: signed, "Livy L. Langdon, Elmira, N. Y., 1869"; also signed, "S. L. Clemens, Buffalo, 1870."
>
> Marginalia: a few notes, of which one in the chapter on Homer reads: "Let us change the form & say: The repudiation of religion is the beginning of wisdom" (*Hunley 1958*). Other marginalia are quoted in *The Twainian*, January-February 1983.
>
> Catalogs: *C1951*, #63c, $12.50, signed by Clemens; *Hunley 1958*, #50, $27.50.

Clemens wrote an indignant public letter in 1872 protesting the fact that Froude, "a distinguished English historian [who] is coming over to visit us," would only be met and honored in New York City by a disgraced and politically corrupt city mayor (Hartford *Evening Post*, 6 December 1872; *MTPP*, p. 47). Howard G. Baetzhold reported Mark Twain's reference to Froude's collection of essays in a marginal note to his manuscript of *A Connecticut Yankee* (1889) (*MT&JB*, p. 343 n. 39).

Surely the Clemenses' copy of this book will surface again. It is likely to be rife with his marginalia; just consider some of Froude's subjects in this miscellany of essays: "The Science of History," "Erasmus, Luther," "The Influence of the Reformation on the Scottish Character," "Criticism of the Gospel History," "Spinoza," "Homer," "The Lives of the Saints," "England's Forgotten Worthies." In an essay titled "Representative Men," Froude offered a pessimistic view of human progress: "We have cast out the Catholic devil, and the Puritan has swept the house and garnished it; but as yet we do not see any symptoms showing of a healthy incoming tenant, and there may be worse states than Catholicism."

———. *Thomas Carlyle: A History of the First Forty Years of His Life, 1795–1835*. 2 vols. Frontispiece portrait. First American edition. 8vo, original plum cloth, brown-coated endpapers, gilt, spines numbered I and II, half blue and half orange morocco slipcase. Wear to the extremities. New York: Charles Scribner's Sons, 1882.

> Inscriptions: the front flyleaves in the first two volumes are signed identically in light blue ink, "Olivia L. Clemens/1882/Hartford."
>
> Marginalia: Volume I is marked on four pages and has one corner turned down. Page 23 has a question mark in Olivia's hand next to a passage regarding university education; page 205 has a pencil mark in an unknown hand by a passage about Carlyle's prose being superior to his poetry; the lower left corner of page 292 is folded over; page 300 was marked by Olivia beside a passage comparing happiness to accomplishments; and on page

302 Olivia made a marginal line next to an observation about Carlyle's inability to write fiction or tell a lie. Volume II has an upper corner folded down at page 76, but no markings in its text.

> Catalogs: *C1951*, D32, $20, listed carelessly as "Thomas Carlyle. 4 vols., signed by Clemens"; *Fleming 1972*, 4 vols; Sotheby Parke Bernet, Sale number 3482 (25 February 1976), "4 vols.," lot 12, "Property of a New York City collector" (John F. Fleming); Second Life Books, Lanesborough, Massachusetts, Catalog 47 (1984), item E, "4 volumes, hinges loose," cloth slip-cases, $1,750; *Sotheby's 2003*, #202, $1,800 (sold with Froude title in the entry below). Offered in 2012 by Charles Parkhurst Rare Books, Prescott, Arizona, with "half blue morocco clamshell," for $4,800 (to be sold with the Froude title below). In 2016 the Charles Parkhurst firm moved to Sun City West, Arizona. This volume remained unsold as of 12 January 2016 (telephone call by Alan Gribben to Charles Parkhurst).
>
> Provenance: a sticker of Brown & Gross Booksellers/Hartford, CT" is on the rear pastedown endpaper; shelfmark numbers of Clara Clemens Gabrilowitsch's private library in Detroit are on the front pastedown endpaper, along with a notation from the 1951 Hollywood auction. Frederick Anderson, then Editor of the Mark Twain Papers in the Bancroft Library at the University of California, Berkeley, examined this volume at the New York City office of John F. Fleming in April 1972 (Anderson to James D. Hart, 17 April 1972, photocopy sent to Alan Gribben). Subsequently the book entered the collection of Nick Karanovich, Fort Wayne, Indiana.
>
> Location: collection of Kevin Mac Donnell, Austin, Texas. Acquired in December 2016 (Mac Donnell to Gribben, 21 December 2016).
>
> Copy examined: Olivia Clemens's copies of Volumes I and II, at the 2003 Sotheby's auction. In addition, Nick Karanovich sent photocopies on 14 December 1984 of the spines, title pages, and inscriptions for Volumes I and II. Kevin Mac Donnell sent Alan Gribben a detailed description (correcting earlier reports of marginalia) on 21 December 2016.

———. *Thomas Carlyle: A History of His Life in London, 1834–1881*. 2 vols. First American edition. 8vo, original plum cloth, brown-coated endpapers, gilt, spines numbered Volumes III and IV. Half orange slipcase. Wear to the extremities. New York: Charles Scribner's Sons, 1884.

> Inscriptions: the front flyleaves of Volumes III and IV are inscribed in light blue ink by Clemens, "Livy L. Clemens/1885."
>
> Marginalia: Volume III contains markings on six pages. On page 23 Clemens changed Froude's syntax. There is a vertical marking in margin of page 47 next to a passage about Carlyle's writing habits. Clemens's underlining of the sentence "Fear nothing but fear" (p. 48) seems notable because of variants of a similar resolve in *A Connecticut Yankee in King Arthur's Court* (1889), *Pudd'nhead Wilson* (1894), and elsewhere; it occurs where Froude quotes from Carlyle's 1835 journal: "What a year this has been! I have suffered much, but also lived much. Courage! hat firmly set on head, foot firmly planted. Fear nothing but fear." Clemens made an exclamation mark at a passage

about boring dinner parties. On page 174 Clemens made a marginal line at Froude's remark that "livers trouble most of us as we advance in life, and his actual constitution was a great deal stronger than that of ordinary men.") Clemens deleted a word in pencil on page 257. All of the marginalia occurs in the first volume (whose spine is stamped Volume III). There are no markings visible in Volume IV except for Clemens's underlining of the phrase "and is a colossus of gossamer" on page 76.

Catalogs: *C1951*, D12, listed among the books signed by Clemens; "New York City Collector,"; Sotheby-Parke-Bernet, Sale 3482, 25 February 1976, "4 vols.," lot #12; Second Life Books, Catalog 47, item E, "4 volumes, hinges loose" $1,750; *Sotheby's 2003*, #202, $1,800 (sold with the above Froude title). Offered in 2012 by Charles Parkhurst Rare Books, Prescott, Arizona, with "half orange morocco slipcase," for $4,800 (to be sold with the Froude title above). In 2016 the Charles Parkhurst firm moved to Sun City West, Arizona. The volumes remained unsold as of 12 January 2016 (telephone call by Alan Gribben to Charles Parkhurst).

Provenance: these volumes bear the sticker of "Brown & Gross/Booksellers/Hartford, CT" on their rear pastedown endpapers. The front pastedown endpapers have the shelf-mark numbers of Clara Clemens Gabrilowitsch's private library in Detroit along with a notation from the 1951 Hollywood auction. Subsequently the volumes entered the collection of Nick Karanovich, Fort Wayne, Indiana.

Location: collection of Kevin Mac Donnell, Austin, Texas. Acquired in December 2016 (Mac Donnell to Gribben, 21 December 2016).

Copy examined: Olivia Clemens's copy, at the 2003 Sotheby's auction. In addition, Nick Karanovich sent photocopies on 14 December 1984 of the spines, title pages, and inscriptions for Volumes III and IV. Kevin Mac Donnell sent a detailed description (correcting the previous reports of marginalia) on 21 December 2016.

FRY, CHARLES WILLIAM (1838–1882). "Lily of the valley" (gospel hymn, written in 1881). Ira D. Sankey (1840–1908, arranger), William Shakespeare Hays (1837–1901, composer). Clemens listed "Lily of the Valley" among his favorite songs in August 1889 (NB 29, *N&J* 3: 513).

FULLER, ANNA (1853–1916). *A Venetian June*. Illustrated by George Sloane (1864–1942). New York: G. P. Putnam's Sons, [cop. 1896]. 315 pp.
Source: MTLAcc, entry #129, volume donated by Clemens.

FULLER, HENRY BLAKE (1857–1929). *The Chevalier of Pensieri-Vani* (published in 1890).
Clemens entered the title, Fuller's name, and the subject "(Italy)" on the rear flyleaf of Notebook 44 in 1901. Fuller's Chevalier, or Cavaliere, as he is called by the narrator, is a bachelor with no permanent home, although he favors Florence. The American viewpoint is represented in this, Fuller's first novel, by a young, bright, prepossessing "barbarian," George W. Occident of Shelby County, who "really had no more business among the minnows that fill the valley of the Po or of the Arno than a deaf man has at a symphony concert, or a paralytic among the diamond-fields of Africa" (Chapter 7). In the end Occident returns to America and marries, but the Chevalier remains, "still sufficient unto himself and enamored only

of that delightful land" (Chapter 13).

FULLER, HORACE WILLIAMS (1844–1901). *Noted French Trials. Impostors and Adventurers*. Boston: Soule & Bugbee, 1882. 264 pp.
Inscription: "S. L. Clemens/Hartford, June 1882."
Catalogs: *A1911*, "12mo, cloth, Bost. 1882," quotes signature, lot 175, sold for $3; *L1912*, #11, $6.
Location: Franklin Meine's Mark Twain Collection, University of Illinois at Urbana-Champaign.
Copy examined: photocopy of the flyleaf inscription.
Soule & Bugbee announced the issue of this book in *Publishers' Weekly* on 10 June 1882; Clemens made a memorandum to look up the volume in his 1882 notebook, although he erred in citing its publisher and title: "Bugbee & Soule—300 Celebrated Cases. Just published" (Notebook 20, *N&J* 2: 484). Fuller chronicled eight court trials—not three hundred, as Clemens had been informed—that resulted from mistaken identification or deliberate imposture. Paraphrasing his judicial sources, Fuller briskly narrated the careers of Collet, Cartouche, Mandrin, and other French scoundrels from four centuries who relied on multiple disguises. Walter Blair believed that Fuller's account of the brazen claimants to the title of Louis XVII ("The False Dauphins") possibly influenced Mark Twain's depiction of the King in *Adventures of Huckleberry Finn* (1885) and that Fuller's first chapter, "The False Martin Guerre," was germinal to the Wilks episode in Twain's novel (*MT&HF* [1960], pp. 327–328). In a previous article, "The French Revolution and Huckleberry Finn" (1957), Blair had analyzed the possible effects of Fuller's book more extensively, emphasizing Fuller's astonishment at the gullibility encountered by all seven "Dauphins" and discussing the final ludicrous claimant to the French throne, Eleazar the Iroquois.
Fuller's opening sentences in his chapter about the "False Dauphins" undoubtedly impressed Clemens: whenever a great historical figure suddenly vanishes, Fuller observed, "there appear on every side counterparts, sometimes dangerous, but more often ridiculous,—doubles of heroes and of kings, whose grotesque courts are composed of fools, always ready to adore an impostor." The author of *The Prince and the Pauper* (1881) and the gestating *Huckleberry Finn* must have concurred with Fuller's opinion that these "celebrated impostors" are "at the same time diverting to the curious and sorrowful to the moralist" (*Noted French Trials*, p. 100).

FULLER, THOMAS (1608–1661). *The Holy State and the Profane State* (originally published in 1642).
Mary Fairbanks received a letter from Clemens written on 9 February 1876 from Hartford that recommended "an old book by Thomas Fuller—I have forgotten its name, but I think Charles Lamb devotes a chapter to it. . . . Just read it—or part of it . . . for the pleasure of searching out what I call 'pemmican sentences.'. . . Old Fuller, who wrote in Charles I's time, boils an elaborate thought down & compresses it into a crisp & meaty sentence. It is a wonderful faculty. When I had the book I purposed searching out & jotting down a lot of these pemmican sentences, . . . but I neglected it, of course" (*MTMF*, pp. 195–196). Most likely Clemens was referring to this British clergyman's collection of character sketches and

moral lessons, *The Holy State and the Profane State* (1642), though Fuller was better known for a posthumous work, *The History of the Worthies of England* (1662). His earlier book is generous in offering witty apothegms ("Memory, like a purse, if it be over-full that it cannot shut, all will drop out of it") and historical examples of both good and bad types: "The Good Husband," "The Good Physician," "The Good Widow," "The Good Solider," and "The True Gentleman." Fuller's credulity regarding witches strikes a discordant note.

FUNK, ISAAC KAUFMAN (1839–1912). *The Psychic Riddle*. New York: Funk & Wagnalls, 1907. 243 pp.

> **Inscription:** "With Compliments/to Samuel L. Clemens/Believing him to be one of the men on earth today who dare to look a fact squarely in the face— however unpopular it may be, holding judgment in abeyance until the fact is duly classified and interpreted—understanding that the personal experience of the humblest of men is entitled to the most careful attention, while the ignorance of the ablest is not worth a moment's thought./Author/March 4, 1907."
>
> **Location:** Mark Twain Library, Redding, Connecticut.
>
> **Copy examined:** Clemens's unmarked copy. Has the red ink Mark Twain Library accession number "3179". Examined in 1970 and again in June 1982.
>
> Clemens was already familiar with Funk's research, for on 4 April 1903 he wrote Olivia a sick-room note about Funk's "furnishing some spiritualism of a most unaccountable & interesting character" (MTP). Twain's "Dr. Loeb's Incredible Discovery" (written in 1905) refers to "Doctor Funk" several times. Funk's *The Psychic Riddle* discussed typical psychic phenomena, admitted fraud in many cases, neither accepted nor rejected spiritualism as a truth, and urged systematic scientific investigation of psychic phenomena.

FURNEAUX, J. H., ed. *Glimpses of India: A Grand Photographic History of the Land of Antiquity, the Vast Empire of the East.* Illus. with 500 photographs. Oblong folio. Bombay: C. B. Burrows, 1895; Philadelphia: Historical Publishing Co., 1895. 544 pp.

> Furneaux was Subeditor of *The Times of India* in Bombay, having been promoted from Chief Reporter in 1887. The second edition of his book, The Imperial Edition—published in London by the International Art Company in 1896—contained a brief letter of endorsement by Mark Twain dated 23 January 1896 in Bombay; the first edition, which must have been the one Twain praised, contained no such letter. (Subsequent undated editions contained Twain's endorsement, and these have sometimes been mistaken for first editions.) Twain wrote in part, "It is worthy of its great subject." The eminent Twain collector Kevin Mac Donnell noticed this evidence of Clemens's reading ("Some New Paths in Twain-Collecting," *Firsts* 8.9 [September 1998]: 41; Mac Donnell to Alan Gribben, 2 August 2004).

FURNISS, GRACE LIVINGSTON (1864–1938). *A Box of Monkeys* (two-act comic farce, published in 1889).

> During a visit by the Clemens family to the home of Frank W. and Mary Bushnell Cheney in Manchester, Connecticut, the Cheneys and their children performed *A Box of Monkeys* (Kym Soper, Hartford *Courant*, 18 February 1999,

quoting David Bush, then director of public information for the Mark Twain House and Museum).

FURTH, EMANUEL (1857–1931). *The Tourist; Outward and Homeward Bound.* Second ed. Illus. by H[enry]. [Nicholas] Moeller (1883–1946). Philadelphia: Gilliam's Sons Co., 1909. 183 pp.

> **Source:** MTLAcc, entry #1375, volume donated by Clemens.
>
> Furth, a Philadelphia attorney and state politician, wrote this guide for Americans traveling to and from Europe on ocean liners.

FYFFE, CHARLES ALAN (1845–1892). *History of Modern Europe.* 3 vols. New York: Henry Holt and Co., 1881–1890.

> Edgar Hemminghaus reported seeing Clemens's copy of this edition of Fyffe's book in the Mark Twain Library at Redding ("Mark Twain's German Provenience" [1945], p. 475 n. 109), but Albert E. Stone did not list the volume in his checklist in 1955 and I was unable to locate it when I visited Redding in 1970. Hemminghaus was usually accurate, and it is quite probable that this book was among those discarded as superannuated by a librarian in the early 1950s.

G

GAGNEUR, LOUISE (MIGNEROT) (1832–1902). *A Nihilist Princess.* Chicago: Jansen, McClurg & Co., 1881. 366 pp.

> **Source:** MTLAcc, entry #2239, volume donated from Clemens's library by Clara Clemens Gabrilowitsch in 1910.
>
> The protagonist of Gagneur's novel, Princess Wanda, is related to the Russian Czar but harbors sympathy for the anti-aristocratic nihilists.

The Galaxy. An Illustrated Magazine of Entertaining Reading (May 1870–October 1870). Contemporary half sheep and marbled boards, extremities rubbed, light foxing. New York: Sheldon & Co., 1870. [*The Galaxy* was published monthly from 1866 until 1878.]

> **Inscription:** the front free endpaper is signed in pencil, "Orion Clemens."
>
> **Marginalia:** passages marked in pencil in the May issue, and a few other passages similarly marked in the June issue. Page 400 was turned down in Titus Munson Coan, M.D.'s discussion of the "science of temperaments" (mental, sanguine, bilious, lymphatic, nervous). See the Catalog entry for Coan. Clemens had a lifelong interest in this concept of human temperaments; see Alan Gribben's "Mark Twain, Phrenology and the 'Temperaments'" (1972). (A revised version of this essay appears as a chapter in Volume One of the present work.)
>
> **Catalogs:** *C1951*, 89c, $12.50, erroneously listed among volumes signed by Clemens; no volume numbers or dates provided; "Property from the Library of Mark Twain," Butterfield & Butterfield, San Francisco, Sale 6613 (16 July 1997), lot 2704.
>
> **Location:** Mark Twain House and Museum, Hartford, Connecticut.
>
> **Copy examined:** Orion Clemens's copy, seemingly consulted and marked by Clemens. Viewed in Hartford in 1997.
>
> Twain contributed "Memoranda" to this periodical between May 1870 and April 1871.

Galignani's Messenger (daily English-language periodical,

published in Paris).

In an 1878 letter to Susan Crane surviving only as a fragment, Clemens described his daily regimen: "After breakfast I lie slippered & comfortable on the sofa, with a pipe, & read the meagre telegrams in the German paper & the general news in Galignani's Messenger" (MTP). During another sojourn on the Continent, Clemens made a memorandum on 26 September 1892: "order Galignani & l'Italy" (NB 32, TS p. 26). In Paris in 1894 Olivia Clemens first saw a published report of the bankruptcy of Charles L. Webster & Company in *Galignani's Messenger*; she experienced "heart-sickness" at reading the "squib" containing this "hideous news," she wrote (*MTB* [1912], pp. 986–987).

Galignani's New Paris Guide, for 1867. Revised and Verified by Personal Inspection. Illus. Paris: A. and W. Galignani and Co., 1867. 612 pp.

Dewey Ganzel found this volume to be Mark Twain's "chief source in rewriting the Paris section of *The Innocents Abroad*" (1869) (*MTAb* [1968], p. 110; see also p. 117). Ganzel quoted parallel passages from *Galignani's New Paris Guide* and *The Innocents Abroad* (1869) describing Notre Dame Cathedral ("Guidebooks" [1965], pp. 83–85).

Gallick Reports; or, An Historical Collection of Criminal Cases, Adjudged in the Supreme Courts of Judicature in France. A Work Equally Instructive and Entertaining. To Which Is Prefixed a Copious Preface, in Relation to the Laws and Constitution of France. 16mo, old sheep (rebacked). London: Printed by J. Applebee for J. Hazard, J. Brindley, J. Joliffe, C. Corbet, Ward and Chandler, E. Withers, 1737. 306 pp. [Publisher and pages conjectured.]

Inscription: signed on the front pastedown endpaper, "S. L. Clemens".

Catalogs: *A1911*, "16mo, old sheep (rebacked; one leaf loose), Lond. 1737, scarce," quotes the signature, lot 176, sold for $3.25; George D. Smith, New York City, "Catalogue of Books" (1911), quotes the signature, item #84, $12.

Here is another title confirming William Dean Howells's recollection that Clemens always relished "some out-of-the-way book" such as "a volume of great trials" (*My Mark Twain* [1910], p. 15). *Gallick Reports* contained the famous identity case of Martin Guerre.

GALLUP, ELIZABETH (WELLS) (1846–1934). *The Bi-Literal Cypher of Sir Francis Bacon Discovered in His Works and Deciphered*. Detroit, Michigan: Howard Publishing Co., [cop. 1901]. 383 pp.

Source: MTLAcc, entry #1397, volume donated by Clemens.

———. *The Bi-Literal Cypher of Sir Francis Bacon Discovered in His Works and Deciphered*. Detroit, Michigan: Howard Publishing Co., 1908. 383 pp.

Source: MTLAcc, entry #1400, volume donated by Clemens.

———. *The Bi-Literal Cypher of Sir Francis Bacon Discovered in His Works and Deciphered*. Detroit, Michigan: Howard Publishing Co., n.d. 229 pp.

Source: MTLAcc, entry #1399, volume donated by Clemens.

———. *The Bi-Literal Cypher of Sir Francis Bacon Discovered in His Works and Deciphered*. Detroit, Michigan: Howard Publishing Co., n.d.

Source: MTLAcc, entry #1401, volume donated by Clemens.

———. *The Bi-Literal Cypher of Sir Francis Bacon Discovered in His Works and Deciphered*. Detroit, Michigan: Howard Publishing Co., n.d.

Source: MTLAcc, entry #1402, volume donated by Clemens.

———. *The Tragedy of Anne Boleyn. A Drama in Cipher Found in the Works of Sir Francis Bacon. Deciphered by Elizabeth Wells Gallup*. Detroit, Michigan: Howard Publishing Co.; London: Gay & Bird, [cop. 1901]. 165 pp.

Location: Mark Twain Library, Redding, Connecticut. Donated by Clemens (MTLAcc, entry #1398).

Copy examined: Clemens's unmarked copy. Contains a red ink accession number: "1398". Examined in 1970 and again on 15 June 1982.

GALTON, (SIR) FRANCIS (1822–1911). *Finger Prints*. London: Macmillan and Co., 1892. 216 pp.

On 10 November 1892 Clemens wrote to Chatto & Windus from Florence: "The Finger-Prints has just arrived, & I don't know how you could have done me a greater favor. I shall devour it" (Berg, NYPL). Anne P. Wigger—"The Source of Fingerprint Material in Mark Twain's *Pudd'nhead Wilson and Those Extraordinary Twins*," *American Literature* 28.4 (January 1957): 517–520—established Twain's indebtedness to "the first published book on methods of fingerprinting and its uses" and demonstrated his reliance upon Galton's book while writing *Pudd'nhead Wilson* in 1892. In a letter to Chatto & Windus on 30 July 1893 he acknowledged that the book they sent had furnished him with an idea for his plot (Wigger, p. 520). A few years later, however, Clemens could no longer accurately recall the author's name. During an interview with a reporter in the summer of 1895 Twain speculated about a blood-stained print left at the scene of a notorious Brooklyn murder: "I should think that they could easily get a handprint from him [the man under arrest] and compare it with that bloody hand print. . . . Galt [*sic*] has made a scientific investigation of this finger marking. . . . He has followed it out persistently and to more purpose than anybody else" (Elmira *Advertiser*, 24 June 1895, quoted in *Mark Twain Society Bulletin* 18.2 [July 1995]: 4–5). Twain informed an unidentified correspondent on 25 June 1895: "My dim impression is that it was called 'Finger Prints.' . . . Mr. Chatto sent it to me when I was writing Pudd'nhead Wilson; & that accident changed the whole plot & plan of my book" (ALS, Harry Ransom Center, University of Texas at Austin). That same day he wrote to an unidentified correspondent that "the name is Galton—Francis Galton. The exact title of the book I am not sure of but I think it was 'Finger Prints.' It is an English publication" (ALS, Detroit Public Library). On 23 February 1897 he wrote to Gertrude Darrall from London about "the finger-mark system of identification," explaining that "it has been quite thoroughly & scientifically examined by Mr. Galt [*sic*], & I kept myself within the bounds of his ascertained facts" (ALS quoted in "Mark Twain," Heritage Bookshop, Los Angeles, 1997, item #130).

The explorer, anthropologist, meteorologist, and inventor

Francis Galton made many scientific inquiries besides fingerprinting. For example, he tested the efficacy of prayer (see the Catalog entry for *The Prayer-Gauge Debate* (1876), investigated human psychology and measurements of human intelligence, and considered forms of eugenics.

John O. West and James M. Day, "Mark Twain's Comedy of Errors in *Pudd'nhead Wilson,*" *Mark Twain Journal* 22.1 (Spring 1984): 43–44; Simon A. Cole, "Twins, Twain, Galton, and Gilman: Fingerprinting, Individualism, Brotherhood, and Race in *Pudd'nhead Wilson,*" *Configurations* 15.3 (2007): 227–265; Ellen Samuels, "Reading Race Through Disability: Slavery and Agency in Mark Twain's *Pudd'nhead Wilson* and 'Those Extraordinary Twins,'" in *The Oxford Handbook of Nineteenth-Century Literature,* ed. Russ Castronovo (Oxford: Oxford University Press, 2012); and Leonard Martinez, "Concentric Failures: Melville, Twain, and Shifting Centers," *Mark Twain Annual 13* (2015): 115–129.

GANE, DOUGLAS M[ONTAGUE]. (1862–1935). *New South Wales and Victoria in 1885.* London: Sampson Low, Marston, Searle & Rivington, 1886. 207 pp.

> **Inscription:** "To Samuel L. Clemens, Esq., with compliments, from Douglas M. Gane, 24. 2. 99" (quoted in *A1911*; the year given, "1899," seems questionable).
>
> **Catalog:** *A1911,* "12mo, cloth, Lond. 1886," quotes the inscription, lot 177, sold for $1.
>
> Mark Twain quotes Gane's description of an Australian dust-storm in Chapter 9 of *Following the Equator* (1897); in Chapter 11 he juxaposes Gane's contradicting accounts of hospitality in Sydney.

GANZ, HUGO [MARKUS] (1862–1922). *The Land of Riddles (Russia of To-day).* Trans. from the German and ed. by Herman Rosenthal (1843–1917). New York: Harper & Brothers, 1904. 331 pp.

> **Source:** MTLAcc, entry #1718, volume donated by Clemens.
>
> Hugo Markus Ganz was a German newspaper journalist who had been stationed in St. Petersburg.

GARDENHIRE, SAMUEL MAJOR (1855–1923). *The Long Arm.* Illustrated by W[illiam]. E[llis]. Mears (1868–1945). New York: Harper & Brothers, 1906. 344 pp.

> **Inscription:** signed on the front pastedown endpaper, "S. L. Clemens, 1906".
>
> **Catalog:** *A1911,* "12mo, cloth, N.Y. 1906," quotes the signature, lot 178, sold for $1.25.
>
> Here is another record of Clemens's interest in detective fiction.

———. *Purple and Homespun; A Novel.* New York: Harper & Brothers, 1908. 371 pp.

> **Source:** MTLAcc, entry #138, volume donated by Clemens.

———. *The Silence of Mrs. Harrold.* New York: Harper & Brothers, [cop. 1905]. 462 pp.

> **Source:** MTLAcc, entry #1092, volume donated Clemens.
>
> Sometime between May and October of 1907 Clemens was photographed on the porch at Tuxedo Park, New York wearing his Oxford University gown and holding a copy of Gardenhire's *The Silence of Mrs. Harrold.* This is one of the very few photographs of Clemens holding a book in which the title can be identified. (Nick Karanovich sent a copy of the photograph to Alan Gribben, 20 June 1984; its original glass print negative was sold at auction

by *Sotheby's 2003*, lot 173.)

GARDINER, SAMUEL RAWSON (1829–1902). *The Thirty Years' War, 1618–1648.* Epochs of History Series. New York: Charles Scribner's Sons, 1887. 237 pp.

> **Catalog:** Ball 2016 inventory, red texture cloth, gilt lettering on the spine, black lettering and design on the covers and the spine.
>
> **Location:** Quarry Farm Library shelves, under the supervision of the Mark Twain Archive, Elmira College, Elmira, New York.
>
> This history work was among the books available to Clemens when he visited Quarry Farm in Elmira.

GARIBALDI, GIUSEPPE (1807–1882).

> Clemens negotiated cautiously for the publishing rights to Garibaldi's autobiography in 1887, but informed Charles L. Webster on 28 May 1887: "Garabaldi [*sic*] is stale enough already; so we shouldn't want to contract for his book for 1892, but for next year—before he gets *too* stale" (*MTBus,* p. 383; *MTLP,* p. 217). Charles L Webster & Company never published Garibaldi's life.

GARLAND, HAMLIN (1860–1940). *The Captain of the Gray-Horse Troop; A Novel.* Spine and signatures loose. New York: Harper & Brothers, 1902. 415 pp.

> **Inscription:** signed on the verso of the frontispiece photograph, "SL. Clemens/1902".
>
> **Marginalia:** no markings, but page 141 was turned down at the beginning of Chapter 14. Page 289, in the middle of Chapter 25, was similarly turned down.
>
> **Location:** Mark Twain Library, Redding, Connecticut. Donated by Isabel V. Lyon, Clemens's secretary (MTLAcc, entry #1004).
>
> **Copy examined:** Clemens's unmarked copy. Examined in 1970 and again in June 1982.
>
> In view of the number of books by Garland that Clemens possessed, it seems very strange that they did not include Garland's *Boy Life on the Prairie* (1899), an account of growing up in rural northeast Iowa. However, one must always bear in mind how many of Clemens's library books were lost, donated, or sold without any record made of their titles.

———. *The Captain of the Gray-Horse Troop.* New York: Harper & Brothers, 1906. 415 pp.

> **Source:** MTLAcc, entry #1557, volume donated by Clemens.

———. *Hesper; A Novel.* New York: Harper & Brothers, 1903. 445 pp.

> **Source:** MTLAcc, entry #1556, volume donated by Clemens.

———. *The Light of the Star; A Novel.* New York: Harper & Brothers, 1904. 278 pp.

> **Source:** MTLAcc, entry #2240, volume donated from Clemens's library by Clara Clemens Gabrilowitsch in 1910.
>
> After Clemens's departure from Florence in June 1904 his business agent there received a package from French, Lemon & Company that contained this and other "Harpers' books"; the books remained in Florence at least until 4 November 1904 (Sebastiano Cecchi to SLC, 30 July, 4 November 1904, Haskard & Co., Bankers, Florence).

———. *The Moccasin Ranch; A Story of Dakota.* New York: Harper & Brothers, 1909. 137 pp.

> **Source:** MTLAcc, entry #1426, volume donated by

Clemens.

———. *Money Magic; A Novel.* Illustrated by J[ohn]. N[orval]. Marchand (1875–1921). New York: Harper & Brothers, 1907. 355 pp.

Source: MTLAcc, entry #2241, volume donated from Clemens's library by Clara Clemens Gabrilowitsch in 1910.

———. "Sanity in Fiction," *North American Review* 176.556 (March 1903): 336–348.

Garland's strong defense of William Dean Howells's literary style against charges that his fiction was too tepid, mild, and similar in characterizations appeared in the same issue of the *North American Review* as an essay by W. D. McCrackan with which Mark Twain registered disagreement; see the Catalog entry for McCrackan.

———. *The Shadow World.* New York: Harper & Brothers, 1908. 295 pp.

Source: MTLAcc, entry #1445, volume donated by Clemens.

———. *The Tyranny of the Dark.* [Illustrated by William E[llis]. Mears (1868–1945).] New York: Harper & Brothers, 1905. 439 pp.

Source: MTLAcc, entry #2242, volume donated from Clemens's library by Clara Clemens Gabrilowitsch in 1910.

On 30 June 1905 Clemens wrote to Garland from Dublin, New Hampshire: "I put in yesterday's holiday [from writing] & up to 2 this morning reading your book—criminal dissipations for a laboring man & slow reader, . . . but I was caught with the last third unread, & had to go on to the end, it was so enthralling. I like that book exceedingly" (ALS, American Academy and Institute of Arts and Letters). Isabel Lyon wrote in her diary on Sunday, 2 July 1905: "Reading Hamlin Garland's 'Tyranny of the Dark'. Mr. Clemens has just finished it. Yesterday he said it was 'good done'" (TS p. 72, MTP). Garland replied to Clemens's letter on 7 July 1905, discussing the treatment of spiritualism in his book (MTP). Garland's correspondence with Clemens is included in *Selected Letters of Hamlin Garland*, ed. Keith Newlin and Joseph B. McCullough (Lincoln: University of Nebraska Press, 1998). Garland provided a prefatory "Appreciation" for *Roughing It* in the so-called Definitive Edition of Twain's works (New York: Gabriel Well, 1922–1925).

Hamlin Garland, "Twain's Social Conscience," *Mark Twain Quarterly* 4.1 (Summer 1940): 8–9 (praises *A Connecticut Yankee*); Oliver Blearsides, "Garland's Twain Anecdotes," *Mark Twain Quarterly* 4.1 (Summer 1940): 13 (recounts two brief jokes that Garland purportedly heard Twain tell); Daniel J. Fuller, "Mark Twain and Hamlin Garland: Contrarieties in Regionalism," *Mark Twain Journal* 17.1 (Winter 1973–1974): 14–18.

———. *The Tyranny of the Dark.* [Illustrated by William E[llis]. Mears (1868–1945).] New York: Harper & Brothers, 1906. 439 pp.

Source: MTLAcc, entry #1087, volume donated by Clemens.

———. *Ulysses S. Grant, His Life and Character.* New York: Doubleday & McClure Co., 1898. 524 pp.

Inscription: on the second flyleaf: "To Samuel M [*sic*] Clemens./Who aided 'The Old Warrior' when he needed it most./From the author/Hamlin Garland/London,

June 14, 99".

Location: Clifton Waller Barrett Collection, Albert and Shirley Small Special Collections Library, University of Virginia, Charlottesville.

Copy examined: Clemens's unmarked copy. Contains the bookstamps and accession number of the Mark Twain Library, Redding, Connecticut.

GARLAND, HERBERT (1880–1921). *Diverse Affections: A Romance of Guernsey.* London: Century Press, 1906. 230 pp.

Source: MTLAcc, entry #1005, volume donated by Clemens.

GARNER, RICHARD LYNCH (1848–1920). *The Speech of Monkeys.* New York: Charles L. Webster & Co., 1892. 217 pp.

Issued by Clemens's publishing firm.

GARNIER, ALBERT. *Scientific Billiards. Garnier's Practice Shots, with Hints to Amateurs.* Oblong volume. Mustard-colored cloth cover with gilt. The front cover is illustrated with a green billiard-table showing diagrams of possible shots involving two silver-colored balls. New York: D. Appleton & Co., 1880. 109 pp.

Inscription: inscribed in black ink on the front free endpaper: "Mr. S. L. Clemens/From his Victim/F. G. Whitmore/Nov. 23rd 1880." (Franklin G. Whitmore [1846–1926] was Clemens's business agent in Hartford.)

Provenance: bookseller's sticker of Brown & Gross, Hartford, Connecticut on the rear pastedown endpaper.

Catalog: ListABP (1910) ("Practice Shots, Garnier").

Location: collection of Alan Gribben, Montgomery, Alabama. A gift in 1992 from an East Coast bookseller who had admired *Mark Twain's Library: A Reconstruction* (1980).

Copy examined: Clemens's unmarked copy. (I will swear that this volume, seldom opened since Clemens's death, gave off a distinct aroma of cigar smoke when I first turned its pages in 1992.)

The French billiards champion Albert Garnier of Paris played in several celebrated tournaments in the United States.

Timothy Long, "Mark Twain's Speeches on Billiards," *Mark Twain Journal* 17.2 (Summer 1974): 1–3.

GARRETT, [FYDELL] EDMUND (1865–1907) and E. J. EDWARDS. *The Story of an African Crisis. Being the Truth About the Jameson Raid and Johannesburg Revolt of 1896, Told with the Assistance of the Leading Actors in the Drama.* New enlarged and revised edition with appendices and introduction. Illus. Original pictorial orange cloth. Westminster: Archibald Constable and Co., 1897. 308 pp.

Marginalia: Clemens annotated the book rather thoroughly in pencil in the introduction and text up to page 122; he also made notes in ink on pages 104–122. No marks or notes thereafter except for pencil marks in the appendices, especially in "The National Union Manifesto," pp. 275, 277, 284. Some of Clemens's notes occur on pages xxx, xxxi, 4 ("But the preparations for force had all been made," he wrote vertically in the margin), 5 ("But the 'populace' wanted to rush out & bring Jim in in triumph," he wrote at the top of the page), 41, 51, 60, 61, 69, 80, 88, 104–105, and 120. There are additional notes.

Location: Albert and Shirley Small Special Collections Library, University of Virginia Libraries, Charlottesville. This was a gift from the collector Clifton Waller Barrett.

Copy examined: Clemens's copy, in 1970. Contains

the bookstamps, accession number, and traces of the charge-slip jacket of the Mark Twain Library, Redding, Connecticut.

On a card sent by Clemens to Chatto & Windus of London on 7 May 1897, Clemens requested a copy of this book , which he had seen "reviewed this morning" (Berg. NYPL). He mentions Garrett's *Story of an African Crisis* in Chapter 65 of *Following the Equator* (1897), characterizing Garrett as "a brilliant writer partial to Rhodes." In Chapter 67 he quotes Garrett's analysis of Jameson's comparatively meager forces and those of the Boers, remarking, "Mr. Garrett's account of the Raid is much the best one I have met with, and my impressions of the Raid are drawn from that." This may have been the book that Twain cited in a 15 September 1899 letter to an unknown correspondent: "As to that South African battle. It isn't I that made the mistake—it is the school history I quote from. It is a text-book down there, & was not written by a Boer, but by a Briton" (ALS, Special Collections, Washington University, St. Louis, Missouri). But see also the Catalog entry for Francis Reginald Statham's *South Africa as It Is* (1897), a less likely but possible referent.

GASKELL, ELIZABETH CLEGHORN (STEVENSON) (1810–1865). *Cranford*. New York: Harper & Brothers, n.d. 329 pp.

  Source: MTLAcc, entry #1845, volume donated from Clemens's library by Clara Clemens Gabrilowitsch in 1910.

  In 1893 Clemens suffered the symptoms of a severe cold during a visit to Chicago, and while he was convalescing Eugene Field came to see him. Clemens wrote to Olivia Clemens on 18 April 1893: "Eugene Field brought me 'Cranford'—I never could read it before; but this time I blasted my determined way through the obstructing granite, slate & clay walls, not giving up till I reached the vein—since then I have been taking out pay ore right along" (*LLMT*, p. 264).

———. *Cranford*. New York: A. L. Burt, n.d. 278 pp.

  Source: MTLAcc, entry #2248, volume donated from Clemens's library by Clara Clemens Gabrilowitsch in 1910.

———. *The Life of Charlotte Brontë* (biography, published in 1857).

  Sometime between 1888 and 1904 Clara Clemens listed the title of Gaskell's much-praised *Life of Charlotte Brontë* in her commonplace book (Paine 150, MTP). Clemens and his daughter often exchanged reading materials.

———. *Ruth* (novel, published in 1853).

  Sometime between 1888 and 1904 Clara Clemens listed the title of Gaskell's novel *Ruth*, the pitiable story of an orphan seduced and later vilified, in her commonplace book (Paine 150, MTP). Clemens and his daughter often exchanged reading materials.

GATTY, MARGARET (SCOTT) (MRS. ALFRED GATTY) (1809–1873). *Parables from Nature*. Illustrated by Paul de Longpré (1855–1911). First edition. Original blue pictorial cloth, gilt. New York: G. P. Putnam's Sons, 1893. 279 pp.

  Catalogs: A1911, "square 8vo, cloth, N.Y. 1893," slip of autograph notes laid in, lot 179, $1.50; sold for $75 at Auction No. 24 (25 January 1968) by Charles Hamilton Autographs, according to *American Book-Prices Current* (New York: Columbia University, 1971), p. 214.

  Location: collection of Kevin Mac Donnell, Austin, Texas.

  Copy examined: Clemens's unmarked copy, in July 2004.

The volume contains the *A1911* sale label with a card signed "Mark Twain" pasted in above that label. A laid-in leaf of manuscript by Clemens refers to "Sunday 17th" and refers to "Great storms Jan 4 in N[ew] Y[ork]—read it yesterday in the Sun."

Gatty's *Parables* consist of stories for children about talking birds, plants, insects, and the wind, with religious overtones.

———. [Identical copy.]

  Source: MTLAcc, entry #544, volume donated by Clemens.

GAULLIEUR, HENRI (OFTEN LISTED AS HENRY) (c. 1843–1898). *The Paternal State in France and Germany*. New York: Harper & Brothers, 1898. 225 pp.

  Source: MTLAcc, entry #677, volume donated by Clemens. Gaullieur, a Swiss novelist, writer, and painter, died suddenly on 20 November 1898 while visiting New York City.

GAY, JOHN (1685–1732). "Sweet William's Farewell to Black-ey'd Susan" (poem, ballad, first published as a poem in 1719), later known as "Black-eyed Susan." Music composed in 1730 by Richard Leveridge (1670–1758).

  In June 1898 Mark Twain had the idea of adding the boy in Felicia Dorothea Hemans's poem "Casabianca" to Huck, Tom, and other "Creatures of Fiction" he planned to assemble in a tale; subsequently Twain added another inspiration: "Make Casabianca sing 'All in the Downs the Ship lay moored' & dance hornpipe" (NB 40, TS p. 27). Gay's poem began, "All in the Downs the fleet was moor'd,/The streamers waving in the wind,/When black-ey'd Susan came aboard./Oh! Where shall I my true love find?" The Downs are in the vicinity of Dover, England.

GAY, MARY ANN HARRIS (1828–1918). *Prose and Poetry. By a Georgia Lady*. Nashville, Tennessee, Privately printed, 1858. 199 pp. [The seventh edition would be titled *The Pastor's Story and Other Pieces; or, Prose and Poetry*. Memphis, Tennessee: Published for the author by Goodwyn & Co., 1871. 266 pp.]

  Hamlin Hill, in "The Composition and the Structure of *Tom Sawyer*," *American Literature* 32.4 (January 1961): 379–392, identified Gay's book as the one from which Mark Twain extracted two essays and a poem for elocutions performed at the graduation ceremony in Chapter 21 of *The Adventures of Tom Sawyer* (1876). In a footnote at the end of the chapter Twain asserts that the "compositions" of Tom's female classmates "are taken without alteration from a volume entitled 'Prose and Poetry, by a Western [*sic*] Lady'—but they are exactly and precisely after the school-girl pattern, and hence are much happier than any mere imitations could be." Hill proved that the pieces "were not then, as Dixon Wecter suggested, Twain's own satiric efforts. On the contrary, the humorist pasted actual pages torn from Mary Ann Gay's book in his manuscript" ("Composition and Structure," pp. 383–384). Hill found that at least seven editions of Gay's book were published between 1858 and 1871, and that the book title varied among its editions. Sydney J. Krause's *Mark Twain as Critic* (1967) grouped these vacuous "compositions" with a long campaign by Twain against the false sentimentality required of young girls' writings, which Krause characterized as "Miltonic ornamentation in a country version of the prose of sensibility" (*MTC*, p. 117). According to Kristina Simms—"Mark Twain and the Lady from Decatur," Atlanta *Journal and Constitution Magazine* (12

November 1972), 48–53—a total of eleven editions of Gay's book were issued between 1858 and 1881. Simms reported that Twain quoted his extracts from the seventh edition, titled *The Pastor's Story and Other Pieces; or, Prose and Poetry* (1871). She also revealed that the piece titled "Is this, then, Life?" was contributed to Gay's volume by her half-sister, Missouria Stokes. Simms reported another hitherto-unnoticed development: Gay's tenth edition, published in 1880, retaliated against "that renowned Bohemian, 'Mark Twain,'" mocking him as "the greatest literary humbug, who could not himself produce a work equal in merit to the one criticized." Gay eventually wrote a more durable work, a memoir titled *Life in Dixie During the War* (1892).

But the discoveries of both Hill and Simms beg the question as to why Twain specifically attributed his examples of insipidity to "Prose and Poetry, by a Western Lady." Only the first, 199-page edition of Gay's book, published in Nashville in 1858, had the similar title *Prose and Poetry. By A Georgian Lady.* The author was bolder on the title page of her second, 233-page edition, published by the South-Western Publishing House in Nashville in 1859, which read *Prose and Poetry. By Miss M. A. H. Gay.* That second edition included the prose effusion "Is This, Then, Life?" (pp. 29–34), not present in the first edition, which Gay credited to "Missouria" of Decatur, Georgia. Gay made her loyalties clear on the dedication page: "To/The Ladies of Georgia,/This Little Volume/Is Most Respectfully Dedicated,/By/A Native Georgian." In summary, then, Twain quoted from a second or later edition of Gay's work, yet he also knew and paraphrased the title of its first edition (a title not mentioned in the second or later editions).

Michelle Gillespie, "Mary Gay (1829–1918): Sin, Self, and Survival in the Post-Civil War South," *Georgia Women: Their Lives and Times.* Ed. Ann Short Chirhart and Betty Wood (Athens: University of Georgia Press, 2009), pp. 199–223.

GEER, GEORGE JARVIS (1821–1885). [Hymn composer.]
"We play euchre every night," Clemens wrote to Susan Crane on 31 March 1869 from Hartford, "& sing 'Geer,' which is Livy's favorite, & . . . a dozen other hymns" (*MTLet* 3: 181). Geer, the rector of St. Timothy's Church in New York City, is credited with providing the tunes for half a dozen popular hymns. Although it is difficult to be certain which hymn had become Olivia Langdon's favorite, four melodies composed by Geer based on lyrics written by others would be leading candidates: John Cawood (1775–1852), "Hark! what mean those holy voices,/Sweetly sounding thro' the skies?/Lo, th' angelic host rejoices,/Heav'nly alleluias rise" (date uncertain); Francis Turner Palgrave (1824–1897), "Thou say'st, 'Take up thy cross/O man, and follow Me';/The night is black, the feet are slack,/Yet we would follow Thee," published in 1869; Henry William Baker (1821–1877), "O what, if we are Christ's/Is earthly shame or loss?/Bright shall the crown of glory be/When we have borne the cross" (published in 1852); and John Leland (1754–1841), "The day is past and gone/The evening shades appear,/O may I ever keep in mind,/The night of death is near" (date uncertain). Different composers other than Geer also set these same

lyrics to music, making the matter more complicated. In addition to composing melodies, Geer compiled a collection of hymns for Protestant-Episcopal churches that went through multiple editions. Allison R. Ensor's "The Favorite Hymns of Sam and Livy Clemens," *Mark Twain Journal* 25.2 (Fall 1987): 21–22 expressed doubts as to which hymn the name "Geer" referred. Various possibilities are discussed in *MTLet* 3: 183–184.

GEER'S HARTFORD CITY DIRECTORY.
On 11 October 1880 Clemens purchased "1 City Directory" from Brown & Gross of Hartford (bill and receipt in MTP). He later bought "1 Copy of Geer's No. 51 July, 1888, Hartford City Directory, $3.00" (receipt dated 7 September 1888 in MTP).

GEIKIE, [JOHN] CUNNINGHAM (1824–1906). *Hours with the Bible; or, The Scriptures in the Light of Modern Discovery and Knowledge.* 6 vols. Illus. New York: James Pott, 1882–1883.
Source: MTLAcc, entries #938–#942, volumes I-V only, donated by Clemens.
On 14 January 1884 Clemens listed his recent reading for Edward H. House; it included "the third volume of Geike's [*sic*] Hours with the Bible" (CWB in ASSSCL).

GEISSE, MARY ALBERTEEN (1866–1935), pseud. "Felix Counop." *Poems.* Philadelphia: Campion & Co., 1904. 80 pp.
Geisse sent poems presumably destined for this volume to Clemens in 1902, but in a reply he gave her no encouragement. She wrote to him bitterly from Philadelphia on 24 May 1902 about his effort to explain that she lacked "that higher quality, which is known as genius" (*DearMT*, pp. 197–198). There is no indication that Clemens saw her eventual book of poetry.

GELLIBRAND, EMMA. *J. Cole.* Every Boy's Library Series. New York: Thomas Y. Crowell & Co., [cop. 1896]. 86 pp.
Source: MTLAcc, entry #871, volume donated by Mrs. Ralph W. Ashcroft (formerly Isabel V. Lyon), Clemens's secretary.
A novella about "the very smallest boy, with the very largest eyes I ever saw," who applies to an advertisement for a servant. He ends up in the clutches of burglars.

GENLIS, COMTESSE DE (*née* Stephanie Félicité du Crest de Saint-Aubin) (1746–1830).
Clemens informed Mary Fairbanks on 6 August 1877 that he recently read "a story by Madame de Genlis . . . in French . . . which [failed to] cast much light upon my subject [the French Revolution] or amounted to much. I would have done well to stop with Carlyle & Dumas" (*MTMF* [1949], p. 208). Genlis played a somewhat equivocal role in the French Revolution. Which of her more than eighty works Clemens read remains unclear.

GENUNG, JOHN FRANKLIN (1850–1919). *The Practical Elements of Rhetoric, with Illustrative Examples.* Boston: Ginn & Co., 1887. 488 pp.
Source: MTLAcc, entry #803, volume donated by Clemens.

GEORGE, HENRY (1839–1897). *The Condition of Labor. An Open Letter to Pope Leo XIII.* New York: Charles L. Webster & Co., 1893. 157 pp.
Issued by Clemens's publishing firm.

———. *The Land Question, What It Involves, and How Alone It Can Be Settled.* New York: Charles L. Webster & Co.,

1893. 87 pp.

Issued by Clemens's publishing firm.

Jim Zwick, "Mark Twain and the Single Tax," *Georgist Journal: News & Views from the International Georgist Movement* 87 (Summer 1997): 5–10. See also the Catalog entries for Henry George's weekly newspaper, *The Standard*, and also for Louis F. Post.

———. *A Perplexed Philosopher, Being an Examination of Mr. Herbert Spencer's Various Utterances on the Land Question, with Some Incidental Reference to His Synthetic Philosophy.* New York: Charles L. Webster & Co., 1892. 319 pp. Issued by Clemens's publishing firm.

———. *Progress and Poverty: An Inquiry into the Cause of Industrial Depression and of Increase of Want with Increase of Wealth: The Remedy.* New York: Charles L. Webster & Co., 1892. 512 pp. Issued by Clemens's publishing firm. There appear to be traces of its influence in the essays read at the Mechanics' Debating Club in Chapters 10 and 14 of *The American Claimant* (1892) as well as in Lord Berkeley's reflections in Chapter 13 and elsewhere in Twain's novel.

———. *Property in Land: A Passage-at-Arms Between the Duke of Argyll [George Douglas Campbell, Duke of Argyll, 1823–1900] and Henry George.* New York: Charles L. Webster & Co., [1892].

Issued by Clemens's publishing firm.

———. *Protection or Free Trade: An Examination of the Tariff Question with Especial Regard to the Interests of Labor.* New York: Charles L. Webster & Co., 189–?.

Clemens's publishing firm intended to publish this book, according to *Publishers' Trade List Annual 1893*, but the Webster edition apparently never appeared. Henry George had first published it in 1886.

———. *Social Problems.* New York: Charles L. Webster & Co., 1893. 342 pp. Issued by Clemens's publishing firm.

"GEORGIE ON THE CARS," Hartford *Courant*, 8 March 1882. Clemens made a note about this newspaper sketch (which had originated in the Boston *Transcript*) in Notebook 20 (*N&J* 2: 450).

GERARD, EMILY (1849–1905), later also known as Emily Laszowska. *The Extermination of Love; A Fragmentary Study in Erotics.* Edinburgh: William Blackwood & Sons, 1901. 313 pp.

Source: MTLAcc, entry #136, volume donated by Clemens.

The Scottish-born Gerard formed a friendship with Mark Twain in Vienna beginning in November 1897. D. M. McKeithan, "Madame Laszowska Meets Mark Twain," *Texas Studies in Literature and Language* 1.1 (Spring 1959): 62–65, reported that she found him "serious almost solemn" and yet "quite fascinating" (p. 65). Her later novel *The Extermination of Love* opened with a dedicatory poem to Twain; its last four lines were adulatory: "And though again the ocean roll between,/Be sure no malice of ungracious fate/Can dim the memory of what has been,/Nor 'love' for thee and thine 'exterminate.'"

On 10 June 1904 she would write him a letter of condolence from Salzburg, Austria about Olivia Clemens's death (Fears, *Day by Day* 3: 1000).

———. *A Foreigner; An Anglo-German Study.* Edinburgh: William Blackwood & Sons, 1896. 526 pp.

Inscription: presented by the author to Clara Clemens, Vienna, 28 January 1898.

Provenance: MTLAcc, entry #2250, volume donated

from Clemens's library by Clara Clemens Gabrilowitsch in 1910.

Catalog: *Mott 1952*, #56, $8.50.

———. *The Land Beyond the Forest: Facts, Figures and Fancies from Transylvania.* Illus. 2 vols. Edinburgh: William Blackwood & Sons, 1888. [Publisher conjectured.]

Inscription: in Volume I, "To Mark Twain with sincerest regards from a humbler worker on the same field so brilliantly occupied by his 'Tramps' and 'Innocents'. Emily Laszowska-Gerard. Vienna, December 19th, 1897."

Catalogs: *A1911*, "Vol. I, illustrated, 12mo, cloth, Edinb. 1888," quotes the inscription, lot 180, sold for $1.50; *C1951*, #24c, presumably Volume II, listed among books signed by Clemens.

Mark Twain wrote that he found a "2 vols." set of this work among "35 cloth-bound books" on a shelf in Kaltenleutgeben in 1898 ("The Great Republic's Peanut Stand," MTP, ms p. 47). *The Land Beyond the Forest* included descriptions of Romani people.

———. *A Secret Mission, A Novel.* Copyright Edition. Collection of British Authors Series. Leipzig: B. Tauchnitz, 1893. 294 pp.

Source: MTLAcc, entry #2249, volume donated from Clemens's library by Clara Clemens Gabrilowitsch in 1910.

———. *The Tragedy of a Nose. (A Brief Delirium).* London: Digby, Long & Co., 1898. 194 pp.

Source: MTLAcc, entry #137, volume donated by Clemens.

———. *The Waters of Hercules.* Edinburgh: William Blackwood & Sons, n.d. 396 pp.

Source: MTLAcc, entry $2251, volume donated from Clemens's library by Clara Clemens Gabrilowitsch in 1910.

GERARD, JOHN (JESUIT, OF STONYHURST). *What Was the Gunpowder Plot? The Traditional Story Tested by Original Evidence.* London: Osgood & McIlvaine, 1897 [cop. 1896]. 288 pp. [Edition conjectured.]

Gerard re-evaluates the evidence against Guy Fawkes (1570–1606), a principal conspirator against James I. Clemens apparently heard about Gerard's controversial book while it was still in press; in London in November 1896 he was aware that "a book is just out by a Cath priest which shows (proves) that history has done some large but awkward & unscientific lying in the G. F. matter" (NB 39, TS p. 20). It may not be coincidental that Tom Sawyer mentions Guy Fawkes in Chapter 2 of "Tom Sawyer's Conspiracy," written 1897–1902 (*HH&T* [1969], p. 173).

German-English, English-German Dictionary. Paris: Neal's, n. d.

Inscription: "Jervis Langdon/Genoa-Milan/April 10, 1898."

Source: list of books transferred from the Quarry Farm library to the Mark Twain Archive by Mark Woodhouse on 9 July 1987.

Provenance: library collection of Jervis Langdon (1875–1952). Conceivably Clemens might have seen this book before or after Langdon married Eleanor Sayles (1878–1971) in 1902.

Location: Mark Twain Archive, Elmira College, Elmira, New York.

GERRARD, ERNEST ALLEN (b. 1873). *France and the Maid. A Drama in Three Acts.* Limited and numbered edition. No. 103. Illus. Original yellow cloth. [Lincoln, Nebraska]: Privately printed [The Ivy Press], 1904. 210 pp.

Inscription: on the front free endpaper, "To Samuel L. Clemens: In admiration of your story woven about 'The Maid,' and with many thanks for happy hours spent on the Mississippi, in the West, and abroad through 'Mark Twain.' Ernest A. Gerrard."

Catalogs: *A1911*, "16mo, cloth, privately printed, [1904], limited and numbered edition," quotes the inscription, lot 182, sold for $1.50; City Book Auction, 21 April 1945, $5.00; "Victor and Irene Murr Jacobs Collection," Sotheby's, New York City, 29 October 1996, lot 313, sold with four other books for a total of $9,321; *Sotheby's 2003*, #217, $4,000 (sold with four other inscribed books).

Provenance: in 1986 Victor Jacobs of Dayton, Ohio owned this book (Jacobs to Alan Gribben, 15 October 1986, a "presentation copy to Clemens"). Subsequently it entered the collection of Nick Karanovich, Fort Wayne, Indiana.

Location: collection of Kevin Mac Donnell, Austin, Texas.

Copy examined: Clemens's unmarked copy, in July 2004. It has the *A1911* sale label.

After graduating from the University of Nebraska, Gerrard had studied literature under George E. Woodbury at Columbia University in New York City.

Gesta Romanorum [Deeds of the Romans]. (A collection of miscellaneous moral tales often dated early in the fourteenth century.)

Homer E. Woodbridge, "Mark Twain and the 'Gesta Romanorum,'" *The Nation* 108.2803 (22 March 1919): 424–425, proposed a curious tale in the *Gesta Romanorum*, "De heremita et pastore et angelo," as a possible source for "the machinery and some of the incidents of 'The Mysterious Stranger.'" (This question is complicated; F. A. O. Cowper saw the influence of Voltaire's *Zadig*.)

Whatever the case, it is indeed tantalizing to speculate about whether Twain possessed or read a copy of these stories, because the one titled "V.—Of Too Much Pride" bears a strong resemblance to the mixed-up identities in *The Prince and the Pauper* (1881). The guardian angel of Emperor Jovinian's soul steals his royal clothes while the emperor is bathing in a stream and assumes the emperor's role in the palace. The now-unrecognized emperor, attempting to assert his prerogatives, is flogged, imprisoned, and dragged by a horse's tale. When the rightful emperor is finally recognized and restored to his imperial status he is a chastened and humbled ruler.

"GET OUT OF THE WILDERNESS" (waltz, arranged by Paul Jones, 1860s).

"Waltz back in the wilderness," Clemens quipped during the *Quaker City* pilgrims' tiring trek through the Holy Land (Notebook 9, 1867, *N&J* 1: 437).

GETTKE, ERNST (1841–1912) and **GEORG ENGEL** (1868–1940). *In Purgatory* (play). German title: *Im Fegefeuer*.

Clemens wrote to Henry H. Rogers from Vienna on 15 March 1898: "Meantime I have arranged to translate a couple of plays—a melancholy one ('Bartel Turaser') and a funny one ('In Purgatory')" (*MTHHR*, p. 326).

Carl Dolmetsch, *Our Famous Guest: Mark Twain in Vienna* (Athens: University of Georgia Press, 1992), p. 128.

GIACOMETTI, PAOLO (1816–1882). *Elizabeth, Queen of England* (historical drama, performed in 1873).

Clemens made a memorandum to see an Italian production

of this play at the Theatre Royal in Drury Lane during his 1873 sojourn in London (*N&J* 1: 529).

GIBBON, EDWARD (1737–1794). *The History of the Decline and Fall of the Roman Empire, with Notes by Dean [Henry Hart] Milman, M. [François] Guizot [1787–1874], and Dr. William Smith [1813–1893]*. 6 vols. New York: Harper & Brothers, 1880. [Gibbon's work was originally published in 1776–1788.]

Inscription: signed "S. L. Clemens, Hartford 1880."

Location: Mark Twain Papers, Bancroft Library, University of California at Berkeley. Bears the *C1951* Hollywood sale label.

Source: University of California at Berkeley Library Catalog, 2006.

Clemens joshed about "The Decline and Fall of the Roman Empire" in a letter of 27 April 1867 to Charles Warren Stoddard, facetiously informing Stoddard that he had "tried and rejected" the idea of contributing an essay of this title to an album Stoddard was editing (*MTLet* 2: 35). In a letter written early in January 1871 to Mollie E. Clemens, Clemens kiddingly attributed the authorship of *The Decline and Fall* to "the lamented Josephus" (*MTLet* 4: 298). He showed renewed interest in the work many years later; when Isabel Lyon entered Clemens's room in his New York City home on 2 January 1906 she found him reading "the first volume of Gibbon's Rome," with "wreaths of smoke" hovering over his head. That night "at dinner he warmed to the subject of Gibbon and his Rome, and Gibbon, the man, whose followings of many creeds made him finally an unbeliever." Clemens then told the story of a "pretty Geneva girl" whom Gibbon spurned, but who later became surprisingly prominent despite his low opinion of her (IVL Journal, TS p. 118, MTP). On 3 November 1909 Clemens told Albert Bigelow Paine: "I have been reading Gibbon's celebrated Fifteenth Chapter . . . and I don't see what Christians found against it. It is so mild—so gentle in its sarcasm" (*MTB*, p. 1535).

———. *The History of the Decline and Fall of the Roman Empire*. 4 vols. Philadelphia: B. F. French, 1880.

Inscription: signed by Asher Tyler, possibly a previous owner.

Catalog: Ball 2016 inventory, 4 vols., brown leather, water stains, fair condition.

Location: Quarry Farm Library, under the supervision of the Mark Twain Archive, Elmira College, Elmira, New York. This work was available to Clemens whenever he visited Quarry Farm in Elmira.

GIBBS, GEORGE FORT (1870–1942). *The Love of Monsieur, A Novel*. New York: Harper & Brothers, 1903. 297 pp.

Source: MTLAcc, entry #1558, volume donated by Clemens.

A historical romance by a prolific author of adventures tales, this one set in seventeenth-century England and on the high seas.

GIBSON, EVA KATHARINE (CLAPP) (1857–1916) [Some sources spell her middle name Katherine, but the title page of *Zauberlinda* and her newspaper obituary spelled it Katharine.]. *Zauberlinda, the Wise Witch*. Illustrated by Mabel Tibbitts. Chicago: R. Smith Ptg. Co., [cop. 1901]. 256 pp.

Source: MTLAcc, entry #455, volume donated by Clemens.

This children's fantasy novel, Gibson's only book written for children, was inspired by L Frank Baum's *The Wonderful*

Wizard of Oz (1900). Her other novels primarily depicted life on the prairies of the Upper Midwest.

GIBSON, WILLIAM HAMILTON (1850–1896). *Camp Life in the Woods and the Tricks of Trapping*. Illustrated by the author. New York: Harper & Brothers, [cop. 1881]. 300 pp.

Source: MTLAcc, entry #792, volume donated by Clemens.

———. *Highways and By-ways; or Saunterings in New England*. Illustrated by the author. 4to. New York: Harper & Brothers, 1883. 157 pp.

Catalogs: *A1911*, "small folio, decorative cloth (a trifle stained), N.Y. 1883," quotes manuscript notes by Clemens on an envelope laid in, lot 184, sold for $5.50; Walpole Galleries (New York City), Catalogue 112 (21 February 1919), item #124.

Location: Mark Twain House and Museum, Hartford, Connecticut. Donated in 1976 by Aileen Harlow, according to Polly Peck, then Library Chairman.

Copy examined: Clemens's copy, unmarked. It has an *A1911* sale label.

———. *Pastoral Days, or Memories of a New England Year*. Illustrated by the author. First edition. Original green cloth, gilt. New York: Harper & Brothers, 1881. 153 pp.

Inscription: laid in is a Christmas package label inscribed by Olivia Clemens: "C[harles]. J[ervis]. L[angdon]. A Merry Christmas." (Charles J. Langdon was Olivia's brother.) Subsequently the author and artist Gibson visited Elmira and inscribed this volume: "W. Hamilton Gibson/Elmira, N. Y./Jan. 5, 1895." No marginalia are visible.

Provenance: the Langdon family library.

Location: collection of Kevin Mac Donnell, Austin, Texas (Mac Donnell to Alan Gribben, 29 November 2011). Purchased from the Langdon family.

The Clemenses ordered two copies of *Pastoral Days* on 20 December 1880, according to a bill they received on 1 January 1881 from Brown & Gross, Hartford booksellers. They paid for the volumes on 17 January 1881 (receipt in MTP).

———. *Pastoral Days, or Memories of a New England Year*. Illustrated by the author. First edition. Original green cloth, gilt; worn at all extremities and shows moderate thumbing. New York: Harper & Brothers, 1881. 153 pp.

Catalog: *A1911*, "small folio, decorative cloth, gilt top and edges (joints somewhat weak, and a fly-leaf missing), N.Y. 1881," quotes an "accompanying . . . verse of four lines" written in Clemens's hand, lot 183, sold for $7.25. René Kelly would publish these same four lines of dialect humor in *Harper's Weekly* 62.3094 (8 April 1916): 372, attributing them to Clemens and reporting that they were "scribbled on a flyleaf" [*sic*] in a copy of W. H. Gibson's *Pastoral Days* "sold at auction in New York a few winters ago." Clemens wrote: "De lady bug hab de golden wing/ De firefly hab de flame/De bedbug doan' hab noth'n 'tall/ But he git dah all de same."

Location: collection of Kevin Mac Donnell, Austin, Texas. Acquired in July 1881 for $125.

Copy examined: Clemens's copy, in July 2004. Has the *A1911* sale label. No annotations except for a blue crayon mark on the front pastedown endpaper and the number "22" penciled on the rear pastedown endpaper. The lines of dialect verse are no longer present, so they must have been laid in and eventually lost.

———. *Pastoral Days, or Memories of a New England Year*. Illustrated by the author. New York: Harper & Brothers, 1886. 153 pp. [Publisher and pages conjectured.]

Catalog: *A1911*, "4to, cloth, gilt edges, N.Y. 1886," sheet of manuscript notes laid in, lot 185, sold for $2.

———. *Sharp Eyes; A Rambler's Calendar of Fifty-Two Weeks Among Insects, Birds, and Flowers*. Illustrated by the author. New York: Harper & Brothers, 1904. 322 pp.

Source: MTLAcc, entry #1180, volume donated by Clemens.

———. [Another identical copy. Original pale green decorated cloth, stamped in silver and letters in gilt, top edge gilt, uncut.]

Inscription: inscribed by Susan Crane to her niece, Ida Langdon (1880–1964) in ink on the front free endpaper: "Ida Langdon/Elmira, N. Y./Christmas/1892." A later inscription was added below this by the author-illustrator during his visit to Elmira: "W. Hamilton Gibson/Elmira, N. Y./Jan 4, 1895." A letter laid in from Susan Crane to Ida expressed a wish that Ida might someday write and illustrate her own book.

Location: collection of Kevin Mac Donnell, Austin, Texas. Purchased from the Langdon family.

Source: supplementary inventory sent to Alan Gribben by Mac Donnell on 28 August 2017. Mac Donnell reported that the text had no markings.

———. *Strolls by Starlight and Sunshine*. Original decorated green cloth, gilt, all edges gilt. New York: Harper & Brothers, 1891. 194 pp.

Inscription: autograph letter from Gibson laid in: "Jan 11, 1895/To Gen. & Mrs. C. J. Langdon/with the grateful remembrance of/The Author/W. Hamilton/Gibson." Gibson sent this book one week after visiting the Langdon home in Elmira.

Location: collection of Kevin Mac Donnell, Austin, Texas. Purchased from the Langdon family.

Source: supplementary information sent by Mac Donnell to Alan Gribben on 28 August 2017. No markings in the text, according to Mac Donnell.

Gibson's drawings display many dozens of flowers that either bloom in the daytime or at night. Could the Langdons have resisted an opportunity to show Clemens this prize when he next visited their home in Elmira?

GIBSON, WILLIS. "Arkansas Fashion," *Century Magazine* 70.2 (June 1905): 276–292. [Illustrated by Walter Jack Duncan (1881–1941).]

Isabel Lyon wrote to Richard Watson Gilder of the *Century* on 1 June 1905 from Dublin, New Hampshire: "Mr. Clemens wishes me to ask you if you will be good enough to send him the address of the author of the delightful story 'Arkansas Fashion,' if you have it" (PH in MTP). Clemens's pleasure in the short story is easily explained: not only does it employ regional dialects and feature a hero from the state of Arkansas, familiar to Clemens from his years as a river pilot, but Gibson repeatedly alludes to the works of Mark Twain in the most flattering manner possible.

The story takes place at Saint's Rest, Minnesota—a railroad depot that gathered no town around it. Humdrum duties at the isolated depot disgust the first telegraph operator, who transfers to Powderly, Iowa. Then Kirby Harbin, a former resident of Arkansas, takes the job at Saint's Rest and is contented. He plays his banjo, smokes a pipe, and savors *Adventures of Huckleberry Finn*. Harbin's cat—named Tom Sawyer—snoozes complacently in the sun beside him. But the I *&* I Railroad engineers and workers go on strike and Harbin's tiny station becomes a battleground over a load of refrigerated peaches bound for Chicago. Scab laborers attempt to deliver the peaches, and strikers gather at Saint's Rest to stop them. A fight ensues, the strikers win out, and the peaches are temporarily returned north to Selby. Kirby Harbin resumes his pipe, his banjo-playing, and his copy of *Huckleberry Finn*. But the battle over the peaches occurs again at Saint's Rest, with the same results. Once more Kirby Harbin repairs the damage to his depot and takes up his reading. But when yet another set-to shapes up over the peaches, the disgusted Arkansan couples the two opposing trains together and uses one locomotive to move the cause of the argument away from his placid domain. The strikers and scabs join forces in an effort to retake the engine from the angry station agent; Harbin retaliates by opening the throttle fully. He refuses to stop the train until he has delivered the peaches south to Division headquarters, quite a feat for someone who has never himself operated a locomotive, but has only observed the engineers. The taciturn young hero brushes aside the superintendent's thanks and simply asks to borrow a copy of *Huckleberry Finn* until he can return to his depot haven at Saint's Rest. Gibson wrote seven other short stories between 1901 and 1905 for *Century*, *Scribner's*, *McClure's*, and the *Saturday Evening Post*.

GIFFORD, EVELYN. *Provenzano the Proud*. London: Smith, Elder & Co., 1904. 331 pp.

Source: MTLAcc, entry #2252, volume donated from Clemens's library by Clara Clemens Gabrilowitsch in 1910. Gifford set her historical novel in Siena, Italy in the years 1267–68.

GIFFORD, FRANKLIN KENT (1861–1948), pseud. "Richard Brinsley Newman." *The Belle Islers; A Novel*. Illustrated by Wallace Goldsmith (1873–1945). Boston: Lothrop, Lee & Shepard Co., 1908. 423 pp.

Source: MTLAcc, entry #868, volume presented by an unknown donor, possibly Clemens. Gifford's fiction took place in Presque Isle and Aroostook County, Maine.

GILBERT, JAMES STANLEY (1855–1906). *Panama Patchwork; Poems, by James Stanley Gilbert*. Intro. by Tracy Robinson (1833–1915). Second ed., revised and enlarged. Panama: Star & Herald Co., 1905. 172 pp.

Inscriptions: inscribed on the front free endpaper in black ink, "'Mark Twain'/A reminder of the 'Ends of the Earth', from one of the 'Ends' where he is admired and esteemed by a 'Band of Brothers'./With the lasting regard of/J. S. Gilbert/Colon 1906". On the front pastedown endpaper is another inscription: "And its me as put Gilbert up to sending this—& its me as put some paper clips to mark some things that did me good & its me that is glad I'm leaving for Home—this 8th of April, 1906/Yours ever/Poultney Bigelow/Colon".

Marginalia: a clipping inside the volume reports Gilbert's death on 15 August 1906; Clemens wrote on the clipping: "Enclosed by Tracy Robinson". (Tracy Robinson was the U. S. vice-consul in Panama.) The obituary

article was clipped from the Colon, Panama *Independent*, 17 August 1906. On page 2 Clemens altered "drank" to "drunk" in black ink in the margin. At page 7 Clemens made a vertical bracket in black ink in the poem titled "Beyond the Changres" next to the lines: "That beyond the Changres River/All paths lead straight to hell!" There is a paper marker inserted between pages 10 and 11 and another placed between pages 38 and 39. Clemens made markings in black ink throughout the poems. He made either "X" marks or vertical lines in black ink on pages 62, 63, 67, 69, 76, 85, 90, 96, 99, 101, 112, 116, 117, 118, 129, 132, 133, 135, 148, and 149. In other places in the book he underlined words or phrases. On page 128 ("The Prayer of a Timid Man") below the lines "Reply to my unspoken questions—/The questions I dare not repeat!," Clemens wrote: "An old, old prayer—& was never yet answered." Someone else, apparently Poultney Bigelow (to judge from the ink), marked additional pages.

Location: Mark Twain Library, Redding, Connecticut. Donated by Clemens (MTLAcc, entry #1690).

Copy examined: Clemens's copy. Has the red ink Mark Twain Library accession number "1690". The rear free endpaper, which contained a note in black ink, has been torn out. A pin in the front flyleaf formerly held a now-missing clipping or note. Examined in 1970 and again in June 1972 and on 8 November 2019.

GILBERT, WILLIAM SCHWENCK (1836–1911). *H. M. S. Pinafore* (operetta, produced in 1878). Music composed by Arthur S[eymour]. Sullivan (1842–1900).

"One day I was there at dinner, and remarked, in a general way, that we are all liars. She was amazed, and said, 'Not *all*?' It was before 'Pinafore's' time, so I did not make the response which would naturally follow in our day, but frankly said, 'Yes, *all*—we are all liars; there are no exceptions'" (Mark Twain's "On the Decay of the Art of Lying," published in 1882). Howard G. Baetzhold pointed out an instance of Twain's borrowing (in Chapter 8 of *A Connecticut Yankee in King Arthur's Court* [1889]) from one of Little Buttercup's songs: "Jackdaws strut in peacock's feathers" (*MT&JB* [1970], p. 116).

———. *Iolanthe* (operetta, produced in 1882). Music composed by Arthur S[eymour]. Sullivan (1842–1900).

Susy Clemens appeared as Phyllis in the Bryn Mawr production that Olivia watched in February 1891. Men were not invited to the performance (*S&MT* [1965], p. 286). *MT&JB* (1970), p. 127.

———. *The Mikado* (operetta, produced in 1885). Music composed by Arthur S[eymour]. Sullivan (1842–1900).

On 18 April 1886 Susy Clemens recorded in her diary that "mama and papa Clara and Daisy [Margaret Warner] have gone to New York to see the 'Mikado'" (*Family Sketch* [2014], p. 158). "Mikado Music," Clemens noted in May 1886 (NB 26, *N&J* 3: 234). In "The Man That Corrupted Hadleyburg" (1899, Part 3), "Somebody wailed in, and began to sing this rhyme . . . to the lovely 'Mikado' tune of 'When a man's afraid of a beautiful maid'; the audience joined in, with joy"; they sing this "Mikado travesty" repeatedly throughout the town meeting. The lines are actually "When a man's afraid,/A beautiful maid/Is a cheering sight to see."

Baetzhold, *MT&JB* (1970), pp. 228–229.

————. *Patience; or, Bunthorne's Bride.* Libretto by Arthur S[eymour]. Sullivan (1842–1900). First edition, No. 15 of 100 copies. Original brown cloth-backed boards with label. New York: Doubleday, Page & Company, 1902. 92 pp.

Inscriptions: the front pastedown endpaper is signed in black ink, "S L. Clemens/Dec. 1902." The front free endpaper is inscribed: "To Paul and Florence with an awful lot of love—*Cause* I know you will appreciate Gilbert—Mark Twain and *ME*. D[add?]y. July 6, 1936."

Catalog: *A1911*, "8vo, boards, cloth back, gilt top, uncut, N.Y. 1902, No. 15 of 100 copies printed," quotes the signature, lot 186, sold for $3.75.

Location: collection of Kevin Mac Donnell, Austin, Texas. He acquired the volume in October 1977 for $85.

Copy examined: Clemens's unmarked copy, in July 2004. The volume bears the *A1911* sale label.

Clemens's household had been familiar with this operetta (produced in 1881) for two decades. Young Susy Clemens wrote to her father during his Mississippi River tour in 1882 about her hearing a visitor to the Hartford home play "some pieces from Patience" (*LLMT* [1949], p. 209).

————. *The Yeomen of the Guard* (operetta, produced in 1888). Music composed by Arthur S[eymour]. Sullivan (1842–1900).

In 1895 Mark Twain praised Gilbert in a newspaper interview for "saying not only the wittiest of things," but for "saying them in verse." He spoke of the "grinning skull" behind Gilbert's humor, and alluded to the jester Jack Point in *Yeomen of the Guard* (Sydney, Australia *Morning Herald*, 17 September 1895; quoted in *MT&JB* [1970], pp. 116, 228, 341 n. 26; also by Scharnhorst, ed., *Complete Interviews*, p. 205).

GILCHRIST, ALEXANDER (1828–1861). *Life of William Blake, "Pictor Ignotus."* 2 vols. Illus. London: Macmillan and Co., 1863. [Author, title, and edition conjectured.]

In November 1878 Clemens noted, "Wm Blake, poet & painter" (NB 17, *N&J* 2: 244). A memorandum on the back flyleaf of the same notebook reminded him to "Return . . . 'Life of Blake'" (*N&J* 2: 281).

GILDER, JEANNETTE LEONARD (1849–1916). *The Tomboy at Work.* Illustrated by Florence Scovel Shinn (1871–1940). Tan cloth. New York: Doubleday, Page & Co., 1904. 252 pp.

Inscription: Gilder inscribed the verso of the front free endpaper in black ink. Clemens signed and inscribed the title page in black ink: "SL. Clemens/1908/From the Author."

Provenance: Antenne-Dorrance Collection, Rice Lake, Wisconsin.

Location: Mark Twain Archive, Gannett-Tripp Learning Center, Elmira College, Elmira, New York.

Copy examined: Clemens's unmarked copy. Examined on 28 May 2015.

Gilder, then the chief editor of *The Critic*, a monthly review of literature, drama, and art, provided this affectionate sequel to her *The Autobiography of a Tomboy* (1900). In thinly disguised autobiographical detail she recounted here the trials and rewards of making a career of journalism and editing.

————. *The Tomboy at Work.* Illustrated by Florence Scovel Shinn (1871–1940). New York: Doubleday, Page & Co., 1904. 252 pp.

Location: Mark Twain Library, Redding, Connecticut.

Copy examined: an unmarked copy that did not belong to Clemens or his family. It has no library stamps or accession number. The book had been added to the Clemens collection sometime after 1970 and before June 1982, when I revisited Redding. I recommended that this book be separated from the volumes donated by Clemens and his daughter Clara Clemens Gabrilowitsch.

GILDER, JOSEPH BENSON (1858–1936). "The Parting of the Ways" (poem), *Harper's Weekly* 44.2256 (17 March 1900): 251.

Mark Twain quotes this entire poem in "The Secret History of Eddypus," written 1901–1902 (*FM*, p. 349). "The Parting of the Ways" pleads with the United States to remember its ideals; the second stanza warns: "Before thy feet the ways divide:/One path leads up to heights sublime;/The other downward slopes, where bide/The refuse and the wrecks of Time." (Twain slightly altered the third line to read, "Downward the other slopes, where bide".) Gilder was the co-founder (1881) and co-editor of *The Critic*. His retrospective article, "Glimpses of John Hay, *The Critic* 47.3 (September 1905): 248–252, recalled an evening Gilder spent with Clemens, John Hay, Richard Watson Gilder, and Henry Adams at Adams' home in Washington, D.C. on 28 January 1886.

GILDER, RICHARD WATSON (1844–1909). *A Book of Music.* Original cloth, rubbing on edges and corners. New York: Century Co., 1906.

Inscription: inscribed by the author in ink on the half-title page, "To Clara Clemens/with the unassailed/regard & admiration of the/author of [title]/on this Xmas Day/1906. R W Gilder His/X/Mark."

Provenance: sold at the 1951 auction in Hollywood, but not listed in the sale sheet.

Location: Mark Twain House and Museum, Hartford, Connecticut.

Copy examined: Clara Clemens's unmarked copy. Viewed in Hartford in 1997.

A Book of Music gathers thirty of Gilder's poems on composers and musicians (Rubinstein, Essipoff, Handel, Paderewski, Wagner, and Beethoven) as well as the general theme of music.

————. *In the Heights.* Original cloth, rubbing on edges and corners. New York: Century Co., 1905.

Provenance: sold at the 1951 auction in Hollywood, but not listed in the sale sheet—a common error owing to the hastiness of the auction arrangements.

Location: Mark Twain House and Museum, Hartford, Connecticut.

Copy examined: Clemens's or Clara Clemens's unmarked copy. Viewed in Hartford in 1997.

Although Gilder was principally known as the editor-in-chief (1881–1909) of *Century Magazine*, he also published more than half a dozen books of poetry, including *In the Heights*. Clemens and Gilder maintained a lengthy social and professional friendship. Joseph B. Gilder's "Glimpses of John Hay," *Critic* 47.3 (September 1905): 248–252, recalled a memorable evening Gilder spent with Clemens, Richard Watson Gilder, John Hay, and Henry Adams at Adams' home in Washington, D.C. on 28 January 1886. In Mark Twain's "King Leopold's Soliloquy" (March 1905) King Leopold remarks that the poet Gilder and his *Century Magazine* led the crusade against the Russian Czar. On 7

December 1905 Isabel Lyon recorded: "This morning Mr. Clemens read me a very great poem by Mr. Gilder in the Times. It is a poem on this terrible massacring of Jews and peasants in Russia. Mr. Clemens said it was difficult to decide—you couldn't decide—if it was satire or not, unless you know your man" (IVL Journal, TS p. 112, MTP).

GILES, CHAUNCEY (1813–1893). *Our Children in the Other Life*. London: James Speirs, 1874. 75 pp.

> Source: MTLAcc, entry #927, volume donated by Clemens.
> Samuel and Olivia Clemens, having lost their son Langdon on 2 June 1972, might naturally have turned to a comforting book such as this one, specifically addressed (in its Introduction) to "bereaved and sorrowing parents" who "have been called upon to part with a most precious treasure." Chapter 7 takes up "How the Death of Children May Become a Ministry of Good to Parents" and "Infants in Heaven, from the Writings of Swedenborg."

GILL, WILLIAM (1842–1919) and HENRY E. DIXEY (1859–1943). *Adonis* (burlesque musical, produced at the Bijou Theatre in New York City in 1884–1885). Music composed by John Eller and Edward Rice (1847–1924).

> Susy Clemens's biography of her father recorded that the family "went to the theater and enjoyed 'Adonis'" (*A Family Sketch* [2014], p. 114).

GILLESPIE, O. CURTIS, comp. *Rumford Fireplaces and How They Are Made, . . . Containing Benjamin, Count of Rumford's Essay on "Proper Fireplace Construction."* Illus. New York: W. T. Comstock, 1906. 199 pp.

> Source: MTLAcc, entry #688, volume donated by Isabel V. Lyon, Clemens's secretary.
> Benjamin Thompson Rumford, inventor of a smokeless fireplace, lived 1753–1814.

GILLETTE, [HOOKER] WILLIAM (1853–1937). *The Professor* (play, produced in 1881). [Gillette's birth year has generally been given as 1855, but his gravesite listed it as 1853 and a number of reputable Connecticut historical sources now accept this revised date.]

> Gillette wrote and produced *The Professor*, and also played the title role of Professor Hopkins. Since Clemens lent financial backing to its production, he presumably saw it or at least read it. On 17 June 1880 he wrote to Susie and Lilly Warner that "it surely ought to succeed" in Madison Square Garden (MTP); in Notebook 24 he mentioned loaning money to Gillette that the actor-playwright intended to repay with proceeds from this play (1885, *N&J* 3: 133 n. 24); and Gillette wrote him about *The Professor* on 29 July 1886 (MTP).

———. *Secret Service* (play, produced in 1895).

> On 2 June 1897 Clemens asked Dr. James Ross Clemens to join him "and help me see Gillette's play, *Secret Service*," which had begun a run at the Adelphi Theatre in London on 15 May 1897 (*MTLW* [1932], p. 81); James Ross Clemens would mistakenly recall their attending this performance at the Strand Theatre, but he added the interesting detail that the two men sat in a stage box as guests ("Reminiscences of Mark Twain" [1929], p. 125). In the top margin of a manuscript page of the unfinished novel "Simon Wheeler, Detective" (written 1877–1898?) Mark Twain noted "Gillette's S S speech," probably referring to Gillette's role as Captain Thorne (*S&B*, pp. 310–311, 424 n. 47). Finley Peter Dunne noted that when Clemens

was in London, Gillette "promptly got up a dinner for him" at the Savoy Hotel with various distinguished guests, and that Clemens and Gillette kidded each other about the quality of their cigars (*Mr. Dooley Remembers: The Informal Memoirs of Finley Peter Dunne* [Boston: Little, Brown, 1963], pp. 248–249). That event took place on 1 July 1897 (Fears, *Day by Day* 3: 54). William Gillette was second on Mark Twain's list of ten nominees for election into the American Academy of Arts and Letters in 1905 (SLC to Robert Underwood Johnson, 28 April 1905, American Academy of Arts and Letters).

GILLIAM, E[DWARD]. W[ILLIAM]. (1834–1925). "Chinese Immigration," *North American Review* 143.356 (July 1886): 26–34.

> "I've read that fellow's article in the North American. With what delicious unconsciousness he gives himself away in his last sentence" (concerning stereotypes of racial superiority), Clemens wrote to William Dean Howells. Gilliam lauded "the Anglo-Saxon's glory" and warned against "the ethnological hell-broth" brewing in the nation (p. 34) (SLC to WDH, Elmira, 15 July 1886, *MTHL*, p. 572). Three years earlier Gilliam had urged the deportation of African Americans ("The African in the United States," *Popular Science Monthly* 22.28 [February 1883]: 433–444).

GILLIAT, EDWARD (1841–1915). *Forest Outlaws; or, Saint Hugh and the King.* Illus. New York: G. P. Putnam's Sons, 1887. 404 pp.

> Inscription: inscribed on the half-title page in black ink, "Clara Clemens/With the love of/Chas. Dudley Warner/ Dec 25 1886."
> Marginalia: there is a pencil mark on page 145. "Get there by Sunday" was written on page 150, not by Clemens.
> Provenance: Donated from Clemens's library by Clara Clemens Gabrilowitsch in 1910 (MTLAcc, entry #2253).
> Location: Mark Twain Library, Redding, Connecticut.
> Copy examined: Clara Clemens's unmarked copy. Has the red ink Mark Twain Library accession number "2253". Both the front free flyleaf and the rear free endpaper have been torn out, which might have contained Clemens's handwriting. The spine and binding are loose. Examined in 1970 and again in June 1982.
> Robin Hood figures prominently in this novel, which the Reverend Gilliat, "Assistant-Master in Harrow School," attested was based on twelfth-century historical documents.

GILLMORE, INEZ (HAYNES) (1873–1970). "The Story That Took," *McClure's Magazine* 25.2 (June 1905): 214–224.

> Gillmore's "The Story That Took," a teasing tale of misunderstandings and a coy courtship, was the last item in the June 1905 *McClure's* issue. Among other things, the story demonstrates that automobiles were beginning to appear in fiction. On 3 June 1905 Gillmore wrote to Clemens from Scituate, Massachusetts: "Mr. S. S. McClure has just sent me a letter quoting the charming and exciting and unforgettable thing that you wrote him about one of my first attempts at fiction, 'The Story That Took' in the June McClure. . . . I am still young enough not to be able to sleep through most of the night that followed that event" (MTP). Already a prolific short story writer for the leading magazines, Gillmore's career would continue in this direction.

GILMAN, CHARLOTTE (PERKINS) (1860–1935).

Gilman's diaries contain several favorable references to Mark Twain, but no confirmation that this feminist author ever met him. Entries on 25 August and 1 September 1881 recorded that she "read Mark Twain" to a young friend (*Diaries*, pp. 75, 76). On 29 August 1883 she would "read Mark Twain's 'Prince & Pauper' during the day, and thoroughly *enjoy* it" (p. 218). Eight years later, on 12 May 1891, she was called on in California by "Mrs. Moffat [*sic*] (sister of 'Mark Twain')," presumably Pamela Moffett (1827–1904) (p. 454). On 16 June 1893, living in Oakland, California, she met Will M. Clemens (1860–1931), whose *Mark Twain, His Life and Work* (1892) had annoyed its subject enormously: "Mr. Will Clemens calls while I'm out—& goes over to Miss Coolbrith's. I go over there. Most interesting evening—most interesting man. He speaks of lodging here" (p. 536). A few days later, on June 22nd, "Mr. Clemens calls to look at rooms. Brings a copy of his 'Life of Mark Twain' to Miss Coolbrith, Delle, & me. Also brings his novel typewritten and leaves it with me" (p. 537). Nearly a decade later, having moved to New York City, Gilman would "go to Macy's & get some small things, including N. A. Review for Mark Twain['] splendid article on Xian science" (p. 829). See *The Diaries of Charlotte Perkins Gilman*, ed. Denise D. Knight. 2 vols. (Charlottesville: University Press of Virginia, 1994). See also the Catalog entry for Will M. Clemens.

[GILMAN, STELLA (SCOTT) (1844–1928).] *Mothers in Council*. New York: Harper & Brothers, 1884. 194 pp.

Source: MTLAcc, entry #395, volume donated by Clemens. With the names disguised, this book recorded the activities of the Mothers' Club of Cambridge, a group formed in 1878 whose forty members met to discuss problems with their children as well as concerns about the welfare of underprivileged children.

GILMORE, PATRICK SARSFIELD (1829–1892), pseud. "Louis Lambert." "When Johnny comes marching home" (song, published in 1863).

In "Answers to Correspondents" (June 1865) Mark Twain recommended poetry that is "spirited—something like 'Johnny Comes Marching Home'"; in "'Mark Twain' on the Ballad Infliction," however, he complained that "a year ago that song was sung by everybody, in every key, in every locality, at all hours of the day and night, always out of tune" (San Francisco *Californian*, 4 November 1865; *MTWY* [1938], p. 194; *ET&S* 2: 186, 194). The pianist in "The Scriptural Panoramist" (*Californian*, 18 November 1865) strikes up, "Oh, we'll all get blind drunk/When Johnny comes marching home!" (*ET&S* 2: 364). Twain mentioned "When Johnny Comes Marching Home" as part of "the popular-song nuisance" (Sacramento *Weekly Union*, 28 April 1866; *LSI* [1938], p. 51). On 1 January 1867 he grumbled about the ship choir's singing these "wretchedest old songs" while afloat among scenic splendors (*MTTMB* [1940], p. 59). In Twain's lamented Whittier Birthday Dinner speech on 17 December 1877, the three literary impostors compel the narrator to sing this song repeatedly—"till I dropped" (*MTB* [1912], p. 1646). The residents of Hope Canyon sing "When Johnny Comes Marching Home" in Chapter 5 of "A Double-Barrelled Detective Story" (1902), and Twain

alludes to "that rollicking frenzy of a tune" in Chapter 13 of "A Horse's Tale" (1906).

GILSON, ROY ROLFE (1875–1933). *In the Morning Glow; Short Stories*. Illus. New York: Harper & Brothers, 1904. 187 pp.

Source: MTLAcc, entry #1496, volume donated by Clemens.

———. *Miss Primrose. A Novel*. New York: Harper & Brothers, 1906. 295 pp.

Source: MTLAcc, entry #142, volume donated by Clemens.

———. *When Love is Young. A Novel*. New York: Harper & Brothers, 1901, 283 pp.

Source: MTLAcc, entry #141, volume donated by Clemens.

GINDELY, ANTON (1829–1892). *Geschichte des dreissigjähri-gen Krieges [History of the Thirty Years' War]*. 4 vols. Prag, 1869–1880.

When Clemens listed his current reading to Edward H. House on 14 January 1884, he included "in German . . . the third volume of The Thirty-Years' War" (ASSSCL). Shortly thereafter the work became available in translation: *History of the Thirty Years' War*. Trans. by A. Ten Broek. 2 vols. (New York: G. P. Putnam's Sons, 1884).

Ginn & Company's Classical Atlas, in Twenty-three Coloured Maps, with Complete Index. Edited by James Cranstoun [1837–1901] after an edition projected and executed by the late A[lexander]. Keith Johnston [1804–1871]. Boston: Ginn & Co., n. d. [Evidently published in 1886. Cranstoun's preface was signed on 1 March 1886 in Edinburgh, where the index and maps were printed.] Each section is paginated separately.

Location: Mark Twain Library, Redding, Connecticut.

Copy examined: very likely Clemens's, unmarked. Has the red ink Mark Twain Library accession number "3884". It was shelved with Clemens's books when I revisited the Mark Twain Library in June 1982 and on 8 November 2019.

This atlas assembles twenty-three ancient maps of Britannia, Hispania, Italia, and other countries.

GIRARDIN, DELPHINE (GAY) DE (1804–1855), pseud. "Mme. Émile de Girardin." *La joie fait pèur; comédie en un acte, par Mme. Émile de Girardin [Joy Frightens; A Comedy in One Act]*. English notes by Ferdinand Bôcher (1837–1902). College Series of Modern French Plays, No. 1. New York: Leypoldt & Holt, 1870. 46 pp.

Inscription: signed on the second flyleaf, "Livy L Clemens/1873".

Location: Mark Twain Library, Redding, Connecticut.

Copy examined: Olivia Clemens's unmarked copy.

Clara Clemens listed this author and title in her commonplace book sometime between 1888 and 1904 (Paine 150, MTP).

GIRDLESTONE, ARTHUR GILBERT (1842–1908). *The High Alps Without Guides: Being a Narrative of Adventures in Switzerland, Together with Chapters on the Practicability of Such Mode of Mountaineering, and Suggestions for Its Accomplishment*. London: Longmans, Green & Co., 1870. 181 pp. [Edition conjectured.]

On 28 August 1878 Clemens noted the title of Girdlestone's book and reminded himself to acquire a copy; he had just seen Girdlestone himself ("a long, wiry, whiskered man"), who was "starting up some new break-neck place with a friend" (NB 16, *N&J* 2: 164–165). While Clemens was working on the Swiss Alps section of *A Tramp Abroad* on

25 April 1879, he wrote to remind Andrew Chatto that he was awaiting his copy of Girdlestone's *High Alps* (TS in MTP). In Chapter 36 of *A Tramp Abroad* (1880) he referred to Girdlestone as "the famous Englishman who hunts his way to the most formidable Alpine summits without a guide."

GLASGOW, ELLEN ANDERSON GHOLSON (1873–1945). *The Ancient Law*. New York: Doubleday, Page & Co., 1908. 485 pp.
    Source: MTLAcc, entry #1006, volume donated by Clemens.
    A convicted financier seeks atonement.
———. *The Voice of the People*. New York: Doubleday, Page & Co., 1900. 444 pp.
    Source: MTLAcc, entry #2254, volume donated from Clemens's library by Clara Clemens Gabrilowitsch in 1910.
    The first of Glasgow's novel set in Virginia, *The Voice of the People* depicted the post-Civil War hardships and social class tensions in the American South. The plot involves the tragedy of a lynching.

GLAZIER, WILLARD (1841–1905). *Three Years in the Federal Cavalry*. Illus. New York: R. H. Ferguson & Co., 1873. 347 pp.
    Provenance: bookplate #654 of the "J. Langdon Family Library" on the front pastedown endpaper.
    Catalog: Ball 2016 inventory, red cloth, gilt lettering, black design, J. Langdon's Family Library #654.
    Location: Mark Twain Archive, Elmira College, Elmira, New York.
    Copy examined: unmarked copy available to Clemens whenever he visited Elmira. Examined on 27 May 2015.

The Globe: A Magazine of Literary Record and Criticism (Buffalo, New York, published 1873–1876).
    In April 1873 Clemens wrote a note to the *Globe's* editor, William C. Cornwell, responding to a critical sketch about Clemens's personality that had appeared in *The Globe* 1 (May 1873): 28–29 (*MTLet* 5: 329).

GLYN, ELINOR (SUTHERLAND) (1864–1943). *Three Weeks* (novel, published in 1907).
    Glyn visited Clemens at the end of 1907 in the hope of gaining a prominent champion for her recently published novel. In his Autobiographical Dictation of 13 January 1908 Clemens gave a lengthy account of their interview and a synopsis of her novel, conceding that "its literary workmanship was excellent," but explaining why he disappointed her by refusing to defend her views publicly. Although his notions about the innate laws of Nature accorded with hers, and he spoke to her "with daring frankness" about adultery ("one of the damnedest conversations I have ever had with a beautiful stranger of her sex"), nevertheless "her book was an assault upon certain old and well-established and wise conventions, and . . . it would not find many friends, and indeed, would not deserve many" (*MTE*, pp. 314–316; *AutoMT* 3: 195–198). Elinor Glyn gave her version of this interview in *Mark Twain on Three Weeks* (privately printed, 1908) and in her 350-page autobiography, *Romantic Adventure* (London: Ivor Nicholson and Watson, 1936). On page 144 of the latter book she recounted Twain's refusal to endorse her controversial novel. See also Charles Henry Meltzer (1853–1936), "Twain Says He Told Her 'Book a Mistake,'" New York *American*, 27 September 1908

(Scharnhorst, *Complete Interviews*, pp. 673–674).
    Vincent L. Barnett, *Elinor Glyn as Novelist, Moviemaker, Glamour Icon, and Businesswoman* (Farnham, Surrey, UK: Ashgate, 2014).

"GO, CHAIN THE LION DOWN" (spiritual).
    Clemens included this spiritual in a list of what appear to be his favorite songs in August 1889 (NB 29, *N&J* 3: 513). Clara Clemens recalled it as one of the songs her father frequently "rendered in a truly impressive way, despite the fact that musically certain lacks were noticeable" (*MFMT* [1931], p. 188). "Go, chain the lion down" was published by J. B. T. Marsh in *The Story of the Jubilee Singers, with Their Songs*. Rev. ed. (Boston: Houghton, Mifflin and Co., 1880), p. 174. Its first stanza repeats the title three times and ends, "Before the heav'n doors close."

[GODDARD, MARTHA (LE BARON) (1829–1888) and HARRIET WATERS PRESTON (1843–1911), compilers.] *Sea and Shore: A Collection of Poems*. Boston: Roberts Brothers, 1874. [Published anonymously.]
    Inscription: on the verso of the front flyleaf, "With the regards of/M. LeB. Goddard". Clemens wrote on the title page: "SL. Clemens/from/Thomas Bailey Aldrich./ Oct. 31, 1905."
    Marginalia: the name "Kingsley" [?] appears on page 77, not in Clemens's hand. There are pencil marks in the index of first lines at the back of the book.
    Provenance: Antenne-Dorrance Collection, Rice Lake, Wisconsin.
    Location: Mark Twain Archive, Gannett-Tripp Learning Center, Elmira College, Elmira, New York.
    Copy examined: Clemens's copy.
    The poems in *Sea and Shore* all have the sea or sailing as their theme; the poets range from Homer, Pindar, and Euripides to Longfellow, Bayard Taylor, and Elizabeth Stuart Phelps.

Godey's Lady's Book (monthly periodical, Philadelphia, published 1830–1898). [Sarah Josepha (Buell) Hale (1788–1879) was the editor from 1837 until 1877. The title varied, and in its middle years the cover sometimes read *Godey's Lady's Book and Magazine*.]
    Godey's published an unflattering ("it does not do full justice to its author") anonymous review of *Mark Twain's (Burlesque) Autobiography and First Romance* (82.492 [June 1871]: 575). Clemens browsed through the February 1834 issue while he lodged in a boarding house in Hamilton, Bermuda with Joseph H. Twichell in May 1877 (NB 13, *N&J* 2: 21). "The House Beautiful" in Chapter 38 of *Life on the Mississippi* (1883) contains the "current number of the chaste and innocuous 'Godey's Lady's Book,' with painted fashion-plate of wax-figure women with mouths all alike—lips and eyelids the same size—each five-foot woman with a two-inch wedge sticking from under her dress and letting-on to be half of her foot." The narrator of "Which Was the Dream?" (written in 1897), imaginatively reliving his life, awakens in the 1850s in a California mining cabin whose walls are graced by "a number of steel engravings from Godey's Lady's Book" (*WWD?*, p. 68). See also the Catalog entry for C. E. S. S. Norton's "The Broken Vow."

"GO DOWN, MOSES" (spiritual, antebellum date).
    Clemens made a list of songs he liked in 1889; it included

"Go Down Moses" (Notebook 29, *N&J* 3: 513).

"GOD SAVE THE KING" (British national anthem, sometimes attributed to Henry Carey, c. 1687–1743).

Clemens noted in Victoria, British Columbia that when nobility entered the hall, "several bars of God Save the Queen played" (NB 35 [August 1895], TS pp. 31–32). Clemens was present in 1907 when Senator Clark of Montana "rose to the tune of . . . 'God Save the King,' frantically sawed and thumped by the fiddlers and the piano" during speeches at the Union League Club (28 January 1907 AD, *MTE* [1940], p. 76; *AutoMT* 2: 389).

GOETHE, JOHANN WOLFGANG VON (1749–1832). *Aus meinem Leben: Dichtung, und Wahrheit [From My Life: Poetry and Truth]*. Illus. 2 vols. Berlin, 1873.

Catalog: *A1911*, "2 vols., 12mo, half calf, Berlin, 1873, with numerous marked paragraphs," with a sheet of notes about German words laid in, lot 188, sold for $4.

———. "Der Erlkönig" (poem, ballad).

Clemens quoted from the poem about the elf king while he was in Munich in December 1878 (NB 17, *N&J* 2: 255). In 1889 he made a memorandum to obtain "3 Erl-Königs" (NB 29, *N&J* 3: 513).

———. *Faust*. Paris: A. Quantin & Cie., 1869. 60 pp. Paperbound.

Source: MTLAcc, entry #390, volume donated by Clemens.

———. *Faust; A Tragedy*. Trans. by Thomas James Arnold (1804–1877). Illustrated by Alexander Liezen Mayer (1839–1898) with ornaments by Rudolf [von] Seitz (1842–1910). Munich: T. Stroefer, 1877. [Publisher conjectured.]

Catalog: *A1911*, "folio, full stamped morocco, gilt edges, Munich, [1877]," with a small sheet of manuscript laid in, lot 191, sold for $3.50.

At the end of December 1878 Clemens wrote from Munich to his mother- in-law: "I want to thank you very sincerely for the magnificent 'Faust' which you sent me Xmas. It is of an edition which has made the most of a stir of any that has ever appeared except for the one with [Wilhelm von] Kaulbach's illustrations. The man who drew the fine pictures for this book . . . is an Austrian with an American wife, & lives in Munich. . . . There are two or three pictures of Margaret in this new Faust which beat Kaulbach to pieces" (MTMH). Olivia Clemens apparently purchased the volume in Munich at her mother's behest: Olivia's account book for 1878 contains an entry for "'Faust' illustrated for Mr Clemens" under the heading of "Mother's account" (MTP).

———. *Faust. A Tragedy*. Translated by Bayard Taylor (1825–1878). 2 vols. Boston: Houghton Mifflin and Co., Riverside Press, 1879.

Catalog: *A1911*, "2 vols., small 4to, full dark brown morocco, gilt edges (a front fly-leaf missing in each volume), Bost.: Riverside Press, 1879," with a manuscript notes laid in, lot 190, sold for $2.75.

On 20 March 1884 Clemens wrote to his business agent in New York City, Charles L. Webster: "I wish you would buy & send to me an *Unbound* copy of Bayard Taylor's translation of Goethe's 'Faust.' I mean to divide it up into 100-page parts and bind each part in a flexible cover—to read in bed" (*MTBus*, p. 242). Accordingly, the statement of Clemens's personal expenses that he received from Webster on 2 September 1884 charged him for the purchase on 10 April 1884 of "1 Taylor's Faust" for $5.80 (MTP).

———. *Faust. Eine Tragödie*. Ed. by William Dwight Whitney (1827–1894). Introduction and notes by William Cook (1842–1882). Whitman's German Texts Series. New York: Henry Holt and Co., 1878. 229 pp.

Catalog: Ball 2016 inventory, green cloth, black lettering and design, good condition.

Location: Quarry Farm library shelves, under the supervision of the Mark Twain Archive, Elmira College, Elmira, New York.

This German language edition was available to Clemens whenever he visited Quarry Farm in Elmira.

———. *Faust: A Tragedy*. 2 vols. Translated from the German by Bayard Taylor (1825–1878). Boston: Houghton, Osgood and Co, 1879.

Inscription: the front flyleaf of Volume I is signed "Ida C. Langdon." Ida Clark Langdon (1849–1934) was married to Charles Jervis Langdon (1849–1916).

Provenance: bookplates of the "J. Langdon Family Library," #585 and #586. This was among the books available to Clemens whenever he visited Elmira, New York.

Catalog: Ball 2016 inventory, green cloth with gilt on the spine and cover.

Location: Mark Twain Archive, Gannett-Tripp Learning Center, Elmira College, Elmira, New York.

The fact that Taylor received only a pittance for his translation never ceased to amaze Clemens. "Bayard Taylor's noble translation of Faust filled the English-speaking world with his fame," Clemens reminded Mary Mason Fairbanks on 31 October 1877, "but he told me his copyright has only yielded him five dollars thus far" (*MTMF* [1949], p. 211). Taylor was Clemens's fellow passenger in 1878 on the *Holsatia* en route to Germany, where Taylor was to begin his duties as the United States ambassador; Clemens later told Henry W. Fisher that he heard Taylor "recite whole acts of his metric translation of Faust" on the ship (*AMT* [1922], p. 139). After Taylor's sudden death, Clemens recalled disgustedly in Munich in January 1879 that despite the popularity of his *Faust* Taylor earned only "$5 for 2 yrs work" on the project (NB 17, *N&J* 2: 268). In September 1887 Clemens noted that Taylor's "royalties in Goethe's Faust were $1,000" (NB 27, *N&J* 3: 321). Toward the end of his life Clemens referred to Taylor as the poet who "made the best of all English translations of Goethe's 'Faust'" (7 July 1908 AD, *AutoMT* 3: 246).

Clemens mentioned *Faust* in July 1897 (NB 42, TS p. 22), and made up a comic English slang translation of a few lines from *Faust* for the amusement of Henry W. Fisher in Vienna (*AMT*, p. 192). Describing his knowledge of German literature in an 1897 newspaper interview in Vienna, Clemens said he read Goethe in the original German, "although he 'just did overcome the second part of *Faust*'" (Odessa *News* [Odesskie *Novosti*], 8 October 1897; translated and reprinted by M. Thomas Inge and George Munro, "Ten Minutes with Mark Twain," *American Literary Realism* 15.2 [Autumn 1982]: 262). In Twain's "Conversations with Satan," written in Vienna in 1898, the devil has the features of "Don Quixotte," Richelieu, or Sir Henry Irving playing Mephistopheles (Paine 155, MTP). In "Which Was It?" (written 1899–1903) Twain describes Deathshead Phillips as "clothed from skull-cap to stockings in dead and lustreless black. . . . The cut of the raiment was not modern, but ancient and mephistophelian" (*WWD?*, p. 268). Goethe is mentioned in "The Secret History of Eddypus" (written 1901–1902) as one of the "extraordinary men" of the nineteenth century (*FM*, p. 357). In 1904 Twain constructed a spoof of *Faust*, "Sold to Satan," in which the soul-seller is surprised that Satan arrives noiselessly without any thunderclap or stench of brimstone—though he is wearing "the well-known and high-bred Mephistophelian smile." The narrator takes it for granted that Goethe ended up in Satan's province, and offers Satan some cigars to take back to the creator of *Faust*. Frederick Augustus Grant Cowper, "The Hermit Story, as Used by Voltaire and Mark Twain," *In Honor of the Ninetieth Birthday of Charles Frederick Johnson*, eds. Odell Shepard and Arthur Adams (Hartford: Trinity College, 1928), p. 336, found in the play and the opera of Goethe's *Faust* numerous "pictorial" details Mark Twain borrowed for his *Mysterious Stranger*.

Coleman O. Parsons, "Background" (1960), p. 62; William M. Gibson, *MSM* (1969), p. 2 n. 4, 17; W. Gerald Marshall, "Mark Twain's 'The Man That Corrupted Hadleyburg' and the Myth of Baucis and Philemon," *Mark Twain Journal* 20.2 (Summer 1980): 7 n. 2.

———. *Faust von Goethe*. Mit Einleitung und fortlaufender Erklärung herausgegeben von [With Introduction and Ongoing Explanation by] Karl Julius Schröer (1825–1900). 2 vols. Heilbronn: Verlag von Gebr. Henninger, 1888.

Inscription: the title page of Volume II is signed "Jervis Langdon".

Marginalia: numerous drawings and notes in Volume II, none by Clemens. On page 250 someone wrote in pencil, below line 2416, "You are both perfect idiots". The same hand underlined line 2418 on page 251, writing in the margin, "Here we are again". Farther down on page 251 the same hand underlined line 2424, writing "once more" in pencil in the margin. The hand resembles Clemens's but certain letters are different from his and after studying the marginalia carefully I do not believe it was he who wrote these words.

Provenance: found on a library shelf at Quarry Farm in 2005 and transferred to the Elmira College campus library.

Catalog: Ball 2016 inventory, dark red cloth, gilt lettering, Volume II only.

Location: Mark Twain Archive, Gannett-Tripp Library, Elmira College, Elmira, New York.

Copy examined: photocopies of the title page and two pages of annotation in Volume II, sent by Mark Woodhouse, Archivist, on 6 December 2005 and again on 25 February 2014. On several visits to Quarry Farm previous to 2005 I inspected these same volumes at Quarry Farm. Some of the marginal notations appear to be by Ida Langdon and others resemble children's drawings and scribblings. None of the jottings appear to be by Clemens, including one that reads "Holy mountain in Spain." However, the lack of his marginalia does not necessarily mean he ignored this title in the Langdons' residential library whenever he visited them during his visits to Elmira.

———. *Female Characters of Goethe, from the Original Drawings of William Kaulbach [Wilhelm von Kaulbach, 1804–1874].* Explanatory Text by G[eorge]. H[enry]. Lewes (1817–1878).

New York: Theodore Stroefer; Munich: Frederick Bruckmann, [1867]. 98 pp.

Catalog: *C1951*, #08.

Lewes' accompanying text contains quotations from the works of Johann Wolfgang von Goethe (1749–1832). In November 1878 Clemens noted in Munich that "the old masters never dreamed of women as beautiful as those of Kaulbach" (NB 17, *N&J* 2: 251).

———. *Gedichte [Poetry]*. Halle a. d. S.: Otto Hendel, 1888. 375 pp.

Edgar Hemminghaus reported seeing Clemens's copy of this volume in the Mark Twain Library at Redding in 1945, but neither Albert E. Stone (in 1955) nor I (in 1970 and thereafter) was able to locate it there ("Mark Twain's German Provenience" [1945], p. 471).

———. *Goethes Werke*. Portrait. 4 vols. Stuttgart, 1887. [Clemens's edition has not been determined, but these four volumes were likely part of the thirty-six-volume set of Goethe's works published in Stuttgart by J. G. Cotta between 1867–1882.]

Catalog: *A1911*, "Portrait, 4 vols., 12mo, cloth, Stuttgart, 1887," with a sheet of manuscript notes laid in, lot 189, sold for $2.75.

———. *Götz von Berlichingen* (play, produced in 1773).

Beverly R. David made a persuasive case for concluding that "most of the Berlichingen text used in *A Tramp Abroad* (1880) came from Mark Twain's fanciful reworking of Goethe's play" ("What's in a Name? Twain's Goethe Hero in *A Tramp Abroad*," *Mark Twain Journal* 26.1 [Spring 1988]: 30–32). "Goethe's drama, not Götz's life, turned the outlaw into a folk hero and attracted Twain's attention" (p. 30).

———. *Illustrations to Goethe's Faust; Twenty-six Etchings by [Friedrich August] Moritz Retzsch [1779–1857] with Illustrative Selections from the Text of Bayard Taylor's Translation*. Boston: Estes and Lauriat, 1877.

Inscription: inscribed as a gift from Clemens to his daughters.

Catalog: *A1911*, "oblong 4to, cloth, gilt edges, Bost. 1877," describes Clemens's "loving inscription" to his daughters, lot 161, sold for $7.

———. *Die Neue Melusine [The New Melusine]* (a literary fairy tale, published in 1817).

Clara Clemens listed this title in her mostly undated commonplace book (Paine 150, MTP).

———. *Reineke Fuchs. [Reynard the Fox]*. Illustrated by Wilhelm von Kaulbach (1804–1874). [Goethe translated this fable in 1794. Kaulbach drew sixty illustrations for the work in 1846. Clemens's edition has not been established.]

Catalog: ListABP (1910), "Reineke Fuchs", no other information supplied.

Clemens wrote to Olivia Clemens's mother Olivia Lewis Langdon from Munich at the end of December 1878: "Take it by & large, it was a very happy & abundant sort of Christmas which we had here. Livy gave me a noble great copy of the 'Reinicke Fuchs' [*sic*], nearly as big as the Faust [the illustrated *Faust* that Mrs. Langdon had given him], & containing the original Kaulbach illustrations" (MTMH). Olivia Clemens had written "Kaulbach's illustrations of Reynard the Fox" in her personal notebook for 1878; later in Munich she recorded an expense of $12.50 for the volume (NB 13a, MTP).

———. "Über allen Gipfeln ist Ruh'" ["Over every mountain-top lies peace"] (poem).

Edgar Hemminghaus identified this as the poem Mark Twain quotes in "Marienbad" (1891). Twain explains that the passage impresses him with Goethe's idea of *Waldeinsamkeit*, i.e., a woodland retreat ("Mark Twain's German Provenience" [1945], p. 471).

———. *Wilhelm Meister's Apprenticeship and Travels.* Translated from the German by Thomas Carlyle (1795–1881). 3 vols. London: Chapman and Hall (Volume I); New York: Scribner, Welford and Co. (Volumes II and III), 1874.

Catalog: Ball 2016 inventory, reddish-brown cloth, gilt lettering on spine, black lettering and design on cover.

Location: Quarry Farm library shelves, under the supervision of the Mark Twain Archive, Elmira College, Elmira, New York.

Copy examined: unmarked copy to which Clemens had access whenever he visited Quarry Farm in Elmira.

———. *Wilhelm Meister's Apprenticeship; A Novel, from the German of Goethe.* Translated from the German by R. Dillon Boylan. London: Bell & Daldy, 1873. 570 pp.

Catalog: Ball 2016 inventory, brown cloth, with marble boards.

Location: Quarry Farm library shelves, under the supervision of the Mark Twain Archive, Elmira College, Elmira, New York.

This was one of the books available to Clemens whenever he visited Quarry Farm in Elmira.

GOFF, GEORGE PAUL. *Nick Baba's Last Drink and Other Sketches.* Illus. Lancaster, Pennsylvania: Inquirer Printing and Publishing Co., 1879. 84 pp.

Source: MTLAcc, entry #143, volume donated by Clemens. In the title story a goblin torments a cobbler who has been resisting liquor.

GOLDSMITH, [JAMES] "JAY" CHARLTON (1844–1887), pseud. "The P. I. Man."

Mark Twain included "Herald P. I. man" in a list of American humorists he compiled in 1881 (NB 19, *N&J* 2: 429). Goldsmith earned that sobriquet among his fellow journalists by being the longtime editor of the "Personal Intelligence" column for the New York *Herald*," where his terse, witty squibs became a prominent feature. One of his better-known longer sketches was "Hints for Farmers." In 1884 he published *Himself Again, A Novel*. His early death at the age of forty-two virtually extinguished his name from the annals of American humor.

GOLDSMITH, OLIVER (1730–1774). *The Citizen of the World* (fictional letters, published in 1762). [A few sources speculate that Goldsmith's birth date may actually have been 1728.]

Clemens wrote to Orion from St. Louis on 18 March 1861 to commend the "quiet style" of a portion of Orion's recent letter; the passage, he stated, "resembles Goldsmith's 'Citizen of the World' and 'Don Quixote,'—which are my *beau ideals* of fine writing" (*MTL*, p. 45 *MTLet* 1: 117). Possibly Clemens absorbed this opinion from a senior river pilot with whom he sometimes served, George Ealer. In Chapter 19 of *Life on the Mississippi* (1883) he recalled of his piloting days that "while we lay at landings I listened to George Ealer's flute, or to his readings from his two Bibles—that is to say, Goldsmith and Shakespeare." Mark Twain imitated Goldsmith's satirical letters purportedly written by a Chinese philosopher residing in London with a series of his own, "Goldsmith's Friend Abroad Again," in the October and November 1870 issues of *The Galaxy*. These were supposedly written by a Chinese immigrant to California named Ah Song Hi who describes his mistreatment in America. Edward H. Weatherly argued that Colonel Sellers of *The Gilded Age* (1873) was a composite characterization based on James Lampton as well as Goldsmith's Beau Tibbs of *The Citizen of the World*. Tibbs and Sellers both tried to conceal their poverty by ludicrous stratagems ("Beau Tibbs and Colonel Sellers," *Modern Language Notes* 59.5 [May 1944]: 310–313). Hemminghaus, *MTG* (1939), pp. 113–114; Krause, *MTC* (1967), pp. 118–120; Baetzhold, *MT&JB* (1970), pp. 271–272; and Richard H. Passon, "Twain and Eighteenth-Century Satire: The Ingenu Narrator in *Huckleberry Finn*," *Mark Twain Journal* 21.4 (Fall 1983): 33–36.

———. *The Deserted Village*. Illustrated by Edwin A. Abbey (1852–1911). New York: Harper & Brothers, 1902.

Inscription: inscribed by Clemens, "Livy Clemens/December/1902."

Catalogs: ListABP (1910), "Deserted Village, Goldsmith"; *C1951*, O26, listed among books containing Olivia Clemens's signature; "Property from the Library of Mark Twain," Butterfield & Butterfield, San Francisco, Sale 6613 (16 July 1997), lot 2700.

Location: Mark Twain House and Museum, Hartford, Connecticut.

Copy examined: Olivia Clemens's unmarked copy. Original cloth, some wear on edges and corners. Viewed in Hartford in 1997.

In "Unfortunate Blunder," a sketch written on 30 August 1863, Mark Twain echoed a line from "The Deserted Village": "They used to go to Goldsmith's church to laugh, and remain to pray, but the Presbyterians here have reversed the thing this morning" (*ET&S* 1: 287, 483). Clemens noted "Deserted Villages" among a series of observations and ideas about Hawaii in 1866 (NB 6, *N&J* 1: 215). In "To Raise Poultry" (1870) he claimed to be such an unusual poultry-raiser that "old roosters that came to crow, 'remained to pray,' when I passed by"—playing on line 180 of Goldsmith's poem, which described the Auburn pastor's powers of persuasion as being so great that "fools who came to scoff, remained to pray" (Buffalo *Express*, 4 June 1870; *MTBE*, p. 208).

——— and RICHARD BRINSLEY SHERIDAN (1751–1816). *Dramatic Works of Sheridan and Goldsmith. With Goldsmith's Poems.* [See the Catalog entry for Sheridan.]

———. *Goldsmith's Natural History; Abridged, for the Use of Schools, by Mrs. [Mary] Pilkington [1766–1839]*. Philadelphia: Johnson & Warner, 1810. 328 pp.

Inscription: the front flyleaf is inscribed in black ink, "Betsey Hill's/Book/Bot Jan. 15th 1818".

Location: Mark Twain Library, Redding, Connecticut.

Copy examined: the descendants of the Hill family of Redding Ridge donated many school books with early imprints to the Mark Twain Library, and this was clearly one of those. It has the purple oval Mark Twain Library stamps but no accession number or markings. This copy definitely did not belong to Clemens or a member of his family, even though there is a description of an animal that might have interested him, the "camelopard," on page 141. In June 1982 this copy was shelved with the books donated by Clemens and his daughter Clara Gabrilowitsch, but I advised the staff that it should be moved elsewhere.

———. *The Good-Natured Man* (comedy, performed in 1768). **Catalog:** *C1951*, J34, listed among the books belonging to Jean and Clara Clemens.

———. *She Stoops to Conquer*. Spine missing. New York: Century Co., 1900.

Inscription: inscribed, "To the Refined Thief/from/Clara Clemens."

Marginalia: a brief passage is underlined on page 134.

Catalog: ListABP (1910), "She Stoops to Conquer, Goldsmith", no other information supplied.

Provenance: shelfmarks of the library numbering system employed by Clara Clemens Gabrilowitsch during her Detroit years.

Catalogs: *C1951*, J16, listed among the books belonging to Jean and Clara Clemens; "Property from the Library of Mark Twain," Butterfield & Butterfield, San Francisco, Sale 6613 (16 July 1997), lot 2712.

Location: Hartford House and Museum, Hartford, Connecticut.

Copy examined: most likely Clemens's copy, inscribed by Clara Clemens. Viewed in Hartford in 1997.

Clemens's familiarity with the plot of *She Stoops to Conquer; or, The Mistakes of a Night*, a comedy first performed in 1773, probably occurred much earlier than 1900. (In Goldsmith's play a family mistakes a private home for a public inn and treats the indignant residents like a landlord and his servants.) Paul Fatout's convincing essay, "Mark Twain's First Lecture: A Parallel," *Pacific Historical Review* 25.4 (November 1956): 347–354, reviewed Mark Twain's familiarity with the works of Washington Irving and Oliver Goldsmith and argued that the *Roughing It* (Chapter 78) account of Twain's first San Francisco lecture in 1866 "strikingly resembles the story of the first night performance of *She Stoops to Conquer* in Washington Irving's biography of Goldsmith" (p. 347). E. W. Kemble remembered that Clemens greatly admired Edwin Austin Abbey's drawings for an illustrated edition of this play (Kemble, "Illustrating *Huckleberry Finn*" [1930]). Clemens noted the title of Goldsmith's comedy on 10 April 1900 while residing in London (NB 43, TS p. 7).

———. *The Vicar of Wakefield, A Tale*. New York: John W. Lovell Co., 1882. 156 pp.

Source: MTLAcc, entry #2255, volume donated from Clemens's library by Clara Clemens Gabrilowitsch in 1910.

Olivia Langdon recorded in her commonplace book the fact that she was reading *The Vicar of Wakefield* in 1868 (MTP). Clemens's contemptuous opinions of *The Vicar* are well known. William Dean Howells recalled in 1910 that "there were certain authors whose names he seemed not so much to pronounce as to spew out of his mouth. Goldsmith was one of these" (*MMT*, p. 15). This must have been a fairly late critical heresy, however, for Jervis Langdon (1875–1952) testified that *The Vicar of Wakefield* was one of Clemens's favorite sources with which he amused the children at Quarry Farm. "Fancy the possibilities lying in scenes devised by sedate old Goldsmith and

interpreted to small children by Mark Twain's fantasy," wrote Langdon (*Some Reminiscences*, p. 15; collected in *Mark Twain in Elmira* [2013], p. 208). Clemens listed Goldsmith's novel among the sources he wished to quote for his proposed appendix to *A Connecticut Yankee in King Arthur's Court* (Howard G. Baetzhold, "Course of Composition" [1961], p. 200).

Sometime between February and June in 1894 Clemens registered the first inkling of profound hostility toward the work: "Now that our second-hand opinions, inherited from our fathers, are fading," he wrote, "perhaps it may be forgivable to write a really honest review of the Vicar of Wakefield & try to find out what our fathers found in it to admire, & what not to scoff at" (NB 33, TS p. 61). In December 1895 (aboard the *Mararoa*) Clemens noted: "In past year have read Vicar of Wakefield & some of Jane Austin [*sic*]. Thoroughly artificial" (NB 36, TS p. 3). On 8 January 1896, having boarded a ship with a superb library, he resolved: "I must read that devilish Vicar of Wakefield again. Also Jane Austin [*sic*]" (NB 37, TS p. 3). His forthcoming *Following the Equator* (1897) provided Clemens the opportunity to vent his disgruntlement with prevailing critical estimates of *The Vicar of Wakefield*. In Chapter 36 of *Following the Equator* Mark Twain likens Goldsmith's "deathless story" to Julia A. Moore's *The Sentimental Song Book*: "I find in it the same subtle touch—the touch that makes an intentionally humorous episode pathetic and an intentionally pathetic one funny." He heaps additional insults on the novel in Chapter 62: "To be fair, there is another word of praise due to this ship's library: it contains no copy of the Vicar of Wakefield, that strange menagerie of complacent hypocrites and idiots, of theatrical cheap-john heroes and heroines, who are always showing off, of bad people who are not interesting, and good people who are fatiguing. A singular book. Not a sincere line in it, and not a character that invites respect; a book which is one long waste-pipe discharge of goody-goody puerilities and dreary moralities; a book which is full of pathos which revolts, and humor which grieves the heart. There are few things in literature that are more piteous, more pathetic, than the celebrated 'humorous' incident of Moses and the spectacles." Twain purports to be quoting from an entry he made in his diary on 10 April [1896], but no such comment appears in his surviving notebooks. Joseph H. Twichell indicated that he agreed with Brander Matthews's defense of Oliver Goldsmith against Twain's cavils in "New Trials for Old Favorites," *Forum* 25 (August 1898): 749–760, to which Clemens replied on 13 September 1898: "I like Brander Matthews. . . . When you say he has earned your gratitude for cuffing me for my crimes against the Leatherstockings & the Vicar, I ain't making any objection" (*LMTJHT* [2017], p. 220).

Blair, *MT&HF* (1960), pp. 330–331; Krause, *MTC* (1967), pp. 109, 120–127, 297; Harris, *Courtship* (1996), p. 26.

GOMEZ, MADELEINE ANGÉLIQUE (POISSON) DE (1684–1770). *La Belle Assemblée: Being a Curious Collection of Some Very Remarkable Incidents Which Happen'd to Persons of the First Quality in France*. [Translated from the French by Eliza (Fowler) Haywood, c. 1693–1756.] 4 vols. London: Dan.

Browne, 1754. [Publisher conjectured.]

Catalog: *A1911*, "Vols. II-IV, copper plates, 3 vols., 12mo, old calf (broken), Lond. 1754," with a small sheet of manuscript laid in, lot 192, vols. 2–4 only.

At one time *La Belle Assemblée* was a very popular French novel. Written in the form of a frame narrative with various story-tellers, it was initially published in stages; the final, fullest version appeared in 1731.

GOODALE, FRANCES ABIGAIL (ROCKWELL) (1839–1934), ed. *The Literature of Philanthropy*. New York: Harper & Brothers, 1893. 210 pp.

Source: MTLAcc, entry #1342, volume donated by Clemens.

A compilation of published reports by women concerning social reform.

Good Literature (New York periodical).

Clemens wrote to Joseph G[allatin]. Hickman (1861–1935) of Florida, Missouri on 24 July 1881 about this "weekly journal published in New York City at 50 cts. per year, devoted to advertising some astonishingly cheap books.... The books are worth much more than the price asked for them" (Monroe [County, Missouri] *Appeal*, 12 August 1881; newspaper clipping courtesy of Ralph Gregory [1909–2015], Marthasville, Missouri). Hickman was a member of a local Florida, Missouri literary club organized in 1880 as the "Mark Twain Literary Society."

GOODMAN, JOSEPH T[HOMPSON]. (1838–1917). *The Archaic Maya Inscriptions*. London: Published for the Editors by R. H. Porter and Dulau & Co., 1897. 149 pp. [Issued as Appendix, Volume 4, in a Series titled Biologia Centrali-Americana. Archælogy, 1889–1902.]

Clemens's good friend from the Virginia City *Territorial Enterprise* later operated a grape ranch in California, but Clemens always considered Goodman one of the mute inglorious Miltons such as Captain Stormfield would see recognized with acclaim in heaven. In a letter written to Olivia Langdon on 10 January 1870 Clemens lamented that "a born poet" like Goodman had been unfortunate in his choice of a wife: "he *could* have been so honored of men, & so loved by all for whom poetry has a charm, but for the dead weight & clog upon his winged genius, of a wife whose soul could have no companionship save with the things of the dull earth" (*MTLet* 4: 17–18).

Consequently Clemens was delighted to receive a letter from Goodman many years later, written on 24 May 1902 from his home in Alameda, California, promising to send "as a curiosity" a copy of his book—a translation of "the inscriptions on the ruins of Central America and Yucatan" issued in London. "There is no hope of profit in it," Goodman added. "Not a thousand persons care anything about the study. The only compensation is that I found out what nobody else could, and that my name will always be associated with the unraveling of the Maya glyphs, as Champollion's is with the Egyptian. But that is poor pay for what will be twenty years' hard work" (MTP). After Clemens got the copy he wrote on 13 June 1902 from Riverdale: "Yesterday I read as much as half of the book, not understanding a word but enchanted nevertheless—partly by the wonder of it all, the study, the erudition, the incredible labor, the modesty ... and partly by the grace and beauty and limpidity of

the book's unsurpassable English" (*MTL*, p. 721). Goodman's study focused on the Maya calendars rather than on their gods or their worship ceremonies. In the book's Preface, dated 1 November 1895, Goodman scoffed at previous "scientists" who kept the materials "sealed to the rest of the world" while indulging in "a deal of learned and pompous knowtowing to each other, but not a single substantial gain toward bottoming [*sic*] the inscriptions." Goodman's "earnest desire," he emphasized, was "that the study may become popularized, instead of being confined to an exclusive and incompetent few" (p. v). In the first Autobiographical Dictation that commenced Mark Twain's long series in 1906, he praised Goodman's "most unpromising and difficult and stubborn study" that had produced "a great <big> book" and established Goodman's status as an expert among European scholars (9 January 1906 AD, *AutoMT* 1: 254). This prediction came true; the discoveries within *The Archaic Maya Inscriptions* were eventually accepted by anthropologists and absorbed into twentieth-century scholarship about Maya achievements. Goodman would recall that in 1910 Twain urged him to "visit me once more before we both get so old we can't hear each other swear" ("Jos. Goodman's Memories of Humorist's Early Days," San Francisco *Examiner*, 22 April 1910, p. 3).

Lawrence I. Berkove, "Life after Twain: The Later Careers of the Enterprise Staff," *Mark Twain Journal* 29.1 (Spring 1991): 22–28; *Insider Stories of the Comstock Lode and Nevada's Mining Frontier 1859–1909: Primary Sources in America's Social History*, ed. Lawrence I. Berkove (Lewiston, New York: Mellen Publishing, 2007) contains Goodman's reminiscence about Clemens.

GOODMAN, JULES ECKERT (1876–1962).

This prolific playwright recalled that as an undergraduate at Columbia University he had the effrontery to approach Mark Twain about a dramatic collaboration on *Joan of Arc*. "He invaded the chamber of a white-maned, white-mustached man in lower Fifth Avenue to ask if he would be outraged over such a plot. Mr. Twain, in his nightshirt, saw nothing heretic in the Goodman scheme, but confessed that he couldn't rouse himself to any active participation. He shifted his pillow, lit a cigar and gave Goodman his benediction" ("The Firm of Goodman & Goodman," New York *Times*, 31 October 1937; this article was kindly brought to my attention by a faculty colleague, Eric Sterling).

GOODRICH, CHARLES AUGUSTUS (1790–1862). *History of the United States*. Paper wrappers. Hartford: Published for Subscribers, 1823. 400 pp.

Catalog: ListABP (1910), "History of the U. S., Goodrich".

Location: Mark Twain Library, Redding, Connecticut.

Copy examined: very possibly Clemens's copy, since Albert Bigelow Paine listed this author and title among the books he was keeping temporarily for the biography he was writing. He could have subsequently donated it to the community library in Redding. The volume that I located and examined in June 1982 has the purple oval Mark Twain Library stamps but no accession number, inscription, or markings. It should be borne in mind that various editions based on this work were published throughout the nineteenth century, so Paine might have been holding another version. However, this copy seems like a candidate for being the one to which he referred.

———. *Lives of the Signers to the Declaration of Independence.* New York: Jonathan Leavitt, 1829.

Inscriptions: signed "Jervis Langdon—Salina [, New York.] July 2, 1833". Also bears a Civil War pass. Subsequently stamped on the title page: "The Park Church, Elmira, N. Y. 1877".

Catalogs: list of books that Mark Woodhouse transferred from the Quarry Farm library to the Mark Twain Archive on 9 July 1987; Ball 2016 inventory, brown cloth, poor condition.

Location: Mark Twain Archive, Elmira College, Elmira, New York.

GOODRICH, CASPAR FREDERICK (1847–1925). *Report of the British Naval and Military Operations in Egypt, 1882.* Maps and illustrations. Washington, D. C. 1885. 340 pp.

Catalog: *A1911*, "8vo, cloth, Wash. 1885," with a sheet of manuscript about feuds laid in, lot 193, sold for $1.25.

GOODRICH, SAMUEL GRISWOLD (1793–1860), pseud. "Peter Parley." *History of All Nations from the Earliest Periods to the Present Time.* Rev. edition. Illus. 2 vols. New York: Miller, Orton & Co., 1857.

Inscriptions: presented to Clemens's brother Orion by William Stotts. Bookplates of Orion Clemens are pasted in. William Stotts (1799–1888) was Orion's father-in-law.

Source: card catalog of the Mark Twain Library, Redding, Connecticut. The volumes were recorded as missing in 1979 and they were still missing when I visited in 1980 and revisited in June 1982.

Under his pen name Goodrich was an enormously popular author of children's educational books. The "Peter Parley" character he invented was an elderly Boston man who relied on a crutch or a cane and delighted in telling stories or explaining geography and history and other subjects to the children who gathered around him. He was often imitated in publications and in fact England alone produced seven other "Peter Parley" figures. See also the Catalog entry for *Parley's Magazine.*

GOODWIN, J[OHN]. CHEEVER (1850–1912). *Evangeline* (musical comedy). Libretto by Goodwin, music composed by Edward E[verett]. Rice (1848–1924).

This burlesque of Longfellow's famous poem *Evangeline: A Tale of Arcadie* was not immediately popular when it opened at Niblo's Garden on Broadway in 1874, but after Edward E. Rice rewrote the songs it had another opening and became a durable hit. In July 1888 Clemens noted that the comic actor George S. Knight had joined Rice in presenting this long-popular entertainment on the stage (NB 28, *N&J* 3: 406).

GORDON, ADAM LINDSAY (1833–1870). *Poems.* Preface by Marcus [Andrew Hislop] Clarke (1846–1881). Melbourne, Australia: A. H. Massina & Co., 1894. 354 pp.

Source: MTLAcc, entry #2031, volume donated from Clemens's library by Clara Clemens Gabrilowitsch in 1910.

Mark Twain quoted from Marcus Clarke's introduction to this volume at considerable length in Chapter 9 of the manuscript for *Following the Equator* (1897), but he deleted this portion before publishing the book in 1897 (Francis Madigan, "MT's Passage to India," pp. 351–353, 358). The final version of *Following the Equator* did include

Gordon among the Australian authors listed approvingly in Chapter 22.

———. *Poems.* Preface by Marcus [Andrew Hislop] Clarke (1846–1881). London: S. Mullen, n.d. 325 pp.

Source: MTLAcc, entry #2030, volume donated from Clemens's library by Clara Clemens Gabrilowitsch in 1910.

GORDON, CHARLES WILLIAM (1869–1937), pseud. "Ralph Connor."

Canadian novelist and clergyman Gordon remembered meeting Mark Twain "on Fifth Avenue, New York, in company with Mr. George Doran, my publisher. . . . In five minutes we were no strangers. Mark Twain had a rare gift of making friends. . . . He was a serious-minded man with depths in his heart, who looked upon humanity with an understanding and sympathetic eye" ("Meeting Mark Twain," *Mark Twain Quarterly* 3.2 [Spring 1939]: 17).

GORDON, (GEN.) GEORGE HENRY (1823–1886). *A War Diary of Events in the War of the Great Rebellion, 1863–1865.* Boston: J. R. Osgood and Co., 1882. 437 pp.

"War Diary of Gen. Geo. H. Gordon," Clemens wrote in Notebook 20 in April 1882 before he left for New Orleans and the Mississippi River (*N&J* 2: 462). He had seen Osgood recently in Boston, so Osgood may have told him about this book, which recounts Gordon's part in Union military operations in Virginia, South Carolina, Florida, and also (pp. 306–331) along the Mississippi River. Gordon's narrative emphasizes the open corruption and collusion with the enemy that he saw practiced by Federal ship officers and their crews, particularly with regard to lucrative cotton shipments.

GORDON-CUMMING, CONSTANCE FREDERICA (1837–1924). *In the Himalayas and on the Indian Plains.* "A new edition with forty-two illustrations." 8vo, original pictorial gray cloth, cover illustrations stamped in silver and black. cloth. London: Chatto and Windus, 1892 (cop. 1886); Bungay: R. Clay and Sons. 608 pp.

Inscription: signed in pencil on the half-title page, "S. L. Clemens, Bombay, 1896."

Marginalia: contains "hundreds" of notes, corrections, and markings in Clemens's hand, according to *A1911*. One note reads: "We must take the position that burial is stuck to merely in the interest of the undertaker (who has his family cremated to save expense)." Sections of leaves have been cut out at pages 135–136 and 269–279. On page 596 Clemens recorded, "Finished in the Indian Ocean four days from Ceylon Jan. 10th 1896. (Well done!)" Other notes and markings are scattered throughout; some of these have been lined through.

Catalogs: *A1911*, "8vo, coth, Lond. 1886," quotes the signature and describes the marginalia and quotes one example, lot 115, sold for $35; George D. Smith, New York City, "Catalogue of Books" (1911), quotes the signature and one marginal note, item #191, $50.

Location: Albert and Shirley Small Special Collections Library, University of Virginia, Charlottesville, Virginia.

Source: online catalog for the Albert and Shirley Small Special Collections Library in 2017.

On 13 June 1895 Clemens wrote from Elmira, New York to his London publisher, Chatto & Windus, ordering "'In the Himalayas, by C F Gordon Cumming.' I see you publish it." He asked that the book be sent to Melbourne, ahead of his arrival there on his worldwide lecture tour. A clerk at Chatto & Windus noted on Clemens's letter, "Sent & chged June 24." Evidently Clemens wanted to read the book before he reached India (ALS advertised in 2005 in James Cummins Bookseller's catalog; copy in the collection of Kevin Mac Donnell). In Chapter 49 of *Following the Equator* (1897) Mark Twain states that the Indian native in a loincloth "answers properly to Miss Gordon Cumming's flash-light picture of him—as a person who is dressed in 'a turban and a pocket hand-kerchief'"; he also repeats her remark—"turban and pocket-handkerchief"—in Chapter 50. Subsequently he uses her statistics (*In the Himalayas*, Chapter 3, p. 63) to document the number of people killed by dangerous wild animals in India (*FE*, Chapter 57).

Madigan, "MT's Passage to India" (1974), p. 358.

GORDON-CUMMING, ROUALEYN GEORGE (1820–1866). *Five Years of a Hunter's Life in the Far Interior of South Africa; With Notices of the Native Tribes, and Anecdotes of the Chase of the Lion, Elephant, Hippopotamus, Giraffe, Rhinoceros, &c.* 2 vols. Illus. London, 1850. The title varied in subsequent editions. An abridged version, *The Lion Hunter of South Africa: Five Years' Adventures in the Far Interior of South Africa, with Notices of the Native Tribes and Savage Animals*, appeared in 1855 and was reprinted by several publishers. This latter edition might have been the one Clemens consulted.

The Scottish adventurer Gordon-Cumming chased game so assiduously in India and Africa that his hunting trophies were displayed in London in 1851 at the Crystal Palace Exposition. In a footnote to Chapter 47 of *Following the Equator* (1897) Mark Twain quotes Gordon-Cumming's account of his deliberate cruelty to an elephant he had wounded in the shoulder, causing the animal to lean against a tree for support; after leisurely brewing himself some coffee, Gordon-Cumming experimented with the elephant's vulnerability to bullets by firing his rifles at various parts of its body, during all of which the animal cried tears of pain and explored the wounds with the tip of its trunk. The worst of the Indian Thuggee chieftains, comments Mark Twain, was only "the Gordon Cumming of his day." Though Twain's excerpt is enclosed within quotation marks, in actuality it is a combined and compressed account of various bull elephant kills that Gordon-Cumming described in excruciating detail in Chapters 17 and 18 of *The Lion Hunter in South Africa*. Twain, however, added no details to make the episode seem more heartless—which would hardly have been possible, anyway.

Madigan, "MT's Passage to India" (1974), pp. 358–359; Welland, *Mark Twain in England* (1978), pp. 183–184.

GORKY, MAXIM (1868–1936). *Orlóff and His Wife. Tales of the Barefoot Brigade.* Trans. by Isabel F[lorence]. Hapgood (1851–1928). Blue cloth. New York: Charles Scribner's Sons, 1905. 485 pp.

Inscription: signed on the front pastedown endpaper in black ink, "SL. Clemens/1906".

Provenance: Antenne-Dorrance Collection, Rice Lake, Wisconsin.

Location: Mark Twain Archive, Gannett-Tripp Learning Center, Elmira College, Elmira, New York.

Copy examined: Clemens's unmarked copy. Examined on

28 May 2015.

Clemens dined with Maxim Gorky, Ivan Narodny, and other anti-Czarists at 3 Fifth Avenue on 11 April 1906. Gorky's adopted son acted as an interpreter, according to Isabel V. Lyon (Fears, *Day by Day* 4: 363). Subsequently the fact that Gorky checked into a hotel with a woman to whom he was not married caused embarrassment for Clemens and other American sympathizers. Joseph H. Twichell thanked Clemens on 18 April 1906 "for your just comment on Gorky's bad mistake. Poor fellow; he didn't understand our bigotry. Too bad!" (*LMTJHT*, p. 384). On 26 August 1906 Isabel Lyon noted that Clemens had defended to Jane Addams his action in dropping his sponsorship of Gorky's visit to the United States after Gorky's marital impropriety came to light (IVL Journals, TS p. 182, MTP). An unpublished manuscript written by Clemens, "A Cloud-Burst of Calamities," recorded his evolving reactions to Gorky's appeals for support (MTP). Louis J. Budd's "Twain, Howells, and the Boston Nihilists," *New England Quarterly* 32.3 (September 1959): 351–371 laid out the background for Mark Twain's initial support of Gorky and reviewed the publications about Russia and the Czarist mines with which Mark Twain and William Dean Howells seem to have been familiar. Gorky's impression of Clemens as he saw him in New York City in 1906 became available in a review of a collection of Gorky's fugitive notes and papers that was published in Moscow in 1941: when Clemens's gray eyes "look up straight at your face, you feel that every wrinkle on your face has been gauged and will remain for ever in the memory of this man" (Alexander Kaun, "Gorky on Literature," *Books Abroad* 16.4 [Autumn 1942]: 396). Gorky added, "He seems very old, yet it is clear that he merely acts the part of an old man, for often his movements and gestures are so powerful, agile, and graceful that for a moment you forget his white head" (p. 397).

———. *Tales from Gorky, Translated from the Russian [by Robert Nisbet Bain (1854–1909)].* New York: Funk and Wagnall's Co., 1902. 285 pp. [Edition conjectured.]

Catalog: ListABP (1910), "Tales from Gorky, Bain", no other information provided.

GORST, HAROLD EDWARD (1868–1950). *The Philosophy of Making Love.* London: Cassell & Co., 1908. 180 pp.

Source: MTLAcc, entry #1467, volume donated by Clemens.

Contemporary reviewers were amused by this attempt to improve the odds of a satisfactory marriage by applying logic, reason, and common sense to romantic relationships. Both the British-educated Gorst and his wife wrote on the subject of language; he also produced books on education, China, the value of laughter, Christ's divinity, and a vision of the future.

"THE GOSPEL TRAIN" (spiritual). Also known as "Get on board." Clemens included "Gospel Train" in what appears to be a list of his favorite songs in August 1889 (NB 29, *N&J* 3: 513).

GOSSE, EDMUND WILLIAM (1849–1928). *Thomas Gray [1716–1771].* English Men of Letters Series. Ed. by John Morley (1838–1923). New York: Harper & Brothers, 1882. 223 pp. [Publisher and pages conjectured.]

Inscription: signed, "S. L. Clemens, Hartford, 1884."

Catalogs: *A1911*, "12mo, cloth, N.Y. 1882," quotes the

signature, lot 201, sold for $1.50; George D. Smith, New York City, "Catalogue of Books" (1911), quotes the signature, item #141, $5.

Clemens wrote "Life of Gray (Morley's English Men of Letters)" in Notebook 22 (*N&J* 3: 50) in 1884. The statement of his personal expenses charged against Charles L. Webster & Company for 1884 included "1 English Men of Letters .50" that was purchased on 28 April 1884 (Charles L. Webster to SLC, 2 September 1884, MTP). Clemens was quite familiar with Thomas Gray's most famous poem, "Elegy Written in a Country Churchyard"; see the Catalog entry for Gray.

———. *Thomas Gray.* New York: Harper & Brothers, n.d. 223 pp.

Source: MTLAcc, entry #1285, volume donated by Clemens.

GOUIN, FRANÇOIS (1831–1896). *The Art of Teaching and Studying Languages.* Translated by Howard Swan and Victor Bétis. London: George Philip & Son, 1892. 407 pp.

Clemens noted the title and publisher in July 1892 (NB 32, TS p. 12).

GOWEN, HERBERT HENRY (1864–1960. *The Paradise of the Pacific. Sketches of Hawaiian Scenery and Life.* London: Skeffington & Son, 1892. 180 pp.

In Chapter 3 of *Following the Equator* (1897) Mark Twain quotes Gowen's account of the plight of Hawaiian lepers and cites his book by its title.

Madigan, "MT's Passage to India" (1974), p. 359.

GOWER, RONALD SUTHERLAND, LORD (1845–1916). *Joan of Arc.* Illus. No. 2 of 208 copies printed. London: John C. Nimmo, 1893. 334 pp.

Marginalia: Clemens marked and annotated both Gower's text and his list of sources with pencil as well as brown and black ink.

Catalogs: ListABP (1910), "Joan of Arc, Gower"; "Retz Appraisal" (1944), p. 8, valued at $20.

Location: Mark Twain Papers, Bancroft Library, University of California at Berkeley.

Copy examined: Clemens's copy.

Mark Twain listed Gower's book among his "authorities examined" for *Joan of Arc* (see the page preceding the "Translator's Preface"). He told Albert Bigelow Paine that he remembered the book as one of his three main sources (*MTB* [1912], p. 958).

Ronald Jenn and Linda A. Morris, "The Sources of Mark Twain's *Personal Recollections of Joan of Arc,*" *Mark Twain Journal* 55.1–2 (Spring/Fall 2017): 55–74; and Linda A. Morris, in "What is 'Personal' about *Personal Recollections of Joan of Arc*?" *American Literary Realism* 51.2 (Winter 2019): 97–110.

GRAHAM, CLEMENTINA STIRLING (1782–1877). *Mystifications, by Clementina Stirling Grahame [sic].* Ed by John Brown, M.D. (1810–1882). Edinburgh: Edmonston and Douglas, 1865. 100 pp.

On 16 June 1896 Clemens noted. "'Mystifications' (Edmonston & Douglas, Edinboro)—1865—ask Chatto to get it for me" (NB 38, TS p. 47). He was aboard the *Norham Castle* off East London, South Africa at the time. Graham was a prominent society hostess known to Walter Scott and the editors and writers connected with the *Edinburgh Review.* One of her whims was to impersonate "Lady Pitlyal," her invented representative of the stubbornest Scots of an older generation. For some reason she spelled her name "Grahame" on the title page and throughout *Mystifications,* a book of prose sketches, reminiscences, and poems recalling her set of friends in Edinburgh and Scotland.

GRAHAME, KENNETH (1859–1932). *Dream Days.* London: John Lane, 1899. 291 pp.

Source: MTLAcc, entry #500, volume donated by Clemens. *Dream Days* (1899) was a sequel of sorts to Grahame's *The Golden Age* (1895). *Dream Days* consists of eight stories (the best-known being "The Reluctant Dragon") involving a parentless family of three boys and two girls who indulge in expeditions and games that combine imaginary adventures and Grahame's childhood reminiscences. The author's masterpiece, *The Wind in the Willows* (1908), was still nearly a decade in the future.

GRAND, SARAH, pseud. of Frances Elizabeth (Clarke) McFall (1854–1943). *Babs, the Impossible.* Illustrated by Arthur I[gnatius]. Keller (1866–1924). New York: Harper & Brothers, 1901. 462 pp.

Source: MTLAcc, entry #2243, volume donated from Clemens's library by Clara Clemens Gabrilowitsch in 1910.

———. *The Heavenly Twins.* Cloth. New York: Cassell Publishing Co., [cop. 1893]. 679 pp.

Marginalia: Clemens made scores of notations on the pages of this novel during a trans-Atlantic voyage in March 1894. He sailed from New York City on 7 March 1894 aboard the *S. S. New York,* bound for Southampton and scheduled to arrive on the 14th (see *MTHHR,* p. 41). Much of his marginalia is quoted in *A1911,* the auction catalog. A note on page 345, dated 9 or 10 March (Clemens is uncertain which day it is) explains why he has so much time to devote to reading and annotating the novel: he has been at sea several days in heavy rain ("How it does pour!") and there is "not a soul on deck," the purser informs him. Clemens penciled another note at the top of pages 556–557 while reading in bed at midnight on 10 March: "Surely there is nothing more delicious than the gentle rolling of a ship in a moderate sea. I wish I could be always at sea."

Clemens's comments about Sarah Grand's novel initially disparage its characters and dialogue, then reveal a grudging admiration for certain aspects of the work, and finally become openly complimentary. By the time he had progressed to page 74 his cavils were beginning: "Thus far, the twins are valueless lumber, & an impertinent & offensive intrusion." At page 149 he recommends that a "blank page in the place of these twins would be a large advantage to the book"; "Are these tiresome creatures supposed to be funny?" he wonders on page 150; "Good-bye, dears. God bless you. Don't come any more," is the adieu he bids them on page 154. He complains: "These disgusting creatures talk like Dr. Samuel Johnson & act like idiots. The authoress thinks that this silly performance of theirs is humorous" (p. 270). His criticisms are sharpest on page 274 ("The art of all this is intolerably bad. It is literary 'prentice-work") and page 275: "This is wretchedly done. A cat could do better literature than this."

Thereafter his tone grows more charitable: "This writer preserves her dignity & her sanity except when she is talking about her putrid twins—then she is vulgar & idiotic." Of Chapter 6 he remarks: "A difficult chapter to write well— but she did it" (p. 283). When slightly more than halfway through the novel he opined: "With the twins left out, this book is more than good, it is great; and packed full of hideous truths powerfully stated. I will not sit in judgment upon the ENGLISH woman who disapproves of this book—she has done that herself. While it is true that the American woman is & always has been a coward & a slave, like her sex everywhere, she has escaped some of the [Clemens turns the page and writes on its verso] degradations of her English sister—degradations whose source is rank & caste, the sacredness of property, & the tyranny of a heartless political Church. Speaking of the sacredness of property—how England does adore the Almighty Farthing" (pp. 340–342).

He recognizes that his attitude toward Grand's novel is changing: "It is very curious. There is nothing but labored & lubberly & unsuccessful attempts at humor concerning the twins up to Chap 7, Book III—but all this about the Boy in this Book IV is very good fun indeed" (p. 417). And, "I can't understand it. The boy *is* humorous now, but as a child he was only disgusting. I think that this part of the book must have been written a long time after the first part—& after severe training" (p. 419). Thereafter his numerous notes generally make grammatical revisions. "Darn the subjunctive—it is always a snare," he observes on page 555, altering a word. Even as far into the volume as page 666 he was improving the style, altering "we should like to have seen" into "we should have liked to see". Before closing the volume he wrote in pencil on the fourth flyleaf, opposite the copyright notice at the front: "*After reading the book*: the grammar is often dreadful—even hideous—but never mind that, it is a strong, good book." The volume contains a great many other notes, including (on the rear pastedown endpaper) several maxims—one of them denigrates the French national character; the other would serve as an epigraph for Chapter 3 of *Following the Equator* (1897): "It is more trouble to make a maxim than it is to do right." On the rear flyleaf Clemens began a comment he never fully completed: "*There's* a curious thing: I am an aristocrat (in the aristocracy of the mind & of achievement) & from my Viscountship look reverently up at all earls, marquises and dukes above me, & superciliously down upon the barons, baronets and Knights below me but I can't find anything endurable in the aristocracy of birth and privilege—*it* turns my stomach. I feel in this way although I. . . ." (the latter note quoted in *MT&JB* [1970], pp. 172—173).

Catalogs: *A1911*, "12mo, cloth, N.Y., n.d., with autograph notes, in pencil, throughout the work," quotes nearly all of the marginalia, lot 195, sold for $55; George D. Smith, New York City, "Catalog of Books" (1911), quotes Clemens's marginalia at length, item #139, $75; Anderson Auction Company, Sale 956, for the library of the late Jordan J. Rollins of New York City (1–3 May 1912), "12mo, cloth, N.Y., n.d., with autograph notes, in pencil, throughout," quotes marginalia, reports the *A1911* sale label, lot 328, sold for $25; George A. Van Nosdall, New York City, List No. 109 (20 November

1923), item #1, $100; Parke-Bernet Galleries, New York City, Sale number 103, 4–5 April 1939, lot 116, "12mo, original cloth; a few small stains on covers, in half blue morocco slip case . . . with autograph notes in pencil by him on the margin of 41 pages . . . comprising about eight hundred words," has the stamp of the Mark Twain Library, Redding, Connecticut, and also the *A1911* sale label, sold for $40.

Location: Henry W. and Albert A. Berg Collection, New York Public Library.

Copy examined: Clemens's copy, one of the most exhaustively annotated volumes in his library. Contains the bookstamps of the Mark Twain Library of Redding on the front pastedown endpaper; it had been donated from Clemens's library by Clara Clemens Gabrilowitsch in 1910 (MTLAcc, entry #2244). Evidently Albert Bigelow Paine retrieved it from that collection for the auction conducted in 1911.

On 27 February 1902 Olivia Clemens included Sarah Grand in the list of guests she had entertained at Riverdale-on-Hudson since October 1901 (OLC's Diary, DV161, MTP). Clemens wrote down the following dialogue between a librarian and a patron in Notebook 48, whose entries span the years 1905–1908 and largely consist of risqué jokes: "'Got the Indiscretions of a Duchess?' 'It's out,—but we have the sequel, "The Heavenly Twins"'" (TS p. 19).

Robert Rowlette, "Mark Twain, Sarah Grand, and *The Heavenly Twins*," *Mark Twain Journal* 16.2 (Summer 1972): 17–18, compared Grand's *The Heavenly Twins* with Twain's *Pudd'nhead Wilson* (1894), which similarly contains "a sub-plot featuring twins." However, Elaine Showalter, in "Mark Twain and Sarah Grand," *Mark Twain Journal* 19.4 (Summer 1979): 21–22, cast doubt on whether "Twain had read this copy of Grand's book early enough to affect his revising of *Pudd'nhead Wilson*." Showalter noted that Clemens seemed comfortable with the feminist messages in the book and the implicit criticism of male sexual behavior that can introduce venereal disease into a home; she incidentally reported that Grand eventually learned of Clemens's marginalia in *The Heavenly Twins*, and in her 1923 edition of the novel she recalled meeting Clemens in 1901 and commended his "open-minded thoroughness" for having "persevered to the end of the book and decided that nevertheless notwithstanding it 'got there.'" See also Kathryn Anne Atkins, "Towards a Critical Edition of the Short Fiction of Sarah Grand," Ph. D. dissertation, University of the West of England, Bristol, 2015.

GRANDGENT, CHARLES HALL (1862–1939). *Italian Grammar*. Rev. and enl. Edition. Boston: D. C. Heath Co., 1902. 132 pp. [Publisher and pages supplied.]

Catalog: *A1911*, "12mo, cloth, Bost. 1902," a small sheet of manuscript notes laid in, lot 196, sold for $1.

Antonio Illiano, "'Italian Without a Master': A Note for the Appreciation of Mark Twain's Undictionarial Translation as Exercise in Humor," *Mark Twain Journal* 17.2 (Summer 1974): 17–20.

GRANGER [Unidentified book].

"I have left the matter of the 'Granger' book alone till Frank [Fuller] shall return. If it is a good thing it will keep" (SLC to Mary F. Fuller, Hartford, 7 April 1874; *MTLet* 6: 101). See the Catalog entry for James Dabney McCabe as one possibility for this reference.

GRANT, PERCY STICKNEY (1860–1927). *Ad Matrem and Other Poems*. New York: Ingalls Kimball, 1905. 61 pp.

Inscription: inscribed on the half-title page, in black ink, "Samuel L. Clemens/from a neighbor and admirer,/ Percy S. Grant."

Location: Mark Twain Library, Redding, Connecticut.

Copy examined: Clemens's unmarked copy. Has the red ink Mark Twain Library accession number "3158". A bookmark advertising *Lippincott's Monthly Magazine* has been inserted between pages 20 and 21. Examined in 1970 and again in June 1982.

———. *The Search of Belisarius, A Byzantine Legend*. New York: Brentano's, 1907. 114 pp.

Source: MTLAcc, entry #2029, volume donated from Clemens's library by Clara Clemens Gabrilowitsch in 1910.

Grant's Farm. Illus. [Author, publisher, date not supplied.]

Source: MTLAcc, entry #1224, volume donated by Clemens.

The Missouri farm in St. Louis County on which Ulysses S. Grant lived with his in-laws the Dents was sketched by landscape artist Walter Staengel for a wood engraving widely reproduced in 1875. However, no record has been located of an illustrated book about the Dent farmhouse and Grant's farm contemporary with Clemens's life.

GRANT, ULYSSES SIMPSON (1822–1885). *Personal Memoirs of U.S. Grant*. Illus. Engraved frontispiece portraits. 2 vols. New York: Charles L. Webster & Co., 1885–86.

Catalog: *A1911*, "Vol. 1 only, 8vo, cloth, N.Y. 1885," original manuscript notes laid in, lot 197, sold for .75¢.

———. [Another identical copy.]

Catalog: *A1911*, "Vol. 1 only, 8vo, cloth, N.Y. 1885," original manuscript notes laid in, lot 198, sold for $1.

———. [Another identical copy.]

Catalog: *A1911*, "Vol. 1 only, 8vo, cloth, N.Y. 1885," original manuscript notes laid in, lot 199, sold for $1.

———. [Another identical copy.]

Provenance: in the collection of Victor Jacobs of Dayton, Ohio in 1986 (Jacobs to Alan Gribben, 15 October 1986, "with Mark Twain's signature in Volume 1"). Jacobs died in 1996 and the Victor and Irene Murr Jacobs Collection was auctioned by Sotheby's on 29 October 1996.

———. [Another identical copy.]

Inscription: "Presented to Mr. Clemens by Mrs. U. S. Grant, 1885; signed by S. L. C." (*C1951*).

Catalog: ListABP (1910), "*Memoirs of Gen. Grant*, 2 v."; *C1951*, #1a, 2 vols., $110, listed among books containing Clemens's marginal notes.

———. [Another identical copy.]

Inscription: Clemens inscribed the front flyleaf of both volumes in ink, "To/Miss Fanny C. Hesse/with kindest regards of/S. L. Clemens/Christmas 1887." Hesse was the sister-in-law of Clemens's friend and neighbor, Charles Warner.

Provenance: acquired by Nick Karanovich of Fort Wayne, Indiana from Paul C. Richards Autographs, Templeton, Massachusetts, for $1,000 on 23 January 1985.

Catalog: *Sotheby's 2003*, #205, $27,500.

Copy examined: presentation copy inscribed by Clemens,

at the 2003 Sotheby's sale. In addition, Nick Karanovich previously had sent photocopies of the spines, title pages, and inscriptions to Alan Gribben on 28 January 1985.

———. [Another identical copy.]

Inscription: Volume 2 inscribed and signed by Clemens: "Miss Fanny C. Hesse with the Christmas greetings of her friend the publisher of this well printed & otherwise admirable book, S. L. Clemens of the firm. 1885." Hesse was the sister-in-law of Clemens's friend and neighbor, Charles Dudley Warner.

Location: Volume 2 only in the Albert and Shirley Small Special Collections Library, University of Virginia, Charlottesville, Virginia. Gift of Clifton Waller Barrett.

Source: University of Virginia Libraries Catalog, March 2006. (Jo Dee Benussi pointed out this listing.)

———. [Another identical copy.]

Inscription: inscribed and signed by Clemens: "To my friend Major Pond./S. L. Clemens/ Publisher." Displays the bookplate of James B. Pond, Mark Twain's lecture agent.

Location: Albert and Shirley Small Special Collections Library, University of Virginia, Charlottesville, Virginia. Gift of Clifton Waller Barrett.

Source: University of Virginia Libraries Catalog, March 2006. (I am grateful to Jo Dee Benussi for noticing this item.)

———. [Another identical copy.]

Inscription: on the front flyleaf of Volume I, in ink, "To/ 'Brer Whitmo'/(otherwise F. G. Whitmore)/ from his friend/S. L. Clemens/(Chief of the firm of C. L. Webster & Co.)/Hartford, Apl. 2, 1887." The front free flyleaf of Volume 2 is inscribed in ink, "To/F. G. Whitmore/from/S. L. Clemens/Apl. 1887".

Location: Mark Twain House and Museum, Hartford, Connecticut.

Copy examined: presentation copy from Clemens to his Hartford friend and business agent, Franklin G. Whitmore. Examined in August 1987.

———. [Another identical copy.]

Location: Mark Twain Papers, Bancroft Library, University of California at Berkeley.

Copy examined: another copy owned by Clemens, unmarked.

———. [Another identical copy.]

Inscription: Clemens inscribed the front flyleaves of both volumes identically in black ink: "To/Theodore Crane/ with the loving regards of/S. L. Clemens/Dec. 2, 1885."

Marginalia: Clemens made a vertical, wavy line in pencil on page 357 at Grant's recollection that after the second day of the Battle of Shiloh "it would have been possible to walk across the clearing, in any direction, stepping on dead bodies, without a foot touching the ground." Scott Dalrymple—"Just War, Pure and Simple: *A Connecticut Yankee in King Arthur's Court* and the American Civil War," *American Literary Realism* 29.1 (Fall 1996): 1–11—made the case that Grant's *Personal Memoirs* (and especially this passage marked by Clemens) had connections with the climactic battle scene in Twain's later novel.

Catalogs: QF Martinez, a list of books in the library when Quarry Farm was donated to Elmira College in 1983; listed among the books that Mark Woodhouse transferred from the Quarry Farm library to the Mark Twain Archive on

9 July 1987; Ball 2016 inventory, inscribed to Theodore Crane, poor condition.

Location: Mark Twain Archive, Elmira College, Elmira, New York.

Copy examined: a presentation copy marked by Clemens and given to Theodore W. Crane in 1885. Brown cloth, half calf, gilt edges. Examined on 11 August 1988 in Elmira. Mark Woodhouse, then curator of the Mark Twain Archive, later furnished photocopies of the inscriptions (Woodhouse e-mail to Alan Gribben, 11 May 2015).

U. S. Grant's military exploits and stature as a public hero awed and fascinated Clemens, and his references to Grant were numerous. Chapter 31 of *The Innocents Abroad* (1869), in which Twain visits the ruins of Pompeii, muses about the "unsubstantial, unlasting character of fame" and jocularly speculates that even "General Grant's great name" may be confused with that of a popular poet "forty centuries hence." In a letter of 23 November 1884 Grant notified George William Childs of the Century Company that he intended to reject their offer and publish his memoirs on "very much more favorable terms by Chas. L. Webster & Co. Mark Twain is the Company." When he thus became Grant's sole publisher Clemens felt that he was truly participating in history—insuring the financial security of Grant's family, recording the dying general's view of the events he had shaped, answering reporters' queries concerning Grant's physical condition, waiting with the nation for the "simultaneous voice" of the bells that would announce Grant's momentarily expected death (NB 23, *N&J* 3: 118). Clemens wrote to Howells on 5 May 1885 from Hartford: "In two days General Grant has dictated 50 pages of foolscap, & thus the Wilderness & Appomattox stand for all time in his own words. This makes the Second volume of his book as valuable as the first" (*MTHL*, p. 528). On 11 December 1885 Clemens joyfully copied Howells's praise for Grant's work into his notebook: "The book merits its enormous success, simply as literature" (NB 25, *N&J* 3: 217). The immense success of this publishing venture was one of the proudest chapters in Clemens's eventful life. Clemens would heatedly defend Grant's prose style in "General Grant's Grammar" (1886). (See the Catalog entry for Caesar's *Commentaries*.) On 20 January 1887 Clemens recommended Grant's *Memoirs* as being among the best reading for young people in a letter to the Reverend Charles D. Crane (ALS, Shapell Manuscript Library, Beverly Hills, California).

Kay Moser, "Mark Twain and Ulysses S. Grant," *Studies in American Humor* n. s. 1.2 (October 1982), pp. 130–141; Rachel Cohen, "A Private History: Moments in the Friendship of Mark Twain and Ulysses S. Grant," *DoubleTake Magazine #21* 6:3 (Summer 2000): n. p.; Mark Perry, *Grant and Twain: The Story of an American Friendship* (New York: Random House, 2004); Forrest G. Robinson, "The General and the Maid: Mark Twain on Ulysses S. Grant and Joan of Arc," *Arizona Quarterly* 61.1 (Spring 2005): 41–56; Joe B. Fulton, *The Reconstruction of Mark Twain: How a Confederate Bushwhacker Became the Lincoln of Our Literature* (Baton Rouge: Louisiana State University Press, 2010); and Jerome Loving, *Confederate Bushwhacker: Mark Twain in the Shadow of the Civil War* (Hanover, New Hampshire: University Press of New England, 2013).

GRAU, ROBERT (1858–1916). *Forty Years Observation of Music and the Drama by Robert Grau. Profusely Illustrated from Photographs and Prints.* Red cloth, decorated. New York: Broadway Publishing Co., 1909. 370 pp.

Marginalia: no signature or markings, but a piece of manuscript approximately six inches square is laid in, containing penciled calculations of the number of words in a two-volume book of 600 pages.

Provenance: Antenne-Dorrance Collection, Rice Lake, Wisconsin.

Location: Mark Twain Archive, Gannett-Tripp Learning Center, Elmira College, Elmira, New York.

Copy examined: Clemens's copy. Examined on 28 May 2015.

Grau's book contains a photograph of Clara Clemens preceding its first page; underneath the portrait is the caption: "Clara Clemens/Contralto (daughter of 'Mark Twain')."

GRAVERT, W[ILHELM]. *Drittes Deutsches Lesebuch. [Third German Reading Book.]* New York: E. Steiger, 1872. 236 pp.

Source: MTLAcc, entry #370, volume donated by Clemens.

———. [Another identical copy.]

Source: MTLAcc, entry #371, volume donated by Clemens.

GRAY, ASA (1810–1888). *Gray's School and Field Book of Botany. Consisting of "First Lessons in Botany," and Field, Forest, and Garden Botany, Bound in One Volume.* New York: Ivison, Phinney, Blakeman & Co., 1869. 236, 386 pp.

Source: MTLAcc, entry #1950, volume donated from Clemens's library by Clara Clemens Gabrilowitsch in 1910.

———. *How Plants Behave; How They Move, Climb, Employ Insects to Work for Them, Etc.* Botany for Young People Series. Part II. Illus. New York: Ivison, Blakeman, Taylor, and Co., 1875. 46 pp.

Source: MTLAcc, entry #514, volume donated by Clemens.

————. *How Plants Grow; A Simple Introduction to Structural Botany; With a Popular Flora.* Botany for Young People and Common Schools Series. Illus. New York: Ivison, Blakeman, Taylor & Co., 1876. 233 pp.

Source: MTLAcc, entry #1949, volume donated from Clemens's library by Clara Clemens Gabrilowitsch in 1910.

GRAY, DAVID (1836–1888). *Letters, Poems and Selected Prose Writings of David Gray.* Edited with a Biographical Memoir by Josephus Nelson Larned (1836–1913). Buffalo, New York, 1888.

Inscription: signed "S. L. Clemens, 1888."

Catalog: *A1911*, "post 8vo, cloth, gilt top, uncut, Buffalo, 1888," quotes the signature, lot 200, sold for $3.

Clemens knew Gray as a newspaperman-poet in Buffalo in the early 1870s and counted him as a close friend. He noted Gray's name for a complimentary copy of *Adventures of Huckleberry Finn* in 1885 (NB 23, *N&J* 3: 115). In 1888 he sent a check to J. N. Larned to assist with the expenses of publishing Gray's collected writings (Thomas J. Reigstad, *Scribblin' for a Livin': Mark Twain's Pivotal Period in Buffalo* [Amherst, New York: Prometheus Books, 2013], pp. 54, 195–196, 293 n. 47). In an Autobiographical Dictation of 22 February 1906 Clemens lamented the "waste" of Gray's writing talents owing to his journalistic editorial responsibilities; "he was a singing bird in a menagerie of monkeys, macaws, and hyenas" (*AutoMT* 1: 375). On 31 July 1906 he recalled Gray's praise for *1601* in 1876

(*MTE*, p. 209; *AutoMT* 2: 156–157).

Martin B. Fried, "Mark Twain as Editor: The *Courier* vs. The *Express*," *Niagara Frontier* (Buffalo and Erie County Historical Society) 19 (Spring 1972): 50–54, explained that the rivalry between their newspapers did not deter the lasting friendship of Clemens and Gray, at whose home Clemens stayed on return visits to Buffalo.

GRAY, GEORGE ZABRISKIE (1838–1889). *The Children's Crusade; An Episode of the Thirteenth Century.* New York: Hurd and Houghton, 1872. 240 pp.

Source: ListABP (1910) ("Children's Crusade, Gray").

Gray was a Protestant Episcopal clergyman in New Jersey when he wrote *The Children's Crusade*; later he became a theology professor. Near the conclusion of this history he summarized the sad outcome: "Sixty thousand families, it is estimated, were by it saddened or bereaved, and in its mad current, nearly a hundred thousand children were carried away to hardships or to death" (p. 281).

GRAY, THOMAS (1716–1771). "Elegy Written in a Country Churchyard" (poem, published 1751).

Clemens quoted from stanza 32 in an early unpublished sketch, "Jul'us Caesar" (TS in DV400, MTP), probably written around 1856. Mark Twain traced "all the grave-yard poetry to Elegy Gray or Wolfe, indiscriminately" in a humorous piece for the *Californian*, 17 June 1865 (*LAMT*, p. 142; *ET&S* 2: 195). In Twain's sketch for the 7 April 1866 issue of the *Californian*, a man who has been drinking on a steamboat quotes from "Elegy" while attempting to remember "Hohenlinden" (*SSix*, p. 209). In 1872 Twain mentioned "Gray who wrote the *Elegy*" in his English journal entry describing the tombs in Westminster Abbey (*MTB*, p. 469; *MTLet* 5: 603); he repeated this same reference in "A Memorable Midnight Experience" (1874). In a speech Twain gave at the Windsor Hotel in Montreal on 8 December 1881 he recalled Major James Wolfe's "remark that he would rather be the author of Gray's 'Elegy' than take Quebec" (*MTSpk*, p. 159). Many years later Clemens quoted from the poem ("Homeward the bandit [*sic*] plods her weary way/And leaves the world to darkness and to me") in a letter to Dorothy Quick written from Tuxedo Park on 12 September 1907 (*Enchantment*, p. 90). Clemens owned a copy of Edmund Gosse's biography of Gray.

Dixon Wecter, ed., *Report from Paradise* (1952), p. xvii.

———. *The Poems of Thomas Gray.* New York: White, Stokes, and Allen, 1883. 167 pp.

Source: MTLAcc, entry #2032, volume donated from Clemens's library by Clara Clemens Gabrilowitsch in 1910.

GRAY, ZENAS J.(1855–1927). *Driftwood.* Harrisburg, Pennsylvania: Patriot Publishing Co., 1884. 86 pp.

Source: MTLAcc, entry #610, volume donated by Clemens. Gray would subsequently attain regional recognition for editing *Prose and Poetry of the Susquehanna and Juniata Rivers* (1893).

———. [Another identical copy.]

Source: MTLAcc, entry #628, volume donated by Clemens.

Great Religions of the World, by Herbert A[llen]. Giles [1845–1935], T[homas]. W[illiam]. Rhys Davids [1843–1922], Oskar Mann [1867–1917], A. C. Lyall, D[elphine]. Menant [b. 1850], Lepel Griffin [1838–1908], Frederic Harrison [1831–1923], E[dward]. Denison Ross [1871–1940], M.

Gasier, Washington Gladden [1836–1918], and Cardinal [James] Gibbons [1834–1921]. First edition. The title page is printed in red and black. Original blue cloth, gilt, spine frayed. New York: Harper & Brothers, 1901. 301 pp.

Inscription: the front free endpaper is inscribed in pencil, "S. L. Clemens/Ampersand/Saranac Lake, N. Y./Sept. 15, 1901."

Marginalia: Clemens made twenty-four mildly critical or negative annotations totaling sixty-seven words, scattered over eighteen pages. Forty other pages contain marginal lines and underlinings. See *The Twainian* 38 (January-February 1979): 1–4; (March-April 1979): 1–3. Most of Clemens's notes occur in the first twenty-nine pages in Giles' chapter on "Confucianism in the Nineteenth Century." Beside Giles' assertion, on page 9, that Protestant missionaries in China have never abused their opportunities, Clemens retorted, "No business there." Following a quotation on page 22 from the Reverend A. Smith's *Chinese Characteristics* that "there is in Confucianism much that is excellent . . . and many points in which the doctrines of Christian revelation are almost echoed," Clemens queried, "Haven't you got it turned around?" Where Giles stated that Christianity cannot accept Confucianism's "dogma that man is born good, and that his lapse into evil is wholly due to his environment" (page 23), Clemens marked the passage and commented, "Most certainly he is not born bad." Marginal markings continue through three subsequent chapters (Rhys Davids on "Buddhism," Oskar Mann on "Mohammedanism in the Nineteenth Century," and Lepel Griffin on "Sikhism and the Sikhs"). The leaves of the three final chapters covering Judaism, Christianity, and Catholicism are largely unopened.

Provenance: has the shelfmark of Clara Clemens Gabrilowitsch's private library in Detroit. In 1970 this volume was in the collection of Chester L. Davis (1903–1987), Executive-Secretary, Mark Twain Research Foundation, Perry, Missouri. Subsequently it joined the collection of Nick Karanovich, Fort Wayne, Indiana.

Catalogs: Christie's, New York City, Sale 7378, including the "Chester L. Davis Estate," 5 December 1991, lot 183, sold for $3,300; *Sotheby's 2003*, lot 203, sold for $3,750.

Location: collection of Kevin Mac Donnell, Austin, Texas.

Copy examined: Clemens's copy, in Perry, Missouri in 1970 (briefly), and in July 2004 in Austin, Texas. It has a *C1951* sale label.

The Greek Romances of Heliodorus [of Emesa, fl. 4th century], Longus [c. 2nd century], and Achilles Tatius [2nd or 3rd century]; Comprising the Ethiopics; or, the Adventures of Theagenes and Chariclea; the Pastoral Amours of Daphnis and Chloe; and the Loves of Clitopho and Leucippe. Translated from the Greek, with Notes, by the Rev. Rowland Smith [1808–1895]. Bohn's Classical Library Series. Original dark green cloth. London: Henry G. Bohn, 1855. 511 pp.

Inscription: title page signed in ink "Saml. L. Clemens/ Hartford, 1875."

Marginalia: According to Kevin Mac Donnell, there is a pencil line in the margin of page xvi of the Preface where Longus is described as an author who wrote about "rustic occupations" and "rural enjoyments." Page 420 is folded down. The front pastedown endpaper carries an *A1911* auction label.

Catalogs: *A1911*, "12mo, original cloth, Lond.: Bohn, 1855," quotes signature, lot 203, sold for $5.50; *Selections from the Library of William E. Boeing, Part II* (2011), comp. Joseph C. Baillargeon, Restoration Books, Seattle, Washington, p. 64.

Location: collection of Kevin Mac Donnell, Austin, Texas (Mac Donnell to Alan Gribben, 29 November 2011).

Robert Klevay, "Mark Twain's Reading in Classical Literature: An Overview," *Mark Twain Journal: The Author and His Era* 57.1 (Spring 2019): 112–132, pointed out that this is one of the few (surviving) books from the Classical Greece period in Clemens's library. Its translator Rowland Smith, a graduate of Oxford College, was the Anglican rector at Ilston, Swansea in Wales from 1854 until 1865; in 1871 he would move to the Swyncombe Rectory at Henley-on-the Thames, Oxford.

GREELEY, HORACE (1811–1872). *Hints Toward Reforms in Lectures, Addresses and Other Writings.* [First published in 1850; variously reprinted in the 1850s.]

Mark Twain jokingly claimed in letter to the *Missouri Democrat* (13 March 1867) that he had sent "the poor savages of the South seas" a copy of "Horace Greeley's speeches and some other cheerful literature" (*MTPP*, pp. 12–13). Greeley had by 1867 developed a national reputation of being a political gadfly, and was becoming an object of ridicule by numerous commentators.

———. *What I Know of Farming: A Series of Brief and Plain Expositions of Practical Agriculture as an Art Based Upon Science.* New York: The Tribune Association, 1871. 335 pp. [Publisher and pages conjectured; an identical edition was published in 1871 by G. W. Carleton & Co. of New York City.]

Inscription: presentation copy inscribed by Greeley: "To Mark Twain, Esq., Ed. Buffalo Express, who knows even less of MY farming than does Horace Greeley. N. York."

Catalog: *A1911*, "first edition, 12mo, cloth, N.Y. 1871," quotes the inscription, lot 204, sold for $22.

Mark Twain ridiculed Greeley's cabbage-raising and notions of a "model garden" in "Private Habits of Horace Greeley" (1868), but conceded that he was "an upright and an honest man—a practical, great-brained man—a useful man to his nation and his generation." On 11 September 1869 Twain alluded in the Buffalo *Express* ("The Last Words of Great Men") to Greeley's interest in political economy; he may have been tipped off that Greeley was bringing out his *Essays Designed to Elucidate the Science of Political Economy, While Serving to Explain and Defend the Policy of Protection to Home Industry, As a System of National Cöoperation for the Elevation of Labor* (Boston: Fields, Osgood, & Co., 1870). At about the same time Olivia Langdon copied a quotation attributed to Greeley into her commonplace book in Elmira (DV161, MTP). Twain poked cruel fun at Greeley's outlandish costume and countenance in "The Tone-Imparting Committee" (February 1871). Much later Twain would recall that he met Greeley only once ("by accident") in 1871, when Twain was looking for John Hay and Greeley snapped at him when he opened Greeley's office door to inquire about Hay (undated AD, *MTE*, pp. 347–348; *AutoMT* 1: 145). In Chapter 20 of *Roughing It* (1872) Twain told and retold the inflated story of Greeley and Hank Monk,

and Chapter 70 of *Roughing It* alluded to Greeley's supposed knowledge of agriculture (specifically the raising of turnips) and made fun of Greeley's supposedly illegible handwriting. Nonetheless, Twain mentioned Greeley as "a man whom I greatly admired . . . and whose memory I still revere" in a letter to the editor of *Harper's Weekly* published in the 21 October 1905 issue (reprinted as "John Hay and the Ballads," in *Mark Twain: Life as I Find It*, ed. Charles Neider [Garden City: Hanover, 1961], p. 274).

Lawrence I. Berkove, "Mark Twain and Horace Greeley: Penpals," *Thalia* 11.2 (1991): 3–11.

GREENAWAY, KATE (1846–1901). *Kate Greenaway's Birthday Book for Children.* 382 illustrations. London: George Routledge and Sons, 1880. [Edition conjectured.]

Catalog: ListABP (1910), "Kate Greenaway's Birthday Book", no other information supplied.

GREEN, JOHN RICHARD (1837–1883). *History of the English People.* 4 vols. New York: Harper & Brothers, 1878–1880. [Edition conjectured; the publisher of Clemens's copy is not confirmed.]

Catalog: *C1951*, D7, $48, listed among books signed by Clemens.

———. *A Short History of the English People.* Maps and Tables [of monarchs and events]. New York: Harper & Brothers, 1875. 823 pp.

Inscription: signed in pencil on the front free flyleaf, "Saml. L. Clemens/Hartford 1875".

Marginalia: Clemens left Green's "Preface" unmarked. The *A1911* catalog reported numerous emendations in Clemens's hand throughout Chapter I, mainly correcting grammatical errors, mixed metaphors, and convoluted sentence structures. His frequent annotations in Chapter I (titled "The English Kingdoms, 607–1013" and comprising pages 39–92) come to a halt at page 87, though Clemens also made vertical lines in the margins of four subsequent pages. All of his notes and markings are in pencil. Clemens pounced on a clause midway down page 46—"Their march led them through a district full of memories of a past which had even then faded from the minds of men"—and pronounced it to be "A meaningless sentence." He then suggested a rewording of it on the opposite blank page: "—full of suggestions of a past which had even then faded from the knowledge of men—(The man had *relic* in his mind—as plainly appears by the next sentence.)" A sentence on page 47 ("When the steady progress of English conquest was stayed for a while by civil wars of a century and a half after Aylesford, the Briton had disappeared from the greater part of the land") caused Clemens to write vertically in the margin: "What *can* that sentence mean?" There are markings or brief objecting notes on pages 49, 50, 51, 52, 53, and 54. The top, bottom, and right-hand margins of page 55 are entirely filled with Clemens's exasperated comments. He bracketed the third sentence and commented, "That sentence is simply turned wrong end first." On the same page 55, where Green states that "The great fabric of the Roman law, indeed, never took root in England," Clemens jeered: "Does a 'fabric' *ever* take root?" Farther down the same page the historian recounted that "the King, however, recovered from his wound, to march on the West-Saxons"; Clemens underlined the statement and

asked, "Did he recover from his wound *merely* for the purpose of marching on the West Saxons?" On pages 55–56 Green writes that the king "slew and subdued all who had conspired against him"; at the top of page 56 Clemens humorously summarized this sequence as "He made corpses of the conspirators & then 'subdued' the corpses." Other corrections appear in the left margin of page 56. Clemens found brief revisions necessary on pages 57, 58, 59 (there are six such corrections, including "not the right word" where Green used the term "divided"), 60, 63, 64, 65, 66, 67, 68, and 69. On page 66 Clemens made a penciled suggestion, writing vertically in the margin: "How would it do to say 'was tied with no string but the sword?'" On page 67 he changed "site" to "base" in the clause, "Earth was brought in boats to form a site".
A few of Clemens's notes spare Green's prose from criticism and instead concentrate on the story he is telling. On page 74, for example, where Green relates the pathos of the Venerable Bede's death as he was using his last breaths to finish translating the Gospel of St. John into English, Clemens wrote vertically in the left margin: "Worthy to stand/with Socrates's/death, & the same". On page 76 Clemens jotted a vertical note to clarify a point about Offa, a Mercian king in Anglo-Saxon England: "(One would suppose that of *course* this miscreant was referring to the Frankish King.)" Passages on pages 77 and 87—(where Clemens queried "(*Whose* horse?)" at the top of the page—seemed to Clemens to require minor revisions. Clemens's marginalia then skip to vertical marks on pages 252 (next to a description of the corruption of the Church in the Middle Ages and Chaucer's barb about "pardons hot from Rome") and 256 (at Wyclif's rejection of the doctrine of transubstantiation) These markings conclude at page 309 in Chapter VI (the period of 1471–1509).
Catalogs: *A1911*, "8vo, cloth, N.Y. 1875," quotes Clemens's signature and various marginalia, lot 205, sold for $16; George D. Smith, New York City, "Catalogue of Books" (1911), quotes the signature and various marginalia, item #142, $35.
Provenance: bookplate of William F. Gable on the front pastedown endpaper. Above that is pasted the bookplate of the George N. Meissner Collection. Below these two bookplates is the *A1911* sale label.
Location: George N. Meissner Collection, Special Collections, Washington University, St. Louis, Missouri. Photocopies of the title page, inscriptions, and representative marginalia were sent to Alan Gribben on 22 January 1981 by Timothy D. Murry, then Curator of Manuscripts, Special Collections, Washington University Libraries. A fuller set of photocopies was later provided by Ms. Kelly Brown of Special Collections (Brown to Alan Gribben, 12 May 2015). Photocopies of the marginalia had also been sent to the Mark Twain Project at the Bancroft Library in Berkeley and were authenticated by the editors there on 20 July 1978, according to a letter on file in the Special Collections at Washington University.
Copy examined: Clemens's heavily annotated copy. Examined in St. Louis on 10 August 2015.
Green's *Short History* contained elaborate "Genealogical Tables" of the "Danish Kings" followed by the "Sovereigns of England" (pp. xxii–xxxv). However, Green took an

unusual approach to his large subject by briefly summarizing the traditional topics of battles and kingships and focusing more extensively on the activities and beliefs of the English people—in other words, he compiled something closer to a social history than merely a military and political chronicle. Clemens wrote to Brown & Gross, Hartford booksellers, on 15 January 1887, requesting Green's one-volume *Short History of the English People* (PH in MTP). On 20 January 1887 Clemens replied to "friend Gross": "As I understand it, you already have Green in ½ calf, & can get a ½ calf Macaulay. . . . That'll do—send 'em along" (ASSSCL, PH in MTP). The textual and explanatory notes for *A Connecticut Yankee in King Arthur's Court*, ed. Bernard L. Stein (Berkeley: University of California Press, 1979) explicated Twain's numerous borrowings from Green's work while composing that novel. A letter from Clara Clemens to Chatto & Windus, written before 15 August 1898, relayed Clemens's request for another copy of this book (Welland, *Mark Twain in England*, p. 189).
Stone, "Mark Twain's *Joan of Arc*" (1959), p. 4; Baetzhold, *MT&JB* (1970), p. 343 n. 39.
GREEN, MARY ANNE EVERETT (1818–1895). *Lives of the Princesses of England from the Norman Conquest.* 6 vols. 1850–1855.
Catalog: *A1911*, "post 8vo, uniformly bound in full polished calf, gilt backs, Lond.," sold as part of the uniformly bound set of Agnes Strickland's *Queens* (26 vols.), lot 441. See the Catalog entry for Strickland.
GREEN, MASON A. (1850–1926). *Springfield [, Massachusetts], 1636–1886; History of Town and City.* Portraits, plans, illustrations. Springfield, Massachusetts: C. A. Nichols, & Co., 1888. 732 pp.
Catalogs: *A1911*, "royal 8vo, cloth, gilt top, Springfield, Mass., 1888," a sheet of notes laid in, lot 206, sold for $3.50; George D. Smith, New York City, "Catalogue of Books" (1911), item #375, $10.
GREEN, NELSON WINCH (1820–1907). *Fifteen Years among the Mormons: Being the Narrative of Mrs. Mary Ettie V. Smith, Late of Great Salt Lake City: A Sister of One of the Mormon High Priests, She Having Been Personally Acquainted with Most of the Mormon Leaders, and Long in the Confidence of the "Prophet," Brigham Young.* New York: H. Dayton, 1859. 408 pp.
Nicole Amare and Alan Manning—"The Mormon Entombed in Mark Twain's Heart: Ina Coolbrith and Samuel Clemens," *Mark Twain Journal* 55.1–2 (Spring/Fall 2017): XXX—establish the fact that the engraved illustration of a Mormon woman on page 118 of Twain's *Roughing It* (1872) was borrowed without credit from the frontispiece of Green's book.
GREENE, BELLE C. [ISABEL CATHERINE (COLTON)] (1844–1926). *Adventures of an Old Maid. By Aunt Ruth.* New York: J. S. Ogilvie, [cop. 1886]. 127 pp. [Greene's first name is sometimes listed as Isabella.]
Greene wrote from Nashua, New Hampshire on 15 January 1887 to inquire whether Clemens had received "a copy of my humorous sketches" that she had sent to him last summer, She asked that he at least read the eleventh of the eighteen stories in the book, "She Goes to the Dentist" (pp. 99–104). Clemens's reply on 17 January 1887 was equivocal at best; he frankly judged that her sketches "are pretty good, but not very good." To soften this blow he

noted that whereas in his opinion John Habberton's *Helen's Babies* was utterly "witless," it had nevertheless enjoyed "a perfectly Biblical circulation" (PH in MTP). JoDee Benussi brought this exchange of letters to my attention after she saw Greene's letter quoted in David H. Fears' *Mark Twain Day by Day*, 2: 125. Evidently Greene stayed in touch with Clemens (or at least with his secretary); see the Catalog entry for H. C. Greene (trans.), *Gospel of the Childhood of Our Lord Jesus Christ*.

————. *A New England Conscience*. New York: G. P. Putnam's Sons, 1885. 196 pp. [Publisher and pages conjectured.]

Source: MTLAcc, entry #2247, volume donated from Clemens's library by Clara Clemens Gabrilowitsch in 1910. This religious novel was somewhat out of Greene's usual line; the Nashua, New Hampshire author generally wrote humorous stories, sketches, and novels about New England rural life. Her books included *A New England Idyl* and *The Hobbledehoy*.

GREENE, HENRY COPLEY (1871–1951), trans. *The Gospel of the Childhood of Our Lord Jesus Christ; Translated from the Latin by Henry Copley Greene, with Original Text of the Manuscript at the Monastery of Saint Wolfgang*. Intro. by Alice Meynell (1847–1922). Illustrated by Carlos Schwabe (1866–1926). New York: Scott-Thaw Co., London: Burns and Oates, 1904. 272 pp.

In Dublin, New Hampshire, Clemens resided in the summer place of "Henry Copley Greene, when I am not occupying his house, which I am doing this season" (SLC to Frederick A. Duneka, 9 October 1905, TS in MTP). On 1 January 1906 Isabel Lyon noted in her journal: "Tonight I took a little book down to Mr. Clemens, a little book sent me by Belle Greene, 'The Childhood of Christ', translated from the Latin of an old monkish manuscript found in a monastery in the Saly Kammergut. Translation by Harry Greene. . . . I . . . read it to its finishing page with delight. Mr. Clemens read a part of it too, and found it delightful, but he was 'afraid it was a lie'" (TS p. 118, MTP). Greene's book was a translation of the Gospel of the Infant According to St. Peter, from the New Testament Apocryphal Books.

GREENE, JACOB LYMAN (1837–1905). *Gen. William B[uel]. Franklin and the Operations of the Left Wing at the Battle of Fredericksburg, December 13, 1862*. Frontispiece, map. Hartford, Connecticut: Belknap and Warfield, 1900. 38 pp.

Source: in a letter written at Dollis Hill House in London and dated 1 September 1900 Clemens thanked "Colonel Greene" for sending "the 'Franklin,' which I have read with amazement & deep concern. I doubt if a thousand men in America know of the infamous wrong that was done to Franklin" (ALS, offered for sale by the Scriptorium, Beverly Hills, California in February 1979, item #20377, priced at $1,500).

At the Battle of Fredericksburg on 13 December 1862 General Franklin commanded a division that failed in assaults against Stonewall Jackson's Confederate right flank. General Ambrose E. Burnside, commander of the Army of the Potomac, blamed Franklin for this failure and Franklin's military career thereafter suffered a series of major and minor misfortunes. The 13,000 casualties at Fredericksburg were one of the reasons that Burnside

was replaced by Joseph Hooker.

General Franklin (1823–1903) retired in Hartford. One of his close friends there, insurance executive and Civil War veteran Jacob L. Greene, endeavored to vindicate Franklin in a paper presented at the Hartford Monday Evening Club and soon thereafter Greene published these same arguments in a brief book (Mark A. Snell, *From First to Last: The Life of Major General William B. Franklin* [Bronx, New York: Fordham University Press, 2000], p. 361).

GREENE, SARAH PRATT (MCLEAN) (1856–1935). *Cape Cod Folks, A Novel*. Boston: A. Williams & Co., 1881. 327 pp.

Source: MTLAcc, entry #214, volume donated by Clemens. McLean (she would not marry Franklin L. Greene until 1887) sent Clemens a complimentary copy of *Cape Cod Folks* (McLean to SLC, 30 November 1881, ALS in MTP). "I hope that you will read it sometime," she added. He praised the book in a letter written to her from Hartford on 12 December 1881 (ALS in MTP), declaring "I have *already* read it—months ago—& vastly enjoyed & admired it, too; as did also the rest of this family" (ALS in the Harry Ransom Center, University of Texas at Austin).

————. [Another identical copy.]

Source: MTLAcc, entry #1259, volume donated by Clemens.

————. *Flood-tide*. New York: Harper & Brothers, 1901. 350 pp. [Publisher and pages conjectured.]

Inscription: the flyleaf is signed "S. L. Clemens, Riverdale, October, 1901."

Catalogs: *A1911*, "post 8vo, cloth, N.Y. 1901," quotes the signature, lot 207, sold for $2; George D. Smith, New York City, "Catalogue of Books" (1911), quotes the signature, item #143, $5.

Flood-Tide, partly a romantic novel and partly a sea adventure, portrayed the lives and adventures of sea-faring folk on the Northeastern coast. Clemens informed William Dean Howells on 29 April 1903 that he had written to Bliss Perry, editor of the *Atlantic Monthly*, "praising [George S.] Wasson's book & Miss McLean's 'Flood Tide,'" and recommending that the two works "be read together, chapter-about." In Clemens's opinion, "Wasson's delightful worldly people & Miss McL's delightful unworldly people belonged together & should mix together on the same stage" (*MTHL*, p. 769). On 26 May 1903 Henry H. Rogers wrote to Clemens from Fairhaven, Massachusetts: "Much obliged for 'Flood tide'[;] I have enjoyed it" (*MTHHR*, p. 529).

————. *Stuart and Bamboo; A Novel*. New York: Harper & Brothers, 1897. 276 pp.

Source: MTLAcc, entry #1595, volume donated by Clemens.

————. *Vesty of the Basins; A Novel*. Illustrated by Otto H. Bacher (1856–1909). New York: Harper & Brothers, 1902. 271 pp.

Source: MTLAcc, entry #1427, volume donated by Clemens.

————. *Winslow Plain*. New York: Harper & Brothers, 1902. 290 pp.

Source: MTLAcc, entry #1007, volume donated by Clemens.

GREENOUGH, JAMES BRADSTREET (1833–1901). *The Queen of Hearts. A Dramatic Fantasia. For Private Theatricals.*

Cambridge, Massachusetts, 1875.

On 28 April 1876, two days after Clemens appeared in a performance of James R. Planché's *The Loan of a Lover*, William Dean Howells inquired: "Did you get the Queen of Hearts?" (*MTHL*, p. 134).

GREENSLET, FERRIS (1875–1959). *The Life of Thomas Bailey Aldrich*. Boston: Houghton Mifflin Company, 1908. 303 pp.

Inscription: the front free endpaper is inscribed by Greenslet in ink: "Samuel L. Clemens with/the grateful acknowledg-ments/of Ferris Greenslet."

Marginalia: no markings. Unopened pages begin on 73 and continue intermittently until the end.

Catalogs: ListABP (1910), "T. B. Aldrich, Greenslet"; *C1951*, #87c, $7.50, listed among books signed by Clemens.

Provenance: sold in August 1987 by Serendipity Books of Berkeley, California for $300; purchased by John L. Feldman.

Location: currently unknown. Purchased by John Feldman of Astoria, New York in 1987 and placed on deposit in the Special Collections at the University of Colorado, but later removed by Feldman.

Aldrich died in 1907. At Greenslet's request William Dean Howells turned over his letters from Aldrich around the same time that Albert Bigelow Paine asked Howells for Mark Twain's letters. On page 157 Greenslet quoted (but misdated) a newspaper interview in Paris in which Twain praised the "inimitable repartee" and "brilliant" wit Aldrich displayed in conversation (see *Complete Interviews* [2006], p. 146 for Twain's correctly dated compliment published on 27 January 1895).

GREENWOOD, GRANVILLE GEORGE (1850–1928). *The Shakespeare Problem Restated*. Frontispiece. London and New York: John Lane Co., 1908. 558 pp.

Marginalia: prolific annotation in both pencil and black ink. Clemens made marginal notes on approximately seventy-five pages. His notes argue against Shakespeare's authorship. On the verso of the half-title page Clemens called Shakespeare "The Arthur Orton of literary 'Claim-ants'"; on the recto he wrote in the same black ink: "Predecessors of Mr. Greenwood have in the course of half a century trimmed <a good deal> several hatfuls of tissue from Arthur Orton Shakespear, & now—as it seems to me—this book reduces him to a skeleton & scrapes the bones" (*Zeitlin 1951*, City Book Auction [1954]). (Arthur Orton [1834–1898] had claimed in 1866 to be the English heir to the Tichborne estates and baronetcy. After a protracted and sensational trial, a jury in 1874 found him to be an impersonator.) On the half-title page and the portrait page Clemens continued his comparison of the Arthur Orton case and that of the defenders of Shakespeare, who refuse to question his identity as the accomplished playwright. Clemens concludes: "S. may have done this; he probably did that; he doubtless did the other. He is The Great Might-Have-Been. Certain people persisted to the end in believing that Arthur Orton was Sir Roger Tichborne. Shakespeare is another Arthur Orton—with all the valuable evidence against him, & not a single established fact in his favor."

The marginalia reveal (e.g., on p. 56) that Clemens is particu-larly impressed that Shakespeare seems not to have written about his own experiences, but only what he discovered in books. On page 75, beside a description of Ben Jon-son's lounging around London, Clemens penciled Huck Finn's name. On page 371 Clemens wrote "The Prairie Belle," apparently referring to John Hay's Pike County dialect ballad, "Jim Bludso, of the Prairie Belle" (1870); his note adds, "Begin Here" and on page 387 (line 19) he wrote, "Stop Here." A few notes are in someone else's handwriting. One of these on page 130 advises skipping the following chapter, which "is not biography but literary argument of the kind that scholars use"; another on pp. 366–367 quotes Francis Bacon's reference to himself as a "concealed poet."

Catalogs: ListABP (1910), "Shakespeare Problem Restated, Greenwood"; *C1951*, #17a, $155; *Zeitlin 1951*, #18, $350; City Book Auction, Sale number 632 (23 and 30 April 1954), "thick 8vo, original cloth, . . . spine faded, small hole in spine, front hinge broken," quotes the margi-nalia, laid in was a *C1951* auction sheet and a typewritten statement by Clara Clemens Samossoud, lot 115.

Location: Henry W. and Albert A. Berg Collection, New York Public Library.

Copy examined: Clemens's copy, one of the most heavily annotated volumes in his library. A typed and signed note by Clara Clemens Samossoud is tipped in to authenticate the marginalia as her father's.

Albert Bigelow Paine reports that Greenwood's book and a work by William S. Booth "added the last touch of convic-tion that Francis Bacon . . . had written the Shakespearean dramas" (*MTB* [1912], p. 1479). Clemens's marginalia in his copy of the book (p. 57) indicate his agreement with the thesis that Bacon would not have wished to be known in court as a playwright, a vocation then associated with vagrant actors. Isabel Lyon noted on 8 March 1909 that Clemens wished to write Greenwood a letter commending the book (Berg, NYPL, TS in MTP). Mark Twain opened Part One of *Is Shakespeare Dead?* (1909) by remarking: "A friend has sent me a new book, from England—*The Shakespeare Problem Restated*—well restated and closely reasoned." In Part Eight Twain quoted nine pages of extracts from Greenwood's volume to demonstrate the inadequacy of Shakespeare's background in law for the writing of certain scenes in the plays. But Twain skirted the issue of Bacon's authorship in *Is Shakespeare Dead?*, merely pointing out in Parts Nine and Ten that Bacon possessed suitable training for the task and that Bacon's contemporaries praised his abilities highly. A minor im-broglio erupted in June 1909 over the fact that Twain's book did not give adequate credit to lengthy extracts from Greenwood's *The Shakespeare Problem Restated*; Twain blamed the matter on a footnote that had somehow got lost in the production of *Is Shakespeare Dead?* A letter that Greenwood wrote in London to his publisher John Lane on 13 June 1909 indicated that Twain's book had made at least three errors, including mixing up the "*quarto*" with the "*Folio!*" (Special Collections, Washington University Libraries, St. Louis, Missouri).

"Can Mark Twain Be a Literary Pirate?," New York *Times*, 9 June 1909; "Twain's Footnote Lost," New York *Times*, 11 June 1909 (www.twainquotes.com); Michael Shelden, *Man in White* (2010), pp. 316–322.

GREENWOOD, JAMES (c. 1832–1929). *The Wilds of London.* Illus. London: Chatto and Windus, 1874. [Publisher conjectured.]
Inscription: signed on the flyleaf, "Saml. L. Clemens, Hartford, 1875."
Catalog: *A1911*, "12mo, cloth, Lond. 1874," quotes the signature, lot 208, sold for $7.
Greenwood wrote a series of exposés about the living and working conditions of the London poor. (See also Clemens's interest in Henry Mayhew's work.)

GREEY, EDWARD (1835–1888). *The Bear-Worshippers of Yezo; And the Island of Karafuto Saghalin. The Adventures of the Jewett Family and Their Friend Oto Nambo.* Illus. Boston: Lee & Shepard, 1884. 304 pp.
Inscription: presented by its author to Jean Clemens.
Provenance: MTLAcc, entry #1887, volume donated from Clemens's library by Clara Clemens Gabrilowitsch in 1910.
Catalog: *Mott 1952*, #59, $4.
As an English officer Greey had served in both China and Japan. He moved to New York City in 1868 and began importing and selling Japanese art and decorative items. His efforts helped promote an American interest in objets d'art from Japan. To augment his income and as an expression of his admiration of the Japanese he also wrote and translated books about Japan. Beset by ill health and financial problems following a return trip to Japan, Greey committed suicide in 1888.

———. *A Captive of Love, Founded Upon Bakin's Japanese Romance Kumono Tayema Ama Yo No Tsuki.* Illus. Boston: Lee & Shepard, 1886. 280 pp.
Source: MTLAcc, entry #2256, volume donated from Clemens's library by Clara Clemens Gabrilowitsch in 1910.

———. *The Wonderful City of Tokio; or, Further Adventures of the Jewett Family and Their Friend Oto Nambo.* Illus. Boston: Lee and Shepard, 1883. 301 pp.
Provenance: MTLAcc, entry #1888, volume donated from Clemens's library by Clara Clemens Gabrilowitsch in 1910.
Inscription: presented by its author to Clara Clemens.
Catalog: *Mott 1952*, #60, $4.

———. *Young Americans in Japan; or, The Adventures of the Jewett Family and Their Friend Oto Nambo.* Illus. Boston: Lee and Shepard, 1882. 372 pp.
Source: MTLAcc, entry #1886, volume donated from Clemens's library by Clara Clemens Gabrilowitsch in 1910.

GREGG, MARY (KIRBY) (1817–1893) and ELIZABETH KIRBY (1823–1873). *Stories About Birds of Land and Water.* London and New York: Cassell, Petter & Galpin, [1873?]. 256 pp.
Source: MTLAcc, entry #1961, volume donated from Clemens's library by Clara Clemens Gabrilowitsch in 1910.

GREGORY, (LADY) AUGUSTA (1852–1932). *A Book of Saints and Wonders, Put Down Here by Lady Gregory According to the Old Writings and the Memory of the People of Ireland.* London: John Murray, 1907. 211 pp. [Publisher conjectured; the book was also issued in New York by Charles Scribner's Sons in 1907 with identical pagination.]
Clemens wrote to Lady Gregory on 8 July 1907 from Tuxedo Park in New York City: "I thank you ever so much for the little book of Saints & Wonders; it was most kind of you to show me by this token that you have not forgotten me" (*Sotheby's 2003*, #118).

———. *Cuchulain of Muirthemne: The Story of the Men of the Red Branch of Ulster. Arranged and Put into English by Lady Gregory.* Preface by William Butler Yeats (1865–1939). London: John Murray, 1902. 360 pp.
Inscription: the front free endpaper is inscribed in black ink: "To Mark Twain—/with kind remembrances/from Augusta Gregory—/Apr 1907." A letter from Lady Gregory is laid in. Someone recorded on the half title page that the volume was "From Mark Twain's Library/ sold in L. A. Calif."
Marginalia: Clemens made favorable pencil notes and markings throughout.
Catalogs: ListABP (1910), "Cuchulain of Muirthemne, Gregory"; *C1951*, #12a, $35, listed among the volumes containing annotation by Clemens. Clipping about Clemens's reading preferences laid in.
Location: Mark Twain House and Museum, Hartford, Connecticut. Donated by Mrs. John L. Martin of Darien, Connecticut.
Copy examined: Clemens's copy. Examined in August 1987.

———. *Gods and Fighting Men: The Story of the Tuatha De Danaan and of the Fianna of Ireland. Arranged and Put into English by Lady Gregory.* Preface by William Butler Yeats (1865–1939). London: John Murray, 1904. 476 pp.
Inscription: the front pastedown endpaper is signed in black ink: "SL. Clemens."
Catalogs: *A1911*, "(Half-title torn.), 8vo, cloth, gilt top, uncut, Lond. 1904," quotes the signature, lot 209, sold for $4.50; *Lexington 1912*, lot 12, sold for $7.50.
Location: Mark Twain House and Museum, Hartford, Connecticut. Donated anonymously in 1974, according to the late Mrs. Dexter B. Peck, then the Library Chairman.
Copy examined: Clemens's unmarked copy. Examined in August 1987. It has an *A1911* sale label.
On 21 February 1904 Lady Gregory wrote to Clemens in concern about Olivia Clemens's health. Lady Gregory mentioned that *Gods and Fighting Men* was finding a favorable reception, for which she was thankful. "It gave me harder work than Cuchulain ... but it was love's labour" (MTP). Clemens replied to her on 16 February 1904: "I wish to thank you for the quaint & beautiful stories, & for remembering us again" (MTP).

———. *Poets and Dreamers: Studies & Translations from the Irish, by Lady Gregory.* Dublin: Hodges, Figgis, & Company, 1903. 254 pp.
Inscription: inscribed in black ink on the front free endpaper: "To 'Mark Twain' with very kind regards from Augusta Gregory, March 1903".
Marginalia: one stray pencil mark at the bottom of page 240. No other markings. Leaves opened.
Catalogs: *C1951*, #61c, $17.50; "The Fine Library of the Late Ingle Barr," Sotheby Parke-Bernet, Los Angeles, Sale No. 68 (18–19 February 1973), item #107, $150; placed on sale by John Howell Books, San Francisco, 24 February 1973, $180.
Location: Mark Twain Papers, Bancroft Library, University of California at Berkeley. Gift of Mr. and Mrs. Kurt E. Appert.
Copy examined: Clemens's copy (at John Howell Books, San Francisco in 1973 and again in the Mark Twain Papers

on 13 June 2002).

In her autobiography Lady Gregory quoted a letter from Mark Twain written to her from Riverdale-on-the-Hudson on 9 March 1903: "I have been marvelling along through your wonderful book again, and trying to understand how those people could produce such a literature in that old day, and they so remote (apparently) from the well-springs and inspirations of such things. . . . But we've got the stories and that is the important thing, and we are grateful to you for that" (*Seventy Years: Being the Autobiography of Lady Gregory* [London: Colin Smythe, 1974], pp. 400–401). See also the Catalog entry for Richard J. O'Duffy, editor and translator, *Oidhe Chloinne Uisnigh: Fate of the Children of Uisneach*.

GREGORY, EDMUND (1832–1913). *Narrative of James Murrells' ("Jemmy Morrill") Seventeen Years' Exile among the Wild Blacks of North Queensland, and His Life and Shipwreck and Terrible Adventures among Savage Tribes; Their Manners, Customs, Languages, and Superstitions; Also Murrells' Rescue and Return to Civilization*. Fifth edition. Brisbane, Australia: Printed by Edmund Gregory, 1896. 43 pp. [Edition conjectured.]

Presumably this was the book to which Clemens was referring in mentioning both "James Murrells" and "Edmund Gregory" in Notebook 35, TS p. 53 (MTP). The name James Murrells (1824–1865) is misspelled as James Murrill or James Morrill in some sources.

GREVILLE, CHARLES CAVENDISH FULKE (1794–1865). *The Greville Memoirs; A Journal of the Reigns of King George IV. and King William IV., by the Late Charles C. F. Greville*. Ed. by Henry Reeve (1813–1895). Second edition. 3 vols. Original blue cloth, gilt. [Volume III was rebacked with the original spine by book repair expert Don Etherington in 1985.] London: Longmans, Green, and Co., 1874.

Inscriptions: Volume I is signed in pencil on the half-title page: "Saml. L. Clemens/Hartford 1875"; the front paste-down endpaper of Volume II is signed "S. L. Clemens" (with an identical signature in another place); the front pastedown endpaper of Volume III is signed "S L. Clemens" in ink in a late hand. The *A1911* sale label is present on the pastedown endpaper in Volume III.

Marginalia: Volume I is annotated in brown ink and pencil; portions of Clemens's marginalia are quoted by Albert Bigelow Paine (*MTB* [1912], pp. 1539–40), and Roger B. Salomon (*TIH* [1961], p. 31). One of Clemens's notes occurs beside Greville's criticism of Byron: "What a man sees in the human race is merely himself in the deep and honest privacy of his own heart" (*MTB*, pp. 1539–40); Paine also quotes other comments. All of Clemens's scattered notes appear to have been made after 1900. The handwriting itself indicates a late period of his life, a penciled remark on page 158 refers to the Spanish-American War, and a note in brown ink on page 386 alludes to an event that Clemens dates as having occurred in 1904. Many pages are folded over. (The amount of annotation in Volume II is unknown.) On the half-title page of Volume III Clemens wrote in ink: "He overworks the word 'that.' Sometimes when he gets to that-ing he doesn't seem to know where to stop." (Below this in another hand are the penciled initials "J. S. D." and a penciled note that possibly reads "Philip Dales/[illegible].") At page 40 in Volume III Clemens crossed out seven "that's" in three sentences.

(In 1909 Clemens made similar textual objections to an abundance of this pronoun in his copy of *Letters of James Russell Lowell*.) The corner of page 128 is dog-eared. On page 130 (Volume III) Clemens made the marginal ink note "an early Browning" beside a passage concerning the German poet Friedrick Gottlieb Klopstock (1724–1803); Greville relates how Klopstock, asked in his old age about the meaning of a passage in one of his books, "looked at it, and then said that he could not then recollect what it was that he meant when he wrote it, but that he knew it was the finest thing he ever wrote, and they could not do better than devote their lives to the discovery of its meaning." At page 145 Clemens wrote "Melbourne's Ashcroft" in ink, referring to Greville's description of one of Lord Melbourne's ministers who had violated a confidence by leaking news to the London *Times*. Clemens felt that Ralph Ashcroft had similarly betrayed him, thereby indicating a date of 1909 or 1910 for this note.

Catalogs: ListABP (1910), "Greville's Journals"; *A1911*, "Vols II and III [only], 2 vols. 8vo, cloth, Lond. 1874," quotes the signatures and Clemens's note on the half-title page of Volume III, lot 210, Vols. II and III only, sold for $1.50 total; *C1951*, #5a, Volume I only, $27.50; Mail Auction, Pennsauken, N.J. (October 1977), Vol. III only, $175 bid recommended; *Sotheby's 2003*, #206, Vol. III only, sold for $1,400.

Provenance: Volume III was formerly in the collection of Nick Karanovich, Fort Wayne, Indiana. He reported on 25 May 1983 that it had the *A1911* auction notation "#210" at the top of its half-title page and some undecipherable names and initials at the bottom of that page; the latter appeared to be post-1951.

Locations: Volume I is in the Mark Twain Papers, Bancroft Library, University of California at Berkeley. Volume II has not been located. Volume III is in the collection of Kevin Mac Donnell, Austin, Texas.

Copies examined: Clemens's copies of Volume I and III. Information about Volume III also derives from a letter from Kevin Mac Donnell to Alan Gribben, 10 September 2009 and from photocopies of the title page, inscription, and marginalia that Nick Karanovich sent to Alan Gribben on 25 May 1983.

On 26 January 1875 Clemens wrote to William Dean Howells from Hartford: "I've been sick abed several days. . . . How little confirmed invalids appreciate their advantages. I was able to read the English edition of the Greville Memoirs through without interruption . . . & smoke 18 cigars a day" (*MTHL*, p. 62). Clemens's marginal annotations, however, seem to date from a much later period. Greville's *Memoirs* were remarkable for their detail and, of course, for his intimate knowledge of his subjects and their activities.

———. *The Greville Memoirs*. Ed. by Richard Henry Stoddard (1825–1903). New York: Scribner, Armstrong & Co., 1875.

Possibly Clemens owned two editions of Greville's *Memoirs*; at any rate he referred to a page number from Stoddard's abridgment in reminding himself in 1880 of a humorous story involving Sydney Smith and the research of Sir John Leslie (1766–1832) about the North Pole: "Sydney Smith (Dn the Equator)/(Greville, page 265" (NB 19, *N&J* 2: 364).

Grew, Edwin Sharpe (1867–1950). *The Romance of Modern Geology, Describing in Simple But Exact Language the Making of the Earth with Some Account of Prehistoric Animal Life.* Illus. Philadelphia: J. B. Lippincott Co., 1909. 308 pp. [Publisher conjectured.]

Inscription: the front pastedown endpaper is signed "S. L. Clemens, 1908." (per Swann Auction Galleries catalog).

Marginalia: lengthy notations on the rear endpapers, as well as three penciled marginal notations (per the Swann Auction Galleries catalog).

Catalog: Swann Auction Galleries (New York City), Sale number 207 (22 April 1948), "thick 8vo, pictorial cloth, Philadelphia, 1909 . . . signature inside front cover—'S. L. Clemens, 1908' and lengthy manuscript notations on rear endpapers, as well as 3 penciled marginal notations," lot 256 (PH in MTP).

Location: currently unknown.

Grey, (Sir) George (1812–1898). *Journals of Two Expeditions of Discovery in North-West and Western Australia, During the Years 1837, 38, and 39, Under the Authority of Her Majesty's Government: Describing Many Newly Discovered, Important, and Fertile Districts, with Observations on the Moral and Physical Condition of the Aboriginal Inhabitants.* 2 vols. London: T. and W. Boone, 1841. [Edition conjectured.]

"Sir George Grey and Mr. Eyre testify that the natives dug wells fourteen or fifteen feet deep" (*FE* [1897], Chapter 22).

Grey described elaborate cave drawings and other facets of aboriginal life.

Grieb, Christoph Friedrich (1810–1861). *Dictionary of the English and German Languages.* Two vols. in one. Stuttgart: P. Neff, 1884. [Publisher conjectured.]

Catalog: *A1911*, "thick imp. 8vo, boards, cloth back (cover loose), Stuttgart, 1884," lot 181, sold for $1.50.

A newspaper interview published on 8 October 1897 reported that "on his table" Clemens had a copy of "an English-German lexicon" (M. Thomas Inge, "Ten Minutes with Mark Twain: An Interview," *American Literary Realism* 15.2 [Autumn 1982]: 262). This might have been Grieb's book.

Griffin, Lepel Henry (1840–1908). *The Great Republic.* [Published in both London and New York in 1884.]

Mark Twain quoted Griffin unfavorably in a speech Twain made on 27 April 1890, "On Foreign Critics" (*MTSpk* [1976], pp. 257–258). He again mentioned Griffin in April 1889 (NB 28, *N&J* 3: 467), February 1890 (NB 29, *N&J* 3: 541), and December 1895 (NB 36, TS p. 4). Evidence that Clemens knew Griffin's *The Great Republic* at first-hand is hazy; see D. M. McKeithan, "The Occasion of Mark Twain's Speech 'On Foreign Critics'" (*CTMT* [1958], pp. 144–145) and *MTHL*, pp. 600–601 n. 1. However, Twain certainly was aware that the book was severely critical of the United States. Griffin was a British colonial administrator in India who wrote *The Great Republic* after traveling in the United States.

Griffis, William Elliot (1843–1928) and others. *Bible Stories for Young People.* Illus. New York: Harper & Brothers, [cop. 1894]. 178 pp.

Source: MTLAcc, entry #1390, volume donated by Clemens.

Grimm Brothers. Jacob Grimm (1785–1863) and **Wilhelm Grimm** (1786–1859). *Grimms' Fairy Tales* (published 1812, 1815).

Thomas J. Reigstad argued that a satirical piece published in the 20 December 1869 issue of the Buffalo *Express* and signed "LITTLE RED RIDING HOOD" has the earmarks of Twain's "being the author." The column "may be a meditation by Twain about fans who intrude on his private time during the lecture trip, about Americans who live vicariously through their celebrity heroes, [and] about the difficult challenge of separating Mark Twain and Samuel L. Clemens" (*Scribblin' for a Livin': Mark Twain's Pivotal Period in Buffalo* [Amherst, New York: Prometheus Books, 2013], pp. 105–107).

Grimm, Herman Friedrich (1828–1901) and **Fanny Elizabeth Bunnett** (c. 1832–1875). *Life of Michael Angelo [1475–1564].* 2 vols. Boston: Little, Brown and Co., 1900.

Inscription: inscribed with the names of Jervis Langdon (1875–1952) and Eleanor Sayles Langdon (1878–1971).

Catalog: Ball 2016 inventory, 2 vols., red leather, good condition.

Location: Quarry Farm Library shelves, under the supervision of the Mark Twain Archive, Elmira College, Elmira, New York.

Conceivably Clemens might have seen this book at the Langdon residence before or after Langdon married Eleanor Sayles (1878–1971) in 1902.

Grimm's Maerchen: Brüder Grimm Kinder und Hausmaerchen. [Grimm Brothers' Fairy Tales. School Edition]. Ed. Charles Pomeroy Otis (1840–1888). First edition. New York: Henry Holt & Co., 1887. 374 pp. [Edition conjectured.]

Source: ListABP (1910) ("Otis, Grimm's Maerchen").

The preface is written in English; the tales are in German.

Grinnell, George Bird (1849–1938). *The Punishment of the Stingy, and Other Indian Stories.* Illus. New York: Harper & Brothers, 1901. 235 pp. [Publisher and pages supplied.]

Inscription: the front flyleaf is signed "S. L. Clemens, Riverdale, October, 1901."

Catalog: *A1911*, "12mo, boards, cloth back, gilt top, uncut, N.Y. 1901," quotes the signature, lot 211, sold for $4.75.

Grinnell avowedly received these Native American tales "from the lips of aged historians." (p. viii). He mentioned the Blackfoot and Pawnee tribes, as well as tribes in "the northwest." Typical story titles are "Bluebird, The Imitator" and "The Girl Who Was the Ring."

Gripenberg, Alexandra, Baroness (1857–1913).

Clemens spent an amiable evening with this Finnish author, editor, and politician at the home of Charles Dudley Warner in June 1888. Clemens told stories and sang spirituals.

Ernest J. Moyne, "Mark Twain Meets a Lady from Finland," *Mark Twain Journal* 11.2 (Summer 1960): 9–10, 25.

Griswold, Louise M. (Roope) (1843–1923), known as "Mrs. Stephen M. Griswold." *A Woman's Pilgrimage to the Holy Land; or, Pleasant Days Abroad. Being Notes of a Tour Through Europe and the East.* Hartford: J. B. Burr & Hyde, 1871. 423 pp.

Griswold and her husband Stephen M. Griswold joined the passengers already aboard the *Quaker City* at Naples, Italy, and her narrative mentions Mark Twain. Surely he would have encountered her book, since it was published in the same city where the publisher of his *The Innocents Abroad* (1869) was located.

Griswold, Stephen Morrell (1835–1916). *Sixty Years*

with Plymouth Church. New York: Fleming H. Revell Co., 1907. 191 pp.

Inscriptions: the flyleaf is inscribed "Samuel L. Clemens/'Mark Twain'/With kind regards of Stephen M. Griswold." Signed in black ink on the front pastedown endpaper: "SL. Clemens/1907."

Marginalia: above and below Griswold's frontispiece portrait Clemens wrote in black ink: "Here is the real old familiar Plymouth-Church self-complacency of 40 years ago. It is the way God looks when He has had a successful season. This is the Griswold that was out in the Quaker City Excursion with us. He was a Beecher-idolater" (quoted in *MTMF* [1949], p. xii, n. 1). Clemens turned down the corner of page 73 and drew a line in black ink beside Griswold's account of Henry Ward Beecher's dramatic purchase of a young enslaved girl during church services he was conducting. (Beecher asked members of his congregation to pledge money to buy the girl from her master and set her free.) The only other notes or markings occur in "The Beecher Trial" chapter (pp. 90–100); there Clemens blames Henry Ward Beecher for maintaining his silence when the charges of adultery were first made, instead of telling "that honorable lie" at once.

Catalogs: ListABP (1910), "Sixty Years with Plymouth Church, Griswold"; "Retz Appraisal" (1944), p. 8, valued at $20.

Provenance: contains the bookstamps of the Mark Twain Library, Redding; apparently it was returned to Clara Clemens Gabrilowitsch after being donated to that library.

Location: Mark Twain Papers, Bancroft Library, University of California at Berkeley.

Copy examined: Clemens's copy.

GROSE, FRANCIS (1731–1791). *A Classical Dictionary of the Vulgar Tongue*. London: Printed for S. Hooper, 1785.

Inscription: the half-title page is signed in black ink "Saml. L. Clemens/Hartford, 1875."

Marginalia: prolific notes and markings by Clemens on virtually every page. All are in pencil. Many of the markings are his usual vertical lines, but there are also horizontal lines and ovals. He adds current usages of certain terms and lists modern replacements for others. "Bilk," he notes, is a "Californian" word. "Blarney" has "changed to flattery." Is "Canterbury Story," he wonders, "from the 'Pilgrims'?" The life and death of Jack o' Legs, a legendarily tall archer and outlaw who robbed the rich in Hertfordshire in the Middle Ages, Clemens observes, was the "same as the legend of Robin Hood." He associates the definition of "Willow" with "Ophelia's song in Hamlet." A transcript of a dozen examples of Clemens's annotations is now in the Mark Twain Papers.

Catalogs: *C1951*, #30a, $55; sold by The Scriptorium, Beverly Hills, 18 December 1967, $135; purchased by Frank Greenagel, Pacific Palisades, California.

Provenance: in the collection of Justin G. Turner (1898–1976), a Los Angeles real estate investor and noted collector of books and manuscripts, in 1970.

Location: currently undetermined.

Copy examined: photocopy of the complete marginalia provided to Alan Gribben in 1979 by Professor Howard G. Baetzhold of Butler University. Justin G. Turner of Turner Investments in Los Angeles had permitted

Baetzhold to make this copy. Baetzhold subsequently (on 4 February 1999) sent his original photocopy to the Mark Twain Papers, Bancroft Library, University of California at Berkeley.

An antiquarian and lexicographer, the Falstaffian-looking Grose compiled a collection of slang that was daring for its day. To obtain its entries he and an assistant spent many hours in slums, shipyards, taverns, brothels, gambling dens, and other locales frequented by the poorest citizens and the criminal underworld. Few words were too crude or sinister to prevent their inclusion in Grose's now-much-praised work.

Howard G. Baetzhold pointed out that while perusing this reference work during the composition of *The Prince and the Pauper*, Twain almost certainly encountered a vulgar term, "Burning shame," that could have reminded him of an indecent tale he heard Jim Gillis tell in 1865 (Baetzhold to Lin Salamo, 4 February 1999, MTP). Oddly, however, Clemens did not mark this particular reference in Grose's book. See also *Adventures of Huckleberry Finn*, ed. Victor Fischer and Lin Salamo (Berkeley: University of California Press, 2003), pp. 438–439.

Baetzhold, *MT&JB* (1970), pp. 52, 331 n. 14.

GRUBE, AUGUST WILHELM (1816–1884). *Charakterbilder aus der Geschichte und Sage, für einen propädeutischen geschichtsunterricht [Character Pictures from History and Legend, for a Propaedeutic History Lesson]*. Three vols. in one. Portraits. Leipzig: Friedrich Brandstetter, 1882. 452 pp. [Publisher conjectured.]

Catalog: *A1911*, "3 vols. in 1, 8vo, cloth, Leipzig, 1882," manuscript notes laid in, lot 212, sold for $1.

Source: Hemminghaus, "Mark Twain's German Provenience" (1945), p. 474. I could not find this volume during my repeated visits to the Mark Twain Library in Redding. Grube collected inspiring and moralistic tales from classical biography and mythology.

GRUMMAN, WILLIAM EDGAR (1854–1925). *The Revolutionary Soldiers of Redding, Connecticut, and the Record of Their Services; with Mention of Others Who Rendered Services or Suffered Loss at the Hands of the Enemy During the Struggle for Independence 1775–1783; Together with Some Account of the Loyalists of the Town and Vicinity, Their Organization, Their Efforts, and Sacrifices in Behalf of Their King, and Their Ultimate Fate*. Hartford, Connecticut: Hartford Press; Case, Lockwood & Brainard Co., 1904. 208 pp.

Inscription: presented to Mark Twain by its author.

Source: described in "Books from Stormfield and Their Annotations," Redding, Connecticut *Pilot*, 15 June 1972, p. 6 (in a section titled "New Mark Twain Library").

Location: Mark Twain Library, Redding, Connecticut.

Local historian Grumman was chosen as the first librarian of the Mark Twain Library in Redding (Paine, *MTB* [1912], pp. 1472–1473. Among other facts, Grumman's book on Redding's part in the American Revolution recounted the winter that General Israel Putnam's army spent in Redding. Grumman also served as Mark Twain's last stenographer (*AutoMT* 3: 628).

GUALDO PRIORATO, GALEAZZO (1606–1678). *The History of the Managements of Cardinal Julio Mazarine [1602–1661], Chief Minister of State of the Crown of France, Translated According*

to the Original. 3 vols. London, 1691.

Catalogs: *A1911*, "Vols. I & III, 2 vols., 12mo, old calf, with the arms of Robert Harley (cracked and much wormed), Lond. 1691," with a sheet of Clemens's German and English notes laid in, lot 243, sold for .75¢; *Lexington 1912*, lot 20, sold for $4.

Provenance: the arms and name of Robert Harley, Earl of Oxford, are on the front and back covers.

The time span of this chronicle extended into the reign of Louis XIV (1638–1715), which commenced in 1643.

GUILLEMIN, AMÉDÉE VICTOR (1826–1893). *The Heavens: An Illustrated Handbook of Popular Astronomy.* An entirely new and revised edition, being the seventh. Ed. by Norman Lockyer (1836–1920). Revised by Richard A[nthony]. Proctor (1837–1888). Illus. London: Richard Bentley & Son, 1878. 436 pp.

Inscription: signed in pencil on the first flyleaf: "S. L. Clemens/Munich, Dec. 1878".

Marginalia: Clemens made penciled notes on pages 144–145 for a story about Captain Ned Wakeman's visiting the moon ("Let Wakeman visit the moon," Clemens wrote at the top of page 144), where he would encounter "groveling," naked "Moonites" who eat lava and "don't breathe or drink." His other idea about these beings (p. 145) would make them "intelligent & with strong telescopes & well informed about us, whom they despise. Their religion & the age (very great) to which they live." Wakeman could have "an interpreter—a former Moonite" (page 145). These musings were evidently triggered by Guillemin's footnote on page 144, which Clemens marked with two vertical lines, expressing an open mind about the possibility of the moon's being inhabited: "Nature is so varied in its modes of action, so infinite in the manifestations of its power, that nothing in Nature can be pronounced by man to be absolutely impossible," Guillemin stated there. Another penciled note by Clemens (written vertically on page 234) projects further space travel: "Wakeman finds that as these various worlds, ex/cept Jupiter, are no denser than water, the people are/very light, & able to walk on water. Jupiter offers/a foothold as good as thick sand." At the top of page 252 Twain jotted down the notion that Wakeman might meet up with a comet last seen in 1680. Above (and extending below) Plate XVIII, which compares the respective sizes of our immense sun and the much smaller planets circling it, Twain wrote: "Showing size of God's footstool/for Wakeman—he thinks it was/not chosen for its bigness since there/are worlds which are 10[,]000 times larger/than our sun, but for some other/virtue." The volume contains a few other notes and numerous pencil markings. Computations in brown ink, blue ink, and pencil cover the rear fly-leaves and the rear pastedown endpaper. The volume was evidently rebound after Clemens made his notes.

Catalog: *C1951*, # 16a, $20.

Location: Mark Twain Papers, Bancroft Library, University of California at Berkeley. Donated by the University of California at Los Angeles, which purchased the book at the 1951 Hollywood auction.

Copy examined: Clemens's copy.

———. *The Sun.* Trans. from the French by Thomas Lamb Phipson (1833–1908) Illus. New York: Scribner, Armstrong & Co., 1872. 297 pp.

Source: MTLAcc, entry #1992, volume donated from Clemens's library by Clara Clemens Gabrilowitsch in 1910.

GUIZOT, FRANÇOIS PIERRE GUILLAUME (1787–1874). *Concise History of France.* Abridged by Gustave Masson (1819–1888). [First issued in 1880.]

Catalog: *C1951*, O24, listed as containing the signature of Olivia Clemens, no edition specified.

———. *History of France.* Illustrated by Alphonse Marie de Neuville (1835–1885). 5 vols.

Clemens described this five-volume set as one of the prizes for a spelling bee held at the Asylum Hill Congregational Church on 12 May 1875 (*MTLet* 6: 662–663). He announced the prizes in the course of his preliminary speech at the event, published in the 13 May 1875 issue of the Hartford *Courant.* Leah A. Strong reprinted Clemens's remarks in "Mark Twain on Spelling," *American Literature* 23.3 (November 1951): 357–359.

Kenneth R. Andrews, *Nook Farm* (1950), p. 50; Fatout, *MTSpk* (1976), pp. 94–95.

———. *A Popular History of England from the Earliest Times to the Reign of Queen Victoria.* Translated from the French by M. M. Ripley. Illus. 5 vols. Boston, 1876. [Quite likely this was the set in the Library of Standard History Series offered by Dana Estes and Charles E. Lauriat of Boston in 1876. Volume 5, added in 1881 and titled *A Popular History of England from the Earliest Times to the Accession of Victoria, 1837–1874*, was prepared from Guizot's notes by Henriette Elizabeth (Guizot) de Witt, 1829–1908, Guizot's eldest daughter.]

Inscription: each volume is signed "S. L. Clemens."

Catalog: *A 1911*, "5 vols., royal 8vo, tree calf (one joint broken) gilt, gilt edges, Bost. [1876]," quotes the signatures, lot 214, sold for $6.75 total.

Location: the front cover of one volume (with a Greek key pattern gilt border on tan tree calf) survives in the collection of Kevin Mac Donnell, Austin, Texas. It remained among Albert Bigelow Paine's effects, and was inherited by his grandson, Bigelow Paine Cushman. No other parts of this set have been located.

Source: description of the detached cover sent to Alan Gribben by Kevin Mac Donnell on 28 August 2017.

———. *A Popular History of France from the Earliest Times.* Illustrated by Alphonse Marie de Neuville (1835–1885). Translated from the French by Robert Black (1830–1915). 6 volumes. Contemporary tree calf, morocco spine labels, marbled endpapers, spine gilt-stamped. Boards loose in several volumes, tape repairs to two volumes, extremities rubbed. Boston: Dana Estes and Charles E. Lauriat, n. d. [187–?].

Inscriptions: each volume is signed "Samuel Clemens" on the front flyleaf.

Marginalia: one short note by Clemens and a few marked passages.

Catalogs: *C1951*, #1c, listed among the volumes signed by Clemens; "Property from the Library of Mark Twain," Butterfield & Butterfield, San Francisco, Sale 6613 (16 July 1997), lot 2674.

Location: Mark Twain House and Museum, Hartford, Connecticut.

Copy examined: Clemens's copy. Viewed in 1997 in Hartford, Connecticut. Volumes V and VI are in need of repair.

A receipt from Estes & Lauriat of Boston, dated 16 May

1874, credits Clemens's account for payments on a serial publication: "2 Each 1st 8 Parts France 8.00" sent on 4 April 1874; and "2 Each Parts 9 & 10 France 2.00" sent on 13 April 1874, making a total of $10. This receipt presumably refers to Guizot's *A Popular History of France from the Earliest Times*, since the envelope in which the receipt was mailed on 16 May 1874 advertises: "Agents Wanted for/GUIZOT'S/POPULAR HISTORY OF FRANCE,/One of the finest Serial Works ever issued in America" (MTP).

GÜMPEL, CARL GODFREY (1835–1921). *Common Salt: its Use and Necessity for the Maintenance of Health and the Prevention of Disease.* London: Swan Sonnenschein & Co., 1898. 380 pp.
    Source: MTLAcc, entry #545, volume donated by Clemens.
    Gümpel had a wide range of interests. An Alsatian manufacturer of trusses and artificial limbs, he also published on public health issues, including the plague in India. His best-known innovation was a chess-playing automaton that was first exhibited in 1878.

GUNN, JOHN C. (1800–1863). *Gunn's Domestic Medicine, or Poor Man's Friend, in the Hours of Affliction, Pain, and Sickness. This Book Points Out, in Plain Language, Free from Doctor's Terms, the Diseases of Men, Women, and Children, and Expressly Intended for the Benefit of Families.* Knoxville, Tenn.: James C. Gunn, 1830. 440 pp.
    Huckleberry Finn notes the presence of this book on a corner of the Grangerford's parlor table: "another was Dr. Gunn's *Family Medicine*, which told you all about what to do if a body was sick or dead" (Chapter 17, *HF* [1885]). Gunn's book became a regional and then national household fixture and was often reprinted, usually in Kentucky or Tennessee, between 1830 and 1842, then in New York between 1843 and 1870. A revised edition was published between 1870 and 1872. A similar but separate work was also brought out during the years between 1857 and 1888, *Gunn's New Domestic Physician; or Home Book of Health.* Gunn, born in Savannah, Georgia, practiced medicine in Louisville, Kentucky.
    Aspiz, "Mark Twain's Reading" (1949), p. 327; Blair, *MT&HF* (1960), p. 230; K. Patrick Ober, *Mark Twain and Medicine: "Any Mummery Will Cure"* (Columbia: University of Missouri Press, 2003), p. 7.

GURNEY, EDMUND (1847–1888), **FREDERIC WILLIAM HENRY MYERS** (1843–1901), and **FRANK PODMORE** (1855–1910). *Phantasms of the Living.* 2 vols. London: Trubner, 1886.
    Phantasms of the Living collected the proceedings of the Society for Psychical Research in London. The book reported upon cases of apparitions, materializations, dematerializations, clairvoyance, telepathy, precognition, and dream experiences. Around Christmas time in 1896 Clemens noted in London: "Been reading Apparitions [*sic*] of the Living—Gladstone suddenly appears—is *solid*—talks, & disappears. Emperor William, Barnum, P. of Wales, &c" (NB 39, TS p. 36). John S. Tuckey identified *Phantasms of the Living* as the work Clemens was reading (*MTSatan* [1963], p. 26).
    Randall Knoper, *Acting Naturally: Mark Twain in the Culture of Performance* (Berkeley: University of California Press, 1995), p. 185; and Randall Knoper, "'Silly creations of an imagination that is not conscious of its freaks': Multiple Selves, Wordless Communication, and the Psychology

of Mark Twain's *No. 44, The Mysterious Stranger,*" *Centenary Reflections on Mark Twain's* No. 44, The Mysterious Stranger, ed. Joseph Csicsila and Chad Rohman (Columbia: University of Missouri Press, 2009), pp. 144–156.

GUTHRIE, CHARLES JOHN (1849–1920). *John Knox and John Knox's House.* Illus. Edinburgh: Oliphant, Anderson, & Ferrier, 1898. 140 pp.
    Catalog: eBay, item #1404041509, 25 January 2001.
    Location: collection of Kevin Mac Donnell, Austin, Texas.
    Source: Mac Donnell to Alan Gribben, 3 May 2005.
    The later, second (1905) edition of this work (published in Edinburgh by T. and A. Constable as well as Oliphant, Anderson & Ferrier) quoted "Critiques of First Edition," including the jocular praise of Mark Twain: "With your *Knox and His House* I can now post myself; for, privately, I don't know so much about Knox as I ought to. In truth, the only really well-settled historical fact of his life hitherto possessed by me is the incident where he threw a campstool in church one morning at a lady of the name of Geddes. Now I shall learn something more." John Knox (1505–1572) met John Calvin in Geneva, wrote religious tracts, preached against the practices of the Roman Catholic Church, promoted Protestantism, and helped organize the Presbyterian Church. Knox's residence is one of the oldest surviving houses in Edinburgh. His biographer Charles Guthrie was a Scottish lawyer and judge.

GUTHRIE, THOMAS ANSTEY (1856–1934), pseud. "F. Anstey." *Vice Versâ; or, A Lesson to Fathers.* Third edition. Original brown cloth, gilt. New York: D. Appleton and Co., 1882. 349 pp. [The first edition was also published in 1882.]
    Inscription: the flyleaf is signed in pencil, "S. L. Clemens/ Hartford, 1882".
    Catalogs: *A1911*, #13, "12mo, cloth, N.Y., 1882," quotes signature, sold for $2.50; *Lexington 1912*, #2, $5; Second Life Books, Lanesborough, Massachusetts, Catalog No. 47 (1984), item F, has the *A1911* auction label, $750.
    Location: collection of Kevin Mac Donnell, Austin, Texas.
    Copy examined: Clemens's copy, in July 2004. Retains the *A1911* sale label on the front pastedown endpaper.
    In this humorous and best-selling novel a boy changes places with his pompous father. The plot of Twain's *The Prince and the Pauper* (1881) had featured a street urchin switching identities with youthful royalty. A review by Brander Matthews in 1885 would declare, "As Mr. F. Anstey understands the English boy, and especially the English boy of the middle classes, so Mark Twain understands the American boy" (Louis J. Budd, *Mark Twain: The Contemporary Reviews* [Cambridge, England: Cambridge University Press, 1999], p. 261). Kevin Mac Donnell pointed out that both *Vice Versâ* and Twain's *Adventures of Huckleberry Finn* (1885) contain similar escape scenes in which a prisoner realizes at some point that he is actually free to simply walk out of his cell. Mac Donnell speculated that both episodes shared a common source (Mac Donnell to Alan Gribben 8 July 2015).

▌H

HABBERTON, JOHN (1842–1921). *Helen's Babies. With Some Account of Their Ways, Innocent, Crafty, Angelic, Impish, Witching and Repulsive. Also, a Partial Record of Their Actions During Ten Days of Their Existence. By Their Latest Victim.* Boston:

Loring, 1876. 206 pp.

In Habberton's novel two mischievous little boys, Budge (age five) and Toddie (age three) try the patience of their uncle Harry Burton, a bachelor. But all turns out well, for Harry's troublesome nephews bring him together with Alice Mayton, a courtship ensues, and their blissful marriage is arranged. Neither the romantic plot nor Habberton's attempts to reproduce the prattle of children probably appealed to Clemens. He apparently offered a vitriolic review of the novel to the *Atlantic Monthly*, for on 30 November 1876 William Dean Howells urged him "to write something better than that about Helen's Babbies [*sic*]. You use expressions there that would lose us all our book-club circulation. Do attack the folly systematically and analytically—write what you said at dinner the other day about it" (*MTHL*, p. 165). In an anonymous review of Edward Payson Hammond's *Sketches of Palestine* published in the *Atlantic Monthly* 39.236 (June 1877): 741, Mark Twain noted that he had refrained from saying that Hammond's book of absurd poetry "is worse than Helen's Babies . . . ; I never went to that length" (quoted by Philip B. Eppard, "Mark Twain Dissects an Overrated Book," *American Literature* 49.3 [November 1977]: 440). Clemens mentioned Habberton's "nauseous & idiotic" novel to Mary Mason Fairbanks on 31 October 1877 (*MTMF*, p. 211). In a letter to Howells on 1 November 1877 he complained that if any story is written "wretchedly & nastily & witlessly" one may expect that "the whole nation of Helen's Baby's admirers will welcome it as a very inspiration of humor & read & copy it everywhere" (*MTHL*, p. 208).

While making notes for his projected anthology of humor in 1881 Clemens noted: "Helen's Babies & The Worst Boy in Town—by the ass Habberton" (NB 19, *N&J* 2: 428). Twice Mark Twain made a joke about the possibility of converting the expletive "Hell" into the socially acceptable book title "—en's Babies": on the margin of the manuscript for "Simon Wheeler, Detective" (written 1877–1898?) and in the text of "1,002d Arabian Night" (written in 1883) (*S&B*, pp. 342, 109). On 14 February 1884 William L. Hughes, seeking Mark Twain's permission to translate into French *Tom Sawyer* and the forthcoming *Huckleberry Finn*, sent him a copy of a work Hughes had recently translated—*Les Bébés d'Hélène* (ALS in ASSSCL). Clemens noted receipt of Hughes' work in Notebook 22 (1884, *N&J* 3: 48).

The financial success of Habberton's novel amazed Clemens. On 17 January 1887 he expressed bewilderment at the continuing sales of "the very worst & most witless book the great & good God Almighty ever permitted to go to press" (SLC to Belle C. Greene, MTP). He mentioned Habberton's mistake in not copyrighting the novel in England to prevent its piracy there ("American Authors and British Pirates" [January 1888]). As late as 1895 Clemens manifested disgust that "when you travel on the Continent . . . the one book which has been translated as the best type of American literature is *Helen's Babies*" ("Mark Twain in Sydney," Sydney, Australia *Argus*, 17 September 1895, clipping in Scrapbook #26, MTP; Scharnhorst, *Complete Interviews*, p. 203).

———. *The Jericho Road: A Story of Western Life*. Square 12mo,

original brown cloth, rubbed, front inner hinge fragile. First edition. Chicago: Jansen, McClurg & Co., 1877. 222 pp.

Inscription: the front free flyleaf is inscribed "With the Author's Compliments."

Marginalia: Clemens made scores of notes and markings in pencil through the first three chapters (pp. 7–37), but only a few comments appear in the margins of fourteen of the remaining twenty-one chapters. His notes on thirty-six pages total approximately 460 words. In the first chapter he quibbles about inaccurate details and terminology ("There is a pretty wide difference between a deck-hand & a roustabout.") that Habberton uses in depicting life aboard a river steamboat (p. 7). Clemens began with the belief that he was reading "a diligent/& determined imitation of Bret/Harte, in style—& also in/ the character of the characters &/their rank in society" (p. 7). Another note in the first chapter declares, "This man is simply an idiot." However, on the last page of the novel he admitted (still writing in pencil) to finding it "a right down good book—with the exception of the first two chapters, which are execrable" (p. 222). The Mark Twain Papers at Berkeley contain a photocopy of Clemens's marginalia. A facsimile of page 7 appeared in the *Mark Twain Journal* 25.2 (Fall 1987) as well as in the 1988 Christie's sale catalog.

Catalogs: ListABP (1910), "Jericho Road"; Christie's, New York City, 1–2 February 1988 auction, lot 456, sold for $3,850.

Provenance: Carrie Estelle Doheny Collection, St. John's Seminary, Camarillo, California. Donated by Mrs. Doheny in 1940 after its purchase from Maxwell Hunley Rare Books of Beverly Hills for $12.20. Auctioned in New York City by Christie's in 1988 on behalf of St. John's Seminary and the Archdiocese of Los Angeles.

Location: collection of Kevin Mac Donnell, Austin, Texas.

Copy examined: Clemens's copy, at St. John's Seminary in 1970 and in Austin, Texas in July 2004.

The title *Jericho Road* is taken from the Biblical story of the Good Samaritan who assisted a man beaten and robbed by thieves on the road from Jerusalem to Jericho. Habberton's novel opens with a "wooding" operation by roustabouts for the steamboat *Helen Douglas* somewhere near the Wabash River. Kevin Mac Donnell observed that Habberton's novel "begins on a steamboat but the action is mostly on the road" and that it "is an entertaining satire of the Biblical story from which it gets its title—except that . . . no Good Samaritan ever puts in an appearance. . . . The musings on heaven and hell (the main character at one point states a preference for hell over heaven—sound familiar?), the episodes with scoundrels encountered along the way, . . . [the record of derogatory references to African Americans], and the portraits of the devout Christians all seem whisperings of another 'road' novel Twain was writing at the time" (Mac Donnell to the Mark Twain Forum, 19 August 2004). Regarding Clemens's marginal reference to Bret Harte, he and Harte had a falling out in 1877 and Clemens would carry a grudge thereafter.

———. *The Worst Boy in Town* (published in 1880).

Mark Twain thought about including a selection from "The Worst Boy in Town—by the ass Habberton" while planning a humor anthology in 1881 (NB 19, *N&J* 2: 428).

But when *Mark Twain's Library of Humor* appeared in 1888 it contained none of Habberton's writings.

The Habits of Good Society: A Handbook for Ladies and Gentlemen. New York: G. W. Carleton & Co., 1879. 320 pp.
Source: MTLAcc, entry #2145, volume donated from Clemens's library by Clara Clemens Gabrilowitsch in 1910.

HADOW, WILLIAM HENRY (1859–1937). *Studies in Modern Music.* London: Seeley and Co., 1893. 335 pp.
Inscription: inscribed on the half-title page in black ink: "To Miss Clemens/From A. Mulligan/'Musik ist die wahre allgemeine/Menschensprache.'/June, 1896/ Durban, Natal."
Marginalia: on page 210 Clara Clemens takes issue with Hadow's view of Robert Schumann. She made pencil marks on pp. 241 and she wrote a contemptuous sentence defending Richard Wagner's *Tannhäuser* in pencil on page 267: "We could not dispense with a *note of it* you dissecting *idiot*!!" Other cynical comments by Clara appear in pencil between 299 and 326. Her notes on pages 318–325 principally object to Hadow's interpretations of Wagner. For example, Clara wrote vertically in pencil in the left margin of page 322, responding to Hadow's observation that "as we listen we forget to criticize": "I wonder that *you* do." On the facing page (323) she objected to Hadow's opinion that the music of *Parsifal* was "less rich than that of *Tristan*" by writing indignantly in pencil in the left margin, "Stilted maniac! It's a marvelous, magnificent overpowering creation." In the right margin of the same page she added: "Spiritual, divine. What's the sense in comparing the two operas. One's red, the other's white." There are penciled notes, underlinings, or vertical marginal notes on pages 263, 267, 277, 279, 281, 282, 287, 293, and 296. Apparently none of this marginalia was made by Clemens.
Location: Mark Twain Library, Redding, Connecticut.
Copy examined: Clara Clemens's copy. Has the Mark Twain Library purple oval stamps and the Library's red ink accession number "2444". Examined in 1970 and again in June 1982 and on 10 November 2019.

HAECKEL, ERNST HEINRICH PHILIPP AUGUST (1834–1919). *The Wonders of Life: A Popular Study of Biological Philosophy.* Trans. by Joseph McCabe (1867–1955). New York: Harper & Brothers, 1905. 483 pp. [Edition conjectured.]
Hyatt Howe Waggoner reported that Clara Clemens Gabrilowitsch recalled her father's reading this book ("Science" [1937], p. 362), but Clemens's copy has never surfaced. Someone other than Clemens wrote that author and title on the rear endpaper of Clemens's copy of Robert Louis Stevenson's *The Pocket R. S. S.* (1904). Haeckel intended *The Wonders of Life* as a supplement to his *Riddle of the Universe* (1899).

HĀFIZ (fl. 14th century). *Odes from the Divan of Hafiz, Freely Rendered from Literal Translations.* Trans. Richard Le Gallienne (1866–1947).
Source: Clara Clemens listed the title and translator in her undated commonplace book (Paine 150, MTP). A 194-page edition of Le Gallienne's translation was copyrighted in Boston in 1903 by the Page Co.

HAGGARD, (SIR) HENRY RIDER (1856–1925). *Allan's Wife.* New York: J. S. Ogilvie, n.d. 180 pp.
Source: MTLAcc, entry #2257, volume donated from Clemens's library by Clara Clemens Gabrilowitsch in 1910.

In a letter to William Walter Phelps (1839–1894) written on 5 August 1892 from Germany, Clemens quoted a poem implicitly critical of Rudyard Kipling that also disparaged Haggard's writings: "When the Rudyards cease from kipling/And the Haggards Ride no more" (ALS, Huntington).

———. *The Brethren.* Illus. New York: McClure, Phillips & Co., 1904. 411 pp.
Source: MTLAcc, entry #1278, volume donated by Clemens.

———. *King Solomon's Mines* (novel, published in 1885).
It is tempting to speculate that Clemens's must have been familiar with Haggard's romantic novels set in Africa, such as the best-sellers *King Solomon's Mines* and *She* (1887). Michael Claxton—"*A Connecticut Yankee* and Victorian Magic," *Philological Review* 30.1 (Spring 2004): 12 n. 1—pointed out that Haggard's *King Solomon's Mines* employed the device of predicting an eclipse to impress gullible natives, somewhat as Mark Twain does in sixth-century England in *A Connecticut Yankee in King Arthur's Court* (1889). However, see also the entries for Christopher Columbus, John Watkins Holden, and Frederick Albion Ober.

Ha! Ha! Ha!: 72 Pages of Fun by Leading Humorists. New York: J. S. Ogilvie & Co., 1882.
On 19 September 1882 Clemens wrote Charles L. Webster to demand copies of a book that he had learned was using the name "Mark Twain": "Get & send me this 'Ha-ha-ha'" (*MTBus*, p. 197).

HAINES, JOHN THOMAS (1799?-1843). *The French Spy; or, The Siege of Constantina. A Military Drama in Three Acts* (melodrama, produced in 1830).
Mark Twain saw Adah Menken play the title role in this play in San Francisco; she was "a frisky Frenchman, and as dumb as an oyster" (13 September 1863 column, *MTEnt*, p. 80).

HALE, EDWARD EVERETT (1822–1909) *The Man without a Country.* New edition. Illus. Boston: Little, Brown and Co., 1907. 59 pp.
Marginalia: vertical line drawn in the margin on page xiii. The bookseller's label of Bretano's in Paris is affixed to the rear pastedown endpaper.
Provenance: shelfmarks on the front pastedown endpaper belong to the library numbering system employed by Clara Clemens Gabrilowitsch during her Detroit years. Sold at the 1951 auction in Hollywood but not listed in the hastily compiled sale sheet.
Catalog: "Property from the Library of Mark Twain," Butterfield & Butterfield, San Francisco, Sale 6613 (16 July 1997), lot 2712.
Location: Mark Twain House and Museum, Hartford, Connecticut.
Copy examined: Clemens's copy. Viewed in Hartford in 1997.
Hale's famous short story about the lonely figure of Philip Nolan, first published in 1863, was often reprinted. Mark Twain listed Hale among those scheduled to receive a complimentary copy of *The Prince and the Pauper* in 1881 (NB 19, *N&J* 2: 385), his first reference to this

clergyman-author. In Chapter 33 of *Life on the Mississippi* (1883) Twain calls the man who owns a mid-river island in the Mississippi "the man without a country." Similarly in Chapter 8 of *Following the Equator* (1897) he refers to two natives who mysteriously appear in a canoe in mid-Pacific as "those Men Without a Country." Following Olivia Clemens's death, Clemens announced to Charley Langdon: "I am a man without a country. Wherever Livy was, that was my country" (Florence, 19 June 1904, MTHM). Edward Everett Hale was third on Mark Twain's list of ten nominees for the American Academy of Arts and Letters in 1905 (SLC to Robert Underwood Johnson, 28 April 1905, American Academy). In "Adam's Soliloquy" (written in 1905) the mother in Central Park exclaims: "You must be the Man Without a Country—the one the story tells about. You don't seem to have any nationality at all" (*The Bible According to Mark Twain*, ed. Howard G. Baetzhold and Joseph B. McCullough [New York: Simon & Schuster, 1995], p. 124). Hale wrote to Clemens in 1906 to reveal that the copyright on his famous story—first published in the *Atlantic Monthly* in its December 1863 issue and then collected in a book in 1868—"expires this year" (IVL Journal, 10 April 1906, TS p. 155, MTP). In his Autobiographical Dictation of 4 February 1907 Mark Twain spoke of the "great and pathetic sensation" Hale's story made "when it issued from the press in the lurid days when the Civil War was about to break out [*sic*]"; Twain went on to assert that Bret Harte was "an invertebrate without a country" (*MTE*, p. 286; *AutoMT* 2: 424).

————. *Susan's Escort, and Others*. Illustrated by W[illiam]. T[homas] Smedley (1858–1920). New York: Harper & Brothers, 1898. 416 pp.

Source: MTLAcc, entry #1559, volume donated by Clemens.

————. *Ten Times One Is Ten, and Other Stories*. Boston: Little, Brown & Co., 1899.

Inscription: signed "Susan L. Crane, Quarry Farm, 1902".

Catalogs: QF Martinez, "Poor Condition"; Ball 2016 inventory, green cloth with gilt lettering, gilt top pages, quotes inscription.

Location: Quarry Farm Library shelves, under the supervision of the Mark Twain Archive, Elmira College, Elmira, New York.

This book was accessible to Clemens whenever he visited Quarry Farm in Elmira.

————— and **SUSAN HALE** (1833–1910). *A Family Flight*.

Catalogs: ListABP (1910) ("Hale, 'A Family Flight'"); *C1951*, D36, listed among the volumes signed by Clemens.

The two Hale siblings published three different books whose titles began with the words "*A Family Flight*": *A Family Flight Through France, Germany, Norway, and Switzerland* (1881), *A Family Flight Over Egypt and Syria* (1882), and *A Family Flight Around Home* (1884). In addition Susan Hale wrote *A Family Flight Through Spain* (1884). Owing to the cryptic 1951 catalog entry it is not clear which of these books Clemens owned and signed.

————. *A Family Flight Through France, Germany, Norway, and Switzerland*. Boston: D. Lothrop & Co., 1881.

Catalog: Ball 2016 inventory, brown cloth, red and gold

lettering, good condition.

Location: Quarry Farm Library shelves, under the supervision of the Mark Twain Archive, Elmira College, Elmira, New York.

This book was accessible to Clemens whenever he visited Quarry Farm in Elmira.

HALE, LUCRETIA PEABODY (1820–1900). *The Peterkin Papers*. Second ed. Illus. Boston: Ticknor and Co, 1886.

Hale's best-selling children's book related the mishaps befalling an eccentric but affluent Boston family. Mark Twain included "The Peterkins Decide to Learn the Languages" in *Mark Twain's Library of Humor* (1888), crediting it to Ticknor & Co. This collection of humorous stories was initially published by James R. Osgood and Co. in Boston in 1880.

HALÉVY, LUDOVIC (1834–1908). *L'abbé Constantin, par Ludovic Halévy. With English Notes by Frederick C. de Sumichrast [1845–1933]*. New York: W. R. Jenkins; Boston: C. Schoenhof, 1888. 203 pp.

Clemens entered the title of this book in Notebook 30 (*N&J* 3: 595) in December 1890. The work, still considered a classic of sorts, was first published in Paris in 1882; W. R. Jenkins brought out French language editions in New York in 1883, 1885, 1886, and 1888. The edition listed above was the most recent one when the book came to Clemens's attention. Halévy's novel, set against the Franco-Prussian War (1870–1871), opened with the curate of a small Catholic church worrying about the sale of the nearby chateau Longueval to a foreigner. Both the abbé and the readers are in for a number of subsequent surprises.

————. *Parisian Points of View*. Translated by Edith Virginia Brander Matthews (1874–1922). Intro. by Brander Matthews (1852–1929). New York: Harper & Brothers, 1894. 195 pp.

Olivia Clemens wrote to her husband from Paris on 27 April 1894, reporting, "I have read the book that Edith Matthews translated. I find it extremely charming. The stories are bright and delightful and the translating is perfect; you could not believe that it was a translation it is so easy flowing" (ALS, formerly in the Mark Twain Research Foundation, Perry, Missouri; quoted in *The Twainian* 37 [May-June 1978]: 4). Edith was Brander Matthews's only child.

HALIBURTON, THOMAS CHANDLER (1796–1865), pseud. "Sam Slick." *The Clockmaker, or Sayings and Doings of Sam Slick* (published in 1837, 1838, 1840).

Haliburton, a Nova Scotia judge and politician before he moved to England in 1856, invented an itinerant Yankee clock-maker named Sam Slick who gained international fame as a humorous character. In *The Clockmaker* a Nova Scotian travels with the Yankee peddler Slick, whose colorful phrasing and keen insights form part of the narrator's satirical examination of Canadians, Americans, and the English. Cyril Clemens reported in 1941 that during "a long talk" with Laura Hawkins Frazer (1837–1928) of Hannibal she told him an anecdote about Sam Clemens's early reading. Supposedly young Clemens haggled with a Yankee pack-peddler before buying a copy of "Judge Haliburton's 'Clockmaker,'" giving the adventures of Sam Slick," a volume that "had a bright yellow cover." Sam Clemens then carried "that old yellow book" about with him everywhere he went, even chuckling over it in church, according to Mrs. Frazer's remembrance more than three-quarters of a century later ("Unpublished Recollections of Original Becky Thatcher," *Mark Twain Quarterly* 4.4 [Summer-Fall 1941]: 20, 23; the table of contents in that issue of the journal titled this article "Unpublished Recollections of the Real Becky Thatcher"). Cyril Clemens repeated this story in *Young Sam Clemens* (Portland, Maine: Leon Tebbetts Editions, 1942), pp. 37–38. Mark Twain listed "Sam Slick" among the humorists he was considering for possible inclusion in an anthology in 1880 (NB 19, *N&J* 2: 363); in 1881 he included "Haliburton" in another compilation of American humorists' names (NB 19, *N&J* 2: 429).

Claude T. Bissell, "Haliburton, Leacock and the American Humorous Tradition," *Canadian Literature* 389 (Winter 1969): 5–19 took the view that Mark Twain was the "great classical embodiment" of American humor.

HALL, ANNA MARIA (FIELDING), "MRS. S[AMUEL]. C[ARTER]. HALL" (1800–1881). "Aileen Mavourneen" (Irish ballad). Alexander D. Roche (c. 1810–1868), composer.

Sheet music published in 1845 credits Hall for writing the lyrics of this wistful ballad, but the song is sometimes assigned to earlier and different sources. In Chapter 3 of "A Dog's Tale" (1903) the narrator explains the name her mother had given her—"Aileen Mavourneen. She got it out of a song."

HALL, BASIL (1788–1844). *Travels in North America, in the Years 1827 and 1828.* 3 vols. First edition. Three-quarter brown calf and marbled boards, marbled endpapers, raised bands, gilt, hand-colored map in Volume I, folding chart in Volume III. Edinburgh: Printed for Cadell and Co., Edinburgh, and Simpkin and Marshall, London, 1829.

Inscriptions: an early owner's name ("W. F. Riesser") is written in ink on the front pastedown endpaper of each volume.

Marginalia: Clemens marked passages in all three volumes, but he primarily concentrated on those in Volume III in which the former British Navy captain Hall described details of Mississippi River navigation. This suggests that Clemens's interest in the book was connected with the composition of *Life on the Mississippi* (1883). In Volume I Clemens made only one marking; he turned down the corner of page 133 and wrote "great city" in the upper margin, drawing a long marginal line beside a passage about the growth of Syracuse, New York. In Volume II he made marginal brackets in the table of contents beside Chapters 14 (Congress and state legislatures, money-making habits, and universal suffrage), 16 (publication of books, the Philosophical Society at Philadelphia, and Benjamin Franklin's tomb), and 18 (the city of Baltimore, and an etiquette book titled *The American Chesterfield* that was published in Philadelphia in 1827). No other markings appear in Volume II. Volume III contains brackets beside several chapters in the table of contents: Chapter 2 (the sale of an enslaved African American, and slavery in the District of Columbia), Chapter 7 (Charleston, a slave market, horse races, and balls), Chapter 9 (the culture of cotton, tasks of slaves, the evils of slavery, proposed remedies for its evils, future prospects of the slavery question), Chapter 14 (a trip to the mouth of the Mississippi, the Spaniards expelled from Mexico, levees, and crevasses), Chapter 15 ("deck-fare" passengers on a

river steamboat, a lively account of a pause at a "wooding" station, a detailed picture of a backwoodsman's farm, an explanation—complete with map—of how steamboat pilots steer while going upstream and downstream, the confluence of the Ohio and Mississippi, and the method of booming off steamboats when they run ashore), Chapter 16 (Louisville, St. Louis, the confluence of the Mississippi and the Missouri Rivers, and rafts), and Chapter 17 (a conversation with an American about England). Pages 319–320 bear Clemens's long marginal lines beside descriptions of the levee at New Orleans (this was quoted by Twain in Chapter 27 of *Life on the Mississippi*). Similar marginal lines are visible on pages 325, 326, 327, 328, 329, 338, 349, 352 (the latter quoted in Twain's Chapter 40), 353, 357, 359, 371, 378, and 388. Clemens turned down the corners of pages 349, 352 (the page from which passages were quoted in Chapter 40), 353, 355, 357, 376, and 378. These indicate Clemens's interest in Hall's first glimpse of the Mississippi River, the rise and fall of the river, descriptions of steamboats and plantations, travel times and distances, a brawl among steamboat crews, the drowning of a deck-hand, the long and lonely stretches of the river, the muddy waters of the rivers, and the method used to free steamboats that run aground. Clemens would presumably have been interested in pages 325–326, where Hall gives an account of a man who jumped from a steamboat and drowned, but these are not marked. At page 359 Clemens drew a line correcting a map of some bends in the river. On page 360 (unmarked) Hall noted that the pilot of his vessel was reluctant to go into any water shallower "than three fathoms or 18 feet," so evidently Hall's pilot did not view "mark twain" (two fathoms) as a safe depth.

Catalog: *A1911*, "map, 3 vols., 12mo, half calf, Edinb. 1829, "some passages marked by Mr. Clemens," lot 215, sold for $1.25.

Location: collection of Kevin Mac Donnell, Austin, Texas. Purchased in 2014 from a seller who advertised the book online.

Source: Kevin Mac Donnell furnished a detailed description of these volumes (Mac Donnell to Alan Gribben, 20 March 2014). Each volume contains an *A1911* sale label, he reported. Four code letters were scribbled on the corner of the final flyleaf following the folding chart four, presumably by a bookseller.

This was one of the "books relating to the river" that Mark Twain requested of his publisher in July 1882. On 22 July 1882 W. Rowlands replied for James R. Osgood that he was sending "a lot of books relating to travel in the U. S. by English people in the first half of the century; twenty-five volumes in all. They include Mrs. Trollope, Basil Hall and Marryatt [sic], &c, &c." (ALS in MTP; partially published in *MTLP*, ed. Hamlin Hill, p. 158 n. 2). Chapter 27 of *Life on the Mississippi* (1883) quotes Hall's reaction to his initial sight of the huge waterway: "Here I caught the first glimpse of the object I had so long wished to behold, and felt myself amply repaid at that moment for all the trouble I had experienced in coming so far. . . . But it was not till I had visited the same spot a dozen times, that I came to a right comprehension of the grandeur of the scene." In another place in Chapter

27 Twain quotes Hall's observation that one could travel "twenty or thirty miles without seeing a single habitation." Chapter 40 of *Life on the Mississippi* quotes Hall's description of the sugar plantations and refers to "grave, honest, intelligent, gentle, manly, charitable, well-meaning Capt. Basil Hall." In the manuscript for an unused portion of *Life on the Mississippi* Twain alluded to Hall as the "starter of the *real* swarm" of British travelers who visited the river. Appendix C of Twain's *Life on the Mississippi* consisted of Frances Trollope's astonished account of the "moral earthquake" in the United States that greeted the publication of Basil Hall's *Travels*, owing, she wrote, to "the exquisite sensitiveness and soreness" of the Americans "respecting everything said or written concerning them." She vigorously defended the fairness of Hall's work. Gretchen M. Beidler—"Huck Finn as Tourist: Mark Twain's Parody Travelogue," *Studies in American Fiction* 20.2 (Autumn 1992): 155–167—asserted that many details in Twain's *Huckleberry Finn* have subtle connections to Basil Hall and other early English visitors to North America.

Barbara Ladd, "'Night after Night and Day after Day': Mark Twain and the Natural World," *Mark Twain Annual 17* (2019): 19.

HALL, FLORENCE MARION (HOWE) (1845–1922). *Social Usages at Washington*. New York: Harper & Brothers, 1906. 166 pp.
  Source: MTLAcc, entry #394, volume donated by Clemens.
  ———. [Another identical copy.]
  Source: MTLAcc, entry #1356, volume donated by Clemens.

HALL, HERBERT BYNG (1805–1883). *The Bric-à-Brac Hunter; or, Chapters on Chinamania*. [First edition published in London in 1875.]
  Catalog: ListABP (1910), "Bric-a-Brac Hunter, Hall", no other information supplied.
  In Chapter 20 of *A Tramp Abroad* (1880) Mark Twain pretends to champion "that elegant Englishman, Byng [*sic*], who wrote a book called 'The Bric-à-Brac Hunter,'" against ignorant people who ridicule Byng "for 'gushing' over these trifles; and for exhibiting his 'deep infantile delight' in what they call his 'tupenny collection of beggarly trivialities'; and for beginning his book with a picture of himself, seated, in a 'sappy, self-complacent attitude, in the midst of his poor little ridiculous bric-à-brac junk shop.'" Clemens was being rather unfair to this collector of rare china specimens; Hall also wrote books on sports, historical sites, travel, and other topics. It seems relevant that Olivia Clemens and her mother were quite interested in porcelain trademarks. See a related entry for William C. Prime, *Pottery and Porcelain* (1878).

HALL, MRS. MATTHEW. *Lives of the Queens of England Before the Norman Conquest*. 2 vols. Boston: Taggard & Thompson, n. d. [1864?].
  Marginalia: a few marginal markings, possibly by Clemens.
  Catalog: Ball 2016 inventory, bookplate #235 of the "J. Langdon Family Library," fair to good condition.
  Location: Quarry Farm library shelves, under the supervision of the Mark Twain Archive, Gannett-Tripp Learning Center, Elmira College, Elmira, New York.
  Copy examined: a copy available to Clemens whenever he visited the Langdons in Elmira. Brown textured cloth, gilt page edges, red and gold lettering. Examined on 26 May 2015.

HALLAM, HENRY (1777–1859). *The Constitutional History of England from the Accession of Henry VII. to the Death of George II.* 2 vols. New York: A. C. Armstrong and Son, 1880.
  Catalog: Ball 2016 inventory, brown leather, marbling, gilt lettering, fair condition.
  Location: Quarry Farm library shelves, under the supervision of the Mark Twain Archive, Gannett-Tripp Learning Center, Elmira College, Elmira, New York.
  Copy examined: a copy available to Clemens whenever he visited Quarry Farm in Elmira. Examined on 26 May 2015.
  ———. *The Constitutional History of England from the Accession of Henry VII. to the Death of George II.* 2 vols.; *Introduction to the Literature of Europe in the Fifteenth, Sixteenth, and Seventeenth Centuries*. 4 vols. in 2 vols. New York, 1880.
  Catalog: *A1911*, "together, 4 vols., 12mo, cloth, N.Y. 1880," a sheet of notes laid in, lot 216, sold for $3.25 total. [These titles were almost certainly published in New York City by A. C. Armstrong and Son.]
  ———. *View of the State of Europe During the Middle Ages.* 2 vols. New York: A. C. Armstrong and Son, 1880.
  Catalog: Ball 2016 inventory, brown leather, marbling, gilt lettering, fair condition.
  Location: Quarry Farm library shelves, under the supervision of the Mark Twain Archive, Gannett-Tripp Learning Center, Elmira College, Elmira, New York.
  Copy examined: a copy available to Clemens whenever he visited Quarry Farm in Elmira. Examined on 26 May 2015.

HALLECK, FITZ-GREENE (1790–1867). "On the Death of Joseph Rodman Drake" (poem, written in 1820).
  The American poet Joseph Rodman Drake died early of tuberculosis. In "Some Thoughts on the Science of Onanism," a bawdy talk Mark Twain delivered at a Stomach Club dinner in Paris in 1879, he jokingly alluded to a "graceful" poem, quoting, "None know it but to love,/ None name it but to praise." As Louis J. Budd noted, Twain was paraphrasing Halleck's tribute to Joseph Rodman Drake (1795–1820): "Green be the turf above thee,/Friend of my better days!/None knew thee but to love thee,/Nor named thee but to praise" (*CTSS&E* 1: 722, 1063).

HALM, FRIEDRICH, pseud. of Eligius Franz Joseph von Münch-Bellinghausen (1806–1871). *Ingomar, the Barbarian* (melodrama, originally titled *Der Sohn der Wildnis*, performed in 1842).
  The best-known English version of this play was Maria Lovell's translation, staged in London in 1851 and shortly followed by an American production featuring Anna Cora Mowatt as Parthenia. From St. Louis, Missouri, young Samuel Clemens wrote to his brother's Muscatine, Iowa *Journal* on 5 March 1855: "[George W.] Jameison, the tragedian, is playing an engagement at the People's Theatre. He appears as Ingomar to-night" (*MTLMusc*, p. 27; *MTLet* 1: 56). Clemens later saw *Ingomar* performed in Virginia City in November 1863; he then wrote a burlesque review, "'Ingomar' Over the Mountains," which was published in the *Territorial Enterprise* and the San Francisco *Golden Era* (*WG*, pp. 58–60; Branch, *LAMT*, p. 288). In Chapter 13 of *The Adventures of Tom Sawyer*

(1876) Tom Sawyer and Joe Harper "were 'two souls with but a single thought,'" echoing a famous sentiment expressed in Halm's play. In 1881 Clemens parodied these closing lines of *Ingomar* in Notebook 19, altering "Two souls with but a single thought,/Two hearts that beat as one" into "Two tramps with but a single shirt,/Two beats that bilk as one" (*N&J* 2: 412).

Branch, *LAMT* (1950), pp. 35, 90–92, p. 288 n. 96; Krause, *MTC* (1967), pp. 47–50.

————. *Wildfeuer [Wild fire]*. Siebente Auflage [Seventh edition]. Green cloth, gilt lettering. Wien: Carl Gerold's Sohn, 1896. 151 pp. [A dramatic poem in five acts.]

Marginalia: note in pencil on the front free endpaper: "3/97".

Location: Mark Twain Library, Redding, Connecticut.

Copy examined: apparently Clemens's copy, unmarked, inspected in 1970 and on 10 November 2019. Has the red ink Mark Twain Library accession number "4087". Hemminghaus, "Mark Twain's German Provenience" (1945), p. 472.

HALSEY, FRANCIS WHITING (1851–1919), ed. *American Authors and Their Homes: Personal Descriptions & Interviews*. Illus. New York: J. Pott & Co. 1901. 302 pp.

Catalog: ListABP (1910), "Authors and Their Homes", no other information provided.

Halsey compiled twenty-two essays by various writers about the homes of such literary figures as Brander Matthews, Thomas Bailey Aldrich, George Washington Cable, Thomas Nelson Page, and William Dean Howells. Mark Twain was not included in that work, possibly because of the peripatetic nature of his household at the turn of the century. However, Halsey's follow-up, 299-page volume, *Authors of Our Day in Their Homes: Personal Descriptions & Interviews* (New York: James Pott & Co., 1902), did contain a chapter on Twain's Hartford house and his Riverdale residence written by Charles T. Sempers (pp. 21–35). Sempers mentioned that Twain declined a request to be quoted for the article. I thank Jo Dee Benussi for noticing the latter publication.

HAMERTON, PHILIP GILBERT (1834–1894). *Chapters on Animals*. Illus. Boston: Roberts Brothers, 1881. 253 pp.

Source: MTLAcc, entry #539, volume donated by Clemens. Hamerton discusses facts, fiction, and folklore associated with horses, cattle, goats, dogs, and cats. One chapter is titled "Animals and Art."

————. *French and English: A Comparison*. Boston: Roberts Brothers, 1889. 480 pp.

In November 1889 Clemens noted: "P Gilbert Hamerton 'French & English.' Roberts Bros. Boston" (NB 29, *N&J* 3: 531). Hamerton's book studied national characteristics; it was based on his seven articles that appeared in the *Atlantic Monthly* in 1886 and 1887.

————. *The Life of J[oseph]. M[allard]. W[illiam]. Turner [1775–1851], R. A.* Illus. Boston: Roberts Brothers, 1879. 404 pp.

Catalog: Ball 2016 inventory, brown boards, gilt lettering, embossed design, bookplate of J. Langdon Family Library #499.

Location: Quarry Farm library shelves, under the supervision of the Mark Twain Archive, Elmira College, Elmira, New York.

This was among the books accessible to Clemens during his visits to the Langdon home in Elmira.

————. *Wenderholme. A Story of Lancashire and Yorkshire*. Boston: Roberts Brothers, 1876. 433 pp.

Source: MTLAcc, entry #2258, volume donated from Clemens's library by Clara Clemens Gabrilowitsch in 1910. An English novel partly treating social class distinctions.

HAMILTON, ANTHONY (1646–1720). *Mémoires du Comte de Gramont*. Paris, 1850.

Catalog: *A1911*, "2 vols in 1, 16mo, half calf (broken), Paris, 1850," with Clemens's note on the verso of a visiting card of W. R. Coe laid in, lot 217, sold for $1.

The Irish-born Count Anthony Hamilton wrote Boswell-like memoirs of his brother-in-law, Philibert Gramont (1621–1707).

HAMILTON, THOMAS (1789–1842). *Men and Manners in America. By the Author of Cyril Thornton, Etc.* Philadelphia: Carey, Lea & Blanchard, 1833. 410 pp.

Marginalia: on page 61 Clemens wrote: "There are several of these fellows who give you a slap, and then turn immediately & kick a member of their family, stupidly imagining that the kick heals the slap. If they had stopped with either the kick or the slap, they wouldn't have offended both parties." Clemens also made additional marginal notations.

Catalogs: *A1911*, "first American edition, 8vo, half calf (a few pages foxed; several defective), Phila: Carey, Lea & Blanchard, 1833," quotes Clemens note on page 61 and reports that "other marginal annotations appear," lot 218, sold for $2; Anderson Auction Company (New York City), Sale number 1113 (8 December 1914), "Library of the Late George W. C. Phillips of Jersey City," "Mark Twain's copy, with the label signed by his literary executor"; American Art Association (New York City), Sale catalogue for the collection of the late William F. Gable of Altoona, Pennsylvania (8 January 1925), "Philadelphia, 1833" edition, has the *A1911* sale label, lot 122, sold for $22.50 (with two other books).

In a chapter deleted from the published version of *Life on the Mississippi* (1883) Mark Twain quotes and ridicules "a countryman" of Mrs. Trollope, "'Author of Cyril Thornton, Etc.,' (no other brand given)," whose book about America "differs from the books of most of the other foreign tourists of that day, in this—that it is not dignified, not brave, and not tolerant." A little farther on, listing the parade of visitors to the United States, Twain again refers to "'Author of Cyril Thornton, etc.,' a now forgotten literary celebrity, 1833–4" (Heritage Press edition [1944], pp. 394–395). Hamilton published his one novel, *The Youth and Manhood of Cyril Thornton*, in 1827. Born and educated in Scotland, he had served as an English officer in warfare against Napoleon in the Peninsula Campaign and was later posted in Canada and France. After retiring in Edinburgh he became friends with Walter Scott, William Wordsworth, and other literary figures. His *Men and Manners in America* appeared in 1833; as Twain noted, its Philadelphia edition merely identified the writer as "the Author of Cyril Thornton, Etc." In twenty-one chapters Hamilton recounted his travels after he entered the United States through Canada and visited New York City, Boston, Philadelphia, Washington, Charleston,

Cincinnati, Louisville, New Orleans, and other cities and towns. He saw Niagara Falls, explored New England, and took passage on both the Ohio River and the Mississippi River. Often sarcastic in describing the inconveniences he endured and the attitudes he encountered, he tended to imply the superiority of England and Scotland. Hartford, Connecticut, for instance, struck Hamilton as "one of the stupidest places on the surface of the globe" (p. 145). He was disgusted with a filthy hotel in New Haven, Connecticut and put off by "the nasty custom" of how Americans chose to eat their eggs (not out of the shell). Hamilton was especially incensed at the continuation of human slavery and the wretched treatment of free African Americans in the North.

Ganzel, "Twain, Travel Books," p. 41 n. 4.

HAMMETT, SAMUEL ADAMS (1816–1865), pseud. "Philip Paxton." *The Wonderful Adventures of Captain Priest: A Tale of But Few Incidents and No Plot in Particular, with Other Legends.* New York: H. Long & Brothers, 1855. 299 pp. [Edition conjectured; another edition was published in New York in 1855 by Redfield.]

> David E. E. Sloane— "Some Twain Sources and How They Affected His Sense of Self," *American Literary Realism* 45.1 (Fall 2012): 48–59—proposed this compendium of comical Down East stories, sketches, and poems as an illustration of "Twain's authorial memory working . . . synthetically with the northeastern literary tradition." Job Priest of Long Island is captain of the small coastal sloop *Sally Ann* when he desperately hails a much larger ship, "*Moro Castle*, three days out from Havana," and pleads for assistance. Sloane perceived similarities with the masterful speech Twain made in Liverpool on 11 July 1907 about the effrontery of the "*Mary Ann*, fourteen hours out from Boston," in hailing "the *Begum*, of Bengal, 142 days out from Canton." See also the Catalog entry for R. H. Dana, *Two Years Before the Mast.*

HAMMOND, EDWARD PAYSON (1831–1910). *Sketches of Palestine Descriptive of the Visit of the Rev. Edward Payson Hammond, M.A., to the Holy Land.* Intro. by the Reverend Robert Knox (1815–1883). Boston: Henry Hoyt, n.d. [The Reverend Knox's Introduction is dated 8 February 1868. Knox was the minister of a Presbyterian Church in Belfast, Ireland.] 180 pp.

> **Inscription:** Clemens wrote in pencil on the front free endpaper: "This book belongs to S. L. Clemens's Library of Literary 'Hogwash.' Hartford 1876." The front pastedown endpaper is signed by Edward P. Judd (1836–1914), the proprietor of a prosperous bookstore founded by his father on Chapel Street in New Haven, Connecticut.

> **Marginalia:** Prolific annotations in pencil by Clemens, uniformly derisive. Choice passages have been scissored from many pages, leaving the volume much mutilated. At the bottom of page 142 Clemens imitated Hammond's verses with a quatrain of his own: "And now I've thought out all the rot/That rhymes with vowel E;/Let not this service be forgot—/Ta-ta, Gethsemane." On page 148 Clemens referred to Hammond as "putrid" and a "humbug." Writing sideways in the margin of page 153 Clemens scoffed: "We have said our little say,/We have sham'd our little sham,/We have prayed our little pray—/Yet how few will care a damn."

> **Location:** Mark Twain Papers, Bancroft Library, University

of California at Berkeley. A typed page of description accompanying the volume explains that it was formerly in the collection of James Westfall Thompson (1869–1941), a history professor at the University of California at Berkeley, who had acquired it from a New Haven, Connecticut book dealer. A note on an index card laid in the book indicates that it was donated to the Mark Twain Papers by Cornelia Beall of Berkeley.

Copy examined: Clemens's copy.

Hammond wrote these "sketches" in the form of four-line poetic stanzas with the rhyme scheme *abab*. On 27 October 1879 Clemens acknowledged in a letter to Albert J. Scott that he had written a review of this "admirable singer" (ALS, Newberry Library, Chicago). Philip B. Eppard— "Mark Twain Dissects an Overrated Book, *American Literature* 49.3. (November 1977): 430–440—reprinted and analyzed this satirical review of Hammond's work that Twain published anonymously in the *Atlantic Monthly* 39.236 (June 1877): 738–741. (It appeared in the "Contributors' Club" column without a separate title.) Twain's review pretends that *Sketches of Palestine*, "an overrated book," has been lavishly praised by eminent literary critics but he predicts that this "frenzy will not last." He insists that "Edward Payson Hammond has been placed too high on the roll of the poets" (p. 738). Still, he denies that he ever claimed Hammond "is worse than Helen's Babies . . . ; I never went to that length" (p. 741). Three of Twain's invented literary authorities— "Hallet," "De Lisle," and "Von Schlecter"—he also cited in another mock-review written around the same time, this one ridiculing S. O. Allen's *Allen Bay, A Story.* See the S. O. Allen entry.

HAMMOND, HENRIETTA HARDY (1854–1888). *The Georgians.* Round-Robin Series, No. III. Boston: James R. Osgood and Co., 1881. [One of the Round-Robin Series of anonymous novels written by "the best writers" that the Osgood firm began publishing and promoting in 1881.]

> **Catalog:** Ball 2016 inventory, green cloth, red and black lettering, signed by Charles Jervis Langdon [Olivia Langdon Clemens's brother, 1849–1916]. Jervis Langdon Family Library bookplate #623.

> **Location:** Quarry Farm Library shelves, under the supervision of the Mark Twain Archive, Elmira College, Elmira, New York.

> Daring for its time, this novel revolves around a love affair between a married French woman and a young Georgia attorney. Clemens might possibly have noticed the book when he visited the Langdons' residence in Elmira.

> Jane Turner Censer, *The Reconstruction of White Southern Womanhood, 1865–1895* (Baton Rouge: Louisiana State University Press, 2003), pp. 48–49.

HAMMOND, NATALIE (HARRIS) (1859–1931). *A Woman's Part in a Revolution.* First edition, 8vo, original red cloth, front hinge cracked, leaves browned. London: Longmans, Green, and Co., 1897. 144 pp.

> **Inscription:** inscribed on the verso of the title page: "To dear Mark Twain who cheered many a weary heart before he reached mine. From the Author, April 1897."

> **Marginalia:** contains marginal notes and underlinings by Clemens on twenty-two pages. His twenty-five comments, ranging from one word to twenty-seven, are generally

favorable and add up to 147 words in ink and pencil. His notes appear on eighteen pages. Eleven pages are turned down. On page 66 Clemens wrote, "$250,000.00 among 64"; on page 120 he noted, "The judge not a citizen." See *The Twainian*, May-June 1954 and January-February 1958 for further details.

Catalogs: ListABP (1910), "A Woman's Part in a Revolution, Hammond"; *C1951*, D69, listed among books signed by Clemens; "Printed Books and Manuscripts," Christie's, New York City, offering the Chester L. Davis collection, 17–18 May 1991, item #78, marginalia described, bid estimate $1,400–1,800; Bauman Rare Books, New York City, Holiday Catalog, December 2019, original red cloth, recased, housed in a custom half-morocco slipcase, copious annotations throughout in both ink and pencil, 150 words written on eighteen different pages, quotes all of Clemens's marginal notations, the leaves are embrowned and a bit fragile, with a bit of soiling to the front board, $15,000.

Provenance: collection of Chester L. Davis (1903–1987), Mark Twain Research Foundation, Perry, Missouri.

Copy examined: Davis would not make this volume available for inspection when I visited Perry, Missouri in 1970.

Mrs. Hammond was the wife of a mining engineer who was Cecil Rhodes's business partner. Twice in Notebook 38 Mark Twain alluded to Mrs. Hammond's serious illness in 1896 (TS pp. 22, 33, MTP). In Chapter 65 of *Following the Equator* (1897) Twain refers to the recently published personal account of "Mrs. John Hays Hammond, a vigorous and vivid diarist, partial to the Reformers" (the English settlers who had revolted against the Boers in Johannesburg); in Chapter 66 he reports her criticism of Doctor Leander Starr Jameson (1853–1917); and in Chapter 67 he summarizes her sympathetic view of the Reform Committee. Mrs. Hammond's husband had been imprisoned after Jameson's raid in Johannesburg, South Africa. On page 152 of Mrs. Hammond's *A Woman's Part in a Revolution* she recounted Twain's visit to the English prisoners held at Pretoria. Eventually her husband would be released from prison rather than executed. John Hays Hammond (1855–1936) later indicated that he resented Twain's jokes about their good treatment in the jail: "You will forgive me, but I am not one of Mark Twain's admirers. . . . Since then I have failed to see anything 'funny' in anything Mark Twain says or does" ("More on Mark Twain in the South African Press," *Mark Twain Journal* 40.1 [Spring 2002]: 48). Years later, however, John Hays Hammond relented, recalling that Twain tried to make amends for his ill-timed humor about the treatment accorded the political prisoners. Mr. Hammond and Twain subsequently reunited at a "delightful luncheon" in New York City (*The Autobiography of John Hays Hammond*. 2 vols. [New York: Farrar & Rinehart, 1935] 2: 398–400. Madigan, "Mark Twain's Passage to India" (1974), p. 359.

HANCOCK, ALMIRA (RUSSELL) (1832–1893). *Reminiscences of Winfield Scott Hancock [1824–1886]. By His Wife*. New York: Charles L. Webster & Co., 1887. 340 pp.

Clemens's publishing firm issued this biography of the army officer who defended key positions in the battle of Gettysburg and was the Democratic candidate for president in 1880, running against James A. Garfield.

Handbook for Travellers in Ireland. Third ed. Revised and edited by J. C. Deane. Maps. London: John Murray, 1871. 358 pp. [Publisher and edition reliably conjectured.]

Catalog: *A1911*, "12mo, cloth, Lond. 1871," sheet of Clemens's notes laid in, lot 261, sold for $4.25.

Hand-Book of Florence and Environs with Views, A Topographical Plan and the Catalogues of Galleries. F. and J. Pineider, eds. Second ed. Illus. Prato, Italy: Contrucci & C., 1868. 152 pp.

Source: MTLAcc, entry #549, volume donated by Clemens.

HANNA, SEPTIMUS JAMES (1844–1921). *Christian Science History*. Boston: Christian Science Publishing Society, 1899.

In *Christian Science* (1907) Mark Twain quotes from page 16 of Hanna's book (*WIM?*, pp. 319, 570).

HANNIBAL *Journal* (12 May 1853).

John Ashmead's "A Possible Hannibal Source for Mark Twain's Dauphin," *American Literature* 34.1 (March 1962): 105–107, quoted the *Journal's* description of a hard-drinking fraud who visits a newspaper office.

HAPGOOD, HUTCHINS (1869–1944). *The Spirit of the Ghetto. Studies of the Jewish Quarter in New York*. New York, 1902.

Inscription: signed "S. L. Clemens, 1902."

Catalog: *A1911*, "12mo, cloth, N.Y. 1902," quotes the signature, lot 220, sold for $3.50.

HAPGOOD, NORMAN (1868–1937).

Journalist, editor, writer, and critic Hapgood's autobiography, *The Changing Years: Reminiscences of Norman Hapgood* (New York: Farrar & Rinehart, 1930), contained a chapter of engaging but generalized and undated recollections of Hapgood's (and his father's) relationship with Samuel L. Clemens. He included a few references to Clemens's reading. Several years later Hapgood would state that his "acquaintance with Mark Twain looms large." He recalled that "the home in Hartford, which I began to visit when I was a Freshman at Harvard, was a warm, cordial center of feeling as well as of thought" ("My Feeling about Mark Twain," *Mark Twain Quarterly* 2.2 [Winter 1937–1938]: 15).

"THE HAPPY LAND OF CANAAN" (song).

Clemens was furious in the mid-1860s when William Gillis and a group of other young men impulsively serenaded him outside his bedroom window in Jackson Hill, California with this and two other songs (William Robert Gillis [1849–1929], *Memories of Mark Twain and Steve Gillis [1838–1918]: Personal Recollections of the Famous Humorist* [Sonora, California: Printed by The Banner, 1924], p. 38; see also *MTLet* 1: 332). There were three songs titled "The happy land of Canaan" current around the 1860s—a Union war song, a Confederate version of it, and a minstrel show tune. It is difficult to know which lyrics Clemens heard that evening, but at this stage in his life the Civil War song with the Union slant would probably have antagonized him the most. See also the Catalog entries for "I'se gwine to de shucking" (song) and Henry Clay Work's "Kingdom coming" (song). Joe B. Fulton's *The Reconstruction of Mark Twain: How a Confederate Bushwhacker Became the Lincoln of Our Literature* (Baton Rouge: Louisiana State University Press, 2010) documented the persistence of Clemens's Southern sympathies.

HARBEN, WILLIAM NATHANIEL (1858–1919).

Evidently Clemens castigated Harben in a letter to William Dean Howells, for on 11 February 1910 Howells replied from New York City: "You seem to require a novelist to be true to the facts and if the facts are not pleasant, to be pleasant himself. That seems rather difficult. . . . But I believe you will end by liking poor old Harben as much as I do. He didn't make North Georgia; he only made a likeness of it. Don't shoot the artist" (*MTHL*, p. 852). Howells published a review, "Mr. Harben's Georgia Fiction," in the March 1910 issue of *North American Review*. During the last months of Clemens's life he entered both censure and praise for Harben in Notebook 49, sometimes writing in German (TS pp. 1–3, 10); generally he seemed to concur with Harben's philosophy but objected to his narrative techniques. Howells recalled in *My Mark Twain* (1910): "In the very last weeks of his life he burst forth, and, though too weak himself to write, he dictated his rage with me for recommending to him a certain author whose truthfulness he could not deny, but whom he hated for his truthfulness to sordid and ugly conditions. At heart Clemens was romantic" (p. 42).

———. *Abner Daniel; A Novel*. New York: Harper & Brothers, 1905. 312 pp.

Source: MTLAcc, entry #1037, volume donated by Clemens.

———. *Ann Boyd; A Novel*. New York: Harper & Brothers, 1906. 390 pp.

Source: MTLAcc, entry #1008, volume donated by Clemens.

On page 51 of Clemens's copy of W. W. Jacobs's *Salthaven* (1908), Clemens paused to write a note of praise: "This book is refreshingly sweet & clean & delicate after one has been floundering through that sewer, 'Ann Boyd,' & scurrying around among its frantic colony of vermin" (marginalia quoted in Dawson's Book Shop, Catalog 479 [June 1985], item #167).

———. [Another identical copy.]

Source: MTLAcc, entry #1434, volume donated by Clemens.

———. *The Georgians; A Novel*. New York: Harper & Brothers, 1904. 338 pp.

Source: MTLAcc, entry #158, volume donated by Clemens.

———. [Another identical copy.]

Source: MTLAcc, entry #1562, volume donated by Clemens.

———. *Gilbert Neal; A Novel*. New York: Harper & Brothers, 1908. 362 pp.

Source: MTLAcc, entry # 1560, volume donated by Clemens.

———. *Mam' Linda; A Novel*. Illus. New York: Harper & Brothers, 1907. 388 pp.

Source: MTLAcc, entry #1561, volume donated by Clemens.

———. *Pole Baker; A Novel*. New York: Harper & Brothers, 1905. 358 pp.

Source: MTLAcc, entry #1010, volume donated by Clemens.

———. [Another identical copy.]

Source: MTLAcc, entry #1258, volume donated by Clemens.

———. *The Redemption of Kenneth Galt*. New York: Harper & Brothers, 1909. 351 pp.

Source: MTLAcc, entry #1421, volume donated by Clemens.

———. *The Substitute*. New York: Harper & Brothers, 1903. 330 pp.

Source: MTLAcc, entry #1009, volume donated by Clemens.

HARDY, ARTHUR SHERBURNE (1847–1930). *But Yet A Woman; A Novel*. Boston: Houghton, Mifflin & Co., 1883. 348 pp.

Source: MTLAcc, entry #2259, volume donated from Clemens's library by Clara Clemens Gabrilowitsch in 1910. Hardy set this romantic novel in Paris during the mid-nineteenth-century Second Empire.

HARDY, E. R. "The Restoration," *Christian Science Journal* 16 (October 1898): 456. In Chapter 6 of *Christian Science* (1907) Mark Twain quoted four excerpts from this article extolling Christian Science (*WIM?*, pp. 238, 242).

HARDY, IZA DUFFUS (1850–1922).

Clemens informed Mary Mason Fairbanks on 6 July 1873 from London that he had met the woman to whom Joaquin Miller was engaged—"rather tall & slender, (about 26) good looking, good hearted, affectionate, frank, honest, cordial, unassuming, educated, intelligent, (she does a little in literature,), thoroughly English" (*MTLet* 5: 403). Hardy had by then published two novels: *Not Easily Jealous* (London, 1872) and *Between Two Fires* (London, 1873). Her engagement to Miller did not last.

HARDY, MARY ANNE (MACDOWELL), LADY HARDY (1824–1891). *A Casual Acquaintance: A Novel Founded on Fact*. London: Low & Co., 1866.

After Clemens conversed with Lady Hardy (who had married the novelist Thomas Hardy in 1850) in London in July 1873 he recorded the gist of their discussion in Notebook 12 (*N&J* 1: 557–559). He wrote to Mrs. Fairbanks on 6 July 1873: "Lady Hardy has written a number of novels & is well known here, but I think not in America. She told us the *facts* upon which her <'Chance'> 'Casual Acquaintance' was founded—a thrilling recital & admirably done" (*MTMF*, p. 176; *MTLet* 5: 403). Lady Hardy's sensation novel involved an actual crime. Subsequently Thomas Hardy would write an unrelated and powerful poem, "The Casual Acquaintance."

HARDY, THOMAS (1840–1928). *Far from the Madding Crowd*. New York, 1874.

Inscription: signed on the title page, "Saml. L. Clemens, Hartford, 1875."

Catalog: *A1911*, "16mo, cloth, N.Y. 1874," quotes the signature, lot 222, sold for $5.

Clemens labeled Hardy's work "haggard, hideous," but included Hardy in the list of eminent authors he constructed to pass the time while snowbound in New York City in March 1888 (NB 27, *N&J* 3: 379). Dr. James Ross Clemens (1866–1918), a distant relative who met Clemens in London in 1897, was responsible for the story that Clemens did not recognize Hardy when they encountered each other one day in a country inn and exchanged literary opinions. Later Clemens was supposedly chagrined to learn that he had attacked Hardy's literary reputation to his face. Dr. Clemens stated that he heard the anecdote from Clemens himself ("Reminiscences of Mark Twain" [1929], p. 105).

———. *Jude the Obscure*. "Thin Paper Edition." Red pliable cloth. Rear endpaper worm-damaged. New York and London:

Harper & Brothers, [cop. 1895]. 488 pp.

Inscriptions: Albert Bigelow Paine noted on the front free endpaper, in black ink: "This book was read by Mark Twain/April 9th—10—11th—1910—in Bermuda./ The last book he ever read through. He/died April 21. When he finished it he/asked me to read it 'so we can talk/about it.' I began it by his bedside,/and continued it on the ship. We/did 'talk about it' more or less, &/never afterwards of any other./A. B. P." (Quoted with slight discrepancies in "A. B. Paine's Part in Boosting Library," Redding, Connecticut *Pilot*, 15 June 1972 [section titled "New Mark Twain Library," p. 18]).

Provenance: inherited by Professor Bigelow Paine Cushman, Department of English, Western Connecticut State College, Danbury, Connecticut. Professor Cushman placed the book on loan to the Mark Twain Library in 1982.

Location: Mark Twain Library, Redding, Connecticut.

Copy examined: Clemens's copy, in June 1982 and March 1985. I was allowed to make a photocopy of Albert Bigelow Paine's inscription on 30 March 1985.

When an aggressive reporter named Mildred Champaign tracked Clemens down in Bermuda in the final stages of his coronary disease, she peered through a glass door and saw how he was occupied: "A number of books were spread out before him on the bed, and he was poring into them" ("Mark Twain at Bermuda," *Mark Twain Journal* 38.1 (Spring 2000): 11; *Complete Interviews* [2006], p. 696). *Jude the Obscure* was likely one of these volumes.

———. *A Laodicean: A Story of To-day.* "Thin Paper Edition." Red pliable cloth. New York: Harper & Brothers, n.d. [The American publisher initially published this title in 1896.]

Location: Mark Twain Library, Redding, Connecticut.

Copy examined: almost certainly Clemens's unmarked copy, since he owned at least one other Hardy title in this American "Thin Paper Edition" series. It has the red ink Mark Twain Library accession number "2419". Albert E. Stone, Jr. did not notice this book in 1955 and I did not see it in 1970. A Mark Twain Library patron last checked it out (according to its charge slip) in 1968, and by the time I returned to Redding in June 1982 it had been (properly) added to the collection of books from Clemens's library.

———. *Poems of the Past and the Present.* 12mo, cloth. New York, 1901.

Inscription: signed "S. L. Clemens, Riverdale, Dec., 1901."

Catalogs: *A1911*, "12mo, cloth (wrinkled), N.Y. 1901," quotes the signature, lot 221, sold for $1.50; George D. Smith, New York City, "Catalogue of Books" (1911), quotes the signature, item #15, $7.50.

———. *Under the Greenwood Tree; or, The Mellstock Quire—A Rural Painting of the Dutch School* (novel, published in 1872).

Cyril Clemens interviewed Thomas Hardy, who reported that Samuel Clemens read this pastoral novel aloud to Olivia Clemens (Cyril Clemens, *My Chat with Thomas Hardy* [Webster Groves, Missouri: Cyril Clemens, 1944], p. 15). Smith and Gibson, eds., *MTHL* (1960), p. 434; Elmo Howell, "Tom Sawyer's Mock Funeral: A Note on Mark Twain's Religion," *Mark Twain Journal* 16.3 (Winter 1972): 16.

Hare, Augustus John Cuthbert (1834–1903). *Memorials of a Quiet Life.* American Edition. New York: George Routledge & Sons, n. d. [Routledge editions with New York imprints appeared in the early and mid-1870s.]

Catalogs: included in the list of books that Mark Woodhouse transferred from the Quarry Farm library to the Mark Twain Archive on 9 July 1987; Ball 2016 inventory, green cloth, gilt, black design, fair to good condition.

Location: Mark Twain Archive, Elmira College, Elmira, New York.

This volume was part of the collection to which Clemens had access during his many summer visits to Quarry Farm in Elmira.

Using family memories and records, Hare constructed this tribute to his mother, Maria Leycester Hare (1798–1870), her husband, and her relatives.

———. *Walks in London.* 2 vols. Illus. London: Daldy, Isbister & Co., 1878. [Edition conjectured; there was also an American edition: New York: George Routledge and Sons, 1878. 500 pp.]

Clemens once recalled how he spent an unspecified period in London: "Nobody in town. Bought [John] Timbs—Walks—[John] Stow— Leigh Hunt, & a lot of other authorities & read about a thing, then went leisurely to see it" (undated MS scrap, DV115, MTP). John Timbs' *Walks and Talks about London* (1865) would seem to be the most likely referent, but Hare's historical guidebook is another possibility.

———. *Walks in Rome.* Fourth American Edition. New York: George Routledge & Sons, 1874. 678 pp. [Publisher and pages supplied.]

Inscription: signed "Saml. L. Clemens, Bateman's Point, Newport, R. I., Aug., 1875." (The Clemenses were spending a five-week vacation at this coastal resort.)

Catalogs: *A1911*, "12mo, cloth, N.Y. 1874," quotes the signature, lot 223, sold for $3; George D. Smith, "Catalogue of Books" (1911), quotes the signature, item #153, $8.50.

Hare recalled as "a great pleasure" his meetings with Clemens and "his most charming wife" in Rome in 1892. Clemens was "a wiry, thin old man, with abundant grey hair. . . . He speaks very slowly, dragging his words and sentences laboriously" (*The Story of My Life*, 6 vols. [London: George Allen, 1900] 6: 281).

———. *Walks in Rome.* 2 vols. London: George Allen, n.d.

Inscription: signed "Mrs. Susan L. Crane/Rome,/April 11/92".

Catalog: Ball 2016 inventory, Volume II only, inscribed by Susan Crane.

Location: Quarry Farm library shelves, under the supervision of the Mark Twain Archive, Gannett-Tripp Learning Center, Elmira College, Elmira, New York.

This copy was available to Clemens whenever he visited Quarry Farm in Elmira.

Harkins, Edward F[rancis]. (1872–1964). *Famous Authors (Men).* Illus. Boston: L. C. Page & Co., 1901. 332 pp.

Harkins was a Boston journalist. His essay about Mark Twain begins on page 43 and ends on page 57. The 1906 printing ("Fourth Impression") of *Famous Authors (Men)* would feature Twain's face on its cover. Quite possibly Twain saw this book, since he owned a copy of Harkins's next publication (see the following entry).

———. *Little Pilgrimages Among the Men Who Have Written Famous Books.* Illus. Boston: L. C. Page & Co., 1902. 332 pp.

Catalog: ListABP (1910), "Little Pilgrimages, Harkins",

no other information supplied.

William Lyon Phelps, "Mark Twain," *Yale Review* 25 (December 1935): 299–300, described Clemens's markings in the sketch of himself in Harkins's book. W. J. Burke, "Mark Twain: An Exhibition," *Bulletin of the New York Public Library* 40: 6 (June 1936): 499–501, reported that an exhibition commemorating Mark Twain opened at the New York Public Library in November 1935 and closed in April 1936. "No catalogue of the exhibition was deemed necessary." Burke mentioned numerous items that were on display, one of them related to Clemens's reading. "In Mark Twain's copy of E. F. Harkins's *Little Pilgrimages Among the Men Who Have Written Famous Books*, he had written some notes at the end of the chapter devoted to him. 'Few biographical sketches contain so many truths,' he observed, and then he tabulated the article and found that it contained twenty-four truths and twenty-six untruths" (p. 500). (I am grateful to Mary Boewe for calling my attention to Burke's article on 19 January 1989.)

Harkins's *Little Pilgrimages* paid tribute to twenty authors, including William Dean Howells (who received the lead-off essay), Bret Harte, George Washington Cable, Joel Chandler Harris, and Thomas Nelson Page. The admiring piece on Mark Twain (pp. 43–57), primarily biographical, asserted that his "career stands unequalled in the literary history of America" (p. 56).

HARKNESS, ALBERT (1822–1907). *A Latin Grammar for Schools and Colleges*. Revised Standard Edition of 1881. New York: D. Appleton and Co., 1886. 430 pp.

Inscription: inscribed in pencil on the front flyleaf in a hand that resembles Olivia Clemens's: "Mary Foote,/ Hartford./ (203 Sigourney St.)" The front pastedown endpaper is inscribed "*Mary Foote & Susy Clemens*". (Mary Foote was Susy Clemens's school classmate.) The front free endpaper is signed "S Clemens." and also "Olivia Susan Clemens"—both signatures apparently in Susy Clemens's hand.

Marginalia: the volume is heavily annotated in pencil throughout. On page 151 Susy Clemens wrote at the top of the page: "Was it about that loving girl with black curls?" Samuel Clemens himself made a note in his unmistakable hand at the top of page 209 in ink: "My dear child, have patience! 'Try, try again!'" The subject matter of that page is the Latin genitive case. One can speculate as to what amusing family scenario produced this jotting.

Location: Mark Twain House and Museum, Hartford, Connecticut.

Copy examined: Susy Clemens's copy, slightly annotated by Clemens. Examined in August 1987. Photocopies of the inscriptions and marginalia had been provided to Alan Gribben by Diana Royce, then Librarian of the Stowe-Day Library, Hartford, Connecticut, on 3 October 1984.

HARLAND, HENRY (1861–1905). *The Cardinal's Snuff-Box*. London: John Lane, 1900. 319 pp.

Catalog: Ball 2016 inventory, red cloth, gilt lettering, good condition.

Location: Quarry Farm Library shelves, under the supervision of the Mark Twain Archive, Elmira College, Elmira, New York.

Cardinal Udeschini's snuff-box, left in a garden, leads to romance for an Englishman visiting Lombardy in northern Italy.

This novel was available to Clemens during his final visits to Quarry Farm in Elmira.

Harper's Bazar (periodical, published 1867–). [The spelling of the magazine's title did not change to *Bazaar* until after Clemens's lifetime.]

On 12 September 1901 Clemens requested Frederick A. Duneka to change his mailing address for *Harper's Bazar* to Riverdale-on-the-Hudson, New York (Berg, NYPL). In June 1904 Clemens asked Isabel Lyon to change his address for "3 Harpers" (*Weekly, Monthly*, and *Bazar*) when he left the Villa di Quarto (MS note in MTP). In 1901 *Harper's Bazar* became a monthly magazine instead of a weekly.

Harper's Guide to Paris and the Exposition of 1900. Illus. New York: Harper & Brothers, 1900. 292 pp.

Source: MTLAcc, entry #1347, volume donated by Clemens.

Harper's Monthly Magazine (periodical, published 1850–).

In a sketch published in the 6 May 1865 issue of *The Californian* Mark Twain alluded to "a neat remark" about Martin Farquhar Tupper "which the editor of *Harper's Magazine* made three years ago" (*ET&S* 2: 154). In 1867 he mentioned the attention to utterances by precocious children shown by the "Editor's Drawer" (NB 10, *N&J* 1: 472). Clemens reminded himself to "get full Harper Monthly for Sue [Crane]" at a secondhand bookstore in New York City in July 1877 (NB 13, *N&J* 2: 38). On 10 August 1878 in Baden-Baden Clemens went "to bed early, with the new home magazines [*Harper's* and *Atlantic*], which I had saved all day & wouldn't cut a leaf" (NB 15, *N&J* 2: 134); a clipping pinned to a leaf in Notebook 14 (*N&J* 2: 91) was taken from the July 1878 issue of *Harper's*. In Chapter 59 of *Life on the Mississippi* (1883) Mark Twain partly burlesqued an anonymous article, "Sketches on the Upper Mississippi," that had appeared in *Harper's Monthly Magazine* 7 (July 1853): 182 (see Rogers, *MTBP*, pp. 91–93; see also the Catalog entry for A. J. Hoeffler).

William Dean Howells took over the "Editor's Study" column for six years beginning in October 1885 (*MTHL*, p. 538 n. 1). In 1888 Clemens wrote of *Harper's* and *Century* that "there is no choice between the two magazines, since they stand equally high" (SLC to Baroness Alexandra Gripenberg, 15 September 1888, quoted by Ernest J. Moyne, "Mark Twain and Baroness Alexandra Gripenberg," *American Literature* 45.3 [November 1973]: 373). Clemens jotted a note in September 1889 about "the train-boy who sold me a September Harper" (NB 29, *N&J* 3: 519). In May 1891 Clemens made arrangements to receive his *Harper's* subscription in Europe (NB 30, *N&J* 3: 628). From Berlin on 9 November 1891 Clemens instructed Franklin G. Whitmore to stop Harper's from sending two copies of the magazine; Whitmore was asked to keep the extra copy (MTHM). In Rome, Italy, Susy Clemens mentioned the March 1892 issue of *Harper's* in a letter she wrote to her college friend Louise Brownell (Hamilton College Archives; Cotton, "Olivia Susan Clemens," p. 140). "Mrs. Clemens fears the subscription to Harper's Monthly has run out—& she wants that magazine," Clemens informed Franklin C. Whitmore on 3 August 1894, while Olivia was in Paris (MTP).

"Of whom do you order the magazine for us?" Clemens grumbled to Whitmore from Rouen on 7 October 1894. "It is *many months* since either a Harper or a Century has arrived" (MTP). From Paris Clemens again complained on 6 November 1894 that "No Harper has arrived yet," and he instructed Whitmore to "give it up" and renew any *Harper's* subscriptions when they expire; he and Olivia were obliged to purchase in Paris the current issue containing a story by Charles Dudley Warner (MTP). In January 1896 Clemens read Edwin Lord Weeks' article on Bombay in the November 1895 issue (NB 36, TS p. 22). He reported to Joseph H. Twichell on 13 September 1898 that he was regularly receiving the *Harper's* issues in Kaltenleutgeben, Austria (*MTL*, p. 666; *LMTJHT*, p. 220). Although Howells had left the "Editor's Study" in 1892, his fiction continued to appear in *Harper's*; on 2 April 1899 Clemens reported from Vienna that he was "waiting for the April Harper" that contained an install-ment of *Their Silver Wedding Journey* (*MTHL*, p. 689). Charles Dudley Warner conducted the "Editor's Study" after Howells resigned until the column was dropped in 1898; Clemens lamented to Howells on 3 January 1899 from Vienna: "I have never gotten over your abandoning the Study to those pathetic stages—famine, water-logged derelict, unlamented submersion. The family feels the same way" (*MTHL*, p. 686). On 12 September 1901 Clemens asked Frederick A. Duneka to change his sub-scription address to Riverdale (Berg, NYPL); on 3 January 1902 he requested Duneka to send another copy of the Christmas 1901 issue, since his was lost (Berg, NYPL). Clemens referred knowledgeably to several pieces in the December 1903 issue when he wrote to Howells on 4 December 1903 from Florence (*MTHL*, pp. 774–775). In June 1904 Clemens directed Isabel Lyon to change the address for his subscriptions to the "3 Harpers" when he left Florence (MS note in MTP). On 2 October 1905 Mark Twain suggested that "A Horse's Tale" (1906) be sold to either the *Ladies' Home Journal* or *Collier's* so that it would reach the audience that "can't afford" *Harper's* (Berg, NYPL), but the story nonetheless appeared in *Harper's Monthly Magazine*. Isabel Lyon wrote to *Harper's* from Dublin, New Hampshire on 29 September 1905 requesting that the mailing department begin sending Clemens's subscription to 21 Fifth Avenue (MTP).

Harper's Monthly Magazine 76 (December 1887–May 1888). New York: Harper & Brothers, 1888. [Bound volume.]
   Location: Mark Twain Library, Redding, Connecticut. Gift of Mrs. William Irelandstair, Mrs. Inez Pennybacker, and Miss Lynn Stone.
   Copy examined: an unmarked volume containing the first printing of "Mark Twain's Letter to the Queen," but this was not Clemens's copy. When I examined it in June 1982 I recommended that it be removed from the shelves holding the books donated to the Mark Twain Library by Clemens and his daughter Clara Gabrilowisch.

Harper's Pictorial History of the War with Spain. Intro. by Major-General Nelson A. Miles (1839–1925). 2 vols. New York: Harper & Brothers, 1899; Harper's History of the War in the Philippines, ed. by Marrion Wilcox (1858–1926). New York: Harper & Brothers, 1899–1900.
   Catalog: *A1911,* "3 vols., folio, half morocco, N.Y.

1899–1900, with a slip of manuscript in Clemens's hand about songs sung by soldiers in the Civil War, lot 439, sold for $9 total.

Harper's Weekly (periodical, published 1857–1916).
   Clemens noticed in 1861 that the houses around Carson City were papered with engravings from *Harper's Weekly* (SLC to Jane Lampton Clemens, 26 October 1861, *MTLet* 1: 138). The library on the *Quaker City* contained two volumes of *Harper's Weekly* (reported by Dr. Abraham R. Jackson, New York *Herald,* 21 November 1867). In November 1872 Clemens congratulated Thomas Nast, the staff artist of the *Weekly,* for his anti-Greeley cartoons during the Grant campaign (*MTL*, p. 202; *MTLet* 5: 249). Touting the illustrator Walter Francis Brown (1853–1929), Clemens referenced Brown's recent work in *Harper's Weekly* in a letter to Frank Bliss on 10 May 1879 (*MTLP*, p. 114; *N&J* 2: 317 n. 55). Clemens mentioned to William Dean Howells on 3 January 1899 in Vienna that "The Weekly has just come" (*MTHL*, p. 686). On 12 September 1901 Clemens asked Frederick A. Duneka to change his mailing address for the *Weekly* to Riverdale (Berg, NYPL). "The Weekly is just received," Clemens informed Howells on 29 April 1903 (*MTHL*, p. 768). While Olivia Clemens lay ill in 1904 Clemens wrote her an undated note to accompany an issue of *Harper's Weekly* containing "not very interesting" war pictures (MTP). In June 1904 Clemens gave instructions to Isabel Lyon about notifying *Harper's Weekly* of his new address in the United States (MS note in MTP). Mark Twain's "King Leopold's Soliloquy" (1905) quoted from a poem published in the 4 February 1905 issue of *Harper's Weekly* (see the Catalog entry for L. M. S. Sill's "To the Czar"). *Harper's Weekly* ran a special insert of text and photographs commemorating George Harvey's dinner for Mark Twain at Delmonico's on 5 December 1905. In December 1906 the magazine published a photograph of Twain reading in bed, accompanied by a poem written by L. J. Bridgman, "To Mark Twain" (*Harper's Weekly* 50.2607 [8 December 1906]: 1748).

HARRADEN, BEATRICE (1864–1936). *Ships That Pass in the Night.* New York: J. S. Ogilvie, 1894.
   In New York City in February 1894 Clemens reminded himself: "Ships that Pass in the Night. Get 2—send one to Paris" (NB 33, TS p. 53). Olivia was then living in Paris. Harraden took her title from a line in Henry Wadsworth Longfellow's "The Theologian's Tale," a poem in *Tales of the Wayside Inn* (1873): "Ships that pass in the night, and speak each other in passing." In Harraden's sentimental novel two lonely individuals meet and fall in love at a Swiss winter resort, but then they part and are never reunited until it is too late.

HARRIS, GEORGE WASHINGTON (1814–1869). *Sut Lovingood: Yarns Spun by a "Nat'ral Born Durn'd Fool."* New York: Dick & Fitzgerald, 1867.
   Mark Twain noticed the issuance of this collection of sto-ries in a brief paragraph published in the 14 July 1867 San Francisco *Daily Alta California;* he referred to the sketches as resembling those "that used to be so popular in the West." Although he thought "the book abounds in humor," he predicted that "the Eastern people will call it coarse and taboo it" (*MTTMB*, p. 221). In 1880

Twain again noted the title and publisher of the edition ("Sut Lovengood [*sic*]—Dick & Fitzgerald") while listing authors for possible inclusion in an anthology of humor (NB 19, *N&J* 2: 362). He jotted down "Sut Lovengood" [*sic*] for the same purpose in 1881 (NB 19, *N&J* 2: 429). When Twain made notes in August 1885 for an "Essay on Humor," he decided to quote from "that forgotten Tennessee humorist" (NB 24, *N&J* 3: 172). *Mark Twain's Library of Humor* (1888) contained one sketch from *Sut Lovingood: Yarns*—"Sicily Burns's Wedding." E. Hudson Long, "Sut Lovingood and Mark Twain's *Joan of Arc*," *Modern Language Notes* 64.1 (January 1949): 37–39, cited Harris's "Sicily Burns's Wedding" sketch in *Sut Lovingood* as the source for the Uncle Laxart and the bull episode in Chapter 36 of Twain's *Joan of Arc* (1896). D. M. McKeithan's "Mark Twain's Story of the Bull and the Bees," *Tennessee Historical Quarterly* 11.3 (September 1952): 246–253 also traced the tale in *Joan of Arc* to Harris's "Sicily Burns's Wedding" tale. Henning Cohen's "Mark Twain's Sut Lovingood," in *The Lovingood Papers*, ed. Ben Harris McClary. Knoxville: University of Tennessee Press, 1962, 1: 19–24, reprinted Twain's 1867 book notice about Harris (as Cohen states, "it could scarcely be called a review"), speculating about Twain's prior knowledge of Harris's work and the discernible effects on Twain's own fiction.

Walter Blair, *NAH* (1937), p. 101; Andrews, *NF* (1950), p. 243; Daniel McKeithan, *CTMT* (1958), pp. 132–140; Blair, *MT&HF* (1960), pp. 242–243; Kenneth S. Lynn, *MT&SH* (1960), pp. 134, 138, 139; Louis H. Harrison, "The Influence of George Washington Harris in the Writings of Mark Twain," Master's thesis, University of Texas at Austin, 1963 (84 pages); Tanner, *Reign of Wonder* (1965), pp. 100–103; Krause, *MTC* (1967), p. 298; Hamada Kassam, "Huck Finn as the Fictive Son of George W. Harris's Sut Lovingood," *Mark Twain Journal* 54.1 (Spring 2016): 125–139.

Harris, Joel Chandler (1848–1908). "At Teague Poteet's: A Sketch of the Hog Mountain Range," *Century Magazine* 26.1–26.2 (May-June 1883): 137–150, 185–194.

David Carkeet—"The Source for the Arkansas Gossips in *Huckleberry Finn*," *American Literary Realism* 14.1 (Spring 1981): 90–92—suggested that this story by Harris could have provided models for Mrs. Hotchkiss and Mrs. Damrell in Chapter 41 of Twain's *Adventures of Huckleberry Finn* (1885). Teague Poteet was depicted as a Georgia moonshiner.

———. *Free Joe and Other Georgian Sketches*. New York: Charles Scribner's Sons, 1887. 236 pp. [Publisher and pages conjectured.]

Inscription: "With the regards of the author, Joel Chandler Harris."

Catalog: *A1911*, "first edition, 12mo, cloth, N.Y. 1887," quotes the inscription, lot 225, sold for $10.50.

The title story recounts the sad dilemma of an emancipated African American; formerly enslaved, he finds that as a supposedly "free" man he no longer has a place in the social order of the Deep South.

———. *Nights with Uncle Remus: Myths and Legends of the Old Plantation*. Boston: James R. Osgood and Co., 1883. 416 pp.

Mark Twain's Library of Humor (1888) credited "The Tar Baby" and "Mr. Fox Victimized" to this collection, though Twain had previously encountered both pieces in *Uncle Remus: His Songs and His Sayings* (1880). In an exchange of letters in December 1881 Harris and Twain had compared versions of one of the tales in *Nights with Uncle Remus*, "A Ghost Story" (SLC to Harris, 12 December 1881, *MTL*, pp. 403–404); Twain called his variant "The Golden Arm."

———. *On the Wing of Occasions; Being the Authorized Version of Certain Curious Episodes of the Late Civil War, Including the Hitherto Suppressed Narrative of the Kidnapping of President Lincoln*. Illus. New York: Doubleday, Page & Co., 1900. 310 pp.

Source: MTLAcc, entry #2260, volume donated from Clemens's library by Clara Clemens Gabrilowitsch in 1910.

———. *Uncle Remus: His Songs and His Sayings. The Folk-Lore of the Old Plantation*. Illus. by Frederick S[tuart]. Church (1842–1924) and James H[enry]. Moser (1854–1913). New York: D. Appleton & Co., 1890. 231 pp.

Inscription: signed in pencil on the flyleaf: "S. L. Clemens/ Hartford, 1890." Signed "Cyril Clemens" on the front pastedown endpaper.

Catalogs: *C1951*, D21, $32.50; *Zeitlin 1951*, #19, $50.

Provenance: shelfmarks of Clara Clemens Samossoud's private library in Detroit on the front pastedown endpaper. Thomas A. Tenney examined (and photocopied) the title page and inscriptions in September 1980 when the book was in Cyril Clemens's collection in Kirkwood, Missouri.

Location: Harry Ransom Center, University of Texas at Austin. Acquired from Cyril Clemens along with six other books on 28 March 1986, for payments of $5,000 to Cyril Clemens and $5,000 to his *Mark Twain Journal*. Thomas A. Tenney, Cyril Clemens, and Alan Gribben (then an English professor at the University of Texas at Austin) negotiated this agreement in an exchange of letters written between 20 August 1985 and 27 April 1986.

Copy examined: photocopies of the title page and inscriptions sent by Thomas A. Tenney of Charleston to Alan Gribben in April 1985. The front pastedown endpaper has the number from the *C1951* auction ("D21") noted at the bottom of the front pastedown endpaper. Confirmed by an examination of the volume in Austin in 1986.

Clemens presumably owned an earlier edition of this book as well. In July 1880 he noted: "<Old Si> (?) Uncle Remus writer of colored yarns" (NB 19, *N&J* 2: 362). On 28 November 1880 Clemens wrote to Fields, Osgood, & Company from Hartford: "Dr Sirs: Please send me 'Uncle Remus's Songs & Sayings.' Yrs. truly, S. L. Clemens" (ALS quoted in an auction catalog, Maxwell Hunley Rare Books [15 July 1958], item #161). In June 1881 when Clemens was inventing comical captions for a Hartford banquet menu he assigned one invented quotation to "Brer Talmage," paying homage to Harris but also ridiculing the Reverend Thomas DeWitt Talmage (Beinecke Rare Book and Manuscript Library, Yale University; Everett Emerson to Alan Gribben, 29 October 1984). Clemens praised the narrator of these tales in a letter to Harris written on 10 August 1881: "In reality the stories are only alligator pears—one merely eats them for the sake of the salad-dressing. Uncle Remus is most deftly drawn, and is a lovable and delightful creation; he, and the little boy, and their relations with each other, are high and fine literature, and worthy to live, for their own sakes; and certainly the stories are not to be credited with *them*" (*MTL*, pp. 401–402).

Of the stories in this collection Clemens favored "Brer Rabbit, Brer Fox, and the Tar Baby." On 27 February 1881 he informed William Dean Howells from Hartford: "I read in Twichell's chapel Friday night, & had a most rattling high time—but the thing that went best of all was Uncle Remus's Tar Baby" (*MTHL*, p. 356). In Chapter 46 of *Life on the Mississippi* (1883) Mark Twain singled out Harris as one of the authors who had abandoned the "old, inflated style" of Southern writers and instead adopted "modern English." The next chapter (47) described Harris's shyness when faced with a public performance. In a manuscript section eventually omitted from Chapter 40 of *Life on the Mississippi* (1883), Twain explained that in parts of the United States people were once called "'Brother' Smith and 'Sister' Jones—a phrase which survives in Uncle Remus's 'Ole Brer Fox' and 'Ole Brer Rabbit.'" Twain noted the story title in 1885 as a possible piece for public reading (NB 23, *N&J* 3: 120, 121), and in October 1889 he planned to "read Tar-Baby at tail-end of Author's Reading in Brooklyn Dec. 16, '89, Academy of Music" (NB 29, *N&J* 3: 523). Meanwhile, he selected this tale and another sketch—"Mr. Fox is Again Victimized"—for inclusion in *Mark Twain's Library of Humor* (1888). (The latter piece Twain published as an extension of "Mr. Rabbit Grossly Deceives Mr. Fox.") "The Tar Baby" was the only selection by another author that Twain planned to read at Bryn Mawr in 1891 (NB 30, *N&J* 3: 604, 608, 616); he also scheduled it for use in his Dresden reading in December 1891 (NB 31, TS p. 16). Notebook 35 reveals that the tar-baby story was part of Twain's repertoire when he began his lecture tour around the world in July 1895 (TS pp. 4, 14). In Chapter 49 of *Following the Equator* (1897) Twain employed a phrase from the tar-baby story: "'Brer fox he lay low,' as Uncle Remus says." During Brer Rabbit's monologue with the silent tar-baby this line is repeated as a refrain: "Tar-Baby stay still, en Brer Fox, he lay low" (*Uncle Remus: His Songs and His Sayings* [New York: D. Appleton Co., 1895], pp. 8–10).

Mark Twain first met Harris in May 1882 in New Orleans, where Harris, Mark Twain, and George Washington Cable read from their writings to neighborhood children at Cable's house; "I read Remus's stories & my own stuff to them," Clemens wrote to Olivia Clemens on 2 May 1882 (*LLMT*, p. 212). In Chapter 47 of *Life on the Mississippi* (1883) Mark Twain mentioned Harris's extreme shyness and praised his ability to write African American dialect ("the only master the country has produced"). Harris praised Twain's books in the Atlanta *Constitution* on 11 June 1882 (*The Stolen White Elephant*) and on 26 May 1885 (*Adventures of Huckleberry Finn*); see Joseph M. Griska, Jr., "Two New Joel Chandler Harris Reviews of Mark Twain," *American Literature* 48.4 [January 1977]: 584–589). In 1888, entertaining a group of specially invited guests in the parlor of the Stanchfields in Elmira, New York, Clemens varied his oral readings of Robert Browning with "selections from 'Uncle Remus'" that "completely won the hearts of his listeners. . . . Mr. Clemens' Negro dialect is so perfect that the darkness may be felt" (*Saturday Tidings* [weekly], Elmira, New

York, 15 September 1888, TS sent to Alan Gribben by Gretchen Sharlow in February 1987). On 5 November 1892 Clemens wrote to Clara Clemens from Florence to describe recent literary readings at Villa Viviani: after laying aside Browning ("too sombre & difficult") and Tennyson ("too tame & effeminate"), he and his circle were "bracing up on Uncle Remus, evenings, for a change" (MTP). From Paris Clemens wrote to Henry H. Rogers on 27 December 1894: "I went to a masked ball blacked up as Uncle Remus, taking Clara along; and we had a good time" (*MTHHR*, p. 112). Harris was one of Clemens's nominations for membership in the American Academy of Arts and Letters in 1905 (SLC to Robert Underwood Johnson, 28 April 1905, American Academy). "Susy and Clara . . . knew his book by heart through my nightly declamation of its tales to them," he later recalled (16 October 1906 AD, *MTE*, p. 136; *AutoMT* 2: 260). When news came that Harris had died, Twain lamented that "Uncle Remus, joy of the child and the adult alike, will speak to us no more. It is a heavy loss" (6 July 1908 AD, MTP; *AutoMT* 3: 243).

Julia Collier Harris, *The Life and Letters of Joel Chandler Harris* (Boston: Houghton Mifflin, 1918); William J. Scheick, "The Spunk of a Rabbit: An Allusion in *The Adventures of Huckleberry Finn*," *Mark Twain Journal* 15.4 (Summer 1971): 14–16; Joseph M. Griska, Jr., "Uncle Remus Correspondence: The Development and Reception of Joel Chandler Harris's Writing, 1880–1885," *American Literary Realism* 14.1 (Spring 1981): 26–37; William R. Bell, "The Relationship of Mark Twain and Joel Chandler Harris," *Atlanta Historical Review* 30.3–4 (Fall-Winter 1986–1987): 97–112.

HARRIS, WILLIAM TORREY (1835–1909), **ANDREW J. RICKOFF** (1824–1899), and **MARK BAILEY** (1822–1904). *The First Reader*. Illus. New York: D. Appleton and Co., 1880. 90 pp.
  Source: MTLAcc, entry #447, volume donated by Clemens. Elementary English words and phrases, with amusing drawings, for elementary school pupils.

HARRISON, AUSTIN (1873–1928). *The Pan-Germanic Doctrine; Being a Study of German Political Aims and Aspirations*. Maps. New York: Harper & Brothers, 1904. 379 pp.
  Source: MTLAcc, entry #1500, volume donated by Clemens.

HARRISON, CONSTANCE (CARY) (1843–1920). *An Edelweiss of the Sierras; Golden-Rod, and Other Tales*. New York: Harper & Brothers, 1892. 209 pp.
  Source: MTLAcc, entry #1485, volume donated by Clemens.

———. *The Story of Helen Troy*. New York: Harper & Brothers, [cop. 1881]. 202 pp.
  Source: MTLAcc, entry # 1173, volume donated by Clemens.
  A novel set on Fifth Avenue, not in ancient Troy, and about the vicissitudes of fate that generally favor a girl named Helen from the family of Troy.

HARRISON, DAVID. *The Melancholy Narrative of the Distressful Voyage and the Miraculous Recovery of Captain David Harrison of the Sloop, Peggy, of New-York, on His Voyage from Fyal, One of the Western Islands, to New-York*. London: Printed for James Harrison, 1766. 67 pp.
  Ann M. Ryan identified Harrison's book as the source of

"Forty-five Days' Sufferings" that Mark Twain encountered in a summary form in *Ocean Scenes; or, The Perils and Beauties of the Deep* (see that Catalog entry). Ryan explored the evidence that Twain knew of Harrison's ordeal and contended that "echoes of the *Peggy's* voyage can be heard throughout *Adventures of Huckleberry Finn*" "(Not) Wanted Dead or Alive: Mark Twain's Literary Autopsy of 'Jim's Ghost Story,'" *Mark Twain Annual 13* (2015): 150–151. Captain Harrison's *Melancholy Narrative of the Distressful Voyage* related how storms tore away his ship's masts and sails, leaving it floating helplessly in rough waters. Famished, the crew resorted to cannibalism, and Harrison gave a gruesome account of how an African American slave became their first victim. They had just selected a fellow crew member as their next meal when they were rescued by the *Susanna*.

Harrison, Frederic (1831–1923). *Theophano: The Crusade of the Tenth Century; A Novel*. New York: Harper & Brothers, 1904. 484 pp.

Source: MTLAcc, entry #1104, volume donated by Clemens.

———. [Another identical copy.]

Source: MTLAcc, entry #2261, volume donated from Clemens's library by Clara Clemens Gabrilowitsch in 1910.

Harrison, Mary St Leger (Kingsley) (1852–1931), pseud. "Lucas Matet." *The Wages of Sin* (novel, published in 1890).

In a letter postmarked in Florence in June 1893 Susy Clemens asked her college friend Louise Brownell, "Have you read 'Wages of Sin' by Lucas Matet? We are all devoted to it. I think it's an excellent illustration of what an artist with a fine purpose ahead of her can venture to put into a book without giving the slightest *shadow* of offence to the reader" (Hamilton College Archives). *Wages of Sin* was written by the daughter of the English author Charles Kingsley. The novel, which inspired Thomas Hardy's *Jude the Obscure*, depicted the moral and masochistic struggles of an artist trapped in a love triangle. He fell in love with a woman after his mistress gave birth to their daughter. Harrison's writings are increasingly seen as neglected precursors of modern fiction and its freedoms.

Hart, Albert Bushnell (1854–1943) and **Blanche E[vans]. Hazard** (1873–1966), eds. *Colonial Children*. Source-Readers in American History, No. 1. New York: Macmillan & Co., 1902.

Clemens joked in a letter to Charles J. Langdon on 25 July 1904 from Lee, Massachusetts: "Ida's 'Colonial Children' are perfectly safe: I only brought it away to hold as security against the return of the [shaving] brush" (MTHM).

Hart, Jerome Alfred (1854–1937). *A Levantine Log-Book*. Illus. New York: Longmans, Green and Co., 1905. 404 pp.

Inscription: inscribed in black ink on the front free endpaper: "Samuel L. Clemens, Esq., with respects and good wishes from an admirer of many years./Jerome A. Hart/January, 1906."

Location: Mark Twain Library, Redding, Connecticut. Donated by Clemens (MTLAcc, entry #587).

Copy examined: Clemens's copy, unmarked. Has the red ink Mark Twain Library accession number "587". Examined in 1970 and again in June 1982.

Hart, editor of the weekly San Francisco *Argonaut*, offered unflinching and sometimes humorous descriptions of famous tourist destinations in Turkey, Egypt, Palestine, Italy, and other regions.

Hart, Joseph (1712–1768). "Come, ye sinners, poor and needy" (hymn, 1759). Originally titled "Come, ye sinners, poor and wretched."

John R. Byers, Jr., "The Pokeville Preacher's Invitation in *Huckleberry Finn*," *Mark Twain Journal* 18.4 (Summer 1977): 15–16 argued that Mark Twain had this hymn in mind when the preacher lines out a hymn for the camp meeting in Chapter 20 of *Adventures of Huckleberry Finn* (1885).

Harte, Bret [Francis Brett Harte] (1836–1902). *"Argonaut Edition" of the Works of Bret Harte*. 25 vols. Illus. New York: P. F. Collier & Son, 1889–1907. "Published under special arrangement with the Houghton Mifflin Company."

Catalog: Ball 2016 inventory, green cloth, gilt lettering, embossed seal on front covers, only 17 vols. The surviving titles are (Vol. 7, 1889) *The Luck of Roaring Camp, Susy, A Story of the Plains*; (Vol. 8, 1902) *The Complete Poetical Works of Bret Harte*; (Vol. 10, 1901) *Under the Redwoods*; (Vol. 11, 1900) *From Sandhill to Pine, A Tourist from Injianny*; (Vol. 12, 1904) *Mr. Jack Hamlin's Mediation, Two Men of Sandy Bar*; (Vol. 13, 1889) *Stories in Light and Shadow, The Argonauts of North Liberty*; (Vol. 15, 1897) *Three Partners*; (Vol. 16, 1903) *Tales of the Argonauts, On the Frontier*; (Vol. 17, 1900) *Mrs. Skaggs's Husbands*; (Vol. 18, 1905) *Clarence, The Story of a Mine*; (Vol. 19, 1894) *The Bell Ringer of Angel's*; (Vol. 20, 1894) *A Protégée of Jack Hamlin's, Jeff Briggs's Love Story*; (Vol. 21, 1893) *Sally Dows, A Phyllis of the Sierras*; (Vol. 22, 1891) *A First Family of Tasajara, The Queen of the Pirate Isle*; (Vol. 23, 1892) *Colonel Starbottle's Client, Flip, Found at Blazing Star*; (Vol. 24, 1907) *Cressy, The Twins of Table Mountain*; (Vol. 25, 1903) *A Sappho of Green Springs, The Four Guardians of Lagrange, Peter Schroeder*.

Location: Quarry Farm Library shelves, under the supervision of the Mark Twain Archive, Elmira College, Elmira, New York.

This set was available to Clemens whenever he visited Quarry Farm in Elmira, New York between 1889 and 1907.

———. *Condensed Novels*. Woodcut frontispiece and one plate by S[olomon]. Eytinge, Jr. (1833–1905). Original purple cloth, gilt, beveled edges, brown-coated endpapers, spine chipped and repaired. Boston: James R. Osgood and Co., 1871. 212 pp. [The first edition of Harte's book appeared in 1867; this revised and expanded edition added two more parodies.].

Inscription: the title page is inscribed at the top in purple ink, "To Samuel L. Clemens/with cordial regards of/Bret Harte."

Marginalia: Clemens made a marginal pencil correction on page 1, altering "For twenty year" to read "For twenty years," and on page 4, correcting "an eight of an inch" to "an eighth of an inch."

Provenance: collection of Nick Karanovich, Fort Wayne, Indiana. Its prior location is unknown.

Catalog: *Sotheby's 2003*, #207, $4,500.

Location: currently unknown.

Copy examined: a presentation copy from Harte to Clemens, viewed at the 2003 Sotheby's sale.

In a portion of Mark Twain's letter of 2 February 1867

that was deleted in publication by the *Alta California* he referred to Harte's "capital *Condensed Novels*," a book then in press (*MTTMB*, p. 284, n. 5). In a letter of 27 January 1871 Clemens praised Harte's "prettiest fancy" in designing the cover for the *Overland Monthly* with a grizzly bear crossing railroad tracks (*MTLet* 4: 317–318).

———. *Drift from Two Shores*. Green cloth. Boston: Houghton, Osgood & Co.; Cambridge: The Riverside Press, 1880. 266 pp.

Marginalia: Mark Twain obviously used this copy to search for materials suitable for the anthology of humor that he was co-editing with William Dean Howells and Charles Hopkins Clark in the 1880s. One or both of his co-editors seem to have previously nominated titles with red and blue pencil markings. On the verso of the first flyleaf Clemens resolved, writing in blue ink, "We must have Clarence/King in full strength./SLC/The Newtys of Pike, for instance." At the top of the volume's "Contents" page he added in blue ink: "We must have the Heathen/Chinee & some other Dia-/lect poems of Harte's." He rated Harte's stories in heavy pencil notes on that "Contents" page, where he bracketed six tales for consideration: "Two Saints of the Foot-hills" was "Good enough" (blue ink); "Roger Catron's Friend" was "Pretty thin" (blue ink); "Who Was My Quiet Friend?" amounted to "Poor stuff" (blue ink); "A Ghost of the Sierras" was "Not humorous" (black pencil); and "The Hoodlum Band (A Condensed Novel)" seemed to Clemens "merely tolerable" (black pencil). The only other story marked on the Contents page was "A Sleeping-Car Experience," which Clemens designated in black pencil as "The best of the lot." Significantly, the pages on which this latter story appears (231–242) were torn out of the book and missing. Clemens made three sarcastic remarks in blue ink in the margins of "Two Saints of the Foot-Hills" on pages 59 (two jibes there) and page 61. The comment on page 59 derides the narrator's reference to Daddy Downey: "This tottering old ass *couldn't* have been 60 by *anybody's* arithmetic but Bret Harte's." On the same page Clemens made three vertical lines and scoffed, "So this story was written in *1896*?" in reference to a town named Rough-and-Ready. At the top of page 61 Clemens objected: "She *couldn't* play Sweetwater on those people— a name that hadn't existed 20 years." (Mammy Downey had alluded to her son Sammy as "taken down with lung fever, at Sweetwater.") Clemens felt impelled to make a stylistic revision on page 71 in blue ink, deleting the word "considerably" in "the circumstances were considerably explained to him". But on page 128, beside the first paragraph of "A Ghost of the Sierras," Clemens took his hat off to one feature of Harte's writing; in blue ink he made a vertical note: "When it comes to Californian scenery, this devil is unsurpassable." The passage that Clemens praised describes a canopy of pine branches that produced "a vast silence . . . , redolent with balsamic breath, and muffled with the dry dust of dead bark and matted mosses." Three other pages (130, 135, and 137) also contain Clemens's notes in "A Ghost of the Sierras." "Good" Clemens wrote vertically in black pencil on page 130 beside an account of the listeners' solicitous desire to lead the Doctor into telling one of his stories ("we all knew that an interruption would be fatal"), a passage resembling "Jim Blaine's Story

of Grandfather's Old Ram" in Mark Twain's *Roughing It* (1872). On page 135 in blue ink Clemens corrected "when" to "where". On 137 in the same story he used black pencil to change "for me to have drawn him out" into "for me to draw him out".

Provenance: Jean Webster McKinney Family Papers. Donated to Vassar College on 12 February 1977.

Location: Special Collections, Library, Vassar College, Poughkeepsie, New York.

Copy examined: photocopies of the pages containing Clemens's marginalia. I am grateful to Frances Goudy, then Special Collections Librarian at Vassar College, for providing these photocopies on 10 October 1980 and identifying Clemens's writing instruments on 27 October 1980. Robert H. Hirst also supplied notes (Hirst to Alan Gribben, 4 February 1981) reporting on Clemens's marginalia. On 15 August 1987 I was able to visit Vassar College and examine the volume myself.

Mark Twain's Library of Humor (1888) included one sketch from this volume, "A Sleeping-Car Experience," on pages 642–648.

———. *Gabriel Conroy* (novel, published in 1876).

Catalog: ListABP (1910), "Gabriel Conroy, Harte", no other information supplied.

Clemens discussed the details of Harte's royalties for this novel, which first appeared in *Scribner's Monthly* and then was issued by the American Publishing Company, in a letter of 5 July 1875 to Howells (*MTHL*, p. 92; *MTLet* 6: 503). "His long novel, 'Gabriel Conroy,'" Clemens declared in an Autobiographical Dictation of 14 June 1906, "is as much like Dickens as if Dickens had written it himself" (*MTE*, p. 267; *AutoMT* 2: 120). In a subsequent Autobiographical Dictation of 4 February 1907 Clemens disparaged Harte's efforts to write the novel as an American Publishing Company subscription book, which turned out to be such a "white elephant" that Elisha Bliss, Jr. ultimately sold it to a magazine (*MTE*, pp. 280–281; *AutoMT* 2: 421).

———. *An Heiress of Red Dog, and Other Tales*. London: Chatto & Windus, 1879. 300 pp.

Source: MTLAcc, entry #2264, volume donated from Clemens's library by Clara Clemens Gabrilowitsch in 1910. "Chatto sent me Harte's new book of Sketches, the other day," Clemens wrote to Howells on 15 April 1879. "1 have read it twice": the first time "through tears of rage over the fellow's inborn hypocrisy & snobbishness, his apprentice-art, his artificialities, his mannerisms, his pet phrases"; nonetheless, on the second reading Clemens became aware of "a most decided brightness on every page of it—& here & there evidences of genius" (*MTHL*, p. 261). Clemens resolved to write a review of Harte's work (*MTHL*, p. 262); he published such a critique as a portion of an anonymous essay in the "Contributors' Club," *Atlantic Monthly* 45.272 (June 1880): 850–851. There he faulted the "inaccuracy" of Harte's efforts to write dialect but praised how "he can *reproduce* Californian scenery so that you see it before you, and hear the sounds and smell the fragrances and feel the influences that go with it." In 1882 Clemens made a memorandum about a story he heard from Harte about a swindle that took place in a restaurant (Notebook 20, *N&J* 2: 509); eventually in an Autobiographical Dictation of 20 December 1906 he told its details (*AutoMT* 2: 324–326). Francis Murphy, "The End of a Friendship: Two Unpublished Letters from Twain to Howells about Bret Harte," *New England Quarterly* 58.1 (March 1985): 87–91 offered additional revelations about Twain's growing contempt for Harte by the year 1877.

———. *In the Carquinez Woods*. Boston: Houghton, Mifflin and Co., 1884. 241 pp.

Source: MTLAcc, entry #2262, volume donated from Clemens's library by Clara Clemens Gabrilowitsch in 1910.

———. "John Burns of Gettysbury" (poem, published in 1864).

Laid in Clemens's copy of G. E. Lewis' *Heart Echoes* (1899) was a newspaper clipping from the Springfield, Massachusetts *Republican* that reprinted Bret Harte's poem "John Burns of Gettysburg." In rhyming couplets Harte's poem told of the bravery in 1863 of the elderly Burns, "The only man who didn't back down/When the rebels rode through his native town." The farmer's stoic courage inspired the Union soldiers and helped turn the tide of the battle.

———. *The Lectures of Bret Harte, Compiled from Various Sources, To which is added "The Piracy of Bret Harte's Fables."* Ed. by Charles Meeker Kozlay (1871–1924). Illus. by Merle Johnson (1874–1935). New York: Charles Meeker Kozlay, 1909. 53 pp.

Inscription: "To Samuel L. Clemens with the compliments of Charles Meeker Kozlay/Oct. 21, 1909."

Location: Mark Twain Library, Redding, Connecticut.

Copy examined: Clemens's copy, unmarked and with several leaves unopened. Has the red ink Mark Twain Library accession number "4124". Examined in 1970 and again in June 1982.

Mark Twain's letter of 20 September 1872 to the editor of the London *Spectator* complaining about the publisher John Camden Hotten is reprinted on pages 48–51 (see Kevin Mac Donnell, "Some New Paths in Twain-Collecting," *Firsts: The Book Collector's Magazine* 8.9 [September 1998]: 42; see also *MTLet* 5: 163–164).

———. *The Luck of Roaring Camp, and Other Sketches*. Illus. Boston: Fields, Osgood & Co., 1870. 239 pp.

Inscription: signed "S. L. Clemens" in pencil on the front free endpaper, written diagonally.

Marginalia: heavily annotated in pencil by Clemens, presumably in the course of recommending pieces for *Mark Twain's Library of Humor* (1888). Clemens quibbled about Harte's terminology on page 2 of "The Luck of Roaring Camp": "They did not gamble at Euchre, & 'bowers' are foreign to poker." Where Harte referred to "the soft summer twilight in "The Luck of Roaring Camp" (p. 14), Clemens opined (writing vertically in pencil): "This must be a mistake—I think there is no twilight on 'the coast.'" However, at the end of "The Luck of Roaring Camp" (on page 18) Clemens pronounced a highly favorable judgment: "This is Bret's very best sketch, & most finished—is nearly blemishless." At the conclusion of the "The Outcasts of Poker Flat" Clemens remarked on page 36: "This ranks next to 'The Luck [of Roaring Camp]' unquestionably." In "Tennessee's Partner" (page 62) Clemens wrote, "This is much more suggestive of

Dickens & an English atmosphere than 'Pike County.'" On page 70 Clemens groused: "This sentimental old miner should have passed away earlier—many, many years earlier." On page 71 of "Tennessee's Partner" Clemens faulted the "gambling slang," pointing out (again) that "bowers . . . do not belong" in poker. "To have said 'a *pair* of *Jacks* & an ace' would have been good enough poker talk, but a wonderfully poor poker *hand* to make a bluster about." Still, he conceded, "In this sketch the 'dialect' is much better done than is usual with Harte" (p. 71). But he derided the author's "knowledge of human nature" for presuming that a man would "welcome back" and forgive someone who stole his wife. "It is new that the human Unpardonable Sin should turn the victim's *love* to rampant adoration" (p. 72). Clemens objected knowledgeably to a piece of dialogue on page 112 in "A Lonely Ride": "One of those brutal Californian stage-drivers could not be polite to a passenger,—& not one of the guild ever 'sir'd['] *anybody*." He noted this at the end of a stagecoach ride, where the driver says, "Must have been asleep sir. [Clemens underlined the "sir".] Hope you had a pleasant nap. Bully place for a nice quiet snooze,—empty stage, sir!" (Clemens again underscored that "sir".) Bradford A. Booth—"Mark Twain's Comments on Bret Harte's Stories," *American Literature* 25.4 (January 1954): 492–495—reported this marginalia. Booth inferred that they dated from "the early 1870's" (p. 492), but it is far more likely that most if not all of these comments were made in the 1880s, when Clemens was reading Harte's volumes in the process of editing *Mark Twain's Library of Humor*. Booth also made a minor error in quoting Clemens's comment at the conclusion of the final sketch, "Boonder," where Booth accidentally italicized the word "vein" instead of "suit"; Clemens actually wrote, "This is Bret's *best* vein—it is his 'strongest *suit*.'"

Catalogs: ListABP (1910), "Luck of Roaring Camp, Harte"; *C1951*, #33a, $200. Purchased by Wilbur Smith, Special Collections librarian at U.C.L.A. (Glen Dawson, "Mark Twain Library Auction," *American Book-Prices Current, 1950–51* [New York: R. R. Bowker, 1951], p. 106).

Location: Mark Twain Papers, Bancroft Library, University of California, Berkeley.

Copy examined: Clemens's copy. A somewhat worn, apparently well read volume.

On 4 December 1903 Clemens related "a curious experience" to William Dean Howells about finding "the bound Blackwood for 1871" and seeing "its surprise & admiration over the Luck of Roaring Camp. . . . There stood his birth!" (*MTHL*, p. 775). Mark Twain came to believe that the title story of this collection "blasted the Heathen Chinee out of the way and opened the road" to literary acclaim for Harte ("John Hay and the Ballads," *Harper's Weekly*, 21 October 1905). In actuality, as Gary Scharnhorst pointed out, Harte's "Plain Language from Truthful James" ("The Heathen Chinee") had appeared in the September 1870 issue of the *Overland Monthly* several years after "The Luck of Roaring Camp" was published in that journal in August 1868 (*MTPP*, p. 203 n. 3). Interviewed by A. E. Thomas for an article that appeared in the New York *Times* on 26 November 1905, Mark Twain used as an illustration of the difficulty of trying to write seriously after beginning comically, "Suppose a man makes a name as a humorist—he may make it at a stroke, as Bret Harte did, when he wrote those verses about the 'Heathen Chinee.' That may not be the expression of the real genius of the man at all. . . . They finally listened [i.e., more completely] to Bret Harte" (*Complete Interviews*, p. 518). In 1906 Clemens recalled that "The Luck of Roaring Camp" was "a loftier grade of literature" than Harte had previously attempted. Sadly, "that Bret Harte died in San Francisco. It was the corpse of Bret Harte that swept in splendor across the continent" (14 June 1906 AD, *MTE*, p. 266; *AutoMT* 2: 120). Clemens would again recall that "when 'The Luck of Roaring Camp' burst upon the world Harte became instantly famous; his name and his praises were upon every lip" (4 February 1907 AD, *AutoMT* 2: 416).

Margaret Duckett's *Mark Twain and Bret Harte* (Norman: University of Oklahoma Press, 1964) sought to correct the prevailing "imbalance" that Twain's well-known views on Bret Harte's character and writings fostered. This is an essential book for anyone interested in understanding the background for Mark Twain's diatribes against his one-time friend. Duckett assembled most of the material spoken or written by either man about the other. Her study was a needed corrective for those who had facilely accepted Twain's character (and literary) judgments of Harte. *Mark Twain and Bret Harte* included a chapter titled "The Question of Influence" (pp. 312–332) that defended Harte against Twain's charges of plagiarism, conceded some of Harte's tendencies toward imitation, traced a few examples of Twain's borrowing from Harte, and discussed Harte's admiration for Twain's work. Gary Scharnhorst's "The Bret Harte-Mark Twain Feud: An Inside Narrative," *Mark Twain Journal* 31.1 (Spring 1993): 29–32 provided another very illuminating appraisal of this famous falling-out between the prominent authors. Leland Krauth, *Mark Twain & Company: Six Literary Relations* (Athens: University of Georgia Press, 2003), detected surprising correspondences between the two writers, including the fact that both "took up arms in the ongoing battle between romance and realism"; however, Harte was "an open sentimentalist" and Twain "a covert one." Blair, *NAH* (1937, 1960), p. 159 n. 3; Benson, *MTWY* (1938), p. 157; Martha Lane Goold, "The Literary and Personal Relationships of Bret Harte and Mark Twain," Master's thesis, University of North Carolina, 1948; Branch, *LAMT* (1950), pp. 152, 298 n. 86; Booth, "Mark Twain's Comments" (1954), p. 493; Robert J. Lowenherz, "Mark Twain on Usage," *American Speech* 33.1 (February 1958): 70–72, quoted Twain's criticisms of Bret Harte's efforts at rendering dialect; Blair, *MT&HF* (1960), pp. 113–114; Krause, *MTC* (1967), pp. 202–220; Gary Scharnhorst, "Mark Twain, Bret Harte, and the Literary Construction of San Francisco," *San Francisco in Fiction: Essays in a Regional Literature*, ed. David Fine and Paul Skenazy (Albuquerque: University of New Mexico Press, 1995), pp. 21–34; Scharnhorst, *Bret Harte: Opening the American Literary West* (Norman: University of Oklahoma Press, 2000).

———. [Identical copy.]

Provenance: bookplate #365 of the "J. Langdon Family

Library" on the front pastedown endpaper.

Catalog: Ball 2016 inventory, reddish cloth, gilt lettering, signature of Mrs. J. Langdon, Jervis Langdon Family Library #365.

Location: Mark Twain Archive, Elmira College, Elmira, New York.

Copy examined: an unmarked copy available to Clemens whenever he visited the Langdon residence in Elmira. Reddish-brown cloth. Examined on 27 May 2015.

———. *Mrs. Skagg's Husbands, and Other Sketches.* Boston: J. R. Osgood & Co., 1873. 352 pp.

Source: MTLAcc, entry #2263, volume donated from Clemens's library by Clara Clemens Gabrilowitsch in 1910.

———, ed. *Outcroppings: Being Selections of California Verse.* San Francisco: A. Roman & Co., 1865.

Mark Twain mentioned this collection of western poets in a letter to the Virginia City *Territorial Enterprise* published on 19 December 1865: "I have to be a little severe, now, because I am a friend to 'Outcroppings'" (*MTCor*, p. 22). Twain gave some thought to editing a burlesque version of Harte's volume (SLC to Jane Lampton Clemens, 20 January 1866, *MTLet* 1: 328–329). *Outcroppings* contained verse by Ina Coolbrith, Charles H. Webb, Charles W. Stoddard, and sixteen others, but Harte aroused resentment among certain poets he excluded. In a letter published in the Virginia City *Territorial Enterprise* on 23 January 1866 Twain alluded to "that legion of California poets who were defrauded of fame in being left out of 'Outcroppings'" (Robert Hirst, "New [Old] Mark Twain Found in Bancroft Scraps," *Bancroftiana* No. 115 [Fall 1999]: 2). See also the Catalog entry for James Linen.

Ben Tarnoff, *The Bohemians: Mark Twain and the San Francisco Writers Who Reinvented American Literature* (New York: Penguin Press, 2014), pp. 117–121, 123, 142, 147–149.

———. *The Poetical Works of Bret Harte.* Complete Edition. Green cloth. Boston: Houghton, Mifflin and Co.; Cambridge: The Riverside Press, 1881. 294 pp.

Marginalia: the table of contents contains markings in black, blue, and red pencil indicating a process of selection for the anthology of American humor that Clemens was preparing with two co-editors in the 1880s. Though Clemens marked sixteen of Harte's poems for his co-editors to consider for the compendium, only two poems in the table of contents—"Plain Language from Truthful James" and "The Society Upon the Stanislaus"—had the (apparently decisive) initials "LA" placed to the left of their titles; all the other poems were marked on the right. These would prove to be the two poems chosen for inclusion in the eventual collection, *Mark Twain's Library of Humor* (1888). A number of poems were torn out of the volume and remain missing—pages 17–20 ("Her Letter"), 37–42 ("Dow's Flat"), 50–58 ("Penelope," "Plain Language from Truthful James," and "The Society upon the Stanislaus"), 79–84 ("The Ballad of the Emeu" and "The Aged Stranger"), 167–172 ("Before the Curtain," "The Stage-Driver's Story"), 199–202 ("A White-Pine Ballad" and "Little Red Riding-Hood"), and 205–210 ("A Moral Vindicator" and "Songs without Sense").

Provenance: Jean Webster McDinney Family Papers.

Donated to Vassar College on 12 February 1977.

Location: Special Collections, Library, Vassar College, Poughkeepsie, New York.

Copy examined: photocopies of the title page and the "Contents" pages, provided on 10 October 1980 by the then Special Collections Librarian, Frances Goudy. Robert H. Hirst also sent notes (Hirst to Alan Gribben, 4 February 1981) describing the missing pages. On 15 August 1987 I was able to visit Vassar College and examine the volume myself.

In the copy of Harte's *Drift from Two Shores* (see the Catalog entry above), Mark Twain urged his co-editors: "We must have the Heathen/Chinee & some other Dia/lect poems of Harte's" (Special Collections, Vassar College), but two poems and two sketches were all that represented Bret Harte in *Mark Twain's Library of Humor*. On 15 January 1871 Twain denied in a letter to the editor of *Every Saturday* that he had written an imitation of Harte's "Heathen Chinee"; in denying the charge Twain simultaneously mocked the obvious errors about card games in Harte's celebrated poem (*MTLet* 4: 304). Twain acknowledged that "Plain Language from Truthful James," generally known as "The Heathen Chinee," made Harte "the most celebrated man in America to-day" and turned Harte's "journey east to Boston" into "a perfect torch-light procession of eclat & homage" (SLC to John Henry Riley, 3 March 1871, *MTLet* 4: 338). Later Twain reflected that the same verse also "stopped his lofty march" to higher literary attainment ("John Hay and the Ballads," *Harper's Weekly*, 21 October 1905). When published, Harte's poem "created an explosion of delight whose reverberations reached the last confines of Christendom," Twain would recall (14 June 1906 AD, *MTE*, p. 266; *AutoMT* 2: 120). In a "Note" added to an Autobiographical Dictation of 16 April 1909 Twain pointed out that "the great public" failed to notice the absurd exaggeration in Harte's "ballad" about Ah Sin's method of cheating at cards because few people knew the game of euchre.

———. *Susy. A Novel.* London: Chatto & Windus, 1893. 304 pp.

Source: MTLAcc, entry #2265, volume donated from Clemens's library by Clara Clemens Gabrilowitsch in 1910.

———. *Tales of the Argonauts, and Other Sketches.* Boston: James R. Osgood and Co., 1876.

Marginalia: contains depreciatory remarks throughout in Clemens's handwriting. The pages following 272 are torn out; they contained "A Jersey Centenarian" (pp. 274–283).

Location: Mark Twain Papers, Bancroft Library, University of California at Berkeley. Donated in 1963 by Mrs. Samuel C. Webster.

Copy examined: Clemens's copy.

Mark Twain's Library of Humor (1888) contained a sketch from this collection, "A Jersey Centenarian."

———. "Tennessee's Partner" (short story).

Mark Twain once referred to "the finer glory of 'The Luck of Roaring Camp,' 'Tennessee's Partner,' and those other felicitous imitations of Dickens" (14 June 1906 AD, *MTE*, p. 266; *AutoMT* 2: 120).

———. *Thankful Blossom, A Romance of the Jerseys, 1779.* Illus. Original green cloth, gilt. Boston: James R. Osgood and Company, 1877. 158 pp.

Inscription: the flyleaf is signed in pencil by Ida C. Langdon (1849–1934), the wife of Charles Jervis Langdon and sister-in-law of Olivia Clemens.

Provenance: Jervis Langdon's bookplate is pasted on the front pastedown endpaper, lettered in blue and bordered in gilt: "J. Langdon's Family Library No. 521." These bookplates were used by Charles Jervis Langdon for many years after his father Jervis's death. Clemens would have had access to this book whenever he visited the Langdons in Elmira.

Location: collection of Kevin Mac Donnell, Austin, Texas (Mac Donnell to Alan Gribben, 29 November 2011, 28 August 2017). Purchased from the Langdon family.

On 5 December 1876 Clemens wrote to George Bentley (1828–1895), editor of the London magazine *Temple Bar*, regarding a "charming little love story" by Bret Harte, which Clemens thought to be "the best piece" of literary art "he has ever done" (University of Illinois, Urbana, TS in MTP). Harte's *Thankful Blossom* was being serialized in the New York *Sun* in December 1876. Perhaps because Harte wrote this tale at Clemens's house in Hartford, Clemens remained convinced "that it belongs at the very top of Harte's literature" (4 February 1907 AD, *MTE*, p. 277; *AutoMT* 2: 419). In July 1904, reported Alice Hegan Rice, "discovering my romantic attachment to Bret Harte, he [Clemens] delighted in recalling incidents that did not redound to that author's credit." But Clemens also told her with some pride the story of Harte's producing "Thankful Blossom" during an early-morning stint while intoxicated at Clemens's home (*The Inky Way*, pp. 78–80).

Duckett, *MT&BH* (1964), pp. 109, 124; Mary Boewe, "Young Mrs. Wiggs Meets the Old Connecticut Yankee," *Filson Club History Quarterly* 56.1 (January 1982): 8–11 (correcting Rice's recollected date of Clemens's anecdote).

———. *The Twins of Table Mountain.* London: Chatto and Windus, n.d. [Publisher's house list at the back is dated 1879.] 123 pp.

Inscription: the paper cover and the first flyleaf are missing.

Marginalia: contains Clemens's penciled marginalia throughout, primarily criticizing Harte's efforts at rendering dialect or derogating certain inconsistencies in the portrayals of his characters. On page 45 Clemens wrote: "That is English—we don't bespeak plays." (This comment refers to Harte's explanation: "The hermit twins of Table Mountain bespoke the chaste performance.") "He drops out of dialect," Clemens noted on page 55. Clemens made a derisive remark on page 88 about Mr. Rand: "One never knows what this nondescript will do next—except that it will be something foreign to human nature." On page 89 Clemens noted a discrepancy: "Girl!—he used to say gal." "Where does the 'dream' leave off & the reality begin?," Clemens wondered on page 121. Sydney J. Krause transcribed Clemens's annotations in *MTC* (1967), pp. 212–220.

Catalogs: ListABP (1910), "Twins of Table Mountain, Harte"; "Retz Appraisal" (1944), p. 8, valued at $35.

Location: Mark Twain Papers, Bancroft Library, University of California at Berkeley.

Copy examined: Clemens's copy.

———. *The Twins of Table Mountain, and Other Stories.* Boston:

Houghton, Mifflin and Co., 1881. 249 pp.

Marginalia: Clemens's caustic marginalia indicate his reasons for rejecting most of Harte's pieces for inclusion in *Mark Twain's Library of Humor* (1888). "I am at work upon Bret Harte," he notified Howells on 23 March 1882, "but am not enjoying it. . . . He is blind as a bat. He never sees anything correctly, except Californian scenery" (*MTHL*, p. 396). Besides the title piece, the volume includes "An Heiress of Red Dog," "The Great Deadwood Mystery," "A Legend of Sammtstadt," and "Views from a German Spion."

Location: Mark Twain Papers, Bancroft Library, University of California at Berkeley. Donated in 1963 by Mrs. Samuel C. Webster.

Copy examined: Clemens's copy.

Mark Twain's *Roughing It* (1872, Ch. 59) alluded to Bret Harte's taking over the editorship of *The Californian* after Charles H. Webb gave up on the literary weekly. On 18 September 1872 the New York *Daily Tribune* noted that the *Hartford City Directory* had listed Bret Harte as a boarder in the Samuel L. Clemens residence. A friendly note from Clemens to Bret Harte written on 13 July 1875 requested a few lines from Harte for an autograph collector (*MTLet* 6: 507–508). That close relationship of goodwill and literary collaboration would not last. The complex reasons for Clemens's increasing hostility toward Harte and his writings involved professional rivalry and personal animosity, among other impulses. He could still could refer to him as "my friend Mr. Harte" in a letter to Chatto & Windus written on 14 September 1876 (when Harte had done him a favor) (Horst E. Meyer, "An Unnoticed Twain Letter," *Mark Twain Journal* 16.3 [Winter 1972]: 25). However, as the years passed Clemens grew more and more furious about what he perceived as Harte's personal traits and moral failings as well as his limitations as a writer. Clemens wrote to Joseph H. Twichell on 29 August 1880 partly to praise a short story by Philander Deming: "I have read 'John's Trial,' & like it very much indeed. It has the advantage of Bret Harte's rot, that it is sincere" (*LMTJHT*, p. 101). Interviewed in Australia in 1895, Mark Twain let loose with extremely candid condemnations such as this one: "It is merely a personal opinion. I detest him, because I think his work is 'shoddy.' His forte is pathos which does not come out of a man's heart. He has no heart, except his name, and I consider he has produced nothing that is genuine. He is artificial" ("Mark Twain in Sydney: A Further Interview," Melbourne *Argus*, 17 September 1895; Scharnhorst, *Complete Interviews*, p. 202). Years later Harte responded: "I always considered that we were friends until that trip of his to Australia, and there it appears he attacked me in a most savage and unprovoked manner—denounced me as a feeble sentimentalist" (Jennifer M. Nader, "Mark Twain in Australia: Two New Interviews," *American Literary Realism* 45.2 [Winter 2013]: 172 n. 3). In a copy of George Trevelyan's *The Life and Letters of Lord Macaulay* (1904) that Clemens inscribed to Isabel V. Lyon in September 1905, Clemens bracketed Macaulay's opinion of Leigh Hunt ("he had no high feeling of independence . . . he had no sense of obligation . . . he took money wherever he could get it . . . he felt no gratitude for it . . . he was

just as ready to defame a person who had relieved his distress as a person who had refused him relief") and wrote, "An absolutely perfect photograph of Bret Harte" (II: 403). Finley Peter Dunne recalled that in Clemens's latter years "another one of his hatreds was Bret Harte. Once Henry James . . . asked him, 'Do you know Bret Harte?' 'Yes,' Mark replied readily, 'I know the son of a bitch'" (*Mr. Dooley Remembers: The Informal Memoirs of Finley Peter Dunne*, ed. Philip Dunne [Boston: Little, Brown, 1963], p. 244). A bitter autobiographical dictation that Twain made on 14 June 1906 characterized Harte as "incapable of emotion" and denounced his "pathetics, imitated from Dickens" (*AutoMT* 2: 119). In another lengthy autobiographical dictation commencing on 4 February 1907 Twain itemized Harte's many failings, characterizing him as "the most contemptible, poor little soulless blatherskite that exists on the planet to-day" (*MTAuto* 2: 415–430). Among an undated set of notes referring to moments of embarrassment, Clemens wrote, cryptically, "Harte White Stockings" (*A1911*, lot 197). Gary Scharnhorst's "The Bret Harte-Mark Twain Feud: An Inside Narrative," *Mark Twain Journal* 31.1 (Spring 1993): 29–32, supplied an illuminating appraisal of this famous falling-out between two prominent literary figures.

————. *Two Men of Sandy Bar* (play, produced in 1876). "The play entertained me hugely, even in its present crude state," Clemens wrote to William Dean Howells on 14 September 1876 (*MTHL*, p. 152).

Hartford, Connecticut *Courant* (newspaper).

In 1869 Clemens thought of becoming a partner in the ownership of this newspaper, but Joseph R. Hawley (1826–1905) declined his offer. The Mark Twain Papers contain a receipt for Clemens's subscription to the *Courant* from 10 October 1872 until 10 May 1873; a note on the receipt also credits payment through 20 January 1874. On 14 September 1876 Clemens referred to Charles Dudley Warner's "good & appreciative review" of Howells's campaign biography of Hayes in the *Courant* (*MTHL*, p. 150). Clemens enclosed a clipping from the *Courant*—a review of Howells's *Yorick's Love*—in his letter of 11 March 1880 to Howells (*MTHL*, p. 292). Clemens received a bill for "Daily Courant from 1 April 1880 to 1 October 1880 $4.00" which he paid on 4 October 1880 (MTP); on 1 January 1881 he paid another bill for the period from 1 October 1880 to 1 January 1881 (MTP); he was billed for a "1 quarter" subscription on 12 June 1885 (MTP). Clemens criticized a *Courant* editorial against Robert G. Ingersoll in 1887 (NB 27, *N&J* 3: 305). A *Courant* editor, Charles Hopkins Clark (1848–1926), assisted in compiling *Mark Twain's Library of Humor* (1888). On 29 September 1892 Clemens complained to Frank G. Whitmore from Florence: "We have not received a Weekly Courant for several weeks. Please see what the matter is" (MTP). When Clemens wrote to William Walter Phelps' daughter Marian (1868–1922) from Florence on 14 February 1893 he referred to a political opinion expressed in the Hartford *Courant* (Henry E. Huntington Library). In February or March 1894 Clemens noted: "Stanley's Interpreter's Account of the Meeting between Stanley and Livingstone—get it out of the Courant" (NB 33, TS p. 56). Pressed by his creditors, Clemens directed

Whitmore on 24 March 1895 to "pay this Courant bill & *stop the paper* for the present" (MTHM).

Jeffrey Steinbrink, *Getting to Be Mark Twain* (Berkeley: University of California Press, 1991), pp. 31–35, 67–70; Henry S. Cohn, "Mark Twain and Joseph Roswell Hawley," *Mark Twain Journal* 53.2 (Fall 2015): 67–84.

HARTLEY, CECIL B. *The Gentlemen's Book of Etiquette and Manual of Politeness; Being a Complete Guide for a Gentleman's Conduct in All His Relations Towards Society. Containing Rules for the Etiquette to be Observed in the Street, at Table, in the Ball Room, Evening Party, and Morning Call; with Full Directions for Polite Correspondence, Dress, Conversation, Manly Exercises, and Accomplishments. From the Best French, English, and American Authorities.* Boston: J. S. Locke & Co., 1873. 332 pp.

> **Source:** MTLAcc, entry #2143, volume donated from Clemens's library by Clara Clemens Gabrilowitsch in 1910.
> Could this book be one of the keys to how rapidly the Wild Humorist of the Pacific Slope managed to acclimate to Eastern society? Hartley's *Gentlemen's Book of Etiquette* offered advice to "the young aspirant for favor in polite and refined circles" (p. 4). Among other prohibitions, it condemned "profane swearing" as hindering one's social and vocational advancement. Hartley was a prolific biographer as well as etiquette expert. His guides regarding male decorum were sometimes paired with Florence Bentley's health and etiquette publications for women, but their relationship is unknown.

HARVEY, GEORGE BRINTON McCLELLAN (1864–1928). *Women, Etc. Some Leaves from an Editor's Diary.* Black cloth. New York: Harper & Brothers, 1908. 232 pp.

> **Inscription:** signed in black ink on the front pastedown endpaper: "SL. Clemens/Stormfield, Jan. 1, 1909."
> **Catalog:** ListABP (1910), "Women, Harvey", no other information provided.
> **Provenance:** Antenne-Dorrance Collection, Rice Lake, Wisconsin.
> **Location:** Mark Twain Archive, Gannett Tripp Learning Center, Elmira College, Elmira, New York.
> **Copy examined:** Clemens's copy, unmarked. Examined on 28 May 2015.
> Harvey was president of the Harper & Brothers publishing company between 1900 and 1916. It was he who had made the arrangements for Clemens's lavish and well-attended Seventieth Birthday Dinner at Delmonico's in New York City on 5 December 1905. *Women, Etc.* collected Harvey's essays, some of them discussing friendship, light reading, and other general topics, others advocating women's suffrage and objecting to taxation rates for unmarried women.

HASKELL, CHARLES COURTNEY (1840–1914). *Perfect Health: How to Get It and How to Keep It, by One Who Has it. True Scientific Living.* Norwich, Connecticut: Published by the author, [cop. 1901]. 209 pp.

> **Source:** MTLAcc, entry #899, volume donated by Albert Bigelow Paine, Clemens's designated biographer. Possibly Clemens saw this book, since the men exchanged reading materials. Haskell, a health reformer in Norwich, Connecticut, promoted the "fasting cure" and was influenced by New Thought ideas in vogue at the turn of the century.

HASKINS, CHARLES WALDO (1852–1903). *How to Keep Household Accounts: A Manual of Family Finance.* New York:

Harper & Brothers, 1903. 116 pp.

> **Source:** MTLAcc, entry #679, volume donated by Clemens.

HASTINGS, THOMAS (1784–1872). "Child of sin and sorrow, filled with dismay" (hymn, published in 1832).

> "Just you hear him [Robert Wicklow] sing: 'Child of sin and sorrow, filled with dismay,/Wait not till to-morrow, yield thee to-day;/Grieve not that love/Which, from above'— and so on" (Mark Twain's "A Curious Experience" [1881]).

HASWELL, CHARLES HAYNES (1809–1907). *Mechanics' and Engineers' Pocket-Book of Tables, Rules, and Formulas Pertaining to Mechanics, Mathematics, and Physics.* New York: Harper & Brothers, 1908. Last leaves missing; 1048 pages intact.

> **Source:** MTLAcc, entry #1819, volume donated by Clemens.

HASWELL, JAMES M. *The Man of His Time. Part I, The Story of the Life of Napoleon III. Part II, The Same Story as Told by Popular Caricaturists of the Last Thirty Years.* Illus. Original red pictorial cloth, gilt, uncut. London: John Camden Hotten, [1871]. 319 pp. [John Camden Hotten (1832–1873) selected and edited the caricatures.]

> **Inscription:** signed in brown ink on the recto of the frontispiece: "S. L. Clemens/Hartford, 1875."
> **Marginalia:** one stray pencil mark in the margin of page 161, and a sheet of rice paper inserted between pages 98–99 (this place marker was present long enough to cause a slight foxing of the pages).
> **Catalogs:** *C1951*, D46; *Zeitlin 1951*, #20, $35.
> **Provenance:** Clara Clemens Gabrilowitsch's shelving numbers from her Detroit period appear on the verso the front free endpaper. There is a bookseller ticket of Hartman's Books of Seattle (c. 1960s) on the recto of the rear free endpaper.
> **Location:** collection of Kevin Mac Donnell, Austin, Texas.
> **Source:** Mac Donnell to Alan Gribben, 14 December 2005.
> Mark Twain discussed Napoleon III (1808–1873) several times in *The Innocents Abroad* (1869), and perhaps had him in mind in Chapter 14 of *Adventures of Huckleberry Finn* (1885) where Huck tells Jim that some members of royalty "gets on the police" to make a living. Pages 163–164 of Haswell's biography recount Napoleon III's period as a policeman in London between 1846 and 1848 following his "orgies" of gambling.

HATCH, P. HENRY (1832–1905). "Oh, charming May!" (song, published in 1844). George Herbert Rodwell (1800–1852), composer.

> Clemens listed this ode to the arrival of spring ("There is peaceful delight, to me ever dear,/In the charming May, the Queen-month of the year") among the songs he heard at the Governor's house in a sketch published in Virginia City on 3 February 1863, "Letter from Carson City" (*ET&S* 1: 197).
> Robert E. Stewart, "Guests and Songs in Twain's 'Letter from Carson City,'" *Mark Twain Journal* 53.2 (Fall 2015): 91.

HATTON, JOHN LIPTROT (1809–1886), ed. *The Songs of England, A Collection of English Melodies, including the Most Popular Traditional Ditties, and the Principal Songs and Ballads of the Last Three Centuries.* London: Boosey & Co., n.d. 240 pp. [Publisher and pages supplied. An edition with this exact title was issued in the mid-1870s.]

> **Marginalia:** contains many notes by Clemens. One reads

"Key of Go down Moses."

Catalog: *A1911*, "royal 8vo, limp leather (one page torn), Lond., n.d., with many autograph notes by Mr. Clemens," lot 354, sold for $2.50.

Clemens purchased a volume on 10 May 1877 titled "Songs of Old England" [*sic*], according to a bill from James R. Osgood & Company of Boston (Scrapbook #10, p. 69, MTP). Mark Twain would refer to several songs in this collection, including "Sally in our alley" and the hymn "Rocked in the cradle of the deep." See also the Catalog entry for Robert Folkestone Williams.

HATTON, JOSEPH (1841–1907). *The Old House at Sandwich. A Novel*. New York: F. M. Lupton Publishing Co., [189–]. 258 pp.

Source: MTLAcc, entry #157, volume donated by Clemens.

HAUFF, WILHELM (1802–1827). "How the Caliph Became a Stork" (fairy tale).

Mark Twain made a partial translation of one of the German poet and novelist's oriental series of stories. See *Tale of the Caliph Stork*, illustrated by Eleanor Simmons (1925–1999). Limited edition of 100 copies. Iowa City: Windhover Press, 1976. 29 pp. (Jo Dee Benussi noticed this item.)

HAUPTMANN, GERHART (1862–1946). *Einsame Menschen [Lonely People]. Drama*. Berlin: G. Fischer, 1903. 136 pp.

Inscription: the half-title page is signed in black ink "Jean L. Clemens/21 Fifth Ave./New York City./April 1905."

Location: Harry Ransom Center, University of Texas at Austin. Purchased from Margarete Willson, who in 1962 sold the Mark Twain portion of a book collection assembled by her husband Frank C. Willson (1889–1960).

Copy examined: Jean Clemens's copy.

HAVEN, GILBERT (1821–1880). *The Pilgrim's Wallet; or, Scraps of Travel Gathered in England, France, and Germany*. New York: Canton and Porter, 1866. 492 pp.

Inscription: the front free endpaper has been torn out.

Location: Mark Twain Library, Redding, Connecticut. Donated by Clemens (MTLAcc, entry #553).

Copy examined: Clemens's copy, unmarked. Has the red ink Mark Twain Library accession number "553".

One wishes for confirmation that Clemens owned and signed this book prior to his *Quaker City* voyage in 1867; it seems quite probable that he did. *The Innocents Abroad* (1869) would have *Pilgrims* in its subtitle.

HAWEIS, HUGH REGINALD (1838–1901). *American Humorists: Lectures Delivered at the Royal Institution*. Third edition. London: Chatto & Windus, 1890. 208 pp.

Inscription: laid in is a calling card with a note: "My Dear Sir, You may know me, by this book. Would much like to see you soon. H R H".

Provenance: shelfmarks of Clara Clemens Gabrilowitsch's library numbering system that she employed during her Detroit years. Sold at the 1951 auction in Hollywood but not listed in the hastily compiled sale sheet.

Catalogs: ListABP (1910), "American Humorists, Haweis"; "Property from the Library of Mark Twain," Butterfield & Butterfield, San Francisco, Sale 6613 (16 July 1997), lot 2712.

Location: Mark Twain House and Museum, Hartford, Connecticut.

Copy examined: Clemens's unmarked copy. Viewed in Hartford in 1997.

Mark Twain was among the half dozen American humorists who received separate essays in Haweis's study. Washington Irving, Artemus Ward, Bret Harte, Oliver Wendell Holmes, and James Russell Lowell were the others.

———. *Mark Twain and Bret Harte*. Maroon morocco over green cloth, raised bands, top edge gilt. New York: John B. Alden, 1900. 192 pp.

Inscriptions: the title page is signed in black ink, "S. L. Clemens/(Mark Twain)". Above that, the signature "Bret Harte" in ink. [The Clemens signature form was highly uncharacteristic of Clemens's habit for inscribing his library books.] The upper corner of the title page is missing, with a note in pencil below the tear: "no fault of mine".

Catalog: Phillip J. Pirages Fine Books and Medieval Manuscripts, McMinnville, Oregon Catalog 63.120 (2014), an item explicitly labeled by the bookseller as another forgery perpetrated by Eugene Field II; priced at $475.

HAWES, CHARLES HENRY (1867–1943) and HARRIET BOYD HAWES (1871–1945). *Crete, The Forerunner of Greece*. Preface by Arthur J[ohn]. Evans (1851–1941). Illus. London and New York: Harper & Brothers, 1909. 157 pp. [Edition conjectured.]

Catalog: *C1951*, Dl6, listed among books signed by Clemens.

HAWKINS, (SIR) ANTHONY HOPE (1863–1933), pseud. "Anthony Hope." *The Intrusions of Peggy*. Illus. New York: Harper & Brothers, 1902. 387 pp.

Source: MTLAcc, entry #1565, volume donated by Clemens.

———. *Sophy of Kravonia; A Novel*. New York: Harper & Brothers, 1906. 332 pp.

Source: MTLAcc, entry #1097, volume donated by Clemens.

HAWTHORNE, JULIAN (1846–1934). *Hawthorne and His Circle*. Illus. New York: Harper & Brothers, 1903. 372 pp.

Source: MTLAcc, entry #1381, volume donated by Clemens.

Julian Hawthorne was the son of the famous novelist Nathaniel Hawthorne (1804–1864). Gary Scharnhorst explored the friendship of nearly forty years that developed between Clemens and Julian beginning around 1872 ("Mark Twain and Julian Hawthorne," *Mark Twain Annual 10* [2012]: 47–54). On 1 September 1908 Joseph H. Twichell sent Clemens a clipping about the speculative mining scandal in which Julian Hawthorne had become ensnared (and for which he would serve a prison sentence for mail fraud); Twichell called it "a melancholy come down" for "a man of his royal descent" (*LMTJHT*, p. 404).

———. *Nathaniel Hawthorne and His Wife, A Biography*. 2 vols. Second edition. Boston: James R. Osgood and Co, 1884.

Inscriptions: Volume I is inscribed, "Merry Xmas to Grandmamma/Hartford 1884 from her loving granddaughter." Volume II is inscribed, "Merry Xmas to Grandmamma/Hartford 1884." This was a gift to Olivia Lewis Langdon (1810–1890) from one of the Clemens daughters.

Catalogs: cataloged in the Quarry Farm library in the 1980s; Ball 2016 inventory, brown boards, good condition.

Location: Quarry Farm Library shelves, under the supervision of the Mark Twain Archive, Elmira College, Elmira,

New York.

Olivia Clemens was clearly familiar with the contents of this biography, because in 1885 Susy Clemens recorded in a sketch of her father that her mother knew of the love letters Hawthorne wrote to Sophia Peabody: "Mamma says she thinks they [the letters Clemens had sent to Olivia Langdon] are the loveliest love-letters that ever were written, she says she thinks that Hawthorne's love-letters to Mrs. Hawthorne are far inferior to these" (*Family Sketch*, p. 110).

———. *Nathaniel Hawthorne and His Wife, A Biography.* 2 vols. Second edition. Boston: James R. Osgood and Co, 1884.

    Inscriptions: Volume I is signed "Susan L. Crane/Elmira, N.Y./Jan. 1885"; Volume II is signed "Susan L. Crane/ Quarry Farm 1887."

    Catalog: Ball 2016 inventory, brown boards, notes on the rear pastedown endpaper list pages reflecting various themes.

    Location: Quarry Farm Library shelves, under the supervision of the Mark Twain Archive, Elmira College, Elmira, New York.

These volumes were available to Clemens whenever he visited Quarry Farm in Elmira, New York.

———. *Noble Blood.* New York: D. Appleton & Co., 1885. 214 pp.

    Source: MTLAcc, entry #2268, volume donated from Clemens's library by Clara Clemens Gabrilowitsch in 1910.

HAWTHORNE, NATHANIEL (1804–1864). "The Christmas Banquet" and "Egotism; or, The Bosom Serpent" (short stories). Clara Clemens discussed both tales in her commonplace book (c. 1888?) (Paine 150, MTP).

———. *The Complete Works of Nathaniel Hawthorne.* 12 vols. Notes by George Parsons Lothrop (1851–1898). Illus. Boston: Houghton, Mifflin Co., 1883–1884.

    Inscription: one volume, *The Marble Faun; or, The Romance of Monte Beni*, is inscribed "Susan L. Crane/Quarry Farm/ Elmira, N. Y./1885".

    Marginalia: pages are marked in *The Marble Faun*, and the marked page numbers occur in notes on the rear pastedown endpaper.

    Catalog: Ball 2016 inventory, green cloth, black spine, gilt lettering, only eleven volumes are listed, good condition.

    Location: Quarry Farm Library shelves, under the supervision of the Mark Twain Archive, Elmira College, Elmira, New York.

This set was accessible to Clemens whenever he visited Elmira, New York.

———. *Doctor Grimshawe's Secret; A Romance.* Ed. with preface and notes by Julian Hawthorne (1846–1934). Boston: J. R. Osgood and Co., 1883. 368 pp.

    Source: MTLAcc, entry #2267, volume donated from Clemens's library by Clara Clemens Gabrilowitsch in 1910.

———. *The House of the Seven Gables, A Romance.* Original cloth, minor wear on edges and corners. Boston: James R. Osgood and Co., 1872.

    Marginalia: a note on the rear free flyleaf might possibly be in Clemens's hand, "61 West 17th/care Mrs. Rufus McHare[?]"

    Provenance: has the shelfmarks of the library numbering system employed by Clara Clemens Gabrilowitsch during her Detroit years. Sold at the 1951 auction in Hollywood

even though it was unlisted in the sale sheet, a frequent occurrence at that bizarre event.

    Catalog: "Property from the Library of Mark Twain," Butterfield & Butterfield, San Francisco, Sale 6613 (16 July 1997), lot 2675.

    Location: Mark Twain House and Museum, Hartford, Connecticut.

    Copy examined: Clemens's copy. Viewed in Hartford in 1997.

In "Eddypus" (written 1901–1902) Mark Twain facetiously predicted that in the future the theatrical producer Charles Frohman would be given credit for writing "a book, presumably upon architecture, called 'The House of the Seven Gables'" (*FM*, p. 335).

———. *The Marble Faun, or The Romance of the Monte Beni.* Illus. 2 vols. Original decorated red cloth with white cloth backstrip. Boston: Houghton, Mifflin and Co., 1890.

    Catalogs: *A 1911*, "2 vols., 12mo, cloth, Bost. 1890," small sheet of autograph notes laid in, lot 226, sold for $2.25; Alta California Catalogue No. 4, two volumes, item #85, $85 (PH in MTP).

    Location: Albert and Shirley Small Special Collections Library, University of Virginia Libraries, Charlottesville. Gift of Clifton Waller Barrett.

    Copy examined: Clemens's unmarked copy, in 1970. Contains an *A1911* auction label on the front pastedown endpaper.

Olivia Langdon copied passages from this novel into her commonplace book in March and October 1867 (DV161, MTP). Mark Twain joked in 1870 that the average reader, less perceptive than Hawthorne's publisher, might simply have "said the 'Marble Faun' was tiresome" ("A General Reply," *The* Galaxy 10.5 [November 1870]: 733; *CG*, p. 97; *CTSS&E* 1, p.487).

———. "The Miraculous Pitcher" (story, published in *A Wonder-Book for Girls and Boys*, 1852).

Carroll D. Laverty, "The Genesis of *The Mysterious Stranger*," *Mark Twain Quarterly* 8.3–4 (Spring-Summer 1947): 17, likened the story of how a magic cat supplies Father Peter's niece with food and drink in *The Mysterious Stranger* to several incidents in Hawthorne's tale.

———. *Mosses from an Old Manse.* New edition, revised. 2 vols. Black cloth, half bound in calf. Spine chipped. Boston: Tichnor and Fields, 1865. [Two volumes bound together as one.]

    Inscriptions: the title pages of both volumes are either signed by Olivia Clemens (or inscribed by a church librarian), in black ink, "Mrs. Clemens." The front pastedown endpaper has a bookplate: "General Library/of the/Park Church/ in/Elmira, N. Y./No. 1457". Both title pages display a bookstamp: "The Park Church/Elmira, N. Y./1877".

    Marginalia: Clemens made pencil marks throughout the first part of "The Old Manse" (pp. 5–21), and also left pencil markings in "Buds and Bird Voices" (pp. 173, 175, 177) and "Feathertop" (p. 285).

    Location: Park Church Library, Elmira, New York. Discovered in the fall of 1987 by Gretchen Sharlow, then the chair of the Historical Committee for Park Church.

    Copy examined: a book marked by Clemens and donated to the library of Park Church by Olivia Clemens. Examined on 12 August 1988.

———. *Mosses from an Old Manse.* 2 vols. New edition, rev.

Boston: Fields, Osgood & Co., 1871. 297 pp.

Source: MTLAcc, entry #2266, Volume 2 only, donated from Clemens's library by Clara Clemens Gabrilowitsch in 1910.

———. *The Scarlet Letter, A Romance.* Brown cloth, gilt spine lettering. Boston: James R. Osgood, 1872. 307 pp.

Inscription: signed twice by Clemens. He wrote "Clemens" in pencil on the flyleaf and signed the title page in black ink: "SL. Clemens".

Marginalia: a pencil mark on page 65. On pages 190–191 Clemens singled out a sentence with penciled brackets: "It is remarkable, that persons who speculate the most boldly often conform with the most perfect quietude to the external regulations of society." An undated newspaper clipping of jokes from *Puck* and the Buffalo *Express* is laid in.

Provenance: Antenne-Dorrance Collection, Rice Lake, Wisconsin, which originated with Katy Leary's selection in 1910 of some volumes from her former employer's library for sentimental keepsakes.

Location: Mark Twain Archive, Gannett Tripp Learning Center, Elmira College, Elmira, New York.

Copy examined: Clemens's copy. Examined on 27 May 2015.

The narrator of "The Loves of Alonzo Fitz Clarence and Rosannah Ethelton" (1878) notes the presence of books by Hawthorne in Aunt Susan's "private parlor of a refined and sensible lady." When Mark Twain compared American and English accomplishments in 1879, he argued that "nobody writes a finer & purer English than Motley[,] Howells, Hawthorne & Holmes" (NB 18, *N&J* 2: 348). But later he complimented William Dean Howells by writing: "You make all the motives & feelings perfectly clear without analyzing the guts out of them, the way George Eliot does. I can't stand George Eliot, & Hawthorne & those people; I see what they are at, a hundred years before they get to it, & they just tire me to death" (SLC to WDH, 21 July 1885, *MTHL*, p. 534). In an 1895 newspaper interview Mark Twain again praised Hawthorne's prose style: "We in the United States, of course, look up to Nathaniel Hawthorne as possessing that something which marks genius and makes a man live forever. It is always remarkable to me that he should have written such incisive English at a time when that was not the prevailing style of authors" ("Mark Twain in Sydney," Sydney, Australia *Argus*, 17 September 1895, clipping in Scrapbook #26, MTP; Scharnhorst, *Complete Interviews*, p. 203). Clemens owned a copy of Felix O. C. Darley's illustrations based on *The Scarlet Letter*; see the Darley entry.

Ann M. Ryan, "Standing in Some True Relation: Mark Twain Visits 'The Custom House,'" *Mark Twain Annual* 15 (2017): 145–161.

———. *The Scarlet Letter, A Romance.* Philadelphia: Henry Altemus, 1893. 348 pp.

Source: MTLAcc, entry #156, volume donated by Clemens.

———. *Selections from the Writings of Nathaniel Hawthorne, Arranged Under the Days of the Year.* Boston: Houghton, Mifflin & Co., 1889. [109 pp.]

Source: MTLAcc, entry #2120a, volume donated from Clemens's library by Clara Clemens Gabrilowitsch in 1910.

———. *The Snow-Image, and Other Twice-Told Tales.* Original cloth, minor wear on the edges. Boston: James R. Osgood and Co., 1872.

Provenance: shelfmarks of the library numbering system that Clara Clemens Gabrilowitsch employed during her Detroit years. Sold at the 1951 auction in Hollywood even though it was not listed in the sale list, an occurrence unfortunately common at that event.

Catalog: "Property from the Library of Mark Twain," Butterfield & Butterfield, San Francisco, Sale 6613 (16 July 1997), lot 2675.

Location: Mark Twain House and Museum, Hartford, Connecticut.

Copy examined: Clemens's copy. Viewed in Hartford in 1997.

———. *Works.* [Unspecified edition.]

Catalog: ListABP (1910), "Hawthorne's Works (marginal notes)," no other information supplied.

Whatever did Albert Bigelow Paine do with this set after he finished his biography of Mark Twain?

HAY, JOHN (1838–1905). *The Bread-Winners: A Social Study.* New York: Harper & Brothers, 1905. 319 pp.

Source: MTLAcc, entry #340, volume donated by Clemens.

Hay's novel was serialized anonymously in 1884. Clemens wrote to Edward H. House from Hartford on 14 January 1884 and mentioned that he was reading "the middle portion" (ASSSCL). "*I* believe John Hay wrote it, but I don't know," Clemens told Mary Fairbanks on 30 January 1884 (*MTMF*, p. 256). Clemens mentioned the book and its anonymous authorship again in a letter of 23 May 1884 to Edward H. House (ASSSCL).

Smith, *Mark Twain's Fable of Progress* (1964), p. 38; Kenton J. Clymer, "John Hay and Mark Twain," *Missouri Historical Review* 67 (April 1973): 397–406, outlined the lengthy Clemens-Hay friendship and summarized their opinions of each other; John Taliaferro, *All the Great Prizes: The Life of John Hay, from Lincoln to Roosevelt* (New York: Simon & Schuster, 2013); Mark Zwonitzer, *The Statesman and the Storyteller: John Hay, Mark Twain, and the Rise of American Imperialism* (Chapel Hill, North Carolina: Algonquin Books of Chapel Hill, 2016).

———. *Castilian Days.* Boston: Houghton, Mifflin and Co., 1899.

Inscription: signed "S. L. Clemens, 1905."

Catalog: *A 1911*, "12mo, cloth, Bost. [1899], . . . passages marked with little crosses on p. 88," quotes the signature, lot 227, sold for $6.75.

Isabel Lyon noted on 21 October 1905, while packing to leave Dublin, New Hampshire, that Clemens "is sitting in the living room now reading John Hay's 'Castilian Days'" (IVL Journal, TS p. 109, MTP). In his "Acknowledgments" preceding "A Horse's Tale" (1906) Mark Twain explains that he has never seen a bull-fight, "but I needed a bull-fight in this story, and a trustworthy one will be found in it. I got it out of John Hay's *Castilian Days*. . . . Mr.. Hay and I were friends from early times, and if he were still with us he would not rebuke me for the liberty I have taken." Mary Boewe traced the extent of Twain's borrowings from Hay's book in "Smouching Towards Bedlam; or, Mark Twain's Creative Use of Some Acknowledged Sources," *Mark Twain Journal* 29.1 (Spring 1991): 8–12.

———. *Pike County Ballads and Other Pieces*. Boston: Houghton, Mifflin & Co., 1871.

Clemens and Hay had met by at least December 1870, perhaps even earlier. In any event, on 14 January 1871 John Hay thanked Clemens for "your generous commendation of my verses" (*MTLet* 4: 300). One of those poems by Hay became extremely popular—"Jim Bludso, of the Prairie Belle," a ballad first published in the New York *Tribune* on 5 January 1871 that recounted in Pike County dialect the courage of a Mississippi River steamboat engineer who heroically held his burning vessel against the river bank until all of passengers had gotten ashore, giving his own life to guarantee their safety. (Clemens had promptly written to remind Hay that a pilot rather than an engineer would have been the more logical figure to perform this deed, but Hay left the poem unrevised [*MTLet* 4: 299].) Clemens praised Hay's "verse" on 25 September 1874 in a letter to William A. Seaver (*MTLet* 6: 246). On 16 December 1874 Hay wrote an extremely complimentary letter to Twain about his first installment of "Old Times on the Mississippi" that had begun running in the *Atlantic Monthly*; "you have the two greatest gifts of the writer, memory and imagination," Hay commented (*MTLet* 6: 325–327). John Hay was one of the trusted dispensers of Twain's ribald *1601* (1880), a spoof of court life in Elizabethan England (*LMTJHT*, p. 98). Hay was among the authors Clemens tried to inveigle into accompanying him on a return trip to the scene of his Mississippi River pilot days (Caroline Ticknor, *Glimpses of Authors* [Boston: Houghton Mifflin Co., 1922], p. 135). Joseph B. Gilder's "Glimpses of John Hay," *Critic* 47.3 (September 1905): 248–252, recalled a congenial evening Gilder spent with Hay, Clemens, Henry Adams, and Richard Watson Gilder at Adams' home in Washington, D.C. on 28 January 1886.

In 1905 Mark Twain published a letter defending Hay against insinuations that his ballads imitated Bret Harte's ("John Hay and the Ballads," *Harper's Weekly* 49 [21 October 1905]: 1530). Twain recalled *Pike County Ballads*, "Jim Bludso, of the Prairie Belle," and Hay's error in making "the engineer of the burning boat the hero" in a "Note" added to an Autobiographical Dictation of 16 April 1909 (*AutoMT* 3: 307). A book that Twain annotated in 1909 (G. G. Greenwood's *The Shakespeare Problem Restated*, 1908) contains a marginal note on page 371 by Twain about Hay's once-popular ballad, "Jim Bludso, of the Prairie Belle"; that jotting ("'The Prairie Belle.' Begin Here.") seems to suggest that Twain intended to incorporate a reference to, or quotation from, Hay's poem in *Is Shakespeare Dead?* (1909). There Twain cited several instances of poems being claimed by various people once those pieces became famous, though Hay's ballad is not mentioned. By 1910 Howells had "forgotten what piece [of poetry] of John Hay's it was that he [Clemens] liked so much" (*MMT*, p. 16). Almost certainly Howells was thinking of "Jim Bludso, of the Prairie Belle."

HAYDN, JOSEPH TIMOTHY (1786–1856). *Haydn's Dictionary of Dates and Universal Information Relating to All Ages and Nations*. Ed. by Benjamin Vincent (1818–1899). New York: Harper & Brothers, 1883. 796 pp.
Catalogs: MTLAcc, entry #731, volume donated by Clemens; ListABP (1910), "Haydn's Dict. Of Dates", no other information provided.

An undated letter from William Winter (1836–1917), the drama critic, essayist, and poet, recalled that Clemens "asked me, in a casual conversation, what book I was reading & (as it happened) I mentioned Haydn's Dictionary of Dates. He said he would read it. He was always watchful of sources of information" (ALS, collection of Kevin Mac Donnell, Austin, Texas). The half-title page of Haydn's compilation promised "remarkable occurrences, ancient and modern, . . . particularly of the British empire."

HAYS, HELEN (ASHE), MRS. W. J. HAYS (1837–1889). *The Adventures of Prince Lazybones, and Other Stories*. Illus. New York: Harper & Brothers, [cop. 1884]. 271 pp.
Source: MTLAcc, entry #434, volume donated by Clemens. Hays published half a dozen successful children's books before she died at fifty-two in New York City. Her artist husband, William Jacob Hays, Sr. (1830–1875), was a recognized painter of pastoral, animal, and frontier scenes.

———. *The Princess Idleways: A Fairy Story*. Illus. New York: Harper & Brothers, 1905. 124 pp.
Source: MTLAcc, entry #424, volume donated by Clemens.

HAZLITT, WILLIAM (1778–1830). *Lectures on the Literature of the Age of Elizabeth, and Characters of Shakespear's Plays*. Two vols. in one. London: George Bell and Sons, 1882. [Publisher conjectured. The spelling of Shakespeare is *sic*.]
Catalog: *A1911*, "12mo, cloth, Lond. 1882," sheet of manuscript notes laid in, lot 228, sold for $4.50.

HEAD, RICHARD (1637?-1686?) and FRANCIS KIRKMAN (1632–c. 1680). *The English Rogue: Described, in the Life of Meriton Latroon, a Witty Extravagant. Being a Compleat History of the Most Eminent Cheats of Both Sexes*. 4 vols. Illus. 8vo, paper-backed boards, broken, covers loose and first quire sprung, spine lacking. N. p: [1874]. [Originally published 1665–1671; this is a reprint of the uniform edition of all four parts as published in 1680.]
Marginalia: there is a penciled note about the reprinting on the title page. Someone wrote ten page numbers on the rear free endpaper identifying some of the more risqué stories in the book.
Catalog: Christie's, New York City, Sale 6382, estate of Phyllis Harrington (11 May 1987), "10 page numbers written on back free endpaper," item #16, sold with two other titles (Primrose and Wallace) for a total of $1,650. (Purchased by John L. Feldman.)
Provenance: Bequeathed by Clara Clemens Samossoud to her friend and secretary Phyllis Harrington in 1962. John L. Feldman of Astoria, New York owned Clemens's copy of this book in 1987, which Feldman described then as a reprint published around 1880 with ten page numbers written on the rear endpaper (Feldman to Alan Gribben, 19 May 1987). For a time Feldman placed the volumes on deposit in the Special Collections at the University of Colorado at Boulder, but by 2003 Feldman had withdrawn the book (Michelle Visser, Special Collections, to Alan Gribben, 10 June 2003).
Location: current whereabouts unknown.
Mark Twain cites "'The English Rogue': London, 1665" as his source for a song of the underworld used in Chapter 17 of *The Prince and the Pauper* (1881). Chapters 18 and 20 of that novel also give evidence of this book's influence. A history of vagabonds and criminals, *The English Rogue*

contains slang, songs, and escapades of London lowlife. Dickinson, "The Sources of *The Prince and the Pauper*" (1949); Stone, *IE* (1961), p. 113; Baetzhold , *MT&JB* (1970), pp. 52–53, 331 n. 14.

Headley, Joel Tyler (1813–1897). *The Great Rebellion: A History of the Civil War in the United States.* Illus. 2 vols. Hartford, Connecticut: American Publishing Co., 1866.

In 1885 Clemens mentioned that "'Headley's History of the War'" sold 200,000 copies in America (NB 24, *N&J* 3: 159).

—————, ed. *Mountain Adventures in Various Parts of the World. Selected from the Narratives of Celebrated Travellers.* Illus. New York: Charles Scribner & Co., 1872. 356 pp.

Source: MTLAcc, entry #2003, volume donated from Clemens's library by Clara Clemens Gabrilowitsch in 1910.

————— and **Willis Fletcher Johnson** (1857–1931). *Stanley's Adventures in the Wilds of Africa: A Graphic Account of the Several Expeditions of Henry M. Stanley.* Illus. [Philadelphia:] Edgewood Publishing Co., [cop. 1889].

Source: MTLAcc, entry #552, volume donated by Albert Bigelow Paine, Clemens's designated biographer. Possibly Clemens saw this book, since the men exchanged reading materials.

Heard, Albert F[arley]. (1833–1890). *The Russian Church and Russian Dissent, Comprising Orthodoxy, Dissent, and Erratic Sects.* New York: Harper & Brothers, 1887. 310 pp.

Source: MTLAcc, entry # 1238, volume donated by Clemens.

Hearn, Lafcadio (1850–1904). *Stray Leaves from Strange Literature; Stories Reconstructed from the Anvari-Soheïli, Baitál Pachísí, Mahabharata, Pantchatantra, Gulistan, Talmud, Kalewala, Etc.* Boston: J. R. Osgood and Co., 1884. 225 pp. [Edition conjectured.]

On 18 October 1886 Clemens urged Edward H. House to obtain this "little book" and read "the Buddhist tale called 'Yamaraja'" (Lord of Death) to find proof that a long poem by Richard Henry Stoddard (1825–1903) did not rely on one of House's stories (ASSSCL). See the related Catalog entry for R. H. Stoddard's "The Brahman's Son."

—————. *Two Years in the French West Indies.* [Edition undetermined; Hearn published this book in 1890].

Catalogs: *C1951*, #31c, $20, listed among books signed by Clemens; Sale of Bradley Martin Collection, Sotheby's, New York City, 30 January 1990, signed by Clemens, notes by Clemens of approximately thirty words, $2,000; D & D Galleries, Somerville, New Jersey, 5 April 1990, annotated by Clemens, $4,000 (notifications to Alan Gribben by collector Nick Karanovich and librarian Diana Royce).

Clemens and this strange literary figure, who was attracted to the exotic, the fantastic, and the supernatural, had in common a first-hand knowledge of the Mississippi River, though they apparently never met. On 2 May 1882 Lafcadio Hearn's "A River Reverie" in the New Orleans *Times-Democrat* reported on Mark Twain's arrival by steamboat on 28 April (Coleman O. Parsons, "Steamboating as Seen by Passengers and River Men, 1875–1884," *Mississippi Quarterly* 24.1 [Winter 1970]: 19–34).

—————. *Youma, Story of a West Indian Slave.* New York: Harper & Brothers, 1890. [Edition conjectured.]

Catalog: *C1951*, O5, listed among books containing Olivia Clemens's signature.

Hearst, William Randolph (1863–1951). [American newspaper publisher.]

Finley Peter Dunne recorded the fact that Hearst was one of the people "of whom he [Clemens] never spoke except with rage. . . . It was against William Randolph Hearst that his wildest rage was directed. . . . His scorn and hatred of Hearst were beyond description. He had never had any business or social relations with the editor and publisher that I know of. . . . At the mention of the laird of San Simeon the old humorist and philosopher would rake his memory for the invective. . . . Mark wrote a lot of scurrilous unprintable doggerel about him which was circulated among his friends" (*Mr. Dooley Remembers: The Informal Memoirs of Finley Peter Dunne*, ed. Philip Dunne [Boston: Little, Brown, 1963], pp. 244–245).

Heaton, Mary Margaret, "Mrs. Charles Heaton" (1836–1883). *Masterpieces of Flemish Art, Including Examples of the Early German and the Dutch Schools, with Memoirs of the Artists. Translation and Introduction by Lafcadio Hearn* [1850–1904]. Twenty-six photographs of paintings. London: Bell & Daldy, 1869. [Publisher conjectured.]

Catalog: *A1911*, "4to, cloth (loose), Lond. 1869," quotes a sheet of Clemens's notes laid in, lot 230, sold for $1.50.

Heber, Reginald (1783–1826). "Missionary hymn," generally known as "From Greenland's icy mountains" (hymn, written in 1819 and published by at least 1821). Lowell Mason (1792–1872) composed the tune in 1823.

Clemens enjoyed Heber's surging "Missionary hymn," though he came to disagree with its message that benighted peoples around the world "call us to deliver/Their land from Error's chain." In "Letter from Carson City," a sketch published in Virginia City on 3 February 1863, Clemens listed "From Greenland's Icy Mountains" among songs he had heard at the Governor's house (*ET&S* 1: 197). The title of this hymn appears amid German sentences in Notebook 27 (September 1887, *N&J* 3: 302). In Chapter 1 of "Those Extraordinary Twins" (1894) Angelo Capello attempts to sing Heber's hymn but Luigi maliciously drowns out the sound "with a rude and rollicking song." On 5 January 1896 Clemens copied the first eight lines into Notebook 36; below the final ones—"They ask us to deliver/Their land from error's chain"—he wrote "NO" (TS p. 17); at the time Clemens was sailing toward Ceylon. On 15 February 1896 Clemens passed the time aboard a train from Calcutta to Darjeeling by constructing an attack on "that most self-complacent of all poems, Greenland's Icy Mountains." Concerning the supposed "call" by native peoples "to deliver their land from Error's chain," wrote Clemens, "The call was never made, never has been made" (NB 36, TS p. 45). Mark Twain quoted from the hymn in Chapter 37 of *Following the Equator* (1897): "'What though the spicy breezes blow soft o'er Ceylon's isle'—an eloquent line, an incomparable line; it says little, but conveys whole libraries of sentiment, and Oriental charm and mystery, and tropic deliciousness." He refers to Heber's hymn in Chapter 55 of *Following the Equator* as "my favorite poem" and quotes the first eight lines that he copied in Notebook 36 in 1896. "Those are beautiful verses," he adds, "and they have remained in my memory all my life"; however, he proceeds to criticize the implied notion that Westerners have an obligation to preach their religion to inhabitants of the Eastern hemisphere. He paraphrased a famous line from the hymn ("Where every prospect pleases & only man is vile") in Notebook 44 in 1901 (TS p. 21). Two lines from the hymn appear in Chapter 11 of "A Horse's Tale" (1906). In Letter VII of Mark Twain's "Letters from the Earth," evidently written in 1909, the microbes within Noah's intestines gleefully sang: "Constipation, O constipation,/The joyful sound proclaim/Till man's remotest entrail /Shall praise its Maker's name" (*LE*, p. 31). The third stanza of Heber's hymn concludes: "Salvation! O salvation!/The joyful sound proclaim,/Till each remotest nation/Has learned Messiah's Name."

John Carlos Rowe, "Mark Twain's Critique of Globalization (Old and New) in *Following the Equator, A Journey Around the World*," *Arizona Quarterly* 61.1 (Spring 2005): 109–135.

————. *The Poetical Works of Reginald Heber, Late Bishop of Calcutta*. Illus. New York, [1875]. [Edition not identified.]

Catalogs: *A1911*, "12mo, stamped morocco, gilt edges, N.Y., n.d.," small sheet of notes by Clemens laid in, lot 231, sold for $1.25; Walpole Galleries (New York City), Catalog 112, 21 February 1919, "Sq. 12mo, stamped morocco. New York, (1875)," item 123.

HECTOR, ANNIE (FRENCH) (1825–1902), pseud. "Mrs. Alexander." *The Wooing o' T; A Novel*. New York: Henry Holt and Co., 1874. 483 pp.

Source: MTLAcc, entry #1832, volume donated from Clemens's library by Clara Clemens Gabrilowitsch in 1910.

HEDGE, FREDERIC HENRY (1805–1890). *Prose Writers of Germany*. Fourth edition. New York: James Miller, 1863.

Edgar Hemminghaus reported seeing Clemens's copy of this volume of translations at the Mark Twain Library in Redding, Connecticut. ("Mark Twain's German Provenience" [1945], pp. 467–469). Albert E. Stone did not include it in his checklist of Clemens's books that he compiled in Redding in 1955, and I was unable to find the book in 1970.

HEINE, HEINRICH (1797–1856). "Du bist wie eine Blume [You are like a flower]" (poem, song, published in 1825).

Mark Twain quoted this poem in "Meisterschaft: In Three Acts" (1888). Its first two lines are rhapsodic: "You are like a flower,/So sweet and fair and pure."

————. *Heinrich Heine's Buch der Lieder. Diamat-Ausgabe. [Heinrich Heine's Book of Songs. Diamond Edition.]* Illustrated by Philipp Grot Johann (1841–1892). Berlin: G. Grote'sche Verlagsbuchhandlung, 1889. 270 pp.

Inscription: signed on the half-title page in black ink, "Clara L. Clemens/June 8th 1894./Paris./Mrs. Willard".

Location: Mark Twain Library, Redding, Connecticut.

Copy examined: Clara Clemens's copy, unmarked. Has the Mark Twain Library red ink accession number "4082". Examined in 1970 and again in June 1982.

Clemens himself owned or borrowed several other copies of *Buch der Lieder*, first published in 1827. In 1883 Clemens copied lines or verses from six poems in this collection (NB 22, *N&J* 3: 36–37). He made a memorandum in 1884: "Heine's Works" (NB 22, *N&J* 3: 49). Henry Fisher remembered hearing Clemens say in London in 1891 that "Heine's songs will make the world happier as long as it stands"; Clemens also told Fisher: "Howells introduced

me to Heine. . . . I am glad he did. . . . I read Heine only for his glittering wit, the scintillating glow of his fancy" (*AMT*, pp. 75, 160–161). Clemens also spoke of "that nimbleness of language," that "airy, fairy lightness" in Heine's verse (*AMT*, p. 138). Describing his knowledge of German literature in an 1897 newspaper interview in Vienna, Clemens said he "grew up with Heine; he is closest to me of them all" (Odessa *News* [Odesskie *Novosti*], 8 October 1897; translated and reprinted by M. Thomas Inge and George Munro, "Ten Minutes with Mark Twain," *American Literary Realism* 15.2 [Autumn 1982]: 262). William Dean Howells loaned Clemens at least one volume of Heine's writings, for on 25 July 1903, explaining the loss of another book that Howells had loaned him, Clemens remarked: "Oh, that volume of Heine! the worrying nights it cost me" (*MTHL*, p. 773).

————. "Ich wollt' meine Lieb' ergösse sich" ["I wish that I could pour my love"] (song). Melody by Felix Mendelssohn (1809–1847).

Mulling over selections for a music box, Clemens made a favorable reference to the English title of this song in Notebook 16 (1878), *N&J* 2: 213); he also jotted down its German title and Mendelssohn's name in Notebook 17 (1878), *N&J* 2: 220).

————. "Die Lorelei" (song). Melody by Friedrich Silcher (1789–1860).

Clemens first heard this song in April 1878, when Bayard Taylor introduced it to the Clemenses and Clara Spaulding on board the *Holsatia* as they sailed for Germany (*MTB*, p. 618). In June 1878 Clemens copied its lyrics into Notebook 14 in German and English (*N&J* 2: 100). He made use of a phrase from its first verse "*Gipfel des Berges*" ("peak of the mountain") in July 1878 in Notebook 15 (*N&J* 2: 118), and he copied the first line into Notebook 15 on 1 August 1878, noting: "Very popular in Germany. 30 years old, but the bands all play it" (*N&J* 2: 125). "Lorelei" was one of the ten tunes Clemens finally selected for the $400 music box he purchased in Geneva in 1878 (SLC to Susan Warner, 20 November 1878, Yale; NB 16, *N&J* 2: 212). Clemens recalled in January 1879 that Bayard Taylor "repeated the Lorelei & a German sang it on ship—first time I heard it" (NB 17, *N&J* 2: 268). In Chapter 16 of *A Tramp Abroad* (1880) Mark Twain quotes and discusses "Die Lorelei," reproducing the musical notes as well as the lyrics. "I could not endure it at first, but by and by it began to take hold of me, and now there is no tune which I like so well," he added. "Lorelei" appears in a list of what appear to be Clemens's favorite songs in August 1889 (NB 29, *N&J* 3: 513). Isabel Lyon recorded on 6 March 1906: "Tonight after Jean played it, Mr. Clemens said: 'The dearest and sweetest lie I ever heard is the Lorelei.' And then he chuckled" (IVL Journal, TS p. 142, MTP).

Scott, *OPMT* (1966), p. 21; Brandi Besalke, "'Ein sehr gluecklicher Kind, you bet': Mark Twain and the German Language," *Mark Twain Annual* 5 (2007): 109–122.

————. "The two grenadiers" (poem, song, 1840). German title: "Die beiden Grenadiere." Melody by Robert Alexander Schumann (1810–1856).

"I'll claim The Grenadiers for sure, dear heart!" Clemens wrote to Clara Clemens from Dublin, New Hampshire on 8 June 1905. "Thank you for remembering" (TS in

MTP). Evidently Clara had offered to sing one of Clemens's favorite pieces at a concert, for on 29 June 1905 Clemens wrote to her: "I am very sorry you are not going to be able to sing the Two Grenadiers" (MTP). Clara quoted Heine's verse in her commonplace book with obvious admiration (Paine 150, MTP, 1888?).

HELM, W[ILLIAM]. H[ENRY]. (1860–1936). *Studies in Style*. London: W. Heinemann, 1900. 195 pp. [Publisher conjectured.]

Catalog: *A1911*, "12mo, cloth, gilt top, uncut, Lond. 1900," small sheet of manuscript notes laid in, lot 232, sold for $3.

Studies in Style is a collection of occult fiction stories. Clemens wrote to Helm on 23 August and 17 September 1900 (MTP).

HEMANS, FELICIA DOROTHEA (1793–1835). "Bird at sea" (song). Melody by C[hristopher]. Meineke (1782–1850).

When Mark Twain saw a land bird hovering over the becalmed *Smyrniote* in 1866, he noted: "he is a long way from home—thought of the old song—'Bird at Sea'" (NB 5, *N&J* 1: 138). He also mentioned this song in Chapter 38 of *Life on the Mississippi* (1883) and "About All Kinds of Ships" (1893).

———. "Casabianca" (poem, published in 1826).

Hemans's often-recited poem became a touchstone item for Clemens because of its lurid scene and sentimental message of dutiful obedience. Mark Twain employed two slightly misquoted lines from this poem in his 5 December 1863 dispatch from Carson City that parodied L. O. Sterns's oratorical style (*MTEnt*, pp. 92–95). He quoted "let the flames that shook the battle's wreck, shine round it o'er the dead"; Hemans wrote "The flame that lit the battle's wreck! Shone round him o'er the dead." In his letter of 14 January 1864 Twain chuckles over the "old-fashioned *impressive* style" of oratorical inflection imposed on school pupils "ever since Mrs. Hemans wrote that verse" (*MTEnt*, p. 135). He also quotes a drunk's rendition of the piece in a column for the 23 August 1864 issue of the San Francisco *Call* (*CofC*, p. 134). Twain's Notebook 5 (*N&J* 1: 146) indicates that he read poems collected in *Ocean Scenes; or, The Perils and Beauties of the Deep* (pp. 381–382, 284–285, 180–184) in the ship library of the S. S. *Smyrniote* when that vessel lay becalmed en route to San Francisco from Honolulu; Hemans' "Casabianca" appeared on pages 306–307 of *Ocean Scenes*. In Notebook 7 on board the *San Francisco* in January 1867 he joked about "what became of the boy that stood on the burning deck" (since "no inquest" was held) (*N&J* 2: 292). Very likely it was Mark Twain who organized the "Country School Exhibition" aboard the *Montana* on 10 July 1868. Part of the evening's entertainment, according to Twain's "Programme," was a "Recitation—The Boy Stood on the Burning Deck, with his Baggage checked for Troy," performed by "Mr. M." (*Alta California*, 6 September 1868; reprinted in *The Twainian* 7 [November-December 1948]: 5). In Chapter 44 of *Innocents Abroad* Twain describes his trek through Syria by invoking a line from the poem: "Tired? Ask of the winds that far away with fragments strewed the sea." Twain displayed a special fondness for John Hay's ballad "Jim Bludso of the Prairie Belle" (1871), and the fiery fate of its heroic steamboat engineer resembled the sacrifice

depicted in Heman's "Casabianca."

In a speech Twain delivered at the Hannibal High School graduation exercises on 30 May 1902 he recalled that "the standby that was never, never absent" from a school exhibition during his boyhood days was "The boy stood on the burning deck." Three years later Twain claimed that "Casabianca" served him as copy for exercises on the first typewriter he purchased in 1873: "At home I played with the toy, repeating and repeating and repeating 'The Boy stood on the Burning Deck,' until I could turn that boy's adventure out at the rate of twelve words a minute" ("The First Writing-Machines" [1905]). That recollection also appeared in an Autobiographical Dictation made in 1904 (and later inserted into a dictation of 27 February 1907), where Twain recalled how he practiced on a new typewriter in the early 1870s by "repeating and repeating and repeating 'The Boy Stood on the Burning Deck'" (*AutoMT*, p. 446; *MTLet* 6: 309).

Those typing rehearsals of Mrs. Hemans's declamatory piece preceded Twain's best-known reference to it in Chapter 21 of *The Adventures of Tom Sawyer* (1876), where a wooden execution of "The Boy Stood on the Burning Deck" is an unavoidable feature of the Examination Evening program at the village schoolhouse. The schoolmaster Mr. Dobbins also listens absent-mindedly to a recitation of the poem in Act 3 of "Tom Sawyer: A Play," written 1875–1884 (*HH&T*, p. 303). In Chapter 31 of *Following the Equator* (1897) Twain quotes a fellow passenger's opinion of Australian railroads: "Goodness knows! Ask of the winds that far away with fragments strewed the sea, as the boy that stood on the burning deck used to say." In June 1898 Twain had the idea of adding the boy in Hemans's poem to Huck, Tom, and other "Creatures of Fiction" he planned to assemble in a tale; later Twain added: "Make Casabianca sing 'All in the Downs the Ship lay moored' & dance hornpipe" (NB 40, TS p. 27). In "Mrs. Eddy in Error" (written 1903), Book 2 of *Christian Science*, Twain again wrote: "As the ballad says: 'Ask of the winds that far away/With fragments strewed the sea'" (*WIM?*, p. 390). No. 44 calls the piece "The Boy Stood on the Burning Deck" and says "It's a poem. It hasn't been written yet, but it's very pretty and stirring. It's English" (Chapter 26, "No. 44, The Mysterious Stranger," written 1902–1908, *MSM*, p. 362). In Chapter 28 of "No. 44" August Feldner intones two lines from this poem (*MSM*, p. 373).

———. *The Forest Sanctuary* (published in 1825).

Clara Clemens listed this work in her commonplace book sometime between 1888 and 1904 (Paine 150, MTP).

———. *Select Poetical Works of Felicia Hemans*. Collection of British Authors Series. Leipzig: B. Tauchnitz, 1865. 342 pp. [Edition conjectured.]

Catalog: *C1951*, D1, $8, listed among the books signed by Clemens.

HENDERSON, ARCHIBALD (1877–1963). "George Bernard Shaw," *North American Review* 185.616 (7 June 1907): 293–305.

Henderson knew Clemens personally toward the end of the author's life. Their friendship began in 1907 when Clemens praised Henderson's sketch of George Bernard Shaw that appeared in the same issue of *North American Review* as Mark Twain's "Chapters from My Autobiography"

North American Review 185.616 (7 June 1907): 241–251, though Clemens kidded Henderson about using so many "fine words, splendid words, magnificent words" in such a short space. (Henderson, for example, had written, "In him rages the dæmonic, half-insensate intuition of a Blake, with his seer's faculty for inverted truism" [p. 305].) The next year Henderson visited Clemens at Stormfield in Redding, Connecticut. In 1909 Clemens read an article that this professor at the University of North Carolina wrote about him, and liked it (IVL to Henderson, February 1909, PH in MTP). This must have been an advance copy of Henderson's "Mark Twain" essay that would appear in *Harper's Monthly* 118 (May 1909): 948–955. Henderson published "Mark Twain—Wie Er Ist. Eine Skizze nach dem Leben" in a German journal in November 1909, and sent a copy to Clemens. "Your article in the Deutsche Revue pleases Mr. Clemens very much indeed," Albert Bigelow Paine assured Henderson from Redding on 15 November 1909 (PH in MTP). The preface to Henderson's subsequent book, *Mark Twain* (London: Duckworth & Co, 1911; New York: Frederick A. Stokes Co., 1912) stated that Clemens had "authorized" Henderson's "writing an interpretation of his life and work" (p. xi). In that 230-page study Henderson emphasized Mark Twain's international appeal. Joe B. Fulton produced the fullest summary of the Twain-Henderson relationship—"Stormfield Scholar: Archibald Henderson," *Mark Twain Journal: The Author and His Era* 58.1 (Spring 2020): 9–20.

HENDERSON, C[HARLES]. HANDFORD (1861–1941). *John Percyfield: The Anatomy of Cheerfulness*. Boston: The Riverside Press, Houghton, Mifflin and Co., 1903. 382 pp.

> **Catalogs:** QF Martinez, "Very Good Condition"; Ball 2016 inventory, blue cloth, gilt lettering, top edges gilt, inscribed "E. S. McAtee/414 W. Gray St.," very good condition.
>
> **Location:** Quarry Farm Library shelves, under the supervision of the Mark Twain Archive, Elmira College, Elmira, New York.
>
> This romantic novel, with settings in France, England, and the United States, was available to Clemens during his final visits to Quarry Farm in Elmira.

HENDERSON, MARY NEWTON (FOOTE) (1842–1931). *The Aristocracy of Health: A Study of Physical Culture, Our Favorite Poisons, and a National and International League for the Advancement of Physical Culture*. New York: Harper & Brothers, 1906. 772 pp.

> **Source:** MTLAcc, entry #401, volume donated by Clemens. Clemens could hardly have endorsed Henderson's call to abstain from tobacco, classifying it with unhealthy habits such as alcohol, tea, coffee, and opium. *The Aristocracy of Health* propounded seven rules for those who hoped to attain longevity. This writer, a wealthy advocate of women's suffrage and other worthy causes and projects in Washington, D. C., should not be confused with Mary (Hallock) Foote (1847–1938), a friend of the Clemenses.

HENDERSON, PETER (1822–1890). *Practical Floriculture; A Guide to the Successful Cultivation of Florists' Plants, for the Amateur and Professional Florist*. Third edition, enlarged. New York: Orange Judd Co., 1882.

> **Inscription:** signed in ink on the front flyleaf, "Olivia L. Clemens/Hartford/4 June 1883." Below this someone else (not Clemens) added in black ink, written over in brown

ink, in a ragged hand: "Presented to/Mr. Dnl Maloy/4 June 1883/Gardner [*sic*]/to S L Clemens/Mark Twain/Farmington Avenue/Hartford /Conn/USA." A photocopy of the flyleaf is in the Mark Twain Papers at Berkeley.

> **Marginalia:** pencil marks throughout.
>
> **Location:** Mark Twain House and Museum, Hartford, Connecticut. Donated by Harry Hinkleman in 1958.
>
> **Copy examined:** Olivia Clemens's copy, given to the family's gardener. Examined in August 1987.

HENDRIK, HANS (c. 1834–1889). *Memoirs of Hans Hendrik, The Arctic Traveller, Serving Under [Elisha Kent] Kane [1820–1857], [Isaac Israel] Hayes [1832–1881], [Charles Francis] Hall [1821–1871] and [George] Nares [1831–1915], 1853–1876. Written by Himself*. Translated from the Eskimo language by Henry [Hinrich Johannes] Rink (1819–1893). Ed. by George Stephens (1813–1895). London: Trübner & Co., 1878. 100 pp.

> **Inscription:** signed and inscribed in pencil on the front flyleaf: "S L. Clemens/Munich, Bavaria,/January, 1879./A very valuable book/—& unique."
>
> **Marginalia:** approximately five penciled comments are scattered through the small volume. On page 22 Clemens wrote: "Only observe these names!"—referring to Joel, Simion, Nathaniel, and Hans in the family of Hans Hendrik. On page 24 Clemens noted about a brief exchange of simple questions and answers, "An Ollendorfian conversation." Clemens wrote "Poor devil" on page 38 where Hendrik describes the death of Umarsuak, who fled from the camp into the snowy hills and whom Hendrik loved like a brother. On page 68 Clemens wrote vertically: "Afloat in mid-ocean for near 6 months in the darkness of the long arctic night." (Clemens seemed moved by various literary passages depicting vessels suspended in time and space, and he explored this motif in his own fiction.) There are a number of vertical pencil marks, including a long one made on page 39 at Hendrik's harrowing sled journey in a snow storm; these marks are present throughout up to page 90.
>
> **Location:** Mark Twain Library, Redding, Connecticut. (Verified by an email exchange with library director Beth Dominianni on 30 January 2013.)
>
> **Copy examined:** Clemens's copy. Has the red ink Mark Twain Library accession number "3129". Examined in 1970 and again in June 1982.
>
> From Hendrik's narrative Mark Twain probably obtained the facts about Eskimo hunting techniques that he employed in "The Esquimau Maiden's Romance" (1893). Hendrik was an Inuk native hunter in Greenland who acted as a guide, dog-driver, and interpreter for several notable Arctic expeditions.

HENESS, GOTTLIEB (1813–1890). *Der Leitfaden für den Unterricht in der deutschen Sprache [The Guideline for Teaching in the German Language]*. New York: H. Holt & Co., [1884?]. 253 pp.

> **Source:** MTLAcc, entry #367, volume donated by Clemens.

HENIGER, ALICE MINNIE (HERTS) (c. 1870–1933). *The Children's Educational Theatre*. New York: Harper & Brothers, 1901.

> Without insisting that Clemens actually read this book by Heniger (whom Clemens knew by her maiden name of Alice Hertz), Joseph Csicsila demonstrated Clemens's

interest in her work as the founder and managing director of the Children's Theatre that was sponsored by the Jewish Educational Alliance in New York City until 1909 ("'The Child Learns by Doing': Mark Twain and Turn-of-the-Century Education Reform," *Mark Twain Annual 6* [2008]: 91–100). The fact that Harper & Brothers published Twain's writings during the last decade of his life makes it likely that he saw her book. One of the children who performed in a dramatization of Twain's *The Prince and the Pauper* at this East Side social center later wrote about the experience—Manuel Komroff, "How I Shook Hands with Mark Twain," *Mark Twain Journal* 11.1 (Summer 1959): 4–5.

Lawrence I. Berkove and Joseph Csicsila, *Heretical Fictions: Religion in the Literature of Mark Twain* (Iowa City: University of Iowa Press, 2010), pp. 171–173.

HENKLE, JOHN FLETCHER (1837–1913). *The National Peacemaker; A Treatise on Present Conditions in the United States.* Chicago: Privately printed, 1904. 140 pp.

Source: MTLAcc, entry #528, volume donated by Clemens. Henkle was a real estate agent residing in Chicago.

HENLEY, WILLIAM ERNEST (1849–1903). *A Book of Verses.* Second edition. Original coarse maroon linen, gilt, uncut. London: David Nutt, 1889. 175 pp.

Inscription: inscribed in black ink on the front free flyleaf: "To Samuel L. Clemens, in admiration of his happy gift of making his fellow creatures happy. From W. E. H./ Glasgow, Sept. 30, '89." (William Angus sent Clemens this volume, along with two Robert Burns books that he requested Clemens to autograph and return.)

Provenance: contains the shelfmark of Clara Clemens Gabrilowitsch's private Detroit library. Later the volume was in the Carrie Estelle Doheny Collection, St. John's Seminary, Camarillo, California. Donated by Mrs. Doheny in 1940 after its purchase from Maxwell Hunley Rare Books of Beverly Hills for $12.20. Auctioned for $935 by Christie's on 21 February 1988 (lot 1760) on behalf of St. John's Seminary and the Archdiocese of Los Angeles. Subsequently it belonged to the collection of Nick Karanovich, Fort Wayne, Indiana.

Catalog: *Sotheby's 2003*, lot #208, $700.

Location: collection of Kevin Mac Donnell, Austin, Texas.

Copy examined: Clemens's copy, with leaves opened, in July 2004. Has the bookplate of "Estelle Doheny."

Pages 56–57 reprint Henley's best-known poem, "Invictus," which concludes: "It matters not how strait the gate,/How charged with punishments the scroll,/I am the master of my fate,/I am the captain of my soul." In the 25 July 1891 issue of the London *Speaker*, Clemens, writing under the pseudonym "Thos. J. Snodgrass, J. P.," pretends not to recognize a reference to "the 'captaincy of our soul,' whatever that may be" (Zachary Turpin, "Thomas Jefferson Snodgrass Goes to England," *American Literary Realism* 49.2 [Winter 2017]: 177).

———. *Hawthorn and Lavender, with Other Verses.* 8vo, original decorated green cloth, small stain on rear cover. First American edition. New York: Harper & Brothers, 1901. 113 pp.

Inscription: inscribed by Clemens in ink on the front free endpaper: "To/Mrs. Olivia L. Clemens—/Nov. 27, 1871 or 2—/Upon the occasion & cele-/bration of one of her early/birth-days, when she did not/mind them so much./

from/SLC./Riverdale-on-Hudson/Nov. 1901."

Catalogs: ListABP (1910), "Hawthorn & Lavender, Henley"; *C1951*, #54a, $40; Christie's, New York City, 1–2 February 1988 auction, lot 457, sold for $2,420 to Heritage Book Shop, Los Angeles.

Provenance: formerly in the Carrie Estelle Doheny Collection, St. John's Seminary, Camarillo, California. Donated by Mrs. Doheny in 1953 after its purchase from Aubrey Davidson on 8 August 1952 for $175. Auctioned in February 1988 by Christie's in New York City on behalf of St. John's Seminary and the Archdiocese of Los Angeles.

Copy examined: Olivia Clemens's copy, unmarked, at St. John's Seminary in 1970.

———. [An identical (or the same, retrieved?) copy.]

Source: MTLAcc, entry #1343, volume donated by Clemens.

HENRY VII, KING OF ENGLAND (1457–1509). *The Statutes of Henry VII in Exact Facsimile, from the Very Rare Original, Printed by [William] Caxton [c. 1422–1491] in 1489.* Edited, with notes and introduction, by John Rae. Large paper. 4to, original half green morocco over glazed red boards, gray-coated endpapers, top edge stained red. Half black calf folding-case. London: John Camden Hotten, 1869.

Catalogs: *A1911*, "4to, boards, morocco back, red top, uncut, Lond. 1869," quotes a riddle written by Clemens on a loose sheet laid in, lot 73, sold for $8; Walpole Galleries (New York City), Catalogue 112, 21 February 1919, item #125, "half roan, uncut," "penciled autograph slip inserted, apparently a riddle; it commences, 'I never speak except when spoken to. I forget a thing as soon as I hear it,'" etc.—the answer is an "echo (or telephone)"; *Sotheby's 2003*, #200, no mention of autograph slip, $3,000 (sold with two other titles about English history and lore); Robert Slotta, Admirable Books, Hilliard, Ohio, undated catalog, item #21, autograph slip no longer present, $1,150.

Provenance: penciled note indicates that the volume was sold on 6 June 1940 by the Brooklyn Public Library to a "Mr. Thomas" for $15. Eventually it entered the collection of Nick Karanovich, Fort Wayne, Indiana.

Location: collection of Kevin Mac Donnell, Austin, Texas.

Copy examined: Clemens's unmarked copy, at the 2003 Sotheby's auction and again in July 2004 at Kevin Mac Donnell's residence. Contains the *A1911* sale label and a Brooklyn Public Library bookplate. The manuscript fragment laid in the volume for the *A1911* auction, a penciled riddle, is no longer present.

William Caxton's edition of these laws was the first collection of English laws to be printed. Conceivably the language may have served as an unacknowledged background source for both *1601* (1880) and *The Prince and the Pauper* (1881). The publisher Hotten, incidentally, was one of Mark Twain's incorrigible and detested British pirates.

HENRY OF HUNTINGDON (c. 1084–1155). *The Chronicle of Henry of Huntingdon, Comprising the History of England, from the Invasion of Julius Caesar to the Accession of Henry II. Also, The Acts of Stephen, King of England and Duke of Normandy.* Translated and ed. by Thomas Forester. London: Henry G. Bohn, 1853. 430 pp.

Inscription: the first flyleaf is signed in pencil: "S L Clemens/

Hartford 1877".

Marginalia: heavily annotated. Black ink markings and notes begin on page 48 and continue throughout, concentrated especially at Henry's credulity about omens. The corners of many pages are folded down for reference. Clemens also read and annotated in ink "The Acts of Stephen, King of England and Duke of Normandy, by an Unknown But Contemporaneous Author" (pp. 321–430).

Catalog: *A1911,* "12mo, cloth (cover somewhat loose), Lond.: Bohn, 1853, . . . numerous marginal notes and marked passages in ink," quotes the signature, lot 256, sold for $2.50.

Location: Henry E. Huntington Library, San Marino, California.

Copy examined: Clemens's copy, on 27 July 1997.

In November 1877 James R. Osgood & Company of Boston billed Clemens for a copy of "Huntingdon's Hist. England," purchased on 24 October 1877 (Scrapbook #10, p. 69, MTP). In his early notes for *A Connecticut Yankee* (1889) Mark Twain made plans to include "remnants of monkish legends. Get them from Wm [*sic*] of Huntingdon" (NB 25 [December 1885], *N&J* 3: 216). In "As Concerns Interpreting the Deity" (written 1905) Twain pokes fun at Henry's notions of Divine Providence: "Whenever God punishes a man, Henry of Huntingdon knows why it was done, and tells us; and his pen is eloquent with admiration; but when a man has earned punishment, and escapes, he does not explain." In the same piece Twain also quotes from *The Acts of Stephen* (*WIM?*, pp. 114–117).

HENRY, PATRICK (1736–1799). "Give me liberty, or give me death!" (the concluding words in Henry's speech to the Second Virginia Convention, 23 March 1775).

Mark Twain recalled in a speech at the Hannibal High School Graduation Exercises on 30 May 1902 that "Give me LIBERTY or give me DEATH!" tended to be "recited every time" at the Hannibal school exhibitions during his boyhood.

HENSCHEL, GEORGE (1850–1934). *Personal Recollections of Johannes Brahms [1833–1897]: Some of His Letters to and Pages from a Journal Kept by George Henschel.* Boston: R. G. Badger, 1907. 95 pp. [Publisher conjectured.]

Catalog: *A1911,* "8vo, boards, gilt top, uncut, Bost. 1907," lot 47, sold for $3.75.

HENSEL, SEBASTIAN (1830–1898). *The Mendelssohn Family (1729–1847) from Letters and Journals.* Eight portraits by Wilhelm Hensel (1794–1861). Translated by Carl Klingemann (1798–1862) and an American collaborator, with a notice by George Grove (1820–1900). 2 vols. New York: Harper & Brothers, 1881. [Publisher conjectured.]

Catalogs: *A1911,* "2 vols., 8vo, cloth, N.Y. [1881]," quotes a small slip laid in containing Clemens's notes, lot 234, sold for $1.25; *Lexington 1912,* lot 15, sold for $5.

Before leaving for Boston and New York City in April 1882, Clemens wrote the title of this book in Notebook 20 (*N&J* 2: 460), probably intending to purchase a copy. Among a group of book titles he listed in September 1887 he included "Mendellsohn's [*sic*] Letters 2 vols." (NB 27, *N&J* 3: 317). The letters in *The Mendelssohn Family* are for the most part those exchanged by Felix Mendelssohn-Bartholdy (1809–1847) and his sister, Fanny Mendelssohn

Hensel (1805–1847).

HENSMAN, HOWARD (1855–1916). *Cecil Rhodes: A Study of a Career.* Portraits. Illus. New York, 1902.

Inscription: on a flyleaf Clemens wrote: "All about the Empire Builder and Pirate . . . S. L. Clemens, Riverdale, Feb., 1902."

Catalog: *A1911,* "8vo, full red morocco, gilt top, uncut, N.Y. 1902," quotes the signature, lot 235, sold for $4.

When visiting South Africa during his lecture tour Clemens developed mixed feelings about Cecil Rhodes (1853–1902).

HENTY, GEORGE ALFRED (1832–1902). *In the Hands of the Cave-Dwellers.* New York: Harper & Brothers, 1904. 205 pp.

Source: MTLAcc, entry #426, volume donated by Clemens.

A romantic tale of early (1830s) Spanish California written for a young adult audience.

———. *St. George for England: A Tale of Cressy and Poitiers.* Illustrated by Gordon [Frederick] Browne (1858–1932). New York: Scribner and Welford, [1887]. 352 pp. [Publication date conjectured but probable.]

Source: MTLAcc, entry #1889, volume donated from Clemens's library by Clara Clemens Gabrilowitsch in 1910. Fourteenth-century battles between the French and English forces are rendered as juvenile fiction.

HEPBURN, THOMAS NICOLL (1861–1930), pseud. "Gabriel Setoun." *Sunshine and Haar; Some Further Glimpses of Life at Barncraig.* New York: Harper & Brothers, 1896. 257 pp.

Source: MTLAcc, entry #1444, volume donated by Clemens.

Hepburn's novel is usually classified in the Kailyard school of the depictions of Scottish life.

HERBERT, EDWARD, FIRST BARON HERBERT OF CHERBURY (1583–1648). *Autobiography* (published in 1764).

Soldier, historian, and philosopher Herbert was the brother of the Metaphysical poet George Herbert (1593–1633). Edward Herbert's candid and encompassing *Autobiography* did not see print until more than a century after his death. Mark Twain intended to cite this work in his proposed appendix to *A Connecticut Yankee in King Arthur's Court* (Baetzhold, "Course of Composition" [1961], p. 200). Lord Herbert's work was available in the "Choice Autobiographies" series edited by William Dean Howells for James R. Osgood & Company of Boston.

HERBERT, GEORGE (1593–1633).

Clemens at least knew of Herbert's devotional writings, for in 1887 he identified him as the "Country Parson," the subtitle of Herbert's posthumously published prose description of a priest's duties, *A Priest to the Temple; or, The Country Parson, His Character and Rule of Holy Life* (1652) (NB 27, *N&J* 3: 314).

HERFORD, OLIVER (1863–1935). *Artful Anticks.* Illustrated by the author. Later printing of the author's first book. Square 8vo. Original pictorial tan cloth, gilt. New York: The Century Co., 1897. 100 pp.

Inscription: inscribed by Herford in black ink on the front free endpaper: "To that from this/in memory of Dec. 25th, 1901." Herford drew a small picture of a cat in ink on the half-title page, with the notation: "Not a good cat/ but my own./By me—/Oliver Herford." (A poem titled "The Audacious Kitten" appears on pages 1–3.)

Provenance: Clara Clemens Gabrilowitsch's private library in Detroit; later in the Carrie Estelle Doheny Collection, St. John's Seminary, Camarillo, California. Donated by Mrs. Doheny in 1940 after its purchase from Maxwell Hunley Rare Books of Beverly Hills for $12.20. Auctioned by Christie's (lot 1178) on 17 October 1988 for $660 (plus commission) on behalf of St. John's Seminary. Offered for sale by Maurice Neville Books, October 1988, $660.

Catalog: *Sotheby's 2003*, #182, $1,100 for this volume and Brander Matthews's *Americanisms and Briticisms*.

Location: collection of Kevin Mac Donnell, Austin, Texas.

Copy examined: presumably Clemens's copy (though it might conceivably have been Clara Clemens's), unmarked. Has the bookplate of "Estelle Doheny." Viewed at St. John's Seminary in 1970, at the Sotheby's sale in 2003, and at the home of Kevin Mac Donnell in July 2004.

Herford's whimsical poems are decorated with his clever sketches of kittens, giraffes, parrots, bees, and other animals, along with a number of forest fairies.

———. *A Child's Primer of Natural History*. Illustrated by the author. New York: C. Scribner's Sons, 1901. 95 pp.

Source: MTLAcc, entry #1890, volume donated from Clemens's library by Clara Clemens Gabrilowitsch in 1910.

————— with ETHEL WATTS MUMFORD (1878–1940) and ADDISON MIZNER (1872–1933). *The Cynic's Calendar of Revised Wisdom for 1903*. Illus. San Francisco: Paul Elder and Co., 1903. [Other similarly titled editions were issued in the following years.]

Catalog: ListABP (compiled in 1910), "Cynic's Calendar", no edition specified.

———. *The Rubáiyát of a Persian Kitten*. Illustrated by the author. First edition. Original printed gray boards. New York: Charles Scribner's Sons, 1904. [75] pp.

Inscription: inscribed by Clemens in black ink on the front pastedown endpaper: "Clara—/from/ Bambino/1904." Bambino was the name of a kitten Clara had adopted during her confinement at a sanitarium while recovering from her mother's death; as she explained in *My Father Mark Twain* (p. 257) it was against the rules to keep pets in the facility, so her father obligingly took the animal and sent reports to her about Bambino's activities during her convalescence. See also Phyllis Harnsberger, *Mark Twain, Family Man*, Chapter 17.

Provenance: Carrie Estelle Doheny Collection, St. John's Seminary, Camarillo, California. Donated by Mrs. Doheny in 1940 after its purchase from Maxwell F Hunley Rare Books of Beverly Hills for $12.20. Sold at auction by Christie's in February 1989 (lot #1761) for $1,650.

Location: collection of Kevin Mac Donnell, Austin, Texas.

Copy examined: Clemens's copy, unmarked, in July 2004. Has the bookplate of "Estelle Doheny."

Herford's was one of the many imitations of Edward FitzGerald's enormously popular *Rubáiyát*, this one accompanied on pages facing the verses by drawings of a playful kitten. Here is a typical stanza: "They say the Early Bird the Worm shall taste./Then rise, O Kitten! Wherefore,/sleeping, waste/The fruits of Virtue? Quick!/the Early Bird/Will soon be on the flutter—O/make haste!"

———. [Identical copy.] Rebacked, preserving portions of original spine. Half-black morocco folding-case.

Inscription: the front pastedown endpaper is inscribed by Clemens in ink, "Clara Clemens/from one of her/principal friends—/her father."

Catalogs: Maurice F. Neville Rare Books, Catalogue Number 8 (1981), item #532, $2,750; *Sotheby's 2003*, #209, $4,750.

Provenance: belonged to Clara Clemens Gabrilowitsch until her death. Bequeathed by her husband Jacques A. Samossoud to Henry and Mary Shisler of Cardiff by the Sea, California in 1966. Entered the collection of Nick Karanovich, Fort Wayne, Indiana in the early 1980s.

Copy examined: Clemens's gift copy to his daughter Clara. Viewed at the Sotheby's sale in 2003. In addition, Nick Karanovich sent a photocopy of the entire book to Alan Gribben on 25 May 1983.

HERNDON, WILLIAM LEWIS (1813–1857) and LARDNER GIBBON (1820–1910). *Exploration of the Valley of the Amazon, Made Under the Direction of the Navy Department*. 2 vols. Washington, D. C.: Part I, Robert Armstrong, Public Printer; Part II, A. O. P. Nicholson, Public Printer, 1853–1854.

Clemens wrote to his brother Henry on 5 August 1856 that Jane and Orion Clemens "have Herndon's Report, now," and he hoped that they can be persuaded of the feasibility of his projected trip to the Amazon (*MTL*, pp. 34–35; *MTLet* 1: 66). (Herndon wrote only Part I of the work. He drowned a few years after the publication of this work while undertaking a heroic sea rescue effort following a hurricane that destroyed his ship.) Mark Twain's Autobiographical Dictation of 29 March 1906 recalled that "I had been reading Lieutenant Herndon's account of his explorations of the Amazon. . . . I made up my mind that I would go to the head-waters of the Amazon and collect coca and trade in it and make a fortune" (*MTA* 1: 461; *AutoMT* 1: 461). Subsequently in "The Turning-Point of My Life" (1910) Twain again described the allurements he found in Herndon's account, especially his "astonishing tale about *coca*, a vegetable product of miraculous powers. . . . I was fired with a longing to ascend the Amazon. Also with a longing to open up a trade in coca with all the world" (*WIM?*, p. 459). Herndon discussed the "coca" crop on pages 88–89 of Part I. See also the Catalog entry for W. G. Mortimer, *Peru*.

HERODOTUS (c. 484–425 BCE). *The History of Herodotus. A New English Version*. Translated and edited by George Rawlinson (1812–1902), Henry Creswick Rawlinson (1810–1895), and John Gardner Wilkinson (1797–1875). Maps and illustrations. 4 vols. New York, 1875. [Two four-volume editions—one by D. Appleton and Company and another by Scribner, Welford and Armstrong—were published in New York in 1875. Which of these sets Clemens owned has not yet been established.]

Marginalia: a few passages marked by Clemens.

Catalogs: *A1911*, "4 vols., 8vo, cloth, N.Y. 1875, a few passages marked by Mr. Clemens," lot 237, sold for $2.25; *Lexington 1912*, lot 16, sold for $7.50.

Mark Twain attributes a (fictitious) quotation to the lauded Greek historian Herodotus at the beginning of the Appendix to *A Tramp Abroad* (1880). In January 1894 Twain made plans to include Herodotus's writings in the projected "Back Number" magazine (NB 33, TS p. 46). "Just like the case recorded by Herodotus," Twain noted alongside a Maori oracle's ambiguous prophecy in F. E. Maning's *Old New Zealand* (1887), presented to Clemens in Dunedin in November 1895. In "Eddypus" (written 1901–1902) Mark Twain assigned to himself the appellation by which Herodotus is generally known, "Father of History." He again assigned a fictitious quotation to Herodotus in the Acknowledgements for "A Horse's Tale" (1907): "Herodotus says, 'Very few things happen at the right time, and the rest do not happen at all: The conscientious historian will correct these defects.'"

———. *Stories of the East from Herodotus.* Translated and edited by Alfred John Church (1829–1912). Illus. New York: Dodd, Mead & Co., n.d. 299 pp.

Source: MTLACC, entry #1878, volume donated from Clemens's library by Clara Clemens Gabrilowitsch in 1910. Herodotus' travels took him through most of the lands that had thus been discovered during his early era.

HERRICK, CHRISTINE (TERHUNE) (1859–1944). *The Expert Maid-Servant.* New York: Harper & Brothers, 1904. 139 pp.

Source: MTLAcc, entry #675, volume donated by Clemens. Instructions about how to hire and train a female housekeeper.

HERRICK, ROBERT (1591–1674). "Greeting to the Violets" (poem).

Olivia Langdon copied this poem on an undated sheet of paper laid in her commonplace book (DV161, MTP).

———. *Selections from the Poetry of Robert Herrick.* Preface by Austin Dobson (1840–1911). Illustrated by Edwin A[ustin]. Abbey (1852–1911). Ivory cloth, faded. Some leaves loose. New York: Harper & Brothers, 1882. 188 pp.

Inscription: the front flyleaf is inscribed by Clemens in blue ink: "Livy L. Clemens/from/S. L. Clemens/Xmas 1882."

Catalog: ListABP (1910), "Selections from Robert Herrick (autograph of M. T.)".

Provenance: in August 1987 it was in the collection of Bigelow Paine Cushman, Deer Isle, Maine. It had previously been in the possession of Albert Bigelow Paine, Clemens's official biographer. (Bigelow Paine Cushman [1928–2003] was the grandson of Albert Bigelow Paine.) On 28 February 1989 Robert T. Slotta of Columbus, Ohio purchased the book from Cushman for $2,000. On 9 July 1990 it was still the property of Robert T. Slotta, then residing in Dublin, Ohio; he informed the staff of the Mark Twain Project that he had obtained it from Cushman.

Location: currently uncertain.

Copy examined: Olivia Clemens's gift copy, unmarked. Viewed in Deer Isle, Maine in August 1987.

E. W. Kemble remembered that Clemens especially praised the drawings that Edwin A. Abbey made for an 1882 edition of Robert Herrick's poems (Kemble, "Illustrating *Huckleberry Finn*" [1930]).

HERRICK, ROBERT (1868–1938).

The American novelist and educator Herrick remembered observing Clemens in August 1902 in York, Maine when he "was living among the pines on a bluff just above the bridge, Sewall's Bridge. He had taken work quarters nearby in Captain Sewall's stark Maine house and I used to see him there on the verandah and on Captain Sewall's float below the bridge. . . . I remember his . . . bushy white hair, tobacco streaked white moustache, and those gleaming dark eyes . . . –and the eternal cigar" ("Mark Twain and the American Tradition," *Mark Twain Quarterly* 2.2 [Winter 1937–1938]: 8).

HERRICK, SOPHIA BLEDSOE (1837–1919). *The Earth in Past Ages.* Illus. 12mo, cloth. New York, 1888. [Presumably this was the edition published by Harper & Brothers, 241 pp.]

Inscription: signed on a flyleaf "S. L. Clemens, 1889."

Catalogs: *A1911*, "12mo, cloth, N.Y. 1888," quotes the signature, lot 238, sold for $1.25; George D. Smith, New York City, "Catalogue of Books" (1911), item #165, $4.50; American Art Association, Sale catalogue (24 February 1925), "12mo, original cloth, New York, 1888, first edition," quotes the flyleaf signature, lot 126, sold for $6.

HERTZ, HENRIK (1798–1870). *King René's Daughter; A Danish Lyrical Drama.* Translated by Theodore Martin. New York: H. Holt and Co., 1880. 100 pp.

Source: MTLAcc, entry #2033, volume donated from Clemens's library by Clara Clemens Gabrilowitsch in 1910. In Bavaria in August 1893 Mark Twain mentioned seeing this play (NB 33, TS p. 25).

HERVEY, GEORGE WINFRED (1821–1908). *A System of Christian Rhetoric, for the Use of Preachers and Other Speakers.* New York: Harper & Brothers, 1873. 632 pp.

Source: MTLAcc, entry #1393, volume donated by Clemens.

HERVEY, MAURICE H. (1853–1940). *Amyas Egerton, Cavalier.* Illustrated by Joseph Ratcliffe Skelton (fl. 1888–1927). New York: Harper & Brothers, 1896. 354 pp.

Source: MTLAcc, entry #1563, volume donated by Clemens.

This historical romance follows the adventures of a defender of King Charles I as the English Civil War unfolds around him.

HERZL, THEODOR (1860–1904). *Der Judenstaat [The State of the Jews]* (published in 1896).

Mark Twain mentions Herzl's "clear insight" regarding a plan to gather Jews of the world together in an independent state in the region of Palestine ("Concerning the Jews" [1889]).

Carl Dolmetsch, *"Our Famous Guest": Mark Twain in Vienna* (Athens: University of Georgia Press, 1992), pp. 129–130.

———. *The New Ghetto [Das Neue Ghetto].* [Four-act drama, performed in Vienna in 1898.]

"I was going to translate a good drama ('The New Ghetto') . . . but shall not contract to do it, yet awhile" (SLC to Henry H. Rogers, Vienna, 22 March 1898, *MTHHR*, p. 334).

Dan Vogel, *Mark Twain's Jews* (Jersey City, New Jersey: KTAV Publishing House, 2006), Chapter 6.

HESSE-WARTEGG, ERNST VON (1854–1918). *Mississippi-Fahrten: Reisebilder aus dem amerikanischen Süden (1879–1880) [Mississippi Rides: Travel Pictures from the American South (1879–1880)].* Leipzig: C. Reissner, 1881. 354 pp.

Mark Twain quoted a translation of this German tourist's description of a yellow fever epidemic in Memphis in Chapter 29 of *Life on the Mississippi* (1883). Possibly Twain translated the passage himself. On 14 March 1891 Hesse-Wartegg wrote to Clemens to express his admiration and gratitude (*DearMT*, pp. 155–156).

Ganzel, "Twain, Travel Books," p. 42 n. 9; Horst H. Kruse, *Mark Twain and "Life on the Mississippi"* (Amherst: University of Massachusetts Press, 1981), pp. 155–156.

HEWLETT, MAURICE HENRY (1861–1923). *Fond Adventures: Tales of the Youth of the World.* Olive green boards. New York:

Harper & Brothers, 1905. 339 pp.

Inscription: signed on the front pastedown endpaper: "SL. Clemens/21—5th Ave./1905."

Marginalia: two words are underlined in the text.

Catalog: *C1951*, D57.

Location: Mark Twain Papers, Bancroft Library, University of California at Berkeley. Donated in 1974 by Professor Robert Falk of the University of California at Los Angeles. Professor Falk had purchased the volume at the *C1951* auction.

Copy examined: Clemens's copy.

Hewlett's *Fond Adventures* contained three romantic novellas and a short story, all of them set in the medieval period. Sometime in 1903 (probably in December) Clemens wrote to F. B. Caulfield, asking for Hewlett's winter address in Florence (ALS, ASSSCL).

———. *The Forest Lovers, A Romance* (novel, published in 1898).

R. Kent Rasmussen, in doing research for his *Mark Twain for Dog Lovers*, noticed that Clemens posed for a photograph in 1904 next to a St. Bernard that his daughter Jean had named Prosper le Gai. This was the name of a gallant young knight in Hewett's dreamlike medieval England (Rasmussen to Alan Gribben, email, 23 January 2016). Clemens usually kept track of what his daughters were reading, even as they grew into adulthood, so he very likely looked into this book.

———. *The Ruinous Face.* New York: Harper & Brothers, 1909.

Catalog: *C1951*, #D68, listed among the books signed by Clemens.

Hewlett's historical novel opens with the siege of Troy and focuses on the fate of Helen.

HEY, [JOHANN] WILHELM (1789–1854). *Fünfzig Fabeln für Kinder. In Bildern gezeichnet nach Otto Speckter [Fifty Fables for Children. Drawn in Pictures by Otto Speckter (1807–1871)].* Neue Ausgabe. Gotha: Friedrich Andreas Perthes, n.d. [1878]. 70 pp.

Inscriptions: inscribed by Clemens on the front free endpaper in black ink: "Susie Clemens/Christmas, 1878/ Fräulein Dahlweiner/ Munich, Bavaria." Clemens wrote "March 10" at the top of the rear free endpaper in pencil. The front pastedown endpaper bears the sticker of Schandri & Wahnschaffe, München."

Location: Mark Twain Library, Redding, Connecticut.

Copy examined: Susy Clemens's copy, unmarked. The binding is loose. The book has the red ink Mark Twain Library accession number "3963". Examined in 1970 and again in June 1982.

Hey's reputation was primarily based on his poems for children.

Hemminghaus, "Mark Twain's German Provenience" (1945), p. 472.

HEYSE, PAUL [JOHANN LUDWIG VON] (1830–1914). *Im Paradiese. Roman in Sieben Büchern [In Paradise. Novel in Seven Books].* Fourth edition. Blue boards with blue morocco spine. 3 vols. Berlin: Verlag von Wilhelm Herz, 1876.

Inscription: all three volumes are inscribed on the title pages by Olivia Clemens: "Saml. L. Clemens/Feb. 2nd 1879/Munich/Bavaria". The volumes were rebound (and the title pages cropped) after she inscribed them, thereby losing portions of the inscriptions. A sticker on the rear

pastedown endpaper of Volume II identifies the bookbinder as the Case, Lockwood & Brainard Company of Hartford, Connecticut.

Catalog: *Zeitlin 1951*, #21, $15.

Location: Mark Twain Papers, Bancroft Library, University of California at Berkeley. Gift of Jake Zeitlin.

Copy examined: Clemens's copy, unmarked. Each volume contains a *C1951* sale label.

———. *Kinder der Welt. Roman in Sechs Büchern [Children of the World. Novel in Six Books].* Fifth edition. 3 vols. Berlin: Berlag von Wilhelm Herz, 1875.

Inscriptions: all three volumes are inscribed by Olivia Clemens on their title pages: "Saml. L. Clemens/Feb. 2nd 1879/Munich". The books were rebound (with title pages cropped) after they were inscribed, thereby losing portions of the inscriptions.

Catalog: *Zeitlin 1951*, #22, $10, Volumes II and III only.

Provenance: Volume I became part of the Mark Twain collection of Frank C. Willson (1889–1960) of Melrose, Massachusetts. In 1962 his widow Margarete sold Volume I to the Humanities Research Center (now the Harry Ransom Center).

Locations: Harry Ransom Center, University of Texas at Austin (Volume I only). Volumes II and III are in the Mark Twain Papers, Bancroft Library, University of California at Berkeley, the gifts of Jake Zeitlin.

Copies examined: Clemens's copies, unmarked. Volumes II and III contain *C1951* sale labels.

———. *Novellen.* 3 vols. Berlin, n.d.

Inscription: Volume I signed "Jean L. Clemens."

Catalogs: *A1911*, "3 vols., 16mo, cloth, Berlin, n.d.," quotes the signature," lot 239, sold for $10 (purchased by the Mark Twain Company); resold at *C1951*, #118, listed among the books belonging to Jean and Clara Clemens.

HEYWOOD, JOHN (1497–1580). *Dialogue of Proverbs* (published in London in 1546).

The Mark Twain Project editors in the Bancroft Library at the University of California at Berkeley traced a phrase Clemens used in a letter of 13 April 1874 written to Jerome B. Stillson ("wrong sow by the ear") to the early dramatist and collector of proverbs John Heywood (*MTLet* 6: 107).

HÉZECQUES, COMTE DE FRANCE D' (CHARLES-ALEXANDRE-FRANÇOIS-FELIX D'HÉZECQUES) (1774–1835). *Recollections of a Page to the Court of Louis XVI.* Translated from the French by Charlotte M[ary] Yonge (1823–1901). London: Hurst and Blackett, 1873. 336 pp.

In July 1873 Clemens noted the title, translator, and publisher of this book (NB 12, *N&J* 1: 559). Hézecques says that he was admitted as a page to the French court at the age of twelve, and his recollections of the characters and intrigues in the Bourbon palaces include portraits of Madame DuBarry. Though faulted for minor inaccuracies (perhaps exacerbated by the translation from French), the authenticity of these memoirs has never been challenged. Twain's off-color *1601* (1880) would imagine the kinds of courtly conversations that might have taken place in Queen Elizabeth's England if they were candidly reported.

HICHENS, ROBERT SMYTHE (1864–1950). *Barbary Sheep; A Novel.* New York: Harper & Brothers, 1907. 253 pp.

Source: MTLAcc, entry #1564, volume donated by

Clemens.

A wealthy English couple travel to the Algerian desert—he to hunt, she (as it turns out) to have her marriage vows tested. A bloody murder ends the affair, and the couple is reunited. Hichens preferred exotic locations for his novels.

———. *The Call of the Blood*. New York: Harper & Brothers, 1906. 484 pp. [Edition conjectured.]

While this Hichens novel was running serially in *Harper's Bazar*, Clemens wrote to Mary Benjamin Rogers on 19 November 1906 to suggest another (unnamed) book: "It is virile and rugged and will make a pleasant change for you after the polished diction of The Call of the Blood" (*MTLM*, p. 89). See the Catalog entry for G. M. V. Long's *The Viper of Milan*, which was likely the work Clemens had in mind. Hichens's *The Call of the Blood* was not exactly tepid reading; set in Sicily, it featured the love of a married man for a Sicilian girl, his deep friendship with a Sicilian boy, and the man's violent death.

———. *The Folly of Eustace, and Other Stories*. First edition. 12mo, original flexible maroon cloth, gilt. New York: Appleton, 1896. 175 pp.

Inscription: Clemens first began to write "truly [yours]" on the pastedown endpaper, but then instead autographed the book ("Mark Twain") in black ink, which was a highly unusual way for him to designate a book for his own library but was his preference when bestowing a book as a gift. Below that he wrote the name of the recipient, "Miss I. V. Lyon."

Catalog: Swann Galleries (New York City), Sale 1148, 26 July [no year], "12mo, cloth, top edge gilt, New York, 1896, Mark Twain's copy, with his signature on the front pastedown endpaper; modern bookplate on flyleaf," item #415 (undated PH of catalog page in MTP).

Provenance: slip of paper laid in shows that the book was at one point purchased from William Kelleher Rare Books in Cliffside, New Jersey; a related pencil note on the endpaper is dated "12/12/52." The front free endpaper displays a subsequent bookplate of Roswell Henderson showing an image of Mark Twain that is dated July 1966. Isabel Lyon sold off some of her Mark Twain materials before she died in 1958 at the age of ninety-five, and this volume was likely among those she parted with.

Location: collection of Kevin Mac Donnell, Austin, Texas.

Copy examined: Isabel V. Lyon's copy presented by Clemens, viewed in July 2004.

The book contains three of Hichens's short stories: "The Folly of Eustace," "The Return of the Soul" (one of his better-known supernatural tales), and "The Collaborators."

———. *The Garden of Allah*. New York: F. A. Stokes Co., [cop. 1904]. 482 pp.

Source: MTLAcc, entry #2270, volume donated from Clemens's library by Clara Clemens Gabrilowitsch in 1910.

The Garden of Allah, among the best-selling novels of 1905, portrayed a troubled woman who embarks on a philosophical trek across the Sahara desert.

———. *A Spirit in Prison*. Illustrated by Cyrus Cuneo (1879–1916). New York: Harper & Brothers, 1908. 664 pp.

Source: MTLAcc, entry #2269, volume donated from Clemens's library by Clara Clemens Gabrilowitsch in 1910.

Love, death, youth, the Bay of Naples—Hichens's sets a romantic novel amid boats and islands in Italy.

HIGGINSON, MARGARET WALDO (1881–1910). *The Drum-Beat*. Cambridge, Massachusetts: Privately printed, 1904. 16 pp.

Higginson's "The Drum-Beat" appeared in *The Outlook* (New York), Saturday, 12 November 1904): 677–679. A dying young soldier is comforted by the sound of a drum as he regresses in his mind to his boyish fantasies of battle. In 1904 Clemens wrote to Margaret's famous father, Thomas Wentworth Higginson, to thank him for sending a specially printed copy of the short short story: "Oh, dear, the pathos of it! the beauty of it! and the winning simplicity. What a pathetic creature is a human being—even in the gayest day of his life; and when we consider his other days—but I must not go into that, for I am the pessimist of pessimists, and irreconcilable" (ALS, 2 pp., on mourning stationery, Occasional List #65 [June 1983], Ximenes Rare Books, New York, New York; I am grateful to Philip Kelley for calling this item to my attention). The next year (1905) Margaret Higginson would marry a surgeon, Dr. James Dellinger Barney (1878–1920).

HIGGINSON, THOMAS WENTWORTH [STORROW] (1823–1911). *Atlantic Essays*. First edition. Original terra cotta cloth, gilt. Boston: James R. Osgood, 1872. 341 pp.

Inscriptions: signed in ink on the front flyleaf, "S. L. Clemens. Hartford, 1876." In the same ink Clemens crossed out a bookplate of the Hartford Young Men's Institute Library that was dated 1872. There is an *A1911* sale label below the library bookplate.

Marginalia: Clemens made pencil marks on page 39 (about John Ruskin's overwriting), 81 (on the use of invented words), 85 (on neglected genius), and on 92 (on living nobly day by day). The marked pages occur in Higginson's essays on "Literature as an Art" and "A Letter to a Young Contributor." (The latter essay is the one that prompted Emily Dickinson to write to Higginson, which led to their meeting.)

Catalogs: *A1911*, "12mo, cloth, Bost. 1871, . . . a few passages marked," quotes the signature, lot 240, sold for $3; George D. Smith, New York City, "Catalogue of Books" (1911), quotes the signature, item #166, $7.50.

Location: collection of Kevin Mac Donnell, Austin, Texas. Acquired in 1975 for $100.

Copy examined: Clemens's copy, in July 2004.

Higginson was well-known in the literary circles of his day, primarily as an author though he also (belatedly) assisted in editing Emily Dickinson's poems. A dedicated abolitionist in his early years, he commanded the first African American military unit in the Civil War. His correspondence and the range of his contemporary acquaintances were extensive.

———. *Cheerful Yesterdays. Contemporaries*. 2 vols. Frontispiece portrait of the author. 12mo. Original blue and maroon cloth, gilt. Boston: Houghton, Mifflin, 1900. [These are the initial two (of seven) volumes of *The Writings of Thomas Wentworth Higginson*; their first edition had appeared in 1898.]

Inscriptions: both volumes signed in ink on the front flyleaf, "Thomas Wentworth Higginson." Isabel V. Lyon, Clemens's secretary, affixed her bookplate to the front pastedown endpapers of both *Cheerful Yesterdays* and *Contemporaries*, and inscribed the front pastedown endpaper of *Contemporaries*: "Dublin, N. H./August, 1905." (That was the summer Clemens rented the home of Henry Copley Greene on Mount Monadnock in Dublin, New Hampshire. Higginson was a neighbor.)

Marginalia: *Cheerful Yesterdays* only has two annotations by Clemens that total thirty-six words. However, sixty-nine pages, primarily in the first three chapters, are extensively marked in pencil and also with marginal ink marks. (In *Cheerful Yesterdays* Higginson mentioned how he was introduced to Twain's "Jumping Frog" story by Charles Darwin, who "said he always kept it by his bedside for midnight amusement.") Isabel V. Lyon recorded on 12 September 1905 at the bottom of one page concerning an anecdote told to Higginson by James Russell Lowell: "A rainy night in Dublin & Mr. Clemens read the above anecdote & said of it: 'One of those things that doesn't mean anything & yet you understand it perfectly.'" (quoted by Robert T. Slotta). On page 118 of *Cheerful Yesterdays*, where Higginson characterized the singing Hutchinson Family as "unconscious *poseurs*," Clemens noted: "Saw a Hutchinson (84 years old) on the train the other day (Aug. '05) with his new bride (aged 35). This old fool was posing all the time, & was an infuriating spectacle." The New Hampshire singing troupe known as the Hutchinson Family had been immensely popular in the mid-nineteenth century. They mainly performed patriotic and sentimental songs, but also sang spirituals and advocated the abolition of slavery. Eventually three of the brothers started their own Hutchinson Family groups with their children, taking up causes such as temperance, women's rights, and the post-war condition of African Americans. Almost certainly Clemens had spotted eighty-four-year-old John Hutchinson (1821–1908), a member of the original group, in that railroad car in August 1905. Hutchinson had married Mrs. Agnes P. (Barnes) Everest (1852–1934) on 24 August 1905 in Portsmouth, New Hampshire. This second wife (John's first wife had died in 1888) was in her early fifties, hardly the "35" that Clemens supposed.

Clemens annotated the volume titled *Contemporaries* much more extensively; twelve pages contain above a dozen notes amounting to a total of 218 words. Some annotations are in pencil, but most are in ink. Thirty-six other pages display Clemens's marginal markings or have underlinings in the text. Isabel V. Lyon made a few notes, mainly recalling people she had met through Clemens. The chapter on Ulysses S. Grant has several page corners folded down. Vertically on page 4 of *Contemporaries* Clemens wrote in ink: "At that very time the men who were to found the country's literature were either already in their cradles or in sight of them, so to speak: Cooper, Irving, Emerson (1803), Whittier (1806), Holmes (1809), Longfellow, Lowell, Hawthorne, Mrs. Stowe (1813), Bryant." (Clemens was answering a prediction in 1807 by the early American essayist, politician, and orator Fisher Ames [1758–1808], quoted by Higginson, that there would never be any such thing as a reputable "American" literature.) Regarding the discovery of anesthetics, Clemens argued that Dr. Charles T. Jackson "got the credit (& a statue in Boston) but Dr. Wells of Hartford was the real discoverer" (*Contemporaries*, page 12). Clemens

was correct about the ongoing disputes regarding the originators of surgical anesthesia; Dr. Charles Thomas Jackson (1805–1880) of Boston had developed ether as an anesthetic, and the Hartford dentist Dr. Horace Wells experimented with nitrous oxide in dental surgery. There were also several other claimants to this medical fame.

On page 74 of *Contemporaries*, where Higginson quotes a pronouncement that foreign admiration produces "a kind of contemporaneous posterity" for an American author, Clemens noted, "Macaulay said it, too, but not so well." Clemens wrote vertically about a grammar point in the margin of page 88: "By a discreet misuse of 'having' & 'being,' one can always hitch two unrelated subjects together in a sentence & give them a quite plausible air of unguiltiness." Clemens recalled in a note on page 183 of *Contemporaries*, "What a delightfully funny Toodles it was! Because drunken men were a familiar sight, then; but it is not so, now, & the bulk of the audience would contemplate poor Toodles's antics with cold resentment." In a chapter on Wendell Phillips that orator is quoted as asking, "Why do people go to lectures?," which (on page 267) prompts Clemens to recall that Petroleum V. Nasby "said to me one night in The Globe Theatre, 'Isn't it amazing that people will come & listen to you & me, when they could come *here*?'" Where Higginson observes how few people, such as the English reformers Thomas Clarkson (1760–1846) and William Wilberforce (1759–1833), are credited by posterity with the abolition of the slave-trade, Clemens agreed: "True. They are remembered, while Zachary Macaulay [1768–1838, father of Thomas Babington Macaulay], who did the real work & the hard work, for 40 years, is never mentioned" (*Contemporaries*, p. 279). Clemens admired Higginson's prose style, remarking of the chapter about Theodore Parker that it represented "Higginson at his very best. And good enough for anybody." Higginson's chapter on Sidney Lanier draws similar approbation: "Finely appreciative & sympathetic, this essay." Higginson alludes in *Contemporaries* to the way he "could at once command the ear . . . of any Englishman by dropping out the fact that I had dined with Mark Twain in his own house and that he had said grace at table."

Provenance: bookplate in both volumes of Isabel V. Lyons, Clemens's private secretary. Sold in 1963 by Seven Gables Bookshop, New York City. In 1986 the volumes belonged to Victor Jacobs of Dayton, Ohio (Jacobs to Alan Gribben, 15 October 1986, "with the bookplate of Isabel Lyon and with numerous comments by Mark Twain"). Jacobs died in 1996. Subsequently these volumes entered the collection of Nick Karanovich, Fort Wayne, Indiana.

Catalogs: Victor and Irene Murr Jacobs Collection, Sotheby's, New York City, 29 October 1996, quotes and reproduces a facsimile of marginalia, lot #293, 2 volumes, $3,737; "Mark Twain and Related Material," Robert T. Slotta, Hilliard, Ohio (November 1998), items #99 and 100, quotes and reproduces facsimiles of marginalia, priced at $3,250 and $6,500, respectively; *Sotheby's 2003*, #210, $7,500 each.

On two small sheets of manuscript tipped into a copy of John L. Motley's *Correspondence* and sold as lot 344 at the 1911 auction, Clemens commented: "Higginson's

Cheerful Yesterdays is one long record of disagreeable services which he had to perform to content his spirit. He was always doing the fine and beautiful and brave and disagreeable thing that others shrank from and were afraid of—and his was a happy life." Higginson had a summer home in the area where Clemens was staying in the summer of 1905, and he wrote Clemens a letter of welcome. "I early learned that you would be my neighbor in the summer & I rejoiced," replied Clemens, "recognizing in you & your family a large asset. I hope for frequent intercourse between the two households" (*MTB*, p. 1237). Along with Moncure D. Conway's *Autobiography* (1904), Higginson's *Cheerful Yesterdays* and *Contemporaries* should be viewed as important influences on Mark Twain's approach to his own *Autobiography*, which he would begin to dictate methodically in 1906.

———. "Emily Dickinson's Letters," *Atlantic Monthly* 68.4 (October 1891): 444–456.

In October 1891 Clemens copied Higginson's description of the Dickinson house in Amherst: "one of those large, square, brick mansions so familiar in our older New England towns, surrounded by trees and blossoming shrubs" (NB 31, TS pp. 8–9).

————— and WILLIAM MACDONALD (1863–1938). *History of the United States from 986 to 1905*. Illus. Original red cloth, gilt. New York: Harper & Brothers, 1905. 632 pp.

Inscription: the front pastedown endpaper is signed in black ink "S L. Clemens/21—5th Ave., 1905."

Marginalia: two penciled notes in Clemens's holograph on pages 548 ("13th") and 568 ("re/Secy/of/State/Fish."). (The American statesman Hamilton Fish [1808–1893] served as Secretary of State from 1869 until 1877.) Several hundred vertical lines, marginal dots (an uncharacteristic notation for Clemens, but apparently his), and underscorings. Clemens's penciled marginalia begin on page 160 and end on page 610, centering on slavery, the Civil War, Reconstruction politics, and statistical data. There are a total of 350 annotations of one type or another.

Catalog: *C1951*, D26, listed among books signed by Clemens.

Location: collection of Kevin Mac Donnell Austin, Texas. Purchased in 1976.

Copy examined: Clemens's copy, viewed in July 2004.

———. *Malbone: An Oldport Romance*. Boston: Fields, Osgood & Co., 1869. 244 pp.

Source: MTLAcc, entry #2271, volume donated from Clemens's library by Clara Clemens Gabrilowitsch in 1910.

———. *Travellers and Outlaws, Episodes in American History*. Boston: Lee and Shepard, 1889 [copyrighted in 1888]. 340 pp.

Clemens noted the title in Notebook 28 (*N&J* 3: 439) in December 1888. Higginson's book included accounts of slave insurrections, including the uprising instigated by Nat Turner in 1831. *Travellers and Outlaws* did not mention John Murrell, the Mississippi River outlaw.

———. *Young Folks' History of the United States*. Boston: Lee and Shepard; New York: C. T. Dillingham, 1875. 382 pp. Reprinted in 1876, 1877, and 1879.

On 13 December 1880 a member of Clemens's household purchased "1 Higginson U. S." for $1.20, according to a bill sent on 1 January 1881 by Brown & Gross, Hartford booksellers (MTP). On that same day Clemens wrote

to the publisher James R. Osgood to request copies of "Questions on Higginson's Young Folks History of the U. States" as well as "Topics to Accompany said History" (TS in MTP). *Questions on Higginson's Young Folks' History of the United States. For the Use of Teachers*. Boston: Rand, Avery & Co., 1875 (35 pp.) and *Topics for the Use of Teachers: To Accompany Higginson's Young Folks' History of the United States*. Boston: Lee and Shepard; New York: C. T. Dillingham, 1877 (21 pp.) must have been intended as learning aids for the Clemens girls.

HILDRETH, RICHARD (1807–1865). *The History of the United States of America*. Revised edition. 6 vols. New York: Harper & Brothers, 1877–1880.

Source: MTLAcc, entries #1288–#1293, complete set donated by Clemens (Vols. I, II, and III published in 1877; Vols. IV and V in 1879; Vol. VI in 1880).

———. *Archy Moore, the White Slave; or, Memoirs of a Fugitive* (novel, published in 1857).

Michael Orth—"*Pudd'nhead Wilson* Reconsidered, or the Octoroon in the Villa Viviani," *Mark Twain Journal* 14.4 (Summer 1969): 11–15—cited striking parallels between this "bitter romance" and Twain's *Pudd'nhead Wilson* (1894).

HILL, FREDERICK TREVOR (1866–1930). *The Accomplice*. New York: Harper & Brothers, 1905. 326 pp.

Source: MTLAcc, entry #2272, volume donated from Clemens's library by Clara Clemens Gabrilowitsch in 1910. In Hill's mystery novel a jury foreman unfolds the story of a murder trial. Isabel Lyon recorded on 6 July 1905: "Mr. Clemens took a novel to bed with him last night. It was 'The Accomplice' by Frederic Trevor Hill, and he didn't go to sleep until past 2 o'clock" (IVL Journal, TS p. 74, MTP).

———. *Decisive Battles of the Law; Narrative Studies of Eight Legal Contests Between the Years 1800 and 1886*. New York: Harper & Brothers, 1907. 268 pp.

Source: MTLAcc, entry #1803, volume donated by Clemens.

———. *The Story of a Street; A Narrative History of Wall Street*. New York: Harper & Brothers, 1908. Illus. 171 pp.

Source: MTLAcc, entry #1719, volume donated by Clemens.

HILL, GEORGE CANNING (1825–1898). *Gen. Israel Putnam. ("Old Put.") A Biography*. Spine broken. Boston: E. O. Libby and Co., 1858. 270 pp.

Location: Mark Twain Library, Redding, Connecticut.

Copy examined: this book had been added to the Clemens collection when I revisited in Redding in June 1982, but there would seem to be no justification for its inclusion among the volumes that were donated by Clemens and his daughter Clara Gabrilowitsch. The unmarked book has no Mark Twain Library stamps, no accession numbers, no inscription or markings, and no apparent connections with Clemens or his family. It had been checked out by library patrons between 1965 and 1970, according to the charge slip at the rear of the volume. I recommended that it be separated from the Clemens collection. General Putnam (1718–1790) was a local Redding hero, having wintered his American Revolutionary forces in the area during the bitter winter of 1778–79.

HILLERN, WILHELMINE (BIRCH) VON (1836–1916).

Geier-Wally: A Tale of the Tyrol. New York: D. Appleton and Co., 1876. 237 pp. [Originally published in German as *Die Geier-Wally; eine Geschichte aus den Tyroler Alpen*. 2 vols. (Berlin, 1875).]

In August 1893, at Krankenheil-Tölz, Clemens inscribed a copy of *The £1,000,000 Bank-Note*: "To Frau von Hillern—/from one who has read with/pleasure & profoundly admires/'Geier-Wally—Mark Twain. . . . (Now I've gone & left the/'Die' out! But I was/born careless [dümm/geboren].)/S L C.'" (*Sotheby's 2003*, #73).

_____. *Am Kreuz; ein Passionsroman aus Oberammergau [On the Cross; Passion novel from Oberammergau]*. Stuttgart: Union deutsche verlagsgesellschaft, 1890. 383 pp.

Source: MTLAcc, entry #377, volume donated by Clemens. Edgar Hemminghaus saw Clemens's copy of this religious romance in the Mark Twain Library at Redding in 1945 ("Mark Twain's German Provenience," p. 473), but it has since disappeared.

HINCHLIFF, THOMAS WOODBINE (1825–1882). *Summer Months Among the Alps; With the Ascent of Monte Rosa*. London: Longman, Brown, Green, Longmans & Roberts, 1857. 312 pp.

Marginalia: pages 18–32 removed; a penciled note by Clemens on the remaining illustration (a map) explains: "See one of my later books of travel for the missing pages./Paris, Apl/1879." Sixteen notes (totaling seventy-words) and numerous markings in pencil throughout; pages 130–135 are marked in brown ink. On page 60, concerning Frutizen, Clemens penciled: "Where we saw the German family." On page 87 he wrote: "Where we saw the girl fall over the precipice" (near the village of Täsch). Opposite page 90 at the top of an illustration of the Matterhorn he noted: "Copy this". At the top of page 128 he observed in pencil: "From the Rizi the lakes & country look like a highly colored 'raised' map."

Catalog: ListABP (1910), "Summer Months among the Alps, Hinchliff", no other information provided.

Provenance: Carrie Estelle Doheny Collection, St. John's Seminary, Camarillo, California. Donated by Mrs. Doheny in 1951 after its purchase from Zeitlin & Ver Brugge Booksellers for $45. Auctioned for $1,540 by Christie's in 1988 on behalf of St. John's Seminary.

Location: the ownership of the volume is currently unknown. The Roy J. Friedman Mark Twain Collection in the Library of Congress contains the holograph manuscript of Chapter 34 of *A Tramp Abroad*, donated by Frances R. Friedman on 15 June 1992. It contains "three printed leaves from T. W. Hinchliff's *Summer Months Among the Alps*, 1857, corrected in Twain's hand for use as quoted descriptions in the printed edition of *A Tramp Abroad*."

Copy examined: Clemens's copy, at St. John's Seminary in 1970. A note on the half-title page recorded the volume's purchase by Zeitlin & Ver Brugge Booksellers at the 1951 auction in Hollywood.

In September 1878 Clemens made references in Notebook 16 to pages 255–256 and 306 of Hinchliff's book (*N&J2*: 194). Chapter 34 of Mark Twain's *A Tramp Abroad* (1880) contains a lengthy extract from Hinchliff's account of his ascent of Monte Rosa. Twain pretends that this narrative is what discourages him from attempting a similar climb.

HINDLEY, CHARLES (1821–1893), ed. *The Old Book Collector's Miscellany; or, a Collection of Readable Reprints of Literary Rarities, Illustrative of the History, Literature, Manners, and Biography of the English Nation During the Sixteenth and Seventeenth Centuries*. Facsimile title pages and woodcuts. 3 vols. London, 1871–1873.

Catalog: *A1911*, "3 vols., 4to, partly uncut (binding poor), Lond. 1871–3, large paper copy, scarce," a sheet of Clemens's notes laid in, lot 241, sold for $5.

Hindley was a bookseller who turned to collecting and editing the popular literature of England, particularly street ballads.

_____, ed. *The Roxburghe Ballads. Collection of Ancient Songs and Ballads, Written on Various Subjects and Printed between the Year MDLX and MDCC*. Woodcuts. 2 vols. London: Reeves and Turner, 1873. [Publisher conjectured.]

Catalogs: *A1911*, "2 vols., 4to, half green morocco, gilt tops, uncut, Lond. 1873," with a sheet of notes by Clemens laid in, lot 413, sold for $5.50; George D. Smith, New York City, "Catalogue of Books" (1911), quotes the signature, item #348, $12.50.

HINGSTON, EDWARD P[ERON]. (c. 1823–1876). *The Genial Showman; Being Reminiscences of the Life of Artemus Ward and Pictures of a Showman's Career in the Western World*. [Published in 1870.]

The editorial team at the Mark Twain Project in Berkeley deduced that Mark Twain obtained information about Artemus Ward (Charles Farrar Browne) from an edition of this biography by Ward's manager (*MTLet* 4: 480 n. 5).

HINMAN, RUSSELL (1853–1912). *Eclectic Physical Geography*. Illus. New York: American Book Co., [1888]. 382 pp.

Hinman sent Jean Clemens a copy of his book on 18 September 1893. The next day Clemens explained to Olivia from New York City that he had met "Hinman the great authority on physical geography" and had told him that the Clemens family—"particularly Jean"—were all interested in geography. "That is how he comes to send her his book" (TS in MTP).

HISLOP, ALEXANDER (1807–1865), comp. *The Proverbs of Scotland; with Explanatory and Illustrative Notes, and a Glossary*. First American edition, from the Third Edinburgh Edition. New York: L. D. Robertson, [cop. 1870]. 367 pp. [Edition conjectured.]

On 14 July 1880 Estes & Lauriat of Boston billed Clemens for twenty-one books, including "1 Scot Proverbs"; he paid on 20 July 1880 (receipt in MTP).

Historical Records of New South Wales. Seven volumes in nine. Vol. I edited by A[lexander]. Britton (1842–1892); Vols. II–VII ed. by F[rank]. M[urcott]. Bladen (1858–1912). Illus. Sydney: Government Printing, 1892–1901.

At the top of page 112 (the first page of "The Seizure of the 'Cyprus'") in Clemens's copy of *The Selected Works of Marcus Clarke*, Clemens wrote: "Copy this, separately, but so mark it as to show that it follows immediately after the 'appendix' account of the trial of Capt. Dennott, from 'Historical Records of New South Wales.' SLC" (MTP).

The History of a Slave.

Clemens discovered this unidentified book in the London Library on 22 October 1896 (NB 39, TS p. 12). The most likely candidate seems to be Henry Hamilton Johnston's *The History of a Slave* (1889); see that Catalog entry.

The History of the Most Remarkable Tryals in Great Britain

and Ireland, in Capital Cases, viz. Heresy, Treason, Felony, Incest, Poisoning, Adultery, Rapes, Sodomy, Witchcraft, Pyracy, Murder, Robbery, Etc., Both by the Unusual Methods of Ordeal, Combat, and Attainder, and by the Ecclesiastical, Civil and Common Laws of These Realms. Faithfully Extracted from Records, and Other Authentick Authorities, as Well [as] Manuscript Printed. 2 vols. London: Printed for A. Bell, in Cornhill; J. Pemberton, in Fleet Street[;] and J. Brown, with Temple Bar, 1715–1716. [Publisher supplied.]

  Catalogs: *A1911,* "12mo, half old calf (cracked), Lond. 1715," Vol. I only, lot 146, sold for $6; George D. Smith, New York City, "Catalogue of Books" (1911), apparently Vol. I only, item #451. $15.

  Here is another work validating William Dean Howells's recollection of Clemens's fondness for "some out-of-the-way book" such as "a volume of great trials" (*My Mark Twain* [1910], p. 15).

HITCHCOCK, RIPLEY (1857–1918), ed. *Decisive Battles of America, by Albert Bushnell Hart [1854–1943], Thomas Wentworth Higginson [1823–1911], et al.* Illus. Blue cloth. New York: Harper & Brothers, 1909. 397 pp.

  Inscription: signed in black ink on the front pastedown endpaper, "SL. Clemens/1909."
  Provenance: Antenne-Dorrance Collection, Rice Lake, Wisconsin.
  Location: Mark Twain Archive, Gannett Tripp Learning Center, Elmira College, Elmira, New York.
  Copy examined: Clemens's copy, unmarked. Examined on 28 May 2015.

HOBBES, THOMAS (1588–1679). *Leviathan; or the Matter, Forme and Power of a Common Wealth Ecclesiastical and Civil* (published in 1651).

  Mark Twain quoted from this political philosophy treatise— "the sudden glory of laughter"—during a newspaper interview in 1895, though he attributed it to Joseph Addison. See Louis J. Budd, "Mark Twain Talks Mostly about Humor and Humorists," *Studies in American Humor* 1.1 (April 1974): 8, and Gary Scharnhorst, *Mark Twain: The Complete Interviews* (Tuscaloosa: University of Alabama Press, 2006), p. 205.

HODGSON, WILLIAM BALLANTYNE (1815–1880). *Errors in the Use of English.* New York: D. Appleton and Co., 1882. 246 pp. [Edition conjectured.]

  Catalog: ListABP (1910), "Errors in Use of English, Hodgson", no other information supplied.

HOEFFLER, ADOLF JOHANN (1825–1898). "Sketches on the Upper Mississippi, by the Author of 'Three Weeks in Cuba,'" *Harper's New Monthly Magazine* 7 (July 1853): 177–190.

  Franklin R. Rogers (*MTBP* [1960], pp. 91–93) deduced that the old panoramist's inflated descriptions in Chapter 59 of *Life on the Mississippi* (1883) partly derived from this anonymously published article. The "sad story" of Winona and the Maiden's Rock, for instance, appears in Hoeffler's essay, together with a pen-and-ink sketch of the site (p. 187). Hoeffler's "Three Weeks in Cuba" had appeared in *Harper's New Monthly Magazine* 6 (January 1853): 161–175. The German-born Hoeffler studied art at the Dusseldorf Academy. He arrived in New Orleans in 1848 and traveled upriver to St. Paul in 1849. Many of his sketches depicted scenes in Minnesota and Wisconsin. Thomas Ruys Smith—"'The Mississippi Was a Virgin

Field': Reconstructing the River Before Mark Twain, 1865–1875," *Mark Twain Journal* 53.2 (Fall 2015): 24–66—did not specifically mention Hoeffler's article, but demonstrated how Twain's magnificent memoir and travelogue followed in the wake of these colorful reports about navigating the Mississippi River.

HOFFMAN, CHARLES FENNO (1806–1884). "Sparkling and Bright" (poem, song, 1830). Melody by James B. Taylor.

  Mark Twain borrowed this title for a limerick he wrote in praise of cigars (NB 5 [1866], *N&J* 1: 157). See also the entry for F. M. Finch.

  Scott, *OPMT* (1966), p. 7 n. 27.

HOFFMAN, ELISHA A[LBRIGHT]. (1839–1929) and HAROLD F[ISKE]. SAYLES (1858–1924), comp. *Battle Hymns of the Church.* Chicago: Evangelical Publishing Co., n. d. 214 pp. [Contains 212 hymns, plus an index.]

  Inscription: "Ruth Reynolds" is written in pencil at the top of the front cover. The front free endpaper, which might have been signed, is missing. The title page is also missing.
  Location: Mark Twain Library, Redding, Connecticut.
  Copy examined: unmarked copy very likely belonging to Clemens. Has a black ink Mark Twain Library accession number, "2894". Albert E. Stone, Jr. included the title of this volume in his checklist of Clemens's books in the Mark Twain Library at Redding, Connecticut in 1955, but provided no additional information. I was unable to locate the volume when I visited Redding in 1970; however, I finally located it when I returned to Redding in June 1982. It was still in the collection on 9 November 2019.

HOFFMANN, HEINRICH (1809–1894). *Der Struwwelpeter* (published in 1847).

  In Berlin in October 1891 Mark Twain translated Hoffmann's verses for children into English, explaining in an introduction that "Struwwelpeter is the best known book in Germany, & has the largest sale known to the book trade, & the widest circulation" (MS in Yale University Library). In October 1893 Clemens mentioned to Clara Clemens that Fred J. Hall had told him the translation "is in the hands of these publishers of baby-books— just lying there—nothing being done about it" (TS in MTP). Clara recalled that her father "frequently . . . brought the old German nonsense rhymes called Struwelpeter [sic] to the lunch table and read them aloud with great emphasis" for his daughters' enjoyment (*MFMT*, p. 56). In 1906 Mark Twain said of *Struwwelpeter* that "crude as the pictures were, and unconventional and fearfully original as the poetry was, they were smart and witty and humorous, and to children they were limitlessly captivating" (22 November 1906 AD, *AutoMT* 2: 285). Twain's translation was finally published in 1935. Dixon Wecter, "Mark Twain as Translator from the German," *American Literature* 13.3 (November 1941): 257–263, commented on Twain's English version of Hoffmann's *Struwwelpeter*, published Twain's original preface of October 1891, and quoted examples of the verses, which increased in vigor and vivacity in Twain's translations.

  John T. Krumpelmann, *Mark Twain and the German Language* (Baton Rouge: Louisiana State University Press, 1953); Gisela M. Cloud, "Mark Twain's Translation of *Der Struwwelpeter* and *Die Schrecken der Deutschen Spreche*," Master's thesis, University of Georgia, 1966; Scott, *OPMT*

(1966), p. 27; J. D. Stahl, "Mark Twain's 'Slovenly Peter' in the Context of Twain and German Culture," *The Lion and the Unicorn* 20.2 (December 1996): 166–180; and Brandi Besalke, "'Ein sehr gluecklicher Kind, you bet': Mark Twain and the German Language," *Mark Twain Annual 5* (2007): 109–122.

HOFMANN, KARL (1836–1916). *A Practical Treatise on the Manufacture of Paper in All Its Branches.* Illus. Philadelphia: H. C. Baird; London: S. Low, Marston, Low & Searle, 1873. 422 pp.

Inscription: a rather shaky signature in black ink on the front free endpaper: "Mark Twain." Obviously forged. Book label of Robert Beall, Bookseller and Stationer, Washington, D.C.

Location: Harry Ransom Center, University of Texas at Austin. (Not part of the Frank C. Willson collection that was purchased in 1962 from his widow Margarete.)

Copy examined: a copy displaying a crude counterfeit signature of Clemens's pseudonym.

HOLCOMBE, RETURN IRA (1845–1916). *History of Marion County, Missouri: Written and Compiled from the Most Authentic Official and Private Sources. Including . . . Reminiscences, Grave, Tragic and Humorous.* St. Louis, Missouri: E. F. Perkins, 1884. 1003 pp.

Catalog: ListABP (1910), "Hist. of Marion Co., Missouri", no other information provided.

Location: Mark Twain Papers, Bancroft Library, University of California at Berkeley.

Copy examined: Clemens's copy, unsigned but containing a pencil mark on page 902. Holcombe wrote to Clemens on 29 August 1883 from Palmyra, Missouri, enclosing a prospectus for the volume and asking for Clemens's assistance in preparing a sketch of John Marshall Clemens (MTP). Clemens sent the letter to Orion Clemens, who contributed to the book.

HH&T (1969), pp. 152–153.

HOLDEN, EDWARD SINGLETON (1846–1914). *Real Things in Nature, A Reading Book of Science for American Boys and Girls.* New York: Macmillan Co., 1903. 443 pp.

Source: MTLAcc, entry #1952, volume donated from Clemens's library by Clara Clemens Gabrilowitsch in 1910. It could be relevant that in October 1904 Clemens inscribed a first edition copy of *Adventures of Huckleberry Finn* "with compliments" to a "Mr. Holden" and autographed it "Mark Twain" (note from Kevin Mac Donnell to Alan Gribben, 1985).

HOLDEN, JOHN WATKINS (1844–1917), known as "The Queen's Magician." *A Wizard's Wanderings from China to Peru.* Illus. London: Dean & Son, 1886. 170 pp.

Michael Claxton ("*A Connecticut Yankee* and Victorian Magic," *Philological Review* 30.1 [Spring 2004]: 12 n. 1) noted that Holden claims on page 117 of *A Wizard's Wanderings* that knowing the date of an eclipse from the almanac saved his life while he was traveling in Egypt, much as the Yankee is rescued by this knowledge in *A Connecticut Yankee in King Arthur's Court* (1889). There seems to be no record that Clemens owned a book of this title. See the Reader's Guide entry for Eclipses to find similar eclipse situations.

HOLDER, CHARLES FREDERICK (1851–1915). *Marvels of Animal Life.* Illus. New York: Charles Scribner's Sons, 1885.

240 pp.

Inscription: inscribed by Olivia Clemens in black ink on the front free endpaper: "Clara L. Clemens/Xmas 1888". A pencil note on the title page ("cover design by/Dan Beard.") was not written by Clemens; it refers to images of an octopus and a frog on the book cover.

Location: Mark Twain Library, Redding, Connecticut. Donated from Clemens's library by Clara Clemens Gabrilowitsch in 1910 (MTLAcc, entry #1951).

Copy examined: Clara Clemens's copy. Has the red ink Mark Twain Library accession number "1951" and the Library's purple oval stamps. Examined in 1970 and again in June 1982.

HOLDSWORTH, ANNIE E[LIZA]. (1860–1917), pseud. "Max Beresford." *Joanna Traill, Spinster.* New York: Charles L. Webster & Co., 1894. 208 pp.

Clemens's publishing firm brought out this work by the London journalist and novelist Holdsworth shortly before Webster & Company foundered. The feminist Holdsworth had previously used the pen name "Max Beresford," but she published *Joanna Traill, Spinster* under her own name. Its protagonist, endeavoring to alter her life in her thirties, meets a sad fate.

HOLLAND, JOSIAH GILBERT (1819–1881). *Bitter-Sweet: A Poem.* New York: C. Scribner, 1862. 220 pp.

Source: MTLAcc, entry #636, volume donated by Clemens.

————, pseud. "Timothy Titcomb." *Plain Talks on Familiar Subjects.* New York, 1866.

Inscription: the flyleaf is signed "S. L. Clemens".

Catalogs: *A1911*, "12mo, cloth, N.Y. 1866," quotes the signature, lot 244, sold for $1.50; George D. Smith, New York City, "Catalogue of Books" (1911), quotes the signature, item #169, $7.50; American Art Association (New York City), Sale catalogue (3–4 March 1925), from the collection of the late William F. Gable of Altoona, Pennsylvania, "first edition, New York, 1866, 12mo, cloth," has the *A911* sale label, lot 101, sold for $10 (with another book included).

Mark Twain informed James Redpath on 18 July 1872 that he planned to criticize "Timothy Titcomb" in a magazine piece (*MTLet* 5: 121). The essay, titled "An Appeal from One That Is Persecuted," was written but not published. Henry Nash Smith, *MTDW* (1962), p. 191 n. 5.20; and *MTLet* 5: 123–124 n. 5.

HOLLAND, WILLIAM JACOB (1848–1932). *The Butterfly Book: A Popular Guide to a Knowledge of the Butterflies of North America.* 48 plates. New York: Doubleday & McClure Co., 1900. 382 pp.

Provenance: has the shelfmarks of the library numbering system employed by Clara Clemens Gabrilowitsch during her Detroit years. Sold at the 1951 auction in Hollywood but not listed in the hastily prepared sale sheet.

Catalog: "Property from the Library of Mark Twain," Butterfield & Butterfield, San Francisco, Sale 6613 (16 July 1997), lot 2712.

Location: Mark Twain House and Museum, Hartford, Connecticut.

Copy examined: a copy most likely belonging to nature-lover Jean Clemens. Viewed in Hartford in 1997.

————. *The Butterfly Book: A Popular Guide to a Knowledge of the Butterflies of North America.* 48 plates. New York: Doubleday

& McClure Co., 1904.

> **Catalog:** Ball 2016 inventory, Nature Library, Vol. VI, in the Quarry Farm library under the supervision of the Mark Twain Archive, Elmira College, Elmira, New York.
> **Location:** current location undetermined.

———. *The Moth Book: A Popular Guide to a Knowledge of the Moths of North America.* Illus. New York: Doubleday, Page & Co. 1904. 479 pp.

> **Catalog:** Ball 2016 inventory, Nature Library, Vol. VII, in the Quarry Farm library under the supervision of the Mark Twain Archive, Elmira College, Elmira, New York.
> **Location:** current location undetermined.

HOLLEY, MARIETTA (1836–1926), pseud. "Josiah Allen's Wife." *Josiah Allen's Wife.* Hartford: American Publishing Company, 1877. 580 pp.

> In 1880 Mark Twain included "Josiah Allen's Wife" in his list of humorists to be considered for inclusion in a projected anthology (NB 19, *N&J* 2: 364). *Mark Twain's Library of Humor* (1888) contained "A Pleasure Exertion" from the *Josiah Allen's Wife* volume.

———. *Samantha at the St. Louis Exposition.* Illus. by Charles Grunwald. New York: G. W. Dillingham Co., 1904. 312 pp.

> **Inscription:** inscribed on the front free endpaper in black ink: "To amuse and cheer/This book was presented/to me by my dear daughter/Isadora L. Jones/Christmas 1904/ Laura [?] Lynt".
> **Copy examined:** an unmarked volume that did not belong to Clemens or his family. It has no library stamps or accession number. Someone added it to the Clemens collection, presumably on account of its early imprint, after 1970 and prior to June 1982, when I revisited Redding. I recommended to the staff that it be shelved elsewhere than with the books donated by Clemens and his daughter Clara Clemens Gabrilowitsch.

HOLLINGSHEAD, JOHN (1827–1904). *Under Bow Bells; A City Book for All Readers.* London: Groombridge and Sons, 1860. 312 pp.

> **Source:** MTLAcc, entry #155, volume donated by Clemens. Twenty-five stories and sketches of London.

HOLMES, MARY JANE (HAWES) (1825–1907). *The Homestead on the Hillside.* New York: Hurst & Co., 1900. 273 pp.

> **Source:** MTLAcc, entry #2273, volume donated from Clemens's library by Clara Clemens Gabrilowitsch in 1910. Three short stories and one longer story, set in New England, depict individuals confronting death.

HOLMES, OLIVER WENDELL (1809–1894). *The Autocrat of the Breakfast-Table.* Plates by Augustus Hoppin (1828–1896). 8vo, original brown cloth, gilt, binding worn and shaken, some signatures loose, brown half morocco slipcase. Boston: Phillips, Sampson & Company, 1858. 364 pp.

> **Inscription:** the first two flyleaves are missing. These no doubt held endearing inscriptions.
> **Marginalia:** Bradford A. Booth transcribed the penciled marginalia in the copy Clemens marked for Olivia Langdon's amusement in 1869 ("Mark Twain's Comments on Holmes's *Autocrat*," *American Literature* 21.4 [January 1950]: 456–463). This was the couple's famous "courting book." Clemens apparently read the book first, then gave it to Olivia. Booth concluded that "the game was unpremeditated," since the early chapters in the first hundred pages contain only scanty annotation. According

to the catalog descriptions by Christie's and Rulon-Miller Books (see below), there are sixty-three separate notes by Clemens consisting of 534 words written on fifty-seven pages. In addition there are penciled underlinings, cross-outs, and other markings on another forty-eight pages. Next to Holmes's caution about private thoughts, Clemens recalls, "I ought not to have said what I did in Wendell Phillips's presence a few days ago, & which produced a blush which touches me yet with distress." (Wendell Phillips, 1811–1884, was a prominent American reformer.) Where Holmes contrasts the lecture audiences in New York and Ohio on page 161, Clemens objects (in a vertical marginal note): "Not true—New York State audiences are much duller and stupider than any other—Ohio audiences are keen, shrewd, & full of life." Next to Holmes's admission that he picks out the best and brightest women's faces toward the front of the audiences and lectures mainly to them, Clemens wrote, "I always do *that*." (page 162). On page 186 Clemens identified a poetic allusion to "the tough old Dean" as referring to "(Swift.)" There is an evocative note by Clemens written vertically in the margin of page 246: "Listening to *any* sound of innocent honest toil when one's abed in the morning is lulling, soothing, pleasant." On page 251 Clemens made another vertical note: "Midnight—March 25, 1869—I wish 'Even Me' to be sung at my funeral."

Next to a passage (p. 258) about falling in love with a woman, Clemens writes: "We fall in love with her when we discover that she is the best & loveliest girl in the world, & maybe we discover that at first—I know instances of it. And the discovery was correct, too: And the name of the same was—Livy." He teasingly jotted a vertical note on page 262: "Conundrum—What is that which a cat has, but no other animal? *Answer*—Kittens." He made a comment about Greek philosophy on page 302, written vertically: "Did you ever read a single paragraph of Aristotle, Livy?—I never did." He playfully alluded to Shakespeare on page 354: "We that have free souls, it touches us not—Hamlet." Clemens praises various poems in the book, writing above "The Deacon's Masterpiece": "This is all good." Holmes's "The Voiceless" poem Clemens declared to be "Incomparable." (page 355). On page 364, below the last sentence of Holmes's text ("I hope you all love me none the less for anything I have told you. Farewell!"), Clemens declared: "Livy—Livy—/ Livy—Livy, je vous aime./—m'aimez-vous?" (quoted in Rulon-Miller Books, List 23).

> **Provenance:** contains the bookstamps of the Mark Twain Library at Redding. Presumably Clara Clemens retrieved the volume from that collection and then later sold it in Hollywood, California. Carrie Estelle Doheny purchased the book from Maxwell Hunley Rare Books of Beverly Hills for $12.20 in 1940. Mrs. Doheny donated the volume to the Carrie Estelle Doheny Collection, St. John's Seminary, Camarillo, California in 1940. Christie's auctioned it in 1988 on behalf of St. John's Seminary and the Archdiocese of Los Angeles.
> **Catalogs:** Christie's, New York City, 1–2 February 1988, lot 458, sold for $5,500 to Rulon-Miller Books, Minneapolis, Minnesota; Rulon-Miller Books, Minneapolis, Minnesota, List 23 (Spring 1988), item #21, "Mark Twain's

'Courting Book'—extensively annotated," $15,000. Listed again in Rulon-Miller Books, Catalog 88, item #64, $15,000 (catalog entries sent to Alan Gribben by Thomas A. Tenney, 15 November 1988).

Location: currently unknown.

Copy examined: Clemens's copy, at St. John's Seminary in 1970.

This is truly a landmark artifact. It was most likely the book that established Clemens's habit of annotating the margins of his readings with witticisms and editorial revisions. Around 1869 Olivia Langdon filled four and a half pages of her commonplace book with prose quotations from *The Autocrat of the Breakfast-Table* (DV161, MS pp. 90–94, MTP). Clemens reported to Olivia Langdon on 8 March 1869 from Hartford, "I went to bed, then, & read the Testament now & then, & now & then the Autocrat of the Breakfast Table, till 3 in the morning" (*MTLet*: 3: 149). Writing from Hartford to Olivia Langdon on 13 May 1869, Clemens joked: "Now, you just cipher out those puns in the Autocrat yourself, Miss" (*MTLet* 3: 223). On 30 September 1869 Clemens wrote to Holmes from Buffalo, stating that he had read *The Autocrat* "two or three times already, when a superior young lady" asked him "to *mark* it & marginal-note it all the way through for her . . . & I did." Clemens added that he then read the book again for his own enjoyment and marked it once more "without a suggestion from anybody" (Library of Congress; *MTLet*: 3: 365). Mary Mason Fairbanks mentioned in a letter to Olivia Clemens of 1 April 1872 that she had been reading to her husband from Holmes's *Poet at the Breakfast Table* (1872), and she urged Clemens to write "one book of *polite literature*" along that line (*MTLet* 5: 75). In a published letter to the Hartford *Evening Post* (6 December 1872), Mark Twain ranked Holmes with Longfellow and Bryant as truly major American poets (*MTPP*, p. 47).

Laura Hawkins requests a copy of *The Autocrat of the Breakfast-Table* while shopping in a bookstore in Chapter 36 of *The Gilded Age* (1873), but the uneducated clerk replies that his shop does not sell cookbooks. Twain sent Holmes a complimentary copy of *Sketches, New and Old* in November 1875 and received a gracious reply complimenting its "humour and its cheerful good-nature and its pictures of life" (*MTLet* 6: 580). In 1879 Clemens punned on Holmes's famous line from Chapter six—"Good Americans, when they die, go to Paris"— in Notebook 18 (*N&J* 2: 320): "Trivial Americans go to Paris when they die." (Holmes had quoted Thomas Gold Appleton, 1812–1884, a Boston writer and art patron.) In the same notebook Clemens observed: "Nobody writes a finer & purer English than [John Lothrop] Motley[,] Howells, Hawthorne & Holmes" (p. 348). On 25 January 1894 Clemens wrote to Olivia from Boston about his having told Holmes how "you & I used the Autocrat as a courting book & marked it all through, & that you keep it in the sacred green box with the love letters" (MTP).

Sherwood Cummings, "*What is Man?*: The Scientific Sources" (1964), pp. 110–111.

———. "The Chambered Nautilus" (poem).

Mark Twain quoted this poem at the Whittier Birthday dinner on 17 December 1877 in his controversial burlesque

of highbrow American poets.

MTB (1912), p. 1644; Smith, "'That Hideous Mistake'" (1955); Bruce Michelson, *Mark Twain on the Loose: A Comic Writer and the American Self* (Amherst: University of Massachusetts Press, 1995), pp. 18–25; Richard S. Lowry, *"Littery Man": Mark Twain and Modern Authorship* (New York: Oxford University Press, 1996), pp. 24–33.

———. "The Deacon's Masterpiece" (poem).

Clemens wrote in pencil above this poem in Chapter 11 of his copy of *The Autocrat of the Breakfast-Table* (p. 295): "This is *all* good" (quoted by Booth, "Mark Twain's Comments" [1950], p. 462). "The Deacon's Masterpiece" was one of the pieces Mark Twain included in his *Library of Humor* (1888). In 1899 Twain referred to "the principle of the 'one-hoss shay'" in a manuscript sketch of the Kellgren treatment (DV13, MTP).

———. *Elsie Venner: A Romance of Destiny* (novel, published in 1861).

Clemens informed Holmes on 30 September 1869 that the young lady [Olivia Langdon] for whom Clemens had recently annotated a copy of *The Autocrat of the Breakfast-Table* would shortly receive from him a similarly marked copy of *Elsie Venner* (*MTLet* 3: 365). This book has not been located.

———. "A Good Time Going!" (poem, published in 1858).

Clemens underscored the three concluding lines in the second stanza, noting "This figure is good." Stanza five he also declared to be "good" in his 1869 marginalia in *The Autocrat of the Breakfast-Table*, reproduced in Bradford A. Booth's "Mark Twain's Comments" (1950), p. 462. Holmes's poem commemorated the departure from the United States of Charles Mackay (1814–1889), a noted Scottish author, editor, and song writer. (One of Mackay's most popular songs was titled "There's a good time coming.")

———. "Grandmother's Story of Bunker Hill Battle" (poem, published in 1875).

In a letter to William Dean Howells of 5 July 1875 Clemens denounced the publication of this centennial poem in the New York *Tribune* without the permission of Holmes's publisher James R. Osgood (*MTHL*, p. 92; *MTLet* 6: 504).

———. *The Guardian Angel* (novel, published in 1867).

Clemens mentioned the title of Holmes's novel about mental health and memory suppression in January 1888 (NB 27, TS p. 48).

———. *The Last Leaf. Poem.* Illustrated by George Wharton Edwards (1859–1950) and F. Hopkinson Smith (1838–1915). First edition thus. Small folio. Original quarter white cloth, gray pictorial cloth sides, gilt, top edge gilt, inserted plates on India paper. Cambridge: Riverside Press, 1886. [Contained a new preface by Holmes relating the story of the poem.]

Inscription: the front pastedown endpaper is signed in ink, "S. L. Clemens".

Catalogs: *A1911*, "folio, decorative boards and vellum, gilt tops, uncut, Cambridge: Riverside Press, 1886," quotes the signature, lot 245, $4; University Archives, Stamford, Connecticut, Catalog 102 (June 1992), item #102, has the *A1911* sale label, priced at $1,500.

Provenance: later signatures of "Oliver M. Zendt" and "J. R. Clemens, 1980" (the latter owner was possibly James

Ross Clemens, the father of Cyril Clemens).

Location: collection of Kevin Mac Donnell, Austin, Texas.

Copy examined: Clemens's unmarked copy, in July 2004. "The Last Leaf" might qualify as Clemens's favorite lyric poem. The lines he quoted in his 30 April 1867 letter from New York City to the San Francisco *Alta California* echoed through his writings thereafter: "The mossy marbles rest/ On the lips that he had pressed/In their bloom;/And the names he loved to hear,/Have been carved for many a year/On the tomb" (*MTTMB*, pp. 164–165). Into Olivia Langdon's commonplace book Clemens himself copied these same lines sometime between 1868 and 1870 (DVI61, MTP). Clemens remarked of his boyhood friend Pet McMurray, whom he saw for the first time in many years in 1885: "Well, see O W Holmes' 'The Last Leaf' for what he is now" (SLC to OLC, 23 January 1885, *LLMT*, p. 233). At an Authors' Reading in 1888 Mark Twain heard Holmes recite "The Last Leaf" so poignantly that the house delivered a standing ovation (26 February 1906 AD, *AutoMT* 1: 384). Clemens returned from Hannibal and St. Louis, Missouri in 1902 with a sense of how rapidly death was winnowing his early friends; amid notes he made then for reassembling Tom Sawyer's gang fifty years after their youth, he twice copied passages he recalled from "The Last Leaf" (NB 45 [May-June 1902], TS pp. 14, 18). In a tribute to his friend's writings, an essay titled "William Dean Howells" (1906), Twain quoted these lines as an example of "the quality of certain scraps of verse which take hold of us and stay in our memories, we do not understand why." Albert Bigelow Paine remembered Clemens's quoting these lines in December 1909; they "put in compact form the thing which we have all vaguely felt," Clemens told Paine (*MTB*, pp. 1555–56).

———. "Mare Rubrum" (poem, published in 1858).

Mark Twain employed lines from this poem in his unfortunate Whittier Birthday Dinner speech in 1877 (*MTB*, p. 1645).

Smith, "'That Hideous Mistake'" (1955).

———. "Ode for a Social Meeting, with Slight Alterations by a Tee-totaler" (poem, published in 1857).

Mark Twain alludes to this piece in Notebook 22 (1884, *N&J* 3: 46). In Holmes's comical poem a teetotaler revises all words favorable to alcohol in a poetic address.

———. *Poems of Oliver Wendell Holmes*. New Revised Edition. Illus. Engraved frontispiece portrait. Thick octavo. Thick 8vo. Original three-quarter tan calf over marbled boards, gilt. Extremities worn. Red morocco folding-case. Boston: Houghton, Mifflin and Co., 1881. 324 pp.

Inscription: the first flyleaf is inscribed by Clemens in blue-black ink: "Livy L. Clemens/from S.L.C./December, 1885".

Catalogs: ListABP (1910), "Poems, Holmes"; *C1951*, #21c, $17.50; Catalogue 174 (1989), Heritage Book Shop, Los Angeles, California, "thick 8vo, contemporary half calf, . . . marbled boards," some wear, "inscribed by Twain in blue ink on a preliminary blank," has the bookplate of Estelle Doheny, item #203, priced at $6,000; "Holiday Miscellany," Heritage Book Shop, Los Angeles, California, Catalog 176, (1989), item #233, "inscribed by Mark Twain to his wife," priced at $6,000; *Sotheby's 2003*, #213, $4,250.

Provenance: Carrie Estelle Doheny Collection, St. John's

Seminary, Camarillo, California. Donated by Mrs. Doheny in 1951 after she purchased the volume from Maxwell Hunley Rare Books of Beverly Hills for $32. Auctioned by Christie's in New York City on 17 October 1988 (lot 1179) for $1,980 on behalf of St. John's Seminary. Subsequently it was in the collection of Nick Karanovich of Fort Wayne, Indiana.

Location: collection of Kevin Mac Donnell, Austin, Texas

Copy examined: Olivia Clemens's unmarked copy, in July 2004. The front pastedown endpaper displays the bookplate of "Estelle Doheny."

———. *The Professor at the Breakfast-Table*. 2 vols. Cambridge, Massachusetts: Houghton Mifflin and Co., 1890.

Catalog: Ball 2016 inventory, 2 vols., green cloth, gilt lettering, gilt top edges, good condition, cloth bookmark attached.

Location: Quarry Farm library shelves, under the supervision of the Mark Twain Archive, Elmira College, Elmira, New York.

One of the works available to Clemens whenever he visited Quarry Farm in Elmira.

———. *Selections from the Writings of Oliver Wendell Holmes, Arranged Under the Days of the Year*. New York: Houghton, Mifflin & Co., 1889.

Source: MTLAcc, entry #2126, volume donated from Clemens's library by Clara Clemens Gabrilowitsch in 1910.

———. *Songs in Many Keys*. Boston: Ticknor and Fields, 1862. [Edition is conjectured.]

Songs in Many Keys gathers poems that Holmes wrote between 1849 and 1861; it did not include "The Last Leaf," but it contained other pieces that Clemens enjoyed—"The Deacon's Masterpiece," "Mare Rubrum," and "The Chambered Nautilus." Ticknor and Fields bound this edition in blue morocco leather embossed with gold lettering. In June 1866, bed-ridden in Honolulu, Clemens passed time by reading the only book in his hotel—"the first volume of Doctor Holmes's blue-and-gold series. . . . I read the book to rags, and was infinitely grateful to the hand that wrote it" (April 1904 AD, *AutoMT* 1: 225). Clemens felt that this prolonged perusal of Holmes's book resulted in accidental plagiarism; the dedication to *The Innocents Abroad* (1869), he was convinced, was virtually identical to Holmes's dedication in *Songs in Many Keys*. There was indeed a general resemblance in sentiment and language. Holmes inscribed his work "To/The Most Indulgent of Readers,/The Kindest of Critics,/My Beloved Mother,/All That Is Least Unworthy of Her/in This Volume/Is Dedicated/By Her Affectionate Son." Mark Twain's book is prefaced by a tribute "To/My Most Patient Reader/and/Most Charitable Critic,/My Aged Mother,/This Volume Is Affectionately/Inscribed." Twain used this similarity as an example of "unconscious plagiarism" in a speech at the *Atlantic Monthly* breakfast for Holmes on 3 December 1879, when he related the circumstances in the Honolulu hotel where he "read and reread Doctor Holmes's poems till my mental reservoir was filled up with them to the brim" (*MTSpk*, p. 135). See also *MTB*, p. 288 and *MTL*, p. 732.

———. *Soundings from the Atlantic*. Boston: Ticknor, 1884. 468 pp. [First published in 1864.]

A short story from this volume, "A Visit to the Asylum for Aged and Decayed Punsters," appeared in *Mark Twain's*

Library of Humor (1888). Mark Twain had included Holmes's name in several lists of humorists he compiled in preparation for editing the anthology (NB 19 [1880], *N&J* 2: 363; [1881], p. 429).

———. "Two Armies" (poem, published in 1858).

Clemens recorded his admiration for this poem in 1869 in his copy of *The Autocrat of the Breakfast-Table*: several lines in "Two Armies" (p. 260) are labeled as "fine," and the last stanza is marked "very fine" (Booth, "Mark Twain's Comments" [1950], p. 462). The medical poem concerns physicians' battle against death.

K. Patrick Ober, *Mark Twain and Medicine: "Any Mummery Will Cure"* (Columbia: University of Missouri Press, 2003) examined some of Holmes's medical views on pages 190, 191, 196, 197, 232, and 321.

———. "The Voiceless" (poem, published in 1858).

Clemens's annotation in his copy of *The Autocrat of the Breakfast-Table* in 1869 declared that "The Voiceless" is "incomparable" (Booth, "Mark Twain's Comments" [1950], p. 461). The poem describes the calamity of genuine grief.

HOLWELL, JOHN ZEPHANIAH (1711–1798). *A Genuine Narrative of the Deplorable Deaths of the English Gentlemen, and Others, Who Were Suffocated in the Black Hole in Fort William, at Calcutta, in the Kingdom of Bengal, in the Night Succeeding the 20th Day of June, 1756, in a Letter to a Friend.* London: A Miller, 1758. 56 pp. [Publisher supplied.]

Mark Twain wrote that "Mr. Holwell's long account of the awful episode was familiar to the world a hundred years ago, but one seldom sees in print even an extract from it in our day. . . . From the middle of Mr. Holwell's narrative I will make a brief excerpt" (Ch. 54, *FE* [1897]). Many defenders of Fort William died of suffocation after they surrendered. Robert Clive became famous for retaking Calcutta with a British force in 1757. (It is now believed that Holwell inflated the number of deaths.)

Mutalik, *Mark Twain in India* (1978), p. 114.

HOME, DANIEL DUNGLAS (1833–1886). *Incidents in My Life.* New York, 1863.

Catalog: *A1911*, "12mo, cloth, N.Y. 1863," a small sheet of notes by Clemens laid in, lot 246, sold for $1.25.

Home was a Scottish spiritualist medium who came to the United States as a boy in 1842 and moved to England in 1855.

Home-Maker: An Illustrated Monthly Magazine (published 1888–1890).

In January 1889 Clemens noted, "Magazine edited by Marion Harland [the pseudonym of Mary Virginia (Hawes) Terhune, 1830–1922], contains something by Annie Trumbull" (NB 28, *N&J* 3: 440). See the Catalog entry for Annie Eliot Trumbull's "Mary A. Twining," in *Home-Maker: An Illustrated Monthly Magazine* 1.3 (December 1888): 168–175. Perhaps Clemens noticed an article in the same issue, "A Boy's Library" by [Catherine Pickens] Kate Upson Clark (1851–1935), suggesting that "Mark Twain's delightful *The Prince and the Pauper*" should have a place in young men's libraries (p. 221).

HOMER (c. 9th-c. 8th century BCE). *The Iliad of Homer.* Translated from the Greek by Alexander Pope (1688–1744). 2 vols. 32mo, original sheep, worn, binding loose in Volume

II. New York: W. Borradaile, 1825.

Inscription: the front flyleaf of Volume II is inscribed in pencil, "Olivia Langdon/Salina/June 6, 1833." [This was Olivia Clemens's mother, Olivia Lewis Langdon (1810–1890), who married Jervis Langdon on 23 July 1832. Salina, New York was a town on the Erie Canal in Onondaga County.]

Provenance: MTLAcc, entry #2079, Volume I only (284 pp.) donated from Clemens's library by Clara Clemens Gabrilowitsch in 1910. Robert H. Hirst, Editor of the Mark Twain Project in the Bancroft Library at the University of California at Berkeley, indicated (Hirst to Alan Gribben, 4 February 1981) that Olivia Lada-Mocarski owned Volume II of this book in 1980.

Catalogs: *A1911*, "Vol. II, 32mo, sheep (cracked), N.Y. 1825," quotes signature, a sheet of notes by Clemens laid in, lot 247, Volume II only sold for $1.75 to the Mark Twain Company; *Sotheby's 2003*, #192, Volume II only, $1,100 (sold with three other Clemens family library books); Robert Slotta, Admirable Books, Hilliard, Ohio, 2006 catalog, item #1, Volume II only, 274 pages (several corners folded over, contains the *A1911* sale label), $1,250. Both volumes of this work would have been available to Clemens in the Langdons' home in Elmira, New York.

———. *The Iliad of Homer.* Translated from the Greek by Alexander Pope (1688–1744). 2 vols. New York: A. S. Barnes & Co., 1858.

Source: MTLAcc, entry #2078, Volume I only (274 pp.) donated from Clemens's library by Clara Clemens Gabrilowitsch in 1910.

See also the Catalog entry for Alexander Pope.

———. *The Iliad of Homer.* Translated into English Blank Verse by William Cullen Bryant [1794–1878]. 2 vols. Boston: Houghton, Mifflin and Co., n.d. [cop. 1870].

Inscription: the front flyleaves of both volumes are inscribed in black ink by Olivia Clemens: "Susy Clemens/Hartford/March 19th 1884/Mamma".

Catalog: *Hunley 1958*, #23, $7.50.

Provenance: sold to the University of Texas in 1962 by Margarete Willson, the widow of Mark Twain collector Frank C. Willson (1889–1960) of Melrose, Massachusetts.

Location: Harry Ransom Center, University of Texas at Austin.

Copy examined: Susy Clemens's copy, unmarked.

Homer, Mark Twain advised those who would be literary "connoisseurs" in 1865, is accountable for "all the heroic poetry, about the impossible deeds done before Troy" (*Californian*, 17 June 1865, *LAMT*, p. 142; *ET&S* 2: 195). In 1867 Clemens was impressed at seeing "the harbor whence Agamemnon's fleet sailed to the siege of Troy" (NB 9, *N&J* 1: 392), as well as the site of ancient Troy itself. In "Political Economy" (1870) Twain referred to "imperial Homer, in the ninth book of the Iliad," quoting Latin verse. To Olivia Clemens on 2 February 1873 Clemens compared an unqualified book reviewer to hiring "Josh Billings to write a critique on the Iliad" (*MTLet* 5: 293). "Aeneas" is P. Dusenheimer's nickname in *The Gilded Age* (1873), because his hotel is located in Ilium, Pennsylvania. The second book of Homer's *Iliad* is mentioned facetiously in "Some Thoughts on the Science of Onanism" (DV200, no. 3, MTP; Fatout, *MTSpk*, p.

125). Clemens wrote to Karl and Hattie Gerhardt on 31 July 1881 to help them find a copy of the *Iliad* in Paris; if Galignani's did not have one, he advised, they should write to Chatto & Windus in London (ALS, Boston Public Library). In a letter written to Andrew Lang around 1890 Mark Twain objected to the common notion that Homer is more valuable to a civilization than "the little everybody's-poet whose rhymes are in all mouths to-day and will be in nobody's mouth next generation" (*MTL*, p. 526). Twain's "A Cure for the Blues" (1893) jokingly predicts that readers will want to keep Samuel Watson Royston's ludicrous novelette "with his Shakspere and his Homer." The same facetious review seriously acknowledges that "There is but one Homer," and mentions Homer's Achilles twice with veneration: "the Achilles of the Florida campaigns" and "See how Achilles woos."

―――. *The Iliad of Homer, Rendered into English Blank Verse. To Which Are Appended Translations of Poems Ancient and Modern.* Translated from the Greek by Edward George Geoffrey Smith Stanley (1799–1869), 14th Earl of Derby. 2 vols. London: John Murray, 1894.

Source: MTLAcc, entry #2053, Volume I only (339 pp.) donated from Clemens's library by Clara Clemens Gabrilowitsch in 1910.

―――. *The Odyssey of Homer. Translated into English Blank Verse by William Cullen Bryant [1794–1878].* 2 vols. Boston: Houghton, Mifflin and Co., 1871–1872. [Edition conjectured.]

Catalog: *C1951*, O9, "Homer's Odyssey," listed as containing Olivia Clemens's signature. Early in 1887 Clemens made a memorandum in Notebook 26: "Get Bryant's Homer (no—only Odyssey)" (*N&J* 3: 272). Presumably this purchase was to be gift to Susy Clemens. One wonders if perhaps the auction agent misread the inscription in compiling the unreliable list for the 1951 Hollywood sale; quite possibly the volumes listed and sold in 1951 actually belonged to Clemens's daughter rather than his wife. Clemens had previously (in 1875) urged Howells to "build an article upon A Boy's Comments Upon Homer" (*MTHL*, p. 105). In September 1880 he copied into Notebook 19 John Sheffield's famous praise—"Read Homer once . . . and Homer will be all the books you need" (*N&J* 2: 371). The Mark Twain Papers contain a fragmentary twenty-five-page (AMS) burlesque review of *The Odyssey* (dated 1883) in which Twain satirizes journalistic "book notices" (Paine 8). The review begins by faulting Homer's decision to write in verse, criticizes his concentration upon "a vanished race," and complains about a surplus of details. Homer obviously exaggerates the facts. Moreover, he ruins his narrative by filching names such as Ithaca and Troy from a New York state map. Twain follows Ulysses into the cave of Polyphemus, but the review breaks off during a discussion of Greek gods. A California gold mine in Twain's "Which Was the Dream?" (written 1897) is named the "Golden Fleece" (*WWD?*, pp. 55, 61). An artist who painted Clemens's portrait in London, probably around 1900, recalled that Clemens entertained him by telling a slightly off-color joke about a lonely scholar who devoted himself solely to the study of Homer (Edwin A. Ward, *Recollections of a Savage* [New York: Frederick A. Stokes Co., 1923],

pp. 248–249). Clemens related the same joke about the scholar in England who wished to be buried with "a small Homer" in each hand "& another one under his Arse" in an undated letter to Joseph H. Twichell (*LMTJHT* [2017], p. 417). Homer is mentioned favorably in "Sold to Satan" (written 1904), "From an English Notebook" (*LE*, p. 172), and a letter from Clemens to Colonel W. D. Mann, 3 January 1906 (MTP). Twain also refers to Homer in Part 6 of "What Is Man?" (1906). In *Extract from Captain Stormfield's Visit to Heaven* (1909) Homer is one of the "prophets" ranked with Shakespeare; nevertheless Homer stands behind the chair of an unknown tailor from Tennessee (*RP* [1952], pp. 67, 73).

Tony Tanner, *Reign of Wonder* (1965), p. 152.

Homes of American Authors, Comprising Anecdotal, Personal, and Descriptive Sketches, by Various Writers. Illus. Original blue cloth, gilt. New York: G. P. Putnam, 1853. 366 pp. Contributors included George William Curtis (1824–1892), William Cullen Bryant (1794–1878), Rufus W[ilmot]. Griswold (1815–1857), and Edward E[verett]. Hale (1822–1909).

Inscription: the front endpaper bears an ink presentation to Olivia Lewis Langdon, Clemens's mother-in-law: "Mrs. Olivia Langdon with the regards of her friend Chas. J. Rand. Jany. 1st, 1853." There are no visible marginalia.

Provenance: Jervis Langdon's bookplate, blue ink within a gilt border, is pasted on the front pastedown endpaper: "J. Langdon's Family Library No. 154." Jervis Langdon, father of Clemens's wife Olivia, lived in a mansion in Elmira, New York.

Location: collection of Kevin Mac Donnell, Austin, Texas (Mac Donnell to Alan Gribben, 29 November 2011). Acquired from the Langdon family.

The homes, portraits, and autographs of seventeen writers are assembled here, including those of Audubon, Dana, Irving, Paulding, Cooper, Emerson, Hawthorne, Longfellow, and Lowell. In some cases their humble birthplaces are contrasted with their later residences, which presumably would have interested Clemens, though there is no confirmation that he ever saw this copy.

Homoselle. Round-Robin Series, No. V. Boston: James R. Osgood and Co., 1881. [One of the Round-Robin Series of anonymous novels written by "the best writers" that the Osgood firm began publishing and promoting in 1881.]

Catalog: Ball 2016 inventory, green cloth, red and black lettering, signed by Charles Jervis Langdon [1849–1916, Olivia Langdon Clemens's brother], Jervis Langdon Family Library bookplate #621.

Location: Quarry Farm library shelves, under the supervision of the Mark Twain Archive, Elmira College, Elmira, New York.

Clemens might have seen this book in the residence of Charles and Ida Langdon.

HOOD, THOMAS (1799–1845). *The Poetical Works of Thomas Hood.* Boston: Crosby, Nichols, Lee & Co., 1860. 480 pp.

Source: MTLAcc, entry #2036, volume donated from Clemens's library by Clara Clemens Gabrilowitsch in 1910.

―――. "Those Evening Bells" (poem, published in 1827).

S. B. Liljegren showed how Mark Twain's "Those Annual Bills" (1875) was based on Hood's parody of Thomas Moore's sentimental poem, "Those Evening Bells" ("Revolt" [1945], pp. 28–30).

————. *Up the Rhine* (published in 1840).

Minnie M. Brashear (*MTSM*, pp. 218–222) suggested this epistolary travel volume as the model with which Clemens compared Orion's style of letter-writing: "It reminds me strongly of Tom Hood's letters to his family (which I have been reading lately)" (18 March 1861, *MTLet* 1: 117, 118 n. 2). Mark Twain makes a reference to *Up the Rhine* in material he discarded from *A Tramp Abroad* (Box 6, No. 47, ms. p. 17, MTP). There Twain describes "the vast feather bed" one encounters in German hotels. "I remember that Hood made many jokes about it."

HOOD, THOMAS (1835–1874), known as Tom Hood.

Mark Twain published "How I Escaped Being Killed in a Duel" in *Tom Hood's Comic Annual for 1873* (London, 1873); another story, "Jim Wolfe and the Cats," appeared in *Tom Hood's Comic Annual for 1874* (London, 1874). "Gone" is "Tom Hood," Clemens noted in July 1899 in London (NB 40, TS p. 60). See *MTLet* 5: 157 n. 10, 868, 952.

M. E. Grenander—"California's Albion: Mark Twain, Ambrose Bierce, Tom Hood, John Camden Hotten, and Andrew Chatto," *Papers of the Bibliographical Society of America* 72.4 (1978): 455–475—provided a useful overview of their mutual acquaintance, principally through Tom Hood.

HOOKER, WORTHINGTON (1806–1867). *The Child's Book of Nature*. New York: Harper & Brothers, 1874. 179 pp.

Source: MTLAcc, entry #1953, volume donated from Clemens's library by Clara Clemens Gabrilowitsch in 1910.

HOOPER, JOHNSON JONES (1815–1862). *Some Adventures of Captain Simon Suggs, Late of the Tallapoosa Volunteers* (published in 1845).

"Simon Suggs," wrote Mark Twain in his list of humorists for an anthology in July 1880 (NB 19, *N&J* 2: 361); but in 1881 he temporarily forgot Suggs's name and wrote "Captain Jones of Alabama" in a similar list (NB 19, *N&J* 2: 428). *Mark Twain's Library of Humor* (1888) contained "Simon Suggs Gets a 'Soft Snap' on His Daddy." Scholarly commentaries have examined similarities between Chapter 10 of *Some Adventures of Captain Simon Suggs*, "The Captain Attends a Camp-Meeting," and Chapter 20 of Twain's *Adventures of Huckleberry Finn* (1885), in which the King invades a Pokeville religious gathering. Twain had alluded to Hooper's sketch— "the man who 'went in on nary pair' (at camp meeting.)"—in a list of humorists and their writings he compiled in 1880 for his projected humor anthology (NB 19, *N&J* 2: 363).

Franklin Meine, *Tall Tales of the Southwest* (1930), pointed out parallels between *Adventures of Huckleberry Finn* and Hooper's "Simon Suggs Attends a Camp Meeting," p. 425; De Voto, *MTAm* (1932), p. 255; Lynn, *MT&SH* (1960), pp. 81–86; Blair, *MT&HF* (1960), pp. 279–284, 326–327, 329; Pascal Covici, Jr., *Mark Twain's Humor: The Image of a World* (Dallas: Southern Methodist University Press, 1962), pp. 3–36; John Rachal, "Scotty Briggs and the Minister: An Idea from Hooper's Simon Suggs?," *Mark Twain Journal* 17.2 (Summer 1974): 10–11; William E. Lenz, "Confidence and Convention in *Huckleberry Finn*," *One Hundred Years of Huckleberry Finn: The Boy, His Book, and American Culture*, ed. Robert Sattelmeyer and J. Donald Crowley (Columbia: University of Missouri Press,

1985), pp. 186–200. Chapter 10 of *Some Adventures of Captain Simon Suggs* was reprinted with commentary in Kenneth S. Lynn, ed., *Huckleberry Finn: Text, Sources, and Criticism* (New York: Harcourt Brace & World, 1961), pp. 144–149; in Hamlin Hill and Walter Blair, eds., *The Art of Huckleberry Finn: Text, Sources, Criticism* (San Francisco: Chandler Publishing Co., 1962), pp. 453–469; and in Bradley, Beatty, and Long, eds., *Adventures of Huckleberry Finn* (1962), pp. 237–243.

HOOVER, BESSIE RAY (b. 1874). *Pa Flickinger's Folks*. Illus. New York: Harper & Brothers, 1909. 274 pp.

Source: MTLAcc, entry #1443, volume donated by Clemens.

Hoover wrote about the Flickingers, a fictional family living in southwest Michigan.

HOPKINS, JOHN HENRY, JR. (1820–1891). *Three Kings of Orient. A Christmas Carol*. Illus. New York: Hurd & Houghton, [cop. 1865].

Source: MTLAcc, entry # 1218, volume donated by Clemens.

On 19 December 1868 Clemens wrote to Olivia Langdon from Fort Plain, New York: "Tunes are good remembrancers. . . . When I hear 'We 3 Kings of Orient' I think of Mrs. Severance" (*MTLet* 2: 334). Hopkins wrote both the words and the music of this carol in 1857.

HOPKINS, MANLEY (1818–1897). *Hawaii: The Past, Present, and Future of Its Island-Kingdom*. London: Longman, Green, Longman, and Roberts, 1862.

Clemens quoted from this book on the front endpaper of Notebook 5 (1866, *N&J* 1: 110) and he also quoted a sentence and summarized Hopkins's comments in Notebook 6 (1866, *N&J* 1: 227).

HOPKINS, MARGARET SUTTON (BRISCOE) (1864–1914). *The Change of Heart; Six Love Stories*. New York: Harper & Brothers, 1903. 172 pp.

Source: MTLAcc, entry #1431, volume donated by Clemens.

Hopkins was acquainted with Clemens and attended his Seventieth Birthday party at Delmonico's in New York City on 5 December 1905.

————. *The Sixth Sense and Other Stories*. Illus. New York: Harper & Brothers, 1899. 274 pp.

Source: MTLAcc, entry #1108, volume donated by Clemens.

The title piece of these nine short stories concerns two men who go to the war; subsequently the women they left behind receive erroneous reports of their fates.

HOPKINS, SAMUEL (1721–1803). *The Life and Character of the Late Reverend, Learned, and Pious Mr. Jonathan Edwards [1703–1758], President of the College of New Jersey. Together with Extracts from His Private Writings & Diary. And Also Seventeen [sic] Select Sermons on Various Important Subjects*. Northampton, Massachusetts: Printed by Andrew Wright, for S. & E. Butler, 1804. 372 pp.

Marginalia: a few pencil marks.

Location: Mark Twain Papers, Bancroft Library, University of California at Berkeley.

Copy examined: Clemens's copy.

In June 1882 Clemens wrote in his pocket notebook: "Life of Jon. Edwards about 1820 Northampton Mass" (NB 20, *N&J* 2: 484). There was no edition published in Northampton in 1820, as he may have learned, so he purchased the 1804 edition instead. This book did not credit Hopkins's authorship of the brief biographical sketch, which precedes eighteen of Edwards's sermons, a few miscellaneous writings, and extracts from his diary.

HOPKINSON, JOSEPH (1770–1842). "Hail, Columbia" (patriotic song, 1789). Melody composed by Philip Phile (c. 1734–1793).

Mark Twain mentioned this song in Notebook 5 (1866), *N&J* 1: 121. The ship's choir "assaulted Hail Columbia" to celebrate the Fourth of July aboard the *Quaker City* (Ch. 10, *IA* [1869]). "Brass bands bray 'Hail Columbia'" as steamboats depart in a race (Ch. 16, *LonMiss* [1883]). "The pride of country rose in his [Alfred Parrish's] heart, Hail Columbia boomed up in his breast" in Twain's "The Belated Russian Passport" (1902).

HOPPIN, AUGUSTUS (1828–1896). *On the Nile*. Illus. Oversized volume. Boston: J. R. Osgood & Co., 1874.

Inscription: inscribed, apparently in Olivia Clemens's hand, "A merry Christmas to C. J. Langdon 1877".

Catalogs: cataloged in the Quarry Farm library in the 1980s; Ball 2016 inventory, green cloth, gilt cover illustration, oversized.

Location: Quarry Farm library shelves, under the supervision of the Mark Twain Archive, Elmira College, Elmira, New York. Available to Clemens during his Elmira visits.

Clemens might have looked at this volume whenever he visited the Langdons in Elmira. Hoppin was a prominent illustrator of humorous books in the nineteenth century. Pen-and-ink sketches record his Egyptian journey.

———. *Ups and Downs on Land and Water*. Illus. Oversized volume. Boston: James R. Osgood & Co., 1871.

Inscription: the front flyleaf is inscribed in black ink by Olivia Clemens: "A very Merry Christmas and Happy New Year/to/C. J. Langdon/Dec 25th 1873. Livy."

Provenance: cataloged in the Quarry Farm library in the 1980s. Found on those shelves by Kevin Mac Donnell in 2005.

Catalog: Ball 2016 inventory, brown cloth, gilt cover illustration, gilt edges, poor condition, damaged spine, loose pages, cover nearly detached.

Location: Mark Twain Archive, Gannett-Tripp Library, Elmira College, Elmira, New York.

Copy examined: photocopies of the title page and inscription in Charles J. Langdon's copy, a gift from the Clemenses. Sent to Alan Gribben by Mark Woodhouse, Archivist, on 6 December 2005.

On 22 December 1873 Olivia Clemens was billed by Brown & Gross, Hartford booksellers, for "1 Ups & Downs $10.00" (MTP). Hoppin's book was the only volume with this title that cost as much as $10. It recounted, with numerous pen-and-ink sketches, the characters he met and the scenes he saw during his travels in England, France, Italy, Germany, and Switzerland.

HORACE, QUINTUS HORATIUS FLACCUS (65–8 BCE). *Odes*.

Mark Twain seemed to know of Horace's line, "dulce et decorum est" (Bk III, ii, 13) when he wrote in 1869: "It is sweet to die for one's native land" ("Ye Cuban Patriot: A Calm Inspection of Him," Buffalo *Express*, 25 December 1869). The cholera germ in Chapter 6 of "Three Thousand Years Among the Microbes" (written in 1905) quotes the

Odes, Book I, Ode 2: "Carpe diem—quam minimum credula postero" (*WWD?*, p. 455). The typical English interpretation is something like "Seize the day, put little trust in tomorrow," but Twain's narrator provides an alcoholic translation of the Latin: "It means, 'Be thou wise: take a drink whilst the chance offers; none but the gods know when the jug will come around again.'"

———. *Q. Horatii Flacci Opera omnia*. Ed. by Johann Gottfried Stallbaum (1793–1861). Leipzig: B. Tauchnitz, 1854. 256 pp.

Source: MTLAcc, entry #372, volume donated by Clemens.

HORNADAY, WILLIAM TEMPLE (1854–1937). *Popular Official Guide to the New York Zoological Park, by William T. Hornaday, Director and General Curator*. Ninth ed. Illus. New York: New York Zoological Society, 1907. 171 pp.

Source: MTLAcc, entry #1982, volume donated from Clemens's library by Clara Clemens Gabrilowitsch in 1910.

HORNE, CHARLES FRANCIS (1870–1942), ed. *Great Men and Famous Women: A Series of Pen and Pencil Sketches of the Lives of More Than 200 of the Most Prominent Personages in History*. 4 vols. Illus. New York: Selmar Hess, 1894. [Publisher conjectured.]

Catalog: *A1911*, "Vols. I and III [only], 2 vols., 4to, cloth, N.Y. 1894," a small sheet of manuscript notes laid in, lot 202, sold for $1.75.

———. *The Technique of the Novel: The Elements of the Art, Their Evolution and Present Use*. New York: Harper & Brothers, 1908. 285 pp.

Source: MTLAcc, entry #860, volume donated by Clemens.

HORNER, SUSAN (1816–1900) and **JOANNA B. HORNER** (1823–1916). *Walks in Florence and Its Environs*. Illus. 2 vols. Frontispiece loose in Volume 2. London: Smith, Elder & Co., 1884.

Inscriptions: two flyleaves were torn from Volume I. The half-title page in Volume II is signed in black ink "Olivia Langdon Clemens/Florence 1892."

Marginalia: in Volume I Clemens made two penciled corrections on page 79; in one of them he drew brackets around a sentence beginning "A long procession . . ." and remarked in the margin: "Of course a procession moves in procession." He also made grammatical revisions in pencil on pages 233, 242, and 244. Pencil markings not in Clemens's hand appear on pages 468, 470, and 471. In Volume II, someone, quite possibly Clemens, made vertical pencil marks in the margins of pages 2, 3, 5, 6, 7, 8, 9, 11, 12, 15, 16, and 17. However, a marginal note about Brunnelleschi's crucifix is definitely not Clemens's and most likely was made by Olivia.

Location: Mark Twain Library, Redding, Connecticut.

Copies examined: Olivia Clemens's copies of Volumes I and II, annotated by Clemens. They have the red ink Mark Twain Library accession numbers "3797" and "3798". Examined in 1970 and again in June 1982.

The Horner sisters, daughters of the prominent Scottish geologist and social reformer Leonard Horner, had deep connections with Italy.

HORNUNG, ERNEST WILLIAM (1866–1921). *A Bride from the Bush* (novel, published in 1890).

A bride from Australia falters in her attempts to enter polite society in England. Mark Twain's "Appendix" to *The American Claimant* (1892) amusingly, as though an afterthought, offers the reader "Weather for Use in This

Book." The sixth of seven extracts Twain took from various books describes a dust-storm in Chapter 18, "The Boundary-Rider of the Yelkin Paddock," in Hornung's novel containing Australian scenes. Twain found this passage reprinted in *Current Literature* 6.4 (April 1891): 630–631 and cut out two paragraphs about the storm from those two pages. See the Catalog entry for that periodical.

———. *The Rogue's March, A Romance.* New York: C. Scribner's Sons, 1903. 403 pp.

Source: MTLAcc, entry #1013, volume donated by Clemens.

Romantic love and marriage miraculously manage to fall into place amid the brutal horrors of convict life and murder in New South Wales in the 1830s.

———. *The Shadow of the Rope.* New York: Charles Scribner's Sons, 1904. 328 pp.

Source: MTLAcc, entry #162, volume donated by Clemens.

Hornung became better known for his Raffles series, featuring a gentleman burglar with charming manners, than for his serious novels such as this one about a woman charged with murder.

Horse-Car Poetry. Republished from the New Monthly Magazine "Record of the Year." New York: G. W. Carleton & Co., 1876. 14 pp.

Inscription: the paper cover is inscribed in pencil by Clemens: "A Centennial gift—from my beloved nephew, W. H. [A?] Marsh, July 4th 1876." Clemens also wrote the name "Mary O. Hayes" vertically on the paper wrapper. Olivia Clemens's first cousins were named Marsh.

Provenance: Carrie Estelle Doheny Collection, St. John's Seminary, Camarillo, California. Donated by Mrs. Doheny in 1953 after its purchase from Aubrey Davidson of Pasadena. Auctioned in 1988 by Christie's for an amount between $130 and $200 at the behest of St. John's Seminary.

Location: currently unknown.

Copy examined: Clemens's copy, at St. John's Seminary in 1970.

This small collection contains Mark Twain's riveting jingle, "Punch, Brothers, Punch!"

Hot Stuff by Famous Funny Men, Comprising Humor, Pathos, Ridicule, Satires, Dialects, Puns, Conundrums, Riddles, Charades, Jokes and Magic . . . with The Philosophy of Wit and Humor by *Melville D. Landon, A. M. ("Eli Perkins").* Chicago: Madison Book Co., 1902. 609 pp. [The publisher also released this title in 1903.]

In an Autobiographical Dictation of 31 July 1906 Mark Twain fumed about the use of his name and image on the cover of "a great, fat, offensive volume" published by a "western pirate" (*AutoMT* 2: 152–153). The Mark Twain Project editors (p. 534) identified *Hot Stuff by Famous Funny Men* and *Library of Wit and Humor by Mark Twain and Others* (see the Catalog entry for that latter book) as versions of the book to which Twain objected. The question of exactly which imprint Twain saw is somewhat complicated. The Chicago publisher Reilly and Britton brought out *Hot Stuff by Famous Funny Men* in 1901 and 1904, as had the Chicago firm George M. Hill Co. in 1900. See also the Catalog entry for *World's Wit and Humor; An Encyclopedia of the Classic Wit and Humor of All Ages and Nations.*

HOUGH, EMERSON (1857–1923). *The Young Alaskans.* Illus. New York: Harper & Brothers, 1908. 292 pp.

Source: MTLAcc, entry #1194, volume donated by Clemens.

HOUGH, ROMEYN BECK (1857–1924). *The American Woods, Exhibited by Actual Specimens and with Copious Explanatory Text.* First edition. Original printed wrappers, original green cloth slipcase, lettered in gilt. Part I. Lowville, New York: The author, 1888.

Inscription: Hough's business card, printed on wood veneer, was laid in—perhaps in an effort to secure an endorsement from Clemens?

Catalog: ListABP (1910), "American Woods Part I, Hough", no other information supplied.

Location: collection of Kevin Mac Donnell, Austin, Texas.

Source: letter from Kevin Mac Donnell to Alan Gribben, 20 March 2014.

Hough's extraordinarily assembled book contained thinly sliced samples of wood from the trees described as growing in New York and adjacent states. Physician-botanist Hough would eventually complete only thirteen of the fifteen volumes he planned for this project; his daughter Marjorie Hough would add a fourteenth volume in 1924.

HOUSE, EDWARD HOWARD (1836–1901). *Japanese Episodes.* Boston: James R. Osgood & Co., 1881. 247 pp.

Source: MTLAcc, entry #572, volume donated by Clemens. Clemens was familiar as early as 10 April 1875 with House's writings about Japan (*MTLet* 6: 444–445). In a postscript to a letter written to James R. Osgood & Company on 6 January 1883 Clemens requested a copy of "Japanese Legends" [*sic*] (*MTLP*, pp. 161–162). House's volume contained four brief sketches intended to portray "the inner life of the Japanese, of their domestic relations, their pleasures, or the gentler romance of their nature" (p. 3). "Little Fountain of Sakanoshita" describes the narrator's vacation in the scenic Sakanoshita region; "A Japanese Statesman at Home" recounted House's visit with an esteemed official, Hirosawa Hiosuké, who was later assassinated; "To Fuziyama and Back" promoted a scenic tour; and "A Day in a Japanese Theatre" explained how a favorite Japanese fable was presented on the stage.

In a letter of 5 February 1890 written to Dean Sage, Mark Twain excoriated House after they had a dispute over the dramatic rights for Twain's *The Prince and the Pauper*, concluding: "Old friendship? Oh dear! . . . It turns out, now, that he didn't write Arrah-na-Pogue (as he always claimed). I thought he was a dramatist" ("Literary Miscellany," Catalog 280, William Reese Company, New Haven, Connecticut, ALS, item #85). See the Catalog entry for D. Boucicault's *Arrah-na-Pogue; or, The Wicklow Wedding.* James Huffman's *A Yankee in Meiji Japan: The Crusading Journalist Edward H. House.* (Lanham, Maryland: Rowman & Littlefield, 2003) sketches the Clemens-House relationship.

HOUSE, EDWARD JOHN (1879–1965). *A Hunter's Camp-Fires.* Illustrated from photographs by the author. New York: Harper & Brothers, 1909. 402 pp.

Source: MTLAcc, entry #1983, volume donated from Clemens's library by Clara Clemens Gabrilowitsch in 1910. House, a resident of Pittsburgh, Pennsylvania, recounts (and provides photographs of) his trophy hunts in East

Africa, Canada, and the American West.

HOUSMAN, ALFRED EDWARD (1859–1936). *A Shropshire Lad*. Illus. New York: Mitchell Kennerley, 1908, 126 pp.

Source: MTLAcc, entry #2034, volume donated from Clemens's library by Clara Clemens Gabrilowitsch in 1910.

A Shropshire Lad contains dozens of poems, including "Loveliest of Trees, the Cherry Now," "When I Was One-and-Twenty," "The Lads in Their Hundreds," "On the Idle Hill of Summer," "Here the Hangman Stops His Cart," and "Terence, This Is Stupid Stuff."

HOWARD, BLANCHE WILLIS, (LATER) BARONESS VON TEUFFEL (1847–1898). *Aunt Serena*. Boston: James R. Osgood and Co., 1881. 358 pp.

Catalog: Ball 2016 inventory, bookplate #616 of the "J. Langdon Family Library", brown cloth with gilt and back lettering, black design, fair condition.

Location: Quarry Farm library shelves, under the supervision of the Mark Twain Archive, Elmira College, Elmira, New York.

Copy examined: unmarked copy to which Clemens had access whenever he visited the Langdons in Elmira. Examined on 26 May 2015.

———. *The Garden of Eden*. New York: Charles Scribner's Sons, 1903. 444 pp.

Source: MTLAcc, entry #159, volume donated by Clemens.

———. *Guenn; A Wave on the Breton Coast, by Blanche Willis Howard*. Boston: James R. Osgood and Co., 1884. 439 pp.

The female protagonist in *Guenn* must choose (tragically, as it turns out) between an exciting but risky life with an impulsive artist or a much duller, pedestrian existence. On 27 January 1894 Clemens wrote to Olivia Clemens from New York City about an artist named Simmons who, Clemens was told "under seal of secrecy . . . is the hero of 'Gwen' [*sic*], and he and Gwen's author were once engaged to marry." The artist Edward E[merson]. Simmons (1852–1931) had lived and painted for a time on the coast of Brittany. The novel's publisher had announced in advance that Simmons would draw the illustrations for *Guenn*, but when the novel appeared there were only a few uncredited pictorial decorations. Clemens informed Olivia Clemens that he had accompanied this same "'fire-escape' Simmons, the inveterate talker, you know," and several other men to watch an exhibition match in Madison Square Garden featuring boxer "Gentleman Jim" Corbett (*MTL*, p. 605).

———. *One Summer*. Boston: James R. Osgood and Co., 1877. 279 pp.

Catalog: Ball 2016 inventory, bookplate #530 of the "J. Langdon Family Library," good condition.

Location: Mark Twain Archive, Elmira College, Elmira, New York.

Clemens had access to these books whenever he visited the Langdon residence in Elmira.

———. *One Year Abroad*. Boston: J. R. Osgood & Co., 1878. 247 pp.

Source: MTLAcc, entry #571, volume donated by Clemens.

———. *Tony, the Maid; A Novelette*. Illus. New York: Harper & Brothers, [cop. 1887]. 166 pp.

Source: MTLAcc, entry #160, volume donated by Clemens.

———. [Another identical copy.]

Source: MTLAcc, entry #1015, volume donated by Clemens.

HOWARD, BRONSON CROCKER (1842–1908).

Mark Twain dined with the playwright Howard and afterward conversed with him at the Savile Club in London in July 1900 (SLC to Brander Matthews, 11 July 1900, Columbia; NB 43, TS p. 22). In 1905 Twain nominated Howard for membership in the American Academy of Arts and Letters (SLC to Robert Underwood Johnson, 28 April 1905, American Academy). Howard is often cited as being the first dramatist to be able to make a living by writing for the stage. *Shenandoah* (1888) was his most successful play.

HOWARD, GEORGE ELLIOTT (1849–1928). *The American Nation: A History. Preliminaries of the Revolution, 1763–1775*. Portrait and maps. New York, 1905.

Inscription: the front pastedown endpaper is signed "S. L. Clemens, Sept. 1905."

Catalogs: *A1911*, "8vo, cloth, N.Y. 1905," quotes the signature, lot 248, sold for $3.50; George D. Smith, New York City, "Catalogue of Books" (1911), quotes the signature, item #173, $7.50.

HOWARD, HATTIE. *Poems*. Hartford, Connecticut: [Press of the Case, Lockwood & Brainard Co.], [cop. 1886]. 108 pp.

Source: MTLAcc, entry #627, volume donated by Clemens. Hattie Howard published other volumes of poetry, including *Later Poems* (1887) and *Poems, Vol. IV* (1904). Her verse was competent and readable. She evidently had connections with Hartford High School and Trinity College, judging from the contents of her books. Additional biographical facts have proven difficult to trace.

HOWARD, H. R., comp. *The History of Virgil A. Stewart [1809–1854], and His Adventure in Capturing and Exposing the Great "Western Land Pirate"[John Andrews Murrell (1806–1844)] and His Gang, in Connexion with the Evidence; Also of the Trials, Confessions, and Execution of a Number of Murrell's Associates in the state of Mississippi During the Summer of 1835, and the Execution of Five Professional Gamblers by the Citizens of Vicksburg, on the 6th July, 1835*. New York: Harper & Brothers, 1836. 273 pp.

In Chapter 29 of *Life on the Mississippi* (1883) Mark Twain quotes extensively from Stewart's narrative of John A. Murrell's life, though the "now forgotten book which was published half a century ago" cited there by Twain was Frederick Marryat's *Second Series of A Diary in America* (1840), because Marryat was in fact quoting from and paraphrasing Stewart's 1835 book. (See the Catalog entry for Virgil A. Stewart.) Howard's biography might have supplemented Twain's notions about Murrell's crimes, which seem to have been exaggerated in the retellings.

HOWARD, LELAND OSSIAN (1857–1950). *The Insect Book: A Popular Account of the Bees, Wasps, Ants, Grasshoppers, Flies, and Other North American Insects*. Illus. New York: Doubleday, Page & Co., 1904. 429 pp.

Catalog: Ball 2016 inventory, Nature Library, Vol. VIII, from the Quarry Farm library.

Location: current location undetermined.

———. *Mosquitoes: How They Live; How They Carry Disease; How They Are Classified; How They May Be Destroyed*. Illus. New York: McClure, Phillips & Co., 1901. 241 pp.

Source: MTLAcc, entry #1954, volume donated from Clemens's library by Clara Clemens Gabrilowitsch in 1910.

HOWE, EDGAR WATSON (1853–1937). *A Moonlight Boy*. Boston: Ticknor and Co., 1886. 342 pp.

> Source: MTLAcc, entry #488, volume donated by Clemens. Howe set this romantic novel in Kansas and (in the middle section) New York City.

————. *The Story of a Country Town*. First state of first edition (without the publisher's name on the spine and with the rubber stamp of "D. Caldwell, Manufacturer" on the front pastedown endpaper). 8vo, original dark brown cloth, ends of spine and covers worn. Illustrated by W. L. Wells. Atchison, Kansas: Howe & Co., 1883. 226 pp.

> Inscriptions: the front free flyleaf is inscribed in pencil: "S. L. Clemens/Hartford/March 1884./Sent by the Author." The front free endpaper bears Clemens's penciled citation to a recent book relating to his favorite poet: "Illustrations/to/Browning's Poems/(With a notice of the Artists and the Pictures)/by Ernest Radford,/published for/The Browning Society/by N. Trübner & Co., 57 & 59 Ludgate Hill,/London E. C."

> Marginalia: only one note on page 3 was reported in *The Twainian* issues of January-February and March-April 1968. On page 3, next to the protagonist's description of his father's "resolve to evangelize in the West on his own account, at the same time putting himself in the way of growing up with the country," Clemens responded in pencil: "Like my father." Clemens also drew vertical pencil lines on six other pages.

> Provenance: the shelfmark of Clara Clemens Samossoud's private library in Detroit; subsequently in the collection of Chester L. Davis (1903–1987), Mark Twain Research Foundation, Perry, Missouri; at a later point the volume joined the collection of Nick Karanovich, Fort Wayne, Indiana.

> Catalogs: "Printed Books and Manuscripts," including the Chester L. Davis collection, Christie's, New York City, 17–18 May 1991, lot #79, bid estimate $1,500–2,000; sold to Nick Karanovich by the Brick Row Book Shop of San Francisco, California in the mid-1990s (John Crichton, Brick Row Book Shop, to Alan Gribben, 27 January 1998 email); *Sotheby's 2003*, #214, $3,500.

> Location: at present unknown.

> Copy examined: Clemens's copy, at the 2003 Sotheby's sale. Spine frayed, corners worn.

> Clemens received Howe's novel while on the lecture tour with George Washington Cable, and he read portions of it to Cable. On 13 February 1884 Clemens responded from Hartford regarding the complimentary copy that Howe had sent from Atchison, Kansas; the letter mixed "public" praise and "private" objections (published by C. E. Schorer in "Mark Twain's Criticism of *The Story of a Country Town*" [1955]). Clemens congratulated Howe on his simple, direct style of writing, but picked a few faults with his grammar, dismissed the preface, suggested more appearances for Big Adam and fewer speeches by Biggs, and rebuked the blatant sentimentality. "I like your book so much that I am glad of the chance to say so," Clemens wrote. "Your style is so simple, sincere, direct, & at the same time so clear & so strong, that I think it must have been born to you, not made. Your pictures of that arid village life, & the insides & outsides of its people, are vivid, & what is more, true; I know, for I have seen it all, lived it all. Your book is a history; your scissors could have turned it into a tale—& that would have been better, maybe. . . . You could have knocked out an obstruction here & there, & then your history would have become a story. . . . You have allowed the tears to plash on the floor once in the preface & thrice in the book. The figure is very striking—& jokes & striking figures should not be repeated. . . . I am talking pretty freely, but I mean no harm. You may have caught the only fish there was in your pond—it's a thing that has occurred before—but I am not able to think so."

> Howe soon found a commercial publisher for *The Story of a Country Town*, but literary critics never saw any match in his later novels of the promise given by this minor masterpiece of American naturalism. Calder M. Pickett's *Ed Howe: Country Town Philosopher* (Lawrence: University Press of Kansas, 1968) quoted Clemens's 1884 letter to Howe and provided related commentary (pp. 75–77 *passim*).

> C. E. Schorer, "Mark Twain's Criticisms of *The Story of a Country Town*" *American Literature* 27.1 (March 1955): 109–112; Claude M. Simpson, "Introduction," *The Story of a Country Town* (Cambridge, Massachusetts: Harvard University Press [Belknap Press], 1961), pp. ix-xviii; Sydney J. Krause, *MTC* (1967), pp. 262–271.

————. *The Story of a Country Town*. Boston: James R. Osgood & Co., 1885. 413 pp.

> Source: MTLAcc, entry #154, volume donated by Clemens. Clemens had influence with James R. Osgood, so Clemens's endorsement of the novel might have been a factor in bringing about this Boston edition.

HOWE, JULIA (WARD) (1819–1910). "The battle hymn of the Republic" (hymn, published in 1862).

> In 1901 Mark Twain wrote a mordant parody of the hymn, "The Battle Hymn of the Republic (Brought Down to Date)" (DV74, MTP, published in Scott, *OPMT* [1966], p. 128). In 1906 Clemens joined Thomas Wentworth Higginson in nominating Julia Ward Howe to be the first female member of the National Institute of Arts and Letters; "it is her earned and rightful place," Clemens wrote. He also sent two letters to Howe in 1906 and 1907 congratulating her on her memberships in the National Institute of Arts and Letters and the American Authors' Club (*Letters and Journals of Thomas Wentworth Higginson, 1846–1906*, ed. Mary Thacher Higginson [Boston: Houghton Mifflin Co., 1921; reprinted later in New York: Negro Universities Press, 1964], p. 235). Clemens recalled that his children enjoyed Howe's hymn (30 November 1906 AD, *AutoMT* 2: 293).

> William M. Gibson, "Mark Twain and Howells, Anti-Imperialists," *New England Quarterly* 20.4 (December 1947): 435–470; Jim Zwick, *Mark Twain's Weapons of Satire: Anti-Imperialist Writings on the Philippine-American War*, ed. Jim Zwick (Syracuse: Syracuse University Press, 1992), pp. 40–41, 240.

HOWE, M[ARK]. A[NTONY]. DEWOLFE (1864–1960). *American Bookmen: Sketches, Chiefly Biographical, of Certain Writers of the Nineteenth Century*. New York: Dodd, Mead and Co., 1898. 295 pp.

> Clemens might have been familiar with this book, since the magazine editor and writer Howe was becoming an

increasingly prominent biographer. His *American Book-men* mentioned Mark Twain briefly but respectfully. In the chapter on American humorists, Howe alluded to "Mark Twain, happily still the living exponent of Amerian humour in its essence" (p. 155). Other humorists, including Artemus Ward, received lengthier treatments. Howe described the careers of a dozen writers, including Irving, Bryant, Poe, Cooper, Hawthorne, Whitman, Lowell, Longfellow, Prescott, and Parkman.

———. *Phillips Brooks.* The Beacon Biographies of Eminent Americans, ed. M[ark]. A[ntony]. DeWolfe Howe (1864–1960). Boston: Small, Maynard & Co., 1899. 120 pp.

Phillips Brooks (1835–1893) was a prominent American Episcopal bishop who held the pastorate of Trinity Church in Boston for more than twenty years. Clemens was surely alluding to this book among others on 18 March 1901 when he wrote to Howe from New York City to "thank you for the books. By the list, I see that they furnish just the kind of reading I am fondest of" (TS in MTP). Howe had shipped sample volumes from the Beacon Biographies series he was editing in an effort to entice Clemens to write a brief biography of Artemus Ward, but Clemens declined.

Unfortunately there seems to be no evidence that Clemens ever received these books, inasmuch as he noted that "evidently they have gone to Hartford" and none of the titles ever surfaced in the records of the Clemenses' library. It seems a pity that this package apparently miscarried, since by March 1901 Howe's series had in print a dozen biographies, including *Frederick Douglass* by Charles Chesnutt, *Nathaniel Hawthorne* by Annie Fields, *James Russell Lowell* by Edward Everett Hale, Jr., *Thomas Paine* by Ellery Sedgwick, *Daniel Webster* by Norman Hapgood, and *James Fenimore Cooper* by William Branford Shubrick Clymer. In 1922 Howe would edit *Memories of a Hostess*, based on the diaries of Annie (Adams) Fields, which contained information about Clemens's reading tastes (see the Critical Bibliography in Volume One of the present work). Howe also mentioned Clemens in *Causes and Their Champions* (Boston: Little, Brown and Co., 1926), pp. 290–291, 330.

———. *Shadows* (poems, published in 1897).

In a letter to Howe written from New York City on 18 March 1901 Clemens testified, "I remember our pleasant conversation at the Tavern Club and also the happy verses" (TS in MTP). Possibly, then, Clemens knew of Howe's *Shadows*.

Howells, Mildred (1872–1966). "At the Wind's Will" (poem), *Harper's Monthly* 112.670 (March 1906): 576.

Isabel Lyon "came across a beautiful little poem by Mildred Howells" on 25 February 1906 and she "took it to Mr. Clemens this morning, he read it aloud to me and then cut it out of the magazine" (IVL Journal, TS p. 138, MTP). She recorded the fact that later the same day he read it to Witter Bynner, "saying that he had wasted a whole chapter to say what she had said in a few lines." In a letter to Mildred's father William Dean Howells written that same evening Clemens complimented the "depth, & dignity, & pathos, & compression, & fluent grace & beauty" of the poem. All day long it had "sung in the ears of my spirit like a strain of solemn music"

(*MTHL*, p. 800).

Howells, William Dean (1837–1920). "After the Wedding" (poem), *Harper's Monthly* 114.679 (December 1906): 64–69.

"I read 'After the Wedding' aloud to Jean & Miss Lyon, & we felt all the pain of it & the truth. It was very moving & very beautiful." The pauses in the poem "furnished me time to brace up my voice, & get a new start" (SLC to WDH, 26 June 1906, *MTHL*, p. 814). Howells had sent Clemens a manuscript copy of the poem in advance of its publication. Albert Bigelow Paine remembered that Clemens read aloud "After the Wedding" and "The Mother," commenting that they "sounded the depths of humanity with a deep-sea lead" (*MTB*, p. 1313).

———. "American Literature," *Literature* (14 May 1898–10 November 1899).

For eighteen months William Dean Howells wrote a column titled "American Literature" for the weekly periodical *Literature*, occasionally discussing Mark Twain's writings. Though Twain was residing in England, it still seems quite probable that he followed Howells's critical opinions in this forum.

———. *Annie Kilburn, A Novel.* New York: Harper & Brothers, 1891. 331 pp.

Catalogs: MTLAcc, entry #1569, volume donated by Clemens; ListABP (1910), "Annie Kilburn, Howells", no other information supplied.

———. *April Hopes.* First edition. Original russet cloth, gilt. New York: Harper & Brothers, 1888. 484 pp.

Marginalia: no markings except for a price of "1.50" in pencil on the front pastedown endpaper. Page 176 is folded down at the beginning of Chapter 21.

Provenance: discovered by Alan Gribben in 1987 in Clara Clemens Gabrilowitsch's former home in Hollywood, California among some Mark Twain association copies and letters that she evidently gave or sold to the next owners of the house. Gribben was inspecting the bookshelves at the request of the Wescoatt family heirs. The *Los Angeles Times Magazine* 3 (10 May 1987): 16–19, 32, provided details about other items that turned up. Nick Karanovich of Fort Wayne, Indiana acquired this volume from the family shortly thereafter in 1987.

Catalog: *Sotheby's 2003*, #215, $1,100 (sold with two other Howells titles).

Location: collection of Kevin Mac Donnell, Austin, Texas.

Copy examined: almost certainly Clemens's unmarked copy, seen in 1987 and again in July 2004. A letter (29 June 1987) from Alan Gribben attesting to its probable authenticity is laid in.

In 1888 Clemens made a memorandum in Notebook 27—"269 Apl Hopes."—contrasting a passage in Howells's *April Hopes* with an incident in Chapter 7 of Walter Scott's *Rob Roy* (*N&J* 3: 378). Also in 1888 Clemens mentioned "Howells" among the authors of "choice and valuable literature" whose English royalties had been effectively protected by their publisher (ALS listed in "Holiday Miscellany," Heritage Book Shop, Catalog 176 [1989], item #232).

———. *Between the Dark and the Daylight: Romances.* Green cloth. New York: Harper & Brothers, 1907. 185 pp.

Inscription: signed in black ink on the front pastedown

endpaper: "SL. Clemens/1908."

Marginalia: markings on page 61 (beside the last three lines) and page 65 (next to lines 20–21).

Provenance: Antenne-Dorrance Collection, Rice Lake, Wisconsin.

Location: Mark Twain Archive, Gannett Tripp Learning Center, Elmira College, Elmira, New York.

Copy examined: Clemens's copy. Examined on 28 May 2015.

This collection of seven short stories contained "Editha," first published in 1905, which would gain increasing respect in the latter-twentieth century for its anti-war sentiment. Another story, "A Case of Metaphantasmia," was one of Howells's ventures into the realm of the supernatural.

———. *Boy Life; Stories and Readings Selected from the Works of William Dean Howells.* Ed. and introduction by Percival Chubb (1860–1960). Illus. First edition. Original mustard cloth. New York: Harper & Brothers, 1909. 190 pp.

Inscription: signed in black ink on the front pastedown endpaper, "S L. Clemens/1909."

Catalogs: ListABP (1910), "Boy Life, Howells"; *C1951*, D71, listed with books signed by Clemens, $15.

Provenance: known to be in Stockton, California in 1981; next in the possession of a Tyler, Texas bookseller, who offered it for sale for $275; then (in 1982) it was briefly in the possession of Theodore Koundajkian of Albany, California, who was considering whether or not to purchase the book (the latter fact confirmed by a letter from Robert H. Hirst to Alan Gribben, 27 August 1982).

Location: collection of Kevin Mac Donnell, Austin, Texas. Acquired in September 1982.

Copy examined: Clemens's unmarked copy, on 9 September 1982 at the Jenkins Company, where Kevin Mac Donnell was then employed, and again in July 2004 at Mac Donnell's residence in Austin, Texas.

Chubb's introduction to *Boy Life* mentions Mark Twain's *Adventures of Tom Sawyer* (1876).

———. *A Boy's Town, Described for "Harper's Young People."* New York: Harper & Brothers, 1890. 247 pp.

Clemens entered the title of Howells's autobiographical reminiscences in Notebook 30 (1890), *N&J* 3: 586. To Howells he wrote: "'A Boy's Town' is perfect—perfect as the perfectest photograph the sun ever made" (27 November 1890, *MTHL*, p. 633).

The most astute analysis of Howells's evocative memories of his years in Hamilton, Ohio appears in Kenneth S. Lynn's *William Dean Howells: An American Life* (New York: Harcourt Brace Jovanovich, 1971), pp. 37–54, which situates *A Boy's Town* within the Boy Book phenomenon. See also Alan Gribben, "Manipulating a Genre: *Huckleberry Finn* as Boy Book," *South Central Review* 5.4 (Winter 1988): 15–21 (a revised version of this essay appears as a chapter in Volume One of the present work).

Stone, *IE* (1961), pp. 70–71; Hunter, "Mark Twain and the Boy-Book" (1963), p. 435; George W. Crandall, "Emperors and Little Empires: The Schoolmaster in Nineteenth-Century American Literature," *Studies in American Humor*, n.s. 2, 5.1 (Spring 1986): 51–61.

———. *Certain Delightful English Towns, with Glimpses of the Pleasant Country Between.* New York: Harper & Brothers, 1906. 289 pp.

Catalog: ListABP (1910), "Certain English Towns, Howells", no other information supplied.

———. *A Chance Acquaintance.* First edition. 12mo, original green cloth, gilt, wear on ends of spine and a corner, stains on pages 68–69. Boston: James R. Osgood and Co., 1873. 279 pp.

Inscription: inscribed by Howells in purple ink on the verso of the front free endpaper: "To S. L. Clemens, with ever so much friendship. W. D. Howells. Cambridge, May 16, 1873."

Catalogs: ListABP (1910), "Chance Acquaintance, Howells"; *C1951*, #81c, $25, listed among the books signed by Clemens; Christie's, New York City, 1–2 February 1988 auction, lot 459, sold for $3,850 to Maurice F. Neville Rare Books, Santa Barbara, California.

Provenance: Carrie Estelle Doheny Collection, St. John's Seminary, Camarillo, California. Donated by Mrs. Doheny in 1951 after its purchase from Maxwell Hunley Rare Books of Beverly Hills for $32. Auctioned by Christie's in New York City for an amount between $2,000 and $3,000 in February 1988 (lot 459) on behalf of St. John's Seminary.

Location: collection of Kevin Mac Donnell, Austin, Texas.

Copy examined: Clemens's unmarked copy, in Austin in July 2004. Has the bookplate of "Estelle Doheny."

Howard K. Bush, Jr. addressed this, Howells's second novel, in "The Mythic Struggle Between East and West: Mark Twain's Speech at Whittier's 70th Birthday Celebration and W. D. Howells's *A Chance Acquaintance*," *American Literary Realism* 27.2 (Winter 1995): 53–73. Twain would include Howells's name among two lists of humorists he made up in anticipation of editing an anthology of humor (NB 19 [1880], *N&J* 2: 363; [1881], p. 429). *Mark Twain's Library of Humor* (1888) eventually included two excerpts from *A Chance Acquaintance*, "Kitty Answers" and "Love's Young Dream."

The approximately ninety William Dean Howells entries in this Annotated Catalog attest to how closely and devotedly Clemens followed and valued his friend's writings. In an interview published in the Johannesburg *Star* on 18 May 1896, he defended Howells as "one of the very best literary men America has produced," and a critic who "delivers his verdicts after weighing the evidence most carefully. . . . Howells is a gentle, kindly spirit; he is too good for this world. In my opinion there is never a trace of affectation or superiority in either the man or his books" (Scharnhorst, *Complete Interviews*, p. 302). Howells would produce an influential memoir of his friend, *My Mark Twain* (1910), and he was one of the members of the American Academy and National Institute of Arts and Letters who spoke at a memorial meeting in Carnegie Hall honoring Clemens on 30 November 1910.

Leland Krauth, *Mark Twain & Company: Six Literary Relations* (Athens: University of Georgia Press, 2003), noted the degree to which Twain and Howells shared a "similarity" in their literary humor. Louis J. Budd judiciously evaluated the mutual admiration of Clemens and Howells in "W. D. Howells and Mark Twain Judge Each Other 'Aright,'" *American Literary Realism* 38.2 (Winter 2006): 97–114. See also Susan Goodman and Carl Dawson, *William Dean Howells: A Writer's Life* (Berkeley: University of California Press, 2005).

Ralph Marx, "The Literary Associations of Mark Twain and William Dean Howells," Master's thesis, De Paul University, 1940; *Mark Twain-Howells Letters: The Correspondence of Samuel L. Clemens and William D. Howells. 1982–1910*, ed. Henry Nash Smith and William M. Gibson (Cambridge: Belknap Press/Harvard University Press, 1960); Kenneth E. Eble, *Old Clemens and W. D. H.: The Story of a Remarkable Friendship* (Baton Rouge: Louisiana State University Press, 1985); Peter Messent, *Mark Twain and Male Friendship: The Twichell, Howells, and Rogers Friendships* (New York: Oxford University Press, 2009); and Kelly L. Richardson, "Contemporary Writers," *Mark Twain in Context*, ed. John Bird (Cambridge, England: Cambridge University Press, 2020), pp. 131–135.

———. *A Chance Acquaintance*. Boston: Houghton, Mifflin and Co., 1882. 271 pp.

Source: MTLAcc, entry #2274, volume donated from Clemens's library by Clara Clemens Gabrilowitsch in 1910.

———. *Christmas Every Day and Other Stories Told for Children*. Illus. New York: Harper & Brothers, [cop. 1892]. 150 pp.

Source: MTLAcc, entry #1596, volume donated by Clemens.

———. "The Christmas Spirit" (poem), *Harper's Weekly* 46.2398 (6 December 1902): 24–25.

"I read to people—& praised—. . . the Santa Claus poem" (SLC to WDH, 24 December 1902, *MTHL*, p. 756). Howells's long poem, written in rhyming couplets, assessed the state of the world as the year 1902 concluded. Mark Twain's "The Belated Russian Passport" appeared in this same issue (pp. 4–5, 8–9).

———. *The Coast of Bohemia*. Illus. New York: Harper & Brothers, 1893. 340 pp.

Source: MTLAcc, entry #1566, volume donated by Clemens.

———. *A Counterfeit Presentment. Comedy*. Boston: J. R. Osgood & Co., 1885. 199 pp. [Play, produced in 1877.]

Source: MTLAcc, entry #2276, volume donated from Clemens's library by Clara Clemens Gabrilowitsch in 1910.

"When does [Lawrence] Barrett open in your piece in N.Y. (or Boston). I calculate to be there," Clemens wrote to Howells on 27 June 1877 (*MTHL*, p. 184). Early the next year, shortly after the Whittier Birthday Dinner in Boston on 17 December 1877 at which Mark Twain gave a criticized speech that strained his friendship with Howells, *A Counterfeit Presentment* played in Hartford. Perhaps partly to make amends for his dinner speech miscalculation, he promptly informed Howells that he had attended the performance: "The play is enchanting. I laughed & cried all the way through it. The dialogue is intolerably brilliant. I cannot remember when I have spent so delightful an evening in a theatre" (4 January 1878, *MTHL*, p. 216).

Numerous books and articles have reflected on the Whittier Birthday speech; among the treatments sensitive to Howells's point of view are Kenneth S. Lynn's *William Dean Howells: An American Life* (New York: Harcourt Brace Jovanovich, 1971), pp. 168–178; Susan Goodman and Carl Dawson's *William Dean Howells: A Writer's Life* (Berkeley: University of California Press, 2005), pp. 190–192; and Gary Scharnhorst's *The Life of Mark Twain:*

The Middle Years, 1871–1891 (Columbia: University of Missouri Press, 2019), pp. 229–240.

———. "The Country Printer," *Scribner's Monthly* 13.5 (May 1893): 539–558.

On 12 May 1893 Clemens wrote from New York: "I forgot to tell you how thoroughly I enjoyed your account of the country printing office, & how true it all was & how intimately recognizable in all its details" (*MTHL*, p. 652). See also the Catalog entry for Howells's *Impressions and Experiences* (1896).

———. "A Difficult Case," *Atlantic Monthly* 86.513 (July 1900): 24–36; (August 1900): 205–217.

"I read the Difficult Situation [*sic*] night before last, & got a world of evil joy out of it" (SLC to WDH, London, c. 1 August 1900, *MTHL*, p. 719). See also the Catalog entry for Howells's *A Pair of Patient Lovers*.

Lawrence I. Berkove, "'A Difficult Case': W. D. Howells's Impression of Mark Twain," *Studies in Short Fiction* 31.4 (Fall 1994): 607–615.

———. *Dr. Breen's Practice* (novel, published in 1881).

Catalog: ListABP (1910), "Dr. Breen's Practice, Howells", no other information provided.

Howells's novel portrays a woman physician who must make difficult choices. In "Mental Telegraphy" (1891) Mark Twain cites the case of a woman who submitted a similar story to *Dr. Breen's Practice* to the *Atlantic Monthly* after Howells's work was already set in type for serialization. "I had read portions of Mr. Howells's story, both in MS. and in proof," Twain adds. In a letter of 14 April 1903 to Howells, he again referred to the coincidence, attributing it to "mental telegraphy" (*MTHL*, p. 767).

———. "Edgar Allan Poe," *Harper's Weekly* 53 (16 January 1909): 12–13.

"I have to write a line, lazy as I am, to say how your Poe article delights me & charms me; & to add that I am in agreement with substantially all you say about his literature" (SLC to WDH, Redding, 18 January 1909, *MTHL*, p. 841, corrected from PH of ALS, MTP). Howells's essay had taken issue with the French tendency to elevate Poe to the stature of a literary genius. Conceding that Poe possessed "great talent" and had mastered a certain "technique," Howells nonetheless argued that his "method is always mechanical, his material mostly unimportant." Unlike the Russian writers, Poe never seemed "sincere." While he could be "subtle" he inevitably failed to be "delicate."

———. *The Elevator: Farce*. Boston: James R. Osgood and Co., 1885. 84 pp. [Edition conjectured, but the most likely one.]

Catalog: ListABP (1910), "The Elevator, Howells", no additional information supplied.

Howells wrote a number of these one-act plays. *The Elevator* had initially appeared in *Harper's Monthly Magazine* 70.415 (December 1884): 111–125.

———. "The Father," Chapter 1 of *The Whole Family* (a composite novel by twelve authors), *Harper's Bazar* 41.12 (December 1907): 1161–70.

In the summer of 1906 the editor of *Harper's Bazar* tried to entice Mark Twain to contribute to *The Whole Family*, a novel narrated by a dozen different characters created by twelve eminent authors, by showing him the first two chapters. "Mr Howells began the composite tale," Twain noted in an Autobiographical Dictation of 29

August 1906. "He held the pen and through it the father delivered his chapter—therefore it was well done" (*MTE*, pp. 243–244; *AutoMT* 2: 190). Twain was less favorably impressed by the second chapter, written by Mary Wilkins Freeman. Uninspired, Twain declined the invitation. *The Whole Family* appeared as twelve monthly installments in *Harper's Bazar* between December 1907 and November 1908. Harper & Brothers issued the book edition in 1908.

———. *A Fearful Responsibility and Other Stories*. Boston: James R. Osgood and Co., 1881. 255 pp.

Inscription: "Mrs. Clemens/With the regards of W. D. Howells. Belmont, July 26, 1881."

Catalogs: ListABP (1910), "Fearful Responsibility, Howells", listed twice; *Zeitlin 1951*, #23, $10.

Clemens noted "July Scribner" in Notebook 19 (1881, *N&J* 2: 396), probably intending to obtain the second installment of Howells's story while the Clemenses were spending their summer in Branford, Connecticut. *A Fearful Responsibility* appeared in the June and July issues of *Scribner's Monthly*. When the story subsequently appeared between covers it was accompanied by two of Howells's short stories, "At the Sign of the Savage" (a tale with a happy ending, about an American and his wife who, arriving in Vienna late at night, are tricked by a driver into staying at the Gasthof zum Wilden Manne (The Sign of the Savage) instead of the highly recommended hotel they had requested) and "Tonelli's Marriage," set in Venice and humorously relating the unusual courtship and marriage of the wealthy Tommaso Tonelli.

———. *Fennel and Rue; A Novel*. Illustrated by Charlotte Harding (1873–1951). New York: Harper & Brothers, 1908. 130 pp.

Source: MTLAcc, entry #2279, volume donated from Clemens's library by Clara Clemens Gabrilowitsch in 1910.

———. *The Flight of Pony Baker; A Boy's Town Story*. Illus. Original pictorial red cloth. New York: Harper & Brothers, 1902. 223 pp.

Inscription: on the first flyleaf: "To S. L. Clemens/Author of 'Huck Finn' and other/Outcast literature/W. D. Howells."

Catalogs: ListABP (1910), "Flight of Pony Baker, Howells"; *C1951*, #65c, $32.50.

Location: Albert and Shirley Small Special Collections Library, University of Virginia Libraries, Charlottesville. Gift of Clifton Waller Barrett.

Copy examined: Clemens's copy, unmarked.

"It is a charming book, & perfectly true" (SLC to WDH, York Harbor, Maine, 3 October 1902, *MTHL*, p. 746). Stone, *IE* (1961), p. 71.

———. [Another identical copy.]

Source: MTLAcc, entry #2278, volume donated from Clemens's library by Clara Clemens Gabrilowitsch in 1910.

———. *A Foregone Conclusion*. Reddish brown cloth. Boston: James R. Osgood and Co., 1875. 265 pp.

Inscription: "Mrs. S. L. Clemens with the best regards of W. D. Howells, Cambridge, Dec. 4, 1874."

Marginalia: two penciled corrections by Clemens on pages 9 and 172. Leaves opened throughout.

Catalogs: ListABP (1910), "Foregone Conclusion, Howells"; "The Fine Library of the Late Ingle Barr," Sotheby Parke-Bernet, Los Angeles, Sale No. 68 (18–19 February 1973), item #291, sold for $125; offered for sale by John

Howell Books, San Francisco, 24 February 1973, $150.

Location: Mark Twain Papers, Bancroft Library, University of California at Berkeley. "From the Appert Collection."

Copy examined: (in 1973, at John Howell Books) Olivia Clemens's copy, read by Clemens.

Howells set his romantic novel in Venice and New York City, inserting comedic touches as well as incidents of pathos within the story of a wealthy young woman with two suitors. Writing from Elmira on 21 June 1874 Clemens declared the first installment of *A Foregone Conclusion* in the *Atlantic Monthly*, upon a "re-reading," to be "such absolute perfection of character-drawing & withal so moving in the matter of <tears> pathos <now, & laughter then> now, humor then, & both at once occasionally, that Mrs. Clemens wanted me to defer my smoke & drop you our thanks" (*MTHL*, pp. 17–18; *MTLet* 6: 165). On 22 August 1874, having read the third installment to Olivia Clemens, Clemens reported: "We think you have even outdone yourself. I should think that this must be the daintiest, truest, most admirable workmanship that was ever put on a story. The creatures of God do not act out their natures more unerringly than yours do" (*MTHL*, p. 21; *MTLet* 6: 209).

Olivia Clemens thanked Howells on 6 December 1874 for the copy of *A Foregone Conclusion* "which reached me yesterday." She reiterated how "thoroughly" she and her husband "enjoyed the story each month as it came to us in The Atlantic," and she joked about a phrase Howells employed in the novel, "operatic pitch" (*MTHL*, pp. 48–49; *MTLet* 6: 306). On 24 April 1875 a letter from Clemens to Howells discussed an actor who might "play your priest [Don Ippolito]—though I doubt if any man can do that justice" (*MTLet* 6: 459). Clemens compared the length of his *The Adventures of Tom Sawyer* in manuscript to "about what the Foregone Conclusion made" in a letter of 5 July 1875 to Howells (*MTLet* 6: 503). In Florence in October 1878 Clemens noted "preserved rose leaves at the Arminian convent" (NB 17, *N&J* 2: 225)—apparently a reference to the "jar of that conserve of rose-leaves" described in Chapter 2 of Howells's novel. Clemens saw a dramatic adaptation of *A Foregone Conclusion* on 12 November 1889 at the Tremont Theatre in Boston (*MTHL*, pp. 620–621).

———. "Frank Norris," *North American Review* 175 (December 1902): 769–778.

"But I *did* read it. And moreover, I found in it . . . a chemist's mastery of analysis & proportion" (SLC to WDH, Riverdale, New York, 24 December 1902, *MTHL*, p. 756). The talented writer Norris had died on 25 October 1902 at the age of thirty-two following an operation for appendicitis.

———. *A Hazard of New Fortunes* (novel, published in 1890).

A Hazard of New Fortunes, depicting Basil March as a middle-aged magazine editor, is considered one of Howells's more daring novels. Clemens wrote supportively to Howells from Hartford on 11 February 1890: "It is a great book; but of course what I prefer in it is the high art by which it is made to preach its great sermon without seeming to take sides or preach at all" (*MTHL*, p. 630).

Henry Nash Smith, *Mark Twain's Fable of Progress*, pp. 20–25.

———. *Heroines of Fiction.* 2 vols. Illustrated by H[oward]. C[handler]. Christy and A[rthur]. I[ignatius]. Keller. New York: Harper & Brothers, 1901.

Inscription: the title page is signed "Olivia L. Clemens. Riverdale, Oct. 1901."

Catalogs: ListABP (1910), "Heroines of Fiction, Howells", listed twice; *C1951,* O1 and O13, the 2 volumes mistakenly listed separately, both grouped with books signed by Olivia Clemens; *Zeitlin 1951,* #24, 2 vols. listed together, $6.

In fifteen chapters Howells discussed famous female characters in the novels of Jane Austen, Walter Scott, Charles Dickens, Nathaniel Hawthorne, and other eighteenth- and nineteenth-century authors.

———. *An Imperative Duty. A Novel.* New York: Harper & Brothers, 1893. 150 pp.

Source: MTLAcc, entry #1567, volume donated by Clemens.

———. *Impressions and Experiences* (essays, published in 1896).

Catalog: ListABP (1910), "Impressions & Experiences, Howells", no other information provided.

In 1893 Clemens had praised one of the pieces collected in this volume, "The Country Printer." On 30 December 1898 he confessed to Howells from Vienna that "the last chance I had at a bound volume of yours was in London nearly two years ago—the last volume of your short things by the Harpers. I read the whole book twice through & some of the chapters several times" and then "lent it to another admirer of yours & he is admiring it yet" (*MTHL,* pp. 684–685).

———. *Indian Summer.* First edition, first state. Original cloth, soiled with minor wear to the extremities. Boston: Ticknor and Co., 1886.

Catalogs: ListABP (1910), "Indian Summer, Howells"; "Property from the Library of Mark Twain," Butterfield & Butterfield, San Francisco, Sale 6613 (16 July 1997), lot 2676.

Provenance: sold at the 1951 auction in Hollywood, but not listed in the sale sheet.

Location: Mark Twain House and Museum, Hartford, Connecticut.

Copy examined: Clemens's unmarked copy. Viewed in Hartford in 1997.

Indian Summer, first published serially in *Harper's Monthly* (Volumes 71–72) between July 1885 and February 1886, elicited Clemens's most fervent praise for any of Howells's novels except perhaps *A Modern Instance*: "You are really my only author; I am restricted to you; I wouldn't give a damn for the rest." Having read the second part twice ("to my mind there isn't a waste-line in it"), Clemens awaited Part One, which the mails had delayed. "I am to read both parts aloud to the family." Howells's theme of the impossibility of recapturing one's youth touched Clemens deeply: "It is a beautiful story, & makes a body . . . feel so old & so forlorn; & gives him gracious glimpses of his lost youth that fill him with a measureless regret, . . . & lord, no chance to ever get back there again! That is the thing that hurts." Clemens especially appreciated the manner in which "you make all the motives & feelings perfectly clear without analyzing the guts out of them" (SLC to WDH, Elmira, 21 July 1885, *MTHL,* p.

533–534). Three years later Clemens amused himself by listing the chief characteristics of prominent authors; for Howells he wrote "truth" (NB 27 [March 1888], *N&J* 3: 379). Howells returned these compliments in 1887, writing that Twain's writings "express a familiar and almost universal quality of the American mind" and "are honest and true" ("The Editor's Study," *Harper's Monthly* 74.444 [May 1887]: 987).

In 1885 George Parsons Lathrop (1851–1898) reported that Howells (usually arriving from Cambridge, Massachusetts) and Clemens were among the guests who would often while away a winter evening at the home of Charles Dudley Warner ("A Model State Capital," *Harper's Monthly Magazine* 71.425 [October 1885]: 726). Tony Tanner, "Mark Twain and Wattie Bowser," *Mark Twain Journal* 12.1 (Spring 1963): 3–4, discussed the implications of Clemens's remarks.

———. *Italian Journeys* (originally published in 1865 and reprinted various times thereafter; revised by Howells and reissued in Boston by Houghton Mifflin & Company in 1901).

Catalog: ListABP (1910), "Italian Journeys, Howells", no other information supplied.

———. "John Hay in Literature," *North American Review* 181.586 (September 1905): 343–351.

In "John Hay and the Ballads," *Harper's Weekly* 49 (21 October 1905): 1530, Mark Twain would quote from Howells's article and try to correct the impression that Hay's *Pike County Ballads* were indebted to Bret Harte's examples.

———. *The Kentons* (novel, published in 1902).

Catalog: ListABP (1910), "The Kentons, Howells", no other information supplied.

———. *The Lady of the Aroostook* (novel), published serially in the *Atlantic Monthly,* Vols. 42–43, between November 1878 and March 1879.

From Munich Clemens reported on 17 November 1878: "We gathered around the lamp, after supper, . . . & tackled the new magazines. I read your new story aloud, amid thunders of applause." Clemens facetiously recommended future plot developments for the novel, which was running in the *Atlantic Monthly* (*MTHL,* pp. 240–241). On 21 January 1879 Clemens added: "Well, I have read-up, now, as far [as] you have got,—that is, to where there's a storm at sea approaching,—& we three think you are clear out-Howellsing Howells. If your literature has not struck perfection now we are not able to see what is lacking.—It is all such truth—truth to the life; everywhere your pen falls it leaves a photograph" (*MTHL,* p. 245). On 30 January 1879 Clemens chaffed in Munich: "Confound that February number. I wish it would fetch along the Lady of the Aroostook" (*MTHL,* p. 250). Howells was experimenting with the possibilities of portraying shipboard emotions and actions on a voyage from Boston to Europe.

———. *The Landlord at Lion's Head.* Original green cloth, gilt. New York: Harper & Brothers, 1908. 408 pp. [A reprint of the first 1897 edition.]

Inscription: in Clemens's hand in black ink on the front pastedown endpaper, "S L. Clemens/1909/An excellent book. *I* believe it is Howells's very best./Stormfield, November '09."

Marginalia: at page 115, where Howells stated that "society is interested in a man's future, not his past, as it is interested in a woman's past, not her future," Clemens underlined that sentence in black ink and drew a line to the top of the page, where he wrote, "Howells is going to get shot one of these days." (That page is also folded over at the upper corner.) Most of the black ink annotations gently edit Howells's syntax or grammar, a reflex that Clemens could seldom control. There are a few notes in black ink, as on page 142 where Clemens underlined "themselves" in the text and queried, "Why plural?—She has been a teacher." On page 394 Clemens made a long vertical line.

Catalogs: Chicago Book and Art Auctions, Sale number 49 (27 March 1935), from the library of the late Charles McA. Willcox of Denver, Colorado, "8vo, cloth, inner front hinge split," inscription quoted, lot 51; Estate of Chester Davis, Christie's, New York City, 17–18 May 1991; offered on eBay, 15 November 1999, "This is a delightful and intriguing piece that I inherited from my father who was a lifelong collector of books and antiques," minimum bid $1,200.

Location: collection of Kevin Mac Donnell, Austin, Texas.

Copy examined: Clemens's copy, in July 2004.

The first version of Mark Twain's "The Turning-Point of My Life," probably written in December 1909, expressed a favorable opinion of this novel that was omitted in its final form; he called Howells's *The Landlord at Lion's Head* ("his latest book," Twain mistakenly wrote) "his masterpiece, as I think," and quoted a sentence from it (*WIM?*, p. 527). Very likely Clemens never read *The Landlord at Lion's Head*, Howells's most deterministic novel, until he received this copy of the reprint edition, possibly when Howells attended Clara Clemens's wedding at Stormfield on 6 October 1909. Clemens had been in London when the book first issued in 1897. The novel has both New England and European settings and is recognized as one of Howells's most intense and accomplished character studies.

———. *Letters Home.* New York: Harper & Brothers, 1903. 299 pp.

Source: MTLAcc, entry #1571, volume donated by Clemens.

Fictitious people write letters to fictitious recipients, with recurring names and sometimes-poignant themes.

———. *Literary Friends and Acquaintances: A Personal Retrospect of American Authorship.* Illus. New York: Harper & Brothers 1900. 287 pp.

Inscriptions: the front free endpaper is inscribed "Herr Gabrilowitsch's friend, with the hope of his continued acquaintance, W. D. Howells, April 27, 1901" (*Hunley 1958*). The front flyleaf is inscribed: "Wishing Herr Gabrilowitsch a safe journey back to Russia, a pleasant stay there & a speedy return to his friends in America. Olivia L. Clemens/April 24th 1901."

Catalogs: ListABP (1910), "Literary Friends & Acquaintances, Howells"; *C1951*, O29, listed among books signed by Olivia Clemens; *Hunley 1958*, #56, $22.50.

Provenance: formerly owned by the Mark Twain Research Foundation, Perry, Missouri. Described in *The Twainian* 34 (May-June 1975): 1, 3–4. *The Twainian's* editor Chester L. Davis (1903–1987) stated that Clara Clemens Samossoud gave him this book.

Location: Mark Twain Papers, Bancroft Library, University of California at Berkeley.

Copy examined: gift copy from Olivia Clemens to Clara Clemens's future husband, Ossip Gabrilowitsch (1878–1936).

———. *Literature and Life: Studies.* Illus. New York: Harper & Brothers, 1902. 323 pp.

Inscriptions: inscribed by William Dean Howells and signed by Olivia Clemens.

Catalogs: MTLAcc, entry #1798, volume donated by Clemens; ListABP (1910), "Literature & Life, Howells".

Provenance: formerly owned by the Mark Twain Research Foundation, Perry, Missouri. Described in *The Twainian* 34 (July-August 1975): 2–4; (November-December): 1–4; 35 (January-February 1976): 1–3; (March-April 1976): 2–4; (May-June 1976): 4; (July-August 1976): 2–4; (September-October 1976): 4; (November-December 1976): 4.

The Twainian's editor Chester L. Davis (1903–1987) stated that Clara Clemens Samossoud gave him this book.

———, ed. *A Little Girl Among the Old Masters.* Introduction and commentary by William Dean Howells. First edition. 54 plates. Original mustard pictorial cloth. Binding soiled, hinges shaken and broken. Black cloth folding-case. Boston: James R. Osgood and Co., 1884. 65 pp.

Inscription: the front flyleaf is inscribed by Howells: "Susy and Clara Clemens, from Pilla's Papa. Hartford, Nov. 13, 1883."

Provenance: the shelfmark is that of Clara Clemens Gabrilowitsch's private library in Detroit. Donated to the Carrie Estelle Doheny Collection, St. John's Seminary, Camarillo, California by Mrs. Doheny in 1940 after she purchased the volume from Maxwell Hunley Rare Books of Beverly Hills for $12.20. Auctioned by Christie's on 21 February 1989 for an amount between $700 and $900 on behalf of St. John's Seminary. Subsequently the book became part of the Nick Karanovich collection in Fort Wayne, Indiana.

Catalogs: ListABP (1910), "Little Girl among the Old Masters, Howells"; *Sotheby's 2003*, #215, $1,100 (sold with two other Howells titles).

Location: collection of Kevin Mac Donnell, Austin, Texas.

Copy examined: Susy and Clara Clemens's copy, seen in July 2004. A photograph of Mildred Howells is laid in.

Howells compiled this book from the drawings that ten-year-old Mildred ("Pilla") Howells (1872–1966) made during a tour of Italy in 1882. (Angels were one of her favorite subjects.) Clemens was familiar with the volume (see WDH to SLC, 28 May 1884, *MTHL*, p. 490).

———. *London Films.* Illus. First edition. Original sage green cloth, gilt. New York: Harper & Brothers, 1905. 241 pp.

Inscription: the front pastedown endpaper is signed in black ink, "S L. Clemens/1905".

Catalogs: ListABP (1910), "London Films, Howells" (listed twice); *C1951*, #58c, $12.

Provenance: at one point this volume was in the collection of Dave Thomson, who supplied a photocopy of the title page and inscription to the Mark Twain Papers, Bancroft Library, University of California at Berkeley.

Location: collection of Kevin Mac Donnell, Austin, Texas.

Copy examined: Clemens's unmarked copy, in Austin in

July 2004.

Employing photographs and prose, Howells pictures scenes in London, Liverpool, Manchester, Sheffield, York, and other English cities and locales.

——. ["Machiavelli,"] *Harper's Monthly* 110.659 (April 1905): 803–806.

In "William Dean Howells" (1906) Mark Twain selected an excerpt from Howells's "Easy Chair" column, a paragraph concerned with Louis Dyer's *Machiavelli and the Modern State* (1904), to illustrate "how clear, how limpid, how understandable" is Howells's prose.

——. "Mark Twain," *Century Magazine* 24.5 (September 1882): 780–783.

On 28 May 1882 Howells kidded Clemens, "I'm going to write your life for The Century. When and why were you born?" (*MTHL*, p. 404). A letter of 16 June 1882 from Clemens to Howells implied that Howells had given Clemens an advance copy of his piece to vet (*MTHL*, p. 405). Howells's appreciative essay concluded insightfully that "in his work evidently the life has everywhere been studied: and it is his apparent unconsciousness of any other way of saying a thing except the natural way that makes his books so restful and refreshing" (p. 783).

——. "Mark Twain: An Inquiry," *North American Review* 172.531 (February 1901): 306–321.

In a probing, perspicacious analysis of Mark Twain's appeal, Howells observed, "Mr. Clemens is the first writer to use in extended writing the fashion we all use in thinking, and to set down the thing that comes into his mind without fear or favor of the thing that went before, or the thing that may be about to follow" (p. 307). Howells especially singled out Twain's manner of employing words for "the plain, straight meaning their common acceptance has given them" (p. 309). Clemens normally followed Howells' publications very closely, but there was another reason he almost certainly saw this essay: on pages 161–176 of the same issue of *North American Review* appeared Mark Twain's "To the Person Sitting in Darkness."

——. *Miss Bellard's Inspiration; A Novel*. New York: Harper & Brothers, 1905. 224 pp.

Source: MTLAcc, entry #1476, volume donated by Clemens.

——. [Another identical copy.]

Catalogs: ListABP (1910), "Miss Bellard's Inspiration, Howells"; MTLAcc, entry #2277, volume donated from Clemens's library by Clara Clemens Gabrilowitsch in 1910.

——. *A Modern Instance*, in *Century Magazine*, Vols. 23–24, published serially between December 1881 and October 1882.

Clemens would have been in a good mood to be receptive to Howells's latest novel, since he had written to his publisher James R. Osgood on 27 October 1881 to express great satisfaction with Howells's review of *The Prince and the Pauper* (1881): "Howells's review pleased me vastly. The praise & the dispraise sound equally candid & sincere. . . . It is a mint-stamp; it will be hard to rub out" (*Sotheby's 2003*, #49). When Clemens saw the March 1882 installment in *Century Magazine*, in which Bartley Hubbard angrily departs from Equity, Maine, is met at the train station by Marcia Gaylord, and elopes with her to Boston, Clemens made a memorandum in his Notebook 20: "Howells, your new book is fine." Clemens

crossed out the entry after he told Howells this opinion (*N&J* 2: 449). Subsequently his admiration increased; on 22 June 1882 he wrote from Hartford: "I am in a state of wild enthusiasm over this July instalment of your story. It's perfectly dazzling—it's masterly— incomparable." Howells's humor was "so very subtle, & elusive" (*MTHL*, p. 407). On 24 July 1882 Clemens confessed to feeling that he himself resembled Bartley Hubbard, "& I enjoy him to the utmost uttermost, & without a pang" (*MTHL*, p. 412). It is not quite clear whether Clemens had yet taken into account the full extent of Bartley's dissipations, including his drinking problem, when he likened himself to Howells's creation. On 30 October 1882 he acclaimed the concluding chapters; they were "prodigious" (*MTHL*, p. 417). Howells's novel, daring for its time, implicitly made a case for divorce. Clemens invariably admired Howells's works, but these reactions to the sequential chapters of *A Modern Instance*, like his eloquent compliments for *Indian Summer*, stand out from even his usual praise.

——. "The Mother" (poem), *Harper's Monthly* 106.631 (December 1902): 21–26.

"I read 'The Mother' aloud [to Jean Clemens and Miss Lyon] & sounded its human deeps with your deep-sea lead. I had not read it before, since it was first published" (SLC to WDH, New York City, 26 June 1906, *MTHL*, p. 814). Four years earlier, on 29 July 1902, Howells had written to say that he was "glad" Clemens liked the poem and to promise that he would soon send a copy to Olivia Clemens (*MTHL*, p. 743). But evidently Clemens was too concerned about his wife's ill health to permit her to read the piece. He wrote to Howells from Riverdale on 24 December 1902: "I read to people—& praised—. . . the deep & moving one which you wrote at York, & which I wanted Mrs. Clemens to see, there, & which I hide from her now—because we guard her against feelings & thinkings all we can" (*MTHL*, p. 756). See also *MTB*, p. 1313 and the Catalog entry for Howells's "After the Wedding" (poem).

——. *The Mother and the Father. Dramatic Passages*. Green cloth. New York: Harper & Brothers, 1909. 55 pp.

Inscription: the front free endpaper is inscribed by Howells in black ink, "S. L. Clemens/from W. D. Howells./May 22, 1909."

Provenance: Antenne-Dorrance Collection, Rice Lake, Wisconsin.

Location: Mark Twain Archive, Gannett-Tripp Learning Center, Elmira College, Elmira, New York.

Copy examined: Clemens's copy, unmarked. Examined on 28 May 2015.

——. *The Mouse-Trap. A Farce*, in *Harper's Monthly* 74.439 (December 1886): 64–75; reprinted in Edinburgh: David Douglas, 1897. 77 pp.

Clemens wrote to Howells from Vienna on 30 December 1898: "At the house of an English friend, on Christmas Eve, we saw the Mouse-Trap played & *well* played. I thought the house would kill itself with laughter" (*MTHL*, p. 684). In Howells's one-act play with three scenes half a dozen women discuss lofty feminist ideals yet display gratitude for the presence of a male, Mr. Campbell, when a mouse makes a brief appearance. This leads to clever repartee between Campbell and Mrs. Somers.

———. "The New Historical Romances," *North American Review* 171.529 (December 1900): 935–948.

Doubtless Mark Twain read here Howells's praise of *A Connecticut Yankee in King Arthur's Court* (1889) and his other romances. "I like Mark Twain's historical fiction above all for this supreme truth [i.e., its commitment to moral law], just as I like Tolstoy's" (p. 946).

———. *An Open-Eyed Conspiracy: An Idyl of Saratoga.* New York: Harper & Brothers, 1897. 181 pp.

Source: MTLAcc, entry #1568, volume donated by Clemens.

———. "Our Spanish Prisoners at Portsmouth," *Harper's Weekly* 42 (20 August 1898): 826–827.

"This morning I read to Mrs. Clemens from your visit to the Spanish prisoners, & have just finished reading it to her again—& lord, how fine it is & beautiful, & how gracious & moving" (SLC to WDH, Kaltenleutgeben, 30 August 1898, *MTHL*, p. 679). Howells had been an early and implacable opponent of the Spanish-American War; his *Harper's Weekly* piece about the Spanish prisoners at the Portsmouth Navy Yard tries to imagine their longing for their homes.

———. *Out of the Question: A Comedy.* Boston: James R. Osgood and Co., 1885 [cop. 1877]. 183 pp.

Catalogs: ListABP (1910), "Out of the Question, Howells"; *A1911*, "12mo, cloth, Bost. 1885," quotes a list of stories that Clemens intended to tell, one of them "at Howells's birthday dinner," laid in the volume, lot 249, $2.75.

When the play was appearing serially in the *Atlantic Monthly* (between February and April 1877) Clemens addressed an undated letter to Howells: "Been reading Out of the ? aloud to the family & have just finished it. All hands bewitched with it. It is wonderful dialogue" (*MTHL*, p. 173). Considered to be one of Howells's most penetrating plays, *Out of the Question* probed issues of social class in depicting a steamboat engineer's efforts to woo an aristocratic woman.

———. *A Pair of Patient Lovers.* Autographed portrait of the author. New York: Harper & Brothers, 1901. 368 pp.

Inscription: presented to Clemens by the author.

Catalogs: ListABP (1910), "Pair of Patient Lovers, Howells"; *C1951*, 48c, $27.50, listed among the books signed by Clemens.

A collection of five short stories: "A Pair of Patient Lovers," "The Pursuit of the Piano," "A Difficult Case," "The Magic of a Voice," "and "A Circle in the Water."

———. *The Parlor Car. Farce.* Boston: Houghton, Mifflin & Co., 1883. 74 pp.

Catalog: MTLAcc, entry #2275, volume donated from Clemens's library by Clara Clemens Gabrilowitsch in 1910.

———. *The Parlor Car. Farce.* Boston: Ticknor and Co., 1886. 74 pp.

Catalog: ListABP (1910), "Parlor Car, Howells", no other information specified.

Location: Mark Twain Papers, Bancroft Library, University of California at Berkeley.

Copy examined: Clemens's copy, unmarked.

Howells's one-act play was initially published in the *Atlantic Monthly* (38.227 [September 1876]: 290–300). On 23 August 1876 Clemens wrote to him from Elmira: "The farce is wonderfully bright & delicious, & *must* make a hit. . . . I read it aloud to the household this morning & it was better than ever" (*MTHL*, p. 147). Clemens added on 14 September 1876 from Hartford: "You may well know that Mrs. Clemens liked the Parlor Car—enjoyed it ever so much." Clemens suggested adding an "odious train-boy" who would sell "foul literature" and candy, and urged Howells to expand the play to full-length (*MTHL*, p. 152). In an undated letter probably written in March 1877 Clemens reminded Howells that "The Parlor Car was as much as 25 times better, in print, than it was when you read it to me" (*MTHL*, p. 173). Mark Twain often felt strong impulses to burlesque what he admired in literature, and Howells's *The Parlor Car* inspired one such effort. A brief manuscript playlet that survives in the Mark Twain Papers (DV322) is titled "Love on the Rail—A REHEARSAL." The two characters in Twain's undated piece discuss the stage problems involved in dramatizing scenes of "Love at First Sight," "The Bridal Trip," and "Three Months After the Marriage." The playlet ends when they realize that "Three Months After" would require more than one parlor car, since by then the husband would more likely be found in the smoker.

———. *A Parting and a Meeting* (novel, published serially in the issues of *Cosmopolitan* between December 1894 and February 1895).

In a letter written from Paris to Henry H. Rogers on 23 January 1895 Clemens showed an awareness that Howells's "story" was then appearing (*MTHHR*, pp. 122–123).

———. *Private Theatricals* (novel, published serially in the *Atlantic Monthly*, Vols. 36–37, between November 1875 and May 1876). It was not published as a book under this title, but was issued in 1921 as *Mrs. Farrell: A Novel.*

"Company interfered last night, & so 'Private Theatricals' goes over till this evening, to be read aloud," Clemens informed Howells from Hartford on 23 November 1875 (*MTHL*, p. 113; *MTLet* 6: 595).

———. *The Quality of Mercy: A Novel.* New York: Harper & Brothers, 1892. 474 pp.

Catalogs: QF Martinez, poor condition; Ball 2016 inventory, red cloth, gilt letter, signed by Charles Jervis Langdon (1849–1916, Olivia Langdon Clemens's brother), Aug. 1, 1892.

Location: Quarry Farm library shelves, under the supervision of the Mark Twain Archive, Elmira College, Elmira, New York.

Available to Clemens during visits to the Langdons' residence in Elmira.

———. *Ragged Lady* (novel, published serially in the issues of *Harper's Bazar* between July and November 1898).

Clemens wrote to Howells from Vienna on 30 December 1898 that he "saved up your last story," but that another Howells admirer had carried away the magazine before he could begin reading it (*MTHL*, p. 684).

———. *Ragged Lady: A Novel.* Illustrated by A[rthur]. I[gnatius]. Keller [1866–1924]. New York: Harper & Brothers, 1899. 357 pp.

Catalogs: QF Martinez, poor condition; Ball 2016 inventory, red cloth, gilt letter, signed by Charles Jervis Langdon (1849–1916) at the Waldorf-Astoria in 1899.

Location: Quarry Farm library shelves, under the

supervision of the Mark Twain Archive, Elmira College, Elmira, New York.

Accessible to Clemens during visits to the Langdons' residence in Elmira.

———. *The Register: Farce*. Green cloth. Boston: James R. Osgood and Co., 1884. 91 pp.

Catalog: ListABP (1910), "The Register, Howells", no other information provided.

Location: Mark Twain Papers, Bancroft Library, University of California at Berkeley.

Copy examined: Clemens's copy, unmarked.

Howells's play originally appeared in *Harper's Monthly* 68.403 (December 1883): 70–86.

———. *The Rise of Silas Lapham*. First edition, first state. Original cloth, soiled and with extremities rubbed. Boston: Ticknor and Co. 1885. 515 pp.

Provenance: sold at the 1951 auction in Hollywood but not listed in the sale sheet, a common occurrence at that strange event.

Catalogs: ListABP (1910), "Rise of Silas Lapham, Howells"; "Property from the Library of Mark Twain," Butterfield & Butterfield, San Francisco, Sale 6613 (16 July 1997), lot 2677.

Location: Mark Twain House and Museum, Hartford, Connecticut.

Copy examined: Clemens's unmarked copy. Viewed in Hartford in 1997.

Howells's *The Rise of Silas Lapham*, which many critics consider to be his best novel, ran serially in the *Century Magazine* (Volumes 29–30) between November 1884 and August 1885. "I was glad & more than glad to meet young Hubbard again . . . ; the story starts most acceptably," Clemens wrote to Howells on 20 October 1884 (*MTHL*, p. 512). "I & madam are clear behind with Silas Lapham, but Clara Spaulding is booming with it," he reported later (26 March 1885, *MTHL*, p. 524). "I read the June instalment in bed a while ago this morning, & found it as great & fine & strong & beautiful as Mrs. Clemens had already proclaimed it to be. You are always writing your best story, & as usual this one is also your best" (SLC to WDH, 5 June 1885, *MTHL*, p. 531). At Quarry Farm, Olivia Clemens noted in her diary on 1 July 1885 that an Elmira acquaintance "read to us . . . the part of Mr Howells['s] Silas Lapham in the July Century that we found also unusual, it seems as if it showed more the moral struggles of mortals than any thing Mr Howells has ever done before. The characters are all so well drawn. You are compelled to like 'Silas' and 'Persis' in spite of their commonness—particularly Silas" (DV161, MTP).

———. *Roman Holidays and Others*. Illus. New York: Harper & Brothers, 1908. 303 pp.

Inscription: the front pastedown endpaper is signed in ink, "S L. Clemens/Jan. 1909".

Catalog: C1951, D44, listed with books signed by Clemens.

Provenance: in 1982 the volume belonged to Mrs. Walter O. Thompson of Turlock, California (letter from Robert H. Hirst to Alan Gribben 27 August 1982).

Copy examined: a photocopy of Clemens's inscription in the Mark Twain Papers, Bancroft Library, University of California at Berkeley that was provided by the owner (who did not wish to be identified) on 29 March 1983.

The volume has a *C1951* sale label pasted in.

Howells painted word pictures of scenes in Spain, Genoa, Naples, Rome, Pompeii, Pisa, and other cities and sites.

———. *Seven English Cities*. Green cloth. Illustrated with photographs. New York: Harper & Brothers, 1909. 201 pp.

Provenance: Antenne-Dorrance Collection, Rice Lake, Wisconsin.

Location: Mark Twain Archive, Gannett-Tripp Learning Center, Elmira College, Elmira, New York.

Copy examined: Clemens's copy, unmarked. Examined on 28 May 2015.

Howells visits York, Manchester, Sheffield, Liverpool, and other cities in England and Wales. The concluding chapter is titled "Glimpses of English Character."

———. *The Shadow of a Dream* (short novel), in *Harper's Monthly* 80.478 (March 1890): 510–529; (April 1890): 766–782; and (May 1890): 865–881.

Howells apparently read the first portion of *The Shadow of a Dream* to the Clemenses in Hartford on 2 and 3 November 1889 (*MTHL*, p. 625).

———. *The Shadow of a Dream; A Story*. New York: Harper & Brothers, 1890. 218 pp.

Source: MTLAcc, entry #1570, volume donated by Clemens.

———. "A Shaker Village," *Atlantic Monthly* 37.224 (June 1876): 699–710.

"We have just finished the Shaker article. . . . The sketch is so full of pathos; I mean all through—in every sentence" (SLC to WDH, Hartford, 12 May 1876, *MTHL*, p. 139). Mark Twain's "Facts Concerning the Recent Carnival of Crime in Connecticut" appeared in this same issue of the *Atlantic Monthly*.

———. *Sketch of the Life and Character of Rutherford B. Hayes. Also a Biographical Sketch of William A. Wheeler*. New York: Hurd and Houghton, 1876. 226 pp.

Source: MTLAcc, entry #830, volume donated by Clemens.

Howells informed Clemens on 8 September 1876: "I finished the book yesterday. . . . Of course I'll send you a copy at once" (*MTHL*, p. 149). On 14 September 1876 Clemens wrote: "I am reading & enjoying the biography. It is a marvelous thing that you read for it & wrote it in such a little bit of a time" (*MTHL*, p. 150). Ohio governor Hayes (1822–1893) would defeat James G. Blaine for the Republican presidential nomination; he would then prevail over the Democratic candidate Samuel L. Tilden in the disputed general election of 1876 owing to Republican concessions made to Southern Democrats. Hayes and his Vice-President, William Almon Wheeler (1819–1887), would serve one term in office.

———. *The Son of Royal Langbrith* (novel), published serially in the *North American Review*, Vols. 178–179, January-August 1904.

"Last night I read your 27 pages in the N.A.R., with vast interest. It stimulated me out of a couple of hours of sleep" (SLC to WDH, Florence, 16 January 1904, *MTHL*, p. 779).

———. *The Son of Royal Langbrith, A Novel*. New York: Harper & Brothers, 1905. 369 pp.

Catalogs: ListABP (1910), "Son of Royal Langbrith, Howells"; MTLAcc, entry #1307, volume donated by Clemens.

———. "Sorrow, My Sorrow" (poem), *Harper's Monthly*

108.643 (December 1903): 147.

Clemens wasted no time in praising "your moving & beautiful poem. How many it comes home to; how many have felt it" (SLC to WDH, Florence, 4 December 1903, *MTHL*, p. 774). Howells's three-stanza poem of rhyming couplets laments that when sorrow becomes an excruciating companion it is then strangely agonizing when it eventually departs, leaving a terrible void. Stanza II concludes by asking, " Sorrow, my treasured grief, my hoarded pain,/Where shall I turn to have you mine again?" Stanza III provides one answer: "Wherever there are other breasts that ache,/Wherever there are hearts are [*sic*] like to break,/Wherever there are hurts too hard to bear,/Turn and look for me, you shall find me there."

———. *Suburban Sketches*. First edition. Original green cloth, gilt, yellow-coated endpapers. New York: Hurd and Houghton, 1871. 234 pp.

Inscription: the front flyleaf is inscribed (in pencil) "S. L. Clemens/1871." The handwriting appears to be that of Olivia Clemens.

Provenance: the shelfmark is that of Clara Clemens Samossoud's private library in Detroit. Subsequently entered the Carrie Estelle Doheny Collection, St. John's Seminary, Camarillo, California, where it was donated in 1940 after Mrs. Doheny purchased the volume from Maxwell Hunley Rare Books of Beverly Hills for $12.20. Auctioned by Christie's with two other titles for $2,040 on 17 October 1988 (lot 1184) on behalf of St. John's Seminary. Then it became part of the Nick Karanovich collection in Fort Wayne, Indiana.

Catalogs: ListABP (1910), "Suburban Sketches, Howells"; *Sotheby's 2003*, #215, $1,100 (sold with two other Howells titles).

Location: collection of Kevin Mac Donnell, Austin, Texas.

Copy examined: Clemens's unmarked copy, in Austin in July 2004. Has an "Estelle Doheny" bookplate.

In a series of nine essays Howells explores the quaint pleasures and minor challenges of living in a small village outside the bustling city of Boston.

———. *Their Silver Wedding Journey* (novel), published serially in *Harper's Monthly* 98–100 (January-December 1899).

At Howells's urging, Clemens promised from Vienna to read this novel when it would begin to appear (SLC to WDH, 30 December 1898, *MTHL*, p. 684). "I am waiting for the April Harper, which is about due now; waiting, & strongly interested," Clemens wrote on 2 April 1899 (*MTHL*, p. 689). After the issue arrived, Clemens informed Howells that he detected in the characters "the weariness & indolence of age; indifference to sights & things once brisk with interest" (5 April 1899, *MTHL*, pp. 689–690). "Day before yesterday the Harper came, & in the evening I hunted it up & was lying on the sofa, & kept interrupting the family's repose with laughter & chuckles" because Clemens recognized Olivia in Mrs. March (SLC to WDH, 12 May 1899, *MTHL*, p. 695). "Your September instalment was delicious—every word of it. You haven't lost *any* of your splendid art" (SLC to WDH, Sanna, Sweden, 26 September 1899, *MTHL*, p. 706).

———. "The Surprise Party to Mark Twain," *Harper's Weekly*

44.2295 (15 December 1900): 1205.

Howells contributed this witty little essay (accompanied by a clever drawing) to a *Harper's Weekly* issue largely devoted to paying homage to Mark Twain, who had returned to the United States from his years abroad. *Harper's Weekly* editorialized that the public should recognize Twain "for his honor, for his integrity" (p. 1204). In "The Surprise Party to Mark Twain" Howells pretends that he is trying to deliver a serious speech at a dinner thrown for Twain by his literary characters.

———. *Their Wedding Journey*. Illustrated by Augustus Hoppin (1828–1896). 8vo, original green cloth, wear at the front joint and ends of the spine. Boston: James R. Osgood and Co., 1872.

Inscription: the front free endpaper is inscribed in brown ink, "To/Mrs. Samuel L. Clemens/with the regards of/W. D. Howells./Cambridge, March 15, 1872."

Marginalia: Olivia Clemens made penciled underlinings and notes in the first thirty-two pages of the text. Page 8: "The perfect taste of Boston" (written beneath an illustration of a stylish couple). Page10: "See picture page 8." She also underlined two lines and altered "officer" to "official". Page 20: "Oh, la, la!" (in the margin). Page 22: "Sweet thing! With his nice cool high hat" (written next to an illustration featuring a man in a top hat). Page 23: "Him awful nice mans to quote pitty po'try on hot morning" (a male character is reciting poetry as he and his wife walk outside). She also guessed that the anonymous poet being quoted was "Probably W. D. H." Page 24: one line of the text is underlined. Page 25: one line of the text is underlined. Page 28: "Oh pish!" and two lines of the text are underlined. Page 32: a line drawn at an angle at the end of a paragraph as though to indicate a stopping point. No markings are visible beyond this.

Catalog: ListABP (1910), "Wedding Journey, Howells", no other information supplied.

Provenance: Carrie Estelle Doheny Collection, St. John's Seminary, Camarillo, California. Donated by Mrs. Doheny in 1940 after she purchased the volume for $12.20 from Maxwell Hunley Rare Books of Beverly Hills. Auctioned by Christie's in New York City (lot 1180) for $3,500 on 17 October 1988 on behalf of St. John's Seminary. A decade later it was offered for sale by Brick Row Book Shop, San Francisco, California, in January 1998, "the first book inscribed by Howells to Clemens," no marginalia, from the library of Estelle Doheny; subsequently sold by Christie's (John Crichton, Brick Row Book Shop, to Alan Gribben, email, 27 January 1998).

Location: collection of Kevin Mac Donnell (Mac Donnell to Alan Gribben, 28 August 2017). A subsequent description sent in August 2017 detailed Olivia Clemens's marginalia.

Copy examined: Clemens's copy, when it was at St. John's Seminary in 1970.

Olivia Clemens mentioned this book to her husband in a letter of 30 December 1871 (MTP). Clemens wrote to Howells several times in 1872, but no surviving letters from Howells to Clemens predated Howells's presentation of this book to Olivia Clemens. On 18 March 1872 Clemens thanked Howells for a complimentary copy of the novel: "We bought it & read it some time ago, but we prize this copy most on account of the autograph" (*MTHL*, p. 10; *MTLet* 5: 58). *Mark Twain's Library of Humor* (1888) would contain four selections from *Their Wedding Journey*: "Trying to Understand a Woman," "At Niagara," "Their First Quarrel," and "Custom House Morals."

————. *Their Wedding Journey*. Illustrated by Clifford Carleton (1867–1946). Original white cloth, gilt, in original tan cloth dust jacket, gilt. Boston: Houghton, Mifflin, 1894. 399 pp.

Inscription: the first free endpaper is inscribed by Olivia Clemens: "From Mr. and Mrs. Clemens/to/Mrs. Haupt [?]/Dec. 25, 1895." On this date the Clemenses arrived in the morning on the *Oceana* at Melbourne (Fears 2: 1095).

Location: collection of Kevin Mac Donnell, Austin, Texas. Acquired from a used bookshop on the West Coast on 8 March 2005.

Source: letter from Kevin Mac Donnell to Alan Gribben, 10 March 2005, and an email from Mac Donnell to Gribben on 19 July 2014.

————. "Thomas Bailey Aldrich."

On 27 March 1907 Isabel V. Lyon, rummaging through cases of books and papers from Charles L. Webster & Company, "ran upon a sketch of Mr. Aldrich's life in ms. written by Mr. Howells which I brought home" (IVL Journal, TS p. 236, MTP).

The Special Collections Library at Penn State University Libraries lists this (presumably) same biographical sketch by Howells, with his corrections, but there is no indication of where the piece was published. Most likely Howells wrote the essay soon after Aldrich's death on 19 March 1907. Susan Goodman and Carl Dawson, in *William Dean Howells: A Writer's Life* (Berkeley: University of California Press, 2005), p. 393, reported that when Aldrich passed away Howells, tired of writing tributes to his elderly friends upon their deaths, "declined to write a commemorative essay for *Harper's Weekly*."

————. *Through the Eye of the Needle: A Romance*. New York: Harper & Brothers, 1907. 232 pp.

Catalog: ListABP (1910), "Through the Eye of the Needle, Howells", no other information supplied.

This utopian novel was the final volume in Howells's Altrurian trilogy.

————. *A Traveller from Altruria*, in *The Cosmopolitan* 14.5 (March 1893): 633–640.

In 1893 Clemens jotted a note about a short story in the March 1893 issue of *The Cosmopolitan* by Ida M. Van Etten (see the Van Etten entry). Chapter 5 of Howells's novel appeared in that same issue, so it seems likely that Clemens read at least that installment of *A Traveller from Altruria*, which would be published in book form by Harper & Brothers in 1894 (whereupon one "*l*" was dropped the word "*Traveler*" in its title).

————. *Tuscan Cities* (published in 1886).

"Lately I was once more reading your incomparable Tuscan Cities—a book whose details I love to forget, so that I can read them again with the pristine relish. If I had a memory I should know the book by heart by this time" (SLC to WDH, Redding, Connecticut, 24 September 1908, *MTHL*, p. 835). Howells's rhapsodic descriptions of Florence, Siena, Pisa, Lucca, and a few other cities are ranked among the best travel writings devoted to this region of Italy.

————. *The Undiscovered Country*. Original decorated brown cloth. Boston: Houghton, Mifflin and Co., 1880. 419 pp.

Inscription: the first flyleaf is inscribed on its verso in purple ink: "S. L. Clemens/with ever so much affection,/W. D. Howells./Belmont,/June 18, 1880."

Marginalia: light pencil marks, possibly not Clemens's, throughout pages 1–65. On page 2 Clemens made a revision in black ink, crossing out "Oh, I don't know that I prefer. . . . the business," marking the rest of the paragraph, and writing in the margin: "from here down to here." On the verso of a flyleaf at the back, someone, perhaps Isabel Lyon, made a note in pencil: "'Bambino makes music more than what it is'—when he sings a chorus to the Wedding March—".

Catalogs: ListABP (1910), "Undiscovered Country, Howells"; *C1951*, D56, "autographed by the author," $30.

Location: Albert and Shirley Small Special Collections Library, Alderman Library, Charlottesville, Virginia. Donated by Clifton Waller Barrett.

Copy examined: Clemens's copy, in 1970.

This novel began to appear serially in the *Atlantic Monthly* in January 1880. Clemens wrote to Howells from Hartford on 8 January 1880: "The Undiscovered starts off delightfully—I have read it aloud to Mrs. C. & we vastly enjoyed it" (*MTHL*, p. 287). "I've read the Feb. Undiscovered, & it is perfectly wrote—as Susy says.— What a master hand you are to jabber the nauseating professional slang of spiritism" (SLC to WDH, Elmira, 24 January 1880, *MTHL*, p. 288). Mark Twain quoted a passage from this novel (see the marginalia above) in "William Dean Howells" (1906) to illustrate Howells's gift for description.

————. *Venetian Life*. New and Enlarged Edition. Original pictorial cloth, boards bumped, cloth soiled. Boston: James R. Osgood and Co., 1874. [First published in book form in 1866.]

Marginalia: a few passages are marked or editorially annotated, apparently in Clemens's hand.

Provenance: displays the shelfmarks of Clara Clemens Gabrilowitsch's library numbering system during her Detroit years. Sold at the 1951 auction in Hollywood but not listed in the sale sheet, a not-uncommon error at that hastily arranged event.

Catalogs: ListABP (1910), "Venetian Life, Howells"; "Property from the Library of Mark Twain," Butterfield & Butterfield, San Francisco, Sale 6613 (16 July 1997), lot 2678.

Location: Mark Twain House and Museum, Hartford, Connecticut.

Copy examined: Clemens's copy. Viewed in Hartford in 1997.

Twenty-two chapters recounted Howells's halcyon days as a U. S. Consul in Venice, the patronage reward for his writing a political campaign biography of Abraham Lincoln in 1860. Sometime before 1870 Clemens copied a passage from *Venetian Life* (describing "the ghost of dead Venice") into Olivia Langdon's commonplace book (DV161, MTP). In Chapter 36 of *The Gilded Age* (1873) Laura Hawkins reads "a familiar passage" in Howells's *Venetian Life* while browsing in a Washington, D.C. bookstore. In "William Dean Howells" (1906) Mark Twain quoted excerpts from the book and recalled: "I read his *Venetian Days* [*sic*] about forty years ago. . . . For forty years his English has been to me a continued delight and astonishment." Afterwards Howells wrote to Clemens good-naturedly about the mistaken title that *Venetian Life* was given in the essay: "You are the only person in the world who may do this and not be destroyed" (1 August 1906, *MTHL*, p. 816).

French, *MT&GA* (1965), pp. 51, 292 n. 50.

————. "The White Mr. Longfellow," *Harper's Monthly* 93.555 (August 1896): 327–343.

"Certainly your White Longfellow is perfect—wholly flawless," Clemens declared (SLC to WDH, Southampton, England, 5 August 1896, *MTHL*, p. 660). Chapters 1–7 of Mark Twain's *Tom Sawyer, Detective* appeared in the same issue of *Harper's Monthly* (pp. 344–361) as Howells's adulatory reflections on his friendship with Henry Wadsworth Longfellow in Cambridge, Massachusetts (pp. 327–343). Longfellow, Howells recalled, possessed a "gentle dignity" (p. 336), "liked people who were acquainted with manners and men" (p. 339), and "disliked after-dinner speaking, and made conditions for his own exemption from it" (p. 342). Howells credited the Norwegian author Björnstjerne Björnson with bestowing the "White Mr. Longfellow" sobriquet on the American poet.

————. *A Woman's Reason* (novel), in *Century Magazine*, Vols. 25–26, published serially in the February-October 1883 issues.

"We have read your two opening numbers in the Century, and consider them almost beyond praise. I hear no dissent from this verdict" (SLC to WDH, Hartford, 1 March 1883, p. 427). "We are enjoying your story with our usual unspeakableness; & I'm right glad you threw in the shipwreck & the mystery— I *like* it" (SLC to WDH, Elmira, 22 August 1883, *MTHL*, p. 439). Howells's romantic story uncharacteristically depended on the return of a fiancé shipwrecked on a remote island in the South Pacific to rescue a refined Boston woman who has suddenly become financially destitute.

————. *A Woman's Reason; A Novel*. Boston: James R. Osgood and Co., 1883. 466 pp. [Edition conjectured.]

Catalog: ListABP (1910), "A Woman's Reason, Howells", no other information supplied.

————, adapt. *Yorick's Love* (play, produced in 1878). Adapted from *Un Drama Nuevo* by Manuel Tamayo y Baus (1829–1898).

"Last night, for the first time in ages, we went to the theatre [in Hartford]—to see Yorick's Love. The magnificence of it is beyond praise. The language is so beautiful, the passion so fine, the plot so ingenious, the whole thing so stirring, so charming, so pathetic!" (SLC to WDH, Hartford, 11 March 1880, *MTHL*, p. 292). The Clemenses saw the prominent actor Lawrence Barrett (1838–1891) perform the leading role (Fears, *Day by Day* 1: 900); Barrett had added Howells's play to his repertoire.

————— and HENRY MILLS ALDEN (1836–1919), eds. *Their Husbands' Wives*. Harper's Novelettes Series. First edition. Original green cloth, gilt. New York: Harper & Brothers, 1906. 181 pp.

Inscription: signed in black ink on the front pastedown endpaper: "S L. Clemens/1906."

Provenance: Carrie Estelle Doheny Collection, St. John's Seminary, Camarillo, California. Donated in 1940 after

Mrs. Doheny purchased the volume from Maxwell Hunley Rare Books of Beverly Hills for $12.20. Sold at auction by Christie's (lot 1173) for $1,430 on 17 October 1988 at the behest of St. John's Seminary.

Location: collection of Kevin Mac Donnell, Austin, Texas.

Copy examined: Clemens's unmarked copy, in Austin in July 2004.

The book contained Mark Twain's "Eve's Diary" (1905) on pages 1–27. Twain had readily consented to Howells's request to include this piece (WDH to SLC, 19 December 1905, *MTHL*, pp. 799–800). Five other fictional contributions came from Elizabeth Stuart Phelps, 1844–1911 ("Covered Embers"), Abby Meguire Roach, 1876–1966 ("Life's Accolade"), [Gilbert] Emery Bemsley Pottle, 1875–1945 ("The Bond"), George A[biah]. Hibbard, 1858–1928 ("The Eyes of Affection"), and Grace Ellery Channing, 1862–1937 ("The Marriage Question"). Clemens often sampled the other contents of books where his writings appeared.

————. [A similar copy issued by the same publisher, also in 1906. Original red cloth.] 181 pp.

Location: Albert and Shirley Small Special Collections Library, University of Virginia Libraries, Charlottesville. Gift of Clifton Waller Barrett.

Source: University of Virginia Libraries online catalog, 12 March 2006: "From the library of Samuel Langhorne Clemens. Personal copy." (I appreciate Jo Dee Benussi's calling this item to my attention.)

————— and HENRY MILLS ALDEN (1836–1919), eds. *Under the Sunset*. Harper's Novelettes Series. New York: Harper & Brothers, 1906. 264 pp.

Source: MTLAcc, entry #2280, volume donated from Clemens's library by Clara Clemens Gabrilowitsch in 1910. Howells and Alden assembled ten works of short fiction set in the American West: Grace Ellery Channing, 1862–1937 ("The End of the Journey"), Charles A[lexander]. Eastman, 1858–1939 ("The Gray Chieftain"), Josiah Flynt [Willard], 1869–1907 ("Jamie the Kid"), Thomas A[llibone]. Janvier, 1849–1913 ("The Sage-Brush Hen"), Maurice Kingsley, 1847–1910 ("Tio Juan"), Marie Manning, 1872–1945 ("The Prophetess of the Land of No-Smoke"), Philip Verrell Mighels, 1869–1911 ("A Little Pioneer"), Elmore Elliott Peake, 1871–1930 ("Back to Indiana"), Elia W[ilkinson]. Peattie, 1862–1935 ("A Madonna of the Desert"), and Zoe Dana Underhill, 1847–1934 ("The Inn of San Jacinto"). Besides providing an excellent collection of Western fiction that was appearing in current magazines, *Under the Sunset* is notable for the percentage (four out of the ten stories) written by women authors—Grace Ellery Channing, Marie Manning, Elia W. Peattie, and Zoe Dana Underhill.

————— and THOMAS SERGEANT PERRY (1845–1928), eds. *Library of Universal Adventure by Sea and Land; Including Original Narratives and Authentic Stories of Personal Prowess and Peril in All the Waters and Regions of the Globe from the Year 70 A.D. to the Year 1888 A.D.* Illus. New York: Harper & Brothers, 1888. [cop. 1887.] 1023 pp.

Location: Mark Twain Library, Redding, Connecticut.

Copy examined: Clemens's copy, unmarked. Has the Mark Twain Library accession number "3293". Examined in

1970 and again in June 1982.

Library of Universal Adventure by Sea and Land should be considered one of the prime "sleeper" volumes in Clemens's personal library. This compendium of notable feats and narrow escapes, organized into four geographical regions ("America" being the first one) contained accounts of historical figures and events that were bound to draw Clemens's attention: John Smith and Pocahontas, Daniel Boone's exploits, Frederick Douglass's escape from slavery, the New York City draft riots, bear and buffalo hunts, Civil War prisoners, American Indian captivities, Cellini's escape from prison, Casanova's imprisonment, Baron Trenck's imprisonment, the French Revolution, the highest recorded balloon ascension, Edward Whymper's fall on the Matterhorn, the Black Hole of Calcutta, the Sepoy Mutiny, hunting lions, elephants, and gorillas, heroic efforts to find and stop slavers in Africa, the death of Captain Cook, and the mutiny on the *Bounty*. These are only a few samples of the dozens upon dozens of stories, condensed from the original narratives, that might have caught Clemens's eye. Howells and Perry supplied abbreviated sources for their material, a courtesy unusual in these types of encyclopedic publications during that era. Especially noteworthy are two reports. The first is an eerie account of what the editors termed The Frozen Ship and titled the phenomenon "A Phantom Ship Manned by a Dead Crew" (pp. 136–137). One thinks of Mark Twain's various depictions of vessels hovering in space or stranded at sea with crews of corpses. The other surprising inclusion, a reprinted narrative about the burning of the *Hornet* and the harrowing ordeal of its survivors, "Forty-Three Days in an Open Boat," is credited to "S. L. Clemens" and dated 2 July 1866 in Honolulu. Clemens often sampled the other contents of books where his writings appeared.

HOWELLS, WILLIAM HOOPER (1844–1918). *The Rescue of Desdemona, and Other Verse.* No. 188 of 1,000 copies. Illustrated by George Wolfe Plank (1883–1965). Philadelphia: Butterfly Press, 1908. 106 pp.

Source: MTLAcc, entry #2035, volume donated from Clemens's library by Clara Clemens Gabrilowitsch in 1910. Clemens very likely acquired this turgid effort as an addition to his "Library of Literary Hogwash," but no comment by him—or the volume itself—survives. Here is a sample of Howells's versifying, titled "Fidelis Paupertas": "In tatters clad my mistress came,/And brought me ample dower of shame./They called her 'Poverty,' and I/In vain essayed her love to fly,/But near me she would still remain" (p. 106).

HOWELLS, WINIFRED ("WINNIE") (1863–1889). Clemens wrote to Olivia Clemens on 18 April 1875 to express his amazement at the poetic and artistic talent of "Winnie Howells, . . . a child of eleven years—daughter of W. D. Howells" (*MTLet* 6: 451). On 23 April 1875 he mentioned to Howells that "Winnie's literature sings through me yet!" (*MTLet* 6: 457).

"HOW FIRM A FOUNDATION" (hymn, published in 1787). Generally attributed to Robert Keene but sometimes to George Keith. The melody was the traditional "Adestes fidelis." Clemens wrote the title of this hymn, which begins "How firm the foundation, ye saints of the Lord," in a copy of *Laudes Domini: A Selection of Spiritual Songs, Ancient and Modern*, compiled by C. S. Robinson. See that

Catalog entry.

HOWITT, MARY (BOTHAM) (1799–1888). *Birds and Flowers; or, Lays and Lyrics of Rural Life.* Illustrated by H[ector]. Giacomelli (1822–1904). Nelson's Series of Juvenile Art-Books. London: T. Nelson and Sons, 1873. 211 pp.

Inscription: the first flyleaf is missing. An *A1911* sale label is affixed to the front pastedown endpaper. A page of Clemens's holograph notes calculating the number of authors and volumes (including books by Abbott, Adams, and Lyman, totaling "515 books by 75 authors") is mounted on the front free flyleaf.

Catalog: *A1911*, "12mo, cloth, some pp. slightly foxed, Lond. 1873," a sheet of Clemens's notes laid in, lot 250, sold for $2.25.

Location: Department of Rare Books and Special Collections, University Library, University of Michigan, Ann Arbor. Donated on 7 October 1940 by Mrs. Barnard Pierce, Mrs. Carl Haessler, Mrs. Howard Luce, and Miss Margaret Knight, from the library of Edward A. Barnes.

Copy examined: photocopy of the Library catalog card sent by then Assistant Rare Book Librarian Karla M. Vandersypen on 3 June 1987.

Rhyming poems by the English author Howitt about wildlife, plants, and seasons, with nearly 100 elaborately engraved drawings.

———. *Hope On! Hope Ever! Or, the Boyhood of Felix Law.* New York: D. Appleton & Co., 1856. 212 pp.

Inscriptions: signed "Olivia Langdon, Elmira, N. Y." and inscribed "Livia [*sic*] Langdon from Lucy Neal, 1857."

Catalogs: list of books transferred by Mark Woodhouse from the Quarry Farm library to the Mark Twain Archive on 9 July 1987; Ball 2016 inventory, blue cloth with gilt lettering, blind cover design, good condition.

Location: Mark Twain Archive, Elmira College, Elmira, New York.

In Howitt's optimistic story, written for a juvenile audience, a Yorkshire lad makes his entrance into London where, among other adventures, he tries to reform a woman addicted to gin. Eventually he returns home, with much experience behind him. Apparently Olivia (Langdon) Clemens (1845–1904) left this book in Elmira when she married Clemens. It would have been accessible to him in the Langdons' home.

———. *Our Four-Footed Friends.* London: S. W. Partridge & Co., [1862?]. 168 pp.

Source: MTLAcc, entry #1891, volume donated from Clemens's library by Clara Clemens Gabrilowitsch in 1910.

HOYOS, CAMILLA, Countess of Austria (1880–1953). *The "Lettre de Cachet" and Other Stories. By C. H.* First edition. Original decorated tan cloth, gilt, uncut. London: Digby, Long & Co., 1900. 188 pp.

Inscriptions: the front flyleaf is inscribed: "To/Mr. Clemens in the hopes of receiving very much more than I have to offer/from Camilla Hoyos. May 24th, 1900." Clemens signed the front pastedown endpaper in black ink, "S L. Clemens/1909."

Provenance: the shelfmark of Clara Clemens Gabrilowitsch's private library in Detroit is visible. Donated to the Carrie Estelle Doheny Collection, St. John's Seminary, Camarillo, California, by Mrs. Doheny in 1940 after she purchased the volume for $12.20 from Maxwell Hunley Rare Books of Beverly Hills. Auctioned by Christie's for $357 on 21 February 1989 (lot 1770) on behalf of St. John's Seminary. Subsequently in the collection of Nick Karanovich, Fort Wayne, Indiana.

Catalog: *Sotheby's 2003*, #216, $3,500 (sold with five other inscribed books).

Location: collection of Kevin Mac Donnell, Austin, Texas. Has the bookplate of "Estelle Doheny."

Copy examined: Clemens's copy, unmarked, in Austin in July 2004.

HOYT, CHARLES HALE (1860–1900). *A Rag Baby* (play, produced in 1884).

"There is a young fellow, playing here [in Boston] in a thing called The Rag Baby, who c'd do Sellers perfectly well. . . . He does an amateur pugilist and walkist, named Sport" (SLC to Charles L. Webster, 10 May 1884, *MTBus*, p. 253). The diminutive comic actor Frank [Albert] Daniels (1860–1935) had created the role of "Old Sport," a drug store clerk and enthusiastic boxing fan, for the American playwright Hoyt's satire of small town life. Daniels's infectious mannerisms would keep the play alive for three years of performances in various cities.

HOYT, JANETTE RALSTON (CHASE) (1847–1925). *Janet and Her Friends*. New York: D. Appleton & Co., 1876. 83 pp. [Edition conjectured.]

Catalog: ListABP (1910), "Janet and Her Friends", no other information provided.

HUBBARD, CHARLES CARROLL (1832–1898).

Hubbard sent a letter to Mark Twain on 25 January 1876 that opened: "I have taken the liberty to forward to you by mail, a little book, not as a sample, nor for review exactly, but to do as you please with" (*Dear Mark Twain*, ed. R. Kent Rasmussen, p. 43). The book has not been identified. Hubbard was a hardware manufacturer and mayor of Middletown, Connecticut. His letter went on to urge Twain to write a book about Florida.

HUBBARD, ELBERT [GREEN] (1856–1915). *Health and Wealth, Wherein Pleasingly Told . . . the Best Methods of Preventing One from Becoming a Burden to Himself, a Weariness to His Friends, a Trial to His Neighbors, and a Reflection on his Maker*. Peeling brown suede cover. East Aurora, New York: The Roycrofters, 1908. 163 pp.

Location: Mark Twain Library, Redding, Connecticut.

Copy examined: Clemens's copy, unmarked. Lacks a library accession number, but it has long been shelved with Clemens's book donations. Examined in 1970 and again in June 1982.

———. *The Man of Sorrows. Being a Little Journey to the Home of Jesus of Nazareth*. Illus. First edition. Original quarter suede, paper covered boards, gilt, blue endpapers, uncut. East Aurora, New York: Roycrofters, 1906. 121 pp.

Inscription: inscribed by Hubbard in ink on the front free flyleaf, "To/Mark Twain/with all kind/wishes/Elbert Hubbard."

Marginalia: caustic annotations on five pages (58, 61, 69, 81, and 87) by Clemens, with pencil markings on another twenty pages (26–27, 32–33, 60–61, 63, 65, 73, 75–76, 79, 82, 90–92, 98, 110, and 114). In black ink on a front flyleaf Clemens altered a printed quotation from the Bible, "What things soever ye desire, when ye pray, believe that ye receive them, and ye shall have them" (Mark, xi, 24–25), changing "ye shall have them" to "ye do have them," and adding underneath: "(Corrected to fit/Christian Science.)" On page 58 Clemens scoffed, "Perhaps this has deceived many persons into believing that God does & will take care of His children & other creatures." Clemens mocked on page 61 Hubbard's implication about a luxurious paradise, writing, "New Jerusalem paved with gold." At Hubbard's admiring reference to Jesus's voice that "was to thunder down the centuries—and affect the destinies of millions yet unborn," Clemens added sarcastically "& spill oceans of innocent blood" (page 87). A laid-in pencil note by Isabel V. Lyon headed "Tuxedo" described how Clemens became disgusted with Hubbard's book, "threw this book on the floor after glancing through it, & . . . declared that he 'despised them both,'" telling Lyon not to send Hubbard a thank-you note (though she says that she did write a note of receipt).

Provenance: in 1986 this volume was in the collection of Victor Jacobs of Dayton, Ohio (Jacobs to Alan Gribben, 15 October 1986). Jacobs sold his collection before he died in 1998, and subsequently the book became part of the collection of Nick Karanovich of Fort Wayne, Indiana.

Catalogs: "Victor and Irene Murr Jacobs Collection," Sotheby's, New York City (29 October 1996), lot 313, sold with four other books for a total of $9,312; *Sotheby's 2003*, $3,500 (sold with a copy of Twain's *Christian Science* (1907) that contains an autograph note).

Location: collection of Kevin Mac Donnell, Austin, Texas.

Copy examined: Clemens's copy, in Austin in July 2004, plus a set of three photocopies sent to Alan Gribben by Robert T. Slotta on 2 June 2001.

Hubbard's Newspaper and Bank Directory of the World. 3 vols. New Haven, Connecticut: H. P. Hubbard, 1882–1884.

"I have 'Hubbard's Newspaper & Bank Directory of the World,' 3 bulky volumes, which you can have for your office" (SLC to Charles L. Webster, n.d., TS in MTP). This enormous directory was compiled by Harlan Page Hubbard (1845–1903).

HUBER, FRANÇOIS (1750–1831). *New Observations on the Natural History of Bees* (first published in 1792; the first English edition appeared in 1806).

In "The Bee" (written in 1902?) Mark Twain mentions this Swiss naturalist as one of "the great authorities" on honeybees (Box 1, no. 1, MTP).

HUC, ÉVARISTE RÉGIS (1813–1860). *Recollections of a Journey Through Tartary, Thibet, and China, During the Years 1844, 1845, and 1846*. New York: D. Appleton & Co., 1852. [The title varied in subsequent editions.]

In November 1889 Clemens made a note concerning the narrative of this French Roman Catholic priest and missionary: "M. Huc's Thibet, Mongolia & China" (NB 29, *N&J* 3: 532).

HUCH, RICARDA OCTAVIA (1864–1947). *Fra Celeste und andere Erzählungen [Fra Celeste and Other Stories]*. Leipzig: H. Haessel, 1899. 273 pp.

Source: MTLAcc, entry #386, volume donated by Clemens. The German historian and intellectual Huch, a pioneer woman in her field of study, also wrote fiction and poetry. Her title story in this collection tempts a priest with earthly carnal love in place of his ethereal love for God.

HUGHES, RUPERT (1872–1956). *Zal, An International Romance*.

New York: Century Co., 1905. 346 pp.

Source: MTLAcc, entry #2281, volume donated from Clemens's library by Clara Clemens Gabrilowitsch in 1910. The story of a struggling Polish immigrant musician who comes to the United States to make a name for himself as a pianist.

HUGHES, THOMAS (1822–1896). *School Days at Rugby. By an Old Boy.* Boston: Ticknor and Fields, 1865. 405 pp.

Provenance: bookplate #97 of the "J. Langdon Family Library" on the front pastedown endpaper.

Catalog: Ball 2016 inventory, brown textured cloth, J. Langdon's Family Library #97.

Location: Mark Twain Archive, Elmira College, Elmira, New York.

Copy examined: unmarked copy available to Clemens whenever he visited the Langdons in Elmira. Examined on 27 May 2015.

———. *The Scouring of the White Horse; or, the Long Vacation Ramble of a London Clerk. By the Author of "Tom Brown's School Days."* Illus. by Richard Doyle (1824–1883). Cambridge, England and London: Macmillan and Co., 1859. 244 pp.

Inscription: the front free flyleaf is inscribed by Olivia Clemens in blue ink: "Clara L. Clemens/Hartford/June 8th 1883".

Provenance: contains the bookstamps of the Mark Twain Library at Redding. Donated from Clemens's library by Clara Clemens Gabrilowitsch in 1910 (MTLAcc, entry #1922).

Catalog: *Mott1952*, #61, $10.

Location: Mark Twain House and Museum, Hartford, Connecticut. Gift of an anonymous donor in 1960.

Copy examined: Clara Clemens's copy, unmarked. Examined in August 1987.

As the title implies, Hughes' subject is the mysterious prehistoric Uppington White Horse chalk figure in the Berkshire Downs of Oxfordshire.

———. *Tom Brown at Oxford.* London: Macmillan & Co., 1882. 546 pp.

Source: MTLAcc, entry #2282, volume donated from Clemens's library by Clara Clemens Gabrilowitsch in 1910.

———. *Tom Brown at Oxford: A Sequel to School Days at Rugby.* Part First. Boston: Ticknor and Fields, 1863. 378 pp.

Inscription: the front flyleaf is signed in pencil, "J. Langdon/1866".

Provenance: bookplate #95 of the "J. Langdon Family Library" on the front pastedown endpaper.

Catalog: Ball 2016 inventory, brown textured cloth, signed by Jervis Langdon in 1866, J. Langdon's Family Library #95.

Location: Mark Twain Archive, Elmira College, Elmira, New York.

Copy examined: an unmarked copy available to Clemens whenever he visited the Langdons' home in Elmira. Examined on 27 May 2015.

———. *Tom Brown at Oxford: A Sequel to School Days at Rugby.* Part Second. Boston: Ticknor and Fields, 1861.

Provenance: bookplate #96 of the "J. Langdon Family Library."

Catalogs: former Archivist Mark Woodhouse's inventory list of the Langdon family library books; Ball 2016 inventory,

brown texture cloth, fair condition.

Location: Quarry Farm library shelves, under the supervision of the Mark Twain Archive, Elmira College, Elmira, New York.

Copy examined: an unmarked copy to which Clemens had access whenever he visited the Langdons' home in Elmira. Examined on 26 May 2015.

———. *Tom Brown's School Days.* New York: Hurst Co., n.d. 233 pp.

Source: MTLAcc, entry #427, volume donated by Clemens.

Mark Twain mentioned "Tom Hughes" in Chapter 15 of *Following the Equator* (1897), but inadvertently conflated the titles of his novels by referring to him as "the author of 'Tom Brown at Rugby.'" Hughes's first novel—*Tom Brown's School Days* (1857)—depicted a pupil's life at Rugby and introduced Flashman, the school bully; its inferior sequel, *Tom Brown at Oxford* (1861), caused Twain's confusion. Hughes's earlier novel contributed the English precedent for the American "boy books" that would follow Thomas Bailey Aldrich's *The Story of a Bad Boy* (1869).

Aidan Chambers, "Letter from England: A Tale of Two Toms," *Horn Book Magazine* 52.2 (April 1976): 187–190; Robert L. Coard, "Tom Sawyer, Sturdy Centenarian," *Midwest Quarterly* 17 (July 1976): 329–349; Alan Gribben, "Manipulating a Genre: *Huckleberry Finn* as Boy Book," *South Central Review* 5.4 (Winter 1988): 15–21 (a revised version of this essay appears as a chapter in Volume One of the present work). See also Alan Gribben, "Boy Books, Bad Boy Books, and *The Adventures of Tom Sawyer*," in *The Adventures of Tom Sawyer*, ed. Beverly Lyon Clark (New York: W. W. Norton, 2007), pp. 290–306.

HUGO, ADÈLE (FOUCHER) (1806–1868). *Victor Hugo, by a Witness of His Life.* Translated from the French by Charles Edwin Wilbour (1833–1896). Original brown cloth, gilt. New York: Carleton, 1863. 175 pp. [This biography was first published in Paris in 1863.]

Inscription: the title page is signed in pencil by Clemens's brother-in-law: "T. H. Crane/1864."

Marginalia: Crane wrote words in pencil on pages 88 and 125 and made marginal lines and underlinings in pencil on forty-six pages. Clemens listed eleven page references on the rear endpaper—30, 47, 55, 67, 73, 81, 98, 99, 102, 115, and 122; of these, pages 73, 81, 98, 99, 102, and 115 display markings by Clemens. Thirteen other pages bear marginal lines and markings characteristic of Clemens's annotations: pages 96, 106, 117, 120, 124, 131, 141, 142, 147, 149, 151, 158, and 166. These markings do not resemble Theodore Crane's. Albert Bigelow Paine's biography described how Clemens and Crane enjoyed passing books back and forth while lying in hammocks and reading at Quarry Farm; this volume might reflect that habit. In any event, Clemens made free use of the Quarry Farm library contents during his many summers there.

Provenance: originally among the books at Quarry Farm in Elmira, New York.

Location: collection of Kevin Mac Donnell, Austin, Texas (Mac Donnell to Alan Gribben, 29 November 2011 and 26 December 2014). Acquired from the Langdon family. "I have read half of Les Miserables, two or three minor works of Victor Hugo & also that marvelous being's biography by his wife" (SLC to Mollie Fairbanks, Elmira, 6 August 1877, *MTMF*, p. 207).

Hugo, Victor Marie, Comte (1802–1885). *Angelo* (play, produced in 1835).

Franklin R. Rogers deduced that the second half of Mark Twain's "Legend of Count Luigi" (Ch. 21, *IA* [1869]) is a burlesque of Hugo's *Angelo* and *Lucrezia Borgia* (*MTBP* [1960], pp. 48–49). Clara Clemens summarized the plot of *Angelo* ("full of satisfactory scenes for the divine Sarah") in her commonplace book, probably in the 1890s (Paine 150, MTP). Clara also listed the title of Hugo's *Hernani* (play, 1830) and *Ruy Blas* (play, 1838).

———. *The Destroyer of the Second Republic, Being Napoleon the Little*. Translated by a clergyman of the Protestant Episcopal Church, from the sixteenth French edition. New York: Sheldon & Co., 1870. 308 pp.

Location: Mark Twain Library, Redding, Connecticut.

Copy examined: Clemens's copy, unmarked. Has the red ink Mark Twain Library accession number "3040". Examined in 1970 and again in June 1982.

Hugo's target was Napoleon III, known as Louis Napoleon (1808–1873), who proclaimed himself Emperor of France in 1852. The unnamed translator signed the preface: "Hartford, Conn., *Nov. 24th, 1870*." This raises the possibility that Clemens knew him.

———. *Fantine, or the Felon and the Fallen*. [Excerpt from *Les Misérables*]. New York: W[illiam]. L. Allison Co., 1893. 195 pp.

Source: MTLAcc, entry #151, volume donated by Clemens.

———. *The Man Who Laughs*. Translated from the French by William Young (1809–1888). New York: D. Appleton and Co., 1869. 351 pp.

In a letter of 13 May 1869 sent from Hartford to Olivia Langdon, Clemens wrote, "I have read Victor Hugo's new story—all that has been published so far [in *Appleton's Journal*]. It is wild, weird—& half the time incomprehensible" (*MTLet* 3: 225). Mark Twain based a burlesque, "L'Homme Qui Rit" (written in 1869), on Young's translation. Portions of Twain's manuscript consist of pages from the book. Franklin R. Rogers (*MTBP* [1960], pp. 40–48, 114–127) discussed Twain's burlesque and demonstrated how the pattern of Gwynplaine's life parallels that of Twain's *The Prince and the Pauper* (1881).

———. *Marius; or, The Son of the Revolution* [Excerpt from *Les Misérables*]. Trans. from the author's latest Paris "Definitive" edition by Lascelles Wraxall (1828–1865), with additions by Charles Edwin Wilbour (1833–1896). New York: William L. Allison Co., [cop. 1893]. 192 pp.

Source: MTLAcc, entry #152, volume donated by Clemens.

———. *Les Misérables*. 2 vols. New York: Carleton, Publisher, 1862.

Inscription: "C. J. Langdon, Aug. 13, 1872."

Catalog: Ball 2016 inventory, brown leather spine with gilt lettering, marbled covers, bookplates of "J. Langdon Family Library," #466 and #467.

Location: Quarry Farm Library shelves, under the supervision of the Mark Twain Archive, Elmira College, Elmira, New York.

Clemens would have had access to these volumes whenever he visited the Langdons' residence in Elmira, New York.

Hugo's novel was first published in France in 1862.

"I have read half of Les Miserables, two or three minor works of Victor Hugo, & also that marvelous being's biography by his wife" (SLC to Mollie Fairbanks, 6 August 1877, *MTMF*, p. 207). A letter from Clemens to Joseph H. Twichell of 10 June 1879 mentioned that "[Hjalmar] Boyesen called on Renan & Victor Hugo" in Paris (*LMTJHT*, p. 91).Clemens's admiration for Hugo was mixed with scorn: in 1885 Mark Twain listed Hugo among the names of Carlyle, Napoleon, Mirabeau, Washington, Emerson, Grant, and others in whom "was allied the infinitely grand & the infinitely little" (NB 23, *N&J* 3: 114). Sometime after 1878, probably in the 1890s, Clemens identified (in ink) Victor Hugo's portrait in a photograph album (Robert T. Slotta to Alan Gribben, 15 August 1997). In a letter postmarked in Franzenbad, Germany on 3 September 1893, Susy Clemens, writing to her college friend Louise Brownell, alluded to "the ten large volumes of 'Les Miserables' in the original which I read in Florence. . . . Superb and supreme as certain of his scenes in 'Les Miserables' are the book as a whole is most trying and unsatisfactory. He is always rushing off far from the purpose and trend of the story to make some theatrical effect which has no bearing on it" (Hamilton College Archives). See also the Catalog entry for E. P. Adams, *Story Sermons from Les Misérables*.

———. *Ninety-Three*. Translated from the French by Helen B[ennet]. Dole (1857–1944). Chicago: M. A. Donohue & Co., n.d. 372 pp.

Source: MTLAcc, entry #150, volume donated by Clemens.

———. *Ruy Blas* (play, produced in 1838).

Clemens's letter to the Keokuk *Saturday Post* on 18 October 1856 mentions Don Caesar de Bazan (*TJS*, p. 14), a possible reference. A jocular pilot's memorandum written by Clemens in August 1860 and published in the St. Louis *Missouri Republican* and the New Orleans *Sunday Delta* claimed to have passed a steamboat named "the Don Caesar de Bazan at the Wood Pile" (Allan C. Bates, "Sam Clemens, Pilot Humorist of a Tramp Steamboat," *American Literature* 39.1 [March 1967]: 102–109). Franklin R. Rogers argued that Twain's *The Prince and the Pauper* (1881) "owes a substantial debt" to Hugo's play or to another play based upon it, *Don Caesar de Bazan* (*MTBP* [1960], pp. 173–174 n. 29). Twain's novel describes Miles Hendon as "a sort of Don Caesar de Bazan in dress, aspect, and bearing." Rogers saw parallels in Miles's protecting Edward from the threatening crowd, Miles's receiving Edward's whipping for him, and—possibly—Twain's using exchanged identities in the novel. Clara Clemens listed *Ruy Blas* in her commonplace book sometime between 1888 and 1904 (Paine 150, MTP).

Hugo's *Ruy Blas* inspired three subsequent stage productions that might have prompted Twain's references. All of them featured the poor but ingenious Spanish nobleman Don César de Bazan. In 1844 a play by Philippe-Francois Pinel (known as "Dumanoir") (1806–1865) and Adolphe Philippe d' Ennery (1811–1899), *Don César de Bazan*, was based on Hugo's play. (American productions of that play often spelled the name Don Caesar or Don Cæsar.) A year later a composer named William Vincent Wallace (1812–1865) wrote an opera, *Maritana*, with words by Edward Fitzball (see the Catalog entry for Fitzball), which relied heavily on *Don César de Bazan*. Then in 1872 Jules Massenet (1842–1912) composed a comic opera titled *Don César de Bazan*, crediting Pinel ("Dumanoir"), d'Ennery, and Jules Chantepie (1833–1904) as the librettists.

———. *Story of the Candlesticks* [Excerpt from *Les Misérables*]. New York: Harper & Brothers, n.d. 158 pp.

Source: MTLAcc, entry #1333, volume donated by Clemens.

———. *Things Seen (Choses Vues)*. Portrait. New York, 1887.

Inscription: the front flyleaf is signed "S. L. Clemens, 1887."

Catalogs: *A1911*, "12mo, boards, cloth back, N.Y. 1887," quotes the signature, lot 253, sold for $1.25; *Lexington 1912*, lot 18, sold for $2.50.

———. *The Toilers of the Sea*. New York: Harper & Brothers, 1866.

Mark Twain spoofed this novel in January 1867 with "Who Was He?," a burlesque written on board the *San Francisco*. Perhaps he found a copy of Hugo's novel in the ship's library. "In an insane moment I ventured to read the opening chapters of the Toilers of the Sea & now I am entangled. My brain is in hopeless disorder." In Twain's burlesque the novelist pauses repeatedly to define and discuss ordinary phenomena and objects—a storm, a man, a windowsill. At every possible juncture he ruminates upon human existence. "Who Was He?" was written in Notebook 7 (*N&J* 1: 280–284; it is published in Rogers's *S&B* [1960], pp. 25–48). In a letter published in the *Alta California* (19 April 1867) Twain claimed that the porter of the Heming House [actually it was the Deming House] in Keokuk brought him a copy of a "romance" entitled *The Toilers of the Sea* (*MTTMB*, p. 153), an incident that so amused him that he repeated the story in Chapter 57 of *The Innocents Abroad* (1869). In Chapter 47 of *The Innocents Abroad* Twain recounted the way in which his pilgrim-companions hailed a boat on the Sea of Galilee and "the toilers of the sea ran in and beached their barque."

Huish, Robert (1777–1850). *Memoirs of George the Fourth, Descriptive of the Most Interesting Scenes of His Private and Public Life, and the Important Events of His Memorable Reign; with Characteristic Sketches of All the Celebrated Men who Were His Friends and Companions as a Prince, and His Ministers and Counsellors as a Monarch*. Portraits. 12mo. Printed wrappers, edges chipped. Cloth case. London: Printed for T. Kelly; New York: Adams, Victor & Co., [1875]. 499 pp. The cover title reads: *The Celebrated Huish "Memoirs." Private and Public Life of George IV and His Court*. [Huish's book was initially published in London in 1830.]

Inscription: the front paper cover is signed in brown ink: "Saml. L. Clemens." Beneath, faintly penciled: "Hartford, 1875."

Catalogs: *A1911*, "12mo, wrappers, N.Y. [1875]," quotes the signature, lot 254, sold for $4.25; George D. Smith, New York City, "Catalogue of Books" (1911), quotes the signature, item #185, $7.50; "First and Other Editions of Samuel L. Clemens," List No. 3, Seven Gables Bookshop, New York City (August 1972), "in cloth case," has the *A1911* sale label, item #139, $100.

Location: Mark Twain House and Museum, Hartford,

Connecticut. Gift of an anonymous donor in 1973, according to the *Mark Twain Memorial Newsletter* 7 (August 1973): 5.

Copy examined: Clemens's unmarked copy. Examined in August 1987 in Hartford.

Hulbert, William Davenport (1868–1913). *Forest Neighbors; Life Stories of Wild Animals*. Illus. New York: McClure, Phillips & Co., 1902. 241 pp.

Source: MTLAcc, entry #1955, volume donated from Clemens's library by Clara Clemens Gabrilowitsch in 1910.

Hullah, Annette. *Theodor Leschetizky*. Living Masters of Music Series. London: John Lane, 1906. [Hullah was an English pupil of Leschetizky.]

Inscription: the front free endpaper is signed ink, "Clara Clemens/December 1906./E.C."

Marginalia: the famous Polish pianist Leschetizky's birth and death dates are written in ink on the title page. (He lived from 1830 until 1915.)

Catalog: ListABP (1910), "Theodor Leschetizky, Hullah", no other information supplied.

Provenance: displays the shelfmark of Clara Clemens Samossoud's private library in Detroit. Subsequently sold at the *C1951* action, although it was not listed in the sale catalog (many volumes were not).

Location: in July 1991 the volume was in the possession of Maxwell R. Keniston of Harvard, Massachuetts. His brother obtained it and other books at the 1951 Hollywood sale (Keniston to Alan Gribben, 22 July 1991).

Copy examined: photocopies of the cover, title page, and inscription of a book belonging to Clara Clemens (sent to Alan Gribben by Maxwell R. Keniston of Harvard, Massachusetts on 22 July 1991; Keniston also enclosed a photocopy of the purchase receipt his brother obtained from W. C. O'Connor, the auctioneer who presided over the 1951 sale).

Artur Schnabel recalled tea parties held in the Clemenses' Hotel Metropole room in Vienna during a period when Schnabel and Ossip Gabrilowitsch were studying under Leschetizky (Cesar Saerchinger, *Artur Schnabel: A Biography* [New York: Dodd, Mead & Co., 1957], p. 27).

———. [Unidentified book.]

Clemens intriguingly thanked Hullah for sending him "that book [unspecified]" on 17 February 1899 (PH in MTP) and added, on 23 March 1899, "that delightful book . . . lights up India like Kipling's masterpieces" (PH in MTP). Not all conundrums can be solved by the first investigator; who will crack this one?

Hume, David (1711–1776). *The History of England, from the Invasion of Julius Caesar to the Revolution of 1688*. 6 vols. New York: Harper & Brothers, 1864. [Publisher conjectured.]

Inscriptions: three of the volumes are signed by Clemens.

Marginalia: passages marked throughout, possibly related to Twain's *The Prince and the Pauper* (1881).

Catalogs: *A1911*, "12mo, half calf, N.Y. 1864," lot 255, sold for $15.50; George D. Smith, New York City, "Catalogue of Books" (1911), "6 vols., small 8vo, half calf, N.Y., 1864," quotes the signature, item #186, $22.50.

"Bring Hume's Henry VIII & Henry VII," Mark Twain reminded himself while traveling toward Hartford from New York City in July 1877 (NB 13, *N&J* 2: 39). Another note refers to Froude's *History of England*, so

Twain evidently intended to take materials from his home library to Quarry Farm for background study preparatory to writing *The Prince and the Pauper* (1881). Twain's working notes cite the page numbers in Hume on which historical events and characters of special interest to him are described—pp. 303, 307, 314, 317, 319, 320, 424 (DV115, MTP). These appear to relate most logically to the court intrigues during the reign of Henry VIII, recounted in the third volume. Five of Twain's notes in *The Prince and the Pauper* quote from this third volume. On 30 September 1896 Clemens again (in London this time) made a memorandum to obtain a copy of "Hume—Henry VIII" (NB 39, TS p. 6).

Salomon, *TIH* (1961), pp. 151–152.

———. "Of Miracles," Section 10 of *An Enquiry Concerning Human Understanding* (published in 1748).

In 1878 Clemens noted "Hume's Essay on Miracles, and Paley's Evidences of Christianity" (NB 17, *N&J* 2: 219). *Mark Twain and Philosophy*, ed. Alan H. Goldman (2017), pp. 74, 83, 126, 129, 186–191.

HUMPERDINCK, ENGELBERT (1854–1921). *Hänsel und Gretel* (opera, produced in 1893).

Humperdinck's opera, based on Grimm's fairy tale, was performed in German at the Metropolitan Opera House in 1905, with Alfred Hertz conducting. Clemens attended "a part of Hansel and Gretel" on 6 December 1905 in New York City, but at Colonel Harvey's insistence left early so that he would not become overtired (IVL Journal, TS p. 112, MTP). Isabel Lyon recorded that he enjoyed the opera. On 15 March 1906 he endorsed a benefit performance of the work by the Metropolitan Opera Company; the chorus of "that lovely masterpiece," he wrote, is "deep and satisfying" (SLC to the Legal Aid Society, *The Twainian* 5 [November 1942]: 3).

HUNEKER, JAMES GIBBONS (1857–1921). *Egoists, A Book of Supermen: Stendhal, Baudelaire, Flaubert, Anatole France, Huysmans, Barrès, Nietzsche, Blake, Ibsen, Stirner, and Ernest Hello*. New York: Charles Scribner's Sons, 1909.

Marginalia: pencil marks on pages 366 and 367. Brentano's of New York bookseller's label is affixed to the rear pastedown endpaper.

Provenance: shelfmarks of the library numbering system employed by Clara Clemens Gabrilowitsch during her Detroit years. Sold at the 1951 auction in Hollywood but not listed in the hastily compiled sale sheet.

Catalog: "Property from the Library of Mark Twain," Butterfield & Butterfield, San Francisco, Sale 6613 (16 July 1997), lot 2712.

Location: Mark Twain House and Museum, Hartford, Connecticut.

Copy examined: copy belonging to Clemens or Clara Clemens. Viewed in Hartford in 1997.

The inclusion of Anatole France (1824–1924), Friedrich Nietzsche (1844–1900), and Henrik Ibsen (1828–1906) make this volume especially interesting.

———. *Iconoclasts, A Book of Dramatists: Ibsen, Strindberg, Becque, Hauptmann, Sudermann, Hervieu, Gorky, Duse and d'Annunzio, Maeterlinck, and Bernard Shaw*. New York: Charles Scribner's Sons, 1905. 430 pp.

Catalogs: QF Martinez, fair condition; Ball 2016 inventory, reddish brown cloth, gilt top edges, rough cut pages,

inscribed "Sayles". (Eleanor Sayles [1878–1971] married Jervis Langdon [1875–1952], the son of Charles Jervis Langdon and Ida B. Clark Langdon, in 1902.)

Location: Quarry Farm library shelves, under the supervision of the Mark Twain Archive, Elmira College, Elmira, New York.

Clara Clemens listed the title of this book in her commonplace book (Paine 150, MTP). It was available to Clemens in his final visits to the Langdons' residence in Elmira.

HUNT, LEIGH (1784–1859). "Abou Ben Adhem" (poem).

Mark Twain employed a phrase from the first line of the poem—"may his tribe increase!"—in Chapter 9 of *The Innocents Abroad* (1869). On 9 February 1876 he quipped about "our mutual Mother,—may whose peace increase!—as those devout Orientals would say" in a letter to Mary Mason Fairbanks (*MTMF*, p. 195). He attempted a parody—"Abou Ben Butler"—in Notebook 19 (1880), *N&J* 2: 372–373. Twain also invented another parody, "Abou Bill Barnum," which he used in a speech in Boston on 6 November 1880 (Cincinnati *Daily Gazette*, 13 November 1880; St. John's *Newfoundlander*, 26 November 1880). In June 1885 he noted: "Perfect: Abou ben Adhem & the Rubiyât [*sic*]" (NB 24, *N&J* 3: 159).

———. *A Day by the Fire; and Other Papers, Hitherto Uncollected*. Ed. Joseph Edward Babson (1830–1875). Boston: Roberts Brothers, 1870. 368 pp.

Inscription: inscribed by Clemens in black ink at the top of the front flyleaf: "Livy L. Clemens". Someone wrote "OLC" on the verso of the front free endpaper.

Location: Mark Twain Library, Redding, Connecticut.

Copy examined: Olivia Clemens's copy. Has a penciled Mark Twain Library accession number, "2779". There is an illegible pencil notation on the front free endpaper: "Brud[?] Thent [?]." Examined in 1970 and again in June 1982.

Could Clemens possibly have resisted opening a collection of essays that discussed, among other things, fairies, *The Arabian Nights*, satyrs, nymphs, mermaids, giants, ogres, cyclops, and other mythological figures of antiquity?

———. *Stories from the Italian Poets. (First Series) Dante Alighieri, With Critical Notices of the Life and Genius of the Author; (Second Series) Bernardo Tasso and Ludovico Giovanni Ariosto, With Critical Notices of the Lives and Genius of the Authors*. Knickerbocker Nuggets Series. 2 vols. New York: G. P. Putnam's Sons, 1888.

Catalog: Ball 2016 inventory, blue cloth, flowered cover with gilt top edges, very good condition.

Location: Quarry Farm library shelves, under the supervision of the Mark Twain Archive, Elmira College, Elmira, New York.

Hunt first published this title in London in 1846. Clemens had access to these volumes whenever he visited Quarry Farm in Elmira.

———. *The Town; Its Memorable Characters and Events. By Leigh Hunt. St. Paul's to St. James's* (published London in two volumes in 1848).

An undated scrap of paper in the Mark Twain Papers contains a note by Clemens: "Nobody in town.—Bought Timbs—Walks—Stow <e >—Leigh Hunt, & a lot of other authorities & read about a thing, then went leisurely to see it" (DV 115). Mark Twain's working notes for *The Prince and the Pauper* (1881) include references to

"Drunken habits of James I & his court—Hunt—413" and "Tom dines in greater state, asking (see Lee [*sic*] Hunt") (DV115 MTP). A footnote to Chapter 16 of Twain's *The Prince and the Pauper* cites Hunt's *The Town* as his source for a "quotation from an early tourist" that describes preparations for the king's meal.

_____ and S. Adams Lee, eds. *The Book of the Sonnet.* 2 vols. Boston: Roberts Brothers, 1867.

Marginalia: light pencil marks and a few pencil notes in Volume I, none of them by Clemens.

Provenance: bookplates #83 and #84 of the "J. Langdon Family Library."

Catalog: Ball 2016 inventory, brown cloth, gilt letter, gilt top edges, fine condition.

Location: Quarry Farm library shelves, under the supervision of the Mark Twain Archive, Elmira College, Elmira, New York.

Copy examined: copy to which Clemens had access whenever he visited the Langdons in Elmira. Examined on 26 May 2015.

Hunt leads off Volume I with a ninety-page, highly insightful analysis of the history and forms of the poetic sonnet. Then follows a lengthy selection of English examples, with (in Volume II) an introduction to the American sonnet by S. Adams Lee and a large number of examples from that nation, with American women poets given their own section. Altogether there are 530 sonnets represented in the two volumes, drawing on 136 poets.

Hunt, Thomas Poage (1794–1876). *Jesse Johnston and His Times.* Philadelphia: Griffith & Simon, 1845. 77 pp.

Inscription: inscribed in black ink on the front free endpaper: "Presented by Mr. Wilson/To/Miss Emily Hill."

Location: Mark Twain Library, Redding, Connecticut.

Copy examined: almost certainly this was one of the many books donated by the descendants of the Hill family. I examined it in June 1982, by which time it had been added to the Clemens collection. It has the purple oval Mark Twain Library stamps but no markings and no accession number. I recommended to the staff that it be separated from the volumes donated by Clemens and his daughter Clara Gabrilowitsch. I could find no basis for concluding that this early temperance work had any association with Clemens or his family.

Hunt, Thornton Leigh (1810–1873). "Shelley. By One Who Knew Him," *Atlantic Monthly* 11.64 (February 1863): 197.

Mark Twain's "In Defence of Harriet Shelley" (1894) quotes the assertion by Leigh Hunt's eldest son Thornton Leigh Hunt that "there is not a trace of evidence or a whisper of scandal against her."

Hunter, Peter Hay (1854–1910). *James Inwick, Ploughman and Elder.* New York: Harper & Brothers, 1896. 194 pp.

Source: MTLAcc, entry #1572, volume donated by Clemens.

The Scottish dialect is so challenging in this novel that the author provides a glossary.

Hunter, William Wilson (1840–1900). *The Indian Empire: Its History, People, and Products.* London: Trübner & Co., 1882. [Second edition published in 1886; a new revised edition appeared in 1893. Mark Twain's edition is undetermined.]

In Chapter 59 of *Following the Equator* (1897) Mark Twain quotes from Hunter's description of the Taj Mahal to

show the "fairy structure" that is often "built by excitable literary people."

Madigan, "MT's Passage to India" (1974), p. 360.

Hurst, John Fletcher (1834–1903). *Indika. The Country and the People of India and Ceylon.* New York: Harper & Brothers, 1891. 794 pp.

Source: MTLAcc, entry #1720, volume donated by Clemens.

———. *Short History of the Reformation.* Illus. New York: Harper & Brothers, 1885. 125 pp.

Source: MTLAcc, entry #1382, volume donated by Clemens.

Hutchings, James Mason (1820–1902). *Scenes of Wonder and Curiosity in California.* First edition, second issue. Ninety-three engraved illustrations. Crimson morocco, gilt, publisher's presentation copy, rebacked. San Francisco: Hutchings & Rosenfield, 1861. 236 pp.

Inscription: the upper margin of the title page is inscribed in ink: "To Saml. L. Clemens from/A. Rosenfield. The Publisher./July 3rd 1868." Clemens was in San Francisco that day, having delivered a lecture at the New Mercantile Library on the previous evening (Fears, *Day by Day* 1.2: 313).

Marginalia: blots of back ink on the front pastedown endpaper; page 180 has been folded down; the corner of the leaf for pages 187–188 has been ripped away; there are blue ink blots on page 187. The torn page described sea lions on the Farallone Islands, located west of the Golden Gate.

Provenance: unknown, but the book nonetheless appears to be an authentic association copy. Owing to his frequent travels Clemens retained very few books prior to his marriage in 1870 and (especially) the construction of his library in the Hartford house. Quite likely Clemens passed this book along to a friend or acquaintance owing to his own upcoming voyage on 6 July 1868 to New York via Panama.

Source: letter from Kevin Mac Donnell to Alan Gribben, 12 December 2012.

Location: collection of Kevin Mac Donnell, Austin, Texas.

Hutchings, a San Francisco journalist and publisher who became an early promoter of the scenic grandeur of Yosemite, arrived in California during the Gold Rush of 1849, leaving his "southern home on the banks of . . . 'the old Mississippi'" (he had been living in New Orleans). *Scenes of Wonder and Curiosity* described the major features of Calaveras County (in three of the ten chapters), the San Francisco Bay area, the San Joaquin Valley, the giant trees, Yosemite Valley and the Sierras, Mount Shasta, and steamboating in the San Francisco Bay, Petaluma Creek, and the Russian River Valley. According to Kevin Mac Donnell, the illustrations on pages 89, 128, 131, and elsewhere that pertain to mountain-climbing in California resembled illustrations about the Swiss Alps that would appear in Twain's *A Tramp Abroad* (1880).

Hutton, Laurence (1843–1904). *A Boy I Knew and Four Dogs.* Illus. New York: Harper & Brothers, 1898. 87 pp.

Source: MTLAcc, entry #1927, volume donated from Clemens's library by Clara Clemens Gabrilowitsch in 1910.

Hutton dedicated his book "TO/MARK TWAIN/THE CREATOR OF/TOM SAWYER/ONE OF THE BEST

BOYS/I EVER KNEW". Much of its contents had appeared originally in *St. Nicholas Magazine*.

On 13 May 1898 Clemens wrote Hutton from Vienna to acknowledge a copy of the book and thank Hutton for "the dedications—both of them [*sic*; Hutton must have inscribed an additional dedication besides the printed one]. I read 36 pages last night before I was ordered to bed, & it was good reading and I enjoyed it." One passage, Clemens averred, gave him his "semi-annual laugh. It is not oftener than twice a year that anything can move me to the explosion-point." Clemens singled out an instance of childish profanity ("the book-incident, p. 21.") and commented that "there has long been a superstition in this family that profanity damages *any* story into which it is injected—a superstition which I have fought against as well as I could, but never with success. I will knock it galley-west from this out" (*Laurence and Eleanor Hutton: Their Books of Association*, pp. 66–67; see that Catalog entry below). In the passage to which Clemens referred, when the young boy's Scottish grandfather gave him a Bible as a gift, he was overheard to mutter, as he climbed the stairs, "Well, he has given me a book! And I wonder how in thunder he thinks I am going to read his damned Scotch!"

———. *A Boy I Knew, Four Dogs, and Some More Dogs*. Illus. New York: Harper & Brothers, [cop. 1900]. 116 pp.

Source: MTLAcc, entry #1597, volume donated by Clemens.

Location: Mark Twain Library, Redding, Connecticut.

Copy examined: Clemens's unmarked copy. I could not locate this book in 1970 but it had been found by the time I revisited the Mark Twain Library in June 1982. No accession number is visible. The Library's check-out slip and envelope have been torn off the rear pastedown endpaper.

This was an augmented edition of Hutton's earlier book (see the previous Catalog entry).

———. *Curiosities of the American Stage*. Red cloth, gilt lettering and decoration. Illus. New York: Harper & Brothers, 1891. 347 pp.

Location: Mark Twain Library, Redding, Connecticut.

Copy examined: Clemens's copy, unmarked. Displays the red ink Mark Twain Library accession number "3553". I could not locate this book in 1970 but when I returned to Redding in June 1982 it had been found and shelved with Clemens's library books. I examined it again on 10 November 2019.

On 3 February 1891 Clemens addressed a letter to "Dear Eddard" to thank him for a book "which could not have come more timely, shut up as I am this rainy morning." He declared that the night before he had felt "a longing for a sight of this very book" (Princeton University Library). Hutton's historical survey, which he dedicated to Brander Matthews, described major and minor figures connected with the American drama, including Edwin Forrest, Frank Mayo, Anna Cora Mowatt Ritchie, Bronson Howard, and Edmund Kean. He includes a discussion of various minstrel performers. On page 43 Hutton pays tribute to the "amusing" Colonel Mulberry Sellers created by Mark Twain and John T. Raymond.

———. *Edwin Booth*. Illus. New York: Harper & Brothers,

1893. 59 pp.

Source: MTLAcc, entry #1767, volume donated by Clemens.

———. *From the Books of Laurence Hutton*. New York: Harper & Brothers, 1892. 182 pp.

Inscription: Laid in is a presentation slip: "S. L. C.—M. T. Nov. 4th '92. Laurence Hutton."

Location: collection of Kevin Mac Donnell, Austin, Texas. Purchased in March 2007 (Mac Donnell to Alan Gribben, 13 March 2007).

Hutton explained in the Preface that "from the books of my own library, comfortably rich in the literature of the seventeenth and eighteenth centuries, I have gathered these oddities and curiosities of Books" (p. v). One chapter, for instance, is devoted to bookplates, another to poetical dedications.

——— and **ELEANOR HUTTON** (1848–1910). *Laurence and Eleanor Hutton: Their Books of Association*. Compiled by Mary Ellen Wood (b. 1858). New York: privately printed (The DeVinne Press), 1905. 208 pp.

Catalogs: ListABP (1910), "Books of Association, Hutton"; *C1951*, #93c, listed among books signed by Clemens.

Pages 66–67 quote the letter that Clemens sent to Hutton about Hutton's *A Boy I Knew and Four Dogs* (see the Catalog entry above for that book).

———. *Literary Landmarks of Florence*. Illus. New York: Harper & Brothers, [cop. 1897]. 81 pp.

Source: MTLAcc, entry #1793, volume donated by Clemens.

It is worth noting that in 1896, 1897, and 1898 Hutton published numerous (and invariably favorable) reviews in *Harper's Monthly* of Mark Twain's writings.

———. *Literary Landmarks of Rome*. Illus. New York: Harper & Brothers, [cop. 1897]. 75 pp.

Source: MTLAcc, entry #1794, volume donated by Clemens.

———. *Literary Landmarks of Venice*. Illus. New York: Harper & Brothers, 1905. 71 pp.

Source: MTLAcc, entry #1795, volume donated by Clemens.

HUXLEY, LEONARD (1860–1933). *Life and Letters of Thomas Henry Huxley [1825–1895], by His Son Leonard Huxley*. 2 vols. New York: Appleton and Co., 1900.

Isabel Lyon noted on 17 October 1905 in Dublin, New Hampshire, that she had "sent back to Library" one volume of Huxley's correspondence (IVL Journal, Mark Twain Archive, Gannett-Tripp Learning Center, Elmira College, Elmira, New York).

HUXLEY, THOMAS HENRY (1825–1895). *Evolution and Ethics* (published in 1893).

Clara Clemens Gabrilowitsch informed Hyatt H. Waggoner that her father read this book ("Science in the Thought of MT" [1937], p. 362), but his copy has evidently not survived.

Waggoner, "Science," pp. 364–367; Cummings, "*What Is Man?:* The Scientific Sources" (1964), p. 114.

———. *Hume*. English Men of Letters series. Ed. by John Morley (1833–1923). New York: Harper & Brothers, 1879.

In Notebook 20 (1882) Clemens simply wrote, "Huxley's Hume" (*N&J* 2: 463).

HYDE, JOHN, JR. (1833–1876). *Mormonism: Its Leaders and*

Designs. New York: W. P. Fetridge & Co., 1857. 335 pp. [Edition conjectured.]

The apostate Hyde's book was one of Mark Twain's sources for details about the Mormons used in *Roughing It* (1872), according to Franklin R. Rogers (*RI* [1972], p. 563). The editors of the subsequent revised edition of *Roughing It*, Harriet Elinor Smith and Edgar M. Branch, also cited Hyde as a Twain source (*RI* [1993], pp. 591, 1040.

HYDE, WILLIAM DE WITT (1858–1917). *The Art of Optimism as Taught by Robert Browning.* New York: T. Y. Crowell & Co., [cop. 1900]. 35 pp.

Source: MTLAcc, entry #870, volume donated by Mrs. Ralph W. Ashcroft (formerly Isabel Lyon), Clemens's secretary.

Hyde, the president of Bowdoin College, quotes liberally from the poetry of Browning in opposition to the philosophical pessimism expressed, for example, by Matthew Arnold's "Dover Beach." Instead, "Browning maintains the militant, active, triumphant air" (p. 31).

Hymnal: According to the Use of the Protestant Episcopal Church in the United States of America. Revised edition. New York: E. & J. B. Young & Co., 1874. 436 pp.

Catalog: Ball 2016 inventory, black leather, gilt edge pages, gilt lettering, good condition.

Location: Quarry Farm library shelves, under the supervision of the Mark Twain Archive, Elmira College, Elmira, New York.

Clemens had access to this volume whenever he visited Quarry Farm in Elmira.

[HYMNS. HAWAIIAN.] *NA HIMENI HOOLEA, HE MAU MELE MA KA UHANE, E HOOLEA AI.* Brown cloth, spine cracked, fragile condition. Honolulu: Paii E H. M. Whitney, 1864. 400 pp. [The volume is a hymnal containing 390 hymns plus an index.]

Inscription: inscribed on the first front flyleaf in pencil: "Sam. L. Clemens/From Rev. S. C. Damon./Honolulu,/March 22/1866./To Annie Moffett." The front free endpaper is torn and adheres to the front pastedown endpaper.

Provenance: Jean Webster McKinney Collection. Donated to Vassar College on 12 February 1977.

Location: Special Collections, Vassar College Library, Vassar College (item B-52).

Copy examined: copy belonging to Clemens that he gave to his niece. Examined on 15 August 1987.

Samuel C. Webster reported that when Clemens returned from the Sandwich Islands in 1866 he presented an Hawaiian Bible as a gift to his niece, fourteen-year-old Annie E. Moffett (1852–1950), Pamela Clemens Moffett's daughter—inscribed "from her venerable Uncle" (*MTBus,* p. 91). In actuality the book was a Christian hymnal in the natives' language.

I

IBSEN, HENRIK (1828–1906). *Hedda Gabler* and *The Master Builder.* Vol. X of Ibsen's *Works.* Trans. by Edmund Gosse (1849–1928) and William Archer (1856–1924). Introduction by William Archer. New York, 1907.

Inscription: signed "S. L. Clemens, 1906" [*sic*], according to *A1911.*

Catalog: *A1911*, "Vol. X of the Works, 12mo, cloth, N.Y.

1907," quotes the signature, lot 257, sold for $4.50.

In 1890 Olivia Clemens mentioned in a letter to Grace King that she was reading Ibsen's *A Doll's House* and planned to read *Ghosts* (*AutoMT* 3: 509). In Berlin around 1891 Henry Fisher understood Clemens to say that Strindberg sought "to out-Ibsen the Norwegian" in harsh portrayals of women (*AMT,* p. 79). Mark Twain mentioned Ibsen noncommittally as a prominent person in "Ancients in Modern Dress" (*FM,* p. 436), written 1896–1897. In an Autobiographical Dictation of 4 September 1907 Twain insisted: "I have not read Nietzsche or Ibsen, nor any other philosopher" (quoted in *WIM?,* p. 17; *AutoMT* 3: 130).

"I DON'T ALLOW NO COONS TO HURT MY FEELINGS" (minstrel song, performed and published in 1898). Written and composed by I. Jones.

In Mark Twain's fragmentary manuscript, "Three Thousand Years among the Microbes" (written in 1905), the narrator-cholera germ twice mentions singing "I don't 'low no Coon to Fool roun' Me" (*WWD?,* p. 462, 464). No song title has been located that exactly matches those words, but this one comes the closest. The deplorable tradition of "coon" songs once thought to be extremely amusing is too complex to address in a catalog entry.

"I HEAR THE HOOFS, OR THE LOST CHILD" (minstrel song, published and performed in 1849).

Clemens entered nine cryptic words in Notebook 30 in December 1890: "They stole, they stole, they stole me child away" (*N&J* 3: 597). A decade later, on 20 April 1900, he noted: "'Lost Child'! Heard it only in Hannibal. Was it never in England or elsewhere?" (NB 43, TS p. 7). In both instances he was thinking of "I hear the hoofs, or the lost child," a dialect song in which a mother plaintively recounts how she put her daughter to bed only to find in the daylight that she had been taken. "They stole, they stole, they stole my child away," she wails. "I hear their hoofs upon the hill/Her voice is growing fainter still." (The implications about the casual sale and separation of enslaved family members are unmistakable.)

"I KNOW THAT MY REDEEMER LIVES" (spiritual). Also known as: "Sinner, please don't let this harvest pass."

Clemens entered this title in Notebook 30 when he heard the Fisk University Jubilee Singers perform in Hartford on 16 December 1890 (*N&J* 3: 593).

ILES, GEORGE (1852–1942). *Flame, Electricity and the Camera; Man's Progress from the First Kindling of Fire to the Wireless Telegraph and the Photograph of Color.* Illus. 8vo, cloth. New York: Doubleday & McClure Co., 1900. 398 pp.

Inscription: "Samuel L. Clemens with the author's high regard. New York, October 27, 1900." Beneath that inscription is a Biblical passage from James 3: 5.

Provenance: MTLAcc, entry #666, volume donated by Clemens. (Listed with a publication date of 1901, possibly an error.)

Catalog: Anderson Auction Galleries, Sale number 1873 (10–11 November 1924), "first edition, autograph presentation copy," quotes Iles' inscription, item #221, $5.

Location: currently unknown.

Clemens wrote to Iles on 28 October 1900 to thank him for an unspecified book that was "just the kind of reading I enjoy the most. There'll not be any skipping done, you may be sure of that" (McGill University Library).

Flames, Electricity, and Camera would seem to be the logical reference here.

———. *Inventors at Work, with Chapters on Discovery*. Original cloth, minor wear. New York: Doubleday, Page & Co., 1906. 503 pp.

Inscriptions: inscribed by the author, "Samuel L. Clemens/from George Iles/with the highest regards and esteem/New York October 9, 1906." Clemens also signed the volume.

Catalogs: *C1951*, 88c, presentation copy, $10, listed among books signed by Clemens; "Property from the Library of Mark Twain," Butterfield & Butterfield, San Francisco, Sale 6613 (16 July 1997), lot 2679.

Location: Mark Twain House and Museum, Hartford, Connecticut.

Copy examined: Clemens's copy. Viewed in 1997 in Hartford.

Illustrated Catalogue of Charles L. Webster Co.'s Publications. New York: Charles L. Webster & Co., 1892. 40 pp.

A list of all books issued by Clemens's publishing firm. Presumably he would have overseen the compiling of this advertising brochure to some extent.

Impressions of Damascus. [Unidentified book.]

Catalog: ListABP (1910), "Impressions of Damascus", no other information provided.

The Independent (weekly magazine, New York City, published 1848–1928).

On 1 January 1874 Geer & Pond, Hartford booksellers, billed Clemens for "Inde from Nov. 1/73 to Jan. 1/74"; on 28 January 1874 they billed him for five additional copies (MTP). In a letter dated only "3 May" Clemens requested the editor to send him a copy of a poem by Caroline Mason "which appeared in the Independent about last August or September" (TS in MTP). See the Catalog entry for Caroline Atherton (Briggs) Mason.

INGELOW, JEAN (1820–1897).

———. "Divided" (poem).

In the month of her wedding—February 1870—Olivia Langdon copied into her commonplace book excerpts from a poem by Ingelow about eternal romantic love (DV161, MTP). Although Olivia titled the excerpt "We Two," the Ingelow poem that best fits the sentiment is "Divided," which employs the phrase "we two" several times. "Divided" opens: "An empty sky, a world of heather,/Purple of foxglove, yellow of broom;/We two among them wading together,/Shaking out honey, treading perfume." The poem takes a melancholy turn toward the end when the lovers find themselves permanently divided, apparently by death: "But two are walking apart forever,/And wave their hands for a mute farewell."

———. *Off the Skelligs: A Novel*. Boston: Roberts Brothers, 1873. 666 pp.

Source: MTLAcc, entry# 2283, volume donated from Clemens's library by Clara Clemens Gabrilowitsch in 1910.

Few authors' family libraries would have been considered complete without including novels and volumes of poetry by the popular British writer Jean Ingelow. The plot of the romantic novel *Off the Skelligs* revolves around the rescue of shipwrecked people near a group of rocky islands known as the Skelligs on the coast of Ireland.

———. *Poems.*

Catalog: *C1951*, O10, edition not supplied, listed among books signed by Olivia Clemens.

———. *The Poetical Works of Jean Ingelow, including the Shepherd Lady and Other Poems*. New York: T. Y. Crowell & Co., [cop. 1863]. 520 pp.

Source: MTLAcc, entry #2037, volume donated from Clemens's library by Clara Clemens Gabrilowitsch in 1910.

———. *A Sister's Bye-Hours*. Boston: Roberts Brothers, 1881. [First published in 1868.]

Catalogs: list of books that Mark Woodhouse transferred from the Quarry Farm library to the Mark Twain Archive on 9 July 1987; Ball 2016 inventory, green cloth, gilt and black lettering, good condition.

Location: Mark Twain Archive, Gannett-Gannett-Tripp Library Elmira College, Elmira, New York.

Clemens would have had access to this volume whenever he visited Quarry Farm in Elmira.

INGERSOLL, ERNEST (1852–1946). *The Ice Queen*. Harper's Young People Series. Illus. New York: Harper & Brothers, [cop. 1884]. 256 pp.

Source: MTLAcc, entry #431, volume donated by Clemens. Three boys and a girl set out on a 100-mile trek across frozen Lake Erie in an effort to reach Cleveland.

———. *Wild Life of Orchard and Field; Papers on American Animal Life*. Illus. New York: Harper & Brothers, 1902. [cop. 1880, 1902]. 347 pp.

Inscription: Inscribed by Olivia Clemens in black ink: "Jean L. Clemens/Riverdale on the Hudson/March 1902".

Location: Mark Twain Library, Redding, Connecticut. Donated from Clemens's library by Clara Clemens Gabrilowitsch in 1910 (MTLAcc, entry #1957).

Copy examined: Jean Clemens's unmarked copy. Has the red ink Mark Twain Library accession number "1957". Examined in 1970 and again in June 1982 and on 8 November 2019.

The American naturalist Ingersoll was an early advocate for the protection of wildlife and their natural habitats.

———. *Wild Neighbors; Out-Door Studies in the United States*. Illus. New York: Macmillan Co., 1902. 301 pp.

Source: MTLAcc, entry #1956, volume donated from Clemens's library by Clara Clemens Gabrilowitsch in 1910.

INGERSOLL, ROBERT GREEN (1833–1899). "The Christian Religion," *North American Review* 133.297 (August 1881): 109–152.

Robert G. Ingersoll, publicly identifying himself as an agnostic but often expressing the freethought views of an outright atheist, became famous for debating those who insisted on literal interpretations of the Christian Bible. On 10 August 1881 Clemens informed Ingersoll that he had "been well entertained by your theological article in the magazine, & Judge Black's ludicrous 'reply' to it" (TS in MTP). Much of Ingersoll's essay questioned the veracity and authority of the Old Testament in the Bible. "No civilized country could reenact its laws, and in many respects its moral code is abhorrent to every good and tender man." Passages in it "are the product of a barbarous people" (p. 111). Following the conclusion of Ingersoll's article on page 128, Jeremiah Sullivan Black (1810–1883) provided a reply. Black argued that in the pre-Christian world, "In every province paganism enacted the same cold-blooded cruelties; oppression and robbery ruled supreme; murder went rampaging and red over all the earth. The Church came, and her light penetrated this moral darkness like a new sun. She covered the globe with institutions of mercy. . . . Her faith was made perfect through suffering, and the law of love rose in triumph from the ashes of her martyrs" (p. 151). Black had served as Chief Justice of the Pennsylvania Supreme Court in the 1850s, had been the U. S. Attorney General in the President James Buchanan administration, and had represented notable political figures in nationally publicized trials in the 1870s. (Jo Dee Benussi contributed substantially to this entry.)

——. *The Ghosts and Other Lectures.* Washington, D.C.: C. P. Farrell, 1879. 232 pp. [The publisher, Clinton P. Farrell, was Ingersoll's brother-in-law.]

Inscription: "Saml Clemens Esq/from his friend/R. G. Ingersoll/Dec 11, 79".

Marginalia: contains Clemens's pencil marks.

Catalogs: The Lincoln Storage Warehouse in New York City recorded in May 1935 the return by Albert Bigelow Paine of a copy of "Robert Ingersoll's Lectures" with an inscription essentially matching the one in *Ghosts*: "Saml. Clemens Esq. from his friend, R. G. Ingersoll, Dec. 11, 79." This storage receipt was in the collection of Bigelow Paine Cushman (1928–2003), grandson of biographer Albert Bigelow Paine, in Deer Isle, Maine in August 1987, when Alan Gribben was allowed to examine it. The "Retz Appraisal" (1944), p. 9, valued at $10 an Ingersoll volume formerly owned by Clemens.

Location: Mark Twain Papers, Bancroft Library, University of California at Berkeley.

Copy examined: Clemens's copy.

Clemens was in awe of Ingersoll's oratorical skills. When Clemens returned from the Chicago reunion of the Army of the Tennessee in November 1879 he called Ingersoll "the most beautiful human creature that ever lived" and declared of the speech he heard Ingersoll deliver: "Its music will sing through my memory always as the divinest that ever enchanted my ears" (SLC to WDH, Hartford, 17 November 1879, *MTHL*, p. 279). He had listened to Ingersoll raise the twelfth toast at the banquet, a tribute to "The Volunteer Soldiers of the Union." Clemens wrote to Olivia on 14 November 1879 describing it as "just the supremest combination of words that was ever put together since the world began" (*MTL*, p. 371). On 9 December 1879 Clemens wrote to Ingersoll from Hartford to request "a perfect copy of your peerless Chicago speech" (TS in MTP). In response Ingersoll sent Clemens copies of *The Ghosts and Other Lectures*, together with other volumes. Clemens thanked Ingersoll on 14 December 1879 "for the books—I am devouring them—they have found a hungry place, and they content it & satisfy it to a miracle. I wish I could hear you *speak* these splendid chapters before a great audience." Reading them to oneself, Clemens explained, "there is a still greater lack, your manner, & voice, & presence" (*MTL*, p. 373; corrected TS in MTP). *The Ghosts and Other Lectures* contained six of Ingersoll's lectures, including "Ghosts," "The Liberty of Man, Woman and Child," and "The Declaration of Independence."

Clemens definitely owned other books by Ingersoll, but most have disappeared. Howells remembered how much "he greatly admired Robert Ingersoll, whom he called an angelic orator, and regarded as an evangel of a new gospel" (*MMT* [1910], p. 27). Grace King noted that "strength always inspires him. He admires Ingersoll. He loves to see Ingersoll knock down his opponents" (undated MS, c. 1888, "Mark Twain, Second Impression," quoted by Robert Bush, "Grace King and Mark Twain" [1972]: 40).

"Mr. Clemens had a profound admiration for Ingersoll," noted Isabel V. Lyon in the margin of her copy of Albert Bigelow Paine's *Mark Twain's Autobiography*, 2 vols. (New York: Harper & Brothers, 1924) 1:16, Victor Jacobs Collection, PH in MTP).

Thomas D. Schwartz—"Mark Twain and Robert Ingersoll: The Freethought Connection," *American Literature* 48.2 (May 1976): 183–193—insisted that "Ingersoll's influence on Clemens . . . must be acknowledged" (p. 184). Schwartz described Clemens's markings in *The Ghosts and Other Lectures* (1879) and discussed the book's impact on his thought. He pointed out that *Ghosts* was the apparent source for a passage in Twain's *The Prince and the Pauper* (1881). Harold K. Bush, Jr., "'Transfigured by Oratory': Thomas Paine, Robert Ingersoll, Mark Twain, and the Roots of American Civil Religion," *Mark Twain Annual 7* (2009): 78–96, reprinted and discussed the Chicago speech that impressed Clemens so greatly. John Bird followed up with an excellent appraisal, "The Mark Twain and Robert Ingersoll Connection: Freethought, Borrowed Thought, Stolen Thought," *Mark Twain Annual 11* (2013): 42–61.

Raymond A. Hall, "Mark Twain's Relation to Robert G. Ingersoll's Program of Frontier Free Thought," Master's thesis (University of Washington, Seattle, 1951); Budd, *MTSP* (1962), p. 116; and Robert Bush, "Grace King and Mark Twain," *American Literature* 44.1 (March 1972): 40.

——. *Lectures.* [Title and edition unidentified.]

In a list of books from Clemens's personal library that Albert Bigelow Paine was allowed to retain temporarily and study after Clemens's death in 1910 there were two separate entries for "Ingersoll's Lectures" ("ListABP"). That list was discovered in 1979 among records donated to the Mark Twain House in Hartford by Jervis Langdon, Jr.

——. *The Philosophy of Ingersoll. . . . Ed. and Arranged by Vere Goldthwaite [1870–1912].* San Francisco: Paul Elder and Co., n.d. [cop. 1906]. 117 pp.

Inscription: "To Mark Twain,/with special reference to the following lines, 'I believe in the medicine of mirth, and in what I might call the longevity of laughter. Every man who has caused real, true, honest mirth, has been a benefactor of the human race'/and with the kind regards of/Vere Goldthwaite/Dec. 1906."

Location: Mark Twain Library, Redding, Connecticut.

Copy examined: Clemens's unmarked copy. Has the red ink Mark Twain Library accession number "3071". Examined in 1970 and again in June 1982.

——. *The Works of Robert G. Ingersoll.* The Dresden Edition. 12 vols. New York: The Dresden Publishing Co./C. P. Farrell, 1900–1902.

On 20 December 1900 Clemens assured a Mr. Griswold: "I shall be very glad indeed to have the Dresden Edition of my old friend's books in my library in this house [at 14 West 10th Street, New York City]. I knew him twenty years, and was fond of him, and held [him] in as high honor as I have held any man living or dead" (TS in MTP). Ingersoll's brother-in-law Clinton P[inckney]. Farrell (1850–1925) collected the Ingersoll materials and arranged for the publication of this memorial edition, which was named for Ingersoll's birthplace, Dresden, New York. Herman Eugene Kittredge (1871–1954) contributed biographical notes.

Budd, *MTSP* (1962), p. 116.

INGLIS, JULIA SELINA (THESIGER), LADY. (1833–1904). *The Siege of Lucknow. A Diary*. London: Osgood & McIlvaine; Leipzig: Bernhard Tauchnitz, 1892. [Edition conjectured.]

Catalog: ListABP (1910), "Siege of Lucknow, Inglis".

Lady Inglis's husband, John B. W. Inglis, commanded the defense of Lucknow during the Sepoy Mutiny in 1857. Susy Clemens informed her college roommate Louise Brownell on 13 October 1892 from Florence, Italy: "I have been reading *'La Siege of Lucknow'* by Lady Inglis—a most touching record" (Hamilton College Archives). In Chapters 58 and 59 of *Following the Equator* (1897) Mark Twain quoted from Inglis's account of events within the besieged garrison.

INGRAHAM, JOSEPH HOLT (1809–1860). *The Prince of the House of David; or, Three Years in the Holy City. Being a Series of Letters of Adina. . . . All the Scenes and Wonderful Incidents in the Life of Jesus of Nazareth*. [First published in 1855 and often reprinted by various publishers.]

Ingraham, an Episcopal priest serving as the Rector at St. John's Church in Mobile, Alabama, produced in *The Prince of the House of David* the first best-seller based on the life of Christ. A fictional Jewish girl writes letters that incorporate the story of Jesus. Mark Twain listed Ingraham's book among the titles that *Quaker City* passengers were instructed to bring with them (*Alta California*, 5 April 1868, *TIA*, p. 303).

INGULF, ABBOT OF CROWLAND (c. 1030–1109). *Ingulph's Chronicle of the Abbey of Croyland, with the Continuations by Peter of Blois [c. 1135–c. 1212] and Anonymous Writers*. Translated from Latin by Henry Thomas Riley (1816–1878). London: Henry G. Bohn, 1854. 546 pp.

Inscription: the half-title page is signed in pencil: "S. L. Clemens, Hartford, 1877".

Marginalia: penciled notes and markings by Clemens.

Catalogs: *A 1911*, "12mo, cloth, Lond. 1854, . . . some passages marked, and a few autograph remarks, all in pencil," quotes the signature, lot 259, sold for $3.25; "The Collection of Alan N. Mendleson," Parke-Bernet Galleries, Sale No. 1719 (December 1956), lot 95; sold for $55, according to *American Book-Prices Current Index 1955–1960* (New York: Bowker, 1961), p. 258.

Location: Albert and Shirley Small Special Collections Library, University of Virginia Library, Charlottesville, Virginia. Listed in their online catalog in 2006.

Clemens purchased this volume on 24 October 1877, according to a bill he received in November 1877 from Osgood and Company of Boston (Scrapbook #10, p. 69, MTP). Ingulf's account of his pilgrimage to Jerusalem and his years as the abbot of Croyland in Lincolnshire is now believed to be a fabrication compiled several centuries later, though the unknown author probably relied on certain now-lost chronicles. Its authenticity began to be questioned half a century before Clemens

acquired this book.

[INSTITORIS, HENRICUS (KRAMER) (1430–1505) and **JAKOB SPRENGER** (c. 1436–1495)]. *Malleus Maleficarum, or Hexenhammer ["Hammer of Witches"]*. (A treatise detailing the exposure and punishment of witches. First published in Germany in 1486).

Henry Fisher reported that Clemens was eager in 1891 to see whether the Imperial Library of Berlin had an edition of *The Witch Hammer*, which had appeared in German and Latin editions up until 1669. Fisher wrote: "I forget now which edition of that murderous book we examined, but I do remember some of the figures we jotted down at the librarian's suggestion. The Witch Hammer, that is, a voluminous 'treatise for discovering, torturing, maiming and burning witches,' was first published, we learned, in 1487" (*AMT*, p. 179). Fisher further recalled that "some years later Mark related the story of our search for the Witch Hammer before a motley crowd of litterateurs at Brown's Hotel" in London. On that occasion Clemens gave Bram Stoker, the author of *Dracula*, a recipe for witch salve—hemlock, mandragora, henbane, belladonna—that Clemens said "Fisher and I dug . . . up at the Berlin Royal Library" (*AMT*, pp. 180–181).

[IOWA.] *The Statute Laws of the Territory of Iowa, Enacted at the First Session of the Legislative Assembly, Held at Burlington, 1838–'39. Published by Authority*. 8vo. Crude half sheep. Worn. One cover loose. Dubuque: Russell & Reeve, Printers, 1839. 600 pages.

Inscription: the title page is signed once by Eugene Field and (purportedly) twice by Clemens: "S. L. Clemens (Mark Twain)."

Catalog: Swann Auction Galleries, New York City, Catalogue number 274 (22 November 1950), lot 155.

Caution: Eugene Field II is known to have forged Twain's autograph in books from his father's and grandfather's personal libraries as well as in additional volumes he obtained. This is almost certainly one of these examples.

IRELAND, ALLEYNE (1871–1951). *The Far Eastern Tropics: Studies in the Administration of Tropical Dependencies: Hong-Kong, British North Borneo, Sarawak, Burma, the Confederated Malay States, the Straits Settlements, French Indo-China, Java, the Philippine Islands*. Boston: Houghton, Mifflin and Co., 1905. 339 pp.

Inscription: signed in black ink on the front pastedown endpaper: "SL. Clemens/1906." Inscribed on the front free endpaper: "To/Samuel L. Clemens Esq./with the author's sincere regards./Alleyne Ireland./1906."

Catalogs: *A1911*, "12mo, cloth, Bost. 1905," quotes the inscription and signature, lot 260, sold for $3.25; George D. Smith, New York City, "Catalogue of Books" (1911), quotes the inscription and signature, item #200, $10.

Provenance: the library bookplate of Jerome Kern is affixed to the front pastedown endpaper.

Location: Mark Twain House and Museum, Hartford, Connecticut.

Copy examined: Clemens's copy, unmarked. Examined in August 1987. Has the *A1911* sale label.

IRELAND, ANNIE ELIZABETH (NICHOLSON) (1839–1893). *Life of Jane Welsh Carlyle [1801–1866], by Mrs. Alexander Ireland*. New York: Charles L. Webster & Co., 1891. 329 pp.

Clemens's publishing firm brought out this biography of

Thomas Carlyle's wife.

IRVING, WASHINGTON (1783–1859). *The Adventures of Captain Bonneville.* Volume 6, Lovell's Library Series, No. 311. New York: John W. Lovell Co., n.d. [1884]. 300 pp.

Marginalia: on the front paper wrapper Clemens penciled: "A narrative poorly & wordily told." He made several other annotations in pencil as well.

Catalogs: ListABP (1910), "Capt. Bonneville, Irving"; "Retz Appraisal" (1944), p. 9, valued at $15.

Location: Mark Twain Papers, Bancroft Library, University of California at Berkeley.

Copy examined: Clemens's copy. Front cover detached.

In a 6 July 1884 letter Clemens started to ask Charles L. Webster for a work by Washington Irving, but changed his mind and deleted the request. The same letter instructed Webster to send him "*personal narratives* of life & adventure out yonder on the Plains & in the Mountains" (*MTBus*, p. 265). The copy of *Captain Bonneville* that Clemens read and annotated was a paperbound edition that cost 20¢. The French-born Benjamin Louis Eulalie de Bonneville (1796–1878) explored what is now Oklahoma and Wyoming, and helped map a portion of what became the Oregon Trail. He would serve in the Mexican-American War and the Civil War as an officer in the U. S. Army. Irving first published this version of Bonneville's journals in 1837.

———. *The Alhambra: A Series of Tales and Sketches of the Moors and Spaniards* (published in 1832).

Before leaving on the *Quaker City* in 1867, Clemens noted: "Irving's Spain/Moors" (NB 8, *N&J* 1: 328). In Chapter 59 of *The Innocents Abroad* (1869) he mentions his disappointment at not being able "to visit the Alhambra at Granada" because of a cholera quarantine.

———. *Astoria; or, Anecdotes of an Enterprise Beyond the Rocky Mountains* (history narrative, published in 1836; revised in 1848).

Clemens wrote "Astoria" among a list of miscellaneous entries in Notebook 22 (*N&J* 3: 56) in 1884, possibly hoping to derive historical details about the Far West for use in "Huck Finn and Tom Sawyer among the Indians" (written in 1884, unpublished until 1969).

———. *A History of the Life and Voyages of Christopher Columbus* (biography, published in 1828).

Mark Twain mentions Columbus repeatedly in his writings, and Irving's work was the premier biography of the explorer during Twain's era. Among many other references, in Chapter 5 of *A Connecticut Yankee in King Arthur's Court* (1889) Hank Morgan recalls how "Columbus, or Cortez, or one of those people, played an eclipse as a saving trump once, on some savages."

———. *The Life of George Washington.* 5 vols. New York: G. P. Putnam, 1864.

Inscriptions: all of the volumes are inscribed in black ink on the verso of the front free endpapers (except for Volume II, which was accidentally inscribed upside down on the rear free endpaper): "Philomathea/from/ Olivia L. Langdon,/Sept. 1866". This could have been the inscription of either Clemens's mother-in-law Olivia Lewis Langdon (1810–1890) or of Clemens's eventual wife, Olivia Louise Langdon (1845–1904). On the front pastedown endpapers a book label identifies the volumes as

the property of the "Philomathea Library," provides their accession numbers from 219 to 223, and indicates that they could be borrowed for one week. Subsequent book labels, charge card slips and charge card pockets indicate that the volumes eventually entered the Elmira College Library, from which they were borrowed in 1932, 1935, 1961, 1964, and 1965.

Catalog: Ball 2016 inventory, 5 vols., brown leather spine with marble cloth cover, gilt lettering, inscribed to Philomathea by Olivia L. Langdon,/Sept. 1866.

Location: Mark Twain Archive, Elmira College, Elmira, New York.

Copy examined: a five-volume book donated to a library before Clemens entered the Langdon family, but nevertheless available whenever he visited Elmira, New York.

———. *The Life of Oliver Goldsmith* (published in 1849).

Paul Fatout's persuasive essay, "Mark Twain's First Lecture: A Parallel," *Pacific Historical Review* 25.4 (November 1956): 347–354, constructed a strong case for believing that Irving's account of the first-night performance of Goldsmith's *She Stoops to Conquer* (1773) materially influenced Twain's description of his first San Francisco lecture (1866) as told in Chapter 78 of *Roughing It* (1872).

———. *Old Christmas and Bracebridge Hall.* Illustrated by Randolph Caldecott (1846–1886). London: Macmillan & Co., 1886. 165 pp. [Edition conjectured.]

Catalog: ListABP (1910), "Old Christmas—Bracebridge Hall, Irving", no other information provided.

———. "Rip Van Winkle" (short story, published in *The Sketch-Book*, 1819–1820).

Catalog: ListABP (1910), "Rip Van Winkle", no other information supplied.

Irving's venerable story repeatedly echoed in Mark Twain's mind. In "A Righteous Judge," an uncredited newspaper sketch published in the Virginia City *Territorial Enterprise* on 23 January 1866, Twain alluded to the "Rip Van Winkle sleep of three generations" undergone by the forgotten word "bilk" (Robert H. Hirst, "New (Old) Mark Twain Found in Bancroft Scraps," *Bancroftiana* Number 115 [Fall 1999]: 10). Under a column headed "Rip Van Winkle" Twain related in a letter published in the 29 September 1867 issue of the *Daily Alta California* how a train whistle at Pompeii "woke me up and reminded me that I belonged to the nineteenth century, and wasn't a rusty mummy, caked with ashes and cinders, eighteen hundred years old" (*TIA*, p. 82). Twain included Irving in two lists of humorists from whom he intended to select representative pieces for an anthology (NB 19 [1880], NB 19 [1881], *N&J* 2: 364, 429). *Mark Twain's Library of Humor* (1888) contained "Rip Van Winkle" and cited an edition of Irving's *Sketch-Book* published by G. P. Putnam's Sons of New York.

Twain was perennially amused by Joseph Jefferson's performances in the stage adaptation of Irving's story (see the Catalog entry for Dion Boucicault); on 6 October 1896 Twain confided to Henry H. Rogers that until Frank Mayo's death he had entertained notions of similarly establishing *Pudd'nhead Wilson* as a popular favorite: "I had begun to think it possible that Mayo would succeed in making the play a permanency, like Rip Van Winkle" (*MTHHR*, p. 239). In "A Postscript," published in the 11

February 1905 issue of *Harper's Weekly*, Twain praised the generosity of "the Putnams" toward Washington Irving during "an earlier day" when authors had often been financially mistreated (*MTPP*, p. 176). When "Bkshp-Huck" of "Three Thousand Years Among the Microbes" (written in 1905) assigns new literary names to his microbe friends, he calls one of them "Rip Van Winkle" (*WWD?*, p. 471). See also the Catalog entry below and the Catalog entry for Sir Herbert Beerbohm Tree.

————. *The Sketch-Book of Geoffrey Crayon, Gent.* Illus. New York: G. P. Putnam, 1860. 465 pp.

Source: MTLAcc, entry #1016, volume donated by Clemens.

This is the collection of short stories and sketches, first published in 1820, that contained Irving's "The Legend of Sleepy Hollow" with its portrayal of the schoolmaster Ichabod Crane. The volume also included "Rip Van Winkle."

George W. Crandall, "Emperors and Little Empires: The Schoolmaster in Nineteenth-Century American Literature," *Studies in American Humor*, n.s. 2, 5.1 (Spring 1986): 51–61.

————. *Works of Washington Irving.* Author's Revised Edition. "Spuyten Duyvil Edition." Illus. 12 vols. New York: G. P. Putnam's Sons, 1881. [Edition and publisher conjectured but likely.]

Catalog: *A1911*, "Author's Revised Edition, Illustrations, 12 vols., post 8vo, cloth, N.Y. 1881," lot 262, sold for $3.75 total.

On 15 October 1881 Clemens wrote to James R. Osgood & Company: "Irving for $13.34 is satisfactory—send her along" (Henry E. Huntington Library, San Marino; TS in MTP).

Rogers, *MTBP* (1960), p. 67; Smith, *MTDW* (1962), p. 53.

IRWIN, WALLACE (1875–1959), pseud. "Hashimura Togo." "Letters of a Japanese Schoolboy," published in *Collier's Weekly* 40–42 (November 1907–February 1909).

(See the Catalog entry below.)

————. *Letters of a Japanese Schoolboy ("Hashimura Togo").* Illustrated by Rollin G. Kirby (1875–1952). First edition. New York: Doubleday, Page & Co., 1909. 370 pp. [The illustrator Rollin Kirby went on to become a noted political cartoonist.]

On 6 July 1908 Mark Twain wrote *Collier's Weekly* to commend Irwin's fractured-English series and to request an early copy of these "Letters" whenever they issued as a book. "That Boy is the dearest & sweetest & frankest & wisest & funniest & delightfulest & loveablest creation that has been added to our literature for a long time. I think he is a permanency & I hope so, too" (ALS in Yale University Library; see "Letter about the Japanese Schoolboy," *Collier's Weekly* 41 [8 August 1908]: 22; reprinted in *AutoMT* 3: 599). Wallace Irwin wrote to thank Clemens for the praise on 8 August 1908 (*AutoMT* 3: 599). A few months later Twain complimented Irwin's schoolboy English ("Observe what Irwin has done. . . . That schoolboy's English is manufactured, yet how forceful it is, how hard it hits, how straight to the mark it goes") because it allows Irwin's character Togo (like Huckleberry Finn?) to be "innocently unconscious" of its effects (22 December 1908 AD, *AutoMT* 3: 290). When Hashimura Togo's broken-English letters appeared in book form in 1909 the rear dust wrapper quoted from Twain's letter to

Collier's: "Hon. Mark Twain. . . . He say, 'When is his book coming out? He is the wisest & funniest & delightfulest creation that has been added to our literature for a long time.'" Doubleday subsequently reprinted Twain's praise in an eight-page pamphlet promoting Irwin's book. Upon receiving a complimentary copy of the book, Clemens responded that he "cannot keep from reading it all the time, & chuckling & enjoying" (*AutoMT* 3: 599). A sequel to Irwin's book, *More Letters of a Japanese Schoolboy* (New York: G. P. Putnam, 1923), would again quote Twain's praise on its dustjacket. Although there are witty observations about American society and other topics in Hashimura Togo's letters, this type of ethnic humor has not worn well in the course of the past century. Perhaps Twain supposed he was responding to letters written in the satiric spirit of Oliver Goldsmith's *The Citizen of the World* (1762), a work he had greatly admired in his younger years.

Aspiz, "MT's Reading" (1949), pp. 110–111 n. 107; Yoshiko Uzawa, "Will White Man and Yellow Man Ever Mix? Wallace Irwin, Hashimura Togo, and the Japanese Immigrant in America," *Japanese Journal of American Studies* 17 (2006): 201–222; Hashimura Uzawa, "From 'Mark Twain's Pet' to ''Merican Jap': The Strange Career of Wallace Irwin's Hashimura Togo," *Mark Twain Studies* (Tokyo) 2 (October 2006): 120–141).

IRWIN, WILLIAM HENRY (1873–1948). *The City That Was; A Requiem of Old San Francisco.* New York: B. W. Huebsch, 1906. 47 pp.

Source: MTLAcc, entry #574, volume donated by Clemens.

ISAACS, ABRAM SAMUEL (1851–1920). *Stories from the Rabbis.* New York: Charles L. Webster & Co., 1893. 201 pp.

Clemens's publishing firm brought out this book, which was advertised as "entertaining tales in popular style from legends of the Talmud and Midrash" (*Publishers' Trade List Annual for 1893*).

"I'SE GWINE TO DE SHUCKIN'" (folk song).

Clemens was furious in the mid-1860s when William Gillis and a group of other young men raucously serenaded him outside his bedroom window in Jackson Hill, California with this and two other songs (William Robert Gillis [1849–1929], *Memories of Mark Twain and Steve* Gillis *[1838–1918]: Personal Recollections of the Famous Humorist* [Sonora, California: Printed by The Banner, 1924], p. 38; see also *MTLet* 1: 332). There were a number of plantation work songs with this or similar titles in the nineteenth century; it would be difficult to determine exactly which one Clemens objected to. See also the Catalog entries for "The happy land of Canaan" (song) and Henry Clay Work's "Kingdom coming" (song).

L'Italie (Rome newspaper).

During a sojourn on the Continent, Clemens made a memorandum on 26 September 1892: "order Galignani & l'Italy" (NB 32, TS p. 26).

"IT CAUSES ME TO TREMBLE" (spiritual). Also known as "Were you there" and "Tremble, tremble, tremble."

Clemens listed several plantation spirituals in Notebook 30 in 1890, including "It Causes me to tremble. (Beautiful)" (*N&J* 3: 594).

J

Jackson, Abraham Reeves (1827–1892).

Numerous scholars have traced the jesting Clemens-Jackson friendship during the *Quaker City* excursion in 1867, but Robert Regan was foremost in pointing out suggestive connections between Mark Twain's *Innocents Abroad* (1869) and Dr. Jackson's letter to the Philadelphia *Press* (22 July 1867) and subsequent travel reports Jackson wrote for the Monroe County *Democrat* published in Stroudsburg, Pennsylvania. See Robert Regan, "Mark Twain, 'The Doctor' and A Guidebook by Dickens," *American Studies* 22.1 (Spring 1981): 35–55, and "The Reprobate Elect in *The Innocents Abroad*," *American Literature* 54.2 (May 1982): 240–257. Dr. Jackson later moved to Chicago where he became a leading gynecologist, surgeon, and medical professor. Page 236 of "Obituary. Dr. A. Reeves Jackson" praised "his humor—for which he was so delightfully known" (*Chicago Clinical Review* [November 1892]: 234–237). See also Jackson's amusing account of the *Quaker City* shipboard life in "The *Quaker City* Pilgrimage—A Malcontent Passenger's Story of the Excursion," *Mark Twain Journal* 47.1–2 (Spring/Fall 2009): 14–20.

Jackson, Edward Payson (1840–1905). *A Demigod; A Novel.* New York: Harper & Brothers, 1887. 337 pp.

Source: MTLAcc, entry #1315, volume donated by Clemens.

Jackson, a Boston teacher of science and classics, imagined the creation of a man with superhuman traits. In Jackson's novel a party of American tourists in Greece encounter (and two of them are rescued from bandits by) an extraordinary figure named Hector Vyr who possesses superior morals and massive strength. He even has the capacity to self-heal from physical wounds. Vyr is not the descendant of ancient titans like Hercules; rather, he is the beneficial product of selective breeding (eugenics). His extraordinary intellect also enables him to develop miraculous processes and inventions.

Jackson, Gabrielle Emilie (Snow) (b. 1861). *Wee Winkles & Her Friends.* Illus. by Rachel [or Rachael] Robinson (1878–1919). New York: Harper & Brothers, 1907. 155 pp.

Source: MTLAcc, entry #1598, volume donated by Clemens.

Annapolis, Maryland author Jackson wrote several successful series of children's books, including Wee Winkles.

———. *Wee Winkles & Snowball.* Illustrated by Mary Theresa Hart (1872–1941). New York: Harper & Brothers, 1906. 147 pp.

Source: MTLAcc, entry #520, volume donated by Clemens.

———. *Wee Winkles & Wideawake.* Illustrated by Mary Theresa Hart (1872–1941). New York: Harper & Brothers, 1905. 153 pp.

Source: MTLAcc, entry #1192, damaged copy donated by Clemens.

———. *Wee Winkles at the Mountains.* Illustrated by Rachael Robinson (1878–1919). New York: Harper & Brothers, 1908. 138 pp.

Source: MTLAcc, entry #1599, volume donated by Clemens.

Jackson, Helen Maria (Fiske) Hunt (1830–1885), pseud. "H. H." and "Saxe Holm." *Cat Stories.* 3 vols. in 1. Illus.

Boston: Roberts Bros., 1886.

Source: MTLAcc, entry #511, volume donated by Clemens. Three stories for children that feature cats as the main characters.

———. *Mercy Philbrick's Choice.* Boston: Roberts Bros., 1876. 296 pp.

Source: MTLAcc, entry #1850, volume donated from Clemens's library by Clara Clemens Gabrilowitsch in 1910.

The daughter of an Amherst College professor, Jackson was encouraged to write poetry and fiction by Thomas W. Higginson. After she traveled to California and then resided in Colorado, she became an implacable champion of Native American rights.

———. *Saxe Holm's Stories.* New York: Scribner, Armstrong and Co., 1877 [cop. 1873]. 350 pp. [Six short stories.]

Catalog: Ball 2016 inventory, red cloth with gilt lettering, J. Langdon's Family Library bookplate #432.

Location: Quarry Farm library shelves, under the supervision of the Mark Twain Archive, Elmira College, Elmira, New York.

Clemens would visit the Langdon residence in Elmira in the summers.

———. *Saxe Holm's Stories.* First Series. New York: Charles Scribner's Sons, 1885. [Six short stories.]

Inscription: "Susan L. Crane/Nov. 21, 1883, Elmira".

Catalogs: QF Martinez, "Poor Condition"; Ball 2016 inventory, green cloth, gilt lettering.

Location: Quarry Farm library shelves, under the supervision of the Mark Twain Archive, Elmira College, Elmira, New York.

This was one of the books available to Clemens during his summers at Quarry Farm.

———. *Verses. By H. H.* Boston: Roberts Bros., 1888. 135 pp.

Source: MTLAcc, entry #2038, volume donated from Clemens's library by Clara Clemens Gabrilowitsch in 1910.

Jackson, Julia (Newell) (1832–1920). *A Winter Holiday in Summer Lands.* Brown cloth. Chicago: A. C. McClurg and Co., 1890. 221 pp.

Inscription: inscribed in black ink on the front pastedown endpaper: "To Mark Twain:/With the kind regards of his old shipmate and friend,/A. Reeves Jackson/Chicago, April 16, 1890."

Provenance: Antenne-Dorrance Collection, Rice Lake, Wisconsin.

Location: Mark Twain Archive, Gannett-Tripp Learning Center, Elmira College, Elmira, New York.

Copy examined: Clemens's copy, unmarked. Examined on 28 May 2015.

Jackson's travel book mainly describes Cuba and Mexico. In 1871 she had married the physician Abraham Reeves Jackson (1827–1892), who had formed a friendship with Clemens (and with her) on the *Quaker City* excursion. Jeffrey A. Churchwell, "The Letters of Julia Newell: Traveling Abroad with Mark Twain," *Wisconsin Academy Review* 42.4 (Fall 1996): 10–14.

Jacob, Samuel Swinton (1841–1917), ed. *Jeypore Portfolios of Architectural Details.*

English engineer Jacob sought to preserve a record of the traditional Indian building arts in the state of Jeypore (now Jaipur) by publishing these portfolios in twelve parts between 1890 and 1913. His illustrations displayed ornamentations of the carved pillars, doors, and other features. In a letter to Richard Watson Gilder written on 12 March 1896 Clemens lauded Jacob's first seven parts depicting the "intricate and exquisite forms and patterns invented by the artists of the great days of the Mogul Empire." Gilder published the letter in "A Gift from India," *The Critic* 28 (25 April 1896): 285. (Jo Dee Benussi helped identify this book.)

JACOBS, HARRIET (1813–1897). *Incidents in the Life of a Slave Girl, Written by Herself* (slave narrative, published in 1861).

Sholom S. Kahn speculated that Mark Twain's frequent use of the phrase "original Jacobs" had something to do with the fact that the formerly enslaved Harriet Jacobs called herself Linda Brent in her autobiography and relied on abolitionist L. Maria Child as her editor ("Mark Twain's 'Original Jacobs': A Probable Explanation," *Mark Twain Circular* 8: 1 [January-March 1994]: 4–6).

JACOBS, WILLIAM WYMARK (1863–1943). *Dialstone Lane*. New York: Charles Scribner's Sons, 1904. 337 pp.

In Jacobs' novel Captain Bowers, retiring from a life on the ocean, moves his parrot and his niece Prudence Drewitt into a seaside cottage on Dialstone Lane, located in the fictional village of Binchester. When Bowers spins a yarn about a buried treasure on a South Pacific island, the colorful characters who frequent his cottage set in motion a plot that contemporary reviewers praised as wholesome comedy. Quite likely the novel's maritime theme and Jacobs' always accurate terminology regarding docks, ships, and sailors appealed to Clemens. He informed Mary Benjamin Rogers on 27 August 1906 from Dublin, New Hampshire that he had just finished dictating an autobiographical chapter that contained "a word about W. W. Jacobs's delightful 'Dialstone Lane'" (*MTLM*, p. 48). In an Autobiographical Dictation of that date Clemens praised its "light and delicate and bubbling and inexhaustible humor" and termed it "the one purely humorous story in our language that hasn't a defect" (*AutoMT* 2: 182). In a letter of 28 October 1908 to Jacobs, Clemens declared: "It is my conviction that Dialstone Lane holds the supremacy over all purely humorous books in our language," and he mentioned that he had kept his copy "moving" among his friends (*MTL*, p. 823). Jacobs would return this favor long after Clemens's passing, writing that Mark Twain was "the foremost humorist America has produced" as well as being "a humorist in the best and fullest meaning of the word. . . . He was a man of his time; a time such as will never occur again and he has left of it an immortal picture" ("An Englishman's Opinion of Mark Twain," *Mark Twain Quarterly* 2.4 [Summer-Fall 1938]: 2).

———. "The Monkey's Paw" (short story, published in *Harper's Monthly* in 1902).

Clemens may have had Jacobs's macabre masterpiece in mind when he jotted "Monkey Tale" and "Doubtful of the Monkey-Tale" in a list he composed sometime around 1902 ("Mark Twain's Travel Trunk: An Impromptu Notebook," *Mark Twain Journal* 42.2 [Fall 2004]: 15–18.

———. *Sailors' Knots*. Illustrated by Will Owen (1869–1957). London: Methuen & Co., 1909. 302 pp.

Inscription: inscribed on the first flyleaf: "To Samuel L.

Clemens/With compliments/W. W. Jacobs/Oct 1909".

Catalogs: ListABP (1910), "Sailors' Knots, Jacobs." In August 1987 Bigelow Paine Cushman's collection in Deer Isle, Maine included a May 1935 memorandum from the Lincoln Storage Warehouse in New York City acknowledging receipt of certain books delivered by Albert Bigelow Paine, including an "autographed presentation copy, 1909" of W. W. Jacobs's *Sailors' Knots* that had belonged to Clemens. (Cushman [1928–2003] was the grandson of Albert Bigelow Paine, Clemens's biographer.) The volume was subsequently included in the "Retz Appraisal" (1944), p. 9, valued at $40.

Location: Mark Twain Papers, Bancroft Library, University of California at Berkeley.

Copy examined: Clemens's copy, unmarked. A few pages opened by tearing.

Sailors' Knots collected a dozen of Jacobs' short stories.

———. *Salthaven*. Illustrated by Will Owen (1869–1957). Original cloth. New York: Charles Scribner's Sons, 1908. 309 pp. [Advertisements in the book are dated August 1908.]

Catalogs: *C1951*, #21a, $65, listed among books containing Clemens's marginal notes; "The Library of Michael D. Hurley, A Second Selection," Dawson's Book Shop, Los Angeles, California, Catalogue 479 (May 1985), item #167; the book sold immediately before Nick Karanovich could purchase it (Karanovich to Alan Gribben, 17 June 1985, enclosing a photocopy of the catalog description). Maurice Neville Books in Santa Barbara, California, had bought the volume (Stephen Tabor, Dawson's Book Shop, to Paul Machlis, Mark Twain Project, 2 July 1985, MTP). In October 2006 the Heritage Book Shop in Los Angeles offered the volume for $17,500: "With a nice inscription by Mark Twain, publisher's cloth, front hinge cracked, slight page staining. . . . Apparently Twain found Chapter V especially praiseworthy. On two pages he has annotated the text with over 90 words. There are numerous small ink corrections throughout the text, most likely by Twain."

Inscriptions: signed "S. L. Clemens 1908" on the front pastedown endpaper. Inscribed in ink on the half-title page, "To Mark Twain/with the author's compliments/Oct. 1908". Clemens wrote in ink below Jacobs's inscription on the half-title page: "It's a delightful book./Mark." [This is a highly unusual use of the first part of his pen name, but definitely authentic. It corroborates his intention (see below) to pass the volume along to someone other than one of his daughters.] Farther down the page Clemens added in ink: "Bay House/Bermuda, March '10/I have read it about 5 times. The above verdict stands."

Marginalia: Dawson's Book Shop gave some details: "In his several readings Twain scratched out a number of words and commas in the text that he considered superfluous. On p. 44 he wrote in the margin, 'This book is refreshingly sweet & clean & delicate after one has been floundering through that sewer, [William N. Harben's] 'Ann Boyd,' & scurrying around its frantic colony of vermin.' [Clemens made] a further note on p. 51: 'I think there is not a defect in this chapter. Even the 'stage directions' are without flaw. In the hands of the literary mechanic, those things are silly & uninforming. Such as 'said he, flipping the ash from his cigar,'—'said he, reaching for a fresh cigar;'— 'said he, fumbling in his vest pocket for a match.' Damn such rubbish! As St. Paul said to the Corinthians.'. . . Two facing pages of the book are rather badly stained, and Jacobs's letter was at one time attached to the front fly [leaf] by two pins. The book is in rather good shape for having been read five times, annotated, and carted to Bermuda and back" (all quotations from the Dawson's Book Shop Catalogue 479 [1985]).

Location: currently unknown.

Copy examined: photocopy of the Dawson's Book Shop catalog, sent to Alan Gribben by Kevin Mac Donnell in June 1985.

Clemens wrote to Jacobs from Redding on 28 October 1908: "I place Salthaven close up next to Dialstone [Lane] because I think it has a fair and honest right to that high position. I have kept the other book moving; I shall begin to hand this one around now. And many thanks to you for remembering me" (*MTL*, p. 823). Notebook 49 contains a reference to Jacobs' *Salthaven* (TS p. 1), entered in January 1910. The same notebook entry observes that while another author "paints with whitewash brush, Jacobs [paints] with camelhair pencil." During the last year of his life Clemens read from "that brilliant book" [*Salthaven*] to a young girl, Helen Allen (MS notes formerly owned by the late Bigelow Paine Cushman, Deer Isle, Maine). Jacobs' drolly humorous novel is set in the shipbuilding seaport town of Salthaven.

JACOBSEN, JENS PETER (1847–1885). *Niels Lyhne.* [Translated from the Danish into the German by Marie Herzfeld (1855–1940).] Illus. Florenz und Leipzig: Eugen Diederichs, 1898. 302 pp.

Source: MTLAcc, entry #374, volume donated by Clemens.

An English translation of this Danish novel, important in the European Naturalist literary movement, would not be available until 1919. *Niels Lyhne* embodied themes of isolation, disillusionment, and atheism; the title character ultimately dies in a pointless war.

JACQUEMART, ALBERT (1808–1875). *History of the Ceramic Art; A Descriptive and Philosophical Study of the Pottery of All Ages and All Nations.* Translated from the French by Fanny (Marryat) Bury Palliser (1805–1878). Second ed. Illus. New York: Scribner, Armstrong and Co., 1877. 627 pp. [The translator was the sister of author Frederick Marryat.]

Catalog: Ball 2016 inventory, brown and marble boards, marbled edges, poor condition, front cover detached.

Location: Quarry Farm library shelves, under the supervision of the Mark Twain Archive, Elmira College, Elmira, New York.

Olivia Clemens had more than a passing interest in the history of pottery and china. This volume would have been available to the Clemenses whenever they visited Quarry Farm in Elmira, New York.

JAMES, ALICE ARCHER (SEWALL) (1870–1955). *An Ode to Girlhood and Other Poems.* New York: Harper & Brothers, 1899. 73 pp.

Source: MTLAcc, entry #1457, volume donated by Clemens.

In addition to her poetry, James became even more prominent as a painter and illustrator. She included her two most-praised poems in *An Ode to Girlhood and Other Poems*, "Sinfonia Eroica" (pp. 16–17) and "The Butterfly" (pp. 33–36), the latter of which begins, "I am not what

I was yesterday."

JAMES, EDMUND JANES (1855–1925). *The Immigrant Jew in America, Edited by Edmund J. James. . . with the Collaboration of Oscar R. Flynn . . . Dr. J. R. Paulding, Mrs. Simon N. Patton (Charlotte Kimball) . . . Walter Scott Andrews . . . Charles S. Bernheimer. . . Henrietta Szold and Other Writers.* Issued by the National Liberal Immigration League. Illus. New York: B. F. Buck & Co., 1907. 403 pp. [Publisher and date conjectured.]

Inscription: "S. L. Clemens, Tuxedo Park, Sept. 1907."

Catalogs: A1911, "12mo, cloth, N.Y. 1907," quotes the signature, lot 258, sold for $1.25; George D. Smith, New York City, "Catalogue of Books" (1911), quotes the signature, item #204, $7.50.

JAMES, GEORGE PAYNE RAINSFORD (1799–1860). *Heidelberg* (novel, published in 1846).

On 2 August 1878, shortly after Clemens left Heidelberg for Baden-Baden, he jotted down a pithy opinion of James's melodramatic novel set in the seventeenth century: "G P R James's 'Heidelberg' is rot" (NB 15, *N&J* 2: 126). Its subject was Frederick V (1596–1632), elector Palatine of the Rhine and briefly (1619–1620) the King of Bohemia, who married the daughter of James I of England. Frederick was inextricably entangled in the Protestant-Catholic wars of his era and spent the remainder of his short life in exile. Coincidentally, James's granddaughter wrote an admiring letter to Clemens on 7 December 1891 (*DearMT*, p. 163).

JAMES, (SIR) HENRY (1803–1877), ed. *Facsimiles of National Manuscripts from William the Conqueror to Queen Anne, Selected [by Sir Thomas Duffus Hardy] under the Direction of the Master of the Rolls and Photozincographed . . . by . . . Sir Henry James, Director of the Ordinance Survey.* With Translations and Notes by W[illiam]. B[asevi]. Sanders (1823–1892). Four parts. Folio, 65 plates. Rebound in black cloth retaining the original brown cloth and gilt-decorated front panel. Some leaves chipped on their edges and restored. Southampton, England: Ordinance Survey Office, 1865–1868.

Inscriptions: on the presentation slip affixed to the front pastedown endpaper Clemens noted: "Presented to S. L. Clemens, 1874,/by Sir Thomas Duffus Hardy." Hardy (1804–1878), a historian, was the "Master of the Rolls" designated in the book title. Below the presentation slip is the A1911 sale label.

Marginalia: two instructions by Clemens to an engraver named "Mr. Anthony" concerning the reproduction of two of the documents. (Almost certainly this engraver was Andrew Stout Varick Anthony, 1835–1906.) One handwritten note that appears on page 60 (Plate no. 31) is signed "S. L. C."; the other, on page 61 is unsigned.

Catalog: A1911, "Part 2 [only], imp. 4to, cloth (stained), quotes the inscription, mentions "two remarks" by Clemens, lot 22, $8.

Provenance: Part 2 only offered for sale on 2 December 2001 by the Bookmark, Salisbury, Connecticut, for $35,000 (Mark Goodman, The Bookmark to Victor Fischer, Mark Twain Papers, 2 December 2001, describing and quoting the title page, marginalia, and other facts about the volume).

Location: Part 2 only, Albert and Shirley Small Special Collections Library, University of Virginia Library, Charlottesville, Virginia. Listed in their online catalog in 2006. Mark Twain used the book, which draws on materials between 1509 to 1553, as a source in writing *The Prince and the Pauper* (1881). Two of the plates in *Facsimiles of National Manuscripts* became frontispieces for Twain's novel.

JAMES, HENRY (1843–1916). *The Ambassadors; A Novel.* New York: Harper & Brothers, 1904. 432 pp.

Source: MTLAcc, entry #1573, volume donated by Clemens.

Leon Edel's *Henry James: The Master, 1901–1916* (London: Rupert Hart-Davis, 1972) mentioned four encounters between James and Mark Twain that occurred in 1879, 1897, 1900, and 1904 (pp. 33–37, 245–246). As Edel put it, "Mark Twain and Henry James were not by nature destined ever to be intimate; there was a newspaperish side to the humorist, the 'lion' side, and the roar of publicity and a love of broad effects, from which James shrank" (p. 35). James' *The Ambassadors* ran serially in two of the same issues (January and February 1903) of the *North American Review* in which Twain's "Christian Science" appeared. Twain also read the March 1903 issue of the *North American Review* that contained the next installment of *The Ambassadors*; see the Catalog entry for W. D. McCrackan.

———. *The American Scene.* New York, 1907.

Inscription: the front pastedown endpaper is signed "S. L. Clemens, 1907."

Catalog: *A1911*, "first edition, 8vo, cloth, gilt top, uncut, N.Y. 1907," quotes the signature, lot 264, sold for $5.50.

———. *The American Scene.* New York: Harper & Brothers, 1907. 443 pp.

Source: MTLAcc, entry #1300, volume donated by Clemens.

———. *The Awkward Age, A Novel.* New York: Harper & Brothers, 1904. 457 pp.

Source: MTLAcc, entry #1106, volume donated by Clemens.

———. *The Bostonians.* First American one-volume edition. Original maroon cloth-backed orange boards, gilt. London and New York: Macmillan and Co., 1886. 449 pp.

Provenance: a *C1951* label is pasted in the book.

Location: collection of Kevin Mac Donnell, Austin, Texas.

Copy examined: Clemens's unmarked copy, in July 2004. James's novel was published serially in the *Century Magazine* in 1885 (the same issues in which Twain's *Adventures of Huckleberry Finn* appeared). From Chicago Clemens reported to his wife on 3 February 1885, during his platform tour with George Washington Cable: "Yes, I tried to read the Bostonians, but couldn't. To me it was unspeakably dreary. I dragged along half-way through it & gave it up in despair" (MTP). He was similarly unequivocal in censuring the novel in a letter of 21 July 1885 to Howells from Elmira: "And as for the Bostonians, I would rather be damned to John Bunyan's heaven than read that" (*MTHL*, p. 534). But Clemens's attitude toward James was variable; in a letter to T. Douglas Murray written on 31 January 1900 he referred to James as "a master" (MTP). Tony Tanner's "The Literary Children of James and Clemens," *Nineteenth-Century Fiction* 16.3 (December 1961): 205–218 asked why the child protagonist suggested itself to authors so different. Also, "what was the child to them, how do they use it?" Tanner's essay focused on Twain's *Adventures of Huckleberry Finn* (1885) and James' *What*

Maisie Knew (1897); however, their mutual concept of innocence led Tanner to discuss characters in *Daisy Miller*, *An International Episode*, *The Bostonians*, and other James novels. "For James innocence is an endearing, sometimes pathetic state, which eventually must be sloughed off if one is to come to know the richness of life. But Clemens saw no dividend in the exchange of innocence for maturity" (p. 216). Tanner did not take up the question of whether they read each other's books, though he does mention that "it is perhaps not surprising that there is no evidence that James ever bothered to read *Huckleberry Finn*" (p. 209). Smith and Gibson, eds., *MTHL*, pp. 160, 161 n. 2; Janet Gabler-Hover, "*Adventures of Huckleberry Finn*, *The Bostonians*, and Henry Ward Beecher: Discourse on the Idealization of Suffering," *South Central Review* 5.4 (Winter 1988): 42–52.

———. *Confidence.* Boston: Houghton, Osgood and Co., 1882.

Inscription: Ida C. Langdon (1849–1934), Charles Jervis Langdon's wife.

Catalogs: inventory list of the Langdon family library books prepared by Mark Woodhouse for the Mark Twain Archive; Ball 2016 inventory, green cloth, gilt lettering, fair condition, bookplate of J. Langdon Family Library #625.

Location: Quarry Farm library shelves, under the supervision of the Mark Twain Archive, Elmira College, Elmira, New York.

Clemens had access to this book whenever he visited the Langdon residence in Elmira.

———. *Daisy Miller: A Study. An International Episode. Four Meetings.* Collection of British Authors Series. Leipzig: B. Tauchnitz, 1879. 288 pp.

Source: MTLAcc, entry #2284, volume donated from Clemens's library by Clara Clemens Gabrilowitsch in 1910.

———. *The Golden Bowl.* 2 vols. New York: C. Scribner's Sons, 1905.

Source: MTLAcc, entries #2286 and #2287, volumes donated from Clemens's library by Clara Clemens Gabrilowitsch in 1910.

On 27 July 1907 Isabel Lyon noted that she was surprised to observe Clemens "stealing quietly up to my study after I was about to get into bed, to get a paper knife to cut the leaves of 'The Golden Bowl' with" (IVL Journal, TS p. 264).

———. *An International Episode.* New York: Harper & Brothers, [cop. 1878]. 136 pp.

Source: MTLAcc, entry #2285, volume donated from Clemens's library by Clara Clemens Gabrilowitsch in 1910.

———. *An International Episode.* Illustrated by Harry W[hitney]. McVickar (1860–1905). Original quarter blue cloth, gilt, gray boards, uncut. New York: Harper & Brothers, 1902.

Inscription: the front pastedown endpaper is inscribed in black ink in Clemens's hand: "Olivia L. Clemens/1903".

Catalogs: ListABP (1910), "International Episode, James"; *Zeitlin 1951*, #25 (misdates the publication date as 1892 by reading the copyright date and overlooking the Roman numerals on the title page), $10.

Provenance: post-1951 bookseller's ticket of Books, Inc., San Francisco on the rear pastedown endpaper.

Location: collection of Kevin Mac Donnell, Austin, Texas.

Acquired in January 2016 (Mac Donnell to Alan Gribben, 21 January 2016).

This would be one of the last books that Clemens gave to his wife.

———. *A Little Tour in France*. Boston: James R. Osgood and Co., 1885. Also issued by Bernhard Tauchnitz of Leipzig. [Edition undetermined.]

"Henry James's Summer trip through Provence," Clemens wrote in Notebook 31 in September 1891 while he was in France (TS p. 5). He noted the correct title of James's travel sketches on the endpaper of Notebook 44 in 1901. Houghton, Mifflin and Company of Boston brought out a new edition in 1900 illustrated by Joseph Pennell (1857–1926).

———. *Nathaniel Hawthorne*. New York: Harper & Brothers, n. d. 177 pp.

Source: MTLAcc, entry #1282, volume donated by Clemens.

———. *Nathaniel Hawthorne*. English Men of Letters Series. New York: Harper & Brothers, 1880. 177 pp.

Catalogs: QF Martinez, good condition; Ball 2016 inventory, dark brown cloth, red lettering, signed by Jervis Langdon (1875–1952).

Location: Quarry Farm library shelves, under the supervision of the Mark Twain Archive, Elmira College, Elmira, New York.

Available to Clemens whenever he visited the Langdons' residence in Elmira.

———. *The Portrait of a Lady*. Boston: Houghton, Mifflin and Co. 1882.

Catalogs: inventory list of the Langdon family library books prepared by Mark Woodhouse for the Mark Twain Archive; Ball 2016 inventory, green cloth, brown and gold lettering, bookplate of J. Langdon Family Library #624, fair condition.

Location: Quarry Farm library shelves, under the supervision of the Mark Twain Archive, Elmira College, Elmira, New York.

Clemens had access to this book whenever he visited the Langdons' residence in Elmira, New York.

———. *The Private Life; Lord Beaupré; The Visits*. New York: Harper & Brothers, 1893. 232 pp.

Marginalia: a penciled notation on the rear endpaper: "R/115". No inscription or other markings.

Provenance: a *C1951* label in the book attests that the volume was sold at Clara Clemens Samossoud's 1951 auction in Hollywood.

Location: collection of Kevin Mac Donnell, Austin, Texas. Acquired in 2008 from its owner "in Southern California."

Source: notes supplied to Alan Gribben by Kevin Mac Donnell in 2008.

———. *Washington Square*. Illustrated by George Du Maurier (1834–1896). New York: Harper & Brothers, 1901. 264 pp.

Source: MTLAcc, entry #1433, volume donated by Clemens.

JAMES, ROBERT (1705–1776). *A Medicinal Dictionary; Including Physic, Surgery, Anatomy, Chymistry, and Botany, Together with a History of Drugs*. 3 vols. London: T. Osborne, 1743–1745.

An undated sheet of manuscript contains Mark Twain's notation: "A medicinal Dic. by R. James, M.D. London,

1743" (*A1911*, lot 290a). Twice in 1888 Twain considered using the book in *A Connecticut Yankee in King Arthur's Court*: "Dose of Medicine—Dr James Dict—y" (NB 27, *N&J* 3: 383); "The leech gives him recipes from James's medical Dictionary. Result bedrids him 2 months" (NB 28, *N&J* 3: 415). Twain devoted an entire sketch, "A Majestic Literary Fossil" (1890), to examining this "literary relic. It is a *Dictionary of Medicine*, by Dr. James, of London, assisted by Mr. Boswell's Doctor Samuel Johnson, and is a hundred and fifty years old. . . . For three generations and a half it had been going quietly along, enriching the earth with its slain." Twain quotes extensively from James's textbook to illustrate the ancient/modern contrast he had recently emphasized in *A Connecticut Yankee in King Arthur's Court* (1889), ridiculing the antiquated remedies and antidotes. On 2 December 1892 Twain asked Frederick J. Hall to obtain "an article which I published in Harper's Monthly several years ago about a Curious Old Book. . . . It was about an ancient Medical Dictionary. I want a paragraph from it for the extravagant novel I am writing" (TS in MTP). In Chapter 7 of "Those Extraordinary Twins" (1894) Twain turned to this source for a ludicrous prescription ("Galen's favorite") recommended for Angelo by Dr. Claypool. Twain summarized James' "ancient treatment" again in "Bible Teaching and Religious Practice" (written in 1890), for the book had become to him a comforting emblem of man's undeniable scientific progress in the past century. During his residence in Vienna in 1898 Clemens may have parted with his copy James's multi-volume work; a letter Clemens wrote on 17 May 1898 to Dr. Edward K. Root, a prominent Hartford physician, conveyed the gift: "Yes, the institution can have the old medical dictionary. If you step out to the house . . . it will be delivered to you. . . . Mrs. Clemens thinks the dictionary is in the billiard room. I think there are 2 vols." (PH in MTP).

Nevertheless, Twain continued to make use of the book's deadly prescriptions. Presumably it was James's *Dictionary* that furnished the primitive medical treatments that the befuddled physician administers to George Harrison of Indiantown in Chapter 12 of "Which Was It?" (written 1899–1903, *WWD?*, pp. 285–286). Likewise Twain seemed to be repeating James's medical practices in the outline of early nineteenth-century procedures he supplied in an Autobiographical Dictation of 22 November 1906 (*AutoMT* 2: 284): bleeding accompanied by doses of fat, toad livers, ipecac, calomel, spiders, and other "odious mixtures."

K. Patrick Ober, *Mark Twain and Medicine: "Any Mummery Will Cure"* (Columbia: University of Missouri Press, 2003), pp. 51, 325.

JAMES, U[RIAH]. P[IERSON] (1811–1889). *James' River Guide; Containing Descriptions of All the Cities, Towns, and Principal Objects of Interest on the Navigable Waters of the Mississippi Valley . . . and Many Interesting Historical Sketches of the Country*. Illus., 44 maps. Cincinnati, Ohio: U. P. James, 1857. 128 pp.

William Baker revealed that while Clemens was working for Wrightson's printing shop in Cincinnati the firm "put up" two thousand copies of James's book, "a river pilot's bible," in January 1857 ("Mark Twain in Cincinnati: A Mystery Most Compelling," *American Literary Realism*

12.2 [Autumn 1979]: 305). Wesley A. Britton elaborated on this fact ("Macfarlane, 'Boarding House,' and 'Bugs': Mark Twain's Cincinnati Apprenticeship," *Mark Twain Journal* 27.1 [Spring 1989]: 14–17).

JAMES, WILLIAM (1842–1910). *The Principles of Psychology*. Authorized Edition. 2 vols. New York: Henry Holt & Co., 1890.

In Florence in December 1892 Clemens made a series of notes that seem to indicate he had purchased an unspecified book by William James (NB 32, TS pp. 51, 53). On 18 December 1892 William James wrote to his friend the Harvard professor Josiah Royce from Florence with the news that "Mark Twain is here for the winter. . . . I have seen him a couple of times—a fine, soft-fibred little fellow with the perversest twang and drawl, but very human and good. I should think that one might grow very fond of him, and wish he'd come and live in Cambridge" (*The Letters of William James*, ed. Henry James [Boston: Atlantic Monthly Press, 1920], p. 333). In a letter written to Francis Boott on 30 January 1893 William James mentioned that "Mark Twain dined with us last night. . . . He's a dear man" (*Letters of William James*, pp. 341–342). Clemens stated in a letter to Olivia Clemens written on 27 January 1894 that Elinor Howells "convinced *me*, before she got through, that she and William James are right—hypnotism & mind-cure are the same thing" (*MTHL*, p. 659). On 30 September 1896 in London Clemens included "Prof. Wm. James's psychology book" among works he wished to obtain (NB 39, TS p. 6). Probably he borrowed a copy at the London Library, which he mentions in his notebook; late in October 1896 he referred to a juggler's ability to perform his feats despite a lapse of thirty years in practicing, "so powerful is a habit once acquired. Quoted by Prof. Wm James in his 'Principles of Psychology'" (NB 39, TS p. 11). Clemens and James corresponded in 1900 about the efficacy of Jonas Kellgren's therapeutic treatments (SLC to William James, 17, 23 April 1900, Houghton Library, Harvard). John S. Tuckey, in "Mark Twain's Later Dialogue: The 'Me' and the Machine," *American Literature* 41.4 (January 1970): 532–542, was the first to argue for the relevance of William James's *The Principles of Psychology* to Mark Twain's *Mysterious Stranger*. See also Tuckey, *WWD?*, p. 17 and Tuckey, *MTSatan*, p. 27.

Jason G. Horn, "Figuring Freedom as Religious Experience: Mark Twain, William James, and *No. 44, the Mysterious Stranger*," *Arizona Quarterly: A Journal of American Literature, Culture, and Theory* 52.1 (1996): 95–123; Horn, *Mark Twain and William James: Crafting a Self* (Columbia: University of Missouri Press, 1996); and Lawrence I. Berkove and Joseph Csicsila, *Heretical Fictions: Religion in the Literature of Mark Twain* (Iowa City: University of Iowa Press, 2010), pp. 155–156, 164, 177, 185–186.

————. *The Varieties of Religious Experience; A Study in Human Nature*. "Fourth Impression." London: Longmans, Green, and Co., 1902. 534 pp.

Inscription: the front pastedown endpaper is signed in ink, "S L. Clemens/ 1903".

Marginalia: numerous pages contain Clemens's vertical lines and brackets. Page 9 is turned down, and where on that page James quotes Spinoza as vowing he "will analyze the actions and appetites of men as if it were a question of

lines, of planes, and of solids," Clemens drew a mark and noted: "Motto for my book." Below that, James quotes Hippolyte Adolphe Taine's introduction to his history of English literature (1865): "Whether facts be moral or physical, it makes no matter. They always have their causes. There are causes for ambition, courage, veracity, just as there are for digestion, muscular movement, and animal heat." That statement caused Clemens to write "Another" and draw a vertical line. At the top of page 83, below which James discusses his concept of human temperament, Clemens wrote, "Training, environment & temperament." Clemens made underlinings on pages 106–107 where the text explains notions of evil and James states: "Pessimism leads to weakness. Optimism leads to power" (107). A description of the Christian "mind-cure" on page 113 prompted Clemens to make very heavy markings. On page 159 James describes profound "religious melancholy," citing and quoting from the case of the devoted American evangelist Henry Alline (1748–1784), who reached the point of envying the beasts that have no soul to lose. Clemens made a large bracket there and noted, "I had it." For a discussion of Clemens's lifelong interest in the concept of human temperaments, see Alan Gribben, "Mark Twain, Phrenology and the 'Temperaments': A Study of Pseudoscientific Influence," *American Quarterly* 24.1 (March 1972): 45–68. A revised version of this essay appears in Volume One of the present work.

Catalog: ListABP (1910), "Varieties of Religious Experience", no other information provided.

Location: collection of Judge Harry Pregerson, Los Angeles, California (as of 1976). Information for this entry derives from a photocopy dated 20 December 1976 in the Mark Twain Papers at the Bancroft Library in Berkeley.

Jason G. Horn, "Figuring Freedom as Religious Experience: Mark Twain, William James, and *No. 44, the Mysterious Stranger*," *Arizona Quarterly: A Journal of American Literature, Culture, and Theory* 52.1 (1996): 95–123; Horn, *Mark Twain and William James: Crafting a Self* (Columbia: University of Missouri Press, 1996); and Lawrence I. Berkove and Joseph Csicsila, *Heretical Fictions: Religion in the Literature of Mark Twain* (Iowa City: University of Iowa Press, 2010), pp. 155–157, 160–161, 164, 179.

JAMESON, ANNA BROWNELL (MURPHY) (1794–1860). *Memoirs of the Loves of the Poets. Biographical Sketches of Women Celebrated in Ancient and Modern Poetry*. "From the Last London Edition." Boston: Ticknor and Fields, 1866. 517 pp.

Inscription: bookplate of "J. Langdon's/Family/Library./ No.225" on the front pastedown endpaper.

Marginalia: Herbert A. Wisbey, "Mark Twain on Petrarch: More Quarry Farm Marginalia," *Mark Twain Journal* 24.1 (1986): 21–23, quoted Clemens's penciled annotations, which were restricted to Chapter 7 (describing the Italian poet Petrarch's unrequited love for Laura) and the first page of Chapter 8 (concerning Dante's love for Beatrice Portinari), where Clemens was still focusing on Petrarch and Laura. "The woman capable of listening was far from pure," Clemens asserted about Laura (p. 75), adding that "a pure woman" possesses "sufficient armor against even approach." On page 76 Clemens disagreed with Jameson's sympathetic interpretation of Laura's motives, writing, "This was a foul hearted beast, this married Laura. A true woman would have ended this sick cub's drivelings in short order & sent him about his business." A few pages farther on, where Jameson described Laura as "a woman of calm passions," Clemens objected, "No—only devilish." On page 82 Clemens queried, "What could his [Petrarch's] 'sacred respect' have been founded on?" Again Clemens dissented on page 86 regarding Jameson's use of the phrase "pure-hearted woman" for Laura: "Pure-hearted is not the term." Clemens summed up his opinion of Petrarch on page 87: "Don Quixote before his time, this Petrarch was. One woman wd have inspired him as well as another at first, possibly." The subject matter of Clemens's remarks suggest that this may have been another of the "courting books" exchanged between Sam Clemens and Olivia Langdon.

Catalogs: Emily Schweizer Martinez, a bookdealer in Horseheads, New York, listed this volume ("marginalia on 5 pages by Twain") in an inventory of the library books she prepared when Quarry Farm was donated to Elmira College in 1982. She estimated its value at $150. The title was subsequently listed among the books that Mark Woodhouse transferred from the Quarry Farm library to the Mark Twain Archive on 9 July 1987. Ball 2016 inventory, marbled cloth cover, endpapers and page edges, green leather spine, gilt lettering, Clemens marginalia, J. Langdon Family Library #225.

Location: Mark Twain Archive, Gannett-Tripp Learning Center, Elmira College, Elmira, New York.

Copy examined: Langdon family copy, annotated by Clemens. Examined in November 1986. I also viewed photocopies of Clemens's annotations sent to me by Herbert A. Wisbey, Jr. on 12 December 1984, as well as photocopies in the Mark Twain Papers, Bancroft Library, University of California at Berkeley, on 29 August 1985 and again in August 1987.

———. *Sacred and Legendary Art*. 2 vols. Boston: Ticknor and Fields, 1866. [First published in 1848.]

Provenance: bookplates #224 (Volume I) and #228 (Volume II) of the "J. Langdon Family Library" on the front pastedown endpapers.

Catalog: Ball 2016 inventory, marbled covers and endpapers, spine missing, J. Langdon Family Library #228 and #228.

Location: Mark Twain Archive, Gannett-Trip Learning Center, Elmira College, Elmira, New York.

Copy examined: unmarked copies available to Clemens whenever he visited the Langdon residence in Elmira. Examined on 27 May 2015.

———. *Sketches of Art, Literature, and Character*. Boston: James R. Osgood and Co., 1875. 502 pp.

Source: MTLAcc, entry #665, volume donated by Clemens.

A travel narrative originally published in 1834, *Sketches of Art, Literature, and Character* collected Jameson's prose impressions of German cities, sites, personalities, and celebrities.

"Jan and Dan" (song)

George Washington Cable inquired, in a speech at a celebration of Clemens's Seventieth Birthday in New York City in 1905, "Do you remember, Mark, how [during their reading tour of 1884–85] we sang almost nightly that old Mississippi ditty, 'Jan and Dan'?" ("Mark Twain's 70th Birthday," *Harper's Weekly* 49.2557 [23 December

1905]: 1889; reprinted in Arlin Turner's *MT&GWC* [1960], p. 127).

Jane, Frederick Thomas (1865–1916). *All the World's Fighting Ships*. New York: Harper & Brothers, 1901. 375 pp.

Source: MTLAcc, entry #1367, volume donated by Clemens.

Janvier, Catherine [born Catharine] Ann (Drinker) (1841–1923). *London Mews*. Illus. New York: Harper & Brothers, 1904. [42 pp., 37 of them with drawings and verses.]

Source: MTLAcc, entry #1371, volume donated by Clemens.

Invented children's nursery rhymes about cats, punning on the famous Mews alleyways in certain boroughs in London, accompanied by amusing color drawings. Catherine Janvier, who had married Thomas Allibone Janvier in 1878, was an artist of note.

Janvier, Thomas Allibone (1849–1913). *The Aztec Treasure-House; A Romance of Contemporary Antiquity*. Illus. New York: Harper & Brothers, [cop. 1890]. 446 pp.

Source: MTLAcc, entry #1574, volume donated by Clemens.

Three explorers, one of them a professor from the University of Michigan, undertake a hazardous search for "Mexican antiquities," a field in which the professor is knowledgeable. Many of the historical allusions are true; the adventures are fictional.

———. *The Christmas Kalends of Provence and Some Other Provençal Festivals*. Illus. Green cloth. New York: Harper & Brothers, 1902. 262 pp.

Inscription: signed in black ink on the front pastedown endpaper: "SL. Clemens/1902".

Provenance: Antenne-Dorrance Collection, Rice Lake, Wisconsin.

Location: Mark Twain Archive, Gannett-Tripp Learning Center, Elmira College, Elmira, New York.

Copy examined: Clemens's copy, unmarked. Examined on 28 May 2015.

———. *An Embassy to Provence*. Illus. New York: The Century Co., 1893. 132 pp.

In 1901 Clemens wrote "Embassy to Provence (Janvier)" among a list of books on the rear flyleaf of Notebook 44.

———. *Henry Hudson, A Brief Statement of His Aims and His Achievements, To Which is Added a Newly-Discovered Partial Record, Now First Published, of the Trial of the Mutineers by Whom He and Others Were Abandoned to Their Death*. Illus. New York: Harper & Brothers, 1909. 148 pp.

Inscription: "S. L. Clemens, 1909."

Catalog: *A1911*, "16mo, cloth, N.Y. 1909," quotes the signature, lot 266, sold for $3.25.

In "Official Report to the I.I.A.S." (written in 1909) Mark Twain employs an extract from Hudson's log taken from Janvier's book (*LE*, p. 150).

———. *In Great Waters: Four Stories*. Illus. New York: Harper & Brothers, 1901. 222 pp.

Inscription: the front flyleaf is signed "S. L. Clemens, Riverdale, Nov. 1901."

Catalog: *A1911*, "12mo, cloth, N.Y. 1901," quotes the signature, lot 265, sold for $5.75.

Death finds fictional characters as they test their luck in seas and lakes.

———. *In the Sargasso Sea, A Novel*. New York: Harper &

Brothers, 1898. 293 pp.

Source: MTLAcc, entry #186, volume donated by Clemens. A gale sinks the *Hurst Castle*, stranding the narrator in the tangled seaweed of "a region which every living ship steered clear of and into which never any but dead ships came" (p. 72). His entrapment amid abandoned vessels reminds one of Mark Twain's repeated stories about the entrapment of ships and balloons carrying only corpses.

———. *The Women's Conquest of New York; Being an Account of the Rise and Progress of the Women's Rights Movement, or the Grant of Female Suffrage, of the Formation of the Area League, of the Capture by the Women Voters of the Government of the City of New York by the Election as Mayoress of Bridget O'Dowd, and the Season of Female Despotism Which Thereafter Ensued, and Which Was Ended by an Appeal to Primitive Natural Law. By a Member of the Committee of Safety of 1908.* Harper's Franklin Square Library series, No. 750. "Extra. June, 1894." New York: Harper & Brothers, 1894 [title page dated 1953]. 84 pp.

Laura Skandera Trombley made a convincing case that this anonymously published book, a futuristic novella in which women have seized control of the New York City government, is the one Mark Twain was critiquing in a partially published, now-missing manuscript titled "Comment on Woman & a Certain Book." Twain evidently wrote the piece sometime in the mid-1890s; the essay was quoted from in the St. Louis *Post-Dispatch* on 9 December 1928, but the manuscript itself has never reappeared.

Janvier's story, related as historical fact by an aging grandfather for the edification of his grandchildren, ridiculed the women's rights movement for taking advantage of the financial collapse caused by the Panic of 1893 and installing a government in which "all the worst faults of Tammany were repeated and enlarged a thousand-fold. Tammany, at least, had endeavored to propitiate public sentiment by executing important public works—under cover of which its largest stealings had been effected. . . . But the Area League . . . did its stealing quite frankly, and left the public works to go by the board" (pp. 44–45). The book belittled Irish and Chinese immigrants, among other troubling tendencies. An "excitable" Irish woman, Bridget O'Dowd, formerly the narrator's cook, becomes arrogant and corrupt when installed in the office of mayor. "Murders greatly increased in atrocity and frequency," with the result that "few people cared to venture abroad after dark" (p. 55). Eventually the grandfather and other men formed a "Committee of Safety" and set out "to depose the existing city government." See Laura Skandera Trombley, "Mark Twain's Mother of Invention," *Mark Twain Journal* 31.2 (Fall 1993): 2–10.

JAPANESE COLORED PICTURE BOOK. [Title, publisher, date unknown.]

Catalog: *A1911*, "8vo, wrappers," lot 267, sold for $2.

See the Catalog entry for Emily Sophia Patton's *Japanese Topsyturvydom* (Tokyo, 1896) for a possible identification of this cryptic catalog listing.

JARDINE, DAVID (1794–1860). *Lives and Criminal Trials of Celebrated Men.* Philadelphia: [No publisher listed on the title page], 1835. 520 pp.

Catalog: *A1911*, "12mo, original cloth (binding poor), Phila., 1835," a sheet of Clemens's notes laid in, lot 269,

sold for .75¢.

Here is another "volume of great trials" such as William Dean Howells testified that Clemens enjoyed because the collection "had the root of the human matter in it" (*My Mark Twain* [1910], p. 15). David Jardine was a London barrister and historian of legal practices. His *Lives and Criminal Trials of Celebrated Men* provided biographical sketches and accounts of the public trials of five eminent figures—Sir Nicholas Throckmorton, the Duke of Norfolk, Dr. William Parry, the Earl of Essex, and Sir Walter Raleigh. Jardine's "Introduction" discussed methods of torture employed in that earlier era, with grisly examples. Throckmorton died, possibly by poison, following his trial; the other men were executed.

JARVES, JAMES JACKSON (1818–1888). *History of the Hawaiian or Sandwich Islands, Embracing Their Antiquities, Mythology, Legends, Discovery by Europeans in the Sixteenth Century, Re-Discovery by Cook, with their Civil Religious, and Political History, from the Earliest Traditionary Period to the Present Time.* Second edition. Illus. Boston: James Munroe and Co., 1844. 407 pp.

Marginalia: Clemens penciled a note on the first flyleaf scoffing at the type of education given Hawaiian youths ("translating Greek, &c") when the islands were being compelled to import mechanics owing to a shortage of people with those skills. Clemens also made a few pencil marks in the text. Michael B. Frank of the Mark Twain Project deciphered references to four books related to the Sandwich Islands that Clemens noted on the rear cover of this paperbound volume: "William Root Bliss, *Paradise in the Pacific; a Book of Travel, Adventure, and Facts in the Sandwich Islands* (New York: Sheldon and Company, 1873); Charles Samuel Stewart, *Private Journal of a Voyage to the Pacific Ocean and a Residence at the Sandwich Islands in the Years 1822–25, with an Introduction by Rev. Wm. Ellis.* Second edition (New York: John P. Haven, 1828); Anderson Rufus, *The Hawaiian Islands: Their Progress and Condition Under Missionary Labors.* Third edition (Boston: Gould and Lincoln, 1865); and George Leonard Chaney, *"Alo'ha": A Hawaiian Salutation* (Boston: Roberts Brothers, 1880 [c. 1879]) (see *N&J* 1: 104–105).

Catalog: "Retz Appraisal" (1944), p. 9, valued at $20.

Location: Mark Twain Papers, Bancroft Library, University of California at Berkeley.

Copy examined: Clemens's copy.

Mark Twain quoted from Jarves's book in a letter published in the Sacramento *Weekly Union* (21 July 1866) to show that "the natives have been improved by missionary labor" (*LSI*, p. 103). He credited Jarves for his information about Captain Cook (*LSI*, p. 157). In Twain's letter of 2 March 1867 from New York City he confessed that he "stole a book" from "Father" Samuel Chenery Damon, pastor of the Seaman's Mission in Honolulu. He seems to mean Jarves's *History of the Hawaiian or Sandwich Islands.* On 20 May 1867 he announced that he had mailed the book back to Damon (*MTTMB*, p. 213). Twain used "Mr. Jarves's excellent history" to correct Hawaiian legends in Chapters 65 and 68 of, and to fill out descriptions in, *Roughing It* (1872)—see the Iowa-California Edition of *Roughing It* (1972), pp. 415, 437–441, and 601, and especially the revised Mark Twain Project edition, *Roughing It* (1993),

p. 443, 713, 723, 725, and 943–944, in which Harriet Elinor Smith and Edgar Marquess Branch deduced (on page 711) that the version Twain borrowed from Damon was Jarves's 240-page Third edition (Honolulu: Charles Edwin Hitchcock, 1847). Fred W. Lorch's "Hawaiian Feudalism and Mark Twain's *A Connecticut Yankee in King Arthur's Court*," *American Literature* 30.1 (March 1958): 50–66, reminded scholars that Twain's chief source for Hawaiian customs—Jarves's *History of the Hawaiian or Sandwich Islands*—emphasized a comparison between native taboos and Catholic interdicts.

Ryan Heryford, "'The Breath of Flowers That Perished': Imperial Ecologies in Mark Twain's Early Letters," *Mark Twain Annual 17* (2019): 49–71.

JARVIS, EDWARD (1803–1884). "The Increase of Human Life," *Atlantic Monthly* 24 (October 1869): 495–506; (November 1869): 581–598; and (December 1869): 711–718.

On the basis of two entries Mark Twain made in Notebooks 28 and 29 (*N&J* 3: 412, 503, 506), James D. Williams ("Use of History" [1965]) and subsequently the editors in the Mark Twain Project at the Bancroft Library in Berkeley deduced the extensive borrowings Twain made from Jarvis's article for Chapter 23 of *A Connecticut Yankee in King Arthur's Court* (1889), titled "Sixth-Century Political Economy." Jarvis discussed sixteenth-century (and later) statistics, so Twain's figures were speculative. Jarvis, a physician interested in medical history, left behind a detailed account of how he compiled these figures in an autobiography eventually edited and published by Rosalba Davico in 1992.

JAY, EDITH KATHERINE SPICER (1846–1901), pseud. "E. Livingston Prescott." *The Apotheosis of Mr. Tyrawley.* New York: Harper & Brothers, 1896. 248 pp.

Source: MTLAcc, entry #1643, volume donated by Clemens.

After rescuing two children from drowning a vagabond gambler endeavors to turn his life around.

JAYNE, DAVID (1799–1866). *Jayne's Medical Almanac and Guide to Health.* Illus. (1854[?] edition).

One of two books that Clemens found on 16 July 1855 in the "reading room" of the only hotel in Paris, Missouri was "Jayne's Med. Almanac" (NB 1, 1: 37). David Jayne, a Philadelphia patent drug manufacturer, began publishing his *Medical Almanac* annually in the mid-1840s as an advertising circular.

JEAFFRESON, JOHN CORDY (1831–1901). *A Book About Doctors.* 2 vols. Leipzig: B. Tauchnitz, [date not supplied].

Catalog: *C1951*, D1, $8 ea. vol., listed among books signed by Clemens, misspelled as "Jefferson."

Non-practicing attorney Jeaffreson here collected anecdotes about English physicians; in similar volumes he did the same for lawyers and clergy.

JEFFERSON, JOSEPH, III (1829–1905). *The Autobiography of Joseph Jefferson.* New York: The Century Co., 1890. 501 pp.

Clemens notified Charles L. Webster from Hartford on 11 May 1887: "Joe Jefferson has written his Autobiography! . . . I will read the MS for 'literary quality,' . . . & meantime you can be thinking of the terms to offer him" (*MTBus*, p. 382). On 28 May 1887 Clemens informed Webster: "Joe Jefferson's MS is delightful reading, & I see that it has this additional great advantage: it is quite largely a book

of *foreign travel*, & the illustrations can be made to show up that feature prominently" (*MTBus*, p. 383). But on 20 October 1887 Jefferson notified Webster that on account of Clemens's "long silence" negotiations were underway with another publisher (TS in MTP). As Clemens later recalled the series of events, "Joe Jefferson wrote me and said he had written his autobiography and he would like me to be the publisher. Of course I wanted the book. . . . Webster did not decline the book. He simply ignored it" (2 June 1906 AD, *MTE*, pp. 187–188; *AutoMT* 2: 76). In a letter to Susy Clemens written on 27 December 1893, Clemens praised his friend Thomas Bailey Aldrich as "fine in heart, fine in mind, fine in every conceivable way, sincere, genuine, & lovable beyond all men save only Joe Jefferson" (quoted in Christie's, New York City, 11 May 1987, item 23). Sometime in 1903 Clemens jokingly made some comically generic sketches of people's faces, one of which he claimed "reproduces Mr. Joseph Jefferson, the common friend of the human race," and another supposedly depicting William Dean Howells (*Sotheby's 2003*, #109). See also the Catalog entry for Dion Boucicault's adaptation of *Rip Van Winkle*.

Randall Knoper, *Acting Naturally: Mark Twain in the Culture of Performance* (Berkeley: University of California Press, 1995), pp. 6, 55, 66–69, 73, 75–76.

JENKINS, EDWARD (1838–1910). *Ginx's Baby: His Birth and Other Misfortunes. A Satire.* 12mo, printed wrappers. Toronto: The Canadian News and Publishing Co., 1871. 168 pp. [The paper wrapper was imprinted by a different publisher—Baltimore: The Baltimore News Co., 1871. That wrapper lacks its front corner.]

Inscription: the title page is inscribed in brown ink: "Life is no joke/When I am broke!/Mark Twain". Beneath the inscription, also in brown ink, is a drawing labeled "Tear-Jug" that resembles the illustration in Chapter 20 of *A Tramp Abroad.*

Catalog: City Book Auction, Catalogue number 311 (26 May 1945), "12mo, original printed wrappers, lacks corner of the front wrapper. . . . Toronto, 1871, inscribed by Clemens on the title page. 'Life is no joke When I am broke!' Mark Twain the optimist in a sad moment," item #118.

Location: Special Collections, University Research Library, University of California at Los Angeles. Wilbur Smith, former Special Collections Librarian at U.C.L.A., reportedly purchased the volume because it was priced cheaply since the bookseller could not guarantee the authenticity of Clemens's signature.

Copy examined: a copy supposedly signed by Clemens but which appears to be a forgery. The volume contains the tipped-in 1945 auction description; a price is marked in red pencil—$15. Clemens rarely signed the title pages of volumes (generally preferring the flyleaves), and almost never used his *nom de plume*—with a few exceptions when the book was intended for someone else. A "Mark Twain" signature could easily have been traced from one of the volumes in his "Authorized Edition" of works. The sophomoric rhyming couplet is scarcely worthy of the writer who would later devise the acidic Pudd'nhead Wilson maxims, and the letters "f," "b." and "k" are not characteristic of Clemens's handwriting. The tear-jug sketch is an anachronism, since it would not appear in Chapter 20 of *A Tramp Abroad* until 1880. Stranger and even less profitable instances of fakery have been perpetrated.

————. *Ginx's Baby: His Birth and Other Misfortunes. A Satire.* Boston: J. R. Osgood & Co., 1871. 125 pp.

Source: MTLAcc, entry #533, volume donated by Clemens. Robert Regan turned up evidence that Clemens definitely was familiar with Jenkins's book. In a column titled "British Benevolence" that appeared in the 27 January 1873 issue of the New York *Daily Tribune*, Mark Twain wrote: "I could reel off instances of prodigal charity conferred by stealth in that city [London] till even THE TRIBUNE'S broad columns would cry for quarter. 'Ginx's Baby' could not satirize the national disposition toward free-handed benevolence—it could only satirize instances of foolish and stupid methods in the application of the funds by some of the charitable organizations. But in most cases the great benevolent societies of England manage their affairs admirably" (Regan to Gribben, 22 July, 4 November 1972). In *Ginx's Baby* Jenkins reveals that only a fraction of the funds collected for a foundling baby are left for the baby's keep after the collection committee deducts its expenses. Jenkins moralizes: "In an age of luxury we are grown so luxurious as to be content to pay agents to do our good deeds for us; but they charge us three hundred per cent. for the privilege" (p. 103).

Jericho and the Jordan.

Mark Twain listed this unidentified book among those the pilgrims were instructed to obtain for the *Quaker City* voyage, but he supplied no author's name (*Daily Alta California*, 5 April 1868; McKeithan, *TIA* [1958], p. 303). The best candidate for this vague reference would seem to be David Austin Randall's *The Handwriting of God in Egypt, Sinai, and the Holy Land* (1862), for two reasons: Twain alludes to Randall's book in *The Innocents Abroad* (see the Catalog entry for Randall); and Randall's travel narrative described in detail what remains of "Jericho of Joshua" (pp. 223–229) and also recounted the sights around "Jordan and the Dead Sea" (pp. 216–222). See also the Catalog entry for John Murray's *Handbook for Travellers in Syria and Palestine*.

JEROME, IRENE ELIZABETH (1858–1945). *One Year's Sketch-Book.* Illustrated by the author. Engraved by George T. Andrew. Green cloth, brown and gilt cover, gilt edges. Boston: Lee and Shepard, 1886. 6 pp. of text, 44 leaves of black and white illustrations.

Source: MTLAcc, entry #1223, volume donated by Clemens.

A collection of seasonal sketches by Jerome accompanied by brief verses from the poetry of various authors.

JEROME, JEROME K[LAPKA] (1859–1927). *Three Men in a Boat (To Say Nothing of the Dog).* Illustrated by Alfred Fredericks (1835–1926). New York: H. Holt & Co., 1890. 298 pp.

Source: MTLAcc, entry #2288, volume donated from Clemens's library by Clara Clemens Gabrilowitsch in 1910.

In *My Life and Times* (New York: Harper and Brothers, 1926), Jerome recalled his first meeting with Clemens in the 1890s. "Hardly anyone knew he was in London. He was living poorly, saving money to pay off the debts of a publishing firm with which he had been connected. . . .

Our children had met at a gymnasium. I found there were two Mark Twains: the one a humorist, the other a humanitarian reformer poet" (pp. 129–130). (Richard H. Cracroft called this item to my notice.) Clemens sat across from Jerome at a dinner in March 1907 at Robert Collier's (Clemens to Jean Clemens, 5 March 1907, quoted in Christie's, New York City, 11 May 1987, item #30). British humorist, novelist, magazine editor, and playwright Jerome published a tribute to Clemens shortly after the American died—"Mark Twain: Some Personal Recollections and Opinions" *Bookman* (London) 38.105 (June 1910): 116–119.

JERROLD, WILLIAM BLANCHARD (1826–1884).

Clemens mentioned meeting the novelist, playwright, and editor Jerrold at a dinner in 1873 several times, once to Mrs. Fairbanks on 6 July 1873 (*MTLet* 5: 402) and again in Notebook 13 (1873, *N&J* 1: 552), Notebook 23 (*N&J* 3: 87), and Notebook 41 (MTP).

JESSE, JOHN HENEAGE (1815–1874). *London: Its Celebrated Characters and Remarkable Places.* 3 vols. London: Richard Bentley, 1871.

Inscription: the flyleaf of Volume I is signed in brown ink: "Saml L. Clemens/London 1873".

Marginalia: Volume I contains Clemens's penciled corrections and markings on pages 150, 215, 216, with many leaves cut and torn open. Volume II is heavily annotated in pencil, with a few notes in purple ink concerning London Bridge and its houses and accidents (pp. 278–283), and pencil markings and notes in the Table of Contents as well as on pages 88 and 215 (Horace Walpole's criticisms of Garrick's acting "were perfectly just, at the time, for he was really in his apprenticeship then"). Volume III contains a purple ink mark beside a description of the founding of Christ's Hospital, but many other pages are unopened.

Catalog: *C1951*, D17, 3 vols.

Location: Henry E. Huntington Library, San Marino, California. The three volumes were purchased from Zeitlin & Ver Brugge of Los Angeles in 1951.

Copies examined: Clemens's copies, much worn from repeated use, on 27 July 1997.

In Chapter 33 of *The Prince and the Pauper* (1881) Mark Twain cites Jesse's *London* as the source from which he obtained information about Christ's Hospital.

Baetzhold, *MT&JB* (1970), p. 52.

The Jest Book: The Choicest Anecdotes and Sayings, ed. Mark Lemon. Green cloth. Cambridge [England]: Sever and Francis, 1866. 389 pp.

Inscriptions: the half-title page is signed in black pencil, "Sibyl F. Hubbard,/1872". The title page is signed at the top in black pencil, faintly and rather unconvincingly, "S. L. Clemens".

Provenance: purchased by the Elmira College Library on 24 October 1956 from Bodley Bookshop, 223 East 60th Street, New York City, from Catalogue 148, item #365, $12.50. Sold as "Mark Twain's copy."

Location: Mark Twain Archive, Elmira College, Elmira, New York.

Copy examined: the alleged signature is very suspicious for numerous reasons, and the book had no recorded provenance prior to 1956. This unmarked compendium of English jokes almost certainly was not part of Clemens's library. Examined on 12 August 1988 in Elmira.

JEWETT, JOHN HOWARD (1843–1925), pseud. "Hannah Warner." *The Easter Story*. Illus. New York: Harper & Brothers, 1904. 20 pp.

Source: MTLAcc, entry #450, volume donated by Clemens. A children's book in which the story of Easter and the Resurrection is first related to fairy children, and then this rendition is followed by Biblical excerpts from the Books of John and Luke.

———. [Another identical copy.]

Source: MTLAcc, entry #1705, volume donated by Clemens.

JEWETT, SARAH ORNE (1849–1909). *The Queen's Twin, and Other Stories*. Boston: Houghton, Mifflin & Co., 1900. 232 pp.

Source: MTLAcc, entry #2289, volume donated from Clemens's library by Clara Clemens Gabrilowitsch in 1910.

———. *Tales of New England*. Boston: Houghton, Mifflin and Co., 1890. 276 pp.

Source: MTLAcc, entry #2290, volume donated from Clemens's library by Clara Clemens Gabrilowitsch in 1910.

Tales of New England collected eight of Jewett's short stories, including the tender "A White Heron," "The Courting of Sister Wisby" (depicting an unorthodox approach to marriage), and the benignly supernatural "Miss Tempy's Watchers." Clemens was acquainted socially with this influential regional writer. In May 1892 in Venice he recalled trying to explain his "driveway-loop" puzzle (concerning the side of a carriage from which a passenger would alight) to Jewett and Mrs. James T. Fields (NB 31, TS p. 47; Fears, *Day by Day* 2: 708–709). On 25 January 1894 Jewett and her sister attended a dinner for Oliver Wendell Holmes—at Mrs. Fields' house—where Clemens was present (SLC to OLC, Boston, 25 January 1894, *MTL*, p. 602; ALS in MTP).

———. *York Garrison—1640*. [Unidentified edition.]

Source: MTLAcc, entry #1892, volume donated from Clemens's library by Clara Clemens Gabrilowitsch in 1910. Listed as "destroyed in circulation."

Jewett's narrative poem of rhyming quatrains (*abcb*) portrays a deadly raid by Native Americans. Historians point out that there are inaccuracies in her dating, but she does evoke the fear of death or captivity felt by early settlers.

JEWITT, LLEWELLYN [FREDERICK WILLIAM] (1816–1886) and S[AMUEL]. C[ARTER]. HALL (1800–1889). *The Stately Homes of England*. Illus. Original pictorial terra cotta, gilt. Philadelphia: Porter and Coates, [1870]. 399 pp. 210 wood engravings.

Inscription: the front flyleaf is inscribed in ink by Olivia Clemens, "T. W. Crane/Christmas/1874/The Clemenses." This gift to Clemens's brother-in-law joined the books at Quarry Farm that Clemens often borrowed and read during his summers in Elmira, New York. No marginalia are visible.

Location: collection of Kevin Mac Donnell, Austin, Texas (Mac Donnell to Alan Gribben, 29 November 2011). Acquired from the Langdon family.

At the time that the Clemenses made a present of these pictures of facades, libraries, drawing rooms, conservatories, ceiling decorations, architectural details, stairways, hallways, hearths, and landscapes, they had just been finishing the construction of their Hartford house that had embellishments somewhat similar to a few of these homes.

"JINNY GIT DE HOECAKE DONE" (minstrel song, c. 1840).

The enslaved Jim sings this song in jail after he becomes more cheerful in Chapter 9 of "Tom Sawyer's Conspiracy" (*HH&T*, p. 234).

JOB, HERBERT KEIGHTLEY (1864–1933). *Among the Water-Fowl: Observation, Adventure, Photography*. Illus. New York: Doubleday, Page & Co., 1902. 224 pp.

Source: MTLAcc, entry #1958, volume donated from Clemens's library by Clara Clemens Gabrilowitsch in 1910.

———. *Wild Wings: Adventures of a Camera-Hunter Among the Larger Wild Birds of North America on Sea and Land*. Intro. by Theodore Roosevelt (1858–1919). Illustrated with 160 photographs by the author. Boston: Houghton, Mifflin & Co., [cop. 1905]. 341 pp.

Inscription: inscribed by Clemens in black ink on the front pastedown endpaper, "Jean L. Clemens/with the love of her/Father./21 Fifth Avenue/ November 27, 1904." [Clemens must have misdated this inscription, since the book's preface was dated 1 April 1905 and the work was not issued until May 1905, as JoDee Benussi pointed out (Benussi to Alan Gribben, email, 18 April 2008). Moreover, Clemens would not move from the Grosvenor Hotel to 21 Fifth Avenue until two days later in 1904 (Fears, *Day by Day* 3: 1053), whereas he was definitely living at 21 Fifth Avenue in 1905 and in fact returned to this New York City address on 27 November 1905 after visiting with Theodore Roosevelt in Washington, D. C. (*Day by Day* 4: 203). It hardly seems coincidental that Roosevelt had written the introduction to Job's book.

Location: Mark Twain Library, Redding, Connecticut. Donated from Clemens's library by Clara Clemens Gabrilowitsch in 1910 (MTLAcc, entry #1959).

Copy examined: Jean Clemens's unmarked copy. Has the red ink Mark Twain Library accession number "1959". Examined in 1970 and again in June 1982 and on 8 November 2019.

"JOHN BROWN'S BODY" (song, published in 1861). Lyrics attributed variously; the tune is "Glory, glory, hallelujah."

The loser of a bet in Virginia City would carry a sack of flour "with a brass band at his heels playing 'John Brown'" (SLC to Jane Lampton Clemens and Pamela A. Moffett, 17 May 1864, *MTEnt*, p. 187; *MTLet* 1: 282). Twain heard the muleteers in the Azores sing this song in 1867 (NB 8, *N&J* 1:346). He included "Chorus—Old John Brown had One little Injun" in a burlesque "Country School Exhibition" he organized aboard the *Montana* on 10 July 1868 (*Alta California*, 6 September 1868, reprinted in *The Twainian* 7 [November-December 1948]: 5). In Chapter 6 of *The Innocents Abroad* (1869) Mark Twain reported hearing "the irrepressible muleteers" of Fayal sing "'John Brown's Body' in ruinous English." Clemens praised the Jubilee Singers' rendition of the song in a letter written on 8 March 1875, requesting that they sing it that night and recalling "an afternoon in London, when their 'John Brown's Body' took a decorous, aristocratic English audience by surprise & threw them into a volcanic eruption of applause" (Willard E. Martin, Jr., "Letters and Remarks by Mark Twain from the Boston *Daily Journal*," *Mark Twain Journal* 18.1 [Winter 1975–1976]: 3; *MTLet* 5:

317 n. 2; *MTLet* 6: 406). In 1887 Clemens jotted "John Brown" in Notebook 27 (*N&J* 3: 309).

JOHN, EUGENIE (1825–1887), pseud. "Eugenie Marlitt" or "E. Marlitt." *Das Geheimnis der Alten Mamsell [The Secret of the Old Mamsell]. Roman von E. Marlitt.* [German novel, first published in 1868 in Leipzig; Clemens's edition has not been determined.]

In May 1878 Mark Twain quoted in German a sentence from this novel (NB 14, *N&J* 2: 83), a work from which he would translate (citing "'The Old Mamselle's Secret,' by Mrs. Marlitt") in Appendix D, "The Awful German Language," of *A Tramp Abroad* (1880). When he listed his current reading for Edward H. House on 14 January 1884, he included "in German . . . the concluding chapters of Das Geheimniss der Alten Mamsell" (ASSCL).

Horst Kruse, "The Old Mamsell and the Mysterious Stranger: Mark Twain's Encounter with German Literature and the Writing of 'No. 44, The Mysterious Stranger,'" *American Literary Realism* 39.1 (Fall 2006): 64–73; and Kruse, "Chamisso's Peter Schlemihl and Mark Twain's Mysterious Stranger: German Literature and the Composition of the Mysterious Stranger Manuscripts," *Centenary Reflections on Mark Twain's No. 44, The Mysterious Stranger*, ed. Joseph Csicsila and Chad Rohman (Columbia: University of Missouri Press, 2009), pp. 71–87.

JOHN, THOMAS (1824–1874). *Turn Him Out!: A Farce in One Act* (first performed at the Royal Strand Theatre in London, 1863).

The Hartford *Courant* reported on 27 April 1876 that when Samuel Clemens had a role in a one-act play staged locally on 26 and 27 April 1876, James Planché's *The Loan of a Lover*, the after piece was *Turn Him Out!*

JOHNSON, BURGES (1877–1963).

Burges Johnson recalled how angry Mark Twain became when Harper & Brothers tried to "revise and extend" *Mark Twain's Library of Humor* (1888) into several volumes of extracts from American writers, retaining the original title. Johnson was assigned the editorial task of preparing the three volumes, but Twain "started in cussing me" because he had not been consulted about the project ("When Mark Twain Cursed Me," *Mark Twain Quarterly* 2.1 [Fall 1937]: 8–9, 24). Johnson would go on to become a distinguished journalist, editor, writer, humorist, and college instructor.

JOHNSON, CLIFTON (1865–1940). *Highways and Byways of the Mississippi Valley.* Illustrated by the author. New York: Macmillan Co., 1906. 287 pp.

Source: MTLAcc, entry #603, volume donated by Clemens.

JOHNSON, OWEN MCMAHON (1878–1952). *The Eternal Boy, Being the Story of the Prodigious Hickey.* First edition. Original red decorated cloth. New York: Dodd, Mead & Co., 1909. 335 pp.

Inscription: "To Mark Twain/from one who has loved Tom Sawyer and Huckleberry Finn and has humbly tried to find something of them in the modern boy/Owen Johnson, 1909."

Provenance: contains the shelfmark from Clara Clemens Gabrilowitsch's personal library in Detroit, Michigan. She sold the volume to Maxwell Hunley Rare Books of Beverly Hills; Miles Standish Slocum of Pasadena,

California purchased it in October 1940.

Location: collection of Kevin Mac Donnell, Austin, Texas.

Copy examined: Clemens's unmarked copy, in July 2004.

Owen, the son of Clemens's good friend Robert Underwood Johnson (1853–1937), would become best known for chronicling the fictional adventures of Dink Stover.

———. *In the Name of Liberty; A Story of Terror.* New York: Century Co., 1905. 406 pp.

Source: MTLAcc, entry #187, volume donated by Clemens. A romantic story is set against the Reign of Terror during the French Revolution.

JOHNSON, ROBERT UNDERWOOD (1853–1937) and **CLARENCE C[LOUGH]. BUEL** (1850–1933), eds. *Battles and Leaders of the Civil War.* 4 vols. New York: The Century Co., 1887–1888.

Clemens attempted to secure publication rights for the magazine series that formed this book, but failed (Charles L. Webster to SLC, 16 March 1885, *MTBus*, p. 307). Nevertheless Clemens became friends with Johnson, a member of the *Century Magazine* staff. In May 1892 Johnson spent some time with Clemens in Venice, heard Clemens give a Robert Browning poetry reading, and recalled how fascinated Clemens was with the story of a perpetual lamp near St. Mark's in Venice that commemorated the wrongful execution of a baker's boy falsely accused of murder (*Remembered Yesterdays* [Boston: Little, Brown, and Co., 1923], p. 321).

Fears, *Day by Day* 2: 709.

JOHNSON, SAMUEL (1709–1784). *Letters of Samuel Johnson, LL.D.* Ed. by George Birkbeck [Norman] Hill (1835–1903). 2 vols. New York: Harper & Brothers, 1892.

Inscription: the front pastedown endpaper of Volume I is signed "S. L. Clemens, 1909"; Volume II was unsigned.

Marginalia: Clemens corrected one of Johnson's sentences on page 184 in Volume I.

Catalogs: A1911, "Vol. I, 8vo, cloth, N.Y. 1892," . . . at p. 184, a correction by Mr. Clemens to a sentence of Johnson," quotes the signature in Vol. I, lot 270, sold for $2.25; George D. Smith, New York City, "Catalogue of Books" (1911), quotes the signature, "Vol. I only, roy. 8vo, cloth, uncut," item #206, $12.

Location: Volume II only in the Mark Twain Library, Redding, Connecticut.

Copy examined: Clemens's unmarked copy of Volume II only. Volume II has the red ink Mark Twain Library accession number "3811". Examined in 1970 and again in June 1982 and on 10 November 2019.

Possibly Clemens had read Johnson's *Letters* by March 1894, when he noted in his copy of Sarah Grand's *The Heavenly Twins* that her chief characters "talk like Dr. Samuel Johnson" (p. 270). Around 1896, however, Clemens supposedly denied to Bram Stoker and Henry Fisher that he had ever read "a written word" of Johnson's; instead, Clemens reportedly said in a London restaurant, "I gauge Johnson's character by his talks with that sot Bozzy" (*AMT*, p. 151). Yet when the teenage Clemens temporarily edited the Hannibal, Missouri *Journal* in May 1853 he had employed the pseudonym "Rambler"—presumably in homage to Johnson's *Rambler*, a bi-weekly periodical that appeared between 1750 and 1752.

———. *The Lives of the Most Eminent English Poets* (published

1779–1781).

Johnson's biographical record and critical assessment of fifty-two poets was one of the "biogs of Milton" that Clemens listed in Notebook 27 (*N&J* 3: 328) in September 1887.

Johnston, Alexander (1849–1889). *Connecticut: A Study of a Commonwealth Democracy.* American Commonwealth Series. Boston: Houghton, Mifflin Co., 1887. 409 pp.

In April 1887 Clemens noted the author, title, and publisher of this work in Notebook 26 (*N&J* 3: 288).

Johnston, Alexander Keith (1804–1871). *The Home Atlas of Astronomy.* Star charts and maps. New York: G. P. Putnam's Sons, 1885.

Inscription: "Susan L. Crane/Quarry Farm/Jan 1885".

Catalog: Ball 2016 inventory, oversize volume, blue leather, gilt lettering, spine cover missing, "poor condition."

Location: Quarry Farm library shelves, under the supervision of the Mark Twain Archive, Elmira College, Elmira, New York.

Clemens had access to this atlas at Quarry Farm in Elmira.

Johnston, Alexander W. *Strikes, Labour Questions, and Other Economic Difficulties: A Short Treatise of Political Economy.* London: Bliss, Sands, and Foster, 1895. 128 pp. [Publisher and pages conjectured.]

Source: MTLAcc, entry #529, volume donated by Clemens.

Johnston, (Sir) Henry ("Harry") Hamilton (1858–1927). *The History of a Slave, with 47 Full-page Illustrations Engraved Facsimile from the Author's Drawings.* London: Kegan Paul, Trench, & Co., 1889. 168 pp.

Clemens discovered a book titled *The History of a Slave* in the London Library on 22 October 1896 (NB 39, TS p. 12). The most likely candidate seems to be Johnston's fictionalized but riveting account of an enslaved man's life in Western Sudan. Johnston was a notable British explorer, linguist, and colonial administrator of Africa. The African slave who related his personal history belonged to a master named Sidi Abd-al-Ghirha. Johnston explained in the Preface that this slave's story was actually a composite of the lives of countless slaves he has encountered. The slave evinced no self-pity or resentment; he simply resigned himself to his fate and carried out his assigned tasks. The illustrations were highly realistic and the slave's story revealed Johnston's familiarity with dozens of tribes and their customs.

Johnston, Mary (1870–1936). *Prisoners of Hope. A Tale of Colonial Virginia.* Boston: Houghton, Mifflin & Co., 1900. 378 pp.

Source: MTLAcc, entry #188, volume donated by Clemens.

Johnston, an increasingly successful Virginia novelist, would become a strong advocate for women's rights. One of her close friends would be Margaret Mitchell, the eventual author of *Gone with the Wind.*

———. *Sir Mortimer. A Novel.* Illus. New York: Harper & Brothers, 1904. 350 pp.

Source: MTLAcc, entry #189, volume donated by Clemens.

This novel about colonial life in Virginia had been serialized in *Harper's Monthly.*

Johnston, Richard Malcolm (1822–1898). *Dukesborough Tales.* Illus. New York: Harper & Brothers, 1883. 93 pp.

Scholars of American humor classify Johnston's rural Georgia narratives as a blend of A. B. Longstreet's earlier, rougher sketches and the emerging regional school of realistic

fiction. On 29 November 1884 Clemens wrote to Olivia from Baltimore: "R. M. Johnston, author of The Dukesboro Tales has called—I will see him presently" (MTP). In April 1888 Mark Twain jotted down "'Dukesboro' Tales" in Notebook 27 (*N&J* 3: 382). He included a story from *Dukesborough Tales*, "The Expensive Treat of Colonel Moses Grice" (which had first appeared in *Scribner's Monthly* 21 [January 1881]: 370–376) in *Mark Twain's Library of Humor* (1888). This tale is widely believed to have influenced the drunk's bareback riding act that so astonishes Huckleberry Finn in Chapter 21 of *Adventures of Huckleberry Finn* (1885). In March 1888 Johnson's name appeared in Twain's list of authors whose works he generally liked (NB 27, *N&J* 3: 379). When Clemens heard that Johnston would visit the Warners in Hartford in 1888, Clemens wrote on 9 November to invite him to stay over two additional days with the Clemenses (Enoch Pratt Free Library). In a letter written from Hartford on 4 January 1889 Mark Twain planned a benefit reading with Johnston to help "poor" Thomas Nelson Page (Enoch Pratt Free Library). Henry P. Goddard—in "Anecdotes of Mark Twain," *Harper's Weekly* 50.2566 (24 February 1906): 280—reported authoritatively that Mark Twain turned over to Johnston the "several hundred dollars" that was Twain's share for their joint reading in Baltimore; Twain had replaced Thomas Nelson Page on the program, and he wished to assist the financially needy Johnston. Goddard was present at a dinner after the reading at the University Club of Baltimore when Twain, upon being toasted, "paid a loving tribute to Colonel Johnston" (p. 280).

Blair, *NAH* (1937), p. 154; Blair, *MT&HF* (1960), pp. 315–316; Kenneth S. Lynn, ed., *Huckleberry Finn* (1961), pp. 149–156; Hamlin Hill and Walter Blair, eds., *The Art of Huckleberry Finn* (1962), pp. 471–483; Dewey Ganzel, "Twain, Travel Books" (1962), p. 53.

———. *Mr. Absalom Billingslea, and Other Georgia Folk.* Illus. New York: Harper & Brothers, 1888. 414 pp.

Source: MTLAcc, entry #2291, volume donated from Clemens's library by Clara Clemens Gabrilowitsch in 1910.

———. [Another identical copy.]

Source: MTLAcc, entry #2293, volume donated from Clemens's library by Clara Clemens Gabrilowitsch in 1910.

———. *Mr. Billy Downs and His Likes.* Fiction, Fact, and Fancy Series, ed. Arthur Stedman. Frontispiece by Dan[iel Carter] Beard (1850–1941). New York: Charles L. Webster & Co., 1892. 232 pp.

Clemens's publishing firm issued this collection of six stories, though earlier it had declined another work by Johnston. On 5 April 1887 Clemens wrote Johnston to explain how "our wheels are now clogged with existing contracts" (Enoch Pratt Free Library).

———. *Old Mark Langstan; A Tale of Duke's Creek.* New York: Harper & Brothers, 1883. 338 pp.

Source: MTLAcc, entry #2292, volume donated from Clemens's library by Clara Clemens Gabrilowitsch in 1910.

John Van Buren, Politician; A Novel of To-day. New York: Harper & Brothers, 1904. 288 pp.

Source: MTLAcc, entry #15, volume donated by Isabel V. Lyon, Clemens's secretary.

This anonymously published novel explored Tammany Hall, municipal graft, and New York State politics.

John Van Buren, Politician; A Novel of To-day. New York: Harper & Brothers, 1905. 288 pp.

Source: MTLAcc, entry #1503, volume donated by Clemens.

JOKAI, MAURUS (MÓR JÓKAI) (1825–1904). *Black Diamonds, A Novel*. Translated by Frances A. Gerard [pseudonym of Geraldine Fitzgerald]. New York: Harper & Brothers, 1898.

Provenance: has the shelfmarks of the library numbering system employed by Clara Clemens Gabrilowitsch during her Detroit years. Sold in 1951 at the Hollywood auction but not listed in the hastily prepared sale sheet.

Catalog: "Property from the Library of Mark Twain," Butterfield & Butterfield, San Francisco, Sale 6613 (16 July 1997), lot 2712.

Location: Mark Twain House and Museum, Hartford, Connecticut.

Copy examined: Clemens's unmarked copy. Viewed in Hartford in 1997.

Jókai, sometimes called "the Mark Twain of Magyar literature," visited Clemens at his apartment suite in the Hotel Metropole in Vienna. In a 1904 letter Clemens would mention the Hungarian novelist as a friend who had recently died.

JOLINE, ADRIAN HOFFMAN (1850–1912). *The Diversions of a Book-Lover*. New York: Harper & Brothers, 1903. 323 pp.

Source: MTLAcc, entry #848, volume donated by Clemens. Of the thousands of books that have disappeared from Clemens's library, his copy of *The Diversions of a Book-Lover*, quite likely annotated, ranks among the more lamentable losses. This is because the bibliophile Joline discussed a wide range of topics that would have caused Clemens to reach for a nearby pen or pencil. Joline described his own library, urged book enthusiasts to avoid gas-logs and tall book-cases, discouraged rebinding antique books, and gave advice to beginning book collectors by suggesting less-expensive genres for collecting. His views of literary plagiarism accorded those of Clemens: "To be entirely candid, most of my ideas are only the thoughts of other people, borrowed without blushes, and in all likelihood those people had borrowed them also" (pp. 10–11). Literary criticism accounts for a surprising proportion of Joline's book. "The [Robert Louis] Stevenson worship has always puzzled me as much as the worship of the golden calf" (p. 122). "I . . . venture to predict that the popularity of Stevenson, already on the wane, will not be enduring" (p. 123). If these passages did not provoke Clemens to insert marginalia, he almost certainly would have reacted to Joline's taking Mark Twain to task for deciding "to ridicule Cooper elaborately and unmercifully" (p. 117). "I cannot refrain from making my indignant if ineffective protest," wrote Joline (p. 118). "Cooper nodded often, but . . . we cannot resist the sweep and power of his best work" (p. 114). Explaining that "I admire Mark and I love Cooper," Joline brought up a painful memory for Twain: "He sometimes errs, as he did in his famous speech at the banquet in honor of Whittier's seventieth birthday. We do not think less of him for these escapades" (p. 118).

———. *Meditations of an Autograph Collector*. Illus. Front flyleaf very loose. New York: Harper & Brothers, 1902. 315 pp.

Inscription: the front flyleaf is signed in pencil in a large scrawl: "Clemens/1902".

Location: Mark Twain Library, Redding, Connecticut. Donated by Clemens (MTLAcc, entry #849).

Copy examined: Clemens's unmarked copy. Has the red ink Mark Twain Library accession number "849". Examined in 1970 and again in June 1982.

As the recipient of frequent autograph requests, Mark Twain would have had a natural interest in Joline's topic. *Meditations of an Autograph Collector* contained reproductions of letters and manuscript pages of famous authors, including Alexander Pope, Sir Walter Scott, and Alfred Lord Tennyson. Joline defended the truly assiduous autograph-seeker: "The mere fondness for autographs has nothing dreadful or feverish about it. . . . The true collector ought not to be vilified because the methods of pseudo-collectors are often objectionable" (pp. vi–vi). On page 101 Joline passingly complimented Twain for his immense popularity, but did not refer to his autograph.

———. [Another identical copy.]

Source: MTLAcc, entry #1701, volume donated by Clemens.

JOMINI, [ANTOINE] HENRI, BARON DE (1779–1869). *Jomini's Handbook of Military Etiquette*.

Mark Twain listed the 1905 West Point Edition of this work as one of his sources of "knowledge about military minutiae" in "A Horse's Tale" (1906). Jomini published many volumes devoted to warfare but none with this exact title; however, sections of his works do describe proper military etiquette for the ceremonial presentation of swords and so forth.

———. *Précis de l'Art de la Guerre* (published in 1838).

In Mark Twain's "Lucretia Smith's Soldier" (1864), the narrator claims that "I have drawn largely on *Jomini's Art of War* . . . so necessary for reference in building a novel like this." The Swiss-born strategist Jomini advised and participated in military campaigns waged by both France and Russia. His theories became enormously influential.

JONAS, ROSALIE M. (1861?–1953). "Timed to an African Chant" (poem, 1906).

Isabel Lyon reported that on 17 January 1906 "a Miss Jonas, a southerner, came with a letter of introduction from E. C. Stedman. She had a little poem she had written, a negro mother's tragic cry over the lynching of her son." Clemens read the piece aloud to Lyon to test its oral effect: "He sat up in bed and reached out his arms with all the tragic feeling of the negro mother, and he was wonderful to behold" (IVL Journal, TS p. 124). The poem Clemens received was Jonas's "Timed to an African Chant," which would appear in *McClure's Monthly* 27.2 (May 1906): 146. Perhaps its most horrifying line occurs midway: "Christ! What dey gwine do/Wid *Rope an To'ches*?" Jonas had moved from New Orleans to New York City; she would go on to become a minor figure in the Harlem Renaissance as well as a promoter of women's suffrage, and her poems and short stories appeared in magazines as diverse as *Harper's*, *Century*, and *Smart Set*.

JONES, CHARLES COLOCK (1831–1893). *Negro Myths from the Georgia Coast, Told in the Vernacular*. Boston: Houghton, Mifflin and Co., 1888. 171 pp.

"I read the 'Negro Myths' several years ago, & they have vanished out of my memory, leaving nothing but an impression—the impression that they were of but small value" (SLC to "Dear Sir," 27 November 1891, PH in MTP; ALS sold by Christie's, New York City, 1–2 February 1988 auction, lot 472).

Jones, Claude P[erry]. (1870–1945) and A. L. Sykes. *Banduk jaldi banduk!: (Quick, My Rifle!).* Illus. by Eliot Keen. New York: J. J. Little & Co., 1907. 313 pp.

Source: MTLAcc, entry #190, volume donated by Isabel V. Lyon, Clemens's secretary.

Fictional adventures ensue in Tibet and China after free-lance mercenaries parachute from a balloon for a rescue mission.

Jones, [Eudora] Dora Duty (1858–1913). *The Technique of Speech: A Guide to the Study of Diction According to the Principles of Resonance.* New York: Harper & Brothers, 1909. 331 pp.

Inscription: inscribed by Clemens in black ink on the front pastedown endpaper: "Clara/1909". A bookmark advertising a book—Margaret Cameron's *The Involuntary Chaperon* (New York: Harper & Brothers, 1909)—was laid between pages 60 and 61.

Location: Mark Twain Library, Redding, Connecticut.

Copy examined: Clara Clemens's unmarked copy. Has the red ink Mark Twain Library accession number "3779". Examined in 1970 and again in June 1982.

Clemens wrote to Clara Clemens from Bermuda on 6 March 1910, referring to a book Clara had championed: "Oh, by George I *am* glad to know of the success of Miss Jones's book" (ASSSCL). Born in North Carolina, Jones would die in 1913 in England.

Jones, Hamilton C[hamberlain]. (1798–1868). "Cousin Sally Dilliard" (burlesque sketch, published in 1831).

Jones' brief, well-constructed yarn about a digressive witness in a law case originally appeared in a Philadelphia newspaper; thereafter it appeared in numerous other newspapers and magazines, including William Trotter Porter's *The Spirit of the Times.* Reportedly Jones' piece became a favorite of Abraham Lincoln. Henry Watterson published the sketch in *Oddities in Southern Life and Character* (Boston: Houghton, Mifflin, 1882), pp. 474–478, Franklin J. Meine reprinted "Cousin Sally Dilliard" in *Tall Tales of the Southwest* (New York: Alfred A. Knopf, 1930), pp. 41–43, and Walter Blair and Raven I. McDavid, Jr. included it in their *The Mirth of a Nation: America's Great Dialect Humor* (Minneapolis: University of Minnesota Press, 1983), pp. 33–36. The sketch recounted the courtroom testimony of Mr. Harris, "a fat, shuffy old man, a 'leetle' corned," who is questioned about a fight he supposedly witnessed by a stuffy attorney, Mr. Chops. (Jones himself was a North Carolina lawyer as well as a state politician and newspaper editor.) Like Mark Twain's Simon Wheeler, Mr. Harris is prone to circumlocution; after lengthy and often-interrupted testimony he turns out not to know anything whatever about the fight. The exasperated Mr. Chops has succeeded only in establishing the irrelevant fact that Cousin Sally Dilliard came by Harris's home to ask whether his wife could go to a nearby party. In a letter to Orion written on 13 April 1862 from Esmeralda, Clemens quipped: "And, as Cousin Sally Dillard [*sic*] says, this is all that I know about the fight" (*MTLet* 1: 185). Later Mark Twain considered including the piece in his projected anthology of humor; in 1880

the name "Cousin Sally Dillard" [*sic*] appeared in a list of possible selections (NB 19, *N&J* 2: 363), and the same title appeared in 1887 as an entry in Notebook 27 (*N&J* 3: 328). *Mark Twain's Library of Humor* (1888), however, did not contain Jones's sketch.

Jones, Henry Arthur (1851–1929).

In 1906 Clemens "had a stag dinner party (Howells, Aldrich, [George] Harvey, & Andrew Carnegie) to meet the English dramatist Henry Arthur Jones" (SLC to Jean Clemens, New York City, 13 November 1906, TS in MTP). Clemens did not indicate which plays by Jones—who wrote *The Liars* (1897) and many other comedies—he had seen.

Jones, Joseph Stevens (1809–1877). *The People's Lawyer, A Comedy* (play, performed in 1839). Also known as *Solon Shingle.*

Mark Twain hoped his *Colonel Sellers* play might "run twenty years, in this country, like Jo Jefferson's 'Rip Van Winkle' & John E. Owens's 'Solon Shingle'" (SLC to Mr. Watt, Hartford, 26 January 1875, Berg Collection, NYPL). John Edmond Owens (1823–1886) first played Solon Shingle in 1856; he came to be identified with this character, performing the role for many years.

Jonson, Ben (1572–1637).

Though Mark Twain alluded to Jonson several times in print, it was not until 1908 that he mentioned seeing and enjoying ("two pleasant and exciting hours") one of Jonson's dramatic works—a masque performed at the New York Plaza Hotel (19 February 1908 AD; *AutoMT* 3: 211). Jonson's praise for Shakespeare is one piece of evidence that Twain had to overcome in proving the thesis of his *Is Shakespeare Dead?* (1909): in Part 3 he notes that Jonson "waited seven years" before he penned his encomium; in Part 5 he reiterates that it was only in 1623 that "Ben Jonson awoke out of his long indifference and sang a song of praise and put it in the front of the book" of Shakespeare's plays; in Part 10 Twain quotes from *Timber; or, Discoveries Made Upon Men and Matters* (1640) Jonson's laudatory remarks about Francis Bacon's oratorical speech.

Jònsonn, Jòn (1829–1868). "Jòn Jònsonn's Saga: The Genuine Autobiography of a Modern Icelander," ed. by George Ralph Fitz-Roy Cole. *Littell's Living Age* 132.1705 (17 February 1877): 407–430. Reprinted from *Fraser's Magazine* (London, 1877).

Casting about in January 1894 for materials to use in a proposed (but never-founded) magazine to be called "Back Number," Clemens noted: "John Johnson (Iceland) in old Littell. Susy Crane has it" (NB 33, TS p. 47). Clemens refers to an autobiographical sketch by an Icelandic farmer who taught himself English after a fashion. Jònsonn's diction is simple and his words frequently misspelled, but his earnestness and his sincere enjoyment of small pleasures breathe life into the account. He described his childhood, his efforts to educate himself, his reading, his farm labors, his fishing, his residence for a time in Copenhagen, his violin-playing ("I am the sole person in the shire Thingosissel in Icland, that can have the name of a musical, for the people on the northward Icland have not the least understanding of music . . . and one cannot gain a farthing by playing" [p. 412]). Jònsonn supported himself by haymaking, farming, and painting churches.

His life was arduous: a volcano threatened his town; his animals starved for want of winter provender; he tried with some success to cultivate potatoes and cabbage despite the cold; he fished often for trout. In 1858 he observed: "So this year passed away, so monotonously as the others, in our farms on Icland. We have very few pleasures or divertisements" (p. 420). He visited with English travelers whenever possible.

Jònsonn's tale is fascinating partly because he holds nothing back. He was admittedly ashamed when he drank too much in a strange village and allowed himself to be robbed by a fellow traveler whom he knew only as "Jack," but he doggedly tracked down the culprit and recovered his ring and most of his money where Jack buried it in the snow. At the conclusion of Jònsonn's journal its editor added that Jònsonn died shortly after finishing "this quaint, simple record of a man's life, a genuine modem saga, simple and true" (p. 430).

Albert Bigelow Paine recorded the fact that "a story of an Iceland farmer, a human document, . . . had an unfading interest" for Clemens and Theodore Crane during the pleasant summer of 1874 (though it was obviously later, presumably in 1877) at Quarry Farm (*MTB*, p. 510). In May 1887 Clemens jotted a memorandum: "Novel about the Esquimaux nabob who owned 5 flints. Told by Jahn in that old Icelander's English" (NB 26, *N&J* 3:295). This suggests that Jònsonn's narrative contributed something to Twain's "The Esquimau Maiden's Romance" (1893), but even though Lasca the Eskimo girl leads a harsh existence, Twain's tale is of an altogether different order.

JORDAN, DAVID STARR (1851–1931) and **BARTON WARREN EVERMANN** (1853–1932). *American Food and Game Fishes: A Popular Account of All the Species Found in America North of the Equator*. Illustrated and with photographs by A[rthur]. Radclyffe Dugmore (1870–1955). New York: Doubleday, Page & Co., 1905. 572 pp.
  Source: MTLAcc, entry #743, volume donated by Clemens.
  ———. [Identical copy, but with a 1904 imprint date.]
  Catalog: Ball 2016 inventory, Nature Library, Volume V.
  Location: Quarry Farm library shelves, under the supervision of the Mark Twain Archive, Elmira College, Elmira, New York.

JORDAN, ELIZABETH GARVER (1867–1947). *May Iverson—Her Book*. Illus. New York: Harper & Brothers, 1905. 282 pp.
  Source: MTLAcc, entry #1600, volume donated by Clemens.
  May Iverson—Her Book is young adult fiction, narrated in first-person by an excitable teenage girl who attends a Catholic girls' school.
  Jordan, editor of *Harper's Bazaar* between 1900 and 1913, tried unsuccessfully to enlist Mark Twain in contributing to a "composite" novel for which twelve distinguished authors would write a chapter apiece. Twain thought about having a boy tell his assigned chapter, but on 4 August 1906 he informed Jordan that his boy had failed to "report for duty"; indeed, "after this long waiting he has never once rung the bell." As tactfully as possible Twain thereupon withdrew from the project (Earl F. Briden, "Samuel L. Clemens and Elizabeth Jordan: An Unpublished Letter," *Mark Twain Journal* 17.2 [Summer 1974]: 11–13). *The Whole Family* began appearing serially in *Harper's Bazar*

in 1907 and was published in book form by Harper & Brothers in 1908. Elizabeth Jordan was one of its authors. See Elizabeth Jordan's *Three Rousing Cheers* (New York: D. Appleton-Century, 1938), pp. 182–183, 259–160.
  ———. *Tales of the Cloister*. Illus. Marbled covers. New York: Harper & Brothers, 1901. 253 pp.
  Provenance: Antenne-Dorrance Collection, Rice Lake, Wisconsin.
  Location: Mark Twain Archive, Gannett-Tripp Learning Center, Elmira College, Elmira, New York.
  Copy examined: Clemens's unmarked copy. Examined on 28 May 2015.
  Life and drama in a Catholic convent that operates a school for girls.

JOSEPHUS, FLAVIUS (c. 37–100 CE). *The Genuine Works of Josephus*. Translated by William Whiston (1667–1752). 2 vols. Philadelphia, 1829.
  Catalog: *A1911*, "2 vols., 8vo, sheep (cracked), Phila. 1829," a sheet of Clemens's notes laid in, lot 271, sold for $1.75.
  In a letter written early in January 1871 Clemens facetiously attributed the authorship of *The Decline and Fall of the Roman Empire* to a vastly earlier Roman historian, "the lamented Josephus" (*MTLet* 4: 298). Mark Twain's "A Brace of Brief Lectures on Science, II," published in *American Publisher* (October 1871) makes a comical reference: "I simply ask the candid reader that question [about the odd proximity of the bones of ancient men, mastodons, bears, and wolves in a cave] and let him sweat—as the historian Josephus used to say." In Chapter 22 of *Roughing It* (1872), Twain describes his adaptation to the Nevada Territory, "I felt rowdyish and 'bully,' (as the historian Josephus phrases it, in his fine chapter upon the destruction of the Temple)." Clemens jocularly referred to advice about proper behavior in summer heat given by "the great & wise historian Josephus" in a letter of 23 June 1872 to Joseph L. Blamire (*MTLet* 5: 111). In 1878 Clemens made a one-word entry in Notebook 17: "Josephus" (*N&J* 2: 219). Clara Clemens listed Flavius Josephus's *Antiquities of the Jews* in her commonplace book sometime between 1888 and 1904 (Paine 150, MTP).

Journal of American Folklore (1888).
  Robert Regan noticed that Clemens was among the 245 members of the American Folklore Society who were listed in the first volume of the *Journal of American Folklore* in 1888 (*UH*, p. viii).

JOYCE, JOHN A[LEXANDER]. (1842–1915). *Edgar Allan Poe*. Illus. Light brown cloth, cover worn and water-stained, spine chipped and torn, front flyleaves loose. New York: F. Tennyson Neely Co., [cop. 1901]. 218 pp.
  Inscriptions: signed in black ink on the front pastedown endpaper: "Catharine Leary." (She was the longtime housekeeper in the Clemens household, and had been allowed by Clara Clemens Gabrilowitsch to select some library books as mementoes of her employer after he died in 1910.) On the front free flyleaf Katharine Antenne recorded, in blue ink: "This book came to Katharine Leary Antenne through her father, Warren D. Leary, a nephew of Katie Leary who willed it to him. Katie became the owner of the book on the death of Mark Twain." Above that explanation is another inscription in blue ink in Katharine Antenne's hand: "To our good friend Alan

Gribben, who inspired us to a deeper interest in the life of Mark Twain, with our appreciation and very best wishes." That note was signed individually by "Katharine (Katie) Leary Antenne" and by "Robert V. Antenne".

Marginalia: Clemens made sarcastic notes in pencil throughout the entire volume, ridiculing Joyce's grammar and prose style as well as his opinions. The mockery begins on the title page, where Clemens altered "Colonel John A. Joyce" to read "Colonel of Literature John A. Joyce." Joyce states in his "Preface": "In boiling down the life of Poe into one handy volume, I blow off the foam and scum of encomiums, and endeavor to get to the bedrock of a character that may be misunderstood through the coming ages"; Clemens underlined "boiling down" and added at the top of the page: "A new way to boil down—that is, in literature. We use his method with dried apples; we boil down a pint of them & they swell to a bushel." Clemens's comments became still more scornful; at the top of page x in the "Introduction" he observed: "It is a shame that this sentimental hyena should be allowed to disinter Poe's remains & paw them over." On the next page Clemens added: "This book is an impertinence—an affront," and called its contents "old tenth-rate thoughts, triumphs of commonplace—hashed up & warmed over" (p. xi). At the bottom of page xii Clemens was reminded of a favorite foe: Joyce possesses "the style of Mrs. Baker G. Eddy before her polisher has been over her MS." (This remark suggests that Clemens annotated the book during or shortly after his intensive reading in Christian Science publications in 1902 and 1903.) Clemens fixed his view of Joyce at the top of the first page of the text: "If he *had* an idea he couldn't/word it./The most remarkable animal/that ever cavorted around a poet's/grave." Similarly belittling notes, brief ejaculations ("rot!," "bow-wow!"), and underlinings abound throughout the volume. At the top of page 107, above a passage where Joyce demeans Poe's poetry and fiction, Clemens wrote, "He is not a friend of Poe."

Provenance: this was one of the books that Clemens's housekeeper Katy Leary was allowed to depart with after Clemens's death in 1910. Subsequently she bequeathed this and approximately ninety other volumes to her nephew Warren Leary, and eventually these books became the property of Mrs. Frank Stinn, the remarried widow of Warren Leary. Katharine and Robert Antenne took custody of the books after Mrs. Stinn, Katharine's mother, became so ill that the volumes were nearly lost. They then became known as the Antenne-Dorrance Collection, Rice Lake, Wisconsin.

Location: collection of Alan Gribben, Montgomery, Alabama. An unexpected gift on 6 February 1994 from Robert and Katharine Antenne (because, they explained, I had rescued the Katy Leary books when they were about to be disposed of inadvertently in Rice Lake back in 1970).

Copy examined: Clemens's copy.

Born in Ireland, John A. Joyce emigrated to Kentucky, became an attorney, and served in the Civil War, eventually being promoted to Colonel. After the war he moved to Washington where he practiced law and began to write poetry, biographies, and memoirs about his military service. He was briefly imprisoned for his part as a revenue commissioner in the "Whiskey Ring," one of the scandals that beset the Grant presidential administration. Later he claimed authorship of "Laugh and the world laughs with you,/Weep and you weep alone," even though all evidence pointed to the first lines of Ella Wheeler Wilcox's poem "Solitude," published in 1883, as their actual source.

JOYCE, ROBERT DWYER (1836–1883). *Deirdrè*. No Names Series. Boston: Roberts Bros., 1877. 262 pp.

Source: MTLAcc, entry #2006, volume donated from Clemens's library by Clara Clemens Gabrilowitsch in 1910.

Deirdrè was a narrative poem in eight sections based on the Ulster cycle of heroic myths about the Children of Uisneach and the tragic story of Deirdre.

Jubliäums-Feier zur Erinnerung an Die Vor 25 Jahren Durch Die Hinzunahme des "Grünen Waldes" Erfolgte Vergrösserung und Einweihung des Tivoli. Röpke's Tivoli, Hamburg. [Hanover: Schlüter'sche Buchdruckerei, 1890?].

Carl Röpke maintained public concert gardens in Hamburg and Hanover. Most concerts featured printed programs such as this four-page sheet listing performances on June 10th and 11th.

Inscriptions: autographed by the poet Eugene Field and (supposedly) by Mark Twain.

Location: Albert and Shirley Small Special Collections Library, University of Virginia Libraries, Charlottesville. Gift of Clifton Waller Barrett. "Upper half of both leaves wanting."

Source: online catalog of the University of Virginia Libraries, 2006. I am grateful to Jo Dee Benussi for calling my attention to the listing.

This is almost certainly a forgery. Eugene Field II became notorious for selling fraudulent association copies of various books and pamphlets.

JUDD, SYLVESTER (1813–1853). *Margaret. A Tale of the Real and the Ideal, Blight and Bloom.* Boston: Roberts Brothers, 1871. 401 pp.

Source: MTLAcc, entry #191, volume donated by Clemens.

In a letter to Olivia of 22 December 1873 Clemens mentioned that in London he had received a letter "about Dr. Browne's [*sic*] 'Margaret'" (*MTLet* 5: 529). From Hartford on 28 February 1874 Clemens notified Dr. John Brown of Edinburgh: "I shipped the novel ('Margaret') to you from here a *week* ago"; in the same letter he informed Brown that he "shipped to you, from Liverpool, Darley's Illustrations of Judd's 'Margaret'" (*MTL*, p. 215; *MTLet* 6: 53). (See the Catalog entry for Felix O. C. Darley.) In the January 1905 issue of the *North American Review* Mark Twain included Judd in a catalogue of prominent authors that included Cooper, Irving, Poe, and Hawthorne ("Concerning Copyright").

———. [Identical copy.]

Inscription: the front free flyleaf is signed in pencil, "Ida C. Langdon" (1849–1934, Charles Jervis Langdon's wife).

Provenance: bookplate #469 of the "J. Langdon Family Library."

Catalog: Ball 2016 inventory, green cloth, gilt lettering, fair condition.

Location: Quarry Farm library shelves, under the supervision of the Mark Twain Archive, Elmira College, Elmira, New York.

Copy examined: an unmarked volume to which Clemens had access whenever he visited the Langdons' home in

Elmira. Examined on 26 May 2015.

JUDSON, EDWARD ZANE CARROLL (c. 1823–1886), pseud. "Ned Buntline." *The Black Avenger of the Spanish Main; or, The Fiend of Blood* (1847).

A youthful Sam Clemens referred condescendingly to this dime novel in an undated (1855–1856?) character sketch, "Jul'us Caesar" (*ET&S*, 1: 112). Such "instructive and entertaining books" were "food and drink" to a fellow lodger in his boardinghouse, Clemens wrote. Walter Blair observed that Tom Sawyer's creator borrowed his buccaneer's sobriquet ("Tom Sawyer, the Black Avenger of the Spanish Main") in Chapters 8 and 13 of *The Adventures of Tom Sawyer* (1876) from the title of Ned Buntline's book ("On the Structure of *Tom Sawyer*" [1939], p. 77). Clemens conceivably might have seen Judson himself before leaving Hannibal: in the autumn of 1851 Orion Clemens's Hannibal *Journal* announced the arrival of Ned Buntline to lecture on Cuban filibustering, a cause he espoused (*SCH*, p. 195). Clemens conceivably could also have seen a play based on Buntline's thriller that was performed along the Mississippi River (David A. Randall Rare Books, New York City, Catalog 2 [1980], "original manuscript and prompt book of this play," item #233). Mark Valentine outlined the decadent behavior and sensational writings of E. Z. C. Judson ("Ned Buntline") and traced Clemens's acquaintance with him and his dime novels ("Mark Twain's Novels and Ned Buntline's Wildcat Literature," *Mark Twain Journal* 48.1–2 [Spring/Fall 2010]: 29–48). See also Albert Johannsen, *The House of Beadle and Adams and Its Dime and Nickel Novels: The Story of a Vanished Literature*, 2 vols. (Oklahoma City: University of Oklahoma Press, 1950), 2: 294–295; Blair, *MT&HF* (1960), p. 64; Stone, *Innocent Eye* (1961), p. 65; John Q. Reed, *Benjamin Penhallow Shillaber*, Twayne United States Authors Series, No. 209 (New York: Twayne Publishers, 1972), who noted that both Ike Partington and Tom Sawyer read and imitate Buntline's *The Black Avenger of the Spanish Main*; and Joseph Church, "The Slave Glascock's Ben in Mark Twain," *American Literary Resources* 45.1 (Fall 2012): 83 n. 7.

———. *The Convict; or, The Conspirator's Victim*. New York: W. F. Burgess, 1851.

In Notebook 4 Clemens jotted down an idea for a "d——d girl always reading novels like [']The Convict, Or The Conspirator's Daughter,' & going into ecstasies about them to her friends" (*N&J* 1: 76).

JUDSON, EMILY (CHUBBUCK) (1817–1854). *An Olio of Domestic Verses*. New York: Lewis Colby, 1852. 235 pp.

Source: MTLAcc, entry #612, volume donated by Clemens.

JUNIUS (pseud.). *Letters of Junius* (published serially 1769–1772).

The authorship of the anonymous "Junius" letters that appeared in the London *Public Advertiser* between 1769 and 1772 was never determined with any certainty. They created a furor by attacking King George III and other leading political figures of the day. In "The Wild Man Interviewed," a column for the 18 September 1869 issue of the Buffalo *Express*, Mark Twain's wild man claims that he "wrote those crazy Junius letters" (*MTBE*, p. 55). The "implacable Junius" is mentioned in "Letter from the Under-World" (Paine 260, MTP), a manuscript letter concerning Byron that Twain penned in 1869. In Chapter 54 of *Following the Equator* (1897) Twain visits "the place where Warren Hastings and the author of the Junius Letters fought their duel." Twain's autobiographical dictation for 30 January 1907 paraphrased a sentence from the dedication of Junius's *Letters* ("The liberty of the press is the *Palladium* of all the civil, political, and religious rights of an Englishman") as "The press is the palladium of our liberties" and remarked that "it was a true saying" (*AutoMT* 2: 409–410).

JUSSERAND, JEAN ADRIEN ANTOINE JULES (1855–1932). *English Wayfaring Life in the Middle Ages (XIVth Century)*. Trans. by Lucy Toulmin Smith (1838–1911). Illustrated from illuminated manuscripts. New York: G.P. Putnam's Sons, 1889. 451 pp. [Publisher and pages conjectured.]

Inscription: "S. L. Clemens, 1889."

Catalog: *A1911*, "8vo, cloth, N.Y. 1889," quotes the signature, lot 272, sold for $11.50.

The French writer and diplomat Jusserand published *Les Anglais au Moyen Âge* in 1884. His social history relied on diverse documents and literary works (including Chaucer's *Canterbury Tales* and William Langland's *The Vision of Piers Plowman*) to create a picture of medieval roads (many left behind by the Romans) and their diverse travelers, including religious pilgrims and fleeing serfs.

▌K

KALAKAUA, DAVID (1836–1891), King of Hawaiian Islands. *The Legends and Myths of Hawaii: The Fables and Folk-Lore of a Strange People*. Ed. and with an introduction by Rollin Mallory Daggett (1831–1901). New York: Charles L. Webster & Company, 1888. 530 pp.

Clemens reminded himself to discuss Kalakaua's book with Charles L. Webster in October 1886 (NB 26, *N&J* 3: 260), perhaps because Clemens had known its editor, Rollin Mallory Daggett. Albert Bigelow Paine noted that the book "barely paid for the cost of manufacture" after Clemens's firm published it (*MTB*, p. 856). The collaborative editor Daggett had founded the *Golden Era* in San Francisco and then had moved to Virginia City, Nevada where he worked on the *Enterprise* with Joe Goodman and Samuel Clemens.

KALER, JAMES OTIS (1848–1912), pseud. "James Otis." *Ezra Jordan's Escape from the Massacre at Fort Loyall*. Stories of American History Series. Illus. Boston: Dana Estes & Co., [cop. 1895]. 109 pp.

Source: MTLAcc, entry #874, volume donated by Mrs. Ralph W. Ashcroft (formerly Isabel Lyon), Clemens's secretary.

Kaler, a journalist who wrote books for boys, based this narrative on an actual and horrific event. In 1690, near Portland, Maine, a force of 500 French soldiers and their Native American allies massacred 200 men, women, and children who had taken refuge in a nearby British stockade, Fort Loyal.

———. *Left Behind; or, Ten Days a Newsboy*. Illus. New York: Harper & Brothers, [cop. 1884]. 205 pp.

Source: MTLAcc, entry #1613, volume donated by Clemens.

———. *Mr. Stubbs's Brother*. Illustrated by W[illiam]. A[llen]. Rogers (1854–1931). New York: Harper & Brothers, [cop.

1882]. 283 pp.

> **Source:** MTLAcc, entry #505, volume donated by Clemens.

———. *Silent Pete; or, The Stowaways.* Illus. New York: Harper & Brothers, [cop. 1886]. 192 pp.

> **Source:** MTLAcc, entry #425, volume donated by Clemens.

———. *Toby Tyler; or, Ten Weeks with a Circus.* Illus. New York: Harper & Brothers, [cop. 1881]. 265 pp.

> **Source:** MTLAcc, entry #1171, volume donated by Clemens.

KALFUS, BERTHOLD (1849–1904). *Aus zwei Welten. Gedichte [From Two Worlds. Poems].* [Denver, Colorado: Verlag von Berthold Kalfus, 1900.] 115 pp.

> **Source:** MTLAcc, entry #392, volume donated by Clemens. Kalfus was in the publishing business in St. Louis, Missouri.

KANE, ELISHA KENT (1820–1857). *Arctic Explorations: The Second Grinnell Expedition in Search of Sir John Franklin, 1853, '54, '55.* Illus. 2 vols. Philadelphia: Childs & Peterson, 1856. [Edition conjectured; the book was reprinted in 1857 and 1858.]

> In describing to Orion Clemens (on 9 March 1858) the struggle by the steamboat *Pennsylvania* to pass through ice on the Mississippi River, Clemens finally wrote: "But in order to understand our situation you will have to read Dr. Kane" (*MTL*, p. 37; *MTLet* 1: 77). Kane, an American explorer and naval medical officer, took part in several Arctic searches for the famed British explorer Sir John Franklin, who had been lost on his fourth expedition into the Arctic in 1847. Perhaps Kane's account inspired Clemens's depiction of the ice-coated men in the yawl as looking "like rock-candy statuary." In Chapter 7 of Volume I, Kane tells about the narrow escape of his group when a gale lashed their brig as it lay among ice-floes.

KANT, IMMANUEL (1724–1804). *Critique of Pure Reason. In Commemoration of the Centenary of Its First Publication.* Translated by F[riedrich] Max Müller (1823–1900). Intro. by Ludwig Noiré (1829–1889). 2 vols. New York: Macmillan, 1881.

> In April 1882 Clemens made this entry in Notebook 20: "Kant's Critique of Pure Reason—Max Müller's translation. Macmillan, N. Y." (*N&J* 2: 455).

KATHRENS, R[ICHARD]. D[ONLAND] (1867–1950), ed. *Side Lights on Mary Baker Eddy-Glover-Science Church Trustees Controversy. "Next Friends" Suit.* Kansas City, Missouri: Frank T. Riley Publishing Co., 1907. 88 pp.

> **Marginalia:** broad blue pencil marks that are not characteristic of Clemens. Page 14 bears a note that "Ex-senator William E. Chandler is special counsel for the petitioners."
>
> **Catalog:** ListABP (1910), "Side Lights (Christian Science)", no other information supplied.
>
> **Provenance:** contains a catalog label #90, with red borders. These labels appear in other volumes that once belonged to Clemens and formed part of the original Mark Twain Papers.
>
> **Location:** Mark Twain Papers, Bancroft Library, University of California at Berkeley.
>
> **Copy examined:** Clemens's copy, unmarked by him.
>
> Kathrens reviews the legal suit by George Washington Glover II (1844–1915), the formerly estranged son of Mary Baker Eddy (1821–1910), against the Christian Science Church over her properties and financial affairs. Much of the text consisted of letters to Kathrens, and the

volume is not very enlightening. Kathrens was a Kansas City, Missouri industrialist and investment broker who (perhaps oddly) held socialist views and campaigned for more liberal divorce laws.

KAVANAGH, JULIA (1824–1877). *Nathalie; A Tale* (novel, published in 1850).

> Olivia Langdon's commonplace book recorded that she was reading *Nathalie* in 1868.
>
> Irish novelist Kavanagh set this novel in France, where a young teacher, Nathalie Montolieu, struggles with her romantic feelings for M. de Sainville, the master of the castle.
>
> Susan K. Harris, *The Courtship of Olivia Langdon and Mark Twain* (Cambridge: Cambridge University Press, 1996), p. 26.

KEARY, ANNIE (ANNA MARIA) (1825–1879). *Castle Daly: The Story of an Irish Home Thirty Years Ago.* New Edition. London: Macmillan and Co., 1876. 576 pp. Reprinted in 1886.

> Clemens misspelled the names of the author, title, and publisher in a notebook entry of September 1887 (NB 27, *N&J* 3: 316).

——————— and **ELIZA KEARY** (1827–1918). *The Heroes of Asgard: Tales from Scandinavian Mythology.* [First published in 1857; the date of this edition undetermined. Rebound without a title page or other preliminary leaves.]

> **Provenance:** has the shelfmarks of Clara Clemens Gabrilowitsch's library numbering system during her Detroit years. Sold at the 1951 auction in Hollywood but not listed in the hastily prepared sale sheet.
>
> **Catalog:** "Property from the Library of Mark Twain," Butterfield & Butterfield, San Francisco, Sale 6613 (16 July 1997), lot 2712.
>
> **Location:** Mark Twain House and Museum, Hartford, Connecticut.
>
> **Copy examined:** Clemens's unmarked copy. Viewed in Hartford in 1997.
>
> This children's book endeavors to bring to life Thor, Loki, Hela, and other figures from Norse legends.

———. *Janet's Home.* New York: Macmillan Co., 1882. 426 pp.

> **Source:** MTLAcc, entry #2294, volume donated from Clemens's library by Clara Clemens Gabrilowitsch in 1910.
>
> "Anna Keary novels/Jennette's Home [*sic*], Castle Bailey [*sic*], & others. Mc Millan," Clemens noted to himself in September 1887 (NB 27, *N&J* 3: 316).
>
> A coming-of-age novel, set in England, about a London professor's family. As with a number of Keary's books, there is a predominant religious theme.

KEATS, JOHN (1795–1821). *Endymion* (poem, published in 1818).

> "And so you think a baby is a thing of beauty and a joy forever?" Mark Twain wrote in a sketch published on 18 June 1865 (and reprinted on 24 June 1865), "Answers to Correspondents" (*ET&S* 2: 204–205, 542). He collected the piece in *Sketches, New and Old* (1875). Crossing through the jungles of Nicaragua, Twain observed in his letter of 15 March 1867 to the San Francisco *Alta California* that "never did the party cease to consider the wild monkey a charming novelty and a joy forever" (*MTTMB*, p. 42).

———. "On First Looking into Chapman's Homer" (poem, published in 1816).

> Clemens slightly echoed the most famous line from this

sonnet, "Silent, upon a peak in Darien," in the course of insulting a rival editor, "the Unreliable," whom he accused of being "the very lawyer's-cub who sat upon the solitary peak, all soaked in beer and sentiment" ("Ye Sentimental Law Student," 19 February 1863, *ET&S* 1: 217).

———. *The Poetical Works of John Keats.* Ed. by Francis Turner Palgrave (1824–1897). Golden Treasury Series. London: Macmillan and Co., 1889. 284 pp.

Source: MTLAcc, entry #2082, volume donated from Clemens's library by Clara Clemens Gabrilowitsch in 1910.

KEAY, J. SEYMOUR (1830–1909). "The Spoliation of India," *Nineteenth Century* (London) 14–15 (July 1883, April 1884, May 1884).

In April or May 1887 Clemens made a note to himself about "an article in Nineteenth Century . . . on England's rule in India" (Notebook 27, *N&J* 3: 383). The editorial team of the Mark Twain Project in the Bancroft Library at the University of California at Berkeley identified Keay's series as the one Clemens recalled. Keay, who had lived in India for twenty years, provided a detailed criticism of England's activities in that country.

KEDDIE, HENRIETTA (1827–1914), pseud. "Sarah Tytler." *Honor Ormthwaite; A Novel.* New York: Harper & Brothers, 1896. 253 pp.

Source: MTLAcc, entry #1505, volume donated by Clemens.

Henrietta Keddie, a protégé of Clemens's friend Dr. John Brown, was a prolific Scottish author who usually wrote as "Sarah Tytler." Her novels about Scottish society combined accuracy with uncommon sympathy for the characters and their situations.

———, pseud. "Sarah Tytler." *Noblesse Oblige.* New York; H. Holt & Co., 1876. 386 pp.

Source: MTLAcc, entry #1852, volume donated from Clemens's library by Clara Clemens Gabrilowitsch in 1910.

KEELER, RALPH (1840–1873). *Gloverson and His Silent Partners.* Boston: Lee and Shepard, 1869. 372 pp.

Clemens instructed Elisha Bliss to send Keeler a complimentary copy of *The Innocents Abroad* (12 November 1871, ALS in MTP, *MTHL*, p. 8). In a futuristic spoof that Clemens wrote to Olivia Clemens on 16 November 1874 (and also sent the letter to William Dean Howells on 20 November 1874) he announced that "the monument to the author of 'Gloverson & His Silent Partners' is finished" and referred to the novel as a "noble classic" that would, by 1935, be "adored by all nations & known to all creatures" (*MTHL*, p. 40; *MTLet* 6: 291). But according to Clemens's designated biographer, poor Keeler was delighted simply to find a copy of his novel about California mines and stocks in a public library near Boston (*MTB*, pp. 449–450). Evidently Clemens was remembering this pathetic incident when he noted Keeler's name and his novel in December 1897, adding "librarian had a copy" (NB 42, TS p. 50). Mark Twain mentioned Keeler familiarly in "My Boyhood Dreams" (1900). Keeler's name also appears in a list of writers Clemens compiled from those he had known personally on 16 January 1903 (NB 46, TS p. 6). Another reference to *Gloverson* occurs among anecdotes Clemens recalled in 1904 (NB 46, TS p. 34). In part of Twain's *Autobiography* written in 1898 and 1899 he recalls Keeler of "about 1865" as "the modestest young fellow

that ever was. . . . The native sweetness of his disposition had not been marred by cares and disappointments; he was buoyant and hopeful, simple-hearted, and full of the most engaging and unexacting little literary ambitions" (*AutoMT* 1:150). In an Autobiographical Dictation of 12 September 1908 Twain quoted from his 1874 letter that had jokingly alluded to *Gloverson and His Silent Partners* as a "noble classic" (*AutoMT* 3: 262; *MTLet* 6: 294 n. 7). There he recalled Keeler as "a dear good young fellow" who "told me himself that only one copy [of *Gloverson*] was sold." Keeler vanished from the steamer *Cienfuegos* off the coast of Cuba in December 1873. Clemens fretted on 24 March 1874 in a letter to Thomas Bailey Aldrich that there were "still no tidings from poor unnecessary but still delightful Keeler! I am getting well discouraged in that direction" (*MTLet* 6: 91). Those interested in the biography of Keeler can consult Philip Graham's "Ralph Keeler, Journalism's Mystery," *Journalism Quarterly* 40.4 (Winter 1963): 45–52. Graham reported that *Gloverson* "failed almost before it came from the presses"; he could locate only one copy—that of the Library of Congress.

———. "New Orleans," "A Day on a Mississippi Steamboat," "St. Louis," and similar articles, a six-month series titled collectively "On the Mississippi," in *Every Saturday: An Illustrated Weekly Journal,* Second series, nos. 79–102 (1 July 1871–9 December 1871). Illustrated by A[lfred]. R[udolph]. Waud (1828–1891).

In writing *Life on the Mississippi* (1883), Mark Twain consulted this series of fifteen articles, mailed to him from the file of James R. Osgood & Company. (Thomas Bailey Aldrich had been editing *Every Saturday* when the Keeler-Waud series appeared.) W. Rowlands of Osgood's Boston firm acknowledged Twain's return of "the package of 'Every Saturday'" in a letter of 16 September 1882 (Horst H. Kruse, *Mark Twain and "Life on the Mississippi,"* p. 50, citing MTP). Thomas Ruys Smith noted that Keeler's tone "is ironic rather than romantic" in describing the river boats, their passengers, and even their pilots ("'The Mississippi Was a Virgin Field': Reconstructing the River Before Mark Twain, 1865–1875," *Mark Twain Journal* 53.2 [Fall 2015]: 54). Author and journalist Keeler was a friend who kept Clemens company during Clemens's lectures in the Boston vicinity. The English-born illustrator Waud had drawn pictures for the exquisitely illustrated *Picturesque America* series that appeared in *Appletons' Journal* in 1870 and would be collected in the two-volume *Picturesque America; or, The Land We Live In* (1872–1874), edited by William Cullen Bryant.

———. "Owen Brown's Escape from Harper's Ferry," *Atlantic Monthly* 33.197 (March 1874): 342–365.

Clemens would recall that "Keeler went out to Ohio and hunted out one of Ossswatomie [*sic*] Brown's brothers on his farm and took down . . . his adventures in escaping from Virginia after the tragedy of 1859. . . . It was published in the *Atlantic Monthly,* and I made three attempts to read it but was frightened off each time before I could finish. The tale was so vivid and so real. . . . The torture of it all was so sharp that I was never able to follow the story to the end" (*MTAuto* 1: 154).

———. *Vagabond Adventures.* Boston: Fields, Osgood, &

Co., 1870. 274 pp.

In view of Clemens's friendship with Keeler in both San Francisco and Boston (especially when Clemens made lecture trips out of that latter city), it would seem highly improbable that Clemens was unaware of Keeler's account of his peripatetic life, which included a stint in a minstrel show and a long sojourn in Europe. Keeler's experiences on steamboats that plied the Mississippi River would surely have caught Clemens's eye. These youthful experiences had appeared serially in the *Atlantic Monthly* before being collected in *Vagabond Adventures* in 1870.

Thomas Ruys Smith, "'The Mississippi Was a Virgin Field': Reconstructing the River Before Mark Twain, 1865–1975," *Mark Twain Journal* 53.2 (Fall 2015): 52–53.

KEIGHTLEY, (SIR) SAMUEL ROBERT (1859–1949). *The Last Recruit of Clare's; Being Passages from the Memoirs of Anthony Dillon, Chevalier of St. Louis, and Late Colonel of Clare's Regiment in the Service of France*. New York: Harper & Brothers, 1901. 299 pp.

Source: *MTLAcc*, entry #1018, volume donated by Clemens.

A work of fiction, despite its historical-sounding title.

KEIGHTLEY, THOMAS (1789–1872). *An Account of the Life, Opinions, and Writings of John Milton. With an Introduction to Paradise Lost*. London: Chapman and Hall, 1859. 484 pp.

Keightley ("London, '59") was one of the "biogs of Milton" that Clemens listed in Notebook 27 (*N&J* 3: 328) in September 1887 for a project he planned.

KEIM, DE BENNEVILLE RANDOLPH (1841–1914). *Sheridan's Troopers on the Borders: A Winter Campaign on the Plains*. Philadelphia: Claxton, Remsen & Haffelfinger, 1870. 308 pp.

Until he modified his view of Native Americans in his later years, Mark Twain was grateful to discover material that seemed to disprove the existence of the portraits drawn by James Fenimore Cooper. In "The Noble Red Man," a *Galaxy* sketch that appeared in the September 1870 issue, Twain cited "Dr. Keim's excellent book" as his source for Native American atrocities committed during 1868 and 1869 against unoffending whites. "These facts and figures are official," Twain declared, "and they exhibit the misunderstood Son of the Forest in his true character—as a creature devoid of brave or generous qualities, but cruel, treacherous, and brutal" (*CG*, p. 72; also reprinted in *Mark Twain: Life as I Find It*, pp. 107–108). In the 1860s and 1870s the American army commander Philip Henry Sheridan (1831–1888), a Civil War hero owing to his cavalry exploits, led brutal campaigns against Native American tribes who resisted relocation to reservations.

Blair, *HH&T* (1969), pp. 82 n. 1, 331; McNutt, "Mark Twain and the American Indian" (1978); Kerry Driscoll, *Mark Twain among the Indians and Other Indigenous People* (Oakland: University of California Press, 2018), pp. 164–167

KELLER, GOTTFRIED (1819–1890). *Die Leute von Seldwyla [The People of Seldwyla]. Erzählungen von Gottfried Keller*. 2 vols. Dritte Auflage [Third ed.] Stuttgart: O.J. Göschen'sche Verlagshandlung, 1876.

Inscriptions: "Sam¹ L. Clemens/Feb. 2nd 1879/Munich" is written in both volumes in brown ink by Olivia Clemens. These inscriptions were slightly cropped when the books

were rebound.

Marginalia: Clemens wrote the words "I feel" on page 15 of Volume I; he also made a few pencil markings in this volume, particularly on page 105.

Provenance: *C1951* sale labels in both volumes. Bookplates of the University of California at Berkeley identify the books as gifts from Jake Zeitlin.

Catalog: *Zeitlin 1951*, p. 4, item #26. Price $10.

Location: Mark Twain Papers, Bancroft Library, University of California at Berkeley.

Copies examined: Clemens's copy of Keller's first collection of short stories, *The People of Seldwyl*, several of which are considered classics of German Realism.

KELLER, HELEN ADAMS (1880–1968). *Helen Keller Souvenir No. 2 (1892–1899), Commemorating the Harvard Final Examination for Admission to Radcliffe College, June 29–30, 1899*. Illus. Washington, D. C.: Volta Bureau for the Increase and Diffusion of Knowledge Relating to the Deaf, 1900 [cop. 1899]. 65 pp.

Inscription: inscribed "Olivia L. Clemens" in Clemens's hand on the front flyleaf.

Catalogs: ListABP (1910), "Helen Keller"; "Retz Appraisal" (1944), p. 9, valued at $5.

Location: Mark Twain Papers, Bancroft Library, University of California at Berkeley.

Copy examined: Olivia Clemens's copy.

Helen Keller's Souvenir contains essays about Keller's academic studies written by Anne M. Sullivan (1866–1936) and other teachers and supervisors, and by Keller herself. It concludes with a facsimile certificate of her college admission. Clemens was aware of Keller's achievements before he received this book. He had written to Mary M. Keller (1860–1946) on 12 September 1890 to thank her for sending a gift (ALS in Stowe-Day Memorial Library, Hartford, Connecticut). He mentioned and praised Helen Keller's accomplishments in Chapter 61 of *Following the Equator* (1897).

———. *The Story of My Life*. Illus. New York: Doubleday, Page & Co., 1903. [Supplementary essay added by John Albert Macy (1877–1932).] 441 pp.

Inscription: (not actually in Braille, but the letters are raised rather than printed): "To Mr. Clemens/If my book finds favor in thy sight dear Friend I shall count my darkness light and each loss a privilege./Helen Keller/March Tenth/ 1903."

Provenance: Antenne-Dorrance Collection, Rice Lake, Wisconsin.

Location: Mark Twain Archive, Gannett-Tripp Learning Center, Elmira College, Elmira, New York.

Copy examined: Clemens's unmarked copy.

Clemens wrote to Helen Keller on St. Patrick's Day, 1903, from Riverdale: "I am charmed with your book—enchanted." He also complimented Anne M. Sullivan, whose "brilliancy, penetration, originality, wisdom, character, & the fine literary competencies of her pen" were apparent in her own letters (*MTB*, pp. 1198–99; *MTL*, p. 731).

———. *The Story of My Life*. [Another copy.]

Catalog: *C1951*, D25, $27.50, listed among the volumes signed by Clemens.

———. *The World I Live In*. New York: Century Co., 1908.

Inscription: Keller wrote in pencil on the front flyleaf: "Dear

Mr. Clemens, come live in my world a little while/Helen Keller". On the front pastedown endpaper Clemens noted in black ink: "It is a lovely book—& Helen is herself another lovely book./SLC/ 1908."

Provenance: Antenne Collection, Rice Lake, Wisconsin.

Location: Mark Twain Archive, Gannett-Tripp Learning Center, Elmira College, Elmira, New York.

Copy examined: Clemens's copy, unmarked.

Coley Taylor recalled that Clemens gave parties at Stormfield "to benefit the library he was founding." One of these parties also had another purpose—"to publicize Helen Keller's new book, *The World I Live In*. He showed it to everyone. On that occasion there were people there from Danbury, Ridgefield, and elsewhere—newspaper reporters. He presented us to Miss Keller" ("Personal Recollections of Mark Twain," *Perspectivas* [Fall 1982]: 37). Elizabeth Wallace reported that Clemens read aloud from Keller's articles appearing in *Harper's Magazine* [*sic*] in Bermuda in March and April 1908; he and Henry H. Rogers were impressed with her phrasing (*MT&HI*, p. 94). Probably Wallace meant *Century Magazine*, which published several Helen Keller poems and articles in 1908. Keller herself provided a brief but touching synopsis of her encounters with Clemens in "My Friend Mark Twain," *Mark Twain Journal* 10.4 (Spring-Summer 1958): 1; she discussed in detail the pessimism and hostility to religion he exhibited during "the few days that I spent with him in the quiet of Stormfield," when she sensed that his anger was "rather superficial" and masked "perplexity and a longing to believe." She especially appreciated his attitude toward her disabilities: "He entered into my limited world with enthusiasm just as he might have explored Mars. Blindness was an adventure that kindled his curiosity. He treated me not as a freak but as a handicapped woman seeking a way to circumvent extraordinary difficulties."

Amy Chambliss, "The Friendship of Helen Keller and Mark Twain," *Georgia Review* 24.3 (Fall 1970): 305–310, reviewed the Keller-Twain relationship.

KELLEY, AGNES V. "Daughters of the Bright Brigade" and "Sons of the Bright Brigade" (apparently unpublished manuscripts).

A woman named Agnes V. Kelley wrote to Clemens 28 April 1892 to obtain biographical information from him for a projected book, "Sons of the Bright Brigade," which was to be a sequel to her nearly complete "Daughters of the Bright Brigade" (Fears, *Day by Day* 2: 703).

KELLEY, JAMES DOUGLAS JERROLD (1847–1922). *The Ship's Company and Other Sea People*. Illus. New York: Harper & Brothers, 1897. 222 pp.

Source: MTLAcc, entry #1368, volume donated by Clemens.

A highly readable compendium of facts and stories about life at sea—the duties of various members of the crew, their superstitions, language, pets, and ports of call such as Tahiti and other South Sea islands. A somber note is struck by recalling several mysteries and tragedies at sea.

KELLOGG, ROBERT HALE (1844–1922). *Life and Death in Rebel Prisons: Giving a Complete History of the Inhuman and Barbarous Treatment of Our Brave Soldiers by Rebel Authorities, Principally at Andersonville, Ga., and Florence, S. C., Describing Plans of Escape, Arrival of Prisoners, with . . . Anecdotes of Prison Life. By Robert H. Kellogg, Sergeant-Major 16th Regiment*

Connecticut Volunteers. Prepared from His Daily Journal. Illus. Sold by Subscription Agents Only. Hartford, Connecticut: L. Stebbins, 1865. 400 pp. [Edition conjectured.]

Clemens made a memorandum in February 1882: "Get Kellogg's Andersonville experiences through short-hand reporter" (Notebook 20, *N&J* 2: 446). His next notebook entry mentions the sinking of the *Hornet* and the ordeal of her crew in an open boat, which he wrote up from a survivor's journal and published in 1866. Possibly he had something similar in mind for using Kellogg's grim journal about the mistreatment endured by Kellogg and his fellow Union soldiers, or he might have considered incorporating these experiences into the sections of *Life on the Mississippi* (1883) that discuss the Civil War. In 1882 Kellogg was a general agent for the Connecticut Mutual Life Insurance Company in Hartford. Perhaps he or his former publisher still possessed the original journals.

KELLY, FANNY (WIGGINS) (1845–1904). *Narrative of My Captivity Among the Sioux Indians, with a Brief Account of General Sully's Indian Expedition in 1864, Bearing upon Events Occurring in my Captivity*. Hartford, Connecticut: Mutual Publishing Co., 1871. 285 pp. Reprinted in 1873.

On 17 February 1876 Clemens requested Elisha Bliss to send this book and several others to a disabled soldiers' home in Virginia (ASSSCL). The book is now in the Darwin R. Barker Historical Museum, Fredonia, New York. Fanny Kelly and her family were attacked in 1864 while traveling as part of a small wagon train in Wyoming.

KELLY, MICHAEL (1762–1826). *Reminiscences of Michael Kelly, of the King's Theatre, and Theatre Royal Drury Lane, Including a Period of Nearly Half a Century*. 2 vols. London: H. Colburn, 1826.

Clara Clemens listed this book title in her commonplace book (Paine 150, MTP). It contains biographies of once-prominent English actors and singers.

KELLY, MARY (SPENCE) (1846–1929), wrote under the name "Mrs. Tom Kelly." *A Leddy in Her Ain Richt: A Brief Romance Compiled from an Unfinished Manuscript by the Late Robert Graeme, for Many Years Secretary and Librarian at the Castle of Karmore*. London: Hurst and Blackett, 1897. 291 pp.

Source: MTLAcc, entry #192, volume donated by Clemens. Inscribed to Mark Twain by the English author, who was married to the artist and illustrator Tom Kelly.

KELVIN, WILLIAM THOMSON (1824–1907). "The Age of Earth as an Abode Fitted for Life," *Science* 9.228 (12 May 1899): 665–674 and 9. 229 (19 May 1899): 704–711.

Sherwood Cummings—"Mark Twain and Science" (1950), pp. 21–22—suggested this two-part article as the most likely source for Mark Twain's knowledge that Kelvin favored a shorter span of time for the earth's formation than his scientific colleagues theorized. (Kelvin believed it to be one hundred million years, with man inhabiting it for 30,000 years.) Albert Bigelow Paine quoted Clemens on this subject in *Mark Twain: A Biography* (1912), page 1358.

H. H. Waggoner, "Science" (1937), p. 362.

KEMBLE, EDWARD WINDSOR (1861–1933).

Commentary regarding E. W. Kemble's illustrations for Mark Twain's *Adventures of Huckleberry Finn* (1885) has gone through sharply differing stages. At first the drawings were admired for their humorous ingenuity. The boy who posed as a model for Kemble's illustrations of Huck Finn (for $4 a week) later wrote a proud account of the experience (Courtland P. Morris, "The Model for Huck Finn," *Mark Twain Quarterly* 2.4 [Summer-Fall 1938]: 22–23). Forty-five years after *Huckleberry Finn* was published the artist Kemble recalled his pleasure in obtaining this lucrative assignment; he remembered that it was "a small picture of a boy being stung by a bee" that had attracted Twain's attention to him as a potential illustrator for the forthcoming novel ("Illustrating *Huckleberry Finn*," *The Colophon: A Book Collectors' Quarterly* 1 (Part One, 1930); however, no one has been able to identify that particular drawing (Gary Scharnhorst, *Twain in His Own Time: A Biographical Chronicle of His Life* [Iowa City: University of Iowa Press, 2010], p. 140 n. 1). Beverly R. David—"The Pictorial *Huck Finn*: Mark Twain and His Illustrator, E. W. Kemble," *American Quarterly* 26.4 (October 1974): 331–351—established the fact that Twain had seen Kemble's work in *Life*; she also reproduced and discussed many of Kemble's drawings and filled in details about the Twain-Kemble relationship.

Thereafter the critical studies of this problem tilted toward condemnatory conclusions owing to the racial exaggerations Kemble employed and that Twain evidently endorsed. Earl F. Briden's "Kemble's 'Specialty' and the Pictorial Countertext of *Huckleberry Finn*," *Mark Twain Journal* 26.2 (Fall 1988): 2–14 specified that Twain saw Kemble's work in the 3 March 1884 issue of *Life*, prompting him to instruct Charles L. Webster to seek out this artist for *Adventures of Huckleberry Finn*; Briden reprinted samples of Kemble's illustrations, pointed out Kemble's regrettable "comic typification" of black characters, and cited related studies. (Actually Kemble's elaborate cartoon work to which Briden referred, "Some Uses of Electricity," had appeared in *Life's* 13 March 1884 [3.63] issue, pp. 148–149, not 3 March; *Life's* previous issue was published on 6 March 1884, and contained only one sketch by Kemble—a racially stereotypical image of an African American showing off his ice-skating skills.) Other scholars similarly objected to this prejudicial type of graphic humor, including Douglass Anderson, "Reading the Pictures in *Huck Finn*," *Arizona Quarterly* 42.2 (Summer 1986): 101–118; Kelly Anspaugh, "The Innocent Eye?: E. W. Kemble's Illustrations to *Adventures of Huckleberry Finn*," *American Literary Realism* 25.2 (Winter 1993): 16–30)—who shrewdly assessed Twain's motives in selecting Kemble as his illustrator; Henry B. Wonham, *Playing the Races: Ethnic Caricature and American Literary Realism* (New York: Oxford University Press, 2004); and Francis Martin, Jr., "To Ignore Is to Deny: E. W. Kemble's Racial Caricature as Popular Art," *Journal of Popular Culture* 40.4 (2007): 655–682.

KEMBLE, FRANCES ANNE (1809–1893), known as "Fanny Kemble." *Journal of a Residence on a Georgian Plantation in 1838–39*. Original dark brown cloth, spine broken. New York: Harper & Brothers, 1863. 337 pp.

Marginalia: a vertical pencil mark by Clemens on page 236, where Kemble described the low standard of living even among "the proud Southern chivalry." There are other vertical pencil marks on pages 84, 35, and 96, though these markings seem broader and heavier than those Clemens

usually made. The corner of page 100 is turned down at an account of an enslaved woman lamenting the probable imminent sale of her family. Page 317 is folded down at a heart-rending vision of "a Southern Infirmary, such as I saw it," describing the primitive treatment of ailing and child-birthing enslaved women.

Provenance: has the shelfmarks of the library numbering system employed by Clara Clemens Gabrilowitsch during her Detroit years. Sold at the 1951 auction in Hollywood but not listed in the hastily compiled sale sheet.

Catalog: "Property from the Library of Mark Twain," Butterfield & Butterfield, San Francisco, Sale 6613 (16 July 1997), lot 2713.

Location: Mark Twain House and Museum, Hartford, Connecticut.

Copy examined: Clemens's copy. Viewed in Hartford in 1997. There is no inscription in the volume.

British actress and writer Frances Anne "Fanny" Kemble had been unable to publish this account of the years she spent on her American husband's plantation because of threats he made after they separated. Her "Preface," dated 16 January 1863 and written in London, stated that she witnessed these scenes on plantations raising rice and cotton in islands "on the coast of Georgia." Observing that these islands are now "in the power of the Northern troops," she explained that "the following pages" depict "a picture of conditions of human existence which I hope and believe have passed away."

———. *Records of Later Life*. New York: Henry Holt and Co., 1883.

Catalogs: QF Martinez, "Good condition"; Ball 2061 inventory, green cloth, silver flower design, gilt lettering, signed "Susan L. Crane,/Oct. 1884".

Location: Mark Twain Archive, Elmira College, Elmira, New York.

This book, available to Clemens in his summers at Quarry Farm, included the actress's none-too-flattering impressions of the United States in the 1830s.

KEN, THOMAS (1637–1711). "Praise God, from whom all blessings flow" ("The Doxology") (hymn, published in 1695).

This four-line stanza was often sung at the conclusion of "Old Hundred," and its identity has merged with that of William Kethe's longer hymn. In Chapter 17 of *The Adventures of Tom Sawyer* (1876) the minister exhorts the overjoyed congregation to celebrate the three boys' safe deliverance by wholeheartedly singing "Praise God from whom all blessings flow" and "Old Hundred"; they shook the rafters of the village church. Elmo Howell called this "one of the most powerful scenes in the novel—one of the great scenes in American literature. . . . In a moment of great dramatic power the spirit of a whole culture is revealed" ("In Defense of Tom Sawyer," *Mark Twain Journal* 15.1 [Winter 1970]: 19). "The Doxology" formed the text of a telegram celebrating the election returns that Clemens sent to William Dean Howells from Hartford (9 November 1876, *MTHL*, p. 163). In Chapter 25 of *Adventures of Huckleberry Finn* (1885) "somebody over in the crowd struck up the doxolojer, and everybody joined in with all their might."

KENDALL, HENRY CLARENCE (1839–1882). *Poems of Henry Clarence Kendall*. Ed. by Alexander Sutherland (1852–1902).

Red cloth. Melbourne: George Robertson and Co., 1890. 328 pp.

Inscription: inscribed in ink on the front flyleaf: "Miss Clemens,/with the best wishes of/S. Talbot Smith/Adelaide, 15th October, 1895".

Marginalia: ink marks in the "Contents" pages beside seven poem titles. These markings may have been made by Clemens.

Provenance: Antenne-Dorrance Collection, Rice Lake, Wisconsin.

Location: Mark Twain Archive, Gannett-Tripp Learning Center, Elmira College, Elmira, New York.

Copy examined: Clara Clemens's copy. Examined on 28 May 2015.

Mark Twain mentions Kendall in Chapter 22 of *Following the Equator* (1897) among the Australian authors who have built "a brilliant and vigorous literature." Kendall's previous poetry collections included *Leaves from Australian Forests* (1869), which contained his well-received "The Hut by the Black Swamp" and "The Last of His Tribe."
Madigan, "Mark Twain's Passage to India" (1974), p. 360.

KENDALL, WILLIAM ANDREW (1831–1876). *The Voice My Soul Heard.* San Francisco: Privately printed, 1868. 16 pp.

Whether or not Clemens saw this volume of poetry, he knew Kendall in the 1860s as a fellow contributor to the *Golden Era* and the *Californian.* Bret Harte published some of Kendall's poems in the *Overland Monthly.* On 7 January 1872 Clemens vouched for Kendall's character ("a good fellow") when enlisting William Dean Howells's assistance for this victim of "hard luck" (*MTLet* 5: 8). However, on 13 March 1873 Clemens withdrew his endorsement of "this ill-constructed chronic starveling," mentioning that "I have had his poems on hand for a month" (Clemens to Howells, *MTLet* 5: 318). Three years later Kendall would take his own life in San Francisco.

KENDRICK, GEORGIA (AVERY) (1848–1922), pseud. "M. R. Grendel." *Contrasts.* New York: G. P. Putnam's Sons, 1881. 392 pp.

Source: MTLAcc, entry #2245, volume donated from Clemens's library by Clara Clemens Gabrilowitsch in 1910.

In this novel two orphaned girls grow up, first in Massachusetts, and then they are removed to the American South, where they experience the "contrasts" promised by the title. The author was the spouse of the Reverend James Ryland Kendrick (1821–1889), minister of the First Baptist Church in Poughkeepsie, New York. In 1891, following the death of her husband, Georgia Kendrick would be appointed Lady Principal of Vassar College, which placed her in charge of the institution's social life.

KENNAN, GEORGE (1845–1924). *Siberia and the Exile System.* 2 vols. New York: The Century Co., 1891.

These articles originally appeared as a series in *Century Magazine* between 1887 and 1891. Howard G. Baetzhold convincingly proved Mark Twain's familiarity with Kennan's allegations of Russian atrocities and banishment ("The Course of Composition of *A Connecticut Yankee*" [1961], 207–211; *MT&JB* (1970), p. 349 n. 32). In an unpublished letter written in the summer of 1890 and intended for a journal titled *Free Russia*, Twain alluded to "the glare of George Kennan's revelations" (*MTPP*, p. 157). Kennan's sympathies led Clemens to suppose in

1901 that Kennan might collaborate on a book about Southern lynchings (Clemens to Frank Bliss, 8 September 1901, ALS in the Harry Ransom Center, University of Texas at Austin).
Louis J. Budd, "Twain, Howells, and the Boston Nihilists" (1959); *MTSP* (1962), pp. 146–147.

———. *Tent Life in Siberia, and Adventures Among the Koraks and Other Tribes in Kamtchatka and Northern Asia.* New York: G. P. Putnam & Sons, 1870. 425 pp.

Inscription: the upper portion of the front flyleaf has been torn out.

Location: Mark Twain Library, Redding, Connecticut. Donated by Clemens (MTLAcc #597).

Copy examined: Clemens's unmarked copy. It has the red ink Mark Twain Library accession number "597". Examined in 1970 and again in June 1982 and on 10 November 2019.

Kennan went to Siberia in the 1860s to work on a Western Union telegraph line linking Russia, the United States, and much of the world. He encountered ancient indigenous people who had skillfully adapted to their harsh environment.

KENNEDY, CHARLES RANN (1871–1950). *The Servant in the House* (play, performed in 1908, New York City).

Clemens saw a performance of *The Servant in the House* on 6 June 1908 and declared it to be "a noble play"; he dined with its author ("whom I very much wish to know") the next evening (Clemens to Dorothy Quick, 7 June 1908, ALS at Columbia University). A week later it still seemed "a wonderful play" (Clemens to Dorothy Quick, 14 June 1908, ALS at Columbia University). In Dorothy Sturgis Harding's reminiscences about her 1908 visit to Clemens's Stormfield, she recalled the nickname of his business manager, Ralph W. Ashcroft: "Also there was Mr. Ashcroft, known as 'Benares,' because of *The Servant in the House*, a very popular current play" ("Mark Twain Lands an Angel-Fish," *Columbia Library Columns* 16 [February 1967]: 8). Obviously all of this was before Clemens turned against his business manager Ashcroft, since in Kennedy's play the admirable Bishop of Benares cleverly disguises himself as a butler in order to effect a moral revolution in a vicar's parsonage.

———. *The Winterfeast.* Illus. New York: Harper & Brothers, 1908. 159 pp.

Source: MTLAcc, entry #1575, volume donated by Clemens.

KENNEDY, HARRY (1855–1894). "Cradle's empty, baby's gone" (song, cop. 1880).

Clemens heard two African American cabin hands on the *City of Baton Rouge* sing this song to banjo accompaniment in 1882 (NB 21, *N&J* 2: 562). Born in Ireland, Harry Kennedy performed in minstrel shows in the 1870s and 1880s. He also became a ventriloquist, saloon keeper, theater owner, and prolific song writer before succumbing to Bright's disease.

KENNEDY, JAMES MACKINTOSH (1848–1922). *The Scottish and American Poems of James Kennedy.* Edinburgh: Oliphant, Anderson & Ferrier, [cop. 1907]. 228 pp.

Source: MTLAcc, entry #2134, volume donated from Clemens's library by Clara Clemens Gabrilowitsch in 1910.

KENNEDY, JOHN PENDLETON (1795–1870). *Swallow Barn; or,*

A Sojourn in the Old Dominion (novel, published in 1832).
During the autumn of 1851 Orion Clemens published extracts from *Swallow Barn* in the Hannibal *Journal* (*SCH*, p. 240).

Kennedy, Kate (1827–1890). *Doctor Paley's Foolish Pigeons, and Short Sermons to Workingmen*. San Francisco: Cubery & Co., 1906. 272 pp.

Source: MTLAcc, entry #676, volume donated by Isabel V. Lyon, Clemens's secretary.

Posthumously published essays about the advantages of Henry George's single-tax system written by Kate Kennedy, a teacher, reformer, and women's rights advocate

Kennedy, William (1799–1849). "The pirate's serenade" (song, published in 1838). Melody by John Thomson (1805–1841).

Mark Twain associated two lines from Kennedy's poem (which was adapted as a popular song) with the tropical scenery he first viewed in the Sandwich Islands. In 1866 he copied the lines into Notebook 6: "Oh, islands there are/on the face of [the] deep/Where the leaves never fade/ & the skies never weep" (*N&J* 1: 200). Previously he had adapted the second line (as "& skies weep") in copying them into Notebook 5 (*N&J* 1: 163), and he explained in a fragmentary sketch about the Sandwich Islands—begun in 1884 (DV111, MTP)—that "the skies do weep, there, but the leaves never fade." He quoted his favorite lines again in Chapter 15, Book II, of *Christian Science* (1907); there he claimed that Mary Baker Eddy led her followers "to a tropical paradise like that of which the poet sings: 'O, islands there are on the face of the deep/Where the leaves never fade and the skies never weep'" (*WIM?*, pp. 358, 574). Several versions of the song introduce a different line—"where the leaves never change"—but Kennedy's original poem used the phrase "never fade." See also the Catalog entry for "Captain Kidd" (ballad).

Kenney, James (1780–1849). *Raising the Wind* (farce, performed in 1803).

In a letter of 27 June 1878 to William Dean Howells, Clemens called Bret Harte "a swindler, a snob, a sot, a sponge, a coward, a Jeremy Diddler" (*MTHL*, p. 235). Reaching for these insults, Clemens seems to have known that Kenney created Jeremy Diddler as a character who was continually "raising the wind" by borrowing small sums which he never repaid.

Kensal Rise Public Library [unidentified commemorative pamphlet or book].

Catalog: ListABP (1910), "Kensal Rise Public Library", no other information provided.

On 27 September 1900 participated in the opening ceremonies for the Kensal Rise Public Library in London.

[Keokuk.] *City of Keokuk in 1856. A View of the City, Embracing Its Commerce and Manufactures, and Containing the Inaugural Address of Mayor Curtis, and Statistical Local Information; Also, A Sketch of the Black Hawk War, and History of the Half Breed Tract*. Written and edited by Orion Clemens. Keokuk: O. Clemens, Book and Job Printer, 1856.

Clemens helped his brother Orion set type for this descriptive civic directory.

Philip Ashley Fanning, *Mark Twain and Orion Clemens: Brothers, Partners, Strangers* (Tuscaloosa: University of Alabama Press, 2000), pp. 44–46.

Keokuk Directory and Business Mirror for the Year 1857. Ed. by Orion Clemens [1825–1897]. Keokuk, Iowa: Ben Franklin Book and Job Office, 1857.

Provenance: a directory copy formerly owned by W. C. Stripe of Keokuk. It is not clear that Samuel L. Clemens ever possessed this particular copy, which was once part of the book collection of Frank C. Willson (1889–1960) in Melrose, Massachusetts.

Location: Harry Ransom Center, University of Texas at Austin. Acquired in 1962 from the widow of Frank C. Willson, Margarete Willson, along with other books that more definitely belonged to Clemens.

Copy examined: a copy belonging to a resident of Keokuk, Iowa.

Sam Clemens helped his brother Orion prepare the 1856 edition of this publication, but the younger Clemens left Keokuk before the book issued in 1857.

Keppel, (Lady) Caroline (1737–1769). "Robin Adair" (sentimental love song, c. 1750).

In August 1889 Clemens listed "Treu und Herzinniglich" among his favorite songs (NB 29, *N&J* 3: 513); this was the highly popular German translation of "Robin Adair." In Chapter 3 of Mark Twain's "A Dog's Tale" (1903) Robin Adair is a "very handsome and courteous and graceful" Irish setter who belongs to the Scotch minister. Isabel V. Lyon recorded "Robin Adair" as one of the Scottish airs Clemens requested her to play for him on 14 February 1906 (IVL Journals, TS p. 135, MTP).

Ker, David (1842–1914). "From the Sea to the Desert," *Cosmopolitan* 6.5 (March 1889): 466–470.

In March 1889 Clemens expressed abhorrence for Ker's "travel-papers in the Cosmopolitan." Ker had published "Over the Cossack Steppes," in the *Cosmopolitan* 6.4 (February 1889): 343–348, and his "From the Sea to the Desert" appeared in the following issue. "Pity to put that flatulence between the same leaves with that charming Chinese story [by Chin Foo Wong]," Clemens wrote (NB 28, *N&J* 3: 457). Ker's essay in the March number described North Africa, the Sahara Desert, and the city of Constantine. He wrote with much assurance but little dexterity; his prose is everywhere overfreighted with adjectives. For instance, this is how Ker pictures some "jutting crags": "The gaunt, distorted, skeleton trees that cling to them with clawed, twisted roots, might well pass for demons breaking forth from the regions of eternal night" (p. 466). Ker especially enjoys jokes of the international variety, such as his anecdote about an English tourist with poor vision who mistook a silently praying Mohammedan "for the stump of a tree" beside the Ganges, and carved his name on this "ill-starred Brahmin. . . . As it would have been a deadly sin to move before the prayer was finished, it was 'rough' on that Brahmin!" (p. 468).

Kerr, (Lady) Amabel (1846–1906). *Blessed Joan of Arc (1412–1431)*. Third Edition with Postscript. London: Catholic Truth Society, 1909. 175 pp.

Inscription: a penciled note appears on the first flyleaf in handwriting that does not resemble Clemens's: "It's getting to be a habit with me!"

Provenance: contains a *C1951* auction label.

Catalog: *Zeitlin 1951*, item #27, price $15.

Location: Mark Twain Papers, Bancroft Library, University

of California at Berkeley. Gift of Jake Zeitlin, Los Angeles.

Copy examined: Clemens's copy, unmarked.

KESTER, PAUL (1870–1933). *When Knighthood Was in Flower* (play, performed in 1901, New York City). Adapted from Charles Major's novel (published in 1898).

"This family—by special request of Mr. Major, author of the play [*sic*]—are booked for the Criterion Theatre tomorrow night," Clemens wrote to Emilie Rogers on 22 January 1901 (*MTHHR*, p. 458). Clemens had listed Kester's New York City address in a notebook for 1898 (NB 42, TS p. 66). Kester, incidentally, would publish a four-act dramatization of *The Adventures of Tom Sawyer* in 1932.

KETHE, WILLIAM. "Old hundred," also known as "Old hundreth" (hymn, published in 1561). Melody attributed to Louis Bourgeois or Guillaume Franc.

In Mark Twain's "Private Habits of Horace Greeley" (*The Spirit of the Times*, 7 November 1868), Greeley shaves while humming: "He knows part of a tune and takes an innocent delight in regarding it as the first half of Old Hundred." This hymn—beginning "All people that on earth do dwell"—was usually followed in church services by Thomas Ken's "Doxology" ("Praise God, from whom all blessings flow"). The congregation sings both hymns when Tom and his friends return to life in Chapter 17 of *The Adventures of Tom Sawyer* (1876): "Old Hundred swelled up with a triumphant burst, and . . . it shook the rafters." The minister exhorts the people to "put your hearts in it!" Elmo Howell called this "one of the most powerful scenes in the novel—one of the great scenes in American literature. . . . In a moment of great dramatic power the spirit of a whole culture is revealed" ("In Defense of Tom Sawyer," *Mark Twain Journal* 15.1 [Winter 1970]: 19). Arthur M. Kompass, "Twain's Use of Music" (1964), p. 617 n. 2; Scott, *OPMT* (1966), p. 395.

KEY, FRANCIS SCOTT (1799–1843). "The star-spangled banner" (anthem, published in 1814).

Mark Twain and Charles Dudley Warner utilize "this stirring song" in Chapter 16 of *The Gilded Age* (1873). In August 1895 Twain alluded to African American soldiers who sang the song (NB 35, TS p. 23). A military band in Chapter 13 of "A Horse's Tale" (1906) plays Key's anthem "in a way to make a body's heart swell and thump and his hair rise!" Twain also refers to "The Star-Spangled Banner" in an Autobiographical Dictation of 28 January 1907 (*MTE*, p. 76; *AutoMT* 2: 389). See also the Catalog entry for Daniel Bedinger Lucas and J. Fairfax McLaughlin, *Fisher Ames-Henry Clay, Etc.*

KIEFER, F. J. *The Legends of the Rhine from Basle to Rotterdam.* Second edition. Trans. by L. W. Garnham. Mayence: David Kapp, 1869. 313 pp.

Clemens's annotations in pencil occur throughout.

Provenance: on the rear pastedown endpaper is the sticker of a Leipzig bookseller. The volume was listed in "Retz Appraisal" (1944), p. 9, valued at $20.

Location: Mark Twain Papers, Bancroft Library, University of California at Berkeley.

Copy examined: Clemens's copy.

Kiefer's legends were the literary source for some of the stories Mark Twain told in *A Tramp Abroad* (1880). One legend, "The Converted Sceptic," Twain reworked into the legend of Dilsberg Castle, giving a Rip Van Winkle theme to the narrative of a raft captain (Chapter 19). Garnham's translation from the German tickled Twain immensely. In Chapter one of *A Tramp Abroad* he introduces Garnham's "toothsome" book to his readers, describing the translator's "quaint fashion of building English sentences on the German plan," and quoting a legend called "The Knave of Bergen" as an example. In Chapter 16 he quotes Garnham's sorry attempt to translate the song titled "The Lorelei" into English: "I believe this poet is wholly unknown in America and England; I take peculiar pleasure in bringing him forward because I consider that I discovered him." Brandi Besalke, "'Ein sehr gluecklicher Kind, you bet': Mark Twain and the German Language," *Mark Twain Annual* 5 (2007): 109–122.

———. [An identical (or the same?) copy.]

Source: MTLAcc, entry #1866, volume donated from Clemens's library by Clara Clemens Gabrilowitsch in 1910.

"THE KILKENNY CATS" (Irish nursery rhyme).

Mark Twain alluded to this limerick—"the Kilkenny cats, which it resembles in some respects"—in explicating *The Book of Mormon* in Chapter 16 of *Roughing It* (1872).

KILLIKELLY, SARAH HUTCHINS (1840–1912). *Curious Questions in History, Literature, Art, and Social Life. Designed as a Manual of General Information.* 2 vols. Illus. New York: A. B. Hill & Co., 1886.

Catalog: Ball 2016 inventory, Volume I only, maroon cloth, gilt lettering, back cover detached, spine cover missing, signed by Jervis Langdon, poor condition.

Killikelly poses 255 questions to pique the reader's curiosity, and then proceeds to answer these, in numerical sequence. The first one is, "When was Rome a deserted city for forty days?" Answer: 547 CE.

Clemens delighted in these sorts of compendiums, if he ever had a chance to spot it in the Langdons' residential library.

KING, [WILLIAM BENJAMIN] BASIL (1859–1928). *The Inner Shrine; A Novel of Today.* Illus. New York: Harper & Brothers, 1909. 356 pp.

Source: MTLAcc, entry #1420, volume donated by Clemens.

Though published anonymously, this novel has generally been ascribed to the Canadian-born Basil King, who began writing after illness forced his retirement as Anglican rector of Christ Church in Cambridge, Massachusetts. He set most of his fiction, which generally held spiritual implications, in the United States; however, he often inserted Canadian characters within the narratives.

———. *In the Garden of Charity.* New York: Harper & Brothers, 1903. 320 pp.

Source: MTLAcc, entry #1017, volume donated by Clemens.

[———.] *The Wild Olive; A Novel.* Illustrated by Lucius W[alcott]. Hitchcock (1868–1942). New York: Harper & Brothers, 1910. 347 pp.

Source: MTLAcc, entry #1842, volume donated from Clemens's library by Clara Clemens Gabrilowitsch in 1910.

Though published anonymously, this novel has generally been ascribed to Basil King. It seems to have been published in the month following Clemens's death.

KING, CHARLES (1844–1933). *Between the Lines; A Story of the*

War. Illus. New York: Harper & Brothers, [cop. 1888]. 312 pp.
Source: MTLAcc, entry #1576, volume donated by Clemens.
Romantic love blossoms amid glorious Civil War battles in this young adult novel.
————. *Between the Lines; A Story of the War*. Illus. New York: Harper & Brothers, 1898. 312 pp.
Source: MTLAcc, entry #1019, volume donated by Albert Bigelow Paine, Clemens's designated biographer. Possibly Clemens saw this book, since the men exchanged reading materials.
————. *Cadet Days; A Story of West Point*. Illus. New York: Harper & Brothers, [cop. 1894]. 293 pp.
Source: MTLAcc, entry #1601, volume donated by Clemens.
————. *To the Front; A Sequel to Cadet Days*. Illus. New York: Harper & Brothers, 1902. 261 pp.
Source: MTLAcc, entry #522, volume donated by Clemens.
————. *To the Front; A Sequel to Cadet Days*. Illus. New York: Harper & Brothers, 1908. 261 pp.
Source: MTLAcc, entry #201, volume donated by Clemens.
————. *A War-Time Wooing; A Story*. Illus. New York: Harper & Brothers, 1888. 195 pp.
Source: MTLAcc, entry #2295, volume donated from Clemens's library by Clara Clemens Gabrilowitsch in 1910.
KING, CLARENCE (1842–1901). *Mountaineering in the Sierra Nevada*. Boston: J. R. Osgood and Co., 1872. 292 pp. [Publisher and pages conjectured.]
Inscription: signed "S. L. Clemens."
Catalogs: *A1911*, "12mo, cloth, Bost. 1872," quotes the signature, lot 273, sold for $5.50; George D. Smith, New York City, "Catalogue of Books" (1911), quotes the signature, item #213, $10.
"I wish Clarence King would put his Pike County people on [the stage]," Clemens commented in a now-incomplete letter written to William Dean Howells on 7 May 1875 (*MTHL*, p. 82; *MTLet* 6: 474). When Clemens was searching for materials to include in the anthology of humor that he was co-editing with William Dean Howells and Charles Hopkins Clark in the 1880s, he made a note on the copyright page in his copy of Bret Harte's *Drift from Two Shores* (1880 edition): "We must have Clarence King in full strength./SLC/The Newtys of Pike, for instance" (Special Collections, Vassar College; *MTLet* 6: 477 n. 4). King's *Mountaineering in the Sierra Nevada* (1872) included descriptions of people he met in the Sierra Nevada region, and Chapter 5 was titled "The Newtys of Pike." However, King demurred when asked for permission (he no longer wished to be thought of as a humorist) and was not represented by any selections in *Mark Twain's Library of Humor* (1888). Clemens's Notebook 26 (1886) recorded a remark made by King as reported by Kate Jenkins (*N&J* 3: 259). In 1888 Clemens passed the time while snowbound in the Murray Hill Hotel of New York City by listing authors with whom he was familiar; Clarence King's name appears in the generally "favorable" list that Clemens constructed (Notebook 27, *N&J* 3: 379).
Robert Wilson, *The Explorer King: Adventure, Science, and the Great Diamond Hoax: Clarence King in the Old West* (New York: Scribner, 2006).

KING, EDMUND FILLINGHAM (1812–1874), ed. *Ten Thousand Wonderful Things; Comprising the Marvelous and Rare, Odd, Curious, Quaint, Eccentric, and Extraordinary in All Ages and Nations, in Art, Nature, and Science, Including Many Wonders of the World, Enriched with Hundreds of Authentic Illustrations*. Illus. [Initially published as a 684-page volume in London by George Routledge and Sons in 1859, but subsequent editions became available in London and New York. The one that Clemens purchased has not been established.]
On 14 July 1880 Estes & Lauriat of Boston billed Clemens for "1 10,000 Wond Things $1"; he paid on 20 July 1880 (receipts file, MTP).
The topics in this miscellany are too numerous and tantalizing for anyone to make a brief survey of how they might have been useful to Mark Twain in his writing. They included the Crown of Charlemagne, Dervishes Dancing, the Rock of Cashel, the Tomb of St. George, Dungeons and Torture Chambers in Germany, Shakespeare's Jug, May-Poles, the Lord of Misrule, the Great Wall of China, a Turkish Bazaar, Corpse Bearers During the Plague, and Witch-Testing at Newcastle in 1649. Edmund F. King attended Cambridge University and lived in Leicester, Leicestershire, England.
KING, EDWARD (1848–1896). *The Great South: A Record of Journeys*. Illustrated by J[ames]. Wells Champney (1843–1903). Maps. Hartford: American Publishing Co., 1875. 808 pp.
Thomas Ruys Smith, "'The Mississippi Was a Virgin Field': Reconstructing the River Before Mark Twain, 1865–1875," *Mark Twain Journal* 53.2 [Fall 2015]: 44–46, made a potent case for believing that King's book—whose contents began to appear in the July 1873 issue of *Scribner's Magazine* and which mentioned Mark Twain by name in the October 1874 issue—almost certainly had a connection with Twain's abrupt decision in that latter month to write a series of reminiscences about his piloting experiences for the *Atlantic Monthly*. King's magazine chapters would be collected and published by Elisha Bliss' firm, Twain's own publisher at the time. Chapter 26 of *The Great South* (pp. 257–263), written after King boarded *The Great Republic* steamboat in St. Louis, discussed the character and skills of the Mississippi River pilots.
Blair, *MT&HF* (1960), p. 37.
KING, GRACE ELIZABETH (1852–1932). "Earthlings" (novella, published in 1888).
After Clemens read this story in the November 1888 issue of *Lippincott's Magazine*, he wrote to the author on 16 November: "I do suppose you struck twelve on Earthlings. It does not seem possible that you or any one else can overmatch that masterpiece. I cannot find a flaw in the art of it—I mean the art which the intellect put there—nor in the nobler & richer art which the heart put in it. I *felt* the story, just as if I were living it; whereas with me a story is usually a procession & I an outsider watching it go by—& always with a dubious, & generally with a perishing interest. If I could have stories like this one to read, my prejudice against stories would die a swift death & I should be grateful" (quoted by Robert Bush, "Grace King and Mark Twain," *American Literature* 44.1 [March 1972]: 41–42).
————. *Monsieur Motte*. New York: A. C. Armstrong and

Son, 1888. 327 pp.

On 17 June 1888 Olivia Clemens wrote to Grace King (in a letter not sent until 7 August 1888): "Mr. Clemens and I are sitting on the Ombra this hot Sunday afternoon. . . . I have just finished Monsieur Motte, . . . a copy of which Mr. Warner gave me. [King had dedicated *Monsieur Motte* "To Mr. Charles Dudley Warner, whose kindly recognition of the possibilities of Southern literature has been an encouragement to Southern writers."] It is simply charming—every line in the book delighted me. I had never before read the last two sketches in the book. Of course now I read it right through together. I don't believe you can know how fine it all is" (ALS in Louisiana State University Library, Baton Rouge). When Grace King dramatized the novel, Clemens introduced her to playwright-producer Augustin Daly in November 1888 to see whether he might produce it. Daly declined the play on 24 November 1888. King's *Memories of a Southern Woman of Letters* (1932) would record her impressions of Clemens and his home that commenced with a visit in 1887 and led to others thereafter. (See related Catalog entries for Edward Bellamy, John Brougham, Robert Browning, and Francis Parkman.)

Robert Bush, "Grace King and Mark Twain," *American Literature* 44.1 (March 1972): 42–45, published portions of King's manuscripts, notebooks, and letters for the first time. Many contain her observations while she was a houseguest of the Clemenses. Over the ensuing years King became a family friend and occasional companion of the Clemenses. David Fears tracked and summarized their many meetings in *Mark Twain Day by Day*, Volume 2. The most convenient and thoroughly annotated collection of correspondence between Grace King and the Clemenses can be found in *A New Orleans Author in Mark Twain's Court: Letters from Grace King's New England Sojourns*, ed. Miki Pfeffer. Foreword by Steve Courtney (Baton Rouge: Louisiana State University Press, 2019).

———. *Tales of a Time and Place*. New York: Harper & Brothers, 1892. 303 pp.

Source: MTLAcc, entry #2296, volume donated from Clemens's library by Clara Clemens Gabrilowitsch in 1910.

King's collection contained four stories: "Bayou l'Ombre," "Bonne Maman," "Madrilène; or, The Festival of the Dead," and "The Christmas Story of a Little Church." On 10 November 1892 Clemens inscribed a presentation copy of his *The American Claimant* (1892) to King: "Miss Grace King/is requested to try to get as much profit out of this book as the undersigned has gotten out of her & her sister's visit at Villa Viviani—which is requiring the impossible./The Author./Villa Viviani,/Settignano/Near Florence, Nov. 10 '92" (American Art Association Anderson Galleries, Sale 4201, 13–14 November 1935, lot #69; Fears, *Day by Day* 2: 748).

KINGLAKE, ALEXANDER WILLIAM (1809–1891). *Eōthen*. Edinburgh: A. W. Blackwood & Sons, 1892. 371 pp.

Source: MTLAcc, entry #2297, volume donated from Clemens's library by Clara Clemens Gabrilowitsch in 1910.

Henry Nash Smith quoted Kinglake's "historical sublime" treatment of the Sphinx (Chapter 20), showing how Mark Twain's description in *The Innocents Abroad* (1869) was modeled on Kinglake's rhapsodic inventory of scenes witnessed by the Sphinx (*MTDW*, p. 29). In Chapter 42 of *Following the Equator* (1897) Twain notes: "Kinglake was in Cairo many years ago during an epidemic of the Black Death, and he has imagined the terrors that creep into a man's heart at such a time." Twain then quotes a lengthy extract from Chapter 18, which Kinglake had titled "Cairo and the Plague."

Madigan, "Mark Twain's Passage to India" (1974), pp. 360–361; Welland, *Mark Twain in England* (1978), p. 176.

———. *The Invasion of the Crimea; Its Origin, and an Account of Its Progress Down to the Death of Lord Raglan*. Illustrations and maps. 6 vols. New York: Harper, 1863–1888. [Only Vol. I of Clemens's copy is known to exist.]

Catalog: *A1911*, "Vol. I, illustrations and maps, 12mo, cloth, N.Y. 1863," quotes a small sheet of Clemens's notes, lot 274, $1.25.

In February 1888 Mark Twain jotted an entry in Notebook 27: "Get Kinglake's Crimean War—v small vols—Harper" (*N&J* 3: 375). Leon Dickinson reasoned in explanatory notes he prepared for an unpublished edition of *Innocents Abroad* (1869) that Twain used Kinglake's history to visualize (in Chapter 35 of *The Innocents Abroad*) the Siege of Sebastopol during the Crimean War (TS in MTP).

KINGSLEY, CHARLES (1819–1875). *Charles Kingsley: His Letters and Memories of His Life*. Abridged from the London Edition. Ed. by Frances Eliza Kingsley (1814–1891). New York: Scribner, Armstrong & Co., 1877. 502 pp.

Provenance: bookplate #423 of the "J. Langdon Family Library."

Catalog: Ball 2016 inventory, brown cloth, gilt lettering, fair condition.

Location: Quarry Farm library shelves, under the supervision of the Mark Twain Archive, Elmira College, Elmira, New York.

Copy examined: unmarked copy available to Clemens and his wife whenever they visited the Langdon family in Elmira. Examined on 26 May 2015.

Albert Bigelow Paine reported that Kingsley called on Clemens in London in the summer of 1873 (*MTL*, p. 207). On November 1873 Kingsley wrote Clemens to say how "fond of your work" he was; Clemens sent the letter to Olivia Clemens from London and indicated that he would endeavor to visit the Christian Socialist Kingsley. Clemens wrote to Kingsley on 26 November 1873 but the letter apparently has not survived. Clemens evidently did have dinner with Canon Kingsley on 28 November 1873, and Richard Henry Stoddard recorded a memory of that meeting (*MTLet* 5: 485–486). In a letter to Kingsley of 13 February 1874 Clemens declared to Kingsley that his wife was "this long, long time a most appreciative & admiring reader of yours" (*MTLet* 6: 31). Four days later Clemens introduced Kingsley when the English author gave a talk on Westminster Abbey in Boston (*MTLet* 5: 487 n. 5). Olivia Clemens mentioned to her sister-in-law Mollie Clemens on 29 July 1877 that she and Susan Crane "are reading together this summer the Life and Letters of Charles Kingsley" (ALS in MTP). Clemens was probably reading the volume when he noted in July 1877: "The Deity filled with humor. Kingsley. God's laughter" (NB 13, *N&J* 2: 37). On 25 August 1881 Clemens mentioned in a letter to Olivia that he had encountered a man in a smoking car on the train who "had a face strongly resembling Charles Kingsley's; & although he was evidently a laboring man, & was covered with cinders, his face was beautiful because of its sweetness" (ALS sold by Christie's, New York City, 1–2 February 1988 auction, lot 468).

Baetzhold, *MT&JB* (1970), p. 200.

———. *Favorite Poems, by Charles Kingsley, Owen Meredith [pseud. of E. R. Bulwer Lytton], and Edmund Clarence Stedman*. Illus. Boston: J. R. Osgood and Co., 1877.

Scrapbook #10 in the Mark Twain Papers at Berkeley contains a bill from J. R. Osgood & Company of Boston for this book, purchased by Clemens on 6 August 1877 (p. 69).

———. *The Heroes, or Greek Fairy Tales for My Children*. Illus. Chicago: Donohue, Henneberry & Co., [1900?]. 181 pp.

Inscription: Kingsley dedicated his book "To my children/ Rose, Maurice, and Mary." On that dedication page Clemens noted in black ink: "(I knew Rose & Mary.)/ SLC./And the papa."

Marginalia: Clemens wrote in black ink on the front pastedown endpaper: "Of course I shall not deny that a fellow endowed with such overweening self-conceit, when he comes to write about himself[,] will set down much which cannot be taken entirely on trust.—(Remark of John Addington Symons [*sic*] concerning Benvenuto Cellini./S. L. Clemens/1906.)" On page 31 Clemens made a correction, first in ink and then in pencil.

Catalog: ListABP (1910), "Greek Heroes, Kingsley", no other information supplied.

Provenance: Carrie Estelle Doheny Collection, St. John's Seminary, Camarillo, California. Mrs. Doheny donated the volume in 1940 after she purchased it from Maxwell Hunley Rare Books of Beverly Hills. Christie's auctioned the volume for $1,980 in 1988 on behalf of St. John's Seminary and the Archdiocese of Los Angeles.

Location: currently unknown.

Copy examined: Clemens's copy, at St. John's Seminary in 1970.

———. *Hypatia; or, New Foes with an Old Face*. Boston: Crosby and Nichols, 1862. 487 pp.

Source: MTLAcc, entry #2300, volume donated from Clemens's library by Clara Clemens Gabrilowitsch in 1910.

Clemens wrote to Olivia Langdon from Boston on 28 November 1869: "Twichell gave me one of Kingsley's most tiresomest books—'Hypatia'—& I have tried to read it & can't. I'll try no more" (*LLMT*, p. 126; *MTLet* 3: 413). Many readers might agree with Clemens about the difficulty of reading this novel, written in 1853 and set in fifth-century Alexandria, Egypt, owing to its layers of conflicting philosophies, religions, and plotlines. Kingsley's female philosopher heroine was martyred before she could convert to the Christian faith she seemed about ready to accept. The implicit criticism of Catholicism and Judaism is another problem.

———. *Hypatia; or, New Foes with an Old Face*. 2 vols. Illustrated by William Martin Johnson (1862–1942). New York: Harper & Brothers, 1895.

Source: MTLAcc, entries #1130 and #1131, volumes donated by Clemens.

———. *Madame How and Lady Why; or, First Lessons in Earth Lore for Children*. New York: Macmillan & Co., 1888. 321 pp.

Inscription: the second flyleaf is inscribed by Olivia Clemens in black ink: "Jean Clemens/July 26th 1890/ Onteora/Mamma."

Location: Mark Twain Library, Redding, Connecticut. Donated from Clemens's library by Clara Clemens Gabrilowitsch in 1910 (MTLAcc, entry #1960).

Copy examined: Jean Clemens's unmarked copy. Displays the Mark Twain Library accession number "2974". Examined in 1970 and again in June 1982.

Geology lessons for older children about soil, earthquakes, volcanos, ice ages, coral reefs, climate changes, and other subjects.

———. *Song of the River*. Illus. Boston: Estes and Lauriat, 1887. 19 leaves.

Inscription: (on the half-title page) "Clara Clemens/From her Friend/F. C. H. [?]/Xmas 1889".

Catalog: ListABP (1910), "Song of the River", no other information supplied.

Location: Paine 150 in Mark Twain Papers, Bancroft Library, University of California at Berkeley.

Copy examined: Clara Clemens's copy, unmarked.

This small volume consists of line etchings by eight illustrators and decorative drawings by H[iram]. P[utnam]. Barnes (1857–1920), with captions extracted from Kingsley's three-stanza poem.

———. *Two Years Ago*. Boston: Ticknor and Fields, 1864. 540 pp.

Source: MTLAcc, entry #2299, volume donated from Clemens's library by Clara Clemens Gabrilowitsch in 1910.

———. *The Water-Babies. A Fairy Tale for a Land-Baby*. Illustrated by Joseph Noël Paton (1821–1901). Spine loose. Boston: T. O. H. P. Burnham, 1870. 310 pp.

Inscription: Olivia signed the first flyleaf in pencil, "Livy L. Clemens/Aug. 1871/Quarry Farm."

Marginalia: the vertical pencil marks in the margins of pages 42, 63, 75, 76, and 77 give the appearance of being Clemens's.

Provenance: sticker on the rear pastedown endpaper reads "Preswick Morse & Co./Booksellers/114 Water St./ Elmira, N. Y."

Location: Mark Twain Library, Redding, Connecticut. Donated from Clemens's library by Clara Clemens Gabrilowitsch in 1910 (MTLAcc, entry #1893).

Copy examined: Olivia Clemens's copy. Displays the Mark Twain Library accession number written in pencil, "1893". Examined in 1970 and again in June 1982.

A favorite of Victorian parents (and possibly some of their children), Kingsley's didactic tale relates the experiences of a young chimney sweep who falls into a river where, instead of drowning, he becomes an amphibian-like creature protected by river-fairies.

———. *Westward Ho!* New York: Macmillan and Co., 1874. 519 pp.

Source: MTLAcc, entry #2298, volume donated from Clemens's library by Clara Clemens Gabrilowitsch in 1910.

The novel opens in North Devon during the reign of Queen Elizabeth when a restless boy named Amyas is allowed to accompany Sir Francis Drake on a voyage around the world. Many other sea adventures ensue.

Kingsley, Henry (1830–1876). *Ravenshoe*. 2 vols. New York:

Charles Scribner's Sons, 1905.

Inscriptions: the first flyleaf of Volume I (296 pp.) is signed "Clara Clemens/S. S. 'Rosalind'/June 29 1907." (The *Rosalind* would collide with another vessel on 1 July 1907 off the coast of Halifax, Nova Scotia [Fears, *Day by Day* 4: 712].) The front pastedown endpaper of Volume II (291 pp.) is signed in black ink, "Clara Clemens". A sticker on the rear pastedown endpaper identifies the place of Clara Clemens's purchase: "Brentano's/Booksellers & Stationers,/New York."

Marginalia: In Volume I Clara Clemens made penciled notes and markings on pages 15, 46, 125, 236, and 261. Extensive penciled revisions in Volume 2 signal Clara's dissatisfaction with Kingsley's prose style. Clara made notations and pencil markings in Volume II on pages 105, 106, 112, 135, 136, 137 ("absurd"), 147, 148, 156, 157 ("Idiotic style!"), 159, 166, 264, crossing out many passages. Her notes extended onto the rear free endpaper of Volume II. A newspaper clipping laid in described Clemens's activities in England, including his meeting with Marie Corelli and his visit to Shakespeare's tomb.

Location: Mark Twain Library, Redding, Connecticut. Donated from Clemens's library by Clara Clemens Gabrilowitsch in 1910 (MTLAcc, entries #2301 and #2302).

Copies examined: Clara Clemens's copies. Volume I has the red ink Mark Twain Library accession number "2301"; Volume II has the red ink Mark Twain Library accession number "2302". Examined in 1970 and again in June 1982 and on 10 November 2019.

In this novel first published in 1862, Charles Ravenshoe, rightful heir to an estate in Ireland, undergoes various discouragements largely owing to Protestant-Catholic religious conflicts, fights in the Crimean War, nearly dies, and is ultimately restored to his inheritance. Clemens and his daughter often shared books they were reading.

————. *The Recollections of Geoffrey Hamlyn.* Melbourne, Australia: E. W. Cole, n.d. 433 pp.

Source: MTLAcc, enterny #193, volume donated by Clemens.

On 8 January 1896, sailing in the Indian Ocean, Clemens found time to expound discursively on this portrait of Australian life: "Henry Kingsley's book, Geoffrey Hamlin[,] [*sic*] is a curiosity. In places, & for a little while at a time, it strongly interested me, but the cause lay in the action of the story, not in the story's people. All the people are offensive. Some of them might be well enough if they could be protected from the author's intolerable admiration of them. The reader is lost in wonder that any man can be so piteously bewitched & derationalized by his own creations. The book's grammar is bad, its English poor & slovenly, its art of the crudest. There is one very interesting feature: the author is never able to make the reader believe in the things that happen in the tale. It is not that the things are extraordinary, it is merely that the author lacks the knack of making them look natural. . . . And how misty, vague, unreal, artificial the characters are" (NB 37, TS pp. 3–4). Possibly Mark Twain was preparing a criticism for inclusion in *Following the Equator* (1897); at any rate he reminded himself on 1 December 1896: "Slam at Geoffrey Hamlyn" (NB 39, TS p. 29). He did not carry this intention into print.

Krause, *MTC* (1967), p. 235 n. 10.

KINGSLEY, MARY HENRIETTA (1862–1900). *The Story of West Africa.* London: Horace Marshall & Son, [1899]. 169 pp.

Inscription: the title page is inscribed by the author in black ink: "'Mark Twain,' With/M. H. Kingsley's/respect & thanks". Booksticker of "Young's Library,/Kensington, W." on the front pastedown endpaper.

Location: Mark Twain Library, Redding, Connecticut.

Copy examined: Clemens's unmarked copy. Displays the red ink Mark Twain Library accession number "2750". Examined in 1970 and again in June 1982.

KINKAID, MARY HOLLAND (McNEISH) (1861–1948). *Walda; A Novel.* New York: Harper & Brothers, 1903. 312 pp.

Source: MTLAcc, entry #1577, volume donated by Clemens.

The novel follows a prophetess named Walda who leaves a secluded utopian religious community for the love of a stranger. Kinkaid would gain a wide range of newspaper and magazine experience and become active in the movement for women's rights.

KINKEL, JOHANNA (MOCKEL) (1810–1858). *Hans Ibeles in London. Ein Familienbild aus dem Flüchtlingsleben [A Family Portrait of Refugee Life].* 2 vols. Stuttgart: J. G. Cotta, 1860.

Inscriptions: the title pages of both volumes are inscribed by Olivia Clemens: "S. L. Clemens/Feb 2nd 1879/Munich". Afterwards the books were rebound and their title pages were cropped.

Provenance: both volumes contain *C1951* sale labels.

Catalog: *Zeitlin 1951,* item #28, $20.

Location: Mark Twain Papers, Bancroft Library, University of California at Berkeley. Donated by Jake Zeitlin of Los Angeles.

Copies examined: Clemens's unmarked copies.

Kinkel's autobiographical novel depicted the life of political exiles whose families joined them as refugees in London. Although the protagonist is male, the novel's female author introduced a number of women into the narrative to show how they, too, were affected by the necessity of leaving one's homeland.

[KIPLING, ALICE (MACDONALD) (1837–1910) **and ALICE MACDONALD (KIPLING) FLEMING** (1868–1948)]. *Hand in Hand; Verses by a Mother and Daughter.* New York: Doubleday, Page & Co.; London: Elkin Mathews, 1902. 122 pp. [The authors' names did not appear on the title page; they were Rudyard Kipling's mother and sister.]

Inscription: the front pastedown endpaper is inscribed by Clemens in black ink: "From Doubleday/to/SL. Clemens/New York, August 1904/Poems by Kipling's/mother & sister."

Location: Mark Twain Library, Redding, Connecticut. Donated from Clemens's library by Clara Clemens Gabrilowitsch in 1910 (MTLAcc, entry #2017).

Copy examined: Clemens's copy, unmarked. Displays the red ink Mark Twain Library accession number "2017". Examined in 1970 and again in June 1982.

KIPLING, RUDYARD (1865–1936). *Abaft the Funnel.* The Pocket Kipling. Red leather. New York: Doubleday, Page & Co., 1909.

Inscription: the front cover is signed "S. L. Clemens/1910."

Location: in 1986 the volume belonged to A. W. Yeats of

Beaumont, Texas.

Source: letter from Yeats to Alan Gribben, 17 October 1986.

————. "The Absent-Minded Beggar" (poem).

Astonished that Kipling would support conscription for the Boer War in 1902, Mark Twain wrote a parody of this poem and glumly recalled when the "great lines in the 'Absent-Minded Beggar' thrilled the world" (Clemens to F. H. Skrine, 7 January 1902, ALS in National Library of Scotland; a fuller draft of the burlesque exists in the Mark Twain Papers, DV152).

D. M. McKeithan, "A Letter to Francis Henry Skrine in London," *Modern Language Notes* 63.2 (February 1948): 134–135; Scott, *MTAL* (1969), p. 228; Baetzhold, *MT&JB* (1970), p. 359 n. 35.

————. "Back to the Army Again" (poem, published in 1894).

The literary tastes of Clemens and his financial savior, Henry H. Rogers, coincided on only a few writers—of whom Kipling was the most notable. When Rogers offered to send Clemens a new Kipling poem, Clemens responded on 9 December 1894: "Kipling *can't* pad. He's always got a line or two at least that saves each piece that he writes. Remember the 'lousy ulster' line in the poem we read [in Chicago] in the 'L'? All by itself it made a good poem out of an indifferent one" (*MTHHR*, p. 102). As first published in the *Pall Mall Magazine* 3 (August 1894): 589–594, the poem began: "I'm 'ere in a lousy ulster an' a broken billycock 'at,/A-layin' on to the Sergeant I don't know a gun from a bat." Kipling changed the phrase that Clemens applauded to "ticky ulster," however, when the poem was collected in *The Seven Seas* (1896).

————. "The Ballad of the 'Bolivar'" (poem, published in 1892).

On 29 February 1908 Clemens read aloud this poem and others by Kipling to Henry H. Rogers, Isabel Lyon, and a small group gathered in his hotel in Bermuda. "We went from shouting joys to tears over the beauties, the perfections," wrote Lyon (IVL Journals, TS p. 306, MTP). Elizabeth Wallace was present at another informal Kipling reading in Bermuda, and she remembered that "we laughed delightedly" at the comic *Bolivar* ballad (*MT&HI* [1913], pp. 97–99).

————. *Barrack-Room Ballads and Other Verses.* Leipzig: Heinemann and Balestier, 1892. 245 pp.

Source: MTLAcc, entry #2040, volume donated from Clemens's library by Clara Clemens Gabrilowitsch in 1910. This collection contains, among other poems, "Danny Deever," "'Fuzzy-Wuzzy,'" "Gunga Din," "'Snarleyow,'" "Mandalay," "The Ballad of East and West," and "The Ballad of the 'Bolivar.'"

————. "The Bell Buoy" (poem, published in 1896).

On 12 October 1903 Clemens thanked Frank N. Doubleday for sending some books; one of these volumes contained Kipling's "The Bell Buoy," which Clemens said he had been reading "over & over again—my custom with Kipling's work." Clemens added that during nights aboard Henry H. Rogers's yacht the *Kanawha* he had listened to the voice of a bell buoy speaking "in his pathetic & melancholy way . . . & I got his meaning—now I have his words! . . . Some day I hope to hear the poem chanted or sung—with the bell-buoy breaking in, out of the distance" (*MTL*, p. 746; ALS in MTP). See other references to this favorite

poem in the following Catalog entries. Baetzhold, *MT&JB* (1970), pp. 189–190.

————. *The Brushwood Boy* (novelette, published in 1895).

In a letter that Clemens wrote to Dorothy Sturgis (later Harding) on 30 September 1908 he alluded to "the Brushwood Boy's seat" at Stormfield (ALS at Columbia University). Dorothy Sturgis Harding would recall that when she visited Stormfield in 1908 she and Clemens "sat on a rock and read aloud to each other, especially Kipling, and we agreed that our favorite story was 'The Brushwood Boy.' From then on we called each other the 'Major' [Georgie Cottar, the Brushwood Boy] and 'Annie-an-Louise' [the girl in Georgie's dreams]" ("Mark Twain Lands an Angel-fish," *Columbia Library Columns* 16 [February 1967]: 8–9).

————. *Collected Verse of Rudyard Kipling.* New York: Doubleday, Page & Co., 1907. 375 pp.

Inscription: the front pastedown endpaper is signed in black ink: "SL. Clemens/Feb. '08/ from Doubleday".

Marginalia: Clemens marked with black ink the titles of poems in the table of contents that appear on pages 19, 24 ("Anchor Song"), 34 ("M'Andrews Hymn"), 45 ("The 'Mary Gloster'"), 53 ("The Ballad of the 'Bolivar'"), 55, 65 ("The Derelict"), 70 ("The Song of Diego Valdez," a title he marked twice for emphasis), 75, 76, 78, 80 ("The Long Trail," marked emphatically), 131 ("When Earth's Last Picture Is Painted"), 136 ("The Ballad of East and West"), 159, 176 ("The Feet of the Young Men"), 194 ("The Bell Buoy"), 208 ("The Wage-Slaves"), 219 ("Recessional"), 220 ("The Three-Decker"), 241 ("Tomlinson"), 252 ("The Last Rhyme of True Thomas"), 261 (both poems—"To Thomas Atkins" and "Danny Deever"), 265 ("Fuzzy-Wuzzy"), 270 ("Cells"), 271 ("Gunga Din"), 274 ("Oonts," about the military use of camels), 281 ("Belts"—describing a violent street brawl between Irish and English regiments), 285 ("Mandalay"), 305 ("'Soldier an' Sailor Too'"), 333 ("'For to Admire'"), 339 ("Chant-Pagan," which Clemens identified by its refrain—the word "ME"), and 341 ("M. I."). It might be noted that in marking these titles he skipped over page 215, "The White Man's Burden." In the text of the poems themselves Clemens merely marked with black ink a phrase ("A whisper in the Void.") that occurs on page 4 in the fifth stanza of "To the True Romance"; perhaps he was thinking of his now-absent wife Olivia, since Kipling's poem implies that all further deeds are pointless because (as the final line reveals) "My Lady is not there!"

Provenance: Antenne-Dorrance Collection, Rice Lake, Wisconsin.

Location: Mark Twain Archive, Gannett Tripp Learning Center, Elmira College, Elmira, New York.

Copy examined: Clemens's copy. Examined on 28 May 2015.

It seems reasonable to surmise that this is the volume of Kipling's verse from which Clemens repeatedly read aloud to groups of vacationing Americans in Bermuda in 1908. "These people had never, never heard anything of the real Kipling before," an admiring Isabel Lyon commented in her journal. Following a reading on March 27th Lyon heard one of the fifteen people present, a Mr. Chamberlain, declare that "there isn't anyone else in the world who could read between the lines as the King can" (IVL Journals, TS p. 313, MTP). Another account of these Kipling readings appears in Elizabeth Wallace's valuable memoir, *Mark Twain and the Happy Island* (1913), pp. 93–100. Wallace, an instructor of French literature and a college dean at the University of Chicago, heard Clemens entertain Henry H. Rogers and other friends in his hotel room in Hamilton on several occasions in March and April 1908. She remembered that Clemens held his pipe in one hand and gesticulated with it during highly dramatic passages. Rogers urged his friend Clemens not to read "too slowly." One of the poems Clemens marked in the table of contents, "The Long Trail," was among the favorites that Wallace later heard Clemens read at Stormfield in 1909, along with the poem titled "The Three-Decker."

———. "The Courting of Dinah Shadd" (short story) in *The Courting of Dinah Shadd and Other Stories*. Intro. by Andrew Lang (1844–1912). New York: Harper & Brothers, 1890. 182 pp. [Edition conjectured.]

Clemens chose this book for the purpose of comparing the costs of typesetting by the Paige machine ($6.50) and those of ordinary printing compositors ($72.50) in January 1891 (NB 30, *N&J* 3: 600).

———. "Danny Deever" (poem, published in 1890). Set to music by Walter Damrosch (cop. 1897).

On 7 [or 8?] February 1894 Clemens reported to Olivia Clemens that he had heard Richard Harding Davis sing "the hanging of Johnny Deever [*sic*], which was of course good" (ALS in MTP). At a benefit for the Mark Twain Library of Redding on 21 September 1909, David Bispham sang this ballad at Clemens's request (Clemens to Elizabeth Wallace, 22 September 1909, *MT&HI* [1913], pp. 131–133). Clemens also liked to read the piece aloud; he listed "Files on Parade" (one of the two voices in the poem; the other is that of the Colour-Sergeant) as a tentative addition to his program for a reading at Bryn Mawr in 1891 (NB 30, *N&J* 3: 605).

———. *The Day's Work* (short stories, first collected in 1898).

Catalog: C1951, D45, listed among the volumes signed by Clemens. (There is no indication as to whether this was the one- or two-volume edition.)

Clemens included the title of this book in a list that he jotted down around 1902 ("Mark Twain's Travel Trunk: An Impromptu Notebook," *Mark Twain Journal* 42.2 [Fall 2004]: 15–18).

———. *The Day's Work*. The Pocket Kipling. Red leather. New York: Doubleday, Page & Co., 1908.

Inscription: the front pastedown endpaper is signed in black ink, "S. L. Clemens/1908 from Doubleday." The cover was also signed "S. L. Clemens/1908."

Location: in 1986 this volume belonged to the collection of A. W. Yeats of Beaumont, Texas (Yeats to Alan Gribben, 17 October 1986).

———. *Departmental Ditties, Barrack-Room Ballads, and Other Verses*. New York: United States Book Co. (successors to John W. Lovell Co.), [cop. 1890]. 270 pp.

Marginalia: Clemens employed pencil to mark several poems for oral interpretation. He underscored words in the third, fourth, and fifth stanzas of "Tommy" (pp. 61–62): "Then," "aren't," "food," "wait," "rations," "treat," "rational." On page 249 he twice altered the word "heaved"

to read "hove" in the fourth stanza of "The Galley-Slave."

Location: Mark Twain Library, Redding, Connecticut. Donated from Clemens's library by Clara Clemens Gabrilowitsch in 1910 (MTLAcc, entry #2039).

Copy examined: Clemens's copy. I discovered this book on the circulating shelves in the Mark Twain Library in September 1970, and I asked the librarian to add it to their collection of volumes from Clemens's personal library. It has the red ink Mark Twain Library accession number "2039". I examined the volume again in June 1982. There is a sticker on the rear pastedown endpaper of a bookstore that the Clemenses often used: "Brown & Gross, Booksellers/Hartford, Ct."

Isabel V. Lyon reported that Clemens sang a song—"There was a row in Silver Street, begod I wonder why"—in the living room in Dublin, New Hampshire on 20 June 1906 "to clear the atmosphere after his morning rage at the [Miss Josephine] Hobby dictation" (IVL Journal, Harry Ransom Center, University of Texas at Austin). A poem in Kipling's *Barrack-Room Ballads*, "Belts," contains that line, "There was a row in Silver Street—begod, I wonder why!" The poem recounts a bloody clash between Irish and English soldiers in Dublin, Ireland: "It started at Revelly an' it lasted on till dark;/The first man dropped at Harrison's, the last forninst [*sic*] the Park." The brawl only ends after a man is killed and arrests ensue (JoDee Benussi recognized this connection; Benussi to Alan Gribben, email, 1 October 2006).

———. *The Five Nations*. New York: Doubleday, Page & Co., 1903. 215 pp.

Inscription: the front flyleaf is inscribed in ink by Clemens: "From/Frank N. Doubleday/to/S L. Clemens./From/S L. Clemens/to/Livy Clemens/with very great love./New York, Oct. 10 '03."

Marginalia: Clemens made marginal marks (one horizontal mark and four vertical marks) beside each of the five stanzas of "The Bell Buoy" that appeared on pages 6 and 7. At the top of page 49 Clemens noted: "There is no sadder sight than a young pessimist. Except an old optimist./M.T."

Catalogs: ListABP (1910), "Five Nations, Kipling"; C1951, #59c, $25, listed among the books signed by Clemens; *American Book-Prices Current Index 1960–1965* (New York, 1968), p. 368, item #64, $80.

Provenance: in 1982 the volume belonged to Mrs. Walter O. Thompson of Turlock, California (letter from Robert H. Hirst to Alan Gribben, 27 August 1982).

Copy examined: photocopy of the inscription and marginalia sent to the Mark Twain Papers, Bancroft Library, on 3 May 1983. The owner of the volume did not wish to be identified. The book has an Ullman bookplate.

On 12 October 1903 Clemens thanked Frank N. Doubleday for sending some books, including one (*Five Nations*) that contained "The Bell Buoy," a poem Clemens declared that he been reading "over & over again" (*MTL*, p. 746; ALS in MTP). Isabel Lyon reported in a diary entry for 28 July 1904 that Richard Watson Gilder visited the Clemens cottage while Clemens, Jean, and Isabel Lyon were playing euchre. "We kept on with our game, and Mr. Gilder read bits of 'Ponkapog Papers' and Kipling's 'Five Seas'" (IVL Journals, TS p. 25, MTP). She may have meant either collection of Kipling's verse, *The Five*

Nations (1903) or *The Seven Seas* (1896). When Clemens became irritated on 4 January 1908, Lyon recorded, "he reached for Kipling's 'Five Seas' [*sic*] and he read aloud, 'The Bell Buoy.' Gradually his mood changed to his sweet naturalness again" (IVL Journals, TS p. 291, MTP). Besides "The Bell Buoy," *Five Nations* collected "The White Man's Burden," "Recessional," and dozens of other poems.

———. *The Five Nations*. New York: Doubleday, Page & Co., 1907. 215 pp.

Source: MTLAcc, entry #197, volume donated by Clemens.

———. "For to Admire" (poem, published in 1894).

In London in 1896 Mark Twain copied down the opening lines from this poem (NB 39, TS p. 26), and he used them in Chapter 62 of *Following the Equator* (1897): "One of Kipling's ballads has delivered the aspect and sentiment of this bewitching sea correctly: 'The Injian Ocean sets an' smiles/So sof', so bright, so bloomin' blue;/ There aren't a wave for miles and miles/Excep' the jiggle from the screw.'" In Twain's 5 December 1905 speech thanking those who attended his Seventieth Birthday dinner at Delmonico's restaurant he paraphrased a few words from this poem, "a time-expired man" (Kipling had written "a time-expired soldier-man") (*MTSpk*, p. 466).

MT&JB (1970), p. 359 n. 29.

———. *From Sea to Sea: Letters of Travel*. 2 vols. Red cloth. London: Macmillan and Co., 1900. Only Volume II (438 pp.) has been located.

Provenance: Antenne-Dorrance Collection, Rice Lake, Wisconsin (Volume II only).

Location: Mark Twain Archive, Gannett Tripp Learning Center, Elmira College, Elmira, New York.

Copy examined: Clemens's unmarked copy of Volume II. Examined on 28 May 2015.

In 1906 Clemens said that Kipling "came over and traveled about America, maintaining himself by correspondence with Indian journals. He wrote dashing, free-handed, brilliant letters but no one outside of India knew about it" (11 August 1906 AD; *MTE*, p. 309; *AutoMT* 2: 175). Clemens was familiar with the portion of Volume II, "An Interview with Mark Twain," that described their first meeting in Elmira in August of 1889. On 15 August 1906 Clemens wrote to Isabel Lyon from Dublin, New Hampshire: "Please look at Kipling's account of his visit to me at Susy Crane's farm, & see if *Mrs. Clemens* as well as Susy Clemens was present" (ALS in MTP).

Fears, *Day by Day* 2: 402–405.

———. *From Sea to Sea: Letters of Travel*. Two vols. in one. New York: Doubleday, Page & Co., 1907.

Source: MTLAcc, entry #196, volume donated by Clemens.

———. "Gunga Din" (poem, published in 1892).

This replaced the customary Robert Browning poem in Mark Twain's program for a public reading at Bryn Mawr in 1891 (NB 30, *N&J* 3: 605). In Chapter 46 of *Following the Equator* (1897) Twain refers to an Indian Thuggee chieftain "who soils a great name borne by a better man—Kipling's deathless 'Gungadin.'"

———. *The Jungle Book* (published in 1894); *The Second Jungle Book* (published in 1895).

Source: according to a note made by Frederick Anderson, the former Editor of the Mark Twain Papers, in 1969 Bigelow Paine Cushman either owned or had previously owned

an 1896 edition of Kipling's novel, a signed copy (MTP).

Mark Twain mentioned an edition of this book ("200 pages") in an unpublished manuscript he wrote in 1898, "The Great Republic's Peanut Stand" (MTP). The Macmillan Company edition (London and New York, 1897; reprinted in 1898) is closest to the pagination that Twain specified.

Planning a tale of child "Creatures of Fiction" in June 1898, Mark Twain noted that "last comes Mogli [*sic*] on elephant with his menagerie & they all rode away with him" (NB 40, TS p. 27). Sometime prior to 15 August 1898 Clemens requested a copy of *The Second Jungle Book* (SLC per Clara Clemens to Chatto & Windus; Berg Collection, New York Public Library; Welland, *Mark Twain in England*, p. 189). Isabel Lyon's journal for 17 March 1905 reveals that Clemens had written a new story about an Admiral with a cat named Bagheera (TS p. 44, MTP). This tale became Twain's long-unpublished "The Refuge of the Derelicts" (DV309a, MTP). In Chapter 2 of "The Refuge of the Derelicts" the Admiral takes down a volume from his book shelves (a book with a "brown back") and quotes Kipling's description of Bagheera the black panther from Volume VII of Kipling's *Collected Works*. The Admiral declares that *The Jungle Books* are "immortal" and will "outlast the rocks" (*FM*, pp. 173–174). On 30 May 1906 Clemens read aloud to his household "from the first Jungle book" before going to bed (IVL Journal, TS p. 161, MTP). Isabel Lyon noted again on 7 June 1906, also in Dublin, New Hampshire: "Evenings Mr. Clemens reads aloud to us. The Jungle Books now" (TS p. 163, MTP). "The incomparable Jungle Books must remain unfellowed permanently," Clemens said in an Autobiographical Dictation of 13 August 1906 (*MTE*, p. 312; *AutoMT* 2: 177). The Mark Twain Papers at Berkeley contain a bill addressed to Clemens from G. P. Putnam's Sons, New York City, for a purchase Clemens made on 4 March 1909: "1 Jungle Book" and "1 Second Jungle Book"; Clemens paid the bill on 10 April 1909. Subsequently Mark Twain utilized Baloo the bear and Hathi the elephant in his "A Fable," published in the December 1909 issue of *Harper's Magazine*. Elizabeth Wallace recalled that Clemens once declared "we were all Bander-log" (*MTHI*, Ch. 2). At some point Twain scrawled the word "bandar-log" in his copy of Saint-Simon's *Memoires* (Vol. II, Chapter 32) to express his disdain for the Duc d'Orleans's stupidity.

MT&JB (1970), pp. 191–192.

———. *Just So Stories for Little Children*. Illustrated by the author. New York: Doubleday, Page & Co., 1902. 249 pp.

Inscription: Clemens wrote in black ink on the front pastedown endpaper (the first word only is in pencil): "For/ Olivia L. Clemens/1902/from SLC".

Catalog: *C1951*, D38, listed among books signed by Clemens, $27.50.

Provenance: part of the Mark Twain collection assembled by Frank C. Willson (1889–1960) of Melrose, Massachusetts. His widow sold that collection to the University of Texas in 1962.

Location: Harry Ransom Center, University of Texas at Austin.

Copy examined: Olivia Clemens's unmarked copy. Contains a *C1951* sale label.

———. *Kim*. Illustrated with photographic plates. 8vo, original pictorial green cloth, gilt. Rebacked, preserving much of original spine. Green cloth folding-case. New York: Doubleday, Page & Co., 1901. 463 pp.

Inscriptions: the front free endpaper is signed "S L. Clemens/Riverdale/Nov. 1901." The half-title page is signed identically. The lower third of the half-title page is missing. The front pastedown endpaper is signed "S L. Clemens (Reading this great book for the sixth time. May, 1906.)" Clara Clemens Gabrilowitsch inscribed the verso of the front free endpaper to "The Westminster College Library, on the solicitation of Chas. B. Boving, President, for a book that had been her Father's. July 1913." A bookplate of Westminster College, Fulton, Missouri, has been placed over Clara's longer inscription.

Marginalia: Clemens made minor corrections to Kipling's vocabulary or grammar on eight pages: 25, 85, 86, 111, 173, 197, 266, 443. The upper corners of many pages are creased from having been folded down.

Provenance: MTLAcc, entry #194, volume donated by Clemens. Apparently retrieved from the Mark Twain Library by Clara Clemens Gabrilowitsch and presented to a college library in 1913. Eventually it was obtained by Nick Karanovich, Fort Wayne, Indiana.

Catalogs: Waverly Auctions, Sale 109, 3 March 1994, lot 193, suggested price $1,000–1,500; *Sotheby's 2003*, #218, $7,500.

Location: currently unknown.

Copy examined: Clemens's copy, at the 2003 Sotheby's sale.

———. *Kim*. New York: Doubleday, Page & Co., 1908. 463 pp. Half title: The Pocket Kipling.

Inscription: the front cover of soft red leather is signed in black ink, "SL. Clemens/ 1908." The front pastedown endpaper is signed in black ink, "SL. Clemens/1908/from Doubleday."

Marginalia: in Chapter 4 (p. 112) Clemens revised with black ink the phrase "I should have rendered thee some service" so that it reads "I render thee some service." On page 197 of Chapter 7 he corrected "herd-hunters" to "head-hunters," also with black ink.

Catalogs: ListABP (1910), "Kim, Kipling"; *C1951*, item D13; resold by Glen Dawson's Bookshop of Los Angeles in 1952.

Location: Harry Ransom Center, University of Texas at Austin. Donated in 1952 by Ed W. Owen of San Antonio, Texas, who acquired it from Dawson's Bookshop.

Copy examined: Clemens's copy.

"I think it was worth the journey to India to qualify myself to read 'Kim' understandingly and to realize how great a book it is," Clemens announced in an Autobiographical Dictation of 13 August 1906. "The deep and subtle and fascinating charm of India pervades no other book as it pervades Kim. . . . I read the book every year" (*MTE*, p. 312; *MTAuto* 2: 177).

———. *Kipling in Black and White*. India Railroad Library Series, Number 3. Allabad: A. H. Wheeler & Co.; London: Sampson, Low, Marston, Searle and Rivington, [1888]. 96 pp. [Edition conjectured.]

Catalog: ListABP (1910), "In Black and White", no other information supplied.

Mark Twain mentioned Kipling's writings several times in Chapter 54 of *Following the Equator* (1897) in discussing readers' and tourists' impressions of India.

———. *Life's Handicap*. The Pocket Kipling. Red leather. New York: Doubleday, Page & Co., 1908.

Inscription: the front cover is inscribed "S. L. Clemens."

Location: in 1986 this volume was in the collection of A. W. Yeats, Beaumont, Texas.

Source: letter from Yeats to Alan Gribben, 17 October 1986.

———. *The Light That Failed*. New York: National Publishing Co., 1890. 186 pp.

Source: MTLAcc, entry #981, volume donated by Albert Bigelow Paine, Clemens's designated biographer. Clemens very possibly saw this book, since the men exchanged reading materials.

———. *The Light That Failed*. Blue cloth. London: Macmillan and Co., 1899. 339 pp.

Inscription: inscribed in black ink on the front free endpaper: "Jean Lampton Clemens/14 West 10th St./New York City./Christmas, 1900,/from Julie."

Provenance: Antenne-Dorrance Collection, Rice Lake, Wisconsin.

Location: Mark Twain Archive, Gannett-Tripp Learning Center, Elmira College, Elmira, New York.

Copy examined: Jean Clemens's unmarked copy. Examined on 28 May 2015.

After Susy's death, Clemens wrote to Olivia Clemens from Guildford on 26 August 1896: "I am alone with my memories of the Light that Failed" (*LLMT*, p. 325). For a planned biography of Susy, Clemens thought of beginning: "This is the history of a promise—a Light that Failed" (NB39 [London, January 1897], TS p. 58).

———. *The Light That Failed*. Revised ed. The Pocket Kipling. Red leather with Ganesha device in gold on the front cover. New York: Doubleday, Page & Co., 1908.

Inscription: signed in black ink on the front cover, "S. L. Clemens/1908."

Marginalia: brief marginalia on page 252.

Location: Harry Ransom Center, University of Texas at Austin.

Source: letter from A. W. Yeats to Alan Gribben, Beaumont, Texas, 17 October 1986. A. W. Yeats was instrumental in building up the Kipling collection at the University of Texas at Austin while doing his doctoral studies under Harry Ransom (and later under William B. Todd). Yeats obtained this book for Ransom's collection as a donation after it was sold (between 1955 and 1959) by Dawson's Bookshop in Los Angeles.

———. "Mandalay" (poem, published in 1890).

On 7 [or 8?] February 1894 Clemens wrote from New York City to Olivia, then in Paris, telling her he heard Richard Harding Davis sing "that most fascinating (for what reason I don't know) of all Kipling's poems, 'On the Road to Mandalay,' sang it tenderly, & it searched me deeper & charmed me more than the [Danny] Deever" (ALS in MTP). In a newspaper interview of 1895 Mark Twain singled out "Mandalay" as a "poem of mingled pathos and humour [which] had the aroma of the Orient, the sound of the sea on the sand and the breezes among the palms in it" ("Mark Twain Put to the Question," Adelaide *South Australian Register*, Scrapbook #26, p. 121, MTP; Scharnhorst, *Complete Interviews*, p. 236).

———. *Many Inventions*. New York: D. Appleton & Co., 1893. 427 pp.

Source: MTLAcc, entry #2303, volume donated from Clemens's library by Clara Clemens Gabrilowitsch in 1910. In a letter postmarked in Franzenbad, Germany on 3 September 1893 Susy Clemens queried her college friend Louise Brownell: "Have you seen Kipling's last book 'Many Inventions'? It doesn't disappoint. What a vigorous manly spirit he is!" Susy then paraphrased the last sentence of a story appearing in *Many Inventions*, "The Children of the Zodiac": "I am keeping the motto of his last story [actually it is the next to last story in the collection] before my mind, 'Whatever comes or does not come we must not be afraid.' I wish I could learn that" (Hamilton College Archives).

———. *Many Inventions*. New York: Doubleday, Page & Co., 1908. 427 pp.

Location: Mark Twain Library, Redding, Connecticut. Donated by Clemens (MTLAcc, entry #198).

Copy examined: Clemens's copy, unmarked. Has the red ink Mark Twain Library accession number "198". Examined in 1970 and again in June 1982.

———. "The 'Mary Gloster'" (poem, published in 1896).

Elizabeth Wallace, who witnessed one of Clemens's informal Kipling readings in Bermuda in 1908, recalled in *Mark Twain and the Happy Island* (1914) that even the hard-boiled Henry H. Rogers "blinked hard" to suppress tears when Clemens read the most successful poem, "The *Mary Gloster*."

———. *Mine Own People*. Intro. by Henry James (1843–1916). New York: George Munro's Sons, 1896. 108 pp. Paperbound.

Source: MTLAcc, entry #200, volume donated by Albert Bigelow Paine, Clemens's designated biographer. Possibly Clemens saw this book, since the men often exchanged reading materials. In any event Clemens had already known of the collection of short stories—which included "Bimi," "The Incarnation of Krishna Mulvaney," "The Man Who Was," and "At the End of the Passage"—since he wrote to Andrew Chatto on 8 July1891 to request "Kipling's last book, . . .—the book 'Mine Own People'" (American Art Association/Anderson Galleries Catalog, 17 November 1936, item #353).

———. "The Naulahka" (poem), one of the group titled "Chapter Headings."

Albert Bigelow Paine (*MTB*, p. 1502) described how Clemens picked out this verse in the *Saturday Times Review*. "I could stand any amount of that," he said, referring to the lines, "Now it is not good for the Christian's health to hustle the Aryan brown,/For the Christian riles and the Aryan smiles and he weareth the Christian down;/And the end of the fight is a tombstone white with the name of the late deceased,/And the epitaph drear: 'A fool lies here who tried to hustle the East.'"

———. *The Naulahka, A Story of West and East. Written in Collaboration with Wolcott Balestier [1861–1891]*. New York: Doubleday, Page & Co., 1907. 379 pp.

Source: MTLAcc, entry #199, volume donated by Clemens.

———. "The Old Men" (poem, published in 1902).

On 12 October 1903 Clemens thanked Frank N. Doubleday for some books, adding, "I have been reading 'The Bell Buoy' & 'The Old Men' over & over again. . . . 'The Old

Men,' delicious, isn't it? And so comically true. I haven't arrived there yet, [but] I suppose I am on the way" (*MTL*, p. 746; ALS in MTP). When we are aged men, Kipling wrote, "We shall peck out and discuss and dissect, and evert and extrude to our mind,/The flaccid tissues of long-dead issues offensive to God and mankind—/. . . . And whatever we do, we shall fold our hands and suck our gums and think well of it."

———. *The Phantom 'Rickshaw, and Other Tales*. New York: M. J. Ivers & Co., 1890. 207 pp.

Source: MTLAcc, entry #2306, volume donated from Clemens's library by Clara Clemens Gabrilowitsch in 1910. The supernatural tale of "The Phantom 'Rickshaw" related how a man was regarded as mentally ill after he became haunted by a former lover, deceased, whom he had jilted.

———. *Plain Tales from the Hills*. Unabridged ed. New York: M. J. Ivers & Co., 1890. 208 pp.

Source: MTLAcc, entry #2305, volume donated from Clemens's library by Clara Clemens Gabrilowitsch in 1910. Clemens thought that he did not begin reading Kipling's prose until around September 1890; that was when he wrote to Mary E. Keller (1860–1946): "I have just found out that whereas Kipling's stories are plenty good enough on a first reading they very greatly improve on a second" (12 September 1890, ALS in MTHM). In 1895 Clemens declared, "I have devoured what Rudyard Kipling has written. He is wonderful" ("Mark Twain in Sydney: A Further Interview," Melbourne *Argus*, 17 September 1895; Scharnhorst, *Complete Interviews*, p. 203). A few months later, during a different interview published in several Indian newspapers on 23 January 1896 and subsequently, Clemens averred, "I have an amazing fondness for his *Plain Tales*, and I think that some of his ballad work is inimitable" (*Complete Interviews*, p. 276). Surveying English literature in an 1897 newspaper interview in Vienna, Clemens said he considered Kipling to be one of the "good and splendid" contemporary authors (Odessa *News* [Odesskie *Novosti*], 8 October 1897; translated and reprinted by M. Thomas Inge and George Munro, "Ten Minutes with Mark Twain," *American Literary Realism* 15.2 [Autumn 1982]: 262).

At the dinner table on 18 September 1905 Clemens told the story of George Warner's introducing him to the wonderful *Plain Tales* in 1890 (IVL Journals, TS p. l00a, MTP), an anecdote that he repeated in an Autobiographical Dictation of 13 August 1906: "The little book was the 'Plain Tales,' and he left it for me to read, saying it was charged with a new and inspiriting fragrance and would blow a refreshing breath around the world that would revive the nations" (*MTE*, pp. 311–312; *AutoMT* 2: 177). Albert Bigelow Paine gave this same version of Clemens's encounter with *Plain Tales* (*MTB*, p. 881). Twice Clemens alluded to Terence Mulvaney, a literary character who first appeared in Kipling's "The Three Musketeers" in *Plain Tales* (though he also figured in other Kipling stories)—in a letter of 16 June 1906 to Charlotte Teller (ALS in Berg Collection), and in a notebook entry of 1910 (NB 49, TS p. 5).

———. *Plain Tales from the Hills*. New York: National Publishing Co., [1890?]. 287 pp.

Source: MTLAcc, entry #982, volume donated by Albert

Bigelow Paine, Clemens's designated biographer. Possibly Clemens saw this book, since the men frequently exchanged reading materials.

———. *Puck of Pook's Hill.* Illustrated by Arthur Rackham (1867–1939). New York: Doubleday, Page & Co., 1906. 277 pp.

Source: MTLAcc, entry #195, volume donated by Clemens. Isabel Lyon took a copy to Clemens on 1 June 1907, and he fancied he saw in it resemblances to parts of his "Mysterious Stranger" manuscripts (IVL Journals, 2 June 1907, TS p. 248, MTP).

———. *Puck of Pook's Hill.* The Pocket Kipling. Red leather. New York: Doubleday, Page & Co., 1909.

Inscription: the front leather cover is signed "S. L. Clemens/1910."

Provenance: in 1986 this volume was in the collection of A. W. Yeats, Beaumont, Texas.

Location: Special Collections, Cushing Memorial Library, Texas A & M University, College Station, Texas.

Source: letter from Yeats to Alan Gribben, 17 October 1986; Cushing Memorial Library and Archives online website, 17 February 2007 (the latter information was forwarded to Alan Gribben by JoDee Benussi).

———. "Recessional" (poem, published in 1897).

On 21 January 1901 Clemens wrote to William Thomas Stead, editor of *Review of Reviews*, to request a copy of a poem that Clemens called "Lest we forget" (ALS in CWB). Four of the five stanzas of "Recessional" conclude with variants of that refrain: "Lord God of Hosts, be with us yet,/Lest we forget—lest we forget!"

———. "Red Dog" (short story, published in 1895).

On the evening of 11 June 1906 Clemens "read aloud" to his household and a neighbor the Mowgli short story "Red Dog," and praised Kipling's diction in picturing the python, Kaa ("the light seemed to go out of his eyes and leave them like stale opals" was Kipling's phrase). "'Stale opals'—*such* a good description, he said" (IVL Journals, TS p. 164, MTP). Carlyle Smythe, one of Clemens's companions during his lecture tour of 1895–96, had reported in 1898 that Clemens "reads Kipling as much for style as for subject" ("The Real 'Mark Twain,'" p. 31).

———. *The Seven Seas.* Second American edition. Original apricot decorated cloth, gilt, top edge gilt, uncut. New York: D. Appleton and Co., 1896.

Inscription: the front free paper is inscribed by Jervis Langdon (1875–1952) to Clemens's sister-in-law Susan Crane (1836–1924): "I hope that you may have as happy a Christmas as you have tried to make for so many others. From Jervis. 1896."

Marginalia: eight poems are marked in pencil in the Contents, and several of these are dog-eared in the text. No other markings. None of the markings appear to be by Clemens.

Location: collection of Kevin Mac Donnell, Austin, Texas. Acquired in May 2016 (email, Mac Donnell to Alan Gribben, 16 May 2016).

Source: detailed description of the volume sent on 9 June 2016 by Mac Donnell to Gribben.

The twenty-nine poems collected in *The Seven Seas* related to England's domination of the oceans. This volume would have been accessible to Clemens at Quarry Farm.

———. *The Seven Seas.* New York: D. Appleton and Co., 1897.

Catalogs: QF Martinez, "very good condition"; Ball 2016 inventory, gray cloth, gold lettering, gilt top page edges, rough cut pages, ownership indications of Jervis Langdon and Eleanor Sayles Langdon

This volume was available to Clemens at the Langdons' home in Elmira.

———. "Soldier an' Sailor Too" (poem, published in 1896). Subtitle: "(The Royal Regiment of Marines)."

Mark Twain quotes two lines from the poem in his "Was the World Made for Man?" (DV12, MTP), written in 1903; the Pterodacty, he says there, is "a kind of a giddy harumfrodite—soldier an' sailor too!" (*WIM?*, p. 105). He jotted down three words from its text in Notebook 48—"harumfrodite," "cosmopolouse," and "procrastitute" (TS p. 18). Isabel Lyon recorded that on 26 March 1908 Clemens entertained Henry H. Rogers and other friends by reading aloud from Kipling's poetry. "He was never in better spirit—never in a completer understanding," she noted. His rendition of "Soldier an' Sailor Too," Lyon averred, was "a thing never again to be repeated" (IVL Journals, TS p. 313, MTP).

———. *Soldier Stories.* New York: International Book and Publishing Co., 1899. 203 pp.

Source: MTLAcc, entry #2307, volume donated from Clemens's library by Clara Clemens Gabrilowitsch in 1910.

———. "They" (short story, published in 1904).

In the course of a luncheon on 28 January 1907 Isabel Lyon showed Clemens a copy of "They" in book form. "He read it aloud as we sat at the table," she wrote, "and he was deeply moved by its beauty and by the last part of it especially" (IVL Journals, TS p. 222, MTP). Kipling's tender ghost tale relates how a motorist is briefly allowed to reunite with his deceased daughter at a mysterious house in the country.

———. "Tommy," more popularly known as "To Thomas Atkins" (poem, published in 1890). Subtitle: "Prelude to Barrack-Room Ballads."

In February 1891 Mark Twain considered using this poem in his public reading at Bryn Mawr (NB 30, *N&J* 3: 605). "Those barrack-room ballads were true to life," he told a newspaper reporter in 1895. "There had been nothing like them written before. For example, that one of Tommy Atkins," and Twain quoted from the second stanza of the poem, which concludes, "For it's Tommy this and Tommy that, and Tommy wait outside,/But it's special train for Atkins when the trooper's on the tide." Twain added, "In all Kipling's work there was genuine feeling" ("Mark Twain Put to the Question," Adelaide *South Australian Register*, 14 October 1895; Scharnhorst, *Complete Interviews*, p. 236). "Certain of the ballads have a peculiar and satisfying charm for me," Twain said in his Autobiographical Dictation for 13 August 1906 (*MTE*, p. 312; *AutoMT* 2: 177)—though he did not name any titles.

———. *Traffics and Discoveries.* London: Macmillan & Co., 1904. 393 pp.

Source: MTLAcc, entry #2304, volume donated from Clemens's library by Clara Clemens Gabrilowitsch in 1910. Collects eleven short stories, including "The Captive," "They," and "The Army of a Dream."

———. *Traffics and Discoveries.* The Pocket Kipling. Red

leather. New York: Doubleday, Page & Co., 1909.

> **Inscription:** the front cover is signed "S. L. Clemens/1910."
>
> **Location:** in 1986 this volume belonged to A. W. Yeats of Beaumont, Texas.
>
> **Source:** letter from A. W. Yeats to Alan Gribben, 17 October 1986.

————. *The Writings in Prose and Verse of Rudyard Kipling.* Outward Bound Edition. 36 volumes. [Only the first twenty-four volumes were published during Clemens's lifetime, and only eighteen were in print by the time Clemens received this set in December 1900]. Original cloth with maroon spines, gilt, uncut. New York: Charles Scribner's Sons, 1899–1937. This was the first authorized collected edition of Kipling.

> **Inscription:** Volume VI (1899) was inscribed by Clemens in ink on the front free endpaper: "S L. Clemens/14 West 10th St./1901." That volume contains *Under the Deodars, The Story of the Gadsbys,* and *Wee Willie Winkie.* Clara Clemens's library shelfmark ("F/Ls24") appears in pencil on the front pastedown endpaper, which also bears a penciled notation ("D-2") corresponding with a Kipling set offered at the Hollywood auction in 1951.
>
> **Marginalia:** Clemens made a marginal pencil mark on page 19 in Volume VI next to a passage describing how one woman's voice sounded like "an Underground train coming into Earl's Court with the brakes on." In the upper left margin of page 308 in that volume Clemens wrote "7:10" (possibly the hour when he stopped reading?) in pencil.
>
> **Provenance:** Volumes II, VI, XIV, and XVIII bear Clara Clemens Gabrilowitsch's penciled shelf markings from the library numbering system she employed during her Detroit years.
>
> **Catalog:** *C1951,* D2 ("The Works of Rudyard Kipling, 18 volumes," clearly a broken set, no edition specified), $37, includes *Plain Tales from the Hills; Soldiers Three and Military Tales, Parts I and II; In Black and White; The Phantom 'Rickshaw; Under the Deodars and Other Stories; The Jungle Book; The Second Jungle Book; The Light That Failed* (two copies listed); *The Naulahka; Verses, 1889–1896; Captains Courageous; The Day's Work, Parts I and II; From Sea to Sea, Parts I and II; Early Verse; Stalky & Co. & Co.* Another lot sold at the Hollywood auction, D13 ("Rudyard Kipling, 9 vols., leather bound," no edition specified), $72, includes *Abaft the Funnel; Puck of Pook's Hill; Many Inventions; Actions and Reactions; Traffics and Discoveries; Life's Handicaps; The Day's Work, Parts I and II;* and *Kim.* Both lots (D2 and D13) were listed among the books signed by Clemens.
>
> **Location:** four volumes of the Outward Bound Edition were acquired by Kevin Mac Donnell of Austin, Texas in 2007 and 2008. These were Volume VI (described above, 1899), Volume II (*Soldiers Three and Military Tales, Part I,* 1899), Volume XIV (*The Day's Work, Part II,* 1899), and Volume XVIII (*Stalky & Co.,* 1899).
>
> **Source:** letters from Kevin Mac Donnell to Alan Gribben, 21 November 2007 and 25 June 2008, plus an email from Mac Donnell to Gribben, 26 September 2013. Mac Donnell obtained these remnants of a broken set from a man whose grandmother had purchased them at the 1951 Hollywood auction. The four surviving volumes were mildew damaged and Mac Donnell had to have

them professionally washed and stabilized.

On 3 December 1900 New York attorney Augustus T. Gurlitz, who was advising both Kipling and Clemens about protecting their copyrighted works against pirating American publishers, sent Clemens an authorized set of Kipling published by Charles Scribner's as well as an unauthorized set issued by New York publisher R. F. Fenno so that Clemens could compare them: "I thank you quite immeasurably for the Kipling set," Clemens responded on that same day, 3 December 1900, adding that Gurlitz could request the return of "the Fenno lot—whenever you need it" (ALS quoted in "Mark Twain," Heritage Bookshop, Los Angeles, 1997, item #131). Kipling himself wrote Clemens a warm letter on 6 May 1901 thanking him for his support for authors' rights against pirate publishers and for "chasing Fenno through the swampy ground of the Law" (ALS, sold by Christie's, New York City, 1–2 February 1988 auction, lot 474). Of Kipling's writings in general, Clemens once said: "I know them better than I know anybody else's books. They never grow pale to me; they keep their color; they are always fresh" (13 August 1906 AD, *MTE,* p. 312; *AutoMT* 2: 177). Indeed, every kind of evidence indicates his unstinting esteem for Kipling. Clemens's housekeeper Katy Leary recalled that "Mr. Clemens used to love to read him; he used to read aloud from Kipling and right up to the end, just before he died, he had a book of Kipling's that he read from" (*LMT* [1925], p. 161).

Mark Twain complimented Kipling very notably in a speech delivered to the Associated Press in New York City on 19 September 1906. Worldwide members of the press, began Twain, "speak with a million voices; no one can reach so many races, so many hearts and intellects, as you—except Rudyard Kipling, and he cannot do it without your help" (*MTSpk,* p. 522). Clemens told Isabel Lyon that he could understand and appreciate Kipling's viewpoint, for Kipling's training "makes him cling to his early beliefs; then he loves power and authority and Kingship—and that has to show itself in his religion" (IVL Journal, 22 January 1907, TS p. 220, MTP). In 1909 Clemens told the Allen family in Bermuda that "he was always fond of fine-sounding words. . . . Kipling's coinage of words was a delight to him" (Marion Schuyler Allen, "Some New Anecdotes of Mark Twain," *Strand Magazine* [London] 46.272 [August 1913]: 169).

Paine, *MTB* (1912), pp. 1208, 1440, 1540; *MTE* (1940), pp. 54–55, 309; Scott, *OPMT* (1966), p. 24 (merely mentioned Kipling); Baetzhold, *MT&JB* (1970), pp. 187–195 (a careful treatment of the Clemens-Kipling relationship); Angus Wilson, *The Strange Ride of Rudyard Kipling: His Life and Works* (London: Secker & Warburg, 1977) (described Kipling's lifelong admiration of Twain's writings); Leland Krauth, *Mark Twain & Company: Six Literary Relations* (Athens: University of Georgia Press, 2003)—a thoughtful and nuanced discussion of what Kipling meant to Twain; Gregg Camfield, "In the Mirror of the Imagination: Mark Twain's Kipling," *Arizona Quarterly* 61.1 (Spring 2005): 85–107 (included a lengthy analysis of Kipling's "The White Man's Burden"). Louis J. Budd reported to Alan Gribben that Mark Twain mentioned Kipling in the following interviews with reporters:

Minneapolis *Times*, 24 July 1895, p. 2; Melbourne *Argus*, 17 September 1895, p. 5; Melbourne *Age*, 27 September 1895, p. 6; Adelaide *South Australian Register*, 14 October 1895; Durban, Republic of South Africa *Weekly Natal Mercury*, 8 May 1896, p. 5989, also called *Natal Mercury* and reprinted in the *Natal Witness*, 9 May 1896, and the *Pretorian Press*, 15 May 1896, p. 3.

————. *The Writings in Prose and* Verse *of Rudyard Kipling*. 36 vols. New York: Charles Scribner's Sons, 1898. [Complete set published 1898–1926. Scribner's imprinted these sets with different dates as the series progressed; in this set Volume I is dated 1898.]

> **Marginalia:** Volume I contains pencil marks on page 99 next to a passage about Joan of Arc, a fact noticed by Susan K. Harris. (The volume was thereupon transferred to the Mark Twain Archive.)
>
> **Catalog:** Ball 2016 inventory, twelve volumes only, red cloth, gilt lettering, gilt top page edges, rough cut side and bottom pages, embossed gold elephant and swastika motif on the front covers, from the library of Jervis Langdon and Eleanor Sayles Langdon.
>
> **Locations:** Volume I only is in the Mark Twain Archive, Gannett-Tripp Learning Center, Elmira College, Elmira, New York; the other eleven volumes are on the Quarry Farm library shelves, under the supervision of the Mark Twain Archive, Elmira College, Elmira, New York.
>
> Clemens could have seen this set during his final visits to the Langdons' residence in Elmira.

KIRBY, WILLIAM (1817–1906). *The Golden Dog (Le chien d'or). A Romance of the Days of Louis Quinze in Quebec*. Illus. Boston: L. C. Page & Co., 1900. 624 pp. [Publisher conjectured.]

> **Inscription:** signed "Clemens, 1902."
>
> **Catalog:** *A1911*, "12mo, wrappers, Bost. 1900," quotes the signature, lot 275, sold for $1.

————. [An identical (or same?) copy.]

> **Source:** MTLAcc, entry #2308, volume donated from Clemens's library by Clara Clemens Gabrilowitsch in 1910.

KIRBY, WILLIAM EGMONT (1867–1925). *Insects: Foes and Friends*. Adapted from the German. Preface by W[illiam]. F[orsell]. Kirby (1844–1912). Illus. London: S. W. Partridge & Co., 1898. 138 pp.

> **Source:** MTLAcc, entry #1962, volume donated from Clemens's library by Clara Clemens Gabrilowitsch in 1910; subsequently lost, according to the library files.

KIRK, ELLEN WARNER (OLNEY) (1842–1928), pseud. "Henry Hayes." *The Story of Margaret Kent*. Boston: Houghton Mifflin Co., Riverside Press Cambridge, 1886. 444 pp.

> In January 1888 Clemens made notes about a misunderstanding between publishers regarding the rights for publication of this book (NB 27, *N&J* 3: 366). The *Story of Margaret Kent*, by far Kirk's most popular novel, went through dozens of editions. A young writer and her daughter Gladys struggle financially in New York City after her husband deserts her. Several men court Margaret, supposing her to be a widow, which presents her with a moral quandary.

KIRK, JAMES PRIOR (1851–1922), pseud. "James Prior." *Forest Folk* (novel, published in 1901).

> On 6 January 1905 Clemens requested Isabel Lyon to search his library for *Letters of Robert E. Lee* "and a book by Mr. Prior. I haven't seen either of them" (IVL Journals, TS p.

36, MTP). The most logical candidate for this missing volume would be James Prior's third novel, *Forest Folk* (1901), his most popular work. Prior, who was born in Nottingham and lived most of his life in Bingham, was sometimes called "The Thomas Hardy of the Midlands." His *Forest Folk*, set in the Luddite years, featured a female character who had traits of the New Woman, an emerging type in British fiction.

KIRK, JOHN FOSTER (1824–1904). *History of Charles the Bold, Duke of Burgundy*. Portraits and map. 3 vols. Philadelphia: J. B. Lippincott & Co., 1864–68.

> **Catalog:** *A1911*, "3 vols., 8vo, half calf, Phila. 1864," quotes a sheet titled "Grant Interview" laid in, lot 276, sold for $3.50.
>
> Mark Twain refers to the "unspeakable atrocities" of Charles the Bold in Chapter 27 of *The Innocents Abroad* (1869).

KIRKHAM, SAMUEL (1796–1843). *English Grammar in Familiar Lectures, Accompanied by a Compendium; Embracing a New Systematick Order of Parsing, a New System of Punctuation, Exercises in False Syntax, and a System of Philosophical Grammar in Notes: To Which Are Added an Appendix, and a Key to the Exercises: Designed for the Use of Schools and Private Learners*. 105th Ed. Baltimore: Brown paper boards. John Plaskitt, 1835. 228 pp.

> **Inscriptions:** several signatures in pencil and ink, sometimes traced in both media. Two on the front free endpaper read "Saml Clemens/Hannibal, Mo." and "Sammy Clemens/Hannibal, Mo." Another appears on the rear pastedown endpaper: "Sam Clemenses/Book".
>
> **Marginalia:** someone has written other names near the Clemens signatures—"John Bowman," "Lucian Gray," and "Lucien Grays Book" A pencil sketch on the front pastedown endpaper depicts the "TEECHER" threatening an angelic "SAMMY" (over whose head a halo hovers) with a rod. Someone has made a pencil note at the top of the front free endpaper: "I promise to pay $[?] Smith & Co".
>
> **Catalog:** San Francisco Art Gallery, Sale catalogue 21–22 May [no year provided], "calf, Baltimore, 1835. This book owned by Samuel Clemens (Mark Twain) with his signature and letter stating the facts of the book, signed and notarized," lot 513, sold for $18.
>
> **Provenance:** the authenticity and provenance of this volume have been in doubt since its first sale. A notarized letter laid in the volume attests that this copy of Kirkham's *English Grammar* was discovered by a construction worker, Charles Lange, during the remodeling of an old printing office storeroom in La Crosse, Wisconsin. Lange's son, Edward Harving Lange, sold the book to Glen Dawson Bookshop of Los Angeles; the notarized letter, which Charles Lange also signed, was sworn there on 17 March 1923. The younger Lange affirmed in the letter that he had owned the book "for five or six years" and that he had added no notes to it during the time it was in his possession. Lange wrote that the diary of William Yarrington, a printer's apprentice who worked for an employer named Ament in 1875, was found in the same place; an entry in the diary mentions that "Mr. Ament has given me some books on composition which I will make use of if I have time."
>
> **Location:** Mark Twain Papers, Bancroft Library, University of California at Berkeley. Donated in May 1964 by Warren

R. Howell of John Howell Books in San Francisco. A letter of 14 May 1964 from Howell to Frederick Anderson, then Editor of the Mark Twain Papers, is laid in the book.

Copy examined: the volume seems to merit acceptance as one of young Clemens's school textbooks, though one wishes for additional corroboration of its authenticity. True, Clemens once worked in the Hannibal newspaper office of Joseph P. Ament. In 1875 Ament was the city mayor of Muscatine, Iowa, where he and his brother were in business together (information supplied by Ralph Gregory [1909–2015], author of "Joseph P. Ament—Master Printer to Sam Clemens," *Mark Twain Journal* 18.2 [Summer 1976]: 1–4). But the sketch of Clemens and the "TEECHER" seems almost too perfect from a twenty-first-century perspective—the kind of thing that people would expect him to have drawn as a child. And Clemens was not known to use "Sammy" as a form of his name, though anything is presumably possible in schoolroom doodling. The larger fact remains that Clemens remembered his youthful struggles with a copy of Kirkham's *English Grammar*. Moreover, a motiveless forgery in 1923 (the book brought only a few dollars, despite the notarized letter) seems an improbable deed to perpetrate merely for creating a spurious association copy.

There is a slight chance that Samuel Kirkham might have visited Hannibal during Clemens's boyhood following the first publication of *English Grammar in Familiar Lectures* in 1825. Kirkham initially made tours lecturing on grammar and elocution, but beginning in 1838 he switched to lecturing on phrenology and examining heads professionally. In this practice "he was very successful financially, principally at [sic] the South" (Charlotte Fowler Wells, "Sketches of Phrenological Biography," *The Phrenological Journal and Science of Health* 96.5 [November 1893]: 249).

In Chapter 23 of Mark Twain's *A Tramp Abroad* (1880) the character named Harris claims that he recalls "doubled-up have's" and other grammatical lapses in Kirkham's renowned book. While vacationing in Bermuda, Twain referred to Kirkham's *English Grammar* as one of the "schoolbooks" popular "fifty or sixty years ago" in an Autobiographical Dictation of 6 January 1907 (*AutoMT* 2: 360). Albert Bigelow Paine testified that during this 1907 visit to Bermuda with Joseph H. Twichell, Clemens recalled "Kirkham's Grammar" as one of the schoolbooks of his youth (*MTB*, p. 1376).

KIRKMAN, MARSHALL MONROE (1842–1921). *The Romance of Gilbert Holmes: An Historical Novel*. Chicago: The World Railway Publishing Co., 1900. 425 pp.

Inscription: the front free endpaper is signed in pencil, carelessly: "Clemens/1902".

Catalog: *A1911*, "12mo, cloth, Chicago, 1900," quotes the signature, lot 277, sold for $1.70[?].

Location: Beinecke Rare Book and Manuscript Library, Yale University. A bookplate on the rear flyleaf indicates that Walter Francis Frear and Mary E. Dillingham Frear donated the volume in 1942.

Copy examined: Clemens's copy, unmarked, in 1970. Many leaves are unopened. An *A1911* label is affixed to the front pastedown endpaper.

This novel opens on the Mississippi River at New Orleans. Possibly Clemens purchased it to pass the time during his railroad journey to Columbia, Missouri in 1902.

KIRLICKS, JOHN ANSKIES (1851–1923). *I've Got the Blues Tonight & Other Troubles*. Houston, 1896. 38 pp. Wrappers.

Kevin Mac Donnell of Austin, Texas speculated that Isabel Lyon referred to this publication when she wrote to John Kirlicks from New York City on 11 December 1907: "Mr. Clemens asks me to write for him & thank you very much for your pleasant letter & the poem & the little pamphlet. He wishes me also to say that such messages & good wishes as yours are always welcome" (TS copy in the collection of Kevin Mac Donnell, quoted in a letter to Alan Gribben, 7 June 1977). On 18 May 1907 Clemens dictated an autobiographical section reporting that "yesterday's mail brought me from Texas a complimentary poem which is so fine and so sincere—and I hope I may say affectionate—that I want it to live. . . . It is by a judge on the bench." Clemens then quoted the entire three-stanza poetic tribute, "To Mark Twain" (*AutoMT* 3: 52). A few days earlier Clemens had sent a letter to Kirlicks on 15 May 1907 thanking him for the "beautiful poem" and suggesting possible venues for its publication (*AutoMT* 3: 467). Kirlicks, who was born on 2 October 1851 in Lithuania and would die in Houston on 5 April 1923, would reproduce a facsimile of Clemens's 1907 letter in *Sense and Nonsense in Rhyme* (Houston: Rein & Sons Co., 1913).

KIRTLEY, JAMES SAMUEL (1855–1949). *The Young Man and Himself; His Tasks, His Dreams, His Purposes, . . . His Complete Life*. Intro. by Henry Hopkins (1837–1908), president of Williams College. Kansas City, Missouri, 1902. 493 pp.

The Reverend James Kirtley wrote books for the American Baptist Society and the Young People's Union. Some of his writings, such as *The Young Man and Himself* and his *Half-Hour Talks on Character Building by Self-Made Men and Women* (1910), quoted prominent people exhorting youth to strive to their utmost. On 13 November 1902 Kirtley wrote to Clemens: "I have asked the publishers to send you a copy of the book on 'The Young Man.'" He thanked Clemens for "approving my quotations from your Hannibal 'sermon' in the book" (MTP).

KIRWAN, DANIEL JOSEPH (1843–1875). *Palace and Hovel; or, Phases of London Life. Being Personal Observations of an American in London, by Day and Night, with Graphic Descriptions of Royal and Noble Personages, Their Residences and Relaxations, Together with Vivid Illustrations of the Manners, Social Customs, and Modes of Living of the Rich and the Reckless, the Destitute and the Depraved, in the Metropolis of Great Britain, with Valuable Statistical Information, Collected from the Most Reliable Sources*. Illus., map. Hartford: Belknap & Bliss, 1870. 662 pp.

Source: MTLAcc, entry #583, volume donated by Clemens.

Kirwan's vivid depictions of the rich and poor, the well-educated gentlemen and the uneducated tradesmen, the socially prominent women and the streetwalkers, and the curious habits observed in various London districts deserve to be investigated for their potential effect on Clemens as he was starting to discern the literary potential of England as a subject.

KITTON, FRED[ERIC]. G[EORGE]. (1856–1904), comp. *Dickensiana: A Bibliography of the Literature Relating to Charles Dickens and His Writings, Compiled by Fred. G. Kitton*. Portrait.

London: George Redway, 1886. 510 pp.

On 28 October 1886 Kitton invited Mark Twain to contribute one of the "Testimonies" by literary people that he included in *Dickensiana*, but Clemens replied on 8 November 1886 that he had no personal experiences to contribute (Fears, *Day by Day* 2: 97; JoDee Benussi noticed this exchange of letters that seem to increase the likelihood that Clemens subsequently owned or read Kitton's compilation. See *N&J* 3: 302 for an amusing story Clemens told about someone else's brief brush with Dickens).

KITTREDGE, GEORGE LYMAN (1860–1941). *The Old Farmer and His Almanack; Being Some Observations on Life and Manners in New England a Hundred Years Ago.* Illus. Boston: William Ware and Co., 1904. 403 pp.

Source: MTLAcc, entry #800, volume donated by Clemens.

KLEIN, CHARLES (1867–1915). *The Lion and the Mouse* (play, performed in 1905).

Isabel Lyon noted on 6 January 1906 that she and Clemens attended this play at the Lyceum Theatre in New York City. He called it "a clean little play, but so stupid" (IVL Journals, TS p. 120, MTP).

———. *The Music Master* (play, performed in 1904).

Clemens saw David Warfield perform in a matinee of *The Music Master* on Saturday, 7 April 1906. Warfield had the part of a piano-player in a dime museum in New York City who rediscovers his lost daughter. Isabel Lyon recorded Clemens's opinion: he not only enjoyed the drama but thought it to be a better drama than Boucicault's adaptation of *Rip Van Winkle* (a major tribute coming from Clemens, who envied the popularity of that work); moreover, he believed that David Warfield was a finer actor than Joseph Jefferson in his prime (IVL Journal, Harry Ransom Center, University of Texas at Austin). Paine, *MTB* (1912), p. 1305.

———. *Two Little Vagrants* (play, performed in 1896). Adapted from Pierre Decourcelle's *Les Deux Gosses*.

Clemens jotted two entries concerning this play (which he mistakenly called *Two Little Vagabonds*) in Notebook 39 (TS pp. 22, 25) while in London in 1896.

KNAPP, ADELINE (1860–1909). *Upland Pastures, Being Some Out-Door Essays Dealing with the Beautiful Things That the Spring and Summer Bring.* East Aurora, New York: Roycroft Printing Shop, 1897. 62 pp. Number 192 of an edition limited to 600 copies.

Inscription: the front free endpaper has been torn out; it may have been signed by Clemens, the author, or the publisher (Elbert Hubbard). The initials "E H" appear on the front colophon page.

Location: Mark Twain Library, Redding, Connecticut.

Copy examined: Clemens's copy, unmarked. Displays the red ink Mark Twain Library accession number "2893". Examined in 1970 and again in June 1982.

KNEIPP, SEBASTIAN (1821–1897). *My Water Cure* (published in 1886, with many reprintings).

Chatto & Windus sent to Germany to obtain a copy of this book for Clemens in February 1891 (Welland, *Mark Twain in England*, p. 154). Kneipp employed hydrotherapy and dietary changes to heal diseases and maintain health.

Knickerbocker; or, New York Monthly Magazine. New York:

Clark and Edson, 1835.

Inscription: "Mrs. Olivia Langdon, 1838". [Olivia Lewis Langdon, 1810–1890, had married Jervis Langdon, 1809–1870, in 1832.]

Source: list of the books that Mark Woodhouse transferred from the Quarry Farm library to the Mark Twain Archive on 9 July 1987.

Location: Mark Twain Archive, Elmira College, Elmira, New York.

This would have been accessible to Clemens in the Langdon residence.

KNIFE AND FORK CLUB. Kansas City, Missouri. *The Book of the Knife and Fork Club of Kansas City, Covering the Period from December, 1898, to December, 1905.* Compiled by F. N. Tufts, J. M. Lee, J. J. Vineyard. Illus. Kansas City: Printed by the F. P. Burnap Stationery and Printing Co., [1906]. Unpaged. Boxed.

Inscription: the front pastedown endpaper is signed and inscribed in black ink, 'SL Clemens /1906. The illustrations are bright & cunning & gracefully done. (Preserve the book.)" [The volume contains photographs and pen and ink sketches.]

Provenance: the bookplate of the W. T. H. Howe library is affixed above Clemens's inscription on the front pastedown endpaper. A note from Isabel Lyon to Howe, dated 12 July 1936, is laid in the book: 'I remember so well the winter morning at 21 Fifth Avenue, when I carried this little book to Mr Clemens, who studied it carefully as he sat propped against his pillows in the wide Italian bed. Then he inscribed it, wrote a personal note to the sender, & handed the book back to me for safe-keeping.'

Catalogs: *A1911*, ""post 8vo, cloth and boards," quotes the signature and inscription, lot 45, sold for $6.50; American Art Association (New York City), Sale catalogue (5 February 1925), "12mo, original boards, cloth back, no date," quotes Clemens's signature and note, lot 116, sold for $4.

Location: Henry W. and Albert A. Berg Collection, New York Public Library

Copy examined: Clemens's copy, otherwise unmarked, in 1970.

On 24 February 1906 Clemens declined an invitation from Govinier Hall to speak at a program of the Knife and Fork Club, but he thanked Hall for sending the book and praised its illustrations as "bright, graceful, & humorous, & eloquently competent" (ALS in MTP). Most of the speakers listed in this commemorative volume were distinguished men of Kansas and Missouri.

KNIGHT, CHARLES (1791–1873), ed. *London.* Illus. 6 vols. London: Charles Knight & Co., 1841–1844.

Provenance: most of the volumes contain the sticker of "Marshall, Bookseller & Stationer, 21 Edgware Road" on the front pastedown endpapers. An *A1911* auction label is affixed to the front pastedown endpaper of each volume.

Catalog: *A1911*, "6 vols., royal 8vo, cloth, Lond. 1841, many of the illustrations are marked by laid-in slips of paper," lot 278, sold for $1.75.

Location: Mark Twain House and Museum, Hartford, Connecticut. Purchased for $37.50 from the Old Mystic Book Shop in 1966.

Copies examined: Clemens's copies, unmarked. Examined in August 1987. The six volumes display the *A1911* sale label.

Knight's book employed different contributors for each subject, as many as twenty per volume. On 23 May 1881 Clemens queried James R. Osgood about a recent bill for books that Clemens had ordered: "What is the last item—'London, 6 vols?' I have puzzled my dam head of trying to recoleck it" (*MTLP*, p. 136).

———. *The Popular History of England: An Illustrated History of Society and Government from the Earliest Period to Our Own Times*. 8 vols. Illus. Green cloth., gilt. Boston: Estes and Lauriat, 1873.

Inscription: the bookplate of "J. LANGDON'S/FAMILY/ LIBRARY/No. 445" is pasted in Volume I. The other seven volumes continue this numbering through "452" on identical bookplates.

Marginalia: Clemens made two vertical marks in Volume I on page 164 on either side of the illustration of "The Pusey Horn." He also underlined the word "still" in an accompanying sentence concerning the influence of the Normans: "So the lands of the Pusey family are still held by the horn which King Canute bestowed upon their ancestor William."

Catalog: Ball 2016 inventory, pencil line in Volume I at page 164 believed to be Clemens's, J. Langdon's Family Library bookplates #445–452.

Location: Volume I (only) in the Mark Twain Archive, Gannett-Tripp Learning Center, Elmira College, Elmira, New York.

Copies examined: Langdon family copies of Volumes I-VIII, with Volume I slightly annotated by Clemens. Discovered by Alan Gribben in the library room at Quarry Farm, 15 September 1999. Volume I was examined again on 17 May 2002 in the Mark Twain Archive. This set would have been accessible to Clemens whenever he visited the Langdons' residence during his visits to Elmira, New York.

———. *Studies of Shakspere; Forming a Companion to Every Edition of the Text* (published in 1849).

Clara Clemens listed this book in her commonplace book (undated entry, Paine 150, MTP).

KNIGHT, CORNELIA (1757–1837) and Thomas Raikes (1777–1848). *Personal Reminiscences by Cornelia Knight and Thomas Raikes*. Ed. by Richard Henry Stoddard (1825–1903). Bric-a-Brac Series. New York: Scribner, Armstrong, and Co., 1875. 339 pp. [Publisher and pages conjectured.]

Inscription: the front endpaper is signed "Saml. L. Clemens, Hartford, 1875."

Catalog: *A1911*, "12mo, cloth, N.Y. 1875," quotes the signature, lot 279, sold for $2.

The Preface by Richard Henry Stoddard indicated that *Personal Reminiscences* "may be regarded as a sort of companion volume to the 'Greville Memoirs'" (p. x), and the comparison seems fitting. Cornelia Knight recalled her impressions of Oliver Goldsmith, Samuel Johnson, Sir Joshua Reynolds, Thomas Gainsborough, and similar celebrities; Thomas Raikes shared his memories of Beau Brummell, the Duke of Wellington, George IV, Sir Robert Peel, and many other notables.

KNIGHT, EDWARD FREDERICK (1852–1925). *Where Three Empires Meet: A Narrative of Recent Travel in Kashmir, Western Tibet, Gilgit, and the Adjoining Countries*. London: Longmans, Green, and Co., 1893. 495 pp. [A "New Edition" with 528 pages was published in 1894, 1895, and 1897; the edition Clemens perused is undetermined.]

While at sea in April [?] 1896 Clemens made two references to this book in Notebook 37: he cited page 61 ("for English administration in India") and page 64 ("for what India was before the English occupation") (TS p. 47). He could have been reading either the 1893 edition or Knight's subsequent "New Edition"; both of them describe on pages 61 and 64 the endemic corruption and extortion that (British) Indian Civil Service administrators were trying to discourage.

KNIGHT, HELEN (CROSS) (1814–1906). *Saw Up and Saw Down; or, The Fruits of Industry and Self-Reliance*. New York: American Female Guardian Society, 1852. 32 pp.

Source: MTLAcc, entry #1894, volume donated from Clemens's library by Clara Clemens Gabrilowitsch in 1910.

KNIGHTON, WILLIAM (1834–1900). *The Private Life of an Eastern King. By a Member of the Household of His Late Majesty, Nussir-u-Deen, King of Oude*. London: Hope and Co., 1855. 330 pp. Revised edition published in 1856.

Nāsir al-Dīn, King of Oudh, died in 1837. Clemens made a note on 21 January 1896 in Bombay: "Private Life of an Eastern King—Chelsea Library. *Get it*" (NB 36, TS p. 22). On 22 October 1896 he jotted down a memorandum that he had withdrawn this book from the London Library (NB 39, TS p. 12).

KNOTT, JAMES PROCTOR (1830–1911). [Reprinted speech.]

On 9 March 1871 Clemens wrote to thank Samuel S. Cox "for Knott's speech—it is first rate" (*MTLet* 4: 346). As a member of the U. S. House of Representatives, Knott had earned a reputation as one of the leading humorous orators of his day. Clemens probably referred to Knott's speech against further federal funding for the St. Croix and Lake Superior Railroad.

KNOWLES, FREDERIC LAWRENCE (1869–1905), comp. *A Treasury of Humorous Poetry; Being a Compilation of Witty, Facetious, and Satirical Verse Selected from the Writings of British and American Poets*. First edition. Boston: Dana Estes & Co., [1902].

Following the title page, a dedication page reads: "Dedicated/by permission to/Samuel Langhorne Clemens/ ("Mark Twain")."

KNOWLES, JAMES D[AVIS]. (1798–1838). *Memoir of Mrs. Ann H[asseltine]. Judson [1789–1826], Late Missionary to Burmah, Including a History of the American Baptist Mission in the Burman Empire*. Fourth ed. Frontispiece. Original full sheep, morocco label, gilt. Boston: Lincoln & Edmands, 1831. 324 pp.

Inscription: the front free endpaper is inscribed in ink by Olivia Clemens's mother: "Mrs. J. O. Langdon/Salina/ Nov 14th, 1832."

Location: collection of Kevin Mac Donnell, Austin, Texas. Acquired from the Langdon family in May 2016 (email, Mac Donnell to Alan Gribben, 16 May 2016).

Source: detailed description of the volume with "a few dog-ears in text, but no markings" sent on 9 June 2016 by Mac Donnell to Gribben.

This book would have been available to Clemens in the Langdon family library in Elmira.

KNOWLES, JAMES SHERIDAN (1784–1862). *William Tell* (play,

performed in 1825).

Mark Twain referred to this perennial favorite in "The Indignity Put Upon the Remains of George Holland by the Rev. Mr. Sabine" (1871): ten preachers cannot "hold their own against any one of five hundred William Tells that can be raised up upon five hundred stages in the land at a day's notice" (*WIM?*, p. 53).

KNOX, ISA (CRAIG) (1831–1903), writing as "Isa Craig." *The Little Folks' History of England*. Illustrated by R.E. Galindo and others. New York and London: Cassell & Co., n.d. 284 pp. [First published in 1872.]

On 1 January 1881 Brown & Gross, Hartford booksellers, billed Clemens for "1 Craig Knox England" purchased for .80¢ on 24 November 1880. Clemens paid for the book on 17 January 1881 (receipt in MTP). Isa Craig (she married John Knox in 1866) was born in Edinburgh and moved to London. Besides being a poet, journalist, novelist, and playwright, she was a noted social reformer and leading women's rights advocate.

KNOX, THOMAS WALLACE (1835–1896). *Backsheesh! or, Life and Adventures in the Orient. With Descriptive and Humorous Sketches of Sights and Scenes*. Illus. Hartford: A. D. Worthington & Co., 1875. 694 pp.

Source: MTLAcc, entry #584, volume donated by Clemens. Knox was a school teacher turned journalist and world traveler. Although he produced serious travel narratives, many of his other books were aimed at boys and were filled with adventures involving travel to exotic locations. Knox was a member of the Lotos Club in New York City (to which Clemens belonged), but unlike Clemens he often resided there.

———. *The Boy Travellers in Australasia*. Illus. New York: Harper & Brothers, 1899. 538 pp.

Source: MTLAcc, entry #475, volume donated by Clemens.

———. *The Boy Travellers in Central Europe*. Illus. New York: Harper & Brothers, [cop. 1889]. 532 pp.

Source: MTLAcc, entry #477, volume donated by Clemens.

———. *The Boy Travellers in Mexico*. Illus. New York: Harper & Brothers, 1905. 552 pp.

Source: MTLAcc, entry #478, volume donated by Clemens.

———. *The Boy Travellers in Northern Europe*. Illus. New York: Harper & Brothers, 1905. 531 pp.

Source: MTLAcc, entry #476, volume donated by Clemens.

———. *The Boy Travellers in South America*. Illus. New York: Harper & Brothers, [cop. 1885]. 510 pp.

Source: MTLAcc, entry #473, volume donated by Clemens.

———. *The Boy Travellers in the Far East. . . in a Journey to Japan and China*. Illus. New York: Harper & Brothers, [cop. 1879]. 421 pp.

Source: MTLAcc, entry #468, volume donated by Clemens.

———. *The Boy Travellers in the Far East; Part Second, . . . in a Journey to Siam and Java*. Illus. New York: Harper & Brothers, [cop. 1880]. 446 pp.

Source: MTLAcc, entry #469, volume donated by Clemens.

———. *The Boy Travellers in the Far East; Part Third, . . . in a Journey to Ceylon and India*. Illus. New York: Harper & Brothers, [cop. 1881]. 483 pp.

Source: MTLAcc, entry #470, volume donated by Clemens.

———. *The Boy Travellers in the Far East; Part Fourth, . . . in a Journey to Egypt and the Holy Land*. Illus. New York: Harper & Brothers, 1905. 438 pp.

Source: MTLAcc, entry #471, volume donated by Clemens.

———. *The Boy Travellers in the Far East; Part Fifth, . . . in a Journey Through Africa*. Illus. New York: Harper & Brothers, 1905. 473 pp.

Source: MTLAcc, entry #472, volume donated by Clemens.

———. *The Boy Travellers in the Russian Empire*. Illus. New York: Harper & Brothers, 1905. 505 pp.

Source: MTLAcc, entry #474, volume donated by Clemens.

———. *Overland Through Asia; Pictures of Siberian, Chinese, and Tartar Life. Travels and Adventures in Kamchatka, Siberia, China, Mongolia, Chinese Tartary, and European Russia, with Full Accounts of the Siberian Exiles, Their Treatment, Condition, and Mode of Life, a Description of the Amoor River, and the Siberian Shores of the Frozen Ocean*. Map and illustrations. Hartford, Connecticut: American Publishing Co., 1871. 608 pp.

Clemens purchased this volume at the wholesale price of $1.30 on 8 December 1876, according to a bill from the American Publishing Company (Scrapbook #10, p. 77, MTP).

KOCH, ROSALIE (1811–1880). *Der Berggeist im Riesengebirge: Fortsetzung der neuen Sammlung der schönsten Sagen und Märchen vom Rübezahl [The Mountain Spirit in the Giant Mountains: Continuation of the New Collection of the Most Beautiful Legends and Fairy Tales of Rübezahl]*. Illus. Berlin: Winckelmann und Söhne, [186–?]. 249 pp.

Source: MTLAcc, entry #1679, volume donated by Clemens.

Koch's folklore novel was first published in 1845.

KOCK, CHARLES PAUL DE (1793–1871).

Kock was the prolific author of vaudevilles, melodramas, and novels, including *Le Barbier de Paris* (1826). Henry Fisher recalled that Clemens referred to Kock derogatorily when Clemens was in Europe in the mid-nineties (Fisher dates the conversation as the year William Jennings Bryan was defeated in a contest for the U. S. Senate, an event that occurred in both 1893 and 1895). According to Fisher, Clemens remarked that Kock's books ranked even below French novels (*AMT*, p. 116).

KOEBEL, WILLIAM HENRY (1872–1923). *South America. Painted by A[rchibald]. S[tevenson]. Forrest [1869–1963]. Described by W. H. Koebel*. 75 illustrations. London: A[dam]. & C[harles]. Black, [1912]. 230 pp.

Provenance: has the shelfmarks of Clara Clemens Gabrilowitsch's library numbering system during her Detroit years. Sold at the 1951 auction in Hollywood but not listed in the hastily prepared sale sheet.

Catalog: "Property from the Library of Mark Twain," Butterfield & Butterfield, San Francisco, Sale 6613 (16 July 1997), lot 2712.

Location: Mark Twain House and Museum, Hartford, Connecticut.

Copy examined: copy belonging to Clara Clemens. The first edition of this gorgeous volume was published in 1912, two years after Clemens's death, so it should not be considered part of his library.

KONEWKA, PAUL (1840–1871). *Falstaff and His Companions. Twenty-one Illustrations in Silhouette*. Intro. by Hermann Kurz (1813–1873). Translated from the German by Charles Chauncy Shackford (1815–1891). Boston: Roberts Brothers,

1872. [Cop. 1871.]

Olivia Clemens mentioned in a letter to Clemens written on 31 December 1871 that "Clara is looking at Fallstaff [sic] and his friends, (Paul Konewka's Silhouetts [sic] that I gave Mother for Christmas)" (Harris, *Courtship* [1996], p. 158). Excerpts from Shakespeare's plays accompanied the evocative silhouette drawings.

The Koran: Commonly Called the Alkoran of Mohammed. Translated into English from the Original Arabic. With Explanatory Notes. Notes by George Sale (1697–1736). Chandos Library Series. London: Frederick Warne and Co., n.d. 470 pp.

Inscription: a pencil note appears at the top of the title page: "S. L. Clemens signature/in book when received—signature now missing".

Location: Mark Twain Library, Redding, Connecticut. MTLAcc #2667.

Copy examined: Clemens's copy, unmarked. Contains the Mark Twain Library accession number, penciled—"2667". Examined in 1970 and again in June 1982.

The Koran: Commonly Called the Alkoran of Mohammed. Translated into English from the Original Arabic, by George Sale [1697–1736]. New York: American Book Exchange, 1880.

Inscription: originally signed "S. L. Clemens/Hartford, Ct./1880." This signature was later reported on the Mark Twain Library catalog card to be "missing."

Source: card catalog of Mark Twain Library, Redding, Connecticut. In 1979 the volume could not be found, nor could it be located in June 1982. All of the information derives from two cards in the shelf catalog at the Mark Twain Library. Note that the city and publisher differ from the preceding Catalog entry.

Mark Twain mentions the *Koran* in Chapters 9 and 34 of *The Innocents Abroad* (1869) and—politely—in Notebook 28 (March 1889, *N&J* 3: 457). Huckleberry Finn refers to "the Koran, which they think is a Bible," in Chapter 13 of *Tom Sawyer Abroad* (1894). Twain's most extensive comment on this book occurs in "Autobiography of a Damned Fool" (written 1877), where he ascribes to Orion Clemens a brief faith in the Islam religion, along with a conviction that he must assemble a harem. "I had diligently and thoughtfully read the Koran during my sickness," Orion says, "and was now a firm and restful believer in the religion of Mahomet" (*S&B*, p. 145). Mahomet shows up in the paradise Mark Twain depicted in *Extract from Captain Stormfield's Visit to Heaven* (1909).

KOSSUTH, LAJOS (ALSO KNOWN AS LOUIS KOSSUTH) (1820–1894).

Dixon Wecter noted that the Hungarian patriot Louis Kossuth visited Hannibal, Missouri in March 1852 and made a speech about the persecutions underway in Hungary; Orion Clemens's newspaper reported the event somewhat sarcastically (*MTH*, p. 245). An epigram attributed to Kossuth heads Mark Twain's preface to *Personal Recollections of Joan of Arc* (1896): "Consider this unique and imposing distinction. Since the writing of human history began, Joan of Arc is the only person, of either sex, who has ever held supreme command of the military forces of a nation *at the age of seventeen*." On 28 July 1901 Clemens quipped: "Kossuth couldn't raise 30

cents in Congress, now, if he were back with his moving Magyar-tale" (Clemens to Joseph H. Twichell, *MTL*, p. 711; *LMTJHT*, p. 283).

KOTZWARA, FRANTISEK (1730–1791), composer. "The Battle of Prague" (piano solo, c. 1757).

This favorite American parlor piece has no words and therefore does not properly belong in a catalog of Clemens's library and reading, but surely an exception can be made for such an important constituent of his musical knowledge. Mark Twain recorded how he endured a rendition of "The Battle of Prague" while he was in Interlaken on 22 August 1878: a young woman "tackled an old rattle trap piano with such vigor & absence of expression . . . that she soon cleaned out the great reading room" (NB 15, *N&J* 2: 142). Recounting the same incident in Chapter 32 of *A Tramp Abroad* (1880), Twain related the manner in which she "turned on all the horrors of the 'Battle of Prague,' that venerable shivaree, and waded chin deep in the blood of the slain." This musical score was among those he noted on the piano in "The House Beautiful" in Chapter 38 of *Life on the Mississippi* (1883). Huckleberry Finn heard the girls in the Grangerford household play "The Battle of Prague" on their tinny old piano (Ch. 17, *HF* [1885]). "Battle of Prague" was one of the music titles Twain wrote on the front wrapper of a song collection published in 1896, F. B. Ogilvie's *Two Hundred Old-Time Songs, Containing the Words and Music of the Choicest Gems of the Old and Familiar Songs.* Twain was not the first novelist to poke fun at these clattering sounds; the dashing George Osborne implored his sisters to "stop that d----d thing. . . . It makes me mad" in Chapter 21 of William Makepeace Thackeray's *Vanity Fair* (1848).

Joseph Slater, "Music at Col. Grangerford's" (1949), 108–111; Arthur M. Kompass, "Twain's Use of Music" (1964), p. 617 n. 2; Arthur L. Scott, *OPMT* (1966), p. 326; James Howard Richards, "Music and the Reed Organ in the Life of Mark Twain," *American Music* 1.3 (Autumn 1983): 38–47.

KRAATZ, CURT (1857–1925). *The Mountain Climber* (three-act farce, adapted from the German by M[ax]. [Dalhoff] Neal, performed in 1906).

Kraatz was a German playwright who specialized in farces. Charles Frohman produced this play on 5 March 1906 at his Criterion Theatre in New York City (*Best Plays of 1899–1909*, 1: 510). Isabel Lyon probably echoed Clemens's opinion by reporting that on 26 March 1906 "after dinner we went up to see Francis Wilson in 'The Mountain Climbers' [sic]. It was a foolish enough play, but the Vorses are lovely and Rodman Gilder was handsome" (IVL Journals, TS p 152, MTP)

KRAFFT-EBING, RICHARD VON (1840–1902). *Psychopathia Sexualis, with Special Reference to Contrary Sexual Instinct: A Medico-Legal Study* (first published in 1886).

Henry Fisher testified that Clemens had conversations about human behavior with Krafft-Ebing in Vienna (*AMT*, pp. 59, 77–78). Carl Dolmetsch, the leading expert on Clemens's Vienna period, found it "quite unlikely Twain could have escaped reading *Psychopathia Sexualis*, Krafft-Ebing's study of sexual aberrations" (*"Our Famous Guest": Mark Twain in Vienna* [Athens: University of Georgia Press, 1992], p. 264). Dolmetsch noted that Clemens's "frantic" search for treatments for Jean Clemens's epileptic seizures brought him into contact with "many illustrious members of Vienna's medical profession," including Krafft-Ebing (*Mark Twain Encyclopedia*, ed. J. R. LeMaster and James D. Wilson [New York: Garland Publishing, 1993], p. 52). I am grateful to JoDee Benussi for calling my attention to these connections.

KRAUSE, RUDOLF. *Starters and Regulators for Electric Motors and Generators; Theory, Construction, and Connection.* Trans. by C[arl]. Kinzbrunner and N. West. Illus. New York: Harper & Brothers, 1904. 132 pp.

Source: MTLAcc, entry #1374, volume donated by Clemens.

KRAVCHINSKI, SERGIUS MICHAELOVITCH (1852–1895), pseud. "Sergius Stepniak." *Russia Under the Tsars.* Trans. by William Westall (1835–1903). "Authorized Edition." Original cloth, some wear on edges and corners. New York: Charles Scribner's Sons, 1885. 381 pp.

Inscription: inscribed by Clemens, "Livy L. Clemens/ Hartford/1885."

Catalogs: *C1951*, O2, listed among books containing Olivia Clemens's signature, no edition specified; "Property from the Library of Mark Twain," Butterfield & Butterfield, San Francisco, Sale 6613 (16 July 1997), lot 2700.

Location: Mark Twain House and Museum, Hartford, Connecticut.

Copy examined: Olivia Clemens's unmarked copy. Viewed in Hartford in 1997.

————. *Underground Russia: Revolutionary Profiles and Sketches from Life.* Preface by Petr A[lekseevich]. Lavrof (1856–1929). Trans. from the Italian. Second edition. New York: Charles Scribner's Sons, 1885. 272 pp. [Reprinted in 1888. The edition of Clemens's copy has not been determined.]

Inscription: a note to Clemens by the author.

Catalog: *C1951*, #53c, $10, listed among the books signed by Clemens, no edition specified.

William Dean Howells sent Clemens a letter of 11 April 1891 to introduce Kravchinski, a Russian exile who had settled in London (*MTHL*, p. 643). Kravchinski visited the Clemenses in Hartford in April 1891, and Kravchinski's letter of 19 April 1891 to Olivia Clemens mentioned that he had sent Clemens a copy of *Underground Russia* (TS in MTP). Clemens thanked Kravchinski for "the words you wrote in the front of the book" on 23 April 1891 and reported that he had "read Underground Russia through with profound & painful interest. What sublime men & women!" (Russian State Archive, Moscow; PH in MTP). Louis J. Budd, "Twain, Howells, and the Boston Nihilists," *New England Quarterly* 32.3 (September 1959): 351–371.

KREMNITZ, MITE (born Marie Charlotte von Bardeleben) (1852–1916). *Reminiscences of the King of Roumania.* Ed. with intro. by Sidney Whitman (1848–1925). Authorized Edition. New York: Harper & Brothers, 1899. 367 pp.

Source: MTLAcc, entry #1782, volume donated by Clemens.

A biography of Charles Anthony (1839–1914), recognized as Charles I of Romania from 1866 until 1914.

Krippen-Kalender 1899—47. Jahrgang + Jahrbuch für Krippen (1847–1899, zeiter Teil des Krippen-Kalenders). Verlag: Eigenverlag—Wien, 1899. 788 pp. [A Christian nativity almanac.]

Source: MTLAcc, entry #1681, volume donated by Clemens.

KROUT, MARY HANNAH (1851–1927).

In Chapter 3 of *Following the Equator* (1897) Mark Twain quotes from "a sketch by Mrs. Mary H. Krout" that enables him "to perceive what the Honolulu of to-day is, as compared with the Honolulu of my time." He extracted these quotations before Mrs. Krout published *Hawaii and a Revolution; The Personal Experiences of a Newspaper Correspondent in the Sandwich Islands During the Crisis of 1893 and Subsequently* (London and New York, 1898). Francis V. Madigan, Jr.—"Mark Twain's Passage to India" (1974), p. 361—explained that Twain consulted her newspaper columns describing the Hawaiian political turmoil of the 1890s.

KUBINYI, VICTOR VON (1873–1966). *The King of Rome; A Biography.* Illus. New York: Knickerbocker Press, 1907. 116 pp.

Source: MTLAcc, entry #1214, volume donated by Isabel V. Lyon, Clemens's secretary. Fine binding, boxed.

Kubinyi's subject is Napoléon François Charles Joseph Bonaparte (1811–1832), King of Rome and Duke of Reichstadt, called Napoléon II. Twain referred to this Napoleon in *Christian Science* (1907), *Is Shakespeare Dead?*, and in a 1909 speech about Henry H. Rogers. Kubinyi, a Hungarian-born Catholic priest in New Jersey, would later convert to the Episcopal faith before leaving church life altogether and leading a rather chaotic and sometimes impoverished life as an author, painter, and teacher. His name often appears as Victor de Kubinyi, and he is sometimes identified, however accurately, as a Hungarian nobleman and godson of Emperor Franz Joseph of Austria.

————. [Another identical copy.] First edition. Rebound in faux morocco, gilt, raised bands, top edges gilt. Uncut leaves.

Inscription: the initials "I. L." [Isabel Lyon?] were written in ink on the title page above the word "*King*."

The oval stamps of the Mark Twain Library in Redding, Connecticut appear on pages iii, 23, 60, and 105. This appears to be a different copy than the one listed above, since the library accession number "2542" appears in ink below the copyright notice. The library assistants in Redding were generally accurate in recording books donated to the collection.

Location: collection of Kevin Mac Donnell, Austin, Texas. Acquired in December 2016 (Mac Donnell to Alan Gribben, 21 December 2016).

Source: description of the volume provided by Kevin Mac Donnell on 21 December 2016.

KUEHN, HERMAN (1853–1918), pseud. "Evelyn Gladys." *Thoughts of a Fool.* Chicago: E. P. Rosenthal and Co., 1905. 258 pp.

Source: MTLAcc, entry #794, volume donated by Clemens. Kuehn's publisher sent a complimentary copy to Clemens on 7 April 1905, asking his opinion of whether "the fool who thought the thoughts, . . . thought something funny" (E. P. Rosenthal to Clemens, MTP). Rosenthal referred to the author as a woman. Previously Rosenthal's firm had presented Clemens with a copy of Oscar L. Triggs' *Chapters in the History of the Arts and Crafts Movement* (1902). There is no indication that Clemens responded to either Rosenthal or the author.

Kugler, Franz Theodor (1808–1858). *Handbook of Painting: The German, Flemish, and Dutch Schools. Based on the Handbook of Kugler as Revised by Gustav Friedrich Waagen [1794–1868]. A New Edition, Revised by J[oseph]. A[rcher]. Crowe [1825–1896].* 2 vols. Illus. London: John Murray, 1874.

    Catalog: *A1911*, "together, 4 vols., 12mo, cloth, uncut (some joints weak), Lond. 1874," lot 219, sold for $4.50 total (sold with the next Catalog entry here).

————. *Handbook of Painting: The Italian Schools. Based on the Handbook of Kugler as Revised by Charles L[ock]. Eastlake [1793–1865].* Fourth Edition. Revised by Elizabeth (Rigby) Eastlake (1809–1893). 2 vols. Illus. London: John Murray, 1874.

    Catalog: *A1911*, "together, 4 vols., cloth, uncut (some joints weak), Lond. 1874," lot 219, sold for $4.50 total (sold with the preceding entry here).

Kuka, Mehrjibhai Nosherwanji, compiler and translator. *The Wit and Humour of the Persians.* Illus. Blue cloth boards. Bombay: Printed at the Education Society's Steam Press, 1894. 255 pp.

    Inscription: (on the verso of the dedication page) "To/ Samuel Clemens Esquire/alias 'Mark Twain'/with the respectful compliments/of the author/M. N. Kuka". A letter from Kuka to Clemens, Bombay, 25 January 1896, is mounted on the leaf facing the title page.

    Marginalia: Clemens's comments and markings register his distaste for some of the humor represented in this volume; "Witless Rubbish," he remarked on page 33. But on page 37 he pronounced "good" a simile that compares a large city to the setting of a ring designed for holding the turquoise stone of the sky. Clemens made penciled markings and notations on pages 32, 33, 35, 36 ("Perhaps was neat in the original," he wrote), 37, 38 ("Untranslatable"), 39, 40.

    Provenance: carries the bookstamps and accession number of the Mark Twain Library, Redding, Connecticut.

    Catalog: *Mott 1952*, item #62, $37.50.

    Location: Mark Twain Papers, Bancroft Library, University of California at Berkeley.

    Copy examined: Clemens's copy.

L

Labouchère, Henry DuPré (1831–1912), editor of *Truth: A Weekly Journal* (London periodical, published 1877–1957). For a time Mark Twain became fascinated with the weekly column titled "Legal Pillory" that Labouchère compiled for *Truth*. In an unpublished essay, "Labouchère's 'Legal Pillory,'" Twain condemned the English game-poaching laws and the courts that enforced them; he based his remarks on this "most interesting literature—and the most blood-stirring—to be found anywhere in print, it seems to me" (MS in DV72, MTP). From Labouchère he learned that it is better to face a magistrate on charges of wife-beating than to be tried for poaching. Filed with Twain's manuscript is a packet of clippings in an envelope from the Players Club of New York City. Each clipping is marked "A" and details various cases in which the penalties for heinous crimes against persons seem ludicrously lenient. Evidently these were clipped from the "Legal Pillory" column in *Truth*. The only clue to

the dating of the manuscript is Twain's remark within it that Labouchère has cited abuses of legal authority "fifty times a year for the past two years or thereabouts." Around 1891 Twain told Henry Fischer in Berlin that he liked Labouchère because the editor of *Truth* detested the British institution of nobility despite being born into its privileged class (*AMT*, pp. 140–141). Twain mentioned his intention to send a clipping about "Baireuth & the opera" to Labouchère in a letter written to Frederick J. Hall from Berlin on 22 November 1891 (PH in MTP).

Laboulaye, Édouard de (1811–1883). *Laboulaye's Fairy Book; Fairy Tales of All Nations.* Translated by Mary Louise Booth (1831–1889). Illus. New York: Harper & Brothers, [cop. 1866]. 363 pp.

    Source: MTLAcc, entry #1177, volume donated by Clemens.

————. *Last Fairy Tales.* Translated by Mary Louise Booth (1831–1889). New York: Harper & Brothers, [cop. 1884]. 382 pp.

    Source: MTLAcc, entry #1602, volume donated by Clemens.

————. *Last Fairy Tales.* Translated by Mary Louise Booth (1831–1889). New York: Harper & Brothers, 1885. 382 pp.

    Source: MTLAcc, entry #1895, volume donated from Clemens's library by Clara Clemens Gabrilowitsch in 1910.

La Bruyère, Jean de (1645–1696). *The Characters, or The Manners of the Age, with the Character of Theophrastus* (satire, published in 1688).

    Someone other than Clemens wrote the author and title on the rear endpaper of Clemens's copy of Robert Louis Stevenson's *The Pocket R. S. S.* (1904).

Lacombe, Paul (1834–1919). *Arms and Armour in Antiquity and the Middle Ages; Also a Descriptive Note of Modern Weapons.* Trans. from the French, and with a preface, notes, and an additional chapter on arms and armour in England, by Charles Boutell (1812–1877). New York: D. Appleton & Co., 1870. 296 pp.

    Source: MTLAcc, entry #2002, volume donated from Clemens's library by Clara Clemens Gabrilowitsch in 1910.

Lacroix, Paul (1806–1884), pseud. "Bibliophile Jacob." *The Arts in the Middle Ages, and at the Period of the Renaissance.* Illustrated by F[ranz]. Kellerhoven (1814–1872). "Fourth Thousand." New York: D. Appleton and Co., 1875. 520 pp.

    Inscription: the front free endpaper is signed in pencil: "SL. Clemens/Hartford 1876". The auction number "5c" appears in pencil on the front pastedown endpaper.

    Catalog: *C1951*, #5c.

    Location: in the 1980s this book was in the collection of W. C. Attal, Jr., Austin, Texas. He had purchased it from R. Harbey of Houston, Texas.

    Copy examined: Clemens's copy, unmarked, in Austin. The spine is broken.

————. *Manners, Customs, and Dress During the Middle Ages, and During the Renaissance Period.* Illustrated by F[ranz]. Kellerhoven (1814–1872). London: Chapman and Hall, 1874. 554 pp.

    Inscriptions: the front free endpaper is signed in black ink: "Saml. L. Clemens/ London, Nov. 1873." The number "5c" appears in pencil on the front pastedown endpaper.

    Marginalia: "Table of Illustrations" (pp. xiii–xiv) is heavily marked in pencil from (alphabetically) "Anne of Brittany"

to "Butler at his Duties," also from "Cook, The Sixteenth Century" to "Costume of Emperors at Their Coronation." On page 329 Clemens corrected the figure 24,000 francs to read "2,400 francs," adding a vertical pencil line beside the revision. On page 345 he drew double pencil brackets at the fourth line from the bottom, which reads, "The King was forbidden from granting written orders (*praecepta*) for carrying off rich widows, young virgins, and nuns."
Catalog: *C1951*, #5c.
Location: collection of W. C. Attal, Jr., Austin Texas. He had purchased it from R. Harbey of Houston, Texas.
Copy examined: Clemens's copy, in Austin. Broken spine (half of it is missing).

———. *Military and Religious Life in the Middle Ages and at the Period of the Renaissance. . . . Illustrated with Fourteen Chromolithographic Prints by F[ranz]. Kellerhoven [1814–1872], Régamey, and L. Allard, and upwards of Four Hundred Engravings on Wood.* Large red cloth cover, stamped, binding peeling. New York: D. Appleton and Co., 1874. 504 pp.
Provenance: displays the shelfmarks of Clara Clemens Gabrilowitsch's library numbering system during her Detroit years.
Catalog: "Property from the Library of Mark Twain," Butterfield & Butterfield, San Francisco, Sale 6613 (16 July 1997), lot 2712.
Location: Mark Twain House and Museum, Hartford, Connecticut.
Copy examined: Clemens's unmarked copy. Viewed in Hartford in 1997.

The Ladies' Home Journal (Philadelphia periodical, published 1883–).
In April 1891 Clemens mentioned the journal and its founder, Edward W. Bok, in Notebook 30 (*N&J* 3: 619). Clemens was later embarrassed by an article about himself which appeared in the October 1898 issue (he generally disliked these biographical sketches, arguing that they should be withheld during an author's lifetime); he scoffed at the writer of this essay, his former lecture agent James B. Pond, "who emptied that sewage down the back of the Chambermaid's Home Journal" (Clemens to Henry H. Rogers, Vienna, 17 November 1898, *MTHHR*, p. 379).

The Lady's Gift; or, Souvenir of Friendship. Illus. Red cloth, gilt floral decoration. New York: Leavitt & Allen, n.d. 324 pp.
Inscription: the front flyleaf is inscribed in pencil: "Olivia L. Langdon/From/Mrs. James Halsey/1861". Olivia Lewis Langdon (1810–1890) was Clemens's mother-in-law.
Provenance: this volume was donated to the Elmira College Library and at some point was recognized as a Langdon/Clemens association copy and placed in the Mark Twain Archive collection.
Location: Mark Twain Archive, Gannett-Tripp Library, Elmira College, Elmira, New York.
Copy examined: Olivia Lewis Langdon's unmarked copy, Viewed in November 1986 and again on 12 August 1988.
Martin F. Tupper, James T. Fields, Georgina C. Munro, and other (mostly little-known) authors of romantic poetry and prose are collected in this volume, which is adorned with sentimental engraved drawings. In Chapter 38 of *Life on the Mississippi* (1883) Mark Twain recalled that copies of "Tupper, much penciled; also 'Friendship's Offering,' and 'Affection's Wreath,' with their sappy inanities illustrated

in die-away mezzotints" were staple sights in the parlors of the "finest dwelling" in each town along the river.
LA FONTAINE, JEAN DE (1621–1695). *Fables*. Paris, 1890. [Edition undetermined; possibly *Fables avec les dessins de Gustave Dor*. Paris: Hachette et cie, 1890. 864 pp.]
Inscription: inscribed by Jean Clemens in Paris on 2 February 1894.
Catalog: *Mott 1952*, item #63, $3.
———. *Fables de J. de La Fontaine*. Ed. by [Joseph] Décembre (1836–1906) and [Edmond] Alonnier (1828–1871). 100 engraved illustrations by J[ules Marie]. Desandré (c. 1845–) and W[illiam]. H[enry]. Freeman (fl. 1839–1875). Engraved frontispiece. Original green cloth, gilt. Paris: Bernardin-Béchet, 1875. 380 pages.
Inscription: the front flyleaf is signed "Olivia L. Clemens/ Hartford/Ct."
Marginalia: Ink was spilled on pages 88–89. Page 108 ("Le chat et le vieux rat") contains pencil marks that appear to be Olivia Clemens's, including small marginal lines, an underlining, and a textual correction. The name "Rabelais" is written (not in Clemens's hand) next to the title of that story. (The tale concerns a cat that cleverly pretends to be dead, hanging himself upside down, in order to lure rats out of their holes, but one old rat doesn't fall for the ruse and taunts the cat.) The corner of page 238 is folded over at "Le rat et l'éléphant."
Provenance: Gilt monogram on the front cover identifies a Boston importer and bookseller, Schonhof & Mollier, from whom the book was presumably purchased. The volume displays the shelfmark of Clara Clemens Gabrilowitsch's Detroit residential library. Formerly in the Carrie Estelle Doheny Collection, St. John's Seminary, Camarillo, California. Donated to that collection by Mrs. Doheny after she purchased it for $12.20 from Maxwell Hunley Rare Books of Beverly Hills in 1940. Sold by Christie's for $275 on 21 February 1989, lot 1771, on behalf of St. John's Seminary. Subsequently this volume was in the collection of Nick Karanovich of Fort Wayne, Indiana.
Catalogs: *Sotheby's 2003*, #192, $1,100 (sold with three other books from the Clemens family's library); Robert Slotta, Admirable Books, Hilliard, Ohio, 2006 catalog, item #4, $1,500.
Location: collection of Kevin Mac Donnell, Austin, Texas. Acquired in 2006.
Copy examined: Olivia Clemens's unmarked copy, at St. John's Seminary in 1970 and viewed again at the Sotheby's auction. Has the bookplate of "Estelle Doheny."
Minnie M. Brashear correctly noted that despite Mark Twain's efforts to write fables, "no reference to Aesop or La Fontaine is to be found in his [literary] writings" (Brashear, *MTSM*, p. 233).

LAGERLÖF, SELMA OTTILIANA LOVISA (1858–1940). *The Story of Gösta Berling*. Translated from the Swedish by Pauline Bancroft Flach (1869–1966). Boston: Little, Brown and Co., 1898. 473 pp. [Edition conjectured, but this is the most likely one.]
Source: LABP ("Lagerlof, Story of Gosta Berling").
Lagerlöf's first novel incorporated the wild folk legends, harsh winters, and lucrative ironworks of Sweden. The title character, a defrocked Lutheran priest, alcoholic but charming, engages in reprehensible behavior until, viewing

the damage that he and others like him have wrought, begins to rehabilitate his character and adopt new values.

LAIGHTON, ALBERT (1829–1887). *Poems by Albert Laighton.* Boston: Brown, Taggard & Chase; Portsmouth, N.H.: J. H. Foster, 1859. 135 pp.

> Inscription: "To Frank Fuller, with the best wishes of his friend, Albert Laighton."

> Catalog: *A1911*, "first edition, 12mo, cloth, Bost. and Portsmouth, [N.H.], 1859," quotes the inscription, lot 281, sold for .50¢.

> Clemens knew Frank Fuller when he was a prominent political figure in the territories of Utah and Nevada during the Civil War. The men remained friends when Fuller later moved to New York City and operated a soap and health food company. At some point this volume entered Clemens's library collection.

LAMAR, JOHN BASIL (1812–1862). "Polly Peablossom's Wedding" (published in 1842, collected in Lamar's *Homespun Yarns* in 1851).

> John B. Lamar was one of the Georgia frontier humorists. Bernard DeVoto pointed out unmistakable correspondences between Lamar's sketch, which was widely circulated in the frontier press, and Clemens's "Ye Sentimental Law Student." That sketch appeared in the Virginia City *Territorial Enterprise* on 19 February 1863 (*ET&S* 1: 217–219). DeVoto noted that Twain could have encountered Lamar's tale in a collection edited by Thomas A. Burke, *Polly Peablossom's Wedding, and Other Tales* (Philadelphia: A. Hart, 1851) (*MTAm*, pp. 157–158).

LAMARTINE, ALPHONSE MARIE LOUIS DE (1790–1869). "Heloise" (story) in *Memoirs of Celebrated Characters.* 3 vols. New York: Harper & Brothers, 1854, 1: 138. [The edition that Clemens consulted is not known.]

> "Such is the story of Abelard and Heloise. Such is the history that Lamartine has shed cataracts of tears over" (*IA* [1869], Ch. 15). In September 1869 Twain joshed about Lamartine's purported last words (Buffalo *Morning Express, SL*, p. 74). Olivia Langdon's commonplace book contains several quotations attributed to an unidentified work by Lamartine; she copied these around 1866 or 1867 (DV161, MTP). See the Catalog entry for Orlando W. Wight.

———. *Meditations Poétiques* (published in 1820).

> Olivia Clemens quoted two lines from Lamartine's "Invocation" (included in *Meditations Poétiques*) as an inscription she wrote and signed on the half-title page of her husband's *Following the Equator*, a copy that both she and Clemens inscribed on 29 April 1898 in Vienna, Austria and presented to Olivia's friend Leila Gittings (Parke-Bernet Galleries Catalog, 21 November 1938, item #90). The sentiment has been translated as "O thou who hast appeared to me in this worldly desert,/Dweller of the heavens, a mere traveler here." I am grateful to JoDee Benussi for contributing this entry.

———. *A Pilgrimage to the Holy Land; Comprising Recollections, Sketches, and Reflections Made During a Tour in the East, in 1832–1833* (published in 1835). Reprinted in New York by Appleton in 1848.

> In Chapter 55 of *The Innocents Abroad* (1869) Mark Twain predicted that the pilgrims will say they were sorry to leave Palestine, for "they do not wish to array themselves

against all the Lamartines and Grimeses in the world."

———. *Twenty-Five Years of My Life.* Translated by Lady Herbert [Mary Elizabeth Herbert, 1822–1911]. Collected in *Prosper Mérimée's Letters to an Incognita; with Recollections by Lamartine and George Sand* (1874). See the Catalog entry for Prosper Mérimée for bibliographic details. Lamartine's *Twenty-five Years of My Life* appears on pages 137–319 of the book. (JoDee Benussi contributed to this entry.)

LAMB, CHARLES (1775–1834). "A Dissertation Upon Roast Pig," collected in *Essays of Elia. First Series* (published in 1823).

> Mark Twain included "Lamb's Origin of Roast pig" in a list of mostly American humorous writers he was considering for inclusion in an anthology (Notebook 19 [1880], *N&J* 2: 363).

———. *Essays of Elia.* The Temple Edition. Illus. New York: G. P Putnam's Sons, 1884. 501 pp.

> Catalog: Ball 2016 inventory, Red/brown cover with gilt lettering, good condition.

> Location: Quarry Farm Library library shelves, under the supervision of the Mark Twain Archive, Elmira College, Elmira, New York.

> This volume was available to Clemens at Quarry Farm in Elmira.

———. *The Last Essays of Elia.* New York: International Book Co., [1885?]. 163 pp.

> Source: MTLAcc, entry #900, volume donated by Clemens.

———. "Specimens from the Writings of Fuller, The Church Historian," collected in *Rosamund Gray, Essays, Letters, and Poems* (published in 1849).

> Clemens referred to this essay in a letter he wrote to Mary Mason Fairbanks on 9 February 1876: "There is an old book by Thomas Fuller—I have forgotten its name, but I think Charles Lamb devotes a chapter to it. . . . Old Fuller . . . boils an elaborate thought down & compresses it into a single crisp & meaty sentence. It is a wonderful faculty. When I had the book I purposed searching out & jotting down a lot of these pemmican sentences, . . . but I neglected it, of course. . . . I remember that to express pompous & empty show, old Fuller uses a figure something like this: 'They that are many stories high, are usually found to be but indifferently furnished in the cockloft'" (*MTMF*, pp. 195–196). Clemens's version compares well with the sentence Lamb actually quotes in an essay on Fuller (published in 1811) regarding "*Intellect in a very Tall One.*—'Oftimes such who are built four stories high, are observed to have little in their cockloft.'" Lamb offers numerous pithy observations by Fuller because "his works are now scarcely perused but by antiquaries" (*Works of Charles Lamb*, 5 vols. [New York: W. J. Widdleton, 1870], 4: 128).

———————— and **MARY ANN LAMB** (1764–1849). *Tales from Shakespeare.* Illustrated by John Moyr Smith (1839–1912). London: Chatto and Windus, 1879. 270 pp.

> Source: MTLAcc, entry #1929, volume donated from Clemens's library by Clara Clemens Gabrilowitsch in 1910.

———. *The Works of Charles Lamb, With a Sketch of His Life and Final Memorials.* Ed. Sir Thomas Noon Talfourd (1795–1854). 2 vols. New York: Harper & Brothers, 1855.

> Inscription: inscribed "Susie Langdon/July 8, 1856".

> Catalog: Ball 2016 inventory, brown morocco spine, blue

board covers with gilt lettering, fair condition.
Location: Quarry Farm library shelves, under the supervision of the Mark Twain Archive, Elmira College, Elmira, New York.

This collection was available to Clemens at Quarry Farm in Elmira.

———. *The Works of Charles Lamb.* 5 vols. Half sheep, marbled endpapers. New York: H. W. Derby, 1859–61.

Each volume contains an individual title page: (Volume I) *The Life and Letters of Charles Lamb*, ed. by Thomas Noon Talfourd (1795–1854); (Volume II) *The Essays of Elia. A New Edition*; (Volume III) *Rosamund Gray, Essays, Letters, and Poems*; (Volume IV, which is missing) *Specimens of the English Dramatic Poets. A New Edition*; (Volume V) *The Final Memorials of Charles Lamb*, ed. by Thomas Noon Talfourd (1795–1854).

Inscriptions: the flyleaves are torn out of Volumes I and V. The others are blank.

Location: Volumes I, II, III, and V are in the Mark Twain Library, Redding, Connecticut; Volume IV is missing. I discovered these four volumes on the circulation shelves when I visited the Mark Twain Library in September 1970. Because the flyleaves of Volumes I and V were torn out in the same manner as those from other volumes definitely belonging to Clemens's library, and since Clemens's early editions of Lamb's works have never been located, I asked the librarian at Redding to place these volumes in the special bookcase with Clemens's library books, as a precautionary measure.

Copies examined: quite likely Clemens's copies, unmarked. They lack inscriptions or marginalia that might certify the identities of previous owners. The volumes have red ink Mark Twain Library accession numbers "2766, 2767, 2768, and 2770," which are within the range of the Clemenses' book donations. Examined in 1970 and again in June 1982 and on 10 November 2019.

Clemens's references to Lamb are mostly unfavorable in tone. "No, I detest Lamb," Clemens insisted on 25 November 1874 in reply to William Dean Howells's suggestion that the style of Clemens's earlier (16 November 1874) letter resembled Lamb's. Howells had jokingly contended that Clemens's real initials might be "C. L. Clemens," but Clemens responded: "I am named after more obscure but nobler beings" (*MTHL*, pp. 42, 44; *MTLet* 6: 296). Clemens mentioned Lamb in a letter written to Mary Mason Fairbanks on 31 October 1877, merely referring to Lamb's being a famous author (*MTMF*, p. 212).

Rereading Bret Harte's writings on 23 March 1882, Clemens complained to Howells that Harte seemed "as slovenly as Thackeray, and as dull as Charles Lamb" (*MTHL*, p. 396.) In June 1882 Mark Twain made a stern memorandum for his Mississippi River travel book about Lamb's being one of the "passé authors": "Make no end of Chas. Lamb, & people who have been educated to think him readable, & really *do* think him so" (NB 20, *N&J* 2: 489). Lamb is mentioned in a cryptic but adverse connection with Sydney Smith and Thomas Bailey Aldrich (NB 24 [June 1885], *N&J* 3: 163). Paradoxically, Twain alluded to Lamb with esteem in a newspaper interview a decade later: "Look at Lamb, getting the quaintest, most spirit-moving effects with the tears just trembling on the verge of every

jest" ("Visit of Mark Twain," Sydney [Australia] *Morning Herald*, 17 September 1895, pp. 5–6; Scharnhorst, *Complete Interviews*, p. 205). The next year, however, the Reverend Joseph H. Twichell testified otherwise: "He does not much enjoy Charles Lamb," wrote Twichell, who considered this to be a "surprising" literary aversion ("Mark Twain," p. 822).

LAMBERT, B. *The History and Survey of London and Its Environs from the Earliest Period to the Present Time.* 4 vols. Plates, portraits, maps. London: Printed for T. Hughes and M. Jones by Dewick and Clarke, 1806. [Publisher conjectured.]
Catalog: *A1911*, "4 vols., 8vo, calf (rubbed and cracked), Lond. 1806," a list of authors in Clemens's hand laid in, lot 282, sold for $1.50.

LAMON, WARD HILL (1828–1893). *The Life of Abraham Lincoln* (published in 1872).
In Berlin in 1891 Clemens and Henry Fisher met the Lincoln biographer. Lamon told Clemens some anecdotes about Lincoln (*AMT* [1922], pp. xviii, 118). The encounter might have prompted Clemens to read Lamon's book.

LA MOTTE, FRIEDRICH HEINRICH KARL DE, BARON FOUQUÉ (1777–1843). *Undine, Eine Erzählung [Undine, A Romance].* Spine broken, endpapers and leaves loose. Leipzig: Philipp Reclam jun, n. d. 95 pp.
Inscriptions: signed in black ink on the front free endpaper, "Livy L. Clemens/Munich/1879," to which Olivia added in blue ink: "To/Susy Clemens/Hartford/April 1882."
Location: Mark Twain Library, Redding, Connecticut.
Copy examined: Olivia Clemens's copy, later Susy Clemens's. Has the red ink Mark Twain Library accession number "4095" and the purple oval Library stamps. Examined in 1970 and again in June 1982.
Originally published in 1811, this fairy tale relates the story of a mermaid who married a knight.

———. *Undine: A Romance, and Sintram and His Companions.* Illustrated by Heywood Sumner (1853–1940). New York: G. P. Putnam's Sons, [1888]. 384 pp. [Edition conjectured.]
Inscription: presented to a Clemens daughter by Charles Dudley Warner.
Catalog: *A1911*, "16mo, cloth, N.Y., n.d., autograph presentation copy from Charles Dudley Warner to Miss Clemens," lot 171, sold for $3.50.
———. *Undine, A Romance.*
Catalog: *C1951*, #J2, listed among the books of Jean and Clara Clemens. Possibly this was the same copy offered for sale at the 1911 auction, but more likely it was an additional one.

LAMPMAN, ARCHIBALD (1861–1899). *Among the Millet and Other Poems.* Ottawa, Ontario: J. Durie & Son, 1888. 151 pp.
In the summer of 1889 Clemens made a note of "Lampman's Poems" (NB 29, *N&J* 3: 510), presumably referring to the Canadian poet's *Among the Millet and Other Poems*. William Dean Howells had reviewed that volume favorably in the April 1889 issue of *Harper's Monthly*.

LAMPTON, WILLIAM JAMES (1859–1917). *Yawps and Other Things.* Philadelphia: Henry Altemus Co., [cop. 1900]. 196 pp.
Source: MTLAcc, entry #645, volume donated by Clemens.
———. [Another identical copy.]
Source: MTLAcc, entry #1268, volume donated by Clemens.
In a letter to Lampton, Mark Twain scoffed at the sentiments

in a poem from this collection ("Ready—If Needed!") regarding the military's recruitment of soldiers for the American invasion of the Philippines. Twain's letter was published (and criticized) in the *Army and Navy Journal* 28 (23 March 1901); that column was then reprinted in the 24 March 1901 issue of the New York *Times*. Twain mentioned and quoted sarcastically the last stanza from Lampton's poem in "The Stupendous Procession" (*FM* [1972], p. 410). JoDee Benussi assisted in writing this entry.

Landon, Melville De Lancey (1839–1910), pseud. "Eli Perkins." *Saratoga in 1901. Fun, Love, Society & Satire.* Illustrated by Arthur Lumley (1837–1912). Loose spine. New York: Sheldon & Co., 1872. 250 pp.

> **Inscription:** on the flyleaf Clemens wrote in pencil (large, bold script): "Saratoga in 1891/or,/The Droolings of an Idiot."
>
> **Marginalia:** in penciled comments throughout the book Clemens called Perkins a "humbug," "sham" (p. 104), "cur" (p. 129), and "little-minded person" (p. 186), whose jokes and sketches are the "Wailings of an Idiot" (p. 152). "Hear this humbug, this sham, deliver himself," Clemens marveled (p. 104). Clemens wrote and underscored the word "*lie*" beside Perkins' reference to "my old friend, Artemus Ward (whose biography I have written to be published by Carleton)" (p. 98). At the bottom of page 99 Clemens observed smugly: "Evidently there were some people there with brains enough to estimate this foetus at his correct value." On page 124 Clemens accused him of repeating an "Ancient Californian Joke from John Phoenix." On page 129, next to Landon's reference to "the aristocratic young ladies from the Clarendon," Clemens made a diagonal speculation: "Evidently this cur has been kicked out of the Clarendon Hotel some time or other." On pages 131, 134, 135, and 145 Clemens charged him with using material from Artemus Ward ("Stolen—& poorly stolen at that," Clemens sneered on page 134. Writing vertically in pencil on page 182, Clemens noted, "Second use of a poor joke" regarding Eli Perkins boast that his ancestor Nathaniel Perkins played a role in the Battle of Saratoga during the Revolution—"carrying water to the British." Clemens made the identical objection (writing vertically) on page 183. On page 187 Clemens noticed that Perkins is "stealing [Josh] Billings's style." Additional claims of theft appear on pages 94 ("Theft. Theft."), 132, 180, 189, and 190. Clemens's vicious marginal notes qualify this book for inclusion in his hypothetical "Library of Literary Hogwash." The Mark Twain Papers at Berkeley contain photocopies of twenty-seven pages of Clemens's marginalia.
>
> **Location:** Mark Twain Library, Redding, Connecticut. Donated by Clemens (MTLAcc, entry #362).
>
> **Copy examined:** Clemens's copy. Has the red ink accession number "362" and the purple oval Mark Twain Library stamps. Examined in 1970, in June 1982, and again on 10 November 2019.

Although Mark Twain had weightier problems to grapple with in the 1890s, he could not have been pleased (if he ever saw it) with Landon's 570-page *Kings of the Pulpit and Platform: Biographies, Reminiscences and Anecdotes of Noted Americans* (Chicago: Werner Co., 1896), which

Landon began publishing in 1890 and reprinted under variant titles and with different publishers. The section on Twain (pp. 348–359) was a mixed bag; although Landon generously declared that Twain "will go down to posterity as the Dickens of America" (p. 350), Landon also presented lengthy verbatim extracts from Twain's lectures and books, a practice Twain detested. Interviewing a Hannibal resident, R. E. Morris, who said he went to school with Clemens when they were boys, Landon quoted Morris's claim that Clemens "never took any interest in books" (p. 350). In an Autobiographical Dictation of 31 July 1906, Twain mentioned Eli Perkins among the American humorists whose fame passed within a few years (*MTE*, p. 201; *AutoMT* 2: 153).

Landor, Arnold Henry Savage (1865–1924). *The Gems of the East; Sixteen Thousand Miles of Research Travel Among Wild and Tame Tribes of Enchanting Islands.* Illus. New York: Harper & Brothers, 1904. 567 pp.

> **Source:** MTLAcc, entry #1721, volume donated by Clemens.

Landor traveled throughout the Philippines.

Landor, Walter Savage (1775–1864).

> Clemens knew that Professor Willard Fisk's villa in Florence "is the one which the English writer and poet Walter Savage Landor lived in so many years" (NB 32 [May 1892], TS p. 8).

Lane, Elinor (Macartney) (1864–1909). *Katrine, A Novel.* New York: Harper & Brothers, 1909. 315 pp.

> **Source:** MTLAcc, entry #1441, volume donated by Clemens.

Though published posthumously, this last of Lane's three novels became the second-best fictional seller of 1909. An heir to a North Carolina plantation falls in love with an Irish overseer's daughter, Katrine.

Lang, Andrew (1844–1912). *Aucassin and Nicolette.* Translated by Andrew Lang. First edition. London: David Nutt, 1887. 70 pp. [This is a conjectured edition based on the information below.]

> **Source:** LABP (1910), no details specified.

A volume merely titled "Aucassin and Nicolette" was among the books recorded as having been in Albert Bigelow Paine's possession after he completed his biography of Mark Twain; it may have been the Andrew Lang translation, since Clemens and Lang were friends. But see also the Catalog entry for August Rodney Macdonough (trans.), another version of this tale of two determined lovers.

_____, ed. *The Blue Fairy Book.* London: Longmans, Green and Co., 1899. [Clemens's acquaintance with this title is a conjecture based on the following fact.]

> When invited to suggest two stories for inclusion in *Favorite Fairy Tales: The Childhood Choice of Representative Men and Women* (1907), Clemens recommended "Aladdin and the Wonderful Lamp" and "Ali Baba and the Forty Thieves." In reprinting these stories the publisher of *Favorite Fairy Tales* (Harper & Brothers) took their texts from Andrew Lang's *The Blue Fairy Book.*

_____. *The Maid of France, Being the Story of the Life and Death of Jeanne d'Arc.* Portraits. London: Longmans, Green and Co., 1908. 379 pp. Reprinted in 1909. [Edition unknown.]

> **Catalog:** *C1951*, #90c, $15, no edition specified, listed

among the books signed by Clemens.

See also the Catalog entry for Anatole France, *Vie de Jeanne d'Arc* (1908).

———. *A Monk of Fife: A Romance of the Days of Jeanne d'Arc, Done into English from the Manuscript in the Scots College of Ratisbon*. London: Longmans, Green and Co., 1895.

Having "just finished" reading this book in Pretoria, South Africa on 25 May 1896, Clemens wrote to Olivia to say that he was sending it along to her. On 7 June 1896 he mentioned the book in another letter, this one written in King Williams Town, Cape Colony, adding, "Hope you got it" (both ALS in Samossoud Collection, TS in MTP).

———. "Mr. Lang on the Art of Mark Twain," *The Critic* 16.395 (25 July 1891): 45–46. [Reprinted from *The Illustrated News of the World*.]

Clemens admired Lang, so given the topic it seems likely that he read this brief essay. Lang praised *Adventures of Huckleberry Finn* but objected to *A Connecticut Yankee in King Arthur's Court* because "he has not the knowledge which would enable him to be a sound critic of the ideal of the Middle Ages" (p. 45). Lang had earlier praised Twain's "genius" as "mellowing, ripening, widening, and improving," but ranked his travel books as "his least excellent; he is happiest at home, in the country of his own Blue Jay" ("Western Drolls," in *Lost Leaders* [New York: Longmans, Green & Co., 1889], pp. 185–186).

———. *Old Friends: Essays in Epistolary Parody*. Edition limited to 150 copies. London: Longmans, Green and Co., 1890. 205 pp. [Publisher and pages conjectured.]

Catalog: *A1911*, "first edition, frontispiece, 8vo, boards, gilt top, uncut, Lond. 1890, Japan paper, only 150 copies printed," lot 283, sold for $3.

Lang praised "Master Thomas Sawyer and his companion, Huckleberry Finn" for being "real boys" (p. 18). Clemens thanked Lang for the "beautiful book" and the commendation in a letter of 4 May 1891 (MTP).

———. *The Red Book of Animal Stories*. Original cloth, minor wear, rubbed edges and corners. London: Longmans, Green, and Co., 1899.

Inscription: the front flyleaf is inscribed, "Jean L. Clemens/ Dec. 25th, 1899/London/Mamma." [Lifelong animal lover Jean Clemens was nineteen in 1899.]

Provenance: sold as lot J50 at the Hollywood auction in 1951 but not listed on the sale sheet, a common error. The lot number is penciled in the volume.

Catalog: "Property from the Library of Mark Twain," Butterfield & Butterfield, San Francisco, Sale 6613 (16 July 1997), lot 2708.

Location: Mark Twain House and Museum, Hartford, Connecticut.

Copy examined: Jean Clemens's unmarked copy. Viewed in Hartford in 1997.

LANGLAND, WILLIAM (c. 1330–c. 1400).

In *Extract from Captain Stormfield's Visit to Heaven* (1909) Sandy McWilliams reports having "had some talk with one Langland and a man by the name of Chaucer—old-time poets—but it was no use, I couldn't quite understand them, and they couldn't quite understand me" (*RP*, p. 78). *The Vision Concerning Piers Plowman*, an alliterative poem written sometime between 1370 and 1390, is usually attributed to Langland.

LANGMANN, PHILIPP (1862–1931). *Bartel Turaser, Drama in drei Akten*. Leipzig: R. Friese, 1897. 107 pp.

On 15 March 1898 Clemens informed Henry H. Rogers from Vienna that he planned to translate this "melancholy" play, a "dismal but interesting piece" currently enjoying popularity in three European countries. "It's the quaintest thing—doesn't much resemble a play—but it crowds the houses every time it is billed" (*MTHHR*, p. 326). Clemens sent his adaptation to Rogers on 22 March 1898: "With the right actor for the chief part, it is bound to go, I suppose. If it goes in America I will then try it in England" (*MTHHR*, pp. 333–334). Nothing of Clemens's translation is known to survive. See also the Catalog entry for Bram Stoker's *The Mystery of the Sea*.

LANGTREE, LILLIE (EMILY CHARLOTTE LeBRETON) (1852–1929).

Although Clemens did not leave behind evidence that he had read anything Langtree published, apparently the two had a literary discussion of sorts. Noel B. Gerson's biography, *Because I Loved Him: The Life and Loves of Lillie Langtree* (New York: William Morrow & Co., 1971), reported that "Mark Twain, who met her on a number of occasions, was impressed, and wrote at length about her clarity of judgment. He said: 'Contrary to what one would expect of a woman whose fame was based on her beauty, Mrs. Langtry is an exceptionally intelligent person. She must read constantly because she is able to discuss in detail any book, classical or modern, English or American or French, that is mentioned to her. I know she isn't shamming, because I questioned her in some detail, and she KNEW the books. She also reads the newspapers, and doesn't bother with the trivia. . . . It would be hell to be married to her. She's too damned bright." Gearson does not supply a source for this quotation.

Lillie Langtry, *The Days I Knew*. Foreword by Richard le Gallienne. Illus. New York: George H. Doran Co., 1925.

LANIER, SIDNEY (1842–1881). *Select Poems of Sidney Lanier*. Ed. by Morgan Callaway, Jr. New York: Charles Scribner's Sons, 1895. 97 pp.

Catalog: Ball 2016 inventory, red/brown cloth, gilt lettering.

Location: Quarry Farm Library library shelves, under the supervision of the Mark Twain Archive, Elmira College, Elmira, New York.

Clemens had access to this book at Quarry Farm in Elmira.

———. *Shakespeare and His Forerunners: Studies in Elizabethan Poetry and Its Development from Early English*. 2 vols. Illus. Original red cloth, gilt. Red cloth folding-case. New York: Doubleday, Page, 1902.

Inscriptions: Clemens inscribed the front pastedown endpaper of Volume One, "To Susan L. Crane from S. L. Clemens, 1903." The front flyleaf is inscribed "To S L. C. from S L. C., 1903." In Volume Two, the position of the inscriptions is reversed: the front pastedown is inscribed "To S. L. C. from S. L. C., 1903." and the front flyleaf bears the longer inscription, "To Susan L. Crane from S L. Clemens/Quarry Farm/Sept. 1903." To each of the longer inscriptions Susan Crane subsequently added another inscription, "To Olivia Langdon Loomis, September 6, 1922." Susan Crane was of course Clemens's sister-in-law who welcomed the Clemens family to Quarry Farm on East Hill outside of Elmira, New York during numerous summers. Clemens gradually came to have mounting doubts about the attribution of Shakespeare's works, so this is an interesting addition to his known reading on the subject.

Provenance: collection of Nick Karanovich, Fort Wayne, Indiana.

Catalog: *Sotheby's 2003*, #219, $9,000.

Copy examined: gift copy from Clemens. Viewed at the 2003 Sotheby's sale.

LANIGAN, GEORGE THOMAS (1845–1886), pseud. "G. Washington Aesop." *Fables by G. Washington Aesop, Taken "Anywhere, Anywhere, Out of the World."* Illustrated by F[rederick]. S[tuart]. Church (1842–1924). New York: The World, 1878. 52 pp. [Publisher conjectured.]

Inscription: signed in two places "S. L. Clemens, 1877."

Catalog: *A 1911*, "12mo, pictorial wrappers (broken), N.Y. 1878," quotes inscriptions, lot 2, sold for $2.50.

The opening sentence of Mark Twain's "About Magnanimous-Incident Literature," published in the May 1878 issue of *Atlantic Monthly*, states that he has "had the habit of reading a certain set of anecdotes, written in the quaint vein of The World's ingenious Fabulist, for the lesson they taught me and the pleasure they gave me." He then proceeds to write the previously unknown "sequels of those anecdotes" (*CTSS&E* 1: 703).

———. *Fables by G. Washington Aesop, Taken "Anywhere, Anywhere, Out of the World."* Illustrated by F[rederick]. S[tuart]. Church (1842–1924). New York: The World, 1878. 52 pp., plus 12 pages of advertisements.

Inscription: the front pastedown endpaper is signed in black ink: "SL. Clemens's book./Nov. '05." Pasted above the signature is a newspaper clipping of Lanigan's poem titled "A Threnody" ("The Akhoond of Swat"). In the clipping Clemens inserted the date "1878" in black ink beside the date supplied, January 22.

Provenance: formerly in the collection of Professor Bigelow Paine Cushman, Department of English, Western Connecticut State College, Danbury, Connecticut.

Location: currently unknown.

Copy examined: Clemens's copy. Inspected at the residence of Bigelow Paine and Anne Cushman in Deer Isle, Maine in August 1987.

On 14 July 1880 Estes & Lauriat of Boston charged Clemens $1.35 for "1 Aesop"; Clemens paid the bill on 20 July 1880 (receipt in MTP). This presumably referred to Clemens's copy of *Bewick's Select Fables of Aesop*, but it is conceivable that Clemens bought a second copy of *Fables by G. Washington Aesop* at this time. In any event, he repeatedly included Lanigan's book title among lists of materials he intended to evaluate for a proposed anthology of humor; he constructed these lists of humorous works twice in 1880, one of them late in July (Notebook 19); another list in 1881 (Notebook 19); and yet another list in March 1882 (Notebook 20); see *N&J* 2: 365 ("World Fables"), 366 ("The World's Fables"), 429 ("World Fables"), and 450 ("Lanigan's World Fables"). When *Mark Twain's Library of Humor* eventually issued in 1888 it contained eight of Lanigan's fables collected from the New York *World* in his *Fables* (1878): "The Villager and the Snake," "The Grasshopper and the Ant," "The Merchant of Venice," "The Good Samaritan," "The Centipede and the Barbaric

Yak," "The Kind-Hearted She-Elephant," "The Fox and the Crow," and "The Ostrich and the Hen."

———. "A Threnody" (humorous poem, published in 1878). Lanigan wrote humorous rhymes as well as prose "fables." His most popular poem was the often-reprinted "A Threnody," which begins: "What, what, what,/What's the news from Swat?/Sad news,/Bad news/ . . . Your great Akhoond is dead!/That's Swat's the matter!" Lanigan's doggerel was inspired by London newspaper notices of the death on 17 January 1878 of Abdul Ghafur, the aged Akhoond of the territory of Swat on the northwest border of India. Rossiter Johnson soon published Lanigan's jingle in an anthology (*Play-day Poems* [New York: Henry Holt and Co., 1878], pp. 191–192), and it became a favorite item in American newspapers.

Clemens pasted a newspaper clipping of Lanigan's "Threnody" in the copy of *Fables by G. Washington Aesop* he signed in 1905; the poem is introduced there by the editor of "Notes and Queries," who writes: "During the last six months I have been several times asked by different correspondents to publish a correct copy of the late G. T. Lanigan's verses. I now reprint them under their original title" [i.e., "A Threnody"]. Mark Twain evidently intended to include the piece in his anthology of American humor, for he referred to it four times in his notebooks of 1880 and 1881 (NB 19 and NB 20, *N&J* 2: 365, 366, 429, 450), yet for some reason it did not appear in *Mark Twain's Library of Humor* (1888). Later Twain mentioned "the Ahkoond [*sic*] of Swat" among a catalogue of "sounding titles" he enjoyed hearing in Bombay (NB 36 [January 1896], TS p. 21), and in Jeypore he reminded himself to quote the poem in his next travel book (NB 36, TS p. 55). Chapter 39 of *Following the Equator* (1897) did list "the Ahkoond [*sic*] of Swat's" title among the "sumptuous" names of India.

LANOYE, FERDINAND (SOMETIMES TUGNOT) DE (1810–1870), also known as AUGUSTIN FERDINAND. *Rameses the Great; or, Egypt 3300 Years Ago*. Translated from the French. Illus. New York: Scribner, Armstrong & Co., 1872. 296 pp. [Lanoye's title is a variant spelling of Ramses II.]

Source: MTLAcc, entry #1990, volume donated from Clemens's library by Clara Clemens Gabrilowitsch in 1910.

———. *The Sublime in Nature; Compiled from the Descriptions of Travellers and Celebrated Writers*. Illus. New York: Scribner, Armstrong & Co., 1872. 344 pp.

Source: MTLAcc, entry #1993, volume donated from Clemens's library by Clara Clemens Gabrilowitsch in 1910.

Categorizes and describes natural scenery and memorable phenomena around the world.

LARDNER, LENA BOGARDUS (PHILLIPS) (1834–1918). *"This Spray of Western Pine."* New York: Broadway Publishing Co., 1903. 46 pp.

On 23 July 1904 the author wrote to Clemens from her home in Niles, Michigan: "As a mark of loving admiration for our country's best author, I have sent—(thru my publisher) my simple little volumes of prose and verse" (MTP). She also enclosed a small advertising leaflet puffing *"This Spray of Western Pine"* as "a dainty book of dainty verse, daintily produced. Illustrated prettily" (MTP). Clemens wrote on the envelope, "Wait for this book." Lardner's poems, miscellaneous in subject matter, included a poem alluding to Mark Twain and other famous writers ("A Dream of Authors," pp. 3–5), a tribute to Booker T. Washington's autobiography (p. 13), and an encomium to the "kind, generous Scot," Andrew Carnegie (p. 14). The poetic responses to nature seem strained, as "Dowagiac Creek" illustrates: "The red man named thee and the red man loved thee,/In light canoe he skimmed thy surface free;/But driven westward toward the reddening sunset,/Left thee to men less picturesque than he!" (p. 42).

LARIVE ET FLEURY, pseudonyms of Auguste Nicolas Merlette (1827–1889) and André-Hauvion Casimir (1839–1909), also known as Hauvion l'aîné. *La deuxième année de grammaire: revision, syntaxe, style, littérature, histoire littéraire, 380 exercices d'orthographe et de redaction, lexique . . . 80 rédactions nouvelles. . . . Soixante-dix-huitième edition.* Paris: Armand Colin et cie, [1887]. 240 pp. [Originally published in 1877.]

Inscription: signed in pencil on the front pastedown endpaper, "Jean Clemens/Couvent Assomption/Le 10 Janvier 1894/Paris./Couvent de l'Assomption". The front cover is inscribed in pencil, possibly in Olivia's hand: "Jean Clemens/Hartford Con".

Marginalia: childish doodlings.

Location: Mark Twain Library, Redding, Connecticut.

Copy examined: Jean Clemens's essentially unmarked copy. Has the red ink Mark Twain Library accession number "3629" and the Library's purple oval stamps. Examined in 1970 and again in June 1982.

LARKIN, GEORGE (1642–1707). *The Visions of John Bunyan, Being His Last Remains; Giving an Account of the Glories of Heaven, the Terror of Hell, and of the World to Come.* Small pocket-size volume, brown cloth, damaged leather spine. New York: John Tiebout, 1806. 126 pp. [First published in 1711, this plagiarized work is now attributed to the London publisher George Larkin, who borrowed material from Bunyan's *A Few Sighs from Hell, or the Groans of a Damned Soul* (1858).]

Inscription: the front free flyleaf is missing.

Location: Mark Twain Library, Redding, Connecticut.

Copy examined: Quite likely Clemens's unmarked copy, based on its early accession number. Albert E. Stone, Jr.'s catalog of Clemens's books in the Mark Twain Library at Redding, Connecticut included this title in 1955. I could not find the volume when I visited the Mark Twain Library in 1970. However, when I returned to Redding in June 1982 it had been located and it was still in the collection when I revisited the Library on 9 November 2019. It has a black ink Mark Twain Library accession number, "2931" and the purple oval Library stamps.

Baetzhold, *MT&JB* (1970), p. 374 n. 21.

LARNED, JOSEPHUS NELSON (1836–1913), ed. *The Literature of American History: A Bibliographical Guide, in Which the Scope, Character, and Comparative Worth of Books in Selected Lists Are Set Forth in Brief Notes by Critics of Authority.* Preface by George Iles (1852–1942). First edition. Original blue cloth, gilt. Boston: Published for the American Historical Association by Houghton Mifflin Co., 1902. 588 pp.

Inscription: (by Clemens, in black ink) "From/George Iles./S L. Clemens/Riverdale, 1902." Iles not only contributed the preface but also funded the research for this work, donating $10,000 (New York *Times*, 13 July 1901). Clemens had met Iles in Montreal in 1881; since then Iles had moved to New York City and become an editor and science writer. He and Clemens exchanged several letters in 1902.

Catalog: *A1911*, "large 8vo, cloth, Bost. 1902," quotes the inscription, lot 291, sold for $3.40.

Location: collection of Kevin Mac Donnell, Austin, Texas.

Copy examined: Clemens's unmarked copy, in July 2004. Displays the *A1911* sale label. An unused envelope from the Windsor Hotel in Montreal is laid in the volume.

J. N. Larned was, with Clemens, one of the co-owners and co-editors of the Buffalo *Express* during the 1869–1871 period of Clemens's connection with that publication. Clemens thanked Larned on 13 June 1902 "for the big literary-historical book, which arrived last night" (PH in MTP).

Reigstad, *SL* (2013), pp. 45–47.

LAROUSSE, PIERRE ATHANASE (1817–1875). *Grammaire supérieure. Troisième année.* Nouvelle édition (19e). Blue cloth. Paris: Librairie Larousse, n.d. [1901]. 552 pp. [Page 8 of the text mentions the date 26 février 1901.]

Inscription: the front free endpaper is signed in black ink: "Jean L. Clemens/21 Fifth Avenue/New York City./December 1904."

Location: Mark Twain Library, Redding, Connecticut.

Copy examined: Jean Clemens's unmarked copy, which possibly belonged previously to another member of the Clemens family. Has the red ink Mark Twain Library accession number "3633". Examined in 1970 and again in June 1982.

——. *Nouveau Larousse illustré:dictionnaire universel encyclopédique publié sous la direction de Claude Augé [1854–1924].* 7 volumes. Illus., maps. Paris: Libraire Larousse, [1898–1904].

In an interior photograph taken by Jean Clemens in the early 1900s seven volumes of this title are visible in a bookshelf in the background (collection of Kevin Mac Donnell, Austin, Texas).

——. *Petite grammaire du premier âge. Nouvelle edition (91e). . . . Livre de l' Élève.* Paris: Librairie Larousse, 1891. 168 pp.

Inscription: the title page is signed "Jean Clemens/October 1892./Florence/Italie." (Jean's signature is in black ink and the other two lines were added by Olivia Clemens in blue ink.)

Marginalia: a penciled notation not in Clemens's hand appears on the rear pastedown endpaper: "The following verbs are conjugated with être, also all reflective verbs"; a list of twelve French verbs follows.

Location: Mark Twain Library, Redding, Connecticut.

Copy examined: Jean Clemens's unmarked copy (except for the conjugations on the rear pastedown endpaper). Has the red ink Mark Twain Library accession number "3631". Examined in 1970 and again in June 1982.

LARROWE, MARCUS DWIGHT (1832–1896), pseud. "Dr. or Prof. Alphonse Loisette." *Physiological Memory; or, The Instantaneous Art of Never Forgetting. Part IV.* New York: Alphonse Loisette, 1886. 32 pp.

Inscription: Albert Bigelow Paine wrote the words "Loisette Memory" in pencil on a leaflet that accompanied this pamphlet.

Location: Mark Twain Papers, Bancroft Library, University

of California at Berkeley.

Copy examined: Clemens's copy, presumably. No marks.

Professor Loisette's memory-building methods became one of Clemens's many enthusiasms, at least for a time. In 1887 Clemens sent a published broadside that quoted himself to the Reverend John Davis of Hannibal, Missouri; in it he testified that an hour of personal counsel from Loisette gave him confidence worth ten thousand dollars (ASSSCL). Page 2 in the Appendix of Loisette's 1887 edition of *The Loisettian School of Physiological Memory: The Instantaneous Art of Never Forgetting* reprinted a letter Clemens wrote on 4 March 1887 stating that "Prof. Loisette proved to me that I already *had* a memory, a thing which I was not aware of till then. . . . The information cost me but little, yet I value it at a prodigious figure" (TS in MTP; also published in *Harper's Weekly*, 2 April 1887). On 9 July 1887 Clemens sent Franklin G. Whitmore a new draft of his testimonial for "that Loisette circular" (ALS in MTP). Later, however, beset by complications with the Paige typesetter and the details of publishing *A Connecticut Yankee in King Arthur's Court*, Clemens instructed Whitmore on 23 November 1889 to answer inquiries by saying that whereas Clemens formerly believed the Loisette method to be worthwhile, he had changed his opinion "long ago" (ALS in MTP). It would seem to be no coincidence that a 224-page book ridiculing Loisette's methods had appeared in the previous year—George S. Fellows's *"Loisette" Exposed (Marcus Dwight Larrowe, Alias Silas Holmes, Alias Alphonse Loisette). Together with Loisette's Complete System of Physiological Memory, the Instantaneous Art of Never Forgetting, to Which Is Appended a Bibliography of Mnemonics, 1325–1888* (New York: G. S. Fellows, 1888). Albert Bigelow Paine described the sequence of Clemens's opinions in *Mark Twain: A Biography* (1912), pp. 850–851. Incidentally, the pattern of Larrowe's life corresponded somewhat with Clemens's experiences: former attorney Larrowe spent his early years in the territory of Nevada and in 1894 he commenced a tour around the world to tout his memory system.

Thomas M. Walsh and Thomas D. Zlatic, "Mark Twain and the Art of Memory," *American Literature* 53.2 (May 1981): 214–231.

"DE LAS' SACK! DE LAS' SACK" (unidentified work song).

"The half-naked crews of perspiring negroes that worked them [the steamboats] were roaring such songs as 'De Las' Sack! De Las' Sack!'—inspired to unimaginable exaltation by the chaos of turmoil and racket" (*LonMiss* [1883], Ch. 16).

LATHBURY, MARY ARTEMISIA (1841–1913). *The Birthday Week; Pictures and Verse.* New York: R. Worthington, [cop. 1884]. [15 pp.]

Source: MTLAcc, entry #1896, volume donated from Clemens's library by Clara Clemens Gabrilowitsch in 1910.

————. *Twelve Times One, Illustrations of Child Life.* Original quarter cloth and chromolithogaphed boards. Illustrated by the author. New York: Worthington Co., 1888.

Inscription: inscribed in ink on the front free endpaper, "Ida Langdon/With love—Aunt Jose/1887." Ida Langdon (1880–1964) was a playmate of the Clemens daughters.

Location: collection of Kevin Mac Donnell, Austin, Texas.

Purchased from the Langdon family.

Source: supplementary inventory sent from Mac Donnell to Alan Gribben, 28 August 2017. No markings in the text.

This anthology of poems about child life would have been accessible to Clemens and his daughters whenever they visited the Langdons in Elmira.

LATHROP, GEORGE PARSONS (1851–1898). *Would You Kill Him? A Novel.* New York: Harper & Brothers, 1890. 384 pp.

Source: MTLAcc, entry #1578, volume donated by Clemens.

Roger Holsclaw is acquitted of murder by a court but convicted nonetheless by his conscience. He confesses to his wife Alice and nearly commits suicide, but his wife forgives him and he elects to go on living. As a couple they are strengthened by the ordeal.

Clemens began corresponding with Lathrop, who had married Nathaniel Hawthorne's daughter Rose, in 1878. The varied career of Lathrop—magazine editor, newspaper editor, travel writer, poet, and novelist—was capped by his founding the American Copyright League in 1883. Lathrop published in 1885 the fullest, most evocative description of Nook Farm, its environs, and Clemens's place in it ever written by a contemporary ("A Model State Capital," *Harper's Monthly Magazine* 71.425 [October 1885]: 715–734). Profusely illustrated, the essay reproduced Karl Gerhardt's bust of Clemens (p. 721) and provided large sketches of the exterior of Clemens's mansion (p. 724) and an interior view of Clemens's library room (p. 725). Lathrop also devoted a number of pages to portraying Clemens's activities, friends, and daily routines. Daniel A. Wells quoted from Lathrop's article ("An Annotated Checklist of Twain Allusions in *Harper's Monthly*, 1850–1900," *American Literary Realism* 17.1 [Spring 1984]: 119–120), but Lathrop's discerning observations really ought to be far more widely known. One supposes that Lathrop's account of the intellectuality of Clemens's Hartford life must have pleased Clemens immensely.

LAURIE, JAMES STUART (1831–1904). *The Story of Australasia: Its Discovery, Colonisation, and Development.* Map. London: Osgood, McIlvaine & Co., 1896. 388 pp.

In Chapter 10 of *Following the Equator* (1897) Mark Twain quotes briefly from Laurie's account of the heartless treatment received by transported convicts; a much longer extract appears in Chapter 29 of *Following the Equator*, where Twain employs the words of "the historian Laurie, whose book, 'The Story of Australasia,' is just out," to describe the Derwent estuary near Hobart "with considerable truth and intemperance." (Twain counterpoises Laurie's grandiose flights with his own deflating remarks about the scenery.) Dennis Welland—"Mark Twain's Last Travel Book" (1965), p. 44—reported that the manuscript for Chapter 29 of *Following the Equator* originally included two entire pages of quotations from Laurie's book; these were deleted by Mark Twain's publisher. In the manuscript version Twain criticized Laurie's style but praised his "eye for scenery." Twain had jotted "The Story of Austral" among notes he made on a photo-mounting board in preparation for his travel book (collection of Kevin Mac Donnell, Austin, Texas).

Madigan, "Mark Twain's Passage to India" (1974), pp. 164 ff., 361.

LAVEDAN, HENRI LÉON ÉMILE (1859–1940). *The Duel* (three-act play, performed in 1906). Translated by Louis N[apoleon]. Parker (1852–1944).

Charles Frohman produced this play at the Hudson Theatre in New York City in February 1906; it contained only two female roles. Clara Clemens and Isabel Lyon saw a performance on 21 March 1906 (Fears, *Day by Day* 4: 381). One of the actors, Mary Lawton (1870–1945) had become a friend of Clara's and visited the Clemenses (*AutoMT* 2: 466). In an Autobiographical Dictation of 5 April 1906 Clemens predicted that "hers will be a great name some day" (*AutoMT* 2: 18). On 7 May 1906 Clemens hotly defended Mary Lawton's performance as the Duchess de Chailles in *The Duel* (Clemens to Otis Skinner, quoted in Fears, *Day by Day* 4: 381). Lawton had studied singing in New York City, Paris, and London before deciding on a stage career. Clemens was not alone in predicting her future success. The July 1905 issue of *The Critic and Literary World* (New York City) had given this "heroic blonde" a full-length article heralding her arrival as an accomplished actress (pp. 14–15). On 29 January 1910 the New York *Dramatic Mirror* praised her performance at the Hackett Theatre in Rudolph Besier's play, *Olive Latimer's Husband*. George Bernard Shaw directed her Broadway performance of his *The Philanderer* in 1913–1914, and the two would remain friends thereafter. Perhaps the high point of her career was being cast by director George Irving in the film version of *John Glayde's Honor* (1915), a play by Alfred Sutro in which she toured. She remained active on the stage into the early 1920s, after which she wrote several books about musicians. In 1925 she published a book based on interviews with the Clemenses' former housekeeper—*A Lifetime with Mark Twain: The Memories of Katy Leary, for Thirty Years His Faithful and Devoted Servant*.

LAWRENCE, GEORGE ALFRED (1827–1876). *Silverland*. London: Chapman and Hall, 1873. 259 pp.

Clemens made a memorandum on the rear flyleaf of Notebook 17 in November 1878: "Return 'Silverland.'" He may have borrowed this book from his fellow tourists, Mr. and Mrs. August Chamberlaine. Lawrence's travel narrative primarily describes California and Nevada. His accounts of Chinese railroad laborers seem unfeeling. See *N&J* 2: 281.

LAWRENCE, HENRY MONTGOMERY (1806–1857).

In Chapter 58 of *Following the Equator* (1897) Mark Twain writes that the chief cause of the Great Mutiny in India was "the annexation of the kingdom of Oudh by the East India Company—characterized by Sir Henry Lawrence as 'the most unrighteous act that was ever committed.'" Lawrence wrote *Adventures of an Officer in the Service of Runjeet Singh* (1845) and *Adventures of an Officer in the Punjaub* (1846). But Francis V. Madigan, Jr.—"Mark Twain's Passage to India" (1974)—concluded that Twain took the Lawrence quotation from Julia Inglis's *The Siege of Lucknow. A Diary*.

Laws of Tennessee. Nashville, Tennessee, 1860. 708 pp.

Source: MTLAcc, entry #888, volume donated by Clemens.

LAWSON, THOMAS W[ILLIAM]. (1857–1925). *Frenzied Finance*. New York: The Ridgway-Thayer Co., 1905. 559 pp. The first part, "The Story of Amalgamated," was published separately in 1904–1905.

Clemens and Henry H. Rogers exchanged derogatory remarks about the serialized publication of Lawson's muckraking exposé, "Frenzied Finance: The Story of Amalgamated," which commenced in the July 1904 issue of *Everybody's Magazine* and ran through 1905. The earliest installments assailed Rogers as "the big brain, the big body, the Master of 'Standard Oil'" (9 [August 1904]: 158). Rogers joked somewhat prematurely about Lawson's being "played out" in a letter to Clemens of 11 July 1905 (*MTHHR*, pp. 589, 590); Clemens predicted that "it is Lawson's turn, now" on 7 August 1905 (*MTHHR*, pp. 595–596). See also the Catalog entry for Finley Peter Dunne.

LAYARD, AUSTEN HENRY (1817–1894). *Early Adventures in Persia, Susiana, and Babylonia, Including a Residence Among the Bakhtiyari and Other Wild Tribes Before the Discovery of Nineveh*. 2 vols. London: John Murray, 1887. [Edition conjectured.]

On 9 June 1893 Clemens wrote from Florence to Joseph H. Twichell about meeting this English archaeologist and diplomat and reading Layard's narrative of his adventures as a young man (*LMTJHT*, p. 179). Clemens quotes a footnote from Layard's book that might be expected to amuse Twichell. The same footnote is entered in the notebook that Clemens kept for this period (NB 33, TS p. 15); Clemens found it on page 357 in the second volume of Layard's *Early Adventures in Persia, Susiana, and Babylonia*. Describing Mr. Lucas, the plain-spoken old quartermaster of the *Assyria*, Layard noted there: "This same quartermaster was celebrated among the English in Mesopotamia for an entry in the log-book. The 'Assyria' had been left under his care near Basra, when there arose one of those violent tornadoes which occasionally sweep over this part of Arabia. The vessel was in great danger. After the storm was over Mr. Lucas thus recorded the event: 'The windy and watery elements raged. Tears and prayers was had recourse to, but was of no manner of use. So we hauled up the anchor and got round the point.'" Clemens was also impressed by the coincidence of Layard's unexpected appearance in Florence just as Clemens was reading his *Early Adventures*. Twice—on a slip of paper inserted into Notebook 33 and in an entry jotted down on 28 May 1896 (NB 38, TS p. 22)—Clemens recorded his astonishment at being called away from reading this book to go to dinner and then finding Layard himself present there.

———. *Nineveh and Its Remains: With an Account of a Visit to the Chaldæan Christians of Kurdistand, and the Yezidis, or Devil-Worshippers; and an Enquiry into the Manners and Arts of the Ancient Assyrians*. [First published in London in 1849; subsequently issued in several editions under various titles.]

Reporting from Florence to Clara Clemens on 12 March 1893 about his recent activities, Clemens mentioned that "Sir Henry Layard & Lady Layard are here for a few days. . . . Susy & I dined with them a night or two ago. Very pleasant indeed, but no talk about Nineveh—which was a disappointment to me" (*Sotheby's 2003*, lot #71).

LEA, HENRY CHARLES (1825–1909). *An Historical Sketch of Sacerdotal Celibacy in the Christian Church*. Second edition, enlarged. Boston: Houghton, Mifflin and Co., 1884. 682 pp.

[Edition conjectured.]

In February 1888, after making a note regarding the issuance of the first two volumes of Lea's *A History of the Inquisition of the Middle Ages*, Clemens added: "Also, his 'Sacerdotal Celibacy'" (NB 27, *N&J* 3: 376).

———. *A History of the Inquisition of the Middle Ages.* 3 vols. New York: Harper & Brothers, 1888.

"History of the Inquisition—2 vols. ready. (Harper.) Henry C. Lea," Clemens noted in February 1888 (NB 27, *N&J* 3: 376).

Scott, *MTAL* (1969), p. 146.

LEAR, EDWARD (1812–1888). *Letters of Edward Lear, Author of "The Book of Nonsense," to Chichester Fortescue, Lord Carlingford, and Frances, Countess Waldegrave.* Ed. by Constance (Braham) Strachie, Lady Strachey (1855–1936). Second edition. The frontispiece is loose. London: T. Fisher Unwin, 1907. 328 pp.

Inscription: inscribed on the front pastedown endpaper in black ink, "To Mr. S. L. Clemens/with the compliments of/the 'Editor'/Aug. 1908."

Location: Mark Twain Library, Redding, Connecticut.

Copy examined: Clemens's copy, unmarked. Has the red ink Mark Twain Library accession number "3070". Examined in 1970 and again in June 1982.

LEATHERS, JESSE (1846–1887). "An American Earl" (unpublished autobiography, 1881).

Clemens encouraged the eccentric Jesse Leathers to submit his autobiography to James R. Osgood, telling Osgood to expect "a gassy, extravagant, idiotic book that will be delicious reading, for I've read some of his rot. . . . I believe this ass will write a serious book which would make a cast-iron dog laugh" (*MTLP*, pp. 133–134). The 12,000-word manuscript proved to be unpublishable, but Clemens testified that "The Earl's [Jesse Leathers's] literary excrement charmed me like Fanny Hill. I just wallowed in it" (SLC to James R. Osgood, Hartford, 30 March 1881, *MTLP*, p. 136). Leathers claimed to be the Earl of Durham.

Lucius M. Lampton, "Jesse Leathers," *The Routledge Encyclopedia of Mark Twain*, ed. J. R. LeMaster and James D. Wilson (New York: Routledge, 2013), pp. 448–450. (A previous edition of this work was published in 1993 by Garland.)

LEAVITT, LYDIA (BROWN) (1851–c. 1907). *Bohemian Society.* Brockville [Ontario] Times Printing and Publishing Co., [188–]. 65 pp.

Inscription: (On the flyleaf) "To 'Mark Twain,' with the compliments of the author/Toronto Dec. 9th 1884".

Location: Mark Twain Library, Redding, Connecticut.

Copy examined: Clemens's copy, unmarked. Has the Mark Twain Library accession number "2898". Examined in 1970 and again in June 1982.

Ennui alternates with ecstasy in these musings about life and people. Leavitt quotes Joaquin Miller's poem "Is It Worthwhile?" on page 63.

LEBERT, SIEGMUND (1822–1884) and **LOUIS STARK** (1831–1884). *Grand Theoretical and Practical Piano-School for Systematic Instruction in All Branches of Piano-Playing.* Fourth English edition. Ninth German edition. Translated by C. E. R. Müller. Stuttgart: J. G. Cotta, 1880. 134 pp.

[Edition conjectured.]

"1 Leibert [*sic*] & Stark's Piano School Book I. 4.00" reads a bill to Clemens of 1 December 1880 from M. L. Bartlett, Hartford (MTP).

LEBLANC, MAURICE (1864–1941). *The Exploits of Arsène Lupin.* Translated by Alexander Louis Teixeira de Mattos (1865–1921). New York: Harper & Brothers, 1907. 314 pp.

Source: MTLAcc, entry #1114, volume donated by Clemens.

Clemens must have enjoyed these nine crime stories by the French author Leblanc, since they featured a master thief whose urbane manners and witty retorts made this "Gentleman Burglar" the mirror opposite of Arthur Conan Doyle's Sherlock Holmes. Clemens thought Sherlock Holmes to be overrated as a literary creation, and in the ninth short story in this volume, "Holmlock Shears Arrives Too Late," this "great English detective for whom no mystery exists" (p. 275) is outmatched by Leblanc's clever Lupin, who only robs the wealthy and whose criminal talents make him vastly superior to police efforts to halt his notorious heists. Leblanc's stories often end with surprising twists of the Guy de Maupassant sort.

LECKY, WILLIAM EDWARD HARTPOLE (1838–1903). *A History of England in the Eighteenth Century.* 8 volumes. 12mo, cloth. New York: D. Appleton and Co., 1887–1890.

Inscription: the front flyleaf of Volume VI is signed "S. L. Clemens."

Catalogs: *A1911*, "6 vols., 8vo, cloth, N.Y. 1887–8," quotes the signature, lot 285, sold for $3.50; Goodspeed's Book Shop, Boston, Massachusetts, Catalogue 253, 1936[?], item #58, "6 vols., New York, 1888–7, Vols. VII and VIII are wanting, . . . the sale label pasted in each volume and his [Clemens's] signature on the flyleaf of Vol. VI," $10.

Location: currently unknown.

Clemens wrote good-naturedly to his friend William H. Gross of Hartford's Brown & Gross bookstore on 21 July 1887: "Whatinthehelldoyoureckonamancando with a History that begins with volume *V*? (Lecky's History of the 18th Century.) Shove along the other 4 volumes & don't fool around" (Madeleine B. Stern, "Hartford's Oldest Surviving Bookstore," *A B Bookman's Weekly*, 8 November 1982, p. 3174). Notebook 28 (September 1888) contains Clemens's reference to "impressment of sailors & soldiers, Vol. 3, last pages" (*N&J* 3: 416); another entry mentions "584 vol 3—18th Cent." (*N&J* 3: 417). Lecky's book also appears in Mark Twain's tentative appendix for *A Connecticut Yankee in King Arthur's Court* (1889), credited for details about "the woman burnt" and the "mansion house" (NB 29 [1889], *N&J* 3: 503, 506).

Coleman O. Parsons, "Background" (1960), p. 67 n. 32; James D. Williams, "The Use of History" (1965), pp. 103, 104; Howard G. Baetzhold, *MT&JB* (1970), pp. 152–153, 230, 344 n. 48; William M. Gibson, ed. *MSM* (1969), pp. 21, 151–152; Paul Baender, ed. *WIM?* (1973), pp. 540–541; Baetzhold, "Samuel L. Clemens" (1988), pp. 34–47.

———. *A History of England in the Eighteenth Century.* 8 volumes. 12mo, cloth. New York: D. Appleton and Co., 1887–1890. [Six volumes only.]

Inscriptions: the front free flyleaf in each of the first five volumes is inscribed in ink, "T. W. Crane/Quarry Farm/

Sept. 1887" (or some similar variant) in a hand that appears to be Susan Crane's. Volume VI, however, is inscribed more elaborately by Clemens: "T. W. Crane/Quarry Farm,/ Go-as-You-Please Hall/Rest-&-be-Thankful/East Hill/ Elmira, N. Y./Sept. 1887."

Marginalia: Mary Boewe made the following transcriptions of the marginalia on 19 and 17–19 September 1984 at Quarry Farm. Clemens annotated Volumes I, II, III, and VI in pencil; Volumes IV and V have no markings. Volumes I and II have by far the most notes and markings. Volumes I contains Clemens's notes on pages 9, 10, 12, 15, 19, 185, 190, 191, 192, 194, 198, and 620, together with markings visible on 8, 9, 10, 11, 12, 13, 14, 15, 17, 18, 19, 20, 185, 186, 190, 191, 194, 197, 198, 619, 621, 623, 624, and 625. In Volume II Clemens wrote notes on pages 9, 17, 19, 20, 22, 24, 26, 32, 36, 43, 58, 81, 84, 88, 89, 90, 91, 94, and 98. That volume also has pencil markings on pages 3, 9, 13, 15, 16, 17, 18, 19, 20, 22, 24, 25, 26, 27, 28, 29, 30, 31, 32, 33, 34, 35, 56, 37, 39, 40, 42, 43, 44, 46, 49, 50, 54, 57, 58, 62, 63, 64, 65, 66, 73, 74, 75, 78, 79, 81, 82, 84, 86, 87, 88, 89, 90, 91, 92, 93, 94, 95, 96, 97, 98, and 134. In Volume III Clemens only made notes on pages 45 and 587. Pencil markings in that volume can be seen on pages 1, 3, 192, 296, 536, 538, 581, 582, 583, 586, and 587. Clemens's notes in Volume VI were made on pages 168, 232, 233, 258, 259, 262, 263, and 268, with pencil markings such as vertical lines and underlinings made on pages 144, 174, 166, 178–171, 221, 225, 231–233, 235–237, 240, 243, 246–248, 250–253, and 255–271. A few of Clemens's comments stand out from the rest: "Both the American & French Revolu-/tions were precipitated by accidents—&/so indeed was the English Rev." (I, top of page 15); "Within 15 yrs of Salem—that they find/so much fault with—where *nobody* was burnt" (II, top of page 88); "After Salem above 10 years" (II, p. 89); "1704–5" (II, p. 89); "34 yrs after Salem" (II, p. 90); "Confused & obscure—an unusual/fault in Mr. Lecky's English" (III, right margin on page 45); "The idea being drawn from Moses?" (VI, p. 232); and "English liberty was for gentlemen only" (VI, left margin of page 262). Clemens seemed particularly interested in the gruesomeness and relative lateness of the Scottish persecution of alleged witches, but many other topics, such as the brutality of the English treatment of resisting areas of Scotland, also caught his attention.

Provenance: The books were discovered on the shelves in the library at Quarry Farm in 1984. Six volumes of this edition had been listed (with "Twain marginalia") in the appraisal of the library books at the time of the donation of Quarry Farm to Elmira College. On 9 July 1987 Mark Woodhouse transferred the volumes from the Quarry Farm library to the Mark Twain Archive; a list Woodhouse made at the time mentions "fragment of a letter to Twain from Elise Rathbone" laid in Volume V.

Catalog: Ball 2016 inventory, 6 vols., red cloth, gilt letter, blind design on covers, marginal notes.

Location: Mark Twain Archive, Gannett-Tripp Learning Center, Elmira College, Elmira, New York.

Copy examined: photocopies of the title page and inscription from Volume I, along with transcriptions of the

marginalia in all six volumes of Theodore Crane's set, which was read and annotated by Clemens during his visits to Quarry Farm. Sent by Mary Boewe in January 1985 to the Mark Twain Papers, Bancroft Library, University of California at Berkeley.

Mary Boewe's often-cited "Twain on Lecky: Some Marginalia at Quarry Farm," (1985) helpfully described and quoted evidence that Clemens read Lecky's book during the summers spent at his in-laws' home outside Elmira. See also Howard G. Baetzhold, "'Well, My Book Is Written'" (1996), pp. 41–77; and especially Joe B. Fulton, *Mark Twain in the Margins: The Quarry Farm Marginalia and A Connecticut Yankee in King Arthur's Court* (2000), pp. 20–21, 39, 63–81, 85–87, 133–173; Delphine Louis-Dimitrov, "The Democratic Reconfiguration of History in Mark Twain's *Personal Recollections of Joan of Arc*," *American Literary Realism* 51.2 (Winter 2018): 162–179.

———. *History of European Morals from Augustus to Charlemagne.* 2 volumes. 8vo, original green cloth, both volumes worn. New York: D. Appleton and Co., 1874.

Inscriptions: the front flyleaf of Volume I is signed in pencil, "T. W. Crane/1874 New York". (Theodore W. Crane was Clemens's brother-in-law.) Below Crane's signature Clemens signed the same flyleaf in black ink with a shaky hand (or a stubborn pen): "S L. Clemens/1906." The title page of Volume II is signed "T. W. Crane 1877" in pencil; Clemens also signed his name ("S L. Clemens") in black ink on the front pastedown endpaper.

Marginalia: Albert Bigelow Paine quoted a few of Clemens's remarks (*MTB*, pp. 511–512), which Paine tantalizingly described as "notes not always quotable in the family circle." Paine attributed these marginalia to "two volumes of Lecky, much worn" (*MTB*, p. 1539). Chester L. Davis (1903–1987) continued this chaste tradition when he reported Clemens's notations in issues of *The Twainian* between May and December 1955 (also in the issue of November-December 1962); Davis's transcription omitted "those things which . . . are too rough for the eyes of some of our young people," as well as Clemens's "many short corrections of language . . . or short exclamations" (November-December 1955 issue, p. 4). The brevity of Paine's quotations and the unreliability of Davis' transcript created a problem for Mark Twain scholars. Walter Blair— *Mark Twain & Huck Finn* (1960), pp. 134–135, 401 n. 6—pointed out that the few comments quoted by Paine do not match up with any of the marginalia appearing in *The Twainian*. This led Blair to a shrewd speculation that Clemens may have owned or had access to another copy of Lecky's book that Paine consulted in writing *Mark Twain: A Biography* (1912). Blair's theory, however, resulted in confusion, since some commentators therefore mistakenly inferred that Clemens annotated one copy around 1874 (Paine's date for the marginalia) and then wrote in another copy in 1906, the date Davis erroneously supposed Clemens both inscribed and marked his copy. It is clear now that Clemens did have access to—and annotated—two separate copies of *History of European Morals* at Quarry Farm (as well as several other books by Lecky Clemens found there; see Mary Boewe's 1985 article, cited below). We can also assume that Clemens simply never bothered to inscribe the volumes sold in the

1951 auction (and then obtained by Chester L. Davis) until the year 1906 because they already contained the signature of his brother-in-law Theodore W. Crane, who died in 1889. My examination of those volumes at Chester Davis's home in August 1970 and at Kevin Mac Donnell's in July 2004 revealed that Clemens re-read them numerous times; his profuse marginalia display various shades of brown, black, and blue ink—together with many markings and notes in pencil. Clemens's writing instruments sometimes alternate from page to page. The first volume, for instance, contains annotation in brown ink on page 192, pencil marks on page 193, a note and brackets in blue ink on page 194, and a remark in brown ink on page 408. Kevin Mac Donnell and I believe that the pencil notes can be associated with the 1870s, the blue ink notes are consistent with the Clemens's holograph in the 1880s, and the black and brown ink notes probably can be dated post-1900.

Clemens made a total of seventy-eight separate notes in pencil and different shades of ink on sixty-eight pages totaling 929 words, besides marking the margins or underlining places in pencil on 231 pages of the 800 pages of text in the two volumes. Obviously this was one of the most heavily annotated books in his personal library, raising issues he could not resist concerning ethics, slavery, religion, persecution, morality, determinism, and progress (or lack of it) in Western civilization. On the rear endpaper of Volume II Clemens wrote in pencil: "If I have understood this book aright, it proves two things beyond shadow or question: 1. That Christianity is the very invention of hell itself; 2. & That Christianity is the most precious & elevating & ennobling boon ever vouchsafed to the world." Unfortunately there are virtually no dates or topical references among Clemens's marginalia, but he does allude (in pencil) to the "Canadian Indians" of Francis Parkman on page 191 of the second volume. Clemens acquired and read Parkman's histories of North America in the early 1880s. Clemens made notes and marks on the following pages of Volume I: 5 (note in brown ink, a late hand), 6, 115, 175, 176, 191, 192 (grammatical correction), 193, 194, 195–197, 210, 214 (a comment in blue ink concerning theories that death is not actually painful), 215–220 (blue ink markings), 221 (pencil marks), 222 (a lengthy marginal comment in pencil pokes fun at Christ's release from Purgatory, suggesting that Purgatory merely functions to produce revenue), 235 (a brown-ink note laments that money has replaced liberty as the god of the American republic), 262, 267, 269, 293 (the sentence beginning "but they" and concluding "to reveal" is underscored and marked with brown ink; Clemens comments that this satisfactorily explains for him why actors employ exaggerations of style), 299 (a penciled note disputes the notion that 80,000 voices could be heard any better than a single voice), 308, 310–334 (pencil marks), 322 (a penciled annotation regarding slavery in the American South), 325, 326, 328, 329 (both pencil marks and notations), 359 (a minor alteration of diction in black ink), and a remark in brown ink on the last page (408) regarding Lecky's account of the tortures inflicted by the Romans on Christian believers who would not forsake their religion "when one word

would have freed them from their sufferings," to which Clemens noted sarcastically in the bottom margin: "& God did not speak it."

In Volume II Clemens made one long vertical note in dark brown or black ink on page 20 where Lecky discusses our innate moral perceptions concerning humanity versus cruelty: "All moral perceptions are acquired by the influences around us; these influences begin in infancy; we never get a chance to *find out* whether we have any that are innate or not." In dark brown ink Clemens underlined on page 22 Lecky's assertion that Christianity "formed a new standard higher than any which then existed" and wrote beneath that line: "And so nothing of it was innate." Clemens used pencil in writing on page 72: "Christianity, then, did not raise up the slave, but degraded all conditions of men to the slave's level." (This comment was made in response to Lecky's praise of the Christian religion for reversing the pagan values of the Romans.) On page 87 of Volume II Clemens drew two vertical lines and declared: "The Catholics have long gotten over that weakness. They don't even support or assist their own poor, now." Kevin Mac Donnell reports certain of Clemens's notes that responded to Lecky's discussion of the Christian views of suicide in the second volume ("Who Killed Charlie Webster? A Brief Review of the Twain-Webster Relationship," *Mark Twain Journal* 51.1–2 [Spring-Fall 2013]: 26–29). For example, in a brown ink note on page 56 of Volume II apparently jotted later than 1900, Clemens wrote vertically: "I can quite easily imagine myself giving an unhappy person something to kill himself with, but I cannot imagine myself trying to prevent an unhappy person from committing suicide. It gives me a very real pang to read of a prevented suicide, & a very real feeling of gratitude to read of a successful one."

Catalogs: ListABP (1910), "Hist. European Morals 2 vols., Lecky" and also "Hist. European Morals v. I, Lecky"; *C1951*, #36a and #43a (the two volumes were listed separately among books containing Clemens's marginal notes, thereby compounding the confusion about how many copies of this book Clemens possessed), each volume sold for $25; Christie's, New York City, Sale 7378, including the "Estate of Chester L. Davis," 5 December 1991, lot 184, 2 vols., sold for $12,100.

Provenance: for four decades both volumes were part of Chester L. Davis's Mark Twain Research Foundation collection in Perry, Missouri.

Location: both volumes belong to the collection of Kevin Mac Donnell, Austin, Texas. Purchased at auction in 1991 after Chester Davis's death.

Copy examined: Clemens's copy of Volumes I and II, briefly in 1970 and more thoroughly in July 2004. In August 2004 Kevin D. Mac Donnell sent me photocopies of sample pages from both volumes along with a description of the marginalia (Mac Donnell to Alan Gribben, 8 August 2004).

Clemens's notebooks contain only a single explicit reference to *European Morals* (though there are other oblique allusions), possibly because Clemens principally used the margins of Lecky's book as a repository of his own reflections. In a tentative appendix for *A Connecticut Yankee* in Notebook 29 (1889) Mark Twain acknowledged Lecky as his source for "Hermits & Stylites" and "Roman law" (*N&J* 3: 506). An allusion to Lecky himself ("This was at Mr. Lecky's [dinner party]. He is Irish, you know") occurs in a letter Clemens wrote to Joseph H. Twichell from London on 4 March 1900 (*MTL*, p. 697; *LMTJHT*, p. 263).

These mentions hardly suggest the true significance of Lecky in Clemens's intellectual development. No serious student of Mark Twain's works should neglect reading at least a few chapters of Lecky's historical survey. (A facsimile reprint containing C. Wright Mills' introduction [New York: George Braziller, 1955] is used here.) The first part of Volume I is devoted to historical categorizations of moral philosophies; Lecky quickly takes issue with Utilitarianism, pointing out the inconsistencies in its doctrines and disputing Bentham and other Utilitarian advocates. In the course of Lecky's analysis he comments on the reasons and motivations for good (right) or pernicious (wrong) behavior. The problem centers upon the question of whether humans really possess a moral faculty, an innate sense of right and wrong. While inductive Utilitarians answered "no," Lecky took the position that mankind *does* have a natural moral perception (Lecky once studied for the Church of England), and his opening chapter attempts to prove this thesis. Lecky's arguments remind us that Utilitarianism still possessed considerable intellectual force in the mid-1860s; John Mill published his important essays by that name in 1861 (collected as a book in 1863), the same decade in which Lecky's *European Morals* first issued (1869).

Clemens no doubt appreciated Lecky's habit of periodically summing up his points for convenient memorizing. Probably Clemens saw in these pages what one part of him wished to write—anti-Catholic, anti-slavery, pro-(enlightened) military history, buttressed by hundreds of pages of facts drawn from all periods of human life. Lecky's numerous quotations in lengthy footnotes form a kind of anthology of readings in intellectual history and philosophy. To Lecky's way of thinking, events like the victory of Christianity or the conversion of Rome did not simply "happen"; one can find rational, discernible causes for their occurrence.

But Clemens's attitudes toward Lecky are more complex and ambivalent than is sometimes supposed. The student interested in Lecky's influence should approach the problem of moral conscience under the tutelage of helpful commentaries written by Walter Blair, Roger B. Salomon, and Howard G. Baetzhold. Blair provided a full explication of Lecky's impact on Mark Twain's thought and examined Twain's use of Lecky in writing *Adventures of Huckleberry Finn* (1885) (*MT&HF* [1960], pp. 135–144, 338, 401 n. 6). Salomon's elucidating remarks about the reflections in *A Connecticut Yankee* (1889) of Lecky's Whig-Liberal bias against the Roman Church (*TIH* [1961], pp. 98–102) are another good place to begin understanding the Lecky/Twain relationship. Baetzhold studied the intermingling of Lecky's theories with Twain's reasoning. He discussed Lecky's impact on Twain's *A Connecticut Yankee* at length (*MT&JB* [1970], pp. 134–142 and 346–347), and his exposition of Lecky's influence on *What Is Man?* was a lucid analysis of Twain's debating dialogue (*MT&JB*, pp. 59, 218–228). In fact, Baetzhold succeeded in proving that

What Is Man? simply must be read in conjunction with Lecky's *European Morals*, and this finding demonstrated one shortcoming of Twain's philosophical treatise.

These and other excellent treatments of this topic have not yet explored all of the reverberations of Lecky in Twain's later writings. Lecky's diatribe against the doctrine of infant damnation (Volume I, p. 96), for example, seems related to Mark Twain's notebook draft for "The Mysterious Stranger" contained in Notebook 42 (11 November 1898). An alter ego whom Twain created in "Which Was It?," Sol Bailey (known to the Indiantown villagers as "Ham-fat Bailey the Idiot Philosopher"), is a freethinker whose dogma is "that all motives are selfish"; consequently one need only choose between "high" and "low" selfish motives (*WWD?*, p. 302). In formulating Bailey's "Gospel of Self," a denial of the existence of any but selfish impulses, Twain resumed his debate with Lecky (*WWD?*, p. 379; written 1899–1903). In "The International Lightning Trust" (written in 1909) Jasper Hackett credits Lecky's *European Morals* with giving him the original scheme upon which the story hinges (*FM*, pp. 79, 85). In Chapter 2 Jasper quotes from Chapter 3 of Volume I (p. 367) of *European Morals* to provide examples of superstitious fears held by early pagans—Augustus, Tiberius, Caligula. "I'll read you a sentence or two out of Mr. Lecky's History of European Morals. . . . That's the passage that gave me my splendid idea" (*FM*, p. 85).

We can also credit Lecky with bringing the phrenological term "temperament" back to Mark Twain's recollection (see Alan Gribben, "Mark Twain, Phrenology and the 'Temperaments'" [1972]; a revised version of this essay appears as a chapter in Volume One of the present work). Twain constructed much of the dialogue in *What Is Man?* (1906) around the concept of "temperament," which he defines there as "the disposition you were born with." This piece of phraseology clung to his thought and expression to the end of his life, though he had not used the word much after he copied passages from George Sumner Weaver's *Lectures on Mental Science* into Notebook 1 in 1855 (*N&J* 1: 21–33). Repeated exposures to Lecky's writing, however, evidently awakened his memories of this early classification of physical and mental characteristics. Lecky's discussions of human character in *History of European Morals* contain numerous references to "temperaments," "dispositions," "faculty," "organ," "cultivation" of "moral types," and other catchwords of phrenology (see Volume I: 3, 60–61, 88, 156, 157, 172, 187–188, *et passim*; also Volume II: 192–194). Besides using these terms prevalently, Lecky also divides mankind into two loosely-defined "temperaments"—one of which (the temperament Lecky identifies with the Protestant nature) closely fits the "sanguine" temperament (Volume II, p. 124). As a youth of nineteen Clemens had believed that the description of the sanguine temperament accorded with his own disposition and appearance.

Lecky does not specifically mention phrenology in his book, since the currency of its distinctive terminology was outliving its main hypothesis of physically detectable mental traits. But the presence of these classifications in *European Morals* (1869) demonstrates the pervasive residual influence of the jargon popularized by this pseudoscience.

The texts of two other books by Lecky that Clemens is not known to have read—*The Map of Life: Conduct and Character* (1899; revised edition 1900) and *Historical and Political Essays* (1908)—employed still more explicit phrenological vocabulary terms: "bilious temperament," "lymphatic temperament," the "buoyant temperament" of a "sanguine and cheerful spirit," "a singularly equable, happy, and sanguine temperament" (*Map,* rev. ed., p. 11, 66, 238–239; *Essays,* p. 245). Like Lecky, Mark Twain became accustomed at an early date to this convenient method of categorizing character types, much as we today are wont to rely upon terms available to us from current psychological theories. In rereading Lecky after 1895, Twain was reminded (whether consciously or not) of this previous article of his belief, and he incorporated it into a psychological framework suitable for his late treatises on human character. Twain emphasizes the overwhelming determinism of "temperament" in Autobiographical Dictations of 25 June 1906 (*MTAuto* 2: 142–143) and 4 February 1907 (*MTAuto* 2: 427–429); in the latter instance he says it accounts for the plight of Bret Harte's daughter, who reportedly had been committed to a home for the indigent and friendless in Portland, Maine.

Harold Aspiz, in "Lecky's Influence on Mark Twain," *Science and Society* 26 (Winter 1962): 15–25, used the marginalia reported in *The Twainian* to make a close comparison of Lecky's *History of European Morals* (1869) and Twain's *A Connecticut Yankee in King Arthur's Court* (1889). This is an excellent analysis, well-reasoned and well-documented; it would seem mandatory for students of this topic. Rodney O. Rogers, "Twain, Taine, and Lecky: The Genesis of a Passage in *A Connecticut Yankee,*" *Modern Language Quarterly* 34.4 (December 1973): 436–447, demonstrated how a chapter about French feudalism that Mark Twain omitted from the final version of *A Tramp Abroad* (published as "The French and the Comanches" in *Letters from the Earth,* pp. 183–184) found its way into Chapter 13 of *A Connecticut Yankee.* Originally based on H. A. Taine's *L'Ancien Régime,* Twain's new version depended on Lecky's *European Morals* for factual information, bias, and perspective. Striking similarities between the two drafts bespeak Twain's continuing skepticism about the abilities of ordinary mankind to think independently. Many other studies of Twain and Lecky are valuable: Paine, *MTB* (1912), pp. 511–512, 743, 1539; Olin H. Moore, "MT and Don Quixote" (1922), pp. 341–343; Henry A. Pochmann, "Mind of Mark Twain" (1924), pp. 21, 176; Brashear, *MTSM,* p. 244; Harold Aspiz, "Mark Twain's Reading" (1949), pp. 340–347; Blair, *MT&HF* (1960), pp. 134–135, 338, 401 n. 6; Coleman O. Parsons, "Background of *The Mysterious Stranger*" (1960), pp. 63, 70; Roger B. Salomon, *TIH* (1961), pp. 98–102; Hamlin Hill and Walter Blair, eds., *The Art of Huckleberry Finn* (1962), pp. 484–491; Philip Y. Coleman, "Mark Twain's Desperate Naturalism" (1964), pp. 26–30; Sherwood P. Cummings, "*WIM?*: The Scientific Sources" (1964), p. 113; James D. Williams, "The Use of History in Mark Twain's *A Connecticut Yankee*" (1965), p. 103 n. 20, 104; Howard G. Baetzhold, *MT&JB* (1970), pp. 54, 57, 59, 134–143, 331 n. 16, 343 n. 39, 363 n. 13; Paul Baender, ed. *WIM?* (1973), pp. 98–100, 544; Mary Boewe, "Twain

on Lecky: Some Marginalia at Quarry Farm," *Mark Twain Society Bulletin* 8.1 (January 1985): 1–6; Howard G. Baetzhold, "Samuel L. Clemens" (1988), pp. 34–47; Baetzhold, "'Well, My Book Is Written'" (1996), pp. 41–77; Joe B. Fulton, *Mark Twain in the Margins: The Quarry Farm Marginalia and A Connecticut Yankee in King Arthur's Court* (Tuscaloosa: University of Alabama Press, 2000), pp. 19, 29, 44, 53, 64, 76, 104; Delphine Louis-Dimitrov, "The Democratic Reconfiguration of History in Mark Twain's *Personal Recollections of Joan of Arc,*" *American Literary Realism* 51.2 (Winter 2018): 162–179.

————. *History of European Morals from Augustus to Charlemagne.* Third edition, revised. 2 vols. New York: D. Appleton and Co., 1900.

Inscription: the front free flyleaves in both volumes are signed in ink, "Susan L. Crane/Quarry Farm,/1902/Elmira."

Marginalia: Mary Boewe made a transcription of Clemens's marginalia during her visits to Quarry Farm on 19 and 27–29 September 1984. Clemens made penciled markings in both volumes but only wrote notes in Volume I. These notes in pencil were added to pages 7, 9, 10, 11, 12, 13, 15, 16, 17, 18, 20, 21, 48, 95, and 111. At the bottom of page 9, in a note dated "July, 1903," he made several dissenting notes where Lecky defined and discussed the topic of human pity. "*No.* Pity arises merely because the sight of/suffering gives *us* pain. We do not *reason* about it./It is as unthinking as coming in out of the cold is" (p. 9). On the next page he insisted: "All this contemplates *reasoning,* whereas there is no reasoning about it; pity is wholly automatic—*when one feels it.*" At the bottom of page 10 Clemens declared: "*All* our acts,/reasoned *and* unreasoned, are selfish." At the top of page 12 Clemens noted: "There is no such thing as inherent/standards of right & wrong. They are *man/ufactured,* & we change them as/time & place & circumstances elect." At the bottom of page 15 Clemens argued, "The Christian theme/is based entirely upon/selfishness—as here/confessed." Writing sideways in the margin of page 21, Clemens noted: "We are totally indifferent to another's pain except when the/spectacle of it gives *us* pain. Otherwise we care not a rap for it." Similarly he stated in the margin of page 48: "If cruelty to an animal gives *you* pain, you will seek to/stop it, & not otherwise. Your motive is wholly selfish." He summed up his dispute with Lecky on the top and (continuing) in the margin of page 95: "Self-sacrifice is a lying phrase./There is no such thing. All appa-/rent sacrifices *of* self are made/*for* self, primarily. Mr. Lecky's premises being/wrong, his arguments result in crazy confusions." At the bottom of page 111 Clemens emphatically concurred with Lecky's quotation from John Henry Newman about the misplaced priorities of the Church: "The *Church,*" wrote Clemens, "is so fastidious about/it! That blood-drenched & crime-sodden/old harlot." The penciled markings in Volume I occur on pages 5, 7, 9, 10, 11, 12, 13, 15, 16, 17, 18, 19, 20, 48, 49, 94, 95, 96, 97, 98, and 111. In Volume II Clemens made penciled underlings and vertical lines on pages 7, 8, 13, 14, 15, 16, 17, 23, 30, 32, 34, 36, 39, 40, 41, 42, 43, 44, 93, 94, 95, 99, and 100.

Provenance: listed and noted ("marginalia of S. L. Clemens") among the books in the library when Emily Schweizer

Martinez inventoried them at the time that Jervis Langdon, Jr. donated Quarry Farm to Elmira College. She estimated the value of these volumes at $500. Discovered on the shelves of the library at Quarry Farm in 1984, they were listed among the books that Mark Woodhouse transferred from the Quarry Farm library to the Mark Twain Archive on 9 July 1987.

Catalog: Ball 2016 inventory, 2 vols., brown cloth, gilt lettering.

Location: Mark Twain Archive, Gannett-Tripp Learning Center, Elmira College, Elmira, New York.

Copy examined: photocopies of the title page, inscription, and marginalia sent in January 1985 to the Mark Twain Papers, Bancroft Library, University of California at Berkeley.

Mary Boewe, "Twain on Lecky: Some Marginalia at Quarry Farm," *Mark Twain Society Bulletin* 8.1 (January 1985): 1–6 described and quoted evidence that Clemens read Lecky's book at his in-laws' home outside Elmira.

————. *History of the Rise and Influence of the Spirit of Rationalism in Europe.* Revised edition. 2 volumes. New York: D. Appleton and Co., 1884. [This work was first published in 1865.]

Inscription: inscribed at the top of the title page in Volume I: "Susie L Crane/Dec. 1884." Volume II is inscribed "Susie L Crane/Quarry Farm 1888." These inscriptions do not appear to be in Susan Crane's handwriting, Clemens's, or Olivia's.

Marginalia: Mary Boewe made a transcription of Clemens's marginalia on 19 and 27–29 September 1884 at Quarry Farm, the former residence of Theodore and Susan Crane. She reported that Clemens made annotations in purple pencil throughout Volume I. Clemens was especially appalled by the accounts of the ease with which someone could be accused of witchcraft and brought into court, despite the fact that "the trials represent pure and unmingled delusions" (p. 85). At Lecky's recital of some of the persecutions for witchcraft and the tortures employed, Clemens observed, writing vertically in the right-hand margin, "All this results from a remark put into God's mouth by/the lying Scriptures: 'Thou shalt not suffer a witch to live.'" (p. 85). Farther on he added, writing vertically in the right-hand margin, "The modern claim that Chris-/tianity was a blessed boon to poor down/trodden woman seems to be a very/pleasant sarcasm" (p. 99). On page 108, where Lecky described the judicial qualifications and "vast" learning of the French jurist Jean Bodin (1530–1596), who wrote *De la démonomanie des sorciers* (1580), an influential work that encouraged suspending normal legal safeguards when interrogating accused witches, Clemens wrote vertically, in the left-hand margin: "How often the argument is flung at our heads that a thing/must be true because a 'cloud of witnesses,' & all supreme/intellects have for ages believed it!—& what a silly argument/it is, after all." On page 112 he underlined the last eight lines and wrote vertically in the margin: "Think a moment—weigh well the meaning of those eight/lines. They mean that the *entire world*, wise & simple, believed/for ages in a thing—sorcery—which had absolutely *no* existence." (The relevance of this realization to the views that Hank Morgan would encounter in *A*

Connecticut Yankee in King Arthur's Court seems obvious.) Clemens also made a vertical mark on page 113 where Lecky referred to the age when "knowledge was made the bond-slave of credulity, and . . . intellects . . . most shackled by prejudice were regarded as the wisest of mankind." Clemens ridiculed the fallacious logic of that era in the left and top margins on page 135: "There were a million evidences that witchcraft did/exist; & only one solitary argument that it didn't—namely,/its im-/probab-/bility; &/that one/argument/proved/stronger/than the/million/proofs/in the/end." (His additional comments were subsequently canceled with a lead pencil.) Clemens underlined a phrase in Footnote 2 on page 136 regarding the witnesses to witchcraft, wizards, and magicians and wrote underneath it: "The eternal argument that in the concurrent testimony of a multitude of fools lies proof." On page 141, underlining Lecky's observation that the majority of the clergy continued to defend the belief in witchcraft "when the great bulk of educated laymen had abandoned it," Clemens made a vertical note in purple pencil: "The church has never started a good work, & has always been the last/to relinquish an evil one. American slavery's last/& stubbornest friend/& champion in the North was the church." A Clemens note, written vertically on page 143 next to three vertical marks he made where Lecky recounted the superstitions of the "harsh and gloomy" Calvinist Scottish ministers, reads: "There are people, even in this day, who/long for a 'united church.' There never/was a united church which did not usurp the privileges of <hell> tyranny." Clemens made additional notes on pages 85, 99, 108, 109, 134, 136, 140, and 147. On the latter page, which describes a hideous torture machine, Clemens jotted: "These are Scotch, not Iroquois" (presumably he was recalling Francis Parkman's accounts of Native American cruelty toward captives). Someone has excised Clemens's comments in the left margin of page 124. A large number of pages in Volume I bear Clemens's markings: 39 (altering verb tenses), 40, 57, 72, 79, 80, 86, 88, 91, 93, 94, 95, 100, 108, 109, 110, 111, 112–114, 116, 118, 124–126, 128, 130, 132–136, 140, 141, 143–151, 153, 154, 161, 173, 174, 182, 183, 200, 201, 291, 312, 315, 322, 323, 328, 330, 358, and 360–364.

In Volume II Clemens used a standard lead pencil rather than the purple pencil, and merely marked a few pages without making notes—73, 74, 116 (a heavy vertical line on this page that treats Jews), 161, 174–177, 184, 199, and 200.

Six of the longer notes by Clemens were reproduced in facsimile and distributed as a keepsake at the *Connecticut Yankee* conference sponsored by Elmira College in August 1989. Joe B. Fulton's *Mark Twain in the Margins* (2000) fully records Clemens's numerous marks, underlinings, and notes, most of which occurred in the first volume.

Provenance: listed (with "Twain marginalia") in the inventory of books in the library when Quarry Farm was donated to Elmira College in 1982. Emily Schweizer Martinez, a book dealer in Horseheads, New York, prepared this checklist of the library volumes. She estimated the value of this annotated book at $500. Discovered on the shelves of the Quarry Farm library in 1984 after the property was donated to Elmira College, the book was listed among the titles that Mark Woodhouse transferred from the Quarry Farm library to the Mark Twain Archive on 9 July 1987.

Catalog: Ball 2016 inventory, 2 vols., green cloth, gilt letter on spine, blind design on front and rear covers, marginal notes.

Location: Mark Twain Archive, Gannett-Tripp Learning Center, Elmira College, Elmira, New York.

Copy examined: photocopies of the inscription and selected marginalia and a typescript transcription of all marginalia in Susan Crane's copy of a book that Clemens read and annotated during his visits to Quarry Farm (photocopies sent by Mary Boewe to the Mark Twain Papers, Bancroft Library, University of California at Berkeley in January 1985).

William M. Gibson proposed this work as the source for Mark Twain's assertion in "The Chronicle of Young Satan" (written 1897–1900) that the rules for dealing with witchcraft were "all written down by the Pope" (*MSM* [1969], p. 79). Mary Boewe's "Twain on Lecky: Some Marginalia at Quarry Farm," *Mark Twain Society Bulletin* 8.1 (January 1985): 1–6 described and quoted evidence that Clemens read this book at his in-laws' home outside Elmira. Joe B. Fulton convincingly illustrated the significant impact of this work on Twain's *A Connecticut Yankee in King Arthur's Court* (*Mark Twain in the Margins* [2000], pp. 20, 29–47, 50, 64, 69, 75, 105–121). See also Howard G. Baetzhold, "'Well, My Book Is Written'" (1996), pp. 41–77.

LEE, ALBERT (1868–1946). *He, She & They; Being a Faithful Record of the Woful Enjoyments and Joyful Woes of Him & Her.* Illustrated by H[enry]. B[revoort]. Eddy (1872–1935). New York: Harper & Brothers, 1899. 141 pp.

Source: MTLAcc, entry #202, volume donated by Clemens.
Comedy surrounds the efforts to stage an aristocratic wedding, with eventually resolved misunderstandings and disagreements arising between the bride and groom and their families.

LEE, HENRY (1826–1888). *The Octopus; or, The "Devil-Fish" of Fiction and of Fact. By Henry Lee, Naturalist of the Brighton Aquarium.* Illus. London: Chapman and Hall, 1875. 114 pp.

Inscription: (on the flyleaf) "To Saml. L. Clemens Esq/ from his friend/The Author./Henry Lee/Augt. 13th 1879".

Location: Special Collections, University Library, University of Nevada, Reno. Purchased in 1963 from Mrs. Louis A. (Haydee U.) Zeitlin of Santa Monica, California.

Copy examined: Clemens's copy, unmarked but worn by usage.

Clemens sent the naturalist Henry Lee a postcard on 26 September 1873: "You must dine with us that evening [i.e., the next Saturday]" (Christie's auction catalog, 17 October 1981). In a letter written to Elisha Bliss on 5 November 1873, Clemens stipulated that Lee was to receive a "very early" copy of *The Gilded Age* (*MTLet* 5: 461). Clemens noted that Lee was among those "gone" when he returned to London in July 1899 (NB 40, TS p. 60). Lee specialized in ichthyology at the popular Brighton Aquarium.

LEE, JENNETTE BARBOUR(PERRY) (1860–1951). *Uncle William, The Man Who Was Shif'less.* New York: The Century

Co., 1906. 298 pp. Reprinted in 1907.
On 13 February 1908 Isabel V. Lyon noted that "Mrs. Riggs [Kate Douglas Wiggin] recommended a book for the King, 'Uncle William' by Jeanette Lee" (IVL Journals, TS p. 302, MTP). Lee's novel revolved around a crusty old sailor who considers himself "shif'less" in spite of an active and generous life. It opened with a philosophical dialogue between Uncle William and one of the artists who flock to the seashore in the summer.

LEE, ROBERT EDWARD (1843–1914). *Recollections and Letters of General Robert E. Lee [1807–1870], by His Son, Captain Robert E. Lee.* Gray cloth, gilt edges, covers slightly soiled. New York: Doubleday, Page & Co., 1904. 461 pp.

Catalog: Robert F. Lucas Antiquarian Books, Blandford, Massachusetts, March 1980, "signature of S. L. Clemens on front end paper, also signature of later recipient of the book, Clemens' Dublin, N. H. landlord," item #17, priced at $300. (Clemens stayed in Dublin, New Hampshire during certain months in 1905 and 1906.)

Inscription: signed "S. L. Clemens" on the front endpaper. Also signed by a later owner to whom Clemens either gave the book or in whose house he accidentally left it (see the rare book dealer's catalog). I am grateful to Joel Myerson of the University of South Carolina for passing along this catalog in 1980.

Clemens requested Isabel Lyon to search his library for this book on Friday, 6 January 1905, but she noted in her journal that in sorting his books since the move to 21 Fifth Avenue she had not seen this volume (IVL Journals, TS p. 36, MTP).

LEE, SIDNEY (1859–1926).
Clemens met the English writer, critic, and editor Sidney Lee twice in March 1903 (Clemens to Laurence Hutton, 18 March 1903, ALS at Princeton; Notebook 46, TS p. 13). Lee entertained Clemens in England in 1907 (*MTE*, p. 332; *AutoMT* 3: 102–103). Lee, incidentally, was a major scholar and editor of Shakespeare, the literary figure whose status Clemens would begin to question in this same decade.

LEECH, JOHN (1817–1864). *John Leech's Pictures of Life & Character. From the Collection of "Mr. Punch."* London: Bradbury and Evans, n.d.

Inscription: to the Clemens family from the [Theodore W.] Crane family, Christmas 1871.

Catalog: *Mott 1952*, item #64, oblong folio, $7.50.

LE FEUVRE, AMY (1861–1929). *"Probable Sons."* Chicago: Fleming H. Revell Co., [cop. 1896]. 120 pp.

Source: MTLAcc, entry #872, volume donated by Mrs. Ralph W. Ashcroft (formerly Isabel Lyon), Clemens's secretary.

The English author Le Feuvre often wrote stories and novels with Christian themes. In *"Probable Sons"* a committed bachelor is moved to change his life after he becomes responsible for an orphaned niece. In the final chapter, "A Little Child Shall Lead Them," the child's mispronunciation of the Biblical prodigal son as the "probable son," brings Sir Edward Wentworth back to an acceptance of Christian faith and morality.

LEFEVRE, EDWIN (1871–1943). *Sampson Rock, of Wall Street. A Novel.* Illus. New York: Harper & Brothers, 1907. 394 pp.

Source: MTLAcc, entry #1579, volume donated by

Clemens.

———. *Sampson Rock, of Wall Street. A Novel*. Illus. New York: Harper & Brothers, 1908. 394 pp.

Source: MTLAcc, entry #1020, volume donated by Clemens.

LE GALLIENNE, RICHARD (1866–1947). *An Old Country House*. Illustrated by Elizabeth Shippen Green (1871–1954). Original cloth, arts and crafts style binding, spine partially missing, covers nearly detached, some wear to edges and corners. New York: Harper & Brothers, 1902. 143 pp.

Inscription: inscribed by Clemens, "Olivia L. Clemens/Dec. 1902." Clemens's wife was in ill health during this period.

Provenance: sold at the 1951 Hollywood auction as lot "O33," but not listed in the very incomplete sale sheet.

Catalog: "Property from the Library of Mark Twain," Butterfield & Butterfield, San Francisco, Sale 6613 (16 July 1997), lot 2700.

Location: Mark Twain House and Museum, Hartford, Connecticut.

Copy examined: Olivia Clemens's unmarked copy. Viewed in Hartford in 1997.

The narrator and his wife Perdita purchase a large rural residence in order to indulge in whimsy and neighborliness.

———. *An Old Country House*. Illustrated by Elizabeth Shippen Green (1871–1954). New York: Harper & Brothers, 1905. 143 pp.

Inscription: Clemens inscribed an illustration pasted on the front cover: "S. L. Clemens, 1905, to I. V. Lyon, 1908."

Catalog: Swann Galleries, Inc., New York City, 11 June 1970, item #314.

———. *Painted Shadows*. Boston: Little, Brown and Co., 1904. 339 pp.

Isabel Lyon seemingly referred to this book when she recorded on 6 January 1905: "Mrs. Whitmore has sent me Richard Le Gallienne's last book. This morning I took it in to Mr. Clemens and he was glad to see it, saying 'an able cuss and writes deliciously'" (IVL Journals, TS p. 36, MTP). In writing to thank Mrs. Whitmore for the Christmas present on 8 January 1905 (the letter is misdated "1904"), Lyon reported that Clemens, who had been ill for three weeks at 21 Fifth Avenue, "took the book from me—saying of its author— 'An able cuss who writes deliciously'—and today he remarked that the book is 'ever so charming'" (ALS in MTHM). The book title is confirmed in a journal entry for 9 July 1905, when Lyon herself got around to reading the volume; she again recalled then how she "carried my new 'Painted Shadows'" into Clemens's room and heard him pronounce Le Gallienne to be "an able cuss who writes deliciously" (IVL Journals, TS p. 77, MTP).

In this collection of twelve stories the English author, poet, editor, and aesthete Le Gallienne indulged his imagination to the utmost in plots and time period settings.

LEIBNIZ, GOTTFRIED WILHELM VON (1646–1716). [Sometimes spelled Leibnitz.]

At Heidelberg University on 2 July 1878 Clemens heard Professor Kuno Fischer (1824–1907) lecture on Leibniz' life and writings (NB 14, *N&J* 2: 105).

LEIGHTON, ROBERT FOWLER (1838–1892). *Latin Lessons Adapted to Allen and Greenough's Latin Grammar*. [Edition undetermined. Published in 1872 and reprinted a number

of times in the 1870s and early 1880s.]

Catalog: *C1951*, J30, edition unspecified, listed among books belonging to Jean and Clara Clemens.

Brooklyn High School principal Leighton had published *A History of Rome* (1879) as well as other histories and editions related to ancient Greece and Rome.

LELAND, CHARLES GODFREY (1824–1903), pseud. "Hans Breitmann." *Hans Breitmann's Party, with Other Ballads*. New and enlarged edition. Philadelphia: T. B. Peterson & Brothers, 1869. 48 pp.

On 6 July 1873 Clemens wrote to Mary Mason Fairbanks from London to tell her he had met "Hans Breitman" [*sic*] among other "pleasant people" (*MTMF*, p. 173; *MTLet* 5: 402). (Leland lived in London between 1869 and 1879.) *Mark Twain's Library of Humor* (1888) would include two of Leland's verses, "Hans Breitmann's Party" and "Ballad of the Rhine." Leland, a Princeton graduate, had formerly edited *Graham's Magazine* and a humor magazine, *Vanity Fair*. His German dialect ballads (Leland had attended universities in Munich and Heidelberg) gave him a temporary popularity.

———. *The Hundred Riddles of the Fairy Bellaria*. Illus. First edition. Original wrappers, rebacked. Folding-case. London: T. Fisher Unwin, 1892. 149 pp.

Inscription: the front flyleaf is inscribed "A hundred riddles to one who has raised a hundred million peals of laughter all over the world, i e Mark Twain. From/Charles G. Leland/Florence Jan. 26 1893". (Journalist, editor, and humorist Leland began residing in Florence, Italy in 1884.)

Provenance: Carrie Estelle Doheny Collection, St. John's Seminary, Camarillo, California. Mrs. Doheny purchased the volume in 1940 from Maxwell Hunley Rare Books of Beverly Hills. Auctioned by Christie's for $357 on 21 February 1989 (lot 1770) on behalf of St. John's Seminary. Subsequently in the collection of Nick Karanovich, Fort Wayne, Indiana. See Nick Karanovich's "Sixty Books from Mark Twain's Library," *Mark Twain Journal* 25.2 (Fall 1987): 15.

Catalogs: ListABP (1910), "Book of 100 Riddles, Leland"; *Sotheby's 2003*, #216, $3,500 (sold with five other inscribed books).

Location: collection of Kevin Mac Donnell, Austin, Texas.

Copy examined: Clemens's umarked copy, in July 2004.

———, trans. and **JOHN DYNELEY PRINCE** (1868–1945), co-trans. *Kulóskap the Master, and Other Algonkin Poems; Translated Metrically*. Illus. New York: Funk & Wagnalls Co., 1902. 370 pp.

Inscription: the front pastedown endpaper is signed in black ink "Clemens/1902".

Location: Mark Twain Library, Redding, Connecticut. Donated by Clemens (MTLAcc, entry #614).

Copy examined: Clemens's copy, unmarked. Loose pages. Has the red ink Mark Twain Library accession number "614". Examined in 1970 and again in June 1982 and on 8 November 2019.

Leland had many research interests, including folklore.

———. *Legends of Florence; Collected from the People and Re-Told by Charles Leland (Hans Breitmann)*. First Series. Second edition, revised and enlarged. 8vo, original green decorated cloth, gilt, uncut, partly unopened. London: David Nutt,

1896. 280 pp.

Inscription: the front flyleaf is signed "SL. Clemens/Villa di Quarto/ Florence/Xmas/1903/Given to me by Livy." This Christmas gift was very likely the last book that Olivia ever gave her husband.

Marginalia: contains Clara Clemens Samossoud's numbering from the library shelving system she employed during her Detroit years. The *C1951* lot number (43c) is penciled in the volume.

Catalogs: ListABP (1910), "Legends of Florence, Leland"; *C1951*, #43c, $17.50 (purchased by Hollywood director Samuel Fuller and his wife); *Fleming 1972*; the book was later resold by Sotheby Parke Bernet, Sale number 3482 (25 February 1976), "original cloth, in a quarter morocco slipcase. . . . Two notes from his daughters to him loosely inserted," "Property of a New York City Collector" (i.e., John F. Fleming), lot 13, sold for $350 (*American Book Prices Current, 1976*, p. 207).

Provenance: Frederick Anderson, then Editor of the Mark Twain Papers in the Bancroft Library at the University of California, Berkeley, inspected this volume at the New York City firm of John F. Fleming, Inc. in April 1972 and verified its authenticity (Anderson to James D. Hart, 17 April 1972; photocopy sent to Alan Gribben).

Location: collection of Kevin Mac Donnell, Austin, Texas. Acquired in 2009.

Source: letter from Kevin Mac Donnell to Alan Gribben, 31 December 2009. According to Mac Donnell, there are no annotations. The leaves of some of the forty-five legends have been opened, but other chapters are entirely unopened. Laid in the volume are two notes to Clemens, one from Clara Clemens and the other from Jean Clemens, reminding him of appointments in Florence.

Clemens and his family had arrived at the Countess Massiglia's Villa di Quarto in Florence in November 1903, hoping to improve Olivia's health.

———. *Legends of the Birds*. New York: H. Holt & Co., 1874. 16 pp.

Source: MTLAcc, entry #2136, volume donated from Clemens's library by Clara Clemens Gabrilowitsch in 1910.

Twelve poems, illustrated with colored plates. Most have Christian themes and recount legends surrounding the eagle, the parrot, the owl, and others birds.

LELAND, HENRY PERRY (1828–1868). "Frogs Shot Without Powder," *Spirit of the Times: A Chronicle of the Turf, Field Sports, Literature and the Stage*, 26 May 1855.

Bernard DeVoto called this source, a sketch in a New York City weekly, the "likeliest" printed variant of a folk tale about frogs weighted with lead for Clemens to have known. DeVoto published this variant and listed several of its reprintings (*MTAm* [1932], p. 174, 340–342). Blair, *NAH* [1937], p. 156.

LEMAÎTRE, JULES (FRANÇOIS ÉLIE JULES) (1853–1914).

On 7 November 1892 Susy Clemens wrote enthusiastically about Lemaître from Florence to her college friend Louise Brownell: "Jules Lemaître fascinates me endlessly. He has that finish that makes one feel intellectually elegant in reading him" (Hamilton College Archives). The French literary critic, lecturer, poet, and playwright Lemaître was becoming known as an opponent of critical dogmatism, favoring impressionistic approaches.

LE NORDEZ, (MONSEIGNEUR) ALBERT-LÉON-MARIE, ÉVÊQUE DE DIJON (1844–1922). *Jeanne d'Arc, racontée par l'image d'après les sculpteurs, les graveurs et les peintres*. Folio, plates and illustrations, some by F[rank]. V[incent]. DuMond (1865–1951). Original brown calf, rubbed and scuffed, decoratively stamped in gilt and blind. Tan cloth with green leather spine. Edges gilt. Green quarter morocco slipcase. Paris: Hachette & cie, 1898. 396 pp.

Inscription: the half-title page is signed in ink, "S L. Clemens/London, 1899."

Marginalia: Clemens's notes on pages 2, 116, 117, 125, 215, 231, 249, and 267 comment on the illustrations of Joan by Frank Vincent Dumond. Several of the remarks are derogatory. Beside an illustration of a fifteenth-century statue of Joan on page ii, Clemens wrote, "We have a duplicate." One note on page 117 scoffs: "A detestable picture of Joan/SLC." Clemens's note on page 125 [the Heritage catalog says page 215] reads: "Another caricature of Joan, but a fine picture otherwise./I asked Dumond to make her 17, slender & spirituelle, & he said he would. SLC/This is his idea of it." On page 231 Clemens noted, "Another caricature of Joan./SLC." On page 267 Clemens sneered: "Probably a grand-niece of Dumond's/other Joans./SLC."

Catalogs: *C1951*, #3c, listed among books signed by Clemens; *Fleming 1972*; Sotheby Parke Bernet, Sale number 3482 (25 February 1976), "original leather, rubbed, in a quarter morocco case" lot 14, "Property of a New York City Collector," sold for $400 (*American Book Prices Current, 1976*, p. 207); Alan Fox Rare Books, Sherman Oaks, California, Catalog 1 (December 1980), "signed in ink on half-title, item #12, priced at $2,500; Heritage Book Shop, Los Angeles, California, Catalogue 170 (June 1988), item 283, priced at $3,000.

Sources: Frederick Anderson, then Editor of the Mark Twain Papers in the Bancroft Library at the University of California, Berkeley, examined this volume at the New York City office of John F. Fleming, Inc. in April 1972 and verified its authenticity (Anderson to James D. Hart, 17 April 1972, photocopy sent to Alan Gribben). Portions of Clemens's annotations as well as a description of the book were also reported in the Alan Fox Rare Books catalog sent to Alan Gribben by Nick Karanovich in 1980 and Kevin Mac Donnell in 1985, as well as the 1988 catalog issued by the Heritage Book Shop.

Provenance: acquired on 8 August 1988 by Charles (1924–2016) and Mary Boewe (1922–2017), Louisville, Kentucky, from the Heritage Book Shop of Los Angeles (Mary Boewe to Alan Gribben, 15 August 1988). Later the Boewes moved to Pittsboro, North Carolina. Mary Boewe was a recognized Mark Twain scholar.

Location: currently unknown.

The American artist Frank Vincent Dumond was greatly influenced by the contemporary French schools of painting. For decades he was an instructor at the Art Students League in New York City, where his students included Georgia O'Keeffe and Norman Rockwell.

LEONARD, WILLIAM ELLERY (1876–1944). *Sonnets and Poems.* Boston: [F. H. Gilson Co.,] 1906. 67 pp.

Source: MTLAcc, entry #2135, volume donated from Clemens's library by Clara Clemens Gabrilowitsch in 1910.

LEONOWENS, ANNA HARRIETTE (EDWARDS) (1831–1915). *The*

English Governess at the Siamese Court; Being Recollections of Six Years in the Royal Palace at Bangkok. Illus. Boston: James R. Osgood & Co., 1871. 321 pp.

Inscription: signed "Saml L. Clemens/1871."

Source: card catalog of Mark Twain Library, Redding, Connecticut. The book was listed as missing by 1979.

Chapter 7 of Mark Twain's *Roughing It* (1872) contains an anecdote about Siam (which later became Thailand) that mentions "the king, and the sacred white elephant, the Sleeping Idol, and all manner of things." These elements seemingly derived from Leonowens's book (*RI* [1993], pp. 47–48, 582). Leonowens was retained by King Mongkut (1804–1868) as a tutor to the royal children and secretary to the King in his effort to understand and defend against Western powers. She arrived in 1862 and left Siam five years later. Her impressions of the royal court, the influential Buddhist priests, the country's military readiness, and the Angkor Wat temple ruins in nearby Cambodia remain of interest. Quite predictably she expressed indignation at the existence of a royal harem and the general treatment accorded women by the court. In other respects, however, historians have faulted her narrative for fictionalization and exaggeration. A later author would romanticize Leonowens's life in 1944, and the musical *The King and I* (1951), based on that popularized version of events, would further distort the governess's experiences.

LE PILEUR, AUGUSTE (1810–1902). *Wonders of the Human Body. From the French.* Illustrated with 45 engravings by Léveillé [Jean Baptiste François Léveillé, 1769–1829.] New York: Scribner, Armstrong & Co., 1873. 256 pp.

Source: MTLAcc, entry #1996, volume donated from Clemens's library by Clara Clemens Gabrilowitsch in 1910.

LE ROW, CAROLINE BIGELOW (1843–1914), compiler. *English As She Is Taught. Genuine Answers to Examination Questions in Our Public Schools.* New York: Cassell & Co., 1887. 109 pp.

Inscription: (on the front free endpaper) "'Mark Twain,' with the gratitude and admiration of the compiler,/ Caroline B. Le Row,/April, 1887."

Catalogs: ListABP (1910), "Eng. as She is Taught, Le Row", listed twice; "Retz Appraisal" (1944), p. 9, valued at $5.

Location: Mark Twain Papers, Bancroft Library, University of California at Berkeley.

Copy examined: Clemens's copy, unmarked and with some leaves unopened.

———. *English As She Is Taught.* Intro. by Mark Twain. 8vo, original cloth, quarter morocco case. New York: Century Co., 1901. 108 pp.

Inscription: the front endpaper is signed in pencil "S. L. Clemens/Riverdale/Oct. 1901."

Catalogs: *C1951*, #37c, listed among the books signed by Clemens; *Fleming 1972*; Sotheby Parke Bernet, Sale number 3482 (25 February 1976), "With an introduction by Mark Twain. . . . [and] with Clemens's ownership inscription," lot 15, from a New York City collector, sold for $250 (*American Book Prices Current, 1976*, p. 207).

Provenance: Frederick Anderson, then Editor of the Mark Twain Papers in the Bancroft Library at the University of California, Berkeley, examined this volume at the New York City office of John F. Fleming, Inc. in April 1972 and verified its authenticity (Anderson to James D. Hart,

17 April 1972, photocopy sent to Alan Gribben).

Mark Twain offered Le Row, a teacher at the Girls' High School in Brooklyn, the use of his name to protect her teaching position, but she declined. He did encourage the publication of her book, however, and he helped publicize it. Her disclosures furnished Twain with examples for his own essay in *Century Magazine* (33.6 [April 1887]: 932–936), also titled "English As She Is Taught." (This duplication of titles has caused confusion about whether "Caroline Le Row" was really another pseudonym for Samuel L. Clemens.) Twain turned over to her the $250 check he received from the *Century*. In a letter to Le Row written on 4 November 1888 Clemens urged her to continue her crusade in behalf of the "mishandled" pupils (ALS, collection of Mrs. Robin Craven, New York City, PH in MTP). Twain returned to *English As She Is Taught*, "a collection of American examinations made in the public schools of Brooklyn," in Chapter 61 of *Following the Equator* (1897); there he quotes an excerpt, ostensibly to defend the grammatical errors committed by natives of India.

Le Row was a more interesting figure than many commentators have supposed. She taught at Vassar College during the 1870s and from time to time published (only slightly noticed) short stories and novels as well a compilation of others' poetry. She certainly was cagey about her age. The year 1843 is the most commonly accepted birthdate, but other contemporary documents listed it as 1844 or (according to a Federal Census in 1900) 1845. Her obituary in a Brooklyn newspaper in 1914 stated that she was seventy-five years old, having been born in 1839. That obituary also noted that her funeral services would be conducted by a spiritualist, the Reverend Helen T. Bingham.

Paine, *MTB* (1912), p. 841; *MTHL* (1960), p. 587 n. 2; Madigan, "Mark Twain's Passage to India" (1974), p. 361.

———. *The Young Idea"; or, Common School Culture.* New York: Cassell & Co., 1888. 214 pp. [Edition conjectured.]

Catalog: ListABP (1910), "Young Idea, Le Row", no other information provided.

LE SAGE, ALAIN RENÉ, sometimes spelled Lesage (1668–1747). *The Adventures of Gil Blas of Santillane* (novel, published 1715–1735).

"I am now reading Gil Blas," Clemens wrote to Olivia Langdon on 27 December 1869 from New Haven, "but am not marking it. If you have not read it you need not. It would sadly offend your delicacy" (*LLMT*, p. 132; *MTLet* 3: 440–441). He was most likely reading Tobias Smollett's translation, published in 1868 by D. Appleton Company of New York City (764 pages) as well as by J. B. Lippincott & Company of Philadelphia (531 pages). Clemens's copy of this witty picaresque novel apparently does not survive. On 5 July 1875 Clemens remarked in a letter to William Dean Howells that he had decided not to take Tom Sawyer's adventures beyond Tom's childhood because "it would be fatal to do it in any shape but autobiographically—like Gil Blas" (*MTHL*, p. 91; *MTLet* 6: 503). Yet when Brander Matthews pointed out similarities between *Gil Blas* and *Huckleberry Finn* ("an unheroic hero . . . who is often little more than a recording spectator"), Matthews "was not at all surprised when Mark promptly assured me that he had never read 'Gil Blas'; I knew he was not a bookish man" (essay dated 1919, collected in *Tocsin of Revolt* [1921], p. 267). Clara Clemens listed Le Sage's *Gil Blas* among mostly undated entries in her commonplace book (Paine 150, MTP).

The fact that Clemens's copy of *The Adventures of Gil Blas* has unfortunately vanished has dissuaded most scholars from recognizing its many parallels with *Adventures of Huckleberry Finn* (1885) as well as with *The Adventures of Tom Sawyer* (1876) and *The Prince and the Pauper* (1881). Most of Tom Sawyer's fantastical notions of adventures are here—robbers and highwaymen, Turkish pirates, dungeons, a subterranean cave hideout, a faithful servant, and rescued damsels. To take up one obvious similarity to *The Prince and the Pauper*, Don Raphael was flogged as a boy whenever his companion, the son of the Marquis of Leganez, erred in his lessons (*Gil Blas*, Chapter 45). As for the impact of this work on *Adventures of Huckleberry Finn*, from its very title (*The Adventures of Gil Blas*) to its cautionary Preface ("Gil Blas to the Reader," which urges readers to look for "the moral concealed" in "my adventures," perhaps provoking Twain's admonitory "NOTICE" for his readers to do the opposite), to Blas' service as a valet de chambre (Chapter 26), Le Sage's entire novel resonates with incidents that would echo in Twain's masterpiece. Consider the examples of Gil Blas' repeated wrestling matches with his conscience (Chapters 35, 48, 49, and 68), Don Alphonso's hugely coincidental arrival (as unpredicted as Tom Sawyer's) at a castle (Chapter 49), the use of the term "burning shame" (Chapter 54), the praise of the stage as a way of life (Chapter 56), Don Raphael's charade as a long-expected nobleman (accompanied by a roguish servant) only to be exposed and branded an impostor (Chapter 60), Gil Blas' diminishing fund of innocence, Blas and Pedrillo's plot to present a maimed soldier as the "uncle" of a young girl (Chapter 60), Blas' imprisonment in a dungeon cell with only one "little grated window" (Chapters 78–81), and his conclusion about the difficulty of curing an alcoholic ("it is bad policy to lock up a reformed drunkard in a wine cellar"—Chapter 86). Gil Blas' first-person narrative of his travels reflects the uncensored thoughts of a gradually educated young man who grows elderly and retires at the end after having repented of his earlier escapades, which implies that *Huckleberry Finn* in effect could be a read as a comically altered burlesque of this eighteenth-century tale of schemers and scoundrels. In *Huckleberry Finn* a much younger (and therefore more passive) child-narrator scarcely ages during his journey and mainly wants to escape dangers and confinements rather than learn the tricks of the world. Le Sage's incidental observations throughout his novel on the subjects of good and bad writing styles, problems with romances, and diverse other matters are generally those with which Clemens would have concurred. All in all, *The Adventures of Gil Blas* is rich with suggestive characters, actions, and topics that Clemens almost certainly had in mind as he composed *Huckleberry Finn* and several other works. This is a seldom-credited literary resource behind Clemens's inventive genius.

Making the case for another connection, Earl F. Briden, "*Pudd'nhead Wilson* and the Bandit's Tale in *Gil Blas*,"

Mark Twain Journal 19.1 (Winter 1977–78): 16–17, pointed out that in Book 1, Chapter 5 of Le Sage's *Gil Blas*, one of the four bandits tells how he was switched as an infant for the child of a nobleman. Briden noted that Tom Driscoll's fate was similar (it is the bandit's mother who reveals his identity); moreover, Tom resembles the bandit in his behavior—gambling, robbing, murdering. Paine, *MTB* (1912), p. 132; Blair, *MT&HF* (1960), p. 98. Lawrence I. Berkove, "No 'Mere Accidental Incidents': *Roughing It* as a Novel," *Mark Twain Annual 1* (2003): 17 n. 12 passingly but accurately noted that *Gil Blas* has been "underestimated as an influence on Twain."

Leslie, Eliza (1787–1858). *The American Girls' Book; or, Occupation for Play Hours*. New York: R. Worthington, 1879. 383 pp.

    Source: MTLAcc, entry #1897, volume donated from Clemens's library by Clara Clemens Gabrilowitsch in 1910.

Lessing, Gotthold Ephraim (1729–1781). *Fabeln. Drei Bücher. Nebst Abhandlungen mit dieser Dichtungsart verwandten Inhalts [Fables. Three Books. In Addition to Essays with This Kind of Poetry Related Content]*. Blue boards, blue morocco spine. Stuttgart: G. J. Göschen, 1876. 125 pp. [Bound with a copy of Lessing's *Laokoon*.]

    Marginalia: the number "4853" appears in black ink on the blank verso of page 125.

    Location: see the Catalog entry for Lessing's *Laokoon*.

———. *Hamburgische Briefe; Hamburgische Dramaturgie [Hamburg Letters; Hamburg Dramaturgy]*.

    Clara Clemens entered these titles in her largely undated commonplace book (Paine 150, MTP).

———. *Laokoon, oder über die Grenzen der Malerei und Poesie . . . Mit beiläufigen Erläuterungen verschiedener Punkte der alten Kunstgeschichte [Laocoon, or about the Limits of Painting and Poetry . . . with Casual Explanations of Various Aspects of Ancient Art History]*. Blue boards, blue morocco spine. Stuttgart: G. J. Göschen Verlag, 1881. 224 pp. [Bound with a copy of Lessing's *Fabeln*.]

    Inscription: on the first flyleaf in blue ink: "Olivia L. Clemens/May 1885/ Hartford".

    Catalog: *Zeitlin 1951*, item #30, $7.50.

    Location: Mark Twain Papers, Bancroft Library, University of California at Berkeley. A *C1951* label is pasted on the inner front cover. A University of California bookplate acknowledged Jake Zeitlin as the donor.

    Copy examined: Olivia Clemens's unmarked copy.

A Lesson in Love. Round-Robin Series, No. II. Boston: James R. Osgood and Co., 1881. 318 pp. [One of the Round-Robin Series of anonymous novels written by "the best writers" that the Osgood firm began publishing and promoting in 1881.]

    Catalog: Ball 2016 inventory, green cloth, red and black lettering, signed by Charles Jervis Langdon [Olivia Langdon Clemens's brother, 1849–1916], Jervis Langdon Family Library bookplate #618.

    Location: Quarry Farm library shelves, under the supervision of the Mark Twain Archive, Elmira College, Elmira, New York.

    Clemens had access to the book when he visited the Langdons in Elmira.

Lester, Charles Edwards (1815–1890). *The Life of Sam Houston (The Only Authentic Memoir of Him Ever Published)*. Illus. Black cloth (faded). Many leaves are loose. New York: J.

C. Derby; Boston: Phillips, Sampson & Co., 1855. 402 pp.

Inscription: the front free endpaper and the front free flyleaf have been torn out roughly, as has the rear flyleaf.

Marginalia: no markings, but pages 64, 200, and 340 are folded down.

Location: Mark Twain Library, Redding, Connecticut.

Copy examined: very possibly Clemens's copy, unmarked. Has the red ink Mark Twain Library accession number "5488". Examined in 1970 and again in June 1982 and on 8 November 2019.

"LET EACH NOW CHOOSE" (unidentified hymn or song).

In Mark Twain's "Mock Marriage" (written in the early 1900s), "the music struck up 'Let each now choose,' etc." (*FM*, p. 292). Twain could have had in mind a Pentecostal hymn, "Who is on the Lord's side?" written by Franklin Edson Belden (1858–1945) and published in 1893. Its chorus demands, "Choose now,/Choose now,/On the right or wrong side?/False or true?/Where stand you?"

LEWES, GEORGE HENRY (1817–1878). *The Life of Goethe*. London: Smith, Elder and Co., 1864.

Inscriptions: the half-title page is signed in ink, "Clara Gabrilowitsch". The volume also has the name and Pasadena address of "The Busch Family."

Provenance: has the shelfmarks of the numbering system for Clara Clemens Gabrilowitsch's library books during her Detroit years. Sold in 1951 at the Hollywood auction but not listed in the hastily prepared sale sheet.

Catalog: "Property from the Library of Mark Twain," Butterfield & Butterfield, San Francisco, Sale 6613 (16 July 1997), lot 2712.

Location: Mark Twain House and Museum, Hartford, Connecticut.

Copy examined: Clara Clemens's copy. Viewed in Hartford in 1997.

LEWIS, ALFRED HENRY (1857–1914). *Wolfville Days*. Frontispiece by Frederic Remington (1861–1909). New York: F. A. Stokes Co., [cop. 1902]. 311 pp.

Source: MTLAcc, entry #203, volume donated by Clemens. The Old Cattleman spins stories from the early roughneck days of cowboy life. His narratives are based in Texas but mention other Southwestern characters and regions.

————. *Wolfville Nights*. New York, n.d. [Edition undetermined. The book was published in 1902 and 1905 by Grosset & Dunlap, and also published in 1902 by Frederick A. Stokes Co. The frontispiece in both editions was drawn by E. S. Hall.]

Inscription: the front pastedown endpaper is signed in ink "S. L. Clemens, 1905".

Catalogs: *C1951*, D24, $11.50, listed among the books signed by Clemens; *Zeitlin 1951*, item #31, $25, edition unspecified.

Lewis related wild tales of Texas cowboy life—fights, shootings, vendettas, hunts, and bragging.

LEWIS, CHARLES BERTRAND (1842–1924), pseud. "M. Quad." "The Demon and the Fury" (sketch published in the Detroit *Free Press*).

In the humorous "Weather for Use in This Book" appendix to *The American Claimant* (1892) Mark Twain quotes two paragraphs of a sketch in which Lewis describes a furious thunderstorm he witnessed on the plains of the American West. The tremendous thunder-claps reminded Lewis of "the 800 cannon at Gettysburg." (Twain had an affinity

for imagery of lightning and thunder and had himself written vivid depictions of storms in Chapter 16 of *The Adventures of Tom Sawyer*, Chapter 9 of *Adventures of Huckleberry Finn*, and Chapter 51 of *Life on the Mississippi*.) Twain found M. Quad's sketch reprinted in *Current Literature: A Magazine of Record and Review* 6.4 (April 1891): 544–545. See the Catalog entry for that periodical.

Blair, "On the Structure of *Tom Sawyer*" (1939), p. 79.

LEWIS, GEORGE EDWARD (1867–1942). *Heart Echoes*. Illustrated by Marie Jewell Clark. Original gray cloth, gilt. Grand Rapids, Michigan: Press of Tradesman Co., [1899]. 181 pp.

Marginalia: annotated by Clemens on fifty-three pages. There are 141 words, 103 underlinings or lines in the margin, and nine question marks. Clemens did not make any notations beyond 103. The corner of page 104 is turned down.

Clemens corrected Lewis's grammar, changed his words, revised the syntax of one line, and made two revisions of geography. He occasionally made alterations that rendered the poetry more ridiculous or brought out possible hidden meanings; in other instances he merely amused himself by rewording sentences. In one poem he inserted the word "nigger" to invert the implications of referring to the "sunny south." On page 54 he revised the lines "The Governor was idle, his fire was bright,/ His clerks were all gone, it was late in the night" to read instead, "The Governor was idle, his fire was bright,/His jug it was empty (it was late in the night)." On page 79 Clemens wrote "Too much sweet" across the top of the page and underlined the words "sweet," "sweetest," and "sweetly" in the three-stanza poem. Laid in the volume were two newspaper clippings. One reprinted Bret Harte's poem "John Burns of Gettysburg" from the Springfield, Massachusetts *Republican*. The other clipping was a New York *Times* obituary for Col. E. L. Drake.

Catalogs: ListABP (1910), "Heart Echoes, Lewis"; *C1951*, #58a, $17.50, listed among the books containing marginalia by Clemens.

Provenance: the front pastedown endpaper bears the shelfmarks ("Po/H4") of the library system that Clara Clemens Samossoud employed during her Detroit years. One of the *C1951* sale labels is pasted on the same endpaper.

Location: collection of Kevin Mac Donnell, Austin, Texas. Acquired in 2010.

Source: letter from Kevin Mac Donnell to Alan Gribben, 29 June 2010.

Lewis was a native of Michigan, and his poems are set in Grand Rapids, Traverse Bay, and Mackinac Island. His *Heart Echoes* obviously belongs on the shelves of Mark Twain's hypothetical "Library of Literary Hogwash," those examples of wretched poetry and prose that Twain collected and savored. Lewis would go on to write fiction as well as verse. The illustrator listed herself as Mary B. Clark, "Artist," in the Grand Rapids city directories.

LEWIS, HENRY TALIAFERRO (1823–1870). "The Harp of a Thousand Strings" (burlesque sermon).

Still considering material for *Mark Twain's Library of Humor* in the autumn of 1887, Clemens wrote "Harp of 1000 Strings" in Notebook 27, *N&J* 3: 328. Walter Blair reprinted this piece in *Native American Humor* (1937, 1960), crediting Lewis as its author (pp. 388–389), but in *The Mirth of a Nation: America's Great Dialect Humor* (Minneapolis: University of Minnesota Press, 1983), page 106, Blair and Raven I. McDavid, Jr. attributed it instead to William Penn Brannan (1825–1866), who wrote several burlesque sermons. To complicate matters more, Samuel Putnam Avery (1822–1904) compiled a book titled *The Harp of a Thousand Strings; or, Laughter for a Lifetime* (1858) and left the authorship of its title piece so vague that some have assigned it to George Washington Harris. (This latter idea, however, does not seem credible.)

LEYPOLDT, FREDERICK (1835–1884), pseud. "L. Pylodet." *New Guide to German Conversation*. New York: H. Holt & Co., [cop. 1868]. 279 pp.

> **Source:** MTLAcc, entry #381, volume donated by Clemens.

Library of Wit and Humor by Mark Twain and Others. With the Philosophy of Wit and Humor by Melville D. Landon, A. M. (Eli Perkins). Illus. Chicago: Thompson & Thomas, cop. 1893, 1898. 438 pp. [Also published in 1900 and other years, with similar or identical contents but sometimes with differing titles.]

> In an Autobiographical Dictation of 31 July 1906 Mark Twain fumed about the use of his name and image on the cover of "a great, fat, offensive volume" published by a "western pirate" (*AutoMT* 2: 152–153). The Mark Twain Project editors (p. 534) identified *Hot Stuff by Famous Funny Men* (see the Catalog entry for that book) and *Library of Wit and Humor by Mark Twain and Others* as versions of the book to which Twain objected. The same comic material was shared among several Chicago publishers; see the Catalog entry for *Hot Stuff by Famous Funny Men*. See also the Catalog entry for *World's Wit and Humor; An Encyclopedia of the Classic Wit and Humor of All Ages and Nations*.

LICHTENBERG, GEORG CHRISTOPH (1742–1799).

> John S. Tuckey cited the German philosopher, mathematician, scientist, and astronomer Lichtenberg's philosophical writings about dream experiences as part of the background for Mark Twain's "The Great Dark" (written 1898). Tuckey pointed out that "in his working notes Twain planned to have his narrator quote Lichtenberg to convince his wife of the possibility of confusing dream and reality" (*WWD?*, p. 17). Twain's "The Mad Passenger" (*WWD?*, pp. 560–567) might also be indebted to Lichtenberg's ideas. Lichtenberg's works were only available in German in the 1890s, and Twain's precise source remains to be determined.
>
> Chad Rohman, "A Great Dark: Mark Twain's Continuing Voyage into Uncertainty," *Mark Twain Annual 3* (2005): 67–80.

LIECHTENSTEIN, MARIE HENRIETTE NORBERTE, PRINZESSIN VON (1843–1878). *Holland House*. Third edition. London: Macmillan and Co., 1875. 370 pp. [Edition conjectured, given that the earlier recorded editions consisted of two volumes.]

> **Catalog:** *C1951*, #85c, listed among books signed by Clemens, apparently one volume.
>
> The ancient Holland House, set amid eighty acres of gardens in Kensington, belonged to the former Marie Fox, who in 1873 had married the German Prince John of Liechtenstein. Her book described the renovations of the residence over the centuries and the family generations and famous guests associated with Holland House.

The Life and Amours of Owen Tideric, Prince of Wales, Otherwise Owen Tudor, Who Married Catharine Princess of France, and Widow of Our Great King Henry V; from Which Marriage Descended Henry VII, Henry VIII, Edward VII, Queen Mary, and Queen Elizabeth, All of Whom Had from Him the Surname of Tudor; and from Him Likewise Are Descended, by the Eldest Daughter of Henry VII, the Present Royal Family of Great Britain, France, and Ireland. First Wrote in French, and Published Many Years Since at Paris, and Now Translated into English. London: William Owen, 1751. 147 pp.

> **Catalog:** *A1911*, "12 mo, half calf (cracked), Lond. 1751, with a small sheet of notes by Clemens laid in," lot 288, sold for $11.50.
>
> The circumstances behind this historical novel are obscure. It originated in France, appearing in 1677 as *Tideric, Prince de Galles*, credited only to "De Curli." Several authorities have speculated that its Paris publisher, Claude Barbin (c. 1628–1698), may have been the actual author. The 1751 English version, *The Life and Amours of Owen Tideric, Prince of Wales, Otherwise Owen Tudor*, retells the doomed love story of Owen Tudor (c. 1400–1461) and the French princess.

Life Magazine (New York weekly, published 1883–1936).

> Clemens saw a cartoon by E. W. Kemble in an 1884 issue of *Life* and instructed Charles L. Webster to procure the artist's services for illustrating *Adventures of Huckleberry Finn* (*MTBus*, p. 246; see also the Catalog entry for E. W. Kemble). In June 1905 Clemens praised the "very cunning portraits" of Petrarch, Dante, Shakespeare, and Emerson that appeared in *Life* (SLC to Clara Clemens, 18 June 1905, MTP).
>
> Earl F. Briden, "Kemble's 'Specialty' and the Pictorial Countertext of *Huckleberry Finn*," *Mark Twain Journal* 26.2 (Fall 1988): 2–3.

The Life Within. Boston: Lothrop Publishing Co., [cop. 1903]. 385 pp.

> **Source:** MTLAcc, entry #14, volume donated by Clemens.
> ———. [Another identical copy.]
>
> **Source:** MTLAcc, entry #1257, volume donated by Clemens.
>
> Mark Twain referred readers of his *Christian Science* (1907) to this anonymous work: "For a clear understanding of the two claims of Christian Science [healing the body and healing the spirit], read the novel *The Life Within*, published by Lothrops [*sic*], Boston" (Book 2, Chapter 15, footnote, *WIM?*, pp. 358, 575).

LILJENCRANTZ, OTTILIE ADELINA (1876–1910). *Randvar the Songsmith; A Romance of Norumbega*. Illustrated by Troy Kinney (1871–1938) and Margaret West Kinney (1872–1952). New York: Harper & Brothers, 1906. 314 pp.

> **Source:** MTLAcc, entry #1580, volume donated by Clemens.
>
> Liljencrantz combined elements of Norse mythology, a forest romance, and a murderous werewolf ("the Other Shape of Starkad's son") in her fiction about a Viking settlement in North America.

LILLIE, LUCY CECIL (WHITE) (1855–1908). *The Colonel's Money*. Harper's Young People Series. Illus. New York: Harper

& Brothers, 1900. 393 pp.

Source: MTLAcc, entry #423, volume donated by Clemens. The novel is set in London, country manor houses, Exeter Cathedral, and other English locations.

———. *The Household of Glen Holly*. Harper's Young People Series. Illus. New York: Harper & Brothers, [cop. 1888]. 368 pp.

Source: MTLAcc, entry #415, volume donated by Clemens.

———. *Phil and the Baby*. Harper's Young People Series. Illus. New York: Harper & Brothers, 1906. 123 pp.

Source: MTLAcc, entry #445, volume donated by Clemens.

———. *The Story of Music and Musicians for Young Readers*. Harper's Young People Series. Illus. New York: Harper & Brothers, [cop. 1886]. 245 pp.

Source: MTLAcc, entry #1460, volume donated by Clemens.

LINCOLN, ABRAHAM (1809–1865). *An Address Delivered Before the Springfield Washingtonian Temperance Society at the Second Presbyterian Church, on the Twenty-second Day of February, 1842*. Springfield, Ill.: T. J. Crowder, Illinois State Register Press, 1906. 12 pp.

Inscription: the blank verso of the front cover is signed in black ink, "Mark Twain." Clemens almost never signed his pseudonym in books belonging to his personal library. Although the signature is authentic-looking, faint outlines of what could be trace marks are visible here and there among the letters and in the flourish beneath the name. The signature is most likely counterfeit. Eugene Field II forged the autograph "Mark Twain" in various books.

Marginalia: someone made a correction in dark brown ink on page 11, changing "poisons" to "passions"; the hand is not Clemens's. A bookseller has priced the pamphlet at $20 on the back cover.

Provenance: collection of Frank C. Willson (1889–1960) of Melrose, Massachusetts. His widow Margarete sold the Mark Twain books to the University of Texas in 1962.

Location: Harry Ransom Center, University of Texas at Austin. (I did not begin teaching at the University of Texas at Austin until 1974, so I was not involved in this acquisition.)

Copy examined: presumably a spurious association copy.

———. "Gettysburg Address" (speech delivered in 1863).

"Mr. Lincoln's words are simple, tender, beautiful, elevated; they flow as smoothly as a poem. This is probably the finest prose passage that exists in the English language," Mark Twain declared ("Comments on English Diction," written around 1876, quoted by Jervis Langdon in *Some Reminiscences* [1938], p. 21). On 8 February 1885 Clemens wrote to his daughter Susy to recommend that "you must take my Morte Arthur & read it." He quoted a passage on the death of Launcelot, comparing its eloquence to that of Lincoln's Gettysburg Address" (ALS, ASSSCL; copy in MTP). In June 1885 Clemens characterized Lincoln's speech as "perfect" (NB 24, *N&J* 3: 159). He parodied the address ("government of the grafted by the grafter for the grafter shall not perish from the earth") in an observation published in *More Maxims of Mark Twain* (privately printed, 1927), p. 14. The painter Edward Simmons (1852–1931) recalled an afternoon at the Players Club in New York City when "a crowd of us were . . . drinking and making frivolous talk." Clemens abruptly left and then reappeared with a book. He proceeded to read to

them Lincoln's "Gettysburg Address," introducing it as "the greatest piece of prose since the days of Marlowe." Simmons was surprised at the "beautiful sonority" of Clemens's voice. "It was one of the big moments of my life," he remembered (*From Seven to Seventy: Memories of a Painter and Yankee* [New York: Harper & Brothers, 1922], p. 318). Clemens then explicated a remarkable stylistic decision in the speech; he challenged anyone to "try to put an adverb after the word *here*. No one but Lincoln could have thought of using, 'That we here *highly* resolve.' No! No! No one!" (pp. 318–319). Krause, *MTC* (1967), p. 113.

———. "Fourth Annual Message" (delivered in December 1864).

Mark Twain alluded to "the *Message of the President and Accompanying Documents*" in "Lucretia Smith's Soldier" (1864).

———. "Second Inaugural Address" (delivered in March 1865).

Mark Twain quoted and paraphrased a passage from this speech in Notebook 5 (1866, *N&J* 1: 143), declaring it "very simple & beautiful." In 1880 Twain hoped to find "a yarn or two" about Lincoln that would be suitable for inclusion in an anthology of humor (NB 19, *N&J* 2: 364). On 11 February 1901 Twain was a featured speaker at a Carnegie Hall event celebrating Lincoln's birthday; there he called Lincoln "the noblest and best man after Washington that this land, or any other land, has yet produced" (Fears, *Day by Day* 3: 478–481). Twain referred to Lincoln as "that great American" in a speech titled "The Day We Celebrate" he delivered to the American Society in London on 4 July 1907 (*MTSpk*, p. 570). Three scholars ably traced the path by which Twain came to admire Lincoln: Allison R. Ensor, "Lincoln, Mark Twain, and Lincoln Memorial University," *Lincoln Herald* 78.2 (Summer 1976): 43–51; Joe B. Fulton, *The Reconstruction of Mark Twain: How a Confederate Bushwhacker Became the Lincoln of Our Literature* (Baton Rouge: Louisiana State University Press, 2010); and Jerome Loving, *Confederate Bushwhacker: Mark Twain in the Shadow of the Civil War* (Hanover, New Hampshire: University Press of New England, 2013).

LINCOLN, A[LMIRA]. H[ART]. (1793–1884). *Familiar Lectures on Botany, Practical, Elementary, and Physiological*. Loose leather covers, badly foxed. New York: F. J. Huntington & Co., 1838. 246 pp. + 186 pp.

Inscription: the front flyleaf is signed in black ink, "Eloise H. Osborne."

Marginalia: Numerous pencil notes and markings, none of them by Clemens.

Copy examined: Albert E. Stone, Jr. included this volume in his catalog of Clemens's library books in the Mark Twain Library at Redding in 1955, but he questioned whether it really belonged in the bookcase containing Clemens's volumes. I could not find the book when I examined the books in Redding in 1970, but I did locate it when I revisited Redding in June 1982. It has no Mark Twain Library accession number, and I am convinced that it did not belong to Clemens or his family.

LINCOLN, JOSEPH CROSBY (1870–1944). *Cape Cod Ballads, and Other Verse, by Joe Lincoln*. Illustrated by E[dward]. W[indsor]. Kemble (1861–1933). Trenton, New Jersey:

Albert A. Brandt, 1902. 198 pp.

Clemens was especially fond of the poem titled "The Village Oracle," consisting of Old Dan'l Hanks' narrow-minded opinions on travel, education, and religion. "Says I, 'how d'yer know you're right?'/'How do I *know*?' says he;/'Well, now, I vum! I know, by gum!/I'm right because I *be*!'" Clemens kiddingly assigned the nickname "Dan'l Hanks" to Harry Rogers, the son of his friend Henry H. Rogers (SLC to Henry H. Rogers, Florence, 18 December 1903, *MTHHR*, pp. 545, 546 n. 2). In August 1904 Clemens copied the title of Lincoln's book and a stanza from this poem into Notebook 46 (TS p. 33). In 1906 he alluded to the "almost limitless knowledge and daring and placid self-confidence" of "the late Simon Hanks [*sic*], of Cape Cod" and quoted (or, rather, paraphrased) a stanza from the poem in a speech, "Introducing Dr. Henry Van Dyke" (*MTS* [1923], p. 298; *MTSpk*, p. 488). Again, on 28 October 1908, in a letter to W. W. Jacobs, Clemens misquoted his favorite stanza; evidently he depended on memory, for three of the four lines contain errors and he calls the title character "Simon Hanks" (*MTL*, p. 823). The lines Clemens liked so much are these: "The Lord knows all things, great or small,/With doubt He's never vexed;/He, in his wisdom, knows it all,—/But Dan'l Hanks comes next."

LINDAU, RUDOLF (1829–1910).

Was Clemens referring to a work by this German writer of fiction when he urged "Lindau" to "send us that book" in a letter of 24 April 1901 (ASSSCL)?

LINDH, E[RIC]. I[SADORE]. (d. 1944). (Boston *Transcript* article).

In Book 2, Chapter 7 of *Christian Science* (1907), Mark Twain reported: "In the present month (February), Mr. E. I. Lindh, A. M., has communicated to the Boston *Transcript* a hopeful article on the solution of the problem of the 'divided [Christian] church'" (*WIM?*, pp. 311, 569). Twain had found Lindh's views condensed in "The Problem of the 'Divided Church,'" *Literary Digest* 26.7 (14 February 1903): 234, which opened its summary with some of the same words Twain employed: "Mr. E. I Lindh, A. M., contributes to the Boston *Transcript* a timely paper on the problem of the 'divided church'" (p. 243). The Reverend Eric I. Lindh, a Harvard graduate, was minister of the First Baptist Church in Hope Valley, Rhode Island between 1898 and 1905. Subsequently he served as a Congregational minister for churches in Rhode Island, Indiana, and (his final, lengthy pastorate) Quincy, Massachusetts.

LINDSAY, ANNA ROBERTSON (BROWN) (1864–1948). *What Is Worth While?* New York: T. Y. Crowell & Co., [cop. 1893]. 32 pp.

Source: MTLAcc, entry #869, volume donated by Mrs. Ralph W. Ashcroft (formerly Isabel Lyon), Clemens's secretary.

Lindsay was the first woman to earn a doctoral degree in English at the University of Pennsylvania. Her *What Is Worth While?* was an inspirational paper with a Christian theme that she read before the Philadelphia branch of the Association of Collegiate Alumnae.

LINDSAY, (LADY) CAROLINE BLANCHE ELIZABETH (FITZROY) (1844–1912). *From a Venetian Balcony and Other Poems of Venice and the Near Lands*. Illustrated by Clara Montalba (1842–1929). Second edition. London: Kegan Paul, Trench, Trübner & Co.; Venice: Rosen, 1904. 68 pp.

Inscription: the front pastedown endpaper is signed in black ink, "SL. Clemens/June, 1907./London./From Lady Lindsay."

Catalogs: *A1911*, "16mo, cloth, gilt top, Lond. 1904," quotes the inscription, lot 289, sold for $1.75; *Hunley 1958*, item #72, $6.50.

Provenance: collection of Frank C. Willson (1889–1960), in Melrose, Massachusetts. Sold by his widow Margarete to the University of Texas in 1962.

Location: Harry Ransom Center, University of Texas at Austin. Contains the *A1911* sale label. Another label has been removed from the front free endpaper. Priced in pencil on the rear endpaper: "$12.50."

Copy examined: Clemens's copy, unmarked.

———. *Godfrey's Quest: A Fantastic Poem*. Green cloth. London: Kegan Paul, Trench, Trübner & Co., 1905. 128 pp.

Inscription: signed in black ink on the front pastedown endpaper: "SL. Clemens/London, June 1907./From Lady Lindsay."

Marginalia: one pencil scrawl on the final page.

Provenance: Antenne-Dorrance Collection, Rice Lake, Wisconsin.

Location: Mark Twain Archive, Gannett-Tripp Learning Center, Elmira College, Elmira, New York.

Copy examined: Clemens's copy. Examined on 28 May 2015.

LINEN, JAMES (1808–1873). "I Feel I'm Growing Auld, Gude-Wife" (poem).

Linen's poem was included by Bret Harte in the collection of Californian verse titled *Outcroppings* (1865). Its three lugubrious stanzas represent the dying words of an elderly Scotsman, including these lines: "I canna bear the dreary thocht/That we maun sindered be;/There's naething binds my poor auld heart/To earth, gude-wife, but thee." In a letter from San Francisco published in the Virginia City *Territorial Enterprise* (6–7 February 1866), Mark Twain seemed to approve of a parody that soon appeared: "The burlesque of James Linen's 'I Feel I'm Growing Auld,' is the most outlandish combination of untranslatable Scotch phraseology I ever saw. I think it is a pretty good take-off on . . . extravagant Scotchiness." (Taper, *MTSF*, pp. 202–203). After living in California during the Gold Rush era, the Scottish-born Linen moved to New York City and began writing poetry in the New York *Evening Post*.

LINGARD, JOHN (1771–1851). *A History of England from the First Invasion by Romans*. Fifth edition. 8 vols. Paris: Baudry's European Library, 1840. Half-title: Collection of Ancient and Modern British Authors. [Publisher conjectured.]

Catalog: *A1911*, "Vol. II, 8vo, half morocco, Paris, 1840," a sheet of notes by Clemens referring to "A medicinal Dic. by R. James, M.D. London 1743" is laid in, lot 290a, sold for .50¢.

The whereabouts of Clemens's set of Lingard is unknown. Isabel Lyon was informed that Clemens kept these books "near at hand" while writing *A Connecticut Yankee in King Arthur's Court* (1889), and she recalled with indignation how Albert Bigelow Paine "broke up that priceless 20 volume [*sic*] Lingard in order to include in the first sale

... two or three odd volumes rich with Mr. Clemens's notes jotted along the margins" ("Notes Re. *A Connecticut Yankee*," Henry W. and Albert A. Berg Collection, New York Public Library). The *A1911* catalog specified only the second volume of Clemens's copy, though other volumes may have been sold without being listed.

James D. Williams, "Genesis, Composition, Publication" (1961), p. 95; Williams, "Use of History" (1965), p. 104.

LINLEY, GEORGE (1798–1865). "Ever of thee I'm fondly dreaming" (song, published in 1852). Melody composed by Foley Hall (d. 1859).

Clemens's letter published in the 8 February 1863 issue of the Virginia City *Enterprise* reports on a Carson City wedding festivity in which a baritone sang "Ever of thee I'm fondly dreaming" (*MTEnt*, p. 59; *ET&S* 1: 209). The song's lyrics begin, "Ever of thee I'm fondly dreaming,/ Thy gentle voice my spirit can cheer;/Thou wert the star that mildly beaming,/Shone o'er my path when all was dark and drear."

LINTON, ELIZABETH (LYNN) (1822–1898). *The True History of Joshua Davidson, Communist*. Philadelphia: J. B. Lippincott & Co., 1873. 279 pp. [Publisher conjectured.]

Inscription: the front flyleaf is signed "S. L. Clemens, Hartford, 1882."

Catalogs: *A1911*, "12mo, cloth, Phila. 1873," quotes the signature, lot 290b, sold for $1.25; *American Book-Prices Current Index 1960–1965* (New York, 1968), p. 368, item #64, $27, listed (probably erroneously) as an 1883 edition.

In March 1882 Clemens wrote the book title and the author's name in Notebook 20 (*N&J* 2: 452). Perhaps its unusual combination of religion and politics piqued his interest. *Joshua Davidson* is the fictional biography of a young Cornwall carpenter whose religious beliefs determine him to practice Christ's precepts totally. There are explicit parallels between Davidson's life and Christ's, as when the modern man sharply questions his parish clergyman about pious hypocrisy (pp. 4–12). The crude narrative, purportedly written by Davidson's friend and disciple named John, is more of a tract than a novel. Joshua becomes the avowed enemy of "Ecclesiastical Christianity" and "Society"; he moves to London and attempts to bring Christ to the working men. Eventually he concludes that Christ would have taken different actions in nineteenth-century England: "The modern Christ would be a politician." Davidson pledges himself to an organization having "the equalization of classes as its end. It is Communism" (p. 83). He labors to achieve "Christian Communism."

In London, Davidson befriends a prostitute, Mary Prinsep, recognizing her "natural virtue" (p. 106). He denounces the reformatory as "a place of humiliation and penitent degradation" (pp. 122–123). He helps to establish the International Working Men's Association. An aristocrat attempts to cooperate with Davidson's movement, but Lord X's efforts are feeble and short-lived. Around 1871 Davidson goes to Paris to assist the Commune during the war between France and Russia. Mary Prinsep is killed there, and French politicians hostile to Communism ultimately triumph ("for the present, God help this poor sorrowful world of ours!" [p. 247]).

Joshua Davidson and the narrator return to England, where Davidson—now branded a Communist who is "wilfully and willingly guilty of every crime under heaven" (p. 262)—begins a series of lectures to "show how Christ and his apostles were Communists, and how they preached the same doctrines which the Commune of Paris strove to embody" (p. 267). At Lowbridge, where he is denounced by his former clergyman, an incited crowd beats and kicks Davidson to death. The narrator ponders: "Is the Christian world all wrong, or is practical Christianity impossible?" (p. 276).

LIPPARD, GEORGE (1822–1854). *Legends of the American Revolution; or, Washington and His Generals. With a Biography of the Author's Life by C[harles]. Chauncey Burr [1817–1883]*. Philadelphia: T. B. Peterson, [1847]. 538 pp. [Edition conjectured.]

Evidence regarding Clemens's early reading is so scanty that the knowledge that he was familiar with this patriotic book is immensely welcome. Clemens wrote to his brother Orion on 26 October 1853 from Philadelphia, describing a recent sight-seeing excursion: "Geo. Lippard, in his 'Legends of Washington and his Generals,' has rendered the Wissahickon [River] sacred in my eyes" (*MTB*, p. 100; *MTL*, p. 27; *MTLet* 1: 21–22). Lippard, journalist, social reformer, and author of historical and gothic novels, was still living in Philadelphia when Clemens arrived there. The newspaper and magazine editor Charles Chauncey Burr was a friend of Lippard in Philadelphia, where Burr also championed the writings of Edgar Allan Poe.

As with Christopher Columbus, George Washington's name and enduring reputation became a kind of touchstone for Mark Twain. Act 4 of the play Twain co-authored with Bret Harte, *Ah Sin* (produced in 1877), mentions George Washington. In Chapter 5 of *Adventures of Huckleberry Finn* (1885), Huckleberry Finn "took up a book and began something about General Washington and the wars" to prove to Pap Finn that he could read. His father responds furiously by giving "the book a whack with his hand and knocked it across the house." "The deeds of Washington, the patriot, are the essential thing," Twain emphasized in "Switzerland, the Cradle of Liberty" (1892); "the cherry-tree incident is of no consequence." Huck refers admiringly to Washington in Chapter 10 of *Tom Sawyer Abroad* (1894). Chapter 53 of *Following the Equator* (1897) alludes three times to Mount Vernon as a site sacred to Americans, and in Chapter 54 Twain mentions that Hindus in India were familiar with only two American names—"George Washington" and "Chicago." In "The Secret History of Eddypus" (written 1901–1902), however, Washington is barely but ridiculously remembered as "George Wishington" who "drowned at Waterloo" (*FM*, pp. 329–330). Twain dated his savage polemic, "A Defence of General Funston," on February 22nd, "the great Birth-Day," and disparagingly compared Funston to Washington throughout the essay (*North American Review*, May 1902). He also referred to George Washington in Notebook 45 (1902), TS p. 38; Chapter 5 of "A Horse's Tale" (1906); Part 6 of *What Is Man?*, published in 1906 (*WIM?*, p. 200); an interview, "Mighty Mark Twain Overawes Marines" (New York *Times*, 12 May 1907; *Complete Interviews*, p. 603); and an Autobiographical Dictation of 3 July 1908 (*MTE*,

p. 294; *AutoMT* 3: 241). See also the Catalog entry for Mason Locke Weems.

———. *The Quaker City; or, The Monks of Monk Hall* (novel, published in 1845).

Jarrod Roark—"Beneath Mark Twain: Detecting Sensational Residues in Twain's Early Writing," *Mark Twain Annual 12* (2014): 14–29—proposed this author and title among possible sensational novels with which Twain might have been familiar.

Literary Digest (weekly periodical, published 1890–1938). New York: Funk & Wagnalls.

Mark Twain's clipping of an article from the issue of 6 December 1902, "Mrs. Eddy and Contagious Disease," survives in the Mark Twain Papers at Berkeley (DV102b, Box 30, no. 6), with his caustic remarks in its margins. In "Was the World Made for Man?," written in 1903 (*LE*, p. 211; *WIM?*, p. 101), Twain used a quotation from this journal as an epigraph; the excerpt concerned Alfred Russel Wallace's theory about the earth as the only habitable globe. In Book 2, Chapters 7 and 8 of *Christian Science* (1907), Twain quoted from the *Literary Digest* issues (Volume 26) of 25 January 1902 and 14 February 1903 (*WIM?*, pp. 311–312, 335–336, 569, 572). See the Catalog entry for Eric I. Lindh.

Literature (New York weekly magazine, began publication in February 1888).

Clemens's friend William Dean Howells started writing regularly for *Literature* in 1898, when Harper & Brothers took control of the magazine (*MTHL*, p. 687 n. 9). Presumably Clemens had a special interest in its contents after this development. In a letter of 1 and 2 March 1899 written from Vienna, Clemens thanked John Kendrick Bangs and "Mr. Harper" for a complimentary subscription to *Literature*; he also mentioned an article on copyright that appeared in the 10 February 1899 issue (ALS in Berg Collection). Jean Clemens employed this subscription to watch the results of Bangs' poll of his readers' choices for ten favorite living authors, as reported in *Literature* between February and April 1899 (SLC to WDH, 5 April 1899, *MTHL*, p. 691).

Littell's Living Age (American weekly journal, published 1844–1941).

On 1 April 1874 the Hartford magazine and newspaper firm Geer & Pond billed Clemens for "Mar 21 Age Dec. 6/73 to Mar. 21/74 $2.45"; he paid on 3 April 1874 (receipt in MTP). In January 1894 Clemens recollected an article he had read "in old Littell. Susy Crane has it" (NB 33, TS p. 47). He was referring to "Jòn Jònsonn's Saga: The Genuine Autobiography of a Modern Icelander," *Littell's Living Age* 132.1705 (17 February 1877): 407–430. But Clemens did not find these reprinted British materials uniformly interesting. On 2 June 1906 Isabel Lyon noted while he was summering in Dublin, New Hampshire: "There are a lot of old bound volumes of Littell's Living Age in the house and Mr. Clemens has taken them as his reading, but [is] finding about one readable article in a volume. It's a pretty dull collection, and . . . as Mr. Clemens opened one of them he said it was 'like looking at an asphalt pavement' for dull monotony" (IVL Journals, TS p. 161, MTP; repeated in the IVL Journal, Harry Ransom Center, University of Texas at Austin).

Litteratur-institut. Vienna: L. and A. Last, 1896. 474 pp.

Source: MTLAcc, entry #560, volume donated by Clemens.

The Little Folks: A Magazine for the Young. Volume 1. Illus. New York: American News Co., [1872]. 416 pp. [Publication date supplied.]

Source: MTLAcc, entry #466, volume donated by Clemens. The London version of this periodical began in 1871.

Little French Masterpieces: Prosper Mérimée, Gustave Flaubert, Théophile Gautier, Honoré de Balzac, Alphonse Daudet, Guy de Maupassant. Edited by Alexander Jessup (b. 1871). Translated from the French by George Burnham Ives (1856–1930). 6 vols. Original red cloth. New York: G. P. Putnam's Sons, 1909.

Inscription: the Balzac volume is signed "Jean L. Clemens/1909." Each of the four volumes present has an *A1911* sale label affixed to its front pastedown endpaper.

Catalogs: *A1911*, "6 vols., 16mo, gilt, N.Y. 1909," quotes signature, lot 292, sold for $3, purchased by J. O. L. representing the Mark Twain Company; *C1951*, D15, listed among books signed by Clemens, erroneously listed as "8 vols."; Property from the Library of Mark Twain," Butterfield & Butterfield, San Francisco, Sale 6613 (16 July 1997), "4 vols.," lot 2711.

Location: Mark Twain House and Museum, Hartford, Connecticut. Only four volumes are present; the Gautier and Maupassant volumes are missing.

Copies examined: Jean Clemens's unmarked copies of (only) the Mérimée, Flaubert, Balzac, and Daudet volumes. Viewed in Hartford in 1997.

"LITTLE RED RIDING HOOD" (European fairy tale).

Mark Twain's column in the Buffalo *Express* issue of 20 December 1869 was signed "Little Red Riding Hood" and cast her as a celebrity stalker (Reigstad, *SL*, pp. 105–106). When Clemens and his bride moved into their new Buffalo house, Clemens referred to himself in a letter of 9 February 1870 as "Little Sammy in Fairy Land" (*MTLet* 2: 66).

LITTRÉ, ÉMILE MAXIMILIEN PAUL (1801–1881). *Dictionnaire de la langue française* (published in 1873).

In a brief piece, "Adieu, 'Chauffeur!'," published in the 13 January 1906 issue of *Harper's Weekly*, Mark Twain quoted "what Littré says about it" in defining the word "chauffeur."

LIVEING, HENRY GEORGE DOWNING (1861–1947). *Records of Romsey Abbey: An Account of the Benedictine House of Nuns, with Notes on the Parish Church and Town (A. D. 907–1558). Compiled from Manuscript and Printed Records.* Illus. Winchester: Warren and Son, 1906. 342 pp. [Publisher and pages conjectured.]

Inscription: signed "S. L. Clemens, 1906."

Catalog: *A1911*, "8vo, buckram, Winchester, 1906," quotes the signature, lot 293, sold for $2.50.

LIVINGSTONE, DAVID (1813–1873) and CHARLES LIVINGSTONE (1821–1873). *Narrative of an Expedition to the Zambesi and Its Tributaries; and of the Discovery of the Lakes Shirwa and Nyassa. 1858–1864.* Illus. New York: Harper & Brothers, 1886. 638 pp.

Source: MTLAcc, entry #1722, volume donated by Clemens.

See also the Catalog entry for Josiah Tyler, *Livingstone Lost and Found; or, Africa and Its Explorers.*

LLOYD, HENRY DEMAREST (1847–1903). *Man, the Social*

Creator. Ed. Jane Addams (1860–1935) and Anne Withington (1867–1933). New York: Doubleday, Page & Co., 1906. 279 pp.

Source: MTLAcc, entry #799, volume donated by Clemens. From Lloyd's speeches, notebooks, previous publications, and other sources, Addams and Withington gather the social reformer's idealistic call for ending labor unrest by adopting "social love," a "new conscience in industry," an end to traditional political parties, a "new political economy," and a new "religion of labour."

———. *Wealth against Commonwealth*. New York: Harper & Brothers, 1903. 563 pp.

Source: MTLAcc, entry #1700, volume donated by Clemens.

Clemens was proud of the self-restraint he exercised when George Warner tried to talk him into publishing Lloyd's *Wealth and Commonwealth*—a book, promised Warner, "that arraigns the Standard Oil fiends, & gives them unmitigated hell, individual by individual." Henry H. Rogers, a vice-president of Standard Oil, was helping Clemens with his tangled financial affairs (see Justin Kaplan, *Mr. Clemens and Mark Twain* [New York: Simon and Schuster, 1966], pp. 323–324; also SLC to OLC, 15 February 1894, MTP).

Matt Seybold, "The Neoclassical Twain: The Zombie Economics of Col. Sellers," *Mark Twain Annual 13* (2015): 82–83.

LLOYD, JOHN WILLIAM (1857–1940). *Dawn-Thought on the Reconciliation; A Volume of Pantheistic Impressions and Glimpses of Larger Religion*. Wellesley Hills, Massachusetts: Maugus Press, [cop. 1900]. 197 pp.

Source: MTLAcc, entry #909, volume donated by Clemens. On 8 March 1901 Clemens wrote to thank Lloyd "very much for the book" (Fears, *Day by Day* 3: 495). Lloyd put forth a cosmically optimistic message of hope. "Dawn Thought," he explains, is "the absorption of the individual into the Divine" (p. 4). "Matter is but congealed spirit, and spirit but sublimated matter, and each transformable into the other" (p. 5). Consequently, "all things in heaven and earth belong to you, are you; no immortality can be greater, for you are life itself, without beginning or end" (p. 31).

Lloyd's Weekly (London weekly newspaper, published 1843–1918).

In "To the Person Sitting in Darkness" (1901), Mark Twain refers to, and quotes from, an issue of *Lloyd's Weekly* that appeared "some days before the affair of Magersfontein" during the Boer War. A British private speaks there of serving the Boers some mercy "*with the long spoon.*" The Battle of Magersfontein was fought near Kimberley on 11 December 1899 during the Anglo-Boer War.

"LOCH LOMOND" ("The bonnie banks of Loch Lomond") (Scottish air). [Lyrics first published in 1841.]

"When I came away she was singing, 'Loch Lomond.' The pathos of it! It always moves me so when she sings that" ("Was It Heaven? Or Hell?," Ch. 5 [1902]). Isabel Lyon played this song at Clemens's request on 14 February 1906 (IVL Journal, Harry Ransom Center, University of Texas at Austin).

LOCKE, DAVID ROSS (1833–1888), pseud. "Petroleum V. Nasby." *The Struggles (Social, Financial, and Political) of*

Petroleum V. Nasby, Embracing His Trials and Troubles, Ups and Downs, Rejoicings and Wailings. Intro. by Charles Sumner (1811–1874). Illus. by Thomas Nast (1840–1902). Boston: I. N. Richardson and Co., 1872. 720 pp. [Sold by subscription.]

Provenance: bookplate of the "J. Langdon Family Library #628". Clemens had access to this collection whenever he visited the Langdon family's residence in Elmira. Subsequently the book was given by Ida Langdon to Elmira College.

Catalog: Ball 2016 inventory, leather with gilt lettering, cover missing.

Location: Quarry Farm library shelves, under the supervision of the Mark Twain Archive, Elmira College, Elmira, New York.

Clemens was well acquainted with Locke and his writings, yet (curiously) no copies of Locke's books survived in Clemens's own library and Locke was the major omission from *Mark Twain's Library of Humor* (1888). Mark Twain mentioned "Nasby's Post-Office" in "Concerning Gen. Grant's Intentions" (New York *Tribune*, 12 December 1868; *MTPP*, p. 35). On 23 January 1869 Twain gloated over his own lecturing triumph ("came off with flying colors") in the city where Locke edited the Toledo *Blade* (SLC to Joseph H. Twichell; *MTLet* 3: 68; *LMTJHT*, p. 21). Twain met Locke on 9 March 1869 and sat up to converse with him until nearly six o'clock in the morning (SLC to Susan Crane, 9 and 31 March 1869, *MTLet* 3: 180). On 10 March 1869 Clemens testified that he "was perfectly fascinated with Nasby's lecture, & find no flaw in it" (SLC to Olivia L. and Charles J. Langdon, *MTLet* 3: 158). In an undated and apparently unmailed letter excoriating a theater critic for the Jamestown, New York *Journal* who had written an unflattering anonymous review of Twain's lecture there, Twain revealed that sixteen years earlier "Nasby told me it was you, at the time. . . You were ashamed to put your name to it" (ALS sold by Christie's, New York City, 1–2 February 1988, lot 478). There exists a photograph taken in 1869 by the Boston Lyceum Bureau for publicity purposes of Mark Twain standing between Petroleum V. Nasby and Josh Billings (Henry Wheeler Shaw); it is captioned "The American Humorists" (*Sotheby's 2003*, lot 1). Twain's complimentary review of a Nasby lecture ("his humor was enjoyable; his logic was ingenious; his arguments were searching") appeared in the 19 February 1870 issue of the Buffalo *Express* (*MTBE*, p. 153). On 10 May 1870 Twain asked James Redpath to pass along his greetings to "Nasby," who was one of the lecturers Redpath managed. In 1877 Locke proposed to Twain that they write a play together, but the collaboration never took place (SLC to Francis D. Millet, 7 August 1877, Harvard Library). Twain noted Locke's name and address in Notebook 13 (1877), *N&J* 2: 11. He mentioned Locke complimentarily in a speech in Quebec on 31 January 1882, "On After-Dinner Speaking" (*MTSpk*, p. 167). Locke's name appeared prominently among Twain's lists of literary comedians to be considered for inclusion in an anthology of American humor (NB 19 [1880], *N&J* 2: 362; NB 19 [1881], p. 429). Twain also meant to "refer to & quote from Nasby" in a proposed "Essay on Humor" (NB 24 [August 1885], *N&J* 3: 172). Thereafter Twain recalled Locke's name and anecdotes in

1887 (NB 27, *N&J* 3: 308), April 1891 (NB 30, *N&J* 3: 617), January 1903 (NB 46, TS p. 6), and 1906 (NB 48, TS p. 10). In an Autobiographical Dictation of 31 July 1906 Twain alluded to Locke as one of the many American humorists "whose writings and sayings were once in everybody's mouth" but whose renown depended wholly on "an odd trick of speech and of spelling.... Presently the fashion passes, and the fame along with it" (*MTE*, pp. 201–202; *AutoMT* 2: 153).

DeVoto, *MTAm* (1932), p. 219; Turner, *MT&GWC* (1960), p. 73; Holger Kersten, "Mark Twain's 'Assault of Laughter': Reflections on the Perplexing History of an Appealing Idea," *Mark Twain Annual 16* (2018): 69; and David E. E. Sloane, "Literary Comedians," *Mark Twain in Context*, ed. John Bird (Cambridge, England: Cambridge University Press, 2020), pp. 59, 61, 63, 66.

LOCKE, JOHN (1632–1704).
"(Shall I confess it?) I have never read Locke nor any other of the many philosophers quoted by you.... So, all these months I have been thinking the thoughts of illustrious philosophers, and didn't know it" (Clemens to Sir John Adams, Vienna, 5 December 1898, in Lawrence Clark Powell's "An Unpublished Mark Twain Letter," *American Literature* 13.1 [March 1942]: 405–407).

LOCKE, WILLIAM JOHN (1863–1930). *The Morals of Marcus Ordeyne. A Novel*. New York: John Lane, 1905. 303 pp.
Source: MTLAcc, entry #204, volume donated by Albert Bigelow Paine, Clemens's designated biographer. Possibly Clemens saw this book, since the men exchanged reading materials.

LOCKER-LAMPSON, FREDERICK (1821–1895). *London Lyrics*. London: Strahan & Co., 1872. 200 pp.
Source: MTLAcc, entry #2061, volume donated from Clemens's library by Clara Clemens Gabrilowitsch in 1910.
Joaquin Miller had recommended to Clemens a Locker-Lampson book whose name Miller could not quite recall in a letter of 4 July 1873, though he called Locker-Lampson "the best humorous poet living." Clemens replied on 5 July 1873, "I'll get that book" (*MTLet* 5: 398–399). Miller conceivably might have had in mind an anthology that Locker-Lampson edited, *Lyra Elegantiarum: A Collection of Some of the Best Specimens of Vers de Société and Vers d'Occasion in the English Language by Deceased Authors* (1867), rather than Locker-Lampson's exquisitely ironic *London Lyrics* (published in 1857). Subsequently Locker-Lampson would publish *London Rhymes* (1882).

LOCKYER, JOSEPH NORMAN (1836–1920). *Elementary Lessons in Astronomy*. New Edition. Illus. London: Macmillan and Co., 1877. 348 pp. [Publisher and pages conjectured.]
Inscription: signed "S. L. Clemens, Munich, Dec. 1878."
Marginalia: a few passages marked and a note ("A body could buy one") written in reference to a planet.
Catalog: *A1911*, "18mo, cloth, Lond. 1877, . . . a few passages marked," quotes the signature and marginalia, lot 295, sold for $4.
Lockyer wrote to Clemens on 29 November 1902. On 7 July 1907 Clemens had lunch with this astronomer in Tuxedo Park, New York (AD, 30 August 1907, *AutoMT* 3: 121).

LODGE, HENRY CABOT (1850–1924). *The War with Spain*. New York: Harper & Brothers, [cop. 1899]. 288 pp.
Source: MTLAcc, entry # 1723, volume donated by Clemens.

LODGE, (SIR) OLIVER JOSEPH (1851–1940). *The Ether of Space*. Illus. New York and London: Harper & Brothers, 1909. 167 pp. [Publisher and pages conjectured.]
Inscription: the front pastedown endpaper is signed "S. L. Clemens, 1909."
Catalogs: *A1911*, "16mo, cloth, gilt top, uncut, N.Y. 1909," quotes the signature, lot 296, $2; *L1912*, lot 19, sold for $4.
Lodge probes the properties and light-conducting behavior of interstellar ether.

———. *The Substance of Faith Allied with Science; A Catechism for Parents and Teachers*. New York: Harper & Brothers, 1907. 144 pp.
Inscription: the front pastedown endpaper is signed in black ink, "SL. Clemens/1907".
Location: Mark Twain Library, Redding, Connecticut. Donated by Clemens (MTLAcc, entry #917).
Copy examined: Clemens's copy, unmarked. Contains the accession number "917."
The subject matter of this book certainly was Clemens's meat: "Ascent of Man," "Development of Conscience," "Nature of Evil," "The Meaning of Sin," just to name a few chapter titles. Each chapter opens with a question, followed by an answer endeavoring to harmonize science and religion. Clemens must have been terribly weary the day he looked through this volume and decided against marking it.

———. *The Substance of Faith Allied with Science; A Catechism for Parents and Teachers*. New York: Harper & Brothers, [cop. 1907]. 144 pp.
Inscription: the front pastedown endpaper is signed in black ink, "SL. Clemens/1907".
Location: Mark Twain Library, Redding, Connecticut (MTLAcc, entry #1391, volume donated by Clemens).
Copy examined: Clemens's unmarked copy. Has the red ink Mark Twain Library accession number "1391". I could not find this volume in 1970 but it had resurfaced when I revisited Redding in June 1982.

———. "What Is Life," *North American Review* 180.582 (May 1905): 661–669.
Sherwood P. Cummings traced Mark Twain's quotation from Lodge in "Three Thousand Years Among the Microbes" (written in 1905) to page 663 of this article, which illustrates the minute size of atoms (Cummings, "Mark Twain and Science" [1950], p. 32). The narrator remarks, "Take a man like Sir Oliver Lodge, and what secrets of Nature can be hidden from him?" (*WWD?*, p. 447).
Paine, *MTB* (1912), pp. 1663–70.

LOEW, WILLIAM NOAH (1847–1922), trans. *Magyar Songs. Selections from Hungarian Poets*. New York: Samisch & Goldmann, 1887. 248 pp.
Source: MTLAcc, entry #2058, volume donated from Clemens's library by Clara Clemens Gabrilowitsch in 1910.

LOGAN, OLIVE (1839–1909).
As early as 8 January 1870 Clemens scoffed at the manner in which the actress Olive Logan signed an autograph for a family in Troy, New York ("Yours ever, for God & Woman") (SLC to Olivia L. Langdon, *MTLet* 4: 7). Much later, looking back over his career, he derided the inflated reputation of Logan—the author of fiction and

writings on theater and homelife who was popular as a lecturer—in an Autobiographical Dictation of 11 April 1906 (*AutoMT* 2: 43–46). "She wasn't worth ten cents a week. . . . She had built up a great, a commercially valuable name, on absolute emptiness" (p. 44). History has dealt with her more kindly; she is often acknowledged as the first actress to support feminist goals.

LONDON. *Forty-One Coloured Views of London, Designed and Engraved by [Augustus Charles] Pugin [1762–1832] and [Thomas] Rowlandson [1756–1827] and Printed in Aquatint by [Joseph Constantine] Stadler, from "Historic Anecdotes and Secret Memoirs of the Legislative Union Between Great Britain and Ireland."* London, n.d.

> Catalog: *A1911*, "4to, boards (broken), Lond., n.d.," a sheet of Clemens's notes laid in, lot 297, sold for $5.95.

LONDON *Daily Chronicle*.

Clemens quibbled with some grammar he noticed in an October 1896 issue (NB 39, TS p. 14). On 12 October 1898 he requested Chatto & Windus to change his London *Chronicle* subscription address to Vienna (ALS in Berg Collection). He instructed Percy Spalding of Chatto & Windus to stop the mailing of his London *Chronicle* to Vienna on 24 May 1899 (ALS in CWB).

LONDON *Daily Mail*.

Clemens was impressed by the success of the publisher Alfred C[harles]. Harmsworth (1865–1922) with his London *Daily Mail* (SLC to Henry H. Rogers, London, 5 February 1900, *MTHHR*, p. 431).

LONDON *Daily News*.

In Paris in 1879, following a note Clemens made about Josh Billings, Robert Burdette, and the Danbury News Man, he added a memorandum to "see scrap book for Am & English humor" (*N&J* 2: 301). In his 1878/1879 scrapbook is a clipping from the London *Daily News* that comments on the "boldness" American humorists exhibit in treating religious ideas and biblical topics, and their overall "astounding coolness and freedom of manners" (MTP). In a letter to Chatto & Windus written on 5 August 1893 from Krankenheil-Tölz, Bavaria, Clemens complained that his issues of the *Daily News* were not arriving as he had requested. He stated that on 30 July 1893 he had asked Chatto & Windus to take out a six-month subscription in his name (ALS in Lilly Collection, PH in MTP)

LONDON *Illustrated News*.

On 28 April 1902 Henry H. Rogers sent Clemens a clipping that retold "A Riddle of the Sea," the disappearance in the 1860s of the brig *Marie Celeste*, bound from Boston to Mediterranean ports. Clemens jotted his opinion on the envelope: "Wonderful sea-tale" (*MTHHR*, pp. 485–486).

LONDON, JACK (1876–1916). *The Call of the Wild*. Illustrated by Philip R[ussell]. Goodwin (1882–1935) and Charles Livingston Bull (1874–1932). First edition, first printing. Original sage green pictorial cloth, gilt. New York: Macmillan Co., 1903. 231 pp.

> Inscription: the front pastedown endpaper is inscribed in black ink: "For Jean/from/S L Clemens/1903." (The top two lines of the inscription—presenting the book to Jean—appear to have been added later in slightly darker ink than the original "S L Clemens/1903" ownership

signature.)

> Provenance: MTLAcc, entry #1963, volume donated from Clemens's library by Clara Clemens Gabrilowitsch in 1910. Subsequently obtained by Dan Beard, who served as vice-president of the Mark Twain Library at Redding. No red ink accession number is visible, indicating that Beard most likely acquired it soon after it was donated and before it could be processed and shelved. New York City bookseller James F. Drake's description of this volume is laid in.
> Location: collection of Kevin Mac Donnell, Austin, Texas.
> Source: letter from Kevin Mac Donnell to Alan Gribben, 15 March 2013. The volume is unmarked, according to Mac Donnell. It bears four ink stamps of the Mark Twain Library at Redding.

Mark Twain wrote "A Dog's Tale" in the summer of 1903 in Elmira, partly in support of Jean Clemens's feelings about experimental animal vivisection. London's story might have prompted him to adopt the narrative perspective of a dog. A copy of *The Call of the Wild* is visible in a bookshelf in the background of an interior photograph that Jean Clemens took of Clemens and the Reverend Joseph H. Twichell in the 1900s (collection of Kevin Mac Donnell, Austin, Texas).

LONDON *Morning Post* (newspaper).

Clemens placed advertisements in this newspaper while cook-hunting in October 1896 (NB 39, TS p. 7).

LONDON. NATIONAL GALLERY. *A Complete Illustrated Catalogue to the National Gallery*. Ed. by Henry Blackburn (1830–1897). 242 illustrations. London, 1879.

> Inscription: the front flyleaf is signed "S. L. Clemens/ London, Aug. 6 '79".
> Marginalia: several illustrations marked with an "X."
> Catalog: *A1911*, "242 illustrations. 8vo, cloth. Lond. 1879," quotes the signature and characterizes the marginalia, lot 44, sold for $1.

LONDON *Standard* (London morning newspaper, published 1827–1916).

Clemens wrote on 19 October 1873 to Charles Warren Stoddard (1843–1909), instructing him to retain a "huge bundle" of *Standard* issues that Clemens had left behind, and also asking Stoddard to subscribe for all issues dating back to 17 October. Clemens wished to "scrap-book" all reports on the Tichborne Claimant trial for a future sketch he planned to write (*MTLet* 5: 456). In 1888 Clemens cited an unrelated fact that he attributed to the London *Standard* (NB 28, *N&J* 3: 474). The London *Evening Standard*, started in 1860, had the same ownership as the morning London *Standard*.

Henry W. Fisher, *AMT* (1922), p. 194.

LONDON *Times* (newspaper).

The sheer volume of its articles impressed Clemens most about this newspaper. He noted the number of words in an average issue in Notebook 17 (25 January 1879), *N&J* 2: 262, and on the front endpaper of Notebook 18 (1879, *N&J* 2: 290). He mentioned this "grim journal" in Chapter 42 of *A Tramp Abroad* (1880) and in Appendix F of that travel book he referred to the *Times* as "the bulkiest daily newspaper in the world," reporting that it "often contains 100,000 words of reading matter." In September and November 1888 Clemens examined the column space of the *Times* for possible applications of the Paige typesetting machine (NB 28, *N&J* 3: 427, 434). The epigraph to "The Czar's Soliloquy" (1905) consists of a quotation Mark Twain took from the London *Times*. In an Autobiographical Dictation of 24 November 1908 Twain spoke of the *Times* as Lord Northcliffe's journal that for a century had wielded political power with world rulers (*AutoMT* 3: 278–279).

Baetzhold, *MT&JB* (1970), pp. 35–36.

LONDON *World* (newspaper).

Clemens mentioned that George Warner once showed him a copy of the London *World* containing a sketch of Rudyard Kipling; this article formed part of his introduction to the important British writer (13 August 1906 AD, *MTE*, p. 312; *AutoMT* 2: 177). Inasmuch as Clemens and Kipling first met at Quarry Farm on 15 August 1889 in Elmira, New York (Fears, *Day by Day* 2: 402–405), it would seem likely that Warner gave Clemens an issue of either *The Man of the World*, a newspaper published in London between 1888 and 1900 or of the London *News of the World* (published 1843–2011). There is no record of a newspaper called the London *World* existing in the 1880s.

LONG, GABRIELLE MARGARET VERE (CAMPBELL) (1885–1952), pseud. "Marjorie Bowen." *The Master of Stair*. New York: McClure, Phillips & Co., 1907. 376 pp. [Edition conjectured.]

On 25 March 1907 Clemens thanked "Miss Marjorie" for her wish to dedicate *The Master of Stair* to him (*MTLW*, p. 127). When the book issued its dedication page accordingly honored Twain: "To Mark Twain/With deep gratitude for the flattering interest shown by a great man of letters in/the work of a beginner". On 6 May 1907 Clemens recommended the novel to Mary Benjamin Rogers, but he couldn't recall the title and he mistakenly supposed it to be the author's only published work. Clemens at least remembered that Marjorie Bowen had dedicated it to him, adding that this made it difficult for him to read the novel "without prejudice or predilection.... It is based on the Massacre of Glencoe [in the Scottish Highlands in 1692], but it mercifully leaves out (or very gently touches) the main horrors. I think that it is greatly to the girl's credit, for there would naturally be a strong temptation to do the other thing" (*MTLM*, pp. 99–100). Bowen wrote Clemens three letters the month her novel was published (April 1907) and he replied twice. Ralph Ashcroft wrote a third letter for Clemens.

———. *The Viper of Milan: A Romance of Lombardy*. New York: McClure, Phillips & Co., 1906. 362 pp. [Edition conjectured.]

Catalogs: ListABP (1910), "Viper of Milan, Bowen"; *C1951*, #20a, $20, listed among the books containing Clemens's marginal notes, no edition specified.

On 20 November 1906 Clemens wrote a letter from Fifth Avenue addressed to McClure, Phillips & Company in which he expressed appreciation for receiving a complimentary copy of this novel. He also registered disbelief that a mere girl, whether fifteen or even nineteen years old, could write "this extraordinary book"; clearly she must be at least twenty-five, he insisted. Such craftsmanship requires "a regular & exacting apprenticeship to the pen." He added that he concurred with the "high estimate" of *The Viper* that had appeared in the *Times Saturday Review*

(ALS quoted in "Mark Twain," Heritage Bookshop, Los Angeles, 1997, item #132). The publisher wrote back on 23 November 1906 to assure Clemens that Long had written *The Viper of Milan* "between the ages of sixteen and seventeen" (TLS in MTP). Since Clemens thought so highly of the novel, he must have meant *The Viper of Milan: A Romance of Lombardy* when writing to Mary Benjamin Rogers on 19 November 1906 about a "remarkable book ... by a child of fifteen." He praised that unidentified book as "virile and rugged" (*MTLM*, p. 89). In *The Viper of Milan*, her first novel, Long loosely set the historical events in fourteenth-century Italy; a ruthlessly rapacious Duke of Milan hounds the more ethical Duke of Verona, with various subplots. Long would go on to become a prolific author, preferring the genres of Gothic romance and historical fiction, though sometimes venturing into the supernatural.

LONG, JOHN LUTHER (1861–1927). *Madame Butterfly. Purple Eyes. A Gentleman of Japan and a Lady. Kito. Glory*. New York: Century Co., 1898. 224 pp. First edition of this collection of five stories. Original green cloth and pictorial color boards.

Inscription: inscribed by the author to Mark Twain's biographer Albert Bigelow Paine: "O Paine--/Salt of the/ Earth—be/good—die/happy--/J. L. Long." (Beginning in 1905 Paine lived with or near Twain until the latter's death in 1910).

Location: collection of Kevin Mac Donnell, Austin, Texas (Mac Donnell to Alan Gribben, 29 November 2011).

Long's "Madame Butterfly" was the inspiration for Puccini's famous opera that premiered in 1904. An American production staged by David Belasco (1853–1931) opened in 1906. When Isabel Lyon noticed on 10 October 1906 that Clemens was looking about aimlessly for a book to read, she gave him a copy of Long's "Madame Butterfly." (This might have been the book Long inscribed to Paine.) "Tonight at dinner," she reported, "the King said he had read 'that beautiful, beautiful story, and it is perfect. There is no flaw in it. There is no word to be changed. He makes you see a country you are a stranger to, and he makes you suffer as if you had been in the story yourself'" (IVL Journals, TS p. 194, MTP). When Clemens was attempting to demonstrate in 1909 how the Shakespeare/Bacon identity might have been mistaken, Albert Bigelow Paine ventured the observation that "even in this day John Luther Long's 'Madame Butterfly' is sometimes called Belasco's play, though it is doubtful if Belasco ever wrote a line of it." Clemens "considered this view, but not very favorably" (*MTB*, p. 1480). On another occasion Clemens remarked that "John Luther Long's exquisite plays would hardly have been successful without David Belasco to stage them" (*MTB*, p. 1414).

Moved and made melancholy by *Madame Butterfly*, Clemens told Isabel Lyon on 10 October 1906 "that he hadn't read 'Purple Eyes' yet and that he wouldn't read it for anything" (IVL Journals, TS p. 194, MTP). *Purple Eyes* tells the story of Cio-Cio San's daughter.

LONG, THOMAS (1621–1707). *An Exercitation Concerning the Frequent Use of Our Lord's Prayer in the Publick Worship of God. And a View of What Hath Been Said by Dr. [John] Owen [1616–1683] Concerning That Subject*. London: Printed by

J. G. for R. Marriot, 1658. 166 pp.
Clemens copied the title of this book into his notebook in 1873, maybe because of its antiquated phrasing (NB 12, *N&J* 1: 554).

LONG, WILLIAM JOSEPH (1867–1952). *Animal Stories* [Unidentified book].
Catalog: ListABP (1910), "Animal Stories, Long", no other information provided.
———. *Beasts of the Field*. Illustrated by Charles Copeland (1858–1929). New York: Ginn & Co., [cop. 1901]. 332 pp.
Source: MTLAcc, entry #1966, volume donated from Clemens's library by Clara Clemens Gabrilowitsch in 1910.
In 1907 Clemens became extremely interested in a dispute between Theodore Roosevelt, who was fond of hunting, and the Congregational clergyman Long who wrote on, and was an advocate for, wild animal life. Clemens thought Long to be a "pleasant and entertaining" naturalist whose books were mainly popular with children. Although Long's works do not measure up to John Burroughs's, Clemens conceded, at least Long "is equipped with a pleasant and entertaining pen" and writes from his own observations. His only fault is that he may sometimes overestimate the intelligence of the wild creatures he describes (AD, 29 May 1907; *MTE*, p. 20; *AutoMT* 3: 62). On 2 June 1907 Clemens told Isabel Lyon that he wished to write something about the Roosevelt-Long clash over Long's nature books (IVL Journals, TS p. 248, MTP). Later Clemens alluded to Long as the "nature fakir" (Roosevelt's derogatory term for Long) in an Autobiographical Dictation of 18 October 1907 (*MTE*, p. 8; *AutoMT* 3: 173) and in Notebook 48 (TS p. 9).
———. *Fowls of the Air*. Illustrated by Charles Copeland (1858–1929). New York: Ginn & Co., 1902. 310 pp.
Source: MTLAcc, entry #1964, volume donated from Clemens's library by Clara Clemens Gabrilowitsch in 1910.
———. *School of the Woods; Some Life Studies of Animal Instincts and Animal Training*. Illustrated by Charles Copeland (1858–1929). New York: Ginn & Co., [cop. 1902]. 361 pp.
Source: MTLAcc, entry #1965, volume donated from Clemens's library by Clara Clemens Gabrilowitsch in 1910.

LONGFELLOW, HENRY WADSWORTH (1807–1882). "The Day Is Done" (poem, published in 1844).
Mark Twain particularly liked the closing stanza of this poem: "The night shall be filled with music,/And the cares that infest the day/Shall fold their tents, like the Arabs,/And as silently steal away." He quoted from these lines in a letter to the *Alta California* written from the Holy Land in September 1867 (*TIA*, p. 183); twice in Chapter 42 of *The Innocents Abroad* (1869); once in Chapter 45 of *The Gilded Age* (1873); and again in a letter to Francis H. Skrine ("gone silently away like Longfellow's Arab") written in Vienna on 3 November 1897 (ASSSCL).
———. *The Divine Tragedy*. Boston: James R. Osgood and Co., 1871. 150 pp.
Inscription: the front flyleaf is inscribed by Olivia Clemens in ink, "S. L. Clemens/1872".
Provenance: formerly in the Mark Twain Library, Redding, Connecticut. Donated from Clemens's library by Clara Clemens Gabrilowitsch in 1910 (MTLAcc, entry #2056).
Location: Special Collections, Elihu Burritt Library, Central

Connecticut State University, New Britain, Connecticut.
Copy examined: photocopies of the inscription and title page supplied by the Burritt Library in 1979.
———. *The Golden Legend*. Original brown cloth, gilt. Boston: Ticknor and Fields, 1862. 326 pp.
Inscriptions: the front free endpaper is inscribed in ink at the top by Olivia Clemens: "S. L. Clemens/1871". The accession number of the Mark Twain Library of Redding, Connecticut ("2046") is penciled on the rear pastedown endpaper. The volume is also priced there at $1.25 (another later price of $25 has been erased). Someone added in brown ink, "M. Twain's copy."
Marginalia: more than thirty pages display Clemens's penciled marginal marks, and three pages carry his comments. On page 27, where Prince Henry exclaims, "Beneath me I can feel/The great earth stagger and reel," Clemens wrote "Drunk already." ("AGE—A Rubáiyát," Mark Twain's humorous parody probably written in 1898, has similar lines: "Along the Earth's Rotundity I reeled,/And swayed and swung my Random Way afield.") At Lucifer's speech on page 240 about "The Holy Satan, who made the wives/Of the bishops lead such shameful lives," Clemens wrote jauntily in the margin: "I like Satan." There are marginal brackets or long vertical lines by Clemens (all in pencil) on pages 14, 44, 84, 85, 88, 89, 108, 109, 117, 119, 173, 179, 180, 184, 185, 188, 193 (plus a note), 194, 197, 198, 209, 212, 215, 226, 232, 242, 252, 255, 284 (three emphatic vertical lines at Longfellow's reference to the restorative value of a "long ride in the open air"), 286, 291, and 292.
Provenance: MTLAcc, entry #2046, volume donated from Clemens's library by Clara Clemens Gabrilowitsch in 1910.
Location: Parkman D. Howe Collection, Rare Books and Manuscripts, University of Florida, Gainsville.
Copy examined: photocopies of the inscription and marginalia (kindly provided by Kevin Mac Donnell, who examined the book in Gainsville in July 1983 and sent his notes and photocopies to Alan Gribben on 7 August 1983).
"I have read & sent home The Golden Legend," Clemens informed his wife Olivia on 10 January 1872 in a letter written during his lecture tour in Ohio (*MTLet* 5: 15). She had already acknowledged her receipt of the volume on 7 January 1872: "I think the Golden Legend is beautiful. I wonder you did not mark it still more than you have. I do heartily enjoy the books that you have marked" (ALS in MTP; *MTLet* 5: 17). At the end of that same year Mark Twain made a favorable reference to Longfellow in a published letter (Hartford *Evening Post*, 6 December 1872, *MTPP*, p. 47). In Chapter 36 of *The Gilded Age* (1873) Laura Hawkins ranks Longfellow with Hawthorne and Tennyson, "favorites of her idle hours."
LLMT, p. 173 n. 10; Harris, *Courtship* (1996), p. 159.
———. *The Hanging of the Crane*. Illustrated by Mary A[nna]. Hallock (1847–1938) and Thomas Moran (1837–1926). Full morocco, gilt stamped spine, joints rubbed, water damage to covers, marbled endpapers. Boston: James R. Osgood and Co., 1875. 64 pp.
Inscription: inscribed in ink by Olivia Clemens on her

husband's birthday, "Saml L. Clemens/Nov. 30th 1874/ Livy."

Provenance: shelfmarks of Clara Clemens Gabrilowitsch's numbering system for her library books during her Detroit years.

Catalogs: ListABP (1910), "Hanging of the Crane, Longfellow"; *C1951*, 95c, listed (erroneously) among books signed by Clemens, no edition specified, $30; "Property from the Library of Mark Twain," Butterfield & Butterfield, San Francisco, Sale 6613 (16 July 1997), lot 2680.

Location: Mark Twain House and Museum, Hartford, Connecticut.

Copy examined: Clemens's unmarked copy. Viewed in Hartford in 1997.

Longfellow's prophetic poem traces the family fortunes of a couple who follow the custom of commemorating with a ceremonious dinner for guests the installation of an iron cooking crane in the fireplace of their newly constructed home. After undergoing harrowing tribulations, on their fiftieth wedding anniversary the "ancient" couple, seated in the same house, are "smiling contented and serene" at the sight of "their form and features multiplied" in children and grandchildren. Since the Clemenses had taken possession of their new Hartford residence in September 1874, this poem would have had symbolic significance for them.

————. "The Hemlock Tree" (poem, published in1845).

On 13 February 1884 George Washington Cable reported from Hartford that Clemens "went to the piano & sang a German song—one that Longfellow has translated—'O hemlock tree, O hemlock tree,/How faithful are thy branches'" (*MT&GWC*, pp. 31–32).

————. *Hyperion, A Romance* (novel, published in 1839).

Catalog: ListABP (1910), "Hyperion, Longfellow", no other information supplied.

Harris, *Courtship* (1996), p. 17.

————. "The Legend Beautiful," i.e., "Theologian's Tale" in Part II of *Tales of a Wayside Inn*. [Published in 1863.]

Clemens sent Olivia a copy of this poem from Harrisburg, Pennsylvania on 20 January 1872, critiquing it and comparing it to a poem by an unidentified woman who had treated the same subject (*MTLet* 5: 29).

————. "The Legend of Rabbi Ben Levi," poem in *Tales of a Wayside Inn* ("The Spanish Jew's Tale," Part 1). [Published in 1863.]

Olivia Langdon copied this poem into her commonplace book around 1868; only two pages farther on, Clemens himself wrote in the same book (DV1 61, MTP). See the Catalog entry below for Olivia Langdon's copy of *Tales of a Wayside Inn*.

————. "The Light of Stars" (poem, published in 1839).

Clemens quoted the concluding line from this poem ("to 'suffer & be strong'") in a letter of 31 March 1872 to James R. Osgood (*MTLet* 5: 72).

————. *Longfellow's Evangeline with Illustrations by F[elix]. O[ctavius]. C[arr]. Darley.* Boston: Houghton, Mifflin and Co., 1883. 51 leaves with 48 pages of text. [Oversize volume.]

Catalog: Ball 2016 inventory, oversize book, textured paper.

Location: Quarry Farm library shelves, under the supervision of the Mark Twain Archive, Elmira College, Elmira,

New York.

Clemens had access to this volume at Quarry Farm in Elmira. See also the Catalog entry for J. C. Goodwin's musical burlesque, *Evangeline.*

————. *The New-England Tragedies. (I.) John Endicott; (II.) Giles Corey of the Salem Farms.* Original terra cotta cloth, gilt. Boston: Ticknor and Fields, 1868. 179 pp.

Marginalia: typical marginal pencil brackets by Clemens on pages 39, 40, 41, 51, 59, 60, 62, 64, 66, 94, 113, and 140. On page 66 the marked text reads: "In this town/ They put sea-captains in the stocks for swearing,/And Quakers for not swearing. So look out."

Provenance: Mark Twain Library, Redding, Connecticut. Donated from Clemens's library by Clara Clemens Gabrilowitsch in 1910 (MTLAcc, entry #2055).

Location: collection of Kevin Mac Donnell, Austin, Texas. Acquired in 2009.

Source: letter from Kevin Mac Donnell to Alan Gribben, 30 April 2009. Mac Donnell reported that the Mark Twain Library accession number "2055" appears on the rear pastedown endpaper of the volume and the oval Mark Twain Library stamp was used on the front and rear endpapers, half-title page, and page 25.

"I have read & sent home . . . The New England Tragedies," Clemens wrote to Olivia on 10 January 1872 from Steubenville, Ohio (ALS in MTP; *LLMT*, p. 172; *MTLet* 5: 15). During this period Mark Twain was on a five-state tour with his *Roughing It* lectures. He often read books on the train and marked them for Olivia. In "Sociable Jimmy" (1874) Mark Twain states that he kept notes of his conversation with a young African American hotel employee on the flyleaf of a copy of *New England Tragedies*, but none are present in the copy acquired by Mac Donnell in 2009.

Shelley Fisher Fishkin, *Was Huck Black?: Mark Twain and African-American Voices* (New York: Oxford University Press, 1993), pp. 14, 35, 252, and Appendix; Susan K. Harris, *Courtship* (1996), p. 159; Kevin Mac Donnell, "Was Huck Quaker? The Inner Light in *Adventures of Huckleberry Finn*," *Mark Twain Journal: The Author and His Era* 56. 2 (Fall 2018): 50–51, 53, 62 (reproduces two marked passages).

————. *Nuremberg; A Poem.* Illus. Nuremberg: J. L. Schrag, n.d. 15 pp.

Source: MTLAcc, entry #2057, volume donated from Clemens's library by Clara Clemens Gabrilowitsch in 1910.

————. *Poems of Henry Wadsworth Longfellow.* Brown cloth, gilt. Boston: Houghton, Mifflin and Co., 1882. 426 pp.

Inscription: the second front flyleaf is signed in ink: "Catherine Leary/37 West 97th St./New York."

Marginalia: both the text and the index at the rear are marked with pencil, but apparently not by Clemens.

Provenance: Antenne-Dorrance Collection, Rice Lake, Wisconsin.

Location: Mark Twain Archive, Gannett-Tripp Learning Center, Elmira College, Elmira, New York.

Copy examined: evidently a copy once belonging to a member of Clemens's family. Examined on 28 May 2015.

Possibly Clemens intended to buy this edition when he made a memorandum in Notebook 20 in April 1882: "Osgood get a Longfellow for Clara's birthday" (*N&J* 2:

460). Longfellow had died on 24 March 1882, and many eulogies were appearing in the press. Clemens planned to meet publisher James R. Osgood in Boston on 14 April (WDH to SLC, 7 April 1882, *MTHL*, p. 399). Clara's eighth birthday would be on 8 June 1882.

———. *The Poetical Works of Henry Wadsworth Longfellow.* 7 vols. Illus. Boston: Houghton, Mifflin and Co., 1881.

Catalog: Ball 2016 inventory, red leather, gilt lettering and edges.

Location: Quarry Farm library shelves, under the supervision of the Mark Twain Archive, Elmira College, Elmira, New York.

This volume was available to Clemens at Quarry Farm in Elmira.

__________, ed. *The Poets and Poetry of Europe.* New York: James Miller, 1863. 779 pp.

Source: Edgar H. Hemminghaus—"Mark Twain's German Provenience" (1945), pp. 467–468—reported seeing Clemens's copy of these translations, biographies, and critical notices in the Mark Twain Library at Redding, Connecticut, in 1945. Albert E. Stone, Jr. could not find the volume there in 1955, however, and I was unable to locate *Poets and Poetry of Europe* when I visited Redding in 1970 or thereafter.

Herbert S. Gorman, *A Victorian American: Henry Wadsworth Longfellow.* New York: George H. Doran Co., 1926.

———. "A Psalm of Life" (poem, published in 1838).

Clemens concluded a letter of 21 November 1860 to his brother Orion by slightly misquoting the stirring fifth of the poem's nine stanzas: "In the world's great [*sic*] field of battle,/In the bivuac [*sic*] of life,/Be not like dumb, driven cattle—/Be a *hero* in the strife" (*MTLet* 1: 103–105) On 14 October 1874 Clemens used a phrase from the poem ("art is long") in a letter to Louise Chandler Moulton (*MTLet* 6: 257). In Chapter 50 of *The Innocents Abroad* (1869) Mark Twain alluded to the first stanza: "The poet has said, 'Things are not what they seem.'" He employed the seventh stanza of the poem—"Lives of great men all remind us/We can make our lives sublime,/And, departing, leave behind us/Footprints in the sands of time"—in his ill-fated Whittier Birthday Dinner speech on 17 December 1877 (*MTB*, p. 1646; *MTSpk*, p. 114). "Ask me not, in mournful numbers," Twain quipped in Chapter 28 of *Life on the Mississippi* (1883), paraphrasing the opening line of "A Psalm of Life." "This is art, and art is long, as the poet says," he wrote in Chapter 6 of *Following the Equator* (1897); Longfellow's fourth stanza observes that "Art is long, and Time is fleeting."

———. *Selections from the Writings of Henry Wadsworth Longfellow, Arranged Under the Days of the Year.* Boston: Houghton, Mifflin & Co., 1889. [128 pp.]

Source: MTLAcc, entry #2125, volume donated from Clemens's library by Clara Clemens Gabrilowitsch in 1910.

———. *The Song of Hiawatha* (poem, published in 1855).

In Mark Twain's sketch titled "A Memory" (*Galaxy* 10.2 August 1870: 286–287), he pretended that as a boy he wrote a parody of *Song of Hiawatha*—substituting language from a warranty deed of property for the words of his father's favorite poem. Twain quotes six lines from *Song of Hiawatha* and then six lines of his resulting burlesque (*CG*, p. 66; also reprinted in *Mark Twain: Life As I Find It—Essays, Sketches, Tales, and Other Material*, ed. Charles Neider [Garden City, New York: Hanover House, 1961], pp. 100–103). This story is sheer nonsense, of course; Clemens's father, John Marshall Clemens, died in 1847 before *Hiawatha* was even published. "Honor be to Mudjeheewis!/You shall hear how Pau-Puk-Keewis—" intones the imposter in Twain's address at the Whittier Birthday Dinner on 17 December 1877 (*MTB*, p. 1644; *MTSpk*, p. 112). Twain informs the readers of *Life on the Mississippi* (1883) that "the tales in 'Hiawatha' . . . came from [Henry R.] Schoolcraft's book." In Chapter 59 Twain publishes Schoolcraft's version of "Peboan and Seegwun, an Allegory of the Seasons," noting that the tale "is used in 'Hiawatha'; but it is worth reading in the original form, if only that one may see how effective a genuine poem can be without the helps and graces of poetic measure and rhythm."

Aspiz, "MT's Reading" (1949), pp. 116–117; Smith, "'That Hideous Mistake'" (1955).

———. *Tales of a Wayside Inn.* Publisher's half-calf and marbled boards, leather spine snagged, marbled endpapers, extremities rubbed. Boston: Ticknor and Fields, 1863. 225 pp.

Inscription: the front flyleaf is signed in ink, "L. L. Langdon/June 1864".

Marginalia: Clemens made vertical pencil lines in the Preface (pages 3, 5, and 16) and in "Paul Revere's Ride" (on page 22, including the line, "The fate of a nation was riding that night.").

Provenance: has the shelfmarks of Clara Clemens Gabrilowitsch's library numbering system during her Detroit years. Sold at the 1951 auction in Hollywood but not listed in the sale sheet. The 1951 auction lot designation "J47" is recorded on the verso of the half-title page.

Catalog: "Property from the Library of Mark Twain," Butterfield & Butterfield, San Francisco, Sale 6613 (16 July 1997), lot 2705.

Location: Mark Twain House and Museum, Hartford, Connecticut.

Copy examined: Olivia Clemens's copy, with markings by Clemens. Viewed in Hartford in 1997.

See also the Catalog entry for Beatrice Harraden's novel, *Ships That Pass in the Night.*

———. "The Village Blacksmith" (poem, published in 1840).

Mark Twain's speech at the Whittier Birthday Dinner on 17 December 1877 included the lines "Thanks, thanks to thee, my worthy friend,/For the lesson thou hast taught" (*MTB*, p. 1646; *MTSpk*, p. 113).

Smith, "'That Hideous Mistake'" (1955).

Longfellow, Samuel (1819–1892), ed. *Life of Henry Wadsworth Longfellow, with Extracts from his Journals and Correspondence.* 2 vols. Boston: Houghton, Mifflin and Co., 1886.

Catalog: Ball 2016 inventory, 2 vols., red cloth, gilt edges and lettering.

Location: Quarry Farm library shelves, under the supervision of the Mark Twain Archive, Elmira College, Elmira, New York.

A volume available to Clemens whenever he visited Quarry Farm in Elmira.

Longstreet, Abby [Abigail] Buchanan (1834–1899). *Social Etiquette of New York.* New York: D. Appleton & Co.,

1879. 187 pp. Revised, enlarged edition published in 1881.
In Mark Twain's unfinished "Burlesque of Books on Etiquette" (written in 1881) he quotes from and cites Longstreet's book as "one of the ablest of our recent works on Deportment" (*LE*, p. 200); he is especially interested in her dictum about calling cards. The dating of Twain's composition of the manuscript (DV68, MTP) derives from his letter to James R. Osgood of 7 March 1881 ("Yes, send me a collection of etiquette books") and William Dean Howells's letter to Clemens, written on 17 April 1881 ("Why don't you go on with the Etiquette Book?") (both letters quoted in *MTHL*, pp. 360 n. 2, 362). Longstreet also wrote separate manuals on wedding ceremonies, general manners, health care, debutantes, and calling cards. The wife of New York City dentist Christopher S. Longstreet (b. 1832), she had an earlier marriage to Charles Henry Gildersleeve (1821–1866).

LONGSTREET, AUGUSTUS BALDWIN (1790–1870). *Georgia Scenes, Characters, Incidents, &c., in the First Half Century of The Republic. By a Native Georgian.* Illus. New York: Harper & Brothers, 1845. 214 pp.

Inscription: the front free endpaper is signed "James W. Hunt"; below this signature Clemens added his own in pencil: "S. L. Clemens/Hartford, 1876." An *A1911* sale label and the bookplate of W. T. H. Howe are affixed to the front pastedown endpaper. A note to Howe from Isabel V. Lyon, Clemens's one-time secretary (dated 26 August 1938), authenticated Clemens's ownership of the volume. Lyon's note is laid in the book.

Marginalia: Clemens made blue ink marks on pages 9 and 11 of "Georgia Theatrics" and on pages 23 and 31 of "the Horse-Swap." In the same ink he also jotted a few instructions: for the illustration of an imaginary fight captioned "A Lincoln [County] Rehearsal" (opposite page 10) he wrote, "Reproduce & use this picture. SLC". On pages 23 and 24 of "The Horse-Swap" he changed several italicized words to "Rom." in the margins; near the illustration of a horseback rider opposite page 24 he directed, "Make fac-simile of this picture & use it. SLC"; and on page 25 he deleted the words "or hawked" in the sentence reading "If a stick cracked, or if any one moved suddenly about him, or coughed, or hawked, or spoke a little louder than common, up went Bullet's tail like lightning."

Catalogs: *A1911*, "12mo, original cloth (worn, and plates spotted), N.Y. 1845, the second New York edition with the original illustrations," quotes the signature and marginalia, lot 298, sold for $5; George D. Smith, New York City, "Catalogue of Books" (1911), quotes the signature and marginalia, item #130, $25; American Art Association (New York City), Sale catalogue (3–4 March 1925), from the collection of the late William F. Gable of Altoona, Pennsylvania, "from the library of S. L. Clemens, with his autograph signature," has the *A1911* sale label, lot 101, sold for $10 (with another book included); American Art Association-Anderson Galleries (New York City), Catalogue number 4354 (7 December 1937), "12 plates, 12mo, original cloth, covers stained, light stains in text, in half morocco slip case, New York, 1845," front flyleaf signed in Hartford in 1876, has the *A1911* sale label, lot 91.

Location: Henry W. and Albert A. Berg Collection, New York Public Library.

Copy examined: Clemens's copy, in 1970.

Mark Twain clearly intended to include material from *Georgia Scenes* in *Mark Twain's Library of Humor*, published in 1888. The title of Longstreet's book appears in a list of humorists and their works that Twain began in 1880 (NB 19, *N&J* 2: 362). Shortly thereafter he wrote "Hall (Georgia Scenes" (NB 19, *N&J* 2: 362), an allusion to one of the pseudonyms Longstreet signed to his sketches in *Georgia Scenes*; its title page did not name the author, and Longstreet alternates the names "Hall" and "Baldwin" in crediting his tales. In 1881 Twain reminded himself of "Georgia Sketches" (NB 19, *N&J* 2: 429). The two stories Twain annotated in his own copy of *Georgia Scenes* were both ascribed by Longstreet to "Hall." One of them, "Georgia Theatrics," is the first piece in Longstreet's collection (pp. 9–11); it describes a ploughboy's pretended thrashing of a detested opponent. The other, "The Horse-Swap" (pp. 23–31), relates how the boastful Yellow Blossom from Jasper ("I'm a *leetle*, jist a *leetle*, of the best man at a horse-swap that ever trod shoe-leather") trades an ornery swayback called Bullet for the gentle sorrel Kit, owned by a local farmer named Peter Ketch. "I'm for short talk in a horse-swap," declares the seemingly gullible Ketch, and the inequitable exchange takes place hurriedly. A few minutes later Blossom learns to his dismay that he has acquired an animal both blind and deaf. Longstreet's stories were worthy of inclusion in Mark Twain's anthology, and Twain's marginal notes display his intention to use their illustrations as well, yet for some reason Longstreet's work was excluded in 1888 from the final version of *Mark Twain's Library of Humor*. Possibly Charles L. Webster & Company, Mark Twain's publishing firm, encountered difficulties in negotiations with Harper & Brothers, which had reprinted *Georgia Scenes* as recently as 1884. Alan Gribben's "Mark Twain Reads Longstreet's *Georgia Scenes*," *Gyascutus: Studies in Antebellum Southern Humorous and Sporting Writing*, n.s. 5–6 (1978): 103–111—revised as a chapter in Volume One of this present work—explained more fully Twain's plan to utilize two stories and several illustrations in this copy of Longstreet's *Georgia Scenes*.

Blair, *NAH* (1937, 1960), pp. 153, 287–289; Branch, *LAMT* (1950), p. 9; Lynn, *MT&SH* (1959), p. 69; Blair, *MT&HF* (1960), p. 62; Joe B. Fulton, *The Reverend Mark Twain: Theological Burlesque, Form, and Content* (Columbus: Ohio State University Press, 2006), pp. 34, 117–118, 141, 145; and Henry B. Wonham, "Southwestern Humor," *Mark Twain in Context*, ed. John Bird (Cambridge, England: Cambridge University Press, 2020), pp. 49–57, especially pp. 50–55.

LONSDALE, MARGARET (1846–1917). *Sister Dora. A Biography.* Boston: Roberts Brothers, 1880. 290 pp.

Source: MTLAcc, entry #840, volume donated by Clemens.

Dorothy Wyndlow Pattison (1832–1878), known as Sister Dora, was an Anglican nun and nurse renowned for her empathy and self-sacrifice in the town of Walsall in the West Midlands of England.

LORD, JOHN (1810–1894). *Beacon Lights of History.* Lord's Lectures Series. 8 vols. New York: Fords, Howard, and Hulbert, 1884–1896. [Only Clemens's copy of Volume I is known to survive.]

Inscription: the front free endpaper of Volume I is inscribed in purple pencil: "2 vols subscribed for—& the same taken & *paid for*, June 17 '85./S. L. Clemens".

Catalogs: ListABP (1910), "Beacon Lights of Hist., Lord"; *C1951*, #97c, $8, listed among books signed by Clemens; *Fleming 1972*, Volume I only; Sotheby Parke Bernet, New York City, Sale number 3482 (25 February 1976), Volume I only, quotes Clemens's inscription, "Property of a New York City Collector" (John F. Fleming), lot 22 (sold with two other titles).

Provenance: Frederick Anderson, then Editor of the Mark Twain Papers in the Bancroft Library at the University of California, Berkeley, examined and authenticated Volume I and made notes at the New York City office of John F. Fleming, Inc. in April 1972 (Anderson to James D. Hart, 17 April 1972, photocopy sent to Alan Gribben).

The first volume of Lord's work encompassed figures from "Antiquity": Moses, Socrates, Phidias, Julius Caesar, Chrysostom, Saint Ambrose, Saint Augustine, Theodosius the Great, Leo the Great. Albert E. Stone, Jr. suggested that Clemens was familiar with Volume V, which treats "Great Women" in history ("Mark Twain's *Joan of Arc*: The Child as Goddess," p. 4). Lord's history covered The Middle Ages (Volume II), Renaissance and Reformation (Volume III), Warriors and Statesmen (Volume IV), Modern European Statesmen (Volume VI), American Statesmen (Volume VII), and Nineteenth-Century Writers (Volume VIII). Clemens mentioned "Dr. Lord's Lectures and the great subscription sales they had in '79 or so" in discussing copyright profits with Isabel Lyon on 31 August 1907 (IVL Journals, TS p. 274, MTP). The former Congregational minister Lord, born in New Hampshire and educated at Dartmouth College, lectured on history at Dartmouth between 1866 and 1876 and became a renowned public lecturer at large.

————. *The Old Roman World: The Grandeur and Fall of Its Civilization*. New York: Charles Scribner and Co., 1867. 605 pp. [Reprinted throughout the 1860s and 1870s.]

On 28 August 1907 Clemens spoke to Isabel Lyon about "Dr. Lord's Lectures on Roman History—etc. took 200 subscriptions in Hartford in 12 days. Canvassed that book for 26 yrs." (IVL Notebook #3, TS p. 3, MTP).

LORD, JOHN CHASE (1805–1877). *Occasional Poems*. Buffalo: Breed & Lent, 1869. 141 pp.

Source: MTLAcc, entry #2042, volume donated from Clemens's library by Clara Clemens Gabrilowitsch in 1910.

Lord, minister of the Central Presbyterian Church in Buffalo, and his wife Mary E. Johnson Lord, "were valued members of Twain's social circle in Buffalo" (Reigstad, *Scribblin' for a Livin'* (2013), p. 167).

Lords and Commons (London journal, published 11 February-20 May 1899).

Clemens was elated when he placed an essay in this "swell new London political periodical" (SLC to Henry H. Rogers, Vienna, 19 February 1899, *MTHHR*, p. 390). His "The 'Austrian Parliamentary System'? Government by Article 14" appeared in the 25 February 1899 issue of this short-lived journal.

"THE LORD'S PRAYER" (Matthew 6: 9–13, from the Biblical Sermon on the Mount).

Mark Twain observed, "The average clergyman, in all countries and of all denominations, is a very bad reader. One would think he would at least learn how to read the Lord's Prayer, by and by, but it is not so. He races through it as if he thought the quicker he got it in, the sooner it would be answered. A person who does not appreciate the exceeding value of pauses, and does not know how to measure their duration judiciously, cannot render the grand simplicity and dignity of a composition like that effectively" (*TA* [1880], Ch. 36). Bernard DeVoto deduced that Twain wrote "Simplified Spelling" in 1906; that essay employs "The Lord's Prayer"—specifically quoting "Our Father which art in heaven"—in arguing for "a lightning-express reformed alphabet" (*LE*, pp. 160, 161).

LOSSING, BENSON JOHN (1813–1891). *The Empire State: A Compendious History of the Commonwealth of New York*. Illustrated with facsimiles of 335 pen-and-ink drawings by H. Rosa. Hartford, Connecticut: American Publishing Co., 1888. 618 pp. [Publisher and pages conjectured.]

Catalog: *A1911*, "royal 8vo, sheep (back torn), Hartford, 1888," a sheet of Clemens's notes laid in, lot 300, sold for $1.

————. *Harper's Popular Cyclopaedia of United States History*. 2 vols. Illus. New York: Harper & Brothers, 1899.

Source: MTLAcc, entries #1230 and #1231, volumes donated by Clemens.

————. *The Pictorial Field-Book of the War of 1812*. Illus. New York: Harper & Brothers, 1869. 1084 pp.

Source: MTLAcc, entry #1725, volume donated by Clemens.

————. *The Story of the United States Navy for Boys*. Illus. New York: Harper & Brothers, [cop. 1880]. 418 pp.

Source: MTLAcc, entry #1189, volume donated by Clemens.

Lotos Leaves, ed. John Brougham (1810–1880) and John Elderkin (1841–1926). Boston: William F. Gill & Co., 1875. 401 pp.

Inscription: in blue-purple ink: "To My Beloved Wife/ Xmas—'74." The handwriting appears to be authentic. Evidently Clemens received a copy in advance of the publication date because he was a contributor to the volume.

Location: collection of Charles F. Cornman, Redwood City, California (in 1970).

Copy examined: Clemens's copy, though its provenance is unestablished.

Mark Twain was one of the Lotos Club members whose literary contributions appeared in this collection. His sketch was titled "An Encounter with an Interviewer." Meditating revenge in January 1881 against Whitelaw Reid, Twain wrote "W. Reid—'Lotos Leaves'" (NB 19, *N&J* 2: 417). Reid had been another contributor to the volume in the form of an essay, "Some Southern Reminiscences," recollecting several years he spent in the Deep South after the Civil War.

LOUGHRAN, EDWARD BOOTH (1850–1928). *'Neath Austral Skies. Poems*. First edition. Original full dark blue morocco, gilt. Melbourne: Melville, Mullen & Slade, 1894. 204 pp.

Inscription: in black ink on the front free flyleaf: "To Samuel L. Clemens Esq/With the best wishes of one/of the devoted admirers of/'Mark Twain',/E. B. Loughran./

Melbourne/28th October 1895." An attached note has been torn from the verso of the presentation leaf, leaving only a fragment (not in Clemens's handwriting) reading, ". . . nds of affectionate ad . . ." A Mark Twain Library in Redding accession number ("2802") appears in ink on the copyright page.

Provenance: MTLAcc, entry #2060, volume donated from Clemens's library by Clara Clemens Gabrilowitsch in 1910. Eventually obtained by Nick Karanovich, Fort Wayne, Indiana on 30 December 1983 from George Robert Minkoff Rare Books, Great Barrington, Massachusetts, for $300.

Catalogs: *Mott 1952,* item #66, $12.50; *Sotheby's 2003,* #217, $4,000 (sold with four other inscribed books).

Location: collection of Kevin Mac Donnell, Austin, Texas.

Copy examined: Clemens's unmarked copy, in July 2004. In addition, Nick Karanovich supplied photocopies of the most relevant pages when he owned the volume (Karanovich to Alan Gribben, 11 January 1984).

LOUISVILLE, KENTUCKY *Courier.*

Catalog: ListABP (1910), "Louisville Courier, 1906", no issue specified.

LOUISVILLE, KENTUCKY *Evening Post.*

In a portion of manuscript deleted from the final version of *Life on the Mississippi* (1883), Mark Twain quotes "a recent article in the Evening Post" that decried lawless behavior in Kentucky (Heritage Press Edition [1944], p. 415).

LOUNSBERY, GRACE CONSTANT (1876–1964). *L'Escarpolette [The Swing]* (one-act play).

On 18 December 1905 Clemens took part in a benefit for Russian Jews at which Sarah Bernhardt performed in this one-act play; Isabel Lyon thought her performance was "utterly charming" (IVL Journals, TS p. 115, MTP). In *L'Escarpolette* a young man falls in love with a Fragonard painting of a girl in a swing. The wealthy American-born Lounsbery resided most of the time in Paris.

LOUNSBURY, THOMAS RAYNESFORD (1838–1915). *James Fenimore Cooper.* Boston and New York: Houghton, Mifflin and Co., 1882. 306 pp. Fifth edition published in 1885.

Mark Twain quotes Lounsbury's laudatory assessment of *The Pathfinder* and *The Deerslayer* at the beginning of "Fenimore Cooper's Literary Offences" (1895). He intended for the same quotation to head a second comic lecture, "Cooper's Prose Style" (*LE*, pp. 137–145).

————. "A Scholar of the Twelfth Century," three articles appearing in the *The New Englander* issues between November 1878 (37.147) and January 1880 (39.154).

Joseph H. Twichell sent Clemens a collection of these essays about Giraldus Cambrensis (c. 1146–c. 1223) on 17 July 1880 (*LMTJHT,* p. 96). Clemens wrote back from Elmira, New York on 19 July 1880: "Have just finished the Scholar of the 12th Cent. & am delighted with the amusing & pathetic story. . . . I wish I could read the original; those marvels charm me—such as the spring running with milk, the man breached like a bull, & that soldier's immaculate conception of a calf. I will re-mail the pamphlet to you to-day or to-morrow" (*LMTJHT,* p. 98). The Catholic archdeacon Giraldus, called "Gerald of Wales," was a historian who left behind an autobiography about his travels and his political struggles to achieve a degree of Welsh autonomy.

————. *The Standard of Usage in English.* New York: Harper & Brothers, 1908.

Source: MTLAcc, entry #854, volume donated by Clemens.

LOUVET DE COUVRAI, JEAN BAPTISTE (1760–1797). *Les amours du chevalier de faublas.* 5 volumes. Contemporary polished calf, extremities somewhat worn, marbled endpapers. Paris: Librairie des bibliophiles, 1884.

Provenance: sold at the 1951 Hollywood auction, but not listed in the hastily compiled *C1951* sale sheet.

Catalog: "Property from the Library of Mark Twain," Butterfield & Butterfield, San Francisco, Sale 6613 (16 July 1997), lot 2681.

Location: Mark Twain House and Museum, Hartford, Connecticut.

Copy examined: Clemens's unmarked copy. Examined in 1997 in Hartford.

In the autumn of 1885 Clemens noted the author and title of this erotic novel, which was first published 1787–1789 (NB 25, *N&J* 3: 207).

LOVE, ROBERTUS (1867–1930). *Poems All the Way from Pike.* St. Louis, Missouri: Pan-American Press, 1904. 126 pp.

Inscription: (on the title page) "To Mark Twain,/the First Missourian,/from Robertus Love,/one of the latest./Arcadia, Mo.,/May 3, 1906." Tipped in on the front pastedown endpaper and the front free endpaper is a typed poem from the St. Louis *Post-Dispatch,* June 1902, titled "To Mark Twain,/'First Missourian,'/of Hannibal," signed by "Robertus Love."

Location: Mark Twain Library, Redding, Connecticut. Donated from Clemens's library by Clara Clemens Gabrilowitsch in 1910 (MTLAcc, entry #2041).

Copy examined: Clemens's copy, unmarked. Has the red ink Mark Twain Library accession number "2041". Examined in 1970 and again in June 1982.

LOVEJOY, JOSEPH CAMMET (1805–1871) and **OWEN LOVEJOY** (1811–1864). *Memoir of the Rev. Elijah P[arish]. Lovejoy [1802–1837], Who Was Murdered in Defence of the Liberty of the Press at Alton, Illinois, November 7, 1837.* Intro. by John Quincy Adams (1767–1848). New York: J. S. Taylor, 1838. 382 pp.

In the course of planning a book on American lynchings, Mark Twain wrote to Frank Bliss about a historical account that the research assistant whom Bliss was supposed to hire "must be sure to get. . . . Let him examine the life of Owen Lovejoy [*sic*] in the Hartford library or the Boston Public—better still, let him *buy* the book, if he can, by advertising a second-hand book dealer" (ALS, Harry Ransom Center, University of Texas at Austin). Surely Mark Twain meant the martyred newspaper publisher and abolitionist Elijah P. Lovejoy, whose brother Owen was present when a mob killed Elijah in Alton, Illinois. Owen Lovejoy did not publish an autobiography, and no biography existed for that Congregational clergyman and loyal Lincoln supporter until Edward Magdol wrote *Owen Lovejoy: Abolitionist in Congress* (New Brunswick, New Jersey: Rutgers University Press, 1967).

LOW, (SIR) ALFRED MAURICE (1860–1929). *The Supreme Surrender: A Novel.* New York: Harper & Brothers, 1901. 230 pp.

Source: MTLAcc, entry #1581, volume donated by Clemens.

LOWELL, JAMES RUSSELL (1819–1891). *The Biglow Papers.*

Philadelphia: H. Altemus, n.d. 221 pp.

Source: MTLAcc, entry #2137, volume donated from Clemens's library by Clara Clemens Gabrilowitsch in 1910. Clemens exultantly reported to his family in St. Louis that "James Russell Lowell ('Hosea Biglow,') says the Jumping Frog is the finest piece of humorous writing ever produced in America" (19 April 1867, *MTLet* 2: 27). No confirmation of this assertion has been found. In 1873 Clemens was aghast when a reviewer for the *Christian Union* compared Edward Eggleston's "genuineness" to Lowell's "first 'Biglow Papers'" (*MTLet* 5: 347–348). A Longfellow impostor improperly claimed credit for *The Biglow Papers* in Mark Twain's edgy speech at the Whittier Birthday Dinner on 17 December 1877 (*MTB*, p. 1646; *MTSpk*, p. 113). In 1880 and 1881 Twain listed Lowell among the humorists he wished to consider for inclusion in an anthology (NB 19, *N&J* 2: 363, 429). *Mark Twain's Library of Humor* (1888) accordingly contained three pieces from Lowell's *Biglow Papers*: "The Courtin'," "Birdofredom Sawin as a Volunteer," and "Birdofredum Sawin After the War."

Blair, *NAH* (1937), p. 160; Scott, *OPMT* (1966), pp. 11, 81–92; Holger Kersten, "Mark Twain's 'Assault of Laughter': Reflections on the Perplexing History of an Appealing Idea," *Mark Twain Annual 16* (2018): 69.

———. "The First Snowfall" (poem, published in 1847).

In 1867 Olivia Langdon copied Lowell's poem, a poignant reflection on his daughter's death, into her commonplace book (DV161, MTP).

———. *Letters of James Russell Lowell.* Ed. by Charles Eliot Norton (1827–1908). 2 vols. Reprint. 8vo, original black cloth, gilt. New York: Harper & Brothers, 1893.

Inscription: both volumes are signed in black ink, "S L. Clemens/1909."

Marginalia: both volumes are profusely annotated; thirty-nine notes total 629 words on 35 pages. In addition, Clemens canceled the pronoun "that" forty-three times on thirty pages and deleted other words whose usage he found excessive; he also made grammatical corrections and verb tense changes on fourteen pages and drew underlinings and marginal lines on seventeen pages. Clemens observed at one point: "He is much too 'thatful' for me—it annoys a body." Several notes in Volume I (on pages 126, 305, and 357) are dated April 1909. Clemens made a caustic marginal note in pencil on page 337 about God's favor: "So had the struggling Filipino patriots in 1898. He always promises both sides. The history of both sides in all wars will tell you as much. What you know about His nature you must have got from the pulpit, not from observation." Beside Lowell's caution to William Dean Howells in 1865 (Volume I, page 351) about the dangerous "rock"—"carelessness and want of scholarly refinement"—that might knock "our literature" completely "to pieces," Clemens wrote, "Yes, sir, & we *done* it!" Where Lowell alludes to the ability to pick up a narrative and resume writing it after a long hiatus (p. 373), Clemens drew a vertical line in pencil in the margin and noted, "I know all about that, from experience."

On page 375 of Volume I, Clemens folded down the corner and discussed his own suicidal impulse in 1866, defending the bravery of those who actually commit the act; he dated this note 21 April 1909. Lowell had written: "I suppose scarce a young man of sensibility ever grew his shell who didn't, during the process, meditate suicide a great many times. I remember in '39 putting a cocked pistol to my forehead—and being afraid to pull the trigger, of which I was heartily ashamed, and am still whenever I think of it. . . . I am glad now that I was too healthy, for it is only your feeble Jerusalems that fairly carry the thing out and rid the world of what would have been mere nuisances." Clemens drew a slanted square bracket in black ink after the word "trigger" in Lowell's text and responded in the same ink with a lengthy note that started in the left margin, moved to the top, and concluded by filling the right margin: "3 a.m., Apl. 21 '09. Down to 'trigger' I am with him, but no/further. It is odd that I should stumble upon this now, for it/is only two days ago since something called to my/mind *my* experience of 1866 & I told/it at dinner. I put the pistol to/my head but wasn't man enough/to pull the trigger. Many times I have/been sorry I did not succeed, but I was never ashamed/of having tried. Suicide is the only really sane thing the young/or the old ever do in this life. 'Feeble Jerusalems' never kill/themselves; they survive the attempt. Lowell & I are instances" (quoted in "Note Bares Twain Attempt at Suicide," Los Angeles *Times*, 15 April 1951, Part 1, p. 40; text corrected against notes taken by Frederick Anderson, former Editor of the Mark Twain Papers, when he examined the volumes in 1972 in New York City, also corrected against a facsimile reproduced in the 25 February 1976 Sotheby Parke Bernet catalog, and further corrected by a personal inspection of Clemens's note in 2004). Robert H. Hirst and the editorial team at the Mark Twain Project in the Bancroft Library at the University of California, Berkeley have theorized that "Clemens was off by part of a year." Citing a letter that Clemens wrote on 20 October 1865 to his brother Orion ("I am utterly miserable"), they would assign his suicidal impulse to 1865 rather than 1866 (Hirst to the Mark Twain Forum, TWAIN-L@YORKU. CA, 5 March 2004). Hirst's suggested correction seems eminently reasonable.

In Volume II, page 57, Clemens underlined Lowell's words ("If I only had a few cadetships to sell!") regarding the necessity of bribing officials to obtain admission for relatives to West Point and wrote in the margin: "Does that explain why the (afterwards disgraced) [William Worth] Belknap [1829–1890], Secretary of War, wouldn't give me a West Point cadetship (of the ten at large) for my nephew Sam Moffett? I never could understand it before" (quoted and explained by Philip W. Leon, *Mark Twain and West Point* [Toronto, Ontario: ECW Press, 1996], p. 24). Belknap served in President Grant's cabinet, was impeached for malfeasance in office in 1876, and resigned his position.

Catalogs: ListABP (1910), "Letters of J. R. Lowell, Norton"; *C1951*, #14a, $35, 2 vols., listed among books containing Clemens's marginal notations (purchased by Hollywood director Samuel Fuller and his wife); *Fleming 1972*, 2 vols.; Sotheby Parke Bernet, Sale number 3482 (25 February 1976), 2 vols., "with his ownership inscription dated 1909, and his . . . annotations throughout, some dated April 1909," "Property of a New York City Collector" (John F. Fleming), the catalog reproduced a facsimile of page 375 of Volume I, lot 16, sold for $6,000 (*American Book Prices Current, 1976*, p. 207); "American and English Literature from the Library of Mrs. Charles Engelhard," Christie's, 27 October 1995, the catalog reproduced page 375 of Volume I.

Provenance: Frederick Anderson, then Editor of the Mark Twain Papers in the Bancroft Library at the University of California, Berkeley, examined this volume at the New York City office of John F. Fleming in April 1972 (Anderson to James D. Hart, 17 April 1972, photocopy sent to Alan Gribben). Following the 1976 Sotheby Parke Bernet auction, Heritage Books sold the volumes to Mrs. Charles Engelhard for $9,000. Christie's auctioned them for $9,775 on 27 October 1995; Kevin Mac Donnell was the purchaser.

Location: collection of Kevin Mac Donnell, Austin, Texas.

Copy examined: Clemens's copy, in July 2004.

Lowell's *Letters* stirred Clemens deeply as he identified in various passages with a previous generation's responses to authorship, grief, depression, aging, and the past. On 12 April 1909 Clemens wrote to Frederick A. Duneka of Harper & Brothers (publishers of Lowell's *Letters*) to request a copy of page 31 in Volume II; the page contained Lowell's letter to E. L. Godkin in 1869, and Clemens desired to read from it at a political banquet for William T. Jerome (ALS in collection of R. J. Friedman, TS in MTP). On 17 April 1909, at 3 o'clock in the morning (four days before he dated his note about suicide on page 375 of Volume I), Clemens wrote to William Dean Howells: "I am reading Lowell's letters, & smoking. I woke an hour ago & am reading to keep from wasting the time." Clemens was amused to run across Lowell's reference (on page 305 of Volume I) to "young" Howells in a note written to Hawthorne in 1860. "I have just margined a note," Clemens joshed his slightly junior friend: "'*Young* friend! I like *that*! You ought to see him *now*'" (*MTHL*, p. 843). Clemens wrote these exact words in the margin of page 305 of Volume I of Lowell's *Letters*. In April 1909 Clemens recorded a criticism of Lowell's letter-writing while rereading his own letters of 1878: "If it was worth mentioning, it was worth quoting. I am reading Lowell's Letters, & in them he commits that irritating crime all the time, & the compiler of the Letters makes himself an accessory after the fact by not inserting the thing mentioned" (*MTHL*, p. 244).

Paine, *MTB* (1912), p. 1540.

——. "Longing" (poem, published in 1844).

Olivia Langdon copied this poem into her commonplace book on 19 February 1865 (DV161, MTP).

——. *My Study Windows* (essays, published in 1871).

In March 1889 Clemens noted the author and title of these miscellaneous essays (NB 28, *N&J* 3: 450), which treat Thoreau, Lincoln, Chaucer, Emerson, Carlyle, and other subjects.

——. *The Poetical Works of James Russell Lowell*. Diamond Edition. Illus. Boston: James R. Osgood & Co., 1871. 453 pp. [Edition, publisher, and pages conjectured.]

Inscription: signed "S. L. Clemens."

Catalogs: *A1911*, "12mo, cloth, Bost. 1871," quotes the signature, lot 302, sold for $5; George D. Smith, New York City, "Catalogue of Books" (1911), quotes the

signature, item #243, $10.

Clemens remembered Lowell as one of the eminent authors who declined Orion Clemens's invitation in 1853 to write something for the Hannibal *Journal* (10 September 1906 AD, *MTE*, p. 236; *AutoMT* 2: 233). On 15 November 1871 Clemens assured Olivia that he intended to annotate a copy of Lowell's writings for her enjoyment, though he regretted marking "such dainty pages" (*MTLet* 4: 491); perhaps he referred to the volume described here.

——. *Selections from the Writings of James Russell Lowell. Arranged Under the Days of the Year*. Boston: Houghton, Mifflin & Co., 1889. [109 pp.]

Source: MTLAcc, entry #2129, volume donated from Clemens's library by Clara Clemens Gabrilowitsch in 1910.

——. *The Vision of Sir Launfal*. Boston: Ticknor and Fields, 1861. 33 pp.

Source: MTLAcc, entry #2059, volume donated from Clemens's library by Clara Clemens Gabrilowitsch in 1910.

"'What is so rare as a day in June?'" Clemens quoted (from Part One, "Prelude") under the heading for 22 December 1903 in Notebook 46 (TS p. 31). "That is this day, exactly," Clemens added—a sunny, balmy respite from winter at their rented villa in Florence, Italy (Fears, *Day by Day* 3: 929).

——. *The Vision of Sir Launfal. The Cathedral. Favorite Poems*. Modern Classics Series. Illus. Boston: Houghton, Mifflin and Co., 1882. [Each of the three sections is separately paginated. The *Favorite Poems* section contains thirty-one poems, including "The Courtin.'"]

Catalog: Ball 2016 inventory, green cloth, gilt lettering, small book, fair condition.

Location: Quarry Farm library shelves, under the supervision of the Mark Twain Archive, Elmira College, Elmira, New York.

This volume was available to Clemens whenever he visited Quarry Farm in Elmira.

LOWELL, PERCIVAL (1855–1916). *Chosön, The Land of the Morning Calm: A Sketch of Korea*. Illustrated from photographs by the author. Boston: Ticknor and Co., 1886. 412 pp. [Edition conjectured; the book was reprinted in 1888.]

In March 1888 Clemens noted "The Land of the Morning Calm, Ticknor" (NB 27, *N&J* 3: 378).

LOWRIE, JOHN MARSHALL (1817–1867). *Adam and His Times*. Philadelphia: Presbyterian Board of Publication, [cop. 1861]. 291 pp.

Source: MTLAcc, entry #916, volume donated by Clemens.

In thirty-five chapters the Presbyterian minister Lowrie interprets the Biblical account of the Garden of Eden in careful detail and with many Biblical references.

LOWRY, HENRY DAWSON (1869–1906). *Make Believe*. Illustrated by Charles Robinson (1870–1937). London: John Lane, 1896. 177 pp.

Source: MTLAcc, entry #1928, volume donated from Clemens's library by Clara Clemens Gabrilowitsch in 1910.

A figure named the Visitor tells young Doris a number of whimsical stories prompted by ordinary sights and sounds. The exquisite drawings of Charles Robinson set the mood for each brief tale.

LUBBOCK, ALFRED BASIL (1876–1944). *Round the Horn Before the Mast*. Illus. New York: E. P. Dutton & Co., 1902. 375

pp. [Publisher and pages conjectured.]

Inscription: signed "S. L. Clemens, Jan., 1903."

Catalogs: *A1911*, "12mo, cloth, N.Y. 1902," quotes the signature, lot 303, sold for $3.75; George D. Smith, New York City, "Catalogue of Books" (1911), quotes the signature, item #226, $10.

LUBBOCK, (SIR) JOHN (BARON AVEBURY) (1834–1913). *Ants, Bees, and Wasps: A Record of Observations on the Habits of the Social Hymenoptera.* The International Scientific Series. Illus. New York: D. Appleton and Co., 1901. [First published in 1882.]

Inscription: signed "S. L. Clemens, 1902." 448 pp.

Marginalia: "A bee has 7,000 eyes; what it needs is 14,000," Clemens wrote in Chapter ten. There he also commented on the poor hearing ability Lubbock noted in certain bees: "But these were from the asylum," Clemens quipped.

Catalog: *A 1911*, "post 8vo, cloth, N.Y. 1901, quotes the signature and a few annotations, lot 23, sold for $8.

Clemens's admiration for this book is understandable even from Lubbock's first sentence in the Introduction, which begins: "The Anthropoid apes no doubt approach nearer to man in bodily structure than do any other animals; but when we consider the habits of Ants, their social organisation, their large communities, and elaborate habitations; their roadways, their possession of domestic animals, and even, in some cases, of slaves, it must be admitted that they have a fair claim to rank next to man in the scale of intelligence" (p. 1). The implicit anthropomorphism attracted Clemens to this book in the year of its original publication and held his interest throughout his lifetime. In the autumn of 1882 Clemens commented: "Lubbock shows that ants are warriors, statesmen, &c. which led me to think they might have religion," and he suggested how an ant-Bible might read (NB 20, *N&J* 2: 507). Clemens had the notion of quoting a "slave-making ant" in 1888 (NB 28, *N&J* 3: 398).

Between 28 and 31 March 1896, sailing aboard the *Wardha* from Calcutta to Ceylon, Mark Twain concocted in Notebook 37 a burlesque of missionaries that parodied Lubbock's method of scientific investigations. In this brief essay Twain claims that in Jeypore he painted forty-five ants different hues and loosed them among "four miniature houses of worship—a Mohammedan mosque, a Hindu temple, a Jewish synagogue & a Xn cathedral." To his professed disappointment the ants always preferred whatever type of church in which he had placed a cube of sugar; he facetiously deduces that this behavior demonstrates how the ant is "the opposite of man" in religious matters. In one canceled passage Twain wonders why Lubbock respected the ant so highly, since Lubbock's experiments seem to show that man overestimates the ant's intelligence (TS pp. 11–13). Twain's decision not to include this amusing spoof in *Following the Equator* (1897) was unfortunate, but as he wrote to Richard Watson Gilder (who wanted the essay for *Century Magazine*) on 13 January 1897, he feared that a digression on ants might unduly interrupt the travel-narrative structure of *Following the Equator*, and so he removed this passage from the manuscript (ALS in MTP).

During Twain's Indian Ocean voyage he also produced— between 11 and 23 April 1896—profuse notes that index

his thoughts while "reading Sir John Lubbock" (NB 37, TS pp. 38–44, MTP). He begins by remarking that "this is a good time to read up on scientific matters & improve the mind": the ship required twenty-eight days to make its voyage. "To-day I have been storing up knowledge from Sir John Lubbock about the ant." Twain quotes from the first and third sentences of Lubbock's Chapter 6 (*Ants*, p. 119). He is especially interested in Lubbock's findings regarding the ant's ability to recognize members of his own nest, sometimes from a population of 500,000; and he quotes an entire paragraph out of Chapter 6 (*Ants*, pp. 122–123) about an ant's capability of recognizing his friends after a separation of twenty-one months. As Twain reads of the ants' accomplishments, they begin to appear nearly human-size: "We seem to be reading about our own race—some stirring old episode of a field day in heretic time." (This comparison echoes Thoreau's memorable description of a battle of ants in *Walden* [1854], though Twain does not make that connection.) He is gratified when Lubbock concludes that ants know their brethren "just by vision alone." At one point Twain adduces various similarities between ants and men: armies, farms, governments, houses, thieves. He praises the ants' disregard for "the overestimated male."

In January 1897 Twain constructed a burlesque anatomy of the ant; though he does not mention Lubbock, his book is obviously the inspiration (NB 39, TS p. 40). Twain looked forward to meeting Lubbock in London on 5 April 1900, when he was scheduled to have breakfast at Lubbock's London address on St. James Square (NB 43, TS p. 6a). In a piece titled "The Bee" (written around 1902), Twain alluded to Lubbock as one of "the great authorities" on that insect (MS in Box 1, No. 1, MTP). Another of Twain's manuscripts from the period of 1901 and 1902, "The Secret History of Eddypus," refers to Lubbock as one of the "extraordinary men" of the nineteenth century (*FM*, p. 357).

Either Twain's notes from 1896 or a deleted portion of *Following the Equator* (1897) served as his source for the example in Part Six of *What Is Man?* (1906)—ants who rescue their comrades but reject strangers when performing life-saving measures. The Old Man cites John Lubbock's experiments and argues that the ant's abilities at memory and recognition cannot be dismissed as mere instinct (*WIM?*, pp. 196–198). On 6 July 1907 Twain breakfasted as an honored guest at the home of Sir John Lubbock (Lord Avebury) (30 August 1907, *AutoMT* 3: 121). From Lubbock's *Ants, Bees, and Wasps*, Twain may also have learned about the wasps' habit of catching live spiders to feed their young—which figures (along with the female spider's inclination to devour hapless flies or even her husband) in Chapter 13 of "The Refuge of the Derelicts," written in 1905 and 1906 (*FM*, pp. 245–248) as well as in Chapter 1 of "Little Bessie," written in 1908 or 1909 (*FM*, p. 36).

Cummings, "*WIM?*: The Scientific Sources" (1964), 113–114.

LÜBKE, WILHELM (1826–1893). *Ecclesiastical Art in Germany During the Middle Ages.* Translated by Leonard Abercromby Wheatley (1835–1895). Illus. Edinburgh: Thomas C. Jack,

1877. [Publisher conjectured.]

Catalog: *A1911*, "184 illustrations, 8vo, cloth, Edinb. 1877," a sheet of notes by Clemens laid in, lot 304, $2.25.

———. *History of Sculpture from the Earliest Ages to the Present Time*. Translated by Fanny Elizabeth Bunnett (1832–1875). Illus. 2 vols. Rebound. London: Smith, Elder and Co., 1872.

Provenance: shows the shelfmarks of the library numbering system that Clara Clemens Gabrilowitsch employed during her Detroit years. Sold at the 1951 auction in Hollywood but not listed in the sale sheet.

Catalog: "Property from the Library of Mark Twain," Butterfield & Butterfield, San Francisco, Sale 6613 (16 July 1997), lot 2712.

Location: Mark Twain House and Museum, Hartford, Connecticut.

Copy examined: presumably Olivia Clemens's copy, unmarked. Viewed in Hartford in 1997.

———. *Outlines of the History of Art*. Edited by Clarence [Chatham] Cook (1828–1900). 2 vols. Illus. New York: Dodd, Mead, and Co., 1878.

Catalog: Ball 2016 inventory, green cloth, gilt lettering, fair condition, Volume II is signed, "T. W. Crane/1878".

Location: Quarry Farm library shelves, under the supervision of the Mark Twain Archive, Elmira College, Elmira, New York.

Clemens had access to this work at Quarry Farm in Elmira.

———. *Outlines of the History of Art*. Edited by Clarence [Chatham] Cook (1828–1900). 2 vols. Illus. New York: Dodd, Mead, and Co., 1881.

Inscriptions: signed by Olivia Clemens on the half-title page of Volume I in black ink, "Olivia L. Clemens/1886." Identically signed by Olivia on the front flyleaf of Volume II in black ink: "Olivia L. Clemens/1886."

Marginalia: Volume I (571 pp.), which addresses the historical periods of Egyptian art up to the Romanesque style, is unmarked. Volume II (695 pp.), which describes art history from the medieval era to the Gothic influence to the nineteenth-century schools, is one of the few books in the family's library that Olivia annotated extensively. There are numerous penciled check marks, especially on pages 115, 204, 208, 210, 217, 224, 234, 322, 323, 324, 328, 346, 354, 362, 367, 379, and 380 (where Olivia check-marked the bottom paragraph and wrote vertically in the margin, "Look for the Tintoretto's [*sic*]/ in the Dresden Gallery"), 382, 471, 480, 496, 546, 571, 572, 579, 581, and 583. A few markings, such as the one on page 359, are by Clemens.

Location: Mark Twain Library, Redding, Connecticut. The purple oval Mark Twain Library stamps are present in both volumes.

Copies examined: Olivia Clemens's copies. Volume I has a penciled Mark Twain Library accession number "3507"; Volume II is recorded in pencil as "3508". Examined in 1970 and again in June 1982 and on 8 November 2019.

———. *Outlines of the History of Art. A New Translation from the Seventh German Edition*. Edited by Clarence [Chatham] Cook (1828–1900). Illus. 2 vols. Red three-quarter morocco boards, marbled. New York: Dodd, Mead and Co., 1886.

Provenance: displays the shelfmarks of the library numbering system employed by Clara Clemens Gabrilowitsch during her Detroit years. Sold at the 1951 auction in

Hollywood but not listed in the sale sheet.

Catalog: "Property from the Library of Mark Twain," Butterfield & Butterfield, San Francisco, Sale 6613 (16 July 1997), lot 2712.

Location: Mark Twain House and Museum, Hartford, Connecticut.

Copy examined: most likely Olivia Clemens's copy, unmarked, with some leaves uncut at the rear of Volume I. Several photographs and a clipping from the Detroit *News* are laid in the first volume. Viewed in Hartford in 1997.

LUCAS, DANIEL BEDINGER (1836–1909) and J[AMES]. FAIRFAX MCLAUGHLIN (1839–1903). *Fisher Ames-Henry Clay, Etc.* Hour Glass Series. New York: Charles L. Webster & Co., 1891. 241 pp.

Source: Clemens's firm advertised this curious volume in the *Publishers' Trade List Annual for 1893* as "historical epitomes of national interest." It contained historical sketches about Fisher Ames (1758–1808), Henry Clay (1777–1852), Daniel O'Connell, Benjamin Robbins Curtis, John Randolph of Roanoke, Thomas Jefferson's first election, and the origin of "The Star-Spangled Banner." This was Webster & Company's experimental first step toward a projected "Hour Glass Series."

LUCKIE, DAVID MITCHELL (1827–1909). *The Raid of the Russian Cruiser "Kaskowiski": An Old Story of Auckland. With an Introduction and Appendix on Colonial Defence, Etc.* Thin, red leather cover. Wellington, New Zealand: New Zealand Times Co., 1894. 39 pp.

Inscription: the title page is inscribed in red ink: "To Samuel L. Clemens—Better Known as 'Mark Twain'—/with respectful compliments/From D. M. Luckie/21.11.95."

Location: Mark Twain Library, Redding, Connecticut.

Copy examined: Clemens's copy, unmarked. Has the red ink Mark Twain Library accession number "3905" and the purple oval Library stamps. Examined in 1970 and again in June 1982 and on 8 November 2019.

The pamphlet titled *The Raid of the Russian Cruiser "Kaskowiski"* recounted an incident in 1873 when a Russian warship seized a British vessel and extorted gold from a New Zealand town. In Chapter 17 of *Following the Equator* (1897) Mark Twain would credit journalist and editor Luckie for figures concerning Australasian production and exports, though Twain mentions no book title.

LUDLOW, FITZ HUGH (1836–1870). *The Hasheesh Eater; Being Passages from the Life of a Pythagorean*. New York: Harper & Brothers, 1857. 371 pp.

Ludlow, an early chronicler of the emotional and psychedelic effects of hasheesh usage, spent a few days in Virginia City in 1863 and became a contributor to San Francisco's *Golden Era*. After Ludlow praised Mark Twain in that journal on 22 November 1863 ("He imitates nobody. He is a school by himself."), Clemens wrote to Jane Lampton Clemens from Carson City on January 1864: "If Fitzhugh Ludlow, (author of the 'Hasheesh Eater,') comes your way, treat him well. . . He published a high encomium upon Mark Twain, (the same being eminently just & truthful)" (*MTLet* 1: 268).

Donald P. Dulchinos, *Pioneer of Inner Space: The Life of Fitz Hugh Ludlow, Hasheesh Eater* (Brooklyn, New York: Autonomedia, 1998).

———. *Little Brother; and Other Genre-Pictures*. Boston: Lee and Shepard, 1867. 293 pp.

>Catalog: Ball 2016 inventory, red cloth, gilt lettering, fair condition, J. Langdon Family Library bookplate #53.

>Location: Quarry Farm library shelves, under the supervision of the Mark Twain Archive, Elmira College, Elmira, New York.

>Copy examined: an unmarked copy of Ludlow's short stories to which Clemens had access whenever he visited Elmira. Examined on 26 May 2015.

LUDLOW, JAMES MEEKER (1841–1932). *The Captain of the Janizaries, A Story of the Times of Scanderbeg and the Fall of Constantinople*. New York: Harper & Brothers, [cop. 1890]. 404 pp.

>Source: MTLAcc, entry #205, volume donated by Clemens. Ludlow's novel focuses on the siege of Constantinople in 1453 by the Albanian chieftain Scanderbeg (c. 1405–1468), educated as a Moslem, who declared himself a Christian and led Albanians against the Turks.

LUKENS, HENRY CLAY (1838–1909), pseud. "Erratic Enrique." *Jets and Flashes*. Illustrated by René Bache (1861–1933). New York: John W. Lovell Co., [1883]. 200 pp.

>Inscription: (in red ink on front free endpaper) "To Samuel L. Clemens/of Hartford, Conn.,/with the sincere esteem of/Henry Clay Lukens/Oct. 5, 1883./An humble effort, dear Mark Twain,/This volume brief,/To cheer the homes where Love doth reign/And Mirth is chief."

>Location: Mark Twain Library, Redding, Connecticut.

>Copy examined: Clemens's copy, unmarked. Has the Mark Twain Library accession number "3080" and the purple oval Library stamps. Examined in 1970 and again in June 1982 and on 8 November 2019.

Lukens was a New York City journalist whose column "Pith and Point" appeared in various newspapers. He also compiled a compressed chronological survey, "American Literary Comedians," *Harper's Monthly Magazine* 80.479 (April 1890): 783–797, that documented the achievements of over a hundred humorists and the transitory fickleness of their fame. Of all of those who started out as journalists, noted Lukens, Mark Twain was "the one man of all our newspaper harlequins whom Good Luck chose for its pampered idol" (p. 796).

LUMLEY, BENJAMIN (1812–1875). *Reminiscences of the Opera*. London: Hurst and Blackett, 1864. 448 pp.

>Clara Clemens listed the author and title of this book among undated entries in her commonplace book (Paine 150, MTP).

LUNDBERG, ELLEN EMELIE (NYLOM) (1869–1933). *Lyriska stämningar*. Stockholm: Wahlström & Widstrand, [1895]. [Edition conjectured.]

>Catalog: ListABP (1910), "Lyrieken Stamningar, Lundberg".

A volume of Swedish poetry.

LUTFULLAH (1802–1874). *Autobiography of Lutfullah, A Mohamedan Gentleman; and His Transactions with His Fellow-Creatures: Interspersed with Remarks on the Habits, Customs, and Character of the People with Whom He Had to Deal*. Ed. by Edward B[ackhouse]. Eastwick (1814–1883). Copyright Edition. Collection of British Authors Series. Leipzig: Bernhard Tauchnitz, 1857. 342 pp.

>Catalog: *C1951*, D1, $8, listed among volumes signed

by Clemens.

An autobiography dating from the era of the British occupation of India.

LUTHER, MARTIN (1483–1546).

>Mark Twain favorably mentioned "Luther's Chorale" in 1878 (NB 16, *N&J* 2: 213). In Appendix B to *A Tramp Abroad* (1880), Twain states that "Luther's wedding ring was shown me" in Heidelberg Castle. Chapter 1 of *Life on the Mississippi* observes that "when De Soto stood on the banks of the Mississippi, it was still two years before Luther's death." Twain also alludes to Luther in "English As She Is Taught" (1887). In "Which Was It?" (written 1899–1903), Twain refers to Luther as a member of "the world's master-minds" who never examined his belief in witches (*WWD?*, p. 306). Luther and Joan of Arc were "that splendid pair equipped with temperaments not made of butter, but of asbestos," Twain wrote in "The Turning-Point of My Life" (1910). See also the Catalog entry for Andrew D. White *A History of the Warfare of Science with Theology in Christendom*.

LYALL, (SIR) ALFRED COMYN (1835–1911). *Natural Religion in India. Rede Lecture Delivered in the Senate-House on June 17, 1891*. Cambridge: University Press, 1891. 64 pp.

>En route to Ceylon on 4 January 1896, Mark Twain quoted "Sir Alfred Lyall" concerning the religious divisions of Asia (NB 36, TS p. 15).

———. *Verses Written in India*. London: Kegan Paul, Trench & Co., 1889. 138 pp. [Publisher and pages conjectured.]

>Catalog: *A1911*, "16mo, cloth, gilt top, uncut, Lond. 1889," a sheet of notes by Clemens laid in, lot 305, sold for $1.

LYELL, (SIR) CHARLES (1797–1875). *Principles of Geology* (3 vols., published 1830–1833). There is evidence that the young Sam Clemens knew about Lyell's geological theories. For instance, Clemens drew pencil marks around Lyell's works in the list of "Authorities" at the front of his copy of J. L. Comstock's *Elements of Geology* (1851), which Clemens signed in 1856. Clemens remembered "Lyell's 'Geology'" as being the "whole library" of "old Davis," the mate on the Mississippi steamboat *John J. Roe* (31 August 1906 AD, MTP; *AutoMT* 2:212). Lyell, declared Mark Twain in "The Secret History of Eddypus" (written 1901–1902), was one of the "wonderful men" of the nineteenth century. "Lyell contributed Geology and spread the six days of Creation into shoreless aeons of time comparable to Herschel's limitless oceans of space" (*FM*, pp. 357, 379). Lyell visited the United States four times, but no evidence indicates that Clemens was familiar with his *A Second Visit to the United States of North America* (1849).

LYLE, EUGENE PERCY (1873–1961). *The Lone Star*. Illustrated by Philip R[ussell]. Goodwin (1882–1935). New York: Doubleday, Page & Co., 1907. 431 pp.

>Source: MTLAcc, entry #206, volume donated by Clemens. Historical fiction about Texas.

LYLY, JOHN (c. 1554–1606). *Euphues, the Anatomy of Wit* (published in 1578); *Euphues and His England* (published in 1580).

>The English playwright, courtier, and poet Lyly set a new standard for elegant prose style in the sixteenth century. The narrator of Mark Twain's *1601* (1880) overhears "fine words and dainty-wrought phrases from the ladies now, one or two of them being, in other days, pupils of that poor ass, Lille [*sic*], himself." Jonson and Shakespeare are restless at listening to these affected speeches, but they

constrain their remarks from knowledge that the Queen was "ye very flower of ye Euphuists herself" (Franklin J. Meine's edition, privately printed for the Mark Twain Society [Chicago, 1939], pp. 38–39).

LYNCH, GEORGE (1868–1928). *The War of the Civilisations, Being the Record of a "Foreign Devil's" Experiences with the Allies in China.* Illus. London: Longmans, Green, and Co., 1901. 319 pp.

Inscription: the half-title page is signed and inscribed in black ink by Clemens: "SL. Clemens/Riverdale, Nov. 1, 1901,/from George Lynch."

Marginalia: Clemens made stylistic revisions in pencil on page 19, correcting the text to read: "but it certainly would have been next to impossible to <have> construct<ed> a railway across this stretch of land so as to <have> avoid<ed> them." He made penciled markings on page 20.

Catalog: *A1911*, "8vo, cloth, Lond. 1901," quotes the signature, lot 306, sold for $4.25.

Provenance: collection of Frank C. Willson (1889–1960) in Melrose, Massachusetts. Sold by his widow Margarete to the University of Texas in 1962.

Location: Harry Ransom Center, University of Texas at Austin.

Copy examined: Clemens's copy.

In an irate letter to the editor of the New York *Tribune* published on 18 February 1901, Mark Twain quoted "the testimony of Mr. George Lynch, in this morning's Herald," regarding the aftermath of the Boxer Rebellion. "He is recently from China. . . . Mr. Lynch is a war correspondent. . . . Mr. Lynch is in town, to lecture on what he has seen" (*MTPP*, p. 165).

LYTTON, EDWARD GEORGE EARLE BULWER-LYTTON, BARON (often referred to as Edward Bulwer-Lytton) (1803–1873). *The Coming Race; or, the New Utopia.* Repr. from the English edition. New York: Francis B. Felt & Co., 1871. 209 pp.

Source: MTLAcc, entry #37, volume donated by Clemens. The narrator discovers a utopian community deep underground whose inhabitants are the beneficiaries of a mysterious energy source, Vril. Women in this society seem to be the superior gender.

———. *Eugene Aram* (historical novel, published in 1832).

"Read Eugene Aram all day—found it tedious—skipped 4 pages out of 5. Skipped the corporal *all* the time. He don't amount to anything" (Clemens to Olivia Clemens, Milford, Massachusetts, 31 October 1871, *LLMT*, p. 162; *MTLet* 4: 483). In Chapter 55 of *Roughing It* (1872) Mark Twain mentions Lytton's reputation for literary productivity. Based on an actual murder, *Eugene Aram* was one of the popular Newgate crime novels of that era.

———. *Harold, the Last of the Saxon Kings* (historical novel, published in 1848).

Catalog: *C1951*, D8, listed among volumes signed by Clemens.

———. *Kenelm Chillingly: His Adventures and Opinions. A Novel.* Harper's Library Edition. New York: Harper & Brothers, 1873. 511 pp.

Inscription: the front flyleaf is signed in pencil, "Saml. L. Clemens/Hartford, Conn."

Marginalia: considerable penciled annotations by Clemens—mainly brackets, vertical lines, and underscorings. These markings are most frequent in the first half of the

volume, but they continue at intervals as far as page 424. None of Clemens's notations indicate displeasure with either style or content. In the margin of page 140 Clemens discusses a joke from *Punch* that he also jotted down in Notebook 20 in 1882: "Advice to persons about to marry—don't." Clemens employed the half-title page as a temporary substitute for his notebooks, recording there a joke, a criticism of New York City police, an adventure undergone by one of Captain Hall's men in the Arctic (Clemens dated this item 30 April 1872), and other random entries. (Charles Francis Hall [1821–1871] was an Arctic explorer who died there.) Someone placed pencil marks in the house list of Harper & Brothers at the rear of this book beside Boswell's *Johnson* and Motley's *Dutch Republic* and *United Netherlands* (books Clemens owned and read). The verso of the rear flyleaf contains a penciled sketch of a house floorplan; it resembles the first floor of the residence that Clemens built in Hartford in 1874.

Catalog: *C1951*, #24a, $35, listed among volumes containing Clemens's notations.

Location: Mark Twain Papers, Bancroft Library, University of California at Berkeley. Purchased from Maxwell Hunley Rare Books of Beverly Hills, California.

Copy examined: Clemens's copy.

Clemens's extensive marginalia contradict Albert Bigelow Paine's assertion that "Clemens had not read Bulwer—never *could* read him at any length" (*MTB* [1912], p. 428). Lytton, for his part, admired Bret Harte and the American humorists in general, but had no taste for Mark Twain (Amy Cruse, *The Victorians and Their Reading* [Boston: Houghton Mifflin Co., 1935], pp. 257–258).

———. *The Lady of Lyons, or Love and Pride* (play, performed in 1838).

Mark Twain alludes to this popular romantic play in Chapter 12 of *The Innocents Abroad* (1869); there he says that in France he "saw the Lady of Lyons and thought little of her comeliness."

McKeithan, *TIA* (1958), pp. 54–55, 59 n.

———. *The Last Days of Pompeii* (first published in 1834).

Catalog: *C1951*, D8, listed among volumes signed by Clemens.

Chapter 31 of *The Innocents Abroad* (1869), "The Buried City of Pompeii," very likely was influenced by Lytton's celebrated work.

———. *The Last Days of Pompeii.* Boston: Little, Brown & Co., [cop. 1893]. 561 pp.

Source: MTLAcc, entry #4, volume donated by Clemens.

———. *The Last of the Barons* (published in 1843).

Catalog: *C1951*, D8, listed among volumes signed by Clemens.

———. *"My Novel," by Pisistratus Caxton; or, Varieties in English Life.* 2 vols. New York: Harper & Brothers, 1860.

Source: MTLAcc, entry #1146, volume 2 only, donated by Clemens.

———. *Richelieu; or, the Conspiracy* (play, performed in 1839).

Clemens condensed lines from this blank-verse play in a letter written from Carson City on 8 February 1862 to his mother and sister: "In the bright lexicon of youth,/ There's *no such word* as Fail" (*MTL*, p. 65). On 26 January 1885 Olivia Clemens wrote to Clemens, who was on a lecture tour: "Booth plays Richelieu this week in N. Y. I wish we were going together to hear him" (*Twainian* 39.5 [September-October 1980]: 3); she referred to Edwin Booth (1833–1893). Much later, in writing a burlesque of Edward FitzGerald's version of Omar Khayyám's *Rubáiyát* (written around 1898), Mark Twain would experiment with a bawdy pun of the Cardinal's most famous line in *Richelieu*, "The pen is mightier than the sword" (*Mark Twain's Rubáiyát*, ed. Alan Gribben and Kevin Mac Donnell [Austin, Texas: Jenkins Publishing Co., 1983], pp. 26–27).

Allison R. Ensor, "'Mightier Than the Sword': An Undetected Obscenity in the First Edition of *Tom Sawyer*," *Mark Twain Journal* 27.1 (Spring 1989): 25–26.

————. *Rienzi, the Last of the Roman Tribunes* (published in 1835).

Catalog: *C1951*, D8, listed among volumes signed by Clemens.

————, pseud. "Pisistratus Caxton." *What Will He Do with It?* New York, n.d.

Inscription: signed "Livy L. Langdon. Elmira, New York, 1866."

Catalog: *Mott 1952*, #67, $2.50.

————. *Zanoni* (published in 1842).

Zanoni can be classified as both a novel of the occult and a dark fantasy. Clara Clemens copied a quotation from *Zanoni* into her mostly undated commonplace book (Paine 150, MTP).

LYTTON, EDWARD ROBERT BULWER-LYTTON, 1st Earl (1831–1891), pseud. "Owen Meredith." *Chronicles and Characters*. 2 vols. Boston: Ticknor and Fields, 1868.

Source: MTLAcc, entries #2065 and #2066, volumes donated from Clemens's library by Clara Clemens Gabrilowitsch in 1910.

Lytton undertook an enormously ambitious project here—narrating, in verse, the deeds of powerful and talented historical figures from ancient Greece to the present day. Most of the characters are European but he includes Mohammed and Middle Eastern literature.

————. *Leila; or, the Siege of Granada*. Philadelphia: J. B. Lippincott & Co., 1872. 351 pp.

Source: MTLAcc, entry #2176, volume donated from Clemens's library by Clara Clemens Gabrilowitsch in 1910.

————. *Lucile*. Author's Edition. Boston: Ticknor and Fields, 1866. 352 pp.

Source: MTLAcc, entry #2067, volume donated from Clemens's library by Clara Clemens Gabrilowitsch in 1910.

————. *Poems of Owen Meredith*. 2 vols. Blue cloth. Boston: Ticknor and Fields, 1864.

Provenance: bookplate #87 of the "J. Langdon Family Library" on the front pastedown endpaper of Volume I.

Catalog: Ball 2016 inventory, Volume I only, blue cloth, gilt lettering and edges, from Jervis Langdon's Family Library #87.

Location: Mark Twain Archive, Elmira College, Elmira, New York. Only Volume I is present.

Copy examined: an unmarked copy of Volume I available to Clemens whenever he visited Elmira. Examined on 27 May 2015.

❙ M

MABIE, HAMILTON WRIGHT (1846–1916), ed. *Fairy Tales*

Every Child Should Know. New York: Doubleday, Page & Co., 1907. 370 pp.

Source: MTLAcc, entry #484, volume donated by Clemens.

————, ed. *Famous Stories Every Child Should Know*. New York: Doubleday, Page & Co., 1907. 300 pp.

Source: MTLAcc, entry #485, volume donated by Clemens.

————, ed. *Heroes Every Child Should Know*. New York: Doubleday, Page & Co., 1908. 332 pp.

Source: MTLAcc, entries #482–485, volumes donated by Clemens.

————, ed. *Heroines That Every Child Should Know*. New York: Doubleday, Page & Co., 1908. [281 pp.]

Source: MTLAcc, entry #483, volume donated by Clemens.

————. *Nature and Culture*. New York: Dodd, Mead & Co., 1904. 325 pp.

Clara Clemens discussed this work in her mostly undated commonplace book (Paine 150, MTP).

————. *Under the Trees and Elsewhere*. Illus. New York: Dodd, Mead and Co., 1900. 298 pp.

Inscription: the front free endpaper is inscribed by an unidentified hand in ink: "'I remember the first time I saw Rosalind I saw the light of the Arden sky in her eyes, the buoyancy of the Arden air in her step, the purity and freedom of the Arden life in her nature.' June 8th 1901".

Marginalia: vertical pencil markings on pages 2, 3, 15, 22, 23, 55, 86, 87, 202, 203. These marks are not characteristic of Clemens's mode of annotation.

Provenance: contains the bookstamps and charge slip of the Mark Twain Library, Redding, Connecticut. Has a Mark Twain Library accession number, 2899".

Location: Special Collections, Elihu Burritt Library, Central Connecticut State University, New Britain, Connecticut.

Copy examined: photocopies supplied in 1979 of the title page, marked passages, and rear endpapers of a volume belonging to someone in the Clemens household.

————. *William Shakespeare: Poet, Dramatist, and Man*. Illus. Maroon cloth. New York: Macmillan Co., 1902. 345 pp.

Inscription: Clemens inscribed the front pastedown endpaper in black ink: "<SL.> Clara Clemens/ 1902."

Provenance: Antenne-Dorrance Collection, Rice Lake, Wisconsin.

Location: Mark Twain Archive, Gannett-Tripp Learning Center, Elmira College, Elmira, New York.

Copy examined: Clara Clemens's unmarked copy. Examined on 28 May 2015.

On 29 April 1901 Clemens noted that Mabie had finished his Shakespeare book and had assumed the Trumbull lectureship at Johns Hopkins (NB 44, TS p. 9). Mabie, the longtime editor and writer for *The Outlook* and author of *Short Studies in Literature* (1891), had a place reserved for him near Clemens at the Sixty-Seventh Birthday Celebration in honor of Clemens at the Metropolitan Club in New York City on 30 November 1902. Clemens inscribed a note to "Hamilton W. Mabie, With the kindest regards of Mark Twain" as a souvenir of the occasion (*Sotheby's 2003*, #106).

[MABINOGION.] *THE BOY'S MABINOGION; BEING THE EARLIEST WELSH TALES OF KING ARTHUR IN THE FAMOUS RED BOOK OF HERGEST*. Ed., with an intro., by Sidney Lanier (1842–1881). Illustrated by Alfred Fredericks (1835–1926). New York:

Charles Scribner's Sons, 1881. 361 pp.

> **Source:** MTLAcc, entry #1868, volume donated from Clemens's library by Clara Clemens Gabrilowitsch in 1910. (See also the Catalog entry for Thomas Malory, *The Boy's King Arthur.*)

McCabe, James Dabney (1842–1883), pseud. "Edward Winslow Miller." *History of the Grange Movement; or the Farmer's War Against Monopolies, Being a Full and Authentic Account of the Struggles of the American Farmers Against the Extortions of the Railroad Companies. With a History of the Rise and Progress of the Order of Patrons of Husbandry, Its Objects, Present Condition and Prospects. To Which Is Added Sketches of the Leading Grangers.* Illus. Philadelphia: National Publishing Co., 1873. 539 pp. [Reprinted with 544 pages in 1874.]

> The "Granger" crusade pitted angry farmers against monopolistic railroads. Centered in the Midwest but erupting elsewhere, these agricultural disputes were of national interest in the late 1860s and early 1870s. The wide sales of James Dabney McCabe's subscription volume, *History of the Grange Movement*, could possibly be related to Clemens's cryptic reference in a letter in 1874: "I have left the matter of the 'Granger' book alone till Frank [Fuller] shall return. If it is a good thing it will keep" (SLC to Mary F. Fuller, Hartford, 7 April 1874; *MTLet* 6: 101).

McAdoo, William (1853–1930). *Guarding a Great City, by William McAdoo, Police Commissioner, New York City, 1904–1906.* New York: Harper & Brothers, 1906. 349 pp. [Publisher and pages conjectured.]

> **Inscription:** signed "S L Clemens 1906".
>
> **Catalog:** *A1911*, "12mo, cloth, N.Y. 1906," quotes the signature, lot 322, sold for $3.50.

———. [Another identical copy.]

> **Source:** MTLAcc, entry #1361, volume donated by Clemens.

MacAlarney, Robert Emmet (1873–1945). (Also known as Robert Emmet McAlarney.) "Tim Rafferty's Romance: A Story of Christmas among 'The Finest,'" New York *Evening Post* 102 (12 December 1903): Section 2, p. 3.

> Seeking to do a favor for a younger writer, Clemens wrote enthusiastically from Florence to Frederick A. Duneka, general manager of Harper & Brothers, on 30 December 1903: "You & the Colonel [George Harvey, president of Harper & Brothers] will naturally be on the lookout for first-class short-story talent—therefore, seek out the man that wrote the police-story (Irish & New York) in the Evening Post of Dec. 14, & secure him. If that story isn't well told, tell me so & I will take my medicine" (ALS, Special Collections, Washington University Libraries, St. Louis, Missouri). Duneka would have been disappointed if he did try to locate the recommended story in that issue of the *Evening Post*. Clemens must have meant the issue of Saturday, December 12th, which featured MacAlarney's Irish dialect tale of police, love, death, and good deeds. Its ironic style of narration and sentimental ending resembled the fables that O. Henry was beginning to publish during that same period. MacAlarney would go on to become an editor for the New York *Evening Mail* and the New York *Tribune* before becoming a college journalism professor.

McAllister, [Samuel] Ward (1827–1895). *Society As I Have Found It.* New York: Cassell Publishing Co., [cop. 1890]. 469 pp.

> **Marginalia:** Clemens wrote in pencil on the front flyleaf: "There is here nothing but the vulgarity of good society—just that and not another specialty. Unchastity, the bar sinister, greed, swinishness, insolence, arrogance, and many other absolute essentials of a real Aristocracy are wanting" (quoted in *Zeitlin 1951*).
>
> **Catalogs:** ListABP (1910), "Society as I have found it" (note by S. L. C.), McAllister; *C1951*, #19a, $75, listed among books containing Clemens's marginal notes; *Zeitlin 1951*, item #32, $115.

> In an 1895 interview Mark Twain somewhat deferentially alluded to Ward McAllister's societal influence ("Mark Twain on Prohibition," *Licensing Guardian*, New South Wales, 1895; Scharnhorst, *Complete Interviews*, p. 221). "The 400. Ward McAlister" [*sic*] Twain wrote in a notebook entry on 12 April 1900 (NB 43, TS p. 7). (McAllister had coined the phrase "the Four Hundred" to designate the members of New York City's most influential elite.) In an undated manuscript, "The Curse of McAllister . . . A Defence" (DV313, MTP), Twain sought to prove that McAllister "doesn't know what an Aristocracy is." The American "aristocracy," lacking a monarchy, long descent, and hereditary title and privilege, cannot truly qualify for the term. Twain quotes from pages 212–213 and 229–231 of McAllister's *Society As I Have Found It.* He intended to disprove McAllister's methods of analysis, but Twain's enthusiasm flagged and he ended the unfinished piece on the first manuscript page of Chapter 3. Dan Beard reported that Twain told him: "I spent three months writing a satire on that book of Ward McAllister's, and when I got through, I again read McAllister's book, and then my satire, and then tore the blamed thing up. Some things are complete in themselves and cannot be improved upon, and I take off my hat to Mr. McAllister" (quoted by Merle Johnson, comp., *A Bibliography of the Works of Mark Twain* [New York: Harper & Brothers, 1910], p. 159).

"Macallum" (unidentified author).

> In "To the Person Sitting in Darkness" (1901) Mark Twain attributes to Macallum's *History* a description of the Pawnee Indians' sense of justice: retribution was meted out on any whites for damages inflicted by a single white person. Twain's "To My Missionary Critics" (1901) refers to his previous quotation "from Macallum's (imaginary) 'History.'" Almost certainly Twain was thinking of Chapter 15 in Charles A. Murray's *Travels in North America During the Years 1834, 1835, & 1836, Including a Summer Residence with the Pawnee Tribe of Indians, in the Remote Prairies of the Missouri*, where Murray quipped that "the Indian notions of reprisals are very cosmopolitan." If horses were stolen from them, they would retaliate similarly against "the first party or tribe" they thereafter encountered (p. 302).

McCarthy, Justin (1830–1912). *A History of Our Own Times, from the Accession of Queen Victoria to the General Election of 1880.* 2 vols. New York: Harper & Brothers, 1880. [Publisher conjectured.]

> **Inscription:** the front flyleaf is signed "S. L. Clemens, Hartford, 1880."
>
> **Catalog:** *A1911*, "Vol. I, 12mo, cloth, N.Y. 1880," quotes the signature, lot 323, sold for $1.

———. *A History of Our Own Times, from the Diamond Jubilee, 1897 to the Accession of King Edward VII.* 5 vols. Illus. New York: Harper & Brothers, 1901–1905.

Source: MTLAcc, entries #1731 and #1732, volumes 2 (n.d.) and 5 (1905), donated by Clemens.

———. *A History of the Four Georges.* 4 vols. [Edition unidentified; possibly: New York: Harper & Brothers, 1893. Reprinted in 1901.]

Catalog: *C1951*, O22, "The Four Georges, Vol. I & II; and the Four Georges and William IV, Vol. III & IV," listed among volumes signed by Olivia Clemens.

"Human Glory. Laugh at it," wrote Clemens in his notebook for 1901. "Quote the death-beds of the renowned. See George I, Prince Charlie, Robert Walpole, Swift, &c in McCarthy" (NB 44, TS p. 12, entry made under the heading of 10 June 1901). McCarthy was unsparing in his description of Jonathan Swift's death, to pick one example of those Clemens listed. On 19 October 1845 "the greatest mind of the age went grimly out in Ireland. . . . For years he had been but in a living death. Racked with pain, almost wholly bereft of reason, sometimes raging in fits of madness, he wsa a fearful sight to those who watched over him. When the end came it came quietly" (Volume II, page 236).

———. *Portraits of the Sixties.* Illus. New York: Harper & Brothers, 1903. 340 pp.

Source: MTLAcc, entry #1770, volume donated by Clemens.

McCarthy's biographical and historical sketches accompany photographs of British luminaries prominent in the 1860s, including Dickens, Thackeray, Carlyle, Tennyson, political figures in Parliament, music and stage celebrities, and "queens of society." McCarthy concludes that the sixties "may claim to be ranked as a distinctive epoch" (p. 339).

———. *The Reign of Queen Anne.* 2 vols. Original green cloth. New York: Harper & Brothers, 1902.

Inscriptions: the front pastedown endpapers of both volumes are signed in black ink, "S. L. Clemens/1902".

Catalogs: *A1911*, "2 vols., 8vo, cloth, N.Y. 1902," quotes the signatures, lot 324, sold for $4.25; *Hunley 1958*, item #132, $7.50.

Location: Albert and Shirley Small Special Collections Library, University of Virginia, Charlottesville, Virginia. Gift of Clifton Waller Barrett.

Copies examined: Clemens's copies, in 1970.

Queen Anne lived from 1665 until 1714; her reign began in 1702.

———. *Reminiscences.* New York: Harper & Brothers, 1899. 424 pp.

Source: MTLAcc, entry #1362, volume donated by Clemens.

McCarthy delivers vivid impressions of prominent men and women he met throughout his life in both England and the United States (he even had a long conversation with Walt Whitman!).

McCARTHY, JUSTIN HUNTLY (1860–1936). *The Dryad; A Novel.* New York: Harper & Brothers, 1905. 314 pp.

Source: MTLAcc, entry #1622, volume donated by Clemens.

———. *The Duke's Motto; A Melodrama.* New York: Harper & Brothers, 1908. 303 pp.

Source: MTLAcc, entry #209, volume donated by Clemens (erroneously listed as donated by Mrs. Julian Hawthorne, but then corrected in the accession record). See also the Catalog entry for Auguste Anicet-Bourgeois.

———. *Marjorie.* Illus. New York: R. H. Russell, 1903. 292 pp.

Source: MTLAcc, entry #1425, volume donated by Clemens.

———. *Needles and Pins; A Novel.* New York: Harper & Brothers, 1907. 371 pp.

Source: MTLAcc, entry #208, volume donated by Clemens. Fiction about François Villon (1431–1463), the French lyrical poet. (It was Villon who penned the famous query, "Where are the snows of yesteryear?")

———. [Another identical copy.]

Source: MTLAcc, entry #1450, volume donated by Clemens.

———. *The Proud Prince.* Illus. New York: R. H. Russell, 1903. 276 pp.

Source: MTLAcc, entry #211, volume donated by Clemens.

———. *Seraphica; A Romance.* New York: Harper & Brothers, 1908. 304 pp.

Source: MTLAcc, entry #210, volume donated by Clemens.

———. [Another identical copy.]

Source: MTLAcc, entry #1623, volume donated by Clemens.

———. *The Wife of Socrates* (play). Adapted from the French of Théodore de Banville (1823–1891).

Apparently Clemens was alluding to this one-act play when he assured Augustin Daly in the autumn of 1888: "I'll take them [the Clemens family] to The Wife, tonight" (ALS in Houghton Library, Harvard). Daly's theater used *The Wife of Socrates* as a curtain-raiser to precede Daly's *The Lottery of Love* (Joseph Francis Daly, *The Life of Augustin Daly* [New York: Macmillan, 1917], p. 482).

McCASKEY, JOHN PIERSOL (1837–1934), comp. *Franklin Square Song Collection: Two Hundred Favorite Songs and Hymns for Schools and Homes, Nursery and Fireside.* No. 1. New York: Harper & Brothers, 1881. 160 pp.

Clemens noted "Franklin Square Song Collection" in 1883 (NB 22, *N&J* 3: 26). This first volume in the series (which would eventually conclude with No. 8 in 1892) contained some of Clemens's favorite songs and hymns, including the hymn "Even Me" (p. 14). Incidentally, McCaskey seems to be alone in ascribing that hymn to Eliphalet Oram Lyte (1842–1913); most sources give the credit to Elizabeth Codner (see her Catalog entry). Numerous other songs and hymns in the collection would also have enticed Clemens: "Comin' thro' the rye," "Home, sweet home," "I would not live alway," "Jolly old Saint Nicholas," "Long, long ago," "The Old oaken bucket," "Row, row your boat," "Auld lang syne," "Those evening bells," "Bonnie Doon," and dozens more.

MACAULAY, THOMAS BABINGTON, FIRST BARON MACAULAY (1800–1859). *Critical and Miscellaneous Essays.* 7 vols. Original green cloth, stamped, spine ends rubbed with loss, cloth split at joints on a few volumes. New York: D. Appleton and Co., 1869.

Inscriptions: the front flyleaves of all volumes except Volume II are signed in pencil: "Livy L. Langdon/Elmira/1869." Volume II is signed "S L Clemens." in black ink on the front pastedown endpaper.

Marginalia: Clemens made mainly penciled notes and markings (with a few later ones in black ink) in various volumes on a total of approximately sixty pages. His annotations amounted to approximately 175 words. At the bottom of page 22 in Volume I Clemens wrote: "See new edition of New Testament about the woman anointing the Savior's feet." At the top of page 13 in Volume II, regarding the reprinting of Macaulay's review of Boswell's *Life of Johnson*, Clemens objected in pencil: "Macaulay should never have published this in book form, without appending a humble note confessing that nine-tenths of his charges against Croker [John Wilson Croker (1780–1857), a British politician, essayist, and editor] were refuted & blown to the winds in an article in 'Blackwood' before they were six weeks old." Clemens made extensive notes, markings, and page-foldings in Macaulay's essay on Lord Bacon (Volume II, pages 295–414). Some of his marginalia consisted of ammunition for his argument that Shakespeare could not have written the works attributed to him. On page 367 of Volume II Clemens noted that there is no indication that Shakespeare possessed a sense of humor, on page 368 he commented (vertically, in pencil) that Shakespeare never mentioned his contemporary fame, and other notes pertain to similar disqualifications of Shakespeare. Volume III was heavily annotated by Clemens. On the front flyleaf of Volume III, below Olivia Clemens's 1869 signature, Clemens wrote: "'Coward.' Every fool applies that name to suicides. Suicides may sometimes lack moral, but *never* physical courage. [Robert] Clive tried to commit suicide twice. Wallenstein once. See p. 86. [On page 86 Macaulay related how Clive's pistol twice misfired when he tried to take his life. Macaulay also referred there to a suicide attempt by the Bohemian-born Austrian general Albrecht von Wallenstein (1583–1634).] Clive *did* commit it at last, but was of unsound mind at the time—p. 156." On the front flyleaf of Volume VI Clemens commented in black ink on Olivia Clemens's 1869 inscription: "(The year we were engaged.)/S L C, 1907."

Catalogs: *C1951*, #60a, "Macaulay's Miscellaneous Essays [*sic*], Vol. I. through Vol. VII, incl.," listed among books containing Clemens's annotations, $160; "Property from the Library of Mark Twain," Butterfield & Butterfield, San Francisco, Sale 6613 (16 July 1997), lot 2682.

Location: Mark Twain House and Museum, Hartford, Connecticut.

Copies examined: Clemens's and Olivia Langdon Clemens's copies. Viewed in Hartford in 1997.

The stature of the English statesman, orator, and essayist Macaulay was at its height in the latter part of the nineteenth century. In Mark Twain's undated and unpublished essay, "The Walt Whitman Controversy," possibly written in 1882, Twain remarks that Boccaccio "is praised by Macaulay" (DV36, MTP).

———. "Essay on Bacon."

In Part 9 of *Is Shakespeare Dead?* (1909) Mark Twain cites Macaulay's essay for the light it throws on Bacon's "horizonless magnitude" of talent. In Part 10 Twain quotes at length several passages from "Essay on Bacon" to show that Bacon "was competent to write the Plays and Poems." Baetzhold, *MT&JB* (1970), pp. 186, 262.

———. "Essay on Lord Clive."

The names of Clive and Macaulay were intertwined for Clemens. He mentioned Robert Clive (1725–1774) in 1892 as a historical personage (NB 32, TS p. 40). "The famine in India in 1770. See Macaulay's Lord Clive," Clemens wrote in Notebook 34 (TS p. 44) on 30 November 1895. Farther on in the same notebook he added another comment about the natives of India and reminded himself to "see close of Clive." Clemens was surprised to discover that Calcutta had no statues or monuments to Clive or Warren Hastings, though "there's a street or two named for Clive" (NB 36, 13 February 1896, TS p. 43). At sea in April 1896, Clemens alluded to Robert Browning's poem titled "Clive" and then launched into an idealizing essay about the "romance" lived by "the great Clive," who governed Bengal (NB 37, TS 37–38). Mark Twain said that Clive was "a sufficiently crooked person sometimes, but straight as a yardstick when compared with . . . Warren Hastings" ("Edmund Burke on Croker and Tammany," speech at the Waldorf-Astoria in New York City, 17 October 1901; *MTSpk*, p. 404). Clemens told Albert Bigelow Paine that he wrote a poem called "The Derelict" after reading about Lord Clive and Hastings in Macaulay's writings—"how great they were and how far they fell"; Clemens guessed that this was "in '93, I think" (*MTB*, p. 1499).

Scott, *OPMT* (1966), pp. 105–107; Baetzhold, *MT&JB* (1970), p. 186.

———. "Essay on Warren Hastings."

Clemens alluded to this essay in Notebook 34 ("See the horrors of the Robilla War") (TS p. 44, MTP). "Macaulay has a light-throwing passage upon this matter [criminal behavior by Thuggee Indian natives] in his great historical sketch of Warren Hastings," writes Mark Twain in Chapter 43 of *Following the Equator* (1897), and he quotes from Macaulay's essay. "Wherever that extraordinary man [Hastings] set his foot, he left his mark," Twain declares in Chapter 52 of the same work. "Some of his acts have left stains upon his name which can never be washed away, but he saved to England the Indian Empire." In a speech delivered to the Order of the Acorns in New York City on 17 October 1901 ("Edmund Burke on Croker and Tammany"), Twain called Hastings a "fiendish" usurper who governed worse than the New York City politician Richard Croker. "The most of us know no Hastings but Macaulay's," said Twain, "and there is good reason for that: when we try to read the impeachment-charges—merely those—against him we find we cannot endure the pain of the details" (MS in Box 3, No. 1, MTP; *MTSpk*, p. 405).

Krause, *MTC* (1967), p. 237; Baetzhold, *MT&JB* (1970), p. 357 n. 16; Madigan, "MT's Passage to India" (1974), p. 361.

———. *The History of England from the Accession of James II.* 4 vols. Illus. Boston: Phillips, Sampson & Co., 1856.

Source: MTLAcc, entries #605–608, volumes donated by Clemens.

———. *The History of England from the Accession of James II.* 5 vols. Volume V edited by Hannah More (Macaulay) Trevelyan (1810–1873). Philadelphia: J. B. Lippincott & Co., 1869. [A sketch of Macaulay's life and writings in Volume V was written by Samuel Austin Allibone (1816–1889) and a memoir of Macaulay in Volume V was supplied by Henry Hart Milman (1791–1868).]

Inscription: the front flyleaf of Volume V is inscribed with ornate printed letters: "Livy L. Langdon/Elmira 1869."

Catalogs: ListABP (1910), "Hist. of England, Macaulay"; *C1951*, O21, 2 vols. only, listed among books containing Olivia Clemens's signature.

Location: Volume V only is in the Mark Twain Papers, Bancroft Library, University of California at Berkeley.

Copy examined: Olivia Clemens's copy of Volume V only, unmarked.

————. *The History of England from the Accession of James II.* 5 vols. Volume V edited by Hannah More (Macaulay) Trevelyan (1810–1873). Philadelphia: J. B. Lippincott & Co., l869. [A sketch of Macaulay's life and writings in Volume V was written by Samuel Austin Allibone (1816–1889) and a memoir of Macaulay in Volume V was supplied by Henry Hart Milman (1791–1868).]

Inscriptions: the front free flyleaf of Volume III is signed in pencil "T. W. Crane/1870." Volume IV is signed in pencil "Susan L. Crane."

Marginalia: Clemens's annotations alternate between purple and black pencil. Two black pencil marks can be seen on page 4 of Volume I. On page 7 Clemens altered Macaulay's word "entombed" to read "engulfed". Clemens underlined a phrase on page 19 of that volume. On page 37 he drew a marginal line where Macaulay charges the Catholic church with three centuries of having the object "to stunt the growth of the human mind." Joe B. Fulton's book records other marginalia (see the Fulton citation below).

Marginalia: Clemens used both black and purple pencils to mark or underline passages in Volume I, and made black pencil markings and underlinings in Volumes II, III, and IV, which also have pages turned down. Volume II has one note on page 374: "25 miles apart." No marginalia appear in Volume V. Joe B. Fulton meticulously records Clemens's reactions in *Mark Twain in the Margins: The Quarry Farm Marginalia and* A Connecticut Yankee in King Arthur's Court (2000).

Provenance: discovered by Dr. Herbert A. Wisbey, Jr. and Gretchen Sharlow on 14 March 1985 on the shelves in the Quarry Farm library room after the property was donated to Elmira College. Listed among the books that Mark Woodhouse transferred from Quarry Farm to the Mark Twain Archive on 9 July 1987.

Catalog: Ball 2016 inventory, 5 volumes, fair condition, Volume III signed "T. W. Crane/1870," Volume IV signed "Susan L. Crane."

Location: Mark Twain Archive, Gannett-Tripp Learning Center, Elmira College, Elmira, New York.

Copy examined: Susan and Theodore Crane's five-volume set, read and annotated by Clemens during his visits to Quarry Farm in Elmira, New York. Examined on 17 May 2002. I also relied on Joe B. Fulton's 1997 typescript report on the volumes (TS in MTP), and Nathaniel Ball, former Archivist of the Mark Twain Archive at Elmira College, added to this information (Ball to Alan Gribben, email, 8 June 2018).

"Macaulay is present when we follow the march of his stately sentences," Mark Twain observed in Chapter 47 of *The Innocents Abroad* (1869), whereas "the Old Testament writers are hidden from view." In 1870 he began a hoax "review" of *Innocents Abroad* with a tribute to Lord Macaulay (*MTB*, p. 428). "Macaulay lies here" in the Poets' Corner of Westminster Abbey, Twain noted in "A Memorable Midnight Experience" (1874). The character called "Harris" in *A Tramp Abroad* (1880) criticizes Macaulay for sometimes using "doubled-up have's" (Chapter 23). In May 1885, when Clemens wished to compare the sale of Grant's *Memoirs* with other publishing successes, he wondered whether "Macaulay's great Check was for £20,000. . . . Was it for the whole 5 vols?" (NB 24, *N&J* 3: 143).

Clemens wrote to Hartford booksellers Brown & Gross in Hartford on 15 January 1887, requesting Macaulay's *History of England* (ALS sold by Alta California Bookstore, April 1976; purchased by C. A. Valverde, Wahrenbrock's Book House, San Diego, California). On 20 January 1887 Clemens instructed "friend Gross" (of Brown & Gross booksellers): "As I understand it, you already have [John R.] Green in ½ calf, & can get a ½ calf Macaulay from Estes [& Lauriat of Boston] at $11.50. That'll do—send 'em along" (ASSSCL). On that same day, 20 January 1887, Clemens recommended Macaulay's histories and essays as among the best reading for young people in a letter to the Reverend Charles D. Crane (ALS, Shapell Manuscript Library, Beverly Hills, California).

On 16 July 1889 Clemens wrote to Susy Clemens: "For forty years Macaulay's England has been a fascination of mine, from the stately opening sentence to the massacre at Glencoe. I am glad you are reading it. And I hope it is aloud, to Mamma" (quoted in Christie's, New York City, 11 May 1987, item #18; TS in MTP). When a fortunate person dined with Macaulay, Clemens speculated on 10 May 1892, "Macaulay would give you the spectacle of a Vesuvius in eruption, & you would be glad to listen to the explosions & look at the fire-spouts" (NB 32, TS p. 9).

Mark Twain was reading Macaulay's *History of England from the Accession of James II* during an Indian Ocean voyage on 8 and 9 April 1896, for he made notes about the English conspiracy figure Titus Oates (1649–1705), executions, and the Tower of London—details based on incidents described in Chapters 4 and 5 of Volume I (NB 37, TS pp. 32–33). Twain's most extensive comments about Macaulay's *History* appear in a portion of manuscript deleted from the final version of *Following the Equator* (1897): "A library can not justly be called dull which has that in it. In our day people say its style is too studied, too precise, too trim, ornate, dress-paradish; but how do they find that out? For the moment one opens any volume of the five, at any place in the volume, he sinks into a profound unconsciousness of everything this worldly— flights of time, & waiting duties, the pains of disease, of hunger, burdens of life, the encroachments, the insults of age,—everything vanishes out of his consciousness except the sense of being pervasively content, satisfied, happy. I have read that History a number of times, & I believe <it has no dull places in it.>" (MS in Henry W. and Albert A. Berg Collection, New York Public Library; quoted in *MTC* [1967], p. 235). Clemens listed Macaulay's *History* under the heading of "*For Cheap Books*" in July 1899 (NB 40, TS p. 58). Earlier, Clemens had admitted that one good argument for loopholes in the copyright legislation was that "I can buy Macaulay's *History*, 3 vols., bound, for $1.25." If Americans were to read such easily available works, he reasoned, "a generation of this sort of thing ought to make this the most intelligent & the best-read nation in the world" (SLC to WDH, 30 October 1880, *MTHL*, p. 334). But in a much later interview, "Mark Twain on the Law of Copyright," *Sketch* (London), 30 (March 1904): 376, Clemens lamented that Macaulay had been willing to settle for "forty-two rather than the sixty years' limit in copyright" (*Complete Interviews*, p. 494). See also the Catalog entry for George Otto Trevelyan's *The Life and Letters of Lord Macaulay*.

Sydney J. Krause, *MTC* (1967), pp. 7, 229, 235; Howard G. Baetzhold, *MT&JB* (1970), p. 186; Baetzhold, "'Well, My Book Is Written'" (1996), pp. 41–77; Joe B. Fulton, *Mark Twain in the Margins: The Quarry Farm Marginalia and* A Connecticut Yankee in King Arthur's Court (Tuscaloosa: University of Alabama Press, 2000), pp. 21, 47–62, 69.

———. *The History of England from the Accession of James the Second*. 5 vols. New York: Harper & Brothers, 1898–1899.

Source: MTLAcc, entries #1726–1728, Volumes I (1898), II (1898), and V (n.d.) only, donated by Clemens.

———. "Horatius" (poem, published in 1842).

The poem titled "Horatius," which Macaulay included in *Lays of Ancient Rome* (see the Catalog entry below), figures in Chapter 26 of *The Innocents Abroad* ("the bridge which Horatius kept 'in the brave days of old'") and in Chapter 34 of *A Connecticut Yankee in King Arthur's Court* ("the king ordered me to play Horatius and keep the bridge"). In an undated sheet of notes later laid in an unrelated volume, Clemens wrote, "*Horatius*—McCaulay [*sic*]/ Selections of admirable poetry & prose" (see the Catalog entry for Dina M. Mulock Craik's *Songs of Our Youth*, in which Albert Bigelow Paine affixed the manuscript scrap to enhance the value of that volume for the *A1911* auction).

One passage in the stirring poem illustrates its theme of heroic self-sacrifice: "Then out spake brave Horatius,/The Captain of the gate:/'To every man upon this earth/Death cometh soon or late./And how can man die better/Than facing fearful odds,/For the ashes of his fathers,/And the temples of his Gods,/. . . ?/In yon strait path a thousand/ May well be stopped by three./Now who will stand on either hand,/And keep the bridge with me?'"

———. *Lays of Ancient Rome* (collection of poems, published in 1842).

Mark Twain quotes from the poem titled "Ivry: A Song of the Huguenots" in describing the "glimpses of Paradise" he saw in France (*IA* [1869], Ch. 12): "We knew, then, what the poet meant, when he sang of—'thy corn-fields green, and sunny vines,/O pleasant land of France!'" Twain included Macaulay's *Lays of Ancient Rome* among a list Twain planned "*For Cheap Books*" in Notebook 40 (July 1899), TS p. 58. See the Catalog entry above for "Horatius."

Baetzhold, *MT&JB* (1970), p. 186.

———. *Miscellaneous Works of Lord Macaulay*. Ed. by Hannah More (Macaulay) Trevelyan (1810–1873). 5 vols. New York: Harper & Brothers, 1880.

Catalog: Ball 2016 inventory, fair condition, Volumes I and and II have broken covers, brown leather spine, marble covers, gilt lettering.

Location: Quarry Farm library shelves, under the supervision of the Mark Twain Archive, Elmira College, Elmira, New York.

Clemens had access to this set at Quarry Farm in Elmira.

———. *Selections from the Writings of Lord Macaulay*. Ed. George Otto Trevelyan (1838–1928). New York: Harper & Brothers, 1877.

Marginalia: on page 162 Clemens struck out the word "have" in the phrase "could have" in pencil in a historical description of Charles II.

Provenance: discovered on the shelves of the library at Quarry Farm by Joe B. Fulton in April 1995.

Catalog: Ball 2016 inventory, black cloth, gilt lettering, J. Langdon Family Library bookplate No. 420.

Location: Mark Twain Archive, Gannett-Tripp Learning Center, Elmira College, Elmira, New York.

Copy examined: a book accessible to (and marked by) Clemens at the Langdons' home in Elmira. Examined on 17 May 2002. I also relied on Joe B. Fulton's 1997 typescript report about the volume (TS in MTP).

Howard G. Baetzhold, "'Well, My Book Is Written'" (1996), pp. 41–77; Joe B. Fulton, *Mark Twain in the Margins* (2000), pp. 60–61, 132.

———. *Speeches and Poems, with the Report and Notes on the Indian Penal Code*. 2 vols. New York: Hurd and Houghton, 1877.

Inscriptions: both volumes contain a library label on the front pastedown endpaper: "J. LANGDON'S/FAM-ILY/LIBRARY./No. 481"in Volume I and "No. 482" in Volume II.

Marginalia: Volume I contains twenty-four of Macaulay's speeches, and Clemens made no annotations in them. By contrast, the poems in Volume II received much attention from him. The corner of page 163 is folded down and there are light pencil markings in the poem that begins there, "Horatius" from *Lays of Ancient Rome*. Stanza XLII is marked "1"; Stanza XLIV is marked "2"; Stanza XLV is marked "3"; and Stanza XLVI (on page 164) is marked "4." At the end of that latter stanza appears a penciled diagonal mark to indicate an end to that section of Clemens's reading (evidently for an oral performance). Clemens's selection of passages includes "Alone stood brave Horatius,/But constant still in mind;/ Thrice thirty thousand foes before,/And the broad flood behind" (Stanza LVIII, page 164). The markings resume on page 166, still in "Horatius," with double diagonal marks to indicate a resumption and these light, wavy vertical pencil marks proceed from LIII (page 166) through LX (pages 167–168). The corner of page 168 is folded down. Thus, the reading begins, "But hark! The cry is Astur," interrupts at "Gaze on the blasted head," resumes at "But meanwhile axe and lever," and halts at "Could scarce forbear to cheer." All of these markings are definitely Clemens's. See also the Catalog entry above for the poem "Horatius."

Page 243 is folded down in Volume II, where the poem "Ivry. (1824)/A Song of the Huguenots" begins. Likewise folded down is page 249, where "The Battle of Naseby" opens a section titled "Songs of the Civil War." (This poem describes the power of Oliver Cromwell to rally his sagging troops and overcome an anticipated defeat.) Clemens often folded the top corners of pages of books when he wanted to find his place repeatedly, especially for his oral poetry readings. Clemens's nephew Jervis Langdon (1875–1952) remembered that when Clemens conducted fireside poetry readings, his family and friends "invariably demanded," as the climax, "'The Battle of Naseby,' which he delivered with supreme eloquence and emotion" ("Some Reminiscences," collected in *Mark Twain in Elmira*, ed. Robert D. Jerome, Herbert A. Wisbey, Jr., and Barbara Snedecor. Second ed. [Elmira, New York: Elmira College Center for Mark Twain Studies, 2013], p. 208). Clemens also quoted from two of these poems in print (see the Catalog entry for *Lays of Ancient Rome* above). All of Clemens's markings occur in the poems in Volume II; he did not annotate the six speeches by Macaulay's also included in that volume.

Provenance: Alan Gribben found this two-volume book on the shelves of the Langdon family library at Quarry Farm on 16 May 2002.

Catalog: Ball 2016 inventory, 2 vols., green cloth with gilt lettering, good condition, J. Langdon Family Library #481 and #482.

Location: Mark Twain Archive, Gannett-Tripp Learning Center, Elmira College, Elmira, New York.

Copy examined: copy belonging to the Langdon family that Clemens annotated. Examined on 16 May 2002.

Obviously the Langdons allowed Clemens free use of these volumes.

MACBEAN, LACHLAN (1853–1931) and **JOHN BROWN** (1810–1882). *Marjorie Fleming: The Story of Pet Marjorie, Together with Her Journals and Her Letters, by L. Macbean. To Which is Added Marjorie Fleming; A Story of Child-Life Fifty Years Ago, by John Brown, M.D.* Illus. First American edition. 8vo, original blue cloth, extremities a little rubbed, inner hinges cracked. New York: G. P. Putnam's Sons, 1904. 203 pp.

Inscription: the front pastedown endpaper is inscribed in black ink: "To Clara/1904./This enlargement will properly go with the first 'Marjorie Fleming' which Dr. John Brown gave to your mother in Edinburg [*sic*] in 1873./S.L.C."

Marginalia: heavily marked and annotated on seventy pages in both pencil and black ink. Clemens's notes total approximately 125 words, plus numbers. His notes cover the front free endpaper, extend to the rear endpapers, and also occur on eighteen pages of the text. He also folded down the corners of many pages. On the front free endpaper Clemens noted in pencil: "travels/ 8—sea/ 3—land/No journal after 6½? lost?" Pages 8, 10, 12, and 16 are folded down and marked in both pen and pencil. Pages 22–24 contain numerous marks for extracts. Pages 26–29 are marked for sequential renumbering of paragraphs. On page 36 Clemens wrote in black ink in the margin: "Just passed 6 yr." Clemens marveled that she "wrote first letter before 6". Beside Macbean's observation on page 72 that in Marjorie's second journal "the landscape is ashen grey," Clemens added: "in her Presbyterian heaven". Clemens also made other notes on pages 85, 90, 119, 129, and 148, and he bent down the corners of pages 90 and 99. There are many markings throughout the text of Dr. Brown's sketch as well. Clemens made numerous notations on the rear endpapers of the volume; these mainly

concern Marjorie's journals and their correspondences to her age. On the rear pastedown endpaper Clemens listed a column of page numbers from both men's sketches, one labeled "MacB." and the other headed "Dr. B." Clemens also experimented there with variant spellings of the girl's name: "Madgie/jory/jorie".

Provenance: Carrie Estelle Doheny Collection, St. John's Seminary, Camarillo, California. Donated by Mrs. Doheny in 1940 after she purchased the volume from Maxwell Hunley Rare Books of Beverly Hills for $12.20. Auctioned by Christie's in 1988 at the behest of St. John's Seminary and the Archdiocese of Los Angeles.

Catalog: Christie's, New York City, 1–2 February 1988 auction, lot 455, sold for $1,100 to the Heritage Book Shop, Los Angeles.

Location: currently unknown.

Copy examined: Clemens's copy. Viewed at St. John's Seminary in 1970.

The Scottish poet and diarist Marjorie Fleming (1803–1811), who succumbed to illness when she was only eight, was one of the child figures Clemens came to admire greatly. In an undated note that Clemens sent to his wife's sickroom around 1904, he quotes a poem and a diary passage written by "that quaint darling, Marjorie Fleming" (ASSSCL). Because Mark Twain's "Marjorie Fleming, the Wonder Child" (*Harper's Bazaar*, December 1909) employed quotations from her journals that appeared in Macbean's book, Twain asked his publisher (Harper & Brothers) to seek permission from Putnam's to quote these passages (SLC to Miss Jordan, undated ALS, NYPL). A footnote in Twain's published essay credited "Mr. L. Macbean's new and enlarged and charming biography . . . published five years ago" as the source of extracts from Marjorie Fleming's journals. He unquestionably gained factual information from Macbean's book as well (TS in MTP, Box 27, No. 17b).

———. *The Story of Pet Marjorie (Marjory Fleming).* Illustrated with plates, maps, facsimiles. First edition. Original red cloth, gilt. London: Simpkin, Marshall, Hamilton, Kent & Co., 1904. 119 pp.

Inscription: the front pastedown endpaper is signed in brown ink: "S L. Clemens/ 1909."

Marginalia: a pencil underlining in the Table of Illustrations.

Provenance: shows the shelfmark of Clara Clemens Gabrilowitsch's private library in Detroit. Donated to the Carrie Estelle Doheny Collection, St. John's Seminary, Camarillo, California in 1940 after Mrs. Doheny purchased the volume from Maxwell Hunley Rare Books of Beverly Hills for $12.20. Auctioned by Christie's for $1,210 on 21 February 1989 (lot 1765) on behalf of St. John's Seminary. Subsequently in the collection of Nick Karanovich.

Catalog: *Sotheby's 2003*, #221, $9,500 (sold with four other literature titles).

Location: collection of Kevin Mac Donnell, Austin, Texas.

Copy examined: Clemens's copy, in July 2004. Has the bookplate of "Estelle Doheny."

MCCLELLAN, GEORGE BRINTON (1826–1885). *McClellan's Own Story: The War for the Union, the Soldiers Who Fought It, the Civilians Who Directed It, and His Relations to It and to Them.* Ed. by W[illiam]. C[owper]. Prime (1825–1905). New

York: Charles L. Webster & Co., 1887. 678 pp.

> **Catalog:** *A1911*, "thick 8vo, full Russia, gilt edges (cover loose), N.Y. 1887," a sheet of Clemens's notes laid in, lot 325, sold for $1.50.

———. [Identical title]. Polished tree calf leather, gilt-stamped spine and boards, gilt inner dentelles, scarlet silk doublures. Minor rubbing on corners and edges. New York: Charles L. Webster & Co., 1887. 678 pp.

> **Provenance:** has the shelfmarks of the library numbering system employed by Clara Clemens Gabrilowitsch during her Detroit years. Sold at the Hollywood auction in 1951 but unlisted in the sale sheet. A pencil note on the front flyleaf states, "Purchased from/Mark Twain's Library/Tuesday April 10, 1951."
>
> **Catalog:** "Property from the Library of Mark Twain," Butterfield & Butterfield, San Francisco, Sale 6613 (16 July 1997), lot 2686.
>
> **Location:** Mark Twain House and Museum, Hartford, Connecticut.
>
> **Copy examined:** Clemens's specially bound and unmarked copy. Viewed in Hartford in 1997.
>
> *McClellan's Own Story* contains a twenty-four-page biographical sketch of McClellan written by his literary executor, William C. Prime, who had known the deceased General personally. Prime's essay, dated 10 August 1886, sought to defend the battered reputation of the military figure who had run for president against Lincoln during the Civil War. "Of all men I have ever known McClelland was the most unselfish," Prime declared (p. 18). In a letter to Olivia Clemens written on 26 July 1887, Clemens compared McClellan's memoirs unfavorably with those by Prince Metternich (1773–1859): "This difference between him & Gen. McClellan is conspicuous. Metternich's book removes the obloquy from his name; but McClellan's deepens that upon *his*, & justifies it" (*LLMT*, p. 249). Prime, of course, was the "William C. Grimes" whose writings Twain had ridiculed in marginalia and in *The Innocents Abroad* (1869)—see the Catalog entries for William Cowper Prime.

McClelland, Mary Greenway (1853–1895). *St. John's Wooing, A Story*. Illus. New York: Harper & Brothers, 1895. 175 pp.

> **Source:** MTLAcc, entry #1323, volume donated by Clemens.
>
> Sometimes compared to Charles Egbert Craddock (the pseudonym of Mary Noailles Murfree), McClelland (in a short life) never stood out among the Southern writers as anything more than a prolific but minor writer.

McClure, Alexander Kelly (1828–1909). *Our Presidents, and How We Make Them. A Historical Survey of How Each Man Came to Hold the Office*. Portraits. Second edition. Original green decorated cloth, gilt. New York: Harper & Brothers, 1902. 482 pp. [First edition was published in 1900.]

> **Inscription:** the front free endpaper is signed in black ink, "S L. Clemens/Riverdale, <Jan.> Feb. 1902".
>
> **Catalogs:** *A1911*, "12mo, cloth, N.N.[*sic*] 1902," quotes the signature, lot 326, sold for $3.25; George D. Smith, New York City, "Catalogue of Books" (1911), quotes the signature, item #262, $10; *Sotheby's 2003*, #212, $6,000 (sold with five other titles about history and travel).
>
> **Provenance:** listed among books for sale at the 15th International Antiquarian Book Fair, Boston, 8–10 November

1991, "N.Y., 1902, from Mark Twain's library, signed and dated by Twain," *A B Bookman's Weekly*, 4 November 1991, p. 1748; entered the collection of Nick Karanovich, Fort Wayne, Indiana.

> **Location:** collection of Kevin Mac Donnell, Austin, Texas.
>
> **Copy examined:** Clemens's unmarked copy, in July 2004. Contains the *A1911* sale label.

———. *Our Presidents and How We Make Them*. New revised edition. Illus. New York: Harper & Brothers, [cop. 1905]. 509 pp.

> **Source:** MTLAcc, entry #1733, volume donated by Clemens.

McClure, James Baird (1832–1895), ed. *Anecdotes of Abraham Lincoln and Lincoln's Stories, Including Early Life Stories, Professional Life Stories, White House Stories, War Stories, Miscellaneous Stories*. Chicago: Rhodes & McClure, 1879.

> **Inscription:** the title page is signed "S. L. Clemens/Mark Twain."
>
> **Source:** Paul Baender reported in the *Mark Twain Circular* in 1990 that the Lincoln Collection at the University of Iowa contains this "paper cover book . . . provenance unknown" with "no marginalia." Clemens definitely would have been interested in this subject, but given the history of Eugene Field II and his confederate Harry Dayton Sickles in forging prominent people's autographs in nineteenth-century books, many of these connected with Chicago (where this title was published), and in view of the highly unusual signature form for a volume supposedly from Clemens's library, a huge degree of caution is warranted here. It is almost certainly a forged association item.

McClure's Magazine (monthly periodical, New York City, published 1893–1929).

> **Catalog:** ListABP (1910), "McClure's Sept. 1905".
>
> From Vienna, Clemens explained to Richard Watson Gilder on 13 January 1897: "A week ago I subscribed for McClure's Magazine for Jean; two or three copies arrived from London last night"; he was furious upon finding that his publisher Frank Bliss was excerpting passages from *Following the Equator* into *McClure's* (ALS in UCLA Library). On 13 September 1898 Clemens informed Joseph H. Twichell that copies of *McClure's* were reaching his present address in Kaltenleutgeben, Austria (*MTL*, pp. 666; *LMTJHT*, p. 220). "I have been waiting and waiting for that McClure [containing Ida Tarbell's history of the Standard Oil Company]—and yesterday I found it in one of the daughters' rooms; it had been there a fortnight, I judge. They carry off anything that is addressed to me, if it looks interesting" (SLC to Henry H. Rogers, Florence, Italy, 21 March 1904, *MTHHR*, p. 559). Clemens praised a story by Inez Haynes Gilimore that he found in the June 1905 issue (Inez Haynes Gillmore to SLC, Scituate, Massachusetts, 3 June 1905, MTP).

McCook, Henry Christopher (1837–1911). *Ant Communities, and How They Are Governed*. Illus. New York: Harper & Brothers, 1909. 321 pp.

> **Location:** Mark Twain Library, Redding, Connecticut. Donated from Clemens's library by Clara Clemens Gabrilowitsch in 1910 (MTLAcc, entry #1967).
>
> **Copy examined:** Clemens's copy, unmarked. Has the Mark Twain Library accession number "1967". Examined in 1970 and again in June 1982.

———. *Nature's Craftsmen: Popular Studies of Ants and Other Insects*. Illus. First edition. Original mustard cloth, gilt. New York: Harper & Brothers, 1907. 317 pp.

Inscription: the front pastedown endpaper is signed and dated by Clemens in black ink; subsequently Clemens added an inscription above the signature in darker ink to read: "To Miss Lyon/from/S L. Clemens/1907."

Marginalia: a note or clipping, once pinned to the front free endpaper, has been removed. There are pencil marks in the text on page 118 (a word underlined), page 119 (a word underlined), and page 160 (a grammatical correction, changing "owe them" to "owe to them"). Isabel Lyon recorded a conversation held in 1915 in notes on the rear pastedown endpaper: "[Abbreviated name, "R.A.,"underlined]/'You'd know this man was a/parson for he drivels/ psalmody all through the/book.'/[Abbreviated name, "I.A.," underlined] Well somebody must do it—/July 18–15." (The abbreviated names are those of Ralph Ashcroft and Isabel Lyon Ashcroft, according to Kevin Mac Donnell.)

Catalog: George Robert Minkoff Rare Books, Catalog 37 (1977), "8vo, original pictorial cloth, first edition," item #34, priced at $225.

Location: collection of Kevin Mac Donnell, Austin, Texas. Acquired in 1977.

Copy examined: Clemens's copy, in July 2004.

———. *Nature's Craftsmen: Popular Studies of Ants and Other Insects*. Illus. New York: Harper & Brothers, 1907. 317 pp.

Source: MTLAcc, entry #1800, volume donated by Clemens.

McCook, John James (1843–1927).

McCook, a minister and faculty member of Trinity College in Hartford, wrote a number of papers on social reform issues such as alcoholism, care of the indigent, and vagrancy. On 15 July 1888 Clemens acknowledged something that McCook had sent him: "That paper is delicious. I do not often find literature that will bear reading twice, but this does" (PH in MTP).

McCrackan, William Denison (1864–1923). "Mrs. Eddy's Relation to Christian Science," *North American Review* 176.556 (March 1903): 349–364.

Mark Twain wrote a cordial letter to McCrackan on 15 December 1902, thanking him for sending "your N. A. Review articles" and stating that he had read them the previous night "with admiration & with profit" (PH in MTP). Twain's "Christian Science" was running serially in three parts in the *North American Review* in the December 1902, January 1903, and February 1903 issues. However, McCrackan's follow-up article, "Mrs. Eddy's Relation to Christian Science," *North American Review* (176.556 (March 1903): 349–364) altered Twain's initially friendly attitude toward this exponent of Christian Science. In that piece McCrackan reduced Twain's objections to "the financial affairs of Mrs. Eddy herself and of the Christian Science denomination" (p. 358), and then proceeded to defend their book sales and other income. McCrackan mockingly assured readers that "Mark Twain need have no fear the Christian Scientists will so deviate from true Christian Science practice as to 'worship' Mrs. Eddy" (p. 364). "He believes Mrs. Eddy's word," Twain soon scoffed in "Mrs. Eddy in Error," *North American Review*

176.557 (April 1903): 51, an essay he later appended to Twain's *Christian Science* [1907] (collected in *WIM?*, pp. 382–395).

Robert Peel, *Mary Baker Eddy*, pp. 196–205.

McCulloch-Williams, Martha (1848–1934). *Field-Farings; A Vagrant Chronicle of Earth and Sky*. New York: Harper & Brothers, 1892. 242 pp.

Source: MTLAcc, entry #1348, volume donated by Clemens.

McCulloch-Williams, born Susan Martha Ann Collins on a Tennessee plantation, moved to New York City in 1887. She took the name of her (possibly common-law) husband, defying convention by inserting a hyphen. Besides writing several hundred short stories she was the author of books on nature appreciation, household management, and cookbooks (including a groundbreaking narrative cookbook about food recipes in the Old South). *Field-Farings; A Vagrant Chronicle of Earth and Sky* was McCulloch-Williams's first book. Highly personal in tone, with no specific locale designated, the book invites the reader, through word-pictures that resemble prose poetry, to share the sights and scents of outdoor life through the seasonal cycle of one year. Game-hunting is described, but from the point of view of the hunted birds and animals.

McCutcheon, John Tinney (1870–1949). *The Mysterious Stranger and Other Cartoons*. New York: McClure, Phillips & Co., 1905. 161 plates.

Source: MTLAcc, entry #1226, volume donated by Clemens.

McCutcheon was a prominent Chicago newspaper cartoonist for the Chicago *Tribune* and the Chicago *Record-Herald*. Most of McCutcheon's drawings collected here depicted a hyperactive President Theodore Roosevelt, the festivities at the Chicago Centennial Jubilee, and the state delegations arriving at the St. Louis World's Fair. The book's title cartoon, "The Mysterious Stranger," involved national politics, and had no reference to Mark Twain's gestating drafts of a novel that are known collectively by that name. It showed a sheepish figure representing the state of Missouri lining up with Republican voters and leaving the "Solid South" Democratic Party.

MacDonald, A. P. *The Adventures of the Hon. Leo Fantassè (Reprinted from the "People's Friend")*. Edinburgh: Sands & Co., 1906. 168 pp.

Catalog: ListABP (1910), "Adventures of the Hon. Leo Fantasse", no other information provided.

———. *The MacPeever Wrangles (Reprinted from the "People's Friend")*. London and Dundee: John Leng & Co., 1907. 157 pp.

On 30 June 1907 Mark Twain wrote to A. P. MacDonald (*Union Catalog of Clemens Letters*, ed. Paul Machlis [Berkeley: University of California Press, 1986], p. 255). According to the New York *Herald* of 30 June 1907 (Section 1, page 9), Twain was delighted with these six stories about a married couple told in Scottish dialect, and wrote enthusiastically to the author: "I have found time (by stealing it from sleep) to umpire the first four 'squabbles,' and I find them fine, both in spirit and in workmanship, and just to my taste." The *Herald* article cited Leng & Company as the book's publisher. *The People's Friend* was a literary weekly founded by Scottish editor and politician John Leng (1828–1906). I am grateful to Louis J. Budd and Paul Machlis for (separately) directing my attention to this item.

MACDONALD, DONALD (1857–1932). *Gum Boughs and Wattle Bloom, Gathered on Australian Hills and Plains.* London and New York: Cassell & Co., [1887?]. 256 pp.

Inscription: inscribed on the title page in black ink, "To Mark Twain/with the author's compliments/26/11/95."

Location: Mark Twain Library, Redding, Connecticut.

Copy examined: Clemens's copy, unmarked. Has a penciled Mark Twain Library accession number, "3906". Examined in 1970 and again in June 1982.

MACDONALD, GEORGE (1824–1905). *At the Back of the North Wind.* Illustrated by Arthur Hughes (1832–1915). New York: George Routledge and Sons, 1871. 378 pp. [Edition conjectured; the first edition was issued in London in 1871. The Routledge edition was reprinted in 1882.]

Clemens and Olivia attended a garden party at the Scottish author MacDonald's home in Hammersmith on 16 July 1873 (NB 12, *N&J* 1: 564; *MTLet* 5: 414). There are indications that the Clemenses met or possibly entertained the MacDonalds during George MacDonald's lecture tour in the United States in 1872–1873. In 1881 Clemens designated MacDonald to receive a complimentary copy of *The Prince and the Pauper* (NB 19, *N&J* 2: 386). MacDonald's allegorical tale for children, *At the Back of the North Wind,* constituted a common vocabulary for Clemens and his young daughters, particularly Susy. At their urging, Clemens would invent additional stories about little Diamond, the dying coachman's son whom the benevolent North Wind carried among the stars (*MFMT*, p. 25). In an undated letter Clemens posed as Santa Claus, explaining to Susy: "Our last lot of kitchen-furniture for dolls has just gone to a very poor little child in the North Star away up in the cold country above the Big Dipper" (*MFMT*, p. 37).

On 19 September 1882 Clemens wrote to MacDonald from Elmira: "I'll send you the book [*Life on the Mississippi*], with names in it, sure, as soon as it issues from the press. . . . Since I may choose, I will take the *Back of the North Wind* in return, for our children's sake; they have read and re-read their own copy so many times that it looks as if it had been through the wars" (quoted by Greville MacDonald, *George MacDonald and His Wife* [London: George Allen & Unwin, 1924], p. 458). In a letter to MacDonald written from Hartford on 9 March 1883, Clemens thanked him "in advance for the North Wind which is coming," and then added a postscript to report that "The North Wind has arrived; & Susy lost not a moment, but went to work & ravenously devoured the whole of it once more, at a single sitting" (ALS in MTP). After Susy's death Clemens wrote: "I have been moved to-night by the thought of a little old copy in the nursery of *At the Back of the North Wind.* Oh, what happy days they were when that book was read, and how Susy loved it! . . . Death is so kind, benignant, to whom he loves" (*MTB*, p. 1074). (In the final chapter of MacDonald's book, an omniscient, feminine form of the North Wind reappears to the ailing Diamond and takes the little boy on a final journey to "the country at the back of the north wind";

he fails to recognize her as a pleasant image of Death.)

Considering Mark Twain's associations of this work with Susy, who died in 1896; MacDonald, who died in 1905; childhood innocence; blessed death; and visitations of supernatural figures (the North Wind takes different shapes in visionary conversations with the boy named Diamond), *At the Back of the North Wind* should be viewed as another inspirational resource for his "No. 44, the Mysterious Stranger," written between 1902 and 1908. Twain's Satan, called "Forty-four" in that version of *The Mysterious Stranger,* represents a bitter and perverse transmogrification of MacDonald's kindly North Wind, who performs good deeds for an ungrateful human populace and eventually imparts the greatest favor of all—swift and painless death. She possesses the same power as Twain's Satan to render earthlings capable of seeing their existence from the horizonless perspective of distance and time (MacDonald alludes to Herodotus's history on several occasions). Coleman O. Parsons suggested that Twain derived from MacDonald's book the mode of airborne conveyance employed by Satan to transport himself and Theodore Fischer in "The Chronicle of Young Satan" (Parsons, "Background" [1960], p. 64).

MacDonald's book has significant affinities with Satan's explanation of our "dream existence" to August Feldner at the conclusion of "No. 44, The Mysterious Stranger." One need only consider the following excerpts from Chapters 36 and 37 of *At the Back of the North Wind* to recognize correspondences between MacDonald's story and Twain's ending: "'Please, dear North Wind,' he said, 'I am so happy that I'm afraid it's a dream. How am I to know that it's not a dream?' 'What does it matter?' returned North Wind. . . . 'The dream, if it is a dream, is a pleasant one—is it not?'" (Chapter 36). "'I can't bear to find *it* a dream, because then I should lose you. You would be nobody then, and I could not bear that. You ain't a dream, are you, dear North Wind? Do say *No,* else I shall cry, and come awake, and you'll be gone for ever.'. . . 'I'm either not a dream, or there's something better that's not a dream, Diamond,' said the North Wind" (Chapter 36). "'I don't think you could dream anything that hadn't something real like it somewhere'" (Chapter 36). "'Yes,' said North Wind. 'The people who think lies, and do lies, are very likely to dream lies. But the people who love what is true will surely now and then dream true things'" (Chapter 37). "'I suppose it's only the people in it that make you like a place, and when they're gone, it's dead, and you don't care a bit about it'" (Chapter 37). "'I thought that would be it,' said North Wind. 'Everything, dream and all, has got a soul in it, or else it's worth nothing, and we don't care a bit about it'" (Chapter 37).

The fact that we know Clemens to have frequently read these passages to his own children and the indication that they were linked closely in his mind with Susy and her untimely death give the words special significance. He did not borrow any language directly, but it can be argued that the poignant ending of *At the Back of the North Wind* contributed fully as much to the composition of the last-written version of *The Mysterious Stranger* as another novel, Anatole France's *Le Crime de Sylvestre Bonnard.* Did this cherished volume in his library disappear because

Clemens could not bear to pass his family's copy of *At the Back of the North Wind* along to other readers as he did with so many hundreds of other books he donated?

————. *Robert Falconer* (novel published in 1868; the American edition was published in 1870).

In a lengthy criticism of the novel that forms part of Clemens's letter to Mary Mason Fairbanks of 2 September 1870, he declared: "My! but the first half of it is superb! We just kept our pencils going, marking brilliant & beautiful things—but there was nothing to mark, after the middle. Up to the middle of the book we did so admire & like Robert—& after that we began to dislike & finally ended by despising him for a self-righteous humbug, devoured with egotism. . . . Shargar was the only character in the book <worthy to live & worthy of> who was *always* welcome, & of him the author gave us just as little as possible, & filled his empty pages with the added emptiness of that tiresome Ericson & his dismal 'poetry'—hogwash, *I* call it." As for Miss St. John, "well, there never was any interest about *her*, from the first. . . . I just wanted to send her a dose of salts with my compliments." Clemens added, "Mind you, we are not through yet—two or three chapters still to read—& that idiot is still hunting for his father. I hoped that as he grew to years of discretion he would eventually appreciate the efforts of a wise Providence to get the old man out of the way. . . . Nothing would do him, clear from juvenile stupidity up to mature imbecility but tag around after that old bummer." Clemens predicted that the father would eventually turn out to be "a missionary, likely, along with Rev. De Fleuri, & trot him around peddling sentiment to London guttersnipes while *he* continues his special mission upon earth of reclaiming venerable strumpets and exhibiting his little wonders at midnight for the astonishment & admiration of chance strangers like the applauding Gordon." In a postscript Olivia playfully apologized for her husband's intemperate mood, but confirmed that "the last part of the book we have not enjoyed as much as the first part, but the first we did enjoy intensely" (*MTMF*, pp. 134–137; *MTL* 4: 188–189).

French, *MT&GA* (1965), p. 33; Kathryn Lindskoog, "Mark Twain and George MacDonald: The Salty and the Sweet," *Mark Twain Journal* 30.2 (Fall 1993): 26.

————. *A Rough Shaking*. Illustrated by W[illiam]. [Edward] Parkinson (1871–1924). New York: George Routledge and Sons, [1890]. 384 pp.

Inscription: a Christmas present to Jean Clemens from "her loving uncle."

Catalog: *Mott 1952*, item #68, $5.

————. *Sir Gibbie*. Seaside Library Edition. New York: G. Munro, 1879. 75 pp. (paperbound).

In July 1880 J. R. Barlow, Hartford booksellers, billed Clemens for "1 Sir Gibbie .20¢" purchased on 10 May 1880; Clemens paid on 5 July 1880 (receipt in MTP). Munro's paperbound edition cost .20¢.

Kathryn Lindskoog surveyed the Clemens-MacDonald friendship and made a case for viewing *Sir Gebbie* (1879) as "the source for *Huckleberry Finn*" ("*Huckleberry Finn* as Morality Tract, and an Audacious Proposal Regarding Its Origin," *Books & Religion: A Monthly Review* 13.8–9 [November-December 1985]: 13–15). Some of the

parallels are indeed striking, once they are pointed out. Jamie Rankin, "The Genesis of George MacDonald's Scottish Novels: *Edelweiss* Amid the Heather?," *Studies in Scottish Literature* 24.1 (1989): 55, cited Lindskoog's 1985 article in asserting that "there is good reason to believe that the parallels between MacDonald's youthful hero Sir Gibbie and Huckleberry Finn can be traced back to MacDonald's Twain's friendship with Mark Twain and a proposed collaboration." In "Mark Twain and George MacDonald: The Salty and the Sweet," *Mark Twain Journal* 30.2 (Fall 1993): 26–32, Lindskoog subsequently detailed twenty similarities indicating that "perhaps *Huckleberry Finn* was influenced by *Sir Gebbie*." She acknowledged that despite these similarities "*Huckleberry Finn* has won world acclaim and *Sir Gebbie* has been consigned to near oblivion" (p. 30).

One impediment for readers, then and now, is the thick Scottish dialect of MacDonald's characters. A mute boy with an alcoholic father and no mother leaves the city for the Scottish Highlands. His encounters with cruelty as well as benevolence reveal to him the wide range of human morality and behavior.

————. *Thomas Wingfold, Curate*. New York: George Routledge and Sons, 1876. 666 pp. [Publisher and pages conjectured; this was the first edition published in New York.]

Inscription: "S. L. Clemens, Hartford, 1874 [*sic*]," quoted in *A1911* catalog.

Catalog: *A1911*, "12mo, cloth, N.Y. 1876," quotes the signature (dating it as 1874), lot 307, sold for $1.25.

MACDONOUGH, AUGUST RODNEY (1820–1907), translator. *The Lovers of Provence: Aucassin and Nicolette. A MS. Song-Story of the Twelfth Century Rendered into Modern French by Alexandre Bida [1813–1895]. Translated into English Verse and Prose by A[ugust]. Rodney Macdonough.* Introductory note by Edmund Clarence Stedman (1833–1908). Preface by Gaston Paris. Illustrated by Alexandre Bida (1813–1895), Mary Hallock Foote (1847–1938), W[illiam]. H[amilton]. Gibson (1850–1896), and Frederick Dielman (1847–1935). New York: Fords, Howard & Hulbert, [cop. 1880]. 82 pp. [This is a conjectured but almost certain edition, based on the information below and Macdonough's correspondence in the Yale University Library (GEN MSS MISC Group 615).]

Catalog: ListABP (1910), "Aucassin and Nicolette", no edition specified.

Clemens was definitely familiar with these legendary lovers. Brown & Gross, booksellers in Hartford, billed Clemens on 1 January 1881 for "1 Lovers of Provence" purchased for $2.50 on 20 December 1880; Clemens paid his account on 17 January 1881 (receipt in MTP). One of the book's illustrators, Frederick Dielman, would be among the illustrators selected for Mark Twain's *Following the Equator* (1897).

MACFALL, HALDANE (1860–1928). *The Masterfolk, Wherein Is Attempted the Unravelling of the Strange Affair of My Lord Wyntwarde of Cavil and Miss Betty Modeyne.* New York: Harper & Brothers, 1903. 440 pp.

Source: MTLAcc, entry #1110, volume donated by Clemens; subsequently withdrawn from circulation.

The marriage of an English couple is threatened by the husband's decision to taste Bohemian life in Paris.

MACFARLANE (possibly a fictional person).

Mark Twain attributed deterministic philosophical views to "Macfarlane," a boardinghouse acquaintance he supposedly knew in Cincinnati in 1856 and 1857 (Albert Bigelow Paine, *MTB* [1912], pp. 114–115). However, Paul Baender ("Alias Macfarlane: A Revision of Mark Twain's Biography," *American Literature* 38.2 [May 1966]: 187–197) vigorously disputed the existence of such a person. But subsequently William Baker—"Mark Twain in Cincinnati: A Mystery Most Compelling," *American Literary Realism* 12.2 (Autumn 1979): 299–315—turned up evidence that a John M. McFarland [*sic*] was employed as a printer by the same firm as Clemens during his brief stint in Cincinnati. See also Wesley A. Britton, "Macfarlane, 'Boarding House,' and 'Bugs,'": Mark Twain's Cincinnati Apprenticeship," *Mark Twain Journal* 27.1 (Spring 1989): 14–17.

MACGAHAN, JANUARIUS ALOYSIUS (1844–1878). *Campaigning on the Oxus, and the Fall of Khiva. By J. A. MacGahan, Correspondent of the "New York Herald."* Illus., maps. First edition. Original terra cotta cloth, gilt. New York: Harper & Brothers, 1874. 438 pp.

Inscription: signed in pencil on the first blank page, "S. L. Clemens/Hartford 1876." At page 159 a small slip of paper was used as a bookmark; it shows the numbers "563–76" in pencil in Clemens's hand. (Those pages describe how MacGahan arrived at a Russian camp after crossing a desert.) The corner of page 206 was formerly turned down, with foxing on the opposite pages as a result.

Catalog: *A1911*, "8vo, cloth, N.Y. 1874," quotes the signature, lot 308, sold for $1.25.

Location: collection of Kevin Mac Donnell, Austin, Texas (Mac Donnell to Alan Gribben, 19 February 2010). Has an *A1911* sale label. No markings.

Campaigning on the Oxus recounts how MacGahan witnessed the surrender of the desert khanate Khiva to the Russian army in 1873.

———. [An identical copy.]

Source: MTLAcc, entry #1729, volume donated by Clemens.

McGLENNON, FELIX (1856–1943). "Bring my boy back again" (song, published in 1891). Arranged by F[rank]. W[hite]. Meecham (1856–1909).

In "About All Kinds of Ships" (1893) Mark Twain listed a song titled "We are far from home on the stormy main" as an example of "soft sentimentality about the sea." A number of songs and hymns employ the phrase "stormy main" and might be candidates for the tune Twain is citing, but McGlennon's "Bring my boy back again" seems to come closest to the phrases he quotes. The first stanza included these lines: "He was the light of my failing years, he was my only pride;/But *far from his home* he's gone to roam over the treacherous tide." The chorus concludes: "Out on the sea he's roaming, out *on the stormy main*,/ Blow, friendly winds, and bring my boy back again" (italics added).

McGOVERN, JOHN (1850–1917). *The Golden Censer; or, the Duties of To-Day and the Hopes of the Future.* Sold by Subscription Only. Chicago: Union Publishing House, 1884. 448 pp.

Provenance: formerly in the collection of Ralph Gregory (1909–2015), onetime curator of the Mark Twain Birthplace Memorial Shrine in Florida, Missouri (now known as the Mark Twain Birthplace State Historic Site). The volume was a gift from Mrs. Mary Gertrude (Stotts) Shotwell, Graybull, Wyoming, in 1965. Mr. Gregory lived in Marthasville, Missouri until his death. See the Catalog entry for Thomas Dick's *Practical Astronomer* for an explanation of this provenance.

Location: in August 2017 the volume belonged to Ralph Gregory's daughter, Nancy Gregory Kimball, Marthasville, Missouri.

Copy examined: Orion Clemens's copy.

The Golden Censer is a collection of moral advice and apothegms ("The mill will never grind with the water that has passed"—p. 30) mainly directed at young men. Warnings about the possible missteps of youth are organized by topic—courtesy, duty, economy, prudence, courage, temperance, worship, companions, bachelorhood, wedded life, and so forth—and offer exemplars such as George Washington for every virtue.

McGUFFEY, WILLIAM HOLMES (1800–1873). *McGuffey's Eclectic Readers.*

Sydney J. Krause (*Mark Twain as Critic* [1967], pp. 92, 112) suggested that Mark Twain was referring to *McGuffey's Readers* when he wrote that "considering the 'Standard School Readers' and other popular and unspeakably execrable models, the real wonder is . . . that they [the pupils] write at all without bringing upon themselves suspicions of imbecility" ("Report to the Buffalo Female Academy," Buffalo *Express*, 18 June 1870).

MACKARNESS, MATILDA ANNE (PLANCHÉ) (1826–1881), known as "Mrs. Henry S. Mackarness." *Sunbeam Stories.* New York: James Miller, 1863. 410 pp.

Source: MTLAcc, entry #413, volume donated by Clemens.

Sunbeam Stories collected the moral tales of this English author, whose *A Trap to Catch a Sunbeam* (1849) had established her reputation as a children's writer. JoDee Benussi identified this author (Benussi to Gribben, email, 19 December 2007).

MACKAY, ALEXANDER (1808–1852). *The Western World; or, Travels in the United States in 1846–47: Exhibiting Them in Their Latest Development, Social, Political, and Industrial; Including a Chapter on California.* 3 vols. London: R. Bentley, 1849. [A second edition was also published in 1849; third and fourth editions were published in 1850; an American edition (in two volumes) was issued in Philadelphia from the second London edition by Lea & Blanchard in 1849. The edition Mark Twain read has not been established.]

Mark Twain quotes from Volume III of Mackay's book in Chapter 27 of *Life on the Mississippi* (1883) about Mackay's first sight of "the lordly stream": "Here it was then in its reality. . . . I looked upon it with that reverence with which every one must regard a great feature of external nature." Twain also mentions Mackay in a portion of manuscript omitted from the book. Presumably *The Western World* was among the twenty-five "books relating to travels in the U.S. by English people in the first half of the century" that James R. Osgood and Company sent to Mark Twain on 22 July 1882 (W. Rowlands to SLC, ALS in MTP; partially published in *MTLP*, ed. Hamlin Hill, p. 158 n. 2). Presumably Mackay's promise on the book's title page of a chapter devoted to California would have intrigued Twain, but Mackay merely discussed the ethics and advisability of the recent Mexican-American War; he did not visit the West Coast.

Walter Blair, *MT&HF* (1960), pp. 298–299; Dewey Ganzel, "Twain, Travel Books" (1962), pp. 41 n. 4, 42 n. 8, 47, 52.

MACKAY, CHARLES (1814–1889). *Forty Years' Recollections of Life, Literature, and Public Affairs, from 1830 to 1870.* 2 vols. London: Chapman & Hall, 1877.

Mackay was a Scottish-born London journalist, newspaper editor, author, poet, song writer, and compiler of anthologies. In a letter to Olivia Clemens written on 3 December 1876 Clemens enclosed a clipping from a New York *Times* book review of Mackay's *Forty Years' Recollections* discussing a problem confronted by prominent authors: they are inundated with unsolicited presentation copies of other writers' books. Clemens underlined a sentence about the necessity of acknowledging receipt of these gifts and wrote "Coincidence" in the margin (MTP). I am grateful to JoDee Benussi for noticing this connection.

———. *Memoirs of Extraordinary Popular Delusions and the Madness of Crowds* (London, first published in 1841). The title was expanded (adding *and the Madness of Crowds*) in the second edition in 1852.

Clemens may have known Mackay's account of the Children's Crusade to Palestine, a cynical scheme to sell youths into slavery in North Africa. The words "The Children's Crusade to Palestine" appear in Notebook 24 (July 1885, *N&J* 3: 168); Clemens repeated them in the same notebook in August 1885 (*N&J* 3: 173). Mackay relates this sordid story in his chapter titled "The Crusades." It is hard to believe that Clemens did not own and annotate at least one copy of Mackay's historical compilation of mass fads, bizarre follies, and widespread evil-doing, including the European witch mania, alchemy, the Dutch tulip craze and other financial bubbles, fortune-tellers and prophets, haunted houses, medical frauds, famous duels, deadly poisoners, celebrated thieves and murderers, religious relics, and Holy Land crusaders. One can scarcely conceive of any other book containing so many topics likely to pique Clemens's interests, yet no copy of *Popular Delusions* has been traced to him.

MACKAY, KATHERINE (DUER) (1880–1930). *The Stone of Destiny.* New York: Harper & Brothers, 1904. 112 pp. [A novel.]
Source: MTLAcc, entry #1442, volume donated by Clemens.

MACKAYE, JAMES (1872–1935). *The Economy of Happiness.* Boston: Little, Brown and Co., 1906. 533 pp.
Source: MTLAcc, entry #851, volume donated by Clemens.
Mackaye analyzed the foundations and methods of achieving a sense of fulfillment. He referred to the views of a few philosophers in the course of discussing actions to avoid and decisions necessary to make in order to attain successful gratification.

MACKENZIE, (SIR) GEORGE (1636–1691). *The Laws and Customes of Scotland, in Matters Criminal* (Edinburgh, published in 1678). [Second edition published in 1699.]
In a fragmentary manuscript, "The Great Witchcraft Madness" (DV129[4], Box 37, MTP), Mark Twain quotes Sir George Mackenzie's description of a woman who confessed to witchcraft because, "being defamed for a witch, she knew she would starve"—no villager thereafter would

show her any charity or have any intercourse whatever with her. Albert Bigelow Paine dated this manuscript in the 1890s or later. Presumably Twain consulted that fragment in writing about the grandmother's confession and execution in Chapter 4 of "The Chronicle of Young Satan," written between 1897 and 1900 (*MSM*, pp. 79–80). Without being aware of Twain's earlier fragment, Coleman O. Parsons surmised that Twain based the burning of Gottfried's grandmother episode on Sir Walter Scott's account of the burning of two Scottish witches in Scott's *Letters on Demonology and Witchcraft* (1830), Letter 9. Parsons showed that Scott in turn was relying on Mackenzie's book ("The Background of *The Mysterious Stranger*" (1960), pp. 67–68).

MACKENZIE, ROBERT SHELTON (1809–1880).
Clemens wrote to this author on 23 September 1874, mentioning his meeting MacKenzie at a dinner in New York City on 23 February 1872 (*MTLet* 6: 241). James R. Osgood & Company of Boston had published MacKenzie's *Sir Walter Scott: The Story of His Life* in 1871, and MacKenzie had also written a biography of Charles Dickens among other works.

MACKINNON, ALEXANDER. *Prince Charles Edward [1720–1788]; or, the Rebellion of 1745–46.* Charlottetown, P.E.I.: Bremner Brothers, Printers, 1873. 71 pp.
Inscription: the front cover is signed across the top with ink in a large, hurried hand: "Clemens".
Catalog: *A1911*, "16mo, original wrappers, Charlestown [*sic*], P.E.I, 1873," quotes the signature, lot 309, sold for $1.
Provenance: *A1911* sale label on the front pastedown endpaper; above that is affixed a bookplate: "The Edith and Lorne Pierce/Collection of Canadiana/Queen's University at Kingston". A penciled price of $75 is visible at the top of the title page.
Location: University of Alberta.
Copy examined: a photographic reproduction of the volume that is available online at Hathitrust Digital Library. The photograph is dated 1983.
Bonnie Prince Charlie led the unsuccessful Jacobite insurrection in 1745 that culminated in the disastrous Battle of Culloden in 1846.

MACLANE, MARY (1881–1929). *The Story of Mary MacLane, by Herself.* Chicago: H. S. Stone and Co., 1902. 322 pp.
"I subscribe for a weekly paper which gets here [York Harbor, Maine] every two weeks, and I learn from that that Mary MacLane is exploring the East for The World," Clemens told a newspaper reporter in 1902. "'Is the young woman a genie,' he asked, 'or is her book a composite of thoughts that had been written before?'" Clemens was reluctant to accept her own word about her writings. "'I can't,' he said, 'in view of her frank declarations about her own mendacity'" ("My First Vacation and My Last—Mark Twain," New York *World*, 7 September 1902).

MCLAREN, ELIZABETH T. *Dr. John Brown and His Sister Isabella: Outlines.* Edinburgh: David Douglas, 1889. 62 pp. [Isabella Cranston Brown lived 1810–1882.]
Inscription: the front free endpaper is signed "Olivia L. Clemens/Hartford/1890."
Catalog: ListABP (1910), "Dr. John Brown", no other information supplied.
Location: Mark Twain Papers, Bancroft Library, University

of California at Berkeley.

Copy examined: Olivia Clemens's unmarked copy.

John ("Jock") Brown, Dr. Brown's son, wrote to Clemens on 28 December 1889 from Edinburgh: "I think you will like the small book I have sent you. It is written by a Miss McLaren who knew my father very well and understood him" (ALS in MTP). Then on 25 January 1890 he wrote again: "I think it as well to send you by letter post another copy of the little book as you may not get the first. . . . If I do not hear from you I will know you have got one or [the] other copy" (ALS in MTP). Clemens wrote from Hartford to thank Jock Brown on 11 February 1890: "Both copies came, and we are reading and re-reading the one, and lending the other. . . . It is an exquisite book, the perfection of literary workmanship. . . . In this book the Doctor lives and moves just as he was" (*MTL*, p. 529; also quoted in John Brown and D.W. Forrest, *Letters of John Brown* [London, 1907], p. 361). In March 1898 Clemens noted "Recollections of Dr. John Brown" (NB 42, TS p. 61). An Autobiographical Dictation Clemens made on 5 February 1906 retold a humorous story about Dr. Brown's fondness for dogs related in McLaren's memoir (*AutoMT* 1: 329).

MacLaren, Gay Zenola (1881–1952).

MacLaren gave Clemens credit for a recommendation that launched her on the Chautauqua circuit where, from a young age, she gave recitals as an elocutionist and dramatic reader. She had the capacity to perform entire plays, acting every role. According to her memoir, *Morally We Roll Along* (Boston: Little, Brown and Co., 1938), she auditioned for Clemens at 14 West 10th Street (the Clemenses moved there on 1 November 1900 and left that address on 21 June 1901) by impersonating Lillian Russell (pp. 62–68). She would employ Clemens's praise ("an unusually gifted young lady") in her future advertising. Her principal object in meeting Clemens had been to ask his permission to perform scenes from *Pudd'nhead Wilson*, which he granted.

McLellan, Charles Morton Stewart (1865–1916), pseud. "Hugh Morton." *The Belle of New York, A Musical Comedy in Two Acts* (performed in 1897). Music by Gustave Adolph Kerker (1857–1923).

Henry W. Fisher mentioned that he and Clemens saw *The Belle of New York* while it was playing in London (*AMT*, p. xx).

McLennan, William (1856–1904), trans. *Songs of Old Canada*. Montreal: Dawson Brothers, 1886. 83 pp.

Source: MTLAcc, entry #2063, volume donated from Clemens's library by Clara Clemens Gabrilowitsch in 1910. McLennan provides translations of fourteen French-Canadian songs with the French and English versions on facing pages.

———. *Spanish John; Being a Memoir, Now First Published in Complete Form, of the Early Life and Adventures of Colonel John McDonell [sic] [1728–1810], Known as "Spanish John," When a Lieutenant in the Company of St. James of the Regiment Irlandia, in the Service of the King of Spain Operating in Italy.* Illustrated by F[elicien]. de Myrbach (1853–1940). New York: Harper & Brothers, 1898. 271 pp.

Inscription: the front free endpaper is inscribed "S. L. Clemens/from G. Iles/N. Y. Feb. 21, 1902".

Location: Mark Twain Library, Redding, Connecticut.

Copy examined: Clemens's copy, unmarked. Has the red ink Mark Twain Library accession number "2513". Examined in 1970 and again in June 1982.

McLennan's novel is centered on an actual historical figure, John Macdonell (1728–1810). (His name is sometimes, but less commonly, spelled "McDonell.") The adventures are set in Italy, before Macdonell immigrated to North America, fought on the Loyalist side during the American Revolution, and subsequently moved to Canada.

———. [Another copy.]

Inscription: "Jervis Langdon/Christmas/1897."

Catalog: Ball 2016 inventory, red cloth, gilt lettering, black and gilt cover design, very good condition.

Location: Quarry Farm library shelves, under the supervision of the Mark Twain Archive, Elmira College, Elmira, New York.

This book would have been available to Clemens whenever the visited the Langdons' residence.

MacLeod, Norman (1812–1872). *Eastward, by Norman MacLeod, D. D., One of Her Majesty's Chaplains, with Seventy Illustrations from Photographs, Engraved by Joseph Swain [1820–1909]*. First edition. Original apricot cloth, gilt, edges gilt, panoramic folding plate, engravings. London and New York: Alexander Strahan, 1866. 304 pp. [A lavishly illustrated guide to the Holy Land with separate chapters on sites that would be visited by the *Quaker City* passengers.]

Inscriptions: the bookplate of Jervis Langdon's "Family Library No. 533" is affixed to the front pastedown endpaper. On the same endpaper is the ownership signature of his son Charley: "C. J. Langdon/Elmira/New York."

Location: collection of Kevin Mac Donnell, Austin, Texas. Acquired in May 2016 from the Langdon family (email, Mac Donnell to Alan Gribben, 16 May 2016).

Source: detailed description of the volume with "no markings in the text" sent on 9 June 2016 by Mac Donnell to Gribben.

Eastward describes, among other destinations, Malta, Alexandria, Cairo, Jaffa, Jerusalem, Bethlehem, and Palestine. Charley Langdon could have taken this book on the *Quaker City* voyage, in which case Clemens might have consulted its contents.

MacManus, Anna (Johnston) (1866–1902), pseud. "Ethna Carbery." *The Four Winds of Eirinn. Poems by Ethna Carbery*. Ed. by Seumas MacManus (1869–1960). New enlarged edition. Dublin: M. H. Gill, 1906. 154 pp. [First published in 1902.]

On 30 March 1907 Isabel Lyon noted in her diary that "Seumas MacManus has written a sweet note to say he is sending books, 1 for the King [Clemens], 1 for C. C. [Clara] and 1 for me—his late wife's poems" (IVL Journals, TS p. 236, MTP).

MacManus, Seumas (1869–1960). *A Lad of the O'Friel's*. Dublin: M. H. Gill & Son, 1906. 318 pp.

Inscription: the front flyleaf is inscribed: "To Mark Twain, with admiration—/Seumas MacManus/of Donegal/29.3.'07." A clipping or letter, now missing, was formerly pinned to the half-title page.

Marginalia: brown ink underlinings, brackets, and a note quoting Robert Browning ("'And did you once see

Shelley—plain?'"), all on page 70.

Provenance: bookstamps, accession number, and other markings of the Mark Twain Library, Redding, Connecticut.

Catalog: "Retz Appraisal" (1944), p. 10, valued at $5.

Location: Mark Twain Papers, Bancroft Library, University of California at Berkeley.

Copy examined: Clemens's copy.

McNALLY, FRANCIS. *National Geographical Series, No. 4—An Improved System of Geography Designed for Schools, Academies, and Seminaries.* Spine detached. New York: A. S. Barnes & Burr, 1863. 110 pp.

Inscription: signed "Olivia L. Langdon/Sputen Duyvil 1863. Sputen Duyvil was (then) a village in New York state on the Hudson River.

Catalogs: inventory checklist of the Quarry Farm library prepared by Emily Schweizer Martinez when Quarry Farm was donated to Elmira College in 1982; Ball 2016 inventory, poor condition.

Location: Quarry Farm library shelves, under the supervision of the Mark Twain Archive, Elmira College, Elmira, New York.

Evidently this was a school textbook belonging to Olivia Louise Langdon (1845–1904) that she left behind when she married Samuel Clemens. It would have been available to Clemens whenever he visited the Langdons' residence.

McNAUGHTON, JOHN HUGH (1829–1891). "Belle Mahone" (song). Melody also by McNaughton.

In a letter to Harriet Lewis, written on 10 January 1869 from Galesburg, Illinois, Clemens referred to "Sweet Belle Mahone" in mentioning "ghastly old sea-sickening sentimental songs" (*LLMT*, p. 48; *MTLet* 3: 23).

MACPHERSON, JAMES (1736–1796). *The Poems of Ossian, the Son of Fingal. Translated from the Original Gaelic* (first published in Edinburgh, 1762).

Mark Twain included books by Ossian in "The House Beautiful," Chapter 38 of *Life on the Mississippi* (1883). The aborted but often reattempted novel, "Simon Wheeler, Detective" (written 1877–1898?), is set in the "sleepy little Missouri village" of Guilford, where "Ossian and [Jane Porter's] Thaddeus of Warsaw were still read, fire and brimstone still preached" (*S&B*, p. 312). In Chapter 3 of Twain's uncompleted novel, when Judge Griswold rehearsed "the grisly theme" of the Dexter-Burnside feud, "he pictured one after another its valorous encounters and their varying fortunes in all their chivalrous and bloody splendor, his fervor grew, the light of battle was in his eye, and it was as if the spirit of some old Gaelic bard had entered into him and he chanted the glories of a great past and of a mighty race that had departed and left not their like behind them" (*S&B*, p. 336). The authenticity of Macpherson's pseudo-mythological poems, purportedly by a Gaelic bard named Ossian, was questioned almost immediately and today they are regarded as hoaxes based on some folklore poems and songs that Macpherson collected in the Scottish highlands. Maureen T. Kravec, "Huckleberry Finn's Aristocratic Ancestry," *Mark Twain Journal* 18.2 (Summer 1976): 19–20, argued for seeing a connection between Huckleberry Finn's surname and the Ossian poems fabricated by Macpherson.

MACPHILPIN, JOHN. *The Apparitions and Miracles at Knock.*

Also the Official Depositions of the Eye-Witnesses. Prepared and Edited by John MacPhilpin, Nephew of the Archbishop of Tuam. New York: P. J. Kenedy, 1898. 142 pp. [Bound with Mary Francis Cusack's *Three Visits to Knock.* New York: P. J. Kenedy, 1898].

Provenance: Antenne-Dorrance Collection, Rice Lake, Wisconsin.

Location: Mark Twain Archive, Gannett-Tripp Learning Center, Elmira College, Elmira, NY.

Copy examined: Clemens's copy, unmarked.

In 1882 Clemens jotted down the title and publisher of MacPhilpin's book and intended to "compare one of these with a miracle from the Bible—& make a devout old Presbyterian fool contend that the ancient miracle proves the modern one" (NB 20, *N&J* 2: 475–476). See also the Catalog entry for Mary Francis Cusack.

MACREADY, [WILLIAM] CHARLES (1793–1873). *Macready's Reminiscences, and Selections from His Diaries and Letters.* Ed. by Sir William Frederick Pollock (1845–1937). Portraits. New York: Harper & Brothers, 1875. 721 pp. [Publisher and pages conjectured.]

Inscription: the front flyleaf is signed "Saml. L. Clemens, Hartford, 1875."

Catalogs: *A1911*, "post 8vo, cloth, N.Y. 1875," quotes the signature, lot 310, sold for $3.50; George D. Smith, New York City, "Catalogue of Books" (1911), quotes the signature, item #251, $10.

The English actor Macready's fame was still resonating when he died in 1873. Among other major events in his life, his feud with the American actor Edwin Forrest had culminated in the Astor Place Opera House riot in New York City in 1849. Clemens included "Sir Frederick Pollock" in an undated list of names that he wrote (*A1911*, lot 305).

McWILLIAM, ROBERT. *Longmans' Handbook of English Literature. Pt. III. From Ben Jonson to Locke.* London: Longmans, Green & Co., 1889. 116 pp.

Source: MTLAcc, entry #806, volume donated by Clemens.

MADAME LUCAS. Round-Robin Series, No. VIII. Boston: James R. Osgood and Co., 1881. [One of the Round-Robin Series of anonymous novels written by "the best writers" that the Osgood firm began publishing and promoting in 1881.]

Catalog: Ball 2016 inventory, green cloth, red and black lettering, signed by Charles Jervis Langdon [Olivia Langdon Clemens's brother, 1849–1916], Jervis Langdon Family Library bookplate #622.

Location: Quarry Farm library shelves, under the supervision of the Mark Twain Archive, Elmira College, Elmira, New York.

This book would have been available to Clemens whenever he visited the Langdons' residence.

MAETERLINCK, MAURICE (1862–1949). *The Life of the Bee.* Translated by Alfred Sutro (1863–1933). Original green cloth, front hinge cracked, light rubbing to extremities, water damage to rear half of the book, dampstaining. New York: Dodd, Mead and Co., 1902. 427 pp.

Inscription: the front pastedown endpaper is signed in black ink, "S L. Clemens."

Marginalia: profuse annotations by Clemens in pencil amount to approximately 120 words, with notes or marked passages on approximately fifty pages. The notes begin on page 36 of "The Swarm" (where Clemens wrote in pencil,

"Drawing room bee") and end on page 146, where he wrote "in bottle" in pencil. On page 40, Clemens wrote vertically: "Order to the queen: 300 a day wanted now. Later: Reduce the output 25%". On page 51 Clemens noted, "bad morals". Clemens jotted a sentence that he felt Maeterlinck should have inserted before the last sentence of a footnote on page 106: "First they *remove* the reigning queen. Then". On page 107 he added, "This is the place." Page 114 contains another comment: "very good". Vertically on page 115 Clemens objected, "[John] Lubbock says no." (This referred to Maeterlinck's statement about the queen bee that "her people . . . venerate her.") Again on page 127 Clemens noted, "L says no."

Catalogs: *C1951*, #25a, listed among volumes containing Clemens's marginal notes, $30; "Property from the Library of Mark Twain," Butterfield & Butterfield, San Francisco, Sale 6613 (16 July 1997), lot 2683.

Location: Mark Twain House and Museum, Hartford, Connecticut.

Copy examined: Clemens's copy. Viewed in 1997 and 2019 in Hartford.

"It was Maeterlinck who introduced me to the bee. I mean, in the psychical & scientific way, & in the poetical way," Mark Twain wrote around 1902 ("The Bee," MS in Box #1, no. 1, MTP; *DE*, 26: 280). Farther on in this essay, which discusses the bee's habits in a comical but informed manner, Twain alludes to François Huber, Sir John Lubbock, and Maeterlinck as "the great authorities."

Paine, *MTB* (1912), p. 1162.

———. *Monna Vanna, A Play in Three Acts*. Translated by Alexis Irénée DuPont Coleman (1843–1904). New York: Harper & Brothers, 1903. 143 pp. [Also published in Paris in 1902.]

Isabel Lyon recorded in her journal that she and the Clemenses went "to the theatre to see a play by Maeterlinck, acted by his wife" on an unspecified date (probably in February 1904) while the Clemenses resided near Florence (IVL Journals, 28 February 1904, TS p. 14, MTP). *Monna Vanna* was set in fifteenth-century Italy. Odoardo Luchini, who represented Clemens in the lawsuit against the Countess Massiglia, added a postscript to his letter to Clemens of 14 February 1905: "P. S. My daughter wishes to know your exact address, in order to send you back *Maeterlinck's book Monna Vanna*" (ALS in MTP). Lyon replied on behalf of Clemens on 28 February 1905 that "he hopes you will not trouble to return the 'Monna Vanna', for there are no associations connected with the book" (PH in MTP).

———. *Thoughts from Maeterlinck, Chosen and Arranged by E. S. S. [Esther Stella (Isaacs) Sutro (1869–1934)]*, comp. New York: Dodd, Mead and Co., 1903. 283 pp.

Inscription: "To Miss Jean L. Clemens. Dec. 25, 1907."
Catalog: *Mott 1952*, item #69, $2.

MAHAN, ALFRED THAYER (1840–1914).

One of Clemens's ten nominations for the American Academy of Arts and Letters was "A. T. MAHAN (if he is the naval historian)" (SLC to Robert Underwood Johnson, 28 April 1905, ALS in the collection of the American Academy of Arts and Letters). Mahan was the author of *The Influence of Sea Power Upon History, 1660–1783* (Boston: Little, Brown and Co., 1890) and similar works.

MAHONY, FRANCIS SYLVESTER (1804–1866), pseud. "Father Prout." *The Reliques of Father Prout*. Illustrated by Daniel Maclise (1806–1870). New edition, rev. and enlarged. London: Bell & Daldy, 1866. 578 pp. [Publisher and pages conjectured.]

Inscription: the engraved title page is signed "Saml. L. Clemens, Hartford, 1875"; the frontispiece is signed "Saml."
Catalog: *A1911*, "12mo, cloth (engraved title loose), Lond. 1866)," quotes signatures, lot 311, sold for $3.50.

Mahony (pretending to be "Oliver Yorke") humorously discusses numerous topics while quoting ballads, songs, and poems from different nations and eras.

Maile Quarterly (Honolulu, monthly magazine, pub. 1865–). Also issued as *Maile Wreath*.

In Notebooks 5 and 6 (1865) Mark Twain alluded to an article from this journal of the Hawaiian Mission Children's Society, "The Legend of Ai Kanaka" (*N&J* 1: 164, 207).

MAJOR, CHARLES (1856–1913), pseud. "Edward Caskoden." *When Knighthood Was in Flower; or, The Love Story of Charles Brandon and Mary Tudor, the King's Sister*. Indianapolis: Bowen-Merrill Co., 1898. 249 pp.

Major's novel was among the best-sellers of 1900. Clemens knew in advance that he would meet "Mr. Major, author of 'When Knighthood was in Flower'" at a London dinner on 29 March 1900 (NB 43, TS p. 6a). On 22 January 1901 Clemens informed Emilie Rogers from New York City: "The family—by special request of Mr. Major, author of the play—are booked for the Criterion Theatre to-morrow night" (*MTHHR*, p. 458). Actually it was Paul Kester who had made the dramatization of Major's novel.

MALLESON, GEORGE BRUCE (1825–1898). *Dupleix*. Maps. Oxford: Clarendon Press, 1890. 188 pp. [Reprinted in 1892 and 1895. Clemens's edition has not been determined.]

In January 1896 Clemens noted the author, title, and publisher of this "beautiful book" about Joseph François Dupleix (1697–1763) (NB 37, TS p. 1). Dupleix revealed the "supreme characteristic" of the French, Clemens noted on 10 April 1896—"treachery"; the next day Clemens contemplated an essay about whether the human race should even be allowed to continue, and planned to cite Dupleix as a central example (NB 37, TS pp. 35, 36). As a French colonial administrator Dupleix became the governor general of French possessions in India, which put him at odds with the British. Recalled, he lost his fortune.

———. *The Indian Mutiny of 1857*. London: Seely and Co., 1891. 421 pp. [Reprinted repeatedly.]

While approaching Bombay on 18 January 1896, Mark Twain resolved: "'The Indian Mutiny'—Col. G. B. Malleson, C. S. I. Review it. Abuse his spelling of Kahnpur, &c" (NB 36, TS p. 19).

MALLOCK, WILLIAM HURRELL (1849–1923) *A Critical Examination of Socialism*. New York: Harper & Brothers, 1907. 303 pp.

Source: MTLAcc, entry #1359, volume donated by Clemens.

Mallock repudiates Karl Marx' views and points out errors of other socialist theories. He does acknowledge certain economic inequities and hopes these can be assuaged in the future.

———. *The New Republic; or, Culture, Faith, and Philosophy in an English Country House*. [First (anonymous) book publication took place in London in 1877. A New York edition was published in 1878. The edition Clemens read is unspecified and undetermined.]

Catalog: "Title page from *The New Republic*, written in 1878 by Wm. H. Mallock, upon which the owner, apparently on a ship with Clemens also a passenger, began a rather critical review in pencil beginning 'This is a book wh . . .' and then stopped writing; below his beginning, Twain has written in pencil 'Certainly it is./Yrs truly/S. L. Clemens/ Mark Twain/ 'Gallia'/Sept. 1/79'; below the printed title, the owner continues his review, which despite having a portion erased is nevertheless legible and brutal; four small gilt leaf adhesive stars are affixed at top and bottom not affecting content; 7.5 x 4, nice example of Twain's wit! . . . $895" (Edward N. Bomsey Autographs, Annandale, Virginia, List #40 [October 1990], item #81).

Clemens was indeed sailing on the Cunard steam liner *Gallia* from Liverpool to New York City on September 1st in 1879. In pencil he pronounced his view of *The New Republic*: "A book which treats of light things seriously; of serious things, lightly; of all things wittily,—which destroys without remaking, suggests without satisfying, inquires without answering, stops without ending" (Fears, *Mark Twain Day by Day* 1[2]: 867). Mallock's satiric novel, mainly dialogue, skewered aestheticism and Oxford Hellenism and at the time was considered an important contribution to utopian literature.

———. *The Reconstruction of Religious Belief*. New York: Harper & Brothers, 1905. 303 pp.

Inscription: (on the front free endpaper) "S. L. Clemens/ on his seventieth birthday/with the highest regard/and esteem of/G. Iles."

Location: Mark Twain Library, Redding, Connecticut. Donated by Clemens (MTLAcc, entry #923).

Copy examined: Clemens's copy, unmarked. Has the red ink Mark Twain Library accession number "923". Examined in 1970 and again in June 1982.

Although disputing dogmatic clerical and philosophical attacks on science, Mallock argues that some form of Deistic "prearrangements" must be conceded and that Theism is not necessarily invalidated by the latest scientific discoveries. He discusses the current theories of Huxley, Haeckel, Spencer, and others.

———. [Another identical copy.]

Source: MTLAcc, entry #1702, volume donated by Clemens.

MALORY, (SIR) THOMAS (c. 1415–1471). *The Boy's King Arthur; Being Sir Thomas Malory's History of King Arthur and the Knights of the Round Table*. Ed. by Sidney Lanier (1842–1881). Illustrated by Alfred Kappes (1850–1894). New York: Charles Scribner's Sons, 1880. 403 pp.

In "'The Master Hand of Old Malory': Mark Twain's Acquaintance with *Le Morte D'Arthur*," *English Language Notes* 16:1 (September 1978): 32–40 (revised as a chapter in Volume One of the present work), I established the fact that Clemens's introduction to Malory's heroes of the Round Table took place earlier than previously thought. One of his encounters with the Arthurian legend consisted of *The Boy's King Arthur*, a condensation prepared for children by Sidney Lanier that should be counted as a previously overlooked resource for Twain's *A Connecticut Yankee in King Arthur's Court* (1889). On 18 November

1880 someone in the Clemens household purchased "1 Boys King Arthur" for $2.40, according to a bill sent on 1 January 1881 by Brown & Gross, Hartford booksellers. The same statement also records another purchase on 13 December 1880 of "1 Boys King Arthur," also for $2.40. Very likely the latter was intended as a Christmas gift. Clemens paid up his account with the bookstore on 17 January 1881. (See also the Catalog entry for Sidney Lanier's edition of *The Boy's Mabinogion*.)

———. *Le Morte Darthur: Sir Thomas Malory's Book of King Arthur and of His Noble Knights of the Round Table*. The Globe Edition Series. Ed. by Sir Edward Strachey (1812–1901). Dark green cloth, gilt title on spine, gilt embossed globe on the lower spine, spine broken, endpapers and half-title page loose, covers worn. London and New York: Macmillan and Co., 1879. 509 pp. [First issued in 1868.]

Inscription: Clemens wrote "S L. Clemens/1884" in ink at the top of the table of contents. A "Mark Twain" inscription, replete with a flourish, appears in ink in a jerky, unusual script at the top of the half-title page (very likely George Washington Cable's designation of the book as a gift to his friend and fellow lecturer).

Marginalia: Clemens marked fifty-one pages, approximately ten of them with notes in both pencil and ink that total eighty-five words. He wrote "S L. Clemens" vertically in the margin beside the first extract employed in *A Connecticut Yankee in King Arthur's Court* (1889). Page 465 is folded down at the corner. On the rear endpaper Clemens made notes for a lecture reading in black ink: "Huck & Tom/Bluejays/Duel or Frog/Nt. Ride [i.e., Mary's Night Ride]."

Provenance: Clara Clemens Gabrilowitsch's library numbering system when she resided in Detroit is visible on the front flyealf. Apparently Clara sold the book in the 1940s or 1950s to a Los Angeles rare book dealer; probably Maxwell Hunley or Jake Zeitlin would be a good guess. A price of $35 is written in pencil on the verso of the front flyleaf.

Location: The current owners, who live in Connecticut, were given the book in 1985 by someone who has since died. (It was kept in a paper sack in their closet, and luckily survived a burglary in which jewelry and other items were taken from their home.) Taylor Roberts recounted the details of how the existence of this long-missing book finally came to light in "The Recovery of Mark Twain's Copy of *Morte Darthur*," *Resources for American Literary Study* 23.2 (1997): 166–180. Roberts described its title page, text, and annotations, adding a summary of the implications for studies of Twain's *A Connecticut Yankee in King Arthur's Court*.

Copy examined: Clemens's copy, when it was displayed by Taylor Roberts at the "State of Mark Twain Studies" conference on 16 August 1997 at Elmira College.

Alan Gribben, "'The Master Hand of Old Malory': Mark Twain's Acquaintance with *Le Morte D'Arthur*," *English Language Notes* 16:1 (September 1978): 32–40 (revised as a chapter in Volume One of the present work), demonstrated that Twain found his way to Sir Thomas Malory's prose romance earlier than commentators had realized—by at least 1880, in fact. This article also traced several patterns of his allusions, particularly his fondness for Sir Ector de Maris's grieving eulogy for his dead brother, Sir Launcelot.

Albert Bigelow Paine referred to the "little green, cloth-bound book" as the copy of Malory that entranced Clemens (*MTB*, p. 790). Robert H. Wilson—"Malory in the *Connecticut Yankee*," *University of Texas Studies in English* 27.1 (June 1948): 185–206—correctly established Sir Edward Strachey's Globe Edition as the text Mark Twain relied on in *A Connecticut Yankee* (1889, and described how Twain borrowed Malory's characters to burlesque medieval romances. Bernard L. Stein, editor of *A Connecticut Yankee in King Arthur's Court* (Berkeley: University of California Press, 1979), accordingly employed that edition "as copy-text for the extended quotations from Malory" (p. 612). Alan Gribben's *Mark Twain's Library: A Reconstruction* (1980) speculated that Clemens might have cannibalized the pages of his *Morte Darthur* for the lengthy extracts from Malory's work that appear in *A Connecticut Yankee*, since Clemens's copy had never resurfaced. Now, of course, that erroneous theory can be put to rest.

The commonly held assumption that George Washington Cable first introduced Clemens to Malory's *Le Morte D'Arthur* in a Rochester bookstore during the winter of 1884—a story set down by Clemens in 1889 (NB 23, *N&J* 3: 79) and repeated by Cable in 1910 (*MT&GWC*, pp. 135–136)—cannot withstand scrutiny. For one thing, there are the copies of *The Boy's King Arthur* purchased by the Clemenses in 1880 (see the preceding Catalog entry). Equally significant is the letter Clemens wrote to Mrs. Cincinnatus A. Taft on 14 August 1883 when her physician-husband was ill. From Elmira, Clemens urged that no one else be allowed to take up Dr. Taft's practice in Hartford: "For what is Sir Kay in Sir Launcelot's armor, but only Sir Kay, after all, & not Sir Launcelot?" (ALS in MTHM; quoted in *S&MT*, p. 170, where the letter was misdated as 17 August). Clemens and Cable would not begin their reading tour until more than a year after Clemens wrote, dated, and signed this letter. However, there *is* evidence that during their lecture tour Clemens was reintroduced to the Malory's prose translation of various Arthurian legends; he and Cable spoke its archaic dialect in jest to each other. In 1884 Clemens made an entry that anticipated *A Connecticut Yankee* in Notebook 23: "Dream of being a knight errant in armor in the middle ages" (*N&J* 3: 78). Reveling in its tales of chivalry and adventure, Clemens wrote to his daughter Susy during a stop in Indianapolis on 8 February 1885: "When I get home, you must take my Morte Arthur & read it. It is one of the quaintest and sweetest of all books." He quoted a passage on the death of Launcelot, comparing its eloquence to that of Lincoln's Gettysburg address . "In this book," Clemens wrote, "one finds out where Tennyson got the quaint & pretty phrases which he uses in 'The Idyls of the King'" (ALS, ASSSCL; MTP; *Family Sketch*, pp.138–139).

Clemens made various references to Malory's book. He alluded to Sir Ector de Maris's eulogy to Launcelot ("the courtliest knight that ever bare shield") in a tribute to Ulysses S. Grant that he wrote for the Hartford *Courant* (24 July 1885; reprinted in *AutoMT* 2: 218). On 20

January 1887 Twain named Sir Thomas Malory's *Morte D'Arthur* as one of his favorite books in a letter to the Reverend Charles D. Crane (ALS, Shapell Manuscript Library, Beverly Hills, California). In 1892 he again mentioned the "intrepid deeds of Launcelot (shut up in his safety-suit)" (NB 32, TS p. 40). The impact of the Jubilee Singers' majestic performance in Weggis, Switzerland "reminded me of Lancelot [*sic*] riding in Sir Kay's armor & astonishing complacent knights who thought they had struck a soft thing" (SLC to Joseph H. Twichell, 22 August 1897, *LMTJHT*, p. 198). When expressing doubts about the authenticity of the Holy Grail displayed by Archdeacon Basil Wilberforce (1841–1916) (12 September 1907 AD, *MTE*, pp. 343–344; *AutoMT* 3: 133), Twain alluded to King Arthur, Sir Galahad, Sir Bors de Ganis, and Sir Launcelot. Part 9 of Twain's *Is Shakespeare Dead?* (1909) alludes to Francis Bacon as "a Launcelot of the bar, the most formidable lance in the high brotherhood of the legal Table Round." See also the Catalog entry for Tennyson's *Idylls of the King*.

Paine, *MTB* (1912), pp. 790, 891, 1320, 1455, 1540; Olin H. Moore, "Mark Twain and Don Quixote" (1922), pp. 340–341; Henry Pochmann, "The Mind of Mark Twain" (1924), pp. 19, 179; John B. Hoben, "Mark Twain's *A Connecticut Yankee*" (1946), pp. 200–201—an especially lucid essay; Harold Aspiz, "MT's Reading" (1949), pp. 338–358; Howard G. Baetzhold, "'The Autobiography of Sir Robert Smith of Camelot': Mark Twain's Original Plan for *A Connecticut Yankee*," *American Literature* 32.4 (January 1961): 456–61; Henry Nash Smith, *Mark Twain's Fable of Progress: Political and Economic Ideas in "A Connecticut Yankee"* (New Brunswick: Rutgers University Press, 1964); James D. Williams, "The Use of History" (1965), p. 103; Robert Regan, *UH* (1966), p. 175; Howard G. Baetzhold, *MT&JB* (1970), pp. 102, 132–133; Evelyn Schroth, "Mark Twain's Literary Dialect in *A Connecticut Yankee*," *Mark Twain Journal* 19.2 (Summer 1978): 26–29 (examined Twain's alterations in Malory's prose style); Henry Nash Smith, "Introduction," *A Connecticut Yankee in King Arthur's Court*, ed. Bernard L. Stein (Berkeley: University of California Press, 1979), pp. 1–30; Allison R. Ensor, "The Magic of Fol-de-Rol: Mark Twain's Merlin," in *The Figure of Merlin in the Nineteenth Century and Twentieth Centuries*, eds. Jeanie Watson and Maureen Fries (Lewiston, New York: Mellen Press, 1989), pp. 51–63; Bruce Michelson, *Mark Twain on the Loose: A Comic Writer and the American Self* (Amherst: University of Massachusetts Press, 1995), pp. 157–158; Betsy Bowden, "Gloom and Doom in Mark Twain's *Connecticut Yankee*, from Thomas Malory's *Morte Darthur*," *Studies in American Fiction* 28.2 (Autumn 2000): 179–202.

MANDEVILLE, (SIR) JOHN (pseudonym of unknown compiler, fl. 14th century).

Clemens's copy of *Early Travels in Palestine* (1848) contained Mandeville's lengthy account of his putative journey to the Holy Land (see the Catalog entry for Thomas Wright, editor). Mandeville's narrative was one of the chapters Clemens annotated in Wright's book. On page 229 Clemens alluded to Hubert Howe Bancroft, which seems to suggest a post-1874 reading; the mixture of pen and pencil markings (pp. 127–282), however, indicate that he read the chapter attributed to Mandeville several different times. In an Autobiographical Dictation on 30 May 1907, Mark Twain mentioned "Sir John Mandeville" and ancient naturalists (*MTE*, pp. 22–23; *AutoMT* 3: 67).

MANING, FREDERICK EDWARD (1812–1883), pseud. "a Pakeha Maori." *Old New Zealand, A Tale of the Good Old Times; and A History of the War in the North Against the Chief Heke, in the Year 1845. Told by an Old Chief of the Ngapuhi Tribe.* Intro. by George Robert Charles Herbert (1850–1895), 13th Earl of Pembroke. London: R. Bentley and Son, 1887. 278 pp.

Inscription: (in black ink) "To Mr. Clemens, with Malcolm Ross' comps., Dunedin, 7 Nov. 1895."

Marginalia: a few marks and notes in pencil by Clemens, including those on pages 43 (he lines through the words "Be careful not to read *rations*"), 102 and 103 ("This" written in the margins), 107, 109 (marginal scoring), 125, 126 ("Begin here" noted in margin), 129 ("India again" noted at the top), 131 (marginal scoring), 150 ("This"), 158 ("Just like the case recorded by Herodotus," Clemens wrote alongside a Maori oracle's ambiguous prophecy).

Catalog: *Hunley 1958*, item #78, $18.50.

Location: Mark Twain Research Foundation, Perry, Missouri.

Source: Chester Davis (1903–1987) reported on this volume and its marginalia in *The Twainian* 37 (July-August 1978): 2–4 and 37 (September-October 1978): 1.

On 6 November 1895 Clemens noted in Dunedin, New Zealand: "Very valuable books given me by Malcom [*sic*] Ross—among them Old New Zealand" (NB 34, TS p. 32). In Chapter 35 of *Following the Equator* (1897), Mark Twain cites Maning's account of internecine native wars, explaining that Maning was among the "highest class of white men who lived among the Maoris in the earliest time [and who] had a high opinion of them and a strong affection for them."

Madigan, "MT's Passage to India" (1974), pp 361–362.

MANLEY, R. M., pseud. "Hilary Trent." *Mr. Claghorn's Daughter.* New York: J. S. Ogilvie Publishing Co., cop. 1903. 277 pp.

A letter from this author gave Mark Twain an opportunity to grouse in his *Autobiography* about how little he welcomed importuning missives from unknown writers seeking his approval of their efforts (undated dictation, *AutoMT* 1: 181, 520). But on 26 April 1903 (Fears, *Day by Day* 3: 849) Twain nevertheless notified Hilary Trent (Manley's pen name) that he had "read your book with a strong interest, because I am in sympathy with its sermon." (Manley was opposed to the concept of infant damnation implied in the Westminster Confession of Faith, part of the Presbyterian doctrine.) Clemens also praised "the grace & vigor of your style" (Alan C. Fox, Catalog 1 [1980]; copy in the Mark Twain Papers, Bancroft Library, University of California at Berkeley). Barbara Schmidt noticed that the publisher Ogilvie's advertisement in the New York *Sun* on 23 May 1903 cited the Brooklyn *Standard-Union*, which had quoted Twain's praise of his novel: "I have read it with strong interest, because of the grace and vigor of the style and because of the attractions of the story as a story" (Schmidt to Alan Gribben, email, 12 May 2007). I found a similar advertisement quoting Twain's endorsement in *The Literary World* (Boston) 34.9 (September 1903): 244. In *Mr. Claghorn's Daughter* theological problems interfere

in a contorted plot to keep a couple apart until wedding bells can ring in the final chapter. Most of the novel is laid in Germany; the parade of German cities and sights might have evoked pleasant memories for Twain, who had traveled extensively in that country. *The Churchman* (27 June 1903, p. iii) complained that *Mr. Claghorn's Daughter* "masquerades as a novel, but it is in reality a diatribe against religion in general, and the Westminster Confession in particular." Under his real name Manley had written two earlier novels. *Some Children of Adam* (1892), a novel about New York society life, earned praise from *Public Opinion* (13.2 [16 April 1892]: 47) for being "full of humor and sentiment." *Good Housekeeping: A Family Magazine* applauded the "mysteries, plottings, hypnotism, poison, and dramatic situations" of a lost world novel, *The Queen of Ecuador* (1894), in which "villainy is punished and the lovers drive away in the cool moonlight" (19.5 [November 1894]: 233). Manley and his wife seem to have lived abroad beginning in the 1890s; he sent reports to the New York *Times* periodically from Paris and Berlin into the early 1900s.

Joe B. Fulton, "Mark Twain's 'Corn-Pone Opinions,' 'Reflections on a Letter and a Book,' and 'Moral and Intellectual Man,'" *American Literary Realism* 50.2 (Winter 2018): 162–163.

MANN, MARY TYLER (PEABODY) (1806–1887), also known as Mrs. Horace Mann. *Moral Culture of Infancy, and Kindergarten Guide.* New York: J. W. Schemerhorn & Co., 1874. 206 pp.

Source: MTLAcc, entry #811, volume donated by Clemens.

MANNING, ANNE (1807–1879). *Deborah's Diary. A Fragment. By the Author of Mary Powell.* London: Arthur Hall, Virtue & Co., 1860. 140 pp.

Provenance: a bookseller's sticker on the front pastedown endpaper reads "C. Winter'sche/Sortimentsbuchhandlung/Heidelberg". Another bookseller's sticker on the rear endpaper reads "Westleys & Co./London."

Location: Mark Twain Library, Redding, Connecticut.

Copy examined: an unmarked copy that presumably belonged to a member of the Clemens family. Shelved with other volumes donated by Clemens. The binding is loose; some leaves may be missing. Has the Mark Twain Library accession number "3048". Examined in 1970 and again in June 1982.

Manning's historical tale purports to be a journal kept between 1665 and 1680 by John Milton's daughter, Deborah. The diction and spelling are deliberately archaic.

———. *The Household of Sir Thos. More.* New ed., with appendix. New York: Dodd, Mead & Co., [18—?]. 257 pp. [First published in book form in 1860.]

Source: MTLAcc, entry #569a, volume donated by Clemens.

A historical novel, written in deliberately antiquated English, about the fate of Sir Thomas More (1478–1535), beheaded for his refusal to accept Henry VIII as head of the Church of England.

———. *Passages in the Life of the Faire Gospeller Mistress Anne Askew.* New York: Dodd, Mead & Co., 1866. 232 pp. [Edition conjectured.]

Catalog: ListABP (1910), "Faire Gospeller", no other information provided.

A novelistic treatment of the religious persecution of the

Protestant heretic and preacher Anne Askew (1521–1546) during the reign of King Henry VIII. For her beliefs she was tortured on the rack and then burned alive.

MANNING, MARIE (1872–1945). *Judith of the Plains; A Novel.* New York: Harper & Brothers, 1904. 331 pp.

Source: MTLAcc, entry #1023, volume donated by Clemens.

Manning was a newspaper advice columnist (writing as "Beatrice Fairfax") as well as an occasional novelist. The title character Judith Rodney, a postmistress in the rugged Wind River Mountains of Wyoming, becomes acquainted with Mary Carmichael, a recent arrival from Virginia and governess for a sheep rancher. The romantic novel involves cattle rustling, a hanging, and other trademarks of Western frontier life.

MANNING, WILLIAM (d. 1905), comp. *The Year-Boke of the Odd Volumes: An Annual Record of the Transactions of the Sette. Seventeenth Year 1894–95.* Limited Edition. Number 136 of 149 copies. London: Privately printed, 1897. 205 pp.

Inscription: "To/Mr. Samuel L. Clemens/with the best regards/of the compiler/W. Manning/O. V. Seer./21 Radcliffe Gardens/London S. W./July 4, 1899."

Location: Mark Twain Library, Redding, Connecticut.

Copy examined: Clemens's copy, unmarked. Has the red ink Mark Twain Library accession number "4146". Examined in 1970 and again in June 1982.

On 1 July 1899 Clemens attended one of the monthly dinner meetings held by the Sette of Odd Volumes at Limmer's Hotel in London (NB 40, TS p. 57). Clemens wrote to William Manning from London on 5 July 1899 to "thank you most heartily for the book" (PH in MTP). The gift volume that Manning presented to Clemens contained the inaugural address of Francis Elgar, fifteenth president, delivered on 4 May 1894. The Sette of Odd Volumes was a book collectors' club founded in 1878 by the noted London bookseller Bernard Quaritch. Its monthly meetings featured talks by book collectors on their special interests. Manning was an expert on publications about the French magician Jean Eugène Robert Houdin (1805–1871).

MANSFIELD, WALTER EDWARD (1870–1916) and CHARLES HERBERT MANSFIELD (1864–1930), pseud. "Huan Mee." *A Diplomatic Woman.* New York: Harper & Brothers, 1900. 174 pp.

Source: MTLAcc, entry #1625, volume donated by Clemens.

The Mansfield brothers paired up to write a number of novels and short stories. Their melodramatic spy novel *A Diplomatic Woman* recounts the cool exploits of a Parisian, Mademoiselle Aidë Lerestelle.

MANZONI, ALESSANDRO (1785–1873). *I promessi sposi. The Betrothed.* London: George Bell and Sons, 1876. 723 pp.

Inscription: the half-title page is signed in pencil "S. L. Clemens, Hartford, 1876".

Catalogs: *C1951*, D55, listed with volumes signed by Clemens; *Zeitlin 1951*, item #33, $17.50.

Considered one of the classic Italian novels, this romance, set in the early seventeenth century, follows the tribulations of two lovers—Renzo and Lucia—cruelly separated by a lascivious nobleman. Among its memorable scenes is the depiction of Milan during the plague.

MAPES, VICTOR (1870–1943). *The Tory's Guest* (play, produced in 1900).

On 8 November 1900 Clemens noted his intention to attend a "Victor Mapes play" at the Empire Theatre in New York City (NB 43, TS p. 28). Thirty-year-old Victor Mapes was the nephew of Mary Mapes Dodge, editor of *St. Nicholas* magazine. David H. Fears identified Mapes' *The Tory's Guest*, a four-act American history drama, as the play Clemens attended with Henry H. Rogers and Chester Lord (*Day by Day* 3: 416). One of its principal characters was George Washington. Mapes, a Columbia University graduate in 1891, had already gained experience in New York City as a stage manager and dramatic critic.

Maps and Views to Accompany a Message from the President of the United States to the . . . First Session Thirty-third Congress, Dec. 6, 1853. Washington, D. C., 1853–54.

Catalog: *A1911*, "sm. folio, cloth, Wash. 1853–4," lot 313, sold for .25¢. A note by William Stotts, surveyor of the port of Keokuk, Iowa, was laid in the small folio volume; the note is dated May 1861. Also laid in was a list of names written in Clemens's hand that included "Gilder, Millet, Carnegie, Brander Matthews."

President Franklin Pierce had delivered his State of the Union address to Congress on the preceding day, 5 December 1853. William E. Stotts (born c. 1809) was Orion Clemens's father-in-law.

MARBOT, JEAN-BAPTISTE-ANTOINE-MARCELINE, BARON DE (1782–1854). *Mémoires du Général Bon de Marbot.* [First published in 1891; translated into English in 1892.]

Catalog: *ListABP* (1910), "Memoires du Gen. Marbot", no other information supplied.

Marbot's *Mémoires* granted readers a front-row view of the Napoleonic era.

MARCET, JANE (HALDIMAND) (1769–1858). *Conversations on Chemistry, in Which the Elements of That Science Are Familiarly Explained, and Illustrated with Experiments, . . . to Which Are Now Added, Explanations of the Text . . . by J[ohn]. L[ee]. Comstock [1789–1858] and a New and Extensive Set of Questions by J[ohn]. L[auris]. Blake [1788–1857].* Illus. Leather cover, flaking. Hartford, Connecticut: Oliver D. Cooke and Co., 1826. 348 pp.

Inscription: the front free endpaper is inscribed in pencil, "Betsey and Lydia Hill's Book". The rear free endpaper is signed in black ink: "Morris Hill's Book/Wilbraham, Mass. Dec 16th 1827".

Location: Mark Twain Library, Hartford, Connecticut.

Copy examined: in June 1982 this volume was shelved with the books donated to the Mark Twain Library by Clemens and his daughter Clara Gabrilowitsch, but this was in all likelihood merely because of its early imprint. There is every indication that it was among the many old schoolbooks donated by descendants of the Hill family, and that it never belonged to Clemens or his family members. I recommended that it be separated from the Clemens collection.

———. *Conversations on Natural Philosophy; in Which the Elements of That Science Are Familiarly Explained, and Adapted to the Comprehension of Young Pupils . . . Improved . . . by Illustrative Notes and a Dictionary of Philosophical Terms by J[ohn]. L[auris]. Blake [1788–1857].* Illus. Leather cover, flaking. Boston: Lincoln & Edmands, 1826. 252 pp. plus

plates. [Title on spine: *Blake's Natural Philosophy*.]
Inscription: the front free flyleaf is signed in pencil, "Betsey and Lydia Hill's Book."
Marginalia: a few marks that were clearly not made by Clemens.
Location: Mark Twain Library, Redding, Connecticut.
Source: Albert E. Stone's checklist of Clemens's books in the Mark Twain Library at Redding in 1955 included the title of this volume but supplied only its date (1826) and neither the place of publication nor the publisher. I was unable to locate the book in 1970.
Copy examined: this volume had resurfaced by the time I revisited Redding in June 1982 and I was able to determine that it was not one of the books donated by Clemens and his daughter Clara Gabrilowitsch and did not belong to Clemens or his family. The volume has no Mark Twain Library accession number, which is characteristic of the various school books someone donated that had once belonged to the Hill family of Redding Ridge.

MARCHAND, CHARLES M. *New Method of French Conversation*. Boston: Carl Schoenhof, [1887?]. 257 pp.
Source: MTLAcc, entry #1682, volume donated by Clemens.

MARCOSSON, ISAAC FREDERICK (1877–1961), pseud. "John S. Gregory," "Henry H. Rogers—Monopolist," *World's Work* 10.1 (May 1905): 6127–6130.
On 5 April 1905 Clemens read the manuscript of an article by Marcosson about Henry H. Rogers, the next day Clemens conferred with Rogers, and on 6 and 7 April Clemens discussed the article with "Mocasson" [*sic*] (Isabel V. Lyon's Journal, Mark Twain Archive, Gannett-Tripp Learning Center, Elmira College, Elmira, New York). Mary Boewe—"Mark Twain Anonymous," *Kentucky Review* 9.1 (Spring 1989): 42–55—revealed that Clemens contributed significantly to Marcosson's article, almost to the point of co-authorship. The Kentucky journalist Marcosson wrote two subsequent accounts of Clemens's contributions to his character-study of Rogers. Clemens was interested in defending the reputation of his financial savior, the vice-president of Standard Oil, who was under attack by anti-monopolist muckrakers. Boewe traced Twain's efforts between 1905 and 1910 to ameliorate the public image of his wealthy friend.
Isaac Frederick Marcosson, *Adventures in Interviewing* (London: John Lane, 1920), pp. 215–217, 244–247; Marcosson, "Mark Twain as Collaborator," *Mark Twain Quarterly* 2.2 (Winter 1937–1938): 7, 24.

MARCY, RANDOLPH BARNES (1812–1887). *Thirty Years of Army Life on the Border, Comprising Descriptions of the Indian Nomads of the Plains, Explorations of New Territory, A Trip Across the Rocky Mountains in the Winter*. Illus. New York: Harper & Brothers, 1866. 442 pp.
On the verso of Clemens's letter of 10 July 1884 requesting a book by Richard Irving Dodge and other "personal narratives" describing Native Americans in the West, Charles L. Webster noted a book Clemens might want: "Thirty Years of Army Life on the Border/Harper Bros./1866" (PH in MTP).

MARGUERITE D'ANGOULÊME, QUEEN OF NAVARRE (1492–1549). *The Heptameron of Margaret, Queen of Navarre*. Translated from the French, and with a memoir of the author,

by Walter K[eating]. Kelly (d. 1867). Portrait. Blind-stamped brown cloth, gilt lettering on spine. Spine panel separated at the back joint but rejoined by repair. London: Henry G. Bohn, 1864. 427 pp. The half-title page reads: "Bohn's Extra Volume."
Inscription: the recto of the frontispiece portrait of Margaret is signed in pencil, "Saml. L. Clemens/Hartford 1875".
Marginalia: several passages marked by Clemens.
Catalogs: A1911, "12mo, cloth, Lond.: Bohn, 1864, . . . several passages of the text have been marked," quotes the signature, lot 236, sold for $10.25; offered for sale by Restoration Books of Seattle in a list dated 29 November 2012 for $3,000 (list attached to an email from Joseph C. Baillargeon to Alan Gribben, 13 December 2012).
Provenance: Library of William E. Boeing, Seattle, Washington (in 2012). The volume probably entered that collection through a member of Bertha Boeing's New York banking family.
Location: collection of Kevin Mac Donnell, Austin, Texas. Purchased in January 2014 from Restoration Books of Seattle, Washington (email from Mac Donnell to Alan Gribben, 14 January 2014).
Source: I am grateful to Joseph C. Baillargeon of Restoration Books in Seattle for informing me about this volume while he was evaluating and disposing of the Boeing collection (Baillargeon to Alan Gribben, email, 18 October 2012). Baillargeon reported that the A1911 auction label was still present at the foot of the verso of the front free endpaper.
The Heptameron, modeled on Boccaccio's *Decameron* and daringly ribald, was first published shortly after its author's death. It consists of seventy-two old French tales told by travelers who seek to entertain themselves by relating "true" stories while a bridge is completed. In Mark Twain's *1601* (1880), Sir Walter Raleigh relates a bawdy tale of attempted rape which he attributes to "ye ingenious Margrette [*sic*] of Navarre" (Franklin J. Meine's edition, privately printed for the Mark Twain Society [Chicago, 1939], p. 39). In "The Walt Whitman Controversy" (DV36, MTP), a manuscript possibly written in 1882, Clemens says that he owns a copy of Marguérite's collection of tales; he begins to quote ("at random—it is all alike") from Tale 46 to demonstrate its unsuitability for young readers. Clemens also mentions—but does not name—a story from *The Heptameron* that exceeds even Rabelais in "filthiness." Chapter 1 of *Life on the Mississippi* (1883) mentions that "when DeSoto took his glimpse of the river. . . . Margaret of Navarre was writing the 'Heptameron' and some religious books,—the first survives, the others are forgotten, wit and indelicacy being sometimes better literature-preservers than holiness." Hank Morgan recorded that in Arthur's court: "Ladies answered back with historiettes that would almost have made Queen Margaret of Navarre or even the great Elizabeth of England hide behind a handkerchief" (CY [1889], Ch. 17). Baetzhold, *MT&JB* (1970), pp. 82, 83, 337 n. 31.

———. *The Mirror of the Sinful Soul. A Prose Translation from the French of a Poem by Queen Margaret of Navarre, Made in 1544 by the Princess (Afterwards Queen) Elizabeth, Then Eleven Years of Age. Reproduced in Fac-Simile, with Portrait, for the Royal Society of Literature of the United Kingdom*. Ed. by Percy W[illoughby]. Ames (1853–1919). London: Asher and Co., 1897. 65 pp.

    Catalog: *A 1911*, "8vo, half calf, Lond. 1897," with a sheet of notes about prominent authors laid in, lot 335, sold for $9.

    Location: Henry E. Huntington Library, San Marino, California.

    Copy examined: Clemens's copy, unmarked. Inspected on 17 July 1997. Entry #335 from an unidentified rare book catalog (advertising this volume) is affixed to the front pastedown endpaper. Two newspaper clippings about Mark Twain—both dated 25 May 1899—are inserted loose in the book.

Extremely pious but also concerned about Church corruption, Marguerite would gradually begin to support the efforts of religious reformers in her century.

MARIOT DE BEAUVOISIN, AUGUSTE (d. 1879). *A Summary of the French Verbs, Embracing an Entirely New System of Conjugation, by Which the Forms of Any French Verb Can Be Ascertained at a Glance.* First published under this title in 1862; often reprinted thereafter in London.

In Mark Twain's "Playing Courier" (1891), the narrator expects his charges to fetch their *French Verbs at a Glance*.

MARKHAM, EDWIN (1852–1940). *The Man with the Hoe and Other Poems.* New York: Doubleday & McClure, 1899.

    Marginalia: eight pencil ticks are visible in the table of contents. There is one mark on page 43, which contains the four-line poem "Infinite Depths." (That gloomy poem refers to "the silent depths of every heart" and "the awful shadow-form" thrown there by "the Eternal.")

    Provenance: shows the shelfmarks of the library numbering system that Clara Clemens Gabrilowitsch employed during her Detroit years. Sold at the 1951 auction in Hollywood but not listed in the sale sheet.

    Catalog: "Property from the Library of Mark Twain," Butterfield & Butterfield, San Francisco, Sale 6613 (16 July 1997), lot 2712.

    Location: Mark Twain House and Museum, Hartford, Connecticut.

    Copy examined: a book from the Clemens family's library and most likely Clemens's personal copy. Viewed in Hartford in 1997.

Markham's title poem, describing a laborer "stolid and stunned, a brother to the ox," was inspired by Jean-Francois Millet's painting of the same name.

MARKS, JEANNETTE AUGUSTUS (1875–1964) and **JULIA ELEANOR MOODY** (1869–1959). *Little Busybodies; The Life of Crickets, Ants, Bees, Beetles, and Other Busybodies.* Illus. New York: Harper & Brothers, 1909. 182 pp.

    Source: MTLAcc, entry #1185, volume donated by Clemens.

MARLOWE, CHRISTOPHER (1564–1593). *Hero and Leander* (published in 1598).

"In the Hellespont we saw where Leander and Lord Byron swam across, the one to see her upon whom his soul's affections were fixed with a devotion that only death could impair, and the other merely for a flyer" (*IA* [1869], Ch. 33). Clemens once wore a bathing-suit when enacting a parlor-game charade of Leander's separation from Hero (*MFMT*, p. 58). Edward Simmons recalled an afternoon at the Players Club in New York City when Clemens read aloud Lincoln's "Gettysburg Address," introducing it as "the greatest piece of prose since the days of Marlowe"

(*From Seven to Seventy: Memories of a Painter and Yankee* [New York: Harper & Brothers, 1922], p. 318).

MARRIOTT, CRITTENDEN (1867–1932). *Uncle Sam's Business Told for Young Americans.* New York: Harper & Brothers, 1908. 321 pp.

    Source: MTLAcc, entry #1603, volume donated by Clemens.

A basic explanation of the many roles of the United States government in serving the interests of its citizens.

MARRYAT, FREDERICK (1792–1848). *The Children of the New Forest* (novel, published in 1847).

This was a favorite book of the Clemens girls that their father sometimes read aloud to them (*MFMT*, p. 25). A work of historical fiction set in the days of the English Civil War, the novel depicts the plight of the four Beverly children who are orphaned during the ferocious conflict between the Puritans and the Cavaliers. Taken in by a kindly gamekeeper after they flee into the New Forest, they must adjust to cottage life in the woods. *The Children of the New Forest* was one of a series of fictional works, including *Masterman Ready* (1841) and *The Settlers in Canada* (1844) that Marryat aimed largely at youthful readers.

———. *A Diary in America, with Remarks on Its Institutions.* 12mo, cloth (worn and loose). New York, 1839. [Editions of 263 pages were published in New York City in 1839 by both D. Appleton & Co. and William H. Colyer. Clemens owned one or the other of these.]

    Inscription: the title page is signed "S. L. Clemens."

    Marginalia: some passages are marked and there are a few comments in pencil, according to *A1911*.

    Catalog: *A1911*, "12mo, half cloth (label damaged), N.Y. 1839, . . . some passages marked and a few remarks in pencil," quotes the signature, lot 314, sold for $4.50.

Marryat toured Canada and the United States in 1837–1838, producing this meandering, penetrating diary of his impressions. He followed other preceding English travelers, of whom he favored Frances Trollope over Harriet Martineau. See also the Catalog entry below for *Second Series of A Diary in America, with Remarks on Its Institutions.*

Dewey Ganzel, "Twain, Travel Books" (1962), p. 41 n. 4.

———. *Newton Forster; or, The Merchant Service* (novel, published in 1832).

Marryat was a British naval officer during the Napoleonic Wars before he turned to writing fiction. *Newton Forster* relates the adventures of a man who finds himself in the merchant navy. Chapter 1 of Mark Twain's *The Innocents Abroad* (1869) paraphrased this renowned seafaring authority: "Captain Marryatt writes: 'I do not know a spot on the globe which so much astonishes and delights upon first arrival as Madeira.'" JoDee Benussi located this sentence in Chapter 34 of Marryat's *Newton Forster*: "I do not know a spot on the globe which astonishes and delights, upon your first landing, as the island of Madeira" (Benussi to Alan Gribben, email, 1 April 2007).

———. *The Pacha of Many Tales.* Author's Edition. London: George Routledge & Sons, [1874?]. 155 pp. Paperbound.

    Source: MTLAcc, entry #221, volume donated by Clemens.

This collection of stories, first published in London in 1835, features a bored Turkish pacha who searches for entertaining story-tellers. In 1878, ensconced in a gondola being rowed near Venice, "a steady, heavy rain" falling outside, Clemens lit a cigar, propped up his feet, and—"wonderfully snug & cosy"—"got out Marryat's Pacha of Many Tales & read" (13 October 1878, NB 16, N&J 2: 209). (Clemens varied in his spelling of Marryat's name.) In "Villagers of 1840–3" (written 1897), Clemens listed "Marryatt" among the favorite authors of early-day Hannibal residents (HH&T [1969]), p. 34.

———. *Second Series of A Diary in America, with Remarks on Its Institutions*. Philadelphia: T. K. and P. G. Collins, 1840. 300 pp. [Publisher and pages conjectured.]

Marginalia: many passages bear Clemens's markings: he made brief pencil notations on pages 5 (regarding Harriet Martineau); 25 (noting a humorous remark about military life); 34 (correcting the size of the Van Rensselaer estate in New York); 67 (concerning the Yankee propensity for whittling); 71 (the Blue Laws); 118 (favorably commenting on a description); 124 (referring to the martyred abolitionist Elijah P. Lovejoy, killed in 1837); 124 (another note, specifying "20,000 in St. L[ouis]," and underlining a passage that appears in Chapter 22 of *Life on the Mississippi*); and 129 (querying a date). Regarding manners in New York City, Clemens remarked, "Conductors, and even hotel clerks, are almost civil now" (the latter comment quoted in *A1911*).

Catalogs: *A 1911*, "12mo, cloth (worn and loose), Phila 1840," quotes and characterizes the marginalia, lot 315, sold for $4; George D. Smith, New York City, "Catalogue of Books" (1911), "Second Series," quotes a comment about New York City manners, item #256, $12; Edward Morrill & Son Rare and Scholarly Books and Prints, Catalogue No. 132 (Boston, 1967), page 36, item #791, $275, "covers almost loose, lacks most of label," quotes marginalia; described more fully in a letter from Edward Morrill & Son to Theodore H. Koundakjian, 2 February 1967, PH in MTP.

On 22 July 1882 W. Rowlands wrote to Clemens for James R. Osgood to report that he was sending "a lot of books relating to travel in the U. S. by English people in the first half of the century. . . . They include Mrs. Trollope, Basil Hall and Marryatt [sic], &c, &c." (ALS in MTP; partially published in *MTLP*, ed. Hamlin Hill, p. 158 n. 2). Chapter 27 of Mark Twain's *Life on the Mississippi* (1883) quotes "Captain Marryat, R. N., author of the sea tales," about the dangerous look of the river. "It is a furious, rapid, desolating torrent, loaded with alluvial soil, and few of those who are received into its waters ever rise again. . . . Instead of reminding you, like other beautiful rivers, of an angel which has descended for the benefit of man, you imagine it a devil." Dewey Ganzel's "Samuel Clemens and Captain Marryat," *Anglia* 80 (1962): 405–416 compared Captain Marryat's *A Diary in America* with its direct impact on *Life on the Mississippi* (1883) and noted a concomitant effect on *Huckleberry Finn* (1885). For instance, the religious camp meeting episode in Chapter 20 of *Adventures of Huckleberry Finn* (1885) probably drew upon Marryat's description of a revival meeting he attended near Cincinnati (Ganzel, pp. 407–410). Ganzel seemed less successful in his attempts to demonstrate a Colonel Sherburn-Captain Marryat

connection (Ganzel, pp. 411–414).

Ganzel convincingly demonstrated that in Chapter 29 of *Life on the Mississippi* Twain took Marryat's account of the "cruelty, brutality, heartlessness, treachery, and . . . comprehensive vileness and shamelessness" displayed by the outlaw John Murrell (including a lengthy extract Twain attributed to "a now-forgotten book") out of Marryat's *Second Series*, pages 89–92. Horst H. Kruse confirmed this uncredited borrowing from Marryat (*Mark Twain and "Life on the Mississippi"* [Amherst: University of Massachusetts Press, 1981], p. 59). Marryat had referred to "John Murel, the land pirate," as a "consummate villain" (p. 89) and a "cold-blooded villain" (p. 92) in recounting some of his deeds. Marryat cited "an octavo volume, published in the United States" (p. 89) as his source of information about the outlaw, and we now know that this book was Virgil A. Stewart's *History of the Detection, Conviction, Life and Designs of John A. Murel, The Great Western Land Pirate* (see that Catalog entry).

JoDee Benussi traced the verse of a song that Twain quotes in a deleted passage from *Life on the Mississippi* ("Englishman he beat/Two French or Portugee;/Yankee-doodle come down,/Whip them all three") to Marryat's Chapter 11, titled "Patriotism," in *Second Series of A Diary in America* (Benussi to Alan Gribben, email, 1 April 2007). See also the Catalog entry above for *A Diary in America, with Remarks on Its Institutions*.

Albert E. Stone, Jr., *IE* (1961), p. 177 n. 13; Ganzel, "Twain, Travel Books" (1962), p. 41 n. 4; and Barbara Ladd, "'Night after Night and Day after Day': Mark Twain and the Natural World," *Mark Twain Annual 17* (2019): 19.

MARSH, OTHNIEL CHARLES (1831–1899). *Fossil Horses in America* (published in 1874).

Soldier Boy discusses the American discoveries of this Yale paleontologist in Chapter 1 of "A Horse's Tale" (1906). Clemens made notes in July 1907 on the rear endpaper of Brueys's *L'Avocat Patelin* that credited "O. C. Marsh" for finding that "we had the first horse."

MARSH, JAMES BRAINERD TAYLOR (1839–1887). *The Story of the Jubilee Singers, with Their Songs*. [First edition published in 1881, with other editions following.]

Catalog: ListABP (1910), "Jubilee Singers", no other information supplied.

To raise funds on behalf of Fisk University the Jubilee Singers gave a cappela performances of spirituals sung by enslaved American Americans on antebellum plantations. Marsh had been an ardent abolitionist and newspaper editor, fought for the Union in the Civil War, and subsequently traveled as a promoter with the Jubilee Singers in England and Europe. If Clemens owned the 1882 edition of Marsh's book published by Houghton, Mifflin and Company, it would have given him the lyrics and melodies of 128 songs.

On 10 March 1873 Clemens vouched for the authenticity of the Jubilee Singers in a letter he wrote from Hartford to Tom Hood and the Routledge publishing house: "I was reared in the South, and my father owned slaves, and do not know when anything has so moved me as did the plaintive melodies of the Jubilee Singers. It was the first time for twenty-five or thirty years that I had heard such songs, or heard them sung in the genuine old way—and it is a way, I think that white people cannot imitate—and never can, for that matter, for one must have been a slave himself in order to feel what that life was and so convey the Jubilee Singers" (Gustavus D. Pike, *The Singing Campaign for Ten Thousand Pounds; or, The Jubilee Singers in Great Britain*. Rev. ed. [New York: American Missionary Association, 1875], pp. 14–15). Two years later Clemens reiterated his praise in a letter written from Hartford on 8 March 1875, stating, "I am expecting to hear the Jubilee Singers to-night, for the fifth time (the reason it is not the fiftieth is because I have not had fifty opportunities)" (Willard E. Martin, Jr., "Letters and Remarks by Mark Twain from the Boston *Daily Journal*," *Mark Twain Journal* 18.1 (Winter 1975–1976): 2–3; *MTLet* 6: 406). A letter from Clemens to Joseph H. Twichell of 22 August 1897 also lavished praise on the Jubilee Singers, whom he heard perform in Weggis, Switzerland (*LMTJHT*, p. 198). See also the Catalog entries for "John Brown's body" and "We shall walk through the valley."

MARSHALL, EDWARD (1870–1933). *Lizette: A Story of the Latin Quarter*. Illustrated by C[harles].D[avid]. Williams (1875–1954) and J. C. Fireman. New York: Lewis, Scribner & Co., 1902. 295 pp.

    Source: MTLAcc, entry #215, volume donated by Clemens. Marshall set his *vie de Bohème* romance in Paris.

MARSHALL, FRANCES (BRIDGES) (1839–1920), pseud. "Alan St. Aubyn." *Fortune's Gate*. London: Chatto & Windus, 1898. 306 pp.

    Source: MTLAcc, entry #252, volume donated by Clemens. This "Varsity"-type novel, intended to appeal to young women, was set in London and Cambridge and involved a swirl of scientific experiments, potential wealth, priority dilemmas, engagements, and marriages.

MARSHALL, JOHN (1818–1891). *Anatomy for Artists*. Illustrated with 200 anatomical woodcuts by J[ohn]. S. Cuthbert. New York: Macmillan and Co., 1878. 436 pp.

    Inscription: inscribed by Clemens to Karl Gerhardt, the young Hartford sculptor whose Paris studies Clemens supported. The flyleaf inscription is dated February 1881.

    Catalog: unidentified catalog description. A memorandum in the Mark Twain Papers in the Bancroft Library at the University of California at Berkeley noted that this volume was advertised for sale in 1977. Iwaki Meisei University in Fukushima, Japan possesses a photocopy of the inscription, according to a database compiled by the Mark Twain Project in the Bancroft Library at Berkeley.

MARSHALL, NINA LOVERING (1861–1921). *The Mushroom Book. A Popular Guide to the Identification and Study of Our Commoner Fungi with Special Emphasis on the Edible Varieties*. Illustrated with photographs by J. A. and H. C. Anderson. New York: Doubleday, Page & Co., 1901. 167 pp.

    Source: MTLAcc, entry #1222, volume donated by Albert Bigelow Paine, Clemens's designated biographer. Possibly Clemens saw this book, since the men exchanged reading materials.

———. *The Mushroom Book. A Popular Guide to the Identification and Study of Our Commoner Fungi with Special Emphasis on the Edible Varieties*. Illustrated with photographs by J. A. and H. C. Anderson. New York: Doubleday, Page, & Co., 1902. 167 pp.

    Source: MTLAcc, entry #741, volume donated by Clemens.

———. *The Mushroom Book. A Popular Guide to the*

Identification and Study of Our Commoner Fungi with Special Emphasis on the Edible Varieties. Illustrated with photographs by J. A. and H. C. Anderson. New York: Doubleday, Page & Co., 1904.

    Catalog: Ball 2016 inventory, Nature Library, Vol. X, from the Quarry Farm library.

    Location: Quarry Farm library shelves, under the supervision of the Mark Twain Archive, Elmira College, Elmira, New York.

Clemens had access to this book at Quarry Farm in Elmira.

MARSTON, ELLIS. *Of the House of Chloe; A Tale of the Times*. London: Simpkin, Marshall, Hamilton, Kent & Co., 1900. 262 pp.

    Source: MTLAcc, entry #216, volume donated by Clemens. Clemens would have concurred with the theme of this novel, whatever its questionable literary merits. The title character Chloe Mainwaring is reluctant to marry Hugh Fortescue when she learns he is a dedicated vivisectionist (i.e., a scientist who experiments on living animals). Ultimately he gives up the cruel practice, but not before his mother succumbs from the agony of knowing about the suffering her son is inflicting. Marston was among the women who had been active in the London Anti-Vivisection Society since the 1870s.

MARTEL DE JANVILLE, SIBYLLE GABRIELLE MARIE ANTOINETTE (DE RIGUETTI DE MIRABEAU), COMTESSE DE (1849–1932), pseud. "Gyp."

    Henry Fisher reported that Clemens called this French novelist and political satirist "warm, yet not torrid" (*AMT*, p. 198).

MARTIALIS, MARCUS VALERIUS (c. 40 CE–c. 103 CE). *The Epigrams of Martial Translated into English Prose. Each Accompanied by One or More Verse Translations from the Works of English Poets, and Various Other Sources*. Half-title: Bohn's Classical Library. Preface signed by Henry G[eorge]. Bohn (1796–1884). Original dark green cloth. London: Bell & Daldy, 1865. 660 pp.

    Inscription: the half-title page is signed in ink "Saml. L. Clemens/Hartford, 1875." An *A1911* auction label is affixed to the front pastedown endpaper.

    Catalogs: *A1911*, "12mo, cloth, Lond. 1865," quotes the signature, lot 316, sold for $6.25; *Selections from the Library of William E. Boeing, Part II* (2011), comp. Joseph C. Baillargeon, Restoration Books, Seattle, Washington, pp. 63–64.

    Location: collection of Kevin Mac Donnell, Austin, Texas. Acquired in 2011 (Mac Donnell to Alan Gribben, 29 November 2011). No marginalia are visible.

Martial, who benefited from the patronage of the Roman emperors Titus and Domitian, left behind more than a dozen books of epigrams.

MARTIN, BENJAMIN ELLIS (1838–1909). *In the Footprints of Charles Lamb*. Illus. New York: Charles Scribner's Sons, 1890. 193 pp.

    American physician, world traveler, and literary biographer Martin described the residences and other sites associated with the writings of the English essayist Charles Lamb (1775–1834).

MARTIN, EDWARD SANDFORD (1856–1939). *The Courtship of a Careful Man, and a Few Other Courtships*. Illustrated by Howard Chander Christy (1873–1952), T[homas]. K[ing].

Hanna (1872–1951), and Margaret West Kinney (b. 1872). New York: Harper & Brothers, 1905. 185 pp.

Source: MTLAcc, entry #1437, volume donated by Clemens.

A co-founder of *The Harvard Lampoon*, the humorist and essayist Martin was also the first editor of *Life Magazine*.

———. *Lucid Intervals*. Illus. New York: Harper & Brothers, 1900. 263 pp.

Source: MTLAcc, entry #667, volume donated by Clemens.

———. *Poems & Verses*. New York: Harper & Brothers, 1902. 125 pp. [Publisher and pages conjectured.]

Inscription: the front pastedown endpaper is signed "Clemens, 1902."

Catalog: *A1911*, "12mo, cloth, gilt top, uncut, N.Y. 1902," quotes the signature, lot 317, sold for $2.

———. [An identical copy.]

Source: MTLAcc, entry #2062, volume donated from Clemens's library by Clara Clemens Gabrilowitsch in 1910.

MARTIN, HENRI (1810–1883). *A Popular History of France, from the First Revolution to the Present Time*. Translated by Mary Louise Booth (1831–1889) and Abby Langdon Alger (1850–1917). Illus. 3 volumes. Boston: Dana Estes and Charles E. Lauriat, [cop. 1877–1882]. [Publisher and date conjectured.]

Inscription: the front flyleaf of each volume is signed, "S. L. Clemens."

Catalogs: *A1911*, "3 vols., royal 8vo, full polished tree calf, gilt edges, Bost. 1882," quotes the signatures, lot 318, sold for $9 total; Stan. V. Henkels (Philadelphia), Catalogue 1057, 14 May 1912, "3 vols., 8vo, full tree calf, gilt, gilt edges, Boston, n.d. . . . autograph on flyleaf, 'S. L. Clemens,' in each volume," item #119 (PH in MTP); American Art Association, New York City, auction of 15–16 April 1929, lot 235, with *A1911* sale label and "S. L. Clemens" in each volume, "3 vols., royal 8vo, full tree calf, gilt edges (backs repaired), Boston, no date."

MARTIN, JOHN (1846–1876). *A Legacy, Being the Life and Remains of John Martin, Schoolmaster and Poet*. Ed. by Dinah Maria (Mulock) Craik (1826–1887). New York: Harper & Brothers, 1878. 294 pp.

Source: MTLAcc, entry #1137, volume donated by Clemens.

As a favor to John Martin, an unsuccessful and dying writer, the novelist and poet Craik promised to edit and publish his literary efforts. Critics acknowledge that Martin's diary contains certain passages of merit; the rest of his work has passed into oblivion.

MARTIN, MARTHA (EVANS) (1861–1925). *The Friendly Stars*. Intro. by Harold Jacoby (1865–1932). Illus. First edition. Original dark blue cloth, gilt. New York: Harper & Brothers, 1907. 264 pp.

Inscription: the front pastedown endpaper is signed and dated by Clemens in black ink, "S L. Clemens/1907."

Marginalia: Clemens made four "X" marks on page 18 and one "X" mark on page 19, singling out five of what Martin termed "the twenty brightest stars". Clemens's vertical pencil marks occur on pages 23, 25, and 28 where Martin locates constellations visible in the night sky.

Catalogs: *C1951*, D59, listed among volumes signed by Clemens; offered by Randall House Rare Books and Manuscripts, San Francisco, August 1983, $450; *Sotheby's*

2003, #197, $5,500 (sold with two other titles from Clemens's library).

Provenance: has the shelfmark of Clara Clemens Gabrilowitsch's private library collection from the period when she resided in Detroit. Purchased by Nick Karanovich of Fort Wayne, Indiana in August 1983 from Randall House (Karanovich to Alan Gribben, 30 August 1983).

Location: collection of Kevin Mac Donnell, Austin, Texas.

Copy examined: Clemens's copy, in July 2004. In addition Nick Karanovich sent photocopies of the inscription, title page, and markings to Alan Gribben on 30 August 1983.

Here is further evidence of Clemens's growing interest in astronomy in the last decade of his life. His was the first generation to peer deeply enough into space through improved telescopes (a forty-inch refracting telescope had been constructed in 1897) to gain a sense of its immensity. Harold Jacoby, who wrote the introduction to *The Friendly Stars*, was a prominent astronomer who pioneered the use of photography in observing and measuring outer space.

———. [An identical copy.]

Source: MTLAcc, entry #1620, volume donated by Clemens.

MARTIN, ROBERT J[ASPER]. (1846–1905). "Killaloe" and "Ballyhooly" (English and Irish music hall songs).

Clemens referred to and quoted "Killaloe" a number of times in Notebook 29 (*N&J* 3: 450, 492, 496, 511, 513, 569) and also alluded there to "Ballyhooly" (*N&J* 3: 551).

MARTIN, THOMAS COMMERFORD (1856–1924). "Nikola Tesla," *Century Magazine* 47.4 (February 1894): 582–585.

In February 1894 Clemens wrote to Olivia about his meeting "Nikola Tesla, the world-wide illustrious electrician; see article about him in Jan. or Feb. Century" (*MTL*, p. 609).

MARTINE, ARTHUR. *Martine's Sensible Letter-Writer; Being a Comprehensive and Complete Guide and Assistant for Those Who Desire to Carry on an Epistolary Correspondence; Containing a Large Collection of Model Letters*. New York: Dick & Fitzgerald, [cop. 1866]. 206 pp.

Source: MTLAcc, entry #2146, volume donated from Clemens's library by Clara Clemens Gabrilowitsch in 1910.

MARTINEAU, HARRIET (1802–1876). *Autobiography*. Ed. by Maria Weston Chapman (1806–1885). 2 vols. Boston: James R. Osgood & Co., 1877.

Clemens may have been alluding to Martineau's anecdote on page 278 (about the "feminine oaths of a hundred years ago" sworn by Mary and Agnes Berry) when he wrote in Notebook 14 (*N&J* 2: 101) in June 1878: "English swore (Misses Berry?) up to end of last century." [The sisters Mary Berry (1763–1852), a writer, and Agnes Berry (1764–1852), an amateur artist, were popular society figures during the Regency and favorites of Horace Walpole.] The editor of Martineau's *Autobiography*, Maria Weston Chapman, added a substantial biography of Martineau. Chapman had been an ardent abolitionist and was prominent in the mounting crusade for women's rights.

———. *The Hour and the Man. An Historical Romance*. 2 vols. Blue cloth, paper labels. New York: Harper & Brothers, 1841.

Inscriptions: the title page of Volume I is signed in pencil, "Ida C. Langdon/1878." Title page of Volume II is signed in pencil, "Ida C. Langdon/1878". Ida Clark Langdon (1849–1934) was married to Charles Jervis Langdon

(1849–1916).

Provenance: bookplates #430 and #431 of the "J. Langdon Family Library."

Catalog: Ball 2016 inventory list of the Langdon family library books (Mark Twain Archive, Elmira College).

Location: Quarry Farm library shelves, under the supervision of the Mark Twain Archive, Elmira College, Elmira, New York.

Copy examined: a novel available to Clemens whenever he visited the Langdons' home during his numerous trips to Elmira. Examined on 26 May 2015.

Harriet Martineau's name came to Mark Twain's attention when he was discussing the Byron scandal in a 9 September 1869 column for the Buffalo *Express* (*MTBE*, p. 42).

———. *The Peasant and the Prince: A Story of the French Revolution.* New York: D. Appleton and Co., 1841. 180 pp. [Reprinted in 1848.]

Howard G. Baetzhold—"Mark Twain's *The Prince and the Pauper*" (1954)—found it pertinent that Martineau wrote a historical novel by this title and that Mark Twain reminded himself while writing *The Prince and the Pauper* (1881): "Miss Martineau describes a coronation. See 'Little Duke'" (DV115, MTP). Twain was confused: Martineau never published a book with such a title; Charlotte M. Yonge published *The Little Duke*. But the similarity of titles between Mark Twain's novel and Martineau's *The Peasant and the Prince* is suggestive.

———. *Retrospect of Western Travel.* 2 vols. London: Saunders and Otley; New York: Harper & Brothers, 1838.

Inscription: Volume I was signed in ink by Clemens in 1875; the front pastedown endpaper of Volume II was inscribed in pencil in Clemens's hand: "T. W. Crane/to/S. L. Clemens/ Xmas 77."

Marginalia: in Volume I Clemens observed: "No matter whence a man comes, slavery brutalizes him. The hardest overseers were Northerners and Negroes." Clemens heavily annotated (in pencil) pages 5–17 of Volume II, the chapter entitled "Mississippi Voyage." Samples: "Think of this weary slow travel!" (p. 9); "Not like mate of St. Nicholas & man in Va City theatre" (cf. *N&J* 2: 536); and "Snagged & not *know* it!" (p. 12). There are no marks in Volume II beyond page 17.

Catalogs: ListABP (1910), "Retrospect of Western Travel, Martineau"; *A1911*, "2 vols., 12mo, cloth and boards (bindings not uniform), N.Y. 1838," quotes the signatures and one example of the marginalia, lot 319, sold for $6 (though both volumes were advertised, apparently only the first was sold); George D. Smith, New York City, "Catalogue of Books" (1911), "2 vols.[sic], 12mo, cloth and boards (bindings not uniform)," quotes the signature, item #257, $15; Vol. II only listed in "Retz Appraisal" (1944), p. 10, valued at $15.

Location: Volume II only is in the Mark Twain Papers, Bancroft Library, University of California at Berkeley. The number "49" appears in blue pencil on the title page and also on a red label pasted to the title page.

Copy examined: Clemens's copy of Volume II.

Clemens wrote delightedly to Mrs. Jervis Langdon on 25 December 1877 to thank the Langdon family for their Christmas gifts: "Theodore could hardly have sent me a book more to my liking than Miss Martineau's Western Travels—I am charmed with the calm way she sharpens the hob-nails in her No. 13s & walks over our late fellow citizens" (ALS in MTP).

Ganzel, "Twain, Travel Books" (1962), p. 41 n. 4.

———. *Society in America.* 2 vols. The cover of Volume I is embossed red cloth with a floral pattern. There is a paper label on the spine. Volume II has embossed brown cloth with a paper label on the spine. Third edition. New York: Saunders and Otley, 1837. [First American edition. A note in Volume I reports that both volumes were repaired in 1990, using original materials as much as possible.]

Marginalia: Volume I contains pencil marks on pages 109 (a vertical line beside her comments on the "depravity" of American newspapers), 111 (ditto), and 115 (where Clemens draws a vertical pencil line and writes the word "citizenship" in the margin near Martineau's comments on American political activities). The only chapters annotated in the first volume are those titled "Newspapers" and "Apathy in Citizenship." Clemens commented more extensively in Volume II, noting "Horrible" at the top of page 116, a discussion titled "Morals of Slavery" that described the use of enslaved women as mistresses and casual sex partners, and mentioned the quadroon women kept in New Orleans. He wrote "Rebuke of England" in pencil at the top of page 168, where Martineau remarks upon "the English insolence of class to class" (Americans manifest class disdain only toward blacks, whereas the English aristocracy scorn everyone below them); exclaimed "Good heavens!" in pencil at the top of page 209, in which Martineau treats American peculiarities of language, especially the reluctance to use the word "woman," preferring "ladies" and "females"; and marked (with pencil) pages 209 and 210, which concern the Americans' preference for the terms "females" or "ladies" instead of "women." On page 288 Clemens drew a line and commented in pencil ("Murderer of Helen Jewett") where Martineau told about a criminal case in which a young man, though guilty, was acquitted because the jury did not wish to have any more hangings. Clemens was alluding to a famous crime in America that had received sensational newspaper coverage. The suspected murderer of Helen Jewett (1813–1836), a twenty-five-year-old prostitute in a New York City brothel, was acquitted after a trial involving sordid testimony. Clemens added pencil marks and wrote "Literature" at the top of page 300, in which Martineau discussed popular books in America and quoted the *Edinburgh Review* concerning the unfortunate results for any country that lacks an esteemed national literature.

Location: Mark Twain Library, Redding, Connecticut (both volumes).

Copies examined: Clemens's copies of both volumes. Volume I (395 pp.) has a red ink Mark Twain accession number, "3442". Volume 2 is numbered "3443" in red ink. Both display the purple oval stamps of the Mark Twain Library. I examined both volumes in 1970 and again in June 1982 and found that the cover of Volume II was worn and its spine broken. By the time I returned on 9 November 2019 these defects had been repaired. When I made a visit to Redding on 12 August 1987 I learned that Volume I was being kept in a safety deposit box rented by the Mark Twain Library Association; Volume II was still present. In November 2019 these volumes were back together again in the Mark Twain Library collection. Yale University reproduced eighteen pages of Clemens's marginalia on microfilm, and the Mark Twain Papers at Berkeley contains a copy of this microfilm (Box #36) as well as a larger, more usable photocopy.

Evidently this was one of the "books relating to the river" that Mark Twain, preparing to write *Life on the Mississippi* (1883), requested of his publisher in July 1882. On 22 July 1882 W. Rowlands replied for James R. Osgood that he was sending "a lot of books relating to travel in the U. S. by English people in the first half of the century; twenty-five volumes in all. They include Mrs. Trollope, Basil Hall and Marryatt [sic], &c, &c." (ALS in MTP; partially published in *MTLP*, ed. Hamlin Hill, p. 158 n. 2). The portion of the *Life on the Mississippi* manuscript in which Twain discussed *Society in America* (primarily quibbling about the observation of the "usually so clear-visioned and accurate" Martineau that Americans had an aversion to the word "woman") was discarded in the final version of Twain's book, though the passages can still be read in the Heritage Press edition published in 1944. Ganzel, "Twain, Travel Books" (1962), p 41 n 4.

The Martyrs of Madagascar, and Other Books for Children and Youth. Illus. by Edward Bookhout (1823–1910). New York: American Tract Society, n. d. [1855?]. Paged variously.

Inscription: rear pastedown endpaper signed, "Joseph McNulty/McConnellsburg/Fulton/County/1859".

Location: Mark Twain Library, Redding, Connecticut.

Copy examined: a book mistakenly added to the Clemens collection by the time I revisited Redding in June 1982. It has no accession number and no indication that any member of the Clemens family ever owned the volume. I recommended to the staff that it be removed from the shelves containing the donations of Clemens and his daughter Clara Gabrilowitsch.

MARVIN, CHARLES THOMAS (1854–1890). *The Russians at the Gates of Herat.* Illus. Maps. Harper's Franklin Square Library, No. 463. New York: Harper & Brothers, [1885]. 46 pp.

First published in England, this book describes Russian expansion in the 1870s in the direction of India. Marvin prepared this brief, urgent report to alert the British that the Russians might have designs on India. Clemens wrote "The Russians at the Gates of Herat (Franklin Square)" in Notebook 24 (1885), *N&J* 3: 148. Herat is an ancient city in Afghanistan.

"MARY HAD A LITTLE LAMB" (nursery rhyme).

If (as seems likely) Clemens arranged the "Country School Exhibition," amateur theatricals presented on board the *Montana* between San Francisco and Panama on 10 July 1868, then it was he who chose this piece as part of the programme: "Poem—Mary had a little Lamb—Mr. O. G." (*Alta California*, 6 September 1868; reprinted in *The Twainian* 7 [November-December 1948]: 5). In Chapter 22 of *The Innocents Abroad* (1869) Mark Twain refers to St. Mark's "tame lion" which "used to travel with him—and everywhere St. Mark went, the lion was sure to go." In the course of the graduation declamations in Chapter 21 of *The Adventures of Tom Sawyer* (1876), "a little shamefaced girl lisped 'Mary had a little lamb,' etc., performed a compassion-inspiring curtsy, got her meed

of applause, and sat down flushed and happy." John D. Rockefeller, Jr. "thinks Joseph was Mary's little lamb; this is an error," quipped Mark Twain in a humorous letter he included in an Autobiographical Dictation of 20 March 1906 (*MTE*, p. 87; *AutoMT* 1: 423). In the last year of Clemens's life he composed in Notebook 49 a variation of the rhyme in German, which translates as "Mary had a little lamb,/and wanted to get another one—/The lamb has fallen down" (TS p. 2).

MARX, KARL (1818–1883).

What would Clemens have made of Karl Marx's *Das Kapital*? We will presumably never know, unless relevant clues finally surface. As things stand, here is another puzzling gap in the record of his reading. We must remember that many hundreds of titles from Clemens's library were never recorded before they were lost in his travels or donated to libraries.

MASCAGNI, PIETRO (1863–1945), composer. *Cavalleria Rusticana* (one-act opera, performed in 1890). Libretto by Guido Menasci (1865–1925) and Giovanni Targioni-Tozzetti (1863–1934). Based on a short story (and later play) by Giovanni Verga (1840–1922).

Susy Clemens mentioned the *Cavalleria Rusticana* in a poignant story she told her college friend Louise Brownell in a letter of 29 April 1892 written from Rome (Hamilton College Archives). From the Villa Viviani Clemens wrote to Clara on 5 November 1892: "Susy & the Kings [Grace and her sister] are down at the Opera—Cavalleria" (ALS in MTP). On 2 November 1903 Clemens noted that "the band (on the ship) played the Cavalleria Rusticana which is forever associated in my mind with Susy. I love it better than any other, but it breaks my heart" (NB 46, TS p. 29; *MTN*, p. 384). Isabel Lyon recorded how Clemens referred to the "Intermezzo" from this work as "the Susie one" in asking Miss Lyon to play it on 2 March 1906. He told Lyon that he could "*fit* the words" to this piece. "Susy calls to me in the Intermezzo, & her mother in the Largo," he said (IVL Journal, Harry Ransom Center, University of Texas at Austin).

———. *I Rantzu* (four-act opera, performed in 1892).

Clemens wrote to Clara from the Villa Viviani on 5 November 1892: "Susy & the Kings are down at the Opera—Cavalleria. Next Thursday they are going down to see its author fetch out his new opera" (ALS in MTP). Mascagni premiered *I Rantzu* in Florence on 10 November 1892. As it turned out, however, Susy was not able to attend that opening performance (Fears, *Day by Day* 2: 747, 748).

MASON, ALFRED EDWARD WOODLEY (1865–1948). *The Broken Road.* New York: Charles Scribner's Sons, 1907. 419 pp.

Source: MTLAcc, entry #1036, volume donated by Clemens.

In this novel difficulties of race, class, and culture complicate Shere-Ali's education in England and his subsequent return to India.

MASON, CAROLINE ATHERTON (BRIGGS) (1823–1890). "'Only Me'" (poem).

Clemens wrote to *The Independent* sometime in the late 1870s or early 1880s (his letter is dated 3 May) to request a copy of Caroline Mason's poem "which appeared in the Independent about last August or September. I can't recal the title of it: I only remember that a mother calls, 'Is that you, Pet?' & is answered, not by the favorite, but by another of her children, 'It isn't Pet, mamma, it's only me.' There are only 4 stanzas." He explained that he wished to use the verses in a platform performance: "I hate to make a reading entirely out of my own pathos" (TS in MTP). Mason's poem "'Only Me'" had three stanzas, not four. Its appearance in *The Independent*, a weekly New York City religious periodical, has not been traced. Clemens's memory was accurate about its poignant first stanza: "A little figure glided through the hall;/'Is that you, Pet?' the words came tenderly:/A sob—suppressed to let the answer fall—/'It isn't Pet, mamma; it's only me.'" Mason's "Only Me" was included in a posthumous collection of this suffragette's verse, *The Lost Ring and Other Poems* (Boston: Houghton, Mifflin and Co., 1891), p. 121. The 29 November 1884 issue of *The Literary World* (Boston) 15.24: 421 singled out Mason's poem: "Of more recent productions, a touching bit for mothers called "'Only Me'" has received the widest editorial favor."

MASON, EDWARD T[UCKERMAN] (1847–1911), ed. *British Letters Illustrative of Character and Social Life.* 3 vols. New York: G. P. Putnam's Sons, 1888.

Catalog: Ball 2016 inventory, leather bound, gilt spine, gilt edges, fine condition.

Location: Quarry Farm library shelves, under the supervision of the Mark Twain Archive, Elmira College, Elmira, New York.

Volumes available to Clemens whenever he visited Quarry Farm in Elmira, New York. The collection published examples of letters written by such distinguished figures as Wordsworth, Keats, Garrick, Wilberforce, Johnson, and Goldsmith.

MASON, FANNY WITHERSPOON (1848–1901), pseud. "Mary Frances." *Daddy Dave.* New York: Funk & Wagnalls, 1887. 116 pp.

Source: MTLAcc, entry #1848, volume donated from Clemens's library by Clara Clemens Gabrilowitsch in 1910.

An aging African American remains loyal to the family that had enslaved him. Born in South Carolina, Mason moved to Brooklyn, New York.

MASON, LOWELL (1792–1872), comp. *Carmina Sacra; or, Boston Collection of Church Music, Comprising the Most Popular Psalm and Hymn Tunes in General Use* (first published in 1841).

"The '*carminaia sacrae*'" was one of the books Clemens and his friends took to "the Humbolt" (SLC to Jane Lampton Clemens, 30 January 1862, Carson City, *MTLet* 1: 147).

MASSETT, STEPHEN C. (1820–1898). *"Drifting About"; or, What "Jeems Pipes, of Pipesville," Saw-and-Did. An Autobiography.* New York: Carleton, 1863. 371 pp.

In a letter written to Mary Mason Fairbanks from San Francisco on 17 June 1868, Mark Twain enclosed a clipping by "this good-natured, well-meaning ass, 'Pipes,'" whom Twain accused of using his and Artemus Ward's material for readings in Calcutta and Hong Kong (*MTMF*, p. 32; *MTLet* 2: 223). The English-born Massett, a monologist, actor, popular music composer, and author, had performed in San Francisco as early as 1849.

MASSON, DAVID (1822–1907). *The Life of John Milton, Narrated in Connexion with the Political, Ecclesiastical, and Literary History of His Time.* 7 vols. Index. Cambridge, London:

Macmillan & Co., 1859–1894.

"Mason's [*sic*] London '59 '71 (lit hist of the time)" was one of the "biogs of Milton" that Clemens listed in September 1887 (NB 27, *N&J* 3: 328).

Masters in Art: A Series of Illustrated Monographs, Issued Monthly. Part 4. Illustrated. Boston: Bates & Guild Co., 1900. 36 pp. Paperbound.

Source: MTLAcc, entry #403, volume donated by Clemens.

MATHER, COTTON (1663–1728). *Magnalia Christi Americana; or, The Ecclesiastical History of New-England from Its First Planting in the Year 1620, unto the Year of Our Lord, 1698.* 2 vols. Hartford, Connecticut: Silas Andrus; Roberts & Burr, Printers, 1820. [First American edition; an earlier London edition had been published in 1702.]

Inscriptions: both volumes were signed on the front free endpaper, "S. L. Clemens/Hartford Nov. 1881." The front pastedown endpapers of both volumes bear the *A1911* sale label.

Marginalia: on page 41 of the first volume Clemens marked a passage and wrote: "The wise man of one age is the idiot of the next." Beside another passage, where Mather describes how a man recovered from one illness, "but about half a year after this he fell into another sickness, whereof he dy'd," Clemens gibed: "But why didn't they rip out some more prayers and get him up again?" Clemens underscored "his three children" in Mather's account of a fire that killed a man's three children and destroyed his home, noting, "The miserable injustice of it."

Catalogs: *A1911*, "2 vols., 8vo, sheep (rubbed and cracked), Hartford, 1820," quotes the signature and three examples of marginalia, lot 320, sold for $37.50; George D. Smith, New York City, "Catalogue of Books" (1911), quotes the signature, item #261a, $50.

Location: Special Collections, Case Western Reserve University Libraries, Cleveland, Ohio. Donated in 1958 by Willis Thornton. Maureen Neff and Susie Hanson, former Special Collections Librarians, supplied information about these volumes.

Copies examined: photocopies of the title pages and inscriptions provided by Thomas A. Tenney on 29 October 1980.

Clemens underlined a reference to Mather's *Magnalia Christi Americana* on page 22 of J. Hammond Trumbull's *The True-Blue Laws of Connecticut and New Haven* (1876), a volume Clemens inscribed in 1877. Trumbull stated that Dr. Henry More's *Antidote to Atheism* "abounds in marvels, some of which are unsurpassed, as tests of credulity, by any in Mather's *Magnalia*"(Detroit Public Library, PH in MTP). As a facetious demonstration of the infallibility of Providence, Mark Twain cited Mather's *Magnalia Christi Americana* in an Autobiographical Dictation of 13 June 1906: "I remembered that in the Magnalia a man who went home swearing, from prayer-meeting one night, got his reminder within the next nine months. He had a wife and seven children, and all at once they were attacked by a terrible disease, and one by one they died in agony, till at the end of a week there was nothing left but the man himself. I knew that the idea was to punish the man, and I knew that if he had any intelligence he recognized that that intention had been carried out, although mainly at the expense of other people" (*MTE*, p. 261; *AutoMT* 2: 117). Coleman O. Parsons, "Background" (1960), p. 65.

———. *The Wonders of the Invisible World* (first published in 1693 in Boston).

In a fragment sometimes titled "Bible Teaching and Religious Practice" (possibly written in 1890), Mark Twain refers derisively to "the parson" at Salem who "clung pathetically to his witch-text after the laity had abandoned it in remorse and tears" (Baender, ed., *WIM?* [1973], pp. 75, 540). The Eskimos in Twain's "The Esquimau Maiden's Romance" (1893) adopt the Puritans' "trial by water" method of determining guilt. Chapter 4 of "The Chronicle of Young Satan," written between 1897 and 1900, relates the burning of Gottfried Narr's grandmother as a witch, together with another, similar story about eleven girls in a school (*MSM*, pp. 78–80). Frau Brandt is burned as a witch in Chapter 7 of the same work; she defies the villagers, refuses to confess or recant, and dies forgiving them for the sake of their innocent childhoods (*MSM*, p. 133). Twain mentions "the Witch Madness" in "The Secret History of Eddypus" (*FM*, p. 367), written 1901–1902, and reviles the witch burnings in "Three Thousand Years Among the Microbes" (*WWD?*, pp. 529–530), written in 1905. See also the Catalog entry for Samuel P. Fowler (ed.), *Salem Witchcraft* (1865).

William M. Gibson, ed., *MSM* (1969), p. 21.

MATHEWS, FRANCES AYMAR (1865–1925). *The Undefiled: A Novel of To-day*. New York: Harper & Brothers, 1906. 278 pp.

Source: MTLAcc, entry #1022, volume donated by Clemens.

Much of this romance is set in New York City. A woman's double identity is involved.

MATSON, NEHEMIAH (1816–1883). *Pioneers of Illinois, Containing a Series of Sketches Relating to Events That Occurred Previous to 1813; Also Narratives of Many Thrilling Incidents Connected with the Early Settlement of the West, Drawn from History, Tradition, and Personal Reminiscences*. Chicago: Knight & Leonard, Printers, 1882. 306 pp.

Inscription: "Samuel L. Clemens/Compliments of the author" (not in Clemens's hand).

Marginalia: black ink marks characteristic of Clemens appear on pages 186 (beginning of the first paragraph), 187 (beside references to the town of Cahokia in the first and second paragraphs), 188 (mid-page), and 189 (top).

Location: Mark Twain Library, Redding, Connecticut.

Copy examined: Clemens's copy. Has a red ink Mark Twain Library accession number, "3421". Examined in 1970 and again in June 1982.

MATTHEWMAN, LISLE DE VAUX (1867–1904). *Crankisms, by Lisle de Vaux Matthewman. Pictured by Clare Victor Dwiggins*. Illus. Philadelphia: Henry T. Coates & Co., 1901. 100 pp.

Inscription: Clemens inscribed the front free endpaper in black ink: "From the artist./SL. Clemens/Riverdale-on-Hudson/Feb. 1902".

Catalog: *A1911*, "4to, boards, N.Y. 1901," quotes the signature, lot 127, sold for $2.

Provenance: collection of Frank C. Willson (1889–1960) in Melrose, Massachusetts. Sold by his widow Margarete to the University of Texas in 1962.

Location: Harry Ransom Center, University of Texas at Austin.

Copy examined: Clemens's unmarked copy.

Matthewman's *Crankisms* are brief witticisms reminiscent of Mark Twain's Pudd'nhead Wilson maxims, illustrated with drawings of languid women and Gibson-type girls. Matthewman and Dwiggins subsequently published *Brevities: Companion Book to "Crankisms"* (cop. 1903), but Matthewman died of typhoid fever in New York City in 1904 before they could collaborate any further. The illustrator Clare Victor Dwiggins (1874–1958) would later ink a comic strip titled "Huckleberry Finn and Tom Sawyer."

MATTHEWS, BRANDER (1852–1929). "American Authors and British Pirates," *New Princeton Review* 4.2 (September 1887): 201–212.

Mark Twain published a querulous, antagonistic reply to this article in the January 1888 issue of the *The New Princeton Review* (pages 47–54) and Matthews responded with "An Open Letter to Close a Correspondence" in the same issue of the *The New Princeton Review* 5 (January 1888): 54–65. Matthews, a professor at Columbia University, was probably the most influential of the academic literary critics of his day. In 1899 he would supply an introduction to the first uniform edition of Mark Twain's writings; there he ranked Twain with Chaucer, Cervantes, Fielding, and Molière. Matthews also provided a prefatory "Appreciation" for *Europe and Elsewhere* in the so-called Definitive Edition of Twain's works (New York: Gabriel Well, 1922–1925).

See related Catalog entries for *The New Princeton Review* and James King Newton.

———. "American Fiction Again," *Cosmopolitan* 12.5 [March 1892]: 636–640).

Mark Twain occasionally crossed swords with Matthews, but he had to take into account the kind of praise Matthews lavished in this essay, which insisted, "In any list of the ten greatest American stories Huckleberry Finn [sic] must hold a high place" (p. 638). Matthews singled out, "beyond all," Twain's achievement in narration: "the author suppresses himself and makes us see with the eyes of Huckleberry Finn" (p. 638).

———. *Americanisms and Briticisms, with Other Essays on Other Isms*. Frontispiece portrait. First edition. Original green cloth, gilt, inner hinges broken. New York: Harper & Brothers, 1892. 190 pp.

Inscription: the front free flyleaf was inscribed in pencil by Matthews: "Col. Mark Twain/from his friend/B M/Nov 1893/The Players [Club in New York City]".

Marginalia: Clemens penciled the table of contents at the essay on Mark Twain; he also placed pencil marks on pages 5, 12, 14 (folded down), 150 (also folded down—the essay titled "Of Mark Twain's Best Story" begins on the facing page; there Matthews chooses *Adventures of Huckleberry Finn* as Twain's best), 151 (Clemens noted "1884–5" above the title of Matthews's essay), 152 (turned down), 152–153 (brackets penciled around a passage in which Matthews describes the moment in the cave in *The Adventures of Tom Sawyer* when the hand bearing a light turns out to be Injun Joe's as "one of the very finest things in the literature of adventure since Robinson Crusoe first saw a single footprint in the sand of the sea-shore"). There are no further marks, though other page corners are folded down.

Provenance: displays shelfmarks on the front pastedown

endpaper from Clara Clemens Gabrilowitsch's Detroit library collection; subsequently in the Carrie Estelle Doheny Collection, St. John's Seminary, Camarillo, California. Estelle Doheny had purchased the volume from Maxwell Hunley Rare Books of Beverly Hills in 1940. Auctioned by Christie's in New York City for $935 on 17 October 1988 (lot 1181) on behalf of St. John's Seminary.

Catalogs: ListABP (1910), "Americanisms and Britticisms [*sic*], Matthews"; Sotheby's *2003*, #182, $1,100 for this volume and Oliver Herford's *Artful Anticks*.

Location: collection of Kevin Mac Donnell, Austin, Texas.

Copy examined: Clemens's copy, in 1970 at St. John's Seminary and again in July 2004 in Austin, Texas. This collection contains an essay on "The Centenary of Fenimore Cooper"—an author who drew Twain's scorn.

———. [An identical copy.]

Source: MTLAcc, entry #658, volume donated by Clemens.

———. *Aspects of Fiction and Other Ventures in Criticism*. Red cloth. New York: Harper & Brothers, 1896. 234 pp.

Provenance: Antenne-Dorrance Collection, Rice Lake, Wisconsin.

Location: Mark Twain Archive, Gannett-Tripp Learning Center, Elmira College, Elmira, New York.

Copy examined: Clemens's copy, unmarked. Examined on 28 May 2015.

Chapter three of Matthews's book is titled "The Penalty of Humor," in which Matthews paid homage to Mark Twain. See the Matthews entry below for "The Penalty of Humor."

———. *Aspects of Fiction and Other Ventures in Criticism*. New York: Harper & Brothers, 1900. 234 pp.

Source: MTLAcc, entry #859, volume donated by Clemens.

———. "Cervantes, Zola, Kipling & Co.," *The Cosmopolitan* 14.5 (March 1893): 609–614.

In 1893 Clemens jotted a brief note about a short story in the March issue of *The Cosmopolitan* by Ida M. Van Etten (see the Catalog entry for Van Etten). Matthews's literary essay assessing the achievements of innovators in the novel genre directly preceded Van Etten's story, so Clemens could hardly have avoided noticing the essay.

———. *The Historical Novel and Other Essays*. First edition. Original green cloth, gilt. New York: Charles Scribner's Sons, 1901. 321 pp.

Inscriptions: the book was formally dedicated "To/Mark Twain/in Testimony of My Regard for the Man and of My Respect for the Literary Artist." Below that printed dedication, Matthews added in pencil: "Witness my hand: Brander Matthews/Feb. 20th, 1901." On the front free flyleaf Matthews wrote jocularly in ink: "By a recent decision of the Supreme Court the man to whom a book is dedicated is personally responsible for all the opinions in it./B. M./Feb. 20th, 1901."

Catalogs: C1951, #41c, $32.50; Sotheby's 2003, #222, $1,400.

Provenance: Clara Clemens Gabrilowitsch's shelfmark from her private library in Detroit is present. Donated to the Carrie Estelle Doheny Collection, St. John's Seminary, Camarillo, California by Mrs. Doheny after she purchased the volume from Maxwell Hunley Rare Books in 1951 for $44.50. Auctioned by Christie's for $1,210 on 21 February 1989 (lot 1766) on behalf of St. John's Seminary. Subsequently in the collection of Nick Karanovich, Fort Wayne, Indiana.

Location: collection of Kevin Mac Donnell, Austin, Texas.

Copy examined: Clemens's unmarked copy, in July 2004. A few leaves in the essay on Daudet are unopened. Has the bookplate of "Estelle Doheny."

In a letter dated 6 November 1900 Clemens gave his consent ("glad & proud") for Matthews to dedicate this book to him (SLC to Matthews, ALS at Columbia University).

Krause, *MTC* (1967), p. 153.

———. *An Introduction to the Study of American Literature*. New York: American Book Company, 1896. 256 pp.

Matthews designed this as a school textbook. He mentioned Mark Twain in the chronology at the rear and included his portrait on page 233. However, these gestures were not sufficient to spare Matthews from Twain's comedic impulses. An early proof or advance copy of Matthews's *Introduction* was Twain's source for quotations from "the Professor of English Literature in Columbia" that appear as epigraphs at the head of "Fenimore Cooper's Literary Offences' (*North American Review* 161.464 (July 1895): 1–12. Not only does Twain quote the three sentences out of order (they actually appear on pages 63, 62, and 58), but he seems unfair in removing them from the context. In fact, Twain implies their endorsement of the very thesis they reject. In his Cooper chapter, Matthews compares Cooper to Scott, inasmuch as "he was an optimist, an idealizer"; he notes that Cooper did not tell the whole truth about American Indians (p. 67); and he closes by acknowledging that "novelists have a more finished art nowadays" (p. 68). Nonetheless, the American realist Twain accused Matthews of pronouncing "opinions on Cooper's literature without having read some of it."

———. "Mark Twain—His Work," *The Book Buyer* N. s. 13.12 (January 1897): 977–979.

Clemens read most of what Brander Matthews wrote about literary figures—and this essay was about him. It seems likely that he saw this piece, even though he was abroad when it appeared. Matthews here praised much of what Mark Twain wrote, but expressed reservations about *The Prince and the Pauper, A Connecticut Yankee in King Arthur's Court*, and *Tom Sawyer Abroad*.

Terry Oggel, "In His Own Time: The Early Academic Reception of Mark Twain," *Mark Twain Annual 1* (2003): 45–60.

———. "The Penalty of Humor," *Harper's Monthly Magazine* 92.552 (May 1896): 897–900.

Clemens avidly followed Brander Matthews's literary assessments—and this essay concerned the touchy issue of the price writers must pay for introducing humorous material. Matthews ranked Mark Twain above John Phoenix, Artemus Ward, and Orpheus C. Kerr, and other "vendor[s] of comic copy." As an artist capable of "presenting character at a passionate crisis," Twain "has had to pay a higher price" for his abilities to entertain (p. 900). It is probable that Clemens saw this piece, even though he was abroad when it appeared. See the Matthews entry above for *Aspects of Fiction and Other Ventures in Criticism*.

Terry Oggel, "In His Own Time: The Early Academic Reception of Mark Twain," *Mark Twain Annual 1* (2003): 47.

———. "New Trials for Old Favorites," *Forum* 25 (August 1898): 749–760. Matthews defended Goldsmith's *The Vicar of Wakefield* against Mark Twain's disparagements in *Following the Equator* (1897), which Matthews termed "the glad exaggeration of the wanton humorist" (p. 749). Clemens wrote to Joseph H. Twichell on 13 September 1898 from Kaltenleutgeben, a village near Vienna: "I thank you very much for sending me Brander's article. . . . His article is as sound as a nut. Brander knows literature, & loves it; . . . and he can discover & praise such merits as a book has, even when they are merely half a dozen diamonds scattered through an acre of mud. And so he has a right to be a critic" (*MTL*, pp. 666–667; *LMTJHT*, p. 220).

———. *Parts of Speech: Essays on English*. Original cloth, minor wear, the spine has a small abrasion. New York: Charles Scribner's Sons, 1901. 350 pp.

Inscription: signed on the pastedown endpaper by Clemens, "S. L. Clemens/Riverdale, Oct. 1901./From Brander."

Catalogs: *C1951*, #79c, listed among the books signed by Clemens, $10; "Property from the Library of Mark Twain," Butterfield & Butterfield, San Francisco, Sale 6613 (16 July 1997), lot 2685.

Location: Mark Twain House and Museum, Hartford, Connecticut.

Copy examined: Clemens's copy. Viewed in Hartford in 1997.

———. *The Story of a Story, and Other Stories*. Illus. New York: Harper & Brothers, 1893. 234 pp.

Source: MTLAcc, entry #1482, volume donated by Clemens.

———. *Studies of the Stage*. New York: Harper & Brothers, 1894. 214 pp.

Location: Mark Twain Library, Redding, Connecticut. Donated by Clemens (MTLAcc, entry #662).

Copy examined: Clemens's copy, unmarked. Examined in 1970 and again in June 1982.

Matthews discussed masterpieces of English, French, and American drama.

———. *Tales of Fantasy and Fact*. New York: Harper & Brothers, 1896. 216 pp.

Source: MTLAcc, entry #1621, volume donated by Clemens.

Seven short stories written by Matthews.

MATHEWS, F[ERDINAND]. SCHUYLER (1854–1938). *Field Book of American Wild Flowers; Being a Short Description of Their Character and Habits, A Concise Definition of Their Colors, and Incidental References to the Insects Which Assist Their Fertilization*. Illus. New York: G. P. Putnam's Sons, 1903. 552 pp.

Source: Ball 2016 inventory, green cloth, gilt lettering and design, green edge pages, color illustrations, signed "Susan L. Crane,/Quarry Farm,/Sep. 11, 1903," with a letter pasted inside.

Location: Quarry Farm library shelves, under the supervision of the Mark Twain Archive, Elmira College, Elmira, New York.

Another volume available to Clemens and his two surviving daughters whenever they visited Quarry Farm in Elmira, New York.

MATTHEWS, FRANKLIN (1858–1917). *The New-Born Cuba*. New York: Harper & Brothers, 1899. 389 pp.

Source: MTLAcc, entry #1730, volume donated by Clemens.

MAUDSLAY, ALFRED PERCIVAL (1850–1931).

Clara Clemens discussed and summarized "Professor Maudsley's" [*sic*] beliefs about plants in her commonplace book (undated entry, Paine 150, MTP). Conceivably she referred to the English botanist Maudslay, who received botanical training at Cambridge University and traveled throughout the world. He was best known for his works in Mayan archaeology but he always took note of the botanical features of Mexico and the other countries he explored. See also the Catalog entry for Maudsley below.

MAUDSLEY. [Unidentified author and work.]

Clara Clemens discussed and summarized "Professor Maudsley's" beliefs about plants in her commonplace book (undated entry, Paine 150, MTP). Possibly she meant Henry Maudsley, M. D. (1835–1918), who published many works on the organic aspects of psychology but none precisely on plants. See also the Catalog entry for A. P. Maudslay (above).

MAURIS, MAURICE (MARCHESE DI CALENZANO). *French Men of Letters*. New York: D. Appleton & Co., 1880. 263 pp.

Source: MTLAcc, entry #831, volume donated by Clemens.

Brief biographical sketches and critical appraisals of a dozen French authors, including Victor Hugo, Alfred de Musset, Alphonse Daudet, Sainte-Beuve, and Émile Zola.

MAXWELL, WILLIAM HAMILTON (1792–1850). *Life of Field-Marshal His Grace the Duke of Wellington [1769–1852]*. Portraits, illus. English Gentleman's Library Series. 3 vols. London: Bickers and Son, n.d. [Very likely this was the Sixth edition, published around 1862, since engraved title pages in Volumes II and III bear the imprint of Henry H. Bohn's earlier Fifth edition, published 1845–1846, even though the spines of these volumes carry the Bickers imprint. The printer was R. Clay, Son, and Taylor.]

Catalog: *A1911*, "3 vols., 8vo, cloth, (title of Vol. I missing), Lond., n.d.," a sheet of notes by Clemens laid in, lot 321, sold for .50¢.

Location: Z. Smith Reynolds Library, Wake Forest University, Winston-Salem, North Carolina. Information supplied in March 1985 by Richard Murdock, then Rare Books Librarian of the Z. Smith Reynolds Library, and in September 2019 by Megan Mulder, Special Collections Librarian of the Z. Smith Reynold Library.

MAY, GEORGIANA MARIAN (CRAIK) (1831–1895). *Only a Butterfly, and Other Stories*. Copyright Edition. Leipzig: B. Tauchnitz, 1874. 288 pp. [Some bibliographies spell her middle name "Marion."]

Source: MTLAcc, entry #2187, volume donated from Clemens's library by Clara Clemens Gabrilowitsch in 1910.

MAY, SAMUEL JOSEPH (1797–1871). *Some Recollections of Our Antislavery Conflict*. Boston: Fields, Osgood & Co., 1869. 408 pp.

Location: Mark Twain Library, Redding, Connecticut. Donated by Clemens (MTLAcc, entry #567).

Copy examined: Clemens's copy, unmarked. No accession number. Examined in 1970 and again in June 1982.

The book title might mislead a reader into expecting another Civil War memoir; instead these were the recollections of a Unitarian minister and social reformer who traveled throughout New England and New York State in the antebellum years as an abolitionist lecturer and activist. He set down here his impressions of William

Lloyd Garrison, William Wells Brown, John Greenleaf Whittier, Frederick Douglass, and many other figures, and recounted riots in Utica and Syracuse, New York. *Some Recollections of Our Antislavery Conflict* related numerous stories about the persecution of abolitionists, including those who aided the Underground Railroad. May bitterly excoriated President Andrew Johnson for depriving the emancipated African Americans of any ownership of the Southern plantation lands they had cultivated without compensation for centuries.

Mayhew, Henry (1812–1887). *London Labour and the London Poor; A Cyclopaedia of the Condition and Earnings of Those That Will Work, Those That Cannot Work, and Those That Will Not Work.* 2 vols. London: G. Woodfall and Son, 1851.

An entry in Clemens's notebook for 1866 reads: "They need Bishop Staley's Missionary labors more in England than they do in H. I.—See London Labor & London Poor" (NB 5, *N&J* 1: 164). (Thomas Nettleship Staley, 1823–1898, was the first Anglican bishop of Honolulu.) Clemens was also familiar with James Greenwood's similar exposé, *The Wilds of London* (1874). See also the Catalog entry for William De Witt Alexander, *A Review of a Pastoral Address.*

———. *The Wonders of Science; or, Young Humphry Davy (The Cornish Apothecary's Boy, Who Taught Himself Natural Philosophy, and Eventually Became President of the Royal Society). The Life of a Wonderful Boy, Written for Boys.* Illus. Brown cloth, gilt lettering. Fair condition. New York: Harper & Brothers, n.d. [The Preface is dated 1854; Harper & Brothers published the first American edition in 1856.] 452 pp.

Location: Mark Twain Library, Redding, Connecticut. Donated by Clemens (MTLAcc, entry #690).

Copy examined: Clemens's copy. The binding is loose. There are pages missing from the index at the rear. Examined in 1970 and again in June 1982 and on 10 November 2019. The volume displays no red ink accession number, but this minor error on the librarian's part occurred more than once.

The extraordinary career of the self-taught scientist Humphry Davy (1778–1829), especially in the field of chemistry, culminated in his being named president of the Royal Society in 1820.

Mayo, Isabella Fyvie (1843–1914), pseud. "Edward Garrett."

In August 1896 Andrew Chatto sent Clemens "the two books by Edward Garrett which you wished to obtain" (Welland, *Mark Twain in England*, p. 168). The Scottish novelist, poet, and social reformer Mayo, writing under the pen name Edward Garrett, had published books such as *At Any Cost* (1885) and *Sunny Tales for Snowy Days* (1893).

Mayo, William Starbuck (1812–1895). *Kaloolah: Adventures of Jonathan Romer of Nantucket.* New York: G. P. Putnam's Sons, 1872. 514 pp. Repr. 1873, 1878. [Originally published in 1849 as *Kaloolah; or, Journeyings to the Djébei Kumri: An Autobiography of Jonathan Romer.*]

Estes & Lauriat of Boston billed Clemens for twenty-one books on 14 July 1880, including "1 Kaloolah $1"; Clemens paid the bill on 20 July 1880 (receipt in MTP). Africa is the principal setting of Jonathan Romer's fictional autobiography. He encounters and rescues an enslaved white woman who takes him to her tribe, but this is only one of his incredible adventures.

Mead, Edwin Doak (1849–1937). "A Righteous Setting Forth" (1902).

Jim Zwick reported that Clemens received a copy of this anti-imperialist piece, presumably a reprint from the Springfield *Republican* issue of 25 November 1902 ("'Prodigally Endowed with Sympathy for the Cause': Mark Twain's Involvement with the Anti-Imperialist League," *Mark Twain Journal* 32.1 [Spring 1994]: 22 n. 29). Mead was a Boston editor and social reformer.

Means, James (1853–1920). *Oppressive Tariff Taxation.* Rev. ed. Illustrated. Boston: Massachusetts Tariff Reform League, 1888. 30 pp. Paper wrappers.

A political cartoon on the front cover depicts a worker carrying a manufacturer and a heavy load of "Tariff Taxes." In 1889 or 1890 James Means of Boston sent Clemens the pamphlet and an undated letter requesting a document "that our Reform League can circulate throughout the country. Let it appeal to the workingmen." Means wrote because he "read between the lines in your 'Yankee.'" Clemens noted in pencil at the top of Means' letter: "Brer [Whitmore], preserve letter & pamphlet, & write him I am too desperately hard-worked these months, but I will keep his letter & pamphlet to remind me & at a future day will see if I really can write anything worth printing" (letter and pamphlet in MTP).

Meikle, James (1730–1799). *Solitude Sweetened; or, Miscellaneous Meditations on Various Religious Subjects Written in Distant Parts of the World.* New York: John Turney, 1831. 369 pp.

Catalog: Ball 2016 inventory, brown cloth with gilt lettering.

Location: Quarry Farm library shelves, under the supervision of the Mark Twain Archive, Elmira College, Elmira, New York.

Meikle was a Scottish seaman, naval ship surgeon, and devotional writer.

Meiners, Christoph (1747–1810). *Lebensbeschreibungen berühmter Männer aus den Zeiten der Wiederherstellung der Wissenschaften [Life Stories of Famous Men from the Times of the Restoration of the Sciences].* 3 vols. Zurich, 1795–1797.

Clara Clemens alluded to "Meiners' lines of Mirandola and Politian" in her mostly undated commonplace book, begun about 1888 (Paine 150, MTP). Meiners's book included stories of Pico della Mirandola (1463–1494) and Angelus Politianus (1454–1494). In the twentieth century Meiners's work as a philosopher and historian began to be denounced because of the simplistic racial hierarchies to which he subscribed.

Méjan, Maurice (1765?-1823). *Recueil des causes célèbres, et des arrêts qui les ont décidées.* Seconde édition. Tome premier. 21 vols. 8vo, contemporary binder's cloth, gilt, spine lacking, covers detached, now rebacked. Paris: Chez Garnery, 1808–1814. [Only Clemens's copy of Volume I survives.]

Inscription: the front pastedown endpaper of Volume I is signed with black ink, "S L. Clemens". (Judging from the handwriting, one might guess the year as 1907.)

Marginalia: Nine notes, nearly all in pencil, appear on six pages of Volume I plus the rear endpaper. They total approximately seventy-five words; some appear to have been made by Olivia Clemens. Penciled notes by Clemens appear on pages 54 "(See page 32 for answer.)", 105, 117, 195, and the rear pastedown endpaper. Certain of the latter notes suggest that Clemens acquired this volume at auction in 1881 along with two other volumes for $1 each. Volume I also contains penciled markings, mostly uncharacteristic-looking check marks, on seventeen pages, including pages 52 and 214. Chester Davis began to publish Louis J. Budd's report on the marginalia in *The Twainian* 38 (March-April 1979): 3–4.

Catalogs: *A1911*, "Vol. VIII [*sic*], 12mo, cloth, Paris, 1810," a sheet listing names written by Clemens laid in, lot 328, 50¢; Christie's, New York City, Sale 7378, including the "Estate of Chester L. Davis," 5 December 1991, lot 185, Volume I only, sold with another book for $1,320 total; *Sotheby's 2003*, #212, Vol. I only, "spine lost, covers detached, shaken," sold with five other volumes pertaining to history and travel for a total of $6,000.

Provenance: Volume I was for several decades in the collection of Chester Davis (1903–1987), Executive-Secretary, Mark Twain Research Foundation, Perry, Missouri. Subsequently Volume I belonged to the collection of Nick Karanovich, Fort Wayne, Indiana.

Location: Volume I belongs to the collection of Kevin Mac Donnell, Austin, Texas.

Copy examined: Clemens's copy of Volume I (427 pp.), in Austin in July 2004. The verso of the title page bears the ownership label of Charles Clark Temple, whose name was also written in Clemens's copy of Armand Fouquier's compilation of crime stories. This suggests that Clemens purchased both titles at the same time.

Isabel Lyon, Clemens's secretary, recorded on Sunday, 10 March 1907: "Tonight at dinner . . . he told me one or 2 stories which he has been reading from 'Causes Celèbres' [*sic*], one of a set of queer and battered little volumes that he ran across in the library" (IVL Journal, TS p. 230, MTP). Clemens's signature in Volume I of Méjan's work looks as though it could belong to 1907, but his marginalia has the appearance of handwriting from an earlier period. William Dean Howells's *My Mark Twain* (1910) mentioned that Clemens was often "reading some vital book" such as "a volume of great trials." See a possibly related entry, Armand Fouquier's *Causes célèbres de tous les peuples*.

D. M. McKeithan's *CTMT* (1958) thoroughly described the trials occurring in Twain's writings; Edwin Briden's "Law" entry in the *Mark Twain Encyclopedia*—J. R. LeMaster and James D. Wilson, eds. (New York: Garland Publishing, 1993), pp. 445–448—provided an overview of that topic.

MELBOURNE *Age* (newspaper).
"Mr. Edmund Barton called. He is going to get me a full file of the Age containing the Dean case" (NB 35, 10 October 1895, TS p. 58).

MELBOURNE *Punch* (journal).
"Punch (Melbourne) & Bulletin (Sydney) good papers. Good & bright cartoons in both" (October 1895, NB 34, TS p. 14).

MELLER, HENRY JAMES. *Nicotiana; or, the Smoker's and Snuff-Taker's Companion: Containing the History of Tobacco; Culture, Medical Qualities and the Laws Relative to Its Importation and Manufacture: With an Essay in Its Defence. The Whole Elegantly Embellished and Interspersed with Original Poetry and Anecdotes, Being Intended as an Amusing and Instructive Volume for All Genuine Lovers of the Herb.* Third ed. London: Effingham Wilson, 1833. 128 pp. [Edition, publisher, and

pages conjectured.]
Catalog: *A1911*, "16mo, original boards, cloth back, Lond. 1833. . . . With the singular error in the date of the preface. Contains the bookplate of Alfred Buckland," a manuscript sheet of notes by Clemens laid in, lot 329, sold for $5.50.

MELVILLE, HERMAN (1819–1891).
One might expect that at least Melville's early South Sea narratives, *Typee* (1846) and *Omoo* (1847), if not his epic *Moby-Dick* (1851), would have been of interest to Clemens, who relished stories of sea voyages and was enamored of the Sandwich Islands. Moreover, Clemens corresponded for decades with several authors who were familiar with Melville's writings. But of course Melville's literary reputation had steeply declined by the time that the Clemenses began to stock their library shelves in the mid-1870s, and perhaps Clemens simply never heard his name mentioned. Then, too, it should always be borne in mind that no truly complete catalog of Clemens's reading can ever be achieved. Books were lost during his travels, and he also made donations to several libraries that were never recorded. However, until something tangible turns up—and such developments have been encouragingly prevalent in Mark Twain studies—the Catalog entry for Herman Melville must remain a tantalizingly blank spot in our knowledge about the contents of Clemens's library shelves.

David D. Anderson's "Melville and Mark Twain in Rebellion," *Mark Twain Journal* 11.3 (Fall 1961): 8–9, explored correspondences between Melville's *The Confidence Man* and Twain's *The Mysterious Stranger*, and G. R. Thompson followed up this topic more comprehensively in "Ornithorhyncus Platypus Extraordinariensis: Modern Metafiction and the Assault on the Reader in Melville's *The Confidence Man* and Mark Twain's *The Mysterious Stranger*," *Mark Twain Annual* 16 (2018): 124–147. Margaret Myers sketched out what Twain's writings seemed to have in common with Melville's *Moby-Dick* and *Billy Budd* in their shared vision of humans limitations, as well as their differing final philosophies ("Mark Twain and Melville," *Mark Twain Journal* 14.2 (Summer 1968): 5–8. Franklin Walker compared and contrasted Melville's impressions of Palestine with Twain's in *Irreverent Pilgrims: Melville, Browne, and Mark Twain in the Holy Land* (1974). William M. Gibson pointed out an intriguing coincidence: both Melville (in *Redburn: His First Voyage* [1849]) and Twain—in "Affeland (Snivelization), a fragment written in 1892 and not published until 1967 (*S&B*, pp. 170–171)—employed the satiric neologisms "snivilization" and "snivilized" ("Snivilization," *American Speech* 49.3–4 (Autumn/Winter 1974): 303–304. Tom Quirk raised interesting parallels between Melville and Twain in "Life Imitating Art: *Huckleberry Finn* and Twain's Autobiographical Writings," *One Hundred Years of Huckleberry Finn: The Boy, His Book, and American Culture*, ed. Robert Sattelmeyer and J. Donald Crowley (Columbia: University of Missouri Press, 1985), pp. 50–53. Quirk later pointed out that in both Chapter 115 of *Moby-Dick* and Chapter 32 of *Adventures of Huckleberry Finn*, both the Captain of the *Bachelor* and Aunt Sally Phelps show a similar indifference to the loss of human life unlike their own people (*Coming to Grips with Huckleberry*

Finn [Columbia: University of Missouri Pres, 1993], pp. 83–85), and he added something about *Billy Budd* (p. 56). See also Leonard Martinez, "Concentric Failures: Melville, Twain, and Shifting Centers," *Mark Twain Annual 13* (2015): 115–129.

Memorial Concerning Conditions in the Independent State of the Kongo. April 19, 1904. Committee on Foreign Relations. U. S. Senate. 58th Congress, 2d Session. Document No. 282. Conference of Missionary Societies. Washington, D. C.: Government Printing Office, 1904. 136 pp.

 Marginalia: Clemens annotated the paper wrapper and the text with black ink. On the front he noted: "Splendid Progress of our Xn Civilization. Too Cold an Interest taken in it by pulpit & press & public." He belittles Leopold II, "a person of brutal history & infamous character." Of the native soldiers he wrote on page 126: "It is like employing the red Indians of 200 yrs ago—*if* they could have been hired to harry their own people." He made other notes and markings.

 Catalog: "Retz Appraisal" (1944), p. 10, valued at $15.

 Location: Mark Twain Papers, Bancroft Library, University of California at Berkeley.

 Copy examined: Clemens's copy.

On 16 October 1904 E. D. Morel wrote to Clemens from the Murray Hill Hotel in New York City: "I send you by an express messenger a packet of Congo literature"; among other publications, "it includes . . . a special copy of the Memorial, which I would like you to keep and show to any friends as a document of perhaps unique historical interest (together with a rough copy enclosed)" (ALS in MTP). Clemens replied from the Hotel Grosvenor in New York City on the same day: "The Senate Memorial reached me early this a.m., & I have remained in bed to read it." He requested an additional copy of the publication (ALS in the British Library of Political and Economic Science, London).

Memorial to the Fiftieth Congress of the United States. Presented by the State Board of Forestry of California. Sacramento: State Office; J. D. Young, Supt. State Printing, 1888. Paper wrappers. 13 pp.

 Inscription: autographed "Mark Twain" in black ink at the top of the front (title page) wrapper. A price of $10 on the right-hand corner of the same wrapper has been crossed out and a price of $5 written below it.

 Location: collection of Theodore H. Koundakjian of Albany, California in 1982.

 Copy examined: photocopy of the entire pamphlet sent to Alan Gribben by Theodore H. Koundakjian on 13 December 1982. I am grateful for that favor but must express a large degree of skepticism about the authenticity of this purported association copy.

This *Memorial* addressed to the U. S. Congress consisted of a resolution by the American Horticultural Association asking Congress to withdraw all remaining California timber lands from sale or entry, supplemented by four reports documenting the destruction that the present policy has engendered. It would be nice to think that Clemens had such a deep interest in subjects involving California's wilderness ecology, but the autograph appears spurious and it was uncharacteristic of Clemens to use his pen name when signing items in his library.

Memories of Westminster Hall; A Collection of Interesting Incidents, Anecdotes, and Historical Sketches Relating to Westminster Hall, Its Famous Judges and Lawyers and Its Great Trials. Historical introduction by Edward Foss (1787–1870). 2 vols. Boston: Estes & Lauriat, 1874. [Only Volume II of Clemens's copy has been found.]

 Inscription: the front flyleaf of Volume II is signed in pencil, "Saml. L. Clemens/Hartford 1874."

 Marginalia: in Volume II Clemens changed the words "would have lived" to read simply "lived" (p. 14); corrected the name "Gates" to read "Oates" (p. 37); altered the phrase "years past" to form "years passed"; drew marginal brackets to set off passages on pages 7, 9, 41, 42, and 43; and made a few other grammatical revisions. There are no markings beyond page 43. All of Clemens's annotations are in pencil.

 Catalogs: *A1911*, #64, vol. II only, sold with fourteen other vols. for $8.50 total; Stan. V. Henkels (Philadelphia), Catalogue 1057 (14 May 1912), "Vol. 2," item #121; offered for sale in 1963 by John Swingle, Alta California Rare Books, Berkeley, California, Catalogue 22, item #25, priced at $350 for "15 books from Clemens' library, . . . 11 with signatures: "Samuel L. Clemens Hartford 1874."

 Location: Mark Twain House and Museum, Hartford, Connecticut (Volume II only). Gift of an anonymous donor in 1965.

 Source: Diana Royce, former Librarian of the Stowe-Day Memorial Library, initially supplied the facts about Clemens's copy presented in this entry. In August 1987 I examined Volume II in Hartford. It has an *A1911* sale label.

 Memories of Westminster Hall includes a chapter on "The Great Tichborne Case," the trial in 1873 of a claimant to the Tichborne estate whose allegations fascinated Clemens.

MENAULT, ERNEST (1830–1903). *The Intelligence of Animals, with Illustrative Anecdotes.* Translated from the French. Illus. New York: Scribner, Armstrong & Co., 1872. 368 pp.

 Source: MTLAcc, entry #1988, volume donated from Clemens's library by Clara Clemens Gabrilowitsch in 1910.

MENDEL, HERMANN (1834–1876). *Musikalisches Conversationslexicon [Musical conversations lexicon]. Eine Encyklopädie.* 11 vols. Berlin: R. Oppenheim, 1880–1882. [Also published in Leipzig: List & Francke, 1884, repr. 1890–1891.]

 Clara Clemens listed the author and title in her commonplace book without specifying a publisher (undated entry, Paine 150, MTP).

Men of the Time: A Dictionary of Contemporaries, Containing Biographical Notices of Eminent Characters of Both Sexes. Eighth edition. Edited by Thompson Cooper (1837–1904). London: George Routledge and Sons, 1872. 1008 pp.

 Inscription: the title page is signed vertically in pencil by Clemens: "Saml. L. Clemens,/London/ 1874."

 Marginalia: Beside the entry for his own name on page 227, Clemens noted in black ink, writing vertically: "From Routledge's 'Men of the Time'". On the other side of the page, in the right margin, Clemens crossed out the lines beginning "He has continued his labours as a lecturer. . . ." through the end of the entry and wrote vertically, in black ink: "Add the MS., here, in/place of the lines/stricken out. S.L.C." There is no other annotation, even in Bret Harte's entry. Some leaves remain unopened, but others—such as those concerning Henry Ward Beecher on page 74—have been cut apart.

Location: Mark Twain Library, Redding, Connecticut. Donated by Clemens (MTLAcc, entry #895).

Copy examined: Clemens's copy. No red ink accession number. Examined in 1970 and again in June 1982 and on 9 November 2019. Displays the purple oval stamps of the Mark Twain Library.

On 17 September 1872, Mark Twain assured Arthur Locker, who was writing a piece about Twain for the London *Graphic*, "I believe the sketch in 'Men of the Time' is accurate—indeed, I furnished the facts myself" (*MTLet* 5: 161). Locker's article appeared in the *Graphic* on 5 October 1872 (pp. 310, 324). "I haven't any biographical facts—gave them all to Routledge, who put them in 'Men of the Time,'" Clemens explained to Robert Watt on 8 March 1875 (*MTLet* 6: 408).

Men of the Time: A Dictionary of Contemporaries, Containing Biographical Notices of Eminent Characters of Both Sexes. Tenth edition. Edited by Thompson Cooper (1837–1904). Binding loose. London: George Routledge and Sons, 1879. 1070 pp.

Location: Mark Twain Library, Redding, Connecticut. Clemens donated the book (MTLAcc, entry #894).

Copy examined: Clemens's copy, unmarked. This edition was catalogued by Albert E. Stone in 1955 as one of Clemens's library volumes in the Mark Twain Library at Redding, Connecticut. I was unable to locate the volume at Redding in 1970, but when I returned in June 1982 it had been found and placed in the bookshelves containing Clemens's library books. It has the purple oval Mark Twain Library stamp but no red ink accession number. Clemens's biographical sketch appears on pages 241–242; it received no emendations this time. I inspected the volume again on 9 November 2019.

Clemens referred an unidentified correspondent to this reference work—"'Men of the Time'—(London: Geo. Routledge & Sons,)"—in a letter of 5 November 1879 (PH in MTP; Sotheby's sale, 29 October 1996, lot 215). This is the version Clemens reprinted for general distribution, as he informed William Dean Howells from Hartford on 19 October 1880: "The idea of that printed biography is a noble good one: saves me time, rage, excuses, declinations, disgust, humiliation; . . . & besides, it at the same time furnishes to the inquiring idiot connected with the literary society exactly what he has ASKED for" (*MTHL*, pp. 331, 332 n. 2). In May 1889 Clemens reminded himself: "Send Charley Clark [of the Hartford *Courant*] Men of the Time Biog slip" (NB 28, *N&J* 3: 471).

Men of the Time: A Dictionary of Contemporaries, Containing Biographical Notices of Eminent Characters of Both Sexes. Eleventh edition. Edited by Thompson Cooper (1837–1904). London: George Routledge and Sons, 1884. 1,168 pp.

Location: Mark Twain Library, Redding, Connecticut. Donated by Clemens (MTLAcc, entry #893).

Copy examined: Clemens's copy, virtually unopened. Clemens's biographical sketch appeared on page 262 and he made no changes in it. The volume has no red ink accession number. Examined in 1970 and again in June 1982 and on 9 November 2019.

MEREDITH, GEORGE (1828–1909). *Diana of the Crossways*

(novel, published in 1885).

In September 1886 Clemens made a memorandum of the name and author of Meredith's only truly popular novel, mistaking its title as "Diana of the Xroads" (NB 26, *N&J* 3: 253). Clara Clemens remembered that when Olivia read aloud to the family at Quarry Farm, Clemens often expressed his opinion that Meredith was too wordy (*MFMT*, p. 61). Albert Bigelow Paine reported that Olivia and her friends read Meredith's novels "with reverential appreciation." Clemens, however, "found his characters artificialities—ingeniously contrived puppets rather than human beings." When *Diana of the Crossways* was read aloud in 1887 (the date Paine supplied), Clemens remarked: "It doesn't seem to me that Diana lives up to her reputation. The author keeps telling us how smart she is, how brilliant, but I never seem to hear her say anything smart or brilliant. Read me some of Diana's smart utterances" (*MTB*, p. 847). Lecture agent Carlyle Smythe declared in 1898 that "Meredith, perhaps not unnaturally, provokes him to laughter" ("The Real 'Mark Twain,'" *Pall Mall Magazine* 16 [September 1898]: 31). Affecting literary ignorance in June 1909, Clemens told his biographer, Paine: "I never could stand Meredith and most of the other celebrities" (*MTB*, p. 1501). Meredith's novel about the fictional Diana Merion Warwick was loosely based on the publicity surrounding Caroline Norton (1808–1877), whose husband cited Lord Melbourne in a divorce case. See also the Catalog entry for Meredith's *Works*.

———. *The Egoist: A Comedy in Narrative* (novel, published in London in 1879).

Clemens made a note of this novel and its author in April 1888 (NB 27, *N&J* 3: 383).

———. *Poems*. Original decorated green cloth, gilt. New York: Charles Scribner's Sons, 1901.

Inscription: the front free endpaper is inscribed in brown ink: "Clara/from/Marie./January 1902." Clara Clemens Gabrilowitsch's shelfmark from her Detroit library is present on the front pastedown endpaper, "F/LS25."

Marginalia: small brown ink hatch-marks are visible at the heads of poems on pages 2 and 3, and there is a horizontal black ink line at the bottom of the last poem in a sequence titled "Modern Love" on page 52 (this latter mark is the only one that seems characteristic of Clemens's annotations).

Provenance: *Sotheby's* 2003, #223, $7,000, sold with a 16-volume set of Meredith's *Works* (purchased by Robert Slotta).

Location: collection of Kevin Mac Donnell, Austin, Texas. A letter from Mac Donnell to Alan Gribben, 10 September 2009, supplied the information for this entry. (See also the Catalog entry for *Works* below, which supplies more information about this copy.)

———. *The Works of George Meredith*. 16 volumes. 8vo, original green cloth, stamped in dark green ink and gilt with a border of green leaves on the front cover, spines lettered with gilt. Light wear to spines. New York: Charles Scribner's Sons, 1899–1902. Plus a duplicate copy of Meredith's *Poems* (1901).

Inscriptions: Clemens inscribed the front free endpapers of all sixteen volumes identically in black ink, "Olivia L. Clemens." He dated his inscriptions in *The Ordeal of Richard Feverel* and in *Poems* as "1903." Clemens inscribed *Diana of the Crossways* more elaborately around Olivia's name, also in ink: "This is Diana, who so/greatly entertained/Theodore [Crane] & me, years ago/(by help of a game.) S L. C./Olivia L. Clemens/1903./From S. L. C./February." Very probably this set was a gift to Olivia on their thirty-third wedding anniversary, February 2nd. A duplicate copy of *Poems* (1901) is inscribed in brown ink, "Clara from Marie./January 1902." (That was most likely a gift from the poet and novelist Marie Van Vorst [1867–1936].)

Marginalia: Someone, possibly Clara Clemens, made pencil lines in the margins of pages 7, 299 (beside Lady Dunstane's question, "But tell me . . . why men are so much happier than women in laughing at their spouses?"), and 368 of *Diana of the Crossways*. On page 153 of that novel Clara Clemens wrote "Bad taste" at a description of Diana's choice of clothing. A clause on page 295 is bracketed: "Emma wanted, however, to taste them as they cropped". In *The Ordeal of Richard Feverel* Clara Clemens or someone made pencil lines in the margins of pages 101, 109, 124, 126, 178, 232, 242, and 371. These marks are much heavier and wider than those Clemens usually made. On page 413 Clara Clemens canceled the word "simply" in a sentence that reads: "'She shall,' Austin said simply." On page 147 of *The Ordeal of Richard Feverel* Clara Clemens objected in pencil, "And if you traverse the/*whole* world there'll be no heart left to anchor." The baronet had just remarked in the text: "'To anchor the heart by any object ere we have half traversed the world, is youth's foolishness, my son.'" Page 318 of the same volume contains two marginal lines bracketing a passage in the text; the ink matches that of Clemens's inscription in the front of the volume. On page 413 someone, most likely Clemens, struck out a word in pencil. The duplicate copy of *Poems* inscribed to Clara contains brown ink cross-hatches on pages 2 and 3.

Provenance: the shelf marks on the front pastedown endpaper were typical of Clara Clemens Gabrilowitsch's private library in Detroit. Warren Howells's accountant told Nick Karanovich on 5 August 1985 that Keith Kinkade sold the set to Warren Howell of John Howell Books on 3 June 1981 for $800. Nick Karanovich of Fort Wayne, Indiana acquired the set from Swann Galleries in 1985. It was purchased at the 2003 Sotheby's auction by Robert Slotta, Admirable Books, Hilliard, Ohio.

Catalogs: John Howell Books, San Francisco, 24 July 1981, $1,500; Swann Galleries, New York City, "The Inventory of John Howell Books," Sale number 1370, 25 April 1985, item #182, $1,800; *Sotheby's 2003*, #223, $7,000 (including a duplicate copy of *Poems* inscribed to "Clara" by "Marie").

Location: collection of Kevin Mac Donnell, Austin, Texas. Acquired in October 2008.

Copies examined: gift copies from Clemens to his wife, viewed at Sotheby's in 2003 and verified against photocopies. By this point Olivia's health had seriously declined, and Clemens very likely hoped to raise her spirits and entertain her with this purchase. It seems doubtful that she ever felt well enough to read these books. On 24 May 1985 Nick Karanovich sent Alan Gribben a complete

set of photocopies of the spines, covers, front pastedown endpapers, title pages, copyright pages, inscriptions, and pages with markings. Most of the markings do not resemble Clemens's or Olivia Clemens's and most probably were Clara Clemens's. On 21 October 2008 Kevin Mac Donnell sent Alan Gribben a detailed description of the volumes.

Merezhkovsky, Dmitry Sergeyevich (1865–1941). *The Romance of Leonardo da Vinci [1452–1519], the Forerunner, by Dimitri Merejkowski. Exclusively Authorized Translation from the Russian* of *"The Resurrection of the Gods."* Translated by [Frederick] Herbert Trench (1865–1923). New York: G. P. Putnam's Sons, 1902. 463 pp.

On the verso of a "sick-room" note that Clemens sent to Olivia Clemens around 1902 or 1903 she noted the title of this translation of the second of a historical trilogy (MTP).

Mérimée, Prosper (1803–1870). *Prosper Mérimée's Letters to an Incognita; with Recollections by [Alphonse de] Lamartine [1790–1869] and George Sand [1804–1876].* Ed. by Richard Henry Stoddard (1825–1903). Bric-a-Brac Series. New York: Scribner, Armstrong & Co., 1874. 350 pp.

Source: MTLAcc, entry #686, volume donated by Clemens. Mérimée's *Letters to an Incognita* appears on pages 17–135; Lamartine's *Twenty-five Years of My Life* occupies pages 137–319; and George Sand's *Recollections* are reprinted on pages 323–343.

Merivale, Charles (1808–1893). *History of the Romans under the Empire.* 7 vols. (published 1840–1862).

Anxious to compare Ulysses S. Grant with Caesar, Clemens made a note in June 1885: "Merivale's History of the Romans—first 2 vols (Caesar)" (NB 24, *N&J* 3: 160).

Merivale, Herman Charles (1839–1906), pseud. "Felix Dale." *He's a Lunatic: A Farce in One Act* (produced in 1867).

While the Clemenses were vacationing at Newport, Rhode Island on 23 August 1875 Clemens lectured between acts of the Bellevue Dramatic Group, which was presenting Merivale's farce and a two-act comic drama (John Roche, "Making a Reputation: Mark Twain in Newport," *Mark Twain Journal* 25.2 [Fall 1987]: 25). See a related article, Earl F. Briden's "Mark Twain's Rhode Island Lectures," *Mark Twain Journal* 24.1 (Spring 1986): 35–40.

———— and **Frank T[homas]. Marzials** (1840–1912). *Life of W. M. Thackeray.* London: Walter Scott, 1891. 255 pp.

Source: Ball 2016 inventory, blue cloth, gilt lettering, rough cut pages, good condition.

Location: Quarry Farm library shelves, under the supervision of the Mark Twain Archive, Elmira College, Elmira, New York.

Clemens had access to this biography at Quarry Farm in Elmira, New York.

"The mermaid" (traditional sea shanty); also known as "The stormy winds do blow" and "On Friday morn."

On 4 February [1903] Clemens wrote to Olivia: "And now the stormy winds do blow, as the sailor-ballad says" (MTP). Another potential source for Clemens's allusion was Thomas Campbell's stirring poem, "Ye Mariners of England" (see that Catalog entry).

Merriam, George Spring (1843–1914). *A Living Faith.* Boston: Lockwood, Brooks and Co., 1876. 282 pp.

James R. Osgood & Company of Boston listed this title on a bill for books Clemens purchased between 21 January and 24 October 1877 (Scrapbook #10, p. 69, MTP). *A Living Faith* consisted of thirty-seven essays and editorials originally published in *The Christian Union*, plus a lengthy "Postscript" exhortation about the principles behind a well-lived life. Merriam's topics ranged over the Bible, Christ's message, Emerson's and Carlyle's writings, and many other subjects.

MERRICK, GEORGE BYRON (1841–1931). *Old Times on the Upper Mississippi; The Recollections of a Steamboat Pilot from 1854 to 1863.* Portraits and illustrations. 8vo, cloth. Cleveland: A. H. Clark Co., 1909 [cop. 1908]. 323 pp.

  Inscriptions: "Samuel L. Clemens, Pilot, with compliments of the author, Geo. B. Merrick, Madison, Wis., Nov. 30, 1908." Also signed on the front pastedown endpaper, "S. L. Clemens, 1908."

  Catalogs: *A1911*, "8vo, cloth, Cleveland, 1909," quotes the inscription and signature, lot 330, sold for $6; Anderson Auction Galleries, Sale number 1873 (10–11 November 1924), "8vo, cloth, uncut, Cleveland, 1909, first edition," contains the *A1911* sale label, lot 222, sold for $22.

  Clemens piloted on the Mississippi River below St. Louis, but he was always interested in the entire waterway and he had seen the Upper Mississippi in 1882.

MERRITT, ERNEST GEORGE (1865–1948). "The New Element Radium," *Century Magazine* 67 (January 1904): 451–460.

  In "Sold to Satan" (written in 1904), Satan lauds the untapped powers of radium, citing its properties and peculiarities. See also the Catalog entry for Marie Curie. Cummings, "Mark Twain and Science" (doctoral dissertation, 1950); Cummings, "Mark Twain's Acceptance of Science" (1962).

MERWIN, SAMUEL (1874–1936).

  Merwin, the author of such novels as *Calumet "K"* (1901) and *Comrade John* (1907), sent Mark Twain a handsome commendation on 4 August 1903; he wrote that Mark Twain's books "brought something really new into our literature" (*MTL* [1917], pp. 743–744; Stone, *IE* [1961], pp. 275–276). Did Clemens ever reciprocate by looking into Merwin's books?

METCHNIKOFF, ÉLIE (1845–1916). *The Nature of Man; Studies in Optimistic Philosophy, by Élie Metchnikoff.* English translated and edited by Peter Chalmers Mitchell (1864–1945). New York: G. P. Putnam's Sons, 1903. 309 pp.

  Isabel Lyon's journal refers to a conversation about "Metchnikoff's Book" between Clemens and William Dean Howells that took place on 25 March 1906 (TS p. 152, MTP). It was Howells who brought up this topic, one which was "always interesting to Mr. Clemens" (IVL Journal, Harry Ransom Center, University of Texas at Austin). Metchnikoff was a Russian zoologist and bacteriologist, associated with Pasteur, who made microscopic studies of diseases of the blood. *The Nature of Man; Studies in Optimistic Philosophy* discussed the evolution of human physiology, religious responses over the millennia to individual and social needs, the ideas of ancient and modern philosophers, and many other subjects.

METTERNICH-WINNEBURG-BEILSTEIN, KLEMENS WENZEL LOTHAR, FÜRST VON (1773–1859). *Memoirs of Prince Metternich, 1773–1815.* Ed. by Prince Richard [Klemens Lothar Fürst von] Metternich (1829–1895). Comp. by M. A[lfons]. de Klinkowström (1818–1891). Translated by Mrs. Alexander

Napier [Robina Napier]. 5 vols. New York: Charles Scribner's Sons, 1880–1882. [Edition conjectured; Metternich's *Memoirs* were also published by Harper & Brothers in 1881.]

  Metternich was the Austrian foreign minister from 1809 until 1848 and played a role in thwarting Napoleon's eventual aims. Clemens wrote to Olivia on 26 July 1887 from the St. James Hotel in New York City: "I read the 4th volume of Metternich's memoirs all the way down in the cars yesterday—& last night. Apparently no narrative that tells the facts of a man's life, in the man's own words, can be uninteresting. Even this man's State papers are after a fashion interesting, when read by the light of his private remarks & comments. And this difference between him & Gen. [George B.] McClellan is conspicuous. Metternich's book removes the obloquy from his name; but McClellan's deepens that upon *his*, & justifies it" (*LLMT*, p. 249; ALS in MTP).

  James D. Williams, "Genesis" (1961), p. 105.

MEUNIER, VICTOR (1817–1903), comp. *Adventures on the Great Hunting Grounds of the World.* Translated from the French. Illus. New York: Scribner, Armstrong & Co., 1873. 297 pp.

  Source: MTLAcc, entry #1989, volume donated from Clemens's library by Clara Clemens Gabrilowitsch in 1910.

  A collection of brief stories published by various travelers who hunted in Africa, Asia, and North and South America. They relate the sport killing of gorillas, lions, giraffes, elephants, rhinoceroses, tigers, buffalo, bears, and crocodiles, together with anecdotes about the customs and histories of natives the hunters encountered.

MICHAELANGELO DI LODOVICO BUONARROTI SIMONI (1475–1574). *Sonnets.*

  On 7 November 1892 Susy Clemens informed her college friend Louise Brownell from Florence that "Nanny [King] and I have been having a lovely time over Vasari's Lives and Michael Angelo's sonnets. We have sat by the fire these cold afternoons reading aloud to each other" (Hamilton College Archives).

MICHELET, JULES (1798–1874). *The Bird.* Illustrated by Hector Giacomelli (1822–1909). Translated by William Henry Davenport (1828–1891). London: T. Nelson and Sons, 1869. 340 pp.

  Source: MTLAcc, entry #1968, volume donated from Clemens's library by Clara Clemens Gabrilowitsch in 1910. Michelet's venture into the natural sciences with this study of bird-life would far surpass the expectations of any reader anticipating a simple ornithological survey.

———. *Historical View of the French Revolution.* Translated by Charles Cocks. London: H. G. Bohn, 1848. 606 pp.

  Henry W. Fisher recalled how Clemens told him (in Vienna, in the late 1890s) that the Clemens family used Michelet's book in Paris to locate "all the places of horror, made odious during the White Terror" (*AMT*, p. 59).

  Blair, "French Revolution and *Huckleberry Finn*" (1957), p. 24.

———. *Jeanne d'Arc (1412–1432).* Paris: Librairie Hachette et Cie., 1873. 152 pp. [A separate printing of the fifth volume of Michelet's extensive *Histoire de France*, 17 vols., published 1833–1867.]

  Marginalia: annotated throughout by Clemens in pencil and brown ink. Albert E. Stone, Jr. (*IE*, pp. 209, 211–212) and Roger Salomon (*TIH*, pp. 170–173) quoted and discussed a few of Clemens's marginal comments. See also Ronald Jenn and Linda A. Morris, "The Sources of Mark Twain's *Personal Recollections of Joan of Arc*," *Mark Twain Journal* 55.1–2 (Spring/Fall 2017): 64–66.

Catalogs: ListABP (1910), "Jeanne D'Arc, Michelet"; "Retz Appraisal" (1944), p. 10, valued at $20.

Location: Mark Twain Papers, Bancroft Library, University of California at Berkeley.

Copy examined: Clemens's copy. Paper wrappers, pages loose.

Albert E. Stone, Jr.—"Mark Twain's *Joan of Arc*" (1959), p. 3, and *The Innocent Eye* (1961), p. 212—proposed an American edition of Michelet's fifth volume of *Histoire de France* as the book from which young Sam Clemens purportedly found a stray leaf in Hannibal in 1849 (Paine, *MTB* [1912], pp. 81–82; Wecter, *SCH* [1952], p. 211). Ronald Jenn and Linda A. Morris, "The Sources of Mark Twain's *Personal Recollections of Joan of Arc*," *Mark Twain Journal* 55.1–2 (Spring/Fall 2017): 64–65, concurred, adding a specific guess about an 1845 Michelet edition published in New York City. Linda A. Morris, in "What is 'Personal' about *Personal Recollections of Joan of Arc?*" *American Literary Realism* 51.2 (Winter 2019): 98, repeated this assertion, noting that the page Clemens saw "was most likely from the English translation of Jules Michelet's 1845 history of Joan of Arc."

Grace King claimed that it was she who, while Mark Twain was writing *Joan of Arc* in Florence, told him about Michelet's *Histoire de France* "and he promised to get it and read it" (*Memories*, p. 174). On the page preceding Twain's "Translator's Preface" to *Joan of Arc* (1896), he listed Michelet's *Jeanne d'Arc* among the "authorities examined" in preparation for the book. Twain mentions Michelet in footnotes to Chapters 12 and 30 of *Joan of Arc*. Afterward he recalled Michelet as one of his three main sources for the novel (*MTB*, p. 958).

Albert E. Stone, "Mark Twain's *Joan of Arc*" (1959), pp. 8–9; Ronald Jenn and Linda A. Morris, "The Sources of Mark Twain's *Personal Recollections of Joan of Arc*," *Mark Twain Journal* 55.1–2 (Spring/Fall 2017): 55–74; Linda A. Morris, in "What is 'Personal' about *Personal Recollections of Joan of Arc?*" *American Literary Realism* 51.2 (Winter 2019): 97–110; Delphine Louis-Dimitrov, "The Democratic Reconfiguration of History in Mark Twain's *Personal Recollections of Joan of Arc*," *American Literary Realism* 51.2 (Winter 2019): 162–179; and Delphine Louis-Dimitrov, "Nature in Mark Twain's *Personal Recollections of Joan of Arc*," *Mark Twain Annual* 17 (2019): 88–111. .

———. *La Sorcière: The Witch of the Middle Ages* (published in 1862 in Paris).

Coleman O. Parsons—"Background" (1960), pp. 60, 67—speculated about this book's connection with Mark Twain's *The Mysterious Stranger* manuscripts.

MICHIE, ALEXANDER (1833–1902). *Missionaries in China.* London: Edward Stanford, 1891. 107 pp. [Publisher and pages conjectured.]

Inscription: signed "S. L. Clemens, Riverdale, Nov. 1901, from Alexander Michie."

Marginalia: several passages marked in pencil.

Catalog: *A1911*, "8vo, cloth, Lond. 1891, . . . several passages marked with pencil," quotes the signature, lot

331, sold for $1.

MICKIEWICZ, ADAM (1798–1855). *Dziady (Forefathers' Eve)* (Romantic Polish poetic drama in four parts, 1822–1832, never completed).

Louis J. Budd makes a case for considering Part Three, Act I, Scene v of *Dziady* as the possible inspiration for the title of Twain's *No. 44, The Mysterious Stranger*. Clemens and his family were in Vienna in 1898 around the time that the odd numerical name first seems to have occurred to him. In the passage cited by Budd a Polish priest imprisoned by the Russian Czar has a nationalistic vision that a revolutionary Polish hero will emerge who will be named "Forty-four" ("Another Stab at the Origin of No. 44 as a Name," *Mark Twain Circular* 3.7–8 [July-August 1989]: 1–3).

MIGHELS, PHILIP VERRILL (1869–1911). *Bruvver Jim's Baby.* New York: Harper & Brothers, 1905. 265 pp.

Source: MTLAcc, entry #1605, volume donated by Clemens.

Mighels's novel has a plot reminiscent of Bret Harte's short story "The Luck of Roaring Camp" (1868). The sudden appearance of a baby transforms the behavior of the denizens of Borealis, a gold-mining camp in Nevada. Mighels was the son of a Sagebrush School newspaper editor, Henry Rust Mighels (1830–1879) of Carson City. Theodore Dreiser (whose comments about Clemens cannot always be trusted) recalled meeting Clemens and "several acquaintances, if not cronies," in the back parlor of a New York saloon in 1907 or 1908; on that occasion, according to Dreiser, "a forty-year-old dynamic and very positive and argumentative writer whose name I have forgotten, but who had written a book entitled *Bruvver Jim's Baby*," sat on one side of Clemens ("Three Contacts," p. 162A).

———. *Chatwit, The Man-Talk Bird.* Illus. New York: Harper & Brothers, 1906. 265 pp.

Source: MTLAcc, entry #1607, volume donated by Clemens.

A black-and-white magpie bird in Nevada learns to mimic human speech.

———. [Another identical copy.]

Source: MTLACC, entry #1969, volume donated from Clemens's library by Clara Clemens Gabrilowjtsch in 1910.

———. *The Crystal Sceptre; A Story of Adventure.* New York: Harper & Brothers, 1906. 346 pp.

Source: MTLAcc, entry #1604, volume donated by Clemens.

A balloon mishap drops the narrator down in a jungle amid human-sized apes in this science fiction novel.

———. *Dunny, A Mountain Romance.* New York: Harper & Brothers, 1906. 264 pp.

Source: MTLAcc, entry #1606, volume donated by Clemens.

The title of the first chapter of Mighel's novel, "Lost in the Snow," might have caught Mark Twain's attention since he had used that same phrase to describe an episode in *Roughing It* (1872). Here the words applied to the plight of passengers on a train stranded in the Sierra Nevada mountains.

MILL, JOHN STUART (1806–1873). *Autobiography.* New York: Henry Holt and Co., n.d. [Henry Holt and Company first published Mill's *Autobiography* in 1873; the same firm reprinted it several times in subsequent years. The publication date of Clemens's copy is unknown.]

Inscription: signed and dated in 1908 by Clemens.

Catalogs: *C1951*, D42, listed among books signed by Clemens; *American Book-Prices Current Index 1960–1965* (New York, 1968), p. 368, entry #64, $110.

———. *A System of Logic, Ratiocinative and Inductive; Being a Connected View of the Principles of Evidence and the Methods of Scientific Investigation.* New York: Harper & Brothers, n.d. 659 pp. [The Harper & Brothers edition published in 1874 matched this specified number of pages.]

Source: MTLAcc, entry #1804, volume donated by Clemens.

MILLAIS, JOHN GUILLE (1865–1931). *The Life and Letters of Sir John Everett Millais [1829–1896], President of the Royal Academy, by His Son, John Guille Millais.* Illus. 2 vols. London: Methuen Co, 1899.

In London, on 10 November 1899, Mark Twain inserted a quotation from page 316 of Volume II of *The Life and Letters of Sir John Everett Millais* (copied by an unknown assistant) into a manuscript titled "Postscript—Osteopathy" (DV13, MTP). (During 1899 Twain was strenuously advocating Kellgren's treatments to anyone who would listen; see, for instance, *MTHHR*, pp. 403–408, 740.) Twain took the quotation from the artist Lord Frederic Leighton's letter of 19 May 1895 to Sir John Millais, which recommended Jonas Henrik Kellgren's therapy of Swedish massage. Twain's manuscript refers to "the recently published Life & Letters of Sir John Millais" (MS p. 36) and adds: "I think it a pity that Sir John Millais [a victim of throat cancer] did not follow that advice" (MS p. 38). On 24 November 1899 Clemens wrote to J. Y. W. MacAlister, quoting the passage from Lord Frederic Leighton's letter to Millais, and inquiring as to whether Lord Leighton (1830–1896) had actually used the Kellgren system himself (ALS in ASSSCL).

MILLER, ANNIE JENNESS (1859–1935). *Physical Beauty: How to Obtain and How to Preserve It.* Illustrated by May R. Kern. New York: Charles L. Webster & Co., 1892. 246 pp.

Clemens's publishing firm advertised this book for women—a handbook on hygiene, food, sleep, skin, eyes, hair, dress, and "cultivation of Individuality"— in the *Publishers' Trade List Annual for 1893.* Miller, a leader in the reform movement advocating less restrictive dress requirements for women, designed new dress styles, edited a fashion magazine, and lectured on feminine health and beauty.

MILLER, ELIZABETH JANE (1878–1961). *The Yoke: A Romance of the Days When the Lord Redeemed the Children of Israel from the Bondage of Egypt.* Indianapolis, Indiana: Bobbs-Merrill Co., [cop. 1904]. 616 pp.

Source: MTLAcc, entry #220, volume donated by Clemens.

MILLER, GEORGE ERNEST (1855–1928). *Luxilla: A Romance.* [Mobile, Alabama], n.d. [cop. 1885]. 54 pp.

According to a notebook Mark Twain kept during the summer of 1886, he planned to "review 'Luxilla' that hogwash novel from the South" (NB 26, *N&J* 3: 240) Apparently Twain did not carry through with this impulse to ridicule Miller's overwrought novella. Miller turned out a number of other writings, including *Corolene, A Poem* (Mobile, 1886), *Mobilia, A Novel* (Mobile, 1886), and

(in 1915) a novel about alcoholic prohibition, *Colonel Berry's Challenge, A Novel* (self-published by Miller in Covington, Kentucky). George Ernest Miller, the son of a Mobile banker who had been prosperous before the Civil War, married in 1891 in Massachusetts, lived in Nutley, New Jersey for more than a decade, and for the last seventeen years of his life had a magazine advertising agency in Washington, D. C. He was seventy two years old when he died in a Covington, Kentucky hospital after failing to recover from a fall he suffered on a street in Washington, D. C.

MILLER, HARRIET (MANN) (1831–1918), pseud. "Olive Thorne Miller." *Little Folks in Feathers and Fur, and Others in Neither.* New York: E. P. Dutton & Co., 1880. 368 pp.

Source: MTLAcc, entry #1970, volume donated from Clemens's library by Clara Clemens Gabrilowitsch in 1910. "Susie and Clara Clemens's copy," binding worn.

Shortly after Annie Moffett Webster moved from Fredonia to New York City, she wrote to her brother Samuel E. Moffett about her Christmas-gift buying excursion: "We meant to go to Leggat's but I was thankful to stop at Dutton's on Broadway and buy all the books we wanted there. We bought . . . 'Little Folks in feathers and fur' for Susie [Clemens]" (19 December 1881, ALS in MTP).

———. *Little People of Asia.* New York: E. P. Dutton & Co., 1883. 405 pp.

Source: MTLAcc, entry #1898, volume donated from Clemens's library by Clara Clemens Gabrilowitsch in 1910.

Miller describes the lives of children in thirteen Asian cultures, including the young people of China and Japan.

———. *True Bird Stories from My Note-Books.* Illus. First edition. Illustrated by Louis Agassiz Fuertes (1874–1927). Original decorated cream cloth, pictorial color label on the front cover. Boston: Houghton, Mifflin and Co., 1903. 156 pp.

Inscription: the front pastedown endpaper is inscribed by Clemens in black ink: "To/Jean Clemens/with her Father's love/Sept. 1903./[blank space]/It is never too late to mend./There's plenty of time./M.T." The book stamp of the Mark Twain Library in Redding, Connecticut appears above Clemens's inscription. The Mark Twain Library of Redding accession number "1971" appears in red ink twice on the rear pastedown endpaper along with the remnants of a torn library card jacket.

Provenance: MTLAcc, entry #1971, volume donated from Clemens's library by Clara Clemens Gabrilowitsch in 1910. Offered to Christie's in New York City in 2008 (email, Kate Hunter of Christie's to Alan Gribben, 8 November 2008).

Location: collection of Kevin Mac Donnell, Austin, Texas. He obtained it from Christie's in July 2009.

Copy examined: photocopies of the front cover, spine, and endpapers of an unmarked copy belonging to Jean Clemens. A letter from Kevin Mac Donnell to Alan Gribben, 30 July 1989, provided many details.

MILLER, HUGH (1802–1856). *The Cruise of the Betsey; or, A Summer Ramble Among the Fossiliferous Deposits of the Hebrides. With Rambles of a Geologist; or, Ten Thousand Miles Over the Fossiliferous Deposits of Scotland.* Ed. by William Samuel Symonds (1818–1887). Boston: Gould and Lincoln, 1858. 524 pp. [Publisher and pages conjectured.]

Inscription: the front flyleaf is signed "S. L. Clemens, 1908."

On the flyleaf Clemens drew a diagram contrasting the age of the world and the brief period of humans' existence.

Catalog: *A1911*, "12mo, original cloth (a few leaves loose, part of back broken), Bost. 1858," quotes the signature and describes a diagram in Clemens's hand on a flyleaf, lot 332, $5.50.

————. *The Foot-Prints of the Creator.* From the third London edition. Biographical memoir by Louis Agassiz (1807–1873). Illus. Boston: Gould and Lincoln, 1866. 337 pp.

Source: MTLAcc, entry #537, volume donated by Clemens.

————. *The Testimony of the Rocks; or, Geology in its Bearings on the Two Theologies, Natural and Revealed. With Memorials of the Death and Character of the Author.* Boston: Gould and Lincoln, 1857. 502 pp.

Catalog: ListABP (1910), "Testimony of the Rocks, Miller", no other information supplied.

On Saturday, 5 December 1908, Isabel Lyon noted that "at dinner the King talked a lot about Geology, a never failing topic full of interest for him. Just now he is reading Hugh Miller on the Rocks. . . . The wonders and mystery of the earth never lose their mysteries for him" (IVL Journals, TS p. 344, MTP). Clemens made a notation on the front pastedown endpaper of his copy of Alexander Winchell's *Sketches of Creation* (1903): "I had been re-reading Hugh Miller (ed. 1857), & wanted to contrast the geology of to-day with the geology of his day. I discovered no contrast" (MTP). See also Mark Twain's "No Poets in Pittsfield" (MS in Paine 246, MTP).

Cummings, "Mark Twain's Acceptance of Science" (1962).

MILLER, JOAQUIN, I.E. CINCINNATUS HEINE MILLER (1837–1913). *Songs of the Sierras.* Boston: Roberts Brothers, 1871. 299 pp.

Inscription: the front flyleaf is inscribed by Olivia Clemens in pencil, "S. L. Clemens/1871".

Location: Mark Twain Library, Redding, Connecticut. Donated from Clemens's library by Clara Clemens Gabrilowitsch in 1910 (MTLAcc, entry #2064).

Copy examined: Clemens's unmarked copy of Miller's poems. Has a penciled Mark Twain Library accession number, "2064". Examined in 1970 and again in June 1982 and on 9 November 2019.

Songs of the Sierras collected ten of Miller's Western-themed poems, including "Kit Carson's Ride," "The Tale of the Tall Alcalde," and "Californian." A number of the poems are lengthy; all strive for imagery evoking the landscape, as in "Even So": "Where pine-tops toss curly clouds to heaven/And shake them far like to downs of thistle,/. . . Where men wrought gold from the rock-ribbed mountain" (p. 279).

————. *Unwritten History: Life Amongst the Modocs.* Hartford: American Publishing Co., 1874. 445 pp.

Marginalia: a note by Clemens in pencil on page 438 refers humorously to Miller's illegible handwriting. This is the only annotation.

Catalog: *A1911*, "8vo, cloth, Hartford, 1874, first edition," lot 333, sold for $2.50.

Location: California Historical Society Library, San Francisco, California.

Copy examined: Clemens's copy, inspected in 1971. Contains the bookplate of Laurance Irving Scott.

Miller was being accorded the treatment of a literary lion in London when Clemens spent the summer there in 1873. (Clemens had known Miller in the 1860s in San Francisco.) On 1 July 1873 Clemens wrote cordially to Miller (*MTLet* 5: 394–395), and on 6 July 1873 Clemens informed Mary Mason Fairbanks: "We see Miller every day or two, & like him better & better all the time. He is just getting out his Modoc book here [in London, published in 1873 by Richard Bentley & Son] & I have made him go to my publishers in America with it (by letter) & they will make some money for him" (*MTMF*, p. 174; *MTLet* 5: 402). Anthony Trollope fêted Miller at a dinner on 7 July 1873 at the Garrick Club to which Clemens was invited (*MTLet* 5: 406 n. 11). Clemens mentioned Miller's forthcoming book in a letter to Elisha Bliss written on 16 July 1873 (NB 12, *N&J* 1: 567). In 1873, hardly by coincidence, Susy Clemens acquired the nickname "Modoc" because of the cut of her hair (*S&MT*, p. 20). Clemens ordered a copy of Miller's book (and four written by himself, along with three other books) to be shipped to a home for disabled soldiers in Elizabeth, Virginia, on 17 February 1876 (SLC to Elisha Bliss, ALS in ASSSCL). In 1907 Clemens would remember attending a dinner in England in honor of Joaquin Miller: "He was affecting the picturesque and untamed costume of the wild Sierras at the time, to the charmed astonishment of conventional London, and was helping out the effects with the breezy and independent and aggressive manners of that far away and romantic region." Now, Clemens added, "Joaquin Miller is white-headed and mute and quiet in his dear mountains" (19 August 1907 AD, *MTE*, pp. 332–333; *AutoMT* 3: 103).

MILLER, MARY FARRAND (ROGERS) (1868–1971). *The Brook Book; A First Acquaintance with the Brook and Its Inhabitants Through the Changing Year.* New York: Doubleday, Page & Co., 1902. 241 pp.

Source: MTLAcc, entry #1972, volume donated from Clemens's library by Clara Clemens Gabrilowitsch in 1910.

MILLER, SAMUEL (1769–1850). *An Essay on the Warrant, Nature, and Duties of the Office of the Ruling Elder, in the Presbyterian Church.* Philadelphia: Presbyterian Board of Publication, [cop. 1832]. 339 pp.

Inscription: (in Orion Clemens's hand) in brown ink: "Orion Clemens/Christmas Eve/1865". Orion Clemens's bookplate is affixed to the front pastedown endpaper.

Location: Mark Twain Library, Redding, Connecticut. Donated by Clemens (MTLAcc, entry #931).

Copy examined: Orion Clemens's copy. Examined in 1970 and again in June 1982 and on 9 November 2019. Has the purple oval stamp of the Mark Twain Library.

MILLET, FRANCIS DAVIS (1846–1912). *The Expedition to the Philippines.* New York: Harper & Brothers, 1899. 275 pp.

Source: MTLAcc, entry #1734, volume donated by Clemens.

MILLET, PIERRE (1635–1709). *Captivity Among the Oneidas in 1690–91 of Father Pierre Milet [sic] of the Society of Jesus.* Ed. by John Gilmary Shea (1824–1892). Translated and annotated by Emma Augusta (Burbank) Ayer (1845–1932). Number 54 of 75 copies printed. Chicago: Blakely Printing Co., 1897. 72 pp.

Inscription: the front pastedown endpaper has a highly questionable "S. L. Clemens/Mark Twain" autograph in ink. The front free flyleaf displays a dubious inscription, "My Book/Frederic Remington". There is a feeble-looking effort to draw (or trace?) a bucking horse below the Remington inscription. Comparing these two signatures to genuine examples of their autographs reveals significant flaws in virtually every letter. One must be cautious about books originating in Illinois and allegedly signed by "Mark Twain"; Eugene Field II and his confederate Harry Dayton Sickles were active forgers in the Chicago vicinity.

Location: Rare Book and Manuscripts Library, University of Illinois at Urbana-Champaign. Originally this volume belonged to the Franklin J. Meine American Humor and Folklore Collection, as a bookplate on the front pastedown endpaper attests.

Copy examined: Information compiled from an email and photocopy sent on 11 June 2020 by Caroline Szylowicz, Kolb-Proust Librarian, Curator of Rare Book and Manuscripts. I am grateful for her assistance.

MILLHOUSE, JOHN and FERDINANDO BRACCIFORTI. *New English and Italian Pronouncing and Explanatory Dictionary, with Many New Additions.* Eighth edition. 2 vols. Milan: Printed for the Editor F[erdinando]. Bracciforti, 1900.

Inscription: the front free endpaper is inscribed, "To dear Miss Lyon,/with much love/and best wishes for/a Merry Christmas./Jean L. Clemens./Firenze, Dec. 25th 1903."

Marginalia: Volume II contains pencil marks and a note by Isabel Lyon at the top of page 512; there are a few grammar notes at the back of the volume.

Location: Mark Twain House and Museum, Hartford, Connecticut. Donated by Professor Norman Holmes Pearson (1909–1975) of Yale University in 1966.

Copy examined: Isabel Lyon's copy, a gift from Jean Clemens. Isabel V. Lyon was Clemens's secretary-factotum after the death of Olivia Clemens in 1904. Examined in August 1987.

MILLS, S[ALLIE]. M. *Palm Branches.* Sandusky, Ohio: Register Steam Press, 1878. 128 pp.

Marginalia: on the recto of the blank page opposite the copyright notice

Clemens speculated that the writer of this novel must be about fifteen years old. He jotted derogatory remarks throughout the volume, first in black ink, then purple ink, and finally (in the latter half) in pencil. On page 65 he penciled his opinion that "puberty will do much for this authoress." He noted on page 120 that when the character named Daisy remained the same "simple, beautiful maiden" despite Mr. Russell's lavishing every luxury upon her (including "pearls and precious gems that a princess might have coveted"), it was "a school-girl's idea of triumph." He made numerous other sarcastic comments. There were several women named Sallie Mills living in Ohio during this era and it is difficult to determine which of them might have written *Palm Branches.*

Catalogs: ListABP (1910), "Palm Branches, Mills"; "Retz Appraisal" (1944), p. 10, valued at $15.

Location: Mark Twain Papers, Bancroft Library, University of California at Berkeley.

Copy examined: Clemens's copy.

MILLS, WEYMER JAY (1880–1938). *Caroline of Courtlandt Street.* Illustrated by Anna Whelan Betts (1873–1959). New

York: Harper & Brothers, 1905. 291 pp.

Source: MTLAcc, entry #1047, volume donated by Clemens.

Mills set his romantic novel in New Jersey and New York City shortly after the American Revolution.

MILNE, JAMES (1865–1951). *The Romance of a Pro-Consul; Being the Personal Life and Memoirs of the Right Hon. Sir George Grey, K. C. B. [1812–1898].* London: Chatto & Windus, 1899. 214 pp.

Inscription: on the front free endpaper (not in Clemens's hand): "R. W. G. from C L. C."

Marginalia: the first eleven pages (but none beyond those) contain voluminous notes in pencil by Clemens, mainly derogatory. He labeled various passages "meaningless," "unnecessary—& juvenile," and "not simple enough—too affected." Beside the third paragraph on page 11, a passage Milne set off by quotation marks, Clemens noted: "This was taken down short-hand or it would have been bitched." He added: "*This* is English, & plain, simple, respectable." At numerous points Clemens corrected the text as though he were its editor. On a blank leaf at the front of the volume, Clemens made this assessment: "The book is affected, artificial, vulgar, airy, trivial, a mess of wandering & aimless twaddle, a literary puke. Its empty, noisy, assiduous imitation of Carlyle is a comical thing— Carlyle's batteries firing blank cartridges. It is a foolish poor book, & had nothing to say & has accomplished its mission." Clemens concluded this evaluation by explaining how he had "struck out a part of the lavish surplusage," marking with the symbol [a circle with an "x" inside] those "passages which had no discoverable meaning—& no purpose, except to be 'fine,'" and designating as "*c. 1.*" ("cow literature") the prose "which is intelligible but lumbering & clumsy."

Catalogs: ListABP (1910), "Romance of a Proconsul, Milne"; *C1951*, #23a, $17.50, listed among books containing Clemens's marginal notations.

Provenance: collection of Frank C. Willson (1889–1960) in Melrose, Massachusetts. Sold by his widow Margarete Willson in 1962 to the University of Texas at Austin.

Location: Harry Ransom Center, University of Texas at Austin.

Copy examined: Clemens's copy.

Alan Gribben, "Mark Twain Library Books in the Humanities Research Center" (1979), pp. 19–21 (reproduces a facsimile sample of Clemens's marginalia in Milne's book).

MILNER, HENRY M. (fl. 1826–1885). *Mazeppa: A Romantic Drama in Three Acts. Dramatized from Lord Byron's Poem* (performed in London in 1831).

In San Francisco Mark Twain went to see Adah Isaacs Menken (1835–1868), "that manly young female," in this role on 9 September 1863, and wrote a lengthy, sarcastic review of the play on 13 September 1863 (*MTEnt*, pp. 78–80).

Justin Martin, *Rebel Souls: Walt Whitman and America's First Bohemians* (Boston: Da Capo Press, 2014), pp. 142–151; Randall Knoper, *Acting Naturally: Mark Twain in the Culture of Performance* (Berkeley: University of California Press, 1995), pp. 49, 51, 53.

MILNES, RICHARD MONCKTON, LORD HOUGHTON 1ST BARON (1809–1885).

Clemens met this poet and statesman in London in 1873

(NB 12, *N&J* 1: 519, 532–535) and wrote to him on 1 September 1875 (*MTLet* 6: 531) and 10 October 1875 (*MTLet* 6: 558).

MILTON, JOHN (1608–1674). *L'Allegro and Other Poems.* Ed. Horace E. Scudder (1838–1902). Riverside Literature Series, No. 72. Boston: Houghton, Mifflin & Co., 1895. 96 pp.

Catalog: Ball 2016 inventory, green cloth, black lettering, good condition, signed by Ida Langdon in 1920.

Location: Quarry Farm library shelves, under the supervision of the Mark Twain Archive, Elmira College, Elmira, New York.

Since this was a copy owned by Ida Langdon (1880–1964), she presumably acquired it for academic purposes and it is unlikely that Clemens ever had access to the volume.

————. *Milton's Paradise Lost.* Illustrated by [Paul] Gustave Doré (1832–1883). Edited and introduction by Robert Vaughan, D. D. (1795–1868). New York: Cassell Publishing Co., [1866]. 311 pp. 50 plates. [Edition conjectured; four Milton editions illustrated by Doré were published in 1866 alone.]

On 6 January 1870, writing to Olivia Langdon from New York City, Clemens mentioned that Daniel Slote "has already selected a Doré for me (for you) & ordered it to be expressed to Elmira" (*MTLet* 4: 1). He followed up when writing to Olivia from Albany, New York on 10 January 1870: "I suppose the book has reached you by this time" (*MTLet* 4: 19). Clemens wrote to Olivia from Utica on 15 January 1870: "I am so glad the Milton pleases my idol—I am delighted. Oh, we'll read, & look at pictures when we are married!" (*MTLet* 4: 28).

Clemens alluded to *Paradise Lost* frequently. While piloting on the river around 1858, he wrote to Orion: "What is the grandest thing in 'Paradise Lost'—the Arch- Fiend's terrible energy!" (*MTB*, p. 146). On 20 March 1862 Clemens informed his mother from Carson City: "There are no prairies, Ma, because sage-brush deserts don't come under that head, in this portion of Paradise Lost" (*MTLet* 1: 175). In a 10 September 1866 letter from Honolulu to the Sacramento *Weekly Union*, Mark Twain congratulated Hawaii and California on their futures: "We have found the true and only direct route to the bursting coffers of 'Ormus and of Ind'" (*LH*, p. 56; cf. *Paradise Lost*, 2: 2). Twain mocked a Congressman's poetic reference to "wide/ As were the thoughts of Milton's soul" in an 1868 column for the Washington *Intelligencer* (reprinted in the *Mark Twain Quarterly* 5.2 [Summer 1942]: 2). In a letter of 1 April 1870 Clemens alluded to Pandemonium, Lucifer's seat (*MTLet* 4: 547). Two years later he wrote waggishly, "If it had been left to you [the reader], you would have said . . . that even 'Paradise Lost' lacked cheerfulness" ("A General Reply" *Galaxy* 10.5 [November 1870]: 733; *CG*, p. 97; *CTSS&E* 1: 487). Clemens mentioned *Paradise Lost* to Mary Mason Fairbanks on 31 October 1877 (*MTMF*, p. 212). In a speech to the Nineteenth Century Club on 20 November 1900, he quipped: "I don't believe any of you have ever read 'Paradise Lost,' and you don't want to. That's something that you just want to take on trust. It's a classic, just as Professor [Caleb Thomas] Winchester [1847–1920] says, and it meets his definition of a classic—something that everybody wants to have read and nobody wants to read" ("Disappearance of Literature,"

MTB [1912], p. 1120; *MTS1923*, p. 210; Fatout, *MTSpk* [1976], p. 359).

George Peirce Clark, "The Devil That Corrupted Hadleyburg," *Mark Twain Journal* 10.2 (Winter 1956): 1–4; Parsons, "Background" (1960), p. 62; Gibson, *MSM* (1969), p. 32 n. 77; Baetzhold, *MT&JB* (1970), pp. 262–264; Gary Scharnhorst, "Paradise Revisited: Twain's 'The Man That Corrupted Hadleyburg,'" *Studies in Short Fiction* 18.1 (Winter 1981): 59–64.

————. *Milton's Poetical Works : . . Together with the Life of the Author* [written by Elijah Fenton, 1683–1730]. Illus. Marble endpapers. New York: Charles Wells, [183–]. 321 pp. + 232 pp.

Inscription: the first flyleaf is missing.

Marginalia: someone totted up arithmetic figures (totals of 4.38, 39, and 4.96) on the verso of the front free endpaper. A large, ornate letter "C" or "L" has been drawn above them in brown ink. There is a reference to "Ly" (i.e., Lydia?) at the bottom of the same endpaper. Page 46 is turned down in *Paradise Regained*. There are small penciled "x's" uncharacteristic of Clemens beside some stanzas of "The Hymn" (pp. 162–166). Markings on page 166 are not by Clemens. A rear flyleaf contains two more penciled arithmetic figures ("18" repeated twice). No other marks.

Location: Mark Twain Library, Redding, Connecticut.

Copy examined: a highly dubious addition to Clemens's library. The likelihood is much greater that the book was another donation from the Hill family—which included an early resident named Lydia Hill—to the Mark Twain Library. It has no accession number. The only reason that it was originally listed in *Mark Twain's Library: A Reconstruction* (1980) was that previous to 1970 someone had shelved the volume with other books that had belonged to Clemens. I examined it in 1970 and again (far more skeptically) in June 1982 and on 9 November 2019.

————. *Paradise Lost.* New York: J. W. Lovell Co., 1881. 291 pp.

Source: MTLAcc, entry #2072, volume donated from Clemens's library by Clara Clemens Gabrilowitsch in 1910.

————. *Paradise Lost. A Poem in Twelve Books.* Portrait. Engraved frontispiece portrait. Contemporary sheep. London: Printed by C. Whittingham for L. Wayland, [n.d., c. 1825]. Original full sheep, morocco label, gilt. 289 pp.

Inscription: (in pencil on front flyleaf) "Olivia Langdon/ Presented by her/Father/Edward Lewis." This was a gift to Olivia Clemens's mother, Olivia Lewis Langdon (1810–1890), sometime after her marriage in 1832 to Jervis Langdon (1809–1870).

Catalogs: *A 1911*, "24mo, sheep, not returnable, Lond. n.d.," quotes the inscription, lot 334, sold for $3 to the Mark Twain Company; *Sotheby's 2003*, #192, $1,100 (sold with three other books from the Clemens family library).

Provenance: Robert H. Hirst, Editor of the Mark Twain Papers, reported that this volume was owned by Olivia Lada-Mocarski in May 1980 (Hirst to Alan Gribben, 4 February 1981). Subsequently it was in the collection of Nick Karanovich of Fort Wayne, Indiana.

Location: collection of Kevin Mac Donnell, Austin, Texas.

Copy examined: an unmarked copy belonging to Olivia Clemens's mother, viewed in July 2004. It bears the *A1911* sale label.

Clemens had access to this book whenever he visited the Langdon residence in Elmira.

———. *Il Penseroso* (poem, published in 1632).

Mark Twain uses the phrase "dim religious light" in Chapter 23 of *The Innocents Abroad* (1869), and the phrase occurs again in Clemens's dictation of June 1873 concerning the Athenaeum Club in London (NB 12, *N&J* 1: 533). He evoked those words again in describing the Cathedral in New Orleans ("dim with religious light") in Chapter 44 of *Life on the Mississippi* (1883). Lines 159–160 of Milton's poem refer to "Storied windows richly dight,/Casting a dim religious light."

———. *The Poetical Works of John Milton*. Ed. by Sir Samuel Egerton Brydges (1762–1837). Illustrated by John Martin (1789–1854) and J[oseph]. M[allard]. W[illiam]. Turner (1775–1851). Boston: Crosby, Nichols, Lee & Co., 1861. 858 pp.

Source: MTLAcc, entry #2121a, donated from Clemens's library by Clara Clemens Gabrilowitch in 1910. "Cover broken." It is disappointing that this book, possibly one of the earliest volumes he acquired, was discarded or lost.

Mark Twain advised aspiring newspaper critics of literature to assign "all the grand ponderous ditto [i. e., verse], with a solemn lustre as of holiness about it, to Milton" (*Californian*, 17 June 1865; *LAMT*, p. 141; *ET&S* 2: 195). Milton's remains are buried in Westminster Abbey, Twain noted in "A Memorable Midnight Experience" (1872). A footnote to Chapter 16 of *Roughing It* (1872) credits Milton with coining the word "smouched." Petitioning for copyright reform, Twain alluded to "the heirs of . . . Milton" in a paragraph (intended for but possibly not included) in a letter to U. S. Representative Samuel S. Cox on 8 February 1875 (*MTLet* 6: 377). One of Twain's comical menu captions for a Hartford banquet in June 1881 was credited to "John Milton" (Beinecke Rare Book and Manuscript Library, Yale University; Everett Emerson to Alan Gribben, 29 October 1982). In September 1887, inspired by Ignatius Donnelly's *The Great Cryptogram*, Twain constructed an elaborate argument "proving" that John Milton rather than John Bunyan actually wrote *The Pilgrim's Progress*. Twain listed every major event in Milton's life, sometimes referring to page numbers of a biography, and demonstrated that Milton's experiences adequately prepared him to write the work for which Bunyan received credit. In the course of Twain's argument, he alludes to most of Milton's major poems. Although Twain is joshing here (he also claims that Bunyan must have written *Paradise Lost*), Twain's pro-Bacon treatise of 1909, *Is Shakespeare Dead?*, will follow the same logic: Milton traveled more, knew more famous people, possessed a greater reputation among his contemporaries, was a finer scholar, and therefore must have written the "immortal *Dream*" of *Pilgrim's Progress* (NB 27, *N&J* 3: 325–328). Twain listed Milton among the famous personages "materialized" by charlatan spiritualists in Chapter 3 of *The American Claimant* (1892). In December 1892 Twain referred to 'Milton, Sonnet" when devising literary japes in Notebook 32 (TS p. 47). In "My First Lie, and How I Got Out of It" (1899) Twain jocularly attributes the authorship of *The Lay of the Last Minstrel* to Milton. Twain seems momentarily sincere in "About Cities in the Sun" (written in 1901?, DV357, MTP) when he acknowledges what "a wonderful experience" it would

be to stand in the New Jerusalem "& hear Shakspeare & Milton & Bunyan read from their noble works" (MS p. 19). In a letter to "Miss Marjory" of 30 October 1908 Clemens facetiously pretended to confuse Milton with Pontius Pilate (Alan C. Fox, Catalog 1 [1980], item 10). On 9 December 1908 Mark Twain wrote regretfully to decline an invitation to a ceremony in New York City honoring John Milton; had he been able to attend, he wrote, he might have "lifted some of that cloud" from the "solemn & sombre function" and "let in the sunshine" (SLC to Frances Nunnally, ALS in the collection of Mrs. John Goodrich, TS in MTP).

———. *Treasures from the Prose Writings of John Milton*. Ed. by Fayette Hurd (1836–1922). Boston: Ticknor and Fields, 1866. 486 pp.

Source: Ball 2016 inventory, black cloth, faded lettering, fair condition, J. Langdon Family Library bookplate #116.

Location: Quarry Farm library shelves, under the supervision of the Mark Twain Archive, Elmira College, Elmira, New York.

This book was accessible to Clemens when he visited the Langdon house in Elmira.

MINES, JOHN FLAVEL (1835–1891). *A Tour Around New York, and My Summer Acre; Being the Recreations of Mr. Felix Oldboy.* Illus. New York: Harper & Brothers, 1893. 518 pp.

Source: MTLAcc, entry #1735, volume donated by Clemens.

Mines visited, for the reader's benefit, dozens of historic sites in New York City and a few other cities around the state, including Albany. Most of the structures in New York City were still standing, but he also reminisced about the former locations of theaters and other features that had vanished. He embellished his descriptions with humorous anecdotes and asides.

MINING LIFE IN WALES. [Unidentified book.]

Mark Twain intended to include this book in the projected series he planned to title "Royalty & Nobility Exposed" (NB 26, May 1887, *N&J* 3: 295). Unfortunately he did not supply the author's name.

MINSTREL SHOWS.

Edgar M. Branch and Robert H. Hirst cited William Birch as one of Clemens's favorite minstrel performers (*ET&S* 1: 490); they recommended Edward Le Roy Rice's *Monarchs of Minstrelsy* (1911) as a repository of information on the general subject. Eric Lott's *Love and Theft: Blackface, Minstrelsy, and the American Working Class* (New York: Oxford University Press, 1993), a comprehensive study, documented Clemens's fondness for blackface minstrel shows. (See the Reader's Guide entry for Minstrel songs.) Among other useful discussions, see Henry B. Wonham's *Playing the Races: Ethnic Caricature and American Literary Realism* (New York: Oxford University Press, 2004); Sharon D. McCoy's "Cultural Critique in *Tom Sawyer Abroad*: Behind Jim's Minstrel Mask," *Mark Twain Annual* 4 (2006): 71–90; Wonham's "Mark Twain's Last Cakewalk: Racialized Performance in *No. 44, The Mysterious Stranger*," *American Literary Realism* 40.3 (Spring 2008): 262–271—reprinted in *Centenary Reflections on Mark Twain's* No. 44, The Mysterious Stranger, ed. Joseph Csicsila and Chad Rohman (Columbia: University of Missouri Press, 2009), pp. 41–50; Sharon D. McCoy's "'I ain' no dread being':

The Minstrel Mask as Alter Ego," *Centenary Reflections on Mark Twain's* No. 44, The Mysterious Stranger (2009), pp. 13–40; and McCoy's "'The Trouble Begins at Eight': Mark Twain, the San Francisco Minstrels, and the Unsettling Legacy of Blackface Minstrelsy," *American Literary Realism* 41.3 (Spring 2009): 232–248.

THE MISSIONARY HERALD AT HOME AND ABROAD (Boston, Massachusetts, 1805–1951).

Mark Twain recalled that "bound copies of The Missionary Herald" were generally observable in homes of Honolulu in the 1860s (*FE*, Ch. 3, 1897). Old Mrs. Richards of "The Man That Corrupted Hadleyburg" (1899) is "reading the *Missionary Herald* by the lamp" when the malevolent stranger deposits a sack of gold with her (Ch. 1, Part 1).

Susan K. Harris, "'Hadleyburg': Mark Twain's Dual Attack on Banal Theology and Banal Literature," *American Literary Realism* 16.2 (Autumn 1983): 240–252, especially p. 247.

MITCHELL, DONALD GRANT (1822–1908), pseud. "Ik Marvel." *About Old Story-Tellers; Of How and When They Lived, and What Stories They Told.* Illus. New York: Scribner, Armstrong, and Co., 1878. 237 pp.

Source: MTLAcc, entry #1899, volume donated from Clemens's library by Clara Clemens Gabrilowitsch in 1910.

———. *Dream Life.* Leather suede brown cover. New York: H. M. Caldwell Co., [1895]. 265 pp.

Provenance: Antenne-Dorrance Collection, Rice Lake, Wisconsin.

Location: Mark Twain Archive, Gannett-Tripp Learning Center, Elmira College, Elmira, NY.

Copy examined: an unmarked copy shelved with Clemens's library books in Rice Lake. Its original provenance is uncertain but it likely came from the Clemenses' family library. Examined on 28 May 2015.

———. *Dream Life.* New York: Optimus Printing Co., n.d. [1894?]. 234 pp.

Source: MTLAcc, entry #692, volume donated by Albert Bigelow Paine, Clemens's designated biographer. Possibly Clemens saw this book, since the men exchanged reading materials.

———. *Reveries of a Bachelor; or, a Book of the Heart. A New Edition.* Green cloth, gilt lettering on spine. New York: Charles Scribner and Co., 1866. 280 pp.

Inscription: signed in pencil on the front free endpaper, "SL Clemens". The style of the hand is very similar to Clemens's signatures of the 1860s.

Location: Mark Twain Library, Redding, Connecticut.

Copy examined: Clemens's copy, unmarked but worn. It contains a penciled accession number: "2879". I examined this volume in 1970 and again in June 1982 and on 9 November 2019.

On Christmas morning in 1877 Clemens kidded Mrs. Jervis Langdon in a thank-you letter: "I have taken Ida's House Beautiful & Baby Days & Ik Marvel's book, & shall give Livy & the children copies of my works in place of them" (ALS in MTP). (This could have been the copy of *About Old Story-Tellers; Of How and When They Lived, and What Stories They Told*; then, as now, publishers sometimes released books slightly in advance of the publication dates that appeared on their title pages.) The author and newspaperman Henry Perkins Goddard (1842–1916)

recalled giving a dinner for Mitchell in Hartford that Clemens attended around 1879. When Clemens began to explain to the other guests his techniques for public speaking, Goddard reported, "Mr. Mitchell was much interested" ("Anecdotes of Mark Twain," *Harper's Weekly* 50.2566 [24 February 1906]: 280). George William Curtis (1824–1892), illustrating how "ominivorous" autograph collectors can be, reported that a young woman petitioned Mark Twain for his signature because she "had only just read his *Reveries of a Bachelor* [*sic*]" and consequently wanted to retain a token of that memory ("Editor's Easy Chair," *Harper's Monthly Magazine* 72.431 [April 1886]; 807).

MITCHELL, EDWARD CUSHING (1829–1900). *The Critical Handbook of the Greek New Testament.* New and enl. edition. New York: Harper & Brothers, 1896. 270 pp.

Source: MTLAcc, entry #1469, volume donated by Clemens.

MITCHELL, ISAAC (1759–1812). *The Asylum; or, Alonzo and Melissa* (published in 1811). More widely known as *Alonzo and Melissa; or, The Unfeeling Father. An American Tale.* [Authorship was also claimed by Daniel Jackson.]

In a letter of 24 March 1869 to Mary Mason Fairbanks, Mark Twain jocularly proposed the name of this Gothic romance as a title for the book that became *The Innocents Abroad* (1869) (*MTMF*, p. 87; *MTLet* 3: 176). "The House Beautiful" in Chapter 38 of *Life on the Mississippi* (1883) contained a copy of "Alonzo and Melissa."

Brashear, *MTSM* (1934), p. 204 n. 22.

MITCHELL, JOSIAH ANGIER (1812–1876). *The Diary of Captain Josiah A. Mitchell.* N.p., 1866. 110 pp.

In 1898 Mark Twain recalled how he relied on Mitchell's manuscript log—and the diaries kept by the Ferguson brothers—in reconstructing their harrowing experience in "Forty-three Days in an Open Boat" (1866) after the burning of the clipper ship *Hornet* ("My Début as a Literary Person," 1899).

MITCHELL, S[ILAS]. WEIR (1829–1914). *Hugh Wynne, Free Quaker, Sometime Brevet Lieutenant-Colonel on the Staff of His Excellency General Washington.* 2 vols. New York: Century House, 1898.

Catalog: Ball 2016 inventory, gray cloth with red lettering, embosse seal, good condition.

Location: Quarry Farm library shelves, under the supervision of the Mark Twain Archive, Elmira College, Elmira, New York.

A work of fiction by the eminent physician S. Weir Mitchell, set in Revolutionary times and principally taking place in and around Philadelphia. This volume was available to Clemens during his final visits to Quarry Farm in Elmira.

MITFORD, ALGERNON BERTRAM FREEMAN-, BARON REDESDALE (1837–1916). *Tales of Old Japan* (published in 1871).

In the margin of another book—Tamenaga Shunsui and Edward Greey's *The Loyal Ronins: An Historical Romance, Translated from the Japanese* (New York, 1880)—Clemens opined: "Mitford's translation of the Ronin story is better literature than this one. S.L.C." (quoted in *A1911*, #268).

MITFORD, BERTRAM (1855–1914).

This British novelist was a member of London's Savage Club and wrote more than forty books after 1890, most of them set in Southern Africa. R. Kent Rasmussen suggested that Clemens would almost certainly have been aware that Mitford produced a series of novels in the vein of H. Rider Haggard (Rasmussen to Alan Gribben, email, 22 February 2007). In these instances of probable but unprovable circumstances one should always bear in mind how many volumes from Clemens's library were lost during his travels or donated to libraries without any records being made of their titles.

MITFORD, JOHN (1781–1859). *The Life of Milton*. [Published in *The Poetical Works of John Milton, with a Life of the Author*. London: W. Pickering, 1851.]

Mitford's was one of the "biogs of Milton" that Clemens listed in September 1887 (NB 27, *N&J* 3: 328).

MITFORD, MARY RUSSELL (1787–1855). *The Friendships of Mary Russell Mitford as Recorded in Letters from Her Literary Correspondents*. Ed. by Alfred Guy Kingan L'Estrange (1832–1915). New York: Harper & Brothers, 1882. 460 pp.

Source: MTLAcc, entry #1296, volume donated by Clemens.

MODI, (SIR) JIVANJI JAMSHEDJI (1854–1933).

"The model of the Towers [of Silence, where Parsees would dispose of their dead,] shown & explained by Mr. Modi. See his book," noted Clemens on 26 January 1896 in Bombay (NB 36, TS p. 26). Modi published numerous books in Bombay about the ceremonies and religion of the Parsees.

MOFFETT, SAMUEL ERASMUS (1860–1908). "Captains of Industry: Henry Huttleston Rogers," *Cosmopolitan* 33 (September 1902): 532–534.

The wealthy Henry H. Rogers welcomed any positive publicity as he and the Standard Oil Company of which he was a vice-president came under public scrutiny in the early twentieth century. Samuel E. Moffett, Clemens's nephew and a prominent newspaper and magazine reporter and editor, became an editor of *Collier's* before Moffett's death while swimming in the New Jersey surf in 1908. On 24 February 1903 Rogers wrote somewhat cryptically to Clemens, "I have your letters, and will make the appointment for the review of the article in the 'Cosmopolitan'" (*MTHHR*, p. 519).

———. *Suggestions on Government*. Chicago and New York: Rand, McNally & Co., 1894. 200 pp.

On 21 September 1893 Clemens wrote to Pamela Moffett and Annie Webster from New York City: "I will ask Mr. Hall for Sam's book; I shall be very glad to read it" (Webster Collection, TS in MTP). Moffett had earlier published *The Tariff. What It Is and What It Does* (Washington: Potomac Publishing Co., 1892).

"THE MOHAMMEDAN'S PRAYER" (unidentified poem).

In 1870 Olivia Clemens copied this poem into her commonplace book (DV161, MS pp. 99–100, MTP).

MOLANDON, RÉMI BOUCHER DE (1805–1893). *La famille de Jeanne d'Arc* (published in 1880).

See Ronald Jenn and Linda A. Morris, "The Sources of Mark Twain's *Personal Recollections of Joan of Arc*," *Mark Twain Journal* 55.1–2 (Spring/Fall 2017): 55–74, where they straightened out Twain's error in citing his sources for *Joan of Arc*. Twain accidentally conflated the authors and titles of two books; one of them was by Molandon.

MOLIÈRE, JEAN-BAPTISTE POQUELIN (1622–1673). *L'Avare: Comédie en Cinq Actes. Édition Nouvelle [The Miser: A Comedy in Five Acts.] Par M[aurice]. Pellisson [1850–1915]. Cinquieme Édition*. Tan boards. Paris: Librairie Ch. Delagrave, 1891. 114 pp. [First performed in 1668.]

Inscription: Jean Clemens signed the half-title page in black ink: "Jean Clemens/Le 12 Mars 95/Paris."

Location: Mark Twain Library, Redding, Connecticut.

Copy examined: Beth Dominianni, Director of the Mark Twain Library, showed me this book on 9 November 2019. It was the first time I had seen the volume, which definitely belonged to Jean Clemens.

MOLTKE, HELMUTH, GRAF VON (1800–1891). *Essays, Speeches and Memoirs*. Translated by Charles Flint McClumpha (1863–1933), Charles St. Leger Barter (1857–1931), and Mary Herms. 2 vols. New York: Harper & Brothers, 1893.

Source: MTLAcc, entries #1778 and #1779, volumes donated by Clemens.

Moltke was chief of staff of the Prussian Army for thirty years.

———. *Letters of Field-Marshall Count Helmuth von Moltke to His Mother and His Brothers*. Translated by Clara Bell (1834–1927) and Henry W. H. Fischer (1856–1932). Illus. New York: Harper & Brothers, 1893. 309 pp.

Source: MTLAcc, entry #1780, volume donated by Clemens.

Fisher's *Abroad with Mark Twain* (1922) mentions his sending Clemens "my translation of Field Marshal Count Moltke's Letters" (p. 120) and indicates that Clemens read the book. (Fisher sometimes permitted a variant spelling of his name as Fischer.)

MONAHAN, MICHAEL (1865–1933). "Saint Mark," *The Papyrus* 4.3 (December 1904).

Clemens wrote to Monahan from New York City on 28 January 1905: "It is strong & eloquent & beautiful & I thank you very much for giving me an opportunity to read it. The inspiration which tipped your pen with fire is from the Maid" (ALS in MTP). Monahan's article took note of Mark Twain's admiration for Joan of Arc. Monahan eventually would publish *My Jeanne d'Arc: Her Wonderful Story in the Light of Recent Researches; with Notes from a Pilgrimage in France* (New York and London: The Century Co., [cop. 1928]). See also the Catalog entry for *The Papyrus*.

LE MONITEUR (serial publication of the French Revolutionary period).

Clemens supposedly told Henry Fisher in the late 1890s that while in Paris "I was particularly interested in the 'Official Gazette' of the guillotine, 'The Moniteur,' and my girls helped me read and digest many tell-tale pages yellow with age and tattered by usage" (Fisher, *AMT*, p. 59).

Blair, "French Revolution" (1957), p. 22; Blair, *MT&HF* (1960), p. 312; Carl Dolmetsch, *"Our Famous Guest": Mark Twain in Vienna* (Athens: University of Georgia, 1992), p. 264.

MONNIER, MARC (1827–1885). *The Wonders of Pompeii. Translated from the Original French*. Illus. New York: Scribner, Armstrong & Co., 1872. 250 pp.

Inscription: the front free endpaper is signed (in pencil) "Saml. L. Clemens./Hartford, 1874."

Marginalia: a penciled note is visible in the margin of page 51: "2712—913 377—Mon".

Provenance: Mark Twain Library at Redding, Connecticut. Donated from Clemens's library by Clara Clemens

Gabrilowitsch in 1910 (MTLAcc, entry #1991).

Catalog: *Mott 1952*, item #70, $10.

Location: Mark Twain House and Museum, Hartford, Connecticut. Donated anonymously in 1963.

Copy examined: Clemens's copy. The spine is missing. Contains the bookstamps and charge slip of the Mark Twain Library at Redding, Connecticut. Examined in August 1987.

MONTAGU, MARY (PIERREPONT) WORTLEY (1689–1762). *The Letters of Lady Mary Wortley Montagu.* Ed. Sarah Josepha (Buell) Hale (1788–1879). Revised edition. Reddish orange cloth cover, worn, spine broken, pages loose. Boston: Roberts Brothers, 1869. 408 pp.

Inscription: the front free flyleaf is signed in pencil, "Livy L. Clem[ens]/1875". (The page corner is missing, taking with it the last three letters of her name.)

Marginalia: Clemens made penciled corrections, refining Montagu's prose style, on pages 219 ("resist the desire" he altered to "resist the revealment of the desire," "continuation of my spirits" he changed to "continuance of my spirits," and "I have wrote" he revised to "I have written"), 220 ("us, and the eager pursuit" became "us, <and> together with the eager pursuit"), 221 (insertions of the words "eager pursuit" and "that," and "easier" was changed to "more easily"), 222, 223, 225, and 226. All of these revisions occur in her letters to her husband, Edward Wortley Montagu (1678–1761), during her travels in Italy. Clemens did not mark Mary Wortley Montagu's vivid description of receiving a Turkish bath surrounded by Turkish women who were attended by their female slaves (pp. 68–71), though he had ridiculed this hyperbolized ritual in Chapter 34 of *The Innocents Abroad* (1869). It is possible, given the 1869 date of publication, that this was another of the courting books Clemens sent to Olivia Langdon; however, inasmuch as the tender marginalia that characterized those volumes is absent here it seems more likely that this copy of *The Letters of Mary Wortley Montagu* was purchased for the Hartford house library in 1875, when Olivia Clemens signed it.

Catalog: ListABP (1910), "Letters of Lady Montagu, Hale", no other information provided.

Provenance: Clara Clemens Gabrilowitsch's library shelf marks appear on the verso of the front free endpaper. These letters and numbers located books within her collection during her Detroit years.

Location: Mark Twain House and Museum, Hartford, Connecticut. Donated on 30 May 1986 by Yvonne Rogow of Los Angeles. Her father was a friend of Phyllis Harrington, Clara Clemens Samossoud's secretary and friend, and Harrington made Yvonne Rogow the executor of her estate.

Copy examined: Olivia Clemens's copy. Examined on 12 August 1987.

MONTAIGNE, MICHEL EYQUEM DE (1533–1592). *Works of Michael de Montaigne, Comprising His Essays, Journey into Italy, and Letters, with Notes from All the Commentators, Biographical and Bibliographical Notices, Etc.* Ed. by William Hazlitt (1811–1893). New, revised ed. prepared by O[rlando]. W[illiams]. Wight (1824–1888). 4 vols. New York: Hurd and Houghton, 1866.

Inscription: Volume I is signed "Saml. L. Clemens,

Hartford, 1873"; the other volumes are signed "S. L. Clemens."

Marginalia: there are a few remarks by Clemens in pencil.

Catalog: *A1911*, "4 vols., 12mo, cloth, N.Y. 1866, . . . a few pencil autograph remarks in pencil," quotes the signatures, lot 336, sold for $15 total.

Clemens made an equivocal reference ("see Montaigne") to the French courtier and essayist among his annotations in J. G. Wood's *The Uncivilized Races; or, Natural History of Man* (1870); see the Catalog entry for Wood. A letter of 8 January 1875 from Clemens to Louise Chandler Moulton alluded to "my delightful old random encyclopedia, Montaigne" (*MTLet* 6: 343). In Mark Twain's *1601* (1880), Shakespeare recalls feats of sexual prowess as well as other sexual matters discussed by Montaigne (Franklin J. Meine's edition, privately printed for the Mark Twain Society [Chicago, 1939], p. 36).

Blair, *MT&HF* (1960), p. 94.

MONTEITH, JOHN B. (1833–1918). *Parson Brooks: A Plumb Powerful Hard Shell. A Story of Humble Southern Life.* St. Louis: O. H. P. Applegate, 1884. 115 pp.

Source: MTLAcc, entry #1849, volume donated from Clemens's library by Clara Clemens Gabrilowitsch in 1910. The Reverend Monteith set his novel in the southern Missouri Ozarks, where a Union soldier settles after the Civil War and learns about the people of the region.

MONTGOMERY, LUCY MAUD (1874–1942). *Anne of Avonlea.* Boston: L. C. Page & Co., 1909. 367 pp.

Source: MTLAcc, entry #1484, volume donated by Clemens.

———. *Anne of Green Gables.* Boston: L. C. Page & Co., 1908. 429 pp.

On 12 October 1908 Clemens wrote to Frances Nunnally from Redding: "I'll send you a book—'Anne of Green Gables.' It came two days after you went away, & I was to read it & give it to Francis Wilson; but I was at once so taken with it that I thought I would send it to you & get another copy for him. I think Anne [Shirley] is a very pleasant child to know, & that the literary quality of the book is fine" (ALS in collection of Mrs. John Goodrich, TS in MTP). An advertisement in the house list of publications at the rear of the 1909 and subsequent impressions quotes a letter from Mark Twain to Francis Wilson (with a copy sent to the author Montgomery by Isabel V. Lyon): "In 'Anne of Green Gables' you will find the dearest & most moving & delightful child since the immortal Alice." The Canadian author Montgomery would write six sequels to this novel.

MONTI, LUIGI (1830–1914), pseud. "Samuel Sampleton." *Adventures of a Consul Abroad.* Boston: Lee and Shepard, 1878. 270 pp.

Clemens noted the title and publisher in Notebook 20 in March 1882 (*N&J* 2: 450), around the time he was consulting with Ulysses S. Grant about President Arthur's intention to replace William Dean Howells's father as the U. S. consul at Toronto. (The death of President Garfield had jeopardized the elder Howells's consular post.) Monti's *Adventures* narrated the problems that beset a Cape Cod schoolmaster who obtained a consular appointment to the mythical Mediterranean city of Verdecuerno. The inexperienced and underpaid functionary blunders through

MARK TWAIN'S LITERARY RESOURCES

unfamiliar European formalities and bungles his official responsibilities. Monti's book satirized the American spoils system, which changed appointees after every shift of political power in Washington. Monti laments: "Our government sends men abroad, who, after hard labor and long experience, learn a complicated, delicate, and responsible profession; and no sooner have they learned it, and are able to perform creditably . . . , than they are recalled, and replaced by inexperienced men, who have to go through the same ordeal, and never stay long enough to be of real service to their country" (p. 270).

MOODIE, SUSANNAH (STRICKLAND) (1803–1885).

Harold Aspiz—"Mark Twain's Reading" (1949), p. 224—cited a book supposedly by Susannah Moodie, *A Bride from the Bush*, as the source of one of the weather descriptions Twain appended to *The American Claimant* (1892). However, Moodie never published anything by this title, though she did write a narrative called *Roughing It in the Bush* (1852) recounting the seven and a half years she spent in the backwoods of Upper Canada. In reality Twain was being accurate in crediting a book titled *A Bride from the Bush*. The account of a dust-storm that Twain quoted came from Ernest William Hornung's novel by that name, *A Bride from the Bush*. See the Hornung entry in the Catalog.

MOODY, DWIGHT LYMAN (1837–1899).

In Mark Twain's "The Loves of Alonzo Fitz Clarence and Rosannah Ethelton" (1878), books by Moody and evangelist Ira David Sankey are noticeable in the "private parlor of a refined and sensible lady," Aunt Susan. Writing a letter he eventually never sent to the New York *Evening Post* (23 November 1880), Twain jokingly referred to the withered Shakespeare mulberry slip he tried to transplant from Stratford-on-Avon, which continued to decline despite prayer "'requests' to Moody & Sankey" (Scharnhorst, ed., *MTPP*, p. 132). Moody appealed to Clemens on 12 November 1886 to help support his Boys' School in Massachusetts, but Clemens noted on the envelope, "D. L. Moody the Revivalist/No sympathy with the movement" (Fears, *Day by Day* 2: 101). Christian Science "is calculated to strikingly impress a person accustomed to Moody and Sankey and Sam Jones revivals," Twain remarked in *Christian Science* (1907, Book 2, Ch. 7). Twain eventually seemed to take a more lenient view. In Chapter 2 of *Extract from Captain Stormfield's Visit to Heaven* (1909) Sandy explains to Stormfield that an arriving bartender "got converted at a Moody and Sankey meeting, in New York."

MOOKERJEE, MOHINDRONAUTH. *Onoocool Chunder Mookerjee (1829–1871): A Memoir. Fifth Edition. Printed Verbatim from the First Edition.* Calcutta: Thacker, Spink and Co., 1895. 72 pp. [First edition published in 1873, subsequently reprinted in 1876, 1884, and 1889.]

Mark Twain granted a newspaper interview in February 1896 in which he alluded to this "immortal biography," asserting that he read it "when it first came out" and was "coming back to it with fresh zest." He noted that its sentences alternated between "faultless English" and utter "bathos" (Scharnhorst, *Complete Interviews*, pp. 287–288). In Chapter 61 of *Following the Equator* (1897) Twain quotes "from a little book which is famous in India—the

biography of a distinguished Hindoo judge, Onoocool Chunder Mookerjee; it was written by his nephew, and is unintentionally funny—in fact, exceedingly so. I offer here the closing scene."

Rebecca Hooker, "Additions to Mark Twain's Library," *American Literary Realism* 38.3 (Spring 2006): 277.

MOON, GEORGE WASHINGTON (1823–1909). *Learned Men's English: The Grammarians. A Series of Criticisms on the English of Dean [Henry] Alford [1810–1871], Lindley Murray [1745–1826], and Other Writers on the Language. . . . Being the Twelfth Edition of "The Dean's English," and "Bad English Exposed."* London: George Routledge & Sons, 1892. Two parts: 215 and 227 pp.

Inscription: inscribed in black ink on the front free endpaper, "Clara L. Clemens/ from/An arrogant autocrat." The hand appears to be that of Olivia Clemens.

Marginalia: Clemens made several marginal notes and underscorings in pencil. A few other markings are not characteristic of his usual system and may be Clara's. A vertical line on page x seems to be by Clemens but a check mark on the opposite side of the same page does not resemble his typical habit. In "Part I" there are notes by Clemens on pages xiv, 29, 41, 85, 102, 110, 192, 193, 194 (referring to the "silliness" of a sentence), 195 (several notes), 196 ("hopelessly slovenly English"), 198, 200, 201 (a "foolish" sentence), and 202; deletions of words on pages 14, 15, 16, 19, 40, 85, 196, and 201; and vertical marks on pages 65, 74, 78, 80, 87, 193, and 206. On page 87 Clemens wrote at the end of the first paragraph, "The man is an ass." Another note written vertically on page 195 reads: "There is no such thing as 'the Queen's English.' The/property has passed into the hands of a joint stock com-/pany, and we own the bulk of the shares." A note on page 192 is dated "1897". In "Part II" Clemens made two vertical pencil marks and an underlining on page 16 and deleted a letter and a word on page 29. At the top of page 35 he made a pronouncement in black in: "This page is *drunk* with Mr./Moon's incomprehensible English." Chester L. Davis (1903–1987) reported many of these comments and markings in "Mark Twain's Marginal Notes on 'The Queen's English,'" *The Twainian* 25 (March–April 1966): 1–4.

Catalog: *Hunley 1958*, item #107, price $35.

Provenance: formerly in the collection of the Mark Twain Research Foundation, Perry, Missouri.

Location: currently unknown.

Copy examined: this volume was not available for examination when I visited Chester L. Davis in Perry in 1970. However, on 2 September 1980 Davis allowed Thomas A. Tenney to photocopy the inscription, title page, and marginalia; Tenney then sent a set of these photocopies to me.

Moon's *Learned Men's English* collected what he considered to be errors in English language usage and idioms. "Moon couldn't write English," Clemens quipped in April 1909 in the margin of his copy of James Russell Lowell's *Letters* (Volume I, page 372).

MOORE, CLEMENT CLARKE (1779–1863). "The Night Before Christmas" (poem, published in 1822). Also known as "A Visit from St. Nicholas."

On Christmas Eve, Olivia Clemens always recited this poem, and Clemens sometimes impersonated Santa Claus afterwards (*MFMT*, p. 36).

MOORE, GEORGE (1852–1933).

Henry Fisher reported that Mark Twain "was visibly tickled" when Fisher told him about a compliment the Anglo-Irish novelist George Moore paid to his writing. Moore had praised Twain's power of presenting pathetic situations without "slush" (*AMT*, p. 194).

MOORE, HENRY BYRON (1839–1925). *Her Royal Highness Queen Bee: A Story of Fact and Fancy and Other Stories.* Illustrated by Hope S. Evershed. Melbourne: Melville & Mullen, [cop. 1905]. 118 pp.

Source: MTLAcc, entry #441, volume donated by Clemens.

MOORE, JOHN HOWARD (1862–1916). *The Universal Kinship.* Chicago: Charles H. Kerr & Co., 1906. 329 pp.

On 2 February 1907 Clemens wrote to Moore, who had sent him a copy of *The Universal Kinship* on 13 January: "The book has furnished me several days of deep pleasure & satisfaction; it has compelled my gratitude at the same time, since it saves me the labor of stating my own long-cherished opinions & reflections & resentments [about human instincts and morals] by doing it lucidly & fervently & irascibly for me" (quoted in *MTB*, p. 1363; also quoted in *MTL*, p. 804). Moore, a zoology instructor, sought to demonstrate the philosophical obligation of humans to acknowledge their moral, ethical, and biological relationship to other species of animal life.

MOORE, JOHN MURRAY (1843–1914).

On 9 January 1874 Clemens invited Moore to call on him while Clemens's ship was docked in Liverpool (*MTLet* 6: 15–16). Moore, a physician, would later write about New Zealand and other subjects.

MOORE, JULIA ANN (DAVIS) (1847–1920). *Original Poems.* Grand Rapids, Michigan: C. M. Loomis, 1878. 56 pp.

Source: MTLAcc, entry #2071, volume donated from Clemens's library by Clara Clemens Gabrilowitsch in 1910.

———. *The Sentimental Song Book.* Grand Rapids, Michigan: C. M. Loomis, 1877. 60 pp. [The edition Clemens read is conjectured; Moore's first edition was published in 1876.]

It is generally agreed that the didactic doggerel of this farmer's wife inspired Emmeline Grangerford's lugubrious elegies in Chapter 17 of *Adventures of Huckleberry Finn* (1885). In *Following the Equator* (1897) Mark Twain returned to *The Sentimental Song Book* ("forgotten by the world in general, but not by me. I carry it with me always," he declared in Chapter 36), and quoted from different poems in Chapters 8 ("Frank Dutton": "He was drowned on Tuesday afternoon/On Sunday he was found,/And the tidings of that drowned boy/Was heard for miles around"), 36 ("William Upson": "Although she knows not that it was her son,/For his coffin could not be opened—/It might be someone in his place,/For she could not see his noble face"), and 44 ("The Author's Early Life": "It was my heart's delight/To compose on a sentimental subject/If it came in my mind just right"). Moore, Twain wrote, had that "subtle touch" necessary for genuine hogwash—"the touch that makes an intentionally humorous episode pathetic and an intentionally pathetic one funny" (Ch. 36).

The Sweet Singer of Michigan, ed. Walter Blair (Chicago: P. Covici, 1928); Blair, *MT&HF* (1960), pp. 209–213, 406 n. 13; L. W. Michaelson, "Four Emmeline Grangerfords,"

Mark Twain Journal 11.3 (Fall 1961): 10–12; *Huckleberry Finn* (1961), ed. Kenneth S. Lynn, pp. 156–160; *The Art of Huckleberry Finn* (1962), eds. Hamlin Hill and Walter Blair, pp. 445–451; *Huckleberry Finn* (1962), eds. Sculley Bradley, Richmond Croom Beatty, and E. Hudson Long, pp. 253–254; Madigan, "Mark Twain's Passage to India" (1974), p. 362; Greg Sevik, "Poetry, Prosody, Parody: Mark Twain's Rhythmic Thought," *Mark Twain Annual* 13 (2015): 130–148.

———. *The Sweet Singer of Michigan": Later Poems.* Grand Rapids, Michigan: Eaton, Lyon & Co., 1878. 90 pp. [Clemens's association copy, if any, has not been found.]

"Sweet Singer 982" was among the notes that Clemens jotted on a photo-board during his global lecture voyage of 1895–96 in preparation for the travel book he was writing (collection of Kevin Mac Donnell, Austin, Texas). "The Sweet Singer of Michigan, Queen & Empress of the Hogwash Guild" is how Clemens described this versifier to a correspondent in 1906 (SLC to John Horner, 12 January 1906, dictation copy by SLC's secretary, Isabel V. Lyon, MTP). Moore was especially drawn to the subject of death—of individual demise or multiple fatalities by any means, including fire, drowning, illness, or train wreck.

MOORE, THOMAS (1779–1852). "Araby's daughter" (ballad, published c. 1824). [Its lyrics were excerpted from "The Fire-Worshippers" section of Moore's narrative poem *Lalla Rookh* (1817). Irish composer George Kiallmark (1781–1835) provided the melody.]

According to Albert Bigelow Paine, Clemens picked up a guitar and sang this ballad to mollify the upset mother of the "Chapparal Quails" in Jackass Hill, California (*MTB* [1912], p. 269). William Gillis recalled this incident as taking place "upon the occasion of our visit to the young ladies of French Flat"; this was when Clemens "told me that 'music had charms to sooth the savage'" (William Robert Gillis [1849–1929], *Memories of Mark Twain and Steve Gillis [1838–1918]: Personal Recollections of the Famous Humorist* [Sonora, California: Printed by The Banner, 1924], p. 39). The ballad's first stanza expresses an emotional parting from the princess, Lalla Rookh: "Farewell, farewell to thee, Araby's daughter!/(Thus warbled a Peri [a mythical Persian creature] beneath the dark sea.)/No pearl ever lay under Oman's green water/More pure in its shell than thy spirit in thee." The final stanza injects bereavement into the separation: "Farewell!—farewell!—until pity's sweet fountain/Is lost in the hearts of the fair and the brave,/They'll weep for the Chieftain who died on that mountain,/They'll weep for the Maiden who sleeps in the wave." On the front wrapper of a song collection published in 1896, F. B. Ogilvie's *Two Hundred Old-Time Songs, Containing the Words and Music of the Choicest Gems of the Old and Familiar Songs*, Clemens jotted a line from "Araby's daughter": "No pearl ever lay in Omar's green water." See also the entry below for *Lalla Rookh, An Oriental Romance*.

———. *The Epicurean, A Romance.* New York: James Miller, 1875. 262 pp. [Publisher and pages conjectured.]

Inscription: "Saml. L. Clemens, Hartford, 1875."

Catalog: *A1911*, "12mo, cloth, N.Y. 1875," quotes the signature, lot 337, sold for $2.50.

Moore's novel, set in the third century CE, tells of an

Epicurean's journal to Egypt in search of the secret to immortality.

———. "Farewell!—But Whenever You Welcome the Hour" (poem, published in 1823 in *Irish Melodies, National Airs, Sacred Songs, Ballads, Etc.*)

Clemens's letter to Olivia Langdon on 7 January 1869 enclosed a fragment of a letter to him from Mary Mason Fairbanks that paraphrased these concluding lines of Moore's poem: "You may break, you may shatter the vase if you will,/But the scent of the roses will hang round it still" (*MTLet* 3: 21 n. 8).

———. "The harp that once through Tara's halls" (ballad, published in 1807, lyrics written to a traditional tune).

Clemens joking paraphrased the first line of this song in a letter to William Dean Howells on 25 June 1875: "The saddle hangs on Tara's walls down below in the stable" (*MTLet* 6: 499). Moore's patriotic ballad alluded to a vanished castle, Tara, where Irish kings once presided.

———. "Hours there were" (song, published in 1825). Melody composed by Joseph Augustine Wade (1800?-1845).

This piece was among the music on the piano in "The House Beautiful" in Chapter 38 of Mark Twain's *Life on the Mississippi* (1883). In a piece written for the 17 June 1865 issue of the *Californian*, Twain advised any would-be literary "connoisseur" to attribute "all the tender, broken-hearted song-verses to Moore" (quoted in Branch, *LAMT*, p. 141; *ET&S* 2: 195). The lachrymose theme of this particular song can be perceived in its opening lines: "Hours there were to mem'ry dearer/Than the sun-bright scenes of day;/Friends were fonder, joys were nearer,/But alas! They've fled away!"

———. *Lalla Rookh, An Oriental Romance* (published in London, 1817).

Mark Twain's quip at the conclusion of "Lucretia Smith's Soldier" (1864) that "the trail of the serpent is over us all" might refer to Part II of Moore's lengthy and complex narrative poem. (But see also the Catalog entry for Mary Elizabeth Braddon's *The Trail of the Serpent*.) In notes for a projected but never published edition of *The Innocents Abroad* (1869), Leon Dickinson traced Twain's reference in Chapter 55 to "gazelles, of 'soft-eyed' notoriety" to Part 5 of *Lalla Rookh*, "The Fire-Worshippers" (MTP). In Chapter 32 of *Adventures of Huckleberry Finn* (1885) Aunt Sally is reminded of the steamboat explosion of "the old Lally Rook." See also the Catalog entry above for "Araby's daughter."

———. "The Last Rose of Summer" (poem, written in 1805; as a song it was set to a traditional tune and published in 1813).

Mark Twain named this title among songs that "tended to regrets for bygone days and vanished joys," favorites among early-day Hannibal residents ("Villagers of 1840–3," written in 1897, *HH&T* [1969], p. 34). In a column reviewing the Virginia City performance of Friedrich von Flotow's opera *Martha, or the Market at Richmond*, Twain praised the "sweet, home-like strains" of "that enchanting old song, 'The Last Rose of Summer'" (Virginia City *Territorial Enterprise*, 3–5 June 1865, reprinted by Gary Scharnhorst in "Additional Mark Twain Contributions to the Virginia City *Territorial Enterprise* 1863–66," *American Literary Realism* 47.1 [Fall 2014]: 90). Likewise, in "Answers to Correspondents" (3 June 1865) Twain commended "that

exquisite melody, 'The Last Rose of Summer'" (*ET&S* 2: 180). In Chapter 61 of *Roughing It* (1872), Twain made the "poor joke" that he and his fellow gold-miners in the California Sierra Nevada range "remained as centless as the last rose of summer." On 11 August 1878 Clemens observed: "When they play Martha, the liars applaud all along—but when The Last Rose of Summer drops in, they forget & the applause is something tremendous" (NB 15, *N&J* 2: 140). Clemens listed the song in Notebook 16 (1878) among possible choices for a music box he was purchasing in Geneva (*N&J* 2: 212). In "Simon Wheeler, Detective," a novel written between 1877 and 1898, Hugh Burnside "detected the long-drawn, wheezy agony of 'The Last Rose of Summer' on a hand-organ" (*S&B*, p. 398). Clemens marked "The Last Rose of Summer" in his copy of D. H. Morrison's *Treasury of Song for the Home Circle: The Richest, Best-Loved Gems, Sacred and Secular*, a book that entered the Clemens family's library in 1883. On 1 June 1902 Mark Twain expressed his intention to use the song in his next work about Huck and Tom (NB 45, TS p. 15). During a speech at the University of Missouri Commencement on 4 June 1902 Twain sadly likened himself to "The Last Rose of Summer." He explained, "I am that rose, the last rose of my summer, I suppose. I shall not be here any more, I imagine" (*MTSpk* [1976], p. 436). Isabel Lyon noted on 1 December 1904 that this piece was one of Clemens's favorite songs for the orchestrelle (IVL Journals, TS p. 29, MTP). See also the Catalog entry for Friedrich von Flotow.

———. *The Loves of the Angels, A Poem* (book-length poem, published in 1823).

Praising Olivia Langdon, Clemens asked rhetorically in a letter to Mary Mason Fairbanks on 24 March 1869, "How could it be 'The Loves of the Angels, when there's only *one* angel—only one that's fledged, anyway?'" (*MTLet* 3: 176). Jo Dee Benussi made this identification (Benussi to Alan Gribben, 28 December 2007).

———. "Oft in the stilly night" (song, published in 1818). Music from a Scotch air, arranged by Sir John Andrew Stevenson (1761–1833).

Clemens marked "Oft in the Stilly Night" in his copy of D. H. Morrison's *Treasury of Song for the Home Circle: The Richest, Best-Loved Gems, Sacred and Secular*, a book that entered the Clemens family's library in 1883. Susy Clemens's death reminded Clemens in January 1897 of lines 5–10 from the first stanza of Moore's song: "The smiles the tears of childhood [Moore wrote "boyhood's"] years/The words of love then spoken,/The eyes that shone now dim'd & gone/The happy [Moore wrote "cheerful"] hearts now broken" (NB 39, London, TS p. 58). In 1897 Clemens included the song in his list of those popular during his childhood in Hannibal ("Villagers of 1840–3," *HH&T* [1969], p. 34). On 1 June 1902 Clemens made plans to use this song in a future piece about Huck and Tom (NB 45, TS p. 15).

———and **WILLIAM JERDAN** (1782–1869). *Personal Reminiscences by Moore and Jerdan*. Edited by Richard Henry Stoddard (1825–1903). Portraits. Bric-a-Brac Series. First edition. Illus. Original white decorated cloth, gilt. New York: Scribner, Armstrong and Co., 1875. 293 pp.

Inscription: the front flyleaf is signed in ink, "Saml. L.

Clemens, Hartford, 1875."

Marginalia: there are several pencil marks and folded page corners.

Catalogs: *A1911*, "12mo, cloth, N.Y. 1875," quotes the signature, lot 338, sold for $2.75; George D. Smith, New York City, "Catalogue of Books" (1911), quotes the signature, item #275, $7.50; American Art Association (New York City), Sale catalogue for the collection of the late William F. Gable of Altoona, Pennsylvania (8 January 1925), "12mo, cloth, New York, 1875," signed "Saml. L. Clemens, Hartford, 1875," lot 124, sold for $15 (with one other book); American Art Association (New York City), Sale catalogue (18 November 1925), "12mo, original cloth, New York, 1875, first edition, Mark Twain's copy. . . . Twain's signature—'Saml. L. Clemens, Hartford, 1875' on front fly-leaf," has the *A1911* sale label, lot 170, sold for $6.00.

Location: collection of Kevin Mac Donnell, Austin, Texas.

Copy examined: Clemens's copy, in July 2004.

In "Some Rambling Notes of an Idle Excursion" (1877) Mark Twain jokingly refers to Moore's sojourn in Bermuda "more than seventy years ago." In January 1894 Twain wanted to include "Tom Moore's Auto" in the projected "Back Number" magazine (NB 33, TS p. 46).

——. "Those Evening Bells" (poem, published in 1818).

Mark Twain penned a parody titled "Those Annual Bills" that he sent to James T. Fields on 7 January 1875 (*ET&S* 2: 341–342). Twain published it as "A Couple of Poems by Twain and Moore" in *Sketches, New and Old* (1875). S. B. Liljegren, "Revolt Against Romanticism" (1945), pp. 28–30.

——. "This World Is All a Fleeting Show" (poem, published in 1816).

Mark Twain quoted the title in "On Linden, Etc." (7 April 1866 *Californian*; *SSix*, p. 209). He paraphrased its title in "Some Rambling Notes of an Idle Excursion" (1877).

MORE, HANNAH (1745–1833). *Letters*. [Unidentified book.]

Source: Listed in Clara Clemens's commonplace book (undated entry, Paine 150, MTP).

Possibly Clara's entry referred to *Letters of Hannah More to Zachary Macaulay [1768–1838], Esq.: Containing Notices of Lord Macaulay's Youth. Now First Published.* Ed. by Arthur Robers (1801–1886). New York: R. Carter & Brother, 1860. 215 pp.

——. *Moses in the Bulrushes* in *Sacred Dramas* (lengthy poem, published in 1782).

More's four-part, twenty-five-page version of the Biblical story of Moses from the Book of Exodus was well-known in the early nineteenth century. Lines 34–36 of Part One convey her tone: "Did not God/Sometimes withhold in mercy what we ask,/We should be ruined at our own request." The first edition of Mark Twain's *A Tramp Abroad* (1880) gave "Titian's Moses" as a burlesque caption for its comical frontispiece sketch of a tearful infant floating in a basket among bulrushes. In Chapter 1 of *Huckleberry Finn* (1885), the Widow Douglas "got out her book and learned me about Moses and the Bulrushers, and I was in a sweat to find out all about him." In Chapter 8 of Twain's "Tom Sawyer's Conspiracy," written between 1897 and 1902, Huck Finn mentions "the pillar of cloud that led Moses out of the bulrushers" (*HH&T* [1969], p. 226).

Twain made up a joke about Moses in the bulrushes in August 1898 (NB 40, TS p. 30). More's *Moses in the Bulrushes* may be related to these allusions. In recent decades More's poem has been interpreted as an early plea against British slavery.

——. *The Shepherd of Salisbury Plain* (tract, published in 1795).

More's tract encouraged the wealthier class to assist the deserving poor wherever they encounter them. This was one of the books the *Quaker City* voyagers were expected to bring with them, Mark Twain reported (5 April 1868 *Daily Alta California*; *TIA*, p. 303). Twain's unfinished play, "The *Quaker City* Holy Land Excursion" (MS in MTP; *MTLet* 2: 412) suggests that More's tract was in the ship library (Act 2, Scene 1). "The House Beautiful" in Chapter 38 of Twain's *Life on the Mississippi* (1883) contains "two or three goody-goody works—'Shepherd of Salisbury Plain,' etc." In *Christian Science* (1907), Twain scoffs at Mary Baker Eddy for explaining the identity of an author as well known as Hannah More (Book 2, Chapter 1).

MOREL, EDMUND DENE (1873–1924). *King Leopold's Rule in Africa.* Illus. London: W. Heinemann, 1904. 466 pp. [Publisher and pages conjectured.]

Inscription: "S. L. Clemens, 1904."

Catalog: *A1911*, "8vo, cloth," quotes the signature, lot 339, sold for $1.75.

On 16 October 1904 Morel wrote to Clemens to "thank you once again for the privilege and pleasure given me to-night, and . . . for the warm way in which you have taken up this question." He informed Clemens: "I send you by an express messenger a packet of Congo literature—all I have got left here. . . . When I get home, I will send you much other matter, including my book" (ALS in MTP). In Mark Twain's "King Leopold's Soliloquy" (1905) Leopold describes Morel as "a Congo reformer. That sizes *him* up. He publishes a sheet in Liverpool called 'The West African Mail.'" On 8 January 1906 Clemens praised Morel's "splendid equipment of energy, brains, diligence, concentration, persistence" (SLC to Dr. Barbour, ALS in Berg Collection, New York Public Library, Astor, Lennox and Tilden Foundations). But Isabel Lyon recorded how Clemens, declaring that "Morel is a[n auto] mobile, I'm a wheel-barrow," sought on 10 January 1906 to extricate himself from the role of spokesman on Belgian Congo affairs (IVL Journals, TS p. 121, MTP). See also the Catalog entry for R. D. Casement.

——. *Red Rubber; The Story of the Rubber Slave Trade Flourishing on the Congo in the Year of Grace 1906.* Introduction by Sir Harry H[amilton]. Johnston (1858–1927). Maps. London: T. F. Unwin, 1906. 213 pp.

Morel mentioned this book in a letter to Clemens written on 18 January 1907 (ALS in MTP).

MORGAN, EMILY MALBONE (1862–1937). *A Poppy Garden.* Hartford: Belknap & Warfield, 1892. 54 pp.

Inscription: the front free endpaper is inscribed, "Livy L. Clemens/from S. R. D./December 25th/92". The handwriting is neither Olivia's nor Clemens's.

Provenance: Contains the bookstamps of the Mark Twain

Library, Redding, Connecticut.

Catalog: *Mott 1952*, item #71, $6.

Location: Mark Twain House and Museum, Hartford, Connecticut. Donated anonymously in 1963.

Copy examined: Olivia Clemens's copy. Examined in August 1987.

In this novella a poppy garden brings together two people with a resulting marriage.

MORGAN, FORREST (1852–1924). "Austria" (series of articles). Mark Twain's "Stirring Times in Austria" (1898) quotes from an "intelligent sketch" on Austrian affairs written by "Mr. Forrest Morgan, of Hartford." Morgan's description of the history and politics of Austria had appeared in four installments in a Hartford monthly magazine he edited, *The Travelers Record* (30.3 June 1894, 30.6 September 1894, 31.1 April 1895, and 31.3 June 1895). Published by the Travelers Insurance Company, this journal was an odd but readable mixture of literary commentary, insurance news, original poetry, and columns and anecdotes reprinted from various newspapers and magazines. Morgan promised additional articles about events in Austria, but the March 1896 issue of *The Travelers Record* instead announced his dismissal as editor for publishing an article (in another Hartford periodical) denouncing the chief executive of Travelers, James G. Batterson.

MORGAN, SALLIE B. (1853–1925), "Mrs. William S. Green." *Tahoe; or, Life in California. A Romance.* Atlanta, Georgia: J. P. Harrison & Co., 1881. 245 pp.

Source: MTLAcc, entry #222, volume donated by Clemens. The Mississippi-born (and steadfast Lost Cause sympathizer) Sallie B. Morgan wrote her novel about California in the spirit of the regional "Local Color" movement. After her husband died in 1905 she would assume the editorship of his newspaper, the Colusa, California *Daily Sun*.

MORGAN, SYDNEY (OWENSON), LADY (1776–1859). *Lady Morgan's Memoirs: Autobiography, Diaries and Correspondence.* Copyright Edition. Collection of British Authors Series. 3 vols. Leipzig: B. Tauchnitz, 1863.

Catalog: *C1951*, D1, $8 per vol., listed among books signed by Clemens.

Born in Dublin, Morgan expressed sentiments of Irish nationalism in novels such as *The Wild Irish Girl* (1806) and *O'Donnel* (1814). Other books related her impressions of France and Italy. In the late 1830s she moved to London and entered into social life there.

MORIER, JAMES JUSTINIAN (1782–1849). *The Adventures of Hajji Baba, of Ispahan.* First edition. 3 vols. London: John Murray, 1824. [Publisher conjectured.]

Inscription: each volume is signed "S. L. Clemens."

Catalog: *A1911*, "first edition, 3 vols., 16mo, half morocco, Lond. 1824," quotes the signatures, lot 340, sold for $14 total.

———. *The Adventures of Hajji Baba of Ispahan.* London, n.d.

Inscription: the verso of the title page is signed "S. L. Clemens."

Catalog: *A1911*, "16mo, boards (back torn off and covers detached), Lond. n.d.," quotes the signature, lot 341, $1.25.

Morier's satiric picaresque novel, first published in 1824, followed the adventures, follies, lapses, and victories of the son of a Persian barber. The English diplomat Morier had traveled widely in Persia, and his fictional work subtly critiques the culture he encountered there. Clemens dictated a notebook entry to a stenographer in June 1873: "Work upon Persia by a representative of Great Britain at the court of Teheran. Title something like *Ali Baba* in *Arabian Nights*" (NB 12, *N&J* 1: 534). It seems relevant that Nasr-Ed-Din, the Shah of Persia, would visit London in July 1873 and that Mark Twain published five letters concerning that event for the New York *Herald*. By 1881 Twain still had not mastered Morier's name; casting about for humorists to include in an anthology, Twain referred to "'Hajji' Something— written by Morton" (NB 19, *N&J* 2: 428).

MORLEY, JOHN, VISCOUNT MORLEY (1838–1923). *Burke.* English Men of Letters Series. New York: Harper & Brothers, [1879?]. 214 pp.

Source: MTLAcc, entry #1281, volume donated by Clemens.

This biography of the British statesman Edmund Burke (1729–1797) differed from the version that Morley had written in 1867. Clemens included "John Morley" in an undated list of names that he wrote (*A1911*, lot 305).

———. *The Life of Richard Cobden.* 2 vols. Twelfth edition. Portrait. London: T. Fisher Unwin, 1905.

Inscriptions: the presentation inscription reads: "To S. L. Clemens, D. Lit., with grateful memories of his noble work for the downtrodden natives of the Congo. Jane Cobden Unwin. London, 1907." Both volumes signed: "S. L. Clemens, London, July/07. . . . Daughter of Richard Cobden . . . from Mrs. Cobden Unwin." Jane Cobden Unwin was the daughter of Richard Cobden (1804–1865).

Catalogs: *A1911*, "2 vols., 8vo, cloth, gilt tops, uncut, Lond. 1905," quotes inscription and signatures, lot 104, sold for $6.75; Swann Galleries, New York City, Sale number 1363 (28 February 1985), 8vo, white buckram, morocco spine labels, very soiled, top edges gilt, bookplates of Frank A. Vanderlip on the front pastedown endpapers, has the *A1911* auction label, lot 310, pre-auction estimate $350–$500, sold for $770 (according to a note of 1 March 1985 to Alan Gribben from Nick Karanovich, who had made an unsuccessful bid of $675).

MORLEY, MARGARET WARNER (1858–1923). *Wasps and Their Ways.* First edition. 8vo, original green pictorial cloth, gilt. New York: Dodd, Mead and Co., 1900. 316 pp.

Inscription: the front free endpaper is signed in pencil, "Clemens/1902".

Provenance: Donated to the Carrie Estelle Doheny Collection, St. John's Seminary, Camarillo, California, after Mrs. Doheny purchased the volume from Maxwell Hunley Rare Books of Beverly Hills in 1940. Auctioned by Christie's in 1988 on behalf of St. John's Seminary and the Archdiocese of Los Angeles. Subsequently acquired by Nick Karanovich, Fort Wayne, Indiana. (See Karanovich's "Sixty Books from Mark Twain's Library," *Mark Twain Journal* 25.2 (Fall 1987): 16.)

Catalogs: Christie's, New York City, 1–2 February 1988 auction, lot 467, sold with one other book for $1,320 to Randall House, Los Angeles; *Sotheby's 2003*, #246, sold for $3,000 with another volume (by G. W. Peckham and E. G. Peckham, also about wasps).

Location: collection of Kevin Mac Donnell, Austin, Texas.

Copy examined: Clemens's copy, unmarked, in July 2004.

Has the bookplate of "Estelle Doheny."

Morris, Clara (1849–1925). *A Pasteboard Crown: A Story of the New York Stage*. New York: Charles Scribner's Sons, 1902. 370 pp.

Catalogs: ListABP (1910), "Pasteboard Crown, Morris"; *C1951*, #35c, $10, listed among the books signed by Clemens, "given to Mark Twain by the author."

"Clara Morris—at Wallack's," Clemens noted on 20 April 1902 (NB 45, TS p. 10). On that day the Clemenses "went into town (NYC) to hear Clara Morris lecture. . . . Mr. Clemens introduced her," Olivia Clemens recorded in her diary (DVI61, MTP). Morris's novel was based on her theatrical experiences.

———. *A Pasteboard Crown: A Story of the New York Stage*. New York: Charles Scribner's Sons, 1903. 370 pp.

Source: MTLAcc, entry #224, volume donated by Clemens.

Morris, George Pope (1802–1864). "The Oak" (poem and song both published in 1837). Soon better known as "Woodman, Spare That Tree!" Melody composed by Henry Russell (1812–1900).

In 1881 Clemens claimed that he stopped Franklin Chamberlin from chopping trees on a lot adjoining Clemens's by calling out: "Woodman spare that tree,/Forego, forego thy hacks,/And list, oh list, to me,/Lay down thy gory axe" (*S&MT*, p. 136).

Morris, Gouverneur (1752–1816). *The Diary and Letters of Gouverneur Morris, Minister of the United States to France; Member of the Constitutional Convention, Etc.* Ed. by Anne Cary Morris. 2 vols. New York: Charles Scribner's Sons, 1888.

Catalog: Ball 2016 inventory, good condition.

Location: Quarry Farm library shelves, under the supervision of the Mark Twain Archive, Elmira College, Elmira, New York.

Clemens had access to these volumes whenever he visited Quarry Farm in Elmira, New York.

Morris was a witness to many historic events, including the American Revolution and the French Revolution. His granddaughter prepared this edition of his journal and correspondence.

Morris, Gouverneu (1876–1953). *Aladdin O'Brien*. New York: Century Co., 1902. 298 pp. [Publisher and pages conjectured.]

Inscription: signed "S. L. Clemens, Riverdale, Dec. 1902."

Catalog: *A1911*, "12mo, cloth, N.Y. 1902," quotes the signature, lot 342, sold for $2.

On 10 December 1902 Isabel Lyon wrote to Richard Watson Gilder at Clemens's request, reporting that her employer "finds Gouverneur Morris's book 'a charming story and beautifully told'" (ALS in collection of Rosamond Gilder, PH in MTP). In Morris's novel two men in love with the same young woman settle their score on a field of battle during the Civil War. This Morris, the author of short stories and novels, was the great-grandson of the American Revolution statesman of the same name.

Morris, William (1834–1896). *The Earthly Paradise, A Poem*. 4 vols. in 3. Boston: Roberts Brothers, 1871.

Source: MTLAcc, entries #2068–2070, volumes donated from Clemens's library by Clara Clemens Gabrilowitsch in 1910.

———. *Pygmalion and the Image*. Illustrated by Sir Edward Burne-Jones (1833–1898). New York: R. H. Russell, 1903.

35 pp.

Location: Mark Twain Library, Redding, Connecticut. Donated by Clemens (MTLAcc, entry #1685).

Copy examined: Clemens's copy, unmarked, mint condition. Contains a red ink Mark Twain Library accession number, "3147," that does not match the number ("1685") in the accession records. Examined in 1970 and again in June 1982.

———. *Pygmalion and the Image*. Illustrated by Sir Edward Burne-Jones (1833–1898). Damaged covers. New York: R. H. Russell, 1903. 35 pp.

Location: Mark Twain Library, Redding, Connecticut. Donated from Clemens's library by Clara Clemens Gabrilowitsch in 1910 (MTLAcc, entry #2138).

Copy examined: Clemens's copy, unmarked, waterstained and damaged. Has a red ink Mark Twain Library accession number, "3148," that does not accord with the number ("2138") in the accession records. Examined in 1970 and again in June 1982.

———. "Shameful Death" (poem), collected in *The Defence of Guenevere, and Other Poems* (1858).

Shortly after Clemens's death in 1910, William Dean Howells recalled that his friend "had favorite poems which he liked to read to you," and "remembered how he fiercely revelled in the vengefulness of William Morris's *Sir Guy of the Dolorous Blast*, and how he especially exulted in the lines which tell of the supposed speaker's joy in slaying the murderer of his brother: 'I am threescore years and ten,/And my hair is nigh turned gray,/But I am glad to think of the moment when/I took his life away'" (*MMT*, p. 16).

Howells referred to one of the villains in the poem, rather than to the poem's actual title. Sir Guy of the Dolorous Blast and Sir John the knight of the Fen ambushed the newly married Lord Hugh; the speaker, Lord Hugh's brother, tells of his revenge on the cowardly murderers: "I am threescore and ten,/And my hair is all turn'd grey,/But I met Sir John of the Fen/Long ago on a summer day,/And am glad to think of the moment when/I took his life away." In the next, penultimate stanza, the narrator adds: "I am threescore and ten,/And my strength is mostly pass'd,/But long ago I and my men/When the sky was overcast,/And the smoke roll'd over the reeds of the fen,/Slew Guy of the Dolorous Blast" (*A Choice of William Morris's Verse*, ed. Geoffrey Grigson [London: Faber and Faber, 1969], p. 64). George Bernard Shaw "regretted" that Clemens "had not known Morris" (23 August 1907 AD, MTP; *AutoMT* 3: 109).

William Dean Howells, *Literary Friends and Acquaintances*, ed. David F. Hiatt and Edwin H. Cady (Bloomington: Indiana Univ. Press, 1968), pp. 265, 332.

———. *The Story of Sigurd the Volsung and the Fall of the Niblungs*. Boston: Roberts Brothers, 1877. 392 pp.

James R. Osgood & Company of Boston billed Clemens in November 1877 for a volume he purchased on 22 March 1877, "1 Sigurd &c $3.00 discounted to $2.40 plus postage" (receipt in Scrapbook #10, MTP). In 1945 Edgar H. Hemminghaus ("Mark Twain's German Provenience" [1945], p. 468) reported seeing this book in the Mark Twain Library at Redding, but Albert E. Stone, Jr. did not include it in his checklist in 1955 and I was unable to locate Clemens's copy when I visited Redding in 1970 and again in June 1982.

———. *The Well at the World's End* (fantasy novel, published in 1896).

Clemens quoted a passage from Volume II, Book III, Chapter 17 ("They Come Through the Woodland to the Thirsty Desert") of Morris's work in a letter to Elizabeth Robins of 25 March 1904: "And now I have bethought me that if we gain that which we seek for, & bear back our lives to our own people. . . . That we shall be as lonely then as we are this hour, & that the folk round about us shall be to us no much & no more than these trees & the wild things that dwell amongst them." In a follow-up letter to Robins of 31 March 1904 Clemens identified Morris's *The Well at the World's End* as the source of his quotation, and added, "It occurs in the second volume, but I do not know just where, for the book is not now on the premises" (ALS of both letters in the Fales Collection, New York University; PH of both letters in MTP). Morris set his work in a medieval world in which a young prince, Ralph of Upmeads, undergoes adventures while seeking a well that grants supernatural awareness and extends one's youth. I am grateful to Jo Dee Benussi for tracing Clemens's quotation.

MORRISON, ARTHUR (1863–1945). *Martin Hewitt, Investigator.* Illus. New York: Harper & Brothers, 1907. 216 pp.
Source: MTLAcc, entry #226, volume donated by Clemens.
A fictional English detective solves seven cases.

———. [Another identical copy.]
Source: MTLAcc, entry #1255, volume donated by Clemens.

MORRISON, DANIEL H., comp. *The Treasury of Song for the Home Circle: The Richest, Best-Loved Gems, Sacred and Secular.* Philadelphia: Hubbard Brothers, [cop. 1882]. 548 pp.
Inscription: (printed in brown ink on half-title page) "Susie O. Clemens/Hartford, Conn./1883./Uncle Theodore."
Marginalia: on a front flyleaf Clemens penciled the lyrics to one of his favorite songs, a comical parody of a hymn by Andrew Young: "There is a happy land/Far far away,/Where they have ham & eggs,/Three times a day./O how those boarders yell,/When they hear that dinner bell,/They *give* that landlord rats/Three times a day." Clemens's penciled notes throughout the volume supply the proper musical key for various songs. He drew pencil marks beside the titles of several songs, including Thomas Moore's "The last rose of summer" (p. 61) and "Oft in the stilly night" (p. 541) Above the title of "Larboard watch" (p. 22) Clemens wrote "There is a happy land." In the index at the rear of the book Clemens marked with pencil the titles of fifty-five songs that were evidently his favorites.
Catalogs: ListABP (1910) ("Treasury of Song"); "Retz Appraisal" (1944), p. 11, valued at $20.
Location: Mark Twain Papers, Bancroft Library, University of California at Berkeley.
Copy examined: Clemens's copy, worn from usage.

MORRISON, GEORGE ERNEST (1862–1920) *An Australian in China, Being the Narrative of a Quiet Journey Across China to British Burma.* London: H. Cox, 1895. 299 pp.
Mark Twain added a footnote to "The United States of Lyncherdom" (written in August 1901) to substantiate the futility of Christian efforts toward converting the vast population of China "These figures are not fanciful,

all of them are genuine and authentic. . . . See Doctor Morrison's book on his pedestrian journey across China; he quotes them and gives his authorities. For several years he has been the London *Times's* representative in Peking." On 26 August 1901 Clemens queried C. F. Moberly Bell about Morrison's book title—"the copy you gave me is packed up with our stuff in New York" (PH in MTP).

MORRISON, WILLIAM MCCUTCHAN (1867–1918). "Report by W. M. Morrison, American Missionary in the Congo Free State." [Unidentified publication.]
King Leopold reads this report of atrocities "with evil joy" in "King Leopold's Soliloquy" (1905). The American Presbyterian Congo Mission published several books by Morrison.

MORSE, EDWARD SYLVESTER (1838–1925). *Japanese Homes and Their Surroundings.* Illustrated by the author. Boston: Ticknor and Co., 1886. 372 pp. [Publisher and pages conjectured.]
Catalog: *A1911*, "imp. 8vo, cloth, Bost. 1886," with a sheet in Clemens's hand listing prominently authors laid in, lot 343, sold for $4.

MORSE, HARRIET CLARA (b. 1883). *A Cowboy Cavalier.* Illustrated by Samuel [Finley]. B[rown]. Morse (1885–1969) and John Goss (1886–1963). Boston: C. M. Clark Publishing Co., 1908. 294 pp.
Source: MTLAcc, entry #1056, volume donated by Clemens.
A girl from the East moves to a ranch in Texas; romances with cowboys ensue. The level of writing seems directed at a young adult audience. Morse resided in Massachusetts.

MORSE, LIVINGSTON B[URRILL]. (1882–1977). *The Road to Nowhere. A Story for Children.* Illustrated by Edna Morse (b. 1885). New York: Harper & Brothers, 1906. 236 pp.
Source: MTLAcc, entry #420, volume donated by Clemens.
Morse, a professor of history at the College of the City of New York, dedicated his book to *Alice in Wonderland.* His sister Edna's red and black illustrations depicted talking animals and human flowers. Morse later used the name Leighton B. Morse when he was a college instructor in New Jersey.

MORTIMER, JAMES (1833–1911). *The White Fawn; or, The Loves of Prince Buttercup and the Princess Daisy* (extravaganza, performed in 1868).
In a letter written on 1 February 1868, Mark Twain advised his readers: "I have been to New York . . . and on the 21st of January I went with some newspaper men to see the new spectacle at Niblo's [Garden], the 'White Fawn,' the splendid successor of the splendid 'Black Crook.' Everybody agrees that it is much more magnificent than the Crook. . . . I think these hundreds of princely costumes are changed every fifteen minutes during half the night . . . America has not seen anything before that can equal the 'White Fawn.'" But Twain went on to denounce the "appalling" influence these extravaganzas have wrought on young minds, breeding "a species of infamous pictorial literature" (3 March 1868 *Alta California*).

MORTIMER, WILLIAM GOLDEN (1854–1933). *Peru: History of Coca, "The Divine Plant" of the Incas; with an Introductory Account of the Incas, and of the Andean Indians of To-Day.* New York: J. H. Vail & Co., 1901. 576 pp.
Source: MTLAcc, entry #604, volume donated by Clemens.
Mortimer, a New York City physician specializing in diseases

of the eye, ear, nose, and throat and the editor of the *Pharmaceutical Journal* as well as the *New York Journal of Medicine*, wrote to Clemens on 6 December 1905: "I beg to fulfill a deferred privilege, that of presenting to you a copy of my book—Peru: History of Coca—a story of those children of the sun, phenomenal socialists of long ago who enjoyed life and chewed Coca until routed from their dreams by the Spanish [mur?]ders. . . . [I] do not recall that you have ever written of the Incas nor of that marvelous plant which they termed 'divine,' each of which affords an endless fund for solace and romance. Will you be good enough to accept this book from an admirer" (ALS in MTP). Mortimer's book enthusiastically advocated investigation of medical uses for coca. It hardly seems coincidental that Clemens mentioned the coca plant in his Autobiographical Dictation of 29 March 1906 (*AutoMT* 1: 461).

Morton, John Maddison (1811–1891). *Box and Cox* (one-act farce, produced in 1847).

In a letter written in London on 19 January 1897, Clemens responded to a neighbor's complaint about the piano-playing of Clemens's daughter: "I am sure I do not know what to do. <It is Box & Cox in a new form>" (SLC to J. Woulfe Flanagan, ALS in MTP). August Feldner explains in Chapter 24 of "No. 44, The Mysterious Stranger," written between 1902 and 1908: "All our lives we have been what 44 called Box and Cox lodgers in the one chamber . . . never encountering each other save for a dim and hazy and sleepy half-moment on the threshold" (*MSM*, p. 343). See also the Catalog entry for F. C. Burnand.

———. *Our Wife; or, the Rose of Amiens: A Comic Drama in Two Acts* (produced in 1856).

While the Clemenses were vacationing at Newport, Rhode Island on 23 August 1875 Clemens lectured between acts of the Bellevue Dramatic Group, which was presenting Morton's comedy and a one-act farce (John Roche, "Making a Reputation: Mark Twain in Newport," *Mark Twain Journal* 25.2 [Fall 1987]: 25). See also a related article, Earl F. Briden's "Mark Twain's Rhode Island Lectures," *Mark Twain Journal* 24.1 (Spring 1986): 35–40.

Mother Goose; or, The Old Nursery Rhymes. Illustrated by Kate Greenaway (1846–1901). New York: G. Routledge and Sons, [1881?]. 48 pp.

Inscription: in pencil, "Clara Clemens/Hartford, Conn. 1881. Mama."

Provenance: Mark Twain Library, Redding, Connecticut. Donated from Clemens's library by Clara Clemens Gabrilowitsch in 1910 (MTLAcc, entry #1884).

Catalog: *Mott 1952*, #58, $7.50.

In November or December 1880 the Clemenses gave a Mother Goose party modeled on one they had attended in November 1879 in Hartford; Clemens listed the characters and those who acted the parts in Notebook 19 (*N&J* 2: 378–379). Farther on in Notebook 19 (1881) Clemens seemed to refer to J. W. Elliott's collection, *Mother Goose's Nursery Rhymes and Nursery Songs. Set to Music*: "Mother Goose—W A Elliott" (*N&J* 2: 394). Later, in June 1898, Mark Twain proposed to "introduce Mother Goose & her people" into his planned piece on childhood "Creatures of Fiction" (NB 40, TS p. 27).

———. [Another identical copy.]

Source: MTLAcc, entry #1885, volume donated from Clemens's library by Clara Clemens Gabrilowitsch in 1910.

Mother Goose's Melodies for Children, or Songs for the Nursery, with Notes, Music, and an Account of the Goose or Vergoose Family and with Illustrations by Henry L. Stephens [1824–1882] and Gaston Fay. New York: Hurd and Houghton, 1869. 186 pp.

Mark Twain listed *Mother Goose's Melodies* as one of the few secular works available in the *Quaker City* ship library ("The *Quaker City* Holy Land Excursion," uncompleted play written 1867, Act II, Scene 1, MS in MTP).

Motley, John Lothrop (1814–1877). *The Correspondence of John Lothrop Motley.* Edited by George William Curtis (1824–1892). 2 vols. New York: Harper & Brothers, 1889. [Publisher conjectured.]

Catalog: *A1911*, "2 vols., royal 8vo, cloth, N.Y. 1889," with two sheets of Clemens's manuscript mentioning Thomas Wentworth Higginson and William Dean Howells, lot 344, sold for $7.50.

———. [An identical copy.] 2 vols. Green cloth, gilt lettering.

Inscriptions: Volume I was inscribed by Clemens in black ink on the front free endpaper, "Mrs. Olivia Langdon/ from her loving son/S L Clemens/Aug. 19, 1889". Volume II was inscribed by Clemens in black ink on the front free endpaper, "Mrs. Olivia Langdon 1889./Aug. 19." Olivia Lewis Langdon (1810–1890) was Clemens's mother-in-law.

Catalogs: included in the inventory list of the books at Quarry Farm prepared by Emily Schweizer Martinez when Quarry Farm was donated to Elmira College in 1983; Ball 2016 inventory, "good" condition.

Location: Mark Twain Archive, Gannett-Tripp Learning Center, Elmira College, Elmira, New York. Transferred from the Quarry Farm library to the Mark Twain Archive by Mark Woodhouse on 9 July 1987.

Copy examined: Olivia Lewis Langdon's unmarked copy of both volumes, on 12 August 1988. These were available to Clemens whenever he visited his mother-in-law.

———. *The Correspondence of John Lothrop Motley.* Edited by George William Curtis (1824–1892). 2 vols. New York: Harper & Brothers, [cop. 1889].

Source: MTLAcc, entries #1773 and #1774, volumes donated by Clemens.

———. *History of the United Netherlands from the Death of William the Silent to the Twelve Years' Truce—1609.* 4 vols. New York: Harper & Brothers, 1860–1868. [Reprinted frequently; this edition has been conjectured.]

Catalog: *C1951*, J21, 2 vols., listed among books belonging to Jean and Clara Clemens, edition unspecified.

———. *Motley's Dutch Nation, Being the Rise of the Dutch Republic (1555–1584) Condensed, with Introduction, Notes, and a Brief History of the Dutch People to 1908, by William Elliot Griffis [1843–1928].* New Edition. Illus. New York: Harper & Brothers, 1908. 960 pp.

Catalog: *A1911*, "thick post 8vo, cloth, N.Y. 1908," with a sheet of notes written by Clemens, lot 345.

Mark Twain referred deferentially to Motley in a 10 December 1866 column in the San Francisco *Alta California* ("Mark Twain Explains the Mexican Correspondence," *MTPP*, p. 7) while Motley was serving as U. S. minister to the Austrian empire. Olivia Langdon was reading the last volume of Motley's work in 1868, according to her commonplace book (MTP). In "The Coming Man" (1871), Twain wrote: "Think of my dainty Lilliputian [Twain calls him General Dewlap G. Lovel] standing in Brobdingnag [John Lothrop] Motley's shoes, and peeping out smartly over the instep at the Great Powers" (*Galaxy* 11.2 [February 1871]: 313; *CG* [1961], p. 121). (In December 1870 General Robert Cumming Schenck [1809–1890] had replaced Motley as the United States minister to England.) Clemens knew that Motley was in London when Clemens visited England in 1873 (SLC to an unidentified correspondent, 31 July 1873, *MTLet* 5: 423). On 17 May 1877 Clemens "had a lantern hung at my head & read self to sleep with Motley's Netherlands" while aboard the S. S. *Bermuda*. The next evening, however, he "said to myself presently, 'Come it's a recreation trip— *why* should I torture myself to store up knowledge about people dead 300 yrs ago?'" (Notebook 13, *N&J* 2: 16–17). On 6 August 1877 Clemens remarked to Mary Mason Fairbanks, in a letter inveighing against "all shades & forms of republican government," that "I read as much of Motley's Dutch Republic as I could stand, on my way to Bermuda, & would have thrown the book into the sea if I had owned it, it did make me so cordially despise those pitiful Dutchmen & their execrable Republic" (*MTMF*, p. 208). In July 1879 Clemens visited the place near the Hague where Motley had stayed for a time (NB 18, *N&J* 2: 331)—"good portraits of him there," Clemens noted. Later in 1879 Clemens expressed the opinion that Americans need not accede to English notions of superiority in prose: "nobody writes a finer & purer English than Motley, Howells, Hawthorne & Holmes" (NB 18, *N&J* 2: 348).

MOTT, EDWARD HAROLD (1845–1920), better known as "Ed. Mott." *The Old Settler and His Tales of the Sugar Swamp*. Chicago: Belford, Clarke & Co., 1889. 213 pp.

Inscription: the half-title carries Mott's presentation inscription, "To Mark Twain, with the apologies of Ed Mott, Ma. 13, 1889."

Location: Rare Book and Manuscript Library, University of Illinois at Urbana-Champaign, Urbana, Illinois. Purchased in 1969 as part of the collection of Franklin J. Meine (1896–1968).

Source: Email from Julie Christenson, Velde Fellow, Rare Book and Manuscript Library, University of Illinois. 30 September 2015. Laid in the volume are two items: a review cut from a magazine and a two-sheet typed biography of Edward Mott with the heading "Taken from 'Cyclopedia of National Biography.'" The volume contains no marginalia.

Ed. Mott began publishing his "The Old Settler" stories in the New York *Sun* in 1879. *Mark Twain's Library of Humor* (1888) included Mott's "The Old Settler," a tall tale the Old Settler relates about one of his bear hunts (pp. 485–490). Mott also published another book that might have interested Clemens, *Pike County Folks* (New York: J. W. Lovell, 1883), though no association copy apparently survives.

MOTT, LAWRENCE (1881–1931). *To the Credit of the Sea*. Illus. New York: Harper & Brothers, 1907. 296 pp. [Publisher and

pages conjectured.]

Inscription: signed "S. L. Clemens, 1909."

Catalog: *A1911*, "12mo, cloth, N.Y. 1907," quotes the signature, lot 346, sold for $1.50.

Eight short stories about the hazards and satisfactions of life on the sea along the Labrador Coast.

———. [An identical copy.]

Source: MTLAcc, entry #227, volume donated by Clemens.

MOTTELAY, PAUL FLEURY (1841–1920) and THOMAS CAMP-BELL-COPELAND (1845–1891), eds. *The Soldier in Our Civil War: A Pictorial History of the Conflict, 1861–65, Illustrating the Valor of the Soldier as Displayed on the Battle-Field. . . . Illustrated from Sketches Drawn by Forbes, Waud, Taylor, Hillen, Becker, Lovie, Schell, Crane, and Other Eye-Witnesses*. Introduction by Robert B[urns]. Beath (1839–1914). 2 vols. Hartford, 1886.

Catalog: *A1911*, "2 vols., folio, cloth, Hartford, 1886," lot 82, sold for $2.75.

MOULTON, LOUISE (CHANDLER) (1835–1908). "Boston. Literary Notes," New York *Tribune*, 22 October 1874.

Clemens wrote Moulton on 8 January 1875 to say that he had been reading her book review of Walter Besant's *The French Humorists, from the Twelfth to the Nineteenth Century*, which was published by Roberts Brothers of Boston. "I think I must get the book you are writing about" (*MTLet* 6: 343). He added several slighting references to Rabelais.

———. *In the Garden of Dreams: Lyrics and Sonnets*. Boston: Roberts Brothers, 1890. 170 pp.

Catalog: *C1951*, O18, listed among books containing Olivia Clemens's signature.

———. *Some Women's Hearts*. Boston: Roberts Brothers, 1874. 364 pp.

Source: MTLAcc, entry #213, volume donated by Clemens. Moulton wrote to Clemens on 12 October 1874, "I have asked my publishers to send you 'Some Women's Hearts,' in the hope that you may flatter me by sometime idling away a half hour over it. . . . I wanted you to see the *kind* of stories I write" (*MTLet* 6: 257). She asked Clemens to help her "make some money" in the subscription book sales method, and on 14 October 1874 Clemens assured her that he had written to the American Publishing Company on her behalf (*MTLet* 6: 256–257). Clemens added that "your dainty volume came last night & Mrs. Clemens read 'Brains' to me while I smoked." He assured her that he was emotionally touched while listening, and that "we liked the story so much" (*MTLet* 6: 257). On 21 October 1874 Clemens wrote to Elisha Bliss a somewhat equivocal letter ("Mrs. Moulton is a pleasant body") that nevertheless plugged her writings again (Bauman Rare Books, New York City, Holiday Catalog, December 2019; Whitmore Rare Books, Pasadena, California, 30 April 2020). Later, on 8 January 1875, Clemens would casually inquire of Moulton, "What did you & [Elisha] Bliss [, Jr.] do?" (*MTLet* 6: 344). Clemens's efforts were evidently unavailing, since Moulton stayed with Roberts Brothers as her publisher. "Brains," the short story Olivia Clemens read aloud to her husband, was the second of eight stories in Moulton's *Some Women's Hearts* (pp. 131–156). The narrator relates her efforts to help a twelve-year-old girl nicknamed "Brains" whose father has died and whose mother had become incapacitated by grief. "They say I've an old head to be on such young shoulders," explains the girl, Susan Mory (p. 131). In a sentimental conclusion Susan gradually dies of a lung disease, but her illness and her unwavering Christian faith bring together the narrator and the man she loves. A marriage results.

MOWATT. [Unidentified author, title, or subject.]

On 24 December 1880, writing to Pamela Moffett, Clemens remarked, "I am mighty glad you could not find the Mowatt book—I have a special reason for detesting that work" (MTP). Conceivably he referred to Anna Cora (Ogden) Mowatt Ritchie (1819–1870), the playwright, actress, and author whose *Autobiography of an Actress; or, Eight Years on the Stage* appeared in 1853. Ritchie's *Italian Life and Legends* was published in the year of her death. Any connection with her is purely speculative. A more likely candidate might be James Alexander Mowatt (1934–1876), an Irish-born temperance reformer who moved to the United States and continued to deliver motivational lectures. Mowatt published *The Autobiography of a Brewer's Son* (1869) and *Mowatt's Temperance Glee Book No. 1, A Collection of Temperance Songs Adapted to Popular Airs* (1874). He died while he was grieving over the loss of his only daughter, who had died a few months earlier.

MOZART, JOHANN CHRYSOSTOM WOLFGANG AMADEUS (1756–1791). *Le Nozze di Figaro (The Marriage of Figaro)* (opera, performed in 1786). Libretto by Lorenzo Da Ponte (1749–1838).

In Rome in April 1892 Clemens noted: "Monday eve, Marriage of Figaro" (NB 31, TS p. 37).

MUHLENBERG, WILLIAM AUGUSTUS (1796–1877). "I would not live alway" (hymn, copyrighted in 1833). Melody composed by George Kingsley (1811–1884).

A sketch by Clemens titled "Letter from Carson City" that appeared in the 3 February 1863 issue of the *Territorial Enterprise* claimed that the Unreliable abruptly sat at the piano at the Governor's house and "shouted some thing about he 'would not live alway'" (*ET&S* 1: 197). Clemens jokingly changed the original word "lurid" to "lucid" in quoting the Unreliable's version of a line from the first stanza: "I would not live alway; I ask not to stay/Where storm after storm rises dark o'er our way;/The few lurid mornings that dawn on us here/Are enough for life's woes, full enough for its cheer." In Chapter 3 of *Following the Equator* (1897) Mark Twain remembered Muhlenberg's song of "love and sentiment" as one likely to be on music stands in parlors in Honolulu in the 1860s.

MUKERJI, SATYA CHANDRA. *The Traveller's Guide to Agra, Containing an Account of the Past History, the Antiquities, and the Principal Sights of Agra, Together with Some Information about Agra as It Is*. Delhi: Sen & Co., 1892. 162 pp.

In Chapter 59 of *Following the Equator* (1897) Mark Twain relies on a description of the Taj Mahal found in "the excellent little guide-book of Mr. Satya Chandra Mukerji." Twain then quotes the praise of Sir William Wilson Hunter and Bayard Taylor for the Taj Mahal without mentioning that he is still relying on the contents of *The Traveller's Guide to Agra*. His excerpts come from pages 68–73 of Chapter II, "The Principal Sights of Agra," in Mukerji's book.

"MULATTO" [incident in an unidentified book].

In December 1896 Clemens made a cryptic notebook entry: "The mulatto's terrible fate—322 vol. 2 quarto" (NB 39, TS p. 32).

MULFORD, PRENTICE (1834–1891).

Mulford lived in California when Clemens resided there and was part of the bohemian literary circle in San Francisco to which Bret Harte and Clemens belonged. He wrote humorous stories for the *Overland Monthly* and other journals, sometimes using the pen name "Dogberry." Later he moved to Passaic, New Jersey and became a pioneer in writing about spiritual phenomena. Charles Stoddard mentioned Mulford in 1875, and Clemens replied on 17 March 1875: "About Mulford you surprise me. I wonder what has become of him" ("Mark Twain," Heritage Bookshop, Los Angeles, 1997, item #126). On 7 August 1877 Clemens mentioned that "I never hear of Prentice Mulford now-a-days" (SLC to Francis D. Millet, Elmira, ALS at Harvard). Clemens included Mulford in a list of humorists he compiled in July 1880 for a projected anthology (NB 19, *N&J* 2: 366). He mentioned Mulford again on 17 January 1903 (NB 46, TS p. 7). On page 138 of the second volume of Moncure Conway's *Autobiography* (1904) Clemens made a note, probably in October 1905 when he signed and dated the book, trying to remember one of his literary contemporaries: "(imitator of Harte's condensed novels—perished in a canoe. (*Now* I recal [*sic*] his name—Prentice Mulford." Clemens was remembering correctly; the fact that Mulford's body was found in a canoe created newspaper headlines at the time, although foul play was ruled out. He had been traveling from Passaic, New Jersey, where he had lived for nearly two decades, to Sag Harbor, Long Island, his birthplace. He died at the age of fifty-seven.

MÜLLER, FRIEDRICH MAX (1823–1900). *India: What Can It Teach Us?* [Published in London and New York, 1883.]

Catalog: *C1951*, #32c, listed among books signed by Clemens, no edition specified.

In January 1879 Clemens alluded to Müller as an eminent philologist (NB 17, *N&J* 2: 266). *India: What Can It Teach Us?* collects seven lectures Müller delivered at Cambridge University, including "The Lessons of the Veda," "Vedic Deities," and "The Human Interest of Sanskrit Literature." The book showed greater respect for India and the Hindu civilization than was typical in England at the time.

Dwayne Eutsey, "God's *Real* Message: *No. 44, The Mysterious Stranger* and the Influence of Liberal Religion on Mark Twain," *Mark Twain Annual 3* (2005): 53–66.

MÜNCHAUSEN, BARON KARL FRIEDRICH HIERONYMUS VON (1720–1797), popularly known as "Baron Munchausen." [The exaggerated stories assigned to him are now usually attributed to Rudolph Erich Raspe (1737–1794).] *The Adventures of Baron Munchausen*. Illustrated by A[lphonse]. [Adolphe] Bichard (1841–1914), sometimes called Aldophe Bichard. Folio, original pictorial terra cotta cloth, gilt. London: Frederick Warne & Co., [c. 1885].

Inscription: the front endpaper is inscribed in ink by Olivia Clemens: "Jervis Langdon/Dec. 25th 1885/From Uncle Sam and Aunt Livy." Jervis Langdon (1875–1952) was Olivia's nephew, the son of her brother Charles J. Langdon.

No marginalia are visible.

Provenance: initially in the Langdon family library in Elmira, New York.

Location: collection of Kevin Mac Donnell, Austin, Texas (Mac Donnell to Alan Gribben, 29 November 2011). Purchased from the Langdon family.

On 2 January 1886 Jervis Langdon, Jr. wrote to the Clemenses to thank them for "a very beautiful book. . . . The story seems as interesting and funny as the pictures" (Fears, *Day by Day* 2: 2).

————. *The Adventures of Baron Munchausen. A New and Revised Edition.* Introduction by T[homas]. Teignmouth Shore (1841–1911). Illustrated by [Paul] Gustave Doré (1832–1883). Original chromolithographed pictorial boards. Tan cloth folding case. London: Cassell, [n.d., c. 1889]. 216 pp.

Inscription: inscribed in black ink, "To/Jean L. Clemens./ With the love of her sister,/Susy Clemens./Elmira, N. Y. /July 26, '89." (This was the date of Jean Clemens's ninth birthday.)

Catalogs: *C1951*, #92c, listed (erroneously) among books signed by Clemens, $17.50; *Fleming 1972*; Seven Gables Bookshop (New York City) sold this book through Sotheby Parke Bernet of New York City, Sale number 3482 (25 February 1976), "Property of a New York City Collector" (John F. Fleming), "quarter morocco case," place of publication erroneously listed as "New York" rather than London and the inscription identified erroneously as written by "Clemens' daughter Mary to her sister Jean", lot 21 (in a group), $200, with Victor Jacobs the buyer; "Victor and Irene Murr Jacobs Collection," Sotheby's, Sale No. 6904, 29 October 1996, item #294, sold with two other books for $2,300; *Sotheby's 2003*, #194, $1,300 (sold with two other titles from the Clemens family's library).

Provenance: contains the shelf mark of Clara Clemens Gabrilowitsch's private library collection when she resided in Detroit. Frederick Anderson, then Editor of the Mark Twain Papers in the Bancroft Library at the University of California, Berkeley, examined this book in the New York City offices of John F. Fleming, Inc. and made notes in April 1972 (Anderson to James D. Hart, 17 April 1972, photocopy sent to Alan Gribben). In 1986 this volume belonged to Victor Jacobs (Jacobs to Alan Gribben, 15 October 1986, "autograph from Susy to Jean"). Jacobs died in 1996. Subsequently it became part of Nick Karanovich's collection in Fort Wayne, Indiana.

Location: collection of Kevin Mac Donnell, Austin, Texas. Obtained in 2003.

Copy examined: Jean Clemens's unmarked copy, in July 2004.

Mark Twain referred to this work several times: Baron de Munchausen, "the world-famed liar" (6 February 1866 letter, Virginia City *Territorial Enterprise*; *MTCor*, p. 44); "flights of fancy lying that make the inventions of Munchausen seem poor and trifling" (27 October 1866 Sacramento *Weekly Union*; *LSI*, p. 202); "Ananias Twain, alias Baron Munchausen" ("Mark Twain's Burlesque Autobiography" [1871]); to Archdeacon Wilberforce "complete and unquestioning belief in Münchausen's [sic], and in all other conceivable extravagances, must come easy" (6 September 1907 AD, *MTE*, p. 341; *AutoMT* 3: 132).

MUNDT, KLARA (MÜLLER) (1814–1873), pseud. "Luise Mühlbach." *Frederick the Great and His Court. An Historical Romance.* Translated from the German by Ann Mary Butler (Crittenden) Coleman (1813–1891). New York: D. Appleton and Co., 1867. 434 pp. [Edition conjectured.]

Olivia Langdon announced to Alice Hooker on 26 May 1867 that she had "finished 'Frederick the Great and His Court' it is extremely interesting" (Harris, *Courtship* (1996), p. 25).

————. *Berlin and Sans-Souci; or, Frederick the Great and His Friends. An Historical Romance.* Translated from the German by Ann Mary Butler (Crittenden) Coleman (1813–1891). New York: D. Appleton and Co., 1867. 391 pp. [Edition conjectured.]

Olivia Langdon quoted from this novel in her commonplace book (Harris, *Courtship* (1996), p. 128).

————. *Henry VIII. and His Court; or, Catharine Parr. An Historical Novel.* Black cloth. Trans. from the German by Henry Niles Pierce (1820–1899). New York: D. Appleton and Co., 1899. 418 pp.

Provenance: Antenne-Dorrance Collection, Rice Lake, Wisconsin.

Location: Mark Twain Archive, Gannett-Tripp Learning Center, Elmira College, Elmira, New York.

Copy examined: Clemens's copy, unmarked. Examined on 28 May 2015.

MUNGEN, WILLIAM (1821–1887). "To an Absent One" (poem, published in 1868).

Mungen was a Congressman from Ohio who had been a colonel in the Union Army. In 1868 he published a sentimental poem about his wife in the Washington *National Intelligencer* that began, "Time flies, and still its rapid wings/Strikes on my thoughts with constant blows,/ Touches my heart's most secret springs,/And love's fond stream toward thee flows./Flows like Niagara's rushing tide—/True as the needle to the pole:/Clear as the deep blue sea, and wide." In a letter to the Chicago *Republican* Mark Twain ridiculed the effort as "bosh" and "Mungenical poetry" (reprinted in the *Mark Twain Quarterly* 5.2 [Summer 1942]: 3; and in *Washington in 1868*, editor Cyril Clemens [Webster Groves, Missouri: International Mark Twain Society, 1943], pp. 11–14). See also the Catalog entry for "Pop! goes the weasel."

MUNICH. *Münchener Tages-Anzeiger* (newspaper).

Clemens "counted the reading-matter" in the issue of 25 January 1879 (less than that in United States newspapers, he found), and logged it in Notebook 17 (*N&J* 2: 262–263). He analyzed the same issue in "Appendix F" of *A Tramp Abroad* (1880).

MUNICH. PINAKOTHEK, ALTE. *Catalogue of the Paintings in the Old Pinakothek, Munich.* Introduction by Franz von Reber (1834–1919). Translated by Joseph Thacher Clarke (1856–1920). "Unabridged Official Edition." Illus. Munich: Verlaganstalt für Kunst und Wissenschaft, n.d. 303 pp.

In Chapter 16 of *A Tramp Abroad* (1880), Mark Twain declares: "Even Garnham has a rival [as a translator]. Mr. X. had a small pamphlet with him which he had bought while on a visit to Munich. It was entitled 'A Catalogue of Pictures in the Old Pinacotek,' and was written in a peculiar kind of English." Twain quotes nearly two pages of art historian Clarke's clumsy attempts at producing idiomatic English prose.

MUNKITTRICK, RICHARD KENDALL (1853–1911). *The Moon Prince, and Other Nabobs*. Illus. New York: Harper & Brothers, 1893. 340 pp.

Source: MTLAcc, entry #1187, volume donated by Clemens.

Four whimsical children's stories—"The Moon Prince," "A Day in Waxland," "The Hurrishoffer," "Opoponax1/2"— are interspersed with songs and poems in a book dedicated to Munkittrick's son Malcolm. The American poet and humorist Munkittrick was the associate editor of *Puck* and *Judge* magazines. He wrote half a dozen books and also contributed poetry, short stories, and witticisms to many newspapers and journals. In New York City he had been a friend and office mate of Albert Bigelow Paine, who based a character named "Capers" on Munkittrick in Paine's *The Bread Line, A Story of a Paper* (1900). Both Paine and Munkittrick belonged to the "Poets of Printing House Square" group. Munkittrick would attend Clemens's Seventieth Birthday party (information supplied in Alain D. Munkittrick's email to Alan Gribben, 13 August 2003).

MUNN, CHARLES ALLEN (1859–1924). *Three Types of Washington Portraits: John Trumbull, Charles Wilson Peale, Gilbert Stuart*. New York: Privately printed, 1908. 66 pp

Inscription: "'Mark Twain'/with the compliments of/ Charles A. Munn."

Location: Mark Twain Library, Redding, Connecticut.

Copy examined: Clemens's copy, unmarked. Has a red ink Mark Twain Library accession number, "3524". Examined in 1970 and again in June 1982.

MUNRO, BRUCE WESTON (1859–1900). *Groans and Grins of One Who Survived*. Toronto, Canada: Warwick & Sons, 1889. 385 pp.

Source: MTLAcc, entry #361 volume donated by Clemens. Clemens had written an admonitory five-page letter on 21 October 1881 to this Canadian would-be writer. "*Experience of life* (not of books) is the only capital usable in such a book as you have attempted. . . . I do not see how any but a colossal genius can write a readable prose book before he is 30 years old. . . . Moderate talent can produce a readable book at 30 or 40, after a good, honest, diligent, pains-taking *apprenticeship* of 15 or 20 years with the pen; but moderate talent cannot do it without such age & such apprenticeship. You will have to produce & burn as much manuscript as the rest of us have done before your mill will yield something worth printing. Ours is a trade which has to be *learned*. . . . If you have good reason to believe that you possess really great & conspicuous genius, I would advise that you stick to your pen; but if you have reason to believe otherwise, I would advise you to put it aside or use it merely for your amusement. . . . I have been frank: one seldom has a right to be otherwise; but I have been far from meaning to be harsh" (*Sotheby's 2003*, #48). Munro nevertheless went on to publish comedic works that gained no popularity, including *A Blundering Boy: A Humorous Story* (1886) and *Splinters; or, a Grist of Giggles* (1887). Evidently Munro later approached Clemens with one of his manuscripts, possibly *A Blundering Boy*. Clemens replied on 21 April 1886, "We couldn't publish it—we are utterly overwhelmed with work" (*Sotheby's 2003*, #62). Undaunted,

Munro apparently sent Clemens another work in 1887, provoking Clemens to respond, "It is of no use—I give it up. . . . I have no liking for novels or stories—none in the world; & so, whenever I read one—which is not oftener than once in two years . . . distaste for the *vehicle* always taints my judgment of the literature itself" (Clemens to Munro, 15 March 1887, *Sotheby's 2003*, #62). Munro's *Groans and Grins of One Who Survived* (1889) consisted of short stories, sketches, and poems.

MUNRO, NEIL (1864–1930). *Bud; A Novel*. New York: Harper & Brothers, 1907. 315 pp.

Source: MTLAcc, entry #1345, volume donated by Clemens.

———. *Bud; A Novel*. New York: Harper & Brothers, 1908. 315 pp.

Source: MTLAcc, entry #1057, volume donated by Clemens.

MUNROE, GEORGE H. (1826–1903). "The Templeton Letters."

Munroe was an editorial writer for the Boston *Saturday Evening Gazette* and later for the Boston *Herald*. Under the pseudonym "Templeton" he wrote weekly letters from Boston for the Hartford *Courant*. Mark Twain listed "Templeton" among those designated to receive complimentary copies of *The Prince and the Pauper* (NB 19 [1881], *N&J* 2: 386).

MUNROE, [CHARLES] KIRK (1850–1930). *The Blue Dragon, A Tale of Recent Adventure in China*. Illus. New York: Harper & Brothers, 1905. 268 pp.

Source: MTLAcc, entry #1608, volume donated by Clemens.

World traveler, reporter, editor, author, and conservationist, Munroe became enchanted with Florida in the early 1880s and resided there for most of his life. His books were especially popular with young people.

———. *Campmates; A Story of the Plains*. Illus. New York: Harper & Brothers, [cop. 1891]. 333 pp.

Source: MTLAcc, entry #1176, volume donated by Clemens.

This was Munroe's tenth novel to appear in print.

———. *Chrystal, Jack, & Co., and Delta Bixby; Two Stories*. Illus. New York: Harper & Brothers, [cop. 1888]. 221 pp.

Source: MTLAcc, entry #1170, volume donated by Clemens.

———. *Derrick Sterling; A Story of the Mines*. New York: Harper & Brothers, [cop. 1888]. 256 pp.

Source: MTLAcc, entry #410, volume donated by Clemens.

———. *The Flamingo Feather*. Illus. New York: Harper & Brothers, [cop. 1887]. 255 pp.

Source: MTLAcc, entry #467, volume donated by Clemens. Reported as "missing" shortly thereafter.

Set in the sixteenth century, this historical novel introduces a young French boy to the Seminole Indians in the part of the New World that would become Florida.

———. *For the Mikado; or, A Japanese Middy in Action*. Illus. New York: Harper & Brothers, 1905. 270 pp.

Source: MTLAcc, entry # 1609, volume donated by Clemens.

———. *The Painted Desert; A Story of Northern Arizona*. Illus. New York: Harper & Brothers, [cop. 1897]. 274 pp.

Source: MTLAcc, entry #1199, volume donated by Clemens.

———. *Snow-Shoes and Sledges*. Illus. New York: Harper & Brothers, [cop. 1895]. 271 pp.

Source: MTLAcc, entry #1610, volume donated by Clemens.

This novel was a sequel to Munroe's *The Fur-Seal's Tooth: A Story an Alaskan Adventure* (cop. 1894).

———. *Wakulla; A Story of Adventure in Florida*. Illus. New York: Harper & Brothers, [cop. 1885]. 255 pp.

Source: MTLAcc, entry #444, volume donated by Clemens.

MUNRO[-]FERGUSON, [EMMA VALENTINE] (1864–1897), pseud. "V." *Music Hath Charms*. New York: Harper & Brothers, 1894. 300 pp.

Source: MTLAcc, entry #1549, volume donated by Clemens.

Munro-Ferguson was the sister of the Liberal politician Ronald Munro-Ferguson and was for a time engaged to the confirmed Scottish bachelor Richard Haldane, 1st Viscount Haldane (1856–1928). Subsequently her close relationship with the singer Mary Wakefield (1853–1910) became a matter of speculation. Munro-Ferguson's *Music Hath Charms*, a novel set in England, depicts an emotional tug of war between the almost irresistible Victoria and her infatuated but stubborn male suitor, Dawney. The novel's title, of course, echoes William Congreve's famous line, "Music hath charms to soothe a savage breast."

Munsey's Magazine (New York periodical, published 1889–1929).

Walter Besant praised Mark Twain and *Adventures of Huckleberry Finn* in the February 1898 issue (p. 660). Clemens wrote to Besant on 22 February 1898 from Vienna: "I have just read it in Munsey for February" (ALS in Berg Collection, New York Public Library).

MUNSON, JAMES E[UGENE]. (1835–1906). *The Complete Phonographer, and Reporter's Guide: An Inductive Exposition of Phonography, with Its Application to All Branches of Reporting, and . . . Also Intended as a School-Book*. Revised edition. Illus. New York: Harper & Brothers, 1892. [cop. 1866, 1877]. 241 pp.

Location: Mark Twain Papers, Bancroft Library, University of California at Berkeley.

Source: University of California at Berkeley online catalog, 6 December 2006. Identified as "Mark Twain's copy," but no provenance or other information is provided. (Jo Dee Benussi noted this listing.)

MURAI, GENSAI (1863–1927). *Hana, A Daughter of Japan*. Illus. First edition. Original delicate silk covers. Japan-bound with string. Color wood-block frontispiece. Tokyo: The Hochi Shimbun, 1904. 298 pp.

Inscription: signed and dated in black ink on the front pastedown endpaper: "S. L. Clemens/21—5th Ave/1905". The number "94c" (from the *C1951* catalog) is written in pencil twice on the same endpaper.

Catalogs: ListABP (1910), "Hana, Murai"; *C1951*, # 94c, $15, listed among the books signed by Clemens.

Provenance: the shelf number of Clara Clemens Gabrilowitsch's private library in Detroit appears on the front pastedown endpaper.

Location: collection of Kevin Mac Donnell, Austin, Texas. Purchased in November 1985 at the Boston Book Fair (for approximately $400 in book trades).

Copy examined: Clemens's unmarked copy, in December

1985 and again in July 2004.

Kevin Mac Donnell, "Mark Twain and Gensai Murai: A Japanese Inspiration for 'The War-Prayer,'" *Journal of Transnational American Studies* (University of California at Santa Barbara) 1.1 (16 February 2009): https://escholarship.org/uc/item/5zs4253w.

MURFREE, FANNY NOAILLES DICKINSON (1846–1941). *Felicia; A Novel*. Boston: Houghton, Mifflin and Co., The Riverside Press, 1891. 358 pp. [Serialized in the *Atlantic Monthly* in 1890–1891.]

Mark Twain's "Weather" appendix to *The American Claimant* (1892) quotes two sentences about a snowfall from Murfree's *Felicia*. The was the first novel published by the sister of Mary Noailles Murfree (see the Catalog entries below). A New York woman meets an opera singer in a city that seems like Cincinnati and finds that his itinerant life presents problems after they are married.

MURFREE, MARY NOAILLES (1850–1922), pseud. "Charles Egbert Craddock." *Down the Ravine*. Boston: Houghton, Mifflin and Co., 1885. 196 pp.

Source: MTLAcc, entry #2203, volume donated from Clemens's library by Clara Clemens Gabrilowitsch in 1910. One of Murfree's first novels about Appalachian mountain life.

———. *In the "Stranger People's" Country: A Novel*. Illus. New York: Harper & Brothers, 1891. 360 pp.

Mark Twain quotes a purple passage from this local-color novel (citing Murfree's pseudonym) in the "Weather" appendix to *The American Claimant* (1892).

———. *In the Tennessee Mountains*. Boston: Houghton, Mifflin and Co., 1884. 322 pp. [These stories first appeared in the *Atlantic Monthly*.]

In 1884 Clemens noted "Tennessee Mountain Tales, by Craddock. (Houghton.)" (NB 22, *N&J* 3: 50).

———. *The Prophet of the Great Smoky Mountains*. Boston: Houghton, Mifflin and Co., 1885. 308 pp.

On 1 July 1885 Olivia Clemens recorded in her journal a visit to Quarry Farm by Ella Corey and Grace Collin: "Ella read to us from the July Atlantic the last installment of Charles Egbert Craddock's 'Prophet of The Great Smoky.' It was wonderfully fine—I think perhaps the strongest [and] best number that we have yet read although it is all strong and fine" (OLC Diary, DV161, MTP). Olivia surely knew the actual name of "Charles Egbert Craddock"; on 5 June 1885 Clemens had written to William Dean Howells from Hartford to ask the Howellses to visit them on 10 June: "Miss Murfree & her sister are coming that day to stay 24 hours" (*MTHL*, p. 531).

MURPHY, JOHN MORTIMER (1845–1898). *Sporting Adventures in the Far West*. Illus. New York: Harper & Brothers, 1880. 469 pp.

Source: MTLAcc, entry #1612, volume donated by Clemens. Murphy, born in Ireland, was a dedicated game preservationist as well as an avid hunter.

MURRAY, (SIR) CHARLES AUGUSTUS (1806–1895). *Travels in North America During the Years 1834, 1835, & 1836, Including a Summer Residence with the Pawnee Tribe of Indians, in the Remote Prairies of the Missouri, and a Visit to Cuba and the Azore Islands*. 2 vols. New York: Harper & Brothers, 1839. [Publisher conjectured.]

Marginalia: penciled notes, marks, and underscorings in

Volume II.

Catalog: *A 1911*, "Vol. II, 12mo, cloth, N.Y. 1839, "some remarks in pencil in the hand-writing of Mr. Clemens, and several passages underscored or marked in the margins," lot 350, $2.25.

Mark Twain employs a description of early-day St. Louis written by this "unimaginative Scotchman" in Chapter 22 of *Life on the Mississippi* (1883): "The streets are narrow, ill paved and ill-lighted." However, in Chapter 27 Twain quotes Murray more lengthily about the "might and majesty" of the river, "fertilizing a boundless valley, bearing along in his course the trophies of his thousand victories over the shattered forest." Twain would paraphrase a passage from Murray's description of the Pawnee tribe as late as 1901; see the Catalog entry for "Macallum."

Ganzel, "Twain, Travel Books" (1962), p. 41 n. 4.

Murray, David Christie (1847–1907). *The Martyred Fool; A Novel*. New York: Harper & Brothers, 1895. 265 pp.

Source: MTLAcc, entry #1636, volume donated by Clemens.

Murray, Eustace Clare Grenville (1824–1881), pseud. "Trois-Étoiles." *The Member for Paris: A Tale of the Second Empire*. Boston: James R. Osgood and Co., 1871. 206 pp. [Edition conjectured.]

On 9 January 1872 Clemens wrote to Olivia from Steubenville, Ohio: "I am reading 'The Member from Paris' [*sic*] a very bright, sharp, able French political novel, very happily translated. It is all so good & Frenchy that I don't know where to mark!" (*MTLet* 5: 15). Despite Murray's employing a French pseudonym and inserting French phrases here and there in the narrative, this book by the English journalist Murray was not a translation.

———. *Strange Tales*. Collection of British Authors Series. Leipzig: B. Tauchnitz, 1878. 272 pp.

Catalog: *C1951*, D1, Tauchnitz Edition specified, listed among books signed by Clemens, $8.

A collection of twenty-eight short stories by Murray, some of them quite brief.

———. *That Artful Vicar: The Story of What a Clergyman Tried to Do for Others and Did for Himself*. Collection of British Authors Series. 2 vols. Leipzig: B. Tauchnitz, 1879. Paperbound.

Source: MTLAcc, entry #229, Volume 2 only (288 pp.), donated by Clemens.

Murray, John (publishing firm in London owned by successive generations of the Murray family). *Handbook for North Germany, from the Baltic to the Black Forest, and the Rhine, from Holland to Basle*. Nineteenth edition. Maps. London: John Murray, 1877. 448 pp.

Clemens seems to be referring to page 422 of this guidebook in comments he made in July 1878 (NB 15, *N&J* 2: 118).

———. *A Handbook for Travellers in Spain*. Fourth edition. London: John Murray, 1869.

Clemens may have used this guidebook on his visit to Gibraltar (cf. NB 8).

———. *A Handbook for Travellers in Switzerland, and the Alps of Savoy and Piedmont*. Fourteenth edition. London: John Murray, 1871. 557 pp.

Clemens may have used this guidebook in the Swiss Alps, though be remarks that Baedeker "has run Murray out of Europe" (NB 16, *N&J* 2: 193).

———. *A Handbook for Travellers in Syria and Palestine*. Edited by Josias Leslie Porter (1823–1889). 2 vols. London: John Murray, 1858. [New and Revised Edition issued in 1868.]

Clemens's entries in Notebook 9 (1867) suggest his familiarity with the first edition of this work. As a matter of fact, Clemens probably consulted Murray's *Handbooks* regarding most of the countries through which the *Quaker City* pilgrims traveled (*N&J* 1: 380–452).

Leon Dickinson—"Mark Twain's *Innocents Abroad*" (1945)—recognized and documented Twain's dependence on Murray's guidebook (Dickinson credited the editor of the *Handbook*, Porter, rather than John Murray), particularly in Chapters 41, 49, and 53 of *The Innocents Abroad* (1869). Subsequently Dewey Ganzel's "Samuel Clemens, Guidebooks and *Innocents Abroad*" (1965), pp. 78–83, and *Mark Twain Abroad* (1968), pp. 219–22, 266–271, revealed Twain's indebtedness more specifically. Robert H. Hirst informed me, however, that neither Dickinson nor Ganzel took into account the extent to which David Austin Randall's *The Handwriting of God in Egypt, Sinai, and the Holy Land* quoted from the text of Murray's *Handbook*, thus presenting an important alternate source.

Robert H. Hirst, "Making of *The Innocents Abroad*" (1975).

Murray, John O'Kane (1847–1885). *Little Lives of the Great Saints*. Illus. New York: P. J. Kenedy, 1889. 513 pp. [Publisher and pages conjectured.]

Inscription: signed "Clemens."

Catalog: *A1911*, "12mo, cloth, N.Y. 1899," quotes the signature, lot 51, sold for $1.

Murray, Lindley (1745–1826). *English Grammar, Adapted to the Different Classes of Learners*. New York: Collins and Co., 1816. 312 pp.

Inscription: the front flyleaf is signed in ink: "Morris Hill's/ Book/Wrote January 11th, 1819."

Location: Mark Twain Library, Redding, Connecticut.

Copy examined: one of the many books with early imprints given to the Mark Twain Library by the descendants of the Hill family. It has the purple oval Mark Twain Library stamps but no marks and no accession number. When I revisited Redding in June 1982 I pointed out to the staff that I could see no reason to believe this volume had any connection with Clemens or his family, and I recommended that it be removed from their collection of Clemens association copies.

Murray, Ross, comp. *The Modern Householder: A Manual of Domestic Economy in All Its Branches*. Illus. London: F. Warne and Co.; New York: Scribner, Welford, and Armstrong, [1872]. 722 pp. [Publisher and edition conjectured.]

A bill listing twenty-one books from Estes & Lauriat of Boston (14 July 1880) begins with a copy of "Mod Householder" for $1.25; Clemens paid the bill on 20 July 1880 (receipt in MTP).

Murray, T. Douglas (1841–1911), ed. *Jeanne d'Arc, Maid of Orleans, Deliverer of France; Being the Story of Her Life, Her Achievements, and Her Death, as Attested on Oath and Set Forth in Original Documents*. Illustrations and map. 8vo, original blue decorated cloth, gilt, uncut, frontispiece loose. London: W. Heinemann, 1902. 396 pp.

Inscriptions: the front flyleaf is signed in black ink, "S. L. Clemens/September, 1902." Pasted on that front flyleaf below Clemens's signature is a publisher's presentation slip from Mr. Heinemann requesting that no reference to the work be made before September 10th. Also present are the bookplate of William Harris Arnold and a subsequent owner's bookplate tipped above Arnold's.

Catalogs: *A1911*, "8vo, cloth, frontispiece loose, Lond. 1902, . . . early copy presented by Mr. Heinemann, the publisher," lot 352, sold for $6.50; Anderson Auction Galleries, Sale number 1873 (10–11 November 1924), "8vo, cloth, uncut, London, 1902, Mark Twain's copy, with his autograph on the fly-leaf," contains *A1911* sale label, lot 223, sold for $25; Anderson Auction Catalogue No. 3911 (1931), lot 111; offered by Kerkhoff Books, Warsaw, Indiana, 20 September 2002, with *A1911* sale label, signed by Clemens in September 1902, first edition, good condition, priced at $24,500 (email from abebooks. com to Kevin Mac Donnell, 20 September 2002).

Location: collection of Kevin Mac Donnell, Austin, Texas (Mac Donnell to Alan Gribben, 9 March 2005). Mac Donnell reported that the volume contains the *A1911* sale label for lot 352.

Copy examined: a photocopy of the flyleaf containing Clemens's signature and date (sent by Kevin Mac Donnell on 9 March 2005).

Murray's documented biography of Joan of Arc (1902) followed Mark Twain's fictionalized version by six years. In September 1899 Twain had read Murray's book in manuscript after consenting to write an introduction (*MTHHR*, pp. 409–411). Although that arrangement fell through, Heinemann the publisher nevertheless sent Twain a complimentary copy of Murray's book in advance of its issuance, requesting that no public reference be made before 10 September 1902. Twain would make use of the projected introduction in writing an essay he published later, "Joan of Arc" (1904).

MUSSET, ALFRED DE (1810–1857).
The French Romantic playwright and poet Musset had a love affair with George Sand. On 18 November 1892 Susy Clemens wrote from Florence to her college friend Louise Brownell about a new enthusiasm: "I have been reading some of Alfred de Musset's little comedies. They are wonderful to me as illustrating what a delicate touch and perfect refinement of style can do with plots really weak or even common place" (Hamilton College Archives).

MUSSET, PAUL EDME DE (1804–1880). *Mr. Wind and Madam Rain*. Translated from the French by Emily Makepeace. Illustrated by Charles H[enry]. Bennett (1829–1867). New York: Harper & Brothers, n.d. [1864]. 126 pp. [Publication date supplied.]
Source: MTLAcc, entry #1911, volume donated from Clemens's library by Clara Clemens Gabrilowitsch in 1910. *Mr. Wind and Madam Rain* was based on a fairy tale from Brittany.

MYERS, CORTLAND (1864–1941). *Would Christ Belong to a Labor Union? or, Henry Fielding's Dream*. New York: Street & Street, [cop. 1900]. 216 pp.
Source: MTLAcc, entry #1058, volume donated by Albert Bigelow Paine, Clemens's designated biographer. Quite possibly Clemens saw this book, since he and Paine often exchanged reading materials.

MYERS, FREDERIC WILLIAM HENRY (1843–1901). *Human Personality and Its Survival of Bodily Death*. [Ed. by Richard Hodgson (1855–1905) and Alice Johnson (1860–1940)

after Myers' death.] 2 vols. London: Longmans, Green, and Co., 1903.
Clemens long harbored a hope, though often wavering, that some form of communication with the deceased might be possible. A letter addressed to Laura F. McQuiston on 26 March 1901, however, mentioned the recent death of "Mr. Myers, President of the London Psychical Research Society. . . . He was a spiritualist. I am afraid he was a very easily-convinced man" (PH in MTP). In 1907 Clemens identified Myers as "the late president of the British Psychical Society" and quoted a note by Ralph Ashcroft recording Clemens's having met "Mrs. Myers (widow of the author of *Human Personality and Its Survival of Bodily Death*)" (6 September 1907 AD, *MTE*, pp. 339, 342; *AutoMT* 3: 132).

———. *Wordsworth*. English Men of Letters Series. New York: Harper & Brothers, 1899. 182 pp.
Source: MTLAcc, entry #1284, volume donated by Clemens.

MYERS, LOUISA (PALMIER) (1837–1917). *An Idyl of the Rhine*. Illus. New York: F. Tennyson Neely Co., [1901]. 41 pp.
Inscription: (on the title page, in large script) "To Mark Twain with regards of F. T. Neely, Sept. 25." Also signed, "S. L. Clemens, Riverdale, Nov., '01."
Catalog: *A1911*, "12mo, cloth, N.Y. [1901], quotes the inscription and signature, lot 356, sold for $1.50.
Myers' six-part sentimental poem, set along the Rhine River, relates the romantic meeting and inevitable parting of "a simple maiden" named Mary and a "daring youth of high degree," Felix, interspersed with photographs. A resident of St. Louis, Myers would achieve a measure of regional acclaim for her lyrics to a song, "Let us sing of old Missouri" (copyrighted in 1915).

N

NADAILLAC, JEAN-FRANÇOIS-ALBERT DU POUGET, MARQUIS DE (1818–1904). *Pre-Historic America*. Translated by Nancy Regina Emily (Meugens) Bell (1844–1933), pseud. "N. d'Anvers." Ed. by William Healey Dall (1845–1927). New York: G. P. Putnam's Sons, 1884. 566 pp. [Repr. throughout the 1890s.]
Nadaillac's study investigated what was then known about the aboriginal Native Americans who had inhabited North and Central America, including the mound builders. On 6 August 1900 Clemens jotted down the author, title, and publisher of this book (NB 43, London, TS p. 23).

NADAL, BERNARD HARRISON (1850–1929). "A Czar—1905" (poem).
Leopold quotes this poem against the Russian Czar ("it is fine, one is obliged to concede it. . . . The mongrel handles his pen well") in Mark Twain's "King Leopold's Soliloquy" (1905). Twain's footnote specifies the New York *Times* as his source.

NAIRNE, CAROLINA (OLIPHANT), BARONESS (1766–1845). "Bonnie Charlie's Now Awa'" (poem, published pseudonymously in the 1820s and collected in 1845).
Clemens first made note of this stirring Scottish poem in 1895 (NB 34, TS p. 5, MTP). Susy Clemens's death brought to Clemens's mind the lines: "Better lo'ed ye canna be,/Will ye no come back again?"; he referred to them in January 1897 (NB 39, TS pp. 50, 58, MTP).

NANSEN, FRIDTJOF (1861–1930). *Farthest North; Being the Record of a Voyage of Exploration of the Ship "Fram" 1893–96, and of a Fifteen Months' Sleigh Journey.* 2 vols. Illus. New York: Harper & Brothers, [cop. 1897].

Source: MTLAcc, entries #1239 and #1240, volumes donated by Clemens.

In "At the Appetite Cure" (1898) a professor reminds Mark Twain: "Nansen was used to fine fare, but when his meals were restricted to bear-meat months at a time he suffered no damage and no discomfort." Twain mentioned the Arctic explorer Nansen's name in a complimentary manner in a speech delivered to the Whitefriars on 16 June 1899 in London (*MTSpk* [1976], p. 327).

NAPIER, (SIR) WILLIAM FRANCIS PATRICK (1785–1860). *History of the War in the Peninsula and in the South of France, from the Year 1807 to the Year 1814.* 6 vols. London, 1828–1840.

Catalogs: ListABP (1910), "Peninsular War 6 vols., Napier"; *C1951*, #36c, $15, listed among books signed by Clemens.

In 1887 Clemens noted Napier's name, birthdate, and year of death, and quoted from his "Peninsular War" (NB 27, *N&J* 3: 314). Part of the Napoleonic Wars, this struggle in the Iberian Peninsula pitted the French forces against Bourbon Spain.

NAPLES *Observer* (newspaper).

Mark Twain's *The Innocents Abroad* (1869) refers to this newspaper in Chapter 34.

Napoleon's Oraculum, or, Book of Fate. New York, n.d. [First published c. 1822; often reprinted under various titles.]

Inscription: signed "S. L. Clemens, Hartford, 1878."

Catalog: *A1911*, "16mo, wrappers, a leaf damaged, N.Y., n.d.," quotes the signature, lot 358, sold for $2.25.

This brief book of advice and fortune-telling was purportedly discovered in 1801 by M. Sonnini during Napoleon's incursion into Egypt. Its initial publication was attributed to "H[enry]. Kirchenhoffer, Fellow of the University of Pavia."

NAPOLEON THE THIRD, EMPEROR OF THE FRENCH (1808–1873). *History of Julius Caesar.* 2 vols. New York: Harper & Brothers, 1865–1866.

Provenance: bookplates of the J. Langdon Family Library #68 and #69.

Catalog: Ball 2016 inventory, good condition.

Location: Quarry Farm library shelves, under the supervision of the Mark Twain Archive, Elmira College, Elmira, New York.

Clemens had access to these volumes whenever he visited the Langdon residence in Elmira.

Napoleon the Third and His Court, by a Retired Diplomatist. London: John Maxwell and Co., 1865. 348 pp. Preface is merely signed "H. S."

Robert Regan (*UH*, p. 71) suggested that this anonymous memoir of Charles-Louis-Napoléon Bonaparte (1808–1873), nephew of Napoleon Bonaparte and Emperor of the French between 1852 and 1870, "might have come to Mark Twain's attention." If so, Regan speculated, Twain may have reworked the information on page 70 into the admiring biographical sketch of Louis Napoleon in Chapter 13 of *The Innocents Abroad* (1869).

NAST, THOMAS (1840–1902). *The Fight at Dame Europa's School: Showing How the German Boy Thrashed the French Boy; and How the English Boy Looked On.* Thirty-three illustrations. Brown cloth, good condition. New York: Francis B. Felt & Co., 1871. 34 pp.

Inscription: beneath a droll self-portrait that Nast sketched of himself holding a signed book on the front flyleaf, Nast wrote in black ink: "To Mark Twain/From the 'Good little Artist who did not/prosper.'"

Location: in 1985 it was part of the collection of Professor Bigelow Paine Cushman, Deer Isle, Maine.

Copy examined: Clemens's copy, in August 1987 at Bigelow Paine Cushman's residence in Deer Isle, Maine.

See also the Catalog entry for Albert Bigelow Paine's biography of Thomas Nast.

———. [Identical copy, red cloth, gilt.]

Inscription: the front flyleaf is signed in pencil, "C J Langdon/from his friend/C.[?] M. Underhill".

Provenance: bookplate #657 of the "J. Langdon Family Library" on the front pastedown endpaper.

Catalog: Ball 2016 inventory, red cloth, gilt lettering, signed C. J. Langdon from his friend C. M. Underhill, from Jervis Langdon's Family Library #657.

Location: Mark Twain Archive, Elmira College, Elmira, New York.

Copy examined: an unmarked copy that was available to Clemens whenever he visited the Langdons in Elmira. Examined on 27 May 2015.

———. *Nast's Illustrated Almanac for 1873.* New York, 1873.

Clemens liked Nast's cartoon in *Harper's Weekly* so much that he wrote on 10 December 1872: "Nast, you more than any other man have won a prodigious victory for Grant. . . . Those pictures were simply marvels" (*MTL*, p. 202; *MTLet* 5: 249). On 17 December 1872 Clemens notified Nast: "The Almanac has come and I have enjoyed those pictures with all my soul and body" (*MTLet* 5: 251). That edition of Nast's almanac reprinted Twain's "Story of the Good Little Boy" (1870). Nast later declined Twain's offer to join him on a lecture tour. On 26 November 1884 Twain and George Washington Cable stayed overnight at Nast's home in Morristown, New Jersey (Fears, *Day by Day* 1: 1262–1263). It was Albert Bigelow Paine's *Th. Nast, His Period and His Pictures* (1904) that would prompt Twain to select Paine as his own designated biographer.

The Nation (weekly periodical, New York, published 1865–).

Early in 1870 Mark Twain had not yet seen the review of *The Innocents Abroad* (1869) in the *Nation* (SLC to Charles F. Wingate, 31 March 1870, *MTLet* 4: 102). "You know the 'Nation' *always* snarls. It would think it was impairing its reputation as our first critical authority if it failed to do that," Twain remarked in 1875 (SLC to Mr. Watt, 26 January 1875, *MTLet* 6: 359). "Perplexing as a compliment from the Nation newspaper," wrote Twain in 1877 in working notes for a play, "Cap'n Simon Wheeler, The Amateur Detective" (*S&B*, p. 296). Twain tried to imagine a certain situation: "The person who tried to fashion his life according to the New York Nation. The fatal result" (NB 14, 1878, *N&J* 2: 66 n. 51). Twain disapproved of a grammatical usage in the issue of 28 August 1879 (NB 18, *N&J* 2: 341). In 1888 he mentioned the *Nation* in a list of appointments, errands, and anecdotes (NB 28, November 1888, *N&J* 3: 433). "Buy 'Nation'" (NB 29, Elmira, N. Y., June 1889, *N&J* 3: 496). "The 'Nation' stopped coming some time ago. Please start it up again," Clemens requested in 1892 (SLC to Franklin O. Whitmore, Florence, Italy, 29 September 1892, ALS in MTP). Clemens enclosed a clipping from *The Nation* (SLC to William Walter Phelps' daughter Marian Phelps [1868–1922], Florence, Italy, 14 February 1893, ALS in Henry E. Huntington Library, San Marino, California.). "Give change of address to *The Nation*," Clemens reminded Franklin G. Whitmore from Florence in anticipation of moving to Paris (13 June 1893, ALS in MTP).

National Centennial Commemoration. Proceedings on the One Hundreth Anniversary of the Introduction and Adoption of the "Resolutions Respecting Independency" Held in Philadelphia on the Evening of June 7, 1876. Philadelphia: Printed for the Committee, 1876. 89 pp.

> Location: Mark Twain House and Museum, Hartford, Connecticut. Gift of Trinity College Library, 1960.
>
> Copy examined: Clemens's unmarked copy. Examined in August 1987.

Mark Twain attended an event in Philadelphia connected with the Centennial, the Congress of Authors in Independence Hall, on 1 July 1876 (Fears, *Day by Day* 1.2: 716). There he read a sketch titled "Francis Lightfoot Lee of Virginia" (published in 1877).

NAYLOR, JAMES BALL (1860–1945). *Ralph Marlowe; A Novel.* Akron, Ohio: Saalfield Publishing Co., 1901. 412 pp.

> Source: MTLAcc, entry #230, volume donated by Clemens.

Ralph Marlowe, despite or because of its regional elements, was the first book by this Malta, Ohio physician that sold well nationally.

NEAD, BENJAMIN MATTHIAS (1847–1923). *Some Hidden Sources of Fiction: A Paper Read Before the Historical Society of Dauphin County, Pennsylvania.* Philadelphia: Printed for private circulation by George W. Jacobs & Co., 1909. 61 pp.

> Inscription: the front pastedown endpaper is signed in black ink, "S L. Clemens/1909." Book label of the *A1911* sale is affixed below the inscription.
>
> Marginalia: Clemens made a three-line note concerning mythology written in black ink on page 3: "Isn't it the same as Castor & Pollux at L. Regillus, & St. James on a white horse at another battle?--& 40 other instances." A few words were underscored on other pages.
>
> Catalog: *A1911*, "12mo, cloth, Phila.: For private circulation, 1909, . . . autograph mythological note of three lines on p. 3; also a few words underscored," quotes the signature, lot 359, sold for $3.
>
> Source: photocopies supplied to the Mark Twain Papers by Thomas G. O'Brien of The Booksmith in Oak Park, Illinois on 29 July 1981. Robert H. Hirst sent photocopies of the title page and marginalia to Alan Gribben on 29 July 1981.

NEAL, JOSEPH CLAY (1807–1847). *Charcoal Sketches; or, Scenes in a Metropolis* (Philadelphia, 1838).

In 1880 Mark Twain included "Neal, Charcoal sketches" among humorous works to be considered for an anthology (NB 19, *N&J* 2: 363). *Mark Twain's Library of Humor* (1888) contained "'Tis Only My Husband" from Neal's *Charcoal Sketches.*

NEGRI, GAETANO (1838–1902). *Julian the Apostate.* Translated from the Italian by Janie (Perry) Litta Visconti Arese (b. 1865). Introduction by Pasquale Villari (1827–1917). Illus.

2 volumes. New York: Charles Scribner's Sons, 1905.

> Inscriptions: both volumes are signed "S. L. Clemens, 1906."
>
> Marginalia: a few notes and passages are marked. In one margin Clemens wrote, "The human being does certainly seem at his silliest when he is fussing & fuming over religious trivialities. What can God almighty care for those mitred lice & their mephitic little squabbles?" (quoted in the 1917 Anderson auction catalog).
>
> Catalogs: *A1911*, "2 vols., 8vo, cloth, N.Y. 1905, . . . a few passages marked," quotes the signature, lot 360, sold for $3; Anderson Galleries (New York City), Sale number 1289 (19–21 March 1917), "gilt tops, uncut, N.Y., 1905," has the *A1911* sale label in each volume, one marginal note (quoted), lot 469.

Flavius Claudius Julianus (331–363 CE), Emperor of Rome, only ruled between 361 and 363 before he was killed in battle. He had announced his belief in paganism and had become a vigorous enemy of Christianity. Negri was a Milan writer and politician.

NELIGAN, WILLIAM HAYES (1814–1880). *Rome: Its Churches, Its Charities, and Its Schools.* New York: Edward Dunigan & Brother, 1858. 452 pp. [Edition conjectured.]

Mark Twain's information about the Catacombs, employed in Chapter 27 of *The Innocents Abroad* (1869), relied partly on Neligan's book. Twain quotes from three paragraphs by Neligan that tell of miracles—citing an 1858 edition and making only slight alterations. A lengthy footnote in Twain's narrative quotes Neligan's account of how an immense miracle in the sixth century saved Rome from "a fearful pestilence." Although Twain scoffs at "the old gentleman's undoubting, unquestioning" reports of these miracles, Twain acknowledges that he "would gladly change my unbelief for Neligan's faith." Neligan, born in Clonmel, Ireland (the son of Lawrence Blake Neligan, M.D., who died in 1816) and ordained in the Anglican faith, converted to Catholicism and immigrated to New York City in 1854. He held various posts in the Catholic Church, including an assignment in the Bahamas.

Rogers, *MTBP* (1960), pp. 58–59, 169 n. 36; Ganzel, "Guidebooks" (1965), pp. 85, 86–88; and Ganzel, *MTAb* (1968), pp. 158–162. Roseanne T. Sullivan, "Queen of Heaven Rejoice, Alleluia!: Regina Caeli," *Dappled Things: A Quarterly of Ideas, Art, & Faith* (online journal, 2018), corrects certain suppositions of both Neligan and Mark Twain.

NELSON. [Unidentified possible author.]

Clemens apparently referred to library books when noting in December 1892 in Florence: "Nelson—2 of mine—1 Susy & Livy, not [re]turned" (NB 32, TS p. 53).

NESBIT, EDWARD PLANTA (1822–1900). *Christ, Christians, and Christianity. Book I. Jesus an Essene.* London: Simpkin, Marshall, Hamilton, Kent & Co., 1895. 215 pp. [Publisher and date conjectured.]

> Source: MTLAcc, entry #919, no publisher or date supplied, *Book I* only donated by Clemens.

Nesbit was a retired schoolmaster in Adelaide, Australia. On 13 October 1895 Clemens wrote to thank him "for the book & also the pleasant words which you have written on the fly-leaf." Clemens added that was "reading it with keen enjoyment" (PH in MTP).

NESBIT, WILBUR [DICK] (1871–1927). *The Gentleman Ragman: Johnny Thompson's Story of the Emigger*. New York: Harper & Brothers, 1906. 312 pp.

Source: MTLAcc, entry #1325, volume donated by Clemens.

———. *The Land of Make-Believe, and Other Christmas Poems*. Illus. New York: Harper & Brothers, 1907. 99 pp.

Source: MTLAcc, entry #499, volume donated by Clemens.

———. [Another identical copy.]

Source: MTLAcc, entry #1193, volume donated by Clemens.

NEVADA STATE HISTORICAL SOCIETY. *First Biennial Report of the Nevada Historical Society, 1907–1908*. Plates, maps. Original brown morocco, raised bands, marbled endpapers, gilt. Carson City, Nevada: State Printing Office, 1909.

Inscription: the name "Mark Twain" is embossed in gold on the upper front of the brown morocco cover, so this was presumably a presentation copy. Signed by the Hicks-Judd Bindery. Page 92 reported a resolution to declare Mark Twain an honorary member of the Nevada Historical Society, and a letter from Albert Bigelow Paine on Twain's behalf accepting the membership. A portrait of Twain appears on page 149.

Provenance: displays a shelfmark ("HU/H11") on the front pastedown endpaper of Clara Clemens Gabrilowitsch's private library in Detroit. Purchased by Mrs. Estelle Doheny in 1940 from Maxwell Hunley Rare Books of Beverly Hills. Price $12.50. Donated to the Carrie Estelle Doheny Collection, St. John's Seminary, Camarillo, California. Sold by Christie's for $165 in February 1989 (lot #1752) on behalf of St. John's Seminary. Subsequently in the collection of Nick Karanovich, Fort Wayne, Indiana. See Karanovich's "Sixty Books from Mark Twain's Library," *Mark Twain Journal* 25.2 (Fall 1987): 16.

Catalogs: ListABP (1910), "Report Nevada Hist. Society"; *Sotheby's 2003*, #211, $2,250 (sold with four other titles pertaining to history).

Location: collection of Kevin Mac Donnell, Austin, Texas.

Copy examined: Clemens's copy, in July 2004. Has the bookplate of "Estelle Doheny."

NEWCOMB, SIMON (1835–1909). *His Wisdom the Defender; A Story*. New York: Harper & Brothers, 1900. 329 pp.

Source: MTLAcc, entry #1637, volume donated by Clemens.

The eminent scientist, astronomer, and mathematician Newcomb also dabbled in science fiction. In this novel set in the future (the 1940s) a professor makes two discoveries that lead to a peaceful utopia.

———. *A Plain Man's Talk on the Labor Question*. New York: Harper & Brothers, 1886. 195 pp.

Source: MTLAcc, entry #689, volume donated by Clemens.

———. *Side-Lights on Astronomy and Kindred Fields of Popular Science: Essays and Addresses*. Illus. New York: Harper & Brothers, 1906. 349 pp.

Inscription: the front pastedown endpaper is signed in black ink: "S L. Clemens/21 Fifth avenue/New York./1906." There is a *C1951* sale label on the front free endpaper.

Marginalia: Clemens annotated the first seventy pages with black ink; those chapters describe the problems of astronomy and the structure and probable extent of the universe. On the front pastedown endpaper Clemens

computed the distance of a light-year and the distance to the nearest star, Alpha Centauri; he also noted that Newcomb estimates the sun to be "more than 1,000,000 times as large as earth." There are other black-ink computations regarding the distance, size, and speed of celestial bodies. Clemens made a note on page 24. On page 25 he recorded the fact that half of the visible stars are in the Milky Way and marveled at the fact that the light from a new star in the Milky Way, "born with Christ," has arrived only recently—it "might be destroyed 5,000 years ago." There is another note on page 26. Clemens wrote "but a speck" vertically on page 30 to emphasize Newcomb's reference to "the vast nebulous masses in the midst of which our whole solar system would be but a speck." On the verso of an illustration between pages 44 and 45, writing vertically, Clemens noted: "Every star, unless it has a family of planets, floats in an immeasurable solitude like a mustard seed in mid-Atlantic." He made a stylistic revision on page 46. Clemens's handwriting deteriorates to near illegibility on pages 52 and 59, as though he were ill or extremely weary). Pages 45 and 53 are folded down. The leaves are unopened at pages 107–110, probably indicating that he did not read that far in the volume. Chester L. Davis (1903–1987) quoted samples of Clemens's marginalia in *The Twainian* 4.5 (September-October 1981): 1–3 and 40.6 (November-December 1981): 1–3; Davis credited photocopies obtained from the University Library of the University of Nevada at Reno.

Catalog: *C1951*, #18a, $30, listed among volumes containing Clemens's annotation.

Location: Special Collections, University Library, University of Nevada at Reno. Purchased in 1963 from Mrs. Louis A. (Haydee U.) Zeitlin of Santa Monica, California.

Copy examined: Clemens's copy in Reno in 1970, and also a photocopy of the title page and inscription provided to the Mark Twain Papers, Bancroft Library, University of California at Berkeley, by Kenneth J. Carpenter, then the Special Collections Librarian, University of Nevada at Reno, on 17 December 1980.

"He said he would do an eclipse, not a real one, but an artificial one that nobody but Simon Newcomb could tell from the original Jacobs" (Chapter 31 of "No. 44, The Mysterious Stranger," written 1902–1908, *MSM*, p. 388).

———. *Side-Lights on Astronomy and Kindred Fields of Popular Science: Essays and Addresses*. Illus. New York: Harper & Brothers, 1906. 349 pp.

Source: MTLAcc, entry #1805, volume donated by Clemens.

———. *Side-Lights on Astronomy and Kindred Fields of Popular Science: Essays and Addresses*. First edition. Illus. Original green cloth, gilt. New York: Harper & Brothers, 1906. 349 pp.

Inscriptions: the front inside cover is inscribed by Clemens: "Susan L. Crane/from/S. L. C./Oct. '06." Susan Crane added an inscription to her nephew in a very unsteady hand, "Jervis Langdon Jr/Sun Jan 28, 1923." Susan Crane had an interest in astronomy (see the Catalog entry for Richard Proctor).

Marginalia: Clemens bracketed a section of the text at pages 230–235 concerning a maligned astronomer with the improbable name of Father Hell, whose observations were proven true after more than a century of derision.

Newcomb's reference was to Maximilian Hell (1720–1792), a Jesuit priest and Hungarian court astronomer who was falsely accused of altering his data.

Provenance: originally among the books in the Quarry Farm library.

Location: collection of Kevin Mac Donnell, Austin, Texas (Mac Donnell to Alan Gribben, 29 November 2011). Acquired from the Langdon family.

NEWELL, ROBERT HENRY (1836–1901), pseud. "Orpheus C. Kerr." "The Great Fit" (comic poem).

In 1880 Mark Twain included Orpheus C. Kerr in his list of humorists for inclusion in a projected anthology of American humor (NB 19, N&J 2: 364). Still casting about for writers to consider in the fall of 1882, he entered Newell's pen name in Notebook 20 (N&J 2: 504). When Mark Twain's Library of Humor issued in 1888 it included Newell's comic poem, "The Great Fit." On 17 January 1903 Twain listed Newell among literary figures he had known (NB 46, TS p. 7). In Twain's Autobiographical Dictation of 31 July 1906 he included "Orpheus C. Kerr" among a list of American humorists who were formerly well-known but had sunk into oblivion (MTE, p. 201; AutoMT 2: 153).

The New International Encyclopaedia. Edited by Daniel Coit Gilman (1831–1908), Harry Thurston Peck (1856–1914), and Frank Moore Colby (1865–1925). 17 vols. New York: Dodd, Mead and Co., 1902–1904.

Catalog: *C1951*, D27, listed among volumes signed by Clemens

NEWLAND, SIMPSON (1835–1925). *Paving the Way: A Romance of the Australian Brush.* London: Gay & Bird, 1893. 376 pp.

On 1 November 1895 Clemens alluded to how "mercifully swift & horrible" was the extinction of native races "in portions of Australia. (See Paving the Way.)." A few days later he made references to pages 319 and 327 of Newland's book (NB 34, TS pp 24, 29).

NEWMAN, (CARDINAL) JOHN HENRY (1801–1890) *Apologia Pro Vita Sua* (personal spiritual history, published in 1864).

Someone, possibly John Russell Young of the New York *Herald*, wrote the author and title in Mark Twain's Notebook 19 in January 1882 (N&J 2: 417). Since the note appears at the head of Twain's list of invectives directed against Whitelaw Reid, perhaps Newman's *Apologia* was supposed to provide a model for the fake biography of Reid that Twain intended to write. In Book I, Chapter 5 of *Christian Science* (1907) Newman was the "intellectual giant" whom Twain paired with the views of Gladstone.

NEWMAN, MARY WENTWORTH (c. 1831–1899), pseud. "May Wentworth."

Clemens noted her name and San Francisco address in 1866 (Notebook 5, N&J 1: 111), though this does not prove that he read any works by Newman, an editor and journalist for the *Golden Era* who in 1867 would edit a notable collection titled *Poetry of the Pacific: Selections and Original Poems from the Poets of the Pacific States.*

NEW ORLEANS *Times-Democrat* (newspaper).

The editors of this newspaper hosted a dinner for Mark Twain on 2 May 1882 in New Orleans. Following this trip to New Orleans in April and May of 1882, Twain subscribed briefly to the *Times-Democrat*; in Notebook 20 he cited the newspaper concerning the promptness

with which murderers are executed in the South (N&J 2: 486) and made a memorandum to have his subscription address changed to Elmira for the summer (N&J 2: 498). Chapter 26 of *Life on the Mississippi* (1883) refers readers to Appendix A for a "detailed and interesting" account of a terrible flood "written on board of the New Orleans *Times-Democrat's* relief boat." In Chapter 39 of *Life on the Mississippi* Twain quotes a description of a Natchez cotton mill from the 26 August 1882 issue of this newspaper. He originally quoted from the *Times-Democrat* to show the timidity of Southern citizens in dealing with ruffians, but he omitted this passage from the published version of *Life on the Mississippi* (Heritage Press edition [1944], p. 414).

The New Princeton Review (periodical, published 1886–1888).

Mark Twain reminded himself to get several copies of the issue of this quarterly journal that contained an article by Brander Matthews, "American Authors and British Pirates," *The New Princeton Review* 4 (September 1887): 201–212, to which Twain objected: "Get 2 or 3 Sept. New Princetons" (NB 27, January 1888, N&J 3: 368). Twain would publish a response to Matthews in the January 1888 issue. (See the Catalog entry for Brander Matthews.) It seems worth noting that the September 1887 issue of this periodical contained two other items likely to have caught Twain's notice when he looked for Matthews' essay—Richard Henry Stoddard's "Lord Byron" (pp. 145–162) and H. W. Conn's "The Origin of Life" (pp. 163–174). See also the Catalog entry for James King Newton.

NEWSON, THOMAS MCLEAN (1827–1893). *Indian Legends [of Minnesota Lakes].* Illus. 2 vols. Minneapolis: [A. S. Dimond], 1881. Volume 2 has the imprint of Dimond & Ross, 1881.

The first piece in Volume 2 of Newson's book is titled "Indian Legends of White Bear, Lake Pepin, and Lake Elmo." Mark Twain quotes the Legend of White Bear Lake from an unnamed guidebook in Chapter 60 of *Life on the Mississippi* (1883), crediting its author with having a "facile pen." The manuscript of *Life on the Mississippi* reveals that Twain merely inserted pages 63 and 64 from Nelson's *Indian Legends* to reproduce the White Bear Lake legend (MS in the Pierpont Morgan Library, PH in MTP). See also the Catalog entry for Henry Rowe Schoolcraft.

NEW SOUTH WALES. *Blue Book for the Year 1894. Compiled from Official Returns in the Registrar General's Office.* Sydney, 1895. [Government publication, issued 1866–1895.]

In Chapter 17 of *Following the Equator* (1897) Mark Twain cites the *New South Wales Blue Book* as his source for figures regarding annual imports and exports.

NEW SOUTH WALES. Photographs. Oblong folio. N.p., n.d.

Inscription: (on the front flyleaf) "S. L. Clemens Esq./ With kindest remembrances / Presented by the New South/Wales Government/ 21 [?] Dec '95/G. H. Reid".

Marginalia: Clemens marked several pictures with the word "This", presumably intending to use them as illustrations for *Following the Equator* (1897).

Catalog: *Mott 1952*, item #77, $75.

Location: Mark Twain House and Museum, Hartford, Connecticut. Donated anonymously in 1963.

Copy examined: Clemens's copy. Bound in red leather cover. This photograph album was specially prepared to commemorate Mark Twain's visit. It contains no prose or any title page. Examined in August 1987.

NEWTON, ALFRED (1829–1907), assisted by Hans Friedrich Gadow (1855–1928). *A Dictionary of Birds.* Illus. London: A. and C. Black, 1893–1896. 1088 pp. [Publisher and pages conjectured.]

> Catalog: *A1911*, "8vo, cloth (back damaged by nails), Lond. 1893–96," with a sheet of manuscript notes by Clemens laid in, lot 363, sold for $1.50.

> A copy of this book is visible in an interior photograph taken by Jean Clemens in the 1900s (Kevin Mac Donnell collection, Austin, Texas).

NEWTON, ALONZO ELIOT (1821–1889), ed. *The Modern Bethesda, or The Gift of Healing Restored. Being Some Account of the Life and Labors of Dr. J[ames]. R[ogers]. Newton [1810–1883], Healer.* New York: Newton Publishing Co., [cop. 1879]. 322 pp.

> Harold Aspiz—"Mark Twain and 'Doctor' Newton," *American Literature* 44.1 (March 1972): 130–136—discovered that this book enthusiastically described the career of the faith healer who was called upon to cure a young invalid named Olivia Langdon in 1864. Dr. Newton's former secretary, Austin A. Hill, recalled this miraculous incident on page 294 of *The Modern Bethesda*; Hill remembered that Newton went to Elmira to treat "Miss Libbie [*sic*] Langdon, whom he cured, and she has since married the author known as 'Mark Twain.' Dr. N. found her suffering with spinal disease; could not be raised to a sitting posture in her bed for over four years. She was almost like death itself. With one characteristic treatment he made her to cross the room with assistance, and in a few days the cure was complete" (p. 294). In the preface to the book, the editor remarked that Dr. Newton has retired "from his laborious practice" but that he will "continue the treatment of patients at a distance by means of magnetized letters" (p. 4). Aspiz also speculated that Mark Twain may have read this account of Olivia's cure prior to his Autobiographical Dictation of 13 February 1906 that refers to her treatment by a "Dr. Newton" (*AutoMT* 1: 356). Twain mentions there that he "met Newton once, in after years." Aspiz theorized that the pen-and-ink sketches of the Dauphin in the first edition of *Adventures of Huckleberry Finn* (1885) might have been modeled after the frontispiece portrait of Newton in *The Modern Bethesda*.

> Several excellent studies have discussed this episode in Olivia Langdon's life: Laura Skandera Trombley, "Mark Twain's Fictionalizing of Dr. Newton's Miraculous Cure," *American Literary Realism* 26.2 (Winter 1994): 82–92; Skandera Trombley, *Mark Twain in the Company of Women* (Philadelphia: University of Pennsylvania, 1994), pp. 83, 90–92, 93; and K. Patrick Ober, *Mark Twain and Medicine: "Any Mummery Will Cure"* (Columbia: University of Missouri Press, 2003)—see his Chapter 11, "Dr. Newton, The Quack," pp. 129–134.

NEWTON, JAMES KING (1843–1892). "Obligations of the United States to Initiate a Revision of Treaties Between the Western Powers and Japan," *Bibliotheca Sacra* 44.173 (January 1887): 46–70. Also published as a pamphlet in Oberlin, Ohio, 1887.

> In "American Authors and British Pirates," an essay published in the January 1888 issue of *The New Princeton Review*, Mark Twain castigated Newton's essay: "This

queer work is made up of rags and scraps of sense and nonsense, sham and sincerity, theft and butter-mouthed piousness, modesty and egotism, facts and lies, knowledge and ignorance . . . mingled with the wild weird whoop-jamboreehoo of the embattled jackass. Now, part of that strange article is original. The rest of it was 'smouched' from [Edward H.] House's *Atlantic* paper." Twain quotes examples of the plagiarism to illustrate "how exactly Mr. Newton can repeat slathers and slathers of another man's literature without ever missing a trick, when the police ain't around. . . . Brer Newton has issued it in pamphlet form, at a Boston admirer's expense; and has printed up in the corner of the cover, 'With the Author's Compliments'—meaning House, per'aps." Newton was a professor at Oberlin College in Ohio. In 1919 a Tokyo banker would establish an Oberlin College scholarship in Newton's name.

NEWTON, RICHARD HEBER (1840–1914). *Christian Science; The Truths of Spiritual Healing and Their Contribution to the Growth of Orthodoxy.* New York: G. P. Putnam's Sons, 1898. 78 pp. Reprinted in 1899.

> "Appendix E" to Mark Twain's *Christian Science* (1907) consists of an extract from pages 8–12 of this book by Newton, the rector of All Soul's Episcopal Church in New York City (*WIM?*, pp. 377–379, 576).

NEW YORK *American and Journal* (newspaper).

> In a speech Mark Twain delivered in 1906 he referred to "a long and fictitious interview, pretending to come from me" that had appeared as "Mrs. Astor Injures Mark Twain's Feelings" on page 3 of the 10 March 1902 issue of the New York *American and Journal* (Dan Cryer, "Mark Twain's 'Long and Fictitious Interview,'" *American Literary Resources* 45.1 [Fall 2012]: 84–86).

NEW YORK *Christian Advocate* (periodical).

> Mark Twain cites an article from the issue of 8 January 1903 in Book II, Chapter 7 of *Christian Science* (1907).

NEW YORK *Evening Post* (newspaper).

> The Mark Twain Papers in Berkeley contain a receipt for a subscription ($3) from 16 November 1880 to 16 November 1881, dated 18 November 1880, from William C. Bryant & Company. "I read an evening or two ago a notice of 'Monsieur Motte' in the N. Y. Evening Post which I want to send you" (OLC to Grace King, 7 August 1888, ALS at Louisiana State University, Baton Rouge). "Somebody (Willard Fiske, I suppose)—has sent me a file of the N. Y. Eve. Post—my favorite paper—from Nov. 1 to 17th, & the election details & comments are nuts to me" (SLC to Fred J. Hall, Florence, Italy, 7 December 1892, *MTLP*, p. 327).

> "What is it the Evening Post is attacking? We don't see the papers in this remote place" (SLC to Richard Watson Gilder, Vienna, 14 March 1899, New York Public Library). "I have stopped all papers except the Evening Post" (SLC to Henry H. Rogers, 20 April 1903, Riverdale, *MTHHR*, p. 524). Mark Twain's original version of "Corn-Pone Opinions," apparently written in 1903, included two clippings from the 27 April 1903 issue of the New York *Evening Post* (Joe B. Fulton, "The Lost Manuscript Conclusion to Mark Twain's 'Corn-Pone Opinions': An Editorial History and an Edition of the Restored Text," *American Literary Realism* 37.3 [Spring 2005]: 258 n.

29). Clemens praised a "New York police-story (Irish)" in the 14 December 1903 issue of the New York *Evening Post* in a letter of 28 December 1903 to George B. Harvey (MTP). On 30 December 1903 Clemens wrote to Frederick A. Duneka about this "well told" short story he had read in a recent issue of the New York *Evening Post* (ALS, Special Collections, Washington University Libraries, St. Louis)—see the Catalog entry for Robert Emmet MacAlarney. Clemens read about a Chicago fire disaster in the New York *Evening Post* in January 1904 (undated letter fragment, no addressee, MTP). On the evening of 2 January 1906 Isabel V. Lyon noted that in Clemens's room "wreaths of smoke were hovering and he had the *Evening Post* for his reading" (IVL Journals, TS p. 118, MTP). Mark Twain quoted from the *Evening Post's* account of Clara Clemens's public concert (16 April 1909 AD, *AutoMT* 3: 305–306).

NEW YORK *Evening Sun* (newspaper).

An Irish reporter told Mark Twain that his paper, the *Evening Sun*, had cabled him a report that Mark Twain was dead. Clemens told him to reply that "the report is exaggerated" (3 April 1906 AD, *MTE*, pp. 252–253; *AutoMT* 2: 11). See also the Catalog entry for the New York *Sun*.

NEW YORK *Graphic* (newspaper).

Instructing Charles L. Webster to send advance copies of *Adventures of Huckleberry Finn* (1885) to most New York City dailies, Mark Twain on 10 February 1885 admonished from Columbus, Ohio: *"Never* send any to N. Y. Graphic" (*MTBus*, p. 300).

NEW YORK *Herald* (newspaper).

Mark Twain's 26 May 1867 letter to the *Alta California* alludes to an article in the *Herald* (*MTTMB*, p. 229). "He was perfectly frank about it, & said he wanted to go to hell: said he had got so used to reading the N. Y. Herald he couldn't do without it" (entry in NB 34, 1895, TS p. 2). Twain was gratified to discover, in "a New York *Herald* of something more than a month ago," an editorial castigating the Theodore Roosevelt administration (14 July 1908 AD, *AutoMT* 3: 258). In another autobiographical dictation Clemens quoted from the *Herald's* account of a public concert by Clara Clemens (16 April 1909 AD, *AutoMT* 3: 306). Clemens's copy of Samuel G. Bayne's *The Pith of Astronomy* (1907) contains an article about Neptune, clipped from the New York *Herald* of 20 November 1909 and pinned to page 55. In Bermuda in 1909 Clemens obtained copies of the *Herald* and the *Times*, but lacked sufficient interest in world affairs even to open them (SLC to Jean Clemens, 6 December 1909, ALS in MTP).

NEW YORK *Sun* (newspaper).

The proprietor of the San Francisco *Call* in 1865 reminded Mark Twain that the *Call* "was like the New York *Sun* of that day: it was the washerwoman's paper—that is, it was the paper of the poor" (13 June 1906 AD, *MTE*, p. 256; *AutoMT* 2: 115). "I saw in the Sun of Monday, that no provision is made for a wooden barrack for the soldiers who guard General Grant's tomb" (SLC to Charles L. Webster, Hartford, 28 October 1885, *MTBus*, p. 334). "The facts are distorted in that 'Sun' squib. (When you see it in the Sun it ain't so.)" (SLC to Henry H. Rogers, Étretat, 2–3 September 1894, *MTHHR*, p. 72). "The

notice [of *Following the Equator*] in the Sun delighted me all over" (SLC to Henry H. Rogers, Vienna, 29 December 1897, *MTHHR*, p. 311).

In "To My Missionary Critics" (1901), Twain quotes from an article about Chinese missionaries that appeared in the *Sun* "last Christmas Eve." At the beginning of "To the Person Sitting in Darkness" (1901), Twain quotes from the 24 December 1900 issue; in the same essay he also quotes a statement by the Reverend Ament explaining indemnities for the Chinese Boxer damages, also taken from the *Sun*. The *Sun*, edited by Paul Dana (1852–1930), lamented: "We are sorry to say that Mark is on a spree. . . . Wait, and welcome the prodigal as of old on his return. He will be along again in time" (*Pen*, p. 180). During this period a photograph was taken of Twain reading a copy of the New York *Sun*, and the date is legible: Tuesday, 7 May 1901 (Library of Congress). He was residing at 1410 W. 10th in New York City at the time (Fears, *Day by Day* 3: 519). "Thank you very much for the Sun. The first copy arrived yesterday and came very handy, for I was knocked down with gout and needed mental reinforcement" (SLC to Henry H. Rogers, Florence, 28 November 1903, *MTHHR*, p. 543). "I am exceedingly glad to have the Sun. It seems to me that it has very greatly improved" (SLC to Henry H. Rogers, Florence, 16 December 1903, *MTHHR*, p. 545). "The New York Sun says Maurice Hewlett is spending the winter in Florence" (SLC to E. B. Caulfield, Villa di Quarto, late in 1903, CWB). Clemens was receiving the *Sun* in Florence in January 1904, for he learned about a fire disaster in Chicago from this and another newspaper (SLC to unidentified correspondent, undated letter fragment, MTP). "It is pretty hard to write you anything new, for the reason that you take the 'Sun'" (Henry H. Rogers to SLC, New York City, 12 January 1904, *MTHHR*, p. 552). "Gales & snow-storms with you, two weeks ago—I read about it in the Sun this morning" (SLC to WDH, Florence, 16 January 1904, *MTHL*, p. 779). A leaf of manuscript by Clemens laid in an auctioned copy of M. S. Gatty's *Parables from Nature* refers to "Sunday 17th" and "Great storms Jan 4 in N[ew] Y[ork]—read it yesterday in the Sun" (see the Catalog entry for Gatty). Henry H. Rogers noted: "You will have seen in the columns of the 'Sun' ere this reaches you" (Rogers to SLC, New York City, 8 February 1904, *MTHHR*, p. 555). "I was glad to gather from the Sun that you were getting the best of the Montana crowd at last" (SLC to Henry H. Rogers, Florence, 25–26 February 1904, *MTHHR*, p. 557). Clemens mentions items in "day before yesterday's New York *Sun*" in his Autobiographical Dictation of 13 June 1906 (*MTE*, p. 257; *AutoMT* 2: 115). He quotes from the 5 December 1906 issue (regarding the Russian famine) in an Autobiographical Dictation of that date (*AutoMT* 2: 307–308). On 14 January 1907 Clemens expressed approval of [American Episcopal clergyman] Algernon Sidney Crapsey's lecture "in today's 'Sun'" (Isabel V. Lyon Journals, TS p. 216, MTP). [The rebellious Crapsey had been deposed from his ministry after being tried and convicted of heresy.] In an Autobiographical Dictation of 15 January 1907 Clemens quoted from a letter "in this morning's *Sun*" regarding military pensions (*AutoMT* 2: 372–374). An Autobiographical Dictation of 25 February

1907 quoted the *Sun's* account in "this morning's" issue describing the shipwreck of the *Berlin* (*AutoMT* 2: 438–440); the next day he quoted another *Sun* report about the *Berlin's* fate (26 February 1907 AD, *AutoMT* 2: 443–444). Clemens quoted several news articles about William Whiteley from the *Sun* in an Autobiographical Dictation of 27 February 1907 (MTP). Louis J. Budd possessed a photograph of Clemens reading the 7 May 1907 issue of the New York *Sun* (conversation with Louis J. Budd, Modern Language Association convention, New York City, December 1982). See also the Catalog entry for the New York *Evening Sun.* Clemens's copy of Samuel G. Bayne's *The Pith of Astronomy* (1907) contains an article about Jupiter, clipped from the New York *Sun* of 21 January 20 [1910?] and pinned to page 39.

NEW YORK *Times* (newspaper).

Catalog: ListABP (1910), "N. Y. Times, 1906"; no issue specified.

Mark Twain feared the possibility of a lawsuit by Captain C. C. Duncan of the *Quaker City* as the result of a front page article titled "Mr. Mark Twain Excited" in the 10 June 1883 issue of the *Times* (*MTBus*, p. 215). In 1905 Clemens alluded to "a fine and appreciative editorial" concerning Andrew Carnegie (SLC to Carnegie, 28 April 1905, ALS at Washington University). On 23 September 1905 Isabel V. Lyon spoke to Clemens about a New York *Times* article (IVL Journals, TS p. 101, MTP). Back in New York City after spending several months in Dublin, New Hampshire, Clemens on 7 December 1905 read to Miss Lyon "a very great poem by Mr. [Richard Watson] Gilder in the *Times*" of that morning (IVL Journals, TS p. 112, MTP). "I want to read from the commercial columns of the New York *Times*, of a day or two ago" (9 January 1906 AD, *MTA*, 1: 270; *AutoMT* 1: 251). Clemens incorporated a clipping from the *Times* of 16 February 1906 in his Autobiographical Dictation of that same date; the article reported John A. McCall's advice to his son (MTP; *MTE*, pp. 79–80; *AutoMT* 1: 365–366). In an Autobiographical Dictation of 20 March 1906 Clemens quotes from a letter of his that had quoted Rabbi Joseph Silverman's explication of the Genesis story of Joseph, published "Sunday before last" (i.e., 11 March 1906) in the *Times* (MTP; *MTE*, pp. 88–89; *AutoMT* 1: 423–424). On 24 March 1906 Isabel V. Lyon mentioned that Clemens was reading "the morning newspaper, The *Times*" (IVL Journals, TS p. 151, MTP). Clemens used a clipping from the *Times* issue of 3 April 1906 as an epigraph for his Autobiographical Dictation of that date (*AutoMT* 2: 6). "This afternoon when Mr. Clemens picked up the *Times* and noticed the date, he said, 'This is one of my anniversaries'" (Isabel V. Lyon Journals, 26 May 1906 entry, TS p. 160, MTP). "This afternoon . . . Mr. Clemens picked up the Times, & noticed the date" (Isabel V. Lyon Journal, 26 May 1906 entry, Harry Ransom Center, University of Texas at Austin). From the Times—the issue published on 19 June 1906, according to the editorial staff of the Mark Twain Project in the Bancroft Library at the University of California at Berkeley—Clemens clipped a report concerning the massacre of Jews in Bialystok on 15 June 1906; he read it into his Autobiographical Dictation of 22 June 1906 (quoted by Charles Neider, "Reflections,"

pp. 339–340; *AutoMT* 2: 133, 524).

Clemens inserted an article from the *Times* (dated 10 January 1907, headlined "Mrs. Morris's Illness Takes a Serious Turn") in his Autobiographical Dictation of 15 January 1907 (*MTA*, 1: 318–319; *AutoMT* 2:). On 20 January 1907 Clemens "picked up the paper and read a political article from *The Times*" (IVL Journals, TS p. 218a, MTP). On Sunday, 27 January 1907, Clemens read aloud to Miss Lyon "Mr. Dooley's ideas about the Army Canteen which appears in today's *Times*" (IVL Journals, TS p. 221, MTP). Clemens pretended that he was sending an embarrassing letter to the *Times* above the name of William Dean Howells; he sent a copy to Henry H. Rogers (SLC to Rogers, New York City, 4 October 1907, *MTHHR*, pp. 640–641) and to William Dean Howells (SLC to WDH, New York City, 4 October 1907, *MTHL*, p. 827). Clemens pinned a clipping from the 31 December 1908 issue of the New York *Times* (pp. 3–4)—an article describing an earthquake in Messina, Italy—in the back of his copy of Nathaniel S. Shaler's *Aspects of the Earth* (1904), a volume Clemens signed in 1908 (MTHM); the slipcase for this book also contains other New York *Times* clippings about earthquakes—these are dated 1 January 1909 (MTHM). Twain quoted two undated articles from the New York *Times*—using one as the epigraph—in "Dr. Loeb's Incredible Discovery" (1923). Twain relied on an article in the 3 January 1909 issue of the New York *Times*, "New Planet Is Indicated," as the basis for an article titled "The New Planet" that he published in 30 January 1909 issue of *Harper's Weekly* (*MTPP*, p. 183). "As for news of the great world, it does not interest me," Clemens wrote resignedly from Bermuda on 6 December 1909. "The Times & the Herald have lain at my elbow 2 days, now—unopened" (SLC to Jean Clemens, ALS in MTP).

NEW YORK *Tribune* (newspaper).

Paul Baender cited an anecdote in the 24 August 1869 issue as Mark Twain's source for the burlesque "confession" by Byron (Paine 260, MTP) that he had nine illegitimate children and devoured them all (Baender, "Mark Twain and the Byron Scandal," *American Literature* 30.4 [January 1959]: 482 n. 26). In "A Royal Compliment" (1870), Twain quoted an editorial from the *Tribune* that suggested the Spanish seek an American for their next sovereign. Clemens mentioned that he "read the Foster petitions in Thursday's Tribune" (SLC to Whitelaw Reid, Hartford, 7 March 1873, New York Public Library). On 14 October 1874 Clemens mentioned to Louise Chandler Moulton that he and Olivia "have so long read your book reviews in the Tribune" (*MTLet* 6: 257). Clemens complained about a quotation attributed to the actress Kate Field that appeared in the New York *Tribune* on 19 January 1875 (Karl Kiralis, "Two Recently Discovered Letters: Mark Twain on Kate Field," *Mark Twain Journal* 20.2 [Summer 1980]: 1–4). Clemens registered disgust on 5 July 1875 when the *Tribune* published a patriotic poem by Oliver Wendell Holmes without the permission of its publisher James R. Osgood (*MTLet* 6: 504). After William Dean Howells's favorable review of *The Prince and the Pauper* (1881) appeared in the 25 October 1881 issue of the New York *Tribune* (p. 6), Clemens wrote to his publisher James R. Osgood on 27 October 1881 to express satisfaction with Howells's essay: "Howells's review pleased me vastly. The praise & the dispraise sound equally candid & sincere; & both are stated so forcibly & backed up by such clear reasoning, that future reviewers will find it difficult to get away from the influence exerted upon their minds by this critique. It is a mint-stamp; it will be hard to rub out" (*Sotheby's 2003*, #49).

However, in the latter part of 1881 and the early months of 1882 Clemens raged against the *Tribune's* editor and publisher, Whitelaw Reid (NB 19, *N&J* 2: 355–356; Notebook 20, *N&J* 2: 432); during most of January in 1882 he futilely gave the newspaper's columns scrupulous attention to determine the extent of Reid's supposed "slurs" against him (SLC to Charles L. Webster, 21 January 1882, *MTBus*, p. 183). "I began to watch the current numbers, for I had subscribed for the paper" (SLC to WDH, Hartford, 28 January 1882, *MTHL*, p. 388). Clemens examined the *Tribune's* editorials minutely in August 1886 to discern the progress of "that other machine," a typesetter rivaling his own investment (SLC to Edward H. House, Elmira, New York, 11 August 1886, ASSSCL). In 1887, possibly in April, Clemens quoted from an editorial on the jury system (NB 26, *N&J* 3: 282)—he was still watching the *Tribune* to estimate the usefulness of the Paige typesetter in which his money was tied up. He analyzed the issue of 25 January 1888 to compute the practical value of his Paige machine (NB 27, *N&J* 3: 370). Twain's "To the Person Sitting in Darkness" (1901), opens with an ebullient *Tribune* editorial that scolds Yuletide grumblers (*Pen*, p. 60); farther on in the essay he quotes a cautionary *Tribune* dispatch from Tokyo that appeared in the 24 December 1900 issue of the *Tribune* (*Pen*, pp. 63–64). Twain wrote an indignant letter to the editor of the *Tribune* on 18 February 1901 (*MTPP*). Clemens mentioned the *Tribune* in some marginalia at the bottom of a page in which Meredith Townsend—*Asia and Europe* (New York: G. P. Putnam's Sons, 1901), p. 15—reminded readers that "it is hardly a century since torture was disused" in Europe, to which Clemens rejoined: "It is used in New York. See Tribune of to-day (May 9/02)" (MTP).

NEW YORK *Weekly* (newspaper).

In 1867 Mark Twain decided to forgo writing correspondence for this newspaper because, though it pays the writer "splendidly," the *Weekly* "circulates among stupid people and the *canaille*" (*MTL*, p. 126; *MTLet* 2: 50). An editorial about a dental fraud in the *Weekly* of 24 August 1871 conceivably gave Twain the notion for the Duke's tartar-remover (Joseph Jones, "The 'Duke's' Tooth-Powder Racket," *Modern Language Notes* 61 [November 1946]: 468–469).

NEW YORK *Weekly Post* (newspaper).

The manuscript of Mark Twain's "The United States of Lyncherdom" (written in August 1901) contained a clipping of an item reprinted in the New York *Weekly Post* (Budd, *CTSS&E* 2: 1033).

NEW YORK *World* (newspaper).

Catalog: ListABP (1910), "N. Y. World, 1906", no issue specified.

Mark Twain culled twenty sensational headlines and stories from the 2 March 1885 issue of Joseph Pulitzer's paper to illustrate the morality of the journal that had called

Adventures of Huckleberry Finn (1885) "cheap and pernicious stuff" (NB 24, *N&J* 3: 128–130). In April or May of 1888 Twain looked at issues of the *World* to estimate the market value of James W. Paige's typesetting machine (NB 27, *N&J* 3: 384); he checked its column space for the same Paige enterprise in December 1888 (NB 28, *N&J* 3: 437). On the Fourth of July in 1892, Twain arose in his room at the Union League Club in New York City, "ordered breakfast & the paper brought to my room. Ate the breakfast, read the 'World' through" (NB 31, TS p. 58). Twain commented favorably on an article about his financial status that appeared in the 13 December 1896 issue of the *World* (SLC to Henry H. Rogers, Vienna, 29 December 1897, *MTHHR*, p. 311). When Twain stipulated a high price in replying to the *World's* request for a Christmas story, he predicted: "That will put the World's feverish desires on ice—those highly-enterprising concerns have their economies, like other people" (SLC to Henry H. Rogers, Vienna, 2 November 1898, *MTHHR*, p. 371). Shortly before Twain returned to the United States in 1900 he granted the *World* a lengthy interview. Twain said that it was the *World* that had wired its London reporter in 1897: "If Mark Twain dying send five hundred words. If dead send a thousand" (3 April 1906 AD, *MTE*, p. 253; *AutoMT* 2: 11; see also Scharnhorst's *Complete Interviews*, 346–351).

"Three days ago the *World* newspaper convicted him [Mr. Roosevelt], beyond redemption, of having bought his election to the Presidency with money" (13 September 1907 AD, *MTE*, p. 14; *AutoMT* 2: 134). In an Autobiographical Dictation of 18 October 1907 Twain quotes from "this morning's news" in the *World* (*AutoMT* 2: 172). On 31 October 1908 Twain inserted into his Autobiographical Dictation a clipping from the *World* issue of 30 October 1908 reporting Henry Butters' death (*AutoMT* 2: 269). Henry Augustus Butters (1850–1908), a wealthy San Francisco Bay Area industrialist and financier, had been in the news previously owing to his separation from his wife.

NEW ZEALAND. *Guide to the Collections in the Canterbury Museum, Christchurch, New Zealand.* Illus. Christchurch, New Zealand: Printed for the Board of Governors, 1895. 232 pp.

Inscription: the front cover is signed "S. L. Clemens."

Catalogs: *A 1911*, "8vo, wrappers, [Christ Church], 1895," quotes the signature, lot 213, sold for .50¢; *Lexington 1912*, lot 4, erroneously reports the flyleaf as signed "S. L. Clemens, Hartford, 1882" [*sic*], sold for $1.50.

The Niagara Book: A Complete Souvenir of Niagara Falls, Containing Sketches, Stories, and Essays—Descriptive, Humorous, Historical and Scientific, Written Exclusively for This Book. By W[illiam]. D[ean]. Howells [1837–1920], Mark Twain [1835–1910], Prof. Nathaniel S[outhgate]. Shaler [1841–1906], and Others. Original pictorial green cloth. Illus. by Harry Fenn (1838–1911). Buffalo: Underhill and Nichols, 1893. 225 pp. [Contains Mark Twain's "Extracts from Adam's Diary."]

Location: Albert and Shirley Small Special Collections Library, University of Virginia, Charlottesville, Virginia.

Source: the online catalog of Special Collections in the University of Virginia Libraries lists this volume as being "From the library of Mark Twain." No signature or annotations are mentioned. I am grateful to JoDee Benussi for noticing this item.

Nichols, George Ward (1831–1885). "Down the Mississippi," *Harper's New Monthly Magazine* 41:246 (November 1870): 835–845.

> Thomas Ruys Smith—"'The Mississippi Was a Virgin Field': Reconstructing the River Before Mark Twain, 1865–1875," *Mark Twain Journal* 53.2 (Fall 2015): 24–66—cited this article as one of several prominent reports that preceded Mark Twain's "Old Times on the Mississippi" (1875). Twain certainly might have been aware of any such article on a subject that interested him so much.

Nicholson, Eliza Jane (Poitevent) (1849–1896), pseud. "Pearl Rivers." *Lyrics*. Philadelphia: J. B. Lippincott & Co., 1873. 131 pp.

> **Source:** MTLAcc, entry #2083, volume donated from Clemens's library by Clara Clemens Gabrilowitsch in 1910.

Nicholson, Meredith (1866–1947). *The House of a Thousand Candles*. Illustrated by Howard Chandler Christy (1873–1952). Indianapolis, Indiana: Bobbs-Merrill Co., [cop. 1905.] 382 pp.

> **Source:** MTLAcc, entry #232, volume donated by Clemens.
>
> *The House of a Thousand Candles* ranked fourth among the best-selling works of fiction in 1906. Nicholson would provide a prefatory "Appreciation" for *Life on the Mississippi* in the so-called Definite Edition of Twain's works (New York: Gabriel Well, 1922–1925).

———. *The Port of Missing Men*. Illustrated by Clarence F[rederick]. Underwood (1871–1929). New York: A. Wessels Co., 1908. 399 pp.

> **Source:** MTLAcc, entry #231, volume donated by Clemens.

Nicholson, William (1753–1815), ed. *American Edition of the British Encyclopedia, or Dictionary of Arts and Sciences. Comprising an Accurate and Popular View of the Present Improved State of Human Knowledge*. Illus. 12 vols. Philadelphia: Mitchell, Ames and White, 1818. [Publisher conjectured.]

> **Inscription:** the bookplate of Orion Clemens.
>
> **Catalog:** A1911, "12 vols., 8vo, old sheep (in poor condition), . . . Phila. 1818, with the book-label of Orion Clemens," lot 364, $1.
>
> The most valuable items in John Marshall Clemens's personal library, according to the appraisal of his property filed in the Probate Court of Marion County on 21 May 1847 following his death, were "6 [*sic*] volumes Nicholsons Encyclopedia" worth $1.50 (McDermott, "Mark Twain and the Bible" [1968], p. 198; Fred Kaplan, *The Singular Mark Twain: A Biography* [New York: Doubleday, 2003, p. 37). Orion Clemens inherited that set of encyclopedias. He died in 1897 and his wife Mollie died in 1904. Mollie Clemens's legal will referred to "the old Brittanica [*sic*] which was their father's." Samuel Clemens specifically requested from Mollie's executor only his mother's Bible and "the *old* Cyclopedia (my father's—I do not care for any later one)" (SLC to Mr. Carpenter, Florence, Italy, 14 February 1904, ALS in MTP). Those volumes have not reappeared since the 1911 auction. The extent of Nicholson's contributions to this work, aside from lending it his illustrious name in science, has been disputed.

Nicholson, William (1872–1949). *Twelve Portraits. Second Series*. [New York: R. H. Russell, 1902].

> **Marginalia:** Clemens inscribed his own sketched portrait:

"Wm. Nicholson/1902".

> **Catalog:** ListABP (1910), "12 Portraits, Nicholson".
>
> **Location:** Mark Twain Papers, Bancroft Library, University of California at Berkeley.
>
> **Copy examined:** Clemens's copy. This is an unbound set of lithograph sketches of prominent figures: Henrik Ibsen, Queen Alexandra, Pope Leo XIII, Theodore Roosevelt (leading his Rough Riders), Mark Twain, Sada Yacco, the Kaiser, Eleonora Duse, Lord Kitchener, Joseph Chamberlain, Li Hung Chang, and Thomas Edison. The covers are tied with a ribbon. There is no text except the name and title on the cover.
>
> Nicholson had earlier sketched Mark Twain for a portrait that appeared on the cover of an issue of *Harper's Weekly* (44.2295 [15 December 1900]: 1201) that honored Twain's achievements.

Nicols, Arthur. *Wild Life and Adventure in the Australian Bush: Four Years' Personal Experience*. Illustrated by John [Trivett] Nettleship (1841–1902). 2 vols. London: R. Bentley and Son, 1887.

> The reading Clemens undertook in London in November 1896 included "Wild Life & Adventure in the Bush—Nicols" (NB 39, TS p. 26).

Niedergesäss, Robert (1829–1887). *Kinderstubengeschichten. Dreissig Erzählungen für das Kindesalter. . . . Mit Bildern von Fritz Bergen [Nursery Stories]*. 2nd edition. Stuttgart: Gebrüder Kröner, 1887.

> **Inscription:** from Livy Clemens to Jean Clemens at Quarry Farm on 26 July 1887, Jean's fifth birthday.
>
> **Catalog:** *Mott 1952*, item #74, $7.50.
>
> Edgar H. Hemminghaus saw this volume in the Mark Twain Library at Redding, Connecticut, in 1945 ("Mark Twain's German Provenience," p. 472). I could never locate it.

Nieritz, Karl Gustav (1795–1876). *Die Wunderpfeife, oder: Die Kinder von Hameln. Ein geschichtliches Märchen [The Marvelous Piper, or the Children of Hameln]*. Elfte Auflage. Wesel: A. Bagel, [187?]. 115 pp. [Bound with Adelbert von Chamisso, *Peter Schlemihl's wundersame Geschichte*.]

> **Catalog:** *Zeitlin 1951*, item #44, $35.
>
> **Location:** Mark Twain Papers, Bancroft Library, University of California at Berkeley.
>
> **Copy examined:** Clemens's copy, unmarked.
>
> On 11 January 1885 Clemens mentioned in a letter to Olivia Clemens that he had begun a translation of "the German prose version of the Pied Piper of Hamelin" (AL in MTP). JoDee Benussi notified me about this possible connection to Nieritz's book. She also noticed that Clemens enclosed in the letter his Chapter VI ("The Great Loneliness") of a fragmentary manuscript that accords with the desolation experienced by the villagers in Hamelin after their children have disappeared.

Nietzsche, Friedrich Wilhelm (1844–1900). *Thus Spake Zarathustra; A Book for All and None*. Translated by Alexander Tille (1866–1912). New York: Macmillan Co., 1906. 479 pp. [Edition conjectured: *Sprach Zarathustra* was first published 1883–1885; Macmillan Company brought out the first American edition in 1896.]

> On 13 July 1906 (while Clemens was away in New York City), Isabel V. Lyon noted that "'Zarathustra' has arrived!" She began reading the book the next day, and found it "wonderful." Clemens returned home on 25

July 1906. Lyon's journals report that on 8 August 1906 "the King wanted to see my Zarathustra. It pained me to give him up, but I did it. And after the King had looked through it he said, 'Oh damn Nietzsche! He couldn't write a lucid sentence to save his soul.' Somehow I am glad he doesn't like Zarathustra. Very, very glad—but I shall be able to quote some passages to him—some telling passages—for Nietzsche is too much like himself" (IVL Journals, TS pp. 173, 178, MTP). On 10 August 1906 Lyon found that "the King says 'Damn Nietzsche' when I offer a quotation for the King's approval. First he damns—but then he approves with his head on one side in his quaint listening attitude" (TS p. 178, MTP). On 27 August 1906 she wrote: "This morning I said to the King, 'Nietzsche says—' 'Oh, damn Nietzsche.' 'But Mr. Clemens, Nietzsche calls the acts of God, 'divine kicks,' 'Hurray for Nietzsche!' the king shouted, and slapped his leg hard" (TS p. 183, MTP).

Clemens mentioned Isabel Lyon's efforts in a letter to Mary Benjamin Rogers he wrote from Dublin on 27 August 1906: "I can't stand Nietsche [sic], so. . . I think there won't be any more Nietsche to-day" (MTLM, p. 47). "I have not read Nietzsche or Ibsen, nor any other philosopher," Clemens declared in an Autobiographical Dictation of 4 September 1907 (quoted in WIM?, p. 17; AutoMT 3: 130). In the same dictation he also remarked: "Nietzsche published his book, and was at once pronounced crazy by the world—by a world which included tens of thousands of bright, sane men who believed exactly as Nietzsche believed, but concealed the fact, and scoffed at Nietzsche. What a coward every man is!" (quoted in MTE, p. xxix; AutoMT 3: 130).

Gabriel Noah Brahm and Forrest G. Robinson, "The Jester and the Sage: Twain and Nietzsche," Nineteenth-Century Literature 60.2 (September 2005): 137–162, demonstrated that "both writers were brilliant psychologists with a common and compelling interest in the submerged wellsprings of human behavior. . . . Indeed, both were at times disposed to view the world as a madhouse" (p. 140). See also Patrick J. Keane, "Mark Twain, Nietzsche, and Terrible Truths That Can Set Us Free," Mark Twain Annual 11 (2013): 22–41; James Wharton Leonard, "The View from the Raft: Huck Finn's Authentically Nietzschean Perspective," American Literary Realism 46.1 (Fall 2013): 76–85; and Mark Twain and Philosophy, ed. Alan H. Goldman (2017), pp. 67, 77, 185–191.

[NIMES, JOSEPH A.] Aristocracy. A Novel. New York: D. Appleton and Co., 1890. 257 pp.

Source: MTLAcc, entry #955, volume donated by Clemens.

First published in November 1888, Aristocracy cynically mocks the English upper class. Its rather thin plot has Philip Allen, a San Francisco millionaire, traveling to England and marrying Lady Edith Vesey. Nimes presumably published the novel anonymously because it skewers prominent English society figures whose fictitious names hardly disguise their identities. Newspaper and magazine reviewers at the time were justified in wishing for a higher degree of literary artistry by which Nimes might better have achieved his satiric intentions. However, his novel is another manifestation of the resentment building in the 1880s against the rigid class structure then prevailing

in English society. Mark Twain's A Connecticut Yankee in King Arthur's Court (1889) is seen by many literary critics as the product of an American writer sympathetic to that rebellious movement.

Nineteenth Century (London, monthly periodical).

In April or May 1888 Clemens recalled an "article in Nineteenth Century— within 7 years—first article of a certain number—on England's rule in India" (NB 27, N&J 3: 383). See the Catalog entry for J. Seymour Keay. It is worth noting that Matthew Arnold had published "Civilization in the United States" in the April 1888 issue, which Clemens definitely read.

Baetzhold, MT&JB (1970), pp 119, 338–339 n. 54.

NISBET, CHARLES and ELI LEMON SHELDON, pseud. "Don Lemon." Everybody's Writing-Desk Book. Rev. edition. Ed. by James Baldwin (1841–1925). New York: Harper & Brothers, 1903. 310 pp.

Source: MTLAcc, entry #1331, volume donated by Clemens.

An odd library item—would a writer as adept with the English language as Mark Twain need any help with his grammar and style in 1903? Perhaps he wanted to review the most current rules for usage.

NOHL, LOUIS [ACTUALLY LUDWIG] (1831–1885). Life of Beethoven. Translated from the German by John J[oseph]. Lalor (1841–1899). Chicago: A. C. McClurg & Co., 1888. 201 pp.

Inscription: the front free flyleaf is inscribed in black ink by Olivia Clemens: "Clara L. Clemens/2 Feb. 1889."

Location: Mark Twain Library, Redding, Connecticut.

Copy examined: Clara Clemens's unmarked copy. Has the red ink Mark Twain Library accession number "2457". Examined in 1970 and again in June 1982 and on 9 November 2019.

When the Clemenses were leaving the Hartford house for Quarry Farm in June 1889, Clemens made a note to "bring Chopin & Beethoven—in drawing-room—□ square, red-bound" (NB 29, N&J 3: 494). Around 1889 Susy Warner played Beethoven's Seventh Symphony on the piano at Clemens's request, as well as "that other deep, rich, noble Beethoven piece" (S&MT, p. 262; LLMT, p. 252).

———. Life of Liszt. Trans. from the German by George Putnam Upton (1834–1919). Chicago: A. C. McClurg & Co., 1887. 198 pp.

Inscription: the front free flyleaf is inscribed in black ink by Olivia Clemens: "Clara L. Clemens/Feb. 1889."

Location: Mark Twain Library, Redding, Connecticut.

Copy examined: Clara Clemens's unmarked copy. Has the red ink Mark Twain Library accession number "2458" and the purple oval Library stamps. Examined in 1970 and again in June 1982 and on 9 November 2019.

———. Life of Wagner. Translated from the German by George Putnam Upton (1834–1919). Chicago: A. C. McClurg & Co., 1888. 204 pp.

Inscription: the front free flyleaf is inscribed in black ink by Olivia Clemens: "Clara L. Clemens/Feb. 1889."

Location: Mark Twain Library, Redding, Connecticut.

Copy examined: Clara Clemens's unmarked copy. Has the red ink Mark Twain Library accession number "2459". Examined in 1970 and again in June 1982 and on 9 November 2019.

"Nora McCarty" (Irish ballad, composer uncertain).

In a letter written to Francis Boott from Florence on 30 January 1893, William James mentioned that "Mark Twain dined with us last night" and expressed regret that "there was no chance . . . to ask him to sing Nora McCarty" (*The Letters of William James*, ed. Henry James [Boston: Atlantic Month Press, 1920], p. 342). The song James had in mind presents a conundrum. Thomas Bailey Aldrich (1836–1907) published a two-stanza poem titled "Nora McCarty" in *The Knickerbocker* 57.2 (February 1861): 135, but it was a slight piece and there is no indication it was ever set to music. Charles Southworth Hill published the words and melody of a sentimental Irish ballad, "Nora McCarty," in 1895, but that was two years later than James' allusion. Another ballad version with the same title, a song both romantic and winsomely comic, appeared as a poem by Francis Arthur Fahy (1854–1935) in 1887 and had lyrics added by the composer Alicia Adélaïde Needham (1863–1945), but no sheet music for it seems to have been in print before 1898. So which of these was Twain supposed to sing? Until earlier dates for the song lyrics by either Hill or Fahy can be established, the question remains open.

Norris, [Benjamin] Frank[lin] (1870–1902), known as Frank Norris.

William Dean Howells published an essay on Frank Norris's fiction in the December 1902 issue of the *North American Review*, "which I suppose you have not had the decency to read," chided Howells in a letter to Clemens written on 23 December 1902 (*MTHL*, p. 755). "But I *did* read it," Clemens assured him on 24 December 1902. "And moreover, I found in it . . . a microscope's vision, a chemist's mastery of analysis & proportion, & a precision all your own in setting down the details & the accumulated result of the inquisition in English which no man can misunderstand" (*MTHL*, p. 756). The writer who would become Clemens's designated biographer, Albert Bigelow Paine, reviewed Norris's *The Pit* (1903) in the February 1903 issue of *The Bookman* (p. 565). Norris, for his part, posthumously recognized that Mark Twain was "American to the core," but categorized him as more of humorist than a genuine novelist (*The Responsibilities of the Novelist, and Other Literary Essays* [New York: Doubleday, Page & Co., 1903], p. 196). Clemens's copies of Norris's novels, if there were any, have never surfaced.

Norris, Mary Harriott (1848–1919).

Clemens wrote her name in Notebook 24 in July 1885 (*N&J* 3: 166), without indicating that he actually bought or read any of her children's books.

Norris, William Edward (1847–1925). *Billy Bellew; A Novel*. Illus. New York: Harper & Brothers, 1895. 305 pp.

Source: MTLAcc, entry #1094, volume donated by Clemens.

———. *Matrimony; A Novel*. Leisure Hour Series, No. 125. New York: Henry Holt and Co., 1881. 433 pp.

Catalog: Ball 2016 inventory, yellow cloth, gilt and black lettering on cover, fair condition, bookplate #613 of the J. Langdon Family Library.

Location: Quarry Farm library shelves, under the supervision of the Mark Twain Archive, Elmira College, Elmira, New York.

Clemens could have had access to this novel with fictional international settings whenever he visited the Langdons in Elmira.

The North American Review (published 1815–1939).

Catalog: ListABP (1910), "N. A. Review, Jan. 1905".

Daniel Appleton & Company of New York City billed Clemens on 26 January 1881 for "N. A. Review 1881 $5.00"; Clemens paid on 31 January 1881 (receipt in MTP). In an introductory note to "Mental Telegraphy" (1891), Mark Twain recalled that "eight or ten years ago I tried to creep in under the shelter of an authority grave enough to protect the article from ridicule—the *North American Review*." Clemens read and disagreed with an article by E. W. Gilliam about Chinese immigration in the July 1886 issue (*MTHL*, p. 573 n. 3). "Get November North American," Clemens noted in October 1887 (NB 27, *N&J* 3: 342). "Please change mailing address [of the *North American Review*] to Riverdale," Clemens instructed Frederick A. Duneka on 12 September 1901 (ALS in the Berg Collection, NYPL). In Mark Twain's Autobiographical Dictation of 20 June 1906 he assailed an article by Charles Augustus Briggs that appeared in the June 1906 issue (*AutoMT* 2: 131).

Northup, Solomon (1807–c. 1863). *Twelve Years a Slave: A Citizen of New-York, Kidnapped in Washington City in 1841, and Rescued in 1853, from a Cotton Plantation Near the Red River, in Louisiana* (slave narrative, published in 1853).

In an 8 April 2018 Internet posting on the Mark Twain Forum discussion board, Clay Shannon wondered whether Clemens might have read Chapter 2 of *Twelve Years a Slave*, in which Northup recounts how he stayed with his soon-to-be captors at Gadsby's Hotel on Pennsylvania Avenue in Washington, D. C. In 1868 Mark Twain published "The Man Who Put Up at Gadsby's," a sketch he later incorporated into Chapter 26 of *A Tramp Abroad* (1880). One wishes for more evidence that Clemens knew of this celebrated slave narrative.

Norton, Caroline Elizabeth Sarah (Sheridan) (1808–1877). "The Arab's Farewell to His Steed" (poem, published in 1830).

Surely Mark Twain had this poem in mind in recalling his "sentimental" notions in boyhood about "the Arab's idolatry of his horse" in Chapter 45 of *The Innocents Abroad* (1869). Norton's poem begins, "My beautiful, my beautiful! That standest meekly by,/With thy proudly arched and glossy neck, and dark and fiery eye!" At the conclusion of the poem the Arab refuses to sell his steed ("I fling them back their gold") and gallops across the desert on his beloved horse. (L. G. Crossman, professor emeritus at the University of Regina, deserves the credit for first noting this resemblance and calling it to my attention.) The English poet Norton was also an influential social reformer, especially the cause of women's rights.

———. *Bingen on the Rhine*. Illus. Original pale green pictorial cloth, gilt, all edges gilt. Philadelphia: Porter and Coates, [cop. 1883]. 24 leaves.

Inscription: Inscribed to Olivia Lewis Langdon (1810–1890), Olivia Clemens's mother, in ink on the front flyleaf: A merrie Christmas/& a happy New Year/to our dear mother/from her children/1883." A note tipped in by Irene Langdon (1922–2015) identified the recipient. The rear endpaper bears the ticket of an Elmira bookseller.

Location: collection of Kevin Mac Donnell, Austin, Texas. Acquired from the Langdon family in May 2016 (email, Mac Donnell to Alan Gribben, 16 May 2016).

Source: detailed description of the volume with "no markings in the text" sent on 9 June 2016 by Mac Donnell to Gribben.

This book would have been available to Clemens in the Langdon family library.

Louis J. Budd pointed out (*CTSS&E* 1: 1063) that Mark Twain's "Reply to a Boston Girl" (*Atlantic Monthly* 45.272 [June 1880]: 851) alludes to "Bingen on the Rhine who says/'The pale moon rose up slowly, and calmly she looked down,/On the red sands,' etc." The phrases "a soft moon" and "on the red sands of the battlefield" occur in Norton's poem. Twain quoted from the penultimate stanza of this seven-stanza poem in "Marienbad—A Health Factory" (1891). Norton's poem—which repeats the dying words of a young legionnaire who leaves messages for his mother, sister, and sweetheart—is included in an anthology of verse that Clemens owned, William Cullen Bryant's *The Family Library of Poetry and Song* (1870), pp. 521–522.

———. "The Broken Vow" (short story).

Clemens read this piece in the February 1834 issue of *Godey's Lady's Book* while he stayed at a boarding house in Hamilton, Bermuda in May 1877. His reaction was unfavorable: "They were a sad & sentimental lot in those days" (NB 13, *N&J* 2: 21). The story, collected in Norton's *The Coquette and Other Tales and Sketches, in Prose and Verse* (London: Edward Churton, 1835), pp. 129–151, portrayed a woman who wed the wrong suitor, found herself in a wretched marriage, and destroyed the life of her other suitor. Among other sources of her unhappiness, the husband beats his wife (just as Norton's real-life husband mistreated her).

———. "The King of Denmark's Ride" (poem, published in 1857).

See the Catalog entry for *Selected Poems, Illustrated.*

———. *The Lady of La Garaye.* New York: A. D. F. Randolph & Co., [cop. 1865]. 115 pp.

Source: MTLAcc, entry #2073, volume donated from Clemens's library by Clara Clemens Gabrilowitsch in 1910. The subject of Norton's lengthy poem was Marie Marguerite La Motte-Picquet, Comtesse de La Garaye (1681–1757).

NORTON, JOHN PITKIN (1822–1852). *Elements of Scientific Agriculture; or, the Connection Between Science and the Art of Practical Farming. Prize Essay of the New York State Agricultural Society.* Albany: Erastus H. Pease & Co., 1850. 208 pp.

Inscriptions: (in pencil) "Given to Orion Clemens/By John Fry, of/Hannibal Mo./Aug. 28 '69". The rear flyleaf is signed in pencil, "Orion".

Provenance: formerly in the collection of Ralph Gregory (1909–2015) of Marthasville, Missouri. Mr. Gregory was a curator of the Mark Twain Birthplace Memorial Shrine in Florida, Missouri (now called the Mark Twain Birthplace State Historic Site). In 1965 Mrs. Mary Gertrude (Stotts) Shotwell of Greybull, Wyoming gave Mr. Gregory this book. See the Catalog entry for Thomas Dick's *Practical Astronomer* for an explanation of this provenance.

Location: in August 2017 the volume belonged to Ralph

Gregory's daughter, Nancy Gregory Kimball, Marthasville, Missouri.

Copy examined: Orion Clemens's unmarked copy, in 1970.

"NOT A LEAF STIRRED" (humorous sketch, published in 1865).

Presumably it was Mark Twain himself who organized amusing "Country School Exhibition" skits to entertain the passengers aboard the *Montana* on 10 July 1868, an event he reported in the 6 September 1868 *Alta California* (reprinted in *The Twainian* 7 [Nov.- Dec. 1948]: 5; also see http://www.twainquotes.com/18680906.html). The last performance he scheduled on the program was "Recitation-----Not a leaf stirred Mr. W. W. J." This same phrase was echoed in Chapter 14 of *Tom Sawyer* (1876) when Tom awakens on Jackson's Island: "Not a leaf stirred; not a sound obtruded upon great Nature's meditation."

Twain's likely referent was a brief comic sketch widely reprinted in newspapers as a space-filler in the years between 1865 and 1872, "A Boy's Composition on Moonlight." It depicts a boy's dilemma after he begins a school assignment with the words, "'Twas a calm still night, the moon's pale light shown soft o'er hill and dale," but then runs out of ideas. He desperately resorts to a litany: "Not a breeze stirred;/Not a leaf stirred;/Not a dog stirred;/Not a horse stirred;/Not a man stirred;/Not an owl stirred;/Not a hog stirred;/Not a cow stirred;/Not a sheep stirred;/Not a cat stirred;/Not a mouse stirred;/Not a hen stirred;/Not even a goose stirred." The teacher interrupts at this point, observing that his effort "appeared to relate more to agriculture than moonlight." One newspaper gave Carson City as the original place the incident supposedly occurred, but most editors introduced it with this explanation: "The following composition is said to have been read in one of our city schools." I have found "A Boy's Composition on Moonlight" in the Red Bluff, California *Independent* (27 March 1865), the Bloomsburg, Pennsylvania *Star of the North* (10 May 1865), *Cassell's Illustrated Family Paper* (London, 19 August 1865), and the Canton, Missouri *Press* (13 July 1872). Presumably there were numerous other reprintings. From memory Twain evidently recalled a line near the beginning ("Not a leaf stirred") and used it more than once.

Notes and Queries (London scholarly journal, published 1849–).

Unable to recall who wrote the poem "Annette" that Clemens wanted to quote on Susy Clemens's gravestone, he turned to *Notes and Queries.* Its editor soon "furnished me the author's name"; it was the Australian poet Robert Richardson (Autobiographical Dictation of 22 January 1907, published in the *North American Review* 185.612 [5 April 1907]: 678; *AutoMT* 2: 376–377).

NOTOVITCH, NICOLAS (1858–c. 1916). *The Unknown Life of Jesus Christ* (published in 1894).

In November 1896 Clemens entered a title in Notebook 39: "The Unknown Life of Christ—by Nicolas Notovitch. London Lib." (TS p. 26). In *The Unknown Life of Jesus Christ* the Russian (some sources label him Crimean) self-proclaimed journalist and explorer Notovitch tells of finding, in a Tibetan monastery, a carefully guarded manuscript about the life, teachings, and hitherto-unrevealed travels in India of Jesus. A majority of scholars now doubt the veracity of Notovitch's account and presume his discovery to have been fraudulent.

NOYES, RUFUS KING (1853–1942). *Views of Religion, Collected by Rufus K. Noyes, M. D.* Portrait. Boston: L. K. Washburn, 1906. 783 pp.

> **Inscriptions:** (on the front flyleaf) "To Mark Twain—Until ethics changes its name or religion its character, keep them independent and separate; as they are essentially unlike. Rufus K. Noyes." The front pastedown endpaper is signed "S. L. Clemens/1907/Tuxedo."
>
> **Marginalia:** the Parke-Bernet Galleries catalog (1957) quoted some of Clemens's extensive penciled marginalia, estimated at 1,000 words. On the title-page he wrote 'A proof-reader should have been employed. Even a dull one would have been better than none at all." On page 5 he remarked: "There are many slaves. In fact, as many as there are human beings in the world." On page 19: "This was Robert G. Ingersoll's character." On page 119: "After Adam, my ancestor was Cain, who married his sister Mary Ann, & had by her a litter of sons & daughters who were also his nephews & nieces. It made a good deal of talk." Caroline Thomas Harnsberger—Mark *Twain's Views of Religion* (Evanston, IL: Schori Press, 1961), pp. 1–13—quoted previously unpublished marginalia from this book in an effort to prove that Twain was "far from an atheist." She does not supply page numbers for the following quotations. "Gods have always been born out of wedlock—apparently there is no other way to make them respectable." "God runs his worldly business just the same on Sunday as he does on week-days, but if you and I break the Sabbath we get damned for it." "God's lightning strikes more churches than any other property." "Three of our libraries have thrown Huck Finn out as being an unclean book. Next they will be wanting an expurgated Bible." "When religion and science elect to live together, it is a plain case of adultery." Harnsberger scattered additional quotations throughout her book, heedless of the incongruity of mixing opinions from the last period of Clemens's life with others representing his youthful ideas.
>
> **Catalogs:** ListABP (1910), "Views of Religion, Noyes"; *C1951*, #6a, $60, listed among books containing Clemens's marginal notations; Lew David Feldman, House of El Dieff Catalogue (1954), item #229r, sold with two other books for $500; "Mark Twain Items and Other Americana," Parke-Bernet Galleries, Sale on 21–22 May 1957, the "consigner" was Caroline Harnsberger, item #124, $340.
>
> **Location:** currently unknown.

Dr. Noyes practiced medicine in Boston for many years. An independent thinker in many ways, he even became an opponent of all vaccinations.

Lawrence I. Berkove and Joseph Csicsila, *Heretical Fictions: Religion in the Literature of Mark Twain* (Iowa City: University of Iowa Press, 2010), p. 196.

Nuremberg. [Photographs.]

> **Inscription:** by Olivia Clemens in black ink: "For/Katy Leary/August first 1891/in memory of days spent in Nuremberg."
>
> **Provenance:** Antenne-Dorrance Collection, Rice Lake, Wisconsin.
>
> **Location:** Mark Twain Archive, Gannett-Tripp Learning Center, Elmira College, Elmira, New York.
>
> **Copy examined:** Katy Leary's copy. A book of photographs bound in red buckram.

This collection was compiled prior to October 1890, according to information received from independent researcher Winston Kelley in July 2019.

NURSERY RHYMES.

Mark Twain ended a column title "Congressional Poetry" in the Washington *Intelligencer* in 1868 with several nursery rhyme references: "This is the house that Jack built, . . . Pop goes the weasel" (reprinted in the *Mark Twain Quarterly* 5.2 [Summer 1942]: 5). Twain wrote a parody of "Who Killed Cock Robin" for the Hartford *Evening Post* of 23 December 1872 (*MTLet* 5: 262). In New Zealand, on 12 November 1895, Clemens remembered and altered an old verse that began, "The north wind doth blow": "When the *south* wind doth blow,/Then we shall have snow; And what will the robin then do, poor thing" (NB 34, TS p 39).

NYE, EDGAR WILSON (1850–1896), pseud. "Bill Nye." *Bill Nye's History of the United States.* Illustrated by Frederick Burr Opper (1857–1937). London: Chatto & Windus, 1894. 329 pp.

> **Source:** MTLAcc, entry #364, volume donated by Clemens.

———. *Forty Liars, and Other Lies.* Illustrated by [Livingston York Yourtee ("Hop")] Hopkins (1846–1927). Chicago: Belford, Clarke & Co., 1882. 264 pp. [Second edition in 1882 was reprinted throughout the 1880s with 301 pages. The edition Clemens consulted has not been unidentified.]

Forty Liars, and Other Lies compiled dozens of Nye's comical newspaper squibs and sketches, some of them about the rigors of life in Wyoming. His preface facetiously gave thanks that the royalties from his previous book had enabled him "to pay the rent, instead of changing my location each month as formerly." In August 1885 Mark Twain noted that he would "merely refer to & quote from . . . Bill Nye" in a proposed "Essay on Humor" (NB 24, *N&J* 3: 172). When Twain planned his projected anthology of American humorists in September 1887, he noted that "we must have Bill Nye in" (NB 27, *N&J* 3: 321). *Mark Twain's Library of Humor* (1888) contained "A Fatal Thirst" from Nye's *Forty Liars*. On 17 April 1890 Twain proposed that Nye, James Whitcomb Riley, and Joe Goodman get together with him in Hartford "& just have an elegant time" (Nye, *Bill Nye: His Own Life Story* [New York: Century Co., 1926], p. 286). Twain made notes referring to Nye in October 1889 (NB 29, *N&J* 3: 525), 1890 (NB 29, *N&J* 3: 553), and August 1895 (NB 35, TS p. 27). Twain praised Nye in a newspaper interview that appeared in the 24 July 1895 issue of the Minneapolis *Penny Press*, saying, "The general tendency, as the years go by, is for a higher plane of humor. Edgar W. Nye's humor I enjoy for it is frosting on the cake. There is something shining out through it all. This is the true humor that will always prevail" (Scharnhorst, *Complete Interviews*, p. 159). In an Autobiographical Dictation of 17 January 1906, Twain credited Nye for the quip, "I have been told that Wagner's music is better than it sounds" (*MTAuto* 1: 288). Later, on 6 April 1906, Twain spoke of "Bill Nye, poor fellow,—that real humorist, that gentle good soul. Well, he is dead" (*MTAuto* 2: 26) Significantly, Twain did not list Bill Nye among the "mortuary" of humorists he recalled in an Autobiographical Dictation of 31 July 1906 "whose writings and sayings . . . are now heard of no more" (*MTAuto* 2: 153). Oddly, Walt McDougall, "Pictures in the Papers," *American Mercury* 6.21 (September 1925): 67–73, insisted that Twain's jealousy of Nye was so great that Twain disliked meeting him and "was none too genial" when the necessity arose (p. 72).

Louis Hasley, "The Durable Humor of Bill Nye," *Mark Twain Journal* 15.3 (Winter 1970–1971): 7–10.

∎ O

OBENCHAIN, ELIZA CAROLINE (CALVERT) (1856–1935), pseud. "Eliza Calvert Hall." *Aunt Jane of Kentucky*. Illus. Boston: Little, Brown & Co., 1907. 283 pp.

Source: MTLAcc, entry #886, volume donated by Clemens. Obenchain's nine short stories, related by Aunt Jane Parish, reflect the author's strong advocacy of women's rights.

OBER, FREDERICK ALBION (1849–1913). *Amerigo Vespucci*. Heroes of American History Series. Illus. New York: Harper & Brothers, 1907. 258 pp.

Inscription: signed in black ink on the front pastedown endpaper, "S L. Clemens/1907." Above that signature is the oval stamp of the "Mark Twain/Library,/ Redding, Conn."

Marginalia: a few textual corrections by Clemens. On page 87 in black ink Clemens transposed several words in line 32, altering "population of thirteen houses only amounted to" to read instead "population of only thirteen houses amounted to". In the same black ink on page 88 he struck out the word "funeral" in the phrase "of various funeral obsequies." On page 89 in black ink he deleted the final "s" in the word "escapes" in the eighth line.

Catalog: *Mott 1952*, item #75, $12.50.

Provenance: donated by Clemens to the Mark Twain Library, Redding, Connecticut (MTLAcc, entry #565). In September 1980 Thomas A. Tenney made a photocopy of the title page, inscription, and marginalia when the volume was in the collection of Cyril Clemens, Kirkwood, Missouri. Tenney saw the volume there again in April 1985.

Location: Harry Ransom Center, University of Texas at Austin. Acquired from Cyril Clemens along with six other books on 28 March 1986, for payments of $5,000 to Cyril Clemens and $5,000 to his *Mark Twain Journal*. Thomas A. Tenney, Cyril Clemens, and Alan Gribben (then an English professor at the University of Texas at Austin) negotiated this agreement in an exchange of letters written between 20 August 1985 and 27 April 1986.

Copy examined: photocopies of Clemens's inscription and marginalia in a book belonging to him (photocopies sent by Thomas A. Tenney to Alan Gribben in April 1985). Has the oval stamp of the "Mark Twain/Library,/Redding, Conn." on the front pastedown endpaper above Clemens's signature. Confirmed by an examination of the volume in Austin in 1986.

———. [Another identical copy.]

Source: MTLAcc, entry #1247, volume donated by Clemens.

———. *Columbus the Discoverer*. Heroes of American History Series. Illus. New York: Harper & Brothers, 1906. 300 pp.

Inscription: the front pastedown endpaper is signed "SL. Clemens/1906." Black ink.

Catalog: *A 1911*, "12mo, cloth, N.Y. 1906," quotes the signature, lot 367, sold for $2.

Provenance: collection of Frank C. Willson (1889–1960) in Melrose, Massachusetts. Sold by his widow Margarete in 1962 to the University of Texas.

Location: Harry Ransom Center, University of Texas at Austin.

Copy examined: Clemens's copy, unmarked.

The American public's admiration for Christopher Columbus's achievements became nearly worshipful during Mark Twain's lifetime and, like the figure of the biblical Adam, Columbus became a recurrent symbol in Twain's writings. "The historian [is] another Columbus in that he discovered it [the dramatization of *The Gilded Age*]," Twain wrote in a letter addressed (but not sent) to the editor of the Hartford *Post* on 3 November 1874 (*MTL*, pp. 517–518; *MTLet* 6: 267; *MTPP*, p. 84). Columbus is mentioned in Act 1 of *Ah Sin* (produced in 1877). "Why, you'd think it was Christopher C'lumbus discovering Kingdom-Come," declares Huckleberry Finn (*HF* [1885], Ch. 12). In 1886 Twain introduced Henry Stanley in Boston by comparing him to Columbus, for whom "America would discover itself," whereas Livingstone "was hidden away somewhere" (Hartford *Courant*, 11 December 1886; *S&MT*, p. 236; Fatout, *MTSpk*, pp. 214–215). In 1887 Twain "revealed to L" [William M. Laffan?] his project for purchasing the remains of Columbus and reinterring the discoverer at the base of the Statue of Liberty or in the Washington Capitol rotunda (NB 26, *N&J* 3: 252, 334), a scheme he thought of again in October 1889, when he hoped to convey Columbus's remains to New York City in time for that city's Columbian Celebration scheduled for October 1892 (NB 29, *N&J* 3: 523). Hank Morgan in *A Connecticut Yankee in King Arthur's Court* (1889) recalls "how Columbus, or Cortez, or one of those people, played an eclipse as a saving trump once, on some savages" (Ch. 5). (Columbus did indeed practice this stunt on some Native Americans in 1504 when he and his men were in a tight spot during his fourth voyage to the New World—though of course he mistakenly thought he was near China.) Twain's publishing firm, Charles L. Webster & Company, published *Writings of Christopher Columbus* in 1892. In Chapter 5 of *Tom Sawyer Abroad* (1894) the boys drift across the ocean in a balloon, watching for land "like Columbus discovering America." That same year their creator responded to the apparent success of the Paige typesetter by writing from Rouen to Henry H. Rogers on 7 October 1894: "It affects me like Columbus sighting land" (*MTHHR*, p. 83). The "Conclusion" in *Pudd'nhead Wilson* (1894) begins with a rueful Mark Twain maxim: "*October 12, the Discovery*. It was wonderful to find America, but it would have been more wonderful to miss it.—*Pudd'nhead Wilson's Calendar*."

It can hardly be coincidental that Twain's *Personal Recollections of Joan of Arc* (1896) opens with the Sieur Louis De Conte's words, "This is the year 1492." A dinner companion uses the phrase "since Columbus's time" in Chapter 37 of *Following the Equator* (1897). On 23 March 1902 Clemens "visited a church [in Havana] where Columbus's itinerant bones reposed for the first time on their travels" ("Log of the Kanawha," TS p. 6, MTP). Twain mentioned Columbus in Chapter 6 of "The Chronicle of Young

Satan," written 1897–1900 (*MSM*, p. 116); Notebook 46 (1903), TS p. 26; "Sold to Satan" (1904); "The Refuge of the Derelicts," written 1905–1906 (*FM*, p. 225); a letter to Colonel W. D. Mann, 3 January 1906 (MTP); and Autobiographical Dictations of 15 February 1906 (*MTE*, p. 250; *MTAuto* 1:362) and 1 June 1906 (*MTE*, pp. 183, 186; *MTAuto* 2: 71, 73). In the latter instance, Twain declared that "all publishers are Columbuses. The successful author is their America." The next year Twain said that "Mr. Roosevelt is easily the most astonishing event in American history—if we except the discovery of the country by Columbus" in a 13 September 1907 Autobiographical Dictation (*MTE*, p. 15; *MTAuto* 3: 134). Captain Stormfield alludes to Columbus in Chapter 1 of *Extract from Captain Stormfield's Visit to Heaven* (1909). In "The Turning Point of My Life" (1910), Twain remarked of Columbus: "Circumstance revised his plan for him, and he found a new *world*. And *he* gets the credit of it to this day." See also the Catalog entry for C. Columbus, *Writings of Christopher Columbus, Descriptive of the Discovery and Occupation of the New World*.

———. *Ferdinand Magellan*. Heroes of American History Series. Illus. New York: Harper & Brothers, 1907. 300 pp.
Source: MTLAcc, entry #561, volume donated by Clemens.

———. *Hernándo Cortés, Conqueror of Mexico*. Portraits. Heroes of American History Series. New York: Harper & Brothers, 1905. 292 pp. [Publisher and pages conjectured.]
Inscription: the front pastedown endpaper is signed "S. L. Clemens, 1905."
Catalog: *A1911*, "12mo, cloth, N.Y. 1905," quotes signature, lot 366, sold for $2.25.

———. [An identical copy.]
Source: MTLAcc, entry #1355, volume donated by Clemens.

———. *John and Sebastian Cabot*. Heroes of American History Series. Illus. New York: Harper & Brothers, 1908. 300 pp.
Source: MTLAcc, entry #564, volume donated by Clemens.

———. [Another identical copy.]
Source: MTLAcc, entry #1462, volume donated by Clemens.

———. *Juan Ponce de Leon*. Heroes of American History Series. Illus. New York: Harper & Brothers, 1908. 287 pp.
Source: MTLAcc, entry #563, volume donated by Clemens.

———. *Vasco Nuñez de Balboa*. Heroes of American History Series. Illus. New : York: Harper & Brothers, 1906. 285 pp.
Source: MTLAcc, entry #562, volume donated by Clemens.

O'BRIEN, FITZ-JAMES (1828–1862).
A pioneer in the realm of science fiction, the Irish-born Fitz-James O'Brien immigrated to New York City in 1852. Perhaps his best-known story was "What Was It? A Mystery" (1859). He joined the Union Army and was killed in 1862 while fighting in the Civil War. In an Autobiographical Dictation of 31 July 1906, Clemens listed "Smith O'Brien" [*sic*] among American humorists of former fame (*MTE*, p. 201; *AutoMT* 2: 153). Despite the immense number of authors whom Clemens knew personally or at least had read their writings, he rather rarely made mistakes in recalling their names. However, in this instance the editors of *Autobiography of Mark Twain* (p. 535) are likely correct in deducing that he had in mind Fitz-James O'Brien. No other "O'Brien" seems

to have written pieces that might have been included in a collection of wit and humor that Clemens was terming "a cemetery" (*AutoMT*, p. 152). It seems possible that Clemens's stenographer misheard "Fitz O'Brien" as "Smith O'Brien," and that Clemens overlooked the error when proofreading the dictation.

O'BRIEN, RICHARD BARRY (1847–1918). *The Life of Charles Stewart Parnell, 1846–1891*. New York: Harper & Brothers, 1898. 772 pp.
Source: MTLAcc, entry #1786, volume donated by Clemens.
Parnell was the Irish Nationalist who led a sustained and occasionally violent effort to achieve Irish Home Rule.

O'BRIEN, SMITH. [Unidentified author.]
See the Catalog entry for Fitz-James O'Brien (above).

O'BRIEN, WILLIAM DESMOND (d. 1893).
Clemens wrote that he might "read a chapter or so" of O'Brien's two-volume encyclopedia of Ireland in manuscript (SLC to Fred J. Hall, note written on another letter, post 26 September 1887, Webster Collection, TS in MTP). A wealthy New York contractor, O'Brien would never complete or publish his projected work, *Encyclopedia Hibernica*.

Ocean Scenes; or, The Perils and Beauties of the Deep; Being Interesting, Instructive, and Graphic Accounts of the Most Popular Voyages on Record, Remarkable Shipwrecks, Hair-Breadth Escapes, Naval Adventures, the Whales Fishery, Etc., Etc. Illus. New York: Leavitt , Trow & Co., 1847. 492 pp. [Repr. by Leavitt & Allen in 1854 and other years.]
Clemens's Notebook 5 (1866) contains the text of Joseph Rodman Drake's poem titled "The American Flag," an allusion to "A Monkey's Trick," and references to "Forty-Five Days' Sufferings"—all of which appeared in the compilation of poetry and (summarized) sea voyage adventures, *Ocean Scenes; or, The Perils and Beauties of the Deep* (pp. 381–382, 284–285, 180–184). Clemens apparently dipped into *Ocean Scenes* in the ship library of the S. S. *Smyrniote* when that vessel lay becalmed en route to San Francisco from Honolulu; see *N&J* 1: 146, 134, 136. See also the Catalog entry for D. Harrison, *The Melancholy Narrative of the Distressful Voyage and the Miraculous Recovery of Captain David Harrison of the Sloop, Peggy*.

O'CONNOR, JOHN CHARLES (1853–1928), ed. *Esperanto. The Student's Complete Text Book. Containing Full Grammar, Exercises, Conversations, Commercial Letters, and Two Vocabularies*. Revised by Dr. [Ludwik Lejzer] Zamenhof (1859–1917). London: "Review of Reviews" Office, 1904. 175 pp.
Inscription: Clemens inscribed the front paper wrapper in black ink (writing between the lines of the book title): "Jean Clemens/Oct. 1905".
Location: Mark Twain Library, Redding, Connecticut.
Copy examined: Jean Clemens's unmarked copy, in poor condition. The badly torn cover, the front flyleaf, and pages through 15 are missing their lower portions. Has the red ink Mark Twain Library accession number "3496". Examined in 1970 and again in June 1982.
On 22 September 1905 Isabel Lyon "wrote to Chatto & Windus for Esperanto Books—Complete Text Book by J. C. O'Connor & Eng-Esp. & Esp-Eng Dictionaries" (IVL Journal, Antenne Collection, PH in Mark Twain

Archive, Elmira College). The Polish physician Ludwik Lejzer Zamenhof invented the international language Esperanto and published its original version in 1887.

O'CONNOR, WILLIAM DOUGLAS (1832–1889). "The Brazen Android," *Atlantic Monthly* 67.402 (April 1891):433–455 and *Atlantic Monthly* 67.403 (May 1891): 577–600. Collected in O'Connor's *Three Tales: The Ghost, The Brazen Android, The Carpenter*. Boston and New York: Houghton, Mifflin and Co., 1892. 320 pp.

In the "Weather" appendix to *The American Claimant* (1892), Mark Twain quotes a lengthy description of a thunderstorm from O'Connor's "The Brazen Android." O'Connor, who was Walt Whitman's close friend, made the first use of the science fiction term "android" in this posthumously published novella about a metallic head that can report about a past civilization.

O'DUFFY, RICHARD J., editor and translator. *Oidhe Chloinne Uisnigh: Fate of the Children of Uisneach*. Translated with notes and vocabulary by Richard J. O'Duffy. Society for the Preservation of the Irish Language. Dublin: M. H. Gill & Son, 1898. 150 pp. [Edition conjectured.]

Clemens praised this book in a letter to Lady Gregory written on 9 March 1903 while apparently thanking her for a copy of *Poets and Dreamers*: "We should always be grateful, even if you had given us [readers] the Fate of the Children of Usnech [*sic*] alone, that moving & beautiful tale, that masterpiece!" (quoted in Lady Gregory's *Seventy Years: Being the Autobiography of Lady Gregory* [London: Colin Smythe, 1974], pp. 400–401).

OGILVIE, FRANK BURHAM (1875–1937), comp. *Two Hundred Old-Time Songs, Containing the Words and Music of the Choicest Gems of the Old and Familiar Songs We Used to Sing When We Were Young*. No. 97 of The Peerless Series. New York: J. S. Ogilvie Publishing Co., n.d. [cop. 1896]. 176 pp. Paper wrappers.

Marginalia: on the front wrapper Clemens wrote in pencil: "Notes for the Complete Works." Below that he added several song titles in brown ink ("Are we almost there?/"Give me 3 grains of corn"), jotted the lyrics to his favorite nonsense song, "There is a boarding-house, far far away" (the words that Colonel Sellers's phonograph recorded inadvertently in Chapter 17 of *The American Claimant* [1892]), and then wrote: "Battle of Prague/No pearl ever lay in Omar's green water/Twenty years ago." He set down approximate dates of composition or popularity beside many songs listed in the table of contents, noting as "1845," for instance, the piece titled "When we went gypseying." On page 112 he observed "Why, it is very very poor" about the song called "Beautiful Snow" (brown ink). He made other marginalia as well.

Catalog: "Retz Appraisal" (1944), p. 10, valued at $25.

Location: Mark Twain Papers, Bancroft Library, University of California at Berkeley.

Copy examined: Clemens's copy.

The lifelong Brooklyn resident Frank B. Ogilvie was president of the Ogilvie Publishing Company in Manhattan. Ogilvie's twenty-five-cent paperbound volume probably inspired Clemens's recollections of the old songs he listed in "Villagers 1840–3," written in 1897 (*HH&T*, p. 34).

OGLE, ANNE CHARLOTTE (1832–1918), pseud. "Ashford Owen." *Her Second Love*. Philadelphia: T. B. Peterson &

Brothers, 1883. 232 pp.

In 1884 Clemens made a list of books in Notebook 20 and started to enter the title *A Lost Love*, but then he canceled the words "A Lost" and instead wrote "Her Second Love (Peterson, Phila)" (NB 22, *N&J* 3: 50). Clemens's confusion is understandable; Ogle's *Her Second Love* was simply a new title for her first novel, *A Lost Love* (1855), originally published in England.

OGLESBY, J. S. *Cyclopedia of Curious Facts*. [Unidentified book.]

In an explanation of the rules accompanying "Mark Twain's Memory-Builder" game that was dated February 1891, Twain recommended several "Fact-Sources to Draw From," including "J. S. Oglesby's 'Cyclopedia of Curious Facts." Twain is seldom mistaken about authors' names or book titles, but this exact referral cannot be found. There are three books that come to mind as distant possibilities: John Clark Ridpath's *Cyclopedia of Universal History*, 3 vols. (1880–1884); Richard S. Peale's *Peale's Popular Educator and Cyclopedia of Reference* (1885); and George W. Ogilvie's *Ogilvie's Encyclopedia of Useful Information and Atlas of the World* (1891). The name of the latter author at least somewhat resembles the name Twain supplied.

O'HAGAN, JOHN (1822–1890). *Joan of Arc*. London: Kegan Paul, Trench, Trübner & Co., 1893. 98 pp.

Inscription: the front free endpaper is inscribed: "Laid at the feet of/Mark Twain/ by Andrew Chatto/Mar 3 '93".

Marginalia: plentiful annotation by Clemens in blue ink, black ink, and pencil. On page 94 Clemens declared, writing vertically across the margin in pencil: "If the 10 greatest of earth be chosen, she must be of the 10; if 2, she must be of the two; if there is but on[e] supremely great, then she is that one." Someone other than Clemens—seemingly Albert Bigelow Paine—made additional notations in pencil.

Catalogs: ListABP (1910), "Joan of Arc, O'Hagan"; "Retz Appraisal" (1944), p. 10, valued at $3.

Location: Mark Twain Papers, Bancroft Library, University of California at Berkeley.

Copy examined: Clemens's copy.

Mark Twain lists O'Hagan's book as one of his "authorities examined" on the page preceding his "Translator's Preface" to *Personal Recollections of Joan of Arc* (1896).

Salomon, *TIH* (1961), p. 176; Ronald Jenn and Linda A. Morris, "The Sources of Mark Twain's *Personal Recollections of Joan of Arc*," *Mark Twain Journal* 55.1–2 (Spring/Fall 2017): 55–74; Delphine Louis-Dimitrov, "The Democratic Reconfiguration of History in Mark Twain's *Personal Recollections of Joan of Arc*," *American Literary Realism* 51.2 (Winter 2018): 162–179; and Delphine Louis-Dimitrov, "Nature in Mark Twain's *Personal Recollections of Joan of Arc*," *Mark Twain Annual 17* (2019): 88–111.

O'HARA, THEODORE (1820–1867). "The Bivouac of the Dead" (poem, published in 1858).

On 26 April 1882, visiting the National Cemetery in Vicksburg, Mississippi where thousands of men slain in that arena of the Civil War were interred, Mark Twain copied four lines of O'Hara's elegiac verse that adorned the gates and walls: "On fame's eternal camping ground/ Their silent tents are spread,/And glory guards with solemn round/The bivouac of the dead" (NB 21, *N&J* 2: 572). O'Hara had originally written this moving twelve-stanza poem to be read at the dedication of a monument for the Kentuckians who died at Buena Vista in 1847.

Edgar Erskine Hume's *Colonel Theodore O'Hara, Author of the Bivouac of the Dead. No. 6 of Southern Sketches* (Charlottesville, Virginia: The Historical Publishing Co., 1936), pp. 17–24.

ŌHASHI, HYDESABURO (1877–1918).

On 7 January 1902 Ōhashi sent Clemens two poems titled "The Misty Mountain Moon" and "Maude and O-Hana" and invited his judgment of them. In another letter of that date he enclosed a poem titled "Music" (*DearMT*, pp. 195–196). Clemens commended his manuscript poems on 12 January 1902 in a letter written to William Dean Howells from Riverdale. Clemens asked Howells whether he might want "to discover a Japanese poet & introduce him to the public?" Ōhashi's "quaint & pretty" prose also pleased Clemens, who "said so" when he wrote this Harvard student who had immigrated to the United States in 1889 (*MTHL*, p. 739).

OHNET, GEORGES (1848–1918). *Dr. Rameau.* Translated from the French by J. C. Curtin. Chicago and New York: Rand, McNally & Co., 1889. 222 pp. Also published in Philadelphia: J. B. Lippincott Co., 1889. 299 pp. [No edition has been determined.]

In February 1892 Mark Twain received an offer to dramatize his *Colonel Sellers* from Alfred Arnold, who "says he dramatized 'Dr. Rameau' & has had experience" (NB 31, TS p. 32). In Ohnet's novel a Paris physician belatedly discovers that his cherished wife, now dead, had been unfaithful and that his daughter was fathered by another man.

"OL' ARK'S A MOVERIN'" (spiritual).

Clemens entered the titles of several plantation spirituals in Notebook 30 in 1890, including "De old Ark's a Moving" (*N&J* 3: 593).

OLCOTT, HENRY STEEL (1832–1907). *People from the Other World.* Illustrated by Alfred Kappes (1850–1894) and True W. Williams (1839–1897). Hartford: American Publishing Co., 1875. 492 pp.

Catalog: ListABP (1910), "People from the Other World, Olcott", no other information provided.

In 1874 Olcott, a former Union colonel and fraud investigator in the Civil War who had become a New York City attorney, decided to investigate the séances being conducted by mediums known as the Eddy brothers in a farmhouse near Chittenden, Vermont. Supposedly Horatio Eddy (1842–1922) and William Eddy (1832–1932) had rapport with spirit guides and could summon apparitions of the deceased. Olcott became so convinced of the reality of these ghostly manifestations that he shortly thereafter served as the first president of the Theosophical Society, traveled to India, and remained a proponent of spiritualism for the rest of his life. One of the illustrators of *People from the Other World*, True W. Williams, would be selected to illustrate Mark Twain's *Sketches, New and Old* (1875) and *The Adventures of Tom Sawyer* (1876).

Old Abe's Jokes; Fresh from Abraham's Bosom. Containing All His Issues, Excepting the "Greenbacks." To Call in Some of Which, This Book is Issued. New York: T[homas]. R[obinson]. Dawley (1832–1904), 1864. 126 pp.

Ray B. Browne makes a case for considering a humorous anecdote in this joke collection ("Old Abe's 'Slap' at

Chicago") as the type of joshing about admission to the Christian Heaven "which almost surely shaped" Twain's depiction of a barkeeper's glorious reception as an arriving saint in *Extract from Captain Stormfield's Visit to Heaven* (1909) (*Mark Twain's Quarrel with Heaven: "Captain Stormfield's Visit to Heaven" and Other Sketches*, ed. Ray B. Browne [New Haven, Connecticut: College & University Press, 1970], pp. 24–27).

"OLD FOLKS." [Unidentified poem.]

Around 1863 Olivia Langdon copied this poem in her commonplace book (DV161, MTP).

The Old Guard (monthly journal in New York City, published January 1863–December 1870).

Chapter 62 of Mark Twain's *Roughing It* (1872) mentions "The Old Guard," a Copperhead periodical advocating slavery and secession, as the favorite reading matter of the Old Admiral aboard the *Ajax*.

"OLD JOE" (minstrel song).

"Without kicking up behind" (SLC to Mr. Holmes, Buffalo, 30 September 1869, ALS in Library of Congress). "I think of that old Negro song: 'Ole Joe kickin up ahind and afore; Yaller Gal kickin' up ahind Ole Joe,' etc., etc." (SLC to Henry H. Rogers, 11 July 1905, *MTHHR*, p. 590). In 1847 Firth & Hall, publishers in New York City, issued *Old Joe, Sung by the Ethiopian Serenaders* (5 pp.).

The Old London Street. [Unidentified book?]

Clemens entered this notation twice in Notebook 26 in 1887 (*N&J* 3: 280, 281). See the Catalog entry for Andrew W. Tuer, the most likely connection.

"OLD ROSIN THE BEAU" (anonymous song, published in 1835). Variant title: "Old Rosin the bow."

"Rosin the Bow" was among the music on the piano in "The House Beautiful," Chapter 38 of *Life on the Mississippi* (1883).

OLFERS, HEDWIG VON STAEGEMANN VON (1799–1891). *Gedichte [Poems].* (First edition was published in Berlin in 1892).

Catalog: ListABP (1910), "Gedichte, Olfers", no edition specified.

OLIPHANT, MARGARET (OLIPHANT WILSON) (1828–1897). *Chronicles of Carlingford; A Novel.* New York: Harper & Brothers, 1863. 306 pp.

Source: MTLAcc, entry #733, volume donated by Clemens.

———. *Jeanne d'Arc: Her Life and Death.* Heroes of the Nations Series. New York: G. P. Putnam's Sons, 1896: 417 pp.

"I have only two books [about Joan of Arc] here—my own & Mrs. Oliphant's. The latter has not always furnished the facts I wanted" (SLC to T. Douglas Murray, Sanna Rosendala, 3 September 1899, TS in MTP).

———. *The Makers of Florence: Dante, Giotto, Savonarola, and Their City.* Illus. London: Macmillan and Co., 1888. 422 pp.

Inscription: the front flyleaf is inscribed by Olivia Clemens: "Susy Clemens/December twenty fifth/1889/ Mamma".

Marginalia: pencil marks in the table of contents. No other markings.

Provenance: Contains the bookstamps, call number, and other identifying marks of the Mark Twain Library, Redding, Connecticut.

Catalog: *Mott 1952*, item #76, $5.

Location: Mark Twain House and Museum, Hartford,

Connecticut. Donated anonymously in 1963.

Copy examined: Susy Clemens's copy. Examined in August 1987.

———. *The Makers of Venice: Doges, Conquerors, Painters, and Men of Letters.* London: Macmillan and Co., 1892. 410 pp.

Inscription: inscribed "Merry Christmas/To dear Aunt Susie/December 1892." Susan Crane (1836–1924), Olivia Clemens's sister, was the owner of Quarry Farm.

Catalogs: inventory list of the library books prepared by Emily Schweizer Martinez when Quarry Farm was donated to Elmira College in 1982; Ball 2016 inventory, red boards, tan spine, red lettering, gold design, good condition.

Location: Quarry Farm library shelves, under the supervision of the Mark Twain Archive, Elmira College, Elmira, New York.

———. *The Makers of Venice: Doges, Conquerors, Painters, and Men of Letters.* Illus. London: Macmillan and Co., 1892. 410 pp. [No edition specified; the city, publisher, and date are conjectured.]

Catalog: *C1951*, J39, listed among volumes belonging to Jean and Clara Clemens.

———. *Margaret Maitland of Sunnyside.* New York: W. I. Pooley, [187?]. 239 pp.

Source: MTLAcc, entry #233, volume donated by Clemens.

———. *Memoir of the Life of Laurence Oliphant and of Alice Oliphant, His Wife* (biography, published in 1891).

Susy Clemens wrote to her college friend Louise Brownell from Germany in April 1892: "I am finishing *Laurence Oliphant*. It is the most curious [and] the most puzzling record in the world! Oh dear Laurence and his wife were deluded and that is so unsatisfactory" (Hamilton College Archives; Cotton, "Olivia Susan Clemens," p. 132). Mrs. Oliphant's book about her cousin Laurence Oliphant (1829–1888) and his wife Alice (d. 1886) described how they became disciples of a spiritualist named Thomas Lake Harris (1823–1906), who founded a utopian settlement on Lake Erie. Eventually Laurence Oliphant became disillusioned with Harris, withdrew from his community, and instituted a law suit.

OLLENDORFF, HEINRICH GOTTFRIED (1803–1865). *Ollendorff's New Method of Learning to Read, Write, and Speak the French Language.* New York: D. Appleton, 1864. [Edition conjectured. Similar volumes were issued for German, Italian, and English languages.]

In Chapter 30 of Mark Twain's *Roughing It* (1872) the narrator leaves for Carson City and Esmeralda "with Mr. Ballou and a gentleman named Ollendorff, a Prussian—not the party who has inflicted so much suffering on the world with his wretched foreign grammars, with their interminable repetitions of questions which never have occurred and are never likely to occur in any conversation among human beings." In 1878 Twain thought of having Captain Stormfield-Wakeman encounter an Ollendorff in heaven (NB 14, *N&J* 2: 66). Casting about for insults to level at Whitelaw Reid in an abortive biography, Twain claimed that Reid "applied for foreign mission & wrote his application in Ollendorffian French" (NB 20, 1882, *N&J* 2: 439).

———. *Ollendorff's New Method of Learning to Read, Write, and Speak the German Language, To Which is Added a Systematic Outline of German Grammar by G. J. Adler [1821–1868].*

New York: D. Appleton, 1872. 510 pp. [Edition conjectured. Similar volumes were issued for French, Italian, and English languages.]

On 3 September 1879 Mark Twain explained to a New York reporter that he can read German but has difficulty speaking "in my peculiar German" (Scharnhorst, *Complete Interviews*, p. 23). (The reporter had asked how far Twain had got in Ollendorff.) Evidently referring to *A Tramp Abroad* (1880), Twain proposed to "begin chapter with Ollendorff & First German Reader" (NB 14, 1878, *N&J* 2: 60). Twain refers to "that idiotic Ollendorff" in "Meisterschaft: In Three Acts" (1888), remarking that "if you stuck to Ollendorff, it would be all about your sister's mother's good stocking of thread, or your grandfather's aunt's good hammer of the carpenter, and who's got it, and there an end. You couldn't keep up your interest in such topics."

John T. Krumpelmann, *Mark Twain and the German Language* (Baton Rouge: Louisiana State University Press, 1953); Brandi Besalke, "'Ein sehr gluecklicher Kind, you bet': Mark Twain and the German Language," *Mark Twain Annual* 5 (2007): 109–122.

OLNEY, JESSE (1798–1872). *A Practical System of Modern Geography; or, A View of the Present State of the World, Simplified and Adapted to the Capacity of Youth.* Illus. [Many editions followed the 270-page first edition published in Hartford by D. F. Robinson in 1828.]

In an Autobiographical Dictation of 6 January 1907, Mark Twain recalled talking with the Reverend Joseph H. Twichell about "several of his schoolmasters, dwelling with special interest upon the peculiarities of an aged one named Olney. Twichell remarked that Olney, humble village schoolmaster as he was, . . . had published textbooks which had enjoyed a wide currency in America in their day. I said I remembered those books, and had studied 'Olney's Geography' in school when I was a boy" (*AutoMT* 2: 360).

ÖMAN, VICTOR EMANUEL (1833–1904). *Svensk-Engelsk handordbok. Utgifven af V. E. Öman.* Ny upplaga, stereotyperad. Stockholm: F. & G. Beijers, [1897]. 470 pp.

Inscription: the front pastedown endpaper is signed "Clara Langdon Clemens/Sanna/1899."

Provenance: collection of Frank C. Willson (1889–1960) in Melrose, Massachusetts. Sold by his widow Margarete in 1962 to the University of Texas.

Location: Harry Ransom Center, University of Texas at Austin.

Copy examined: Clara Clemens's copy.

OMAN, (SIR) CHARLES WILLIAM CHADWICK (1860–1946). *A History of Greece from the Earliest Times to the Death of Alexander the Great.* Second, enl. edition. Maps, plans. London: Longmans, Green, & Co., 1891. 560 pp.

Marginalia: Greek words and mythological names are underlined in various places.

Catalog: Ball 2016 inventory, red cloth, gold lettering.

Location: Mark Twain Archive, Gannett-Tripp Learning Center, Elmira College, Elmira, New York. The former Archivist, Mark Woodhouse, moved this volume from the Quarry Farm library shelves to the Mark Twain Archive on 13 March 2007 because of the underlinings on its pages.

OMAR KHAYYÁM (1048–1131). *One Hundred Quatrains, from*

the Rubáiyát of Omar Khayyám; A Rendering in English Verse by Elizabeth Alden Curtis. Intro. by Richard [Eugene] Burton (1861–1940). No. 227 of 600 copies. Gouverneur, New York: Brothers of the Book, 1899. 72 pp.

Source: MTLAcc, entry #2021, volume donated from Clemens's library by Clara Clemens Gabrilowitsch in 1910.

Clemens bristled at this attempt to improve upon Edward FitzGerald's 1859 translation, writing incredulously to Joseph H. Twichell on 1 January 1900 from London: "It is the most detailed & minutely circumstantial plagiarism that has yet been perpetrated in any century"; she had committed "sacrilege" upon "a noble poem" by endeavoring to recast it line by line, he declared. The result was "as if a Tammany boss should wreck the Taj & then rebuild it after *his* notions of what it ought to be" (*LMTJHT*, p. 255). Clemens expressed astonishment that "Dick Burton" would supply the volume's introduction. "It took Dick two hours to write that Introduction, & he was in a clean man's hell all the while" (*LMTJHT*, p. 255). Curtis and Burton were both from Hartford, Connecticut, a fact Clemens almost certainly knew.

Elizabeth Alden Curtis, born in 1879, attended Trinity College in Hartford. She translated another Persian work into English verse, *The Lament of Baba Tahir* (1902), published poetry that appeared in a number of magazines, and wrote a play that was apparently never produced. Curtis would have bad luck in her marriages. In 1914 she won a lawsuit in federal court against her former husband, the Reverend Cranston Brenton of Yonkers, New York, for having her involuntarily committed to the Brattleboro Insane Asylum in 1912. By then she had married Frederick Ernest Holman of Waterville, Maine. In 1921 she filled out a passport application while being married to Holman and living in Portland, Maine, and in 1922 she was listed as "Mrs. Elizabeth C. Holman" in Oxford, Maine. On 11 December 1923, however, she married Martin S. Tidd of Norway, Maine, and in 1938 she was recorded as "Mrs. Elizabeth C. Tidd" in Portland, Maine.

———. *A Paraphrase of the Philosophical Quatrains of Omar Khayyám, The Astronomer Poet of Persia. Rendered into English Verse by Frien ch Simpson*. Green cloth, gilt lettering. Houston, Texas: J. V. Dealy Co., for Frienc ch Simpson, 1909. 187 pp.

Location: Mark Twain Library, Redding, Connecticut.

Copy examined: almost certainly Clemens's copy, unmarked. Has the red ink Mark Twain Library accession number "3157" and the purple oval Library stamps. I did not find this volume in 1970, but when I made a return visit to Redding in June 1982 it had been added to the bookcase containing Clemens's donations to the Library. I examined it again on 9 November 2019.

Inasmuch as Clemens was interested in every edition of the *Rubáiyát of Omar Khayyám*, it seems highly likely that someone sent him this book. The translator of this version of the *Rubáiyát*, Friench Simpson (1848–1923), was a banker, former member of the Texas Senate (1893–1897), and civic leader in Hallettsville, Texas. For some reason the volume escaped Clemens's sarcastic comments about translations other than Edward FitzGerald's of his beloved poem.

———. *The Quatrains of Omar Khayyám of Nishapur, Translated from the Persian into English Verse, including Quatrains Now*

for the First Time So Rendered, by Eben Francis Thompson. Introduction by Nathan Haskell Dole (1852–1935). First edition, illustrated. Frontispiece portrait of Thompson. Original quarter white linen and boards, gray endpapers, gilt. [Worcester, Massachusetts:] Privately printed [by the Commonwealth Press], 1906. 290 pp.

Inscriptions: the frontispiece portrait of Eben Francis Thompson (1859–1939) is signed in black ink "Faithfully yours/Eben Francis Thompson." The facing flyleaf is inscribed in black ink: "To/'Mark Twain'/Please accept this book as a/partial payment on account/for the many happy hours and/hearty laughs which you have/given me./With kind regards/Faithfully yours,/James Logan./Worcester, Mass.,/Jany, 19, 1907." James Logan (1852–1929), vice president and general manager of the United States Envelope Company, was a prominent citizen of Worcester, Massachusetts and would be its future (1908–1911) mayor. Clemens signed the verso of the front flyleaf in black ink, "S L. Clemens/1907."

Marginalia: five small stylistic corrections by Clemens in black ink on page iv of the introduction. Clemens used both black ink and pencil to mark thirty-three quatrains with marginal vertical lines or brackets: 21, 23, 24, 25, 26, 27, 28, 37, 39, 41, 44, 45, 55, 58, 60, 62, 67, 73, 104, 109, 113, 140, 141, 142, 148, 150, 164, 173, 258, 300, 301, 302, and 313. There were no further markings although the stanzas are numbered up to 878.

Catalogs: *A1911*, "8vo, cloth, privately printed, 1901, . . . a few corrections by Mr. Clemens," quotes the signature and inscription, lot 369, sold for $7.50; George D. Smith, New York City, "Catalogue of Books" (1911), quotes the signature and inscription, item #292, $25; Maurice Neville Rare Books, Santa Barbara, California, Catalogue No. 4 (May 1979), item #1123, $600; *Sotheby's 2003*, #224, $2,750.

Provenance: in 1982 this volume was in the collection of Nick Karanovich, Fort Wayne, Indiana (Karanovich to Alan Gribben, 29 June 1982).

Location: collection of Kevin Mac Donnell, Austin, Texas.

Copy examined: Clemens's copy, in July 2004. Has an *A1911* sale label affixed to the front pastedown endpaper. On 29 June 1982 Nick Karanovich sent Alan Gribben photocopies of all pages of interest from this volume.

On the afternoon of 26 January 1907, a Saturday, Clemens "sat on the red sofa" and read aloud to Isabel Lyon from a new translation of the *Rubáiyát* he had just received. "Of course it doesn't tally with FitzGerald's exactly," noted Miss Lyon, "which made the King remark that 'Omar had changed his principles'" (IVL Journals, TS p. 221, MTP). Clemens wrote to James Logan on 2 February 1907: "I owe you many thanks for sending me Mr. Thompson's book. I read it with strong interest & pleasure, & shall continue to drink from it, for the more a disciple gets of Omar the thirstier he becomes" (MTP).

———. *Rubáiyát of Omar Khayyám, the Astronomer-Poet of Persia. Rendered into English Verse* by Edward FitzGerald. Boston: Houghton, Mifflin and Co., Printed at the Riverside Press, n.d. [1884]. [Publication date conjectured but highly likely.]

Inscription: the half-title page is signed "S. L. Clemens, Hartford, Conn."

Marginalia: several words and passages are marked with

pencil, and a few remarks are written in pencil.

Catalogs: *A1911*, "16mo, cloth, " Bost., n.d., . . . several passages and words marked with pencil, and a few remarks written in pencil," quotes the signature, lot 371, sold for $5; George D. Smith, New York City, "Catalogue of Books" (1911), quotes the signature, item #293, $15; American Art Association (New York City), Sale catalogue (18 November 1925), "12mo, original cloth, enclosed in half blue morocco slip-case, gilt back, with inlays of crimson morocco, Boston, Riverside Press, no date, on the second half-title appears his autograph signature and address—"S. L. Clemens, Hartford, Conn.," has the *A1911* sale label, lot 173, sold for $19.

On 19 May 1884 Clemens instructed Charles L. Webster: "Send me a copy of the 'Rubayat [*sic*] of Omar Khayam'— published by Osgood" (*MTBus*, p. 254). A statement of Clemens's personal expenses that Charles L. Webster & Company sent to Clemens on 2 September 1884 shows that Clemens purchased "1 Rubayat" [*sic*] for .67¢ on 27 May 1884 (MTP).

Clemens already knew this literary work. On 28 August 1907 Isabel Lyon reported that she had run across an old letter to Clemens ("written about 1877") from the Reverend Joseph H. Twichell, who advised Clemens to read the verses from the *Rubáiyát* appearing in that morning's Hartford *Courant* (IVL Journals, TS p. 273, MTP). Evidently Miss Lyon had turned up Twichell's "long ago" postcard that Clemens discusses in his Autobiographical Dictation of 7 October 1907 (Clemens interpreted its postmark as 22 December and guessed the year was 1879). "Read (if you haven't) the extracts from Omar Khayyam. . . . I think we'll have to get the book. . . . Read it, and we'll talk it over," urged Twichell. "Surely this Omar was a great poet" (*AutoMT* 3: 159; Paine quoted Twichell's note with variant phrasing in *Mark Twain: A Biography*, p. 615 n. 1). Steve Courtney (in 2008) and then Dwayne Eutsey (in 2015) eventually corrected the date of the Hartford *Courant* issue that published and commented on forty-two stanzas from FitzGerald's version of *The Rubáiyát*, showing that the guesses of both Lyon and Clemens were wrong. As Courtney and Eutsey pointed out, the verses actually appeared in the *Courant* on 22 December 1875 and were accompanied by what Eutsey termed "a rather unsympathetic critique of Khayyám's life and poetry." Twichell, on 22 December 1875, then sent the harbinger postcard to Clemens (*LMTJH*, p. 55).

The effect on Clemens was lifelong. As he remarked in his reminiscence of 7 October 1907: "No poem had ever given me so much pleasure before, and none has given me so much pleasure since; it is the only poem I have ever carried about with me; it has not been from under my hand for twenty-eight years" (*AutoMT* 3: 159). This tribute is supreme among Clemens's judgments of poetry. An early allusion appeared in a letter from Clemens to William Dean Howells written on 26 November 1876: "It is no harm to put these words into wise old Omar-Khèyam's [*sic*] mouth, for he would have said them if he had thought of it" (*MTHL*, p. 164). In Appendix A of *A Tramp Abroad* (1880), Mark Twain joked: "Omar Khayam, the poet-prophet of Persia, writing more than eight hundred years ago, has said: 'In the four parts of the

earth are many that are able to write learned books, many that are able to lead armies, and many also that are able to govern kingdoms and empires; but few there be that can keep a hotel.'" An entry in Notebook 24 (1885) reveals that Twain intended to "quote Omar Khayam" for a speech; another entry observes: "Perfect: [Leigh Hunt's] Abou ben Adhem & the Rubiyât [*sic*]" (*N&J* 3: 159). On 20 August 1886 Clemens wrote to Clara Spaulding Stanchfield from Elmira to give her some marriage advice; he quoted "the admonition of the divine Omar": "'A moment's Halt'—a momentary taste/Of Being, at the well amid the waste,/ And lo! the phantom caravan has reached/The *Nothing* it set out from—O, make haste!'" (ALS in collection of Stanchfield Wright, Earleville, Maryland, PH in MTP). "Omar Khayam" was one of the names Twain jotted on a photo-mounting board during his around-the-world lecture tour in 1895–96 in preparation for the travel book he would write (collection of Kevin Mac Donnell, Austin, Texas). In October 1898 Twain tried his hand at composing a burlesque he would eventually title *AGE—A Rubáiyát*, and initially succeeded in writing four quatrains (NB 40, TS p. 47). Twain listed Omar Khayyám's name under the heading of "*For Cheap Books*" in July 1899 (NB 40, TS p. 58). On 18 September 1899 Twain wrote from Sanna to a Mr. Lee, offering "a Boyhood-Dream Sketch" for publication: "There's about 1300 or 1500 words of prose nonsense, & 20 quatrains of Omar poetry—took me two weeks to build them" (ALS in MTP). These verses appeared as part of Mark Twain's "My Boyhood Dreams" (1900); there he titled them "To the Above Old People" (i.e., William Dean Howells, George Washington Cable, Brander Matthews, and others). The twenty-stanza poem begins in the tone of its Persian model, describing old age and "the haunting Pathos of the Might-Have-Been," but then humorously catalogues the ailments that await elderly men. Twain's more complete version of this homage, *AGE—A Rubáiyát*, was published in *Mark Twain's Rubáiyát*, ed. Alan Gribben. Textual intro. by Kevin Mac Donnell (Austin: Jenkins Publishing Co., 1983) and in Alan Gribben's "'Bond Slave to FitzGerald's Omar': Mark Twain and *The Rubáiyát*," *Sufism and American Literary Masters*, ed. Mehdi Aminrazavi (Albany: State University of New York Press, 2014), pp. 245–262.

On 1 January 1900 Clemens castigated a new version of the *Rubáiyát* that Elizabeth Alden Curtis attempted in 1899 (see the first Catalog entry for Omar Khayyám). Clemens obtained two copies of Oliver Herford's playful *The Rubáiyát of a Persian Kitten* (1904)—see the Herford entry—and inscribed them in 1904 to his daughter Clara. On 31 May 1906 Isabel Lyon recorded in Dublin, New Hampshire, that "after our dinner Mr. Clemens read The Rubaiyat to me" (IVL Journal, Harry Ransom Center, University of Texas at Austin; a similar entry for this date occurs in IVL Journals, TS p. 161, MTP). At Stormfield, Clemens named two of his cats "Omar" (SLC to Dorothy Sturgis Harding, 27 October 1908, ALS at Columbia University).

Paine, *MTB* (1912), pp. 614, 1295; Baetzhold, *MT&JB* (1970), pp. 57, 213–218, 332 n. 23, 362 n. 7, n. 8; Everett Emerson, *Mark Twain: A Literary Life* (Philadelphia: University of Pennsylvania Press, 2000), pp. 240–241; Steve

Courtney, *Joseph Hopkins Twichell: The Life and Times of Mark Twain's Closest Friend* (Athens: University of George Press, 2008), pp. 172–173, 294 n. 30 and n. 31); and Dwayne Eutsey, "'An Immense Revelation': The Correct Date and Significance of the Article That Prompted Joseph Twichell's '*Rubáiyát* Note' to Mark Twain," *Mark Twain Journal* 53.1 (Spring 2015): 106–111.

———. *Rubáiyát of Omar Khayyám in English Verse. The Text of the Fourth Edition, Followed by That of the First; With Notes Showing the Extent of His Indebtedness to the Persian Original; and a Biographical Preface*. Translated by Edward FitzGerald (1809–1883). New York and Boston: Houghton, Mifflin and Co., The Riverside Press, Cambridge, 1888. 124 pp.

Inscription: (black ink) "To/'Mark Twain'/from his affectionately/F. D. Millet/Chicago/and/New York/ March/1894". [This was Francis Davis Millet (1846–1912), the prominent painter, sculptor, and author.]

Marginalia: a few notes and textual corrections by Clemens in pencil and black ink. Clemens used pencil in the text to renumber the Roman numerals of most stanzas with Arabic numerals. On page 41 of the Preface by Edward FitzGerald, "Omar Khayyám, The Astronomer-Poet of Persia" (pp. 35–51), FitzGerald stated, "Having failed (however mistakenly) of finding any Providence but Destiny, and any World but This, he set about making the most of it." Clemens deleted the parenthetical phrase, "however mistakenly," and bracketed FitzGerald's observation in the next paragraph that Omar "has never been popular in his own Country." In the same black ink that Clemens used for these markings, he wrote vertically in the margin: "Apparently the same reason which makes it a sin to respect Tom Paine or know of his great service to his race" (p. 41). There are a few other markings in black ink in the volume.

Catalogs: ListABP (1910), "Rubaiyat of Omar Khayyam, FitzGerald"; "Retz Appraisal" (1944), p. 8, valued at $5.

Location: Mark Twain Papers, Bancroft Library, University of California at Berkeley.

Copy examined: Clemens's copy.

———. *Rubáiyát of Omar Khayyám, The Astronomer-Poet of Persia, Rendered into English Verse*. [Translated by Edward FitzGerald, 1809–1883.] London: Macmillan and Co., 1899. 111 pp.

Inscriptions: the front flyleaf is signed in pencil, "S. L. Clemens/Vienna, April '99." Below that is an added signature in pencil: "Clara Clemens".

Marginalia: Clara Clemens made indignant notes in pencil on page 31 ("Ts! Ts!" at the third line in Stanza XIII); on page 35 ("We don't descend. But *ascend*.") at Stanza XXIV; the last two lines of Stanza XXV are marked with a heavy pencil bracket; the word "*lie*" is written in Clara Clemens's hand beside the last line of Stanza LXIIII; she wrote "The Soul couldn't be Hell. But the human *mind is* heaven and hell" next to the last line of Stanza LXVI, which reads, "I myself am Heav'n and Hell"; she bracketed Stanza LXXI and wrote in the margin, "(except by *sublimated thought*.)"; she labeled Stanza LXXIII as "Rubbish"; and she dismissed Stanza LXXVII as "Drunkard" next to a reference to "the Tavern."

Provenance: formerly belonging to Clara Clemens Samossoud when she resided in Hollywood, California; then

in the collection of Dr. William E. Seiler (1909–1978), along with Clara's *Awake to a Perfect Day: My Experience with Christian Science* (the latter volume inscribed "To/ Dr. William Seiler/from/a friendly opponent/Clara Clemens/13 May/1956") and *Mark Twain at Your Fingertips*, ed. Caroline Thomas Harnsberger (Beechurst Press), also inscribed by Clara Clemens Samossoud to Dr. William Seiler ("With best wishes").

Location: in June 2005 this volume belonged to Reita L. Seiler (b. 1932) of San Diego, California (Seiler to Alan Gribben, 28 May 2005). Mrs. Seiler was married to William E. Seiler, M.D., a close friend of Clara Clemens Samossoud and her husband Jacques A. Samossoud (1894–1966).

Copy examined: photocopies of Clemens's signed copy, which was also signed (and annotated) by Clara Clemens. Photocopies of the title page, inscriptions, and marginalia were sent to Alan Gribben by Reita L. Seiler on 3 February 2003.

On 10 April 1899 Clemens wrote from Vienna to his London publisher, Chatto & Windus: "Please send me this 2/6 Omar Khayyam" (ALS, Berg Collection, New York Public Library). Presumably this volume was the prompt result of his letter.

Welland, *Mark Twain in England*, pp. 196–197.

———. *Rubáiyát of Omar Khayyám, The Astronomer-Poet of Persia. Rendered into English Verse by Edward FitzGerald*. "Ninth American Edition." Boston: Houghton, Mifflin and Co., n. d.

Inscription: signed in pencil, "Ida C. Langdon".

Marginalia: someone, quite possibly the book's owner, Olivia Clemens's sister-in-law Ida Clark Langdon (1849–1934), copied stanzas from the *Rubáiyát* in blue ink onto the verso of pages 63 (Stanza C) and 64 (Stanza LXXV); the handwriting is definitely not Clemens's. Clemens occasionally visited the Langdons' home during his summer stays in Elmira, New York, so it seems significant that pencil markings singling out various stanzas in the volume strongly resemble his system of annotation in books of poetry. There are double vertical lines in pencil that appear to be made by Clemens on nearly a dozen pages: 35 (XII), 36 (XVI, XVII), 37 (XIX), 38 (XXII, XXIII), 45 (XLIII, XLIV), 46 (XLV), 52 (LXIV), 53 (LXVI, LXVIII), 58 (LXXXI), 63 (XCVI), and 64 (XCIX).

Catalogs: cataloged in 1982 with the library books at Quarry Farm containing marginalia. Listed among the books transferred by Mark Woodhouse from the Quarry Farm library to the Mark Twain Archive on 9 July 1987.

Location: Mark Twain Archive, Gannett-Tripp Learning Center, Elmira College, Elmira, New York.

Source: photographs of the title page and all pages containing notations. These were sent to Alan Gribben by Nathaniel Ball, former Archivist, Mark Twain Archive, Elmira College, on 30 January 2019.

———. *The Rubáiyát of Omar Khayyám*. Boston: Crowell, n. d.

Inscription: "Ida Langdon—Christmas 1899". Since this volume belonged to Clemens's niece Ida Langdon (1880–1964), herself a great reader and later a college professor, it seems unlikely that he would have had access to it.

Catalog: among the books transferred by Mark Woodhouse from the Quarry Farm library to the Mark Twain Archive

on 9 July 1987.
Location: Mark Twain Archive, Elmira College, Elmira, New York.
———. *Rubáiyát.* Philadelphia, n. d.
Inscription: signed "S. L. Clemens, 1900."
Marginalia: passages are marked in pencil.
Catalog: *A1911,* "16mo, cloth, Phila., n.d., . . . some passages marked with pencil," quotes the signature, lot 370, sold for $5.
This volume has never reappeared since the 1911 auction.
———. *The Rubáiyát of Omar Khayyám.* Translated by Edward FitzGerald (1809–1883). Riverside Press "Red-Line" Edition. Black cloth. Boston: Houghton, Mifflin and Co., n. d. 79 pp.
Marginalia: a large "X" in pencil at verse LXIV (p. 52), "Strange, is it not? . . . we must travel too." No other marks. A prayer written in blue ink on ruled notebook paper (not in Clemens's hand)—titled "Peace of Allah"—is laid in at page 52.
Provenance: formerly in the Antenne-Dorrance Collection, Rice Lake, Wisconsin, among the keepsake books from Clemens's library that Katy Leary bequeathed to her nephew Warren Leary, Sr.
Location: Mark Twain Archive, Gannett Tripp Learning Center, Elmira College, Elmira, New York.
Copy examined: Clemens's copy. Shelved with Clemens's volumes when Ann Cameron Harvey listed the collection in 1966 and when I visited Rice Lake in 1970. Examined again on 28 May 2015 at Elmira College.
———. *Rubáiyát of Omar Khayyám.* Translated by Edward FitzGerald (1809–1883). Frontispiece portrait of FitzGerald. "Ariel Booklets" Series. Original flexible red morocco, green floral endpapers, gilt. Spine repaired. Half red morocco folding-case. New York: G. P. Putnam's Sons, n. d.
Inscription: on the recto of the front free endpaper Clemens wrote, in black ink, "To/Mrs. H. H. Rogers, Jr.—/With a reminder from/S. L. Clemens/entitled/*Superintending the Game (Unasked).*" *Mary Benjamin Rogers (1879–1956)* had married Harry Rogers (1879–1935), the son of Clemens's financial savior Henry H. Rogers (1840–1909), in 1900. On the facing flyleaf, Clemens wrote a lighthearted parody of FitzGerald's Quatrain XLVIII in black ink: "A moment's Pause, a momentary Waste/Of Comment more or less misplaced,/And lo, the Joker & his Mate must light out/While there's time to do it—O, make Haste!"
Marginalia: on page 75, beside FitzGerald's translation of Quatrain XXX, Clemens wrote in ink, "This cannot be correct," but then later noted in pencil, "It is!"
Provenance: unknown until the volume entered the collection of Nick Karanovich, Fort Wayne, Indiana.
Catalog: *Sotheby's 2003,* lot 225, $7,500.
Copy examined: a gift copy to Mary (Benjamin) Rogers, inscribed by Clemens. Viewed at the 2003 Sotheby's auction.
On 28 August 1906 Clemens wrote to Mary Benjamin Rogers from Dublin, New Hampshire to relate a "charade-combination" he had invented for the quatrain beginning "A moment's Halt, a momentary Taste" (*MTLM,* p. 54).
In 1898 Mark Twain had amused himself by composing a forty-five-stanza poem that he titled *AGE—A Rubáiyát.* Employing the stanzas and rhymes of FitzGerald's translation Twain's verses half-humorously lament every elderly man's inevitable mental decline and physical miseries.

Alan Gribben's introduction to the first publication of *AGE—A Rubáiyát* (*Mark Twain's Rubáiyát.* Textual note by Kevin Mac Donnell [Austin, Texas: Jenkins Publishing Co., 1983], pp. 9–30) analyzed Twain's reverence for Edward FitzGerald's version of the *Rubáiyát* and looked at Twain's occasional penchant for lewd writings. See also Alan Gribben's "'Bond Slave to FitzGerald's Omar': Mark Twain and *The Rubáiyát,*" *Sufism and American Literary Masters,* ed. Mehdi Aminrazavi (Albany: State University of New York Press, 2014), pp. 245–262,which reprints Twain's *AGE—A Rubáiyát.*
Lewis Leary, ed., *MTHHR* (1969), p. 575.
One Hundred Songs of Scotland. Words and Music. Boston, n.d.
Inscription: autograph at the head of "Preface": "Mark Twain, 1901."
Catalog: Union Galleries (New York City), Sale number 58 (8 May 1936), "8vo, original boards, cloth back, worn, Boston, n.d.," quotes the signature, lot 50, sold for $2.00.
Assuming that this association item is genuine rather than spurious, the edition is probably the one published in Boston by O. Ditson & Company that was copyrighted in 1859. Clemens hardly ever inscribed his nom de plume in a book he did not write. The early date of its first recorded sale (1936) somewhat argues against a forgery, but even by then a few fraudulent autographs had already been perpetrated.
O'NEILL, ROSE CECIL (1874–1944), also known as "Mrs. H[arry]. L[eon]. Wilson." *The Lady in the White Veil.* Illustrated by the author. New York: Harper & Brothers, 1909. 351 pp.
Source: MTLAcc, entry #1448, volume donated by Clemens.
On the Gridiron and Other Stories of Outdoor Sport, by Jesse Lynch Williams [1871–1929], S. Scoville, Junior, J. Conover, W. J. Henderson, and Paul Hull. Illus. New York: Harper & Brothers, 1909. 224 pp.
Source: MTLAcc, entry #1453, volume donated by Clemens.
On Track and Diamond, by George [Brinton McClellan] Harvey [1864–1928], Van Tassel Sutphen, James M. Hallo well, J. Conover, and S. Scoville, Jr. Harper's Athletic Series. Illus. New York: Harper & Brothers, 1909. 221 pp.
Source: MTLAcc, entry #1191, volume donated by Clemens.
———. [Another identical copy.]
Source: MTLAcc, entry #1454, volume donated by Clemens.
OORT, HENRICUS (1836–1927) and **ISAÄC HOOYKAAS** (1837–1893). *The Bible for Learners.* Authorized translation from the Dutch by Philip Henry Wicksteed (1844–1927), with the assistance of Abraham Kuenen (1828–1891). 3 vols. Maps. Boston: Roberts Brothers, 1878–1879.
Source: MTLAcc, entries #935–937, volumes donated by Clemens.
Clemens sent a copy of this work to his brother Orion, explaining to their sister Pamela Moffett on 18 November 1879: "'The Bible for Learners' may cure him or kill him—a body can't tell which—but I've ordered the publishers to send it to him—let's await the result" (SLC to Pamela Moffett, *MTBus,* p. 131; ALS at Vassar College).
———and **ISAÄC HOOYKAAS** (1837–1893), with the assistance

of Abraham Kuenen (1828–1891). *The Bible for Young People*. Authorized Translation by Philip Henry Wicksteed (1844–1927). 6 vols. London and Edinburgh: Williams and Norgate, 1873–1879.

> Clemens made a memorandum in October 1878: "Bible for the Young. Philip Wickstead [*sic*], translator. Published by the Manchester Sunday School Union.—Dr. Oort of Amsterdam is one of the writers—7 vols." (NB 16, *N&J* 2: 209).

OPIE, AMELIA (ALDERSON) (1769–1853). *Illustrations of Lying, in All Its Branches*. New York, 1828.

> **Inscription:** "S. L. C. Compliments of S. A. Hubbard." Stephen A[shley]. Hubbard (1828–1890) was the managing editor of the Hartford *Courant*.
>
> **Catalogs:** *A1911*, "l6mo, calf, gilt, N.Y. 1828," quotes the inscription, with a sheet of notes by Clemens laid in, lot 372, sold for $1.50; George D. Smith, New York City, "Catalogue of Books" (1911), quotes the signature, item #204. $5.
>
> On 5 May 1886 Olivia Clemens informed her husband: "Today was left a book here for you from S. A. Hubbard 'Opie on Lying'" (*Twainian* 39.6 [November-December 1980]: 2). Opie was a prolific novelist of the British Romantic period. Her book describing lies subdivides the topic into many categories of deceit. The subject of lying was perennially fascinating to Twain, as Hubbard probably knew.

OPPENHEIM, EDWARD PHILLIPS (1866–1946). *A Maker of History*. Illustrated by Fred[erick] Pegram (1870–1937). Boston: Little, Brown and Co., 1906. 305 pp.

> **Source:** MTLAcc, entry #1211, volume donated by Clemens.
>
> The British author Oppenheim set his spy novel largely in Paris, but the consequences of espionage and intrigue involved the nations of England, Germany, Russia, and Japan amid reports of naval maneuvers.

ORCUTT, WILLIAM DANA (1870–1953). *The Spell*. Illustrated by Gertrude Demain Hammond (1862–1952). New York: Harper & Brothers, 1909. 352 pp.

> **Source:** MTLAcc, entry #1428, volume donated by Clemens.

The Order for Daily Evening Prayer: Also the Hymn Called Benedictus, as Set Forth for the Use of the Church by the General Convention of 1886. The Book of Common Prayer, and Administration of the Sacraments; and Other Rites and Ceremonies of the Church, According to the Use of the Protestant Episcopal Church in the United States of America, Together with the Psalter, or Psalms of David. Oxford: University Press, and Sold by Thomas Nelson & Sons, New York. [1886?] 580 pp. [Also known as *The Book of Common Prayer*.]

> **Marginalia:** a calling card for "Mr. Samuel L. Clemens/ Hartford, Conn." was tucked into a pocket in the front black leather cover. On the rear of that card someone (not in Clemens's hand but quite possibly that of Olivia Clemens) listed six colors (for a fabric?) followed by numbers, some of them canceled, ranging from 1 to 5. Perhaps it was Olivia Clemens who noted in pencil at the bottom of the title page, "Mrs. Susan Crane gave [me?]". Susan Crane herself might have been the one who wrote jokingly in pencil on the last page of the Appendix, "To

My Sisier/Susin CRANE."

> **Location:** Mark Twain Archive, Gannett-Tripp Learning Center, Elmira College, Elmira, New York.
>
> **Copy examined:** most likely Susan Crane's copy, with indications that Olivia Clemens handled it, made a note, and enclosed an annotated card. Examined on 16 July 1998 at Elmira College, where Deborah Bangs brought it to my attention.
>
> See also the Catalog entry for *The Book of Common Prayer*.

O'REILLY, BERNARD (1823–1907). *Life of Leo XIII [1810– 1903], from an Authentic Memoir Furnished by His Order; Written with the Encouragement, Approbation and Blessing of His Holiness the Pope*. Illus. New York: Charles L. Webster & Co., 1887. 603 pp.

> "Send latest news about Pope's book," Clemens wrote in 1886 (Notebook 26, *N&J* 3: 229 and *passim*). When the volume issued, Clemens was elated at the prospect of its sales (*MTB*, p. 832); however, the results would not live up to his expectations.

O'REILLY, JOHN BOYLE (1844–1890).

> In "My Boyhood Dreams" (1900), Mark Twain referred to the poet and editor of the Boston *Pilot*, "Boyle O'Reilly, lost to us now these many years." Boyle's life contained many adventures. Prosecuted for his Fenian activities in Ireland, he was transported to Australia but managed to escape from the penal colony. In Boston he became a prominent journalist and civic figure, known for his advocacy of human rights.
>
> A. G. Evans, *Fanatic Heart: A Life of John Boyle O'Reilly 1844–1890* (Boston: Northeastern University Press, 1999); Ian Kenneally, *From the Earth, A Cry: The Story of John Boyle O'Reilly* (New York: Collins Press, 2012).

ORR, ALEXANDRA (LEIGHTON) (1828–1903), known as "Mrs. Sutherland Orr." *Life and Letters of Robert Browning [1812–1889]*. Second ed. London: Smith, Elder, & Co., 1891. 451 pp.

> **Inscription:** "Susan L. Crane/Berlin,/Jan. 1892."
>
> **Catalog:** Ball 2016 inventory, brown cloth, gilt lettering, fair condition.
>
> **Location:** Quarry Farm library shelves, under the supervision of the Mark Twain Archive, Elmira College, Elmira, New York.
>
> This biography was available to Clemens whenever he visited Quarry Farm in Elmira.

ORTHWEIN, EDITH HALL. *Songs of the Beloved*. New York: Dodge Publishing Co, [cop. 1909]. 88 pp.

> **Source:** MTLAcc, entry #2074, volume donated from Clemens's library by Clara Clemens Gabrilowitsch in 1910.
>
> Orthwein, born in St. Louis and married in 1897 to Charles Clemmens Orthwein (b. 1869), was a Kansas City poet and fiction writer.

OSGOOD, FRANCES SARGENT (LOCKE) (1811–1850). *Poems*. New York: Clark, Austin, Maynard & Co., 1861. [252 pp.]

> **Source:** MTLAcc, entry #657, volume donated by Clemens.
>
> In "Letter from Carson City," a sketch published in the *Territorial Enterprise* on 3 February 1863, Clemens mentioned hearing Osgood's "Call me pet names" sung at the Governor's house (*ET&S* 1: 197). Her poem had been set to music by Francis Weiland.

O'SULLIVAN, DANIEL, comp. *The Book of Legends, Containing a Selection of Standard Tales from the Most Esteemed British*

Essayists, to Which Is Prefixed an Abridgment of Dunlop's "History of Fiction.". . . . Preceded by a History of Fiction by D. O'Sullivan. Paris: Pourchet, 1842. 300 pp. [Publisher conjectured.]
> **Catalog:** *A1911*, "l2mo, half bound (cover loose), Paris, 1842," lot 46, sold for $1.50.
> *The Book of Legends* collects accounts of Alexander the Great, Charlemagne, and other heroic figures.

OTIS, CHARLES POMEROY (1840–1888). *Elementary German: An Outline of the Grammar, with Exercises, Conversations, and Readings.* Sixth edition. Arranged and edited by Horatio Stevens White (1852–1934). The Original Two Parts in One Volume. Handbooks for Students and General Readers Series. New York: Henry Holt and Co., 1889.
> **Inscription:** the front flyleaf is signed, "Clara L. Clemens/ Sept. 24th '89/Hartford."
> **Marginalia:** Clara Clemens made notes about the German language on the endpapers, flyleaves, and other blank spaces throughout the volume. On one of the front flyleaves she listed her reading interests and plans: "Read again etc./'Little Dorrit'/'Oliver Twist'/Tale of Two Cities/ Barnaby Rudge/all of the rest of Dickens/Ramona/The Newcombes one or two/More of Thackeray./Precede/with Queens of England./Short history of French/Revolution. A Brief French/History. The S. S. Biographies/of the great men./Zoroaster."
> **Location:** in 1985 this was in the Stowe-Day Memorial Library in Hartford, Connecticut, on loan from the Connecticut State Library in Hartford (Diana Royce to Alan Gribben, 17 June 1985).
> **Copy examined:** Clara Clemens's copy, which was available to Clemens. Photocopies of the title page, inscription, and sample annotations sent to Alan Gribben on 17 June 1985 by Diana Royce, then librarian of the Stowe-Day Memorial Library located adjacent to the Mark Twain Memorial (now the Mark Twain House and Museum) in Hartford. I examined the book itself in August 1987 in Hartford.

OTTO, EMIL. *German Conversation-Grammar; A New and Practical Method of Learning the German Language.* New York, [cop. 1864].
> "A joyous, innocent, good-natured numscull" in Chapter 27 of *A Tramp Abroad* (1880) "carried a German Grammar,—Otto's." He explained: "I'm to enter Harvard next year.—Studying German all the time now. Can't enter till I know German. This book's Otto's Grammar. It's a mighty good book to get the *ich habe gehabt haben's* out of."

Our Children's Songs. Illus. New York: Harper & Brothers, [cop. 1877]. 207 pp.
> **Source:** MTLAcc, entry #1872, volume donated from Clemens's library by Clara Clemens Gabrilowitsch in 1910.
> Many of the songs in this lavishly illustrated volume were suitable for adults, too.

Our Children's Songs. Illus. New York: Harper & Brothers, 1904. 207 pp.
> **Source:** MTLAcc, entry #1372, volume donated by Clemens.
> Many of the songs in this lavishly illustrated volume were also suitable for adults.

Our Stories, by the School Children of the State of New Jersey, Fifteen Years of Age and Under. Written for the George W. Altemus, Jr. Gold Prizes. Portraits of the child authors.

Philadelphia, 1888.
> **Inscription:** "Mark Twain: Best Wishes of Geo. W. Altemus, Jr. 7/20/88."
> **Marginalia:** "The title should have been Literary Thefts"; "There doesn't seem to be an unstolen page in the book." Later Clemens altered the word "Thefts" to "Imitations" and changed "unstolen" to "unborrowed." He concluded: "All things (except the phrasing) in ALL books are borrowed, May, 1908."
> **Catalog:** *A1911*, "Square 12mo, coth, Phila. 1888," quotes inscription and marginalia, lot 77, sold for $3.50.

The Outlook (New York weekly newspaper, 1870–1932).
> In a speech Mark Twain made on 29 April 1901, he mentioned *The Outlook's* objections to his views of missionaries to China: "One must admit that it is frank in its delinquencies, that it is outspoken in its departures from fact, that it is vigorous in its mistaken criticism of men like me" ("Dinner to Hamilton W. Mabie," *MTS1923*, p. 240; see also Paul Fatout, *Mark Twain Speaking*, p. 398). Hamilton Wright Mabie (1846–1916) was *The Outlook's* editor. On 29 May 1907 Twain mentioned in an Autobiographical Dictation that "the other day the President . . . got himself interviewed for the *Outlook*, and launched a devastating assault upon poor obscure little Mr. [William Joseph] Long" (*MTE*, p. 19; *AutoMT* 3: 62).

Out of the World [unidentified book title].
> **Catalog:** ListABP (1910), "Out of the World", no other information provided.

OVID (43 BCE-17 CE). *Art of Love, in Three Books, Together with His Remedy of Love. Translated into English Verse by Several Eminent Hands. To Which Are Added The Court of Love, A Tale from Chaucer, and the History of Love.* Second edition. Four engraved plates. Original cottage style calf. Rebacked. London: Printed for J. T. and Sold by William Taylor, 1716.
> **Catalog:** *Sotheby's 2003*, #220, $900 (sold with four other miscellaneous titles).
> **Provenance:** the title-page has the inscription of J. Longwood. A *C1951* label is affixed to the front pastedown endpaper. (This volume was not listed in the 1951 Hollywood auction checklist, but many of the books sold there never made it onto that sheet, which was put together in a slapdash manner.) Subsequently the book was owned by J. Cheney and then, in April 1991, by Robert T. Slotta (Slotta to Alan Gribben, 23 April 1991). Eventually the volume entered the collection of Nick Karanovich of Fort Wayne, Indiana.
> **Copy examined:** presumably Clemens's copy, unsigned and unmarked (but this was not unusual; Clemens was generally loath to sign or annotate the antique books that he acquired if he admired them). Robert Slotta provided photographs of the cover, front and rear endpapers, title page, and first page of the text to Alan Gribben in April 1991. Also viewed at the Sotheby's sale in 2003.
> In *Ars Amatoria* the Roman poet Ovid offers explicit lessons to male readers in finding, seducing, and keeping a lover. The classical myth of Baucis and Philemon that Ovid related in *Metamorphoses* has been suggested as having "direct and even striking parallels" with Twain's "The Man That Corrupted Hadleyburg" (1899) (W. Gerald Marshall, "Mark Twain's 'The Man That Corrupted Hadleyburg' and the Myth of Baucis and Philemon," *Mark Twain Journal* 20.2

[Summer 1980]: 4–7). Marshall acknowledged that the myth was retold in Jonathan Swift's poem "Baucis and Philemon" and in Goethe's *Faust, Part Two*.

OWEN, ELIZABETH S. (comp.). *The Whittier Birthday Book*. Boston: Houghton, Mifflin and Co., [cop. 1881]. 402 pp. [This copy is a later printing, probably c. 1890.]

    Inscriptions: signed by "Jean Clemens. 1895." under the date of her birthday (26 July) while she was staying at Quarry Farm. A calendar with quotations from various poets, the volume bears the ownership inscription of "Ida Langdon, Elmira, Oct. 15, 1891." Clemens's niece Ida Langdon (1880–1964) was a friend and companion of the Clemens daughters. Ida's other friends also signed the volume, including Edith Sayer Brooks, Ada May Gleason, Crystal Eastman, and Jay Fletcher Slee.

    Location: collection of Kevin Mac Donnell, Austin, Texas. Purchased from the Langdon family.

    Source: supplementary inventory list sent to Alan Gribben by Mac Donnell, 27 August 2017.

OWEN, FRANCIS BROWNING (1830–1910), pseud. "Francis Browning." *Poems: A Holiday Book*. Detroit: Free Press Printing House, 1874. 89 pp.

    Catalog: Swann Galleries (New York City), Catalogue 715 (10 November 1966), "12mo, cloth, first edition, Detroit, 1874, 'S. L. Clemens (Mark Twain)' written at the head of the title, in the humorist's hand," item #62.

    The florid verse of Michigan lawyer Francis Browning Owen (who repeatedly claimed to be closely related to the poet Robert Browning) is only a few degrees better than Julia A. Moore's, and it is tempting to imagine that Clemens was looking for another Sweet Singer of Michigan whose poetry he could ridicule. However, the placement (on the title page) and the form (Clemens's name above his pen name) of the putative autograph do not follow his customary habit of registering ownership of a book and instead resemble the pattern found in a significant number of forged association copies. Given this discrepancy and in view of the volume's abrupt appearance without any preceding mention in catalogs or other records it should be considered a highly dubious addition to his personal library. Nonetheless I am grateful to Linda Moore, Public Services Librarian at Hillsdale College in Hillsdale, Michigan, for helping me turn up information about this obscure literary figure, who prospected in California during the Gold Rush and thereafter resided in three different states while trying his hand as, periodically, a merchant, restaurateur, magazine correspondent, newspaper editor, door-to-door bookseller, and evangelist. Always, however, Owen returned to the practice of law in Michigan. He would die on 16 December 1910 and be buried in Farmington Hills, Michigan.

OZAKI, YEI THEODORA (1871–1932). *Japanese Fairy Tales*. New York: A. L. Burt Co., [1905]. 305 pp. [Author and edition conjectured.]

    Source: ListABP (1910) ("Japanese Fairy Tales" is the entire entry).

❙ P

PACKARD, ALPHEUS SPRING (1839–1905). *Half Hours with Insects*. Illus. Boston: Estes and Lauriat, 1877. 384 pp.

    Source: MTLAcc, entry #1973, volume donated from

Clemens's library by Clara Clemens Gabrilowitsch in 1910.

Packard's Monthly: The Young Men's Magazine (New York periodical).

    Mark Twain mentioned the April 1869 issue in a letter to Mrs. Fairbanks written from Elmira on 24 March 1869: "Did you see 'J. B.'s' able bosh in reply to me ["An Open Letter to Mark Twain," pp. 120–121], in the last Packard? I hate to talk back at such small fry, but *how* can I resist . . . ?" (*MTMF*, pp. 86–87; *MTLet* 3: 176). Twain had criticized Cornelius "Commodore" Vanderbilt (1794–1877).

PADDOCK, CORNELIA ("MRS. A. G. PADDOCK") (1840–1898). *The Fate of Madame La Tour; A Tale of Great Salt Lake*. New York: Fords, Howard & Hulbert, 1881. 352 pp.

    Clemens made note of this anti-Mormon novel about the practice of polygamy: "'The Fate of Madame La Tour. (Ford, Howard & Hulbert)" (NB 19, December 1881, *N&J* 2: 416).

    Jeffrey Nichols, *Prostitution, Polygamy, and Power: Salt Lake, 1847–1918*. Champaign: University of Illinois Press, 2002.

PAGE, THOMAS NELSON (1853–1922). *In Ole Virginia; or, Marse Chan and Other Stories* (collection of six short stories, published in 1887).

    Noticing Isabel V. Lyon's references by June 1903 to her employer as "Marse Clemens," "Marse C.," or sometimes "Marse," Laura Skandera Trombley suggested in 2010 that "the name was likely a pun on Thomas Nelson Page's Marse Chan, the main character in a short story by the same name from his collection entitled *In Ole Virginia*." Skandera Trombley added that "there would have been an edge to Isabel Lyon's pun, as Marse Chan was a slaveholder in the antebellum south" (*Mark Twain's Other Woman: The Hidden Story of His Final Years* [New York: Alfred A. Knopf, 2010], p. 21). Nelson's "Marse Chan. A Tale of Old Virginia" first appeared in the *Century Magazine* 27.6 (April 1884): 932–942. This sentimental story of a formerly enslaved man's lifelong loyalty to his beloved master, killed in the Civil War, is told in dialect to an appreciative stranger (who provides the frame narration) by Sam, who tends the family's graves.

———. *Pastime Stories*. Illustrated by A[rthur]. B[urdett]. Frost (1851–1928). New York: Charles Scribner's Sons, 1903. 220 pp.

    Source: MTLAcc, entry #236, volume donated by Clemens. In January 1889 Mark Twain went to Baltimore to fill in for "poor Page" at an authors' reading after Page's wife died. Twain wrote to Aleck Badlam on 9 February 1889 from Hartford, giving details about the unexpectedness of Mrs. Page's death. "This is all I have heard," Twain explained, "for I have not seen Page nor had any correspondence with him. It broke him all up" (TS in MTP). In 1905 Page was one of Twain's ten choices for membership in the American Academy of Arts and Letters (SLC to Robert Underwood Johnson, New York City, 28 April 1905, ALS in American Academy of Arts and Letters). Page appeared with Twain before the Congressional copyright committee on 7 December 1906 (*MTS1923*, p. 323; Fatout, *MTSpk*, p. 533).

    Edward L. Tucker, "A Thank-You Message from Samuel Clemens to Thomas Nelson Page," *ANQ* 16.3 (Summer

2003): 44.

———. *Two Prisoners.* Illustrated by Virginia Keep (1878–1962). New York: R. H. Russell, 1903. 82 pp.

Source: MTLAcc, entry #1115, volume donated by Clemens.

PAGET, VIOLET (1856–1935), pseud. "Vernon Lee." *Miss Brown, A Novel* (published in 1884).

Susy Clemens wrote to her college friend Louise Brownell from Florence on 13 November 1892 to report that she had met Vernon Lee. "Gauche, homely, atrociously dressed. . . . There was a pathetic approachable quality about her personality, a humanness. . . . Of course she's a brilliant woman [and] she carried that about with her somewhere in some very subtle way." Susy continued, "You offer to send me 'Miss Brown'. I should be very glad dearest to read it" (Hamilton College Archives). Lee's novel had stirred up controversy by satirizing the Pre-Raphaelites such as Burne-Jones and Rossetti and the aesthetic circles that had sprung up in England in the 1880s. Another letter from Susy to Brownell postmarked in Florence on 31 December 1892 mentioned that she "met Vernon Lee on horseback the other day, but I was late in recognizing her and it seems she never recognizes anyone" (Hamilton College Archives). In a letter from Florence postmarked on 8 June 1893 Susy stated that she "just finished 'Miss Brown' and my feelings about it are rather chaotic. . . . Her style seems amateurish to Mamma and me. But the book does teach a lesson and I should never think of calling it 'dirty'" (Hamilton College Archives).

PAIGE, ELBRIDGE GERRY (1816–1859), pseud. "Dow, Jr."

Clemens included Paige in the list of humorists he assembled in 1881 in Notebook 19 (*N&J* 2: 429), although he erroneously referred to "Dow, Jr." as "Page." Paige was the author of *Short Patent Sermons, by "Dow, Jr."* (New York, 1845).

PAINE, ALBERT BIGELOW (1861–1937). *The Bread Line: A Story of a Paper.* New York: The Century Co., 1900. 228 pp.

Inscription: the front free endpaper is inscribed "To/Mark Twain/whose 'Innocents' was/my first temptation./From/ Albert Bigelow Paine".

Provenance: Antenne-Dorrance Collection, Rice Lake, Wisconsin.

Location: Mark Twain Archive, Gannett-Tripp Learning Center, Elmira College, Elmira, New York.

Copy examined: Clemens's copy, unmarked.

Paine joined three other writers in New York City in publishing *Youth and Home*, a journal that lasted only four issues. He then wrote an account of the doomed venture as *The Breadline* and sent copies of the book to Thomas Nast and Mark Twain (see Firmin Dredd, "Mark Twain's Biographer" [1910], p. 363).

———. *Captain Bill McDonald, Texas Ranger. A Story of Frontier Reform.* Introductory letter by Theodore Roosevelt. Special Subscription Edition. Illus. New York: J. J. Little & Ives Co., 1909. 448 pp.

Inscription: presented by Albert Bigelow Paine to Jean L. Clemens.

Catalogs: *C1951*, D48; "An Omnibus of Western Americana," Catalogue 14 (1971), Bennett & Marshall, Los Angeles," item #189.

———. [Identical copy.]

Inscription: inscribed by McDonald to Albert Bigelow Paine.

Provenance: collection of Bigelow Paine Cushman, who inherited the volume from Albert Bigelow Paine.

Location: collection of Kevin Mac Donnell, Austin, Texas (Mac Donnell to Alan Gribben, email, 27 February 2012). This is another copy of the Texas Ranger book that would have been available to Clemens.

Mark Twain apparently depended on the manuscript of Paine's book in arraigning Theodore Roosevelt (1858–1919) for mishandling the racially charged Brownsville Affair in 1906 (14 July 1908 AD, MTP). "By the testimony of Captain McDonald, Texas Ranger, a man whose character for veracity is well established," asserted Twain, "the government and its agents acted in a shabby and dishonest and dishonorable way from the beginning to the end" (*MTE*, p. 32; *AutoMT* 3: 258). William Jesse McDonald (1852–1918) endured notoriety for taking his position on the incident.

Michael Shelden, *Man in White* (2010), pp. 180–182.

———. "Christmas Luck," *Harper's Weekly* 46.2398 (6 December 1902): 24–25.

Mark Twain praised a poem by William Dean Howells, "The Christmas Spirit," that appeared in this same issue of *Harper's Weekly*, separated from Paine's short story by only by two illustrated pages; therefore it seems almost certain that he would have read "Christmas Luck." Twain's "The Belated Passport" was also published in this 6 December 1902 issue (pp. 4–5, 8–9).

———. *From Van Dweller to Commuter. The Story of a Strenuous Quest for a Home and a Little Hearth and Garden.* Green cloth. Illus. New York and London: Harper & Brothers, 1907. 416 pp.

Inscription: the front pastedown endpaper is signed in black ink, "SL. Clemens/1907."

Provenance: Antenne-Dorrance Collection, Rice Lake, Wisconsin.

Location: Mark Twain Archive, Gannett-Tripp Learning Center, Elmira College, Elmira, New York.

Copy examined: Clemens's copy, unmarked. Examined on 28 May 2015.

———. [An identical copy.]

Source: MTLAcc, entry #1639, volume donated by Clemens.

———. *The Little Lady—Her Book, for Girls and Boys.* Illustrated by Mabel Humphrey (fl. 1885–1905) and others. Philadelphia: Henry Altemus Co., [1901]. 315 pp.

Inscription: "To the Mark Twain Library/from Albert Bigelow Paine/Dec 1908".

Location: unknown at present.

Copy examined: none. Albert E. Stone, Jr. included the volume in his catalog of Clemens's books in the Mark Twain Library at Redding in 1955, but the book was missing when I visited Redding in 1970 and in subsequent years.

———. *The Ship-Dwellers: A Story of a Happy Cruise.* Illustrated by Thomas Fogarty (1873–1938). New York: Harper & Brothers, 1910. 394 pp.

Paine formally dedicated *Ship-Dwellers*, about a cruise in the Mediterranean, "To/Mark Twain/Hero of My Youth/ Friend of These Later Years." Clemens probably saw this book or at least its manuscript before his death on 21 April 1910.

———. *The Tent Dwellers*. Illustrated by Hy. [Henry Sumner] Watson (1868–1933). New York: The Outing Publishing Co., 1908. 280 pp.

Inscription: inscribed on the front free endpaper in black ink: "To/The Mark Twain Library/From/Albert Bigelow Paine/Nov 10, 08".

Location: Mark Twain Library, Redding, Connecticut.

Copy examined: presentation copy to the public library founded by Clemens. Has the Mark Twain Library accession number "790" and the purple oval Library stamps. The title page was loose when I examined the volume in 1970. When I examined it again in June 1982 the title page was missing.

The well-known illustrator Hy. Watson was nicknamed "the dog's Norman Rockwell" for his *Field and Stream* magazine covers.

———. *Th. Nast, His Period and His Pictures*. Illus. First edition. Large 8vo, original blue cloth, gilt, quarter morocco slip case. New York: Macmillan Co., 1904. 603 pp.

Inscription: the front free endpaper is inscribed in black ink: "To 'Mark Twain'/from Albert Bigelow Paine/With love and gratitude—/Dec. 1905".

Marginalia: a few brief textual corrections on pages 162 and 163, perhaps by Albert Bigelow Paine but more likely by Clemens. They seem characteristic of Clemens in that they were purely stylistic.

Catalogs: *C1951*, #100c, erroneously listed among volumes signed by Clemens, $17.50; *Fleming 1972*; Sotheby Parke Bernet, New York City, Sale number 3482 (25 February 1976), "Property of a New York City Collector" (John F. Fleming), lot 18, sold for $325 (*American Book Prices Current, 1976*, p. 207); bought by Fleming; sold to Kevin Mac Donnell.

Provenance: Frederick Anderson, then Editor of the Mark Twain Papers in the Bancroft Library at the University of California, Berkeley, examined this book in the New York City offices of John F. Fleming, Inc. and made notes in April 1972 (Anderson to James D. Hart, 17 April 1972, photocopy sent to Alan Gribben).

Location: collection of Kevin Mac Donnell, Austin, Texas.

Copy examined: Clemens's slightly annotated copy, on 15 December 1983 and again in July 2004. A letter to Clemens from an admirer is laid in. Clara Clemens Gabrilowitsch's penciled shelf numbers from her Detroit period are visible. The Hollywood sale number "100c" is written in pencil on the front pastedown endpaper.

The book titled *Th. Nast* emphasized Nast's lack of formal education and his popularity among the common people. By 1871, wrote Paine, "it was not only in the market-place that his name and achievements were recognized. In the most isolated farmhouse of the West, in the woodsman's hut and in the miner's cabin, cartoons of Tweed and his fellows decorated the walls" (p. 204). Paine also underscored Nast's "originality of idea, . . . absolute convictions and splendid moral courage" (p. 204). Nast's "great triumph had been accomplished in spite of his lack of early study and academic training" (pp. 204–205). If these descriptions were compatible with Mark Twain's self-opinion, he might also have approved of the way Paine focused

on another aspect of Nast's character: "Primarily, and before all, Thomas Nast was a moralist. . . . He was in the fullest sense the arch enemy of evil in every form, never letting pass an opportunity to strike it down. He saw in a straight line and aimed accordingly" (p. 576). Consequently "it was natural that such a man should make enemies as well as friends. . . . Preeminently Thomas Nast was a man to be honored for the friends and loved for the enemies he had made" (p. 577). As a writer involved in various reformist crusades in 1906, Twain might have liked Paine's characterization of Nast's opponents: "Men concerned in political intrigue and the practices of corruption, men seeking to ride down and disregard the rights of their fellow men, those who would cloak ill-doing with a mantle of righteousness—in a word, every intruder upon human privilege and the pursuit of happiness—these were his enemies" (p. 577). Paine's biography had much to say about Boss Tweed and Tammany Hall.

Paine's biography of Nast was profusely illustrated with drawings, mostly by Nast, and photographs to the extent that it resembled Twain's travel narrative *Following the Equator* (1897). By the end of his life Twain was so great an admirer of the graphic arts that it was probably he who arranged for his own biography—which would be completed by Paine in 1912—to employ numerous photographs, facsimiles, and drawings. Louis J. Budd speculated that Twain must have liked the way that *Th. Nast* stressed "his self-tutored genius, popularity with the common folk, and combatively firm moralism in politics" (*Our Mark Twain* [1983], pp. 202–203). To these appeals might be added Paine's casting of Nast as a great-hearted statesman-artist figure (Budd, *MTSP* [1962], pp. 202–203).

Th. Nast, His Period and His Pictures quoted several letters from Mark Twain to Nast. According to the earliest account of how Paine came to have "the biggest Boswellian opportunity of modern times," Firmin Dredd's "Mark Twain's Biographer," *The Bookman* (New York) 31 (June 1910): 363–365, Paine managed to obtain Twain's consent to use his letters in the Nast biography because Twain liked Paine's published writings. Later, when the biography issued, Twain was "one of its most appreciative readers." Through David Munro, editor of the *North American Review*, Twain sent Paine "a gratifying message and invited him to a little dinner . . . at The Players Club." (Dredd, "Mark Twain's Biographer," p. 364). Paine himself recalled corresponding with Twain while preparing Nast's biography; two years later, according to Paine's account, on 3 January 1906 Paine and Twain came together at the Players Club dinner for Twain (Fears, *Day by Day* 4: 256–257). At that event Paine asked permission to call on Twain for a talk about Twain's own biography. On 6 January 1906 he discussed the project with Twain, who was propped up in bed "as was his morning custom" at 21 Fifth Avenue. Twain then expressed his approval of the Nast book (Paine, "Mark Twain—Boy and Man: The Story of His Life," *Mentor* 12 (May 1924): 18–19). Paine told Isabel V. Lyon on 9 January 1906, the day he moved in with Clemens, that "it had always been his dream, ambition to write Mr. Clemens's biography, but [he] never came close to the prospect of it until Mr. Clemens said to Mr. David Munro that Paine's book on Thomas Nast was 'damn good' and Munro told Paine. Then his courage flowed" (IVL Journals, TS p. 212, MTP).

Paine's not-always-reliable biography and his authority over Mark Twain's manuscripts and editions have presented problems for later commentators. However, the circumstances that brought about his expanded role ought to be borne in mind. Inhabiting the palace of a dying king can prove to be a perilous, treachery-filled experience. In the instance of Samuel L. Clemens, an exceedingly precarious climate suffused the household of this celebrity writer ensconced in a faux Italian villa on a scenic hill in rural Connecticut. The volatility in the mansion of that grief-stricken writer must have been palpable, what with a maneuvering mixture of two daughters, a loyal longtime housekeeper, a private secretary who would have married Clemens without hesitation if he could have forsaken the memory of his cherished wife, a devoted and dutiful biographer, and several other hangers-on. Isabel Lyon held a losing hand in this dangerous game, and perhaps Albert Bigelow Paine's occasional slipperiness with the truth served him well in that milieu of emotional intrigues. In any event, he managed to survive this trying phase, and ended up assisting Clara Clemens Samossoud in constructing an image of Twain that would dominate scholarship and the popular mind for decades to come.

Let me raise three cautionary points. The first concerns the tendency of many scholars to judge and condemn Paine by our contemporary editorial practices. Naturally we wish that Paine had enjoyed the benefit of a twenty-first-century graduate school education and had grasped what we today view as the sacrosanct nature of an author's final versions of his manuscripts—however incomplete and unsatisfying those might seem. This time-warp approach of imposing modern-day editing standards on Paine's work seems unfair to him. Paine was selected in the normal "men-of-letters" tradition prevalent at the turn of the last century. The designated biographer became in fact or in effect the literary executor of the author's estate and was expected to put the best possible face on the writer's life and works, shepherd the reprinting of his publications, oversee the safekeeping and potential use of unpublished materials, and ensure that any surviving family members profited from these activities. Trimming and expurgating an author's writings were not yet viewed as the horrendous crimes that our emerging PhDs are taught to locate and revile; they were the countenanced and anticipated responsibilities of the person chosen in advance by an author to carry out solemn posthumous duties. I am hardly saying that these practices were commendable or beneficial—indeed, I myself have published more than one article deploring several of Paine's decisions that have misled generations of readers and scholars. I am merely urging a recognition that, like the rest of us, Paine was caught like an unaware specimen in the amber of his generation's social history.

Paine's fate was not entirely enviable. True, he did struggle free of a no doubt stultifying life as a photographer and wholesale supplier in a small Midwestern town, eventually entering the more stimulating atmosphere of urban opportunities in St. Louis and then New York City. But after he succeeded in elevating his professional standing he found himself, somewhat like the hapless Isabel Lyon, primarily known for his association with celebrated people and never acclaimed as one of them. He fortunately possessed more writerly instincts than Isabel Lyon, and he did produce novels, poems, essays, travelogues, and biographies that pulled him up to the status of being quasi-known, of having a vaguely recognizable name, but he was denied entrance to the upper echelon of national personalities. It must have been frustrating at times to be so close to being truly famous, to have entrée to the homes and families of such famous figures as Thomas Nast, Mark Twain, and Lillian Gish, to see into the lives of many other prominent people of their era, and yet be viewed as little more than a useful tool for shoring up and making permanent their fame.

Here is a pertinent question for future scholars to consider. If Paine had lost at that hazardous poker game underway among the Stormfield relationships, if the document that was discovered decades later in an attorney's safe had been called the Albert-Dora Manuscript instead of the Ashcroft-Lyon Manuscript, if Paine had been erased from the seething firmament of Mark Twain's final constellation, what would have been the outcome? Those of us who resent Paine's habits of meddling with the integrity of the papers under his supervision, who would eagerly join Hamlin Hill's 1973 denunciation in *Mark Twain: God's Fool* of Paine's efforts to exclude others from tinkering with the carefully crafted image of Twain he cast in brittle plaster, might give thought to what could have occurred without Paine's presence in the aftermath of the literary lion's death. Clara presumably could have attempted to fill in as a literary executor, but she hardly had her departed sister Susy Clemens's gifts as a writer or interpreter. Moreover, Clara still would have installed a protective sheath around her father's memory, perhaps even a more antiseptic version than the one we ended up with. Twain's aging friend William Dean Howells might have been asked to step in as a substitute biographer-executor, but it's not likely that Howells would have accepted, given his always intense publication schedule. Isabel Lyon, if she had somehow survived the Stormfield purge, was a helpful journal-keeper but clearly had no inclination to write a full-length study, nor would Clara have accorded her the authority necessary to dictate the disposition of Twain's writings. There were a few young writers who had caught Mark Twain's fancy and had visited him, but it is highly doubtful that they could have acquitted themselves any better than (or nearly as well as) Paine.

No, we are stuck with the obstinate and irritating shield thrown up in places by Paine, yet the situation definitely could have become more challenging. Paine, after all, is penetrable rather than entirely opaque. Furthermore, Paine proved to be a talented, complex, and engaging figure for us to investigate in his own right. We could have done much worse. Much worse. And if Twain's chosen biographer had to forget in Grand Central Station any particular manuscript belonging to the Mark Twain estate, let us be glad it was poor Orion Clemens's pitiable narrative. Paine's unconscious forgetfulness happily spared us from studying that pathetic document.

A doctoral dissertation by Dennis W. Kennedy, "Mark Twain's 'Particular Friend': A Study of the Relationship Between Samuel Langhorne Clemens and Albert Bigelow Paine" (University of Massachusetts, 1987), investigated this crucial friendship between Twain and his chosen biographer, answering a number of questions. The *Mark Twain Journal: The Author and His Era* 56.1 (Spring 2018): 203–295 published a special section edited by Terry Oggel that contained six incisive essays examining the Twain-Paine relationship. Additional revealing essays about the final Stormfield years appeared in the Spring 2020 (58.1) issue of the *Mark Twain Journal: The Author and His Era*. See also Terry Oggel's "Paine Offers to Purify Duneka, Summer 1913," *Mark Twain Journal: The Author and His Era* 58.2 (Fall 2020).

PAINE, THOMAS (1737–1809). *The Age of Reason*. New York: Truth Seeker Co., [cop. 1898].

    Inscription: the verso of the front flyleaf is inscribed in black ink, "S L. Clemens/Tyringham, Mass.,/August 1904."

    Catalog: *C1951*, D37, listed among volumes signed by Clemens, $22.50.

    Provenance: Donald I. Bender notified the Mark Twain Papers at the Bancroft Library in 1993 about his ownership of the volume (Kenneth M. Sanderson to Donald I. Bender, 28 October 1993, MTP). According to Bender, the best guess is that Heritage Books had the copy at one time and sold the book to the popular author Irving Wallace. Bender subsequently purchased the volume from a private party in 1993.

    Location: on 17 June 2002 a telephone call verified that this book was still in the collection of Donald I. Bender, Berkeley, California. Bender reported the presence of a *C1951* auction label in the volume.

In Chapter 1 of *Those Extraordinary Twins* (1894), "Luigi, with Paine's 'Age of Reason' in his hand, sat down in one chair . . . while Angelo took his 'Whole Duty of Man' [a devotional work by Richard Allestree], and both began to read." The eminent painter, sculptor, and author Francis D. Millet (1846–1912) presented Clemens with a copy of Omar Khayyám's *Rubáiyát* in 1894; on page 41 of Edward FitzGerald's biographical introduction to the book, Clemens compared Omar's poor reception in his own country to Paine's unpopularity: "Apparently the same reason which makes it a sin to respect Tom Paine or know of his great services to his race," Clemens wrote in brown ink. Where FitzGerald compared Omar and Lucretius on page 43 ("men . . . passionate for Truth and Justice; who justly revolted from their Country's false Religion"), Clemens drew a line beside the sentence and noted in ink: "Tom Paine over again" (volume in MTP). In May 1908 Clemens spoke of *The Age of Reason* with Albert Bigelow Paine: "That seems a mild book now. I read it first when I was a cub pilot, read it with fear and hesitation, but marveling at its fearlessness and wonderful power. I read it again a year or two ago, for some reason, and was amazed to see how tame it had become. It seemed that Paine was apologizing everywhere for hurting the feelings of the reader" (*MTB*, p. 1445). Subsequently Clemens observed that both the Catholic and Protestant churches "turn upon Thomas Paine and charge *him*

with irreverence" (*Is Shakespeare Dead?* [1909], Part 12). Sherwood Cummings insisted, "It is nearly impossible to exaggerate the impact of *The Age of Reason* on the mind of Mark Twain" ("Mark Twain's Theory of Realism; or The Science of Piloting," *Studies in American Humor* 2.3 [January 1976]: 209–221).

Brashear, *MTSM* (1934), pp. 247–248; Waggoner, "Science" (1937), p. 369; Cummings, "*WIM?*: The Scientific Sources" (1964), p. 110; *The Bible According to Mark Twain*, ed. Howard G. Baetzhold and Joseph B. McCullough (New York: Simon & Schuster, 1995), pp. 313–314; David Shapiro-Zysk, "The Separation of Church and Twain: Deist Philosophy in *The Innocents Abroad*," *Mark Twain Annual* 4 (2006): 25–32; Roger D. Lund, "Philosophic Drollery in *Letters from the Earth*," *Mark Twain Annual* 4 (2006): 104–126 (discusses the Paine-Twain connection in detail); Lawrence I. Berkove and Joseph Csicsila, *Heretical Fictions: Religion in the Literature of Mark Twain* (Iowa City: University of Iowa Press, 2010), pp. 5, 10–11, 154; and Harold K. Bush, "Religion," *Mark Twain in Context*, ed. John Bird (Cambridge, England: Cambridge University Press, 2020), pp. 171–172.

———. *The Crisis* (pamphlet, No. 1 in the American Crisis series, published in December 1776).

Minnie M. Brashear noticed that by 1853 Clemens already knew Paine's famous opening words, "These are the times that try men's souls" (*MTSM,* p. 162). Brashear was quoting from Clemens's excitedly patriotic letter to Orion and Henry Clemens written from Philadelphia, in which he referred to "the days that tried men's souls" (*MTLet* 1: 23).

———. *Common Sense* (pamphlet, published in January 1776).

Wesley Britton—"Tom Paine and Mark Twain: 'Common Sense' as a Source for 'The War Prayer,'" *CCTE Studies* 54 (September 1989): 13–19—summarized the evidence of Twain's interest in Thomas Paine and argued that the Bible and "the writings of Thomas Paine, in particular his pamphlet 'Common Sense,' are plausible origins for the classic, posthumously published political statement that Twain wrote in February or March of 1905."

Harold K. Bush, Jr. "'Transfigured by Oratory': Thomas Paine, Robert Ingersoll, Mark Twain, and the Roots of American Civil Religion," *Mark Twain Annual* 7 (2009): 78–96.

PALEY, WILLIAM (1743–1805). *A View of the Evidences of Christianity* (published in 1794 in London).

In 1878, probably in Venice, Clemens wrote: "Hume's Essay on Miracles, and Paley's Evidences of Christianity" (NB 17, *N&J* 2: 219). Under his heading for 13 March 1903 in Notebook 46, Clemens quipped: "Paley discovered that the watch was not made by accident but design, & it immortalized him. Bk named for him" (TS p. 12).

PALFREY, SARAH HAMMOND (1823–1914), pseud. E. Foxton. *Herman; or, Young Knighthood*. 2 vols., Boston: Lee and Shepard, 1866.

    Inscription: "Chas. Langdon". Charles Jervis Langdon (1849–1916) became Clemens's brother-in-law in 1870.

    Catalog: Ball 2016 inventory, 2 vols., brown textured cloth, embossed lettering, J. Langdon Family Library bookplates #127 and #128.

    Location: Quarry Farm library shelves, under the

supervision of the Mark Twain Archive, Elmira College, Elmira, New York.

Despite its misleading title, this novel was set in the United States and advocated the abolition of slavery. The poet and novelist Palfrey was the daughter of a noted Unitarian clergyman in Massachusetts. The author explained in her Preface, dated 1865 in Boston, that she wrote the novel in 1857 and 1858, several years before "traitors" struck against the Union (p. 3). The volumes would have been available to Clemens whenever he visited the Langdons' home during his many stays in Elmira.

PALGRAVE, (SIR) FRANCIS (1788–1861). *Handbook for Travellers in Northern Italy.* Fourth edition. London: John Murray, 1852.

Explanatory notes that Leon Dickinson once prepared for a projected edition of *The Innocents Abroad* demonstrated how Mark Twain relied on Palgrave's guidebook for Chapters 27 and 28 of *The Innocents Abroad* (1869) (MTP).

PALGRAVE, FRANCIS TURNER (1824–1897), comp. *The Golden Treasury of the Best Songs and Lyrical Poems in the English Language.* Revised and enlarged edition. 12mo, contemporary olive green polished calf, raised bands, gilt. London: Macmillan and Co., 1894. 381 pp.

Inscriptions: the front free endpaper is inscribed in black ink: "Clara Clemens/from/Carlyle Smythe/London/17: VIII: 96". Clara Clemens wrote a date in pencil on the rear flyleaf: "Sept. 2nd '97." Smythe (1865–1925) had been Mark Twain's lecture manager during a large portion of his recent global tour.

Marginalia: numerous markings by Clemens in pencil on thirty pages throughout (though Clara Clemens may have made a few of these): 6, 24–25, 34–35, 38, 40, 42–43, 54, 55, 172, 217, 220, 229, 231–233, 255, 262, 305, 327–329, 331, 333–334, 339–340. Stanzas in the following poems contain pencil markings (usually brackets) that appear to be in Clemens's hand: Shakespeare's "A Madrigal," "Memory," "Revolutions," "Blow, blow, thou winter wind," and several sonnets; Thomas Moore's "Echoes"; Byron's "To a Distant Friend"; Keats' "The Terror of Death" (p. 229), with its final couplet, "Of the wide world I stand alone, and think/Till Love and Fame to nothingness do sink"; Shelley's "One word is too often profaned" (p. 233); and Byron's "Elegy" (p. 262). The first stanza of Byron's "Elegy on Thyrza" (pp. 231–233)—"And thou art dead, as young and fair/As aught of mortal birth;/And forms so soft and charms so rare/Too soon return'd to Earth!"—was marked. The following lines received heavy double brackets: "To gaze, how fondly! on thy face,/To fold thee in a faint embrace,/Uphold thy drooping head;/And show that love, however vain,/Nor thou nor I can feel again"; the pronoun "I" there is underscored. Several other poems are lightly marked in pencil. Most of the markings occur beside passages about the implacability of death, and it seems relevant that Susy Clemens had died of spinal meningitis on 18 August 1896, only one day after Clara Clemens was made a present of this volume. Clara and her mother had already sailed for America on 15 August after getting the news of Susy's serious illness, so Smythe undoubtedly gave this book to Clemens to pass along to Clara. However, Clara would not return from the United States until 9 September 1896 and until then Clemens could have read and marked *The*

Golden Treasury of the Best Songs and Lyrical Poems while he was in England grieving, house-hunting, and playing billiards until his family rejoined him three weeks later.

Provenance: Contains the shelfmark from Clara Clemens Gabrilowitsch's private library collection when she resided in Detroit. Subsequently in the Carrie Estelle Doheny Collection, St. John's Seminary, Camarillo, California. Mrs. Doheny had purchased the volume from Maxwell Hunley Rare Books in 1940 for $12.20. Auctioned by Christie's in New York City on 17 October 1988 (lot 1185) with one other title for a combined $1,320 on behalf of St. John's Seminary. Acquired at that time or later by Nick Karanovich of Fort Wayne, Indiana; see Karanovich's "Sixty Books from Mark Twain's Library," *Mark Twain Journal* 25.2 (Fall 1987): 16.

Catalog: *Sotheby's 2003*, #193, $3,000 (sold with four other titles from the Clemens family's library).

Location: collection of Kevin Mac Donnell, Austin, Texas.

Copy examined: Clara Clemens's copy, apparently annotated by Clemens. Viewed in July 2004. Has the bookplate of "Estelle Doheny." The volume contains no sale labels.

Despite the reference to "Songs" in its title, *The Golden Treasury of the Best Songs and Lyrical Poems in the English Language* is a poetry collection.

———, comp. *The Golden Treasury, Selected from the Best Songs and Lyrical Poems.* Second series. London: Macmillan and Co., 1898. 275 pp.

Source: MTLAcc, entry #2081, volume donated from Clemens's library by Clara Clemens Gabrilowitsch in 1910.

———, comp. *The Treasury of Sacred Song, Selected from the English Lyrical Poetry of Four Centuries.* Oxford: Clarendon Press, 1890. 374 pp.

Source: MTLAcc, entry #2080, volume donated from Clemens's library by Clara Clemens Gabrilowitsch in 1910.

Although the lyrics of Isaac Watts and other hymn-writers are collected here, Palgrave provides no musical melodies. *The Treasury of Sacred Song* is thus a collection of Christian poetry and hymn lyrics.

Pall Mall Gazette (London newspaper).

Responding to an article in the *Pall Mall Gazette*—"Mark Twain as an Inventor" (18 January 1889)—Twain published a letter in the 16 February 1889 issue to explain that James W. Paige, not Twain, had invented the typesetter in which Twain had invested (*MTPP*, pp. 153–154).

PALMER, FREDERICK (1873–1958). *The Ways of the Service.* Illustrated by Howard Chandler Christy (1873–1948). New York: Charles Scribner's Sons, 1904. 340 pp.

Source: MTLAcc, entry #238, volume donated by Clemens.

Palmer was an American war correspondent who, though having gained a reputation for his daring, steadfastly refused to glorify the various military conflicts he covered.

PALMER, JOHN (1742–1818). *Journal of Travels in the United States of North America, and in Lower Canada, Performed in the Year 1817.* Map. London: Sherwood, Neely, and Jones, 1818. 456 pp. [Publisher and pages conjectured.]

Inscription: "To Samuel L. Clemens, Esqr—A trifling recognition of the many happy hours his writings have marked. Ch. P. Green, Malvern, England, Novr. 29, 1886."

Catalog: *A1911*, "8vo, original boards (good portion of back missing), uncut, Lond. 1818," quotes the inscription, lot

374, sold for $4.

Charles P. Green sent a letter to Clemens with this book on 29 November 1886 (American Art Association-Anderson Galleries Catalogue, UCLC 43112), and Clemens thanked him on 26 December 1886 (MS: MT-H, UCCL 3503). Twain had quoted and cited early-day British travelers in *Life on the Mississippi* (1883), so his interest in these journals was well known.

PALMER, JOHN WILLIAMSON (1825–1906), ed. *Folk Songs.* New edition, revised and enlarged. Illus. Original full brown morocco, heavily decorated, gilt, raised bands, inner dentilles gilt, marbled endpapers, all edges gilt. New York: Charles Scribner and Co., 1867. 596 pp.

Inscription: the front flyleaf is inscribed by Clemens's brother-in-law: "A Merry Christmas to/My dear Ida/1872/CJL." Charles Jervis Langdon (1849–1916) gave this gift to his wife Ida B. (Clark) Langdon (1849–1934), whom he had married in 1870.

Location: collection of Kevin Mac Donnell, Austin, Texas. Purchased from the Langdon family.

Source: a supplementary description sent to Alan Gribben by Mac Donnell on 28 August 2017. A silk page marker is laid in the volume.

The title of this book is misleading; it is an immense collection of lyrics primarily by eminent British poets such as Keats and Tennyson from the English Renaissance to the 1860s. Longfellow, Holmes, Poe, and a few other American poets are also included. Clemens might have seen this parlor table volume when he visited the Langdons in Elmira.

PALMER, RAY (1808–1887). "My faith looks up to Thee" (hymn, published in 1830). Lyrics written by Palmer; melody composed by Lowell Mason (1792–1872).

Clemens wrote the title of this hymn, which begins, "My faith looks up to Thee, thou Lamb of Calvary," in a copy of *Laudes Domini: A Selection of Spiritual Songs, Ancient and Modern*, compiled by C. S. Robinson. See that Catalog entry.

The Papyrus: A Magazine of Individuality. Edited by Michael Monahan (1865–1933). Mount Vernon, New York (published 1903–1912).

In a letter written to Michael Monahan on 28 January 1905, Mark Twain referred approvingly to Monahan's article on "Saint Mark" that appeared in the issue of December 1904. Monahan had discussed Twain's devotion to Joan of Arc. *The Society of the Papyrites* published Twain's letter in its March 1905 (4: 3) issue. See also the Catalog entry for Michael Monahan.

PARDON, GEORGE FREDERICK (1824–1884). *Routledge's Guide to London and Its Suburbs: Comprising Descriptions of All Its Points of Interest.* New edition, revised and improved. London: George Routledge and Sons, 1866. 206 pp.

Marginalia: profuse notations by Clemens in pencil. On page 109, writing vertically in the margin, Clemens characterized James I as "England's most commonplace King." Across the text of that same page Clemens reminded himself: "Get Pepys." Pardon's volume contains an index, but Clemens made another one, consisting of landmarks and events and the pages where they are described, on the recto and verso of the rear free endpaper and on the

rear pastedown endpaper.

Catalog: ListABP (1910), "Guide to London", no other information supplied; "Retz Appraisal" (1944), p. 11, valued at $15.

Location: Mark Twain Papers, Bancroft Library, University of California at Berkeley.

Copy examined: Clemens's copy. Cover and map are now loose.

PARIS, LOUIS-PHILIPPE-ALBERT D'ORLÉANS, COMTE DE (1838–1894). *History of the Civil War in America.* Ed. by Henry Coppée (1821–1895) and John Page Nicholson (1842–1922). Translated from the French by Louis Fitzgerald Tasistro (1808–1886). Maps. 4 vols. Philadelphia: Porter & Coates, 1875–1888. [Volume I appeared in 1875; Volume II was published in 1876.]

Inscriptions: Volumes I and II signed "S. L. Clemens, Hartford, 1877."

Catalogs: *A1911*, "2 vols., title page of vol. 2 loose and a leaf damaged, Phila. 1876," quotes the signatures, lot 375, sold for $3.25.

Paris served as captain of volunteers on General George B. McClellan's staff. *Histoire de la Guerre Civile en Amérique* appeared first in France.

PARKER, ARTHUR (1858–1935). *A Hand-Book of Benares, by the Rev. Arthur Parker, London Missionary Society.* Map. Benares: E. J. Lazarus and Co., 1895. 89 pp.

Catalog: ListABP (1910), "Hand-Book of Benares, Patton [*sic*], no other information supplied.

Mark Twain refers to the "Rev. Mr. Parker's compact and lucid Guide to Benares" in Chapter 50 of *Following the Equator* (1897); a page farther on he comments sarcastically on Parker's "hope and confidence" about the prospects for Christianizing the Hindus of Benares, and then he quotes "Mr. Parker's touching picture" of Hindu devotion to Benares as a holy place. "I got some of the facts [about religious rites] from conversations with the Rev. Mr. Parker and the others from his Guide to Benares; they are therefore trustworthy," Twain writes in Chapter 51. "Mr. Parker said that [Indian] widows would burn themselves now if the government would allow it," he reports in Chapter 52. One of the living gods of Hinduism "would receive Rev. Mr. Parker at any time. I think he is sorry for Mr. Parker, and I think Mr. Parker is sorry for him; and no doubt this compassion is good for both of them."

Coleman O. Parsons, "Mark Twain: Sightseer in India," *Mississippi Quarterly* 16.2 (Spring 1963): 76–93. In a detailed day-by-day calendar of Twain's activities during his 1895–1896 visit to India, on page 84 Parsons mentioned Parker's book as an example of Twain's reading. See also Susan K. Harris, "My Life with Mark Twain: Chapter One—Hinduism," *Mark Twain Annual 15* (2017): 1–21.

PARKER, (REVEREND) EDWIN POND (1836–1920). [Unidentified work.]

"I have read it all & enjoyed it all, & I will go bail that Hawthorne's account is less beautiful than yours—it *must* be so; both cannot be perfect. Mrs. Clemens is reading it now, & we both thank you for sending it" (SLC to Parker, 14 October 1903, ALS in ASSSCL). It seems probable that a sketch by Parker, the minister of the Second Congregational Church of Christ in Hartford, had described Venice. Nathaniel Hawthorne's *The French and Italian Notebooks* (1858–1859) served as a sourcebook for his romance *The Marble Faun* (1860). The Clemenses were preparing to leave for Italy in hopes of improving Olivia's health.

PARKER, (SIR) GILBERT (1862–1932). *A Ladder of Swords; A Tale of Love, Laughter and Tears.* Illus. New York: Harper & Brothers, 1905. 291 pp.

> **Source:** MTLAcc, entry #1422, volume donated by Clemens.

> Clemens was introduced to Winston Churchill on 26 March 1900 at the home of Parker, a Canadian-born novelist (including *The Lane That Had No Turning* [1900]) and dramatist as well as a member of Parliament (NB 43, TS p. 6; 17 August 1907 Autobiographical Dictation, *AutoMT* 3: 102). In 1905 Clemens wrote: "Sir Gilbert Parker, M. P./Trevelyan" (NB 48, TS p. 1). Clemens dined at Parker's home again in 1907 (17 August 1907 AD, MTP; *AutoMT* 3: 101). *A Ladder of Swords*, set in the Elizabethan era, told the story of some Huguenots who fled France to England.

———. *Northern Lights.* Illus. New York: Harper & Brothers, 1909. 352 pp.

> **Source:** MTLAcc, entry #1436, volume donated by Clemens. The book was subsequently lost while in circulation.

> Parker set these seventeen short stories in the Canadian provinces of Alberta and Saskatchewan. In 1909 Clemens presented Parker with a photographic portrait of Clemens wearing his signature white suit and smoking a cigar, inscribing it in black ink, "To/Sir Gilbert Parker/with the love of/Mark Twain/April/09." (*Sotheby's 2003*, #133).

PARKER, JANE (MARSH) (1836–1913), pseud. "Jenny Marsh Parker." "Archie Dean" (poem) and "What I Did, Gail Hamilton" (poem).

> Around 1863 Olivia Langdon copied these lightweight pieces near the front of her commonplace book (DV161, MTP).

PARKER, THEODORE (1810–1860).

> In 1869 or 1870 Olivia Langdon copied several quotations attributed to Parker, an American Unitarian minister, into her commonplace book (DV161, MTP).

PARKHURST & WILKINSON (undated advertising flier).

> **Inscription:** signed in ink on the upper right-hand corner, "S. L. Clemens/(Mark Twain). The signature is crudely executed and highly uncharacteristic of Clemens in every respect. Another signature, that of "Eugene Field.", appears in the center of the flier at the top.

> **Provenance:** offered for sale to Kevin Mac Donnell in June 1998.

> **Source:** photocopies of the recto and verso of the flier sent to Alan Gribben by Kevin Mac Donnell of Austin, Texas on 18 August 2005. The Clemens/Twain autograph is obviously spurious.

PARKIN, (SIR) GEORGE ROBERT (1846–1922). *Round the Empire; for the Use of Schools.* Preface by the Earl of Rosebery [Archibald Philip Primrose (1847–1929), Fifth Earl of Rosebery]. Illus. London: Cassell and Co., 1893. 263 pp.

> **Source:** MTLAcc, entry #569b, a mutilated copy donated by Clemens.

> In Chapter 19 of *Following the Equator* (1897), Mark Twain cites Parkin's book as his source for figures about

telegraph wires.

> Pochmann, "Mind of MT" (1924), p. 184; Madigan, "MT's Passage to India" (1974), p. 363.

PARKMAN, FRANCIS (1823–1893). *The Conspiracy of Pontiac and the Indian War After the Conquest of Canada.* Maps. 2 vols. Ninth edition, rev. Stamped green cloth, brown endpapers. Boston: Little, Brown, and Co., 1880.

> **Marginalia:** Clemens made marginal notes and marked passages.

> **Catalog:** *A1911*, "2 vols., 12mo, cloth, Bost. 1880, . . . two vols. . . . with numerous marked paragraphs and marginal notes," lot 376, sold with two other vols., $22.50 total.

> **Location:** Mark Twain Papers, Bancroft Library, University of California at Berkeley. Acquired in November 2016. Has the *A1911* sale label.

> Mark Twain met Parkman at the *Atlantic Monthly's* Seventieth Birthday breakfast for Oliver Wendell Holmes on 3 December 1879; this was the occasion at which Twain made a brief, clever speech about how easily one falls into unconscious plagiarism (Fatout, *MTSpk*, p. 134). Twain's remarks were well received, but in December 1897 Twain guiltily recollected the "Breakfast to Holmes, when I made 3 blunders—the last with a man I worshiped—Francis Parkman" (NB 42, TS p. 50). *What* faux pas in his conversation with Parkman could have been so egregious that Twain was still haunted by it twenty years later? On 20 January 1887 Clemens named Parkman's histories among the literary favorites he listed in a letter to the Reverend Charles D. Crane (ALS, Shapell Manuscript Library, Beverly Hills, California).

———. *Count Frontenac and New France Under Louis XIV.* Boston: Little, Brown & Co., 1877. 463 pp. [Publisher and pages conjectured.]

> **Inscription:** signed by Clemens in light blue ink: "SL Clemens/Hartford 1881."

> **Marginalia:** numerous markings and notes. Five pages contain notations totaling fifty-five words. Fifteen other pages contain markings. Of the Catholic rule in Canada, Clemens says: "It was as degraded and iron clad a slavery as the early Puritanism." In another context he wrote: "Here is French villainy to offset the French heroism of the missionaries."

> **Catalog:** *A1911*, "12mo, cloth, Bost. 1880, . . two vols. . . . with numerous marked paragraphs and marginal notes," quotes two examples of Clemens's marginalia, lot 376, sold with three other vols., $22.50 total.

> **Location:** Mark Twain Papers, Bancroft Library, University of California at Berkeley. Acquired in November 2016.

> Clemens referred to this volume in a canceled part of the postscript to his letter of 28 November 1881 to Olivia (ALS in MTP). See the Catalog entry for Parkman's *The Old Régime in Canada*.

———. *The Jesuits in North America in the Seventeenth Century.* Fifteenth edition. Boston: Little, Brown, and Co., 1880. 463 pp.

> **Inscription:** "S. L. Clemens/Hartford, 1881."

> **Marginalia:** annotated throughout in blue ink, black pencil, and purple pencil. "What manner of men *were* these?" he wrote on page 256. Elsewhere he remarked: "That men should be willing to leave happy homes & endure what the missionaries endured, in order to teach the Indians the

road to hell, would be rational, understandable; but why they should want to teach them the way to heaven is a thing which the mind cannot somehow grasp" (*MTB*, p. 1538).

Catalog: *C1951*, #29a, listed among volumes containing marginalia, $35.

Location: Mark Twain Papers, Bancroft Library, University of California at Berkeley.

Copy examined: Clemens's copy.

"You must read about the early Jesuit missionaries in Canada," Clemens urged Olivia from Montreal on 29 November 1881. "Talk about self-abnegation! heroism! fidelity to a cause! It was sublime, it was stupendous. Why what these men did & suffered, in trying to rescue the insulting & atrocious savages from the doom of hell, makes one adore & glorify human nature as exemplified in those priests—yes, & despise it at the very same time. In endurance & performance they were gods; in credulity, & in obedience to their ecclesiastical chiefs, they were swine" (*LLMT*, p. 206). About this same time, Clemens tried rather half-heartedly to construct a humorous sketch that would contrast modern-day irritations and mock-heroics against the martyred agony and death of Father Brébeuf at the hands of his Native American captors; the sketch is based on page 389 of Parkman's book (NB 19, *N&J* 2: 411). In "What Is Man?" (1906), the Old Man argues: "Many a missionary, sternly fortified by his sense of duty, would not have been troubled by the pagan mother's distress—Jesuit missionaries in Canada in the early French times, for instance; see episodes quoted by Parkman" (*WIM?*, p 146). Albert Bigelow Paine categorized *The Jesuits in North America in the Seventeenth Century* as one of the books that Clemens "read periodically" (*MTB*, p. 1538).

Williams, "Genesis" (1961), p. 105.

———. *La Salle and the Discovery of the Great West*. Boston: Little, Brown, and Co., 1879. 483 pp. First published as *The Discovery of the Great West* (1869).

Twice in Notebook 20 (1882) Mark Twain resolved to consult this book: "Get. . . . something about La Salle's trip out of Parkman"; "Get La Salle's discovery of Mississippi" (*N&J* 2: 472, 482). In the same notebook he also made a memorandum to send Parkman a copy of *Life on the Mississippi* (1883) when it issued (p. 514). Chapter 2 of *Life on the Mississippi* explicitly cites Parkman's "fascinating narrative" about the explorations of La Salle, Joliet, and Marquette as Twain's source of information. In Chapter 27 of *Life on the Mississippi* Twain concludes a set of quotations from early travelers with Parkman's version of La Salle's descent down the Mississippi and his claiming, in 1682, the river and its regions for the King of France. Kenneth M. Sanderson, then an editorial associate at the Mark Twain Project at the University of California at Berkeley, shared with me his research indicating that Mark Twain employed the revised version of 1879 (*La Salle*) rather than the first edition of 1869 (titled *Discovery*); out of ten variants, Twain's text agreed with the 1879 edition in eight instances.

Krause, *MTC* (1967), p. 163 n. 17; Barbara Ladd, "'Night after Night and Day after Day': Mark Twain and the Natural World," *Mark Twain Annual 17* (2019): 19.

———. *Montcalm and Wolfe*. 2 vols. France and England in North America Series. Sixth edition. Green cloth. Boston: Little, Brown, and Co., 1885.

Inscriptions: the front free flyleaves of both volumes were inscribed identically by Olivia Clemens in black ink: "Saml. L. Clemens/Hartford/Conn./Nov. 30th 1885". That was the date of Clemens's fiftieth birthday.

Marginalia: there is a long vertical pencil mark typical of Clemens in Volume I beside an account of the lenient treatment of Acadians by the English (p. 96).

Location: Mark Twain Library, Redding, Connecticut.

Copy examined: Clemens's copy. Volume I (514 pp.) has a penciled Mark Twain Library accession number, "3804". Volume II has a penciled accession number that is reversed—"3840". (Should it be mentioned that Volume II has a distinct odor of cigar smoke?) Examined in 1970 and again in June 1982.

———. *The Old Régime in Canada*. Ninth edition. Boston: Little, Brown and Co., 1880. 448 pp.

Inscription: the front free endpaper is signed in ink, "S. L. Clemens/Hartford, 1881." At the top of the title page Clemens wrote in black ink: "Very interesting. Tells how people, religiously & otherwise insane, came over from France & colonized Canada. January, 1908" (corrected from Albert Bigelow Paine's version quoted in *MTB* [1912], p. 1538).

Marginalia: Sixteen pages contain ink notes or markings by Clemens. All of these seem to be in a very late hand. Clemens made double vertical marks on page 5 beside Parkman's statement that "if the Iroquois have their hidden designs, so, too, has God." On page 51 he drew another set of vertical marks next to an account of a runaway girl who "immured herself in a convent." Writing vertically in the margin, Clemens made an observation on that same page: "The Adult Jesus, & the Infant Jesus, were both alive at the same time, according to these pleasant liars." In the margin of page 55 he wrote vertically: "So did the Immaculate Conception in our own superior day." (This latter note referred to a voice that admonished the Iroquois for killing an innocent French colonist, a story that "found believers among the most intelligent men of the colony.") Regarding the brave Major Closse, who welcomed his death from the Iroquois, Clemens wrote vertically on page 58: "Of all the millions of Gods that have lived & died, I have never heard of one that possessed any dignity. Without any doubt this one was proud to have the 'service' of this bacillus." A similar remark came from Clemens's pen on page 64: "Some more of His 'service.'" And on page 67: "How curiously trivial a Deity it is!" Also on page 104: "Insanity is a sufficient excuse for being pious." On page 166, where Parkman explains, by quoting a sermon preached at Montreal, the importance to the Jesuit faithful that the state must submit to the policies of the Pope and the church: "The damned scoundrel!" Clemens's ejaculation on page 178 was a familiar sentiment expressed in his final decade: "What a trivial invention is the human race!" Another withering opinion of humankind appears on page 180, vertically: "It seems to be established that God prefers a Christian to a monkey, but probably not even He knows why." (This comment was elicited by Parkman's account of the missionaries' efforts to convert the Huguenots.) Where

Parkman describes the campaign "against the Iroquois, enemies of God and tools of the devil" as being perceived as "a holy war, all for the glory of God," Clemens scoffed: "All concerned, all mentioned, have died, rotted, stunk & long ago disappeared & become wandering gases—what went with the glory?" A similar note was begun but not finished on page 196. Parkman recounts the fate of Prae-textata, whose hands withered before she "died suddenly five months after, and was precipitated into hell," merely because she dressed her niece in "a worldly fashion": Clemens was moved to leave a sarcastic marginal note: "Rather a mild punishment for so serious an offense. But God is always just so soft-hearted thataway." On page 198 he wrote "pathetic"; on page 358, "This is just too sweet" next to the story of a religious recluse who abandoned her family; and on page 363, concerning Saint Joachim of Floris, an Italian mystic, "This is evidently the grandfather. I never heard of him before."

Catalog: *C1951*, #52a, listed among volumes containing marginalia, $35.

Location: Gloria Grace Griffen Western Americana Collection, Special Collections, Library, University of Nevada at Reno.

Copy examined: photocopies of Clemens's inscriptions and marginalia supplied to the Bancroft Library on 22 December 1981 by Robert E. Blesse, then Head, Special Collections, Library, University of Nevada at Reno (MTP).

On 28 November 1881 Clemens added a postscript to a letter written to Olivia from Montreal: "On the piano, (I think) you will find Parkman's 'The Old Regime' <or 'New France Under Louis XIV'—can't remember the title, exactly, but I think it is a *double* title & am quite sure that at least the words '*under Louis XIV*' form *part* of it.>. Well, won't you direct it to this hotel & send Patrick immediately to the post-office with it? I brought away 3 volumes of Parkman, but by day after to-morrow I shall have finished them. These three begin with 1498 & sketch French, Spanish, <&> English & Dutch occupation in America down to 1701—fourteen years before Louis XIV's death. I *suppose* the 'Old Regime' treats of Canada under Louis XV" (ALS in MTP; postscript omitted from Paine's *MTL*, p. 407, where the body of the letter is published). In 1877 Parkman had published *Count Frontenac and New France Under Louis XIV*. Albert Bigelow Paine reported: "Francis Parkman's *Canadian Histories* [*sic*] he had read periodically, especially the story of the *Old Régime* and of the *Jesuits in North America*" (*MTB*, p. 1538).

———. *The Oregon Trail: Sketches of Prairie and Rocky-Mountain Life*. Boston: Little, Brown, and Co., 1880. [Publisher conjectured.]

Inscription: signed in pencil "SL Clemens/Hartford".

Marginalia: notations by Clemens total seventy-one words on twenty-two pages. Twenty-nine pages contain only markings. Corners are turned down at pages 107, 137, and 232. Four bookmarks are laid in.

Catalog: *A1911*, "12mo, cloth, Bost. 1880," lot 376, sold with three other vols., $22.50 total.

Location: Mark Twain Papers, Bancroft Library, University of California at Berkeley. Acquired in November 2016.

Walter Blair noted that in "Huck Finn and Tom Sawyer among the Indians" (written in 1884) "the names of two characters mentioned in Twain's narrative come from Parkman's book—old Vaskiss, the trader, and Roubidou, the blacksmith of Fort Laramie" (*HH&T*, p. 85). When young Dorothy Quick (1896–1962) expressed a desire to become a writer, Isabel V. Lyon recorded the fact that Clemens suggested several pen names for her to adopt, including "Oregon Trail" (*AutoMT* 3: 523).

Smith, *MTDW* (1962), p. 53.

———. *Pioneers of France in the New World*. Boston: Little, Brown, and Co., 1865. The eleventh edition was published in 1874. 427 pp. [Clemens's edition has not been unidentified.]

Clemens made a series of four notes about this work in November 1881, en route by rail to Montreal (NB 19, *N&J* 2: 404–406). One notebook entry mentions his reading the book on a smoking car "somewhere out of Concord"; another records that when Clemens got off the train at a stop, the overcast sky and snow "helped me realize the times of Champlain & others in Canada." Upon arriving in Montreal, Clemens informed Olivia on 28 November 1881: "I brought away 3 volumes of Parkman, but by day after to-morrow I shall have finished them. These three begin with 1498 & sketch French, Spanish, <&> English & Dutch occupation in America down to 1701" (ALS in MTP).

———. "Some of the Reasons Against Woman Suffrage" (essay, first published between 1878 and 1880 and thereafter reprinted by various organizations).

In 1880 Mark Twain copied into Notebook 19 (*N&J* 2: 359) two sentences from Francis Parkman. He employed these quotations in a talk delivered on 5 April 1880 at the Hartford Monday Evening Club, "On the Decay of the Art of Lying," which he later published in *The Stolen White Elephant* (1882): "Parkman, the historian, says, 'The principle of truth may itself be carried into an absurdity." Twain went on in that chapter to quote another sentence from the same Parkman essay: "'The saying is old that truth should not be spoken at all times; and those whom a sick conscience worries into habitual violation of the maxim are imbeciles and nuisances.' It is strong language, but true." Twain did not supply his specific source, probably because of its polemical nature. Between 1878 and 1880 Francis Parkman had carried on a vigorous campaign against the concept of women's suffrage in a series of three articles in the *North American Review*. Julia Ward Howe wrote a spirited retort to his second piece. At some point during this period Parkman released a more strongly worded essay than his *North American Review* pieces, "Some of the Reasons Against Woman Suffrage," that contained the nearly verbatim sentences Twain extracted in his notebook and utilized in his speech and his story. Parkman's argument would be reprinted by several organizations over the ensuing decades. The context of Parkman's statements that Twain copied is worth examining: "Rights may be real or unreal. Principles may be true or false; but even the best and truest cannot safely be pushed too far, or in the wrong direction. The principle of truth itself may be carried into absurdity. The saying is old that truth should not be spoken at all times; and those whom a sick conscience worries into habitual violation of the maxim are imbeciles and nuisances. Religion may pass into morbid enthusiasm or wild fanaticism, and turn from a blessing to a curse. So the best of political principles must be kept without bounds of reason, or they will work mischief." This basic topic of truthfulness versus lying, of course, held an endless fascination for Twain.

———. *Works* (unidentified edition).

    Catalog: ListABP (1910), "Parkman's Works" listed twice, no other information provided.

    Miki Pfeffer, an authority on Grace King's life, informed me that King "sent a set of Parkman's Histories as a thank you for hospitality. She read them, and I think Livy was trying to make her way through them" (Pfeffer to Alan Gribben, email, 10 July 2019).

Parley's Magazine (Boston, later moved to New York City, children's periodical, published 1833–1844).

    Samuel Griswold Goodrich (1793–1860), whose pen name was "Peter Parley," founded *Parley's Magazine*, but William Alcott soon took over the editorship in 1834. Goodrich himself contributed very few pieces to the magazine. The circulation was never large; its borderline success resulted from its numerous engraved drawings. (Periodicals struggled in the United States until postal distribution improved and the transcontinental railroad opened up vast new territories.) In 1844 *Parley's* merged with *Robert Merry's Museum for Boys and Girls.* During Clemens's childhood, his father "subscribed for *Peter Parley's Magazine,* a marvel of delight to the older children" in his family, Albert Bigelow Paine reported in 1912 (*MTB*, p. 14). See the Catalog entry for S. G. Goodrich.

    Stone, *IE* (1961), p. 18.

PARR, HARRIET (1828–1900). *The Life and Death of Jeanne d'Arc, Called the Maid*. 2 vols. London: Smith, Elder & Co., 1866.

    Parr's work ("Life and Death of Joan of Arc. S. & E. 6/—") was among six books listed for Clemens's consultation in 1892; the note is not in Clemens's hand, and probably was prepared for him by Chatto & Windus of London (MS notes formerly in the collection of Barry Bingham, Sr., Louisville, Kentucky; PH in Box 36, No. 6, MTP).

    Welland, *Mark Twain in England* (1978), p. 158.

PARSONS, ALBERT ROSS (1847–1933). *Parsifal; The Finding of Christ Through Art: A Wagner Study*. New York: The Metaphysical Publishing Co., 1893. 113 pp.

    Inscription: "Susan L. Crane/Quarry Farm 1893".

    Catalog: Ball 2016 inventory, blue cloth, gilt lettering and design, good condition.

    Parsons viewed Richard Wagner (1813–1883) partly as a theologian, leading audiences to Christian interpretations. Clemens had access to the Quarry Farm library.

PARSONS, ALFRED (1847–1920). *Notes in Japan*. Illustrated by the author. New York: Harper & Brothers, 1896. 223 pp.

    Source: MTLAcc, entry #1738, volume donated by Clemens.

    This, the only book that the English artist Parsons published, resulted from his visit to Japan between 1892 and 1894.

PARSONS, FRANK (1854–1908), **FRED ERASTUS CRAWFORD** (1857–1950), and **H. T. RICHARDSON**. *The World's Best Books: A Key to the Treasures of Literature*. Boston: Little, Brown and Co., 1889. 134 pp.

    Source: MTLAcc, entry #853, volume donated by Clemens.

PARTON, JAMES (1822–1891). *The Life and Times of Aaron Burr*. Enlarged edition. Portraits. 2 vols. Boston: Houghton,

Mifflin and Co., 1886. [Publisher conjectured.]

    Inscriptions: the flyleaves of both volumes are signed "S. L. Clemens, 1886."

    Catalogs: *A1911*, "2 vols., 8vo, cloth, gilt tops, Bost. 1886," quotes the signatures, lot 377, sold for $7; George D. Smith, New York City, "Catalogue of Books" (1911), quotes the signatures, "2 vols.," item #47, $20.

    In January 1897 Clemens reflected: "I seem like poor old Aaaron Burr [*sic*] standing in the mists of the early morning gazing out to sea for the ship that had long ago gone down" (NB 39, TS p. 56). Writing to Joseph H. Twichell from Ampersand [Saranac Lake], New York on 28 July 1901, Clemens joked that he named some squirrels that were congregating on the front porch "Blennerhasset [*sic*], from Burr's friend" (*MTL*, p. 711). He was referring to Harman Blennerhassett (1765–1831), Burr's tragic co-conspirator in a doomed military attempt to establish an empire. Clemens also mentioned Burr ironically in Notebook 45 (14 October 1902), TS p. 31.

———. *Life of Voltaire*. Portrait. 2 vols. Boston: Houghton, Mifflin and Co., 1881. [Publisher conjectured.]

    Inscriptions: both volumes are signed "S. L. Clemens."

    Marginalia: numerous markings and marginal notes. One notation reads: "Sara[h] Bernhardt has peculiar reason to be fond of playing the part of Adrienne Lecouvreur."

    Catalog: *A 1911*, "2 vols., 8vo, cloth, gilt tops, Bost. 1881, . . . numerous marked paragraphs and marginal notes in Clemens' handwriting," quotes the signatures and one example of the marginalia, lot 469, sold for $9.

    Williams, "Genesis" (1961), p. 105.

PARTON, SARAH PAYSON (WILLIS) (1811–1872). *Little Ferns for Fanny's Little Friends, by the Author of "Fern Leaves."* [First published in 1853, with numerous editions following. The Clemenses's edition has not been identified.]

    Catalog: ListABP (1910), "Little Ferns", no other information supplied.

Pastels in Prose. From the French. Edited and translated by Stuart Merrill (1863–1915). Illustrated by H[arry]. W[hitney]. McVickar (1860–1905). Introduction by William Dean Howells (1937–1920). New York: Harper & Brothers, [1890].

    Provenance: has the shelfmarks of the library numbering system employed by Clara Clemens Gabrilowitsch during her Detroit years. Sold at the 1951 auction in Hollywood but not listed in the hastily compiled sale sheet.

    Catalog: "Property from the Library of Mark Twain," Butterfield & Butterfield, San Francisco, Sale 6613 (16 July 1997), lot 2712.

    Location: Mark Twain House and Museum, Hartford, Connecticut.

    Copy examined: Clemens's unmarked copy. Viewed in Hartford in 1997.

    In his Introduction to the volume, William Dean Howells praised the literary form "known as a Prose Poem." The editor and translator, Stuart Merrill, presented selections from Baudelaire, Mallarmé, and nearly twenty other French authors.

The Paston Letters, 1422–1509 A. D. A New Edition. Ed. by James Gairdner (1828–1912). 3 vols. Westminster: A. Constable, 1896. [Edition conjectured.]

    Fifteenth-century English correspondence involving the Paston family and their neighbor, Sir John Fastolf, became known as *The Paston Letters*. Clemens discovered that the amount he was charged for using the London Library late in October 1896 was "just the rent of an unfurnished house suitable for a family of 4 persons & 5 servants in Henry IVs time, according to the Paston letters" (NB 39, TS p. 12). Shortly thereafter, also in Chelsea, Clemens copied a quotation into Notebook 39: "1477. I, John Paston, Knyght, will, graunt & bequeth my sowle to All Myghty God, & to the holy Marye, Seint John Baptist, Seint Gorge, Seint Cristofer & Seint Barbara" (TS p. 16). In the preface to "The Ashcroft-Lyon Manuscript" of 1909 Clemens referred to "the Paston Letters . . . of four & a quarter centuries ago" and wished that they had been "free-spoken" enough to reveal "domestic life in England in that old day" (*AutoMT* 3: 329).

PATERSON, ANDREW BARTON (1864–1941). *The Man from Snowy River and Other Verses*. First edition. 12mo, original maroon buckram, spine gilt-lettered, top edge gilt, uncut. Sydney, Australia: Angus and Robertson, 1895.

Inscription: on the day Clemens left Sydney for Ceylon he recorded the receipt of this gift copy of bush ballads in ink on its front free endpaper: "From Mr. Carruthers/to/S. L. Clemens./In memory of December/22, most pleasantly/spent at Port Hackin[g] Bay,/Sydney, N. S. W., Dec. 23, '95." The most likely presenter of this volume was Sir Joseph Hector Carruthers, who would serve as Premier of New South Wales from 1904 to 1907.

Catalogs: *A1911*, "12mo, cloth, Sydney, 1895," quotes the inscription, lot 378, sold for $1.75; Dawson's Book Shop, Catalogue number 35 (October 1924), "12mo, cloth, gilt top, uncut, Sydney, 1895, with an autograph inscription by Clemens, on the fly-leaf" (quoted), contains the *A1911* sale label, item #124, $15; *Sotheby's 2003*, #227, $1,400.

Provenance: in 1983 this volume was part of the collection of Nick Karanovich, Fort Wayne, Indiana. Offered for sale on eBay on 5 October 2007, with this explanation: "Bought from James Cummings, Bookseller [of New York City] . . . a few years ago. Purchase price was $3750. . . . First Edition. Original maroon buckram, spine a bit faded, slightly rubbed at extremities, overall a good, sound copy. . . . I am selling this copy, since I still have another Mark Twain library book I will keep for myself, and I need to pay off a guitar." The eBay description included a photograph of Clemens's inscription.

Location: collection of Kevin Mac Donnell, Austin, Texas. Acquired in October 2007 (Mac Donnell to Alan Gribben, 23 October 2007).

Copy examined: Clemens's copy, at the 2003 Sotheby's auction. Contains the *A1911* sale label. Nick Karanovich had sent Alan Gribben photocopies of the endpaper, inscription, and title page on 25 May 1983.

Australian journalist, author, and poet Andrew Barton Paterson would write the famous "Waltzing Matilda" poem (1917) which, set to music, would become immensely and enduringly popular.

PATMORE, COVENTRY KERSEY DIGHTON (1823–1896). *The Angel in the House* (published in London, 1854–1856). Book One: "The Betrothed"; Book Two: "The Espousals." [These two principal sections initially appeared in four installments.] Clemens and Olivia Langdon read and shared allusions to Patmore's poetic celebration of marriage throughout

1868 (see *MTLet* 2: 274, 310, 313–314, 343, 369). "Ladies don't usually like those books, Livy, I don't know why—because those same books praise them so much, maybe," Clemens speculated in a letter to Olivia Langdon written on 23 and 24 December 1868 (*MTLet* 2: 343). A letter from Clemens to Olivia Langdon on 13 and 14 January 1869 refers to Patmore's work as "the 'exquisite'" and "a vivid echo of my own sentiments" (*MTLet* 3: 3). On 25 December 1873 Clemens wrote to Olivia from Salisbury, England, mentioning Patmore's tribute to marriage: "To-day I attended the grand Christmas service in Salisbury Cathedral. . . . And then we drove by Old Sarum—all day I was thinking lovingly of my 'Angel in the House,'—for Old Sarum & Salisbury naturally recall Coventry Patmore's books" (*MTLet* 5: 534).

Harris, *Courtship* (1996), pp. 95–96, 99, 108; Leland Krauth, *Proper Mark Twain* (Athens: University of Georgia Press, 1999), pp. 84–85.

PATON, WILLIAM AGNEW (1848–1918). *Picturesque Sicily*. Illus. New York: Harper & Brothers, 1902. 384 pp. [Publisher and pages conjectured.]

Inscription: the front pastedown endpaper is signed "S. L. Clemens, 1903."

Marginalia: the first section is considerably underscored. On one page Clemens makes a cross reference.

Catalog: *A1911*, "8vo, cloth, gilt top, uncut, N.Y. 1902," quotes the signature and characterizes the marginalia, lot 379, sold for $4.50.

PATTERSON, THOMAS MACDONALD (1839–1916). According to Jim Zwick, Clemens received a copy of Colorado Senator Patterson's speech to the U. S. Senate on 27 March 1902 that was critical of the conduct of American military forces in the Philippines ("'Prodigally Endowed with Sympathy for the Cause': Mark Twain's Involvement with the Anti-Imperialist League," *Mark Twain Journal* 32.1 [Spring 1994]: 22 n. 29).

PATTISON, JOHN NELSON (1845–1905), arranger. "Guide me, O Thou great Jehovah" (hymn, published in 1863). Clemens noted Pattison's arrangement of this eighteenth-century hymn in Notebook 19 (1881): "Guide me, O thou Great Jehovah by J N Pattison, (Wm A Pond & Co.[)]" (*N&J* 2: 394). The lyrics were originally written in Welsh by William Williams (1717–1791) in 1745 and translated into English by Peter Williams (1722–1796) in 1771.

PATTON, EMILY SOPHIA (1831–1912). *Japanese Topsyturvydom*. Soft crepe paper wrappers and text. Illus. Tokyo: T. Hasegawa, 1896.

Catalog: *A1911*, "Japanese Colored Picture Book, 8vo, wrappers," lot 267, sold for $2. [Patton's publication appears to be the best candidate for this cryptic entry in the 1911 auction catalog.]

Kevin Mac Donnell first noticed the dedication page of this small book of twenty double-fold leaves: "Dedication/To/'Mark Twain'/In grateful acknowledgment of the amusement his/works have for many years past afforded/The Writer./Yokohama." (Mac Donnell to Alan Gribben, 2 August 2004). It would seem likely that Clemens received a copy of this small book of twenty double-fold pages. Patton urged Westerners to avoid "narrow-minded prejudice" in viewing Japanese customs. She fondly described the food, table etiquette, gardens, social habits, bells, funerals, and other aspects of Japanese life.

Kevin Mac Donnell, "Mark Twain and Gensai Murai: A Japanese Inspiration for 'The War-Prayer,'" *Mark Twain Studies* (Japan) 2 (2006): 41–44.

PAYN, JAMES (1830–1898). "An Adventure in a Forest; or, Dickens's Maypole Inn," *Harper's New Monthly Magazine* 57.338 (July 1878): 298–302.

In May 1878 Clemens pinned a clipping from this essay to a leaf in Notebook 14 (*N&J* 2: 91 n. 86). Payn comically described his futile search for Epping Forest and the famous Maypole Inn of Dickens's *Barnaby Rudge*.

———. *High Spirits: Being Certain Stories Written in Them* (first published in London, 3 vols., 1879).

Clemens noted "In High Spirits—by James Payn" in Notebook 22 (1883, *N&J* 3: 17). *High Spirits* collected novellas and short stories by the English journalist, editor, and novelist Payn. One of them qualifies as science fiction and another novella incorporates elements of science fiction with utopian fiction.

———. *Some Literary Recollections*. New York: Harper & Brothers, [1884]. 205 pp. [Date of publication supplied.]

Source: MTLAcc, entry #1354, volume donated by Clemens.

Payn shared here his lighthearted reminiscences about Dickens, Thackeray, Harriet Martineau, and other literary figures.

PAYNE, JOHN HOWARD (1791–1852). "Home, sweet home" (from the operetta *Clari; or, the Maid of Milan*)" (song, published in 1823). Arranged by Sir Henry Rowley Bishop (1786–1855).

In 1864 Mark Twain recalled as an "outrage" the efforts of an amateur violinist to play "Sweet Home" (*ET&S* 2: 95–99; *CTSS&E* 1: 97–101). Twain mentioned this song in Notebook 5 (1866, *N&J* 1: 146); he also singled it out as part of "the popular-song nuisance" in the 28 April 1866 Sacramento *Weekly Union* (*LSJ*, p. 51). In 1885 Twain noted that this "commingling, healing, unifying song" was one that both Union and Confederate soldiers joined together in singing on the Rapidan in Virginia (NB 25, *N&J* 3: 201). He repeated that incident in an undated note he set down (*A1911*, lot 439).

PAYNE, WILL (1865–1954). *Jerry the Dreamer*. New York: Harper & Brothers, 1896. 299 pp.

Source: MTLAcc, entry #1640, volume donated by Clemens.

The Chicago journalist Payne wrote his first novel, *Jerry the Dreamer*, about a young man who leaves his small Illinois town to make his mark in the city. The corruption he encounters and the limitations of his personal character place a strain on his marriage. Payne is ranked with Henry Blake Fuller, Robert Herrick, and other Midwestern writers whose Realistic narratives contained elements of the impending school of Literary Naturalism.

PAYSON, WILLIAM FARQUHAR (1876–1939). *Barry Gordon*. Illustrated by Harry Townsend (1879–1941). New York: The McClure Co., 1908. 341 pp. [Publisher and pages supplied.]

Inscription: "To Saml. L. Clemens, Esq. Dear Mr. Clemens: May I inscribe this copy of my latest novel to you with glowing recollections of the dinner on your seventieth birthday. As Huck Finn, Tom Sawyer, and the rest have been my intimate friends for over twenty years, perhaps

you will grant at least a bowing acquaintance to *my* black sheep—Barry Gordon. With all esteem, Yours very sincerely, William Farquhar Payson, December 28th, 1908, Kingsthorpe, Bristol, R. I."

Catalog: *A1911*, "12mo, cloth, N.Y. 1908," quotes the inscription, lot 380.

Payson's eponymous hero, who displays traits of both Tom Sawyer and Huckleberry Finn, grows from boyhood into a young man who falls in love and endures hardships and adventures in Morocco. The journalist and author Payson had been an editor on the staffs of the New York *Times* and *Vogue* during the 1890s.

———. *The Triumph of Life; A Novel*. New York: Harper & Brothers, 1903. 425 pp.

Source: MTLAcc, entry #1112, volume donated by Clemens.

A young writer named Enoch Lloyd is distracted by two women who exert opposing influences on his character and actions.

PEABODY, FREDERICK WILLIAM (1862–1938). *A Complete Exposé of Eddyism or Christian Science and the Plain Truth in Plain Terms Regarding Mary Baker G. Eddy, Founder of Christian Science*. Boston, 1901. 68 pp. [An address delivered at the Tremont Temple in Boston on 1 August 1901.]

Provenance: this item was sold at the *C1951* Hollywood auction, although the catalog for that sale did not list it.

Location: in 1980 this pamphlet was in the private collection of Mrs. Mac Benoff, Beverly Hills, California.

Peabody was an attorney who wrote several books criticizing Christian Science. This pamphlet served Mark Twain for numerous examples, and he also corresponded with Peabody (see Paul Baender, *WIM?*, pp. 557–558). In Twain's "Portraits of Mrs. Eddy," written in 1903 but not published then, Twain recommended Peabody's "hostile portrait" to readers. "It is bitter, unsparing, fiendishly interesting" and well worth its price of 25 cents, he wrote (*WIM?*, p. 515). In Book 2 (Chapter 4) of "Christian Science" (1907), Twain refers to "Mr. Peabody's book *(Eddyism, or Christian Science*. Boston: 15 Court Square, price twenty-five cents)." See also the Catalog entry for Eddy's *Manual of the Mother Church*.

Robert Peel, *Mary Baker Eddy: The Years of Authority* (New York: Holt, Rinehart and Winston, 1977), 3: 194–202.

PEACOCK, THOMAS LOVE (1785–1866). "Memoirs of Percy Bysshe Shelley," in *Fraser's Magazine* (June 1858); "Memoirs of Shelley," in *Fraser's Magazine* (January, March 1860); and "Percy Bysshe Shelley" (supplementary notice), in *Fraser's Magazine* (January, March 1860); Collectively known as *Memoirs of Shelley*. [Repr. in *Thomas Love Peacock: Memoirs of Shelley and Other Essays and Reviews*, ed. Howard Mills (New York: New York University Press, 1970), pp. 15–89.]

Mark Twain's "In Defence of Harriet Shelley" (1894) quotes from Peacock's praise of Harriet as a wife.

PEARD, FRANCES MARY (1835–1923). *An Interloper; A Novel*. New York: Harper & Brothers, 1894. 315 pp.

Source: MTLAcc, entry #1641, volume donated by Clemens.

The English traveler and novelist Peard set her romantic story in the chateaus of rural France.

PEARS, (SIR) EDWIN (1835–1919). *The Fall of Constantinople, Being the Story of the Fourth Crusade*. New York: Harper &

Brothers, 1886. 422 pp.

Source: MTLAcc, entry #1458, volume donated by Clemens.

PECK, CHARLES HENRY (1838–1922). *The Jacksonian Epoch.* New York: Harper & Brothers, 1899. 472 pp.

Source: MTLAcc, entry #1501, volume donated by Clemens.

PECK, GEORGE WILBUR (1840–1916). *Peck's Bad Boy and His Pa* (published in Chicago, 1883).

From Hartford on 26 February 1884 Clemens informed William Dean Howells about Peck's royalties for the stage adaptation of *Peck's Bad Boy and His Pa* (*MTHL*, p. 476). Stone, *IE* (1961), p. 72; Hunter, "MT and the Boy-Book" (1963), p. 435. Cyril Clemens reported a meeting of Peck and Clemens ("The Unknown Mark Twain," *Hobbies: The Magazine for Collectors* 77.2 [March 1972]: 150–151).

———. *Peck's Fun: Being Extracts from the "LaCrosse Sun," and "Peck's Sun," Milwaukee. The Cream of Mr. Peck's Writings of the Past Ten Years.* Compiled by V. W. Richardson. Tan cloth, decorated. Chicago: Belford, Clarke & Co., 1880. 248 pp.

Marginalia: pencil mark on page 9.

Provenance: Antenne-Dorrance Collection, Rice Lake, Wisconsin. These were the books that Katy Leary, the Clemenses' longtime housekeeper, was given as keepsakes following Clemens's death in 1910.

Location: Mark Twain Archive, Gannett-Tripp Learning Center, Elmira College, Elmira, New York.

Copy examined: quite possibly Clemens's copy. However, Mary Evans Leary, the first wife of Warren Leary, Sr. (Katy Leary's nephew, who inherited her library), was from LaCrosse, Wisconsin, so this volume conceivably could have belonged to her. Examined on 28 May 2015.

PECK, WALLACE. *The Golden Age of Patents: A Parody of Yankee Inventiveness.* Illustrated [by Walter Hugh McDougall]. New York: Frederick A. Stokes, 1888. 55 pp. [Edition conjectured.]

In March of 1891 Clemens intended to "ask Wallace Peck" of New York City "who made the pictures for 'How to Run a Railroad' [*sic*]. Want him for my book" (NB 30, *N&J* 3: 610). Peck's *The Golden Age of Patents* contained a six-page chapter devoted to "The Multum in Parvo Train" of the future that Peck humorously envisioned as pulling vegetable garden cars, barnyard cars, Lyceum cars, laundry cars, shopping cars, lawn-tennis cars, bathing cars, and even divorce cars, (to guarantee the "comfort of mismated mates"). Peck's title page did not credit the illustrator for his whimsical book, but a number of the cartoons were signed by Walt [Walter Hugh] McDougall (1858–1938), who would become a prominent newspaper cartoonist.

PECKHAM, GEORGE WILLIAMS (1845–1914) and **ELIZABETH (GIFFORD) PECKHAM** (1854–1940). *Wasps, Social and Solitary.* Introduction by John Burroughs (1837–1921). Illustrated by James H. Emerton (1847–1930). First edition. 8vo, original red cloth, gilt, small tear in the spine. Boston: Houghton, Mifflin and Co., 1905. 311 pp.

Inscription: the front pastedown endpaper is signed in black ink, "S L. Clemens,/21—5th Ave/1905."

Provenance: Donated to the Carrie Estelle Doheny Collection, St. John's Seminary, Camarillo, California, after Mrs. Doheny purchased the volume from Maxwell Hunley Rare Books of Beverly Hills, California in 1940 for $12.20. Auctioned by Christie's on 1 February 1988 on behalf of St. John's Seminary and the Archdiocese of Los Angeles. Subsequently acquired by Nick Karanovich, Fort Wayne, Indiana; see Karanovich's "Sixty Books from Mark Twain's Library," *Mark Twain Journal* 25.2 (Fall 1987): 16–17.

Catalogs: Christie's, New York City, 1–2 February 1988 auction, lot 467, sold with one other book for $1,320 to Randall House, Los Angeles; *Sotheby's 2003*, #246, $3,000 for this and another volume on wasps by M. W. Morley.

Location: collection of Kevin Mac Donnell, Austin, Texas.

Copy examined: Clemens's unmarked copy in 1970 at St. John's Seminary in Camarillo, California, and later in Austin, Texas in July 2004. Has the bookplate of "Estelle Doheny."

It was in the Peckhams' book (Chapter 9, "The Spider-Hunters," pp. 196–247) that Mark Twain learned how wasps leave live spiders as food for young wasps, a practice Twain cites in "The Refuge of the Derelicts" (written 1905–1906) to illustrate the absurdity of believing in the benevolence of Nature (*FM*, p. 247). In "Little Bessie" (written 1908–1909), the title character is appalled that "the wasps catch spiders and cram them down their nests in the ground—alive, mamma!—and there they live and suffer days and days and days" while young wasps devour them (*FM*, p. 36).

Peirce School, Philadelphia. Annual Graduating Exercises of Peirce School of Business and Shorthand . . . 1882 to 1892. Philadelphia: Thomas May Peirce, 1893. 524 pp.

Source: MTLAcc, entry #890, volume donated by Clemens.

PEMBERTON, MAX (1863–1950). *Sir Richard Escombe; A Romance.* New York: Harper & Brothers, 1908. 351 pp.

Source: MTLAcc, entry #877, volume donated by Mrs. Ralph W. Ashcroft (formerly Isabel Lyon), Clemens's secretary.

PENDLETON, LOUIS BEAUREGARD (1861–1939). *Bewitched: A Tale.* New York: Cassell & Co., [cop. 1888]. 288 pp. Also contains a separate story, "Ariadne in the Wire-Grass," pp. 241–269.

Clemens wrote to the Georgia author on 4 August 1888 from Elmira, reporting that an hour ago he had found and read Pendleton's book. "Ariadne is a beautiful and satisfying story; and true, too." Since Pendleton had invited Clemens's criticism, he picked a few faults "which one may notice also in my books, and in all books whether written by man or God: trifling carelessness of statement or expression." Clemens also pointed to one instance of error "in that other not-small matter—selection of the exact single *word*." Clemens concluded: "I save the other stories for my real vacation—which is nine months long [i.e., when he is away from Quarry Farm], to my sorrow" (*MTL*, pp. 497–499).

———. *In the Wire Grass: A Novel.* Appleton's Town and Country Library, No. 29. New York: D. Appleton and Co., 1889. 245 pp.

Pendleton addressed a letter to Clemens on 3 June 1889, enclosing his newly published novel and reminding Clemens of his "kind, encouraging letter last summer" (Machlis, *UCLC*, p. 267; Fears, *Day by Day* 2: 383).

PENNINGTON, JAMES W. C. (1807–1870). *The Fugitive Black-smith; or, Events in the History of James W. C. Pennington . . . Formerly a Slave in the State of Maryland.* Second ed. London: C. Gilpin, 1849. 87 pp. Third ed., 1850. [Clemens's edition, if any, is undetermined.]

William L. Andrews, "Mark Twain and James W. C. Pennington: Huckleberry Finn's Smallpox Lie," *Studies in American Fiction* 9.1 (Spring 1981): 103–112, pointed out a number of similarities between Pennington's description of his escape from enslavement in *The Fugitive Blacksmith* (first published in 1849) and Huckleberry Finn's smallpox lie that saves Jim from the slave-hunters in Chapter 16 of *Adventures of Huckleberry Finn* (1885). Pennington's book recounted how he told some (temporary) captors in Maryland that his former master, a slave-trader, had died of smallpox; the farmers promptly drew back from him in apprehension. Subsequently Pennington, who became a minister following his emancipation, argued the circumstances of his "great moral dilemma" regarding the ethics of telling this untruth.

Lucinda H. MacKethan, "Huck Finn and the Slave Narratives: Lighting Out as Design," *Southern Review* 20.2 (April 1984): 247–264, especially 252–257.

The Pennsylvania Magazine of History and Biography 1.3 (1877): 343–347.

This issue contains Mark Twain's tribute to Francis Lightfoot Lee (1734–1797), a signer of the Declaration of Independence. Other contributors to the first volume included Charles Francis Adams, Richard H. Dana, Jr., Robert C. Winthrop, Charles H. Hart, and Wayne MacVeagh. On 1 July 1876 Twain had attended an event in Philadelphia connected with the Centennial, the Congress of Authors in Independence Hall, and read there his sketch titled "Francis Lightfoot Lee of Virginia" (Fears, *Day by Day* 1.2: 716).

PENZANCE, (SIR) JAMES PLAISTED WILDE (1816–1899). *Lord Penzance on the Bacon-Shakespeare Controversy. A Judicial Summing-Up*. Edited by M. H. Kinnear. Biographical Note by Frederick Andrew Inderwick (1836–1904). London: S. Low, Marston & Co., 1902. 200 pp.

"We read the praises bestowed by Lord Penzance and the other illustrious experts upon the legal condition and legal aptnesses, brilliancies, profundities, and felicities so prodigally displayed in the Plays" (Part 9, Mark Twain's *Is Shakespeare Dead?* [1909]).

PEPPER, CHARLES MELVILLE (1859–1930). *To-morrow in Cuba*. New York: Harper & Brothers, 1899. 362 pp.

Source: MTLAcc, entry #1737, volume donated by Clemens.

PEPYS, SAMUEL (1633–1703). *Diary and Correspondence of Samuel Pepys, Esq., F. R. S., from His MS. Cypher in the Pepysian Library, with a Life and Notes by Richard [Griffin,] Lord Braybrooke [1783–1858]. Deciphered, with Additional Notes, by Rev. Mynors Bright [1818–1883]*. Illus. 6 vols. London: Bickers and Son, 1875–1879.

Catalogs: Ball 2016 inventory, 5 volumes (Volume I is missing), brown leather, gilt design and lettering, gilt page edges. Laid in is a New York City clipping dated 10 December 1890 regarding the pronunciation of Pepys' name.

Location: Quarry Farm library shelves, under the supervision of the Mark Twain Archive, Elmira College, Elmira, New York.

In August 1879 Clemens noted in England: "New Pepy's [*sic*] Diary" (NB 18, *N&J* 2: 339). Mynors Bright's was the most recent edition of Pepys in print. The Cranes'

set was available to Clemens during his visits to Quarry Farm in Elmira.

———. *The Diary of Samuel Pepys*. 10 vols. [Edition and dates unknown.]

Marginalia: "There was not much room for comment on the narrow margins of the old copy of Pepys, which he had read steadily since the early seventies; only here and there a few crisp words, but the underscoring and marked passages are plentiful enough to convey his devotion to that quaint record which, perhaps next to Suetonius, was the book he read and quoted most" (Albert Bigelow Paine, *MTB* [1912], p. 1538).

Catalog: *C1951*, D9, listed among the volumes signed by Clemens, Volumes I-X inclusive, no edition specified, $80.

Albert Bigelow Paine wrote that Pepys' *Diary* was one of the "few books that [Clemens] read regularly every year or two" (*MTL*, p. 489). "Get Pepys," Clemens scrawled in pencil across the text of page 109 in George F. Pardon's *Routledge's Guide to London* (London, 1866); this page describes the palace of Whitehall (volume in MTP). "Am luxuriating in glorious old Pepys' Diary & smoking," Clemens wrote contentedly to the Reverend Joseph H. Twichell from the Langham Hotel in London on 29 June 1873 (*MTL*, p. 207; *MTLet* 5: 393; *LMTJHT*, p. 43). Clemens entered the title "*Pepys Diary*" in his stenographic notebook in June 1873 (NB 12, *N&J* 1: 528). In July 1873 Clemens could not help wondering why Pepys failed to mention such a famous English dramatist as Shakespeare (NB 12, *N&J* 1: 563, 568); Clemens also mentions a calculating machine invented "in 1664 by Sir Sam'l Morland," a device to which Pepys refers (NB 12, *N&J* 1: 565). (Sir Samuel Morland, 1625–1695, was an English inventor.) Paine reported that Pepys' *Diary* was one of the "reliable favorites" of Clemens and Theodore Crane in the summer of 1874 at Quarry Farm (*MTB*, p. 511). According to Paine, Clemens perused the work again during the summer of 1876, which he also spent at Quarry Farm (*MTB*, pp. 579–580). Mark Twain's prefatory note to *1601* (written in 1876) acknowledges Pepys as his model: "The following is supposed to be an extract from the diary of the Pepys of that day, the same being Queen Elizabeth's cup-bearer" (Franklin J. Meine's edition, privately printed for the Mark Twain Society [Chicago, 1939], p. 32). In 1878 Twain noted "Queer names—Sir Harbottle Grimstone" (NB 14, *N&J* 2: 59), a name Pepys mentioned in his 26 April 1660 entry. In a biography he signed in 1879 (Moritz Busch's *Bismarck*), he wrote a name in the margin of page 98: "Pepys." Mark Twain referred to Grimstone again in his working notes for *The Prince and the Pauper* (DV1 15, MTP), which contain Pepys' name and indications that Pepys' diary supplied archaic language. Clemens reread "the second volume of Pepys" in January 1884 (SLC to Edward H. House, 14 January 1884, ALS in ASSSCL). "'But Lord,' as Pepys says," Clemens remarked to William Dean Howells in a letter of 2 June 1884 (*MTHL*, p. 491). While sketching some ideas for "Picturesque Incidents in History & Tradition (of all countries)" in August 1885, Twain noted "Plague & Fire of London. Copy from Pepys" (NB 24, *N&J* 3: 173). In January 1894 Pepys' *Diary* would have been one of Twain's first selections for the "Back Number" magazine he then envisioned (NB 33, TS p. 46).

The Reverend Joseph H. Twichell's sketch of Clemens (1896) stated that "books like Pepys' *Diary*, that afford the means of looking narrowly and with human sympathy into the life and manners of bygone generations, have a peculiar charm to him" (p. 822). On 6 October 1900 Twain claimed in London: "There has never been an autobiography or biography or diary or whatever you like to call it that has been written with quite the detachment from all anxiety about what the readers may think of it or its writer as this one of mine. Pepys, you might be disposed to think, was a miracle of candor even at his own expense, but even Pepys wrote with the consciousness that his contemporaries were looking over his shoulder, and despite all he could do he was fettered by a sense of restraint that consciousness produced" ("Mark Twain, the Greatest American Humorist, Returning Home, Talks at Length," New York *World*, 14 October 1900). On 8 November 1906 Clemens wrote to Jean Clemens from 21 Fifth Avenue about a pleasurable experience: "Percy Grant came up to my room at 5 & I made him stay till 7. We had good talk about Pepys' Diary, & about Howells" (TS in MTP). Isabel V. Lyon recorded in Bermuda (in an entry dated 6 January 1907) that Clemens "sat off in a corner most of the time when he wasn't in his cabin—& mostly he read Vols. V & VI of Pepys's Diary" (IVL's Secretarial Notebook, MTP). Albert Bigelow Paine recalled Pepys' *Diary* as one of perhaps five books that Clemens "read steadily" during the last four years of his life (*MTB*, p. 1540). During Clemens's final stay in Bermuda, which commenced in November 1909 and ended in April 1910, his hostess observed that Pepys's *Diary* was one of the books that entertained Clemens in the mornings (Marion Schuyler Allen, "Some New Anecdotes of Mark Twain," *Strand Magazine* [London] 46.272 [August 1913]: 168). See also Scharnhorst, *Mark Twain: The Complete Interviews*, pp. 346–351, especially page 349.

Williams, "Genesis" (1961), p. 105; *MT&JB* (1970), pp. 80–87, 335 n. 26 and n. 27.

————. *The Diary of Samuel Pepys, 1662–1663*. [Introduction by Henry Morley (1822–1894).] New York: Cassell & Co., 1886. 192 pp.

Source: MTLAcc, entry #974, volume donated by Clemens.

————. *Memoirs of Samuel Pepys, Esq., F.R.S. Comprising His Diary from 1659 to 1669, and a Selection from His Private Correspondence*. Edited by Richard [Griffin,] Lord Braybrooke (1783–1858). Chandos Library Edition. London: Frederick Warne and Co.; New York: Scribner, Welford, and Armstrong, n. d. 815 pp.

Inscription: originally inscribed "T W Crane/New York Feby 1878." Clemens later added a note in ink below that line: "Stolen from/Mrs. Susan L. Crane,/by/her most loving & almost only/brother-in-law/S L. Clemens/Riverdale, October, 1901."

Marginalia: Clemens annotated the volume throughout in pencil.

Catalog: ListABP (1910), "Pepys' Memoirs", no other information provided.

Location: Mark Twain House and Museum, Hartford, Connecticut. A gift from Jervis Langdon of Elmira, New

York in 1981.

Copy examined: Clemens's copy, in August 1987.

The Percy Anecdotes, Collected and Edited by Reuben and Sholto Percy [Thomas Byerly (1788–1826) and Joseph Clinton Robertson (1788–1852)]. A Verbatim Reprint of the Original Edition, with a Preface by John Timbs [1801–1875]. "Chandos Classics" edition. 4 vols. London and New York: F. Warne and Co., [1887]. [Publisher and date conjectured.]

Inscription: Volume I is signed "S. L. Clemens, 1895."

Marginalia: some humorous notes by Clemens. When Clemens read, for instance, that Cassius Scaeva had 130 arrows sticking in his shield, he observed: "St. Sebastian had 200 in his body and never cracked a smile" (quoted in *A1911*). (Marcus Cassius Scaeva, a Roman centurion during Julius Caesar's civil war with Gnaeus Pompey, held a fortress despite receiving terrible wounds. Shown Cassius Scaeva's shield that bore more than 100 arrows, Julius Caesar promoted the soldier and gave generous rewards to him and his men.)

Catalogs: *A1911*, "4 vols., 12mo, cloth, leaf of a volume cut off, Lond., n.d., . . . with humorous autograph notes by Mr. Clemens," quotes the signature and quotes one example of the marginalia , lot 381, sold for $6 total; George D. Smith, New York City, "Catalogue of Books" (1911), "4 vols.," quotes the signature, item #305, $12 total.

Clemens resolved to obtain a copy of these anecdotes drawn from various time periods and categorized by topics. "Get 'Percy Anecdotes' for Black Hole of Calcutta," Clemens advised himself on 10 November 1895 in Timaru, New Zealand (NB 34, TS p. 37). On 30 November 1895, Clemens made another entry about India: "Black Hole—(Percy Anec)" (NB 34, TS p. 44).

How unfortunate that these four volumes containing Clemens's marginalia disappeared after 1911. Initially issued in twenty-four parts between 1820 and 1823, *The Percy Anecdotes* consisted of briefly told stories loosely assembled without regard to historical eras under general topics such as Humor, Crime and punishment, Travelling, War, Music Pulpit, Shipwreck, Heroism, and so forth. Clemens's reprint edition added somewhat unreliable indexes to the four volumes.

PERCY, THOMAS (1729–1811), ed. *Reliques of Ancient English Poetry, Consisting of Old Heroic Ballads, Songs, and Other Pieces of Our Earlier Poets; Together with Some Few of Later Date*. 3 vols. Philadelphia: Gebbie & Co., 1890.

Catalogs: Ball 2016 inventory, 3 volumes , reddish-brown cloth, pages largely uncut.

Location: Quarry Farm library shelves, under the supervision of the Mark Twain Archive, Elmira College, Elmira, New York.

The antiquarian and cleric Percy (he was the Bishop of Dromore) collected these English ballads and songs that prompted a national interest in these forms of poetry and influenced the Romantic movement. These volumes were available to Clemens at Quarry Farm whenever he visited Elmira.

PERRONET, EDWARD (1721–1792). "All hail the power of Jesus' name" (hymn, published in 1779). Later added to a melody by Oliver Holden (1765–1844), known as "Coronation" (hymn, 1793).

"It is a good tune," Mark Twain wrote of "Coronation" in

Chapter 4 of *The Innocents Abroad* (1869); the hymn was included in Henry Ward Beecher's *Plymouth Collection of Hymns and Tunes*. Annie Fields (1834–1915) remembered that Clemens told a story about an old clergyman who mistakenly sang the first verse of "Coronation" after it was to have been omitted (*Memories of a Hostess*, p. 254). Clemens listed "All Hail the Power of Jesus' Name" among "Selections of admirable poetry and prose" on an undated scrap of manuscript (*A1911*, lot 348; Chicago Book and Art Auctions, Sale number 7 (14–15 April 1931), lot 92). Allison R. Ensor, "The Favorite Hymns of Sam and Livy Clemens," *Mark Twain Journal* 25.2 (Fall 1987): 21–22.

Perry, Matthew Calbraith (1794–1858). *Narrative of the Expedition of an American Squadron to the China Seas and Japan, Performed in the Years 1852, 1853, and 1854*. Compiled by Francis L[ister]. Hawks (1798–1866). Illus. New York: D. Appleton and Co., 1856. 624 pp. [Edition conjectured.]

Mark Twain's letter of 10 September 1866 to the Sacramento *Weekly Union* quoted Perry's report on sugar production in Mauritius from Chapter 6 (page 133) of Perry's *Narrative* (*MTH*, pp. 257–258, 398).

Petersen, Marie (1816–1859). *Prinzessin Ilse. Ein Märchen aus dem Harzgebirge [Princess Ilse. A Fairy tale from the Harz Mountains]*. Leipzig: P. Reclam, [1890]. 57 pp. [Publisher and date conjectured.]

Source: MTLAcc, entry #380, volume donated by Clemens.

Peterson, Franklin Sievewright (1861–1914). *An Introduction to the Study of Theory: A Sequel to the "Elements of Music," and Intended to Prepare the Student for Professor Prout's Series of Theoretical Works*. London: Augener & Co., [1897]. 87 pp.

Source: MTLAcc, entry #810, volume donated by Clemens. Peterson was the organist and choirmaster of the Palmerston Place Church in Edinburgh.

Les Petits Bergers, ou Les Avantages de l'instruction. Par G. H. Traduit de Schmidt. Illus. Rouen: Mégard et Cie, 1858. 103 pp.

Inscription: bookplate of E. Serein, 1859, Écoles Chrétiennes des Frères.

Location: Mark Twain Library, Redding, Connecticut.

Copy examined: why was this volume shelved with Clemens's library books when I revisited the Mark Twain Library in June 1982? It has no accession number, no purple Mark Twain Library stamps, and no indication of ownership by Clemens or any member of his family. I recommended that it be moved elsewhere.

Petrarch (Francesco Petrarca) (1304–1374).

In 1878 Clemens mentioned Petrarch as one of the "names familiar to every school-boy" (NB 17, *N&J* 2: 228). Petrarch was identified as a great Italian writer in "Three Thousand Years Among the Microbes" (written 1905, *WWD?*, p. 529). See also the Catalog entry for Anna Brownell Jameson, *Memoirs of the Loves of the Poets*.

Petrie, (Sir) William Matthew Flinders (1853–1942). *Personal Religion in Egypt Before Christianity*. New York: Harper & Brothers, 1909. 174 pp.

Source: MTLAcc, entry #1349, volume donated by Clemens.

Petronius Arbiter (Gaius Petronius) (fl. 1st century CE). *The Satyricon*.

In Mark Twain's "The Walt Whitman Controversy" (DV36,

MTP), an undated manuscript possibly written in 1882, Twain writes of *The Satyricon* as an accepted masterpiece that contains obscene matter, and states that he himself owns a copy of the work. He did indeed possess this work: see the Catalog entry for Sextus Propertius, *Erotica: The Elegies of Propertius, The Satyricon of Petronius Arbiter* (1874).

Ed Folsom and Jerome Loving, "Mark Twain: 'The Walt Whitman Controversy,'" *Virginia Quarterly Review* 83.2 (Spring 2007): 123–138.

Pflüger's Archiv für die gesammte Physiologie des Menschen und der Thiere (journal). Edited by Eduard Friedrich Wilhelm Pflüger (1829–1910).

In Vienna Mark Twain referred to *Pflüger's Archiv* on 26 May 1899 while writing an article on vivisection (Hemminghaus, "Mark Twain's German Provenience," [1945], p. 476).

Phelips, Harry Vivian Majendie (1860–1939), pseud. "Philip Vivian." *The Churches and Modern Thought; An Inquiry into the Grounds of Unbelief and an Appeal for Candour*. Second and revised edition. London: Watts & Co., 1907. 418 pp.

Inscription: the front pastedown endpaper is signed in brown ink, "S L. Clemens/London, July 1907."

Marginalia: in brown ink Clemens bracketed a passage on page 389 that reads, "The Egyptian cross or 'life' sign is a fashionable ornament. . . . Its pious wearers are, of course, quite unaware that it is the phallic emblem!" Below this, using brown ink, Clemens underlined in a footnote a reference to Thomas William Doane's *Bible Myths and Their Parallels in Other Religions* (New York: The Commonwealth Company). Clemens would sign his copy of Doane's book in 1908.

Location: Mark Twain Library, Redding, Connecticut. Donated by Clemens (MTLAcc, entry #915).

Copy examined: Clemens's copy. Has the red ink Mark Twain Library accession number "915". Examined in 1970 and again in June 1982 and on 9 November 2019.

The English socialist and journalist Phelips argued that the Christian religion is neither valid nor essential.

Phelps, Edward John (1822–1900). *Orations and Essays of Edward John Phelps, Diplomat and Statesman*. Ed. by John Griffith McCullough (1835–1915). Memoir by John Wolcott Stewart (1825–1915). Portrait. New York: Harper & Brothers, 1901. 475 pp.

Catalog: *A1911*, "thick 8vo, cloth, gilt top, uncut, N.Y. 1901," with a sheet of Clemens's notes laid in, lot 382, sold for $3.25.

———. [An identical copy.]

Source: MTLAcc, entry #1771, volume donated by Clemens.

Phelps, Elizabeth Stuart (1844–1911), later also known by her married name, Elizabeth Stuart (Phelps) Ward. *The Gates Ajar* (novel, published in 1868).

Mark Twain's "The Story of Mamie Grant, the Child-Missionary," written in Notebook 11 in July 1868, owed its characters and structure to *The Gates Ajar* (*N&J* 1: 499–506). An unsigned column by Twain for the Buffalo *Express* (13 September 1869) conceded that "so long as there are death and bereavement in this world, and the necessity for books of consolation, it will have a permanent, intrinsic value," but quibbled about its "defect in logic" (*MTBE*, pp. 51–53). Twain undoubtedly took part in lampooning Phelps' novel with poems that appeared in the October 1870 *Galaxy* (*CG*, p. 86). Olivia Clemens evidently shared a vision of heaven similar to the one discussed in *The Gates Ajar*; in her diary for 12 July 1885 she noted that she "cannot help wondering" if Mrs. Henry W. Sage of Ithaca—a longtime friend of her father and mother—"will see father and tell him all about us" (OLC Diary, DV161, MTP).

In London in January 1897 Twain referred to "Capt. Stormfield's Visit to Heaven? (begun in the winter of 1867–8 as a satire upon the 'Gates Ajar' & still in MS.)" (NB 39, TS p. 55). On 13 June 1906 Twain told Isabel Lyon that his "Captain Stormfield's Visit to Heaven" actually "was intended as a satire on 'The Gates Ajar'" (IVL Journals, TS p. 165, MTP). Elizabeth Wallace reported from her conversations with Twain during his last years that he found Phelps' picture of Heaven to be "a sentimental and foolish idea. He resolved to satirize it, and wrote the first draught of Captain Stormfield" (Wallace, *MT&HI*, p. 24). Twain testified that in 1868 he wrote one version of "Captain Stormfield's Visit to Heaven": "I had turned it into a burlesque of 'The Gates Ajar,' a book which had imagined a mean little ten-cent heaven about the size of Rhode Island—a heaven large enough to accommodate about a tenth of 1 per cent of the Christian billions who had died in the past nineteen centuries. I raised the limit" (29 August 1906 AD, *MTE*, p. 247; *AutoMT* 2: 194). But Robert A. Rees—in a commendable note, *"Captain Stormfield's Visit to Heaven* and *The Gates Ajar,"* *English Language Notes* 7.3 (March 1970): 197–202—pointed out that in *The Gates Ajar* Mary Cabot's aunt, Winifred Forceythe, actually ridiculed the notion of heaven as the abode of white-robed souls forever singing praises. Aunt Winifred's concept of heaven was commonsensical and unelaborate. She even scoffed at attempts to estimate the geographical dimensions of the afterlife, which accords with the perspective of heaven Eli Stormfield discovers upon his arrival at the pearly gates. Rees and Franklin R. Rogers (*S&B*, pp. 31–32) both speculated that Mark Twain confused his target with that of an earlier, closer satire of his—"The Story of Mamie Grant, the Child-Missionary." Wecter, *RP* (1952), p. xiii.

———. *Trixy.* Boston: Houghton, Mifflin & Co., 1904. 299 pp.

Source: MTLAcc, entry #240, volume donated by Clemens. A small white dog named Trixy is abducted for the purpose of training medical students. The novel endeavors to show that the cruel practice of experimenting on live animals is detrimental for the future physicians as well as amounting to torture for the hapless canine victims. Ward became a strong advocate for women's rights, temperance, the labor struggle, and the campaign against vivisection. The similarity of *Trixy* to Mark Twain's "A Dog's Tale" (1903) should be obvious.

Emily E. Vandette, "Animals and Animal Rights," *Mark Twain in Context*, ed. John Bird (Cambridge, England: Cambridge University Press, 2020), pp. 270–271.

——— and **HERBERT DICKINSON WARD** (1861–1932). *The Master of the Magicians*. Boston: Houghton, Mifflin and Co., 1890. 324 pp.

Catalog: Ball 2016 inventory, yellow boards with black

lettering and design, good condition, bookseller's label of Hossmer H. Billings.

Location: Quarry Farm library shelves, under the supervision of the Mark Twain Archive, Elmira College, Elmira, New York.

After Elizabeth Stuart Phelps married Herbert Dickinson Ward in 1888 they collaborated in writing a number of historical novels set in Biblical times. *The Master of the Magicians* takes place in ancient Babylon. Clemens had access to this work whenever he visited Quarry Farm in Elmira, New York.

PHELPS, WILLIAM LYON (1865–1943). *A Dash at the Pole*. Illustrated by John Goss (1886–1963). Boston: Ball Publishing Co., 1909. 72 pp.

Inscription: inscribed by the author in black ink on the front free endpaper, "S L Clemens/from/Wm Lyon Phelps/Dec 1909".

Location: Mark Twain Library, Redding, Connecticut.

Copy examined: Clemens's copy, unmarked. Has the red ink Mark Twain Library accession number "3088" and the purple oval Library stamps. Examined in 1970 and again in June 1982 and on 9 November 2019.

Phelps' fictional narrative burlesqued the expeditions that were racing each other to the North Pole. On 13 December 1909 Jean Clemens wrote to Phelps from Redding, Connecticut: "When I found your book, 'Dash at the Pole,' I neglected my duty until I had read it through, thereby getting much entertainment and I believe that father will surely enjoy it when he gets back" (typed letter, formerly in the collection of Cyril Clemens, Kirkwood, Missouri; photocopied by Thomas A. Tenney in 1980 and sent to Alan Gribben in September 1982; now in the Mark House and Museum in Hartford; published in "A Page of Tributes," *Mark Twain Journal* 6.4 [Winter-Spring 1945]: 10). Clemens was in Bermuda at the time. Jean Clemens would die a few days later on 24 December 1909. Clemens wrote to Phelps on 12 March 1910: "I knew my poor Jean had written you" (*MTL*, p. 840; *MTB*, p. 1562).

In 1939 Phelps would finally summon the courage to reveal that as a twelve-year-old boy in Hartford he had shot Clemens's prize white ducks in Nook Farm, thinking that they were wild; Clemens had offered a reward for the "miscreant" who had killed his five ducks. "I never dared to tell him of this particular episode," Phelps admitted ("Mark Twain's White Ducks," *Mark Twain Quarterly* 3.2 [Spring 1939]: 4).

——— *Essays on Modern Novelists.* New York: Macmillan Co., 1910. 293 pp.

Inscription: the front free endpaper is inscribed in black ink (not Clemens's hand): "S. L. Clemens/from/Wm Lyon Phelps/2 March 1910".

Marginalia: Clemens's black ink notations are scattered throughout. (This was quite possibly the last book he annotated.) In the first essay, "William De Morgan," Clemens made ink marks on pages 2, 4, 18, and 22; at the top of page 2 he also wrote "patent-office 'interferences.' Morse, Henry, the Munich man"; in the margin of the same page, beside the statement that genius will win out, he simply objected "no." In Phelps' second essay, "Thomas Hardy," Clemens jotted "Ganz gut" [Quite good] near this sentence: "To him the Christian religion and what we call the grace of God have not the slightest shade of meaning; he is as absolute a Pagan as though he had written four thousand years before Christ." On page 53, beside Phelps' comment that Hardy believed men and women are morally superior to God, Clemens wrote "Vrai."; below, concerning the cause of Hardy's pessimism, he observed: "repetition (it is temperamental)." Clemens then drew a line beside the final, lengthy paragraph, wrote *"all* temperamental," and continued the line on the next page to the end of the paragraph. There are no marks in the third essay, whose subject is William Dean Howells. The fourth essay concerns Bjørnstjerne Bjørnson: on page 89 Clemens drew an "X" at the mention of Bjørnson's "natural optimism of his temperament," and added, "Because he was *born* an optimist; & not even God could have changed him." Clemens made numerous ink markings on this page. On page 90 Clemens protested "Nein!" regarding Bjørnson's decline, making him "farther off from heaven" in his work. "Gut," Clemens noted on page 94 beside a sentence that states: "Religion is of no importance in comparison with conduct, nor have the two things any vital or necessary connexion[*sic*]." Clemens made only two markings in the fifth chapter, "Mark Twain": on page 106 he made double vertical marks beside Phelps' statement that he has never known anyone frivolous "who really enjoyed or appreciated Mark Twain"; on page 110 Clemens drew a single vertical mark beside Phelps' assurance that one cannot outgrow *Tom Sawyer:* "The eternal Boy is there, and one cannot appreciate the nature of boyhood properly until one has ceased to be a boy."

In essay VI, "Henryk Sienkiewicz," Clemens wrote "Harben" vertically in the margin of page 124. (Clemens disapproved of Will Harben's novels about Georgia; see Harben's entry in the Annotated Catalog.) In the seventh essay, "Hermarin Sudermann," Clemens drew double vertical marks beside a comparison between Sudermann's young boy-hero, Paul, and Tom Sawyer. "Robert Louis Stevenson," the ninth essay, contains an ink mark on page 179 beside disparaging remarks about the stylistic shortcomings of Walter Scott and James Fenimore Cooper. There are also ink marks on page 192 (at a list placing Mark Twain in a class with Tolstoi, Ibsen, Anatole France, Rostand, Kipling, and others); page 199 (around a statement that a humorist knows life is a tragi-comedy); and page 257 (beside a list of good writers for teachers—including Mark Twain). Clemens heavily annotated a poem published in 1907 by Thomas Hardy titled "New Year's Eve," in which the speaker questions God's preparing yet another year for humans "who in/This tabernacle groan" (pp. 258–259). He underscored the last line of stanza three ("'If ever a joy be found herein,/Such joy no man had wished to win/If he had never known!'"), and wrote "Gut!" next to the poem's last stanza: "He sank to raptness as of yore,/And opening New Year's Day/Wove it by rote as theretofore,/And went on working evermore/In his unweeting way." In the unmarked pages Phelps discussed William Dean Howells, Alfred Ollivant, Mrs. Humphry Ward, and Richard Blackmore's *Lorna Doone: A Romance of Exmoor.*

Catalog: *C1951*, #26c, listed erroneously among books signed by Clemens, $20.

Location: Clifton Waller Barrett Collection, Albert and Shirley Small Special Collections Library, University of Virginia, Charlottesville.

Copy examined: Clemens's copy.

On 12 March 1910 Clemens wrote to Yale professor Phelps: "I thank you ever so much for the book, which I find charming—so charming, indeed, that I read it through in a single night & did not regret the lost night's sleep. I am glad if I deserve what you have said about me; & even if I don't I am proud & well contented, since you *think* I deserve it" (*MTL*, p. 840; *MTB*, p. 1562). Phelps, incidentally, had spoken on the topic "Mark Twain" to the Teacher's Club in Hartford on 23 February 1907, thereby becoming quite likely the first English professor of note to devote an entire lecture to this author ("Some Unpublished Phelps Letters," *Mark Twain Journal* 6.4 [Winter-Spring 1945]: 9).

———. "Introduction," *The Novels and Letters of Jane Austen.* Edited by Reginald Brimley Johnson (1867–1932). Introduction by William Lyon Phelps (1865–1943). Illustrated by C. E. and H. M. Brock. 12 vols. "Chawton Edition." New York: F. S. Holby, 1906. [Only 1,250 sets printed.] Number 18 of fifty separately printed copies of Phelps' preface to Austen's works. First edition. Original flexible blue cloth, gilt, uncut.

Inscriptions: the front pastedown endpaper is inscribed in black ink: "To/S. L. Clemens/as a slight memorial/of his hearty dislike/for Jane Austen/from one of his/heartiest admirers/Wm. Lyon Phelps/Yale College/23 Dec. 1906". The front flyleaf and the title page have been removed.

Provenance: red ink accession number ("2792") and six purple stamps of the Mark Twain Library in Redding, Connecticut. Eventually obtained by Nick Karanovich, Fort Wayne, Indiana.

Catalogs: *Mott 1952*, 3 July 1951, $15; *Sotheby's 2003*, #216, "two front flyleaves excised," $3,500 (sold with five other inscribed books).

Location: collection of Kevin Mac Donnell, Austin, Texas.

Copy examined: Clemens's unmarked copy of Phelps' separately bound Introduction. Viewed in July 2004. (There is no indication that Clemens owned or read the twelve-volume Jane Austen set itself.)

In this Introduction to the privately printed Chawton Edition of Jane Austen's writings Phelps diplomatically (and perhaps preemptively, to deflect any response by Mark Twain) acknowledged Twain's "hearty dislike" of her novels.

Philadelphia Exhibition of 1876. Treasures of Art, Industry and Manufacture Represented in the American Centennial Exhibition at Philadelphia. Color plates. Philadelphia, 1876.

Catalog: *A1911*, "folio, half morocco (rubbed), Phila. 1876," with a sheet of notes by Clemens laid in, lot 383, sold for .50¢.

PHILADELPHIA *Public Ledger* (newspaper, published 1836–1942).

Clemens wrote a letter from Philadelphia dated 3 February 1854 to Orion Clemens's newspaper that joked about the funeral verse appearing in the Philadelphia *Public Ledger.* After quoting a stanza he asked, "What do you think of that? Will not Byron lose some of his popularity now?" (Edgar M. Branch, "Three New Letters by Samuel Clemens in the Muscatine *Journal, Mark Twain Journal* 22.1 [Spring 1984]: 2). Clemens chuckled in a letter to

Olivia Langdon written on 6 September 1869 about some terrible poetry he had received from George W. Elliott (see his Catalog entry) that "is equal to anything I have ever seen in the death column of the Philadelphia Ledger" (*MTLet* 3: 336). In "Post-Mortem Poetry" (1870), Mark Twain ridiculed the imitative doggerel appended to death notices in this newspaper. "In that city death loses half its terror because the knowledge of its presence comes thus disguised in the sweet drapery of verse." On 9 April 1885, addressing the Actors Fund Fair in Philadelphia, Twain joshed that "more than once I have been accused of writing obituary poetry in the Philadelphia *Ledger*. I wish right here to deny that dreadful assertion" (*MTSpk*, p. 194).

Philanthropy Dissected: The so-Called "Act for the Further Protection of Seamen" Reviewed, Prepared for the "Seamen's Boarding House Keepers' Benevolent Association of the City of New York. New York: Bunce & Co., Printers, 1872. 23 pp. [Published by Morris & Wilder, Attorneys at Law, 69 Wall Street, New York City.]

Continuing to feud with Captain Charles C. Duncan, captain of the *Quaker City* excursion, Mark Twain referred to how "that infamous law was most ably dissected and its purpose exposed four or five years ago, in a pamphlet published by Messrs. Morris and Wilder, attorneys, of New York" ("Mark Twain Once More," New York *World*, 25 February 1877, *MTPP*, p. 104).

PHILLIMORE, CATHERINE MARY (1847–1929). *Dante at Ravenna: A Study.* London: Elliot Stock, 1898. 219 pp.

Catalogs: QF Martinez, fair condition; Ball 2016 inventory, red cloth, gilt lettering. Laid in is a note by a Mark Twain scholar.

Location: Quarry Farm library shelves, under the supervision of the Mark Twain Archive, Elmira College, Elmira, New York.

A work available to Clemens during his later Elmira visits.

PHILIPPI, FELIX (1851–1921). *As'ra* (play).

Clemens dined on 6 April 1900 with a South African millionaire, Adolf Goerz (1857–1900), a mining engineer who had founded a lucrative gold mining company. Afterward they went to see a performance of Philippi's play at the German Theatre in London (NB 43, TS p. 6a; London *Times*, 6 April 1900). Goerz would die a few months later, on 28 July 1900.

PHILIPPINE INFORMATION SOCIETY. *A Period of Guerrilla Warfare, November 1899, to September 1900.* Facts About the Filipinos Series. Vol. 1, No. 9 (1 August 1901). Boston. 67 pp.

Location: Paine 89aa, Mark Twain Papers, Bancroft Library, University of California at Berkeley.

Copy examined: Clemens's copy of a paperbound pamphlet, unmarked but with a few pages folded over.

PHILLIPPS, SAMUEL MARCH (1780–1862), ed. *Famous Cases of Circumstantial Evidence. With an Introduction on the Theory of Presumptive Proof.* Fourth ed., enlarged and revised. Jersey City: F. D. Linn & Co., 1879. 540 pp. [The edition is conjectured; previous editions had been published by Estes & Lauriat in Boston (1873) and by J. Cockcroft & Co. in New York (1873, 1874).]

On 17 July 1880, Estes & Lauriat, Boston publishers and booksellers, notified Clemens: "Famous Cases Circum. Evidence out of print. Cannot supply at present" (written on a receipt for Charlotte Yonge's *Young Folks' History of*

England, MTP). If Clemens was eventually able to obtain a copy of this book, virtually any of its seventy-one cases might have intrigued him; each documented an erroneous verdict that resulted from seemingly conclusive circumstantial evidence. Some of the narratives, such as "Case of Martin Guerre," involved mistaken identities. Phillipps did not supply the sources for his stories, which spanned several centuries of legal history and included the courts of England, Europe, and America. Perhaps the most significant was the "Case of Sören Qvist," a miscarriage of justice that became the basis for Mark Twain's *Tom Sawyer, Detective* (1896), whose exact source has been a matter of conjecture by scholars. Phillipps told how Sören Qvist, a Danish clergyman, was wrongly convicted and executed for the murder of a farm servant who turned up alive twenty-one years after the supposed crime. See also the Catalog entry for Steen S. Blicher, *The Minister of Veilby.*

PHILLIPS, MARY ELIZABETH (1857–1945), ed. *Laurel Leaves for Little Folk.* Illustrated by the editor. Boston: Lee & Shepard, 1903. 148 pp.

Catalogs: ListABP (1910), "Laurel Leaves, Phillips"; *C1951*, #96c, listed among books signed by Clemens, $12.50.

Laurel Leaves for Little Folk collected poems and stories suitable for children written by authors such Eugene Field, Edward Everett Hale, and James Whitcomb Riley. On 16 February 1901 Clemens had thanked Phillips for sending him a copy of an unidentified book (PH in MTP). Perhaps this was her *Reminiscences of William Wetmore Story, The American Sculptor and Author* (1897); Clemens was familiar with Story's writings—see the Catalog entries for Story.

PHILLIPS, STEPHEN (1868–1915). *Herod: A Tragedy.* London and New York: John Lane, 1901. 126 pp.

Inscription: the front flyleaf is signed, "Clara Clemens/New York/1901."

Catalogs: *C1951*, J26, listed among volumes belonging to Jean and Clara Clemens; "Property from the Library of Mark Twain," Butterfield & Butterfield, San Francisco, Sale 6613 (16 July 1997), lot 2711.

Location: Mark Twain House and Museum, Hartford, Connecticut.

Copy examined: Clara Clemens's unmarked copy. Viewed in Hartford in 1997.

Reproduces the blank verse script of a Biblical play as performed at Her Majesty's Theatre on 31 October 1900.

———. *Paolo & Francesca: A Tragedy in Four Acts.* Cloth, wear on edges and corners. London and New York: John Lane, 1900. 120 pp.

Inscription: the front flyleaf is inscribed by Olivia Clemens, "Clara L. Clemens/Dec. 25th, 1899/London/Mamma."

Catalogs: *C1951*, J38, listed among volumes belonging to Jean and Clara Clemens; "Property from the Library of Mark Twain," Butterfield & Butterfield, San Francisco, Sale 6613 (16 July 1997), lot 2709.

Location: Mark Twain House and Museum, Hartford, Connecticut.

Copy examined: Clara Clemens's unmarked copy. Viewed in Hartford in 1997.

The script of a play written in blank verse and set in Rimini, Italy.

PHILLIPS, WENDELL (1811–1884).

Phillips used his oratorical powers on behalf of abolitionism before the Civil War, and then took up a number of social reform causes after that conflict. In August 1895 Clemens quoted Phillips's praise of Canada (NB 36, TS p. 26). (Phillips approved of the antebellum reception Canada provided for runaway enslaved African Americans, which might have been Clemens's reference; however, Phillips also commended other Canadian activities in later decades.) Clemens's Autobiographical Dictation of 10 October 1907 praised Phillips's mastery of the art of public speaking on behalf of a cause (*MTE*, p. 215; *AutoMT* 2: 282).

PHILLPOTTS, EDEN (1862–1960). *The Human Boy Again*. Illustrated by L[eonard]. Raven- Hill (1867–1942). First edition. Original red cloth, gilt. London: Chapman and Hall, 1908. 307 pp.

Inscription: the front pastedown endpaper is inscribed and signed by Clemens in black ink: "From the author./S L. Clemens/1908."

Catalog: *A1911*, "12mo, cloth, Lond. 1908," quotes the signature, lot 384, sold for $5.50.

Location: collection of Kevin Mac Donnell, Austin, Texas. Acquired in 1977 for $125.

Copy examined: Clemens's unmarked copy, in 1985 and again in July 2004. Contains the *A1911* auction label.

On New Year's Day, 1908, Clemens thanked the British writer Phillpotts for offering to dedicate a forthcoming book to him; Clemens signed the letter to Phillpotts, "Your sincere friend & persistent admirer these many years" (MTP). Clemens approved the wording of the dedication on 12 February 1908 (ALS, ASSSCL). "The Human Boy Again has arrived, & I have just begun it & am greatly enjoying it," Clemens wrote to Phillpotts from New York City on 26 April 1908 (ALS in ASSSCL). Phillpotts dedicated his book "TO MY DEAR FRIEND,/ MARK TWAIN,/FATHER OF 'TOM SAWYER' AND/'HUCKLEBERRY FINN,'/THESE HUMAN BOYS,/WITH SINCEREST REGARD." The title page of *The Human Boy Again* quotes Mark Twain's maxim from "Pudd'nhead Wilson's New Calendar" (in Chapter 12 of *Following the Equator* [1897]), which Twain attributed to "the school-boy who said, 'Faith is believing what you know ain't so.'"

The Human Boy Again (1908) contained twelve short stories and was a sequel to Phillpotts's popular *The Human Boy* (1900), which consisted of eleven stories. They are both set in an English boarding school in the fictional town of Merivale. The aptness of dedicating this second book to Mark Twain stems from the fact that Phillpotts' stories are related, sometimes not too grammatically, by different boys who possess varied backgrounds and viewpoints. Each tells of an adventure at the school, ranging from playing pirates (in *The Human Boy*) to pretending to be detectives (in *The Human Boy Again*).

———. *The Mother of the Man*. New York: Dodd, Mead & Co., 1908. 455 pp.

As Clemens was beginning to read *The Human Boy Again*, he informed Phillpotts that "meantime (in Bermuda) I read—& re-read—The Mother of the Man, with high admiration. A great book!" (SLC to Eden Phillpotts,

New York City, 26 April 1908, ALS in the Albert and Shirley Small Special Collections Library, University of Virginia, Charlottesville).

———. *The River; A Novel*. Black cloth, decorated. New York: Frederick A. Stokes Co., [cop. 1902]. 394 pp.

Inscription: the front free endpaper is signed in pencil "Clemens/1892" [*sic*]. The handwriting resembles Clemens's.

Provenance: Antenne-Dorrance Collection, Rice Lake, Wisconsin.

Location: Mark Twain Archive, Gannett-Tripp Learning Center, Elmira College, Elmira, New York.

Copy examined: Clemens's copy, unmarked. Examined on 28 May 2015.

Clemens met Phillpotts at a dinner in London on 29 March 1900 (NB 43, TS p. 6a). In 1907 Clemens noted: "Eden Phillpotts sends happy New Year, speaks of the splendid English welcome" (NB 48, TS p. 16). *The River* was set in southwest England where deep river valleys wind through the wild uplands of Dartmoor in the county of Devon. Phillpotts depicted the sometimes brutal struggles of farmers in this lonely landscape.

Phrenological Journal and Science of Health (published in Philadelphia, 1838–1841; then in New York City, 1841–1911). Issued 1838–1869 as the *American Phrenological Journal* (its subtitle varied). Ed. by Orson Squire Fowler (1809–1887) and Lorenzo Niles Fowler (1811–1896); from 1855 until 1875 it was edited by Samuel Roberts Wells (1820–1875).

Around 1869 Olivia Langdon copied a brief quotation from this journal into her commonplace book (DV161, MTP). See also the Catalog entry for Samuel Roberts Wells.

PHYFE, WILLIAM HENRY PINKNEY (1855–1915). *Seven Thousand Words Often Mispronounced: A Complete Hand-Book of Difficulties in English Pronunciation, Including an Unusually Large Number of Proper Names and Words and Phrases from Foreign Languages*. Third edition. New York, London: G. P. Putnam's Sons, 1890. 491 pp.

Marginalia: Clemens wrote notes in brown ink on pages 18, 37, and 93; he also made notes in pencil on pages 20–21. On page 93 he noted in exasperation: "This author is an ass. The word *ask* has no established pronunciation."

Provenance: contains the red-ink accession number and call number of Mark Twain Library, Redding, Connecticut.

Catalog: *Mott 1952*, #78, $35.

Location: Mark Twain Papers, Bancroft Library, University of California at Berkeley.

Copy examined: Clemens's copy.

PIATT, SARAH MORGAN (BRYAN) (1836–1919). *A Voyage to the Fortunate Isles, Etc.* Illus. Boston: J. R. Osgood & Co., 1874. 180 pp.

Source: MTLAcc, entry #2076, volume donated from Clemens's library by Clara Clemens Gabrilowitsch in 1910. Piatt's book contains fifty-one poems, including the title poem.

PIER, ARTHUR STANWOOD (1874–1966). *The Sentimentalists; A Novel*. New York: Harper & Brothers, 1901. 425 pp.

Source: MTLAcc, entry #1039, volume donated by Clemens.

A novel of manners contrasting, among other things, the families and attitudes of Boston versus those of Gage City, a "Western" metropolis.

———. [Another identical copy.]
Source: MTLAcc, entry #1059, volume donated by Isabel V. Lyon, Clemens's secretary.
———. [Another identical copy.]
Source: MTLAcc, entry #1276, volume donated by Isabel V. Lyon, Clemens's secretary.

PIERCE, EDWARD LILLIE (1829–1897). *Memoir and Letters of Charles Sumner [1811–1874].* 4 vols. Boston: Roberts Brothers, 1878–1893.
Provenance: bookplates #518 (Volume I) and #517 (Volume II) of the "J. Langdon Family Library." Clemens had access to these books whenever he visited the Langdon residence in Elmira.
Catalog: Ball 2016 inventory, marble with cloth, gilt lettering, brown leather spine, Volumes I and II are in poor condition, Volumes III and IV are in fair condition and these latter lack bookplates.
Location: Quarry Farm library shelves, under the protection of the Mark Twain Archive, Elmira College, Elmira, New York.
Copy examined: unmarked copies to which Clemens had access whenever he visited the Langdon residence in Elmira. Examined on 26 May 2015.
U. S. Senator Charles Sumner of Massachusetts was known as an unyielding force for abolishing human slavery, and in 1856 a pro-slavery zealot assaulted and badly injured him on the Senate floor. Later Sumner advocated the granting of full civil rights to formerly enslaved African Americans. He also championed other causes and opposed various national political policies, eroding his popularity with his colleagues.

PIERSON, HAMILTON WILCOX (1817–1888). *In the Brush; or, Old-Time Social, Political, and Religious Life in the Southwest.* Illustrated by William Ludwell Sheppard (1833–1912). New York: D. Appleton and Co., 1881. 321 pp. [Edition conjectured.]
In March or April 1882, Mark Twain wrote in his pocket notebook: "In the Brush. by Pierson" (NB 20, *N&J* 2: 453). Twain would soon depart on a trip to revisit the Mississippi River and gather literary material; evidently he wanted to compare the present-day scenes with these sketches of poor-white settlements visited by this Presbyterian clergyman before the Civil War. Pierson's pietistic memoirs related his experiences as an agent for the American Bible Society in the Old Southwest region (he never named the exact states). To the earnest Pierson, the camp-meeting revivals, isolated plantations, and vernacular backwoods characters constituted an exotic society. He was alternately amused and scandalized by the dress, manners, and speech of the Southern frontier settlers to whom he sold Bibles and preached the gospel.
If Twain obtained a copy of *In the* Brush he would have appreciated Pierson's accounts of a revival camp meeting with split-log seats (pp. 62–66); calico sun-bonnets, linsey-woolsey and calico dresses, and butternut-colored woolsey coats (pp. 29, 98, 119, 160); the preachers' platforms (pp. 65, 160); the congregations' exclamatory shouts (pp. 175–176); and the origin of the word "or'nery" (p. 181). No doubt Twain had witnessed similar examples of local color; his "The Holy Children," an undated manuscript, opens with a camp-meeting scene similar to those pictured

by Pierson: "I can remember seeing sixty-four saddle horses tied to . . . [the] farm-fence at one time; I often saw thirty and forty tied there. Such persons as came in wagons often camped in the woods and fields near by and staid several days" (*FM*, p. 70). Pierson described a method of hitching horses to tree limbs: "It has often been a pleasant sight to me to see scores or hundreds of horses hitched in this manner, and standing comfortably in the shade of forest trees, surrounding a church, preaching-stand, or camp-ground" (*In the Brush*, pp. 174–175).
In Chapter 32 of *Adventures of Huckleberry Finn* (1885), Huck approaches "one of these little one-horse cotton plantations," home of the Phelpses: "When I got half-way, first one hound and then another got up and went for me. . . . And such another pow-wow as they made! In a quarter of a minute I was a kind of hub of a wheel." He is rescued when an enslaved woman "come tearing out of the kitchen with a rolling-pin in her hand. . . . And here comes the white woman running from the house." Pierson explained that only "the most untraveled and inexperienced" would dismount and approach the door of an isolated farmhouse. Near the Mississippi River one night, Pierson shouted a greeting from horseback. "A large pack of hounds and various other kinds of dogs responded with a barking chorus, a group of black pickaninnies rushed from the adjacent kitchen, followed to the door by their sable mother, with arms a-kimbo and hands fresh from mixing the pone or corn-dodger for the family supper." When "the mistress of the incipient plantation" arrived at the door, "stockingless and shoeless," she invited the preacher to come inside. "The dogs . . . obeyed their instructions not to harm me, and granted me a safe entrance as a recognized friend." (Huckleberry Finn's hounds "come back, wagging their tails around me and making friends with me.") Pierson concluded: "Such was the universal training of the dogs, and such was the uniform method of approaching and gaining admittance to the houses of the people in the Brush" (p. 50).

PIKE, MARSHALL SPRING (1818–1901). "Home again" (song, published in 1850). Words and music by Pike; arranged by J. P. Ordway.
The pet parrot on a Mississippi River tugboat applied his "ear-splitting" laugh "to every pathetic song. He cackled it out with hideous energy after 'Home again, home again, from a foreign shore,' and said he 'wouldn't give a d—for a tug-load of such rot.' . . . So the singing and talking presently ceased." The first stanza of Pike's sentimental song begins, "Home again, home again, from a foreign shore/And oh, it fills my soul with joy, to meet my friends once more."

PILGRIM, JAMES (d. 1879). *The Limerick Boy; or, Paddy's Mischief. An Original Farce, in One Act* (first performed in 1856?).
Mark Twain saw William M. ("Billy") O'Neil perform this farce in 1864: "Billy O'Neil was so successful in keeping the house in a roar as the Limerick Boy, and especially as the Irish Schoolmaster, that he was frequently driven from his own masterly gravity," Twain reported (letter from Carson City, 13 January 1864, *MTEnt*, p. 132).

PINDAR, SUSAN (1820–1891), afterwards Mrs. Embury. *Legends of the Flowers*. New York: D. Appleton & Co., 1873. 178 pp.

Source: MTLAcc, entry #443, volume donated by Clemens. Moral stories for children, including fairy tales. Originally published in 1852.

———. *Midsummer Fays; or, The Holidays at Woodleigh*. New York: D. Appleton & Co., 1878. 233 pp.

Source: MTLAcc, entry #842, volume donated by Clemens. Fairy tales, originally published in 1850.

PINERO, (SIR) ARTHUR WING (1855–1934). *The Gay Lord Quex: A Comedy in Four Acts* (play, performed in 1899).

Mark Twain intended to see this comedy in New York City on 14 November 1900 (NB 43, TS p. 29). In London, on 9 June 1900, Twain's toast preceded the English playwright Pinero's at a dinner for Sir Henry Irving held at the Savoy Hotel. Twain said of Pinero: "He has not written as many plays as I have, but he has had the God-given talent, which I lack, of working them off on the manager." Clemens also referred to Pinero's "fine work" (*MTS1923*, p. 194; *MTSpk*, p. 339).

PINKERTON, ALLAN (1819–1884). *Mississippi Outlaws and the Detectives. Don Pedro and the Detectives. Poisoner and the Detectives*. New York: G. W. Carleton & Co., 1879. 377 pp. [Edition conjectured.]

Mark Twain's "Cap'n Simon Wheeler, The Amateur Detective. A Light Tragedy," a play written in 1877, burlesques Pinkerton's detective tales. Wheeler declares in Act 3: "When I've finished working up this case it'll be worthy a chapter in one of Allan Pinkerton's great detective books!" (*S&B*, p. 272). Seated on a seemingly dead man (whom Wheeler mistakes for a log), Wheeler explains that an old glove, a footprint, even a cigar stub—merely "3 or 4 little clues like that, they just lead him [a shrewd detective] as dead straight to his man as the poles would an *ord*'nary man to the telegraph office" (*S&B*, pp. 231–232). Wheeler brags to his wife, Jenny: "*There*, old girl, I'll bet a doughnut Allan *Pinkerton* couldn't do it better, himself" (*S&B*, p. 272). Wheeler remarks that "in the stories, the detectives most always notice that the wound is made in a way that couldn't be made only by a left-handed man" (*S&B*, p. 240).

Twain's novel titled "Simon Wheeler, Detective," written between 1877 and 1898 and unpublished until 1967, also burlesqued Pinkerton and his detective agency. Simon Wheeler introduces his associates—three men named Baxter, Billings, and Bullet; they wear silver disks "with a staring human eye engraved upon it, surrounded by the modest legend, 'WE NEVER SLEEP.'" Wheeler speaks of these men as "the most celebrated detectives in America—all belong to Inspector Flathead's celebrated St. Louis Detective Agency—Flathead that writes the wonderful detective tales, you know" (*S&B*, pp. 384, 382). After Wheeler read a book called "Tales of a Detective," it "became his Bible. He read and re-read it until he knew it by heart; . . . he marveled over its cheap mysteries and trivial inventions. . . . It was natural for this kindly, simple-natured, transparent old infant to fall down and worship that detective rubbish and its poor little tuppenny hero" (*S&B*, pp. 437–438).

Twain again made fun of Pinkerton's detective stories in "Tom Sawyer's Conspiracy," written 1897–1900; Walter Blair explained that "the eye which Tom uses as an insignia

in his reversed woodcuts is based upon the insignia of the Pinkerton agency, which bore a similar eye with the motto 'We Never Sleep' beneath it" (Chapter 4, *HH&T*, p. 159). In "Which Was it?" (written 1899–1903), Sol Bailey—who resembles the good-hearted Simon Wheeler—hires Allen Osgood ("one of the best detectives"), even though Bailey's wife feels that Osgood "couldn't follow the telegraph wire and find the office" (*WWD?*, pp. 351, 352). Howard G. Baetzhold—"Of Detectives and Their Derring-Do: The Genesis of Mark Twain's 'The Stolen White Elephant,'" *Studies in American Humor* 2.3 (January 1976): 183–195—astutely sketched the public's familiarity with Allan Pinkerton's books.

Rogers, *MTBP* (1960), pp. 132–133, 175 n. 40; Blair, *MT&HF* (1960), pp. 224–225; *S&B* (1967), p. 10.

———. *The Spy of the Rebellion; Being A True History of the Spy System of the United States Army During the Late Rebellion. Revealing Many Secrets of the War Hitherto Not Made Public*. New York: G. W. Carleton & Co., 1883. 688 pp.

In "Tom Sawyer's Conspiracy," written 1897–1900, Tom's invention of "The Sons of Freedom" may derive its name and tendencies from Chapter 18 of this Pinkerton novel (see Walter Blair, *HH&T*, p. 159).

PINKLEY, VIRGIL A[LONZO] (1852–1914). *Essentials of Elocution and Oratory*. Cincinnati: Cranston & Stowe; New York: Phillips & Hunt, 1888. 471 pp.

Source: MTLAcc, entry #804, volume donated by Clemens.

The Pioneer Mail and Indian Weekly News (Allahabad, published 1874–1931).

Citing the Indian natives' penchant for mendacity, Mark Twain writes in Chapter 43 of *Following the Equator* (1897): "An article in one of the chief journals of India (the *Pioneer*) shows that in some respects the native of to-day is just what his ancestor was" more than a century before. Twain quotes the opinion that "India in especial is the home of forgery" and that some districts "have earned notoriety for skilled perjury."

PITMAN, (SIR) ISAAC (1813–1897). *A Manual of Phonography; or, Writing by Sound* (New York, 1842).

In "A Simplified Alphabet" (written in 1899), Mark Twain reproduces a phonographic alphabet from Burnz' *Phonic Shorthand,* "arranged on the basis of Isaac Pitman's *Phonography*. Isaac Pitman was the originator and father of scientific phonography. . . . It was a memorable invention. He made it public seventy-three years ago. The firm of Isaac Pitman & Sons, New York, still exists, and they continue the master's work." In 1910 Clemens jotted, "Harper send me a Pittman [*sic*], right away" (NB 49, TS p. 1), probably referring to *Isaac Pitman's Shorthand Instructor*, enlarged and revised edition (New York: Isaac Pitman & Sons, 1905).

PITTMAN, HANNAH (DAVIESS) (1840–1919). *The Belle of the Bluegrass Country. Studies in Black and White*. Illus. Boston: C. M. Clark Publishing Co., 1906. 424 pp.

Source: MTLAcc, entry #243, volume donated by Clemens. In this novel a young civil engineer building a bridge in Kentucky in the 1870s encounters the aftermath of the Civil War in the lives of whites and African Americans. The novel's implicit attitudes belong to the Myth of the Old South tradition of depicting the formerly enslaved (whose speech is rendered in vernacular dialect) as still unwaveringly loyal to their former masters. Chapter 3, "'Uncle Dave'—Faithful unto Death," seems deeply beholden to Thomas Nelson Page's short story, "Marse Chan. A Tale of Old Virginia" (1887).

[PITZER, ALEXANDER WHITE (1834–1927)]. *Ecce Deus-Homo; or, The Work and Kingdom of the Christ of Scripture.* Philadelphia: J. B. Lippincott, 1868. 207 pp.

Source: MTLAcc, entry #903, volume donated by Clemens.

PLANCHÉ, JAMES ROBINSON (1796–1880). *The Loan of a Lover: A Vaudeville in One Act* (performed in London, 1834).

Catalog: ListABP (1910), "Loan of a Lover, Planche", no other information supplied.

On 26 and 27 April 1876, Clemens played the role of Peter Spyk in a Hartford production of Planché's play (H. B. Langdon to SLC, Hartford, 27 April 1876, MTP; Fears, *Day by Day* 1.2: 703–704). Annie Fields saw his second performance and reported that his part "was a creation. . . . It is really amazing to see what a man of genius can do beside . . . his legitimate sphere" (*Memories of a Hostess*, pp. 246–247). William W. Ellsworth, a member of the dramatic club in Hartford, recalled that Clemens injected off-the-cuff remarks into the script. His ad-libbing was hilarious to the audience, but the other members of the cast, lacking Clemens's ease before the footlights, found his additions nerve-wracking as they tried to remember lines and cues (*A Golden Age of Authors*, p. 223). Clemens declined a proposal to perform the one-act play in New York City. "By rewriting Peter Spyk, I managed to change the language & the character to a degree that enabled me to talk the one & represent the other after a fashion—but I am not equal to the metropolitan boards yet," Clemens wrote to Augustin Daly on 4 May 1876 (Joseph Francis Daly, *The Life of Augustin Daly*, p. 146).

The silly romantic plot—relying on overheard conversations and lovers hiding behind props representing bushes—probably benefited from Clemens's impromptu additions. Peter Spyk learns too late that he actually would prefer to wed Gertrude (played by Miss Helen Smith in the Hartford production), whom he has known since childhood. But she is pledged to Captain Amersfort. By the play's end everyone living in this villa on a canal near Utrecht is satisfied, however; the betrothal of Gertrude and the Captain was merely a ruse to frighten the Captain's lover, Ernestine Rosendaal, into wedding him—and to make Peter Spyk aware of his jealousy concerning Gertrude. Ernestine promises to marry Amersfort and admits that she was foolish to "loan" him to Gertrude; she had become convinced that she had permanently lost her lover. For Gertrude's assistance in bringing Ernestine to her senses, Amersfort gives Gertrude 2,000 crowns, which becomes her dowry to wed Peter Spyk.

MTHL (1960), p. 130 n. 1; Salsbury, *S&MT* (1965), p. 49.

PLATO (428 or 427 BCE–348 or 346 BCE). *The Dialogues of Plato.* Trans. by Benjamin Jowett (1817–1893). 4 vols. New York: Scribner, Armstrong, and Co., 1873. [Jowett's translation of Plato was first published in 1871.]

Inscriptions: Clemens inscribed the half-title page of each volume "For Livy Clemens/Dec. 1874./S. L. C."

Catalog: *C1951*, D6, listed among volumes signed by Clemens, $40 total.

Location: Special Collections, University Library, University

of Nevada, Reno. Purchased in 1963 from Mrs. Louis A. (Haydee U.) Zeitlin of Santa Monica, California.

Copies examined: Olivia Clemens's unmarked copies.

Plato, whose best-known work is the *Republic*, was a student of Socrates in ancient Athens. In 1867 Clemens wrote that "Plato & Diogenes were captured by pirates & publicly sold as slaves in the market place of Athens—Plato brought $500. by the way of ransom" (NB 9, *N&J* 1: 392). Olivia Clemens commenced a letter to her mother on 9 May 1875 from Hartford: "Mr. Clemens is reading aloud in 'Plato's Dialogues'—so if I write incoherently you must excuse it" (MTHM, Hartford). In a letter to the Reverend Charles D. Crane written on 20 January 1887, Clemens listed "Jowett's Plato" among his favorite books (Shapell Manuscript Library, Beverly Hills, California). On 2 February 1905 Isabel Lyon noted that "Miss [Clara] Clemens sent down for Plato and the Iliad & Byron" while recuperating from an illness (IVL Journal, Mark Twain Archive, Elmira, New York.). See also the Catalog entry for Socrates.

Alicia Tromp, "Platonic Parody: Mark Twain and the Quest for the Idea(l) in 'My Platonic Sweetheart,'" *American Literary Realism* 46.1 (Fall 2013): 58–75.

PLATT, ISAAC HULL (1853–1912). *Bacon Cryptograms in Shakespeare, and Other Studies.* Boston: Small, Maynard and Co., 1905. 123 pp.

Inscription: (on half-title page) "As a slight token of appreciation and admiration of Mark Twain's knock-down blow to the old impostor William Shaxpur, the perpetrator of this feeble effort to the same end (an ill favored thing but his own) begs its acceptance and—if he may dare hope it—its perusal by the mightier champion./To Samuel L. Clemens Esq./with the compliments of/Isaac Hull Platt,/Challingford, Pennsylvania,/May 1909."

Marginalia: on page 121 someone (not Clemens) altered the Latin verb "tuitor" in red ink to read "tueor." Uncut leaves in the volume have been opened.

Provenance: contains accession number 3549, traces of a charge-slip pocket, and a call number on the spine—presumably those of the Mark Twain Library, Redding, Connecticut. Curiously, there are no Mark Twain Library bookstamps in the volume.

Location: Special Collections, University Library, University of Nevada, Reno. Purchased in 1963 from Mrs. Louis A. (Haydee U.) Zeitlin of Santa Monica, California.

Copy examined: Clemens's copy.

Platt's book contended that evidence about the plays showed Francis Bacon "was in some manner concerned in their production or associated with them." Platt did not claim that he can absolutely prove Bacon's authorship (p. 2).

The Players. [*By-laws and Membership List of the Players Club, New York City.*] New York: Gilliss Press, 1892. 73 pp.

Location: Mark Twain Papers, Bancroft Library, University of California at Berkeley.

Source: the online catalog of the University of California at Berkeley Library, 12 June 2006. Jo Dee Benussi supplied this information.

PLETSCH, OSCAR (1830–1888). *Shnik-Shnak.* Leipzig: L. Grumbach, n.d.

Source: MTLAcc, entry #1931, volume donated from

Clemens's library by Clara Clemens Gabrilowitsch in 1910.

In Munich in 1878 Olivia Clemens recorded in her account book an outlay of .75¢ for "Pletch [*sic*] (illustrated book[)]" (NB 13a, MTP). *Shnik-Shnak* contained sketches drawn of children with accompanying brief verses.

PLINIUS CAECILIUS SECUNDUS, GAIUS ("The Younger," 62–113 CE). *The Letters of Gaius Plinius Caecilius Secundus.* Translated by William Melmoth (1710–1799). First published in 1746.

Pliny's description of Vesuvius erupting on 9 November 79 CE fascinated Mark Twain. He quoted from the account of events in Pompeii set down by Pliny the Younger in a letter published in the 29 September 1867 issue of the *Daily Alta California* (*TIA*, pp. 82–83). Twain quoted from William Melmoth's translation of Pliny's letter to Tacitus in Chapter 31 of *The Innocents Abroad* (1869). In Rome, Twain quipped in November 1878: "It is always safe to say a thing was mentioned by Pliny. He was the father of reporters—he mentioned everything" (NB 17, *N&J* 2: 246). "I thought I would get the account by the Younger Pliny of the overwhelming of Herculaneum and Pompeii in CE 79 and put it in this book" to compare it with the recent eruption of Vesuvius, he remarked in 1906, but the newspapers quickly did the same thing (11 June 1906 AD, *AutoMT* 2: 110). In 1908 Twain made a notation on page 56 of Nathaniel S. Shaler's *Aspects of the Earth* (1904) beside a quoted passage from *Pliny's Letters*, Book VI, describing the eruption of Vesuvius: "The interest of this excellent narrative never fades. In my lifetime I believe I have read it twenty-five times."

PLINIUS SECUNDUS, GAIUS ("The Elder," 23–79 CE). *The Natural History of Pliny.*

Twain's Autobiographical Dictation on 30 May 1907 refers to Pliny as one of the respected "students of animal nature." Twain adds, however, "Natural history is . . . not an exact science, and thus no naturalist can pose as an 'unassailable authority'"—not even Aristotle, Pliny, or Sir John Mandeville (30 May 1907 AD, *MTE*, pp. 22–23; *AutoMT* 3: 67).

PLOETZ, KARL JULIUS (1819–1881). *Epitome of Ancient, Mediaeval, and Modern History.* Translated, with extensive additions, by William Hopkins Tillinghast (1854–1913). Boston, New York: Houghton, Mifflin and Co., 1884. 618 pp. [Publisher and pages conjectured.]

Inscription: signed "S. L. Clemens, 1886."

Catalog: *A1911*, "12mo, half morocco, Bost. 1884," quotes the signature, lot 387, sold for $2.

Ploetz concisely surveys world history from the ancient Egyptians to Europe of the mid-nineteenth century, with many lists of historical dates linked to the narratives.

PLUTARCHUS (c. 46 CE-c. 120 CE). *The Boys' and Girls' Plutarch. Being Parts of the "Lives" of Plutarch.* Edited and with an introduction by John Stuart White (1847–1922). Illus. New York: G. P. Putnam's Sons, 1883. 468 pp.

Inscription: the front flyleaf is inscribed (not in Clemens's hand) "Clara L. Clemens./Christmas 1883./Aunt Sue."

Provenance: bookstamps, charge-slip pocket, and call number (on spine) of the Mark Twain Library, Redding, Connecticut. Donated from Clemens's library by Clara

Clemens Gabrilowitsch in 1910 (MTLAcc, entry #1937).

Catalog: *Mott 1952*, item #93, $4.50.

Location: Mark Twain House and Museum, Hartford, Connecticut. Gift of an anonymous donor in 1963.

Copy examined: Clara Clemens's unmarked copy. Examined in August 1987.

On 20 January 1887 Clemens recommended Plutarch's *Lives* as among the best reading for young people in a letter to the Reverend Charles D. Crane (ALS, Shapell Manuscript Library, Beverly Hills, California).

———. *The Children's Plutarch: Tales of the Greeks.* Intro. by W[illiam]. D. Howells (1837–1920). Illustrated by Walter Crane (1845–1915). New York: Harper & Brothers, 1910. 167 pp.

Location: Mark Twain Library, Redding, Connecticut.

Copy examined: almost certainly an unmarked copy from Clemens's Stormfield library collection. Has the red ink Mark Twain Library accession number "2501." I did not see this volume in 1970 but it was grouped with Clemens's library books when I revisited Redding in June 1982.

———. *Plutarch's Lives & Writings.* 10 volumes. Collector's Edition. Octavo, three-quarter morocco, extra gilt, dentelles. New York: Colonial Co., 1905. [Only 200 sets of this edition were published.]

Inscription: "S. L. Clemens/(Mark Twain)".

Provenance: offered by Serendipity Books, Berkeley, California, 6 September 1983, explaining that "this came from a gentleman's library given to a Midwestern institution," priced at $2,000.

Caution: Kevin Mac Donnell inspected this set in 1983 and came away convinced that the signature is a forgery and that the set should be considered a faked association copy. The signature certainly is extremely uncharacteristic for Clemens in his library collection and resembles the forgeries perpetrated by Eugene Field II in various books.

———. *Plutarch's Lives of Alcibiades & Coriolanus, Aristides & Cato the Censor [234 BCE-149 BCE].* Trans. by John Langhorne (1735–1779) and William Langhorne (1721–1772). No. 26 of Cassell's National Library Series. Ed. by Henry Morley (1822–1894). New York: Cassell & Co., [1886]. 192 pp.

Location: Mark Twain Papers, Bancroft Library, University of California at Berkeley.

Copy examined: Clemens's unmarked copy, paperbound. The paper wrapper is dated 24 July 1886 and priced at .10¢.

———. *Plutarch's Lives of Illustrious Men. Translated from the Greek by John Dryden [1631–1700] and Others.* "Reprinted from the Latest English Editions." 3 vols. Cloth, cracked hinges, spine ends rubbed. New York: John Wurtele Lovell, [c. 1880, no copyright date].]

Marginalia: Clemens's annotations amount to about forty-five words; approximately fourteen pages have his pencil or black ink notes or marked passages. All three volumes give evidence, including folded page corners, of having been read. Volume I contains only one pencil mark on page 271 (about Pericles), but its leaves have been cut and page 242 (about Pericles) is folded over, as is page 317 (concerning Alcibiades). On the title page of Volume II Clemens complained (in black ink) that the work was translated from the Greek "into rotten English . . . by an ass." He added, in black ink, writing vertically on that title page: "When you come across the pronouns he & him in this slovenly book, you will never know to whom they refer. But never mind—neither does God." Pages 114 and 115 of Volume II display Clemens's vertical lines in black ink in the margins. Next to a passage on page 115 in the life of Sylla, Clemens jotted in black ink, "Interpretations of God." In Volume III Clemens made a penciled grammar correction on page 47 and penciled two similar verb corrections on page 49. He revised the verb "were" to read "was" in the last line on page 63. All three volumes have small penciled "x's" in their "Contents" pages, and these were very likely made by Clemens.

Catalog: ListABP (1910), "Plutarch's Lives", no other information supplied; also "Plutarch's Lives v. 2", no other information supplied.

Provenance: displays the purple ink stamp of the Mark Twain Library in Redding, Connecticut on page 354 of Volume III (and a library charge slip loaning the book to a patron until "Ap. 15, [19]11"). However, Clara Clemens evidently retrieved all three of the volumes; the front flyleaf of Volume I displays Clara Clemens Gabrilowitsch's library numbers from her system of shelving volumes in Detroit. Subsequently she sold these volumes at the 1951 Hollywood auction, though they were not listed in the hastily compiled sale sheet for that event (which happened in numerous instances).

Catalog: "Property from the Library of Mark Twain," Butterfield & Butterfield, San Francisco, Sale 6613 (16 July 1997), lot 2687.

Location: Mark Twain House and Museum, Hartford, Connecticut.

Copies examined: Clemens's copies, in Hartford in 1997. There are no inscriptions at the front of the volumes.

On 14 July 1880 Estes & Lauriat of Boston billed Clemens for "1 Plutarch 3 vol $3"; Clemens paid on 20 July 1880 (receipt in MTP). Ridiculing several supporters of presidential candidate James Blaine in a letter to William Dean Howells written on 31 August 1884, Clemens used a phrase—"Man, 'Know thyself'"—which Plutarch attributed to the Delphic oracle in "Consolation to Apollonius" (*MTHL*, p. 501). At 1:30 p.m. on Friday, 15 March 1907, Isabel Lyon "slipped down to his room to see him lying asleep with his glasses on and his hands clasped over his breast and over a volume of 'Plutarch's Lives'" (IVL Journals, TS p. 232, MTP). Albert Bigelow Paine listed Plutarch's *Lives* among Clemens's favorite books toward the end of his life: "A volume of Plutarch was among the biographies that showed usage" (*MTB*, p. 1540).

———. *Plutarch's Lives of Illustrious Men. The Translation Called [John] Dryden's [1631–1700]; Corrected from the Greek and Revised by A[rthur]. H[ugh]. Clough [1819–1861]. The Athenaeum Society.* 5 vols. Philadelphia: John C. Winston and Co., 1905.

Catalog: Ball 2016 inventory, green cloth, 5 vols., paper label.

Location: Quarry Farm library shelves, under the supervision of the Mark Twain Archive, Elmira College, Elmira, New York.

Available to Clemens in the Quarry Farm library got his final visits to Elmira.

———. *Plutarch's Lives of Illustrious Men. The Translation Called*

[John] Dryden's [1631–1700]; Corrected from the Greek and Revised by A[rthur]. H[ugh]. Clough [1819–1861]. The Athenaeum Society. 5 vols. Boston: Little, Brown, and Co., 1905.

Catalog: Ball 2016 inventory, 4 vols. only, red cloth, gilt lettering and gilt paper edges, good condition.

Location: Quarry Farm library shelves, under the supervision of the Mark Twain Archive, Elmira College, Elmira, New York.

Available to Clemens in the Quarry Farm library for his final visits to Elmira.

———. *Plutarch's Morals. Translated from the Greek by Several Hands. Corrected and Revised by William W[atson]. Goodwin [1831–1912].* Intro. by Ralph Waldo Emerson (1803–1882). 5 vols. New York: Athenaeum Society, 1905.

Catalog: Ball 2016 inventory, 5 vols., green cloth with paper label, good condition.

Location: Quarry Farm library shelves, under the supervision of the Mark Twain Archive, Elmira College, Elmira, New York.

Available to Clemens in the Quarry Farm library for his final visits to Elmira.

PLYMPTON, ALMIRA GEORGIA (1850–1938). *Dear Daughter Dorothy.* Illustrated by the author. Boston: Roberts Brothers, 1891. 190 pp.

Source: MTLAcc, entry #1901, volume donated from Clemens's library by Clara Clemens Gabrilowitsch in 1910.

In this novel a motherless baby grows up and resolves to assist her father, who has been unjustly accused of embezzlement. Plympton, born in Boston, resided in Dover, Massachusetts.

POE, EDGAR ALLAN (1809–1849).

For an overview of Mark Twain's connections with Poe, see Alan Gribben's "'That Pair of Spiritual Derelicts': The Poe-Twain Relationship," *Poe Studies* 18.2 (December 1985): 17–21, which pointed out parallels in the fiction of two seemingly very dissimilar authors. A revised version of this essay appears in Volume One of the present work.

———. "Annabel Lee" (poem, published in 1849).

"It is many and many a year since" goes a phrase in the third paragraph in Chapter 33 of *The Adventures of Tom Sawyer* (1876). Burton R. Pollin detected this possible echo of Poe's poem (Pollin to Alan Gribben, 24 July 1987).

———. "The Balloon Hoax" (short story, published in 1844).

Standing on the crater of the dead volcano of Haleakala, Mark Twain remarked in Chapter 76 of *Roughing It* (1872): "Formerly, when I had read an article in which Poe treated of this singular fraud perpetrated upon the eye by isolated great altitudes, I had looked upon the matter as an invention of his own fancy." Franklin R. Rogers noted that in Poe's piece Mr. Ainsworth, the narrator, observes: "The sea does not seem convex (as one might suppose) but absolutely and most unequivocally concave" (*Roughing It*, Iowa-California Edition (1972), pp. 613–614; see also *Roughing It*, Works of Mark Twain Edition (1993), p. 738). Poe's story should also be remembered in connection with *Tom Sawyer Abroad* (1894) and Twain's other treatments of balloon ascents.

———. "The Bells" (poem, published in 1849).

In Chapter 36 of *Tramp Abroad* (1880), Mark Twain states that "Mr. Poe's poem of the 'Bells' stands incomplete to this day; but it is well enough that it is so, for the public reciter or 'reader' who goes around trying to imitate the sounds of the various sorts of bells with his voice would find himself 'up a stump' when he got to the church bell."

———. "The Black Cat" (short story, published in 1843).

Alan Gribben ("'That Pair of Spiritual Derelicts': The Poe-Twain Relationship," *Poe Studies* 19.2 [December 1985]: p. 19) and Richard Bridgman—*Traveling in Mark Twain* (Berkeley: University of California Press, 1987), p. 110—both pointed out the gruesome similarity between the actions of Poe's narrator who, angry at his wife, "buried the axe in her brain," and Mark Twain's anecdote in Chapter 30 of *Life on the Mississippi* (1883) about a "Captain Poe" who, trying to save his wife from a sinking steamboat, accidentally "clove her skull" with an axe.

———. "The Cask of Amontillado" (short story, published in 1846).

Jack Scherting, "Poe's 'The Cask of Amontillado': A Source for Twain's 'The Man That Corrupted Hadleyburg,'" *Mark Twain Journal* 16.2 (Summer 1972): 18–19, traced "Poe's seminal influence" on Twain's story. Both protagonists seek revenge for an unspecified insult, both are "willing to defer vengeance," and both "exploit human vanity by challenging the reputation of their victims."

———. "A Descent into the Maelström" (short story, published in 1841).

Margaret Augur—"Mark Twain's Reading" (1939), p. 65—believed that Mark Twain's picturesque and thrilling description in Hawaii (*RI* [1872], Ch. 76) bears a resemblance to Poe's story. Steven E. Kemper held the view that Twain was parodying Poe's tale by writing "The Invalid's Story" (1882) ("Poe, Twain, and Limburger Cheese," *Mark Twain Journal* 21.1 [Winter 1981–1982]: 13–14).

———. "Four Beasts in One; or, the Homo-cameleopard," (Originally published in 1836, then included in *Tales of the Grotesque and Arabesque* [1845]).

Walter Blair offered this tale as a "possible literary source" for "The King's Cameleopard or the Royal Nonesuch" in Bricksville (*HF* [1885], Ch. 22), though Blair conceded that many particulars differ (*MT&HF* [1960], pp. 319–320).

Pascal Covici, Jr., *Mark Twain's Humor: The Image of a World* (Dallas: Southern Methodist University Press, 1962), pp. 148–156.

———. "The Gold Bug" (short story, published in 1843).

Tom Sawyer's treasure-digging in Chapter 25 of *The Adventures of Tom Sawyer* (1876) may owe details to Poe's story. Pochmann, "Mind" (1924), p. 186; Ferguson, *MTM&L* (1943), p. 26; Blair, *MT&HF* (1960), p. 61; *HH&T* (1969), p. 159 n. 15.

———. "The Imp of the Perverse" (short story, published in 1845).

See Michael Kiskis, "'Hadleyburg' and 'The Imp of the Perverse': Twain, Poe, and the Insanity of Revenge," *Notes on American Literature* 20 (April 2011): 20–30.

———. "The Masque of the Red Death" (short story, published in 1842).

In Chapter 10 of Mark Twain's "Which Was It?" (written 1899–1903) a mute, "dismal guest," the "sombre apparition" of Deathshead Phillips, "upright and rigid," clothed in "dead and lustreless black," its raiment "ancient and mephistophelian," its face "ghastly white, dead and lustreless . . . . wholly white and horrible," stares ominously at George Harrison (*WWD?*, p. 268). Critics have understandably associated this figure with Twain's admiration for Adolf von Wilbrandt's *The Master of Palmyra*, but one can also recognize similarities between Twain's dramatic figure and the sense of awe and dread created by the skeletal intruder at the conclusion of Poe's story.

———. *The Murders of [sic] the Rue Morgue and Other Tales.* [Bound with *The Narrative of A. Gordon Pym.*] Chicago: Belford, Clarke & Co., [1886?]. 349 pp.

Source: MTLAcc, entry #1064, volume donated to the Mark Twain Library in Redding by Albert Bigelow Paine, Clemens's designated biographer. Possibly Clemens saw this book, since the men exchanged reading materials.

On 1 June 1896, in Bloemfontein, Orange Free State, Clemens noted: "What a curious thing a 'detective' story is. And was there ever one that the author needn't be ashamed of, except 'The Murders in the Rue Morgue?'" (NB 38, TS p. 32). Clemens listed Poe's name in a projected catalogue of works "For Cheap Books" in July 1899 (NB 40, TS p. 58). Clemens's caustic marginalia in John A. Joyce's *Edgar Allan Poe* (cop. 1901) characterize that biographer as "the most remarkable animal that ever cavorted around a poet's grave." Poe's books lived at least forty-two years, Clemens pointed out to a Congressional committee on copyright reform on 7 December 1906 (*MTS1923*, p. 327; *MTSpk*, pp. 533–539). Clemens commented on page 110 of Frank Moore Colby's *Imaginary Obligations* (1906) about the hazing practices at West Point that "made the place unsatisfactory to Whistler & to Edgar A. Poe." But on 18 January 1909, Clemens expressed indifference to Poe's tales in a letter to William Dean Howells: "I *have* to write a line, lazy as I am, to say how your Poe article [*Harper's Weekly*, 16 January 1909] delights me & charms me; & to add that I am in agreement with substantially all you say about his literature. To me his prose is unreadable—like Jane Austin's [sic]. No, there is a difference. I could read his prose on salary, but not Jane's. . . . Another thing: you grant that God & circumstances sinned against Poe, but you also grant that he sinned against himself—a thing which he couldn't do & didn't do" (*MTHL*, p. 841).

MTL (1917), p. 830; Pochmann, "Mind" (1924), p. 130; Stone, *IE* (1961), p. 191.

———. *The Narrative of Arthur Gordon Pym of Nantucket* (novel, published in 1838). [See also the preceding entry, bound with it.]

Kenneth S. Lynn saw "Poe-like" parallels in the "weird symbolism and psychological atmosphere" of Mark Twain's projected novel, "The Great Dark," written in 1898 (*MT&SH*, pp. 274–276). See also James D. Wilson, "'The Great Dark': Invisible Spheres, Formed in Fright," *Midwest Quarterly* 23.2 (Winter 1982): 229–243.

———. "The Purloined Letter" (short story, published in 1845).

Walter Blair suggested that perhaps Dupin's observations gave Tom Sawyer the inspiration in "Tom Sawyer's Conspiracy" (written 1897–1902) to follow up a search in unlikely locations by hunting "in the likely places" (*HH&T*, p. 159).

———. "The Raven" (poem, published in 1845).

Around 1864 Mark Twain wrote a clumsy, racist burlesque,

"The Mysterious Chinaman" (published in *The Twainian* 6 [July-August 1947]: 3; reprinted in Scott's *OPMT*, p. 53). Possibly Twain was thinking of Rufus Griswold's depiction of Poe in December 1866, when he wrote in Notebook 7: "Geniuses are people who dash off wierd [*sic*], wild, incomprehensible poems with astonishing facility, & then go & get booming drunk & sleep in the gutter." Farther on, Twain observed that a man who "wears out the affection & the patience of his friends & then complains in sickly rhymes of his hard lot, & finally . . . persists in going up some <infamous> back alley & dying in rags & dirt, he is beyond all question a genius" (*N&J* 1: 250–251). (Twain had been reading books aboard the *America*.) Minnie M. Brashear pointed out that the conscience perching atop the narrator's bookcase in Twain's "Concerning the Recent Carnival of Crime in Connecticut" (1876) could be construed as a burlesque of Poe's "The Raven" (*MTSM* [1934], p. 213 n. 39). For Twain's evolving opinion of Poe, see also the Catalog entry for John A. Joyce, *Edgar Allan Poe* (cop. 1901).

Duckett, *MT&BH* (1964), pp. 54–55; Scott, *OPMT* (1966), p. 6.

———. "To Helen" (poem, published in 1845).

In Chelsea, late in October 1896, Mark Twain copied into Notebook 39 the line "The glory that was Greece & the grandeur that was Rome" (TS p. 16). A decade later he employed this line to illustrate that "when the right words are conspicuous . . . they thunder" ("William Dean Howells" [1906]). In defending an extension of the Copyright Bill, Twain quoted "the stately line—'The glory that was Greece, and the grandeur that was Rome'" (19 December 1906 AD, MTP, *AutoMT* 3: 323).

———. "The Unparalleled Adventure of One Hans Pfaall" (short story, published in 1835).

Burton R. Pollin found traces of this tale in Twain's *Roughing It* (1872). See *The Collected Writings of Edgar Allan Poe: The Imaginary Voyages* (Boston: Twayne/G. K. Hall, 1981), p. 478 n. 37A.

———. "William Wilson" (story, published in 1839).

Minnie M. Brashear suggested this story of dual personalities (at the end of which the central figure murders his conscience, and thus himself) as having been inspirational for Mark Twain's "Concerning the Recent Carnival of Crime in Connecticut" (1876) (*MTSM* [1934], p. 213 n. 39). In Chapter 25 of "No. 44, The Mysterious Stranger" (written between 1902 and 1908), August Feldner comes to a chilling observation that echoes the conclusion of Poe's "William Wilson": "Good heavens! In trying to ruin the Duplicate, I had only ruined myself" (*MSM*, p. 353).

Other commentators have pursued correspondences between the stories: Robert C. Comeau, "Reading Poe on Salary: Mark Twain's Use of 'The Raven,' 'Hop Frog,' and 'William Wilson' in the 'The Facts Concerning the Recent Carnival of Crime in Connecticut,'" *Southern Literary Journal* 29.1 (Fall 1996): 26–34; Patricia L. Bradley, "Mark Twain's 'Carnival of Crime' and Anxieties of Influence," *Kentucky Philological Review* 12 (March 1997): 20–28; and (especially) Lawrence I. Berkove, "Poe, Twain, and the Nature of Conscience," *ESQ* 46.4 (2000): 239–253. See also the Catalog entry for Robert Louis Stevenson's *The Strange Case of Dr. Jekyll and Mr. Hyde* (1886).

———. *Works of Edgar Allan Poe*. The Raven Edition. 5 vols. New York: P. F. Collier & Sons, 1904.

Catalog: Ball 2016 inventory, 4 vols., lacking only Volume Five, back cloth, gray lettering, good condition, has a Sayles bookplate. [In 1902 Jervis Langdon (1875–1952) married Eleanor Sayles (1878–1964).]

Location: Quarry Farm library shelves, under the supervision of the Mark Twain Archive, Elmira College, Elmira, New York.

Conceivably Clemens could have noticed this edition in the Langdons' home during one of his last visits to Elmira.

———. *The Works of the Late Edgar Allan Poe with a Memoir by Rufus Wilmot Griswold [1815–1857] and Notices of His Life and Genius by N[athaniel]. P[arker]. Willis [1806–1867] and J[ames]. R[ussell]. Lowell [1819–1891]*. Preface by Maria Clemm (1790–1871). 4 vols. New York: [J. S.] Redfield, 1850. [The first three volumes appeared in 1850; Volume IV was added in 1856.]

Dennis W. Eddings—"Sam Clemens Reads Edgar Poe," *Mark Twain Journal: The Author and His Era* 56.2 (Fall 2018): 124–133—made a convincing case that this was the edition in which Clemens initially encountered the majority of Poe's writings while living in Keokuk, Iowa in 1856. It could be relevant that residents of Keokuk, Iowa recalled Clemens's carrying about "the tales of Edgar Allan Poe" in 1856 or 1857 (*MTB*, p. 106).

The Poet and the Painter; or, Gems of Art and Song. Folio. Full brown morocco, elaborately embossed, heavily gilt, raised bands, gilt, all edges gilt. Steel engravings. New York: D. Appleton, 1869.

Inscription: inscribed in ink on the front flyleaf by Clemens's brother-in-law to his fiancée: "Merry Christmas/to/Ida Clark/December 25th, 1868/C. J. L." Olivia Clemens's brother Charles Jervis Langdon (1849–1916) would wed Ida B. Clark (1849–1934) in 1870.

Location: collection of Kevin Mac Donnell, Austin, Texas. Purchased from the Langdon family.

Source: supplementary inventory sent by Mac Donnell to Alan Gribben, 28 August 2017. No markings in the text.

This was the type of literary gift book for which Mark Twain sometimes expressed disdain. Did he ever see this one in the Langdons' parlor?

Poetry of the Woods; Passages from the Poets Descriptive of Forest Scenes, Etc. Illus. Philadelphia: E. H. Butler & Co., 1857. 128 pp.

Inscription: "Mrs. Susan L. Crane, From her Brother and Sister, 'Charlie' & Libbi Langdon, Elmira Dec. 26, 1859".

Catalogs: cataloged among the library books at Quarry Farm in the 1980s (inventory card in the Mark Twain Archive, Elmira College); listed among the books that Mark Woodhouse transferred from the Quarry Farm library to the Mark Twain Archive on 9 July 1987; Ball 2016 inventory, brown cover, gilt lettering, broken cover, inscribed to Susan L. Crane in 1859.

Location: Mark Twain Archive, Elmira College, Elmira, New York.

This volume would have been accessible to Clemens whenever he visited the Quarry Farm in Elmira, New York.

POLE, WILLIAM (1814–1900). *The Theory of the Modern Scientific Game of Whist*. London: Longman & Co., 1884. 144 pp.

Source: MTLAcc, entry #693, volume donated by Clemens.

Pollard, Rebecca (Smith) (1831–1917), pseud. "Kate Harrington." Portrait. 12mo, cloth. *Centennial and Other Poems.* Portrait. Philadelphia: J. B. Lippincott & Co., 1876. 252 pp.

Inscription: signed "S. L. Clemens, Hartford, 1876."

Marginalia: Clemens marked certain passages and made several penciled comments.

Catalogs: *A1911*, "12mo, cloth, Phila. 1876, . . . some passages marked, and a few autograph remarks in pencil," quotes the signature, lot 224, sold for $1.50; George D. Smith, New York City, "Catalogue of Books" (1911), quotes the signature, "some passages marked, and a few autograph remarks in pencil," item #154, $7.50; AAA-A (New York City), Catalogue number 4351 (23 November 1937), "12mo, original cloth, worn at corners and top and bottom of the backstrip, Philadelphia, 1876, first edition, copy once owned by Samuel L. Clemens, with a number of marginal annotations in his handwriting, in pencil, giving the names of earlier poems that inspired or suggested seven of the poems in this volume," has the *A1911* sale label, lot 94.

Clemens obviously knew poetry well enough that he could detect imitations.

Pond, James Burton (1838–1903). *Eccentricities of Genius; Memories of Famous Men and Women of the Platform and Stage.* Frontispiece portrait and illustrations. First edition. Original crimson cloth, gilt. Shaken and with soiling and loose signatures. In a slipcase. New York: G. W. Dillingham Co., 1900. 564 pp.

Inscription: lengthily inscribed to Olivia Clemens by Pond on 17 November 1900, with a warm tribute to the genius of her husband. It reads in part: "To Mrs. S. L. Clemens, with kind regards of the one who made this book . . . and who has written of her husband,—the only man whose make-up contains much that is best in every friend he has written about in this book."

Marginalia: Clemens made vertical pencil marks on seven pages within the section (pages 197–233) devoted to him and on three pages (246–247 and 249) about him and James Whitcomb Riley. In addition he turned down the corners of several pages.

Provenance: Frederick Anderson, then Editor of the Mark Twain Papers in the Bancroft Library at the University of California, Berkeley, examined this book in the New York City offices of John F. Fleming, Inc. and made notes in April 1972 (Anderson to James D. Hart, 17 April 1972, photocopy sent to Alan Gribben). Subsequently the volume belonged to Victor Jacobs of Dayton, Ohio in 1986 (Jacobs to Alan Gribben, 15 October 1986, "presentation copy" to Olivia Clemens). Jacobs died in 1996. Nick Karanovich then acquired the book.

Catalogs: ListABP (1910), "Eccentricities of Genius, Pond"; *C1951*, D41, listed erroneously among the books signed by Clemens; *Fleming 1972*; Sotheby Parke Bernet, Sale number 3482 (25 February 1976), "Property of a New York City Collector" (John F. Fleming), lot 21 (a group of titles); acquired in 1976 by Seven Gables Bookshop, New York City, $60; Victor and Irene Murr Jacobs Collection sale, Sotheby's, 29 October 1996, lot 294, sold with two other volumes for a total of $2,300; *Sotheby's 2003*, #228, $3,000 (sold with an archive of materials related to the Clemens-Pond relationship, including letters

and a photograph).

Location: collection of Kevin Mac Donnell, Austin, Texas.

Copy examined: Clemens's copy, in July 2004 in Austin, Texas.

James B. Pond , known as "Major Pond" owing to his heroic record in the Civil War, was the lecture agent who managed the North American leg of Twain's global lecture in 1895, and the two men hit it off quite well. "I found every line of your boyhood article in the magazine well said & interesting," Clemens wrote to Pond from London on 19 October 1899 (ALS, Berg Collection, NYPL). However, on 14 September 1900 Clemens objected strenuously to Pond's suggestion that he be allowed to publish portions of Clemens's letters in the forthcoming book. "Leave them [these notions] to men of the Will M. Clemens breed," Clemens admonished from London (Berg Collection, NYPL). William W. Ellsworth stated that it was he who told Clemens about Pond's book shortly after *Eccentricities* issued, and that Clemens said "he would read it" (*A Golden Age of Authors*, p. 226). Clemens wrote Pond on 3 December 1900: "I find your book well written & distinctly interesting" (Berg). On 20 May 1901 Clemens showed enthusiasm, addressing Pond from New York City: "Your book is making friends all the time, & I am glad for it deserves it" (Berg Collection, NYPL).

Overland with Mark Twain: James B. Pond's Photographs and Journal of the North American Lecture Tour of 1895, ed. Alan Gribben and Nick Karanovich. Elmira, New York: Center for Mark Twain Studies at Quarry Farm, Elmira College, 1992.

———, ed. *A Summer in England with Henry Ward Beecher; Giving the Addresses, Lectures, and Sermons Delivered by Him in Great Britain During The Summer of 1886; Together with an Account of the Tour, Expressions of Public Opinion, etc.* Illus. New York: Fords, Howard & Hulbert, 1887. 707 pp.

Inscription: "Yours, my dear Mrs. Crane/to the end of [illegible] volume,/J. B. Pond/Sept. 15, 1895,/The day that good news came from Australia."

Catalog: Ball 2016 inventory, brown textured cloth, gilt lettering on the spine, top page edges gilt, fine condition.

Location: Mark Twain Archive, Gannett-Tripp Library, Elmira College, Elmira, New York.

This book was available to Clemens in the Quarry Farm library in Elmira.

Pool, Marie Louise (1841–1898). *Roweny in Boston, A Novel.* New York: Harper & Brothers, 1900. 348 pp.

Source: MTLAcc, entry #1642, volume donated by Clemens.

Roweny in Boston, a novel about an opera singer who loses her voice and eventually takes up painting and moves to Paris, was first published in 1892.

Poole, John (c. 1786–1872). *Little Pedlington and the Pedlingtonians* (London, published in 1839).

In November 1878 Clemens made an entry in Notebook 17: "Little Pedlington" (*N&J* 2: 281). E. Cobham Brewer called Pedlington "an imaginary place, the village of quackery and cant, egotism and humbug, affectation and flattery" (*The Reader's Handbook* [1919], p. 619).

Poole, Robert. *Marian Grantham's Child, Margaret Le Boutilier, and Rene Le Rossignol.* Chicago: Thomas Gilmartin,

Printer, 1894.

Inscriptions: the title page has "Mark Twain" written at the top in black ink, one of the more obvious forgeries that have been on the market. The front flyleaf bears an explanatory inscription in black ink: "This pamphlet/came from the/library of my father/Eugene Field./Nov 9, 1931./Eugene Field II."

Provenance: offered for sale by a book dealer in Michigan in the 1980s.

Location: currently unknown.

Copy examined: Kevin Mac Donnell of Austin, Texas has identified this book as a forged association item, and after viewing a photocopy of the title page and the front flyleaf (kindly sent by Mac Donnell) I completely concur. Eugene Field II had sold off the genuine contents of his father's library by the early 1920s. Subsequently he began buying miscellaneous books at second hand stores and forging various signatures in them, sometimes accompanied by statements of authentication like the one in this volume.

POPE, ALEXANDER (1688–1744). "Eloisa to Abelard" (poem, published in 1717).

Chapter 15 of *The Innocents Abroad* (1869) possibly borrowed details from Pope's poem for Mark Twain's version of the story of the tragically separated lovers, Abélard and Héloïse.

Henry A. Pochmann, "The Mind of Mark Twain" (1924), p. 186.

———. *An Essay on Criticism* (poem, published in 1711).

Pope's phrase "In the ages that have dragged their slow length along" appears in Chapter 26 of Mark Twain's *The Innocents Abroad* (1869). "A cat may err—to err is cattish," Twain quipped in "A Cat Tale" (written in 1880; DeVoto, *LE* (1962), p. 134; Budd, *CTSS&E*, 1: 772).

———. *An Essay on Man* (poem, published 1732–1734).

In a letter to his mother on 20 March 1862, Clemens parodied lines from this poem in describing Nevada. "Lo! the poor Indian, whose untutored mind," was the first line Clemens invented (*MTLet* 1: 174). On page 224 of Henry H. Breen's *Modern English Literature* (1857), Clemens noted in 1876: "The thought is nothing—it has occurred to everybody; so has every thought that is worth fame. The *expression* of it is the thing to applaud, and there Pope is best" (quoted in *MT&HF* [1960], p. 60). When devising comical menu captions for a Hartford banquet held in June 1881, Clemens referred to "the noblest work of God" (Beinecke Rare Book and Manuscript Library, Yale University; Everett Emerson to Alan Gribben, 29 October 1982). In an Australian interview published on 17 September 1895 (Sydney *Morning Herald*, pp. 5–6), Mark Twain spoke of Pope as "one of the wittiest writers who ever put pen to paper," but added that "most of us agree that he was 'artificial.' Now, humor is never artificial" (*MT&JB* [1970], p. 274; Scharnhorst, *Complete Interviews* [2006], p. 206). "A wiser observer than you," says the Young Man of Twain's *What Is Man?* (1906), "has recorded the fact that 'an honest man's the noblest work of God'" (*WIM?*, p 164).

———, translator. *The Iliad of Homer.* [Published 1715–1720.]

In Rome, the Oracle of the *Quaker City* declared that "the Pope was a noble-looking old man, but he never *did* think much of his Iliad" (*IA* [1869], Ch. 32). Clemens joked

when writing Mary Fairbanks, "If Helen's Babies & Pope's translation of Homer, & Paradise Lost, & Lamb's works, had been submitted to me, I would have burned them with a <savage> maniacal joy & scalped their authors" (31 October 1877, *MTMF*, p. 212).

See the Catalog entry for Homer, *The Iliad of Homer.*

———. *The Works of Alexander Pope, Esq., with Notes and Illustrations, by Himself and Others, To Which Are Added, a New Life of the Author, an Estimate of his Poetical Character and Writings, and Occasional Remarks by William Roscoe [1753–1831], Esq.* 8 vols. London: Longman, Brown and Co., 1847.

Catalog: Ball 2016 inventory, brown marble cloth, leather binding, 8 vols.

Location: Quarry Farm library shelves, under the supervision of the Mark Twain Archive, Elmira College, Elmira, New York.

This set of volumes would have been accessible to Clemens whenever he visited Quarry Farm in Elmira, New York.

POPE, (GENERAL) JOHN (1822–1892). "The Second Battle of Bull Run," *Century Magazine* 31.3, n.s. 9 (January 1886): 442–474.

Amid notebook entries about U. S. Grant's *Memoirs*, Clemens wrote in 1885: "Pope mentions &c &c" (NB 24, *N&J* 3: 158). Possibly Clemens had been shown an advance copy of General Pope's detailed battlefield account.

"POP! GOES THE WEASEL" (children's song).

In 1868 Mark Twain's letter to the Chicago *Republican* suggested adding "Pop goes the weasel" at the end of a feeble poem, "To an Absent One," published by Congressman William Mungen in the Washington *National Intelligencer* (reprinted in *Washington in 1868*, ed. Cyril Clemens [Webster Groves, Missouri: International Mark Twain Society, 1943], p. 14). In a sketch published in the *Galaxy* 10.5 (November 1870): 731, "A Reminiscence of the Back Settlements" (later published in *Sketches, New & Old* [1975] as "The Undertaker's Chat"), Twain recalled an undertaker's praise for a corpse who led his funeral mourners in choruses of "Pop Goes the Weasel"—"because he'd always liked that tune when he was down-hearted."

Popular Fiction. 3 vols. [Unidentified book.]

On 14 July 1880 Estes & Lauriat of Boston billed Clemens $2 for "1 Popular Fiction 3 v."; Clemens paid on 20 July 1880 (receipt in MTP).

Popular Science Monthly (magazine, New York, published 1872–).

Daniel Appleton & Co. of New York City billed Clemens on 26 January 1881 for "Science Mo 1881 5.00"; Clemens paid his "Club rates" ($5 less .50¢) on 31 January 1881 (receipt in MTP). In May 1891 Clemens made an entry in Notebook 30 about forwarding his *Popular Science* subscription to Europe (*N&J* 3: 628).

PORTER, EVELINA (ANDERSON) (1791–1871). "Thou hast wounded the spirit that loved thee" (song).

In "Letter from Carson City," a sketch published in the *Territorial Enterprise* on 3 February 1863, Clemens included this song among those he had heard at the Governor's house (*ET&S* 1: 197). He waggishly claimed that he "wept at the recollection of the circumstance which he was singing about."

PORTER, GEORGE. "The Maid, A Drama in Five Acts" (typescript of a play).

George Porter of Bridgeport, Connecticut copyrighted "The Maid, A Drama in Five Acts" on 27 February 1904 (*Dramatic Compositions Copyrighted in the United States* [Washington, D. C.: Library of Congress Copyright Office, 1918], p. 1370). On 20 February 1905 Isabel Lyon recorded: "This evening Mr. Clemens began the reading of a Joan of Arc play by Mr. Geo. Porter." He "finished reading" it on 22 February (IVL Journal, Mark Twain Archive, Elmira, New York.). Porter went to see Clemens in Dublin, New Hampshire about this play on 23 July 1905, according to Clemens's note on a letter from Porter of 19 July 1905 (TS in MTP). The same George Porter would copyright another play, *The Lindseys*, on 14 June 1906. This would-be playwright could have been the prominent Bridgeport physician George Loring Porter (1838–1919), who principally wrote medical articles. He had attained an early prominence by being present at the death of John Wilkes Booth and serving as the attending physician to the other conspirators during their trials.

PORTER, JANE (1776–1850). *The Scottish Chiefs* (historical novel, published in 1810).

In the summer of 1885 the Clemens children named their Quarry Farm playhouse "Ellerslie" from this novel (*MTB*, p. 824; *S&MT*, p. 204). When Clemens was interviewed at Quarry Farm in September 1886 by Edwin J. Park of the Chicago *Tribune*, Clemens explained: "My three daughters have had that stony place fenced off, and they live there about all the time in that building. They call it Ellerslie, and at present they are living retired lives, which they spend in reading *Scottish Chiefs*" (Scharnhorst, *Complete Interviews*, p. 94). Porter's novel was principally the tragic story of the Scottish rebel chieftain William Wallace (c. 1272–1305), legendarily associated with a vicinity in Scotland purportedly known as Ellerslie. In Porter's narrative Wallace's estate, located below rocky cliffs, had the name Ellerslie (though current historians doubt the accuracy of this) and Porter made it the site where Wallace's pregnant wife is cruelly murdered and his manor house destroyed. See the next Catalog entry for additional information about the Clemens children's devotion to *The Scottish Chiefs*. See also the contradictory account by Albert Bigelow Paine in the Catalog entry for Grace Aguilar's *The Days of Bruce* (1834).

———. *Thaddeus of Warsaw* (historical novel, published in London, 1803).

According to two biographers, a tangle of vines and bushes on Quarry Farm was granted to the Clemens and Langdon children, "and the place was named Helen's Bower, for they were [in 1885] reading *Thaddeus of Warsaw* and the name appealed to Susy's poetic fancy" (Paine, *MTB*, p. 824; Salsbury, *S&MT*, p. 203). Either Paine or Clemens was confused about this reference; the "bower" of the virtuous Lady Helen Mar was mentioned in Porter's *The Scottish Chiefs*, not in *Thaddeus of Warsaw*. For instance, Chapter 38 of *The Scottish Chiefs* is titled "The Bower, or Ladies' Apartment," referring to Helen's retiring to "an inner apartment" in Snowdoun Palace. *Thaddeus of Warsaw*, by contrast, portrayed the plight of a fugitive from the failed Polish uprising of 1794 against Russian and Austrian invaders, Thaddeus Sobieski, who takes refuge

in London. Mark Twain set an attempted novel, "Simon Wheeler, Detective" (written 1877–1898?) in "a sleepy little Missouri village" called Guilford where "Ossian and Thaddeus of Warsaw were still read, fire and brimstone still preached" (*S&B*, p. 312).

PORTER, MARY WINEARLS (1886–1980). *What Rome Was Built With: A Description of the Stones Employed in Ancient Times for Its Building and Decoration*. Green cloth, gilt lettering. London and Oxford; New York and Toronto: Henry Frowde, 1907. 108 pp.

Inscription: the front free endpaper is inscribed in black ink, "Mark Twain/with my affectionate good/wishes,/ Polly Porter."

Marginalia: Clemens wrote "they?" in black ink in the margin of page 77, apparently criticizing the syntax.

Location: Mark Twain Library, Redding, Connecticut.

Copy examined: Clemens's copy. Has the red ink Mark Twain Library accession number "3913". Examined in 1970 and again in June 1982 and on 9 November 2019.

Porter wrote to Clemens on 11 August 1907 (ALS in MTP).

PORTER, WILLIAM TROTTER (1809–1858). "Letter from Billy Patterson Himself," in *Big Bear of Arkansas, and Other Sketches*. Philadelphia: T. B. Peterson and Brothers, 1843. [Edition conjectured; the book was reprinted in subsequent years by various firms.]

In Rome, on 29 October 1878, Mark Twain jotted down the humorous proposal that the Ecumenical Council, having solved the question of Immaculate Conception, ought to "decide once & forever . . . who it was that struck Billy Patterson" (*N&J* 2: 235). On page 115 of a sketch included in *The Big Bear of Arkansas, and Other Sketches* (1843), "Letter from Billy Patterson Himself," the title character alludes to "a vilent blo reseaved long sense by some anonymus person." In Appendix A to *A Tramp Abroad* (1880), Twain declared: "You ask the [hotel] portier . . . 'who struck Billy Patterson.' It does not matter what you ask him: in nine cases out of ten he knows, and in the tenth case he will find out for you before you can turn around three times."

The Portfolio, An Artistic Periodical (London, published 1870–1893). Edited by Philip Gilbert Hamerton (1834–1894).

Clemens wrote to Charles L. Webster on 30 December 1882 from Hartford: "Here is the usual bill for the 'Portfolio.' I subscribed for it for one year, and ordred that year to be paid for. I never subscribed a second time, but have done my best to keep them from throwing away that excellent work upon me. I do not want to have to refuse to receive the publication from the post-man. . . . I wish you would explain the case to Mr. Bouton and have the periodical stopped before bloodshed" (*MTBus*, p. 206). Webster indicated on 2 January 1883 that he had attended to this matter. But on 22 February 1883 Clemens wrote from Hartford about further dunning: "Bouton's understanding with you does not seem to have been permanent. . . . If one subscription has never been paid, I am willing that you shall pay for one and close up the controversy. But if any year has already been paid, Mr. Bouton will have to sue me as long as I live, and then I won't pay" (*MTBus*, p. 210). On 9 March 1883 Clemens capitulated: "Pay this check over to Bouton & let him give you a receipted bill. I can't find the half of those Portfolios" (*MTBus*, p. 211).

PORT LOUIS, MAURITIUS *Merchants' and Planters' Gazette.*
From the issue of 20 April 1896 Mark Twain quoted "the article of a regular contributor, 'Carminge,'" concerning the death of a prominent citizen's nephew (*FE* [1897], Ch. 63).

POSCHINGER, MARGARETE [ALSO MARGARETHA] MARIA VIKTORIA FREIIN (VON LANDAU) VON (1861–1911). *Life of the Emperor Frederick.* Ed. and intro. by Sidney Whitman (1848–1925). Portrait. New York: Harper & Brothers, 1901. 459 pp. [Publisher and pages conjectured.]
  Catalog: *A1911*, "8vo, cloth, gilt top, uncut, N.Y. 1901," with a sheet of Clemens's notes laid in, lot 388, sold for $1.25.
  The subject was the German Emperor Frederick III (1831–1888). His Prussian-born biographer, married to Heinrich Joseph Karl Ludwig von Poschinger, died in Alpes-Maritmes, France.

POST, EMILY (1872–1960).
  Emily Post, then better known as a fiction author than as an authority on etiquette, was among the guests at Mark Twain's Seventieth Birthday dinner at Delmonico's on 5 December 1905. In a letter to Cyril Clemens written on 2 June 1953 she told of meeting Twain twice, the first time when F. Hopkinson Smith introduced her to him at a banquet held in Twain's honor. At the second encounter she was surprised that he remembered her as well as the phrase used when they had met ("Emily Post and Edna Ferber Recollect," *Mark Twain Journal* 19.2 (Summer 1978): Back cover.

POST, LOUIS FREELAND (1849–1928). *Documentary Outline of the Philippine Case.* Pamphlet No. 7. Chicago: The Public Publishing Co., [1900]. 47 pp. [Appeared as an article in the 19 May 1900 issue of *The Public*, a weekly Chicago review of current events.]
  Marginalia: Mark Twain heavily annotated pages 12–41 in pencil and black ink. At the top of page 39 he wrote in black ink (concerning the provisional government): "a gov't of universal acceptance by its people—Spain dead—the whole country in their hands—nobody with a claim upon it."
  Location: Mark Twain Papers, Bancroft Library, University of California at Berkeley.
  Copy examined: Clemens's copy, a paperbound pamphlet.
  Mark Twain's Weapons of Satire: Anti-Imperialist Writings on the Philippine-American War, ed. Jim Zwick (Syracuse: Syracuse University Press, 1992), p. 86.
———. *Ethics of Democracy: A Series of Optimistic Essays on the Natural Laws of Human Society.* New York: Moody Publishing, 1903. 374 pp.
  Mark Twain's Weapons of Satire: Anti-Imperialist Writings on the Philippine-American War, ed. Jim Zwick (Syracuse: Syracuse University Press, 1992), p. xxvi mentioned that Louis F. Post sent Mark Twain a copy of *Ethics of Democracy* (which quoted Twain's advocacy of self-governance); Zwick cited a letter from Post to Twain written on 21 December 1903. Twain praised the book in a letter to Post of 7 January 1904, which was published in *The Public* 7 (10 September 1904): 367. See also Jim Zwick, "'Prodigally Endowed with Sympathy for the Cause': Mark Twain's Involvement with the Anti-Imperialist League," *Mark Twain Journal* 32.1 (Spring 1994): 22 n. 29. Post

had earlier collaborated with the economic philosopher Henry George (1839–1897). In August 1891 Post took over the editorship of the weekly newspaper that George founded and edited, *The Standard* (Dominic Candeloro, "Louis F. Post and the Single Tax Movement," 1872–98," *American Journal of Economics and Sociology* 35.4 [October 1976]: 415–430). See the Catalog entries for Henry George and for *The Standard.*

POST, MELVILLE DAVISSON (1869–1930). *The Man of Last Resort; or, The Clients of Randolph Mason.* New York: G. P. Putnam's Sons, 1907. 284 pp.
  Source: MTLAcc, entry #1061, volume donated by Clemens.
  The online Hathitrust listings give Melville Davisson Post's birth date as 1871, but the majority of biographical sources now point toward the year 1869. In *The Man of Last Resort* (originally published in 1897) and two other collections of Randolph Mason short stories, Post depicts the shenanigans of a Perry Mason-like (some readers would say unscrupulous) attorney who solves crimes and outwits the legal system on behalf of his clients.
———. *The Strange Schemes of Randolph Mason.* New York: G. P. Putnam's Sons, 1907. 280 pp. [Edition conjectured.]
  Source: MTLAcc, entry #241, volume donated by Clemens, listed only as "Randolph Mason" by the librarian who entered the title, publisher, date, and pages in the Mark Twain Library accession book.
  The number of pages listed by the librarian fit the G. P. Putnam's Sons edition of *The Strange Schemes of Randolph Mason,* a collection of short stories Putnam's first published in 1896. It seems clear that Clemens owned an edition of this Post title.

POSTON, CHARLES DIBRELLE (1825–1902). *The Parsees: A Lecture.* "For Private Circulation." Binding loose. N.p., [1870?]. 100 pp.
  Inscription: the front free endpaper is inscribed in black ink "Mark Twain/with the Author[']s Complts/London/1872". 113 pp.
  Marginalia: the frontispiece illustration depicts the plump Poston with a mustache, his hands crossed, dressed in the garments of a Rajah. Someone, possibly Clemens (but not Poston), wrote "The Author" in ink below this sketch. A bit of loose newspaper print was laid in at pages 94–95.
  Location: Mark Twain Library, Redding, Connecticut.
  Copy examined: Clemens's copy, unmarked. Has the red ink Mark Twain Library accession number "3449". Should I mention a distinct cigar odor wafting from this volume? Examined in 1970 and again in June 1982 and on 9 November 2019.
  Poston had been an early pioneer and politician in the Arizona Territory. After he traveled to India and lived among the Parsees he became a convert to Zoroastrianism.

POTTER, BEATRIX (1866–1943). *The Tale of Peter Rabbit.* Illus. New York: F. Warne & Co., n.d. 85 pp.
  Source: MTLAcc, entry #440, volume donated by Clemens; reported as being in "practically worn out" condition on 15 March [1910?].
———. [Four identical copies.]
  Source: MTLAcc, entries #1251–1254, volumes donated by Clemens. One copy was subsequently sold to a Mrs. E. T. Field for .25¢.

Potter, Frances Boardman (Squire) (1867–1914). *The Ballingtons, A Novel*. Boston: Little, Brown & Co., 1905. 445 pp. Mrs. Potter, a native Elmiran, wrote from London in 1904 or 1905 (the letter is undated) asking Clemens to send her publishers "a line" to help the sales of her first novel (MTP). There is no indication as to whether he complied. Little, Brown & Company wrote to Clemens on 27 October 1905, addressing the letter in care of Thomas Bailey Aldrich: "We are taking the liberty of sending you a copy of our most prominent fall novel, 'The Ballingtons,' by Francis Squire [*sic*]. (Frances Squire had married Winfield S. Potter in Elmira in 1891.) Some time ago a copy of this book was sent you addressed to Tarrytown, New York, together with a note from the author. The Post Office Department now informs us that the book remains unclaimed at the Post Office in that place, but we trust you received the letter" (MTP).

Potter, Margaret Horton (1881–1911), "Mrs. John D. Black." *The Genius*. New York: Harper & Brothers, 1906. 449 pp.
Source: MTLAcc, entry #242, volume donated by Clemens.
———. *The Golden Ladder, A Novel*. New York: Harper & Brothers, 1908. 434 pp.
Source: MTLAcc, entry #1089, volume donated by Clemens; subsequently withdrawn from circulation.
———. *The Princess*. New York: Harper & Brothers, 1907. 386 pp.
Source: MTLAcc, entry #1060, volume donated by Clemens.
———. [Another identical copy.]
Source: MTLAcc, entry #1269, volume donated by Clemens.
———. *A Star of Babylon. A Phantasy*. New York: Harper & Brothers, 1902. 494 pp.
Source: MTLAcc, entry # 1324, volume donated by Clemens.
In a letter dated 23 December that was most likely written in 1902 (it was signed "Margaret Potter Black," and Potter had married attorney John D. Black on 1 January 1902), the author assured Clemens that "there has been no joy in my life that you have not made richer, no sorrow that your work has not show[n] me how to bear—*best*" (*DearMT*, p. 207). Potter would attend the Seventieth Birthday banquet that Harper & Brothers arranged for Clemens in 1905.

Pötzl, Eduard (1851–1914). *Bummelei. Neue Gelammelte Skizzen [Loafing. New Collected Sketches]*. Illustrated by Koloman Moser (1868–1918). Wien: Robert Mohr, 1896. 181 pp.
Location: Mark Twain Library, Redding, Connecticut.
Copy examined: Clemens's copy, unsigned and unmarked. The front free endpaper is loose. Has a red ink Mark Twain Library accession number "4089". Examined in 1970 and again in June 1982 and on 9 November 2019. Clemens and Pötzl, a feature writer and editor for the Vienna newspaper *Neues Wiener Tagblatt*, became friends during Clemens's long sojourn in Vienna in the late 1890s. On 2 October 1897 Clemens wrote from the Hotel Metropole "to offer my sincerest thanks for the books" (MTP).
———. *Hoch vom Kahlenberg. Heitere nd ernste Skizzen aus dem Wiener Leben [High from the Kahlenberg. Serious and Cheerful Sketches from Old Vienna]*. Leipzig: Philipp Reclam

jun., n.d. 95 pp. + 32.
Inscription: (on the title page) "Xmas 1898./Yours truly/ Edward Pötzl".
Location: Mark Twain Library, Redding, Connecticut.
Copy examined: Clemens's copy, unmarked. Has a red ink Mark Twain Library accession number, "4092". Examined in 1970 and again in June 1982 and on 9 November 2019.
———. *Landsleute. Kleine Beobachtungen eines Wieners [Small Observations of a Viennese Compatriot]*. Original green cloth. Wien: Verlag von Robert Mohr, 1899. 133 pp.
Inscription: the front free endpaper is inscribed "Seinem verehrten Meister/Mark Twain/Weihnacten 1898/Ed Pötzl".
Marginalia: on page 59 someone—possibly Clemens—translated "Beobachter" as "observer" in ink.
Provenance: contains a red-ink accession number and other catalog markings of the Mark Twain Library at Redding.
Catalog: *Mott 1952*, item #21, $95.
Location: Clifton Waller Barrett Collection, Albert and Shirley Small Special Collections Library, University of Virginia, Charlottesville.
Copy examined: Clemens's copy.
———. *Launen. Neue Sammlung augewählter Skizzen [Whims. New Collection of Selected Sketches]*. Zweite Auflage. Illus. Wien: Robert Mohr, 1897. 189 pp.
Location: Mark Twain Library, Redding, Connecticut.
Copy examined: Clemens's copy, unsigned and unmarked. Has the red ink Mark Twain Library accession number "4088". Examined in 1970 and again in June 1982 and on 9 November 2019.
———. *Stadtmenschen. Ein Wiener Skizzenbuch [Townspeople. A Vienna Sketchbook]*.
Edgar H. Hemminghaus—"Mark Twain's German Provenience" (1945), p. 470—reported seeing Clemens's copy of these humorous sketches in the Mark Twain Library at Redding, Connecticut. Albert E. Stone, Jr. did not include the volume in his checklist of Clemens's books at Redding in 1955, however, and I was unable to find this title when I visited the Mark Twain Library in 1970 or revisited it thereafter.

Powell, John Wesley (1834–1902). *Third Annual Report of the Bureau of American Ethnology to the Secretary of the Smithsonian Institution, 1879–1880*. Washington: United States Government Printing Office, 1884. 606 pp.
Source: MTLAcc, entry #898, volume donated by Clemens. Explorer of the Grand Canyon and respected scientist John Wesley Powell would warn that the arid lands of the Western United States should be viewed as fragile, water-starved regions far less suitable for intensive farming and large populations than the lusher, rain-rich Eastern areas. For this realistic prophecy he would be made to forfeit his directorship of the United States Geological Survey.

Power, Susan (Dunning) (c. 1843–1922), pseud. "Shirley Dare." *The Ugly-Girl Papers; or, Hints for the Toilet*. New York: Harper & Brothers, [cop. 1874]. 283 pp.
Source: MTLAcc, entry #547, volume donated by Clemens. Power here collected her columns from *Harper's Bazar*. The daughter of a Presbyterian minister in Vernon, Indiana, she would become the women's department editor at the New York *Tribune* before moving to Boston.

Powers, (Mrs.) O. A. *High-Toned Sprees: A Series of Temperance*

Legends. Fifth ed. Middletown, N. Y.: Stivers & Slauson, Printers, 1875. 80 pp.

> Source: MTLAcc, entry #2124, volume donated from Clemens's library by Clara Clemens Gabrilowitsch in 1910.

———. *The Maple Dell of '76*. Philadelphia: J. B. Lippincott Co., 1889. 95 pp.

> Source: MTLAcc, entry #611, volume donated by Clemens. *The Maple Dell of '76* tells a story in verse of how a home was destroyed and a wife made to suffer owing to the ravages of alcohol. Mrs. O. A. Powers, who seems never to have used any other name, moved from town to town, selling this book to support herself and her children.

PRAED, ROSA CAROLINE (MURRAY-PRIOR), "MRS. CAMPBELL PRAED" (1851–1935). *Australian Life, Black and White*. Illus. London: Chapman and Hall, 1885. 276 pp.

> Mark Twain took (and altered) extracts from a book by Mrs. Praed to illustrate the clash between white settlers and black natives, and the treachery (such as the arsenic poisoning of aborigines by a squatter) occasionally practiced by the whites (*FE* [1897], Ch. 21). Dennis Welland, "Mark Twain's Last Travel Book" (1965), p. 45, revealed that other quotations about aborigines from Mrs. Praed's book were deleted before the publication of *Following the Equator*. Madigan, "MT's Passage to India" (1974), p. 363.

PRATT, FRANCES LEE (1831–1905). "Captain Ben's Choice" (short story).

> *Mark Twain's Library of Humor* (1888) included this piece, crediting the *Atlantic Monthly* as the original publisher and Houghton, Mifflin & Co. of Boston as the possessor of copyright.

PRATT, MAGEE (1845–1916). *The Orthodox Preacher and Nancy; Being the Tale of the Misfortunes of a Minister who Tried to Do as Jesus Would. A Story of Ministerial Life as It Is*. Frontispiece portrait. Hartford, Connecticut: Connecticut Magazine Co., 1901. 191 pp.

> Source: MTLAcc, entry #244, volume donated by Clemens. Magee was an English-born Congregational minister who lived in Hartford in 1901. In 1909 he would become pastor of the First Congregational Church in North Granby, Connecticut.

The Prayer-Gauge Debate, by Prof. [John] Tyndall [1820–1893], Francis Galton [1822–1911], and Others, Against Dr. [Richard Frederick] Littledale [1833–1890], President [James] McCosh [1811–1894], the Duke of Argyll, Canon Lyddon, and "The Spectator." The "Introductory" is signed by John O. Means (1822–1883). Boston: Congregational Publishing Society, 1876. 311 pp.

> Inscription: the front flyleaf is signed "Saml. L. Clemens/ Hartford, 1876." A bookplate on the front pastedown endpaper reads, "Liber Edvardi/Wheelock quem/qui celaverit/anathema sit./MCMXII."
>
> Marginalia: a few passages were marked or briefly annotated by Clemens. There is a tipped-in comment by Clemens on the second flyleaf concerning page 142.
>
> Catalog: *A1911*, "12mo, cloth, Bost. 1876," . . . a few passages marked," quotes the signature, lot 389, sold for $3.
>
> Location: Mark Twain House and Museum, Hartford, Connecticut. Purchased in 1966 for $100.
>
> Copy examined: Clemens's copy. Examined in August 1987. It has an *A1911* sale label on the front endpaper.
>
> The contested subject of this prolonged debate was the

value of prayer on behalf of the sick. One of the debaters, Francis Galton, would publish a book, *Finger Prints*, that influenced Mark Twain's plot in *The Tragedy of Pudd'nhead Wilson* (1894). Among Galton's many scientific interests, he pursued statistical data concerning the efficacy of prayer.

PRENDERGAST, THOMAS (1806–1886). *The Mastery Series*. New York: D. Appleton and Co., 1868–1882.

> "Prendergast—Appleton," Clemens wrote in 1890 (NB 29, TS p. 47). Thomas Prendergast published handbooks for learning the French, German, Spanish, Hebrew, and Latin languages. His French *Mastery* handbook might be a good conjecture here, since Susy Clemens started her college studies at Bryn Mawr in October 1890. But the German one could also be a possibility.

PRENTISS, ELIZABETH (PAYSON) (1818–1878). *Little Susy's Little Servants*. New York: A. D. F. Randolph & Co., [cop. 1856]. 111 pp.

> Source: MTLAcc, entry #1900, volume donated from Clemens's library by Clara Clemens Gabrilowitsch in 1910.

———. *Little Susy's Six Birthdays*. Cloth, wear on edges and corners. New York: Anson D. F. Randolph & Co. [1856].

> Inscription: the front free endpaper is inscribed in ink by Olivia Clemens: "Susie Clemens/March 19th 1877/5th Birthday/(Mamma)." To the right of this inscription Olivia Clemens made a large (quite competent) pen-and-ink sketch of a farmyard doorway, including stone steps.
>
> Catalogs: *C1951*, J31, listed among volumes belonging to Jean and Clara Clemens; "Property from the Library of Mark Twain," Butterfield & Butterfield, San Francisco, Sale 6613 (16 July 1997), lot 2710.
>
> Location: Mark Twain House and Museum, Hartford, Connecticut.
>
> Copy examined: Susy Clemens's unmarked copy, subsequently in the possession of Clara Clemens. Viewed in Hartford in 1997.

———. *Little Susy's Six Teachers*. Cloth, wear on edges and corners. New York: Anson D. F. Randolph & Co., [1856].

> Inscription: inscribed by Olivia Clemens on the front free endpaper, "Susie Clemens/5th Birthday/19 March 1877/ Hartford/(Mamma)." To the right of the inscription Olivia Clemens added a charming pen-and-ink sketch of a small plant and a cattail.
>
> Catalogs: *C1951*, J27, listed among volumes belonging to Jean and Clara Clemens; "Property from the Library of Mark Twain," Butterfield & Butterfield, San Francisco, Sale 6613 (16 July 1997), lot 2710.
>
> Location: Mark Twain House and Museum, Hartford, Connecticut.
>
> Copy examined: Susy Clemens's unmarked copy, subsequently in the possession of Clara Clemens. Viewed in Hartford in 1997.

Presbyterian Observer (Baltimore journal, published 1872–1895).

> In Emmeline Grangerford's scrapbook she "used to paste obituaries and accidents and cases of patient suffering in it out of the *Presbyterian Observer*, and write poetry after them out of her own head" (*HF* [1885], Ch. 17). Given the fact that Mark Twain's novel is set prior to the Civil War, he may have meant the *Presbyterian Magazine* (Philadelphia, published 1851–1860), if he had any specific journal in mind at all. There were a dozen similar

titles in the nineteenth century.

PRESCOTT, WILLIAM HICKLING (1796–1859). *History of the Conquest of Peru, with a Preliminary View of the Civilization of the Incas* (2 vols., published in 1847).

During a sea voyage on the *Havel* to New York City, Clemens wrote to Olivia Clemens in June 1892: "I've been reading the *Conquest of Peru*. It is interesting—hideously interesting—and the diction is smooth, flowing, graceful, happy—but!! Mr. Prescott's English is not exact enough—it is devilish inexact in lots of places. Sometimes his grammar is bad; and now and then he reels you off a sentence that makes you think of Ben Hur Wallace, it is so slovenly and obscure" (*MFMT*, p. 99, quoting an undated letter). In "Some National Stupidities," written 1891–1892, Mark Twain quotes Prescott's description of the messenger courier service devised by the Incas for linking parts of their empire (*Conquest*, Vol. 1, Ch. 2). He facetiously uses this extract to buttress his contention that Americans had "a businesslike and effective postal and express service" 325 years before Europe saw it.

Pressburger Zeitung, Erstes stuct. Sonnabend, 1764. Avertissement.

Location: this facsimile of the first issue of the first newspaper published in Hungary, annotated by Clemens, is shelved with Clemens's library books in the Mark Twain Papers, Bancroft Library, University of California at Berkeley.

PRIME, WILLIAM COWPER (1825–1905). *Boat Life in Egypt and Nubia.* New York: Harper & Brothers, 1866. 498 pp.

Marginalia: Clemens made occasional pencil marks and underlinings and wrote brief notes in the initial thirty-five pages and then did the same between pages 294 and 313 of the volume. For example, on page 22 he scoffed: "What a wonderful person he is. He goes about astonishing the world." On page 26: "Soliloquizes in foreign languages—being particular to be overheard doubtless." On page 35: "What a braggart and liar the man is." On page 307: "And so he goes about, being mistaken everywhere for God." On page 311: "Here's God again!" Clemens made additional pencil notes on pages 28, 294, 301, 303 (two notes), 309, 310, 312 (three notes), and 313. Clemens's marginalia are nearly disparaging enough to qualify this book for inclusion in his hypothetical "Library of Literary Hogwash."

Provenance: *Boat Life* was one of the books from the estate of Ida Langdon (1880–1864) that were donated in 1965 to the Mark Twain Memorial in Hartford, Connecticut (later renamed the Mark Twain House and Museum).

Location: Mark Twain House and Museum, Hartford, Connecticut.

Copy examined: Clemens's annotations in a volume that Charley Langdon apparently took with him on the *Quaker City* excursion. Mallory Howard, Museum Assistant at the Mark Twain House and Museum, supplied photocopies of the title page and marginalia to Alan Gribben in August 2011. She and Patti Philippon, the chief curator, were doing an inventory and cleaning of the books in the library at the Mark Twain House and Museum when they discovered the previously unrecorded marginalia.

Mark Twain altered the author's name (calling him "Grimes") and the book title (he referred to "Scow Life in Egypt") in quoting and ridiculing Prime's book in

Chapter 50 of *The Innocents Abroad* (1869). Yet Henry Nash Smith—in *Mark Twain: Development of a Writer* (1962), p. 28—showed how Twain's own description of the Sphinx (*IA*, Ch. 58) resembled that drawn by Prime.

———. *I Go A-Fishing.* New York: Harper & Brothers, [cop. 1873]. 365 pp.

Source: MTLAcc, entry #1376, volume donated by Clemens.

I Go A-Fishing endeavored to be a nineteenth-century equivalent of Izaak Walton's *The Compleat Angler* (1653) as Prime pursued the wily trout in Connecticut, New Hampshire, and New York. He closely observed the natural scenery but his efforts at philosophizing were interrupted by mundane dialogue and his frequent boasting about his travels to exotic foreign lands.

———. *Pottery and Porcelain of All Times and Nations. With Tables of Factory and Artists' Marks for the Use of Collectors.* Illus. Wood-engraved frontispiece. Original green cloth, green-coated endpapers, gilt. Half-green morocco folding-case. New York: Harper & Brothers, 1878. 531 pp.

Inscription: the front flyleaf is inscribed by Clemens in purple ink: "Livy Clemens/from S.L.C./Nov. 27, 1877./Hartford." This date was Olivia Clemens's thirty-second birthday.

Catalogs: *C1951*, #86c, $20; *Sotheby's 2003*, #229, $2,250.

Provenance: displays the shelfmark of Clara Clemens Gabrilowitsch's private library in Detroit; subsequently the book was in the collection of film producer Robert Daley, Burbank, California; eventually it entered the collection of Nick Karanovich, Fort Wayne, Indiana.

Copy examined: Olivia Clemens's copy, a gift from her husband. Viewed at the 2003 Sotheby's sale.

The narrator of "The Loves of Alonzo Fitz Clarence and Rosannah Ethelton" (1878) stipulates that Aunt Susan's apartment, "the private parlor of a refined and sensible lady," contains "books about all kinds of odious and exasperating pottery, of course." The idea for this story appeared in Clemens's notebook on 23 November 1877, a few days before he presented Prime's book as a gift (*N&J* 2: 49). On 13 January 1887 Olivia Clemens mentioned in a letter to her mother Olivia Lewis Langdon that she had "looked a little in Mr Primes book to find the mark" in two porcelain dishes her mother had given her that day (ALS, MTHM). See also the Catalog entry for Herbert Byng Hall, *The Bric-à-Brac Hunter* (1875).

———. [Identical copy, but with blue cloth.]

Catalogs: checklist of Quarry Farm library books prepared by Emily Schwizer Martinez when Quarry Farm was donated to Elmira College in 1982; Ball 2016 inventory, blue cloth with gilt top edges and cover lettering, fair condition.

Location: Quarry Farm library shelves, under the supervision of the Mark Twain Archive, Elmira College, Elmira, New York.

This volume was available to Clemens in the Quarry Farm library in Elmira.

———. *Tent Life in the Holy Land.* Illus. New York: Harper & Brothers, [cop. 1857]. 498 pp.

Inscriptions: signed in ink on the front free endpaper, "C. J. Langdon/Elmira/New York". Diagonal pencil notes above this signature repeat the date "1867" four times and add the month "June". Below the signature seventeen-year-old Charles Jervis Langdon recorded in pencil his date of his departure for the *Quaker City* excursion: "Left Elmira,/4:38 a.m. June 5th 1867." The book plate of "J. Langdon's/Family/Library./No. 513" is affixed to the top of the front pastedown endpaper.

Marginalia: Clemens borrowed the book and made numerous derogating notes and underlinings, all in pencil. For example, Prime's habitual reliance on the words "dim" or "dimly" caused Clemens to underline and denote these repetitions on pages 2, 56, 60, 66, 76, and 82. A similar word that caught his attention was "weary," as in "weary limbs" and "wearily" (p. 22),"weary eyes" (p. 54), "weary eyes" (p. 55), and "weary eyes" (p. 66). His labels for Prime were uniformly demeaning; he termed him a "sham" (p. 14), a "sickly infant" (p. 22), a "Border Ruffian" (p. 27), "the Grand Mogul" (p. 34), "Grand Mogul Big Injun" (p. 84), "a terrible man" and a "liar" (p. 86), an "ignoramus" (p. 88), "Big Injun" (p. 114), a "thief" (p. 120, also p. 121), and "This terrible hero!" (p. 135). Clemens categorized Prime's prose as "lie" (p. 14),"nauseating drivel" (p. 23), melodramatic" (p. 24), "Bosh" (p. 29), "lie" (p. 38), "Hogwash" (p. 60), and "Old bosh" (p. 114). On page 32 Clemens stated his opinion of Prime succinctly: "Always picturesque. Always an ass." Prime's snide remarks about "the religion of the camel driver of Mecca," whom Prime referred to as a "haughty Turk," caused Clemens to ask at the bottom of page 84: "The charity and the gentleness that Christ taught?" Where Prime promised on page 118 to recount an anecdote "hereafter," Clemens pleaded, "*Please* don't/forget it." Clemens expressed disgust at Prime's admission on page 120 that he had borrowed a hammer and chisel to chip off souvenirs from the age-old columns in the Valley of Jehoshaphat. On page 299 Clemens scoffed at Prime's theories about the Jerusalem gateway: "This *is* cheek. This fellow, after swelling around ten days, knows more about it than old Robinson, who *studied* those ruins 30 years." The annotations conclude on page 306, two-thirds of the way into the volume. See the Catalog entry for Edward Robinson (1794–1863), *Biblical Researches in Palestine, and in the Adjacent Regions. A Journal of Travels in the Years 1838 & 1852.*

Provenance: presented to the Mark Twain Archive at Elmira College on 11 October 2008 in a Hamilton Hall ceremony by Irene Langdon (1922–2015), the widow of Jervis Langdon, Jr. (1905–2004), during a Centennial Symposium on Mark Twain's *The Mysterious Stranger* sponsored by the Center for Mark Twain Studies. This book has to rank among the dozen most significant volumes surviving from Clemens's literary resources, and one of the most important recent additions. Mark Woodhouse, then the curator of the Mark Twain Archive, was instrumental in facilitating this gift by Mrs. Langdon.

Catalog: Ball 2016 inventory, brown cloth, gilt lettering, signed by C. J. Langdon, Elmira, New York, bookplate of the J. Langdon's Family Library #513.

Location: Mark Twain Archive, Gannett-Trip Learning Center, Elmira College, Elmira, New York.

Copy examined: Charlie Langdon's copy that Clemens heavily annotated. Examined on 11 October 2008 when it was presented to Elmira College. Subsequently Mark Woodhouse, then the curator of the Mark Twain Archive at Elmira College, scanned and transmitted by email on 19 February 2013 copies of the inscription, title page, and marginalia to Alan Gribben.

The clichéd idioms and affected tone of Prime's *Tent Life in the Holy Land* irritated Mark Twain so much that it would not be overstating the case to say Twain wrote his account of travels in the Holy Land in part to expose and defeat Prime's pious precedent. Twain's unfinished play—"The *Quaker City* Holy Land Excursion" (MTP), written in 1867—suggests that Prime's book was one of the tiresome volumes in the ship library (Act II, scene 1). In a travel letter published in the *Daily Alta California* of 1 March 1868, Twain alludes to *Tent Life* by its author and title, then comments: "No man ever enjoyed a funeral as Prime did his Sentimental Journey through the Holy Land" (*TIA*, p. 265). Prime's *Tent Life* was one of the books that *Quaker City* passengers were instructed to bring along on the trip (*Daily Alta California*, 5 April 1868; *TIA*, p. 303). In Chapter 46 of *The Innocents Abroad* (1869), Twain diplomatically renamed Prime (as "Wm. C. Grimes") and Prime's book (as "*Nomadic Life in Palestine*") and then proceeded to scoff at the author's "hairbreadth escapes from Bedouins." Chapter 48 of *Innocents Abroad* quotes "Wm. C. Grimes" at length in order to ridicule his sentimentality about the desolate landscape at the Sea of Galilee. In Chapter 49 Twain refers to the actual title—"*Tent Life in the Holy Land*." Prime's book also figures in Chapter 50, where Twain quotes an inflated excerpt that was "written by whom? Wm C. Grimes." Twain winds up Chapter 50 by explaining that "*Nomadic Life in Palestine* is a representative book—representative of a class of Palestine books—and a criticism upon it will serve for a criticism upon them all."

In an odd twist of fate, Twain found himself having to negotiate with Prime in 1885 and 1886 about the rights for Charles L. Webster and Company to publish an autobiography of General George B. McClellan that Prime, as McClellan's literary executor, had edited (*AutoMT* 1: 481) (See the Catalog entry for George B. McClellan.) Nonetheless, in January 1886 (when Prime was a professor of art history at Princeton University) Twain was still belittling his style: "Say 'Cemetery' instead of 'Appendix'—Mr. Prime's accidental characterization. Therefore, he say, 'further in this connection, will be found in the Cemetery at the end of this volume'" (NB 25, N&J 3: 220). Twain's Autobiographical Dictation of 31 October 1908 recounts a joke about Prime's receiving the news of Edwin M. Stanton's death when Prime and J. Hammond Trumbull were together on the Nile. "Prime was a gushing pietist; religion was his daily tipple; he was always under the influence. Seldom actually and solidly drunk with holiness, but always on the verge of it, always dizzy, boozy, twaddlesome," Twain added (*MTE*, pp. 349–351; *AutoMT* 3: 269–270). In an undated note Clemens referred again to Prime: "Wm. C. Prime bought book at auction" (*A1911*, lot 468).

Leon T. Dickinson's "Mark Twain's Revisions in Writing *The Innocents Abroad*," *American Literature* 19.2 (May 1947): 139–157 examined on pages 155–156 Twain's alterations in his treatment of William C. Prime while revising the

Alta California letters to produce *The Innocents Abroad*. Mark Woodhouse's "'Innocents' and Experience: Mark Twain's Marginalia in William Prime's *Tent Life in the Holy Land: The Innocents Abroad* and the Resilience of Literature," *International Journal of the Book* 8.2 (2011): 171–186, and Woodhouse's "Rough Compassion and Self-Restraint: Samuel Clemens and *Tent Life in the Holy Land*," *American Literary Realism* 45.1 (Fall 2012): 77 thoroughly discussed Twain's reliance on Prime's book.

Leon T. Dickinson, "Mark Twain's *Innocents Abroad*" (1945), p. 109 n. 6 ; Franklin R. Rogers, *MTBP* (1960), pp. 59–61, 169 n. 37; Robert H. Hirst, "Making of *The Innocents Abroad*" (1975); Eleftheria Arapoglou, "Mark Twain's 'Spatial Play': Venice and the Holy Land in *The Innocents Abroad*," *Mark Twain Annual 6* (2008): 101–117.

PRIMROSE, ARCHIBALD PHILIP (1847–1929), fifth earl of Rosebery. *Lord Randolph Churchill*. Portrait. New York: Harper & Brothers, 1906. 201 pp. [Publisher and pages conjectured.]

Inscription: signed "S. L. Clemens, 1906."

Marginalia: a few corrections by Clemens.

Catalog: *A1911*, "8vo, cloth, N.Y. 1906, . . . a few autograph corrections," quotes the signature, lot 410, sold for $3.50.

Lord Churchill (1849–1895), best known as the father of the far more famous Winston Churchill (1874–1965), was a Conservative MP for Woodstock, a small town near Blenheim Palace. He had a checkered career as a politician and statesman in terms of his political standing and influence.

———. *Napoleon: The Last Phase*. New York: Harper & Brothers, 1901. 282 pp.

Inscriptions: the front pastedown endpaper is signed in pencil, "Isabel Ashcroft." She also wrote: "The few markings in this book were/made by SLC, who gave me the/volume as he owned 3 copies of it./Isabel Ashcroft." Below that notation R. J. Rebman identifies "SLC" as "Mark Twain" and Mrs. Ashcroft (the former Isabel V. Lyon) as Clemens's one-time secretary from whom Rebman received the book in "1945."

Marginalia: pages 134–220 contain pencil markings characteristic of Clemens. There are a few notes and signs of close reading: "in a hut" is written in the margin of page 168 beside the underscored words "gold and silver plate"; "chess" appears in the margin of page 173; the corner of page 192 is turned down; the word "suicide" marks the corner of page 202; "true" is noted on page 220 near the opinion that "Russia is the power that marches most surely, and with the greatest strides, towards universal dominion, . . . for now there is no France and, therefore, no equilibrium."

Location: Mark Twain House and Museum, Hartford, Connecticut. Donated by Professor Norman Holmes Pearson (1909–1975) of Yale University in 1964.

Copy examined: Clemens's copy. Examined in August 1987.

———. [An identical copy.] Red cloth, stamped gilt. Covers slightly faded, front hinge tender.

Marginalia: Clemens made brief grammatical or stylistic corrections on five pages—for example, on page 2 he wrote in the margin that Primrose's verb "undertake" should instead be "achieve" or "accomplish," and there are similar recommended revisions on pages 3, 4, 5, and 23. He made marginal "X's" beside perceived stylistic lapses

on pages 2, 7, and 45 and vertical lines next to stylistic shortcomings on pages 4, 27, and 28. The corners are folded down on pages 87, 176, and 246.

Catalogs: Christie's, New York City, Sale 6382, Estate of Phyllis Harrington, 11 May 1987, three titles (Primrose, Head, and Wallace), Clemens's "penciled underlinings, crossings-out and words inserted in the margins on pages 2, 3, 4, 5, 7, 23, 27, 28, 45 . . . totaling 10 words," lot 16, sold for a total of $1,650. Purchased by John L. Feldman.

Provenance: this book became the property of Phyllis Harrington, Clara Clemens Samossoud's friend and secretary, after Clara died on 19 November 1962. In 1987 this book was in the possession of John L. Feldman of Astoria, New York. He described it then as "*Napoleon: The Last Phase*. 1901. Penciled underlinings and words inserted throughout" (Feldman to Alan Gribben, 19 May 1987). Feldman placed the volume on deposit in the Special Collections at the University of Colorado at Boulder, but by 2003 he had withdrawn it (Michelle Visser, Special Collections, to Alan Gribben, 10 June 2003).

Location: currently unknown.

Prize Essays on "Billiards as an Amusement for all Classes." Stamped green cover, gilt lettering, black design. Manchester: James Galt & Co., 1873. 113 pp. [Published for "Let Us to Billiards. Orme & Sons, Manchester. Billiard Table Makers. Established 1845."]

Inscription: inscribed in black ink on the first advertising page at the front: "Samuel Clemens/from Frank Finlay/Belfast, 30 Aug. 1873". [Francis Dalzell Finlay (1832–1917), owner of the Belfast *Northern Whig*, met Clemens in Belfast in August 1873 (*MTLet* 5: 432).] Clemens would eventually reciprocate this gift by inscribing a copy of *Adventures of Huckleberry Finn* to Finlay's daughter Mary when she visited Hartford in 1899 (Sotheby's Catalogue, lot 118, 24 November 2015).

Location: Mark Twain Library, Redding, Connecticut.

Copy examined: Clemens's copy. Has a penciled Mark Twain Library accession number, "3536". Examined in 1970 and again in June 1982 and on 8 November 2019.

PROCTER, ADELAIDE ANNE (1825–1864). *The Poems of Adelaide A. Procter*. Boston: Ticknor and Fields, 1866. 416 pp.

Inscription: the front free endpaper is stenciled or stamped in ink, in Gothic-style script: "Olivia L. Langdon/Elmira". The front free flyleaf is inscribed in pencil, "Livy L. Langdon/Elmira/Dec. 25th 1865/From Charlie". [Charles Jervis Langdon (1849–1916) was Olivia's brother.]

Marginalia: there are slanting (diagonal) pencil marks at the poem titles on pages 16, 17, 23, 28, 30, 44, 50, 72, 73, 111, 174, 275, and 414. An ink marking on page 16 calls attention to the poem "Judge Not."

Location: Mark Twain Library, Redding, Connecticut. Donated from Clemens's library by Clara Clemens Gabrilowitsch in 1910 (MTLAcc, entry #2077).

Copy examined: Olivia Clemens's copy. Has a penciled Mark Twain Library accession number, "2077". Examined in 1970 and again June 1982 and on 9 November 2019. See also a relevant Catalog entry for G. A. Stevens, "Storm" (song).

PROCTOR, CHARLES HAYDEN (1850–1890). *The Life of James Williams, Better Known as Professor Jim, for Half a Century Janitor of Trinity College*. Purple cloth, gilt lettering. Hartford,

Connecticut: Case, Lockwood & Brainard, 1873. 79 pp.

Inscription: unknown; the front free endpaper has been torn out.

Location: Mark Twain Library, Redding, Connecticut. Donated by Clemens (MTLAcc, entry #834).

Copy examined: Clemens's copy, unmarked. Examined in 1970 and again in June 1982.

James Williams (c. 1790–1878), the African American custodian and "general factotum" at Trinity College in Hartford, had boyhood recollections of his and his enslaved mother's being owned by a prominent New York family. After his mother was emancipated James ran away to sea. He became such a beloved figure at Trinity College that he took part in the graduation ceremonies and received annual gifts from the students. Charles Hayden Proctor graduated from Trinity in 1873. As an Episcopal priest he would serve as rector of St. James Church in New Bedford, Massachusetts between 1878 and 1885. His early death from an illness occurred while he was Dean of Trinity Cathedral in Little Rock, Arkansas.

PROCTOR, RICHARD (1837–1888). *A New Star Atlas for the Library, the School, and the Observatory, in Twelve Circular Maps.* Third edition. Original red cloth. London: Longmans, Green, and Co., 1873. 27 pp. 13 double plates, maps, and diagrams.

Inscription: The half-title page is signed by Clemens's sister-in-law: "Susan L. Crane/Quarry Farm/1884." Laid in is a Quarry Farm envelope enclosing a gift tag indicating that this was an Easter present to Susan Crane from "Norman." Clemens freely used the Quarry Farm library whenever he and his family summered there.

Marginalia: The star chart for the northern hemisphere has pencil drawings in the margin showing the relative positions of the Big Dipper and the Little Dipper, probably made by Susan Crane.

Provenance: originally on the library shelves at Quarry Farm in Elmira, New York. Susan Crane may have had a special interest in astronomy; Clemens would inscribe a copy of Simon Newcomb's *Side-Lights on Astronomy* to her in 1906.

Location: collection of Kevin Mac Donnell, Austin, Texas (Mac Donnell to Alan Gribben, 29 November 2011).

PROPERTIUS, SEXTUS (c. 50 BCE-c. 16 BCE). *Erotica: The Elegies of Propertius, The Satyricon of [Gaius] Petronius Arbiter [fl. 1st century CE], and The Kisses of Johannes Secundus [1511–1536] Literally Translated [the Elegies by P. J. F. Gantillon], and Accompanied by Poetical Versions [by G. F. Nott and C. A. Elton] from Various Sources. To Which Are Added the Love Epistles of Aristaenetus [fl. c. 500 CE] Translated by R[ichard]. Brinsley Sheridan [1751–1816] and Mr.[Nathaniel Brassey] Halhed [1751–1830].* Ed. by Walter K[eating]. Kelly (d. 1867). Bohn's Classical Library Series. Original dark green cloth. London: George Bell and Sons, 1874. 500 pp.

Inscription: signed in pencil on the half-title page "Saml. L. Clemens/Hartford, 1875."

Catalogs: *A1911*, "12mo, cloth, Lond. 1874," quotes the signature, lot 391, sold for $10.50; *Selections from the Library of William E. Boeing, Part II* (2011), comp. Joseph C. Baillargeon, Restoration Books, Seattle, Washington, p. 65.

Location: collection of Kevin Mac Donnell, Austin, Texas. He reported that the corner of page 259 is folded down. An

A1911 auction sale label is affixed to the front pastedown endpaper. (Mac Donnell to Alan Gribben, 29 November 2011). No marginalia are visible. See also the Catalog entry for Petronius Arbiter.

PROUDFIT, DAVID LAW (1842–1897). *Love Among the Gamins, and Other Poems.* Illus. New York: Dick & Fitzgerald, 1877. 144 pp.

Source: MTLAcc, entry #631, volume donated by Clemens.

PROYART, LIÉVAIN BONAVENTURE (c. 1743–1808). *Vie de M. D'Orléans De La Motte. Évêque d'Amiens, par M. L'Abbé Proyart.* Paris, Limoges: Martial Ardant Frères, 1846. 260 pp.

Location: unknown; formerly in Mark Twain Library, Redding, Connecticut.

Copy examined: none. Information supplied from the card catalog of the Mark Twain Library, Redding. The provenance of this volume is unclear, and it might not have belonged to Clemens. The volume was no longer present when I looked for it in 1970 and it was still missing when I returned to Redding in June 1982.

Louis-François-Gabriel d'Orléans de la Motte (1683–1774) was the Bishop of Amiens.

————. *Vie de M. D'Orléans De La Motte. Évêque d'Amiens, par M. L'Abbé Proyart.* Lille et Paris: Librairie De L. Lefort, 1865. 183 pp.

Inscription: the bookplate on the front pastedown endpaper reads: "Ernest Sorin, Écoles Chrétinnes des Frères."

Location: Mark Twain Library, Redding, Connecticut.

Copy examined: possibly Clemens's unmarked copy, but a very problematical entry. It was shelved with books from Clemens's library when Albert E. Stone, Jr. made his checklist in 1955 and when I visited Redding in 1970. It has no accession number and no Mark Twain Library stamps. I examined the volume again in June 1982 and could not detect why it was once placed with Clemens's library books other than its early date of publication.

PRYM, JERUSHA. "Familiar Letter on Art" (sketch).

Orion Clemens's Hannibal *Journal* of 4 March 1852 reprinted this sketch from Benjamin P. Shillaber's *Carpet-Bag* (17 January 1852) (Edgar M. Branch, "A Chronological Bibliography of the Writings of Samuel Clemens to June 8, 1867," *American Literature* 18.2 [May 1946]: 114; Wecter, *SCH* [1952], p. 246).

The Publishers' Trade List Annual, 1907. 35th Year. New York: Publishers' Weekly, 1907. [Subsequent to Clemens's lifetime *Publishers Weekly* would drop the apostrophe from its title.]

Source: MTLAcc, entry #1829, volume donated from Clemens's library by Clara Clemens Gabrilowitsch in 1910.

PUCCINI, GIACOMO (1858–1924). *Tosca* (opera, performed in Rome, 1900).

On 8 January 1906 Clemens related "how he had left the opera—'Tosca'— where they had gone after dinner, & found Dr. Quintard in the lobby" (IVL Journal, Harry Ransom Center, University of Texas at Austin). Hill, *MTGF* (1973), p. 123.

Puck (New York, weekly magazine, published 1877–1918). Ed. by Henry Cuyler Bunner (1855–1896).

"The very feature that keeps it [Mardi-Gras] alive in the South—girly-girly romance—would kill it in the North or in London. *Puck* and *Punch*, and the press universal, would fall upon it and make merciless fun of it, and its first exhibition would be also its last" (*LonMiss* [1883], Ch. 46).

PULITZER, WALTER (1878–1926). *Cozy Corner Confidences.* New York: Dodge Publishing Co., 1904. 71 pp.

Isabel V. Lyon, writing on behalf of Clemens on 7 September 1906, thanked Pulitzer for "the little book; it is bright" (MTP). Pulitzer specialized in sarcastic aphorisms about romantic love and marriage; *Cozy Corner Confidences* followed his earlier *A Cynic's Meditation* (1904).

PULLEN, ELISABETH (JONES) (1849–1926), pseud. "Elisabeth Cavazza," after 1894 sometimes known as "Mrs. Stanley T. Pullen." *Don Finimondone: Calabrian Sketches.* Fiction, Fact, and Fancy Series, general ed. Arthur Stedman. New York: Charles L. Webster & Co., 1892. 179 pp. Frontispiece by Dan[iel Carter] Beard (1850–1941).

Clemens's publishing firm advertised this work as providing pictures of Italian life among the Calabrian peasants (*Publishers' Trade List Annual for 1893*).

PUMPELLY, RAPHAEL (1837–1923). *Explorations in Turkestan, with an Account of The Basin of Eastern Persia and Sistan. Expedition of 1903.* Publication No. 26. Washington, D. C.: Carnegie Institute of Washington, 1905. 324 pp.

Pumpelly was an American geologist and explorer who customarily spent his summers near Mount Monadnoch in New Hampshire. Clemens wrote from Dublin, New Hampshire to his daughter Clara on 16 July 1905, mentioning that "we sup with Raphael Pumpelly this evening" (*Sotheby's* 2003, #113). Isabel Lyon noted on 17 July 1905 that Clemens and his daughter Jean dined with "Mr. & Mrs. Raphael Pumpelly" (IVL Journal, Mark Twain Archive, Elmira, New York.). Having dined with Pumpelly twice, Clemens talked with Miss Lyon on 5 August 1905 "about Mr. Pumpelly's book and about his account of the Japanese" (IVL Journals, TS p. 84, MTP). Thirty-five years earlier, Pumpelly had published *Across America and Asia; Notes of a Five Years' Journey Around the World, and of Residence in Arizona, Japan, and China* (New York: Leypoldt & Holt, 1870).

Punch (London, weekly magazine, published 1841–).

In July 1873, while in London, Clemens noted "Punches [*sic*] jokes" (NB 12, *N&J* 1: 570). He conjectured that "Punch's Advice to Persons about to Marry—Don't—was 1000 yrs old when Punch was born" (NB 20, *N&J* 2: 482). Mark Twain conceived of *Punch* as a corrective pressure against human foolishness; in *Life on the Mississippi* (1883) he declared that the "girly-girly romance" of the Mardi-Gras would doom it in the American North or in London. "*Puck* and *Punch*, and the press universal, would fall upon it and make merciless fun of it, and its first exhibition would be also its last" (Ch. 46). "*Punch* caricatured me! Yes, I was a made man now; my place was established. I might be joked about still, but reverently, not hilariously, not rudely; I could be smiled at, but not laughed at. The time for that had gone by" (Twain's "The £1,000,000 Bank-Note" [1893]). In Twain's final Lotos Club speech, he mentioned *Punch* as "the greatest periodical in the world on its own soil" (11 January 1908, *MTSpk*, 608). See also the Catalog entry for Francis Cowley Burnand (1836–1917), editor of *Punch* from 1880 until 1906, as well as the Catalog entry for *Cartoons from "Punch"* (1906).

PURRINGTON, WILLIAM ARCHER (1852–1926). *Christian Science; An Exposition of Mrs. Eddy's Wonderful Discovery, including Its Legal Aspects. A Plea for Children and Other Helpless Sick.* New York: E. B. Treat & Co., 1900. 194 pp.

Purrington was a lawyer who lectured on the legal aspects of medical practice. In a letter of 25 January 1903, Purrington mentioned sending Clemens a copy of his book (*WIM?*, pp. 558–559).

PUTLITZ, GUSTAV HEINRICH GANS, EDLER HERR VON UND ZU (1821–1890). *Was sich der Wald erzählt [What Was Said in the Woods].* Berlin: Gebrüder Paetel, 1886.

Inscription: presented to Clemens by L. Waldstein in Marienbad in August 1891.

Location: currently unknown.

Copy examined: none. Edgar H. Hemminghaus saw this volume in the Mark Twain Library at Redding ("Mark Twain's German Provenience" [1945], p. 473), but Albert E. Stone, Jr. did not include it in his checklist of Clemens's books still there in 1955. I was unable to find it when I visited Redding in 1970 or thereafter.

PYLE, HOWARD (1853–1911). *Men of Iron.* Illustrated by the author. New York: Harper & Brothers, [cop. 1891]. 328 pp.

Source: MTLAcc, entry #1644, volume donated by Clemens.

———. *The Merry Adventures of Robin Hood of Great Renown, in Nottinghamshire. Written and Illustrated by Howard Pyle.* New York: Charles Scribner's Sons, 1883. 296 pp.

Catalog: *C1951*, D34, listed among the books signed by Clemens, $27.50.

On 13 February 1884 George Washington Cable reported from Hartford that "Mrs. Clemens is reading aloud to Mark & the children Howard Pyle's beautiful new version of Robin Hood. Mark enjoys it hugely; they have come to the death of Robin & will soon be at the end" (*MT&GWC*, p. 32).

———. [Another copy.]

Inscriptions: the first front flyleaf shows traces of a vigorously erased inscription written in blue or black ink. It appears to read "Merry Christmas/to/Clara L. Clemens/ Hartford 1883/Mamma," though some of the letters are practically illegible; the handwriting was large. The front flyleaf is inscribed in black ink: "To Elsie Leslie Lyde./ This book is for *you*, my dear, &/you will like it./Mark Twain". An undated note from Elsie Leslie (Lyde) Milliken is laid loose in the volume, attesting: "One day Mr. Clemens told me the story of Robin Hood & I was so enchanted with it, he sent me this copy of the book. Its [poor] condition shows how often I read it." She refers readers to Paine's *Mark Twain: A Biography* (1912), page 883, adding that she still has the slippers and the letter described there; they "are my most cherished possessions." An original pen-and-ink sketch, autographed by Howard Pyle, is laid loose in the front of the book.

Marginalia: the word "goodliness" on page 145 is deleted in pencil and altered to "godliness." (The hand resembles Clemens's.)

Catalogs: "Mark Twain Items and Other Americana," Parke-Bernet Galleries, New York City, sale of 21–22 May 1957, item #121, sold for $70; Lew David Feldman, "House of El Dieff, Inc." (1957), p. 1, offered along with three other books for a total of $2,850.

Provenance: collection of Frank C. Willson (1889–1960) in Melrose, Massachusetts. Sold by his widow Margarete in 1962 to the University of Texas.

Location: Harry Ransom Center, University of Texas at Austin.

Copy examined: copy once belonging to Clara Clemens, subsequently given to Elsie Leslie Lyde.

———. [Another copy.]

Inscription: in Olivia Clemens's handwriting, in blue ink, on the front flyleaf: "A Merry Christmas/to/Jervis Langdon/1883/From Uncle Sam & Aunt Livy."

Provenance: formerly in the collection of Jervis Langdon (1875–1952), Elmira, New York.

Location: Mark Twain House and Museum, Hartford, Connecticut. Gift of Jervis Langdon, Jr. (1905–2004). The gift was announced in 1980.

Copy examined: photocopies of the title-page and the inscription in the Mark Twain Papers, Bancroft Library, University of California at Berkeley. Described in detail by Jervis Langdon, Jr. (Langdon to Alan Gribben, 6 November 1980). I examined the volume in Hartford in August 1987.

Clemens sent an accompanying letter with this book to young Jervis on 19 December 1883 from Hartford: "I hope you will like the Robin Hood. I have been reading it, to see if it still possessed for me the fascination which it had when I was your age—a fascination so great that it paled the interest of all other books & made them tame & colorless. I find, to my utter astonishment & delight, that a very large part of the old charm still remains in the book." Clemens writes that he has rediscovered the Sherwood Forest of his imagination, "fragrant & woodsy," with its "matchless society" of "darling sweet rascals." He concludes: "I have always regretted that I did not belong to Robin Hood's gang" (ALS, formerly in the collection of Jervis Langdon, Jr., Elmira, New York, PH in MTP). Tom Sawyer and Joe Harper play Robin Hood with lath swords in Chapter 8 of *The Adventures of Tom Sawyer* (1876), using an earlier story book as their text; see the Catalog entry for Joseph Cundall, *Robin Hood and His Merry Foresters* (1841).

———. *Otto of the Silver Hand*. Illustrated by the author. New York: Charles Scribner's Sons, 1888. 173 pp.

Inscriptions: a small card on the front flyleaf is inscribed in ink by Olivia Clemens, "Merry Christmas/to/Jervis/from/his loving cousin/Clara/1888". Jervis Langdon (1875–1952) was the son of Charles Jervis Langdon and Ida B. Clark Langdon.

Provenance: found on the Quarry Farm library bookshelves by Kevin Mac Donnell in 2005.

Catalog: Ball 2016 inventory, green cloth, lettering in red, white, gold, and back, inscribed to Jervis Langdon, binding missing.

Location: Mark Twain Archive, Gannett-Tripp Library, Elmira College, Elmira, New York.

Copy examined: photocopies of the title page and the inscription in a copy that belonged to Jervis Langdon sent to Alan Gribben by Mark Woodhouse, Archivist, on 6 December 2005.

———. *Otto of the Silver Hand*. Illustrated by the author. New York: Charles Scribner's Sons, 1888. 173 pp.

Source: MTLAcc, entry #1932, volume donated from Clemens's library by Clara Clemens Gabrilowitsch in 1910.

———. *Pepper & Salt; or, Seasoning for Young Folk*. Illustrated by the author. New York: Harper & Brothers, 1906. 121 pp.

Source: MTLAcc, entry #1933, volume donated from Clemens's library by Clara Clemens Gabrilowitsch in 1910. Verses and fairy tales enlivened by Pyle's drawings.

———. *Rejected of Men; A Story of To-day*. New York: Harper & Brothers, 1903. 268 pp.

Inscription: the front pastedown endpaper is inscribed in black ink "To Samuel L. Clemens/with the best regards/of the author/Howard Pyle/Chadd's Ford/July 1st 1903".

Marginalia: annotated throughout in pencil. Clemens's underscorings and vertical lines are more carelessly scrawled than usual. He wrote "good" next to the dialogue on page 28 in which a group of clergymen decide to appoint a committee to investigate some unorthodox baptisms being conducted by a man who calls himself John the Baptist. But Clemens noted "No" next to a passage that followed. On page 32, where Dr. Caiaphas observes the crowed encampments of "the commoner sort" of people gathering for the next mass baptism, Clemens observed: "Naturally they would take up with a new religion, old ones having nothing for the poor."

Catalog: "Retz Appraisal" (1944), p. 10. Valued at $25.

Location: Mark Twain Papers, Bancroft Library, University of California at Berkeley.

Copy examined: Clemens's copy.

Pyle wrote to Clemens on 7 January 1903: "I am not really and truly a literary man, you know. So, when a master workman is pleased to praise my work, I feel at once surprised and very grateful" (Fears, *Day by Day*, 3: 803). On 9 January 1903, evidently while leaving home, Clemens noted to himself: "Take 'Rejected of Men'" (NB 46, TS p. 5).

———. [Another identical copy.]

Source: MTLAcc, entry #1111, volume donated by Clemens.

———. *The Ruby of Kishmoor*. Illustrated by the author. First edition. Original pale green pictorial cloth, gilt. New York: Harper & Brothers, 1908. 73 pp.

Inscription: the front pastedown endpaper is signed in ink, "S. L. Clemens/Stormfield, Jan. 1, 1909." The front flyleaf also bears a gift inscription from Thomas A. Buckner to Miss Dorothy Perkins.

Catalog: *A1911*, "8vo, cloth, N.Y. 1908," quotes the signature, lot 394, sold for $6.

Provenance: in 1988 the volume was in the possession of Alan C. Wasserman of New Haven, Connecticut: "While my Howard Pyle collection is not . . . extensive, I do have several beautiful items. I have. . . . a first edition of *The Ruby of Kishmoor*, signed by Samuel Clemens" (Alan C. Wasserman, "Illustration: A Collector's Profile of N. C. Wyeth," *A B Bookman's Weekly* 82: 12 [19 September 1988]: 993).

Location: collection of Kevin Mac Donnell, Austin, Texas (Mac Donnell to Alan Gribben, 25 February 2012). Displays the *A1911* sale label. The book is unmarked.

Pyle's fanciful story involves a beautiful pirate captain's daughter hiding in Jamaica and a Quaker merchant who kills her father's murderers and restores a famous gem to her.

———. *Stolen Treasure*. Illustrated by the author. New York:

Harper & Brothers, 1907. 254 pp.

Source: MTLAcc, entry #1645, volume donated by Clemens.

Pirate stories, told by a man who claims he sailed with the infamous buccaneer Henry Morgan (c. 1635–1688).

———. *Yankee Doodle, An Old Friend in a New Dress. Pictured by Howard Pyle.* [The text is the traditional song.] Gray paper boards. New York: Dodd, Mead and Co., 1881. 31 pp.

Inscription: the front flyleaf is inscribed by Clemens in blue ink, "Merry Christmas/to the Only Jean/from/Papa/ 1884."

Catalog: "Retz Appraisal" (1944), p. 10. Valued at $30.

Location: Mark Twain Papers, Bancroft Library, University of California at Berkeley.

Copy examined: Jean Clemens's copy.

In an undated note about a Civil War incident that occurred on the Rapidan River in Virginia, Clemens mentioned that "the Yanks began to sing 'Yankey [*sic*] Doodle'" (*A1911*, lot 439).

———. [Another identical copy.]

Inscription: inscribed in Olivia Clemens's hand in brown ink: "Merry Xmas/to/Ida Langdon/from her loving cousin/Jean Clemens." [Both Ida Langdon (the daughter of Charles Jervis Langdon and Ida B. Clark Langdon) and Jean Clemens were born in 1880.]

Location: collection of Kevin Mac Donnell, Austin, Texas. Purchased from the Langdon family in May 2016 (email, Mac Donnell to Alan Gribben, 16 May 2016).

Source: detailed description of the first edition with Pyle's illustrations sent on 9 June 2016 by Mac Donnell to Alan Gribben.

PYRNELLE, LOUISE (CLARKE) (1850–1907). *Diddie, Dumps, and Tot; or, Plantation Child-Life.* Illus. New York: Harper & Brothers, [cop. 1882]. 217 pp.

Source: MTLAcc, entry #433, volume donated by Clemens.

This once-popular novel offered a romanticized vision of antebellum plantation life in the Deep South. Though set in Mississippi, Pyrnelle's story relied largely on recollections of her parents' plantation in in Perry County, Alabama in depicting three while girls who have the companionship of three enslaved African girls—Riar, Chris, and Dilsey. Pyrnelle's book was especially praised for its depiction of the enslaved people's dialect. Harper & Brothers reprinted the book several times as late as the early twentieth century. If the copy owned by Clemens was the original first edition (1882), as seems likely, it could be viewed as another literary resource for *Adventures of Huckleberry Finn* (1885). Unfortunately that volume does not seem to have survived its donation to the Mark Twain Library at Redding. Most of his books that went there were worn out by the library patrons, exactly as he had intended.

❚ Q

QUACKENBOS, GEORGE PAYN (1826–1881). *A Natural Philosophy, Embracing the Most Recent Discoveries in the Various Branches of Physics, and Exhibiting the Application of Scientific Principles in Everyday Life.* Revised edition. New York, Cincinnati: American Book Co., [cop. 1899]. 455 pp. Originally published in New York: D. Appleton and Co., 1859. 450 pp.

On Wednesday, 12 February 1908, Isabel Lyon noticed that Clemens was reading "Quackenbores [*sic*] book on Natural Philosophy" in bed with "a cigar between his teeth" (IVL Journals, TS p. 301, MTP).

QUACKENBOS, JOHN DUNCAN (1848–1926). *Hypnotic Therapeutics in Theory and Practice, with Numerous Illustrations of Treatment by Suggestion.* New York: Harper & Brothers, 1908. 335 pp.

Inscription: the front pastedown endpaper is signed in ink "SL. Clemens/1909."

Marginalia: somewhat surprisingly, Clemens did not mark Quackenbos's criticisms of Mary Baker Eddy on pages 100–103. On page 115 Clemens drew a long vertical line in ink beside the various ailments that "reputable physicians" employ "suggestion" to relieve or cure— "occupation neuroses (like telegrapher's arm, writer's, violinist's, and ballet dancer's cramp). . . . Indeed, there is no rational sufferer who may not be benefited in some degree by such treatment." Clemens turned down the corner of this page in a permanent fold. Seeking a cure for Jean Clemens, Clemens drew two ink marks beside Quackenbos's comments on epilepsy. These observations are not optimistic, beginning with the admission that "nothing can be hoped for in cases where the mental faculties are seriously impaired as the result of organic brain conditions" (p. 119). Page 120 is folded over at the corner to call attention to Quackenbos's further discussion of hypnotism for epilepsy. Clemens underscored in ink and marked in the margin Quackenbos's contention that suggestion could be helpful "in hysterical contractions and torticollis, *with painful spasms of the neck muscles*" (Clemens's added italics). Clemens also marked the chapter on "Speech Defects: Stammering." On page 256 he made double brackets at the sentence: "If an adult patient could be made to forget that he ever stammered, he never would stammer again." He bracketed a paragraph on page 257 that recommended repeated treatment, "a hundred times if necessary, preferably by some forceful member of the family at night, when the patient is asleep. I have seen the most obstinate cases yield to such persistence." Clemens bent down the corner of page 257 for future reference and wrote in black ink in the margin: "Peter Piper picked a peck of pickled peppers &c (Exercise.)" There are no other notations.

Catalogs: *A1911*, "8vo, cloth, gilt top, uncut, N.Y. 1908, . . . containing numerous marked paragraphs and marginal notes in Clemens' handwriting," quotes the signature and quotes a marginal note, lot 395, sold for $6; Stan. V. Henkels (Philadelphia), Catalogue 1057 (14 May 1912), "8vo, cloth, New York, 1908. . . . Containing numerous marked paragraphs and marginal notes in Clemens' handwriting," item #122.

Location: Mark Twain Papers, Bancroft Library, University of California at Berkeley. Acquired in September 1971 from the John M. Tufts Collection, San Francisco, California.

Copy examined: Clemens's copy.

QUESNAY DE BEAUREPAIRE, JULES (1838–1923), pseud. "Jules de Glouvet." *The Woodman; A Novel.* Translated from the French by Mrs. John Simpson (née Senior). New York: Harper & Brothers, 1892. 223 pp.

Source: MTLAcc, entry #1674, volume donated by

Clemens.

A French peasant living in his beloved forest fights against the Prussians in 1870.

QUESNÉ, JACQUES SALBIGOTON (1778–1859). *Lettres de la Vallée de Montmorency, publiées par J. S. Quesné*. Paris: Delaunay, 1816. 180 pp.

> Catalog: *A1911*, #286, "l2mo, unbound," .50¢.
>
> La Vallée de Montmorency was an ancient community in a region northwest of Paris.

QUICHERAT, JULES ÉTIENNE JOSEPH (1814–1882), comp. *Procès de condamnation et de réhabilitation de Jeanne d'Arc, dite La Pucelle, publiés pour la premiere fois d'après les manuscrits de la Bibliothèque Royale*. 5 vols. Paris: J. Renouard et cie, 1841–1849.

> When Mark Twain became interested in the history of Joan of Arc, Andrew Chatto suggested the "5 good-sized volumes published in Paris in the years 1841–9 by Quickery [*sic*]" because they contained "just the sort of *minute contemporary evidence*" (Welland, *Mark Twain in England*, p. 158). Twain listed Quicherat's work at the head of the list of "authorities examined" in writing *Joan of Arc* (1896). (The list appears in front of Mark Twain's "translator's preface.") Albert Bigelow Paine identified Quicherat as one of Mark Twain's three central sources for *Joan of Arc* (MTB, p. 958). In a footnote at the beginning of Twain's brief essay, "Saint Joan of Arc" (1904), Twain stated: "The true story remained in the official archives of France from the Rehabilitation of 1456 until Quicherat dug it out and gave it to the world two generations ago, in lucid and understandable modern French. It is a deeply fascinating story."
>
> Albert E. Stone, Jr., "Mark Twain's *Joan of Arc*" (1959), p. 3; Stone, *IE* (1961), p. 205. See especially Ronald Jenn and Linda A. Morris, "The Sources of Mark Twain's *Personal Recollections of Joan of Arc*," *Mark Twain Journal* 55.1–2 (Spring/Fall 2017): 55–74.

QUINCY, JOSIAH PHILLIPS (1829–1910). *The Peckster Professorship; An Episode in the History of Psychical Research*. Boston and New York: Houghton, Mifflin and Co., 1888. 310 pp.

> In this novel Professor Hargrave valiantly investigates "work in the transcendental sphere" (p. 308) at great personal cost to his academic reputation. Clemens twice entered the title of Quincy's work in Notebook 28 (*N&J* 3: 438, 439) in December 1888.

R

RABELAIS, FRANÇOIS (c. 1494–1553). *The Works of Francis Rabelais, Translated from the French. With Variorum Notes, and Numerous illustrations by [Paul] Gustave Doré [1832–1883]*. London: John Camden Hotten, [1872]. 640 pp. [Publisher, date, and pages are conjectured, based on Clemens's remarks in "The Walt Whitman Controversy" (see below).]

> Catalog: *A1911*, "12 mo, cloth, (worn), Lond., n.d.," with a sheet of notes by Clemens laid in, lot 396, sold for $4.
>
> Location: this volume has never reappeared since the 1911 auction.
>
> Walter Blair showed how closely the fossilized figure in Mark Twain's "The Petrified Man" (1862) imitated Panurge's offensive gesture in Chapter 19 of *The Second Book of Gargantua and Pantagruel*, where Panurge argues with Thaumastes entirely by gestures, some of them obscene

("The Petrified Man and His French Ancestor," *Mark Twain Journal* 19.1 (Winter 1977–1978): 1–3). Clemens referred to "my pet detestation, Rabelais" in a letter of 8 January 1875 to Louise Chandler Moulton, adding that "I have often had more than half a mind to go over & dig up Rabelais & throw his bones away" (*MTLet* 6:342). (Decades later he would make a similar threat, equally ludicrous, regarding the bones of Jane Austen.) In May 1878 Mark Twain envied the freedom of Boccaccio and Rabelais to write about "the very funniest things" that are currently "unprintable" (NB 14, N&J 2: 87). Writing in Paris in 1879, Twain observed: "It depends on who writes a thing whether it is coarse or not. Rabelais." Twain then tells of the scandalized reaction of a magazine editor to whom he showed *1601*: "But that man was a praiser of Rabelais, & had been saying, O that we had a Rabelais—I judged I could furnish him one" (NB 18; N&J 2: 303). In an undated manuscript, "The Walt Whitman Controversy," possibly written in 1882, Twain argues that Whitman's poetry is innocuous compared to a passage in the thirteenth chapter of *The Life of Gargantua and Pantagruel*. Twain pretends to quote from Rabelais' novels, but he omits words in the sentences, blaming this censorship on the editor of the *Evening Post*. In the same sketch, Twain remarks: "Hotten's London edition is illustrated by Doré, and the pictures have carried it all over the world" (DV36, MTP). Chapter 1 of *Life on the Mississippi* (1883) mentions that "when DeSoto stood on the banks of the Mississippi, . . . Rabelais was not yet published." In a newspaper interview in 1903, Twain waxed ecstatic when the name was mentioned: ""But Rabelais! Ah, my dear young sir, I know Rabelais from the head down to the end of his toes and from his toes to the top of his head. Yes, I know Rabelais, and if I had lived in the fifteenth century I would have been Rabelais" (New York *Evening Journal*, 24 October 1903; Scharnhorst, *Complete Interviews*, pp. 484–485). Twain's Autobiographical Dictation of 31 July 1906 characterized the speech in most "ancient English books" as seeming to have been "merely . . . Rabelaisian—exaggerated, artificial, made up by the author for his passing needs." In Twain's *1601* (written in 1876), however, "I put into the Queen's mouth, and into the mouths of those other people, grossnesses not to be found outside of Rabelais, perhaps" (*MTE*, pp. 206–207; *AutoMT* 2: 155–156).

> Ed Folsom and Jerome Loving, "The Walt Whitman Controversy: A Lost Document," *Virginia Quarterly Review* 83.2 (Spring 2007): 123–138, published Twain's manuscript about Whitman.

RACINE, JEAN BAPTISTE (1639–1699). *Phaedra, A Tragedy in Five Acts. French and English*. New York: F. Rullman, 1905. 31 pp.

> Source: MTLAcc, entry #2124a, volume donated from Clemens's library by Clara Clemens Gabrilowitsch in 1910.
>
> On 22 December 1905 Isabel Lyon recorded in New York City: "Tonight we went to see [Sarah] Bernhardt in Phedre, Mr. Clemens, Dorothea Gilder, Francesca [Frances Nunnally], Jean and I. Mr. Clemens was pretty well bored" (IVL Journals, TS p. 115, MTP). Bernhardt had made her New York debut in this tragedy in 1880. Clara Clemens listed the author and title of the play in her

mostly undated commonplace book (Paine 150, MTP). Racine's drama *Phèdre* had first been performed in 1677.

RACINET, [ALBERT CHARLES] AUGUSTE (1825–1893). *Le costume historique. Cinq cents planches, trois cents en couleurs, or et argent, deux cents en camaïeu. Types principaux du vêtement et de la parure.* 6 vols. Paris: Firmin-Didot et cie, 1888. [Volumes I-VI published in installments, 1876–1888.]

On the rear flyleaf of Notebook 17 (1878–1879), Clemens jotted down, probably in Munich: "Racinet's 'Le Costume Historique' $100 Paris, Didot" (*N&J* 2: 283). The painter and illustrator Racinet had undertaken a monumental survey of dress and style throughout the world from the togas of antiquity to the tailcoats of the mid-nineteenth century. The Paris publisher of *Le costume historique* printed many of the illustrations in color. Such a literary resource would be obviously useful to an author who was working on *The Prince and the Pauper* (1881) and possibly contemplated other historical novels as well.

RADAU, RODOLPHE (1835–1911). *Wonders of Acoustics; or, The Phenomena of Sound.* Translated from the French by Robert Ball. Illus. New York: Scribner, Armstrong & Co., 1872. 267 pp.

Source: MTLAcc, entry #1999, volume donated from Clemens's library by Clara Clemens Gabrilowitsch in 1910.

Wonders of Acoustics endeavored to treat all aspects of sound on the human ear, often alluding to classical authors' descriptions. Radau surveyed in Chapter 1 the sounds made by wildlife, even alluding to "the croaking frogs"—but failing by far to match Mark Twain's marvelously onomatopoeic "the bull-frogs a-cluttering," a detail of early-morning sounds on the river that would appear in Chapter 19 of *Adventures of Huckleberry Finn* (1885). *Wonders of Acoustics* also examined the potentially therapeutic effects of certain sounds. Twain might have been especially interested in Chapter VI, "Reflection of Sound," which described in detail (with illustrations) various tests applied to the phenomenon of echoes.

"THE RAGING CANAL" (poem and song, published 1844), also known as "The Raging Canawl" or "The Ragin' Can-all." Lyrics and melody by its frequent performer, the comic singer Pete Morris (b. 1821).

In Chapter 51 of *Roughing It* (1872), Mark Twain credits this "old song" for suggesting his comical poem about the Erie Canal, "The Aged Pilot Man," but he adds that he "cannot remember now." Roger L. Brooks, "A Second Possible Source for Mark Twain's 'The Aged Pilot Man,'" *Revue de littérature comparée* 36 (July-September 1962): 451–453, disputed Twain's speculation that the poem in *Roughing It* was suggested by "The Raging Canal." Brooks pointed out that "the poetic form and certain lines of 'The Aged Pilot Man' bear a greater similarity to Coleridge's 'The Ancient Mariner'" (pp. 451–452).

Baetzhold, *MT&JB* (1970), p. 277; *Granger's Index to Poetry*, ed. William James Smith. Sixth edition (New York and London: Columbia University Press, 1973), p. 1118; *Roughing It* (1993), ed. Harriet Elinor Smith and Edgar Marquess Branch, pp.681–682; and R. Kent Rasmussen, *Critical Companion to Mark Twain* (2007) 1: 18.

RAILWAY AGE (Chicago; New York, journal, published 1876–). Clemens once mentioned this periodical as part of a possible business transaction (SLC to Charles L. Webster, Hartford

14 May 1881, *MTBus*, p. 155).

RALEIGH, (SIR) WALTER (c. 1554–1618). Raleigh was one of the favored aristocratic writers who joined the Queen's court for conversation in *1601* (written in 1876). The remarks of "ye damned windmill" (as the narrator calls him) about sexual practices in America are consonant with Raleigh's sensational narrative about the discovery of Guiana. On 6 August 1877 Clemens cited Raleigh as one of those who had the *"best* of opportunities for working. . . . solitary imprisonment, by compulsion" (SLC to Mollie Fairbanks, *MTMF*, pp. 206–207). Clemens mentioned Raleigh jestingly as a pipe-smoker in a letter written on 15 August 1908 to William Henry Watts (1836–1923), an amateur English antiquarian who lived in Tewkesbury (*MTL*, p. 812; PH in MTP). In *Is Shakespeare Dead?* (1909), Mark Twain alluded to Raleigh among "the other distinguished literary folk of Shakespeare's time."

RALPH, JULIAN (1853–1903). *Alone in China, and Other Stories.* Black cloth, decorated. London: Osgood, McIlvaine & Co., 1897. 388 pp.

Inscription: the front free endpaper is inscribed in black ink: "To S. L. Clemens Esq/With the warm regards of/Julian Ralph/35 Courtfield Road S. W./March 18 '97".

Provenance: Antenne-Dorrance Collection, Rice Lake, Wisconsin.

Location: Mark Twain Archive, Gannett-Tripp Learning Center, Elmira College, Elmira, New York.

Copy examined: Clemens's copy, unmarked. Examined on 28 May 2015.

———. *Alone in China, and Other Stories.* Illustrated by C[harles]. D[ater]. Weldon (1855–1935). New York: Harper & Brothers, 1906. 282 pp.

Source: MTLAcc, entry #1493, volume donated by Clemens.

———. *Dixie; or, Southern Scenes and Sketches.* Illus. New York: Harper & Brothers, 1896. 412 pp.

Source: MTLAcc, entry #1302, volume donated by Clemens.

———. *Harper's Chicago and the World's Fair.* New York: Harper & Brothers, 1893. 245 pp.

Source: MTLAcc, entry #1739, volume donated by Clemens.

Twain did not attend this exposition, but his *Following the Equator* (1897) alludes to it.

———. *The Making of a Journalist.* New York: Harper & Brothers, 1903. 200 pp.

Source: MTLAcc, entry #1466, volume donated by Clemens.

———. *Our Great West: A Study of the Present Conditions and Future Possibilities of the New Commonwealths and Capitals of the United States.* Illus. New York: Harper & Brothers, 1893. 478 pp.

Source: MTLAcc, entry #1233, volume donated by Clemens.

———. [Another identical copy.]

Source: MTLAcc, entry #1301, volume donated by Clemens.

RAMSAY, ALLAN (1686–1758). "Bonny Bessy" (Scottish air, published in 1724). Tune: "Bessey's Haggies."

One of the tunes Clemens requested Isabel Lyon to play

on 14 February 1906 was "Bonnie Sweet Bessie" (IVL Journals, TS p. 135, MTP).

RANDALL, DAVID AUSTIN (1813–1884). *The Handwriting of God in Egypt, Sinai, and the Holy Land: The Records of a Journey from the Great Valley of the West to the Sacred Places of the East.* Two volumes in one. Philadelphia: John E. Potter & Co., 1862.

Provenance: bookplate #554 of the J. Langdon Family Library. Robert Jerome found this volume in a yard sale on 17 October 1984 and donated it to the collection that became the Mark Twain Archive. Clemens had access to these books whenever he visited Elmira.

Catalogs: inventory list of the Langdon family library books compiled by Mark Woodhouse in 2013; Ball 2016 inventory, brown cloth, leather spine, gilt lettering, fair condition.

Location: Mark Twain Archive, Elmira College, Elmira, New York.

Prior to his Holy Land excursion in 1867, Mark Twain made historical and geographical background notes in Notebook 10; many of these quoted or paraphrased Randall's book. He may have condensed these passages from a copy of Randall's book in the ship library of the *Quaker City* (or, conceivably, he consulted the Langdon family's copy if young Charles Jervis Langdon took it with him to the Holy Land). Twain quoted from *The Handwriting of God* in Chapter 52 of *The Innocents Abroad* (1869). Aside from the edition published in Philadelphia (which was reprinted in 1866), other editions appeared in Columbus, Ohio (Randall and Aston, 1862) and New York (Sheldon & Co., 1862). Randall's book seems like a logical candidate for the vaguely identified *Jericho and the Jordan* title that Twain reported the pilgrims were instructed to obtain for the *Quaker City* voyage. Twain supplied no author's name for that book (*Daily Alta California*, 5 April 1868; McKeithan, *TIA* [1958], p. 303), but see the Annotated Catalog entry for *Jericho and the Jordan*. See also the Catalog entry for John Murray, *Handbook for Travellers in Syria and Palestine.*

Robert H. Hirst, "Making of *The Innocents Abroad*" (1975).

RANDALL, JAMES RYDER (1839–1908). *Maryland, My Maryland, and Other Poems.* New York: John Murphy Co., [cop. 1908]. 180 pp.

Source: MTLAcc, entry #2085, volume donated from Clemens's library by Clara Clemens Gabrilowitsch in 1910.

In February or March 1885 Mark Twain sent a copy of *Adventures of Huckleberry Finn* (1885) to Randall, a journalist and poet on the staff of the Augusta, Georgia *Chronicle* (*MTBus*, p. 304).

Rand, McNally & Co's General Atlas of the World, Containing . . . A Ready Reference Marginal Index. Chicago: Rand, McNally & Co. [published in 1897 and in other years thereafter].

A photograph of Jean Clemens and her father taken in Dublin, New Hampshire in the summer of 1906 shows her holding a copy of this atlas (Geoffrey C. Ward, Dayton Duncan, and Ken Burns, *Mark Twain: An Illustrated Biography* [New York: Alfred A. Knopf, 2001], pp. 228–229). Jo Dee Benussi noticed this detail.

RANDOLPH, ANSON DAVIES FITZ (1820–1896), comp. *The Changed Cross, and Other Religious Poems.* New York: Anson

D. F. Randolph & Co., 1865. 228 pp.

In 1866 Olivia Langdon copied the title poem from this collection into her common place book. The authorship of "The Changed Cross," like most of the verses in this volume, was uncredited. As the compiler explained, they had simply been "gathered from magazines and newspapers." Harris, *Courtship* (1996), p. 15.

_____, comp. *The Changed Cross, and Other Religious Poems.* New York: Anson D. F. Randolph & Co., 1867. 228 pp.

Catalog: Ball 2016 inventory, brown boards, gilt lettering, gilt edge pages, cover detached, poor condition, contains a note from Pompeii dated 20 May 1874 as well as pressed flowers and leaves.

Inscription: "Ida Clark,/Elmira, N. Y./Merry Christmas 1869". [Ida B. Clark (1849–1934) would marry Charles Jervis Langdon in 1870.]

Location: Quarry Farm library shelves, under the supervision of the Mark Twain Archive, Elmira College, Elmira, New York.

Copy examined: Clemens had access to this book whenever he visited the Langdon house in Elmira.

_____, comp. *The Shadow of the Rock, and Other Religious Poems.* New York: Anson D. F. Randolph, 1867. 224 pp.

Inscription: "Merry Christmas/1867". [Ida B. Clark (1849–1934) would marry Charles Jervis Langdon in 1870.]

Catalog: Ball 2016 inventory, brown boards, gilt lettering, gilt edge pages, cover detached, poor condition.

Location: Quarry Farm library shelves, under the supervision of the Mark Twain Archive, Elmira College, Elmira, New York.

Copy examined: Clemens had access to this book whenever he visited the Langdon house in Elmira.

These poems "have been selected from many sources. . . . The publisher has designed it as a companion book to *The Changed Cross*" (p. 3).

RANKE, LEOPOLD VON (1795–1886). *Deutsche Geschichte im Zeitalter der Reformation [German History in the Age of the Reformation].* Siebente Auflage. 6 vols in 3. [Volumes One and Two bound together, making 391 pp.; Volumes Three, Four, Five, and Six are bound as three volumes.] Original three-quarter tan morocco and marbled boards, gilt, edges stained red, rebacked with original spine preserved. Leipzig: Duncker & Humblot, 1894.

Inscription: the front free endpapers of Volumes One and Two (bound together) are signed in black ink: "Jean L. Clemens/21 Fifth Ave./New York City/1905."

Provenance: sold in 1963 by Maxwell Hunley of Beverly Hills, California. In 1986 Victor Jacobs of Dayton, Ohio reported that he owned a "book in German signed by Jean L. Clemens, 21 5th Ave., New York City, 1905" (Jacobs to Alan Gribben, 15 October 1986). No other book except the Ranke volumes contains this exact inscription.

Catalogs: *C1951*, J19, 3 vols., listed among books belonging to Jean and Clara Clemens; "Victor and Irene Murr Jacobs Collection," Sotheby's, New York City, Sale of 29 October 1996, "2 volumes in 1, half sheep, worn," item 294, sold with two other books for $2,300; *Sotheby's 2003*, #194 (presumably Volumes One and Two only), $1,300 (sold with two other titles from the Clemens family's library).

Locations: Volumes One and Two in the collection of Kevin Mac Donnell, Austin, Texas. Volumes Three, Four, Five, and Six of the six-volume set, bound as three volumes, are in the Mark Twain Papers, Bancroft Library, University of California at Berkeley. The latter were donated in 1970 by Theodore Koundakjian of Albany, California.

Copies examined: unmarked copies belonging to Jean Clemens. Stickers on the rear pastedown endpapers identify the bookseller-importer as G. E. Stechert & Co., New York City. Penciled sale markings on the front endpapers resemble those in other volumes sold at the *C1951* auction. The two volumes in the Mac Donnell collection were viewed in July 2004.

———. *The History of the Popes, Their Church and State, and Especially of Their Conflicts with Protestantism in the Sixteenth and Seventeenth Centuries.* Translated by Elizabeth Foster. Bohn's Standard Library Series. 3 volumes. Engraved frontispiece portraits. 12mo, original embossed green cloth, spines gilt-lettered, corners bumped, Volume I split at its hinge. London: George Bell and Sons, 1876.

Marginalia: a few pages throughout the work bear Clemens's penciled brackets and underlinings. The three volumes are largely unopened, but several leaves in the front of each volume, particularly in Volume I, have been roughly opened.

Catalogs: *A1911*, "3 vols., 12mo, cloth, Lond. 1876," with a small sheet of notes by Clemens laid in, lot 397, sold for $4.25; Victor and Irene Murr Jacobs collection sale, Sotheby's, 29 October 1996, 3 volumes, lot 208, sold for $2,185; Sotheby's, 19 June 2003, 3 volumes, #230, $1,700.

Provenance: these volumes contain the bookplate of Edward S. Marsh. Seven Gables Bookshop, New York City, offered the books in 1971. They were owned by Victor Jacobs of Dayton, Ohio in 1986 (Jacobs to Alan Gribben, 15 October 1986). Subsequently the three volumes became part of the collection owned by Nick Karanovich, Fort Wayne, Indiana.

Copy examined: Clemens's copy of the three volumes, at the 2003 auction. Volume I has the *A1911* sale label; above it a holograph manuscript fragment written by Clemens in black ink (in a late hand) was tipped in on the front pastedown endpaper by Albert Bigelow Paine for the 1911 auction. It reads, "History. Read more of it than anybody, yet don't know as much about it as I do about multipli'n table, & I never can say *that* without breaking down at 9 x 6 is 35."

Clemens reminded himself in Rome on 6 November 1878: "See death of Alexander VI in vol 3 of History of Popes. 1st chap Appen" (NB 17, *N&J* 2: 244). Clemens was referring to Section One of the Appendix in Volume III, which recounted how a cardinal escaped murder and poisoned his would-be murderer, Pope Alexander VI, instead. In Napier, New Zealand, Clemens noted the title on 1 December 1895: "Ranke's History of the Popes" (NB 34, TS p. 45).

RANSFORD, EDWIN (1805–1876). "In the Days When We Went Gypsying" (poem and song), collected in *Jottings, by Edwin Ransford.* London: Ransford and Son, [1863?]. 84 pp.

"Can anybody furnish me the poem 'In the days when we went gipsying, a long time ago?'" Clemens queried in New York City in January 1894 (NB 33, TS p. 45). He marked this song (dating it "1845") in his copy

of Frank B. Ogilvie's *Two Hundred Old-Time Songs, Containing the Words and Music of the Choicest Gems of the Old and Familiar Songs* (1896). On 6 January 1897, in London, Clemens thought of quoting the poem in "a farce or sketch" about an enchanted fairy palace in which Chaucer would appear and write songs. One of Clemens's notes reads: "Song—young people grown old, 'In the days when we went gipsying'" (NB 39, TS p. 43). The poem came readily to mind in January 1897 when Clemens grieved in London over Susy Clemens's death; he included his favorite line in his notes for a biographical sketch of Susy; he recalled that one of "the two most pathetic, most moving things in the Eng tongue to me" was "the refrain of a long-ago forgotten song [Ransford wrote the poem in 1837] familiar to me in my earliest boyhood: [']In the days when we went gypsying, a long time ago'"; and he subsequently associated the song title again with Susy's death (NB 39, TS pp. 50, 52, 58). On 30 December 1898, writing to William Dean Howells from Vienna, Clemens again quoted "The days when we went gipsying/A long time ago" in connection with his memories of Susy (*MTHL*, p. 685). Henry Nash Smith and William M. Gibson have commented that the fragmentary refrain "had powerfully incantatory and talismanic values for Clemens"; they report that Clemens first quoted it in a dispatch from San Francisco to the Virginia City *Territorial Enterprise* on 11 December 1865 (*MTHL*, p. 686 n. 6, citing Yale Scrapbook). On 1 June 1902 Mark Twain indicated that he intended to use the line in his next Huck and Tom story (NB 45, TS p. 15).

RANSOME, STAFFORD (1860–1931). *Japan in Transition: A Comparative Study of the Progress, Policy, and Methods of the Japanese Since Their War with China.* Illus., maps. New York: Harper & Brothers, 1899. 261 pp.

Source: MTLAcc, entry #1459, volume donated by Clemens.

RAWLINSON, (SIR) HENRY CRESWICKE (1810–1895).

"Sir Henry Rawlinson, who is a Persian scholar and talks to the Shah in his own tongue" ("O'Shah," London, 18 June 1873). In "As Concerns Interpreting the Deity" (written in 1905 and unpublished during Clemens's lifetime), he alluded to Rawlinson's work on the Rosetta Stone.

RAWSON, [ALICE] MAUD (FIFE) STEPNEY (1865–1945). *A Lady of the Regency.* New York: Harper & Brothers, 1901. 352 pp.

Source: MTLAcc, entry #1646, volume donated by Clemens.

In 1894 Alice Maud Fife married an English amateur footballer, William Stepney Rawson (1854–1932), and thereafter wrote novels under the name "Mrs. Maude Stepney Rawson."

RAYMOND, GEORGE LANSING (1839–1929). *The Psychology of Inspiration; An Attempt to Distinguish Religious from Scientific Truth.* New York: Funk & Wagnalls, 1908. 340 pp.

Source: MTLAcc, entry #850, volume donated by Clemens.

RAYMOND, RICHARD JOHN (fl. 1818–1847) and WILLIAM EVANS BURTON (1802–1860). *The Toodles. A Domestic Drama in Two Acts* (first performed under this title in New York City in 1848).

On 13 January 1864 Mark Twain wrote from Carson City after seeing the R. G. Marsh Juvenile Troupe in this drama: "They played here last night—'Toodles,' you know"

(*MTEnt*, p. 131). Twain mentioned several characters— Toodles, Mrs. Toodles, a sailor boy, a lovely girl, a ratty old gentleman, and a reformed pirate. In "Private Habits of Horace Greeley" (1868), Twain joked that Greeley's cravat is so askew that one of its ends "goes after his eye, in the good old Toodles fashion." Twain's *Roughing It* (1872) related an incident in a California bar-room that "was nothing but a bit of acting, but it seemed to me a perfect rendering, and worthy of Toodles himself" (Ch. 55). Twain stipulated in 1877 that his chief character in "Cap'n Simon Wheeler, The Amateur Detective: A Light Tragedy" should have the mannerisms of Toodles (*S&B*, p. 248 n. 19). In marginalia that Clemens apparently made in 1900, he recalled the "delightfully funny" Toodles (see the Catalog entry for T. W. S. Higginson's *Cheerful Yesterdays. Contemporaries*). On 12 February 1903 Clemens reminisced about "the time in St. Louis in '53, aged 17 1/2, that I took the shy pretty girl from up country to Ben de Bar's theatre <to see Toodles>" and then Clemens could not get his tight-fitting shoes on again after the performance (NB 46, TS p. 10). The *Toodles* was an adaptation by the London-born actor and editor William Evans Burton of Raymond's *The Farmer's Daughter of the Severn Side; or, Mr. and Mrs. Toodles, A Domestic Drama*, first performed in London in 1832.

RAYNER, SIMEON (1832–1886). *The History and Antiquities of Pudsey*. Edited by William Smith (1832–1907). London: Longmans, Green, and Co., 1887. 313 pp.

Inscription: the half-title page is inscribed "S. L. Clemens, Esq./with the Editor's/Sincere/regards/Morley, Aug 16 '87."

Marginalia: there is a pencil mark on page 22 at a description of the immense power wielded by feudal lord over his chattels; Clemens made pencil marks on page 25 beside the bondage agreement of John, son of Ellis de Pudsey.

Location: Mark Twain Library, Redding, Connecticut.

Copy examined: Clemens's copy. Has the red ink Mark Twain Library accession number "3452". Examined in 1970 and again in June 1982.

The editor, William Smith, had also sent Clemens a copy of his *Morley: Ancient and Modern* (see that Catalog entry).

READ, THOMAS BUCHANAN (1822–1872). "Come, Gentle Trembler" (poem) [Collected in *The Poetical Works of Thomas Buchanan Read*. 3 vols. Philadelphia: J. B. Lippincott, 1866.]

Viewing the nearly deserted wharf at St. Louis in 1882, Mark Twain was reminded of the penultimate stanza of Read's six-stanza poem: "The old, old sea, as one in tears,/ Comes murmuring, with foamy lips,/And knocking at the vacant piers,/Calls for his [Read wrote "its"] long-lost multitude of ships" (*LonMiss* [1883], Ch. 22). Burton Stevenson first identified Twain's source in *The Home Book of Quotations, Classical and Modern* (New York: Dodd, Mead & Co., 1934), p. 1774. Twain quoted the same four lines of personification in "Three Thousand Years Among the Microbes," written in 1905 (*WWD?*, p. 518).

———. *The Wagoner of the Alleghanies. A Poem of the Days of Seventy-Six*. Philadelphia: J. B. Lippincott & Co., 1863. 276 pp. [Read's introductory "Advertisement" states that "the scenes of this poem are chiefly laid on the banks of the Schuylkill, between Philadelphia and Valley Forge; the time, somewhat previous to and during a great part of the war of Independence."]

Inscription: the yellow bookplate of Orion Clemens is affixed to the front pastedown endpaper.

Marginalia: On the front free endpaper someone (not Clemens) wrote in pencil, "Charing Cross means 'dear/ Queen's Cross.'" Someone other than Clemens wrote on the title page, in pencil, "Page 59". On page 59 brackets are drawn around several lines of verse.

Location: Mark Twain Library, Redding, Connecticut Donated by Clemens (MTLAcc, entry #659).

Copy examined: Orion Clemens's copy, later Samuel Clemens's. The volume has no Mark Twain Library accession number. Examined in 1970 and again in June 1982.

READE, CHARLES (1814–1884). *Bible Characters*. London: Chatto & Windus, 1888. 106 pp.

Source: MTLAcc, entry #929, volume donated by Clemens.

———. *Bible Characters*. New York: Harper & Brothers, 1889. 106 pp.

Source: MTLAcc, entry #1129, volume donated by Clemens.

———. *The Cloister and the Hearth; or, Maid, Wife, and Widow: A Matter-of-Fact Romance*. Chicago: M. A. Donohue & Co., n. d. 524 pp. Paperbound.

Source: MTLAcc, entry #248, volume donated by Clemens. Clemens enjoyed this picaresque novel about the father of the prominent Dutch scholar Desiderius Erasmus (c. 1466–1536), first published in 1861. The Reverend Joseph H. Twichell "recommended Chas. Reade's 'Hearth & Cloister' [*sic*] & I bought it & am enchanted. You shall have it if you have not read it. I read with a pencil by me, sweetheart, but the book is so uniformly good that I find nothing to mark" (SLC to Olivia Langdon, Boston, 28 November 1869, *LLMT*, p. 126; *MTLet* 3: 413). Walter Blair (*MT&HF* [1960], pp. 129–130) pointed out that Chapter 63 of Reade's historical novel, set in fifteenth-century Holland, contains the same "lap-test" for determining someone's sexual identity that Judith Loftus uses in Chapter 11 of *Adventures of Huckleberry Finn* (1885). Baetzhold, *MT&JB* (1970), pp. 201–202.

———. *The Cloister & the Hearth; or, Maid, Wife, and Widow: A Matter-of-Fact Romance*. 2 vols. Spine missing from first volume. Illustrated by William Martin Johnson (1862–1942). New York: Harper & Brothers, 1894.

Marginalia: markings on pages 259, 313, and 317 in Volume I. A postcard dated 2 April 1927 is laid in Volume II; it is addressed to Nina Gabrilowitsch from a Detroit friend ("Aileen").

Provenance: has the shelfmarks of Clara Clemens Gabrilowitsch's library numbering system during her Detroit years. Sold at the 1951 auction in Hollywood but not listed in the hastily prepared sale sheet.

Catalog: "Property from the Library of Mark Twain," Butterfield & Butterfield, San Francisco, Sale 6613 (16 July 1997), "2 vols.," lot 2712.

Location: Mark Twain House and Museum, Hartford, Connecticut.

Copy examined: Clemens's copy, later in the possession of Clara Clemens. Viewed in Hartford in 1997.

———. *The Cloister and the Hearth; or, Maid, Wife, and Widow: A Matter-of-Fact Romance*. New York: Harper & Brothers,

1904. 440 pp.

Source: MTLAcc, entry #1123, volume donated by Clemens.

_____ and DION BOUCICAULT (1820–1890). *Foul Play; A Novel.* Chicago: M. A. Donahue Co., n. d. 260 pp. Paperbound.

Source: MTLAcc, entry #247, volume donated by Clemens.

_____ and DION BOUCICAULT (1820–1890). *Foul Play; A Novel.* New York: Harper & Brothers, 1902. 245 pp.

Source: MTLAcc, entry #1122, volume donated by Clemens.

_____ and DION BOUCICAULT (1820–1890). *Foul Play.* Bound with Charles Reade's *It Is Never Too Late to Mend; A Matter-of-Fact Romance.* New York: Harper & Brothers, n. d. 650 pp.

Source: MTLAcc, entry #1648, volume donated by Clemens.

——. *Good Stories.* Illus. New York: Harper & Brothers, 1898. 319 pp.

Source: MTLAcc, entry #1128, volume donated by Clemens.

_____. *Griffith Gaunt; or, Jealousy* (novel, published 1866; also dramatized).

In a letter of 30 April 1867 to the *Alta California,* Mark Twain relates a story about the President of the Society for the Prevention of Cruelty to Animals, who protested the treatment of a pig used in the last act of this play. Twain saw the play at Wallack's Theatre in New York City (*MTTMB,* p. 160).

——. *Griffith Gaunt; or, Jealousy.* New York: Harper & Brothers, 1904. 225 pp.

Source: MTLAcc, entry #1118, volume donated by Clemens.

——. *Griffith Gaunt; or, Jealousy.* Bound with *A Simpleton* and *The Wandering Heir.* New York: Harper & Brothers, n. d. 519 pp.

Source: MTLAcc, entry #1649, volume donated by Clemens.

——. *Hard Cash; A Matter-of-Fact Romance.* Illus. New York: Harper & Brothers, 1904. 415 pp.

Source: MTLAcc, entry #1126, volume donated by Clemens.

——. *"Love Me Little, Love Me Long."* New York: Harper & Brothers, 1902. 230 pp.

Source: MTLAcc, entry #1119, volume donated by Clemens.

Along with C. H. Webb, Mark Twain and others on the staff of the Virginia City *Weekly Occidental* burlesqued Reade's novel, which had appeared in 1859 (*MTBP,* p. 77). Twain recalled the group novel and mentioned *"Love Me Little, Love Me Long"* in Chapter 51 of *Roughing It* (1872). *Roughing It* (1993), ed. Harriet Elinor Smith and Edgar Marquess Branch, pp. 680–681.

——. *Peg Woffington, Christie Johnstone, and Other Stories.* New York: Harper & Brothers, 1904. 353 pp.

Source: MTLAcc, entry #1120, volume donated by Clemens.

——. *Peg Woffington, Christie Johnstone, and Other Stories.* Bound with *A Terrible Temptation.* New York: Harper & Brothers, n.d. 603 pp.

Source: MTLAcc, entry #1651, volume donated by Clemens.

——. *A Perilous Secret.* Bound with *The Cloister and the Hearth; or, Maid, Wife, and Widow: A Matter-of-Fact Romance.* New York: Harper & Brothers, n. d. 600 pp.

Source: MTLAcc, entry #1652, volume donated by Clemens.

——. *Put Yourself in His Place. A Novel.* Illus. New York: Harper & Brothers, 1902. 319 pp.

Source: MTLAcc, entry #1124, volume donated by Clemens.

Clemens surely remembered that the *Galaxy* had serialized this novel from March 1869 to July 1870.

——. *A Terrible Temptation.* Bound with *Peg Woffington, Christie Johnstone, and Other Stories.* Illus. New York: Harper & Brothers, n. d. 250 pp.

Source: MTLAcc, entry #1125, volume donated by Clemens.

——. *White Lies.* Bound with *Good Stories.* New York: Harper & Brothers, n. d. 598 pp.

Source: MTLAcc, entry #1647, volume donated by Clemens.

——. *White Lies.* New York: Harper & Brothers, 1904. 280 pp.

Source: MTLAcc, entry #1127, volume donated by Clemens.

——. *A Woman-Hater. A Novel.* Bound with *Put Yourself in His Place.* New York: Harper & Brothers, n. d. 570 pp.

Source: MTLAcc, entry #1650, volume donated by Clemens.

——. *A Woman-Hater. A Novel.* New York: Harper & Brothers, 1900. 251 pp.

Source: MTLAcc, entry #1121, volume donated by Clemens.

——. *A Woman-Hater. A Novel* (3 vols., published in 1877).

On 9 June 1870 Clemens informed Elisha Bliss that Edward H. House "is a nephew of Charles Reade the novelist & comes of a fine literary breed" (*MTLet* 4: 148; ALS in MTHM). "The touchy Charles Reade can sue English newspapers and get verdicts; he would soon change his tactics here," Clemens remarked in a speech before the Monday Evening Club of Hartford on 31 March 1873 ("License of the Press," *MTS1923,* p. 47). "I am just finishing Charles Reade's Woman Hater, which has a handful of diamonds scattered over every page" (SLC to Mary Mason Fairbanks, Elmira, 6 August 1877, *MTMF,* p. 209). During his lecture tour in Australia Mark Twain observed that "Charles Reade, in writing about anything he's witnessed or felt, does it with remarkable success, but when he gets his matter second-hand he makes an awful botch of it" (Sydney, Australia *Bulletin,* 4 January 1896; Scharnhorst, ed., *Complete Interviews,* p. 266). While Clemens was in London in July 1899, he reflected that Charles Reade was among those "gone" (NB 40, TS p. 60). Few scholars or biographers have noticed the surprisingly large number of Reade's writings on the shelves of Clemens's library.

Baetzhold, *Mark Twain and John Bull* (1970), pp. 200–201.

READE, CHARLES L[ISTON] (1848–1917) and COMPTON READE (1834–1909). *Charles Reade [1814–1884], D.C.L., Dramatist, Novelist, Journalist. A Memoir Compiled Chiefly from His Literary Remains.* New York: Harper & Brothers,

1887. 448 pp.

    Source: MTLAcc, entry #837, volume donated by Clemens. Charles Liston Reade was Charles Reade's illegitimate son whose mother died in childbirth; Reade eventually acknowledged his paternity. Compton Reade was Charles Reade's nephew.

REED, ANDREW (1787–1862). "Holy Ghost! With light divine" (hymn, melody composed by Louis Moreau Gottschalk [1829–1869]; arranged by Edwin Pond Parker [1836–1925]).

    Either Clemens or his wife Olivia marked this hymn in their copy of *Laudes Domini: A Selection of Spiritual Songs, Ancient and Modern* (1884), compiled by C. S. Robinson. (See that Catalog entry.) Its first line implores, "Holy Ghost! With light divine/Shine upon this heart of mine."

REED, MYRTLE (1874–1911). *The Book of Clever Beasts; Studies in Unnatural History.* Illustrated by Peter Newell (1862–1924). New York: G. P. Putnam's Sons, 1904. 231 pp.

    Source: MTLAcc, entry #456, volume donated by Clemens. "Whimsical" is not exactly the word for these eight stories about imaginary animals, and "weird" comes only a little closer. "Bizarre" is better, perhaps. The plots, one of which involves a suicide, hardly seem designed for reading to children. The author names as her inspirations John Burroughs and half a dozen other naturalists, but in actuality her tales parody their efforts to document animal behavior. Reed had already written her most famous romance, *Lavender and Old Lace* (1902). In 1911 she would take her own life with a sleeping medication.

———. *The Master's Violin.* New York: G. P. Putnam's Sons, 1905. 315 pp.

    Source: MTLAcc, entry #246, volume donated by Clemens. Reed's novel was first published in 1904. Clara Clemens criticized *The Master's Violin* for "much badly expressed sentiment" (undated entry in her commonplace book, Paine 150, MTP), and subsequent readers have agreed with her opinion of this once immensely popular author. However, Marion Schuyler Allen, whose daughter Helen became one of Clemens's Angelfish aquarium girls and in whose Bermuda house Clemens stayed more than once, revealed that in 1910 Clemens marked a copy of Reed's *The Master's Violin* and found comfort in the following passage spoken by the Master in Chapter 20 on page 282: "I do not think of heaven as the glittering place with the streets of gold and the walls of pearl, but more like one quiet wood, where the grass is green and the little brook sings all day. I have thought of heaven as the place where those who love shall be together, free from all misunderstanding or the thought of parting" (Allen, "Some New Anecdotes of Mark Twain," *Strand Magazine* [London] 46.272 [August 1913]: 169; her slightly misquoted text has been corrected).

A Reference Catalogue of Current Literature Containing the Full Titles of Books Now in Print and On Sale with the Prices at Which They May be Obtained of All Booksellers. London: Joseph Whitaker, 1874.

    On a bill for William H. Rule's *History of the Inquisition* dated 5 June 1874, Scribner, Welford & Armstrong of New York City notified Clemens: "'Whittaker's [*sic*] Reference Catalogue' is not yet ready, we will forward when published." Clemens returned the statement with his payment (that statement was later sent back as his receipt), noting his reply: "All right. Many thanks/Yrs Truly/Mark Twain" (receipt in MTP; *MTLet* 6: 154).

Reglement für die Verheirathung der Officiers [Regulations for Marriage of the Officers]. Leipzig: Carl Reigner, 1884. 62 pp. Paperbound.

    Source: MTLAcc, entry #388, volume donated by Clemens.

REICH, EMIL (1854–1910). *Success Among Nations.* New York: Harper & Brothers, 1904. 293 pp.

    Source: MTLAcc, entry #1465, volume donated by Clemens.

    The title of *Success Among Nations* hardly does justice to its sweeping survey of governments and religions from the era of ancient Egypt up to the then-current state of political, economic, church, and social affairs in Germany, Britain, and the United States.

REID, MAYNE (1818–1883). *The Quadroon; or, A Lover's Adventures in Louisiana* (novel, published in 1856).

    Michael Orth cited this anti-slavery novel as "one that I suspect led . . . directly to *Pudd'nhead Wilson*" ("*Pudd'nhead Wilson* Reconsidered, or the Octoroon in the Villa Viviani," *Mark Twain Journal* 14.4 [Summer 1969]: 12–13). Reid's novel, Orth wrote, "relied for its appeal more on sentiment and melodramatic adventure than on any special abolitionist tone, but its basic message questioned the foundations of Southern civilization" (p. 12). No copy owned by Clemens has turned up yet, nor did he allude to it in his writings.

REID, STUART JOHNSON (1848–1927). *Lord John Russell [1792–1878].* New York: Harper & Brothers, 1895. 381 pp.

    Source: MTLAcc, entry #1280, volume donated by Clemens.

———. *A Sketch of the Life and Times of the Rev. Sydney Smith [1771–1845], Rector of Combe-Florey, and Canon Residentiary of St. Paul's. Based on Family Documents and the Recollections of Personal Friends.* Portrait and illustrations. First American edition. 8vo, original blue cloth, gilt. New York: Harper & Brothers, 1885. 409 pp.

    Inscription: the front pastedown endpaper is signed "S. L. Clemens" and also signed and dated on the front flyleaf "Olivia L. Clemens/Dec. 1884."

    Catalogs: *A 1911,* "8vo, cloth, N.Y. 1885," quotes the signatures, lot 398, sold for $5.50 (sold to the Mark Twain Company); *C1951,* #19c, listed among books signed by Clemens; Alan Fox, Catalog 1, 1980, item #15, has the *A1911* label, "fine copy," $450, sold to Nick Karanovich; *Sotheby's 2003,* #231, sold with three other books for $2,500

    Provenance: an (erased) shelfmark of Clara Clemens Gabrilowitsch's private library in Detroit is still visible. The book eventually was acquired by Nick Karanovich of Fort Wayne, Indiana for $450.

    Location: collection of Kevin Mac Donnell, Austin, Texas.

    Copy examined: Clemens and Olivia Clemens's unmarked copy, in July 2004. Displays the *A1911* sale label.

    The Anglican clergyman, writer, and co-founder of *The Edinburgh Review* Sydney Smith exerted an immense influence on his generation. His public lectures on moral philosophy drew much applause, as did his appeals for Roman Catholic emancipation and better treatment for the London poor. It is believed that his witty political observations and his social reform tendencies cost him an appointment as a bishop, though he was made canon of St. Paul's Cathedral in London.

REID, (SIR) WEMYSS (1842–1905). *Memoirs and Correspondence of Lyon Playfair [1818–1898], First Lord Playfair of St. Andrews.* New York: Harper & Brothers, 1899. 487 pp.

> Source: MTLAcc, entry #1787, volume donated by Clemens.

———. *William Black [1841–1898], Novelist: A Biography.* Original cloth, gilt. New York: Harper and Brothers, 1902. 352 pp.

> Inscription: the front free endpaper is signed carelessly, in large letters: "S L. Clemens/1902". The front pastedown endpaper is signed at the top, "Cyril Clemens".
> Provenance: formerly in the Mark Twain Library, Redding, Connecticut. It has the oval Mark Twain Library stamp centered on the front pastedown endpaper and there is a library call number on the lower spine. The copyright page displays a Mark Twain Library accession number: "2692". Thomas A. Tenney inspected this volume in 1980 when it was in the collection of Cyril Clemens of Kirkwood, Missouri.
> Catalog: *Mott 1952*, #79, $5.
> Location: Harry Ransom Center, University of Texas at Austin. Acquired from Cyril Clemens along with six other books on 28 March 1986, for payments of $5,000 to Cyril Clemens and $5,000 to his *Mark Twain Journal.* Thomas A. Tenney, Cyril Clemens, and Alan Gribben (then an English professor at the University of Texas at Austin) negotiated this agreement in an exchange of letters written between 20 August 1985 and 27 April 1986.
> Copy examined: photocopies of the covers, endpapers, and title page of Clemens's copy, sent to Alan Gribben by Thomas A. Tenney in 1985. Confirmed by examination of the volume in Austin in 1986.

All biographies that Clemens acquired during this period when he was conceiving the possibility of designating his own biographer (eventually Albert Bigelow Paine) should be considered as potentially significant.

REID, WHITELAW (1837–1912). *Ohio in the War: Her Statesmen, Generals, and Soldiers.* Illus. 2 vols. Cincinnati: Wilstach, Baldwin, 1872. [Publisher supplied.]

> Catalog: *A1911*, "2 vols., royal 8vo, cloth, Cinn. 1872," with a sheet of Clemens's notes laid in, lot 399, sold for $1.25.

As the managing editor of Horace Greeley's New York *Tribune*, Reid opposed the nomination of the scandal-tainted Ulysses S. Grant for a second presidential term in 1872 and instead supported Greeley's bid for the office. Clemens seems never to have forgotten or forgiven that decision by Reid. In November 1877 Clemens noted cryptically: "Biography of Whitelaw Reid' (NB 14, *N&J* 2: 49). Later Clemens became convinced that Reid's newspaper was publishing derogatory remarks about him. Fishing for insults in January 1882, Clemens claimed that Reid carried *Ohio in the War* around in his boots to read to people who would listen (NB 19, *N&J* 2: 423). Clemens's tirade against Reid in Notebook 20 (*N&J* 2: 443) alluded to Reid's "double-facedness & treachery toward Grant, whose biography he wrote." Clemens may have meant an unidentified campaign biography; Reid's well-respected *Ohio in the War* included a biographical sketch of U. S. Grant, but it was reserved about Grant's merits.

———. "Schools of Journalism," *Scribner's Monthly* 4.2 (June 1872): 194–204.

Looking for revenge against Reid in January 1882, Clemens made a memorandum to read this article (NB 19, *N&J* 2: 418). Reid's innocuous essay merely recommended that universities consider adding a School of Journalism for professional training of graduates and suggested some readings and types of preparation for that career. Eventually Clemens would conclude that the reports claiming Reid was insulting him in the *Tribune* were unfounded, and he dropped his idea of a launching a counter-attack.

———. "Some Southern Reminiscences," in *Lotos Leaves*, ed. John Brougham (1810–1880) and John Elderkin (1841–1926). Boston: William F. Gill & Co., 1875, pp. 3–17.

Concluding (erroneously, as it turned out) that Whitelaw Reid was conducting a vendetta against him, Clemens made a memorandum to read Reid's essay, "Some Southern Reminiscences," which had appeared in the *Lotus Leaves* volume published in 1875 (Notebook 19, *N&J* 2: 417). In that brief sketch Reid recalled the years he spent after the Civil War trying (to no avail) to make his fortune by raising cotton in the Deep South. He gave his impressions of the scenes and society in Louisiana, Alabama, and Georgia, focusing on the difficult living conditions endured by the emancipated African Americans.

REINTZEL, MARGARET (b. 1845), comp. *The Musician's Year Book.* New York: E. P. Dutton & Co., 1895. 195 pp.

> Source: MTLAcc, entry #678, volume donated by Clemens.

A compendium of important dates in musical history and in musicians' lives.

REMINGTON, FREDERIC (1861–1909). *Crooked Trails.* Illustrated by the author. New York: Harper & Brothers, 1899. 151 pp.

> Source: MTLAcc, entry #1614, volume donated by Clemens.

E. W. Kemble recalled that Clemens included Remington among "a little group of shining lights undimmed by time" (Kemble, "Illustrating *Huckleberry Finn*" [1930]).

———. *Stories of Peace and War.* New York: Harper & Brothers, 1899. 98 pp.

> Source: MTLAcc, entry #1338, volume donated by Clemens.

These stories and sketches were extracted from Remington's *Pony Trails* (1895) and *Crooked Trails* (1898).

RÉMUSAT, CLAIRE ÉLISABETH JEAN GRAVIER DE VERGENNES, COMTESSE DE (1780–1821). *Memoirs of Madame de Rémusat, 1802–1808.* Preface and notes by Paul de Rémusat (1831–1897). Translated from the French by Frances Sarah (Johnston) Hoey (1830–1908) and John Lillie. 3 vols. New York: D. Appleton and Co., 1880. [Publisher conjectured.]

> Inscription: the front pastedown endpaper of Volume III is signed "S. L. Clemens, Hartford, Jan. 1880."
> Catalog: *A1911*, "Vol. 3, 8vo, wrappers, N.Y. 1880," quotes the signature, lot 401, sold for $1.

Mary Baker Eddy is "just a Napoleon as Madame de Rémusat saw him, a brass god with clay legs" (Book 2, Chapter 12, *Christian Science* [1907]). Rémusat was lady-in-waiting to the Empress Josephine. Cf. the Book of Daniel 2: 3 1–33: "thighs of brass . . . his feet part of iron and part of clay."

RENAN, [JOSEPH] ERNEST (1823–1892). *L'Abesse de Jouarre*

(five-act philosophical drama, published in Paris in 1886). Clara Clemens listed this author and title in her undated commonplace book (Paine 150, MTP).

———. *The Apostles. Translated from the Original French.* Blind stamped black boards, spine lettered in gilt. New York: Carleton, Publisher, 1866. 353 pp.

Marginalia: several lines, question marks, and other marginalia are written in pencil throughout the book.

Catalogs: *A1911*, "post 8vo, original cloth, N.Y. 1866," with a slip containing notes by Clemens laid in, lot 400, sold for $1; offered on eBay on 31 October 2019 by an owner in West Chester, Pennsylvania, "some damage, signs of repair to spine, rubbing, wear, foxing, some previous owner's markings, else in good condition," has the *A1911* bookplate, priced at $12,000. (I am grateful to R. Kent Rasmussen for noticing the latter listing.)

A letter from Clemens to Joseph H. Twichell of 10 June 1879 mentioned that "[Hjalmar] Boyesen called on Renan & Victor Hugo" in Paris (*LMTJHT*, p. 91). In this 1866 sequel to his humanistic *Life of Jesus* (1863), Renan applies the methods of the German higher criticism of the Bible to the aftermath of Christ's crucifixion.

The Report of the Commission of Inquiry on the Belgian Congo. [Unidentified publication.]

"The Report . . . is a curious document. I sent you a copy of my presentation of it. I trust you received it, but I fear it will have been too long to wade through" (Edmund D. Morel to SLC, 27 November 1905, MTP). Morel might be referring to a version of Robert David Casement's *Treatment of Women and Children in the Congo State; What Mr. Casement Saw in 1903*; see the Catalog entry for Casement.

Report of the Commission of 1906 to Investigate the Condition of the Blind in the State of New York. Illus. Albany, New York: J. B. Lyon Co., State Printers, 1906. 586 pp.

Source: MTLAcc, *Condition of the Blind*, entry #889, volume donated by Clemens.

REPPLIER, AGNES (1855–1950). *Essays in Miniature.* Fiction, Fact, and Fancy Series, General ed. Arthur Stedman. New York: Charles L. Webster & Co., 1892. 217 pp.

Olivia Clemens wrote to Frederick J. Hall, the manager of Clemens's publishing firm, to request Repplier's "Essays in Literature" and two other books for Christmas gifts (Philip C. Duschnes, Catalogue No. 30 [June 1938], item #143, date of letter not supplied). Presumably she meant *Essays in Miniature*, which discusses novels.

REUTER, FRITZ (1810–1874). "Dörchläuchting," in *Olle Kamellen* (published in 1865).

An approximate translation of *Olle Kamellen* might be "old but useful tales of bygone days." In February 1879 Clemens quoted from "Dörchläuchting" in the sixth (final) volume of Reuter's collected stories about the Mecklenburg area (NB 17, *N&J* 2: 278). Olivia Clemens informed her mother on 2 February 1879 that she would return from Europe with "a translation of one of Fritz Reuter's books I intend not to read until I can read it with you" (MTP). Mark Twain observed that "quite indifferent students of German can read Fritz Reuter's charming platt-Deutsch tales with some little facility because many of the words are English" (*TA* [1880], Ch. 18).

Review of Reviews (London, monthly periodical, published 1890–1932).

"Don't go on sending the 'Review' to Dollis Hill, but if you are minded to continue your benevolence, send it to . . . my present home" (SLC to William Thomas Stead, Editor, New York City, 21 January 1901, ASSSCL). See also the Catalog entry for William T. Stead.

Revue des deux mondes (Paris, journal, published 1829–).

The *Revue des deux mondes* published Marie-Thérèse Blanc's translation of "The Celebrated Jumping Frog." Mark Twain mentioned the journal by name in 1894 in his sketch on the "Private History of the 'Jumping Frog' Story" for the *North American Review*. Madame Blanc (Thérèse Bentzon) was offended by Twain's "retranslation," but he refused to apologize to her through Grace King in a letter to King written on 30 April 1894. "The French character. . . . hasn't a shred of humor in it," he complained (Robert Bush, "Grace King and Mark Twain" *American Literature* 44.1 [March 1972]: 48).

Mark K. Wilson, "Mr. Clemens and Madame Blanc," *American Literature* 45.4 (January 1974): 537–556; James C. Austin, *American Humor in France* (Ames: Iowa State University Press, 1978), pp. 5–7.

REYNOLDS-BALL, EUSTACE ALFRED (1858–1928). *Mediterranean Winter Resorts. A Practical Hand-book to the Principal Health and Pleasure Resorts on the Shores of the Mediterranean. With Special Articles on the Principal Invalid Stations by Resident English Physicians.* [First published in London in 1888; successive editions followed until 1908.]

On 22 February 1892 an ailing Clemens, writing from Berlin, thanked Reynolds-Ball for a copy of his book (Christie's, 27 September 1995 sale, lot #7). I am grateful to JoDee Benussi for noting this item.

RHOADES, JAMES (1841–1923). "Artemus Ward," London *Spectator* 40.2020 (16 March 1867): 299 (poem, reprinted in *Littell's Living Age* 93.1194 [20 April 1867]: 177).

Charles Farrar Browne, "Artemus Ward," died in Southampton on 6 March 1867. Mark Twain usually closed his lectures in 1871 and 1872 by reading Rhoades' memorial poem about Ward's passing (Fatout, *MTLC* [1960], p. 160; Fatout, *MTSpk* [1976], pp. 46–48; *MTLet* 4: 493 n. 4)."I end with the poetry, every time," Clemens wrote to Olivia (*MTLet* 4: 491), and he provided the *Littell's Living Age* citation to her on 3 December 1871 (*MTLet* 4: 503). The third and final stanza of this poem is worth quoting here: "He came with a heart full of gladness/From the glad-hearted world of the West,/Won our laughter, but not with mere madness/Spake and joked with us, not in mere jest:/For the Man in our heart lingered after,/When the merriment died from our ears,/And those who were loudest in laughter/Are silent in tears" ("On the Death of Artemus Ward," *Poems by James Rhoades* [London: Macmillan and Co., 1870], p. 84).

Scott, *OPMT* (1966), p. 18.

RICARD, ANTOINE (1834–1895). *Jeanne d'Arc, La Vénérable, d'après les documents verses au procès de sa canonisation en cour de Rome. Avec une preface de Monseigneur [Xavier] Gouthe-Soulard [1819–1900, Archbishop of Arles].* Paris: E. Dentu, [1894]. 294 pp. [The preface is dated 9 March 1894.]

Marginalia: Clemens made comments in pencil throughout; a few are in French. On page 37 he noted in the margin: "One of her famous speeches." Beside some dialogue on page 223 he wrote "You lie" and "shut-up!" Roger Salomon quoted marginalia from pages 23, 167, and 213–234 (*TIH* [1961], pp. 174, 177–178). Ronald Jenn and Linda A. Morris, "The Sources of Mark Twain's *Personal Recollections of Joan of Arc*," *Mark Twain Journal* 55.1–2 (Spring/Fall 2017): 55–74, quoted and discussed Clemens's marginalia, concluding that he "was deeply engaged by Ricard's Joan of Arc" (p. 68).

Catalogs: ListABP (1910), "Jeanne d'Arc, Ricard"; "Retz Appraisal" (1944), p. 11, valued at $20.

Location: Mark Twain Papers, Bancroft Library, University of California at Berkeley.

Copy examined: Clemens's copy, in such fragile condition that it is in danger of falling into pieces.

Ricard was Prélat de la Maison de sa Sainteté, Vicaire Général Honoraire de Monseigneur l'Archevêque d'Aix. Mark Twain listed this work among his "authorities examined" in writing *Joan of Arc* (1896); see the page preceding the "Translator's Preface." In Chapter 11 he quoted from page 197 of Ricard's book, identifying the author as "Honorary Vicar-General to the Archbishop of Aix."

RICE, ALICE (CALDWELL) HEGAN (1870–1942). *Mr. Opp.* Illustrated by Leon Guipon (1872–1910). New York: The Century Co., 1909. 326 pp. [Edition conjectured. The book's copyright date was 1908.]

In Mrs. Rice's autobiography, *The Inky Way* (1940), she reproduced in facsimile an undated note from Clemens acknowledging some newspaper clippings that became the genesis for *Mr. Opp.* Clemens wrote: "I am glad to have those samples. There is hope for the saddest of us when we note that a brother with an atrophied lung & a petrified brain can still be modestly gay" (p. 77). Presumably Rice later sent Clemens a presentation copy of the book, because in a 1909 "Note" to his *Autobiography* Clemens declared that "a writer who ventures to use the professional technicalities . . . of a trade which he has not served . . . will never fail to make mistakes. . . . Chapter X of Alice Kegan [*sic*] Rice's new book ('Mr. Orr') [*sic*] opens with a scene on a Mississippi steamboat which . . . will sorely befog the trained steamboatman" (*AutoMT* 3: 307). Mary Boewe noted that Clemens's criticism suggests a careless reading; Rice's steamboat hauled local traffic on the Ohio River (Boewe to Alan Gribben, 13 November 1987).

———. *Mrs. Wiggs of the Cabbage Patch.* New York: The Century Co., 1901. 153 pp. [Edition conjectured.]

Rice's novel was among the best sellers in 1903. Sometime in 1903 Clemens slipped Olivia Clemens a "sick-room note" that read: "Now I will go to bed & read the Cabbage-Patch & forget the 'wars of life' & my work—if I can." In a subsequent note to his wife, Clemens criticized "the poverty & crudeness & vulgarity" of the book, comparing it unfavorably with Adelaide Sartoris's *A Week in a French Country-House* ("it's the difference between Emerson & [a slang term for minstrel shows]" (MTP). Isabel Lyon made a diary entry for 26 July 1904, when the remnant of the Clemens family was finishing the summer at Richard Watson Gilder's place near Lee, Massachusetts: "Mrs. Alice Hegan Rice who wrote *Mrs. Wiggs of the Cabbage Patch* came in with Mr. [Cale Young] Rice this evening for a little farewell call. They have been visiting the Gilders. I ought not to say I was disappointed in Mrs. Rice, but

I was. She seemed very unliterary and inconsequent. Mr. Clemens says that "Mrs. Wiggs" is not literature so there is less need than might be for a literary flavor to Mrs. Rice" (IVL Journals, TS p. 25, MTP). When Rice visited Richard Watson Gilder in July 1904 she was pained by Clemens's grumblings against the universe. "I have an amusing recollection of Mr. Gilder leading me protectingly into the house on one of these occasions, and whispering, 'Don't listen to that blasphemous and unhappy old man!'" (*The Inky Way*, p. 80). Rice's husband, the poet Cale Rice, recalled Clemens's bitterness over his wife Olivia's death: "'God,' he would exclaim then, 'is a mere jester who pulls our heart-strings to see us squirm'" (Boewe, "Young Mrs. Wiggs," p. 10). In Mrs. Rice's diary she recorded her impression of Clemens in 1904: "He talks a great deal with a slow deliberateness that emphasizes the humor of his remarks. He is not a monopolist but listens attentively to what you say and gives every remark courteous attention" (Boewe, *Beyond the Cabbage Patch*, p. 59). After Clemens died she fondly recalled his "mane of snowy hair, his beetling eyebrows overhanging the bluest and most mischievous pair of eyes" (Boewe, p. 58). Mary Boewe's "Young Mrs. Wiggs" (1982) quoted from Rice's journal and valuably corrected some of her dates and recollections.

Cale Young Rice, *Bridging the Years* (New York: D. Appleton-Century Co., 1939); Alice Hegan Rice, *The Inky Way* (New York: D. Appleton-Century Co., 1940), contained a description of her friendship with Clemens and a few references to his awareness of her books; Hamlin Hill, *MTGF* (1973), p. 97; Mary Boewe, "Young Mrs. Wiggs Meets the Old Connecticut Yankee," *Filson Club History Quarterly* [Louisville, Kentucky] 56.1 (January 1982): 5–13; and Boewe, *Beyond the Cabbage Patch: The Literary World of Alice Hegan Rice* (Louisville, Kentucky: Butler Books, 2010). Mary Boewe's "Bewildered, Bothered, and Bewitched: Mark Twain's View of Three Women Writers," *Mark Twain Journal* 45.1 (Spring 2007): 17–23 summarized Clemens's opinion of Alice Hegan Rice.

RICHARDS, ALFRED BATE (1820–1876). *Religio Animae, and Other Poems.* London: Edward Moxon & Co., [1866?]. 309 pp.

Source: MTLAcc, entry #2087, volume donated from Clemens's library by Clara Clemens Gabrilowitsch in 1910.

RICHARDSON, ABBY (SAGE) (1837–1900). *Pebbles and Pearls for the Young Folks.* Illus. Hartford, Connecticut: American Publishing Co., 1868. 298 pp.

A year after this volume of children's stories appeared its author would be involved in a love triangle with tragic consequences; see the Catalog entry below for Albert Deane Richardson. Jane Lampton Clemens wrote to Sam and Olivia on 11 April 1874, asking whether Clemens and Charles Dudley Warner would donate some books to the reading room established by the Women's Christian Temperance Union in Fredonia, New York. According to the 9 December 1874 issue of the Fredonia *Censor*, Clemens gave his mother sixteen volumes to present to the newly opened reading room. Accession records in the Darwin R. Barker Library, which succeeded the WCTU reading room and acquired its book collection, indicated that a copy of Richardson's *Pebbles and Pearls* was one of Clemens's gifts. Most of these books were publications of the American Publishing Company. On 2 February 1890 Mark Twain would draft a letter to theatrical producer Daniel Frohman complaining that Richardson's dramatization of Twain's *The Prince and the Pauper* "carefully & deliberately got as far away from the book as she could"; moreover, "she changed the language--& degraded it." The result was a "mess of idiotic rubbish & vapid twaddle." There is no evidence that Twain actually mailed this letter (ALS, sold by Christie's, New York City, 1–2 February 1988 auction, lot 471). In an Autobiographical Dictation on 28 August 1907 Twain recalled that "she hadn't ever dramatized anything, but knew she could." He gave credit to Daniel Frohman's stage-manager, who "took it in hand and reformed it" (*AutoMT* 3: 115).

RICHARDSON, ALBERT DEANE (1833–1869). *Beyond the Mississippi: From the Great River to the Great Ocean. Life and Adventure on the Prairies, Mountains, and Pacific Coast. . . . 1857–1867.* Illus. Hartford, Connecticut: American Publishing Co., [cop. 1867]. 572 pp. [Publisher and pages conjectured but virtually certain.]

Catalog: *A1911*, "8vo, half morocco (slightly rubbed), Hartford, n.d.," with a sheet of Clemens's notes laid in, lot 403, sold for $4.75.

For his second subscription book Richardson undertook a geographically immense subject. Mark Twain alluded to Richardson's forthcoming book in a letter of 2 February 1867 to the *Alta California* (*MTTMB*, p. 284 n. 5). In a letter to Elisha Bliss written on 22 July 1869 Twain pointed out that the priority given by the publisher to "the 'Mississippi'" delayed *The Innocents Abroad* and "damaged my interests" (*MTLP*, p. 23). On 2 December 1867 Twain wrote to Elisha Bliss: "I know Richardson, & learned from him, some months ago, something of an idea of the subscription plan of publishing" (*MTLet* 2: 119). Two years later, as the climax of a notorious love triangle case, Richardson would be murdered in the offices of the New York *Tribune* on 25 November 1869 by Daniel McFarland, the alcoholic former husband of actress Abby Sage McFarland. Richardson lived for only a few days, but that was long enough for him to wed the actress, who thereafter kept his name and became known as Abby Sage Richardson. On 29 October 1870 Clemens wrote to Elisha Bliss, Jr. from Buffalo, saying that he was "suffering for" a copy of *Beyond the Mississippi* from its publisher (*MTLet* 4: 217). Twain passingly mentioned Richardson's book in Chapter 20 of *Roughing It* (1872), but the Explanatory Notes prepared by Harriet Elinor Smith and Edgar Marquess Branch for the 1993 edition of that work made clear Twain's extensive indebtedness throughout *Roughing It* to Richardson's *Beyond the Mississippi*. In 1876 Clemens wanted two of Richardson's books—*Beyond the Mississippi* (1867) and *Secret Service* (1865)—sent to a disabled soldiers' home in Elizabeth, Virginia, along with three other books and his own works (SLC to Elisha Bliss, 17 February 1876, ASSSCL). These are now in the collection of the Darwin R. Barker Historical Museum, Fredonia, New York.

On 1 February 1877 the American Publishing Company billed Clemens $1.30 for a copy of *Beyond the Mississippi*, "del'd at house," ordered by Clemens on 8 December 1876 (Scrapbook #10, p. 77, MTP). Albert E. Stone, Jr.

believed that Mark Twain "probably consulted" this book between 1884 and 1889 while reading western lore for "Huck Finn and Tom Sawyer among the Indians" (*IE*, p. 176 n. 13). Clemens would eventually credit Richardson with giving him excellent advice about publishing *The Innocents Abroad* (1869): "I consulted A. D. Richardson and he said 'take the royalty.' I followed his advice and closed with Bliss" (21 May 1906 AD, *MTE*, p. 146; *AutoMT* 2: 48).

Richardson's *Beyond the Mississippi* recounted his travels across the continent. Some of his anecdotes are grisly—such as the story of the Montana trapper who amputated his own leg with a hunting knife (p. 485). Twain would have been especially interested in Richardson's opinion of the Native Americans he encountered. In Oregon, "near a little road-side grocery, supported by a post and flanked by an empty cask, stood a Noble Red Man. Indifferent to his tattered clothing, which afforded no protection from the sharp, wintry nights—with his long black locks flying in the wind—his whole soul was wrapped in a whisky bottle. He regarded it with a fixed stare, in which satisfaction at the quality of its contents and pensive regret at their diminishing quantity were ludicrously blended. Mr. Cooper died too early. I think one glimpse of *this* Aboriginal would have saved his pen much labor, and early American literature many Indian heroes" (*Beyond the Mississippi* [Ch. 41], p. 512).

———. *A Personal History of Ulysses S. Grant.* Hartford, Connecticut: American Publishing Co., 1868. 560 pp. Revised by R. H. Fletcher, 1885. 607 pp.

"They only publish two books at a time, & so my book & Richardson's Life of Grant will fill the bill for next fall & winter" (SLC to Jane Lampton Clemens and Pamela Moffett, Hartford, 24 January 1868, *MTL*, pp. 145–146; *MTLet* 2: 160–161). When Elisha Bliss pushed Richardson's book to the front of the line, Clemens objected on 22 July 1869 that "the delay for 'Grant' damaged my interests" (*MTLP*, p. 23). In 1885 Clemens was furious that the American Publishing Company was again marketing this book, "written by the late A. D. Richardson," as though it were written recently and by Grant himself (undated letter to the reading public, TS in MTP). Clemens's own publishing firm, of course, was marketing Grant's *Personal Memoirs of U. S. Grant* (1885).

———. *The Secret Service: The Field, the Dungeon, and the Escape.* Hartford, Connecticut: American Publishing Co., 1865. 512 pp.

Richardson's first subscription book, *The Secret Service* (1865), described his coverage of the Civil War as a newspaper correspondent, his capture by the Confederates, and his escape from a Southern prison. Clemens wanted two of Richardson's books—*Beyond the Mississippi* (1867) and *Secret Service* (1865)—sent to a disabled soldiers' home in Virginia, along with three other books and his own works (SLC to Elisha Bliss, 17 February 1876 (ASSSCL). These are now in the collection of the Darwin R. Barker Historical Museum, Fredonia, New York.

RICHARDSON, GEORGE TILTON (1863–1938) and WILDER DWIGHT QUINT (1863–1936), joint pseud. "Charles Eustace Merriman." *Letters from a Son to His Self-Made Father; Being the Replies to Letters from a Self-Made Merchant to His Son.*

Illus. Boston: New Hampshire Publishing Co., 1903.

These fictional letters purporting to be from a Harvard undergraduate reflected rural humor, with the son reporting to his sausage-manufacturing father details about his student life away from home. Actually the book was spoofing *Letters from a Self-Made Merchant to His Son; Being the Letters Written by John Graham, Head of the House of Graham & Company, Pork-Packers in Chicago, Familiarly Known as "Old Gordon Graham," to His Son, Pierrepont, Facetiously Known to His Intimates as "Piggy"* (Boston: Small, Maynard & Co., 1902), a popular book written under the pseudonym "John Graham" by George Horace Larimer (1867–1937), who edited the *Saturday Evening Post* from 1899 until 1936. An infuriated Larimer sued Richardson (who was a drama critic and editor for the Boston *Traveler*) and the poet Quint, alleging misrepresentation and copyright infringement, but the court ruled against Larimer. What all of this has to do with Samuel L. Clemens is that Richardson and Quint had dedicated their pseudonymously published parody "To/ Mark Twain/A Ready-Made Wit"—meaning that there is a chance that Clemens looked at a copy of *Letters from a Son to His Self-Made Father*. Kevin Mac Donnell first noticed the dedication to Twain (Mac Donnell to Alan Gribben, 2 August 2004).

RICHARDSON, ROBERT (1850–1901). "Annette" (poem, also known as "To Annette" or "Requiem"), published in *Willow and Wattle: Poems*. Edinburgh: John Grant, 1893. 88 pp.

Catalog: ListABP (1910), "Willow and Wattle Poems, Richardson", no other information supplied.

Susy Clemens died on 18 August 1896 at the age of twenty-four. In December 1896, in Chelsea, Clemens copied some lines of verse by the Australian poet Robert Richardson into Notebook 39: "'Warm summer sun, shine friendly here;—/Warm southern wind [Richardson had written "western wind"], blow kindly here—/Green sod above, rest light, rest light—/Goodnight, dear heart, goodnight, goodnight.' (Robt. Richardson[)]" (TS p. 33). Richardson's version of the last line differed: "Good-night, Annette! Sweetheart, good-night." A similar version of these lines ("rest light" became "lie light") was inscribed on Susy's gravestone in Woodlawn Cemetery in Elmira, New York (*MTB*, p. 1024). "Annette" had appeared on pages 33–35 of Richardson's volume. Another line in the poem about the lost girl's youth probably also appealed to Clemens in thinking of his beloved Susy's unlived years: "Dead, and only twenty-one!"

On 6 January, probably in 1903, Clemens imitated a stanza from the poem to send to Olivia Clemens, a sick-room patient: "Good-night, sweetheart, goodnight—/The stars are shining bright,/The snow is turning [becoming?] white,/Dim is the failing light,/Fast falls the glooming night,/All right!/Sleep tight!/Goodnight" (ALS in MTP). Before sailing for Italy, Clemens recorded on 3 October 1903: "To-day I placed flowers on Susy's grave—for the last time, probably; & read the words—'Good night, dear heart/Good-night'" (NB 46, TS p. 25). In an Autobiographical Dictation of 22 January 1907 published in the *North American Review* 185.612 (5 April 1907): 678, Twain explained that at first he was unable to identify the authorship of the lines. "We had found them in a book

in India, but had lost the book, and with it the author's name. But in time an application to the editor of *Notes and Queries* furnished me the author's name, and it has been added to the verses upon the gravestone" (*AutoMT* 2: 376–377).

See *The Home Book of Quotations*, comp. Burton Stevenson (New York: Dodd, Mead & Co., 1934), p. 570; John Bartlett, *Familiar Quotations*, 11th edition, revised (Boston: Little, Brown and Co., 1947), p. 702; Salsbury, *S&MT* (1965), p. 393. Barbara Schmidt located a copy of *Willow and Wattle*, which enabled a comparison of Clemens's wording (Schmidt to Alan Gribben, e-mail, 3 August 2003).

RICHARDSON, SAMUEL (1689–1761). *Clarissa; or, The History of a Young Lady*. New and Abridged Edition. 8vo, cloth, quarter morocco case. London: G. Routledge, n.d. [1868 is the likely date].

Inscription: signed, "Saml. L. Clemens/Cabin 55 & 56/ Steamer—City of Chester/(Please return it.)" Previously signed, "Harriet Ward, London, October 23rd, 1868." Clemens sailed from New York City to England on the *City of Chester* on 8 November 1873 (Fears, *Day by Day* 1: 554). After seven days at sea, he wrote to Olivia Clemens on 14 November 1873: "I have read all night during this [rough] weather—sleep would only tire me" (*MTLet* 5: 475).

Catalogs: ListABP (1910), "Clarissa Harlowe, Richardson"; *C1951*, D67, listed among volumes signed by Clemens; *Fleming 1972*; Sotheby Parke Bernet, Sale number 3482 (25 February 1976), "8vo, original cloth, quarter morocco case," "Property of a New York City Collector" (John F. Fleming), lot 19, sold for $375 (*American Book Prices Current, 1976*, p. 207).

Provenance: Frederick Anderson, then Editor of the Mark Twain Papers at Berkeley, examined this copy and made notes in April 1972 at the New York City office of John F. Fleming, Inc.

Location: currently undetermined.

On 14 January 1884 Clemens informed Edward H. House that he had recently read "all of Clarissa Harlowe" (ALS in University of Virginia Libraries, *MT&JB*, p. 374 n. 30). Samuel Richardson would have been quoted ("where printable") in Mark Twain's proposed appendix to *A Connecticut Yankee in King Arthur's Court* (1889). Richardson's epistolary novel about Clarissa Harlowe and her rakish seducer, Robert Lovelace, first appeared in book form in 1748.

Baetzhold, "Course of Composition" (1961), p. 200.

———. *Pamela; or, Virtue Rewarded* (epistolary novel, published in 1740).

From Hartford, on 14 January 1884, Clemens informed Edward H. House that he had recently read "the closing chapters of Pamela" (ALS, ASSSCL). Around January 1887, Mark Twain projected "a story wherein pantaletted little children talked the stilted big-word sentimental hifalutin of Walter Scott's heroes & the other & older novels (Pamela &c)" (*N&J* 3: 268). In 1894 Twain avowed that he would relish the chance to review *Pamela* and other "old-time literary mud idols" (NB 33, TS p. 61).

Krause, *MTC* (1967), p. 123.

RICHMOND, GRACE LOUISE (SMITH) (1866–1959). *The

Indifference of Juliet. Illustrated by Henry Hutt (1875–1950). New York: Doubleday, Page & Co., 1905. 307 pp.

> **Source:** MTLAcc, entry #1052, volume donated by Clemens.

RIDDLE, WILLIAM (1837–1926) *Nicholas Comenius; or Ye Pennsylvania Schoolmaster of Ye Olden Time.* Second edition. Original brown cloth, gilt. Illus. Lancaster, Pennsylvania: T. B. & H. B. Cochran, 1898. 469 pp.

> **Inscription:** the front free flyleaf is inscribed by Riddle in black ink: "'Mark Twain'/Compliments of/The Author/Lancaster Pa./Jan. 28,/1902".
>
> **Provenance:** contains the accession number ("2820") and purple stamps of the Mark Twain Library, Redding, Connecticut. Eventually the volume became part of Nick Karanovich's collection in Fort Wayne, Indiana.
>
> **Catalogs:** *Mott 1952,* item #80, $6; *Sotheby's 2003,* #216, $3,500 (sold with five other inscribed books).
>
> **Location:** collection of Kevin Mac Donnell, Austin, Texas.
>
> **Copy examined:** Clemens's unmarked copy, in July 2004.

RIDENBAUGH, MARY YOUNG. *The Biography of Ephraim Mc-Dowell, M. D. [1771–1830], "The Father of Ovariotomy."* New York: Charles L. Webster & Co., 1890. 558 pp.

> "I have not seen the Biography, but I would walk several miles for a chance to read it, for Dr. McDowell was so great a man, & so picturesque, eccentric & extraordinary a personality, that nobody, howsoever gifted with dulness [*sic*], could make a book about him that would not be interesting" (SLC to an unidentified correspondent, undated ALS, MTP). This physician should not be mistaken for the Kentucky-born Dr. Joseph McDowell , who taught in a St. Louis medical school and owned McDowell's Cave near Hannibal. (Joseph McDowell was, however, the nephew of Ephraim McDowell and did practice with him in Kentucky for a number of years before turning against his uncle and seeking thereafter to damage his medical reputation.) Dr. Ephraim McDowell was born in Virginia, practiced in Kentucky, and traveled internationally to demonstrate his surgical discoveries and techniques. Mary Young Ridenbaugh was his granddaughter. She had become known as the author of a popular novel set in Kentucky, *Enola; or, Her Fatal Mistake* (1886). In 1890 she was residing in St. Louis, Missouri; the next year she was listed in the New York City directory.
>
> Blair, ed., *HH&T* (1969), p. 358; K. Patrick Ober, "The Body in the Cave: Dr. Joseph McDowell's Influence on Mark Twain," *Mark Twain Journal* 41.2 (Fall 2003): 6, 14.

RIDGE, WILLIAM PETT (1859–1930). *By Order of the Magistrate.* New York: Harper & Brothers, 1901. 276 pp.

> **Source:** MTLAcc, entry #1655, volume donated by Clemens.
>
> When Alice Hegan Rice sojourned in London in 1909, she heard a story that was current there about the meeting of Mark Twain and Ridge, an English humorist and novelist: "Some tactless person, introducing him to Mark Twain, said: 'This is the Mark Twain of England.' Whereupon Pett Ridge said, with a twinkle, 'And you, sir, I presume, are the Pett Ridge of America?'" (*The Inky Way* [1940], p. 136). The London *Times* reported a similar version of this quip in Ridge's obituary in 1930. Ridge typically set his fiction in London's East End and was classified as one of the "Cockney novelists." *By Order of the Magistrate* was

a good example of his knowledge of London street life and its gangs of youths.

——. *The Second Opportunity of Mr. Staplehurst; A Novel.* New York: Harper Brothers, 1896. 283 pp.

> **Source:** MTLAcc, entry #1653, volume donated by Clemens.
>
> Witty social satire directed at elite clubs and other London institutions.

——. *Secretary to Bayne, M.P.; A Novel.* New York: Harper & Brothers, 1898. 263 pp.

> **Source:** MTLAcc, entry #1654, volume donated by Clemens.

RIDLEY, JAMES KENNETH (1736–1765), pseud. "Sir Charles Morell." *The Tales of the Genii; or, The Delightful Lessons of Horam, the Son of Asmar. Faithfully Translated from the Persian Manuscript.* Illus. 2 vols. London, 1764.

> **Inscription:** Volume II is 2 signed "S. L. Clemens, London, 1873."
>
> **Catalog:** *A1911,* "2 vols., 8vo, old calf (covers loose), Lond. 1764," quotes the signature, lot 404, sold for $3.75.
>
> Ridley invented a narrator ("Sir Charles Morell") and a fictional Imam ("Horam"), together with fantastic elements borrowed from *The Arabian Nights,* to produce this moralistic imitation of Persian literature. This pastiche was first published in 1764.

RIGUTINI, GIUSEPPI (1829–1903) and **PIETRO FANFANI** (1815–1879). *Vocabolario Italiano della lingua parlata, compilato da G. Rigutini e P. Fanfani.* Firenze, n.d. 1,648 pp. [Pages conjectured.]

> **Inscription:** signed "Jean L. Clemens."
>
> **Catalog:** *A1911,* "4to, cloth, Firenze, n.d.," quotes the signature, lot 263, sold for $1 to the Mark Twain Company.
>
> Antonio Illiano, "'Italian Without a Master': A Note for the Appreciation of Mark Twain's Undictionarial Translation as Exercise in Humor," *Mark Twain Journal* 17.2 (Summer 1974): 17–20.

RILEY, HENRY THOMAS (1816–1878). *Memorials of London and London Life in the Thirteenth, Fourteenth, and Fifteenth Centuries* (published in London in 1868).

> Liam Purdon noted that in conducting research for *The Prince and the Pauper* (1881) Mark Twain might have run across some fourteenth-century models for the King and Duke of *Adventures of Huckleberry Finn* (1885) in Riley's meticulously edited compendium of historical records ("Early Predecessors of the King and the Duke in Mark Twain's *Adventures of Huckleberry Finn,*" *Mark Twain Journal* 54.1 [Spring 2016]: 116–124).

RILEY, JAMES WHITCOMB (1849–1916). "The Absence of Little Wesley" (poem, published in 1888).

> Mark Twain included "The Absence of Little Wesley" in his program of readings at Smith College in Northampton, Massachusetts on 21 January 1889 (*N&J* 3: 437). Most of the other poems he chose were by Robert Browning. A grieving farmer's lament for his deceased grandson—with its opening line, "Sence little Wesley went, the place seems all so strange and still"—could surely be counted on to choke up the sternest audience.
>
> Mary Boewe, "On Stage and Off with James Whitcomb Riley and Mark Twain," *Traces of Indiana and Midwestern History* 7.4 (Fall 1995): 18; Harold K. Bush, Jr., "Broken Idols': Mark Twain's Elegies for Susy and a Critique of

Freudian Grief Theory," *Nineteenth-Century Literature* 57.2 (September 2002): 248–249. I wish to thank Jo Dee Benussi for drawing my attention to this poem.

———. *Armazindy*. Indianapolis, Indiana: Bowen-Merrill Co., 1894. 169 pp.

Source: MTLAcc, entry #2086, volume donated from Clemens's library by Clara Clemens Gabrilowitsch in 1910. The title poem describes a heroic woman whose father died on the steamboat *Sultana* returning from the Civil War; she refused to accept charity as she grew up and took over the farm. A large number of the seventy-three poems in this collection, like "A Barefoot Boy" (p. 134), hark back to a carefree stage of boyhood that Clemens largely missed out on after his father died in debt.

———. *The Book of Joyous Children*. Illustrated by Will Vawter (1871–1941). New York: Charles Scribner's Sons, 1902. 176 pp.

Inscription: "To—/Samuel L. Clemens, Esq.—/With hale greetings and acclaims,/—James Whitcomb Riley./Indianapolis:/Oct. 30—1902./Though you find no 'Jim' within,/'Tom,' nor 'Huckleberry Finn,'/You'll find friends of theirs, I know,/and gay pards of Long Ago."

Location: Mark Twain House and Museum, Hartford, Connecticut.

Copy examined: Clemens's unmarked copy. Examined in August 1987 in Hartford.

Clemens thanked Riley belatedly on 27 July 1903 for a "delightful book" and quoted portions of Riley's flyleaf inscription (Lilly Library, Indiana University, PH in MTP).

———. *A Child-World*. Original cloth, minor wear. Indianapolis: Bowen-Merrill Co., 1897. 209 pp.

Inscription: inscribed, "For/Samuel L. Clemens, Esq./With all good greetings and esteem/James Whitcomb Riley/Indianapolis, Oct./1896."

Catalogs: *C1951*, 33c, listed among books signed by Clemens, $25; "Property from the Library of Mark Twain," Butterfield & Butterfield, San Francisco, Sale 6613 (16 July 1997), lot 2688.

Location: Mark Twain House and Museum, Hartford, Connecticut.

Copy examined: Clemens's unmarked copy. Viewed in Hartford in 1997.

———. "Erasmus Wilson" (poem, published in 1891), collected in *Neighborly Poems* (1891).

On 2 February 1891, only a few days after this poem first appeared in the Pittsburgh *Commercial Gazette* on 30 January 1891, Clemens complimented Riley: "In the fine 'Ras Wilson poem you've flung in some more of those things which make my mouth water for an Elder Time, and a big toe with a rag around it. One time or another you've got them *all* in, I believe—except, perhaps, p'simmons & p'cons; and maybe red haws" (*Letters of James Whitcomb Riley*, ed. William Lyon Phelps [Indianapolis: Bobbs-Merrill, 1930], pp. 329–330). Clemens refers to a long list of plants and animals native to the region of Little Bethel that the persona of Riley's poem would like to discuss with his boyhood friend, Erasmus Wilson; these include pennyrile, peppermint, calamus-root, ginseng, watermelons, muskrats, and raccoons. The speaker is addressing in Wilson a man who became celebrated, yet remained "common, like you allus was/Afore you went

to town and s'prised/The world by gittin' 'reckonized.'" Erasmus Wilson stayed "what all mankind had ort to be—/Jest *natchurl*, and the more hurraws/You git, the less you know the cause."

———. *Home-Folks*. Indianapolis: Bowen-Merrill Co., [1900]. 166 pp.

Inscription: the front free flyleaf is inscribed, "For—/Samuel L. Clemens, Esq./With hale Hoosier greetings of his old friend/James Whitcomb Riley./Indianapolis, Nov. 12: 1900/Mostly, poets is all star-gazin'/And moanin' and groanin' and paraphrasin'!"

Catalogs: ListABP (1910), "Home-Folks, Riley"; *C1951*, D70, erroneously listed with volumes signed by Clemens.

Provenance: Carrie Estelle Doheny Collection, St. John's Seminary, Camarillo, California. Donated by Mrs. Doheny in 1951 after she purchased it from Maxwell Hunley Rare Books of Beverly Hills for $44.50. Auctioned by Christie's in New York City (lot 1182) for $5,280 on 17 October 1988 on behalf of St. John's Seminary.

Location: currently unknown.

Copy examined: Clemens's copy, at St. John's Seminary.

———. "Honest Old Sam Hungerford" (poem, written in 1891, published in 1930).

Riley sent this poem to Clemens from Pittsburgh on 30 January 1891; it is a "dialect" piece about "the prince of honest men," someone who "never earnt a dollar, ner he didn't give a dam!" Riley wrote that he wanted to hear Clemens recite the short poem "in some deep, reposeful state of satirical exasperation." Clemens replied from Hartford on 2 February 1891: "It's a darling poem, and I thank you ever so much for it. But—when it comes to reciting it, I can't even remotely approach you. You are the only man alive that can read your poems exactly right. . . . I take off my hat to you, my boy; you *do* know how" (*Letters of James Whitcomb Riley*, ed. William Lyon Phelps [Indianapolis: BobbsMerrill, 1930], 329–330; Phelps' edition indicates that the Twain-Riley correspondence was unvaryingly complimentary).

———. "The Old Soldier's Story" (humorous story).

Around 1883 Riley began telling lecture audiences the tale of a private who rescued a wounded comrade from the battlefield, which Mark Twain praised in "How to Tell a Story" (1895) as "about the funniest thing I have ever listened to." In Riley's rendition of the tale, a "dull-witted old farmer" narrates mixed-up details, unconscious that his audience is exhausted with laughter (see Marcus Dickey, *The Maturity of James Whitcomb Riley* [Indianapolis: Bobbs Merrill Company, 1922] pp. 187, 247. Dickey quotes several encomiums bestowed on Riley by Mark Twain).

———. *"The Old Swimmin'-Hole," and 'Leven More Poems, by Benj. F. Johnson, of Boone*. Indianapolis, Indiana: George C. Hitt & Co., 1883. 50 pp. [Publisher and pages supplied.]

Riley sent this small volume, his first book, to Mark Twain from Indianapolis on 25 February 1885, writing: "Your sketches in which real characters and their varied dialects occur have interested and delighted me for many years; and in thanking you, as I want to now, I beg you to accept as well the little book of Hoosier dialect I mail with this" (*Letters of James Whitcomb Riley*, p. 54; corrected text in R. Kent Rasmussen's *Dear MT*, p. 110). Mary Boewe, "On Stage and Off with James Whitcomb Riley and

Mark Twain," *Traces of Indiana and Midwestern History* 7.4 (Fall 1995): 18, quoted a letter from Twain to Riley on 11 March 1885 about Riley's title poem: "I could feel the pathetic great deeps which your verse has sounded in the 'Old Swimmin' Hole,' & know what a strong text it was & how well you have handled it." Riley replied to Twain on 17 March 1885. During this period Twain began to think of speaking with Riley in England on a lecture tour (NB 23, *N&J* 3: 89). Twain and Riley participated in public readings on behalf of the American Copyright League in Washington, D. C. on 17 March and 19 March 1888. They also met at a farewell dinner at Delmonico's in New York City for actors Henry Irving and Ellen Terry given by Augustin Daly on 26 March 1888. On 24 August 1888 Twain recommended one of Riley's illustrators—Mary Catherine McDonald (1852–1897)—to Richard Watson Gilder of *The Century* (ALS, American Academy and Institute of Arts and Letters). On 3 October 1888, when Twain declined (owing to necessary work on *A Connecticut Yankee*) an invitation to appear at a dinner held in Riley's honor by the Western Association of Writers, Twain referred emphatically to "the strong love and admiration which I feel for Riley" (Dickey, *The Maturity of James Whitcomb Riley* [1922], p. 231).

Clemens echoed Riley's Hoosier phrasing in a letter written to Susy Clemens on 16 July 1889: "Sometimes I have a feeling which... is either the malady called homesickness or is a something which is 'jist contaagious' to it," quoted in Christie's catalog, New York City, 11 May 1987, item #18). In Mark Twain's famous letter to Andrew Lang—the "Belly and the Members" manifesto of 1890—he declared that overly rigid adherence to artistic standards "requires Whitcomb Riley to sing no more till he can sing like Shakespeare." Farther on in the letter, Twain argues that "the passing rhymester of their day leaves them higher than he found them" (*MTL*, pp. 526–527). Twain and Riley appeared in a series of duet performances at Madison Square Garden in New York City on 26 and 27 February and 3 March 1894 (Fears, *Day by Day* 2: 892–895, plus "Addenda & Errata—Vol. II). Twain praised Riley in an interview published in the 24 July 1895 issue of the Minneapolis *Times* (p. 2), according to information sent to me by Professor Louis J. Budd. In December 1897 Riley sent Twain an admiring tribute to *Following the Equator* (1897): "For a solid week—night sessions—I have been glorying in your last book—and if you've ever done anything better, stronger, or of wholesomer uplift I can't recall it" (*Letters of James Whitcomb Riley*, p. 223). Riley visited Elmira, New York in March 1899 during a lecture tour and expressed "his personal fondness and intense admiration for Mark Twain, the author and the man, whom he regards as an Elmiran" (see Mary Boewe's "Mark Twain's 'Dear Old Friend': James Whitcomb Riley and His 1899 Elmira Lecture," *Mark Twain Society Bulletin* 18: 2 [July 1995]: 1–2, 4). On 27 July 1903, acknowledging receipt of a book of poetry with a special message from Riley on the flyleaf, Twain wrote, "Thank you cordially, dear old friend, & may we yet meet again!" (Lilly Library, Indiana University).

Aspiz, "MT's Reading" (1949), p. 157; Mary Boewe, "On Stage and Off with James Whitcomb Riley and Mark Twain," *Traces of Indiana and Midwestern History* 7.4 (Fall 1995): 16–25.

———. *Poems Here at Home*. Illustrated by E[dward]. W[indsor]. Kemble (1861–1933). New York: Century Co., 1893. 187 pp.

"Thanks in advance for the Riley poems—I shall watch the mails; I want them very much" (SLC to Henry H. Rogers, Paris, 11 November 1894, *MTHHR*, p. 95). Clemens confided to Henry H. Rogers that his praise for Riley's work came with a qualification: "There were good things in Riley's book, but you have noticed, of course, that there's considerable padding in it, too. Also in his other books, as per the indexes advertised in this one. A little padding can be allowed to pass, no doubt, but Riley must certainly damage himself if he keeps his ratio up. He is unwise— in fact one may say reckless. But Kipling *can't* pad" (SLC to Henry H. Rogers, Paris, 9 December 1894, *MTHHR*, p. 102).

———. *Rhymes of Childhood*. Indianapolis: Bowen-Merrill, 1890. 186 pp.

Mark Twain praised *Rhymes of Childhood* in a letter to Riley of 29 December 1890, acknowledging that it captured his "own lost youth" better than he himself could do (Lilly Library, Indiana University). Riley wrote to Twain on 31 December 1890 from Indianapolis: "Your comment on the Child's book is the prize gift to me of all this uncommonly considerate Christmas," especially Twain's "own indorsement [*sic*] of the general grade of children and child-character the book so affectionately embraces." In the same letter Riley described how he encountered Mark Twain's "Celebrated Jumping Frog" as a boy setting type in his uncle's printshop, and he alluded to "my rare fortune of meeting you and knowing you even for the briefest two or three times we have glimpsed by [*sic*] each other" (*Letters of James Whitcomb Riley*, pp. 115–116).

———. *Rubáiyát of Doc Seifers*. Illustated by Charles M. Relyea (1863–1932). Original cloth, spine darkened and stained. New York: Century Co., 1897. 111 pp.

Inscription: inscribed in ink "To/Samuel L. Clemens, Esq./With all hale greeting,/James Whitcomb Riley/Indianapolis, USA,/Dec. 1, 1897." Below that inscription Riley added an eight-line poem: "Doc's own war-rickord wuzn't won/so much in line o' fight/As line o' work and nussin'done/the wounded, day and night.—/His wuz the hand, through dark and dawn,/'at bound their wounds, and laid/As soft as their own Mother's on/their forreds when they prayed."

Provenance: displays the shelfmarks of Clara Clemens Gabrilowitsch's library during her Detroit years.

Catalogs: ListABP (1910), "Rubaiyat of Doc Sifers, Riley"; *C1951*, 34c, "with author's signature and verse to Mark Twain," $50; "Property from the Library of Mark Twain, Butterfield & Butterfield, San Francisco, Sale 6613 (16 July 1997), lot 2689.

Location: Mark Twain House and Museum, Hartford, Connecticut.

Copy examined: Clemens's unmarked copy. Viewed in Hartford in 1997.

Mark Twain's high opinion of Riley was apparent in the address he placed upon an envelope mailed from Vienna on 16 January 1898: "Mr. James Whitcomb Riley/Poet

& a dern capable one, too,/Indianapolis, Indiana,/U. S. of America" (quoted by Marcus Dickey, *Maturity of James Whitcomb Riley*, p. 165; Lilly Library, Indiana University). The letter inside Twain's envelope expressed gratitude for receipt of "a lovely book" that possesses "your delicious felicities of phrase—& your old effective X-ray is present, too, & penetrating to the deep places" (Lilly Library, Indiana University). It seems likely that Twain was referring to Riley's *Rubáiyát of Doc Seifers*.

RILEY, JOHN HENRY (c. 1830–1872).

Riley was a literary resource to Mark Twain in various ways. They became friends in San Francisco when they were both newspaper reporters. Twain praised his wit and bravado in a sketch that appeared in the Buffalo *Express* in October 1870 and he used Riley as a fictionalized character (the "mendicant Blucher") in Chapter 59 of *Roughing It* (1872) and in Chapter 26 of *A Tramp Abroad* (1880, "The Man Who Put Up at Gadsby's"). In 1870 Twain persuaded Riley to travel to South Africa (in January 1871) to explore the diamond fields and obtain information for Twain to use in a projected literary work (and for Riley to utilize in lectures). Riley did make the journey; however, before he and his taskmaster could benefit, the unfortunate Riley died of cancer in September 1872.

RIMMER, ALFRED (1829–1893). *Ancient Streets and Homesteads of England*. Introduction by John Saul Howson (1816–1885). 150 engravings by James Davis Cooper (1823–1904), after drawings by the author. London: Macmillan and Co., 1877. 340 pp. [Publisher and pages conjectured.]

Inscription: the verso of the frontispiece is signed "S. L. Clemens, Hartford, 1877."

Catalog: *A1911*, "8vo, cloth, gilt top, uncut (joints weak), Lond. 1877," quotes the signature, lot 405, sold for $3.75.

In November 1877 James R. Osgood & Company of Boston billed Clemens for a volume purchased on 27 February 1877: "1 Anct Streets &c. of England $7.50," discounted to $6 (Scrapbook #10, p. 69, MTP). This has to be counted among Mark Twain's literary resources for composing *The Prince and the Pauper* (1881).

"RIOLA" [pseudonym of an unidentified author.]

A dramatist whose pseudonym was "Riola" called on Mark Twain in South Africa on 27 May 1896 (NB 38, TS p. 19).

"RISE AND SHINE" (spiritual). Also known as "Oh, rise an' shine."

When Clemens sang this song "he gave out so much fervor of spirit that one could never forget it," his daughter Clara recalled (*MFMT*, p. 188).

Salsbury, *S&MT* (1965), p. 181.

RIZAL, JOSÉ (1861–1896). *An Eagle Flight: A Filipino Novel, Adapted from "Noli Me Tangere."* New York: McClure, Phillips & Co., 1900. 256 pp.

Marginalia: a pencil bracket is visible at the poem "My Last Thought" in the "Introduction" (p. xiii); pencil marks at pages 3, 54, and 55; corners are folded down at pages 112, 151, 153, 156, 187, and 220.

Location: Mark Twain Papers, Bancroft Library, University of California at Berkeley.

Copy examined: Clemens's copy.

On 4 January 1906 Isabel Lyon noted: "Mr. Clemens read aloud to me José Rizal's wonderful poem 'My Last Thought' written the night before his execution [in Manila

in 1896] as a traitor, and then he read the poem *he* wrote after reading Rizal's beautiful work" (IVL Journals, TS p. 119, MTP). Rizal's poem appears on pages xii–xiii of *An Eagle Flight*. Mark Twain's version, dated May 1901 in New York City, uses the same title as Rizal's poem; Twain suggests that the stars on the American flag are beginning to resemble a skull and crossbones. Originally Twain laid the manuscript loose in his copy of Rizal's novel; his version is now in Paine 6, Mark Twain Papers at Berkeley. Scott, *OPMT* (1966), pp. 129–131.

ROACH, ABBY MEGUIRE (1876–1966). *Some Successful Marriages*. Illustrated by Alice Barber Stephens (1858–1932). New York: Harper & Brothers, 1906. 285 pp.

Source: MTLAcc, entry #1424, volume donated by Clemens.

Twelve short stories by the Louisville, Kentucky author Abby Meguire Roach present fictional case histories of marital situations. One of these, "Life's Accolade," also appeared in *Their Husbands' Wives* (New York: Harper & Brothers, 1906), a collection edited by William Dean Howells (1837–1920) and Henry Mills Alden (1836–1919) that contained Mark Twain's "Eve's Diary."

ROBBINS, ROYAL (1787–1861). *Outlines of Ancient and Modern History on a New Plan*. Illus. New edition, revised and enlarged. 2 vols. in 1 Hartford, Connecticut: William J. Hamersley, 1865.

Catalog: *A1911*, "12mo, half roan (worn), Hartford, 1865," with a small sheet containing Clemens's notes laid in, lot 406, sold for .25¢.

Provenance: collection of Frank C. Willson (1889–1960) in Melrose, Massachusetts. Sold by his widow Margarete in 1962 to the University of Texas.

Location: Harry Ransom Center, University of Texas at Austin.

Copy examined: Clemens's copy, unmarked. Sale label of the *A1911* auction on the front pastedown endpaper.

Robbins concentrates on the "ancient" eras rather than anything remotely "modern."

ROBERTS, (SIR) CHARLES GEORGE DOUGLAS (1860–1943). *The Kindred of the Wild; A Book of Animal Life*. Illustrated by Charles Livingston Bull (1874–1932). Green cloth, gilt lettering and design. Boston: L. C. Page & Co., 1902. 374 pp.

Inscription: inscribed by Clemens on the front pastedown endpaper in black ink, "To/Jean Clemens/from her Father/Sept. '03." An instrument of some type poked through the front cover and damaged the "e" in Jean. Someone traced in pencil an outline of a moose onto the title page, using the tissue paper of the frontispiece.

Location: Mark Twain Library, Redding, Connecticut Donated from Clemens's library by Clara Clemens Gabrilowitsch in 1910 (MTLAcc, entry #1976).

Copy examined: Jean Clemens's unmarked copy. Has the red ink Mark Twain Library accession number "1976". Examined in 1970 and again in June 1982 and on 9 November 2019.

ROBERTS, EDWARDS (1855–1926). *Shoshone and Other Western Wonders*. Preface by Charles Francis Adams (1907–1886). Illus. New York: Harper & Brothers, 1888. 275 pp.

Source: MTLAcc, entry #249, volume donated by Clemens.

Roberts describes the Rocky Mountains, Denver, the Mormons, Salt Lake City, Yellowstone, and other Western scenes and populations.

———. [Another identical copy.]

Source: MTLAcc, entry #601, volume donated by Clemens.

ROBERTS, FREDERICK SLEIGH, EARL (1832–1914). *Forty-One Years in India. From Subaltern to Commander-in-Chief. By Field-Marshal Lord Roberts of Kandahar*. 2 vols. New York: Longmans, Green, 1897. [Edition conjectured.]

In a letter to the Reverend Joseph H. Twichell written on 2 February 1902 Clemens refers to the "opening sentence of all translations of letters passing between Lord Roberts & Indian princes & rulers" (*LMTJHT*, p. 300).

ROBERTS, MORLEY (1857–1942). *Lord Linlithgow, A Novel*. New York: Harper & Brothers, 1900. 319 pp.

Source: MTLAcc, entry #250, volume donated by Clemens.

———. [Another identical copy.]

Source: MTLAcc, entry #1704, volume donated by Clemens.

ROBERTS, WILLIAM CULVER, JR. ("BOBS ROBERTS"). *The Boy's Account of It: A Chronicle of Foreign Travel by an Eight-Year-Old. Translated by a Patient Printer from the Manuscript of "Bobs" Roberts (William Culver Roberts, Jr.)*. Illustrated with photographs. New York: Waterloo Press, 1909. 70 pp.

Inscription: the front free endpaper is inscribed in ink "This little books [*sic*] is presented/to my distinguished contemporary author, Mark Twain,/with the compliments of/the little writer, and the/friend of the big writer/Bobs Roberts". Clemens wrote in black ink below the inscription: "It is the handwriting of a boy of 15, & <so is> the literature is as old."

Provenance: Donated from Clemens's library to the Mark Twain Library in Redding by Clara Clemens Gabrilowitsch in 1910 (MTLAcc, entry #1902). A bookstamp of the Mark Twain Library, Redding, Connecticut, appears on the front pastedown endpaper.

Location: Special Collections, University of Nevada at Reno. Purchased in 1963 from Mrs. Louis A. (Haydee U.) Zeitlin of Santa Monica, California.

Copy examined: Clemens's copy, unmarked, in 1971.

The boy's travels approximate those Mark Twain recounted in *The Innocents Abroad* (1869).

ROBERTSON, FREDERICK WILLIAM (1816–1853). *Life, Letters, and Addresses of Fredk. W. Robertson, M.A., Incumbent of Trinity Chapel, Brighton, 1847–53*. Ed. by Stopford Augustus Brooke (1832–1916). New York: Harper & Brothers, n.d. 840 pp.

Source: MTLAcc, entry #1387, volume donated by Clemens. Cover loose.

An Anglican divine, Frederick W. Robertson distinguished himself by the force of his sermons and lectures advocating social reform on behalf of the working poor and Christian missionary efforts in India.

———. *Sermons*. 2 vols. Portrait. Boston: Fields, Osgood & Co., 1869. [Publisher conjectured.]

Inscription: the flyleaf is signed "Livy L. Langdon, Jan. 1870."

Catalog: *A1911*, "Vol. I, Portrait, 12mo, cloth, Bost. 1869," quotes the signature, with a sheet of Clemens's notes laid in, lot 407, sold for $1 to Mark Twain Company.

———. *Sermons*. 2 vols. Boston: Fields, Osgood & Co., 1869.

Source: MTLAcc, entry #905, Volume 2 only (696 pp.), donated by Clemens.

In "Advice to Youth," a speech Mark Twain made on 15

April 1882, he urged young people to read only "good" books to improve their minds—works such as Robertson's *Sermons*, Baxter's *Saints' Rest*, and Mark Twain's *Innocents Abroad* (*MTSpk*, p. 171). "Robertson's Sermons" was among the volumes visible in Aunt Susan's apartment, "the private parlor of a refined and sensible lady" ("The Loves of Alonzo Fitz Clarence and Rosannah Ethelton" [1878]).

———. *Sermons*. New York: Harper & Brothers, n.d. 838 pp.

Source: MTLAcc, entry #1237, volume donated by Clemens.

ROBERTSON, HARRISON (1856–1939). *The Inlander*. New York: Charles Scribner's Sons, 1901. 320 pp. [A novel.]

Source: MTLAcc, entry #251, volume donated by Clemens.

ROBERTSON, JOHN MACKINNON (1856–1933).

Clemens quoted the British politician, lecturer, and author Robertson in 1897 (NB 39, TS p. 40). Robertson was associated with the Free Thought movement. He endeavored to apply secular rationalism against religious myths, including even the birth of Christ.

ROBERTSON, MORGAN (1861–1915). *Sinful Peck; A Novel*. New York: Harper & Brothers, 1903. 355 pp.

Source: MTLAcc, entry #1657, volume donated by Clemens.

———. *Spun-Yarn; Sea Stories*. New York: Harper & Brothers, 1898. 215 pp.

Source: MTLACC, entry #1066, volume donated by Clemens.

ROBERTSON, THÉODORE (1803–1871). *The Whole French Language*. Edited by Louis Ernst. Half-title: The Robertsonian System. New York: R. Lockwood & Son 1855. 605 pp. [Edition conjectured.]

In an unsigned gossip column ("Oh, You Robinson!") that Mark Twain most probably wrote for the 6 November 1865 issue of the San Francisco *Dramatic Chronicle*, he quipped: "The 'Robertsonian method of teaching French' is very good, but the Robinsonian method of getting divorces is rather too brash" (*ET&S* 2, p. 488). Alexander H. Monteith had edited a similarly titled series: *The Robertsonian Method: A Course of Lessons in the French Language* (London, 1842).

ROBERTSON, WILLIAM (1721–1793). *An Historical Disquisition Concerning the Knowledge Which the Ancients Had of India; And the Progress of Trade with That Country*. New York: Harper & Brothers, 1855. 146 pp. [Bound with *The History of Scotland*; see the Catalog entry below.]

Source: MTLAcc, entry #1741, *Scotland and India* (606 total pp.), donated by Clemens.

———. *The History of Scotland During the Reigns of Queen Mary [Stuart, 1542–1567] and of King James VI [1567–1625] Till His Accession to the Crown of England*. New York: Harper & Brothers, 1855. 460 pp. [Bound with *An Historical Disquisition Concerning the Knowledge Which the Ancients Had of India*; see the Catalog entry above.]

Source: MTLAcc, entry #1741, *Scotland and India* (606 total pp.), donated by Clemens.

———. *The History of the Discovery and Settlement of America*. Examination questions furnished by John Frost, LL.D. New York: Harper & Brothers, 1855. 570 pp.

Did Clemens keep these volumes from his youthful years? The date of publication leads one to speculate that this Scottish historian's writings were part of Clemens's early reading.

ROBINS, ELIZABETH (1862–1952), pseud. "C. E. Raimond." *The Magnetic North.* New York: Frederick A. Stokes Co., 1904. 417 pp.

On 25 March 1904 Clemens wrote to Robins from Florence about her novel, whose setting was the Yukon Territory: "I thank you ever so much. 'The Magnetic North' is a great book, & heart-breakingly true. True in so many ways: in the wild strange life depicted; in the characters, feelings & ambitions of the people in the book; in the eternal & frank sordidness of the human race . . . . in the tragic & unfulfilled ending of the story" (ALS in MTP). See also the Catalog entry for William Morris's *The Well at the World's End.*

———. *The Open Question; A Tale of Two Temperaments.* New York: Harper & Brothers, 1899. 522 pp.

Albert Bigelow Paine reported that Clemens read this book in 1899 during his stay in Sweden. Clemens wrote to Robins, evidently on 30 July 1899: "A relative of Matthew Arnold lent us your 'Open Question' the other day, & Mrs. Clemens & I are in your debt. I am not able to put in words my feeling about the book—my admiration of its depth & truth & wisdom, & courage; & the fine & great literary art & grace of the setting." He concluded: "I have not been so enriched by a book for many years, nor so enchanted by one" (*MTB*, p. 1089; text corrected against PH in MTP). Robins replied on 6 August 1899, thanking Clemens for his "beautiful letter." On her envelope Clemens noted: "From Miss Robins, author of 'An Open Question.' Keep it" (MTP). Olivia Clemens and Clara Clemens wrote to Chatto & Windus, 20 August 1899, requesting "a copy of 'The Open Question' by Miss Robbins. . . . (C. E. Raimond)" (MTP). At the novel's beginning the Maryland plantation-owning Gano family is ruined by the Civil War and must move West, despite the loyal willingness of their enslaved African Americans to stay and help them eke out a living. A murky ending takes place in a storm at sea near the Golden Gate in California.

ROBINSON, CHARLES SEYMOUR (1829–1899), comp. *Laudes Domini: A Selection of Spiritual Songs, Ancient and Modern. With Music.* New York: Century Co., [1884]. [Publisher conjectured.]

Inscription: signed in pencil "Chas. Dudley Warner." Editor and author Charles Dudley Warner (1829–1900) was a Nook Farm friend and neighbor of the Clemenses.

Marginalia: in the rear of the volume, Clemens noted in pencil four page numbers and referred to the songs appearing there. He also wrote the beginning of two hymns—"How firm a foundation" and Ray Palmer's "My faith looks up to Thee."

Catalog: *A1911,* "8vo, morocco, N.Y. [1884]," quotes the signature and describes and quotes the marginalia, lot 284, sold for $1.

———. *Laudes Domini: A Selection of Spiritual Songs, Ancient and Modern. With Music.* Original morocco-grain maroon cloth, gilt, bound divinity style on thin Bible paper, edges red. New York: Century Co., [1884]. [First edition.]

Marginalia: there are notes in at least two hands. A marginal double line in purple ink at page 488 marks the Lord's Prayer, and two penciled page references (to 234 and 458) on the rear endpaper appear to be in Clemens's

handwriting. The partial title ("Beyond the smiling") of a hymn by Horatio Bonar is written in pencil, apparently by Olivia Clemens, on the rear end paper. Marginal lines and numbers in pencil occur at pages 8, 134, 138, 233, 234, 388, and 458. An ink spillage at page 79 cannot be identified. The upper corners at pages 135 and 137 were deliberately folded over, and the corners of several other pages appear to be either folded or accidentally turned down. The two hymns marked in Clemens's other copy of this book (see the preceding Catalog entry) were not marked in this volume. The hymns marked in this copy include Isaac Watts' "How pleasant, how divinely fair," Charles Wesley's "Hark! The herald angels sing," Cecil Frances Alexander's "Once in royal David's city," Andrew Reed's "Holy Ghost! With light divine," Isaac Watts' "Eternal Spirit, we confess," Sarah Flower Adams's "Nearer, my God to thee," and Horatius Bonar's "Beyond the smiling and the weeping."

Catalog: *A1911,* "8vo, cloth, N.Y., n.d.," with a sheet of notes by Clemens laid in, lot 353, sold for $3.50.

Location: collection of Kevin Mac Donnell, Austin, Texas. Acquired in October 2015.

Source: letter from Mac Donnell to Alan Gribben, 26 October 2015. Mac Donnell reported the presence of an *A1911* sale label in the book, and an auction lot slip laid in. The manuscript leaf mentioned in the *A1911* catalog is no longer present, however.

ROBINSON, EDWARD (1794–1863). *Biblical Researches in Palestine, and in the Adjacent Regions. A Journal of Travels in the Years 1838 & 1852. By Edward Robinson, Eli Smith [1801–1857, joint author], and Others.* Second ed. 3 vols. London: John Murray, 1856. [Also published in 1856 by Crocker and Brewster in Boston, with a second edition in 1860. Clemens's edition is undetermined.]

In Notebook 9 (1867) Mark Twain wrote of "the Pool of Siloam discovered by Dr Robinson" (*N&J* 1: 434). Twain's letter in the 5 April 1868 issue of the *Daily Alta California* reported that "Robinson's Holy Land" was one of the volumes the *Quaker City* travelers were instructed to obtain. Twain apparently used Robinson's book title to invent a fictitious book in the list: "Dusenberry's Researches in Palestine" (*TIA*, p. 303). Twain concluded *The Innocents Abroad* (Ch. 61, 1869) by quoting his own New York *Herald* article, which reported that "the pilgrims played dominoes when too much Josephus or Robinson's Holy Land Researches, or book-writing, made recreation necessary." In thanking Twain on 26 September 1869 for a complimentary copy of *The Innocents Abroad,* Oliver Wendell Holmes remarked that Twain had looked at Palestine and Egypt "in a somewhat different way . . . from Dr Robinson or [Karl Richard] Lepsius [1810–1884]" (*MTLet* 3: 365 n. 1).

ROBINSON, LUCY CATLIN (BULL) (1861–1903). *A Child's Poems, from October to October, 1870–1871.* Portrait. Privately printed. Hartford, Connecticut: Case, Lockwood & Brainard, 1872. 171 pp.

Inscription: the front flyleaf is signed, "Saml. L. Clemens/ Hartford, Dec. 1874."

Catalogs: *A1911,* "16mo, cloth, gilt edges, Hartford, 1872, a privately printed and scarce volume," laid in is a letter from William Cullen Bryant sent from New York City in 1871, quotes Clemens's signature, lot 54, sold for $9.25; Anderson Auction Company (New York City), Sale catalogue for the library of the late Michael Pardee of New York City (19–20 October 1911), "16mo, cloth, gilt edges, Hartford, 1872," quotes Clemens's flyleaf inscription, a W. C. Bryant letter of 1871 is laid in, lot 105, sold for $4; Parke-Bernet Galleries, New York City, "Collection of the Late John Gribbel, Philadelphia," Sale number 662 (16–17 April 1945), "original cloth, inner hinges cracked," has the *1911* sale label, no mention of the Bryant letter, lot 96.

The rhyming poems by this Hartford ten year old range from playful to meditative as she moves through the seasons of a year. Her poem on December 20, 1870, "Santa-Claus' Visit," marks the traditional approach of Christmas, but others explore a wide range of emotions about human experiences and changing perspectives. Lucy Robinson's mother provided a Preface assuring the public that Lucy's parents have not placed any pressure on her to produce these heartfelt verses. An introductory "Note" by William Cullen Bryant, himself once something of a young poet prodigy, testified, "I do not think I have seen any thing produced at the same age at all comparable to them."

———. [An identical copy.]

    Source: MTLAcc, entry #2052, volume donated from Clemens's library by Clara Clemens Gabrilowitsch in 1910.

ROBINSON, ROBERT (1735–1790). "Come thou fount of every blessing" (hymn, published in 1758).

    On 31 December 1871 Clemens quoted four lines in satirizing a minister's manner of reading this hymn (SLC to Olivia Clemens, Paris, Illinois, *MFMT*, p. 10; *MTLet* 4: 528).

ROBINSON, WILLIAM (1838–1935). *The Wild Garden; or, Our Groves and Gardens Made Beautiful by the Naturalisation of Hardy Exotic Plants; Being One Way Onwards from the Dark Ages of Flower Gardens, with Suggestions for the Regeneration of the Bare Borders of the London Parks.* Illustrated by Alfred Parsons (1847–1920). London: The Garden Office; New York: Scribner and Welford, 1881. 179 pp.

    Source: MTLAcc, entry #1975, volume donated from Clemens's library by Clara Clemens Gabrilowitsch in 1910.

ROCHE, JAMES JEFFREY (1847–1908). *Her Majesty the King; A Romance of the Harem, Done into American from the Arabic.* Illustrated by Oliver Herford (1863–1935). New York: R. H. Russell, 1905. 149 pp.

    Source: MTLAcc, entry #358, volume donated by Clemens.

ROCHE, REGINA MARIA (DALTON) (1764–1845). *The Children of the Abbey. A Tale* (novel, published in 1796).

    Aboard the *Mararoa* in December 1895, Clemens wrote about reading Roche's romance about Amanda and Oscar, two lovers swindled of their inheritance by a forged will: "Have begun Children of the Abbey. It begins with this 'impromptu' from the sentimental heroine: 'Hail, sweet asylum of my infancy! Content and innocence reside beneath your humble roof, & charity unboastful of the good it renders. Here unmolested may I wait, till the rude storm of sorrow is overblown, & my father's arms are again expanded to receive me.' Has the earmarks of preparation" (NB 36, TS p. 3; quoted in *MTB*, p. 1016).

"ROCK-A-BYE BABY" (nursery lullaby).

    In Chicago in November 1879, Mark Twain reminded the soldiers at the Army of the Tennessee banquet that they once "tried to *sing!*—'Rock-a-by baby in the tree-top,' for instance. And what an affliction for the neighbors" (*MTSpk*, p. 132). The cub pilot who oversleeps in Chapter 6 of *Life on the Mississippi* (1883) endures mockery: "Give him some sugar in a rag and send for the chambermaid to sing 'rock-a-by baby,' to him."

ROE, EDWARD PAYSON (1838–1888). *Barriers Burned Away.* New York: Dodd & Mead, 1873. 488 pp.

    Inscription: the front free endpaper is signed in pencil, "Ida C. Langdon/March 28, '73." [Ida B. Clark (1849–1934) had married Charles Jervis Langdon in 1870.]

    Provenance: bookplate #635 of the "J. Langdon Family Library."

    Catalog: Ball 2016 inventory, green cloth, gilt lettering and design, fair condition, quotes inscription.

    Location: Quarry Farm library shelves, under the supervision of the Mark Twain Archive, Elmira College, Elmira, New York.

    Copy examined: unmarked copy to which Clemens had access whenever he visited the Langdon house in Elmira. Examined on 26 May 2015.

    Roe produced a fictionalized account of the calamity and aftermath of the Great Chicago Fire of 1871.

ROGERS, CHARLES (1825–1890), ed. *The Centenary Garland; Being Pictorial Illustrations of the Novels of Sir Walter Scott, in Their Order of Publication. By George Cruikshank [1792–1878], and Other Artists of Eminence, With Descriptions, Memoir, Etc.* 36 plates. Edinburgh: W. P. Nimmo, 1871. 71 pp.

    Inscription: inscribed by Frank Finlay to Olivia Clemens, Belfast, 30 August 1873.

    Provenance: formerly in the Mark Twain Library, Redding, Connecticut.

    Catalog: *Mott 1952*, item #46, $3.50.

    Location: currently unknown.

ROGERS, JULIA ELLEN (1866–1958). *The Shell Book: A Popular Guide to a Knowledge of the Families of Living Mollusks, and an Aid to the Identification of Shells Native and Foreign.* Illustrated with photographs by Arthur Radclyffe Dugmore (1870–1955). New York: Doubleday, Page & Co., 1908. 485 pp.

    Source: MTLAcc, entry #742, volume donated by Clemens.

———. *The Tree Book: A Popular Guide to a Knowledge of the Trees of North America and to Their Uses and Cultivation.* Illustrated with photographs by Arthur Radclyffe Dugmore (1870–1955). New York: Doubleday, Page & Co., 1906. 589 pp.

    Source: MTLAcc, entry #740, volume donated by Clemens.

ROGERS, SAMUEL (1763–1855). "Venice," Part X, collected in *Italy, A Poem* (published 1822–1828).

    In Chapter 22 of *The Innocents Abroad* (1869), Mark Twain quotes seventeen lines of Rogers's verse to show that in the moonlight Venice resembles the picture in his poem. See also the Catalog entry for *The Book of Pleasures.*

ROGET, PETER MARK (1779–1869). *Thesaurus of English Words and Phrases.* Revised and edited by Barnas Sears (1802–1880). Boston: Gould and Lincoln; New York: Sheldon and Co., 1874. 567 pp. [Publisher and pages conjectured.]

    Inscription: the front flyleaf is signed, "Saml. L. Clemens, Hartford, 1875."

    Catalog: *A1911*, "12mo, cloth, Bost. 1874," quotes the

signature, lot 408, sold for $3.50.

"When a word is so near the right one that a body can't quite tell whether it is or isn't, it's good politics to strike it out and go for the Thesaurus" (SLC to Louis Pendleton, Elmira, 4 August 1888, *MTL*, pp. 498–499). In March 1890 Clemens noted, "Roget's Thesaurus" (NB 29, TS p. 43). Clemens wrote Robert Barr twice, once on 18 September and again on 29 September 1897 to thank Barr for remembering to send "the Thesaurus" (PH in MTP). "A couple of nights ago Mr. Clemens was speaking of the way in which certain words always elude him. . . . The word never reaches him when he is most in need of it and he cannot always have a thesaurus at his elbow" (IVL Journals, 26 March 1905, TS p. 48, MTP).

———. *Thesaurus of English Words and Phrases*. New edition, enlarged. Edited by John Lewis Roget (1828–1908). New York: Thomas Y. Crowell & Co., n. d. [The preface is dated 1879].

Inscription: the front pastedown is endpaper signed, "SL. Clemens, 1903."

Catalogs: *C1951*, #22c; *Zeitlin 1951*, item #35, $17.50.

Location: collection of Robert Daley, Burbank, California. Mr. Daley supplied information to me about this volume in 1978. He reported that the front pastedown endpaper bears a sale label from the 1951 Hollywood auction.

———. *Thesaurus of English Words and Phrases, Classified and Arranged So As to Facilitate the Expression of Ideas and Assist in Literary Composition. . . . New Edition, Enlarged and Improved, Partly from the Author's Notes, and with a Full Index by John Lewis Roget [1828–1908]*. Boston: De Wolfe, Fiske, & Co., [1886?]. 429 pp. [The publisher, date, and pages are conjectured.]

Inscription: the front flyleaf is inscribed by Clemens: "Susy Clemens, Hartford, 1890."

Catalog: *A1911*, "12mo, cloth, Bost. n.d.," quotes the signature, lot 409, sold for $3 to Mark Twain Company.

ROHLFS, ANNA KATHARINE (GREEN) (1846–1935). *Hand and Ring*. Illus. New York: G. P. Putnam's Sons, 1883. 608 pp.

Source: MTLAcc, entry #2246, volume donated from Clemens's library by Clara Clemens Gabrilowitsch in 1910.

Anna Katharine Green (she married Charles Rohlfs in 1884 and then moved to Buffalo, New York) was a pioneer in detective fiction. This novel features vivid courtroom scenes in the process of solving a murder case that has several suspects. Her posthumous reputation has been injured by her opposition to women's suffrage.

ROLFE, WILLIAM JAMES (1827–1910). *Shakespeare the Boy, with Sketches of the Home and School Life, the Games and Sports, the Manners, Customs and Folklore of the Time*. New York: Harper & Brothers, 1896. 251 pp.

Inscription: Clemens inscribed the front pastedown endpaper in black ink: "The title is a lie; it has not a fact in it concerning Shakespeare, but a multitude of imbecile guesses. It should have been called Manners & Customs in Rural England in the Sixteenth Century./SL Clemens/1909." In pencil he added below: "There is one important fact stated in a sentence on p. 106—a very damaging one." On page 106 Rolfe stated: "No English was taught in the Stratford school then, or for many years after." Clemens underscored this sentence with pencil.

Marginalia: pencil marks and notes up to page 109; none thereafter. He disagreed with statements on virtually every page. Examples: "Sho!" (pp. 17, 18); "dung" and "dung-heap sentence" (p. 25); and "A chapter of damned rot" (p. 80). He might well have consigned Rolfe's biography to his hypothetical "Library of Literary Hogwash."

Provenance: Antenne-Dorrance Collection, Rice Lake, Wisconsin.

Location: Mark Twain Archive, Gannett-Tripp Learning Center, Elmira College, Elmira, New York.

Copy examined: Clemens's copy.

"Rolfe's Shakspeare for Elsie Leslie./—See Harpers," Clemens noted in February 1890 (NB 29, *N&J* 3: 541). Rolfe's multi-volume edition of Shakespeare was published between 1871 and 1884.

"ROLL A MAN DOWN" (sea chantey). Also known as "Blow the man down," "As I was a-walking," and "Come all ye young fellows."

In "The Great Dark," written in 1898, the sailors chant while reefing the sheet: "If you get there, before I do—/Hi-ho-o-o, roll a man down;/If you get there before I do,/O, give a man time to roll a man down!" (*WWD?*, p. 109).

ROLLIN, CHARLES (1661–1741). *The Ancient History of the Egyptians, Carthaginians, Assyrians, Babylonians, Medes and Persians, Grecians and Macedonians*. 4 vols. New York: John W. Lovell Co., n. d. [c. 1880).

Catalog: QF Martinez, Vols. III and IV only, top edge gilt, poor condition.

Available to Clemens at Quarry Farm.

"ROLL, JORDAN, ROLL" (spiritual, published in 1867).

Clemens included this spiritual in his list of favorite songs in August 1889 (NB 29, *N&J* 3: 513). It is contained in *Slave Songs of the United States* (1867); see the Catalog entry for William Francis Allen (comp.).

"ROLL ON, SILVER MOON" (song, published in 1841). [There are several claimants to this song, but its most likely composer was the singer Jane Sloman (b. 1824); the most popular arrangement was that of Nathan Barker (1820–1885).]

From Carson City, on 2 April 1862, Clemens jokingly complained to his mother about Orion Clemens's whistling: "I have got to sit still and be tortured with his infernal discords, and fag-ends of tunes which were worn out and discarded before 'Roll on—Sil-ver Moo-oon' became popular" (*MTBus*, p. 65; *MTLet* 1: 181). Mark Twain used the song title as a subheading in his eighteenth letter to the Sacramento *Weekly Union*, 1 July 1866 (*MTH*, p. 366). On 23 December 1866 Twain vowed that if the ship choir "attempted that outrage I would have scuttled the ship" (*MTTMB*, pp. 28–29). He alluded to "Roll on Silver Moon" in his annotations in E. C. E. M. S. Wortley's *Travels in the United States, Etc., During 1849 and 1850* (see that Catalog entry). In Twain's description of "The House Beautiful" in Chapter 38 of *Life on the Mississippi* (1883), a visitor would see, "spread open on the rack, where the plaintive singer has left it, *Ro*-holl on, silver *moo*-hoon, guide the *trav*-el-lerr his *way*, etc." The Honolulu parlors of the 1860's contained "Roll on Silver Moon, . . . and other songs of love and sentiment" on music stands (*FE* [Ch. 3], 1897). As depicted by Twain, in a Missouri village in 1849–1850 Hale Dexter "won Milly's deep regard" by singing this song "and several other villainous ditties of a like sort" ("Simon Wheeler, Detective," unfinished novel, written sporadically 1877–1898?, *S&B*, p. 335).

ROOD, HENRY EDWARD (1867–1954). *Hardwicke; A Novel.* New York: Harper & Brothers, 1902. 312 pp.

Source: MTLAcc, entry #1658, volume donated by Clemens.

Rood gently depicts contemporary religious differences in a rural community.

———. *In Camp at Bear Pond.* Illustrated by W[illiam]. E. Mears (1868–1945). New York: Harper & Brothers, 1904. 263 pp.

Source: MTLAcc, entry #1615, volume donated by Clemens.

Two fictional boys have adventures while hunting and fishing in a Pennsylvania forest. Rood was born in Pennsylvania but lived in upstate New York.

ROOSA, DANIEL B[ENNETT]. ST. JOHN (1838–1908). *A Doctor's Suggestions to the Community, Being a Series of Papers Upon Various Subjects from a Physician's Standpoint.* New York: Putnam's Sons, 1880. 234 pp.

Inscription: signed "Susan L. Crane/Mch 1881".

Catalogs: QF Martinez, "Poor Condition"; Ball 2016 inventory, brown cloth, gilt lettering, quotes the inscription.

Location: Mark Twain Archive, Gannett-Tripp Learning Center, Elmira College, Elmira, New York.

K. Patrick Ober, "Mark Twain and Family Health in Nook Farm," *Mark Twain Journal* 56.1 (Spring 2018): 23–71, discussed medical concerns that bedeviled the Clemenses.

ROOSEVELT, THEODORE (1858–1919). *Good Hunting: In Pursuit of Big Game in the West.* Illustrated with frontispiece and fifteen plates. 12mo, original pictorial tan cloth. First edition. New York: Harper & Brothers, 1907. 106 pp.

Inscription: the front pastedown endpaper is signed in black ink "S L. Clemens/1907."

Marginalia: the upper corner of page 23 (concerning an elk-hunt) is folded down.

Provenance: displays the shelfmark of Clara Clemens Gabrilowitsch's private library in Detroit. Donated to the Carrie Estelle Doheny Collection, St. John's Seminary, Camarillo, California, after Mrs. Doheny purchased this book for $12.20 from Maxwell Hunley Rare Books of Beverly Hills in 1940. Auctioned by Christie's on 1 February 1988 on behalf of St. John's Seminary. Subsequently the volume became part of the collection of Nick Karanovich; see Karanovich, "Sixty Books from Mark Twain's Library," *Mark Twain Journal* 25.2 (Fall 1987): 17.

Catalogs: Christie's, New York City, 1–2 February 1988 auction, lot 460, sold for $1,210 to Randall House, San Francisco; *Sotheby's 2003*, #233, $10,000.

Copy examined: Clemens's copy, unmarked, at St. John's Seminary. Has the bookplate of "Estelle Doheny."

Clemens found "Roosevelt the man" to be likeable in person, but as "Roosevelt the statesman & politician I find him destitute of morals & not respect-worthy" (Clemens to Joseph H. Twichell, 16 February 1905, *MTB*, p. 1231). Roosevelt's *Good Hunting* described his adventures with elk, bear, deer, wolves, antelope, and mountain goats. Clemens ridiculed Roosevelt's latest bear hunt ("the chase of the frightened creature lasted three hours, and reads like a hectic chapter in a dime-novel") in an Autobiographical Dictation on 21 October 1907 (*MTE*, pp. 10–14; *AutoMT 3*: 174–176). In a book that Clemens signed in June 1909 (George Gordon Coulton's *From St. Francis to Dante* [1907]), Clemens noted on page 318, in a passage about St. Dominic's plucking alive a sparrow that interrupted his studies, "Another heroic hunter like Roosevelt."

———. *A Square Deal.* Allendale, New Jersey: Allendale Press, n. d. [cop. 1906]. 206 pp. [A collection of selected passages from Roosevelt's speeches.]

Inscription: signed in black ink on the front pastedown endpaper, "S L. Clemens/1907."

Marginalia: using black ink, Clemens crossed out the title of the book and replaced it (in all capital letters) with one word: 'BANALITIES'. Similarly on page 5 he crossed out the word "FOREWORD" and in black ink substituted "A PUKE/BY A DISINTERESTED PUBLISHER". Clemens made a grammatical correction on page four (striking out the "ly" in "garrulously") and other black ink marginal markings on pages 86, 87, and 89 of a chapter titled "The Nobility of Parenthood." On page 115 he wrote "Not true" beside Roosevelt's assertion that "great corporate fortunes" were mainly due "to natural causes in the business world." He drew a line in the margin of page 200 about the duties of Christians. Pages 86 and 200 were folded down.

Catalog: *C1951*, #27c, listed among books signed by Clemens, $32.50.

Location: Mark Twain Papers, Bancroft Library, University of California at Berkeley. Purchased for $2,000 and donated as a gift to the Mark Twain Papers in December 1988 by Mrs. Kurt (Violet) Appert.

Copy examined: a typescript of the inscription and marginalia (MTP). The book bears the *C1951* auction number (27c) in pencil on the front pastedown endpaper. Above that is the penciled shelfmark number of Clara Clemens Samossoud's private library during her years in Detroit.

"I think he is as distinctly and definitely the representative American gentleman of today as was Washington the representative American gentleman of his day," Clemens declared in an Autobiographical Dictation of 3 April 1906 (*MTE*, p. 33). In a later diction on 13 September 1907 he called Roosevelt to "the most colossal" earthquake in history and said he made the San Francisco earthquake disaster seem like "but a poor thing, and local" (MTP).

ROOT, GEORGE FREDERICK (1820–1895). "The battle cry of freedom" (better known as "Rally round the flag") (patriotic song, published in 1862). Words and music by Root.

A gifted musician who was making a name for himself in the 1850s, Root in the next decade became the best-known composer of anthems and songs supporting the Union cause but also sympathizing with the losses the Civil War inflicted on all American families. Chapter 13 of "A Horse's Tale" (1906) refers to this song, which begins, "Yes, we'll rally round the flag, boys/We'll rally once again/Shouting the battle cry of freedom." Similar but inferior lyrics were written in 1862 by James T. Fields (1817–1881) and set to music by William B. Bradbury (1816–1868), but Root's original song remained the popular version.

———. "Just before the battle, Mother" (song, published in 1863). Words and music by Root.

Music critics can safely attribute "all the nauseating rebellion mush-and-milk about young fellows who have come home to die—just before the battle, mother—to George F. Root and kindred spirits" (17 June 1865 San

Francisco *Californian*, quoted in *LAMT*, p. 142; *ET&S* 2: 195). The title of Root's song is also its first line; the chorus goes: "Fare-well, Mother, you may never, you may never, Mother,/Press me to your heart again;/But/ Oh, you'll not forget me, Mother, you will not forget me,/If I'm numbered with the slain." In "'Mark Twain' on the Ballad Infliction" (San Francisco *Californian*, 4 November 1865), he referred to "You'll Not Forget Me, Mother" as "a still more malignant distemper than 'When Johnny Comes Marching Home,'" and he disparaged its "lugubrious strains" (*MTWY*, p. 194). In the Sacramento *Weekly Union* (28 April 1866) Twain again mentioned it as part of "the popular-song nuisance" (*LSI*, p. 51). On the *America* in December 1866, it was one of the "d—dest, oldest, vilest songs" rendered by the ship choir (NB 7, *N&J* 1: 262). Again on 1 January 1867 Twain mentioned this as one of the "wretchedest old songs in the world" and wondered why the ship choir insisted on singing it amidst breathtaking surroundings (*MTTMB*, p. 59).

———. "Tramp! tramp! tramp!" (song, published in 1864). Words and music by Root.

In "The Last Words of Great Men" (Buffalo *Express*, 11 September 1869), Mark Twain absurdly claimed that the last words of Joan of Arc were "Tramp, tramp, tramp, the boys are marching" (*MTBE*, p. 46). Twain's working notes for "Cap'n Simon Wheeler, The Amateur Detective" (written in1877) contain a four-line parody of the song (*S&B*, p. 297). In Chapter 13 of Twain's "A Horse's Tale" (1906), "Everybody's excitement rose to blood-heat" when the bands played this song.

ROPES, ARTHUR REED (1859–1933) and MARY EMILY ROPES (1842–1932). *On Peter's Island.* New York: Charles Scribner's Sons, 1901. 478 pp.

Source: MTLAcc, entry #1067, volume donated by Clemens.

Writing under the stage name "Adrian Ross," Arthur Reed Ropes was becoming a highly successful lyricist writer for the musical theater in London and New York City. In *On Peter's Island*, Ropes and his sister Mary Emily Ropes, both of them born in Russia, set their novel in St. Petersburg during the era of Emperor Alexander III (1845–1894), who reigned from 1881 until 1894. Secret societies were at work to undermine his regime.

ROPES, JOHN CODMAN (1836–1899). *The First Napoleon. A Sketch, Political and Military.* Second ed. Boston: Houghton, Mifflin and Co., 1886. 347 pp.

Source: Mark Twain Library card catalog (1977), which records the donation of a volume signed "S. L. Clemens" to the Mark Twain Library at Redding, Connecticut at an unspecified date. Subsequently the book disappeared.

In December 1885 or January 1886, Clemens entered "'The First Napoleon' by John Ropes" in Notebook 25 (*N&J*: 3: 218).

ROSE, GEORGE (1817–1888), pseud. "Arthur Sketchley." *Mrs. Brown Series.*

Rose's books had titles such as *Mrs. Brown in America* (London, 1868) and *Mrs. Brown up the Nile* (London, 1869). In 1880 Clemens referred disparagingly to Rose's "Mrs. Brown" in a list of humorists to be considered for an anthology: "Arthur Rose ('Mrs. Brown') (rot)" (NB 19, *N&J* 2: 363).

ROSEGGER, PETER (1843–1918). *Stoansteirisch.* N.p., 1896. 356 pp.

Source: MTLAcc, entry #378, volume donated by Clemens. *Stoansteirisch* described the Bavarian dialect of the state of Styria in Austria.

ROSENTHAL, RICHARD S. *The Meisterschaft System: A Short and Practical Method of Acquiring Complete Fluency in the French Language.* Fifteen Parts. Boston: Estes and Lauriat, 1882. Paperbound. [Edition conjectured.]

Source: On 17 January 1886 Clemens wrote from Hartford: "Dear Sirs: Please send me a French Meisterschaft" (American Art Association, New York City, Sale catalogue, 1 April 1926, lot 77).

———. *The Meisterschaft System: A Short and Practical Method of Acquiring Complete Fluency of Speech in the German Language.* Fifteen Parts. Boston: Estes and Lauriat, 1882. Paperbound. 473 pp.

Marginalia: heavy black ink markings can be seen in the exercises in Part I. These seem to be in Clemens's hand.

Catalogs: ListABP (1910), "Meisterschaft", listed twice, no other information provided; "Retz Appraisal" (1944), p. 11. Part I only. Valued at $15.

Location: Part I only (53 pp.) in the Mark Twain Papers, Bancroft Library, University of California at Berkeley.

Copy examined: Clemens's copy, an extremely worn paper pamphlet. Part I only.

Rosenthal's books advocated (and necessitated) memorizing conversational sentences before approaching the rules of grammar. Clemens mentioned the Meisterschaft system textbooks in 1883 (NB 22, *N&J* 2: 25). In an introductory footnote to "Meisterschaft: In Three Acts" (1888), Mark Twain urges his readers to change the foreign language portions of his play "from language to language," to "knock the German Meisterschaft sentences out of the first scene, and replace them with sentences from the French Meisterschaft." One of his characters, Margaret, complains that "if you stick to Meisterschaft, it would change the subject every two minutes." Farther on, she resolves that "whosoever may ask us a Meisterschaft question shall get a Meisterschaft answer—and hot from the bat!" Much of the play purportedly derives from Rosenthal's primers.

Brandi Besalke, "'Ein sehr glueclicher Kind, you bet': Mark Twain and the German Language," *Mark Twain Annual* 5 (2007): 109–122.

ROSS, HENRY JAMES (1820–1902). *Letters from the East by Henry James Ross, 1837–1857.* Ed. by Janet Ann (Duff-Gordon) Ross (1842–1927). Illus. London: J. M. Dent & Co., 1902. 332 pp.

Inscriptions: the front pastedown endpaper is signed in black ink, "S L. Clemens/1902/from [August F.] Jaccaci." Below a sketch of Henry James Ross (after a drawing of 1860 by G. F. Watts) opposite the title page, Clemens wrote in black ink: "It was 30 years later that we knew him 10 months in Settignano. A fine man."

Marginalia: a pencil mark is visible on page vii; the page number of page 53 is circled in pencil; "wisdom" is written on page 141; there is a pencil mark on page 142; the corner of page 210 is turned down.

Catalogs: *A1911*, "square 8vo, buckram, gilt top, uncut, Lond. 1902, . . . a few marginal notes," quotes the signature and one note by Clemens, lot 411, $3.75; American Art Association (New York City), Sale catalogue for the collection of the late William F. Gable of Altoona, Pennsylvania (8 January 1925), "8vo, cloth, gilt top, uncut, London, 1902, signed "S. L. Clemens, 1902. From Jaccaci.", has the *A1911* sale label, a three-page Clemens letter laid in, lot 126, listed for $17; American Art Association (New York City), Sale catalogue, 18 November 1925, "8vo, original cloth, gilt top, uncut, London, 1902, first edition. . . . Mark Twain's copy, . . . autograph signature," has the *A1911* sale label, lot 171, listed for $5.00; American Art Association (New York City), Sale catalogue, 1 April 1926, "8vo, original cloth, gilt top, uncut, London, 1902, first edition, Mark Twain's copy, with his autograph signature and date inside front cover—"S. L. Clemens, 1902. From Jaccaci.", has the *A1911* sale label, lot 92, listed for $6.00; Chicago Book and Art Auctions, Sale number 30 (25 January 1933), lot 64.

Location: Henry W. and Albert A. Berg Collection, New York Public Library, Astor, Lenox and Tilden Foundations.

Copy examined: Clemens's copy, on 4 September 1970.

Janet Ross had married Henry James Ross in 1860. They resided in Italy for many years. Ross' *Letters from the East* described his travels in Turkey and Iraq. August Florian Jaccaci (1857–1930), a French-born art critic and historian, was briefly the art editor for *McClure's Magazine*.

ROSS, JANET ANN (DUFF-GORDON) (1842–1927), ed. *Three Generations of English Women: Memoirs and Correspondence of Susannah Taylor [1755–1823], Sarah Austin [1793–1867], and Lady [Lucie] Duff Gordon [1821–1869]. A New, Revised and Enlarged Edition.* 8vo, original light green cloth, red morocco slipcase. London: T. Fisher Unwin, 1893. 571 pp.

Inscription: the front flyleaf is inscribed, "To S. L. Clemens from Janet Ross, Dec. 1892."

Marginalia: Clemens made numerous marginal markings and notes in pencil and black ink in this memoir of Ross' mother, grandmother, and great-grandmother. The thirty-seven notes total 242 words. On page 14, beside a letter of 23 November 1776 from Susannah Cook to Judith Dixon, he wrote vertically in the margin: "It is a far call between these stilted, affected school-girl 'effusions' & Lady Duff Gordon's virile, straightforward, compact eloquence. However, she is only a child of 21." He underscored two words in a sentence on page 15—"I am soon to be *indissolubly united!*'—and then added wryly, "*married*, she means." On page 20 he observed: "Lady Duff would have slammed all this into four sentences—& they would be *pemmican*." Beneath a funeral poem written in 1798 by Anna Letitia Barbauld: "What a sing-song sentimental goody-goody age it was" (p. 23). Clemens became admiring: "She improves" (p. 24); "She's improving" (p. 27); "This whole letter is good. It's a prophecy of Lady Duff herself" (p. 29); "She has learned to write, now" (p. 31); "She is a very superior woman" (p. 33); similar comments appear on pages 39, 40, and 53. Of Sarah Austin, Clemens noted in black ink on page 56: "But *this* is a child of 21, too, yet there are no slops in her style." Clemens encountered another poem by Mrs. Barbauld ("To Sarah Taylor") on page 57; "It must be a good deal of a trial to have this kind of a poet always squirting at you," he remarked in black ink. On page 59 he underlined a reference to Lord Byron's "most secret depravity," and wrote in pencil: "Mrs. [Harriet Beecher]

Stowe." (Clemens's marginalia vary between ink and pencil, a stretch of each at a time.)

To the (underscored) suggestion that Anne Adkins "had gipsy blood in her veins" (p. 88), Clemens responded: "This accounts for Lady Duff." At page 218, beside a mention of "the deification of money by a whole people," Clemens observed: "America to-day, largely." "Well said," Clemens noted on page 242 where Sarah Austin dismissed the French language for imparting "an air of meaning to no meanings." Clemens labeled Sarah Austin's missive to Barthélemy St. Hilaire, 23 December 1859: "A beautiful & eloquent letter." Clemens commented "True" on page 349 concerning the comment that marriage avoids solitude. "How great she was!" he wrote on page 364. Clemens made pencil marks in the section devoted to Lady Duff-Gordon, especially in pages 529–560. *"She didn't know them,"* Clemens remarked on page 546 regarding Arabs. There are many other notes and markings. An empty envelope is laid loose in the volume; Clemens wrote "35 x 12" on it in pencil.

Catalogs: ListABP (1910), "Three Generations of Englishwomen, Ross"; *C1951*, #10a, $30; Catalogue 174 (1989), Heritage Book Shop, Los Angeles, California, " 8vo, original light green cloth, bit rubbed, . . . in a Chinese-red morocco slipcase," has the bookplate of Estelle Doheny, quotes the marginalia, item #205, priced at $6,000; Heritage Book Shop, Los Angeles, California, "Holiday Miscellany," Catalog 176 (1989), item #234, "Twain has made extensive comments in the margins," the volume derives "from the library of Estelle Doheny, with her bookplate on the front pastedown," $6,000.

Provenance: Carrie Estelle Doheny Collection, St. John's Seminary, Camarillo California. Donated by Mrs. Doheny in 1951 after she purchased it for $42 from Maxwell Hunley Rare Books of Beverly Hills. Christie's auctioned the volume (lot 1183) in New York City on 17 October 1988 for $2,750 on behalf of St. John's Seminary.

Location: currently unknown.

Copy examined: Clemens's copy, at St. John's Seminary in 1970.

Witter Bynner quoted a letter from Janet Ross that reported, "I am expecting Mr. Clemens here next month." He supplied no date (Bynner, *Prose Pieces*, ed. James Kraft [New York: Farrar Straus Giroux, 1979], p. 39). Ross edited her husband's *Letters from the East by Henry James Ross, 1837–1857* (1902) and also edited Lady Lucie Duff Gordon's *Letters from Egypt* (1904); see those Catalog entries. In *The Fourth Generation: Reminiscences by Jane Ross* (London: Constable, 1912) she would recall assisting Clemens with rental properties in Florence in 1892 and quoted from their correspondence. She also mentioned his singing spirituals and his tender regard for his wife Olivia.

ROSS, MALCOLM (1862–1930).

In Chapter 30 of *Following the Equator* (1897) Mark Twain says: "The population [of Dunedin, New Zealand] is stated at 40,000, by Malcolm Ross, journalist; stated by an M. P. at 60,000. A journalist cannot lie." Ross, a noted mountaineer, athlete, and journalist, moved from Otago, New Zealand (where he was a reporter for the Otago *Daily Times*) to Wellington, New Zealand in 1897. From there he wrote dispatches for various newspapers.

Scharnhorst, *Complete Interviews*, pp. 246–249.

ROSS, MARGARET ANN (1860–1939), pseud. "Emanda M'Kittrick Ros." *Delina Delaney*. Original glazed yellow decorated paper-covered boards, rebacked. Belfast, Ireland: R. Aickin, [n.d., cop. 1898]. 259 pp.

Inscription: the front pastedown endpaper is signed in ink "S L. Clemens/1906." Clemens or someone else heavily crossed out this signature at a later date.

Marginalia: notes and markings indicate Clemens's close reading of pages 51 ("He" changed to "She"), 170 ("plight" altered to "flight"), and 178 and 179 (ink X marks). Clemens made pencil marks at pages and 7–8, highlighting overwrought passages. Red pencil markings, possibly by Clemens, are present on twenty-three pages between pages 10 and 48, and also in a few other places. Tipped in at the front of the volume is a six-page typed copy of a hostile review of an earlier Ross novel written by Barry Pain that John Horner included when he sent Clemens this present book. (Ross caustically responded to Pain's criticisms in her preface to *Delina Delaney*.)

Catalog: ListABP (1910), "Delina Delaney (autograph of M. T.), Ros".

Provenance: displays Clara Clemens Gabrilowitsch's shelfmark from the period when she lived in Detroit; sold to a private buyer in June 1970 by the Seven Gables Bookshop, New York City.

Location: collection of Kevin Mac Donnell, Austin, Texas.

Copy examined: Clemens's copy, in July 2004.

Ross was an Irish poet and novelist. Emboldened by Clemens's delight with Ross' *Irene Iddesleigh*, John Horner of Belfast, Ireland mailed him a copy of another of her works, *Delina Delaney*, on 21 April 1906 (Horner's ALS in MTP). Horner requested a signed photograph of Clemens in return.

———. *Irene Iddesleigh*. Belfast, Ireland: W. & G. Baird, 1897. 189 pp.

Inscription: the bookplate of John Horner, Belfast, is affixed to front pastedown endpaper.

Marginalia: there are numerous pencil and black ink annotations by Clemens up to page 55. John Horner of Belfast sent the volume to him on 15 December 1905; Horner's accompanying letter is pinned to the front free endpaper.

Provenance: the volume contains the bookstamps and accession number of the Mark Twain Library, Redding, Connecticut.

Catalog: "Retz Appraisal" (1944), p. 11. Valued at $10.

Location: Mark Twain Papers, Bancroft Library, University of California at Berkeley.

Copy examined: Clemens's copy.

In a letter written to the book's sender on 12 January 1906, Clemens expressed immense pleasure in the "enchanting" volume, and speculated that Julia A. Moore's reign as undisputed Empress of the Hogwash Guild might finally be at an end (dictation copy of a TLS sent by Isabel V. Lyon, MTP). On 21 April 1906 Horner sent Clemens a copy of Ross' *Delina Delaney*, together with a copy of Barry Pain's humorous criticism of *Irene Iddesleigh* that had appeared in *Black and White* (ALS in MTP). See also the Catalog entry for Thomas Dagless, *The Light in Dends Wood, and Other Stories*.

ROSSETTI, CHRISTINA GEORGINA (1830–1894). "Rest" (poem, written in 1849).

Clara Clemens quoted a poem titled "Rest" in her commonplace book, possibly around 1888 (Paine 150, MTP). The speaker in the poem invites death to take charge of an ill person and end her suffering: "O Earth, lie heavily upon her eyes;/Seal her sweet eyes weary of watching Earth." Clara Clemens and her father often shared their reading.

ROSSETTI, DANTE GABRIEL (1828–1882), ed. and trans. *Dante and His Circle, with the Italian Poets Preceding Him (1100–1200–1300). A Collection of Lyrics*. Revised edition. London: Ellis and White, 1874. 468 pp.

Clemens showed cognizance of the Pre-Raphaelite School in 1890: "'Dante & his Circle' by Dante Rosetti" [*sic*], he wrote in Notebook 30 (*N&J* 3: 586).

———. *Hand and Soul*. Second ed. Limited edition of 450 copies. Tan cloth. Portland, Maine: The Germ, Thomas B. Mosher, 1900. 54 pp.

Provenance: Antenne-Dorrance Collection, Rice Lake, Wisconsin.

Location: Mark Twain Archive, Gannett-Tripp Learning Center, Elmira College, Elmira, New York

Copy examined: presumably Clemens's copy. Examined on 28 May 2015. See also the odd entry for Browning's *Rabbi Ben Ezra*.

———. *The Poetical Works of Dante Gabriel Rossetti. A New Edition in One Volume*. Ed. with preface by William M[ichael]. Rossetti (1829–1919). London: Ellis and Elvey, 1895. 380 pp.

Inscription: the half-title page is inscribed in ink: "To Clara L. Clemens/from/Carlyle Smythe" followed by an inscription in Greek. [Smythe was Mark Twain's lecture agent during part of his 1895–96 global lecture tour.]

Marginalia: someone marked many poem titles in the Table of Contents; these check-marks are not characteristic of Clemens. Pencil marks occur on page 130 (in "Rose Mary"), page 225 (in "A Superscription"), page 378, and page 380. The volume contains the sale label of the *C1951* auction.

Catalog: *Zeitlin 1951*, item #36, $3.

Location: Mark Twain Papers, Bancroft Library, University of California at Berkeley.

Copy examined: Clara Clemens's copy.

Rossetti was one of Susy Clemens's favorite poets when she was twelve and thirteen years old (*MFMT*, p. 66).

ROSSETTI, MARIA FRANCESCA (1827–1876). *A Shadow of Dante: An Essay Towards Studying Himself, His World and His Pilgrimage*. London: Rivingtons, 1871. 296 pp.

In 1890 Clemens noted: "'Shadow of Dante' by Miss Rossetti" (NB 30, *N&J* 3: 586).

ROSSINI, GIOACCHINO ANTONIO (1792–1868). *Il Barbiere di Siviglia [The Barber of Seville]* (opera, performed in Rome, 1816). Based on the comedy of Pierre Beaumarchais (1732–1799).

In a letter published in the *Daily Alta California* (22 September 1867), Mark Twain jokingly claimed to have located the Barber of Seville only to find that "with all that fellow's reputation, he was the worst barber on earth" (*TIA*, p. 55). "The comic basso [at concerts] . . . always sings the Barber" (*GA* [1873], Ch. 31).

———. *Elisabetta, Regina d'Inghilterra [Elizabeth, Queen of*

England] (opera, performed in Naples, 1815).

Clemens made notes for seeing this opera on 18 June 1873 at the Theatre Royal in Drury Lane, London (NB 12, *N&J* 1: 529). The London *Times* of 17 June 1873 advertised Madame Ristori in the role of Elizabeth (p. 8).

———. *Guillaume Tell [William Tell]* (opera, performed in Paris, 1829).

Clemens made a favorable reference to this opera in Notebook 16 (1878, *N&J* 2: 213).

ROSTAND, EDMOND (1868–1918). *L'Aiglon [The Eaglet]*. Green cloth, gilt design and lettering. Binding is damaged; the front leaves are loose. New York: Brentano's; Paris: Charpentier et Fasquelle, 1900. 260 pp.

Inscriptions: the bookplate of Helen Willoughby Underwood is affixed to the front pastedown endpaper. The front free endpaper is signed in black ink, "Helen Willoughby Underwood/June 4, 1901." Helen Willoughby Underwood (b. 1883) moved to Redding, Connecticut in 1902. The rear endpapers have been torn out.

Location: Mark Twain Library, Redding, Connecticut

Copy examined: conceivably a copy Clemens somehow obtained or was given, but the provenance makes this seem very dubious. The volume has no accession number or Mark Twain Library stamps. It was shelved with Clemens's books when Albert E. Stone, Jr. formed his checklist in 1955 and when I visited Redding in 1970, in June 1982, and on 9 November 2019.

ROUBAUD, E. *A French and English Dictionary*. 711th thousand. Later quarter cloth, with original gilt cloth spine cut down and used as a spine label. London: Cassell, [1904]. 1,122 pp.

Inscription: there is a barely visible signature (because of the rebinding job), "Clara Clemens/[illegible, possibly a date]/NY".

Marginalia: Clara Clemens's pencil notes appear on the verso of a front advertising leaf and the facing half-title page. The volume is well worn.

Provenance: bookplate of Nick Karanovich, Fort Wayne, Indiana, stating that he acquired this volume from Maurice Neville Books in 1983.

Location: collection of Kevin Mac Donnell, Austin, Texas.

Copy examined: Clara Clemens's copy, in July 2004.

ROUGET DE LISLE, CLAUDE JOSEPH (1760–1836). "La Marseillaise" (French national anthem, published in 1792). Words and music by Rouget de Lisle.

Clemens listed "the Marseilles Hymn in French" among the songs he had listened to at the Governor's house in "Letter from Carson City" published in the *Territorial Enterprise* on 3 February 1863 (*ET&S* 1: 197). He referred to "where they . . . sing March on march on ye brave, the 'venging sword unsheath' & so on" in Act I, scene 1 of "The *Quaker City* Holy Land Excursion," an unfinished play written in 1867 (MTP; *MTLet* 2: 406–414). "Tunes are good remembrancers. Almost every one I am familiar with, summons instantly a face when I hear it. It is so with the Marseillaise" (SLC to Olivia Langdon, Fort Plain, N. Y., 19 December 1868, *MFMT*, p. 23; *MTLet* 2: 334). "These Marseillaise make Marseillaise hymns," Twain quipped in Chapter 11 of *The Innocents Abroad* (1869). "La Marseillaise" was among the piano music in "The House Beautiful" (*LonMiss* [1883], Ch. 38). "Last night [in June 1894] a mob surrounded our hotel, shouting, howling,

singing the 'Marseillaise,' and pelting our windows with sticks and stones; for we have Italian waiters" ("A Scrap of Curious History" [published in 1914]). On 28 July 1906, in Dublin, New Hampshire, Isabel Lyon heard Clemens "singing the Marseillaise in lusty tones as he is drawing a bath for himself"; she added that "when the King sings very hard it means a perturbation of spirit; . . . it never stands for happiness" (IVL Journals, TS p. 175, MTP).

ROUSSEAU, JEAN JACQUES (1712–1778). *Les Confessions* (published in 1781 and 1788).

"The 'sights' of Geneva are not numerous. I made one attempt to hunt up the houses once inhabited by those two disagreeable people, Rousseau and Calvin, but had no success" (*TA* [1880], Ch. 47). "Rousseau confesses to masturbation, theft, lying, shameful treachery, & attempts made upon his person by Sodomites. But he tells it as a man who is *perfectly aware* of the shameful nature of these things, whereas your coward & your failure should be happy & sweet & unconscious" (SLC to Orion Clemens, 26 February 1880, *MTBus*, p. 144). "There are things in the Confessions of Rousseau which one must believe," Clemens wrote in 1886 (NB 26, *N&J* 3: 239), then added: "What is biography? Unadorned romance." Mark Twain planned to use Rousseau's *Confessions* as a source in his *Connecticut Yankee* appendix (Howard G. Baetzhold, "Course of Composition" [1961], p. 200). He included "Rousseau's Confession" [*sic*] among the literary items he would use in his projected "Back Number" magazine (NB 33, January 1894, TS p. 46). On Sunday, 14 January 1906, Clemens told Isabel Lyon that his autobiography "was going to be frank—not once but many times. (There were Rousseau confessions, but I am going to leave that kind alone, for Rousseau had looked after that end—)" (IVL Journals, TS p. 123, MTP; repeated in the IVL Journal, Harry Ransom Center, University of Texas at Austin). An Autobiographical Dictation that Clemens made on 23 February 1906 alluded to the lack of guilt detectable in "Rousseau and his 'Confessions'" (*AutoMT* 1: 378).

Stone, *IE* (1961), p. 270.

———. "Days of absence" (song, written in 1775). Words and music by Rousseau.

Mark Twain included "Days of Absence" among music on the piano in Chapter 38, "The House Beautiful," of *Life on the Mississippi* (1883).

ROUSSELET, LOUIS-THÉOPHILE MARIE (1845–1929). *India and Its Native Princes: Travels in Central India and in the Presidencies of Bombay and Bengal*. Revised and edited by Charles Randolph Buckle (1835–1920). [An illustrated travel book.]

Catalog: ListABP (1910), "India, Rousselet", no other information supplied.

Rousselet's *L'Inde des Rajas: Voyage dans l'Inde Central* was published in 1875 and Buckle's translation appeared in the next year. Both were profusely illustrated.

ROWELL, GEORGE PRESBURY (1838–1908). *American Newspaper Directory, 1888*. New York: George P. Rowell & Co., 1888.

Catalog: ListABP (1910), "Amer. Newspaper Directory, '88, Rowell".

———. *Forty Years an Advertising Agent, 1865–1905*. Portrait. New York: Printers' Ink Publishing Co., 1906. 517 pp.

Inscriptions: the front pastedown endpaper is signed "S L. Clemens/1906/ 21 Fifth Ave." Above Clemens's inscription," Rowell's widow added her own later inscription: "Presented to R. M. Kauffmann/by/Mrs. George P. Rowell/Christmas 1924/Below is Mark Twain's/autograph!/(and address)." Mrs. Rowell drew an arrow pointing to the *A1911* sale label that was signed by Albert Bigelow Paine, noting, "(Paine himself a well-known author)".

Catalog: *A1911*, "8vo, cloth, gilt top, N.Y. 1906," quotes the signature, lot 412, sold for $3.75.

Marginalia: no annotations, but three page corners are turned down as follows: pages 100–101, where Rowell discusses A. W. Fairbanks of Cleveland, the husband of Clemens's friend "Mother" Mary Mason Fairbanks (1828–1898); pages 104–105, where Rowell describes his encounter with Mark Twain early in Twain's career ("I remember him as a youthful, sandy complexioned person, not appearing to be particularly impressed with his surroundings at the moment, but very much in earnest in a resolve to ascertain whether or no, in the City of Hartford, such a much needed staple as a bottle of Bass's ale could be procured"); and pages 266–267, where Rowell discusses Petroleum V. Nasby (David Ross Locke) and a conversation at the Lotus Club, of which Clemens was a member.

Provenance: on the front free endpaper R. W. Kauffmann inscribed the book in 1949 to "Godfrey," his "advertising son".

Location: collection of Kevin Mac Donnell, Austin, Texas. Acquired in 2009.

Source: letter from Kevin Mac Donnell to Alan Gribben, 31 December 2009.

Rowell owned a large advertising agency. In 1905 he wrote a total of fifty-two reflective columns for *Printers' Ink*, a house organ he had initiated in 1888, and then collected these recollections in this volume. They describe many prominent newspapers and magazines with which he did business over the decades.

ROWLANDSON, MARY (c. 1637–1711). *The Narrative of the Captivity and the Restoration of Mrs. Mary Rowlandson* (captivity narrative, first published in 1682; the title varied among later editions).

Robert Tindol wondered if Mark Twain might have had this early American best-seller in mind in depicting Injun Joe in *The Adventures of Tom Sawyer* (1876) ("Tom Sawyer and Becky Thatcher in the Cave: An Anti-Captivity Narrative?," *Mark Twain Annual 7* [2009]: 118–126).

ROWLEY, CHARLES (1839–1933), comp. *Brotherhood with Nature: A Treasury.* Manchester: Sherratt & Hughes, 1904. 57 pp.

Source: MTLAcc, entry #2084, volume donated from Clemens's library by Clara Clemens Gabrilowitsch in 1910.

Rowley was a social reformer who founded the Ancoats Brotherhood to improve the emotional life of the industrial workers of Manchester by exposing them to art and literature. He caught the attention of many intellectuals of the day. *Brotherhood with Nature: A Treasury* collected English lyrical poems.

ROY, JUST JEAN ÉTIENNE (1794–1872). *Hugues Capet et Son Époque.* Troisième edition. Tours: Ad Mame et Cie, Imprimeurs Libraires, 1861. 187 pp.

Inscription: the bookplate of Ernest Lorine, 1862 is present.

Location: Mark Twain Library, Redding, Connecticut.

Copy examined: conceivably Clemens's copy, but the evidence is slim. No accession number or Library stamps. It was shelved with the Clemens family's library books when I revisited Redding in June 1982, but the reason for this was unclear and unconvincing.

ROYSTON, SAMUEL WATSON. (1815–1879). *An Address Delivered at Cumming, Georgia, February, 1844, on the Rise and Progress of Society and the Formation of Government.* New Haven, Connecticut: Printed for the Author, 1844. 16 pp.

Mark Twain quoted a line—"like the topmost topaz of an ancient tower"— in ridiculing this speech in Twain's "A Cure for the Blues" (1893).

———. *The Enemy Conquered; or, Love Triumphant. By S. Watson Royston, Author of "An Address," &c. Delivered at Cumming, Georgia, and Member of the Yale Law School.* New Haven, Connecticut: T. H. Pease, 1845. 31 pp.

Marginalia: two copies once owned by Clemens are extant. One lacks the paper wrappers and contains numerous markings in brown ink and pencil; the other has pencil markings throughout. Clemens cut out sentences, paragraphs, and entire pages from both copies, leaving the volumes much mutilated.

Location: two copies in the Mark Twain Papers, Bancroft Library, University of California at Berkeley.

Copies examined: Clemens's copies.

Clemens displayed a special brand of animosity whenever he detected inflated rhetoric in the writings of Southern authors. (See, for example, his infuriated excoriations of Belton O'Neall Towsend's *Plantation Lays and Other Poems* [1884].) Professor Francis Bacon of Yale College purportedly loaned a copy of this novelette to George Washington Cable, and Cable then introduced Clemens to the tale of Indian fighter Major Elfonzo's courtship of Ambulinia Valeer, a Southern belle. This sequence of events was established in Charles V. S. Borst's preface to *A Cure for the Blues* (Rutland, Vemont: Charles E. Tuttle, 1964), pp. vii-viii, which mistakenly dated the incident as occurring in February 1884. Albert Bigelow Paine also provided a version of how Clemens came to know this book (*Mark Twain: A Biography* [1912], pp. 765–767), but Paine changed the names of the author and title. On 29 January 1884 Clemens requested Charles L. Webster to procure him a copy of *The Enemy Conquered*, instructing Webster to "pay two or three dollars if necessary" (*MTBus*, p. 233). Charles V. S. Borst, accepting Paine's account, stated that the Reverend Joseph H. Twichell subsequently obtained six copies of *The Enemy Conquered* in New Haven for Clemens's private amusement, but that Clemens somehow misplaced these and appealed to Cable for another copy in 1889. "They are lost! I have searched everywhere & cannot find a vestige of that pamphlet," Clemens wrote to Cable. "I possess not a single book which I would not sooner have parted with" (*Cure*, p. viii). It was Cable who, in 1889, came through with more copies of the book for which Clemens hungered; and on the blue envelope in which he kept them Clemens wrote, "Cable's precious pamphlet/Ambulinia, written by a jackass" (MTP). Clemens made a note to remind himself to return "one of those old New Haven pamphlet novels" to Cable in 1889 (NB 29, *N&J* 3: 47, 490), and in 1891 he again referred to "Cable's New Haven Idiot's

Romance" (NB 31, TS p. 17).

Mark Twain then developed the idea of writing a satiric introduction and reprinting the entire novelette for the delectation of readers like himself who enjoyed examples of exquisitely bad literary efforts. However, Twain encountered trouble in convincing editors of its potential for humor. He sent the effort to *Harper's Monthly* in January 1892, titling it "A Curious Book" (*MTLP*, pp. 322–323), but Henry M. Alden declined it (*MTLP*, pp. 326–327). Twain next offered it to *The Century*, which recommended that Twain take the precaution of altering Royston's name and town (*MTLP*, p. pp. 329–330). Twain complied by changing Samuel Watson Royston to "G. Ragsdale Mc-Clintock," but *The Century* passed on the piece anyway. In the end Twain included the entire novelette, together with his mocking introduction, as "A Cure for the Blues" in *The £1,000,000 Bank-Note* (1893). Its publication drew scarcely any public attention.

Guy A. Cardwell's "Mark Twain's Failures in Comedy and *The Enemy Conquered*," *Georgia Review* 13.4 (Winter 1959): 424–436 corrected Albert Bigelow Paine's misinformation in *Mark Twain: A Biography* about Twain's interest in Samuel Watson Royston's novelette, sketched what little was then known about Royston's life, analyzed Twain's criticism of *The Enemy Conquered*, and linked Twain's assault on it to his ambivalent feelings toward George Washington Cable. In Cardwell's opinion, Twain's satirical "A Cure for the Blues" was far too lengthy and too "shrill." See also Cardwell's *Twins of Genius* (East Lansing: Michigan State College Press, 1953), p. 110.

Many additional facts have since emerged about Samuel Watson Royston. He never attempted another literary effort, but this had nothing to do with Twain's 1893 derision of Royston's feeble venture in 1845. Royston's mother, Elizabeth Watson (who died on 23 October 1860), was the daughter of the Reverend Samuel Watson. She married Joshua Royston on 25 June 1802 in South Carolina. Her son Samuel Watson Royston was born in Wilkes County, North Carolina, on 6 February 1815. The family moved to Tennessee when the boy was two years old. He graduated from the Yale law school in 1844, returned to his home state of Tennessee, was admitted to the bar in 1845, and became an attorney in Athens, Tennessee. A Yale alumni publication confused researchers by erroneously reporting that he was from Tuscaloosa, Alabama and that he had died in 1855. In reality he had received B.A. (in 1841) and M.A. degrees from Tusculum College (which had recently merged with Greeneville College) in Greeneville, Tennessee. In April 1848 Royston married Elizabeth "Lizzie" Parshall (born on 27 September 1826) and shortly after that he give up the practice of law and began farming four miles west of Athens. He was mentioned in legal deeds of 25 March 1851 (conveying the estate of his wife's deceased parents to him), 25 May 1867 (conveying his deceased sister-in-law's land to him), and 18 April 1873 (conveying a Deed of Trust from Royston and his wife to J. H. Gaut of Bradley County), as well as in a County Court lawsuit decree on 2 December 1867 in which Royston served as an administrator. His wife Elizabeth passed away on 24 January 1874, according to Athens, Tennessee newspapers. At the time of Royston's death

on 30 November 1879 he was still residing in McMinn County, Tennessee near Athens. Four of his children had preceded him in death but four others were still living. In brief, then, this unoffending lawyer-turned-farmer had quickly given up whatever youthful fantasy he once held of earning a literary reputation and instead dropped into a rural existence of hard work and family responsibilities.

RUGGLES, DAVID (1810–1849. *The Abrogation of the Seventh Commandment by the American Churches*. New York: David Ruggles, 1835. 23 pp. [Includes an illustration of an enslaved man being whipped. See the Catalog entry for William E. Channing's *Letter to J. G. Birney*, with which this and six other pamphlets were bound.]

Ruggles was an African American abolitionist in New York City who served as secretary of the New York Vigilance Society and assisted Frederick Douglass and many others who escaped from enslavement.

RULE, WILLIAM HARRIS (1802–1890). *History of the Inquisition from Its Establishment in the Twelfth Century to Its Extinction in the Nineteenth*. 2 vols. London: Hamilton, Adams and Co.; New York: Scribner, Welford and Co., 1874. [Edition conjectured.]

Catalog: *C1951*, D29, 2 vols., listed among books signed by Clemens, $25.

On 5 June 1874 Scribner, Welford & Armstrong of New York City sent Clemens a bill for "1 Rule's Inquisition 2v 1050 $8.40" (*MTLet* 6: 154); he paid for these volumes on 9 June 1874 (receipt in MTP).

RUNKLE, BERTHA (1879–1958). *The Helmet of Navarre*. Illustrated by André Castaigne (1861–1929). New York: Century Co., 1901. 470 pp.

Source: MTLAcc, entry #1065, volume donated by Clemens.

Runkle's novel of intrigue about sixteenth-century Paris and King Henry IV (1553–1610) was a romantic bestseller. She was also a contributor to *A House Party*, the composite novel edited by Paul Leicester Ford (see that Catalog entry).

RUSKIN, JOHN (1819–1900). *Letters to M. G. and H. G. [Mary Gladstone (1847–1927) and Helen Gladstone (1849–1925)]*. Preface by George Wyndham (1863–1913). New York: Harper & Brothers, 1903. 149 pp.

Source: MTLAcc, entry #1236, volume donated by Clemens.

———. *Modern Painters* (published in 1843–1860).

On 11 August 1878 Clemens decided that J[oseph]. M[allord]. W[illiam]. Turner's famous painting, "The Slave Ship" (1840), "is a manifest impossibility—that is to say, a lie." Yet he acknowledged: "Mr. Ruskin is educated in art up to a point where that picture throws him into as mad an ecstasy of pleasure as it throws me into one of rage" (NB 15, *N&J* 2: 139). In Chapter 24 of *A Tramp Abroad* (1880) Mark Twain elaborated: "Mr. Ruskin is educated in art up to a point where that picture throws him into as mad an ecstasy of pleasure as it used to throw me into one of rage, last year, when I was ignorant. . . . The most of the picture is a manifest impossibility,—that is to say, a lie; and only rigid cultivation can enable a man to find truth in a lie. But it enabled Mr. Ruskin to do it, and it has enabled me to do it, and I am thankful for it." Clemens's rejection of this particular painting never abated. "Slave Ship—Cat having a fit in a platter of tomatoes" (NB 14 [June 1878], *N&J* 2: 96). "What a red rag is to a bull, Turner's 'Slave Ship' is to me" (NB 15 [11 August 1878], *N&J* 2: 139). "There are pictures here [in Milan] as bad as the Slave Ship. They give you the belly-ache" (NB 16 [September 1878], *N&J* 2: 192). "Turner soon makes one sick at the stomach—it is partly intense admiration & partly the color" (NB 18 [1879], *N&J* 2: 337). In a footnote in Chapter 24 of *A Tramp Abroad* (1880), Twain remarked, "The Turners which attracted me most [in the National Gallery in London] did not remind me of the Slave Ship." He added, "What a red rag is to a bull, Turner's 'Slave Ship' was to me, before I studied art" (Ch. 24, *TA* [1880]). Clemens ridiculed the painting in a letter from Hartford to Elsie Leslie Lyde, 5 October 1889 (*Europe and Elsewhere* [1923], pp. 87–91). "It is just like his 'Slave Ship,' that immortal work. . . . A Boston reporter said it reminded him of a yellow cat dying in a platter of tomatoes" (Twain's "A Wonderful Pair of Slippers" [*St. Nicholas Magazine* 17.4 (February 1890): 390–312; *Europe and Elsewhere* (1923), pp. 87–91]). One has to wonder whether the subject of Turner's painting—human slavery—possibly pricked Clemens's conscience, reminding him of his early and later regretted support of a barbarous practice.

In any event, what exactly *did* Ruskin have to say about "The Slave Ship"? In Chapter 3 ("Of Water, As Painted by Turner"), Section 5, Part II of Volume I, *Modern Painters*, 5 vols. (London: Smith, Elder and Co., 1873), pp. 376–377, Ruskin declared: "But, I think, the noblest sea that Turner has ever painted, and, if so, the noblest certainly ever painted by man, is that of the Slave Ship. . . . The fire of the sunset falls along the trough of the sea, dyeing it with an awful but glorious light, the intense and lurid splendour which burns like gold, and bathes like blood. The tossing waves. . . . [are] lighted with green and lamp-like fire. . . . Purple and blue, the lurid shadows of the hollow breakers are cast upon the mist of night, which gathers cold and low, advancing like the shadow of death upon the guilty ship as it labours amidst the lightning of the sea, its thin masts written upon the sky in lines of blood." Ruskin concluded: "I believe, if I were reduced to test Turner's immortality upon any single work, I should choose this. Its daring conception, ideal in the highest sense of the word, is based on the purest truth, and wrought out with the concentrated knowledge of a life; its colour is absolutely perfect, not one false or morbid hue in any part or line, and so modulated that every square inch of canvas is a perfect composition."

Mark Twain's extended burlesque of art criticism in Chapter 48 of *A Tramp Abroad* (1880), especially his mockery of Leandro Bassano's painting, seems directed at Ruskin even though his name is not mentioned. Likewise, Twain may have been referring to Ruskin in Chapter 50 of *A Tramp Abroad* when he alluded to "the most famous of all the art critics" in discussing Titian's "Moses."

————, ed. *Roadside Songs of Tuscany*. Translation and illustrations by Francesca Alexander (1837–1917). 10 vols. Original buff boards, uncut. First American edition. New York: John Wiley & Sons, 1884–1885.

    Catalog: *A 1911*, "Parts I to IX (not consecutive), together

7 vols., 8vo, boards, uncut, N.Y. 1884–85," with a portion of a sheet of notes by Clemens, lot 414, sold for $3.75.

    Location: six volumes only (Parts I, II, V, VII, VIII and IX) acquired in 2010 by Kevin Mac Donnell of Austin, Texas. The *A1911* sale label is present in each volume.

    Source: letter to Alan Gribben from Kevin Mac Donnell, 29 March 2010; Mac Donnell sent a full description on 28 August 2017.

The prose stories are entirely in English, but the folk songs and poems are printed in parallel Italian and English texts.

————. *Sesame and Lilies: Three Lectures*. Complete Edition. Orpington: George Allen, 1899.

    Inscription: the front flyleaf is inscribed in black ink, "To/my dear Highness." [Isabel V. Lyon's pet names for Clemens were often variations of "The King."]

    Location: Mark Twain Library, Redding, Connecticut

    Copy examined: possibly Clemens's book (unmarked).

In *Sesame and Lilies* Ruskin expatiated on the responsibilities of men ("King's Treasuries") and the duties of women to guide men morally ("Queens' Gardens")." I found this volume on the circulation shelves of the Mark Twain Library when I visited Redding in 1970, and at my request the librarian added *Sesame and Lilies* to the collection of books believed to have belonged to Clemens.

————. *The Stones of Venice*. 3 vols. Illus. New York: John W. Lovell Co., [cop. 1884].

    Source: MTLAcc, entries #976–978, set of volumes donated by Clemens.

Olivia Clemens twice wrote "Ruskin's Stones of Venice (illustrated)" in Notebook 13a while she was in Venice in 1878 (TS p. 1, MTP). In 1878 (NB 16) Clemens referred to Ruskin's book in scoffing at Tintoretto's "The Magdalen"; disliking Tintoretto's "St. Mary of Egypt"; admiring Tintoretto's "Flight into Egypt"; and studying the Casa Grimini (*N&J* 2: 202–205). Cf. *The Stones of Venice*, 3 vols. (London: Smith, Elder and Co., 1873–1874), 3: 330, 331, and 328. In January 1882 Clemens entered in Notebook 20 an off-color joke that occurred to him about Whitelaw Reid: "He envied the stones of Venice" (*N&J* 2: 441).

————. *The True and the Beautiful in Nature, Art, Morals, and Religion*. With a notice of the author by Louisa C[aroline]. Tuthill (1798–1879). Third ed. Illus. New York: John Wiley and Son, 1859. 452 pp.

    Inscription: "Susie L. Crane, Elmira, June 18, 1860".

    Catalog: Ball 2016 inventory, brown textured cloth, gilt lettering and design, poor condition.

    Location: Quarry Farm library shelves, under the supervision of the Mark Twain Archive, Elmira College, Elmira, New York.

Clemens had access to this book at Quarry Farm in Elmira.

————. *The True and the Beautiful in Nature, Art, Morals, and Religion*. With a notice of the author by Louisa C[aroline]. Tuthill (1798–1879). Illus. New York: John Wiley and Son, 1868. 452 pp.

    Provenance: displays bookplate #436 of the "J. Langdon Family Library."

    Catalog: Ball 2016 inventory, brown textured cloth, gilt lettering and design partly fallen off or removed, fair condition, marginalia.

    Location: Quarry Farm library shelves, under the

supervision of the Mark Twain Archive, Elmira College, Elmira, New York.

Copy examined: an unmarked copy to which Clemens had access whenever he visited Elmira. Examined on 26 May 2015. (The Ball 2016 inventory reported marginalia, but I did not spot any.)

RUSSELL, CHARLES TAZE (1852–1916). *Millennial Dawn: The Plan of the Ages.* [6 vols.] Allegheny, Pennsylvania: Watch Tower Bible and Tract Society, 1904.

Source: MTLAcc, entry #920, Volume I only (374 pp.) donated by Clemens.

On 30 September Clemens received and annotated a twenty-two-page tract from the Watch Tower Society (CU-MARK, UCLC 24192).

RUSSELL, GEORGE WILLIAM ERSKINE (1853–1919). *An Onlooker's Note-book.* New York: Harper & Brothers, 1902. 310 pp.

Source: MTLAcc, entry #1808, volume donated by Clemens.

Russell gathers here forty-three columns he published in the Manchester *Guardian* consisting of history and commentary about the English social classes, religion, monarchy, and political history.

RUSSELL, MICHAEL (BISHOP OF GLASGOW AND GALLOWAY) (1781–1848). *Polynesia; or, an Historical Account of the Principal islands of the South Sea including New Zealand; the Introduction of Christianity; and the Actual Conditions of the Inhabitants.* New York: Harper & Brothers, 1843. 362 pp. [Edition conjectured.]

In Chapter 6 of *Following the Equator* (1897) Mark Twain disparagingly quotes Russell's Manifest Destiny vision of civilizing the Pacific islands, calling it a "hand-painted rhapsody." Russell's book urged reliance on missionaries. Madigan, "MT's Passage to India" (1974), p. 364.

RUSSELL, MORRIS CRAW (1840–1913). *Uncle Dudley's Odd Hours; Being the Vagaries of a Country Editor. Also , as an Appendix, J[ames]. Proctor Knott's [1830–1911] Famous Speech on Duluth.* Duluth, Minnesota: Compiled and Published by Susie M. Russell, 1882. 296 pp.

Source: MTLAcc, entry #845, volume donated by Clemens.

RUSSELL, ROBERT (1843–1910). *Natal, the Land and its Story.* Pietermaritzburg: P. Davis and Sons, 1891.

"Also, quote what Russell ('Natal') says about reserving worthless lands for natives" (NB 38 [May 1896], TS p. 5). "I will cull some details of it [the Boer British war of 1881] from trustworthy sources—mainly from 'Russell's Natal.' Mr. Russell is not a Boer, but a Briton. He is inspector of schools, and his history is a text-book whose purpose in the instruction of the Natal English youth" (*FE* [1897], Ch. 67).

Madigan, "MT's Passage to India" (1974), p. 364.

RUSSELL, WILLIAM CLARK (1844–1911). *Alone on a Wide Wide Sea: A Novel.* 3 vols. London: Chatto & Windus, 1892.

On 16 July 1899 Clemens asked Chatto & Windus to "send a couple of the *very best* of Clark Russell's sea-tales that you've got in stock" (CU-MARK, UCCL 10570). Percy Spalding of Chatto & Windus wrote to Clemens on 20 July 1899: "In reply to your letter I am sending you two of Clark Russell's sea stories, 'Wide Wide Sea' & 'Convict Ship,' both of which I think you will like" (ALS in MTP).

———. *The Convict Ship.* 3 vols. London: Chatto & Windus,

1895. See the previous Catalog entry.

———. *Representative Actors. A Collection of Criticisms, Anecdotes, Personal Descriptions, Etc., Etc., Referring to Many Celebrated British Actors from the Sixteenth to the Present Century; With Notes, Memoirs, and a Short Account of English Acting.* "The Chandos Classics" Series. Decorated green cloth, gilt lettering. London: Frederick Warne and Co.; New York: Scribner, Welford and Armstrong, [1888]. 496 pp. [Initially published in 1872; a new edition had appeared in 1875.]

Inscription: the front free endpaper is signed in black ink, "Clara L. Clemens/Adelaide Oct. 1895/ Australia." A bookseller's sticker is affixed to the front pastedown endpaper: "Cole's Book Arcade/67, Rundle Street."

Marginalia: no markings, but page 223—"Miss Linley (Mrs. Sheridan)"—is turned down. Page xv is loose.

Location: Mark Twain Library, Redding, Connecticut

Copy examined: Clara Clemens's unmarked copy. Has the red ink Mark Twain Library accession number "3716" and the purple Library stamps. Examined in 1970 and again in June 1982 and on 9 November 2019.

———. *Round the Galley Fire.* New ed. London: Chatto & Windus, 1893. 308 pp.

On 3 January 1895 Clemens asked Andrew Chatto to compare "the paper, binding & printing costs" of two books published by Chatto & Windus—"Pudd'nhead Wilson' & Clark Russell's 'Round the Galley Fire.' Is this blue cover of the latter *cloth*? It looks like some kind of leather" (ALS, Mark Twain Boyhood Home and Museum, Hannibal, Missouri). The same letter thanked Chatto for sending the Clemens family "a charming variety" of books.

———. *Sailors' Language: A Collection of Sea-Terms and Their Definitions.* London: Sampson Low & Co., 1883. 164 pp.

Mark Twain parodied this work with his own "Glossary of Sea-Terms" (DV332, MTP), possibly written in 1898, in which he claimed that his absurd definitions were "carefully examined by Mr. W. Clark Russell [,] the best living expert in sea terminology" (*WWD?*, p. 15).

———. *A Sailor's Sweetheart. An Account of the Wreck of the Sailing Ship "Waldershare," from the Narrative of Mr. William Lee, Second Mate.* No. 142, Franklin Square Library Series. New York: Harper & Brothers, 1880. 81 pp.

Shortly after noting the title of Russell's *Wreck of the "Grosvenor"* in Notebook 19 (1881), Clemens added "Sailor's Sweetheart 142" (*N&J2*: 393, 395). "Please send me No's 68 and 142 of Harper's Franklin Square Library (Green Hand [by George Cupples] and Sailor's Sweetheart.)," Clemens directed James R. Osgood on 23 May 1881 (*MTLP*, p. 136). Albert B. Stone, Jr. (*IE* [1961], p. 161) and Walter Blair (*HH&T* [1969], p. 145) suggested that Clemens utilized these stories as sources for the undated fragment, "Tom Sawyer's Gang Plans a Naval Battle."

———. *The Wreck of the "Grosvenor." An Account of the Mutiny of the Crew and the Loss of the Ship When Trying to Make the Bermudas.* No. 301, Franklin Square Library Series. New York: Harper & Brothers, [1883]. 64 pp. [Novel, first published in 1877.]

Clemens noted the title in Notebook 19 (1881, *N&J2*: 393). Around 1895 Mark Twain produced an uncompleted essay which he intended to form part of the critical series begun with two critiques of James Fenimore Cooper ; he titled this one "Studies in Literary Criticism/Lecture IV.

'The Wreck of the Grosvenor'" (DV 6, MTP). He opens his essay by complimenting Russell, and then never gets around to any objections. The persona, "Mark Twain, M. A., Professor of Belles Lettres in the Veterinary College of Arizona," writes in a mode of burlesque criticism, half serious and half facetious. Russell's tale "has no superior in the literature of the sea, and perhaps no equal"; it contains "truthful and marvelously vivid sea-pictures." Twain recounts the various plot developments, and then prepares to point out the one defect in seamanship in "this thoroughly charming story"—the handling of the ship by Royle, the navigator, after its abandonment by the mutinous crew. But here the essay stops.

Whatever literary icons Twain admired—such as Thomas Malory's *Morte d'Arthur*—he itched to imitate and burlesque. On Regina notepaper associated only with Twain's writings of June 1895, he began a fragmentary manuscript of fourteen-and-a-half pages, titled by Albert Bigelow Paine, "Burlesque Sea Story" (DV331, MTP). All the details of this fanciful narrative accord with those in *The Wreck of the "Grosvenor."* A young girl named Gwendolen is wooed by Albert, the mate on a mutineers' ship at sea. Twice Gwendolen alludes to "Russell's enchanting descriptions" of sea life (Twain later cancelled her second reference to Russell). The mate's technical directions about trimming the sails repeatedly interrupt the lovers' intimate, romantic talks. Several descriptions of ocean scenes are modeled on purple passages in Russell's prose. The tale breaks off when the ship's crew mysteriously vanishes, though the girl notes optimistically that Russell always saves the lives of his heroes and heroines.

In November 1896, in London, Twain recalled that "the officers of the Warrimoo said Clark Russell didn't know anything about ships. I doubt it" (NB 39, TS p. 22). John S. Tuckey suggested that Twain's abortive draft, "Statement of Captain Murchison" (DV 332, MTP), written around 1898, owed its comic nautical terminology to Twain's impulse to burlesque Russell (*WWD?*, pp. 15–16).

▌ S

Saadi [Sa 'dī], Musharrif al-Dīn ibu Muslih-al-Dīn, known as Saadi of Shiraz (c. 1213–1291). *The Gulistan; or, Rose Garden, by Musle-Huddeen Sheik Saadi, of Shiraz.* Translated by Francis Gladwin (c. 1745–1812). Biographical essay by James Ross (1759–1831). Preface by Ralph Waldo Emerson (1803–1882). First edition, first binding. 12mo, original terra cotta cloth, lettered gilt on supper cover and spine, beveled edges, top edge gilt, pale blue coated endpapers. Boston: Ticknor and Fields, 1865. 379 pp.

 Inscription: the front free endpaper is signed in black ink, "Saml L. Clemens/Hartford, 1875." A price of "$20.00" is written on the rear free endpaper.

 Catalogs: *A1911*, "first edition, 12mo, original cloth, gilt top, Bost. 1865," quotes the signature, lot 153, sold for $8.50; Christie's, New York City, 20 May 1988, "extremities slightly rubbed, front inner hinge tender, half-morocco slipcase," lot 158, price estimate $400–600. Purchased by John L. Feldman"; "The James S. Copley Library," Sotheby's auction, New York City,17 June 2010, lot 555, sold with five other titles for $4,250.

 Provenance: at one time owned by Willard S. Morse and

later (prior to 1988) by Lazare M. Kauffman. John L. Feldman of Astoria, New York placed this volume on deposit in the Special Collections at the University of Colorado, but later withdrew it.

 Location: collection of Kevin Mac Donnell, Austin, Texas. Acquired in 2010.

 Source: letter from Kevin Mac Donnell to Alan Gribben, 29 June 2010. Mac Donnell reported that the volume contains no annotations. It has the *A1911* auction label.

 One section of *The Gulistan; or, Rose Garden,* "On the Morals of Kings," collects forty-one short parables illustrating the wisdom of rulers. Another section consists of 106 "Rules for the Conduct of Life." Other sections of short stories depict the effects of old age, youth, love, and other human conditions. Twain's later affection for Omar Khayyám's *Rubáiyát* seems relevant to this entry.

Sabin, Oliver Corwin (1840–1914). *Christology—Science of Health and Happiness; or, Metaphysical Healing Exemplified—Through Rules, Formulas and Incidents.* Washington: News Letter Press, 1901. 315 pp.

 Source: MTLAcc, entry #487, volume donated by Clemens. Sabin was a proponent of Christian Science whose *Washington News Letter* approved of its beliefs, but independently he was also the president and chief instructor of the International Metaphysical University of Washington, D. C. and the author of numerous pamphlets and books that advocated spiritual healing.

Sach, August (1837–1929). *Die Deutsche Heimat. Landschaft und Volktstum [The German Homeland. Landscape and Folklore].* Spine broken, poor condition. Halle: Weisenhauses, 1885. 660 pp.

 Inscription: the half-title page was inscribed in black ink by Olivia Clemens: "Susy Clemens/Dec 25th 1885/ Mamma". The bookseller's stamp of "Gustave Stechert, 766 Broadway, New York" was placed on the front pastedown endpaper.

 Catalog: *Mott 1952*, item #81, $4.50.

 Location: Mark Twain House and Museum, Hartford, Connecticut. Donated anonymously in 1963.

 Copy examined: Susy Clemens's unmarked copy. Examined in August 1987.

Sadler, James (1860–1935). *Lyrics and Rhymes, by Ab. Original.* Adelaide: E. S. Wigg, 1890. 163 pp.

 Catalog: ListABP (1910), "Lyrics and Rhymes, Sadler", no other information supplied.

 Born in Adelaide, the journalist and poet James Sadler became a London correspondent but traveled often to Australia. Sadler published this volume under the pseudonym "Ab. Original." Clemens wrote to Sadler while visiting Adelaide on 16 October 1895 to thank him for the book and a "most pleasant hour" they spent together," adding that Olivia has pasted "the poem 'To Mark Twain' in it" (Fears, *Day by Day* 2: 1069).

Sadlier, Mary Anne (Madden) (1820–1903), "Mrs. James Sadlier." *The Spanish Cavaliers: A Tale of the Moorish Wars in Spain.* Translated from the French. Illus. New York: D. & J. Sadlier & Co., 1866. 203 pp.

 Inscription: a bookplate was torn off the front pastedown endpaper, leaving only a fragment of it visible. The bottom corner was torn off the illustration facing the half-title page.

Location: Mark Twain Library, Redding, Connecticut.

Copy examined: very likely Clemens or Olivia Clemens's very worn copy, unmarked. It has the red ink Mark Twain Library accession number "3110" and the purple oval Library stamps. Examined in 1970 and again in June 1982 and on 9 November 2019.

SAGE, DEAN (1841–1902). *The Ristigouche and Its Salmon Fishing. With a Chapter on Angling Literature.* Illus. Edinburgh: D. Douglas, 1888. 275 pp. [Publisher and pages conjectured.]

   Catalog: *A1911,* "finely illustrated with full-page etchings on Japan paper, photogravure plates, etc., imp. 8vo, original dark green buckram, uncut, Edinb. 1888, only 105 copies printed," lot 416, sold for $105.

———. "Ten Days' Sport on Salmon Rivers," *Atlantic Monthly* 36.214 (August 1875): 142–151.

   Clemens informed Sage on 22 April 1875 that William Dean Howells had Sage's manuscript, and that Howells "has long been praying" for someone "who could write about wood & water sports without being dreary" (*MTLet* 6: 452). To Howells on 14 May 1876 Clemens praised another of Sage's nature sketches (one which Howells decided not to accept for the *Atlantic*); Clemens wrote that he and Olivia Clemens read Sage's works "not because we care 2 cents about hunting & fishing," but because of Sage's "admirable gift in narrative-writing." Clemens declared: "The simplicity, the frozen truth, the homely phraseology—no use talking, this is the best & the happiest narrative-talent that has tackled pen since Thoreau" (*MTHL,* p. 138). An installment of Mark Twain's "Old Times on the Mississippi" appeared on pages 190–196 of the same August 1875 issue of the *Atlantic Monthly* in which Howells published Sage's salmon-fishing essay.

"SAIL AWAY, LADIES" (traditional folk song).

   Clemens seems to have improvised some stanzas that converted this folk song into an invented plantation spiritual in 1887. The original lyrics begin: "Ain't no use to sit and cry/Sail away, ladies, sail away./You'll be an angel by and by,/Sail away, ladies, sail away." Clemens's version differed considerably; it opened, "No use for to weep & cry in de morn,/*You*'ll be an angel by & by,/Dig up de *ta*ters, hoe *up* de corn,/You'll be—" (NB 27, *N&J* 3: 310).

SAINT-AMAND, [ARTHUR-LÉON] IMBERT DE (1834–1900). *La Jeunesse de l'Impératrice Joséphine.* [First published in Paris in 1883.]

   Jean Clemens read aloud to Isabel V. Lyon from this book (in French) on one occasion while Clemens was away visiting Clara (IVL Journal, 16 August 1905, TS p. 89, MTP).

SAINTE-BEUVE, CHARLES AUGUSTIN (1804–1869). *Memoirs of Mme. Desbordes-Valmore.* Translated. from the French by Harriet W[aters]. Preston (1836–1911). Boston: Roberts Brothers, 1873. 227 pp.

   Catalog: *C1951,* D52, "Memoirs of Madame Desbordes-Valmore."

   Sainte-Beuve's biography of the French poet, actress, and woman of letters Marceline Félicité Josèphe Desbordes-Valmore (1786–1859) reprinted a number of her poems as well as extracts from her letters to eminent literary figures.

———. *Monday-Chats, Selected and Translated from the "Causeries du Lundi," with an Introductory Essay on the Life and Writings of Sainte-Beuve, by William Mathews [1818–1909].*

Chicago: S. C. Griggs and Co., 1877. 298 pp. [Publisher and pages conjectured.]

   Inscription: signed, "S. L. Clemens, Hartford, 1878."

   Marginalia: some passages marked with pencil.

   Catalog: *A1911,* "12mo, cloth, Chicago, 1877," quotes the signature and describes the marginalia, lot 417, sold for $6.50 to Jervis Langdon.

   William Mathews provides a lengthy appraisal of Sainte-Beuve's career and then presents the literary critic and historian's essays on Louis XIV, Fenelon, Bossuet, Massillon, Pascal, Rousseau, Madame Geoffrin, Joubert, Guizot, the Abbé Galiani, and Frederick the Great, King of Prussa.

SAINT-GAUDENS, AUGUSTUS (1848–1907).

   Trying to encourage the young sculptor Karl Gerhardt (1853–1940), who had become his protégé, Clemens name-dropped in a letter of 30 May 1881 from Hartford: "St. Gaudens called the other day, but we were out. His Farragut has received boundless praise, from the press & from everybody. No statue in America has had the like good fortune before, so we are all delighted" (*Sotheby's 2003*). Saint-Gaudens's statue of Admiral David G. Farragut stood on a pedestal designed by Stanford White in Madison Square in New York City.

SAINT-GERMAIN, (COMTE) C. DE (C.1710–1784), comp. and ed. *Practical Hypnotism: Theories and Experiments.* Original blue pictorial boards, with the spine badly chipped and badly taped. Half blue morocco folding-case. Chicago: Laird & Lee, [1901]. 260 pp.

   Inscription: the front flyleaf is inscribed in blue ink, possibly by Clara Clemens Gabrilowitsch in her later years, "This book was the property of Mark Twain/C. C." (The "C. C." initials were added with a ball point pen in blue ink.) The handwriting does not convincingly resemble Clara's.

   Marginalia: vertical pencil marks, conceivably by Clemens but much heavier than his usual ones, on pages xvii and xviii of the preface.

   Catalogs: *Fleming 1972;* Sotheby Parke Bernet, Sale number 3482 (25 February 1976), "8vo, original binding, quarter morocco slip case," from a New York City collector, lot 20; "Victor and Irene Murr Jacobs Collection," Sotheby's, New York City, 29 October 1996, lot 313, sold with four other books for a total of $9,312; *Sotheby's 2003,* #231, $2,500 (sold with three other titles).

   Provenance: the book's whereabouts are unknown until it was listed for sale by John F. Fleming in New York City in March 1972. In 1986 it belonged to Victor Jacobs of Dayton, Ohio (Jacobs to Alan Gribben, 15 October 1986, "inscribed on front flyleaf: This book was the property of Mark Twain. Signed C. C."). Eventually the volume was purchased from Robert Slotta by Nick Karanovich of Fort Wayne, Indiana.

   Location: collection of Kevin Mac Donnell, Austin, Texas.

   Copy examined: purportedly Clemens's copy, in July 2004. A plausible but still somewhat dubious association copy. Clemens and his wife cast about desperately for therapies to alleviate Jean Clemens's epilepsy, so this book would be a possible acquisition. But why did it not show up anywhere until 1972, and then with such unconvincing inscriptions?

SAINTINE, JOSEPH XAVIER BONIFACE (1798–1865). *The Myths of the Rhine.* Translated from the French by Maximilian Schele de Vere (1820–1898). Illustrated by [Paul] Gustave Doré

(1832–1883). Original pictorial cloth. Spine ends rubbed with loss, cloth split at joints, tape stains on the binding, hinges badly cracked. New York: Scribner, Armstrong, and Co., 1875. 423 pp.

Inscription: inscribed by Olivia Clemens, "Merry Christmas to Papa/From Susie and 'Ba'/1874." (That was the Clemenses' first Christmas in their new Hartford house.)

Provenance: has the shelfmarks of the library numbering system employed by Clara Clemens Gabrilowitsch during her years in Detroit.

Catalogs: *C1951*, 59a, listed among volumes containing Clemens's marginalia, $35; "Property from Mark Twain's Library," Butterfield & Butterfield, San Francisco, Sale 6613 (16 July 1997), lot 2690.

Location: Mark Twain House and Museum, Hartford, Connecticut.

Copy examined: Clemens's unmarked copy. Viewed in Hartford in 1997.

———. *Picciola* (novel, published in 1836). [Subsequent English editions were published with the titles *Picciola; or, The Prison Flower. A Tale* as well as *Picciola; The Prisoner of Fenestrella*.]

"I . . . have also begun Picciola in French" (SLC to Mollie Fairbanks, Elmira, 6 August 1877, *MTMF*, p. 209). Much of Saintine's novel is set in a mountaintop dungeon where the morale and sanity of a political prisoner, the Comte de Charney, are salvaged by a stray seed that drifts into his cell and, under his watering and nurturing, grows into a plant capable of blooming. In Chapter 38 of Mark Twain's *Huckleberry Finn* (1885), Tom Sawyer urges Jim to plant a flower in the corner of his prison cell, "and don't call it mullen, call it Pitchiola—that's its right name, when it's in a prison. And you want to water it with your tears." Walter Blair revealed that Twain originally intended for Tom to instruct Jim to arise early every morning to tend his plant—but he deleted this passage from the manuscript of the novel (Blair, "French Revolution," pp. 23–24). While the Clemenses vacationed for Olivia Clemens's health in York Harbor, Maine, in 1902, a news reporter noted that Clemens's room displayed "an author's carelessness. An edition of Saintine's *Picciola* lay on a table in the centre of the room. One of the villainous-looking cigars had been left on it" ("'My First Vacation and My Last'—Mark Twain," New York *World Magazine*, 7 September 1902; reprinted in Charles Neider, ed. *Mark Twain: Life as I Find It* [1961], p. 363; and by Gary Scharnhorst, ed., *Complete Interviews* [2006], p. 473).

ST. LOUIS *Republican* (newspaper).

In "A General Reply" (*Galaxy* 10.5 [November 1870]: 732), Mark Twain recalls writing several pieces for the *Republican* when he was sixteen or seventeen—but he lost his nerve when he went to the editor's office with his manuscripts (a *Galaxy* piece reprinted in Charles Neider, ed., *Mark Twain: Life as I Find It* [1961], p. 70; Budd, *CTSS&E* 1 [1992], pp. 484–485). While Twain was collecting stories of lynchings in the American South in 1901, he advised Frank E. Bliss that "the *best* & fullest source will always be the *principal* paper in the *chief city* of the State where a lynching has occurred." Accordingly, he urged Bliss to hire someone to search the files of the St. Louis *Republican* for 1835 and 1849 (SLC to Bliss, 26 August 1901, ALS,

Harry Ransom Center, University of Texas at Austin).

SAINT MAUR, KATE (VANDENHOFF) (1866–1942). *The Earth's Bounty*. With many illustrations from photographs. Green decorated cloth. New York: Macmillan & Co., 1909. 430 pp.

Marginalia: Clemens severely edited (in pencil) Chapter 13, "Dogs"; his pencil marks and comments occur between pages 362 and 378. He crossed out much of the chapter as superfluous; these deletions did not result from prudishness, since he retained many observations about dog breeding. On page 378 he wrote the word "end" in the margin, and there are no further markings. Clemens pinned something to page 372—the pin is still stuck in the page.

Location: Mark Twain Library, Redding, Connecticut.

Copy examined: Clemens's copy. No red ink accession number, but it displays the purple oval Mark Twain Library stamps. Examined in 1970 and again in June 1982 and on 9 November 2019.

Kate Vandenhoff, born in Seneca Falls, New York, had a stage career before she married the English actor Harry Saint Maur in 1894. They eventually moved to West Redding, Connecticut, where her huband died in 1907. In 1908 she met a newly arrived Redding resident, Samuel L. Clemens. She would become one of the librarians for the community library that Clemens helped found in Redding.

The Earth's Bounty offered practical advice on the breeding, raising, and marketing of various crops and animals. Her subjects ranged from winter violets, orchards, and wood-lots to cattle, horses, quail, goats, and even toy dogs.

St. Nicholas: A Magazine for Boys and Girls (New York, published 1873–1940).

On 24 March 1874 Clemens praised a story by Thomas Bailey Aldrich, "The Little Violinist," that appeared in the April 1874 issue of the magazine Mary Mapes Dodge (1831–1905) edited from 1873 until 1905 (*MTLet* 6: 91). In a letter to Frank E. Bliss written on 10 May 1879, Clemens mentioned the recent illustrations that Walter Francis Brown (1853–1929) did for *St. Nicholas* (*MTLP*, p. 114; *N&J* 2: 317 n. 55). Brown would be one of the illustrators for Twain's *A Tramp Abroad* (1880). The Mark Twain Papers in the Bancroft Library at Berkeley contain a receipt dated 23 December 1879 from Scribner & Company of New York City, crediting Clemens with payment for a subscription to *St. Nicholas* from January 1880 through December 1880. It is probably only a coincidence that Clemens disparaged the hermit St. Nicholas ("he has ranked for ages as the peculiar friend of children, yet it appears he was not much of a friend to his own") in Chapter 31 of *A Tramp Abroad* (1880). Clemens admired the clever art-work of Reginald Bathurst Birch (1856–1943) "in the St. Nicholas for January last" (SLC to Frederick J. Hall, 2 July 1889, MTP).

ST. PAUL *Pioneer Press* (newspaper).

In Chapter 55 of *Life on the Mississippi* (1883) Mark Twain quotes statistics about St. Paul's commercial growth taken from "a recent number of the leading St. Paul paper, the 'Pioneer Press.'"

SAINT-PIERRE, JACQUES-HENRI BERNARDIN DE (1737–1814). *Paul et Virginie* (novel, published in 1788).

In Chapter 62 of Mark Twain's *Following the Equator* (1897), Twain explains that Mauritius is the "scene of the sentimental adventure of Paul and Virginia." Their "romantic sojourn" was the only prominent event in the history of Mauritius, he says; however, it "didn't happen." A citizen informs Twain that this book "is the greatest story that was ever written about Mauritius, and the only one." A tragic "pastorale," the novel recounted the tale of two lovers kept apart by their mothers. Virginie dies in a shipwreck, Paul from grief over her fate, and the two mothers succumb to sorrow.

SAINTSBURY, GEORGE EDWARD BATEMAN (1845–1933). *The Earl of Derby.* New York: Harper & Brothers, 1892. 223 pp.

Source: MTLAcc, entry #1788, volume donated by Clemens.

The English historian and literary critic Saintsbury wrote this biography about the wealthy British statesman Edward George Geoffrey Smith Stanley, the Fourteenth Earl of Derby (1799–1869), who served as Prime Minister three times.

SAINT-SIMON, LOUIS DE ROUVROY, DUC DE (1675–1755). *The Memoirs of the Duke of Saint-Simon on the Reign of Louis XIV [1638–1715] and the Regency.* Translated from the French by Bayle St. John (1822–1859). 3 vols. London: Bickers and Son, [c. 1880]. [The publisher's house list at rear of Volume I is dated July 1880.]

Inscriptions: the front free endpaper of Volume I is signed in blue ink "S. L. Clemens/Hartford, Nov. 1881." The front pastedown endpapers of Volumes II and III are signed in blue ink: "SL. Clemens".

Marginalia: on the front free endpaper of Volume I, above Clemens's signature, he commented in blue ink: "This, & Casanova & Pepys, set in parallel columns, would afford a good coup d'oeil of French & English high life of that epoch" (quoted in *MTB*, p. 1536, where Albert Bigelow Paine characterized Clemens's marginalia and gave six examples). Walter Blair (*MT&HF* [1960], p. 283), Roger Salomon (*TIH* [1961], pp. 23–24), and Arthur L. Scott (*MTAL* [1969], p. 134) also quoted marginalia. On page 86 of Volume I Clemens remarked in pencil, "The Court is a family of cats & dogs who are always quarreling over scraps of offal." On page 125 (pencil): "Louis the Louse, King of the Lice." Page 157 (pencil): "Still, God made these vermin, & by this we know that to Him they were dear. We all have our tastes." Page 200 (black ink): "Persistence in making French people is but little creditable to God." Page 375 (purple pencil): "From the year AD 300 to the year 1800 may be described as the age of pious W——s." Clemens added a penciled subtitle to the half-title page in Volume II: "A Record of Interesting Incidents illustrating Life in the royal sty in the days of Louis XIV, the Favorite of God." Page 117 of Volume II contains additional invectives in the margin: "These low scoundrels, these shams, these play-acting sentimental pukes!/How French it all is!" In Volume III Clemens dated a note in black ink on page 9 as written on 30 December 1908; he referred to Nathaniel Shaler's *Aspects of the Earth.* On page 25 (in purple pencil) Clemens called the court "gilded lice." Page 256 (pencil): "Oh, selfishness and general hellfiredness is [*sic*] not confined to the poor & the lowly." A note in brown ink on page 313 is dated 29 July 1909. The three volumes contain numerous other notes and markings.

Catalogs: ListABP (1910), "Memoirs of Duke of St. Simon

3 v., St. John"; *C1951*, #13a, 3 vols., $60. Purchased by Wilbur J. Smith, Special Collections Librarian, University of California at Los Angeles.

Location: Mark Twain Papers, Bancroft Library, University of California at Berkeley. Presented by Wilbur J. Smith of the University of California at Los Angeles.

Copies examined: Clemens's copies.

An entry Clemens made in Notebook 19 in November 1881 reads, "St Simon in French" (*N&J* 2: 402). On 14 January 1884 Clemens informed Edward H. House from Hartford that he had just read "the third volume of Saint-Simon" in English and "the tenth volume of Saint-Simon" in French (ALS in CWB). In 1886 Clemens wrote cryptically: "Studies for that article: Balzac, Shakspeare, Saint Simon," adding, "One believes St. S. & Benvenuto." He then asked: "What is biography? Unadorned romance" (NB 26, *N&J* 3: 239). In May 1887, flushed with the success of Grant's *Memoirs,* Clemens made plans to "publish the Memoirs of Saint-Simon, elaborately & beautifully illustrated—4 big vols at $8 to $12 the set, according to binding"; this work was to form part of a series titled "Royalty & Nobility Exposed" (NB 26, *N&J* 3: 295). Clara Clemens attempted to discuss Saint-Simon's *Memoirs* in her commonplace book (Paine 150, MTP), but she soon exclaimed: "These Memoirs are impossible to read for they are only a series of vulgar anecdotes about people so low and meaningless that all one can do is blush and regret," whereupon she returned to her comments about George Eliot's characters and beliefs (undated entry, possibly 1888).

Clemens intended to draw upon Saint-Simon, as reflected in his proposed appendix to *A Connecticut Yankee* (Howard G. Baetzhold, "Course of Composition" [1961], p. 200). Saint-Simon would have been included in Clemens's projected "Back Number" magazine (NB 33 [January 1894], TS p. 46). "I read three large volumes containing, it is to be supposed, the best things he [Saint-Simon] said and wrote. . . . To me it was a work of despair. Those three big volumes! And I did not find them witty! That's going back a good ways" ("Mark Twain in Paris," New York *Sun,* 27 January 1895, third section, p. 4; reprinted by Louis J. Budd, "Mark Twain Talks Mostly About Humor and Humorists," *Studies in American Humor* 1 [April 1974]: 8, and by Scharnhorst, ed., *Complete Interviews* [2006], p. 146). When Charlotte Teller began writing her "Mirabeau" play in 1906, Clemens insisted on loaning her a four-volume [*sic*] edition of Saint-Simon's *Memoirs* (Teller's preface to a privately printed pamphlet of letters from Twain to Teller, Berg Collection, NYPL, TS in MTP). In an undated letter written to Teller in the summer of 1906, Clemens reported: "Last night I read myself to sleep with Saint-Simon, & was again astonished at that man's facility in dashing off vivid & delightful portraits with his felicitous pen" (Berg Collection). Albert Bigelow Paine noted that Clemens said he had read the three volumes of Saint-Simon "no less than twenty times" (*MTB*, p. 1536). Williams, "Use of History" (1965), p. 106.

SAITO, H. *Love and Spring: Selections from the "Kokinshū."* Translated by H. Saitō. Tokyo: Kobunsha, n.d. [Published prior to 1890, when the Kobunsha firm changed its name to T. Hasegawa & Co.] 101 pp.

Source: MTLAcc, entry #2097, volume donated from Clemens's library by Clara Clemens Gabrilowitsch in 1910. The *Kokinshū* are tenth-century anthologies of revered Japanese poems. Many of them anonymous, they were collected by Imperial decree and organized by topic into twenty books.

SALA, GEORGE AUGUSTUS (1828–1895). *Under the Sun: Essays Mainly Written in Hot Countries.* London: Vizetelly & Co., 1884. 397 pp. [First published by Tinsley Brothers in London, 1872; Clemens's edition is undetermined.]

In New Zealand, Clemens noted: "*Timaru,* Sunday, Nov. 10. . . . Lying abed reading Sala's brilliant & breezy 'Under the Sun'" (NB 34 [1895], TS p. 34). Sala was a travel correspondent for the London *Daily Telegraph.* His *Under the Sun* recounted a voyage to, and sojourn in, Havana, Cuba during the Civil War in the United States. The book, reminisicent of Laurence Sterne's style, is suffused with literary allusions and anecdotes drawn from Sala's visits to various countries. Clemens mentioned Sala in a speech on 16 June 1899 at the Whitefriars Club Dinner in London (*MTSpk,* p. 325).

SALEEBY, CALEB WILLIAMS (1878–1940). *The Cycle of Life According to Modern Science: Being a Series of Essays Designed to Bring Science Home to Men's Business and Bosoms.* Diagrams by Richard Muir. New York: Harper & Brothers, 1904. 342 pp.

Inscription: unsigned, but something written in pencil has been erased from the top of the front free endpaper.

Marginalia: Clemens made markings on page 34, a diagram on page 35, and a note on page 38—all in brown ink. The note reads: "'Helium atom is twice as heavy as the hydrogen atom & the radium atom is 200 times as heavy as the hydrogen atom.' Here is Arcturus with a brave new speed—more than three times that of Mercury. Astronomers & geologists do not seem to agree often." Jottings in brown ink on the rear flyleaf also appear to be Clemens's: "Drp-glb./ Mole/Atm.—/Elect—". Someone drew a circle in brown ink on the rear pastedown endpaper.

Catalogs: ListABP (1910), "Cycle of Life, Saleeby"; *C1951,* 61a, $30; *Zeitlin 1951,* item #37, $50.

Provenance: collection of Frank C. Willson (1889–1960) in Melrose, Massachusetts. Sold by his widow Margarete in 1962 to the University of Texas.

Location: Harry Ransom Center, University of Texas at Austin.

Copy examined: Clemens's copy.

A note by Henry J. Lindborg—"A Cosmic Tramp: Samuel Clemens' *Three Thousand Years Among the Microbes,*" *American Literature* 44.4 (January 1973): 652–657—was devoted to parallels between Mark Twain's later concepts of microscopic life and a few of the "materials which would have been available to him from popular sources" (p. 652). Lindborg concentrated on C. W. Saleeby's *The Cycle of Life.* H. H. Waggoner, "Science in the Thought of Mark Twain" (1937), p. 362.

———. *Evolution, the Master-Key: A Discussion of the Principle of Evolution as Illustrated in Atoms, Stars, Organic Species, Mind, Society and Morals.* London and New York: Harper & Brothers, 1906. 359 pp.

Inscription: the front pastedown endpaper is signed in black

ink, "SL. Clemens/1906."

Catalog: *C1951,* D47.

Provenance: collection of Frank C. Willson (1889–1960) in Melrose, Massachusetts. Sold by his widow Margarete in 1962 to the University of Texas.

Location: Harry Ransom Center, University of Texas at Austin.

Copy examined: Clemens's copy.

The views of physician and freelance journalist Saleeby ultimately came to embrace certain aspects of eugenics.

SALTER, WILLIAM MACKINTIRE (1853–1931). *The Cure for Anarchy. A Lecture Delivered Before the Society for Ethical Culture, by W. M. Salter, Sunday, October 30, 1887, at the Grand Opera House, Chicago.* Chicago: Press of H. M. Shabad & Co., 1887. 14 pp.

Henry Nash Smith and William M. Gibson (*MTHL,* p. 599 n. 3) deduced that this may have been one of the books to which Clemens referred when he wrote to William Dean Howells on 31 March 1888: "I'll return the Anarchist pamphlets by & by" (*MTHL,* p. 597). Salter's lecture made a plea on behalf of the principles of socialism and the motives of seven imprisoned anarchists.

Salvation Through Grace [or] Salvation by Grace. [Unidentified book.]

Mark Twain claimed that this volume in the paltry contents of the *Quaker City's* library was the only reading available to the pilgrims after they left the ship in the Holy Land. A lazy cabin-boy had selected all the volumes from the same shelf—a shelf containing only this one title (*Daily Alta California,* 5 April 1868; *TIA,* p. 303). Twain gives two variants of the title and does not supply the name of its author. There are a number of books with these or very similar titles dating from the 1770s to the 1850s, and it is difficult to guess the one to which Twain was alluding.

SAMPSON, HENRY (1841–1891). *A History of Advertising from the Earliest Times.* Illus. London: Chatto and Windus, 1874. 616 pp.

Inscription: the half-title page is signed, "Saml. L. Clemens, Hartford, 1875."

Catalog: *A1911,* "colored frontispiece and facsimiles, 12mo, cloth, uncut, Lond. 1874," quotes the signature, lot 418, sold for $3.75.

SAMUEL, HERBERT LOUIS.

On 26 December 1905 Clemens wrote to Thomas Bailey Aldrich on stationery of 21 Fifth Avenue: "I am very glad you thought to send me Mr. Samuel's article. It is able and to the point. It will be difficult to unseat Leopold, but it is worth trying and we shall go on trying" (Houghton Library, Harvard University). Very likely Clemens referred to Herbert [Louis] Samuel (1870–1963), a liberal Member of Parliament who was becoming increasingly identified with the crusade to oust King Leopold from the Belgian Congo. Samuel had published an article about the Congo situation in the 29 May 1903 issue of E. D. Morel's *West African Mail.*

SAMUELS, MAURICE VICTOR (1873–1945). *The Florentines: A Play.* Red cloth, gilt design and lettering. New York: Brentano's, 1904. 153 pp.

Inscription: Samuels inscribed the front free endpaper in black ink: "To S. L. C./You have often made us glad—/ Yes, Mark Twain!/And have sometimes made us sad—/

Without pain!/But there never will be one/Who when your last work is done/Of an unkind touch or bad/Will complain!/Maurice V. Samuels/New York/Dec. 15 '04."

Location: Mark Twain Library, Redding, Connecticut.

Copy examined: Clemens's copy, unmarked. Has the red ink Mark Twain Library accession number "3152". Examined in 1970 and again in June 1982 and on 9 November 2019.

SANBORN, FRANKLIN BENJAMIN (1831–1917), ed. *The Life and Letters of John Brown [1800–1859], Liberator of Kansas and Martyr of Virginia*. Illus. Boston: Roberts Brothers, 1885. 645 pp. [Publisher conjectured.]

Inscription: signed, "S. L. Clemens, 1885."

Marginalia: Clemens made notes totaling fifty-eight words on pages 34, 35, 36, and 60 and made pencil marks throughout the volume. Paragraphs of the text were cut out of pages 21 and 147.

Catalogs: *A1911*, "8vo, cloth (somewhat stained), Bost. 1885," quotes the signature, lot 51, sold for $5.50; American Art Association (New York City), sale catalogue for the collection of the late William F. Gable of Altoona, Pennsylvania (8 January 1925), "Boston, 1885," signed by Clemens, reports his marginalia, lot 122, sold for $22.50 (with two other books).

In 1885 George Parsons Lathrop (1851–1898) reported that Sanborn (usually arriving from Concord, Massachusetts) and Clemens were among the guests who would often while away a winter evening at the home of Charles Dudley Warner ("A Model State Capital," *Harper's Monthly Magazine* 71.425 [October 1885]: 726).

SANBORN, JOHN WENTWORTH (1848–1922). *Legends, Customs and Social Life of the Seneca Indians of Western New York*. Gowanda, New York: Horton & Deming, [cop. 1878]. 76 pp.

Catalog: ListABP (1910), "Seneca Indians (notes laid in)", no other information provided.

Location: currently unknown.

Beginning around 1873 Sanborn wrote Clemens half a dozen letters, the first of which jokingly warned how people might get their fingers stuck on Clemens's self-pasting scrapbooks (*DearMT*, pp. 55–57). Sanborn sent Clemens a copy of *Indian Legends, Customs and Social Life* and Clemens responded from Elmira on 1 October 1879: "I have read the little book through, & greatly enjoyed it. I like the straightforward simplicity of its language. The Indian idea of creation is more picturesque & poetical than the Biblical one." Clemens compared an American Indian female figure who obtained children miraculously to Christianity's concept of immaculate conception. "Many thanks for the entertaining little volume," Clemens concluded (quoted by Sanborn in *Distinguished Authors Whom I Have Known* [Friendship, New York: Privately printed, 1920], p. 9).

———. *The Method of Teaching the Elements of the Latin Language as Employed at Phillips Academy, Exeter, New Hampshire*. Tabulated by John Wentworth Sanborn. Boston: J. S. Cushing, Printer, 1881. 22 pp.

Location: currently unknown.

Sanborn sent Clemens a copy of this small volume on 8 November 1881 (Sanborn, *Distinguished Authors Whom I have Known* [1920], p. 9). A letter to Clemens from Sanborn dated 18 February 1882 mentioned "the little book I sent you on the Tabulation of the Exeter Academy

Method of Teaching Latin. I am glad I warmed your heart by my modest execrations on the Adjective" (MTP).

SANBORN, KATHERINE ABBOTT (1839–1917), comp. *Indian Summer Calendar*. Hartford, Connecticut: Case, Lockwood & Brainard Co., 1905.

Source: MTLAcc, entry #541, volume donated by Clemens.

A collection of uplifting observations about old age, *Indian Summer Calendar* offered daily inspirational messages for the elderly in prose or poetry by Socrates, Jonathan Swift, Oliver Wendell Holmes, Walt Whitman, Helen Hunt Jackson, Thomas Bailey Aldrich, and dozens of other commentators from every era. (Mark Twain was not included.) Sanborn dedicated the volume to Julia Ward Howe.

———. *The Wit of Women*. New York: Funk & Wagnalls, 1885. 215 pp. [Edition conjectured; in 1895 the publisher released a "Fourth edition."]

A copy of *The Wit of Women* belonging to Clemens has never surfaced, but given his inclination to investigate as many humor collections as possible (and in light of the fact that he was preparing *Mark Twain's Library of Humor* for publication in 1888), such an association copy could logically have been one of the numerous books he lost or gave away without retaining any record of his ownership. Sanborn's "Introduction" alluded to a character Mark Twain had launched in *The Gilded Age* (1873): "I feel a cheerful and Colonel Sellers-y confidence in the success of the book," Sanborn declared, "for every woman will want to own it, as a matter of pride and interest, and many men will buy it just to see what women think they can do in this line" (p. 3). Sanborn discussed and quoted examples of humor by British and American female authors, including Aphra Behn, Phoebe Cary, Rose Terry Cooke, Mary Mapes Dodge, Kate Field, Sarah Orne Jewett, Anna Cora Mowatt, Frances Miriam Whitcher ("Widow Bedott"), and Constance Fenimore Woolson. The collection even included a punning poem written by Caroline B. Le Row, whom Twain knew in 1887 as a Brooklyn school teacher (see the Catalog entry for Le Row). *The Wit of Women* was so generous in quoting extracts by the various writers that it qualifies as an anthology as well as a study in gender humor.

SAND, GEORGE, pseud. of Amandine Aurore Lucile [Dupin] Dudevant (1804–1876). *Les Lettres d'un Voyageur* (travel narrative and personal reflections, published 1834–1836).

Clara Clemens listed the author and title of this work in her commonplace book (undated entry, Paine 150, MTP). Sand's *Recollections* are reprinted on pages 323–343 of *Prosper Mérimée's Letters to an Incognita; with Recollections by Lamartine and George Sand* (1874). See the Catalog entry for Prosper Mérimée.

SANDERS, CHARLES WALTON (1805–1889) and JOSHUA CHASE SANDERS (1815–1905). *Bilder Fibel [Pictorial Primer]*. [First published in 1846, this pictorial primer went through many editions.]

Catalog: ListABP (1910), "Bilder Fibel, Sanders", no other information provided.

SANDERS, DANIEL (1819–1897). *Wörterbuch deutscher Synonymen [Dictionary of German Synonyms]*. Hamburg: Hoffmann & Campe, 1882. 681 pp. [The publisher and pages are conjectured.]

Catalog: *A1911*, "12mo, half morocco (rubbed). Hamburg, 1882," quotes the signature, lot 419, sold for $1.50.

SANFORD, ELIAS BENJAMIN (1843–1932), ed. *A Concise Cyclopedia of Religious Knowledge, Biblical, Theological, Historical, and Practical.* New York: Charles L. Webster & Co., 1891. 700 pp.

Clemens's publishing firm advertised that this work included contributions by Edward Everett Hale (1822–1909), was "absolutely unsectarian," and covered "all religious knowledge" (*Publishers' Trade List Annual for 1893*).

SAN FRANCISCO *Morning Call* (newspaper).

Clemens recalled that in 1865 the publisher of the newspaper told him "that the *Call* was like the New York *Sun* of that day: it was the washer-woman's paper—that is, it was the paper of the poor; it was the only cheap paper. The Irish were the poor. They were the stay and support of the *Morning Call*" (13 June 1906 AD, *MTE*, p. 256; *AutoMT* 2: 115).

SANGER, WILLIAM W[ALLACE]. (1819–1872). *The History of Prostitution: Its Extent, Causes, and Effects Throughout the World.* New York: Harper & Brothers, 1876. 685 pp. [Publisher, date, and pages conjectured.]

Olivia Clemens's account book of 1878 included this entry: "Get Sanger's History of Prosti." (NB 13a, MTP). Sanger received criticism when he first published his study in 1858 because of its controversial subject and the blame he placed on males for causing this persistent social problem. In more recent years his book has been faulted for its moralistic tone and its reductionist approaches.

SANGSTER, MARGARET ELIZABETH (MUNSON) (1838–1912). *Little Knights and Ladies; Verses for Young People.* New York: Harper & Brothers, 1904. 148 pp.

Source: MTLAcc, entry #451, volume donated by Clemens. Dedicated "To/the Children's Order/of/'The Round Table,'" these seventy poems portrayed the personalities, habits, and situations of various children. A number of the pieces celebrated holidays from the youngsters' point of view.

———. *Winsome Womanhood. Illustrated by Studies from Life by William Buckingham Dyer.* New York: F. H. Revell, [1901]. 260 pp. [Publisher conjectured.]

Catalog: American Art Association, Sale catalogue (24 February 1925), "8vo, original gilt decorated cloth, gilt top, uncut, New York [1901], first edition, large handmade paper edition," limited edition, copy No. 17, signed by the author, has the *A1911* sale label, lot 127, sold for $6. The magazine editor (among journal assignments, she edited *Harper's Bazaar* between 1889 and 1899), author, and poet Sangster often wrote works of advice and inspiration for young women. *Winsome Womanhood* contained twelve chapters of moralistic and religious prose encouraging her readers to persevere and retain their sense of worth. In her last decade Sangster would embrace feminist goals. William Buckingham Dyer (1860–1931) was an accomplished illustrator.

SANKEY, IRA DAVID (1840–1908).

Clemens mentioned "a Moody and Sankey meeting" in Hartford in a letter to Jane Lampton Clemens and Pamela A. Moffett, 7 April 1878 (MTP). The narrator of Mark Twain's "The Loves of Alonzo Fitz Clarence and Rosannah Ethelton" (1878) notes the presence of books by "Moody and Sanky" [*sic*] in the "private parlor of a refined and sensible lady"—Aunt Susan. Twain facetiously referred to his prayer "requests" to Moody & Sankey on behalf of an ailing mulberry tree from Stratford-on-Avon in an unsent letter to the editor of the New York *Evening Post* dated 23 November 1880 (*MTPP*, p. 132). "I have always avoided the Moody & Sankey revivals," Clemens avowed (SLC to Augustin Daly, 30 November 1888, Houghton Library, Harvard University). "Singing the Moody & Sankey," Clemens noted in January 1897 (NB 39, TS p. 46). Twain mentioned Moody and Sankey revivals in Chapter 7, Book II of *Christian Science* (1907). Captain Stormfield learns about a new arrival in Heaven: "This barkeeper got converted at a Moody and Sankey meeting, in New York (*Extract from Captain Stormfield's Visit to Heaven* [1909], Ch. 2). See also the Catalog entry for Dwight Lyman Moody.

SARASWATI, SRI SWAMI BHASKARANANDA (OF BENARES), trans. *Upanishad Prasada, i.e., An Easy Translation of 10 Upanishads.* Benares: Bharat-jiwan, 1894.

Catalog: ListABP (1910), "Upanishad Prasada", no other information supplied.

Mark Twain showed this book of Hindu philosophy and the photograph of its translator to a reporter in India, describing his visit with Saraswati in a half-serious, half-jesting interview ("Mark Twain Interviewed: First Impressions of India," *Englishman* [Calcutta], 8 February 1896; reprinted in *Complete Interviews*, ed. Gary Scharnhorst [2006], pp. 284–285, 286 n. 4). Subsequently he recounted the session he had with this holy man in Chapter 53 of *Following the Equator* (1897): "He proposed an exchange of autographs. . . . He wrote his in his book, and I have a reverent regard for that book, though the words run from right to left, and so I can't read it. It was a mistake to print [it] in that way. It contains his voluminous comments on the Hindoo holy writings, and if I could make them out I would try for perfection myself. I gave him a copy of Huckleberry Finn."

Rebecca Hooker, "Additions to Mark Twain's Library," *American Literary Realism* 38.3 (Spring 2006): 277; Dwayne Eutsey, "Waking from This Dream of Separateness: Hinduism and the Ending of *No. 44, The Mysterious Stranger*," *Mark Twain Annual* 7 (2009): 66–77; and Susan K. Harris, "My Life with Mark Twain: Chapter One—Hinduism," *Mark Twain Annual* 15 (2017): 1–21.

SARDOU, VICTORIEN (1831–1908).

Sometime after 1878 and probably during the 1890s Clemens identified forty authors (in ink) in a photograph album. Victorien Sardou was one of them (Robert T. Slotta to Alan Gribben, 15 August 1997). Sardou was a successful French playwright who also claimed to be a spiritualist medium.

SARGENT, EPES (1813–1880). "A life on the ocean wave" (song, published in 1838). Melody by Henry Russell (1812–1900).

In a sketch Mark Twain published in the 18 November 1865 issue of the *Californian* a pianist for a scriptural panoramist inappropriately bangs out "Oh, a life on the ocean wave,/And a home on the rolling deep!" (*ET&S* 2: 365). In 1866 Twain resolved to "show up Life at Sea & abuse 'Life on the Ocean Wave'" (NB 5, *N&J* 1: 134); he was aboard the *Smyrniote* bound for San Francisco from Honolulu. He referred to the song twice more in the same notebook (pp. 148, 162). Sargent's song was one of the "villainous ditties" that Hale Dexter sang to win the regard of some Missouri villagers in Twain's unfinished novel, "Simon Wheeler, Detective," written sporadically between 1877 and 1898 (*S&B*, p. 335). The sentimental music on the piano in "The House Beautiful" (Ch. 38, *LonMiss* [1883]) included "A Life on the Ocean Wave, a Home on the Rolling Deep." Twain quoted this song ("A life on the ocean wave/And a home on the rolling deep,/Where the scattered waters rave/And the winds their revels keep!") in "About All Kinds of Ships" (1893) to illustrate the kind of "soft sentimentality about the sea" that had vanished. Around 1906 he wrote in Notebook 48: "'A Life on the Ocean Wave'—old pianist. Nicholson" (TS p. 12). Twain recalled it as one of the "sentimental songs" in the later minstrel shows (30 November 1906 AD, *MTE*, p. 114; *AutoMT* 2: 296).

Sartain's Union Magazine of Literature and Art (New York, Philadelphia, published 1847–1852).

Clemens recalled that in 1853 [*sic*] "a Philadelphian, Homer C. Wilbur," had become "a regular and acceptable contributor to *Sartain's Magazine* and the other first-class periodicals" (10 September 1906 AD, *MTE*, p. 236; *AutoMT* 2: 234). See also the Catalog entry for Homer C. Wilbur.

SARTORIS, ADELAIDE (KEMBLE) (1815–1879). *A Week in a French Country-House*. London: Smith, Elder and Co., 1867. 200 pp. There was also another edition: Illustrated by Lord Frederic Leighton (1830–1896). Preface by Anne Thackeray Ritchie (1837–1919). New York, London: Macmillan Co., 1902. 221 pp. [The edition Clemens owned is currently undetermined.]

Catalog: *C1951*, #51c, listed among books signed by Clemens, no edition specified, $12.

Sartoris, the younger daughter of the actor Charles Kemble, was an English opera singer who left the stage when she married in 1843. Her son wed the daughter of President Ulysses S. Grant in 1874. Late in 1902 or early in 1903 Clemens wrote to the ailing Olivia Clemens: "I have been reading that book 'A Week in a French Country House' right on top of [Mrs. Rice's] the 'Cabbage Patch,' & my! what a contrast between the richness & brilliancy & finish of the one & the poverty & crudeness & vulgarity of the other! It's an experience!" Here, he asserted, was "the difference" between Emerson and a minstrel show (MTP).

The protagonist in *A Week in a French Country-House*, a twenty-eight-year-old woman named Bessy, travels to Madame Olympe de Caradec's home in Marny-les-Monts to see if the French climate will restore her health; she is to stay only a single week. Bessy (or Bessie, as her new French friends spell her name) is amazed that merely by crossing a narrow channel of water one suddenly encounters altogether strange manners, speech, sports, customs, and mores. The household of the widowed Madame de Caradec consists of nobility who paint after Corot, play the music of Beethoven, and dine mainly for the sake of conversation. Enchanting October foliage surrounds her small park carved out of a forest. Bessy notices a romantic intrigue between Miss Ursula Hamilton and Monsieur Jacques. Ursula, who hunts boars and performs in public as a singer, also attracts the attentions of a cad, René de

Saldes, who thinks of marrying her; she refuses: "I cannot marry you, for I cannot love you" (p. 190). (Ursula once loved him for four years, but he spurned her then and courted Madame de Malan in Florence.) Bessy returns to London to wed William L'Estrange, a curate whose poverty had compelled them to postpone their marriage since she was seventeen; still, "I have not lost these eleven years, since I have passed them in loving the best and noblest human creature that I ever knew" (p. 170). After Bessy returns to London she receives a letter from Ursula in Paris conferring a living as rector of her parish at Holt upon L'Estrange. Ursula determines to enter London society with her rich aunt's bequest; she will bring her friend Jacques along as a servant. Bessy is thus enabled to marry within a month, and on the last page of the novel she wishes Ursula similar good fortune: "I have seen her reject the wrong casket—may she choose the right one when the time comes!"

Saturday Review of Politics, Literature, Science and Art (weekly London periodical, published 1855–1938).

The *Saturday Review* took notice of Mark Twain's *The Innocents Abroad* in its 8 October 1870 issue. Twain thereupon fabricated a jesting review of his own book—*Galaxy* 10.6 (December 1870): 876–878—attributing it to the *Saturday Review*; he then admitted the hoax in the *Galaxy* 11.1 (January 1871): 158–159. On 28 January 1885 Twain urged Charles L. Webster to "see the fine notice [of *Huckleberry Finn*] in London Saturday Review—get it at Brentano's for your scrapbook" (*MTBus*, p. 298).

SAUZAY, ALEXANDRE (1804–1870). *Wonders of Glass-Making in All Ages*. Library of Wonders Series. Illus. New York: Scribner, Armstrong & Co., 1872. 325 pp.

Source: MTI Acc, entry #1994, volume donated from Clemens's library by Clara Clemens Gabrilowitsch in 1910.

SAVAGE, MINOT JUDSON (1841–1918).

On 21 December 1902 the Reverend Minot Judson Savage, a Unitarian clergyman, provoked a theological dispute by preaching a sermon in the Church of the Messiah in New York City that argued against the divinity of Jesus and disputed the doctrine of virgin birth. In January 1903 Mark Twain referred to this "warm dispute" (Book II, Ch. 7, *Christian Science*, *WIM?*, p. 309). Perhaps that allusion by Twain was what later prompted the Reverend Savage to send Twain a copy of one of his sermons. Isabel Lyon noted on 17 January 1906: "The morning mail brought a little book—a sermon by Minot J. Savage, sent by the publisher. Mr. Clemens stroked the soft leather binding & said,: 'Just the thing to sharpen my razor on,' so the publisher has done a good deed after all" (IVL Journal, Harry Ransom Center, University of Texas at Austin; a similar entry in IVL Journals, TS p. 124, MTP). Five of Savage's recent sermons were published individually in 1906 by W. B. Perkins in New York City, all of them bound in "limp Persian calf." Given Clemens's immediate dismissal of the sermon's content (in favor of using its leather cover to strop his razor), the most likely candidate would be the pamphlet titled *Religion: Its Changing Forms and Its Eternal Essence* (30 pp.); however, another possibility might be *Immortality: Some Reasons for Belief* (35 pp.). The other sermons by the Reverend Savage published by W. B. Perkins in 1906 were *The Blessedness of Work*

(Preface by Helen Keller, 38 pp.), *The Companionship of Friends* (Preface by Lyman Abbott, D. D., 39 pp.), and *The Jew in Christendom* (Preface by the Reverend Joseph Silverman, 31 pp.). All five of these pamphlets contained a frontispiece portrait of the Reverend Savage.

———. *Can Telepathy Explain? Results of Psychical Research.* First edition. 12mo. Original green cloth, gilt. New York: G. P. Putnam's Sons, 1902. 243 pp.

Inscription: the front free endpaper is inscribed and signed by Clemens: "From Rev. Minot J. Savage./Riverdale, Jan. 1903./S L. Clemens."

Catalogs: *A1911*, "12mo, cloth, N.Y. 1902," quotes the inscription, lot 420, sold for $2.50; American Art Association (New York City), Sale catalogue of the library of Oscar Haywood, D. D. (13 March 1918), "12mo, original cloth," quotes Clemens's inscription, has the *A1911* sale label, lot 80; "First and Other Editions of Samuel L. Clemens," Seven Gables Bookshop, New York City, List No. 3 (August 1972), has the *A1911* sale label, item #140, $125; *Sotheby's 2003*, #234, $1,900.

Provenance: Sotheby's sale, 3 June 1997, lot 59; subsequently in the collection of Nick Karanovich, Fort Wayne, Indiana.

Location: collection of Kevin Mac Donnell, Austin, Texas.

Copy examined: Clemens's unmarked copy, in July 2004. Has the *A1911* auction label.

One would have expected Clemens to annotate at least a few pages of a work on one of his favorite subjects, but other concerns must have intervened. The Reverend Savage wrote a number of books expressing his beliefs in Darwin's theories, the probability of an afterlife, and (to a degree) psychics and spiritualism.

SAVILE, FRANK MACKENZIE (1865–1850). *Beyond the Great South Wall: The Secret of the Antarctic, with Sundry Graphic Illustrations Painted by One Robert Lindsay Mason [1874–1952].* New York: New Amsterdam Book Co., 1901. 322 pp.

Source: MTLAcc, entry #1072, volume donated by Albert Bigelow Paine, Clemens's designated biographer. Possibly Clemens saw this book, since the men exchanged reading materials. In this work of science fiction, Savile imagined a lost Mayan world guarded in the Antarctic by a prehistoric creature.

SAWYER, CHARLES CARROLL (1833–1891). "Weeping, sad, and lonely; or, when this cruel war is over" (song, published in 1863). Melody by Henry Tucker (1826–1882).

Clemens heard this song "thrice encored" in the Carson City Opera House (letter of 13 January 1864, *MTEnt*, p. 132).

SAXE, JOHN GODFREY (1816–1887).

In 1880 Mark Twain included this poet—known for his humorous verse— among writers to be considered for an anthology of American humor (NB 19, *N&J* 2: 364).

SAXTON, ROBERT (fl. 1870), ed. *Mental Photographs: An Album for Confessions of Tastes, Habits, and Convictions.* New York: Leypoldt & Holt, 1869. 78 pp.

Inscription: signed by Clemens.

Marginalia: questionnaire completed in Clemens's handwriting.

Source: Beineke Library, Orbis Yale University Library Catalog.

In "Mental Photographs" (Buffalo *Express* 2 October 1869) Mark Twain described and joshed about this album of blank spaces in which friends were to submit photographs, names, dates, and answers to questions. He filled in his imaginary version of the album, providing absurd responses.

Jeffrey Steinbrink, *Getting To Be Mark Twain* (Berkeley: University of California Press, 1991), p. 54; Harold K. Bush, Jr., *Mark Twain and the Spiritual Crisis of His Age* (Tuscaloosa: University of Alabama Press, 2007), pp. 88–90.

Jo Dee Benussi provided materials for this entry.

SAYERS, HENRY J. (1854–1932). "Ta-ra-ra-boom-de-ay!" (song, copyrighted and published in 1891). Also spelled: "Tah-rah-rah-boom-de-aye!" Words and music by Sayers.

The Canadian-born Henry J. Sayers was an Army bandmaster and later the manager of minstrel shows. It has been alleged that there was an African American precedent for this infectious song. "Ta-ra-ra-boom-de-ay!" became wildly popular after an English music-hall singer, Lottie Collins, reintroduced it to American audiences in 1894. Clemens condemned the song in October or November of 1895 (NB 35, TS p. 64). This was one of the songs he mentioned as becoming "wearisome through repetition (Book II, Ch. 7, *Christian Science* [1907], *WIM?*, p. 323). Paul Baender also noted that Clemens originally included "Tah-rah-rah boom-de-aye" among the Young Man's examples of songs that are soon tiring in Chapter 5 of "What Is Man?" (1906) (*WIM?*, p. 178). In 1931 Sayers would compose an encouraging song during the Great Depression, "Hard times will soon be over." He died at the age of seventy-seven on 20 February 1932 in New York City.

SAYLES, JAMES M[ASON]. (1837–1900). "Star of the evening" (song, published in 1855). Also known as "Beautiful star." Words and music by Sayles. Arranged by Henry Tucker (1826–1882).

Steamboat captain George F. Carvell recalled that when Clemens was aboard the *Alfred T. Lacey* in 1859, "Sam had an old guitar and could play one song, 'Star of the Evening, Beautiful Star.' Our voices joined in singing it" (Branch, "A New Clemens Footprint," p. 505). "Star of the Evening" is one of the songs "of love and sentiment" that Mark Twain lists in Chapter 3 of *Following the Equator* (1897) as belonging on music stands in the Honolulu parlors of the 1860s. The sentimentality of "Star of the Evening" was parodied by the Mock Turtle in Lewis Carroll's *Alice in Wonderland* (1865). The composer Sayles was born (30 March 1837), married (1861), and died (24 December 1900) in Albany, New York. His other songs and hymns, such as "When the roses bloom," "The golden grain was waving," and "The trumpet sounds the challenge," like the better-known "Star of the evening," had only passing vogues.

Edgar M. Branch, "A New Clemens Footprint: Soleather Steps Forward," *American Literature* 54.4 (December 1982): 497–510.

"A SCENE ON THE OHIO," Bloomington *Herald*, 13 February 1849. [The sketch was credited to "The Elephant."]

Fred W. Lorch—"A Source for Mark Twain's 'The Dandy Frightening the Squatter," *American Literature* 3.3 (November 1931): 309–313—thought that this sketch might have suggested young Sam Clemens's earliest published sketch, "The Dandy Frightening the Squatter" (1852). However, Bernard Devoto (*MTAm* [1932], p. 244 n. 5) and Walter Blair (*NAH* [1937, 1960], p. 154) cast doubt on that speculation.

SCHAFF, PHILIP (1819–1893), ed. *The Revision of the English Version of the New Testament.* Intro. by Philip Schaff. 3 vols. in 1. New York: Harper & Brothers, 1873. 634 pp.

Source: MTLAcc, entry #1814, volume donated by Clemens.

This is an *extremely* detailed account of the process involved in revising the New Testament by committees.

SCHEFER, LEOPOLD (1784–1862). *The Artist's Married Life; Being That of Albert Dürer.* Translated from the German by Jemima Henrietta (Brown) Stodart (1807–1875), "Mrs. John Riddle Stodart." Rev. edition, with memoir. Boston and Cambridge: J. Munroe and Co., 1861. 204 pp.

Olivia Langdon copied a passage from this historical novel into her commonplace book around 1869 or 1870 (DV161, MTP). The great German Renaissance engraver and court painter Albrecht Dürer lived from 1471 until 1528.

SCHERER, GEORG (1824–1909). *Die schönsten Deutschen Volkslieder mit ihren eigenthümlichen singweisen. [The most beautiful German folk songs with their singular ways of singing.]* [Edition undetermined.]

Scherer was a German compiler and publisher of German *volkslieder* (people's songs). F. W. Christern, a New York City importer of foreign books, billed Clemens on 21 April 1881 for "1 Scherer Volkslieder $2.20"; Clemens paid on 22 April 1881 (receipt in MTP).

Schermerhorn's Boy (minstel farce, performed in New York City, 1860s).

Christy's Minstrels performed *Schermerhorn's Boy* as early as 1859, with George Christy featured as Julius Schermerhorn; Christy revived the farce in 1862 and it had engagements in various theaters throughout the early 1860s. In a letter published in the Virginia City *Enterprise* on 8 February 1863, Clemens alluded to a Carson City saloon proprietor named Lytle as "Schermerhorn's Boy" (*MTEnt*, p. 58; *ET&S* 1: 208), which seemingly alluded to Christy's show. However, Edgar M. Branchand Robert H. Hirst raised the possibility that the allusion might have been to a local celebrity in Carson City (*ET&S* 1: 465). Nevertheless, the attachment of the word "Boy" to the name appears to indicate a familiarity with Christy's immensely popular minstrel character.

SCHERR, JOHANNES (1817–1886). *Deutsche Kultur-und Sittengeschichte [History of German Culture and Customs].* Leipzig, 1852–1853. [Edition undetermined.]

Clara Clemens listed the author and title in her commonplace book (undated entry, Paine 150, MTP).

SCHEVICHAVEN, HERMAN DIEDERIK JOHAN VAN (1827–1918), pseud. "Jacob Larwood" and JOHN CAMDEN HOTTEN (1832–1873). *The History of Signboards, from the Earliest Times to the Present Day.* Illustrated by Schevichaven. Sixth edition. Original purple cloth, gilt. London: John Camden Hotten, [1875]. 536 pp.

Inscription: the front free flyleaf is signed in black ink, "Saml L. Clemens/1875/Hartford."

Catalogs: ListABP (1910), "Hist. Of Sign Boards"; *C1951*, #17c, listed among volumes signed by Clemens, no edition specified, $15.

Location: collection of Kevin Mac Donnell, Austin, Texas. Acquired in 1985.

Copy examined: Clemens's unmarked copy, in July 2004.

The History of Sign Boards surveyed the designs and names of shop-door sign boards from classical Greek and Roman references through Shakespeare and into the nineteenth century, quoting Swift, Longfellow, and many other authors.

SCHICK, LOUIS (1842–1892), comp. *Schick's humoristische Bibliothek [Library of Humor].* 11 vols. Illus. Chicago: L[ouis]. Schick, 1886–1889. [Each of the eleven paperbound numbers sold for .25¢].

Clemens made a memorandum in May 1888: "Collection Schick/ L. Schick, publisher, Chicago. Get it of C. Schoenhof, 144 Tremont St Boston" (NB 27, *N&J* 3: 391). The Hamburg-born Schick had established a publishing firm in Chicago.

SCHILLER, JOHANN CHRISTOPH FRIEDRICH VON (1759–1805). *Ausgewählte Briefe von Friedrich von Schiller [Selected Letters by Friedrich von Schiller].* Ed. by Eugen Kühnemann (1868–1946).

Edgar H. Hemminghaus saw Clemens's copy of this book (which Clemens acquired "in his later years") in the Mark Twain Library at Redding ("Mark Twain's German Provenience" [1945], p. 470), but Albert E. Stone, Jr. could not find it in 1955 and I was unable to locate it in Redding in 1970 or thereafter.

———. *The Fight with the Dragon. A Romance. [Der Kampf mit dem Drachen.]* Translated by John Payne Collier (1789–1883). Sixteen engravings from designs by [Friedrich August] Moritz Retzsch (1779–1857). Boston, 1877.

Inscription: the front flyleaf was signed (on Clemens's birthday), "Saml. L. Clemens, Nov. 30th, 1884."

Catalog: *A1911*, "oblong, 4to, cloth (back worn), Bost. 1877," quotes the signature, lot 424, sold for $2.50.

The British translator of this poem was famously accused of Shakespearean forgeries.

———. *Die Jungfrau von Orleans [The Maid of Orleans]: eine romantische tragödie* (play, first performed in 1801).

"Susy [Clemens] is reading aloud to me Schillers 'Yungfrau von Orleans,'" Olivia Clemens wrote in her journal at Quarry Farm on 2 July 1885. "She reads it very well and it is delightful to read it with her" (OLC Diary, DV 161, MTP; *Family Sketch*, p. 100). Clemens quoted a line from Act III, Scene 6 in an Autobiographical Dictation of 2 October 1906: "Against the stupid even the gods strive in vain" (*MTE*, pp. 390–391; *AutoMT* 2: 239).

Stone, *IE* (1961), p. 206.

———. *Maria Stuart: ein Trauerspiel [Mary Stuart, A Tragedy].*

Edgar H. Hemminghaus reported that Clemens's copy of this play about Mary, Queen of Scots (1542–1587) was in the Mark Twain Library at Redding ("Mark Twain's German Provenience" [1945], p. 470). He may have meant the edition included in Schiller's collected works; see the Catalog entry for *Schiller's Sämmtliche Werke.*

———. *Schiller's Complete Works. Edited, with Careful Revisions and New Translations, by Charles J[ulius]. Hempel [1811–1879].* 2 vols. Philadelphia: I. Kohler, 1861.

Catalog: Ball 2016 inventory, bookplates #60 and #61 of the "J. Langdon Family Library," marbled board, gilt lettering, black leather spine, fair to poor condition.

Location: Quarry Farm library shelves, under the supervision of the Mark Twain Archive, Elmira College, Elmira, New York.

Copies examined: unmarked copies available to Clemens during his visits to the Langdon residence in Elmira. Examined on 26 May 2015.

———. *Schiller's Pegasus im Joche [Pegasus in Harness].* Nebst Andeutungen zu den Umrissen von [Friedrich August] Moritz Retzsch [1779–1857]. Stuttgart, n.d. [The date of Clemens's edition of this poem is undetermined.]

Catalog: *A1911,* "oblong 4to, morocco (rubbed), Stuttgart, n.d.," with a sheet of notes by Clemens laid in, lot 402, sold for .75¢.

———. *Schiller's Sämmtliche Werke in Zwölf Bänden [Schiller's Complete Works in Twelve Volumes].* Mit Einleitungen von Karl Goedeke [1814–1887]. 12 volumes in 6. Stuttgart: J. G. Cotta, 1881.

Inscriptions: the verso of the front free endpapers in the joint binding of Volumes 5 and 6 were inscribed in ink by Clemens: "Livy L. Clemens/from/S. L. Clemens/1884." The front endpapers in Volumes 9 and 10 (bound together) were inscribed by Clemens identically.

Provenance: Maxwell Hunley of Beverly Hills, California offered Volumes 9 and 10 (bound together) on 19 November 1963 for $15, "purchased at the Mark Twain sale in Hollywood in 1951." In 1986 Victor Jacobs of Dayton, Ohio reported that he owned "Schiller's Poems (in German). Presentation copy from Clemens to Olivia Clemens" (Jacobs to Alan Gribben, 15 October 1986). Presumably Jacobs meant that he had two volumes of the set bound as one volume. Jacobs died in 1996, and the "Victor and Irene Murr Jacobs Collection" was subsequently auctioned by Sotheby's on 29 October 1996.

Location: Mark Twain House and Museum, Hartford, Connecticut (partial set, Volumes 5 and 6 bound together). The whereabouts of Volumes 9 and 10, bound together, are currently unknown. The other missing four volumes (bound as Volumes 1–2, 3–4, 7–8, and 11–12) have never been recorded.

Copy examined: Olivia Clemens's copy of Volumes 5 and 6, bound together, presented by her husband. Spine missing, poor condition. Examined in August 1987. Contains *Maria Stuart, Die Jungfrau von Orleans, Wilhelm Tell, Die Huldigung der Künste,* and *Die Braut von Messina.*

Chapter 27 of *A Tramp Abroad* (1880) describes "a massy pyramidal rock eighty feet high, devised by Nature ten million years ago against the day when a man worthy of it should need it for his monument. The time came at last, and now this grand remembrancer bears Schiller's name in huge letters upon its face." Early in 1884 Clemens made a memorandum to "get a good Schiller" (NB 22, *N&J* 3: 47). Listing his current reading for Edward H. House on 14 January 1884, Clemens mentioned, "& in German, the second volume of Schiller (the poems, I mean)" (ASSSCL). Describing his knowledge of German literature in an 1897 newspaper interview in Vienna, Clemens said he "read Schiller in the original" (Odessa *News* [Odesskie *Novosti*], 8 October 1897; translated and reprinted by M. Thomas Inge and George Munro, "Ten Minutes with Mark Twain," *American Literary Realism*

15.2 [Autumn 1982]: 262).

———. "Der Verbrecher aüs verbrener Ehre. Eine wahre Geschichte" (tale, 1786, known in English as "The Criminal of Lost Honor: A True Story").

Clemens wrote to Dr. E. K. Root on 8 June [no year] in German to state that [in translation] "this evening we have made a change—the lecture consists only of 1_ pages of Schiller's 'Der Verbrecher aüs verbrener Ehre,' and did not start at the beginning, but with the 7th paragraph of the story where one reads the following: 'Christian Wolf Warder owner of a restaurant. . . .'" (*Sotheby's 2003,* #134).

———. *Wilhelm Tell, Schauspiel* (play, written in 1804).

Mark Twain mentioned William Tell several times in *A Tramp Abroad* (1880); see Chapter 31, for instance. In "Switzerland, the Cradle of Liberty" (1892), Twain makes reference to the encouragement of Stauffacher's wife to her husband; Professor Robert Regan of the University of Pennsylvania informed me that the probable source was *Wilhelm Tell,* I, ii.

Schillings, Karl Georg (1865–1921). *In Wildest Africa.* Translated from the German by Frederic Whyte (1867–1941). Illustrated with "over 300" photographs by the author. New York: Harper & Brothers, 1907. 716 pp.

Inscription: the front pastedown endpaper is inscribed by Clemens in black ink: "The/Adventures of an Assassin/for Jean Clemens/from/her Father/Xmas, '07."

Location: Mark Twain Library, Redding, Connecticut.

Copy examined: Jean Clemens's unmarked copy. Has the red ink Mark Twain Library accession number "2467". Examined in 1970 and again in June 1982 and on 9 November 2019.

———. *With Flash-light and Rifle; Photographing by Flash-light at Night the Wild Animal World of Equatorial Africa.* Translated from the German and abridged by Henry Zick. Spine broken and loose. New York: Harper & Brothers, 1905. 421 pp.

Inscription: the front pastedown endpaper is inscribed by Clemens in black ink, "Jean Clemens/1905/Nov. 27".

Location: Mark Twain Library, Redding, Connecticut. Donated from Clemens's library by Clara Clemens Gabrilowitsch in 1910 (MTLAcc, entry #1977).

Copy examined: Jean Clemens's unmarked copy. Has the red ink Mark Twain Library accession number "1977". Examined in 1970 and again in June 1982 and on 9 November 2019.

Inasmuch as Schillings had gained a reputation as a big game hunter in Africa, this might seem like an odd gift for Clemens to give his animal-loving daughter on what would have been her mother's birthday if Olivia had not died the previous year. However, Schiller had now been converted to the cause of game conservation, was a leader in the new field of animal photographers, and Jean greatly enjoyed books of nature photography.

Schlegel, Friedrich von (1772–1829). *The Philosophy of History; in a Course of Lectures, Delivered at Vienna.* Translated from the German by James Burton Robertson (1800–1877). 2 vols. London: Saunders and Otley, 1835. [Often reprinted. Clemens's edition is unknown.]

"Speaking of Mahomet, Schlegel, the German historian, tells us, 'Even the prohibition of wine was, perhaps, not so much intended as moral precept. . . .'" ("Mark Twain on Prohibition," *Licensing Guardian,* New South Wales,

1895; Scharnhorst, ed., *Complete Interviews*, p. 222). In Volume II, Schlegel, writing of "the infancy of the Mohametan faith" and those who sought refuge in Ethiopia (p. 89), speculated that "even the prohibition of wine was perhaps so much intended for a moral precept, . . . as for answering a religious design of the founder" (p. 90).

SCHLESSING, ANTON (1828–1910). *Deutscher Wortschatz oder Der passende Ausdruck [German Vocabulary; or, The Appropriate Expression].* [Clemens's edition is unknown.]

Edgar H. Hemminghaus saw this pronunciation study aid in the Mark Twain Library at Redding ("Mark Twain's German Provenience" [1945], p. 467), but neither Albert E. Stone, Jr. (in 1955) nor I (in 1970) was able to locate the volume.

SCHMID, CHRISTOPH VON (1768–1854). *Genovefa* (religious children's book, published in 1810. Based on a medieval legend, Genevieve of Brabant).

F. W. Christern, foreign book importers of New York City, billed Clemens on 21 April 1881 for "1 Genovefa .75"; Clemens paid the amount on 22 April 1881 (receipt in MTP).

———. *Der gute Fridolin und der böse Dietrich. Eine lehrreiche Geschichte für Aeltern und Kinder [The Good Fridolin and the Evil Dietrich: An Instructive Story for Parents and Children]. . . . Sechste, einzig rechtmässige Original-Auflage.* München: Louis Finsterlin, 1874. 242 pp.

Catalog: *Zeitlin 1951*, item #38, $2.

Location: Mark Twain Papers, Bancroft Library, University of California at Berkeley, California.

Copy examined: Clemens's copy, unmarked. A sale label of the *C1951* auction is affixed to the front pastedown endpaper.

Schmid was an extremely popular writer of religious children's stories.

SCHMIDT, WILLIAM A. (d. 1905), known as "The Only William." *The Flowing Bowl: When and What to Drink: Full Instructions How to Prepare, Mix, and Serve Beverages.* New York: Charles L. Webster & Co., 1892. 294 pp.

Clemens's publishing firm brought out this collection of cocktail recipes by a bartender who had learned his craft over more than thirty years while he was employed in hotels and bars in Chicago and New York City. *The Flowing Bowl* concluded with twelve pages of poetry—including verse by Shakespeare, Robert Burns, and have a dozen German writers (including Friedrich von Schiller)—extolling the pleasures of alcoholic beverages.

SCHNECKENBURGER, MAX (1819–1849), pseud. "Max Heimthal." "Die wacht am Rhein" ["The watch on the Rhine"] (patriotic poem, published in 1840). Melody composed by Karl Wilhelm (1815–1873) in 1854.

Clemens listed "Die Wacht am Rhein" among his favored songs in August 1889 (NB 29, *N&J* 3: 513). In an unpublished seven-page sketch written during his period of residence at Riverdale, New York, "A Song Composed in a Dream," Mark Twain hears in a dream an English version of "Die wacht am Rhein" ("The watch on the Rhine") and remarks that he has "dreamed in verse with a strange frequency" (John Spalding Gatton, "Catalog of the Peal Exhibition," *Kentucky Review* 4.1 [1982]: 219–220).

SCHOOLCRAFT, HENRY ROWE (1793–1864). *Algic Researches, Comprising Inquiries Respecting the Mental Characteristics of the North American Indians. First Series. Indian Tales and Legends.* 2 vols. New York: Harper & Brothers, 1839. [No more published in this series.] A later edition, with additions and omissions, appeared as *The Myth of Hiawatha, and other Oral Legends, Mythologic and Allegoric, of the North American Indians.* Philadelphia: J. B. Lippincott & Co., 1856. 343 pp. [Clemens's edition has not been determined.]

In Chapter 59 of *Life on the Mississippi* (1883), Mark Twain tells of meeting a panorama lecturer on a Mississippi River steamboat in 1882; he purportedly told Twain "that if I would hunt up Mr. Schoolcraft's book, published near fifty years ago, and now doubtless out of print, I would find some Indian inventions in it that were very far from being barren of incidents and imagination; that the tales in 'Hiawatha' were of this sort, and they came from Schoolcraft's book. . . and that the contributors to Schoolcraft's book had got them directly from Indian lips, and had written them down with strict exactness, and without embellishments of their own." Twain continues: "I have found this book. The lecturer was right. There are several legends in it which confirm what he said. I will offer two of them—'The Undying Head' [published as Appendix D to *Life on the Mississippi*], and 'Peboan and Seegwun, an Allegory of the Seasons.' The latter is used in 'Hiawatha'; but it is worth reading in the original form, if only that one may see how effective a genuine poem can be without the helps and graces of poetic measure and rhythm." Twain then quotes the legend. See also the Catalog entry for Thomas McLean Newson's *Indian Legends*.

Rogers, *MTBP* (1960), pp. 91, 171, n. 62; McNutt, "Mark Twain and the American Indian" (1978): 223–242; Richard Lettis, "The Appendix of *Life on the Mississippi*," *Mark Twain Journal* 21.2 (Summer 1982): 10–12; Richard Bridgman, *Traveling in Mark Twain* (Berkeley: University of California Press, 1987), pp. 106, 118–119; and Driscoll, *Mark Twain among the Indians and Other Indigenous Peoples* (2018), pp. 30–31.

SCHOPENHAUER, ARTHUR (1788–1860). *Essays of Arthur Schopenhauer.* Selected and translated from the German by Thomas Bailey Saunders (1860–1928). New York: A. L. Burt Co., [no copyright date, c. 1892]. 455 pp.

Inscription: the front flyleaf is signed in pencil, "Clara Clemens/Atlantic City."

Marginalia: annotated by both Clemens and Clara Clemens. On pages 8–9 Clemens observed in black ink, "He is totally ignorant/of what a man *is*./Man is a machine which is operated/wholly by circumstances beyond his/control./A machine *can't* choose—& a man/is merely a machine" (p. 8). "Since he is ignorant of what a man *is*, he can't discuss him sanely" (p. 9). Clemens made no other notes. Very similar phrasing would appear in Mark Twain's "What Is Man?" (1906).

Catalogs: *C1951*, J23, listed among the volumes belonging to Jean and Clara Clemens; "Property from the Library of Mark Twain," Butterfield & Butterfield, San Francisco, Sale 6613 (16 July 1997), lot 2691.

Location: Mark Twain House and Museum, Hartford, Connecticut.

Copy examined: Clara Clemens's copy shared with Clemens. Viewed in 1997 in Hartford.

Henry W. Fisher reported that in the early 1890s (in Berlin)

Clemens expressed interest in three unpublished essays by Schopenhauer, whom Clemens termed "the arch-misogynist"—"Tetragamy," "Fragments of Philosophy," and "Pandectes et Spicilegia," all still in manuscript in the Royal Library of Berlin (*AMT*, pp. 78–81).

Schreiner, Olive (1855–1920) and **Samuel Cron Cronwright-Schreiner** (1863–1936). *The Political Situation [in Cape Colony].* London: T. Fisher Unwin, 1896. 148 pp.

Source: MTLAcc, entry #531, volume donated by Clemens. On 24 December 1896 Clemens sent a postcard to Chatto & Windus, his London publisher: "I would like to have a copy of Olive Shreiner's [*sic*] (& her husband's) little book (political)—forgotten the name of it—published a couple of months or such a matter ago—by Fisher Unwin" (Berg Collection, New York Public Library).

Baetzhold, *MT&JB* (1970), p. 380 n. 9.

———, pseud. "Ralph Iron." *The Story of an African Farm. A Novel* (published in 1883).

Clemens entered the title in Notebook 28 in December 1888 (TS p. 37). Among several other book titles, Clemens noted on 20 November 1895 in New Zealand: "Story of an African Farm" (NB 34, TS p. 40). The 18 May 1896 issue of the Johannesburg, South Africa *Times* published an interview—"Mark Twain on the Rand/He Gives a Few Opinions"—in which he discussed Schreiner's novel (Scharnhorst, ed., *Complete Interviews*, p. 308). In that interview Twain said that he had read the novel "when it first came out, in a casual sort of way, yet it left a definite impression upon me, which was chiefly derived from the first chapter. The book is good literary art, and gives a clear, definite picture, I believe, of the country where the scene is laid." However, "I read the book again on the ocean, this time as the literary critic examining the workmanship, and found the greater part to be written crudely, and to be formless and without any distinct aim." On 1 June 1896 Clemens referred to Schreiner's unfavorable view of the Boer's industry: "according to Olive Shreiner [*sic*]—quote her" (NB 38, TS p. 25); on 4 June 1896 he called the Boer "dirty," "indolent," and "solemn," and reminded himself to "See African Farm" (NB 38, TS p. 35). Chapters 67 and 68 of Twain's *Following the Equator* (1897) allude to Olive Schreiner and her writings. In the latter chapter Twain describes the Boer in generalities, then adds: "I think that the bulk of those details can be found in Olive Schreiner's books, and she would not be accused of sketching the Boer portrait with an unfair hand." In Chapter 68 Twain also praises the scenery and climate of South Africa in June: "The vigor and freshness and inspiration of the air and the sun—well, it was all just as Olive Schreiner had made it in her books."

Madigan, "MT's Passage to India" (1974), pp. 364–365.

Schubert, Franz Peter (1797–1828). "Impromptu." This was "Jean's favorite," Clemens stated (24 December 1909 AD, *AutoMT* 3: 318).

———. "Symphony in B minor" ("Unfinished symphony"). After dinner on Sunday, 11, March 1906, Clemens stayed downstairs only long enough to listen to "the andante movement of the Schubert Unfinished Symphony" (IVL Journals, TS p. 146, MTP).

———. "Das wandern" (song). Clemens mentioned the song titled "Wanderer" favorably

in 1878 (NB 16, *N&J* 2: 212).

Schultz, Christian (c. 1770–c. 1814). *Travels on an Inland Voyage Through the States of New-York, Pennsylvania, Virginia, Ohio, Kentucky, and Through the Territories of Indiana, Louisiana, Mississippi, and New-Orleans, Performed in the Years 1807 and 1808; Including a Tour of Nearly Six Thousand Miles.* 2 vols. Maps and plates. New York: Printed by Isaac Riley, 1810.

Peter G. Beidler—"Christian Schultz's *Travels*: A New Source for *Huckleberry Finn*?," *English Language Notes* 28.2 (December 1990): 51–61—believed that Schultz's book was very likely among those Mark Twain read as background sources for *Life on the Mississippi* (1883). Beidler also cited a number of correspondences between Schultz's letters to a friend and certain incidents and descriptions in *Adventures of Huckleberry Finn* (1885).

Schultz, James Willard (1859–1949). *My Life as an Indian; The Story of a Red Woman and a White Man in the Lodges of the Blackfeet.* Illus. New York: Doubleday, Page & Co., 1907. 426 pp.

Source: MTLAcc, entry #489, volume donated by Clemens. As a young man Schultz lived among the Blackfeet and married a Native American woman. Later, after the tribe was moved onto a reservation, he became an insistent advocate for their welfare.

Schumann, Robert Alexander (1810–1856). *Music and Musicians. Essays and Criticisms.* Trans., ed., and annotated by Fanny Raymond Ritter (1840–1890). New York: E. Schuberth & Co., 1877. 418 pp. Second series: 1880, 540 pp.

In September 1889 Clemens made an entry in Notebook 29: "Schumann's 'Musical Criticism'" (*N&J* 3: 518). See also the Catalog entry for Heinrich Heine, "The two grenadiers" (song). Ritter was an accomplished musician and music authority in her own right.

Schurz, Carl (1829–1906). *American Imperialism: The Convocation Address Delivered on the Occasion of the Twenty-Seventh Convocation of the University of Chicago, Jan. 4, 1899.* Boston: Dana Estes, 1899. 31 pp.

Source: Jim Zwick reported that Clemens received a copy of this address ("'Prodigally Endowed with Sympathy for the Cause': Mark Twain's Involvement with the Anti-Imperialist League," *Mark Twain Journal* 32.1 [Spring 1994]: 22 n. 29).

Clemens introduced Schurz at a Mugwump political meeting in Hartford on 20 October 1884 (*MTHL*, p. 511 n. 3). In 1905 Clemens nominated him for the American Academy of Arts and Letters, and then added: "Carl Schurz should have been elected at the *recent* meeting—& *should not fail this time*" (SLC to Robert Underwood Johnson, 28 April 1905, American Academy of Arts and Letters). When Schurz died, Clemens wrote to his family: "I am one of those who loved Carl Schurz & revered him" (14 May 1906, MTP). "Carl Schurz, that marvelously ready and fluent and felicitous handler of our great English tongue on its highest planes," Clemens declared in an Autobiographical Dictation (19 August 1907 AD, *MTE*, p. 337; *AutoMT* 3: 105).

Brook Thomas, "*Adventures of Huckleberry Finn* and Reconstruction," *American Literary Realism* 50.1 (Fall 2017): 15.

———. *For Truth, Justice and Liberty.* New York: Anti-Imperialist

League of New York, 1900. 32 pp.
Jim Zwick indicated that Clemens received a copy of Schurz' speech in this pamphlet form ("'Prodigally Endowed with Sympathy for the Cause': Mark Twain's Involvement with the Anti-Imperialist League," *Mark Twain Journal* 32.1 [Spring 1994]: 22 n. 29).
———. *Life of Henry Clay*. 2 vols. American Statesmen Series. Third ed. Boston: Houghton, Mifflin (Riverside Press), 1887.
Catalogs: QF Martinez, good condition; Ball 2016 inventory, blue cloth, gilt lettering, gilt top edges.
Location: Quarry Farm library shelves, under the supervision of the Mark Twain Archive, Elmira College, Elmira, New York.
A work available to Clemens during his visits to Quarry Farm in Elmira.
SCHUYLER, EUGENE (1840–1890). *Turkistan; Notes of a Journey in Russian Turkistan, Khokand, Bukhara, and Kuldja.* Illus. Maps. 2 vols. New York: Scribner, Armstrong & Co., 1876. [Publisher conjectured.]
Catalog: *A1911*, "2 vols. 8vo, cloth, N.Y. 1876," with a sheet of notes by Clemens about Leopold II laid in, lot 421, sold for $2.
SCHWARTZ, JOZUA MARIUS WILLEN VAN DER POORTEN (1858–1915), pseud. "Maarten Maartens." *My Lady Nobody; A Novel.* New York: Harper & Brothers, [cop. 1895]. 413 pp.
Source: MTLAcc, entry #1308, volume donated by Clemens.
SCHWOB, MARCEL (1867–1905). *The Children's Crusade.* Translated from the French by Henry Copley Greene (1871–1951). Two limited editions were available: Boston: Small, Maynard, 1898 (83 pp., 500 copies); and Portland, Maine: Thomas B[ird]. Mosher, 1905 (86 pp., 425 copies). Clemens's edition, if any, has not been determined.
The translator Greene paraphrased Mark Twain's unflattering remark about an early short story Schwob wrote ("a peculiarly unpleasant little production"—see the Catalog entry below), so Twain's attention might have been drawn to Schwob's later publication depicting a child's view of the medieval Children's Crusade. Jo Dee Benussi noticed this fact and relayed it to me on 9 May 2007.
———. "'Terrifiante histoire de mes dents', un pastiche de Mark Twain" (story, published in 1888).
The twenty-one-year-old Schwob sent Clemens a copy of his story soon after it appeared in France. Clemens apparently misunderstood the gesture and assumed the story was being attributed to him. On 4 November 1888 Clemens responded indignantly from Hartford: "You seem to think me the author of the original of this singularly unpleasant production. But I assure you you have been deceived. I do commit crimes, but they are not of this grade" (*Sotheby's 2003*, lot 64). Schwob would become associated with the French Symbolist movement, especially on account of his *Vies imaginaires* (1896).
SCIDMORE, ELIZA RUHAMAH (1856–1928). *Jinrikisha Days in Japan.* Illus. New York: Harper & Brothers, 1904. 386 pp.
Source: MTLAcc, entry #596, volume donated by Clemens. Scidmore's title alludes to the rickshaw, once a common passenger vehicle in Japan.
Scientific American (New York magazine, commenced publication in 1859).
In an issue of this journal published on 12 December 1891

(Vol. 65), Mark Twain probably read a short illustrated article about the Tocci conjoined twins— Giovanni and Giacomo (1877–1940)—who toured the United States in 1891. See Robert A. Wiggins, "The Original of Mark Twain's *Those Extraordinary Twins*," *American Literature* 23.3 (November 1951): 355–357.
Christine Quigley, *Conjoined Twins: An Historical, Biological, and Ethical Issues Encyclopedia* (Jefferson, North Carolina: McFarland & Co., 2003).
SCOLLARD, CLINTON (1860–1932). *On Sunny Shores.* Illustrated by Margaret Barker (Landers) Randolph (1848–1938), later Sanford. New York: Charles L. Webster & Co., 1893. 237 pp.
Clemens's publishing firm advertised this prose travel narrative (with poems interspersed) as descriptive of a journey along the Wye River, down the Neckar, through the Tyrol, over the Splugen, to Belaggio, Verona, then to Greece and Syria (*Publishers' Trade List Annual for 1893*).
———. *Under Summer Skies.* Illustrated by Margaret Barker (Landers) Randolph (1848–1938), later Sanford. New York: Charles L. Webster & Co., 1892. 290 pp.
"A poet's itinerary through Egypt, Palestine, Italy, and the Alps. Also, Arizona and Bermudas" (*Publishers' Trade List Annual for 1893*). In the "Weather" appendix to *The American Claimant* (1892), Mark Twain quoted three lines of verse from Scollard's "Easter-Eve at Kerak-Moab."
SCOT, REGINALD (1538–1599). *The Discoverie of Witchcraft, Wherein the Lewde Dealing of Witches and Witchmongers is Notablie Detected* (self-published in 1584).
In June 1885 Clemens mentioned the name of this work in Notebook 24: "Reginald Scott's [*sic*] Discovery of Witchcraft: 1584" (*N&J* 3: 163). Scot was an Englishman who lived on his family estates in Kent. Despite the implications of its title, *The Discoverie of Witchcraft* actually expressed a skepticism toward belief in magic or witches that was rare for the sixteenth century. To make his case against these pernicious and deadly superstitions, Scot reported a number of supposed witch manifestations and sought to disprove them. He blamed the Inquisition for this "extreme and intolerable tyranny."
SCOTT, CATHARINE AMY (DAWSON) (1865–1934). *The Agony Column.* London: Chapman & Hall, 1909. 310 pp.
In or after November 1909, Clemens listed *The Agony Column* along with other book titles in the jottings he made in purple ink on the same envelope that carried his famous dictum about his reading preferences: "I like history, biography. . . . And I detest novels, poetry & theology" (Fragments file, MTP). Presumably Clemens meant that he especially abhorred this particular novel, written by the woman who (in 1921) would found and become the first president of the PEN Club, an international organization for writers. *The Agony Column* opens with an epigraph attributed to Clemens's former antagonist, Paul Bourget: "*Mon ami, quelle comédie que la vie, et quelle sottise d'en faire un drame.*" After coming to know a young Jewish man named Theodore Higham, Frances Morgan feels that her marriage of ten years to Colonel Morgan of Fair Lawns is unbearable. "Though discontented with her lot, Mrs. Morgan had hitherto endured its monotony without overmuch complaint— certainly without making more than tentative efforts in the direction of change. Now, though she did not know what she must do, she

had been brought to the edge of revolt" (p. 4). Colonel Morgan wants a male heir (he has a daughter) to inherit his estate near Bath. He charges Frances with adultery with Higham, and the couple arrange a marital separation. But Frances Morgan finds herself pregnant; since the child is her husband's, she resolves to return to Fair Lawns for its birth. Colonel Morgan joins some friends on an expedition to Lake Chad in Africa. During his absence Frances incurs progressive optic atrophy, requiring her to remain in darkness. By the time her daughter is born she has become blind.

One day a friend read the "Agony Column" to her from the daily newspaper— the column containing distressful messages to friends and missing relatives. A certain line seems directed to Frances and inspires her to live on: "Rupert has obeyed you and they are on their way to India. He asked me to give you this message:—The outer courts are for the uses of life the inner shrine holds that which is sacred, and of the existence of which none will ever know save the priest, who worships" (p. 289). She now finds solace in the belief that Theodore Higham did not rank her with those women whose "calls of the flesh were loud in his ears"; with Frances alone he "had obeyed the call of the spirit" (p. 290). Colonel Morgan returns triumphantly from Africa, though several in his party succumbed to disease and dangers. He saved the life of Dicky Barnes, the son of his former love, Laura Gillespie. His wife is bitter that he did not hasten his return from Central Africa on account of her illness. She insists that he accept the newborn girl, Honoria, as his own child. He refuses to acknowledge Frances's assurance that he is the actual father. "I will take you back for the child's sake— and as my housekeeper—that certainly. I have no wish to take back as my wife another man's mistress," Morgan declares (p. 220). She repudiates him as her husband, but they live on together for the sake of their children and appearances. The final chapter reveals that it was Theodore Higham's brother who placed the "Rupert" advertisement on the first of each January in accordance with a promise. The self-pitying Frances derives from this knowledge "a solitary gleam of happiness. I sit here in the dark, remembering each one that I have had and looking forward to the next." Though her life is lonely, "at least I have consistently lived up to the highest that I knew" (p. 310). Clemens might have disliked the theme of infidelity, even though the affair is imaginary, or he may have been disgusted at the way Frances brings misery upon several people, especially her husband.

Alan Gribben, "'I Detest Novels, Poetry & Theology': Origin of a Fiction Concerning Mark Twain's Reading," *Tennessee Studies in Literature*, 22 (1977): 154–161—revised and reprinted in Volume One of this present work.

SCOTT, HENRY WILSON (1866–1935). *Distinguished American Lawyers, with Their Struggles and Triumphs in the Forum.* Introduction by John J[ames]. Ingalls (1833–1900). New York: Charles L. Webster & Co., 1891. 716 pp.

Clemens's publishing firm advertised that this work included sketches of Abraham Lincoln, Chauncey Depew, Grover Cleveland, and Benjamin Harrison (*Publishers' Trade List Annual for 1893*).

SCOTT, HUGH STOWELL (1862–1903), pseud. "Henry Seton Merriman." *Dross.* Illus. Chicago: H. S. Stone & Co., 1899. 330 pp.
Source: MTLAcc, entry #1212, volume donated by Clemens.

———. *From One Generation to Another.* New York: Harper & Brothers, 1900. 256 pp.
Source: MTLAcc, entry # 1626, volume donated by Clemens.

———. *The Grey Lady.* New York: Macmillan and Co., 1897. 377 pp.
Source: MTLAcc, entry #219, volume donated by Clemens.

———. *The Phantom Future; A Novel.* New York: Harper & Brothers, 1897. 239 pp.
Source: MTLAcc, entry #1627, volume donated by Clemens.
In 1889 the first edition of *The Phantom Future*, a romance set in coastal England, launched the career of this English novelist.

———. *The Sowers; A Novel.* New York: Harper & Brothers, 1900. 390 pp.
Source: MTLAcc, #1628, volume donated by Clemens.
The Sowers was the most popular of Scott's novels.

———. *With Edged Tools; A Novel.* New York: Harper & Brothers, [cop. 1894]. 340 pp.
Source: MTLAcc, entry #1447, volume donated by Clemens; subsequently destroyed while in circulation from the Mark Twain Library at Redding.

SCOTT, JAMES WINFIELD (1867–1944). *Jack Hardin's Rendering of the Arabian Nights; Being a New Translation in Up-to-Date English: With Wise Comments, Explanations, &c., by This Eminent Linguist.* Illus. Boston: H. B. Turner & Co., 1903. 260 pp.
Source: MTLAcc, entry #363, volume donated by Clemens.
A folksy narrator, Jack Hardin, provides slangy summaries of the best-known tales from *The Arabian Nights*. James Winfield Scott was a lawyer and journalist who worked for newspapers in Colorado, Nevada, and Montana and practiced law in Nevada, California, and Montana.

SCOTT, JOHN (1820–1907). *Partisan Life with Col. John S. Mosby.* Illus. New York: Harper & Brothers, 1867. 492 pp.
Scott writes a near-worshipful account of the Confederate commander of the Virginia Cavalry, John Singleton Mosby (1833–1916). Clemens owned very few military books about the Southern side in the Civil War.
Source: MTLAcc, entry #1789, volume donated by Clemens.

SCOTT, MICHAEL (1789–1835). *The Cruise of the Midge* (published 1836).
"Would also like to get hold of 'Tom Cringle's Log' and 'The Cruise of the Midge,' if they are still in print" (SLC to James R. Osgood, 23 May 1881, *MTLP*, p. 137).
Stone, *IE* (1961), p. 161; Blair, *HH&T* (1969), p. 145.

———. *Tom Cringle's Log.* London: F. Warne & Co., n.d. 455 pp.
Source: MTLAcc, entry #253, volume donated by Clemens.
See the previous Catalog entry.

SCOTT, (SIR) WALTER (1771–1832).
Clemens's well-known animosity toward Scott could have been a reaction against—and an attempt to obliterate—the worshipful view of Scott he held in his youth. Throughout his life Clemens inveighed against the "romantic" and chivalric notions that he himself indulged in as a boy. In

1897 Clemens remembered Sir Walter Scott as one of the authors idolized by the "Villagers of 1840–3," when "Pirates and Knights [were] preferred to other society. Songs tended to regrets for bygone days and vanished joys. . . . The gushing Crusaders [were] admired; the serenade was a survival or a result of this literature" (*HH&T* [1969], p. 34). "All that sentimentality and romance among young folks seem puerile, now," Clemens wrote, "soft, sappy, melancholy" (*HH&T*, p. 35). Newspapers of the 1850s reveal that the St. Louis & Keokuk Packet line, which served the Mississippi River port of Hannibal, named their steamboats exclusively from Scott's fictional nomenclature (for instance, the *Diana Vernon* from *Rob Roy* and the *Jeanie Deans* from *The Heart of Midlothian*). Clemens's first roommate in St. Louis, Jacob H. Burrough, "was fond of Dickens, Thackeray, Scott & Disraeli, & was the only reading-man in the establishment" (SLC to Frank E. Burrough, 15 December 1900, Southeast Missouri State College, Cape Girardeau, Missouri). In a speech delivered on 20 November 1900 Twain conceded that "when you're eighteen you can read *Ivanhoe*" (*MTB* [1912], p. 1120; *MTS 1923*, p. 210; *MTSpk* [1976], p. 359).

In the 17 June 1865 *Californian*, Mark Twain advised literary experts to attribute "all the scouring, dashing, descriptive warrior rhymes to Scott" (*LAMT*, p. 141; *ET&S* 2: 195). Twain mentioned Scott's immense canon in *Roughing It* (Ch. 55, 1872). "If your genuine stories can die," Clemens wrote to William Dean Howells from Elmira, New York after finishing Howells's *A Foregone Conclusion* on 22 August 1874, "I wonder by what right old Walter Scott's artificialities shall continue to live" (*MTHL* [1960], p. 21; *MTLet* 6: 209). Howells replied from Cambridge on 2 September 1874: "I shall yet make immortality bitter to the divine Walter—as the French would call the Waverley man" (*MTHL*, p. 23). In a paragraph intended for a letter to U. S. Representative Samuel S. Cox (but possibly not included in what was sent), Clemens on 8 February 1875 alluded to "the heirs of one Scott or Burns or Milton in a hundred years" as the targets of lawmakers who severely restricted literary copyrights" (*MTLet* 6: 377).

Twain's "Comments on English Diction," probably written in 1876, contained strictures against Walter Scott (*MT in Elmira* [2013], pp. 212–213). Twain's objections to Scott's themes and style would become so virulent that twentieth- and twenty-first-century classroom teachers often cited his criticisms as symbolic of the tensions between authors associated with rising American Realist movement and their receding Romantic predecessors. Tom Sawyer embodied the false romanticism that Twain associated with Scott and the American South; in *The Adventures of Tom Sawyer* (1876) and *Adventures of Huckleberry Finn* (1885), Tom is steeped in history, ritual, social codes, and absurd notions of "glory." Chapters 40, 45, and 46 of *Life on the Mississippi* (1883) poured abuse upon Walter Scott's reputation, partly blaming the American Civil War on Scott's influence. Twain there referred to "his fantastic heroes and their grotesque 'chivalry' doings and romantic juvenilities," echoing an earlier chastisement of Will Bowen that he had delivered in 1876 for sentimentalizing the past—"the melancholy, the romance, the heroics, of sweet but sappy sixteen" (*Mark Twain's Letters to Will Bowen*, ed. Theodore

Hornberger [Austin: University of Texas Press, 1941], pp. 23–25). In Chapter 46 of *Life on the Mississippi* Twain condemned "the silliness and emptiness, sham grandeurs, sham gauds, and sham chivairies of a brainless and worthless long-vanished society. . . . Most of the world has now outlived [a] good part of these harms, though by no means all of them." Scott, he proclaimed, "did measureless harm" with his "dreams and phantoms" and his "decayed and swinish forms of religion"—"more real and lasting harm, perhaps, than any other individual that ever wrote." In Chapter 13 of *Huckleberry Finn* (1885), the wrecked and doomed steamboat *Walter Scott* nearly finishes off Huck and Jim; the vessel's name hardly seems coincidental. Twain's "Private History of a Campaign That Failed" (1885) ridicules a recruit named Dunlap: "He was young, ignorant, good-natured, well-meaning, trivial, full of romance, and given to reading chivalric novels and singing forlorn love- ditties." On the other hand, Scott's phenomenal sales long fascinated Clemens. Gloating over the success of U. S. Grant's *Memoirs* in June 1885, Clemens noted that "Sir Walter Scott paid debts amounting to £120,000 out of his numerous copyrights, but not out of one or two volumes" (NB 24, *N&J* 3: 159).

Late in 1886 or early in 1887 Mark Twain thought of creating "a story wherein the pantaletted little children talked the stilted big-word sentimental hifalutin of Walter Scott's heroes & the other & older novels (Pamela &c)" (NB 26, *N&J* 3: 268). On 22 August 1887 he wrote to Howells from Elmira about how one's perceptions and literary tastes change: "They would not say that of Dickens's or Scott's books. *Nothing* remains the same" (*MTHL*, pp. 595–596). Clemens mentioned Scott in Notebook 27 in March 1888 (*N&J* 3: 379). "Suppose Sir Walter, instead of putting the conversations into the mouths of his characters, had allowed the characters to speak for themselves? We should have had talk from Rebecca and Ivanhoe and the soft lady Rowena which would embarrass a tramp in our day" (*CY* [1889], Ch. 4). When Rudyard Kipling visited Clemens in Elmira on 15 August 1889, he reported that Clemens took Scott's novels as an example while discoursing on copyright reforms (*From Sea to Sea* [1899], 2: 173–174; Scharnhorst, ed., *Complete Interviews* [2006], p. 121). At Rowena-Ivanhoe College in *The American Claimant* (1892) the young ladies move among "castellated college-buildings—towers and turrets and an imitation moat—and everything about the place named out of Sir Walter Scott's books and redolent of royalty and state and style." They do not learn "a single blessed thing but showy rubbish and un-American pretentiousness," one character asserts (Ch. 4). In Chapter 5 a few of their college buildings are mentioned: Kenilworth Keep, Redgauntlet Hall, Rob Roy Hall. Tom Sawyer's adventures in *Tom Sawyer Abroad* (1894) are again indebted to his familiarity with Walter Scott's works, especially *The Talisman* (see Stone, *IE* [1961], p. 183).

Mark Twain commented on Scott's elaborate style in a newspaper interview, "A Ramble with Mark Twain: His Views on Men and Things," Sydney, Australia *Daily Telegraph,* 17 September 1895, p. 5 (Scharnhorst, *Complete Interviews*, p. 208). At a dinner of the Nineteenth Century Club on 20 November 1900, Twain challenged

Scott's reputation: "I'd be willing to take my chances with Mr. Scott to-morrow evening in selling a piece of literature to the Century Publishing Company" (NB 43, TS p. 29; speech reported in the New York *Tribune*, 21 November 1900; Fatout, *MTSpk*, pp. 358–359). A newspaper interviewer in 1902 recorded a rare instance of Clemens relenting in this attitude toward Scott, though the exception involved character rather than literary judgement: "He sat there smoking his fourth cigar. In the advertising papers of a monthly on the table before him was a picture of Sir Walter Scott. Looking at the picture with evident affection, he said: 'There never was a man in the history of all literature who was confronted by so gigantic a task as that undertaken by Scott in his magnificent effort to rid himself of a mountain of debts for which he was not responsible.' Yet, but a few years before," commented the reporter, "the man who had paid this tribute to Sir Walter Scott had himself won the admiration of the world for a transaction similar in almost every detail" ("My First Vacation and My Last—Mark Twain," New York *World Magazine*, 7 September 1902; *Complete Interviews*, p. 473).

Clemens's most complete commentaries on Scott's novels appear in two letters written to Brander Matthews from Riverdale on 4 May and 8 May 1903 (*MTL* [1917], pp. 737–739; the second letter was not mailed until June 1910, when it was discovered). In the first letter Clemens complained, "Brander, I lie here dying, slowly dying, under the blight of Sir Walter"; in the second he approved of a single book by Scott: "I wonder who wrote *Quentin Durward*?" In Chapter 1 of Twain's "The $30,000 Bequest" (1904), the Fosters pass their evenings in Lakeside by "reading romances to each other, dreaming dreams, comrading with kings and princes and stately lords and ladies in the flash and stir and splendor of noble palaces and grim and ancient castles." Their children are named Clytemnestra and Gwendolen, whose "names betray the latent romance-tinge in the parental blood." The classical character Clytemestra figured in the background of Scott's historical novel *Woodstock; or, The Cavalier* (1826); Gwendolen appeared in Scott's *The Bridal of Triermain; or, The Vale of St. John: In Three Cantos* (1818), a poem relating three stories set in the Lake District. In Chapter 6 of "The $30,000 Bequest" the couple's penchant for romance reading is replaced by their equally unfruitful daydreaming about "fictitious finances." In a book by Anatole France that Clemens read and enjoyed in 1891 and again in 1906, *The Crime of Sylvestre Bonnard* (1881), a young scholar named Henri Gélis called Scott's work "rococo, troubadourish, and only fit to inspire somebody engaged in making designs for cheap bronze clocks." In fact, said Gélis, historical novels are altogether "false" because "one cannot possibly know just how men used to live five or ten centuries ago." Old Bonnard disputed this harsh judgment and the dialogue is suggestive of Twain's colloquy titled "What Is Man?" (1906). In an Autobiographical Dictation of 21 March 1906 Twain rather fondly recalled that Joseph H. Twichell and his wife Harmony "were devotees of Scott" who spent several days "ransacking Edinburgh for things and places made sacred by contact with the Magician of the North" (*MTA*,

2: 224; *AutoMT* 1: 430).

In sum, then, Clemens's mixed comments about Sir Walter Scott over a lifetime indicate that in his youth he joined in idolizing the vaunted Scottish author, but he gradually shifted his opinion to the point where he perceived Scott as the epitome of the ornate stylists against whom he and other American Realists were rebelling. He thereafter came to associate Scott with the falsely inflated beliefs of American Southerners that he himself had shared in his youth (and saw as contributing to the disastrous Civil War). He always remained in awe of Scott's immense sales figures achieved in spite of the imperfect copyright laws, and eventually, following his own bankruptcy, he was willing to admire Scott's heroic determination to repay his financial creditors. During all this time, he and members of his family were nevertheless assembling a very substantial collection of Scott's writings.

An ongoing discussion about Mark Twain's contempt for Scott's writings soon commenced after Clemens's death. William Dean Howells wrote that except for Twain "no one has ever poured such scorn upon the second-hand, Walter Scotticized, pseudo-chivalry of the Southern ideal" (*MMT* [1910], p. 30). Brander Matthews continued to defend Scott by suggesting that Twain's criticism was limited by his insistence on applying the standards of his own day to fiction of the past. Moreover, wrote Matthews, he had "the realist's abiding abhorrence for romanticism, wilful, arbitrary and high-flown, for its striving after vivid external effects, and for the departure from veracity which this seeking entails" (*Essays on English* [1921], pp. 262–263). The English historical novelist Maurice Hewlett—"Mark on Sir Walter," *Sewanee Review Quarterly* 29.2 (April 1921): 130–133—quoted Twain's opinions of Scott found in *Mark Twain's Letters* (1917) and criticized his "easy line of attack." Twain "was in a rage, and . . . undiscerning"; he did not allow for historical conventions, Hewlett argued. Hamilton James Eckenrode, "Sir Walter Scott and the South," *North American Review* 206.743 (1917): 595–603, neatly summarized Twain's celebrated cavils against the Scottish novelist. G. Harrison Orians, in "Walter Scott, Mark Twain, and the Civil War," *South Atlantic Quarterly* 40.4 (October 1941): 342–359, wrote the most frequently cited rebuttal of Mark Twain's views, an article that invalidated some then-common assumptions. He used Twain's charges in *Life on the Mississippi* as the starting-point for a revisionist assessment of Scott's influence on the South that considered Scott's popularity, feudal psychology, militarism, tournaments, the eighteenth-century English origins of American plantation culture, rural economy, slavery, and cotton agriculture in order to show that the tendencies noted by Twain (and many others) resulted from more complex factors than the maligned Walter Scott. Orians deplored the Gilded Age, "the fatuity of an industrial era," which was supplanting what Twain criticized. Orians's was a spirited, intelligent essay that challenged glib generalizations.

Friedrich Schönemann (1925), condensed in Edgar H. Hemminghaus's *MTG* (1939), pp. 106–109; Grace Warren Landrum, "Sir Walter Scott and His Literary Rivals in the Old South," *American Literature* 2.3 (November 1930): 256–276—an extensive survey of Scott's literary

influence in the Deep South; S. B. Liljegren, "Revolt
Against Romanticism" (1945), p. 35; Floyd Stovall, ed.,
The Development of American Literary Criticism (Chapel
Hill: University of North Carolina Press, 1955), pp.
131–132; Walter Blair, *MT&HF* (1960), pp. 118, 292,
299; Roger B. Salomon, *TIH* (1961), p. 83; Edward
Wagenknecht, *MTMW* (1967), p. 38; Sydney J. Krause,
"The Sir Walter Disease," a chapter in *MTC* (1967),
pp. 148–189—arguably the best analysis; Howard G.
Baetzhold, *MT&JB* (1970), p. 71; Baetzhold, "Samuel
L. Clemens" (1988), pp. 34–47.
See also the Catalog entry for Charles Rogers, ed., *The
Centenary Garland* (1871).
———. *The Abbot.* Copyright Edition. Collection of British
Authors Series. Leipzig: Bernhard Tauchnitz, 1860. 451 pp.
Inscription: "Jean Clemens. Aix les Bains. July, 1891."
Provenance: formerly in the Mark Twain Library, Redding,
Connecticut.
Catalog: *Mott 1952*, item #82, $3.50.
———. *Anne of Geierstein.* Collection of British Authors Series.
Half calf covers. Leipzig: Bernhard Tauchnitz, 1871. 419 pp.
Inscription: inscribed by Olivia Clemens in black ink on the
front free endpaper: "Jean Clemens/Ouchy./Sept. 1891".
Location: Mark Twain Library, Redding, Connecticut.
Copy examined: Jean Clemens's unmarked copy. Has the
Mark Twain Library accession number "2711". Examined
in 1970 and again in June 1982 and on 9 November 2019.
———. *The Betrothed* (novel, published in 1825–1826).
On 12 July 1885 Olivia Clemens noted in her diary at
Quarry Farm: "Susy is reading Scott's 'Betrothed,' tonight
she said to me Scott has a cool way of writing—even when
the event is exciting he writes of it cooly" (DV161, MTP;
Family Sketch, pp. 100–101).
———. *Christmas in the Olden Time.* Illustrated by E[dmund].
H[enry]. Garrett (1853–1929), Harry Fenn (1838–1911),
Childe Hassam (1859–1935), and others. Engraved and
printed under the supervision of George T. Andrew. New
York: Cassell and Co., 1887. 62 pp.
Catalogs: *A1911*, "royal 8vo, decorated cloth, gilt edges,
N.Y. 1887," with a sheet of notes by Clemens laid in, lot
423, sold for $1.50; *Lexington 1912*, lot 23, sold for $5.
Provenance: in the collection of Victor Jacobs of Dayton,
Ohio in 1986 (Jacobs to Alan Gribben, 15 October 1986).
Jacobs reported then that the volume contains the *A1911*
sale label. Jacobs's collection was mostly sold in 1996.
Location: currently unknown.
Copy examined: photocopies of the title page and the
front pastedown endpaper provided by Victor Jacobs to
the Mark Twain Papers, Bancroft Library, University of
California at Berkeley, in December 1984. The volume
has the *A1911* sale label.
———. *Count Robert of Paris* (historical novel, published
in 1831).
This, the last of the "Waverley Novels," was set in the years
1081–1118 among the first Crusaders. Tom Sawyer refers
to "Godfrey de Bulleyn" (i.e., Geoffrey de Bouillon), who
"hacked and hammered at the paynims." Huckleberry
Finn deduces that "Tom got all that notion out of Walter
Scott's book, which he was always reading" (*Tom Sawyer
Abroad* [1894], Ch. 1). See also the Catalog entry for
Scott's *The Talisman.*

———. *The Fair Maid of Perth.* Illus. New York: Harper &
Brothers, n.d. 466 pp.
Source: MTLAcc, entry #1117, volume donated by
Clemens.
———. *The Fortunes of Nigel* (historical novel, published in
1822).
After Annie Fields and her husband visited Clemens in
Hartford, she recorded his remarks in her diary on 6
April 1876: "He was very interesting and told J[ames].
the whole story of his life. . . . He described the hunger
of his childhood for books, how the *Fortunes of Nigel*
was one of the first stories which came to him while he
was learning to be a pilot on a Mississippi boat. He hid
himself with it behind a barrel, where he was found by
the Master, who read him a lecture upon the ruinous
effects of reading" ("Bret Harte and Mark Twain in the
'Seventies: Passages from the Diaries of Mrs. James T.
Fields," ed. M[ark]. A[ntony]. DeWolfe Howe, *Atlantic
Monthly* 130.3 [September 1922]: 345). In study notes
Mark Twain made for *The Prince and the Pauper* (1881)
around 1879, Twain wrote: "Alsatia (or White-friars) was
legal refuge (See Nigel, introduction[)]"; he also jotted
down page numbers from the novel (DV114, DV115,
MTP). Scott's novel was set in the days of King James I
and related Nigel Olifaunt's struggle in London to reclaim
his ancestral estate.
Howard G. Baetzhold, *MT&JB* (1970), p. 330 n. 7.
———. *Guy Mannering; or, The Astrologer.* Illus. New York:
Harper & Brothers, n.d. 440 pp.
Source: MTLAcc, entry #1659, volume donated by
Clemens.
Scott's *Guy Mannering*, published in 1815 and set in
eighteenth-century Scotland, involved the kidnapping
of Harry Bertram, the theft of his rightful estate, and his
encounter with Colonel Guy Mannering, whose daughter
he wished to marry.
———. *Guy Mannering; or, The Astrologer.* New Century
Library. Blue leather. London: Thomas Nelson and Sons,
n.d. 532 pp.
Provenance: Antenne-Dorrance Collection, Rice Lake,
Wisconsin.
Location: Mark Twain Archive, Gannett-Tripp Learning
Center, Elmira College, New York.
Copy examined: probably Clemens's unmarked copy,
though his ownership of this volume is not established.
It might have belonged to Mary T. Evans of LaCrosse,
Wisconsin, the first wife of Warren Leary, Sr. Examined
on 28 May 2015.
In "Comments on English Diction," an essay written
around 1876, Mark Twain turned to *Guy Mannering*
for an example ("This proposal seemed to dispose most
of the assembly instantly to evacuate the premises") of
high-flown prolixity: "Sir Walter Scott and Mr. Dickens
were distressingly given to using too many words," he
remarked. "One should suit his language to his theme;
and not be always riding the high horse like Sir Walter"
(quoted by Jervis Langdon, *Some Reminiscences* [1938], pp.
20, 21; reprinted in *MT in Elmira* [2013], pp. 212–213).
"I finished Guy Mannering—that curious, curious book,
with its mob of squalid shadows jabbering around a single
flesh-and-blood being—Dinmont; a book crazily put

together out of the very refuse of the romance-artist's stage properties" (SLC to Brander Matthews, Riverdale, 8 May 1903, *MTL*, pp. 738–739; Clemens neglected to mail the letter and it did not reach Matthews until after Clemens had died).

During a newspaper interview published on 10 April 1904 in the New York *Times*, Mark Twain said that he had read *Guy Mannering* and then "wrote to Brander Matthews and asked him if he would be good enough to point out to me the literary and stylistic merits of the work, for I could not find them" (Scharnhorst, *Complete Interviews* [2006], p. 495). Choosing from among his favorite literary characters (including Don Quixote and Sancho Panza), "Huck-Bkshp" renames his microbe companions in "Three Thousand Years Among the Microbes" (written in 1905). Surprisingly, he calls one Guy Mannering, and Twain originally wrote "Meg Merrilies" in the list of a dozen literary figures, though he subsequently deleted the name of this aged gypsy-nurse who recognizes Colonel Mannering when he returns as Henry Bertram (*WWD?*, p. 472).

Krause, *MTC* (1967), pp. 113–114.

———. *The Heart of Midlothian* (historical novel, published in 1818).

Catalog: ListABP (1910), "Midlothian, Scott", no other information provided.

Scott titled his novel after an Edinburgh prison known in the eighteenth century as the "Heart of Midlothian." In 1866 Clemens wrote in Notebook 5: "Simple and Touching Eloquence— <Effie> Jeanie Deans pleading for her sister before the Queen" (*N&J* 1: 143), an episode that takes place in Chapter 37 of Scott's narrative.

Baetzhold, *MT&JB* (1970), p. 330.

———. *Ivanhoe; A Romance* (historical novel, published in 1819).

Scott set this novel in medieval England during the reign of Richard I. Some critics have pointed out its thematic resemblance to the Robin Hood legend. A Saxon knight, Sir Wilfred of Ivanhoe, returns from the Crusades to claim him rightful inheritance and win his beloved Rowena from Athelstane of Coningsburgh, to whom she has been betrothed. On 10 January 1870 Clemens wrote in jest to Olivia Langdon from Albany while he was touring the lecture circuit: "I am reading Ivanhoe. Ivanhoe was a knight in Sir Walter Scott's time. He is dead, now. He married Cedrick the Saxon, & the fruit of this union was a daughter by the name of Reginald Front-de-Boeuf. The whole six fell in battle at Ashby de la Zouche. . . . You know all that it is necessary to know about this romance, now, Livy darling" (*Let* 4: 15–16). Mark Twain mentioned "the amiable Bois-Guilbert and the pleasant Front-de-Boeuf" in a sketch for the July 1870 *Galaxy*, "The 'Tournament' in A.D. 1870." He included page numbers from *Ivanhoe* in study notes for *The Prince and the Pauper* (1881).

"Maybe 'Ivanhoe'" was among the "several books, piled and disposed, with cast-iron exactness," on a parlor table in the antebellum "House Beautiful" that Twain itemized in Chapter 38 of *Life on the Mississippi* (1883). Twain recalled that in a few American villages the "puerility" of tournaments was re-enacted: "It was a kind of two-cent, tin-imitation of Ashby-de-la-Zouche; where a lot of

young gentlemen disguised themselves in stage armor, called themselves Brian de Bois-Gilbert, The Disinherited Knight, and so on, and gravely tilted at each other in a ring" (a passage omitted from Chapter 40 of *Life on the Mississippi*, published in the Heritage Press edition [1944], p. 411). "A curious exemplification of the power of a single book for good or harm is shown in the effects wrought by 'Don Quixote' and those wrought by 'Ivanhoe.' The first swept the world's admiration for, the mediaeval chivalry-silliness out of existence; and the other restored it. As far as our South is concerned, the good work done by Cervantes is pretty nearly a dead letter, so effectually has Scott's pernicious work undermined it" (*Life on the Mississippi*, Ch. 46). Twain appeared to borrow details of Scott's description of the tournament at Ashby-de-la-Zouch from Chapter 12 of *Ivanhoe* in depicting the well-attended tournament in Chapter 9 of *A Connecticut Yankee in King Arthur's Court* (1889). In "The Disappearance of Literature," a speech Twain made to the Nineteenth Century Club on 20 November 1900, he commented: "The fact of the business is, you've got to be one of two ages to appreciate Scott. When you're eighteen you can read *Ivanhoe*, and you want to wait until you're ninety to read some of the rest" (*MTB* [1912], p. 1120; *MTS* 1923, p. 210; *MTSpk* [1976], p. 359).

In *Mark Twain as Critic* (1967) Sydney Krause primarily dealt with *Life on the Mississippi* (1883) in explicating Twain's opinions of Sir Walter Scott; in an earlier article, "Twain and Scott: Experience versus Adventures," *Modern Philology* 62.3 (February 1965): 227–236, Krause focused on *Adventures of Huckleberry Finn* (1885). Krause's essay assigned Twain's hostility to his belief that Scott's books represented history as adventures, and thus were contrary to Twain's dichotomy between "realism" and "romance." Krause examined Chapters 12 and 13 of *Huckleberry Finn* (the *Walter Scott* episode) and identified analogues between *Huckleberry Finn* and Scott's *Ivanhoe*.

Pochmann, "Mind of MT" (1924), p. 191; Baetzhold, *MT&JB* (1970), pp. 49, 133–134, 330 n. 7.

———. *Ivanhoe; A Romance*. 3 vols. Edinburgh: Archibald Constable and Co., 1820.

Source: eBay listing, item 7033145257, 18 May 2006, starting bid $4,750, bids ending on 24 May 2006, "1st Edition, 1820, "first volume of this complete three-volume set has the Clemens library auction plate on the inside front cover, front cover of volume 2 is detached, leather covers, no foxing, clean and tight inside." The set was described as originating from a "Long Island estate," and was accompanied by nineteen other Walter Scott volumes "boxed together and in storage for 78 years, since the newspaper they were wrapped in were from 1928. There is no mold and no foxing, and the pages are clean, although there is substantial spine brittleness." (JoDee Benussi noticed this eBay listing and generously sent it to me on 18 May 2006.)

Here is a somewhat problematical addition to Clemens's known library contents. First of all, this *Ivanhoe* edition was not listed in the catalog provided for the 1911 sale by the Anderson Auction Company of New York City. That fact in itself does not preclude its authenticity, since a number of books have turned up over the years that were not included in that sale catalog and yet have the *A1911* label signed by Albert Bigelow Paine and give every evidence of having belonged to the Clemens family's library. The *A1911* auction label at the bottom of the front pastedown endpaper in this volume certainly looks authentic in the photograph provided for the eBay listing. On the other hand, it appears to be pasted over part of an earlier bookplate (picturing a black raven holding a pennant) of one "Osman Ricardo." Did that person own this *Ivanhoe* set before Clemens acquired it? It is also puzzling that these were not part of the Abbotsford Edition of Scott's *Waverley Novels* (1842) that Clemens took pride in acquiring. Still, it would be quite conceivable that Clemens obtained in Edinburgh or London another, earlier edition of *Ivanhoe* that was never recorded anywhere. The verdict making the most sense in this case is a slightly qualified vote for acceptance of the three volumes' genuineness as Clemens association copies.

————. *The Journal of Sir Walter Scott, from the Original Manuscript at Abbotsford.* Ed. David Douglas (1823–1916). 2 vols. Illus. Edinburgh: David Douglas, 1890.
"Sir Walter Scott's Diary—David Douglas, Edinburgh," Clemens wrote in Notebook 28 in March 1889 (TS p. 44). A little farther on he repeated the entry: "Diary of Scott (Douglas)" (TS p. 45).

————. *The Journal of Sir Walter Scott, from the Original Manuscript at Abbotsford.* Ed. David Douglas (1823–1916). 2 vols. Illus. Edinburgh: David Douglas, 1891.
Inscription: signed in ink on the page of advertisements following the front flyleaf: "Ida C. Langdon". Ida Clark Langdon (1849–1934) was married to Charles Jervis Langdon (1849–1916).
Marginalia: R. Kent Rasmussen noticed a small marginal marking on page 60 next to a passage where Scott explains his word count and productivity.
Catalog: Ball 2016 inventory, blue cloth, gilt lettering on the spine.
Location: Quarry Farm library shelves, under the supervision of the Mark Twain Archive, Elmira College, Elmira, New York.
These volumes were accessible to Clemens whenever he visited the Langdons' home in Elmira.

————. *The Journal of Sir Walter Scott, from the Original Manuscript at Abbotsford.* Ed. David Douglas (1823–1916). 2 vols. Illus. Edinburgh: David Douglas, 1891.
Inscription: signed by "Ida C. Langdon". Ida Clark Langdon (1849–1934) was married to Charles Jervis Langdon (1849–1916).
Catalog: Ball 2016 inventory, blue cloth, gilt lettering, good condition.
Location: Mark Twain Archive, Gannett-Tripp Learning Center, Elmira College, Elmira, New York.
These volumes were accessible to Clemens whenever he visited the Langdons' home in Elmira.

————. *Kenilworth; A Romance.* Illus. Boston: DeWolfe, Fiske & Co., n.d. 448 pp.
Source: MTLAcc, entry #1246, volume donated by Clemens. [The historical novel was first published in 1821.]
Olivia Clemens wrote to her mother on 5 July 1873, "I am reading Kenilworth and enjoying it very much. We shall go to Kenilworth castle [in Warwickshire] before long

and I shall try to fancy how it looked when prepared to recieve [*sic*] Queen Elizabeth—If you have not read the book I think it would be pleasant for you to read it, then you can realize better what I am seeing at least in that one instance" (MTHM). Around 1879 Mark Twain's study notes for *The Prince and the Pauper* (1881) contained citations to *Kenilworth*: "lady's dress—20, Kenilworth"; "A building—28 Ken"; "Prince dress—p. 131 Ken" (DVI 14, MTP). Twain seemingly borrowed proper names from Scott's novel when writing *Pudd'nhead Wilson* (1894); Scott wrote about Cecil Burleigh and the Earl of Leicester, while *Pudd'nhead Wilson* contains characters named Colonel Cecil Burleigh Essex and York Leicester Driscoll.

————. *The Lady of the Lake.* With notes and index. Edinburgh: John Ross & Co., 1871. 216 pp.
Source: MTLAcc, entry #2099, volume donated from Clemens's library by Clara Clemens Gabrilowitsch in 1910.
A little boy in *The Gilded Age* (1873) is named Roderick Dhu, after Scott's rebel Highland chief; a footnote in the novel explains: "In those days the average man called his children after his most revered literary and historical idols" (Chapter 11). Henry Pochmann—"The Mind of Mark Twain" (1924), p. 190—suggested that Book I, Canto III of Scott's poem gave Twain the notion for Tom Sawyer to send a boy to run about town with a blazing stick as a signal for his gang to convene (*HF* [1885], Ch. 3); Walter Blair corroborated this source (*MT&HF* [1960], pp. 117–118). In "English as She Is Taught" (1887), Twain quotes six lines of rhyming couplets from Scott's poem, then presents a schoolchild's effort to paraphrase the passage. Chapter 61 of *Following the Equator* (1897) includes "a Brooklyn public-school boy's attempt to turn a few verses of the 'Lady of the Lake' into prose."

————. *The Lady of the Lake.* Boston: J. R. Osgood & Co., 1885. 273 pp.
Source: MTLAcc, entry #2089, volume donated from Clemens's library by Clara Clemens Gabrilowitsch in 1910.

————. *The Lay of the Last Minstrel* (poem, published in 1805).
Mark Twain parodied Scott's famous line (Canto 6, i) in a letter written on 30 December 1863 from Virginia City: "Breathes there a man with soul so dead that he wouldn't take hold under such seductive circumstances? Scasely" (*MTEnt*, p. 120). In 1866 Twain jokingly referred to the lay (i.e., share) of the last crew member on a whaling vessel as the 'Lay of the Last Minstrel" (Sacramento *Weekly Union*, 26 May 1866; *LSI*, p. 64). Planning a speech in 1885, Twain jocularly attributed Scott's narrative poem to Tennyson (NB 24, *N&J* 3: 138). In "My First Lie, and How I Got Out of It" (1899), Twain pretends to believe that Milton wrote the poem.

————. *A Legend of Montrose* (historical novel, published in 1819).
Mark Twain, comparing British and American humor in August 1885, acknowledged: "Major Dalgetty (good on stage, no doubt)"—as though he found Scott's comical Sir Dugald Dalgetty of Drumthwacket less than satisfying in the pages of the novel (NB 24, *N&J* 3: 172).

————. *Letters on Demonology and Witchcraft, Addressed to J[ohn]. G[ibson]. Lockhart, Esq.* (published in London in 1830).
Walter Scott addressed ten letters to his son-in-law,

the Scottish writer and critic John Gibson Lockhart (1794–1854); in these Scott surveyed purported instances of demonology and witchcraft from the earliest times to his own day. He took a rational approach that explained away all of the hysterical illusions of supernatural events. Coleman O. Parsons—"The Background of *The Mysterious Stranger*" (1960), pp. 67–68—used parallel columns to demonstrate the "connection" between Mark Twain's account of Gottfried's grandmother's death by burning in Chapter 4 of the Eseldorf version ("The Chronicle of Young Satan") of *The Mysterious Stranger* and Scott's description of the burning of a bewildered beldam in Scotland. See also the Catalog entry for George Mackienzie's *The Laws and Customes of Scotland, in Matters Criminal.* Baetzhold, *MT&JB* (1970), p. 365.

———. *The Poetical Works of Sir Walter Scott.* 5 vols. Philadelphia: J. Maxwell, 1827.

Source: MTLAcc, entry #2088, Volume IV only (266 pp.) donated from Clemens's library by Clara Clemens Gabrilowitsch in 1910. The last pages of this volume were missing in 1910.

———. *The Poetical Works of Sir Walter Scott.* 5 vols. Engraved frontispiece in Volume I. Green roan-backed spines, marbled boards, very worn. Philadelphia: J. Maxwell, 1827.

Inscription: the flyleaf of Volume V is signed, "J. Langdon/Salina" (this was Jervis Langdon, father of Olivia Clemens). Salina, New York was a town on the Erie Canal in Onondaga County.

Catalogs: *A1911,* "Vols. 1–3 and 5, 4 vols., 24mo, half leather, . . . Phila. 1827," quotes the signature, with a sheet of notes by Clemens laid in, lot 422, sold for $1.75 to the Mark Twain Company; *Sotheby's 2003,* #192, Volumes I and V only, $1,100 (sold with three other titles from the Clemens family library); Volumes I and V only listed by Admirable Books, *Twainucopia* (2006), p. 5, item #2.

Copy examined: Jervis Langdon's unmarked copies of Volumes I and V, at the Sotheby's auction in 2003. Robert H. Hirst had inspected these volumes in May 1980 when they were in the possession of Olivia Lada-Mocarski (Hirst to Alan Gribben, 4 February 1981).

———. *The Poetical Works of Sir Walter Scott, Bart. Complete in One Volume.* Boston: Crosby, Nickols, Lee and Co., 1861. 840 pp.

Catalog: Ball 2016 inventory, red cloth, gilt lettering, gilt-edged pages, spine broken, covers detached, poor condition.

Location: Quarry Farm library shelves, under the supervision of the Mark Twain Archive, Elmira College, Elmira, New York.

This book was available to Clemens whenever he visited Quarry Farm in Elmira.

———. *The Poetical Works of Sir Walter Scott. With Life by William Chambers, LL.D. [1800–1883].* Embossed blue-gray cloth cover, decorated endpapers. New York: R. Worthington Co., 1886. 629 pp.

Inscription: inscribed by Olivia Clemens on the verso of the frontispiece in black ink: "Clara L. Clemens/Sept. '87/Elmira."

Location: Mark Twain Library, Redding, Connecticut. Donated from Clemens's library by Clara Clemens

Gabrilowitsch in 1910 (MTLAcc, entry #2090).

Copy examined: Clara Clemens's unmarked copy. Displays the red ink Mark Twain Library accession number "2090" and the purple oval Library stamps. The front endpapers, front flyleaf, title page, and spine are loose. Laid in at the rear of the volume is a child's essay on Scott—not Clara's but rather the effort of a later Library patron—that earned a grade of "B-". Examined in 1970 and again in June 1982 and on 9 November 2019.

———. *Quentin Durward* (historical novel, published in 1823). Mark Twain alluded to this novel in his study notes for *The Prince and the Pauper* (1881). Besides noting the title in one place, he also wrote: "(Dress of arms about p. 54 Q. Durward)"; he additionally copied out some archaic phrases from this source (DV115, MTP). Howard G. Baetzhold (*MT&JB*, p. 134) saw an indebtedness to Chapter 4 of *Quentin Durward* in Twain's depiction of Hank Morgan's horsemanship in *A Connecticut Yankee* (1889). On 8 May 1903 Clemens stated in a letter to Brander Matthews written from Riverdale that he had recently finished reading *Quentin Durward.* After grappling with *Guy Mannering,* he averred, "it was like leaving the dead to mingle with the living: it was like withdrawing from the infant class in the College of Journalism to sit under the lectures in English literature in Columbia University." He concluded incredulously, "I wonder who wrote Quentin Durward?" (*MTL,* p. 739). Clemens neglected to mail the letter and it did not reach Matthews until after Clemens had died. Baetzhold, *MT&JB* (1970), pp. 94, 330 n. 7, 338 n. 51.

———. *Rob Roy* (historical novel, published in 1818). Clemens made an entry in Notebook 27 in March 1888 concerning Scott's novel about the Scottish outlaw Rob Roy MacGregor: "7th chap. Rob Roy—/269 Apl Hopes," suggesting a contrast between an incident in *Rob Roy* and a similar one in William Dean Howells's 1888 novel, *April Hopes* (see *N&J* 3: 378). Clemens would have used these examples in a projected (but never undertaken) study of prose styles (*N&J* 3: 379). To Brander Matthews Clemens complained in 1903: "I have read the first volume of Rob Roy. . . . Lord, it's all so juvenile! so artificial, so shoddy; and such wax figures and skeletons and spectres. . . .And oh, the poverty of the invention!" Clemens reported that he "can't find the rest of Rob Roy," so he doubted that he would finish reading the novel (SLC to Matthews, Riverdale, 4 May 1903, *MTL* [1917], p. 738).

———. *Roderick Dhu; or, The Lady of the Lake: Opera Libretto.* Yellow wrappers. San Francisco: Francis, Valentine, & Co., 1881. A musical adaptation of Scott's novel composed by J[ohn]. McCulloch. The title celebrates Scott's rebel Highland chief, Roderick Dhu.

Inscription: the signature "Mark Twain" is on the front cover.

Provenance: Appert Collection.

Location: Mark Twain Papers, Bancroft Library, University of California at Berkeley.

Source: University of California at Berkeley online catalog, 28 November 2007. I wish to thank JoDee Benussi for calling my attention to this acquisition.

It was highly unusual for Clemens to label additions to his library with his pen name. The lack of information about this item's earlier provenance raises questions about its authenticity.

———. "St. Leon's Toast" (also known as "The Knight's Toast," poem).

In February 1870 Olivia Langdon Clemens (who had married Clemens that month) copied this sentimental poem into her commonplace book (DV161, MS pp. 95–98, MTP). St. Leon, a "gallant knight," rises at a banquet and proposes his heartfelt toast to "to one, whose love for me shall last,/When lighter passions long have passed." The final words of the poem reveal the woman's identity to be "My mother!" Jo Dee Benussi identified this poem for me.

———. *Tales of a Grandfather: History of Scotland.* Illustrated Library Edition. Six volumes bound as three. Three-quarter tan calf, raised bands, gilt compartments, double labels, marbled boards and endpapers, gilt edges. Boston: James R. Osgood, 1879–1881.

Inscriptions: all three volumes were inscribed in ink by Clemens: "Livy L. Clemens/1886."

Provenance: the pastedown endpapers of each volume display Clara Clemens Gabrilowitsch's library shelf numbering system from her Detroit years—"HE Music Room Shelf." Evidently she retained these volumes when she sold so many other books in 1911 and 1951, but their ownership after Clara's death is not known.

Location: collection of Kevin Mac Donnell, Austin, Texas.

Source: email from Mac Donnell to Alan Gribben, 1 November 2005.

———. *The Talisman* (historical novel, published in 1825).

In Chapter 1 of *Tom Sawyer Abroad* (1894), Tom Sawyer "got all that notion" about setting off on a new Crusade, like Richard the Lion-Hearted, "out of Walter Scott's book, which he was always reading." Huckleberry Finn adds: "I took the book and read all about it, and as near as I could make it out, most of the folks that shook farming to go crusading had a mighty rocky time of it." Baetzhold, *MT&JB* (1970), p. 338 n. 50.

———. *Waverley; or, 'Tis Sixty Years Since.* Blue leather. London: Thomas Nelson and Sons, 1906. 571 pp.

Provenance: Antenne-Dorrance Collection, Rice Lake, Wisconsin (a family collection inherited from Katy Leary, the Clemenses's housekeeper).

Location: Mark Twain Archive, Gannett-Tripp Learning Center, Elmira College, Elmira, New York.

Copy examined: possibly Clemens's unmarked copy, though his ownership of this volume is not established. It may have belonged to Mary T. Evans of LaCrosse, Wisconsin, the first wife of Warren Leary, Sr. (Leary was the nephew of the Clemenses' housekeeper Katy Leary, and she bequeathed her book collection to him.) Examined on 28 May 2015.

James Birchfield—"Jim's Coat of Arms," *Mark Twain Journal* 14.4 (Summer 1969): 15–16—suggested that Tom Sawyer's grandiose notion of a coat of arms for the enslaved Jim (*Adventures of Huckleberry Finn* [1885], Chapter 38) could have derived from Scott's novel *Waverley,* published in 1814.

———. *The Waverley Novels.* Abbotsford Edition. 12 vols. Illus. Edinburgh: Robert Cadell, 1842–1847.

Inscriptions: Volumes I and III signed by Miss Ida Langdon.

Location: formerly in the collection of the Mark Twain House and Museum, Hartford, Connecticut. Reported as "missing" in August 1987 by the adjacent Stowe-Day Library, which was then housing the Clemens association

copies.

Copy examined: copy purchased by Clemens in 1873 for the Langdon family. Examined in 1970. This set was supposedly identical to the one Clemens acquired for his own library at the same time. The Langdons' copy was given to the (then-named) Mark Twain Memorial in Hartford.

In a postscript to a letter Olivia Clemens wrote from Edinburgh on 6 August 1873 to her mother, Mrs. Langdon, Clemens added: "Our books have come—a rare thing we have been on the track of for ten days—got it at last—the famous 'Abbotsford Edition' of Scott's works—12 huge volumes elaborately illustrated. Pretty scarce book" (*MTLet* 5: 428). Mark Twain's page references in his working notes for *The Prince and the Pauper* (DV 115) correspond to the pagination of the Abbotsford Edition. Rudyard Kipling interviewed Twain in August of 1889, and during a discussion of copyright reform Twain alluded to Scott's novels: "When the copyright notes protected them, I bought editions as expensive as I could afford, because I liked them. At the same time the same firms were selling editions that a cat might buy" (*From Sea to Sea* [1899], 2: 174; Scharnhorst, *Complete Interviews,* p. 121). On 27 June 1893 Twain made a note while traveling by train to Berlin: "Article—'The Unfinished Novel.' If it were continued, how sad it would be. Thackeray finishing the Waverley novels was on track of a truth" (NB 33, TS p. 20).

———. *The Waverley Novels.* 25 vols. Illus. Edinburgh: Adam and Charles Black, 1854.

Catalog: Ball 2016 inventory, brown leather, gilt lettering, two volumes only, Volume I lacks a cover, Volume II is in fair condition.

Location: Quarry Farm library shelves, under the supervision of the Mark Twain Archive, Elmira College, Elmira, New York.

Presumably this set was still complete when it was available to Clemens at Quarry Farm in Elmira.

SCOTT, WILLIAM BELL (1811–1890). *Autobiographical Notes of the Life of William Bell Scott, H. R. S. A., LLD. And Notices of His Artistic and Poetic Circle of Friends 1830 to 1882.* Ed. by W[illiam]. Minto (1845–1893). 2 vols. Illus. New York: Harper & Brothers, 1892.

Source: MTLAcc, entries #1775 and #1776, volumes donated by Clemens.

The Scottish artist, art teacher, and poet Scott resided periodically in London. He left behind his intimate impressions of the Pre-Raphaelite circle.

Scribner's Magazine (New York, published 1887–1939).

After halting the publication of *Scribner's Monthly* in 1881 (see the following Catalog entry), the Scribner's firm started a new journal in 1887 whose cover billed itself as *Scribner's Magazine: Publishing Monthly with Illustrations.* Evidently Clemens referred to this latter magazine on 13 September 1888 when he complained to Franklin O. Whitmore that some numbers of Scribner's "illustrated Art-monthly" had never arrived in Elmira (MTP).

Scribner's Monthly (New York, published 1870–1881; in November 1881 it became *Century Magazine*).

"No such pictures in Europe as you get in Scribner," Clemens observed in 1878 (NB 14. *N&J* 2: 57). There is a receipt in the Mark Twain Papers in the Bancroft

Library at Berkeley for Clemens's subscription to *Scribner's Monthly* from January 1880 to December 1880; it is dated 23 December 1879. See the Catalog entry for Richard Malcolm Johnston's *Dukesborough Tales* for a reference to Johnston's "The Expensive Treat," which appeared in the January 1881 issue. In 1881 Clemens wrote "July Scribner" in Notebook 19 (*N&J* 2: 396)—referring to an issue that contained writings by William Dean Howells and George Washington Cable.

SCRIVENER, A. E. "Instances of Belgian Cruelty in Africa," *Missionary Review of the World* 27 (September 1904): 678–680.

In Mark Twain's "King Leopold's Soliloquy" (1905), Leopold reads from "Report of a Journey Made in July, August and September, 1903, by Rev. A. E. Scrivener, a British Missionary." King Leopold complains that such missionaries "spy and spy, and run into print with every foolish trifle." A. E. Scrivener's *Missionary Review of the World* article was Twain's probable source.

SCUDDER, HORACE ELISHA (1838–1902). *Doings of the Bodley Family in Town and Country*. Illus. New York: Hurd and Houghton, 1878. 250 pp.

Source: MTLAcc, entry #1869, volume donated from Clemens's library by Clara Clemens Gabrilowitsch in 1910. Between 1875 and 1887 the Boston author and editor Scudder published a "Bodley Books" children's series that combined travel sketches, stories, poems, and songs.

———. *The Bodleys Telling Stories*. New York: Hurd and Houghton, 1878. 236 pp.

Source: MTLAcc, entry #1870, volume donated from Clemens's library by Clara Clemens Gabrilowitsch in 1910.

SEAMAN, LOUIS LIVINGSTON (1851–1932). *The Real Triumph of Japan: The Conquest of the Silent Foe*. Illus. New York: D. Appleton and Co., 1906. 291 pp. [Publisher and pages conjectured.]

Inscription: the front pastedown endpaper is signed, "S. L. Clemens, 1906."

Catalogs: *A1911*, "12mo, cloth, N.Y. 1906," quotes the signature, lot 425, sold for $3; George D. Smith, New York City, "Catalogue of Books" (1911), quotes the signature, item #202, $10.

Japan had prevailed against Russia in the Russo-Japanese War of 1904–1905.

———. *The Real Triumph of Japan: The Conquest of the Silent Foe*. Illus. First edition, third printing. Original olive green pictorial cloth, gilt, top edge gilt, untrimmed, red silk marker. New York: D. Appleton and Co., 1907. 291 pp.

Inscription: the front free flyleaf is inscribed in ink, "Miss Lyons [Isabel V. Lyon, Clemens's secretary]/With the hope that she is/in sympathy with the motif/that inspired this little volume/and with the regards of the/Author./New York/May 11th, 1908."

Marginalia: annotations in Lyon's hand on pages 40, 143, and 166. The first 166 pages contain markings, including fifty lines and four question marks in the margins of forty-two pages. Grammatical correctons and stylistic changes on pages 25, 28, and 153 are characteristic of Clemens's habits of marking books. The text beyond page 166 is wholly unmarked and mostly unopened.

Location: collection of Kevin Mac Donnell, Austin, Texas.

Source: Mac Donnell to Alan Gribben, 3 September 2005.

SEARS, EDMUND HAMILTON (1810–1876). "Calm on the

listening ear of night" (hymn, 1834). Also known as "The Christmas hymn."

Clemens quoted the last two lines of the fourth stanza in a letter written to Orion Clemens from Esmeralda, California on 7 August 1862: "And the poet dreamt of Nevada when he wrote: 'and Sharon waves, in solemn praise,/Her silent groves of palm'" (*MTL*, p. 84; *MTLet* 1: 234). In 1866 Clemens was reminded of this hymn by scenery in the Sandwich Islands; in Notebook 6 he copied the lines: "And Sharon waves/In silent praise/Her sacred groves of palm" (*N&J* 1: 214).

The Secret Out; or, One Thousand Tricks with Cards, and Other Recreations. By the Author of "The Sociable; or, One Thousand One Home Amusements," "The Magician's Own Book," Etc., Etc. Illus. Brown cloth, stamped, gilt. New York: Dick & Fitzgerald, [cop. 1859]. 398 pp. [Wiljalba Frikell (1818–1903) is sometimes credited as the author.]

Inscription: the front flyleaf is signed in brown ink: "Charles Langdon/Elmira/N. Y./Dec 4th 1863" [Charles Jervis Langdon (1849–1916) was Olivia Langdon's brother], to which was added in pencil, "No 4" and then below that (in ink) "B. W. H. A. M".

Provenance: bookplate #567 of the "J. Langdon Family Library" on the front pastedown endpaper.

Catalog: Ball 2016 inventory, brown cloth, gilt lettering, signed by Charles Langdon in 1863, Jervis Langdon Family Library #567.

Location: Mark Twain Archive, Elmira College, Elmira, New York.

Copy examined: unmarked copy available to Clemens whenever he visited Elmira. Examined on 27 May 2015.

SEDGWICK, ARTHUR GEORGE (1844–1915). "International Copyright by Judicial Decision," *Atlantic Monthly* 43.256 (February 1879): 217–230.

This article prompted Clemens to enter several comments about copyright in Notebook 17 in February 1879 (*N&J* 2: 270–271).

SEEBERG, REINHOLD (1859–1935). *Revelation and Inspiration*. Harper's Library of Living Thought. New York: Harper & Brothers, 1909. 135 pp.

Source: MTLAcc, entry #1491, volume donated by Clemens.

Seeberg, a University of Berlin scholar, lays out a reformed Christian belief system that cultivates personal growth and "the inspired mind."

SEELEY, (SIR) JOHN ROBERT (1834–1895). *Ecce Homo; A Survey of the Life and Work of Jesus Christ*. Boston: Roberts Brothers, 1866. 373 pp.

Source: MTLAcc, entry #902, volume donated by Isabel V. Lyon, Clemens's secretary.

———. *The Expansion of England; Two Courses of Lectures*. London: Macmillan and Co., 1883. 309 pp. Repr. in 1891.

Reading at the London Library, Clemens wrote down a title on 22 October 1896: "The Expansion of England—J R Seeley" (NB 39, TS p. 12). Seeley's *Expansion of England* largely describes the colonization of India.

SEEMANN, BERTHOLD CARL (1825–1871). *Viti: An Account of a Government Mission to the Vitian or Fijian Islands, in the Years 1860–61*. Cambridge: Macmillan & Co., 1862. 447 pp.

In the list of Clemens's reading in London during November 1896 appears this author and title: "Seeman's *Viti*" (NB

39, TS p. 26).

Madigan, "MT's Passage to India" (1974), p. 365.

SEEMÜLLER, ANNE MONCURE (CRANE) (1838–1872). *Emily Chester. A Novel.* Boston: Ticknor and Fields, 1864. 367 pp. [Published anonymously.]

Assembling evidence of coincidental phenomena in "Mental Telegraphy" (1891), Mark Twain quotes from a Boston *Post* article that notes striking parallels between *Emily Chester* and Louisa May Alcott's first novel, *Moods* (1864). These similarities occurred even though "Miss Anna M. Crane, of Baltimore" and Miss Alcott were strangers who lived hundreds of miles apart. Twain does not indicate that he has read either work. Crane's (she was not yet married in 1864) first novel depicted the suffering of a woman married unhappily to a man whom she admired intellectually but did not love.

SÉGUR, SOPHIE (ROSTOPCHINE), COMTESSE DE (1799–1874). *The Adventures of a Donkey.* Translated from the French by "P. S." Illus. Baltimore, Maryland: Baltimore Publishing Co., [1880], 274 pp. [Other available editions: Philadelphia: H. L. Kilner & Co., 1880. 274 pp. Also: Baltimore, Maryland: J. P. Piet, 1881. 274 pp. The Clemens family's edition is undetermined.]

Olivia Clemens's journal for 28 June 1885 records that the Clemens children gave their donkey the name Patience Cadichon (pronounced "Kaditchon") (DV 161, MTP). Clara Clemens recalled that the girls called their donkey "'Kadichan' (named after the delightful book, *Adventures with a Donkey*)" (*MFMT*, p. 76). Beaten cruelly by his first master, Cadichon runs away into a sheltering forest. In his subsequent adventures this "learned donkey" finds kinder masters.

SEIDEL, HEINRICH (1842–1906). "Der Tausendmarkschein" (story, published in 1886; collected in *Der Tausendmarkschein und andere Erzählungen [The Thousand-Mark Bill and Other Narrations]*, a collection published in 1900). [The edition of the story that Clemens read has not been undetermined.]

Edgar H. Hemminghaus evidently saw Clemens's copy of a book by Seidel in the Mark Twain Library at Redding; he commented that Clemens "enjoyed the charm, the natural flow, and the refreshingly delicate humor of his stories. The tale *Der Tausendmarkschein* in particular appealed to him" ("Mark Twain's German Provenience" [1945], p. 470). That volume has since disappeared.

SEITZ, DON CARLOS (1862–1935). *Discoveries in Every-day Europe; Vagrant Notes of a Rapid Journey.* Illustrated by Maurice Ketten (1875–1965), birth name Prosper Fiorino. New York: Harper & Brothers, 1907. 69 pp.

Source: MTLAcc, entry #591, volume donated by Clemens.

Clemens might have enjoyed this curious little book of miscellaneous information and amusing cartoons. *Discoveries in Every-day Europe* has no table of contents or index, but simply reported on what the traveler might expect to encounter in Gibraltar, England, France, Germany, Switzerland, and Italy. It compared and contrasted the clothing, shopping, trolleys, beggars, restaurant cleanliness, train coaches, dining cars, newspapers, college campuses, mail services, and dozens of other topics.

Selected Poems, Illustrated. From Arnold, Burns, Schiller, Tennyson, [Adelaide A.] Procter, [James] Shirley, Shelley, Keats, [Francis Turner] Palgrave, Mrs. Browning, Longfellow,

[Thomas] Gray, Campbell, [Winthrop Mackworth] Praed, Herrick, R. Browning, Wordsworth, Moore, Dryden, [Caroline] Norton, [Thomas] Percy, Mrs. Barbauld [Anna Laetitia (Aikin) Barbould], [Richard Harris] Barham [, pseud. "Thomas Ingoldsby"]. Illus. New York: Kilbourne Tompkins, 1875. [The pages are not numbered.]

Inscription: the front flyleaf is signed in pencil, "Saml. L. Clemens/Hartford, 1875."

Catalogs: A1911, "12mo, cloth, N.Y. 1875," quotes the signature, lot 426, sold for $2; *Hunley 1958*, item #135, $6.50.

Location: Mark Twain House and Museum, Hartford, Connecticut. Gift of Professor Norman Holmes Pearson (1909–1975) of Yale University in 1958.

Copy examined: Clemens's copy, unmarked. Examined in August 1987. There is a sale label from the *A1911* auction on the front pastedown endpaper.

This book was acquired and signed when Clemens and his wife were stocking their new home's library shelves. Most of the poets are British, though Longfellow is accorded two poems ("Midnight Mass for the Dying Year" and "Song of the Silent Year"). Percy Bysshe Shelley and Thomas Gray get two poems, and Robert Burns and Alfred Lord Tennyson have three; all of the others are restricted to a single poem apiece. Among the famous pieces are Tennyson's "'Break, Break, Break,'" Shelley's "To the Skylark," Keats' "Ode on a Grecian Urn," Elizabeth Barrett Browning's "Sonnet from the Portuguese," Gray's "Elegy Written in a Country Churchyard," and Robert Browning's "How They Brought the Good News from Ghent to Aix." Some of the selections are now obscure, such as Caroline Norton's "The King of Denmark's Ride" and Richard Harris Barham's "Look at the Clock!" The lack of pagination probably stems from the insertion of so many full-page engraved illustrations; blank pages surround most of these, and the printer must have therefore decided not to bother with page numbers. There is no index at the rear of the volume, but the table of contents does list all of the poets and poems in sequence.

SELKIRK, ALEXANDER (1676–1721).

Mark Twain knew the identity of this original for Defoe's Robinson Crusoe character. "I feel as Alexander Selkirk felt, who had to cheer himself with sorrowful poetry because there was no other way to put in the time," Twain remarked in his Autobiographical Dictation on 11 June 1906 (*AutoMT* 2: 109). See also the Catalog entries for Daniel Defoe's *Robinson Crusoe* (1719) and William Cowper's "Verses Supposed to Be Written by Alexander Selkirk" (1782).

Scott, *OPMT* (1966), p. 37.

SELMER, LOUIS. *Boer War Lyrics.* Original cloth, spine soiled, edges and corners worn. New York: Abbey Press, [1903]. 105 pp.

Inscriptions: inscribed by the author to Clemens. Laid in is a letter from Selmer to Clemens on which Clemens jotted a caustic note: "Preserve this rhymed slush & also this ass's letter. S L C."

Provenance: has the shelfmarks of the library system that Clara Clemens Gabrilowitsch employed for her books during her Detroit years.

Catalogs: ListABP (1910), "Boer War Lyrics (letter laid in),"

Selmer"; *C1951*, 46a, listed among volumes containing marginal notations by Clemens, "includes a personal letter to Clemens by the author," $27.50; "Property from the Library of Mark Twain," Butterfield & Butterfield, San Francisco, Sale 6613 (16 July 1997), lot 2692.

Location: Mark Twain House and Museum, Hartford, Connecticut.

Copy examined: Clemens's unmarked copy. Viewed in Hartford in 1997.

Clemens's sympathies did not lie with the Boers' side in this struggle, but Selmer's poetic efforts were unlikely to please him anyway. The opening stanza of "Sine Die" furnishes a sample: "Full zodiacs three the fiery sun,/Thro' maze of stars, his web has spun,/Since War's late grimy page begun/To blaze its line—the bloody hand/Whose lurid strokes bade Peace to stand" (p. 103). Clemens's derogatory opinion qualifies *Boer War Lyrics* for a place in his hypothetical "Library of Literary Hogwash." Selmer is not known to have published any other books.

SEPET, MARIUS (1845–1925). *Jeanne d'Arc*. Deuxième Edition Revue. Illus. Tours: Alfred Mame et Fils, 1887. 535 pp.

Marginalia: Clemens made extensive markings and annotations in pencil and violet and brown ink. "Use this?" he inquired in pencil on page 217. "The trap that caught her at last," he noted on page 322 in pencil. "Must dress & undress in the presence of these men who were so outraged by her male attire," he wrote in pencil on page 371. There are no marks beyond page 385, and many leaves are unopened after that point.

Catalogs: ListABP (1910), "Jeanne D'Arc, Sepet"; "Retz Appraisal" (1944), p. 11, valued at $25.

Location: Mark Twain Papers, Bancroft Library, University of California at Berkeley.

Copy examined: Clemens's copy. Paper wrappers. Poor condition; the spine is broken.

In France in September 1891 Mark Twain made a memorandum: "Sepet. Jeanne d'Arc gr. in—8° M. 20 fr" (NB 31, TS p. 6). One entry farther on, he indicated that the London firm of Chatto & Windus was supposed to send him books about Joan of Arc. Sepet's *Jeanne d'Arc* was fourth in the list of "authorities examined" that Twain placed on the page preceding the "Translator's Preface" of *Personal Recollections of Joan of Arc* (1896).

Ronald Jenn and Linda A. Morris, "The Sources of Mark Twain's *Personal Recollections of Joan of Arc*," *Mark Twain Journal* 55.1–2 (Spring/Fall 2017): 55–74; and Linda A. Morris, "What is 'Personal' about *Personal Recollections of Joan of Arc*?" *American Literary Realism* 51.2 (Winter 2019): 97–110.

SERAO, MATILDE (1856–1927). *The Ballet Dancer, and On Guard*. Trans. from the Italian. New York: Harper & Brothers, 1901. 266 pp.

Source: MTLAcc, entry #1660, volume donated by Clemens.

Two tragic novellas, the first set in Naples about the frustrations of a ballet dancer, Carmela Minino, and the second about the convict Sciurrillo in a Piedmontese prison.

———. *The Conquest of Rome*. First American edition. Trans. from the Italian. Original decorated gray/tan cloth, gilt. Half green morocco folding-case. New York: Harper & Brothers,

1902. 317 pp.

Inscription: the front pastedown endpaper is signed in ink, "S L. Clemens/1903".

Catalogs: *C1951*, D64, listed among volumes signed by Clemens; *Zeitlin 1951*, item #39, $15; *Sotheby's 2003*, #232, $3,250 (sold with two other titles about ancient Rome).

Provenance: has the shelfmark (erased) of Clara Clemens Gabrilowitsch's private library in Detroit. During the 1970s the volume belonged to the film producer Robert Daley of Burbank, California, but eventually it became part of the collection of Nick Karanovich, Fort Wayne, Indiana.

Location: collection of Kevin Mac Donnell, Austin, Texas. Incidentally, this volume is visible in a photograph that Jean Clemens took of her cat sitting in a chair; the title can be detected in a bookcase on the second shelf from the bottom.

Copy examined: Clemens's unmarked copy, in July 2004. Serao set this novel about political intrigue and marital infidelity in Rome in the 1880s.

SERVISS, GARRETT PUTNAM (1851–1929). *Astronomy with the Naked Eye; A New Geography of the Heavens*. New York: Harper & Brothers, 1908. 246 pp.

Catalog: *C1951*, D63, listed among volumes signed by Clemens, $9.

———. *Curiosities of the Sky. A Popular Presentation of the Great Riddles and Mysteries of Astronomy*. Illus. New York: Harper & Brothers, 1909. 264 pp.

Inscription: the front pastedown endpaper is signed in brown ink, "SL. Clemens/1909/ Stormfield".

Catalog: *C1951*, D43, listed among volumes signed by Clemens.

Provenance: collection of Frank C. Willson (1889–1960) in Melrose, Massachusetts. His widow Margarete sold the Mark Twain items to the University of Texas in 1962.

Location: Harry Ransom Center, University of Texas at Austin.

Copy examined: Clemens's copy, unmarked.

———. *The Moon Metal*. New York: Harper & Brothers, 1900. 164 pp.

Source: MTLAcc, entry #1069, volume donated by Clemens.

In this early science fiction novel a new metal is obtained from the moon and becomes the new international standard of currency.

SETON, ERNEST THOMPSON (1860–1946). *Wild Animals I Have Known, and 200 Drawings*. Illus. New York: Charles Scribner's Sons, 1901. 359 pp. [cop. 1898]. [Edition conjectured.]

Clemens's copy of this book, if he obtained one, has never surfaced. The likelihood that he owned *Wild Animals I Have Known* seems very great inasmuch as he attended Seton's lecture by that title at Carnegie Hall on 1 January 1902 (Fears, *Day by Day* 3: 610). Seton would later recall that Clemens was present when Seton and John Burroughs quarreled at the home of Andrew Carnegie after Burroughs questioned Seton's credentials as a "naturalist" in an *Atlantic Monthly* essay; however the approximate date that Seton reports (between March and July 1904) does not jibe with Clemens's known biographical facts (Seton, *Trail of an Artist-Naturalist: The Autobiography of Ernest Thompson Seton* (New York: Charles Scribner's Sons,

1940), pp. 367–371). Seton studied in England and Paris and lived at times in the United States, but he spent his formative young years in Ontario, Canada and his literary and artistic subjects often derived from those memories.

SÉVIGNÉ, MARIE DE RABUTIN-CHANTAL, MARQUISE DE (1626–1696). *The Letters of Madame De Sévigné to Her Daughter and Friends*. Ed. by Sarah Josepha (Buell) Hale (1788–1879). Revised edition. 8vo, maroon cloth. Boston: Roberts Brothers, 1878. 438 pp.

Inscription: the front flyleaf is signed in blue ink "S. L. Clemens,/Hartford, 1880."

Marginalia: there are many notations in blue ink and a few markings in pencil. Clemens's notes in blue ink total approximately 580 words on thirty-eight pages. He also made extensive marginal markings, underlinings, and grammatical corrections, nearly all in the same blue ink, on eighteen of the annotated pages and nineteen other pages. Chester Davis (1903–1987) transcribed Clemens's marginalia in the columns of *The Twainian*, extracting more quotations from Sévigné than from Clemens. Davis commenced his report in the November-December 1972 issue (Volume 31), and continued publishing her text and Clemens's comments in every subsequent issue through that of September-October 1974 (Volume 33). According to Davis, Clemens marked the entire book and its index. Some of the marginalia were also quoted in the 1991 Christie's catalog, which revealed that on page 181 Clemens observed, writing sideways in the margin: "It was a sordid time—they wail over/a friend's 'disgrace' one moment, & the next they set about seeing what/profit they can gather from it." On page 276—beside a letter of 21 February 1689—Clemens wrote: "Madame de Sevigne is even more nauseating here than when she is adoring her daughter. She is a pretty offensive old cat, in all, or nearly all, her aspects" (*Twainian* 32 [July-August 1973]: 2). On page 292 Clemens pondered: "A strange & villainous system, where an ignorant infant like this [eighteen-year-old youth] is placed in command of a regiment, with no merit to back him but high birth." Of Sévigné's last letter to her daughter, written on 26 February 1690, Clemens commented in ink at the bottom of page 296: "Being hungry, I drank this/barrel of feeble soup in the/hope of getting the bean in/the bottom, but there was no/bean. These Letters have/not even the common/French merit of being/indecent" (*Twainian* 32 [July-August 1973]: 4; a facsimile reproduction of this note was included in the 1991 Christie's catalog). "What is the value of this letter? Why is it considered worth preserving 200 years?" Clemens asked on page 321 (*Twainian* 33 [January-February 1974]: 3—however, Christie's 1991 catalog said that this remark occurs on page 342).

Clemens also objected to Hale's editing: "What this book mainly lacks, is notes which convey information which we lack" (p. 352). At the top of page 368 Clemens complained: "The idea of arranging these letters by massing those to each *person*, instead of massing them by *date*, was certainly the inspiration of an idiot" (*Twainian* 33 [May-June 1974]: 3). On page 361 Clemens underlined and numbered five words, demanding in the margin, "1. What prince? 2. What prince? 3.What prince? 4. What loss? 5. What disgrace?" He continued his irritated questions in

the margin of page 362, ending with the number "18. What prince?" and adding, "If this book had 2/pages of notes to each/page of matter, it would run the/risk of being intelligible." Clemens theorized about Madame Sévigné's fame on page 363: "Apparently the scarcity of women of rank who are not fools—(in history—) has made this woman renowned, by contrast. Why else she should be conspicuous, is not sharply perceptible." Beside one of Hale's footnotes on page 372, Clemens carped: "Who cares to know this? The notes in this book are beneath contempt." Davis resumed his report of marginalia in *The Twainian* issues of September-October 1985 and November-December 1985 (Volume 44.5: 1–4 and Volume 44.6: 1–4), reproducing four pages of Clemens's comments (181, 296, 361, and 362) in facsimile.

Catalogs: ListABP (1910), "Letters of Mme De Sevigne, Hale"; *C1951*, 42a, $25; Christie's, New York City, estate of Chester Davis, 17 May 1991, "essentially disbound, maroon cloth sides and two-thirds of spine present (the latter loose), some upper corners and fore-edges chipped, many leaves loose and out of order, a tear in one page with word loss, some edges a bit brittle. . . . Its disconcerting condition aside, this is one of the most extensively annotated volumes by Twain to appear on the market in recent years," lot 80, price estimate $2,500–3,500.

Provenance: formerly in the possession of Chester L. Davis's Mark Twain Research Foundation, Perry, Missouri.

Location: currently unknown.

Copy examined: none. I was not allowed to inspect this volume when I visited Chester Davis's home in Perry in 1970.

Estes & Lauriat of Boston billed Clemens on 14 July 1880 for "1 de Sevigne .85¢"; he paid on 20 July (receipt in MTP). Henry Fisher reported that while Clemens was staying at the Hotel Metropole in Vienna he told Fisher that if Princess Pauline Metternich (1836–1921) "were to write her memoirs, the world would gain a book as bright as Mme. de Sévigné's Letters" (*AMT*, p. 43). Susy Clemens informed Clara Clemens on 10 April 1893 that she was amusing herself in Venice by "conscientiously translating a little life of Mme. de Sévigné" (TS in Harnsberger Collection, *S&MT*, p. 329).

Paine, *MTB* (1912), p. 1540.

SEWELL, ANNA (1820–1878). *Black Beauty: The Autobiography of a Horse* (novel, published in 1877).

Just at the time that the automobile was beginning to eliminate horses as a means of transportation, Mark Twain published a novella titled *A Horse's Tale* (1906). He unquestionably meant for this story to reach the same wide audience that Sewell had found previously. Her book, also narrated by a horse, chronicled a lifetime of kindnesses and blows, pettings and whippings, imposed upon a brave-hearted animal that lacked the power of speech. Finally reduced to dragging heavy carts up steep hills, Black Beauty is purchased by a man who operates a fleet of cabs; when the horse collapses from overwork he is sold along with other broken-down nags. Black Beauty is rescued by Mr. Thoroughgood, restored to health, and finally recognized by his original masters, who rejoice at finding him again and rename him "Black Beauty."

Stone, *IE* (1961), p. 253.

SEWELL, MARY (WRIGHT) (1797–1884). *"Our Father's Care"*

(A Ballad). From the twentieth London edition. Illus. Green cloth, gilt lettering on the spine. Philadelphia: American Sunday-School Union, New York, n.d. [1867?]. 34 pp.

> **Inscription:** the front free endpaper is torn out.
>
> **Location:** Mark Twain Library, Redding, Connecticut. Donated from Clemens's library by Clara Clemens Gabrilowitsch in 1910 (MTLAcc, entry #2010).
>
> **Copy examined:** an unmarked copy belonging to the Clemens family. Has the red ink Mark Twain Library accession number "2010". Examined in 1970 and again in June 1982 and on 9 November 2019.

Shafroth, John Franklin (1854–1922). "Speech of Hon. John F. Shafroth, of Colorado, in the House of Representatives, Tuesday, December 17, 1901." Two parts. Unbound reprint from the *Congressional Record*. 31 pp.

> **Marginalia:** Shafroth's speech criticized a Philippine tariff bill that was before Congress; he argued that "the [United States] policy of forcibly annexing and holding the Philippine Islands is a violation of the moral law itself." Clemens's numerous penciled comments and underscorings attest to his concurrence. At the top of page 5 in Part 1 Clemens noted: "The Great Republic became The Great Despotism." Another marginal note implies his approval of Emilio Aguinaldo's role in developing Philippine independence.
>
> **Location:** Paine 89aa, Mark Twain Papers, Bancroft Library, University of California at Berkeley.
>
> **Copy examined:** Clemens's copy.

Shakespeare, William (1564–1616). *All's Well That Ends Well* (comedy, written between 1595 and 1604).

> In a 17 February 1869 letter written to Mary Mason Fairbanks from Titusville, Pennsylvania, Clemens punned on the play's title: "Oils well that ends well" (*MTMF*, p. 75; *MTLet* 3: 107). Following Mark Twain's first lecture in San Francisco, as he recalled, "All the papers were kind in the morning; my appetite returned; I had abundance of money. All's well that ends well" (*Roughing It* [1872], Ch. 78).

———. *Antony and Cleopatra* (historical tragedy, probably written around 1606–1607).

> Leaving Ephesus, Mark Twain recalled, Antony and Cleopatra "sailed on pleasure excursions, in galleys with silver oars and perfumed sails" (letter of 8 September 1867, published in the *Daily Alta Californian*, 24 November 1867; *TIA*, p. 174); cf. Act II, Scene ii, 198–199: "Purple the sails, and so perfumed that/The winds were love-sick with them./ The oars were silver." Clara Clemens included a synopsis of numerous scenes from Acts I and III, interspersed with dialogue, in her undated commonplace book that she began in 1888 (Paine 150, MTP). The tale of the Sydney-bound sailing vessel *Duncan Dunbar*, wrecked on rocks in a disaster that cost nearly 200 lives, "will never grow old, custom cannot stale it" (*FE* [1897], Ch. 9); cf Act III, Scene ii, 240: "Age cannot wither her, nor custom stale/Her infinite variety."

———. *As You Like It*. New York Cassell & Co., 1887. 192 pp. (comedy, probably performed around 1599).

> **Source:** MTLAcc, entry #969, volume donated by Clemens. Mark Twain's "Official Physic" sketch in the New York *Sunday Mercury* (21 April 1867) quoted the phrase "good in everything" (cf. Shakespeare's play, II.i.17; Louis J. Budd,

ed., *CTSS&E* 1: 228, 1039). "All the world's a stage & everybody is writing plays for it," Clemens remarked in a letter of 7 August 1877 to Francis D. Millet, listing his friends who were turning dramatists (ALS in Houghton Library, Harvard). In "A Presidential Candidate" (New York *Evening Post*, 9 June 1879), casting himself as suitably a coward in character, Twain paraphrased *As You Like It* (Act 2, Scene ii, 152–153) when averring that "the bubble reputation can be obtained only at the cannon's mouth" (Louis J. Budd, ed., *CTSS&E* 1: 725, 1063). Clemens entered the title of Shakespeare's play among addresses of 1903–1904 (NB 46, TS p. 2, MTP).

———. *The Comedy of Errors* (comedy, performed by at least 1594).

> Charmed by any instance of double identity, Mark Twain referred to twin servants in November 1877 as "The two Dromios" (NB 14, *N&J* 2: 51). In 1882, contemplating the idea of a novel that featured two strangers coincidentally wearing the same signal, Twain noted: "& then comes the comedy of errors" (NB 20, *N&J* 2: 453).

———. *The Complete Works of William Shakespeare: Comprising His Plays and Poems, with Dr. [Samuel] Johnson's Preface*. 928 pp. With a 178-page Supplement *"Comprising the Seven Dramas Which Have Been Ascribed to His Pen, But Which Are Not Included with His Writings in Modern Editions."* Philadelphia: James B. Smith & Co., 1855. 1104 total pp. The famous preface by Samuel Johnson (1709–1784) came from his Shakespeare edition of 1765. The seven doubtful plays, most notably *The Two Noble Kinsmen*, now believed to be mostly the work of John Fletcher (1579–1625) with probable collaboration by Shakespeare, were edited with notes and introductions by William Gilmore Simms (1806–1870).

> **Source:** MTLAcc, entry #2122a, volume donated from Clemens's library by Clara Clemens Gabrilowitsch in 1910. This might be an early edition that Clemens kept for a lifetime.

———. *The Complete Works of William Shakespeare*. London: Western Mail, Limited, 82, Fleet Street. Cardiff: Tudor Printing Works, 1897. 365 pp.

> **Source:** MTLAcc, entry #2123a, a volume donated from Clemens's library by Clara Clemens Gabrilowitsch in 1910.

> Set in triple columns with a small type font, this compact edition managed to include virtually all of Shakespeare's known plays and poems.

———. *Cymbeline* (historical drama, performed in 1610 or 1611).

> From Washington, D. C. Clemens wrote to Olivia Clemens on 14 January 1891: "I have avoided encountering people, by clinging as a rule to my room & reading. I have read four acts of Cymbeline. There are but two characters in it, apparently—Cloten [intended by the King and Queen to be Imogen's husband] and Imogen [the daughter of the King of Britain, Cymbeline]. The former is my darling, though Imogen is very well. Cloten is an admirably complete & fascinating hog. Imogen's speech is beautiful & pathetic where she insists that Pisanio [servant to Posthumus Leonatus, Imogen's husband] shall carry out his orders & kill her" (ALS in MTP). On 22 October 1906 Isabel Lyon recorded that "the King and C[lara] C[lemens] went to see a first performance of 'Cymbeline'"

(IVL Journals, TS p. 198, MTP).

———. *Hamlet* (tragedy, probably performed before 1603 or 1604).

On 14 March 1857 Clemens wrote a letter for the Keokuk *Daily Post* that began, "It mought be that some people think your umble sarvant has 'shuffled off this mortal quile' and bid an eternal adoo" (*TJS*, p. 37). "Let it [a law to tax the mines] go hence to that undiscovered country from whose bourne no traveler returns (as hath been remarked by the gentleman from Washoe, Mr. Shamp)" (letter from Carson City, 5 December 1863, *MTEnt*, p. 94). "Mr. Musser—'Mr. President: To be, or not to be—that is the question'" (13 December 1863 letter from Carson City, *MTEnt*, p. 108). "O, woman, thy name is humbug!" declared Mark Twain, playing on Shakespeare's "Frailty, thy name is woman!," in "Just 'One More Unfortunate,'" a sketch that appeared between 27 and 30 June 1865 in the Virginia City *Territorial Enterprise* (*ET&S* 2: 238). In Twain's "Earthquake Almanac," published in the San Francisco *Dramatic Chronicle* on 17 October 1865 (*ET&S* 2: 299) and reprinted in the San Francisco *Golden Era* (22 October 1865, *WG* [1938], p. 91), he recommended that on November 6th one should "prepare to shed this mortal coil," echoing Act III, Scene i, 67. In a 25 August 1866 sketch for the Sacramento *Weekly Union*, Twain produced a rhyming paraphrase of Polonius's advice to Laertes, "a passage full of wisdom, which I thought I might remember easier if I reduced it to rhyme." This version causes Mr. Brown to vomit (*LSI*, pp. 142–143). "All he had to do was to shed his mortal coil," Twain remarked in the Sacramento *Weekly Union*, September 1866 (*LSI*, p. 177). On the rear flyleaf of Notebook 5 (1866), Clemens wrote: "'Give thy thoughts no tongue'—Polonius to his Son" (*N&J* 1: 177). In December 1866 Clemens made notes—apparently about his fellow ship passengers—in Notebook 7. One woman had reminded him of "Hamlet's ghost. (with the flabby dead, expressionless, Hamlets ghost's countenance & dingy white veil)" (*N&J* 1: 262).

On 7 January 1869 Clemens amusingly quoted "Oh, my prophet soul!" (Hamlet's remark in listening to the ghost's story in Act I, Scene v, line 27) when writing to Olivia Langdon about her lack of cooking skills (*LLMT*, p. 45; *MTLet* 3: 12). Chapter 22 of *The Innocents Abroad* (1869) contains the phrase "speak by the card" (cf. *Hamlet*, V, i, 148), and in Chapter 26 Twain claims that as a newspaper drama critic, "I was often surprised to notice how much more I knew about Hamlet than [the eminent actor Edwin] Forrest [1806–1872] did." In the Capuchin Convent in Rome the monk-guide speaks of Brother Thomas: "He took a skull and held it in his hand, and looked reflectively upon it, after the manner of the grave-digger when he discourses of Yorick" (*IA*, Ch. 28). "I was no more like him [his cabinmate] than I am like Hercules" (*IA*, Ch. 35); cf. *Hamlet*, I, ii, 152–153. Twain draws on *Hamlet*, III, ii, 251 in Chapter 41 of *Innocents Abroad*, where the narrator declares: "We that have free souls, it touches us not." In annotating his copy of Oliver Wendell Holmes's *Autocrat of the Breakfast-Table* in 1869, Clemens again quoted "We that have free souls, it touches us not.—Hamlet" on page 354 of Chapter 12, where Holmes described "the great procession of the

UNLOVED" (Bradford A. Booth, "Mark Twain's Comments on Holmes's *Autocrat*" [1950], p. 463). "High on a rough and dismal crag,/Where Kean [Edmund Kean, 1787–1833, famous for his Shakespearean roles] might spout, 'Ay, there's the rub'" ("The Miner's Lament," "Memoranda," *Galaxy* 11.1 (January 1871): 155; *OPMT*, pp. 59–60). The minister in Virginia City tries to comprehend Scotty Briggs' request for a service at the funeral of Buck Fanshaw by resorting to Hamlet's famous soliloquy in III, i, 18–19: "Ah— has departed to that mysterious country from whose bourne no traveler returns"; Scotty replies that Buck "kicked the bucket," that "he's *dead*" (*RI* [1872], Ch. 47). Chapter 55 of *Roughing It* (1872) mentions how "I cudgeled my brain" (cf. *Hamlet*, V, i, 56). "I speak by the card," Clemens quipped in a letter to Whitelaw Reid written on 5 December 1872 (*MTLet* 5: 242). The Clemenses saw Edwin Booth perform *Hamlet* in New York City on 3 November 1873 (*MTLet* 5: 460). One of the compositions read aloud at the "Examination" Day in *The Adventures of Tom Sawyer* (1876) includes the phrase "the observed of all observers," referring to *Hamlet*, III, i, 157. "I am at this moment leaving for that bourne from whence no traveler returns when sober (Elmira, N. Y.)" (SLC to Augustin Daly, 15 August 1877, postcard, published in Joseph F. Daly, *Life of Augustin Daly* [1917], p. 147). When Tom Hooker wore his cap on backwards, "it was as significant, too, as Ophelia's straws" ("Simon Wheeler, Detective," novel written intermittently from 1877 to 1898, *S&B*, p. 391).

In June 1878 Clemens wrote "Ponderous & marble jaws" in Notebook 14 (*N&J* 2: 100), a quotation from Act I, iv, 39. Clemens punned on Hamlet's opening line ("A little more than kin, and less than kind," I, ii, 65–66, which was echoed by Alexander Pope as well as David Garrick) in December 1878 (NB 17, *N&J* 2: 255). Mocking his brother Orion's poems, Clemens alluded to "a taste of his quality" in a letter to William Dean Howells written on 9 October 1879 (*MTHL*, p. 273; cf. *Hamlet*, II, ii, 431–432, "a taste of his quality"). In December 1880 Clemens wrote to the Reverend Edwin Pond, imploring Parker to "compose a certain piece of music"; its theme was to be a passage from Tennyson's poem *The Princess*. Clemens described for Parker how the instruments' notes could reproduce the effects of certain lines, explaining " I have *imagined* it all the morning" and adding, "It sounds well when it is fading & receding in my mind's ear Horatio," alluding to the scene in Act I, ii, 185 as Hamlet reveals where he has seen his father's ghost: "In my mind's eye, Horatio" (ASSSCL; PH in MTP). Clara Clemens recalled parlor productions of *Hamlet* that took place in 1881 (*MFMT*, p. 88). Clemens wrote to Charles L. Webster on 31 August 1881 from Elmira: "If anything happened to the 4 acting copies of Hamlet, buy them again, of Samuel French, Nassau St., . . . & mail them to me" (*MTBus*, p. 167).

Twice Mark Twain undertook burlesques of *Hamlet*, once in 1872 and again in 1881; his intention was to insert a humorous character in the play, a man ignored by the other players. The first time he experimented with a country cousin who arrives to enliven the lugubrious court, but Twain destroyed this version. He resolved in Munich in

January 1879 to "try Hamlet again, & make free with Shakspere" (NB 17, *N&J* 2: 261). A fragment survives from the later effort (DV320, MTP), which Twain wrote at Quarry Farm in late August and early September 1881. See Clemens's letter to William Dean Howells, Elmira, 3 September 1881 (*MTHL*, pp. 370, 371 n. 2). In the second version, a subscription-book salesman, Basil Stockmar, is a foster brother to Hamlet; at the court Basil is out of his element, baffled by the stately blank verse addresses and unappreciative of the drama unfolding before him (*S&B*, pp. 49–87). Onto this manuscript Twain pasted in speeches from the acting copies of *Hamlet* that he had Charles L. Webster purchase from Samuel French and send to Elmira (*S&B*, p. 52). Clemens corresponded with Joseph T. Goodman of Fresno, California in the early 1880s about the idea of Hamlet's having a brother (*S&B*, pp. 51, 53).

In Chapter 28 of *Life on the Mississippi* (1883) Mark Twain recalls passing scows "bearing a humble Hamlet and Co. on an itinerant dramatic trip." Chapter 51 of *Life on the Mississippi* describes a bit-part actor: "Poor devil, he had been patiently studying the part of Hamlet for more than thirty years, and he lived and died in the belief that some day he would be invited to play it!" In a chapter omitted from *Life on the Mississippi*, Twain quotes from Mrs. Trollope's disparaging review of Edwin Forrest's Hamlet (Heritage Press edition [1944], p. 393). Walter Blair (*MT&HF* [1960], pp. 302–303) published Twain's facetious pastiche of lines from *Hamlet* and *Macbeth* that he wrote on a note of 19 March 1883 from Charles L. Webster; this became the Duke's ludicrous soliloquy in Chapter 21 of *Huckleberry Finn* (1885). On 2 January 1884 Twain directed Webster to find out "where N. C. Godwin is playing. This is a young fellow who made something of a strike as the grave-digger in Hamlet at the Cincinnati festival a year or two ago" (*MTBus*, p. 231). In 1884 Twain wrote "Hamlet's Soliloquy" in Notebook 22 (*N&J* 3: 60). Chapters 20 and 21 of *Huckleberry Finn* (1885) contain burlesque Shakespearian recitations by the King and the Duke. Anthony J. Berret's "The Influence of *Hamlet* on *Huckleberry Finn*," *American Literary Realism* 18.1–2 (Spring-Autumn 1985): 196–207 is the most detailed examination of these Shakespeare burlesques, and well worth reading.

A cryptic entry in Notebook 25—"5 Exp Hamlets"—may indicate the number of expurgated copies Clemens wished to order for his family in October 1885 (*N&J* 3: 206). "Say the kind word for it, Horatio.—Hamlet, Act 2, Sc. v.," Clemens jotted in Notebook 27 (September 1887, *N&J* 3: 318). When making up his projected appendix for *A Connecticut Yankee in King Arthur's Court* (1889), Mark Twain twice listed "Ophelia's burial" as a source (NB 29, *N&J* 3: 502, 506). *A Connecticut Yankee* contains a line, "Even so! already it falleth trippingly from my tongue" (Ch. 15); cf. *Hamlet*, III, ii, 1–2. Chapter 39 of *A Connecticut Yankee* includes a reference to "Hamlet's ghost." Henry Fisher reported that in 1891 Twain said, after he arrived in the carriage of the Marquis of Lorne, "I must have walked into the hall with the strut of Larry Barrett [American actor Lawrence Barrett, 1838–1891] playing the Ghost in Hamlet" (*AMT*, p. 210). Sometime

in 1895 or 1896 Twain made a reference to Yorrick in his working notes for *Following the Equator* (1898; collection of Kevin Mac Donnell, Austin, Texas). "I am old, & will get me to a nunnery" (SLC to Robert Barr, Vienna, 29 September 1897, PH in MTP; cf. *Hamlet*, III, i, 122). Twain misquoted Act V, ii, 10, when he wrote in March 1898: "There's a divinity rough-hews our ends, smooth-shape them as we may" (NB 42, TS p. 60). Making the case in "About Play-Acting" (1898) that "New York ought to have one theatre devoted to tragedy," Twain recalls that "thirty years ago Edwin Booth played 'Hamlet' a hundred nights in New York. With three times the population, how often is 'Hamlet' played now in a year? . . . The tragedians are dead; but I think that the taste and intelligence which made their market are not."

Clemens paraphrased a Hamlet speech in annotating Lew Wallace's *The First Christmas, from "Ben Hur,"* a volume Clemens signed in 1902, quipping, "To what trivial uses may we come at last" (cf. *Hamlet*, V, i, 223). George Harrison of "Which Was It?" (written 1899–1903) echoes Hamlet's speech in Act III, ii, 317, when Harrison declaims: "Look at man, in his right and proper estate: how nobly gifted, intellectually, how graciously endowed" (*WWD?*, p. 376); Shakespeare is twice mentioned reverently in this story (*WWD?*, pp. 306, 401). On 20 July 1900 Clemens played with some lines in Act V, ii, 10–11: "There is a divinity that roughs our ends, smooth-hew them how we will" (NB 43, TS p. 22a). "The first witness testifies that . . . he had 'nearly all the ills that flesh is heir to'" (*Christian Science* [1907], Book I, Ch. 6); cf. *Hamlet*, III, i, 62–63. After Henry H. Rogers died in 1909, Clemens wrote to Elizabeth Wallace, who had met both men in Bermuda: "Here we shall not look upon his like again" (26 May 1909, *MT&HI*, p. 128); cf. *Hamlet*, I, ii, 187. Walter Blair, *NAH* (1937), p. 148; Blair, *MT&HF* (1960), pp. 296, 301; E. Bruce Kirkham, "Huck and Hamlet: An Examination of Twain's Use of Shakespeare," *Mark Twain Journal* 14.4 (Summer 1969): 17–19; John D. Reardon, "'Shakespearan Revival!!!': Satire of American Elizabethans," *Mark Twain Journal* 21.4 (Fall 1983): 36–38; Jeffrey Kahan, *The Cult of Kean* (Burlington, Vermont: Ashgate Publishing Co., 2006), pp. 103–114; and Amy M. Green, "Huck and Jim at the Bare Bodkin's Point: *Hamlet's* Mangled Soliloquy as Textual Commentary," *Mark Twain Annual 5* (2007): 69–81. Joseph Church—"An End of Metaphysics in Mark Twain's 'A Carnival of Crime,'" *American Literary Realism* 43.2 (Winter 2011): 103–104—discerned "a half-comical, half-serious version of Hamlet's sexually laden engagement with his mother" in Twain's furious confrontation with his fictional aunt Mary.

———. *Henry IV. Parts First and Second. With Introduction, and Notes Explanatory and Critical. For Use in Schools and Families.* Edited by Henry N[orman]. Hudson (1814–1896). Boston: Ginn, 1889.

Inscription: Part Second is signed, "Olivia S. Clemens/ Oct. 1st 1890/Radnor Hall." (Olivia Clemens inscribed an entire set of Shakespeare plays to Susy Clemens at Bryn Mawr in 1890.)

Provenance: Part Second acquired by the Harry Ransom Center on 27 July 1981 from Henry and Mary Shisler, to whom the volume had been bequeathed in 1966 by

Clara Clemens Samossoud's second husband, Jacques A. Samossoud.

Location: currently unknown. This volume was listed as "Lost" in 1984. The information for this entry derives from its original accession card in the Harry Ransom Center and from a handwritten list supplied to Alan Gribben by Mary Shisler on 17 September 1980 prior to the sale transaction.

"Like the hero of Agincourt, he [the King of the Sandwich Islands] renounced his bad habits and discarded his Falstaffs when he became King" (Sacramento *Weekly Union*, 23 June 1866; *LSI*, p. 94). In Mark Twain's *1601* (1880), "Master Shaxpur did rede a part of his King Henry IV., ye which, it seemeth unto me, is not of ye value of an arseful of ashes, yet they praised it bravely, one and all" (Franklin J. Meine's edition, privately printed for the Mark Twain Society [Chicago, 1939], p. 38). Twain credited Shakespeare for some of the obsolete phrases he copied into his study notes for *The Prince and the Pauper* around 1880 (DV114, DV115, MTP). He cites one phrase— "Known as well as Pauls"—as coming from "K. Henry 4." *Henry IV* is one of the books whose "heroes" Tom Sawyer recommends to Huckleberry Finn (*HF* [1885], Ch. 35). "She could depend on us and on herself for valor, but discretion is the winning thing in war, after all; discretion is the rarest and loftiest of qualities" (*JA* [1896], Ch. 5); cf. *I Henry IV*, V, iv, 122.

In Chapter 50 of *Following the Equator* (1897) Mark Twain describes the appearance of "a minor native prince from the backwoods somewhere," with his guard of honor: "when this Falstaff and his monkeys marched through it one saw that that seeming impossibility [of exhausting variety] had happened" (cf. *II Henry IV*, III, 2). "Sir John Oldcastle is a person whom we do not know very well by that name, nor much care for; but we know him well and adore him, too, under his other name— Sir John Falstaff. . . . That old tun of sack and godless ruffler, Sir John Oldcastle, . . . fat-faced, purple with the spirit of bygone and lamented drink, smiling his hospitable, wide smile upon all the world, leering at the women, wallowing about in his saddle, proclaiming his valorous deeds as fast as he could lie . . . —the most inhuman spectacle in England, a living, breathing outrage, a slander upon the human race" ("Queen Victoria's Jubilee" [1897]). In a newspaper interview in 1906, "when reminded that the Senate, as a body, is sadly lacking in humor and needs livening up, Mr. Twain said, smilingly:—'Well, as "Falstaff to the Senate" I guess I could fill the bill and earn my salary'" ("Mark Twain Too Lazy for a United States Senator," New York *Herald*, 11 March 1906; *Complete Interviews*, p. 537). Twain mentions the country justice (and foolish liar) Robert Shallow in Part 4 of *Is Shakespeare Dead?* (1909). Baetzold, *MT&JB* (1970), pp. 52, 259–260.

———. *Henry V* (historical drama, performed in 1599).

Olivia Langdon's commonplace book indicates that she read this play in 1867 (Paine 150, MTP). Acording to Henry W. Fisher, "Mark Twain, when speaking of a king, was fond of quoting Shakespeare's: 'I have an humour to knock you indifferently well.' (Henry V)" (*AMT*, p. 219). On 5 August 1899 Clemens thought of Act II, iii, 9 in describing the movements Jean Clemens made with her

hands when she was ill: "It is not the same thing as the picking at the bed clothes by the doomed, but makes me think of Falstaff's doing that, what time he 'babbled o' green fields'—that pathetic picture" (MS in DV13, MTP; cf *Henry V*, II, iii, 15). "Mrs. Clemens . . . is booked for Henry V with the children to-morrow evening" (SLC to Emilie Rogers, New York City, 13 November 1900, *MTHHR*, p. 454).

———. *Henry VIII* (historical drama, performed in 1613).

Without seeing any of the performances, Twain applauded Frank Mayo's success in "such parts as 'Henry VIII'" (24 or 26 December 1865, Virginia City *Territorial Enterprise*; *ET&S* 2: 339). Concerning the promise Clemens's made to Olivia, "When the anchor is down, then I shall say: 'Farewell—a long farewell—to *business*! I will *never* touch it again!'" (27–30 January 1894; quoted in *Mark Twain's Correspondence with Henry Huttleston Rogers*, p. 20), was he perhaps paraphrasing *Henry VIII*, III, ii, 351, a famous "set speech" in Clemens's day? Wolsey's soliloquy ruefully philosophizes: "So farewell to the little good you bear me!/Farewell, a long farewell, to all my greatness!" (this possibility was suggested to me by L. G. Crossman (Crossman to Alan Gribben, 3 January 1987).

———. *History of King John. Plays of Shakespeare, Selected and Prepared for Schools, Clubs, Classes and Families*. Three volumes. Ed. andwith an introduction by Henry N. Hudson (1814–1886). Boston: Ginn, Heath & Co., 1884–1885. One title page is dated 1884, the others 1885.

Inscriptions: the front free flyleaf of the first volume is signed in black ink, "Olivia L. Clemens/Hartford/June 1886." The bookseller's sticker of Brown & Gross of Hartford appears on the rear pastedown endpaper of two of the volumes.

Provenance: Clara Clemens Samossoud held back these volumes from the 1951 Hollywood sale. Her second husband, Jacques A. Samossoud, bequeathed them to Henry and Mary Shisler of Cardiff by the Sea, California when he died in1966. The Shislers had possession of the books until 1981, when they sold them to the Humanities Research Center (now the Harry Ransom Center).

Location: Harry Ransom Center, University of Texas at Austin.

Copy examined: Olivia Clemens's copy, in 1984.

Determined to work Shakespeare's "really apt and beautiful" phrase ("To 'gild refined gold, to paint the lily'") from *King John* (IV, ii, 11) into some type of description, Mark Twain employs a paraphrase of it ludicrously in Chapter 18 of *Roughing It* (1872) by referring to the thirst of a mule team after a long haul. Several decades later Twain referred to another line: "When he is King John, with a nephew to render untroublesome, he uses a red-hot iron" ("Man's Place in the Animal World," written in 1896, *WIM?*, p. 83; cf. *King John*, IV, i, 58). See also the Catalog entry below for *King Richard the Second*.

Baetzhold, *Mark Twain and John Bull* (1970), p. 372 n. 12.

———. *Julius Caesar*. New York: S. French & Son, n.d. 66 pp. [tragedy, probably performed in 1599).

Source: MTLAcc, entry #2129a, volume donated from Clemens's library by Clara Clemens Gabrilowitsch in 1910.

———. *The Tragedy of Julius Caesar*. New York: Harper &

Brothers, 1891. 199 pp.

Source: MTLAcc, entry #2128a, volume donated from Clemens's library by Clara Clemens Gabrilowitsch in 1910. Clemens's first Thomas Jefferson Snodgrass letter (18 October 1856) to the Keokuk *Saturday Post* burlesques this play (*TJS*, pp. 5–16). In a column appearing in the Virginia City *Territorial Enterprise*, "The Illustrious Departed," Clemens referred comically to Dan De Quille's departing words as "'Et tu Brute,'" whereupon he "gave us his pen" (*ET&S* 1: 173; cf. III, i, 77). The 3 February 1863 issue of the *Territorial Enterprise* contained Clemens's letter from Carson City in which he alluded to "my prophetic soul" (*ET&S* 1: 197, whose editors trace these words to Act I, Scene v, line 40). Mark Twain rewrote the tragedy *Julius Caesar* in comically journalistic style, partly citing "William Shakespeare, who saw the beginning and the end of the unfortunate affray," in "The Killing of Julius Caesar Localized" (San Francisco Californian, 11 November 1864; *ET&S* 2: 110–115). "Oct 31 [1878]—Evening—Wood fire in Mr. Chamberlain's room—C[hamberlain] sketched, Mrs. C darned, Livy & Clara crotched [*sic*], & I read Julius Caesar aloud" (NB 17, *N&J* 2: 239); this domestic scene occurred in Rome. "He said he was cast for a part in 'Julius Caesar,' for that night, and if I should come I would see him" (*LonMiss* [1883], Ch. 51). Twain's Satan brought events to life when he told stories, especially when "he saw Caesar's death" ("The Chronicle of Young Satan," written 1897–1900, *MSM*, p. 50). Twain wrote to Joseph H. Twichell from Kaltenleutgeben on 13 September 1898 about the manner in which he had learned of the assassination of the Empress of Austria: "Why, it brings the giant event home to you, makes you a part of it & personally interested; it is as if your neighbor Antony should come flying & say 'Caesar is butchered—the head of the world is fallen!'" (*MTL* [1917], p. 667; *LMTJHT* [2017], p. 221). Twain mentioned Julius Caesar's death in "The Memorable Assassination" (1898). Isabel Lyon recorded on 9 October 1906: "Tonight after dinner he wanted Shakespeare. I took him the 4 volumes I had brought up here and he selected 'Julius Caesar' and read to us for an hour and a half. It was fine. The King acts the characters with modified gestures and inflections of voice" (IVL Journals, TS p. 193, MTP). "Tonight he read 'Julius Caesar' again and . . . he was lost in the wonder of the play and unconsciously acted it" (IVL Journals, 11 October 1906, TS pp. 194–195, MTP). On 12 October 1906 Clemens wrote to Mary Benjamin Rogers from Dublin to report that he had "finished reading the first half of Shakespeare's Julius Caesar aloud to Jean and Miss Lyon—that tremendous poem!" (*MTLM*, p. 71). "As famous as the assassination of Caesar," Twain wrote in *Christian Science* (1907), Book II, Appendix F, "Mrs. Eddy in Error." In an Autobiographical Dictation of 26 September 1907 Clemens employed the phrase "with none so poor to do it honor," paraphrasing *Julius Caesar*, Act III, Scene ii, line 25—"none so poor to do him reverence" (*AutoMT* 3: 138, 515).

———. *King Lear* (tragedy, performed in 1606).

In February 1871 Mark Twain insisted in his *Galaxy* column: "Where was ever a sermon preached that could make filial ingratitude so hateful to men as the sinful play of 'King Lear'?" ("The Indignity Put Upon the Remains of George Holland," *Galaxy* 11.2 [February 1871]: 320; *MTB*, p. 1625; *CG* [1961], p. 128). Twain described the Roman Coliseum as "that 'looped and windowed' bandbox" (*IA* [1869], Ch. 26); cf. *King Lear*, III, iv, 31: "Your loop'd and window'd raggedness." Clemens made notes about a performance of *King Lear* in the German language that he attended in Mannheim on 24 May 1878; "Lear's great speeches sounded mighty flat" in German (NB 14, *N&J* 2: 85–86). "One day we took the train and went down to Mannheim to see King Lear played in German. It was a mistake. We sat in our seats three whole hours and never understood anything but the thunder and lightning. . . . It is a pain to me to this day, to remember how that old German Lear raged and wept and howled around the stage, with never a response from that hushed house, never a single outburst till the act was ended" (*TA* [1880], Ch. 9). "The huge ruin of Heidelberg Castle, with empty window arches, ivy-mailed battlements, moldering towers—the Lear of inanimate nature,—deserted, discrowned, beaten by the storms, but royal still, and beautiful" (*TA* [1880], Ch. 2). "Gone stark mad as any Tom o'Bedlam" (*P&P* [1882], Ch. 4); cf. *Lear*, I, ii, 148 and II, iii, 114. The Duke dressed Jim "in King Lear's outfit— it was a long curtain-calico gown, and a white horse-hair wig and whiskers" (*HF* [1885], Ch. 24). In Chapter 16 of *A Connecticut Yankee* (1889) the Yankee remarks "how louder and clearer than any tongue, does dumb circumstantial evidence speak," which Howard G. Baetzhold identified as "a prosaic echo of Lear's "how sharper than a serpent's tooth" (*MT&JB*, p. 372 n. 12). To an Australian interviewer in 1895 Twain favorably compared Thackeray's and Dickens's techniques for injecting humor into pathos with Shakespeare's handling of the Fool in *King Lear* (Sydney *Morning Herald*, 17 September 1895; *Complete Interviews*, p. 205). In "The Chronicle of Young Satan," written 1897–1900, Satan, annoyed by the weeping and praying emitted by his miniature population, "mashed all those people into the earth just as if they had been flies, and went on talking just the same" (*MSM*, p. 50); cf. Gloucester's "As flies to wanton boys, are we to the gods;/They kill us for their sport" (noted by William M. Gibson, *MSM*, p. 22). Twain believed William Stone Booth's claim in *Some Acrostic Signatures* that "through the last page of King Lear is scattered Francis Bacon's acrostic 'Verulam,' spelled backwards" (11 January 1909 AD, *AutoMT* 3: 300). In "The Ashcroft-Lyon Manuscript," written in 1909, Clemens speculated that Isabel V. Lyon and Ralph Ashcroft intended to leave him "another stripped & forlorn King Lear" (*AutoMT* 3: 347).

Robert L. Gale, "*The Prince and the Pauper* and *King Lear*," *Mark Twain Journal* 12.1 (Spring 1963): 14–17, found parallels in two works about royalty.

———. *King Richard the Second. Plays of Shakespeare, Selected and Prepared for Schools, Clubs, Classes and Families.* Three volumes. Ed. and with an introduction by Henry N. Hudson (1814–1886). Green cloth. Boston: Ginn, Heath & Co., 1884–1885. One title page is dated 1884, the other two 1885.

Inscriptions: the front free endpaper of the first volume is signed in black ink, "Olivia L. Clemens/Hartford/June 1886. The sticker of Hartford bookseller Brown & Gross

is affixed to the rear pastedown endpapers of two volumes.
Provenance: Clara Clemens Samossoud held these volumes
back from the 1951 Hollywood auction. Her second hus-
band, Jacques A. Samossoud, died in 1966 and bequeathed
them to Henry and Mary Shisler of Cardiff by the Sea,
California. The Shislers sold them to the Humanities
Research Center (now the Harry Ransom Center) at the
University of Texas at Austin in 1981.
Location: Harry Ransom Center, University of Texas at
Austin.
Copy examined: Olivia Clemens's copy, in 1984.
"*Richard II*, in prison listening to a poor minstrel outside,"
Clemens noted in July 1873 (NB 12, *N&J* 1: 568). In
May or early June 1885 Clemens made a memoran-
dum: "Ginn, Heath & Co/New York/ (Expurgated
Shakspeare./3-vol Shak \$1.20 per vol." (NB 24, *N&J*
3: 159). He must have meant the edition prepared by
Hudson, an American Shakespearean scholar who was a
professor at Boston University and an ordained priest of
the Protestant Episcopal Church.

————. *The Leopold Shakspere. The Poet's Works in Chronological
Order, from the Text of Professor [Nicolaus] Delius [1813–1888]*.
Introduction by Frederick James Furnivall (1825–1910). Illus.
New York: Cassell and Co., n.d. [1883]. 1056 pp.
Source: MTLAcc, entry #2125a, volume donated from Cle-
mens's library by Clara Clemens Gabrilowitsch in 1910.
This book's title is explained by the fact that the collection
was dedicated to Queen Victoria's youngest son, Prince
Leopold, the Duke of Albany (1853–1884).

————. *Macbeth*. New York: Cassell & Co., 1886. 192 pp.
(tragedy, probably written around 1606).
Source: MTLAcc, entry #972, volume donated by Clemens.
Scoffing at the name of Lake Tahoe in a sketch published
in the Virginia City *Territorial Enterprise* either on 4 or
5 September 1863, Mark Twain referred to "the view-
less spirits of the air," a phrase recalling Shakespeare's
"sightless couriers of the air" (*Macbeth*, I, vii, 23; this
echo was identified by Edgar M. Branch and Robert H.
Hirst, *ET&S* 1: 290). Twain paraphrased "the lamented
J. W. Macbeth, Thane of Cawdor, Scotland," from Act
III, Scene iv, 78–79—"The time has been,/That, when
the brains were out, the man would die"—in "Those
Blasted Children" (New York *Sunday Mercury*, 21 February 1864; reprinted in the San Francisco *Golden Era*,
27 March 1864; *WG* [1938], p. 21; *ET&S* 1: 355). In
Chapter 15 of *The Innocents Abroad* (1869) Twain found
the *grisettes* of Paris disappointing in appearance: "Aroint
thee, wench!"; cf. *Macbeth*, I, iii, 6. When Twain wrote
in Chapter 17 of *The Innocents Abroad* that the houses of
Genoa "might 'laugh a siege to scorn,'" he was drawing
on *Macbeth*, V, v, 3. Chapter 26 of *The Innocents Abroad*
alludes to "golden opinions" (cf. *Macbeth*, I, vii, 33). In
a letter of 12 June 1870 to Pamela Moffett, Clemens
praised inventors of machines as possessing "that 'round
& top of sovereignty,'" alluding to a line in *Macbeth*, IV,
i, 88–89 (identified in *MTLet* 4: 152): "[He] wears upon
his baby brow the round/And top of sovereignty." In 1875
Twain quoted a letter containing a line in *Macbeth*, Act
III, Scene iv, 78–79: "The times have been that when
the brains were out the man would die & there an end"
("'Information' from 'Professor A.B.,'" Hartford *Courant*,

25 October 1875, *MTPP*, p. 93).
Clemens jokingly alluded to "my sere & yellow leaf" in
a letter of 28 January 1882 to William Dean Howells
(*MTHL*, p. 387); cf. *Macbeth*, V, iii, 24. Walter Blair
published a 19 March 1883 note from Charles L. Webster
on which Mark Twain rehearsed the Duke's soliloquy for
Chapter 21 of *Huckleberry Finn* (1885); in this pastiche
of lines from *Hamlet* and *Macbeth* the language from
Macbeth came mainly out of the soliloquy in Act III, Scene
ii (*MT&HF* [1960], pp. 302–303). Clemens directed
Charles L. Webster in December 1885 to "buy 8 acting
Macbeths—pamphlets" at Samuel French's bookstore,
"& mail to me" (*MTBus*, p. 344). Clara Clemens recalled
that parlor productions of *Macbeth* took place in 1885
(*MFMT*, p. 88). In one version of Twain's *American
Claimant* play, Colonel Sellers says, "Take my girl and
my earldom both. I will be like Banquo, not a King, but
the father of a line of Kings" (MS in ASSSCL, quoted
in Robert Regan's *Unpromising Heroes*, pp. 204–205).
Clemens wrote to Olivia Clemens from Guildford on 30
August 1896: "Poor Susy, it is now eleven days. 'After
life's fitful fever she sleeps well.' And will wake no more
for me." Later Clemens would choose this same line—
adapted from *Macbeth*—as the gravestone epitaph for Jean
Clemens (*LLMT*, p. 327). He used lines 33–34 of Act V,
Scene viii, to illustrate a system of spelling reform in "A
Simplified Alphabet" (written in 1899): "La on, Makcduf,
and damd be he hoo furst krys hold, enuf!" Marginal notes
in the copy of *The Works of Tacitus* that Clemens signed in
1905 quoted Malcolm from *Macbeth*: "Nothing in his life
became him like the leaving of it." While Twain worked
on the manuscript for *Is Shakespeare Dead?* (1909), he
intermittently read aloud from *Macbeth* to Isabel Lyon
on 10 February 1909 (IVL's Notes, Berg Collection,
NYPL, TS in MTP). In Part One of *Is Shakespeare Dead?*,
George Ealer, "an idolator of Shakespeare," burlesques a
speech from *Macbeth*, III, iv, 99–107, by interlarding
it with shouted steamboat commands. A small sheet of
manuscript sold at the 1911 auction of Clemens's library
books reads: "The audience thought you had washed your
hands and couldn't get over the novelty of it. No public
person has ever centered so much interest in his hands
since Macbeth's wife" (*A1911*, lot 396). Jean Clemens's
tombstone, arranged for by Clemens after her death on
24 December 1909, reads, "After life's fitful fever she
sleeps well," echoing Lady Macbeth's lines in *Macbeth*,
III, ii, 22–23: "Duncan is in his grave;/After life's fitful
fever he sleeps well."
Blair, *MT&HF* (1960), pp. 302–303. E. Bruce Kirham,
"Huck and Hamlet: An Examination of Twain's Use of
Shakespeare," *Mark Twain Journal* 14.1 (Summer 1969):
17–19, analyzed the Duke's garbled soliloquy in Chapter
21 of *Adventures of Huckleberry Finn*. See also Anthony J.
Berret, "The Influence of *Hamlet* on *Huckleberry Finn*,"
American Literary Realism 18.1–2 (Spring-Autumn
1985): 196–207, an essential analysis; Jeffrey Kahan, *The
Cult of Kean* (Burlington, Vermont: Ashgate Publishing
Co., 2006), pp. 103–114; and Amy M. Green, "Huck
and Jim at the Bare Bodkin's Point: *Hamlet's* Mangled
Soliloquy as Textual Commentary," *Mark Twain Annual*
5 (2007): 69–81.

———. *Merchant of Venice*. New York: Cassell & Co., 1886. 192 pp. (comedy, probably written about 1596).

Source: MTLAcc, entry #971, volume donated by Clemens. Clemens saw this play performed ("I had always thought that this was a comedy, until they made a *farce* out of it") by the St. Louis Dramatic Association of St. Louis, Missouri (SLC to the Muscatine, Iowa *Journal*, 16 February 1855; *MTLMusc* [1942], p. 25; *MTLet* 1: 48). In January 1862 Clemens joked about an obstinate mule in a letter to Orion Clemens's wife Mollie: "If I had the 'Paint Brush' here, Mollie, I would 'feed fat the ancient grudge I bear him'" (*MTLet* 1: 145; cf. *Merchant of Venice*, I, iii, 47–48: "If I can catch him once upon the hip,/I will feed fat the ancient grudge I bear him"). Mark Twain utilized Portia's speech in Act IV, i, 184–185 to burlesque L. O. Sterns' oratory in a dispatch from Carson City on 5 December 1863: "Ah, sir, the quality of mercy is not strained, so to speak (as has been aptly suggested heretofore), but droppeth like the gentle dew from Heaven, as it were" (*MTEnt*, p. 94). In the California Art Union "the first thing that attracts your attention when you enter is a beautiful and animated picture representing the Trial Scene in the *Merchant of Venice*" ("An Unbiased Criticism," *Californian*, 18 March 1865; *Ssix*, p. 164; *MTLet* 2: 142). Olivia Langdon devoted part of her day on 7 March 1867 to copying extracts from *The Merchant of Venice* (III, ii; IV, i) into her commonplace book (DV161, MTP). Twain quoted, "It was a pleasure excursion— . . . it was so nominated in the bond—but it surely hadn't the general aspect of one" in Chapter 2 of *The Innocents Abroad* (1869); cf. Shylock's line in *Merchant*, IV, i, 159: "Is it so nominated in the bond?" In the moonlight Twain found it easy to envision "Shylocks in gaberdine and sandals, venturing loans upon the rich argosies of Venetian commerce" (*IA*, Ch. 22). "I dock your bill about $25 to feed fat an ancient grudge I bear," Clemens kidded in a letter to James Redpath and George L. Fall (7 March 1872; *MTLet* 5: 54), paraphrasing Act I, Scene iii, line 48 of *The Merchant of Venice*. (The same line—"that hatred has 'fed fat its ancient grudge'"—occurs in Appendix A of *Roughing It* [1872].) Chapter 28 of *Roughing It* contains another reference: "I observed, then, that 'all that glitters is not gold'" (cf. *The Merchant of Venice*, Act II, vii, 65). Margaret Duckett noticed that Mrs. Plunkett's romantic rhapsody in Bret Harte and Mark Twain's *Ah Sin* (performed in 1877) parodies the dialogue between Lorenzo and Jessica in *Merchant of Venice*, V, i, 1–28 (*MT&BH*, p. 317). Into Notebook 19 (September 1880), Twain copied the abridged passage that would soon become the verse epigraph for *The Prince and the Pauper* (1881): "The quality of Mercy . . . . . is twice bless'd;/ It blesseth him that gives & him that takes;/'Tis mightiest in the mightiest; it becomes/The thronèd monarch better than his crown" (*N&J* 2: 371; cf. *Merchant of Venice*, IV, i, 184–189). In Chapter 12 of *The American Claimant* (1892) Howard Tracy (Lord Berkeley) observes of Mr. Marsh the landlord: "At table he is Sir Oracle, and when he opens his mouth not any dog in the kennel barks"; cf. *Merchant of Venice*, I, i, 93–94: "I am Sir Oracle,/And when I ope my lips, let no dog bark!" (Gratiano). Twain asked, in "Concerning the Jews" (1899), "In time would his [Joseph's] name come to be familiarly used to express that character—like Shylock's?" Twain used Shylock's defense ("Hath not a Jew eyes? . . . If you poison us, do we not die?" [III, i, 64, 69]) as an epigraph for "Randall's Jew Story," a sympathetic piece written in the 1890s (*FM*, p. 284). George Harrison laments in Chapter 6 of "Which Was It?" (written 1899–1903): "Ah, Moral Law, you are a hard trader; Shylock of the Shylocks, you exact your pound of flesh a hundred fold!" (*WWD?*, p. 236; cf. *Merchant of Venice*, IV, i, 231). "Thank my 96 creditors, only one of whom was a Shylock—Thos. Russell & son" (NB 43 [21 May 1900], TS p. 12). "By God I might as well have pleaded with Shylock himself!" Clemens remarked of Marie Corelli, who had extracted his promise to stop in Stratford for a luncheon (16 August 1907 AD, *MTE*, p. 325; *AutoMT* 3: 99).

———. *The Merry Wives of Windsor* (comedy, probably written in 1600–1601).

Clemens surely saw Susy and Clara Clemens perform the second part of this play in August 1885 for the widowed Olivia Lewis Langdon's seventy-fifth birthday party in Elmira (OLC's Diary, DV161; *S&MT*, p. 210; Fears, *Day by Day*, pp. 1059–60).

———. *A Midsummer Night's Dream* (comedy, written in 1595 or 1596).

"When I see such a thing as this [production of] 'Midsummer Night's Dream,' I wish to 'gush,'" wrote Mark Twain, declaring the scenic production at Selwyn's Theatre in Boston to be "enchantingly beautiful." Twain pronounced "this whole spectacle . . . the finest thing I ever saw" ("Browsing Around," Buffalo *Express*, 27 November 1869, p. 2; *MTBE*, pp. 95–96). Twain remarked in a newspaper interview published in the St. Paul *Dispatch* on 24 July 1895 that his lecture tour (echoing Puck in Act II) was "putting a girdle around the earth as it were" (*Complete Interviews*, p. 160). In June 1909 Clemens attended a private girls' school production of the play (SLC to Elizabeth Wallace, 7 June 1909, *MT&HI*, p. 129). Blair, *MT&HF* (1960), p. 311.

———. *Midsummer Night's Dream*. Illustrated by Alfred Fredericks (1835–1926). New York: D. Appleton and Co., 1874.

Catalog: Ball 2016 inventory, leather with embossed designed, gilt lettering, fair condition.

Location: Quarry Farm library shelves, under the supervision of the Mark Twain Archive, Elmira College, Elmira, New York.

This was another potential literary resource for Clemens whenever he visited Quarry Farm in Elmira.

———. *Mottoes and Aphorisms from Shakespeare. Arranged Alphabetically*. Philadelphia: J. B. Lippincott & Co., 1870.

Inscription: signed in pencil, "S. L. Clemens, Buffalo, N. Y., 1871".

Catalogs: ListABP (1910), "Mottoes from Shakespeare"; *C1951*, D18, listed among volumes signed by Clemens, $25; *Zeitlin 1951*, item #40, "hinge broken," $35.

If only we could inspect this volume for the probable notations next to Clemens's favorite lines. Perhaps the book will turn up someday.

———. *Much Ado about Nothing* (comedy, probably performed in 1598–1599).

For the December 1870 *Galaxy*, Mark Twain wrote a column

entitled "Dogberry in Washington" that deplored the obtuse reasoning of Post Office bureaucrats (*CG* [1961], pp. 105–106; Reigstad, *SL* [2013], p 183). Decades later, Twain's "Bkshp," renaming his fellow microbes after his favorite literary characters, calls one of them Dogberry after Shakespeare's officious constable ("Three Thousand Years among the Microbes," written in 1905, *WWD?*, p. 472). Clark Griffith's "*Pudd'nhead Wilson* as Dark Comedy," *ELH* 43.2 (Summer 1976): 209–226 perceived parallels between Shakespeare's comedy and Twain's novel.

———. *Othello* (tragedy, performed in 1604).

Writing to the Muscatine *Journal* on 18 February 1854 from Washington, D. C., Clemens mentioned that "Mr. [Edwin] Forrest played Othello at the National Theatre last night, to a good audience" (*MTLMusc* [1942], p. 22; *MTLet* 1: 42). Clemens quoted "nor set down aught in malice" (*Othello*, V, ii, 43) in a letter to Orion Clemens written on 6 February 1861 (*MTLet* 1: 111). "I have given you almost her [Madame Caprell's] very language to me, and nothing extenuated, nor set down aught in malice" (SLC to Orion Clemens, Cairo, Illinois, 6 February 1861, *MTBus*, p. 56); cf. *Othello*, V, ii, 342–343: "Speak of me as I am; nothing extenuate,/Nor set down aught in malice" (Othello speaking). A letter from Mark Twain published in the 30 July 1863 issue of the San Francisco *Morning Call* alluded to a political feud between two judges as having "a lame and impotent conclusion" (*ET&S* 1: 260)—a phrase he would employ again a few years later. A sketch for the San Francisco *Morning Call* of 24 August 1864 that Edgar M. Branch attributed to Twain, "A Dark Transaction," alludes to Desdemona and Othello (*ET&S* 2: 460). In San Francisco in 1865 Twain noted: "The Tragedy of Othello—first part seen from dress circle—last part from private box" (NB 4, *N&J* 1: 84). A phrase in Chapter 4 of *The Innocents Abroad*—"so lame and impotent a conclusion"—occurs in *Othello*, II, i, 162. Venice by moonlight brought to Twain's mind "Othellos and Desdemonas, with Iagos and Roderigos" (*IA* [1869], Ch. 22).

Mark Twain burlesqued *Othello* in a newspaper hoax, "Shocking Results of Miscegenation and Jealousy" (Buffalo *Express*, May 1870). The next year he asked his readers, "Where was there ever a sermon that could so convince men of the wrong and the cruelty of harboring a pampered and unanalyzed jealousy as the sinful play of 'Othello'?" ("The Indignity Put Upon the Remains of George Holland," *Galaxy* 11.2 [February 1871: 320; *MTB* [1912], p. 1625; *CG* [1961], p. 128). At the end of Chapter 6 of *The Adventures of Tom Sawyer* (1876), the love-addled Tom makes multiple mistakes in geography class "till chaos was come again" (cf. *Othello*, III, iii, 93–94: "And when I love thee not/Chaos is come again."). At the beginning of Chapter 12 of *Tom Sawyer*, Becky Thatcher is absent from school and Tom tries unavailingly to "whistle her down the wind," echoing *Othello*, III, iii, 262: "I'd whistle her off, and let her down the wind" (Baetzhold, *Mark Twain and John Bull* [1970], p. 373 n. 14). A sketch Twain published in 1882 told "everything just as it happened; nothing extenuated, and naught set down in malice" ("The McWilliamses and the Burglar Alarm"). Twain recalled an apprentice blacksmith in Hannibal

who became stage-struck after some English actors performed; later, in St. Louis, he stood on a street corner, "face bowed and frowning, slouch hat pulled down over his forehead— imagining himself to be *Othello* or some such character" (*LonMiss* [1883], Ch. 51). Michael Patrick Hearn detected an allusion to *Othello* in the description of Jim as "*harmless when not out of his head*" (*The Annotated Huckleberry Finn* [1981], p. 230).

In 1885 Twain recorded: "Oct. 26. Saw [the Italian actor Tommaso] Salvini [1829–1915] in Othello. His was a grand performance, but his support was wretchedly poor. They might as well *all* have talked Italian—or Sanscrit, for that matter—nobody could understand what they said" (NB 25, *N&J* 3: 205). (Twain would meet Salvini in person in Italy in 1893.) Twain commented that Samuel Watson Royston's literary travesty, *The Enemy Conquered*, contained the motive of jealously merely as "a pretext to drag in a plagiarism of his upon a scene or two in 'Othello'" ("A Cure for the Blues" [1893]). Susy Clemens wrote excitedly from Venice in 1893 after visiting "the house of my beloved Othello and his statue" (Salsbury, *S&MT* [1965], p. 328). In a letter postmarked in Italy on 5 March 1893 Susy quoted a line spoken by Desdemona in a letter to Louise Brownell, a college friend (Hamilton College Archives).

———. *The Plays and Poems of Shakespeare, According to the Improved Text of Edmund Malone [1741–1812], Including the Latest Revisions, with a Life, Glossarial Notes, an Index, and One Hundred and Seventy Illustrations, from Designs by English Artists*. Ed. by A[braham]. J[ohn]. Valpy (1787–1854). Illus. 15 vols. London: Henry G. Bohn, 1853.

Inscription: the front flyleaf is signed, "S. L. Clemens/ (Mark Twain)". This was a highly uncharacteristic form for Clemens to inscribe books. Eugene Field II faked the autographs of Clemens and other prominent figures in various nineteenth-century books, and this is unquestionably another one of his forgeries.

Location: currently unknown. Formerly in the Special Collections, Michigan State University Library. Donated to that collection on 29 September 1952 by Charles G. Munn of Jackson, Michigan. The volumes were then appraised at $225. In 2014 the set could no longer be found in the Michigan State University Library.

Source: "Update: Mark Twain, Eugene Field, and a Skeptical Odyssey in the Stacks," *Adversaria: Special Collections at Michigan State University*, 23 September 2014.

———. *Plays of Shakespeare. Introduction and Notes Explanatory and Critical. For Use in Schools, Clubs, Classes and Families*. Edited and with an introduction and notes by Henry N[orman]. Hudson (1814–1886). 28 vols. Boston: Ginn & Co., 1884–1890.

Inscriptions: the front flyleaf of each of the twenty-two surviving volumes is inscribed in black ink (now faded to brown): "Olivia S. Clemens/Oct 1st 1890/Radnor Hall/ Mamma." In the copy of Shakespeare's *Twelfth Night* she varied this wording, writing (by habit, no doubt), "From O. L. C." instead of "Mamma." In the copy of *Romeo and Juliet* she added "Bryn Mawr" on a separate line after "Radnor Hall". The handwriting of these inscriptions is very careful and precise, as though she felt the gift to be of importance. Radnor Hall was (and still is, at last report) a small residence hall. That is where Susy had received her living assignment.

Marginalia: all of the volumes bear penciled brackets, underlinings, and study notes. The copies of *Julius Caesar* and *Othello* contain the most extensive annotations, but other volumes are also marked with thoroughness. Although this set was not purchased for Clemens, he apparently borrowed it. His characteristic penciled brackets and underlings are visible in its copies of *King Richard the Third* (at Richmond's lines, "True hope is swift, and flies with swallow's wings/Kings it makes gods, and meaner creatures kings"); in *Romeo and Juliet* (pencil and black ink notions on the front pastedown endpaper refer to pages 69, 109, and 153; underlinings in black ink on page 74 designate "The more I give to thee,/The more I have"); in *King Henry the Eighth* (an underlining of the editor Hudson's awkward phrasing on page 7, underlinings of "my hopes in Heaven do dwell" on page 133 and "their virtues we write in water" on page 142, and penciled brackets on pages 10, 16, 44, 65, 78, 80, 90, 110, 111, 120, 122, 127, 129, 130, 136, 143, 150, and 172). Possibly Clemens annotated other plays as well—the volumes are often so heavily marked that it is difficult to distinguish his markings from those by Susy and (apparently) others.

Provenance: Clara Clemens Samossoud held back these volumes from the *C1951* sale, perhaps out of sentiment. Her second husband, Jacques A. Samossoud, outlived his wife; when he died in 1966 he bequeathed these books to Henry and Mary Shisler of Cardiff by the Sea, California. The Shislers had possession of them from 1968 until 1981, when they decided to sell them to the Humanities Research Center (now the Harry Ransom Center), at University of Texas at Austin. (Many other Clemens association items owned by the Shislers were purchased at that time by a book dealer in Santa Barbara, California, Maurice Neville.)

Location: Harry Ransom Center, University of Texas at Austin.

Copies examined: Susy Clemens's personal copies, in 1984.

When the Clemenses visited New York City with Susy Clemens on 29 September 1890 (Fears, *Day by Day* 2: 39), they bought her a complete set of Shakespeare, and on 1 October in Bryn Mawr, Pennsylvania, Olivia Clemens sat down and fondly inscribed each of the volumes to her daughter. Susy Clemens's father recalled, "I cannot remember when she first began to carry around a vast Shakespeare. She was never without it. It was a trouble in traveling, but she had to have it" (Notebook 39 [London, January 1897], TS p. 48, MTP). There may have been a single-volume work, now lost, that Clemens was describing, but the worn and annotated condition of the Shakespeare set in the Harry Ransom Center makes it probable that these twenty-two volumes constituted the "vast Shakespeare" that Susy insisted on toting around Europe.

For many more details about this Shakespeare set, the circumstances surrounding this gift to the college-bound daughter, and the family's veneration of Shakespeare, see Alan Gribben, "Susy Clemens' Shakespeare: An Addition to the Twain Library Books in the Harry Ransom Humanities Research Center," *The Library Chronicle* (University of Texas at Austin) n. s. No. 27 (1984): 94–103—revised

and reprinted in Volume One of this present work. That essay looks in detail at Samuel Clemens's veneration for Shakespeare, his markings in the twenty-eight-volume set inscribed for Susy Clemens 1890, and the family's fondness for amateur theatricals that these books suggest. (See also the Catalog entry below for another set owned by Susy Clemens, *The Works of Shakespeare*.)

———. *Richard III* (historical tragedy, probably produced in 1594).

Mark Twain quoted from Act I, i, 15–16 in a piece he wrote about James White's museum of freaks for the San Francisco *Dramatic Chronicle* 21 (October 1865): 3: he praised the "three-quartered dog" as "a most wonderful freak of nature. Poor fellow! Richard III was—'Cheated of feature by dissembling nature,/ Deformed, unfinished,' but this dog is actually cheated of a quarter by dissembling nature" (quoted by Edgar M. Branch, "'My Voice is Still for Setchell': A Background Study of 'Jim Smiley and His Jumping Frog,'" *PMLA* 82.7 [December 1967]: 595, 599). "I was born without teeth—and there Richard III. had the advantage of me; but I was born without a humpback, likewise, and there I had the advantage of him," Twain joked in "A Burlesque Autobiography" (1871). In a brief speech before an amateur theatrical production in Hartford on 12 November 1875 Twain spoke of how an actor should deliver King Richard's line in Act V, Scene iii, line 177, "A horse, a horse!" (Hartford *Courant*, 13 November 1875, quoted in *MTLet* 6: 590). Chapter 51 of *Life on the Mississippi* (1883) contains a related anecdote: "When he was an apprentice-blacksmith in our village, and I a schoolboy, a couple of young Englishmen came to the town and sojourned a while; and one day they got themselves up in cheap royal finery and did the Richard III. sword-fight with maniac energy and prodigious pow-wow, in the presence of the village boys." In Chapters 20 and 21 of *Adventures of Huckleberry Finn* (1885) the King and the Duke prepare the sword fight from *Richard III* as one of three theatrical performances in Bricksville. The Duke also paraphrases a line from the opening speech of *Richard III*—"And all the clouds that lowered o'er our housetops"—in his garbled soliloquy in Chapter 21. Michael Patrick Hearn detected another *Richard III* allusion—to the murder of George Duke of Clarence in a butt of malmsey wine—in Chapter 23 of *Adventures of Huckleberry Finn* (*The Annotated Huckleberry Finn* [1981], p. 227). Clemens wrote to Charles L. Webster on 20 June 1887 to advocate action "in these piping times of pious pow-wow," very likely an echo of Glouster's "Now is the winter of our discontent" opening speech (I, i, 1) that contains the phrase "This weak piping time of peace" (I, i, 24; Berg Collection, NYPL; Webster, *MTBus*, p. 347).

Another (faint) echo occurs in Chapter 23 of Twain's *The American Claimant* (1892): "The thing which he [Tracy-Berkeley] had made prominent was the opportunity now so happily afforded to reconcile York and Lancaster, graft the warring roses upon one stem, and end forever a crying injustice which had already lasted far too long." According to Edward T. Perrine, who stayed at the Hotel Kranz in Vienna in 1898, Twain liked to tell an anecdote about his playing the title role in this play for an impromptu performance in Nevada. When he cried "A horse, a horse, my kingdom for a horse," a dejected nag was dragged onto the stage ("Long Evenings of Rich Talk with Mark Twain," Hartford *Daily Courant* [22 September 1935]: Section E, p. 3, TS in MTP). Twice Twain thought of burlesquing lines 1–2 from Act I, Scene i, in a sketch about the Tammany Hall machine; the second entry in Notebook 44 reads: "Now is the winter of our discontent made glorious summer by this sun of New York; & all the clouds that Seth Lowered o'er our housetops are in the deep bosom of the ocean buried" (20 June 1901, TS pp. 14, 17).

Blair, *MT&HF* (1960), pp. 302–303; E. Bruce Kirkham, "Huck and Hamlet: An Examination of Twain's Use of Shakespeare," *Mark Twain Journal* 14.4 (Summer 1969): 17–19. See also Anthony J. Berret, "The Influence of *Hamlet* on *Huckleberry Finn*," *American Literary Realism* 18.1–2 (Spring-Autumn 1985): 196–207; Jeffrey Kahan, *The Cult of Kean* (Burlington, Vermont: Ashgate Publishing Co., 2006), pp. 103–114; and Amy M. Green, "Huck and Jim at the Bare Bodkin's Point: *Hamlet's* Mangled Soliloquy as Textual Commentary," *Mark Twain Annual* 5 (2007): 69–81.

———. *Romeo and Juliet* (romantic tragedy, produced 1594–95).

There are similarities between *Romeo and Juliet*, II, ii, 43–44 and Mark Twain's "Dysentery-Dusenberry" confusion (*Golden Era*, 28 February 1864; *WG* [1938], p. 69). In Verona, Twain in Chapter 21 of *The Innocents Abroad* (1869) resists the urge to write about the "Montagues and Capulets, their famous balconies and tombs of Juliet and Romeo et al." Katy Leary recalled that during the mid-1880s the Clemens children "frequently played the balcony scene from 'Romeo and Juliet'" (*MTB*, p. 837). On 1 May 1882 Clemens was present in New Orleans when six-year-old Birney and four-year-old Laura Guthrie, the children of attorney James B. Guthrie, "played the balcony scene in Romeo & Juliet" (NB 21, *N&J* 2: 552). Clemens wrote to Olivia Clemens about their performance, done "in the quaintest most captivating way, with good emphasis, elocution, earnestness, & perfect simplicity & unconsciousness. I never have seen anything that moved me more. They required prompting only once. There was an audience of twenty-five ladies & gentlemen" (2 May 1882, *LLMT*, p. 212). The King and the Duke ludicrously get up the *Romeo and Juliet* balcony scene for Bricksville performances (*HF* [1885], Chs. 20, 21). In his early (October-November 1892) working notes for *Pudd'nhead Wilson* (1894), Mark Twain intended for the twins to "play Romeo & Juliet"; subsequently he added details: "They play piano, sing duets & do Romeo & Juliet—balcony scene" (Florence, NB 32, TS pp. 35, 36). As a tourist in Verona in June 1893, Clemens "passed house of the Capulets" (NB 33, TS p. 18). On 14 September 1906 Isabel Lyon found that Clemens had taken her copy of the play with him to Fairhaven for his visit (IVL Journals, TS p. 186, MTP). Clemens's nephew Jervis Langdon remembered Clemens "turning to his companion at a performance of 'Romeo and Juliet,' on one of his last visits to the theatre," and remarking: "That's one of the greatest things Bacon ever wrote" (Langdon, *Samuel Langhorne Clemens: Some Reminiscences* [1938], p. 12; reprinted in

Mark Twain in Elmira [2013], p. 206).

Blair, *MT&HF* (1960), pp. 225, 296–297.

———. [*Romeo and Juliet*.] *Maude Adams Acting Edition of Romeo and Juliet*. Illustrated by Ernest Haskell (1876–1925) and C[harles]. Allan Gilbert (1873–1929). Published with the authorization of Charles Frohman (1856–1915). First edition. Art nouveau gray cloth decorated cover designed by R. K. Richardson, stamped in white. New York: R. H. Russell, 1899. 110 pp.

Inscription: a label is inserted at the front: "With the compliments of Maude Adams." The front flyleaf is inscribed in ink, "With my best love, in memory of the time we saw Juliet together. S. L. G." [The "G" appears distinct and does not seem to be a "C".]

Provenance: from the library of Susan Crane. It would have been in the Langdon library at Quarry Farm at the time of Clemens's visit there in 1903.

Location: collection of Kevin Mac Donnell, Austin, Texas.

Source: letter from Kevin Mac Donnell to Alan Gribben, 27 October 2014, which states that the volume is unmarked.

Charles Frohman's production of *Romeo and Juliet* starred the popular Maude Adams (1872–1953) in the Juliet role, but it ran for only sixteen performances.

———. "Sonnet 144."

An entry in Notebook 22 (1883–1884) reads: "CXLIV. *Shaks.* 'Fire him out!' last line" (*N&J* 3: 45). Shakespeare's poem begins, "Two loves I have of comfort and despair"; its last lines are these: "Yet this shall I ne'er know, but live in doubt,/Till my bad angel fire my good one out."

———. *The Taming of the Shrew* (comedy, probably written around 1594).

John Drew remembered that Clemens saw him in the play in 1875 and spoke at a dinner honoring the production of *The Taming of the Shrew* that starred Ada Rehan as Katharina and Drew as Petruchio (*My Years on the Stage* [1922], pp. 75, 90). Clemens delivered remarks at this dinner on 13 April 1887 to commemorate the one hundredth night of the comedy at Augustin Daly's theatre (Joseph Francis Daly, *Life of Augustin Daly* [1917], pp. 432–434; Fatout, ed., *MTSpk* [1976], pp. 222–224). On 13 March 1889 Clemens wrote to Augustin Daly from Hartford to say that he and his family would appreciate receiving good seats for Saturday night: "They wish to see the taming done again" (Houghton Library, Harvard; see also SLC to Daly, 5 April 1889).

———. *The Tempest*. New York: Cassell & Co., 1887. 192 pp. (romantic drama, probably written in 1611).

Source: MTLAcc, entry #970, volume donated by Clemens. Thirty pages were reported missing in 1910.

Olivia Langdon read *The Tempest* in 1867 (Harris, *Courtship* [1996], p. 24). Mark Twain quoted Prospero's valedictory speech ("The cloud-capt towers. . . .") in his 1872 English journals upon visiting Westminster Abbey (*MTLet* 5: 603). He quoted it again in "A Memorable Midnight Experience" (1874), crediting the inscription on the scroll of Shakespeare's statue in Westminster Abbey. In reply to Clemens's query, William Dean Howells informed him on 13 March 1876 from Cambridge: "The 'great globe,' etc., is in the Tempest, Scene I, Act 4., Prospero speaking" (*MTHL*, p. 127). Twain quoted Prospero's valedictory ("The cloud-capp'd towers. . . .") and proclaimed the speech "sublime and tremendous" in "Comments on English Diction," perhaps written in 1876 (Jervis Langdon, *Some Reminiscences* [1938], p. 22; repr. in *Mark Twain in Elmira* [2013], p. 215). Twain echoed the lines in Chapter 17 of *A Connecticut Yankee in King Arthur's Court* (1889): "Recal the commandment, or he will dissolve the castle and it shall vanish away like the instable fabric of a dream!" The assemblage flees, "before I should change my mind and puff the castle into the measureless dim vacancies of space." John S. Tuckey (*Mark Twain and Little Satan* [1963], p. 69) noted that Twain was referring to Prospero's valedictory speech (Act V, Scene i, lines 50–57) in a 1905 letter to Clara about breaking his bow and burning his arrows. Coleman O. Parsons recognized the implications of Prospero's haunting speech for Twain's dream musings, particularly Satan's revelation in "No. 44, The Mysterious Stranger" (written between 1902 and 1908) that the entire bitter spectacle of life is a dream (Parsons, "Background" [1960], p. 72). Twain quoted at length from Prospero's famous speech (IV, i, 152–158) in *Is Shakespeare Dead?* (1909) to remind readers that the author of *The Tempest* "was a genius without a mate." In Part 7 of the same essay Twain considers the seaman's language from Act I, Scene i, 1–47. Twain credulously accepted John Macy's demonstration of the claim by G. G. Greenwood that the Epilogue to *The Tempest* concealed the Latin acrostic of "Francisco Bacono" (11 January 1909 AD, *AutoMT* 3: 300).

Parsons, "Background" (1960), pp. 71–72; Baetzhold, *MT&JB* (1970), pp. 231–232; Gibson, *MSM* (1969), pp. 31, 32 n. 77, 33.

———. *The Temple Shakespeare*. Ed. Israel Gollancz (1864–1930). Text from the Cambridge Edition. 41 vols. London: J. M. Dent and Co., 1898.

Catalog: Ball 2016 inventory, red leather, gilt edged pages, fair to poor condition, 41 vols.

Location: Quarry Farm library shelves, under the supervision of the Mark Twain Archive, Elmira College, Elmira, New York.

This set was available to Clemens during his few remaining visits to Quarry Farm in Elmira.

———. *Titus Andronicus* (tragedy, performed in 1594).

Clemens inscribed (but abbreviated and altered) lines from Act I, Scene i, lines 150–156 as a handwritten epigraph for the guest book that visitors signed at Stormfield (1908): "In peace and honor rest you here, my guest; repose you here,/ Secure from worldly chances and mishaps!/Here lurks no treason, here no envy swells,/Here grow no damned grudges; here are no storms,/No noise, but silence and eternal sleep:/In peace and honor rest you here, my guest!" Clemens omitted line 151 that welcomed "Rome's readiest champions" and twice he changed the words "my sons" to read instead "my guest." (Kevin Mac Donnell, "Stormfield: A Virtual Tour," *Mark Twain Journal* 44.1–2 [Spring/Fall 2006]: 33). (In light of the imminent Isabel V. Lyon-Ralph Ashcroft fiasco, Clemens's hope for "no damned grudges" and "no storms" seems futile as well as ironic.) "Rightly viewed," Mark Twain wrote in Part 4 of *Is Shakespeare Dead?* (1909), "Calf-butchering accounts for 'Titus Andronicus,' the only play—ain't it?—that the Stratford Shakespeare ever wrote."

———. *Twelfth Night* (comedy, probably performed in 1600 or 1601).

"Time brings its revenges," Mark Twain quipped in Chapter 51 of *Roughing It* (1872), and he paraphrased the same Shakespearean line ("Thus the whirligig of time brings in his revenges"—Act V, Scene i) in a letter of 10 April 1875 to Elisha Bliss predicting "that 'whirligig of time' will bring round *another* revenge by & by, I suspect" (*MTLet* 6: 445). Clemens had made a note of the same *Twelfth Night* line on the envelope of a letter from Charles H. Webb (*MTLet* 6: 443 n. 1).

———. *The Two Gentlemen of Verona* (comedy, probably performed in 1594–1595).

Mark Twain alluded to this play in one of his *Quaker City* letters as he approached Verona in July 1867 (*Alta California*, 22 September 1867; McKeithan, *TIA* [1958], p. 55). In the margin of William J. Rolfe's *Shakespeare the Boy* (published in 1896; inscribed by Clemens in 1909), where Rolfe asserted on page 24 that Shakespeare must have had the Avon River in mind when he wrote the simile of a river that Rolfe quotes from *The Two Gentlemen of Verona*, Clemens objected: "No enamelled stones, & you couldn't make that drowsy current rage, anyway. *Does it go to the ocean?*"

———. *Venus and Adonis* (poem, published in 1593).

In Mark Twain's bawdy *1601* (1880), Shakespeare "did rede a portion of his 'Venus and Adonis,' to their prodigious admiration," but the attendant cup-bearer "did deme it but paltry stuff" (Franklin J. Meine's edition, privately printed for the Mark Twain Society [Chicago, 1939], p. 38). Twain's "The Walt Whitman Controversy" (DV36, MTP), probably written around 1882, pretends to quote lines from *Venus and Adonis*, which "every creature in every household in America has the opportunity to read." The (ostensibly) six lines begin "'The boar!' quoth she; whereat a sudden pale," but the editor of the *Evening Post* supposedly intervenes to delete most of the remainder of the passage. Twain states that he owns a copy of this poem, though it and other works in Shakespeare's canon might well be judged indecent and obscene. "Is there an educated young fellow of nineteen, in the United States, who has not read Venus and Adonis?," he asks. In Part 4 of *Is Shakespeare Dead?* (1909), Twain protests that Shakespeare could not have written "that graceful and polished and flawless and beautiful poem" at the mere age of twenty-two. As proof one need only look at its "smooth and rounded and flexible and letter-perfect English."

Ed Folsom and Jerome Loving, "'The Walt Whitman Controversy': A Lost Document," *Virginia Quarterly Review* 83.2 (Spring 2007): 123–127.

———. *The Works of Shakespeare: The Text Carefully Restored According to the First Editions*. Ed. by Henry N[orman]. Hudson (1814–1886). Revised edition, with additional notes. Red cloth, darkened to brown color. Worn bindings. 12 vols. Boston: Estes and Lauriat, n. d. [copyright 1871].

Marginalia: there is a pencil notation on the rear flyleaf of Volume I that is not in Clemens's hand: "349. 12th Night". No other markings are discernible, nor do the volumes bear any inscriptions. On 21 November 1977 John W. Berry, then the Public Services Coordinator for the Gannett Tripp Learning Center, discovered a letter (dated 28 June 1895) from Frank Pratt, president of Century Publishers, to Clemens that was laid in Volume I at pages 68–69 in *The Tempest*. This perhaps suggests that Clemens was reading these books at Quarry Farm prior to his global lecture tour.

Catalog: Ball 2016 inventory, [only] 6 vols., brown cloth, gilt lettering on cover and spine, publication date 1851 [*sic*].

Location: Mark Twain Archive, Gannett-Tripp Learning Center, Elmira College, Elmira, New York. Six volumes [only] donated by Jervis and Irene Langdon in 1977.

Copies examined: these six volumes are quite possibly Clemens association copies. Examined in November 1986 and again on 11 August 1988. The 28 June 1895 letter from Frank Pratt is no longer laid in Volume I, but in that book there is still laid in part of a letter in Clemens's hand, probably intended for James B. Pond, written in pencil and then black ink and numbered as page 2: "Look here—that program which I sent you is a good deal too long. Here is a full enough bill of fare for *one* night:" (the fragment ends here).

———. *The Works of Shakespeare.* 20 vols. Volume I, *Titus Andronicus, Henry VI, Part 1*; Volume II, *Henry VI, Part 2, Henry VI, Part 3*; Volume III, *Richard III, Love's Labour's Lost*; Volume IV, *Comedy of Errors, Two Gentlemen of Verona*; Volume V, *Midsummer Night's Dream, Romeo and Juliet*; Volume VI, *King John, Richard II*; Volume VII, *Merchant of Venice, Taming of the Shrew*; Volume VIII, *Henry IV, Part 1, Henry IV, Part 2*; Volume IX, *Henry V, Merry Wives of Windsor*; Volume X, *Twelfth Night, Much Ado about Nothing*; Volume XI, *As You Like It, All's Well That Ends Well*; Volume XII, *Measure for Measure, Troilus and Cressida*; Volume XIII, *Hamlet, Julius Caesar*; XIV, *Macbeth, Othello*; Volume XV, *King Lear, Antony and Cleopatra*; Volume XVI, *Coriolanus, Timon of Athens*; Volume XVII, *Pericles, The Tempest*; Volume XVIII, *Cymbeline, Winter's Tale*; Volume XIX, *Henry VIII, Two Noble Kinsmen*; Volume XX, *Poems, Sonnets*. Edited by William J[ames]. Rolfe (1827–1910). Friendly Edition. Original half calf and marbled boards, a few boards detached but present (including the back cover of Volume XIII and the front cover of Volume XVIII), rubbed edges and corners. New York: Harper & Brothers, 1884.

Inscriptions: Volume II is inscribed in black ink, "Olivia S. Clemens/Christmas 1885/Mamma." Volume III is inscribed identically. Clemens similarly inscribed Volumes IV through XX as gifts to Susy Clemens: "Susy Clemens/Xmas 1885."

Marginalia: Volume V (*Midsummer Night's Dream, Romeo and Juliet*) contains a penciled note, possibly by Susy Clemens, referring to *Romeo and Juliet*: "Act IV Scene III. J. P. /Act III Scene V (Father)." The passages singled out in Act III occur on pages 104, 105, and 106; those in Act IV appear on pages 114, 115, and 116. The latter involve Juliet and her parents, Capulet and Lady Capulet. A few speeches are marked in pencil in the text. Both *The Merchant of Venice* and *The Taming of the Shrew* (Volume VII) have passages marked for actors to read; the latter play is much more heavily marked, and includes numerous speeches that are to be read or to be "cut." In Volume XVII (in *The Tempest*) Clemens made notes while trying to deduce whether Francis Bacon left any acrostic clues

of his authorship.

Catalogs: *C1951*, J1, listed among volumes belonging to Jean and Clara Clemens; "Property from the Library of Mark Twain," Butterfield & Butterfield, San Francisco, Sale 6613 (16 July 1997), lot 2706.

Location: Mark Twain House and Museum, Hartford, Connecticut.

Copies examined: Susy Clemens's first Shakespeare set, subsequently in the possession of Clara Clemens. Viewed in Hartford in 1997.

"Get Susy a Shakspre," Clemens wrote in November 1885 (NB 25, *N&J* 3: 212). (See also the Catalog entry above for another set owned by Susy Clemens, *Plays of Shakespeare*.)

———. *The Works of Shakespeare.* Ed. Charles Harold Hereford (1853–1931). Eversley English Classics Series. London: Macmillan and Co., 1899–1902. Volume I, *Love's Labour Lost, Comedy of Errors, Midsummer Night's Dream*; Volume II, *Taming of the Shrew, Merchant of Venice, As You Like It*; Volume III, *Much Ado about Nothing, All's Well That Ends Well*; Volume IV, *Pericles, Cymbeline, The Winter's Tale, The Tempest*; Volume V, *Henry VI, Parts 1 and 2, Richard III*; Volume VI, *King John, Richard II, Henry IV, Parts 1 and 2*; Volume VII, *Henry V, Henry VIII, Titus Andronicus, Romeo and Juliet*; Volume VIII, *Julius Caesar, Hamlet, Othello*; Volume IX, *King Lear, Macbeth, Antony and Cleopatra*; Volume X, *Coriolanus, Timon of Athens, Poems*. [Edition conjectured but almost certain.]

Catalog: *C1951*, D10, listed among volumes signed by Clemens, edition unspecified, $80 for the set.

Mark Twain publicly endorsed Hereford's edition in 1903: "I am of the unlearned and to me the Notes and Introduction are invaluable; they translate Shakespeare to me and bring him within the limits of my understanding. Most people have limits similar to mine, and need these generous helps; here they have their opportunity to supply their lack" (advertisement in *Collier's Weekly* 32.10 [5 December 1903]: 42; discussed in Lawrence W. Levine's *Highbrow/Lowbrow: The Emergence of Cultural Hierarchy in America* [Cambridge, Massachusetts: Harvard University Press, 1988], p. 72).

Mark Twain's endorsement of the pro-Bacon faction in 1909 has sometimes confused readers about his true feelings regarding the plays. All of the surviving evidence—including the numerous entries above—suggests that Twain's attitude toward Shakespeare approached worshipful veneration, surpassing his admiration for any other author. Shakespeare's phrases resounded throughout his writings and speeches.

In Mark Twain's *Life on the Mississippi* (1883) and in his 1909 study, *Is Shakespeare Dead?*, Twain depicted a Mississippi River pilot named George Ealer as the person who introduced him to Shakespeare's works. Albert Bigelow Paine, Clemens's designated biographer, followed this version of events, reiterating the importance of Ealer's influence; according to Paine, Sam and Henry Clemens "spent a good deal of their leisure with the other pilot, George Ealer, who . . . quoted Shakespeare and Goldsmith" (*MTB* [1912], p. 134). R. Kent Rasmussen, in *Critical Companion to Mark Twain: A Literary Reference to His Life and Work* (New York: Facts on File, 2007), 2: 675, provided information about Ealer (1829–1866), who piloted the *Pennsylvania* and relished literature.

Entering a gold miner's cabin in Jackass Hill, California in January 1865, Mark Twain observed in Notebook 4 that the dwelling had no planking on its floor, yet he could see "Byron Shakspeare, Bacon Dickens, & every kinds of only first class Literature" (*N&J* 1: 70). That same year Twain recommended that the "literary connoisseur" should attribute "all the royal blank verse, with a martial ring to it, to Shakespeare" (*Californian*, 17 June 1865, *LAMT*, p. 141; *ET&S* 2: 195). Twain received much advice about what supplies to take on the *Quaker City* sightseeing excursion, whereas, he wrote, "I wouldn't give a cent for anything but a Shakespeare, and a deck of cards, and a couple of shirts" (Letter 18, New York City, 18 May 1867, *MTTMB*). He compared Shakespeare to the anonymous authors of the Old Testament in Chapter 47 of *The Innocents Abroad* (1869), observing that by comparison "Shakespeare is always present when one reads his book." "The world's great teacher—it is Shakespeare," he declared in 1872 ("From an English Notebook," *LE*, p. 172).

Clemens and his wife visited Stratford-on-Avon in July 1873 in the company of Moncure Conway (see *MTB*, p. 647); Clemens made notes about the trip in Notebook 12, where he wondered about several facts: "It is curious there is not scrap [*sic*] of manuscript in the shape of a letter or note of Shakespeare in the present day" (*N&J* 1: 562). Mainly he was amused by the extent of the idolatry he witnessed and by the chicanery of men such as the entrepreneur who supplied a never-ending number of wooden items supposedly manufactured from a mulberry tree cut down at Shakespeare's home in the eighteenth century. Shakespeare was one of the authors who gathered at the royal fireside in *1601*, written in 1876 and published in 1880. Around 1876 Twain suggested in "Comments on English Diction" that the Bible, Shakespeare, and Lincoln used the English language forcefully (quoted in *Mark Twain in Elmira* [2013], pp. 213–216). In the margin of Clemens's copy of Henry H. Breen's *Modern English Literature* that Clemens signed in 1876 he declared: "Shakespeare took other people's quartz and extracted gold from it—it was a nearly valueless commodity before" (MTP) One line in a play that Twain wrote in 1877 reads, "I bet it'll crack me up till I wouldn't swap graves with Shakespeare!" ("Cap'n Simon Wheeler, The Amateur Detective," *S&B*, p. 274).

On 21 January 1879 Clemens predicted that William Dean Howells might not be recognized as a writer of classics until a century after his death: "It is the fate of the Shakespeares & of all genuine prophets" (SLC to Howells, Munich, *MTHL*, p. 246). Mulling over ideas for a burlesque toast in 1879, Twain thought of "illustrating & backing up remarks by quotations from Shakspeare et al which they never uttered, & which do not apply, anyhow" (Notebook 18, *N&J* 2: 332). In an unsent letter (a sketch, really) addressed to the New York *Evening Post*, Twain alluded to "Shakspeare's immortality" (23 November 1880, MTHM, Scharnhorst, ed., *MTPP* [2014], p. 133). On 7 April 1882 Howells vetoed that same sketch, titled "The Shakespeare Mulberry," for inclusion in *The Stolen White Elephant* (1882). In this piece Twain scoffs at the slips from this hallowed tree that the mayor of Stratford-on-Avon is sending to New York City for a

city park. Seven years ago, writes Twain, the Stratford mayor gave *him* one of the flourishing slips, but it soon drooped and grew primarily "downwards & sideways." An orchard of such trees in Central Park will "look like a currant patch in winter time" (MTHM; *MTPP*, p. 133).

Twain's "The Walt Whitman Controversy" (DV36, MTP), probably written in 1882, states that he owns a copy of Shakespeare's works. Recalling his days as a Mississippi river pilot, Twain wrote that "while we lay at landings I listened to George Ealer's flute, or to his readings from his two Bibles—that is to say, Goldsmith and Shakespeare" (*LonMiss* [1883], Ch. 19). In Notebook 23 (1884), Twain noted: "Write a criticism of one of Shakspere's plays in the modern style—'nothing new in situation, or plot or anything—all worn-out'—quote whence this that & the other incident was stolen. Write in modern English, *then reduce it to quaint old English*" (*N&J* 3: 78). "Studies for that article: Balzac, Shakspeare, Saint Simon," Twain jotted in 1886 (NB 26 [May? 1886], *N&J* 3: 239). On 20 January 1887 Twain listed Shakespeare's plays among his favorite reading in answering an inquiry from the Reverend Charles D. Crane (ALS, Shapell Manuscript Library, Beverly Hills, California).

In September 1887, having returned to Hartford from Elmira, Twain entered the names "Bacon-Shakspere" in Notebook 27 (*N&J* 3: 309)—the first indication of his interest in the controversy. (He was irked that Charles L. Webster & Company had not published Ignatius Donnelly's *The Great Cryptogram*.) In the same notebook, Twain adumbrated his Baconian argument with a burlesque "cipher" of Milton's career and works in which he proved that Milton's travel, abilities, and education better qualified him to have written *Pilgrim's Progress* than did John Bunyan's (NB 27 [September 1887], *N&J* 3: 325). While Twain commenced the exercise as an amusing pastime, his mounting pages of "evidence" show how much this type of argument appealed to him. In Twain's initial concept of *A Connecticut Yankee in King Arthur's Court* (1889) the Yankee was supposed to win a contest among the bards by reciting from Shakespeare and Tennyson (manuscript in the Berg Collection, New York Public Library; cited by James D. Williams, "Revision and Intention in Mark Twain's *A Connecticut Yankee*," *American Literature* 36.3 [November 1964]: 288–297). Clemens recorded a major event in January 1889: "*Monday, Jan. 7*—4:45 p.m. The first proper name ever set by this new [James W. Paige typesetter] key-board was *William Shakspeare* [*sic*]. I set it, at the above hour" (NB 28, *N&J* 3: 443). Around 1890 Clemens declared that Paige was "a poet, a most great and genuine poet, whose sublime creations are written in steel. He is the Shakespeare of mechanical invention" (*MTA*, 1: 72–73; *AutoMT* 1: 102). Henry Fisher reported that Clemens was amused by the German translations of Shakespeare: "They think them classic—they get my eyes in flood with laughter" (*AMT*, p. 193). Clemens mentioned Shakespeare around December 1892 in Notebook 32 (TS p. 47). Samuel Watson Royston's awful novelette, *The Enemy Conquered*, Mark Twain promised, is a book which—once read—the reader "will keep it by him, with his Shakspere and his Homer," even though "there is but one Homer, there is but one Shakspere" ("A Cure for the

Blues" [1893]).

As early as 1894 Clemens was attempting to account for Shakespeare's anonymity: "Now what *was* the accident that brought Shakspeare into notice after two centuries of neglect & oblivion—was it a chance remark of a monarch?" (NB 33 [1894], TS p. 61). In Chapter 44 of *Following the Equator* (1897), Twain deprecatingly compares Julia A. Moore's poetry to Shakespeare's, the highest standard. Recalling his travels, Clemens observed, "An excellent profile of Shakspeare looks out from a crag on the border of Lake Tahoe. I saw a perfect face of Shakspeare once on the face of a rock wall . . . under . . . Mont Blanc" (NB 42 [1897], TS p. 12). Tom Sawyer guarantees Huck Finn that when they free Jim in England they will "see the Tower and Shackspur's [*sic*] grave" ("Tom Sawyer's Conspiracy," Ch. 8, written 1897–1900, *HH&T*, p. 227).

"No doubt Shakspeare knew what was in the Shaksperean parts which he *played*; but as to the contents of the rest of the piece there is more than one Shaksperean scholar to-day who could teach him" (SLC to Sir Walter Besant, Vienna, 22 February 1898, Berg Collection, NYPL). Carlyle Smythe wrote of Twain: "I have heard him quote both Shakespeare and Tennyson purely out of a delight for the melody of the words, because, as he says, the phrase 'tastes good in the mouth'" ("The Real 'Mark Twain,'" *Pall Mall Magazine* [London] 16.65 [September 1898]: 31). "The intellectual snow-summits built by Shakespeare and those others," was the way Twain phrased it ("About Play-Acting," *The Forum* 26 [October 1898]: 151). Still, Twain explained to a correspondent, "Shakespeare and [James] Watt, and we others can't even *combine* our idea-catchers on plans original with ourselves, but that even the combination-scheme must come from the outside—gathered from reading and experience" (SLC to Sir John Adams, Vienna, 5 December 1898, published by Lawrence Clark Powell, "An Unpublished Mark Twain Letter" *American Literature* 13.4 [January 1942]: 407). The spiritualist medium in Twain's "Schoolhouse Hill" (written in 1898) conjures up Shakespeare, but he only "did some rather poor things" in poetry (*MSM*, p. 206). Twain observed that Shakespeare was one of the "masterminds" who accepted the pervasive belief in witches ("Which Was It?" [written 1899–1903], *WWD?*, p. 306). In a discarded fragment, "Trial of the Squire," written in the summer of 1899 and intended for inclusion in Twain's "Which Was It?," a lawyer argues in court: "'*You—godless—villain.*' It is lofty—it is stately—it is theatrical—it is melodramatic. . . . Shakspeare could have built the phrase, but that ignorant German low-wage mill-hand *never* did!" (*WWD?*, p. 582). In tragedy, "Shakespeare is a standard," Twain was certain ("Corn-Pone Opinions," written in 1901, *WIM?*, p. 95). In Twain's sarcastic "About Cities in the Sun" (DV357, MTP), written around 1901, he seems sincere in referring to the "wonderful experience" it would be to stand in the New Jerusalem "& hear Shakspeare & Milton & Bunyan read from their noble works" (MS p. 19). On 23 January 1903 Twain mentioned Shakespeare along with Washington as belonging among mankind's "giants," and in April 1903 he noted Shakespeare's birthday (NB 46, TS pp. 8, 14). In January 1905 Twain alluded to "the Shakespeares of the inventor-tribe, so to

speak" ("Concerning Copyright"). Shakespeare was an "intellectual giant" and a "splendid name," Twain wrote in 1905 in "Proposal for Renewal of the Adam Monument Petition" (*FM*, p. 452). There is a complimentary allusion to Shakespeare in Clemens's letter to Colonel W. D. Mann, 3 January 1906 (ALS in MTP).

"It had not seemed to me that the blushful passages in Shakspeare were of a sort which Shakspeare had actually heard people use," Twain speculated, "but were inventions of his own—liberties which he had taken with the facts, under the protection of a poet's license" (31 July 1906 AD, *MTE*, p. 206; *AutoMT* 2: 155). The Old Man in Part 1 of "What Is Man?" (1906) claims that "Shakspeare created nothing. He correctly observed, and he marvelously painted," but he was merely an imitator—a "*machine*" (*WIM?*, p. 130) and in Part 5 he reiterates that "the elaborate Shaksperen play was the final outcome" of a long historical process (*WIM?*, p. 183). Twain jokingly referred to Shakespeare as a writer, like Chaucer and Spenser, who couldn't spell modern English ("Spelling and Pictures," speech at the Associated Press dinner, 19 September 1906, *MTS1923*, p. 322; *MTSpk*, p. 526). Twain alluded to Shakespeare admiringly in Book I, Chapter 5 of *Christian Science* (1907). The subject of Twain's "The Little Tale," the Reverend Elliot B. X., discovers a rare edition of Shakespeare that contains a Shakespeare signature (30 January 1907 AD, *MTE*, pp. 91–96; *AutoMT* 2: 411). Twain's "Extract from Captain Stormfield's Visit to Heaven" (1907) supposes that while Shakespeare was a prophet, he is compelled "to walk behind a common tailor from Tennessee" in the Hereafter; nonetheless, Twain ranks Shakespeare with Homer (*RP*, p. 67). In an Autobiographical Dictation of 14 February 1908 Twain recounted Dorothy Quick's recent visit to 21 Fifth Avenue, when she "read Shakspeare aloud, always selecting from each play her favorite passages" (*AutoMT* 3: 208).

Mark Twain's doubts about Shakespeare's authorship gradually became manifest. On the rear flyleaf of Notebook 48 (1908) Clemens noted: "Shaksperidolater/Stratfordolater." Around November 1908 he wrote in the same notebook: "2 most celebrated imposters—Sh[akespeare] & Sat[an]" (NB 48, TS p. 23). In a late essay, "Satan and Shakespeare" (DV371, MTP), Twain tried to make something out of the "close parallel" between these figures—namely, that almost nothing is known about either, despite their historical prominence. "From away back towards the very beginning of the Shakspear-Bacon controversy I have been on the Bacon side, and have wanted to see our majestic Shakespear unhorsed. . . . It always seemed unaccountable to me that a man could be so prominent in Elizabeth's little London . . . yet leave behind him hardly an incident for people to remember him by." Indeed, "not even a distinguished horse could die and leave such biographical poverty behind him." (At this time Twain's own designated biographer was hard at work constructing an authorized literary monument that Twain had prudently arranged.) Twain was anticipating that a forthcoming book, William S. Booth's *Some Acrostic Signatures of Francis Bacon* (1909) "would unhorse Shakspeare permanently and put Bacon in the saddle" (11 January 1909 AD, *AutoMT* 3: 298). In a letter to Jean

Clemens written at Stormfield on 26 February 1909, her father explained that his forthcoming book-length essay was simply "throwing bricks at Shakespeare" that he had laid up fifty years ago, when he decided that Shakespeare "didn't write a line of the Plays & Poems that pass under his name." He declared that Shakespeare is a humbug, like Mary Baker Eddy (TS in MTP). "I've been reading half a dozen Shakespeare-Bacon controversy books," he wrote to Jean on 3 March 1909. They left him ashamed that the "so-called great intellects" allowed such a sham to remain on his pedestal (TS in MTP). "The truth is, we don't know *who* wrote Shakespeare. There is no evidence at all that S. did it; & as there was only one alive that *could* have done it . . . the plausibilities favor the suspicion that *he* did it," Twain wrote on 25 April 1909 to James M. Beck, an admirer of Shakespeare and a friend of Henry H. Rogers (MTP). Subsequently invited to Stormfield to "discuss and discuss" the authorship of Shakespeare, Beck was astonished to hear Twain "burst into a volley of profanity, worthy of his early days on the Mississippi, and [he] cursed and reviled Shakespeare with a virulence of phrase." In Beck's opinion, the incident "shows how a strong and vigorous mind, when infected with the virus of the Baconian theory, can lose all sense of proportion." Sadly, "it became an obsession with him" to the point that "he lost alike his humor and poise when his mind dwelt upon this subject" (Dunbar Plunket Barton, *Shakespeare and the Law*, pp. xvii, xx, -xxi; see a full citation below this Catalog entry). To M. B. Colcord, Twain insisted on 18 May 1909 that the actual identity of the author was not his concern; he merely wanted to persuade readers that Shakespeare was not the writer (Folger Library).

On 4 June 1909 Clemens added marginal comments to a letter of 5 March 1909 from Jean Clemens, explaining that he did not mean Shakespeare was a scoundrel ("only his apologists") and correcting her assumption that he meant Shakespeare had stolen Bacon's work ("No, he is not chargeable with theft") (ALS in MTP). Clemens admitted to Helen Keller on 29 June 1909 that his book and those of the other revisionists would have no effect on men's minds: "Shakspeare the Stratford tradesman will still be the divine Shakspeare to our posterity a thousand years hence" (PH in MTP). Mark Twain's *Is Shakespeare Dead?* (1909) is more comprehensible when we recall his lifelong desire to make an exclusive "find," to demonstrate to the world that some cherished assumption was in reality a falsehood, to discover a well-kept secret of the ages. Henry W. Fisher reported that Clemens once thought he might have turned up such a bombshell in 1894, when he asked Fisher to assist him in gathering evidence to prove that Queen Elizabeth was in fact a man (*AMT*, pp. 47–54). English history, with its hallowed names and fixed reputations, particularly attracted Clemens's historical sleuthing. The Shakespeare-Bacon controversy was almost an inevitable snare for him. The very mention of Shakespeare's name became in his view a sign of human stupidity; in the texts of various volumes in his library he underlined references to the Bard of Stratford-on-Avon and gloatingly set down derogatory opinions of these authors' faulty knowledge. "As silly & empty as the 'arguments' in favor of the claim that Shaks wrote Shaks,"

he wrote in 1910 (NB 49, TS p. 4).

James M. Beck, "Foreword," Dunbar Plunket Barton, *Shakespeare and the Law* (Boston: Houghton Mifflin Co., 1929), xvi-xxxix); Brashear, *MTSM* (1934), p. 216; Aspiz, "Mark Twain's Reading" (1949), pp. 265, 271–276; Salomon, *TIH* (1961), p. 172; Krause, *MTC* (1967), p. 289; Baetzhold, *MT&JB* (1970), pp. 255–262, 271–273; and Edward Mendelsohn, "Mark Twain Confronts the Shakespeareans," *Mark Twain Journal* 17.1 (Winter 1973–1974): 20–21. See especially James Hirsh, "Samuel Clemens and the Ghost of Shakespeare," *Studies in the Novel* 24: 3 (Fall 1992): 251–272, and Anthony J. Berret, *Mark Twain and Shakespeare: A Cultural Legacy* (Lanham, Maryland: University Press of America, 1993), the fullest studies of Twain's admiration for the Bard. Joe Falocco reviewed some possible reasons for Clemens's "odd" sympathy for the Baconians in "Is Mark Twain Dead?: Samuel Clemens and the Question of Shakespearan Authorship," *Mark Twain Annual 2* (2004): 25–40. Ed Folsom and Jerome Loving looked carefully into the dating of a relevant essay—"'The Walt Whitman Controversy': A Lost Document," *Virginia Quarterly Review* 83.2 (Spring 2007): 123–127.

SHALER, NATHANIEL SOUTHGATE (1841–1906). *Aspects of the Earth: A Popular Account of Some Familiar Geological Phenomena*. Illus. New York: Charles Scribner's Sons, 1904. 344 pp.

Inscriptions: a bookplate on the front pastedown endpaper reads: "To the King/ with/the affectionate homage/of Betsy." The half-title page is signed, "S L. Clemens/1908/ from Betsy Wallace." [This was Elizabeth Wallace (1865–1960), who would write *Mark Twain and the Happy Island* (1913) about her friendship with Clemens.]

Marginalia: beside a passage on page 56 quoted from *Pliny's Letters*, Book VI, 20, describing the eruption of Vesuvius, Clemens noted in pencil: "The interest of this excellent narrative never fades. In my lifetime I believe I have read it twenty-five times." At the top of page 69 in the chapter on volcanoes (page 68 discusses Aetna's magnitude), Clemens wrote in pencil: "*Dec. 29, 1908.* I was reading these volcanic pages in bed when the morning paper brought this account of AEtna's yesterday performances." In the rear of the volume, laid in loose, is a clipping (pages 3–4) from the New York *Times* of 31 December 1908; it describes the force of an earthquake in Italy, especially in Messina. Something was once pinned to the index pages at the rear—the pin holes and yellowed imprint still remain. Page 341 shows chemical traces of the ink with which Clemens wrote on whatever was once pinned there; most of the words are undecipherable except for "intelligence," "earthquake," and the final sentence: "Oh hear this ass brag!" The slipcase for this volume contains articles from the 31 December 1908 and 1 January 1909 issues of the New York *Times* (pp. 1–4) concerning earthquake-devastated Sicily and Calabria. The Mark Twain Papers at Berkeley contain photocopies of Clemens's marginalia and the Christmas gift card from Betsy Wallace that accompanied the book.

Catalogs: ListABP (1910), "Aspects of the Earth, Shaler"; *C1951*, #91c, $12.50; Lew David Feldman, "House of El Dieff" Catalogue (1954), item #229r, sold for $500 together with two other books; "Mark Twain Items and

Other Americana," Parke-Bernet Galleries, New York City, 21–22 May 1957 sale, item #123, sold for $60; *American Book-Prices Current Index 1955–1960* (New York, 1961), p. 258, resold in 1959 for $50.

Location: Mark Twain House and Museum, Hartford, Connecticut. Donated anonymously in 1959.

Copy examined: Clemens's copy, in August 1987.

SHARP, WILLIAM (1855–1905). *Flower O' the Vine: Romantic Ballads and Sospiri di Roma.* Introduction by Thomas A[llibone]. Janvier (1849–1913). Portrait. New York: Charles L. Webster & Co., 1892. 188 pp.

Catalog: *A1911*, "12mo, cloth, gilt top, N.Y. 1892," with a sheet of notes by Clemens laid in (including a reference to the mate of the *Alec Scott*, who "stood with pistol, over life boat"), lot 427, sold for $3.

———. *Life of Robert Browning.* Original blue cloth, minor wear. London: Walter Scott, 1890. 219 pp.

Inscription: signed in black ink, "Olivia L. Clemens/ Onteora [New York], 1890".

Marginalia: Clemens objected to the convoluted and digressive syntax of a sentence on page 54, writing in pencil: "This beastly mess of incoherence is not English." There are no other notes.

Provenance: shelfmarks of the numbering system that Clara Clemens Gabrilowitsch employed for her library books during her Detroit years.

Catalogs: *C1951*, O28, listed among volumes signed by Olivia Clemens; "Property from the Library of Mark Twain," Butterfield & Butterfield, San Francisco, Sale 6613 (16 July 1997), lot 2693.

Location: Mark Twain House and Museum, Hartford, Connecticut.

Copy examined: Olivia Clemens's copy, shared with Clemens. Viewed in Hartford in 1997.

SHARPE, SAMUEL (1799–1881). *The History of the Hebrew Nation, and Its Literature.* Original green cloth, light wear to edges and corners. London: Elliot Stock, 1908. 451 pp.

Inscriptions: the front pastedown endpaper is inscribed, "To Him/who has told to the world the story/of the pilgrimage of the 'Innocents Abroad'/this copy of an account of an/earlier journey is offered with/the best wishes of an/ Old Friend/Jan. 1909." Clemens also signed the front pastedown endpaper in black ink: "S L. Clemens/1909."

Catalogs: ListABP (1910), "Hist. Hebrew Nation, Sharpe"; *C1951*, 82c, presentation copy from the author, $15; "Property from the Library of Mark Twain," Butterfield & Butterfield, San Francisco, Sale 6613, 16 July 1997, lot 2694.

Location: Mark Twain House and Museum, Hartford, Connecticut.

Copy examined: Clemens's unmarked copy. Viewed in Hartford in 1997.

SHAW, FLORA LOUISA, (LATER) LADY LUGARD (1852–1929). *Castle Blair: A Story of Youthful Days.* Boston: Roberts Brothers, 1878. 308 pp. Reprinted in 1881. [Clemens's edition is undetermined.]

Clemens entered the author, title, and publisher of this book in Notebook 19 (1881, *N&J* 2: 402). Susy Clemens wished for *Castle Blair* while she was consigned to a "*read, sew, read, sew*" routine in Venice, she wrote to Clara on 29 April 1893 (TS in Harnsberger Collection; *S&MT*,

p. 331). In the novel a nineteenth-century heroine is sent to live on the estate of her elderly uncle in Ireland; there she encounters young cousins she never knew she had and they gradually and mutually influence each other.

———. *Hector: A Story.* Boston: Roberts Brothers, 1881. 340 pp.

Clemens entered the author, title, and publisher of this work in Notebook 19 (1881, *N&J* 2: 402). Shaw was a British journalist and author who traveled widely, especially in Africa and Australia. In *Hector: A Story* two children in France, Zélie (the narrator) and Hector, try to rectify an adult error in anticipated nuptials. In the process they fall in love with each other and seem destined themselves to marry someday, even though Hector must leave for England.

SHAW, GEORGE BERNARD (1856–1950). *John Bull's Other Island.* London: A. Constable & Co., 1907. 293 pp.

Source: MTLAcc, entry #530, volume donated by Clemens.

Clemens's secretary Isabel V. Lyon explored Shaw's works frequently. On 18 July 1907, for instance, she mentioned that she had read the preface of *John Bull's Other Island* to her mother (IVL Journals, TS p. 263, MTP). Since Lyon often shared her enthusiasms with Clemens, she may have loaned this book to him.

———. *Plays.*

Clara Clemens wrote Shaw's name and the word "Plays" in her mostly undated commonplace book (Paine 150, MTP). Henry Fisher recorded that Mark Twain "sometimes spoke with near-admiration of Bernard Shaw, 'whose plays[, Twain said,] are popular from London to St. Petersburg, from Christiania to Madrid, from Havre to Frisco, and from Frisco to the Antipodes, while mine are nowhere'" (*AMT*, p. xix). Twain met Shaw briefly in the London railway station on 18 June 1907: "Both told each other how glad the one was to meet the other. . . . After agreeing upon another meeting they shook hands again" (New York *Herald*). "I like his face," Twain told reporters afterward. "I want to see more of him" ("Mark Twain Tells Sea Tales," New York *Sun*, 19 June 1907). Archibald Henderson interviewed Shaw about Mark Twain in June 1907; during their hansom cab ride Shaw declared, "I consider Mark Twain America's greatest writer by far. America's two greatest and most precious literary assets are Poe and Twain." Henderson reported that "several days later" Shaw wrote Twain that "the future historian of America will find your works as indispensable to him as the French historian finds the political tracts of Voltaire" ("Mark Twain and Bernard Shaw," *Mark Twain Journal* 9.4 [Summer 1954]: 3). In Twain's Autobiographical Dictation of 25 July 1907, he recalled his conversation with "that brilliant Irishman, Bernard Shaw. . . . I lunched at Mr. Shaw's house a week or two afterward, and expanded the acquaintanceship" (MTP; *AutoMT* 3: 73). Shaw himself recollected going to meet his biographer Archibald Henderson "at the railway station, and found that Mark had come over in the same boat and was in the same train. There was a hasty introduction. . . . Some days later he walked into our flat in Adelphi Terrace. . . . [Then or later] he did do lunch with us, and told us stories of the old Mississippi storekeepers" ("Excerpts from Letters Written by Thomas A. Edison and G. Bernard Shaw,"

Overland Monthly 87 [April 1929]: 102). In a letter written to Cyril Clemens in 1937, Shaw testified that Twain "presented me with one of his books. . . . He had a complete gift of intimacy. . . . He was himself, and exactly what I expected. We got on together perfectly" (George Bernard Shaw, "My Encounters with Mark Twain," *Mark Twain Journal* 9.4 [Summer 1954]: 24; reprinted and extended in "Bernard Shaw Meets Mark Twain," *Mark Twain Journal* 20.1 [Winter 1979–1980]: 22). Twain said essentially the same of the playwright: "Shaw is a pleasant man; simple, direct, sincere, animated; but self-possessed, sane, and evenly poised, acute, engaging, companionable, and quite destitute of affectations. I liked him" (23 August 1907 AD, MTP; *AutoMT* 3: 109). Twain was aghast that Shaw's biographer "wildly imagined a lot of resemblances" between Shaw's philosophy and Twain's "What Is Man?" (1906) (2 November 1908 AD, MTP; *AutoMT* 3: 271). Carl Van Doren, "Mark Twain and Bernard Shaw," *Century Magazine* 109.5 (March 1925): 705–710, compared the two men but paid no attention to mutual influence. Van Doren tried to account for the differences in temperament and culture that caused Twain to be more cautious than the audacious Shaw, and so much less learned and penetrating. Archibald Henderson took credit for introducing Twain to Shaw, noted that "each tried to be natural," and recalled that after Shaw invited Twain to lunch and the car failed to come at once, Twain "pranced up and down like a caged lion" (*Bernard Shaw: Playboy and Prophet* [New York: D. Appleton and Co., 1932], pp. 737–738). See also Howard G. Baetzhold, *MT&JB* (1970), p. 250.

SHAW, HENRY WHEELER (1818–1885), pseud. "Josh Billings."
Everybody's Friend, or Josh Billings's Encyclopedia and Proverbial Philosophy of Wit and Humor. Illustrated by Thomas Nast and others. Hartford, Connecticut: American Publishing Co., 1874. 617 pp.

On 17 February 1876 Mark Twain added this book to four by himself (together with three by other authors) that Elisha Bliss was supposed to send to a home for disabled soldiers in Elizabeth, Virginia (SLC to Bliss, ALS in ASSSCL).

Twain mentioned Billings humorously in a column ("People and Things") in the 23 August 1869 issue of the Buffalo *Express* (Thomas J. Reigstad, *Scribblin' for a Livin': Mark Twain's Pivotal Period in Buffalo* [Amherst, New York: Prometheus Books, 2013], p. 241). In "Last Words of Great Men" (Buffalo *Express*, 11 September 1869), Twain labeled Benjamin Franklin "the Josh Billings of the eighteenth century," but added that Billings excelled his predecessor's "proverbial originality as much as he falls short of him in correctness of orthography" (McCullough and McIntire-Strasburg, *MTBE*, p. 46). A photograph taken for publicity purposes by the Boston Lyceum Bureau in 1869 shows Twain standing between Petroleum V. Nasby (David Ross Locke) and Josh Billings; it is captioned "The American Humorists" (*Sotheby's 2003*, lot 1). Twain asked Billings's lecture manager James Redpath to pass along his greetings to "Billings" on 10 May 1870 and later wrote to Redpath on 8 November 1870 to joke about Billings's amusing lecture, "Milk and Natural History" (*MTLet4*, pp. 128, 227). In marginalia Twain wrote in M. de L. Landon's *Saratoga in 1901* (1872), Twain accused

Landon of "stealing Billings's style." A tongue-in-cheek letter (intended for publication) that Twain wrote to Shaw in 1873, probably in March, complimented Shaw as "a personal friend, of long standing" and "an honest man," assured him "that in the dominion of natural history, you stand without a peer," but admonished Shaw about his spelling: "It is out of all reason that a man, seventy-five years of age, should spell as you do. Why do you not attend a night-school?" (*MTLet* 5: 304–306). Clemens was amused by the antiquated orthography in a court record of 1636 that J. Hammond Trumbull reproduced in *The True-Blue Laws of Connecticut* (1876), a volume Clemens signed in 1877; in the margin of page 143 Clemens wrote: "As for culture, Josh Billings could spell all around them & give them points." In 1879 Clemens noted in Paris: "Speech in 3d person is detestable—only the exact word has point—Could you 3d person Josh Billings', or Robert Burdette's or the Danbury News' happy remarks [?]" (NB 18, *N&J* 2: 300).

Mark Twain included "Josh Billings" in his review of American humorists for possible inclusion in an anthology, noting Shaw's pseudonym twice (NB 19, *N&J* 2: 363, 364). In Twain's proposed "Essay on Humor," he meant to "merely refer to & quote from" Josh Billings and others (NB 24 [August 1885], TS p. 36). Six pieces by Josh Billings appeared in *Mark Twain's Library of Humor* (1888); see the Catalog entry below. In 1906, reflecting on the disappearance of so many literary comedians whose names were once "conspicuous and popular," Twain mused, "Humor is only a fragrance, a decoration. Often it is merely an odd trick of speech and spelling, as in the case of Ward and Billings and Nasby . . . and presently the fashion passes, and the fame along with it" (31 July 1906 AD, *MTE*, p. 202; *MTAuto* 2: 152, 153). David Kestersen, "The Mark Twain-Josh Billings Friendship," *Mark Twain Journal* 18.1 (Winter 1975–1976): 5–9, noted that this dismissal considerably underrated Shaw's brand of humor and ignored their friendship, whereas Shaw steadfastly admired Twain's achievements (p. 8). Twain would again mention Josh Billings's poor spelling in Book II, Chapter 3 of *Christian Science* (1907).

DeVoto, *MTAm* (1932), p. 219. David E. E. Sloane (*Mark Twain as a Literary Comedian*, 1979) included Josh Billings among the northeastern Literary Comedians who had an impact on Twain's humor.

———. *Josh Billings' Farmer's Allminax for the Year 1870* [later annual editions were titled *Josh Billings' Old Farmer's Allminax.*] New York: G. W. Carleton, [1870].

On 14 February 1870 Shaw mentioned in a letter to Mark Twain that his *Allminax* had already sold 80,000 copies, a success which "came near ravishing me" (*MTLet* 4: 210 n. 3). Twain later wrote to his own publisher, Elisha Bliss, Jr., to express his hope that "a Christmas volume will out-pay Josh Billings' Allminax" (*MTLet* 4: 209). In the Buffalo *Express* Twain praised the *Allminax* as "a pleasant conceit and happily executed. . . . The pamphlet is selling handsomely and profitably" (Milton Meltzer, *Mark Twain Himself* [New York: Thomas Y. Crowell Co., 1960], pp. 116–117).

———. *Josh Billings: His Works, Complete. (Four Volumes in One).* Illustrated by Thomas Nast (1840–1902) and others.

Biographical introduction. New York, 1876.

Inscription: "To my very good friend Mark Twain, from his very good friend, Josh Billings, with the affection of the author. New York, Sept. 25, 1876."

Catalog: *A1911*, "8vo, cloth, N.Y. 1876," quotes the inscription, lot 429, sold for $23.

——. *Josh Billings: His Works, Complete. (Four Volumes in One).* Engraved frontispiece portrait of Shaw, numerous wood-engraved illustrations. Original pebble-grain russet cloth, decorated and lettered in black and gilt, brown endpapers. New York: G. W. Carleton & Co., 1881.

Catalogs: *A1911*, "8vo, cloth, N.Y. 1881," with a small sheet of notes about Fulton laid in, lot 428, sold for $2; *Sotheby's 2003*, #235, $700.

Provenance: contains the morocco bookplate of Hugo J. Lion. Eventually part of the collection of Nick Karanovich.

Copy examined: Clemens's copy, unmarked, at the 2003 Sotheby's auction. Has the *A1911* sale label.

Mark Twain's Library of Humor (1888) contained six sketches by Josh Billings: "To Correspondents," "The Alligator," "Natral and Unnatral Aristokrats," "The Neat Person," "The Bumble Bee," and "Ants, Etc."

SHEFFIELD, JOHN, DUKE OF BUCKINGHAM (1648–1721). *An Essay on Poetry.* In September 1880 Clemens copied into Notebook 19 Sheffield's famous quatrain: "Read Homer once, & you can read no more/ . . . And Homer will be all the books you need" (*N&J* 2: 371).

SHELDON, ELI LEMON (1849–1892), comp. *Everybody's Pocket Cyclopedia of Things Worth Knowing, Things Difficult to Remember, and Tables of Reference.* New York: Harper & Brothers, [cop. 1892]. 214 pp.

Catalogs: MTLAcc, entry #1330, volume donated by Clemens; ListABP (1910), "Pocket Remembrancer", no other information provided.

SHELDON, GEORGE WILLIAM (1843–1914). *Hours with Art and Artists.* New York: Appleton & Co., [cop. 1882]. 184 pp.

Source: MTLAcc, entry #1229, volume donated by Isabel V. Lyon, Clemens's secretary. Most likely this is the copy of Sheldon's book that was inscribed (according to a card in the book catalog of the Mark Twain Library at Redding): "A Merry Christmas/to Uncle Sam & Aunt Livy/ from Annie & Charlie [Webster] 1882." The inscribed volume could no longer be found in 1977.

SHELLEY, MARY WOLLSTONECRAFT (GODWIN) (1797–1851). *Frankenstein; or, The Modern Prometheus* (novel, published in 1818).

In Chapter 48 of Mark Twain's *Life on the Mississippi* (1883), a pet parrot on a river tugboat "had also a superabundance of the discordant, ear-splitting, metallic laugh common to his breed—a machine-made laugh, a Frankenstein laugh, with the soul left out of it." Twain sketched a "burlesque Frankenstein" in Notebook 22 in 1884 (*N&J* 3: 49, 50); eventually he employed some of these ideas—a hotel fire, mistaken identification—for Viscount Berkeley's plight in *The American Claimant* (1892). In Twain's story titled "Luck" (1891) the name appears again: "I felt as guilty and miserable as Frankenstein." Twain declared that Edward Dowden's *Life of Percy Bysshe Shelley* was "the strangest book that has seen the light since Frankenstein. Indeed, it is a Frankenstein itself [*sic*]; a Frankenstein with the original infirmity supplemented by a new one;

a Frankenstein with the reasoning faculty wanting" ("In Defence of Harriet Shelley" [1894]). In Twain's "Little Bessie," written 1908–1909, Hollister argues that God's creation of the cat which tortures a mouse is "just the case of Frankenstein and his Monster over again. . . . Frankenstein took some flesh and bones and blood and made a man out of them; the man ran away and fell to raping and robbing and murdering everywhere, and Frankenstein was horrified and in despair, and said, *I* made him, without asking his consent, and it makes me responsible for every crime he commits. *I* am the criminal, he is innocent. . . . It's just the case of God and man and you and the cat over again" (*FM*, p. 38).

SHELLEY, PERCY BYSSHE (1792–1822). *The Poetical Works of Percy Bysshe Shelley.* 2 vols. Contemporary polished half calf and marbled boards, gilt-decorated spines, morocco labels, rubbed edges and corners. Boston: Houghton, Mifflin and Co., 1883.

Inscriptions: both volumes were inscribed by Clemens, "Livy L. Clemens/Hartford/1887."

Provenance: displays the shelfmarks of Clara Clemens Gabrilowitsch's numbering system for her library books during her Detroit years. Sold at the 1951 Hollywood auction as "O36" but was not listed in its hastily compiled and unreliable sale sheet.

Catalog: "Property from the Library of Mark Twain," Butterfield & Butterfield, San Francisco, Sale 6613 (16 July 1997), lot 2695.

Location: Mark Twain House and Museum, Hartford, Connecticut.

Copy examined: Olivia Clemens's unmarked copy. Viewed in Hartford in 1997.

——. [An identical title.]

Catalog: *C1951*, J3, listed among the volumes belonging to Jean and Clara Clemens.

——. *A Selection from the Poems of Percy Bysshe Shelley.* Ed. with a memoir by Mathilde Blind (1841–1896). Collection of British Authors Series. Leipzig: B. Tauchnitz, 1872. 334 pp.

Catalog: *C1951*, D1, listed among volumes signed by Clemens, $8.

Shelley, Dryden, and Cowper were responsible for "all the poetry that everybody admires and appreciates, but nobody ever reads or quotes from," Mark Twain wrote in 1865 (*Californian*, 17 June 1865; *LAMT*, p. 142). Shelley was one of Susy Clemens's favorite poets when she was twelve and thirteen years old (*MFMT*, p. 66). In 1888 Twain composed the first of his criticisms of Shelley's biographers (DV49, MTP). In December 1892 Twain, then living in Florence, noted "Shelley—Löesche's," and then added: "Return damaged book [by William James?] to Loesches & get Shelley—we got 2 copies" (NB 32, TS p. 51). Twain made a memorandum in Chicago in April 1893: "Material [?] about Shelley article" (NB 33, TS p. 11). In the summer of 1893 Twain wrote to Fred J. Hall from Krankenheil, Bavaria: "Where is Shelley? If still on hand, keep it and I will tell you what to do with it" (undated letter in pencil, G. A. Van Nosdall, List No. 61 [October 1938], item #3). Twain's "In Defence of Harriet Shelley" (1894) quotes from seven poems by Shelley in the course of castigating Edward Dowden's *The Life of Percy Bysshe Shelley*: "To Harriet"; "Ever as Now with

Love and Virtue's Glow"; "Evening, to Harriet"; "Thy
Dewy Looks Sink in my Breast"; "Stanzas: April, 1814";
"To Harriet: May, 1814"; and "To Mary Wollstonecraft
Godwin: June, 1814." In 17 and 30 July 1901 Twain hotly
defended Harriet Shelley and criticized Shelley and his
biographer Edward Dowden (Richard Cary, "In Further
Defence of Harriet Shelley: Two Unpublished Letters
by Mark Twain," *Mark Twain Journal* 16.4 [Summer
1973]: 13–15).

On 14 February 1907 Clemens wrote to Jean Clemens from
21 Fifth Avenue in New York City: "I am to read Shelley's
Skylark. I have never done anything of quite so serious
a nature before" (TS in MTP; quoted in Christie's, New
York City, 11 May 1987, item 29). Isabel Lyon recorded
on 14 February 1907 that Mark Twain "read Shelley's
'Skylark' at the Shelley-Keats Memorial at the Waldorf.
He was bored to extinction and hated it all" (IVL Journals,
TS p. 224, MTP). "I have come to be quite entirely satisfied with my Shelley Skylark of the other day, much as I
was depressed about it at first. . . . I saw more than fifty
women crying," Clemens informed his daughter Clara on
5 March 1907. He offered "to recite it & you play a soft
accompaniment" (SLC to Clara Clemens, TS in MTP;
ALS quoted in *Sotheby's 2003*, #117). When Elizabeth
Wallace sent Francis Thompson's book on Shelley to Clemens, he responded with a letter to her on 22 September
1909 that pronounced it "a lovely little book, and as rich
in sumptuous imagery as is Shelley himself. The reading
so moved me & charmed me that I read some Shelley
under the inspiration of it" (*MT&HI*, pp. 131–133).

Paine, *MTB* (1912), p. 988; Paul Baender, "Mark Twain
and the Byron Scandal," *American Literature* 30.4 (January
1959): 467–485; Baetzhold, *MT&JB* (1970), pp. 284, 377
n. 17; Alex Brink Effgen, "Mark Twain's Defense of Virtue
from the Offense of English Literature: Matthew Arnold
and Percy Shelley," *Mark Twain Annual 11* (2013): 77–95.

SHELTON, FREDERICK WILLIAM (1814–1881). *Up the River.*
Illus. New York: Charles Scribner's Sons, 1853. 335 pp.
Mark Twain's Library of Humor (1888) contained "A Victim
of Hospitality" from Shelton's book.

SHEPPARD, (REVEREND) W. H. [Unidentified author.]
King Leopold quotes a report by this "meddlesome missionary" ("King Leopold's Soliloquy" [1905]).

SHERIDAN, PHILIP HENRY (1831–1888). *Personal Memoirs
of P. H. Sheridan, General, United States Army.* 2 vols. Illus.
New York: Charles L. Webster & Co., 1888.
Inscription: inscribed on the front flyleaf of Volume I,
"To/Fred Whitmore/with the regards of his friend/S L
Clemens/ Dec. 25 '88."
Catalog: ListABP (1910), "*Memoirs of General Sheridan* 2
v.", no other information provided.
Location: Mark Twain House and Museum, Hartford,
Connecticut (two volumes).
Copy examined: copies inscribed by Clemens, unmarked.
Examined in August 1987.
Clemens had sent Sheridan a "full morrocco" [*sic*] copy of
U. S. Grant's *Personal Memoirs* on 19 November 1885
(NB 25, *N&J* 3: 212). Clemens wrote and then canceled
an entry about Sheridan's *Personal Memoirs* in Notebook
28 (December 1888, *N&J* 3: 439): "Send 2d Vol to Ida."
He had evidently intended to send both volumes to his

in-laws, Charles and Ida Langdon. Sheridan's *Personal
Memoirs* recounted his impressions of his fellow com-
manding officers in the Civil War, President Abraham
Lincoln, and the outcome of numerous battles. He also
included his postwar experiences with Native American
tribes, including the Cheyenne and the Yakima.

SHERIDAN, RICHARD BRINSLEY BUTLER (1751–1816). *The
Rivals* (play, performed 1775).
Sheridan lies buried in Westminster Abbey, Mark Twain
noted in "A Memorable Midnight Experience" (1874).
Frederick Anderson pointed out "Mrs. Plunkett's obvious
descent from Mrs. Malaprop" in Mark Twain and Bret
Harte's play titled *Ah Sin* (performed in 1877); Anderson
also noted that Twain particularly claimed the authorship
of "my old Plunkett family" (*Ah Sin* [San Francisco: Book
Club of California, 1961], p. xi). In a letter to Joseph H.
Twichell written on 13 September 1898 from Kaltenleutgeben, Clemens mentioned "a noble dame in Vienna"
who misused French phrases; "but these Malaproperies
are always inventions—they don't happen" (*MTL* [1917],
p. 668; *LMTJHT* [2017], p. 221).

_____ and **OLIVER GOLDSMITH** (1728–1774). *Dramatic
Works of Sheridan and Goldsmith. With Goldsmith's Poems.* 2
vols. Miniature boxed set. Blue cloth. London: Cassell &
Co., [1886].
Provenance: Antenne-Dorrance Collection, Rice Lake,
Wisconsin.
Location: Mark Twain Archive, Gannett-Tripp Learning
Center, Elmira College, Elmira, New York.
Copies examined: Clemens's copies, unmarked. There is a
bookseller's sticker on the front pastedown endpaper of
Volume I: "Loescher & Seeber/ Firenze/ 20 Via Tornabu-
oni 20." Examined on 28 May 2015.

SHERLEY, [GEORGE] DOUGLAS (1857–1917).
Sherley, an author of fiction and poetry, was a wealthy resident of Louisville, Kentucky who worked as a journalist
for the Louisville *Courier-Journal* despite having studied
law. He had most recently published a volume of short
stories, *A Few Short Sketches* (1892) when he joined James
Whitcomb Riley in his national tour in 1893. Mark Twain
appeared with both men in Madison Square Garden in
New York City on 26 and 27 February and 3 March 1894.

SHERMAN, ELLEN BURNS (1867–1956). *Taper Lights.* Spring-
field, Massachusetts: Gordon Flagg Co., 1904. 253 pp.
Source: MTLAcc, entry #846, volume donated by Clemens.
Sherman, a Springfield resident and the author of *Why Love
Grows Cold* (1903), here collected her essays that had ap-
peared in *The Critic, The Lamp*, and elsewhere. Their titles
are intriguing: "Modern Letter Writing," "Our Comédie
Humaine," "The Root and Foliage of Style," and "When
Steel Strikes Punk," as examples. She was a member of
the Massachusetts Equal Suffrage Association.

SHERMAN, WILLIAM TECUMSEH (1820–1891). *Memoirs of
General William T. Sherman. By Himself.* 2 vols. Blue cloth,
gilt. New York: D. Appleton and Co., 1875.
Inscription: both volumes are signed by Clemens in
pencil on the front free endpapers: "Saml L. Clemens/
Hartford 1875."
Marginalia: both volumes bear the *C1951* sale number
"9-c" on the lower left front pastedown endpapers. Clemens's penciled annotations in Volume I consist of eleven

marginal lines on eleven pages, one initial corrected in a name on page 118, and one marginal note. That latter note occurs on page 118 where Sherman mentioned that the San Francisco *Herald* was the only newspaper that did not support the Vigilance Committee; Clemens then added, "This killed the Herald in a single day. It was the most prosperous paper there." Clemens made marginal lines at pages 66 (at Sherman's admiration for the African Americans in California), 67 (the deep mud on Montgomery Street in San Francisco), 68 (a description of 600 ships in San Francisco Bay), 79 (the California Constitution's exclusion of slavery), 87 (hearing Daniel Webster speak in the United States Senate), 99 (surviving the sinking of a schooner near the Golden Gate), 119 (threatening to throw a printer out a window), 136 (recounting the rescue of passengers from a ship that sank with a heavy loss of life), 139 (meeting Senator [William Morris] Stewart), 140 (setting up practice as an attorney), and 168 (his anger after a meeting with President Lincoln). The corners of pages are folded down at pages 108, 282, and 367. Pages 221–224 have a deliberate vertical fold. Volume II only contains a calculation of word counts on page 490, the last page of the text, that are obviously related to Twain's decision to publish this memoir. The corner of page 149 is folded down in Volume II.

Catalog: *C1951*, #9c, 2 vols., listed among books signed by Clemens, $40.

Location: collection of Kevin Mac Donnell. Acquired in January 2019.

Source: description furnished by Mac Donnell to Alan Gribben, emails, 29 and 30 January and 1 and 3 February 2019.

Mark Twain facetiously quoted equivocal praise by Sherman for Twain's ridiculous battle map initially published in the Buffalo *Express* (17 September 1870, *MTBE*, p. 229), a sketch later reprinted as "Fortifications of Paris" (1870). On 18 September 1887 Twain mentioned in a letter to Charles L. Webster that Sherman's book had sold 25,000 copies for Appleton and earned Sherman $25,000 in royalties (*MTLP*, p. 234).

———. *Memoirs of General W. T. Sherman, Written by Himself.* Fourth edition, revised, corrected, and complete. 2 vols. New York: Charles L. Webster & Co., 1891. [Includes an appendix organized and written by James G[illespie]. Blaine (1830–1893). This edition was reprinted by Webster & Co. in 1892.]

Sherman's name appeared in Clemens's Notebook 25 (1885, *N&J* 3: 202); shortly thereafter Clemens determined to send Sherman a "full morrocco" [*sic*] copy of U. S. Grant's *Personal Memoirs* (*N&J* 3: 212). In a letter from Hartford written on 9 October 1889 Clemens alluded to "Sherman, author of the brisk & delightful memoirs" (SLC to Mr. Bowker, New York Public Library, PH in MTP). On 27 February 1891 Clemens wrote to Fred J. Hall to say he was "feeling better" about the prospects for publishing a new edition of Sherman's *Memoirs*; Hamlin Hill explained that the Sherman family had agreed to obtain an essay by James G. Blaine and subsidize the costs of a new edition in the amount of $3,500 (*MTLP*, p. 269 n. 2).

SHERWOOD, MARY ELIZABETH (WILSON) (1826–1903). *Manners and Social Usages.* New York: Harper & Brothers, 1884. 337 pp. [Edition conjectured; other editions followed this one.]

Catalog: ListABP (1910), "Manners and Social Usages", no other information provided.

———. *A Transplanted Rose; A Story of New York Society.* Illus. New York: Harper & Brothers, 1900. 307 pp.

Source: MTLAcc, entry #1041, volume donated by Clemens.

SHILLABER, BENJAMIN PENHALLOW (1814–1890). *Life and Sayings of Mrs. Partington and Others of the Family* (first published in New York, 1854).

Sam Clemens's first printed sketch—"The Dandy Frightening the Squatter"—appeared in Shillaber's Boston journal, *The Carpet Bag* (1 May 1852; *ET&S* 1: 63–65), where the humorous monologues of Mrs. Partington also had their initial publication. Orion Clemens's Hannibal *Journal* (15 July 1852) mentioned a fictional character from *The Carpet Bag* (see the Catalog entry for "Ensign Jehiel Stebbings"). On 7 February 1870 Shillaber wrote a fulsome poem ("To Mark Twain") congratulating the author on his marriage; this poem appeared in the Virginia City *Territorial Enterprise*, was published in the Buffalo *Express*, and was later included in Shillaber's *Lines in Pleasant Places. Rhythmics of Many Moods and Quantities. Wise and Otherwise* in 1874 (Lawrence I. Berkove, "B. P. Shillaber Congratulates Mark Twain," *Mark Twain Journal* 32.2 [Fall 1994]: 10). From Buffalo, Clemens wrote a friendly thank-you letter to Shillaber for his subsequent "hearty words & good wishes" on 28 May 1870 (*MTLet* 4: 142). In Chapter 27 of Twain's *Roughing It* (1872), the character Mr. Ballou's "one striking peculiarity was his Partingtonian fashion of loving and using big words *for their own sakes*, and independent of any bearing they might have upon the thought he was purposing to convey." On 9 March 1874 Twain wrote to his publisher, Elisha Bliss, Jr.: "Damnation! Please send a cloth 'Roughing It' to B. P. Shillaber, Chelsea, Mass.," presumably to keep a promise (*Sotheby's 2003*, #23). Walter Blair sketched the striking resemblances between Aunt Polly of Twain's *Tom Sawyer* (1876) and Shillaber's Ruth Partington, a widow addicted to nostrums (*NAH* [1937], pp. 150–152; *MT&HF* [1960], pp. 62–64). On 13 March 1882 Mary Mason Fairbanks alluded familiarly to Shillaber's characters in a letter to Clemens written from Cleveland: "I know I am only a kind of Mrs. Partington, but you are not Ike [her precocious nephew], and my apron string is no check to you" (*MTMF*, p. 250). Oddly and perhaps significantly, nothing of Shillaber's appeared in *Mark Twain's Library of Humor* (1888). Twain wrote down Shillaber's name on 28 January 1903 (NB 46, TS p. 9). On 31 July 1906 Twain recalled that *Mark Twain's Library of Humor* (1888) "has no mention of Ike Partington, once so welcome and so well known" (Autobiographical Dictation, *MTE*, p. 202; *MTAuto* 2: 153).

Howard S. Mott, Jr., "The Origin of Aunt Polly," *Publishers' Weekly* 134 (19 November 1938): 1821–23, further established the surmise that Shillaber's Mrs. Partington was the model for Tom Sawyer's aunt. A modified portrait of Shillaber's character even appeared as an illustration in *Tom Sawyer*. See also DeVoto, *MTAm* (1932), p. 88; Stone, *IE* (1961), pp. 72, 120, and 137; Krause, *MTC* (1967), p. 93; Howard H. Kerr, *Mediums, and Spirit-Rappers, and*

Roaring Radicals (1972), p. 172. John Q. Reed, *Benjamin Penhallow Shillaber*. Twayne United States Authors Series, No. 209 (New York: Twayne Publishers, 1972), pp. 86–87, 91–92, and 128, reviewed similarities between Shillaber's books and Twain's writings, especially in regard to the characters of Isaac ("Ike") Partington and Tom Sawyer. David E. E. Sloane's *Mark Twain as a Literary Comedian* (1979) made the case for including Shillaber among the literary comedians who had an influence on Twain's humor; see also Sloane's "Literary Comedians," *Mark Twain in Context*, ed. John Bird (Cambridge, England: Cambridge University Press, 2020), pp. 60–1, 63, and 66.

SHIPP, J[ESSE]. A[LLISON]. (1864–1934) and ALEX ROGERS (1876–1930). *Abyssinia* (musical comedy, two acts, performed in 1906). Music by Will Marion Cook (1869–1944) and Bert A. Williams (1874–1922).

On Saturday, 10 March 1906, Isabel Lyon noted that "Mr. Rogers came at 12:30 and took him off to luncheon and to the matinee, 'Abbysinia' [*sic*] at the Majestic Theatre" in New York City (IVL Journals, TS p. 144, MTP). The musical was notable for being written and performed by African Americans. One of the lead actors was George Walker (1872–1911).

Shitakari Suzume (Japanese fairy tale, also known as "The Tongue-Cut Sparrow").
  Catalog: ListABP (1910), "Shitakiri Suzume", no edition specified.
  In this morality tale about kindness and generosity, an old man rescues an injured sparrow, but his wife becomes angry and cuts its tongue. When the old man ventures into the bamboo forest to seek the sparrow's forgiveness, he finds an inn where the sparrows stay; he is forgiven and offered his choice of a large basket or a small basket to take home. The old man chooses the small basket, which angers his wife when she discovers that it is filled with gold and valuables. She makes her way to the same sparrows' inn and asks for the large basket, but to her horror it turns out to be filled with monsters.

SHORTER, DORA (SIGERSON) (1866–1918). *The Collected Poems of Dora Sigerson Shorter*. Introduction by George Meredith (1828–1909). New York: Harper & Brothers, 1907. 292 pp.
  Source: MTLAcc, entry #1688, volume donated by Clemens.
  ———. [Another identical copy.]
  Source: MTLAcc, entry #2093, volume donated from Clemens's library by Clara Clemens Gabrilowitsch in 1910.
  ———. *The Story and Song of Black Roderick*. New York: Harper & Brothers, 1906. 90 pp.
  Source: MTLAcc, entry #257, volume donated by Isabel V. Lyon, Clemens's secretary.
  ———. [Another identical copy.]
  Source: MTLAcc, entry #1043, volume donated by Clemens.
  ———. [Another identical copy.]
  Source: MTLAcc, entry #1275, volume donated by Clemens.

SHORTHOUSE, JOSEPH HENRY (1834–1903). *John Inglesant: A Romance*. 2 vols. London: Macmillan and Co., 1882.
  Catalog: *A1911*, "Vol. I, 12mo, cloth, Lond. 1882," with a sheet laid in containing a list of names of individuals to receive a complimentary copy of Mark Twain's "Eve's Diary," lot 431, Volume I only, sold for $1.
  Shorthouse's historical novel, told in the first person, takes place during the times of Charles I.

SHUNSUI, TAMENAGA (1790–c. 1844). *The Loyal Ronins: An Historical Romance, Translated from the Japanese . . . by Shiuichiro Saito [1855–1910] and Edward Greey [1835–1888]*. Plates after Kei-Sai Yei-Sen. First edition in English. 8vo, original pictorial boards, rebacked with original spine preserved, floral-printed endpapers, white buckram folding-case. New York: G. P. Putnam's Sons, 1880. 275 pp.
  Marginalia: on page iv of the preface Clemens marked the first paragraph and observed in brown ink: "Mitford's translation of the Ronin story [in *Tales of Old Japan*, 1871] is better literature than this one. SLC." (Clemens was refuting the translator Saito's assertion that "in 'Mitford's Tales of Old Japan,' something has been related of the social conditions of the people; but as an example of Japanese literature, the book possesses little value.") On page viii Clemens noted in the same brown ink, "It was silly to anglicize the proper names. SLC." In the margin of page 95 Clemens queried in pencil, "Which of the pair took the bath?"; this referred to the sentence, "After he had refreshed himself and taken a bath, the visitor was ushered into his presence." On page 143 Clemens marked out an indefinite article, thereby altering "How a few vows stand the test of years" to read instead, "How few vows stand the test of years."
  Catalogs: *A1911*, "small 4to, boards, N.Y. 1880," quotes a marginal note by Clemens, lot 268; Waverly Auctions, Bethesda, Maryland, Sale No. 60, 22 September 1988, "front cover detached, spine loosening, some wear & soil to binding," item #547; *Sotheby's 2003*, #236, $2,000.
  Provenance: collection of Nick Karanovich, Fort Wayne, Indiana. Acquired from the 19th Century Shop of Baltimore, Maryland on 25 September 1988 for $2,000. The bookseller's receipt acknowledged "a fair copy only. Front cover detached, spine clipped and loose, some wear and soiling."
  Location: collection of Kevin Mac Donnell, Austin, Texas.
  Copy examined: Clemens's copy, in Austin in July 2004. Has the *A1911* sale label on the front pastedown endpaper. In addition, Nick Karanovich sent Alan Gribben photocopies of the cover, *A1911* sale label, title page, marginalia, and related auction catalog listings and bookseller's receipt on 6 October 1988.
  Saito and Greey here translated a ninjoban version of the *Chushingura*. Saito insisted that the works of Japanese authors "have been sealed to American and English readers."

SHUTE, HENRY AUGUSTUS (1856–1943). *The Real Diary of a Real Boy*. Illus. Boston: Everett Press Co., 1906. 200 pp.
  Source: MTLAcc, entry #1905, volume donated from Clemens's library by Clara Clemens Gabrilowitsch in 1910.
  Henry Shute was equivocal about whether he had actually found a diary he kept as a boy in Exeter, New Hampshire in 1867–68, but the antics and pranks he supposedly found there caused early-twentieth-century readers to forgive the labored cacography and remain eager to read sequels to *The Real Diary of a Real Boy*.
  Tim Prchal, "The Bad Boys and the New Man: The Role of Tom Sawyer and Similar Characters in the Reconstruction of Masculinity," *American Literary Realism* 36.3 (Spring

2004): 187–205, esp. 194 and 200.

SHUTTLEWORTH, PHILIP NICHOLAS (1782–1842). *The Consistency of Revelation with Itself and with Human Reason.* New York: Harper & Brothers, 1856. 267 pp.

Source: MTLAcc, entry #908, volume donated by Clemens. An Anglican churchman here vigorously defended the concept of Biblical revelation against the emerging breed of skeptics.

SIDGWICK, ARTHUR (1840–1920). *Introduction to Greek Prose Composition, with Exercises.* London: Rivingtons, 1876. 255 pp. Repr. Throughout the 1870s and 1880s).

In a footnote to "Private History of the 'Jumping Frog'" (1894), Mark Twain quotes from and cites Sidgwick's version (in English) of "The Athenian and the Frog." As Louis J. Budd noted, Twain's story had actually been adapted by Sidgwick for use in his *Introduction to Greek Prose Composition* (*CTSS&E* 2: 154 and 1022).

SIDNEY, (SIR) PHILIP (1554–1586).

In January 1894 Clemens made a memorandum in New York City: "Sir Philip Sidney. Return to [William Mackay] Laffan" (NB 33, TS p. 44).

SIENKIEWICZ, HENRYK (1846–1916). *"Quo Vadis": A Narrative of the Time of Nero.* Translated from the Polish by Jeremiah Curtin (1838–1906). New edition, with maps of ancient Rome. 2 vols. Boston: Little, Brown and Co., 1897. [Historical novel, first published in 1896. The conjectured Little, Brown edition had a two-volume format like the copy retained from the Clemens family's library by Albert Bigelow Paine.]

Catalogs: ListABP (1910), "Quo Vadis 2 v., Sienkiewicz"; *C1951*, J24, listed among volumes belonging to Jean and Clara Clemens.

In an interior photograph that Jean Clemens took in the 1900s a copy of this book is visible in a bookshelf in the background (collection of Kevin Mac Donnell, Austin, Texas).

SIGOURNEY, LYDIA HOWARD (HUNTLEY) (1791–1865). *Memoir of Mary Ann Hooker [1796–1838].* Philadelphia: American Sunday-School Union, [cop. 1840]. 177 pp.

Source: MTLAcc, entry #928, volume donated by Clemens.
Location: Mark Twain Library, Redding, Connecticut.
Copy examined: Clemens's unmarked copy. Has the red ink Mark Twain Library accession number "928". I could not find this volume in 1970 but located it on a return visit in June 1982.

Mary Ann (Brown) Hooker was the wife of the Reverend Horace Hooker (1793–1864). They resided in Connecticut and she wrote a series of children's scriptural biographies.

———. *Sketches.* Dark brown cloth, blind stamped, gilt lettering on the spine. Amherst, Massachusetts: J. S. & C. Adams, 1844. 216 pp.

Location: Mark Twain Library, Redding, Connecticut.
Copy examined: very possibly a copy belonging to the Clemens family. It is unmarked. The volume was shelved with Clemens's volumes when Albert E. Stone, Jr. compiled his checklist in 1955, and was still among them when I visited Redding in 1970, 1977, June 1982, and on 9 November 2019. It bears the red ink accession number "5471," which seems well beyond the numbers assigned to other donations by Clemens or his daughter Clara. However, there are apparently no surviving accession

records for books assigned numbers above 2315, so who can say how many more volumes Clara later sent to the community library?

Sigourney's *Sketches* consisted of six character sketches of the members of an unnamed family, outlining their tendencies, roles, and experiences. These include "The Father," "The Intemperate," and "The Patriarch."

Andrews, *NF* (1950), pp. 146–147.

SILL, LOUISE MORGAN (SMITH) (1867–1961). *In Sun or Shade, Poems.* New York: Harper & Brothers, 1906. 226 pp.

Provenance: MTLAcc, entry #901, volume donated by Clemens.
Location: Special Collections, Elihu Burritt Library, Central Connecticut State University, New Britain, Connecticut.
Source: information provided to Alan Gribben by Ewa Wolynska, Head of Special Collections, 13 January 2020.
———. [Another identical copy.]
Source: MTLAcc, entry #2091, volume donated from Clemens's library by Clara Clemens Gabrilowitsch in 1910.
———. *Sunnyfield, The Adventures of Podsy and June.* Illus. New York: Harper & Brothers, 1909. 228 pp.
Source: MTLAcc, entry #1178, volume donated by Clemens.
———. "To the Czar," *Harper's Weekly* 49.2511 (4 February 1905): 171.

Combining two causes he was supporting, Mark Twain employed this poem advocating the overthrow of the Russian Czar in Twain's polemical essay protesting the atrocities committed in the Belgian Congo. In Twain's "King Leopold's Soliloquy" (March 1905), Leopold quotes extracts from Sill's "To the Czar," noting how "it fits me—and rather snugly too"; Twain's footnote cites *Harper's Weekly* as his source. Sill's six-stanza poem opens on a note of outrage—"Imperial minion, swollen with a pride/That reeks to Heaven"—and closes by imploring Heavenly assistance: "Thou God who seest these things/ Help us to blot this terror from the earth."

SILVER, CHARLES W. *A Secular Anathema on Fakery in Business, Social and Professional Life; or, Twentieth Century Conduct.* London: Privately published, 1901. 528 pp.

Source: MTLAcc, entry #852, volume donated by Clemens. Silver opened his book with a quotation from Mark Twain deploring the U. S. policies toward China regarding immigration policies and missionaries and toward the treatment of Japan during the Russo-Japanes War. But Silver's book was far less concerned with foreign policies than with demonstrating the ubiquity of unfair and unethical practices in early-twentieth-century society. He deplored the prevalence of greed, competitiveness, ignorance, wealth disparities, and materialism. The solution, he felt, was for more people to read the English journal *Mind* (founded in 1876) and to appreciate the spiritual nature of life. "We are blindly groping in a malformed condition of thought. Let us seek the truths of Mind and Soul Realms. Let us become one with the Sublime and the Universal Mind whose dictates are for goodness, truth, justice, beauty, love, health and happiness" (p. 528).

SILVERMAN, JOSEPH (1860–1930).

Mark Twain quotes an account of Joseph in the Book of Genesis from "the very learned and able Dr. Silverman," terming it "Dr. Silverman's bank statement—all painted and gilded and ready for the inspector." Twain added that Silverman's explication was carried in the New York *Times*, "Sunday before last" (20 March 1906 AD, *MTE*, pp. 88–89; *AutoMT* 1: 424). The date Twain specified would be Sunday, 11 March 1906.

Silverman was the rabbi of the Temple Emanu-El on Fifth Avenue.

SIMCOX, GEORGE AUGUSTUS (1841–1905). *A History of Latin Literature from Ennius to Boethius*. 2 vols. New York: Harper & Brothers, 1906.

Source: MTLAcc, entries #1796 and #1797, volumes donated by Clemens.

SIMMS, WILLIAM GILMORE (1806–1870), ed. *War Poetry of the South*. New York: Richardson & Co., 1867. 482 pp.

Catalog: *A1911*, "first edition, 12mo, cloth (name cut from title), N.Y. 1867," with a slip containing Clemens's notes laid in, lot 432, sold for $2.

Clemens's library collection included relatively few Civil War voices from the American South. This volume was one of the exceptions.

SIMON, CHARLES (1850–1910) and PIERRE FRANÇOIS SAMUEL BERTON (1842–1912). *Zaza, A Comedy Drama in Five Acts*. Adapted from the French by David Belasco (1853–1931). (Performed in New York City, 1899).

Clemens saw *Zaza* at the Garrick Theatre in London on 20 April 1900 (NB 43, TS p. 7).

Simple Stories. Boston: Lothrop & Co., n.d.

Source: MTLAcc, entry #1915, volume donated from Clemens's library by Clara Clemens Gabrilowitsch in 1910.

A good candidate for the librarian's cryptic entry might be this children's book: Abby Morton Diaz (1821–1904), *Simple Traveller: Little Stories for Little Folks*. Illus. Boston: D. Lothrop and Co., cop. 1880. 93 pp.

Simplicissimus; Illustrierte Wochenschrift (German satirical magazine in Munich, published 1896–1944). Ed. by Albert Langen (1869–1909).

G. E. Stechert & Company, New York City importers and dealers in books and periodicals, notified Clemens on 12 July 1905: "We are pleased to receive your order [of 10 July] for 'Simplicissimus', which we have entered to begin with July 1st and will continue sending the numbers regularly to your present address [in Dublin, New Hampshire] until November, when we will forward them to the city address. Enclosed please find bill for the year's subscription to same" (MTP). Isabel Lyon noted how much Clemens cheered up on 24 March 1906: "He saw and received the copy of Simplicissimus that I brought in to him. He enjoys it. He calls it his 'Darling Simplicissimus'" (IVL Journals, TS p. 151, MTP; similar entry in the IVL Journal, Harry Ransom Center, University of Texas at Austin). On Sunday, 1 September 1907, Lyon recorded: "This morning the King had discovered a marvelous Mona Lisa in *Simplicissimus*—the only satisfactory Mona Lisa he has ever seen. Of course it was in caricature, and he was so happy over it, that he carried it over to the Mortimers, and they were very much amused by it" (IVL Journals, TS p. 275, MTP). Clemens wrote from Tuxedo Park on the same day, 1 September 1907, to praise Ragnvald Blix' comic drawings of old masterpieces, then appearing in the German humor magazine *Simplicissimus* (Nils Erik Enkvist, *British and American Literary Letters*

in Scandinavian Public Collections [Abo, 1964], p. 88). See also the Catalog entry for Blix.

SIMS, GEORGE ROBERT (1847–1922). *Tinkletop's Crime, and Other Stories*. Illus. New York: Charles L. Webster & Co., 1891. 315 pp.

Clemens's publishing firm advertised this volume as a collection of "mostly humorous" stories (*Publishers' Trade List Annual for 1893*).

SINCLAIR, MARY AMELIA ST. CLAIR (KNOWN AS "MAY") (1863–1945). *The Divine Fire*. New York: Henry Holt and Co., 1904. 597 pp.

Elizabeth Jordan—*Three Rousing Cheers* (New York: D. Appleton-Century Co., 1938), pp. 182–183—tells about a weekend party Clemens attended at Jorjalma, the country home of the prominent editor George Harvey (1864–1928). She seated Clemens next to Sinclair. "Like the rest of us, Mr. Clemens was fascinated by the amazing contrast between the passion and power of that novel and the personality of the prim, tucked-in little woman who had written it" (p. 183).

———. *The Judgment of Eve, and Other Stories*. Illus. New York: Harper & Brothers, 1908. 123 pp.

Source: MTLAcc, entry #261, volume donated by Clemens.

SINCLAIR, UPTON BEAU (1878–1968). *The Jungle*. New York: Doubleday, Page & Co., 1906. 413 pp. [Publisher and pages conjectured.]

Inscription: "To Mark Twain with the Compliments of the Author." The front pastedown endpaper is signed "S. L. Clemens, 1906."

Catalog: *A1911*, "post 8vo, cloth, N.Y. [1906]," quotes the inscription and the signature, lot 433, sold for $6.

The Jungle became a best-seller in 1906. In an Autobiographical Dictation of 13 June 1906, Mark Twain alluded to "to-day's lurid exposure, by Upton Sinclair, of the most titanic and death-dealing swindle of them all, the Beef Trust" (*The Autobiography of Mark Twain*, ed. Charles Neider [New York: Harper & Brothers, 1959], p. 121; *AutoMT*: 2: 116). Later that same month Twain wrote to Sinclair about "the magnitude and effectiveness of the earthquake which 'The Jungle' has set going under the Canned Polecat Trust of Chicago" (*AutoMT* 2: 515). Isabel V. Lyon conveyed Clemens's sentiment and thanked Sinclair "for your book" (MTP).

Sinclair, however, left behind an uncharitable opinion of Mark Twain's lack of courage when it came to risking his reputation and his income: "He was full of understanding, and would agree with everything we [muckraking radicals] said; yes, he was one of us. But when we asked him for a public action, a declaration, he was not there. 'The Jungle' was published, and he wrote me a letter. . . . I recall only one statement: he had had to put the book down in the middle, because he could not endure the anguish it caused him. Naturally I had my thoughts about such a remark. . . . Think what the uncrowned king of America could have done, in the way of backing a young author." Sinclair recalled another incident when "Mark Twain was visiting Bermuda, and came to see me. He had taken to wearing a conspicuous white costume, and with his snow-white hair and mustache he was a picturesque figure. He chatted about past times, as old men like to do. I saw that he was kind, warm-hearted, and also full of rebellion against capitalist greed and knavery; but he was an old man, and a sick man, and I did not try to probe the mystery of his life" (Upton Sinclair, *Mammonart: A Essay in Economic Interpretation* [Pasadena, California: Published by the author, 1925], p. 328). Sinclair likewise arraigned William Dean Howells and other writers of that era who had failed to lend their voices forcefully to reformist political movements.

SINGLETON, ESTHER (1865–1930). *The Furniture of Our Forefathers*. 2 vols. Illus. Critical descriptions of plates by Russell Sturgis (1836–1909). New York: Doubleday, Page and Co., 1901.

Catalog: *C1951*, 6c, listed among books signed by Clemens, $26.

Singleton would prove to be a prolific author of books on the history of European art, music, and architecture as well as guides to cities and primers on natural history.

SĪRAFĪ, ABŪ ZAYD HASAN IBN YAZĪD (10th century) and AL-TĀJR SULAYMĀN (9th century). *Ancient Accounts of India and China, by Two Mohammedan Travellers, Who Went to Those Parts in the 9th Century. Translated from the Arabic, by the Late Learned Eusebius Renaudot* [Eusèbe Renaudot, 1646–1720]. *With Notes, Illustrations, and Inquiries by the Same Hand*. London: Printed for Sam. Harding at Bible and Anchor on the Pavement in St. Martins-Lane, 1733. 273 pp. [Edition conjectured, but this one seems very probable.]

On 22 October 1896 Clemens entered the title and call number (I2511R) of a book he had found in the London Library: "Travels of 2 Mohamedans thro India & China in the 9th c." (Notebook 39, TS p. 12).

SISMONDI, JEAN CHARLES LÉONARD SIMONDE DE (1773–1842). *Historical View of the Literature of the South of Europe*. Translated from the French with notes and a life of the author by Thomas Roscoe (1791–1871). "Fourth edition, including all the notes from the last Paris edition." Half-title: Bohn's Standard Library. 2 vols. Contemporary marbled boards with polished calf backstrip. London: George Bell & Sons, 1881.

Inscription: the front flyleaf of Volume II is inscribed by Clemens, "Livy L. Clemens/from S L C/Hartford/1883".

Catalogs: *C1951*, O17, Volume II only; *Hunley 1958*, item #136, Volume II only, $7.50.

Location: Volume II only is in the Albert and Shirley Small Special Collections Library, University of Virginia, Charlottesville, Virginia. Gift of Clifton Waller Barrett. .

Copy examined: Olivia Clemens's unmarked copy of Volume II, in 1970.

"SIXTUS," pseud. of unidentified author. *Progressive Protestantism*. New York: Charles L. Webster & Co. [189?].

Clemens's publishing firm listed this twenty-five-cent pamphlet in *Publishers' Trade List Annual for 1893*.

———. *A Review of Professor Briggs' Inaugural Address*. New York: Charles L. Webster & Co., [189?].

Clemens's publishing firm listed this twenty-five-cent pamphlet in *Publishers' Trade List Annual for 1893*.

The Biblical scholar Charles Augustus Briggs (1841–1913) had become the focus of a heated religious controversy. After being appointed to the Edward Robinson Chair of Biblical Theology at Union Theological Seminary, Briggs delivered an inaugural address, "The Authority of the Holy Scripture," on 20 January 1891 that shocked and offended many Presbyterian clergy. In 1892 he was

charged with heresy and urged to retract his conclusions and recant, but he remained obdurate. Owing to his continued intransigience the General Assembly of the Presbyterian Church excommunicated Briggs in 1893. He thereafter became a Protestant Episcopal priest and went on to receive several distinguished honorary degrees for his scholarship.

SKELTON, GLADYS (WILLIAMS), LATER BENDIT (1889–1975), pseud. "John Presland." *Joan of Arc: A Historical Drama in Five Acts [and in Verse]*. London: Simpkin, Marshall & Co., [1909]. 184 pp.

Catalog: *C1951*, D50, listed among books signed by Clemens.

The Australian novelist and poet Skelton would later contribute to the science fiction genre.

SKINNER, CHARLES RUFUS (1844–1928). *Manual of Patriotism, for Use in the Public Schools of the State of New York*. [Albany, N. Y.: Brandow Printing Co.,] 1900. 470 pp.

Source: MTLAcc, entry #732, volume donated by Clemens.

SKRINE, FRANCIS HENRY BENNETT (1847–1933). *Fontenoy and Great Britain's Share in the War of the Austrian Succession 1741–48*. Introduction by Field-Marshal Earl Roberts (1832–1914). Illus. Red cloth, gilt lettering. Edinburgh and London: William Blackwood and Sons, 1906. 393 pp.

Inscription: the half-title page is inscribed in black ink, "Mr. S. L. Clemens/with the author's affectionate/ regards."

Location: Mark Twain Library, Redding, Connecticut.

Copy examined: Clemens's copy, unmarked. Has the red ink Mark Twain Library accession number "3457". Examined in 1970 and again in June 1982 and on 9 November 2019.

The consequential Battle of Fontenoy was fought in 1745 in Belgium.

———. *An Indian Journalist: Being the Life, Letters, and Correspondence of Dr. Sambhu C. Mookerjee [1839–1894]*. Illus. Calcutta: Thacker, Spink & Co., 1895. 477 pp.

In a newspaper interview published on 1 April 1896, Mark Twain said, "I have recently read a book by Mr. Skrine . . . dealing with the merits of a Hindu friend of the higher caste. Mr. Skrine makes certain quotations from letters written by his friend and that Hindu was so much a master of our language. . . . His English was flowing, easy and ever so idiomatic. This great aptitude on the part of the native of this country to excel in the English language is what one is confronted with all the time" (Gary Scharnhorst, ed., *The Complete Interviews*, pp. 294–295).

———. *Life of Sir William Wilson Hunter [1840–1900]*. Portraits and illustrations. London and New York: Longmans, Green, and Co., 1901. 496 pp. [Publisher and pages conjectured.]

Inscriptions: presented by the author to Clemens, who added in pencil: "From Skrine, whom we all knew so pleasantly in Calcutta, S. L. Clemens, Riverdale, Feb. 1902."

Catalog: *A1911*, "8vo, cloth, Lond. 1901," characterizes the inscription and quotes the signature, lot 434, sold for $1.25.

Clemens recommended this book to William Dean Howells, who replied on 31 July 1901 from York Harbor: "I will try to keep the Hunter book in mind; I wish it were out now, for I need a text" (*MTHL*, pp. 728, 729 n. 2). On 7 January 1902 Clemens wrote to Skrine from Riverdale on the Hudson: "Although the Sir William biography, through the (possibly criminal) neglect of your publishers continues to not arrive, *that* doesn't prevent these Clemenses from shouting Happy New Year in the most cordial voice across the Atlantic to those well-loved Skrines" (ALS in the National Library of Scotland). The next month Clemens sent a copy to Howells (WDH to SLC, New York City, 3 February 1902, *MTHL*, p. 741). In a letter that Clemens wrote sporadically between 7 and 13 February 1902 while he was reading the Hunter biography, Clemens had nothing but praise: "It was a noble life & most nobly lived. The beauty & cheer & pathos of it move hand in hand together through it all. . . . The book stirs every emotion & throbs with every interest that human beings feel; you have done your work well" (photocopy of a California rare book dealer's 24 October 1984 flier; sent to Alan Gribben by Nick Karanovich, 16 November 1984). On 17 December 1903 Clemens addressed Skrine from Florence about another, unidentified title: "It is a charming young lady. She brought the book , & I have dipped into it with satisfaction" (University of Wisconsin, Madison).

D. M. McKeithan, "A Letter to Francis Henry Skrine in London," *Modern Language Notes* 63.2 (February 1948): 134–135.

————— and [SIR] E[DWARD]. D[ENISON]. Ross (1871–1940). *The Heart of Asia: A History of Russian Turkestan and the Central Asian Khanates from the Earliest Times*. Illus. London: Methuen & Co. 1899. 444 pp. [Edition conjectured.]

Clemens wrote to Skrine from Sweden in 1899 to thank him for promising to send an inscribed copy of a book; *The Heart of Asia* seems like the most likely referent (Dennis Welland, *Mark Twain in England*, p. 221).

SLATER, [GEORGE HENRY] ERNEST (c. 1869–1942), pseud. "Paul Gwynne." *The Pagan at the Shrine*. New York and London: Macmillan Co., 1903. 478 pp.

Under the heading for 24 June 1903 in Clemens's appointment book, he wrote: "Spanish proverb quoted in Gwynne's 'The Pagan at the Shrine': 'Whom God loves, his bitch litters sucking pigs'" (NB 46, TS p. 19). Slater, who lived and wrote in London, set his work of fiction in rural Southern Spain during a period of resentment against the Jesuits.

SLEEMAN, (SIR) WILLIAM HENRY (1788–1856). *A Journey Through the Kingdom of Oude, in 1849–1850*. 2 vols. London: R. Bentley, 1858. [Edition conjectured.]

Francis V. Madigan, Jr., listed this work as one of Mark Twain's sources for *Following the Equator* (1897) ("Mark Twain's Passage to India: A Genetic Study of *Following the Equator*," doctoral dissertation, New York University, 1974, p. 365). The Kingdom of Oude was located in northern India; today it is known as Uttar Pradesh.

—————. *Rambles and Recollections of an Indian Official*. Ed. by Vincent Arthur Smith (1848–1920). New edition. 2 vols. Westminster: Archibald Constable and Co., 1893. [This edition seems certain, since in Chapter 49 of *Following the Equator* Mark Twain refers to "Major Sleeman's editor, Mr. Vincent Arthur Smith." *Rambles and Recollections* was initially published in 1844.]

Mark Twain's account in *Following the Equator* (1897, Ch. 48) of an Indian wife's insistence on sacrificing herself after her husband's death—a *Suttee*—is taken from Chapter 4 of

Volume I of *Rambles*, entitled "A Suttee on the Nerhudda" (pp. 22–37). Twain quotes from pages 24–27, incorrectly giving the date as 1828 instead of 1829 and merely stating that Major Sleeman provides the case "in one of his books." In Chapter 49 of *Following the Equator* Twain writes: "Major Sleeman reveals the fact that the trade union and the boycott are antiquities in India"; he then quotes from page 60 (Volume I) of *Rambles*, and he also quotes from "a footnote by Major Sleeman's editor, Mr. Vincent Arthur Smith." The latter citation indicates that it was the 1893 edition that Twain was using. In Chapter 49 of *Following the Equator* Twain refers to Sleeman's observations about the killing of girl babies in India—"one of Sleeman's casual electrical remarks"; he additionally refers to the "division of labor" in Indian villages that Sleeman discusses in *Rambles*, Volume I, Chapter 10. Chapter 50 of *Following the Equator* quotes Sleeman's ironic remark about differing standards of modesty that prevailed with Indian and European women. "Major Sleeman wrote forty or fifty years ago (the italics are mine): 'I would here enter my humble protest against the *quadrille and lunch parties* which are sometimes given to European ladies and gentlemen of the station at the imperial tomb [the Taj Mahal]; drinking and dancing are no doubt very good things in their season, but they are sadly out of place *in a sepulchre*'" (*FE*, Ch. 53).

—————. *Report on the Depredations Committed by the Thug Gangs of Upper and Central India, from the Cold Season of 1836–37, Down to Their Gradual Suppression, Under the Operation of the Measures Adopted Against Them by the Supreme Government, in the Year 1839*. Calcutta: G. H. Huttmann, Bengal Mily. Orphan Press, 1840. 549 pp.

This is the book Mark Twain cites and quotes from in *Following the Equator* (1897), Chapters 46 and 47. There Twain identifies its author as "Major Sleeman," whose "Official Report" on Thuggee was published in Calcutta in 1840. This report provides the basis for Mark Twain's extended discussion of Thuggee in Chapters 43, 46, 47, and 49. In Chapter 46 Twain quotes a comment by Captain Vallancey that appears on p. vi of the "Preface" to Sleeman's *Report*; Twain repeats the same quotation in Chapter 47: "The day that sees this far-spread evil eradicated from India and known only in name, will greatly tend to immortalize British rule in the East."

Francis V. Madigan, Jr., "MT's Passage to India" (1974), p. 365; Keshav Mutalik, *Mark Twain in India* (1978), pp. 113–114.

—————. *The Thugs or Phansigars of India; Comprising a History of the Rise and Progress of That Extraordinary Fraternity of Assassins, and a Description of the System Which It Pursues and of the Measures Which Have Been Adopted by the Supreme Government of India for Its Suppression, Compiled from Original and Authentic Documents Published by W. H. Sleeman*. 2 vols. Philadelphia: Carey & Hart, 1839.

Francis V. Madigan, Jr., listed this work as one of Mark Twain's sources for *Following the Equator* (1897) ("Mark Twain's Passage to India: A Genetic Study of *Following the Equator*," doctoral dissertation, New York University, 1974, p. 365).

SLOANE, WILLIAM MILLIGAN (1850–1928). *Life of Napoleon Bonaparte*. Illus. 4 volumes. Original half leather and boards.

Joints cracked, spine and extremities rubbed. New York: Century Co., 1896.

Catalogs: ListABP (1910), "Napoleon Bonaparte 4 v., Sloane"; not listed in *C1951* but sold at that Hollywood auction in 1951—a common occurrence owing to the hastily compiled and sloppily edited sale sheet; "Property from the Library of Mark Twain," Butterfield & Butterfield, San Francisco, Sale 6613 (16 July 1997), lot 2696.

Provenance: Mark Twain House and Museum, Hartford, Connecticut.

Copy examined: Clemens's copy, unmarked but worn on the extremities as though used. Viewed in Hartford in 1997.

Clemens participated in a meeting of the Thursday Evening Club at the home of Sloane on 7 March 1901 (New York *Times*, 8 March 1901). Suggesting suitable guests for a cruise on Henry H. Rogers's steam yacht, Clemens wrote to Rogers from Saranac Lake, New York on 17 July 1901: "There's Professor Wm. Sloane of Columbia, a perfectly delightful man—would you like to have him? . . . He wrote the big History of Napoleon that appeared in the Century" (*MTHHR*, pp. 466–467). Sloane, however, declined to join the cruise. Clemens wrote Sloane's name and academic affiliation in a list of addresses on an undated slip of paper, mistakenly referring to him as "Professor Wm. A. Sloane" (*A1911*, lot 6).

SLOCUM, JOSHUA (1844–1909). *Voyage of the Liberdade*. Illus. Boston: Roberts Brothers, 1894. 160 pp.

Source: MTLAcc, entry #513, volume donated by Albert Bigelow Paine, Clemens's designated biographer. Possibly Clemens saw this book, since the men exchanged reading materials. Clemens generally enjoyed narratives of sea adventures.

SLOSSON, ANNIE (TRUMBULL) (1838–1926). *Dumb Foxglove, and Other Stories*. New York: Harper & Brothers, 1898. 218 pp.

Source: MTLAcc, entry #465, volume donated by Clemens. The American entomologist Slosson lived in Hartford during her years of education. Her books generally had natural history as their subject. The stories and sketches in *Dumb Foxglove* contain revelations about the useful plants growing in the White Mountains region of New Hampshire and Maine as well as a plea for animal rights. Slossom was a niece of the author Annie Eliot Trumbull (1857–1949).

———. *Seven Dreamers*. New York: Harper & Brothers, 1903. 281 pp.

Source: MTLAcc, entry #259, volume donated by Clemens.

SMALL, SAMUEL W[HITE]. (1851–1931).

In 1880 Clemens wrote and then canceled the name of Small's African American narrator, "Old Si," replacing it with a reference to Joel Chandler Harris' character, Uncle Remus (*N&J* 2: 362). Small, who was born on a Tennessee plantation and joined the Confederate army toward the end of the Civil War, wrote humorous dialect sketches for the Atlanta *Constitution* in the persona of "Old Si," an elderly African American who shared his frank opinions about life, family, politics, and friends. When Small left the Atlanta *Constitution*, Joel Chandler Harris and his "Uncle Remus" character replaced Small's column. Small would collect his humorous columns in *Old Si's Sayings* (1886) and *Humorous Sketches of "Old Si"* (1886).

SMALLEY, GEORGE WASHBURN (1833–1916).

In 1886 Clemens considered publishing a book by Smalley: "I should think a book on England from Smalley would sell. It would be exceedingly interesting— that I *know*" (SLC to Charles L. Webster, Hartford, 17 November 1886, *MTBus*, p. 367). Smalley was the European correspondent for the New York *Tribune;* he would write *London Letters and Some Other Things*, 2 vols. (New York: Harper & Brothers, 1891), published in London by Macmillan and Co. in 1890.

SMILES, SAMUEL (1812–1904). *Josiah Wedgwood, F.R.S., His Personal History*. New York: Harper & Brothers, 1895. 330 pp.

Source: MTLAcc, entry #1790, volume donated by Clemens.

Josiah Wedgwood (1730–1795) founded a famous pottery industry. The Scottish journalist and author Smiles was a proponent of free market ideas who advocated the benefits of sound character traits.

———. *Life and Labor; or Characteristics of Men of Industry, Culture and Genius*. New York: Harper & Brothers, 1904. 448 pp.

Source: MTLAcc, entry #1143, volume donated by Clemens.

———. *Robert Dick [1811–1866], Baker of Thurso, Geologist and Botanist*. Illus. New York: Harper & Brothers, n.d., 436 pp.

Source: MTLAcc, entry #1144, volume donated by Clemens.

———. *Thrift*. New York: Harper & Brothers, 1899. 404 pp.

Source: MTLAcc, entry #1616, volume donated by Clemens.

Smiles showed the advantages accruing to those who save and invest money.

SMILIE, ELTON R[OMEO]. (1819–1889), pseud. "R. Elton Smile." *Investigations and Experience of M. Shawtinbach, at Saar Soong Sumatra. A Set or Sequel to "The Manatitlans."* San Francisco, California: Joseph Winterrurn & Co., 1879. 263 pp.

Source: MTLAcc, entry #556, volume donated by Clemens.

It is conceivable that Clemens met or at least knew of this dentist-author (he was a co-discoverer of the efficacy of anesthesia for dental extractions) in California. Smilie had moved there from Massachusetts soon after the Gold Rush. He published an earlier science fiction work, *The Manatitlans*, in 1877. His epistolary novel *Investigations and Experience of M. Shawtinbach* bizarrely combined missionaries, Jesuits, pirates, and primitive half-humans (who still possess a tail appendage) in a science fiction version of Sumatra.

SMITH, ALBERT RICHARD (1816–1860). *The Story of Mont Blanc*. London: D. Bogue, 1853. 219 pp.

In 1878 Clemens mentioned Smith as "the Creator" of Mont Blanc (NB 16, *N&J* 2: 172). "Balmat and De Saussure discovered Mont Blanc—so to speak—but it was Smith who made it a paying property. His articles in Blackwood and his lectures on Mont Blanc in London advertised it and made people as anxious to see it as if it owed them money" (*TA* [1880], Ch. 43).

SMITH ALEXANDER (1830–1867). *Edwin of Deira*. Boston: Ticknor and Fields, 1861. 191 pp.

Source: MTLAcc, entry #2092 volume donated from Clemens's library by Clara Clemens Gabrilowitsch in 1910.

"Livy old sweetheart, sent you another book to-day—Edwin

of Deira" (SLC to OLC, Dayton, Ohio, 4 January 1872, *MTLet* 5: 5). Six days later Clemens confirmed that "I have read & sent home … Edwin of Deira" (SLC to OLC, Steubenville, Ohio, 10 January 1872, *LLMT*, pp 172–173; *MTLet* 5: 15). The hero of Smith's romantic poem is Edwin (c. 585–633), King of Northumbria, the son of Aella, King of Deira. Edwin was converted to Christianity by Paulinus (d. 644), whom he made Archbishop of York. Book I of Smith's poem opens dramatically: "With hasty rein from off the bloody field/ Prince Edwin with a score of followers fled/Toward King Redwald's border,—thither drawn/By hope, which was twin-brother to despair."

SMITH, CHARLES HENRY (1826–1903), pseud "Bill Arp."
"Bill Arp" was the first name that came to Clemens's mind when projecting an anthology of humor in July 1880 (NB 19, *N&J* 2: 361). However, none of Smith's work—published in the Atlanta *Constitution* after the Civil War and collected in such volumes as *Bill Arp, So Called* (New York, 1866) and *Bill Arp's Peace Papers* (New York, 1873)—appeared in *Mark Twain's Library of Humor* (1888).
James E. Ginther, "Charles Henry Smith, the Creator of Bill Arp," *Mark Twain Journal* 10.3 (Summer 1955): 11–12 and 23–24.

Smith College Commencement Poems, '79–'86. These Poems, Reprinted with the Consent of the Authors, Are Published for the Benefit of the Gymnasium Fund. North Brookfield, Massachusetts: H. J. Lawrence, Printer, 1888. 61 pp.
Source: MTLAcc, entry #2075, volume donated from Clemens's library by Clara Clemens Gabrilowitsch in 1910. Mark Twain would have recognized some of the poets' names in this volume: Elizabeth Stuart Phelps, "Victurae Salutamus" (p. 3), Rose Terry Cooke, "The Flower Sower" (pp. 16–22); Paul Hamilton Hayne, "A Poem" (pp. 34–43); and Richard Watson Gilder, "Mors Triumphalis" (pp. 57–61).

SMITH, FRANCIS HOPKINSON (1838–1915). "Colonel Carter of Cartersville," *Century Magazine* 41.6 (April 1891): 885–891. Shortly thereafter the novel was released as *Colonel Carter of Cartersville*. Illus. by the author and E[dward]. W[indsor]. Kemble (1861–1933). New York: Grosset & Dunlap, 1891. 208 pp.
An unreconstructed, once-wealthy Virginia colonel manages to demonstrate genuine affection and concern for his African American servant and displays additional signs of genuine kindness and humanity toward his acquaintances. Section 6 of this novel appeared in the same *Century Magazine* issue in which Clemens marked T. Cole's "Adoration" notes and engraving. See the Catalog entry for T. Cole.

———. "Editor's Drawer: Ginger and the Goose," *Harper's New Monthly Magazine* 64.382 (March 1882): 638–640. [Credited simply to "F.Y.P.," with four unsigned, racially exaggerated drawings by Francis Hopkinson Smith.]
In June 1888, at a social gathering in the Warners' house in Hartford to greet the visiting Finnish author and social reformer Baroness Alexandra Gripenberg, Clemens "in his incomparable way," employed "a Virginia dialect" in telling "a condensed version" of Smith's story about the preposterous efforts of a plantation cook to explain why a drumstick was missing from a roast goose (Ernest J. Moyne, "Mark Twain Meets a Lady from Finland,"

Mark Twain Journal 11.2 [Summer 1960]: 10, 25). At the beginning of "Private History of the 'Jumping Frog' Story" (1894), Twain states that he once told a woman from Finland "one of Hopkinson Smith's negro stories, and gave her a copy of *Harper's Monthly* containing it."
Alexandra Gripenberg, *A Half Year of Travel in the United States.* Translated and edited by Ernest J. Moyne (1916–1976) (Newark, Delaware: University of Delaware Press, 1954); Ernest J. Moyne, "Mark Twain and Baroness Alexandra Gripenberg," *American Literature* 45.3 (November 1973): 370–378.

———. *Peter: A Novel of Which He Is Not the Hero.* Illustrated by A[rthur]. I[gnatius]. Keller (1866–1924). First edition. Original green decorated cloth, gilt. New York: Charles Scribner's Sons, 1908. 482 pp.
Inscription: the front pastedown endpaper is signed in black ink, "S L. Clemens/1908".
Marginalia: Clemens made several caustic marginal notes in black ink on three pages that total fifty-one words. On page 150, where Smith describes the exact monetary value ("30 per cent. to the ton") of the "tailings" of a gold mine, Clemens objected, "I am a miner, but I don't understand this." Two pages farther on, beside the story of an English prospector duped by two con men, Clemens observed, "Verily there's been no such miner as this since Bret Harte! Still, it's a mighty good story all the same." An account of a lavish dinner party replete with oysters, truffles, claret, and cigars drew this comment from Clemens on page 147: "This entire chapter was written with one sole & only purpose: to show off Hop. Smith's familiarity with 'high life.'" Clemens also made ink underlinings or other marks on three pages, and several other leaves are creased from having been folded down. A note or clipping was formerly pinned to the front free endpaper.
Catalogs: ListABP (1910), "Peter, Smith"; *Sotheby's 2003,* #237, $2,500.
Provenance: displays the shelfmark of Clara Clemens Gabrilowitsch's private library in Detroit. Donated to the Carrie Estelle Doheny Collection, St. John's Seminary, Camarillo, California, by Mrs. Doheny in 1940 after she purchased it for $12.20 from Maxwell Hunley Rare Books, Beverly Hills, California. Auctioned on 21 February 1989 for $1,870 by Christie's (lot 1767) on behalf of St. John's Seminary. Subsequently acquired by Nick Karanovich, Fort Wayne, Indiana.
Location: collection of Kevin Mac Donnell, Austin, Texas.
Copy examined: Clemens's copy, July 2004, in Austin, Texas. Has the bookplate of "Estelle Doheny."
Peter was among the best-selling novels of 1908. Clemens did not comment on Smith's title, which was presumably a homage to William Makepeace Thackeray's *Vanity Fair: A Novel Without a Hero* (1848). Smith and Clemens met at a Tile Club dinner in New York City on 20 December 1880 (*MTHL*, p. 340 n. 2). In 1935 Emily Post (1872–1960) recalled being introduced to Mark Twain by F. Hopkinson Smith at a banquet given in Twain's honor; she was impressed that Twain later remembered her when they encountered each other again, even though she was "a single person among the several hundred who met him at the banquet" ("Emily Post and Edna Ferber Recollect," *Mark Twain Journal* 19.2 [Summer 1978]: 30).

SMITH, GEORGE BARNETT (1841–1909). "The Growth of London," *Cornhill Magazine* 39.229 (January 1879): 41–60. Clemens preserved and annotated a clipping of this article ("observe the absurdity of these figures") in Notebook 17 early in 1879 (*N&J* 2: 277).

SMITH, GERTRUDE (1860–1917). *Little Ned Happy and Flora.* Illustrated by Henrietta Adams. New York: Harper & Brothers, 1908. 214 pp.
Source: MTLAcc, entry #516, volume donated by Isabel V. Lyon, Clemens's secretary.
Henrietta Adams (1877–1946), later Mrs. McClure of Philadelphia, was a student of Howard Pyle. She became a prominent illustrator of children's books.
———. *Little Precious.* Illus. New York: Harper & Brothers, 1906. 147 pp.
Source: MTLAcc, entry #498, volume donated by Clemens.
———. *The Loveable Tales of Janey and Josey and Joe.* Illustrated by E[thel]. Mars (1876–1959) and M[aud]. H[unt]. Squire (1873–1954). New York: Harper & Brothers, 1902. 158 pp.
Source: MTLAcc, entry #1373, volume donated by Clemens.
Ethel Mars and Maud Hunt Squire, life partners, lived by turns in France and the United States. They would become friends of Gertrude Stein and her circle and would later be prominent in the Provincetown artists and printmakers group.
———. *The Roggie and Reggie Stories.* Illustrated by E[thel]. Mars (1876–1959) and M[aud]. H[unt]. Squire (1873–1954). New York: Harper & Brothers, [cop. 1900]. 95 pp.
Source: MTLAcc, entry #1617, volume donated by Clemens.
———. *The Stories of Peter and Ellen.* Illustrated by E[thel]. Mars (1876–1959) and M[aud]. H[unt]. Squire (1873–1954). New York: Harper & Brothers, 1903. 138 pp.
Source: MTLAcc, entry #1618, volume donated by Clemens.

SMITH, GOLDWIN (1823–1910). *Three English Statesmen [John Pym (1584–1643), Oliver Cromwell (1599–1658), William Pitt (1759–1806)]: A Course of Lectures on the Political History of England.* New York: Harper & Brothers, 1867. 298 pp.
On 14 January 1869 Clemens wrote to Olivia Langdon from Davenport, Iowa, recounting his activities on 3 January in Fort Wayne, Indiana: "I lay abed till 1 P.M[.], . . . and read Prof. Goldwin Smith's lecture on Cromwell" (*MTLet* 3: 39).

SMITH, HARRY BACHE (1860–1936). *Little Nemo* (musical comedy in three acts, perf. in 1908). Music by Victor Herbert (1859–1924).
Clemens, Isabel Lyon, and other members of his household attended a matinee performance of *Little Nemo* at the New Amsterdam Theatre in New York City on Wednesday, 2 December 1908 (IVL Journals, TS p. 343, MTP).
———. *The Soul Kiss* (musical, two acts and two scenes, perf. in 1908). Music by Maurice Levi, Paul Linche, Burkhardt, Hirsch, and Woodward.
On 9 May 1908 "the King, Ashcroft and I went to see 'The Soul Kiss'—a horrid sort of play, but [Adeline] Genee the Danish dancer was beautiful and wonderful," Isabel Lyon recorded (IVL Journals, TS p. 323, MTP). Florenz Ziegfeld produced this entertainment at the New York Theatre.

SMITH, HASKETT (1857–1906).
In 1895 Mark Twain alluded to a humorous conversation he had with this British clergyman (Wellington, New Zealand *Mail*, 12 December 1895; Scharnhorst, *Complete Interviews*, p. 261).

SMITH, MOSES. *Plain Truths about Stock Speculation. How to Avoid Losses in Wall Street. With a Visitor's Directory in and Around New York.* Brooklyn, New York: Printed by E. V. Smith, 1888. 290 pp. [Smith's first edition was copyrighted and published in 1887. *Plain Truths* mixed practical explanations and advice with dire warnings.]
Source: MTLAcc, entry #589, volume donated by Clemens.
Biographers and critics view Samuel L. Clemens's business ventures ruefully, reasonably assuming that he cheated his readers of additional literary masterpieces by squandering his time and talents on deleterious commercial enterprises. Clemens's surviving letters and correspondence encourage this response. In January 1894, beside himself with anxiety about his investments in the Paige typesetter and a publishing firm, Clemens invoked one of the ship-reaching-port-in-a-storm images that pervaded his letters and manuscripts for more than a decade: "When the anchor is down," he promised his wife Olivia, "then I shall say: 'Farewell—a long farewell—to *business!* I will *never* touch it again!' I will live in literature, I will wallow in it, revel in it, I will swim in ink! Joan of Arc—but all this is premature; the anchor is not down yet."[1] Hardly by coincidence, becalmed vessels, mutinous crews, and shipwreck debris would float about in his subsequent writings, for Clemens's frequent voyages between his family's temporary home in Europe and his business headquarters in New York City proved futile, as everyone knows, and he was obliged to endure the ignominy of public exposure as a financial failure.
However, a succession of commentators has filled out the record of Clemens's business affairs with fascinating fullness, and their findings afford improved perspectives on this often-unappealing side of Clemens's life. Samuel C. Webster interwove a family biography among the extant letters he chose to publish in an influential book titled *Mark Twain, Business Man* (1946),[2] principally a good-natured defense of Webster's father, Charles L. Webster, at one time the manager of Clemens's publishing firm, against charges Clemens had raised in autobiographical dictations that appeared in *Mark Twain in Eruption* (1940). Hamlin Hill complicated the matter by editing *Mark Twain's Letters to His Publishers* (1967) and noting in the introduction that "the fact is that Charles L. Webster's letters to his uncle, which Samuel Webster unfortunately did not examine while editing his volume, become increasingly dictatorial, overweening, and almost hysterical. . . . An accurate portrait of Charley Webster lies somewhere between the one in *Mark Twain in Eruption* and the one in *Mark Twain, Business Man*."[3]
Whatever the case, Clemens's relationships with his publishers and business agents were conducive to financial mismanagements and misunderstandings. They certainly began inauspiciously. In a study of Clemens's first publisher, *Mark Twain and Elisha Bliss* (1964), Hamlin Hill argued that Bliss "was coldly calculating, he was happy to cheat both authors and customers with a repertory of the

worst tricks of salesmanship, and he apparently juggled books with the skill of a master accountant."[4] In brief, Clemens learned the rudiments of literary business under the tutelage of a tougher, less ethical, more opportunistic taskmaster than Horace Bixby had ever been in teaching a cub pilot the course of the Mississippi River. That harsher education began on 21 November 1867 with a letter from Bliss soliciting "a work of some kind" from newspaper correspondent Clemens (*MT&EB*, p. 23). Although Clemens flirted with the idea of changing publishers during the mid-1870s, Bliss managed to sell 337,902 volumes for Mark Twain between 1869 and 1879 (p. 157); it was only Bliss' death on 28 September 1880 that truly freed Clemens, for the next fourteen years, from the American Publishing Company.

Dennis Welland's book about the English publication and reception of Clemens's works, *Mark Twain in England* (1978), also shed light on Clemens's view of the publishing field. From the correspondence files of Chatto & Windus, Welland pieced together an image of Clemens as an impatient author who wanted his books manufactured and distributed as instantaneously as every writer always desires, but who found his match in the canny Andrew Chatto, who parted Clemens from Routledge & Sons and kept him mollified if not entirely content for more than thirty-five years. Glancing over a list of Clemens's publishers, one can only conclude that their lot hardly seems enviable. Charles H. Webb (1834–1905) brought out the *Jumping Frog* volume in 1867, but mainly earned Clemens's later execrations. Clemens never trusted Elisha Bliss (1822–1880), who managed the American Publishing Company with which Clemens was associated from 1869 until 1881. James R. Osgood (1836–1892), an ambitious but scrupulously ethical man miscast in the subscription trade, accompanied Clemens on his 1882 trip to the Mississippi River and published three of Clemens's books; nonetheless, he disappointed Clemens with the sales of *Life on the Mississippi* and lost him as a house author. Andrew Chatto (1841–1913), guided by Moncure Conway,[5] signed Clemens to an initial contract on 24 May 1876, and his Chatto & Windus firm published at least 910,000 volumes for Clemens, yet their relations were always delicate. Charles L. Webster (1851–1891), who had married Clemens's niece Annie E. Moffett (1852–1950) in 1875, fatefully entered Samuel Clemens's employment in 1881, became his partner in a publishing firm in 1884, retired because of his nerves and health in 1888, and died in 1891, with his posthumous reputation besmirched by Clemens's accusations of incompetence. Fred J. Hall (1860–1926) had the misfortune to administer Charles L. Webster & Company while it labored to survive the Panic of 1893 and attempt to bring forth *A Library of American Literature*. Francis E. "Frank" Bliss (1843–1915), more easily intimidated by Clemens than his father Elisha had been, succeeded in obtaining *Pudd'nhead Wilson, Following the Equator*, and a uniform edition of Clemens's collected writings after his bankruptcy, yet ultimately failed to retain this valued author. Finally, Frederick A[therton]. Duneka (1863–1919), a former newspaper editor who became the general manager of Harper & Brothers when George Harvey (1864–1928) assumed its presidency,

helped Harvey negotiate long-term contracts for acquiring Clemens's writings but had to weather bruising differences of opinion with the headstrong writer. As Hamlin Hill wrote, "The author 'Mark Twain' was dragged into this world by businessman Samuel L. Clemens; and there were some obvious internal conflicts with resulting rages (whose blasts frequently singed the publisher who happened to be standing by)." According to Hill, "Clemens's antagonism toward his publishers was merely an antagonism toward the commercial aspect of his own personality. . . . Having sacrificed genteel approval by stubbornly choosing subscription publication, Clemens blamed his publishers (in arduously intemperate language) when a volume failed or a promotion scheme fell through" (*MTLP*, p. 3). The emerging picture of Clemens's attitudes toward his publishers suggests something else as well: either the publisher owned Clemens, or Clemens owned the publisher; this author was incapable of respecting and heeding any publisher who lacked the steel to come off well in a close encounter with him. Osgood, Webster, Hall, and Frank Bliss quailed beneath Clemens's withering scorn; Elisha Bliss, Andrew Chatto, Frederick A. Duneka (whom Clemens habitually distrusted but ultimately obeyed), and George Harvey fought the prominent author toe-to-toe, earning his grudging approval and cooperation.

There is another conclusion that needs acknowledgement. Essentially Clemens's efforts at finagling lucrative contracts for his prose were efficacious; he realized vastly more income than most of his contemporaries who wrote, and he even succeeded in keeping Elisha Bliss more watchful and honest than he might otherwise have been. Clemens's London publisher proved especially diligent in procuring and promoting his works. His relations with most of his publishers were stormy and he wrote more letters querying points in his contracts and demanding additional concessions (and more of his letters have survived) than was typical for his day, but a large percentage of authors—then and now—undergo periods of unhappiness or open dispute with their publishers. Besides, Clemens was more prolific than many writers, and he had to attend to wearisome details regarding new material.

As a publisher himself, moreover, Clemens was not exactly the unmitigated disaster that many people suppose. One biographer conceded, "For the first five years of its existence, the Webster company was a well-to-do concern. . . . Had Mark [Twain] confined his business speculations to publishing, he would not have got into very serious trouble."[6] Hamlin Hill explained that the multi-volume *Library of American Literature*, a worthy but expensive project, required massive subsidies, but "it is untrue that Clemens drained badly needed capital from the [Webster] Company to finance the Paige typesetter, although such a statement has often been accepted" (*MTLP*, p. 6). The impoverishment of rural book-buyers, trends toward urbanization, greater availability of trade bookstores, increases in public education—these and other reasons shrank the subscription-book market, and Charles L. Webster & Company, strapped by its costly *Library of American Literature* undertaking, was unable to switch smoothly to the retail book trade. Clemens's sojourn in Europe beginning in 1891 was ill-timed, since he "knew the subtleties and intricacies of subscription publication from over twenty years of personal experience," and yet he "helped choose (or veto) [no] more than a handful of the new books" that Webster & Company issued toward the end (*MTLP*, p. 300).

Of course it was indisputably unwise for an author of Clemens's productivity and gifts, susceptible to fits and starts of inspiration, to occupy so many of his waking hours with the mundane worries of a publishing enterprise. And once having made that commitment, he unquestionably should have lavished all of his remaining energies on that single business, forsaking other temptations. For it was not his publishing company that placed his name in the annals of colossal, heart-breaking financial failures. He was a competent if not brilliant strategist, and his company had several stunning successes—the publication in 1885 of General Grant's *Memoirs*, most notably—that would have satisfied the appetites of a normal business entrepreneur.

When people deplore Clemens's inclinations toward "business," they really mean something other than his close attention to his publishing arrangements; they are speaking of his repeated, risk-taking investments in companies and inventions that drained off so much of his authorial earnings. And what a sad inventory of misplaced confidence this is. The epitome of these gambles was his purchase in February 1880 of what he believed to be the controlling interests in the patent for a chalk-plate process to engrave illustrations, Kaolatype (*MTBus*, p. 142)—an invention combining his affection for the printing trade (representing a heritage of his earliest livelihood) and his interests as an author of illustrated books; an innovation requiring endless amounts of "final" outlays for perfecting the remaining flaws to render the method commercially marketable; a product that encountered sales resistance from clients he had presumed to be "definite" purchasers and incurred constant, maddening delays in production; a company that required Clemens to fight off attempts to reorganize and recapitalize its investments, and threatened to leave him and the original investors out in the cold; and finally, all of these factors culminating in a gradual relinquishing of his hopes, despite sporadic efforts to revitalize those once-brilliant prospects. The jubilant letter that Clemens wrote to Elisha Bliss on 20 March 1880 could stand as the prototype of numerous other schemes, foremost the Paige typesetter: "I own near four-fifths of the [Kaolatype] stock—paid cash for it," Clemens boasted, "and have agreed to lend the Co a liberal and sufficient sum every month for 3 months to get the thing going. (But I did this latter thing after I had myself hit upon a new application of the patent which I think puts non-success about out of the question.)" (*MTLP*, p. 121).

On 9 December 1881, Clemens's sister Pamela Moffett (1827–1904) wrote ominously to her son Samuel E. Moffett (1860–1908) that Clemens's Kaolatype process "is very small indeed, compared to another enterprise Sam has set Charley [Webster] to work on. This is some new invention. They want to start with a capital of five hundred thousand dollars, a stock company. Charley took a lot of prominent men to Hartford the other day to examine the machines" (*MTLP*, p. 187 n. 1). There is no need to rehearse here the dreary chronicle of Clemens's

rising hopes in that typesetting machine and its precipitous defeat in 1894, a ghastly exercise in self-delusion that outlasted, but failed to rescue, Clemens's beleaguered publishing firm, which declared bankruptcy on 18 April 1894. Henry H. Rogers concluded that the Paige project was hopeless in December 1894, and by 2 January 1895 Clemens was writing that he must "soberly realize that my ten-year dream is actually dissolved" (*MTHHR*, p. 115).

These two large disappointments, coupled with his failure as a publisher, were only the most visible objects in Clemens's stream of investment adventures; others bobbed along in the eddies and floods of his surplus funds: the Independent Watch Company of Fredonia, New York ($3,500 in 1881), whose directors he later designated as "the Watch thieves" (*MTBus*, p. 199), the Crown Point Iron Company, the Denver & Rio Grande Railroad (*MTBus*, p. 178), a patented bed-clamp to keep children from kicking off their covers at night, the design for which Clemens excitedly fretted about in 1884 and 1885 (*MTBus*, pp. 279–280, 291, 296 *passim*), a history game, the Jewell Pin Company, whose stock returned a measly dividend of $44.90 in 1904 (*MTHHR*, p. 569), and a self-pasting scrapbook, generally cited as his one eminently successful business speculation. Incorrigible, he never learned a lesson about financial investing; in March 1898 he tried to convince an advisor that the American patent rights would be worth acquiring (at $1,500,000) for Jan Szczepanik's textile-designing machine, which Clemens had seen in Vienna (*MTHHR*, pp. 327–332). He plunged heedlessly into a Plasmon health food craze while still dripping wet from his nightmarish dunking in the Paige fiasco. By 1900 he was elected a director of the Plasmon syndicate and was promoting its stock in the United States; six years later, two "rascals" had formed a new company that would eliminate Clemens.

While under the guidance of Standard Oil tycoon Henry H. Rogers, Clemens's stock-portfolio began to swell handsomely with blue-chip dividends: Brooklyn Union Gas, American Smelting Company, U.S. Steel, Borden's Condensed Milk, International Navigation Company, Anaconda Copper Mining Company, Union Pacific (26 May 1904, *MTHHR*, pp. 392, 568–569). Yet in 1905 Clemens considered investing in the unpromising Insole Company, and in 1905 he invested $5,000 in the Hope-Jones Organ Company, urged on by his nephew-by-marriage Jervis Langdon (1875–1952), its president and treasurer (*MTHHR*, pp. 623, 624 n. 1). He also bought shares in the Tabard Inn Corporation, the Formaline Company, the American Mechanical Cashier Company, Koy-lo Company, and the International Spiral Pin Company (*MTHHR*, p. 623)—all without significant returns. On 3 August 1902 he elatedly reported to Henry Rogers a sterling offer: he could buy $50,000 worth of bonds in the Kansas City, Mexico and Orient Railroad. Two days later Rogers replied with admirable restraint: "In the first place, it would seem quite natural to inquire as to the Kansas City, Mexico & Orient Railroad. In view of the fact that Poor's Manual makes no reference to the railroad, it is reasonably fair to assume that it is not of any great prominence. I certainly would never undertake to enter into the arrangement for myself. . . . Do be careful. It is much easier to keep out of trouble than it is to get out. You and I know that of old," he added tiredly (*MTHHR*, pp. 494–495).

What is the pattern of these pathetic gambles? Apparently Clemens sought opportunities to get in at the middle stage of a new undertaking, wanting to play the improbable part of a moderately wealthy capitalist who underwrites the final expenses for polishing up a new invention or project, and then reaps tremendous dividends. But he always got called on for "just a little more" investment—and so he would throw away good money after bad. Nonetheless, it is necessary to remember that the Paige machine was not exactly a crackpot venture; virtually every knowledgeable person in the printing industry in the 1880s and 1890s expected that the burgeoning technologies in keyboards and metals would eventually devise a machine to replace the tedious labor of setting type by hand. Clemens's fault lay in greedily consenting to contribute so *much* capital in order to obtain a lion's share of anticipated returns, and in not pressing the Mergenthaler team for a reciprocal trade-off in stock that would have enabled everybody to win the race one way or another. Let it also be said in Clemens's defense that at least he had the good sense to consult Henry Rogers about his troubles, and to heed Rogers's words whenever his financial mentor was able to advise him on business affairs.

All of Clemens's monetary dealings—his publishing company and his stock-purchases alike—are punctuated throughout by intermittent, discerning desires to retire from such risky enterprises. In February 1867 his tone was only half jocular when scolding his brother Orion for placing "business in my hands when he knows I abhor everything in the nature of business & don't even attend to my own."[7] "I *won't* talk business," he adjured Charles L. Webster on 29 June 1883, "I will perish first. I hate the very idea of business, in all its forms" (*MTBus*, p. 217). To the same manager he wrote on 19 January 1885, concerning the bed-clamp that he had been so anxious to manufacture: "Dear Charley—No, it is *business*—and so I don't want anything to do with it. You are there to take care of my business, not make business for *me* to take care of. Your security is perfect, but I want no business that I must look personally after" (*MTLP*, p. 180). Webster would no doubt have jeopardized his "security" if he had taken this injunction at its face-value. Clemens meant that he didn't wish to be bothered by questions at that particular moment; actually he demanded minute accounts of expenditures and decisions for nearly every transaction. Too late, on 2 June 1893, Clemens plaintively begged Fred J. Hall: "Get me out of business! And I will be Yours forever gratefully" (*MTLP*, p. 344).

Most of his adult life Clemens searched after, scolded, and abandoned a series of these "loyal assistant" figures like Webster and Hall. Their duties were usually much more onerous than Charles Warren Stoddard's secretarial assignment to paste clippings about the Tichborne Clairmont trial into scrapbooks in 1873 and 1874. Clemens's habit of relying on business agents began with pitiable "Dear Bro" Orion, who by the 1870s had proven that he could never make a living without close supervision. The necessity of overseeing Orion's every move established Clemens's lifelong practice of supervising each trivial aspect of a business operation, and of refusing to trust and delegate responsibilities to his own appointed manager. Orion Clemens, a bereaved parent and broken man early in his life, sought advice and reassurance from his younger brother at every stage—business negotiations seemed foreign to his visionary nature. But Orion was at least a devoted if unimaginative automaton.[8] After Orion moved back to Keokuk, Iowa, bewildered and uncertain about his brother's opinion of his aptitudes, Charles L. Webster took his turn in Clemens's fire-pit of errand-running and contract-shuffling. (Kevin MacDonnell tracked the details of the sad trajectory of Webster's health and career.)[9] Fred J. Hall, who took over as manager in 1888, fared a little better but had the ignominious task of managing Clemens's publishing firm (in which Hall had himself invested) as it writhed and succumbed in 1894, in the process earning Clemens's contempt.

Only in the realm of fiction, understandably, did Clemens find his ideal of a business agent, Clarence, described in Chapter 10 of *A Connecticut Yankee in King Arthur's Court* (1889): "Clarence was twenty-two, now, and was my head executive, my right hand. He was a darling; he was equal to anything; there wasn't anything he couldn't turn his hand to."[10] As a result, when the Boss discovers another man with "loyalty to one's country, not to its institutions or its office-holders" (Chapter 13), he "wrote on a piece of bark—*Put him in the Man-Factory*— and gave it to him, and said—'Take it to the palace at Camelot and give it into the hands of Amyas le Poulet, whom I call Clarence, and he will understand.'" Clarence has charge of "the beginnings of all sorts of industries" and of "training a crowd of ignorant folk into experts—experts in every sort of handiwork and scientific calling." These endeavors were conducted as surreptitiously as Clemens's stealthy efforts to combat a stock take-over or to perfect Paige's typesetting machine; the populace was unaware: "Unsuspected by this dark land, I had the civilization of the nineteenth century booming under its very nose! It was fenced away from the public view, but there it was, a gigantic and unassailable fact—and to be heard from, yet, If I lived and had luck."

In real life, however, in 1889 Clemens only had the services of the fallible Fred J. Hall. By at least 1887 he had also begun to employ Franklin G. Whitmore (1846–1926), a Hartford real estate and insurance agent, to take care of everything from the Clemens family's magazine subscriptions to the sale of the Hartford house in 1903. Isabel V. Lyon's tenure of service after 1904 demonstrated just how far Clemens could go in expecting "business" assistance from his personal secretaries. Curiously, the procession of factotum figures in Clemens's fiction often hark back to his earliest print-shop days, when he himself was an assistant, first to Joseph Ament and then to Orion Clemens. Secrecy is frequently stressed; in "No. 44, The Mysterious Stranger," written between 1902 and 1908, sixteen-year-old August Feldner is an apprentice to Heinrich Stein, who discreetly operates a printing shop in the moldering Rosenfeld castle. "My master was a printer. His was a new art, being only thirty or forty years old, and almost unknown in Austria. Very few persons in our secluded region had ever seen a printed page, few had any very clear idea about the art of printing. . . . We had to conduct our business with some degree of privacy, on account of the Church. The Church was opposed to the cheapening of books and the indiscriminate dissemination of knowledge."[11] The person to whom Clemens addressed confidential queries and directives during the final decades of his life was a most unlikely candidate for this role: millionaire Wall Street financier Henry H. Rogers (1840–1909). As Hamlin Hill noted, "The most puzzling aspect of his relationship with Rogers was Clemens's apparently total insensitivity about his demands on the oil magnate's time and energies. Almost as if Rogers and his executive secretary, the tall, bespectacled Katharine I. Harrison (c. 1867–1935), were office boys, Clemens requested them to make stock purchases and sales, collect dividends, and engage in complicated business manipulations for him. Harrison had access to Clemens's safety-deposit box; she and Rogers both had powers of attorney and negotiated literary contracts for Clemens as well as purely financial investments."[12] These arrangements amounted to another, if more dependent, version of the kind of business association Clemens had preferred since he first utilized his brother's otherwise wasted years. In this instance, however, Clemens gave ungrudging credit to Rogers: "You and I are a team: you are the most useful man I know, and I am the most ornamental" (*MTHHR*, p. 310). More than a trace of humility, resignation, and self-knowledge is recognizable in that remark, which suggests Clemens's awareness that he lacked the expertise and the qualifications for a full-time business career.

Considering these occasional glimmers of insight, and in view of Olivia Clemens's nervousness about her husband's tangled finances, what would drive a respected, affluent author to take those repeated risks? In the first place, Clemens thought of his business moves as logical extensions of his authorship; encouraged by his training in typesetting and then journalism, he became accustomed to conceiving of his literary craft as a type of commercial product rather than an artistically inspired creation. After all, he had been paid by the "em" as a printing compositor in St. Louis and New York City,[13] by the trip or month as a pilot on the river, by the ounce as a miner, by the column as a newspaperman, by the letter as a travel correspondent, and by the public appearance as a platform lecturer; this background prepared the way for his concept of the author as a monied capitalist. Even more significant, perhaps, was the reality of how seldom he been free of financial concerns since his earliest teens. Only someone schooled by one of his nation's severe financial recessions or depressions can probably appreciate what amount of funds it would take to placate Clemens's anxiety after the ghastly series of experiences that seared his memory beginning in 1843, when the Clemenses' Hannibal property was auctioned off to satisfy creditors and the family had to rely on the generosity of John Marshall Clemens's distant cousin, the affluent James Clemens, Jr., of St. Louis. Upon the death of John Marshall, the family became literally dependent on James' good favor in providing them a place to live, and they pinned much hope on his benefactions; very likely Samuel Clemens was therefore mortified in 1855

when his elder relative refused to help him become a river pilot and advised him instead to "stick to his present trade or art" (*N&J* 1: 26, 36). There would *never* be sufficient enough, or reliable enough, income to erase those bitter memories of vulnerability in Hannibal and St. Louis, or to allow the peace of mind that would encourage Clemens to envelop himself in a purely literary atmosphere. Haunted by the harrowing experiences that followed his father's bankruptcy and death, Clemens pursued a line of conduct that, ironically, brought him to a point strangely reminiscent of those sad, early days, when again in 1894 and 1895 he had to rely on the goodwill of his creditors and the benevolence of a benefactor, Henry H. Rogers. Four decades had brought him back to the same anguished conversations that probably took place around widow Jane Lampton Clemens's dining table. Small wonder that Clemens's fiction began to probe the possibility of cycles of dreams.

The amounts of money that his insecurity demanded were far from being satisfied by the publishing industry. Few huge fortunes had been made in American publishing up until then, and even as the twentieth century approached, the profit on books was generally uncertain and slow in accruing. Meantime, such entrepreneurs as Gould, Fisk, Vanderbilt, Pullman, Rockefeller, Colt, Remington, Carnegie, and numerous others had given the process of fortune-making the appearance of utter feasibility. Someone with Clemens's psychological needs and hyperactive temperament found it excruciating to sit on the sidelines while major technological and financial events took place all around him.

Another earlier influence can be mentioned as well: Clemens's mining-camp days in Nevada and California between 1861 and 1865 had taught him to view his livelihood as a sort of *gamble*, and he would always be repeating the pattern of those freer years—watching for his chance to buy shares in a potentially big strike, a bonanza. To his mind, therefore, the notion of gaining financial security of an impregnable amount would always seem to be strictly a matter of *timing*. This partially accounts for the urgency with which he pushed each investment project, and the anger he manifested at any delay. Virtually monomaniacal regarding each new venture, he promptly abandoned preceding enterprises; this latest one would assuredly make his permanent fortune, if he could only push people along *in time*. Significantly, he seemed to take pleasure in the very element of risk involved in each adventure in speculation, as though the situation recreated for his psyche the carefree days he spent in miners' cabins. Bored by the routine, conservative policies of money-making, he liked his reputation as a high-stakes roller. Unfortunately, while his friends were often willing to let him win at games of skill such as billiards in his own house, less indulgent strangers gladly took his money in the business world.

A number of recurrent, compulsive behavioral patterns characterized his decisions in both publishing and investing, not all of them detrimental. A partial survey might look at the following tendencies. Clemens keenly relished the clash of competing business interests, the surprise raids on astonished, complacent rivals, the jubilation after a seemingly successful coup. His metaphors in business correspondence are frequently militaristic. For one thing, he was convinced that cheating was rampant among the men with whom he had financial dealings; he suspected that they were providing him with figures arrived at dishonestly, or that they were holding back crucial information, as Elisha Bliss sometimes did. He was implacable in repudiating those like Charles H. Webb, "liar and thief," Edward H. House, "gigantic liar . . . & . . . inconceivable hound," and James W. Paige, whom he wished to catch in a steel trap "and watch that trap till he died," men whom he suspected of taking advantage of his gullible nature. Possibly for this reason, he invariably tried to convince his personal friends to join in his investment schemes, needing this reassurance of shared risk but putting a strain on his social relationships with importunities to cash in on these offers.

In all of this activity, Clemens spread his energies too thinly again and again, attempting not only to be an author but a publisher as well, not only a publisher but a major backer of inventors, a Wall Street expert, *and* a celebrated public performer. Considering the range of these responsiblities, he never sufficiently surrounded himself with competent advisors in Nook Farm, where he actually had no adequate office. Instead he persisted in hiring "yes-men" of the Charley-Clarence stamp, and stationing them in New York City. Worse yet, he played superstitious hunches as though he were gambling on a steamboat race or a mine-shaft sinking. His main surprise at news of the Paige machine failure was that "it reverses my horoscope. The proverb says, 'Born lucky, *always* lucky,' and I am very superstitious. . . . All my life I have stumbled upon lucky chances of large size. . . And so I have felt entirely certain that that machine would turn up trumps eventually. . . I couldn't shake off the confidence of a life time in my luck."[14] He had counted on that infallible luck to deliver his version of the American Dream, which was larger and more spectacular than most people's—Tom Sawyerish in its proportions and longed-for showiness. After all, he could always bank on an unfailing income from his pen and his platform tours after 1867, and that confidence encouraged fatal tendencies to accept unwarranted risks in business.

These habits of thought were compounded by Clemens's delight in the expanding technology and literacy of the nineteenth century. The optimism expressed in Clemens's famous letter in honor of Walt Whitman, dated 24 May 1889, and his "Queen Victoria's Jubilee" sketch (1897) is a sincere note; it gratified him to laud the progress in industry, science, and education that the nineteenth-century population had witnessed. He was incapable of following the quiet logic of Thoreau's rejection of materialism, mass manufacturing, and organized commerce, and he toyed uneasily with Howells' socialistic theories. Complicating Clemens's thinking about economics was his dependence on his wife Olivia's lucrative dividends that arrived regularly from the J. Langdon & Company coal company. He got a glimpse of supply-and-demand capitalism at work when he was briefly allowed to attend that firm's annual meeting in 1869, but a scholar who studied the Langdon family's business interests concluded that in the long run they regarded Clemens "as an outlier

and a cipher"—in other words, unreliable in his judgments.[15] Louis J. Budd's *Mark Twain: Social Philosopher* (1962) found that even as early as 1869 Clemens was sympathetic with "the case for capitalists in general"; that by 1877, "teetering between his old awe and a rising sense of being an insider, he mixed socially with the local titans of finance and industry"; that after 1900, "Twain still found it hard to think that free enterprise could go seriously wrong," and "likewise found it easy to believe still that—'taken by and large'—success in business is proof of a man's honesty"; and that he resolutely defended Henry H. Rogers and the Standard Oil Company against public opinion and Ida Tarbell's muckraking journalism, telling Rogers and his wealthy friends: "You men have won your places . . . not by family influences or extraneous help, but only by the natural gifts God gave you at your birth, made effective by your own energies."[16] These views echoed the attitudes he had encountered in Hartford, where the Nook Farm writers, "as they acquired experience in an industrial culture, . . . attacked abuses but continued to assume that the good of the whole nation was being served by expanding capitalism. . . . The excesses in its exploitation by the unscrupulous were controllable. Industrial democracy was a successful experiment."[17]

George Orwell, while serving as a literary editor for the London political magazine *Tribune*, described the result caustically: "He gave himself up to the prevailing fever. . . . He even for a period of years deserted writing for business; and he squandered his time on buffooneries, . . . for instance, . . . a book like *A Connecticut Yankee*, which is a deliberate flattery of all that is worst and most vulgar in American life. The man who might have been a kind of rustic Voltaire became the world's leading after-dinner speaker, charming alike for his anecdotes and his power to make businessmen feel themselves public benefactors."[18] Lewis Leary noted that "Samuel Clemens had always wanted to be a millionaire, and now he was, vicariously. . . . One part of him hated it; the other part lapped it up greedily: he became more and more spoiled—a kind of private jester to the Rogerses and the Rockefellers and the Flaglers and their friends. He called Andrew Carnegie St. Andrew, and Carnegie called him St. Mark, and each knew that the joke of it was that neither was saintly at all. . . . It was good for these wealthy men to be seen with a person so popularly loved as Mark Twain. . . . Surely, no man could be all bad, if Mark Twain liked him."[19]

Reviewing these patterns and faults of Clemens's business methods, and observing their generally unpleasant consequences on his financial well-being and his family's security, the student of literature might be moved to ask if anything, then, stands in the other column of that ledger—any benefits to balance the many losses Clemens and his readers discerned in totting up the red ink and black ink of these financial transactions. The answer could be a qualified "yes." Clemens's infatuation with business predictably carried over into a comfortableness with economics as a literary metaphor, for business language as amusing slang, and for business occurrences as important parts of literary plots. Imagery of the commercial marketplace permeates Mark Twain's writings, providing humor by the incongruity of its application.

Business deals occur in stories involving misrepresentation of merchandise by sellers. In "A Visit to Niagara" (1869), as a simple example, the narrator naively believes that the Irish immigrants wearing Indian costumes and selling souvenir bead-baskets and moccasins are authentic specimens of the romantic Noble Red Man. A similarly fooled narrator in Chapter 24 of *Roughing It* (1872) looks forward to an auctioneer's funeral after he finds out what kind of horse a "Genuine Mexican Plug" really is. Other tales, novels, and sketches incorporate business philosophies—including "The Curious Republic of Gondour" (1875), *The American Claimant* (1892), and "When in Doubt, Tell the Truth" (1906). Despite Clemens's allegiance to the subscription-book industry, several stories make fun of door- to-door salesmen; the narrator of "The Canvasser's Tale" (1876) commences by noticing a portfolio under his visitor's arm and saying to himself, "Behold, Providence hath delivered his servant into the hands of another canvasser," and ends, despairingly, by writing, "You know the result perfectly well, because you know that when you have once opened the door to a canvasser, the trouble is done and you have got to suffer defeat"; he purchases three "echoes" for which he has little use. In a fragmentary manuscript known as "Burlesque *Hamlet*" (written in 1881), Twain introduced "Basil Stockmar, book agent (with a canvassing copy), weary with tramping," into the Danish castle to stumble about during the soul-searching of Hamlet and the plotting of King Claudius—thus producing a slang-talking predecessor to his Connecticut Yankee, who would be mired anachronistically in another ancient kingdom.

One type of commercial exchange found no sympathy in Mark Twain's writings—the trafficking in human slaves. He derogatorily remembered William Beebe, "rich man and slave trader," in a number of late reminiscences about early-day Hannibal,[20] connecting Beebe and his son with heartless cruelty and the Clemens family's monetary decline. Huckleberry Finn finds it impossible to forget the enslaved Jim's tangible value to his rightful owner or anyone who wishes to capture and sell him. In a different strain, the narrator of *The Innocents Abroad* (1869) links Wall Street capitalism with immorality, reporting that the "slave girl market report" in Constantinople would indicate that "stocks are up, just at present," on account of reluctance on the part of the girls' parents—"an unusual abundance of breadstuffs . . . enables them to hold back for high prices" (Ch. 34). In *A Connecticut Yankee*, the selling of human beings into slavery symbolizes the grossest corruption of which people are capable as a society. The scenes of a man beating and auctioning slaves in *A Connecticut Yankee* remind one of the poignant tale that won Mark Twain an *Atlantic Monthly* audience, "A True Story" (1874). But the Yankee is at least able to see a little humor in the mistaken identities that send Arthur and the Boss into slavery: "Yes, we were sold at auction, like swine. In a big town and an active market we should have brought a good price; but this place was utterly stagnant," comments the Yankee, with a New Englander's appreciation for a bargain, "and so we sold at a figure which makes me ashamed, every time I think of it. The king of England brought seven dollars, and his

prime minister nine; whereas the king was easily worth twelve dollars and I as easily worth fifteen. . . . If you force a sale on a dull market, I don't care what the property is, you are going to make a poor business of it" (Ch. 34). The town-hall scene in "The Man That Corrupted Hadleyburg" sarcastically inverts this situation, staging a mock-auction in which the destroyed reputations of Hadleyburg's leading citizens (mostly businessmen) are bid upon in reverse-scale. This "value" of an individual fascinated Twain as a concept: in one installment of "Old Times on the Mississippi" (1875), he related how a steamboat pilot named Stephen succeeded in bringing around a parsimonious captain who had hired him at half-wages, $125 a month; steering the boat steadily into the river's current, Stephen convinces the captain that he needs one of those "two-hundred-and-fifty-dollar pilots!" In notebooks and letters, Clemens would constantly try to check his own financial worth over the years.

A pair of tales—"The £1,000,000 Bank-Note" (1893) and "The $30,000 Bequest" (1904)—reveal the two sides of Clemens's feelings about business (and reflect, unintentionally, the erosion of his optimism after the collapse of the Paige typesetter hopes). In the earlier piece, a romance of youthful aspirations, an American obtains financial credit in London on the strength of possessing a bank-note of such large denomination that it cannot be cashed without complicated arrangements; thereby he saves his friend's investments, gains a lucrative career for himself, and wins the hand of a lovely heiress. But the other short story portrays the darker, obverse side of this fairy tale; a happy but somewhat reverse-gendered couple are destroyed by an old man's promise to leave them a bequest; they squander it in fantasized steps to improve their social standing and their amount of capital, then hesitate too long to sell their day-dreamed stock on Wall Street, with their "imaginary brokers . . . shouting frantically by imaginary long-distance, 'Sell! sell! for Heaven's sake *sell!* . . .' The very next day came the historic crash, the record crash, the devastating crash, when the bottom fell out of Wall Street, and the whole body of gilt-edge stocks dropped ninety-five points in five hours. . . . Then . . . the man in her [Aleck] was vanquished, and the woman in her resumed sway. She . . . wept, saying: 'I am to blame, do not forgive *me*, I cannot bear it. We are paupers!'" The maudlin story, not one of Mark Twain's finest, is memorable for the nightmarish "dream" linkings of money, family, status, recklessness, and remorse.

Less obviously, motifs in the narrative diction of certain other pieces develop the theme of business, often for comic purposes. Here Twain perhaps took his cue for figurative language from Bret Harte, who pioneered the humorous tensions possible between a genteel, fastidious narrator, and a mining-camp of Forty-niners whose chief vernacular is poker slang; Harte's gambler John Oakhurst solemnly "struck a streak of bad luck on the 23rd. of November, 1850, and handed in his checks," while the character named "Tennessee" surrenders to an opponent holding "two bowers and an ace . . . two revolvers and a bowie knife." (Twain exploited this same vein vividly in his story of Scotty Briggs and Buck Fanshaw's funeral in Chapter 47 of *Roughing It*.) Twain extended the possibilities of this verbal irony, perceiving that business phraseology could be amusingly incongruous out of its customary context. An example winds up the fantastic "Carnival of Crime in Connecticut" (1876), at the conclusion of which the victorious narrator nonchalantly offers to sell already dispatched tramps "by the gross, by cord measurement, or per ton," advising shoppers to "examine the lot in my cellar before purchasing elsewhere, as these . . . can be had at a low rate, because I wish to clear out my stock and get ready for the spring trade." A number of Twain's animal stories draw upon this commercial vocabulary, which thereby gain an added dimension of incongruity. Dick Baker's supposedly wise cat named Tom Quartz disapproves of the more efficient system of blasting for quartz instead of using picks and shovels on the hillside: "That cat, you know, was *always* agin new fangled arrangements—somehow he never could abide 'em. . . . He'd get the blues, . . . knowin' as he did, that the bills was runnin' up all the time an' we warn't makin' a cent" (*Roughing It*, Ch. 61). The jay in "Baker's Blue-jay Yarn" (*A Tramp Abroad*, 1880), like an unwary investor, momentarily puzzles over the immensity of an acorn-hole he has decided to fill, then "finally says, 'Well, it's too many for *me*, that's certain; must be a mighty long hole; however, I ain't got no time to fool around here, I got to 'tend to business.'"

Infatuation with the making of fortunes reveals itself in various stories. Cecil Rhodes, the narrator of *Following the Equator* (1897) informs us, arrived in Sydney penniless but had the good sense to sell a vital piece of information to "the richest wool-broker in Sydney," who categorizes men into three kinds—"'Commonplace Men, Remarkable Men, and Lunatics. I'll classify you with the Remarkables, and take the chances.' The deal went through, and secured to the young stranger the first fortune he ever pocketed" (Ch. 13). Another such tale in *Following the Equator* (Ch. 28) recounts the fluke that made Ed Jackson the agent of Commodore Vanderbilt in developing a tobacco-commerce depot in Memphis, "in supreme command of that important business"—an inadvertent but happy consequence of his being the butt of a practical joke by his Memphis pals, who had forged a letter of introduction soliciting an interview with the millionaire. Ed Jackson—previously only a wharfboat clerk at the Memphis landing—is thereby empowered to appoint his own loyal "assistants; choose them yourself—and carefully. . . . All things being equal, take the man you know, in preference to the stranger," advises Vanderbilt. "The $30,000 Bequest" is naturally filled with allusions to wealth and commerce; for instance, Sally is impressed with Aleck's plans for their daughters' matrimonial prospects: "'I get the idea. Instead of finding fault with the samples on view, thus hurting feelings and obstructing trade without occasion, you merely offer a higher class of goods for the money, and leave nature to take her course.' . . . They must look the market over—which they did." In "How to Make History Dates Stick" (published in 1914), Twain mentions the manner in which Henry VI "lost the throne and ended the dynasty which Henry IV had started in business with such good prospects." "To the Person Sitting in Darkness" (1901) takes high-finance as its controlling metaphor, pretending to be a prospectus

for setting up a new sales approach to the marketing of a "business"—"The Blessings-of-Civilization Trust." The narrator proposes that "we should throw in a little trade-taffy about the Blessings of Civilization," and then "it will take in the Persons who are Sitting in Darkness, and we can resume Business at the old stand."[21]

A Connecticut Yankee in King Arthur's Court is of course the *locus classicus* for this sort of economic imagery, and the Yankee instinctively relies on the slang of commerce. Deciding to undertake the task of telling a funny story to the monks gathered for dinner at the monastery in the Valley of Holiness, Hank Morgan must repeat it twelve times before overcoming their ingrained British reserve, and fifteen until "they disintegrated, and I got a broom and swept them up. This language is figurative. Those islanders—well, they are slow pay, at first, in the matter of return for your investment of effort, but in the end they make the pay of all other nations poor and small by contrast" (Ch. 22). When he undertakes an easier task—pumping the miraculous waters from the holy fountain—he opines that "as a matter of business it was a good idea to get the notion around that the thing was difficult. Many a small thing has been made large by the right kind of advertising." In Chapter 42, Clarence relates the doleful tale of the fall of Arthur's kingship: "Three miles of the London, Canterbury & Dover were ready for the rails, and also ready and ripe for manipulation in the stock market. It was wildcat, and everybody knew it. The stock was for sale at a give-away. What does Sir Launcelot do, but—" The Yankee can finish the sorrowful events in his own imagination: "He quietly picked up nearly all of it, for a song; then he bought about twice as much more, deliverable upon call." Clarence adds that Launcelot "skinned them alive, and they deserved it." The imposition of real-world business transactions onto the lofty deeds in a misty, legendary romance struck Twain as the essence of literary burlesque, and many critics have agreed about its deftness since 1889. It *is* an amusing premise, a salubrious antidote to the mellifluous, enshrining qualities of Tennyson's idealistic verse.

But the most pixilated usage of an inappropriate business idiom occurs not in *A Connecticut Yankee* but in Mark Twain's famous though viciously unfair dissection of *The Deerslayer*, his exercise in drollery titled "Fenimore Cooper's Literary Offenses" (1895). Scoffing at the futile efforts of six hostile Native Americans to drop onto the deck of a houseboat carrying the Hutter girls as it passes beneath a tree when approaching Lake Glimmerglass, Twain demands: "Did the Indians notice that there was going to be a tight squeeze there? Did they notice that they could make money by climbing down out of that arched sapling and just stepping aboard when the ark scraped by? No, other Indians would have noticed these things, but Cooper's Indians never notice anything." All of them leap from the tree but somehow miss the objective; five of them land in the water instead, and one falls unconscious in the stern of the boat.

These humorous verbal devices and plot ideas are admittedly small recompense for the suffering that Clemens inflicted on himself, his family, and his friends by indulging in business speculations, and every serious reader of Clemens's writings will inevitably wish that he had restricted his activities to the world of letters. But we must keep in mind the disposition of the Samuel Clemens who emerged from Hannibal, Missouri in 1853 and matured on the Mississippi River and in the Far West. His tremendous vitality was bound to lead him into other endeavors besides writing; no single occupation could contain his energies or gratify his longings. Like Charles Dickens, who persistently wore himself out under the labors of magazine editing and the arduous challenges of author's readings and amateur theatricals, for Clemens the act of writing literature was in itself an insufficient outlet; he craved a greater participatory role in his era. And the historical period in which his adulthood took place was the Gilded Age of technological advances, stock speculations, and mass industrialism (and sometimes overnight ruination). The urge to develop and market his own products was as strong and insistent a part of Clemens's temperamental makeup as was his conviction that he could invest in a mine or a publishing house or a typesetter or a railroad and make the sudden fortune that had eluded his father, who had ill-advisedly speculated on worthless land in Tennessee. Though it is often assumed (as Clemens claimed in his autobiographical dictations) that he merely fell prey in the mid-1880s to a smooth-talking inventor-adventurer and to his own logical wish as an author to print and distribute his writings without any interference or profit-taking by an intervening publisher, in actuality a side of Clemens's imagination had ever been attracted toward the enticing power and income potentially afforded by investments, manufacturing, and commerce. His literary works—principally *A Connecticut Yankee*—mirrored these business preoccupations and simultaneously provided him with workshops in which to sort out his confusing experiences. We can empathize with his remorse over his missteps and we can admire the literature he managed to construct from language and situations he borrowed from his contacts with factories, banks, and board-of-directors meetings. More than that, we should accept with apprehending tolerance the combination of genius and victim, sagacity and dupery, success and failure, that made Clemens an enigma to many of his contemporaries and a revealing symbol of his age to our own.

NOTES

1 Clemens to Olivia Clemens, 27–30 January 1894, New York City, quoted in *Mark Twain's Correspondence with Henry Huttleston Rogers*, ed. Lewis Leary (Berkeley: University of California Press, 1969), p. 20—hereafter cited in the text as *MTHHR*.

2 *Mark Twain, Business Man*, ed. Samuel C. Webster (Boston: Little, Brown and Co., 1946), p. 378, for example—hereafter cited as *MTBus*.

3 *Mark Twain's Letters to His Publishers*, ed. Hamlin Hill (Berkeley: University of California, 1967), p. 6—hereafter cited as *MTLP*. Hill referred to *Mark Twain in Eruption*, ed. Bernard DeVoto (New York: Harper & Brothers, 1940).

4 *Mark Twain and Elisha Bliss* (Columbia: University of Missouri Press, 1964), p. 18—hereafter cited as *MT&EB*.

5 Dennis Welland, *Mark Twain in England* (London: Chatto

& Windus, 1978), p. 76.

6 DeLancey Ferguson, *Mark Twain: Man and Legend* (Indianapolis: Bobbs-Merrill, 1943), p. 233.

7 Clemens to Mollie Clemens, New York City, February 1867, *MTBus*, p. 90.

8 Philip Ashley Fanning provided a poignant portrait of this tortured relationship in *Mark Twain and Orion Clemens: Brothers, Partners, Strangers* (Tuscaloosa: University of Alabama Press, 2003).

9 "Who Killed Charlie Webster?," *Mark Twain Journal* 51.1–2 (Spring/Fall 2013): 9–37.

10 *A Connecticut Yankee in King Arthur's Court*, ed. Bernard L. Stein and Henry Nash Smith (Berkeley: University of California Press, 1979), pp. 129–130.

11 *Mark Twain's Mysterious Stranger Manuscripts*, ed. William M. Gibson (Berkeley: University of California Press, 1969), pp. 229–230.

12 "Hamlin Hill, *Mark Twain: God's Fool* (New York: Harper & Row, 1973), p. xx.

11 *Mark Twain's Notebooks & Journals*, ed. Frederick Anderson et al. (Berkeley: University of California Press, 1975), 1: 39—hereafter cited as *N&J*.

14 Clemens to Henry H. Rogers, Paris, 2 January 1895, *MTHHR*, p. 115.

15 Thomas J. Reigstad, "Mark Twain and the Coal Question," *Mark Twain Journal: The Author and His Era* 56.2 (Fall 2018): 43.

16 Louis J. Budd, *Mark Twain: Social Philosopher* (Bloomington: Indiana University Press, 1962), pp. 42, 67, 192, and 196.

17 Kenneth R. Andrews, *Nook Farm: Mark Twain's Hartford Circle* (Cambridge: Harvard University Press, 1950), p. 126.

18 "Mark Twain—The Licensed Jester," *Tribune*, 26 November 1943, reprinted in *The Collected Essays, Journalism and Letters of George Orwell*, 4 vols., ed. Sonia Orwell and Ian Angus (New York: Harcourt, Brace & World, 1968), 2: 328. Orwell castigated "that flaw in his own nature, his inability to despise success" (2: 328).

19 Lewis Leary, *Southern Excursions: Essays on Mark Twain and Others* (Baton Rouge: Louisiana State University Press, 1971), pp. 80–81.

20 *Mark Twain's Hannibal, Huck & Tom*, ed. Walter Blair (Berkeley: University of California Press, 1969), pp. 39, 344. See also Dixon Wecter, *Sam Clemens of Hannibal* (Boston: Houghton Mifflin, 1952), pp. 111–113.

21 *North American Review* 172.531 (February 1901): 165, 172, 176. The essay was reprinted in *A Pen Warmed-up in Hell*, ed. Frederick Anderson (New York: Harper & Row, 1972), pp. 59–76.

The foregoing is a revised and updated version of my essay, "Mark Twain, Business Man: The Margins of Profit," *Studies in American Humor* N. s. 1.1 (June 1982): 24–43. (In reprinting it here I have taken the opportunity of removing a racial epithet the journal editors inserted without my permission, a customary usage then gratuitously common in academic discussions of *Adventures of Huckleberry Finn*.) See also Charles H. Gold's indispensable *"Hatching Ruin" or Mark Twain's Road to Bankruptcy* (Columbia: University of Missouri Press, 2003) as well as Peter Krass' upbeat and oddly formatted *Ignorance, Confidence & Filthy Rich*

Friends: The Business Adventures of Mark Twain, Chronic Speculator and Entrepreneur (Hoboken, New Jersey: John Wiley & Sons, 2007) and Lawrence Howe's concisely summarized "Business and Economics" in *Mark Twain in Context*, ed. John Bird (Cambridge, England: Cambridge University Press, 2020), pp. 161–170. In 2017 a comprehensive study of the attraction of business matters for Clemens appeared: *Mark Twain and Money: Language, Capital, and Culture*, ed. Henry B. Wonham and Lawrence Howe (Tuscaloosa: University of Alabama Press, 2017) contained twelve essays probing nearly every aspect of Twain's business ventures—real property, brand management, the Panic of 1893, bankruptcy, and other topics.

Smith, R[obert]. A. *Philadelphia As It Is in 1852; Being a Correct Guide to All the Public Buildings; Literary, Scientific, and Benevolent Institutions; and Places of Amusement; Remarkable Objects; Manufactures; Commercial Warehouses; and Wholesale and Retail Stories in Philadelphia and Its Vicinity.* Illustrations and map. Philadelphia: Lindsay and Blakiston, 1852. 452 pp.

Fred W. Lorch—"Mark Twain's Philadelphia Letters in the Muscatine *Journal*," *American Literature* 17.4 (January 1946): 348–352— demonstrated that Clemens made "liberal use" of R. A. Smith's *Philadelphia As It Is in 1852* when writing letters of 4 December 1853 (*MTLet* 1: 30–31) and 24 December 1853 (*MTLet* 1: 34–35) to the Muscatine newspaper. Clemens's use of this material, Lorch noted, explains Clemens's stereotyped phrasing and guidebook techniques. Lorch's valuable note mostly consists of juxtaposed columns from Clemens's 1853 letters and Smith's *Philadelphia As It Is in 1852*. Robert A. Smith is listed as a "map colourer" in the Philadelphia City directory for 1852; he seems likely to have been the compiler of *Philadelphia As It Is in 1852*.

Smith, Samuel Francis (1808–1895). "America" (anthem, published in 1832). Tune: "God Save the King," attributed to Henry Carey (c. 1687–1743).

Clemens mentioned the song titled "America" favorably in 1878 (NB 16, *N&J* 2: 212).

Smith, Seba (1792–1868), pseud. "Major Jack Downing."

Mark Twain mentioned "Maj. Jack Downing" in his list of books and authors to be considered in 1880 for an anthology (NB 19, *N&J* 2: 363). *Mark Twain's Library of Humor* (1888) reprinted two letters by Jack Downing— "Uncle Joshua Downing in Boston" and "Jack Downing in Portland."

L. W. Michaelson, "Four Emmeline Grangerfords," *Mark Twain Journal* 11.3 (Fall 1961): 10–12.

Smith, Solomon Franklin ("Sol") (1801–1869). *The Theatrical Journey-Work and Anecdotical Recollections of Sol. Smith, Comedian, Attorney at Law, Etc., Etc.* Philadelphia: T. B. Peterson, cop. 1854. 254 pp.

Howard G. Baetzhold pointed out that Sol Smith told how an elocutionist, irked by the inattention of his audience, injected the "seven ages of man" speech into an address— a trick that brings to mind both the Duke's burlesque monologue in Chapter 21 of Mark Twain's *Adventures of Huckleberry Finn* (1885) and Twain's depiction of George Ealer's interruptions while declaiming from *Macbeth* in *Is Shakespeare Dead?* (1909) (*Mark Twain and John Bull* [1970], pp. 258, 372 n. 9). The comic actor and theater manager Sol Smith not only owned theaters in St. Louis

and New Orleans but his traveling troupes also produced plays in towns along the Mississippi River and in other parts of the South. He is credited with building the first steam showboat.

Smith, Sydney (1771–1845). *Essays Social and Political. First and Second Series.* Memoir of the author by Samuel Orchart Beeton (1831–1877). Blue and brown cloth. London and New York: Ward, Lock, and Co., [1882]. 539 pp.

Provenance: Antenne-Dorrance Collection, Rice Lake, Wisconsin.

Location: Mark Twain Archive, Gannett-Tripp Learning Center, Elmira College, Elmira, New York.

Copy examined: presumably Clemens's copy, unmarked. Examined on 28 May 2015.

Mark Twain resolved in 1883 to contrast Smith and Aldrich in an anthology of wit and humor (NB 22, *N&J* 3: 40). In June 1885 Clemens recalled the "bitter enmity" stemming from Smith's famous query, "Who reads an American book?" (NB 24, *N&J* 3: 163). Clemens alluded to Sydney Smith again in August 1885 (NB 24, *N&J* 3: 172) and December 1887 (NB 27, *N&J* 3: 355). Clara Clemens wrote "Sidney [*sic*] Smith, Letters" in her mostly undated commonplace book (Paine 150, MTP).

Smith, (Sir) William (1813–1893), ed. *A Concise Dictionary of the Bible, Comprising Its Antiquities, Biography, Geography, and Natural History: Being a Condensation of the Larger Dictionary.* Boston: Little, Brown, and Co., 1865. 1039 pp.

Inscription: the front flyleaf is inscribed (seemingly in Clemens's hand, though he spelled his bride's name the way her family often had, rather than his preferred "Livy") in purple ink "Livie L. Langdon/ Feb 2d 1870"; this was the date of her wedding.

Provenance: contains the bookstamps and other markings of the Mark Twain Library, Redding, Connecticut.

Catalog: *Mott 1952*, item #83, $5.

Location: Mark Twain House and Museum, Hartford, Connecticut. Donated anonymously in 1963.

Copy examined: Olivia Clemens's unmarked copy. Examined in August 1987.

———. *A Smaller History of England, from the Earliest Times to the Year 1862.* Assisted by Philip Smith (1817–1885). Illus. Original black cloth. New York: Harper & Brothers, 1879. 357 pp.

Inscription: lacks the front free endpaper and the half-title page, either of which might have contained a signature or inscription.

Marginalia: several pencil notes, seemingly by Clara, are scattered throughout the volume. There are pencil brackets such as Clemens habitually made on pages 70, 71 (regarding Edward I), 97, 101, 104 (Henry VI), 107, 108, and 111 (concerning Richard III). "X's" resembling Clemens's were made across entire paragraphs on page 65, especially in the second paragraph. Pencil marks in the Table of Contents call attention to the contents of Chapter 11 and 12 in a manner such as Clemens often did. A marking in the Table of Contents regarding Chapter 25 looks more like Clara's hand.

Provenance: there is an ownership inscription of "H. G. Corwin" on the front pastedown endpaper. The rear pastedown endpaper is signed in pencil: "S. & C. C." (Susy and Clara Clemens?). This volume was found by

Alan Gribben in 1987 in the Hollywood residence formerly belonging to Clara Clemens Samossoud. Gribben's advice had been sought by the owners of the property, the Wescoatt family. A typed letter to Nick Karanovich signed by Alan Gribben on 29 June 1987 attested to the probability of the book's having been part of the Clemens family library. Nick Karanovich, Fort Wayne, Indiana had obtained the volume by then.

Catalog: *Sotheby's 2003*, #211, $2,250 (sold with four other history titles).

Copy examined: almost certainly a copy that was in the Clemens family library. This book should be considered another potential historical source for Twain's *The Prince and the Pauper* (1881).

———. *A Smaller History of Greece, from the Earliest Times to the Roman Conquest.* Student's Smaller Series. Illus. New York: Harper & Brothers, 1887. 248 pp.

Marginalia: penciled study notes on the verso of the two rear free endpapers are not by Clemens.

Provenance: Oval purple stamps of the Mark Twain Library at Redding, Connecticut are visible on the front and rear pastedown endpapers. The accession number "3733" appears in red ink at the bottom of the publisher's advertisement page and at the top of the rear pastedown endpaper.

Location: Special Collections, Elihu Burritt Library, Central Connecticut State University, New Britain, Connecticut. Listed as a Clemens association copy.

Copy examined: photocopies of the endpapers, title page, and publisher's advertisement page were provided to Alan Gribben by Ewa Wolynska, Head of Special Collections, on 13 January 2020.

SMITH, WILLIAM (1832–1907). *Morley: Ancient and Modern.* Illus. London: Longmans, Green and Co., 1886. 322 pp.

Inscription: "To S. L. Clemens, Esq./with the Author's kind regards/Morley, Aug. 1886."

Location: Mark Twain Library, Redding, Connecticut.

Copy examined: Clemens's copy, unmarked. Has the Mark Twain Library accession number "3460". Examined in 1970 and again in June 1982.

On 18 October 1886 Clemens thanked Smith ("under great obligations to you") for mailing him this book (MTP). Smith would also send Clemens a copy of Simeon Rayner's *The History and Antiquities of Pudsey*; see that Catalog entry.

———, ed. *Old Yorkshire.* New Series. Introduction to Volume I by Will Carleton (1845–1912). Introduction to Volume II by James W[illiam]. Davis (1846–1893). Introduction to Volume III by Isabella (Varley) Banks (1821–1897). 3 vols. Illus. London: Longmans, Green & Co., 1889–1891.

Inscriptions: in Volume I of the New Series: "With the Editor's sincere regards, Morley, March, 1889." In Volume II of the New Series: "With the editor's kind regards, Morley, Nov. 28, 1889" (the latter volume is dated 1890).

Catalogs: *A1911*, "Vol. II, New Series, 3 vols., numerous portraits and illustrations, 4 vols., 8vo, cloth, Lond. 1889–91," quotes the inscription, lot 436, sold for $1.75; *C1951*, D33, Vols. I and III only, inscribed by the editor to Clemens, $24.

———————, ed. *The Registers of Topcliffe, and Morley in the W. R. of the County of York. Baptisms, 1654–1830. Burials, 1654–1888.* London: Longmans, Green and Co., 1888.

228 pp.

Inscription: the front free endpaper is inscribed, "For S. Clemens, Esq./with the Editor's kind regards/May Day, 1888."

Location: Mark Twain Library, Redding, Connecticut.

Copy examined: Clemens's copy, unmarked. Has the red ink Mark Twain Library accession number "3459". Examined in 1970 and again in June 1982.

SMOLLETT, TOBIAS GEORGE (1721–1771). *The Adventures of Roderick Random* (picaresque novel, published in 1748).

From this novel written in the vein of Le Sage's earlier *Gil Blas* (1715–1735) Mark Twain borrowed a name—Tom Bowling—for a character in "Some Rambling Notes of an Idle Excursion" (1877). In Twain's opinion, Fielding's *Tom Jones* was "Roderick Random over again," especially in the way that Tom Jones' "magnificent father" fortuitously "turns up" (NB 18, *N&J* 2: 294). Twain was struck by the hypocrisy he perceived in Victorian-era literary tastes: "People praise Tom Jones & Rod. Random (beastly[,] witless, poverty) & dispraise [Edward Eggleston's ']Mystery of Mechanicsville' [*sic*] whereas their argument fits both. . . . It depends on who writes a thing whether it is coarse or not" (NB 18 [entry written in Paris], *N&J* 2: 303). In Chapter 50 of *A Tramp Abroad* (1880), Twain observes that "Fielding and Smollett could portray the beastliness of their day in the beastliest language," whereas "the privileges of Literature in this respect have been sharply curtailed within the past eighty or ninety years." In "The Walt Whitman Controversy" (DV36, MTP), possibly written in 1882, Twain declares that he owns various "old bad books," including "Smollet's [*sic*] Works." Hank Morgan remarks: "Many of the terms used . . . by this great assemblage of the first ladies and gentlemen in the land would have made a Comanche blush. . . . However, I had read 'Tom Jones,' and 'Roderick Random,' and other books of that kind, and I knew that the highest and first ladies and gentlemen in England had remained little or no cleaner in their talk, and in the morals and conduct which such talk implies, clear up to a hundred years ago; in fact clear into our own nineteenth century" (*CY* [1889], Ch. 4). In 1894 Twain hoped to write "a series of reviews of old-time literary mud idols," including *Roderick Random* (NB 33, TS p. 61).

Brashear, *MTSM* (1934), p. 235 n. 18; Ed Folsom and Jerome Loving, "The Walt Whitman Controversy: A Lost Document," *Virginia Quarterly Review* 83.2 (Spring 2007): 123.

———. *The Expedition of Humphry Clinker* (novel, published in 1771).

Clemens owned and annotated a copy of William Makepeace Thackeray's *The English Humourists* (collected in *Thackeray's Lectures* [1868]). Where Thackeray asserted on page 213 that "the novel of 'Humphry Clinker' is, I do think, the most laughable story that has ever been written since the goodly art of novel-writing began," Clemens noted in pencil in the margin: "It seemed to me the most insufferably dull." Clemens almost certainly owned a copy of this epistolary novel but it has not turned up.

———. *Travels Through France and Italy* (published in 1766).

It is tempting to speculate that Mark Twain might have known, and even benefited from, Smollett's *Travels*

Through France and Italy, in which the grumpy, often-dissatisfied narrator disparages the inconveniences of foreign travel ("Of Sienna I can say nothing . . . but that we were indifferently lodged in a house that stunk like a privy, and fared wretchedly at supper") and is equally critical of his fellow English tourists: " I have seen in different parts of Italy a number of raw boys, whom Britain seemed to have poured forth on purpose to bring her national character into contempt: ignorant, petulant, rash, and profligate, without any knowledge or experience of their own, without any director to improve their understanding, or superintend their conduct." Since Clemens's association copies of Smollett's novels have never been found, his copy of this travel book could have met the same fate.

SMYTH, ROBERT BROUGH (1830–1889). *The Aborigines of Victoria: With Notes Relating to the Habits of the Natives of Other Parts of Australia and Tasmania.* 2 vols. Melbourne: George Robertson, 1878. Another edition: London: John Ferres, 1878.

Mark Twain relied on Smyth's *The Aborigines of Victoria* in several places in Chapters 21 and 22 of *Following the Equator* (1897). "Mr. Brough Smyth saw the feat [performed by an aborigine with a *weet-weet*] and did the measuring, and set down the facts in his book about aboriginal life, which he wrote by command of the Victorian government" (*FE*, Ch. 21). In Chapter 22 of *Following the Equator* Twain quoted examples of the Australian aborigine's fortitude "recorded by the Rev. Henry N. Wolloston [*sic*], of Melbourne, who had been a surgeon before he became a clergyman." (Wollaston's name was spelled correctly in the British edition of Twain's book, *More Tramps Abroad*.) Twain found this material in Volume II of *The Aborigines of Victoria*, where Smyth writes, "The following interesting narratives in illustration of the wonderful powers of endurance of bodily pain were related to me by the Rev. Henry N. Wollaston, of Trinity Church, Melbourne, who was formerly an Assistant Colonial Surgeon in Western Australia" (p. 254). One of the stories described the surgical removal of a spear point without any anesthesia, during which the aboriginal displayed no sensation of pain. See also the Catalog entry for Wollaston.

Madigan, "Mark Twain's Passage to India" (1974), p. 366.

SMYTHE, ALBERT ERNEST STAFFORD (1861–1947). *Poems, Grave and Gay.* Toronto: Imrie & Graham, 1891. 184 pp.

Source: MTLAcc, entry #2094, volume donated from Clemens's library by Clara Clemens Gabrilowitsch in 1910. The Irish-born Canadian journalist Smythe introduced Theosophy into Canada and founded the Toronto Theosophy Society. The Theosophy Society, established by Helena Petrovina Blavatsky (1831–1891) and Henry Steel Olcott (1832–1907) in New York City in 1875, sought to explore the individual's spiritual and psychic powers.

SNAITH, JOHN COLLIS (1876–1936). *Broke of Covenden.* Boston: H. B. Turner & Co., 1904. 52 pp.

Source: MTLAcc, entry #1318, volume donated by Clemens.

Snaith's novel about the matrimonial prospects of the Broke family's daughters was one of the English author's most popular works.

SNEDEKER, FLORENCE WATTERS (1857–1893). *A Family Canoe Trip.* Illus. New York: Harper & Brothers, [cop. 1892]. 137 pp.

Source: MTLAcc, entry #1206, volume donated by Clemens.

SNELL, EBENEZER STRONG (1801–1876). *The Gyroscope, with Experiments and Explanations.* 8vo, paper wrappers, tear to corner of front wrapper. Hartford, Connecticut: Holbrook Apparatus Co., 1857. [This advertising promotion touting the gyroscope as a "Mechanical Paradox" reprints Snell's scholarly explanation from *Barnard's American Journal of Education.* Snell was identified in the pamphlet as a professor of Natural Philosophy at Amherst College in Massachusetts.]

Inscription: the first page of the text following the advertisements is signed in black ink, "Truly Yours/Mark Twain". The autograph does not appear to be genuine in either its outline or its interior points of form.

Provenance: offered for sale to Nick Karanovich in 1985 by Second Life Books, Lanesborough, Massachusetts, priced at $500. On 30 January 2001 the book was listed as lot #310 in the Oinonen Book Auction, Sunderland, Massachusetts, Sale 276.

Copy examined: photocopies of the front wrapper, advertisement pages, inscription, seven sample pages of the text, and the rear wrapper were sent to Alan Gribben by Nick Karanovich on 22 August 1985. Karanovich elected not to purchase this book in 1985, suspecting that the autograph was one of the forgeries perpetrated by Eugene Field II and Harry Dayton Sickles that Charles Hamilton described in *Great Forgers and Famous Fakes: The Manuscript Forgers of America and How They Duped the Experts* (1980). This scholar is inclined to agree. The fact that the pamphlet was published in Hartford (long before Clemens moved there) is not sufficient evidence to offset the major problems with the autograph.

SNYDER, CARL (1869–1946). *New Conceptions in Science, with a Foreword on the Relationship of Science and Progress.* Illus. New York: Harper & Brothers, 1903. 361 pp. [Place, publisher, date, and pages conjectured.]

Catalog: *C1951*, 74c, listed among books signed by Clemens, $7.

Soard's New Orleans Directory for 1882.

Mark Twain made a request of George Washington Cable in a letter written from Hartford on 11 November 1882: "P. S. Please send me a New Orleans directory of this or last year. I do not know the price but inclose five dollars at random" (Cardwell, *TG* [1953], p. 88). In a passage eventually deleted from the final version of *Life on the Mississippi* (1883), Twain wrote: "I take four pages, at random, from the city directory for the present year—1882. It 'samples' the book, and affords one a sort of bird's-eye view of the nationalities of New Orleans"; then he added: "(Insert the 4 pages, [772 A B & C]—reduce them in fac simile & crowd them onto a single page of my book, to be read by a magnifier.)" (TS in Houghton Library, Harvard; Heritage Press Edition, *LonMiss* [1944], p. 416).

SOCIETY FOR PSYCHICAL RESEARCH (LONDON). *First Report of the Committee of the Society for Psychical Research Appointed to Investigate the Evidence for Marvelous Phenomena Offered by Certain Members of the Theosophical Society.* London: Privately circulated, 1885. 130 pp.

Richard Hodgson directed this inquiry, which concluded that Helena Petrovna Blavatsky (1831–1891) and the

Theosophical Society had manufactured illusions of spirit visitors in India. Clemens almost certainly encountered this report, which within a few years was widely reprinted. He had corresponded with a founder of the Society for Psychical Research, William Fletcher Barrett (1844–1925), and on 4 October 1884 agreed to become a member and receive their publications (MTP; *AutoMT* 3: 510). He went further than this; he allowed his letter from Hartford to be published in the *Journal of the Society for Psychical Research* 9 (October 1884) under the title "Mark Twain on Thought-transference" (pp. 166–167). He explained, "I should be very glad indeed to be made a Member ... for Thought-transference, as you call it, ... has been a very strong interest with me for the past nine or ten years." Six years later he added, "Ever since the English Society for Psychical Research began its investigations of ghost stories, haunted houses, and apparitions of the living and the dead, I have read their pamphlets with avidity as fast as they arrived" (postscript to "Mental Telegraphy" [1891]). Clemens wrote the address of the "Psychical Society, London" in Notebook 26 in October 1886 (*N&J* 3: 260). He somewhat skeptically discussed Lady Stanley's affiliation with the "British Psychical Society" in an Autobiographical Dictation of 6 September 1906 (*AutoMT* 3: 130). Clara Clemens recalled that her mother Olivia became interested in spiritualism in London around 1896 or 1897, and that Clemens knew Frederic William Henry Myers (1843–1901) of the *Journal of the Society for Psychical Research* (*MFMT*, p. 184).

Walter E. Prince, "An Incident by 'Mark Twain' Verified," *Journal of the American Society for Psychical Research* 15.1 [January 1921]: 29–31 (cited two letters from Twain in the Society's files); Lester M. Hirsch, "Mark Twain and ESP," *Mark Twain Journal* 21.3 (Spring 1983): 35–36.

SOCRATES (c. 470–399 BCE, classical Athenian philosopher).
   Catalog: ListABP (1910), "Socrates," no edition specified.
Plato was Socrates's most famous student. Olivia Clemens began a letter to her mother on 9 May 1875 from Hartford: "Mr. Clemens is reading aloud in 'Plato's Dialogues'—so if I write incoherently you must excuse it" (MTHM, Hartford). In a book that Clemens acquired and signed in 1875, J. R. Green's *A Short History of the English People*, Green's account on page 74 of the pious death of the Venerable Bede reminded Clemens of another famous man's dying scene: "Worthy to stand with Socrates's death," Clemens wrote in the margin. Writing to George Cumming from Hartford on 15 May 1875, Clemens referred to a joke by an author "who was dead ... before Socrates's time" (*MT-Let* 6: 480). In a posthumously published sketch, "Sold to Satan" (1923), Mark Twain referred to "the renowned and lamented—Goethe, and Homer, and Socrates, and Confucius." See also the Catalog entry for Plato.
   Marvin Klotz, "Mark Twain and the Socratic Dialogue," *Mark Twain Journal* 11.1 (Summer 1959): 1–3; Alicia Tromp, "Platonic Parody: Mark Twain and the Quest for the Idea(l) in 'My Platonic Sweetheart,'" *American Literary Realism* 46.1 (Fall 2013): 63.

SOMERVILLE, EDITH ANNA ŒNONE (1858–1949), comp. *Mark Twain Birthday Book*. London: Remington, 1885.
   Somerville collected quotations from Mark Twain's works on the occasion of his fiftieth birthday.

_____ and VIOLET FLORENCE MARTIN (1862–1915), pseud. "Martin Ross." *Some Experiences of an Irish R.M.* Illus. London: Longmans, Green and Co., 1901. 309 pp.
   Source: MTLAcc, entry #1070, volume donated by Clemens.
Somerville and her second cousin Violet Martin jointly wrote a series of successful Irish novels and other works.

SOMERVILLE, MARY (FAIRFAX) (1780–1872). *Personal Recollections, from Early Life to Old Age, of Mary Somerville. With Selections from Her Correspondence.* Edited by Martha Somerville (1813–1879). Binding loose. Boston: Roberts Brothers, 1874. 377 pp.
   Inscription: the frontispiece has been torn out.
   Marginalia: pencil marks on pages 46, 67, 70, 93, 97, 102, 111, 119, 131, and 140. Beside a footnote on page 6 regarding the eleventh Lord Fairfax, Clemens wrote in pencil: "I knew this one, in California & Nevada, 1862–3. SLC." Clemens drew a vertical pencil mark on page 46 where Somerville declared that she has "always considered a highly-educated aristocracy essential, not for government, but for the refinement of a people." On page 59 Clemens wrote vertically with pencil in the margin: "Yes, one does need an aristocracy 'for the refinement of a people.' Page 46." (Somerville made this assertion on page 46, acknowledging, "I have never been a republican.") Clemens made a pencil bracket on page 67 at Somerville's page of grief over a pet goldfinch her servants had allowed to die of hunger. On page 70 he drew double brackets at her story of how her brother died of sun-stroke in India just as his new appointment as a writer (freeing him from the military) arrived. Clemens commented on page 125 about her boast of smuggling excavated Italian statues out of Pompeii: "Evidently Mrs. S. thinks there are kinds of immorality which are not immoral." On page 140 he made a vertical pencil mark at her descriptions of Mr. [Charles] Babbage's calculating machine. Beside a reference on page 225 to an authoress who was unfriendly to Somerville in Florence, Clemens speculated in black ink: "Harriet Beecher Stowe? I think likely. SLC". The Mark Twain Papers at the University of California at Berkeley contain photocopies of Clemens's marginalia, citing the Beinecke Collection at Yale University as their source.
   Location: Mark Twain Library, Redding, Connecticut. (Its location was verified on 30 January 2013. This, then, is not the same copy as the one listed in the entry below, despite similarities in Clemens's marginalia.)
   Copy examined: Clemens's copy. Has the red ink Mark Twain Library accession number "3056". Examined in 1970 and again in June 1982.
Despite many discouragements, the Scottish-born, self-educated Somerville became one of the leading British scientists of her day, recognized with prestigious awards and memberships for her knowledge in the fields of mathematics, astronomy, geology, botany, and geography. Her major publications were *The Connection of the Physical Sciences* (1834) and *Physical Geography* (1848). She moved to Italy in 1838 because of her husband's precarious health. Somerville's daughter Martha edited her mother's *Personal Recollections* in 1873. In Mark Twain's "The New Planet" (*Harper's Weekly*, 30 January 1909), his published response to the news that a ninth planet had been discovered in

our solar system, he recalled, "I was eleven years old in 1846, when Leverrier and Adams and Mary Somerville discovered Neptune" (*MTPP*, p. 183).

———. [An identical copy.]

Marginalia: Clemens made notes in pencil on seven pages. On page 181 he meditated about the idea of dividing up property to prevent poverty. Mathematical discoveries caused him to make a note on page 182. On both page 192 and 194 he noted, "French politeness." Where the author tells about an "American authoress" who ignored her efforts at conversation, Clemens wondered, "Mrs. Stowe?" On page 242 he joked about the reported superstition that one should avoid meeting a monk or priest when first going out in morning: "How do they avoid it? There's hardly any other sort of people to meet." A note on 251 identifies a Canadian figure. On page 290 Clemens commented about astronomical discoveries. He also made pencil marks on pages 70, 106, 125–126, 129, 131, 184–185, 203, 205, 207, 217, 223, 227, 293–294, 295, 297, 300–301, 303, 305, 307, 310, 312, 316, 320, 325, 327, and 335–336.

Provenance: donated to (what was then called) the Mark Twain Memorial in Hartford from Ida Langdon's estate in 1965.

Location: Mark Twain House and Museum, Hartford, Connecticut.

Copy examined: email scans of marginalia sent to Alan Gribben by Mallory Howard, then a Museum assistant, Mark Twain House and Museum, on 16 September 2011. Howard and Patti Philippon, the Chief Curator, were performing an inventory and cleaning of the books when they discovered the previously unrecorded marginalia. Obviously Clemens read and annotated this book while it was at Quarry Farm.

The Song of Roland [La Chanson de Roland] (Old French epic poem, c. 1100).

The stranger "lifted up the most noble and pathetic voice that was ever heard, and began to pour out the great Song of Roland. . . . And when the last verse was reached, and Roland lay dying, all alone, with his face to the field and to his slain, lying there in heaps and winrows, and took off and held up his gauntlet to God with his failing hand, and breathed his beautiful prayer with his paling lips, all burst out in sobs and wailings" (*JA* [1896], Ch. 3).

SONNENSHEIN, WILLIAM SWAN (1855–1931), comp. *The Best Books: A Reader's Guide to the Choice of the Best Available Books (about 50,000) in Every Department of Science, Art, and Literature*. London: S. Sonnenschein & Co., 1891. 1009 pp.

Inscription: "S. L. Clemens Esq. from R. Whiting, London, April 23, '97, with admiration for the writer, respect for the man." Presumably this was Richard Whiteing (1840–1928), an English journalist and novelist.

Catalog: *A1911*, "4to, cloth, Lond. 1891," quotes the inscription, lot 437, sold for $1.

SONNICHSEN, ALBERT (1878–1931). *Ten Months a Captive among Filipinos; Being a Narrative of Adventure and Observation During Imprisonment on the Island of Luzon, P. I.* New York: Charles Scribner's Sons, 1901. 383 pp.

"I thank you very much for the book. We all take a high pleasure in seeing our theories vindicated and supported. One of my theories is, that the hearts of men are about alike, all over the world, no matter what their skin-complexions may be. . . . Your book goes far to persuade me that the infusion of bastard and un-American civilization which we have injected into the Filipino has been [done?] a good deal of a damage to him" (SLC to Albert Sonnichsen, New York City, 18 March 1901, ALS in collection of Roy J. Friedman in 1979, TS in MTP).

SONREL, [MARIE JEAN BAPTISTE] LÉON (1839–1870). *The Bottom of the Sea*. Translated from the French and edited by Elihu Rich (1819–1875). Illus. New York: Scribner, Armstrong & Co., 1872. 402 pp.

Source: MTLAcc, entry #1997, volume donated from Clemens's library by Clara Clemens Gabrilowitsch in 1910. Sonrel's book described the latest efforts to construct diving suits and submarines to explore the ocean depths. He also explained what was then known of deep-water currents, fisheries, coral reefs, and other marine life. *The Bottom of the Sea* emphasized that the earth's hot core is continually reshaping the ocean depths.

SOULÉ, FRANK[LIN] (1811–1882).

Clemens was fond of the college-educated Frank Soulé, who had moved to California from Freeport, Maine in 1849, but he harbored major doubts about Soulé's poetic talent. Soulé had briefly edited the *Daily Alta California* in 1851 and the *California Chronicle* from 1853 until 1856. He was one of the three co-authors of *The Annals of San Francisco, Containing a Summary of the First Discovery, Settlement, Progress, and Present Condition of California* (New York, 1855, 824 pp.). He worked with Mark Twain on the San Francisco *Call* (Paine, *MTB* [1912], p. 259). In the mid-1860s Soulé held a federal appointment as Collector of Internal Revenue, a fact Twain spoofed in a December 1865 sketch, "A Graceful Compliment," pretending that the Collector wrote Twain's tax notice in "some happy blank verse" (*ET&S*: 2: 391, 563). Samples of Soulé's poetry appeared in *Poetry of the Pacific: Selections and Original Poems from the Poets of the Pacific States*, ed. May Wentworth (San Francisco: Pacific Publishing Co., 1867), p. 69. A poem he titled "Labor" begins: "Despise not labor! God did not despise/The handiwork which wrought this gorgeous globe,/That crowned its glories with yon jeweled skies/And clad the earth in nature's queenly robe." Years later, when Twain had become influential, Soulé sought his assistance in finding a publisher for his verse. Twain turned to William Dean Howells on 3 September 1880 for an opinion, though Twain's endorsement was half-hearted: "Frank Soulé believes himself a poet (& many others believe it, too) & it is sad enough to see him on the street begging for the charity of mere notice" (*MTHL*, p. 326).

SOUTHEY, ROBERT (1774–1843). *The Complete Poetical Works of Robert Southey, LL.D. (Late Poet Laureate.) Collected by Himself*. New York: D. Appleton and Co., 1860.

Provenance: bookplate #58 of the "J. Langdon Family Library."

Catalog: Ball 2016 inventory, gilt edges, brown leather with gilt lettering, good condition.

Location: Quarry Farm library shelves, under the supervision of the Mark Twain Archive, Elmira College, Elmira, New York.

Copy examined: unmarked copy to which Clemens had

access whenever he visited the Langdons in Elmira. Examined on 26 May 2015.

———. *Poems*. New York: Leavitt & Allen, 1853. 288 pp.

Source: MTLAcc, entry #649, volume donated by Clemens.

SOUVESTRE, ÉMILE (1806–1854). *Un Philosophe sous les toits: Journal d'un homme heureux [A Philosopher Under the Roof: Journal of a Happy Man]*. Paris: Michel Lévy Freres, 1858. 257 pp. [An alternate translation of the title: *An Attic Philosopher: Diary of a Happy Man*.]

Marginalia: Clemens translated a large number of French words and sentences.

Catalog: *A1911*, "l2mo, half leather (rubbed), Paris, 1888 [*sic*], with translation of a large number of words or sentences in the handwriting of Mr. Clemens," lot 438, sold for $1.25.

Location: Mark Twain House and Museum, Hartford, Connecticut. The volume was in need of repairs in 2006.

Source: "Support the Book Conservation Fund," internet message to members, Mark Twain House and Museum, 1 October 2006.

SOWDEN, WILLIAM JOHN (1858–1943). *Chips from China*. Illus. Adelaide: Printed by W. K. Thomas for W. J. Sowden, 1901. 50 pp.

Sowden wrote to Clemens from the Adelaide *South Australia Register* on 26 August 1901, stating that he was "sending you a copy of a little book of sketches written by me for private circulation after a visit to China." Clemens noted on the envelope: "China Sketches" (MTP). Kevin J. Hayes—"Mark Twain at Home and Abroad," *Canadian Review of American Studies* 47.3 (2017): 430—identified this small book of travel sketches that Sowden had contributed to the *Register* and then collected in privately published form.

SOWERBY, JOHN G. (1850–1914) and HENRY HETHERINGTON EMMERSON (1831–1895). *Afternoon Tea: Rhymes for Children with Original Illustrations*. New York: Rhodes and Washburn, 1881. [Edition conjectured.]

Source: ListABP (1910). "Afternoon Tea, Sowerby & Emmerson," no other information.

SOYER, BLANCHE AUGUSTINE ANGÈLE (1843–1911), pseud. "Baroness Staffe." *The Lady's Dressing-Room (Le cabinet de toilette)*. Translated from the French by Lady Colin Campbell [Gertrude Elizabeth (Blood) Campbell, 1857–1911]. London: Cassell & Co., 1893. 366 pp.

Location: Mark Twain Library, Redding, Connecticut. Donated by Clemens (MTLAcc, entry #399).

Copy examined: unmarked copy belonging to a member of the Clemens family. Has the red ink Mark Twain Library accession number "399". Examined in 1970 and again in June 1982. Laid in between pages 338 and 339 are three newspaper clippings providing beauty advice about wrinkles, foot problems, facial astringents, and remedies for "enlarged pores." Apparently the source of these articles was a Connecticut newspaper, perhaps a Hartford one, since the verso of one clipping contains a news article about New London, Connecticut.

The Lady's Dressing-Room offered recommendations for attaining physical beauty and attractive dress. It addressed each facial and bodily feature separately—the face, hair, mouth, eyes, nose, ear, hand, and feet—with additional advice about toilet waters, perfumes, and pomades as well

as pointers about how to take care of jewelry.

SPAMER, FRANZ OTTO (1820–1886), pseud. "Franz Otto." *Männer eigner Kraft [Men's Own Power]*. Illus. 12mo, cloth. Leipzig, 1875.

Catalogs: *A1911*, "8vo, cloth, Leipzig, 1875," with a sheet of notes by Clemens laid in, lot 373, sold for $1.25; Anderson Auction Galleries (New York City), Sale number 941 (27–29 February 1912), the library of the late Captain J. F. Hinckley of St. Louis, "12mo, cloth, Leipzig, 1875," has the *A1911* sale label, lot 224; American Art Association (New York City), Sale catalogue for the library of Oscar Haywood, D. D. (13 March 1918), "Leipzig, 1875," has the *A1911* sale label, lot 70.

A self-help guide intended to inspire boys and young men with illustrative examples.

SPEARMAN, FRANK HAMILTON (1859–1937). *Doctor Bryson, A Novel*. New York: Charles Scribner's Sons, 1904. 308 pp.

Source: MTLAcc, entry #263, volume donated by Clemens.

Henry Elwood Bryson, M. D., a stickler for protocol, is offered the position of Surgeon-in-Chief for the Eye at a large Chicago clinic for the eye and ear. At the end of the novel he has become humbled and human as well as having been appointed dean of the faculty.

Spectator (London journal, published 1828–).

Two letters by George Nicolson and Henry Woodall in the *Spectator* 81 (9 July 1898): 47, provided Mark Twain's character called the Old Man with examples of animal intelligence in Part 6 of "What Is Man?" (1906).

Baender, *WIM?* (1973), pp. 191–192.

Speeches at the Lotos Club, ed. John Elderkin (1841–1926), Chester S[anders]. Lord (1850–1933), and Horatio N[elson]. Fraser (1851–1942). New York: Privately printed, 1901. 441 pp.

Catalog: ListABP (1910), "Speeches at the Lotos Club", no other information supplied.

This volume included Mark Twain's speech of 10 November 1900 at the Lotos Club Dinner given in his honor, along with talks delivered at various times by Robert G. Ingersoll, Ulysses S. Grant, Bayard Taylor, William Winter, Oliver Wendell Holmes, and other notables.

Fatout, *MTSpk* (1976), pp. 349–353.

SPENCER, HERBERT (1820–1903).

Clemens informed Mary Mason Fairbanks on 6 July 1873 that he had met the English sociologist and philosopher Herbert Spencer at a dinner in London (*MTLet* 5: 402). Watchful for new manuscripts to publish with Charles L. Webster & Company, Clemens noted in 1887: "The Unitarian Herald says Herbert Spencer has deter[mined] to autobi-" (NB 26, *N&J* 3: 273). Sometime during the early 1900s Mark Twain listed Spencer among the "intellectual giants" ("Proposal for Renewal of the Adam Monument Petition," *FM*, p. 452). In a sarcastic summary of mankind's entire existence and achievements written in 1901 and 1902, Twain recorded that Spencer was one of the "wonderful men" of the nineteenth century "who was introducing his wonderful all-clarifying law of Evolution, a law which he claimed was in force throughout the universe" ("The Secret History of Eddypus," *FM*, p. 357). (Spencer's notions of natural selection and survival of the fittest, generally referred to as social Darwinism, held great sway for decades.) In Book II, Chapter 3 of

Christian Science (1907), Twain indicated that he was familiar with Spencer's prose style. Clara Clemens listed Herbert Spencer's name and the title "Universal Postulate" in her undated commonplace book (Paine 150, MTP).

Spenser, Edmund (c. 1552–1599). *The Faerie Queene. To Which Is Added His Epithalamion.* Green cloth. London and New York: George Routledge and Sons, n.d. 820 pp.

> **Provenance:** Antenne-Dorrance Collection, Rice Lake, Wisconsin.
>
> **Location:** Mark Twain Archive, Gannett-Tripp Learning Center, Elmira College, Elmira, New York.
>
> **Copy examined:** probably Clemens's copy, unmarked. Examined on 28 May 2015.

Spenser, wrote Mark Twain in 1865, is noted for his "broken-English poetry" that resembles Chaucer's (*Californian*, 17 June 1865, *LAMT*, p. 142; *ET&S* 2: 195). Twain recorded the fact that Spenser was buried in Westminster Abbey ("A Memorable Midnight Experience" [1874]). "Chaucer is dead, Spenser is dead, so is Milton, so is Shakespeare," he joked in a speech to the Savage Club in London on 9 June 1899 (*MTSpk*, p. 321). "Chaucer and Spenser and Shakespeare and a lot of other people who did not know how to spell anyway" (speech at the Associated Press dinner, 19 September 1906, *MTSpk*, p. 526). "No one can write perfect English. . . . It has never been done. It was approached in the 'well of English undefiled'" (Book II, Chapter 2, *Christian Science* [1907], *WIM?*, p. 273); cf. *Fairie Queen*, IV, Canto ii, stanza 32: "Dan Chaucer, well of English undefiled." In *Is Shakespeare Dead?* (1909), Twain alluded to "Spenser, and Raleigh, and the other distinguished literary folk of Shakespeare's time."

———. *Spenser for Children.* Ed. by M. H. Towry. Illustrated by W[alter]. J[enks]. Morgan (1847–1924). London: Chatto & Windus, 1878. 177 pp.

> **Source:** MTLAcc, entry #1935, volume donated from Clemens's library by Clara Clemens Gabrilowitsch in 1910.

Among the 21 books Estes & Lauriat of Boston charged Clemens for on 14 July 1880 was "1 Spenser .90"; Clemens paid the bill on 20 July 1880 (receipt in MTP). The title and edition were not specified.

Spenser, Mary Clare (1842–1923). *The Benefit of the Doubt.* New York: G. P. Putnam's Sons, 1885. 371 pp.

> **Source:** MTLAcc, entry #269, volume donated by Isabel V. Lyon, Clemens's secretary.

Spenser's romantic novel opens in Milan, Italy but moves between Europe and the United States.

Spielhagen, Friedrich (1829–1911). *Problematische Naturen: Roman [Problematic Characters: A Novel].* 2 vols. Leipzig: Staackmann, 1876.

> **Marginalia:** Numerous pencil markings, especially in the first half of Volume 1. Page 13 of Volume 1 contains eight words in Clemens's hand. Page 88 has eight more words.
>
> **Provenance:** sold at the 1951 Hollywood auction, though not listed in the sale sheet.
>
> **Catalog:** *Zeitlin 1951*, item #42, "small 8vo, 3/4 morocco, . . . few leaves loose," $3.
>
> **Location:** Mark Twain Papers, Bancroft Library, University of California at Berkeley.
>
> **Source:** UCB Library Online Catalog, 12 June 2006. The volumes contain labels certifying that they were sold at the 1951 Hollywood auction.

———. *In Reih' und Glied: Roman [In Rank and File: A Novel].* 4. Aufl. 2 vols. Leipzig: L. Staackmann, 1876.

> **Provenance:** sold at the 1951 Hollywood auction, though not listed in the sale sheet.
>
> **Catalog:** *Zeitlin 1951*, item #41, "small 8vo, 3/4 blue morocco," $3.
>
> **Location:** Mark Twain Papers, Bancroft Library, University of California at Berkeley.
>
> **Source:** UCB Library Online Catalog, 12 June 2006. The volumes contain labels certifying that they were sold at the 1951 Hollywood auction.

Spindler, Karl (1796–1855). *Der Jude, historischer Roman [The Jew, A Historical Novel]* (published in 1827).

In Frankfort in 1878 Clemens made an entry in Notebook 14: "Der Jude, by Carl Spindler" (*N&J* 2: 75).

The Spirit of the Times: A Chronicle of the Turf, Field Sports, Literature and the Stage (New York weekly, published 1831–1858). Ed. by William Trotter Porter (1809–1858).

David E. E. Sloane—*The Literary Humor of the Urban Northeast, 1830–1890* (Baton Rouge: Louisiana State University Press, 1983), pp. 7–8—pointed to an item reprinted in the *Spirit of the Times* 17 (16 October 1847): 396 (where it was credited to "Gamboge" in the *Yankee Blade*) as "the actual source" of the carpet-weaving tragedy in Jim Blaine's "Story of the Old Ram" in Chapter 53 of Mark Twain's *Roughing It* (1872). Similarly, Henry P. Leland's "Frogs Shot without Powder," an earlier version of Twain's "Celebrated Jumping Frog" (1865), appeared in *Spirit of the Times*, 26 May 1855.

DeVoto, *MTAm* (1932), pp. 340–342; Blair, *NAH* (1937), p. 156; Blair, *MT&HF* (1960), pp. 245–247. See also the Catalog entries for William Trotter Porter's "Letter from Billy Patterson Himself" and Hamilton C. Jones' "Cousin Sally Dilliard" for other references to *The Spirit of the Times.*

Spirituals (religious songs of enslaved African Americans).

Clemens may have heard the Jubilee Singers of Fisk University when they performed in Hartford in 1872, but in any event he attended their performances twice while he was in England in 1873. On 10 March 1873 Clemens declared in an open letter to the press that "they reproduce the true melody of the plantations. . . . One must have been a slave himself in order to feel what that life was & so convey the pathos of it in the music" (*MTLet* 5: 315–316). In a letter written to the Jubilee Singers' musical director on 8 March 1875 Clemens claimed he was going to hear the Jubilee Singers "for the fifth time" (*MTLet* 5: 316–317 n. 2).

In June 1888, at the home of Charles Dudley Warner, Clemens was cajoled into singing in a "clear tenor voice several Negro songs. Most of the songs were spiritual and told about Moses and Pharoah, Saul and David, David and Goliath, and so forth. One song as the interpreter of Pharoah's dreams was rather playful. There were many references in it to seven fat cows and seven lean cows. Otherwise, even though they were monotonous and sad, they were endowed with emotional, wild poetry, which Mark Twain interpreted very well" (Ernest J. Moyne, "Mark Twain Meets a Lady from Finland," *Mark Twain Journal* 11.2 [Summer 1960]: 25; *Alexandra Gripenberg's A Half Year in the New World: Miscellaneous Sketches of Travel in the United States* (1888), translated and ed. by Ernest J.

Moyne [Newark: University of Delaware Press, 1954], p. 71). On 16 November 1890 Clemens attended a concert given by the Fisk University Jubilee Singers in the Asylum Hill Congregational Church in Hartford; he made entries in Notebook 30 about several of the spirituals they sang (Fears, *Day by Day* 2: 555). In *The Fourth Generation: Reminiscences by Jane Ross* (London: Constable, 1912), Janet Ann (Duff-Gordon) Ross (1842–1927) would recall assisting Clemens with rental properties in Florence in 1892. She also mentioned his singing spirituals.

Henry B. Wonham, "Mark Twain's Last Cakewalk: Racialized Performance in *No. 44, The Mysterious Stranger*," *Centenary Reflections on Mark Twain's* No. 44, The Mysterious Stranger, ed. Joseph Csicsila and Chad Rohman (Columbia: University of Missouri Press, 2009), pp. 44–48.

SPITZKA, EDWARD ANTHONY (1876–1922). "Contributions to the Encephalic Anatomy of the Races," *American Journal of Anatomy* 2.1 (29 November 1902): 25–71.

"Nearly a month ago there came to me from one of the universities a tract by Dr. Edward Anthony Spitzka on the 'Encephalic Anatomy of the Races'"; Mark Twain then quotes a paragraph from page 49, unintelligible to the layman, and compares it to Mary Baker Eddy's *Science and Health* (*Christian Science* [1907], Ch. 3, *WIM?*, p. 231). Paul Baender traced Mark Twain's source to Spitzka's article (*WIM?*, p. 556).

SPOFFORD, AINSWORTH RAND (1825–1908) and **CHARLES GIBBON** (1843–1890), eds. *Library of Choice Literature; Prose and Poetry, Selected from the Most Admired Authors, Edited with Biographical and Critical Notes*. Illus. 8 vols. Philadelphia: Gebbie & Co., 1883–1884.

Inscriptions: presented to S. L. Clemens by the publishers.

Catalog: *A1911*, "8 vols., 8vo, cloth, gilt edges, Phila. 1883–84, presentation copy from the publishers to S. L. Clemens," lot 287, sold for $3.50.

Ainsworth Rand Spofford was the sixth Librarian of the Library of Congress, serving from 1864 until 1897.

_____ and **RUFUS EDMONDS SHAPLEY** (1840–1906), eds. *The Library of Wit and Humor, Prose and Poetry, Selected from the Literature of All Times and Nations. Edited, with Biographical and Critical Notes, by A. R. Spofford, Librarian of Congress, Washington, D. C., and Rufus E. Shapley, Author of "Solid for Muhooly."* Illus. 5 vols. Philadelphia: Gebbie & Co., 1884–1894.

Inscriptions: presented to S. L. Clemens by the publishers (in the two extant volumes).

Provenance: two volumes formerly in the Mark Twain Library, Redding, Connecticut.

Catalog: *Mott 1952*, item #65, 2 vols. only, $12.50.

In 1880 the Philadelphia publisher George Gebbie (1832–1892) proposed that Mark Twain edit this compendium of humor, but the negotiations were fruitless. Gebbie's prospectus for the volumes is in the Mark Twain Papers, Bancroft Library, University of California at Berkeley. The eventual collection included Mark Twain's "Story of the Bad Little Boy Who Didn't Come to Grief," "The Scriptural Panoramist," "The Celebrated Jumping Frog of Calaveras County," and two passages from Twain and Charles Dudley Warner's *The Gilded Age*.

SPOFFORD, HARRIET PRESCOTT (1835–1921). "Down the River," *Atlantic Monthly* 16.96 (October 1865): 468–490.

R. J. Ellis—"'No Authority at All': Harriet Prescott Spofford's 'Down the River' and Mark Twain's *Huckleberry Finn*," *Mark Twain Annual 4* (2006): 33–53—presented such a detailed and nuanced comparison of Spofford's fourth published short story and Twain's masterpiece that one must concede striking correspondences (Ellis refers to "some type of literary debt"), in spite of the wide span of years between the two works. A young enslaved woman is influenced by an older, formerly enslaved man, a maroon who has hidden out in a swamp. Her arduous journey to the coast where the Union army can liberate her has its share of hazards and terrors.

SPRING, GARDINER (1785–1873). *Fragments from the Study of a Pastor*. New York: John S. Taylor, 1838.

Inscription: signed in pencil, "Olivia Langdon". Gift of Nancy Dout.

Catalog: Ball 2016, brown cloth, gilt lettering, signed by Olivia Langdon (1810–1890).

Location: Mark Twain Archive, Gannett-Tripp Learning Center, Elmira College, Elmira, New York.

Copy examined: a volume of Presbyterian sermons belonging to Clemens's mother-in-law and available to Clemens in the Langdons' home. Viewed on 17 May 2002.

SPRINGER, WILLIAM MCKENDREE (1836–1903). *Tariff Reform, the Paramount Issue. Speeches and Writings on the Questions Involved in the Presidential Contest of 1892*. Introductory sketch of the author by Alexander J. Jones (1860–1909). New York: Charles L. Webster & Co., 1892. 420 pp.

Clemens's publishing firm issued this political opinion statement. The United States presidential election of 1892 pitted Grover Cleveland (Democrat) against Benjamin Harrison (Republican). Alexander J. Jones, an Illinois journalist (and later a prominent Chicago attorney) was a partisan of Cleveland, who had previously given him a political appointment.

The Standard (weekly newspaper, New York City, 1887–1892).

There is little question that Clemens would have been familiar with *The Standard*, since he had a lengthy association with its founder and editor, the economic philosopher Henry George (1839–1897), and was sympathetic to reform efforts such as George's that addressed income inequality. Notable Mark Twain scholars have gone further, however, and have accepted Twain's authorship of an essay inveighing against private land ownership, "Archimedes," that appeared in the 27 July 1889 issue of *The Standard* under a preposterous pseudonym, "Twark Main." Jim Zwick, for example, partly based an article, "Mark Twain and the Single Tax," *Georgist Journal: News & Views from the International Georgist Movement* 87 (Summer 1997): 5–10, on the assumption that Twain wrote "Archimedes." In my opinion, this is wishful thinking. I can detect hardly anything genuinely Twain-like in the piece, and it seems far more likely that George himself wrote "Archimedes" and merely implied that the famous and popular Mark Twain was responsible. (See the Catalog entries for Henry George and Louis F. Post.)

A Standard Dictionary of the English Language Upon Original Plans. Isaac K[aufman]. Funk (1839–1912), Editor-in-Chief. 2 vols. New York: Funk & Wagnalls Co., 1900.

On 6 February 1900 Mark Twain endorsed this edition of

the dictionary: "In my experience I have found that one can do without principles, but not without the Funk & Wagnalls Standard Dictionary." The publisher used Twain's words in an advertisement in the 14 April 1900 issue of the New York *Sun* (Barbara Schmidt, "Dictionary," www.twainquotes.com). Around 1901, writing a devastating book review, "About Cities of the Sun" (DV357, MTP), Twain noted: "It was high time to go to the dictionary, now, and so I did it. . . . His [George Woodward Warder's] furlongs make his city 1200 miles square; the Standard's furlongs make it 1500" (MS p. 13). On 7 February 1910 Clemens made a request of Albert Bigelow Paine from Bermuda: "Please send me the *Standard Unabridged* that is on the table in my bedroom. I have no dictionary here" (collection of Kevin Mac Donnell, quoted but misdated in *MTB*, p. 1560).

Joe B. Fulton, "Mark Twain's New Jerusalem: Prophecy in the Unpublished Essay 'About Cities in the Sun,'" *Christianity and Literature* 55.2 (Winter 2006): 173–194.

Standards of Length, ed., George M[eade]. Bond (1852–1935). Illus. Hartford, Connecticut: Pratt & Whitney Co., 1887. 180 pp.

Source: MTLAcc, entry #892, volume donated by Clemens.

STANDRING, GEORGE (1855–1924). *The People's History of the English Aristocracy*. London: Robert Forder, 1887. [The preface to the first edition is dated 1 February 1887. A second edition was issued by the same publisher in 1891.]

Standring was a printer for the Fabian Society and the editor of *The Radical*. He called for replacing the British monarchy with a republic, but his efforts at social reform extended in many other directions as well. On 25 August 1886 Mark Twain wrote to Standring from Elmira asking about rates for composition in London printing houses; he added: "I thank you in advance for the book, & shall welcome it when it comes" (PH in MTP). Twain entered Standring's London address in Notebook 26 (October 1886, *N&J* 3: 260). James D. Williams—"The Use of History" (1965), pp. 107–108—speculated that Twain "may have read" one of Standring's shorter pamphlets such as "Does Royalty Pay?," first issued in *The Atheistic Platform* (London) 10 (1884), 160–174. Standring wrote to Twain on 7 May 1887 to say that he was sending a copy of *The People's History of the English Aristocracy* (MTP). In May 1887 Twain made a memorandum to "hand the 'Nobility' book to a publisher" (NB 26, *N&J* 3: 293). Another note explains that Saint-Simon's *Memoirs*, Twain intended to "add the English printer's little book as another volume, & call the whole 'Royalty & Nobility Exposed'" (NB 26 [May 1887], *N&J* 3: 295).

The preface to Standring's first edition of *People's History* vows to "show in its true light the aristocracy of this country. This has never been done by the courtly chorus of sycophantic history-mongers. Hence it arises that, to-day, thousands of Englishmen bow the knee before the fetish of nobility, oblivious or ignorant of the fact that the aristocracy of to-day differs from that of Charles II. only in its hypocrisy." (The Mark Twain Papers at Berkeley contain a photocopy of the second edition [1891], which reprinted Standring's preface from the first edition.) In September 1887 Twain copied Standring's figures concerning the overabundance of highly paid commissioned

officers in the British army and navy (Notebook 27, *N&J* 3: 306). In an undated manuscript, "A Defence of Royalty & Nobility" (DV 313a, MTP), Twain quotes from pages 24–32 of an essay titled (he says) "Kingship & Nobility" that he claims was "clipped from a magazine article"; Standring's writings are probably the actual source. In January 1889 Twain wrote Standring's name and address in Notebook 28 (*N&J* 3: 440). Standring, Twain wrote, differed from the Englishmen who prefer to criticize America; Standring alone provides "An Englishman on England" (NB 28 [April 1889], *N&J* 3: 467). Twain designated Standring to receive a complimentary copy of *A Connecticut Yankee in King Arthur's Court* (NB 29 [1889], *N&J* 3: 500).

Mark Twain's *A Connecticut Yankee* (1889) was unquestionably influenced by Standring's radical views; originally Twain intended to cite *People's History of the English Aristocracy* in an appendix to the novel. "Carry down George —'s Exposure of English society & publish at 25 cents," Twain proposed in April 1889 (NB 28, *N&J* 3: 468). In October 1889 Twain wished to "write to Standring for particulars" about the "earl of Galoway rape-case. Oc. '89. Scotland" (NB 29, *N&J* 3: 523). On 24 November 1889 Twain wrote to Frederick J. Hall of Charles L. Webster & Co.: "I send you a little book by George Standring"; Twain wanted to publish Standring's work as a cheap paperback simultaneously with the issuance of *A Connecticut Yankee* (*MTLP*, p. 257). He drafted a title-page for the projected book: "ENGLISH ROYALTY AND NOBILITY. By George Standring . . . Authorized American Edition . . . New York: Charles L. Webster & Co., 1889" (*A1911*, lot 47). Standring's writings were pertinent to the speech that Viscount Berkeley of Twain's *The American Claimant* (1892) hears at the Mechanics Club, a ringing assault on "the shams of monarchy and nobility." Twain copied Standring's London address on 18 July 1900 and reminded himself to write to George Standring, "printer" (NB 43, TS p. 22). He sent Standring a complimentary copy of *The Man That Corrupted Hadleyburg and Other Stories and Essays* (NB 43 [1900], TS p. 33). On a letter from Standring written on 5 December 1905, Twain noted, presumably for biographer Albert Bigelow Paine's benefit: "Standring is a practical printer & a radical in politics & religion. I have known him 30 years—a fine man" (MTP).

Baetzhold, "Course of Composition" (1961), p. 200; Budd, *MTSP* (1962), p. 124; Baetzhold, *MT&JB* (1970), pp. 111–113, 126, 340 n. 17, 344 n. 45, and 345 n. 52.

STANHOPE, PHILIP DORMER, FOURTH EARL OF CHESTERFIELD (1694–1773). *Letters to His Son* (published in 1774).

The 11 September 1869 issue of the Buffalo *Express* carried Mark Twain's humorous sketch, "The Last Words of Great Men," in which Twain facetiously attributed to Lord Chesterfield the final words, "Shin around John, and get the gentleman a chair" (*MTBE*, p. 317). As any Internet search for famous quotations will show, Chesterfield, in keeping with his gentlemanly reputation, supposedly uttered the polite request, "Give [Solomon] Dayrolles a chair." He and Dayrolles had been closely connected in their political careers. Later, Clemens paraphrased a piece of advice by Lord Chesterfield in Notebook 12 in the summer of 1873: "Something better than <gold and

silver> gold and [illegible word]. Lord Chesterfield" (*N&J* 1: 556). One of Chesterfield's letters had pointed out that "in common life, one much oftener wants small money, and silver, than gold."

STANHOPE, PHILIP HENRY, FIFTH EARL (1805–1875), pseud. "Lord Mahon." *History of England, Comprising the Reign of Queen Anne until the Peace of Utrecht*. 2 vols. Leipzig: Bernhard Tauchnitz, 1870.

Catalog: *C1951*, Dl, listed among books signed by Clemens, 2 vols., $16.

————. *Joan of Arc*. London, 1853. New edition, London: John Murray, 1854. 88 pp.

A six-book bibliography compiled for Clemens, probably by Chatto & Windus of London in 1892, listed "Earl Stanhope, Joan of Arc (in Miscellanies). A good account of the trial. Murray 12/6" (MS notes formerly in the collection of Barry Bingham, Sr., Louisville, Kentucky; PH in Box 36, no. 6, MTP). However, contrary to what is implied in these notes, neither the First Series (London: John Murray, 1863) nor the Second Series (London: John Murray, 1872) of Stanhope's *Miscellanies* contained any essay on Joan of Arc. Someone must have confused that collection with his book on Joan.

STANLEY, ARTHUR PENRHYN (1815–1881). *Historical Memorials of Westminster Abbey*. Fifth edition. London: John Murray, 1882. [Edition uncertain; the first edition was published in London in 1869.]

Mark Twain alluded to the symbolic floral crowning of Henry III—described by Stanley on pages 47–48—in Notebook 24 (July 1885, *N&J* 3: 167). Twain then went on to describe other historical events treated by Stanley on pages 44, 58, 88; these involved Henry II, Richard II, and George III (*N&J* 3: 167–168). Twain believed it was from Stanley's *Memorials* that he gained facts about the Interdict during King John's reign (NB 29 [1889], *N&J* 3: 504, 506). He listed Stanley's book in a tentative appendix for *A Connecticut Yankee in King Arthur's Court* (1889). Salomon, *TIH* (1961), p. 110 n. 9.

STANLEY, (LADY) DOROTHY (TENNANT) (1855–1926). *London Street Arabs*. Eighth thousand. Illus. (28 plates). London: Cassell & Co., 1890. 12 pages of text and 28 leaves. [Contains more than forty drawings of impoverished children and, in some pictures, their families.]

Inscription: the verso of the front free endpaper is inscribed, "With Dorothy Stanley's affectionate love/to Jean./1891.—"

Provenance: formerly in the Mark Twain Library, Redding, Connecticut.

Catalog: *Mott 1952*, item #84, $6.

Location: Mark Twain House and Museum, Hartford, Connecticut. Donated anonymously in 1963.

Copy examined: Jean Clemens's copy, unmarked but with evidence of having belonged to the Mark Twain Library at Redding. Examined in August 1987.

Dorothy Tennant was a painter when she married the African explorer Henry Stanley in 1890. Twain said of her: "She is an intense spiritualist. . . . To me, who take no interest in other-worldly things, and am convinced that we know nothing whatever about them, and have been wrongly and uncourteously and contemptuously left in total ignorance of them, it is a pleasure and a refreshment

to have converse with a person like Lady Stanley, who uncompromisingly believes in them" (August? 1907 AD, *MTE*, p. 339; *AutoMT* 3: 130).

STANLEY, (SIR) HENRY MORTON (1841–1904). *The Autobiography of Sir Henry Morton Stanley*. Edited by Dorothy Stanley (1855–1926). Illus. Boston and New York: Houghton Mifflin Co., 1909. 551 pp. [Edition conjectured.]

When Stanley died in 1904, Clemens wrote to his widow, recalling how he and Stanley met in 1867: "I have known no other friend & intimate so long, except John Hay" (11 May 1904, ALS in MTP). During Clemens's visit to England in 1907 he "found that Stanley had left behind him an uncompleted autobiography. It sets forth freely and frankly the details of his childhood and youth and early manhood, and stops with his adventures in our Civil War, if I remember rightly" (6 September 1907 AD, *MTE*, p. 340; *AutoMT* 3: 131). On 11 February 1910 William Dean Howells wrote from New York City to urge Clemens to "get the life of Stanley," which Howells termed "about the livest book I ever read" (*MTHL*, p. 852).

————. *In Darkest Africa; or, the Quest, Rescue, and Retreat of Emin, Governor of Equatoria*. 2 vols. Illus. New York: Charles Scribner's Sons, 1890. [Edition conjectured.]

In November 1886 Clemens declined to introduce Stanley for his lecture in Hartford ("I am common & valueless here"), but arranged for Stanley to stay with the Clemens family (SLC to James B. Pond, 18 November, 30 November 1886, Berg Collection, NYPL). On 9 December 1886 Clemens introduced Stanley in Boston for a lecture titled "Through the Dark Continent" (*MTHL*, p. 574 n. 1). Having previously entered Stanley's name and London address in Notebook 30 (1890), Clemens wrote "Stanley's book at Scribner's" (*N&J* 3: 587, 588). Several compliments follow this entry, apparently in preparation for a speech. Olivia Clemens wrote to her mother from Hartford on 26 October 1890: "Our life here goes on just as usual. . . . Mr. Clemens is reading aloud to me Mr. Stanley's new book which we are enjoying very much indeed" (MTHM). Clemens had tea with the Stanleys at Max O'Rell's in London on 30 June 1899 (NB 40, TS p. 57). Stanley and his wife received a complimentary copy of Mark Twain's *The Man That Corrupted Hadleyburg and Other Stories and Essays* in 1900 (NB 43, TS p. 33; Lady Stanley to SLC, 16 September 1900, MTP).

————. *Slavery and the Slave Trade in Africa*. Illus. New York: Harper & Brothers, 1893. 86 pp.

Source: MTLAcc, entry #1207, volume donated by Clemens.

————. *Through the Dark Continent; or, The Sources of the Nile, Around the Great Lakes of Equatorial Africa, and Down the Livingstone River to the Atlantic Ocean*. 2 vols. Illus., maps. New York: Harper & Brothers, [cop. 1906]. [Stanley first published this work in 1878. Harper & Brothers published early editions, but the Mark Twain Library accession record specified that the donated edition was the one copyrighted in 1906.]

Source: MTLAcc, entries #1743 and #1744, volumes donated by Clemens.

Clemens noted approvingly in 1872 that "when Stanley discovers Livingstone, England does him honor through some graceful personal attentions from the queen of the empire" (letter to the Hartford *Evening Post*, 6 December 1872, *MTPP*, p. 47). In March 1879 Clemens predicted in Paris: "Stanley is almost the only man alive to-day whose name & work will be familiar 100 yrs hence" (NB 18, *N&J* 2: 304). On 26 July 1900 Lady Stanley wrote to Olivia Clemens, while the Clemenses were in England: "I will send Mr. Clemens the second volume of *Through the Dark Continent*. Pray give him my love and tell him that when I read *Through the Dark Continent* I felt anxious to meet the author and marry him, so my Heart's Desire was given me" (quoted by Caroline T. Harnsberger, *Mark Twain, Family Man* [New York: Citadel Press, 1960], p. 121).

Judith Yaross Lee, *Twain's Brand: Humor in Contemporary American Culture* (Jackson: University Press of Mississippi, 2012), pp. 89 and 189 n. 36.

STANTON, ELIZABETH (CADY) (1815–1902), ed. *The Woman's Bible*. Ed. by Stanton and others.

"Eliz Cady Stanton & daughter gone to Europe to write 'Woman's Version of the Bible,'" Clemens noted (NB 26 [October 1886], *N&J* 3: 261). The American feminist Stanton and a committee of twenty-six women would collect and publish gender-based commentaries on the Christian Bible in two parts in 1895 and 1898. Their essays questioned conventional interpretations and compared the Bible to the sacred writings of other religions.

The Statesman's Year-Book: Statistical and Historical Annual of the States of the World. Ed. by Frederick Martin (1830–1883) from 1864 until 1882. London: Macmillan and Co., 1864– .

In 1878 Clemens's first entry in Notebook 16 was: "Fred'k Martin's Statesman's Year Book—15 years" (*N&J* 2: 158).

STATHAM, FRANCIS REGINALD (1844–1908). *South Africa as It Is*. London: T. Fisher Unwin, 1897. 311 pp. [Edition conjectured.]

In Chapter 66 of *Following the Equator* (1897), Mark Twain mentions this as a recently published book "by Mr. Statham, an able writer partial to the Boers." Twain cites the book in a footnote in Chapter 67 to document an officer's prediction (in 1881) that "the Boers would turn tail at the first beat of the big drum." (Francis V. Madigan, Jr.—"Mark Twain's Passage to India" (1974), p. 366—corrected Twain's page citation, which should be to page 98 instead of page 82.) This may have been the book that Twain cited in a 15 September 1899 letter to an unknown correspondent: "As to that South African battle. It isn't I that made the mistake—it is the school history I quote from. It is a text-book down there, & was not written by a Boer, but by a Briton" (ALS, Special Collections, Washington University, St. Louis, Missouri). But see also the Catalog entry for F. Edmund Garrett's *Story of an African Crisis* (1897), seemingly an even more likely referent. Statham was an often-controversial figure because of a scandal in his past and his anti-imperialist views. On 24 April 1901 Twain recommended the author to James B. Pond as a promising lecturer: "Mr. Statham wrote an admirable history of the troubles in South Africa, from the Boer point of view" (PH in MTP).

STEAD, WILLIAM THOMAS (1849–1912). "Character Sketch: Mark Twain," *Review of Reviews* (London) 16 (August 1897): 122–133.

Clemens wrote to Chatto & Windus on 15 September 1897: "Mrs. Clemens would like a copy of the Review of Reviews

containing Stead's recent article on me" (MTHM). (Jo Dee Benussi called my attention to this letter.) The English editor Stead's article praised Twain's writings, described his life, and recounted several meetings with him. Seven photographs of Twain accompanied the article, including a photograph of his birthplace home in Florida, Missouri (which would, incidentally, seem further to authenticate that structure). Subsequently M. A. DeWolfe Howe (1864–1960) reproduced in facsimile a joshing note from Twain to Stead: "The Czar is ready to disarm. I am ready to disarm" (*Causes and Their Champions* [Boston: Little, Brown and Company, 1926], p. 291).

_____, ed. *Portraits and Autographs: An Album for the People*. Illus. London: Review of Reviews, 1890. 160 pp.

Source: MTLAcc, entry #1220, volume donated by Clemens.

Stead reproduced (on page 63) a facsimile of a letter from Clemens thanking Stead "for giving my Yankee such a handsome amount of space."

———. "A Suggested Test Reading," *Borderland: A Quarterly Review and Index* 1.5 (July 1894): 463; and "Test Readings of Mark Twain's Hands," *Borderland: A Quarterly Review and Index* 1.6 (October 1894): 558–560.

Stead's *Borderland*, published in London, reported on claims of palmistry, clairvoyance, telepathy, spiritualist mediums, haunted houses, premonitions, astrology, and various other manifestations of the occult and the paranormal. In July 1894 he published photographs of the front and back of Mark Twain's right hand and invited palmists to deduce his life and character. *Borderland* published the experts' opinions in the October issue. Twain discussed the mixed results in a letter to Stead written from Paris on 30 November 1894 (ASSSCL). In an undated manuscript titled "Palm Readings," Twain reported that seven British palmists were unable to deduce his occupation as a humorist from photographs they examined (Mark Twain Papers, Bancroft Library, University of California at Berkeley). In an Autobiographical Dictation he again recounted how Stead photographed his hand while they were "on board a ship bound for Europe" and then published the deductions of "six or seven" palmists "in his magazine" (26 December 1906 AD, *AutoMT* 2: 336–337).

Joseph O. Baylen, "Mark Twain, W. T. Stead, and 'The Tell-Tale Hands,'" *American Quarterly* 16.4 (Winter 1964): 606–612.

"STEAL AWAY TO JESUS" (spiritual).

Clemens included "Steal Away" in a brief list of plantation spirituals he made in 1890 in Notebook 30 (*N&J* 3: 593). In Chapter 9 of "Tom Sawyer's Conspiracy" (written 1897–1900), Jim's "mournfulness all went away . . . and 'stead of singing 'Ain't got long to stay here' he sung 'Jinny git de hoecake done,' and the gayest songs he knowed" (*HH&T*, p. 234).

"STEBBINGS, ENSIGN JEHIEL" (fictional character).

On 15 July 1852 Orion Clemens's newspaper, the Hannibal *Journal*, commended to Hannibal youths the 'Carpet Bag's' great hero, Ensign Jehiel Stebbings" (*SCH*, p. 246). Sam Clemens's *jeu d'esprit* on 16 September 1852, "Blabbing Government Secrets," also referred to Jehiel Stebbings (*MSM* [1934], pp. 117–118; *SCH* [1952], p. 314 n. 46). The staff of the *Carpet Bag* in Boston had entered this fictional candidate (conceived by Benjamin Drew) in the presidential contest of 1852 to satirize the Scott-Pierce campaign. A number of newspapers throughout the nation publicized the invented candidate.

John Q. Reed, *Benjamin Penhallow Shillaber* (1972), pp. 24–25.

STEDMAN, ARTHUR [GRIFFIN] (1859–1908), ed. "Short Biographies of All Authors Represented in This Work," an excerpt of pages 467–614 from Volume XI of *A Library of American Literature from the Earliest Settlement to the Present Time*, ed. Edmund Clarence Stedman and Ellen Mackay (Hutchinson) Cortissoz. No. 8 of 100 copies. Portrait. New York: Charles L. Webster & Co., 1891.

> Inscription: inscribed by the editor, "To Samuel L. Clemens with the author's compliments. New York, January 1, 1891."
>
> Provenance: formerly in the Mark Twain Library, Redding, Connecticut.
>
> Catalog: *Mott 1952*, item #85, $65.
>
> Location: Albert and Shirley Small Special Collections Library, University of Virginia, Charlottesville, Virginia. Gift of Clifton Waller Barrett.
>
> Source: the online catalog for the Albert and Shirley Small Special Collections Library in 2017.

Arthur Stedman wrote the multitudinous short biographies that were included at the rear of the final, eleventh volume of Charles L. Webster & Company's costly set, *A Library of American Literature*. His brief sketch of "Samuel L. Clemens, 'Mark Twain'" concluded by stating that Clemens "founded the New York publishing firm of Charles L. Webster & Co. in 1884" (p. 493). Arthur Stedman also edited the twelve-volume "Fiction, Fact, and Fancy Series" that Clemens's publishing firm issued in 1891–1892. Clemens wrote to Stedman from Florence, Italy on 8 December 1892—misspelling his name in the salutation as Dear Mr. Steadman—about the first volume in the series, *Merry Tales by Mark Twain* (NYPL). In January 1894 Clemens noted: "Set Arthur Stedman to work on 'Justice as She is Administered in England'" (NB 33, TS p. 46). At approximately the same time, Clemens recorded in New York City that he had enjoyed an anecdote told by Arthur Stedman (NB 33, TS p. 47). Jo Dee Benussi noticed that Clemens sent a humorous letter to Stedman on 10 July 1906 (quoted by Elizabeth Lindley, *The Diary of a Book-Agent* [New York: Broadway Publishing Co., 1912], p. 11).

STEDMAN, EDMUND CLARENCE (1833–1908) and ELLEN MACKAY (HUTCHINSON) CORTISSOZ (1851–1933), eds. *A Library of American Literature, from Earliest Settlement to the Present Time*. 11 vols. Illus. Biographies of authors written by Arthur [Griffin] Stedman (1859–1908). New York: Charles L. Webster & Co., 1888–1890.

> Source: MTLAcc, entries #721–730, volumes donated by Clemens.
>
> ———. [Another identical set.]
>
> Source: MTLAcc, entries #2147–2158, volumes donated from Clemens's library by Clara Clemens Gabrilowitsch in 1910.

On 1 March 1887 Clemens fretted in Hartford, "I think well of the Stedman book, but I can't somehow bring myself to think *very* well of it" (SLC to Charles L

Webster, *MTBus*, p. 377). Clemens's publishing firm issued the work in eleven volumes by subscription only; prices ranged from $3 to $7 per volume. The eleventh volume comprised biographical sketches of the authors written by Arthur Stedman (1859–1908) and a topical index. Mark Twain (along with John Greenleaf Whittier and Thomas Wentworth Higginson) provided a letter of endorsement for the prospectus that was carried by the sale agents. Charles L. Webster & Company touted *A Library of American Literature* as a study that traced "the growth of a national literature, a literature keeping pace with our wonderful material prosperity. . . . Strictly a work for the whole people, not for a class" (*Publishers' Trade List Annual for 1893*). In a note of 13 December 1890 on the letterhead stationery of The Players Club, Twain requested his business manager Fred J. Hall: "Also send vol. 9, L. A. L., to C. J. Langdon, Elmira. His copy never arrived or has been lost" (Berg Collection, NYPL). In Twain's Autobiographical Dictation of 2 June 1906, he mentioned that "Stedman, the poet, had made a compilation, . . . called 'The Library of American Literature'—nine or ten octavo volumes"; Clemens blamed Webster for its mismanagement and Hall for its failure as a publishing investment (*MTE*, pp. 191–192; *AutoMT* 2: 78). Most Mark Twain biographers agree that *A Library of American Literature*, though a commendable project, was one of the slow-selling weights that dragged Clemens's publishing company into bankruptcy as a consequence of the financial Panic of 1893. Still, Stedman was "a valued friend" of thirty-five years, Twain declared on the day of Stedman's death (MT to the New York *Times*, 18 January 1908, MTP). (The next day the *Times* published Twain's brief remarks, which concluded, "His loss stuns me, and unfits me to speak" [Fears, *Day by Day* 4: 868]). To an unidentified correspondent Twain testified, "I am grieved to the heart, for we were close friends for more than a generation" (18 January 1908, *Day by Day* 4: 869).

———. *Lyrics and Idylls, with Other Poems*. London: C. Kegan Paul & Co., 1879. 238 pp.

> Source: MTLAcc, entry #2095, volume donated from Clemens's library by Clara Clemens Gabrilowitsch in 1910.

On 26 January 1883 Stedman wrote Clemens to say that in return for a complimentary copy of *The Prince and the Pauper* (1881), he was sending Clemens "a copy which I find of my English (& eclectic) edition of verse. It goes by mail" (TS in MTP). Clemens replied from Hartford on 6 February 1883, explaining that he had been ill. "But if I couldn't write, I have been able to read; & so I have enjoyed your poems, & with sincerest pleasure. And I found old friends among them—particularly among the war poems" (Lehigh University). A three-poem section in *Lyrics and Idylls* (pp. 191–201) was titled "In War-Time"; its second poem, "The Sergeant's Tale" somewhat prefigured Rudyard Kipling's verse. A section titled "American Lyrics and Idylls" commemorated notable events in American history, such as "How Old Brown Took Harper's Ferry" (p.33), "Kearny at Seven Pines" (p. 46), and "Custer" (p. 48). Other poems in the collection were more miscellaneous in their subject matter.

———. *The Poetical Works of Edmund Clarence Stedman*. Household Edition. Boston: Houghton, Mifflin and Co.,

1885. 422 pp. [Edition conjectured.]
Clemens noted Edmund C. Stedman's address in 1885 (NB 25, N&J 3: 179) Also in 1885, George Parsons Lathrop (1851–1898) reported that Stedman (usually arriving from New York City) and Clemens were among the guests who would often while away a winter evening at the home of Charles Dudley Warner ("A Model State Capital," *Harper's Monthly Magazine* 71.425 [October 1885]: 726). *Mark Twain's Library of Humor* (1888) would include "The Diamond Wedding" from Stedman's *Poetical Works*. On 8 October 1901 Clemens wrote to Stedman from Riverdale: "Yes indeed, I shall read that poem, & so will your appreciative friend Mrs. Clemens" (ASSSCL). After Stedman died, however, Twain recalled that Thomas Bailey Aldrich "had very nearly as extensive an appreciation of himself and his gifts as had the late Edmund Clarence Stedman, who believed that the sun merely rose to admire his poetry and was so reluctant to set, at the end of the day, and lose sight of it, that it lingered and lingered and lost many minutes diurnally. . . . Stedman was a good fellow; Aldrich was a good fellow; but vain?—bunched together they were as vain as I am myself" (3 July 1908 AD, *MTE*, p. 294; *AutoMT* 3: 241).

STEDMAN, S[AMUEL]. O[LIVER]. *Allen Bay, A Story*. Philadelphia: J. B. Lippincott & Co., 1876. 152 pp.
On 23 November 1877 William Dean Howells asked Clemens, "Didn't you once read me some passages out of an idiot novel called Allen Bay?" (*MTHL*, p. 209). Clemens undoubtedly *had* singled out certain parts of the novel for Howells's amusement, but the copy of *Allen Bay* from which he had read was then no longer in existence; he had torn many pages from the volume in the course of writing a thirty-nine-page unpublished manuscript, "Burlesque Review of Allen Bay" (Paine 9, MTP). He used purple ink and Crystal Lake Mills ruled paper in writing the undated manuscript, a paper-and-ink combination that mainly occurred during 1876 and 1877. It is one of Mark Twain's fullest book reviews, inspired in this case by his disgust with Stedman's style. He begins by listing some of the prominent (but fictitious) literary critics whose favorable opinion of Stedman's "sweet melancholy" he disputes: De Lisle, Von Schlecter, Hallett, Lovejoy, Sumner, Turner. (Three of these fictitious authorities—De Lisle, Von Schlecter, and Hallett—also turn up as purported champions of another book Twain mocked during this period, Edward Payson Hammon's *Sketches of Palestine*. See the Catalog entry for Hammond, where Twain uses the spelling "Hallet.")
Twain claims to have reread Stedman's book seven times after a first reading, and launches into a stylistic analysis of its mixed metaphors, marrings of tone, poor transitions, faulty diction, and other flaws. Gradually it dawns upon the reader that Twain is spoofing the vocabulary and clichés of book reviewers as well as the reprehensible tastes of the readers and writers of such sentimental trash. Moreover, in many instances Twain's purple-ink revisions of the extracts he removed from the book distort the original wording and punctuation to heighten Stedman's already-woeful problems with syntax, diction, sense, and image. Twain tore out pages 143–150 to demonstrate the fatuity of Stedman's highflown bathos, and plundered other pages

for shorter extracts. The narrative—about a misanthropic hermit who adopted a baby girl, Judith, only to watch her (as a teenager) die of grief over her boyfriend's drowning in a millpond—was undeniably atrocious, but Twain's revisions emphasize its ludicrous qualities by compressing, italicizing, and isolating them. Stedman's preface recounted his memories of growing up in coastal Virginia near the Dismal Swamp canal. His introductory sketch of the setting of the novel, "Hamburg," described "my father's farm and place of business" near the seaport of Norfolk, Virginia.

STEEL, FLORA ANNIE (WEBSTER) (1847–1929). *On the Face of the Waters; A Tale of the Mutiny*. London: William Heinemann, [1896]. 432 pp.
Mark Twain "rashly described Miss Steele's [*sic*] *On the Face of the Waters* as 'the finest novel ever written by a woman'" (Edward Wagenknecht, *MTMW* [1967], p. 39, no source supplied). Her work was set during the Sepoy Mutiny of 1857–1858 in India.

STEELE, ANNE (1716–1778). "O for a sweet, inspiring ray" (hymn, published in 1760). The melody is often attributed to Thomas Tallis (c. 1505–1585).
"He gave out another hymn, beginning—'O for a sweet, inspiring ray—'. . . . The choir raved & roared around that victim, & pulled & hauled it & rent & flayed it" (SLC to OLC, Paris, Illinois, 31 December 1871, *MFMT*, p. 11; *MTLet* 4: 528). The fourth stanza of Steele's hymn conveys its fervor: "He smiles,—and seraphs tune their songs/To boundless rapture, while they gaze;/Ten thousand, thousand joyful tongues/Resound his everlasting praise" (*The Church Hymn Book, with Tunes*, comp. Edwin F. Hatfield [New York: Ivison, Blakeman, Taylor & Co., 1873], p. 320).

STEELE, JOEL DORMAN (1836–1886). *Fourteen Weeks in Natural Philosophy*. Illus. New York: A. S. Barnes & Co., 1869. 320 pp.
Source: MTLAcc, entry #805, volume donated by Clemens. Steele was a member of the Elmira College faculty.

STEELE, THOMAS SEDGWICK (1845–1903). *Canoe and Camera: A Two Hundred Mile Tour Through the Maine Forests*. Illus. New York: Orange Judd Co., 1880. 139 pp.
Source: MTLAcc, entry #550, volume donated by Clemens.
———. *Paddle and Portage, from Moosehead Lake to the Aroostook River, Maine*. Illus. Boston: Estes and Lauriat, 1882. 148 pp.
Source: MTLAcc, entry #551, volume donated by Clemens.

STEERS, FANNY (d. 1861). "The last link is broken" (song, c. 1834). The melody is usually credited to William Clifton.
This duet song was visible among the music on the piano in Chapter 38 of *Life on the Mississippi* (1883). The young ladies in the Grangerford household sang it ("nothing was ever so beautiful") in Chapter 17 of *Adventures of Huckleberry Finn* (1885). Tom Sawyer suggests that Jim play "The Last Link is Broken" on a jews-harp to his rats in Chapter 38 of that same novel. Clemens remembered it as one of the "songs that tended to regrets for bygone days and vanished joys" in "Villagers of 1840–3," written 1897 (*HH&T*, p. 34). The woman to whom its lyrics are generally attributed was a respected painter and composer who belonged to the Pre-Raphaelite circle in England. The opening lines of the song convey the lachrymose message of a spurned lover: "The last link is broken,/That

bound me to thee,/And the words thou hast spoken,/ Have render'd me free./That bright glance misleading/ On others may shine." Both of its two stanzas conclude: "I have not loved lightly,/I'll think on thee yet,/I'll pray for thee nightly,/Till life's sun is set."

STENHOUSE, THOMAS BROWN HOLMES (1825–1882). *The Rocky Mountain Saints: A Full and Complete History of the Mormons, from the First Vision of Joseph Smith to the Last Courtship of Brigham Young; . . . and the Development of the Great Mineral Wealth of the Territory of Utah*. Illus. New York: D. Appleton and Co., 1873. 761 pp. [Edition conjectured.]

Mark Twain mentioned Stenhouse as a Salt Lake visitor to New York City in a letter published in the 6 September 1868 issue of the San Francisco *Alta California* (www.twainquotes.com). Dan De Quille seemingly became concerned that Stenhouse, the owner and editor of the Salt Lake *Daily Telegraph*, might next take up the mining subject that De Quille was writing about (see *MTLet* 6: 440–441). On 29 March 1875, coaching Dan De Quille about how to write *The Big Bonanza*, Clemens assured him, "Don't be afraid of Stenhouse's book. Bosh!" (*MTLet* 6: 437). The index to Stenhouse's *The Rocky Mountain Saints* rather frankly referred readers to nearly forty pages that discussed "Polygamy." Stenhouse's wife Fanny Stenhouse (1829–1904) published several exposés of Mormon polygamy, including *A Lady's Life Among the Mormons* (1872) and *"Tell It All": The Story of a Life's Experience in Mormonism* (1874).

STENNETT, SAMUEL (1727–1795). "On Jordan's stormy banks I stand" (hymn, words published in 1787). Music composed by George Kingsley (1811–1884).

In Chapter 55 of *The Innocents Abroad* (1869), Mark Twain quotes the hymn's first four lines sung by the *Quaker City* pilgrims as they waded in the Jordan River: "On Jordan's stormy banks I stand,/And cast a wistful eye/To Canaan's fair and happy land,/Where my possessions lie." (Twain notes gleefully that "the water was so fearfully cold that they were obliged to stop singing and scamper out again.") Subsequently, in an article written for the New York *Tribune* (6 January 1873), Twain recalled that a typical native of the Sandwich Islands "knows all the hymns you ever heard in your life, and he sings them in a soft, pleasant voice, to native words that make 'On Jordan's stormy banks I stand' sound . . . grotesquely and sweetly foreign to you" (*MTLet* 5: 561; *MTPP*, p. 52).

STEPHEN, JAMES KENNETH (1859–1892). *Lapsus Calami*. New edition. Cambridge: Macmillan and Bowes, 1891. 92 pp.

In a letter to William Walter Phelps (1839–1894) written on 5 August 1892 from Germany, Clemens quoted a poem, "To R. K." (ALS, Huntington). Jo Dee Benussi traced that title to Stephens' *Lapsus Calami* (Benussi to Gribben, 25 January 2008 email message).

Many of the poems in Stephens's collection had cryptically abbreviated titles ("To C. S. C.," "To A. S.," "Of T. G.," and so forth) and registered a cynical outlook on the literary world and on human endeavor in general. To "R. K.," the second poem in the volume, was presumably directed at Rudyard Kipling, against whom Stephens seemed to contrast the poetry of Robert Browning (an epigraph from Browning opened "To R. K."). The poem longed for deliverance from "a season/. . . Of a prose which

knows no reason/And an unmelodious verse." "To R. K." concluded by hoping for a day "When the Rudyards cease from kipling/And the Haggards Ride no more."

STEPHENS, JOHN LLOYD (1805–1852). *Incidents of Travel in Greece, Turkey, Russia, and Poland*. 2 vols. New York: Harper & Brothers, 1875.

Source: MTLAcc, entries #1706 and #1707, volumes donated by Clemens.

Stephens first published this travel narrative in 1839. It had several reprintings.

STEPHENS, ROBERT NEILSON (1867–1906). *Philip Winwood; A Sketch of the Domestic History of an American Captain in the War of Independence . . . Written by His Enemy in War, Herbert Russell, Lieutenant in the Loyalist Forces*. Illustrated by E[dward]. W[ilbur]. D[ean]. Hamilton (1864–1943). Boston: L. C. Page & Co., 1900. 412 pp.

Source: MTLAcc, entry #1098, volume donated by Clemens.

Stephens's historical novel principally tells a love story.

STEPHENSON, ELIZA (TABOR) (1835–1914). *St. Olave's. A Novel*. Quarter brown morocco, gilt, mottled boards. New York: Harper & Brothers, 1871. [A reprint of the 1863 first American edition.]

Inscription: pencil ownership signature on title-page: "Susie L. Crane Sept 21st/Quarry Farm/1872." No marginalia are visible.

Provenance: originally in the library of Theodore and Susan Crane at Quarry Farm in Elmira, New York.

Location: collection of Kevin Mac Donnell, Austin, Texas (Mac Donnell to Alan Gribben, 29 November 2011).

This was the second of British author Stephenson's more than thirty novels. A large percentage of these incorporated religious themes. Clemens often perused and read from the contents of the Cranes' Quarry Farm library shelves.

STERN, CAROLINE (1868–1920). "Mark Twain (A Nocturne of the Mississippi)."

On 11 January 1906 Isabel Lyon recorded: "After luncheon I took him a little poem written by Caroline Stern of Greenville, Miss. He . . . read aloud the first verse of it. 'Who speaks of care, of toil, of time?'" (IVL Journal, Harry Ransom Center, University of Texas at Austin; entry repeated in IVL Journals, TS p. 121, MTP).

Caroline Stern, born in Hale, Alabama, was a public school teacher in Greenville, Mississippi for more than thirty years. William Alexander Percy's autobiography, *Lanterns on the Levee* (1941), recalled Stern's literary influence on generations of students. She would eventually collect her poems in *At the Edge of the World* (1916). "Who speaks of care, of toil, of time?" was the first line in a six-stanza poetic tribute to Mark Twain. The speaker in the poem imagined herself to be aboard a steamboat on the Mississippi River at night, and wondered, "Is that Huck Finn's low signal made?" The fourth stanza was representative of the whole: "His spell is mingled with the night,/The phantoms roll in changing line—/A cabin on Sierra's hight,/A castle on the storied Rhine./The out-worn East, the new-born West—/Like wind-reefs on the river's breast./Mark Twain,/Mark Twain, 'tis!" (*The Edge of the World* [Boston: Gorman Press, 1916], pp. 49–51).

Anne Franklin Lamar, "'The Multitude of Thronging Thoughts and Baseless Dreams': The Diary of Caroline

Stern," master's thesis, University of Alabama at Tuscaloosa, 2011.

Stern, Julius, pseud. of Julius Karl Reinhold Sturm (1816–1896). "Translation from the German of Julius Stern" (poems).

Around 1863 Olivia Langdon copied a piece with this title into her commonplace book, misspelling the author's name as "Sterne" (DV161, MTP). Julius Stern was a German religious poet and songwriter. His *Fromme Lieder* (1852) had been translated and published as *Devout Songs and Poems* in 1858.

Harris, *Courtship* (1996), p. 15.

Sterne, Laurence (1713–1768). *The Life and Opinions of Tristram Shandy, Gentleman* (novel, published 1759–1767).

In a letter written to Olivia Langdon on 23 and 24 December 1868, Clemens recalled Sterne's "Uncle Toby & the wounded soldier" (from Volume VI, Chapter 8), but added that "the book is coarse, & I would not have you soil your pure mind with it." For that matter, "I don't know what reminded me of Sterne," Clemens wrote. But "when everything else that Lawrence [*sic*] Sterne wrote shall have been forgotten, that one little paragraph [regarding Toby's oath that rose up to Heaven] will still secure to him an enduring fame—a fame that shall last while English is written & noble impulses still stir in the human heart" (*LLMT*, p. 34; *MTLet* 2: 344–345). Clara Clemens listed this novel in her undated commonplace book (Paine 150, MTP). William Dean Howells's last letter to Clemens (11 February 1910, *MTHL*, p. 852) reported that Howells was "slowly plowing through 'Tristram Shandy.' How tough is the humor that our poor ancestors battened on! But I *will read* it."

Harris, *Courtship* (1996), pp. 92–93, 100.

———. *A Sentimental Journey Through France and Italy*. Illustrated by Maurice Leloir (1853–1940). New York: J. W. Bouton, 1884. 210 pp.

Catalog: Ball 2016 inventory, oversize volume in protective case, good condition.

Location: Quarry Farm library shelves, under the supervision of the Mark Twain Archive, Elmira College, Elmira, New York.

Clemens had access to this whimsical travel masterpiece, written in 1768, at Quarry Farm.

"No man ever enjoyed a funeral as [William C.] Prime [, author of *Tent Life in the Holy Land*,] did his Sentimental Journey through the Holy Land," Mark Twain quipped (*Daily Alta California*, 1 March 1868; *TIA*, p. 265). John Irwin Fischer made the case that Sterne's book affected the way Twain told an amusing story about buying gloves in Gibraltar ("How to Tell a Story: Mark Twain's Gloves and the Moral Example of Mr. Laurence Sterne," *Mark Twain Journal* 21.2 [Summer 1982]: 17–21). In William Dean Howells's last letter to Clemens (11 February 1910, *MTHL*, p. 852), Howells conceded that "The 'Sentimental Journey' is all right, though nasty."

Rogers, *MTBP* (1960), pp. 31, 33.

Stevens, Abel (1815–1897). *Sketches & Incidents; or, A Budget from the Saddle-Bags of a Superannuated Itinerant*. 2 vols. in 1. New York: G. Lane & P. P. Sandford for the Methodist Episcopal Church, 1844. 166 pp.

Inscription: the title page is signed twice in black ink: John

R. Hills Book/J R Hills Book."

Location: Mark Twain Library, Redding, Connecticut.

Copy examined: almost certainly a copy donated by a Redding resident other than Clemens. The Hill family contributed numerous books to the Mark Twain Library. This book contains neither an accession number nor any of the usual oval Library stamps. There are no signs of Clemens's ownership, yet the volume was shelved—probably accidentally—with his former library volumes in 1970. I examined it again in June 1982 and still could see no reasons to connect the book with Clemens's personal library collection.

Stevens, Edward Thomas (1828–1878). *Flint Chips. A Guide to Pre-Historic Archaeology, as Illustrated by the Collection in the Blackmore Museum, Salisbury*. Illus. London: Bell and Daldy, 1870. 593 pp.

Inscription: the recto of the frontispiece is inscribed in brown ink (not in Clemens's hand): "Saml. L. Clemens/ Christmas 1879/In recollection of Salisbury, England/ Wm. Blackmore/Edward T. Stevens."

Location: Mark Twain Library, Redding, Connecticut.

Copy examined: Clemens's copy, unmarked. Numerous leaves are unopened. Has a penciled Mark Twain Library accession number, "3835". Examined in 1970 and again in June 1982.

Stevens was the curator of the Blackmore Museum, founded in Salisbury in 1867 by the English lawyer and investor William Henry Blackmore (1827–1878), who had traveled throughout the American West. Clemens visited the museum on 24 December 1873 (*MTLet* 5: 535). Its exhibits featured stone implements and weapons devised by Native Americans. Discouraged by the death of his wife in 1872, faltering investments, and personal problems, Blackmore would commit suicide on 12 April 1878. The inscription written at the front of the volume in December 1879 was probably placed there by Dr. Humphrey Purnell Blackmore (1835–1929), a practicing physician who had gained a reputation as an archaeologist for his excavations in England and had donated his fossil collection to the Blackmore Museum. Humphrey became the Museum's director in 1878 after the deaths of both his brother William and the curator Edward Thomas Stevens.

Stevens, George Alexander (1710–1784). "The storm" (song). (Melody from an English tune, "Welcome, Brother Debtor.")

Mark Twain categorized a song titled "The storm at sea" (without identifying its author) as belonging to the "soft sentimentality about the sea" ("About All Kinds of Ships" [1893]). Louis J. Budd suggested that Twain was referring to Stevens's song, inasmuch as it appeared in a book that Clemens owned—William Cullen Bryant's *The Family Library of Poetry and Song* (*CTSS&E* 3: 1021). It is conceivable, though, that Twain instead meant Adelaide Anne Procter's "The Storm" (also known as "The Tempest Rages"), whose melody was composed by John P. Hullah (1812–1884). Olivia Langdon received a book of poems by Procter (1825–1864) for Christmas in 1865 and it entered the Clemenses' library after their marriage. In Procter's poem an earnest child's bedtime prayer saves a distant ship being tossed on the ocean when "a tempest rages wild and high."

STEVENS, HORACE J[ARED]. (1866–1912). *The Copper Handbook: A Manual of the Copper Industry of the World.* Volume VIII. Houghton, Michigan: Horace J. Stevens, 1908. 1500 pp.
  Source: MTLAcc, entry #1232, Volume VIII donated by Clemens.
  Quite likely Clemens acquired this volume for investment reasons, since it surveyed the current outlook for this metal and listed all copper mines operating in 1908. (The book was copyrighted and actually issued in 1909, despite the 1908 date on its title page.)
STEVENS, WILLIAM BACON (1815–1887). *The Parables of the New Testament Practically Unfolded.* Philadelphia: J. M. Stoddart & Co., [cop. 1871]. 382 pp.
  Provenance: bookplate #390 of the "J. Langdon Family Library."
  Catalog: Ball 2016 inventory, brown textured cloth, gilt design, fair condition, Langdon bookplate #390.
  Location: Quarry Farm library shelves, under the supervision of the Mark Twain Archive, Elmira College, Elmira, New York.
  Copy examined: unmarked copy to which Clemens had access whenever he visited the Langdon residence in Elmira. Examined on 26 May 2015.
STEVENSON, ROBERT LOUIS (1850–1894). *An Inland Voyage.* London: Chatto & Windus, 1896. 238 pp.
  Inscription: "Jean Clemens/Vienna/Dec 25th 1897/ Mamma".
  Catalogs: C1951, J5; *Fleming 1972*; Sotheby Parke Bernet, New York City, Sale number 3482 (February 1976), "Property of a New York City Collector" (John F. Fleming), "ownership inscription by Clemens' daughter Jean, dated Vienna, 25 December 1897, from 'Mamma,'" lot 22 (sold with two other titles).
  Provenance: Frederick Anderson, then Editor of the Mark Twain Papers in the Bancroft Library at the University of California, Berkeley, examined this book in the New York City offices of John F. Fleming, Inc. and made notes in April 1972 (Anderson to James D. Hart, 17 April 1972, photocopy sent to Alan Gribben).
  Location: unknown at present.
In 1876 Stevenson and a friend paddled a canoe through Belgium and northern France, using canals and the Oise River. The Clemenses indicated their interest in Stevenson's account of this trip that had appeared in 1878; Olivia Clemens wrote to Chatto & Windus in November 1897 to request copies of both *An Inland Voyage* and *Travels with a Donkey* (Berg Collection, NYPL).
Numerous other signs of their familiarity with the Scottish author's works are on record. Clemens wrote Stevenson's New York City hotel address in Notebook 27 in 1888 (*N&J* 3: 301). In April 1888 Clemens and Stevenson sat on a bench in Washington Square in New York City and spoke of fellow writers and books (Baetzhold, *MT&JB*, pp. 203–204). Clemens recalled their talk in an Autobiographical Dictation made in Florence; Stevenson's eyes, Clemens said, "burned with a smouldering rich fire . . . and they made him beautiful" (*AutoMT* 1: 229). Clara Clemens briefly quoted Stevenson in her undated commonplace book, perhaps around 1888 (Paine 150, MTP). It must have gratified Clemens when Brander Matthews reported: "Robert Louis Stevenson told me he considered

Huckleberry Finn the strongest book which has appeared in our language in its decade" ("American Fiction Again," *Cosmopolitan* 12.5 [March 1892]: 638). A letter from Clemens to Franklin G. Whitmore (Munich, 3 July 1893) alluded to a letter from Stevenson to Clemens (MTP). "What was said of Stevenson would apply to her," Clemens wrote of Susy Clemens in January 1897 in London: "A soul of flame in a body of gauze" (NB 39, TS p. 60). In Chapter 7 of *Following the Equator* (1897) Mark Twain quoted Stevenson's directions to Arthur Conan Doyle and J. M. Barrie for finding Samoa: "You go to America, cross the continent to San Francisco, and then it's the second turning to the left." Carlyle Smythe remarked in 1898 that Clemens "is a thorough admirer of Stevenson" ("The Real 'Mark Twain,'" p. 31). "Louis Stevenson—Submerged Fame," Clemens wrote in Notebook 48 (1907), TS p. 15. In 1909 Clemens jotted a note about Stevenson's religion of kindness: "He is evidently as ignorant as a priest or a Bible—or a god" (see the Catalog entry for W. J. Dawson [co-ed], *The Great English Letter-Writers*). The Twain-Stevenson connections deserve more attention than they have received, but an excellent introduction to this topic was made by Leland Krauth in his *Mark Twain & Company: Six Literary Relations* (Athens: University of Georgia Press, 2003).
———. *Kidnapped; Being Memoirs of the Adventures of David Balfour in the Year 1751* (novel, published in 1886).
"Prince Otto, by author of Kidnapped," Clemens wrote in September 1886 (NB 26, *N&J* 3: 253). "Stephenson [*sic*] (Kidnapped)," he noted in March 1888, listing authors and his opinions of them; the reference seems favorable (NB 27, *N&J* 3: 379). In a letter of 15–17 April 1888 inviting Stevenson to visit Hartford, Clemens expressed his willingness to travel to the St. Stephens Hotel to "see you & thank you for writing Kidnapped & Treasure Island. . . . Those two great books! how we bathed in them, last summer, & refreshed our spirits" (John Howell Papers, Silverado Museum, St. Helena, California, PH in MTP). Clemens made a memorandum about Stevenson's plan to stay from 19 to 26 April 1888 at "St. Stephen's Hotel East 11th" (Notebook 27, *N&J* 3: 301).
———. *The Letters of Robert Louis Stevenson to His Family and Friends.* Ed. by (Sir) Sidney Colvin (1845–1927). 2 vols. New York: Charles Scribner's Sons, 1899.
  Inscription: inscribed, "Susan Crane/Quarry Farm".
  Catalog: Ball 2016 inventory, red cloth, gold lettering, gilt top edges, good condition, signed by Susan Crane.
  Location: Quarry Farm library shelves, under the supervision of the Mark Twain Archive, Elmira College, Elmira, New York.
These *Letters* were available to Clemens during his remaining visits to Quarry Farm in Elmira.
———. *A Lowden Sabbath Morn.* Illustrated by A[lexander]. S[tuart]. Boyd (1854–1930). Green cloth, gilt stamped. London: Chatto & Windus, 1898. 125 pp.
  Inscription: inscribed by Clemens in black ink "To Livy/ on her next birthday./ SL Clemens/ Kaltenleutgeben [Austria], August '98."
  Catalogs: ListABP (1910), "A Lowden Sabbath Morn (inscription by M. T.), Stevenson"; "Retz Appraisal" (1944),

p. 11, valued at $10.

Location: Mark Twain Papers, Bancroft Library, University of California, Berkeley.

Copy examined: Olivia Clemens's copy, unmarked.

Stevenson's poetic picture of Sunday morning in a rural Scottish parish is so powerfully evocative as to utterly transcend the dialect spellings.

———. *The Pocket R. L. S.; Being Favourite Passages from the Works of Stevenson*. Marbled covers, leather spine. London: Chatto & Windus, 1904. 217 pp.

Inscription: the front flyleaf contains a foreign-language inscription of two lines.

Marginalia: passages have been marked with vertical pencil lines on pages 57, 81, 89, 100, 122, 137, 140 (beside "Words are for communication, not for judgment"), 144, 145, 146, 148, 158, 161 (the word "steadfast" is underscored in line 7), and 197. Someone other than Clemens—probably Clara Clemens—listed book titles on the rear flyleaves in pencil; these include Blase de Bury, *The Spiritualization of Thought in France*; Ernst Haeckel, *The Wonders of Life*; Jean de La Bruyère, *Characters*; and Charles Wagner, *L'Ame des Choses*. The pencil markings in the text resemble Clara's, too.

Provenance: Antenne-Dorrance Collection, Rice Lake, Wisconsin.

Location: Mark Twain Archive, Gannett-Tripp Learning Center, Elmira College, Elmira, New York.

Copy examined: Clemens's (and Clara Clemens's) copy. Examined on 28 May 2015.

The Pocket R. L. S. compiles passages from Stevenson's poetry, stories, novels, and nonfiction writings. An index at the rear supplies the sources of these excerpts.

———. *Prayers Written at Vailima*. Introduction by Mrs. [Fanny (Van de Grift) Osbourne Stevenson, 1840–1914]. Calf, gold stamped, top edge gilt, hinges loose. New York, 1904.

Inscription: "Yrs. Truly Mark Twain". This is a very odd inscription. Clemens never signed his own library copies in this manner. Clemens genuinely admired and was knowledgeable about Stevenson's writings, but skepticism seems warranted about the lack of knowledge about the book's provenance and such an uncharacteristic inscription.

Catalog: Second Life Books, Lanesborough, Massachusetts, Catalog No. 47 (1984), item L, priced at $450.

Source: Kevin Mac Donnell and another rare book specialist examined the inscription in this book and became convinced that it is a forgery. Among other problems with the signature, this autograph was not Clemens's customary way of either conferring gifts or designating his own library books.

———. *Prince Otto: A Romance* (novel, published in 1885).

"Prince Otto, by the author of Kidnapped," reads a Clemens memorandum (Notebook 26 [September 1886], NB 26, *N&J* 3: 253). In the Indian Ocean on 8 January 1896, Clemens recorded: "On this voyage I have read a number of novels. Prince Otto—full of brilliances, of course—plenty of exquisite phrasing—an easy-flowing tale, but—well, my sympathies were not with any of the people in it. I did not care whether any of them prospered or not. There was a fault somewhere; it could have been in me" (NB 37, TS p. 3).

———. *The Strange Case of Dr. Jekyll and Mr. Hyde* (novel, published in 1886).

Stevenson's novel, along with Edgar Allan Poe's short story "William Wilson" (1839), naturally interested Mark Twain, a writer fascinated by instances of doubleness and twin identities. Angelo and Luigi of *Those Extraordinary Twins* (1894) were two of Twain's best-known creations in this vein. In Notebook 40 (January 1898) Twain mused in London about the resemblances in Stevenson's tale to his own story of 1876, "Concerning the Recent Carnival of Crime in Connecticut": "Presently Stevenson published Dr. Jekyll & Mr. Hyde. That was nearer the thing. J & H were the dual persons in one body—quite distinct in nature & character; & presumably each with *a conscience of its own*. Nearer, yes, but not near enough" (TS p. 2). Twain went on to object to Jekyll's and Hyde's knowing each other: "Stevenson was wrong, for the two persons in a man are wholly unknown to each other & can never in this world communicate with each other in any way" (TS p. 3). Among the characters in Twain's posthumously published writings, Harry, the twin brother with a "sound good heart" and Allen, his "temptation-ridden irreclaimable lost sheep" brother, exemplify dual personalities in "Which Was It?" (written 1899–1903, *WWD?*, p. 264). Following Olivia Clemens's death in 1904, Clemens reflected in Notebook 47: "God, so atrocious in the Old Testament, so attractive in the New—the Jekyll & Hyde of sacred fiction romance. Stevenson plagiarized it?" (TS p. 18). In Chapter 25 of "No. 44, The Mysterious Stranger" (written between 1902 and 1908), August Feldner comes to a terrible observation that echoes Poe's "William Wilson" (1839) as well as Stevenson's novel: "Good heavens! In trying to ruin the Duplicate, I had only ruined myself" (*MSM*, p. 353). See also the Catalog entry for Edgar Janes Bliss' *The Peril of Oliver Sargent*.

———. *Travels with a Donkey in the Cévennes* (travel narrative, published in 1879).

Cévennes is a mountainous region in southern France. Mark Twain visited a Trappist monastery in Natal in April 1896; subsequently he noted: "For the Trappists draw on Louis Stephenson's [sic] Travels with a Donkey in the Cevennes" (NB 38 [26 June 1896, Grahamstown, South Africa], TS p. 54). In November 1897 Olivia Clemens wrote to Clemens's English publisher, Chatto & Windus, to request "Louis Stevenson's 'Travels with a Donkey' and 'An Inland Voyage'" (Berg, NYPL).

———. *Treasure Island* (novel, published in 1883).

In 1888 Clemens wrote to Stevenson to express his desire to "see you & thank you for writing Kidnapped & Treasure Island. . . . Those two great books! how we bathed in them, last summer, & refreshed our spirits" (SLC to Stevenson, Hartford, 15–17 April 1888, John Howell Papers, Silverado Museum, St. Helena, California, PH in MTP). One wonders if Twain noticed how much young Jim Hawkins's close call—when he falls asleep in an apple barrel and overhears the pirates plotting—resembles Chapter 31 of Twain's earlier *The Adventures of Tom Sawyer* (1876), in which Tom Sawyer and Huckleberry Finn, hiding in the attic of the haunted house, become terrified as Injun Joe starts up the stairs to see if anyone has overheard them, much as one of Stevenson's pirates begins to reach for an apple where Jim Hawkins is hiding.

_____ and LLOYD OSBOURNE (1868–1947). *The Wrecker*. First edition. London: Cassell & Co., 1892. 427 pp. [Edition conjectured. The novel had appeared serially in *Scribner's Magazine* from August 1891 to July 1892.]

An international novel with episodes in Paris, Edinburgh, and San Francisco, *The Wrecker* largely describes daring salvage operations at sea. In a newspaper interview published in Australia in 1895, the reporter testified that "as regards Robert Louis Stevenson's books, Mr. Clemens says that he is a very great favorite in America. He had read *The Wrecker*—which depicts the commercial and social life of San Francisco in such daring colors—but so long ago that he had almost forgotten it, but he remembered that part especially." Clemens added that "a man often oversteps the limits of probability in describing national characteristics," but that "Stevenson was a great, a very great writer" (Louis Becke [presumably the interviewer], "Mark Twain: A Talk about His Books," Sydney *Evening News*, 21 September 1895, Supplement p. 3, reprinted in *Mark Twain: The Complete Interviews*, ed. Gary Scharnhorst, p. 215).

Rebecca Hooker, "Additions to the Mark Twain Library," *American Literary Realism* 38.3 (Spring 2006): 276.

_____ and LLOYD OSBOURNE (1868–1947). *The Wrong Box*. New York: Charles Scribner's Sons, 1889. 244 pp.

Marginalia: the figure "3,501,249" is written in pencil on page 43, possibly by Clemens; "commence" is changed to "commune" in pencil by Clemens on page 187; "of" is inserted between the words "disposing them," in pencil, probably by Clemens, on page 199. Page 29 is turned down.

Location: Mark Twain Library, Redding, Connecticut.

Copy examined: Clemens's copy. Has the red ink Mark Twain Library accession number "2587". Examined in 1970 and again in June 1982.

The Wrong Box, a darkly humorous novel about men trying to outlive each other to collect a tontine, was one of several works Stevenson wrote with his stepson Osbourne.

STEWART, CHARLES DAVID (1868–1960). *The Fugitive Blacksmith*. New York: Century Co., 1905. 321 pp.

Inscription: the front cover is embossed in gold letters: "SAMUEL L. CLEMENS".

Provenance: contains the bookstamp and traces of a charge-slip jacket of the Mark Twain Library, Redding, Connecticut.

Catalog: *Mott 1952*, item #86, $3.50.

Location: Mark Twain House and Museum, Hartford, Connecticut. Donated anonymously in 1963.

Copy examined: Clemens's copy, unmarked. Examined in August 1987.

William W. Ellsworth of the Century Company wrote to Clemens on 4 March 1905: "Have you read 'The Fugitive Blacksmith' yet? Do, if you haven't. You see the N. Y. Evening Post likens it to some of your work. We sent you a copy some time ago" (MTP). Ellsworth enclosed a clipping from the New York *Evening Post*; that review praised Stewart's first book, the story of a blacksmith wrongly accused of murder whose flight takes him along the Mississippi River in the region of Memphis. The *Evening Post* singled out Finerty, keeper of a sandhouse and coal bunker in the Memphis railyards, as a character

who speaks a convincing dialect. It is presumably a mere coincidence that Stewart chose the same title for his fictional work as James W. C. Pennington's much earlier *The Fugitive Blacksmith; or, Events in the History of James W. C. Pennington . . . Formerly a Slave in the State of Maryland* (1849).

_____. *Partners of Providence*. Illustrated by C[harles]. J[ay]. Taylor (1855–1929). New York: Century Co. 1907. 538 pp.

William W. Ellsworth of the Century Company ruefully recalled in his memoirs, *A Golden Age of Authors: A Publisher's Recollection* (Boston: Houghton Mifflin Co., 1919), that in Stewart's second novel, "'Partners of Providence,' he utilized his experience on the river itself, and the book has always seemed to me a companion volume to Mark Twain's 'Life on the Mississippi.' When 'Partners of Providence' came out [in March 1907] I sent a copy to Mark Twain, but he never acknowledged it or spoke of it" (p. 196). Clemens seldom applauded works that seemed to emulate his life and writings, and very likely Stewart's novel came a little too close to Clemens's river memories for comfort. Stewart had dropped out of school, served as a crew member on Mississippi and Missouri River steamboats, worked as a ranch hand in Texas, and, in 1907, moved to a town near Hartford, Connecticut. His *Partners of Providence* was a vernacular narrative related by a boy only fourteen years old about the adventures he had when he was thirteen on the Mississippi and Missouri Rivers. C. J. Taylor's well-executed drawings throughout the volume blended the styles of E. W. Kemble and A. B. Frost.

STEWART, CHARLES SAMUEL (1795–1870). *Private Journal of a Voyage to the Pacific Ocean and Residence at the Sandwich Islands, in the Years 1822, 1823, 1824, and 1825*. Intro. by William Ellis (1794–1872). Second edition. New York: John P. Haven, 1828. 406 pp.

Clemens listed Stewart's book on the rear cover of James J. Jarves's *History of the Hawaiian or Sandwich Islands* (*N&J* 1: 105).

STEWART, JAMES E. (b. 1843). "Farewell, Annie darling" (minstrel song, published in 1872).

On 31 May 1876 Mark Twain gave a reading at the Asylum Hill Congregational Church. The audience was also entertained by vocalists who sang "Farewell, Annie Darling" (Andrews, *Nook Farm* [1950], p. 50). Stewart, a white Detroit, Michigan musician, was a prolific composer and lyricist of songs, many of them sentimental, for the touring minstrel troupes. His pieces included "I want to see the old home," "Close the shutters, Willie's dead," "Ella Ree" (published in 1880), and "Only to see her face again."

_____. "Mary's gone with a Coon" (minstrel song, published in 1880).

Clemens heard two African American cabin hands sing "Mary's gone away wid de coon"—a racially derogatory song considered comical in that era—aboard the *City of Baton Rouge* in 1882 (NB 21, *N&J* 2: 562). The lyrics express an African American father's disappointment in his daughter's choice of a mate. Jo Dee Benussi identified this piece as one of the many minstrel pieces composed by James E. Stewart (Benussi to Alan Gribben, email, 6 July 2006). Benussi learned that it was popularized by Billy Kersands (c. 1842–1915), an African American singer, dancer, comedian, and acrobat who had great success in black minstrel shows. Charles Dudley Warner witnessed a much-applauded public performance of this song by a formerly enslaved African American woman before a mixed audience in the South (*On Horseback: A Tour in Virginia, North Carolina and Tennessee* [1888]). The song title vaguely occurred to Mark Twain in 1905 when writing a fragmentary manuscript, "Three Thousand Years among the Microbes"; the cholera germ-narrator belts out his "Sally [*sic*] and the Coon-song," but it quickly wears out its welcome (*WWD?*, p. 462).

Stewart, James M[onroe] (fl. 1870s-1880s). *Legend of the Castle of Drachenfels.* Author's proofs. Washington, D.C.: C. P. Farrell, 1881. 100 pp. Paperbound.

Source: MTLAcc, entry #2098, volume donated from Clemens's library by Clara Clemens Gabrilowitsch in 1910.

Clemens was asked to look over this volume of poetry written by a friend of Robert G. Ingersoll named James M. Stewart. Clemens wrote to Ingersoll from Elmira on 10 August 1881, explaining that he found nothing to say to Stewart, "further than to thank him for his courtesy in sending me his book. I am not bold enough to express an opinion about it, for I never read poetry, & a criticism from me would be a thing which I should laugh at, myself" (TS in MTP). (This is a pose Clemens often adopted when pressed about his tastes in *belles-lettres*.) Only Clemens's admiration for Ingersoll must have checked him from giving a more candid opinion of stanzas such as this one on page 17 of Stewart's eventually published 112-page book: "When the minstrels sing of the 'good old time,[']/We love the tune and endure the rhyme;/But the claim is a canting hypocrisy—/Like a proud but decayed aristocracy./The phrase is a humbug,—a lie per se,/And herein do history and I agree" (*Roland and Hildegarde, A Legend of the Castle of Drachenfels, in Humorous Verse; and Other Poems* [Baltimore, Maryland: Commercial Printing House, 1884]. Stewart would also publish a melodrama, *Disenchanted* (1889).

Stewart, Virgil A. (1809–1854), pseud. "Augustus Q. Walton." *A History of the Detection, Conviction, Life and Designs of John A. Murel [sic], The Great Western Land Pirate. . . . To Which is Added, a Biographical Sketch of Mr. Virgil A. Stewart.* Athens, Tennessee: Printed at the Journal Office; repr. by G. White, 1835. 75 pp. [Reprinted in Cincinnati, Ohio in the mid-1850s.]

While Clemens was working for Wrightson's printing shop in Cincinnati in 1856 and 1857 the firm reprinted Stewart's book under his pseudonym, "Augustus Q. Walton" (see William Baker, "Mark Twain in Cincinnati: A Mystery Most Compelling," *American Literary Realism* 12.2 [Autumn 1979]: 305). In *The Adventures of Tom Sawyer* (1876), Tom and Huck recover more than $12,000 buried by "Murrel's gang" (Chapters 26 and 34). One entire paragraph in Virgil A. Stewart's book (a portion of John A. Murrell's confession to Stewart) accords exactly with Twain's quotation in Chapter 29 of *Life on the Mississippi* (1883) of "a now forgotten book which was published half a century ago." But see the Catalog entry for Marryat's *A Diary in America* (1840), which presents a complication; Twain's direct source was Marryat's *Diary*, and Marryat was quoting from and paraphrasing Stewart. Also see the

Catalog entry for H. R. Howard (comp.), *The History of Virgil A. Stewart* (1836). Twain's notes for "Tom Sawyer's Conspiracy" (written 1897–1902) mention "Murrel's gang" (*HH&T*, p. 385). Renamed "Burrell's Gang," these same desperadoes figure in the fears of the townspeople in Chapter 8 of Twain's resulting novella (*HH&T*, pp. 156 n. 11, 229–230). The exploits of John Andrews Murrell (1806–1844) seem to have been exaggerated in Stewart's account.

Ganzel, "Samuel Clemens and Captain Marryat" (1962); Edwin A. Miles, "The Mississippi Slave Insurrection Scare of 1835," *Journal of Negro History* 42.1 (January 1957): 48–60; Lee Sandlin, *Wicked River: The Mississippi When It Last Ran Wild* (New York: Pantheon Books, 2010), pp. 142–147, 150, 156, 160–168, 171, and 176; Michael Butter, *Plots, Designs, and Schemes: American Conspiracy Theories from the Puritans to the Present* (Berlin: Walter de Gruyter GmbH, 2014), pp. 201–209.

Stewart, William Frank. *Pleasant Hours in an Eventful Life.* San Francisco: John H. Carmany & Co., 1869. 94 pp.

Edgar M. Branch and Robert H. Hirst informed me that Mark Twain praised this book in an unsigned review in the 16 October 1869 issue of the Buffalo *Express*: "His little volume of 'Spare Hours' [*sic*] contains a number of short poems that are all well conceived and happily rendered. We are indebted to the author for a copy, he being his own publisher. His 'Past Pliocene,' 'The Great Cedar Tree,' 'Saltillo,' and 'The Ballad of Sir John Franklin,' are all good; but, as might have been expected, he is most at home and most felicitous on his heart's specialty, the earthquake." Twain then quotes a stanza from "Temblor Muy Terrible" that begins and ends with the ominous line, "There's trouble in the land!" Jo Dee Benussi, citing Chapter 8 of Eugene Taylor Sawyer's *History of Santa Clara County, California, with Biographical Sketches of the Leading Men and Women of the County* (Los Angeles: Historic Record Co., 1922) turned up the fact that Twain's favorable review of Stewart's poetry was an effort to mollify this acquaintance he had known in Virginia City, Nevada (and later in San Jose, California in 1866) because Twain had mocked him in the Buffalo *Express* for purporting to be an expert on earthquakes (Benussi to Gribben, email 12 June 2006). Actually Stewart was prescient in repeatedly warning that the brick buildings in downtown San Francisco would topple over when a truly large earthquake struck. Stewart led a peripatetic life, later moving back to Nevada, serving in the state senate from 1876 until 1880, and then becoming the state mineralogist. According to published reports he was active as late as 1895.

Stiles, Charles Wardell (1867–1941).

Mark Twain mentions this authority on medicine and health in Letter 7, "Letters from the Earth" (*LE*, p. 34). Stiles, who had obtained his Ph.D. degree at Leipzig, served for thirty years as chief of the Division of Zoology at the forerunner of the National Institute of Health. He also became the medical director of the United States Public Health Service.

Still, William (1821–1902). *The Underground Rail Road. A Record of Facts, Authentic Narratives, Letters, &c., Narrating the Hardships, Hair-breadth Escapes, and Death Struggles of*

the Slaves in Their Efforts for Freedom, as Related by Themselves and Others, or Witnessed by the Author; Together with Sketches of Some of the Largest Shareholders, and Most Liberal Aiders and Advisers, of the Road. Illus. "Sold Only by Subscription." First edition. Original quarter morocco and mottled boards, gilt. Philadelphia: Porter & Coates, Publishers, 1872. 780 pp. 70 engravings.

> **Inscription:** a gold and blue library bookplate reads, "J. Langdon's Family Library No. 384." Jervis Langdon's family was active in the abolitionist cause and co-founded the Park Church in Elmira, New York when the congregation of the Presbyterian Church in Elmira split over this issue. No marginalia are visible, though page 289 has a corner folded down, perhaps by accident. An old piece of paper marks page 176 where a story about Elmira's role in the underground railroad is recounted.

> **Provenance:** originally in the Langdon family library, to which Clemens had access. The book appears to have been much handled; the original spine survives only in fragments and the front cover was detached and has been rebacked.

> **Location:** collection of Kevin Mac Donnell, Austin, Texas (Mac Donnell to Alan Gribben, 29 November 2011). Obtained from members of the Langdon family.

> Elmira, New York served as an important stop on the Underground Railroad. Mark Twain's "A True Story, Repeated Word for Word as I Heard It" (1874) reflected his awareness of the pain inflicted by the separation of enslaved families and the joy resulting from occasional successes in reuniting family members.

————. *The Underground Rail Road: A Record of Facts, Authentic Narratives, Letters, &c., Narrating the Hardships, Hair-breadth Escapes, and Death Struggles of the Slaves in Their Efforts for Freedom, as Related by Themselves and Others, or Witnessed by the Author; Together with Sketches of Some of the Largest Shareholders, and Most Liberal Aiders and Advisers, of the Road.* Illustrated and with an engraved frontispiece portrait of the author. Revised edition. Original pebbled maroon cloth, covers elaborately gilt, maroon endpapers, gilt edges, half maroon morocco slipcase. Philadelphia: William Still, 1883. 780 pp.

> **Marginalia:** Clemens recorded an anecdote running to 154 words in black ink on the front free flyleaf: "Mrs. Luckett was a slave in Richmond, with a daughter 3 years old. Her brother, Jones, an escaped slave, lived in Elmira (1844). He cut two duplicate hearts out of pink paper, & wrote on one, 'When you see this again, you will know.' No other word accompanied it. After a while a white man went [to] Richmond with the other heart, called on the woman's mistress on some pretext which brought in the slaves: Mrs. L. saw & recognized the duplicate heart; she escaped, with her child in the night, joined the man at a place appointed, (Annapolis,) & thence got through safely to Elmira. She lives in Canada, now (whither she had to flee when the fugitive slave law was passed (1850,) & the child is also married & lives in Binghamton, N. Y. (1884.) This account given by Mother [Olivia Lewis Langdon, Clemens's mother-in-law], who knew the several parties." Clemens made numerous marginal black-ink markings (but no comments) in the story of Seth Concklin (pages 24–38), which bears some resemblances to Clemens's earlier "A True Story, Repeated Word for Word as I Heard

It" (1874). He did not annotate the book beyond page 38. Elmira, New York is mentioned on page 393.

> **Catalogs:** ListABP (1910), "Underground Railroad, Still"; *C1951*, #2a, $75; *Sotheby's 2003*, #238, $21,000; The 19th Century Shop, Baltimore, Maryland, Catalogue 104 (2006), "Original maroon cloth gilt-extra, all edges gilt. . . . A lengthy anecdote in his hand about an escaped slave on the front flyleaf. . . . Full-page, 146-word anecdote in Twain's handwriting," priced at $45,000.

> **Provenance:** displays the shelfmark of Clara Clemens Gabrilowitsch's private library in Detroit. Donated to the Carrie Estelle Doheny Collection, St. John's Seminary, Camarillo, California, by Mrs. Doheny in 1951 after she purchased the volume for $87 from Maxwell Hunley Rare Books of Beverly Hills. Auctioned by Christie's for $4,180 on 21 February 1989 (lot 1768) on behalf of St. John's Seminary. Subsequently in the collection of Nick Karanovich, Fort Wayne, Indiana.

> **Location:** currently unknown.

> **Copy examined:** Clemens's copy, at St. John's Seminary in 1970. Has the bookplate of "Estelle Doheny." A photocopy of Clemens's flyleaf narrative is in the Mark Twain Papers, Bancroft Library, University of California at Berkeley, obtained from St. John's Seminary.

> William Still was born free, but his parents had known the hazards of escape from enslavement and he himself was deeply involved in the Underground Railroad activities in the Philadelphia area. Clemens's holograph note indicates his awareness that merely escaping to a "free" state would not guarantee an enslaved person's safety after the passage of the Fugitive Slave Act in 1850.

STILLSON, FLORENCE GEORGEANNA MERCHANT (1856–1890). *Doris: A Story of 1778.* Blue cloth. Danbury, Connecticut: Published for Private Circulation, [1891]. 96 pp.

> **Inscriptions:** the second front flyleaf is inscribed in pencil, "Mrs. Henry H. Barroll [?]/343 Main St./Danbury/ Conn." The title page is inscribed in blue ink, "Gift of Elsie Hill/1316." On the verso of the title page, written in the same blue ink: "Forence Stillson born in Redding 1856".

> **Copy examined:** an unmarked copy belonging to a member of the Hill family, who donated many books to the Mark Twain Library. This book had been added to the Clemens collection when I revisited Redding in June 1982, and I recommended to the staff that it be removed and shelved elsewhere. It clearly had no connection with Clemens or his family.

STINDE, JULIUS ERNST WILHELM (1841–1905). *Die Familie Buchholz. Aus dem Leben der Hauptstadt [The Buchholz Family. From the Life of the Capital].* Berlin: Freund & Jeckel, 1886. 210 pp. Paperbound.

> **Source:** MTLAcc, entry #393, volume donated by Clemens.

STIRNER, MAX (1806–1856), born Johann Kaspar Schmidt. *The Ego and His Own.* Preface by James L. Walker (1845–1904). Translated from the German by Steven T[racy]. Byington (1868–1957). New York: Benjamin R. Tucker, 1907. 506 pp. [This was the first English edition of Stirner's book, originally published in 1844.]

> The German philosopher Stirner's work was an early exposition of ideas now categorized as nihilism, individual anarchism, and existentialism. "I am sending you by post a complimentary copy of 'The Ego and His Own,'

by Max Steiner [*sic*]. Whatever you, Mr. Clemens, may think of the book, I am sure that pp. 395–405 will commend themselves to Mark Twain" (Benjamin R. Tucker to SLC, 7 April 1907, MTP). In the specified pages Stirner examined the relative morality inherent in such slippery concepts as "truth" or "lying." He cited Martin Luther among historical examples. Clemens's dictated reply, written on the verso of Tucker's letter, is in Josephine Hobby's shorthand and is undecipherable. Isabel V. Lyon noted on the letter: "Answd Apr 24, '07." Tucker would move to France shortly after his uninsured New York City bookshop burned in 1908. James L. Walker, the American who wrote the Preface, was known as a radical egoist anarchist.

STOCKTON, FRANK RICHARD (1834–1902). *A Bicycle of Cathay. A Novel.* Illustrated by Orson [Byron] Lowell (1871–1956). New York and London: Harper & Brothers, 1900. 239 pp.

> While this novel was being serialized in *Harper's Magazine*, Clemens joked on 26 September 1900: "Better 60 days of Dollis/Than a cycle of Cathay" (NB 43, TS p. 26). Clemens was enjoying an extended vacation in Dollis Hill House, a historic residence in a suburb north of London. Both Stockton and Clemens were punning on a line uttered by the speaker in Alfred Lord Tennyson's dramatic monologue, "Locksley Hall" (1842), who is bitter over an unrequited love: "Better fifty years of Europe than a cycle of Cathay." (Kevin J. Hayes—"Mark Twain at Home and Abroad," *Canadian Review of American Studies* 47.3 (2017): 430—noticed this allusion.)

———. "Mark Twain and His Recent Works," *Forum* 15 (August 1893): 673–679. Quite possibly Clemens read this complimentary article, which declared that "his faculty and range of expression are wonderful," but "it is his courage which gives to his expressions, as well as his inventions, their force and unique effect" (p. 674).

> Jensen, "Mark Twain's Comments on Books and Authors" (1964), p. 49.

———. *Mrs. Cliff's Yacht.* New York: Charles Scribner's Sons, 1896. 314 pp.

> **Catalog:** Ball 2016 inventory, green cloth, gold lettering, pirate-themed cover design by Margaret Neilson Armstrong (1867–1944) in black and gold ink, fair condition.
> **Location:** Quarry Farm library shelves, under the supervision of the Mark Twain Archive, Elmira College, Elmira, New York.
> After a widow inherits money she is persuaded to purchase a yacht and take a cruise with some ministers. This novel was available to Clemens during his few remaining visits to Quarry Farm in Elmira.

———. *Rudder Grange.* New York: Charles Scribner's Sons, 1904. 292 pp.

> **Source:** MTLAcc, entry #270, volume donated by Clemens.
> A married couple finds adventures and happiness in a renovated canal boat they call *Rudder Grange*.

———. *Stockton's Stories. Second Series. The Christmas Wreck and Other Stories.* New York: Charles Scribner's Sons, 1886. 242 pp.

> This volume collected Stockton's amusing "The Remarkable Wreck of the 'Thomas Hyke'" (1884), which would appear in *Mark Twain's Library of Humor* (1888). In January 1888 Clemens mentioned Stockton as a writer who was

protected by his publisher in matters of copyright and royalties (NB 27, *N&J* 3: 363). He repeated this comment about Stockton's good fortune in an unpublished essay he wrote in January 1888, "Concerning the British Pirates" (ms. offered for sale in "Holiday Miscellany," Heritage Book Shop, Catalog 176 [1989], item #232); there he listed Stockton among the authors of "choice and valuable literature" published by *The Century*. Clemens referred to Stockton again in October 1889 (NB 29, *N&J* 3: 525). Twain's "My Boyhood Dreams" (1900) alludes to Stockton in a context indicating esteem and affection; he jokingly claims that Stockton originally hoped to be a barkeeper (MS in DV390, MTP, written in September 1899 in Sanna, Sweden).

STODDARD, CHARLES WARREN (1843–1909). *A Cruise Under the Crescent; From Suez to San Marco.* Chicago: Rand, McNally & Co., 1898. 358 pp.

> On 1 February 1875 Clemens wrote to Stoddard from Hartford: "I have cut your delightful article about San Marco out of a New York paper (Joe Twichell saw it & brought it home to me with loud admiration) & sent it to Howells. It is too bad to fool away such good literature in a perishable daily journal" (*MTL*, p. 249; *MTLet* 6: 364). The next month Clemens tried to encourage Stoddard, writing, "I feel persuaded that your book would sell, by subscription. When you've got it ready, call here on one of your journeys, & I think we'll find a Hartford publisher" ("Mark Twain," Heritage Bookshop, Los Angeles, 1997, item #126). Howells, however, faulted Stoddard's newspaper piece, and Clemens replied: "*I* didn't enjoy his *gush*, but I thought a lot of his similes were ever so vivid & good" (SLC to WDH, Hartford, 10 February 1875, *MTHL*, p. 65). Stoddard eventually expanded his book about a Mediterranean Sea cruise until it included impressions of Athens, Damascus, Jerusalem, and other sites in the Holy Land.

———. *Exits and Entrances: A Book of Essays and Sketches.* Boston: Lothrop Publishing Co., [1903]. 375 pp.

> In November 1902 Clemens assisted Stoddard in obtaining the advance that the Lothrop Publishing Company had paid to Stoddard's unscrupulous literary agent (*MTHL*, pp. 750–755). Stoddard's book discussed Joaquin Miller, Robert Louis Stevenson, Bret Harte, and other literary figures. Stoddard had attended a dinner with the Kiplings and Clemens in New York City on 7 April 1893 (NB 33, TS p. 6). Around 1907 Clemens made a note: "Dolby—C. W. Stoddard" (NB 48, TS p 2). George Dolby (1831–1900) was an English theatrical agent who managed Mark Twain's reading tour.

———. *The Lepers of Molokai.* Notre Dame, Indiana: Ave Maria Press, [cop. 1885]. 80 pp.

> Stoddard described the labors of Joseph Damien de Veuster (1840–1889), known as "Father Damien," who worked at the Kalaupapa leper colony on the island of Molokai. On 16 March 1886 Clemens wrote to Stoddard from Hartford: "It is your best piece of work; & well nigh faultlessly done. And what a sublime hero is your priest the good father"; Clemens urged Stoddard to "write the case of [Bill] Ragsdale" (ALS in Scripps College Library). William Phileppus Ragsdale (c. 1837–1877) had impressed Clemens greatly when he visited Honolulu in

1866 (see *Mark Twain's Letters from Hawaii*, ed. A. Grove Day [Honolulu: University Press of Hawaii, 1966], pp. 110–111). In 1873 Ragsdale contracted leprosy and banished himself to the Kalaupapa colony, where he served as its superintendent.

———. *Poems.* Original blue cloth. San Francisco: A. Roman and Co., 1867. 123 pp.

Inscription: the front free endpaper is inscribed in black ink, "Mark Twain/with the love of his/faithful friend—/ Chas. Warren Stoddard." Following the inscription someone added in pencil, "Mary—". The latter hand may be Clemens's.

Location: Location: Albert and Shirley Small Special Collections Library, University of Virginia, Charlottesville, Virginia. Donated by Clifton Waller Barrett.

Copy examined: Clemens's copy.

Stoddard acted as Clemens's secretary in England in 1873. In 1876 Clemens sought political office for Stoddard, whom he termed one of the "stainless literary incapables" (SLC to WDH, Hartford, 21 September 1876, *MTHL*, p. 153). "O dear, dear, it is dreadful to be an unrecognized poet," Clemens remarked to Howells from Hartford on 24 October 1880, "How wise it was in Ch—W— Stoddard to take in his sign & go for some other calling while still young" (*MTHL*, p. 333).

———. *South-Sea Idyls.* Boston: James R. Osgood and Co., 1873. 354 pp.

"Charley Warren Stoddard made quite a name for himself with his South-Sea Idyl. He was here the other day" (SLC to Mrs. Mary Mason Fairbanks, 31 October 1877, *MTMF*, p. 211). Clemens went on in the letter to smile about the royalties Stoddard had earned on the book— only "six dollars" in the past two years.

STODDARD, JOHN L[AWSON]. (1850–1931). *John L. Stoddard's Lectures.* 10 vols. Boston: Balch Brothers Co., 1898. [Volume IX only: Lectures on Scotland, England, and London. Profusely illustrated with photographs of the sites Stoddard describes.]

Catalog: Ball 2016 inventory, green cloth, gold lettering.

Location: Quarry Farm library shelves, under the supervision of the Mark Twain Archive, Elmira College, Elmira, New York.

Clemens would have had access to this travel commentary at Quarry Farm.

STODDARD, RICHARD HENRY (1825–1903). "The Brahman's Son," *Harper's New Monthly Magazine* 73.437 (October 1886): 738–745.

Clemens got pulled into a small contretemps about the literary source for Stoddard's lengthy poem depicting a grief-stricken father who finds comfort in a mystical vision. On 18 October 1886 Clemens assured Edward H. House from Hartford: "No, sir, Stoddard didn't borrow 'The Brahman's Son' from your story." Clemens directed House instead to Lafcadio Hearn's *Stray Leaves from Strange Literature* (ALS in ASSSCL).

STODDARD, WILLIAM O[SBORN]. (1835–1925). *Inside the White House in War Times.* Illustrated by Dan[iel Carter] Beard (1850–1941). New York: Charles L. Webster & Co., 1890. 244 pp.

Clemens's publishing firm issued this book. Stoddard, who served as one of the secretaries assigned to President

Lincoln from 1861 until 1864, later became an author and inventor.

———. *In the Open: Stories of Outdoor Life.* Illus. New York: Harper & Brothers, 1908. 192 pp.

Source: MTLAcc, entry #411, volume donated by Clemens. There is a little bit of everything in this nature narrative, from fishing advice to an encounter with a bear.

———. *The Red Mustang, A Story of the Mexican Border.* Illus. New York: Harper & Brothers, 1890. 284 pp.

Source: MTLAcc, entry #416, volume donated by Clemens.

———. *Two Arrows: A Story of Red and White.* New York: Harper & Brothers, [cop. 1886]. 239 pp.

Source: MTLAcc, entry #1904, volume donated from Clemens's library by Clara Clemens Gabrilowitsch in 1910.

STOKER, BRAM (1847–1912). *Dracula.* Westminster: Archibald Constable and Co., 1897. 390 pp.

Inscription: the front free endpaper is inscribed in black ink, "Mark Twain/from/Bram Stoker/1 June 1897".

Marginalia: no markings, but page 11 is folded down. Leaves in the second half of the volume were unopened as recently as 1972, though they have since been cut apart.

Catalog: "Retz Appraisal" (1944), p. 11. Valued at $75.

Location: Mark Twain Papers, Bancroft Library, University of California at Berkeley.

Copy examined: Clemens's copy.

On 23 October 1897 Clemens instructed Chatto & Windus, the British publisher of his *More Tramps Abroad* (titled *Following the Equator* in the United States), to send "an early copy to . . . Bram Stoker" (*Sotheby's 2003*, #90). Stoker's *Dracula*, the Gothic novel about supernatural forces that overcome humans and make them predatory, issued in that same year, 1897. In Chapter 14 of Stoker's novel, Professor Van Helsing tells Dr. Seward that he "must believe in things that you cannot. Let me illustrate. I heard once of an American who so defined faith: 'that faculty which enables us to believe things which we know to be untrue.' For one, I follow that man." Mark Twain had affixed a humorous Pudd'nhead Wilson maxim as the epigraph for Chapter 12 of *Following the Equator* (1897): "There are those who scoff at the schoolboy, calling him frivolous and shallow. Yet it was the schoolboy who said 'Faith is believing what you know ain't so.'" In Twain's "The Chronicle of Young Satan," written between 1897 and 1900, Felix Brandt, who lived in Eseldorf, Austria, "had seen the great bat that sucks the blood from the necks of people while they are asleep, fanning them softly with its wings and so keeping them drowsy till they die" (*MSM*, p. 44).

See also the Catalog entry for H. Wachenhusen, *Vampyr. Novelle aus Bulgarien.*

———. *The Jewel of Seven Stars.* New York: Harper & Brothers, 1904. 311 pp.

Source: MTLAcc, entry #1310, volume donated by Clemens.

Stoker's supernatural thriller, his eighth novel, depicted the efforts to resurrect an ancient queen of Egypt.

———. *The Mystery of the Sea; A Novel.* Green cloth. New York: Doubleday, Page & Co., 1902. 498 pp.

Inscription: the front free endpaper is inscribed in black ink, "Mrs. Clemens/from Bram Stoker/22–3 [?]-02". The front pastedown endpaper is signed in black ink,

"Catharina [sic] Leary/ Reading [sic]/Conn."

Provenance: Antenne-Dorrance Collection, Rice Lake, Wisconsin.

Location: Mark Twain Archive, Gannett-Tripp Learning Center, Elmira College, Elmira, New York.

Copy examined: Olivia Clemens's copy, unmarked. Examined on 28 May 2015.

Stoker combined a supernatural mystery with a romance between an Englishman and an American heiress. A secret code, pirates, and a treasure hunt figured in the plot.

A story that Stoker once told Clemens stuck in his memory for years. "Bram Stoker's yarn about the Irish christening," Clemens noted in 1885 (NB 25, *N&J* 3: 195). Clemens would tell this anecdote in a speech on 14 May 1908 (*MTS1923*, p. 380; *MTSpk*, pp. 624–625): a clergyman christens an infant, praising his future potential ("greater than Caesar"), and then learns that the child's name is MaryAnne. In 1886 Clemens thought about using Stoker's story for an upcoming speech, but did not (Notebook 26, *N&J* 3: 268). Stoker's story "of the christening" again occurred to Clemens in November 1887 (NB 27, *N&J* 3: 353). On 25 December 1893, writing to Olivia Clemens from The Players Club, Clemens mentioned that he planned to "go to Mrs. Laffan's Xmas dinner this evening—where I shall meet Bram Stoker" (Bauman Rare Books, Holiday Catalog, December 2019). Stoker was one of the unfortunate investors in the Paige typesetter that Clemens promoted in 1894 (*MTHHR*, p. 40). "Write Bram Stoker about stock," Clemens reminded himself in January 1894 (NB 33, TS p. 46). (Stoker was an agent for Sir Henry Irving, who also invested in Clemens's machine.) In London Clemens dined "Sunday, Nov. 15 [1896]. At Bram Stoker's" (NB 39, TS p. 25). Clemens intended to present Stoker with a complimentary copy of *Following the Equator* (SLC to Chatto & Windus, Vienna, 23 October 1897, TS in MTP); Clemens made a memorandum to remind himself to give this volume to Stoker (NB 42, TS p. 74). In February 1898 Stoker consented to act as an agent for Mark Twain's dramatic works (NB 40, TS p. 12). Clemens consulted Stoker in September 1898 about staging Clemens's adaptation of Phiipp Langmann's *Bartel Turaser* (NB 40, TS p. 46). On 27 February 1902 Olivia Clemens listed Bram Stoker among the guests who had visited Riverdale since October 1901 (OLC's Diary, DV161, MTP).

STOKES, CAROLINE PHELPS (1854–1909), pseud. "A. B." *Travels of a Lady's Maid. By "A. B."* Boston: L. C. Page & Co., 1908. 336 pp.

Source: MTLAcc, entry #1050, volume donated by Clemens.

Stokes and her sister Olivia, wealthy through inheritance, lived together and were generous philanthropists to Christian churches and educational institutions for African Americans and Native Americans. Caroline based *Travels of a Lady's Maid* on her extensive travel journals; she died soon after her only novel saw print.

STOKES, FREDERICK ALEXANDER (1857–1939). *College Tramps: A Narrative of the Adventures of a Party of Yale Students During a Summer Vacation in Europe, with Knapsack and Alpenstock, and the Incidents of a Voyage to Rotterdam and Return, Taken in the Steerage.* Illus. New York: G. W. Carleton & Co.,

1880. 295 pp.

Stokes wrote to Mark Twain for advice about writing a travel book but went ahead and published his imitation of *The Innocents Abroad* before receiving Twain's response. On 17 April 1880 he sent Twain a complimentary copy "for your kindness and courtesy." Twain's *A Tramp Abroad* appeared in March 1880, too late to have influenced Stokes' *College Tramps*. Twain noted on Stokes's letter, "Not much of a book" (Rasmussen, ed., *DearMT*, pp. 69–70).

STONE, WITMER (1866–1939) and **WILLIAM EVETT CRAM** (1871–1947). *American Animals.* New York: Doubleday, Page & Co., 1904.

Catalog: Ball 2016 inventory, Nature Library, Vol. IV, from Quarry Farm, current location undetermined.

STORY, WILLIAM WETMORE (1819–1895). "Cleopatra" (poem, published in 1865 in *Blackwood's Magazine* [Edinburgh]).

Writing from New York City, Mark Twain slightly misquoted lines from the lengthy poem's fifth stanza ("I don't suppose I have quoted that right, because remembering verses is not my strong suit") in his letter of 19 May 1867 to the San Francisco *Alta California*. "It is good poetry, though, and carries well the idea of that impatient Egyptian wench, Cleopatra" (published on 30 June 1867, *MTTMB*, p. 196). The first line of "Cleopatra" was arresting: "Here, Charmian, take my bracelets." The poem's erotic imagery raised some eyebrows in the United States, but the sculptor, poet, and writer Story was an expatriate living in Italy by then. He had carved a marble statue of Cleopatra in 1858 that was much admired.

———. *Roba di Roma* . 2 vols. London: Chapman and Hall, 1863. Numerous reprintings and editions would follow.

Clemens read and wrote about this collection of essays on the history and culture of Rome while he was staying in Florence in October 1878: "Roba di Roma. Rome seems to be a great fair of shams, humbugs, & frauds. . . . Read the chapter 'Christmas' [actually titled "Holidays"]—& think of this Bambino rot existing in 19th century" (NB 17, *N&J* 2: 230). He made additional notes about superstition and religious gullibility. Possibly Clemens had borrowed a copy of the book, for in late October 1878, following his notes about Story's work, he wrote in Notebook 17: "Send to Chatto [& Windus, of London] for Roba di [sic] & Benvenuto" (*N&J* 2: 234). In Rome on 31 March or 1 April 1892 Clemens again wrote in his notebook: "Get Roba di Roma" (NB 31, TS p. 35). Clemens wrote to Charlotte Teller on Sunday, 17 June 1906, describing his indecision about how to pass some time in bed in Dublin, New Hampshire: "No—I think I will read. Roba di Roma; a good rainy-weather book" (Berg Collection, NYPL).

STOW, JOHN (1525–1605). *A Survey of London* (published in 1598 and again in 1603; later revised by the ecclesiastical historian John Strype (1643–1737), who corrected, updated, and enlarged the work in 1720).

On an undated sheet of paper Clemens recalled in pencil, probably between 1876 and 1880, a tour he made in London: "Nobody in town.—Bought [John] Timbs—[A. J. C. Hare's] Walks—[John] Stow<e>—Leigh Hunt, & a lot of other authorities & read about a thing, then went leisurely to see it" (DV 115, MS fragment, MTP). He mentioned Stow's *Survey of London* in his working notes for *The Prince and the Pauper* (1881) (DV115, MTP).

STOWE, CALVIN ELLIS (1802–1886). *Origin and History of the Books of the Bible, Both the Canonical and the Apocryphal, Designed to Show What the Bible Is Not, What It Is, and How to Use It.* Illus. Hartford: Hartford Publishing Co., 1867. 587 pp. [Edition conjectured; repr. in 1868 and 1869.]

In September 1886 Clemens noted that "Prof. Stowe says . . . [in] his 'History of the Books of the Bible' that a facsimile of no part of the *New Testament* (Vatican Bible) has ever been permitted to be taken"; Clemens reasoned that it would be a "good thing if we could get a scrap for the Pope's Life" (i.e., for Bernard O'Reilly's *Life of Leo XIII*, to be published by Charles L. Webster & Company 1887). Clemens read on to discover that "Stowe adds that (1867) Prof. Tischendorff [sic] was about to issue the Vatican B. parts of *both* Testaments to be in facsimile" (NB 26, N&J 3: 256). Contantin von Tischendorf (1815–1874) of Leipzig, Germany was a leading Biblical scholar.

STOWE, HARRIET ELIZABETH (BEECHER) (1811–1896). *Betty's Bright Idea. Also, Deacon Pitkin's Farm, and the First Christmas of New England.* Illus. New York: J. B. Ford & Co., 1876. 121 pp.

Inscription: (in brown ink) "Mrs. Samuel Clemens/from/H B Stowe". Clemens made penciled notes in the German language on the front endpaper: "Hat der Bauer das Bauer, oder gebte er es mit das Bund zu der Bund? Der Chor ist niel besser als das Chor. Der Erbe hat erhaltet das Erbe."

Location: Mark Twain Library, Redding, Connecticut.

Copy examined: Olivia Clemens's unmarked copy. Inspecting the book in June 1982, I noticed that the handwritten red ink accession number "2704" had replaced a deleted accession number, "2717".

————, pseud. "Christopher Crowfield." *The Chimney-Corner.* Boston, 1884.

Inscription: Clemens inscribed the front endpaper "Susie Clemens, Mch. 19, 1887."

Catalog: *Hunley 1958*, item #144, $5.

————. *A Dog's Mission; or, the Story of the Old Avery House. And Other Stories.* Illus. Contemporary half calf and marbled boards, gilt decorated spines, marbled endpapers, rubbed edges and corners. Boston: Houghton and Co., 1886. 131 pp.

Inscription: the front free endpaper has been removed, presumably because it bore a family inscription. The binding of this volume matches four other Stowe books that Clemens inscribed to Susy Clemens at Christmas in 1886.

Provenance: shelfmarks of Clara Clemens Gabrilowitsch's library numbering system during her Detroit years. Sold at the 1951 Hollywood auction as lot J41 but not listed in the hastily compiled sale sheet.

Catalog: "Property from the Library of Mark Twain," Butterfield & Butterfield, San Francisco, Sale 6613 (16 July 1997), lot 2707.

Location: Mark Twain House and Museum, Hartford, Connecticut.

Copy examined: Susy Clemens's unmarked copy, later in the possession of Clara Clemens. Viewed in Hartford in 1997.

This was one of Stowe's books set in Oldtown and featuring Sam Lawson. It evoked the New England of an earlier generation, in which every household owned a yellow dog and "your yellow dog had an important part to act in life, as much as any of his masters" (Ch. 3).

————. *Dred: A Tale of the Great Dismal Swamp.* Boston: Houghton, Mifflin and Co., 1885. 607 pp.

Inscription: inscribed in ink by Olivia Clemens on the front flyleaf, "Susy Clemens/Xmas, 1886."

Provenance: the title page displays the shelf markings of a catalog system employed by Clara Clemens Samossoud for her personal library during her years in Detroit. A label of the *C1951* auction appears on the front flyleaf.

Location: Mark Twain House and Museum, Hartford, Connecticut.

Copy examined: photocopies of the title page and the inscription, provided by Diana Royce, then Librarian of the Stowe-Day Memorial Library, on 3 October 1984. I examined the volume in person in August 1987 in Hartford. No marginalia are present.

Abigail Ann Hamblen, in "Uncle Tom and 'Nigger Jim': A Study in Contrasts and Similarities," *Mark Twain Journal* 11.3 (Fall 1961): 15, 17 n. 19, pointed out that Stowe depicts religious camp meetings in both *Uncle Tom's Cabin* (1852) and *Dred* (1856) that bear resemblances to the gathering in the woods that the King exploits in Chapter 20 of Twain's *Adventures of Huckleberry Finn* (1885). Judie Newman, in her introduction to an edition of *Dred: A Tale of the Great Dismal Swamp* (Edinburgh: Edinburgh University Press, 1998) and in "Was Tom White? Stowe's *Dred* and Twain's *Pudd'nhead Wilson*," *Soft Canons: American Women Writers and Masculine Tradition*, ed. Karen L. Kilcup (Iowa City: University of Iowa Press, 1999), pp. 67–81, discerned parallels with Twain's novel regarding racial identity. In editing a new edition of Twain's novel, Victor Fischer and Lin Salamo included Chapter 23 of *Dred* among the literary antecedents that possibly reminded Twain how religious camp-meetings were conducted (*HF* [2003], p. 550).

————. *Flowers and Fruit from the Writings of Harriet Beecher Stowe.* Comp. by Abbie H. Fairfield (1863–1942). Boston: Houghton, Mifflin and Co., 1888. 198 pp.

Inscription: the front free endpaper is inscribed in black ink, most likely by Olivia Clemens, "Clara L. Clemens/Xmas 1888,/Hartford".

Marginalia: vertical pencil marks or notes on pages 2, 3, 5, 6, 7, 8, ("Simply grand"), 9, 10, 11, 12 ("Simply grand"), 13 ("Simply grand"), and 14. The notes are not in Clemens's hand but some of the pencil markings might be.

Location: Mark Twain Library, Redding, Connecticut. Donated by Clemens (MTLAcc, entry #997).

Copy examined: Clara Clemens's copy. There is no Mark Twain Library accession number in this volume, a rare slip-up by those conscientious early librarians. However, the book does display the purple oval Mark Twain Library stamps. Examined in 1970 and again in June 1982.

Fairfield arranged excerpts from Stowe's fiction and nonfiction by topic.

————, pseud. "Christopher Crowfield." *House and Home Papers.* Illus. Boston: Houghton, Mifflin and Co., 1883. 333 pp.

Provenance: library shelf marks on the title page accord with the system Clara Clemens Samossoud employed during her Detroit years. There is a label denoting the *C1951* auction pasted on the front flyleaf.

Location: Mark Twain House and Museum, Hartford,

Connecticut.

Copy examined: photocopies of the front flyleaf and the title page were provided by Diana Royce, then Librarian of the Stowe-Day Memorial Library, on 3 October 1984. I examined the volume myself in Hartford in August 1987 and found no marginalia.

These essays and stories chronicle especially the domestic shifts necessitated by the Civil War and its aftermath.

————, pseud. "Christopher Crowfield." *House and Home Papers.* Boston, 1883. [Most likely this was the Houghton, Mifflin illustrated edition, 333 pages.]

Catalog: M & S Rare Books, Providence, Rhode Island, Catalog 12 (April 1994), with an *A1911* sale label on the flyleaf, "no inscriptions or annotations," three-quarter calf binding, front cover detached, item #201, priced at $25. No inscription or marginalia.

————. *Lady Byron Vindicated: A History of the Byron Controversy, from Its Beginning in 1816 to the Present Time.* Boston: Fields, Osgood & Co., 1870. 482 pp.

Inscription: the front flyleaf is signed in pencil, "Saml. L. Clemens/Hartford 1875."

Marginalia: pencil marks throughout pages 326–350 in Chapter five, "The Direct Argument to Prove the Crime." On page 337 Clemens used pencil to alter "were" to "was" in the phrase "'Manfred' were so appalling." A bookmark of white string is laid in at pages 192–193.

Catalog: *C1951,* D66, $16.

Location: Mark Twain House and Museum, Hartford, Connecticut.

Copy examined: Clemens's copy. Examined in August 1987. Paul Baender—"Mark Twain and the Byron Scandal," *American Literature* 30.4 (January 1959): 467–485—argued convincingly that Mark Twain wrote a series of unsigned editorials in the Buffalo *Express* in 1869 concerning Stowe's controversial "The True Story of Lady Byron's Life" that had appeared in the *Atlantic Monthly* 24.143 (September 1869): 295; it charged that Byron was guilty of incest with his half-sister. Joseph B. McCullough and Janice McIntire-Strasburg's *Mark Twain at the* Buffalo Express (2000), reprinted Twain's seven columns on this subject; they had been published in the *Express* between 18 August and 11 September 1869 (*MTBE,* pp. 8–51 *passim*). Thomas J. Reigstad observed that in these columns Twain "was almost always sympathetic to Stowe and critical of Byron" (*SL,* p. 75), but this is perhaps putting it too categorically about Twain's humorous and often-equivocal statements. Twain's "Last Words of Great Men" (Buffalo *Express,* 11 September 1869) facetiously claimed: "Byron made a poor business of it, and could not think of anything to say, at the last moment, but 'Augusta—sister—Lady Byron—tell Harriet Beecher Stowe'—etc., etc." (*MTBE,* p. 46). Twain again alluded to the scandal in "The 'Wild Man'" (Buffalo *Express,* 18 September 1869), where "SENSATION" is assigned "TO DIG UP THE BYRON FAMILY" (*MTBE,* p. 55–56). To "Dear Sir," Twain wrote on 7 October 1869 from Elmira: "Well I like the Stowe article, too, for it is good. But see how tastes run—I think the Humboldt one ever so much better. . . . Maybe it is because I am prejudiced against the Byron business—because I tried to burlesque it, & had my labor for my pains—our stove got the article"

(*MTLet* 3: 366). In a fragmentary sketch dating from 1869 or 1870 ("Letter from the Under-World," Paine 260, MTP), Twain's shade of Lord Byron professes interest in "the Byron-Scandal lately stirred up on earth by Mrs. Harriet Beecher Stowe.

————, pseud. "Christopher Crowfield." *Little Foxes.* Twenty-first edition. Boston: Houghton, Mifflin and Co., 1886. 287 pp.

Inscription: inscribed by Clemens in black ink, "Susy Clemens/From Mamma./Christmas, 1886."

Provenance: a sale label of the *C1951* auction is pasted above Clemens's inscription. Sold as item J42. Subsequently part of the Mark Twain collection assembled by Frank C. Willson (1889–1960) of Melrose, Massachusetts. Sold by Willson's widow Margarete in 1962 to the University of Texas.

Location: Harry Ransom Center, University of Texas at Austin.

Copy examined: Susy Clemens's unmarked copy. Stowe was a Nook Farm neighbor and friend of the Clemenses in Hartford, Connecticut.

————. *Little Pussy Willow. Also, The Minister's Watermelons.* Illus. Contemporary half-calf with marbled boards, gilt-decorated spines, marbled endpapers, rubbed edges and corners. New York: Fords, Howard, and Hulbert, [1880]. 161 pp.

Inscription: the front flyleaf has been removed, presumably because it contained a family inscription. The binding matches that of four other books given to Susy Clemens by her father at Christmas in 1886.

Provenance: has the shelfmark of Clara Clemens Gabrilowitsch's numbering system for her library books during her Detroit years. Sold at the 1951 auction but not listed in the hastily compiled sale sheet.

Catalog: "Property from the Library of Mark Twain," Butterfield & Butterfield, San Francisco, Sale 6613 (16 July 1997), lot 2707.

Location: Mark Twain House and Museum, Hartford, Connecticut. Obtained at the San Francisco auction in 1997.

Copy examined: Susy Clemens's unmarked copy, subsequently in the possession of Clara Clemens. Viewed in Hartford in 1997.

————. *The May Flower, and Miscellaneous Writings.* Twenty-fourth edition. Boston: Houghton, Mifflin and Co., 1884. 471 pp.

Inscription: unknown; the front flyleaf has been torn out.

Provenance: a *C1951* sale label is pasted on the remaining front flyleaf. The penciled "J42" on the verso of the front free endpaper designates the lot for the Hollywood auction, and also suggests that the book may have been inscribed to one of Clemens's daughters.

Location: Harry Ransom Center, University of Texas at Austin. Acquired in August 1978 from Robert Dawson Wallace of Ft. Myers, Florida for $100. Mr. Wallace had purchased the volume in 1952 from Dawson's Bookshop in Los Angeles. Alan Gribben assisted with this transaction on behalf of the Harry Ransom Center.

Copy examined: an unmarked copy belonging to a member of the Clemens family, possibly one of Clemens's daughters.

This volume collects thirty-five short stories and sketches from Stowe's early writing period. The title refers to a flower, not the Puritans' ship of 1620.

———. *The Minister's Wooing*. Brown cloth, spine torn, leaves loose. New York: Derby and Jackson, 1859. 578 pp.

Inscription: the front free endpaper is signed in pencil, "J. Langdon/Nov 1859."

Provenance: the bookplate #119 of the "J. Langdon Family Library" is affixed to the front pastedown endpaper.

Catalog: Ball 2016 inventory, brown cloth, spine missing, inscribed "J. Langdon/Nov 1859", J. Langdon Family Library bookplate #119.

Location: Mark Twain Archive, Elmira College, Elmira, New York.

Copy examined: an unmarked copy, examined on 27 May 2015. Pages 14 and 23 are folded down.

This copy of Stowe's historical novel, set in eighteenth-century New England, was available to Clemens whenever he visited the Langdon residence in Elmira. As the title suggests, *The Minister's Wooing* is principally a romantic love story but it also captures the heavy legacy of Puritan beliefs.

———. *The Minister's Wooing*. Boston, 1885.

Inscription: the front free endpaper is inscribed by Clemens, "Susy Clemens, Xmas, 1886."

Catalog: *Hunley 1958*, item #145, $5.

Location: presumably this copy was sold (but not listed) at the Hollywood auction in 1951. It has never reappeared in any records.

———. *My Wife and I: or, Harry Henderson's History*. Four wood-engraved plates. 8vo, brown half roan over marbled boards, marbled endpapers and edges, gilt spine, a bit worn, front outer hinge cracking. Boston: Houghton, Mifflin and Co., [cop. 1871]. 474 pp.

Provenance: displays the shelfmark of Clara Clemens Gabrilowitsch's numbering system for her private library in Detroit. Contains a *C1951* sale label on the front flyleaf. (The title was not listed in the 1951 auction checklist, but that list was notoriously incomplete.) For four decades the volume belonged to the collection of Chester L. Davis (1903–1987), Executive-Secretary, Mark Twain Research Foundation, Perry, Missouri. Subsequently it was in the Mark Twain collection amassed by Nick Karanovich, Fort Wayne, Indiana.

Catalogs: Christie's, New York City, Sale 7378, including the "Estate of Chester L. Davis," 5 December 1991, lot 185, sold with another book for a total of $1,320; *Sotheby's 2003*, lot 220, $900 (sold with four other miscellaneous titles).

Location: currently unknown.

Copy examined: Clemens's copy, unmarked. Viewed in Perry, Missouri in 1970 when owned by Chester L. Davis and again at the 2003 Sotheby's sale.

Stowe's novel was ahead of its time in portraying without moral condemnation a young man of good health and excellent reputation who succumbs to alcoholism and sinks in social status and self-respect. As he comes to realize in Chapter 29, "In short, the use of a stimulant to the brain-power brings on a disease . . . for whose manifestations the world has no pity" (p. 314).

———. *Oldtown Fireside Stories* (published in 1872).

Clemens's publishing firm credited an undated Houghton, Mifflin and Company edition published in Boston as the source for "The Parson's Horse-Race," which appeared in *Mark Twain's Library of Humor* (New York: Charles L. Webster & Co., 1888), pp. 315–323.

Claude R. Flory, in "Huck, Sam and the Small-Pox," *Mark Twain Journal* 12.3 (Winter 1964–1965): 1–2, 8, observed that in *Oldtown Fireside Stories* (1872) Sam Lawson relates "the same trick" Huckleberry Finn used to mislead two slave-catchers in Chapter 16 of *Huckleberry Finn* (1885).

———. *Oldtown Folks*. Twenty-eighth edition. Boston: Houghton, Mifflin and Co., 1885. 608 pp.

Inscription: inscribed by Clemens on the front flyleaf, "Susie Clemens/Mch 19, 1887."

Provenance: contains a *C1951* sale label above Clemens's inscription.

Catalog: Bruce Gimelson, Autographs, 5 October 1972 auction, Royal Manhattan Hotel, New York City, item #44, $150 suggested as a bidding price.

Location: Mark Twain House and Museum, Hartford, Connecticut. Verified on 3 October 1984 by Diana Royce, then Librarian of the Stowe-Day Memorial Library in Hartford.

Copy examined: Susy Clemens's unmarked copy. I was able to examine the book in Hartford in August 1987. It has no annotations.

Around February 1870 Olivia Clemens copied a passage from *Oldtown Folks* into her commonplace book (DV161, MS p. 94, MTP). Mark Twain included "Stowe (Sam Lawson)" among notes he made about English and American authors in March 1888 (NB 27, *N&J* 3: 379). In "The Man That Corrupted Hadleyburg" (1899, Part 2), newspaper reporters made "damnable portraits" of Hadleyburg residents—"even of Jack Halliday, who was the loafing, good-natured, no-account, irreverent fisherman, hunter, boys' friend, stray-dogs' friend, typical 'Sam Lawson' of the town." Stone, *The Innocent Eye* (1961), pp. 9–11.

———. *Pink and White Tyranny: A Society Novel*. Boston: Roberts Brothers, 1871. 331 pp.

Catalog: Ball 2016 inventory, red cloth, gilt lettering, embossed cover design, top edges dyed black, fair condition, bookplate #368 of the J. Langdon Family Library.

Location: Quarry Farm library shelves, under the supervision of the Mark Twain Archive, Elmira College, Elmira, New York.

Copy examined: an unmarked copy displaying the bookseller's sticker of "Preswick Morse/& Co./Booksellers/114 Water St./Elmira, N. Y." Examined on 26 May 2015.

Stowe departed from her previous subjects in this novel about a wealthy man in New England who gets more than he bargained for by marrying a seemingly angelic young woman. Clemens had access to this work whenever he visited the Langdons' residence in Elmira.

———. *Poganuc People: Their Loves and Lives*. Illus. Contemporary half calf and marbled boards, gilt-decorated spines, marbled endpapers, rubbed edges and corners. Boston: Houghton, Mifflin and Co., 1884. 375 pp.

Inscription: inscribed by Clemens, "Susy Clemens/Xmas, 1886."

Catalogs: *C1951*, J20, listed among volumes belonging to Jean and Clara Clemens; "Property from the Library of Mark Twain," Butterfield & Butterfield, San Francisco,

Sale 6613 (16 July 1997), lot 2707.

Location: Mark Twain House and Museum, Hartford, Connecticut.

Copy examined: Susy Clemens's unmarked copy, later in the possession of Clara Clemens. Viewed in Hartford in 1997. Stowe's childhood memories of Litchfield, Connecticut welled up in this, her last novel.

———. *Queer Little People*. Illus. Boston: Houghton, Mifflin and Co., 1885. 191 pp.

Inscriptions: the front free flyleaf has been removed, presumably because it bore a family inscription. What remains on another flyleaf is a poetic inscription by Stowe: "Not a sparrow falleth to the/ground without your Heavenly Father/Harriet Beecher Stowe/December 6, 1886." The book's binding matches other Stowe volumes that Clemens gave his daughter Susy at Christmas in 1886.

Provenance: has the shelfmarks of Clara Clemens Gabrilowitsch's library numbering system from her Detroit days. Sold at the 1951 Hollywood auction, but not listed in the often-inaccurate sale sheet.

Catalog: "Property from the Library of Mark Twain," Butterfield & Butterfield, San Francisco, Sale 6613 (16 July 1997), lot 2707.

Location: Mark Twain House and Museum, Hartford, Connecticut.

Copy examined: Susy Clemens's unmarked copy, subsequently in the possession of Clara Clemens. Viewed in Hartford in 1997.

Stowe gathered here a potpourri of enhanced fables, personal observations, and biographical stories about animals (one chapter is titled "Sir Walter Scott and His Dogs").

———. *Religious Poems*. Illus. Contemporary half calf and marbled boards, gilt-decorated spines, marbled endpapers, rubbed edges and corners. Boston: Ticknor and Fields, 1867. 107 pp.

Inscription: the front free flyleaf has been removed, presumably because it bore a family inscription. The binding of this volume matches those of four other books given to Susy Clemens by her father at Christmas in 1886. On the remaining flyleaf Stowe inscribed a passage from her own text: "Think not when the waking/winds of autumn/Drive the shivering leaflets/from the tree./Think not all is over: spring returneth/Buds & leaves & blossoms thou/shalt see./Page 34/H. B. Stowe/Dec. 16, 1886."

Provenance: has the shelfmark of the library numbering system that Clara Clemens Gabrilowitsch employed during her Detroit years. Sold at the 1951 Hollywood auction, although this title was not listed in the hastily compiled sale sheet.

Catalog: "Property from the Library of Mark Twain," Butterfield & Butterfield, San Francisco, Sale 6613 (16 July 1997), lot 2707.

Location: Mark Twain House and Museum, Hartford, Connecticut.

Copy examined: Susy Clemens's unmarked copy, subsequently in the possession of Clara Clemens. Viewed in Hartford in 1997.

———. *Uncle Tom's Cabin; or, Life Among the Lowly*. New Edition. Illus. Boston: Houghton, Mifflin and Co., 1886. 529 pp.

Inscription: the front free endpaper is inscribed in black ink: "Precious in the sight of the Lord is the death of his

saints/Harriet Beecher Stowe. Dec. 16 1886".

Provenance: Antenne-Dorrance Collection, Rice Lake, Wisconsin, a group of books that Katy Leary was allowed to select as keepsakes in 1910.

Location: Mark Twain Archive, Gannett-Tripp Learning Center, Elmira College, Elmira, New York.

Copy examined: copy presented by the author to the Clemens family, unmarked. Viewed in 1970 in Rice Lake and again on 28 May 2015 in Elmira.

Mark Twain recalled that a play based on Stowe's novel "was in full blast" when he lived in New York City in 1853; "everybody went there in elegant toilettes and cried over Tom's griefs" (2 February 1867 letter to San Francisco *Alta California*, *MTTMB*, p. 84). Twain met Stowe at Henry Ward Beecher's residence in Brooklyn at a dinner on 5 January 1868 (SLC to Jane Lampton Clemens and Pamela Moffett, Washington, D. C., 8 January 1868, *MTL*, p. 143; *MTLet* 2: 144). In "Mr. and Mrs. Byron" (Buffalo *Express*, 11 September 1869), Twain claimed to have overheard a conversation in which an ignorant woman referred to Mrs. Stowe as "an authoress; she wrote 'Uncle Tom's Cabin,' the Emancipation Proclamation, the Dred Scott Decision, and I believe several other colored works" (*MTBE*, p. 49). In 1874 Twain compared the sales of *The Gilded Age* (1873) to those of *Uncle Tom's Cabin* (SLC to Dr. John Brown, Hartford, 28 February 1874, *MTL*, p. 215; *MTLet* 6: 53). "Uncle Tom's Cabin sold 200,000 in this country," Twain noted in June 1885, anticipating huge sales for U. S. Grant's *Memoirs* (NB 24, *N&J* 3: 159).

Around 1885 George Parsons Lothrop (1851–1898) sat in on an evening Stowe spent as a guest at Twain's house. Stowe described to the group in vivid detail the horrendous, always anonymous threats she received after *Uncle Tom's Cabin* appeared. One of the "fire-eaters" even mailed her an ear chopped off an enslaved African American ("A Model State Capital," *Harper's Monthly Magazine* 71.425 [October 1885]: 730). Stowe also took the opportunity to propose a number of unrelated incidents "as deserving literary treatment" (p. 731). Twain wrote to a literary manuscript-seeker on 12 November 1885 that Mrs. Stowe "hasn't a scrap. She asked me to say this for her & save her the labour of writing; she is older & feebler now than she was when she gave *Uncle Tom's Cabin* to the world" (SLC to James F. Gluck, ALS sold by Christie's, New York City, 1–2 February 1988 auction, lot 469).

In October 1886 Twain reminded himself to "ask Webster if he sent 2 Uncle Toms"; following several intervening entries, he wrote: "Get a tree calf Uncle Tom from Charley" (NB 26, *N&J* 3: 262). On 25 April 1887, delighted to learn that Stowe was reading *The Prince and the Pauper* (1881) for the fourth time, Twain directed Charles L. Webster to have a tree-calf copy marked with her name in gilt letter as a gift (Berg Collection, NYPL). In 1887, at a neighborhood celebration of the ten thousandth dramatic performance of *Uncle Tom's Cabin*, Twain said, "Mrs. Stowe, you have made a book and you have given to the stage a drama which will live as long as the English tongue shall live" (Francis Johnson, *Musical Memories of Hartford* [Hartford: Witkower's, 1931], p. 243). Among a list of Twain's favorite punch lines for anecdotes, he listed (in December 1887): "Mrs. S. 'Ever read Uncle Tom?'

Tried to" (NB 27, *N&J* 3: 356). Twain jotted down notes about authors while he waited out a snowstorm in New York City in March 1888; of Stowe he wrote: "Uncle Tom (earlier, & dialect)"—he seemed to be comparing this novel with Stowe's *Oldtown Folks*, to which he had alluded previously (NB 27, *N&J* 3: 379). In June 1888, at a gathering in the Warners' house in Hartford, Twain compared "how she changed our Lord's order in the world" by writing *Uncle Tom's Cabin* to the impact of "Copernicus and Galileo" (Ernest J. Moyne, "Mark Twain Meets a Lady from Finland," *Mark Twain Journal* 11.2 [Summer 1960]: 10). In May 1891 Twain twice repeated that punch line of a joke about *Uncle Tom's Cabin* ("*tried* to!") in Notebook 30 (*N&J* 3: 625, 646). "It don't seem right and fair that Harriet Beacher Stow [*sic*] and all them other second-handers gets all the credit of starting that war and you never hear Tom Sawyer mentioned in the histories," says Huck Finn in "Tom Sawyer's Conspiracy" (*HH&T*, p. 167, written 1897–1900). Twain mentioned *Uncle Tom's Cabin* in his B-2 working notes for "The Secret History of Eddypus," a manuscript written in 1901–1902 (*FM*, p. 470). Twain pointed out in 1905 that "the profits on 'Uncle Tom's Cabin' continue to-day; nobody but the publishers get them—Mrs. Stowe's share ceased seven years before she died; her daughters receive nothing from the book" ("Concerning Copyright" [January 1905]). Stowe's book lived at least forty-two years, Twain reminded a Congressional committee on copyright reform on 7 December 1906 (*MTS1923*, p. 327; *MTSpk*, p. 535).

Stowe's significant effect on Mark Twain has long been recognized; see E. K. Maxfield, "Goody-goody Literature and Mrs. Stowe," *American Speech*, 4 (February 1920), 201; Blair, "On the Structure of *Tom Sawyer*" (1939), p. 77; Andrews, *Nook Farm* (1950), pp. 150–151, 167–172, and 198–204; Lynn, *MT&SH* (1959), pp. 111, 240–241, and 265–266; Abigail Ann Hamblen, "Uncle Tom and 'Nigger Jim': A Study in Contrasts and Similarities," *Mark Twain Journal* 11.3 (Fall 1961): 13–17; Richard Beale Davis, "Mrs. Stowe's Characters-in-Situations and a Southern Literary Tradition," *Essays on American Literature in Honor of Jay B. Hubbell*, ed. Clarence Gohdes (Durham: Duke University Press, 1967), pp. 108–125; and James M. Cox, "Humor and America: The Southwestern Bear Hunt, Mrs. Stowe, and Mark Twain," *Sewanee Review* 83.4 (Fall 1975): 573–601 (moving next door to Stowe in Nook Farm helped Clemens commence "his personal reconstruction"). Ellen Moers, in *Harriet Beecher Stowe and American Literature* (Hartford: Stowe-Day Foundation, 1978), asserted Stowe's influence on Twain and her profound impact on *Adventures of Huckleberry Finn*. Anthony J. Berret, "Huck Finn's Library: Reading, Writing, and Intertextuality," *Making Mark Twain Work in the Classroom*, ed. James S. Leonard (Durham: Duke University Press, 1999), p. 209, likewise explained how *Uncle Tom's Cabin* was one of the likely "paradigms in *Huckleberry Finn*." Leland Krauth, *Mark Twain & Company: Six Literary Relations* (Athens: University of Georgia Press, 2003) seemed justified in identifying Stowe as the unseen force who "haunted" many of Twain's writings. The substantial number of her works in the Clemenses' family library underscores Krauth's contention.

———. *Uncle Tom's Cabin; A Tale of Life Among the Lowly.* Illus. Large red cloth. Philadelphia: John C. Winston & Co., 1897. 680 pp.

   Inscription: the front free endpaper is inscribed in black ink, "Addis N. Shelton/Foxbury Sta/Conn./Dec 25th 1905./From Mrs. Norton/Danbury/Ct."

   Location: Mark Twain Library, Redding, Connecticut.

   Copy examined: why was this unmarked volume added to the Clemens collection sometime between 1970 (when I first visited the Mark Twain Library) and June 1982, when I revisited Redding? It has no accession number or library stamps. I advised the staff to remove this book from the shelves holding the donations by Clemens and his daughter Clara Clemens Gabrilowitsch, since it obviously had no connection with the Clemens family.

———. *We and Our Neighbors; or, the Records of an Unfashionable Street. A Novel.* Thirty-sixth edition. Boston: Houghton, Mifflin and Co., n.d. [cop. 1873]. 480 pp.

   Inscription: unknown; the second flyleaf has been torn out.

   Marginalia: a few stray pencil marks throughout.

   Provenance: there is a *C1951* auction label on the second flyleaf. (The book was not listed in the sale sheet, but this was hardly unusual at that chaotic auction.)

   Catalog: "A Mark Twain Collection," The Bookman, List No. 25 (1970), item #331.

   Location: Wake Forest University, Winston-Salem, North Carolina. Given by Mrs. Nancy Susan Reynolds in 1970.

   Copy examined: a volume belonging to the Clemens family.

   A sequel to *My Wife and I: or, Harry Henderson's History* (1871), this novel discarded the first-person voice of the earlier work. Its plot encompassed a range of topics in which Stowe was interested, including prostitution, women's suffrage, and the respect that housekeeping is due.

STRACHEY, LIONEL (1864–1927). "Progressional" (satirical poem).

   Clemens pinned this anti-imperialist poem—a parody of the hymn "Onward, Christian Soldiers"—to the front free endpaper of G. L. Dickinson's *Letters from a Chinese Official* (1904, volume in MTP). He clipped the poem from a New York City newspaper. At the point on page 7 where Dickinson's book described Western civilization as "progressive," Clemens underscored this word and wrote in pencil at the top of the page: "See the poem pinned to fly leaf." Sabine Baring-Gould was the author of the lyrics for the original hymn; its melody was composed by Arthur S. Sullivan (1842–1900).

STRAUSS, DAVID FRIEDRICH (1808–1874). *The Life of Jesus, Critically Examined.* Translated from the fourth German edition by George Eliot [pseud. of Marian Evans (1819–1880)]. 3 vols. London, 1846. [Strauss' *Leben Jesu* had first been published in 1835. The edition that Clemens read of George Eliot's English translation is unknown; it might have been the 784-page second edition with an introduction by Otto Pfleiderer (1829–1920), published in London by Swan Sonnenschein & Company in 1898.]

   Twenty-seven-year-old theologian David Strauss had shocked Europe with his interpretation of Jesus as a historical figure rather than a divine being and his rereading of Christ's miracles as mythical inventions. Eliot's translation of the work in 1846 renewed the controversy. On 11 October 1906 Isabel Lyon recorded: "The King has been reading George Eliot's translation of Straus's [*sic*] Life of Jesus, & is amazed at the great care taken by Straus [*sic*] to trace the genealogy of Christ (Jesus) back through 14 generations on the father's side. No one—apparently—not even George Eliot remembered that on the father's side he had God, & as the King said he could so easily say 'Papa up there, is enough for me'" (IVL Journals, MTP).

STREAMER, VOLNEY (1850–1915), comp. *In Friendship's Name.* Fourteenth edition. New York: Brentano's, 1904. Sixty-eight leaves.

Source: MTLAcc, entry #620, volume donated by Clemens. Steamer gathers excerpts from various writers over the ages defining and praising friendship.

_____, comp. *Voices of Doubt and Trust.* New York: Brentano's, 1897. 215 pp.

Inscription: the front free endpaper is inscribed in black ink, "Samuel L. Clemens,/from George Iles,/with the highest esteem/and regard./New York, Feb. 12, 1902."

Marginalia: pencil brackets enclose the last four lines of William Gilmore Simms' "The Lost Pleiad" (p. 48). Pencil marks bracket the first two stanzas of "The Pantheist's Song of Immortality" by Constance Caroline Woodhill Naden (p. 67). Clemens wrote the words "re-existence after death" in pencil on page 81, and drew a line to the phrase "a higher morality" in John Morley's "Explanation, Not Attack," from *On Compromise.* At the bottom of page 98, below Anatole France's seven-sentence assertion that evil exists to balance good, titled "Evil Is Necessary," Clemens retorted: "Then, except heaven be a repetition of this, you will find it foolish, & God's pet idea a mistake?" (France had declared: "It is because of evil and suffering that the earth may be inhabited and that life is worth living. For every vice that you destroy there is a corresponding virtue that perishes with it.") Clemens made a pencil mark beside Thomas Bailey Aldrich's "Sleep" (p. 102). He drew a pencil line around the last four verses of Matthew Arnold's "Self-Dependence" (p. 108). On page 112 he made a pencil mark at "Infidelity" by Minot Judson Savage. On page 114 Clemens exclaimed (writing vertically in pencil in the margin) of Bryant's "Thanatopsis": "Written at 19!" He drew a penciled bracket around the first two sentences from Herbert Spencer's "Scientific Grounds for Right Conduct" (p. 117), a preface to Spencer's *The Data of Ethics.*

Location: Mark Twain Library, Redding, Connecticut. Donated from Clemens's library by Clara Clemens Gabrilowitsch in 1910 (MTLAcc, entry #2096).

Copy examined: Clemens's copy. Has a red ink Mark Twain Library accession number ("2096") and the purple oval Library stamps. Examined in 1970 and again in June 1982.

————. [An identical copy. Green cloth. 215 pp.]

Inscription: the front pastedown endpaper is signed in black ink, "S. L. Clemens/Dec. 1905./21—5th Ave."

Marginalia: on page 98 Clemens bracketed Anatole France's brief opinion, "Evil Is Necessary," and wrote in black ink (vertically) in the margin: "Anatole France is not an idiot; yet if an idiot had written that, it would still be no credit to the idiot." At the bottom of the same page Clemens added, also in black ink: "Evil is the crime of an immoral God. With a moral God it could not exist." There are no

other annotations. The corner of page 29 is folded down.

Provenance: Antenne-Dorrance Collection, Rice Lake, Wisconsin.

Location: Mark Twain Archive, Gannett-Tripp Learning Center, Elmira College, Elmira, New York.

Copy examined: Clemens's copy. Examined on 28 May 2015.

Clemens received this volume from Volney Streamer: "He is Librarian of the Players Club. He called here to bring me a book which he has published, and, in a general way, to make my acquaintance" (16 January 1906 AD, *MTA*, 1: 328; *AutoMT* 1: 283–284). In an undated note Clemens made a memorandum: "Invite Volney Streamer historian of the Players" (*A1911*, lot 192).

STRICKLAND, AGNES (1796–1874) and ELIZABETH STRICKLAND (1794–1875). *Lives of the Queens of England, from the Norman Conquest; With Anecdotes of Their Courts, Now First Published from Official Records and Other Authentic Documents, Private as Well as Public.* New edition, with Corrections and Additions. 12 vols. Engraved frontispieces. Contemporary full tan polished calf, double morocco labels, raised bands, gilt compartments, inner dentilles gilt, marbled endpapers and edges, one spine missing. London: Henry Colburn, 1844–1848.

Marginalia: Clemens made corrections of names, dates, and grammar on pages 7, 9, 22, 39, 48, 54, 56, and 57 of Volume I. He questioned the identity of "Robert" in pencil on page 7. On page 54 he used pencil in correcting the date "1608" to "1068" and in altering the Stricklands' word "palladium" to read "folly" in their reference to "that great palladium of English liberty, the right of trial by jury." Clemens also made a penciled grammatical correction in the second footnote on page 56 of Volume I and then wrote at the bottom of the page, "This book needs editing in spots." No other markings are visible in Volume I. (Robert T. Slotta supplied photographs of most of these annotations to Alan Gribben on 23 April 1991.) There is also a correction on page 64 of Volume IV, according to Kevin Mac Donnell. A funeral notice for George Thorndike Angell (5 June 1823–16 March 1909), founder of the American Humane Education Society and the Massachusetts Society for the Prevention of Cruelty to Animals, was laid in Volume IX as a bookmark at pages 156–157, according to Robert T. Slotta.

Catalogs: *A1911*, "post 8vo, uniformly bound in full polished calf, gilt backs, Lond." sold as a set of twelve together with fourteen other uniformly bound volumes, lot 441, sold for $27.50 total; *Sotheby's 2003*, #211, Volumes I, II, IV, VII, and IX only, $2,250 (sold with four other history titles).

Provenance: Volumes I, II, IV, VII, and IX only acquired by Robert T. Slotta, Dublin, Ohio (Slotta to Alan Gribben, 23 April 1991). Subsequently these same volumes entered the collection of Nick Karanovich, Fort Wayne, Indiana.

Location: collection of Kevin Mac Donnell, Austin, Texas. Mac Donnell described the five volumes to Alan Gribben in an inventory sent on 28 August 2017.

Copy examined: copies of five volumes belonging to the Clemens family library. Viewed at the 2003 Sotheby's sale. Estes & Lauriat of Boston billed Clemens on 28 July 1882 for "1 Strickland's Queens/6 vols [$]110.00"; Clemens paid the bill on 4 August 1882 (receipt in MTP). Presumably the set included the Stricklands' eight-volume *Lives of the Queens of Scotland* (see that Catalog entry) as well as Mary Anne Everett Green's *Lives of the Princesses of England*, a six-volume work (see the Catalog entry for Green).

———. *Lives of the Queens of England from the Norman Conquest, with Anecdotes from Their Courts.* New Edition. 12 vols. Boston: Taggard & Thompson, n. d. [1864?].

Provenance: bookplates #236 (Volume I), #697 (Volume IV), #238 (Volume VIII), #239 (Volume X), and #240 (Volume XII) of the "J. Langdon Family Library."

Catalog: inventory list of the Langdon family library books (Mark Twain Archive, Elmira College).

Location: Quarry Farm library shelves, under the supervision of the Mark Twain Archive, Elmira College, Elmira, New York.

Copies examined: unmarked copies that Clemens had access to whenever he visited the Langdon residence in Elmira. Only five volumes appear to be present. Examined on 26 May 2015.

———. *Lives of the Queens of Scotland and English Princesses Connected with the Regal Succession of Great Britain.* 8 volumes. First edition. Contemporary full tan polished calf, double morocco labels, marbled endpapers and edges. Edinburgh and London: William Blackwood & Sons, 1850–1859.

Catalog: *A1911*, "post 8vo, uniformly bound in full polished calf, gilt backs, Lond." sold as a set with eighteen other uniformly bound volumes, lot 441, sold for $27.50 total.

Provenance: in 1980 this set belonged to Margaret Sherman of North Muskegon, Michigan (Sherman to Alan Gribben, 24 November 1980; 9 December 1980). It had no annotations and appeared unread but contained the *A1911* sale labels.

Location: collection of Kevin Mac Donnell, Austin, Texas (Mac Donnell to Alan Gribben, 25 February 2012). The *A1911* sale labels are present in Volumes I, II, V, and VII only. There are no markings in the texts, according to Mac Donnell.

STRINDBERG, AUGUST (1849–1912).

The Clemenses were aware of this notable Swedish dramatist and novelist. Clara Clemens listed Strindberg's *Plays* in her undated commonplace book (Paine 150, MTP). In Berlin, perhaps in 1891, Clemens purportedly told Henry Fisher that he had read books and dramas of "queer Strindberg," whose women are "hard-faced, sullen, cold-blooded, cheeky, grasping, vindictive, hell-raising, unvirtuous, unkind vixens, all of them." Fisher recalled Clemens's remark that "a writer who sees no good in women confesses that he was found out by the sex he wars on." The women portrayed by Strindberg, said Clemens, "are all compounds of vile ingredients—hideous hags with or without angel-faces—wife-beater Strindberg whipping dead mares" (*AMT*, pp. 78–79). Strindberg translated a short story and a sketch by Mark Twain for a Swedish humor anthology published in 1878, but there is no indication that Twain knew of this fact (Harry Bergholz, "Strindberg's Anthologies of American Humorists, Bibliographically Identified," *Scandinavian Studies* 43.4 (Autumn 1971): 335–343. See also the Catalog entry for H. Ibsen, *Hedda Gabler*.

STRIPLING, ALGERNON BYRON (1845–1916). *The Poet in Embryo; Being the Meditations of Algernon Byron Stripling.* Illustrated by Maud Sherman Cowles (i.e., Maude Alice Cowles, 1871–1905). New York: E. P. Dutton and Co., 1905. 18 pp.

Source: MTLAcc, entry #1903, volume donated from Clemens's library by Clara Clemens Gabrilowitsch in 1910.

A very young schoolboy attempts to write poems, with countless comical phonetical misspellings.

STRONG, AUSTIN (1881–1952). *The Toymaker of Nuremberg; A Play in Three Acts and Two Scenes* (play, produced by Charles Frohman at the Garrick Theatre in 1907).

Albert Bigelow Paine recorded that Clemens attended a performance of this play on his birthday, 30 November 1907, commenting afterward: "It is a fine, delicate piece of work. . . . I wish I could do such things as that" (*MTB*, pp. 1413–14).

Aspiz, "MT's Reading" (1949), pp. 263–264.

STRUTT, JOSEPH (1749–1802). *The Sports and Pastimes of the People of England, Including the Rural and Domestic Recreations, May Games, Mummeries, Shows, Processions, Pageants, and Pompous Spectacles, from the Earliest Period to the Present Time.* Ed. by William Hone (1780–1842). Illus. London: Chatto and Windus, 1876. 530 pp.

Inscription: the half-title page is signed "S. L. Clemens."

Catalogs: *A1911*, "12mo, cloth, Lond. 1876," quotes the signature, lot 442, sold for $2.25; Stan. V. Henkels (Philadelphia), Catalogue 1057 (14 May 1912), "12mo, cloth, uncut, London, 1876," item 123.

This work seems like it has the potential to be an unduly overlooked source of Twain's knowledge about England at play. To put it another way, Twain's literary characters Tom Sawyer and Tom Canty would have devoured any such compendium of "*Shows, Processions, Pageants, and Pompous Spectacles.*"

STUART, (LADY) LOUISA (1757–1851). *Lady Louisa Stuart: Selections from Her Manuscripts.* Ed. by James Archibald Home (1837–1909). New York: Harper & Brothers, 1899. 310 pp.

Source: MTLAcc, entry #1045, volume donated by Clemens.

Lady Louisa Stuart was the granddaughter of Lady Mary Wortley Montagu (1689–1762), whose letters had become famous as witty records of the personalities and events of her time. (The Clemens family's library included an 1875 edition of Lady Montagu's *Letters.*) Lady Stuart was herself a brilliant member of the elite London social circle. *Lady Louisa Stuart: Selections from Her Manuscripts* contained extracts from her memoirs and several fictional sketches as well as previously unpublished correspondence with her close friend Sir Walter Scott (pp. 217–260) and other eminent figures.

STUART, RUTH (McENERY) (1856–1917). *The Second Wooing of Salina Sue, and Other Stories.* Illustrated by E[dward]. W[indsor]. Kemble (1861–1933) and A[rthur]. B[urdett]. Frost (1851–1928). New York: Harper & Brothers, 1905. 236 pp.

Inscription: the front pastedown endpaper is signed, "S. L. Clemens/21—5th Ave., 1905".

Catalog: *A1911*, "12mo, cloth, N.Y. 1905," quotes the signature, lot 443, sold for $3.

The narrator of these dialect stories wrote in standard English about African Americans' lives on an unspecified Southern plantation in a nebulous, apparently post-slavery era. While the author probably intended the tone of these stories to seem tender and poignant, to a later age they come off as patronizing. In the title story, an African American woman frets about merely being a common-law wife instead of having the religious blessing of an evangelical church.

———. [An identical copy.]

Source: MTLAcc, entry #1344, volume donated by Clemens.

———. *The Story of Babette, A Little Creole Girl*. Illus. New York: Harper & Brothers, [cop. 1894]. 209 pp.

Source: MTLAcc, entry #1661, volume donated by Clemens.

Stuart's sentimental novel involved romantic love, parentage, and secrets. Set in New Orleans, its dialogue was interspersed with French language expressions.

STUDER, JACOB HENRY (1840–1904), ed. *The Birds of North America; One Hundred and Nineteen Artistic Colored Plates, Representing the Different Species and Varieties, Drawn and Colored from Nature* [*by Theodore Jasper* (1814–1897), *revised by John Graham Bell* (1812–1889)], *Including a Copious Text*. New York: Natural Science Association of America, 1888. 192 pp. [Edition conjectured.]

Catalog: *C1951*, D75, listed among volumes signed by Clemens, "Birds of North America, with illustrations," no author supplied, $37.50.

In Jean Clemens's diary at the sanitarium in Katonah, New York, she recorded among her gifts on 25 December 1906: "Father's 'Birds of North America' is a beautiful book and will prove very useful indeed" ("Extracts from Diary of Jean L. Clemens," TS in DV13a, MTP).

STURGE, JOSEPH (1793–1859). *A Visit to the United States in 1841*. Boston: Dexter S. King, 1842. 235 pp.

Mark Twain consulted this book in writing an unpublished portion of *Life on the Mississippi* (1883); among the "irruption of tourists," he mentioned "Mr. Joseph Sturge, 1841" (Heritage Press edition [1944], p. 402).

Sturge had little time for the usual sight-seeing of a British tourist. This Quaker activist from Birmingham, England principally came to the United States to establish firmer connections with its abolitionist societies and meet with government officials to press for legislation opposing African American enslavement. As he stated in his Preface, "For obvious reasons, *the abolition of slavery in the United States* is the most prominent topic in my narrative" (p. vii). In a petition to the President he called slavery a "monstrous and wicked assumption of power by man, over his fellow man" (p. 111). Sturge visited a slave-trading establishment in Alexandria, Virginia where thousands of enslaved families routinely became victims of "unfeeling separation" through heartless sales practices (pp. 100–101). During large parts of his tour of the American South he traveled in the company of the poet-abolitionist John Greenleaf Whittier. A dozen appendixes to Sturge's narrative publish correspondence with fellow abolitionists and cite the horrific treatment of enslaved people in Georgia and other states, such as gagging individuals who resist the placement of manacles on their ankles and wrists. Scholars and biographers should calculate the impact of Sturge's book in assessing the literary resources that lay behind Mark Twain's masterpiece,

Adventures of Huckleberry Finn (1885).

Dewey Ganzel, "Twain, Travel Books" (1962), p. 41 n. 4.

STURT, CHARLES (1795–1869). *Narrative of an Expedition into Central Australia, Performed Under the Authority of Her Majesty's Government, During the Years 1844, 5, and 6. Together with a Notice of the Province of South Australia, in 1847*. 2 vols. London: T. and W. Boone, 1849.

In Chapter 9 of *Following the Equator* (1897), Mark Twain mentioned that "Captain Sturt, the great explorer, gives us a sample of the heat." Sturt "wondered *the very grass did not take fire*," and claimed that his thermometer broke after reaching 125° Fahrenheit. Twain took this quotation and the thermometer incident from Volume II of Sturt's *Narrative*, pages 90–91, adding italics.

Madigan, "MT's Passage to India," (1974), p. 366.

Success Magazine (New York journal, published 1897–1911).

Theodore Dreiser, sometimes an unreliable source, reported that in November 1900 Clemens said to him: "You say you're from *Success Magazine*? Don't think I ever heard of it. But the name is sort of comforting" (Dreiser, "Three Contacts" [1935], p. 162A). On 12 October 1906 Clemens parried a request by *Success Magazine* to lend his name to an unnamed cause (Berg, NYPL).

SUCKLING, (SIR) JOHN (1609–1642). *The Poems, Plays and Other Remains of Sir John Suckling. A New Edition, with a Copious Account of the Author, Notes, and an Appendix*. Ed. by William Carew Hazlitt (1834–1913). 2 vols. London: F. & W. Kerslake, 1874. [Edition conjectured.]

Below Clemens's reminder to look up Robert Burns' *Merry Muses*, he wrote a note about an English Cavalier poet and playwright: "Unexpurgated Sir John Suckling" (NB 18 [1879], *N&J* 2: 335).

SUDERMANN, HERMANN (1857–1928). *Frau Sorge, Roman* [*Mrs. Worry, Novel*]. Stuttgart: J. G. Cotta, 1897. 292 pp.

Source: MTLAcc, entry #384, volume donated by Clemens.

———. *Das Glück im Winkel; schauspiel in drei Akten von Hermann Sudermann* [*The Happiness in the Corner; Acting in Three Acts*]. Stuttgart, 1896. 128 pp.

Clara Clemens listed this work in her undated commonplace book (Paine 150, MTP).

SUE, EUGÈNE, actually Joseph Marie Sue (1804–1857). *The Wandering Jew (Le Juif errant)* (published 1844–1845).

Mark Twain bestowed the sobriquet "Wandering Jew" upon a nuisance passenger aboard the *America* in January 1867 (NB 7, *N&J* 1: 268). Chapter 54 of *The Innocents Abroad* (1869) includes Twain's account of the suffering endured by this figure who must live and wander forever, "longing to stop, in city, in wilderness, in desert solitudes, yet hearing always that relentless warning to march—march on!" (Twain had rehearsed this woeful tale in a letter published in San Francisco *Daily Alta California* issue of 29 March 1868—see *TIA*, pp. 283–285.) In a humorous Buffalo *Express* column published on 2 October 1869 in which Twain pretended to answer questions posed in a book titled *Mental Photographs: An Album for Confessions of Tastes, Habits, and Convictions* (see the Catalog entry for Robert Saxton, its editor), he answered "The Wandering Jew, with a nice annuity" to the query about whom he would rather be (*MTBE*, p. 63).

In Chapter 46 of *Following the Equator* (1897) Twain recalled that Sue's novel revived interest in the murderous

Thugs of India "fifty years ago" in the Mississippi River Valley: "Then Eugene Sue's 'Wandering Jew' appeared, and made great talk for a while. One character in it was a chief of Thugs—'Feringhea'—a mysterious and terrible Indian who was as slippery and sly as a serpent, and as deadly; and he stirred up the Thug interest once more. But it did not last. It presently died again—this time to stay dead." Chapter 47 of *Following the Equator* described the stratagem by which the real-life version of "Eugène Sue's famous Feringhea" was captured. The French novelist Eugene Sue's best-selling *The Wandering Jew* carried an implicitly anti-Catholic message as well as a direct attack on the Jesuit order. Sue merely used the Christian legend about a Jew who had taunted Christ and was cursed to wander the earth endlessly as a hook for the title; the novel's murkily Gothic plot barely made any reference to that medieval legend and instead depicted a family about to come into a fortune if the dastardly Jesuits could be blocked by the family's supernatural protectors.

SUETONIUS [GAIUS OR CAIUS SUETONIUS TRANQUILLUS] (c. 69–122 CE). *The Lives of the Twelve Caesars. By C. Suetonius Tranquillus.* Translated from the Latin in 1796 by Alexander Thomson (1763–1803). Revised and corrected by T[homas]. Forester. Bohn's Classical Library Series. London: George Bell and Sons, 1876. 557 pp.

Inscriptions: the front pastedown endpaper is signed in black ink, "SL. Clemens." Clemens inscribed the verso of the half-title page (opposite the title page) in black ink: "Translated into Cowboy English". Albert Bigelow Paine noted in pencil on the half-title page: "This was a favorite book of Mark Twain's—one of the very last that he tried to read. (See my biography of him; account of his last days.) A. B. P."

Marginalia: Clemens made notes and marks in pencil and black ink on the front and rear endpapers. He selectively crossed out entire portions of the catalogue of Bohn's Libraries with pencil at the rear of the volume. Throughout the book he annotated and underscored the text in pencil, black ink, and brownish-black ink. Dixon Wecter quoted some of this marginalia in *Sam Clemens of Hannibal* (1952, p. 1). Paine stated that "there were not many notes in the Suetonius, nor in the Carlyle *Revolution*, though these were among the volumes he read oftenest" (*MTB*, p. 1537). However, Clemens's notes in *Lives of the Twelve Caesars* are more numerous than Paine suggests. On page 31 Clemens observed in pencil: "People have always preferred the old, it seems." In brownish-black ink he remarked at the top of page 150: "He reels from tense to tense like a Scot going home from a Burns banquet." On the same page Clemens underscored the words "little," "seems," "proof," "all," "was," and wrote "Drunk again!" in brownish-black ink. Clemens's penciled note on page 162 is scrawled crudely, as though he were ill or else traveling in a moving vehicle: "This from a man who believes in the miracles of the New Testament." On page 164 he remarked in brownish-black ink: "Why so gravely & so solemnly analyse a miracle? No miracle will bear examination."

Clemens recognized a general decline in the ancient Romans; on page 261 he wondered (in pencil): "Was it the Roman Emperors who taught their people to accept gratuities

without shame?" Albert Bigelow Paine added (in black ink): "Caesar was murdered on the *suspicion* that he was not good for the Empire, yet Caligula went *unhung*" (p. 269). In brownish-black ink Clemens noted on page 281: "Leopold *robs* his daughters." Annotation on pages 290 and 291 also refers to Leopold and the Belgian Congo. In the same ink Clemens commented on page 318: "It is not to be doubted that the Crucifixion did not make a hundredth part of the stir that the death of Mrs. Eddy would create to-day. Nor the ten thousandth, for that matter." Clemens employed the same ink on page 341 to underscore twenty-four usages of "he" and "his," remarking: "Some more pronouns out on a drunk." On page 480 Clemens made a penciled note in large script: "This book is one mass of chuckle-headed construction & idiotic grammar." In black ink he referred to Flavius Clemens on page 492: "I guess this is where our line starts. It will end with another kind of line, probably."

Catalogs: ListABP (1910), "Lives of the Caesars"; "Retz Appraisal" (1944), p. 11, valued at $35.

Location: Mark Twain Papers, Bancroft Library, University of California at Berkeley.

Copy examined: Clemens's copy.

Clemens began reading this copy of Suetonius at least as early as November 1878, when he wrote an Italian phrase ("Quanto fiamato? How long do we stop") on the front flyleaf [in Italian it should be *per quanto tempo ci fermiamo*], and then commented in Notebook 17: "Had several books—wrote Quanto firmato [English translation: *as signed*] in one—train always left before I could find it" (*N&J* 2: 247). On Sunday, 11 June 1905, Isabel Lyon recorded: "Mr. Clemens is reading Suetonius on the Caesars, finding it very interesting too. Today he said that he'd just been reading how Caesar's mother came into possession of a serpent-like scar at the time of Caesar's birth" (IVL Journals, TS p. 65, MTP). Clara Clemens received a letter Clemens wrote to her from Dublin, New Hampshire on 18 June 1905: "I'm reading Suetonius again, oh, good land! This country is not Rome-in-the-days-of-the-early-Caesars, but—there are resemblances. And they are increasing" (MTP; *MFMT*, p. 273). On Saturday, 24 June 1905, Lyon again reported: "After he had rested a bit down stairs, he took his Suetonius and went up stairs to sleep a little" (IVL Journals, TS p. 69, MTP). Mark Twain repeatedly quoted from *Lives of the Caesars* in "As Concerns Interpreting the Deity" (written in 1905), citing pages 138, 139, and 141 of "Bohn's Suetonius" (*WIM?*, pp. 111–112). Twain probably drew on Suetonius when he mentioned Nero and Caligula as killers ("Twain Calls Leopold Slayer of 15,000,000," New York *World*, 3 December 1905; *Complete Interviews*, p. 529).

Describing homely and largely contrived miracles to Jean Clemens on 25 February 1907, Clemens claimed: "If these marvels had happened in Caesar's time it would have meant nothing less than the caving-in of the Universe" (TS in MTP). "If he [Theodore Roosevelt] should die now, he would be mourned as no ruler has been mourned save Nero" (29 May 1907 AD, *MTE*, p. 22; *AutoMT* 3: 63). Speaking about Roosevelt's selection of William Howard Taft as his successor, Mark Twain seemed to rely on Suetonius when commenting on 12 September 1908 in an Autobiographical Dictation: "Things will go on well enough under this arrangement, so long as a Titus succeeds a Vespasian, and we shall best not trouble about a Domitian until we get him" (*MTE*, p. 34; *AutoMT* 3: 260). In "No. 44, The Mysterious Stranger," written between 1902 and 1908, Forty-Four explains the art of prophecy: "Here in Suetonius is an instance. He is speaking of Atia, the mother of Augustus Caesar: 'Before her delivery she dreamed that her bowels stretched to the stars, and expanded through the whole circuit of heaven and earth.'" When "the dream-messages had become loose and rickety and indefinite," however, "Rome had to give up dream-messages, and the Romans took to [chicken] entrails for prophetic information" (*MSM*, pp. 384–385). On 16 August 1909 Albert Bigelow Paine recorded: "he is reading Suetonius, which he already knows by heart" (*MTB*, p. 1516). In October and November 1909 Twain wrote "Letters from the Earth," which includes a reference to Titus's assembling animals for Roman shows (*WIM?*, pp. 421, 578; cf. *Lives of the Twelve Caesars*, p. 470). Late in 1909 Twain paraphrased and quoted from Suetonius's account of the decision Caesar made on the banks of the Rubicon: "Perhaps the most celebrated turning-point recorded in history was the crossing of the Rubicon" ("Turning-Point of My Life" [1910], *WIM?*, pp. 456–457). Paine, recalling the period between 1906 and 1910, stated: "In the days I knew him he read steadily not much besides Suetonius and Pepys and Carlyle" (*MTB*, p. 1540). Several decades later, in a letter to Hyatt Howe Waggoner, Paine restated this recollection: "The only book he kept by him was not a scientific work: it was Suetonius' *Lives of the Caesars*. He loved the drama and wonder of science, but the pageant of history more" (Waggoner, "Science in the Thought of Mark Twain" [1937], p. 362).

Williams, "Genesis" (1961), p. 105.

SULLIVAN, MARION DIX (1802–1860). "The blue Juniata" (song, 1844). Words and music by Sullivan.

"Songs tended to regrets for bygone days and vanished joys," Clemens recalled in "Villagers of 1840–3" (written in 1897), citing "Bright Alforata" [*sic*] (*HH&T*, p. 34). In 1906 Clemens remembered "The Blue Juniata" as a "sentimental" song sung by the later minstrel troupes (30 November 1906 AD, *MTE*, p. 114; *AutoMT* 2: 296). The Juniata is a river in Pennsylvania. The first two lines of the song begin, "Wild roved an Indian girl,/Bright Alfarata." Kerry Driscoll, *Mark Twain among the Indians* (2018), p. 26.

A Summer in Africa. [Unidentified book title.]

Mark Twain quoted from page 148 of Volume One of this apparently fabricated book in a discarded chapter of *A Tramp Abroad* (1880) that describes courtship and marriage practices: "The Bakalodolo, like the French, do their watching before the marriage, seldom after it" (verso of MS p. 75, Box 6, no. 7, MTP). (A people known as the Bakololo did live in the Botswana region of Africa.) He may have been disguising the name and title of Charles Chaillé-Long's *Central Africa: Naked Truths of Naked People* (1877). That one-volume book mentioned (on page 150) the explorer and his guards receiving from an African tribal chieftain an unsolicited gift of eight nude young women for them to marry. Twain additionally cited in the manuscript an apparently fictional author, "Syme," and

Syme's *Central Africa*. Possibly Twain felt delicate about naming such a recently published book as Chaillé-Long's, especially with its somewhat provocative title.

Summer Sketches [Unidentified book.]

On 4 December 1874 Estes & Lauriat of Boston sent Clemens two receipts for two copies of this work ($6 each); one book had been sent to the Reverend Joseph H. Twichell and the other to Clemens. The bill was dated 2 December 1874 (receipts in MTP).

SUMNER, WILLIAM GRAHAM (1840–1910). *What Social Classes Owe to Each Other*. New York: Harper & Brothers, [cop. 1883]. 169 pp.

Source: MTLAcc, entry #542, volume donated by Clemens.

A Yale professor of sociology, Sumner accepted the concept of Social Darwinism but urged that the talented and motivated individuals among the poor should be assisted in their efforts to better themselves.

Sunday School Times (Philadelphia weekly periodical, published 1859–1966).

"Those two unspeakable shams, buttermouthed hypocrites, John Wanamaker [1838–1922] & his Sunday School Times" (NB 28 [July 1888], *N&J* 3: 407–408).

SUTERMEISTER, OTTO (1832–1901), comp. *Dichtungen in Luzerner Mundart [Seals in Lucerne Dialect]*. Zürich: Dress, Zugli & Co., n.d. 112 pp.

Source: MTLAcc, entry #389, volume donated by Clemens.

SUTHERLAND, HOWARD VIGNE (1868–1943). *Idylls of Greece*. Boston: Sherman, French & Co., 1908. 175 pp.

"At the suggestion of the author, we are sending you a complimentary copy" (Sherman, French & Co. to SLC, 4 December 1908, TLS in MTP). Sutherland's four long poems were inspired by ancient Greek sites and myths. The poet, playwright, and journalist Sutherland, born in Cape Town, South Africa, had been a gold miner in the Klondike and now lived in Alameda, California. He would later move to Honolulu.

SUTPHEN, [WILLIAM GILBERT] VAN TASSEL (1861–1945). *The Doomsman*. Illus. New York: Harper & Brothers, 1906. 295 pp.

Source: MTLAcc, entry #264, volume donated by Clemens. Set in New York City in the year 2015, Sutphen's novel projects a dystopian state of chaos.

———. *The Gates of Chance*. Illustrated by Charles Johnson Post (1873–1956). New York: Harper & Brothers, 1904. 303 pp.

Source: MTLAcc, entry #1073, volume donated by Clemens.

In this collection of linked short stories a detective named Winston Thorp matches wits with diverse malefactors.

———. *The Golficide, and Other Tales of the Fair Green*. Illus. New York: Harper & Brothers, 1898. 228 pp.

Source: MTLAcc, entry #1350, volume donated by Clemens.

Among his attainments, the novelist, editor, playwright, and American Episcopalian minister Sutphen became a leading expert on the sport of golf. In 1902 he would be invited to Mark Twain's birthday celebration arranged by George Harvey at the Metropolitan Club.

SWAN, HOWARD (fl. 1890–1916). *Travellers' Colloquial Italian. A Handbook for English-Speaking Travellers and Students. Idiomatic Italian Phrases, with the Exact Pronunciation*. London:

D. Nutt, 1892. 107 pp. [Edition conjectured.]

Catalog: ListABP (1910), "Colloquial Italian", no other information supplied.

Antonio Illiano, "'Italian Without a Master': A Note for the Appreciation of Mark Twain's Undictionarial Translation as Exercise in Humor," *Mark Twain Journal* 17.2 (Summer 1974): 17–20.

SWEDENBORG, EMANUEL (1688–1772). *Heaven and Hell.* New York: General Convention of the New Jerusalem Church in the United States, 1858. 379 pp. [Originally published in 1758 as *Heaven and Its Wonders and Hell from Things Heard and Seen.*]

Source: MTLAcc, entry #932, volume donated by Clemens. William Dean Howells inquired of Clemens on 3 April 1891 whether he had received "the little Swedenborg book?" (*MTHL*, p. 640). The next day Clemens responded, "The little book is charmingly written, & it interested me. But it flies too high for me. Its concretest things are filmy abstractions to me" (*MTHL*, p. 641). Clemens added that he would try to remember to "mail it back to you." Albert Bigelow Paine noted that Swedenborg was "an author in whom the Boston literary set was always deeply interested" (*MTL*, p. 545). Swedenborg's book assured readers of an afterlife that begins in a spirit world. Mark Twain mentions Swedenborgianism approvingly in Book I, Chapter 6 of *Christian Science* (1907).

SWEET, ALEXANDER EDWIN (1841–1901) and JOHN ARMOY KNOX (1851–1906). *On a Mexican Mustang, through Texas, from the Gulf to the Rio Grande.* Hartford, Connecticut: S. S. Scranton & Co., 1883. 672 pp.

Mark Twain at least knew about this book title. When he asked his publishing firm to send him books about Native American life, Charles L. Webster replied from New York City on 9 July 1884, assuring Clemens that several were in the mail. Webster was hesitant about "a book entitled 'On a Mexican Mustang from the Gulf to Rio Grande'" that contained "only a very few" American Indian adventures. "It is published by 'Texas Siftings.' Generally, the book would be of no use so I have not sent it" (ALS in MTP). On 10 July 1884 Clemens agreed with Webster's decision: "Don't want the Texas Siftings book" (*MTBus*, p. 266). Clemens was conducting research for a novel that would ultimately remain unfinished, "Huck and Tom among the Indians."

SWETT, SOPHIE MIRIAM (1858–1912). *Captain Polly.* Illus. New York: Harper & Brothers, 1905. 306 pp.

Source: MTLAcc, entry #1168, volume donated by Clemens.

The Massachusetts author Swett wrote young adult fiction, usually with New England, often coastal, settings. Her novels typically had an upbeat, inspiring message.

———. *Flying Hill Farm; A Story.* Illus. New York: Harper & Brothers, 1892. 263 pp.

Source: MTLAcc, entry #1040, volume donated by Clemens.

———. *The Mate of the "Mary Ann"; A Story.* Illus. New York: Harper & Brothers, 1894. 235 pp.

Source: MTLAcc, entry #1662, volume donated by Clemens.

SWIFT, JONATHAN (1667–1745). *Gulliver's Travels into Several Remote Nations of the World. First American Edition Illustrated, with a Life of the Author by Rev. John Mitford [1781–1859],*

and Copious Notes by W[illiam]. C[ooke]. Taylor[1800–1849]. Original slate cloth, gilt. Philadelphia: J. B. Lippincott & Co. 1866. 431 pp.

Inscription: the front flyleaf is signed in pencil, "J. Langdon." Jervis Langdon's bookplate reads, "J. Langdon's Family Library No. 357" in blue within a gilt border.

Marginalia: "28 charter" written in pencil by Clemens on the front free endpaper even though no "charter" is mentioned on page 28; the corner of page 117 is folded down and Clemens noted in blue ink in the margin: "The elf would pack it full."; the corner of page 147 is folded down; there is a note by Clemens in blue ink in the lower margin of page 164 below a footnote: "Why the book is brim full of them!" (evidently referring to Swift's grammar errors or to W. C. Taylor's notes pointing them out); a note in blue ink on page 168 appears in the lower margin below a footnote: "The blind leading the blind" (alluding to a grammar error in a W. C. Taylor footnote citing a grammatical slip by Swift); on page 191 a marginal line in pencil was drawn beside a footnote; the corner of page 221 is folded down; a pencil note on page 239 in the bottom margin observes: "If this ass had restricted his labor to calling attention to the scattering instances where good ["good" underlined] grammar has been used in this work, he could have saved a deal of ink"(again referring to another Taylor footnote pointing out an instance of poor grammar); a pencil note in the margin of page 249 comments, "It was a poor invention. All he really needed was a permanent platform 8 feet high with a chair on it, placed 20 feet distant from the page. The letters were an inch high & easily read at that distance" (this concerned Gulliver's use of a scaffold-like platform to read the gigantic books in the library of Glumdalditch, king of the Brobdingnagians, leaning it against one page at a time in order to read one line of text at a time).

Provenance: this volume was in the Langdon family's library, whose shelves Clemens could peruse whenever he visited their residence in Elmira, New York.

Catalog: ListABP (1910), "Gulliver's Travels", no other information provided.

Location: collection of Kevin Mac Donnell, Austin, Texas (Mac Donnell to Alan Gribben, 29 November 2011). Purchased from the Langdon family.

Clemens's personal copy of *Gulliver's Travels* is not known to survive, though he definitely owned the work. A bill for twenty-one books from Estes & Lauriat of Boston, dated 14 July 1880, included one copy of "Gulliver" priced at $1.25; Clemens paid the bill on 20 July 1880 (receipt in MTP). In addition, in November or December 1885, Clemens noted, "Scribner & Welford— Gulliver,—not cloth" (NB 25, *N&J* 3: 215). However, at least we now have evidence that he also had access to, and annotated, a copy in the Langdons' library in Elmira.

Evidently Swift's 1726 satire was one of Sam Clemens's earliest reading experiences. He nicknamed a young playmate, Norval "Gull" Brady, after Lemuel Gulliver ("Recollections of Norval L. ['Gull'] Brady," Hannibal *Courier-Post*, 6 March 1935, cited in *SCH*, p. 141). In 1854 Clemens wrote that the buildings in Washington, D. C. are "strewed about in clusters. . . . They look as though they might have been emptied out of a sack by some Brobdignagian [*sic*] gentleman, and when falling, been scattered abroad by the winds" (SLC to the Muscatine *Journal*, 24 March 1854, *MTLMusc* [1942], p. 19; *MTLet* 1: 40). In "The Great Earthquake in San Francisco," New York *Weekly Review*, 25 November 1865, Mark Twain described seeing "a brick warehouse mashed in as if some foreigner from Brobdignag [*sic*] had sat down on it" (*ET&S* 2: 308). Clemens annotated *Thackeray's Lectures* (1868) in the section on Swift (see Coley B. Taylor, *Mark Twain's Margins on Thackeray's "Swift"* [New York: Gotham House, 1935]). On 2 March 1869 Clemens informed Olivia Langdon from Rochester, New York: "I have been reading—I *am* reading—Gulliver's Travels, & am much more charmed with it than I was when I read it last, in boyhood—for now I can see what a scathing satire it is upon the English government, whereas, before, I only gloated over its prodigies & its marvels. Poor Swift—under the placid surface of this simply-worded book flows the full tide of his venom—the turbid sea of his matchless hate. . . . If you would like to read it . . . I will mark it & tear it until it is fit for your eyes—for portions of it are very coarse & indelicate" (ALS in MTP, *LLMT*, p. 76; *MTLet* 1: 132). In "The Coming Man" (1871), Mark Twain wrote: "Think of my dainty Lilliputian [Twain calls him General Dewlap G. Lovel] standing in Brobdingnag [John Lothrop] Motley's shoes, and peeping out smartly over the instep at the Great Powers" (*Galaxy* 11.2 [February 1871]: 313; *CG* [1961], p. 121). (In December 1870 General Robert Cumming Schenck [1809–1890] had replaced Motley [1814–1877] as the United States minister to England.) The narrator in Chapter 3 of *Roughing It* (1872) recalls lying under a sagebrush that resembled a miniature live oak tree, "fancying that the gnats among its foliage were lilliputian birds, and that the ants marching and counter-marching about its base were lilliputian flocks and herds, and myself some vast loafer from Brobdingnag waiting to catch a little citizen and eat him." On 25 September 1873 Twain wrote to Dr. John Brown from London: "I read Gulliver all over again at Condover (*first* edition)" (*MTLet* 5: 440). Howard G. Baetzhold pointed out that Twain's "The Curious Republic of Gondour" (1875) seems influenced by Swift's satire (*MT&JB*, p. 266). An idea for an imaginary orator's pronouncement that occurred to Twain in 1879 ("The man who causes 2 dates to grow in French history where only one date grew before, is his country's benefactor") paraphrased the pronouncement by the King of Brobdingnag that "whoever could make two ears of corn, or two blades of grass, to grow upon a spot of ground where only one grew before, would . . . do more essential service to this country, than the whole race of politicians put together" (Notebook 17, *N&J* 2: 276). In Chapter 38 of *A Tramp Abroad* (1880) Twain marveled, "All the circling horizon [surrounding Monte Rosa] was piled high with a mighty tumult of snowy crests. One might have imagined he saw before him the tented camps of a beleaguering host of Brobdingnagians." In Twain's undated manuscript, "The Walt Whitman Controversy" (DV36, MTP), possibly written around 1882, he states that *Gulliver's Travels* is one of the "old bad books" he owns; to make his point about the indecencies in accepted classics, he purports to quote a passage from

Chapter 5 of the second part of this "book which is in everybody's house," but omits most of the words following "neither did they at all scruple, while I was by"—putting this pretended censorship upon the *Evening Post* editor. In the same manuscript Twain began but then canceled a quotation from Chapter 5 of the first part of Swift's work: "<The heat I had contro>".
Clara Clemens much later testified: "Now and again Father entertained us at dinner—when no guests were present—by relating the contents of books he was reading, such as *Gulliver's Travels*" (*MFMT*, p. 56). "Your other characters are good," Clemens wrote to Edgar Watson Howe on 13 February 1884 concerning Howe's *The Story of a Country Town*, "but when Big Adam strides by, it is Gulliver in Lilliput" (ALS in MTP, *MTC*, p. 265). On 20 January 1887 Clemens recommended Swift's *Gulliver's Travels* as among the best reading for young people in a letter to the Reverend Charles D. Crane (ALS, Shapell Manuscript Library, Beverly Hills, California). In a letter written from Hartford on 14 March 1887 to Joseph H. Twichell, Clemens discussed Henry Ward Beecher's adultery trial: "What a pity—that so insignificant a matter as the chastity or unchastity of an Elizabeth Tilton could clip the locks of this Samson & make him as other men, in the estimation of a nation of Lilliputians creeping & climbing about his shoe-soles" (Joseph H. Twichell's Journal, 5: 121, Yale; *NF*, p. 52; *LMTJHT*, p. 141).
It seems likely that Mark Twain hoped to produce in *A Connecticut Yankee in King Arthur's Court* (1889) a modern satire meriting comparison with *Gulliver's Travels* and *Don Quixote*. For instance, Hank Morgan observes that he is a "giant among pygmies" (see Liela Goldman's article, below). Henry Fisher reported that while Twain was in Berlin in 1891 he denounced critic-biographers who write "highfalutin' tommy-rot about the Dean's vagaries in erotics and small beer politics. There must be a considerable library on the subject, every new author threshing the old straw a tenth time, and adding mystery trimmings of his own"; Twain's own notion (according to Fisher) was that "Swift's character can be explained on the theory that he was a Sadist and a Masochist in one," judging from his cruelties to Stella, Vanessa, and the rest (*AMT*, p. 184). In August 1892 Twain wrote the title of *Gulliver's Travels* at the conclusion of a series of working notes for a new Huckleberry Finn story to be set in Africa (NB 32, TS p. 18); this suggests that *Tom Sawyer Abroad* (1894) owes something to Swift's narrative. Twain's "The Lowest Animal" (written around 1897, *LE*, pp. 222–232) seems indebted to Swift's view of mankind. Satan awes three Austrian boys by creating clay animals and tiny, castle-building Lilliputian figures in "The Chronicle of Young Satan," written 1897–1900 (*MSM*, pp. 46–52). Larry Carver of the University of Texas at Austin pointed out to me a palpable connection between Swift's Houyhnhnms and the reasonable horse to whom Satan compares Yahooish mankind in Chapter 7 of "Young Satan" (*MSM*, p. 130). Carroll D. Laverty—"The Genesis of *The Mysterious Stranger*," *Mark Twain Quarterly* 8.3–4 (Spring-Summer 1947): 17–18—explored this "comparison of men with animals, especially with horses." In 1901 Clemens alluded to Swift's painful death; see the

Catalog entry for Justin McCarthy's *A History of the Four Georges*. Clemens wrote to Olivia Clemens on 23 March 1902 to speculate that the explosion of the battleship *Maine* resembled "a brobdignagian [*sic*] tarantula in its death-squirm" (ALS in MTP). "Huck" or "Bkshp," the cholera germ who narrates "Three Thousand Years among the Microbes" (written in 1905) renames his microbe friends after his favorite literary figures; he calls two of them "Lemuel Gulliver" and "Lurbrulgrud" [*sic*] (*WWD?*, p. 471). Lorbrulgrud, a city of 600,000 and the capital of Brobdingnag, was called the "Pride of the Universe" (*Gulliver's Travels*, Part 2). In an Autobiographical Dictation of 8 November 1906, Clemens said that his imaginary mind's-eye landscapes "seem close by, but they look as they would look to a Gulliver in Lilliput" (MTP).

Brashear, *MTSM* (1934), p. 240; Hemminghaus, *MTG* (1939), p. 103; Warren M. Briggs, "Gulliver's Travels on the Mississippi River: A Question of Mark Twain's Satire (and Jonathan Swift's Humor)," Master's thesis, Columbia University, 1954 (156 pp.); Rogers, *MTBP* (1960), p. 32; Rogers, *PRI* (1961), pp. 23–24; Salomon, *TIH* (1961), p. 105; Stone, *IE* (1961), p. 260; Joseph R. Zweig, "Jonathan Swift and Mark Twain: A Study in Methods of Satire," Master's thesis, University of Pittsburgh, 1962; Wagenknecht, *MTMW* (1967), p. 63; Gibson, *MSM* (1969), p. 22; Baetzhold, *MT&JB* (1970), pp. 265–268; W. Gerald Marshall, "Mark Twain's 'The Man That Corrupted Hadleyburg' and the Myth of Baucis and Philemon," *Mark Twain Journal* 20.2 (Summer 1980): 7 n. 2; Liela Goldman, "'A Giant among Pygmies,'" *Mark Twain Journal* 21.4 (Fall 1983): 14–17; Richard H. Passon, "Twain and Eighteenth-Century Satire: The Ingenu Narrator in *Huckleberry Finn*," *Mark Twain Journal* 21.4 (Fall 1983): 33–36; and Ed Folsom and Jerome Loving, "The Walt Whitman Controversy: A Lost Document," *Virginia Quarterly Review* 83 [Spring 2007]: 123–127].

SWINBURNE, ALGERNON CHARLES (1837–1909). *The Age of Shakespeare*. New York: Harper & Brothers, 1908. 302 pp.

Source: MTLAcc, entry #1791, volume donated by Clemens.

———. *The Duke of Gandia*. New York: Harper & Brothers, 1908. 57 pp.

Inscription: the front pastedown endpaper is signed "S. L. Clemens, 1908."

Catalogs: *A1911*, "8vo, cloth, N.Y. 1908," quotes the signature, lot 444, sold for $3; American Art Association (New York City), Sale catalogue (5 February 1925), "8vo, original cloth, gilt top, uncut, first American edition, with autograph signature "S. L. Clemens, 1908" on the front pastedown flyleaf," has the *A1911* sale label, lot 115, sold for $4.

Swinburne's play about the powerful Borgia family is set in Rome in 1497.

———. *Love's Cross-Currents; A Year's Letters*. New York: Harper & Brothers, 1905. 245 pp.

Source: MTLAcc, entry #1116, volume donated by Clemens.

Swinburne's convoluted novel begins with a thirty-seven-page Prologue that eventually introduces thirty letters exchanged by half a dozen fictional (aristocratic) characters. In Mark Twain's mock letter to the New York *Evening Post*, "The Walt Whitman Controversy" (DV36, MTP), possibly written around 1882, he classes Swinburne's poetry with "the new bad books" of Wilde and Whitman, and avers that he does not own copies of any of them. Clemens mentioned Swinburne in an anecdote in 1884 (SLC to WDH, Elmira, 7 August 1884, *MTHL*, p. 498). Swinburne was one of Susy Clemens's favorite poets when she was around twelve or thirteen years old (*MFMT*, p. 66). In Mark Twain's unpublished letter about the Russian Czar written in the midsummer of 1890, he concluded: "If I am a Swinburnian—& clear to the marrow I am—I hold human nature in sufficient honor to believe there are eighty million mute Russians that are of the same stripe, & only one Russian family that isn't" (*MTL*, p. 538; *MTPP*, p. 158). King Leopold remarks that of all the Russian Czar's detractors, "the finest and capablest of the pack, and the fiercest, are Swinburne (English, I think) and a pair of Americans" ("King Leopold's Soliloquy" [March 1905]). Clemens underlined Swinburne's name in James Russell Lowell's *Letters* (Volume I, page 357) and noted that Swinburne "died two or three days ago (April, 1909.)"

Williams, "Genesis" (1961), p. 105; Ed Folsom and Jerome Loving, "Mark Twain: The Walt Whitman Controversy,'" *Virginia Quarterly Review* 83.2 (Spring 2007): 123–138.

———. *Three Plays of Shakespeare*. Harper's Library of Living Thought Series. Red cloth. New York: Harper & Brothers, 1909. 85 pp. [Essays on *King Lear*, *Othello*, and *King Richard II*.]

Inscription: the front pastedown endpaper is signed in black ink "SL. Clemens/1909." (The hand seems unusually small and clumsy.)

Marginalia: at the top of the first page in Swinburne's essay on *King Lear* (p. 3), Clemens noted in black ink: "Throughout this Essay, for 'Shakespeare' read 'Bacon.'" There are no other notes or marks.

Provenance: Antenne-Dorrance Collection, Rice Lake, Wisconsin.

Location: Mark Twain Archive, Gannett-Tripp Learning Center, Elmira College, Elmira, New York.

Copy examined: Clemens's copy. Examined on 28 May 2015.

"SWING LOW, SWEET CHARIOT" (African American spiritual). Clara Clemens remembered this as one of Clemens's cherished songs; he liked to sing it solo (*MFMT*, p. 188). Clemens listed the title among his favorite songs in August 1889 (NB 29, *N&J* 3: 328).

SWINTON, WILLIAM (1833–1892). *Rambles Among Words; Their Poetry, History, and Wisdom*. Revised ed. New York: Ivison, Blakeman, Taylor & Co.,1872. 302 pp.

Inscription: "Susan L. Crane/Elmira, N. Y./Aug. 21, 1872".

Catalog: Ball 2016 inventory, fair condition.

Location: Quarry Farm library shelves, under the supervision of the Mark Twain Archive, Elmira College, Elmira, New York.

Swinton affectionately explores the etymology of English words and phrases such as "Bon-mot," "Marriage," and "Mausoleum," categorizing them into chapters titled "Words of Abuse," "Verbal Ethics," "The Growth of Words," and so forth. This was one of the many books available to Clemens during his visits to Quarry Farm in Elmira.

————. *Outlines of the World's History, Ancient, Medieval, and Modern. . . . for Use in the Higher Classes in Public Schools, and in High Schools, Academies, Seminaries, Etc.* American Educational Series. Green cloth, red spine (broken). New York and Chicago: Ivison, Blakeman, Taylor and Co., 1874. 498 pp.

Inscription: in pencil on the front pastedown endpaper: "Susy Clemens./S S—S S S/Susan Clemens."

Marginalia: Many penciled (and a few black ink) brackets, notes, and markings throughout the volume, most apparently in a young hand although a few could be by an older person. Those that most resemble Clemens's habitual methods are vertical penciled brackets on pages 155–161 (relating to the history of ancient Rome), 427 (regarding Napoleon Bonaparte) and 441 (on the French Constitution). Susy Clemens's jottings of historical dates on the rear endpapers cover the period 1547–1603. There is also a note: "Read Don Quixote/Read Essays of Montaigne."

Provenance: there is a booksticker on the rear paste-down endpaper of "Brown & Gross,/BOOKSELLERS/Hartford, Ct."

Location: Mark Twain House and Museum, Hartford, Connecticut. Donated on 30 May 1986 by Yvonne Rogow of Los Angeles. Originally from the collection of Phyllis Harrington, Clara Clemens Samossoud's secretary and friend. Rogow's father was a friend of Phyllis Harrington, and Harrington made Yvonne Rogow the executor of her estate.

Copy examined: Susy Clemens's school textbook, worn. Examined on 12 August 1987.

SWISSHELM, JANE GREY (CANNON) (1815–1884). *Half a Century.* Third edition. Chicago: Jansen, McClurg & Co., 1880. 360 pp.

Swisshelm wrote to Mark Twain on 19 January 1880 to apologize for allowing her publishers to employ Twain's praise in advertisements for the third edition of her autobiography (MTP). Twain had been lavish in complimenting her memoir: "This whole nation ought to thank you for writing it. It is the record, bravely set down, of a most brave life—and excellent life, a high and great life. . . . I read it when it first came out, and am not wholly quieted down yet; neither do I wish to be, for it is wholesome to be stirred, so I shall read it again now" (quoted from an advertisement in Joaquin Miller's *Shadows of Shasta* [1881], another title by the same publisher). Notebook 19 contained a reminder Twain made for himself: "Write Mrs. Swisshelm" (*N&J* 2: 387). Newspaper journalist and editor Swisshelm had been a fiery abolitionist before the Civil War and then a volunteer nurse during the conflict; she also gained prominence as a writer and public speaker on behalf of women's rights and the temperance movement.

SYBEL, HEINRICH VON (1817–1895). *The Founding of the German Empire by William I. Based Chiefly upon Prussian State Documents.* Translated from the German by Marshall Livingston Perrin (1855–1935), assisted by Gamaliel Bradford (1863–1932), Jr. 7 vols. New York: Thomas Y. Crowell & Co., [1890–1898].

Location: Volumes I-V only, Albert and Shirley Small Special Collections Library, University of Virginia, Charlottesville, Virginia. Gift of Clifton Waller Barrett.

Copies examined: presumably Clemens's copies of five volumes, though the books bear no inscriptions, marginalia,

auction labels, or other confirmation that they belonged to Clemens. However, because these books came to the University of Virginia from Clifton Waller Barrett, and inasmuch as Barrett was known to be a highly knowledgeable collector, they ought to be viewed as authentic association copies.

————. [Identical set of volumes.]

Catalog: Ball 2016 inventory, 5 vols., 1890 publication date, black cloth with blue and marble boards, gilt lettering on spine, good condition.

Location: Quarry Farm library shelves, under the supervision of the Mark Twain Archive, Elmira College, Elmira, New York.

A set of volumes available to Clemens during his visits to Quarry Farm in Elmira.

SYDNEY, AUSTRALIA *Bulletin.*

"Punch (Melbourne) & Bulletin (Sydney) good papers. Good & bright cartoons in both; Bulletin bright enough to hold its own in any country" (NB 34 [October 1895], TS p. 14).

SYME. *Central Africa.* [Unidentified author and title.]

Mark Twain quotes from a work with this name in a discarded chapter from *A Tramp Abroad* (1880) that compares French courtship and marriage practices with the rituals of African tribes (MS p. 99, Box 6, no. 7, MTP). He seems to have been disguising the name of Charles Chaillé-Long, who published *Central Africa: Naked Truths of Naked People* in 1877. See also the Catalog entry for *A Summer in Africa.*

SYMMONS, CHARLES (1749–1826). *The Life of John Milton.* London, 1810.

Clemens cited this book among other "biogs of Milton" in Notebook 27 (September 1887, *N&J* 3: 328).

SYMONDS, JOHN ADDINGTON (1840–1893).

Susy Clemens described seeing Symonds's "poor daughter" and alluded to "her father's death" in a letter to Louise Brownell postmarked in Florence on 12 June 1893: "It was altogether a most horrible and tragic death, and he was so in the prime of his mental vigor" (Hamilton College Archives). Essayist, biographer, literary critic, and poet Symonds wrote daringly about themes involving homosexual attraction.

▌T

Tableaux de la Révolution Française; An Historical Reader. Edited, with Notes, by T[homas]. F[rederick]. Crane [1844–1927] and S[amuel]. J[acquis]. Brun. Intro. by Andrew D[ickson]. White (1832–1918). New York: G. P. Putnam's Sons, 1884. 311 pp.

Catalog: Ball 2016 inventory, red cloth with black design and lettering, good condition.

Location: Quarry Farm library shelves, under the supervision of the Mark Twain Archive, Elmira College, Elmira, New York.

The text, prepared by two Cornell University professors, is in French; their explanatory notes are in English. Andrew D. White was then the president of Cornell University. Clemens had access to this book during his visits to Quarry Farm in Elmira.

TACITUS, PUBLIUS CORNELIUS (56 C.E.-c. 120 C.E.). *The Works of Tacitus. The Oxford Translation, Revised. With Notes.*

Harper's New Classical Library Series. 2 vols. 8vo, original blue cloth, the rear cover of Volume II is somewhat spotted and the endpaper is cracked at the front inner hinge. New York: American Book Co., n.d.

Inscriptions: the front pastedown endpaper of Volume I is signed in black ink, "S L. Clemens/November, 1905./21—5th Ave." On its title page Clemens twice underscored with black ink the word "Revised" and wrote beneath it: "What, the English of it? If so, in the name of God what was it like *before* it was 'revised'?" (A few editions of "The Oxford Translation" credited J. L. Kingsley as the translator, but Clemens's copy does not identify a translator.) Clemens signed the front pastedown endpaper of Volume II in black ink, "S. L. Clemens/Nov. 1905/21 Fifth Avenue."

Marginalia: Clemens made approximately a dozen notations in Volume I, using black ink and pencil; he wrote comments and corrections in Volume II in the same black ink and pencil. He folded down corners of pages throughout both volumes. Numerous marginalia seek to improve the prose; on page 34 of Volume I, for instance, Clemens changed (in pencil) the phrase "if they disobeyed" to read "if (the soldiers) disobeyed"; on page 2 he employed black ink to delete one word and a letter in the sentence, "Nor were there wanting authors of distinguished genius to <have> compose<d> the history of the times." Clemens left a trail of exasperated notes in black ink on the leaves of Volume I: "Execrable English" (p. 122); "Doubtless this translator can read Latin, but he can't write English" (p. 202); "'pidgin' English" (p. 205); "To *quote* a man puts the man's remark in the first person, but this fossil doesn't know that" (p. 215, where Clemens underlined usages of the pronoun *he*); and "What does this ass mean by that?" (p. 242). Clemens marked with black ink a passage on page 225 of Volume I that discussed the opinion "that the gods take no interest in the beginning or the end of our course, or in short, in humanity in any aspect: and thence so eternally calamities afflict the upright, while prosperity attends the wicked"; Clemens observed: "Apparently they were not all fools in that early day." Volume II contains extensive additional corrections and markings, mostly in black ink but a few in pencil. His notes in black ink on seventeen pages total 169 words. Several pages have corners turned down. Beside the assertion that the Roman people learned that "the gods are not concerned about the protection of the innocent, but the punishment of the guilty," Clemens commented in black ink, "They found out that indisputable fact so early as that" (p. 3). In Volume II Clemens continued his black-ink cavils about the translation: "This book's English is the rottenest that was ever/puked upon paper" (p. 100, a note written vertically). On the same page he attempted to repair the grammar with nine revisions in black ink in the second paragraph. Other objections followed: "Could the baggage bring corn?" (p. 221); "He probably means a hog" (p. 235, deleting the word "swine"); "But this more recent ass believes it" (p. 266, concerning omission of the miraculous passage through the Red Sea); "How would you expiate a prodigy?" (p. 276); "O, hear the pot calling the kettle black!" (p. 276). Regarding the death of the Roman emperor Otho, Clemens quoted Malcolm from

Macbeth: "Nothing in his life became him like the leaving of it'" (p. 101, black ink). (Emperor Marcus Salvius Otho [32 C.E.-69 C.E.] committed suicide after leading an ill-advised military campaign that ended in defeat.) Where Tacitus mentioned on page 247 that Arretinus Clemens was both a Roman senator as well as a commander of the praetorian guards, Clemens joked: "An error of judgment. There was never yet a Clemens who could creditably fill two stations at the same time" (black ink). (Though formerly a friend of Domitian, Arretinus Clemens became one of the Domitian's early victims after he was named Emperor.) On page 326 Clemens noted in black ink, "In this great eulogy he paints the opposite of the Romans without noticing that he is doing it." At the top of page 338 Clemens wrote, "Calls it a 'globe'—at that early day" (black ink).

Catalogs: ListABP (1910), "Tacitus 2 v."; *C1951*, D22, Vol. I only, $17.50; Christie's, New York City, 1–2 February 1988 auction, lot 461, Volume II only, sold for $3,300 to Dawson's Book Shop of Los Angeles.

Provenance: for nearly half a century Volume II only was in the Carrie Estelle Doheny Collection, St. John's Seminary, Camarillo, California, having been donated by Mrs. Doheny in 1940 after she purchased it from Maxwell Hunley Rare Books of Beverly Hills for $12.20. Christie's auctioned Volume II (only) in 1988 on behalf of St. John's Seminary and the Archdiocese of Los Angeles.

Locations: Volume I only, Henry E. Huntington Library, San Marino, California; donated by Robert F. Sisk in November 1959. The whereabouts of Volume II is currently unknown.

Copies examined: Clemens's copies of both volumes. I examined Volume I at the Henry E. Huntington Library on 27 July 1997. I had inspected Volume II at St. John's Seminary in 1970.

Twain's first reference to the Roman historian, orator, and public official Tacitus seems to have occurred in an 1895 interview: "In those German forests where the British constitution was reared, beer, according to Tacitus [,] was popular" ("Mark Twain on Prohibition," September, October, or November 1895, *Licensing Guardian*, New South Wales, in Gary Scharnhorst, *Mark Twain: The Complete Interviews*, p. 222). By the final half decade of Clemens's life, Tacitus had become one of his favorite historians. Clemens returned home on 12 April 1906 "so tired he couldn't eat any dinner. . . . Later [Isabel Lyon] slipped into the room to find him reading 'Tacitus' and very tired" (IVL Journal, Harry Ransom Center, University of Texas at Austin). Isabel Lyon's journal for Monday, 16 April 1906 related how she found Clemens in his room after dinner, "reading Tacitus and oh, so tired and so dear and *so* beautiful" (TS p. 157, MTP). She recorded on Sunday, 12 August 1906 that Clemens "lay in his bed smoking and reading Roman History" (IVL Journals, TS p. 179, MTP). On 5 August 1909 Clemens told Albert Bigelow Paine, "When I read Tacitus and know that I am reading history I can accept it [bloody violence] as such and supply the imaginary details and enjoy it" (*MTB*, p. 1516).

TAINE, HIPPOLYTE ADOLPHE (1828–1893). *The Ancient Régime*. Translated from the French by John Durand (1822–1908). Octavo. Original green cloth, gilt lettering, brown-coated endpapers. New York: Henry Holt and Co., 1876. 421 pp.

Inscription: the front free endpaper is signed in pencil, "Saml. L. Clemens/Hartford 1876."

Marginalia: there are pencil marks and annotations by Clemens on pages 8, 43, 53, 56, 87, 104, 105, 116, and 402. Apparently he read the book at least twice; on the final leaf of the text he noted, "Finished Jan 29th" and beneath that he later added, "Finished Sept. 10th."

Catalogs: *A1911*, "l2mo, cloth, N.Y. 1876, . . . with several annotations in Mr. Clemens' autograph," quotes the signature, lot 447, $5.50; Robert T. Slotta's Admirable Books, Dublin, Ohio, "Clemens' own copy with his ownership signature and his annotations in pencil, purple ink, and brown ink through the book" (advertised in *AB Bookman's Weekly*, 16 September 1991, clipping sent to Alan Gribben by Joel Myerson); *Sotheby's 2003*, #211, $2,250 (sold with four other history titles). In 2007 (for $22,000) and again in 2012 (for $22,500) Charles Parkhurst Rare Books of Prescott, Arizona offered the volume, "water staining to about the last 20 leaves, binding somewhat worn, hinges cracked but holding well, housed in a custom leather backed clamshell." In 2016 the Charles Parkhurst firm moved to Sun City West, Arizona. This volume remained unsold as of 12 January 2016 (telephone call by Alan Gribben to Charles Parkhurst). The volume reappeared in the Holiday Catalog of Bauman Rare Books, New York City, December 2019, quoting the inscription and Clemens's two notations, reporting light dampstain to the final few leaves, wear to the spine ends, inner paper hinges tender, an *A1911* auction label is present, priced at $25,000.

Provenance: William Duncan Cheney, San Francisco, inscribed the *A1911* auction label, which is affixed to the front pastedown endpaper. Robert T. Slotta of Dublin, Ohio obtained the volume in April 1991 (Slotta to Alan Gribben, 23 April 1991). Subsequently it entered the collection of Nick Karanovich, Fort Wayne, Indiana.

Location: currently undetermined.

Copy examined: Clemens's copy, briefly examined at the 2003 Sotheby's sale.

On 6 August 1877 Clemens referred to this book, along with works by Carlyle and Dumas, as histories that helped clear up his confusion about French events (SLC to Mary Mason Fairbanks, *MTMF*, p. 208). In May 1887 Mark Twain made plans to incorporate *L'Ancien Régime* in a projected series to be titled "Royalty & Nobility Exposed" (NB 26, *N&J* 3: 295). Twain intended to cite Taine's *L'Ancien Régime* as a supporting source in the proposed appendix for *A Connecticut Yankee* (1889; Notebook 29, *N&J* 3: 505–506). The duchess at King Arthur's royal banquet (*CY* [1889], Ch. 17) "could have sat in advance for the portrait of the young daughter of the Regent d'Orleans, at the famous dinner whence she was carried, foul-mouthed, intoxicated, and helpless, to her bed, in the lost and lamented days of the Ancient Regime." The 10 September 1891 issue of *The Youth's Companion* (Boston) reprinted a story from an unidentified issue of the Buffalo *Courier* about an amusing incident that occurred when Olivia Clemens and a friend tried to purchase a copy of Taine's *Ancient Régime* in "a bookstore in New York." The sales clerk, unfamiliar with

either the author or the title, insisted that "you have the name a little wrong. You mean Twain—not Taine" (Kevin Mac Donnell to Alan Gribben, 6 June 2007). Sherwood Cummings called *The Ancient Régime* "the sixth and last of the books which fundamentally influenced the evolution of his philosophy" and deduced that Twain "borrowed liberally from it for material and incidents in both *The Prince and the Pauper* and *A Connecticut Yankee*" (*Mark Twain and Science*, p. 76).

Howard G. Baetzhold, "Course of Composition" (1961), p. 200; James D. Williams, "Genesis" (1961); Williams, "Use of History" (1965), pp. 102–110; Rodney O. Rogers, "*A Tramp Abroad*, *A Connecticut Yankee*, and Taine's *L'Ancien Régime*: An Instance of Source Adaptation in Mark Twain's Writings" (Master's thesis, University of Virginia, 1965); Baetzhold, *MT&JB* (1970), pp. 30–31, 344 n. 50; Rodney O. Rogers, "Twain, Taine, and Lecky: The Genesis of a Passage in *A Connecticut Yankee*," *Modern Language Quarterly* 34 (December 1973): 436–447; and Sherwood Cummings, *Mark Twain and Science* (1988), pp. 76–80, 112–118, 162. Everett Emerson specified some of the details that Twain borrowed from Taine for *The Prince and the Pauper* ("Afterword," *The Prince and the Pauper* [New York: Oxford University Press, 1996], p. 4).

———. *History of English Literature. A New Edition.* Translated from the French by Henri Van Laun (1820–1896). 2 vols. London: Chatto & Windus, n.d. [The translator's preface is dated 1871.]

Inscription: the front free endpaper of Volume I is inscribed by Clemens in pencil, "Olivia L. Clemens". Volume II is not inscribed.

Marginalia: both Clemens and Olivia Clemens made pencil marks throughout Volume I. Olivia Clemens wrote "Beautiful Manners" on page 72 of that volume. In Volume II, Clemens changed "hung" to "hanged" in black ink on page 51. There are no other notes. Some of the pencil marks in Volume II—on pages 6, 206, and 367—are distinguishable as Clemens's. The leaves have not been opened beyond page 367 in Volume II.

Catalogs: *C1951*, #020; *Zeitlin 1951*, item #43, 2 vols., $30.

Location: Volumes I and II, Mark Twain Papers, Bancroft Library, University of California at Berkeley. Donated by Jake Zeitlin.

Copies examined: Clemens's copies of both volumes.

On 14 July 1880 Estes & Lauriat, Boston publishers and book dealers, billed Clemens for "1 Taine's Lit 2 vol $3"; Clemens paid the bill on 20 July 1880 (receipt in MTP). In August 1885 Clemens made notes while assembling "Picturesque Incidents in History & Tradition," a project he never began; one of his entries reads, "Plague & Fire of London. Copy from Pepys. Also see 315 Taine's English Literature" (NB 24, *N&J* 3: 173). In "The Brazilian Republic," a piece Twain published in the Boston *Herald* (29 December 1889), p. 12, he employed a phrase— "monarchical fripperies" that appeared in Taine's chapter on John Milton in *History of English Literature* (Gary Scharnhorst, "Mark Twain on the Brazilian Revolution: A Recovered Essay," *American Literary Realism* 50.1 [Fall 2017]: 90, 93). Henry Fisher recalled that in London, possibly in 1896, Clemens dubbed Taine "the Father of English literature . . . because he made so many people read serious books which without his advice and encouragement they would never have tackled" (*AMT*, p. 138). Rodney O. Rogers, "Twain, Taine, and Lecky" (1973), pp. 436–447.

———. *Notes on England. Translated, with an Introductory Chapter, by W[illiam]. F[raser]. Rae [1835–1905].* New York: Holt & Williams, 1872. 377 pp.

Inscription: the first flyleaf is signed in pencil, "Livy L. Clemens/1873/Hartford." The second flyleaf is signed in brownish-black ink, "Saml. L. Clemens/Hartford, 1873."

Marginalia: pencil marks in Clemens's hand appear on pages 110, 111, 117, and 139. The book contains no notes.

Catalog: *C1951*, #62c, $13.

Provenance: Mrs. Louise Halley of Santa Barbara, California purchased this volume for .50¢ from a second-hand bookstore in Santa Barbara in May 1972. She became curious about the signatures and eventually contacted the Mark Twain Papers in the Bancroft Library at the University of California at Berkeley.

Location: Mark Twain Papers, Bancroft Library, University of California at Berkeley. Acquired in September 1972 for $75 from Mrs. Louise Halley of Santa Barbara, California. The transaction was arranged in Santa Barbara by Alan Gribben on behalf of Frederick Anderson, then the Editor of the Mark Twain Papers.

Copy examined: Clemens's copy, belonging jointly to Olivia Clemens.

Taine based this book on visits he made to England and Scotland between 1861 and 1871. His impressions of English society were wide-ranging: the governing classes, clergy, working classes, theatres, *Punch* magazine, street preachers, English poetry, life at the university, and dozens of other topics. His observations on "French Wit and English Humour" (Chapter 30) would surely have intrigued Mark Twain. In Chapter 36 of *The Gilded Age* (1873) Laura Hawkins buys a copy of Taine's *Notes on England*—"an American reprint of an English translation"—during her first visit to a bookstore in Washington, D.C. It is, she says, "a volume that is making a deal of talk just now, and is very widely known." (Bryant Morey French, *MT&GA* [1965], p. 62, listed Chapter 36 of *The Gilded Age* among those written by Twain without Charles Dudley Warner's collaboration.)

Williams, "Use of History" (1965), p. 106.

———. *A Tour Through the Pyrenees.* Translated from the French by John Safford Fiske (1837–1907). Illustrated by [Paul] Gustave Doré (1832–1883). New York: Henry Holt and Co., 1874. 349 pp. [Publisher and pages conjectured.]

Inscription: the front free endpaper is signed, "S. L. Clemens, Hartford, 1875."

Catalogs: *A1911*, "square 8vo, cloth, gilt edges, N.Y. 1874," quotes the signature, lot 446, sold for $3.50; *Lexington 1912*, item #24, sold for $6.50.

The formidable Pyrenees mountain range extends for nearly 300 miles along the border between France and Spain.

———. *A Tour Through the Pyrenees.* Translated from the French by John Safford Fiske (1837–1907). Illustrated by [Paul] Gustave Doré (1832–1883). Original green pictorial cloth, gilt. New York: Henry Holt and Co., 1875. 349 pp.

Inscription: the front flyleaf is inscribed in ink by Olivia Clemens, "Merry Christmas/to/C. J. Langdon/1874/

Livy." Charles Jervis Langdon was Olivia's brother who had introduced Clemens to her.

Provenance: originally in the Langdon family library.

Location: collection of Kevin Mac Donnell, Austin, Texas (Mac Donnell to Alan Gribben, 29 November 2011 and 30 August 2017). Purchased from the Langdon family.

TALBOT, ETHELBERT (1848–1928). *My People of the Plains.* Illus. New York: Harper & Brothers, 1906. 265 pp.

Source: MTLAcc, entry #559, volume donated by Clemens.

Talbot recounts his experiences as an Episcopal missionary in the regions that later became Idaho and Wyoming. He began as a minister to the Shoshone and Arapaho tribes on the Wind River Reservation. His descriptions of the Native Americans, like his testimony about the Mormons he encounters, are calmly matter-of-fact in tone.

———. [Another identical copy.]

Source: MTLAcc, entry #1703, volume donated by Clemens.

TALIAFERRO, H[ARDY]. E[DWARDS]. (1811–1875).

When Mark Twain made notes in August 1885 for a projected essay on wit and humor, he planned to quote from "that forgotten Tennessee humorist" (NB 24, *N&J* 3: 172). Although Taliaferro wrote comic sketches mainly about North Carolina, where he was born, and Alabama, where he spent his middle years, Twain may have been aware that Taliaferro moved to Roane County, Tennessee in 1829 and lived there for six years before moving to Talladega, Alabama. In 1873 he returned to Tennessee, where he died.

George Washington Harris is of course another possibility for the "forgotten Tennessee humorist" Clemens had in mind, but in earlier notebooks (see the G. W. Harris entry) he had easily recalled the names of Harris and his character Sut Lovingood. Opie Read (1852–1939), by comparison, was hardly "forgotten" in 1885—in fact was a rising humorist and author. Taliaferro, then, would seem like the best candidate for being the Tennessee humorist whose name Clemens could not recall.

TALLEYRAND-PÉRIGORD, CHARLES MAURICE DE (1754–1838).

Clemens mentioned Talleyrand in a newspaper interview ("Mark Twain in Paris," New York *Sun*, 27 January 1895): "There was Talleyrand. . . . Every brilliant thing he said was repeated and recorded because Talleyrand said it. Suppose somebody else had said these same things, people would have paid no attention to them" (Louis J. Budd, "Mark Twain Talks Mostly About Humor and Humorists," *Studies in American Humor* 1 [April 1974]: 8; also reprinted in Scharnhorst, *Complete Interviews* [2006], pp. 146). Thomas Bailey Aldrich's biographer Ferris Greenslet later paraphrased this interview but mistakenly dated it as occurring in 1885: "Mark Twain was telling a Parisian interviewer: 'Thomas Bailey Aldrich has said fifteen hundred if not fifteen thousand things as brilliant as the things Talleyrand said, which are labelled "French Wit"'" (Greenslet, *The Life of Thomas Bailey Aldrich* [Boston: Houghton Mifflin Co., 1908], p. 157).

TALMAGE, THOMAS DE WITT (1832–1902). *Crumbs Swept Up.* Philadelphia: Evans, Stoddard & Co., 1870. 445 pp. [Edition conjectured.]

Mark Twain's best-known assault on Talmage's notion of Christianity was "About Smells," a column published in the *Galaxy* 9.5 (May 1870): 721–722 (*WIM?*, pp. 48–50). A few months later Twain apparently referred to *Crumbs Swept Up*, a collection of essays and stories, mentioning on 22 December 1870 "De Witt Talmage's new book of rubbish" to Elisha Bliss, Jr. (*MTLet* 4: 281). Joe B. Fulton, *The Reverend Mark Twain: Theological Burlesque, Form, and Content* (Columbus: Ohio State University Press, 2006), pp. 57, 58, 98–100, and 196; Harold K. Bush, Jr., *Mark Twain and the Spiritual Crisis of His Age* (Tuscaloosa: University of Alabama Press, 2007), pp. 73–75.

———. *Daily Thoughts*. New York: Dodd, Mead & Co., 1877. 496 pp.

Source: MTLAcc, entry #906, volume donated by Clemens.

———. *Old Wells Dug Out. Third Series*. New York: Harper & Brothers, [cop. 1874]. 432 pp.

Source: MTLAcc, entry #934, volume donated by Clemens.

———. *Sermons. Second Series*. New York: Harper & Brothers, 1877. 416 pp.

Source: MTLAcc, entry #933, volume donated by Clemens.

One sign of the low esteem in which Mark Twain held Talmage's views is that "Talmage's Sermons" appears among a list of works by humorists that Twain considered for an anthology in 1880 (NB 19, *N&J* 2: 362). Talmage figures prominently in an unfinished satire Twain began in 1881, "The Second Advent" (*FM*, pp. 50–68). To a reporter in 1895 Twain complained that when he "bought his [Talmage's] book of sermons," intending to write a burlesque, they had been "edited carefully" and seemed too "reasonable" to make fun of (Melbourne *Age*, 27 September 1895, *Complete Interviews* [2006], p. 234). Twain remarked in another interview in February 1896 that the face of a holy man in Benares reminded him of "Dr. DeWitt Talmage. But the head is more intellectual than that of Talmage" (*Complete Interviews*, p. 286). Sandy McWilliams explains in *Extract from Captain Stormfield's Visit to Heaven* (1909): "There's a Brooklyn preacher by the name of Talmage, who is laying up a considerable disappointment for himself [by expecting to embrace Abraham, Isaac, and Jacob]. . . . They ain't any fonder of kissing the emotional highlights of Brooklyn than you be" (*RP*, p. 61).

TAMMEN, HARRY HEYE (1856–1924). *Objects of Interest from the Plains and Rocky Mountains*. Denver, Colorado: H. H. Tammen, 1886. "Price 10 cents." 33 pp.

Inscription: the front wrapper is signed at the top in black ink, "Mark Twain."

Catalog: "A Check List of the Theodore H. Koundakjian Collection of Native American Humor of the Nineteenth Century." Part One: Mark Twain. Twenty copies, privately printed. Berkeley, California, 1970, p. 2.

Location: in the private collection of Theodore H. Koundakjian, Albany, California in 1982.

Copy examined: a photocopy of the entire pamphlet that was sent to Alan Gribben by Theodore H. Koundakjian on 13 December 1982.

Tammen assembled here a catalog of artifacts and mounted animals plundered or purchased in the Rocky Mountains. The modestly priced offerings included clay figures and pottery from "the Moki Pueblos" of New Mexico, various mineral specimens, "rare Indian arrow points," stuffed prairie dogs (replete with their burrows), "Indian bead-work, war-clubs, blankets, etc.," stuffed owls, woodpeckers, hawks, and dozens of other bird species, mounted elk, buffalo, and antelope heads, and so forth.

Clemens had been interested in acquiring books about Native Americans and the Far West in 1884 when he was trying to extend Huckleberry Finn's adventures in that direction, but even if his interest carried over into 1886 and took the form of perusing bizarre mail order catalogs, there are still problems with this item. The autograph does not appear to be authentic in execution; the "rhythm" of it is vaguely wrong, and the individual letters seem heavy and clumsy-looking. Moreover, it was highly unusual for Clemens to employ his pseudonym in his library books. This is a highly dubious association item.

TANNENBAUM, SAMUEL AARON (1873–1948). *Was William Shakespeare a Gentleman? Some Questions in Shakespeare's Biography Determined*. Illus. New York: Tenny Press, 1909. 29 pp. [Edition conjectured but presumed to be correct.]

Catalog: ListABP (1910), "Wm. Shakespeare, Gentleman, Tannenbaum", no other information provided.

Was William Shakespeare a Gentleman? examined a coat of arms. The Hungarian-born Tannenbaum was one of the first psychoanalysts to practice in the United. He was also an authority on Shakespeare and a proponent of socialized medicine.

TANSWELL, JOHN (1800–1864). *The History and Antiquities of Lambeth*. Illus. First edition. Original purple cloth, gilt, rebacked with original spine preserved. London: Frederick Pickton, 1858. 245 pp., plus "List of Subscribers."

Inscription: "Mark Twain, with much respect, from Canon Benham, D.D., of Trinity College, Hartford, U.S.A." William Benham (1831–1910), an Honorary Canon of Canterbury Cathedral, had been awarded the D. D. degree by Trinity College of Hartford, Connecticut in 1898. (JoDee Benussi made this identification.)

Catalogs: *A1911*, "8vo, cloth, Lond. 1858," quotes the inscription, lot 448, sold for $1.25; *Sotheby's 2003*, #217, $4,000 (sold with four other inscribed books).

Provenance: formerly in the collection of Nick Karanovich, Fort Wayne, Indiana.

Location: collection of Kevin Mac Donnell, Austin, Texas.

Copy examined: Clemens's unmarked copy, in July 2004. Contains the *A1911* sale label.

TAPPAN, EVA MARCH (1854–1930). *Robin Hood, His Book*. Color plates. Boston: Little, Brown & Co., 1903. 267 pp.

Catalogs: QF Martinez, good plus condition; Ball 2016 inventory, green cloth, black embossed lettering and design.

Location: Quarry Farm library shelves, under the supervision of the Mark Twain Archive, Elmira College, Elmira, New York.

This book written for juveniles was available to Clemens during his remaining Quarry Farm visits. The Robin Hood legend endured as one of his favorite subjects.

TARBELL, IDA MINERVA (1857–1944). *The History of the Standard Oil Company*. 2 vols. Illus. New York: McClure, Phillips & Co., 1904.

On 26 December 1901 Henry H. Rogers complained to Clemens about Tarbell's unsympathetic attitude toward the Standard Oil Company (*MTHHR*, p. 478). From Riverdale, Clemens subsequently arranged meetings between Tarbell and Rogers through the assistance of the art editor and art historian August F[lorian]. Jaccaci (1857–1930) (*MTHHR*, p. 480). Tarbell's book ran serially in *McClure's Magazine* from October 1902 until October 1904. "Miss Tarbell always gives you a good character, as a man . . . but she gives you no rank as a conspirator," Clemens wrote gloatingly to Rogers from Florence, Italy on 21 March 1904 (*MTHHR*, pp. 559–560).

———. *The Life of Abraham Lincoln, Drawn from Original Sources.* 2 vols. Illus. New York: McClure, Phillips & Co., 1908.
   Source: MTLAcc, entries #823 and #824, volumes donated by Clemens.
   Henry Fisher reported that "when Ida M. Tarbell's 'Life of Lincoln' was running in McClure's during the late nineties, Mark said at luncheon at the Cafe Ronacher, Vienna, one afternoon: 'That woman is writing a wonderfully good and accurate, intimate and comprehensive book'" (*AMT*, p. 147). After 1908, Tarbell was one of Clemens's neighbors in Redding, Connecticut (*MTGF*, p. 206).

TARKINGTON, BOOTH (1869–1946). *Beasley's Christmas Party.* Illustrated by Ruth Sypherd Clements (1887–1924). Red cloth. New York: Harper & Brothers, 1909. 100 pp.
   Provenance: Antenne-Dorrance Collection, Rice Lake, Wisconsin.
   Location: Mark Twain Archive, Gannett-Tripp Learning Center, Elmira College, Elmira, New York.
   Copy examined: Clemens's copy, unmarked. Examined on 27 May 2015.
   Under an entry in Clemens's notebook for 7 December 1901, he wondered about a detail concerning a dinner at the Metropolitan Club with Colonel Harvey: "Has Tarkington a wife?" (NB 44, TS p. 19). Clemens wrote a letter about *Beasley's Christmas Party* ("I don't like Christmas stories, but this one is an exception") to Harper & Brothers on 3 November 1909; his note was reproduced in the 18 December 1909 issue of *Harper's Weekly Magazine* and then echoed by Albert Bigelow Paine, who recorded that on 10 November 1909 Clemens, who was reading *Beasley's Christmas Party* while propped up in bed, remarked: "I seldom read Christmas stories, but this is very beautiful. It has made me cry. I want you to read it. . . . Tarkington has the true touch, . . . his work always satisfies me" (*MTB*, p. 1535). On 10 November 1909 Clemens wrote to Elizabeth Wallace: "I sent you Booth Tarkington's little Xmas tale the other day. I hate Christmas stories, but this one is bright and felicitous, and hasn't any religion in it, and I like it" (*MT&HI*, p. 134). The admiration was certainly mutual; Tarkington supplied a prefatory "Appreciation" for *The Adventures of Tom Sawyer* in the so-called Definitive Edition of Twain's works (New York, Gabriel Wells, 1922–1925), and in an Introduction for the Limited Editions Club's *Adventures of Huckleberry Finn* (New York, 1933), Tarkington averred that "time has not shaken it, nor will shake it" (p. 7). Tarkington set the novella *Beasley's Christmas Party* in the American Midwest. A young reporter becomes curious about the private life of David Beasley, a local politician with statewide appeal. Beasley's mysterious Christmas party reveals his caregiving responsibilities for an ill, disabled, and orphaned boy, and the reporter learns

much more, besides.

———. *The Conquest of Canaan: A Novel.* Illustrated by Lucius W[alcott]. Hitchcock (1868–1942). New York: Harper & Brothers, 1905. 389 pp.
   Source: MTLAcc, entry #1483, volume donated by Clemens.
   Stepbrothers Joe Louden and Eugene Bantry receive altogether different treatments by the self-righteous citizens of Canaan, Indiana.

———. *The Gentleman from Indiana.* New York: Doubleday & McClure, 1900. 384 pp.
   Source: MTLAcc, entry #297, volume donated by Clemens.

———. *His Own People.* Illustrated by Lawrence Mazzanovich and F. R. Gruger. New York: Doubleday, Page & Co., 1907. 150 pp.
   Source: MTLAcc, entry #298, volume donated by Clemens.

———. *Monsieur Beaucaire.* Illustrated by C[harles]. D[avid]. Williams (1875–1954). Front hinge cracked at the title page. New York: McClure, Phillips & Co., 1900. 128 pp.
   Provenance: has the shelfmarks of Clara Clemens Gabrilowitsch's library numbering system during her Detroit years. Sold at the 1951 auction in Hollywood but not listed in the hastily prepared sale sheet.
   Catalog: "Property from the Library of Mark Twain," Butterfield & Butterfield, San Francisco, Sale 6613 (16 July 1997), lot 2712.
   Location: Mark Twain House and Museum, Hartford, Connecticut.
   Copy examined: Clemens's unmarked copy. Viewed in Hartford in 1997.
   In this novella a French barber's impersonation leads to romantic complications in England. Clemens generally enjoyed tales employing impersonation.

TASMAN, ABEL JANSZOON (1603–1659). [Diary.]
   The Dutch explorer Tasman was the first European to reach New Zealand, in 1642. On 6 November 1895 Clemens noted in Dunedin, New Zealand: "Livy, Clara & I went to Dr. Hochen's house, saw his wife & young daughter & *him*. Noble collection of books relating to N. Z. Gave me his translation of Tasman's diary" (NB 34, TS p. 30). Hochen was a Dunedin physician who had excelled in collecting materials and writing about the history of New Zealand. It was actually Dr. Hocken's wife Bessie (Elizabeth Mary [Buckland] Hocken), his partner in all his activities, who had translated Tasman's diary; her husband then made its contents available to historians.

TASSO, TORQUATO (1544–1595). *Amyntas, A Sylvan Fable.* Translated by Frederic Whitmore (1852–1954). Illustrated by William R. Whitmore (1854–1907). Springfield, Massachusetts: Ridgewood Press, 1900. 72 pp.
   Source: MTLAcc, entry #2108, volume donated from Clemens's library by Clara Clemens Gabrilowitsch in 1910.
   On 13 January 1901 Clemens praised an unidentified "translation" that he had showed to William Dean Howells; "He was fervent in his praises of that translation. . . . I told him I thought the authors had made & printed other translations in their private press in Springfield, or were purposing to do it" (SLC to Harriet E. Whitmore, ALS, MTP). See also the Catalog entry for Frederic Whitmore's *A Florida Farm.*

———. *La Gerusalemme Liberata; con Note Raccolte et Ordinate per Cura di Eugenio Camerini*. Milan, 1898.

> **Catalog:** *A1911*, "post 8vo, three-quarter red polished morocco, gilt top, uncut, Milan, 1898," with a slip of notes by Clemens laid in, lot 449, sold for $2.
>
> This was Tasso's most celebrated poem, a heroic epic about Godfrey Bouillon and the first crusade of 1099. Published in 1581, it was later translated in English as *Jerusalem Delivered*.

TAUTPHOEUS, JEMIMA (MONTGOMERY), BARONESS VON (1807–1893). *Quits, A Novel*. Two volumes in one. Philadelphia: J. B. Lippincott & Co., 1865.

> **Catalogs:** inventory list of the Langdon family library books compiled by the then-Archivist Mark Woodhouse in 2013; Ball 2016 inventory, brown textured cloth, blind text and design, J. Langdon Family Library bookplate #378, fair condition.
>
> **Location:** Quarry Farm library shelves, under the supervision of the Mark Twain Archive, Elmira College, Elmira, New York.
>
> The Irish-born Tautphoeus lived in Bavaria after her marriage and wrote about the scenery and customs of her adopted country. *Quits* (first published in 1857) is set in the uplands of the Bavarian and Styrian Alps and describes one of the *Oberammergau Passion Plays*. Leonora, the principal character, is a strong and intellectually curious figure. Clemens had access to the Langdons' books whenever he visited their residence in Elmira.

TAVERNIER, JEAN BAPTISTE (1605–1689). *Travels in India*. Edited and translated by Valentine Ball (1843–1895). 2 vols. London, New York: Macmillan and Co., 1889.

> Mark Twain's *Following the Equator* (1897, Ch. 49) reports: "Tavernier, the French traveler (17th century), notes that Ganges water is often given at weddings, 'each guest receiving a cup or two, according to the liberality of the host; sometimes 2,000 or 3,000 rupees' worth of it is consumed at a wedding.'"

TAYLEURE, CLIFTON W. (1831–1887). *East Lynne* (play).

> Clemens wrote a letter about this play for the San Francisco *Call* from Virginia City in 1863. He called the dramatization of the sensation novel *East Lynne* "the sickest of all sentimental dramas" and recalled watching "San Franciscans whine and snuffle and slobber all over themselves" during a performance at Maguire's Theatre (quoted in *MTC*, p. 29). After a career of acting in and writing melodramas, Tayleure managed several Broadway theaters. The English novelist Ellen (Price) Wood (1814–1887), who wrote as "Mrs. Henry Wood," was the author of other successful books, but none as popular as *East Lynne* (1861), which employed the device of double identities.
>
> Branch, *CofC* (1969), p. 8.

TAYLOR, BAYARD (1825–1878). *At Home and Abroad: A Sketch-Book of Life, Scenery, and Men*. First Series, Second Series. 2 vols. New York: G. P. Putnam and Son, 1866–1867.

> **Inscription:** signed, "C. J. Langdon/13th August 1871". Charles Jervis Langdon (1849–1916) was Olivia Clemens's brother.
>
> **Provenance:** bookplates #456 and #457 of the J. Langdon Family Library.
>
> **Catalog:** Ball 2016 inventory, brown cloth, marble board and edges. One volume is in fair condition; the cover has

fallen off the other volume.

> **Location:** Quarry Farm library shelves, under the supervision of the Mark Twain Archive, Elmira College, Elmira, New York.
>
> Taylor outdid himself in these volumes, covering every sight from Niagara Falls to the big trees of California, and discussing topics that ranged from ghosts and mediums to the staff writers of *Punch*, together with travels in Canada, the United States, and Europe. Clemens had access to this book whenever he visited the Langdons' residence in Elmira.

———. "Bedouin Love-Song" (poem, published in 1855).

> After thirty years, Clemens noted in 1908, only two of Taylor's poems were still remembered; one of them was "the tremendously inspiriting love song of an Arab lover to his sweetheart" (7 July 1908 AD, *MTE*, p. 308; *AutoMT*: 3: 246).

———. *By-Ways of Europe*. Illus. New York: G. P. Putnam and Son, 1869. 436 pp.

> **Inscription:** inscribed, "C. J. Langdon/13th August 1871".
>
> **Catalog:** Ball 2016 inventory, marble and leather boards, marble side edges, bookplate #461, J. Langdon Family Library, poor condition, front cover detached.
>
> **Location:** Quarry Farm library shelves, under the supervision of the Mark Twain Archive, Elmira College, Elmira, New York.
>
> Clemens had access to this book whenever he visited the Langdon residence in Elmira.
>
> Richard S. Lowry, *"Littery Man": Mark Twain and Modern Authorship* (New York: Oxford University Press, 1996), p. 52.

———. *Egypt and Iceland in the Year 1874*. New York: G. P. Putnam, [cop. 1874]. 282 pp. [Edition conjectured.]

> **Catalog:** ListABP (1910), "To Egypt", no other information supplied.
>
> Given Clemens's appetite for Bayard Taylor's travel writings, *Egypt and Iceland in the Year 1874* would be a logical candidate for anyone trying to decipher Albert Bigelow Paine's cryptically abbreviated title in the list of books he kept to consult while writing Clemens's biography.

———. *Eldorado; or, Adventures in the Path of Empire; Comprising a Voyage to California via Panama, Life in San Francisco and Monterey, Pictures of the Gold Region, and Experiences of Mexico Travel*. New York: G. P. Putnam and Son, 1868.

> **Inscription:** signed, "C. J. Langdon/13th August 1871".
>
> **Catalog:** Ball inventory 2016, marble boards and leather, marbled-edge pages, bookplate #459 of the J. Langdon Family Library. poor condition, front cover loose, rear cover detached.
>
> **Location:** Quarry Farm library shelves, under the supervision of the Mark Twain Archive, Elmira College, Elmira, New York.
>
> Clemens had access to this book whenever he visited the Langdons' residence in Elmira.

———. *Hannah Thurston: A Story of American Life*. New York: G. P. Putnam, 1864. 464 pp.

> **Inscription:** the front flyleaf is inscribed in brown ink, "Mrs. J. Langdon/N. B. Feby. 1864".
>
> **Provenance:** bookplate #133 of the "J. Langdon Family Library" is affixed to the front pastedown endpaper.
>
> **Catalog:** Ball 2016 inventory, brown cloth, white lettering,

J. Langdon Family Library bookplate #133.

Location: Mark Twain Archive, Elmira College, Elmira, New York.

Copy examined: unmarked copy available to Clemens whenever he visited the Langdon residence in Elmira. Examined on 27 May 2015.

Taylor showed his skill at writing fiction rather than his usual travelogues in this diverting novel. Chapter 9 features a séance in which believers and nonbelievers gather around a spiritualist medium and his table, with comic results.

————. *Home Ballads.* Illus. Original brown calf, gilt, marbled endpapers, maple panels inlaid on both covers. Boston: Houghton, Mifflin and Co., 1882. 61 pp. First separate edition.

Inscription: Olivia Clemens inscribed this elaborately bound volume in ink to her mother, Olivia Lewis Langdon: "Merry Christmas to Grandmama, from Jean & Clara Clemens, Dec. 25th, 1881." No marginalia are visible.

Location: collection of Kevin Mac Donnell, Austin, Texas (Mac Donnell to Alan Gribben, 29 November 2011). Acquired from the Langdon family.

Bayard Taylor was born in Chester County, Pennsylvania. His parents were Quaker farmers. In these five poems Taylor returned to those scenes: "The Quaker Widow," "The Holly-Tree," "John Reed," "Jane Reed," and "The Old Pennsylvania Farmer."

————. *A Journey to Central Africa; or, Life and Landscapes from Egypt to the Negro Kingdoms of the White Nile.* Household Edition. Illustrated by the author. New York: G. P. Putnam and Son, 1870. 522 pp.

Catalog: Ball 2016 inventory, marble and leather boards, marble-edged pages, bookplate #464, poor condition.

Location: Quarry Farm library shelves, under the supervision of the Mark Twain Archive, Elmira College, Elmira, New York.

Clemens had access to this book whenever he visited the Langdons' residence in Elmira.

————. *The Lands of the Saracens; or, Pictures of Palestine, Asia Minor, Sicily, and Spain.* Household Edition. New York: G. P. Putnam and Son, 1870. 451 pp.

Inscription: inscribed, "C. J. Langdon/13th August 1871".

Catalog: Ball 2016 inventory, marble and leather boards, marble-edge pages, bookplate #465, J. Langdon Family Library.

Location: Quarry Farm library shelves, under the supervision of the Mark Twain Archive, Elmira College, Elmira, New York.

Clemens had access to this book whenever he visited the Langdons' residence in Elmira.

————. *The National Ode: The Memorial Freedom Poem.* Illus. Boston: William F. Gill & Co., 1877. 74 pp.

Inscription: the verso of the front free endpaper is inscribed in violet ink, "To Livy L. Clemens/from S. L. ditto/Hartford 1876."

Provenance: the shelfmark on the front pastedown endpaper accords with Clara Clemens Samossoud's numbering system for her personal library in Detroit. This volume was part of the Carrie Estelle Doheny Collection, St. John's Seminary, Camarillo, California, to which the book was donated by Mrs. Doheny after she purchased it in 1940 for $12.20 from Maxwell Hunley Rare Books, Beverly Hills. Auctioned by Christie's in February 1989 for $2,860 on behalf of St. John's Seminary. Purchased by the 19th Century Shop in Baltimore, Maryland.

Catalogs: ListABP (1910), "National Ode, Taylor"; 19th Century Shop, Baltimore, Maryland, 22 January 1990 advertisement in *AB Bookman's Weekly,* "Bayard Taylor, *The National Ode.* Boston, 1876. Inscribed by Twain to his wife Livy."

Location: currently unknown.

Copy examined: Olivia Clemens's copy, a gift from her husband. Viewed at St. John's Seminary in 1970.

On 21 January 1877 Clemens purchased a copy of *"Centennial Ode.* illd," discounted to $3.20; he paid James R. Osgood & Company for this and other volumes on 13 November 1877 (receipt in Scrapbook #10, p. 69, MTP). Most likely this purchase was Taylor's poem, which was riding a crest of popularity owing to the recent centennial celebrations throughout the United States.

Mark Twain mentioned Bayard Taylor in Chapter 20 of *Roughing It* (1872). In a letter of 17 January [1877] to Norwegian author and scholar Hjalmar Hjorth Boyesen, Clemens mentioned, "I wrote & asked Bayard Taylor to be our guest (he is to lecture here presently) & he has accepted. I was glad to hear what you said about him" (*Sotheby's 2003,* #32). Aboard the *Holsatia* Clemens discovered that his fellow-passenger "Bayard Taylor is a really lovable man" (SLC to WDH, Frankfort, 4 May 1878, *MTHL,* p. 227). On 20 December 1878, in Munich, Clemens wrote in his journal upon learning of Taylor's death: "He was a very loveable man" (NB 17, *N&J* 2: 254). See the Catalog entry under Goethe for Taylor's translation of *Faust* (1879), which Clemens would call "the best of all English translations" (7 July 1908 AD, MTP; *AutoMT* 3: 246). In January 1879 Clemens reflected on Taylor's death and remembered that "at our house once he told some more anecdotes about animals" (NB 17, *N&J* 2: 269). Clemens expressed indignation at the paltry amount of financial assistance the United States government provided for its ministers like Bayard Taylor (NB 18 [1879], *N&J* 2: 297). In Chapter 18 of *A Tramp Abroad* (1880), Mark Twain describes "a poor old tailless raven" in Hirschhorn, Germany: "I never have seen another dumb creature that was so morbidly sensitive. Bayard Taylor, who could interpret the dim reasonings of animals, and understood their moral natures better than most men, would have found some way to make this poor old chap forget his troubles for a while, but we had not his kindly art, and so had to leave the raven to his griefs." In May 1891 Twain had a literary notion: "Remember Bayard Taylor in the Holsatia" (NB 30, *N&J* 3: 621). On 14 January 1906 Clemens told Isabel Lyon "that so few—no autobiographies were ever very frank. Bayard Taylor was—'so self-satisfied, & sat back & licked his chops'—but it was all delightful" (IVL Journals, TS p. 123, MTP; a virtually identical entry can be found in the IVL Journal, Harry Ransom Center, University of Texas at Austin). In 1908 Twain described Taylor as "a genial, lovable, simple-hearted soul. . . . He was a poet and had written voluminously in verse"; however, "all his poetry is forgotten now except two very fine songs"—"The Song of the Camp" and "Bedouin Love-Song" (7 July 1908 AD,

MTE, pp. 307–308; *AutoMT* 3: 246).

———. *Northern Travel: Summer and Winter Pictures of Sweden, Denmark, and Lapland*. New York: G. P. Putnam and Sons, 1869. 436 pp.

Inscription: inscribed, "C. J. Langdon/13th August 1871".

Catalog: Ball 2016 inventory, marble and leather boards and spine, bookplate #460 of the "J. Langdon Family Library," fair condition.

Location: Quarry Farm library shelves, under the supervision of the Mark Twain Archive, Elmira College, Elmira, New York.

Copy examined: unmarked copy to which Clemens had access whenever he visited the Langdons in Elmira. Examined on 26 May 2015.

———. *The Picture of St. John*. First edition. Original terra cotta cloth, gilt. 2,190 copies printed. Boston: Ticknor and Fields, 1866. 220 pp.

Provenance: the bookplate of Jervis Langdon's "Family Library No. 80) is affixed to the front pastedown endpaper.

Location: collection of Kevin Mac Donnell, Austin, Texas. Acquired in May 2016 from the Langdon family (email, Mac Donnell to Alan Gribben, 16 May 2016).

Source: detailed description of the volume sent on 9 June 2016 by Mac Donnell to Gribben.

Clemens had access to this volume whenever he visited the Langdons' residence in Elmira. Taylor's lengthy verse narrative related the travels, experiences (sometimes hardly chaste), and philosophizing of an artist preparing to paint a profound religious subject.

———. *Prince Deukalion: A Lyrical Drama* (published in 1878). This would turn out to be Bayard Taylor's last work. Upon Taylor's death, Clemens wrote to William Dean Howells on 21 January 1879 that he was glad "there was not a single sting & so many good praiseful words in the Atlantic's criticism of Deukalion" (*MTHL*, p. 246). The *Atlantic* review, while it warned that "the allegorical veil and nomenclature of this poem will daunt the casual reader," nonetheless it urged that "he will do well to overcome his fears. The ideal is so maintained by Mr. Taylor's imaginative force that its story is unbroken and its personages become living and well defined" (*Atlantic Monthly* 43.255 [January 1879]: 118). *Prince Deukalion* offered moral and religious philosophizing in the form of a blank verse drama.

———. "The Song of the Camp" (poem, published in 1856). "All his poetry is forgotten now except two very fine songs, one about the Scotch soldiers singing 'Annie Laurie' in the trenches before Sebastopol [*sic*]" (7 July 1908 AD, *MTE*, pp. 307–308; *AutoMT* 3: 246). The Crimean War reached its climax in the ordeal of the Siege of Sevastopol (1854–1855). Clemens was recalling the fifth verse of Taylor's moving poem: "They sang of love, and not of fame;/Forgot was Britain's glory:/Each heart recalled a different name,/But all sang 'Annie Laurie.'"

———. *Travels in Greece and Russia, with an Excursion to Crete*. First Series, Second Series. New York: G. P. Putnam and Son, 1870. 426 pp.

Inscription: inscribed, "C. J. Langdon/13th August 1871".

Catalog: Ball 2016 inventory, marble and leather boards, marble-edge pages, bookplate #462 of the J. Langdon

Family Library, fair condition.

Location: Quarry Farm library shelves, under the supervision of the Mark Twain Archive, Elmira College, Elmira, New York.

Clemens had access to this book whenever he visited the Langdons' home in Elmira.

———. *Views A-Foot; or, Europe Seen with Knapsack and Staff*. Household Edition, Revised. New York: G. P. Putnam and Son, 1870. 506 pp.

Catalog: Ball 2016 inventory, bookplate #458 of the J. Langdon Family Library, poor condition.

Location: Quarry Farm library shelves, under the supervision of the Mark Twain Archive, Elmira College, Elmira, New York.

Clemens had access to this book whenever he visited the Langdons in Elmira.

Richard S. Lowry, *"Littery Man": Mark Twain and Modern Authorship* (New York: Oxford University Press, 1996), p. 52.

———. *A Visit to India, China, and Japan, in the Year 1853*. New York: G. P. Putnam and Son, 1870. 539 pp.

Inscription: inscribed, "C. J. Langdon/13th August 1871".

Catalog: Ball 2016 inventory, marble and leather boards, marble-edge pages, bookplate #463 of the J. Langdon Family Library, good condition.

Location: Quarry Farm library shelves, under the supervision of the Mark Twain Archive, Elmira College, Elmira, New York.

Clemens had access to this book whenever he visited the Langdons' home in Elmira.

Noting how much the Hoogli River of India reminded him of the Louisiana stretch of the Mississippi River, Clemens wrote in March 1896: "The illusion has remained—I am leaving La & the Miss behind, not India & the Hoogli. See Bayard Taylor" (NB 36, TS p. 62). In Chapter 59 of *Following the Equator* (1897) Mark Twain quotes a paragraph from Taylor's description of the Taj Mahal to demonstrate that although Taylor's lavish praise is technically merited, the net result is "a noble big lie." The passage Twain quotes appears in Chapter 10 (p. 133) of the American edition of Taylor's work.

Madigan, "MT's Passage to India," (1974), p. 366.

TAYLOR, BENJAMIN FRANKLIN (1819–1887). "The Isle of the Long Ago" (poem), often reprinted as "The Long Ago."

In a grieving letter about Susy's death, written to Olivia Clemens from Guildford on 30 August 1896, Clemens quoted ten lines of Taylor's poem, slightly altered (*LLMT*, p. 327). Taylor's opening lines understandably appealed to the ex-river pilot: "Oh, a wonderful stream is the River Time,/As it flows through the realm of Tears." The third of the poem's seven stanzas continues this metaphor: "There's a magical Isle up the River Time,/Where the softest of airs are playing;/. . . . And the Junes with the roses are staying." Stanza four delivers the central image, "And the name of this Isle is the Long Ago,/And we bury our treasures there" (*Old-Time Pictures and Sheaves of Rhyme*. Chicago: S. C. Griggs & Co., 1874, p. 188). Taylor was a Chicago newspaper editor who later covered the Civil War as a correspondent before becoming popular as a poet and giving public readings.

TAYLOR, CHARLES D. (1826–1900). "Ye Olde Militia Muster"

(unpublished farce, written in 1892).

Charles D. Taylor wrote to Clemens from Kingston, Rhode Island on 24 May 1892: "Although a stranger to you, I venture to enclose to you a farce I have written entitled 'Ye Old Militia Muster'" (Fears, *Day to Day* 2: 709). A man named Charles D. Taylor, most likely this would-be playwright, was born in 1826 and died in 1900 in Kingston, Rhode Island.

TAYLOR, ELIZABETH (1831–1879). *Quixstar; A Novel.* 3 vols. Edinburgh: Edmonston & Douglas, 1873.

Source: MTLAcc, entries #4–6, set donated by Clemens.

Taylor, who grew up in Dalkeith, a small town near Edinburgh, left behind two respected novels depicting Scottish life of the middle and lower classes, *Blindpits; A Story of Scottish Life* (Edinburgh, 1868) and *Quixstar; A Novel* (Edinburgh, 1873). Literary critics liked *Quixstar* but preferred *Blindpits*. According to an admiring obituary published in *Lippincott's Monthly Magazine* 24.33 (November 1879): 637–640 after her unexpected death on 13 August 1879, the author Dr. John Brown (1810–1882) called Taylor "the Scottish Jane Austen." Clemens and Olivia passed the latter part of July 1873 and most of August 1873 in Scotland, mainly spending those weeks in Edinburgh. While there they had several pleasant meetings with Dr. John Brown, who held Taylor in high esteem (Fears, *Day by Day* 1: 545–547).

TAYLOR, ISAAC (1787–1865). *Fanaticism, By the Author of Natural History of Enthusiasm.* 12mo, original boards. New York: J. Leavitt; Boston: Crocker & Brewster, 1834. 386 pp.

Inscriptions: in ink at the top of the title page: "Mark Twain 1880" and below the title, in pencil: "Taylor is the Author of this work. M. T." In pencil at the bottom of the front free endpaper: "Beverly Chew—Geneva, N. Y."

Catalogs: Union Galleries (New York City), Sale number 50 (19 September 1935), from the collection of Nicholas Orlando, with additions, "12mo, original boards, cloth back, paper label, uncut, binding worn, New York, 1834," quotes the inscriptions, lot 75; City Book Auction (New York City), Sale number 292 (9 December 1944), "12mo, original boards, worn, chipped, front cover loose, parts of spine chipped away, lacks front flyleaf, stained, N. Y., 1834. Mark Twain's copy," lot 62.

While this subject matter obviously might have been of interest to Clemens, both the date of publication and the inscriptions make this a dubious addition to Clemens's personal library. He very seldom employed his *nom de plume* in inscribing his library books. Furthermore, the book was first sold in 1935 along with another association copy that had suspect credentials; see the Catalog entry for Ralph Waldo Emerson's *Miscellanies; Embracing Nature, Addresses, and Lectures* (1858). Until someone experienced in identifying Clemens's handwriting can examine this copy of *Fanaticism* closely it should not be listed among the contents of Clemens's library.

TAYLOR, JANE (1783–1824) "The Mysterious Stranger" (story, published in 1824).

Carroll D. Laverty—"The Genesis of *The Mysterious Stranger*," *Mark Twain Quarterly* 7.3–4 (Spring-Summer 1947): 15–19—proposed this brief moral tale as "the germinal idea" for Mark Twain's *The Mysterious Stranger* manuscripts. According to Laverty, Taylor's story was included in *McGuffey's Rhetorical Guide and Fifth Reader* (1840, rev. 1844, pp. 298–302) and *McGuffey's New Sixth Eclectic Reader* (1867, pp. 206–211). "In both, a mysterious stranger comes from a supernatural realm, is accepted by some of the people of the town, and then makes known what he thinks of human nature. Each thinks that . . . man is trivial, . . . and that death is a blessing often." Coleman O. Parsons ("Background of *The Mysterious Stranger*" [1960], pp. 55–56) located three other possible sources for Mark Twain's title, and the "mysterious stranger" phrase appeared in additional literary texts and titles of the nineteenth century. However, Laverty did raise several fundamental similarities beyond the titles.

———— and **ANN (TAYLOR) GILBERT** (1782–1866). *Little Ann, and Other Poems.* Illustrated by Kate Greenaway (1846–1901). London, New York: George Routledge & Sons, [1883]. 64 pp.

Catalogs: ListABP (1910), "Little Anne [*sic*], Greenaway"; C1951, J36, listed among the volumes belonging to Jean and Clara Clemens.

TAYLOR, [PHILIP] MEADOWS (1808–1876). *Confessions of a Thug.* 3 vols. London: R. Bentley, 1839. [Edition conjectured.]

In the introduction to *Confessions*, Taylor summarized the social and travel conditions in India that encouraged the rise of Thuggee. Mark Twain reviewed the same facts in Chapter 43 of *Following the Equator* (1897). The narrator of Taylor's book is Ameer Ali, a former Thug, now an informer on his old confederates. He is addressing an Englishman mentioned only as "Sahib," who is taking notes "for the information of those in England" (*Confessions of a Thug*, Chapter 1). Ameer Ali narrates "a faithful portrait of a Thug's life, his ceremonies, and his acts" (final chapter). In Chapter 43 of *Following the Equator* (1897), Twain writes that a murder trial which took place in Bombay while he was there "brought back the forgotten days of Thuggee and made them live again; in fact, even made them believable. . . . The thing reads like a Meadows-Taylor [*sic*] Thug-tale of half a century ago, as may be seen by the official report of the [Bombay] trial." This recent murder exhibited the same "cold business-like depravity, absence of fear, absence of caution, destitution of the sense of horror, repentance, remorse." Twain added a comment about Thuggee: "One of the chiefest wonders connected with it was the success with which it kept its secret. The English trader did business in India two hundred years and more before he ever heard of it; and yet it was assassinating its thousands all around him every year, the whole time."

Chapter 46 of *Following the Equator* opens with an entry from Twain's diary on 28 January 1896: "I learned of an *official* Thug-book the other day. I was not aware before that there was such a thing. I am allowed the temporary use of it." Twain begins Chapter 47 of *Following the Equator* with a quotation from the first chapter of Taylor's *Confessions of a Thug*: "How many of you English are passionately devoted to sporting! . . . How much higher game is a Thug's!" This same "joy of seeing killing done" is a trait of the entire human race, Twain concludes; therefore "we white people are merely modified Thugs." The twenty-nine-year-old Taylor selected the incidents from an official inquiry as well as from his personal knowledge of Thuggee.

Madigan, "MT's Passage to India" (1974), p. 366.

TAYLOR, (GENERAL) RICHARD (1826–1879). *Destruction and Reconstruction: Personal Experiences of the Late War.* New York: D. Appleton and Co., 1879. 274 pp.

Before Mark Twain left for New Orleans in 1882, he wrote "Gen Dick Taylor's book" in Notebook 20 next to the title of General George H. Gordon's *A War Diary*, a Northerner's views (*N&J* 2: 462). Taylor's book recounted Confederate military operations in Louisiana and Mississippi. He died soon after the publication of these memoirs, but his indictments of Reconstruction policies helped the sales of *Destruction and Reconstruction* in both America and England.

TAYLOR, TOM (1817–1880). *The Bottle: A Drama in Two Acts* (first performed in London in 1847).

Mark Twain dismissed *The Bottle*, a temperance vehicle, as "rather overwrought in the misery line" (Branch, *CofC* [1969], p. 97; Randall Knoper, *Acting Naturally: Mark Twain in the Culture of Performance* [Berkeley: University of California Press, 1995], p. 36). Taylor was an English playwright who later edited the humorous magazine *Punch.*

———. *Dundreary, A Four-Act Comedy* (first performed in London in 1875). [Originally titled *Our American Cousin,* first performed in 1858.]

In a letter to Taylor written on 5 January 1874 in London, Clemens apologized for missing an appointment and claimed that Taylor had written "the only play I ever appeared in on any stage" (*MTLet* 6: 10). James R. Sturdevant, "Mark Twain's Unpublished Letter to Tom Taylor—An Enigma," *Mark Twain Journal* 14.1 (Winter 1967–1968): 8–9, speculated that Clemens possibly had a role in an amateur production of *Our American Cousin.*

Edward A. Sothern (1826–1881) created the role of Lord Dundreary in this comedy. His son Edward H. Sothern (1859–1933) revived the play and continued the character. On 25 April 1908 Isabel Lyon noted that "Mrs. Collier, the King and I went to see Sothern in Dun Dreary [*sic*]" (IVL Journals, TS p. 320, MTP). Clemens wrote that he liked the younger Sothern's interpretation of Lord Dundreary as well as the performance of that role by the elder Sothern; Clemens had seen the father play the same part "a generation ago" (SLC to Dorothy Sturgis, 25 April 1908, ALS, Columbia University Library). In an Autobiographical Dictation of 28 April 1908, Clemens said that he last saw the senior Sothern as Lord Dundreary twenty-five years ago in Hartford, when Clemens laughed so constantly that he felt obliged to leave the theatre so as not to distract from Sothern's acting. "In those days it was the funniest thing I had ever seen on the stage, and I find that it is just as funny now as it was then. I saw it yesterday [*sic*]. I am old & intelligent now, and by earnest and watchful effort was able to keep from going into hysterics over it." Clemens said that Daniel Frohman had explained to him the extent to which Edward A. Sothern had expanded the Dundreary role until "he was become the chief figure on the stage." Consequently, "the piece's name, 'The American Cousin' [*sic*], sank out of sight. . . . The piece came to be called 'Lord Dundreary' . . . and nobody cares for anything in it but the idiotic

and fascinating nobleman" (MTP; *AutoMT* 3: 225).

Randall Knoper, *Acting Naturally: Mark Twain in the Culture of Performance* (Berkeley: University of California Press, 1995), pp. 56, 67, 69, 70, 76.

———. *An Unequal Match. A Comedy in Three Acts* (first performed in 1857).

In 1865 Clemens saw this play at Maguire's Academy of Music and criticized its characterizations (*LAMT*, p. 139).

Catherine Coffin Phillips, *Cornelius Cole, California Pioneer and United States Senator* (San Francisco: John Henry Nash, 1929), pp. 140–141; Aspiz, "MT's Reading" (1949), p. 259.

TCHAIKOVSKY, PETR ILICH (1840–1893). *Textbook on Harmony.*

Clara Clemens listed this author and music instruction title in her undated commonplace book (Paine 150, MTP).

TEGG, WILLIAM, COMP. (1816–1895). *The Last Act: Being the Funeral Rites of Nations and Individuals.* London: W. Tegg & Co., 1876. 404 pp. [Edition conjectured.]

Catalog: *C1951*, D20, $15, listed among the books signed by Clemens.

The London publisher Tegg compiled many other factual works, including *The Knot Tied: Marriage Ceremonies of All Nations* (1877) and *Shakespeare and His Contemporaries; Together with the Plots of His Plays* (1879).

TEGNÉR, ESAIAS (1782–1846). *Frithiof's Saga; A Legend of Ancient Norway.* Translated from the Swedish by Lucius Adelno Sherman, Ph.D. Illus. Boston: James R. Osgood and Co., [cop. 1877]. 237 pp.

James R. Osgood and Company billed Clemens $1.20 for "1 Frithioff's Saga" purchased on 20 March 1877; Clemens paid on 13 November 1877 (receipt in Scrapbook #10, p. 69, MTP).

———. *Fridthjof's Saga; A Norse Romance.* Translated from the Swedish by Thomas Addis Emmett Holcomb and Martha A. Lyon Holcomb. Chicago: S. C. Griggs and Co., 1877. 213 pp.

Source: MTLAcc, entry #623, volume donated by Clemens.

See also the Catalog entry for R. B. Anderson and J. Bjarnason (trans.), *Viking Tales of the North.*

TELLER, CHARLOTTE ROSE (1876–1953), later Mrs. [Gilbert J.] Hirsch. *The Cage.* New York: D. Appleton and Co., 1907. 340 pp.

Charlotte Teller had married Frank Minitree Johnson (1872–1944) in 1902, but the couple soon separated and eventually divorced. Clemens encountered Charlotte Teller in 1906 at a meeting of people who sympathized with notable Russian revolutionaries. Teller afterwards recalled of Clemens, who resided near her in New York City, "I saw him almost every day for nearly three months. He read all the manuscript of my novel, 'The Cage,' and made on the margin his critical suggestions." In letter of 24 September 1906 Clemens wrote to Teller: "Mr. Sears [Joseph Hamblen Sears, 1965–1946, the president of D. Appleton and Company] has been here, & we chatted an hour & I told him what a high opinion . . . I hold of the book, & he spoke highly of it himself. When it is all ready to submit to magazines he will carry out your desire & let the magazine have it that will pay you the best price" (ALS, Berg Collection, NYPL). As soon as Appleton and Company had accepted the novel, Clemens wrote a letter to be used as a publisher's notice over his own name, addressed to Maude Adams. But when Clemens became alarmed about gossip concerning Teller's relationship with him, Teller returned the letter and never saw Clemens again (privately printed pamphlet of Clemens's letters to Teller, Berg Collection, New York Public Library, TS in MTP; Hill, *MTGF*, pp. 156, 172–173; *Mark Twain Encyclopedia*, p. 729).

Teller set her novel about class struggle in the Chicago of the 1880s, still in 1907 associated with the Haymarket Square Riot in 1886. Woven into Teller's narrative was a woman's growing consciousness of her individual rights and sexual freedom. Laura Skandera Trombley discussed with discernment the Clemens-Teller relationship, which seemed to threaten the interests of both Isabel Lyon and Clara Clemens (*Mark Twain's Other Woman: The Hidden Story of His Final Years* [New York: Alfred A. Knopf, 2010], pp. 102–105, 123–125).

———. "Mirabeau: A Play in Five Acts." 106 TS pp. Copyrighted 3 July 1906 (*Dramatic Compositions Copyrighted in the United States* [Washington, D.C.: Library of Congress, 1918], p. 1493).

In a letter of 11 June 1906, Clemens apologized to Teller for "that foolish letter" criticizing her play. "You that can do that wonderful thing—forecast & map out a great & intricate drama clearly, sharply, intelligently & intelligibly from beginning to end—why should you doubt that you can . . . make it stable & beautiful?," Clemens wrote, encouraging Teller to take a vacation of several months from the strain of writing (ALS, Berg Collection, NYPL). Clemens again read the play manuscript titled "Mirabeau" in Dublin, New Hampshire on 15 June 1906, covering two acts before lunch and finishing all five acts before dinner; "Mr. Clemens has to read aloud anything like a play, to get at its values," noted Lyon (IVL Journal, Harry Ransom Center, University of Texas at Austin; virtually identical entry in IVL Journals, TS, p. 166; MTP). On 16 June 1906 Clemens wrote to Teller: "It is a beautiful play, Charlotte. . . . Mirabeau is greatly portrayed; you have missed no detail of his rich & varied nature; he stands forth clear, winning, worshipful, a majestic & benignant colossus"; Clemens could see no reason to "doubt that it will also *play*" (ALS, Berg Collection, NYPL). Clemens informed Clara Clemens that Teller's play "is fine and strong and brisk. Five acts. I read it aloud to Miss Lyon Friday" (ALS, 20 June 1906, MTP). Teller later recalled that Clemens was so interested in the "Mirabeau" play that "he loaned me his own copy of the French Revolution, and sent me a 4 volume [*sic*] edition of 'Saint Simon'" (privately printed pamphlet of Twain's letters to Teller, Berg Collection, New York Public Library, TS in MTP). The scandal-plagued French adventurer, politician, and orator Honoré-Gabriel Riquet, comte de Mirabeau (1749–1791) played a prominent role in the early phases of the French Revolution.

———— and **MARTHA S. BENSLEY.** "Sociological Maid. A Play in One Act," 25 TS pp. (*Dramatic Compositions Copyrighted in the United States*, p. 2170). (Unperformed play.)

In a letter to Charlotte Teller apparently dated 5 July 1906, Clemens praised an unidentified work: "If you will let me say it, it is well beyond what I thought you could do. Your manner is mature, facile, practised, confident, & you

have the sure touch of a seasoned old professional. . . . Let Margaret have a show when you can—I mean the sixteen-year-older over the way" (ALS, Berg Collection, NYPL). Isabel V. Lyon reported that Clemens discussed Teller's play on 6 April 1906, and Lyon remarked that Maude Adams would perform the role of Joan of Arc (IVL Journals, TS p. 154, MTP). Judging from Lyon's reference to Joan, apparently Clemens also took an interest in the play Charlotte Teller copyrighted on 24 February 1906, an unperformed work she co-authored with Martha S. Bensley, "Sociological Maid." Clemens referred to Teller's Joan of Arc play in a letter to Isabel Lyon on 20 September 1906; he told Teller, he said, "frankly, & in detail our judgment of the Joan play, & she took it in good part" (MTP).

THE TEMPERANCE ADVOCATE & SEAMEN'S FRIEND (Honolulu, monthly newspaper, published 1843–). Edited by the Reverend Samuel Chenery Damon from 1843 until 1885. [In 1845 the periodical changed its name to *The Friend*.]

In 1866 Mark Twain sketched an admiring if somewhat inaccurate version of the history of this periodical (NB 6, *N&J* 1: 199–201 n. 37). Clemens was in Honolulu at the time. Many years later, in Chapter 3 of *Following the Equator* (1897), Twain would list "Father Damon's Seaman's [*sic*] Friend" among the reading materials to be found on the parlor tables of the typical cottages in Honolulu in 1866.

TEMPLE BAR: A LONDON MAGAZINE FOR TOWN AND COUNTRY READERS (London monthly periodical, published 1860–1906).

A footnote in Mark Twain's "Lionizing Murderers" (1872, collected in *SN&O* in 1875) quotes an extract from an 1866 issue of *Temple Bar* to demonstrate that people's sympathizing with men convicted of heinous crimes "is not confined to the United States." Twain wrote to the editor of *Temple Bar*, George Bentley (1828–1895), nearly half a dozen times during the 1870s about publishing matters.

TEMPLE, (LADY) DOROTHY (OSBORNE) (1627–1695). *The Love Letters of Dorothy Osborne to Sir William Temple, 1652–54*. Ed. by [Sir] Edward Abbott Parry (1863–1943). 8vo, original cloth, in a quarter morocco case. New York: Dodd, Mead & Co., 1901. 349 pp.

Inscription: the front pastedown endpaper is signed "S L. Clemens/Tuxedo Park,/Aug. '07."

Marginalia: Clemens wrote a note of seventeen lines on the front flyleaf, recommending ideal qualities for letters; they should be "easy & strong & full of wit, & sense, & goodness, & high principle, & a gracious & kindly spirit . . . charm." Clemens made brief notations and markings on pages 100 ("It's a prophecy of the kaleidoscope"), 110, 112, 124, 167, 171, 177 ("have relieved" altered to "relieve"), 253 ("servant" changed to "suitor"), 298 ("1600" altered to "1650?"), and 324.

Catalogs: ListABP (1910), "Love Letters of Dorothy Osborne"; C1951, #26a, $35; *Fleming 1972*; Sotheby Parke Bernet, New York City, Sale number 3482 (25 February 1976), "a17-line note on the front flyleaf, and several brief marginal notes or corrections," "Property of a New York City Collector" (John F. Fleming), lot 17, sold for $375 (*American Book Prices Current, 1976*, p. 207).

Provenance: Frederick Anderson, then Editor of the Mark

Twain Papers in the Bancroft Library at the University of California, Berkeley, examined this book in the New York City offices of John F. Fleming, Inc. and made notes in April 1972 (Anderson to James D. Hart, 17 April 1972, photocopy sent to Alan Gribben).

Location: unknown at present.

The love letters of William Temple (1628–1699) to Dorothy Osbourne apparently do not survive, but he kept two years' worth of her letters that she wrote during their courtship before they married in 1655, despite the opposition of both their families and amid political dangers.

TEMPLE, (SIR) RICHARD (1826–1902). *India in 1880*. Third edition. London: John Murray, 1881. 524 pp.

The British politician Richard Temple had served as the Finance Minister of India. His *India in 1880* delivered a sobering assessment of the Indian economy. Twain wrote, "There are trustworthy statistics furnished by Sir Richard Temple and others, which show that the individual Indian's whole annual product . . . is worth in gold only $7.50" (*FE* [1897], Ch. 17).

TEMPLE, (SIR) WILLIAM (1628–1699). "Upon the Gardens of Epicurus" (essay, published in 1685).

After the English statesman Sir William Temple retired he wrote an influential essay, "Upon the Gardens of Epicurus." It surveyed various philosophies through the ages, traced the brutal attitudes of powerful men (and the dangers of human nature in general), and advocated the virtues of the ethical thinking promoted by the Greek philosopher Epicurus (341–270 BCE), who resolved to live and teach within his gardens. Temple then proceeded to prescribe the plants best suited to deliver the most pleasure, best food, and greatest sense of serenity in the English climate. William Makepeace Thackeray quoted from Temple's "Essay on Gardens" in a footnote to Thackeray's essay on Jonathan Swift, and Clemens commented approvingly: "There isn't an ill-balanced sentence or a jagged, uneven place in this smoothly-worded paragraph" (Coley B. Taylor, *Mark Twain's Margins on Thackeray's "Swift"* [1935], p. 37).

TENNYSON, ALFRED, FIRST BARON TENNYSON (1809–1892). *Ballads and Other Poems*. Boston: James R. Osgood & Co., 1880. 112 pp.

Source: MTLAcc, entry #2104, volume donated from Clemens's library by Clara Clemens Gabrilowitsch in 1910.

———. *Beauties of Tennyson*. Illustrated by Frederic B. Schell (1838–1905). Philadelphia: Porter & Coates, [cop. 1885].

Source: MTLAcc, entry 651, volume donated by Clemens.

Beauties of Tennyson has no table of contents or page numbers. It collected a dozen brief excerpts from the poet's longer poems and six complete shorter poems, "Break, Break, Break," "The Brook," "The Charge of the Light Brigade," "A Farewell," "Lilian," and "Ring Out, Wild Bells."

———. *Becket* (costume drama, published in 1884, performed in 1893).

Clemens and William Dean Howells saw Henry Irving play the title role at Abbey's Theatre in New York City on 16 November 1893 (*MTHL*, p. 654). From the Players Club in New York City, Clemens wrote to Joseph H. Twichell on 20 November 1893 after dining with Irving; "You *must* see it, Joe. It's an ideal picture of what we all imagine the England of seven and a half centuries ago to have been"

(*LMTJHT*, p. 181). Thomas à Becket (c. 1118–1170), the Archbishop of Canterbury, was canonized in 1172 after he was murdered by four knights for resisting the king during the reign of Henry II.

———. "Break, Break, Break" (poem, published in 1842).

Clemens mentioned this title in Notebook 28 in September 1888, apparently planning for Hank Morgan to vanquish King Arthur's bards with a recitation of "Tennyson, with a touch of Shak & Browning" (*N&J* 3: 420). On 29 August 1896 Clemens wrote to Olivia Clemens from Guildford, England, grieving over Susy Clemens's death; he quoted, "O for the touch of a vanished hand/And the sound of a voice that is still" (*LLMT*, p. 327).

———. "Charge of the Light Brigade" (poem, published in 1854).

"Cannon to the right of them, cannon to the left of them, cannon in front—it was Balaclava come again" (*The American Claimant* [1892], Ch. 17). Balaclava was a small seaport on the Crimea, scene of the famous cavalry charge.

———. "The Day-Dream" (poem, published in 1842).

Albert Bigelow Paine recalled that Richard Watson Gilder recited four lines from this Tennyson poem as Ossip and Clara Clemens Gabrilowitsch drove away from their wedding in an automobile on 6 October 1909. Gilder was paraphrasing a portion of Stanza IV ("The Departure") from Tennyson's "The Day-Dream": "Over the hills and far away,/Beyond the utmost purple rim,/Beyond the night, beyond the day,/Through all the world she followed him" (*MTB*, p. 1524). Tennyson's actual lines are very close to the Gilder/Paine version: "And o'er the hills, and far away/Beyond their utmost purple rim,/Beyond the night, across the day,/Thro' all the world she follow'd him." (Robert H. Hirst identified this poem in an e-mail to the Mark Twain Forum, 23 September 1998.)

———. *A Dream of Fair Women*. Illustrated by A[ndrew]. V[arick]. S[tout]. Anthony (1835–1906). Boston: James R. Osgood & Co., [cop. 1880]. 103 pp.

Source: MTLAcc, entry #2100, volume donated from Clemens's library by Clara Clemens Gabrilowitsch in 1910.

In a letter written in February 1885 Olivia Clemens reported that "the children have been reading to me from their private books tonight, Susy from 'Dream of Fair Women. . . . I do wish that Lord Tennyson could hear Susy talk of him and of his work. . . . Some of the finest verses in 'The Dream of Fair Women' she read me tonight" (*Twainian* 39.5 [September-October 1980]: 3).

———. *Enoch Arden* (narrative poem, published in 1864).

Dennis Welland inspected the manuscript of Mark Twain's *Following the Equator* (1897) and reported that Twain continued the "theme of the outcast" in Chapter 8 by "a long quotation from Tennyson that he had intended including for its description of a wilderness; he struck it out, but significantly the poem from which it comes is 'Enoch Arden'" ("Mark Twain's Last Travel Book" [1965], p. 45). Baetzhold, *MT&JB* (1970), p. 286.

———. *Harold; A Drama. Author's Edition, from Advance Sheets*. Red cloth, embossed. Boston: James R. Osgood and Co., 1877. 170 pp.

Inscription: the front free endpaper is signed in pencil, "S. L. Clemens/Hartford 1876".

Marginalia: on page 13 Clemens underscored "What's up is faith, what's down is heresy." Clemens marked the speech of Wulfnoth, Act II, Scene 2, beginning, "And deeper still the deep-down oubliette" (p. 64). On page 65 he underlined "To the very Devil's horns" and "To the very feet of God." Clemens also drew penciled vertical lines and underscorings on pages 83, 84–85 (heavily underlined), 86, 90, 96–97, 125 (brackets enclose "no—the childish fist/That cannot strike again"), 141 (a bracket around "Were the great trumpet blowing doomsday dawn"), and 143 (a line next to Harold's speech, beginning "I die for England then, who lived for England"). On pages 84–85 Clemens marked the speech of Leofwin: "Good brother,/ By all the truths that ever priest hath preach'd,/Of all the lies that ever men have lied,/Thine is the pardonablest." He underscored the word "pardonablest" and commented in pencil: "Even the wise and witty Leofwin is too sodden with narrow teaching, not to know that when a man lies to save his brother's life & liberty & the life & liberty of his country, he can *not* have sinned. Harold would have richly deserved to be damned if he had not *lied*."

Provenance: Antenne-Dorrance Collection, Rice Lake, Wisconsin.

Location: Mark Twain Archive, Gannett-Tripp Learning Center, Elmira College, Elmira, New York.

Copy examined: Clemens's copy. Examined in 1970 and again on 28 May 2015.

———. *Idylls of the King*. Volume V of *The Works of Alfred Tennyson, Poet Laureate*. Green cloth, gilt lettering. 10 vols. Boston: James R. Osgood and Co., 1871. 158 pp.

Inscription: Clemens inscribed the front free endpaper of Volume V in black ink, "Susie Clemens/from her father/ March 19/'84."

Location: Mark Twain Library, Redding, Connecticut. (MTLAcc, entries #2109, 2110, and 2111, 3 volumes [Volumes IV, V, and VI of the ten-volume *Works of Alfred Tennyson, Poet Laureate* edition issued by James R. Osgood and Company in 1871], donated from Clemens's library by Clara Clemens Gabrilowitsch in 1910.)

Copy examined: Susy Clemens's unmarked copy of Volume V, a gift from Clemens. Has the red ink Mark Twain Library accession number "2110". Examined in 1970 and again in June 1982 and on 9 November 2019. The other volumes of *Idylls of the King* in this edition have not been found.

In Clemens's English journals of 1872 he expressed his delight in visiting the Gustave Doré Gallery and seeing "Dore's original studies for his Tennyson [*Idylls of the King*] & other books" (*MTLet* 5: 621) On 20 July 1873 Clemens referred to "King Arthur and his knights and their bloody fights with Saxon oppressors" in a letter written to Mrs. Jervis Langdon (*MTL*, p. 207; *MTLet* 5: 419). In Chapter 11 of *A Tramp Abroad* (1880), "A round-table as large as King Arthur's stood in the centre of the room" of an inn in Heilbronn, Germany. Writing to Susy Clemens on 8 February 1885, Clemens urged that she "take my Morte Arthur & read it. It is one of the quaintest and sweetest of all books." He added, "In this book one finds out where Tennyson got the quaint & pretty phrases which he uses in 'The Idylls of the King'" (ALS, ASSSCL; copy in MTP).

Mark Twain originally planned for the narrator of *A Connecticut Yankee* to recite "some exploit of Launcelot, (to curry favor with Queen) from Idyls [*sic*]" (NB 28 [September 1888], *N&J* 3: 420). Tennyson's "Merlin and Vivien" prepared Mark Twain's readers of *A Connecticut Yankee* (1889) to accept Merlin's position as counselor to Arthur (see *MT&JB*, p. 145). In October 1892, probably at Villa Viviani, Clemens noted the title "Idylls of the King" (NB 32, TS p. 33). From Florence, Clemens informed Clara Clemens on 5 November 1892: "Browning was too sombre & difficult, Tennyson proved too tame & effeminate after Browning; so now we are bracing up on Uncle Remus, evenings, for a change" (ALS in MTP). In Chapter 2 of *Joan of Arc* (1896), Mark Twain refers to "a prophecy of Merlin's, more than eight hundred years old . . . that in a far distant time France would be lost by a woman and restored by a woman." See also the Catalog entries for Thomas Malory.

Wilson, "Malory in the *Connecticut Yankee*" (1948), pp. 186 n. 2, 189 n. 17; Williams, "Use of History" (1965), p. 103; Baetzhold, *MT&JB* (1970), pp. 118, 132, 348 n. 27.

———. *In Memoriam*. Volume VII of *The Works of Alfred Tennyson, Poet Laureate*. 10 vols. Boston: James R. Osgood & Co., 1871. 218 pp.

Source: MTLAcc, entry #2112, volume donated from Clemens's library by Clara Clemens Gabrilowitsch in 1910.

On 15 December 1873 Clemens wrote to invite Tennyson to a lecture he was giving, adding, "I do not expect you to come . . . but . . . what I am trying to do now is only homage, & therefore ought not to be offensive" ("Mark Twain," Heritage Book Shop, Los Angeles, 1997, item #125). Clemens reported to Olivia from London on 22 December 1873: "We met a lady whom [Frank] Finlay knew. . . . We walked with her an hour, then went to her house in Harley street (the 'Long, unlovely street' of Tennyson's In Memoriam) to drink a glass of wine" (*LLMT*, p. 188; *MTLet* 5: 530).

Susy Clemens's death in 1896 gave her parents an impelling reason to revisit this elegy. "I have read part of In Memoriam again. It *is* a noble poem. Mrs. Clemens reads it persistently, & thanks you all the time for the healing it brings her" (SLC to J. Y. W. MacAlister, Weggis, 20 July 1897, ASSSCL). In November 1897 Olivia Clemens wrote to the London publisher Chatto & Windus: "The In Memoriam has just arrived and is entirely satisfying. We thank you for the care and thought which gave us this result" (ALS in MTP).

Harold K. Bush, Jr., in "'Broken Idols,': Mark Twain's Elegies for Susy and a Critique of Freudian Grief Theory," *Nineteenth Century Literature* 57.2 (September 2002): 237–268, and in *Mark Twain and the Spiritual Crisis of His Age* (Tuscaloosa: University of Alabama Press, 2007), pp. 241–250, noted Twain's probable indebtedness to Tennyson's *In Memoriam* in composing poems about the death of Susy Clemens.

Harold K. Bush, "'Nature Shrieking' and Parasitic Wasps: Mark Twain, Theodicy, and the War of Nature," *Mark Twain Annual 17* (2019): 112–113.

———. *Lady Clare*. 23 leaves, 22 illustrations by Alfred Fredericks (1835–1926), Frederic B. Schell (1838–1905), Granville Perkins (1830–1895), Edmund H[enry]. Garrett (1853–1929), F[rederick]. S[tuart]. Church (1842–1924), and Harry Fenn (1838–1911). Original light green pictorial cloth, gilt. Philadelphia: Porter & Coates, [cop. 1884]. First separate American edition.

Inscription: the front flyleaf is inscribed in pencil: "Susie from cousin Lucie, Christmas, 1884." No marginalia are present.

Location: collection of Kevin Mac Donnell, Austin, Texas (Mac Donnell to Alan Gribben, 29 November 2011, with follow-up description sent on 28 August 2017). Purchased from the Langdon family.

In February 1885 Olivia Clemens informed her husband that "the children have been reading to me from their private books tonight. . . . At supper she [Susy] quoted all but two or three lines of 'Lady Clair' [*sic*], simply from having read it so much. She has never attempted to learn it. I was all choked up hearing her and had to look steadily at my plate" (*Twainian* 39.5 [September-October 1980]: 3). Tennyson's poem begins, "It was the time when lilies blow,/And clouds are highest up in air./Lord Ronald brought a lily-white doe/To give his cousin, Lady Clare."

———. "Locksley Hall" (poem, published in 1842).

When Clemens wrote "Better 60 days of Dollis/Than a cycle of Cathay" (NB 43 [September 1900], TS p. 26), he echoed Tennyson's rejected suitor in the dramatic monologue titled "Locksley Hall," who declared, "Better fifty years of Europe than a cycle of Cathay." Clemens's reference was also topical, however; see the Catalog entry for Frank R. Stockton's *A Bicycle of Cathay* (1900). In an Autobiographical Dictation of 6 January 1907 Clemens said that the Reverend Joseph H. Twichell had quoted "those striking verses of Tennyson's which forecast a future when air-borne vessels of war shall meet and fight above the clouds" (*AutoMT 2*: 360). The bitter speaker in "Locksley Hall" momentarily envisions an apocalyptic vision of the future: "Heard the heavens fill with shouting, and there rain'd a ghastly dew/From the nations' airy navies grappling in the central blue."

———. "Mariana" (poem, published in 1830).

In 1902 Clemens reacted to his bill from the Players Club with a gesture that later reminded him of a quotation from Tennyson: "I was aweary, aweary, and I put it in the waste-basket" (21 March 1906 AD, *MTA*, 2: 228; *AutoMT* 1:432). The seven stanzas in Tennyson's poem end in the same refrain (with a only slight variation in the last stanza): "She only said, 'My life is dreary./He cometh not,' she said;/She said, 'I am aweary, aweary,/I would that I were dead!'"

———. *Maud, and Other Poems*. Volume IX of *The Works of Alfred Tennyson, Poet Laureate*. 10 vols. Boston: James R. Osgood & Co., 1871. 177 pp.

Source: MTLAcc, entry #2114, volume donated from Clemens's library by Clara Clemens Gabrilowitsch in 1910.

———. *Miscellaneous Poems*. Volumes I and II of *The Works of Alfred Tennyson, Poet Laureate*. 10 vols. Boston: James R. Osgood & Co., 1871.

Source: MTLAcc, entries #2106 and #2107, 2 volumes donated from Clemens's library by Clara Clemens Gabrilowitsch in 1910. [Volume III (also titled *Miscellaneous Poems*) of this edition was not recorded as having been received by the Mark Twain Library at Redding.]

———. *The Poetical Works of Alfred Tennyson, Poet Laureate,*

Etc. Complete in One Volume. Boston: Ticknor and Fields, 1859. 524 pp.

Inscription: "Susan L. Crane/1860/C.C.H./S[illegible] 1, 1860."

Catalog: Ball 2016 inventory, navy boards, gilt edged pages, fair condition.

Location: Quarry Farm library shelves, under the supervision of the Mark Twain Archive, Elmira College, Elmira, New York.

Clemens had access to this book whenever he visited Quarry Farm in Elmira.

———. *The Poetical Works of Alfred Tennyson*. Leipzig: Bernhard Tauchnitz, 1860. 276 pp.

Source: MTLAcc, entry #2105, volume donated from Clemens's library by Clara Clemens Gabrilowitsch in 1910.

Among various (mostly facetious and fictional) items that Mark Twain listed as "entrusted articles" he was carrying for delivery from San Francisco to his friends' relatives on the East Coast was "1 volume Tennyson" ("Important to Whom It May Concern," 13 June 1868, San Francisco *Newsletter and California Advertiser*, MTLet 2L 224; *MTPP*, p. 33).

———. *The Poetical Works of Alfred Lord Tennyson*. Blue cloth. Boston and New York: Houghton, Mifflin and Co., 1886. 757 pp.

Inscription: front flyleaf inscribed in black ink, "Katie Leary/March 17, 1889, Hartford, Conn."

Provenance: Antenne-Dorrance Collection, Rice Lake, Wisconsin.

Location: Mark Twain Archive, Gannett-Tripp Learning Center, Elmira College, Elmira, New York.

Copy examined: an unmarked copy inscribed in an unidentified hand for Katy Leary, the housekeeper for the Clemens family. Examined on 27 May 2015.

———. *The Poetical Works of Alfred, Lord Tennyson, Poet Laureate*. 2 vols. New York: Thomas Y. Crowell & Co., [cop. 1885].

Inscriptions: the front flyleaf of Volume I and the verso of the frontispiece in Volume II are inscribed in black ink: "From/Orion to Molly/Christmas/1893".

Marginalia: a few pencil marks in Volume I on pages iii, iv, v, 39, 84, and 107; none of these appear to be by Clemens. There are no markings in Volume II.

Location: Mark Twain Library, Redding, Connecticut. These volumes were donated from Clemens's library by Clara Clemens Gabrilowitsch in 1910 (MTLAcc, entries #2101 and #2141). (I discovered both volumes on the circulation shelves in 1970, and requested the librarian to place them in the special bookcases with the other books from Clemens's personal library.)

Copies examined: copies belonging to Clemens's sister-in-law. Volume I (462 pp.) has the red ink Mark Twain Library accession number "3154" and Volume II (933 pp.) has the red ink number "3155". (It was rare for the librarians to make such errors in transcribing numbers, but in this case the numbers written in the volumes do not match those in the accession record.) Examined in 1970 and again in June 1982 and on 9 November 2019.

In Chapter 36 of *The Gilded Age* (1873), one of the chapters Mark Twain wrote by himself without collaboration, Laura Hawkins ranks Tennyson (one of the "favorites of her idle hours") with Hawthorne and Longfellow. Tennyson's

works were represented among the numerous books in "the private parlor of a refined and sensible lady," Aunt Susan, in Twain's "The Loves of Alonzo Fitz Clarence and Rosannah Ethelton" (1878). Tennyson was one of Susy Clemens's favorite poets when she was twelve or thirteen years old (*MFMT*, p. 66). On 20 January1887 Twain recommended Alfred Lord Tennyson's poetry as among the best reading for young girls in a letter to the Reverend Charles D. Crane (ALS, Shapell Manuscript Library, Beverly Hills, California). Carlyle Smythe stated: "I have heard him quote both Shakespeare and Tennyson purely out of a delight for the melody of the words, because, as he says, the phrase 'tastes good in the mouth'" ("The Real 'Mark Twain'" [1898], p. 31). See also the Catalog entry for *Selected Poems, Illustrated* (1875).
Budd, *MTSP* (1962), p. 29; Baetzhold, *MT&JB* (1970), p. 286.

——. *The Poetical Works of Alfred Lord Tennyson, Poet Laureate*. Black pebbled leather, covers detached. London: Macmillan and Co., 1893. 535 pp.
Inscription: the half-title page is inscribed by Olivia Clemens in black ink: "Jean Clemens/Sept. 11th 1896/London/from Mamma."
Marginalia: there are pencil marks in *In Memoriam*. Clemens made double brackets beside the first two stanzas of section LI, which begin, "Do we indeed desire the dead/ Should still be near us at our side?" and remind the reader that those in the grave can now detect our "baseness," "vileness," and "hidden shame."
Provenance: Antenne-Dorrance Collection, Rice Lake, Wisconsin.
Location: Mark Twain Archive, Gannett-Tripp Learning Center, Elmira College, Elmira, New York.
Copy examined: Jean Clemens's copy. Examined on 28 May 2015.

——. *The Princess, A Medley*. Volume VIII of *The Works of Alfred Tennyson, Poet Laureate*. 10 vols. Boston: James R. Osgood & Co., 1871. 213 pp.
Source: MTLAcc, entry #2113, volume donated from Clemens's library by Clara Clemens Gabrilowitsch in 1910.
Clemens especially liked the introductory poem to Part 4, "The Bugle Song." He wrote to Olivia Langdon on 12 January 1869 about the pleasure they would enjoy after they were "serene & happy old married folk" and he "will read: 'The splendor falls on castle walls,/And snowy summits old in story'" (*MT&JB* [1970], p. 148; *MTLet* 3: 26). Tom Sawyer's reverie in Chapter 7 of *The Adventures of Tom Sawyer* (1876)—"The drowsing murmur of the five and twenty studying scholars soothed the soul like the spell that is in the murmur of bees"—recalls the lines in Tennyson's song, "Come down, O maid": "The moan of doves in immemorial elms,/And murmuring of innumerable bees." Clemens wrote to the Reverend Edwin Pond Parker in December 1880, imploring Parker to "compose a certain piece of music"; its theme was to be "The Splendor falls on Castle walls, & snowy summits old in story," and Clemens intricately described the sounds, ranging from "male voices" to "bugle notes" to "flute" echoes, that could express each line, quoting selected words from the next eight lines of the poem down to "the horns of Elfland

faintly blowing!" (ASSCL, PH in MTP).
Surely Mark Twain's description of Morgan le Fay's castle in Chapter 15 of *A Connecticut Yankee in King Arthur's Court* (1888), "whose gray towers and battlements were charmingly draped with ivy, and whose whole majestic mass was drenched with splendors flung from the sinking sun," owes something to Tennyson's verse. In a letter of 22 and 23 March 1893 written to Jean Clemens while Clemens was aboard the *Kaiser Wilhelm II*, he remarked that "in this ship they call you to meals with a bugle" and quoted Tennyson's "O sweet & far from cliff & scar,/The horns of elfland faintly blowing." (PH of ALS, MTP). In "Queen Victoria's Jubilee" (1897) Twain used the poem respectfully, argued Howard G. Baetzhold (*MT&JB*, p. 348 n. 28). Twain copied some lines—"The splendor falls on castle walls/And snowy summits old in story" in a satiric verse diatribe he wrote in Vienna in September 1898 (NB 40, TS p. 43). Howard G. Baetzhold maintained that Twain alludes to the lines again in "Three Thousand Years Among the Microbes" (*WWD?*, p. 464), a piece written in 1905 (*MT&JB*, pp. 348–349 n. 28). Twain again showed familiarity with lines from the Introductory Song to Part 4 of *The Princess* in some humorous notes he made on the rear endpaper of Brueys' *L'Avocat Patelin* (1905); the translator, Samuel F. G. Whitaker, inscribed *L'Avocat Patelin* to Clemens in 1907.

——. *The Princess, A Medley*. Boston: Houghton, Mifflin and Co., 1894. 190 pp.
Source: MTLAcc, entry #2103, volume donated from Clemens's library by Clara Clemens Gabrilowitsch in 1910.

——. *Queen Mary, A Drama. Author's Edition, from Advance Sheets*. Boston: James R. Osgood and Co., 1875. 263 pp. [Publisher and pages conjectured.]
Inscription: the front flyleaf is signed, "Saml. L. Clemens, Hartford, July, 1875."
Catalog: *A1911*, "12mo, cloth, Bost. 1875," quotes the signature, lot 450, sold for $4.

——. *Tennyson's Suppressed Poems, Now for the First Time Collected*. Edited by Joseph Charles Thomson (b. 1867). New York: Harper & Brothers, 1903. 203 pp.
Source: MTLAcc, entry #2102, volume donated from Clemens's library by Clara Clemens Gabrilowitsch in 1910.
TENNYSON, HALLAM (1852–1928). *Alfred, Lord Tennyson; A Memoir by His Son*. 2 vols. London: Macmillan and Co., 1897. [Edition conjectured but almost certainly correct.]
Catalog: ListABP (1910), "Memoir of Tennyson, 2 vols., Tennyson," no other information supplied.
There was a request for this title from Clemens per Olivia Clemens addressed to Chatto & Windus, 13 September 1898 (MTP).
Welland, *Mark Twain in England* (1978), p. 189.
TERHUNE, MARY VIRGINIA (HAWES) (1830–1922), pseud. "Marion Harland." *Breakfast, Luncheon and Tea*. New York: Scribner, Armstrong & Co., 1875. 459 pp.
Catalog: *C1951*, #019, listed with volumes signed by Olivia Clemens.
Recipes for griddle cakes, broiled oysters, potatoes, fried chicken, preserved fruits, cakes, and other delicacies are interspersed with advisory "Familiar Talks" and fictional sketches and short stories.

——. *Common Sense in the Household: A Manual of Practical*

Housewifery. Revised edition. New York: Charles Scribner's Sons, [cop. 1880]. 546 pp.

Clemens's statement of account from Brown & Gross, Hartford booksellers, recorded the purchase on 13 November 1880 of "1 Common Sense H. M." for $1.40; the bill is dated 1 January 1881 and Clemens paid it on 17 January 1881 (receipt in MTP). Clemens obtained his customary 20% discount; the volume normally sold for $1.75. See also the Catalog entry for Annie Eliot Trumbull's "Mary A. Twining." Terhune, a Virginia-born novelist who moved to New Jersey after her marriage, believed that efficiency with household responsibilities could free women for outside activities.

Terry, Frederick Battell (1874–1890). *Stories*. New York: De Vinne Press, 1890. 78 pp.

In a letter to Annie E. Trumbull written on 11 January 1891 Clemens praised "'Stony Lonesome,' which is in more than one respect a remarkable performance for a lad; it is really Kiplingish in its straightforward, unembroidered style& its familiar handling of the technical colloquialisms of the railway. He must have served a term on the rails" (TS in MTP). Terry had grown up in Connecticut and had recently died of a mysterious illness on 30 July 1890 at the age of fifteen. The story Clemens singled out (on pages 49–55) was a ghost tale told at the Hartford depot by a locomotive engineer about a train wreck he witnessed at "a sharp bend around a precipitous face of rock" called Stony Lonesome.

Teskey, Adeline Margaret (1853–1924). *Where the Sugar Maple Grows; Idylls of a Canadian Village*. Illustrated by John]. S[loane]. Gordon (1868–1940). New York: R. F. Fenno & Co., 1901. 268 pp.

Source: MTLAcc, entry #307, volume donated by Albert Bigelow Paine, Clemens's designated biographer. Possibly Clemens saw this book, since the men exchanged reading materials.

Teskey lived in Welland, Ontario. The series of stories in *Where the Sugar Maple Grows* are set in the fictional Canadian town of Mapleton.

Tewkesbury. *The Official Guide to Tewkesbury*.

Having received a souvenir handbook describing the 1471 battle at Tewkesbury from William Henry Watts (1836–1923), an amateur English antiquarian who lived in Tewkesbury, Clemens wrote on 15 August 1908: "I thank you for . . . the official guide, which I read through at a single sitting" (*MTL*, p. 813; PH in MTP).

Thackeray, William Makepeace (1811–1863). *The Adventures of Philip on His Way Through the World; Showing Who Robbed Him, Who Helped Him, and Who Passed Him By. To Which Is Now Prefixed A Shabby Genteel Story*. Illustrated by Frederick Walker (1840–1875). Household Edition. New York: Harper & Brothers, n.d. 442 pp.

Inscription: the initials "S. C." are written in pencil on the front flyleaf, possibly in Olivia Clemens's hand. (A similar designation appears in Clemens's copy of E. L. Voynick's *The Gadfly*.)

Location: Mark Twain Library, Redding, Connecticut. (MTLAcc, entry #301, volume donated by Clemens).

Copy examined: Clemens's copy. Has the red ink Mark Twain Library accession number "301". I could not locate this book in 1970 but it had turned up by the time

I revisited Redding in June 1982.

The last complete novel Thackeray published, *The Adventures of Philip on His Way Through the World*, appeared in 1861–1862 and reintroduced characters Thackeray had earlier described in "A Shabby Genteel Story" (1840). On 14 July 1880 Estes & Lauriat, publishers and booksellers in Boston, billed Clemens for "1 Thackeray 11 vol. $23"; Clemens paid on 20 July 1880 (receipt in MTP). The reliable HathiTrust Digital Library dates an eleven-volume edition published by Harper & Brothers as first appearing in 1869. Three other volumes from this set were donated to the Mark Twain Library in Redding (see the Catalog entries below).

———. *Ballads*. Illus. Boston: James R. Osgood and Co., 1882. 374 pp.

Source: MTLAcc, entry #2115, volume donated from Clemens's library by Clara Clemens Gabrilowitsch in 1910. Thackeray's "Little Billee" ballad is included on pages 185–188.

———. *The Diary of Jeames de la Pluche, Esq., with His Letters* (novella, published serially in *Punch*, 1845–1846).

The Mark Twain Project editors identified this reference in Clemens's disillusioned description of Ralph Ashcroft as "a lackey, in England" who possessed "the Jeames style" (*AutoMT* 3: 352).

———. *The History of Henry Esmond* (novel, published in 1852).

As with so many literary topics, the evidence regarding Clemens's definitive view of Thackeray seems somewhat contradictory. Carlyle Smythe reported that "when . . . Mr. [William Dean] Howells entreated him [Clemens] to read 'Esmond,' he could find no scene to interest him." Smythe added that Clemens "has never been able to find a line in Thackeray which interested him," the result, Smythe believed, of Clemens's addiction to newspaper reading ("The Real 'Mark Twain'" [1898], p. 31). After luncheon on 7 October 1906, Isabel Lyon recorded, Clemens "went up to bed—to read 'Henry Esmond' and finds that it drags—and to smoke and loaf to his heart's content" (IVL Journals, TS p. 191, MTP). Clemens informed Clara Clemens on 9 October 1906, in a letter written from Dublin, New Hampshire: "I have just finished Henry Esmond. There are very fine passages in it. On the whole I liked it. Its close is dramatically great. But I had a surprise: from the beginning to the end I found nothing that was familiar to me. It turns out—per the [Isabel] Lyon—that I've not read this book before, but was mistaking 'The Virginians' for this one" (ALS in MTP, quoted by Joseph Gardner, "MT and Dickens" [1969], p. 97).

———. *History of Pendennis, His Fortunes and Misfortunes, His Friends and His Greatest Enemy* (novel, published in 1848–1850).

During a newspaper interview published on 10 April 1904 in the New York *Times*, Mark Twain remarked, "Is there a more tiresome and unnatural book than *Pendennis*? All the people are exaggerated, caricatures, with no intention of being so. . . . I dare say it is wonderful, for its time; but its time is past" (Scharnhorst, ed., *Complete Interviews*, p. 495). Isabel Lyon recorded Clemens's reminiscing on 18 September 1905 about Kipling's first trip to Elmira, when Kipling found him in the Langdons' library. Kipling asked Clemens "what he thought of 'Pendennis,' and Mr. Clemens replied 'Oh I don't know—what's his other name?' (He can't abide Thackeray)" (IVL Journals, TS p. 100, MTP).

———. *A Legend of the Rhine* (burlesque novel, first published in 1845).

Franklin R. Rogers insisted that the first half of Mark Twain's "Legend of Count Luigi" in Chapter 21 of *The Innocents Abroad* (1869) "seems most indebted to Thackeray's *Legend of the Rhine*, a burlesque of Dumas's *Otto, l'archer*" (*MTBP* (1960), p. 48).

Smith, *MTDW* (1962), p. 35; Baetzhold, *MT&JB* (1970), p. 294.

———. "Little Billee" (ballad, published in 1849).

"All that I remember about Madagascar is that Thackeray's little Billie [*sic*] went up to the top of the mast and there knelt him upon his knee, saying 'I see/Jerusalem and Madagascar,/And North and South Amerikee'" (*FE* [1897], Ch. 64). Twain's memory was accurate here. In Thackeray's "Little Billee," first published as "The Three Sailors," two starving sailors in a boat from Bristol are about to kill and eat young Billee, but just then Billee catches sight of an approaching British warship: "When up he jumps—'There's land I see!/Jerusalem and Madagascar/And North and South Amerikee.'" The murderous sailors are thereupon hanged and young Billee is made the captain of a ship.

———. *The Memoirs of Barry Lyndon. Esq.* (fictional autobiography, first published in 1844, revised in 1856).

"When Professor Brander Matthews recommended him [Clemens] 'Barry Lyndon' as a monumental work . . . he could find no scene to interest him," reported Carlyle Smythe ("The Real 'Mark Twain'" [1898], p. 31).

———. *Miscellanies.* Illus. New York: Harper & Brothers, n.d. 442 pp.

Source: MTLAcc, entry #302, volume donated by Clemens. One wishes that the accession record were more detailed about the title page and contents of this book. Harper & Brothers brought out a Household Edition of Thackeray's *Miscellanies* in two volumes in 1877. This book might have been one of those volumes.

———. *The Newcomes; Memoirs of a Most Respectable Family* (novel, published in 1853–1855).

Carlyle Smythe wrote that Clemens "could not finish 'The Newcomes' without showing signs of distress" ("The Real 'Mark Twain'" [1898], p. 31).

———. *Sketch Books. The Paris Sketch Book of Mr. M. A. Titmarsh. The Irish Sketch Book of a Journey from Cornhill to Grand Cairo.* Illustrated by the author. New York: Harper & Brothers, n. d. 590 pp.

Source: MTLAcc, entry #299, volume donated by Clemens.

———. *Thackeray's Complete Works.* 20 vols. De Luxe Edition. Limited to 250 copies. No. 139. India proof illustrations. Boston: Estes and Lauriat, 1882–1883.

Catalog: Ball 2016 inventory, 20 vols., no inscriptions, red cloth, paper label on spine, rough cut pages.

Location: Quarry Farm library shelves, under the supervision of the Mark Twain Archive, Elmira College, Elmira, New York.

Clemens had access to this set whenever he visited Quarry Farm in Elmira.

———. *Thackeray's Lectures. The English Humorists. The Four Georges. Complete in One Volume.* Blue cloth, gilt lettering. New York: Harper & Brothers, 1868. 449 pp. [The spine reads "Thackeray's Works."]

Inscription: there is no flyleaf signature or inscription. A virtually illegible note on the rear free endpaper seems to read "However [?] bet [?] goes to the Wll/J. F. U. T. B!!"

Marginalia: profusely annotated in pencil (and only pencil) between pages 6 and 185, with a few additional pencil markings and notes up to page 219. Clemens made vertical lines, brackets, and many notes. There are no marginalia in "The Four Georges" section. Coley B. Taylor published the comments that Clemens wrote in Thackeray's essay about Jonathan Swift (*Mark Twain's Margins on Thackeray's "Swift,"* Limited edition of 1000 copies [New York: Gotham House, 1935]). Besides the remarks in the Swift essay, Clemens also annotated pages about Congreve, Addison, Steele, Prior, Gay, Pope, Hogarth, Smollett, Fielding, Sterne, and Goldsmith.

"A neat portrait of Johnson," Clemens observed on page 9. Clemens, who had long been interested in the pseudoscience of phrenology, scoffed on page 9: "Possibly it was some poor parish idiot's skull they got instead [in 1835, when Swift's skeletal remains were reportedly examined in St. Patrick's Cathedral in Dublin]—'medics' are seldom very authentic. Think of these learned, spectacled, Doctors of Phrenology gravely getting up an 'opinion' of Swift's intellect by examining another man's skull!" Clemens was amused by Thackeray's attempts to sanitize the reputation of Swift, remarking in a vertical pencil note on page 11: "A happy sketch of a hideous character." On page 22 Clemens wrote a vertical commiseration about Swift's painful demise: "The sorrowful story, & the humbled pride, of even *Swift*, who pitied nobody, himself, compels compassion." At the bottom of page 25 Clemens observed, in pencil: "The character of Swift seems to have been a curious medley of startling contrasts—of goodness & badness, of worth & unworthiness, of greatness & littleness, of towering pride & cringing baseness, of feeble love & fickle hate, of imperial genius<,> & groveling vulgarity & obscenity." Clemens seems to address Olivia Langdon as his audience on page 30 where he advises: "Exquisite—pray put it in the Book of Extracts—it is a picture that is worthy." The Thackeray passage to which Clemens refers reads: "Through the storms and tempests of his furious mind, the stars of religion and love break out in the blue shining serenity, though hidden by the driving clouds and the maddened hurricane of his life" (pages 29–30). On page 40 Clemens commented, "And so she was the English Heloise--& he as base as Abelard." He followed this on page 45 with a similar remark: "What a charming sort of a sweetheart this Mr. Swift must have been." On page 47 he summarized his impression, writing vertically: "Swift was heartless." At the bottom of the next page he declared of Swift: "And he might have added that he has as prurient a taste as Rabelais, also, & was only a little less bestial in its expression" (p. 48). Thackeray wrote that "thinking of him is like thinking of an empire falling" (p. 49). At the end of the chapter on Swift, Clemens noted: "Void of every tender grace, every kindly humanizing element, what a bare, glittering iceberg is mere *intellectual* greatness—& such was Swift's" (bottom of p. 49, in pencil).

Of William Congreve (on page 54) Clemens lamented, "Alas, that this 'equal of Shakespeare' [as Dryden had declared him] should have been forgotten so soon—for such seems to be the case." Pages 63–64 and 65–66 have been cut out of the volume in the Congreve and Addison chapter, and the lower half of pages 83–84, also about Congreve and Addison, were similarly scissored; these mutilations were noted by "E. G." on 9 March 1937. Since this seems to have been one of the "courting books" that Clemens exchanged with Olivia Langdon, Clemens himself possibly cut out the missing parts of the pages because they contained matter he deemed too coarse for her pre-marital eyes.

On page 69 Clemens wrote: "What an infamous affectation are these fancy names: Stella, Varina, Vanessa, Pastora, &c." Of Addison, Clemens wrote in pencil on page 90: "As noble & beautiful a nature as Swift's was ignoble & deformed." At the end of Thackeray's second lecture, titled "Congreve and Addison," Clemens observed at the bottom of page 91: "What a pity it is that Thackeray did not sketch Sir Philip Sidney." Below that, Clemens added: "Swift's [*sic*—Clemens presumably meant Addison here] writings were at times touched on some degree with indelicacy—Swift's were coarse, often, & often obscene—worse than Fielding or Smollett." At the bottom of page 137, the end of Lecture Three (titled "Steele"), Clemens noted in pencil, "The next hundred pages of this book are tolerably dull, *I* think." On page 174 Clemens wrote in pencil: "*How* can any one conceive of Swift being fat?" Where Thackeray asserted on page 212 that "the novel of 'Humphry Clinker' is, I do think, the most laughable story that has ever been written since the goodly art of novel-writing began," Clemens opined in the margin: "It seemed to me the most insufferably dull."

Location: Mark Twain Library, Redding, Connecticut.

Copy examined: Clemens's copy. Good condition. Has the red ink Mark Twain Library accession number "4526". Examined in 1970 and again in June 1982 and on 9 November 2019.

Clemens apparently acquired this book more than a decade before obtaining the eleven-volume set of Thackeray's writings in 1880 (see the Catalog entry above for *The Adventures of Philip on His Way Through the World*). Sometime between November 1867 and February 1870, Olivia Langdon copied several comments by Thackeray about Jonathan Swift into her commonplace book (DV161, MTP), citing Thackeray's *English Humorists*; this must have been while she and Clemens were reading the book together. Later, writing to Olivia Clemens from London on 22 December 1873, Clemens promised, "I'll look up the Thackeray & Dickens" (*MTLet* 5: 529).

Sam Clemens's boardinghouse roommate in 1853, a journeyman chair-maker named Jacob Burrough, "was fond of Dickens, Thackeray, Scott & Disraeli; & was the only reading-man in the establishment" (SLC to Frank E. Burrough, New York City, 15 December 1900, ALS, Southeast Missouri State College, Cape Girardeau). "Thackeray's bust" is in Westminster Abbey, Clemens remarked ("A Memorable Midnight Experience" [1874]).

Compelled to reread Bret Harte's writings for a projected anthology of humor, Clemens complained to William Dean Howells on 23 March 1882 that he found Harte's work "as slovenly as Thackeray, and as dull as Charles Lamb" (*MTHL*, p. 396). In March 1882, shortly before Clemens departed from Hartford for the Mississippi River Valley, he reminded himself to "criticise Thackeray. Calling [Christian Bernhard] Tauchnitz a pirate" (NB 20, *N&J* 2: 449). (One would suppose that Clemens might be interested in "A Mississippi Bubble," Thackeray's account in *Roundabout Papers* [1864] of his voyage from New Orleans to St. Louis on "a huge, tall, white, pasteboard castle of a steamer"—though there is no evidence that Clemens read this essay.) On 27 June 1893, musing about "how sad it would be" to complete "the Unfinished Novel," Clemens wrote: "Thackeray finishing the Waverley novels was on track of a truth" (NB 33, TS p. 20). In Vienna, according to Henry Fisher, Clemens conceived the idea of writing a book on the Three Charleses (Charles William Ferdinand of Brunswick [1735–1806] and Charles I and II of England), but he discarded the project because of its similarity to Thackeray's *Four Georges* (*AMT*, p. 157). In 1906 and again in 1909 Clemens told how "humiliated" Olivia Clemens felt in confessing to Sergei M. Kravchinski (pseud. "Stepniak") that her husband had not read Thackeray, Balzac, and other prominent authors—and thus had no opinions about their writings (*MTB*, pp. 1350, 1500).

Krause, *MTC* (1967), p. 14; Gardner, "MT and Dickens" (1969), p. 97.

———. *Vanity Fair, A Novel Without a Hero* (novel, published 1847–1848).

Chapter 44 of Mark Twain and Charles Dudley Warner's *The Gilded Age* (1873) presumably alludes to Thackeray's title: "This was by contrast the maddest Vanity Fair one could conceive." (But see also the Catalog entry for John Bunyan's *Pilgrim's Progress*.) One wishes for more evidence that Clemens was familiar with Thackeray's satirical novel. To an Australian interviewer in 1895 Twain favorably compared Thackeray's and Dickens's techniques for injecting humor into pathos with Shakespeare's handling of the Fool in *King Lear* (Sydney *Morning Herald*, 17 September 1895; Scharnhorst, ed., *Complete Interviews*, p. 205). Surveying English literature in an 1897 newspaper interview in Vienna, Clemens said he "loves Thackeray" (Odessa *News* [Odesskie *Novosti*], 8 October 1897; translated and reprinted by M. Thomas Inge and George Munro, "Ten Minutes with Mark Twain," *American Literary Realism* 15.2 [Autumn 1982]: 262).

———. *The Virginians; A Tale of the Last Century*. Illus. New York: Harper & Brothers, n.d. 542 pp.

Source: MTLAcc, entry #300, volume donated by Clemens.

Clemens read this book (and evidently disliked it) sometime prior to 9 October 1906, when he wrote to Clara Clemens after reading *Henry Esmond*: "I've not read this book before, but was mistaking 'The Virginians' for this one" (ALS in MTP). See the Catalog entry above for *The History of Henry Esmond*.

THAYER, WILLIAM MAKEPEACE (1820–1898). *Marvels of the New West: A Vivid Portrayal of the Stupendous Marvels in the Vast Wonderland West of the Missouri River. Six Books in One*

Volume. Comprising Marvels of Nature, Marvels of Race, Marvels of Enterprise, Marvels of Mining, Marvels of Stock-Raising, and Marvels of Agriculture, Graphically and Truthfully Described. Sold Only by Subscription. Illus. Norwich, Connecticut: Henry Bill Publishing Co., 1888. 715 pp.

Mark Twain, financially dependent on the subscription method of selling books, could hardly afford (at least in public) to rebuff subscription sales canvassers who approached him. E. W. Abell, a student at Yale University in New Haven, wrote an excited letter to his employer, the Henry Bill Publishing Company of Norwich, Connecticut, on 1 July 1889. Abell described how he followed Chauncey M. Depew into a railroad car, sold him a copy of *Marvels of the New West*, and then recognized Clemens nearby. "I sat on the foot stool before him, took out my prospectus, told him just what the work was, pointed to Chauncey Depew's name and handed him the pen. He put his name right down. I then asked him to comment on the engravings that I might tell people how pleased he was with the work; but he was trying to drink some wine, and said in his slow, droll way, 'you tell people what you think I thought about it'" (PH in MTP). Clemens wrote to the college student on 22 September 1889 from Hartford: "My Dear Mr. Abell:/The book has arrived & I would have made the due acknowledgment sooner but have been hindered one way or another" (PH in MTP).

———. *The Pioneer Boy, and How He Became President.* Boston: Walker, Wise, 1863. 310 pp. [A biography of Abraham Lincoln.]

Inscription: "Charles Langdon from his Mother/June 29, 1863/Elmira N. Y." [Charles Jervis Langdon was Olivia Langdon's brother.]

Catalogs: listed among the books that Mark Woodhouse transferred from the Quarry Farm library to the Mark Twain Archive on 9 July 1987; Ball 2016 inventory, dark green cloth with gilt lettering and design, fair condition.

Location: Mark Twain Archive, Elmira College, Elmira, New York.

Clemens had access to this book whenever he visited the Langdons' residence in Elmira.

THEAL, GEORGE McCALL (1837–1919). *South Africa: The Cape Colony, Natal, Orange Free State, South African Republic, and All Other Territories South of the Zambesi.* The Story of the Nations Series. London: T. Fisher Unwin, 1894. 397 pp.

On 20 November 1895 Clemens noted, among a list of books, "Theal's 'South Africa'" (NB 34, TS p. 40).

"THERE'S A MEETING HERE TO-NIGHT" (spiritual).

Clemens included this title ("There's a Meeting here to-night") in a brief list of plantation spirituals he set down in Notebook 30 (1890, *N&J* 3: 593).

"THERE WAS A WOMAN IN OUR TOWN" (folk ballad).

Henry Nash Smith and William M. Gibson discussed Mark Twain's repeated use of this song (*MTHL* [1960], Appendix, p. 874). He employed the ballad in a fragmentary farce that survives in the Mark Twain Papers (Paine 115) from his newspaper days in San Francisco. Annie Moffett Webster recalled this as a song that Clemens sang for comic entertainment at the time of his wedding trip to Buffalo: "There was an old woman in our town,/In our town did dwell,/She loved her husband dearily/But another man twicet as well,/Another man twicet as well" (*MTBus*, p.

109). Webster referred to this song as "Johnny Sands." (A ballad of that title recounts how Johnny Sands married Betty Hague, a wealthy woman, and then engineered her death by drowning.) "There was a woman in our town" likewise concludes with a wealthy wife (this one a devious, murderous woman) drowning in a river. Mark Twain's character named Brummel lustily sings "There was a woman in our town" while he is intoxicated in the "Brummel-Arabella Fragment" (written in 1870) of the Simon Wheeler sequence of plays (*S&B*, p. 211). Miles Hendon sings a version of four lines from the song in Chapter 13 of *The Prince and the Pauper* (1881): "There was a woman in our town/In our town did dwell—/She loved her husband dearilee,/But another man he loved she." A raftsman in the so-called "Raft Passage" omitted from Chapter 16 of *Adventures of Huckleberry Finn* and published instead in Chapter 3 of *Life on the Mississippi* (1883) bellows out two verses of this folk tune; Huck Finn mentions that "it wasn't a nice song—for a parlor, anyway," and that it had "fourteen verses." The raftsman's version goes: "There was a woman in our towdn,/In our towdn did dwed'l,/She loved her husband dear-i-lee,/But another man twyste as wed'l"; he breaks off from singing when another raftsman complains that "it was the tune the old cow died on," and still another man urges,"Oh, give us a rest."

THOMAS À KEMPIS (c. 1380–1471). *The Imitation of Christ* (attributed) (written c. 1418–1427).

On 12 July 1885 Olivia Clemens alluded to this early devotional work when characterizing a list of resolutions to do good that young Clara Clemens had written: "It has to me a real à Kempis ring about it" ("Quarry Farm Diary," *Family Sketch*, p. 102). On 24 December 1909, in the closing section of Mark Twain's autobiography, he punned on words attributed to Thomas à Kempis: "Man proposes, Circumstances dispose" (*AutoMT* 3: 311). The original maxim was "Man proposes, God disposes."

THOMAS, AUGUSTUS (1857–1934). *Editha's Burglar* (performed as a one-act play in 1883; performed as a four-act play, *The Burglar*, in 1887 and 1889). Adapted from a story by Frances Hodgson Burnett (1849–1924).

On 2 January 1902 William Dean Howells invited Clemens to lunch with him in New York City "next Thursday. . . . Thomas, the dramatist, whom you like, will be there" (*MTHL*, p. 736). In 1905 Thomas was among ten writers whom Clemens nominated for membership in the American Academy of Arts and Letters (SLC to Robert Underwood Johnson, New York City, 28 April 1905, ALS, American Academy of Arts and Letters, PH in MTP). In 1906 Clemens listed Thomas first among the "literatics" whom he hoped to organize into a group for entertaining "the visiting literary stranger" (SLC to WDH, New York City, 10 April 1906, *MTHL*, p. 804). Isabel V. Lyon noted on 23 April 1908 that Clemens attended a performance of *Editha's Burglar* at the Educational Alliance, where he spoke afterwards on behalf of the Educational Theatre (IVL Journals, TS p. 319, MTP; *MTSpk*, pp. 620–621).

———. *The Witching Hour.* Illus. New York: Harper & Brothers, 1908. 249 pp.

Source: MTLAcc, entry #1477, volume donated by Clemens.

THOMAS, BERTHA (1845–1918). *In a Cathedral City. A Tale.* New Edition. London: Chatto & Windus, 1900. 350 pp.

> **Source:** MTLAcc, entry #304, volume donated by Clemens. Thomas wrote seven novels. This one, set in Bury St. Martin's, involves a scheming, blackmailing former husband who victimizes a young woman.

THOMAS, BRANDON (1856–1914). *Charley's Aunt* (farce, performed 1892).

> As Shelley Fisher Fishkin made clear in "Mark Twain and the Stage," Twain's play titled *Is He Dead?* (written in 1898) was greatly indebted to Thomas's enormously popular *Charley's Aunt*, especially in its reliance on cross-dressing as a plot device (*A Companion to Mark Twain*, ed. Peter Messent and Louis J. Budd [Malden, Massachusetts: Blackwell Publishing, 2005], pp. 262–272). The confused narrator of "The Secret History of Eddypus" (written 1901–1902) puzzles over an allusion to *Charley's Aunt*. "We search the old writers in vain to find out who she was. . . . Charley's Aunt once filled the ancient world with her fame; and where is it now? . . . Dear idol of the perished Great Republic, Charley's Aunt!" (*FM*, p. 335).

THOMAS, CHARLES G. *Johannesburg in Arms 1895–96, Being the Observations of a Casual Spectator.* Illus. London: Smith, Elder & Co., 1896. 120 pp.

> **Inscription:** the front free endpaper is signed, "S. L. Clemens/Cape Town, July 13 '96".
>
> **Catalogs:** *A1911*, "12mo, cloth, Lond. 1896," quotes the signature, lot 452, sold for $3; George D. Smith, New York City, "Catalogue of Books" (1911), quotes the signature, item #430, $7.50; Parke-Bernet Galleries, Sale No. 1719 (December 1956), lot 130 (Alan N. Mendelson's collection), sold for $50.

THOMAS, EDWIN. "A warrior bold" (song, published in 1875). Melody composed by Michael Maybrick (1844–1913), aka "Stephen Adams."

> "A Warrior Bold" begins, "In days of old, when knights were bold,/And barons held their sway." Katy Leary remembered that Clemens "used to sing one song that was so lovely that I always used to sneak in and listen to it: 'In the [*sic*] Days of Old When Knights Was [*sic*] Bold'" (*LMT*, p. 73). The lyricist Thomas dropped from sight after writing several songs, but Maybrick was a noted English vocalist as well as a composer of popular light songs.

THOMAS, FREDERICK WILLIAM (1806–1866). "'Tis Said That Absence Conquers Love" (poem, published in 1831). Subsequently set to music as a song by E. Thomas.

> Clowning about an abscess in his ear, Clemens wrote to the Reverend Joseph H. Twichell from Quarry Farm on 29 August 1880: "'Tis said that abscess conquers love,/But O believe it not'" (*MTL*, p. 384; *LMTJHT*, p. p. 101). Except for the absence/abscess pun, this is an exact quotation from Thomas's poem. The American novelist, poet, and journalist Thomas was a friend of Edgar Allan Poe.

THOMPSON, DENMAN (1833–1911) [assisted by GEORGE W. RYER (1843–1902)]. *The Old Homestead* (four-act play, performed in 1886).

> Thompson himself starred in the role of the kindly old farmer named Joshua Whitcomb, the character in this rural drama who worries about his absent son and the mortgage on the homestead. On 14 January 1898 Clemens reminisced in Vienna: "Uncle John Quarles who

was very like the Yankee farmer in Old Homestead"; he then resolved: "Write an Old Homestead of the South" (NB 42, TS p. 53).

THOMPSON, FRANCIS (1859–1907). "From the Night of Forebeing. An Ode after Easter" (poem). [Collected in *New Poems*, London, 1897.]

> Robert Regan solved a long-puzzling literary allusion in Mark Twain's "Queen Victoria's Jubilee" (1897) where the "spirit correspondent," an interior narrator, describes Henry V's entry into London in 1415 after the battle of Agincourt. In this account the brilliant sunlight, reflected on the lifted shields of Henry's knights, "lit up that dappled sea of color with a glory like 'the golden vortex in the west over the foundered sun.'" The "golden vortex" quotation comes from Thompson's poem, which appeared in the same year as Twain's essay (letter from Robert Regan to Alan Gribben, 29 August 1996). The Catholic mystical poet and opium addict Francis Thompson produced visionary verse that impressed or baffled readers of his time. The lines Twain quoted from are these: "The thing from which I turn my troubled look/Fearing the gods' rebuke;/That perturbation putting glory on,/As is the golden vortex in the West/Over the foundered sun."

———. *Shelley.* Introduction by George Wyndham (1863–1913). Notes by Wilfred Meynell (1852–1948). Original green buckram gilt. Half green morocco folding-case. New York: Charles Scribner's Sons, 1909. 91 pp.

> **Inscription:** the front pastedown endpaper is signed in ink, "S L. Clemens/1909/from Betsy". Priced in pencil at $350 on the front free endpaper.
>
> **Marginalia:** annotations by Clemens total more than fifty words. At the foot of page 37, where Thompson discusses the love of a wife, Clemens wrote, poetically: "Love is a clay vase in a/furnace. When it comes out/& cools down, it is perfect,/& permanently precious &/beautiful." Clemens made vertical marks beside two passages on page 38 in which Thompson describes the love of Shelley's second wife and compares her to Browning's Elizabeth. Where Thompson praised Shelley's imagery (page 53), Clemens noted, "And what a wonder-worker/with imagery he is, himself!" At Thompson's lamenting the "utter desolation" of Shelley's pantheism (page 63), Clemens objected, writing vertically and marking the passage: "Still it is better than a heaven/cluttered up with Christians." And next to Thompson's assurance on page 68 that he is hardly blind to the "evil side" of Shelley's life, Clemens marked that paragraph and wrote vertically, "What a strange mixture Francis Thompson is,/of splendid mentality & crass assfulness."
>
> **Catalogs:** ListABP (1910), "Shelley, Thompson"; *C1951*, #40c; *Sotheby's 2003*, #239, $6,500.
>
> **Provenance:** the shelfmark of Clara Clemens Samossoud's private library in Detroit is present. Later the book belonged to film producer Robert Daley of Burbank, California. Subsequently it entered the collection of Nick Karanovich in Fort Wayne, Indiana.
>
> **Copy examined:** Clemens's copy, at the 2003 Sotheby's auction. There is a photocopy of Clemens's inscription and marginalia that Robert Daley provided on 1 March 1977 to the Mark Twain Papers, Bancroft Library, University

of California at Berkeley.

On 22 September 1909 Clemens wrote from Redding, Connecticut to his friend Elizabeth Wallace to thank her for this copy of Thompson's book: "It's a lovely little book, and as rich in sumptuous imagery as is Shelley himself. The reading so moved and charmed me that I read some Shelley under the inspiration of it. Thank you ever so much for sending it" (MT&HI, pp. 131–132). Francis Thompson wrote his essay on Percy Bysshe Shelley (1792–1822) in 1889; it was found among Thompson's papers after his death in 1907.

THOMPSON, GEORGE (1823–c. 1873). *City Crimes; or, Life in New York and Boston: A Volume for Everybody, Being a Mirror of Fashion, a Picture of Poverty, and a Startling Revelation of the Secret Crimes of Great Cities* (novel, published in 1849).

Jarrod Roark cited this author and title in his study of Mark Twain's interaction with sensational novels ("Beneath Mark Twain: Detecting Sensational Residues in Twain's Early Writing," *Mark Twain Annual 12* [2014]: 14–29).

———. *Venus in Boston and Other Tales of Nineteenth-Century City Life* (1849).

Jarrod Roark named this lurid short novel as another example of sensation fiction in "Beneath Mark Twain: Detecting Sensational Residues in Twain's Early Writing," *Mark Twain Annual 12* (2014): 14–29.

THOMPSON, HENRY S. (born c. 1824). "Lilly Dale" (song, published in 1852). Words and music by Thompson.

In a column dated 10 June 1865 Mark Twain urged, "Don't sing 'Lilly Dale,'" which is "a lugubrious ditty" (ET&S 2: 183). Twain called it one of the "wretchedest old songs in the world" (letter to *Alta California*, written on 1 January 1867, published in the 17 March 1867 issue; *MTTMB*, p. 59). Two years later he mentioned it again as one of the "ghastly old sea-sickening sentimental songs" (SLC to Harriet Lewis, Galesburg, Illinois, 10 January 1869, *LLMT*, p. 48; *MTLet* 3: 23). Thompson, born in Massachusetts, composed music for minstrel troupes. The dying Lilly Dale in this song asks that she be buried "Neath the chestnut tree,/Where the wild flowers grow."

THOMPSON, [JAMES] MAURICE (1844–1901). *Songs of Fair Weather*. First edition. Original pictorial vegetable vellum, uncut. Half brown morocco folding-case. Boston: James R. Osgood and Co., 1883. 99 pp.

Inscription: the front free endpaper is signed in pencil, "S. L. Clemens/Hartford, 1883."

Catalogs: *A1911*, "first edition, 12mo, vellum (soiled), uncut, Bost. 1883," quotes the signature, lot 453, sold for $2; *Lexington 1912*, item #25, $7.50; American Art Association (New York City), sale catalogue for the collection of the late William F. Gable of Altoona, Pennsylvania, "Boston, 1883, 8vo, signed "S. L. Clemens, Hartford, 1883", has the *A1911* sale label, lot 125, sold for $9 (with one other book); *Sotheby's 2003*, lot 197, $5,500 (sold with two other titles from Clemens's library).

Provenance: in the collection of Robert Daley, Burbank, California in the 1970s. Subsequently in the collection of Nick Karanovich, Fort Wayne, Indiana.

Location: collection of Kevin Mac Donnell, Austin, Texas.

Copy examined: Clemens's unmarked copy, in July 2004. A newspaper clipping about Clemens's fiftieth birthday

has been tipped in.

Clemens noted the title of this book in 1883 in Notebook 22 (N&J 2: 39). A collection of thirty-three poems, most of them about the sights and sounds of nature, *Songs of Fair Weather* was Thompson's first book of poetry.

———. *Tallahassee Girl*. Round-Robin Series, No. IX. Boston: James R. Osgood and Co., 1881.

Catalog: Ball 2016 inventory, green cloth, red and black lettering, signed by Charles Jervis Langdon [Olivia Langdon Clemens's brother, 1849–1916], displays the Jervis Langdon Family Library bookplate #620.

Location: Quarry Farm library shelves, under the supervision of the Mark Twain Archive, Elmira College, Elmira, New York.

In 1881 the Osgood firm began publishing and promoting its Round-Robin Series of anonymous novels, written by "the best writers." Thompson, a Crawfordsville, Indiana writer who bore certain Southern sympathies from his early days on a Georgia plantation, originally published this novel anonymously; however, after his literary reputation became established he listed his name as the work's author. This was another book available to Clemens whenever he visited the Langdons' residence.

THOMPSON, JEAN MAY (FOWLER) (b. 1865), also known as Mrs. Henry W. Thompson. *Water Wonders Every Child Should Know; Little Studies of Dew, Frost, Snow, Ice and Rain*. Illus. New York: Doubleday, Page & Co., 1907. 233 pp.

Source: MTLAcc, entry #486, volume donated by Clemens. The Connecticut-born author Jean M. Thompson resided in Yonkers, New York. She worked for magazines and wrote children's books and songs.

THOMPSON, WILLIAM TAPPAN (1812–1882), pseud. "Major Joseph Jones." *Major Jones's Courtship. Detailed, with Humorous Scenes, Incidents, and Adventures*. Revised and enlarged. Illustrated by F[elix]. O[ctavius]. C[arr]. Darley, 1822–1888) and Carey. Philadelphia: T. B. Peterson & Brothers, [cop. 1879]. 190 pp.

Clemens included the title of this book in 1880 for consideration while selecting material for an anthology of humor (NB 19, N&J 2: 363). Shortly after Thompson died on 24 March 1882, Clemens wrote the title of these Georgian sketches in Notebook 20 (N&J 2: 455). One of Major Jones' humorous letters, "Christmas in Pineville," appeared in *Mark Twain's Library of Humor* (1888); Twain's anthology credited the edition published by T. B. Peterson & Brothers as its source for the sketch. *Major Jones's Courtship* was first published in 1843, with enlarged editions appearing subsequently.

DeVoto *MTAm* (1932), p. 254; Blair, *MT&HF* (1960), pp. 240–243, 304–305, and 315; Ganzel, "Twain, Travel Books" (1962), p. 53.

———. *Major Jones's Sketches of Travel* (published in 1847).

D. M. McKeithan—"Mark Twain's Letters of Thomas Jefferson Snodgrass," *Philological Quarterly* 32.4 (October 1953): 353–365—demonstrated that Clemens was familiar with William Tappan Thompson's *Major Jones's Sketches of Travel* as early as 1856 and borrowed from Thompson for comic letters of 1856–1857 to the Keokuk *Saturday Post* and in a few later works. The efforts to point up parallels between *Sketches of Travel* and Mark Twain's *Innocents Abroad*, *Roughing It*, and *Tramp Abroad* seem less persuasive. (McKeithan's *Court Trials in Mark Twain* [1953], pp. 353–365, collected this essay.) A promising subject remains unexplored: the possible effect of *Major Jones's Sketches* on Mark Twain's rendition of Southern dialect, especially Thompson's early efforts in 1847 to render the conversation of enslaved (and therefore, by law, uneducated) African Americans. In Thompson's first chapter of *Major Jones's Sketches*, for instance, a representative dialogue begins: "'Ki,' ses Prissy, lookin' like she was half scared out of her senses, 'den I ain't gwine to no New York.'"

DeVoto, *MTAm* (1932), p. 101; McKeithan, *CTMT* (1953), pp. 117–131.

Thomson, (Sir) Basil Home (1861–1939). *The Diversions of a Prime Minister.* Illus. Edinburgh and London: W. Blackwood and Sons, 1894. 407 pp.

Clemens found the title—"Diversions of a Prime Minister"—in the London Library on 22 October 1896 (NB 39, TS p. 12).

Thomson delivers a detailed account of the installations (and deposings) of office-holders in the South Sea nation of Tonga.

Thomson, James (1700–1748). *The Seasons: With the Castle of Indolence.* New York: W. B. Gilley, 1817. 287 pp. [*The Seasons* was first published in 1730.]

Inscription: "Mary A. B. Rogers/Norwich/Connecticut".

Catalogs: this volume was among the books transferred from the Quarry Farm library shelves to the Mark Twain Archive by Mark Woodhouse on 9 July 1987; Ball 2016 inventory, green cloth, gilt lettering and design, poor condition.

Location: Mark Twain Archive, Elmira College, Elmira, New York.

The provenace of this volume is unclear, but Clemens still might have had access to it at Quarry Farm in Elmira.

Clemens referred to Thomson's blank verse poems on nature in 1865, advising the literary critic to attribute "all the sleepy, tiresome, rural stuff, to Thomson and his eternal *Seasons*" ("Literary Connoisseur," in "Answers to Correspondents," *Californian,* 17 June 1865, quoted in *LAMT,* p. 141; *ET&S* 2: 195). At Thomson's grave in Richmond Park in July 1873, Clemens dictated to his secretary eighteen lines of a memorial poem, "Lines on James Thomson, the Poet of Nature" (NB 12, *N&J* 1: 561). In Chapter 6 of *Following the Equator* (1897) Mark Twain quotes "an invocation from Thomson" he found in a book [titled *Polynesia*] by the Reverend Michael Russell: "Come, bright Improvement! on the car of Time,/And rule the spacious world from clime to clime." Twain then comments: "Very well, Bright Improvement has arrived, you see, with her civilization, and her Waterbury, and her umbrella, and her third-quality profanity, and her humanizing-not-destroying machinery, and her hundred-and-eighty-death-rate, and everything is going along just as handsome!" In actuality this poetic couplet came from Thomas Campbell's "The Pleasures of Hope" (1799) rather than from something Thomson wrote, and Twain's error was corrected in later editions of *Following the Equator.*

Thomson, Mortimer Neal (1831–1875), pseud. "Q. K. Philander Doesticks."

Thomson moved from Michigan to New York City, where his satiric newspaper sketches introduced an innocent character named Doesticks to urban problems, vices, and entertainments. Mark Twain instructed Elisha Bliss , Jr. to send a copy of *Innocents Abroad* (1869) to "my friend Mortimer Thomson," better known as "'Q. K. Philander Doesticks, P. B.'" (SLC to Bliss, Buffalo, 28 October 1870, *MTLet* 4: 215). Twain's column for the Buffalo *Express* on 24 December 1870, "Mean People," alluded to "my ancient comrade, 'Doesticks'" (*MTBE*, p. 280). Thomson's pseudonym appeared among the list of humorists Twain was considering in 1880 for inclusion in an anthology (NB 19, *N&J* 2: 363). Twain included "Doesticks" in a list of authors he made up in March 1888 (NB 27, TS p. 61). *Mark Twain's Library of Humor* (1888) did reprint "A New Patent Medicine Operation," citing *Doestick's Letters* published by T. B. Peterson & Brothers of Philadelphia as its source. In an Autobiographical Dictation of 31 July 1906, Twain noted that a recent compilation of humorists "has no mention of Doesticks" (*MTE*, p. 202; *AutoMT* 2: 153).

Ed Piacentino, "Two Perspectives on Racial Oppression: Doesticks and Mark Twain," *Studies in American Humor,* New Series 3, No. 22 (2010): 69–90.

Thomson, William Hanna (1833–1918). *The Parables and Their Home. The Parables by the Lake.* New York: Harper & Brothers, 1895. 159 pp.

Source: MTLAcc, entry #1388, volume donated by Clemens.

The son of William McClure Thomson (see the Catalog entries below), William Hanna Thomson drew on his years in the Holy Land (and his father's writings about Syria and Palestine) to situate and explicate Christ's parables such as those about the pearl, the mustard-seed, and the hid treasure. Thomson became a physician and was appointed President of the New York Academic of Medicine. As an author he was best known for his book *Brain and Personality; or, The Physical Relations of the Brain to the Mind* (1906). Subsequently he became intrigued by concepts of the Hereafter; he contributed (along with William Dean Howells and other prominent American writers) to a volume titled *In After Days: Thoughts on the Future Life* (1910) and in 1911 Thomson published *Life, Death, and Immortality* (1911).

Thomson, William McClure (1806–1894). *Central Palestine and Phoenicia.* Illus. New York: Harper & Brothers, 1882. 689 pp.

Source: MTLAcc, entry #1745, volume donated by Clemens.

From 1832 until 1876 the Ohio-born Thomson served (except for one interval) as a Presbyterian missionary to Syria and Palestine. In 1859 he published the first edition of *The Land and the Book*, and in the succeeding years he would revise and update this work through numerous editions that carried varying titles. Although Mark Twain would disparage Thomson's efforts (see the Catalog entry below), the book in its several formats was nevertheless detailed and comprehensive, describing the foods, clothing, rituals, shrines, religious sects, coins, architecture, legends, and tombs of the people Thomson encountered, as well as the villages, rivers, trees, birds, and animals he observed in the countries they inhabited.

———. *The Land and the Book; or, Biblical Illustrations Drawn*

from the Manners and Customs, the Scenes and Scenery of the Holy Land. Illus. London: Thomas Nelson and Sons, 1872. 718 pp.
  Source: MTLAcc, entry #579, volume donated by Clemens.
  In Chapter 48 of *The Innocents Abroad* (1869) Mark Twain suggests that Thomson "smouched" language for his *The Land and the Book* from William C. Prime's book. Twain also mentions Thomson's book title (without alluding to its author) in Chapter 49 of *The Innocents Abroad.*
  Ganzel, *MTAb* (1968), p. 224; Hirst, "The Making of *The Innocents Abroad*" (1975).

———. *The Land and the Book; or, Biblical Illustrations Drawn from the Manners and Customs, the Scenes and Scenery, of the Holy Land: Lebanon, Damascus and Beyond Jordan.* Illus. New York: Harper &. Brothers, 1886. 711 pp.
  Source: MTLAcc, entry #1746, volume donated by Clemens.

THOREAU, HENRY DAVID (1817–1862). "Civil Disobedience" (essay, originally published in 1849).
  See the Catalog entry below for Thoreau's *A Yankee in Canada, with Anti-Slavery and Reform Papers,* which contains "Civil Disobedience" (pp. 123–151).
  Robert C. Evans inventoried the number and degree of acts "of genuine civil disobedience" in Mark Twain's most prominent novel ("Civil Disobedience and the Ending of Mark Twain's *Adventures of Huckleberry Finn*," *Civil Disobedience,* ed. Harold Bloom and Bake Hobby. Bloom's Literary Themes Series. [New York: Bloom's Literary Criticism, 2010], pp. 21–29). Evans did not directly trace these displays of courage to Thoreau's defiant essay.

———. *The Maine Woods.* Eleventh edition. Boston: Houghton, Mifflin and Co., 1881. 328 pp.
  Inscription: the front pastedown endpaper is signed in pencil, "Clemens".
  Location: Mark Twain Library, Redding, Connecticut.
  Copy examined: Clemens's copy, unmarked. Has the red ink Mark Twain Library accession number "2904" and purple oval Mark Twain Library stamps. Examined in 1970 and again in June 1982 and on 9 November 2019.
  In Clemens's opinion, Dean Sage was "the best & happiest narrative-talent that has tackled pen since Thoreau" (SLC to WDH, 15 May 1876, date supplied from the MTP letter files, *MTHL,* p. 138).
  J. Mark Baggett, "'Practicing in the Wild': Twain and Thoreau at the Lakes," *Mark Twain Annual 17* (2019): 28–48; and Barbara Ladd, "'Night after Night and Day after Day': Mark Twain and the Natural World," *Mark Twain Annual 17* (2019): 11–27.

———. *Walden; or, Life in the Woods* (nature narrative, published in 1854).
  Clemens almost certainly must have owned a copy of *Walden,* but this is another one of those frustrating lacunae in the surviving records of his library. Sometime between 1888 and 1904, Clara Clemens listed this author and title in her undated commonplace book (Paine 150, MTP).
  Roger Asselineau, "A Transcendentalist Poet Named Huckleberry Finn," *Studies in American Fiction* 13.2 (Autumn 1985): 217–226; and J. Mark Baggett, "'Practicing in the Wild': Twain and Thoreau at the Lakes," *Mark Twain Annual 17* (2019): 28–48.

———. *A Yankee in Canada, with Anti-Slavery and Reform Papers.* Boston: Houghton, Mifflin & Co., 1881. 286 pp.
  Marginalia: penciled check marks on pages 124, 125, 127, 128, 129, 130, 131, 133, 134, 135, 137, 138, and elsewhere.
  Location: Mark Twain Library, Redding, Connecticut.
  Copy examined: Clemens's copy, although the volume lacks his signature and the penciled check marks throughout the book are not at all characteristic of his annotation. Albert E. Stone, Jr. did not include this volume in his checklist of Clemens's library books in 1955, but I found *A Yankee in Canada* shelved with Clemens's collection when I visited Redding in 1970. It has the red ink Mark Twain Library accession number "2905", which makes it consecutive with Clemens's copy of *The Maine Woods* and well within the recorded numbers of Clara Clemens Gabrilowitsch's donations; the volume also displays the purple oval Mark Twain Library stamps. I examined the book again in June 1982 and on 9 November 2019 and concluded that it was an authentic association copy.

THORNTON, JAMES (1862–1938). "My sweetheart's the man in the moon" (song, published in 1892). Words and music by Thornton.
  In July or August 1892 Clemens noted: "The Man in the Moon—never heard of this one till lately—now everyone has heard of him" (NB 32, TS p. 16). Surely Clemens referred to the effect of Thornton's newly popular song, since Henry F. Reddall called the notion of the Man in the Moon "one of the oldest superstitions in the world" (*Fact, Fancy, and Fable* [Chicago: A. C. McClurg & Co., 1889], p. 339).

THORPE, ROSE (HARTWICK) (1850–1939). "Curfew Must Not Ring To-night" (poem, published in 1870).
  The most famous publication by this American poet, novelist, editor, and supporter of the women's suffrage movement had reached print the year before she married Edmund Thorpe in 1871, yet it lacked the copyright protection that could have earned her royalties. Clemens marveled in 1896 about the fact that "this old stager has gotten a new lease on life. They exhibit life size photos while the recitation is going on" (Notebook 38, TS p. 16, an entry that Clemens later crossed out). In 1906 Clemens recalled hearing "over-impassioned recitations of 'Curfew Shall Not Ring To-night,' with other worn and ancient distresses," frequently performed during amateur theatricals on board ocean vessels (3 September 1906 AD, *AutoMT 2:* 215). For several decades it seemed like American writer Thorpe's poem might prove to be deathless. All ten stanzas concluded with resounding variations of its title. The melodramatic piece, set in seventeenth-century England, narrated the frantic efforts of young Bessie to prevent an evening curfew bell from ringing—the signal for the scheduled execution by Oliver Cromwell's soldiers of her imprisoned lover, Basil Underwood. Heroically Bessie climbed a ladder and clung to the clapper of the bell in the parish church, painfully silencing its peal; then she pled for and obtained a pardon from Cromwell for the despairing prisoner. "'Go! your lover lives,' said Cromwell,/'Curfew shall not ring to-night.'" The poem's historical setting and circumstances bear a resemblance to Twain's short story titled "The Death Disk" (1901), in which a seven-year-old girl named Abby Mayfair must

choose which of Cromwell's prisoners will be executed. By proudly giving her father the prettiest token—a disk colored red to signify the prisoner's doom—Abby unknowingly condemns her father to be killed. As in Thorpe's poem, Cromwell ultimately relents and releases the man.

THORPE, THOMAS BANGS (1815–1878). "The Big Bear of Arkansas" (story, published in 1841).

Kenneth S. Lynn speculated that this comic tale lay behind Mark Twain's discovery of "the poetic potentiality of the vernacular" (*MT&SH*, pp. 89–99). However, no one has yet produced direct evidence that Clemens knew Thorpe or his famous story, even though it seems highly likely that he did. Thorpe edited newspapers in Louisiana, where he gained an appreciation for the folk humor of the Mississippi River region. A New York sporting newspaper he co-edited, *Spirit of the Times*, reprinted his backwoods sketches.

THRING, EDWARD (1821–1887). *Addresses*. Ed. with a preface by Sarah E[liza]. Thring (1856–1946). London: T. Fisher Unwin, 1887. 203 pp.

Source: MTLAcc, entry #809, volume donated by Clemens.

———. *Poems and Translations*. Ed. with a preface by Sarah E[liza]. Thring (1856–1946). London: T. Fisher Unwin, 1887. 150 pp.

Source: MTLAcc, entry #635, volume donated by Clemens.

———. *Uppingham School Songs and Borth Lyrics*. Ed. with a preface by Sarah E[liza]. Thring (1856–1946). London: T. Fisher Unwin, 1887. 79 pp.

Source: MTLAcc, entry #622, volume donated by Clemens.

Thring was the headmaster of the influential Uppingham School in England from 1853 until 1887.

H. D. Rawnsley, *Edward Thring: Teacher and Poet* (London: T. Fisher Unwin, 1889).

THURSTON, KATHERINE CECIL (1875–1911). *The Gambler, A Novel*. Illus. New York: Harper & Brothers, 1905. 499 pp.

Source: MTLAcc, entry #308, volume donated by Clemens.

Though the Irish novelist Katherine Thurston died at the early age of thirty-six during an epileptic seizure, several of her novels had already become best-sellers in both England and the United States.

THWAITES, REUBEN GOLD (1853–1913). *France in America, 1497–1763*. Volume 7. The American Nation Series. 27 vols. Portrait and maps. New York: Harper & Brothers, 1905. 320 pp.

Catalog: *A1911*, "Vol. 7, 12mo, cloth, N.Y. 1905," with a slip containing notes by Clemens laid in, lot 454, sold for $5.

TICKNOR, GEORGE (1791–1871). *Life, Letters, and Journals of George Ticknor*. Edited by George S[tillman]. Hillard (1808–1879). 2 vols. Brown cloth. Boston: James R. Osgood and Co., 1876.

Inscriptions: the front free endpaper of Volume I is signed in pencil, "T. W. Crane/Elmira,/N.Y." The front flyleaf is signed in pencil, "SL Clemens/Hartford 1876". The front pastedown endpaper is inscribed "1877" in pencil and then signed in pencil, "S. L. Clemens/Hartford,/Conn./April, 1877." The second flyleaf of Volume II is signed in pencil, "S. L Clemens/Hartford 1876". A sale label of the *A1911* auction is affixed to the front pastedown endpaper of Volume II.

Marginalia: Chester L. Davis transcribed Clemens's

marginalia from Volume I in consecutive issues of *The Twainian* 27 (July-August 1968): 4 through 28 (November-December 1969): 1–3. Davis commenced with the second volume of Ticknor's book in *The Twainian* 28 (November-December 1969): 4 and concluded in *The Twainian* 29 (March-April 1970): 1–4. These marginalia were reprinted, starting with Volume I, in *The Twainian* beginning with the January-February 1986 issue. Clemens made penciled underscorings, vertical lines, brackets, and notes in both volumes. His annotation is far more profuse in Volume I; that in Volume II ends on page 301, which is heavily marked. On page 14 Clemens remarked, "Doubtless true." at the observation that a democracy "cannot end in a quiet ripe old age." "Ticknor is a Millet who makes all men fall in love with him," Clemens noted on page 317 of Volume I. On page 15 of Volume II, Clemens wrote in pencil in the margin: "America has to-day, for President, *Grant*; Secry of War, little Don Cameron; Navy, poor Robeson; Interior, P. M. General &c., unknown men. In Congress, nothing but nobodies. We have not one single statesman connected with affairs—or elsewhere." Twain's allusions are interesting. The well-respected American painter, author, and translator Francis Davis Millet (1846–1912) would tragically be lost on the *Titanic*. Pennsylvanian politician James Donald Cameron (1833–1918) only served briefly (1876–1877) as Secretary of War under President Grant and then went into the U. S. Senate where he remained for the next two decades. George Maxwell Robeson (1829–1897), a New Jersey attorney and politician, was President Grant's Secretary of the Navy from 1869 until 1877; his scandal-plagued term in office was marked by charges of bribes and corruption. Zachariah Chandler (1813–1879), a Michigan politician who was appointed Secretary of the Interior by Grant in 1869, served until 11 March 1877. Chandler had been zealously anti-slavery prior to the Civil War and was never associated with anything illicit in his career. Another Grant appointee, James Noble Tyner (1826–1904), an attorney from Indiana, held the office of Postmaster General for less than a year (12 July 1876–12 March 1877) before President Rutherford B. Hayes replaced him; Tyner stayed on in the U. S. Post Office administration and would later be accused of a number of misdeeds.

Catalogs: ListABP (1910), "Life of Geo. Ticknor"; *A1911*, "Vol. II, Portrait, 8vo, cloth, Bost. 1876, . . . several passages underscored," quotes the signature and one example of marginalia concerning the "unknown men" and "nobodies" in American political life, lot 455, withdrawn from sale; *C1951*, #39a, unspecified number of volumes, $45.

Provenance: Volumes I and II belonged to Chester L. Davis's Mark Twain Research Foundation, Perry, Missouri by at least 1969.

Location: currently uncertain. *Life, Letters, and Journals of George Ticknor* was not among the titles listed in either of the two Christie's sales (on 5 December 1991 and 9 June 1993) that disposed of the estate of Chester L. Davis (1903–1987).

Copies examined: Clemens's copies of both volumes, briefly, in Chester L. Davis's residence in 1970. Volume I was extremely worn.

Clemens wrote to William Dean Howells from Elmira on 29 August 1877: "I am re-reading Ticknor's diary, & am charmed with it; though I still say he *refers* to too many good things when he could just as well have *told* them" (*MTHL*, p. 200). Clemens would make a similar criticism of James Russell Lowell's *Letters* in 1909 (*MTHL*, p. 244).

———. *Life of William Hickling Prescott*. First edition. Original dark green cloth, gilt. Boston: Ticknor & Fields, 1864. 491 pp.

Provenance: attested by the accession number "2821" and the oval purple stamps of the Mark Twain Library of Redding, Connecticut on the front pastedown endpaper and several pages in the text.

Location: collection of Kevin Mac Donnell, Austin, Texas

Source: letter from Mac Donnell to Alan Gribben, 5 October 2005: "Here's the description of the possible Twain ex libris I bought for $15." Mac Donnell reported that the volume contains no annotations or other ownership marks; still, this seems like a good candidate for being a copy that once belonged to Clemens. The library accession number fits within the range of the many other book donations in Redding that Clemens made in 1909. William Hickling Prescott (1796–1859) was an American historian who resided in Massachusetts and became notable for his judicious use of historical evidence, especially in his studies of the rise and fall of the Spanish empire.

TIDBALL, MARY LANGDON (DANA) (1846–1904). *Barbara's Vagaries*. New York: Harper & Brothers, 1886. 175 pp.

Source: MTLAcc, entry #1049, volume donated by Clemens.

A girl from the mountains of North Carolina, Barbara Dexter, finds herself at a formidable disadvantage when she moves to Washington, D. C. She overcomes her social detractors before returning home. Tidball herself was born in Louisiana, married a military officer, and died in New Jersey.

TIERNAN, FRANCES CHRISTINE (FISHER) (1846–1920), pseud. "Christian Reid." "Regret" (poem).

In the last (June 1902) pages that Olivia Clemens kept in her diary (DV161, MTP) she laid a newspaper clipping of this poem. Written in 1861 when the poet was only fifteen, it expressed grief over the unexpected death of a male friend. The first of its seven stanzas captures the message and meter: "If I had known, O loyal heart,/ When hand to hand, we said farewell,/How for all time our paths would part,/What shadow o'er our friendship fell,/I should have clasped your hand so close/In the warm pressure of my own,/That memory still would keep its grasp,/If I had known."

TILDEN, SAMUEL JONES (1814–1886). *Letters and Literary Memorials of Samuel J. Tilden*. Edited by John Bigelow (1817–1911). 2 vols. New York: Harper & Brothers, 1908.

Catalogs: *A1911*, "2 vols., 8vo, cloth, N.Y. 1908," with a small sheet of notes by Clemens laid in, lot 456, sold for $2; *Lexington 1912*, lot #26, sold for $6.

Tilden (1814–1886), the former governor of New York state, ran as the Democratic candidate against Rutherford B. Hayes in the disputed presidential election of 1876.

———. *The Writings and Speeches of Samuel J. Tilden*. Edited by John Bigelow (1817–1911). 2 vols. New York: Harper &

Brothers, 1885.

Source: MTLAcc, entries #1234 and # 1235, volumes donated by Clemens.

TIMBS, JOHN (1801–1875). *Clubs and Club Life in London, with Anecdotes of Its Famous Coffee Houses, Hostelries, and Taverns, from the Seventeenth Century to the Present Time*. Illus. London, n.d. [Two London publishers brought out editions with this title in 1872—John Camden Hotten and Chatto and Windus; both of the imprints had 544 pages. Either of these would seem to be a likely candidate for the copy Clemens obtained.]

Inscription: the half-title page is signed, "Saml. L. Clemens/ Hartford, 1875."

Catalogs: *A1911*, "12mo, cloth, Lond. n.d.," quotes the signature, lot 457, sold for $2.75; George D. Smith, New York City, "Catalogue of Books" (1911), quotes the signature, item #439, $10.

Provenance: acquired by the rare book dealer Robert Slotta, who explained in an email of 1 September 2001 to Alan Gribben about the book's condition: "I don't know precisely what happened, . . . but I can tell you that Clubs and Club Life in London by Timbs (i.e., catalog *A1911*, #457) was at some time the victim of a fire. When I obtained it, the covers and spine were missing, as were some pages of the book, and the edges of the text were charred, and there was a marked odor of smoke present. Also, the half title inscribed by Sam [Clemens] was in pieces (yet the inscription was largely able to be reassembled like a jig saw puzzle). . . . The person who sold it to me told me she also acquired it in the mutilated condition. In any event, the current owner is Martin Zehr."

Location: collection of Martin Zehr, Kansas City, Missouri ("I have the remnants," email, Martin Zehr to the Mark Twain Forum, 20 July 2011).

———. *Curiosities of London, Exhibiting the Most Rare and Remarkable Objects of Interest in the Metropolis; With Nearly Sixty Years' Personal Recollections. A New Edition, Corrected and Enlarged*. Engraved frontispiece portrait of Timbs. Polished and ribbed calf, elaborate gilt stamped, morocco spine label, green-coated endpapers, outside joints cracking, brown cloth slipcase. London: John Camden Hotten, [1871]. 872 pp. [A note of clarification is needed here: Alan Gribben's *Mark Twain's Library: A Reconstruction* (1980) speculated erroneously about the probable edition and publisher of this Timbs book, which has since caused confusion in the rare book market. The book listed above is in fact the only edition Clemens is known to have owned. *Mea culpa*.]

Inscription: the third front free flyleaf (the recto of the frontispiece portrait) is signed boldly and diagonally in pencil, "S. L. Clemens—/Hartford, Conn."

Marginalia: Clemens made more than 200 penciled annotations and markings in the volume. The marginal notes in pencil total some 780 words on forty-six pages and the rear endpapers; 127 other pages are heavily marked with penciled marginal rules, underlinings, and other marks. On page 41 Clemens wrote vertically in the margin, in pencil, "What St. Paul's (or say Parliament House) needs is whitewashing." Clemens's notes on page 42 refer to "Lucifer droppers." Beside Timbs' explanation of the Guildhall (page 386), Clemens noted, "So-&-so, spectacle-maker, does not signify that he *is* one but simply belongs to that guild. The Prince of Wales is a Fishmonger that don't sell fish." Clemens noted on page 390, "They don't do anything in England without a dinner nor we without a mass meeting and resolutions." On page 395 Clemens marked a description of the loving-cup ceremony that would be burlesqued (without acknowledging Timbs) in Chapter 10 of *The Prince and the Pauper* (1881). Timbs states on page 483 that only twelve Jews resided in England in 1663, and Clemens reminded himself to use this fact: "A Jew could have been exhibited for money as a curiosity—picture it and describe." But when Timbs goes on to claim that London's first synagogue was built in 1656, Clemens objected: "This old fool is unreliable. 12 couldn't build a synagogue." "All the histories are compiled in the [British] Museum," Clemens noted on page 587, "—and all the Ministers cabbage sermons there." At the bottom of the same page Clemens jotted: "Drink? Yes, too early—besides I've just had one." At Timbs' recital of Richard III's responsibility for the deaths of Edward V and the Duke of York in the Tower of London (page 792), Clemens observed, "It is pleasant to believe these old traditions, & hanged if I don't believe *all* of them. They have found *2* sets of bones of the young Princes." On the rear free endpaper Clemens wrote a lengthy note about "a *real* curiosity in the British Museum"—an autograph letter dated 10 July 1553 from Lady Jane Grey, concluding, "Poor girl, was only queen 9 or 10 days, & perished within the only enclosure that knew her as such."

Catalogs: *A1911*, "thick 8vo, cloth (loose), Lond., n.d., . . . a few autograph remarks, and some passages marked," quotes the signature, lot 458, sold for $6; Alan Fox Rare Books, Sherman Oaks, California, Catalog 1 (December 1980), item #13, priced at $4,500, sold to Irving Wallace; Jeffrey Thomas Fine and Rare Books, San Francisco, September 1996, "extensively annotated . . . and loaded with notes and comments," item #10, $12,500; *Sotheby's 2003*, #240, $29,000; Christie's, 23 June 2011 sale, "polished calf, top edges, gilt, green endpapers, Clemens's signature and annotations in pencil, $30,000.

Provenance: in the collection of Nick Karanovich in the 1990s.

Copy examined: Clemens's copy, at the 2003 Sotheby's sale. "Nobody in town," Clemens recorded in an undated, penciled manuscript fragment. "Bought Timbs—Walks—Stow—Leigh Hunt, & a lot of other authorities & read about a thing, then went leisurely to see it" (DV115, MTP). Mark Twain's English journals of 1872 depended on Timbs' *Curiosities of London* for information about "drinking the 'loving-cup' at the banquet, &c." (*MTLet* 5: 612). Twain explicitly cited Timbs' *Curiosities of London* in two notes to *The Prince and the Pauper* (1881), documenting historical facts mentioned in Chapter 4 of the novel. Various additional borrowings he made from Timbs went unacknowledged.

Dickinson, "Sources of *The Prince and the Pauper*" (1949), 103–106; Baetzhold, *MT&JB* (1970), p. 51; Iowa-California Edition of *P&P* (1979).

———. *Things Not Generally Known, Familiarly Explained. A Book for Old and Young.* London, 1867. [No publisher is specified in the catalogs.]

Inscription: the front free endpaper is inscribed in ink, "S.

L. Clemens, Hartford." *Hunley 1958* reports that Olivia Clemens made this inscription.

Marginalia: Clemens used ink to write on pages 8 ("And heaven, according to Revelation, has a frontage on each side of only 1500 miles!"), 12 ("Evidently his [the French astronomer and mathematician Pierre Simon de Laplace, 1749–1827] fine mind decayed toward the last"), and 36 ("Oh dear!" of a quotation by François Arago [the French scientist, 1786–1853] regarding the unpredictability of weather). The sale catalogs state that Clemens made no other notes.

Catalogs: ListABP (1910), "Things Not Generally Known (autograph of S. L. C.), Timbs"; *C1951*, D72; *Zeitlin 1951*, item #45, $25; *Hunley 1958*, item #147, $17.50.

This book might be pertinent to Clemens's detailed discussion in 1870 regarding the age of the earth and the size of the universe (SLC to Olivia Langdon, Troy, N.Y., 8 January 1870, *LLMT*, pp. 133–134; *MTLet* 4: 12–13).

———. *Walks and Talks about London.* London: Lockwood & Co., 1865. 310 pp. [Edition conjectured.]

Clemens almost certainly meant Timbs' *Walks and Talks about London* when he recalled on an undated scrap of manuscript: "Nobody in town. Bought Timbs — Walks——[John] Stow—Leigh Hunt, & a lot of other authorities & read about a thing, then went leisurely to see it" (DV115, MTP). However, it is conceivable that he referred to Augustus J. C. Hare's *Walks in London* (1878) instead.

TIREBUCK, WILLIAM EDWARDS (1854–1900). *Meg of the Scarlet Foot; A Novel.* New York: Harper & Brothers, 1898. 420 pp.

Source: MTLAcc, entry #1075, volume donated by Clemens.

A girl named Meg is born with a red birthmark amid unpromising conditions in a Lancaster mining village. *Publishers' Weekly* (2 July 1898) reported that "romantic mysticism" can be detected in a novel about a rural community where "simple superstition and fatalism" prevail. Tirebuck was an English journalist, author, and critic.

TISSOT, JAMES [JACQUES JOSEPH] (1836–1902). *The New Testament.* 2 vols. New York: Idem Publishing Co., 1887.

Catalog: Ball 2016 inventory, two volumes.

Location: Quarry Farm library shelves, under the supervision of the Mark Twain Archive, Elmira College, Elmira, New York.

This set of 500 paintings by Tissot depicting the life of Christ was printed in Europe by the chromo-lithography process. The two volumes with gilt page tops sold for the (then-expensive) price of $65.

TITCOMB, SARAH ELIZABETH (1841–1895). *Aryan Sun-Myths: The Origin of Religions.* Introduction by Charles Morris (1833–1922). Troy, New York: Nims and Knight, 1888. 192 pp.

Marginalia: approximately fifty-five penciled notations in Clemens's hand, comprising around 260 words. One note reads: "Crishna's era was nine or ten hundred years B.C. His career & Christ's were about identical. Promoted to godship 300 or 400 B.C." Another notation on page 60 remarks, "All the Christs seem to run the same career & have the same adventures." After observing at the top of page 79 that "Saviors have no originality," Clemens softened his stance in the margin: "I seem to be throwing slurs at these various Saviors. I did not mean to do that. I feel an honest reverence for every one of them—on account of their *motives*. I was only meaning to slur those dull liars their followers." On page 85 he resumed his blasphemous tone, however: "There has manifestly been a large family of Only Begotten Sons." He commented on page 97, "Christ, then[,] was a Buddhist first & afterwards a Christian?" Pages 103 and 104 contain remarks by Clemens critical of "your pulpit" and "theology's method." The Mark Twain Papers at Berkeley contain photocopies of eight pages of Clemens's marginalia, including a note on page 78, sent by Victor Jacobs on 22 May 1967.

Catalogs: *C1951*, #31a, $22.50; Lew David Feldman, "House of El Dieff" Catalog (1954), item #229r, sold with two other volumes for $500; "Mark Twain Items and Other Americana," Parke-Bernet Galleries, New York City (21–22 May 1957 Sale), item #122, sold for $160; "Victor and Irene Murr Jacobs Collection," Sotheby's, Sale No. 6904, 29 October 1996, "hammered down" for a telephone bid of $6,000 (source: Robert T. Slotta).

Provenance: in 1986 the volume was in the private collection of Victor Jacobs, Akron, Ohio (Jacobs to Alan Gribben, 15 October 1986). Jacobs died in 1996.

Copy examined: photocopies of Clemens's marginalia in the Mark Twain Papers, Bancroft Library, University of California at Berkeley.

Titcomb's investigative urges took her in various directions; in addition to studying comparative religions, she wrote about the genealogical roots of early New Englanders and in 1885 published *Mind Cure on a Material Basis*, an effort to extract the beneficial power of mental healing from any religious context such as that of Christian Science. The author of the Introduction to Titcomb's book, Charles Morris, wrote a study of Indo-European cultures titled *The Aryan Race: Its Origins and Its Achievements* (1888).

TOCQUEVILLE, ALEXIS CHARLES HENRI MAURICE CLÉREL DE (1805–1859). *Democracy in America* (travel narrative, published in 1835).

In a discarded portion of the manuscript for *Life on the Mississippi* (1883) Mark Twain listed "De Toqueville [*sic*], 1835" among the "irruption of foreign tourists" in America (Heritage Press edition [1944], p. 402). Tocqueville's *Democracy in America* candidly and famously assessed the strengths and problems (including the enslavement of African Americans) he observed in the young Republic.

TODD, CHARLES BURR (1849–1928). *The History of Redding, Connecticut*. Second edition, enlarged and revised. Original green cloth, gilt. New York: Grafton Press, cop. 1906. 303 pp. [The first edition had appeared in 1880.]

Provenance: the personal library of Albert Bigelow Paine, Clemens's designated biographer. Clemens would have had opportunities to see this volume because Paine and Clemens shared their library books.

Location: collection of Kevin Mac Donnell, Austin, Texas.

Source: letter from Mac Donnell to Alan Gribben, 11 April 2013.

Todd notified Mark Twain on 28 May 1906 that he was bringing out a new edition of his Redding history and inquired about Twain's plans to locate there (Fears, *Day by Day* 4: 390). He also asked for a photograph of Twain, but evidently Twain did not comply with that part of the request. *The History of Redding, Connecticut* mentioned that Twain had purchased "nearly one hundred acres of land" in 1906 with the intention to build a "costly stone villa of the Italian order of architecture" as a permanent residence in Redding (p. 182). On pages 183–186 Todd discussed "The Literary Colony" that was assembling in the Redding area, including such prominent figures as Richard Watson Gilder, Joseph Gilder, Jeanette Gilder, Ida Tarbell, and Albert Bigelow Paine. Todd briefly summarized Twain's writings in heralding his imminent arrival as a Redding resident (p. 184). *The History of Redding, Connecticut* took special note of the Hill family among Redding's earlier settlers. In the ensuing decades librarians of the Mark Twain Library would intermix books donated by the Hills with the volumes given by Clemens and his daughter Clara, owing to the early imprints of those titles. One needs to be cautious about this problem of attribution.

Paine, *MTB* (1912), p. 1473.

TODD, HENRY JOHN (1763–1845). *Some Account of the Life and Writings of John Milton[1608–1674], Derived Principally from Documents in His Majesty's State-Paper Office, Now First Published*. London: C. and J. Rivington [and others], 1826. 370 pp., plus a 57-page "Appendix Containing an Inquiry into the Origin of Paradise Lost." [Edition conjectured.]

In September 1887 Clemens cited "Todd" as one of the "biogs of Milton" to be consulted (NB 27, *N&J* 3: 328).

TODD, MARGARET GEORGINA (1859–1918), pseud. "Graham Travers." *Windyhaugh; A Novel*. London: William Blackwood & Sons, 1908. 446 pp.

Source: MTLAcc, entry #313, volume donated by Clemens. Todd was a pioneering female physician in Edinburgh as well as the author of five impressive novels set in Scotland. She was also an earnest advocate for women's rights. Blackwood first published *Windyhaugh* in 1898.

To Egypt. [Unidentified book.]

Catalog: ListABP (1910), "To Egypt", no other information supplied.

The Token and Atlantic Souvenir. A Christmas and New Year's Present. Ed. by Samuel Griswold Goodrich (1793–1860). Boston: Gray and Bowen, 1833. 354 pp.

Inscription: presentation page signed from "Catherine Herriman" [?] and dated "1837"—both in pencil

Location: Mark Twain Library, Redding, Connecticut.

Copy examined: an unmarked volume of poetry and prose belonging to someone other than Clemens or his family members. It has a red ink accession number, "5752". When I revisited Redding in June 1982 this book had been added to the shelves containing donations from Clemens and his daughter Clara Clemens Gabrilowitsch, presumably on account of its early imprint or perhaps because it contains a prose sketch of Joan of Arc (pp. 185–200), credited to "F. I." However, there are no signs of any connection with Clemens and I recommended to the staff that it be separated from the Clemens collection.

TOLAND, JOHN (1670–1722). *The Life of John Milton [1608–1674]*.

"Toland" was one of the "biogs of Milton" that Clemens jotted down, presumably to consult, in September 1887 (NB 27, *N&J* 3: 328). John Toland, an Irish philosopher, wrote *The Life of John Milton* in 1698. He followed it with *Amyntor; or, a Defense of Milton's Life* in 1699.

Tolstoy, (Count) Lev (Leo) Nikolaevich (1828–1910). *Ivan the Fool; or, the Old Devil and the Three Small Devils. Also, A Lost Opportunity, and Polikushka.* Translated from the Russian by Count Adolphus Norraikow (1844–1892). Illustrated by Valerian Gribayédoff (1858–1908). New York: Charles L. Webster & Co., 1891. 172 pp.

> Olivia Clemens wrote to Frederick J. Hall, probably in 1894, to request this and two other books for Christmas gifts (Philip C. Duschnes, Catalog No. 30 [June 19381, item #143). "Bring down Tolstoi," Clemens reminded himself before leaving for Elmira in June 1886 (NB 26, TS p. 9a). "I can't get *him* [Tolstoi] in focus yet, but I've got Browning" (SLC to WDH, Elmira, 22 August 1887, *MTHL*, p. 596). Henry Fisher reported that in Berlin in 1891 Clemens approvingly mentioned Tolstoi's kindness to animals (*AMT*, p. 75). On another, unspecified occasion, Clemens congratulated Fisher for having "broken bread with the man who commands, and almost monopolizes, the thought of the world" (*AMT*, p. xix). In 1899 Clemens fled from a tea reception in Vienna where an American girl was expounding on her visit with Tolstoi (SLC to WDH, 2 April 1899, *MTHL*, p. 692).

> For a revealing account of the translator Adolphus Norraikow's life, see Nick Mount, *When Canadian Literature Moved to New York* (Toronto: University of Toronto Press, 2005), especially pages 87–89.

———. *Life is Worth Living, and Other Stories.* Translated from the Russian by Count Adolphus Norraikow (1844–1892). Illustrated by Valerian [Michaelovich] Gribayédoff (1858–1908). New York: Charles L. Webster & Co., 1892. 208 pp.

> Clemens's publishing firm advertised this book as "stories written to teach the middle and lower classes of Russia some great moral truths, such as temperance, kindness, honesty" (*Publishers' Trade List Annual for 1893*).

———. *Sebastopol.* Translated from the French by Francis Davis Millet (1846–1912). Introduction by William Dean Howells (1837–1920). New York: Harper & Brothers, [cop. 1887]. 241 pp.

> **Source:** MTLAcc, entry #1663, volume donated by Clemens.

———. *The Teaching of Jesus.* Translated by Louise (Shanks) Maude (1855–1939) and Aylmer Maude (1858–1938). New York: Harper & Brothers, 1909. 120 pp.

> **Source:** MTLAcc, entry #1385, volume donated by Clemens.

> Tolstoy's "Preface" explained that this booklet came from his efforts to teach the four Gospels to "a class of village children," after which he concluded that "its perusal, chapter by chapter . . . cannot but be beneficial to children" (pp. viii-viii). Isabel Lyon noted on 2 November 1908: "The King regrets so that Tolstoy is a Christian—'A Hell of a Christian'" (IVL Journals, TS p. 340, MTP).

Tomes, Robert (1817–1882). *The Bazar Book of Decorum. The Care of the Person, Manners, Etiquette, and Ceremonials.* New York: Harper & Brothers, [cop. 1870]. 282 pp.

> **Source:** MTLAcc, entry #397, volume donated by Clemens.

> The weekly magazine *Harper's Bazar* (a spelling retained into the 1920s) spun off books on women, health, and fashion.

Tom Hood's Comic Annual (London).

> The 1873 issue contained Mark Twain's "How I Escaped Being Killed in a Duel," and a version of his "Jim Wolfe

and the Cats" appeared in *Tom Hood's Comic Annual, for 1874*. In June 1882 Clemens made a memorandum to "write Chatto send me Hood's Annual for 73, 74, 75" (*N&J* 2: 485). On 10 June 1882 Clemens sent this request to Chatto & Windus of London (Berg Collection, NYPL). Tom Hood (1835–1874) edited this annual compilation of wit and humor. After his death the engravers George Dalziel (1815–1902) and Edward Dalziel (1817–1905) continued it briefly.

Tooke, Thomas (1774–1858). *A History of Prices, and of the State of the Circulation, from 1793 to 1837.* 6 vols. London, 1838–1857. Also: New York, 1857.

> In Clemens's Autobiographical Dictation of 15 January 1906 he recalled perusing "Tooke on Prices" in the Library of Congress in Washington before writing "Facts in the Case of the Great Beef Contract" (*Galaxy*, May 1870); Ainsworth Rand Spofford (1825–1908), sixth Librarian of the Library of Congress, obtained the book for him (*MTA*, 1: 325; *AutoMT* 1: 282).

Toole, John Lawrence (1830–1906).

> "Tomorrow I lunch with Mr. Toole & a member of Parliament—Toole is the most able comedian of the day" (Clemens to Olivia Clemens, London, 15 September [1872]; *Sotheby's 2003*, #20, ALS). English comedian Toole, a close friend of Henry Irving, played in *Thespis* (1871), the first Gilbert and Sullivan collaboration.

Torrens, William Torrens McCullagh (1813–1894). *Empire in Asia, How We Came by It: A Book of Confessions.* London: Trübner & Co., 1872. 426 pp.

> "Torrens's book on India," Clemens wrote in Notebook 27 (TS p. 64) late in April 1888, presumably referring to this description of the British occupation of India.

Tourgée, Albion Winegar (1838–1905). *Bricks Without Straw. A Novel.* Frontispiece. New York: Fords, Howard, & Hulbert, [cop. 1880]. 521 pp.

> **Inscription:** the flyleaf is signed, "S. L. Clemens, Hartford, Oct. 1880."

> **Catalog:** *A1911*, "12mo, cloth, N.Y. n.d. [1880]," quotes the signature, lot 459, sold for $2.25.

> According to a bill of 1 January 1881 from Brown & Gross, Hartford booksellers, Clemens purchased this novel on 6 October 1880 for $1.20; he paid the bill on 17 January 1881 (receipt in MTP).

> As a former Union officer from Ohio who moved to North Carolina after the Civil War, Tourgée witnessed at first hand the continued subjugation of African Americans in the South. *Bricks Without Straw* was a fictionalized effort to depict the plight of these formerly enslaved people. It seems noteworthy that Tourgée, like Mark Twain, was dedicated to rendering with accuracy the dialect of uneducated characters (before the war it was illegal to allow enslaved people to learn to read or write in nearly all of the slave states). Here is evidence that Twain owned a work in 1880 that grappled with orthographic devices to capture this dialect. "Yes, ma'am, I hears; but whar you gwin, Miss Mollie? . . . Dey'll kill you, sure," warns a character named Nimbus in *Bricks Without Straw* (p. 157). More scholarly attention should be directed toward Jim's literary antecedents prior to *Adventures of Huckleberry Finn* (1885).

> Brook Thomas's *Civic Myths: A Law-and-Literature Approach*

to Citizenship (Chapel Hill: University of North Carolina Press, 2007) included a comparison of Twain and Tourgée; see also Thomas, "*Adventures of Huckleberry Finn* and Reconstruction," *American Literary Realism* 50.1 (Fall 2017): 18.

———. *A Fool's Errand, by One of the Fools: The Famous Romance of American History. . . . To Which Is Added, by the Same Author, Part II. The Invisible Empire: A Concise Review of the Epoch in Which the Tale Is Based.* Marbled boards, black leather spine, gilt lettering. New York: Fords, Howard, & Hulbert, 1880. 521 pp.

> **Inscription:** bookplates #60, 61, "Jervis Langdon Family Library."
> **Catalogs:** first inventoried in the Quarry Farm library by Emily Schweizer Martinez in 1982; inventory list of the Mark Twain Archive prepared in 2013 by the then-Archivist Mark Woodhouse.
> **Location:** Mark Twain Archive, Gannett-Tripp Learning Center, Elmira College, Elmira, New York.
> In *A Fool's Errand* Tourgée, drawing on his experiences in North Carolina, attempted to show in fiction the utter failure of Reconstruction policies for both black and white Southerners. Corruption and ignorance defeated every good intention. Tourgée tried to be accurate in his dialogues involving African American characters: "Wal, putty much de same way you did, I spects," answers a character named Andy in *A Fool's Errand* (p. 98). Clemens had access to this book whenever he visited the Langdon residence in Elmira.
> Brook Thomas, "*Adventures of Huckleberry Finn* and Reconstruction," *American Literary Realism* 50.1 (Fall 2017): 18.

———. *The Invisible Empire: Part I. A New, Illustrated, and Enlarged Edition of a Fool's Errand, by One of those Fools . . . Part II. A Concise Review of Recent Events. Two Parts Complete in One Volume.* Sold Only by Subscription. New York: Fords, Howard, & Hulbert, [cop. 1880]. 521 pp.

> **Inscription:** the title page is signed in pencil "Mark Twain/1882." Clemens hardly ever signed books belonging to his library with his nom de plume, reserving "Mark Twain" for autographing books he wrote himself; moreover, there is a curious evenness of pressure throughout the signature, as though it were traced. It was also highly unusual for him to inscribe the title page of a volume. A note appears on the front pastedown endpaper: "Autographed copy by Mark Twain—bought by my father in N. Y. City/Oct 1, 1907—F. Barrett Jr/Newton N. Y." A price of $17.50 is marked on the front pastedown endpaper. The front free endpaper is signed, "Barrett./Newton/Sussex Co. N. Y."
> **Provenance:** formerly in the collection of Ralph Gregory (1909–2015), a curator of the Mark Twain Birthplace Memorial Shrine in Florida, Missouri (now named the Mark Twain Birthplace State Historic Site). He purchased the book from a visitor to the Shrine in the 1960s. Mr. Gregory lived in Marthasville, Missouri.
> **Location:** in August 2017 the volume belonged to Ralph Gregory's daughter, Nancy Gregory Kimball, Marthasville, Missouri.
> **Copy examined:** unmarked copy that purportedly belonged to Clemens. The signature is uncharacteristic of Clemens, but the fact that Clemens purchased another novel by

Tourgée (that one acquired in 1880 and signed "S. L. Clemens") makes his acquisition of this book a little more plausible. Conceivably he intended it as a gift to someone? The provenance of this item remains dubious.

Endeavoring to build upon the success of *A Fool's Errand*, Tourgée set aside the requirements of a novel and in this nonfiction sequel that exposed the rise of the Ku Klux Klan, the terror this clandestine organization generated, and the reassertion of white domination.

TOWER, DAVID B. (1808–1868) and **CORNELIUS WALKER.** *North American First Class Reader; The Fifth Book of Tower's Series.* Second edition. Leather cover, flaking. New York: Cady and Burgess; Boston: Benjamin B. Massey & Co., 1850. 426 pp.

> **Location:** Mark Twain Library, Redding, Connecticut.
> **Copy examined:** a book once belonging to someone other than Clemens or a member of his family. It has the purple oval Mark Twain Library stamps but no accession number, inscription, or markings. When I revisited Redding in June 1982 this volume had been discovered and placed with the Clemens collection, even though there is no discernible reason to associate it with the donations by Clemens and his daughter Clara Gabrilowitsch. I recommended that the staff remove it from that collection.

TOWNSEND, ANNIE (LAKE) (1857–1926), pseud. "Philip Shirley." *On the Verge; A Romance of the Centennial.* San Francisco: A. L. Bancroft & Co., 1879. 295 pp.

> **Source:** MTLAcc, entry #256, volume donated by Clemens.
> A romantic novel with breezy dialogue pits the charms of San Francisco against the lure of the New York Centennial and Exposition. Townsend, born in San Francisco and a contributor to *The Argonaut*, would die in Utica, New York. *On the Verge* was her only long work of fiction to see print. Consult also the Catalog entry (below) for Edward Waterman Townsend.

TOWNSEND, BELTON O'NEALL (1855–1891). *Plantation Lays and Other Poems.* Dark brown cloth, gilt. Custom-made light brown cloth box. Columbia, South Carolina: C. A. Calvo, Jr., Printer, 1884. 106 pp. plus one page of "Notes."

> **Inscriptions:** a lengthy presentation inscription in brown ink on the third front flyleaf explains how Clemens came to possess this volume: "Mr. Sam'l L. Clemens,/(Mark Twain),/May 22, 1884./With the compliments of the au/thor, who has spent so many/delightful hours over 'Mark Twain's'/writings, that he sincerely hopes/Mr. Clemens will spare a half hour/to glance over this little volume,/& (if worthy) lend a word of/encouragement or a helping hand/to an ambitious young author." At the top of the second front flyleaf Clemens declared in pencil: "A volume of/unspeakable rot." Subsequently Clemens added a note in black ink in a late hand: "1884?/April, 1908. Think of it! Less/than a quarter of a century/ago Howells & Longfellow/were charitably (& bitterly/against their consciences),/lying to this idiot, & pretending/that they wanted him to continue his literary dysentery. (See/'Dedication.')/It seems impossible that/those two admirable men/could ever have been so/abandoned, so wicked, so/conscienceless, so rotten!" The front pastedown endpaper is signed "Alan Gribben" in blue ink. A bookplate on the front free endpaper contains a record in blue ink: "Alan Gribben/Austin, Texas/Acquired from/John F. Hunter of/Hillsboro,

N. H./November 15, 1982."

Marginalia: Clemens made pencil marks on page 88 and wrote disparaging notes in pencil on pages 91, 99, 104, 105, and in Townsend's "Notes."

Provenance: contains several blue-black stamps of the Mark Twain Library, Redding, Connecticut. At the top of the rear pastedown endpaper is the Mark Twain Library accession number in red ink: "3156". A library charge slip and a charge-card jacket have been removed from the rear free endpaper and the rear pastedown endpaper.

Catalog: offered for sale for $500 on 28 October 1982 by John F. Hunter, NECCo Art, Numismatics, Photography, Hillsboro, New Hampshire. Hunter indicated in a letter to Alan Gribben of 9 November 1982 that the volume "was purchased by me a few years ago, along with a rather strange assortment of other books," from an elderly woman "in a nearby town where she had been the librarian."

Location: collection of Alan Gribben, Montgomery, Alabama. Acquired on 15 November 1982. (After my *Mark Twain's Library: A Reconstruction* was published in 1980, I finally allowed myself to make my first and only purchase of a book from Clemens's library collection.)

Copy examined: Clemens's copy.

Clemens wrote with amazement to William Dean Howells on 24 May 1884 from Hartford: "Good land, have you seen the 'poems' of that South Carolinian idiot, 'Belton O'Neall Townsend, A. B. & Attorney at Law?'—& above all, the dedication of them to you? . . . He deserves hanging any-way & in any & all cases—no, boiling, gutting, brazing in a mortar—no, no, there *is* no death that can meet his case. Now think of this literary louse dedicating his garbage to you, & quoting encourageing compliments from you & poor dead Longfellow. Let us hope there is a hell, for this poet[']s sake, who carries his bowels in his skull, & when they operate works the discharge into rhyme & prints it. Ah, if he had only dedicated this diarrhea to Aldrich, I could just howl with delight; but the joke is lost on you—just about wasted" (*MTHL*, p. 488). Belton was a prominent South Carolina planter and attorney. Clemens was especially critical of any Southern writers in whose poetry or prose he detected inflated language and false ideals.

TOWNSEND, EDWARD WATERMAN (1855–1942). *Days Like These; A Novel.* New York: Harper & Brothers, 1901. 444 pp.
  Source: MTLAcc, entry #1113, volume donated by Clemens.
  Townsend, the husband of Annie (Lake) Townsend (see the Catalog entry above), published half a dozen novels, most of them set in New York City, as was *Days Like These.*

TOWNSEND, GEORGE ALFRED (1841–1914), pseud. "Gath." *Tales of the Chesapeake.* New York: American News Co., 1880. 285 pp.
  Source: MTLAcc, entry #310, volume donated by Clemens.
  The title of this collection of short stories and poetry alludes to the Delaware and Maryland shores of the Chesapeake Bay. Clemens was generous in his praise to the journalist and novelist Townsend in a letter written in 1880: "Many thanks for the book. I got it yesterday evening and gave it a chance toward bedtime, but it failed to put me to sleep or even make me drowsy. Few books treat me so unkindly. I read it more than halfway through, picking out the plums,

such as 'The Big Idiot,' 'The Circuit Preacher,' etc., and greatly enjoyed the entertainment" (Ruthana Hindes, *George Alfred Townsend: One of Delaware's Outstanding Writers* [Wilmington, Delaware: Privately printed, 1946], p. 50). Townsend's publisher placed a condensed version of the last sentence of Clemens's letter at the top of a long list of quoted compliments by various authors for *Tales of the Chesapeake* in the third edition of Townsend's stories and poems. "The Circuit Preacher" (pp. 167–170) is a humorous poem about an aging minister seeking a permanent church appointment. (Townsend's father was a minister who often relocated.) Townsend set his short story "The Big Idiot" (pp. 171–193) in the early colonial days.

TOWNSEND, JOHN DRAKE (1835–1896). *New York in Bondage.* New York, 1901. 251 pp.
  Source: MTLAcc, entry #580, volume donated by Clemens.
  Townsend, a prominent New York City lawyer, served as the attorney for William "Boss" Tweed, the politician convicted in 1873 who died in prison in 1878. Townsend's daughter, Margaret Townsend Tagliapietra (she married the opera baritone Giovanni Tagliapietra in 1900) undertook the posthumous publication of her father's bold exposé of Tammany Hall graft and corruption that chronicled how an elite political group had gained (and retained) control of New York City. Margaret Tagliapietra would die in 1942.

TOWNSEND, MEREDITH WHITE (1831–1911). *Asia and Europe: Studies Presenting the Conclusions Formed by the Author in a Long Life Devoted to the Subject of the Relations Between Asia and Europe.* New York: G. P. Putnam's Sons, 1901. 388 pp.
  Inscription: the front free endpaper has been torn out.
  Marginalia: Clemens filled the front pastedown endpaper with many notes in black ink, but half of these annotations have been canceled with a darker black ink. Only fragmentary phrases are still legible, as, for example: "Palmist says <——.> Have taken out fire insurance, being admonished <———.>" There is no writing on the rear endpapers or flyleaves. Clemens folded down numerous pages throughout the volume. His penciled comments extend through page 132, and he marked other passages with pencil beyond that point. Someone whose pencil markings are broader and heavier than Clemens's joined him in annotating the text on page 121 and thereafter.
  On page 14 Clemens noted "Jonathan Edwards" beside a quotation characterizing the Mahommedan Moollah: "These to hell and I care not, these to heaven and I reck not." At the bottom of page 15 he jotted a notation about Europe's abandonment of torture: "It is used in New York. See Tribune of to-day (May 9/02)". He marked Townsend's assertion that, "As yet all that Europe has effected in China is to create an impression that the white peoples are intolerably fierce and cruel, that they understand nothing but making money, and that from them there is nothing intellectual or moral to be gained" (p. 27). Clemens both underscored and marked Townsend's observation on page 29 that the European is essentially secular, as proven by the fact that the mythology of Greece and Rome "died away utterly, there being on earth now not one man who believes in Jupiter." On page 60 he wrote vertically in the margin: "The Christian conversions in India are 3,300 a year"—meaning that this is an insignificant number; he

repeated the statement in the margin of page 63. Clemens made a few brief notes on pages 121–122. For instance, beside a diplomat's description of the total lack of social obligations in Turkey—no calling cards, RSVPs, no thank-you letters—Clemens quipped, "I want to live in Turkey" (p. 122). He made a note about "the monarchs of England" on page 132. On page 280 Clemens marked a passage in which Townsend compares the Po River and the Mississippi.

Catalogs: ListABP (1910), "Asian and Europe, Townsend"; *C1951*, #63a, $35; Bruce Gimelson Autographs, catalog for public auction, New York City (1 March 1973), item #185; purchased by Charles W. Sachs, The Scriptorium, Beverly Hills, California, $200.

Location: Mark Twain Papers, Bancroft Library, University of California at Berkeley, California. Purchased from The Scriptorium of Beverly Hills on 13 March 1973. See letter, Charles W. Sachs to Frederick Anderson, 8 March 1973 (MTP). Alan Gribben, who had visited The Scriptorium, arranged this acquisition.

Copy examined: Clemens's copy.

TOWNSHEND, RICHARD BAXTER (1846–1923) and [**LETITIA JANE**] **DOROTHEA** (**BAKER**) **TOWNSHEND** (1846–1930). *The Bride of a Day*. London: George Allen, 1905. 295 pp.

Inscription: the front free endpaper is inscribed: "To M. T./Oh dweller in the Fairy lands/Where every fairy flower blows,/Accept a weed from cowboy hands/That have not skill to bring a rose./D. T."

Provenance: formerly in the Mark Twain Library, Redding, Connecticut.

Catalog: *Mott 1952*, item #87, $12.50.

Location: Mark Twain House and Museum, Hartford, Connecticut. Donated anonymously in 1963.

Copy examined: Clemens's copy. Examined in August 1987. Born and educated in England, Richard Townshend spent an adventurous decade (1869–1879) roving throughout Colorado, New Mexico, and Texas. He returned to England, married Dorothea in 1881, and settled down to a far more sedate life of teaching and tutoring in Oxford. Their novel *The Bride of a Day* depicted Navajo Indians and Mexican settlers in New Mexico during the 1850s.

T. P.'s Weekly (London, journal, published 1902–1916).

Henry Fisher reported that Clemens bought a copy of this literary magazine in Cork, Ireland (*AMT*, p. 213). On 10 July 1907 Clemens went to Liverpool with its editor, Thomas Power ("Tay Pay") O'Connor (1848–1929), for a banquet at the Town Hall (*MTB*, pp. 1399, 1401). Clemens invited O'Connor to visit Redding, Connecticut on 26 October 1909 (ALS in MTP).

TRACY, LOUIS (1863–1928). *The Captain of the Kansas*. New York: Edward J. Clode, [cop. 1906]. 336 pp.

Source: MTLAcc, entry #1077, volume donated by Clemens.

Tracy was a prolific British novelist. In *The Captain of the Kansas*, sabotage imperils a ship on the South American coast, with other adventures in store.

———. *The Pillar of Light*. New York: E. J. Clode, 1904. 339 pp.

Source: MTLAcc, entry #309, volume donated by Clemens.

———. *The Red Year; A Story of the Indian Mutiny*. New York: E. J. Clode, [cop. 1907]. 328 pp.

Source: MTLAcc, entry #1076, volume donated by

Clemens. Subsequently sold to Lt. Bauer, 15 October [1908?], according to the Mark Twain Library records.

———. [Another identical copy.]

Source: MTLAcc, entry #1256, volume donated by Clemens.

———. *The Wings of the Morning*. New York: Grosset & Dunlap, [cop. 1903]. 354 pp.

Source: MTLAcc, entry # 1309, volume donated by Clemens.

TRAILL, HENRY DUFF (1842–1900). *The Marquis of Salisbury*. New York: Harper & Brothers, 1901. 224 pp.

Source: MTLAcc, entry #1295, volume donated by Clemens.

Biographer Traill chronicles the life of the British statesman and Prime Minister, Robert Cecil (1830–1903), Marquess of Salisbury.

———. *Sterne*. English Men of Letters Series. New York: Harper & Brothers, 1901. 173 pp.

Source: MTLAcc, entry #1286, volume donated by Clemens.

This life of Laurence Stern (1713–1768) was Traill's second biography in the English Men of Letters Series; he had previously written one on Samuel Taylor Coleridge.

TRAIN, GEORGE FRANCIS (1829–1904).

Mark Twain's column in the 18 December 1867 issue of the New York *Tribune* took the form of a letter to the editor (titled "Information Wanted"), seeking news about the American writer, orator, international businessman, and publicity-seeking social reformer George Francis Train; Twain claimed that his uncle was interested in Train's scheme to "buy Ireland for those persons they call the Fenians." A follow-up letter to the New York *Tribune* (22 January 1868) inquired about Train's safety (it was well known that Train was briefly incarcerated in the Cork County Jail for entering Ireland with pro-Fenian pamphlets and newspapers). Twain mentioned Train humorously in a column in 1868 that appeared in the Washington *Intelligencer* (reprinted in the *Mark Twain Quarterly* 5.2 [Summer 1942]: 16). In "A Daring Attempt at a Solution of It" (*Galaxy*, July 1870), Twain belittled this Fenian "Champion." Twain also made fun of Train in letters to the Virginia City *Enterprise* (30 January 1868) and the Chicago *Republican* (21 February 1868) (see *MTLet* 2 n. 158 n. 5).

TRASK, KATRINA (**BIRTH NAME KATE**) (**NICHOLS**) (1853–1922). *John Leighton, Jr.; A Novel*. New York: Harper & Brothers, 1898. 252 pp.

Source: MTLAcc, entry #312, volume donated by Clemens.

The novelist, poet, and dramatist Katrina Trask was married to a wealthy Wall Street banker, financier, and railroad magnate. As a philanthropist she helped sponsor an artist's community called Yaddo in Saratoga Springs, New York.

———. *Lessons in Love*. New York: Harper & Brothers, 1900. 138 pp.

Source: MTLAcc, entry #311, volume donated by Clemens.

TRAUBEL, HORACE (1858–1919), ed. *Camden's Compliment to Walt Whitman, May 31, 1889: Notes, Addresses, Letters, Telegrams*. Edited by Horace L. Traubel. Philadelphia: D. McKay, 1889. 74 pp.

Traubel included a letter from Mark Twain in this laudatory

collection (pp. 64–65).

Inscription: autographed in black ink, "Walt Whitman/ Dec. 16 '89". Below that, in a different hand, also in black ink: "With autograph with/kind regards of/C. G. Garrison/Christmas 1897".

Provenance: this volume was part of a book collection assembled by Mrs. Louis (Haydee) Zeitlin of Santa Monica, California. It was purchased, along with six books that once belonged to Clemens's personal library, by the University of Nevada, Reno in 1963. However, the University Library accession record indicates that *Camden's Compliment to Walt Whitman* was listed then under the rubric "Books with Letters" rather than with the other listed "Books That Belonged to Mark Twain," which leaves its provenance quite vague. Jacob Zeitlin's bookshop was of course a well-known fixture for decades in Southern California book circles. (All of this information was supplied in an email to Alan Gribben on 8 April 1998 by Robert E. Blesse, then Head, Special Collections, University Library, University of Nevada, Reno.)

Location: Special Collections Department, University Library, University of Nevada, Reno.

Copy examined: photocopies of the title page and signatures, sent to Alan Gribben on 8 March 1998 by David K. Parsons, then a student at the University of Nevada at Reno, who recognized that this might be a Clemens association item. It is true that Clemens usually obtained (or was presented with) copies of works that contained any of his writings, however minor. But this copy has such a clouded origin that on the basis of the known facts it cannot be included in a reconstruction of Clemens's library.

Travelers Record (magazine, Hartford, Connecticut, published 1865–1906). Issued by the Travelers Insurance Company of Hartford.

In 1885 Clemens made a memorandum to "Send Huck to Traveler's Record. Hartd " (NB 25, *N&J* 3: 133). See also the Catalog entry for Forrest Morgan.

TREE, (SIR) HERBERT BEERBOHM (1853–1917), adapt. *Rip Van Winkle* (play).

Clemens mentioned this play—and perhaps saw it—on 31 May 1900, the day it opened in London (NB 43, TS p. 13a). See also the Catalog entry for Dion Boucicault, *Rip Van Winkle*.

TRELAWNY, EDWARD JOHN (1792–1881). *Adventures of a Younger Son* (published in London, 1831).

Clemens noted the title of this book in 1879 while he was in England (NB 18, *N&J* 2: 337). The incredible feats related in this Englishman's semi-fictional autobiography are now viewed with skepticism, but few readers at the time of its publication doubted Trelawny's veracity. One reason was that this seaman-adventurer had ingratiated himself into the so-called Pisan Circle, becoming friends with Shelley, Byron, and other figures associated with the Romantic movement.

———. *Records of Shelley, Byron, and the Author.* 2 vols. London: Basil Montagu Pickering, 1878. [An enlarged version of Trelawny's *Recollections of the Last Days of Shelley and Byron*, published in 1858.]

In England, possibly at Cholmondeley's Condover Hall, Mark Twain wrote in 1879: "Trelawney's [*sic*] Adventures of a Younger Son & Reminiscences [*sic*] of Shelley &

Byron" (NB 18, *N&J* 2: 337). Twain would quote from Trelawny's latter book in the essay titled "In Defence of Harriet Shelley" (1894). A surviving note in the Notebook Fragments file in the Mark Twain Papers at the Bancroft Library at the University of California at Berkeley, apparently in Isabel Lyon's handwriting, reads: "Records of Shelly [*sic*], Byron & the Author by Ed. John Trelawny—London/Basil Montagu Pickering—1878".

TRENCK, (BARON) FRIEDRICH VON DER (1726–1794). *The Life of Baron Frederic Trenck.* Translated from the German. 3 vols. (Published in London, 1788–1793; American editions followed.)

It would be difficult to exaggerate the adventures or the misfortunes of this Prussian officer, a sometime favorite of Frederick the Great. Lengthy imprisonments, replete with ingenious attempts at escape, were eventually followed by years of liberty that Robespierre brought to an end by ordering Trenck's beheading in July 1894. "Baron Trenck" was one of the "best authorities" on prison escapes whom Tom Sawyer recommends to Huck Finn in Chapter 35 of *Adventures of Huckleberry Finn* (1885). As early as 1924, Henry A. Pochmann noticed parallels between Trenck's adventures—he tamed a mouse, used a penknife to dig with, made a rope from bedsheets and a leather portmanteau, sawed a bed-leg, encountered a moat—and the methods advocated by Tom Sawyer to free Jim ("The Mind of Mark Twain," pp. 15, 201). Pochmann also cited Trenck's work as a source for Chapter 18, "In the Queen's Dungeons," of Mark Twain's *A Connecticut Yankee* (1889). A newspaper interview published on 8 October 1897 reported that "on his table" Clemens had a copy of *Merkwurdige Lebensgeschichte* [*Marvelous Adventures*] *of Freiherr von der Trenck of Spilberg* (M. Thomas Inge, "Ten Minutes with Mark Twain: An Interview," *American Literary Realism* 15.2 [Autumn 1982]: 262).

Olin H. Moore, "MT and Don Quixote" (1922), pp. 334–335.

TRESCOTT, LEWIS ELMER (1883–1910).

On 28 February 1907 the educator, editor, and author Ossian Herbert Lang (1865–1945), who lived in Mount Vernon, New York, informed Mark Twain that a Long Island poet, Lewis E. Trescott, had been good-naturedly chosen as the latest "Poet Lariat," a title originally coined by Twain. Lang wrote again on 16 and 17 August 1907 to inquire about Twain's reaction to Trescott's verses. Twain obligingly read over his effusions, but found that they fell short in crucial areas. He explained to Lang on 21 August 1907 why Trescott was not an entirely satisfactory successor to Bloodgood H. Cutter, the "Poet Lariat" whose strained verse Twain had celebrated in *The Innocents Abroad* (1869). Trescott's poems lacked "incoherency," "idiocy," "windy emptiness," and "putrid & insistent bastard godliness" (MTP).

The background for Twain's exchange of letters with Lang is more complicated, and sadder, than it might initially appear. Bloodgood H. Cutter died on 26 September 1906. In November 1906 a humor columnist for the Brooklyn *Daily Eagle*, Willis Brooks Hawkins (1852–1928), commenced a tongue-in-cheek search for another Long Island poet worthy of the "Poet Lariat" label Twain had invented for Cutter. In the 20 February 1907 issue of the *Daily*

Eagle Hawkins (who wrote under the pseudonym "Willis Brooks" or sometimes employed the pen name "Quills") announced the winner of his contest: a self-nominated twenty-three-year-old school principal from Glenwood Landing, Long Island—Lewis Elmer Trescott. The young man had submitted some stanzas from a lengthy poem titled "The Wrath of Winter," portions of which Hawkins quoted. In his letter applying for the Poet Lariatship, Trescott testified that he had been a personal friend of Bloodgood H. Cutter and was therefore "the logical successor." It was hard for the readers then (or even now) to decide whether Tresnott was simply making a bid for attention or whether he really had a poor opinion of his own poetic efforts. Taking note of Trescott's effort to obtain this notoriety, *The School Bulletin and New York State Educational Journal* 33.388 (December 1906): 77 expressed its hope that "his letter . . . was probably intended to be humorous." (In 1906 Trescott had managed to sell a six-page song, "My Highland Brunette," to the Success Music Company in Chicago, so he evidently had some degree of talent.) In any event, this newly anointed Poet Lariat caught pneumonia and died on 18 May 1910 at the age of only twenty-seven. His obituary in the *Long Island Daily Farmer* mentioned that he left behind more than 500 poems.

TREVELYAN, (SIR) GEORGE OTTO (1838–1928). *Cawnpore.* Fourth edition reprint. 8vo, original dark blue cloth, blue-coated endpapers, gilt, dampstain on the rear cover. London: Macmillan and Co., 1899. 280 pp.

Inscription: the half-title page is signed in pencil, "S L Clemens/1903/No, this is/Clara Clemens's/book."

Marginalia: Clemens made a few pencil markings on pages 273 and 275 and penciled three words concerning "The Massacre." Several page corners are turned down, including those of 272 and 274. A number of leaves remain uncut in the middle section of the volume; judging from the fact that only the first few and the last few gatherings have been opened, it would appear that Clemens jumped to the final two chapters, "The Treachery" and "The Massacre."

Catalogs: Christie's, New York City, 1–2 February 1988 auction, lot 462, sold for $1,100 to Randall House of Los Angeles; *Sotheby's 2003*, #241, $1,700.

Provenance: the shelfmark of Clara Clemens Gabrilowitsch's private library in Detroit is present. Donated to the Carrie Estelle Doheny Collection, St. John's Seminary, Camarillo, California, by Mrs. Doheny after she acquired the volume in 1940 for $12.20 from Maxwell Hunley Rare Books of Beverly Hills. Auctioned by Christie's in 1988 on behalf of St. John's Seminary and the Archdiocese of Los Angeles. Subsequently acquired by Nick Karanovich, Fort Wayne, Indiana.

Location: collection of Kevin Mac Donnell, Austin, Texas.

Copy examined: Clemens's copy, in July 2004. It has the bookplate of "Estelle Doheny."

Mark Twain obviously had access to an earlier edition of this book about the 1857 Sepoy Mutiny in Kanpur. "I had read, in the histories, that the June marches made between Lucknow and Cawnpore by the British forces in the time of the Mutiny were made in that kind of weather—138 in the shade—and had taken it for historical embroidery," Twain writes in *Following the Equator* (1897, Ch. 54). In Chapter 58 of *Following the Equator* Twain quotes at length Trevelyan's account of the indignities and hardships faced by English families fleeing the outlying stations during the Great Mutiny; he also quotes Trevelyan's version of the massacre of English soldiers by Nana Sahib as well as the massacre of English women and children at Cawnpore. In Twain's "Which Was It?," written between 1899 and 1903, Sol Bailey exultantly reads to George Harrison from Trevelyan's account. (Twain also planned to insert an extract describing the atrocities committed by British soldiers to avenge the rebel Indians' massacre of English women and children during the Cawnpore mutiny.) In the opinion of freethinker Bailey, "That's man, all over!" Bailey is pleased to run across this confirmation of his pessimistic views; he is "cutting its leaves and devouring its contents" eagerly (*WWD?*, pp. 375–376). During the night of 26 January [1904], Clemens dispatched a note to Olivia Clemens's secluded sick-room while they were residing in Florence: "I am where the Mutiny is approaching, Livy dear—April 22—then the 30th—then May 8th— that awful shadow creeping upon them stage by stage, & they don't know it. May the 9th, & they are easy & comfortable, & think it was a trifling flurry & has blown over. On May the *10th* & they are junketing—& the slaughter & the butchery & the burning is raging at Meerut, & they don't suspect.—by gracious there is something immensely moving & dramatic about that creeping shadow & those poor self-satisfied people's unconsciousness of it!" (ALS in MTP, quoted in *MFMT*, p. 229).

Baetzhold, *MT&JB* (1970), p. 357 n. 13; Madigan, "MT's Passage to India" (1974), pp. 366–367.

———. *The Life and Letters of Lord Macaulay, by His Nephew G. Otto Trevelyan.* 2 volumes. Engraved frontispiece portrait of Macaulay in Volume I. 8vo, original black cloth, gilt, brown-coated endpapers, the spine has largely perished, the front cover and first eighty pages are detached.] New York: Harper & Brothers, 1876. [Volume I only.]

Marginalia: The approximately sixty-five separate pencil annotations in Volume I total more than 300 words on forty-four pages; thirty-two additional pages are marked with penciled marginal rules, underlinings, and other markings. At Trevelyan's reference (page 45) to Macaulay's "habitual overestimate of the average knowledge possessed by mankind," Clemens underlined that sentence and wrote, "A *schoolboy* would know better." Clemens disapproved of the style of two letters Macaulay wrote at fifteen: "What a contrast with his former simplicity"; Macaulay "has become a prig—ineffable" (p. 64); "This is delicious priggishness" (pp. 64–65). Where one of Macaulay's letters described the *Decameron* as "elegant, amusing, and . . . strikingly delicate," Clemens responded on page 65, "This Boccaccio business is a perfect enigma. He must have read an expurgated edition." Chester Davis reported on the marginalia in this work in three issues of *The Twainian* 10 (July-October 1951), mentioning only Volume I. On page 116, next to Macaulay's observation that "every magazine must contain a certain quantity of mere ballast, of no value but as it occupies space," Clemens noted, "Send that to Howells with next article." On page 150 Davis wrote that Clemens twice noted, "America today—1876." The same page contains another note by

Clemens prompted by Trevelyan's description of the state of public affairs in England in 1830: "Susie's aphorism (aged 4) 'How easy it is to break things.' Her first remark in the morning—sitting up in bed."

Catalogs: *C1951*, #4a, listed under books containing Clemens's marginalia, $35; also #14c, listed among volumes signed by Clemens, $7. Presumably these two volumes were part of the same work, but were sold separately by accident; Christie's, New York City, Sale 7378, including the "Estate of Chester L. Davis," 5 December 1991, lot 186, Volume I only, sold for $3,850; *Sotheby's 2003*, lot 242, Volume I only, $6,000.

Provenance: the shelfmark in Volume I of Clara Clemens Gabrilowitsch's private library in Detroit is present. Volume I only (apparently) became part of the Mark Twain Research Foundation collection in Perry, Missouri; Chester Davis (1903–1987) was reluctant to show me this book when I visited his residence in Perry in 1970. Eventually the book entered the collection of Nick Karanovich, Fort Wayne, Indiana.

Location: the whereabouts of both volumes are currently unknown.

Copies examined: Clemens's copy of Volume I, prior to the Sotheby's auction in 2003.

The English statesman, orator, and writer Thomas Babington Macaulay lived from 1800 until 1859. Shortly after Trevelyan's work appeared in 1876, Clemens prepared a paper, "Life of Lord Macaulay," for the Saturday Morning Club in Hartford (lecture program in MTP). Clemens's talk focused particularly on Macaulay's precocious intellectual development. In a conversation on 9 September 1905 about "the value of keeping a journal—especially to a literary man," Clemens alluded to "Macaulay's journal" (Isabel V. Lyon Journals, TS p. 96, MTP). On Sunday, 25 March 1906, Isabel Lyon recorded: "It was a delight to hear Mr. Clemens & Mr. Howells talk of Macaulay & Trevelyan's life & letters" (IVL Journal, Harry Ransom Center, University of Texas at Austin; a similar entry appears in IVL Journals, TS p. 152, MTP). "So far as I know, only one author has ever made a memorable speech before a law-making body in the interest of his trade—that was Macaulay. I think his speech is called great to this day, . . . whereas the speech is so exhaustively ignorant of its subject, and so trivial and jejune in its reasonings. . . ." (24 November 1906 AD, *MTE*, pp. 374–375; *AutoMT* 2: 289). After dinner on 25 August 1907 Isabel Lyon "found him lying with his beautiful feet uncovered and reading Macaulay's 'Life & Letters.' He dropped it on his breast and chatted for a few minutes" (IVL Journals, TS p. 272, MTP).

Krause, *MTC* (1967), p. 229; Baetzhold, *MT&JB* (1970), p. 186.

———. *The Life and Letters of Lord Macaulay, by His Nephew G. Otto Trevelyan.* 2 volumes. Engraved frontispiece portrait of Macaulay in Volume I. Original black cloth, brown-coated endpapers, the spine has largely perished. New York: Harper & Brothers, 1876.

Marginalia: Clemens made a vertical pencil line in Volume I on page 55 at lines 3–8 about Macaulay's mother urging commendable behavior whether it was rewarded or not. On pages 106 and 107 he corrected the phrasing in a sentence, crossing out "have said" so that it reads "to say" and crossing out "have" in another phrase. Where the text on page 164 discusses the conduct toward opponents on the floor of Parliament, Clemens wrote "They still wear their hats" in pencil in the margin. He made a pencil line at the top of page 174 (lines 2–6) regarding a journal kept by Macaulay's sister Margaret Macaulay in which she expressed her sense of his becoming "extremely cold" toward her. One of Clemens's characteristic pencil brackets appears in the margin in the middle of page 190 concerning a man's strategy for seating himself so as not to be asked to give up his chair for arriving ladies. A vertical line on page 325 sets off a passage about the limited opportunities for reading books in India. No notes or markings are visible in Volume II. Joe B. Fulton's *Mark Twain in the Margins* (2000) reported the marginalia in detail.

Provenance: the bookplate of "J. Langdon Family Library/ No. 398" is pasted in Volume I. An identical bookplate, numbered 399, is affixed to the front endpaper of Volume II. Joe B. Fulton discovered these volumes on the shelves of the library at Quarry Farm in April 1995.

Catalog: Ball 2016 inventory, 2 vols., black cloth, gilt lettering, J. Langdon Family Library bookplates #398 and #399.

Location: Mark Twain Archive, Gannett-Tripp Learning Center, Elmira College, Elmira, New York.

Copy examined: a two-volume work that was available to Clemens (and was annotated by him) at the Langdons' residence in Elmira. Examined on 17 May 2002 in the Mark Twain Archive.

Howard G. Baetzhold, "'Well, My Book Is Written'" (1996), pp. 41–77; Joe B. Fulton, *Mark Twain in the Margins: The Quarry Farm Marginalia and* A Connecticut Yankee in King Arthur's Court (Tuscaloosa: University of Alabama Press, 2000), pp. 60–61.

———. *The Life and Letters of Lord Macaulay.* 2 vols. Engraved frontispiece portrait of Macaulay in Volume I. Original black cloth, the spines are gilt lettered. New York: Harper & Brothers, 1904.

Inscriptions: Clemens inscribed the front free endpapers of both volumes, "To Miss Isabel V. Lyon my private secretary with kindest regards of S L. Clemens, Sept. '05"; to the same inscription in the second volume Clemens added an endorsement, "It is a great book about a great & most interesting personality."

Marginalia: thirty-one pages have some thirty separate annotations by Clemens totaling more than 430 words; thirty additional leaves are marked with ink and pencil, and a score of other leaves have been folded down. On page 204 of Volume I, where Macaulay debated the correct terminology for the drinking vessels next to Zeus's throne, Clemens gave his own whimsical view: "They were jugs. One contained generous Scotch, the other that green-complected deadly French drink whose name, for the moment, fails me. (An hour later. Oh, damnation, absinthe!)" (Mark Twain's "AGE—A Rubàiyàt," probably written in 1898, had alluded to the "subduing Draught of tender green/and kindly Absinth, with its wimpling Sheen/Of dusky half-lights" (*Mark Twain's Rubàiyàt*, p. 42). On page 211 of that same volume, an anecdote about Talleyrand prompts Clemens to muse about his daughter Clara's aspirations for a musical career: "This is the equivalent of Clara's idea of a similar change of place which is to come soon: people will stop speaking of her in the newspapers as my daughter, & I shall come to be known & referred to as Clara Clemens's father." Regarding Jephthah, the Israelite general who kept a vow to sacrifice his only daughter to God (Judges 11, 29–38), Clemens scoffed, "Jeptha was a carrot. The pulpit admires him, but he ought to have been skinned alive for being scoundrel enough to keep his pledge." (Jephthah first allowed his daughter, an only child, two months to roam the hills and say goodbye to her friends, after which she dutifully returned to him to be sacrificed.) Isabel Lyon made a penciled note on the rear free endpaper of Volume I: "Mr. Clemens said tonight that if he weren't so lazy he'd write to Lord Trevelyan & ask him to append notes to chapter 3 mentioning the vast improvements or the great progress in the world since that time when Macaulay wrote so complacently."

In Volume II, Clemens drew a vertical line next to the entire text of page 208, which described the cheap editions of Macaulay's works sold in the United States, France, and Belgium, and wrote in ink: "This reads like a complaint; it ought to—& does—grieve us that there should have been occasion for the grief, still, the grief is modified by the fact that Macaulay was the assassin of copyright." Macaulay praised Jane Austen, causing Clemens to object, "He is praising those odious books again" (II: 394). As for Macaulay's effort to resolve one of Austen's sometimes puzzling punctuations, Clemens remarked that attempts to correct it would prove futile: "What did he do? You could not confuse the meaning if you removed *all* of the punctuation-marks; or even if you rearranged them at random" (II: 395). Clemens rebuked Macaulay for his 1853 criticism of Harriet Beecher Stowe because it was "published while Mrs. Stowe was still alive" (II: 302). Where Macaulay lamented that he had "just begun to understand how to write" even though "I have very nearly done writing," Clemens noted, "My condition at 72; his at 57" (II: 380). Next to Macaulay's account of Leigh Hunt as a person who "had no high feeling of independence . . . no sense of obligation . . . took money wherever he could get it . . . felt no gratitude for it . . . was just as ready to defame a person who had relieved his distress as a person who had refused him relief" (II: 403), Clemens wrote, "An absolutely perfect photograph of Bret Harte." Trevelyan's description of the dignity of Macaulay's death and the void it left caused Clemens to recall the death of Olivia Clemens: "With almost no important emendations this could apply to June 5, 1904." Lord Macaulay's opinions of American institutions provoked Clemens to predict, at the beginning of the appendix: "These are interesting letters, but they put off the destruction of the Republic until we shall have a population of seven or eight hundred millions. I think it will happen very much sooner. All that is required is just one more Roosevelt, I think. We have learned to expect him, & also to long for him."

Provenance: displays the bookplate of Isabel V. Lyon; at some point this volume joined the collection of Nick Karanovich, Fort Wayne, Indiana.

Catalog: *Sotheby's 2003*, #243, quotes the marginalia

extensively, $8,500.

Location: unknown at present.

Copy examined: Isabel V. Lyon's copy, annotated by Clemens. Viewed prior to the Sotheby's auction in 2003.

Trials of Mutinous Convicts. [Unidentified book.]

When Clemens listed various topics about Australia and New Zealand on 1 December 1896 in Chelsea, he also wrote, "Trials of Mutinous Convicts (Book[)]" (NB 39, TS p. 28). Possibly he was thinking of Marcus Clarke's *For the Term of His Natural Life.*

TRIGGS, OSCAR LOVELL (1865–1930). *Chapters in the History of the Arts and Crafts Movement.* Illus. Chicago: Bohemia Guild of the Industrial Arts League, 1902. 198 pp.

Inscription: the front pastedown endpaper is signed, "SL. Clemens, 1902."

Catalog: *A1911*, "8vo, boards, cloth back, Chicago, 1902," quotes the signature, lot 461, sold for $1.25.

E. P. Rosenthal, of E. P. Rosenthal and Company in Chicago, wrote to Clemens on 7 April 1905: "The time I sent you our volume, 'Chapters in History of the Arts and Crafts Movement,' you told us that by registering the same we anchored it. Today I am sending you another volume [Herman Kuehn's *Thoughts of a Fool*] and . . . I am anxious for you to get it as quickly as possible" (MTP).

TRIMMER, SARAH (KIRBY) (1741–1810). *The History of the Robins. In Words of One Syllable.* Ed. by Charles Swete. Illustrated by Harrison Weir (1824–1906). New York: G. Routledge & Sons, n.d. 246 pp.

Source: MTLAcc, entry #428, volume donated by Clemens.

British author Trimmer's long-popular book first appeared (under a different title) in 1786. Through the story of a family of birds she endeavored to teach children to treat birds and other small creatures humanely. The Reverend Charles Swete simplified its vocabulary.

TRIPP, ALONZO (1818–1891), pseud. "Willie Triton." *The Fisher Boy.* Boston: Whittemore, Niles & Hall, 1862. 362 pp.

Inscription: C. J. A. [?] Langdon/from his mother/Dec 25th 1862" [Charles Jervis Langdon, 1849–1916, Clemens's future brother-in-law].

Catalogs: listed among the books transferred by Mark Woodhouse from the Quarry Farm library to the Mark Twain Archive on 9 July 1987; Ball 2016 inventory, brown cloth, gilt design and lettering, fair condition, inscribed to C. J. A. Langdon by his mother in 1862.

Location: Mark Twain Archive, Elmira College, Elmira, New York.

Tripp set his novel on the Cape and Island shores of New England. This copy was accessible to Clemens whenever he visited the Langdons' home in Elmira.

TROLLOPE, ANTHONY (1815–1882). *Australia and New Zealand.* 2 vols. London: Chapman & Hall, 1873.

The reading that Clemens undertook in London in November 1896 included "Australia & N. Z. 2 Vls A. Trollope" (NB 39, TS p. 26).

———. *An Autobiography.* New York: J. W. Lovell Co., [cop. 1883]. 264 pp.

Source: MTLAcc, entry #841, volume donated by Clemens.

Clemens met Anthony Trollope in 1873 at the Garrick Club in London at a dinner honoring the flamboyant Joaquin Miller. In 1907 Clemens recalled attending this dinner that Trollope had hosted in London thirty-four years earlier: "Trollope was voluble and animated" and he was "pouring forth a smooth and limpid and sparkling stream of faultless English" (19 August 1907 AD, *MTE*, pp. 332–333; *AutoMT* 3: 103). He had mentioned meeting Trollope in a letter of 6 July 1873 to Mary Mason Fairbanks (*MTLet* 5: 402). Harold Aspiz, "Mark Twain and Anthony Trollope, Equestrians," *Mark Twain Quarterly* 9.1 [Winter 1951]: 14–15, related how, at the Joaquin Miller dinner, Trollope endeavored to converse with Clemens about horses.

———. *Barchester Towers*. Ed. Ernest [Percival] Rhys (1859–1946). Everyman's Library Series. London: J. M. Dent & Sons, 1912. 462 pp.

Inscriptions: the initials "S. C." are penciled on the front pastedown endpapers, and the same initials are written in black ballpoint pen on the title page.

Location: Mark Twain Library, Redding, Connecticut.

Copy examined: an unmarked copy belonging to someone other than Clemens or any member of his family. It has a red ink accession number, "5104". This Everyman's Library edition of Trollope's 1857 novel was first published in 1906, but the verso of the title page states that this particular reprinting was issued in 1912—two years after Clemens died. A Mark Twain Library volunteer had added this volume to the Clemens collection by the time I revisited Redding in June 1982. I recommended to the staff that it be removed from the shelves containing the books donated by Clemens and his daughter Clara Clemens Gabrilowitsch.

———. *Phineas Finn* (novel, published in 1869) and *Phineas Redux* (novel, published in 1874).

At a circulating library in Weggis, Switzerland on 2 August 1897 Clemens "took a couple of Trollope's— 2 vols each" for a fee of two francs (NB 42, TS p. 23). Howard G. Baetzhold makes a case for supposing that these two Parliamentary novels were the books borrowed (*MT&JB* [1970], pp. 202–203).

Krause, *MTC* (1967), p. 14 (surmised that "he does not seem to have read" Trollope); Madigan, "Mark Twain's Passage to India" (1974), p. 367.

TROLLOPE, FRANCES (MILTON) (1779–1863). *Domestic Manners of the Americans. Complete in One Volume.* London: Printed for Whittaker, Treacher, & Co.; New York: Reprinted for the Booksellers, 1832. 325 pp.

Inscription: the title page is signed in ink at the top: "T. [?] J. [?] Brener [?]/July 1832."

Provenance: Caroline Ticknor, the daughter of Benjamin H. Ticknor, a partner in James R. Osgood & Company of Boston, explained the provenance of the volume in a handwritten note on its front flyleaf, listing the pages that Twain annotated. She added a similar note on the rear flyleaf, attesting that the words "Annotated by Mark Twain" at the top of the same flyleaf were "made by/Benjamin H. Ticknor/to whom 'Mark Twain'/sent the book."

Marginalia: Caroline Ticknor twice revealed to the public some of Mark Twain's several dozen penciled notes ("'Mark Twain's' Missing Chapter," *The Bookman: A Magazine of Literature and Life* 39 [May 1914]: 298–309; and Chapter 10 of her *Glimpses of Authors* [Boston: Houghton Mifflin Co., 1922], pp. 132–151). She did this in the course of publishing Chapter 48 from Twain's manuscript for *Life on the Mississippi* (1883), which she labeled "The Suppressed Chapter" (a misnomer that would prevail thereafter) and disclosing Twain's proof revisions. She quoted Twain's marginalia from the copy of Trollope's *Domestic Manners of the Americans* that Twain marked and sent to James R. Osgood & Company for quotations to be used in *Life on the Mississippi* and which in 1914 still remained in Ticknor's library. Until this volume eventually became available to scholars, Caroline Ticknor's transcription provided our only glimpse of Twain's comments.

Caroline Ticknor quoted Twain's comments without citing page numbers, but these can be added now that the book itself has surfaced. Trollope acknowledged that she was surprised to encounter a milliner who was highly valued in society, but resolved on page 30 not to surmise that this was necessarily a "national" trait; Twain noted, writing vertically, "She is very fair & thoughtful." Where Trollope on page 34 describes the Memphis-bound *Belvidere*, a Mississippi steamboat with worn carpets in her cabin, Twain quipped at the foot of the page: "This is the boat I saw." (His description in Notebook 21 of the steamboat *Fannie Tatum*, which he tried to board in 1882 in St. Louis—"This boat built by Fulton; has not been repaired since" [*N&J* 2: 523]—accords with her comment that the condition of its carpet "requires the pen of Swift to do it justice.") He also marked on page 34 her reference to the "incessant, remorseless spitting of Americans." Regarding the uncouth table manners of the boat passengers, Twain conceded at the top of page 37: "This was still true in a large/measure, 25 yrs ago." On that same page he made heavy vertical lines at her account of "the graceful and luxuriant palmetto" and other tropical-looking plants above New Orleans. On page 38 he marked and noted "Natchez" at her vivid description of that vicinity. "Copy," Twain wrote on a page he marked on page 39 about the depredations of enormous man-eating crocodiles. On page 41 he wrote "Memphis" at the top of the page and drew vertical marks alongside the account of her experiences there. At her description of an island covered with tall trees near Memphis, he noted "Island gone, now" on page 42 and drew long vertical marks along most of the page. At the top of page 49 he wrote "Cincinnati" and marked the first paragraph where she praised its appearance. He marked a passage on page 56 concerning "the total and universal want of manners, both in males and females." Twain declared, "She hit it" on page 57 at her assertion that Americans lacked refinement. On page 60 he marked a passage about the crudity of American life (and death). In Ohio, Trollope observed on page 61, there is great difficulty in "getting servants, or, as it is called in that region, 'getting help,'" which Twain called "A fair shot!" Trollope claimed great fidelity in transcribing conversations on page 62, to which Twain added a vertical comment: "But your memory was wo[e]fully defective, as to details." Twain drew a vertical line at Trollope's complaint on page 63 about how unreasonably a female maid in Cincinnati treated her by leaving her employment despite "very high wages" and "several expensive articles of dress." Her chronicle of dismal dinner parties in Cincinnati on page 66 apparently reminded Twain of his Western years; he wrote vertically, "Ball at Jackass Gulch." He marked and made a note—"True then, no doubt, but the thing is reversed now"—about the wretched fruit available in Cincinnati. "This is changed, too," Twain noted at the foot of page 72 where Trollope discussed the crowd attracted by the sensation of hearing a learned female lecturer. On page 73 Trollope lamented Thomas Jefferson's hypocrisy in owing slaves and repeated the rumor that he had fathered children by enslaved females; Twain admitted, "It is within/the pos/sibilities/at any/rate." Her detailed account on page 78 of a preacher's hell-and-brimstone sermon caused Twain to write "Talmage" vertically in the margin. Her rendition on page 79 of the preacher's exhortations resemble the camp-meeting call for conversion in Chapter 20 of Twain's *Adventures of Huckleberry Finn* (1885): "We will clear the bench for anxious sinners to sit upon. Come, then! come to the anxious bench, and we will show you Jesus! Come! Come! Come! . . . Young girls arose. . . . Several came tottering out, their hands clasped, their heads hanging on their bosoms, and every limb trembling, and still the hymn went on; but as the poor creatures approached the rail their sobs and groans became audible." Twain made a vertical pencil mark beside that excited scene. On page 94 he marked her observation about the frequency with which the term "woman" was employed. "Changed,/now" Twain wrote near her description on page 95 of the Americans' casualness about dropping by unannounced for a social call and their vulgar parlor manners. However, on page 98 he admitted that her conclusion that in the United States "freedom . . . is enjoyed solely by the disorderly at the expense of the orderly" was "True yet." She asserted on page 99 that it was essential to belong to one of "an almost endless variety of religious factions" in order "to be well received in society," but Twain wrote that this requirement had "Changed."

Chapter 31, titled "Reception of Captain Basil Hall's Book in the United States" (pages 282–291), Twain marked very heavily for insertion in *Life on the Mississippi*, giving the publisher instructions for deleting certain passages and including others in "Appendix C." He wrote "A change coming?" next to a passage he omitted on page 286 in which Trollope lauded the Church of England as protection against "fanatic superstition on one side, and the still more dreadful inroads of infidelity on the other." On page 291 he marked with heavy triple brackets her statement that "it may, perhaps, be long before any justice is done to Capt. Hall's book in the United States," but eventually he drew vertical lines through that passage to signify that it should not be copied. He made a note at the foot of page 321 about the length and locations of Trollope's visit. At the foot of page 322 he made a retaliatory rejoinder after her comment that "the original stock of the white population now inhabiting the United States were persons who had banished themselves, or were banished from the mother country"; Twain wrote, "Mrs. T. then married a French *valet*." (Twain was mistaken here; perhaps he was thinking of Auguste Hervieu, 1794–1858, the French drawing teacher and artist who devotedly accompanied Trollope and her children to the United States and illustrated many of her works.) Twain jotted approving notes beside Trollope's concluding statement, "In all my travels, both among heathen and among Christians, I have never

encountered any people by whom I found it so difficult to make myself understood as by the Americans." Twain's notes suggest that he annotated Trollope's book following his trip to the Mississippi River in April and May of 1882.

Location: Arents Collections, Rare Books and Manuscripts Division, New York Public Library.

Copy examined: photocopy of the title page and marginalia provided on 8 May 1984 by the then-Curator of the Arents Collections to the Mark Twain Papers, Bancroft Library, University of California at Berkeley. I made notes from the photocopy in August 1984.

In response to a request from Mark Twain, W. Rowlands replied for publisher James R. Osgood on 22 July 1882 that he was sending "a lot of books relating to travel in the U. S. by English people in the first half of the century; twenty-five volumes in all. They include Mrs. Trollope, Basil Hall and Marryatt [sic], &c, &c." (ALS in MTP; partially published in *MTLP*, ed. Hamlin Hill, 1967], p. 158 n. 2). In Chapter 27 of *Life on the Mississippi* (1883) Twain quoted Mrs. Trollope's initial impression as she approached the mouth of the Mississippi, where "its muddy mass of waters" mingled "with the deep blue of the Mexican Gulf. I never beheld a scene so utterly desolate." Twain concludes Chapter 29 with a picture drawn by the "once renowned and vigorously hated Mrs. Trollope" of hotel patrons in Memphis gobbling their victuals. Twain originally intended to follow this with another chapter based on her visit to Cincinnati; there he would have defended her views as those of "a humane spirit against inhumanities; of an honest nature against humbug; of a clean breeding against grossness; of a right heart against unright speech and deed" (Heritage Press edition [1944], p. 392). He was impressed by the fact that "she lived three years in this civilization of ours; in the body of it—not on the surface of it."

Blair, *MT&HF* (1960), pp. 293, 296; Ganzel, "Twain, Travel Books" (1962), p. 41 n. 4; Guy A. Cardwell, "Mark Twain, James R. Osgood, and Those 'Suppressed' Passages," *NEQ* 46.2 (June 1973), 163–188; Horst H. Kruse, *Mark Twain and Life on the Mississippi* (Amherst: University of Massachusetts Press, 1982); Gretchen M. Beidler, "Huck Finn as Tourist: Mark Twain's Parody Travelogue," *Studies in American Fiction* 20.2 (Autumn 1992): 155–167; and Barbara Ladd, "'Night after Night and Day after Day': Mark Twain and the Natural World," *Mark Twain Annual 17* (2019): 19.

TROLLOPE, THOMAS ADOLPHUS (1810–1892). *A History of the Commonwealth of Florence, from the Earliest Independence of the Commune to the Fall of the Republic in 1531.* 4 vols. London: Chapman and Hall, 1865.

In March 1882 Clemens entered in his pocket-notebook: "A History of the Florentine Commonwealth—A. Trollope" (NB 20, *N&J* 2: 452). Thomas Trollope, the older brother of Anthony, settled in Florence and wrote this book, as he announced in its introduction, to justify naming Florence "the future capital of Italy" (1: v). Trollope dutifully chronicled the sufferings of an ancient city and the many wrongs perpetrated by its rulers, but he retained a nineteenth-century progressivist faith that "amelioration *is* the universal law" of history (4: 554).

TROUBETZKOY, (PRINCESS) AMÉLIE (RIVES) CHANLER

(1863–1945), pen name "Amélie Rives." *A Brother to the Dragons, and Other Old-Time Tales.* New York: Harper & Brothers, 1888. 230 pp.

Olivia Clemens wrote a note that accompanied Clemens's letter to Frederick J. Hall of 1 June 1894; she requested Amélie Rives' *Brother to the Dragons* and two other books for Christmas gifts (Philip C. Duschnes, Catalog No. 30 [June 1938], item #143). Princess Troubetzkoi would be one of the guests at Mark Twain's Seventieth Birthday Dinner in 1905 at Delmonico's in New York City. At a supper and ball at Sherry's, Clemens realized that the wife of "Prince Troubetskoi" [*sic*] was "Amélie Rives, the poet" (19 February 1908 AD, *AutoMT* 3: 210). Following a scandalous divorce, she had married Prince Pierre Troubetzkoy (1864–1936), a painter and a member of the Russian royal family. She was not only a social celebrity but also a novelist, poet, and playwright.

———. *Seléné.* New York: Harper & Brothers, 1905. 89 pp. [A poem.]

Source: MTLAcc, entry #2139, volume donated from Clemens's library by Clara Clemens Gabrilowitsch in 1910.

———. *Trix and Over-the-Moon.* Illustrated by F[rank]. Walter Taylor (1874–1921). First edition. Quarter cloth and pictorial boards, lettered in argent and gilt. New York: Harper & Brothers, 1909. 165 pp.

Inscription: the front pastedown endpaper is signed in black ink: "S L. Clemens/1909/Stormfield, October."

Provenance: shelfmark of Clara Clemens Gabrilowitsch's private library in Detroit. Donated to the Carrie Estelle Doheny Collection, St. John's Seminary, Camarillo, California, by Mrs. Doheny after she purchased the volume in 1940 from Maxwell Hunley Rare Books, Beverly Hills, California, for $12.20. Auctioned by Christie's on 17 October 1988 (lot 1184) with two other titles for $2,040 on behalf of St. John's Seminary. Subsequently in the collection of Nick Karanovich, Fort Wayne, Indiana.

Catalog: *Sotheby's 2003*, #221, $9,500 (sold with four other literature titles).

Location: collection of Kevin Mac Donnell, Austin, Texas.

Copy examined: Clemens's copy, unmarked, in July 2004. The last pages are uncut.

———. *Virginia of Virginia, A Story.* Illus. New York: Harper & Brothers, 1901. 222 pp.

Source: MTLAcc, entry #1656, volume donated by Clemens.

The author of this novel had been born in Richmond, Virginia, and though she lived for a time with her first husband in New York City she would eventually return to the state where her family was prominent. Her portrayals of strong women with erotic impulses were considered daring for the time, *The Quick or the Dead?* (1888) being perhaps her most controversial novel.

TROWBRIDGE, JOHN TOWNSEND (1827–1916). *The Book of Gold, and Other Poems.* Illus. New York: Harper & Brothers, 1878. 81 pp.

Source: MTLAcc, entry #621, volume donated by Clemens.

Trowbridge was associated with the magazine *Our Young Folks* from 1865 until 1873, the last three years as its editor. Subsequently he became a prolific novelist, writer, and poet. In June 1908 Clemens would greet Trowbridge at the Thomas Bailey Aldrich Memorial Museum in Portsmouth, New Hampshire, by saying, "Trowbridge, are you still alive? You must be a thousand years old. Why, I listened to your stories while I was being rocked in the cradle" (*MTB*, p. 1456).

———. *Cudjo's Cave.* Boston: J. E. Tilton and Co., 1864. 504 pp.

David E. E. Sloane illustrated how Twain quite likely borrowed from this antislavery novel for young adults in depicting Pap Finn's rants about enslaved African Americans ("Some Twain Sources and How They Affected His Sense of Self," *American Literary Realism* 45.1 [Fall 2012]: 49–59).

———. *The Emigrant's Story, and Other Poems.* Boston: James R. Osgood and Co., 1875. 173 pp.

Inscriptions: signed in pencil on the second flyleaf, "Saml. L. Clemens/Hartford 1875." The front free endpaper bears the initials "A. M. '27"—i. e., Arthur Milliken 1927 (see below).

Catalogs: *A1911*, "12mo, cloth, Bost. 1875," quotes the signature, lot 462, sold for $1.75; George D. Smith, New York City, "Catalogue of Books" (1911), quotes the signature, item #452, $7.50.

Provenance: formerly in the collection of Arthur Milliken, the longtime headmaster of the Westminster School for Boys in Simsbury, Connecticut.

Location: Mark Twain House and Museum, Hartford, Connecticut. Donated by the son of Arthur Milliken on 10 December 1982.

Copy examined: photocopies of the front pastedown endpaper, flyleaf, and title page were supplied by Margaret S. Cheney, then Museum Coordinator, on 10 December 1982, and another set of the photocopies was provided by Diana Royce, then Librarian of the Stowe-Day Memorial Library, on 3 October 1984. No marginalia were visible when I had the opportunity to examine the book itself in August 1987. An *A1911* auction label is affixed to the front pastedown endpaper. Above that label is pasted a New Year's Eve Reservation card for "Mr. S. L." for a party of "16" at "Table No. 41" at the Elks Club, West Forty-third Street, New York City.

———. *Neighbor Jackwood.* Boston: J. E. Tilton and Co., 1865. 414 pp.

Inscription: front flyleaf signed in pencil, "Charles J. Langdon/1865". [Charles (1849–1916) was Olivia Clemens's brother.]

Provenance: bookplate #558 of the "J. Langdon Family Library."

Catalog: Ball 2016 inventory, brown textured cloth, gilt lettering on the spine, J. Langdon Family Library bookplate No. 558, fair condition.

Location: Quarry Farm library shelves, under the supervision of the Mark Twain Archive, Elmira College, Elmira, New York.

Copy examined: a book to which Clemens had access whenever he visited the Langdon residence in Elmira. Examined on 26 May 2015.

In *Neighbor Jackwood*, an adult anti-slavery novel first published in 1856, a fugitive enslaved young woman named Camille finds romantic love but remains in danger of recapture. Her husband eventually must purchase her from her master. Trowbridge also turned the novel into a play.

———. *My Own Story, with Recollections of Noted Persons.* Illus. Boston: Houghton, Mifflin and Co., The Riverside Press, 1903. 482 pp.

Catalogs: QF Martinez, "Good plus condition"; Ball 2016 inventory, green cloth, gilt letter, gilt top edges.

Location: Quarry Farm library shelves, under the supervision of the Mark Twain Archive, Elmira College, Elmira, New York.

Clemens had access to this autobiography at Quarry Farm after 1903.

———. *The Vagabonds, and Other Poems.* Boston: Fields, Osgood and Co., 1869. 172 pp. [Collects the humorous poem "Darius Green and His Flying Machine," published in 1867.]

When Mark Twain began a list of humorists in July 1880 for a projected anthology, he included, "Trowbridge—Darius Green" (NB 19, *N&J* 2: 361). *Mark Twain's Library of Humor* (1888) would contain "Darius Green and His Flying Machine," credited to Trowbridge's *The Vagabonds, and Other Poems.*

Trow's Business Directory of Greater New York. New York: Trow Directory, Printing, & Bookbinding Co., [published annually].

In 1885 and 1889 Clemens assumed that John Fowler Trow's publishing firm would be interested in James W. Paige's typesetter (NB 25, *N&J* 3: 187, 189, 199; NB 29, *N&J* 3: 508). "Get a N.Y. Directory through B. & Gross [Hartford booksellers], or Chly [Webster]," Clemens noted in October 1887 (NB 27, *N&J* 3: 335).

TRUMBULL, ANNIE ELIOT (1857–1949), pseud. "Annie Eliot." *Haman: A Tragedy.* Paper wrapper. Hartford, Connecticut: Lockwood & Brainard, 1907. 63 pp.

Marginalia: Clemens marked the text in black ink in six places. Page 31 is folded over.

Location: Mark Twain Papers, Bancroft Library, University of California at Berkeley.

Copy examined: Clemens's copy.

Trumbull was a Hartford author and friend. "Do you think you love me well enough to read a tragedy in blank verse?, . . . That is what Doctors of Letters are *for*—to read tragedies in blank verse written by their intimate friends," she wrote to Clemens on 11 August 1907 (MTP). Isabel Lyon's notes on Trumbull's letter indicate the gist of Clemens's reply: "'Not competent to sit in judgment on a printed tragedy [.] Would have to see it on the stage, but glad she let me read it,' and he finds poetry all through. Good poetry—fine poetry—& some he read to me." Annie Trumbull had written a memorial poem to Susy Clemens (SLC to Franklin G. Whitmore, London, 14 September 1896, MTHM). Trumbull stayed the weekend of 17–20 May 1902 at Riverdale with the Clemenses (OLC's Diary, DV161, MTP). On 9 December 1905 Clemens wrote to her from 21 Fifth Avenue: "I thank you most cordially for that fine and strong poem *now*—I was so irretrievably dull & weary & muddy-headed the other night that I couldn't, then" (MTHM).

———. *An Hour's Promise.* New York: Cassell & Co., 1889. 265 pp. Paperbound.

Source: MTLAcc, entry #126, volume donated by Clemens. Trumbull addressed the discouraging situation experienced by many African Americans in this novel.

———. *Life's Common Way.* First edition. New York: A. S.

Barnes and Co., 1903. 420 pp. [Edition conjectured as the most likely one.]

Catalog: ListABP (1910), "Life's Common Way, Trumbull", no other information provided.

———. "Mary A. Twining," *Home-Maker: An Illustrated Monthly Magazine* 1.3 (December 1888): 168–175.

In January 1889 Clemens noted, "Magazine edited by Marion Harland [the pseudonym of Mary Virginia (Hawes) Terhune, 1830–1922], contains something by Annie Trumbull" (NB 28, *N&J* 3: 440). Trumbull's sketch pondered a young woman's journal from the 1770s. If Clemens found his way to this issue of the short-lived *Home-Maker* (1888–1890), he might have noticed that an article titled "A Boy's Library" by [Catherine Pickens] Kate Upson Clark (1851–1935) recommended that "Mark Twain's delightful *The Prince and the Pauper*" should be included in the ideal collection of books for young men (p. 221).

———. *A Masque of Culture.* Second edition. Hartford, Connecticut: Case, Lockwood & Brainard Co., 1894. 54 pp.

In an undated letter written from the Players Club in New York City, Clemens promised an unidentified woman (presumably Annie Trumbull) that he would attend her play on 10 January 1894: "I'll be occupying that reserved seat when the curtain goes up" (ASSSCL). This was a production by the Saturday Morning Club of Hartford. On 11 January 1894 Clemens wrote to Olivia Clemens from Hartford: "I saw Annie's play, last night, & it was just as cute & delightful as its large merit & my partiality could make it"; he mentioned the roles of Confucius and "old Socrates," Lady Jane Grey, Zenobia, Cassandra, Hypatia, and Gertrude (TS in MTP).

LLMT, p. 291; *S&MT,* p. 345.

———. *The Wheel of Progress* (play, published in 1897).

On 4 February 1899 Clemens wrote to Joseph H. Twichell from Vienna: "Annie Trumbull's a duck—she does certainly turn out the cunningest and sparklingest dialogue of anybody I know. The play cost me a day's work, for I lay abed till into the afternoon reading it; but no matter, it paid" (*LMTJHT,* p. 229). The lighthearted nature of this play is suggested by the newspaper review of an amateur production staged by the juniors and seniors of the Brooklyn Heights Seminary on 30 April 1898. Its dialogue "sparkled with wit." The cast of characters included Cleopatra, Boadicea [queen of the ancient Britons], Joan of Arc, Queen Elizabeth, the Goddess of Liberty, and a spiritual medium. "They go to a cycle [bicycle] academy and after their first ride emerge with crowns battered, trains torn and looking generally demolished," the reviewer explained. "At the conclusion of the play the appearance of the Goddess of Liberty evoked a burst of patriotism, the audience joining in by rising and singing 'America'" (Brooklyn *Daily Eagle,* 1 May 1898, p. 13).

———. *White Birches. A Novel.* New York: Harper & Brothers, 1893. 356 pp.

Complicated romantic games ensue among residents and visitors in a rural village near Shadow Pond in Trumbull's *White Birches.* Before leaving on a sea voyage, Clemens wrote to William Dean Howells from New York City on 12 May 1893 about the complimentary copy he received from J. Hammond Trumbull's daughter: "Annie Trumbull has sent me her book" (*MTHL*, pp. 652–653). In New York City in 1893 Clemens made a memorandum, "*Friday, Dec. 15*, Annie Trumbull" (NB 33, TS p. 40).

TRUMBULL, JAMES HAMMOND (1821–1897), ed. *The Memorial History of Hartford County Connecticut 1633–1884. Projected by Clarence F[rederick]. Jewett [1852–1909]*. 2 volumes. Illus., map. Boston: Edward L. Osgood, Publisher, 1886. [Preface is dated June 1886.]

In October 1886 Clemens wrote "Hist Hartford" in Notebook 26 (*N&J* 3L 259). On 14 December 1886 the publisher Edward L. Osgood wrote to Clemens from Hartford to apologize for the delay in sending a copy of Trumbull's *Memorial History of Hartford County Connecticut* to the English historian William Smith as Clemens had directed ("Literary Miscellany," Catalog 280, William Reese Company, New Haven, Connecticut, ALS, item #83). Volume I of Trumbull's book treated the history of Hartford county and the city of Hartford; Volume II described the history of other towns in the county. Each chapter was prepared by a different author. Trumbull was the President of the Connecticut Historical Society.

In 1885 George Parsons Lathrop (1851–1898) reported that Trumbull and Clemens were among the guests who would often while away a winter evening at the home of Charles Dudley Warner ("A Model State Capital," *Harper's Monthly Magazine* 71.425 [October 1885]: 726).

_____, ed. *The True-Blue Laws of Connecticut and New Haven and the False Blue-Laws Invented by the Rev. Samuel Peters [1735–1826], to Which Are Added Specimens of the Laws and Judicial Proceedings of Other Colonies and Some Blue-Laws of England in the Reign of James I*. Hartford, Connecticut: American Publishing Co., 1876. 360 pp.

Inscription: signed, "Saml. L. Clemens/Hartford 1877".

Marginalia: Profusely marked and annotated by Clemens with vertical marks, brackets, underlinings, and a few unusual diagonal hook-like marks—all apparently made in pencil. The Mark Twain Papers in the Bancroft Library at the University of California at Berkeley contain photocopies of fifty-nine pages with Clemens's marginalia. On page 14, for example, Clemens noted: "a tramp's second offense was death, up to Anne's time." Of court records from 1636 reproduced on page 143, Clemens, writing vertically in the margin, quipped: "As for culture, Josh Billings could/spell all around them & give them points." In a section devoted to "Religion" on page 332, Clemens wrote vertically: "Evidently the law <en> empowered magistrates to marry people, & then fined them for doing it." Regarding Thomas Morton's 1630 sentence to have his house burned and some of his goods given to the Native Americans "for many wrongs hee hath done them," Clemens marked the passage on page 333 and noted, "Served him right." Clemens declared the fine and threat of whipping imposed on a man named Nicholas Knopp for a worthless patent medicine ("a water of noo worth nor value, which he solde att a very deare rate") to be "Good" (p. 334). He marked two other cases on that page and referred back to page 332 in a note. He marked page 336 heavily and wrote vertically, "This partly explains the low price/of tobacco in Virginia. P. 329—2d paragraph." He commented on page 342: "A repealed law still in force."

Catalog: ListABP (1910), "Blue Laws, True and False,

Trumbull", no other information provided.

Location: Detroit Public Library, Detroit, Michigan.

Copy examined: photocopies of Clemens's signature and marginalia (MTP).

Hartford antiquarian and librarian J. Hammond Trumbull supplied the multi-language chapter epigraphs for *The Gilded Age* (1873). Mark Twain based events in Chapters 15, 23, and 27 of *The Prince and the Pauper* (1881) on facts he obtained from Trumbull's *True-Blue Laws of Connecticut and New Haven*, according to Twain's citations; in addition, he added a "General Note" to *The Prince and the Pauper* documenting the relative mildness of Connecticut Blue-Laws when measured against the severity of penal codes in England at the time, and he referred the reader to Trumbull's book for proof. In a projected appendix Twain assembled for *A Connecticut Yankee in King Arthur's Court* (1889), he cited "Blue Laws" as his source for "Boil in Oil" (NB 29, *N&J* 3: 506).

Dickinson, "Sources of *The Prince and the Pauper*" (1949), pp. 103–106; Stone, *IE* (1961), p. 112; Williams, "Use of History" (1965), p. 105; Baetzhold, *MT&JB* (1970), pp. 52–53; and Gregg Camfield, "History," *Mark Twain in Context*, ed. John Bird (Cambridge, England: Cambridge University Press, 2020), pp. 256–257.

Truth: A Weekly Journal (London periodical, published 1877–1957).

Henry Fisher testified that Clemens told him in Berlin, probably in 1891, that he approved of the editor of *Truth*, Henry DuPré Labouchère, because he was a member of the nobility by birth who nonetheless detested the institution of nobility (*AMT*, pp. 140–141). In 1894 Poultney Bigelow sent Clemens "a copy of 'Truth' for April 5 with the article 'Notes from Paris' marked" where it mentioned Clemens (SLC to OLC, New York City, 15 April 1894, MTP). Clemens made a note regarding the English penal system in October 1895: "Now quote from the present Pillory of *Truth*" (NB 35, TS p. 57). After Clemens wrote about Australian penal atrocities in Notebook 34, he added on 2 November 1895: "The *spirit* of the old brutalities remains in England, where they still punish poaching heavier than brutal wife-beating. (Insert from 'Pillory.')" (TS p. 25). Sailing toward Ceylon on New Year's Day, 1896, Clemens took time to note: "Truth, Nov. 14 '95, contains a clear statement of the unfair treatment of Surgeon Lea of the Navy by the Admiralty" (NB 36, TS p. 14). The court martial of Dr. Francis J. Lea on 30 April 1895 had drawn much interest in medical circles. Dr. Lea, concluding that S. A. Johnson, Captain of H. M. S. *Ringarooma*, was "mentally deranged and unfit for duty," attempted to place the captain on the sick list and remove him from command. Despite twelve years of unblemished service in Her Majesty's Navy, Surgeon Lea was subsequently dismissed from service on the grounds of "insubordination and contempt." "Get bound vols. of 'Truth,'" Clemens wrote on 18 June 1896 in Port Elizabeth, South Africa (NB 38, TS p. 49). See also the Catalog entry for Henry DuPré Labouchère.

The Truth Seeker (reform magazine, 1873–present).

During Mark Twain's lifetime this controversial periodical was published in New York City (in the mid-twentieth century its editorial office moved to San Diego, California).

The Truth Seeker has long claimed Mark Twain as one of its subscribers, and George E. Macdonald (1857–1944), who edited the magazine from 1908 until 1937, asserted that Twain had renewed his subscription in 1910 (*Fifty Years of Freethought; Being the History of "The Truth Seeker," with the Natural History of Its Third Editor.* 2 vols. [New York: The Truth Seeker Co., 1929]: 2: 361–362). *The Truth Seeker* championed many intellectual figures and social movements, including Robert G. Ingersoll (especially), Thomas Paine, women's rights, secularist objections to Christian assumptions, and Darwin's evolutionary theories. See also the Catalog entry for Benjamin Franklin Underwood.

TUCKER, MARY ELIZA (PERINE), LATER LAMBERT (1838–1896). *Life of Mark M. Pomeroy ("Brick" Pomeroy, Editor of the Lacrosse, Wis., Democrat, and of the Democrat, Daily, New York City), A Representative Young Man of America: His Early History, Character, and Public Services in Defence of the Rights of States, Rights of the People, and Interests of Working Men. Prepared from Materials Furnished by Mr. Pomeroy and Others, by Mary E. Tucker.* Portrait. New York: G. W. Carleton, 1868. 230 pp.

If Clemens read the articles written by Frank M. Thorn and signed "Carl Byng" in the Buffalo *Express*, then he would have seen Tucker's biography mentioned in "That Book Agent," Buffalo *Express*, 7 January 1871. Marcus Mills ("Brick") Pomeroy (1833–1896) wrote numerous books for Carleton's firm, including *Nonsense; or, Hits on the Follies of the Day* (1868). Following her divorce from John M. Tucker, Mary Eliza Tucker would marry a close friend of Pomeroy, Colonel Charles H. Lambert.

TUCKERMAN, HENRY THEODORE (1813–1871) *The Criterion; or, The Test of Talk about Familiar Things. A Series of Essays.* Boston: Hurd and Houghton, 1866. 377 pp.

Source: MTLAcc, entry #532, volume donated by Clemens. Tuckerman gave his readers a dozen musing essays on random topics such as "Holidays," "Lawyers," "Authors" (mostly humorous in treatment, mostly laudatory of the classic English writers and mocking of their upstart imitators), "Newspapers," "Preachers," "Actors," and "Inns" (the latter of which he complained were becoming obsolete).

———. "The Old Bankers of Florence," *Atlantic Monthly* 24.145 (November 1869): 629–636.

Roger Salomon (*Twain and the Image of History* [1961], p. 111 n. 9) traced two references in Twain's tentative appendixes prepared for *A Connecticut Yankee* (NB 29, N&J 3: 503, 506) to this Tuckerman article.

TUCKEY, JANET. *Joan of Arc, "The Maid."* The New Plutarch Series: Lives of Men and Women of Action. London: Marcus Ward & Co., 1880. 224 pp.

Marginalia: numerous notes and marks in black ink occur on pages 14 and 28–34 only; profuse penciled notes and marks are scattered throughout the volume. Essentially Clemens's annotations indexed the events of Joan's life. On page 14 he wrote at the top of the page (in black ink): "What was left of France". Page 126 bears a typical note in pencil, "Here is that villain priest." On page 160 he penciled, "The dress-trap again." Other notes and markings abound.

Catalogs: ListABP (1910), "Joan of Arc, Tuckey"; "Retz Appraisal" (1944), page 11, valued at $20.

Location: Mark Twain Papers, Bancroft Library, University of California at Berkeley.

Copy examined: Clemens's copy.

In 1892 Andrew Chatto sent Mark Twain a copy of "Mr. [*sic*] Tuckey's life in the new Plutarch series" (Welland, *Mark Twain in England* [1978], p. 158). The Mark Twain Papers at Berkeley in the Bancroft Library contain a copy of a six-book bibliography for Joan of Arc (the original document is not in Twain's hand) that Chatto & Windus prepared, probably at Twain's request; the list included Tuckey's "Joan of Arc. Popular based Quicherat New Plutarch Series. M. Ward 2/6" (Box 36, no. 6, MTP; MS notes then in the collection of Barry Bingham, Sr., Louisville, Kentucky). Albert Bigelow Paine stated that Tuckey's work was "apparently the first book he read with the definite idea of study" (*MTB* [1912], p. 958). Twain listed Tuckey's *Joan of Arc* among the "authorities examined" for his *Joan of Arc* (1896)—see the page preceding his "Translator's Preface."

Stone, "MT's *Joan of Arc*" (1959), p. 9; Stone, *IE* (1961), pp. 212–213. See especially Ronald Jenn and Linda A. Morris, "The Sources of Mark Twain's *Personal Recollections of Joan of Arc*," *Mark Twain Journal* 55.1–2 (Spring/Fall 2017): 55–74.

TUDOR, HENRY (1846–1913). *The Ghost of Kisheneff and Other Poems.* First edition. 12mo. Cloth. [Shrewsbury, Missouri: Camelot,] 1905. 100 pp. The title page identified Henry Tudor as employed in the "Mo. Pacific Central Offices—Gould System." He dedicated the book to his son, Henry Plantagenet Tudor.

Inscription: inscribed in ink underneath a portrait of the poet, "To dear/Mark Twain,/with the gratitude of nearly half a/century—all the sounder for growing old/in battle--/Henry Tudor/Christmas 1905."

Provenance: formerly in the Mark Twain Library, Redding, Connecticut. Donated to that community library from Clemens's personal library by Clara Clemens Gabrilowitsch in 1910 (MTLAcc, entry #2140).

Catalogs: *Mott 1952*, item #88, $17.50; Edward S. Mott, Sale catalog No. 166 [1957?], item 73, $37.50.

Location: Colson Hall Library, West Virginia Library, Morgantown, West Virginia.

Copy examined: photocopies of the front endpaper, frontispiece, and title page were sent to Alan Gribben by Thomas A. Tenney in September 1981. Displays the oval stamp of the Mark Twain Library at Redding, Connecticut on the front endpaper.

Newspapers of the period report that Tudor was called the Oliver Goldsmith of St. Louis. After each workday he went home from his position in the freight claim office of the Missouri Pacific Railroad to Shrewsbury Park, a St. Louis suburb, where his wife and five children lived in the large house he had named Camelot Cottage. *The Ghost of Kisheneff and Other Poems* collected twenty-five of his poems. Many were religious in theme, and a number had pacifist messages such as "The Rage of the King Bell" that he dated 2 January 1905: "The poet listened, with lute unstrung,/Eager to hear what words of fear/Should sum up the scroll of the dying year,/What wrathful edicts the king bell sung" (p. 85). Somehow Tudor's amateur versifying escaped Clemens's ridiculed "Library of Literary Hogwash."

TUER, ANDREW WHITE (1838–1900). *The Follies and Fashions of Our Grandfathers.* Illus. London: Field & Tuer, 1887. 366 pp. [Publisher and pages conjectured.]

Catalog: *A1911*, "8vo, half leather, Lond. 1887," with a sheet of Clemens's notes laid in, lot 463, sold for $6.

Follies and Fashions of Our Grandfathers is a digest of material from magazines flourishing in 1807. Tuer was a London publisher and writer.

———. *Old London Street Cries and the Cries of To-Day, with Heaps of Quaint Cuts.* London: Field & Tuer, Printed at the Leadenhall Press, 1885. 137 pp.

Twice in 1887 Clemens entered the title "The Old London Street" in Notebook 26 (*N&J* 3: 280, 281), and Tuer's book seems the most likely reference. A New York reprint of Tuer's book was "Published for The Old London Street Company, 728 Broadway, 1887"; possibly this was the edition that caught Clemens's attention.

TUFTS, WILLIAM WHITTEMORE (1832–1901). *A Market for an Impulse. A Novel.* Boston: Arena Publishing Co., 1895. 234 pp.

Inscription: the top of the title page is inscribed in brown ink, "Samuel L. Clemens, Esq/with the compliments of/William Whittemore Tufts"; at the bottom of the title page, in the same ink and the same hand, appears "p. 205". (Page 205 of the novel mentioned Mark Twain.) A bookplate on the front pastedown endpaper identifies the George Buell Aloord Collection.

Location: Beinecke Rare Book and Manuscript Library, Yale University.

Copy examined: Clemens's copy, unmarked, in 1970.

Tufts' love story is set in the New England town of Skye. On page 205 a sophisticated character with the name of Mollestone remarks, "So, when I am not impelled, I read L'Allegro, Twain, Kipling, Harte, and the rest."

TUPPER, MARTIN FARQUHAR (1810–1889). *Proverbial Philosophy: A Book of Thoughts and Arguments, Originally Treated.* First Series. New York: Wiley & Putnam, 1847. 154 pp.

Catalogs: inventory list of the Langdon family library books compiled by Mark Woodhouse, then the Archivist, in 2013; Ball 2016 inventory, red cloth, gilt lettering, J. Langdon Family Library No. 86.

Location: Quarry Farm library shelves, under the supervision of the Mark Twain Archive, Elmira College, Elmira, New York.

Clemens had access to the Langdons' collection of books whenever he visited their home in Elmira.

Tupper's moralizing verse without rhyme or meter was initially published in 1838 with a Second Series issuing in 1842. In a sketch of 6 May 1865 for *The Californian*, Mark Twain alludes to "a neat remark which the editor of *Harper's Magazine* made three years ago. . . . 'Don't poor Martin Farquhar Tupper fondle his platitudes and think they are poems?'" (*SSix*, p. 172). A "literary connoisseur," Twain advised, may safely assign "all the harmless old platitudes, delivered with a stately and oppressive pretense of originality, to Tupper" (*The Californian*, 17 June 1865; *LAMT*, p. 142; *ET&S* 2: 195). Naturally, Twain recorded, the earnest passengers brought "Tupper's Poems" aboard the *Quaker City* (*Daily Alta California*, 5 April 1868, *TIA*, p. 303). Twain's marginalia in Chapter 12 of Oliver Wendell Holmes's *Autocrat of the Breakfast-Table* (p. 361) noted in 1869 that the handwritten inscription

on a copy of "Tupper's Poems" is "splendid" (Bradford A. Booth, "MT's Comments on Holmes's *Autocrat*" [1950], p. 463). In Chapter 33 of *The Gilded Age* (1873), a dog has the name Martin Farquhar Tupper—a lapdog that "was sickly, and died young, but he was the sweetest disposition." Laura Hawkins complains in Chapter 36 of *The Gilded Age* that ignorant peanut boys in the railway cars often try to sell one "Tupper or a dictionary or T. S. Arthur if you are fond of poetry." Clemens remarked to William Dean Howells in a letter written in Hartford on 15 January 1875: "I have noticed that a little judicious profanity helps out an otherwise ineffectual sketch or poem remarkably. I attribute the feebleness of many of Tupper's noblest efforts to the lack of this element" (*MTHL*, p. 59; *MTLet* 6: 350). In November 1881 Clemens joked in Montreal about Tupper's bromides: "Tupper called in England Solomon-&-Water. <Brandy & soda.>" (NB 19, *N&J* 2: 408). In *Life on the Mississippi* (1883), Mark Twain remembered that "The House Beautiful" of ante-bellum days contained "Tupper, much penciled" on its parlor table (Ch. 38). In Chapter 3 of *Following the Equator* (1897), Twain recalled that in the 1860s Tupper's *Proverbial Philosophy* was one of the "books of a tranquil sort" invariably lying on the center table of a well-appointed parlor in "the Honolulu of my time."

———. *Washington: A Drama, in Five Acts.* New York: James Miller, 1876. 67 pp.

Source: MTLAcc, entry #629, volume donated by Clemens. Tupper wrote this commemoration of George Washington (1732–1799) for the nation's Centennial celebrations.

TURGENEV, IVAN SERGIEEVICH (1818–1883).

Turgenev called on Clemens in London during the summer of 1873 (*MTL*, p. 207). Clemens visited him in Paris on 8 May 1879 in the company of Hjalmar Boyesen "& had a cup of tea out of his Samovar" (Notebook 18, *N&J* 2: 308). On 12 May 1879 Clemens recorded: "Tourgènieff called & spent evening. Brought me one of his books. Gave him Tom Sawyer" (NB 18, *N&J* 2: 309). Clemens requested Andrew Chatto to send "Monsieur Ivan Tourguèneff" of Paris a complimentary copy of *Roughing It* (SLC to Chatto, Paris, 29 May 1879, Berg Collection, NYPL). A letter from Clemens to Joseph H. Twichell of 10 June 1879 mentioned that "[Hjalmar] Boyesen spent a pleasant evening with Tourgueneff" (*LMTJHT*, p. 91). In a discarded portion of Mark Twain's *A Tramp Abroad* manuscript, he mentioned "the illustrious Tourguènef, great in literature & equally great in brave & self-sacrificing patriotism" (MTP).

———. *First Love* (novella, published in 1860).

Clemens wrote the German title of this story ("Erster Liebe") in Notebook 24 in May 1885 (*N&J* 3: 147). At the same time he also entered in Notebook 24 the German words "Ein Tochter Russlands," which could be translated as "A Daughter of Russia" (*N&J* 3: 147). Perhaps he meant the type of Russian woman Turgenev became known for portraying; no work by Turgenev approximating this title has been found.

———. "The Nobleman of the Steppe," *Scribner's Monthly* 14.3 (July 1877): 313–338.

In Mark Twain's working notes for a play titled "Cap'n Simon Wheeler, The Amateur Detective" (written in

1877), he mentioned that "Wakeman is Nobleman of Steppe" (*S&B*, p. 291). (The title of Turgenev's short story has more often been translated as "The Lear of the Steppes" or "King Lear of the Steppes.")

———.*Smoke* (novel, published in 1867).

Catalog: ListABP (1910), "Smoke, Turgenef", no other information supplied.

———. *The Torrents of Spring* (novel, published in 1872). Clemens wrote the German title of this novel ("Fruhlings-fluten") in Notebook 24 in May 1885 (*N&J* 3: 147).

———."Visions, A Phantasy," *Galaxy* 14.1 (July 1872): 108. In November 1878 Clemens noted "Turganieff's Visions" and "Visions, a Phantasy, by Tourganieff—in the Galaxy" in Notebook 17 while in Rome (*N&J* 2: 244, 247).

TURNBULL, FRANCESE HUBBARD (LITCHFIELD) (1844–1927), also known as "Mrs. Lawrence Turnbull." *The Golden Book of Venice: A Historical Romance of the 16th Century.* New York: Century Co., 1900. 399 pp.

Catalogs: QF Martinez, "Good plus condition"; Ball 2016 inventory, red cloth, gilt lettering and illustration, gilt top edges, rough cut pages.

Location: Quarry Farm library shelves, under the supervision of the Mark Twain Archive, Elmira College, Elmira, New York.

Turnbull's novel, with its many vivid word-paintings of scenes in Venice, was available to Clemens during his remaining visits to Quarry Farm.

TURNER, ETHEL MARY "SYBIL" (1870–1958), afterward Mrs. H. R. Curlewis. *Seven Little Australians.* Illus. by A[lfred]. J. Johnson (fl. 1878–1894). London: Ward, Lock & Bowden, 1894. 191 pp. [Edition conjectured.]

On 19 September 1895 Clara Clemens wrote to "Miss Turner" on behalf of Clemens "to thank you most heartily for 'Seven Little Australians' which he is greatly pleased to receive. He has not yet had an opportunity to read it but hopes to have this pleasure later as do I also" (ALS, Mitchell Library, State Library of New South Wales, Sydney, Australia). From Sydney on 24 September 1895, Clemens himself wrote to "Miss Turner": "I have stolen a moment & had a glimpse, & now I know I am going to enjoy your book" (ALS, Mitchell Library, State Library of New South Wales, Sydney, Australia). Turner's children's novel would become a classic of Australian literature, never going out of print, and would be followed by several sequels including *The Family at Misrule* (1895).

Turner's Comic Almanac. Boston: James Fisher; Philadelphia, Turner & Fisher, 1842.

Georgianne McVay wondered if Mark Twain might have seen a later reprinting of an item from the 1842 edition of this humorous collection of jests and drawings. The sketch noticed by McVay was a parody of romantically idealized descriptions of young girls, much in the manner in which Twain describes in Chapter 9 of *A Tramp Abroad* (1879) an "enchanting" and "sweet and bewitching" girl at the Mannheim opera who suddenly remarked, "Auntie, I just *know* I've got five hundred fleas on me!" ("Mark Twain's Girl with 500 Fleas and Her Literary Ancestor," *Mark Twain Journal* 20.4 [Summer 1981]: 24–25).

TWICHELL, JOSEPH HOPKINS (1838–1918). *John Winthrop, First Governor of the Massachusetts Colony.* Makers of America Series. Original red cloth. New York: Dodd, Mead and Co.,

[cop. 1891]. 245 pp.

Inscription: the front free endpaper is inscribed, "To Mark Twain,/with the unbounded love/of his ancient (and modern) friend./Joseph H. Twichell/Hartford./ Nov. 1891".

Provenance: contains the bookstamps of the Mark Twain Library, Redding, Connecticut.

Catalog: *Mott 1952*, item #89, $25.

Location: Albert and Shirley Small Special Collections Library, University of Virginia, Charlottesville. A gift of Clifton Waller Barrett.

Copy examined: Clemens's copy, unmarked, in 1970.

Twichell wrote to Clemens on 18 November 1891: "I am mailing you today a copy of the poor little baby book of which I have been guilty. You will not read it, of course: [*sic*] and I do not expect you to. . . . The opinion you hold of the people of whom I write is, to say the least, not a flattering one" (*LMTJHT*, pp. 167–168).

Twichell's enduring friendship with Clemens has been verified in many sources. One example can illustrate the many contexts in which they met and talked: in 1885 George Parsons Lathrop (1851–1898) reported that the Reverend Twichell and Clemens were among the casual drop-in guests who would often while away a winter evening at the home of Charles Dudley Warner ("A Model State Capital," *Harper's Monthly Magazine* 71.425 [October 1885]: 726).

Leah Strong, *Joseph Hopkins Twichell: Mark Twain's Friend and Pastor* (Athens: University of Georgia Press, 1966); and *The Letters of Mark Twain and Joseph Hopkins Twichell*, ed. Harold K. Bush, Steve Courtney, and Peter Messent (Athens: University of Georgia Press, 2017).

"TWINKLE, TWINKLE, LITTLE STAR" (nursery rhyme).

If (as seems likely) it was Clemens who arranged the "Country School Exhibition" aboard the *Montana* on the evening of 10 July 1868, then it was he who chose as part of the program "Poem—Twinkle, twinkle, little Star—Mr. H. M. T." (*Alta California*, 6 September 1868, reprinted in *The Twainian* 7 [November-December 1948]: 5).

Two—and an Indian. N.p., n.d. [Unidentified book.]

Source: MTLAcc, entry #1846, volume donated from Clemens's library by Clara Clemens Gabrilowitsch in 1910, described as "A typographical curiosity."

Let's try a long shot here. Joseph Sabin, in *A Dictionary of Books Relating to America, from Its Discovery to the Present Time.* Volume VI (New York: J. Sabin & Sons, 1873), described a translation of the New Testament prepared and published (in 1661) by John Eliot (1604–1690), a New England clergyman and missionary to the Massachusetts Native Americans, as "an extremely rare book. . . . Among the many points of interest which this book possesses, not the least is the fact that it is the language of a nation no longer in existence, and is almost the only monument of the race. . . . It is certainly a very great typographical curiosity; and, it is said, that there are not now more than two persons living who can read the language in which it is written" (p. 138).

TYLER, JOSIAH (1823–1895). *Livingstone Lost and Found; or, Africa and Its Explorers.* Illus. Maps. First edition. Publisher's three-quarter morocco, raised bands, gilt. Hartford,

Connecticut: Mutual Publishing Co., 1873. 782 pp.

Inscription: the front flyleaf is signed in ink "S. L. Clemens."

Marginalia: Clemens's only marking is a pencil line on page 135 beside a passage about whipping Africans to make them "believe the words of Christ." There is also an undated House of El Dieff appraisal signed by Lou David Feldman, who valued the volume at $25.

Catalog: *A1911*, "8vo, half leather (rubbed), Hartford, 1873," quotes the signature, lot 465, sold for $1.

Location: collection of Kevin Mac Donnell, Austin, Texas. (Mac Donnell to Alan Gribben, emails, 17 February 2015, 24 February 2015). According to Mac Donnell, an *A1911* sale label is pasted on the first flyleaf.

Published by a Hartford subscription house that competed with the American Publishing Company, *Livingstone Lost and Found* contained the first printing of Twain's speech on Stanley and Livingstone in which he claims to have found Livingstone himself but nobly let Stanley take the credit (pages 641–642). Chapter 46 described African diamond mines (a subject that Twain intended to write about) and Chapter 47 investigated the slave-trade.

TYNDALL, JOHN (1820–1893). *Fragments of Science for Unscientific People: A Series of Detached Essays, Lectures, and Reviews.* Original cloth, minor wear on the extremities. New York: D. Appleton and Co., 1871. 422 pp.

Inscription: the front flyleaf has been removed, presumably because it contained an inscription.

Provenance: the volume presents a strange combination of surviving clues: an erasure of names on the front pastedown endpaper, an ownership stamp of "GEO. B. LATHROP," and the label of "Geo. A. Collins, Bookseller and Stationer, 110 N. Main St., Hannibal, Mo." George B. Lathrop (1867–1920) was born in Hannibal but moved to Chicago, where he became a banker. The sale sheet of the 1951 auction in Hollywood does not list this Tyndall title, but then that document was notoriously unreliable.

Catalog: "Property from the Library of Mark Twain," Butterfield & Butterfield, San Francisco, Sale 6613 (16 July 1997), lot 2697.

Location: Mark Twain House and Museum, Hartford, Connecticut.

Copy examined: almost certainly Clemens's copy, though there are no confirming details that survive in the book itself. Viewed in Hartford in 1997. See also the Catalog entry for *The Prayer-Gauge Debate* (1876), to which Tyndall was a contributor.

Tyndall discussed subjects in this collection that assuredly would have enticed Clemens: "Miracles and Special Providences" (Chapter III), "Dust and Disease" (Chapter XI), and, in Chapter XIV, "Shorter Articles," the topics of "Death by Lightning" (p. 397), "Science and Spirits" (p. 402, including Tyndall's skeptical participation in a medium's séance), and "Additional Remarks on Miracles" (p. 418).

————. *Sound. A Course of Eight Lectures Delivered at the Royal Institution of Great Britain.* [First published in London in 1867, with numerous reprintings thereafter; Clemens's edition is unknown.]

In a letter to Hyatt Howe Waggoner, Clara Clemens Gabrilowitsch listed Tyndall's *Sound* among the books on science her father often read; she did not mention

the edition or the whereabouts of Clemens's copy (Waggoner, "Science in the Thought of Mark Twain" [1937], p. 363). Tyndall's eight lectures scarcely left undiscussed *any* aspect of the phenomenon of sound: how sound enters the ear, the male and female human voice, vocal chords, distinctions between noise and music, harmonics, the diatonic scale, sympathetic vibrations—he even described the effect of echoes.

TYNG, STEPHEN HIGGINSON (1800–1885). *The Office and Duty of a Christian Pastor.* New York: Harper & Brothers, 1874. 178 pp.

Source: MTLAcc, entry #1470, volume donated by Clemens.

In a series of five lectures, Tyng, Rector of St. George's Church in New York City, offered advice, anecdotes, and lessons to students in the School of Theology at Boston University about what they could expect to encounter as Christian pastors. St. George's was an Episcopal church, whereas the School of Theology was Methodist in its orientation, so the Reverend Tyng offered broad guidelines rather than denominational doctrines.

❚ U

UHLIG, THEODOR (1822–1853).

Mark Twain's "At the Shrine of St. Wagner" (1891) quotes a defense of Richard Wagner's musical principles from "a letter written by Uhlic [sic] thirty-three years ago." Wagner (1813–1883) maintained a close relationship with the musician and music critic Uhlig, who steadfastly championed Wagner's music. The composer dedicated a major essay, *Oper und Drama* (1852), to Theodor Uhlig.

ULBACH, LOUIS (1822–1889). *Madame Gosselin.* New York: D. Appleton and Co., 1878. 366 pp.

Source: MTLAcc, entry #314, volume donated by Clemens. The French author Louis Ulbach was a friend of Victor Hugo. Ulbach's novel *Madame Gosselin* had been published in Paris in 1877.

UMSTED, JUSTUS T[HOMAS]. (1820–1896). *A Plea for the Priority of Domestic Missions; A Discourse Delivered Before the Synod of Iowa, in Burlington, Oct. 12, 1856.* Keokuk, Iowa: O. Clemens, Book and Job Printer, 1856. 28 pp.

Catalog: The 19th Century Shop, Baltimore, Maryland, List No. 31, "Mark Twain," item #1, unmarked copy of a "rare relic of Samuel Clemens's early days as an itinerant printer," $450. Most items in this catalog are "from the library John C. Gerber, the noted Mark Twain scholar."

The Presbyterian minister Justus T. Umsted held pastorates over his lifetime in Indiana, Iowa, Alabama, Delaware, and Pennsylvania. Between 1853 and 1858 he was pastor of the Westminster Church in Keokuk, Iowa. Samuel L. Clemens was employed in his brother Orion's printing shop in Keokuk during much of 1855 and 1856, so it is likely that he at least read this pamphlet (and perhaps even set the type for it).

UNDERHILL, IRVING S[EARS]. (1866–1937). [Unidentified poem.]

"I like that poem ever so much, & so does Mrs. Clemens. I mean to show it to some friends & see if they confirm our judgment" (SLC to Irving S. Underhill, London, 23 May 1900, Berg Collection, NYPL, PH in MTP). Underhill, a resident of Buffalo, New York, was president of the Underhill Coal Company. He was also an avid book collector who would leave behind an extensive assemblage of Mark Twain first editions. Little of Underhill's poetry ever saw print; an exception was "To the Modern Girl," which appeared in *The Banner Weekly* 11.529 (31 December 1892): 3.

The Unfathomable Mystery. Benedictine Sisters of Perpetual Adoration. Clyde, Missouri: Privately printed, 1902.

In Chapter 8 of "No. 44, The Mysterious Stranger" (1969), August Feldner "wanted the prayers of the Sisters of Perpetual Adoration." Twain pinned clippings from a pamphlet about this religious order published in Clyde, Missouri in 1902 to the manuscript for Chapter 10 of "No. 44," noting that it was "an institution devoted to good and charitable works and rest from intellectual activity." The clippings provided textual copy for Father Peter's sermon.

Mark Twain's Mysterious Stranger Manuscripts, ed. William M. Gibson (Berkeley: University of California Press, 1969), pp. 260, 272, 515–516; Sholom J. Kahn, *Mark Twain's Mysterious Stranger: A Study of Manuscript Texts* (Columbia: University of Missouri Press,, 1978), p. 116; Rebecca Johnston, "The Sisters of Perpetual Extortion: Historical Parallels in *No. 44, The Mysterious Stranger*," *Mark Twain Journal* 55.1–2 (Spring/Fall 2017): 228–239.

UNDERWOOD, BENJAMIN FRANKLIN (1839–1914). *Essays and Lectures*. New York: D. M. Bennett, [1883?]. 366 pp.

Source: MTLAcc, entry #907, volume donated by Clemens. Newspaper and magazine editor Underwood was a close friend of the agnostic writer and speaker Robert G. Ingersoll. Underwood himself was a lecturer on women's rights, Dawinism, Thomas Paine, atheism, spiritualism, and other radical Free Thought ideas. He was elected to an office in the Free Religious Association and edited *The Truth Seeker* for more than a decade (see the Catalog entry for that magazine). Underwood was married to the prominent author, journalist, lecturer, feminist, and spiritualist Sarah A. Francis Underwood (1838–1911). *Essays and Lectures* collected a number of his pamphlets that were also available separately.

[UNIDENTIFIED BOOK, 1903.]

Writing to "Dear sir" from Quarry Farm in Elmira, New York on 1 October 1903, Clemens requested "a little book" promised by a letter-writer "from Brazil." He added, "I seldom use the books that are sent me by strangers, but this time it is different!" (Cyril Clemens Collection, Mark Twain House and Museum, Hartford, Connecticut).

[UNIDENTIFIED BOOK, 1907.]

Clemens wrote to Jean Clemens on 15 November 1907: "You may return that unpleasant book & we will put it out of sight. It lacks the ring of truth; lacks it so prominently that it fell flat, & made not a ripple on the surface of the human sea; whereas if its statements had been believed it would have created a cyclone. Evidently the world saw in it only an expression of the spite of some disgruntled persons of the servant class, who had suffered from blighted little ambitions & were drunk with the spirit of unreasoning revenge. I think it is nothing but a hotch-potch of libels & slanders, & not worth anyone's serious attention" (Christie's, New York City, "Printed Books and Manuscripts, including Miniature Books,"

11 May 1987, lot 32).

UNION PACIFIC RAILWAY COMPANY (undated invitation).

Inscriptions: a large invitation, signed in ink on the upper right corner, "S. L. Clemens/(Mark Twain)". On the verso, in ink, appears an attestation: "This original invitation came/from the library of my father,/Eugene Field./Lit. Executor/Eugene Field II/April 29, 1934". The recto invitation reads, in varied fonts of type: "U.P.Ry.E.D./ The Union Pacific Railway Company Eastern Division/ invites you to be present as per letter of/Mr. Samuel Hallett/to celebrate the opening of the/First Section of Forty Miles/of their/Road West from the Missouri River." The invitation also bears the purported signatures of "Eugene Field" and "Bret Harte".

Provenance: offered for sale in June 1998, when a photocopy of both sides was sent to Kevin Mac Donnell, bookman and collector, of Austin, Texas.

Copy examined: photocopies of both the recto and verso of the invitation were sent to Alan Gribben by Kevin Mac Donnell on 18 August 2005. The Clemens/Twain autograph is clearly one of the many forgeries committed by Eugene Field II.

Unitarian Herald (Manchester, England, weekly newspaper, published 1861–1889).

Early in 1887 Clemens referred to a report about Herbert Spencer that appeared in this periodical, citing its title (NB 26, *N&J* 3: 273).

UNITED STATES CONGRESS. HOUSE COMMITTEE ON PATENTS. *Arguments Before the Committee on Patents.* Washington, D.C.: Government Printing Office, 1878. 460 pp.

Source: MTLAcc, entry #891, volume donated by Clemens.

United States Constitution.

In San Francisco in 1865 Clemens wrote "Constitution U. S, Whole Duty of Man & other light reading" (NB 4, *N&J* 1: 83).

UNITED STATES WAR DEPARTMENT. *Regulations for the Army of the United States, 1904.* Document No. 230, War Department, Office of the Chief of Staff. Washington, D.C.: Government Printing Office, 1904. 302 pp.

Among Mark Twain's acknowledgments of sources at the beginning of "A Horse's Tale" (1906) he names *"Army Regulations,* ed. 1904" as one of his guides for describing military operations.

UNWIN, [EMMA] JANE COBDEN (1851–1947). *The Hungry Forties: Life Under the Bread Tax. Descriptive Letters and Other Testimonies from Contemporary Witnesses.* Illus. First edition. Original red cloth, gilt. London: T. Fisher Unwin, 1904. 274 pp.

Inscription: the front pastedown endpaper is signed in black ink: "S. L. Clemens/London, July 1907./From Mrs. Unwin."

Catalog: *A1911*, "12mo, cloth, Lond. 1904," quotes the signature, lot 466, $1.75.

Location: collection of Kevin Mac Donnell, Austin, Texas.

Copy examined: Clemens's unmarked copy, on 15 December 1983 and again in July 2004. Has the *A1911* sale label. Jane Cobden Unwin was married to the publisher Thomas Fisher Unwin. *The Hungry Forties* described the hardships of an earlier era in England.

UPHAM, THOMAS C[OGSWELL]. (1799–1872). *The Life of Faith; in Three Parts, Embracing Some of the Scriptural Principles or*

Doctrines of Faith. Original black cloth, gilt. Boston: Charles H. Peirce, 1847. 480 pp.

> **Inscription:** the blue and gold bookplate of Jervis Langdon is present: "J. Langdon's Family Library No. 148." The rear endpaper is signed "Jervis Langdon." (Jervis Langdon [1809–1870] was Olivia Clemens's father.)
>
> **Marginalia:** Clemens made pencil marks in the margins of pages 182 and 282. (Jervis Langdon or some other family member made markings at pages 286–287; those passages pertained to self-control and a quiet spirit.) The passage that Clemens marked on page 182 concerned divine order and divine will and the predestination of all things that occur except sin. (Is it relevant that in Chapter 5 of Mark Twain's *The Adventures of Tom Sawyer* [1876] a village minister delivers a tedious sermon involving the "predestined elect"?) On page 282 Clemens marked a passage stating that ordinary men can attain a level of good character equal to "a Paul or an Apollos." (Apollos was a first-century Christian preacher.) The corner of page 358 is folded down.
>
> **Location:** collection of Kevin Mac Donnell, Austin, Texas (Mac Donnell to Alan Gribben, 29 November 2011).

Clemens could make free use of the Langdon family library whenever he visited their residence in Elmira.

An ordained minister who had attended Andover Seminary and been the pastor of a Congregational church, Thomas C. Upham became a professor of moral and mental philosophy at Bowdoin College between 1825 and 1867. His many publications reflected in part his efforts to reconcile the intellect with a yearning for the spiritual. Upham held strong anti-slavery and anti-war views. He befriended Harriet Beecher Stowe during the period when she was writing *Uncle Tom's Cabin*.

UPTON, GEORGE PUTNAM (1834–1919). *The Standard Operas: Their Plots, Their Music, and Their Composers*. New Edition, Revised. Chicago: A. C. McClurg & Co., 1907. 495 pp.

> **Inscription:** the front free endpaper is signed in black ink, "Clara Clemens/New York".
>
> **Location:** Mark Twain Library, Redding, Connecticut.
>
> **Copy examined:** Clara Clemens's unmarked copy. Has the red ink Mark Twain Library accession number "2462" and the purple oval Library stamps. Examined in 1970 and again in June 1982.

UPWARD, ALLEN (1863–1926). *The Slaves of Society. A Comedy in Covers: By the Man Who Heard Something*. New York: Harper & Brothers, 1900. 253 pp.

> **Source:** MTLAcc, entry #1504, volume donated by Clemens.

Unable to find a producer for this play about the English aristocracy, Upward turned it into fiction even though it still retained stage directions, set descriptions, rapid-fire dialogue, and other earmarks of drama. Born in Wales and educated in Dublin, Upward maintained a frenetic career as a journalist, editor, author, political reformer, traveler, and poet. He would shock his literary circle by committing suicide in 1926.

URUSOV, SERGEI DMITRIEVICH (1862–1937). *Memoirs of a Russian Governor*. Translated from the Russian and edited by Herman Rosenthal (1843–1917). Authorized Edition. New York: Harper & Brothers, 1908. 181 pp.

> **Source:** MTLAcc, entry #1777, volume donated by

Clemens.

V

VĂCĂRESCU, ELENA (1864–1947). *Kings and Queens I Have Known, by Hélène Vacaresco*. Illus. New York: Harper & Brothers, 1904. 320 pp.

This was one of four "Harper's books" that Clemens's business agent in Florence received for him "from Messrs. French, Lemon & Co." (Sebastiano V. Cecchi, Haskard & Co., Bankers, to SLC, Florence, 30 July 1904, MTP). Clemens left this book in Florence in a parcel containing three other books (Sebastiano V. Cecchi, Haskard & Co., Bankers, to SLC, Florence, 4 November 1904, MTP).

The memoirs of the Romanian-French aristocrat Elena Văcărescu conveyed her impressions of numerous royalty with whom she had associated, including Queen Victoria and Edward VII of England, Victor Emmanuel II, King of Italy, Wilhelmina, Queen of the Netherlands, and Franz Joseph I, Emperor of Austria.

VADERS, HENRIETTA (b.1857), pseud. "Yam." *Wikkey: A Scrap, by Yam*. New York: E. P. Dutton & Co., 1888. 75 pp.

> **Source:** MTLAcc, entry #1865, volume donated from Clemens's library by Clara Clemens Gabrilowitsch in 1910. Vaders, an eminent American actor often cast in tragic parts, published *Wikkey: A Scrap* as a novella. She had gained a degree of notoriety in September 1885 when her actor husband, Harry Thompson, attempted suicide after they had a row in Syracuse, New York over his suspected infidelity.

VALLERY-RADOT, RENÉ (1853–1933). *The Life of Pasteur*. Translated from the French by Henriette Caroline (Vulliamy) Devonshire (1864–1949), "Mrs. R. L. Devonshire." 2 vols. New York: McClure, Phillips and Co., 1902.

> **Inscriptions:** the front free endpaper of Volume I is signed in black ink, "SL. Clemens/ Riverdale-on-Hudson/ <Feb.> Jan. 1902./From [Auguste F.] Jaccaci/of McClure's". Below this, Clemens noted in pencil: "Admirably written—this book." In black ink he then added: "And ably translated, too." On the front pastedown endpaper Clemens wrote in black ink: "SL. Clemens/Among Biographies this one is surely entitled to rank as the Taj Mahal ranks among marble memorials." The front free endpaper of Volume II is signed in black ink, "SL. Clemens/Jan. 1902./ Riverdale."
>
> **Marginalia:** pencil marks and underscorings (and a few in black ink) throughout Volume I up to page 181. On a front flyleaf Clemens observed: "A past-master of the pathetic, this author; he keeps one's tears near the surface all the time, yet hides his machinery so well that he never seems to be trying to do it." On page 14 Clemens noted in black ink: "1828–1908. Seventy years have gone by and now there is a Pasteur installation in every city in the civilized world. To foreknow this could have amazed the boy that dismal morning." Chester L. Davis (1903–1987) reported a few other annotations in "Mark Twain's Copy 'Life of Pasteur,'" *The Twainian* 18 (November-December 1959): 1–4.
>
> **Catalogs:** *C1951*, # 8c, listed among books signed by Clemens, $4; also #11a, listed among books annotated by Clemens, $40 (evidently the two volumes were sold separately by mistake); *Hunley 1958*, item #153, 2 vols.,

$42.50.

Provenance: both volumes were formerly in Chester L. Davis's Mark Twain Research Foundation, Perry, Missouri.

Location: currently unknown.

Copies examined: Clemens's copies of both volumes, in 1970, in Perry, Missouri.

Mark Twain mentioned Louis Pasteur (1822–1895) as an expert on bacteriology in "Three Thousand Years among the Microbes," written in 1905 (*WWD?*, p. 513). In "Dr. Loeb's Incredible Discovery" (published in 1923), Twain referred to "Pasteur and his majestic honor roll of prodigious benefactions!" He added: "They shortened his life by their malignities and persecutions; and thus robbed the world of the further and priceless services of a man who—along certain lines and within certain limits—had done more for the human race than any other one man in all its long history."

VANBRUGH, (SIR) JOHN (1664–1726). *The Provok'd Wife. A Comedy* (first performed in 1697).

Where Mark Twain stipulated that "Wheeler shall *play drunk* like Garrick," a note on his manuscript for the novel "Simon Wheeler, Detective" (written sporadically 1877–1898?), Franklin R. Rogers speculated that Twain meant David Garrick's simulation of drunkenness as Sir John Brute (*S&B*, p. 392 n. 40). Garrick (1717–1779) was noted for this comic role in Vanbrugh's *The Provok'd Wife*.

VAN BUREN, ALICIA (KEISKER) (1860–1922). *As Thought Is Led; Lyrics and Sonnets.* Boston: Richard G. Badger/The Gorham Press, 1904. 48 pp.

Source: MTLAcc, entry #619, volume donated by Isabel V. Lyon, Clemens's secretary.

Alicia Van Buren lived in Brookline, Massachusetts and was prominent in the Boston literary scene.

VANCE, WILSON J. (1845–1911). *Big John Baldwin; Extracts from the Journal of an Officer of Cromwell's Army, Recording Some of His Experiences at the Court of Charles I and Subsequently at That of the Lord Protector and on the Fields of Love and War and Finally in the Colony of Virginia, Edited with Sparing Hand by Wilson Vance.* New York: Henry Holt and Co., 1909. 375 pp.

Source: MTLAcc, entry #1479, volume donated by Clemens.

A fictional memoir set in seventeenth-century England.

———. *God's War.* New York and London: F. Tennyson Neely, [cop. 1899]. 348 pp. Paperbound.

Source: MTLAcc, entry #315, volume donated by Clemens. The Ohio-born Vance certainly had the credentials to write a Civil War novel; he had been awarded the Medal of Honor for valor he displayed at the Battle of Stone River in Tennessee in 1862.

VAN DYKE, HENRY (1852–1933). *The Americanism of Washington.* New York: Harper & Brothers, 1906. 72 pp.

Source: MTLAcc, entry #1337, volume donated by Clemens.

Van Dyke pondered the character traits of George Washington and disputed some of the false impressions that had arisen.

———. [Identical copy.]

Provenance: has the shelfmarks of Clara Clemens Gabrilowitsch's library numbering system during her Detroit years. Sold at the 1951 auction in Hollywood but not listed in its hastily prepared sale sheet.

Catalog: "Property from the Library of Mark Twain," Butterfield & Butterfield, San Francisco, Sale 6613 (16 July 1997), lot 2712.

Location: Mark Twain House and Museum, Hartford, Connecticut.

Copy examined: Clemens's unmarked copy. Viewed in Hartford in 1997.

———. *The Blue Flower.* Illus. New York: Charles Scribner's Sons, 1902. 299 pp.

Inscription: the front free endpaper is inscribed in black ink by Van Dyke to Mark Twain in the form of a long, fulsome poem signed, "Nov 30th/1835–1902./Henry van Dyke". Van Dyke had delivered this poetic tribute on 27 November 1902 at a dinner in the Metropolitan Club in New York City celebrating Twain's sixty-seventh birthday.

Catalog: ListABP (1910), "Blue Flower, Van Dyke", no other information provided.

Provenance: in August 1987 this volume was in the private collection of Bigelow Paine Cushman, Deer Isle, Maine. Cushman had inherited the book.

Location: currently unknown.

Copy examined: Clemens's copy, in August 1987.

The Blue Flower was among the top ten best-sellers in 1902.

———. [An identical copy.]

Source: MTLAcc, entry #887, volume donated by Clemens.

Mark Twain presented Van Dyke to a public audience in March 1906, "not to praise his delicious books, they praise themselves better than any words of mine could do it for them" ("Introducing Doctor Van Dyke," *MTS1923*, p. 296; *MTSpk*, p. 487). (On 20 February Twain had explained to Gertrude Natkin that "Dr. Van Dyke" could not speak "next Sunday," i. e., 25 February, so the engagement was postponed until March [Fears, *Day by Day* 4: 304].) Van Dyke was then a professor of English literature at Princeton. In an Autobiographical Dictation (actually a holograph manuscript) of 29 April 1908 relating a good-natured theological dispute Clemens had with Van Dyke, Twain inserted a clipping of Van Dyke's account of catching a land-locked salmon, remarking: "Last night I read in the *Atlantic* a passage from one of Rev. Dr. Van Dyke's books. . . . I like Van Dyke, and I greatly admire his literary style—this notwithstanding the drawback that a good deal of his literary product is of a religious sort" (*AutoMT* 3: 226). The clipping that Twain quotes (by pinning it to his manuscript) is scissored out of Henry Bradford Washburn's "Shall We Hunt and Fish? The Confessions of a Sentimentalist," *Atlantic Monthly* 101.5 (May 1908): 672–679, where Washburn opens his essay with a quotation from Van Dyke's "Some Remarks on Gulls, with a Foot-note on a Fish," *Scribner's Magazine* 42.2 (August 1907): 129–142. Van Dyke's piece endeavored to help people appreciate a coastal bird always taken for granted, the sea gull, in the course of which he described several unsportsmanlike ways humans use to catch fish and contrasted them with the thrill of angling for salmon in a lake and landing one after a long tussle with the fish. Henry Van Dyke was an officiating clergyman and delivered an emotional eulogy at the funeral services for Clemens at Brick Presbyterian Church in New York City, along with the Reverend Joseph H. Twichell

(*MFMT*, p. 292). Van Dyke was also one of the members of the American Academy and National Institute of Arts and Letters who spoke at a memorial meeting in Carnegie Hall honoring Clemens on 30 November 1910. Van Dyke would provide a prefatory "Appreciation" for *Joan of Arc* in the so-called Definitive Edition of Mark Twain's works (New York, Gabriel Wells, 1922–1925).

———. *The Christ-Child in Art; A Study of Interpretation.* Illus. New York: Harper & Brothers, 1904. 236 pp.

Source: MTLAcc, entry #1693, volume donated by Clemens.

———, ed., assisted by Hardin Craig (1875–1968). *Little Masterpieces of English Poetry, by British and American Authors.* 6 volumes. New York: Doubleday, Page & Co., 1905. Volume I, *Ballads Old and New*; Volume II, *Idyls and Stories in Verse*; Volume III, *Lyrics*; Volume IV, *Odes, Sonnets, and Epigrams*; Volume V, *Descriptive and Reflective Verse*; Volume VI, *Elegies and Hymns.*

Inscriptions: the front pastedown endpaper of Volume I is signed, "S L. Clemens/1905." The front pastedown endpaper of Volume III is signed, "S L. Clemens/1905." The front pastedown endpaper of Volume IV is inscribed, "Jean Clemens/from SLC." The front pastedown endpaper of Volume V is inscribed, "To Jean Clemens from S L. Clemens/1905." The front pastedown endpaper of Volume VI is signed, "S L. Clemens/1905." All of the inscriptions are in black ink. Only Volume II was missing when Ann Cameron Harvey recorded these inscriptions in 1966. (See below for the signature in Volume II.)

Marginalia: in Volume I, Clemens revised line 334 of Coleridge's "Rime of the Ancient Mariner" (p. 165), altering "To see those dead men rise" to read "To have seen those dead men rise." The table of contents in Volume III contains some markings. In Volume V Clemens drew lines in the table of contents beside the poems on pages 39, 93, 118, 144, 165, 167, 177, 184, 191, 240, 247, 249, 260, 271, and 282. Volumes IV and VI are unmarked. The second volume was missing when Ann Cameron Harvey examined the set in 1966.

Provenance: in 1966 all of the volumes except Volume II were in the Antenne-Dorrance Collection, Rice Lake, Wisconsin. The entire set had been temporarily misplaced when I visited Rice Lake in 1970.

Location: the whereabouts of Volumes I and II are currently unknown. Volumes III, IV, V, and VI are in the Mark Twain Archive, Elmira College, Elmira, New York.

Copy examined: copies shared by Clemens and Jean Clemens. I examined Volumes III, IV, V, and VI in Elmira on 28 May 2015.

———. *Little Masterpieces of English Poetry, by British and American Authors.* 6 volumes. New York: Doubleday, Page & Co., 1907. 286 pp.

Inscription: the front free endpapers of Volumes IV and V are signed "S L. Clemens/1907."

Catalogs: *C1951*, D15, "8 [*sic*] vols., by famous authors"; Catalogue 174 (1989), Heritage Book Shop, Los Angeles, California, Volume V only, "original brown morocco spine laid down, . . . bit scuffed, joints cracked, joints repaired with tape, in a half green morocco box," item #209, priced at $1,000; unidentified bookseller's catalog, December 1993, Volume II only, half leather, marbled

boards, signed "S L. Clemens/1907," $1,650 (note in the collection of Kevin B. Mac Donnell, Austin, Texas).

Location: Volumes IV and V only, collection of Kevin Mac Donnell, Austin, Texas. They have marbled boards, gilt lettering, and the *C1951* notation "D15." The two volumes are unmarked other than Clemens's signature and Clara Clemens Samossoud's library shelf mark "Po/H4." (which has been partly erased in Volume IV). Volume V was acquired in 2019 (Mac Donnell to Alan Gribben, 22 November 2019); Volume IV was acquired by him in 2020 (emails, MacDonnell to Alan Gribben, 7 March 2020, 13 March 2020).

Volume IV consists of "Odes, Sonnets, and Epigrams." Its contents range from Shakespeare's sonnets and Milton's "Ode on the Morning of Christ's Nativity" to Wordsworth's "Ode on the Intimations of Immortality," Keats' "Ode on a Grecian Urn," and Shelley's "To a Skylark." Two poems by Emily Dickinson, "Our Share of Night to Bear" and "Heart, We Will Forget Him," appear among miscellaneous pieces printed at the end of Volume IV. Volume V includes poems by Milton, Wordsworth, Tennyson, Browning (five poems), Arnold, Longfellow, Emerson, and others.

———. *Ships and Havens.* New York: T. Y. Crowell & Co., [cop. 1897]. 37 pp.

Source: MTLAcc, entry #875, volume donated by Mrs. Ralph W. Ashcroft (formerly Isabel V. Lyon), Clemens's secretary.

———. *The Story of the Other Wise Man.* Illus. New York: Harper & Brothers, [cop. 1895]. 83 pp.

Location: Mark Twain Library, Redding, Connecticut. Donated by Clemens (MTLAcc, entry #464).

Marginalia: pencil marks on page 17 underlined the word "welcome" and crossed out "to Ahura-Mazda", adding a period to precede the deleted name.

Copy examined: Clemens's copy. Has the red ink Mark Twain Library accession number "464". Examined in 1970 and again in June 1982.

In Van Dyke's novella a fourth wise man, Artaban of Persian, sets out to worship the newborn Christ as did the three whom the Gospel of Matthew would describe in the New Testament. However, Artaban is delayed and his valuable gifts sacrificed by good deeds he performs along the way. As he dies after devoting thirty years to his quest, he receives assurance that he has found his own salvation even though he never saw the savior he sought.

———. *The Story of the Other Wise Man.* New York: Harper & Brothers, [cop. 1899]. 75 pp.

Source: MTLAcc, entry #1336, volume donated by Clemens.

Van Dyke, John Charles (1856–1932). "The Lotto Portrait of Columbus," *Century Magazine* 44.6 (October 1892): 818–822.

The frontispiece for the October 1892 issue of *Century Magazine* was the recently discovered Lorenzo Lotto portrait of Columbus, owned by James W. Ellsworth. Van Dyke's appraisal in the accompanying article was equivocal: "The history of this portrait is . . . about as unsatisfactory as any of the other Columbuses" (p. 818). After discussing the antiquity of the canvas, colors, techniques, costume, and symbols, Van Dyke suggested that Lotto merely painted from a sketch by someone else. Clemens complained bitterly to United States Vice- Consul-General Hogue of Frankfort, Germany regarding "the article in the Century about the Columbus portrait." Clemens wrote that he "lost my temper over the article. It merely throws cold water, as far as I can see. I wish the man had kept his article to himself" (SLC to Hogue, 14 October 1892, ASSSCL, PH in MTP). See also the Catalog entry for Lockwood De Forest. Clemens's indignation may been prompted by the fact that his Charles L. Webster publishing firm brought out *The Writings of Christopher Columbus* this same year, 1892.

VANE, FLORENCE. "Are we almost there?" (sentimental ballad, published in 1845). Lyrics and melody both composed by Vane.

Clemens wrote the title of this song on the front wrapper of a song collection published in 1896, F. B. Ogilvie's *Two Hundred Old-Time Songs, Containing the Words and Music of the Choicest Gems of the Old and Familiar Songs*. Vane's ballad consisted of questions and recollections of a dying young woman as her friends make an effort to take her home before she expires. The piece was so popular that it inspired another song, this one with lyrics by James H. Brown and music by Isaac Baker Woodbury (1819–1858), "We are almost there!" (published in 1847), which told of arriving at the destination just as the ill woman passed away.

VAN EEDEN, FREDERICK (1860–1932). "Curing by Suggestion," *The World's Work* 18.5 (September 1909): 11993–11999.

In "The Ashcroft-Lyon Manuscript" of 1909 Clemens stated that an article "on hypnotic suggestion" by the Dutch psychologist Dr. Van Eeden provided an explanation for how Clemens had been manipulated by Ralph Ashcroft and Isabel V. Lyon (*AutoMT 3*: 438).

VAN ETTEN, IDA M. (c. 1837–1894). "The House of the Dragons," *The Cosmopolitan* 41.5 (March 1893): 615–625.

In December 1893 Clemens noted, "Cosmo[n] story by Miss Van Etten. Get & send to Mrs. C." (NB 33, TS p. 42). Ida M. Etten, born into an affluent family in Chemung County, New York, taught school in Elmira in the mid-1870s before moving to New York City and managing the collection of data for a city directory. Gradually she became recognized as a notable social reformer for the welfare of working women. As a writer she specialized in stories and articles about the downtrodden and forgotten urban poor. In this short story a young girl named Mary, struggling to find housing and employment in New York City, receives a dismal prediction from a sex worker in a house of prostitution: "You will come to the House of the Dragons—there will be nothing else to do." At the story's end, having exhausted all other possibilities for survival, Mary finds herself fulfilling that prophecy as she climbs "up the steps and through the open door, which closed quickly upon her." Etten would die of heart failure in March 1894, a year after this short story appeared, while doing research in Paris on the appeal of socialism among the impoverished populations of Europe.

Vanity Fair (New York humor magazine, published 1859–1863).

Lectures that Mark Twain delivered in 1871 and 1872 paid tribute to Artemus Ward's efforts as editor and contributor

to save this doomed periodical, which "had already entered upon that rapid decline which every American comic journal seems destined to. . . . He had always been of the opinion that an occasional joke improved a comic paper" (Paul Fatout, ed., *MTSpk* [1976], pp. 44–45).

A century and a half later this short-lived magazine became part of a perennial, or one should say recurrent, debate within Mark Twain studies concerning the origins of his famous pen name. The ultimate cause for this disagreement partly lies in the untruthful explanation Clemens came up with during his lifetime, which left the door open for optional theories. Every now and then a prominent scholar attempted to put the matter to rest once and for all, as Guy Cardwell did in his authoritative essay, "Samuel Clemens' Magical Pseudonym," *New England Quarterly* 48.2 (June 1975): 175–193. Nonetheless, the same or related differences of opinion have sprung up again every decade or two. Carolyn Grattan Eichin's "From Samuel Clemens to Mark Twain: Sanitizing the Western Experience," *Mark Twain Annual 12* (2014): 113–135 articulated one of the two leading ideas. In 2017 a leading Twain collector and scholar, Kevin Mac Donnell, proposed an entirely different source—a sketch titled "The North Star" that appeared in the 26 January 1861 issue of *Vanity Fair*—in "How Samuel Clemens Found 'Mark Twain' in Carson City," *Mark Twain Journal: The Author and His Era* 50.1–2 (Spring/Fall 2012): 8–47. Mac Donnell elaborated on this theory in "Mark Twain at Ten Paces: Facts Versus Fictions in the Origin of 'Mark Twain' as a Nom de Plume, *Mark Twain Journal: The Author and His Era* 57.1 (Spring 2019): 77–111. The respected Twain biographer Gary Scharnhorst disputed that explanation in "Mark Twain's *Nom de Plume* Redux: A Reply to Kevin Mac Donnell," *Mark Twain Journal: The Author and His Era* 57.2 (Fall 2019): 21–27, defending the alternative hypothesis Scharnhorst had offered in *The Life of Mark Twain: The Early Years* (Columbia: University of Missouri Press, 2018), pp. 190–192—that "Mark Twain" was the method by which Clemens's bar-tab was calculated in Virginia City. Kevin Mac Donnell answered Scharnhorst's objections in "Mark Twain Did Read *Vanity Fair*—in Nevada," *Mark Twain Journal: The Author and His Era* 58.1 (Spring 2020): 146–156. This dispute is hardly a trivial concern, cutting, as does, to the very heart of Twain's public and professional identity and throwing open to question the origin of one of the most famous names associated with American literature and culture.

VAN NADA, L. BELLE (1845–1891). *Poems*. Indianapolis, Indiana: Carlon & Hollenbeck, Printers, 1881. 151 pp.

Source: MTLAcc, entry #637, volume donated by Clemens. The inflated sentimentality of these twenty-five poems somehow escaped any record of their consignment to Mark Twain's hypothetical Library of Literary Hogwash. Van Nada was the proprietor of a lodging house in Petersburg, Indiana.

VAN NORTWICK, WILLIAM H. *Yanks and Johnnies; or, Laugh and Grow Fat*. New York: Charles L. Webster & Co., 1888.

Clemens mentioned the schedule for publication of Van Nortwick's book in a letter to Charles L. Webster written from Elmira on 5 September 1887 (*MTLP*, p. 228). *Yanks and Johnnies* collected humorous stories about the

Civil War.

Van Vorst, Bessie (McGinnis) (1873–1928), "Mrs. John Van Vorst," and **Marie Van Vorst** (1867–1936). *Bagsby's Daughter*. Illus. New York: Harper & Brothers, 1901. 338 pp.
Source: MTLAcc, entry #317, volume donated by Clemens. The setting of this romantic novel shifts from Chicago to London.

_____ and **Marie Van Vorst** (1867–1936). *The Woman Who Toils; Being the Experiences of Two Ladies as Factory Girls*. Illus. New York: Doubleday, Page, & Co., 1903. 303 pp.
Source: MTLAcc, entry #594, volume donated by Clemens. The authors formally dedicated this exposé of working conditions "To Mark Twain/In loving tribute to his genius, and to his human sympathy, which in Pathos and Seriousness, as well as in Mirth and Humour, have made him kin with the whole world:—/this book is inscribed by/Bessie and Marie Van Vorst." The two women took employment in New York, Chicago, and other cities to see firsthand how working class women labored in industrial factories.

Van Vorst, Marie Louis (1867–1936). *Philip Longstreth; A Novel*. New York: Harper & Brothers, 1902. 396 pp.
Source: MTLAcc, entry #318, volume donated by Clemens. The social distance between a factory girl and a suave upper-class suitor proves to be formidable.

Van Zandt, George Harrison (1832–1889). *Poems of George Harrison Van Zandt*. Philadelphia: Jay & Co., 1886. 256 pp. [Edition conjectured.]
In 1887, while Clemens was managing the business affairs of Charles L. Webster & Company, the Philadelphia lawyer Van Zandt approached the publishing firm with a proposal to write a historical romance. In an undated letter to Charles L. Webster, Clemens recommended that Webster consult with Van Zandt about the project (ALS in Berg Collection, NYPL). At the top of a letter of 21 June 1887 from Van Zandt, however, Clemens advised Fred J. Hall, his representative at Charles L. Webster & Company, not to dispel Van Zandt's delusion that he could write another *Ben-Hur*, but neither to encourage his proposals. "His volume of alleged 'poems,'" Clemens assured Hall, "is mere hogwash" (quoted from Philip C. Duschnes Catalog No. 49, item #125). Clemens was no doubt thinking of labored verses such as "Sonnet" in Van Zandt's 1886 collection, which begins, "Ah! Thou didst lead me to the river's brink,/And to me, standing on the sands, didst say:/Let us take boat and seaward sail away;/But as I heeded, thou aback didst shrink./And when mine eyes did thy beauty drink,/As rose a wave, thou, tow'rd the shore straightway/Didst turn, as if some fear did thee betray,/While I was left alone of thee to think" (p. 43). Van Zandt would die in his mid-fifties, on 11 April 1889, only two years after he wrote to Clemens's publishing firm.

Van Zile, Edward S[ims] (1863–1931). *With Sword and Crucifix; Being an Account of the Strange Adventures of Count Louis de Sancerre, Companion of Sieur de la Salle, on the Lower Mississippi in the Year of Grace 1682*. Illus. New York: Harper & Brothers, 1900. 299 pp.
Source: MTLAcc, entry #1664, volume donated by Clemens.
Historical fiction about the explorer, René-Robert Cavelier, Sieur de La Salle (1643–1687), who claimed the entire Mississippi River waterway for France.

Vasari, Giorgio (1511–1574). *Lives of the Most Excellent Painters, Sculptors, and Architects, from Cimabue to Our Times* (first published in 1550, enlarged in 1568).
Susy Clemens wrote to her college friend Louise Brownell from Florence, Italy on 7 November 1892 to report that "Nanny [King] and I have been having a lovely time over Vasari's Lives" (Hamilton College Archives).

Vedder, Henry Clay (1853–1935). *American Writers of To-day*. New York, Boston: Silver, Burdett and Co., 1894. 326 pp.
Source: ListABP (1910), "American Writers of To-Day, Vedder".
Clemens reminded himself late in April 1892 to "cable Vedder" and then to "send Vedder's book home" from Florence (NB 31, TS pp. 38, 39). Vedder's *American Writers* would contain essays on Mark Twain, William Dean Howells, Henry James, and sixteen other major and minor literary figures. Presumably Clemens was cooperating with a request by Vedder for information.

Velazquez, Loreta Janeta (1842–1897). *The Woman in Battle: A Narrative of the Exploits, Adventures, and Travels of Madame Loreta Janeta Velazquez, Otherwise Known as Lieutenant Harry T. Buford, Confederate States Army. In Which Is Given Full Descriptions of the Numerous Battles in Which She Participated as a Confederate Officer; of Her Perilous Performances as Spy; . . . Her Mining Adventures on the Pacific Slope; Her Residence among the Mormons; Her Love Affairs, Courtships, Marriages, &c., &c.* Ed. by C. J. Worthington. Illus. Richmond, Virginia: Dustin, Gilman & Co., 1876. 606 pp.
Velazquez wrote to Clemens several times in 1874, seeking assistance in publishing her memoirs about her Civil War spy activities, some of them undertaken as the cross-dressing "Harry T. Buford." On 9 October and 13 October 1874 Clemens expressed resentment that she was implying he had endorsed her manuscript (*MTLet* 6: 250–256). Cuban-born, she had married an American and tended to use her married name, Mrs. E. H. Bonner, except for the title page of her book. There is an ongoing dispute concerning the veracity of her alleged escapades as a Confederate soldier and spy. Her adventures after the war, equally astounding, took her to Europe, South America, and the American West.

Venable, William Henry (1836–1920). *Tom Tad*. Illus. New York: Dodd, Mead, & Co., 1902. 287 pp.
Source: MTLAcc, entry #493, volume donated by Clemens.
"I have only been able to steal time enough to read the first chapter, but if the rest is up to that standard it is a good boy-book. I thank you very much for sending it to me" (SLC to Venable, Riverdale, 27 October 1902, Ohio Historical Society, PH in MTP). Clemens was preoccupied at the time with Olivia Clemens's illness. Chapter I of Venable's book, "Boys in the Woods," consisted of reckless dialogue between Tom Tadmore and "Charley" followed by the bragging of five other boys whom they encounter in the Big Woods. If Clemens ever finished this novel set in the Ohio Valley, he discovered a comforting Christmas family scene and Tom's intellectual and spiritual growth at the conclusion. Though clearly conceived as an homage to Mark Twain's Tom Sawyer and Huckleberry Finn characters, *Tom Tad* lacked the riveting interest of Twain's narratives.

"Veni creator spiritus" ("Come creative spirit") (Catholic hymn).

"Then came a body of priests singing the *Veni Creator*" (*JA* [1896], Ch. 13).

VENNOR, HENRY GEORGE (1840–1884).

Clemens mentioned this Canadian naturalist and geologist in November 1881 (NB 19, *N&J* 2: 407, 411). He also alluded to Vennor in a speech at the Windsor Hotel on 8 December 1881 (New York *Times*, 10 December 1881; *MTSpk*, p. 158).

VERDI, GIUSEPPI (1813–1901). *Un Ballo in Maschera (A Masked Ball)* (opera, performed in 1859).

On 19 May 1904 Isabel Lyon made an entry in her diary: "We went to hear some opera in the Verdi Theatre. The Verdi is a splendid building and the music was the Bal Masque, not a very good opera, and the baritone Battisini is not so good as Sulli seems to think" (IVL Journals, TS p. 17, MTP). Unfortunately Lyon does not explain whether "we" referred to her mother or to one or more of the Clemenses. Mattia Battisini (1856–1928) was an Italian baritone. Giorgio M. Sulli, a prominent New York City voice teacher, gave vocal lessons to Clara Clemens.

———. *Rigoletto* (opera, performed in 1851).

Clemens made a favorable reference to *Rigoletto* in 1878 (NB 16, *N&J* 2: 213), choosing its "Introduction" as one of the melodies for his expensive music box.

———. *La Traviata* (opera, performed 1853). Libretto by Francesco Marie Piave (1810–1876).

Mark Twain boasted that after "I had got myself cultivated" he could "close one eye in an opera and tell . . . 'Traviata' from 'Trovatore'" (Virginia City *Territorial Enterprise*, 3–5 June 1865; reprinted by Gary Scharnhorst, "Additional Mark Twain Contributions to the Virginia City *Territorial Enterprise*, 1863–66," *American Literary Realism* 47.1 [Fall 2014]: 90).

———. *Il Trovatore (The Troubador)* (opera, performed in 1853). Libretto by Salvadore Cammarano (1801–1852).

Mark Twain bragged that he could now "close one eye in an opera and tell . . . 'Traviata' from 'Trovatore'" (Virginia City *Territorial Enterprise*, 3–5 June 1865; reprinted by Gary Scharnhorst, "Additional Mark Twain Contributions to the Virginia City *Territorial Enterprise*, 1863–66," *American Literary Realism* 47.1 [Fall 2014]: 90). Twain lengthily burlesqued a production of this opera performed by Bianchi's Grand Italian Opera Company on 24 August 1866 at Maguire's Opera House in San Francisco (NB 5, *N&J* 1: 167–172); he ridiculed its acting, scenery, direction, music, and bathos. In 1867 he heard "the loveliest air from 'Trovatore'" at Zion Protestant Episcopal Church in New York City (18 February 1867 letter to *Alta California*, *MTTMB*, p. 96). "I am enchanted with the airs in Trovatore & other old operas which the hand organ & the music box have made entirely familiar to my ear—I am carried away with delighted enthusiasm when they are sung at the Opera—but O, how far between they are!" (NB 14, 30 May 1878, *N&J* 2: 93). Clemens picked "Miserère" from this opera for the repertoire of his $400 Geneva music box (NB 16, *N&J* 2: 212; SLC to Susan Warner, 20 November 1878, Yale University). When conversing with Henry Fisher, Clemens once alluded to "an exchange of babies, as in the old-time operas,

Troubador and the rest" (*AMT*, p. 48).

Rogers, *S&B* (1967), pp. 19–24.

VERNE, JULES (1828–1905). *Five Weeks in a Balloon; or, Journeys and Discoveries in Africa, by Three Englishmen. Compiled in French by Jules Verne, from the Original Notes of Dr. Ferguson [pseud.]; and Done into English by William Lackland*. New York: D. Appleton and Co., 1869. 345 pp. ["William Lackland" is now believed to have been the pseudonym of an unknown translator.]

Sometime after this American edition issued in the spring of 1869, Mark Twain returned to Notebook 11 and added an explanation for why he left uncompleted and unpublished the story of a Frenchman's aerial voyage to Illinois that he began aboard the *Henry Chauncey* in 1868: "*Mem.*—While this was being written, Jules Verne's 'Five Weeks in a Balloon' came out, & consequently this sketch wasn't finished" (*N&J* 1: 511). In April 1876 Twain returned to the idea of depicting a balloon trip from France to the American Midwest in "A Murder, a Mystery, and a Marriage" (MS in the Harry Ransom Center, University of Texas at Austin; TS in DV411, MTP). In Chapter 8 of this posthumously published novella (2001), Jean Mercier recounts how Jules Verne "bought an old second-hand balloon and sent me up in it. The old bladder collapsed, and I fell in a brick-yard and broke my leg. The literary result of that trip was the book called 'Five Weeks in a Balloon'" (TS p. 25). Mercier eventually throws Verne from the balloon basket ("I hope it killed him") and sails to Deer Lick, Missouri; he predicts that Verne, roasting in hell, will write an exaggerated account titled "Eighteen Months in the Furnace" (TS pp. 26, 28). In this sketch as in his spoofs of Sherlock Holmes, Twain registers both impatience with, and jealousy of, successful writers who discover infallible formulas for producing popular novels. In February or March 1878, criticizing a manuscript by Orion Clemens, Twain wrote: "One should not call Verne harsh names. His crime should be sarcastically *suggested*, rather than *told*" (DV415, MTP).

By 1882 Twain's fascination with balloon stories had taken a turn toward the macabre: he made entries in Notebook 20 for a tale about "mummified (frozen) corpses" of balloonists drifting in a stratum from which escape was impossible (*N&J* 2: 492). In the manuscript for *Life on the Mississippi* (1883) Twain developed this tale about grinning corpses hovering perpetually in a "stratum of dead air," but he omitted that passage from the published book. D. M. McKeithan, "Mark Twain's *Tom Sawyer Abroad* and Jules Verne's *Five Weeks in a Balloon*," *University of Texas Studies in English* 28 (1949): 257–270 (collected in *Court Trials in Mark Twain* [1958], pages 156–168), persuasively demonstrated how Twain returned again in 1892 to Verne's story about three men crossing central Africa in a balloon in thirty-six days; the result was *Tom Sawyer Abroad* (1894), in which Tom and Huck Finn drift away from Missouri. In 1896 Twain again employed the situation of trapped vessels—this time ocean-going ships—in "The Enchanted Sea-Wilderness" (*WWD?* [1969], pp. 7–8, 74–86).

Parsons, "Background of *The Mysterious Stranger*" (1960), pp. 63–65; Stone, *IE* (1961), p. 180.

———. *A Journey to the Centre of the Earth* (novel, published in 1864; the first English translation was published in 1871). In 1878 Orion Clemens labored on a narrative about an expedition into the core of the earth (*MTHL*, p. 226 n. 2). On 21 February 1878 Clemens warned Orion from Hartford that he was "poaching upon Verne's peculiar preserve" by "writing this sort of story" about a "trip to the interior world." Clemens suggested that Orion rewrite the tale as a parody: "I think the world has suffered so much from that French idiot that they could enjoy seeing him burlesqued—but I doubt if they want to see him imitated" (MTP). When Clemens wrote to Orion again on 23 March 1878 he was still dissatisfied with Orion's effort: "You should not publish it in book form at all—for this reason: it is only an imitation of Verne, at last—it is not a burlesque. But I think it may be regarded as proof that Verne cannot *be* burlesqued" (ALS in MTP; *MTL*, p. 322). Clemens alluded to Orion's "travesty Jules Verne" in a letter written to William Dean Howells on 9 February 1879 (*MTHL*, p. 255). Philip A Fanning's *Mark Twain and Orion Clemens* (2003) offered insights into the strange relationship that grew up between these two siblings.

———. *The Mysterious Island* (novel, published in 1870).

During the American Civil War five escapees from a Confederate prison camp float in a balloon to a remote island. Pirates are only one of the hazards they must overcome in Verne's novel. Mark Twain's character Jean Mercier complains: "He [Verne] patched up his miserable balloon, and set me on one more trip. I stuck fast in the clouds over Paris without budging, for three days, waiting for a wind, and then slumped down into the river, caught a fever and was abed upwards of three months. . . . He put into my hands his distortion of my last trip—a book entitled 'The Mysterious Island'!" Jean Mercier is so repulsed by this gross misrepresentation that he attempts to murder his employer Verne by heaving him from a floating balloon ("A Murder, A Mystery, and a Marriage" [written in 1876, posthumously published in 2001], MS in Harry Ransom Center, University of Texas at Austin; TS in DV411, MTP, TS pp. 25–26).

———. *Stories of Adventure*. Illus. New York: Scribner, Armstrong & Co., 1874. 305 pp. [Includes *Meridiana* and *A Journey to the Centre of the Earth*.]

Inscription: the front free endpaper is signed in pencil at the top: "le J. Langdon/Montreal/Aug. 3, 1874".

Provenance: bookplate #637 of the "J. Langdon Family Library" on the front pastedown endpaper.

Location: Mark Twain Archive, Elmira College, Elmira, New York.

Copy examined: unmarked copy available to Clemens whenever he visited the Langdons in Elmira. Examined on 27 May 2015.

———. *The Tour of the World in Eighty Days*. Trans. George M[akepeace]. Towle (1841–1893). The Saunterer's Series. Green buckram, red edges. Boston: James R. Osgood and Co., 1874. 291 pp.

Inscription: the front flyleaf is inscribed in pencil, "Theodore, pay/$1.50 for this &/ give it to Livy/S. L. Clemens". Clemens had started to sign the front paste-down endpaper in pencil, but found that the initial "S" did not show up well on the dark brown paper and abandoned the effort. The volume is priced at "1[.]50" in pencil on

the front pastedown endpaper. There is a fern leaf pressed at pages 214–215.

Location: Mark Twain Library, Redding, Connecticut.

Copy examined: Clemens's copy, unmarked. Has the Mark Twain Library accession number "2830" ("2998" has been crossed out). Examined in 1970 and again in June 1982.

The adventures of Phileas Fogg and his French valet in their effort set a record for circling the globe include hasty sightseeing, unforeseen setbacks, and discouraging delays in India, China, Japan, North America (where they are attacked by Sioux Native Americans) and other countries. Mark Twain's character named Jean Mercier explains in Chapter 8 of "A Murder, a Mystery, and a Marriage," written in 1876: "By and by he [Jules Verne] sent me from Paris all the way to a beggarly town at the very tail end of Spain, in an ox-cart. I was nearly a year on the road, and almost died of low spirits and starvation before I got back. What was the result? Why, 'Around the World in Eighty-five [*sic*] Days'!" (MS in Harry Ransom Center, University of Texas, Austin; TS p. 25, DV411, MTP).

———. *The Tour of the World in Eighty Days*. Reddish-brown cloth, gilt. Boston: James R. Osgood and Co., 1874.

Inscription: "From [illegible] Feb 21st, 1874—C. J. Langdon" [Charles Jervis Langdon, 1849–1916].

Provenance: the bookplate #522 of the "J. Langdon Family Library" is affixed to the front pastedown endpaper.

Catalog: Ball 2016 inventory, red cloth, gilt lettering, inscribed on 21 February 1874 by C. J. Langdon, J. Langdon Family Library #522, Mark Twain Archive.

Location: Mark Twain Archive, Elmira College, Elmira, New York.

Copy examined: an unmarked copy available to Clemens whenever he visited the Langdons in Elmira. Examined on 27 May 2015.

———. *Twenty Thousand Leagues Under the Sea* (published in 1870).

By 1876 Mark Twain was familiar with at least four of Verne's books, including this one. In Chapter 8 of Twain's "A Murder, a Mystery, and a Marriage" (Harry Ransom Center, University of Texas, Austin; TS in DV411, MTP), Jean Mercier confesses to a murder, but pleads that "murder comes easy to a man whose mind has been unsettled by tortures such as M. Verne has inflicted upon me" (TS p. 27). Verne sent Mercier on adventures for a salary, then wrote them up in books. "This man sent me down the Seine in a leaky sand-barge; when I came back, he listened to my tale and went to work and spread it out into that distressed book called 'Twenty Thousand Leagues Under the Sea'" (TS p. 25).

VERSEN, MAXIMILIAN VON (1833–1893). *Reisen in Amerika und der Südamerikanische Krieg [Travel to America and the South American War]*. Breslau: M. Mälzer, 1872. 220 pp. [Edition conjectured.]

Versen's book presents an account of travel in South America and a version of the Paraguayan War, 1865–1870. In Germany, on 20 February 1892, Clemens mentioned dining at the home of General von Versen. In a prior notebook entry, Clemens wrote: "This is genuine modesty. . . . You will find it in his literature. His account of his perilous running the gauntlet 25 yrs ago between the Brazilian & Paraguayan lines reads as modestly and unconsciously as a Sunday School Pleasure excursion. . . . He got about a page of literature out of that daring performance—just the mere bald unadorned *facts*" (NB 31, TS pp. 28, 31). See also the Catalog entry for Freiherr von Werthern, *General von Versen* (1898).

VIARDOT, LOUIS (1800–1883). *Wonders of Italian Art.* Illus. New York: Scribner, Armstrong & Co., 1872. 343 pp.

Source: MTLAcc, entry # 1995, volume donated from Clemens's library by Clara Clemens Gabrilowitsch in 1910.

VICTOR, METTA VICTORIA (FULLER) (1831–1886). *A Bad Boy's Diary.* New York: J. S. Ogilvie & Co., 1880.

"I would not be the author of that witless stuff (Bad Boy's Diary) for a million dollars" (SLC to Charles L. Webster, 19 September 1882, *MTBus*, p. 197). There was good reason for Clemens's resentment. Eight-year-old Georgie Hackett's first-person narrative, despite his inept schoolboy's efforts at spelling, became a best-seller in the 1880s.

VICTORIA, QUEEN OF GREAT BRITAIN AND IRELAND (1819–1901). *The Letters of Queen Victoria: A Selection from Her Majesty's Correspondence Between the Years 1837 and 1861. Published by Authority of His Majesty the King.* Ed. by Arthur Christopher Benson (1862–1925) and Reginald Baliol Brett Esher (1852–1930). 3 vols. New York: Longmans, Green and Co., 1907.

Inscriptions: all three volumes are signed, "S. L. Clemens".

Marginalia: a few marginal corrections in Volume II; no report of markings in Volume III.

Catalogs: *A1911*, lot 468, "2 vols. [apparently these were Volumes I and II], 8vo, cloth, gilt tops, uncut, N.Y. 1907. Both volumes autographed by S. L. Clemens, and a few marginal corrections," sold for $7.50; *C1951*, D35, Volume III only, listed among books signed by Clemens, $7.50.

On the flyleaf of Clemens's copy of Albert S. Evans's *Our Sister Republic* (1870), Clemens had penciled: "Every great man ^personage^ must be shadowed by a parasite who is infinitely little.—Johnson had his Boswell, Seward his Evans, Victoria her 'John'" (quoted in *A1911*, lot 159).

Vienna Neue Freie Presse (Vienna newspaper, published 1864–1939).

In a footnote to "Stirring Times in Austria" (1898), Mark Twain quotes from "the opening remark of an editorial in this morning's Neue Freie Presse, December."

VIETT, GEORGE FREDERIC (1868–1943). *The Deeper Harmonies and Other Poems; A Book of Verses, Essays and Selections.* Norfolk, Virginia: Free-Lance Publishing Co., [cop. 1905]. 304 pp.

Source: MTLAcc, entry #644, volume donated by Clemens. Viett wrote melancholy verse that capitalized nouns to suggest profundity. His "Love Transcendent" illustrates the emotional tone of what *The Deeper Harmonies* offered: "Phantom shapes that come and go,/Breaking hearts that burst in song;/Memories of the 'Long Ago,'/But all save Love will fade anon." Viett resided in Norfolk, Virginia until his death in 1943. Clemens's copy of the book evidently did not survive.

Viewpoints Against Vivisection from Some Great Minds. New York: Anti-Vivisection Society, n. d.

A pamphlet compilation of statements by prominent international and American figures, including Henry Ward Beecher, Robert Browning, Thomas Carlyle, Lewis Carroll, Harriet Beecher Stowe, Alfred Lord Tennyson,

and dozens of others, *Viewpoints Against Vivisection from Some Great Minds* condemned the cruelty of "scientific" experiments on conscious animals. Mark Twain's own objection—reading, in part, "The pain which it inflicts upon unconsenting animals is the basis of my enmity toward it"—appeared on page 23.

Location: Isabel V. Lyon's copy is in the collection of Kevin Mac Donnell, Austin, Texas.

Copy examined: photocopy of Isabel V. Lyon's copy, sent to Alan Gribben by Kevin Mac Donnell in 1984. Photographs of Clemens and William James appear on the front page of the pamphlet. Lyon was Clemens's private secretary during his brief campaign against the inhumane practice of vivisection.

VILAS, WILLIAM FREEMAN (1840–1908).

Clemens heard Colonel Vilas raise the fourth toast ("Our First Commander, General U. S. Grant") at the meeting of the Army of the Tennessee in Chicago in November 1879. On 13 October 1909 Clemens thanked Mrs. Vilas for sending him a "Memorial" to Colonel Vilas (ALS, Wisconsin Historical Society, PH in MTP).

VILLARI, PASQUALE (1827–1917). *The Life and Times of Niccolò Machiavelli.* Translated from the Italian by Linda (White) Mazini Villari (1836–1915). Illus. "A New Edition, Revised by the Translator." 2 vols. London: T. Fisher Unwin, 1892.

Marginalia: Clemens annotated ten pages, at one point noting that "we have barnstormers for this" and elsewhere alluding to "a use for aristocracy." In a margin Clemens called attention to this passage: "This rich, industrious, intelligent people, before whom all Europe stood, as it were, in ecstasy of admiration—this people was rapidly becoming corrupt. Everywhere liberty was disappearing, tyrants were springing up." A few pages farther on Clemens commented: "Here is the social world of Europe revealed under a lightning flash." Farther on he wrote: "Here was a Pope & a Church claiming authority to dictate to men what they should think, whereas even God himself has no authority (in that sense) over the human reason."

Source: offered for sale on eBay on 14 January 2011 with an opening bid of $15,000. The seller supplied these details: "Frontispiece portraits and 30 full-page illustrations. . . . This set was originally sold at the Clara Clemens Samossoud sale in 1951. . . . Two volumes. Thick octavo, original maroon cloth gilt, top edges gilt. Housed in a custom clamshell box." (Not all of the 1951 auction lots were listed on its sale sheet, so it is indeed entirely possible that even a book of this importance was galeved down without any record of the transaction.)

Copy examined: photocopy of the eBay listing sent to Alan Gribben by Kevin Mac Donnell of Austin, Texas on 15 January 2011. To all appearances, the book should be considered a legitimate addition to Clemens's known library. Certainly the sentiments expressed in the reported annotations have an authentic ring to them.

Linda Villari had previously written *On Tuscan Hills and Venetian Waters* (1885) and would soon publish *Here and There in Italy* (1893). In a 1903 Italian interview conducted in Florence, Mark Twain declared, "Machiavelli? I don't like him! Theoretically, Machiavelli could rule the universe, but in practice, he could never manage anything very cunning, except a change, more or less advantageous, of masters. . . . When you have no end other than that of serving efficiently, it is much better to live obscure and content without annoyance or disturbance. The smoke of glory is not worth the smoke of a pipe" ("An Interview with Mark Twain," Milan *Corriere della Sera*, 12 November 1903; reprinted by Robert Luscher, "Italian Accounts of Mark Twain: An Interview and a Visit from the *Corriere Della Sera*," *American Literary Realism* 17.2 [Autumn 1984]: 220). Twain's essay on William Dean Howells for *Harper's Monthly* in 1906 would mention that "what Machiavelli beheld round him in Italy was a civic disorder in which there was oppression with statecraft, and revolt without patriotism."

VINCENS, CÉCILE, "MME. CHARLES VINCENS" (1840–1908), pseud. "Arvède Barine." *Alfred de Musset*. Les grands écrivains français series. Original three-quarter morocco-grained olive-green cloth and marbled boards, gilt. Paris: Librairie Hachette et Cie, 1893. 182 pp.

Inscription: the front free endpaper is inscribed in black ink, "Clara Langdon Clemens/from/Marie Pichaud./June 8th 1893/Berlin."

Provenance: Has a shelfmark from Clara Clemens Gabrilowitsch's private Detroit library collection. Subsequently the volume became part of the Carrie Estelle Doheny Collection, St. John's Seminary, Camarillo, California. Donated in 1940 after Mrs. Doheny purchased the volume for $12.20 from Maxwell Hunley Rare Books, Beverly Hills, California. Auctioned by Christie's for $275 on 21 February 1989 on behalf of St. John's Seminary. Acquired by Nick Karanovich (1938–2003) of Fort Wayne, Indiana.

Catalog: *Sotheby's 2003*, #193, $3,000 (sold with four other titles from the Clemens family library).

Location: collection of Kevin Mac Donnell, Austin, Texas. Has the bookplate of "Estelle Doheny."

Copy examined: Clara Clemens's unmarked copy, in July 2004.

The French poet, fiction author, and playwright [Louis Charles] Alfred de Musset (1810–1857) based some of his poems on his celebrated affair in 1833 and 1834 with George Sand (1804–1876).

VINCENT, FRANK (1848–1916). *The Land of the White Elephant: Sights and Scenes in South-eastern Asia. A Personal Narrative of Travel and Adventure in Farther India, Embracing the Countries of Burma, Siam, Cambodia, and Cochin-China*. Illus. New York: Harper & Brothers, 1874. 316 pp.

Inscription: the front flyleaf is inscribed in black ink, "Samuel L. Clemens, Esq./With the compliments of the Author./Feb. 24th, 1877."

Location: Mark Twain Library, Redding, Connecticut.

Copy examined: Clemens's copy, unmarked. Has the red ink Mark Twain Library accession number "3394". Examined in 1970 and again in June 1982.

Chapter 7, entitled "The White Elephant," described the royal custom of possessing at least one such animal. Mark Twain's "The Stolen White Elephant" would appear in 1882.

VINOGRADOFF, (SIR) PAUL (1854–1925). *Roman Law in Mediaeval Europe*. Harper's Library of Living Thought Series. London and New York: Harper & Brothers, 1909. 136 pp.

Inscription: the front pastedown endpaper is signed in black ink, "SL. Clemens/ 1909."

Provenance: Antenne-Dorrance Collection, Rice Lake, Wisconsin.

Location: Mark Twain Archive, Gannett-Tripp Learning Center, Elmira College, Elmira, New York.

Copy examined: Clemens's copy, unmarked. Examined on 28 May 2015.

VIRGIL (OR VERGIL) (70–19 BCE). *The Works of Virgil*. Translated from the Latin by Joseph Davidson. London: George Bell & Sons, 1891. 404 pp. [Pages conjectured.]

Catalog: Ball 2016 inventory, blue cloth, gilt lettering, fair condition.

Location: Quarry Farm library shelves, under the supervision of the Mark Twain Archive, Elmira College, Elmira, New York.

Clemens had access to this volume during his later visits to Quarry Farm in Elmira.

In 1872 Mark Twain mentioned the Roman poet Virgil with veneration in "From an English Notebook" (*LE*, p. 172). "Perhaps a thousand times he [Dusenheimer] had heard the remark, 'Ilium fuit [i.e., Troy is no more],' followed in most instances by a hail to himself as 'Aeneas,' with the inquiry, 'Where is old Anchises?'" (*GA* [1873], Ch. 29). Twain referred to Virgil in Part 9 of *Is Shakespeare Dead?* (1909).

VITALI, GAETANO. *Manuel de la Conversation et du style épistolaire*. Paris: Garnier Freres, n.d. 354 pp.

Source: MTLAcc, entry #391, volume donated by Clemens.

In their Guides Polyglottes Series the publisher Garnier Freres offered various European language translations. This might have been the Français-Italien volume, but it is impossible to know, since the book apparently did not survive.

VOLTAIRE, FRANÇOIS MARIE AROUET DE (1694–1778). *L'A, B, C, ou dialogues entre A, B, C* (published in 1768–1769).

In 1860 or 1861 Clemens copied the title—"Si l'homme est né méchant et enfant du diable"—of *le troisième entretien* of this series of dialogues into Notebook 3 (*N&J* 1: 59). Such dialogues later became a favored type of discourse for the writer Mark Twain; conversations between a learned tutor and his puzzled pupil take the form of Tom Sawyer's lectures to the less-literate Huckleberry Finn, Huckleberry Finn's discussions with Jim about kings and biblical figures, and, most noticeably, Twain's characters in "What Is Man?" (1906).

Roger D. Lund, "Philosophic Drollery in *Letters from the Earth*," *Mark Twain Annual* 4 (2006): 104–126.

———. *The Age of Louis XIV* (history, published in 1751).

Clemens wrote to his publisher James R. Osgood from Hartford on 31 October 1881: "Would like to have Voltaire's 'Age of Louis XIV' if you can scare it up in the English tongue" (ALS, University of Pennsylvania).

———. *Candide* (published in 1759).

Clara Clemens listed the author and title in her undated commonplace book sometime between 1888 and 1904 (Paine 150, MTP).

———. "Dialogue entre un philosophe et un contrôleur général des finances" (published in 1751).

Clemens quoted (in French) the first remarks of the philosopher in the 1861 portion of Notebook 3 (*N&J* 1: 56–57).

———. "Dialogue entre un plaideur et un avocat" (published

in 1751).

Clemens copied the opening passages from this dialogue (in French) into his second piloting notebook (NB 3, *N&J* 1: 51–53), following several French exercises. He broke off abruptly to record a voyage he undertook on the *Alonzo Child* in November 1860. Voltaire's dialogue implicitly criticized the French system of litigation.

———. *Letters Concerning the English Nation (Lettres philosophiques sur les Anglais)* (published in 1733).

Clemens implied that he had read this work when he told Henry Fisher that he did not remember any reference to Samuel Johnson in Voltaire's English letters (*AMT*, p. 152). Voltaire's brilliant letters to his friend Nicolas-Claude Thirot, written after he visited England from 1726 to 1728, incisively described the religions, government, science, and literature he had encountered. The resulting book was banned in France.

———. *Mémoires pour servir à la vie de M. de Voltaire, écrits par lui-même.* Berlin, 1784.

Catalog: *A1911*, "16mo, wrappers, uncut, Berlin, 1784," with a small sheet containing notes by Clemens laid in, lot 468, sold for $1.25.

Clemens mentioned to Henry Fisher that "Voltaire got his start in literature by the library he bought as a youngster out of Ninon de l'Enclos' two thousand livres bequest" (*AMT*, p. 153). Fisher also reported that he and Clemens found a volume of verse by Voltaire in the Berlin Royal Library; the book was addressed to Frederick the Great and contained "grossly indecent" poetry. Fisher copied one stanza for Clemens to take with him to show Krafft-Ebing in Vienna. Clemens said he "would blush to remember any of these stanzas" (*AMT*, pp. 77–78). In Mark Twain's "Sold to Satan" (1923), the narrator offers a cigar to Satan, who says, "With permission I will save it for Voltaire"; the narrator refers to Voltaire as "a great man."

———. "Micromégas: A Comic Romance; Being a Severe Satire Upon the Philosophy, Ignorance and Self-Conceit of Mankind" (short story, published in 1752).

Clara Clemens listed the author and title in her undated commonplace book (Paine 150, MTP). In Voltaire's brief science fiction satire, two outer space aliens bring unwelcome news to earthlings.

———. *Zadig* (published in 1747).

In 1928 Professor Frederick Augustus Grant Cowper proposed that Chapter 20 ("L'Hermite") of *Zadig* was "was probably the chief source" for Mark Twain's *Mysterious Stranger* as published in 1916. Both works feature supernatural visitors who visit earth and impart wisdom ("The Hermit Story, as Used by Voltaire and Mark Twain," *In Honor of the Ninetieth Birthday of Charles Frederick Johnson*, eds. Odell Shepard and Arthur Adams. [Hartford: Trinity College, 1928], pp. 313–337).

Brashear, *MTSM* (1934), p. 247; Parsons, "Background of *The Mysterious Stranger*" (1960), pp. 59, 63, and 69; Gibson, ed., *MSM* (1969), p. 2 n. 4.

VOYNICH, ETHEL LILIAN (BOOLE) (1864–1960). *The Gadfly*. New York: Henry Holt and Co., 1897. 373 pp.

Inscription: the front free endpaper has been torn out. The initials "S. C." were written in pencil on the front pastedown endpaper and with a modern ballpoint pen on the title page. (There is a similar designation in Clemens's

probable copy of Thackeray's *Adventures of Philip*.)

Location: Mark Twain Library, Redding, Connecticut.

Copy examined: very likely Clemens's copy, unmarked. Has the red ink Mark Twain Library accession number "2595". I found this volume on the circulating shelves of the Mark Twain Library in 1970; I requested the librarian to remove it from circulation because of the probability that the missing endpaper once bore Clemens's signature or the author Voynich's inscription. I examined the volume again in June 1982.

The Gadfly is set in a revolutionary period of the 1840s in Italy.

W

W., M. Y. *A Wreath of Remembrance. By M. Y. W. Author of "At Rest," Etc., Etc.* London: Henry J. Drane, [1900?]. 260 pp.

Inscription: the front pastedown endpaper is inscribed, "Mark Twain/from M. Y. W."

Marginalia: markings and notes in black ink (none of these appear to be by Clemens) on pages 50, 55, 63, 81, 84, 93, 95, 97 ("tears" crossed out and replaced with "sobs"), 128, 133, 134, 150, 154, 158 (the name "Justin McCarthy," without any apparent relevance), and 182.

Location: Mark Twain Library, Redding, Connecticut. Donated by Clemens (MTLAcc, entry #1377).

Copy examined: Clemens's copy, unmarked by him. Has the red ink Mark Twain Library accession number "1377". Examined in 1970 and again in June 1977.

A collection of religious and secular poems.

WACHENHUSEN, HANS (1823–1898). *Der Vampyr. Novelle aus Bulgarien.* Stuttgart und Leipzig: Eduard Hallberger, 1878. 235 pp.

Catalog: *Zeitlin 1951*, item #46, $2.

Location: Mark Twain Papers, Berkeley, California. Donated by Jake Zeitlin.

Copy examined: Clemens's unmarked copy. There is a *C1951* sale label on the front pastedown endpaper.

Wachenhusen's was hardly the first German treatment of vampire tales. In this novel the creature was once an Eastern Orthodox priest. Wachenhusen, who had traveled in the Bulgarian region, evoked the atmosphere of the final phases of the Ottoman empire. Romani, here called gypsies, figured in his version of the legend. See also the Catalog entry for Bram Stoker's *Dracula*, which would not appear until 1897.

WACK, HENRY WELLINGTON (1869–1854). *The Story of the Congo Free State: Social, Political, and Economic Aspects of the Belgian System of Government in Central Africa.* Illus., maps. Frontispiece portrait of Leopold II. 101 photographs. Original pictorial brown cloth, spine with original brown morocco lettering, gilt. New York: G. P. Putnam's Sons, 1905. 634 pp.

Inscription: the front pastedown endpaper is signed, "S L. Clemens, 1905."

Marginalia: Above the frontispiece portrait of King Leopold, Clemens wrote in black ink: "A bucket of whitewash for the miscreant King Leopold."

Catalogs: *A1911*, "8vo, cloth, gilt top, uncut, N.Y. 1905," quotes an inscription on the portrait page, lot 470, sold for $4; Sloan, 18 November 1999, #489; *Sotheby's 2003*,

#244, $3,500.

Provenance: collection of Nick Karanovich (1938–2003), Fort Wayne, Indiana.

Copy examined: Clemens's unmarked copy. Viewed in 2003 at the Sotheby's auction.

Mark Twain wrote a polemical pamphlet in 1905 about King Leopold's documented atrocities in his African colony. Wack's apologia attempted to defend Leopold's stewardship of the Congo Free State (now Zaire) against "stories of cruelty and oppression" in a "campaign of calumny." Three years later the Belgium parliament, buffeted by a global humanitarian movement, would take control of the colony.

WADDEVILLE, MADAME DE (fl. 1870s-1880s). *Le monde et ses usages.* Nouv. édition. Paris: Librairie du Magasin des Demoiselles, 1875. 306 pp.

Mark Twain quotes extensively from this French etiquette book (citing its title but not its author) in a discarded chapter of *A Tramp Abroad* (1880) (Box 6, no. 7, MTP). Paula Harrington and Ronald Jenn, *Mark Twain & France: The Making of a New American Identity* (Columbia: University of Missouri Press), pp. 113 and 224–228.

WADE, JOSEPH AUGUSTINE (1796–1845). "Meet me by moonlight" (song, published in 1830). Melody also by Wade.

Clemens mentioned hearing this romantic ballad sung at the Governor's house in a sketch published in the *Territorial Enterprise* on 3 February 1863 (*ET&S* 1: 197). Its first lines plead with a female lover, "Meet me by moonlight alone/And then I will tell you a tale/Must be told by the moonlight/In the grove at the end of the vale."

WADLEIGH, FRANCES E. (1842–1908). *'Twixt Wave and Sky.* New York: Authors' Publishing Co., 1878. 261 pp.

Source: MTLAcc, entry #319, volume donated by Clemens.

The moral message of Wadleigh's novel *'Twixt Wave and Sky* supported the Catholic Church's position against divorce. Later in the 1880s the Boston-born author moved to the Washington, D. C. area and produced humorous stories and verses imitating the Southern dialect of African Americans in a manner that would be considered offensive to readers of later generations.

WAGHORNE, ARTHUR. *Through a Peer Glass: Winnie's Adventures in Wastemonster.* Illustrated by David Wilson (1873–1935). London: Hodder & Stoughton, 1908. 183 pp.

Source: MTLAcc, entry #495, volume donated by Clemens.

As the title implies, this political satire takes a young Winston Churchill ("Winnie") on a visit to the House of Lords, evoking Lewis Carroll's *Alice in Wonderland* and *Through the Looking-Glass.*

WAGNALLS, MABEL (1871–1946). *The Palace of Danger; A Story of La Pompadour.* Illustrated by John Ward Dunsmore (1856–1945). New York: Funk & Wagnalls Co., 1908. 311 pp.

Source: MTLAcc, entry #1096, volume donated by Clemens.

"We take pleasure in sending you by today's mail a complimentary copy of 'The Palace of Danger.' (A Story of La Pompadour)" (Funk & Wagnalls Co. to SLC, New York City, 18 December 1908, TLS in MTP). The letter mentioned "the inscription which we have written under your name in the book" and requested "a word of commendation, with your permission to use it in public." Mabel Wagnalls, a concert pianist and author, was the

only child of the publisher Adam Wagnalls (1843–1924), founder of Funk & Wagnalls. *Palace of Danger*, a novel, was based on the life of the gifted Jeanne-Antoinette Poisson (1721–1764), Madame de Pompadour, a member of the French court and mistress of Louis XV.

WAGNER, CHARLES (1852–1918). *L'Âme des Choses [The Soul of Things].*

Someone other than Clemens wrote the author and title of this book on the rear endpaper of Clemens's copy of Robert Louis Stevenson's *The Pocket R. S. S.* (1904). Wagner was a liberal French theologian and minister, independent in his sometimes mystical views. His son's death inspired *L'Âme des Choses.*

WAGNER, RICHARD (1813–1883). *Richard Wagner to Mathilde Wesendonck.* Ed. and trans. William Ashton Ellis (1852–1919). New York: Charles Scribner's Sons, 1905. 386 pp. [Edition conjectured but almost certain.]

Clara Clemens listed this title in her undated commonplace book, probably in 1905 (Paine 150, MTP).

Wagner's infatuation with the German poet Mathilde Wesendonck (1828–1902), wife of the wealthy silk merchant Otto Wesendonck (1815–1896), caused the rupture of Wagner's first marriage but also inspired some of his music.

———. *Lohengrin, Son of Parsifal* (opera, performed in 1850).

Wagner based his opera on the anonymous German epic of The Swan Knight. Clemens wrote "The Lohengrin" in pencil at the top of page 291 in F. J. Kiefer's *The Legends of the Rhine* (1870), which was the first page of the legend of The Swan Knight. In May 1878 Clemens attended a performance of *Lohengrin* in Mannheim; he reported on 30 May 1878 that the opera gave him the first headache of his life, though he enjoyed the "martial & stirring" bugle blasts. "I recognized nothing I had ever heard before, except the bridal song," he noted; this piece alone he found "very sweet & beautiful" (NB 14, *N&J* 2: 92–93). "The Wedding March" from *Lohengrin* was one of ten tunes that Clemens selected in 1878 for the $400 music box he purchased in Geneva (NB 16, *N&J* 2: 213; SLC to Susan Warner, 20 November 1878, Yale University). In Chapter 9 of *A Tramp Abroad* (1880), Mark Twain wrote: "We went to Mannheim and attended a shivaree—otherwise an opera,—the one called Lohengrin"; he criticized the lack of action ("there-was not much really done, it was only talked about; and always violently"). "We only had one brief little season of heaven and heaven's sweet ecstasy and peace," added Twain; "this was while a gorgeous procession of people marched around and around, in the third act, and sang the Wedding Chorus. To my untutored ear that was music,—almost divine music." Henry Fisher recalled that in Berlin around 1891 Clemens remarked of Wagner: "I like his Wedding March hugely and very little else he has done. . . . While Livy and the kids went to pieces [in Bayreuth] over Tristan and Isolde and the [Der Ring des] Nibelungen, I visited the grave of the Margravine" (*AMT*, p. 76). On 12 November 1891 Susy Clemens wrote from Berlin to her college friend Louise Brownell: "I saw Lohengrin the other night for the first time. It is delicate, exquisite, painful beyond words" (Hamilton College Archives; Cotton, "Olivia Susan Clemens," p. 127). In London in January 1897 Clemens remembered that he had been told Susy Clemens's soprano voice was competent for *Lohengrin, Tannhäuser,* and *Tristan und Isolde* (NB 39, TS p. 53). In June 1897 Clemens pretended to think Bach or Mendelssohn wrote the "Wedding March," then corrected himself (NB 42, TS p. 1). Isabel Lyon recorded on 1 December 1904 that "The Wedding March" was one of Clemens's favorite tunes on his orchestrelle (IVL Journals, TS p. 29, MTP). On 16 November 1906 Lyon "played the Lohengrin Wedding March for him twice" (IVL Journals, TS p. 203, MTP). A pianist "softly" played Wagner's "The Wedding March" (more properly "The Bridal Chorus" or "*Treulich geführt*") at Clara Clemens's wedding on 6 October 1909 (*MTB* [1912], p. 1523).

Clemens's pronouncements about Wagner's operas are noteworthy. "I *hate* the opera," Clemens swore in a letter to William Dean Howells from Munich on 30 January 1879. "I have got in two or three chapters [in *A Tramp Abroad*] about Wagner's Operas & managed to do it without showing temper—but the strain of another such effort would burst me" (*MTHL*, p. 249). "I wish I could see a Wagner opera done in pantomime once," Twain wrote in Bayreuth. "Then one would have the lovely orchestration unvexed to listen to and bathe his spirit in, and the bewildering beautiful scenery to intoxicate his eyes with, and the dumb acting couldn't mar these pleasures" ("At the Shrine of St. Wagner" [1891]). In Pisa in March 1892 Clemens made a complimentary reference to the "orchestral combinations in Wagner with silver horns in it" (NB 31, TS p. 33). "When they play Wagner in Paris they get mobbed," he noted in 1892 (NB 32, TS p. 16). "Wagner's house" was among the notes that Clemens jotted on a photo-board during his global lecture of 1895–96 in preparation for the travel book he would write (collection of Kevin Mac Donnell, Austin, Texas). "W's music is better than it sounds," Clemens remarked in July 1899 in Notebook 40 (TS p. 59); he attributed this quip—"I have been told that Wagner's music is better than it sounds"—to the humorist Bill Nye in a speech at the University of Missouri Commencement on 4 June 1902 and in an Autobiographical Dictation of 17 January 1906 (*AutoMT* 1: 288). That same year Clemens said, "I have witnessed, and greatly enjoyed, the first act of everything which Wagner created, but the effect on me has always been so powerful that one act was quite sufficient; whenever I have witnessed two acts I have gone away physically exhausted; and whenever I have ventured an entire opera the result has been the next thing to suicide" (30 November 1906 AD, *MTE*, p. 110; *AutoMT* 2: 294).

———. *Parsifal* (opera, performed in 1882).

Mark Twain related an ordeal: "This present opera was 'Parsifal.' . . . The first act of the three occupied two hours, and I enjoyed that in spite of the singing. . . . When we reached home [in Bayreuth] we had been gone more than seven hours. Seven hours at five dollars a ticket is almost too much for the money." Twain then describes "a hermit named Gurnemanz who stands on the stage in one spot and practices by the hour, while first one and then another of the cast endures what he can of it and then retires to die" ("At the Shrine of St. Wagner" [1891]). Katy Leary recalled that the Clemens family "liked *Parsifal* and they thought Parsifal himself was good

and that old Kundry—she was wonderful! Clara was mad about Parsifal." As for Clemens, he purportedly said "that old Kundry was good 'if she'd only get up more and walk around'" (*A Lifetime with Mark Twain* [1925], p. 118).

———. *Siegfried* (opera, performed in 1876).

On 9 September 1892 Susy Clemens reported to her college friend Louise Brownell that "in Frankfurt we went to see Siegfried" (Hamilton College Archives).

———. *Tannhäuser* (opera, performed in 1845).

Clemens considered choosing a melody from this opera as one of the ten tunes allowable on the $400 music box he bought in Geneva in 1878 (NB 16, *N&J* 2: 212). Among a list of errands in February or March 1889, Clemens set down "Tannhäuser tickets—4" (NB 28, *N&J* 3: 449). In August 1891 Mark Twain declared: "Yesterday they played the only operatic favorite I have ever had—an opera which has always driven me mad with ignorant delight whenever I have heard it—'Tannhäuser.' I heard it first when I was a youth; I heard it last in the last German season in New York." From the first notes of "that noble chorus of men's voices . . . until the closing of the curtain it was music, just music—music to make one drunk with pleasure, music to make one take scrip and staff and beg his way round the globe to hear it" ("At the Shrine of St. Wagner" [1891]). Susy Clemens wrote from Berlin to her college friend Louise Brownell on 31 October 1891: "We went to Tannhaüser the other night; a thrilling touching performance. . . . It was much more impressive than at Bayreuth" (Hamilton College Achives; Cotton, "Olivia Susan Clemens," p. 125).

Carlyle Smythe testified of Clemens: "He is no musician, although a fervid lover of music; but beyond a strong and natural affection for the simple negro melodies of his native land, his taste runs to Wagner. He once told me that he would walk twenty miles to hear *Tannhäuser*" ("The Real 'Mark Twain'" [September 1898], p. 30). In "Queen Victoria's Jubilee" (1897) Twain alluded to the Tournament of Song procession from Act II ("rich and adorable costumery"). He made a complimentary reference to "the Overture to Tannhauser" in a letter written to Joseph H. Twichell from London on 1 January 1900 (*LMTJHT*, p. 255). "It took me some time to get myself educated up to the point where I could enjoy Wagner," Twain remarked in a speech at University of Missouri Commencement on 4 June 1902. Isabel Lyon played the *Tannhäuser* overture for Clemens on Saturday, 24 February 1906, apparently at his request (IVL Journals, TS p. 137, MTP; a similar entry occurs in another IVL Journal, Harry Ransom Center, University of Texas at Austin).

———. *Tristan und Isolde* (opera, performed in 1865).

In August 1891 Mark Twain reported from Bayreuth: "Yesterday the opera was 'Tristan and Isolde.'" He scoffed at the devoutly pious attitude of the worshipers in attendance, but admitted that he "enjoyed both of these operas" ("At the Shrine of St. Wagner" [1891]).

WAITE, CATHARINE (VAN VALKENBURG) (1829–1913). *The Mormon Prophet and His Harem; or, an Authentic History of Brigham Young, His Numerous Wives and Children.* Cambridge, Massachusetts: Riverside Press, 1866. 280 pp. [Edition conjectured; a 318-page edition of the book was reprinted in

Chicago by J. S. Goodman and Co. in 1867.]

In Chapter 17 of *Roughing It* (1872) Mark Twain states that "it was not until Mrs. Waite's book, *The Mormon Prophet*, came out with Judge Cradlebaugh's trial of the accused parties in it," that the truth about the Mountain Meadows Massacre was revealed: "the Mormons *were* the assassins." Twain's Appendix B relies on "Mrs. C. V. Waite's entertaining book" to correct the historical record. After quoting from "her interesting detail of the great massacre," he closes with her summary of evidence implicating Brigham Young and his Mormons, a conclusion Twain finds to be "concise, accurate, and reliable." Herman Nibbelink, "Mark Twain and the Mormons," *Mark Twain Journal* 17.1 (Winter 1973–1974): 1–5.

WAKEFIELD, CLARK B. (1881–1905).

On 11 November 1902 William Dean Howells sent Clemens an unprintably obscene tale by this young Texas writer (*MTHL*, p. 749). Evidently the story has not survived. The Illinois-born Wakefield was then a newspaper reporter in Dallas, Texas; the next year he became an assistant night editor. Two years later he would die of typhoid fever in Brooklyn, New York, where he had sought employment with newspapers.

WAKEFIELD, WILLIAM, M. D. (1840–1884). *The Baths, Bathing, and Attractions of Aix-les-Bains, Savoy: Its History, Geology, Mineral Waters, and the Places of Interest in Its Neighbourhood; With Other Useful Information for Visitors.* London: Sampson Low & Co., 1886. 223 pp.

Mark Twain repeatedly quotes from Dr. Wakefield's "interesting local guide" in "Aix, the Paradise of the Rheumatics" (1891).

WAKEMAN, EDGAR (1813–1875). *The Log of an Ancient Mariner; Being the Life and Adventures of Captain Edgar Wakeman. Written by Himself and Edited by His Daughter [Minnie Wakeman-Curtis].* Illus. San Francisco: A. L. Bancroft & Co., 1878. 378 pp.

Clemens and Wakeman corresponded in March and April 1874 about Wakeman's publications plans (*MTLet* 6: 82–83, 119–120).

WALKER, JEROME (1846–1924). *Anatomy, Physiology, and Hygiene: A Manual for the Use of Colleges, Schools, and General Readers. . . . With Original and Carefully Selected Illustrations.* New York: A. Lovell & Co., 1887 [cop. 1883]. 415 pp. [Edition conjectured but highly likely.]

Marginalia: notes by Clemens.

Catalog: *A1911*, "12mo, cloth, N.Y. 1887, .. with marginal notes by Mr. Clemens and thirteen pages of original manuscript in pencil relating to the nerves feeding the brain," lot 471, sold for $3.50.

Dr. Jerome Walker had worked in battlefield hospitals in the Civil War, was chosen to guide Abraham Lincoln through a field hospital at City Point, Virginia, and served on the newly formed United States Sanitary Commission. After the war he practiced medicine in Brooklyn, New York and lectured on the subjects of physiology and hygiene in schools and hospitals in the New York City area.

WALKER, KATHERINE KENT (CHILD) (1833–1916), "Mrs. Edward Ashley Walker." "The Total Depravity of Inanimate Things," *Atlantic Monthly* 14.83 (September 1864): 357–364.

Mark Twain reprinted this comical sketch in *Mark Twain's Library of Humor* (1888).

"WALK TOGETHER CHILDREN" (spiritual).

Clemens listed the titles of several plantation spirituals in Notebook 30 in 1890, including "Walk Together Children" (*N&J* 3: 593). The song begins, "Walk together children/Doin you get weary"; each of the three stanzas concludes with a promise, "There's a great camp meeting in the promised land."

WALL, OSCAR GARRETT (1844–1911). *Recollections of the Sioux Massacre: An Authentic History of the Yellow Medicine Incident, of the Fate of Marsh and His Men, of the Siege and Battles of Fort Ridgely, and of Other Important Battles and Experiences. Together with a Historical Sketch of the Sibley Expedition of 1863.* Lake City, Minnesota: Printed at "The Home Printery," M. C. Russell, Proprietor, 1909. 282 pp. plus index.

Clemens wrote from Stormfield on 8 November 1909 to endorse Wall's book: "I find your history of the Great Massacre blood-curdlingly & most pathetically interesting. I . . . 'highly commend the literary excellence of the book'" (ALS in the collection of Kevin Mac Donnell, Austin, Texas). An uprising of Native Americans in Minnesota in the summer of 1862 resulted in the deaths of between 400 and 500 white settlers. Thirty-eight Dakota Sioux warriors were subsequently executed and many others were imprisoned.

WALLACE, ALFRED RUSSEL (1823–1913). *Australasia.* Volume I, *Australia and New Zealand. By Alfred R. Wallace. New Issue.* Maps, illus. Stanford's Compendium of Geography and Travel. London: Edward Stanford, 1893. 505 pp. Volume II, *Malaysia and the Pacific Archipelagoes. By F[rancis]. H[enry]. H[ill]. Guillemard [1852–1933].* London: Edward Stanford, 1894. 574 pp. [Volume I was first published in 1878.]

Among several other titles that Clemens noted in New Zealand on 20 November 1895, appears: "Alfred Russell [*sic*] Wallace's Australasia (get only the 1st vol.)" (NB 34, TS p. 40). In November 1896 Clemens listed his recent reading in London, which included, "Australasia <vol 1> (in one volume) A R Wallace" (NB 39, TS p. 26).

———. *Man's Place in the Universe: A Study of the Results of Scientific Research in Relation to the Unity or Plurality of Worlds.* New York: McClure, Phillips & Co., 1903. 326 pp.

Wallace also published an essay titled "Man's Place in the Universe," *Independent* 55 (26 February 1903): 473–483; it evoked reactions in the *Literary Digest*. Mark Twain discussed Wallace's article and quoted (as an epigraph) a comment from the *Literary Digest* in "Was the World Made for Man?" (DV12, MS p. 2, MTP), a piece Twain wrote in 1903: "'Alfred Russell [*sic*] Wallace's revival of the theory that this earth is at the centre of the stellar universe, & is the only habitable globe, has aroused great interest in the world.' —*Literary Digest.*" Twain, identified as a "scientist & theologian," professes guarded agreement with Wallace's supporters, but actually indicates sarcastic skepticism "that the world was made for man, & that the universe was made for the world" (*WIM?*, pp. 101–106). William Dean Howells wrote from New York City on 20 December 1903 to recommend Wallace's *Man's Place in the Universe* to Clemens, who was in Florence: "Wallace gives us back the old earth of our boyhood and more, too. . . . You ought to read that book; then you would not swear so much at your own species" (*MTHL*, p. 776).

———, William Ramsay, et al. *Progress of the Century.*

New York: Harper & Brothers, 1901. 582 pp. [Publisher and pages conjectured.]

Inscription: the front flyleaf is signed, "S. L. Clemens, Feb. 1902."

Catalog: *A1911*, "small 8vo, cloth, N.Y. 1901," quotes the signature, lot 390, sold for $2.50.

A number of experts appraised 100 years of progress in fourteen areas. Alfred Russel Wallace (1823–1913) treated the topic of Evolution, William Ramsay (1852–1916) surveyed gains in Chemistry, Joseph Norman Lockyer (1836–1920) summarized progress in Astronomy, Sir Charles Wentworth Dilke (1843–1911) was assigned the status of War, Andrew Lang (1844–1912) looked at Literature, and other prominent figures examined Archaeology, Electricity, Engineering, Medicine, Naval Ships, Philosophy, Physics, Religion, and Surgery.

——. *The Wonderful Century; Its Successes and Its Failures.* New York: Dodd, Mead & Co., [cop. 1898]. 400 pp.

On 7 December 1906 Frederic Whyte sent Clemens an excerpt—Wallace's continued advocacy of phrenology—from Wallace's *The Wonderful Century*; Whyte asked for Clemens's response, which he then published in the London *Daily Graphic*. See Madeleine Stern's "Mark Twain Had His Head Examined," *American Literature* 41.2 (May 1969): 216–217.

WALLACE, CHARLES WILLIAM (1865–1932). "New Shakespeare Discoveries: Shakespeare as a Man among Men," *Harper's Monthly* 120.718 (March 1910): 489–510.

According to Marion Schuyler Allen, during Clemens's final visit to Bermuda (and shortly before his return as an ill man to Connecticut on 12 April 1910) he "much underscored" a certain passage in Wallace's article. Professor Wallace's "New Shakespeare Discoveries" reported on public records pertaining to Shakespeare that Wallace had recently located in London. The sentences Clemens singled out on page 510 concerned human mortality: "It has sometimes been said that a man's last will and testament best expresses his character. Does it? Do we not rather know a man best from the simple act, look, or speech of daily life when the consciousness is unaware?" (Marion Schuyler Allen, "Some New Anecdotes of Mark Twain," *Strand Magazine* [London] 46.272 [August 1913]: 167; text corrected from the original article). I am grateful to Jo Dee Benussi for identifying this source.

WALLACE, LEWIS (1827–1905). *Ben-Hur: A Tale of the Christ.* 8vo, olive-green beveled cloth, rubbed, gilt, brown coated endpapers, rebacked, hinges reinforced, front free endpaper torn. New York: Harper & Brothers, [cop. 1880]. First edition, later issue, but with the early form of Wallace's dedication to "the wife of my youth." Second state binding.

Inscription: the front free flyleaf is signed in blue ink: "S. L. Clemens/Hartford, 1881."

Marginalia: there is a horizontal mark, possibly a stray one, midway in the margin of page 53. The top corners of four pages—53, 203, 395, and 410—are folded down.

Catalogs: ListABP (1910), "Ben Hur, Wallace"; Christie's, New York City, Sale 6382, estate of Phyllis Harrington, 11 May 1987, "cover nearly detached, front free endpaper loosening," lot 16, sold with two other books (by Head and Primrose) for a total of $1,650. Purchased by John L. Feldman; "The James S. Copley Library," Sotheby's

auction, New York City, 17 June 2010, lot 555, "faint dampstaining along top margin," sold for $3,500 to Kevin Mac Donnell.

Provenance: Clara Clemens Samossoud, who died on 19 November 1962, bequeathed this book to her friend and secretary Phyllis Harrington. It entered the collection of John L. Feldman of Astoria, New York in 1987. He described the edition as having been published around 1880 (Feldman to Alan Gribben, 19 May 1987). Subsequently Feldman placed this book on deposit in the Special Collections at the University of Colorado at Boulder, but by 2003 he had withdrawn it (Michelle Visser, Special Collections, to Alan Gribben, 10 June 2003).

Location: collection of Kevin Mac Donnell of Austin, Texas (Mac Donnell to Alan Gribben, 29 June 2010). "There are no marks of provenance in this volume—no sale labels, no marks by Clara Clemens Samossoud, no marks from the Mark Twain Library in Redding," reported Mac Donnell.

Copy examined: photocopy of the title page, copyright page, inscription, and page 53 provided by Special Collections at the University of Colorado to the Mark Twain Papers, Bancroft Library, University of California at Berkeley. The title page and inscription were reproduced in facsimile in the Sotheby's auction catalog (17 June 2010).

——. *Ben-Hur: A Tale of the Christ.* 2 vols. Illustrated by William Martin Johnson (1862–1942). New York: Harper & Brothers, 1900. 438 pp. (paged continuously).

Source: MTLAcc, entries #1677 and #1678, volumes donated by Clemens.

——. [Another identical copy.]

Inscription: both volumes are signed, "S. L. Clemens, 1900."

Catalog: *A1911*, "2 vols., 12mo, cloth, N.Y. 1900," quotes the signatures, lot 472, sold for $6.50.

Clemens mentioned Wallace in a letter addressed to Susy Clemens on 23 November 1884: "He has an article in this month's Century about the great Victory at Fort Donelson." Clemens added that he had met Wallace at the home of General U. S. Grant: "Gen. Lew Wallace was there. . . & when I told him Mamma was at the reading the other night & was sorry I didn't make her acquainted with the author of Ben Hur, he was very sorry I was so heedless himself. Mrs. Grant got up & stood between Gen. Wallace & me, & said, 'There's many a woman in this land that would like to be in my place & be able to tell her children that she had stood once elbow to elbow between two such great authors as Mark Twain & General Wallace.' We all laughed" (*LLMT*, p. 220). In July 1885 Clemens meant to "inquire for Gen Wallace" about a Turkish railroad investment; Wallace was minister to Turkey between 1881 and 1885 (NB 24, *N&J* 3: 170). In 1891 or 1892 Clemens wrote an undated letter to Olivia Clemens concerning William H. Prescott's *Conquest of Peru*: "Sometimes his grammar is bad; and now and then he reels you off a sentence that makes you think of Ben Hur Wallace, it is so slovenly and obscure" (*MFMT*, p. 99). Above all Clemens was impressed with the publishing success of Wallace's novel. In an interview in 1896 Clemens marveled at the sales of Bellamy's *Looking Backward*, comparing that "record" to the best-sellers *Ben-Hur* and Du Maurier's *Trilby* (Johannesburg *Star*, 18 May 1896; *Complete Interviews*, p. 303).

———. *Ben-Hur: A Tale of the Christ. By Lew. Wallace. Illustrated with Scenes and Characters from the Play*. The Player's Edition. Original green pictorial cloth, light green and apricot decorations, gilt. New York: Harper & Brothers, 1901. 552 pp.

Inscription: signed in black ink, "S L. Clemens/14 W. 10th, New York City, 1900."

Provenance: Dorothy Quick told the story of being given this copy by Clemens, who called it "one of the greatest books that was ever written." According to Quick, she was reading the book in Clemens's home in 1907 when he walked in and made her a gift of the volume she was holding. She added, "I still have the Players Edition of *Ben Hur* with 'S. L. Clemens' written on the back of the cover, for he wouldn't hear of my returning it as he said it was the kind of book one should reread as one grew older" (*Enchantment: A Little Girl's Friendship with Mark Twain* [1961], p. 148). When Quick died in March 1962 she owned homes on Park Avenue and in East Hampton; her copy of *Ben-Hur* surfaced at an East Hampton garage sale in March 1997, priced at $5.

Location: collection of Kevin Mac Donnell, Austin, Texas. Acquired in September 2016.

Source: Kevin Mac Donnell to Alan Gribben, 17 September 2016. Mac Donnell reported that there are no markings in the text; indeed, the book appears to be unread. Many pages after page 52 are uncut and unopened.

———. *Ben-Hur: A Tale of the Christ. By Lew. Wallace. Illustrated with Scenes and Characters from the Play*. The Player's Edition. New York: Harper & Brothers, 1904. 552 pp.

Source: MTLAcc, entry #1316, volume donated by Clemens.

———. *The Boyhood of Christ*. Illus. Original purple cloth, stamped with gilt lettering on front cover and spine, the spine faded. New York: Harper & Brothers, [1888].

Marginalia: Clemens wrote approximately 107 words on four pages. He registered a dislike for Wallace's style as well as his treatment of religion. "All *this* unspeakable silliness to show that God Almighty & His family were *respectable* while down here!" he noted, writing vertically in black ink on page 74. Clemens wrote vertically on page 76, "Hear him drool!" On page 78, which is the blank verso of a picture of the young Christ, Clemens commented: "It is curious 'literature.' The aged fool drivels complacently along (it is Wallace himself) . . . , yet all the time he notices, unoffended & unashamed, that the children are laughing at him. It is delicious, the way he keeps pumping complimentary lies out of these poor bored children. . . . And it is charming the way he airs his cheap & squalid learning before them to astonish them & the reader." On page 82 Clemens added, "How he does admire himself!"

Provenance: has a library accession number in red ink ("2999") on the rear pastedown endpaper and contains the purple stamps of the Mark Twain Library at Redding, Connecticut on the front pastedown endpaper and elsewhere (the check-out slip at the rear of the volume records a borrowing due back on 15 June 1912). Evidently Clara Clemens retrieved the volume because it also bears the shelfmarks of her library numbering system from her Detroit days. Later the book was sold at the 1951 Hollywood auction but not listed in the sloppily compiled

sale sheet for that event.

Catalog: "Property from the Library of Mark Twain," Butterfield & Butterfield, San Francisco, Sale 6613, 16 July 1997, lot 2698.

Location: Mark Twain House and Museum, Hartford, Connecticut.

Copy examined: Clemens's copy, in Hartford in 1997.

The presumptuousness of the complacently confident Wallace, coupled with his celebrity and unctuousness, apparently made him seem like fair game for Clemens's private gibes.

———. *The Boyhood of Christ*. Illus. New York: Harper & Brothers, 1900. 101 pp.

Source: MTLACC, entry #1370, volume donated by Clemens.

———. *The Chariot-Race from Ben-Hur*. Illustrated by Sigismond Ivanowski (1875–1944). New York: Harper & Brothers, 1908. 132 pp.

Inscription: the front pastedown endpaper is signed, "S. L. Clemens, Stormfield, Jan. 1, 1909."

Catalogs: *A1911*, "8vo, cloth, N.Y. 1908," quotes the signature, lot 473, sold for $4; Lew David Feldman, Catalog of "House of El Dieff" (1954), item #248, price $50; Lew David Feldman, "American Books," Catalog of "House of El Dieff" (1955), item #254, price $35.

———. *The Fair God; or, The Last of the 'Tzins. A Tale of the Conquest of Mexico*. Boston: James R. Osgood & Co., 1874. 586 pp.

Source: MTLAcc, entry #320, volume donated by Clemens.

———. *The First Christmas, from "Ben-Hur."* Illustrated by William Martin Johnson (1862–1942) and by photographs. New York: Harper & Brothers, 1902. 109 pp.

Inscription: the front pastedown endpaper is signed in black ink, "S. L. Clemens/1902". The front free endpaper is also signed in black ink, "SL. Clemens/York Harbor, Maine,/October 1902."

Marginalia: next to the last nine lines of page vi of Wallace's preface Clemens wrote in black ink: "Ah—the finger of God in it. How nice." At the end of the preface (page vii) he commented: "In this fairy tale we have a curiously grotesque situation: God, ambushed in a Pullman sleeper, surreptitiously & unfairly <employing> betraying an unsuspecting good & honest infidel [Robert G. Ingersoll] into converting Lew Wallace. To what trivial uses may we come at last." The book contains no other notes. The leaves beyond page 57 are uncut. Robert G. Ingersoll (1833–1899), a nationally prominent agnostic, often debated clergymen in public forums; see the Catalog entry for Ingersoll.

Catalogs: ListABP (1910), "First Christmas, Wallace"; *C1951*, #41a, $55.

Provenance: collection of Frank C. Willson (1889–1960) in Melrose, Massachusetts. Sold by his widow Margarete in 1962 to the University of Texas.

Location: Harry Ransom Center, University of Texas at Austin.

Copy examined: Clemens's copy. Contains a *C1951* sale label.

Gribben, "Mark Twain's Library Books in the Humanities Research" (1979), pp. 24–25 (reproduced a facsimile of page vii of Wallace's book).

———. *The First Christmas, from "Ben-Hur."* New York: Harper & Brothers, 1903. 140 pp.

Source: MTLAcc, entry #1335, volume donated by Clemens.

———. *The First Christmas, from "Ben-Hur."* New York: Harper & Brothers, 1906. 140 pp.

Source: MTLAcc, entry #1334, volume donated by Clemens.

———. *Lew Wallace: An Autobiography.* 2 vols. Illus. New York: Harper & Brothers, 1906. 1028 pp. (paged continuously).

Inscription: Volume I is signed and inscribed in black ink on the front pastedown endpaper, "S L Clemens/1906./ The English of this book is incorrect &/slovenly, & its diction, as a rule, barren of/distinction. I wonder what 'Ben Hur' is like." Volume II contains no inscription.

Marginalia: Clemens made a note in black ink at the end of Chapter 5: "Nobody's English is perfect, but his would have been better if he had served a term in a printing office" (p. 59). On page 140 Clemens made a pencil correction, altering "to have walked with you" to read "to walk with you." At the end of Chapter 14 Clemens wrote in pencil: "In keeping the secret wasn't he a party to the theft?" (p. 142). This comment referred to Wallace's account of a doctor who stole a venerated skull of the religious founder of a cathedral in Mexico as "'a lovely piece of furniture in my office. What good was it doing there? . . . You'll say nothing, of course.' I kept his secret." On page 291 Clemens used pencil to alter "it had passed unnoticed" to "it would have passed unnoticed". On page 294, also in pencil, he changed "it had not been possible for me to have held my position" to read "it would not have been possible for me to hold my position." In black ink on page 332 he revised "It don't suit me" into "It doesn't suit me."

Location: two volumes, Mark Twain Library, Redding, Connecticut. Donated by Clemens (MTLAcc, entries #826 and #827).

Copies examined: I examined both volumes in 1970 and again in June 1982 and on 9 November 2019. Volume I (502 pp.) has the red ink Mark Twain Library accession number "826" and Volume II shows the red ink number "827".

———. *The Prince of India; or, Why Constantinople Fell.* 2 vols. New York: Harper & Brothers, 1906.

Source: MTLAcc, entries #321 and #322, volumes donated by Clemens.

———. *The Wooing of Malkatoon. Commodus.* Illustrated by [Frank Vincent] DuMond (1865–1951) and [John Reinhard] Weguelin (1849–1924). Green cloth, decorated. New York: Harper & Brothers, 1898. 168 pp.

Provenance: Antenne-Dorrance Collection, Rice Lake, Wisconsin.

Location: Mark Twain Archive, Gannett-Tripp Learning Center, Elmira College, Elmira, New York.

Copy examined: Clemens's copy, unmarked. Examined on 28 May 2015.

Contains a long narrative poem ("The Wooing of Malkatoon") and a play about Lucius Aelius Aurelius Commodus (171–192 CE), Emperor of Rome.

WALLER, MARY ELLA (1855–1938). *The Wood Carver of 'Lympus.* Boston: Little, Brown & Co., 1906. 311 pp.

Source: MTLAcc, entry #323, volume donated by Clemens. An injured Vermont farmer learns that a different life is still worthwhile.

WALLING, WILLIAM ENGLISH (1877–1936). *Russia's Message, The True World Import of the Revolution.* New York: Doubleday, Page & Co., 1908. 476 pp.

Inscription: signed, "S. L. Clemens, 1908".

Catalogs: *C1951*, item #12c; *Zeitlin 1951*, item #47, $10.

WALLON, HENRI ALEXANDRE (1812–1904). *Jeanne d'Arc, par H. Wallon.* 2 vols. Paris: L. Hachette & cie, 1860. [Reprinted repeatedly in the 1870s, 1880s, and 1890s by Hachette. Clemens's edition has not been determined.]

Mark Twain listed Wallon's *Jeanne d'Arc* third in order of the "authorities examined" for his research on Joan of Arc; see the page preceding his "Translator's Preface."

Ronald Jenn and Linda A. Morris, "The Sources of Mark Twain's *Personal Recollections of Joan of Arc*," *Mark Twain Journal* 55.1–2 (Spring/Fall 2017): 55–74.

WALPOLE, HORACE (1717–1797), fourth earl of Oxford. *The Letters of Horace Walpole, Earl of Oxford. Edited by Peter Cunningham [1816–1869]. Now First Chronologically Arranged.* 9 vols. English Gentleman's Library Series. London: Henry G. Bohn, 1861–1866.

Marginalia: certain passages in Volumes I–VIII are marked with pencil. There are extensive pencil annotations (and one black ink mark on page 161) in Volume IX. Pages 247, 278, 295, 296 (horrors of the guillotine), 302 (beside a derogatory remark about "coarse" Thomas Paine), 305, 306, 308, 310, 319 (at a comment on Samuel Johnson's "brutal" remarks) of Volume IX contain Clemens's pencil markings. On page 242 of Volume IX Clemens noted: "There was a proposition, once, to make the Bishop of Osnaburg King of *America*." Of Lord Mount-Edgcumbe's remark that "Mademoiselle D'Eon is her own widow" (p. 321), Clemens responded in pencil: "That is mighty good." George Edgcumbe, First Earl of Mount Edgcumbe, lived from 1720 until 1795. Chevalier d'Éon (1727–1810) also identified openly as Mademoiselle d'Éon after s/he immigrated to England in 1763. It was said that Chevalier d'Éon was known to fight duels wearing women's clothing. On page 356 Clemens commented on Madame du Barry, writing vertically next to an account of how the King of England subtly snubbed a court member: "Good, then she got snubbed." He wrote "Gospel truth" near a characterization of the French, "so innate is their savage barbarity" (p. 398). (On page 386 he had noted "Amen" beside a prior reference to French barbarity.) "See legend in the Peerage," Clemens jotted on page 401. In the margin of page 404 he wrote vertically in pencil: "The princess would have sacrificed her life to save one she *loved*—not so great a merit as to do it for one she *hated*. Did the savior love the world, or hate it? What is the measure of the merit of his sacrifice?"

Provenance: Volume IX only was sold at the *C1951* auction, though the book was omitted from the sale catalog.

Catalogs: *A1911*, "Vols. I-VIII, portraits, 8 vols., 8vo, cloth, Lond. 1861–66, some passages marked with pencil by Mr. Clemens," lot 474, sold for $1 total; *Zeitlin 1951*, item #12, Vol. IX only, price $10.

Location: volume IX only, American Literature Collection,

Beinecke Rare Book Library, Yale University, New Haven, Connecticut.

Copy examined: Clemens's copy of Volume IX only. Displays the bookplate of George Buell Aloord on the front pastedown endpaper. A pencil note on the front free endpaper states that the volume was sold in Hollywood at the *C1951* auction. The Mark Twain Papers, Bancroft Library, University of California at Berkeley, possesses photocopies of the annotations in Volume IX, and these were examined also.

In Mark Twain's "The Walt Whitman Controversy" (DV36, MTP), an undated manuscript possibly written in 1882, Twain mentions that he owns a copy of Walpole's *Letters* and groups it among the classics that contain obscenity. Interviewed in Australia in September 1895, Clemens quoted a Walpole letter that defined life as "a tragedy to those who feel—a comedy to those who think" (Gary Scharnhorst, *Complete Interviews*, p. 204). In June 1899 Clemens referred publicly to his early reading: "I, for instance, read the *Walpole Letters* when I was a boy. I absorbed them, gathered in their grace, wit, and humor, and put them away to be used by and by. One does that so unconsciously with things one really likes. I am reminded now of what use those letters have been to me" ("Author's Club Dinner Speech," *MTSpk* [1976], p. 323).

Baetzhold, *MT&JB* (1970), p. 29.

———. *Letters of Horace Walpole, Selected and Edited by Charles Duke Yonge [1812–1891].* 2 vols. Illus. London: Swan Sonnenschein & Co., 1891.

Catalog: Ball 2016 inventory, 2 vols., blue cloth, gilt lettering, gilt top edge pages, good to fair condition.

Location: Quarry Farm library shelves, under the supervision of the Mark Twain Archive, Elmira College, Elmira, New York.

Clemens had access to these volumes whenever he visited Quarry Farm in Elmira.

WALSH, JOHN JOHNSTON (1820–1884). *A Memorial of the Futtehgurh Mission and Her Martyred Missionaries, with Some Remarks on the Mutiny in India.* Illus. Spine loose. Philadelphia: Presbyterian Board of Publication, n.d. [Preface is dated 1858.] 338 pp. Cover title: *The Martyred Missionaries.*

Inscriptions: a small pink bookplate of "Orion Clemens" is pasted on the front pastedown endpaper. The front flyleaf is inscribed in brown ink: "Presented to/Mary E. Clemens,/by/Dr. C. L. Anderson,/Carson City,/Nevada." There are pressed stains of maple leaves on pages 74–75, 94–95, and 210–211.

Location: Mark Twain Library, Redding, Connecticut. Donated by Clemens (MTLAcc, entry #839).

Copy examined: Orion Clemens's unmarked copy. Has the red ink Mark Twain Library accession number "839". Examined in 1970 and again in June 1982. Clemens and his brother sometimes exchanged reading materials, so Clemens might have seen this book.

Eight Christian missionaries at the Mission at Futtehgurh were executed in 1857 during the Sepoy Rebellion.

WALSH, WILLIAM SHEPARD (1854–1919), pseud. "William Shepard." *Authors and Authorship.* The Literary Life Series. New York: G. P. Putnam's Sons, 1882. 258 pp. [Publisher and pages conjectured.]

Inscriptions: inscribed, "Compliments of William Shepard Walsh." Signed "S. L. Clemens, Hartford, 1882."

Catalogs: *A1911*, "16mo, cloth, N.Y. 1882," quotes the signature and the inscription, lot 430, sold for $2; George D. Smith, New York City, "Catalogue of Books" (1911), quotes the signature and inscription, item #18, $8.50.

On pages 43–48 Walsh reprinted "Mark Twain's General Reply" from the November 1870 issue of the *Galaxy*. On page 80 Walsh stated: "As to Mark Twain, it is well known that that genial gentleman has found a bonanza mine in literature—$300,000 has been named as the sum realized from 'The Innocents Abroad'— as well as in the drama." In the chapter titled "First Appearance in Print," Walsh reported: "Mark Twain was not only surprised at having his early articles accepted (they were in the form of letters addressed from the mining districts to the *Virginia City Enterprise*), but from that time his good opinion of the editors steadily declined. 'It seemed to me they might have found something better to fill up with than my literature.' A cheerful modesty not an innate quality of every aspiring author" (p. 171).

WALTERS, WILLIAM THOMPSON (1820–1894). *Oriental Ceramic Art; Illustrated by Examples from the Collection of W. T. Walters.* Preface by William M[ackay]. Laffan (1848–1909). Text and notes by Stephen W[ootton]. Bushell (1844–1908). 116 color plates. 400 black and white illustrations. 10 vols. Edition limited to 500 copies. New York: D. Appleton and Co., 1897. 942 pp.

Clemens wanted his own publishing firm to issue an elaborate catalog of Walters's art collection. On 13 January 1887 Clemens wrote to Charles L. Webster from Hartford, predicting "that book is a greenback-mine" (*MTBus*, p. 374). Later Clemens would recall how Webster neglected to follow up on this tip, even though "William M. Laffan told me that Mr. Walters, of Baltimore, was going to have a sumptuous book made which should illustrate in detail his princely art collection" (2 June 1906 AD, *MTE*, pp. 189–190; *AutoMT* 2: 77).

WALTON, IZAAK (1593–1683). *Lives of John Donne, Henry Wotton, Richd Hooker, George Herbert, &c.* Ed. by H[enry]. A[ustin]. Dobson (1840–1921). The Temple Classics Series. General editor, Sir Israel Gollancz (1864–1930). 2 vols. Black leather, covers detached. London: J. M. Dent, 1898. [Facsimile edition.]

Inscriptions: the front free endpapers of both volumes are inscribed identically in ink: "To Mr. and Mrs. Clemens/A little souvenir of a short visit to Izaak Walton and Charles Cotton's country, Beresford Dale, the Dove and Manyfold from/Thomas Wardle/ Swainsley/November 29th 1899."

Provenance: Antenne-Dorrance Collection, Rice Lake, Wisconsin.

Location: Mark Twain Archive, Gannett-Tripp Learning Center, Elmira College, Elmira, New York.

Copies examined: Clemens's unmarked copies of both volumes. Examined on 28 May 2015.

In Mark Twain's "The Secret History of Eddypus," written 1901–1902, "Sir Izaac [sic] Walton" is bizarrely remembered as the man who "discovered the law of the Attraction of Gravitation" (*FM*, p. 357).

WÄLZEL, CAMILLO (1829–1895) and **FRANZ FRIEDRICH RICHARD GENÉE** (1823–1895). *Fatinitza* (operetta in three acts, performed in Vienna, 1876). Music composed by Franz

MARK TWAIN'S LITERARY RESOURCES

von Suppé (1819–1895).

In October 1880 Clemens received a bill from Hawley, Goodrich & Company of Hartford for one ticket to "Fatinitza," sold on 27 May 1880 (receipt in MTP). The first American production took place at the Fifth Avenue Theatre in New York City on 14 April 1879; it starred Jennie Winston. The scene is a Bulgarian military outpost in 1877 during the Russo-Turkish War. "Fatinitza" is the name Lt. Vladimir Michailoff assumes when he disguises himself as a young Turkish girl; to his embarrassment, the Russian General Count Timofay Gabrilovitsch Kantschakoff falls in love with him.

WARD, HERBERT (1863–1919). *My Life with Stanley's Rear Guard*. Map by F. S. Weller. New York: Charles L. Webster & Co., 1891. 151 pp.

Clemens's publishing firm issued this book, written by a captain of the Rear Guard who knew Henry M. Stanley. It describes the Congo.

WARD, MARY AUGUSTA (ARNOLD) (1851–1920), also known as "Mrs. Humphry Ward." *Fenwick's Career*. Illustrated by Albert Sterner (1863–1946). First American edition. Original red cloth, gilt. New York: Harper & Brothers, 1906. 367 pp.

Source: MTLAcc, entry #1666, volume donated by Clemens.

A painter leaves his wife and child behind in rural Westmoreland in order to enter the London scene and seek fame.

———. [Another identical copy.]

Inscription: the front pastedown endpaper is signed in black ink, "S L. Clemens/1906."

Marginalia: a few notes in the text. Clemens made vertical pencil lines on pages 24 and 25 (where the landscape of Westmoreland is described), and on pages 80, 85, 114, 150, 216, 218, and 278. He underlined the word "naughtiness" on page 85. Pages 113 and 137 are folded down. Clemens altered the syntax in pencil on page 153. On page 278 he made a vertical mark next to a quotation from Omar Khayyám about "One thing is certain and the rest is lies—/The flower that once is born forever dies."

Catalog: *A1911*, "12mo, cloth, N.Y. 1906," quotes the signature, lot 475, sold for $2.25.

Provenance: the bookplate of Charles Dexter Allen is signed in pencil, "Mary A. Ward/August, 1916." (The envelope in which she returned the autographed bookplate is tipped in.) Post-1916 newspaper clippings about Ward are pasted on the front and rear flyleaves.

Location: collection of Kevin Mac Donnell, Austin, Texas. Acquired in October 1983.

Copy examined: Clemens's copy, examined in Austin on 15 December 1983 and again in July 2004. Has the *A1911* sale label, #475.

———. *Fenwick's Career*. Illustrated from drawings by Albert Sterner (1863–1946) on Japan paper. 2 vols. 498 copies printed. New York: Harper & Brothers, 1906.

Inscription: Volume I autographed by the author.

Catalog: *A1911*, "2 vols., 8vo, half cloth, gilt tops, uncut, N.Y. 1906, only 498 copies issued, Volume I is signed by the author," a sheet of Clemens's writing laid in, lot 476, $3.25.

———. *The History of David Grieve* (novel, published in 1892).

Susy Clemens wrote to her college friend Louise Brownell from Rome on 29 April 1892 about this tale of two English

orphans: "I have just finished 'David Grieve' and it *is* so great I think. . . . Do read it" (Hamilton College Archives).

———. *Lady Rose's Daughter, A Novel*. Illustrated by Howard Chandler Christy (1873–1952). 2 vols. New York: Harper & Brothers, 1903. 491 pp. [Paged continuously.]

Inscriptions: Clemens inscribed the front pastedown endpaper of Volume I in black ink, "Livy L. Clemens/1903/ from SLC". He inscribed the front pastedown endpaper of Volume II in black ink, "L. Clemens/1903".

Location: Mark Twain Library, Redding, Connecticut. Donated by Clemens (MTLAcc, entries #1478 and #1665).

Copies examined: Olivia Clemens's unmarked copies. Many leaves are unopened in both Volume I and Volume II. The Library accession numbers do not accord with the recorded donations; Volume I has a red ink Mark Twain Library accession number "2723" and Volume II has a red ink number 2724". This was unusual but not unprecedented; evidently the librarian entering the donations into the accession record was occasionally distracted. Examined in 1970 and again in June 1982 and on 9 November 2019.

———. *Lady Rose's Daughter, A Novel*. Illustrated by Howard Chandler Christy (1873–1952). New York: Harper & Brothers, 1903. 491 pp.

Source: MTLAcc, entry #1303, volume donated by Clemens.

———. *The Marriage of William Ashe*. Illustrated by Albert Sterner (1863–1946). New York: Harper & Brothers, 1906. 563 pp.

Source: MTLAcc, entry #1054, volume donated by Clemens.

———. *Robert Elsmere*. London and New York: Macmillan and Co., 1888.

Robert Elsmere portrayed a clergyman caught between his unshakable desire to serve a congregation and the new scientific and critical readings of the Bible. Clemens admitted to Rudyard Kipling on 15 August 1889 that he had succumbed to social pressures ("when people plague me to know what I think of the last book that every one is reading") and sat down with this book. "I read it, of course, for the workmanship. . . . The effect on me was exactly as though a singer of street ballads were to hear excellent music from a church organ. I didn't stop to ask whether the music was legitimate or necessary. I listened and I liked what I heard. I am speaking of the grace and beauty of the style. . . . You have my private opinion about that book. I don't know what my public ones are exactly. They won't upset the earth" (published a year later in "Rudyard Kipling on Mark Twain," New York *Herald*, 17 August 1890; collected in Kipling's *From Sea to Sea: Letters of Travel* [1899], 2: 180).

Howard G. Baetzhold, *MT&JB* (1970), pp. 120–123, 187, 343–344 n. 39, n. 40, 358 n. 18; Scharnhorst, ed., *Complete Interviews* (2006), p. 123; David H. Fears, *Day by Day* (2009) 2: 402–405.

——— and **CHARLES EDWARD MONTAGUE** (1867–1928). *William Thomas Arnold, Journalist and Historian*. Manchester, England: Manchester University Press, 1907. 136 pp.

Source: MTLAcc, entry #1772, volume donated by Clemens.

Mary Augusta Ward was the sister of William Thomas Arnold (1852–1904); Montague had been Arnold's colleague at the Manchester *Guardian*.

Warden, William (1777–1849). *Letters Written on Board His Majesty's Ship the Northumberland, and at Saint Helena; in Which the Conduct and Conversations of Napoleon Buonaparte, and His Suite, During the Voyage, and the First Months of His Residence in That Island, Are Faithfully Described. By William Warden, Surgeon on Board the Northumberland*. Philadelphia: M. Thomas, 1817. [The title was published earlier in London in 1816, but this edition seems more probable as the one Clemens read.]

In 1887 Clemens was fascinated to learn from "Surgeon Warden of the Northumberland" that "Napoleon's pulse never actually rose above 62 when he was in health." Below that notation in Notebook 26 Clemens then cited Warden's "little book of Letters, published 1817," as the source for a quotation attributed to Napoleon: "I found a crown in the kennel, I cleansed the filth from it & placed it on my head" (NB 26, *N&J* 3: 280). On page 96 Warden reported that "his pulse never exceeds sixty-two" and on page 168 he quoted Bonaparte's explanation for his seizing power: "I found a crown in the kennel; I cleansed it from its filth, and placed it on my head."

Warder, George Woodward (1848–1907). *The Cities of the Sun*. 12mo, New York: G. W. Dillingham Co., 1901. 320 pp. [Paperbound, wrappers missing.]

Marginalia: approximately two hundred words of marginal notations by Clemens; most comments and underlinings occur in Chapter 12. Clemens connects Warder's cosmology with the teachings of Mary Baker Eddy.

Catalog: Goodspeed's of Boston, Catalogue No. 326 (1940), "12mo (wrappers wanting, title-page defective), in cloth slipcase. . . . With numerous penciled marginal notations in his hand. . . . Most . . . occur in the pages dealing with the relation of mind and matter. . . . Many pages have been underlined," $25.

Location: University of Rochester Library, Rochester, New York. Purchased in 1940 from Goodspeed's Book Shop in Boston.

Copy examined: photocopy of the title page and a description of Clemens's marginalia, supplied to Alan Gribben by the University of Rochester Library in 1979. The fragile condition of this volume did not permit the photocopying of its annotations.

A disparaging review—"About Cities in the Sun"—survives in the Mark Twain Papers at Berkeley (DV357) to demonstrate Mark Twain's amusement with the book. He planned to publish this piece, and even penciled notes to the editor in the margins of his manuscript, but it never appeared in print. Mainly he pokes fun at the Kansas City attorney and investor for taking literally St. John's vision of the New Jerusalem as located in the sun (Book of Revelation, 21: 1–27), especially Warder's efforts to construct a precise picture of the heavenly city. Twain's essay also derides Senator Chauncey M. Depew for endorsing "this turbulent philosopher." Warder's cosmology theories led him to write other books with titles such as *The Stairway to the Stars* (1902) and *The Universe a Vast Electric Organism* (1903).

Wecter, *RP* (1952), pp. ix–x; Joe B. Fulton, "Mark Twain's New Jerusalem: Prophecy in the Unpublished Essay 'About Cities in the Sun,'" *Christianity and Literature*

55.2 (Winter 2006): 173–194.

Wardman, Ervin (1865–1923). *The Princess Olga*. New York: Harper & Brothers, 1906. 315 pp.

Source: MTLAcc, entry #324, volume donated by Clemens. This was the first novel for Harvard graduate Wardman, Editor-in-Chief of the New York *Press* and former reporter for the New York *Tribune*.

———. [An identical copy.]

Source: MTLAcc, entry #1271, volume donated by Clemens.

Wardwell, Simon Willard (1849–1921), pseud. "Simon Durst." *Bub and Sis: A 20th Century New England Story*. Illus. Woonsocket, Rhode Island: Woonsocket Publishing Co., 1903. 144 pp.

Source: MTLAcc, #633, volume donated by Clemens. Wardwell was a highly successful Rhode Island inventor of textile looms and sewing machines. Over the years he published—under the pseudonym "Simon Durst"—a series of small volumes of poetry. Quite possibly Wardwell himself sent this volume to Clemens, but it is also conceivable that someone else passed it on, hoping to add to Clemens's hypothetical Library of Literary Hogwash. Wardwell wrote this volume in rhymed couplets, as a sample will display: "This is a story true that may not halt/For rime or reason, though they show a fault/On every page, according to the rules/Of all the medio-critics of the schools" (p. 5).

Ware, Eugene Fitch (1841–1911), pseud. "Ironquill." *Some of the Rhymes of Ironquill. (A Book of Moods)*. New York: G. P. Putnam's Sons, [cop. 1902]. 373 pp. [Edition conjectured but likely.]

Catalog: *C1951*, #49c, "Moods in Rhymes" [*sic*], no edition specified, listed among books signed by Clemens, $15.

On Saturday, 2 February 1907, Albert Bigelow Paine gave a luncheon at the Players Club for Clemens and Ware; Isabel Lyon noted that "Ware wrote in the King's volume of poems—Ironquill poems—'The man that is frozen to death dies hard.' It delighted me—but the King didn't find it clever at all" (IVL Journals, TS p. 223, MTP). Paine recorded that "Clemens had put in most of the day before reading Ware's book of poems, *The Rhymes of Ironquill* [*sic*], and had declared his work to rank with the very greatest of American poetry—I think he called it the most truly American in flavor." Paine cited Ware's "Fables" and "Whist" as two poems that "especially impressed" Clemens (*MTB*, p. 1374). Many of Ware's folksy poems referred to the history and locales of Kansas, the state to which he moved in 1867 after fighting on the Union side in the Civil War and where he would reside until his death in 1911. There he became a newspaper editor and lawyer, and gained influence in the state Republican party. Ware viewed his poetry as largely a whimsical sideline and much of his verse has not worn well over the years. Clemens must have been in a charitable frame of mind when he admired "Fables" (pp. 224–243), which consisted of eighteen poems that strained to imitate Aesop's *Fables*. The other poem Clemens singled out, "Whist," has more merit. In 1907 Clemens would have approved of its fatalistic second stanza: "Life is a game of whist. From unseen sources/The cards are shuffled and the hands are dealt;/Blind are our efforts to control the forces/That, though unseen, are no less strongly felt." The concluding third stanza would also have appealed to him: "I do not like the way the cards are shuffled,/But yet I like the game and want to play;/ And through the long, long night will I, unruffled,/Play what I get until the break of day."

WARE, THOMAS (1758–1842). *Sketches of the Life and Travels of Rev. Thomas Ware, Who Has Been an Itinerant Methodist Preacher for More Than Fifty Years. Written by Himself. Revised by the Editors*. New York: T. Mason and G. Lane, for the Methodist Episcopal Church, 1839. 264 pp.

Inscription: only a stray black ink mark on the front pastedown endpaper.

Location: Mark Twain Library, Redding, Connecticut.

Copy examined: it is unlikely that this unmarked volume ever belonged to Clemens or his family. Albert E. Stone, Jr. found the leather-bound volume shelved with books from Clemens's personal library in 1955, and it was still among them when I visited Redding in 1970 and in June 1982. The book displays no Library accession number, which is unusual. In view of its extremely early date (1839) and the other facts, this is an extremely dubious addition to the Clemenses' library collection.

WARE, WILLIAM (1797–1852), pseud. "Lucius M. Piso." *Probus; or, Rome in the Third Century. In Letters of Lucius M. Piso from Rome, to Fausta, the Daughter of Graccus, at Palmyra*. 2 vols. New York: C. S. Francis; Boston: Joseph H. Francis, 1838.

Location: Mark Twain House and Museum, Hartford, Connecticut. A gift from "Miss Mildred Cooper" in 1962.

Copy examined: Clemens's unmarked copy, apparently, though there is no indication as to how Mildred Cooper knew that this volume belonged to Clemens. The entry below for another novel by the same publisher seems connected to this purported association copy. Examined in August 1987.

———. *Zenobia: or the Fall of Palmyra. An Historical Romance. In Letters of Lucius M. Piso from Palmyra, to His Friend Marcus Curtius at Rome*. 2 vols. New York: C. S. Francis; Boston: Joseph H. Francis, 1838.

Inscription: reported as "S L Clemens".

Location: unknown. Formerly in the Mark Twain Library, Redding, Connecticut.

Copy examined: none. I have based this entry on a card in the files of the Mark Twain Library at Redding; it records that a copy of *Zenobia* ("N.Y., Boston, Francis, 1838") signed "S L Clemens" once belonged to its collection.

———. *Zenobia, Queen of Palmyra. A Tale of the Roman Empire in the Days of the Emperor Aurelian*. Green buckram cover, embossed, gilt lettering and design. London: Frederick Warne & Co., n.d. [1881?]. 494 pp.

Inscription: the front free endpaper is inscribed ornately in black ink (in a hand other than Clemens's), "S L Clemens."

Location: Mark Twain Library, Redding, Connecticut.

Copy examined: supposedly Clemens's copy, unmarked. There is no red ink Mark Twain Library accession number, though it displays the purple oval Library stamps. Examined in 1970 and again in June 1982 and on 9 November 2019. One wishes for far more information about all three copies of these Ware novels that are supposed to have belonged to Clemens. Their connection with him seems quite tenuous.

WARING, GEORGE EDWIN, JR. (1833–1898). *Whip and Spur*.

Boston: James R. Osgood and Co., 1875. 245 pp. [Edition conjectured. Much of the book appeared originally as a series in the *Atlantic Monthly*, Volume 36, in 1875.]

Mark Twain likely met Waring at the Parker House dinner for *Atlantic* contributors held on 15 December 1874 (*MT-Let* 6: 319). On 14 July 1875 he offered to meet Waring in Newport, Rhode Island later that month (*MTLet* 6: 512). In a note that seems relevant to the composition of *A Connecticut Yankee in King Arthur's Court* (1889), Twain wrote in May 1888: "An English hermit of the Middle Ages—'Whip & Spur,' Waring, 191" (NB 27, *N&J* 3: 384).

The first four chapters of Waring's *Whip and Spur* pertained to his military service in the American Civil War, and these chapters were named after a succession of four horses he owned: Vix (in full, Vixen), Ruby, Wellstein, and Max. He acquired the first of these horses in 1858 for $75 from a clam-peddler who had nearly worked the animal to death hauling a heavy wagon. Initially thin and worn out, the black mare soon became, with better care, a "prancing" and "beautiful" mount. Unfortunately during the first months of the Civil War in 1861 she developed brain fever, and while she was still recovering a nearby horse kicked and severely injured Vix. Waring reluctantly allowed someone to shoot her to end her pain. He carved the initials "VIX" in an oak tree near her burial site. In "A Family Sketch," primarily written in 1901–1902, Mark Twain recalled that at Quarry Farm his children named one of their riding horses "Vix" after "Col. Waring's war horse, whose pathetic and beautiful history . . . won the children's worship, and broke their hearts and made them cry."

The last two chapters of *Whip and Spur* described Waring's subsequent travels in England, including the experience of fox-hunting on horseback. In Chapter 7, "In the Gloaming," Waring reverently recounted his visit to Stow Pool and the parish church of St. Chad, named after a seventh-century religious figure who initially lived a hermit life but later became the Bishop of Lichfield. Page 191 of the Osgood 1875 edition of *Whip and Spur* related how this pious saint converted the brutal King of the Mercians to the Christian faith and marveled at how Chad's burial shrine became a holy (and, purportedly, a healing) destination for countless pilgrims.

A Family Sketch and Other Private Writings, ed. Benjamin Griffin (Oakland: University of California Press, 2014), p. 42; K. Patrick Ober, "Mark Twain and Family Health in Nook Farm," *Mark Twain Journal: The Author and His Era* 56.1 (Spring 2018): 62 and 71.

WARNER, ANNA BARTLETT (1824–1915). *The Melody of the Twenty-third Psalm*. New York: Anson D. F. Randolph and Co., 1869. 135 pp.

Inscription: inscribed "Susan L. Crane".

Catalog: Ball 2016 inventory, brown cloth, gilt edge pages, poor condition, newspaper review taped in.

Location: Quarry Farm library shelves, under the supervision of the Mark Twain Archive, Elmira College, Elmira, New York.

Clemens had access to this interpretive study of an Old Testament psalm whenever he visited Quarry Farm in Elmira.

WARNER, CHARLES DUDLEY (1829–1900). "The Adirondacks

Verified," *Atlantic Monthly*, published in installments that appeared between January and June in 1878.

Editor and author Charles Dudley Warner was a Nook Farm neighbor of Clemens and co-authored *The Gilded Age* (1873) with him. From Heidelberg, Clemens wrote to William Dean Howells on 26 May 1878: "While Livy & Miss Spaulding have been writing at this table, I have sat tilted back, nearby, with a pipe & the last Atlantic, & read Charley Warner's article with prodigious enjoyment. I think it is exquisite. I think it must be the roundest & broadest & completest short essay he has ever written. It is clear, & compact, & charmingly done" (*MTHL*, p. 230). On the same day Olivia Clemens wrote to Mrs. Langdon: "Mr Clemens sits [on] the other side of the table reading Mr Warner's Adirondack sketch, he is perfectly convulsed with laughter—this evening Clara & I will read it" (Mark Twain House and Museum). Henry Nash Smith and William M. Gibson deduced that the article in "The Adirondacks Verified" series Clemens enjoyed so particularly was "A Character Study," *Atlantic Monthly* 41.247 (May 1878): 636–646 (*MTHL*, p. 231 n. 4). That essay described a guide named Orson Phelps, also known as Old Mountain Phelps, a pipe-smoking, log-sitting fixture of the region who "loved his mountains." To Warner he seemed "a natural growth amid primal forces." Warner's *In the Wilderness* (1878) would contain this chapter.

———. *As We Go.* Black cloth, decorated. New York: Harper & Brothers, 1894. 195 pp.

Inscription: the front free endpaper is inscribed in black ink: "Mrs. Livy Clemens/with affectionate greetings/Chas. Dudley Warner/For/Dec 25, 1893".

Provenance: formerly in the Antenne-Dorrance Collection, Rice Lake, Wisconsin, which derived from Katy Leary's having selected volumes from Clemens's library as keepsakes after his death.

Location: Mark Twain Archive, Gannett-Tripp Learning Center, Elmira College, Elmira, New York.

Copy examined: Olivia Clemens's unmarked copy. Viewed in 1970 in Rice Lake.

———.[An identical copy.]

Source: MTLAcc, entry #664, volume donated by Clemens. Listed as a "damaged copy."

French, *MT&GA* (1965), pp. 56–57, 192–193.

———. *As We Were Saying.* Illustrated by [Harry] Whitney McVickar (1860–1905) and others. New York: Harper & Brothers, 1891. 219 pp.

Catalog: Ball 2016 inventory, blue-green cloth, gilt and black lettering, good condition.

Location: Quarry Farm library shelves, under the supervision of the Mark Twain Archive, Elmira College, Elmira, New York.

In these essays Warner's whimsical topics ranged from "The Burden of Christmas" to "The Responsibility of Writers." Clemens had access to this book whenever he visited Quarry Farm in Elmira.

———. *As We Were Saying.* Illustrated by [Harry] Whitney McVickar (1860–1905) and others. New York: Harper & Brothers, 1903. 219 pp.

Source: MTLAcc, entry #1341, volume donated by Clemens.

———. *Backlog Studies.* Twenty-one illustrations by Augustus

Hoppin (1828–1896). Original pictorial green cloth. Boston: James R. Osgood and Co., 1873. 281 pp.

Marginalia: considerable annotation in pencil, but neither the markings nor the few notes appear to be in Clemens's hand. The pencil marks are lighter and differently patterned than Clemens's usual ones. The notes occur on pages 18 ("boozy"), 20 ("A true Yankee should not think so"), 21 ("Spoken so like C. D. W."), 25 ("So true").

Provenance: contains the bookstamps and accession number of the Mark Twain Library, Redding, Connecticut. Donated by Clemens (MTLAcc, entry #687).

Catalog: Mott 1952, "Clemens's copy with marginal scorings throughout and a few notes," $65.

Location: Albert and Shirley Small Special Collections Library, University of Virginia, Charlottesville. Gift of Clifton Waller Barrett.

Copy examined: copy belonging to Clemens or a member of his family.

Installments of Warner's "Back-log Studies" (with a hyphen in the title that was later omitted when the series was collected as a book) began running in the February 1872 issue of *Scribner's Monthly*. "We have read two Back-logs aloud since we came here [to Elmira], & a thoroughly grateful audience have insisted both times that I write & cordially thank the author" (SLC to Warner, 22 April 1872, *MTLet* 5: 79). On 17 April 1873 Clemens informed the New York *Daily Graphic*: "During the last two months my next-door neighbor, Chas. Dudley Warner, has dropped his 'Back-Log Studies,' & he & I have written a bulky novel [*The Gilded Age*] in partnership" (published on 22 April 1873, *MTL*, p. 205; *MTPP*, pp. 70–71). Two selections from Warner's conversational essays in *Backlog Studies*—"Brilliant Drunkards" and "Pie"—would appear in *Mark Twain's Library of Humor* (1888).

Earl F. Briden, "Tom Sawyer's Funeral—Shades of Charley Warner?," *American Notes and Queries* 4 n.s. (April 1991): 75–78, speculated about a connection between an episode in *Backlog Studies* and Chapter 17 of Twain's *Adventures of Tom Sawyer* (1876).

———. *Backlog Studies.* Cloth, mild wear on edges and corners. Boston: Houghton, Mifflin and Co., 1885.

Inscription: inscribed by Olivia Clemens to her daughter Susy, "Olivia Susan Clemens/Christmas, 1885."

Provenance: sold at the 1951 Hollywood auction as lot J14 but inadvertently omitted from the sloppily compiled sale sheet. Has the shelfmarks of the numbering system that Clara Clemens Gabrilowitsch employed for her library volumes during her years in Detroit.

Catalog: "Property from the Library of Mark Twain," Butterfield & Butterfield, San Francisco, Sale 6613 (16 July 1997), lot 2710.

Location: Mark Twain House and Museum, Hartford, Connecticut.

Copy examined: Susy Clemens's unmarked copy, later in the possession of Clara Clemens. Viewed in Hartford in 1997.

———. *Being a Boy.* Illus. Boston: James R. Osgood & Co., 1878. 244 pp.

Source: MTLAcc, entry #1936, volume donated from Clemens's library by Clara Clemens Gabrilowitsch in 1910.

For a discussion of the relevance of this work to Mark Twain's writings about youth, see Alan Gribben, "Manipulating a Genre: *Huckleberry Finn* as Boy Book," *South Central Review* 5.4 (Winter 1988): 15–21 (a revised version of this essay appears in Volume One of this present work). See also Alan Gribben, "'I Did Wish Tom Sawyer Was There': Boy-Book Elements in *Tom Sawyer* and *Huckleberry Finn*" (1985); Marcia Jacobson, *Being a Boy Again: Autobiography and the American Boy Book* (1994); Ryuichi Asayama, "Mutual Influences: Mark Twain's and Charles Dudley Warner's Views of Children in Their Early Works," *Mark Twain Annual 2* (2004): 61; Tim Prchal, "The Bad Boys and the New Man: The Role of Tom Sawyer and Similar Characters in the Reconstruction of Masculinity," *American Literary Realism* 36.3 (Spring 2004): 187–205; and Alan Gribben, "Boy Books, Bad Boy Books, and *The Adventures of Tom Sawyer*," in *The Adventures of Tom Sawyer*, ed. Beverly Lyon Clark. Norton Critical Edition Series. New York: W. W. Norton, 2007), pp. 290–306.

———. [Identical copy.]

Provenance: bookplate #515 of the "J. Langdon Family Library" on the front pastedown endpaper.

Location: Mark Twain Archive, Elmira College, Elmira, New York.

Catalog: Ball 2016, red cloth, gilt and black lettering, J. Langdon Family Library #515, Mark Twain Archive.

Copy examined: unmarked copy available to Clemens whenever he visited Elmira. Examined on 27 May 2015.

———. "Editor's Drawer," *Harper's Monthly Magazine* 84.502 (March 1892): 490–510.

Susy Clemens praised "Mr. Warner's answer to Mr. Howells in the last Harper" in a letter written to Louise Brownell in April 1892. She referred to Warner's sign-off column as he left the "Editor's Drawer" and took over the "Editor's Study" from William Dean Howells in *Harper's Monthly* (Hamilton College Archives; Cotton, "Olivia Susan Clemens," p. 140). Warner replaced Howells in the "Editor's Study" from 1892 until 1898, when the magazine discontinued the column. In Clemens's opinion Warner proved to be no substitute for Howells; Clemens wrote to Howells from Vienna on 3 January 1899: "I have never gotten over your abandoning the Study to those pathetic stages—famine, water-logged derelict, unlamented submersion" (*MTHL*, p. 686).

———. *The Golden House. A Novel.* Illustrated by W[illiam].T[homas]. Smedley (1858–1920). New York: Harper & Brothers, 1902. 346 pp.

Source: MTLAcc, entry #1667, volume donated by Clemens.

Olivia Clemens wrote to her husband from Paris on 31 July 1894: "Mr Warner's Golden House I like very much" (TS in MTP). Installments of the novel had begun running that month in the July issue of *Harper's Monthly*. When Part IV (Chapters XIV-XVIII) of *The Golden House* appeared in *Harper's Monthly* 89.533 (October 1894): 733–760, Clemens complained to Franklin O. Whitmore that the subscription issues were failing to reach him in Paris: "We had to buy the Harper's containing Warner's story" (6 November 1894, MTP). E. W. Kemble would recall that Clemens placed the illustrations of William Thomas Smedley among "a little group of shining lights undimmed by time" (Kemble, "Illustrating *Huckleberry Finn*" [1930]). *The Golden House*, known for its social satire of the

privileged classes, would be the last of Warner's novels.

———. *In the Levant.* Boston: James R. Osgood & Co., 1877. 374 pp.

Source: MTLAcc, entry #555, volume donated by Clemens. Warner dedicated this travel narrative to William Dean Howells. *In the Levant* describes Jerusalem, Bethlehem, Damascus, and other sites in the Middle East.

———. *In the Wilderness.* Boston: Houghton, Mifflin and Co., 1881. 226 pp.

Inscription: the front flyleaf is inscribed in purple pencil, "Mrs. S. L. Clemens/from her friend/Chas. Dudley Warner/Dec. 25th 1880". A scrap of newspaper dated 17 August 1906 is laid in between the front endpapers.

Location: Mark Twain Library, Redding, Connecticut.

Copy examined: Olivia Clemens's unmarked copy. Has a penciled Mark Twain Library accession number, "4140". Examined in 1970 and again in June 1982.

Warner's name came to Clemens's mind immediately in July 1880 when he began his list of humorists for an anthology (NB 19, *N&J* 2: 361). In 1881 Clemens set down Warner's name among another list of humorists (NB 19, *N&J* 2: 429). *Mark Twain's Library of Humor* (1888) reprinted two pieces from *In the Wilderness*, "How I Killed a Bear" and the droll sketch, "A Fight with a Trout." (Warner made his frantic shooting of a bear that was eating berries and then started toward him seem entirely unheroic.)

———. *My Summer in a Garden.* First edition. Original terra cotta cloth, gilt, spine restored, brown-coated endpapers, half maroon morocco slipcase. Boston: Fields, Osgood, and Co., 1871. 183 pp.

Inscription: the front free flyleaf is inscribed by Olivia Clemens in black ink, "S. L. Clemens/Buffalo 1871".

Marginalia: some underscoring in pencil, mainly of single words. On page 109 Clemens altered the phrase "have all the toads hop in any direction" to read, "have all the toads hop in one direction". He also changed the text slightly on page 116 ("an armed man and a legged dog" rendered into "an armed man and a long-legged dog") and made pencil marks on eleven other pages, including vertical lines on pages 94 and 95 and underlined words on page 108. An admiring bracket on page 76 locates Warner's aphorism, "Lettuce is like conversation: it must be fresh and crisp, so sparkling that you scarcely notice the bitter in it."

Provenance: contains a partially erased shelfmark from Clara Clemens Gabrilowitsch's private library system in Detroit; at one point the book entered the Ingle Barr Collection; subsequently it joined the collection of Nick Karanovich (1938–2003), Fort Wayne, Indiana.

Catalogs: ListABP (1910) ("My Summer in a Garden, Warner"); *Sotheby's 2003*, #245, $3,250.

Location: collection of Kevin Mac Donnell, Austin, Texas.

Copy examined: Clemens's copy, in July 2004.

On 19 December 1870 Clemens expressed surprise in writing to the Reverend Joseph H. Twichell from Buffalo: "I didn't know Warner had a book out" (*MTL*, p. 180; *MTLet* 4: 276; *LMTJHT*, p. 26). (*My Summer in a Garden* was Warner's first book.) On 3 January 1871 Clemens wrote to the Reverend Joseph H. Twichell in praise of Warner's *Summer in a Garden*: "I tell you it is magnificent!—rich, delicious, fascinating, brim full of meat,—the humor transcends anything I have seen in print or heard from a stage this many a day,—& every page glitters like a cluster-pin with many-sided gems of fancy— . . . it is splendid" (*MTLet* 4: 294; *LMTJHT*, pp. 26–27). Olivia Clemens likewise enjoyed Warner's book, writing to Alice Hooker Day on 25 January 1871: "Mr Clemens and I read with a great deal of pleasure Mr Warners book—I came very near writing Mrs Warner and telling her of the two or three exceedingly pleasant evenings that the book gave us" (*MTLet* 4: 312). Two years later Warner and Mark Twain would collaborate on a first novel for both men, *The Gilded Age*. Twain would reprint "Plumbers," "The Garden and Its Enemies," and "Boy the Destroyer" from Warner's *Summer in a Garden* in *Mark Twain's Library of Humor* (1888).

Upon Warner's death in 1900, Clemens lamented: "I feel the stroke. He was one of the old, old friends" (SLC to Charles H. Clark, New York City, 21 October 1900, TS of undated clipping from the Hartford *Courant*, MTP). Annie Fields' biography of Warner quoted Clemens's praise for "the sunshine shed by his personality" (*Charles Dudley Warner* [New York: McClure, Phillips & Co., 1904], p. 40).

Andrews, *NF* (1950), pp. 151–156, 172–182, and 204–206; French, *MT&GA* (1965), p. 293 n. 64; Ryuichi Asayama, "Mutual Influences: Mark Twain's and Charles Dudley Warner's Views of Children in Their Early Works," *Mark Twain Annual 2* (2004): 59–62.

———. *My Winter on the Nile, Among the Mummies and Moslems*. Hartford: American Publishing Co., 1876. 477 pp.

Catalog: ListABP (1910), "Mummies and Moslems, Warner."

"Warner's book is mighty readable, I think," Clemens wrote from Elmira to William Dean Howells on 9 August 1876 (*MTHL*, p. 145). Warner's book was initially titled *Mummies and Moslems*, which was soon altered to *My Winter on the Nile, Among the Mummies and Moslems* to correspond with his earlier work, *My Summer in a Garden* (1871). "Please send me 2 cloth copies of Warner's book," Clemens instructed per postcard from Elmira on 1 August [1876] (New York State Library, PH in MTP). On 3 August 1876 the American Publishing Company shipped two copies of Warner's "Mummies and Muslims" [*sic*] to Clemens at Elmira ($2.50 total price); Clemens circled these and some other books on the bill dated 1 February 1877 and noted, "These are just about half retail rates, Charley [Webster], so you should always buy through me. Sam." (Scrapbook #10, p. 77, MTP). Olivia Clemens wrote to Mrs. Langdon on 26 December 1877 that "Mr. Warner gave me his book" (Mark Twain House and Museum).

———. *The Relation of Literature to Life*. New York: Harper & Brothers, [cop. 1896]. 320 pp.

A collection of essays.

Source: MTLAcc, entry #858, volume donated by Clemens.

———. *The Relation of Literature to Life*. New York: Harper & Brothers, 1896. 320 pp.

Source: MTLAcc, entry #1273, volume donated by Clemens.

———. *The Relation of Literature to Life*. New York: Harper & Brothers, 1897. 320 pp.

Source: MTLAcc, entry #857, volume donated by Clemens.

———. *A Roundabout Journey*. Boston: Houghton, Mifflin and Co., 1884. 360 pp.

Inscription: the front flyleaf is inscribed by the author in ink: "Mrs. Livy Clemens/With the affectionate regards/of/Chas. Dudley Warner/Dec 25 1883."

Provenance: contains the bookstamps of the Mark Twain Library, Redding, Connecticut.

Location: Special Collections, Elihu Burritt Library, Central Connecticut State University, New Britain, Connecticut.

Copy examined: photocopies of the flyleaf and title page provided by the Elihu Burritt Library in 1979. The book is not annotated.

Roundabout Journey takes the reader through parts of France, the Spanish Mediterranean coast, northern Africa (particularly Morocco), and ends with a reverent account of a Wagner opera (*Parsifal*) at Bayreuth that differs considerably from Mark Twain's impressions.

———. *Saunterings*. Purple cloth. Boston: James R. Osgood and Co., 1872. 289 pp.

Inscription: the title page is signed at the top in pencil, "Ida C. Langdon" [1849–1934, wife of Charles Jervis Langdon].

Provenance: bookplate #582 of the "J. Langdon Family Library" on the front pastedown endpaper.

Catalog: Ball 2016, purple cloth, gilt lettering, signed by Ida C. Langdon, J. Langdon Family Library #582.

Location: Mark Twain Archive, Elmira College, Elmira, New York.

Copy examined: unmarked copy available to Clemens whenever he visited the Langdons in Elmira. Examined on 27 May 2015.

Warner wanders throughout Europe in *Saunterings*, supplying vivid descriptions of London, Paris, Holland, Switzerland, Italy, Rome, and many other destinations. His travelogue is hardly up to the high standard set by Mark Twain, but it does strike this reader as being unduly neglected by scholars and collectors of travel writings.

———. *Studies in the South and West, with Comments on Canada*. Green cloth. New York: Harper & Brothers, [cop. 1889]. 484 pp.

Inscription: the front pastedown endpaper is signed in black ink, "Catharine Leary/Reading [*sic*], Conn."

Provenance: Antenne-Dorrance Collection, Rice Lake, Wisconsin.

Location: Mark Twain Archive, Gannett-Tripp Learning Center, Elmira College, Elmira, New York.

Copy examined: almost certainly Clemens's copy, unmarked. Examined on 28 May 2015.

Warner lacked Mark Twain's narrative gift for compelling prose, but his travels in the 1880s from Louisiana to Minnesota, from New Orleans to Chicago to Canada, and from Kansas City to St. Louis, Cincinnati, Memphis, and Louisville offer an underrated glimpse at local customs. Warner is especially interested in racial relations in the South. Visiting Nashville, Tennessee in 1887, he assembled "eight or ten" African American men considered to be "solid, sensible business men," and posed a question: "What do you want here in the way of civil rights that you have not?" They answer that they long for access to public conveyances, hotels, theaters, and places of amusement "without loss of self-respect" (p. 117).

———. *Their Pilgrimage*. Illustrated by C[harles]. S[tanley]. Reinhart (1844–1896). New York: Harper & Brothers, [cop. 1886].

Clemens had strong praise for this impressionistic tour of the main tourist meccas of the Northeast, ranging from the Catskill Mountains to Niagara Falls to the White Mountains, Atlantic City, Bar Harbor, Saratoga, and other sites. "It's got everything in it: pervasive & continuous interest, charming humor, flashing wit, noble scenery-painting, a perennially-bubbling happy life & the reader right in it & part of it. . . . It's a rounded, symmetrical & masterly performance altogether" ("Mark Twain," Heritage Bookshop, Los Angeles, 1997, item #128). *Their Pilgrimage* was Warner's first attempt to write a novel since he had co-authored *The Gilded Age* (1873) with Mark Twain (Warner would go on to write three more novels). The plot had Stanhope King pursuing Irene Benson as she moved from one Northeastern summer resort to another.

WARNER, J. "Down in Alabam' (or Ain't I glad I got out de wilderness)" (minstrel song, published in 1858). Arranged by Walter Meadows.

In 1866 Mark Twain pretended to despise a flutist who varied the time of "Get out of the wilderness," and was "always skipping the first note in the second bar" (Sacramento *Weekly Union*, 23 June 1866, *LSI*, pp. 86–87). Twain's little joke is that he is critiquing a raucous minstrel song as though it were a fine concert piece.

J. Warner was a member of the blackface "Bryant's' Minstrels troupe who primarily performed in New York City. Music historians suggest that Warner merely reworked a traditional tune that had obscure origins. His repetitious chorus concluded "Ain't I glad I got out de wilderness,/ Down in Alabam.'" The final verse resembled in sentiment a number of antebellum minstrel songs such as "I never will leab de old plantation,/Down in Alabam.'"

WARNER, SUSAN BOGERT (1819–1885). *The Hills of the Shatemuc. By the Author of the "Wide, Wide World."* New York: D. Appleton and Co., 1856. 516 pp.

Catalog: Ball 2016 inventory, green marble boards and leather, covers torn, poor condition, J. Langdon Family bookplate #438.

Location: Mark Twain Archive, Gannett-Tripp Learning Center, Elmira College, Elmira, New York.

Copy examined: an unmarked copy to which Clemens had access whenever he visited the Langdon residence in Elmira. Examined on 26 May 2015.

Warner's novel depicted the rising tensions within a family over hard farm work versus a university education. Among the characters is a young African American woman named Clam. Chapter 10 features a huckleberry-picking expedition. "Shatemuc" was the Algonquin name for the river later called the Hudson.

———. *Queechy*. Two vols. in one. Philadelphia: J. B. Lippincott & Co., 1882.

Catalog: Ball 2016 inventory, red cloth, gilt and black lettering and design, good condition.

Location: Quarry Farm library shelves, under the supervision of the Mark Twain Archive, Elmira College, Elmira, New York.

Clemens had access to this volume whenever he visited Quarry Farm in Elmira.

WARNER, WILLIAM JOHN (1866–1936), pseud. "Cheiro." He also adopted the names "Count Louis Hamon," "Leigh Warner," and Count Leigh de Hamong." *Cheiro's Language of the Hand*. [Self-published in 1894; Eighth edition, New York: F. Tennyson Neely, 1897; Ninth edition, London: Nichols & Co., 1897. There were also other editions.]

Very likely Clemens owned or read this book, the first of several manuals written by the Irish-born astrologer and occultist who practiced under the name "Cheiro," since Clemens consulted him in 1894 when "he examined my hand, took a print of it for his book, then told me some things about my character" (Clemens to Susy Clemens, 8 August 1894, quoted by Christie's, New York City, 11 May 1987, item #24). Later in London there was another session with Cheiro. Reportedly Clemens wrote in Cheiro's visitor's book, "Cheiro has exposed my character to me with humiliating accuracy." In a letter to Henry H. Rogers of 12 November 1898 the once-bankrupt Clemens recalled Cheiro's reassuring prediction that "I am to be rich when I am 68" (*MTHHR*, p. 378). "Cheiro is coming to New York by and by," he remarked to Rogers. "I wish you would see him personally when he comes, and get him to reduce the time-limit on that fortune of mine" (8–13 December 1898, *MTHHR*, p. 381). "I think Cheiro is beginning to realize that his reputation is at stake and that he had better begin to hump himself," Clemens quipped (SLC to HHR, 27 December 1898, *MTHHR*, p. 383). As Clemens's financial picture began to improve, he jokingly asked, "Do you believe Cheiro can come on me for commission?" (SLC to HHR, 3 January 1899, *MTHHR*, p. 385). Rogers was in charge of Clemens's investments in 1899, and Clemens quipped that "Cheiro can work his prophecy-mill very well when you stand behind him and turn the crank" (10 May 1899, SLC to HHR, *MTHHR*, 395). In Notebook 36 Clemens made reference to the accuracy of Cheiro's prediction that he would recover his fortunes in 1903: "I am superstitious. I kept the prediction in mind and often thought of it. When at last it came true, Oct. 22,/03, there was but a month and 9 days to spare" (TS p. 15, quoted in *MTHHR*, p. 540 n. 1). "For my sixty-eighth birthday," Clemens informed a newspaper interviewer in Italy, "a fortune teller has predicted good fortune for me. In fact, I have signed a contract with the house of Harper, by means of which I have assured myself of a lifetime annuity for me, my wife, and my children. I believe more in palmistry than in medicine or politics" ("An Interview with Mark Twain," Milan *Corriere della Sera*, 12 November 1903; reprinted by Robert Luscher, "Italian Accounts of Mark Twain: An Interview and a Visit from the *Corriere della Sera*," *American Literary Realism* 17.2 [Autumn 1984]: 219). Cheiro attributed his clairvoyant powers to his intensive study of mysticism in India. *Cheiro's Language of the Hand* reproduced a print of Clemens's right hand.

WARREN, WILLIAM FAIRFIELD (1833–1929). "Homeward bound" (hymn, published in 1857). Melody by Calvin Sears Harrington (1826–1886). Arranged by John William Dadmun (1819–1890).

Clemens thought this hymn to be "pretty, & touched a chord in every breast" when sung by a men's choir on the *America* in December 1866 (NB 7, *N&J* 1: 262). Its first lines begin, "Out on an ocean, all boundless we ride,/We're homeward bound, homeward bound." He did not mind the ship's choir singing "Homeward Bound" aboard the *Quaker City*, he explained on 1 January 1867, because at least it was "in keeping with our surroundings" (*MTTMB*, p. 59). A letter of 24 March 1874 to Thomas Bailey Aldrich contained some musical notes resembling the first line of "Homeward Bound," with the hymn's title following these but then deleted (*MTLet* 6: 90). Perhaps the hymn title contributed two words—the climactic pitch—to Mark Twain's magnificent Liverpool speech on 10 July 1907: "I am the *Begum of Bengal*, a hundred and twenty-three days out from Canton—homeward bound!" (*MTSpk*, p. 583). (Richard Henry Dana's *Two Years Before the Mast* supplied other details Twain employed in the speech.) Ganzel, *MTAb* (1968), p. 28.

Warton, Joseph (1722–1800). *An Essay on the Genius and Writings of Pope*. Second ed. London: R. and J. Dodsley, 1762. 335 pp.

> **Catalog:** Ball 2016 inventory, brown leather, gilt-edge pages, ribbon bookmark, very good condition, bookplate of Chillingham Castle No. 130.

> **Location:** Quarry Farm library shelves, under the supervision of the Mark Twain Archive, Elmira College, Elmira, New York.

> Clemens was familiar with the writings of Alexander Pope (1688–1744), so he might have glanced into this volume, which was available to him whenever he visited Quarry Farm in Elmira.

Washburn, Henry Bradford (1869–1962). "Shall We Hunt and Fish? Confessions of a Sentimentalist," *Atlantic Monthly* 101.5 (May 1908): 672–679.

> The Reverend Washburn, a Harvard graduate, was professor of ecclesiastical history at the Episcopal Theological School in Cambridge, Massachusetts. In 1920 he would become the dean of that institution. Washburn opened his essay by quoting a passage from Henry Van Dyke's "Some Remarks on Gulls, with a Foot-note on a Fish," *Scribner's Magazine* 42.2 (August 1907): 129–142. Clemens clipped the Van Dyke excerpt and pinned it (as a quotation) in the text of his Autobiographical Dictation of 29 April 1908; he said that he had read Washburn's article "last night . . . in the Atlantic" (*AutoMT* 3: 226–228). Clemens used the extract in debating with Van Dyke about theology.

Washburn, Henry S[tevenson] (1813–1903). "The grave of Bonaparte" (song), also known as "On a lone barren isle." Melody by Lyman Heath (1804–1870). [First published in 1843.]

> Stevenson was a Boston manufacturer who became an insurance executive and a Massachusetts state senator. On the side he wrote poems and hymns. His poem "The Vacant Chair" (1861) touched many hearts during the Civil War. One of the pieces of music on the piano in "The House Beautiful" (*LonMiss*, Ch. 38) is "On a Lone Barren Isle (St. Helena)." Clemens included "Grave of Napoleon" [*sic*] in a list of what appear to be his favorite songs in August 1889 (NB 29, *N&J* 3: 513).

Washburne, Elihu Benjamin (1816–1887). *Recollections of a Minister to France, 1869–1877*. 2 vols. Illus. New York: Charles Scribner's Sons, 1887.

> Amid notes about Prussian nobility and wars, Clemens

wrote in July 1888: "Also, Washburne's book (Scribner)" (NB 28, *N&J* 3: 404).

Washington *National Intelligencer.*

> In 1868 Clemens wrote deprecatingly: "The Intelligencer woke up in the most astonishing way this morning & told the world that there had been an eruption at Vesuvius. It is a wonderful paper" (SLC to John Russell Young, Washington, 1 February 1868, PH in MTP). In a story written in 1899 Clemens set the scene seventy years earlier in Indiantown, Missouri: "Two or three copies of the National Intelligencer (weekly) came tired from Washington bringing political tidings three weeks old" ("Indiantown," *WWD?*, p. 155).

Wasson, George Savary (1855–1932). *Cap'n Simeon's Store*. Boston: Houghton, Mifflin and Co., 1903. 287 pp.

> Cap'n Simeon's Store is the gathering point for the mariners and fisherman of Killick Cove on a rugged coast in the state of Maine. Many sea tales are told and retold there. "Please don't let the firm forget to send me Wasson's book. I want to read again those delicious things that tasted so good in my mouth last summer," Clemens wrote from Riverdale to the editor of the *Atlantic Monthly*, Bliss Perry, on 12 January 1903 (Houghton Library, Harvard). *Cap'n Simeon's Store* collected Wasson's stories that had appeared in *Atlantic Monthly, Scribner's, Century*, and *Harper's Weekly*. Clemens informed William Dean Howells from Riverdale on 29 April 1903: "Five days ago I wrote Bliss Perry praising Wasson's book & Miss McLean's 'Flood Tide' [Sarah Pratt (McLean) Greene's *Flood-Tide*], & said they ought to be read together, chapter-about; that Wasson's delightful worldly people & Miss McL's delightful unworldly people belonged together & should mix together on the same stage" (*MTHL*, pp. 768–769). Clemens was pleased that Howells liked Wasson's book, but seemed puzzled by Howells's suggestion in *Harper's Weekly* that it be read with Grace L. Collins's *Putnam Place*.

Watson, Aaron (1850–1907). *The Savage Club: A Medley of History, Anecdote, and Reminiscence by Arron Watson, With a Chapter by Mark Twain*. Illus. London: T. Fisher Unwin, 1907. 327 pp.

> **Inscription:** Clemens wrote "1872+" in brown ink on the cream-colored front cover.

> **Catalog:** ListABP (1910), "Savage Club, Watson", no other information provided.

> **Location:** Mark Twain Papers, Bancroft Library, University of California at Berkeley.

> **Copy examined:** Clemens's unmarked copy. Chapter 12 is titled "Mark Twain's Own Account" (pp. 131–135).

> Mark Twain spoke at this London club and was honored by it several times.

Watson, Henry Brereton Marriott (1863–1921). *The Adventurers; A Tale of Treasure Trove*. Illustrated by A[rthur]. I[gnatius]. Keller (1866–1924). New York: Harper & Brothers, 1900. 298 pp.

> **Source:** MTLAcc, entry #1084, volume donated by Clemens.

> The Australian-born Watson lived in New Zealand until 1885, when he commenced a career in journalism in London. His output of fiction was prolific in a variety of subgenres, including romance and historical novels, treasure-seeking sea adventures, and supernatural Gothic

tales. He formed literary friendships with Stephen Crane, H. G. Wells, and James M. Barrie, among many notables.

WATSON, HENRY COOD (1816–1875). "The prodigal son" (sacred song, published in 1853). [Some, but fewer, sources list Watson's birth date as 1818.]

Clemens remarked in a letter to Olivia Langdon written on 19 December 1868 from Fort Plain, New York: "Tunes are good remembrancers. . . . Whenever I hear the 'Prodigal' I shall as surely think of you, my loved & honored Livy" (*MTLet* 2: 334). Was Clemens identifying here with a straying sinner who had found salvation? The key verse in the "The Prodigal Son" strikes that chord: "Afflictions though they seem severe/In mercy oft are sent/They stopp'd the prodigal's career/And caus'd him to repent." The London-born Watson moved to the United States in 1840 after a notable musical career in England. In New York City he gained a reputation as a music critic and also composed and performed various types of music. In the mid-1840s he was associated with Edgar Allan Poe in founding *The Broadway Journal*.

WATSON, JOHN (1850–1907), pseud. "Ian Maclaren."

When William Dean Howells asked Clemens about the lecture profits that James B. Pond paid to Ian Maclaren, Clemens replied from London on 3 July 1899: "Maclaren is a Scotchman & a Christian—a combination hard to beat in business" (*MTHL*, p. 703). Watson was a Scottish minister who wrote novels set in rural Scotland that captured the Scottish dialect.

WATSON, JOHN WHITTAKER (1824–1890). "Beautiful Snow" (poem, published in 1865).

Several people claimed the authorship of this anonymously published and highly popular poem, the portrait of a respectable woman driven compulsively to drink and prostitution and thus (in the last lines) "To lie and to die in my terrible woe,/ With a bed and a shroud of the beautiful snow!" Clemens may have read an article, "Who Wrote 'Beautiful Snow,'" *Galaxy* 8 (July 1869): 143–144, which credited William A. Sigourney with writing the poem that had made "the rounds of the periodical and newspaper press for the past four winters." But William Cullen Bryant's *The Family Library of Poetry and Song* (a book in Clemens's library) and most other authorities have attributed the poem to John Whittaker Watson, who published *Beautiful Snow, and Other Poems*. Fifth edition. Philadelphia: Turner Brothers & Co., [1869].

Writing to the Langdons at the end of March 1870, Clemens possibly had this then-popular poem in mind when describing an ongoing Buffalo snowstorm as "very beautiful when falling," but "its loveliness passes away very shortly afterward. The grand unpoetical result is merely chilblains & slush" (*MTLet* 4: 98; Reigstad, *SL*, p. 135). In a speech delivered to some Republicans on 16 October 1879 Mark Twain facetiously referred to the politician and Hartford *Courant* editor Joseph R. Hawley as the "author of 'Beautiful Snow'" who "has given us a poem which has added a new pang to winter" (*MTSpk*, p. 128). Clemens labeled the song version of the poem as "very very poor" in his copy of Frank B. Ogilvie's *Two Hundred Old-Time Songs* (1896). On 14 April 1903 Clemens wrote William Dean Howells: "I don't regard as frauds the several claimants to Beautiful Snow"; rather, he interpreted such disputes

as additional evidence of "mental telegraphy" (*MTHL*, p. 767). In Part 9 of *Is Shakespeare Dead?* (1909), Mark Twain asks, "Do you remember 'Beautiful Snow'?," and recalls that it had numerous claimants to authorship.

Henry S. Cohn, "Mark Twain and Joseph Roswell Hawley," *Mark Twain Journal* 53.2 (Fall 2015): 67–84.

WATSON, THOMAS EDWARD (1856–1922). *The Story of France, from the Earliest Times to the Consulate of Napoleon Bonaparte.* 2 vols. New York: Macmillan Co.; London: Macmillan & Co., 1904.

Inscriptions: the front pastedown endpapers of both volumes are signed in black ink: "SL. Clemens/21—Fifth ave/1905."

Marginalia: many markings by Clemens in pencil in both volumes and a few notes by him in brown ink and black ink. On page 120 of Volume I Clemens used black ink to alter the words "Just as paganism defiled Christianity" to read "Just as Christianity defiled itself." In the margin of that page he noted in brown ink: "The entire Christian religion came from older (but probably not 'grosser') religions. It is quite sufficiently gross, in morals, facts, & language." A few pencil notes are in the hand of someone else.

Catalogs: *C1951*, #47a, Volume I only, $25; #D40, Volume II only; *Zeitlin 1951*, item #48, 2 vols., $75.

Provenance: collection of Frank C. Wilson (1889–1960) in Melrose, Massachusetts. Both volumes were sold by his widow Margarete in 1962 to the University of Texas.

Location: Harry Ransom Center, University of Texas at Austin.

Copy examined: Clemens's copy of both volumes.

WATT, ROBERT (1837–1894), trans.). "For Lud og koldt Vand" (translation into Danish of a Mark Twain short story, 1874).

Source: ListABP (1910), "For Log of Koldt Vand, Watt", no other information provided.

This was a Danish translation of "The Frog of the Calaveras District" [*sic*], the first of a series of translations Robert Watt made of Mark Twain's writings. Watt was a writer and theater director in Denmark. The Danish phrase "koldt Vand" loosely translates as "cold water," "out in the cold," or "be neglected."

WATTERSON, HENRY (1840–1921). *The Compromises of Life, and Other Lectures and Addresses, Including Some Observations on Certain Downward Tendencies of Modern Society.* New York: Fox, Duffield & Co., 1903. 477 pp.

Catalogs: QF Martinez, fair condition; Ball 2016 inventory, blue cloth, gilt lettering.

Location: Quarry Farm library shelves, under the supervision of the Mark Twain Archive, Elmira College, Elmira, New York.

This volume was available to Clemens after 1903 at Quarry Farm in Elmira.

Since Mark Twain included "newspaper paragraphists" among the humorists he intended to read in 1881 or 1882 for his *Library of Humor* (NB 19, *N&J* 2: 429), he may have looked up the writers of the Old Southwest represented in *Oddities in Southern Life and Character*, ed. Henry Watterson. Illustrated by W. L. Sheppard and F. S. Church (Boston: Houghton, Mifflin Co., 1882). Twain, acting as master of ceremonies, introduced Watterson at a celebration of Abraham Lincoln's birthday at Carnegie

Hall on 11 February 1901 (see Allison R. Ensor, "The House United: Mark Twain and Henry Watterson Celebrate Lincoln's Birthday, 1901," *South Atlantic Quarterly* 74.2 [Spring 1975]: 258–268). On 11 October 1907 Isabel Lyon recorded: "I told him [Clemens] that I had picked up a little clipping in the hall & it voices—in part—his own feelings [about Theodore Roosevelt]. I'll copy it for he wants it again. Henry Watterson wrote it" (IVL Journals, TS, MTP). Watterson was one of the members of the American Academy and National Institute of Arts and Letters who spoke at a memorial meeting in Carnegie Hall honoring Mark Twain on 30 November 1910.

WATTS, ISAAC (1674–1748). "Against idleness" (hymn, published in 1715).

A spoofing sketch by Clemens, "City Marshall Perry," which apparently appeared in the 4 March 1863 issue of the Virginia City *Territorial Enterprise*, quoted from Watts' *Divine and Moral Songs for the Use of Children*: "How doth little busy bee/Improve each shining hour,' etc.—'" (*ET&S* 1: 236, 471). In October 1887 Clemens paraphrased four lines, "How doth the little busy bee/Improve each shining hour,/Gathering honey all the day/From many a lovely flower," adding a comic "b'gosh" to the second and fourth lines (NB 27, *N&J* 3: 334).

———. "Against quarrelling and fighting" (hymn, published in 1715), also known as "Let dogs delight to bark and bite."

In a sketch that apparently appeared in the *Territorial Enterprise* on 4 March 1863, Clemens claimed that the recently re-elected City Marshall of Virginia City had written "his last great poem, beginning: 'Let dogs delight to bark and bite,/For God hath made them so—/Your little hands were never made/To tear out each other's eyes with—'" (*ET&S* 1: 237). In an 1873 speech Mark Twain jokingly attributed to Cleopatra the lines "Let dogs delight to bark & bite,/For God hath made them so" ("Speech at the Scottish Banquet in London," *MTS1923*, p. 44; Fatout, *MTSpk* [1976], p. 80; *MTLet* 5: 489); he was again quoting from Watts' *Divine and Moral Songs for Children* (1715), xvi, "Against quarrelling and fighting."

———. "Alas, and did my Saviour bleed!" (hymn, 1707).

John R. Byers, Jr. made a case for Mark Twain's having had this hymn in mind when he wrote certain lines of Emmeline Grangerford's poetic effusions, particularly "Ode to Stephen Dowling Bots, Dec'd.," in *Adventures of Huckleberry Finn* (1885). See "Miss Emmeline Grangerford's Hymn Book," *American Literature* 43.2 (May 1971): 259–263.

———. "Am I a soldier of the cross?" (hymn, published in 1709).

Among the "luxuries" that Clemens and his comrades packed into their wagon in Nevada—Dickens's *Dombey and Son*, two dogs, and fourteen decks of cards—they also took "Watt's [*sic*] Hymns" (SLC to Jane Lampton Clemens, Carson City, 30 January 1862, Rogers, *PRI* [1961], p. 30; *MTLet* 1: 147). "And tell them anecdotes and lies, and quote Watts's hymns to them" wrote Mark Twain in "The Reception at the President's" (*Galaxy*, October 1870). In the February 1871 *Galaxy*, Twain playfully attributed the authorship of "Watts's hymns" to Professor Thomas Henry Huxley ("A Book Review," *CG*, p. 123).

In Chapter 5 of *The Adventures of Tom Sawyer* (1876) "the minister gave out the hymn, and read it through with a relish. . . . Shall I be car-ri-ed toe the skies, on flow'ry *beds*/of ease,/Whilst others fight to win the prize, and sail thro' *blood-/y* seas?" The second stanza of Watts' hymn reads: "Must I be carried to the skies/On flowery beds of ease?/While others fought to win the prize,/And sailed through bloody seas?"

———. "Eternal spirit, we confess" (hymn, written c.1707–1709).

Either Clemens or his wife Olivia marked this hymn in their copy of *Laudes Domini: A Selection of Spiritual Songs, Ancient and Modern* (1884), compiled by C. S. Robinson. (See that Catalog entry.) Its first line is humble: "Eternal spirit, we confess/And sing the wonders of Thy grace."

———. "How pleasant, how divinely fair" (hymn, first published in 1719; set to music in 1738 by William Knapp [1698–1768]).

Either Clemens or his wife Olivia marked this hymn in their copy of *Laudes Domini: A Selection of Spiritual Songs, Ancient and Modern* (1884), compiled by C. S. Robinson. (See that Catalog entry.) Its first line expresses satisfaction: "How pleasant, how divinely fair/O Lord of hosts, Thy dwellings are!"

———. *The Improvement of the Mind*. Green cloth, gilt. Baltimore: Bayly and Burns, 1838.

Inscription: "Mrs. Olivia Langdon/Nov. 1838" [1810–1890, Jervis Langdon's wife].

Catalogs: included among the books that Mark Woodhouse transferred from the Quarry Farm library to the Mark Twain Archive on 9 July 1987; Ball 2016 inventory, green cloth, gilt lettering, fair condition.

Location: Mark Twain Archive, Elmira College, Elmira, New York.

This was among the many books available to Clemens whenever he visited the Langdon residence in Elmira.

WATTS-DUNTON, THEODORE (1832–1914). *Aylwin*. New York: Dodd, Mead and Co., 1899. 460 pp.

Inscription: the front free endpaper is inscribed, "C. C./1907." There is a booksticker on the rear pastedown endpaper: "BRENTANO'S/Booksellers & Stationers,/New York."

Marginalia: on page 69 Clara Clemens changed (in pencil) "one who is loved" to read "one who loves".

Location: Mark Twain Library, Redding, Connecticut.

Copy examined: Clara Clemens's hardly marked copy. Has the Mark Twain Library red-ink accession number "2417". Examined in 1970 and again in June 1982.

A disabled boy in northern coastal England whose stepfather subscribes to mystical beliefs forms a friendship with a girl who has close alliances with Romani people. The narrative turns into a romantic novel as the couple mature.

WAUGH, ARTHUR (1866–1943). *Alfred, Lord Tennyson: A Study of His Life and Work*. Third edition. New York: Charles L. Webster & Co., 1894. 268 pp.

Clemens's publishing company brought out this title shortly before the firm folded.

Waverley Magazine (Boston periodical, published 1850–1909).

In the margin of Chapter 4 of Oliver Wendell Holmes's *The Autocrat of the Breakfast-Table* (p. 144), Clemens amused Olivia Langdon in 1869 by comparing those who send short pieces to the "Pactolian" with authors whom Clemens termed "Waverley Magazine contributors" (Bradford A. Booth, "Mark Twain's Comments on Holmes's *Autocrat*" [1950], p. 460).

WAWN, WILLIAM T[WIZELL]. (1837–1907). *The South Sea Islanders and the Queensland Labour Trade: A Record of Voyages and Experiences in the Western Pacific, from 1875 to 1891*. Edited by W[illiam]. D[elisle]. Hay (b. 1851). Illus. London: Swan Sonnenschein & Co., 1893. 440 pp.

In Chapter 5 of *Following the Equator* (1897) Mark Twain is critical of Wawn's "pleasant" viewpoint, and quotes from Wawn's book "of very recent date" to show the unpopularity among the natives of labor recruiters for the Queensland plantations. Wawn, born in Durham, England, spent most of his life on the sea; after he became a ship captain he gained a reputation for his knowledge of the Pacific islands.

The Way into Print. Ridgewood, New Jersey: The Editor Co., n. d. [1906?]. 47 pp.

Catalog: ListABP (1910), "The Way into Print", no further information provided.

This small booklet reprinted the contents of a special issue of *The Editor: The Journal of Information for Literary Workers* 24.2 (1906), which had included an essay titled "The Way into Print" by the prolific Christian author Amos Russel Wells (1862–1933), an article by Jack London on "Getting into Print," and a piece by Albert Bigelow Paine, "In the Literary Market."

WAYLAND, JOHN ETON (1860–1932).

Attorney and minor poet and playwright Wayland and his wife Isabel S. Wayland were among the first guests to sign Clemens's guest book at Stormfield. They received a signed receipt (for donating to the Mark Twain Library) and an autographed picture of Clemens (*Sotheby's 2003*, #126, #127).

"THE WEARING OF THE GREEN" (song, published c. 1798). Words and music of anonymous Irish origin.

"In another week, maybe, all San Francisco will be singing 'Wearing of the Green,'" Mark Twain predicted in 1865; he declared that "three repetitions of this song will produce lunacy, and five will kill—it is that much more virulent than its predecessors. . . . It is Wheatleigh's song. He sings it in [Dion Boucicault's] *Arrah-na-Pogue*, with a sprig of shamrock in his hat. . . . It is doled out slowly, and every note settles deliberately to its place on one's heart like a solid iceberg" ("Mark Twain on the Ballad Infliction," San Francisco *Californian*, 4 November 1865, *MTWY* [1938], pp. 194–195). "Wearing of the Green" was part of the "popular-song nuisance" that Twain discussed in the 28 April 1866 issue of the Sacramento *Weekly Union* (*LSJ* [1938], p. 51). Boucicault's version of this song remained the most popular adaptation. See also the Catalog entry for Dion Boucicault.

WEATHERLY, FREDERIC EDWARD (1848–1929). "Nancy Lee" (song, published in 1840). Melody composed by "Stephen Adams," pseud. of Michael Maybrick (1844–1913).

Clara Clemens Gabrilowitsch recalled that when she and her sisters were young, Clemens often requested a Mr. Beattie to sing "Nancy Lee," which ended, "A sailor's wife his star shall be" (Ralph Holmes, "Mark Twain and Music" [1922], p. 846). The refrain of Weatherly's song

goes "The sailor's wife the sailor's star shall be, Yeo ho!"

WEAVER, GEORGE SUMNER (1818–1908). *Lectures on Mental Science According to the Philosophy of Phrenology. Delivered Before the Anthropological Society of the Western Liberal Institute of Marietta, Ohio, in the Autumn of 1851*. Illus. New York: Fowlers and Wells, 1852. 225 pp. [Reprinted several times during the mid-1850s.]

Alan Gribben's "Mark Twain, Phrenology and the 'Temperaments': A Study of Pseudoscientific Influence" (1972) revealed that Clemens copied Weaver's four classifications of human appearance virtually verbatim into Notebook 1 (1855), adding a few details to his own "sanguine temperament" description, and also copied from Weaver's book a skull diagram illustrating the "mental groups" of organs (*N&J* 1: 21–33). George Sumner Weaver was a Universalist minister in St. Louis, where Clemens was living at this period. It is worth noting that this book was one of Clemens's earliest reading experiences that can be conclusively documented.

After 1855 Clemens occasionally employed the doctrines and jargon of phrenology. In Notebook 4 (1865) he wrote down the report of "Prof. G." about the Great Vide Poche Mine: "An expert can tell no more about what kind of rock is underneath by the croppings on the surface here than he can tell the quality of a man's brain by the style & material of the hat <that covers his head.> he wears" (*N&J* 1: 88). On 7 January 1866, aboard the *America* between San Francisco and New York City, Clemens recorded a story in Notebook 7: "Kingdom's [Hector J. Kingman's] fellow who went on stage & examined prof's head & said it was first time he ever saw such a peculiar head—ever saw ignorance & pusillanimousness so remarkably combined—prettiest fight there in about a minute you ever saw" (*N&J* 1: 288). In San Francisco during the sixties Clemens was acquainted with Frederick Coombs, a colorful character who had opened a successful phrenological office in 1860 (Robert Ernest Cowan, Anne Bancroft, and Addie L. Ballou, *The Forgotten Characters of Old San Francisco* [San Francisco: Ward Ritchie Press, 1964], pp. 4–7). In 1867 Mark Twain invented a letter purportedly written by "Mrs. Zeb Leavenworth," an angry exponent of women's suffrage who vows vengeance on Twain: "If I get my hands on that whelp I will snatch hair out of his head till he is as bald as a phrenological bust" ("Female Suffrage," St. Louis *Daily Missouri Democrat*, 13 March 1867; *LAMT* [1950], p. 192; also reprinted in *Life As I Find It* [1961], p. 13). Twain utilized a phrenological term to describe General U. S. Grant in a letter to the *Alta California* written from Washington, D.C. on 14 February 1868: "His head is large, square of front and perpendicular in the rear, where the selfish organs of the head lie." In the same letter Twain also mentioned "Uncle Freddy Coombs," the phrenologist who left San Francisco in 1867 and was then living in Washington, D.C.: "This serene old humbug still infests the Eastern cities," wrote Twain. In 1878 Twain pretended to worry about his own organ of Self-Esteem: "The fact is, I am spoiled by 10 years' petting.—I needed to come to a country where I was unknown to get the tuck taken out of my self-complacency" (NB 16, *N&J* 2: 163).

Will M. Clemens, *Mark Twain: His Life and Work, A*

Biographical Sketch (San Francisco: Clemens Publishing Co., 1892), pp. 176–180, introduced a phrenologist's opinion of Twain that had appeared in a newspaper: "Some years ago in making a phrenological examination of Mark Twain, Professor Beall of Cincinnati" found Twain's temperament to be "mental-motive, which is favorable to hard sense, logic, general intelligence and insight into human nature." Beall also discovered indications of Wit, Mirth, Secretiveness, Memory, and Approbation, with small organs of Self-Esteem, Music, and those devoted to love of gain or the supernatural. Twain had undergone Beall's examination in 1885 when he and George Washington Cable visited Cincinnati during a lecture tour. Ozias Pond, the brother of lecture agent James B. Pond, recorded in his diary that Twain was analyzed by a phrenologist there on 3 January 1885 ("Extracts from the Diary of Ozias W. Pond," TS copy in the Cable Collection, Tulane University, New Orleans; cited by Guy A. Cardwell, *Twins of Genius* [East Lansing: Michigan State College Press, 1953], p. 33). Dr. Edgar Charles Beall (1853–1930) wasted no time in publicizing the humorist's visit to his office; the 4 January 1885 issue of the Cincinnati *Commercial Gazette* carried an article titled "Mark Twain's Head Analyzed/What Mr. Beall, the Cincinnati Phrenologist, Thinks of His Many-Sided Faculties" (Victor Fischer located this report; Robert H. Hirst to Alan Gribben, 4 February 1981). Beall was gaining a reputation as the leading phrenologist in the nation, partly because of his editorship of *The Phrenological Journal* but also owing to his mounting publications on the subject. (See the Catalog entry for Edgar Charles Beall.)

In Chapter 21 of *The American Claimant* (1892) Colonel Sellers pontificates on "the difficult science of character-reading"; some of his terms—"moon-faced," "the shape of the head," "superhuman firmness," "concealment," "protuberant simplicity," "a colossal sense of humor"—seem related to Twain's interest in phrenology. In the penultimate "Next Day" section of "Extracts from Adam's Diary" (1893), Adam observes that Cain talks like a parrot, "having the imitative faculty in a highly developed degree." In Chapter 6 of "A Double-Barrelled Detective Story" (1902), the residents of Hope Canyon watch Holmes admiringly: "He's got his thumb on the bump on the near-corner of his forehead, and his forefinger on the off one. His think-works is just a-*grinding* now." Twain remarked in 1906 that "from the beginning of my sojourn in this world there was a persistent vacancy in me where the industry ought to be" (21 May 1906 AD, *MTE*, p. 143; *AutoMT* 2: 46). Frederic Whyte wrote to Twain on 7 December 1906, asking for a contribution on the subject of phrenology for the London *Daily Graphic*; the starting point was to be Alfred Russel Wallace's endorsement of phrenology in *The Wonderful Century* (1898). Whyte's request led Twain to talk at length about his encounters with phrenology in an Autobiographical Dictation of 26 December 1906 (*MTAuto* 2: 334–336). On 10 January 1907 Whyte sent Twain a copy of the *Daily Graphic* issue containing Twain's comments, and thanked him for his cooperation. Twain then dictated a letter to Isabel Lyon on 29 January 1907, complaining that he had not "supposed" Whyte would use his "private answer in a public

way. It has made him [Mark Twain] violate a contract with his publisher, which he naturally regrets" (IVL's copy in MTP). Twain also added a footnote to his earlier 26 December 1906 Autobiographical Dictation, criticizing but not naming Whyte (MTP). In another Autobiographical Dictation of 28 January 1907 Twain recalled how, posing as "John B. Smith," he once went to the London office of Lorenzo N. Fowler, who "found no humor in me." Returning "three months later as 'Mark Twain,'" Twain was amused that Fowler then found "a pyramid" of humor on his skull (*MTAuto* 2: 391). In a speech for the Society of the Pilgrims luncheon at the Savoy Hotel in London on 25 June 1907, Twain claimed that seven years earlier Bishop Wilberforce accidentally took Twain's hat upon leaving. Therefore Twain was left with Wilberforce's clerical hat. "My head was not the customary size just at that time. I had been receiving a good many very nice and complimentary attentions, and my head was a couple of sizes larger than usual, and his hat just suited me. The bumps and corners were all right intellectually. There were results pleasing to me—possibly so to him" (*MTS1910*, p. 37; *MTSpk* [1976], pp. 560–561).

Mark Twain would remain a favorite subject for phrenologists. William Windsor's *Phrenology: The Science of Character*. Intro. by Woodbridge N. Ferris (Big Rapids, Michigan: Ferris-Windsor Co., 1921), for example, contained two photographs of Twain taken from different angles to show his strengths in Ideality, Imitation, Wit, Language, and Expression (p. 337).

Alan Gribben, "Mark Twain, Phrenology and the 'Temperaments': A Study of Pseudoscientific Influence," *American Quarterly* 24.1 (March 1972): 45–68. A revised version of this essay appears in Volume One of the present work. See also Tom Quirk, *Mark Twain and Human Nature* (Columbia: University of Missouri, 2007), pages 24–30. Stanley Finger's "Mark Twain's Life-Long Fascination with Phrenology, *Journal of the History of the Behavioral Sciences* 55.2 (April 2019): 99–121 was largely based on, but extended, Gribben's findings.

WEBB, CHARLES HENRY (1834–1905), pseud. "John Paul." *Arrah-na-Poke! Or, Arrah of the Cold Pomme de Terre* (farce, produced in 1865; a burlesque of Dion Boucicault's *Arrah-na-Pogue*, which was produced in 1864).

Mark Twain wrote about Webb's farce in "Mark Twain on the Ballad Infliction" (reprinted from the Virginia City *Enterprise* in the San Francisco *Californian*, 4 November 1865, *MTWY*, pp. 194–195). The comedian Dan Setchell starred in this production. See also the Catalog entry for the song "The Wearing of the Green."

———. *John Paul's Book, Moral and Instructive; Consisting of Travels, Tales, Poetry, and Like Fabrications.* Illus. Hartford, Connecticut: Columbian Book Co., 1874. 621 pp.

Webb's often-topical burlesques ran the danger of becoming dated. "I never hear of Webb's book, & I don't believe it sells *at all*," Clemens remarked in a letter to Charles Stoddard written on 17 March 1875 (*MTLet* 6: 416).

———. *Liffith Lank; or, Lunacy.* New York: Carleton, 1866. 48 pp.

Mark Twain and Webb were dramatic critics at the same time in San Francisco. Twain referred to Webb's parody of Charles Reade's novel *Griffith Gaunt* in a letter written to the *Alta California* on 2 February 1867, but that portion of the letter was not printed (*MTTMB* [1940], p. 284 n. 5). Webb also wrote a fifty-nine-page travesty of Augusta J. Evans's sentimental novel *St. Elmo* (1867), titled *St. Twel'mo; or, the Cuneiform Cyclopedist of Chattanooga* (New York: C. H. Webb, 1867). In 1867 Twain made a note about "Webb & his books & mag. articles" (NB 8, *N&J* 1: 325).

———. *Our Friend from Victoria* (farce, produced in 1865). In "Mark Twain's Jenkins," *Mark Twain Journal* 21.3 (Spring 1983): 7–8, Harold Aspiz persuasively established links between Twain's sketch of 1865, "After Jenkins," and a minor character in Charles Henry Webb's farce *Our Friend from Victoria*. Aspiz noted that Webb founded and edited the *Californian*, in which writings by both Twain and Bret Harte appeared. Twain mentioned Webb as the editor of "a very excellent literary weekly called the *Californian*" in Chapter 59 of *Roughing It* (1872).

———. *Parodies. Prose and Verse.* Illus. New York: G. W. Carleton & Co., 1876. 227 pp.

Mark Twain copied Webb's political satire, "Aboo Ben Butler," adding improvisations to the poem, into Notebook 19 in September 1880; he began, "Abou [sic] Ben Butler—(May his tribe decrease/surcease!)" (*N&J* 2: 372). Around July or August 1889, Twain wrote "C. H. Webb's Poems" (NB 29, TS p. 18), possibly a reference to Webb's *Parodies. Prose and Verse*, which collected *Poems. By "John Paul."* Twain's memories of Webb became increasingly bitter over the years. In 1905 Clemens declared, "I hate both the name and memory of Charles Henry Webb, liar and thief" (SLC to Mr. Buell, New York City, 29 December 1905, dictated to IVL, ASSSCL; PH in MTP). In 1906 Twain devoted portions of two Autobiographical Dictations to his impressions of Webb; in one summary Twain recalled, "His prose was enchantingly puerile, his poetry was not any better; yet he kept on grinding out his commonplaces at intervals until he died, two years ago, of over-cerebration" (23 May 1906 AD; *MTE* [1940], p. 151; *MTAuto* 1: 50). In the other Autobiographical Dictation (on 17 July 1906) he referred to "my disastrous adventures with Charles H. Webb, my first publisher" (*AutoMT* 2: 143). Webb had published Twain's *The Celebrated Jumping Frog of Calaveras County, and Other Sketches* (1867), which failed to sell many copies.

Rogers, *MTBP* (1960), pp. 17–25, 71.

WEBSTER, DANIEL (1782–1852). *The Private Correspondence of Daniel Webster.* Ed. by [Daniel] Fletcher Webster (1813–1862). 2 vols. Boston: Little, Brown and Co., 1875. [This edition is conjectured as the one Clemens may have read; the book was first published in 1857.]

Clemens jokingly attributed one line of a parody of a poem by Alexander Pope to "Daniel Webster" in a letter to Jane Lampton Clemens written on 20 March 1862 (*MTLet* 1: 174). "On 29 August 1880 Clemens wrote to Joseph H. Twichell from Quarry Farm: "Been reading Daniel Webster's Private Correspondence. Have read a hundred of his diffuse, conceited, 'eloquent,' bathotic (or bathostic) letters, written in that dim (no, vanished) Past, when he was a student. . . . The only *real* thing about the whole shadowy business is the sense of the lagging dull & hoary lapse of time that has drifted by since then, a vast empty

level, it seems, with a formless spectre glimpsed fitfully through the smoke & mist that lie along its remote verge" (first quoted in Twichell's "Mark Twain" [1896]; see also Paine, *MTB* [1912], p. 683; Paine, ed., *MTL* [1917], p. 384; and *LMTJHT* [2017], p. 102). The editor of these Webster letters, Fletcher Webster, served the Union as a Colonel in the Civil War and was mortally wounded in the Second Battle of Bull Run.

WEBSTER, JEAN (1876–1916), actually Alice Jane Chandler Webster. *Jerry Junior.* Illustrated by Orson [Byron] Lowell (1871–1956). New York: Century Co., 1907. 282 pp.

Source: MTLAcc, entry #1085, volume donated by Clemens.

In *Jerry Junior*, Webster's third novel, two young Americans visiting Italy, Jerry and Constance, amusingly flirt, dissemble, and fall in love. Webster had been a guest at Mark Twain's Seventieth Birthday dinner at Delmonico's in New York City on 5 December 1905. Besides *Jerry Junior* she wrote seven other novels before dying in 1916 from childbirth complications.

———. *When Patty Went to College.* Illustrated by C[harles]. D[avid]. Williams (1875–1954). New York: Century Co., 1903. 280 pp.

In an undated "sick-room" note to Olivia Clemens written in 1903, Clemens reported: "I read the most of Jean Webster's book to-day; & the most of what I read greatly pleased me—the workmanship, I mean. It is limpid, bright, sometimes brilliant; it is easy, flowing, effortless, & brimming with girlish spirits; it is light, very light, but so is its subject, therefore its lightness is not a fault; its humor is genuine, & not often overstrained. There are failures in the book, but that happens with all books" (ALS in MTP). Clara Clemens was mistaken in supposing that Clemens referred to Jean Webster's *Daddy-Long-Legs*; Webster's highly successful novel about orphan asylums would not appear until 1912 (*MFMT*, p. 249). Jean Webster's *When Patty Went to College*, her first novel, was published in March 1903. It reflected her enjoyable years at Vassar College, from which she had graduated in 1901. Born in Fredonia, New York, Jean Webster was Charles L. Webster's daughter and hence Clemens's great-niece. Mary Boewe's "Bewildered, Bothered, and Bewitched: Mark Twain's View of Three Women Writers," *Mark Twain Journal* 45.1 (Spring 2007): 17–23 summarized Clemens's opinion of Jean Webster.

WEBSTER, NOAH (1758–1843). *An American Dictionary of the English Language.* Springfield, Massachusetts: George & Charles Merriam and Co., 1891. 2118 pp.

Source: MTLAcc, entry #1827, volume donated from Clemens's library by Clara Clemens Gabrilowitsch in 1910.

On 7 March 1891 Clemens wrote from Hartford to George and Charles Merriam & Company, paying a glowing tribute to the complimentary copy of the Merriam-Webster *Dictionary* the firm had sent him: "This one is to me the most awe-inspiring of all Dictionaries, because it exhausts knowledge, apparently. It has gone around like a sun, & spied out everything & lit it up. This is a wonderful book—the most wonderful that I know of." He was particularly impressed by the fact that "a hundred" men had labored on the edition. He concluded, "I thank you very sincerely for the majestic volume" (ALS in the collection of G. and C. Merriam & Co., PH in MTP; quoted by C. Merton Babcock in "Mark Twain and the Dictionary" *Word Study* 42 [October 1966]: 1–6).

———. *The Elementary Spelling Book.* New York, 1829. 168 pp.
Aunt Polly distractedly butters and then bites into "the little Webster spelling book" in Mark Twain's "Tom Sawyer's Conspiracy," written 1897–1900 (*HH&T* [1969], p. 194). In one of Twain's late writings, near a Kentucky schoolhouse "Thomas X" comes upon a girl named Alison, "the dearest and prettiest little thing I had ever seen. . . In one hand she had a Webster spelling-book and first reader" ("Which Was the Dream?," *WWD?* [1969], p. 36). Krause, *MTC* (1967), p. 92.

———. *Webster's Dictionary.*
At John Marshall Clemens's death in 1847 he owned a "Webster's Dictionary" valued at .12½¢, according to the appraisal of his personal property filed on 21 May 1847 in the Marion County Probate Records at Palmyra, Missouri (John Francis McDermott, "Mark Twain and the Bible" [1968], p. 198).

———. *Webster's International Dictionary . . . The Authentic Unabridged, Revised and Enlarged.* [Edition not determined.]
In an interior photograph that Jean Clemens took in the 1900s this book is visible in a bookshelf in the background (collection of Kevin Mac Donnell, Austin, Texas).

———. *Webster's Practical Dictionary of the English Language.*
Green cloth. New York: Ivison, Blakeman & Co., [cop. 1884]. 634 pp.
Marginalia: stray pencil marks.
Provenance: Antenne-Dorrance Collection, Rice Lake, Wisconsin.
Location: Mark Twain Archive, Gannett-Tripp Learning Center, Elmira College, Elmira, New York.
Copy examined: quite possibly Clemens's copy. Examined on 28 May 2015.
On 8 February 1862 Clemens facetiously remarked in a letter written from Carson City to Jane Lampton Clemens and Pamela Moffett that Daniel [*sic*] Webster "wasn't a natural poet. He used to say himself, that unabridged dictionaries was *his* strong suit" (ALS in MTP, quoted in *PRI* [1961], p. 35). On 18 February 1867 Mark Twain described a typesetting machine he viewed in New York City: "The little machine could prepare Webster's Unabridged for the press in a space no larger than a common bath-room" (letter to *Alta California*, *MTTMB* [1940], p. 99). In a humorous Buffalo *Express* column published on 2 October 1869 in which Twain pretended to answer questions posed in a book titled *Mental Photographs: An Album for Confessions of Tastes, Habits, and Convictions* (see the Catalog entry for its editor, Robert Saxton), he answered "Noah Webster, LL.D." to the query about his favorite author (*Mark Twain at the Buffalo Express: Articles and Sketches by America's Favorite Humorist*, ed. Joseph b. McCullough and Janice McIntire-Strasburg [DeKalb: Northern Illinois Press, 2000], p. 63). Listing nine words in a letter of 14 March 1871, Clemens challenged Susan Crane "to correctly pronounce these italicized words without referring to a dictionary. . . Webster *is* an old fool" (*MTLet* 4: 358).
Mark Twain's "Concerning the American Language" (1882) compares the pronunciation that "Mr. Webster's

Dictionary" of 1847 prescribed for "basket" with the same "English Dictionary to-day." In Twain's undated "A Cat Tale," the cat says: "We have authority for it, you see—Mr. Webster; and he is dead, too, besides. It would be a noble good thing if his dictionary was, too. But that is too much to expect" (*LE* [1962], p. 127; Budd, *CTSS&E* 1: 764–765). On 8 November 1902 Twain noted that "Books should bear *all* the copyrights—Webster Dic." (NB 45, TS p. 33). The narrator of "Three Thousand Years Among the Microbes" (written in 1905) lambastes the "Unabridged" dictionary: "Oh, that worthless, worthless book, that timid book, that shifty book, that uncertain book, that time-serving book, that exasperating book, that unspeakable book, the Unlimited Dictionary! that book with but one object in life: to get in more words and shadings of the words than its competitors"; the result is that "a good old useful word" such as "*unique*" now means "everything in general and nothing in particular" (*WWD?* [1969], p. 439). See also the Catalog entry for *Standard Dictionary.*

WEBSTER, SIDNEY (1828–1910). *Two Treaties of Paris and the Supreme Court.* New York: Harper & Brothers, 1901. 132 pp. [Publisher and pages conjectured.]
Inscription: the front flyleaf is signed, "S. L. Clemens, Riverdale, Oct. 1901."
Catalog: *A1911*, "12mo, half cloth (waterstained and warped), N.Y. 1901," quotes the signature, lot 478, sold for .50¢.

WEEKES, ROSE KIRKPATRICK (1874–1956). *Love in Chief. A Novel.* New York: Harper & Brothers, 1904. 289 pp.
Source: MTLAcc, entry #326, volume donated by Clemens.

WEEKS, EDWIN LORD (1849–1903). "Recent Impressions of Anglo-Indian Life," *Harper's Monthly* 91 (November 1895): 903–922.
"*Wed., Jan 22, '96.* Read Edwin Lord Weeks's article on Bombay in Nov. Harper" (Notebook 36 [a note made in Bombay], TS p. 22). Weeks' essay provided a detailed account of his third visit to Bombay.

WEEMS, MASON LOCKE (1759–1825), better known as "Parson Weems." *The Life and Memorable Actions of George Washington* (various editions were published, beginning in 1800).
George Washington's reputation for veracity became a humorous reference point for Mark Twain. "A Touching Story of George Washington's Boyhood" (collected in *The Celebrated Jumping Frog of Calaveras County, and Other Sketches*, 1867) relies on tales like the one about the cherry tree that the Reverend Weems successfully disseminated in his influential biography. In Chapter 20 of *Roughing It* (1872), weary from hearing the too-familiar story of Horace Greeley and the stagecoach driver Hank Monk, Twain implores the next tale-spinner, "Spare me only just this once, and tell me about young George Washington and his little hatchet for a change." Judge Thatcher alludes to "George Washington's lauded Truth about the hatchet!" when praising Tom in Chapter 35 of *The Adventures of Tom Sawyer* (1876). On 16 March 1876 Twain joked in a letter to Richard McCloud published that same day in the Hartford *Courant* about "the symbol of Truth—George Washington's little hatchet" (Fears, *Day by Day* 1: 694, 695). A letter to William Dean Howells, written on 11 October 1876, jokingly refers to Washington's probity as

a "fault" (*MTHL*, p. 158). "The deeds of Washington, the patriot, are the essential thing," Twain emphasized in "Switzerland, the Cradle of Liberty" (1892); "the cherry-tree incident is of no consequence." "A 'high-principled' boy should always do the 'right and righteous thing' and follow George Washington's example after stealing a watermelon, Twain joked in a speech at the University of Missouri Commencement on 4 June 1902. In a speech at the Manhattan Dickens Fellowship Dinner on 7 February 1906 Twain wove a comical interpretation into "the story about George Washington and his little hatchet" *MTSpk* [1976], pp. 483–484). See also the Catalog entry for George Lippard's *Legends of the American Revolution; or, Washington and His Generals*.

Gregg Camfield, "The Art of Judicious Lying," *Mark Twain Annual 16* (2018): 109.

Weihnacht Abend (Christmas Eve). [Unidentified work.]
F. W. Christern, New York City importers of foreign books, billed Clemens on 21 April 1881 for "1 Weihnachts abend .55¢"; Clemens paid on 22 April 1881 (receipt in MTP).

WEISS, JOHANNES (1863–1914). *Paul and Jesus.* Translated from the German by H[enry]. J[ohn]. Chaytor (1871–1954). New York: Harper & Brothers, 1909. 131 pp.
Source: MTLAcc, entry #1492, volume donated by Clemens.
Weiss was a German Protestant biblical scholar at Heidelberg. The Reverend Chaytor was the headmaster of Plymouth College in England.

WELCH, FLETCHER G. (1833–1907), pseud. "F. G. W." *That Convention; or, Five Days a Politician.* Illustrated by Frank Beard (1842–1905). Frontispiece and woodcuts. 12mo, cloth. New York: F. G. Welch & Co., 1872. 184 pp.
Inscriptions: on a flyleaf Clemens wrote, "They seem to have been satisfied with pretty poor stuff in those days. M. T." He also noted, "'A Jumping Frog' was published in 1867 through The American News Company. Mark Twain." The content, tone, and signature in these inscriptions would seem to indicate that Clemens was obliging a fan by autographing a book published decades earlier. Why would he sign notes that he made in a book he owned? And why sign them "M. T." rather than his customary "S. L. C."? An altogether odd association copy.
Catalogs: Anderson Auction Company (New York City), Sale number 380 (14 April 1905), "first edition, comic illustrations, post 8vo, cloth, New York, 1872, "Mark Twain's copy, with MS. notes on fly-leaf," lot 84; Anderson Auction Company (New York City), Sale number 440 (6 March 1906), "first edition, comic illustrations, post 8vo, cloth, New York, 1872, "Mark Twain's copy, with MS. notes on fly-leaf," lot 163; Anderson Auction Galleries (New York City), Sale number 965 (14–15 October 1912), "12mo, cloth, New York, 1872," lot 121, sold for $10 (PH in MTP). The inscriptions derive from this latter catalog.
Location: collection of Kevin Mac Donnell, Austin, Texas.
Source: notification from Mac Donnell to Alan Gribben, 28 August 2017.
The Ohio-born businessman Welch lived in Chicago in 1872. Pages 147–155 of Welch's humorous account of the 1872 Liberal Republican convention in Cincinnati (which nominated Horace Greeley for president) reprinted Mark Twain's spoof about Greeley's handwriting from Chapter

70 of *Roughing It* (1872). Ulysses S. Grant easily gained re-election by defeating Greeley. By 1880 Fletcher G. Welch had moved to Williamsburg, Kansas and as late as 1900 listed himself as a real estate broker there.

WELCKER, ADAIR (1858–1926). *A Dream of Realms Beyond Us.* Eighth edition. Original purple printed wrappers. San Francisco: [Cubery and Company, Printers,] 1904. 30 numbered leaves (printed on the recto side only), plus an 8-page "Supplement".
Inscription: effusively inscribed to Clemens by the author, who included a copy of a letter from someone claiming that Clemens had praised an earlier edition.
Provenance: MTLAcc, entry #2116, volume donated from Clemens's library by Clara Clemens Gabrilowitsch in 1910. Eventually obtained by Nick Karanovich (1938–2003), Fort Wayne, Indiana.
Catalogs: *Mott 1952*, item #91, $100; *Sotheby's 2003*, #217, $4,000 (sold with four other inscribed books).
Location: collection of Kevin Mac Donnell, Austin, Texas.
Copy examined: Clemens's unmarked copy, in July 2004. A Mark Twain Library accession number written in ink is visible on the verso of the title page.
Welcker self-published numerous poems, plays, and other works, often laying in these copies favorable correspondence promoting his writings. He was a frequent target of Ambrose Bierce, who ridiculed Welcker's literary abilities. His *A Dream of Realms Beyond Us* is a verse drama.

WELLBY, MONTAGU SINCLAIR (1866–1900). *'Twixt Sirdar and Menelik; An Account of a Year's Expedition from Zeila to Cairo Through Unknown Abyssinia.* Intro by J[ohn]. L[ane]. Harrington (1864–1927). Illustrated with plates and maps. First edition. Original tan pictorial cloth, gilt. New York: Harper & Brothers, 1901. 409 pp.
Inscription: the front free flyleaf is signed in black ink, "S L. Clemens/1903."
Provenance: MTLAcc, entry #1299, volume donated by Clemens. I. R. Brussel of Brooklyn offered the book for $10 on 8 September 1960. In 1986 the book belonged to Victor Jacobs of Dayton, Ohio (Jacobs to Alan Gribben, 15 October 1986, "signed by S. L. Clemens"); subsequently it became part of the collection of Nick Karanovich (1938–2003), Fort Wayne, Indiana.
Catalogs: "Collection of Victor and Irene Murr Jacobs," Sotheby's, New York City, 29 October 1996, lot 313, sold with four other books for a total of $9,312; *Sotheby's 2003*, #212, $6,000 (sold with five other history and travel titles).
Location: collection of Kevin Mac Donnell, Austin, Texas.
Copy examined: Clemens's unmarked copy, in July 2004. No sale labels are visible.
Wellby was killed in military action in South Africa shortly before this book was published.

WELLS, CAROLYN (1869–1942). *A Phenomenal Fauna.* Illustrated by Oliver Herford (1863–1935). New York: R. H. Russell, 1902. [90 pp.]
Source: MTLAcc, entry #1906, volume donated from Clemens's library by Clara Clemens Gabrilowitsch in 1910.
Wells provided nonsensical rhymes about, and Herford drew fantastical pictures of, odd-looking animals. Birds, monkeys, frogs, snakes, and other bizarre-looking creatures strut around on the pages.

———. *The Rubáiyát of Bridge.* Illustrated by May (Wilson)

Preston (1873–1949). New York: Harper & Brothers, 1909. [No page numbers, 19 illustrations.]

Source: MTLAcc, entry #1486, volume donated by Clemens.

Wells imitated Edward FitzGerald's translation of *The Rubáiyát* while giving instructions for playing the card game of bridge: "A Book of Bridge Rules underneath the Bough,/A Score Card, Two new Packs of Cards, and Thou," and so forth. The illustrator May Wilson Preston, an early and ardent supporter of the women's rights movement, provided twenty (tinted) pen-and-ink sketches of fashionably dressed ladies languidly indulging in this pastime.

WELLS, CATHERINE BOOTT (GANNETT) (1838–1911). *About People*. Boston: J. R. Osgood and Co., 1885. 233 pp.

Source: MTLAcc, entry #674, volume donated by Clemens. A book of essays by a woman who, though known as a social reformer, nevertheless opposed the notion of women's suffrage.

WELLS, HENRY PARKHURST (1842–1904). *City Boys in the Woods; or, A Trapping Venture in Maine*. Illus. New York: Harper & Brothers, 1903. 277 pp.

Source: MTLAcc, entry #515, volume donated by Clemens. The New York City attorney Wells was an avid fisherman and outdoorsman.

WELLS, H[ERBERT]. G[EORGE]. (1866–1946). *Anticipations of the Reaction of Mechanical and Scientific Progress Upon Human Life and Thought*. New York: Harper & Brothers, 1902. 342 pp.

Catalog: *A1911*, "12mo, boards, gilt top, uncut, N.Y. 1902," a small sheet of notes about the Russian-Japanese war laid in, lot 480, sold for $4.

Location: Henry E. Huntington Library, San Marino, California.

Copy examined: Clemens's copy, unmarked, on 27 July 1997. Many leaves are unopened, beginning with pages 10–11. The sale label of the *A1911* auction is affixed to the front pastedown endpaper.

Wells' generally optimistic predictions for a dawning new world would require, he speculated, new types of institutions and modifications in human behavior. On 6 April 1906 William Dean Howells invited Clemens to lunch in New York City with "H. G. Wells, the man from Mars and other malign planets" (*MTHL*, p. 803). Isabel Lyon recorded that Clemens attended a luncheon for Wells on 8 April 1906 (IVL Journals, TS p. 155). On that same day Clemens wrote to Clara from New York City: "I lunched with Howells to-day to meet H. G. Wells" (ALS, School of the Ozarks, Point Lookout, Missouri, PH in MTP). Cyril Clemens reported that Wells and Clemens later met in 1907 at a dinner given by Sir Arthur Quiller-Couch. Wells was impressed then by Clemens's "extraordinarily picturesque phraseology" and his clever method of delivery in telling a story ("Tea with H. G. Wells," *Hobbies: The Magazine for Collectors* 51 (November 1946): 141–142). This latter meeting seems to have only Cyril Clemens's word as corroboration that it occurred. The details appear plausible, however.

———. [An identical copy.]

Source: MTLAcc, entry #1468, volume donated by Clemens.

———. *The Future in America; A Search After Realities*. Illus.

8vo, original cloth, gilt top, uncut. New York: Harper & Brothers, 1906. 259 pp.

Inscription: the front pastedown endpaper is signed in black ink, "S L. Clemens/1906."

Marginalia: on page 27 Clemens used brown ink to cross out the word "less" and substitute "fewer". In brown ink Clemens underscored the first three lines on page 79 and noted "True" in the margin; there Wells declared: "Patriotism has become a mere national self-assertion, a sentimentality of flag cheering, with no constructive duties." Across the tops of pages 80–81 Clemens wrote in brown ink: "We have a bastard Patriotism, a sarcasm, a burlesque; but we have no such thing as a public conscience. Politically we are just a joke." In the last sentence on page 115 ("One million seven hundred children, practically uneducated, are toiling"), Clemens inserted the word "thousand" in brown ink between "hundred" and "children."

Catalogs: *A1911*, "12mo, cloth, gilt top, uncut, N.Y. 1906," quotes the signature, lot 479, sold for $2.50; American Art Association (New York City) sale catalogue (8 January 1925), quotes marginalia, has the *A1911* sale label, lot 122, sold for $22.50 (with two other books); American Art Association, Anderson Galleries (New York City), sale number 4201 (13–14 November 1935), quotes marginalia, lot 72, sold for $210.

Location: Henry W. and Albert A. Berg Collection, New York Public Library, Astor, Lenox, and Tilden Foundations.

Copy examined: Clemens's copy, in 1970.

———. *The Future in America; A Search after Realities*. Illus. New York: Harper & Brothers, [cop. 1907]. 259 pp.

Source: MTLAcc, entry #1747, volume donated by Clemens.

———. *The Invisible Man. A Grotesque Romance*. New York: Harper & Brothers, [cop. 1897]. 278 pp.

In February 1898 Mark Twain had an inspiration: "The <Invisible Salve> Magic Ointment. A finger-touch with it makes the entire object invisible & keeps it so for 8 days" (NB 40, TS p. 12). The Young Man of Mark Twain's "What Is Man?" (1906) alludes to "Mr. Wells's man who invented a drug that made him invisible" (Part 5, *WIM?*, p. 179).

———. *The Time Machine* (novel, published in 1895).

This is one of those frustrating gaps in what got recorded about Clemens's library books. Surely Clemens would have been attracted to the subject of Wells' book, no matter how much his financial worries weighed on him in the 1890s. We can only remain aware of the many hundreds of volumes missing from this inventory of his library and reading, despite every effort to identify them.

Philip Klass ("An Innocent in Time: Mark Twain in King Arthur's Court," *Extrapolation* 16.1 [December 1974]: 17–32) reminded readers that Twain's time-travel novel antedated Wells' epochal work by six years. Twain also anticipated some of the anachronisms as well as the paradoxes in social values that became relevant to later science fiction. Klass wrote that Wells "perfected" what Twain initiated, leaving "little for late-comers to do." James S. Leonard noted "a suspicious resemblance" between numbers used in *The Time Machine* and Twain's last major work of fiction ("*No. 44, The Mysterious Stranger*: The Final Soliloquy of a 'Littery Man,'" *Centenary Reflections on Mark Twain's* No. 44, The Mysterious Stranger, ed. Joseph Csicsila and Chad Rohman [Columbia: University of Missouri Press, 2009], pp. 172–173).

———. *The War of the Worlds.* Illus. New York: Harper & Brothers, 1900. 291 pp.

Inscription: the front pastedown endpaper has penciled initials that appear to be made by Olivia Clemens—"S. C." (She made similarly hurried designations in some other volumes presumably belonging to Clemens, such as Thackeray's *Adventures of Philip*.)

Marginalia: no notes, but page 186 in Book II is turned down, one of Clemens's reading habits.

Location: Mark Twain Library, Redding, Connecticut. (MTLAcc, entry #1668, volume donated by Clemens.)

Copy examined: Clemens's copy, unmarked. Has a black ink Mark Twain Library number, "4566" and the oval purple Library stamps. I could not find this book in 1970 but when I returned to Redding in June 1982 it had been located and placed with Clemens's other library books.

———. *When the Sleeper Wakes.* Illus. New York: Harper & Brothers, 1906. 329 pp.

Source: MTLAcc, entry #1699 a, volume donated by Clemens.

A man named Graham sleeps for more than two hundred years, awakening in a dystopian London in which he is both revered and hated.

———. *The Wonderful Visit.* New York: Macmillan Co., 1895. 251 pp.

Source: MTLAcc, entry #1481, volume donated by Clemens.

In this satirical fantasy an angel arrives at a small English village and is mistakenly wounded by a vicar who collects birds. Recovering, the creature from a more ideal realm passes satirical judgments upon the obvious faults of human society.

WELLS, JOSEPH (1855–1929). *Oxford and its Colleges.* Illustrated by Edmund H[ort]. New (1871–1931). Seventh edition. London: Methuen & Co., [1906]. 342 pp.

Marginalia: one word and a suffix crossed out to correct the grammar in black ink on page 137, thereby changing "to have benefited Lincoln" to read instead "to benefit Lincoln". Pages turned at 12 and 220 (the latter at an etching of the staircase at Christ Church).

Location: Mark Twain Library, Redding, Connecticut.

Copy examined: Clemens's copy, unmarked. It has the red ink Mark Twain Library accession number "4119". (Judging by the advanced number, this might have been one of the later donations from Stormfield.) Examined in 1970 and again in June 1982.

WELLS, SAMUEL ROBERTS (1820–1875). *Wedlock; or, the Right Relation of the Sexes; Disclosing the Laws of Conjugal Selection, and Showing Who May, and Who May Not Marry.* New York: S. R. Wells, 1869. 238 pp.

On 21 August 1869 Clemens wrote indignantly to Olivia Langdon about a book that had arrived at the Buffalo *Express* offices: "Among the books sent us to review was one called 'Wedlock,' which I siezed [*sic*] & read, intending to mark it & take it to you, but it was nothing but a mass of threadbare old platitudes & maudlin advice shoveled together without rhyme or reason, & so I threw it away

& told [Josephus N.] Larned to embody that opinion in his notice (he was reviewing the books)" (*LLMT*, pp. 104–105; *MTLet* 3: 317). Wells was a partner in the Fowler & Wells publishing firm of New York City and from 1855 until 1875 would edit and publish the *American Phrenological Journal*; see also the entries for Orson Squire Fowler and for George Sumner Weaver.

"WE'LL SING THE WINE-CUP AND THE LASS" (unidentified song).
In Mark Twain's "The Chronicle of Young Satan" (written 1897–1900), Father Adolf "was rolling along down the road . . . braying 'We'll sing the wine-cup and the lass' in his thundering bass" (*MSM*, p. 37). This might refer anachronistically to Thomas Moore's "The Wine-Cup Is Circling" (published in 1835), sung to the air of the tune "Michael Hoy."

WELSH, HERBERT (1851–1941).
Jim Zwick reported that Clemens was familiar with *City and State*, a weekly that this political reformer edited from 1895 until 1904, as well as a book, *Stranger Than Fiction*, compiled from *City and State* and other periodicals ("'Prodigally Endowed with Sympathy for the Cause': Mark Twain's Involvement with the Anti-Imperialist League," *Mark Twain Journal* 32.1 [Spring 1994]: 22 n. 29).

WENCKEBACH, CARLA (1853–1902). *Deutsche Grammatik für Amerikaner. Nach einer neuen praktischen Methode.* Fourth edition. New York: Henry Holt and Co.; Boston: C. Schoenhof, [cop. 1887]. 291 pp.

Before going to a bookstore in Boston, Clemens wrote: "'German Grammar for Americans' by Carla Wenckebach—same place" (NB 27 [May 1888], *N&J* 2: 392).

WENTWORTH, GEORGE ALBERT (1835–1906). *A Text-book of Geometry.* Boston: Ginn & Co., 1889. 437 pp.

Source: MTLAcc, entry #815, volume donated by Clemens.

WERTHERN, FREIHERR VON (ALFRED HERMANN THILO) (1842–1908). *General von Versen: ein militärisches Zeit- und Lebensbild: aus hinterlassenen Briefen und Aufzeichnungen zusammengef. Von Frhr. Von Werthern.* Portrait. Berlin: E. S. Mittler und Sohn, 1898. 254 pp.

Inscription: a presentation inscription at the top of the title page contains names and a date that are now mostly illegible (at least in a photocopy) except for the words "R. M. Cle[mens?]/from his Sister/Alice" and "Berlin". The handwriting does not resemble that of Samuel Clemens or any members of his immediate family.

Provenance: cataloged by Thomas A. Tenney in 1980 in the collection of Cyril Clemens (1902–1999) in Kirkwood, Missouri.

Location: undetermined at present.

Copy examined: photocopy of the title page sent to Alan Gribben by Thomas A. Tenney in September 1980 from Kirkwood, Missouri. Clemens's travels in Austria in 1897, 1898, and 1899 (and, more briefly, in Germany in 1899) gave him opportunities to acquire this biography of Maximilian von Versen (1833–1893). He had met Versen in 1892 and was familiar with his travels in South America (see the Catalog entry for Maximilian von Versen, *Reisen in Amerika* [1872]). However, the fact that pages 189–216 discuss this German military officer's ties with the Clemens family make it conceivable that the book came to Cyril Clemens through his own family.

"WE SHALL WALK THROUGH THE VALLEY" (spiritual).

George Washington Cable noted on 14 November 1884 in Boston: "It isn't easy to write as Mark Twain is singing 'We shall walk through the Valley'" (*MT&GWC* [1960], p. 59). This spiritual was collected in J. B. T. Marsh's *The Story of the Jubilee Singers, with Their Songs*, revised edition (Boston: Houghton, Mifflin and Co., 1880), pp. 194–195. Its first lines are "We shall walk thro' the valley of the shadow of death,/We shall walk thro' the valley in peace."

WESLEY, CHARLES (1707–1788). "Hark! the herald angels sing" (Christmas carol, published in 1739; its lyrics were adapted by George Whitefield [1714–1770] in 1753). Melody by Felix Mendelssohn-Bartholdy (1809–1847).

Either Clemens or his wife Olivia marked this hymn in their copy of *Laudes Domini: A Selection of Spiritual Songs, Ancient and Modern* (1884), compiled by C. S. Robinson. (See that Catalog entry.)

————. "Son of the Carpenter! receive" (hymn, published in 1739).

In Mark Twain's "About Smells" (*Galaxy*, May 1870), he demanded of the Reverend Thomas De Witt Talmage whether Talmage's church choir did not sing, "Son of the Carpenter! receive/This humble work of mine" (*WIM?*, p. 50). These are the first two lines of Wesley's hymn; the next two lines continue, "Worth to my meanest labor give,/By joining it to Thine." Wesley was inspired by the question, "Is this not the carpenter's son?" (Matthew 13.55).

WESLEY, JOHN (1703–1791). *A Collection of Hymns, for the Use of the People Called Methodists*. London: John Mason, n.d. 734 pp.

Source: MTLAcc, entry #924, volume donated by Clemens.

John Mason published numerous editions of this work during the first half of the nineteenth century; the 1833 edition matched the specified number of pages recorded by the Mark Twain Library. The majority of these hymns were written by Charles Wesley (1707–1788).

WESSELY, IGNAZ ÉMANUEL (1841–1900). *A New Pocket Dictionary of the English and Italian Languages*. Fourteenth edition. Rewritten by Giuseppi Rigutini and George Payn. Tauchnitz New Pocket Dictionaries Series. Leipzig: Bernhard Tauchnitz, 1891. 217 pp.

Inscriptions: the front free endpaper is signed in ink, "Clara Langdon Clemens./Italia/April 1892." The half-title page is signed in ink, "Clara Langdon Clemens/Roma/April 1892."

Provenance: formerly in the Mark Twain Library, Redding, Connecticut.

Catalog: *Mott 1952*, item #92, $2.50.

Location: Mark Twain House and Museum, Hartford, Connecticut. Donated anonymously in 1963.

Copy examined: Clara Clemens's copy. Worn condition; spine missing. Examined in August 1987.

WEST, (SIR) ALGERNON EDWARD (1832–1921). *Recollections, 1832 to 1886*. Illus. New York: Harper & Brothers, 1900. 442 pp.

Source: MTLAcc, entry #1783, volume donated by Clemens.

West was private secretary to William Ewart Gladstone (1809–1898), the four-time prime minister of Great Britain.

WESTBROOK, RICHARD BRODHEAD (1820–1899). *Girard's Will and Girard College Theology*. Frontispiece portrait. 12mo, original plum cloth, spine spotted and with wear at top, one signature nearly loose. Philadelphia: Published by the author, 1888. 183 pp.

Marginalia: Clemens annotated Westbrook's book extensively, writing approximately 465 words (mainly in pencil) on thirty-one of its 183 pages. He also bracketed certain paragraphs, crossed out others in ink, marked the text with vertical lines, and used pencil to write numerals in the margin. The corners of nine pages have been folded down. It would appear that he was preparing an essay or speech about the College Trustees' imposing a religious viewpoint on the institution. On page 40 he wrote, "It makes the indignant blood rise to see a good man [i.e., Girard] so used; to see his corpse crawled over & defiled by these slimy worms." Farther on he commented: "But they are doing a good work: they are proving Christianity a breeder of shams & rascals" (p. 41). Clemens filled every margin of page 43 with sarcastic taunts, such the one at the top of that page: "I object to the selling of whisky to boys. Suppose my fam[ily] should use my money to *give* it to them." On page 44 he wrote, "There isn't anybody connected with it [the College] that has *any* moral character--& *so they have no right* to remain" as Trustees. "Is all Phila. a den of inane scoundrels? The whole city is smirched" (p. 52). On page 53 Clemens wrote: "This is not a good time—for few people are now Christians privately." Chester L. Davis reported on Clemens's annotation in *The Twainian* 27 (May-June, July-August 1968).

Provenance: formerly in the collection of Chester L. Davis's Mark Twain Research Foundation, Perry, Missouri.

Catalogs: ListABP (1910), "Girard's Will, Westbrook"; Christie's, New York City, estate of Chester Davis, 17 May 1991, lot 81, quotes marginalia and reproduces page 43 in facsimile, price estimate prior to auction $2,500–3,500.

Location: currently unreported.

Copy examined: none. Chester Davis (1903–1987) did not show me this volume when I visited Perry in 1970.

In Chapter 29 of *Following the Equator* (1897) Mark Twain would mention Girard as one of the "first American marsupials." The wealthy Philadelphia merchant Stephen Girard (1750–1831) left an estate to establish Girard College, intended for the education of fatherless boys. (The name was a misnomer, since Girard College served boys younger than college-age.) Girard, a devout atheist, had specified in his legal will that no clergy or religious teachings should be tolerated in the institution. Richard Brodhead Westbrook was hardly a disinterested commentator about the periodic efforts to test this prohibition. A former Presbyterian clergyman, he had forsaken that religious calling to become a lawyer, judge, and investor. In 1889 he would serve as the president of the American Secular Union, and he also had connections with the American Theosophist movement.

WESTCOTT, EDWARD NOYES (1846–1898). *David Harum: A Story of American Life*. Pearson's Colonial Library Series. Red cloth. London: C. Arthur Pearson, 1900. 392 pp.

Provenance: Antenne-Dorrance Collection, Rice Lake, Wisconsin.

Location: Mark Twain Archive, Gannett-Tripp Learning

Center, Elmira College, Elmira, New York.

Copy examined: Clemens's copy, unmarked. Examined on 28 May 2015.

Westcott's posthumously published novel, set in the upstate New York village of Homeville, featured a fictitious banker and horse trader who dispensed homespun philosophy and practiced secret philanthropy. A young protegee of Harum, John Lenox, furnished the romance in the story by almost hopelessly pursuing a society girl, Mary Blake. The folksy David Harum figure struck a chord with the public and the novel became a best-seller after it first appeared in 1898.

WESTRUP, MARGARET (1875–1922), later (after 1910), "Mrs. W. Sidney Stacey." *The Coming of Billy*. New York: Harper & Brothers, 1906. 267 pp.

Source: MTLAcc, entry #1619, volume donated by Clemens.

A young boy is sent back to England to recuperate from the Indian climate with his four aunts.

———. *The Greater Mischief; A Novel*. New York: Harper & Brothers, 1908. 377 pp.

Source: MTLAcc, entry #327, volume donated by Clemens.

WETMORE, ELIZABETH (BISLAND) (1861–1929). *A Candle of Understanding, A Novel*. New York: Harper & Brothers, 1903. 306 pp.

Source: MTLAcc, entry #1093, volume donated by Clemens.

WEYMAN, STANLEY JOHN (1855–1928). *The Red Cockade. A Novel* (published in 1895).

During the sea voyage from Mauritius, Mark Twain read several of Weyman's historical romances, including this one set in revolutionary France. He alluded to them in the manuscript (MS pp. 153 ff., Berg Collection, NYPL) for *Following the Equator* (1897), but deleted that passage before its publication (Krause, *MTC* [1967], p. 235).

———. *Under the Red Robe* (novel, published in 1896).

In a passage deleted from the manuscript of *Following the Equator* (MS pp. 153 ff., Berg Collection., NYPL), Mark Twain criticized this novel about a gentleman rogue in France for carelessness with facts and national characterizations (Krause, *MTC* [1967], p. 235).

WEYMOUTH, JOHN (1874–1944), pseud. "Nat Prune." *College Chaps*. Illustrated by [Isaac Brewster] Hazelton (1875–1943). Boston: Mutual Book Co., 1902. 95 pp. [Illustrator, publisher, and pages conjectured.]

Inscription: presented by the author.

Catalog: *A1911*, "12mo, cloth, gilt top, uncut, Bost. 1902, presentation copy," a small sheet of Clemens's notes laid in, lot 392, sold for $1.25.

John Weymouth, a resident of Hampton, Virginia and a graduate of the College of William and Mary, was the pseudonymous "Nat Prune" listed as the author in the *A1911* catalog. Weymouth also wrote *Wedding Bells and Other Sketches* (New York: Abbey Press, 1901). He later became a prominent lawyer specializing in corporate litigation and eventually served as a district judge.

WHARTON, EDITH NEWBOLD (JONES) (1862–1937). *The House of Mirth*. Illustrated by A[lbert]. B[eck]. Wenzell (1864–1917). Red cloth. New York: Charles Scribner's Sons, 1905. 533 pp.

Inscription: the front pastedown endpaper is signed with black ink in a hand that is loose and wavering,

but definitely Clemens's: "S. L. Clemens./21—5th Avenue/N. Y."

Marginalia: on page 142 Clemens drew a vertical pencil line beside the sentence: "It is almost as stupid to let your clothes betray that you know you are ugly as to have them proclaim that you think you are beautiful." On the rear flyleaf Isabel V. Lyon began an unfinished remark in pencil, evidently quoting Clemens: "The rarest & sweetest lie I ever heard in the". There are no other markings. The leaves of the book have been opened to the very end, tearing some pages.

Provenance: Antenne-Dorrance Collection, Rice Lake, Wisconsin.

Location: Mark Twain Archive, Gannett-Tripp Learning Center, Elmira College, Elmira, New York.

Copy examined: Clemens's copy. This volume was missing when I inspected the collection in 1970, but subsequently Katharine Antenne discovered the book was in Eau Claire, Wisconsin and had it returned to the collection in Rice Lake. I examined the volume on 28 May 2015 at Elmira College.

Edith Wharton wrote a letter in 1904 declining a dinner invitation at Colonel George Harvey's at which Clemens and Henry James would be present; she stated that she especially regretted missing the chance to meet Clemens, but that her work had to take priority (Terry L. Gellin to Alan Gribben, 30 June 1989, citing Leon Edel's biography). *The House of Mirth* became a best-selling novel in 1905. Clemens and Isabel V. Lyon often exchanged literary opinions, so it may be significant that on 18 March 1906 Lyon wrote of "the great horror" she felt toward all works of fiction after attempting three times to read the "dreadfulnesses" in Wharton's *House of Mirth* (IVL Journals, TS p. 149, MTP). Clemens was dissatisfied with Upton House in Dublin, New Hampshire; on 10 June 1906 he sarcastically referred to the residence as "The House of Mirth" (IVL Journals, TS p. 164, MTP). Laura Skandera Trombley provided a sensitive analysis of Lyons's emotional reaction in *Mark Twain's Other Woman: The Hidden Story of His Final Years* (New York: Alfred A. Knopf, 2010), pp. 100–103.

WHEATLEY, HENRY B[ENJAMIN]. (1838–1917). *Samuel Pepys and the World He Lived In*. Second ed. London: Bickers and Son, 1880. 311 pp.

Catalog: Ball 2016 inventory, brown leather, gilt lettering design, gilt top edges.

Location: Quarry Farm library shelves, under the supervision of the Mark Twain Archive, Elmira College, Elmira, New York.

This biography of Samuel Pepys (1633–1703) was available to Clemens whenever he visited Quarry Farm in Elmira.

WHEELER, ANDREW CARPENTER (1835–1903), pseud. "J. P. Mowbray." *A Journey to Nature*. Illus. New York: Doubleday, Page and Co., 1901. 315 pp. [Publisher and pages conjectured.]

Inscription: the front free endpaper is signed, "Clemens, 1902".

Catalogs: *A1911*, "12mo, cloth, N.Y. 1901," quotes the signature, lot 347, sold for $1.50; *Lexington 1912*, lot 21, sold for $4.

On a doctor's advice a stockbroker leaves his frenetic urban life and lives for a year in the country. Twenty-five chapters record his experiences as he learns to appreciate the simpler pleasures of bird songs, animal antics, streams, foliage, and snowfalls.

———. *The Making of a Country Home*. Illustrated by Charles Edward Hooper (1867–1920). First edition. Original light green pictorial cloth, gilt, pictorial endpapers. New York: Doubleday, Page and Co., 1901. 258 pp.

Inscriptions: the front free endpaper is signed in pencil, "Clemens/1902"; the half-title page is signed identically.

Provenance: contains the shelfmark of Clara Clemens Gabrilowitsch's private library collection from the period when she lived in Detroit. Belonged to the Carrie Estelle Doheny Collection, St. John's Seminary, Camarillo, California. Donated by Mrs. Doheny in 1940 after she acquired the volume for $12.20 from Maxwell Hunley Rare Books, Beverly Hills, California. Auctioned by Christie's in New York City with two other titles (lot 1184) for $2,040 on 17 October 1988 on behalf of St. John's Seminary. Subsequently it belonged to the collection of Nick Karanovich (1938–2003), Fort Wayne, Indiana.

Catalog: *Sotheby's 2003*, #197, $5,500 (sold with two other titles from Clemens's library).

Location: collection of Kevin Mac Donnell, Austin, Texas.

Copy examined: Clemens's unmarked copy, in 2003 and again in July 2004. Some leaves are ripped open. It has the bookplate of "Estelle Doheny."

This story follows a man who decides to build a home in the country. One wonders whether this combination of fact and fiction, part of a "back to nature" sentiment discernible in American literature during the first decade of the twentieth century, had any bearing on Clemens's eventual decision to build an Italianate villa in the hilly woods of Connecticut.

WHEELER, CANDACE (THURBER) (1827–1923). *Prize Painting Book: Good Times. Pictures by Dora Wheeler*. New York: White & Stokes, [cop. 1881]. 62 pp.

Source: MTLAcc, entry #1907, volume donated from Clemens's library by Clara Clemens Gabrilowitsch in 1910.

A coloring book for young readers, with cash prizes offered by the publisher for winning entries. The black and white outline drawings are by Dora Wheeler (1856–1940, later Dora Keith); the accompanying verses were written by Dora's mother, the textile designer Candace Wheeler.

WHEELER, EDWARD L[YTTON]. (c. 1854–1885).

Gary P. Henrickson—"Out on a Limb with Deadwood Dick: A Possible Source for *Huckleberry Finn*," *Twainian* 50: 2 (30 June 1994): 1–4—argued that dime novels have been largely overlooked as lowbrow reading fare with which Mark Twain might have been familiar. Edward L. Wheeler was an especially popular author in this strata; Wheeler wrote *Deadwood Dick, The Prince of the Road; or, The Black Rider of the Black Hills* (1877) and many other Beadle and Adams titles. Henrickson singled out *Deadwood Dick's Dream; or The Rivals of the Road* (1881) as having "situations, dialogue, and illustrations" similar to the Sherburn-Boggs episode in Chapter 22 of *Adventures of Huckleberry Finn* (1885), particularly the facing down of a lynch mob.

WHEELER, J[AMES]. TALBOYS (1824–1897). *The Life and Travels of Herodotus [c. 484–425 BCE] in the Fifth Century Before*

Christ: An Imaginary Biography Founded on Fact, Illustrative of the History, Manners, Religion, Literature, Arts, and Social Condition . . . in the Days of Pericles and Nehemiah. 2 vols. Half sheep, marbled endpapers and edges, spine is loose. New York: Harper & Brothers, 1856.

Location: Mark Twain Library, Redding, Connecticut.

Copy examined: very likely Clemens's copy, unsigned and unmarked. Has the red ink Mark Twain Library accession number "3256" in Volume 1 (445 pp.) and the number "3257" in Volume 2 (466 pp.). I did not see this book in 1970 but it had been shelved among Clemens's library books when I revisited Redding in June 1982.

This book might have been among the small personal library collection that survived from Clemens's youthful days.

WHEELER, MARIANNA (b. 1856). *The Baby; His Care and Training*. Illus. New York: Harper & Brothers, [cop. 1901]. 189 pp.

Source: MTLAcc, entry #671, volume donated by Clemens. Wheeler was the superintendent of the New York Babies Hospital.

WHEELER, POST (1869–1956). *Love-in-a-Mist*. Blue cloth, decorated. New York: Camelot Co., 1901. 216 pp.

Inscription: the front flyleaf is inscribed in black ink: "To/ Samuel L. Clemens,/with an admiration that/dates from the birth of/Tom Sawyer./Post Wheeler/New York, May 26, 1901".

Provenance: Antenne-Dorrance Collection, Rice Lake, Wisconsin.

Location: Mark Twain Archive, Gannett-Tripp Learning Center, Elmira College, Elmira, New York.

Copy examined: Clemens's unmarked copy. This volume of poems was missing when I inspected the collection in 1970, but subsequently Katharine Antenne found the book in Eau Claire, Wisconsin and returned it to the collection in Rice Lake. I examined the book on 28 May 2015 in Elmira, New York.

Poetry by a Princeton graduate, world traveler, and newspaper writer.

———. [An identical copy.]

Source: MTLAcc, entry #615, volume donated by Clemens.

WHITAKER, HERMAN (1867–1919). *The Planter; A Novel*. New York: Harper & Brothers, 1909. 536 pp.

Source: MTLAcc, entry #1429, volume donated by Clemens.

WHITCHER, FRANCES MIRIAM (BERRY) (1811–1852), pseud. "Widow Bedott." *The Widow Bedott Papers*. Introduction by Alice B[radley]. Neal (1827–1863), also known as Mrs. Alice Haven. New York: J. C. Derby, 1856.

Catalogs: a bookdealer from Horseheads, New York, Emily Schweizer Martinez, listed this book in an inventory of the library she prepared when Quarry Farm was donated to Elmira College; Ball 2016 inventory, green cloth, embossed silver lettering on the spine, fair condition, inscribed "Clark". Ida B. Clark married Charles Jervis Langdon in 1870.

Location: Quarry Farm library shelves, under the supervision of the Mark Twain Archive, Elmira College, Elmira, New York.

Clemens had access to the Langdon's library whenever he visited Elmira in the summers.

In 1880 Mark Twain twice listed "Widow Bedott" among the humorists to be considered for a projected anthology

(NB 19, *N&J* 2: 363, 364). He again included this fictional character in another compilation of humorists in 1881 (NB 19, *N&J* 2: 429). Nevertheless, *Mark Twain's Library of Humor* (1888) contained no selections written by Whitcher. (In some cases these omissions occurred because of difficulties in obtaining publication rights.) In 1895 the author of *The Widow Bedott Papers* (1856) was the only woman Mark Twain could recall who dealt capably in American humor. "The book was a good one, and it lived for say 15 years, or possibly 20 years, and it is a good long life for a book" ("Mark Twain: Arrival in Auckland," New Zealand *Herald*, 21 November 1895, p. 5, quoted by Louis J. Budd, "Mark Twain Talks Mostly About Humor and Humorists," *Studies in American Humor* 1 [April 1974]: 8; interview reprinted in Scharnhorst, *Complete Interviews*, p. 256). In 1906 Twain commented that Elmira, New York was "the town where was also born the first distinctly and rollickingly humorous book that was ever written by an American woman, 'The Widow Bedott.' That book was written by a girl eighteen years old. It is now forgotten, but it swept this continent with a hurricane of laughter when it first came out" (11 April 1906 AD, *AutoMT* 1: 45). (In actuality Whitcher was born in Whitesboro, New York in Oneida County, much closer to Utica, New York than to Elmira.)

The Widow Bedott Papers collected Whitcher's classic dialect sketches that lampooned rural provincialism and yet captured universal truths about humanity. A few chapter titles can convey the flavor of these pieces: "The Widow Discourses of Pumpkins," "The Widow Trades with a Peddler," and "The Widow 'Sets Her Cap.'" One of the chapters, "The Widow Essays Poetry," could be an overlooked inspiration for Emmeline Grangerford's verses in Chapter 17 of Twain's *Adventures of Huckleberry Finn* (1885). Take, for example, the paean to her deceased husband: "Whiskey and rum he tasted not—/He thought it was a sin—/I thought so much o' Deacon Bedott/I never got married agin" (p. 29). Whitcher's early death from tuberculosis at the age of forty prevented the full development of her portrayals of the foibles and strengths of human nature.

Alan Gribben, "The Importance of Mark Twain," *American Humor*, ed. Arthur Power Dudden (New York: Oxford University Press, 1987), p. 30.

WHITCOMBE, MARY ELIZABETH (JOCE) (c. 1835–1887), also known as "Mrs. Henry Pennell Whitcombe." *Bygone Days in Devonshire and Cornwall, with Notes of Existing Superstitions and Customs.* London: Richard Bentley and Son, 1874. 276 pp.
Inscriptions: signed in pencil on the half-title page, "S. L. Clemens/ Hartford, 1874". The front pastedown endpaper has an *A1911* sale label at the bottom.
Marginalia: Clemens marked a few passages with pencil. On page 41 he drew a vertical line beside a paragraph describing the custom of informing the bees of their owner's death and placing wine and honey before the bee hives on the day of the funeral. Clemens also made two corrections in the text on page 72 at the sentence "So truly aimed it was that it shot up right through the globe, dashed through the roof of the church and fell with a loud explosion between the lady and her intended bridegroom," deleting "roof" and "fell" and substituting

"floor" and "landed". The following pages were unopened: 177–184, 185–192, 217–224, 237–240, 241–248, 249–256, 257–264, and 265–272.
Catalogs: *A1911*, "12mo, cloth, Lond. 1874, . . . with a few passages marked in pencil and two autograph corrections," quotes the signature and two notations, lot 482, sold for $2.50; *Lexington 1912*, lot 27, sold for $5; American Art Association (New York City), sale catalogue for the collection of the late William F. Gable of Altoona, Pennsylvania (8 January 1925), "London, 1874," half-title page signed by Clemens, has the *A1911* sale label, lot 123, sold for $15 (with another book).
Provenance: in September 1980 the volume was in the collection of Cyril Clemens, Kirkwood, Missouri. At that time Thomas A. Tenney sent photocopies of the cover, half-title page, title page, and marginalia to Alan Gribben.
Location: undetermined at present.

Whitcombe consulted various published sources for her reports of apparitions, legends, fairies, and witches associated with Devonshire and Cornwall. King Arthur is among the closely held beliefs.

WHITE, ANDREW DICKSON (1832–1918). *Autobiography of Andrew Dickson White.* Portraits. 2 vols. New York: Century Co., 1906.
Inscription: Volume II was signed by Clemens.
Catalogs: ListABP (1910), "Autobiography of Andrew D. White"; *C1951*, 7c, 2 vols., listed among books signed by Clemens, $6; *Zeitlin 1951*, item #51, 2 vols., inscription, $15.
Location: Neither volume has reappeared since 1951.
In March or April 1879, in Paris, Clemens alluded approvingly to an anecdote told by White, the United States minister to Germany who succeeded Bayard Taylor (NB 18, *N&J* 2: 305). On 3 February 1906 Clemens, talking with Isabel Lyon about books, "said that Andrew D. White's autobiography is too expensive, which it is at $7.50, but good to have of course" (IVL Journals, TS p. 130, MTP). On 8 March 1906 Clemens dined with Moncure D. Conway and White, "those 2 autobiographists," as Lyon called them (IVL Journals, TS p. 143, MTP). The memoirs of both men, Conway and White, should be counted as potential influences on the form and scope of Mark Twain's in-progress *Autobiography*. In Clemens's Autobiographical Dictation of 10 April 1906, he quipped: "I have been reading another chapter or two in Ambassador White's autobiography, and I find the book charming, particularly where he talks about me"; Clemens said that he had read up to the Willard Fiske-Cornell University episode (*AutoMT* 2:). White served as Cornell's first president; Fiske was a professor and librarian there until he resigned during White's presidency. Albert Bigelow Paine testified that White's memoirs "gave him [Clemens] enjoyment" (*MTB*, p. 1540).

———. *A History of the Warfare of Science with Theology in Christendom.* 2 vols. New York: D. Appleton & Co., 1901.
Inscriptions: the front free endpaper of Volume I is signed in brownish-black ink, "SL. Clemens/Feb. 22, 1902." The front free endpaper of Volume II is signed in brownish-black ink, "SL. Clemens/ 1902"; below this, Clemens wrote in pencil: "SL. Clemens/Riverdale, March, 1902". Clemens subtitled Volume II: "Being an Exposure of the

most Grotesque & Trivial of all Inventions, Man."

Marginalia: Volume I is annotated throughout in pencil and black ink, sometimes (as on page 319) overlapping. On page 99 he noted in black ink, writing vertically: "Mr. White is constantly & deliberately forcing his reader to say 'God damn theology & everything connected with it'; but I think it would be fairer & more honorable in him if he would come out & say it himself instead of tricking the reader into it." Clemens wrote vertically on page 124, using pencil: "The Bible was (& is) able to addle the ablest intellects in the world." He asserted on page 142 in black ink: "The average human being is always an ass" (regarding the devotion of Parisian mobs to Martha Brossier, a girl supposedly possessed by the devil). On page 161, in pencil (concerning the effect of holy water upon demons): "X The *human* style of argument—(human & ass being equivalent terms always)." Page 204 (black ink): "What is the order of theological evolution: does a person first become an idiot & then a theologian, or is it the other way about?" Page 205 (black ink): "Doubtless theology & dysentery are two of the most enervating diseases a person can have." Page 207 (black ink): "It [White's summary] is delightful. Shingle by shingle, brick by brick, he has carted the edifice to the dump-pile & now he can't contain his joy to see how much more precious the cellar is than the whole property was before." Page 208 (black ink): "A summary written to show that the abolishing of *all* truth from the Bible has mightily improved the book's value. Queer idea." Page 287 (pencil): "Apparently the pulpit has attacked each & every thing that is classifiable under the term 'progress'—& in each & every case has suffered defeat & been obliged (in the words of the song) to 'Go way back & set down.'" (Clemens was quoting the title of a then-popular tune by Elmer Bowman; see the Bowman entry in the Catalog.) Volume I contains numerous other notes, underscorings, vertical lines, and brackets. Clemens jotted pencil and black-ink marginalia throughout Volume II. He also opened all of its leaves. On page 54 he wrote vertically in pencil: "Adams [*sic*] invented 30 names a day—200 a week—10,000 a year—400,000 separate breeds of animals & insects in 40 years, & then quit, tired. Said he must have a fleet of arks for Mastodons, &c". On page 80 (pencil): "We have the words of Rev. Hodge, Duffield, Wilberforce & many others of like authority that 'the Scriptures are false.' It is odd." At the bottom of page 319 Clemens noted in black ink: "Amherst lately refused the missionary-ticket to two young candidates who doubted that *all* the B. C. pagans are roasting in hell." On page 321 he commented in black ink: "But, after all, the only really important question is, how to be a Christian yet not a fool." Page 400 (black ink): "Francis Bacon, who wrote the plays & poems attributed to Shakespeare." At the top of page 409 Clemens used black ink to note, "Pasteur threw pious sops to the Church." Page 410 (bottom, black ink), at White's reference to "that most mistaken of all mistaken ideas: the conviction that religion and science are enemies," Clemens scoffed: "Now Dr. White *you* know it *isn't a* mistake. You know they *are* enemies, & ought forever to remain so." On the verso of the rear free endpaper of Volume II, Clemens noted in black ink: "This book burdens with new difficulties a great question which has for ages been languishing for an answer: How to be an Ass Yet Not a Christian." These volumes contain some of Clemens's most unrestrained assaults on the reluctance of religious hierarchies to accept the findings of scientific research. Roger Salomon quoted from Clemens's marginalia in demonstrating how Clemens found a theory of moral progress in White's comparison of historical ages (Salomon, *TIH* [1961], pp. 22–23).

Catalogs: ListABP (1910), "Warfare of Science, White"; *C1951*, #15a, 2 vols., $105.

Location: Mark Twain Papers, Bancroft Library, University of California at Berkeley. Presented by the U.C.L.A. Library in memory of Dixon Wecter.

Copies examined: Clemens's copies (both volumes).

White's *History of the Warfare of Science with Theology in Christendom* was first published in 1896. Hiram S. Maxim, the inventor of the Maxim machine gun, mentioned the book in the postscript to a letter written to Clemens from London on 8 May 1901. Maxim remarked that the book provides "a full account of the fables regarding Saint Francis Xavier in the 2nd Vol."; Clemens noted in pencil at the bottom of the letter, "Send me this" (MTP). On 16 February 1902 Clemens wrote to Frederick A. Duneka of Harper & Brothers, requesting a copy of White's *Warfare of Science with Theology* together with any "up-to-date books" Duneka could find "on the *half-dozen great sciences*" (TS in MTP). In "The Secret History of Eddypus," written 1901–1902, Mark Twain sided with science against theology in writing about Martin Luther's "discovery of the Lord's baked miniature models for Creation" (*FM*, pp. 370–376). John S. Tuckey termed White's book "a main source" for the final chapters of Book 2 of "The Secret History of Eddypus" (*FM*, p. 25). White wrote to Willard Fiske on 20 April 1904 about meeting Twain in Florence, Italy: "We had a pleasant afternoon with Mark Twain at his Villa . . . and two admirable luncheons at Mr. Cannon's—at one of which we met the Twains; that is, father and daughter" (Horatio Stevens White, *Willard Fiske: Life and Correspondence, A Biographical Study* [New York: Oxford University Press, 1925], p. 470). On 21 June 1909 Clemens engaged Albert Bigelow Paine in a discussion of this "most amusing book of White's. When you read it you see how those old theologians never reasoned at all" (*MTB*, p. 1506). Paine included *History of the Warfare of Science with Theology in Christendom* among Clemens's favorite books—"a chief interest for at least one summer" (*MTB*, p. 1539). Indeed, Clemens found much that he could endorse in White's historical survey of an age-old conflict.

Parsons, "Background," p. 67; Cummings, "Mark Twain's Acceptance of Science" (1962), p. 254; Horst H. Kruse, "Mark Twain's *Pudd'nhead Wilson*: From Farce to Satire: The Unrecorded Contributions of Elizabeth E. and Edward P. Evans," *American Literary Realism* 50.3 (Spring 2018): 236.

WHITE, CARLOS (1842–1901). *Ecce Femina: An Attempt to Solve the Woman Question. Being an Examination of Arguments in Favor of Female Suffrage by John Stuart Mill and Others, and a Presentation of Arguments Against the Proposed Change in the Constitution of Society.* Hanover, New Hampshire: Published by the Author. Boston: Lee

& Shepard, 1870. 258 pp.

Source: MTLAcc, entry #680, volume donated by Clemens. A graduate of Dartmouth College, White would leave Hanover, New Hampshire in 1871 for San Francisco, where he began to publish a weekly newspaper, the *Home Standard*.

WHITE, CHARLES (1821–1891). "Old Bob Ridley" (minstrel song, 1855).

"'Bob Ridley' is a common rackety slam-bang secular song, one of the rippingest and rantingest and noisiest there is" (Mark Twain's *Those Extraordinary Twins*, Ch. 2 [1894]).

WHITE, GILBERT (1720–1793). *The Natural History and Antiquities of Selborne. With Notes by Frank Buckland.* Illustrated by P[hilip]. H[enry]. Delamotte (1821–1889). London, 1875.

Inscription: the half-title page is inscribed, "Saml. L. Clemens, Hartford, 1876".

Marginalia: several pencil marks.

Catalog: *A1911*, "8vo, cloth, gilt top, uncut, Lond. 1875, . . . several pencil marks," quotes the signature, lot 483, sold for $2.75.

Location: the volume has apparently not been recorded anywhere since 1911.

In Montreal, Canada, Clemens noted in November 1881: "Gilbert White, bees & idiots" (NB 19, *N&J* 2: 408). White's letter #27 to the Honourable Dames Barrington described an idiot boy who viewed bees as "his food, his amusement, his sole object." In Notebook 19 Clemens repeated "Gilbert White's bees & idiots" (*N&J* 2: 408).

The English clergyman Gilbert is recognized as one of the earliest and greatest naturalists, even though he merely studied the plants, animals, and birds in his local vicinity. *The Natural History and Antiquities of Selborne* has never been out of print since its first publication in 1789.

————. *The Natural History of Selborne. With a Naturalist's Calendar and Additional Observations.* Preface by Richard Jefferies (1848–1887). Illustrated by P[hilip]. H[enry]. Delamotte (1821–1889). The Camelot Series, General editor Ernest Rhys (1859–1946). London: Walter Scott, 1887. 366 pp.

Marginalia: a penciled check mark on page 104 is not characteristic of Clemens. There are pencil marks on two pages at the end of the book that advertise other books of the publisher.

Location: Mark Twain Library, Redding, Connecticut.

Copy examined: very likely Clemens's copy, though there is no ownership signature, accession number, or purple oval Mark Twain Library stamps. Albert E. Stone, Jr. reported that an 1887 edition of White's book was among the volumes from Clemens's library collection in the Mark Twain Library at Redding in 1955, but I was unable to find the book in 1970. When I revisited Redding in June 1982 I was able to locate the volume that Stone had seen, though Stone's assertion is still the principal corroboration. However, I lean toward its authenticity.

Richard Jefferies, author of the preface, was himself a noted English naturalist and novelist.

WHITE, HORACE (1834–1916).

"Horace White, old and famous and able journalist" (19 August 1907 AD, *MTE*, p. 334; *AutoMT* 3: 104). White was editor-in-chief of the Chicago *Tribune* and later filled the same position with the New York *Evening Post*.

WHITE, RICHARD GRANT (1821–1885). "London Streets,"

Atlantic Monthly 43.256 (February 1879): 230–241.

Clemens made a series of entries in Notebook 17 in Munich in February 1879 after reading White's article (*N&J* 2: 271). White praised London for its lack of shop signs, beggars, and streets named with mere numbers; he contrasted London with New York City.

————, ed. *Poetry Lyrical, Narrative, and Satirical of the Civil War.* Green cloth, spine torn. New York: American News Co., 1866. 334 pp.

Provenance: bookplate #45 of the "J. Langdon Family Library" on the front pastedown endpaper.

Catalog: Ball 2016, green cloth, gilt lettering, J. Langdon Family Library #45, Mark Twain Archive.

Location: Mark Twain Archive, Elmira College, Elmira, New York.

Copy examined: an unmarked copy available to Clemens whenever he visited the Langdons in Elmira. Examined on 27 May 2015.

The haste with which this collection was compiled is evident. Certain pieces one would expect, and they are here—"Battle Hymn of the Republic" and "Sheridan's Ride," for instance. Other well-known verses lack attributions to their authors—"When Johnny Comes Marching Home" and "When This Cruel War Is Over," as examples. There are odd omissions of poems that were popular during the conflict, such as "All Quiet on the Potomac Tonight." The best service performed by *Poetry Lyrical, Narrative, and Satirical of the Civil War* was the inclusion of ephemeral newspaper poems that eluded later editors, including "Left on the Battle Field" and "The Drummer-Boy's Burial."

This volume was accessible to Clemens whenever he visited the Langdons in Elmira.

————. *Words and Their Uses, Past and Present. A Study of the English Language.* New York: Sheldon & Co., 1872. 437 pp.

Inscriptions: signed, "Saml. L. Clemens" in two places and "Mark Twain, 1873" in another. It was extremely unusual for Clemens to autograph his personal library books with his pen name. This rare exception might have been occasioned by his loaning the book to someone.

Catalog: *A1911*, "12mo, cloth, N.Y. 1872," quotes the signatures, lot 484, sold for $6.50.

If only Clemens's copy of this work had survived! The annotations of a writer with such stylistic instincts would have been enlightening. *Words and Their Uses, Past and Present* takes up "Newspaper English" (Chapter 1), "British English and 'American' English" (Chapter 2), "Style" (Chapter 3), "Misused Words" (Chapter 5), "Words That Are Not Words" (Chapter 7), "Grammar, English and Latin" (Chapter 9), and "Formation of Pronouns" (Chapter 8). White's Chapter 11 ("Is Being Done") discusses the fluid shifting of fashions in language. A thorough index leads the reader to every subject from "Dr. Johnson" to "riparian" to "tenses" to (even) "wash-tub."

It seems extremely peculiar that nothing has turned up to indicate that Clemens owned any copies of White's work on, or editions of, William Shakespeare—endeavors considered at the time to have been White's most notable achievements. Clemens's copies of these may well have been among the hundreds of his books donated or lost without any surviving record of their titles. The journalist, editor, author, and critic White was the father of the prominent architect Stanford White (1853–1906).

David Sewell, "We Ain't All Trying to Talk Alike: Varieties of Language in *Huckleberry Finn*," *One Hundred Years of Huckleberry Finn: The Boy, His Book, and American Culture*, ed. Robert Sattelmeyer and J. Donald Crowley (Columbia: University of Missouri Press, 1985), pp. 205–207.

WHITE, WILLIAM ALLEN (1868–1944). *The Court of Boyville*. Illus. New York: McClure, Phillips, & Co., 1904. 358 pp.

Source: MTLAcc, entry #508, volume donated by Clemens. White's first book consisted of six nostalgic stories about the pleasures and pangs of boyhood, each preceded by a poem.

———. *In Our Town*. Illustrated by F[rederic]. R[oderigo]. Gruger (1871–1953) and W[illiam]. Glackens (1870–1936). New York: McClure, Phillips & Co., 1906. 369 pp.

Inscriptions: the front pastedown endpaper is signed, "S. L. Clemens/1906". The first flyleaf is inscribed: "For Samuel L. Clemens/with gratitude for/many happy hours/from W. A. White/Emporia, Kansas/May 26, 1906".

Catalogs: ListABP (1910), "In Our Town, White"; *C1951*, #30c, presentation copy, $32.50.

Location: Albert and Shirley Small Special Collections Library, University of Virginia, Charlottesville. A gift of Clifton Waller Barrett.

Copy examined: Clemens's copy, in 1970.

William Dean Howells recommended White's book to Clemens on 24 May 1906: "It is like all the middling-sized towns you ever lived in. It is a series of photographs taken with Roentgen rays" (*MTHL*, p. 808). The Emporia, Kansas newspaper editor White sent an autographed copy to Clemens on 26 May 1906. Clemens wrote to White from Dublin, New Hampshire on 24 June 1906: "Howells told me that 'In Our Town' was a charming book, and indeed it is. All of it is delightful when read [to] one's self, parts of it can score finely when subjected to the most exacting of tests—the reading aloud"; he singled out pages 197 and 212–216 as passages suitable "to fetch any house of any country," and urged White to "talk again—the country is listening" (TS in MTP; *MTL*, pp. 797–798). Clemens informed Howells from New York City on 26 June 1906: "I like 'In Our Town,' particularly that Colonel, of the Lookout Mountain Oration, & *very* particularly pages 212–16. I wrote & told White so" (*MTHL*, p. 814). Page 197 of Chapter 13, "A Pilgrim in the Wilderness," begins the tale of a lawyer named Adoneran P. Balderson, a scoundrel who drifts from town to town and state to state, appropriating fictitious titles for himself ("Colonel," "Judge," and "Governor," among others) and taking advantage of the citizens until their patience with him reaches an end and they banish him. Wherever he goes he finds some public event at which he can deliver his stock oration, "The Battle of Look Out Mountain," an address featuring his own heroic actions as a climax. (In reality he merely served in the commissary during the Civil War and was in fact dishonorably discharged from that post.) The Balderson story ends with his death in an avalanche near Boise, Idaho, whereupon his obituary in a gullible Boise newspaper declares, "Heaven's angel gained is Roosevelt's hero lost" (p. 216).

White supplied a prefatory "Appreciation" for *Adventures of Huckleberry Finn* in the so-called Definitive Edition of Twain's works (New York, Gabriel Wells, 1922–1925).

White would later critically summarize the literary career of Albert Bigelow Paine, who had once resided in Fort Scott, Kansas; after his great success with Mark Twain, White wrote, Paine "became official biographer of the rich and passing great. . . . He wasn't a Kansan. He was a bird of passage" ("Albert Bigelow Paine, *Mark Twain Quarterly* 1.4 [Summer 1937]: 15).

Paine, *MTB* (1912), p. 1313.

WHITE, WILLIAM HALE (1831–1913), pseud. "Mark Rutherford." *The Autobiography of Mark Rutherford, Dissenting Minister. Edited by His Friend, Reuben Shapcott*. New York: G. P. Putnam's Sons, 1881. 218 pp.

Inscription: the first front flyleaf is signed in purple pencil, "SL Clemens/1886".

Marginalia: "Mardon's" altered to "K's" on page 89. "nation" changed to "nature" on page 217. Both corrections are in black pencil.

Catalog: *A1911*, "12mo, cloth, N.Y. 1881," quotes the signature, lot 415, sold for $3.

Provenance: collection of Frank C. Willson (1889–1960) in Melrose, Massachusetts. Sold by his widow Margarete in 1962 to the University of Texas at Austin.

Location: Harry Ransom Center, University of Texas at Austin.

Copy examined: Clemens's copy. Priced in pencil ($20) at the rear of volume.

The English novelist White composed this fictional autobiography (replete with a fictional editor) to depict the theological dilemma of a man searching for a set of beliefs beyond what Protestant Christianity offered him. Rutherford struggled with religious and romantic decisions amid the confusions and temptations of sprawling London.

———, pseud. "Mark Rutherford." *Mark Rutherford's Deliverance; Being the Second Part of His Autobiography. Edited by His Friend, Reuben Shapcott*. London: Trübner & Co., 1885. 210 pp.

Source: MTLAcc, entry #254, volume donated by Clemens.

WHITEHEAD, CHARLES (1804–1862). *Lives and Exploits of the Most Noted Highwaymen, Robbers and Murderers, of All Nations, Drawn from the Most Authentic Sources and Brought Down to the Present Time*. Illus. Hartford, Connecticut: Silas Andrus & Son, 1843. 287 pp.

Catalog: *A1911*, "12mo, foxed and binding missing, Hartford, 1843," a sheet of Clemens's notes laid in, lot 294, sold for $4.

Whitehead enthusiastically recounted the careers (and usually the trials and executions) of thirty-four British malefactors, including Dick Adams, Eugene Aram, and Jack Shepherd. One of the miscreants, James Porter, moved to the United States to continue his depredations. William Dean Howells would recall Clemens's appetite for "some out-of-the-way book" that "had the root of the human matter in it," such as "a volume of great trials" (*My Mark Twain* [1910], p. 15).

WHITESIDE, MURIEL (McCULLEN). *Mizpah; or, Drifting Away, by Mrs. M. McCullen Whiteside, ("Muriel")*. St. Louis, Missouri: A. R. Fleming & Co., 1885. 142 pp.

On 11 January 1885 Clemens wrote to Olivia Clemens from St. Louis, describing a letter he had written after reading "a young woman's (married, but a mere child), MS book through." Her fiction was "a moral essay, &

an earnest & heartfelt essay, but more an essay than a story." It was "crude" and "too wordy, too diffuse"; "with the exception of Malcolm's letter to his wife, the whole book ought to be carefully & painstakingly re-written." Clemens criticized "little blemishes" such as allowing "your hero" to "descend" a rain-water pipe "with a woman in his arms" (*LLMT*, pp. 227–228). Obviously Muriel Whiteside ignored Clemens's advice regarding her temperance novel. The Biblical "Mizpah" in her title alluded to references in the Old Testament to God's protection as well as to lookout towers and towns situated on elevations for safety. Much of the novel was set in the milieu of New Orleans, especially in its theaters.

WHITING, LILIAN (1847–1942). *After Her Death; The Story of a Summer*. Boston: Roberts Brothers, 1897. 137 pp.

Source: MTLAcc, entry #685, volume donated by Isabel V. Lyon, Clemens's secretary.

Whiting recounted how she learned, while in Paris and through a delayed cablegram, of the death two weeks previous of her close friend and companion Kate Field (1838–1896). At that moment "I seemed to actually know that she stood by me,—that her hand was on me" (pp. 28–29). Her grief leads her toward an even more optimistic faith in unseen presences. "Psychic science is steadily conquering new territory and reclaiming the vague and the unknown to the realm of rational and intelligent comprehension" (p. 128).

———. *The World Beautiful. Second Series*. Boston: Roberts Brothers, 1896. 291 pp

Source: MTLAcc, entry #684, volume donated by Isabel V. Lyon, Clemens's secretary.

Whiting's five essays explored the dimensions of a Christian spiritual philosophy that merged with mysticism and the occult to discern the potentialities of an unseen world. Essentially she insisted upon the supremacy of the spiritual over the physical. Whiting's books quite probably belonged to one of the Clemenses; Isabel V. Lyon was carrying out Clemens's and Clara's wishes in transferring selected books from the family library to the new Mark Twain Library in Redding, and the librarian may have merely set down Lyons's name as the person who delivered these volumes.

WHITLOCK, WILLIAM M. "BILLY" (1813–1878), comp. *Whitlock's Collection of Ethiopian Melodies as Sung with Great Applause by William Whitlock at the Principal Theatres in the United States* (published in 1846).

On 12 August 1902 Clemens wrote to William Dean Howells: "I was very glad you sent me the Whitlocks. I enjoyed it" (collection of Kevin Mac Donnell, Austin, Texas). Given Clemens's fondness for the minstrel shows of his youth, this compilation by a blackface banjo performer could be a likely candidate for Clemens's cryptic reference.

WHITMAN, WALT (1819–1892). *Autobiographia; or, the Story of a Life. By Walt Whitman. Selected from His Prose Writings*. Fiction, Fact, and Fancy Series, General editor, Arthur [Griffin] Stedman (1859–1908). New York: Charles L. Webster & Co., 1892. 205 pp.

Clemens's publishing firm advertised that these passages from Whitman's prose works, "chosen with his approbation, are arranged so as to give a consecutive account of the old poet's career in his own picturesque language"

(*Publishers' Trade List Annual for 1893*).

In 1884 Clemens told an anecdote that grouped together Whitman, James, Swinburne, and Howells (SLC to WDH, Elmira, 7 August 1884, *MTHL*, p. 498). On 26 August 1885 Clemens sent ten dollars to a fund that was set up to acquire a horse and buggy for the infirm Whitman. "I have great veneration for the old man," wrote Clemens, and offered to add more to the sum (Thomas Donaldson, *Walt Whitman the Man* [New York: Francis P. Harper, 1896], p. 174). Early in 1887 Clemens reminded himself: "Send $20 to Walt Whitman, poet" (NB 26, *N&J* 3: 269). On 28 May 1887 Clemens wrote from Hartford to Sylvester Baxter of the Boston *Herald*, enclosing $50 for the Whitman fund and offering further help if needed; "What we want to do," Clemens added, "is to make the splendid old soul comfortable, & do what we do heartily & as a privilege. . . . There couldn't & wouldn't be any lack of people ready & willing to build a cottage for Walt Whitman; & as long as a rope-walk, if he wants it" (ALS, Boston Public Library, PH in MTP). Clemens requested that no specific sum be placed beside his name. The fund was for a small summer cottage in the woods at Timber Creek near Kirkwood, New Jersey, described by Whitman in *Specimen Days*.

Clemens was unable to attend a birthday dinner in honor of Whitman but contributed a congratulatory letter of 24 May 1889 to *Camden's Compliment to Walt Whitman*, ed. Horace L. Traubel (Philadelphia: D. McKay, 1889), pp. 64–65. Some critics have mocked the manner in which this letter slights Whitman's poetic works, but actually Clemens's enthusiastic inventory of nineteenth-century achievements (which resembled the catalogue Clemens would later parade in "Queen Victoria's Jubilee" [1897]) reflected Whitman's own exuberant sentiments and seems to confirm rather than deny Clemens's familiarity with his verse. Clemens's birthday felicitations to Whitman match the optimistic, expansive attitude of their recipient: "Man at almost his full stature at last!— and still growing, visibly growing, while you look." (Clemens almost surely was aware that his letter would be read aloud at the congratulatory dinner, as Kevin Mac Donnell pointed out (Mark Twain Forum, Internet discussion board, 7 April 2006.)

Whitman's opinion of Clemens was equivocal, however. In 1889 he remarked: "I think he mainly misses fire: I think his life misses fire: he might have been something: he comes near to being something: but he never arrives." Whitman acknowledged Clemens's occasional financial assistance, but characterized their relationship as one of caution: "I have always regarded him as friendly, but not warm: not exactly against me: not for me either" (Ed Folsom and Jerome Loving, "The Walt Whitman Controversy: A Lost Document," *Virginia Quarterly Review* 83.2 [Spring 2007]: 123).

Clemens set down Whitman's name among those scheduled to receive a complimentary copy of *A Connecticut Yankee in King Arthur's Court* (NB 29 [1889], *N&J* 3: 503). While traveling from Chicago to New York City between 29 June and 4 July 1892, Clemens noted: "KENNEDY'S WALT WHITMAN. (Letter)"; evidently William Sloane Kennedy (1850–1929) had contacted Clemens about an in-progress biography Kennedy would publish in 1896,

Reminiscences of Walt Whitman with Extracts from His Letters and Remarks on His Writings. But Clemens could be defensive on the topic of Whitman. Isabel Lyon inserted a paper slip loose into her notepad of letters dictated to her by Clemens in 1906 and 1907; this piece of paper recorded Clemens's reply on "Feb. 23" to "a woman who had sent him Extracts from Whitman but he never rec'd it." Clemens responded (according to Lyon's notes): "If I've become a Whitmanite I'm sorry—I never read 40 lines of him in my life—but I contributed $200 toward building a cottage for the old man to die in" (IVL's Dictation Notepad, MTP). Maxwell Geismar propagated a fallacy in *Mark Twain: An American Prophet* (Boston: Houghton, Mifflin Co., 1970), p. 2, by alluding to "Walt Whitman, whom Twain in effect never knew or mentioned."

Scott, *OPMT* (1966), p. 18.

———. *Leaves of Grass by Walt Whitman, Including a Fac-simile Autobiography, Variorum Readings of the Poems, and a Department of Gathered Leaves.* Green cloth, decorated. Philadelphia: D. McKay, 1900. 496 pp.

Inscription: the front pastedown endpaper is inscribed with black ink in a hand that appears to be Clemens's: "Katie Leary. N. Y. C."

Marginalia: a hand that looks like that of Clara Clemens marked poems in pencil on pages 288 ("All Is Truth"), 398 ("Quicksand Years"), 400 ("Pensive and Faltering"), and 474 (Section 4, second sentence of "Says"). There are no further markings.

Provenance: Antenne-Dorrance Collection, Rice Lake, Wisconsin.

Location: Mark Twain Archive, Gannett-Tripp Learning Center, Elmira College, Elmira, New York.

Copy examined: presumably Clemens's copy, since it seems unlikely that his housekeeper Katy Leary would have acquired this book for herself. Examined on 28 May 2015.

———. *Leaves of Grass.* Original green cloth, gilt. New York: D. Appleton and Co., 1908. 455 pp.

Inscription: the front pastedown endpaper is signed in blue ink, "Clara Clemens".

Marginalia: Clara Clemens made marginal pencil lines throughout the text, plus a few annotations reflective of close reading. Several parallel lines drawn in certain margins could possibly be in the hand of Clemens.

Provenance: Clara Clemens Samossoud's second husband, Jacques A. Samossoud, bequeathed this book and others to Henry and Mary Shisler of Cardiff by the Sea, California in 1966. A subsequent bookplate affixed by Nick Karanovich (1938–2003) of Fort Wayne, Indiana states that he obtained this volume from Maurice F. Neville Rare Books in 1983.

Location: collection of Kevin Mac Donnell, Austin, Texas.

Copy examined: Clara Clemens's copy, in July 2004.

British publisher John Camden Hotten (1832–1873) had published Whitman's poems in 1868, so Clemens might have encountered that edition of the book when he visited England in 1872 and 1873. He seems to have been familiar with Hotten's titles. Wesley Britton pointed out in 1998 that both Mark Twain and Walt Whitman worked as apprentice printers, had sympathy for underdogs, championed American idioms and speech, and celebrated the individual against a conformist society. Around 1882

Twain began, but did not complete, an expository essay he titled "The Walt Whitman Controversy" (DV 36, MTP). The portion Twain managed to write does not discuss Whitman's poetry. Though the ostensible purpose of the piece is to aid Whitman against charges of prurience, Twain's logic hardly helps Whitman's cause. Essentially Twain argues that *Leaves of Grass* is more innocuous than it seems because "in the matters of coarseness, obscenity, and power to excite salacious passion," it had been surpassed by numerous predecessors. This putative letter to the New York *Evening Post* actually appears to express the views of a worried family man who wants to plead for literary freedoms yet anxiously frets about the "defilement" (Twain's word) of young people's minds. He notes in passing that he himself does not own any "new bad books," as he terms the poetry of Whitman, Wilde, and Swinburne. At one point in his argument he pretends to quote several "erotic" lines of Whitman's verse, but a censor supposedly deletes them. Twain feels that they should not be "handy for the average young man or Miss to get at," an ambivalent position for a supposed defender of Whitman's authorial rights.

Mims Thornburgh Workman, "The Whitman-Twain Enigma," *Mark Twain Quarterly* 8.2 (Summer-Fall 1948): 12–13; Herbert Bergman, "The Whitman-Twain Enigma Again," *Mark Twain Journal* 10.2 (Winter 1956): 22–23; Herbert Bergman, "The Whitman-Twain Enigma Again," *Mark Twain Journal* 10.3 (Fall-Winter 1957): 3–9; Wesley Britton, "Clemens and Whitman," *Walt Whitman Encyclopedia,* ed. J. R. LeMaster and Donald D. Kummings (New York: Garland Publishing, 1998), p. 131; Ed Folsom and Jerome Loving, "The Walt Whitman Controversy: A Lost Document," *Virginia Quarterly Review* 83 [Spring 2007]: 123–127); Jerome Loving, *Mark Twain: The Adventures of Samuel L. Clemens* (Berkeley: University of California Press, 2010), pp. 2, 4, 7, 67, 72, 81, 85, *passim.*

———. *Selected Poems, by Walt Whitman.* Fiction, Fact, and Fancy Series, General editor, Arthur [Griffin] Stedman (1859–1908). New York: Charles L. Webster & Co., 1892. 179 pp.

Clemens's publishing firm advertised that Whitman had granted "special permission" for selecting these poems (*Publishers' Trade List Annual for 1893*).

WHITMORE, FREDERIC (1852–1954). *A Florida Farm.* Illustrated by William R. Whitmore (1854–1907). Springfield, Massachusetts: Ridgewood Press, [cop. 1903]. 115 pp.

Source: MTLAcc, entry #588, volume donated by Clemens.

Whitmore wrote books of prose and verse that were issued—usually with illustrations by William R. Whitmore—from the Ridgewood Press of Springfield, Massachusetts. Isabel V. Lyon wrote to Harriet E. Whitmore on 8 March 1904 from Florence: "Mr. Clemens wants me to write for him to thank you for the book that you sent Mrs. Clemens some time ago. He wants me to tell you 'how charming he found it; how delightful the literary style of it is; in fact he could find no defect in it,' and I am thinking how glad Mr. Frederick [*sic*] Whitmore will be, of a criticism like that" (MTHM). See also the Catalog entry for Torquato Tasso, *Amyntas, A Sylvan Fable.*

WHITNEY, ADELINE DUTTON (TRAIN) (1824–1906). *Hitherto: A Story of Yesterdays.* Brown cloth, gilt. Boston: Loring, [cop.

1869]. 473 pp.

Catalog: Ball 2016 inventory, bookplate #440 of the J. Langdon Family Library, brown cloth, gilt lettering, fair condition.

Location: Quarry Farm library shelves, under the supervision of the Mark Twain Archive, Elmira College, Elmira, New York.

Social historians generally categorize Whitney as a hearth-and-home, anti-suffrage traditionalist, but a number of her works offered supportive perspectives to young women and had feminist implications. In this novel a young woman struggles with a growing dissatisfaction stemming from her stifling marriage to a farmer. Clemens had access to this book whenever he visited the Langdon residence in Elmira.

Joanne Dobson, *Dickinson and the Strategies of Reticence: The Woman Writer in Nineteenth-Century America* (Bloomington: Indiana University Press, 1989), pp. 120–121.

———. *Mother Goose for Grown Folks*. New York: Carleton, 1866. 111 pp.

Source: MTLAcc, entry #2007, volume donated from Clemens's library by Clara Clemens Gabrilowitsch in 1910. The original nursery rhyme is followed by a more elaborate (but rhymed) version for older readers.

———. *A Summer in Leslie Goldthwaite's Life*. Illustrated by Augustus Hoppin (1828–1896). Boston: Ticknor & Fields, 1867. 230 pp.

Source: MTLAcc, entry #331, volume donated by Clemens. An "almost beautiful" (p. 20) fifteen-year-old girl on vacation tries to look ahead in her life. She receives guidance from an older woman, Miss Craydocke.

———. *A Summer in Leslie Goldthwaite's Life*. Boston: Houghton, Mifflin and Co., 1881.

Inscription: "Julia Olivia Langdon/from her father,/ November 21, 1882". This was the birthday of Charles Jervis and Ida B. Langdons' daughter, Julia Olivia Langdon (1871–1948).

Catalog: Ball 2016 inventory, red cloth, gilt and black lettering, dyed top edges, inscribed to Julia Olivia Langdon by her father, good condition.

Location: Quarry Farm library shelves, under the supervision of the Mark Twain Archive, Elmira College, Elmira, New York.

This book would have available to the Clemenses whenever they visited the Langdons' home.

WHITNEY, CASPAR (1862–1929). *On Snow-Shoes to the Barren Grounds. Twenty-Eight Hundred Miles After Musk-Oxen and Wood-Bison*. Illustrated by Frederic Remington (1861–1909). New York: Harper & Brothers, 1896. 324 pp.

Inscriptions: the front free endpaper is signed, "My Book/ Frederic Remington." The title page is signed at the bottom, "S. L. Clemens/(Mark Twain)." Clemens very seldom used this form except to autograph books he had written.

Location: formerly in the private collection of John and Estelle Winkler, Hannibal, Missouri. Purchased in 1947 along with a painting by Frederic Remington from Mc-Caughen & Burr, St. Louis art dealers. The book cost $90.

Location: at present unknown.

Copy examined: possibly a personal copy of the illustrator, Frederic Remington (1861–1909), autographed by Clemens. Inspected in 1970. One is always aware of the many forgeries perpetrated by Eugene Field II.

Whitney provided a vigorous narrative of his venture into remote northwestern Canada, describing the Native Americans, the sled dogs, and the animals he pursued—carribou, musk-ox, and wood-bison.

WHITNEY, HELEN (HAY) (1875–1944). *Sonnets and Songs*. Black cloth, decorated. New York: Harper & Brothers, 1905. 81 pp.

Inscription: the front pastedown endpaper is signed in black ink, "S L. Clemens/1905."

Provenance: Antenne-Dorrance Collection, Rice Lake, Wisconsin.

Location: Mark Twain Archive, Gannett-Tripp Learning Center, Elmira College, Elmira, New York.

Copy examined: Clemens's copy, unmarked. Examined on 28 May 2015.

During a supper and ball given by Robert Collier at Sherry's Restaurant in New York City on 13 February 1908 (*Day by Day* 4: 890), Clemens met "John Hay's poet-daughter, Mrs. Payne Whitney. I had not seen her since she was a little child. Neither her mother's nor her husband's limitless millions have smothered her literary gift or beguiled her into neglecting it" (19 February 1908 AD, *AutoMT* 3: 210). Helen Hay had married the wealthy William Payne Whitney (1876–1927) in 1902.

———. [An identical copy.]

Source: MTLAcc, entry #650, volume donated by Clemens.

WHITNEY, HENRY M[ARTYN]. (1824–1904). *The Tourists' Guide Through the Hawaiian Islands, Descriptive of Their Scenes and Scenery*. Second ed. Illus. Honolulu: Honolulu *Gazette* Company's Press, 1895. 176 pp.

Whitney opened his book with Mark Twain's ecstatic description of the islands, including his assertion that "for me its balmy airs are always blowing." On 30 November 1895 Twain wrote to Whitney from Napier, New Zealand: "I thank you ever so much for your beautiful 'Tourist [*sic*] Guide Through Hawaii,' which arrived by recent mail." Twain had become acquainted with Whitney in Hawaii in 1866.

Gary Scharnhorst, "A Recovered Mark Twain Letter to Henry M. Whitney in 1895," *American Literary Realism* 39.1 (Fall 2006): 87–88.

WHITNEY, LOUISA (GODDARD) (1819–1883). *The Burning of the Convent. A Narrative of the Destruction, by a Mob, of the Ursuline School on Mount Benedict, Charlestown[, Massachusetts], as Remembered by One of the Pupils*. First edition. Original brown cloth, stamped and lettered in black and gilt, green-coated endpapers, a signature loose. Boston: James R. Osgood and Co., 1877. 198 pp.

Inscription: the half-title page is signed in pencil in large script, "S L Clemens/1877".

Provenance: displays the shelfmark of Clara Clemens Gabrilowitsch's private library in Detroit. Donated to the Carrie Estelle Doheny Collection, St. John's Seminary, Camarillo, California, by Mrs. Doheny in 1940. She had acquired the volume for $12 from Maxwell Hunley Rare Books, Beverly Hills, California. Auctioned by Christie's in 1988 on behalf of St. John's Seminary and the Archdiocese of Los Angeles. Eventually it became part of the collection assembled by Nick Karanovich (1938–2003), Fort Wayne, Indiana.

Catalog: Christie's, New York City, 1–2 February 1988

auction, lot 465, sold (with three other books) for $2,750 to Randall House, Los Angeles.

Location: collection of Kevin Mac Donnell, Austin, Texas.

Copy examined: Clemens's copy, unmarked. Viewed in July 2004.

Whitney's book recounted the fallacious rumors and escalating events in 1834 that led an anti-Catholic mob to destroy a convent school near Boston.

WHITNEY, WILLIAM DWIGHT (1827–1894), ed. *The Century Dictionary: An Encyclopedic Lexicon of the English Language.* 6 vols. New York: Century Co., 1889.

Catalog: Ball 2016 inventory, 6 vols., brown leather, gilt lettering, gilt edge pages, poor condition.

Location: Quarry Farm library shelves, under the supervision of the Mark Twain Archive, Elmira College, Elmira, New York.

Clemens had access to this set whenever he visited Quarry Farm in Elmira.

———. *French Grammar.* [1886 or later.]

Catalog: ListABP (1910), "French Grammar, Whitney", no other information supplied.

Whitney published a series of variously titled French grammars beginning in 1886.

WHITTIER, JOHN GREENLEAF (1807–1892). *At Sundown.* Illustrated by E[dmund]. H[enry]. Garrett (1853–1929). Boston: Houghton, Mifflin and Co., 1892. 70 pp.

Source: MTLAcc, entry #2118, volume donated from Clemens's library by Clara Clemens Gabrilowitsch in 1910.

———. "Burns. On Receiving a Sprig of Heather in Blossom" (poem, published in 1854).

Clemens copied the first stanza of Whittier's poetic tribute to Burns onto the front endpaper of Volume I of a gift set of *The Works of Robert Burns*, dating the inscription as 1889. He also copied the nineteenth stanza from Whittier's twenty-nine-stanza poem onto the front flyleaf of a gift copy of Allan Cunningham's *The Life of Robert Burns*, likewise dating his inscription as 1889. See the Catalog entries for the set of Burns and for Cunningham's book.

———, ed. *Childlife: A Collection of Poems. Edited by John Greenleaf Whittier.* Illus. First edition. Original green pictorial cloth, gilt. Boston: James R. Osgood and Co., 1872. 263 pp.

Inscription: (not in Clemens's hand, apparently written by Olivia Clemens) "Langdon Clemens/Nov. 7th 1871". Clemens's infant son, born in 1870, would die in 1872.

Marginalia: a few stray pencil and ink marks throughout.

Provenance: collection of Frank C. Willson (1889–1960) in Melrose, Massachusetts. Sold by his widow Margarete in 1962 to the University of Texas.

Location: Harry Ransom Center, University of Texas at Austin.

Copy examined: a copy belonging to the Clemens family. This anthology of poetry written for or about children includes verse by the New England luminaries Longfellow, Whittier, Holmes, Lowell, Bryant, and Emerson, but also samples the works of Edward Lear, Maria Lowell, Celia Thaxter, Fitz-Hugh Ludlow, George MacDonald, William Blake, Elizabeth Barrett Browning, and Alfred Lord Tennyson.

———, ed. [An identical copy.]

Inscription: inscribed by Olivia Clemens on behalf of her son Langdon, then just over a year old: "A Merry Christmas

to Little Lady Langdon from her cousin Langdon Clemens, 1871." The "Little Lady" was Julia Olivia Langdon (1871–1948), the newborn daughter of Olivia Clemens's brother, Charles Jervis Langdon. (The Clemenses' son Langdon would die a few months later in 1872.)

Catalog: *Sotheby's 2003,* #247, $6,000.

Provenance: formerly in the collection of Nick Karanovich (1938–2003), Fort Wayne, Indiana.

Location: collection of Kevin Mac Donnell, Austin, Texas.

Copy examined: copy belonging to the Langdon family. Viewed in July 2004.

———, ed. *Child Life in Prose.* Illus. Boston: J. R. Osgood and Co., 1874. 301 pp. [Edition conjectured.]

Source: MTLAcc, entry #1908, volume donated from Clemens's library by Clara Clemens Gabrilowitsch in 1910. Lacks the title page.

Whittier's book collected stories about children written by Nathaniel Hawthorne ("Little Annie's Ramble"), Thomas Bailey Aldrich ("The Cruise of the Dolphin"), Mary Lamb ("A Young Mahometan"), Horace Scudder ("The Prince's Visit"), Charles Lamb ("Dream-Children: A Revery"), Harriet Beecher Stowe ("The Hen That Hatched Ducks"), and others authors.

———. *The Complete Poetical Works of John Greenleaf Whittier.* Household Edition. Brown cloth, decorated, gilt. Boston: Houghton, Mifflin and Co., 1883. 450 pp.

Inscription: the front flyleaf is inscribed by Olivia Clemens in brown ink: "Clara L. Clemens./ Hartford, Ct./June 8th '84."

Marginalia: penciled "X's" were inserted beside various poems in table of contents.

Provenance: Antenne-Dorrance Collection, Rice Lake, Wisconsin.

Location: Mark Twain Archive, Gannett-Tripp Learning Center, Elmira College, Elmira, New York.

Copy examined: Clara Clemens's copy. Examined on 28 May 2015.

———. "The Eternal Goodness" (poem, published in 1865).

In August 1870 Olivia Clemens copied portions of this poem into her commonplace book (MS pp. 101–103, DV161, MTP). A newspaper clipping of the poem is laid loose in the commonplace book; she wrote on the clipping: "Father sent May 29th 1870". Jervis Langdon died on 6 August 1870.

Decades later, Olivia Clemens's commonplace book (DV161, MTP) contained two loose sheets of paper that resemble the cross-barred paper her husband used in Weggis in 1897; on these she twice copied the second half of Whittier's inspirational Christian poem, beginning with the lines "I know not what the future hath,/Of marvel or surprise," and ending "Forgive me if too close I lean/ My human heart on Thee." On 28 March 1902 Clemens made an entry (within quotation marks) in Notebook 45 during an excursion from Cuba to Jamaica: "'Where'er thy holy islands lift their fronded palms in air'" (TS p. 7). Clemens was striving to recall the lines from the twentieth quatrain of this poem: "I know not where His islands lift/ Their fronded palms in air;/I only know I cannot drift/ Beyond His love and care."

———. "Maud Muller" (poem, published 1854).

In 1884 Clemens twice experimented with German

translations of lines 105–106 of Whittier's poem, "For of all sad words of tongue or pen,/The saddest are these: 'It might have been!'" An outline of an eerie tale about families trapped for generations inside an iceberg then follow (NB 22, *N&J* 3: 55). In April 1887 Clemens noted: "Whittier's drown [*sic*] climax" (NB 26, *N&J* 3: 287).

———. *Poems*. Boston: Houghton, Mifflin and Co., 1882. 450 pp.

Source: MTLAcc, entry #2117, volume donated from Clemens's library by Clara Clemens Gabrilowitsch in 1910. Among a group of undated manuscript notes, Clemens mentioned "Whittier's 2 Old Maids" (*A1911*, lot 432).

———. *Poems*. [Unidentified multi-volume edition.]

Catalog: ListABP (1910), "Whittier v 2", no other information provided.

———. "Rantoul" (poem, written in 1852).

Whittier's antebellum poem honored the passionately abolitionist Congressman and orator Robert Rantoul, Jr. (1805–1852) upon his unexpected death. Mark Twain paraphrased and altered four of Whittier's lines in describing Jack Van Nostrand in a dinner speech for the Society of Illustrators in New York City on 21 December 1905 (*MTSpk*, p. 476). Whittier's original text read: "For he had sat at Sidney's feet,/And walked with Pym and Vane apart;/And through the centuries, heard the beat/Of Freedom's march in Cromwell's heart." Twain omitted the references to Pym and Vane, and also made other more minor changes.

———. *Selections from the Writings of John Greenleaf Whittier, Arranged Under the Days of the Year*. Boston: Houghton, Mifflin & Co., 1889. [109 pp.]

Source: MTLAcc, entry #2127, volume donated from Clemens's library by Clara Clemens Gabrilowitsch in 1910.

———. *Snow-Bound. A Winter Idyl*. Boston: Ticknor and Fields, 1869. 51 pp.

Inscriptions: the half-title page is inscribed by Clemens, "Livy/Nov. 27, 1870./From S. L. C." (November 27th was Olivia Clemens's birthday.) The front flyleaf is inscribed by Clemens, "Mrs. S. L. Clemens."

Catalogs: ListABP (1910), "Snow Bound, Whittier"; *C1951*, #71c, $22.50; *Zeitlin 1951*, item #52, "somewhat rubbed, hinge cracking," quotes inscriptions, $50.

The varied reactions to Mark Twain's speech at the Whittier Birthday Dinner on 17 December 1877 would trouble Twain throughout the rest of his life. See, for one interpretation, Bruce Michelson, *Mark Twain on the Loose: A Comic Writer and the American Self* (Amherst: University of Massachusetts Press, 1995), pp. 18–25.

The Whole Family; A Novel by Twelve Authors: William Dean Howells, Mary E. Wilkins Freeman, Mary Heaton Vorse, Mary Stewart Cutting, Elizabeth Jordan, John Kendrick Bangs, Henry James, Elizabeth Stuart Phelps, Edith Wyatt, Mary R. Shipman Andrews, Alice Brown, Henry Van Dyke. Illus. New York: Harper & Brothers, 1908. 315 pp.

Source: MTLAcc, entry #1053, volume donated by Clemens.

During the spring and summer of 1906 Elizabeth Jordan, editor of *Harper's Bazar*, patiently tried to persuade Mark Twain to join other prominent authors—including William Dean Howells, Henry James, and Mary E. Wilkins Freeman—in writing a collaborative novel. The

Whole Family appeared serially in *Harper's Bazar*, each installment the product of a different writer, but Twain never received sufficient inspiration from the initial contributions—produced by Howells and Freeman—to contribute his assigned chapter. See Elizabeth Jordan's *Three Rousing Cheers* [New York: D. Appleton, 1938], pp. 258–260. See also the Catalog entries for William Dean Howells, "The Father," and Mary E. (Wilkins) Freeman, "The Old-Maid Aunt."

Earl F. Briden, "Samuel L. Clemens and Elizabeth Jordan" (1974); *The Whole Family: A Novel by Twelve Authors*. Intro. by Alfred Bendixen (New York: Ungar Publishing Co., 1986), p. xv.

WHYMPER, EDWARD (1840–1911). *Scrambles Amongst the Alps in the Years 1860–69*. Illus. London: John Murray, 1871. 432 pp.

Whymper was an English engraver who climbed mountains in the Alps; he found a route up the Matterhorn in 1865 and climbed many peaks in the Mont Blanc group. *Scrambles Amongst Alps* describes assaults on the Matterhorn. On 28 August 1878 Mark Twain made a note to get Girdlestone's "book.—& Whymper's" (NB 16, *N&J* 2: 164). Twain wrote from Paris to Andrew Chatto on 25 April 1879: "Can't you send me *immediately* Mr. Wymper's [*sic*] book? It contains his ascent of the Matterhorn (about 1865) when young Lord Douglas & a guide or two lost their lives. I don't know who published it" (TS in MTP). From Paris on 15 May 1879 Twain informed Mary Mason Fairbanks: "I can't burlesque Mr. Whymper & the other fantastic Alp-climbers with a solemn underpinning to my thought—it would be a failure" (*MTMF*, p. 230).

In *A Tramp Abroad* (1880) Mark Twain relied on Whymper's book to inject the heroic flavor of mountain climbing into his own cowardly account; supposedly Whymper's narrative inspires the narrator to attempt the Riffelberg (though he merely moves to a slightly higher tourist hotel). "I closed my readings with a fearful adventure which Mr. Whymper once had on the Matterhorn when he was prowling around alone, 5,000 feet above the town of Briel" (*TA*, Ch. 36); Twain quotes more than a page directly from Whymper's tale of his fall and his miraculous survival. In Chapter 40 of *A Tramp Abroad*, Twain quotes at length from Whymper's description of glacier formations. In Chapter 41 Twain refers to the 1865 catastrophe on the Matterhorn: "The details of it are scarcely known in America. To the vast majority of readers they are not known at all. Mr. Whymper's account is the only authentic one. I will import the chief portion of it into this book partly because of its intrinsic interest, and partly because it gives such a vivid idea of what the perilous pastime of Alp-climbing is." Twain then quotes lengthily from "Mr. Whymper's graphic and thrilling narrative." Beverly R. David, "Tragedy and Travesty: Edward Whymper's *Scrambles Amongst the Alps* and Twain's *A Tramp Abroad*," *Mark Twain Journal* 27.1 (Spring 1989): 2–8, carefully collated Twain's quotations from Whymper, recording numerous alterations, and documented the uses Twain made of the drawings in Whymper's book.

Katherine E. Bishop, "'A Wilderness of Oil Pictures': Reframing Nature in *A Tramp Abroad*," *Mark Twain Annual* 17 (2019): 72–87.

WHYTE-MELVILLE, G[EORGE]. J[OHN]. (1821–1878). *Holmby House; A Tale of Old Northamptonshire*. Illustrated by G. H. Jalland (fl. 1888–1908). London: W. Thacker & Co., 1901. 427 pp.

    Catalog: Ball 2016 inventory, red cloth, gold lettering, rough cut pages, gilt edge page tops, fair to good condition.

    Location: Quarry Farm library shelves, under the supervision of the Mark Twain Archive, Elmira College, Elmira, New York.

    The novel begins and ends with a scene Whyte-Melville sets in a fairy ring under an oak tree. Clemens had access to this book during his final visits to Quarry Farm in Elmira.

WIDMANN, JOSEPH VIKTOR (1842–1911). *Johannes Brahms in Erinnerungen [Reminiscences of Johannes Brahms]*. Berlin: Gebrüder Paetel, 1898. 180 pp.

    Source: MTLAcc, entry #1680, volume donated by Clemens.

WIESENTHAL, THOMAS VAN DYKE (1790–1833). "The sailor-boy's dream, an admired ballad" (song, published in 1819).

    In "About All Kinds of Ships" (1893) Mark Twain commented on the loss of romantic "soft sentimentality about the sea" owing to improvements in vessels and navigation aids. He included "The Sailor Boy's Dream" among the one-time "favorites" ensuring that "everybody on a farm lived chiefly amid the dangers of the deep in those days." Indeed, "The sailor-boy's dream" did embody the lachrymose forebodings Twain cited: "Oh Sailor-boy, Sailor-boy, never again/Shall home, love or kindred thy wishes repay;/Unblest and unhonor'd, down deep in the main/Full many a score fathom thy frame shall decay."

WIGGIN, JAMES HENRY (1836–1900).

    This American clergyman revised Mary Baker Eddy's writings. On 12 October 1899 Clemens thanked Wiggin from London for a letter which confirmed "that a smooth Bible & rough miscellaneous literature indicate the presence of a polisher around the establishment somewhere" (ALS in the private collection of Robert C. Grossman, Chicago in 1979; PH in MTP). See also the Catalog entry for Livingston Wright.

WIGGIN, KATE DOUGLAS (SMITH) (1856–1923), "Mrs. George Christopher Riggs." *Rose o' the River*. Illustrated by George [Hand] Wright (1872–1951). Boston: Houghton, Mifflin & Co., 1905. 176 pp.

    Clemens wrote to the author on 9 December 1905: "I didn't know until last night (Dec. 8) that you had sent me a book & a letter, dear Mrs. Riggs. I am enjoying them this afternoon, in place of working" (Yale, TS in MTP). The book she sent might have been either of her recent best-selling novels, *Rebecca of Sunnybrook Farm* (1903) or *Rose o' the River* (1905). The latter was the only work she published in 1905. She set that romantic novel along the banks of the Saco River in the state of Maine. Also set in Maine, the less-idealized *Rebecca of Sunnybrook Farm* would prove to be Wiggin's more durable work.

    Wiggin's fame as a children's author began with two privately printed novels, *The Story of Patsy: A Reminiscence* (1883) and *The Birds' Christmas Carol* (1887); Houghton, Mifflin soon made these two books popular. Wiggin's succession of last names sometimes causes confusion. Born Kate Douglas Smith, she married Samuel Bradley Wiggin in 1881. He died in 1889. Subsequently she married George Christopher Riggs in 1895 and for social purposes took his name, though her books continued to be published under the name she had established as an author, Wiggin. Riggs proved to be a great supporter of her career. Clemens came to know her by both names.

Mark Twain participated in a New York City reading with Wiggin on 4 November 1893 (Fears, *Day by Day* 2: 832). In January 1894 Twain made a memorandum in New York City: "Mrs. Hutton's—Kate Douglas Wiggin—Jan. 18th?" (NB 33, TS p. 47). Subsequently Twain noted: "Charming debate last night (Jan. 18) at Hutton's between Mrs. Kate Douglas Wiggin & Mrs. Bisland Wetmore on kindergartens. It was delightful" (NB 33, TS p. 48); Twain's summary of the arguments seemed to favor Wiggin's viewpoint. On 2 December 1900 in New York City, Twain was scheduled for a "dinner—Mrs. Kate Douglas Riggs" (NB 43, TS p. 30). Twain made a note on 13 January 1901 from conversation: "Kate Douglas W—'I'm a lady, & I have to be so d—d particular'" (NB 44, TS p. 3). Writing from 1410 W. 10th Street in New York City on 8 February on 8 February 1901, Twain teased "Mrs. Riggs": "You are just as bright as you can be, and you are just as fascinating as you can be, and also don't swear, in company" (Kenneth W. Rendell, Inc., Rare Books and Manuscripts, South Natick, Massachusetts [2010], priced at $7,500).

On 27 February 1902 Olivia Clemens recorded among her visitors at Riverdale-on-the-Hudson since October 1901 "Mr. & Mrs. George Riggs (she was Kate Douglas Wiggin)" (OLC's Diary, DV161, MTP). A photograph taken at Mark Twain's Seventieth Birthday dinner, 30 November 1905, shows Kate Douglas Wiggin seated at Twain's left hand (Albert Bigelow Paine, "Mark Twain—Boy and Man" [1924], p. 14). In 1906 Twain worked with her on behalf of copyright legislation; Isabel Lyon recalled that they exchanged dinners between 1905 and 1907 in New York City, and that Twain liked her (IVL's TS, MTP, filed with a letter from SLC to Kate Douglas Wiggin, 7 or 8 December 1906). On 22 November 1907, writing from 21 Fifth Avenue, Twain thanked Wiggin for "a noble feed & noble company" (Mary Boewe, "How to Preserve a Mark Twain Letter," *Mark Twain Journal* 21.3 [Spring 1983]: 16). "That rare bird & darling of mine, Kate Douglas Wiggin Riggs," Twain remarked in a letter (SLC to "Julie dear," 16 January 1908, MTP). Wiggin supplied a prefatory "Appreciation" for *The Prince and the Pauper* in the so-called Definitive Edition of Twain's works (New York, Gabriel Wells, 1922–1925). Mary Boewe's "Bewildered, Bothered, and Bewitched: Mark Twain's View of Three Women Writers," *Mark Twain Journal* 45.1 (Spring 2007): 17–23 summarized Twain's opinion of Kate Douglas Wiggin.

———. *Timothy's Quest: A Story for Anybody, Young or Old, Who Cares to Read It*. First edition. Original quarter green cloth, red cloth sides, gilt. Boston: Houghton, Mifflin, 1890. 201 pp.

    Inscription: inscribed in ink on the front free endpaper by Clemens's sister-in-law Susan Crane (1836–1924) to Clemens's niece Ida Langdon (1880–1964): "Ida Langdon/Merry Christmas/'Aunt Susie' 1890."

    Location: collection of Kevin Mac Donnell, Austin, Texas.

Purchased from the Langdon family.

Source: supplementary inventory sent by Mac Donnell to Alan Gribben, 28 August 2017. Mac Donnell pointed out that Wiggin's subtitle somewhat echoed Mark Twain's subtitle for *The Prince and the Pauper* (1881).

This would have been one of the books available to Clemens whenever he visited the Langdons in Elmira. An undated ten-word fragment in Clemens's hand begins with the title of Wiggin's novel—"Timothy Quest" (Lilly Library, Indiana University, pointed out by Mary Boewe in a letter to Alan Gribben, 13 November 1987).

WIGHT, ORLANDO WILLIAMS (1824–1888). *Lives and Letters of Abelard and Heloise.* Second edition. New York: M. Doolady, 1861. 319 pp.

Franklin R. Rogers—Mark Twain's *Burlesque Patterns* (1960), pp. 44–47, 167 n. 17—demonstrated that Twain relied upon this book (and this edition) in writing about the legend of Abelard and Heloise in Letter 31 of his *Quaker City* series (1867). The story also appeared in Chapter 15 of Mark Twain's *The Innocents Abroad* (1869). Both versions vilify Pierre Abelard, eschew sentimentality, and use similar quotations from Abelard's testimony. See also the Catalog entry for Alphonse Lamartine.

Ganzel, *MTAb* (1968), p. 104.

WILBERFORCE, REGINALD GARTON (1838–1914) and ARTHUR RAWSON ASHWELL (1824–1879). *Life of the Right Reverend Samuel Wilberforce [1805–1873], D. D., Lord Bishop of Oxford and Afterwards of Winchester; With Selections from His Diary and Correspondence.* 3 vols. London: John Murray, 1880–1882. Second edition published in 1883. Rev. edition issued in 1888. [The Clemenses' edition is undetermined.]

Clara Clemens listed "Life of Wilberforce" in her undated commonplace book between 1888 and 1904 (Paine 150, MTP). Ashwell wrote Volume I; Wilberforce's son Reginald wrote Volumes II and III.

WILBRANDT, ADOLF VON (1837–1911). *The Master of Palmyra. A Dramatic Poem. (Der meister von Palmyra; dramatische dictung in fünf aufzügen).*

In Mark Twain's "About Play-Acting" (October 1898), he hailed Wilbrandt's "remarkable play" performed in Vienna as "a great and stately metaphysical poem, and deeply fascinating." Twain promised that the work would make the playwright's "name permanent in German literature," and added that "the play gave me the sense of the passage of a dimly connected procession of dream- pictures." He summarized the plot of the play, quoted some lines, and urged Americans to see it: "You will not need to translate it: its story is as plain as a procession of pictures." When Clemens saw the play in Vienna for what was at least the second time, he wrote to William Dean Howells on 30 December 1898 about the associations it had for him with Susy Clemens's death: "We saw the 'Master of Palmyra' last night. How Death, with his gentleness and majesty, made the human grand-folk around him seem little & trivial & silly!" (*MTHL*, p. 685). In Chapter 10 of Mark Twain's "Which Was It?" (written 1899–1903) he tried to duplicate the sense of inevitability and dread he experienced from Wilbrandt's allegorical characterizations; the "sombre apparition" of Deathshead Phillips, "upright and rigid," appears to the guilt-ridden George Harrison. Clothed in "dead and lustreless black," its raiment "ancient

and mephistophelian," its face "ghastly white, dead and lustreless .... wholly white and horrible," the mute, "dismal guest" stares prophetically at Harrison for half an hour (*WWD?*, p. 268). (See also the Catalog entry for E. A. Poe's "The Masque of the Red Death.")

Carroll D. Laverty, "The Genesis of *The Mysterious Stranger*," *Mark Twain Journal* 8.3–4 (Spring-Summer 1947): 16; Coleman O. Parsons ("Background" [1960], p. 59); and John S. Tuckey (*MT&LS* [1963], p. 95 n. 254) noted resemblances between Wilbrandt's *The Master of Palmyra* and Mark Twain's *Mysterious Stranger* manuscripts.

Friedrich Schönemann, "Mark Twain and Adolf Wilbrandt," *Modern Language Notes* 34.6 (June 1919): 372–374, was the earliest to examine (though briefly) Twain's admiration for Wilbrandt's dramatic works. See also Max Lederer, "Mark Twain in Vienna," *Mark Twain Quarterly* 7.1 (Summer-Fall 1945): 10–12; Hemminghaus, "Mark Twain's German Provenience" (1945), p. 472; *MTHL* (1960), p. 686 n. 7; Krause, *MTC* (1967), pp. 284, 285, 299; and Gibson, ed., *MSM* (1969), p. 17.

WILBUR, HOMER C. [Unidentified author.]

In 1906 Clemens recalled that Orion Clemens sought a contribution by a professional writer for his Hannibal newspaper in 1853 [*sic*]. "At last a celebrity of about the third degree took him up—with a condition. This was a Philadelphian, Homer C. Wilbur, a regular and acceptable contributor to *Sartain's Magazine* and the other first-class periodicals. He said he could not write an original story for the sum offered—*which was five dollars*—but would translate one from the French for that sum. My brother took him up" (10 September 1906 AD, *MTE*, p. 236; *AutoMT* 2: 234). Twain's timeline in this story seems somewhat mistaken; *Sartain's Union Magazine of Literature and Art* ceased publication in 1852. Was it merely coincidental that "Parson Homer Wilbur, A.M., Pastor of the First Church of Jaalam" was one of James Russell Lowell's pseudonyms? Parson Wilbur functioned as the purported editor of the fictional Hosea Biglow's writings.

WILCOX, EARLEY VERNON (1869–1955) and CLARENCE BEAMAN SMITH (1870–1948). *Farmer's Cyclopedia of Agriculture: A Compendium of Agricultural Science and Practice on Field, Orchard, and Garden Crops, Spraying, Soils, and Feeding and Disease of Farm Animals, Dairy Farming, and Poultry in the United States and Canada.* Illus. New York: Orange Judd Co., 1905. 619 pp.

Inscription: the front free endpaper is signed in black ink, "Jean L. Clemens./Hickory Farm./1909."

Provenance: contains the bookstamps of the Mark Twain Library, Redding, Connecticut.

Catalog: *Mott 1952*, item #94, $3.

Location: Mark Twain House and Museum, Hartford, Connecticut. Donated anonymously in 1963.

Copy examined: Jean Clemens's copy. Examined in August 1987.

Jean Clemens had a great love of animals and the outdoors, and Clemens gave her a small farm adjacent to Stormfield in Redding, Connecticut.

WILCOX, GEORGE A[UGUSTUS]. (1830–1928). *A Christian Philanthropist. A Sketch of the Life of Mr. Daniel Hand, and of His Benefaction to the American Missionary Association, for the Education of the Colored People in the Southern States of America.*

New York: American Missionary Association, 1889. 32 pp.

Mark Twain concludes the posthumously published "You've Been a Dam Fool, Mary. You Always Was!" (written in December 1903 and January 1904) by asserting that he based his fictionalized story on an oral "tradition" about an actual incident. Then he adds: "Since writing the above tale a friend in America has procured for me a 'Sketch of the Life of Daniel Hand,' prepared by Mr. George A. Wilcox, of Detroit, for the *Magazine of American History*, and from it I quote this eloquent passage: 'Rarely is there an instance of more implicit mutual commercial faith and confidence than is shown in these transactions; a faith preceding, living through and surviving a war that swept men and fortunes away like chaff, yet in this instance survived to point the moral that *honesty and honor are not sectional but national American traits*'" (*FM*, p. 278). Wilcox's article in the *Magazine of American History* had been titled "Evolution of a Philanthropist of a Puritan Type"; his book *A Christian Philanthropist. A Sketch of the Life of Mr. Daniel Hand* was a slightly condensed and revised version of that essay. Since Twain mentioned the principal incident as early as May or June 1895 in Notebook 34, he could have been familiar with its outlines as presented in Wilcox's *A Christian Philanthropist* (1889). Daniel Hand (1801–1891) was a wealthy resident of Madison, Connecticut who had lived in Augusta, Georgia before and during the Civil War. He became immensely sympathetic to the plight of emancipated African Americans in the South and established the Hand Fund to help alleviate their impoverished condition. Hand's nephew, George A. Wilcox, resolved to obtain public recognition of Hand's benefactions by publishing an account of his generous charity. Wilcox, a Yale graduate, practiced law in Detroit from 1853 until 1892, when he returned to Madison, Connecticut.

Matthew D. Klauza, "Mark Twain's Recovered Comic Voice in 'You've Been a Dam Fool/Damfool, Mary,'" *Mark Twain Journal* 52.1 (Spring 2014).

WILDE, OSCAR (1854–1900). *De Profundis* (public letter, published in 1905).

Catalog: ListABP (1910), "De Profundis, Wilde", no other information provided.

Mark Twain's "The Walt Whitman Controversy" (written around 1882?) classified Wilde's poetry with the "new bad books" of Whitman and Swinburne; he owned none of these works, Twain claimed (DV3 6, MTP). (We can never verify this assertion, since Clemens and his daughter Clara donated many hundreds of books from his library whose authors and titles were never recorded in a surviving document.) Clemens called on the Wildes in London in the late 1880s and signed Constance's autograph book (Joseph B. McCullough to the Mark Twain Forum, 18 February 2006). Susy Clemens wrote Louise Brownell in October 1891, probably from Berlin, to report that ""Oscar Wilde was over here the other day in a suit of soft brown with a pale pink flowered vest, a blue necktie and some strange picturesque white flowers in his button hole" (Hamilton College Archives; Linda Morris to the Mark Twain Forum, 18 February 2006; Cotton, "Olivia Susan Clemens," p. 108). Clara Clemens recalled that Clemens met Wilde at a hotel during their European

health-hunting sojourn, when Wilde wore "a carnation as large as a baby sunflower"; she seemed to set the encounter at Bad Nauheim (*MFMT*, p. 113).

———. *The Picture of Dorian Gray* (fantasy novel, published in 1891).

Richard Bridgman made a case that a series of elaborate puns in Chapter 50 of *Following the Equator* (1897) subtly alluded to the title of Wilde's novel, his homosexuality, and his imprisonment (*Traveling in Mark Twain* [Berkeley: University of California Press, 1987], pp. 137–138).

WILDER, MARSHALL PINCKNEY (1859–1915). *The People I've Smiled With: Recollections of a Merry Little Life*. Illus. New York, 1889.

Wilder's book contained a story (on pages 194–198) that Mark Twain told at a reception at Daly's Fifth Avenue Theatre on 13 April 1887 and which Twain would recount in Chapter 45 of *Following the Equator* (1897). It concerned Twain's difficulties in getting past an Irishman guarding the backdoor entrance to Daly's theatre. Almost certainly Twain was familiar with Wilder's version of his anecdote, in which Twain solved his problem by feigning an expertise in dogs.

———. *Smiling 'Round the World*. Illus. New York: Funk & Wagnalls Co., 1908. 330 pp.

Source: MTLAcc, entry #557, volume donated by Clemens.

———. *The Sunny Side of the Street*. Illustrated by Bart Haley (fl. 1900–1920). Cover illustration by Charles [S.] Graham (1852–1911). New York: Funk & Wagnalls Co., 1905. 359 pp.

"I am just mailing you my book. I know just how busy you are but you have always been such a good friend to me I wanted you to know I did not forget you" (Wilder to SLC, New York City, 11 July 1905, MTP). Wilder had left behind the expected limitations of dwarfism by becoming a popular monologist, actor, humorist, and author. A resilient optimism was his trademark.

WILDERMUTH, OTTILIE (1817–1877). *Für Freistunden; Erzählungen für die Jugend [For Free Time: Stories for Young People]* (children's stories, published in 1860).

Catalog: ListABP (1910), "Fur Freiftunden [*sic*], Wildermuth", no other information provided.

Wildermuth, a prominent German author of literature for children, lived with her husband in Tübingen.

WILDMAN, EDWIN (1867–1932). *Aguinaldo: A Narrative of Filipino Ambitions*. Boston: Lothrop Publishing Co., [1901]. 374 pp.

Inscription: the front free endpaper is inscribed in black ink, "Compliments of/Edwin Wildman/Spt 7 1901/To/ Samuel L. Clemens Esq".

Marginalia: Clemens's profuse pencil markings and notations begin on page 5 of "A Note to the Reader" and continue to page 172; except for some figures and a marginal mark on page 310, they do not resume until page 319. Thereafter the final section is annotated as thoroughly as the first part of the volume. All of the marginalia are in pencil. On page 46 Clemens noted, "Reads like truth." At the head of Chapter 6 he commented: "This is a disastrous friend: he always defends us by making us out idiots. It is a comical book. The gov't ought to gag the author or drown him. Still, it is the very book that is needed—it tells the dismal truth without intending to" (page 92). He observed on page 93, writing vertically:

"Another confession. Ag's intentions were notorious, but no man could find out what ours were—they wouldn't bear the light." At the top of page 95: "Always scoffing because Ag. couldn't write his own state papers. The King of Eng. can't do it. But Ag could do *other* things." Top of page 105: "He never quotes an authority—his own quite sufficient for his purposes." On the margin of page 107: "The U. S. hates patriots". Clemens made penciled notes stating that a political and military leader should possess humanity, fidelity ("keeper of pledges"), probity, magnetism, faith, fortitude, and "the quality that enables a man to concentrate upon himself the love of a people & belief in the purity of his motives." There are numerous other notes.

Location: Mark Twain Papers, Bancroft Library, University of California at Berkeley.

Copy examined: Clemens's copy.

Emilio Aguinaldo (1869–1964) incited Filipino revolutionary movements against Spain and later against the American occupation. In his eventual role as a military leader Aguinaldo was captured and imprisoned in 1901 by General Frederick Funston. Mark Twain's "To the Person Sitting in Darkness" (February 1901) referred to Aguinaldo as "their leader, their hero, their hope, their Washington." Twain employed Wildman's *Aguinaldo* in a mocking essay, "A Defence of General Funston" (May 1902), to reveal the subterfuge by which Aguinaldo was vanquished: "Now came his capture. An admiring author shall tell us about it"; he quotes from pages 356–361 of Wildman's book, deleting a few less-relevant sentences. A footnote cites the author, title, and publisher. Farther on in the essay, Twain quotes a passage in *Aguinaldo* (p. 360) gloating over the clever, treacherous ruse (begging food from the rebel troops) that caught Aguinaldo's bodyguards unprepared.

Twain's main response to Wildman's book remains unpublished, however. Twenty-three typescript pages survive in the Mark Twain Papers at Berkeley (Paine 89aa) from a book review that Twain produced about *Aguinaldo: A Narrative of Filipino Ambitions.* The last page breaks off in mid-sentence. Despite Wildman's "prejudices—which are almost over-frank and cordial," Twain felt that "a vivid and living" portrait of the rebel leader emerged from the book. Using lengthy extracts, Twain constructs a detailed biographical sketch of Aguinaldo, seeking to familiarize Americans with his career and aspirations. In Twain's interpretation, Aguinaldo becomes a valiant modern counterpart of Joan of Arc, with whom Twain repeatedly compares him. Aguinaldo is opposed by the government, harassed by military officers, and betrayed by Catholic priests. Twain also likens him to an oppressed young black man in Alabama. Twain's narrative ends before Aguinaldo's capture is described; conceivably Twain elected to use this missing last portion for his essay titled "In Defence of General Funston" (1902).

Philip S. Foner, *Mark Twain: Social Critic* (New York: International Publishers, 1958), p. 289.

WILHELM II. FRIEDRICH WILHELM VIKTOR ALBERT (1859–1941), Emperor of Germany and King of Prussia. *The Kaiser's Speeches, Forming a Character Portrait of Emperor William II.* Trans. and ed. with notes by Wolf von Schierbrand

(1851–1920). Comp. by Anton Oskar Eugen (1851–1916). Portrait. New York: Harper & Brothers, 1903. 332 pp.

Catalog: *A1911*, "8vo, cloth, gilt top, uncut, N.Y. 1903," with a sheet of notes about *Roughing It* and *Adventures of Huckleberry Finn*, lot 487, sold for $3.25.

———. [An identical copy.]

Source: MTLAcc, entry #1499, volume donated by Clemens.

WILHELMINA, FREDERICA SOPHIA (1709–1758), Margravine of Bayreuth. *Memoirs of Frederica Sophia Wilhelmina, Princess Royal of Prussia, Margravine of Baireuth, Sister of Frederick the Great. With an Essay by William D. Howells.* 2 vols. Choice Autobiographies Series. Boston: James R. Osgood and Co., 1877.

Inscription: the front free endpaper of Volume I is inscribed "S. L. Clemens,/ from his friend/W. D. Howells./Cambridge,/Oct. 7, 1877".

Marginalia: Clemens marked Volume I in pencil throughout. However, he wrote only one note, on page 58: "See Pepys' Diary—the first Russian embassy."

Catalogs: ListABP (1910), "Autobiog.—Margravine of Baireuth, Howells"; "RetzAppraisal" (1944), p. 8, Volume I only, valued at $10.

Location: Volume I only, Mark Twain Papers, Bancroft Library, University of California at Berkeley.

Copy examined: Clemens's copy of Volume I only.

Wilhelmina was the sister of Frederick the Great (1712–1786). William Dean Howells notified Clemens from Cambridge on 21 December 1877: "I sent you on Tuesday by express the 2 vols. of the Margravine" (*MTHL*, p. 211). On 2 August 1878 Clemens noted in Baden-Baden: "1725 is just the time of the Margravine of Baireut, who was born 1707 [*sic*] (NB 15, *N&J* 2: 127). In 1886 Clemens commented, "One . . . partly believes the Margravine of Bayreuth" (NB 26, *N&J* 3: 239). Henry Fisher stated that when James R. Osgood sent him Howells's two-volume edition of the Margravine's *Memoirs* for Christmas (in 1891?), Fisher took the book to Clemens, who was recuperating from illness in Berlin. When Fisher returned the next day, Clemens remarked, "I am reading this book for the second time . . . and it actually makes me forget that I am sick" (*AMT*, p. 74). "I most heartily admire her," Clemens added. "They thought I went to Bayreuth to hear Wagner. . . . Nothing of the kind. . . . I visited the grave of the Margravine and looked at the temples and grottoes and houses she built, the statues and fountains she set up, the beauty she lavished on the landscape!" (*AMT*, p. 76). In Mark Twain's "At the Shrine of St. Wagner" (1891), he relates how he avoided the opera one day in Bayreuth in August 1891 and "went hunting for relics and reminders of the Margravine Wilhelmina, she of the imperishable 'Memoirs.' I am properly grateful to her for her (unconscious) satire upon monarchy and nobility, and therefore nothing which her hand touched or her eye looked upon is indifferent to me. I am her pilgrim; the rest of this multitude here are Wagner's." For a proposed magazine, Twain hoped in January 1894 to "buy a set of Howells's Autobiographies for the Back Number" (NB 33, TS p. 46). In a letter to Clemens written from New York City on 12 April 1904, Henry W. Fischer (a variant spelling of Fisher's name) mentioned that "you once told me of your great and lasting fondness for the Margravine of Bayreuth" (MTP).

———. *Memoirs of Wilhelmine, Margravine of Baireuth*. Translated and ed. by Helena Augusta Victoria (1846–1923), Princess Christian of Schleswig-Holstein. First edition of this translation. 8vo, original two-toned cloth, worn, inner hinges broken. London: David Stott, 1887. 452 pp.

Marginalia: numerous notes (119, totaling approximately 144 words) and markings, mostly in pencil but a few in black ink. The annotations in pencil mainly occur on pages 214–448. Fifty-four pages in the second half of the book bear Clemens's underlinings or other markings. Beside a reference on page 248 to Dr. Stahl, who maintained that illnesses are caused by powers of the imagination, Clemens queried "mind-cure?" On page 258 he noted, "Ought to have saved the powder for traveling expenses." At the top of page 264 he wrote: "Across the principality is half a day's journey on a crippled horse." Along the bottom of page 265: "The expense of a governess would not have been above $2 a month." At the top of page 270: "Paupers, from the King down. Even the husband was not around." On page 288 he observed, "No doctor for a King" and "How could *they* lose their minds?" On page 295 he wrote, "See St. Simon for the explanation of this" (why the king rose every morning at 4 a.m. to review his regiment's parade, evidently). Of an interview between the King and his daughter (p. 297), Clemens scoffed: "Passage between the two humbugs." Clemens jotted exclamation marks on page 299 and labeled it "Specimen of the translator's English". On page 300 he noted, "W. gives frequent evidence of lacking common sense herself." On page 306 he wrote "The old blister," referring to M. von Stocker, lover of the Duchess of Brunswick. Of the Queen, Clemens noted at the bottom of page 307: "The old slut". In the margin of page 310 he observed: "A rat of to-day is better off than was a royal princess of that time." At the top of page 311: "W. has a settled superstition that her health is bad. She knew how to make the most of a stomach-ache." On page 312: "No royal box" and (at the bottom) "Was it like Shak's theatre? Next page"; on page 313 he wrote "Here it is" beside the description of a theatre. At the top of page 365 he noted, "Examine Carlyle's Fred. Compare 5, 1"; at the bottom of the same page he added, "Fred the Great is at this time a boy of 22." Concerning Wilhelmina's brother, Clemens commented on page 366: "He knew himself, this dissipated Hal, the true Prince. He is Hal over again." Farther down the page he noted, "He was the sort of tonic the sentimental girl needed. *He* could have cured her." Regarding the death of Wihelmina's father-in-law, he jotted on page 375: "Takes the old reptile a tiresome long time to die." On page 394: "cats & dogs". On page 410: "They are all lunatics apparently." Many other brief comments are not reported here.

Catalogs: *C1951*, #8a, $22.50; Christie's, New York City, 1–2 February 1988 auction, lot 463, sold for $2,200.

Provenance: Donated to the Carrie Estelle Doheny Collection at St. John's Seminary in 1951 after she purchased the volume for $34.50 from Maxwell Hunley Rare Books, Beverly Hills, California. Auctioned by Christie's in 1988 on behalf of St. John's Seminary and

the Archdiocese of Los Angeles.

Location: currently unknown.

Copy examined: Clemens's copy, when it was at St. John's Seminary in Camarillo, California in 1970.

Mark Twain intended to add Wilhelmina's *Memoirs* to his projected series titled "Royalty & Nobility Exposed" (NB 26 [May 1887], *N&J* 3: 295). He also wished to cite the work in his proposed appendix to *A Connecticut Yankee in King Arthur's Court*, published in 1889 (Baetzhold, "Course of Composition" [1961], p. 200).

On cross-barred paper associated with Twain's sojourn in Weggis in 1897, Twain wrote out a draft of twenty-four manuscript pages, plus thirteen pages of densely packed notes, toward a historical novel based on Wilhelmina's life; he never got beyond the manuscript page labeled simply "Chapter 2" (Paine 212, MTP). His working notes are keyed to page numbers that do not correspond with the pagination of Howells's 1877 edition of *Memoirs of Frederica Sophia Wilhelmina*. Twain's story would have opened in January 1732 and would have revealed various castle intrigues. Wilhelmina's bout with smallpox was to be a central event in the book. The manuscript has no title, and probably could best be referred to as "The Margravine of Bayreuth." In the opening character sketch Twain lauds her intelligence, frankness, sympathy, loyalty, patience, and—most important—her humor. He concedes that she was proud and ambitious, but claims that these were not her dominant traits. He quotes from the journal she kept. The surviving chapter concludes with her entry into tawdry Bayreuth, where she was unimpressed by its populace, ceremony, or sights. "Judged by the standards of her time she was refined & delicate in feeling & expression; judged by our standards she was not," Twain wrote.

WILKINSON, FLORENCE, LATER MRS. FLORENCE (WILKINSON) EVANS (b. 1878). *The Silent Door*. New York: McClure, Phillips & Co., 1907. 436 pp.

Inscription: the front free endpaper is signed in black ink "Jean L. Clemens./July 26th '07./From Aunt Sue."

Provenance: in August 1987 Alan Gribben was shown the collection of Bigelow Paine Cushman (1928–2003) in Deer Isle, Maine. It included a list of books used by Cushman's grandfather Albert Bigelow Paine in writing his biography of Mark Twain, including an entry for Florence Wilkinson's *The Silent Door*, "with 'Jean Clemens' signature." Subsequently the Mark Twain Papers at Berkeley acquired much of this collection, a transaction I helped facilitate.

Location: Mark Twain Papers, Bancroft Library, University of California at Berkeley.

Copy examined: Jean Clemens's unmarked copy, in the Mark Twain Papers.

In this novel a door in the basement of the Penrith House is keep locked until the very last chapter. Its hardly revelatory interior seems (to this reader, at least) rather anti-climactic.

———. *The Strength of the Hills; A Novel*. New York: Harper & Brothers, 1901. 395 pp.

Catalog: *C1951*, D61, listed among volumes signed by Clemens.

In the third part of Mark Twain's "What Is Man?" (1906), titled "Instances in Point," the Young Man reports that he "examined many fine and apparently self-sacrificing deeds in romances and biographies" and finally found one in an (unnamed) novel "which seems to promise." But the Old Man's searching analysis of the plot exposes the basic selfishness of what appeared to be an altruistic act, and he chortles: "The authoress quite innocently and unconsciously gives the whole business away." Paul Baender identified the novel being discussed as Wilkinson's *The Strength of the Hills*; he also explained that Twain took liberties with the plot and the supposed quotations (*WIM?*, pp. 148–151, 548). In "Which Was It?" (written 1899–1903), Twain had introduced a still more detailed analysis of the selfish motives underlying the Adirondack lumberjack's missionary efforts in the East Side of New York City as related by Wilkinson in *The Strength of the Hills* (*WWD?*, pp. 379–383). John S. Tuckey observed that this dialogue between George Harrison (representing the intuitive viewpoint) and Sol Bailey (a spokesman for utilitarian arguments) follows an early draft of "What Is Man?" (*WWD?*, p. 383). Bailey argues: "Whenever you read of an unselfish act, or of an act of self-sacrifice, or of a duty done for *duty's* sake, take it to pieces and look for the selfish motive," but Harrison terminates the debate by falling asleep (*WWD?*, p. 383).

WILKINSON, GEORGE THEODORE. *The Newgate Calendar Improved; Being Interesting Memoirs of Notorious Characters, Who Have Been Convicted of Offences Against the Laws of England, During the Seventeenth Century; and Continued to the Present Time, Chronologically Arranged*. 6 vols. Illus. London: Printed for Thomas Kelly, 1836. [Only Volume V was dated by the publisher, who there specified the year as 1836.]

Marginalia: a few penciled check marks in the indexes of Volume II (entries for "Jefferies, Elizabeth, Murderer"; "Origin of the Gibbet in England"; and "Williams, Renwick, the Monster") and of Volume VI ("Angelini, Edmund, an Italian, volunteered to suffer death in the place of Henry Fauntleroy" and all of the entries for "Fauntleroy, Henry"). In the list of plates at the rear of Volume V, all but four are preceded by small penciled check marks.

Provenance: a bookseller's stamp appears on the front pastedown endpaper: F. H. Thomas & Co./LAW BOOKSELLERS/St. Louis, Mo."

Catalogs: *A1911*, "Plates (one stained), 6 vols., 8vo, half cloth, imperfect, Lond.: Velly [*sic*] & Co., n. d.," with a sheet of notes by Clemens laid in, lot 486, sold for $4.50; *Lexington 1912*, lot 28, 6 vols., sold for $12.50.

Provenance: Horace G. Commin, Ltd., Bournemouth, England, letter to John Winkler, 12 May 1960, "6 vols., in poor condition, a great portion missing from the text has been replaced by leaves from another edition, 7 quires of Vol. 6 missing, 38 ex 50 plus one, upper covers of vols. 1, 4 & 6 loose and lower covers of Vol. 6 loose. London: Thomas Kelly, n. d., £4.10.0 ($13.00)." I am grateful to Henry Sweets, then the director of the Mark Twain Boyhood Home and Museum, for locating this information on 12 December 1978 and sending it to me.

Location: Mark Twain Boyhood Home and Museum, Hannibal, Missouri. Purchased in May 1960 from Horace G. Commin, Ltd., Bournemouth, England. John Winkler was then the director of the Hannibal historical site.

Copies examined: Clemens's copies of six volumes, in 1979.

Seven quires were omitted from Volume VI; for example, the pagination skips from page 48 to 73.

"In England, long ago, . . . a gentleman could commit all the crimes and bestialities known to the Newgate Calendar," Twain mentioned in "Introducing Dr. Henry Van Dyke," a speech he delivered in February or March 1906 (*MTSpk* [1976], p. 488).

WILLARD, EMMA (HART) (1787–1870). "Rocked in the cradle of the deep" (hymn, published in 1840), sometimes known as "Sailor's Hymn." Melody composed by Joseph Philip Knight (1812–1887).

Mark Twain quoted from this hymn in "About All Kinds of Ships" (1893).

WILLARD, JOSIAH FLYNT (1869–1907), pseud. "Josiah Flynt." *Tramping with Tramps: Studies and Sketches of Vagabond Life*. Preface by Andrew D[ickson]. White (1832–1918). Illus. Loose frontispiece. New York: Century Co., 1901. 398 pp.

Inscription: inscribed in black ink on the front free endpaper, "To Mr. Clemens/with the sincere regards/of the Author".

Location: Mark Twain Library, Redding, Connecticut.

Copy examined: Clemens's copy, unmarked. Has the red ink Mark Twain Library accession number "2524". Examined in 1970 and again in June 1982.

Mark Twain made so many references to "tramps" and so often depicted the roving life that one would have been surprised if *Tramping with Tramps* were missing from his library. Willard camped with homeless men until he became an expert on their ways. His resulting essays appeared in *Atlantic Monthly*, *Century Magazine*, and *Harper's Monthly* before being collected in *Tramping with Tramps* in 1899. Willard did not beautify the life he experienced, and Chapter 2, "The Children of the Road," depicted the parental neglect and mistreatment that drove young people into the hobo jungles, detailed the rough life that awaited them there, and recommended the establishment of humane reformatories to turn children away from this path. Other chapters described the tramps' attire and meals, the differences between city and rural tramps, and the tramps' dependence on the railroad system. Wallace even provided a glossary of their jargon.

Axel Nissen's "A Tramp at Home: *Huckleberry Finn*, Romantic Friendship, and the Homeless Man," *Nineteenth-Century Literature* 60.1 (2005): 57–86 discussed Willard's book in the course of analyzing the King and the Duke in Twain's *Adventures of Huckleberry Finn* (1885), including certain homosexual implications.

WILLCOX, LOUISE (COLLIER) (1865–1929). *The Human Way*. New York: Harper & Brothers, 1909. 305 pp.

Source: MTLAcc, entry #1461, volume donated by Clemens.

Willcox's *The Human Way* collected ten of her more introspective essays; they have titles such as "The Service of Books," "Out-of-Doors" (she was an enthusiastic traveler in the Canadian Rockies), "Human Relations," "The Hidden Life," "Solitude," and "Memorat Memoria." Willcox was an influential advocate for women's equality and suffrage.

WILLIAMS, FRANCIS CHURCHILL (1869–1945). *J. Devlin—Boss: A Romance of American Politics*. Illustrated by Clifford Carleton (1867–1946). First edition. Boston: Lothrop

Publishing Co., 1901. 520 pp. [Edition conjectured.]
> **Catalog:** ListABP (1910), "J. Devlin, Boss, Williams", no other information supplied.
> A romance is wrapped into a novel about a political boss and a presidential convention.

WILLIAMS, HENRY SMITH (1863–1943). *The Story of Nineteenth-Century Science.* Illus. New York: Harper & Brothers, 1900. 475 pp.
> **Source:** MTLAcc, entry #1379, volume donated by Clemens.
> Williams assessed the progress that was accomplished during the preceding century in the fields of astronomy, geology, paleontology, physics, medicine, biology, and chemistry.

———. *The Story of Nineteenth-Century Science.* New York: Harper & Brothers, 1904. 475 pp.
> **Source:** MTLAcc, entry #1807, volume donated by Clemens.

WILLIAMS, JOHN D. (1829–1871) and **SILAS SADLER PACKARD** (1826–1898). *Guide to Williams & Packard's System of Penmanship for Teachers and Adepts.* Illus. New York: Slote, Woodman & Co., 1869. 59 pp., plus plates.
> An unsigned column in the 19 March 1870 Buffalo *Express* mentioned that the publisher, "Dan Slote," was "our stateroom-mate in the 'Quaker City' excursion." It praised this "handsome volume, a graceful green bound thing, fit for the centre-table. And in it appears to be concentrated all the information about penmanship that a man could need" (McCullough and McIntire-Strasburg, *MTBE*, pp. 170–171). The publisher of this work would be engaged for years in exasperating courtroom battles to prove that a competing book on penmanship had plagiarized its contents.

WILLIAMS, ROBERT FOLKESTONE (c. 1805–1872). "Good-bye, sweetheart, good-bye" (song, published in 1863). Music by John Liptrot Hatton (1809–1886).
> On 3 October 1872 Clemens lovingly ended a letter to Olivia with these words: "Good-bye, Sweetheart, good-bye. Good-bye, Sweetheart, good-bye" (*MTLet* 5: 189).

WILLIAMS, THOMAS (1815–1891) and **JAMES CALVERT** (1813–1892). *Fiji and the Fijians.* Volume I, *The Islands and Their Inhabitants. By Thomas Williams.* Volume II, *Mission History. By James Calvert.* Ed. by George Stringer Rowe. 2 vols. London: A. Heylin, 1858. Second edition, 1860. Third edition, 1870. [Clemens's edition is undetermined.]
> Clemens's reading in London in November 1896 included "Fiji & the F.'s, 2 vols James Calvert" (NB 39, TS p. 26). Chapter 7 of *Following the Equator* (1897) discusses the efforts of Christian missionaries in Fiji.
> Madigan, "MT's Passage to India" (1974), p. 367.

WILLIAMS, THOMAS E. (d. 1864). "The larboard watch" (song, published in 1859, lyrics and melody by Williams, a London composer).
> Clemens quoted the last line of the chorus ("The Larboard Ahoy!") while on board the *Smyrniote* in 1866 (NB 5, *N&J* 1: 149). Clemens explained on 1 January 1867 that he could tolerate this song on board a ship; at least it is "in keeping with our surroundings" (*MTTMB*, p. 59); therefore, "Larboard Watch ahoy!" was *appropriate* for the men's choir to sing on the *America.* He noted "Larboard Watch ahoy" again on 2 January 1867 (NB 6, *N&J* 1: 262, 269). In January 1867 he again copied

the title, "Larboard Watch" (NB 7, *N&J* 1: 299). "And call the larboard watch," Clemens quipped to Emily A. Severance on 24 December 1867 from Washington, D.C. (*Journal and Letters of Emily A. Severance* [Cleveland: Gates Press, 1938], p. 218). Clemens marked "Larboard Watch" in his copy of D. H. Morrison's *Treasury of Song for the Home Circle: The Richest, Best-Loved Gems, Sacred and Secular,* a book that entered the Clemens family's library in 1883. In August 1889 Clemens included "Larboard Watch" in a list of what appeared to be his favorite songs (NB 29, *N&J* 3: 513). Mark Twain's "About All Kinds of Ships" (1893) quotes from "Larboard Watch." In 1906 Twain mentioned "The Larboard Watch" as one of the "sentimental songs" of the later minstrel shows (30 November 1906 AD, *MTE*, p. 114; *AutoMT* 2: 296). The song's chorus begins, "But who can speak the joy he feels/While o'er the foam his vessel reels,/And his tir'd eye-lids slumb'ring fall,/He rouses at the welcome call/Of 'Larboard Watch, A-hoy!'"

"WILLIE REILLY" (Irish folk ballad, probably dating from the late eighteenth century).
> The piano player in Mark Twain's "The Scriptural Panoramist" (1865) bangs out "Come rise up, William Ri-i-ley,/And go along with me!" In the ballad's opening stanza, a young girl offers to run away with Willie Reilly: "Oh rise up, Willie Reilly, and come along with me,/I mean to go along with you and leave this country." This attempted elopement lands Reilly in jail, and the rest of the song describes the courtroom arguments.

WILLING, WILLIAM (fl. 1850s-1870s). "Twenty years ago" ("I've wander'd to the village, Tom") (song). Words and music generally attributed Willing. (Published in 1856.)
> "Twenty Years Ago" was one of the songs Clemens listed on the front wrapper of his copy of Frank B. Ogilvie's *Two Hundred Old-Time Songs, Containing the Words and Music of the Choicest Gems of the Old and Familiar Songs* (1896). In the last year of Clemens's life he quoted this nostalgic song during a conversation with Albert Bigelow Paine ("I have wandered through [*sic*] the village, Tom, and sat beneath the tree") and spoke of the author's ability to "put in compact form the thing which we have all vaguely felt" (*MTB*, pp. 1555–56). The sentimental ballad was reputedly one of Abraham Lincoln's favorites as well. Its opening lines emphasize the rapid effects of time: "I've wandered to the village, Tom/I've sat beneath the tree/Upon the schoolhouse playing ground/Which sheltered you and me./But none were there to greet me, Tom/And few were left to know/That played with us upon the grass/Some twenty years ago." After reminding Tom of their many classmates who have passed away, including the singer's schoolyard sweetheart, he concludes the song with the hope that "when our time shall come, dear Tom/And we are called to go/I hope they'll lay us where we played/Just twenty years ago." (Many readers told Mark Twain that his *The Adventures of Tom Sawyer* [1876] evoked for them essentially this same sentiment in prose.)

WILLIS, HENRY PARKER (1874–1937). *Our Philippine Problem; A Study of American Colonial Policy.* Maps. New York: Henry Holt and Co., 1905. 479 pp.
> **Inscription:** inscribed by Clemens in black ink across both the front pastedown endpaper and the front free endpaper:

"S. L. Clemens, 1905—from Charles Francis Adams."

Marginalia: annotated in black ink up to page 6. On page 2, regarding Professor Burgess's notion of the "manifest mission of the Teutonic nations. . . . of organising the world politically," Clemens queried in the margin: "Our Indians, for instance?" On page 3 Willis discussed the ambiguity of the United States' philosophy of international relations; Clemens noted in the margin: "Why don't [they] capture & take care of the Russians? Is there any reason except that they dasn't try?" He made black-ink marks on page 5. Where Willis described President McKinley's railroad journey through the American West in 1898, a trip which convinced him that Americans wished him to acquire the Philippines (p. 6), Clemens rejoined: "If McK had opposed it, these empty heads would have applauded *that*. He put imperialism into them, & they *responded*."

Location: Mark Twain Library, Redding, Connecticut. Donated by Clemens (MTLAcc, entry #568).

Copy examined: Clemens's copy. Examined in 1970 and again in June 1982.

WILLIS, NATHANIEL PARKER (1806–1867). *The Poems, Sacred, Passionate, and Humorous, of Nathaniel Parker Willis.* Complete edition, rev. and enl. Spine broken. New York: Clark, Austin, Maynard & Co., 1861. 352 pp.

Inscription: the front flyleaf is inscribed (not in Olivia Langdon's hand) in black ink: "Livie L. Langdon/Feby 1864/New York".

Location: Mark Twain Library, Redding, Connecticut. Donated from Clemens's library by Clara Clemens Gabrilowitsch in 1910 (MTLAcc, entry #2120).

Copy examined: Olivia Clemens's unmarked copy. Has the Mark Twain Library accession number "2120". A piece of white cloth at pages 220–221 was used as a bookmark. I examined this volume in 1970 and again in June 1982.

WILLIS, SARA PAYSON (1811–1872), later Mrs. Sara Payson (Willis) Parton, pseud. "Fanny Fern."

Olivia Langdon copied a passage about "little things" by Fanny Fern into her commonplace book around 1869 or 1870 (DV161, MTP).

WILLS, WILLIAM GORMAN (1828–1891). *Charles the First: An Historical Tragedy. In Four Acts* (play, performed in 1872).

Charles I, written by the British bohemian artist, dramatist, and poet Wills, opened 28 September 1872 at the London Lyceum, with Henry Irving in the title role. Clemens referred to the play unfavorably ("a curious literary absurdity") in an unpublished piece he wrote in 1872, "London Notes." In a letter written to Mary Mason Fairbanks on 6 July 1873 from London, Clemens mentioned that "we have met many pleasant people at dinners—. . . Wills (who wrote the two great dramatic successes of the period, Chas. I & Miss [Kate Josephine] Bateman's Medea [*in Corinth*, performed in 1872]" (*MTMF*, p. 173; *MTLet* 5: 402). "I think it was at [Hezekiah Linthan] Bateman's, thirty-five years ago, that I told [Henry] Irving and [William Gorman] Wills, the playwright, about the whitewashing of the fence by Tom Sawyer," Clemens would recall (19 August 1907 AD, *MTE*, p. 331; *AutoMT* 3: 102).

———. *The Man o' Airlie: A Drama of the Affections* (play, performed in London in 1867; produced in New York City in 1871).

This play was Wills' first major success on the stage. Clemens

recognized "Man of Airlie" [*sic*], a ballad sung repeatedly in Wills' play, as one of the pieces played in June 1873 by a marching band during a military review in honor of the Shah of Persia's visit to London (NB 12, *N&J* 1: 544). Clemens's familiarity with the song raises the possibility that he heard Lawrence Barrett (1838–1891) sing it in the American production of *The Man o'Airlie* in 1871; Barrett had the role of James Harebell, a fictional Scottish poet resembling Robert Burns. Wills wrote the lyrics, and some sources credit Barrett as composer of the melody. The plot of the melodrama, set in 1790, revolves around the financial ruin and mental suffering of Harebell, whose genius is only recognized and celebrated after he has lost his mind and is dying. The opening lyrics of the ballad strike a poignant tone: "Oh! There above yon heather hill,/Where footfall comes but rarely,/There is a house they point at still,/Where dwelt the Man o' Airlie." The song's last stanza begins: "He's dead and gone, this Prince of Fife,/Mute is his burly laughter,/But ah! The music of his life,/That bides with us long after."

———, adapt. *Olivia* (four-act play, performed in 1873, revived in 1900).

An entry in Notebook 43 on 16 June 1900 indicates that Clemens may have seen Sir Henry Irving open this play on that night at the Lyceum Theatre in London (TS p. 16a). Irving played Dr. Charles Primrose in this adaptation of Oliver Goldsmith's *The Vicar of Wakefield*; Ellen Terry performed the role of Olivia (London *Times*, 15 June 1900, p. 8).

WILLSON, MARCIUS (1813–1905). *Mosaics of Bible History; The Bible Record with Illustrative Poetic and Prose Selections from Standard Literature.* 2 vols. New York: Harper & Brothers, 1883.

Source: MTLAcc, entry #1389, Volume 2 only (442 pp.) donated by Clemens.

WILMANS, HELEN (1831–1907), later Helen (Wilmans) Post. *Back Numbers/Wilmans Express, Condensed* (Douglasville, Georgia, 1890?).

In Paris Olivia Clemens quoted a lengthy extract from a chapter titled "I can and I will" into her journal, crediting Helen Wilmans ("A Mental Scientist") and dating the quotation 17 February 1894 (DV161, MTP). However, at the end of the extract Olivia Clemens gave her source as Ada Wilmans Powers.

Helen Wilmans had left an abusive husband and commenced a career as a newspaper columnist; gradually she found a national platform as an author, magazine editor, and proponent of writings about the power of spiritual healing. Her daughter Ada Wilmans Powers (1858–1958) was sometimes listed as a co-author of Wilmans's publications. Olivia Clemens was quoting from *Back Numbers/ Wilmans Express, Condensed* (1890?), on the first page of which Wilmans emphatically stated: "*Mental science does heal the sick when everything else fails.*" Her essay titled "I Can and I Will" explained: "To take sides with the spirit and against the flesh, is the way to be strong. . . . Let me tell you about the two voices within you. One voice says, 'I can't,' and the other voice says, 'I can and I will'" (p. 84). The names of both Wilmans and Powers appeared on the title page of *Back Numbers/Wilmans Express, Condensed*. An advertisement at the rear of the volume stated that

Ada Wilmans Powers was the editor of *Wilmans Express*, which (according to that notice) had begun publication in April 1888. Wilmans wrote a number of books before she had to fight fraud charges filed by the United States Post Office in 1905.

WILSON, AUGUSTA JANE (EVANS) (1835–1909). *Beulah, A Novel*. New York: Carleton, 1863. 510 pp.

Source: MTLAcc, entry #127, volume donated by Clemens. In this second novel published in 1859, Wilson (at that time writing as "Evans" and having moved to Mobile, Alabama) achieved her first success as a writer. A young orphan named Beulah Benton wrestles with a profound skepticism that challenges her religious faith while above all she resolves to attain intellectual independence. Despite these avant-garde tendencies, *Beulah* is rarely classified with women's rights writings, mainly because in the looming Civil War Evans would prove to be an ardent secessionist and later she would oppose women's suffrage. In 1868 she would marry Lorenzo Madison Wilson (1808–1891).

WILSON, BINGHAM THOBURN (1867–1937). *Ye Mountaineer*. Illustrated by J. Arthur Day. New York: F. Tennyson Neely Co., 1901. 233 pp.

Source: MTLAcc, entry #648, volume donated by Clemens. Wilson's poems described landmarks and incidents in American colonial history. A resident of Brooklyn and an editorial writer for the New York *World*, Wilson would become well known on the Chautauqua lecture circuit and would move to Los Angeles.

WILSON, FLOYD BAKER (1845–1934). *Paths to Power*. New York: R. F. Fenno & Co., 1901. 229 pp.

Inscription: inscribed, "To Samuel L. Clemens, LL.D., with the compliments and best wishes of the author.—Floyd B. Wilson. New York, June 17, 1902."

Marginalia: on page 10, where Wilson states, "Let one declare repeatedly and openly as he may his inability to control his own atmosphere, his whole existence is full of proofs of his efforts to do that very thing," Clemens circled the word "efforts" and wrote: "The idea of reforming his atmosphere[,] however, must come from the outside; he cannot originate it. You seem to think he can." The volume contains several underscorings.

Catalog: *A1911*, "12mo, cloth, gilt top, uncut, N.Y. 1901, . . . several . . . underscorings are in the volume," quotes the inscription and Clemens's notation, lot 488, sold for $1.75.

Wilson touted the London Society for Psychical Research and praised those who believe that "the soul can speak directly with the Infinite" (p. 67). He exhorted his readers to access their inner psychic power and to "believe in yourselves, believe in your own divinity" (pp. 76–77). Wilson was a wealthy New York City attorney and investor.

———. [An identical copy.]

Source: MTLAcc, entry #681, volume donated by Albert Bigelow Paine, Clemens's designated biographer. Possibly Clemens saw this book, since the men exchanged reading materials.

WILSON, HARRY LEON (1867–1939). *The Spenders; A Tale of the Third Generation*. Illustrated by O'Neill Latham [Rose C. O'Neill, 1874–1944]. Boston: Lothrop Publishing Co., 1902. 512 pp.

On 13 June 1902 Richard Burton of Lothrop Publishing Company notified Clemens that he was sending an autographed copy of Wilson's *The Spenders*, "which I think you will enjoy for its idiomatic freshness and flavor of Americanism and especially for its humorous presentation of Western types" (MTP). Wilson himself wrote to Clemens on 19 June 1902, reminding him that they had met eight or nine years previously. "I am asking you to accept a copy of my novel 'The Spenders,'" he announced. "The publishers told me to slather them around. They want to sell a lot, I reckon. I don't ask you to read the book. . . . Just accept it, please, as a mark of the very warm liking of one who's [*sic*] chief treasure was once 'Tom Sawyer', and who, as a boy, read 'Roughing It' over and over and over for years and years, until it was so far gone you couldn't tell it had been 'Stolen from the Oregon [, Illinois] Public Library'" (MTP). Clemens replied on 23 June 1902: "Read it? Indeed I will, & with great pleasure." Clemens informed Wilson that the Clemens family was leaving the next day for a summer vacation at York Harbor, "but the book will go thither. I went to Harpers to-day to get it, but I had too many bundles, so I told them to ship it to me. With many thanks for the book" (ALS in the Bancroft Library, University of California, Berkeley). A photograph in the collection of the Mark Twain House and Museum at Hartford shows Clemens holding a copy of an elaborately decorated book titled *The Spenders*. On 28 June 1902 Clemens informed Wilson: "Between you & me & the gatepost, I think it's a *damnation* good book! It cost me my day, yesterday: You owe me $400. But never mind it, I forgive you, for the book's sake" (ALS in the Bancroft Library, University of California, Berkeley). In Wilson's *The Spenders* a romantic love resulting (at the conclusion) in marriage is combined with characters and tales from the early days of California gold mining, prospecting for silver in the Washoe Valley of Nevada, a family's generational fortune, and bold new ventures to make money in New York, Chicago, and the growing American cities. Wilson would go on to write the humorous novel *Ruggles of Red Gap* (1915). The illustrator of *The Spenders*, incidentally, married Wilson in 1902, the year that best-selling novel came out; later (after they divorced) she earned a small fortune in the 1920s making the famous "Kewpie Doll" based on cartoons she had drawn.

WILSON, HENRY (1740–1810). *Wonderful Characters; Comprising Memoirs and Anecdotes of the Most Remarkable Persons of Every Age and Nation. Collected from the Most Authentic Sources*. Louisville, Kentucky: Morton & Griswold, 1854. 510 pp.

Inscription: the front flyleaf is inscribed at the top by Olivia Clemens in pencil, "S. L. Clemens/1870".

Location: Mark Twain Library, Redding, Connecticut.

Copy examined: Clemens's copy, unmarked. Has the red ink Mark Twain Library accession number "3060". Examined in 1970 and again in June 1982.

Although published in 1854, this volume was not inscribed until 1870, when the Clemenses set up housekeeping as a married couple. It seems likely that it had long belonged to Clemens and should be counted among his early reading. Wilson provided biographical sketches of more than eighty personages notable for their marvelous adventures, freakish feats, or miraculous achievements. Included in his compilation was a skeptical yet sympathetic chapter (pp. 354–373) about "Joan d'Arc," whom he referred to as an "unfortunate woman." There was also a description of Thomas Parr (pp. 211–215), so Clemens may have been reading or rereading *Wonderful Characters* when he wrote to Olivia Clemens on 18 August 1871 about his wish "to write an Autobiography of Old Parr, the gentleman who lived to be 153 years old & saw the reigns of 8 English kings" (*MTLet* 4: 446). Wilson credited Parr with living "one hundred and fifty-two years and odd months (p. 211) and having been the subject of English monarchs from Edward IV to Charles I. The long chapter on "Baron Frederick Trenck" (pp. 395–412) recounts so many details about Trenck's lengthy dungeon imprisonment that it probably contributed to the requirements Tom Sawyer imposes on the captive Jim at the Phelps farm (Tom alludes to "Baron Trenck" in Chapter 35). Among other figures treated in *Wonderful Characters* are the Admirable Crichton (p. 229), Lady Godiva (p. 423), Old Boots, whose protruding nose reached down to his mouth (p. 281), and Peter the Wild Boy (p. 418).

WILSON, JAMES GRANT (1832–1914), pseud. "Allan Grant," ed. *Love in Letters; Illustrated in the Correspondence of Eminent Persons; with Biographical Sketches of the Writers by Allan Grant*. Green cloth. New York: G. W. Carleton & Co., 1867. 336 pp.

Inscription: inscribed on the front flyleaf in Clemens's handwriting: "Livy Langdon"; below, in larger script, "Livy Clemens/1872". Both inscriptions are in pencil.

Provenance: Antenne-Dorrance Collection, Rice Lake, Wisconsin.

Location: Mark Twain Archive, Gannett Tripp Learning Center, Elmira College, Elmira, New York.

Copy examined: Olivia Clemens's unmarked copy. Examined on 28 May 2015.

Wilson collected thirty-five examples of letters written to lovers, about lovers, or about passionate feelings. The authors of these letters included Abelard (to Heloise), Henry VIII (to Anne Boleyn), Madame de Sévigné, Samuel Pepys, Dr. Samuel Johnson, Hannah More, Lord Nelson (to Lady Hamilton), Napoleon (to Josephine), Charles Lamb, John Keats, and Sir Walter Scott. Each writer is represented by only a single letter.

WILSON, JAMES HARRISON (1837–1925). *The Life of Charles A. Dana*. New York: Harper & Brothers, 1907. 545 pp.

Source: MTLAcc, entry #828, volume donated by Clemens. Charles A[nderson]. Dana (1813–1897) edited the New York *Sun* from 1868 until 1897.

———. *The Life of Charles A. Dana*. First edition. Original maroon cloth, gilt. New York: Harper & Brothers, 1907. 545 pp.

Inscriptions: inscribed in black ink by Dan Beard on the front free endpaper: "This book is from/Mark Twain's private/library, Stormfield, Redding,/Conn./Dan Beard/Vice-President/Mark Twain Library." (Beard similarly inscribed other volumes for book sales to benefit the Mark Twain Library in Redding, Connecticut.)

Marginalia: the Mark Twain Library accession number "1781" appears in red ink on the rear pastedown endpaper. The first 106 pages, covering Dana's education and early journalism career, have been opened, as well as pages 438–455 (the chapter describing President Grant's second

term), but there are no markings.

Catalog: MTLAcc, entry #1781, volume donated by Clemens.

Location: collection of Kevin Mac Donnell, Austin, Texas.

Source: Mac Donnell to Alan Gribben, 3 September 2005.

WILSON, JOHN GROSVENOR (1866–1948). *Lyrics of Life*. New York: Caxton Book Concern, 1886. 190 pp.

Inscription: the front flyleaf is inscribed in brown ink, "Samuel L. Clemens Esq./With compliments of/The Author".

Location: Mark Twain Library, Redding, Connecticut. Donated from Clemens's library by Clara Clemens Gabrilowitsch in 1910 (MTLAcc, entry #2119).

Copy examined: Clemens's copy, unmarked. Has the red ink Mark Twain Library accession number "2119". Examined in 1970 and again in June 1982.

Seven of these poems composed in a romantic vein are based on characters and symbols in Malory's and Tennyson's tellings of the Camelot legend, including "Ballad of Sir Launcelot," "The Death of Guinevere," "Excaliber," "Morgain," and "Sir Boris." Owing to the date (1886), this volume conceivably could have been among Mark Twain's fund of memories as he began to write *A Connecticut Yankee in King Arthur's Court* (1889).

WILSON, JOSEPH T[HOMAS]. (1836–1891). *The Black Phalanx; A History of the Negro Soldiers of the United States in the Wars of 1775–1812, 1861–'65*. Illus. Hartford, Connecticut: American Publishing Co., 1888. 528 pp.

Source: MTLAcc, entry #558, volume donated by Clemens.

WILSON, WILLIAM HUNTINGTON (1869–1915). *Rafnaland; The Strange Story of John Heath Howard*. New York: Harper & Brothers, 1900. 352 pp.

Source: MTLAcc, entry #1671, volume donated by Clemens.

A balloon voyager discovers a lost colony of Vikings at the North Pole.

WILSON, WOODROW (1856–1924). *A History of the American People. Illustrated with Portraits, Maps, Plans, Facsimiles, Rare Prints, Contemporary Views, Etc.* 5 vols. New York: Harper & Brothers, 1902.

Inscriptions: the front pastedown endpaper of each volume is signed in black ink "S L. Clemens/1902".

Marginalia: vertical pencil lines, some underscorings, and a few notes. Volume I contains pencil markings on pages 23, 34, 50, 52, and 142. In Volume III Clemens wrote "In 1780" on the margin of page 4 where Wilson described international military movements during the period of the American Revolution; there are no other marks in that volume. Page 17 of Volume IV contains pencil marks and corrections.

Catalog: C1951, #20c, 5 vols., $20.

Provenance: formerly in the private collection of Charles W. Sachs, Beverly Hills, California (5 volumes). On 23 February 1987 the set was reported to be in the bookshop of John Fleming, New York City (TS note in MTP). Fleming had apparently owned them since 1984 and offered them for sale for $3,500 (note in Kevin Mac Donnell's collection).

Copies examined: Clemens's copies of all five volumes, when Charles W. Sachs owned them.

On 25 October 1902 Clemens marched in the procession

at Princeton University to install Woodrow Wilson as its president (Hill, *MTGF* (1973), p. 51).

———. [An identical set, also published in 1902.]

Catalog: Ball 2016 inventory, 5 vols., blue cloth, gilt top, rough cut edges, fine condition.

Location: Quarry Farm library shelves, under the supervision of the Mark Twain Archive, Elmira College, Elmira, New York.

This set was available to Clemens during his final visits to Quarry Farm.

———. *Mere Literature, and Other Essays.* Boston: Houghton, Mifflin and Co., 1896. 247 pp.

On Saturday, 4 April 1908, in the excursion boat *Euryalus* off Bermuda, Isabel Lyon noticed that Clemens, despite a rough sea, "sat in a corner of the cabin reading Woodrow Wilson's 'Mere Literature'" (IVL Journals, TS p. 315, MTP). Clemens saw Wilson in Bermuda in 1909, when the two men were photographed together on a golf course (*MFMT*, p. 287, photographs opposite page 222).

Wilson's essays largely consist of truisms. His chapter titled "A Calendar of Great Americans" opens with Alexander Hamilton and Benjamin Franklin and diplomatically concludes with the generation of James Russell Lowell, thereby avoiding the risk of offending by omission any subsequent author.

Michael Shelden, *Mark Twain: Man in White, The Grand Adventure of His Final Years* (New York: Random House, 2010), includes a valuable glimpse of Woodrow Wilson.

WINCHELL, ALEXANDER (1824–1891). *Sketches of Creation: A Popular View of Some of the Grand Conclusions of the Sciences in Reference to the History of Matter and of Life. Together with a Statement of the Intimations of Science Respecting the Primordial Condition and the Ultimate Destiny of the Earth and the Solar System.* Illus. New York: Harper & Brothers, 1903. 445 pp.

Inscription: the front pastedown endpaper is signed and inscribed in black ink: "SL. Clemens/1908/I sent for the 'most recent' geology (this theological treatise is the result), for I had been rereading Hugh Miller (ed. 1857), & wanted to contrast the geology of to-day with the geology of his day. I discovered no contrast. *Now* I find the reason: these 'Sketches' are only recent on the *title-page* (1903); the copyright date shows that they were written in the carboniferous period—a time when grown-up children were still trying to mix fact & fiction: Geology & Theology." Below the copyright notice on the verso of the title page, Clemens underscored in pencil the year 1898 and noted: "A renewal for 14 years."

Marginalia: annotated in pencil and black ink. On page 160 Clemens noted in black ink: "And man was on the earth 200,000 years before God remembered whom it was He built the coal for." Clemens used black ink to comment (on page 161), "This flapdoodle is put forth as 'reasoning.'" On the same page Clemens also wrote: "Yes, all those ages upon ages & aeons upon aeons were spent in preparing the world as a habitation for Man, but that was not the final object in view. The object in view from the very start was to prepare a habitation for the microbe. Man is that habitation. He was only an incident in the majestic plan." In the Appendix (p. 436), Clemens identified Dr. T. S. Hunt ("I knew him") and a scientist named Ramsay ("I know Ramsay"). (Thomas Sterry Hunt [1826–1892]

was an expert in economic geology and applied chemistry. The British chemist William Ramsay [1852–1916] would be awarded the Nobel Prize in 1904.) On the rear free endpaper Clemens commented in pencil: "This would be a very valuable book if its rotten & rancid theology could be squashed out of it" There are numerous other notes and markings. Caroline T Harnsberger quoted the marginalia in *Mark Twain's Views on Religion* (Evanston, Illinois: Schori Press, 1961), p 27. Roger Salomon (*TIH* [1961], p. 50) and Sherwood Cummings ("Mark Twain's Acceptance of Science' [1962]) also reported portions of the marginalia.

Catalog: *C1951*, #28a, $60.

Location: Mark Twain Papers, Bancroft Library, University of California, Berkeley.

Copy examined: Clemens's copy.

Winchell set himself the formidable task of guessing at the origins of the solar system and Earth, tracing the prehistoric periods and ice ages, and pondering whether the Sun will eventually cool. However, a firm belief that an omnipotent and omniscient intelligence keeps alive the massive cycles of life offered comfort to this American geologist. Winchell held professorships in geology, zoology, and botany at the University of Michigan, Vanderbilt University, and other institutions.

J. Michael Pratt, "A Fossil Guide to Mark Twain's Essay 'Was the World Made for Man?,'" *Mark Twain Annual* 3 (2005): 81–89.

WINNER, SEPTIMUS (1827–1902), pseud. "Alice Hawthorne." "What is home without a mother?" (song, published in 1854). Words and music by Winner.

This was one of the "d-------dest, oldest, vilest songs" favored by the ship's choir on board the *America* in December 1866 (NB 7, *N&J* 1: 262). On 23 December 1866 Clemens mentioned hearing "What Is Home Without a Mother?" and other "venerable melodies" (*MTTMB* [1940], p. 28).

WINSLOW, KENELM (1863–1951), ed. *The Home Medical Library.* 6 vols. Illus. New York: Review of Reviews Co., 1907.

Source: MTLAcc, entries #404–409, complete set donated by Clemens.

Dr. Winslow practiced medicine in Boston until 1901, when he moved to Seattle. He led the fight to require the pasteurization of milk. Winslow was the general editor of *The Home Medical Library*, but many other medical specialists contributed chapters.

WINTER, WILLIAM (1836–1917). "The Chieftain" (poem). Clemens wrote to Winter from Hartford on 5 December 1879 to praise "the rhythm, the music, the pathos, the affection, the noble eloquence" of this poem, which "moves me out of all self-control." He tried to read it to Olivia Clemens—"as I do with all things that seem perfect to me—but in each verse there is a rock upon which my voice would be wrecked" (ASSSCL, PH in MTP). Winter noted on the letter that Clemens referred to "The Chieftain." The poet replied to Clemens on 9 December 1879 (MTP).

It is no wonder that "The Chieftain," read at a commemoration of Oliver Wendell Holmes's seventieth birthday that the *Atlantic Monthly* held at the Hotel Brunswick in Boston, nearly brought Clemens to tears; Holmes's *Autocrat of the Breakfast-Table* had been a courting book exchanged between Clemens and Olivia Langdon.

Moreover, the poem acknowledged that Holmes was (mistakenly) classified initially as a lightweight humorist, a situation with which Clemens could identify: "At first we thought him but a jest,/A ray of laughter, quick to fade;/We did not dream how richly blest/In his pure life our lives were made" (Stanza II).

———. *Gray Days and Gold in England and Scotland*. [First edition published in 1892; Clemens's edition has not been established.]

Catalog: ListABP (1910), "Gray Days and Gold, Winter", no additional information provided.

As the title implies, Winter records here his rambles around historical sites, old ruins, and literary landmarks.

———. "Love's Queen" (poem), *Atlantic Monthly* 20.121 (October 1868): 475.

When Clemens wrote to Mary Mason Fairbanks about Olivia Langdon on 13 March 1869, he quoted "that poem in the Atlantic—representing her out of reach—'And all my life shall lift its hands/In earnest longing toward thy face'—/I wasn't going to regard her at *that* distance" (*MTMF*, pp. 85–86; *MTLet* 3: 169).

———. *Old Shrines and Ivy*. New York: Macmillan Co., 1901. 296 pp.

Inscription: presented to Clemens by the author, with a letter from Winter laid in.

Catalogs: ListABP (1910), "Old Shrines and Ivy, Winter"; "Retz Appraisal" (1944), p. 12. Valued at $5.

Provenance: this volume was reported missing before the Mark Twain Papers were removed from Cambridge, Massachusetts ("Deficiencies of Lincoln Warehouse Inventory," Henry E. Huntington Library, San Marino, 3 April 1947, TS copy in MTP).

Location: currently unknown.

A combination of travel narrative and literary criticism, *Old Shrines and Ivy* described literary sites and also discussed prominent authors. The greatest amount of space was devoted to William Shakespeare, but Winter also analyzed the works of Sheridan, Farquhar, Cooper, and Longfellow.

———. *The Poems of William Winter*. Boston: J. R. Osgood and Co., 1881. 169 pp.

Source: MTLAcc, entry #2142, volume donated from Clemens's library by Clara Clemens Gabrilowitsch in 1910.

———. *Shakespeare's England*. [First edition published in 1892; Clemens's edition has not been identified.]

Catalog: ListABP (1910), "Shakespeare's England, Winter", no other information provided.

———. *The Trip to England*. Second edition, revised and enlarged. Illustrated by Joseph Jefferson (1829–1905). Boston: James R. Osgood and Co., 1881. 167 pp. First edition: New York, 1879. [Edition conjectured.]

Evidently Clemens knew about the admiring tribute to Whitelaw Reid—first published in the New York *Tribune*—that Winter included in this book. "Winter's Dedication to Reid," Clemens noted in January 1882 (NB 19, *N&J* 2: 420). It is a little-known fact that the celebrated actor Joe Jefferson was also a talented artist and illustrator. William Winter would publish *The Life and Art of Joseph Jefferson* in 1894.

———. *Wanderers: The Poems of William Winter. New Edition.*

Portrait. New York: Macmillan and Co., 1893. 268 pp.

Inscription: inscribed to Clemens by the author.

Catalogs: ListABP (1910), "Wanderers, Winter"; *C1951*, #80c, listed among volumes signed by Clemens, edition unspecified, $5.

Wanderers included Winter's poetic tributes to Oliver Wendell Holmes, Edgar Allan Poe, Edwin Booth, Lawrence Barrett, Henry Wadsworth Longfellow, Henry Irving, and (two poems) Whitelaw Reid. Mark Twain's Autobiographical Dictation of 11 January 1906 recalled the banquet-speaking abilities of "Willie Winter," dramatic editor of the New York *Tribune*. " During a matter of twenty years I was seldom at a banquet where Willie Winter . . . did not read a charming poem written for the occasion." Twain added some impressions: "There was never any vigor in his poetry, but it was always smooth, wavy, and dainty, happy, choicely phrased, and as good to listen to as music." Winter recited his poems more entertainingly after a sip of champagne, Twain indicated (*AutoMT* 1: 265).

WINTERBOTTOM, THOMAS MASTERMAN (1765–1859). *An Account of the Native Africans in the Neighbourhood of Sierra Leone*. Illus. 2 vols. London: Printed by C. Whittingham and sold by J. Hatchard, 1803. [Publisher conjectured.]

Catalogs: *A1911*, "2 vols., 8vo, calf (rubbed and cracked), Lond. 1803," with a small sheet of notes by Clemens laid in, lot 489, sold for $1.25; *Lexington 1912*, lot 29, sold for $5.

WIRTH, BETTINA (1849–1917), pseud. "August Lienhardt."

Clemens came to know this Austrian journalist and novelist in Vienna in 1897. She was a correspondent for the London *Daily News* and translated some of Bret Harte's stories, but evidently Clemens forgave her for this latter deed. On 17 October 1898 Clemens wrote her a letter explaining certain American idiomatic greetings (ALS, Admirable Books, Hilliard, Ohio, undated catalog, item #13).

Dan Vogel, *Mark Twain's Jews* (Hoboken, New Jersey: KTAV Publishing House, 2006); David H. Fears, *Mark Twain Day by Day*, 3: 96, *passim*.

WISE, JOHN (1808–1879). *Through the Air: A Narrative of Forty Years' Experience as an Aeronaut. Comprising a History of the Various Attempts in the Art of Flying by Artificial Means from the Earliest Period Down to the Present Time. With an Account of the Author's Most Important Air-Voyages and His Many Thrilling Adventures and Hairbreadth Escapes*. Illus. Philadelphia: To-Day Printing and Publishing Co., 1873. 650 pp. [This entry is theoretical; no copy of Wise's book connected to Clemens has survived.]

In Notebook 20 (1882) Clemens wrote about "that (fabled) stratum where, once in, you remain—going neither up nor down for years—forever." Clemens then sketched a yarn about discovering two perpetually hovering balloons, one basket containing the corpse of "Prof. Wise," the other the bodies of "Donaldson & the journalist" (*N&J* 2: 492). Wise disappeared over Lake Michigan during a balloon voyage in 1879. Four years earlier, the balloonist Washington Harrison Donaldson (1840–1875) had died while crossing Lake Michigan with a reporter for the *Chicago Evening Journal*. Clemens was interested in balloon feats, so he may have read Wise's *Through the Air*,

Chapter 21 of which quotes James Glaisher's account of an ascent from Wolverhampton, England in 1862. Glaisher reported that he and his companion were overcome by "total insensibility" for seven minutes when their balloon briefly rose to 37,000 feet (pp. 212–216). Wise's own account of a voyage in 1859 from St. Louis, Missouri to Henderson, New York could have given Mark Twain some details for *Tom Sawyer Abroad* (1894). Wise and his three companions delighted in hallooing the farms they passed over in Illinois during the night, listening to the country watch-dogs "bow-wow" in reply (p. 499). In Chapter 2 of *Tom Sawyer Abroad*, "the moonshine made everything soft and pretty, and the farm-houses looked snug and homeful, and we could hear the farm sounds."

WISEMAN, (CARDINAL) NICHOLAS PATRICK STEPHEN (1802–1865). *Fabiola; or, The Church of the Catacombs. A New Edition.* Popular Catholic Library Series. London: Burns and Oates, 1877. 385 pp.

> **Location:** Mark Twain Library, Redding, Connecticut. Donated from Clemens's library by Clara Clemens Gabrilowitsch in 1910 (MTLAcc, entry #1844).
> **Copy examined:** Clemens's copy, unmarked. Green buckram cover. Has the Mark Twain Library accession number "2917" (the previous number "1844" has been crossed out).
> Wiseman was an English Roman Catholic prelate. His *Fabiola; or, The Church of the Catacombs* recounted the history of early Christian martyrs, including St. Sebastian.

———. *Fabiola; or, The Church of the Catacombs.* New York, Montreal: D. & J. Sadlier & Co., 1878. 385 pp.

> **Location:** currently unknown. Formerly in the Mark Twain Library, Redding, Connecticut.
> **Copy examined:** none. This volume was missing when I inventoried Clemens's books at Redding in 1970. I have relied upon a library card in the files of the Mark Twain Library at Redding in constructing this entry; the card is not specific about whether this volume definitely belonged to Clemens himself or to someone else in his family.

Wise Sayings of the Great and Good. London: Whittaker and Co., 1864. 339. [Another London publisher, George Routledge and Sons, brought out *Wise Sayings of the Great and Good* in an almost identical edition in 1867. The publisher and pages can only be conjectured, since Clemens's copy has never resurfaced.]

> **Inscription:** the front flyleaf is signed, "S. L. Clemens, 1892".
> **Catalog:** *A 1911*, "12mo, cloth, Lond. (ca. 1871)," quotes the signature, lot 490, sold for $3.
> Quotations extracted from the works of famous writers are arranged by topic, such as "Accidents," "Ambition," "Angels," "Families," "Fashions," "Uprightness," "Youth," and "Zeal of the Early Christians." The volume has no index.

WISTER, OWEN (1860–1938). *The Dragon of Wantley, His Rise, His Voracity, and His Downfall: A Romance.* Illustrated by John Stewardson (1858–1896). Philadelphia: J. B. Lipincott Co., 1892. 149 pp. [This burlesque romance promptly went through several additional Lipincott editions; the exact year of Clemens's edition is not known.]

> On 4 August 1895 Clemens wrote to Wister from Helena, Montana during the first stage of his around-the-world lecture tour: "I have taken the Dragon of Wantley away

from my wife & daughter—by violence—& am reading it with a delicate & tingling enjoyment which goes searching & soothing & tickling & carressing [*sic*] all through me everywhere like the balm of Gilead with a whit of Apollinaris in it" (ALS in the Library of Congress; this letter was noticed by Barbara Schmidt, who sent a transcript of it to Alan Gribben on 14 January 2002). Subsequently Ying Xu reprinted Clemens's letter in "Additions to the Mark Twain Library (*American Literary Realism* 46.2 [Winter 2014]: 187–188). Wister wrote in 1928 of his wonderment that his medieval fantasy "brought, as from the sky, a letter from Mark Twain" (Ying Xu, p. 188). *The Dragon of Wantley,* set at Christmastime in the thirteenth century, was a far cry from the best-selling Western novel that would bring Wister his fame, *The Virginian* (1902). Stewardson, an architect who would die a few years later in a skating accident, supplied eye-catching Gothic-styled woodcut illustrations throughout the volume. Later, in the twenty-first century, John Stewardson's ferocious-looking dragon on the front cover of Wister's novel became a vintage image on posters, sweatshirts, and other marketable items.

———. *Lin McLean.* New York: Harper & Brothers, 1908. 304 pp.

> **Source:** MTLAcc, entry #1672, volume donated by Clemens.
> This was Wister's first Western novel. Wister had been in contact with Clemens socially. Clemens's calendar in New York City recorded on 19 December 1900: "Owen Wister coming, 10:30" (NB 43, TS p. 31a). On 2 June 1902 Clemens noted: "Wister will call at 5.30" (NB 45, TS p. 15).

———. *The New Swiss Family Robinson: A Tale for Children of All Ages.* Cambridge, Massachusetts: S. W. Sever and Co., 1882.

> Clemens sent Wister a letter praising these burlesque sketches that Wister had originally written for the Harvard *Lampoon* (Ying Xu, "Additions to the Mark Twain Library," *American Literary Realism* 46.2 [Winter 2014]: 187–188).

WITT, HENRIETTE ELIZABETH (GUIZOT) DE (1829–1908). *Monsieur Guizot in Private Life, 1787–1874. By His Daughter, Madame de Witt.* Authorized Edition. Translated by Mary Charlotte Mair (Senior) Simpson (1825–1907). Illus. Boston: Estes & Lauriat, 1881. 357 pp.

> Brown & Gross, Hartford booksellers, billed Clemens on 1 January 1881 for a purchase made on 22 December 1880: "1 Life Guizot $2.20." Clemens paid the bill on 17 January 1881 (receipt in MTP). The French historian and statesman François Pierre Guillaume Guizot (1787–1874) served as the premier of France prior to the Revolution of 1848. Henriette Elizabeth (Guizot) de Witt was his eldest daughter.

———. [Identical copy.]

> **Inscription:** the front free endpaper is signed in pencil, "Ida C. Langdon/June 25th 1881". [Ida C. Langdon, 1849–1934, was the wife of Charles Jervis Langdon.].
> **Provenance:** bookplate #544 of the "J. Langdon Family Library."
> **Catalog:** Ball 2016 inventory, brown textured cloth, gilt lettering, fair condition, inscribed by Ida C. Langdon.
> **Location:** Quarry Farm library shelves, under the

supervision of the Mark Twain Archive, Elmira College, Elmira, New York.

Copy examined: unmarked copy available to Clemens whenever he visited the Langdon's residence in Elmira. Examined on 26 May 2015.

———. *Motherless; or, A Parisian Family.* Translated from the French by Dinah Maria (Muloch) Craik (1826–1887). New York: Harper & Brothers, 1871. 253 pp.

Source: MTLAcc, entry #1525, volume donated by Clemens.

———. *An Only Sister.* Translated from the French by Dinah Maria (Mulock) Craik (1826–1887). Illus. New York: Harper & Brothers, 1904. 251 pp. [Harper & Brothers first published this book in 1873.]

Source: MTLAcc, entry #504, volume donated by Clemens.

WOLF, KARL (1848–1912). *Geschichten aus Tirol [Stories from Tyrol].* Dritte Auflage. Innsbruck: A. Edlinger's Verlag, 1895. 282 pp.

Inscription: the half-title page is inscribed by Olivia Clemens in ink, "S. L. Clemens/Vienna/1898".

Location: Mark Twain House and Museum, Hartford, Connecticut.

Copy examined: photocopies of the inscription and title page were provided to Alan Gribben by Diana Royce, then Librarian of the Stowe-Day Memorial Library, Hartford, Connecticut, on 3 October 1984. In August 1987 I examined the volume in Hartford. It has no marginalia.

Tirol, also spelled Tyrol, is located in the Austrian Alps.

WOLFE, CHARLES (1791–1823). "The Burial of Sir John Moore after Corunna" (poem, published in 1817).

Minnie M. Brashear discovered and reprinted in 1930 a parody, "The Burial of Sir Abner Gilstrap, Editor of the Bloomington *Republican*," that Clemens published on 23 May 1853 in the Hannibal *Daily Journal.* Mark Twain employed the second line of Wolfe's famous piece to burlesque L. O. Sterns in a dispatch from Carson City on 5 December 1863 (*MTEnt* [1957], pp. 92–95). Because Wolfe wrote this "Burial" poem, Twain classified him in 1865 with "Elegy Gray" and "the grave-yard" poetry (17 June 1865 *Californian*, *LAMT* [1950], p. 142; *ET&S* 2: 195). Twain mentioned Sir John Moore in Notebook 6 (1866, *N&J* 1: 225). In June 1866 Twain combined lines from Wolfe's poem with lines from Byron's "The Destruction of Sennacherib" to construct a jumbled yet vaguely comprehensible creation, "The Burial of Sir John Moore and other parties, subsequently to the Destruction of the Sennacherib," in a letter to the Sacramento *Union* (*MTH* [1947], pp. 411–412). Twain's parody appeared in the 25 October 1866 issue of the Sacramento *Union*, causing Mr. Brown to vomit (*LSI* [1938], pp. 199–200). In "My First Literary Venture" (*Galaxy*, April 1871), Twain related how, as a youth, he wrote an outrageous calumny against a rival newspaper editor, "putting the article into the form of a parody on the 'Burial of Sir John Moore'—and a pretty crude parody it was, too" (*CG* [1961], p. 131).

Lieutenant-General Sir John Moore (1761–1809) heroically engineered a strategic British victory in 1809 against the French army on the Spanish coast during the Peninsular War. Near the end of what became known as the Battle of Corunna, however, Moore was mortally wounded by a cannon ball. His British forces, finding it necessary to

retreat from Napoleon's massive and rapidly advancing infantry, had no choice but to bury him without any ceremony. An Irish country parson, Charles Wolfe, wrote a powerful poem about that scene. This is the concluding stanza: "Slowly and sadly we laid him down,/From the field of his fame fresh and gory;/We carved not a line, and we raised not a stone,/But left him alone with his glory."

Brashear, "Mark Twain's Juvenilia" (1930), pp. 48–49; Brashear, *MTSM* (1934), pp. 135–139; Frear, *MTH* (1947), pp. 411–412; Scott, *OPMT* (1966), pp. 44, 54.

———. "Go! forget me" (song, published in 1845). Melody composed by Joseph Philip Knight (1812–1887).

Among the music on the piano in "The House Beautiful," Chapter 38 of *Life on the Mississippi* (1883), Mark Twain listed "Go, Forget Me, Why Should Sorrow O'er That Brow a Shadow Fling." Those were the first two lines of Wolfe's poem, followed by these: "Go forget me, and to-morrow/Brightly smile and sweetly sing."

WOLLASTON, (REVEREND) HENRY NEWTON (1822–1907).

In Chapter 22 of *Following the Equator* (1897), Mark Twain quotes examples of the Australian aborigine's fortitude "recorded by the Rev. Henry N. Wolloston [*sic*], of Melbourne, who had been a surgeon before he became a clergyman." (Wollaston's name was spelled correctly in the British edition, *More Tramps Abroad*.) Twain found this material in Robert Brough Smyth's *The Aborigines of Victoria* (1878). See the Catalog entry for Smyth's book.

WOLTMANN, ALFRED FRIEDRICH GOTTFRIED ALBERT (1841–1880) and KARL WOERMANN (1844–1933). *History of Ancient, Early Christian, and Mediaeval Painting.* Illus. 2 vols. Volume I was edited by Clara Bell (1834–1927); Volume II was edited by Sidney Colvin (1845–1927). New York: Dodd, Mead & Co. 1880–1885.

Catalog: *A1911*, "Vol. I, imp. 8vo, cloth, N.Y. 1880," with a small sheet of notes by Clemens about the German language laid in, lot 491, Volume I only, sold for $4.50.

Women of the Bible, by Twelve Eminent Divines. Illus. New York: Harper & Brothers, 1902. 188 pp. Includes essays by John White Chadwick (1840–1904), Henry Van Dyke (1852–1933), and others.

Source: MTLAcc, entry #1816, volume donated by Clemens.

WONG CHIN FOO (dates unknown). "Wu Chih Tien, the Celestial Empress: A Chinese Historical Novel," *Cosmopolitan* 6.4 (February 1889): 327–334; 6.5 (March 1889), 477–485; continued serially in monthly installments through the September 1889 issue. In March 1889 Clemens criticized an article by David Ker that appeared in *Cosmopolitan*: "Pity to put that flatulence between the same leaves with that charming Chinese story" (NB 28, *N&J* 3: 457). The March installment of Chin Foo Wong's novel, like the previous chapter, was illustrated by Dan Beard (1850–1941). Set in ancient China, the tale relates how Wu Chih Tien dominates her husband Tung Ko Sung and takes charge of his palace at Chung Ang. Eventually he dies of shame and humiliation at having allowed a woman to come to power. At her court "the flash of gems, the sheen of silks, the glow of jeweled fans, and the waving of many-hued plumes met the eye wherever it turned, and the air throbbed with sensuous music and was stirred with continual song" (pp. 479–480). "From the trees hung festoons of colored lanterns like luminous fruit, and the senses of the revelers reeled and became drunk" (p. 480). She closed the temples and the schools of Con Fu Chi; she increased taxes to support the royal parties; and she tortured and killed dissenters. Eventually a claimant to the usurper's throne appears in Li Sing Ming, a young son of the deceased king.

Dan Beard traced Clemens's admiration for his drawings to this story, recalling that "Mr. Fred Hall, Mark Twain's partner in the publishing business, came to my studio . . . and told me that Mark Twain wanted to meet the man who had made the illustrations for a Chinese story in the *Cosmopolitan* and he wanted that man to illustrate his new book, *A Connecticut Yankee in King Arthur's Court*" (*Hardly a Man Is Now Alive: The Autobiography of Dan Beard* [New York: Doubleday, Doran & Co., 1939], p. 336).

For a helpful analysis of the story and its author, see Hsuan L. Hsu, "A Connecticut Yankee in the Court of Wu Chih Tien," *Commonplace: the journal of early American life* 11:1 (October 2010), accessed 22 March 2020, URL: http://commonplace.online/article/a-connecticut-yankee-in-the-court-of-wu-chih-tien/

WOOD, CHARLES ERSKINE SCOTT (1852–1944). *A Masque of Love*. 500 copies printed. Chicago: W. M. Hill, 1904. 87 pp.

Source: MTLAcc, entry #2127a, volume donated from Clemens's library by Clara Clemens Gabrilowitsch in 1910.

Joseph H. Twichell sent Clemens an unidentified "periodical containing an article by our friend Lt. Wood" [Wood was an officer at West Point] on 17 April 1881 (*LMTJHT*, p. 108). In 1882 Wood assisted in the discreet publication of Mark Twain's bawdy *1601*. Clemens wrote to Wood on 7 June 1901 from New York City, lamenting, "I am so sorry you interred that noble poem in an obscure publication" (ALS, Huntington). Possibly Clemens referred to Wood's "Ode to Freedom," a poem published in 1901. A former railroad attorney, Wood became, among other things, an anti-imperialist activist, an advocate for Native Americans (especially the Nez Perce), and a painter of landscapes and Native Americans.

On 31 October 1904 Clemens wrote to Wood again: "I have read 'A Masque of Love' with strong pleasure. It is a beautiful poem & wise & deep. What Alp shall you subdue next? You were an able instructor of West Point lads in the science of war; then you took up the law & distinguished yourself in that profession; & now you have proven that you are a poet" (ALS, Bancroft Library, University of California, Berkeley). Wood's *A Masque of Love* was a dramatic poem (written as much in prose as in poetry) consisting of three parts in which speakers ruminated about life, death, and love. The work asserted that death, like life and love, is "blessed," and that dreams and books enable us to outlive our mortal limitations. Clemens wrote to Joseph H. Twichell on 1 June 1905 about Wood, whom Clemens had met in Portland, Oregon in 1895. "He has written some poetry, & it is good and on a high plane." Twichell had sent Clemens an article by Wood, and Clemens responded that he had "read a little of his article which you sent. . . . I like it" (*LMTJHT*, pp. 365–366).

Robert Hamburger's *Two Rooms: The Life of Charles Erskine Scott Wood* (Lincoln: University of Nebraska Press, 1998) portrayed the "genteel anarchism" (p. 143) of this gifted raconteur of the Far West (he resided in Portland, Oregon

and later Los Gatos, California) who strongly espoused free speech and individual rights. Page 73 alluded to Clemens.

WOOD, CHARLOTTE DUNNING (1859–1898), later Charlotte Dunning (Wood) Morse, pseud. "Charlotte Dunning." *Upon a Cast*. New York: Harper & Brothers, 1885. 330 pp.

Source: MTLAcc, entry #114, volume donated by Clemens.

Wood's biographical facts have proved difficult for literary scholars to trace, owing to her pseudonym, her marriage to Edwin Lind Morse (1857–1923), and her relatively early death. In addition to her society novel *Upon a Cast*, Wood wrote two other books, *A Step Aside* (1886) and *Cabin and Gondola* (1886).

WOOD, EUGENE (1860–1923). *Back Home*. Illustrated by A[rthur]. B[urdett]. Frost (1851–1928). New York: McClure, Phillips & Co., 1905. 286 pp.

Source: MTLAcc, entry #233, volume donated by Clemens.

A representative of McClure, Phillips & Company wrote to Clemens in 1905: "Have you any time to read books nowadays? If you have, would you give a little of it to this book, BACK HOME, by Eugene Wood, which we are sending to you? It is a series of reminiscent sketches dealing with any American rural village about twenty years ago; and the reviewer of the New York Sun said: 'We are sure that no one will read Mr. Wood's sketches with greater delight than that infallible authority on the American boy. the author of Huckleberry Finn and Tom Sawyer" (Vivian Burnett to SLC, New York City, 27 September 1905, MTP). Wood's *Back Home* contained chapters titled "The Old Red School-house," "The Sabbath-School," "The Swimming Hole," and "The County Fair."

WOOD, FRANCES FISHER. *Infancy and Childhood*. New York: Harper & Brothers, 1897. 154 pp.

Source: MTLAcc, entry #1384, volume donated by Clemens.

Infancy and Childhood instructed expectant parents about setting up the nursery, avoiding contagious diseases, using milk as a food, developing a sleep system, and other related subjects.

WOOD, JOHN GEORGE (1827–1889). *Common Shells of the Sea-shore* (published in London in 1865).

Clemens notified Olivia from London on 9 December 1873 that he had "put matters in motion about the Wood 'Shells'"—evidently an effort to help Elisha Bliss, Jr. explore the idea of publishing an American edition of Wood's monograph (*MTLet* 5: 497). There was no progress with that idea.

———. *Nature's Teachings; Human Invention Anticipated by Nature*. Boston: Roberts Brothers, 1885. 533 pp.

Source: MTLAcc, entry #1978, volume donated from Clemens's library by Clara Clemens Gabrilowitsch in 1910.

———. *Our Living World; An Artistic Edition of the Rev. J. G. Wood's Natural History of Animate Creation. Revised and Adapted to American Zoology by Joseph B. Holder [1824–1888]*. 83 engraved plates, 42 chromolithographed plates by Louis Prang (1824–1909). Original half red morocco over marbled boards, gilt, marbled endpapers, edges stained red. Red cloth slipcase. 3 vols. New York: Selmar Hess, 1885. [Three volumes are bound as six. Volumes V-VI are rebacked with remnants of the original spines; one front free endpaper has been repaired. Each volume contains the bookbinder's ticket of Case, Lockwood & Brainard Company, Printers and Binders,

Hartford, Connecticut.]

Inscription: the first four volumes are inscribed by Clemens, "Clara Clemens/Christmas/1885/From Papa." Volumes V and VI are not inscribed; perhaps the bookbinder could not finish their extensive restoration before Christmas. Clara Clemens Gabrilowitsch's library system number (during her residence in Detroit) is visible on the front free endpapers of all six volumes.

Catalogs: *C1951*, #2c, listed among books signed by Clemens, edition unspecified; *Sotheby's 2003*, #248, $3,500.

Provenance: purchased by Nick Karanovich (1938–2003) of Fort Wayne, Indiana from Randall House Rare Books, San Francisco, California, on 18 October 1983 for $3,300 (photocopy of the invoice sent to Alan Gribben by Nick Karanovich in January 1984). Acquired by bookseller Robert Slotta at or after the Sotheby's 2003 auction. Slotta sold the volume to Kevin Mac Donnell in 2008.

Location: collection of Kevin Mac Donnell, Austin, Texas (email, Mac Donnell to Alan Gribben, 5 August 2008).

Copy examined: Clara Clemens's copy, a gift from Clemens. Viewed in 2003 prior to the Sotheby auction.

Though ordained as an Anglican priest, Wood turned to a career as a writer and lecturer on natural history. His books were part of a movement popularizing science, especially the fields of zoology and anthropology.

———. *The Uncivilized Races; or, Natural History of Man; Being a Complete Account of the Manners and Customs, and the Physical, Social, and Religious Condition and Characteristics, of the Uncivilized Races of Men, Throughout the Entire World. With Over 700 Fine Illustrations.* 2 vols. Tall, thick 8vo, half dark brown morocco. Hartford, Connecticut: American Publishing Co., 1870.

Marginalia: Clemens made numerous penciled notes and markings throughout Volume I; he made some pencil markings (but no notes) in Volume II. There are several ink markings in Volume I—pages 267 and 268 (purple-ink marks beside the description of a Bosjesman tribesman), and page 654 (brown-ink mark at marriage customs among the Dahomans). Clemens's penciled markings in Volume I are the most prolific in pages 1–129, where they often occur on nearly every other page. He deleted with large penciled "X's" some portions of the text on pages 83, 84, 85, and 89. Notes appear in Volume I on pages 3, 4, 7 (concerning the Kaffirs's hospitality and desire for company), 10, 38, 65, 73, 90, 124, 408, 411, 419, 425, 445, 446, 447, and 608. On page 3, Clemens noted "opinion of color" and "*affectation*" beside Wood's statement that Europeans have difficulty admiring white skin upon their return home after living with Kaffir tribes. Wood asserted on page 4 that "the newly-born infant of a Kaffir is nearly as pale as that of a European," but Clemens expressed skepticism, marking the sentence and writing, "a lie, no doubt". Below that Clemens wrote "Kaffir *not* a Negro" beside Wood's description of the Kaffirs' hair. On that same page, next to Wood's report that the missionaries' advice "to take no thought for the morrow" had no effect on the natives, Clemens wrote "good." Clemens made five vertical marks and brackets down the margin of page 38, and near Wood's description of the Kaffirs's smearing themselves with rancid grease, unbothered by the powerful odor, Clemens wrote, "See Montaigne."

Clemens made note (writing "both sexes valuable" in the margin) of Wood's observation that female children are respected, unlike their treatment in many other societies. Regarding the luxuries enjoyed by "millionaire" Kaffirs who owned cattle (p. 65), Clemens quipped, "Warwick. Vanderbilt." (The wealthy Vanderbilt family dominated Warwick, Rhode Island and built enormous summer homes in nearby Newport, Rhode Island.) Wood reported on page 90 that a Kaffir man's "praise-name" repeatedly changes, and Clemens noted in the margin, "names change in Japan also." "The ingenious King", Clemens wrote on page 408 where Wood related how a Balonda tribal king kept his population in check by periodically destroying villages and enslaving their inhabitants. On page 419 Wood depicted a Balonda ritual he witnessed, and Clemens jotted, "All Africans imbibe[?] each other's blood to cement friendship." Wood's description on page 425 of the wailing at funerals reminded Clemens of his visit to the Sandwich Islands; "like the S. I.," he jotted. There are many notes by Clemens on page 445, including the word "hideous" about a bizarre funeral ceremony and (next to an exaggerated account of lions guarding one tribe): "This is very human egotism." He made two notes on pages 446: "The idea of their believing power to abide in such things" and "After idea of beauty—& Chinese." "At a description of the corpulence admired in Wahuman women on page 447, Clemens drew three vertical lines and wrote, "obesity". "Absurd & impossible," Clemens pronounced on page 608 regarding Wood's statement that the gorilla produces a booming sound by beating on a hollow tree trunk before attacking. The index of Volume I contains a pencil mark at the subject of marriage among the Bubes (referring to p. 682).

Two pages of manuscript are pasted in Volume I: that on the front free endpaper is written in French, probably by one of Clemens's daughters; the other, labeled "K," is in Clemens's hand and outlines information to be found on two specified pages about the Kaffir's military organization: "119—Deformed infants are usually killed"; "120—Army made up in 2 great divisions—married men and 'boys.' (How about the 'boy' whose wife watched his arms for the shadows?)"; "120—Regiments are formed & named according to physical characteristics of the men. Elephant, lion, springbok, &c.—stature, daring, activity, &c."; "120—Concerning the uniform of the 26 regiments & the harem guard"; "120—The K's have several military ranks—not one mere chief, like our poor stupid Indians."

Catalogs: *A1911*, "2 vols., royal 8vo, half morocco, Hartford, 1870, . . . many marginal notes and marked paragraphs by Mr. Clemens, chiefly those relating to the marriage customs and rites of the tribes," with two pages of notes by Clemens laid in, one in French and one in English, lot 492, sold for $4.50; Walpole Galleries (New York City), Sale 332, 8 July 1924, "2 vols.," lot 10; American Art Association (New York City), Anderson Galleries, Sale 492 (5 February 1925), "2 vols., thick 8vo, half dark brown morocco," has the *A1911* sale label, lot 114, sold for $20.

Location: Special Collections, University Library, University of Nevada, Reno. Purchased in 1963 from Mrs. Louis A.

(Haydee U.) Zeitlin of Santa Monica, California.

Copies examined: Clemens's copies, worn from his usage, in Reno, Nevada. The *A1911* sale label is affixed at the foot of the front pastedown endpaper. Photocopies of the title page and Clemens's marginal notes are on file in the Mark Twain Papers, Bancroft Library, University of California at Berkeley, sent in May 1976 by the Special Collections curator at the University of Nevada, Reno.

Elisha Bliss, Jr. was remiss about supplying Clemens with Wood's book as well as others; on 29 October 1870 Clemens wrote from Buffalo to remind Bliss that he was suffering "*especially* for the 'Uncivilized Races,' and [you] never say 'boo' about sending them" and he urged Bliss at least to send this particular book (*MTLet* 4: 217). In Chapter 19 of *Roughing It* (1872) Mark Twain denounced the Goshoot Indians as the wretchedest type of mankind I have ever seen. . . . Indeed, I have been obliged to look the bulky volumes of Wood's *Uncivilized Races of Men* clear through in order to find a savage tribe degraded enough to take rank with the Goshoots. I find but one people fairly open to that shameful verdict. It is the Bosjesmans (Bushmen) of South Africa." In that same chapter of *Roughing It,* Twain also mentions "the Kytches of Africa"; Wood had declared: "It is hardly possible to conceive a more miserable and degraded set of people than the Kytch tribe" (*Uncivilized Races,* 1: 439). In a chapter discarded from *A Tramp Abroad* (1880), Twain relied heavily on Wood's book in writing about courtship and marriage practices among primitive tribes (see *N&J* 2: 314 n. 46); he may also have been citing *Uncivilized Races* when (in the same abandoned chapter) he quoted from page 84 of the second volume of a book he referred to as "Kaffir Life" (MS p. 88, Box 6, No. 7, MTP). Chapter 21 of *Following the Equator* (1897) quotes from Wood's account of the Australian aboriginal's feats at throwing the *weet-weet*; the quotation comes from *Uncivilized Races,* 1: 730. Twain misspells Wood's name there, alluding to "Rev. J. G. Woods."

Rogers, ed., *Roughing It* (Iowa-California Edition, 1972), p. 567; McNutt, "Mark Twain and the American Indian" (1978); Smith and Branch, eds., *Roughing It* (Works of Mark Twain Edition, 1993), pp. 605–606.

WOOD, JOHN TURTLE (1821–1890). *Discoveries at Ephesus, Including the Site and Remains of the Great Temple of Diana.* Illus. London: Longmans, Green, 1877. 285 pp. [Edition conjectured.]

David Roessel ("Mark Twain at Ephesus," *Mark Twain Journal* 27.1 [Spring 1989]: 27–31) described Mark Twain's interest in the excavations of the amateur archaeologists John Turtle Wood and Heinrich Schliemann (1822–1890) as reflected in Twain's letters to the *Alta California* and his later account of visiting Ephesus in *The Innocents Abroad* (1869). However, there is no tangible evidence that Clemens followed up by purchasing or reading Wood's eventual book explicating the finds they had unearthed. If the book ever subsequently come to his attention he probably would have acquired it, but that is all that can be said. See also the Catalog entry for Edward Falkener's *Ephesus and the Temple of Diana.*

WOOD, ROBERT WILLIAMS (1868–1955). *Animal Analogues. Verses and Illustrations.* Denatured Series, No. 24. San Francisco and New York: Paul Elder and Co., [cop. 1908]. 28 pp.

Inscription: signed and inscribed "S. L. Clemens, 1909, Stormfield. A cunning book."

Catalog: *A1911,* "square 12mo, boards, uncut, San Fran. [1908]," quotes the signature, lot 493.

Verses and drawings of humorous nonsense. For example, a doggerel poem accompanies whimsical cartoons likening "The Puss/The Octo-pus."

WOOD, WILLIAM (1774–1857). *General Conchology; or, A Description of Shells, Arranged According to the Linnean System.* Illus. London: Printed for John Booth, 1835.

Inscription: Clemens inscribed the flyleaf, "Susie Clemens, Oct. 1881/from Papa."

Provenance: formerly in the Mark Twain Library, Redding, Connecticut. Its card catalog supplied the inscription.

Catalog: *Mott 1952,* item #95, $27.50.

WOODBERRY, GEORGE EDWARD (1855–1930). "The Orator" (poem), *Century Magazine* 57.4 (February 1899): 630.

"And is it the Booth-Memorial poet that did 'The Orator?' It's good; & contains a nut which will break the teeth of any religion that tries to crack it" (SLC to Richard Watson Gilder, Vienna, 2 February 1899, private collection of Rosamond Gilder, PH in MTP). Woodberry's poem consisted of only four lines: "I saw him stand upon the Judgment-Day/Who in his life all human wrath had braved,/The appealing angel in his voice, and say:/'If but one soul be lost, how is man saved?'"

WOODBRIDGE, WILLIAM CHANNING (1794–1845) and **EMMA (HART) WILLARD** (1787–1870). *Woodbridge and Willard's Universal Geography . . . Accompanied by Modern and Ancient Atlases.* New edition, revised and enlarged. Illus. Hartford, Connecticut: Belknap and Hammersley, [1844]. [Edition conjectured. The first edition was published in 1824; the tenth edition appeared in 1842. The edition owned by Clemens's father is undetermined.]

John Marshall Clemens's library included a copy of "Woodbridge & Williams [*sic*], Geography" valued at .12½¢, according to the appraisal of his personal property filed with the Marion County Probate Court on 21 May 1847 (McDermott, "Mark Twain and the Bible" [1968], p. 198).

WOODBURY, W[ILLIAM]. H[ENRY]. (1809–1888). *A New Method of Learning the German Language: Embracing Both the Analytic and Synthetic Modes of Instruction; Being a Plain and Practical Way of Acquiring the Art of Reading, Speaking, and Composing German.* New York: Ivison, Phinney, Blakeman & Co., 1864. 523 pp. [Publisher and pages conjectured but virtually certain.]

Inscription: the flyleaf is signed, "S. L. Clemens."

Catalog: *A1911,* "12mo, half roan (back torn off, loose), N.Y. 1864," quotes the signature, lot 494, sold for .75¢.

WOODHEAD, GERMAN SIMS (1855–1921). *Bacteria and Their Products.* Illus. The Contemporary Science Series, Volume 14. London: Walter Scott Publishing Co.; New York: Charles Scribner's Sons, [1903]. 459 pp.

Marginalia: the text contains no annotations, but some-one drew vertical pencil lines beside seven titles in The Contemporary Science Series booklist at the rear of the volume: P. Mantegazza, *Physiognomy and Expression*; Havelock Ellis, *The Criminal* and *Man and Woman;*

Albert Moll, *Hypnotism*; Sidney E. Hartland, *The Science of Fairy Tales*; J. M. Guyan, *Education and Heredity*; and Cesare Lombroso, *The Man of Genius*. On the rear free endpaper Clemens or someone else computed figures in pencil. Other fragmentary notes in pencil on the same end-paper do not appear to be Clemens's.

Provenance: unknown. This volume contains none of the markings—blue-penciled numbers, red labels, or black-penciled notes—by which the executors of the Mark Twain Estate customarily designated Clemens's library books. It also seems curious that the "Retz Appraisal" (1944) did not refer to this book. Moreover, it was unusual for Clemens not to sign or annotate a work of this nature.

Location: Mark Twain Papers, Berkeley, California.

Copy examined: a copy presumably belonging to Clemens, although corroborating proof does not exist.

This book might have been one of the sources for Mark Twain's list of bacterial species and human diseases in his working notes evidently related to "Three Thousand Years Among the Microbes," a manuscript written in 1905 (Paine 88, MTP). Twain incorporated many details about bacteria in that fragmentary piece (see, for example, *WWD?*, pp. 517–528). He also referred in other works to the attributes as well as the ill effects of bacteria.

WOODMAN, H[ANNAH]. REA (1870–1951). *The Noahs Afloat; An Historical Romance.* New York: Neale Publishing Co., 1905. 323 pp.

Source: MTLAcc, entry #509, volume donated by Clemens.

Woodman took a whimsical look at the problems confronting the Biblical Noah's family, including Japheth and Ham, as they transported their ark of animals through incessant rains. As a child Woodman was captured (and released) by Arapaho Native Americans near Wichita, Kansas. She went on to earn a master's degree in English, undertake additional graduate studies, and teach at various colleges before moving back to Wichita in 1927.

WOODS, MARGARET LOUISA (BRADLEY) (1856–1945). *The Invader; A Novel.* New York: Harper & Brothers, 1907. 319 pp.

Source: MTLAcc, entry #1213, volume donated by Clemens.

An English writer of poetry and novels, Woods was married to Henry George Woods, the President of Trinity College in Oxford. Here she produced an eerily disturbing science fiction novel about mysterious and monstrous transformations.

WOODWORTH, SAMUEL (1785–1842). "The bucket" (song, published in 1826). Better known as "The old oaken bucket." Melody from an earlier ballad, "Araby's daughter" (c. 1824), composed by George Kiallmark (1781–1835).

Around 1873 or 1874 Clemens parodied this song in an undated letter to Charles Warren Stoddard, replacing the line "How dear to my heart are the scenes of my childhood" with "How sick to my soul are the scenes of my beer-hood" (Huntington, TS in MTP). On 6 September 1901 Clemens wrote to Henry H. Rogers, suggesting a parody which would begin, "The old broken Mugwump,/ The iron-bound Mugwump," and asked Rogers, "Do you remember the words of the Old Oaken Bucket? If you do, and I were near you, I'd milk you. By and by I will send to Harper for it" (*MTHHR*, pp. 469–470). On 30 November 1902 Clemens recalled his parody: "The old

broken Mugwump, the iron-clad M, the Moss-covered M that's pointed for—" (NB 45, TS p. 34).

WOOLSEY, JANE STUART (1830–1891). *Hospital Days.* "Printed for Private Use." New York: D. Van Nostrand, 1868. 180 pp. [Edition conjectured; the same publisher reprinted the book anonymously in 1870.]

Woolsey's book recounted her experiences in a Union field hospital improvised in a former divinity school during the Civil War. Though some scenes are amusing, she also quoted the poignant last words and letters of dying soldiers. In a letter of 22 September 1875 (*MTLet* 6: 542) Clemens complained to William Dean Howells about "an entirely gratuitous addition by Mr. Bliss" to the proofs for *Sketches, New and Old* (1875). Clemens wrote to Elisha Bliss, Jr. on 5 November 1875 from Hartford to ask, "Didn't you make that correction of the paragraph smouched from 'Hospital Days?'" (*MTLet* 6: 586). This apparent misunderstanding between the author and his publisher provoked a series of efforts by scholars to get to the bottom of the problem. The manuscript of Mark Twain's "From 'Hospital Days'" credits Woolsey as his source, although her name has been crossed through (MS, Yale University, PH in MTP). Twain's sketch relates a soldier's public account of an errant life, capped by his attributing the catalogue of sins to his flabbergasted friend who is seated nearby. Twain wrote the piece from a third-person point of view that underscores his dependence on Woolsey's narrative; the second sentence of the manuscript, for instance, reads: "I was present when a Defender <of his Country> rose (her customary name for Uncle Sam's soldier-lads). . . ." In an instructive note, Jacob Blanck—"Mark Twain's 'Sketches New and Old.'" *Publishers' Weekly* 132 (30 October 1937): 1740–41—disclosed that the first state of the first edition of Twain's *Sketches, New and Old* (1875) contained a passage from page 77 of Woolsey's book; as a consequence, Twain's publisher apologized in an erratum slip and withdrew the entire sketch from subsequent editions. Blanck also convincingly argued that Woolsey's linking of the Capitol dome in Washington with the splendor of a February ice-storm (*Hospital Days*, p. 84) later resulted in Twain's mental association of the breath-taking architectural achievement of the Taj Mahal with nature's ice-storms (*FE* [1897], Ch. 23), though Twain could not recall the source of this suggestion. Henry Nash Smith and William M. Gibson discussed the facts known about Woolsey's book and Mark Twain's sketch (*MTHL*, pp. 863–864). See also *Early Tales & Sketches* 1: 633, 643–644, 649, 673; *Early Tales & Sketches* 2: 581; *MTLet* 6: 587 n. 7.

WOOLSEY, SARAH CHAUNCEY (1835–1905), pseud. "Susan Coolidge." *Last Verses.* Boston: Little, Brown, and Co., 1906. 167 pp.

Inscription: the front pastedown endpaper is signed, "S. L. Clemens, 1907."

Catalog: *A1911*, "12mo, cloth, gilt top, uncut, Bost. 1906," quotes the signature, lot 111.

Provenance: offered for sale on eBay, item number 7025757352, April 2006, contains the *A1911* sale label, "separation starting between inside front cover and end sheet, . . . water staining on the inside front cover and the inside end sheet," nine photographs of the volume are provided, starting bid $3,750.

Location: currently unknown.

Clemens praised and quoted from a poem in this posthumous collection, "Helen Keller," in his Autobiographical Dictation of 17 January 1907. Susan Coolidge, he said, caught "with such subtle pathos and charm" the young Helen Keller's habitation of "a happy and benignant spot/ Where kindness reigns, and jealousy is not." However, since that earlier period, Clemens deduced, Keller has "lost that gracious world, and now inhabits the one we all know—and deplore" (*AutoMT*, p. 375).

———. [An identical copy.]

Source: MTLAcc, entry #2049, volume donated from Clemens's library by Clara Clemens Gabrilowitsch in 1910.

———. *The New Year's Bargain*. Illus. Boston: Roberts Bros., 1872. 231 pp.

Source: MTLAcc, entry #442, volume donated by Clemens.

———. *Nine Little Goslings*. Original tan pictorial cloth, gilt. Boston: Roberts Brothers, 1892.

Inscription: "1893/A Merry Christmas to/My dear daughter Ida/C. J. Langdon." [A gift from Clemens's brother-in-law Charles Langdon to Clemens's niece Ida Langdon.]

Location: collection of Kevin Mac Donnell, Austin, Texas. Purchased from the Langdon family (Mac Donnell to Alan Gribben, 30 August 2017). No markings reported.

———. *What Katy Did: A Story*. Boston: Roberts Brothers, 1872. [Edition conjectured.]

This was the first of five books that Woolsey wrote about the eldest daughter, high-spirited Katy, in the motherless family of a physician father who was aided in rearing his children by a housekeeper, Izzie, and an invalid, Cousin Helen. Mark Twain pointed out in a letter of December 1872 to the *Literary World* the resemblance of a passage in Woolsey's novel for girls to Twain's comical depiction of a boy's journal in Chapter 59 of *The Innocents Abroad* (1869) (*MTLet* 5: 232).

WOOLSON, CONSTANCE FENIMORE (1840–1894). *Jupiter Lights; A Novel*. New York: Harper & Brothers, 1900. 347 pp.

Source: MTLAcc, entry #1673, volume donated by Clemens.

One wishes that Clemens had left behind some comments about this surprisingly unsentimental (for its era) novel. Eve Bruce confronts alcoholism, mental illness, domestic abuse, and post-Civil War race relations.

Caroline Gebhard, "Romantic Love and Wife-Battering in Constance Fenimore Woolson's *Jupiter Lights*," in *Constance Fenimore Woolson's Nineteenth Century: Essays*, ed. Victoria Brehm (Detroit: Wayne State University Press, 2001), pp. 83–96.

WORCESTER, JOSEPH EMERSON (1784–1865). *A Dictionary of the English Language*. Philadelphia: J. B. Lippincott & Co., 1882. 2058 pp.

Source: MTLAcc, entry #1828, volume donated from Clemens's library by Clara Clemens Gabrilowitsch in 1910.

WORDSWORTH, WILLIAM (1770–1850). "I Travelled among Unknown Men" (poem, published in 1807).

"Mighty glad to hear old Twichell is back. I want to hear him howl about the <for> 'strange, strange lands beyond the sea'" (SLC to OLC, Haverhill, Massachusetts, 15 November 1871, *MTLet* 4: 491). Wordsworth's poem opens with the lines "I travelled among unknown men,/

In lands beyond the sea."

———. "Lines Composed a Few Miles above Tintern Abbey" (poem, published in *Lyrical Ballads* in 1798).

Early in May 1856 Sam Clemens wrote a good-natured spoof of this poem, titling it "Lines Suggested by a Reminiscence, and Which You Will Perhaps Understand" and addressing it to Ann Virginia Ruffner. The Hannibal, Missouri *Evening Courier-Post* eventually published the piece on 6 March 1935, referring to a copy discovered in an autograph album (*ET&S* 1: 120).

———. "Ode on the Intimations of Immortality" (poem, published in 1807).

Mark Twain echoed Wordsworth's phrasing ("The child is father of the Man") in the closing sentence of "The Babies" toast at the 13 November 1879 banquet to General Ulysses S. Grant at the Chicago Palmer House—"And if the child is but a prophecy of the man" (SLC to OLC, 14 November 1879, *MTL* [1917], p. 371; *MTSpk* [1976], p. 133).

Liljegren, "Revolt Against Romanticism" (1945), pp. 31–35, 58–59; Stone, *IE* (1961), p. 270; Baetzhold, *MT&JB* (1970), pp. 278–279, 376 n. 5.

———. "On the Power of Sound" (poem, published in 1828).

Clara Clemens listed this title in her undated commonplace book (Paine 150, MTP).

———. *Poems of Nature and Sentiment*. Illus. 8vo, full tan morocco, gilt back, raised bands, gilt and blind stamping on sides, gilt edges. Philadelphia: E. H. Butler & Co., 1867. 124 pp.

Inscription: the half-title page is inscribed "S. L. C." in pencil in the upper left-hand corner. It appears to be an early hand of Clemens or possibly Olivia Langdon. Below that someone else has written in pencil, "Presented 1887". A bookseller's description is pasted in at the front of the book identifying it as belonging to Mark Twain's personal library. A bookplate has been removed from the front pastedown endpaper.

Catalog: Union Galleries, Sale 52, 17 December 1935, "From the library of Mark Twain, bearing, on half-title, the following in his handwriting: 'S. L. C. Presented 1887.' Choice copy, in a handsome binding," lot 63, sold for $2.50.

Source: photocopies and an email sent to Alan Gribben on behalf of "a patron" by Henry Sweets of the Mark Twain Boyhood Museum in Hannibal, 9 November 2006.

Location: collection of Kevin Mac Donnell, Austin, Texas. Purchased in March 2007 (Mac Donnell to Alan Gribben, 13 March 2007).

Source: supplementary description sent to Alan Gribben by Mac Donnell on 28 August 2017. Mac Donnell reported no markings in the text.

———. *The Poetical Works of Wordsworth*. New York: Hurst & Co., n.d. 707 pp. [Hurst & Co. published an edition with this specified number of pages (707) in 1898. It seems probable that this was the date of Clemens's edition.]

Source: MTLAcc, entry #2121, volume donated from Clemens's library by Clara Clemens Gabrilowitsch in 1910.

———. "She Dwelt among the Untrodden Ways" (poem, published in 1800).

In a letter Clemens wrote in July 1907 to Miss Joy Agnew, he quoted from this "Lucy" poem, "Fair as a star when only one/Is shining in the sky" (*MTL*, p. 808). He inserted that letter into his Autobiographical Dictation of

31 August 1907 (*AutoMT* 3: 125).

Baetzhold, *MT&JB* (1970), p. 279.

WORK, HENRY CLAY (1832–1884). "Grandfather's clock" (song, cop. 1876). Words and music by Work.

"'Grandfather's Clock' & 'The Sweet By & By' were sweet & pretty & were able to move one—at first; but when everybody & every*thing* persecuted you with them you learned to loathe the originals as well as the copies" (NB 17 [November 1878], *N&J* 2: 240). Work's enormously popular song repeated two lines so often they became familiar: "But it stopped, short, never to go again/When the old man died."

———. "Marching through Georgia" (song, published in 1865).

Mark Twain was ambivalent and sometimes antagonized by the enduring popularity of this song. "'Mark Twain' on the Ballad Infliction" (San Francisco *Californian*, 4 November 1865) mentions this song (*MTWY*, p. 195). While Twain was visiting the (pro-Union) Sandwich Islands in 1866, he jotted an entry in Notebook 6: "I wish Sherman had marched through Alabama" (*N&J* 1: 228). Work's song, Twain declared in the 28 April 1866 issue of the Sacramento *Weekly Union*, is "a calamity"; even the natives in Honolulu are "singing it in their own barbarous tongue!" (*LSI* [1938], p. 51). In December 1866 he complained in Notebook 7 about the ship's choir on the *America*, who sang this and other of the "d—dest, oldest, vilest songs" (*N&J* 1: 262). On 23 December 1866 he reported the agony of hearing the ship's choir sing "When We Go Marching Through Georgia" and other "venerable melodies" (*MTTMB* [1940], p. 28). Chapter 65 of Mark Twain's *Roughing It* (1872) recalls his hearing the tune sung in Honolulu in the Hawaiian language. When Twain "heard the thousand voices lift that chorus" on 14 November 1879 at the Army of the Tennessee banquet for General U. S. Grant, however, he wrote William Dean Howells that it was "grand times, my boy, grand times!" (SLC to WDH, Hartford, 17 November 1879, *MTHL*, p. 280). Work died in Hartford in 1884; in 1887 the sculptor Karl Gerhardt inquired whether Twain and others would sponsor his creating a civic statue to honor the songwriter (Notebook 27, *N&J* 3: 335). The bands play "When We Were Marching Through Georgia" in Chapter 13 of "A Horse's Tale" (1906). In 1906 Twain said, "I remember how General Sherman used to rage and swear over 'When we were marching through Georgia,' which was played at him and sung at him everywhere he went" (2 December 1906 AD, *MTE*, p. 128; *AutoMT* 2: 302).

S&B (1967), p. 39.

———. "Kingdom coming," also known as "Say, Darkies, hab you seen Ole Massa?" (Civil War song, words and music by Work.)

Clemens was furious when William Gillis and a group of other young men mischievously serenaded him outside his bedroom window in Jackass Hill, California with this song and two other tunes popular in the mid-1860s (William Robert Gillis [1849–1929], *Memories of Mark Twain and Steve Gillis [1838–1918]: Personal Recollections of the Famous Humorist* [Sonora, California: Printed by The Banner, 1924], p. 38; see also *MTLet* 1: 332). Clemens, then still sympathetic to the Confederate cause, would

have been offended by Work's lyrics, which portrayed enslaved African Americans (kept illiterate by laws prevailing in most Southern states) as gloating because their plantation owner had disappeared when the Union troops approached. One chorus exults: "De massa run, ha, ha!/De darkey stay, ho, ho!/It mus' be now de kingdom coming,/An' de year ob Jubilo!" Another chorus is similarly celebratory: "De oberseer he make us trouble,/An' he dribe us round a spell;/We lock him up in de smokehouse cellar,/Wid de key trown in de well." See also the entries for "Happy land of Canaan" (song) and "I'se gwine to de shuckin'" (song). Joe B. Fulton's *The Reconstruction of Mark Twain: How a Confederate Bushwhacker Became the Lincoln of Our Literature* (Baton Rouge: Louisiana State University Press, 2010) analyzed the persistence of Clemens's Southern sympathies.

The World of Wonders; A Record of Things Wonderful in Nature, Science, and Art. Illus. Pittsburgh: J. R. Foster & Co., 1873. 416 pp. [No author is credited.]

Catalog: Ball 2016 inventory, red cloth, gilt lettering, fair condition, bookplate of J. Langdon Family Library #397.

Location: Quarry Farm library shelves, under the supervision of the Mark Twain Archive, Elmira College, Elmira, New York.

Clemens had access to this book whenever he visited the Langdons' home in Elmira. Its contents would have appealed to his inborn curiosity. *The World of Wonders* contained, among dozens of other subjects, brief essays on "Wonderful Impostors" (p. 351), "Wonders of the Alps" (p. 257), "Curious Stories of Highwaymen" (p. 60), "Volcanoes" (pp. 188, 217, 242, and 321), "The Female Pirates" (p. 37), "Man with the Iron Mask" (p. 41), "Wild Man in London" (p. 30), "White Elephants" (p. 346), "Australian Explorers" (p. 147), and "Astronomical Wonders" (pp. 103, 211, 172, 290, 323, 340, and 384). Someone should give thought to whether this book should be counted among the resources reflected in any of Twain's post-1873 writings.

The World's Wit and Humor; An Encyclopedia of the Classic Wit and Humor of All Ages and Nations. Ed. by Joel Chandler Harris (1848–1908), Andrew Lang (1844–1912), Brander Matthews (1852–1929), and William Hayes Ward (1835–1916). Lionel Strachey (1864–1927), Managing editor. 15 vols. New York: Review of Reviews Co., 1905–1906.

Source: MTLAcc, entries #342–356, complete set donated by Clemens.

A joint editorial effort of American and British literary critics, this set of volumes unfortunately disappeared from the Mark Twain Library at Redding before Clemens's annotations, if any, could be examined. Each volume was dedicated to a specific nation or culture (a number of these occupied multiple volumes) and had an editor who specialized in that literature—Joel Chandler Harris (American), Andrew Lang (British), William Hayes Ward (Greek, Roman, and Oriental), and Brander Matthews (Continental European).

Curiously, although Mark Twain's signed portrait served as the frontispiece of Volume II, his writings were only awarded two selections totaling fifteen pages ("Colonel Mulberry Sellers" and "The Notorious Jumping Frog of Calaveras County"). By comparison, for example, Artemus

Ward (Charles Farrar Browne) was represented by eleven of his sketches. Finley Peter Dunne ("Mr. Dooley") was awarded six pieces, Eugene Field had five, and three of Charles Dudley Warner's essays were included. Even Albert Bigelow Paine earned two slots.

Volume 2 of the Mark Twain Project's edition of *Autobiography of Mark Twain* (2013) logically proposed that Twain's fulminations on 31 July 1906 about the perishability of most American humorists in contrast to his own lasting reputation (pp. 152–153) were prompted by the publication in a Chicago piracy titled *Hot Stuff by Famous Funny Men* or (variously) *Library of Wit and Humor by Mark Twain and Others* (see the Catalog entries for those books.) It would seem equally plausible—given the 1905 publication date of Volumes I-V devoted to American humor and edited by Joel Chandler Harris—that *The World's Wit and Humor; An Encyclopedia of the Classic Wit and Humor of All Ages and Nations*, which paid homage to 124 American authors plus a large number of anonymous pieces grouped as "College Humor," could additionally have triggered Twain's reflections about his durability versus his competitors' rapid extinction.

The World's Work (New York, monthly periodical, published 1900–1932). Edited 1900–1913 by Walter Hines Page (1855–1918).

The Mark Twain Papers at Berkeley contain a published broadside photograph that shows Clemens reading the July 1906 issue of *The World's Work* while propped up in his Italian mahogany bed, cigar protruding from beneath his mustache, wire spectacles dangling halfway down his nose. He appears to be reading the magazine avidly. The printed caption on the broadside reads: "Mark Twain writes:—'Two days overdue and THE WORLD'S WORK has not yet reached me. Pray make a note of this. I would rather not have to resort to violence.'" The advertisement is copyrighted by "Brown Bros." In "The Ashcroft-Lyon Manuscript" that Twain composed in 1909 he alluded to "an article [by Dr. Frederick Van Eeden] in the September number of *The World's Work* on hypnotic suggestion" to explain how he was misled by his two former assistants (*AutoMT* 3: 438).

WORTLEY, (LADY) EMMELINE CHARLOTTE ELIZABETH (MANNERS) STUART-WORTLEY (1806–1855). *Travels in the United States, Etc., During 1849 and 1850*. Blue cloth, gilt lettering and design. New York: Harper & Brothers, 1851. 463 pp.

Inscription: the front free endpaper has been torn out. Presumably it displayed Clemens's signature.

Marginalia: very profuse penciled notes and vertical markings by Clemens begin at Chapter 20, the section describing Wortley's travel on the Mississippi River and her visit to New Orleans (pages 113–162). The first page of this portion is turned down where Wortley found the Mississippi River to be "sublimity itself" (p. 113). Clemens's annotations include (all in pencil): (p. 113) "Scenery"; (p. 114) "floating 'palace'"; (top of pp. 116–117) "Snagged, going *down*-stream! It was drift-logs, of course"; (p. 121) "Mosquitoes"; (p. 126) "Cemeteries"; (p. 127) "<Stealing> Claiming a corpse, for the jewels & money,—the Todd-Galleries, Munich"; and (p. 129) "Pompano." At the top of page 139, where Wortley disparagingly described a bragging boy in Boston, "his hat so knowingly on one

side," who likes to chew and smoke, Clemens noted, "antismoke". On page 142 Clemens commented, "Each tourist blackguards his predecessor." On that same page he made a vertical pencil mark at her observation that Americans "uniformly" respect and honor their churchyard dead. He noted on page 157, "Telegraph.—no telephone"; on page 162 he jotted, "Roll on Silver Moon"; and on page 248 he drew a line next to a complimentary reference to Bayard Taylor. The Mark Twain Papers, Bancroft Library, University of California at Berkeley, contain photocopies of twenty-two pages that Clemens annotated, as well as a microfilm of this marginalia (Microfilm Box #36).

Location: Mark Twain Library, Redding, Connecticut.

Copy examined: Clemens's copy. Has the red ink Mark Twain Library accession number "3395". Examined in 1970 and again in June 1982 and on 9 November 2019.

Mark Twain referred to Lady Wortley's *Travels in the United States* in a portion of the manuscript eventually omitted from *Life on the Mississippi* (1883); see Dewey Ganzel, "Twain, Travel Books" (1962), p. 41 n. 4.

WRIGHT, HENRIETTA CHRISTIAN (1854–1899). *The Princess Liliwinkins, and Other Stories*. Illus. New York: Harper & Brothers, 1889. 220 pp.

Source: MTLAcc, entry #1909, volume donated from Clemens's library by Clara Clemens Gabrilowitsch in 1910.

The life of this New Jersey children's author was cut short by tuberculosis, but not before she wrote more than half a dozen history books and novels.

WRIGHT, LIVINGSTON. *How Reverend Wiggin Rewrote Mrs. Eddy's Book*. Brookline, Massachusetts, n.d. [1906 or 1907].

Clemens read Wright's book in manuscript form; he was elated that Wright "proves" that Mary Baker Eddy did not write *Science and Health* (SLC to Wright, Riverdale, 17 April 1903, TS in MTP; Clemens's letter quoted in Wright's book, pp. 9–10). Wright argued that the Reverend James Henry Wiggin shaped Mrs. Eddy's work more than was supposed.

Peel, *Mary Baker Eddy* (1977).

WRIGHT, MABEL (OSGOOD) (1859–1934). *Birdcraft: A Field Book of Two Hundred Song, Game, and Water Birds*. Illustrated by Louis Agassiz Fuertes (1874–1927). New York: Macmillan Co., 1903. 317 pp.

Inscription: the front pastedown endpaper is inscribed by Clemens in black ink, "To/ Jean Clemens/with the love of/her Father/Sept. '03".

Location: Mark Twain Library, Redding, Connecticut. Donated from Clemens's library by Clara Clemens Gabrilowitsch in 1910 (MTLAcc, entry #1981).

Copy examined: Jean Clemens's unmarked copy. Has the red ink Mark Twain Library accession number "1981". Examined in 1970 and again in June 1982.

————— and ELLIOTT COUES. *Citizen Bird; Scenes from Bird-Life*. Illustrated by Louis Agassiz Fuertes (1874–1927). New York: Macmillan Co., 1900. 430 pp.

Source: MTLAcc, entry #1980, volume donated from Clemens's library by Clara Clemens Gabrilowitsch in 1910.

—————. *Four-Footed Americans and Their Kin*. Ed. by Frank Michler Chapman (1864–1945). Illustrated by Ernest Thompson Seton (1860–1946). New York: Macmillan Co., 1901. 432 pp.

Inscription: inscribed by Clemens to Jean Clemens, Sept.

1903.

Provenance: formerly in the Mark Twain Library, Redding, Connecticut. Donated from Clemens's library by Clara Clemens Gabrilowitsch in 1910 (MTLAcc, entry #1979).

Catalog: *Mott 1952*, item #96, $30.

Frank Michler Chapman would become one of the most respected naturalists in America. At the American Museum of Natural History, where he held the post of Associate Curator in 1901, his special area of expertise was ornithology. The wildlife artist Ernest Thompson Seton was one of the founders of the Boy Scouts of America.

WRIGHT, THOMAS (1810–1877), ed. *Early Travels in Palestine, Comprising the Narratives of Arculf, Willibald, Bernard, Saewulf, Sigurd, Benjamin of Tudela, Sir John Maundeville, De La Brocquière, and Maundrell.* Bohn's Antiquarian Library Series. London: Henry G. Bohn, 1848. 517 pp.

Inscription: the half-title page is signed in pencil, "S L Clemens/Hartford 1877".

Marginalia: vertical lines, brackets, underscorings, and notes in pencil and black ink. While the penciled annotations occur throughout the volume, the black-ink marginalia begin on page 184 in Sir John Maundeville's chapter. Mainly Clemens was comparing then-and-now scenes and artifacts. On page 8, referring to the twelve stones that Joshua ordered taken out of the Jordan River, Clemens noted, "More perishable things have been preserved, & the 12 stones lost." (The stones were formerly housed in a church.) "The 'Wailing-Place' of to-day," Clemens observed on page 83. On page 221 Clemens wrote "The original Magellan" in black ink beside Maundeville's description of a voyager. At the top of page 229 he penciled: "This can be done by some Indians on our Northwest Coast. (See Bancroft.)"; the passage describes a practice of stretching the upper lip. On the same page, next to the description of an island where people purportedly "have ears so long that they hang down to their knees" and the males possess thin beards and few hairs on their heads, Clemens bracketed the sentence and noted in pencil, "Vision of a modern Congress." Vertically on page 230, beside an account of how the "religious men" eat the meat that is cooked as a sacrifice, Clemens noted, "The same trick played by the Jewish priests—&, metaphorically, by *all* priests." Clemens did not annotate any pages beyond page 280, and many leaves remain unopened thereafter.

Catalogs: ListABP (1910), "Early Travels in Palestine"; "Retz Appraisal" (1944), p. 12. Valued at $20.

Location: Mark Twain Papers, Bancroft Library, University of California at Berkeley.

Copy examined: Clemens's copy.

Clemens purchased Wright's *Early Travels* on 24 October 1877 for $1.50, according to a bill sent to him by James R. Osgood and Company of Boston in November 1877 (Scrapbook #10, p. 69, MTP). Wright's book may have influenced Chapter 54 of *The Innocents Abroad* (1869), according to a typescript copy of Leon Dickinson's draft of an unpublished introduction of Mark Twain's travel narrative (MTP). In 1881 Twain wrote "Compass, 1322. Rotundity of earth, 132[2]/Sir John Mandeville" (NB 19, *N&J* 2: 417); Twain marked Maundeville's comments about the rotundity of the earth on page 219 of Wright's *Early Travels*. Twain mentioned "Sir John Mandeville"

as an expert on animal behavior in an Autobiographical Dictation of 30 May 1907 (*AutoMT* 3: 67).

Scott, *MTAL* (1969), p. 61. See also the Catalog entry for John Mandeville.

———. *The Homes of Other Days: A History of Domestic Manners and Sentiments in England, from the Earliest Known Period to Modern Times.* Illus. New York: D. Appleton & Co., 1871. 511 pp. [Publisher and pages conjectured.]

Catalog: ListABP (1910), "Homes of Other Days", no other information provided.

Wright here provides a cultural history of a very comprehensive nature. Among the hundreds of topics he describes are these: food, cooking methods, furniture, servants, hunting, minstrels, gambling, lighting methods, inns, education, pet animals, dancing, drunken brawls, punishments, gallows, and literature. There is a thorough index. *Homes of Other Days* might have provided Mark Twain with historical details for a variety of his writings.

———. *Narratives of Sorcery and Magic, from the Most Authentic Sources.* New York: Redfield, 1852. 420 pp. [The publisher and pages are conjectured. The first edition of this work was published in London in 1851.]

Inscription: the front flyleaf is signed, "S. L. Clemens, Hartford, 1885".

Catalogs: *A1911*, "12mo, cloth, N.Y. 1852," quotes the signature, lot 495, sold for $2.75; *Lexington 1912*, lot 30, sold for $5.

Wright recounts stories of sorcerers and magicians that have caught the public's attention over the centuries in England, Scotland, and Europe. The greater proportion of his stories, however, have to do with allegations and purported practices of witchcraft. Chapter 31 is devoted to "The Doings of Satan in New England." This volume merits more intense investigation from Mark Twain scholars than it has received.

Coleman O. Parsons, "Background" (1960), p. 67.

WRIGHT, WILLIAM (1829–1898), pseud. "Dan De Quille." *History of the Big Bonanza: An Authentic Account of the Discovery, History, and Working of the World-Renowned Comstock Silver Lode of Nevada; Adventures with Mining, the Indians, and the Country.* Introduction by Mark Twain. Illus. Half tan morocco over marbled boards, marbled endpapers and edges, spine lettered gilt. Upper joint rubbed and starting. Hartford, Connecticut: American Publishing Company, 1876.

Inscription: the front flyleaf is inscribed, "Compliments of E. Bliss Jr."

Catalog: "The James S. Copley Library," Sotheby's auction, New York City, 17 June 2010, lot 556. Sold with five other volumes for $4,250.

Location: collection of Kevin Mac Donnell, Austin, Texas.

Source: letter from Kevin Mac Donnell to Alan Gribben, 22 July 2014. This volume almost certainly belonged to Clemens, since it was a presentation copy from Clemens's publisher.

Beginning in March 1875 Mark Twain was extensively involved in the evolution and publication of *The Big Bonanza* (see *MTLet* 6: 424 *passim*). Twain included "Dan de Quille" among the American humorists listed in Notebook 19 in 1881 (*N&J* 2: 429). In Twain's "Mental Telegraphy" (1891), he recounts the coincidental timing of his own letter of encouragement to Wright and Wright's inquiry about writing such a book.

The Mark Twain-Dan De Quille relationship has received much scholarly discussion: Branch, *LAMT* (1950), pp. 63, 105–109; Blair, *MT&HF* (1960), pp. 121–127; Bradley, Beatty, and Long, eds. *Huckleberry Finn* (1962), p. 243 (reprinted Chapter 72 of *The Big Bonanza*); Hill and Blair, *The Art of Huckleberry Finn* (1962), pp. 404–415 (reprinted Chapter 38 of *The Big Bonanza*); Walter Blair and Hamlin Hill, *America's Humor: From Poor Richard to Doonesbury* (New York: Oxford University Press, 1978), pp. 243–248; David W. Toll, "Princes of the Fourth Estate," *Nevada Magazine* 39 (Winter 1979): 12–14 (disparaged the reputation Clemens had while in Nevada); Lawrence I. Berkove, "A Neglected Memoir of Mark Twain," *Quarterly Newsletter of the Book Club of California* 46 (Spring 1981): 31–33; Berkove, "The Literary Journalism of Dan De Quille," *Nevada Historical Society Bulletin* 28.4 (Winter 1985): 249–261; Berkove, "Dan De Quille and 'Old Times on the Mississippi,'" *Mark Twain Journal* 24.2 (Fall 1986): 28–35; Berkove, "New Information on Dan De Quille and 'Old Times on the Mississippi,'" *Mark Twain Journal* 26.2 (Fall 1988): 15–20; Berkove, "'Nobody Writes to Anybody Except to Ask a Favor': New Correspondence between Mark Twain and Dan De Quille," *Mark Twain Journal* 26.1 (Spring 1988): 2–21; Berkove, "Life after Twain: The Later Careers of the *Enterprise* Staff," *Mark Twain Journal* 29.1 (Spring 1991): 22–28; Berkove, "'Assaying in Nevada': Twain's Wrong Turn in the Right Direction," *American Literary Realism* 28.3 (Spring 1995): 64–79; Berkove, *Dan De Quille*. Western Writers Series No. 136 (Boise, Idaho: Boise State University Press, 1999)—a valuable treatment of the De Quille-Twain friendship; Kerry Driscoll, *Mark Twain among the Indians and Other Indigenous Peoples* (2018), pp. 60, 64, 65, and 82–83.

———. *History of the Big Bonanza: An Authentic Account of the Discovery, History, and Working of the World-Renowned Comstock Silver Lode of Nevada; Adventures with Mining, the Indians, and the Country*. Introduction by Mark Twain. Illus. Original light blue-gray cloth, gilt. Laid in a half morocco slipcase. Hartford, Connecticut: American Publishing Co., 1877. 569 pp.

Inscription: On the front endpaper of this copy Mark Twain testified, writing in ink, that he helped Wright with the work through what Twain would later term "mental telepathy": "Is there any truth in the newspaper story that you planned this book for the author before you knew he had written it?" reads a question posed by the owner of the volume. "Yes, it is true. Mark Twain." responded Twain. He was recording this message in a copy of *History of the Big Bonanza* for an early collector; this copy was not part of Clemens's personal library.

Catalogs: "The Powers Collection . . . of Samuel L. Clemens," Merwin-Clayton Sales Co., Sale 385, 4–7 April 1911, lot #261, sold for $15.50; Jenkins Company, Austin, Texas, Catalog 203, September 1987, item #182, priced at $2,250.

Provenance: The 1911 Merwin-Clayton Sales catalog asserted that "this copy came from the estate of Elisha Bliss, owner of American Publishing Company." However, the volume instead appeared to be one of the several batches

of books that the Reverend Levi M. Powers of Haverhill, Massachusetts sent to Mark Twain between 1902 and 1909 with a question about each book written on a front endpaper of each volume. Twain initially wrote complete replies to the questions, but as these repeated interrogations became annoying his patience wore thin and his answers became briefer. Later the minister apparently cashed in some of these autographed books at an auction in 1911. Kevin Mac Donnell of Austin, Texas briefly owned this copy of Wright's book in 1987, but traded it to rare book dealer John Jenkins of Austin for Olivia Clemens's well-used Bible in red morocco.

Location: currently unknown.

———. "Washoe Rambles" (serial narrative, published in 1861).

Without insisting upon any direct influence, Kerry Driscoll noted certain similarities in Clemens's reports about the Paiutes and the details furnished by De Quille in his account of a prospecting trip he undertook in Nevada in the summer of 1861. De Quille's "Washoe Rambles" ran weekly in the *Gold Era* between 28 July and 1 December 1861 (Driscoll, *Mark Twain among the Indians and Other Indigenous Peoples* [2018], pp. 60, and 78–79).

WUICHET, CHARLES (1846–1947). *The Sunny Side of a Busy Life*. Illus. [Dayton, Ohio: privately published, 1906]. 86 pp.

Source: MTLAcc, entry #357, volume donated by Clemens.

Wuichet related stories and history of early days in Dayton, Ohio.

WYATT, EDITH FRANKLIN (1873–1958). *Every One His Own Way*. Decorative designs by William James Jordan (1871–1955). New York: McClure, Phillips and Co., 1901. 290 pp.

On 22 July 1903 William Dean Howells wrote to Clemens from Kittery Point, Maine, requesting the return of Wyatt's collection of short stories, from which Howells had "read some sketches" to Clemens when the latter was ill in May 1903. Clemens had subsequently borrowed the volume. Howells joked: "Is there *no* crevice in your brazen armor through which one can get a borrowed book out of you? . . . That book was very precious to us all, especially Mrs. Howells" (*MTHL*, pp. 772–773). The short stories in *Every One His Own Way* have whimsical titles—"The Fox and the Stork," "Jack Spratt," "Beauty and the Beast," "The Brave Tin Soldier," "Queen for a Day," "Daffy-Down-Dilly," "The Story of a Way Side Inn"—that bear little resemblance to their settings or plots, yet fit their offbeat endings.

WYETH, JOHN ALLAN (1845–1922). *Life of General Nathan Bedford Forrest*. Illus. New York: Harper & Brothers, 1904. 657 pp.

Source: MTLAcc, entry #1784, volume donated by Clemens.

Clemens did not own many books about Confederate figures who distinguished themselves in the Civil War, but this was one of the few exceptions. General Forrest (1821–1877) became renowned for his cavalry tactics. A major blot on his war record was the merciless treatment his troops displayed in massacring African American Union soldiers after the Battle of Fort Pillow. Following the war he served as the first grand wizard of the newly formed Ku Klux Klan.

Wyman's Comic Almanac for the Times, 1856. New York: T.

W. Strong, 1855.

    Location: Mark Twain Papers, Bancroft Library, University of California, Berkeley.

    Copy examined: presumably Clemens's copy, unmarked. Although the "Retz Appraisal" (1944) did not include this small paperbound pamphlet, a former Editor of the Mark Twain Papers, Frederick Anderson, informed me that it had been part of the collection since at least the year he assumed his office in 1964.

    Bound with thread, the pamphlet consisted of unpolished brief jokes and sketches interspersed with crude woodcuts and arranged around almanac charts of the months for 1856. Clemens was always fascinated with the pseudoscience of phrenology, so it is interesting that midway through the unnumbered pages appeared a short lampoon of the Fowlers's phrenology office in Clinton Hall in New York City; in this sketch, a woman took her son to Fowler to determine the boy's proper vocation, but "for all Bill's goods there're two bads, and for every bad there's two goods"—so the mother simply allowed the boy's father to bind him over as an apprentice to a shoemaker.

WYNKOOP, MARTIN L., pseud. "Martin L. Ware." *A Condensed Manual on Patented Inventions: What to Do and What Not to Do to Insure Success to the Inventor.* New York: [Funk & Wagnalls Co.,] 1897. 166 pp.

    Source: MTLAcc, entry #576, volume donated by Clemens. Clemens was very attracted to the idea of providing financial resources for an inventor—most notably, of course, James W. Paige, but he also backed others.

WYSS, JOHANN DAVID (1743–1818). *The Swiss Family Robinson. A New Translation.* Ed. by William Henry Giles Kingston (1814–1880). Illus. New York: G. Routledge & Sons, [cop. 1882]. 323 pp.

    Source: MTLAcc, entry #1930, volume donated from Clemens's library by Clara Clemens Gabrilowitsch in 1910. Presumably this book, first published in German in 1812, was obtained for the Clemens children. They no doubt enjoyed the Swiss clergyman Wyss' tale of a shipwrecked family who find themselves marooned on a tropical island. Wyss borrowed ideas from Daniel Defoe's *Robinson Crusoe* (1719) in explaining how the group improvises and adapts to their surroundings.

    ———. *The Swiss Family Robinson; or, The Adventures of a Shipwrecked Family on an Uninhabited Island Near New Guinea.* Illus. New York: A. L. Burt Co., n.d. 292 pp. [A. L. Burt published an edition in 1894 that had 292 pages, as specified by the recording librarian here.]

    Source: MTLAcc, entry #494, volume donated by Clemens.

❙ Y

"YANKEE DOODLE" (song, patriotic versions emerged in the 1770s). Traditional tune, with an English origin. Words anonymous, American in origin.

    "As Philip fell, the orchestra struck up 'Yankee Doodle' in the liveliest manner" (Mark Twain and Charles Dudley Warner, *GA* [1873], Ch. 31). A manuscript passage eventually omitted from Chapter 29 of Twain's *Life on the Mississippi* (1883) related Frances Trollope's disgust at the audience behavior when she attended a performance of Shakespeare's *Hamlet* in Cincinnati; periodically the crowd would break into a chorus of "Yankee Doodle."

In 1885 Twain noted that Northern troops sang "Yankee Doodle" to goad the nearby Confederates (NB 25, *N&J* 3: 201). See also the Catalog entry for Howard Pyle, *Yankee Doodle* (1881).

YEATS, WILLIAM BUTLER (1865–1939). *Stories of Red Hanrahan.* 500 copies printed. 8vo, linen back, leaves uncut. Dundrum, Ireland: Dun Emer Press, 1904. 56 pp.

    Inscription: the front pastedown endpaper is signed "S. L. Clemens, 1908."

    Catalogs: *A1911,* "8vo, boards, linen back, uncut, Dundrum (Ireland), 1905, . . . Limited edition," quotes the signature, lot 143, $4.25; George D. Smith, New York City, "Catalogue of Books" (1911), quotes the signature, item 108, $12; American Art Association (New York City), Sale catalogue for the collection of the late William F. Gable (8 January 1925), "first edition, 8vo, linen back," has the *A1911* sale label, lot 124, sold for $15 (with one other book); American Art Association (New York City), Sale catalogue (18 November 1925), "8vo, original boards, cloth back, paper labels, uncut, Dundrum: The Dun Emer Press, 1904, Mark Twain's copy, with . . . his autograph signature—'S. L. Clemens, 1908' inside front cover," has the *A1911* sale label, lot 172, sold for $10.

    Inscription: the front pastedown endpaper is inscribed, "S. L. Clemens, 1908".

    Clemens wrote to Lady Augusta Gregory on 16 February 1904: "I hope Mr. Yeats is being well treated in our country. . . . We keep him most pleasantly in mind" (MTP). On 21 February 1904 Lady Augusta Gregory wrote to assure Clemens: "Yes, Mr. Yeats has been very well treated, indeed, . . . I wrote. . . and gave him your kind message." Lady Gregory mentioned her *Gods and Fighting Men* (1904), for which Yeats provided a preface (ALS in MTP). Late in his life Yeats wrote, "I knew Mark Twain slightly. Lady Gregory and I dined with him many years ago, and I remember vividly his talk and his stories, always admirable in matter and manner" ("W. B. Yeats Receives the Mark Twain Medal," *Mark Twain Quarterly* 1.4 [Summer 1937]: 21).

YONGE, CHARLES DUKE (1812–1891). *The Life of Marie Antoinette [1755–1793], Queen of France.* New York: Harper & Brothers, 1876. 473 pp.

    In 1877 Clemens read "Mr. Yonge's recent 'Life of Marie Antoinette,' which is without exception the <worst> blindest & slovenliest piece of literary construction I ever saw, & is astounding in another way; it starts out to make you a pitying & lamenting friend of Marie, but only succeeds in making you loathe her all the way through & swing your hat with unappeasable joy when they finally behead her" (SLC to Mary Mason Fairbanks, 6 August 1877, *MTMF,* p. 207). Mark Twain was still fuming when he wrote Chapter 26 of *A Tramp Abroad* (1880): "Martyrdom made a saint of the trivial and foolish Marie Antoinette, and her biographers still keep her fragrant with the odor of sanctity to this day, while unconsciously proving upon almost every page they write that the only calamitous instinct which her husband lacked, she supplied,—the instinct to root out and get rid of an honest, able, and loyal official, wherever she found him." In Chapter 19 of Twain's *Adventures of Huckleberry Finn* (1885) the rapscallion King claims to be the son of "Marry Antonette."

Blair, "French Revolution" (1956), pp. 22, 24; Baetzhold, *MT&JB* (1970), p. 30.

YONGE, CHARLOTTE MARY (1823–1901). *A Book of Worthies, Gathered from the Old Histories and Now Written Anew.* Golden Treasury Series. London: Macmillan and Co., 1869. 405 pp.

Marginalia: Clemens wrote in the margin of one page, "She meant to make him presentable, but she ran out of whitewash."

Provenance: formerly in the Mark Twain Library, Redding, Connecticut.

Catalog: *Mott 1952*, item #97, $15.

Yonge offered brief biographical sketches of thirteen men she deemed heroes from Biblical, Greece, and Roman times, including Joshua, David, Hector, Aristides, Alexander the Great, and Julius Caesar.

Stone, *IE* (1961), pp. 116 and 268.

————. *The Caged Lion.* Illus. New York: Macmillan and Co., 1892. 287 pp.

Source: MTLAcc, entry #881, volume donated by Mrs. Ralph W. Ashcroft (formerly Isabel Lyon), Clemens's secretary.

A novel about James I (1304–1437), King of Scotland.

————. *Cameos from English History. The Wars in France.* Second Series. London: Macmillan and Co., 1871. 415 pp.

Inscription: the half-title page is signed in pencil, "Mark Twain, Hartford." Clemens probably purchased the book during his pleasant sojourn in London in 1872; the fact that he was living abroad may account for the use of his pen name, an extremely rare signature in books belonging to Clemens's library. He wrote the name and city in uncharacteristically large script, turning the book so that his autograph is nearly vertical. There is an *A1911* sale label on the front pastedown endpaper.

Marginalia: numerous underscorings and a few notes in Clemens's hand. Where Yonge wrote that Wat Tyler's followers wanted "to destroy all lawyers, that no one might be left to make laws," Clemens underlined the phrase "to destroy all lawyers" and noted, "Shibboleth" (p. 130). Albert E. Stone quoted marginalia from page 134, including Clemens's observation that "Slavery still exists by (obsolete) law in England" (*IE*, pp. 115–116). "Old-time elections for Lord Mayor," Clemens jotted on page 167. His pencil marks appear on pages 115–119, 123–124, 126, 135–136, 139, 146, 148–149, 255 (on this latter page Prince Hal, crowned King Henry V, began his reign with generous gestures). It should be noted that Yonge recited the career of Joan of Arc, a historical figure who fascinated Clemens, in considerable detail (pp. 362–385).

Catalog: *A1911*, "Second Series, 12mo, cloth, Lond. 1871," quotes signature and describes marginalia, lot 63, sold for $4.25.

Location: Special Collections, Elihu Burritt Library, Central Connecticut State University, New Britain, Connecticut.

Copy examined: photocopies of the title page, inscription, and marginalia in 1979.

"See 'Cameos,'" Mark Twain wrote in his study notes for *The Prince and the Pauper* (1881) around 1879 (DV115, MTP). Late in August or early in September 1898 Twain noted: "Write some more Cameos of [*sic*] English History" (NB 40, TS p. 32).

————. *Child's History of France.* New York: Syndicate Trading Co., n.d. 279 pp.

Source: MTLAcc, entry #463, volume donated by Clemens.

————. *The Heir of Redclyffe.* 2 vols.

Catalog: *C1951*, O4, listed among books signed by Olivia Clemens.

————. *The Lances of Lynwood.* Illustrated by "J. B." New Edition. Yellow-green buckram, stamped. London: Macmillan and Co., 1882. 286 pp.

Inscription: the recto of the frontispiece is inscribed in black ink, "Jean Clemens/July 26th '89./Clara."

Location: Mark Twain Library, Redding, Connecticut.

Copy examined: Jean Clemens's unmarked copy. Has the red ink Mark Twain Library accession number "2947". Examined in 1970 and again in June 1982.

This fictional story of chivalry is set in the England of King Edward III, who lived from 1312 until 1377.

————. *Landmarks of History.* 3 vols. New York: Leypoldt & Holt and Co., 1868.

Edgar H. Hemminghaus saw Clemens's copy of this edition in the Mark Twain Library at Redding ("Mark Twain's German Provenience" [1945], p. 475 n. 109). Albert E. Stone, Jr. did not list the book when he catalogued the collection in 1955, and I was unable to locate it in Redding in 1970 or thereafter. If it ever turns up, there should be three parts (Ancient History, Medieval History, and Modern History) in its three-volume format.

————. *The Little Duke; or, Richard the Fearless* (novel, published in 1854).

Yonge's *Little Duke*, recounting the exploits of Richard I (933–996), was the first of her history stories written for children. In Clemens's study notes for *The Prince and the Pauper* (1881) he wrote: "Miss Martineau [*sic*] describes a coronation. See 'Little Duke'" (DV115, MTP). He included Charlotte Yonge in the list of people scheduled to receive complimentary copies of *The Prince and the Pauper* (NB 19 [1881], *N&J* 2: 385). In a well-known letter written from Redding on 27 August 1908 to the Reverend F. V. Christ of New York City, Clemens revealed that the notion of writing *The Prince and the Pauper* (1881) "came to me from the outside—suggested by that pleasant and picturesque little history-book, Charlotte M. Yonge's 'Little Duke'" (ALS in MTP). Albert Bigelow Paine added a note when publishing Clemens's letter (*MTL*, p. 814), pointing out that Clemens presumably meant Yonge's *The Prince and the Page.* But Leon Dickinson—"The Sources of *The Prince and the Pauper*" (1949), p. 103—and other commentators proved that Clemens's recollection in 1908 was correct. Howard G. Baetzhold, in particular, demonstrated that *The Prince and the Pauper* has many more features in common with *The Little Duke* than with Yonge's other novel, *The Prince and the Page* ("Mark Twain's *The Prince and the Pauper*," *Notes and Queries* 199 [September 1954]: 401–403).

Stone, *IE* (1961), pp. 114–115, agreed with Paine's theory that Clemens was confused about Yonge's book titles; Baetzhold, *MT&JB* (1970), pp. 48–49, 329–330, contended otherwise.

————. *A Parallel History of France and England; Consisting of Outlines and Dates.* First edition. Oblong octavo, brown half calf over marbled boards, morocco spine labels, marbled endpapers, red-sprinkled edges, double labels, gilt, spine scuffed, corners rubbed, marginal tear mended on verso of title page and recto of the Preface page, quarter red morocco slipcase. First edition. London: Macmillan and Co., 1871. 53 pp.

Inscription: the front free flyleaf is inscribed by Olivia Clemens in black ink, "S. L. Clemens/Christmas/1874/ Livy". (This was the Clemenses' first Christmas in their Hartford house on Farmington Avenue.)

Marginalia: a note in pencil in the left hand column on page 9 refers to page 15, where Clemens underlined the name "Louis VI" in the left hand column and drew a pencil line to a marginal comment: "See page 15." On page 15 he again underscored Louis VI's name and noted, "I suppose it should be Louis X."

Catalogs: Christie's, New York City, 1–2 February 1988 auction, lot 464, sold for $1,100 to the Heritage Book Shop, Los Angeles; Heritage Book Shop, Los Angeles, Catalogue 170 (June 1988), item #62, priced at $1,750; *Sotheby's 2003*, #200 (sold with two other titles about English history and lore), $3,000.

Provenance: contains the shelfmark of Clara Clemens Gabrilowitsch's private library in Detroit. Donated to the Carrie Estelle Doheny Collection, St. John's Seminary, Camarillo, California by Mrs. Doheny in 1940 after she acquired the volume for $12.20 from Maxwell Hunley Rare Books, Beverly Hills, California. Auctioned by Christie's in 1988 on behalf of St. John's Seminary and the Archdiocese of Los Angeles. Acquired by the Heritage Book Shop of Los Angeles in February 1988. Purchased on 20 June 1988 by Nick Karanovich (1938–2003), Fort Wayne, Indiana.

Location: collection of Kevin Mac Donnell, Austin, Texas.

Copy examined: Clemens's copy, in July 2004. Has the bookplate of "Estelle Doheny."

———. *The Prince and the Page: A Story of the Last Crusade* (novel, published in 1865).

Catalog: ListABP (1910), "Prince and Page, Yonge", no other information provided.

Yonge's *The Prince and the Page* is set in 1270 during the eighth Christian crusade. Albert Bigelow Paine attributed Mark Twain's inspiration for *The Prince and the Pauper* (1881) to this "little juvenile volume, an English story of the thirteenth century," which Clemens "picked up among the books" at Quarry Farm (*MTB*, p. 596). Arthur Hobson Quinn—*American Fiction: An Historical and Critical Survey* (New York: D. Appleton-Century Co., 1936), p. 250—noted that in Yonge's novel the cousin of Edward I "dwelt in disguise as a blind beggar for a period of years" and inferred that from this device Twain devised the "correlative idea" of disguising a prince as a beggar, and a beggar as a prince. Leon Dickinson, however, observed that Yonge's novel is highly dissimilar to Twain's ("The Sources of *The Prince and the Pauper*" [1949]). Howard G. Baetzhold's "Mark Twain's *The Prince and the Pauper*," *Notes and Queries* 199 (September 1954): 401–403 proposed another novel as the "chief stimulus" for *The Prince and the Pauper*—Charlotte M. Yonge's *The Little Duke* (1854)—and erased the status of Yonge's *The Prince and the Page* as Twain's main inspiration, though Baetzhold conceded that it may have given "the final form" to Twain's book title.

———. *Young Folks' History of England*. Original cloth, mild wear on edges and corners. Boston: Estes & Lauriat, [1879]. 415 pp. [One of Yonge's series of five history books: *Germany* (1878), *Greece* (1878), *England* (1879), *Rome* (1879), and *France* (1879).]

Inscription: inscribed by Olivia Clemens: "Clara Langdon Clemens/Hartford/June 8th, 1885/Mamma." [This was Clara Clemens's eleventh birthday.]

Catalogs: *C1951*, J28, one volume, listed among books belonging to Jean and Clara Clemens; "Property from the Library of Mark Twain," Butterfield & Butterfield, San Francisco, Sale 6613 (16 July 1997), lot 2709.

Location: Mark Twain House and Museum, Hartford, Connecticut.

Copy examined: Clara Clemens's unmarked copy. Viewed in Hartford in 1997.

On 17 July 1880 Estes & Lauriat, Boston publishers and book dealers, billed Clemens for "5 vol Yonge's Hist" costing $5.62, sent to Hartford. Clemens paid on 27 July 1880 (receipt in MTP). The disposition of the France and Greece volumes in this set seems not to have been recorded.

———. *Young Folks' History of Germany*. Title page loose. Boston: Estes & Lauriat, [cop. 1878]. 447 pp.

Inscription: inscribed by Olivia Clemens on the front flyleaf in black ink: "Olivia Susan Clemens/March 19th 1886/ Hartford/Mamma."

Location: Mark Twain Library, Redding, Connecticut.

Copy examined: Susy Clemens's unmarked copy. See information in the preceding entry. Has a black (not red) ink Mark Twain Library accession number, "2786".

———. *Young Folks' History of Rome*. Boston: Estes & Lauriat, [cop. 1879]. 443 pp.

Source: MTLAcc, entry #1910, volume donated from Clemens's library by Clara Clemens Gabrilowitsch in 1910.

YORK MINSTER. *An Accurate Description and History of the Cathedral and Metropolitan Church of St. Peter, York, from its First Foundation*. Illus. Third edition, with additions. York, England, 1790.

Inscription: signed "Saml. L. Clemens, York, July 19, 1873."

Catalog: *A1911*, "12mo, half cloth, uncut, York, 1790," quotes the signature, lot 498, sold for $1.25.

YOUMANS, ELIZA ANN (1826–1914). *The First Book of Botany*. Illus. New York: D. Appleton & Co., 1870. 183 pp.

Source: MTLAcc, entry #812, volume donated by Clemens.

YOUNG, ANDREW (1807–1889). "There is a happy land" (Sunday-school hymn, published in 1843).

As reprinted in Amos R. Wells' *A Treasure of Hymns* (Boston: W. A. Wilde Co., 1945), pp. 221–222, Young's hymn begins: "There is a happy land,/Far, far away,/Where saints in glory stand,/Bright, bright as day./O, how they sweetly sing,/'Worthy is our Saviour King,/Loud let His praises ring,/Praise, praise for aye'"; it has two other stanzas. Susy Clemens announced on 12 February 1886 that "Papa has written a new version of 'There is a Happy Land'" (MS in ASSSCL; Box 31, MS p. 92, PH in MTP); Clemens noted beside his daughter's statement: "No, it was Billy Rice's new version. . . . — S.L.C." (*S&MT*, p. 222). Clemens's parody began, "There is a boarding-house/Far, far away." In an Autobiographical Dictation of 30 November 1906, Clemens explained: "It was not I that wrote the song. I heard Billy Rice sing it in the negro-minstrel show, and

I brought it home and sang it—with great spirit—for the elevation of the household. The children admired it to the limit, and made me sing it with burdensome frequency. To their minds it was superior to the 'Battle Hymn of the Republic'" (S&MT, p. 222; AutoMT 2: 293). The white comedian Billy Rice (William H. Pearl, 1844–1902) played in New York City with Thatcher, Primrose and West's Minstrels in February and October 1883 (George C. D. Odell, Annals of the New York Stage [New York: Columbia University Press, 1940], 12: 48, 255). In 1883 Clemens wrote the humorous lyrics to Rice's song in Notebook 22 (N&J 2: 38) and also copied them into (and wrote "There is a happy land" above the title of another song in) D. H. Morrison's Treasury of Song for the Home Circle, a book that entered the Clemens family's library in 1883. Mark Twain would use this parody in Chapter 17 of The American Claimant (1892), where Colonel Sellers demonstrates his "cursing phonograph" to Washington Hawkins; that song begins, "There is a boarding-house, far far away,/Where they have ham and eggs, 3 times a day." Mild (implied) profanity then follows: "O, how the boarders yell,/When they hear that dinner bell—/They give that landlord —/Three times a day." Twain transferred these portions of the chapter from the earlier "Colonel Sellers as a Scientist" play (MS pp. 63, 64, MTP). He also copied Rice's version onto the front wrapper of his copy of Frank B. Ogilvie's Two Hundred Old-Time Songs (1896).

The Young Artists, and Other Stories. Illus. Original red cloth, gilt, with hand-colored plates. New York: Philip J. Cozans, n.d. 128 pp.

Inscriptions: the front flyleaf is inscribed, "Presented to/Jennie Clemens/by/Judge George Turner/Chief Justice/of/Nevada Territory/Carson City." Below that inscription Mollie Clemens added, in purple ink: "in 1863." The front free endpaper is inscribed, probably in Mollie Clemens's hand, "For Clara/from Uncle Orion & Aunt Mollie/Christmas, 1880." (Clara was then six years old.)

Provenance: for decades this volume belonged to the Carrie Estelle Doheny Collection, St. John's Seminary, Camarillo, California, having been donated by Mrs. Doheny in 1940 after she purchased the volume for $12.20 from Maxwell Hunley Rare Books, Beverly Hills, California. It was auctioned by Christie's on 21 February 1989 for $275 on behalf of St. John's Seminary. Subsequently it belonged to the collection of Nick Karanovich (1938–2003), Fort Wayne, Indiana.

Catalogs: ListABP (1910), "Young Artists", no other information provided; Sotheby's 2003, #193, $3,000 (sold with four other titles from the Clemens family library).

Location: collection of Kevin Mac Donnell, Austin, Texas.

Copy examined: Clara Clemens's unmarked copy, in Camarillo and again in July 2004 in Austin, Texas. Contains the bookplate of "Estelle Doheny."

Jennie Clemens, Orion and Mollie's daughter, died at the age of eight in 1864. The publishing firm of Philip J. Cozans issued numerous books of moral stories for children written by various authors, including Cozans himself.

YOUNG, CHARLES AUGUSTUS (1834–1908). *A Text-Book of General Astronomy for Colleges and Scientific Schools.* Revised edition. Boston: Ginn & Co., [1904]. 630 pp. [Preface dated August 1904.]

Inscription: an initial note at the top of the front flyleaf note is signed "Yrs, etc, (seriously)/Saml. Clemens." Then at the foot of the flyleaf appears another signature: "Mark Twain,/(who never wrote a book on/the sub. of Astronomy)/Gramercy Park, N. Y. City, [month obliterated by mending tape] 30/1907." A lengthy note above this latter signature advises "Friend Cole" to "read 'Huckleberry Finn' once again, & then if you are still in the dark, call upon me personally at any time"; it furthermore argues that the science of geometry "has "failed to arrive" and remains a "pure pastime." Neither the note nor the signature is in Clemens's hand.

Marginalia: numerous facetious remarks are scattered throughout the volume; these comments are signed "Saml. Clemens," "Samuel Clemens," "S. C.," "Saml.," and "Saml. C." Most are addressed to "Friend Cole." None are in Clemens's handwriting.

Location: Kelley Memorial Library, St. Dunstan's University, Charlottetown, Prince Edward Island, Canada. Grace E. Schillich, Reference Librarian of the Kelley Memorial Library, noticed the signature and marginalia while re-cataloguing volumes (Schillich to Frederick Anderson, then Editor of the Mark Twain Papers, 23 February 1969, MTP).

Copy examined: photocopy of the title page and marginalia in the Mark Twain Papers, Bancroft Library, University of California at Berkeley. At first I considered the possibility that a Mark Twain scholar, perhaps George Hiram Brownell, founding editor of The Twainian and long-time collector of Mark Twain material, might have transcribed marginalia from Clemens's actual copy into another copy of the astronomy textbook. But I have concluded that these annotations are entirely spurious, the work of a prankster who possessed a rudimentary knowledge of Clemens's biography and interests. The arguments against authenticity are these: (1) the notes are not in Clemens's hand; (2) "Cole" seems to be fictional, since Clemens had no close acquaintance by this name in the 1900s; (3) Clemens's comments display skepticism regarding science, ignorance concerning mathematics, and scorn about astronomical discoveries—highly uncharacteristic attitudes for him; (4) the style and vocabulary of the notes (and the unlikely admonition for Cole to read Huckleberry Finn, nonsensical in the context) differ markedly from Clemens's marginalia in other books; (5) the contents of the brief notes are trivial, far beneath Clemens's usual level of discourse during this decade; and (6) the greatest contradiction is the employment of the youthful "Saml." form of signature within three years of Clemens's death. This problem—a counterfeit signature in a volume that Clemens might logically have owned—also arises with Edward Jenkins's Ginx's Baby (1871) and Albion W. Tourgée's The Invisible Empire (1880).

YOUNG, EDWARD (1683–1765). *Complaint; or, Night Thoughts on Life, Death, and Immortality* (lengthy blank verse poem, published 1742–1745).

Young's Night Thoughts is often credited with inspiring the so-called "Graveyard" school of poetry. Although Samuel and Olivia Clemens' copies of Night Thoughts seem not to have survived (or at least not to have reappeared yet), both Clemenses were definitely familiar with Young's work. Olivia Langdon quoted from it in her common place book in 1867 (MTP). On 17 May 1869 Clemens wrote to Olivia Langdon from Hartford: "Let Mrs. Sue be troubled no more about her memoir [for Henry Babcock Noyes, a neighbor who died in 1866 at the age of twenty]. *I* will write it"; Clemens made light of the task, promising to include "tasty" congratulations from famous personages, "and I'll have some poetry in—some of those sublime conundrums from Young's Night Thoughts which only Livy can cipher out the meaning of" (*LLMT*, pp. 95–96; *MTLet* 3: 241). Mark Twain employed a line from Young's poem in Chapter 40 of *The Innocents Abroad* (1869): "Procrastination is the thief of time." That same adage appeared in Twain's "Last Words of Great Men" (Buffalo *Express*, 11 September 1869), though facetiously attributed to Benjamin Franklin. Twain adapted Young's line of verse on 29 April 1900 in London: "Punctuality is the thief of time" (NB 43, TS p. 9). In 1908 he thought up another variation: "Procreation is the thief of time/ Nobody objects to it" (NB 48, TS p. 22).

Harris, *Courtship* (1996), p. 22.

———. *Night Thoughts on Life, Death, and Immortality*. Flaking leather cover. Brunswick, Maine: printed by Joseph Griffin, for T. Bedlington, 1822. 270 pp.

Inscription: the front free endpaper is signed in pencil, "Mary Hill's book" to which is added, in blue ink, "Mary Hill, Redding Ridge/Conn."

Location: Mark Twain Library, Redding, Connecticut. (Many early donations to this library contained the signatures of members of the Hill family, early-day residents of Redding.)

Copy examined: not a copy belonging to Clemens or his family. Albert E. Stone, Jr. included this volume in his checklist of Clemens's library books in 1955, but I was unable to locate the volume when I visited Redding in 1970. By the time I revisited Redding in June 1982 the book had been located and placed with Clemens's library books. Its date and inscriptions suggest that this book, like many other Hill family donations, was given to the Mark Twain Library by someone other than Clemens or Clara Clemens Gabrilowitsch. The volume has no accession number but bears the purple oval Library stamps.

YOUNG, JOHN RUSSELL (1841–1899). *Around the World with General Grant in 1877, 1878, 1879*. Illus. Map. 2 vols. New York: American News Co., [1879]. [The publisher and edition are conjectured.]

Inscription: "To Mark Twain, honoring his genius; and remembering the friendship of many, many years. Jno. Russell Young, N. Y., January 26, 1882."

Catalog: *A1911*, "2 vols., imp. 8vo, half calf, N.Y. [1897 (*sic*)]," quotes the inscription, lot 499, listed erroneously as an 1897 edition, sold for $3.50.

John Russell Young was a prominent journalist, editor, and foreign minister. As a correspondent for the New York *Herald* he accompanied U. S. Grant on his journey. Numerous notebook entries testify to Clemens's esteem for Young; in 1881, for instance, Clemens wrote in Notebook 19: "Russell Young ought to change & go to China" (*N&J* 2: 390). Young sent Clemens another work in 1890; Clemens replied to Young from Tannersville, New York

in the Catskill Mountains on 6 August 1890: "You sent it to Hartford, but it will be forwarded to me, & then I shall read it with pleasure" (PH in MTP).

———. *Men and Memories: Personal Reminiscences by John Russell Young. Edited by His Wife May D[ow]. Russell Young*. 2 vols. New York, London: F. Tennyson Neely, [1901].

Inscription: the flyleaf of Volume II is signed, "S. L. Clemens, Feb. 1902."

Catalogs: *A1911*, lot 500, "Vol. II, 12mo, cloth, N.Y. [1901]," quotes the signature, sold for $1.75; *C1951*, #60c, presentation copy inscribed by Young, erroneously listed as "Men and Memoirs," one volume only, sold for $5. Russell's memoir alluded to Mark Twain on pages 327 and 335 of Volume II.

The Youth's Companion; An Illustrated Weekly for Young People and the Family (Boston, published 1827–1929). Ed. by Daniel Sharp Ford (1822–1899) from 1857 until 1899.

The issue of 18 May 1882 contains a letter from Clemens to an unnamed person, facetiously condemning the notion of a "Society for the Prevention of Cruelty to Children" ("I have a baby downstairs that kept me awake several hours last night") and offering his services to any "society for the prevention of cruelty to fathers" (*The Twainian* [April 1944]: 6). Projecting lucrative history games in 1883, Clemens planned to "advertise games in Youth's Companion, Boston" (NB 22, *N&J* 3: 37). In 1896 he pleaded, "I want a copy of that Youth's Companion account of Helen [Keller]. My copy of it got lost in India & I very much want another one" (SLC to Mrs. Laurence Hutton, London, 26 November 1896, ALS at Princeton University, PH in MTP).

Krause, *MTC* (1967), p. 91.

YSAGUIRRE (pseud.) and **LA MARCA** (pseud.). *Cold Dishes for Hot Weather*. New York: Harper & Brothers, 1896. 126 pp.
Source: MTLAcc, entry #672, volume donated by Clemens.

Z

ZANGWILL, ISRAEL (1864–1926). *Children of the Ghetto*. London: William Heinemann, 1905. 212 pp.
Source: MTLAcc, entry #234, volume donated by Clemens.

The novel *Children of the Ghetto* (1892), followed by other novels and writings, had made the London-born Zangwill the most prominent Jewish literary figure in England and the United States. Basil Tozer would recall that he introduced Zangwill to Mark Twain in Paris when the Clemenses were staying at the Hotel Brighton, "but for some reason Mark Twain never took to Zangwill" (*Recollections of a Rolling Stone* [New York: Dutton, 1923], p. 40). Members of the Clemens family lived in the Brighton (visited by Clemens periodically) beginning in December 1893 and ending in May 1895 (Fears, *Day by Day* 2: 843–990). In London on 11 November 1896 Clemens "heard Zangwill on the Jewish Ghetto. Very fine & bright. Knowledge boiled down. Pemmican in fact. Substance enough in it to furnish forth 5 ordinary lectures" (NB 39, TS p. 23).

———. *The Master; A Novel*. Illus. New York: Harper & Brothers, 1906. 523 pp.
Source: MTLAcc, entry #236, volume donated by Clemens.

On 8 January 1896 Clemens evaluated the novels he had recently read during a cruise on the Indian Ocean; he wrote in Notebook 37: "Zangwill's 'Master' is done in good English—what a rare thing good English is! & the grammar is good, too—& what a very very rare thing that is! The characters are real, they are flesh & blood, they are definite; one knows what they will do in nearly any given set of circumstances. And when there is an incident, an episode, it comes about in a natural way, & happens just as it would happen in actual life" (TS pp. 4–5). Clemens's appraisal disparages Henry Kingsley's *The Recollections of Geoffrey Hamlyn* for its failures to match Zangwill's standards.

Krause, *MTC* (1967), p. 235 n. 10.

ZECHMEISTER, ALEXANDER VICTOR (1817–1877), pseud. "Alexander Victor Wilhelmi." *Einer muss heiraten! [One of Them Must Get Married!]* (one-act comedy).

A bill of 6 February 1890 from Gustave E. Stechert, Foreign Bookseller and Importer, New York City, charges Olivia Clemens $3.50 (.35¢ each) for "10 Wilhelmi, Einer muss heiraten". The Clemenses paid the bill on 12 February 1890.

Zechmeister's characters Jacob and Wilhelm Zorn resemble the famous Grimm Brothers in this gentle comedy.

ZHUKOVSKIĬ, VASILIL ANDREEVICH (1783–1852). "Russian national hymn" (national anthem of Imperial Russia). Variant title: "God save the Czar." Melody by Aleksei Fyodorovich Lvov (1799–1870).

"Russian National Hymn" was one of Clemens's selections for the repertoire of his new Geneva music box in 1878 (SLC to Susan Warner, 20 November 1878, Yale University; NB 16, *N&J* 2: 211–213).

ZILLIACUS, KONNI (1855–1924). *The Russian Revolutionary Movement. Translated by the Authority and at the Request of the Author.* Original yellow cloth, 8vo. New York: E. P. Dutton and Co., 1905. 366 pp.

Provenance: has the shelfmarks of Clara Clemens Gabrilowitsch's library numbering system during her Detroit years. Sold at the 1951 auction in Hollywood but not listed in the hastily compiled sale sheet.

Catalog: "Property from the Library of Mark Twain," Butterfield & Butterfield, San Francisco, Sale 6613 (16 July 1997), lot 2712.

Location: Mark Twain House and Museum, Hartford, Connecticut.

Copy examined: Clemens's unmarked copy. Viewed in Hartford in 1997.

ZOGBAUM, RUFUS FAIRCHILD (1849–1925). *"All Hands"; Pictures of Life in the United States Navy.* Illus. New York: Harper & Brothers, 1897. (36 p1.)

Source: MTLAcc, entry #1365, volume donated by Clemens.

ZOLA, ÉMILE (1840–1902). *Assommoir [The Drinking Place].* Illus. Paris: Marpon & B. Flammarion, [187?].

"Get copy of *L'Assommoir* [*sic*] illustrated—" Clemens noted in Paris in July 1879 (NB 18, *N&J* 2: 326). Zola's novel about alcoholism and working class life in Paris had been published in 1877.

———. *L'Attaque du Moulin [The Attack on the Mill].* Notes and exercises by F. Julien. London: Librairie Hachette, 1897 (novella, first published in 1880).

Catalog: Ball 2016 inventory, brown cloth, black lettering,

good condition.

Location: Quarry Farm library shelves, under the supervision of the Mark Twain Archive, Elmira College, Elmira, New York.

Clemens had access to this fictional work about the Franco-Prussian War during his later visits to Quarry Farm in Elmira.

———. *Labor: A Novel (Travail).* Illus. New York: Harper & Brothers, 1901. 604 pp.

Source: MTLAcc, entry #237, volume donated by Clemens.

———. *Lourdes* (novel, published in 1894).

Around 1894 Olivia Clemens wrote from Bourges to Clemens, who was in the United States: "The enclosed notice of 'Lourdes' may interest you. You never saw a book so much advertised as this one is in all the shop windows of every little town. Even the little town of Neris-les-Bains had great placards announcing it and there were rows and rows of copies in the book-store windows" (*MFMT*, p. 108).

———. *Rome.* A New Edition. Trans. by Ernest Alfred Vizetelly (1853–1922). Red cloth, decorated. London: Chatto & Windus, 1896. 587 pp.

Marginalia: Clemens's penciled annotations on the front and rear endpapers ruminate about the dearth of cheap American books. There are no annotations in the text. On the verso of the front free endpaper Clemens computed the numbers of words per page with different varieties of type; he mentions *Rome, Entombed in Flesh, The Jungle Book, Natural Law in the Spiritual World, Amiel's Journals,* and *The Land Beyond the Forest.* The rear endpaper is covered with similar figures and with penciled notes: "No way to sell a 25¢ book in Am. that I know of, except in stores—not on stands nor in railways without giving pretty much all the profit to News Cos. Why don't we have cheap editions now? I spose because of News Cos & this is one reason why there is merely a momentary raid of pirates when a book dies—they can't sell it. What are the books that survive? Poetry—Philosophy—History[,] Bancroft—Biography (Franklin)—Religious ([Albert] Barnes' Notes) Novel (Stowe) Cooper[.] Mainly *solid* things. We could produce 60 authors per century."

Catalog: ListABP (1910), "Rome, Zola".

Provenance: Antenne-Dorrance Collection, Rice Lake, Wisconsin.

Location: Mark Twain Archive, Gannett-Tripp Learning Center, Elmira College, Elmira, New York.

Copy examined: Clemens's copy. Examined on 28 May 2015.

In 1886 Mark Twain complained: "We do get cheap alien books—and not of one kind only. We get . . . an ounce of wholesome literature to a hundred tons of noxious. . . . The hundred tons represent the vast editions of foreign novels consumed here—including the welcome semiannual inundation from Zola's sewer" (published in "Topics of the Time: Open Letters," *Century Magazine* 31.4 [February 1886]: 634). Twain intended to refer to Zola in the proposed appendix to *A Connecticut Yankee* "to show that modern French are the same yet" (Howard G. Baetzhold, "Course of Composition" [1961], p. 200). While the Clemenses lived in Paris in the 1890s, however, Zola became a hero to Clemens for his efforts to right the injustice done to Alfred Dreyfus (*MFMT* [1931], p.

130). On 19 January 1898 in Vienna Clemens made a notebook entry condemning "ecclesiastical & military courts" and praising "a Joan of Arc & a Zola" (NB 42, TS p. 54). In Kaltenleutgeben in1898 Clemens used "a translation" of Zola's *Rome* that he found among "35 cloth-bound books" on a "shelf" in "this little Austrian village" as he contemplated a scheme for bringing out a series of cheap books in reduced-size type. "This Englished Rome" provided an example of what he might be able to market "at 25 cents." The book was "near 600 pages" ("The Great Republic's Peanut Stand," unpublished manuscript, pp. 47–48, MTP).

———. *La Terre [The Soil]* (novel, published in 1887).
In December 1887 Mark Twain noted: "La Terre. Zola. N. Y. W. R. Jenkins" (NB 27, *N&J* 3: 357). Although in the 1880s the New York City publisher W. R. Jenkins brought out many of Zola's novels in inexpensive translations costing $1.25, *La Terre* was not one of them. A six-page undated and untitled manuscript written by Twain opens with the question: "Have you read Zola's fearful book, *La Terre*?" This brief essay is further evidence of Twain's never-resolved ambivalence toward the unvarnished sort of Naturalism produced by Zola. *La Terre* seemed to Twain "a tumultuous & ghastly nightmare, through which you were being whirled & buffeted helpless." It "does beat any French book I ever saw before" in its "filthy" subject and details; moreover, "there are five hundred & eighteen pages of it" in Twain's copy. (A Paris publishing house, G. Charpentier et cie, issued a 519-page edition of *La Terre* in 1887.) Nevertheless the people in this novel "resemble the community" in American villages. Indeed, concludes Twain, "how strange it is to reflect that that book is true. But it is. You have to confess it at last" (DV35, MTP; *LE*, pp. 172–174). In Twain's "Down the Rhone" he both attacks and defends *La Terre* as a novel that represents the literary Naturalism movement (Box 28, no. 1, MTP).
Owen Wister listened to Mark Twain discuss Zola in New York City when Twain was around "sixty years old" (Wister stated that it was after Twain came back from his global lecture tour with his debts "paid off"). Although Wister remembered the date as "during the nineties," the conversation most likely took place following Twain's return to the United States in 1900. "Mark Twain was striding up and down again, whirling on me once in a while, scowling fiercely at me, his blue eyes burning beneath the scowl, and the mound of hair all of a piece with the electric total of the man. . . . Zola was the subject, he was wholly serious, very concentrated." Wister summarized Twain's comments: "It was not about Zola's merits or defects or his position in literature; it was the latitude which French conventions allowed novelists. Did I remember the beginning of *La Terre*, where a young girl takes a cow to a bull in the presence of a man? Did I remember this and that and the other in the same book? Such doings couldn't be described here. That sort of thing wasn't confined to France; it was human, universal in rustic life; but American taste wouldn't stand its being so much as hinted at" (Owen Wister, "In Homage to Mark Twain," *Harper's Magazine* 171.1025 [October 1935]: 547–556; Wister reported Twain's opinions about Zola

on pages 548 and 553).
Krause, *MTC* (1967), pp. 274–276; Terry Oggel, "Zola and Mark Twain's Public Writing," *Excavatio* 10 (1997): 34–39.

ZSCHOKKE, JOHANN HEINRICH DANIEL (1771–1848). *Meditations on Death and Eternity*. Translated from German by Frederica Maclean Rowan (1814–1882) (published in London, 1862; reprinted in Boston, 1863). [The edition Clemens looked at is undetermined.]
Clemens was amused at the circumstances in which he encountered (but presumably did not read) these essays in Bermuda in May 1877: "Couldn't sleep—got to feeling low & far from home—went into next room to find a cheerful book—got one in the dark—'Meditations on Death & Eternity.' Looked again & found books better suited to my mood" (NB 13, *N&J* 2: 19–20). Clemens and Joseph H. Twichell were lodging at a boarding house in Hamilton, Bermuda.

ZUEBLIN, CHARLES (1866–1924). *The Religion of a Democrat*. Original quarter cloth and boards, rubbed edges and corners. New York: B[enjamin]. W. Huebsch, 1908. 192 pp.
Provenance: has the shelfmarks of the library numbering system that Clara Clemens Gabrilowitsch employed during her Detroit years. Sold at the 1951 auction in Hollywood but not listed in the sale sheet, which was a common problem owing to the hasty arrangements for that event.
Catalog: "Property from the Library of Mark Twain," Butterfield & Butterfield, San Francisco, Sale 6613 (16 July 1997), lot 2699.
Location: Mark Twain House and Museum, Hartford, Connecticut.
Copy examined: Clemens's unmarked copy. Viewed in Hartford in 1997.
On 5 July 1909 Albert Bigelow Paine recorded in his notebook that "Clemens read aloud from a book which Professor Zubelin [*sic*] left here a few days ago—*The Religion of a Democrat*" (*MTB*, pp. 1508–09). Zueblin's book criticized conventional notions of Christianity and called for a new "impersonal immortality" and "democratic religion." He declared, "When we come to understand religion and democracy and life, may we not discover that Walt Whitman means more for humanity than many captains of industry?" (p. 174). He was convinced that "democratic religion will eliminate prejudice" (p. 190).

ZURCHER, FRÉDÉRIC (1816–1890) and **ÉLIE MARGOLLÉ** (1816–1884). *Meteors, Aërolites, Storms, and Atmospheric Phenomena*. Translated from the French by William Lackland. Illus. New York: D. Appleton and Co., 1870. 324 pp.
Source: MTLAcc, entry #2004, volume donated from Clemens's library by Clara Clemens Gabrilowitsch in 1910.
Meteors, Aërolites, Storms, and Atmospheric Phenomena sought to be comprehensive, offering descriptions and explanations (many of them of course now outdated) for clouds, precipitation, fog, tornadoes, and glaciers as well as shooting stars, aurora borealis, and various sights in the heavens. Mark Twain might have been especially intrigued by Chapter V, devoted entirely to the thunderstorms and lightning that figure so frequently in his writings.

Covers, Title Pages, and Illustrations from the Clemens Family's Books

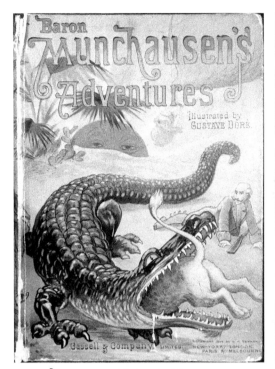

(Continued)

WONDERFUL

BALLOON ASCENTS:

OR,

The Conquest of the Skies.

A HISTORY OF

BALLOONS AND BALLOON VOYAGES.

From the French of F. Marion.

WITH ILLUSTRATIONS.

NEW YORK:
CHARLES SCRIBNER & CO.
1871.

Preceding page: Munchausen,
Adventures. *Illus. by Gustave
Doré; Alvan Bond,* Young
People's Illustrated Bible History,
*inscribed by Grandmother
Langdon to Olivia Susan
Clemens, 1879; Melville Landon,
Saratoga in 1901; Samuel Clarke,
A Mirror, possibly the oldest book
in Clemens's library.*

*This page: N. C.
Flammarion,* Wonderful Balloon
Ascents; *and Henry Wilson,*
Wonderful Characters.

A Reader's Guide to the Annotated Catalog

Because this Reader's Guide grew organically alongside the Annotated Catalog, the Reader's Guide became a large tail of more than 10,000 entries and 187,000 words that almost wags the dog. In addition to the titles of the books, stories, essays, poems, songs, plays, and other works listed in the Catalog, here one can also find the names of co-authors, editors, co-editors, pseudonyms, illustrators, translators, compilers, adaptors, writers of introductions and prefaces, composers of melodies, and other individuals who contributed to the listed items. Authors, titles, and topics of Samuel Clemens's marginalia can often be located under subject and genre headings such as Literary guides and criticism, Parapsychology, Diaries, Slavery, American politics, Letters, Silver mining, San Francisco, New York City, Italian language, Native Americans, English grammar, usage, and style, Hunting, Balloon ascents, Health and fitness, English history, Medical advice and topics, American history, Spiritualism and spiritual healing, Finance and business, Civil War, Children's and young adult literature, and dozens of other categories. Since in many instances a book title barely hints at its actual subject matter, the Reader's Guide can clarify matters by classifying it in a genre like Detective fiction. Although a major attempt was made to determine the topic or theme of works and Clemens's marginalia, the effort to analyze nearly 6,000 entries inevitably could not be complete.

THE JERICHO ROAD.

CHAPTER I.

IN WHICH THE HERO IS INTRODUCED.

"LIVELY, boys, lively! Trot along! 'Taint no time to try the turtle-step. While you're a-creepin' along like an angle-worm funeral, the Wabash is a-fallin', and if we get stuck way up the river, so's we have to lay up all summer, and you have to hoof it to deep water, you can blame your own lazy legs for it."

The speaker was Captain Sam Bates, of the river packet "Helen Douglas," and his hearers were the deck hands, or "roustabouts," who were engaged in the operation of "wooding up." To the passengers, the men seemed to move with great alacrity, and the large pile of wood on the bank appeared literally to melt under their touch, but to the captain, anxious to get up the Wabash for a load of freight, and to get out again before the river, tempo-

Marginalia in John Habberton, The Jericho Road.

A

"A. B." (pseud.): see C. P. Stokes.

Abaft the Funnel (short stories). R. Kipling.

Abaft the Funnel (short stories): see R. Kipling, *Writings in Prose and Verse*.

Abbé Constantin. L. Halévy.

Abbey, Edwin Austin (illus.): see
  W. Black, *Judith Shakespeare; Her Love Affairs and Other Adventures*.
  H. A. Dobson (ed.), *Quiet Life. Verses by Various Hands*.
  O. Goldsmith, *Deserted Village*.
  O. Goldsmith, *She Stoops to Conquer* (play, entry).
  R. Herrick, *Selections from the Poetry of Robert Herrick*.

Abbot. W. Scott.

Abbott, Edwin Abbott (pref.): see F. Bacon, *Promus of Formularies and Elegancies (Being Private Notes, Circ. 1594, Hitherto Unpublished) by Francis Bacon. Illustrated and Elucidated by Passages from Shakespeare*.

Abbott, Lyman (ed.): see (ed.) *Christian Union*.

A, B, C, ou dialogues entre A, B, C. F. M. A. de Voltaire.

Abelard and Heloise: see
  A. M. L. de Lamartine, Heloise" (story).
  W. M. Thackeray, *Thackeray's Lectures. The English Humorists. The Four Georges* (marginalia).
  O. W. Wight, *Lives and Letters of Abelard and Heloise*.
  J. G. Wilson (ed.), *Love in Letters; Illustrated in the Correspondence of Eminent Persons; with Biographical Sketches of the Writers*.

Abesse de Jouarre. [J.] E. Renan.

Abner Daniel; A Novel. W. N. Harben.

Abolitionist movement: see the Reader's Guide entry for Slavery.

"Aboo Ben Butler" (poem). C. H. Webb.

Aborigines of Victoria: With Notes Relating to the Habits of the Natives of Other Parts of Australia and Tasmania. R. B. Smyth.

"Abou Ben Adhem" (poem). L. Hunt.

About Old Story-Tellers; Of How and When They Lived, and What Stories They Told. D. G. Mitchell.

About People. C. B. G. Wells.

Abraham Lincoln. C. C. Coffin.

Abroad. T. Crane and E. B. Houghton.

Abrogation of the Seventh Commandment by the American Churches. D. Ruggles.

"Absence of Little Wesley" (poem). J. W. Riley.

"Absent-Minded Beggar" (poem). R. Kipling.

Absinthe (liquor): see G. O. Trevelyan, *Life and Letters of Lord Macaulay* (marginalia).

Abyssinia (musical comedy). J. A. Shipp and A. Rogers.

Acadians: see
  F. S. Cozzens, *Acadia; or, a Month with the Blue Noses*.
  F. Parkman, *Montcalm and Wolfe* (marginalia).

Acadia; or, a Month with the Blue Noses. F. S. Cozzens.

Accomplice. F. T. Hill.

Account of the Life, Opinions, and Writings of John Milton. T. Keightley.

Account of the Native Africans in the Neighbourhood of Sierra Leone. T. M. Winterbottom.

Accurate Description and History of the Cathedral and Metropolitan Church of St. Peter, York, from its First Foundation. York Minster.

Achilles Tatius: see
  Greek Romances of Heliodorus, Longus, and Achilles Tatius.

Acoustics: see
  R. Radau, *Wonders of Acoustics; or, The Phenomenon of Sound*.
  J. Tyndall, *Sound. A Course of Eight Lectures Delivered at the Royal Institution of Great Britain*.

Across Africa. V. L. Cameron.

Across America and Asia; Notes of a Five Years' Journey Around the World: see R. Pumpelly, *Explorations in Turkestan, with an Account of The Basin of Eastern Persia and Sistan. Expedition of 1903*.

Acts of Stephen: see Henry of Huntingdon, *Chronicle*.

Acts of the Apostles. A. Barnes.

Adam and Eve: see
  J. H. Friswell, "Story of Adam and Eve."
  B. W. Howard, *Garden of Eden*.
  J. M. Lowrie, *Adam and His Times*.
  A. D. White, *History of the Warfare of Science with Theology in Christendom* (marginalia).

Adam and His Times. J. M. Lowrie.

Adam Bede. G. Eliot.

Adams, Abigail: see J. Adams, *Familiar Letters of John Adams and His Wife Abigail Adams, During the Revolution*.

Adams, Charles Francis: see
  (ed.) J. Adams, *Familiar Letters*.
  (pref.) E. Roberts, *Shoshone and Other Western Wonders*.
  (inscr.) H. P. Willis, *Our Philippine Problem; A Study of American Colonial Policy* (marginalia).

Adams, Dick (British criminal): see C. Whitehead, *Lives and Exploits of the Most Noted Highwaymen, Robbers and Murderers, of All Nations*.

Adams, Henrietta (illus.): see G. Smith, *Little Ned Happy and Flora*.

Adams, John Quincy: see
  G. Berkeley, "On the Prospect of Planting Arts and Learning America" (poem) (Catalog entry).
  (intro.) J. C. Lovejoy and O. Lovejoy, *Memoir of the Rev. Elijah P. Lovejoy, Who Was Murdered in Defence of the Liberty of the Press*.

Adams, Maude (actress): see
  J. M. Barrie, *Peter Pan, or the Boy Who Wouldn't Grow Up* (play).
  A. Davies, *Maude Adams*.
  W. Shakespeare, *Romeo and Juliet* (play).
  C. R. Teller, *Cage* (Catalog entry).
  C. R. Teller, "Sociological Maid. A Play in One Act" (Catalog entry).

Adams, Sarah Taylor (illus.): see E. P. Adams, *Story Sermons from Les Misérables*.

"Adams, Stephen" (pseud. of M. Maybrick, composer): see
  E. Thomas, "Warrior bold" (song).
  F. E. Weatherly, "Nancy Lee" (song).

Adamson, Sydney (illus.): see J. K. Bangs, *R. Holmes & Co.*

Addictions: see

S. H. Adams, "Great American Fraud: The Scavengers" (article).

F. H. Ludlow, *Hasheesh Eater; Being Passages from the Life of a Pythagorean*.

J. J. McCook (Catalog entry).

H. E. B. Stowe, *My Wife and I; or, Harry Henderson's History*.

Addison. W. J. Courthope.

Addison, Joseph: see

L. Cornaro, *Art of Living Long* (includes a *Spectator* piece).

W. J. Courthope, *Addison*.

W. M. Thackeray, *Thackeray's Lectures. The English Humorists. The Four Georges*.

Address Delivered at Cumming, Georgia, February, 1844, on the Rise and Progress of Society and the Formation of Government. S. W. Royston.

Addresses. E. Thring.

"Adeler, Max" (pseud.): see C. H. Clark.

Adirondack Region. V. Colvin.

Adirondacks: see F. Wilkinson, *Strength of the Hills; A Novel*.

Adirondack Stories. P. Deming.

"Adirondacks Verified" (essay). C. D. Warner.

Adler, G. J. (contr.): see H. G. Ollendorff, *Ollendorff's New Method of Learning to Read, Write, and Speak the German Language*.

Ad Matrem and Other Poems. P. S. Grant.

Admiral George Dewey; A Sketch of the Man. J. Barrett.

Adonis (burlesque musical). W. Gill and H. E. Dixey.

Advanced Course in Yogi Philosophy and Oriental Occultism. W. W. Atkinson.

Adoption: see the Reader's Guide entry for Orphans.

"Adventure in a Forest; or, Dickens's Maypole Inn" (essay). J. Payn.

Adventurers; A Tale of Treasure Trove. H. B. M. Watson.

Adventures du Chevalier de Faublis. J. Louvet de Couvrai.

Adventures in Kamtchatka and Northern Asia. G. Kennan.

Adventures of a Consul Abroad. L. Monti.

Adventures of a Donkey. S. R. Ségur.

Adventures of a Fair Rebel. M. J. Crim.

Adventures of a Nice Young Man; A Novel, by Aix. F. Bausman.

Adventures of an Old Maid. By Aunt Ruth. B. C. Greene.

Adventures of a Younger Son. E. J. Trelawny.

Adventures of a Young Naturalist. L. Biart.

Adventures of Baron Munchausen. B. Münchausen.

Adventures of Buffalo Bill. W. F. Cody.

Adventures of Captain Bonneville. W. Irving.

Adventures of Count Louis de Sancerre. E. S. Van Zile.

Adventures of Gil Blas of Santillane. A. R. Le Sage.

Adventures of Hajji Baba, of Ispahan. J. J. Morier.

Adventures of Jimmy Brown, Written by Himself. W. L. Alden.

Adventures of M. D'Haricot. J. S. Clouston.

Adventures of Mr. Verdant Green. E. Bradley.

Adventures of Philip on His Way Through the World; Showing Who Robbed Him, Who Helped Him, and Who Passed Him By. W. M. Thackeray.

Adventures of Podsy and June. L. M. Sill.

Adventures of Prince Lazybones, and Other Stories. H. A. Hays.

Adventures of Roderick Random (novel). T. G. Smollett.

Adventures of Sherlock Holmes: see A. C. Doyle (Catalog entry).

Adventures of the Hon. Leo Fantassé. A. P. MacDonald.

Adventures on the Great Hunting Grounds of the World. V. Meunier (comp.).

Advertising: see

G. P. Rowell, *Forty Years an Advertising Agent*.

H. Sampson, *History of Advertising from the Earliest Times*.

H. D. J. van Schevichaven and J. C. Hotten, *History of Signboards, from the Earliest Times to the Present Day*.

Aegyptische Königstochter. Historischer Roman. G. M. Ebers.

"Aesop, G. Washington" (pseud.): see G. T. Lanigan.

Aesop's Fables. Aesop.

Aesop's Fables: see E. F. Ware, *Some of the Rhymes of Ironquill. (A Book of Moods)*.

Aetna (volcano): see N. S. Shaler, *Aspects of the Earth: A Popular Account of Some Familiar Geological Phenomena* (marginalia).

Afghanistan: see

C. T. Marvin, *Russians at the Gates of Herat*.

R. Pumpelly, *Across America and Asia; Notes of a Five Years' Journey Around the World*: see R. Pumpelly, *Explorations in Turkestan, with an Account of The Basin of Eastern Persia and Sistan. Expedition of 1903*.

Africa and its explorers:

S. Bonsal, *Morocco As It Is*.

V. L. Cameron, *Across Africa*.

C. Chaillé-Long, *Central Africa: Naked Truths of Naked People*.

P. B. Du Chaillu, *Country of the Dwarfs*.

P. B. Du Chaillu, *Wild Life Under the Equator*.

A. A. B. Edwards, *Thousand Miles Up the Nile*.

R. G. Gordon-Cumming, *Five Years of a Hunter's Life in the Far Interior of South Africa*.

J. T. Headley, *Stanley's Adventures in the Wilds of Africa: A Graphic Account of the Several Expeditions of Henry M. Stanley*.

E. J. House, *Hunter's Camp-Fires*.

W. D. Howells (co-ed.), *Library of Universal Adventure by Sea and Land*.

H. H. Johnston, *History of a Slave* (enslaved Africans in Western Sudan).

D. Ker, "From the Sea to the Desert" (article).

M. H. Kingsley, *Story of West Africa*.

T. W. Knox, *Backsheesh! or, Life and Adventures in the Orient*.

D. Livingston and C. Livingstone, *Narrative of an Expedition to the Zambesi and Its Tributaries*.

W. S. Mayo, *Kaloolah: Adventures of Jonathan Romer of Nantucket* (novel).

V. Meunier (comp.), *Adventures on the Great Hunting Grounds of the World*.

W. C. Prime, *Boat Life in Egypt and Nubia*.

K. G. Schillings, *In Wildest Africa*.

K. G. Schillings, *With Flash-light and Rifle;*

Photographing by Flash-light at Night the Wild Animal World of Equatorial Africa.

H. M. Stanley, *Autobiography of Sir Henry Morton Stanley.*

H. M. Stanley, *In Darkest Africa; or, the Quest, Rescue, and Retreat of Emin, Governor of Equatoria.*

H. M. Stanley, *Slavery and the Slave Trade in Africa.*

H. M. Stanley, *Through the Dark Continent; or, The Sources of the Nile, Around the Great Lakes of Equatorial Africa, and Down the Livingstone River to the Atlantic Ocean.*

Summer in Africa (unidentified book).

Syme. *Central Africa* (unidentified book).

B. Taylor, *Journey to Central Africa; or, Life and Landscapes from Egypt to the Negro Kingdoms of the White Nile.*

J. Tyler, *Livingstone Lost and Found; or, Africa and Its Explorers.*

H. Ward, *My Life with Stanley's Rear Guard.*

M. S. Wellby, *'Twixt Sirdar and Menelik; An Account of a Year's Expedition from Zeila to Cairo Through Unknown Abyssinia.*

T. M. Winterbottom, *An Account of the Native Africans in the Neighbourhood of Sierra Leone.*

J. G. Wood, *Uncivilized Races; or, Natural History of Man; Being a Complete Account of the Manners and Customs, and the Physical, Social, and Religious Condition and Characteristics, of the Uncivilized Races of Men, Throughout the Entire World.*

See also the Reader's Guide entries for Congo, for Slavery, and for South Africa.

African Americans: see

G. Ade, *Pink Marsh. A Story of the Streets and Town.*

C. C. Brush, *Colonel's Opera Cloak.*

A. M. Buckner, *Towards the Gulf; A Romance of Louisiana.*

G. W. Cable (various Catalog entries).

A. R. Colquhoun, *Greater America.*

C. W. Dilke, *Greater Britain: A Record of Travel in English-Speaking Countries During 1866 and 1867.*

T. Dixon, *Leopard's Spots: A Romance of the White Man's Burden—1865–1900.*

P. L. Dunbar, *Majors and Minors: Poems.*

R. M. Jonas, "Timed to an African Chant" (poem).

C. C. Jones, *Negro Myths from the Georgia Coast, Told in the Vernacular.*

E. W. Kemble (Catalog entry).

T. N. Page, *In Ole Virginia; or, Marse Chan and Other Stories.*

H. D. Pittman, *Belle of the Bluegrass Country. Studies in Black and White.*

W. Reid, "Some Southern Reminiscences" (essay).

W. T. Sherman, *Memoirs of General William T. Sherman. By Himself* (marginalia).

J. A. Shipp and A. Rogers, *Abyssinia* (musical comedy).

S. W. Small ("Old Si" dialect sketches).

F. H. Smith, *Colonel Carter of Cartersville* (novel).

F. H. Smith, "Editor's Drawer: Ginger and the Goose" (story).

R. M. Stuart, *Second Wooing of Salina Sue, and Other Stories.*

A. W. Tourgée, *Bricks Without Straw. A Novel.*

A. W. Tourgée, *Fool's Errand, by One of the Fools.*

A. E. Trumbull, *Hour's Promise* (novel).

F. E. Wadleigh, *'Twixt Wave and Sky* (novel) (Catalog entry).

C. D. Warner, *Studies in the South and West, with Comments on Canada.*

G. A. Wilcox, *Christian Philanthropist. A Sketch of the Life of Mr. Daniel Hand, and of His Benefaction to the American Missionary Association, for the Education of the Colored People in the Southern States of America.*

J. T. Wilson, *Black Phalanx; A History of the Negro Soldiers of the United States in the Wars of 1775–1812, 1861–'65.*

African American enslavement: see the Reader's Guide entry for Slavery.

African American spirituals: see the Reader's Guide entry for Spirituals.

"After" (poem). R. Browning.

After Her Death; The Story of a Summer. L. Whiting.

Afterlife: see

F. P. Cobbe, *Peak in Darien, with Some Other Inquiries Touching Concerns of the Soul and the Body. An Octave of Essays.*

M. D. Conway, *Sacred Anthology: A Book of Ethnical Scriptures, Collected and Edited by Moncure Daniel Conway* (marginalia).

H. Drummond, *Natural Law in the Spiritual World.*

A. F. Eastman, "Dose of Paradise" (short story).

C. Giles, *Our Children in the Other Life.*

E. G. Hubbard, *Man of Sorrows. Being a Little Journey to the Home of Jesus of Nazareth* (marginalia).

A. A. S. James, *Ode to Girlhood and Other Poems.*

L. Macbean and J. Brown, *Marjorie Fleming: The Story of Pet Marjorie* (marginalia).

F. W. H. Myers, *Human Personality and Its Survival of Bodily Death.*

H. S. Olcott, *People from the Other World.*

Old Abe's Jokes; Fresh from Abraham's Bosom.

Omar Khayyám, *Rubáiyát of Omar Khayyám, The Astronomer-Poet of Persia, Rendered into English Verse* (Clara Clemens Samossoud's marginalia).

E. S. Phelps, *Gates Ajar.*

M. Reed, *Master's Violin.*

C. T. Russell, *Millennial Dawn: The Plan of the Ages.*

M. J. Savage, *Can Telepathy Explain? Results of Psychical Research.*

V. Streamer (comp.), *Voices of Doubt and Trust* (marginalia).

E. Swedenborg, *Heaven and Hell.*

F. Thompson, *Shelley* (marginalia).

W. H. Thomson, *Parables and Their Home. The Parables by the Lake* (Catalog entry).

J. Timbs, *Things Not Generally Known, Familiarly Explained* (marginalia).

C. Wagner, *Âme des Choses.*

G. W. Warder, *Cities of the Sun.*

A. D. White, *History of the Warfare of Science with Theology* (marginalia).

L. Whiting, *After Her Death; The Story of a Summer*.

L. Whiting, *World Beautiful. Second Series*.

J. H. D. Zschokke, *Meditations on Death and Eternity*. See also the Reader's Guide entries for Agnosticism, for Atheism, for Christianity, and for Death.

Aftermath; Part Second of "A Kentucky Cardinal." J. L. Allen.

Afternoon Tea: Rhymes for Children with Original Illustrations. J. G. Sowerby and H. H. Emmerson.

"After the Wedding" (poem). W. D. Howells.

"Against idleness" (hymn). I. Watts.

"Against quarrelling and fighting" (hymn). I. Watts.

Agamemnon, La Saisiaz, Dramatic Idyls, and Jocoseria. R. Browning.

Agamemnon of Aeschylus. R. Browning.

Agassiz, Louis: see

  E. C. Agassiz (ed.), *Louis Agassiz, His Life and Correspondence*.

  (contr.): see H. Miller, *Foot-Prints of the Creator*.

Aging: see the Reader's Guide entry for Old age.

Age of Chivalry; or, Legends of King Arthur. T. Bulfinch.

"Age of Earth" (article). W. T. Kelvin.

Age of Fable; or, Beauties of Mythology. T. Bulfinch.

Age of Louis XIV. F. M. A. de Voltaire.

Age of Reason. T. Paine.

Age of Shakespeare. A. C. Swinburne.

Agitator; A Novel. C. M. Black.

Agnes. J. Abbott.

Agnes Grey: see E. Brontë and Anne Brontë, *Wuthering Heights and Agnes Grey*.

Agnosticism: see

  C. Darwin, *Journal of Researches into the Natural History and Geology of the Countries Visited During the Voyage of the H.M.S. Beagle Round the World* (marginalia).

  S. Dill, *Roman Society in the Last Century of the Western Empire* (marginalia).

  T. W. Doane, *Bible Myths and Their Parallels in Other Religions: Being a Comparison of the Old and New Testament Myths and Miracles with Those of Heathen Nations of Antiquity*.

  V. Goldthwaite, *Philosophy of Ingersoll*.

  H. C. Greene, *Gospel of the Childhood of Our Lord Jesus Christ* (Catalog entry).

  R. G. Ingersoll, "Christian Religion."

  R. G. Ingersoll, *Ghosts and Other Lectures*.

  R. G. Ingersoll, *Lectures*.

  R. G. Ingersoll, *Works of Robert G. Ingersoll*.

  R. K. Noyes, *Views of Religion, Collected by Rufus K. Noyes, M. D.*

  [J.] E. Renan, *Apostles. Translated from the Original French*.

  M. J. Savage (Catalog entry).

  V. Streamer (comp.), *Voices of Doubt and Trust*.

  Tacitus, *Works of Tacitus* (marginalia).

  F. Thompson, *Shelley* (marginalia).

  L. N. Tolstoy, *Teaching of Jesus* (Catalog entry).

  Truth: A Weekly Journal (London periodical).

  Truth Seeker (magazine).

  M. A. A. Ward, *Robert Elsmere*.

W. H. White, *Autobiography of Mark Rutherford, Dissenting Minister* (novel).

W. H. White, *Mark Rutherford's Deliverance; Being the Second Part of His Autobiography* (novel).

A. J. E. Wilson, *Beulah, A Novel*.

G. E. Woodberry, "Orator" (poem).

T. Wright (ed.), *Early Travels in Palestine* (marginalia).

C. Zueblin, *Religion of a Democrat*.

See also the Reader's Guide entries for Afterlife, for Atheism, and for Christianity.

Agony Column. C. A. Scott.

Agra: see S. C. Mukerji, *Traveller's Guide to Agra, Containing an Account of the Past History, the Antiquities, and the Principal Sights of Agra*.

Aguinaldo: A Narrative of Filipino Ambitions. E. Wildman.

Aguinaldo, Emilio: see

  J. F. Shafroth, "Speech of Hon. John F. Shafroth, of Colorado, in the House of Representatives, Tuesday, December 17, 1901" (marginalia).

  E. Wildman, *Aguinaldo: A Narrative of Filipino Ambitions*.

  See also the Reader's Guide entry for Philippines.

Agriculture: see

  B. Barney, *The Bright Side of Country Life*.

  H. Greeley, *What I Know of Farming: A Series of Brief and Plain Expositions of Practical Agriculture as an Art Based Upon Science*.

  P. G. Hamerton, *Chapters on Animals*.

  J. P. Norton, *Elements of Scientific Agriculture*.

  K. V. Saint Maur, *Earth's Bounty*.

  E. V. Wilcox and C. B. Smith, *Farmer's Cyclopedia of Agriculture: A Compendium of Agricultural Science and Practice*.

Ahn's First German Book, Being the First Division of Ahn's Rudiments of the German Language. J. F. Ahn.

Ahn's Second German Book. J. F. Ahn.

Aiglon. E. Rostand.

Aikin, Lucy (ed.): see D. Defoe, *Robinson Crusoe in Words of One Syllable*.

"Aileen Mavourneen" (song). A. M. F. Hall.

"Ain't I glad I got out de wilderness": see J. Warner, "Down in Alabam'" (minstrel song).

"Aix" (pseud.): see F. Bausman.

Akenside, Mark (author): see *Book of Pleasures*.

"Akhoond of Swat": see G. T. Lanigan, "Threnody" (poem).

Alabama: see

  J. G. Baldwin, *Flush Times of Alabama and Mississippi*.

  L. C. Pyrnelle, *Diddie, Dumps, and Tot; or, Plantation Child-Life*.

  H. E. Taliaferro (Catalog entry).

  J. Warner, "Down in Alabam'" (minstrel song).

  E. Wildman, *Aguinaldo: A Narrative of Filipino Ambitions* (Catalog entry).

  H. C. Work, "Marching through Georgia" (song).

Aladdin O'Brien. G. Morris.

Alan Ransford, A Story. E. D. Deland.

Alaska: see

  C. A. Adams, *Pete's Devils*.

  A. Badlam, *Wonders of Alaska*.

F. Bancroft, *Life of William H. Seward*.

E. Hough, *Young Alaskans*.

C. K. Munroe, *Snow-Shoes and Sledges*.

"Alas, and did my Saviour bleed!" I. Watts.

"Alas! those chimes, so sweetly pealing" (aria): see E. Fitzball, *Maritana* (opera).

Albany, New York: see J. F. Mines, *Tour Around New York, and My Summer Acre;Being the Recreations of Mr. Felix Oldboy*.

Albums: see

Carnan d'Ache (pseud.), *Bric à Brac; Album par Carnan d'Ache*.

Favorite Album of Fun and Fancy.

R. Saxton (ed.), *Mental Photographs: An Album for Confessions of Tastes, Habits, and Convictions*.

W. T. Stead, *Portraits and Autographs: An Album for the People*.

Alcibiades (Athenian general): see

Plutarch's Lives of Alcibiades & Coriolanus, Aristides & Cato the Censor.

Plutarchus, *Plutarch's Lives of Illustrious Men*.

Alcoholic beverages: see the Reader's Guide entries for Addictions, for Bar-Tending, for Drunkenness, for Liquor, and for Temperance literature.

Alcoholism: see the Reader's Guide entries for Addictions, for Drunkenness, and for Temperance literature.

Alden, Henry Mills (co-ed.): see

W. D. Howells (co-ed.), *Their Husbands' Wives*.

W. D. Howells (co-ed.), *Under the Sunset*.

Aldin, Cecil Charles Windsor (illus.): see

W. L. Emanuel, *Dog Day; or, The Angel in the House*.

W. L. Emanuel, *Dogs of War*.

Aldine, Henry (evangelist): see W. James, *Varieties of Religious Experience; A Study in Human Nature* (marginalia).

Aldrich, Thomas Bailey: see

M. L. Goddard (co-comp.), *Sea and Shore: A Collection of Poems* (inscr.).

F. Greenslet, *Life of Thomas Bailey Aldrich*.

W. D. Howells, "Thomas Bailey Aldrich" (biographical sketch).

"Nora McCarty" (ballad).

S. Smith, *Essays Social and Political. First and Second Series* (Catalog entry).

V. Streamer (comp.), *Voices of Doubt and Trust*.

C. M. de Talleyrand-Périgord (Catalog entry).

J. T. Trowbridge, *Book of Gold, and Other Poems* (Catalog entry).

Alec Scott (steamboat): see W. Sharp, *Flower O' the Vine: Romantic Ballads and Sospiri di Roma* (sheet of notes laid in).

Alexander III (Emperor of Russia): see A. R. Ropes and M. E. Ropes, *On Peter's Island* (novel).

Alexander VI (Pope): see L. von Ranke, *History of the Popes, Their Church and State*.

Alexander, Francesca: see (trans., illus.) J. Ruskin, *Roadside Songs of Tuscany*.

"Alexander, Mrs." (pseud.): see A. F. Hector.

Alexander the Great: see

T. A. Dodge, *Great Captains*.

C. W. C. Oman, *History of Greece from the Earliest Times to the Death of Alexander the Great*.

D. O'Sullivan (comp.), *Book of Legends, Containing a Selection of Standard Tales from the Most Esteemed British Essayists*.

C. M. Yonge, *Book of Worthies, Gathered from the Old Histories and Now Written Anew*.

Alford, Henry: see G. W. Moon, *Learned Men's English: The Grammarians*.

Alfred de Musset. C. Vincens.

Alfred, Lord Tennyson; A Memoir by His Son. H. Tennyson.

Alfred, Lord Tennyson: A Study of His Life and Work. A. Waugh.

Alger, Abby Langdon (co-trans.): see H. Martin, *Popular History of France, from the First Revolution to the Present Time*.

Algeria: see

R. S. Hichens, *Barbary Sheep; A Novel*.

D. Ker, "From the Sea to the Desert" (article).

Algic Researches, Comprising Inquiries Respecting the Mental Characteristics of the North American Indians. H. R. Schoolcraft.

Alhambra: A Series of Tales and Sketches of the Moors and Spaniards. W. Irving.

Alice-For-Short: A Dichronism. W. F. De Morgan.

Alice's Adventures in Wonderland. C. L. Dodgson.

Allan's Wife. H. R. Haggard.

All Around a Palette. E. Champney.

Allegro and Other Poems. J. Milton.

Allen, Alexander Viets Griswold, *Life and Letters of Phillips Brooks*: see M. B. Cheney (ed.), *Life and Letters of Horace Bushnell* (commentary).

Allen Bay, A Story. S. O. Stedman.

"Allen, Jennie" (pseud.): see G. Donworth.

"Allen, Josiah" (fictional character): see M. Holley, *Josiah Allen's Wife*.

Allen, Mary Augusta (Wood) (co-author): see C. B. Allen and M. A. W. Allen, *Man Wonderful in the House Beautiful: An Allegory Teaching the Principles of Physiology and Hygiene, and the Effects of Stimulants and Narcotics*.

"All hail the power of Jesus' name" (hymn). B. Perronet.

"All Hands"; Pictures of Life in the United States Navy. R. F. Zogbaum.

Allibone, Samuel Austin (contr.): see T. B. Macaulay, *History of England from the Accession of James II*.

All in a Garden Fair. W. Besant.

Allingham, Helen (co-ed.): see W. Allingham, *William Allingham, A Diary*.

"All in the Downs the fleet was moor'd" (line from poem and ballad): see J. Gay, "Sweet William's Farewell to Black-ey'd Susan" (poem, ballad).

"All people that on earth do dwell" (hymn). W. Kethe.

"All Quiet on the Potomac Tonight" (poem, song): see E. L. Beers, "Picket-Guard" (poem, song).

All Sorts and Conditions of Men; An Impossible Story. W. Besant.

All's Well That Ends Well (play). W. Shakespeare.

All the World's Fighting Ships. F. T. Jane.

Almanacs: see

J. H. Carter, *Commodore Rollingpin's Humorous Illustrated Almanac*.

B. Franklin, *Poor Richard's Almanack*.

D. Jayne, *Jayne's Medical Almanac and Guide to Health*.

G. L. Kittredge, *Old Farmer and His Almanack; Being Some Observations on Life and Manners in New England a Hundred Years Ago*.

Krippen-Kalender 1899–47.

T. Nast, *Nast's Illustrated Almanac for 1873*.

H. W. Shaw, *Josh Billings' Farmers' Allminax for the Year 1870*.

Turner's Comic Almanac.

Wyman's Comic Almanac for the Times, 1856.

See also the Reader's Guide entry for Calendars.

"Alo'ha!": A Hawaiian Salutation. G. L. Chaney.

Alone in China, and Other Stories. J. Ralph.

Alone on a Wide Wide Sea: A Novel. W. C. Russell.

Alonnier, Edmond (co-ed.): see J. de La Fontaine, *Fables de J. de La Fontaine*.

Alonzo and Melissa; or, The Unfeeling Father. An American Tale. I. Mitchell.

Alps: see the Reader's Guide entry for Mountain climbing.

Alroy. A Romance. B. Disraeli.

Altemus, George W., Jr. (inscr.): see *Our Stories*.

Alter ego stories: see the Reader's Guide entries for Double identities and for Twins.

Amazon River: see W. L. Herndon, *Exploration of the Valley of the Amazon*.

Ambassadors; A Novel. H. James.

Âme des Choses. C. Wagner.

"America" (anthem). S. F. Smith.

America, Historical, Statistic, and Descriptive. J. S. Buckingham.

American Animals. W. Stone (co-author).

American Annual Cyclopaedia: see *Appletons' Annual Cyclopedia and Register of Important Events of the Year*.

"American Authors and British Pirates" (article). B. Matthews.

American Authors and Their Homes: Personal Descriptions & Interviews. F. W. Halsey (ed.).

American Bookmen: Sketches, Chiefly Biographical, of Certain Writers of the Nineteenth Century. M. A. D. Howe.

American Colonial Policy. H. P. Willis.

American Colonization Society: see *Am. Col. N. E. Society, Dec. 22, 1886*.

American Dictionary of the English Language. N. Webster.

American drama: see

D. Belasco (Catalog entry).

J. Bernard, *Retrospections of America, 1797–1811*.

E. T. Booth (Catalog entry).

D. Boucicault (various play titles).

G. H. Brennan, *Bill Truetell, A Story of Theatrical Life*.

A. Davies, *Maude Adams*.

J. M. Field, *Drama in Pokerville, The Bench and Bar of Jurytown, and Other Stories*.

L. Hutton, *Curiosities of the American Stage*.

L. Hutton, *Edwin Booth*.

J. Jefferson, *Autobiography of Joseph Jefferson*.

G. Z. MacLaren (Catalog entry).

B. Matthews, *Studies of the Stage*.

C. Morris, *Pasteboard Crown: A Story of the New York Stage* (novel).

F. S. Smith, *Theatrical Journey—Work and Anecdotical Recollections of Sol Smith*.

H. Vaders, *Wikkey: A Scrap, by Yam*.

See also the Reader's Guide entry for Theatrical history.

"American Earl" (unpublished autobiography). J. Leathers.

American Edition of the British Encyclopedia, or Dictionary of Arts and Sciences. W. Nicholson (ed.).

American Far West: see the Reader's Guide entry for the American West.

"American Fiction Again" (essay). B. Matthews.

"American Flag" (poem). J. R. Drake.

"American Flag" (poem): see *Ocean Scenes; or, The Perils and Beauties of the Deep*.

American Folklore: see *Journal of American Folklore*.

American Food and Game Fishes: A Popular Account of All the Species Found in America North of the Equator. D. S. Jordan (co-author).

American Girl in London. S. J. D. Cotes.

American Girls' Book; or, Occupation for Play Hours. E. Leslie.

American history (including early Canadian history): see

American Nation: A History from Original Sources by Associated Scholars. A. B. Hart (ed.).

W. Archer, *America To-Day: Observations and Reflections*.

G. M. Asher (ed.), *Henry Hudson the Navigator*.

A. F. de Bacourt, *Souvenirs of a Diplomat: Private Letters from America*.

J. Barnes, *Loyal Traitor: A Story of the War of 1812*.

A. B. Berard, *Berard's History of the United States*.

J. Bonner, *Child's History of the United States*.

A. Brown, *Genesis of the United States*.

W. C. Bryant (co-author), *Popular History of the United States, from the First Discovery of the Western Hemisphere by the Northmen, to the End of the Civil War*.

C. C. Coffin, *Old Times in the Colonies*.

F. O. C. Darley, *People of America*.

S. A. Drake, *Heart of the White Mountains, Their Legend and Scenery*.

E. Eggleston, *First Book in American History*.

T. D. English, *Boy's Book of Battle-Lyrics: A Collection of Verses Illustrating Some Notable Events in the History of the United States of America*.

C. H. Farnham, *Life of Francis Parkman*.

J. Fiske, *Beginnings of New England; or, The Puritan Theocracy*.

J. Fiske, *Discovery of America, with Some Account of Ancient America and the Spanish Conquest*.

J. W. Forney, *Anecdotes of Public Men*.

C. A. Goodrich, *History of the United States*.

P. G. Hamerton, *French and English: A Comparison*.

A. B. Hart, *Colonial Children*.

T. W. S. Higginson, *History of the United States from 986 to 1905* (marginalia).

R. Hildreth, *History of the United States of America*.

R. Hitchcock (ed.), *Decisive Battles of America*.

G. E. Howard, *American Nation: A History. Preliminaries of the Revolution, 1763–1775.*

T. A. Janvier, *Henry Hudson, A Brief Statement of His Aims and His Achievements.*

M. Johnston, *Prisoners of Hope. A Tale of Colonial Virginia* (novel).

M. Johnston, *Sir Mortimer. A Novel.*

J. O. Kaler, *Ezra Jordan's Escape from the Massacre at Fort Loyall* (novel).

F. A. Kemble, *Records of Later Life.*

J. N. Larned (ed.), *Literature of American History: A Bibliographical Guide.*

B. J. Lossing, *Harper's Popular Cyclopaedia of United States History.*

B. J. Lossing, *Pictorial Field-Book of the War of 1812.*

D. B. Lucas and J. F. McLaughlin, *Fisher Ames-Henry Clay, Etc.*

J. McCarthy, *Reminiscences.*

C. Mather, *Magnalia Christi Americana; or, The Ecclesiastical History of New-England.*

W. J. Mills, *Caroline of Courtlandt Street* (novel).

F. A. Ober, *Amerigo Vespucci.*

F. A. Ober, *Columbus the Discoverer.*

F. A. Ober, *Ferdinand Magellan.*

F. A. Ober, *John and Sebastian Cabot.*

F. A. Ober, *Juan Ponce de Leon.*

F. A. Ober, *Vasco Nuñez de Balboa.*

F. Parkman, *Conspiracy of Pontiac and the Indian War after the Conquest of Canada.*

F. Parkman, *Count Frontenac and New France Under Louis XIV.*

F. Parkman, *Jesuits in North America in the Seventeenth Century.*

F. Parkman, *La Salle and the Discovery of the Great West.*

F. Parkman, *Montcalm and Wolfe.*

F. Parkman, *Old Régime in Canada.*

F. Parkman, *Oregon Trail: Sketches of Prairie and Rocky-Mountain Life.*

F. Parkman, *Pioneers of France in the New World.*

J. Parton, *Life and Times of Aaron Burr.*

C. H. Peck, *Jacksonian Epoch.*

Pennsylvania Magazine.

K. J. Ploetz, *Epitome of Ancient, Mediaeval, and Modern History.*

W. Robertson, *History of the Discovery and Settlement of America.*

W. Swinton, *Outlines of the World's History, Ancient, Medieval, and Modern.*

R. G. Thwaites, *France in America, 1497–1763.*

T. Thomas, *History of Prices, and of the State of the Circulation, from 1793 to 1837.*

G. A. Townsend, *Tales of the Chesapeake.*

G. O. Trevelyan, *Life and Letters of Lord Macaulay* (marginalia).

United States Constitution.

E. B. Washburne, *Recollections of a Minister to France, 1869–1877.*

S. Webster, *Two Treaties of Paris and the Supreme Court.*

B. T. Wilson, *Ye Mountaineer.*

J. T. Wilson, *Black Phalanx; A History of the Negro Soldiers of the United States in the Wars of 1775–1812, 1861–'65.*

W. Wilson, *History of the American People.*

See also the Reader's Guide entries for American politics, for American Revolution, for Civil War (American), and for North American travel writings.

American humorists:

C. F. Adams, *Leedle Yawcob Strauss, and Other Poems.*

G. Ade, *Fables in Slang* (and five other titles).

W. L. Alden, *Shooting Stars as Observed from the "Sixth Column" of the Times* (and four other titles).

T. B. Aldrich, "Friend of My Youth."

G. W. Bagby, *Week in Hepsidam; Being the First and Only True Account of the Mountains, Men, Manners and Morals Thereof.*

J. M. Bailey (pseud. "Danbury News Man"), *Life in Danbury.*

O. Bainbridge, *Devil's Note Book.*

J. G. Baldwin, *Flush Times of Alabama and Mississippi.*

J. K. Bangs (numerous titles).

J. Barber, *War Letters of a Disbanded Volunteer, Embracing His Experiences as Honest Old Abe's Bosom Friend and Unofficial Adviser.*

A. Bierce, *Cobwebs from an Empty Skull.*

N. Brooks and I. Bromley, "Punch, Brothers, Punch" (newspaper jingle).

C. F. Browne, *Artemus Ward, His Book.*

C F. Browne, *Artemus Ward in London, and Other Papers.*

H. H. Brownell (poet).

R. J. Burdette, *Rise and Fall of the Mustache and Other "Hawk-Eyetems."*

G. Burgess, *Are You a Bromide? or, The Sulphitic Theory Expounded and Exemplified.*

E. P. Butler, *Pigs Is Pigs.*

E. P. Butler, "Reformation of Uncle Billy" (short story).

W. A. Butler, *Nothing to Wear: An Episode of City Life* (humorous poem).

G. W. Cable, "Frowenfeld's Clerk" in *Grandissimes. A Story of Creole Life.*

J. H. Carter (pseud. "Commodore Rollingpin").

C. H. Clark (pseud. "Max Adeler"), *Elbow-Room; A Novel without a Plot.*

C. H. Clark (pseud. "Max Adeler"), *Fortunate Island and Other Stories.*

G. M. Cooke, *Their First Formal Call.*

F. S. Cozzens, *Acadia; or, a Month with the Blue Noses.*

F. S. Cozzens, *Sparrowgrass Papers; or, Living in the Country.*

G. W. Curtis, *Potiphar Papers.*

G. W. Curtis, *Prue and I.*

S. P. Davis, *Short Stories.*

G. H. Derby, *Phoenixiana; or, Sketches and Burlesques.*

M. E. M. Dodge, "Miss Malony on the Chinese Question" (sketch).

G. Donworth, *Letters of Jennie Allen to Her Friend Miss Musgrove.*

F. P. Dunne, *Dissertations by Mr. Dooley.*

E. Field, *Little Book of Profitable Tales.*

J. M. Field, *Drama in Pokerville, The Bench and Bar of Jurytown, and Other Stories.*

M. I. T. Fisk, *Monologues.*

M. I. T. Fisk, *Talking Woman (Monologues).*

J. C. Goldsmith, pseud. "P. I. Man" (Catalog entry).

B. C. Greene, *Adventures of an Old Maid. By Aunt Ruth.*

L. P. Hale, *Peterkin Papers.*

T. C. Haliburton, *Clockmaker, or Sayings and Doings of Sam Slick.*

G. W. Harris, *Sut Lovingood: Yarns Spun by a "Nat'ral Born Durn'd Fool."*

J. C. Harris, "At Teague Poteet's: A Sketch of the Hog Mountain Range" (story).

J. C. Harris, *Nights with Uncle Remus: Myths and Legends of the Old Plantation.*

J. C. Harris, *Uncle Remus: His Songs and His Sayings.*

W. B. Hawkins ("Quills"): see the Catalog entry for L. E. Trescott.

M. Holley, *Josiah Allen's Wife.*

O. W. Holmes, *Autocrat of the Breakfast-Table.*

J. J. Hooper, *Some Adventures of Captain Simon Suggs, Late of the Tallapoosa Volunteers.*

M. A. D. Howe, *American Bookmen: Sketches, Chiefly Biographical, of Certain Writers of the Nineteenth Century.*

W. Irving, "Legend of Sleepy Hollow" (short story).

W. Irving, "Rip Van Winkle" (short story).

R. M. Johnston, *Dukesborough Tales.*

R. M. Johnston, *Mr. Absalom Billingslea, and Other Georgia Folk.*

R. M. Johnston, *Mr. Billy Downs and His Likes.*

R. M. Johnston, *Old Mark Langstan; A Tale of Duke's Creek.*

R. M. Johnston, *Two Gray Tourists: From Papers of Mr. Philemon Perch.*

H. C. Jones. "Cousin Sally Dilliard" (sketch).

H. Kuehn, *Thoughts of a Fool.*

J. B. Lamar, "Polly Peablossom's Wedding" (sketch).

M. D. L. Landon (pseud. "Eli Perkins"), *Saratoga in 1901. Fun, Love, Society & Satire.*

G. T. Lanigan, *Fables by G. Washington Aesop, Taken "Anywhere, Anywhere, Out of the World."*

A. Lee, *He, She & They; Being a Faithful Record of the Woful Enjoyments and Joyful Woes of Him & Her.*

C. G. Leland, *Hans Breitmann's Party, with Other Ballads.*

H. P. Leland, "Frogs Shot Without Powder" (sketch).

C. B. Lewis ("M. Quad"), "Demon and the Fury" (sketch).

H. T. Lewis, "Harp of a Thousand Strings" (mock sermon).

D. R. Locke, *Struggles (Social, Financial, and Political) of Petroleum V. Nasby.*

A. B. Longstreet, *Georgia Scenes, Characters, Incidents, &c., in the First Half Century of The Republic.*

J. R. Lowell, *Biglow Papers.*

H. C. Lukens ("Erratic Enrique"), *Jets and Flashes.*

J. T. McCutcheon, *Mysterious Stranger and Other Cartoons.*

E. S. Martin, *Courtship of a Careful Man, and a Few Other Courtships.*

E. S. Martin, *Lucid Intervals.*

S. C. Massett, *"Drifting About"; or, What "Jeems Pipes, of Pipesville," Saw-and-Did. An Autobiography.*

L. de V. Matthewman, *Crankisms, by Lisle de Vaux Matthewman.*

P. Mulford (Catalog entry).

J. C. Neal, *Charcoal Sketches; or, Scenes in a Metropolis.*

R. H. Newell (pseud. "Orpheus C. Kerr"), "The Great Fit" (comic poem).

E. W. Nye (pseud. "Bill Nye"), *Forty Liars, and Other Lies.*

O'Brien, Fitz-James (Catalog entry).

Old Abe's Jokes; Fresh from Abraham's Bosom.

E. G. Paige (pseud. "Dow, Jr.") (Catalog entry).

G. W. Peck, *Peck's Bad Boy and His Pa.*

G. W. Peck, *Peck's Fun.*

W. T. Porter, "Letter from Billy Patterson Himself."

W. T. Porter (ed.), *Spirit of the Times.*

F. L. Pratt, "Captain Ben's Choice" (short story).

O. Read: see H. E. Taliaferro (Catalog entry).

G. Rose, *Mrs. Brown Series.*

K. A. Sanborn, *Wit of Women.*

J. G. Saxe (Catalog entry).

J. W. Scott, *Jack Hardin's Rendering of the Arabian Nights; Being a New Translation in Up-to-Date English.*

H. W. Shaw, *Everybody's Friend, or Josh Billings's Encyclopedia and Proverbial Philosophy of Wit and Humor.*

H. W. Shaw, *Josh Billings' Farmers' Allminax for the Year 1870.*

H. W. Shaw, *Josh Billings: His Works, Complete.*

F. W. Shelton, *Up the River.*

B. P. Shillaber, *Life and Sayings of Mrs. Partington and Others of the Family.*

G. R. Sims, *Tinkletop's Crime, and Other Stories.*

S. W. Small ("Old Si" dialect sketches).

C. H. Smith (pseud. "Bill Arp") (Catalog entry).

F. H. Smith, "Editor's Drawer: Ginger and the Goose" (story).

S. Smith (pseud. "Major Jack Downing") (Catalog entry).

F. R. Stockton, "Remarkable Wreck of the 'Thomas Hyke.'"

H. E. Taliaferro (Catalog entry).

W. T. Thompson, *Major Jones's Courtship.*

W. T. Thompson, *Major Jones's Sketches of Travel.*

M. N. Thomson (pseud. "Q. K. Philander Doesticks") (Catalog entry).

T. B. Thorpe, "Big Bear of Arkansas" (story).

J. T. Trowbridge, *Vagabonds, and Other Poems.*

Turner's Comic Almanac.

W. H. Van Nortwick, *Yanks and Johnnies; or, Laugh and Grow Fat.*

F. E. Wadleigh, *'Twixt Wave and Sky* (novel) (Catalog entry).

K. K. C. Walker, "Total Depravity of Inanimate Things" (sketch).

E. F. Ware, *Some of the Rhymes of Ironquill. (A Book of Moods).*

H. Watterson, *Compromises of Life, and Other Lectures and Addresses, Including Some Observations on Certain Downward Tendencies of Modern Society* (Catalog entry).

C. Wells, *Phenomenal Fauna*.

J. Weymouth, *College Chaps*.

F. M. B. Whitcher (pseud. "Widow Bedott"), *Widow Bedott Papers*.

M. P. Wilder (three titles).

R. W. Wood, *Animal Analogues. Verses and Illustrations*. *Wyman's Comic Almanac for the Times, 1856*.

See also the Reader's Guide entries for Humor collections and for Humor studies.

American Imperialism. C. Schurz.

American Indians: see the Reader's Guide entry for Native Americans.

Americanism of Washington. H. Van Dyke.

Americanisms and Briticisms, with Other Essays on Other Isms. B. Matthews.

American Journal of Anatomy: see E. A. Spitzka.

American literature (criticism): see

S. A. Allibone,. *Critical Dictionary of English Literature and British and American Authors*.

S. K. Bolton, *Famous American Authors*.

Cyclopædia of American Literature, Embracing Personal and Critical Notices of Authors, and Selections from Their Writings.

W. D. Howells, *Literary Friends and Acquaintances: A Personal Retrospect of American Authorship*.

B. Matthews, "American Fiction Again" (essay).

B. Matthews, *Americanisms and Briticisms, with Other Essays on Other Isms*.

B. Mathews, *Aspects of Fiction and Other Ventures in Criticism*.

B. Matthews, *Introduction to the Study of American Literature*.

B. Matthews, *Historical Novel and Other Essays*.

B. Matthews, "New Trials for Old Favorites" (article).

B. Matthews, *Studies of the Stage*.

E. C. Stedman (co-ed.), *Library of American Literature, from Earliest Settlement to the Present Time*.

H. C. Vedder, *American Writers of To-day*.

See also the Reader's Guide entries for American drama, for Literary guides and criticism, and for Theatrical history.

American Nation: A History from Original Sources by Associated Scholars. A. B. Hart (ed.).

American Nation: A History. Preliminaries of the Revolution, 1763–1775. G. E. Howard.

American Newspaper Directory: see G. P. Rowell, *American Newspaper Directory*.

American Notes for General Circulation. C. Dickens.

American Notes for General Circulation: see also the Catalog entry for C. Dickens, *Pictures from Italy and American Notes*.

American patriotism: see

J. R. Drake, "American Flag" (patriotic poem).

E. E. Hale, "Man without a Country" (story).

O. W. Holmes, "Grandmother's Story of Bunker Hill Battle" (poem).

J. Hopkinson, "Hail, Columbia" (patriotic song).

H. Pyle, *Yankee Doodle, An Old Friend in a New Dress*.

C. F Skinner, *Manual of Patriotism, for Use in the Public Schools of the State of New York*.

S. F. Smith, "America" (anthem).

H. G. Wells, *Future in America; A Search after Realities* (marginalia).

"Yankee Doodle" (song).

American Phrenological Journal: see *Phrenological Journal and Science of Health*.

American politics: see

J. A. Altsheler, *Candidate; A Political Romance*.

A. F. de Bacourt, *Souvenirs of a Diplomat: Private Letters from America*.

A. P. Bettersworth, *John Smith, Democrat: His Two Days' Canvass*.

T. Campbell-Copeland (ed. and comp.), *Cleveland and Stevenson: Their Lives and Record. The Democratic Campaign Book for 1892*.

T. Campbell-Copeland (ed. and comp.), *Harrison and Reid: Their Lives and Record. The Republican Campaign Book for 1892*.

W. D. Howells, *Sketch of the Life and Character of Rutherford B. Hayes*.

A. K. McClure, *Our Presidents, and How We Make Them. A Historical Survey of How Each Man Came to Hold the Office*.

U. B. Sinclair, *Jungle*.

W. M. Springer, *Tariff Reform, the Paramount Issue. Speeches and Writings on the Questions Involved in the Presidential Contest of 1892*.

J. D. Townsend, *City in Bondage*.

S. Webster, *Two Treaties of Paris and the Supreme Court*.

F. G. Welch, *That Convention; or, Five Days a Politician*.

F. C. Williams, *J. Devlin—Boss: A Romance of American Politics* (novel).

T. Wright (ed.), *Early Travels in Palestine* (marginalia).

See also the Reader's Guide entry for Political science.

American Revolution: see

J. Adams, *Familiar Letters of John Adams and His Wife Abigail Adams, During the Revolution*.

J. Barnes, *For King or Country. A Story of the American Revolution*.

C. T. Brady, *For Love of Country: A Story of Land and Sea in the Days of the Revolution*.

C. T. Brady, *Grip of Honor: A Story of Paul Jones and the American Revolution*.

E. S. Brooks, *Chivalric Days, and the Boys and Girls Who Helped to Make Them*.

T. Campbell, *Gertrude of Wyoming; or, the Pennsylvanian Cottage*.

C. C. Coffin, *Boys of '76. A History of the Battles of the Revolution*.

C. C. Coffin, *Old Times in the Colonies*.

C. A. Goodrich, *Lives of the Signers to the Declaration of Independence*.

W. E. Grumman, *Revolutionary Soldiers of Redding, Connecticut, and the Record of Their Services*.

O. W. Holmes, "Grandmother's Story of Bunker Hill Battle" (poem).

G. E. Howard, *American Nation: A History. Prelimi-naries of the Revolution, 1763–1775.*

R. G. Ingersoll, *Ghosts and Other Lectures.*

W. Irving, *Life of George Washington.*

W. E. H. Lecky, *History of England in the Eighteenth Century* (marginalia).

G. Lippard, *Legends of the American Revolution.*

S. W. Mitchell, *Hugh Wynne, Free Quaker, Sometime Brevet Lieutenant-Colonel on the Staff of His Excellency General Washington.*

G. Morris, *Diary and Letters of Gouverneur Morris.*

T. Paine, *Common Sense.*

T. Paine, *Crisis.*

J. Parton, *Life and Times of Aaron Burr.*

T. B. Read, *Wagoner of the Alleghanies. A Poem of the Days of Seventy-Six.*

R. N. Stephens, *Philip Winwood; A Sketch of the Domestic History of an American Captain in the War of Independence* (novel).

W. M. Thackeray, *Virginians; A Tale of the Last Century.*

H. Van Dyke, *Americanism of Washington.*

J. T. Wilson, *Black Phalanx; A History of the Negro Soldiers of the United States in the Wars of 1775–1812, 1861–'65.*

See also the Reader's Guide entry for American history.

American Scene. H. James.

American social classes: see

E. A. G. Glasgow, *Voice of the People* (novel).

W. D. Howells, *Out of the Question: A Comedy* (play).

S. W. McAllister, *Society As I Have Found It.*

H. Martineau, *Society in America* (marginalia).

San Francisco *Morning Call.*

M. E. W. Sherwood, *A Transplanted Rose; A Story of New York Society.*

W. G. Sumner, *What Social Classes Owe to Each Other.*

F. M. Trollope, *Domestic Manners of the Americans* (marginalia).

M. Van Vorst, *Philip Longstreth; A Novel.*

C. D. Warner, *Golden House.*

E. N. J. Wharton, *House of Mirth.*

C. D. Wood, *Upon a Cast.*

C. Zueblin, *Religion of a Democrat.*

See also the Reader's Guide entries for Economics and labor issues, for English social classes, and for French social classes.

American South: see

A. C. Artman, *Glimpses of the Sunny South.*

J. G. Baldwin, *Flush Times of Alabama and Mississippi. A Series of Sketches.*

V. F. Boyle, *Devil Tales.*

C. C. Brush, *Colonel's Opera Cloak.*

A. M. Buckner, *Towards the Gulf; A Romance of Louisiana.*

F. H. Burnett, *Louisiana.*

K. Chopin (speculative Catalog entry).

P. H. Coggins, "Old Sile's Clem" (short story).

M. E. Davis, *Elephant's Track and Other Stories.*

N. Davis, *Wallace Rhodes, A Novel.*

C. W. Dilke, *Greater Britain: A Record of Travel in English-Speaking Countries During 1866 and 1867.*

G. A. Kendrick, *Contrasts.*

J. P. Kennedy, *Swallow Barn; or, A Sojourn in the Old Dominion.*

E. King, *Great South: A Record of Journeys.*

G. King, *Balcony Stories.*

G. King, *Monsieur Motte.*

G. King, *Tales of a Time and Place.*

E. M. Lane, *Katrine, A Novel.*

M. G. McClelland, *St. John's Wooing, A Story.*

J. B. Monteith, *Parson Brooks: A Plumb Powerful Hard Shell. A Story of Humble Southern Life.*

New Orleans *Times-Democrat* (Catalog entry).

H. W. Pierson, *In the Brush; or, Old-Time Social, Political, and Religious Life in the Southwest.*

H. D. Pittman, *Belle of the Bluegrass Country. Studies in Black and White.*

L. C. Pyrnelle, *Diddie, Dumps, and Tot; or, Plantation Child-Life.*

J. Ralph, *Dixie; or, Southern Scenes and Sketches.*

W. Reid, "Some Southern Reminiscences" (essay).

E. Robins, *Open Question; A Tale of Two Temperaments.*

R. M. Stuart, *Second Wooing of Salina Sue, and Other Stories.*

J. Sturge, *Visit to the United States in 1841.*

J. M. Thompson, *Tallahassee Girl.*

M. L. D. Tidball, *Barbara's Vagaries.*

A. W. Tourgée, *Bricks Without Straw. A Novel.*

A. W. Tourgée, *Fool's Errand, by One of the Fools.*

B. O. Townsend, *Plantation Lays and Other Poems.*

C. D. Warner, *Studies in the South and West, with Comments on Canada.*

See also the Reader's Guide entries for New Orleans, for Slavery, and for individual states.

American West: see

M. M. Austin, *'Cension. A Sketch from Paso Del Norte.*

J. G. Bourke, *On the Border with Crook.*

C. T. Brady, *Bishop; Being Some Account of His Strange Adventures on the Plains.*

F. T. Clark, *Mistress of the Ranch; A Novel.*

A. G. Clarke, Jr., *Arickaree Treasure, and Other Brief Tales of Adventurous Montanians.*

W. F. Cody, *Adventures of Buffalo Bill.*

W. F. Cody, *Life of the Hon. William F. Cody, Known as Buffalo Bill.*

Cow-Boys Ballads.

C. A. Curtis, *Captured by the Navajos.*

T. J. Dimsdale, *Vigilantes of Montana; or, Popular Justice in the Rocky Mountains.*

R. I. Dodge, *Our Wild Indians: Thirty-Three Years' Personal Experience among the Red Men of the Great West.*

R. I. Dodge, *Plains of the Great West and Their Inhabitants, Being a Description of the Plains, Game, Indians, &c. of the Great North American Desert.*

J. P. Dunn, *Massacres of the Mountains: A History of the Indian Wars of the Far West.*

W. Glazier, *Three Years in the Federal Cavalry.*

E. J. House, *Hunter's Camp-Fires.*

W. D. Howells (co-ed.), *Library of Universal Adventure by Sea and Land.*

W. D. Howells (co-ed.), *Under the Sunset*.

W. Irving, *Adventures of Captain Bonneville*.

W. Irving, *Astoria; or, Anecdotes of an Enterprise Beyond the Rocky Mountains*.

D. B. R. Keim, *Sheridan's Troopers on the Borders: A Winter Campaign on the Plains*.

M. Manning, *Judith of the Plains; A Novel*.

R. B. Marcy, *Thirty Years of Army Life on the Border, Comprising Descriptions of the Indian Nomads of the Plains*.

V. Meunier (comp.), *Adventures on the Great Hunting Grounds of the World*.

J. Miller, *Songs of the Sierras* (poems).

J. Miller, *Unwritten History: Life Amongst the Modocs*.

S. B. Morgan, *Tahoe; or, Life in California. A Romance*.

C. K. Munroe, *Campmates; A Story of the Plains*.

C. K. Munroe, *Painted Desert; A Story of Northern Arizona*.

J. M. Murphy, *Sporting Adventures in the Far West*.

F. Parkman, *Oregon Trail: Sketches of Prairie and Rocky-Mountain Life*.

J. W. Powell, *Third Annual Report of the Bureau of American Ethnology to the Secretary of the Smithsonian Institution, 1879–1880*.

J. Ralph, *Our Great West: A Study of the Present Conditions and Future Possibilities*.

F. Remington, *Crooked Trails*.

F. Remington, *Stories of Peace and War*.

A. D. Richardson, *Beyond the Mississippi: From the Great River to the Great Ocean*.

E. Roberts, *Shoshone and Other Western Wonders*.

E. Robins, *Open Question; A Tale of Two Temperaments*.

T. Roosevelt, *Good Hunting: In Pursuit of Big Game in the West*.

T. B. H. Stenhouse, *Rocky Mountain Saints: A Full and Complete History of the Mormons, . . . and the Development of the Great Mineral Wealth of the Territory of Utah*.

E. T. Stevens, *Flint Chips. A Guide to Pre-Historic Archaeology, as Illustrated by the Collection in the Blackmore Museum, Salisbury*.

E. Talbot, *My People of the Plains*.

B. Taylor, *Eldorado; or, Adventures in the Path of Empire; Comprising a Voyage to California via Panama, Life in San Francisco and Monterey, Pictures of the Gold Region, and Experiences of Mexico Travel*.

W. M. Thayer, *Marvels of the New West: A Vivid Portrayal of the Stupendous Marvels in the Vast Wonderland West of the Missouri River*.

R. B. Townshend, *Bride of a Day*.

L. J. Velazquez, *Woman in Battle: A Narrative of the Exploits, Adventures, and Travels of Madame Loreta Janeta Velazquez, Otherwise Known as Lieutenant Harry T. Buford, Confederate States Army*.

H. L. Wilson, *Spenders; A Tale of the Third Generation*.

W. Wright, "Washoe Rambles" (articles).

See also the Reader's Guide entries for Mormonism, for Native Americans, for North American travel writings, for the Rocky Mountains, and for individual Native American tribes and individual states.

American Woods, Exhibited by Actual Specimens and with Copious Explanatory Text. R. B. Hough.

American Writers of To-Day. H. C. Vedder.

America To-Day: Observations and Reflections. W. Archer.

Amerigo Vespucci. F. A. Ober.

Ames, Fisher: see
    T. W. S. Higginson, *Cheerful Yesterdays. Contemporaries* (marginalia).
    D. B. Lucas and J. F. McLaughlin, *Fisher Ames-Henry Clay, Etc.*

Ames, Percy Willoughby (ed.): see Marguerite d'Angoulême, *Mirror of the Sinful Soul*.

"Am I a soldier of the cross?" (hymn). I. Watts.

Amicis, Edmondo de: see E. De Amicis.

Amiel's Journal: The Journal Intime of Henri-Frédéric Amiel. H. F. Amiel.

Am Kreuz; ein Passionsroman aus Oberammergau. W. B. von Hillern.

Among the Millet and Other Poems. A. Lampman.

Among the Water-Fowl: Observation, Adventure, Photography. H. K. Job.

Amours du chevalier de faublas. J. B. Louvet de Couvrai.

Amphibians: see the Reader's Guide entries for Frogs, for Natural history, and for Toads.

Amyas Egerton, Cavalier (novel). M. H. Hervey.

Amyntas, A Sylvan Fable. T. Tasso.

Amyntor; or, a Defense of Milton's Life: see J. Toland, *Life of John Milton*.

Analytic Index. D. M. Matteson (comp.): see *American Nation: A History from Original Sources by Associated Scholars*, ed. A. B. Hart.

Ananias (Biblical figure): see E. Sue, *Wandering Jew*.

Anatomy: see
    C. Cutter, *Anatomy and Physiology*.
    J. Marshall, *Anatomy for Artists*.
    J. Walker, *Anatomy, Physiology, and Hygiene: A Manual for the Use of Colleges, Schools, and General Readers*.
    See also the Reader's Guide entry for Physiology.

Anatomy and Physiology. C. Cutter.

Anatomy for Artists. J. Marshall.

Anatomy, Physiology, and Hygiene: A Manual for the Use of Colleges, Schools, and General Readers. J. Walker.

Ancestors; A Novel. G. F. H. Atherton.

Ancient Accounts of India and China, by Two Mohammedan Travellers. A. Z. H. Y. Sīrāfī.

Ancient history: see
    C. A. B. Bloss, *Bloss' Ancient History, for the Use of Families and Schools*.
    I. Donnelly, *Atlantis: The Antediluvian World*.
    J. Lord, *Beacon Lights of History*.
    E. R. B. Lytton. *Chronicles and Characters*.
    E. Reich, *Success Among Nations*.
    R. Robbins, *Outlines of Ancient and Modern History on a New Plan*.
    C. Rollin, *Ancient History of the Egyptians, Carthaginians, Assyrians, Babylonians, Medes and Persians, Grecians and Macedonians*.
    C. M. Yonge, *Landmarks of History*.

Ancient History of the Egyptians, Carthaginians, Assyrians, Babylonians, Medes and Persians, Grecians and Macedonians. C. Rollin.

Ancient Law (novel). E. A. G. Glasgow.

Ancient Mariner. S. T. Coleridge.

Ancient Mariner. S. T. Coleridge: see also E. Wakeman, *Log of an Ancient Mariner; Being the Life and Adventures of Captain Edgar Wakeman. Written by Himself and Edited by His Daughter.*

Ancient Régime. H. A. Taine.

Ancient Streets and Homesteads of England. A. Rimmer.

Anderson, J. A. and H. C. (illus. with photographs): see N. L. Marshall, *Mushroom Book. A Popular Guide to the Identification and Study of Our Commoner Fungi.*

Anderson, Jesse Sylvester "Vet" (illus.): see O. Bainbridge, *Devil's Note Book.*

Anderson, John Jacob: see (ed.) C. A. B. Bloss, *Bloss' Ancient History, for the Use of Families and Schools* (Catalog entry).

André, Richard (illus.): see J. H. G. Ewing, *Dolls' Wash.*

"Andrea del Sarto" (poem). R. Browning.

Andrews, M. R. S. (co-author): see *Whole Family; A Novel by Twelve Authors.*

Andrews, Walter Scott, (co-author): see E. J. James, *Immigrant Jew in America.*

Anecdotes: see *Percy Anecdotes.*

Anecdotes of Public Men. J. W. Forney.

Anecdotes; Religious, Moral, and Entertaining. C. Buck (comp.).

Angel: see H. G. Wells, *Wonderful Visit.*

Angel in the House. C. K. D. Patmore.

Angelo (play). V. M. Hugo.

Anger (of Clemens): W. R. Hearst (Catalog entry).

Anglican Church: see the Reader's Guide entry for Church of England.

Animal Analogues. Verses and Illustrations. R. W. Wood.

Animal intelligence: see *Spectator* (London journal).

Animal Life. C. G. D. Roberts.

Animal rights: see

J. H. Moore, *Universal Kinship.*

A. T. Slossom, *Dumb Foxglove, and Other Stories.*

B. Taylor, *National Ode* (Catalog entry).

S. K. Trimmer, *History of the Robins. In Words of One Syllable.*

See also the Reader's Guide entries for Ecology, nature appreciation, and land usage and for Vivisection.

Animals: see the Reader's Guide entry for Natural history.

Animal Stories (unidentified book). W. J. Long.

"Annabel Lee" (poem). E. A. Poe.

Anna Karenina (novel): see L. N. Tolstoy, *Anna Karénine.*

Anna Karénine (novel). L. N. Tolstoy.

Ann Boyd; A Novel. W. N. Harben.

Anne of Avonlea. L. M. Montgomery.

Anne of Geierstein. W. Scott.

Anne of Green Gables. L. M. Montgomery.

Anne, Queen: see

J. McCarthy, *Reign of Queen Anne.*

P. H. Stanhope, *History of England, Comprising the Reign of Queen Anne until the Peace of Utrecht.*

J. H. Trumbull (ed.), *True-Blue Laws of Connecticut and New Haven* (marginalia).

"Annette" (poem). R. Richardson.

Annie Kilburn, A Novel. W. D. Howells.

"Anstey, F." (pseud.): see T. A. Guthrie.

Antarctic: see F. M. Savile, *Beyond the Great South Wall: The Secret of the Antarctic.*

Ant Communities, and How They are Governed. H. C. McCook.

Anthologies:

H. Abbey (comp.), *Bright Things from Everywhere: A Galaxy of Good Stories, Poems, Paragraphs, Wit, and Wisdom.*

American Miscellany. A Magazine of Complete Stories (periodical).

J. M. Chapple (comp.), *Heart Throbs in Prose and Verse Dear to the American People.*

M. E. Phillips (ed. and illus.), *Laurel Leaves for Little Folk.*

Poet and the Painter; or, Gems of Art and Song.

K. A. Sanborn (comp.), *Indian Summer Calendar.*

J. G. Whittier (ed.), *Child Life in Prose.*

See also the Reader's Guide entries for Literary anthologies and for Poetry collections.

Anthony, Andrew Stout Varick (illus. and engraver): see

C. Dickens, *Christmas Carol in Prose.*

H. James (ed.), *Facsimiles of National Manuscripts from William the Conqueror to Queen Anne.*

A. Tennyson, *Dream of Fair Women.*

Anthropology:

S. A. Arrhenius, *Life of the Universe as Conceived by Man from the Earliest Ages to the Present Time.*

H. H. Bancroft, *Native Races of the Pacific States of North America.*

C. D. W. Brownell, *Indian Races of North and South America.*

E. J. Eyre, *Journals of Expeditions of Discovery into Central Australia, and Overland from Adelaide to King George's Sound, in 1840–1, Including an Account of the Manners and Customs of the Aborigines.*

G. Grey, *Journals of Two Expeditions of Discovery in North-West and Western Australia, During the Years 1837, 38, and 39, Under the Authority of Her Majesty's Government: Describing Many Newly Discovered, Important, and Fertile Districts, with Observations on the Moral and Physical Condition of the Aboriginal Inhabitants.*

R. B. Smyth, *Aborigines of Victoria: With Notes Relating to the Habits of the Natives of Other Parts of Australia and Tasmania.*

J. G. Wood, *Our Living World; An Artistic Edition of the Rev. J. G. Wood's Natural History of Animate Creation.*

See also the Reader's Guide entry for Archeology.

Anticipations of the Reaction of Mechanical and Scientific Progress Upon Human Life and Thought. H. G. Wells.

Anti-slavery Catechism. L. M. Child.

Anti-war literature: see the Reader's Guide entries for Philippines, for Spanish-American War, and for Warfare.

Antony and Cleopatra (play). W. Shakespeare.

Ants: see the Reader's Guide entry for Insects.

Ants, Bees, and Wasps: A Record of Observations on the Habits of the Social Hymenoptera. J. Lubbock.

"Anvers, N. d'" (pseud. of translator), N. R. E. M. Bell: see J. F. A. du P. Nadaillac, *Pre-Historic America.*

Apaches (Native American tribe): see
> J. R. Browne, *Adventures in Apache Country: A Tour Through Arizona and Sonora.*
> J. C. Cremony, *Life Among the Apaches.*
> C. A. Curtis, *Captured by the Navajos* (novel).

Apocrypha: see
> Bible. New Testament.
> H. C. Greene (trans.), *Gospel of the Childhood of Our Lord Jesus Christ.*

Apologia Pro Vita Sua. J. H. Newman.

Apollinaris Sidonius: see
> S. Dill, *Roman Society in the Last Century of the Western Empire* (marginalia).
> O. Wister, *Dragon of Wantley, His Rise, His Voracity, and His Downfall: A Romance* (Catalog entry).

Apollo (early Christian preacher): see T. C. Upham, *Life of Faith; in Three Parts, Embracing Some of the Scriptural Principles or Doctrines of Faith* (marginalia).

Apostles. Translated from the Original French. [J.] E. Renan.

Apotheosis of Mr. Tyrawley. E. K. S. Jay.

Apparitions and Miracles at Knock. J. MacPhilpin.

"Apparitions of the Living" [*sic*]: see E. Gurney *Phantasms of the Living.*

Appeal to the People in Behalf of Their Rights as Authorized Interpreters of the Bible. C. E. Beecher.

Appleton, Thomas Gold: see O. W. Holmes, *Autocrat of the Breakfast-Table.* (marginalia).

April Hopes (novel). W. D. Howells.

Arabic Bible: see the Catalog entry for Bible. Arabic.

Arabian literature: see the Reader's Guide entry for Persian literature.

Arabian Nights: see
> *Favorite Fairy Tales: The Childhood Choice of Representative Men and Women.*
> L. Hunt, *Day by the Fire; and Other Papers, Hitherto Uncollected* (Catalog entry).
> J. K. Ridley, *The Tales of the Genii; or, The Delightful Lessons of Horam, the Son of Asmar.*
> J. W. Scott, *Jack Hardin's Rendering of the Arabian Nights; Being a New Translation in Up-to-Date English.*
> See also the Reader's Guide entry for Persian literature.

"Arab's Farewell to His Steed" (poem). C. E. S. S. Norton.

"Araby's daughter" (song). T. Moore.

Arago, François: see J. Timbs, *Things Not Generally Known, Familiarly Explained* (marginalia).

Aram, Eugene (British criminal): see
> E. G. E. B. Lytton, *Eugene Aram.*
> C. Whitehead, *Lives and Exploits of the Most Noted Highwaymen, Robbers and Murderers, of All Nations.*

Arapaho (Native American tribe): see
> E. Talbot, *My People of the Plains.*
> H. R. Woodman, *Noahs Afloat; An Historical Romance* (Catalog entry).

Archaeology: see
> I. Donnelly, *Atlantis: The Antediluvian World.*
> L. Figuier, *Primitive Man.*
> J. T. Goodman, *Archaic Maya Inscriptions.*
> E. T. Stevens, *Flint Chips. A Guide to Pre-Historic Archaeology, as Illustrated by the Collection in the Blackmore Museum, Salisbury.*
> A. R. Wallace, William Ramsay, *et al. Progress of the Century.*
> See also the Reader's Guide entry for Anthropology.

Archaic Maya Inscriptions. J. T. Goodman.

Archer, William (co-trans., intro.): see H. Ibsen, *Hedda Gabler* (play).

"Archie Dean" (poem). J. M. Parker.

"Archimedes" (article): see *Standard* (newspaper).

Architecture: see
> *American Architect and Building News.*
> *Artistic Houses; Being a Series of Interior Views of a Number of the Most Beautiful and Celebrated Homes in the United States.*
> T. A. Cook, *Old Touraine: The Life and History of the Famous Chateâux of France.*
> C. S. Farrar, *History of Sculpture, Painting, and Architecture.*
> J. Fergusson, *History of Architecture in All Countries from the Earliest Times.*
> O. C. Gillespie, *Rumford Fireplaces and How They Are Made.*
> S. S. Jacob (ed.), *Jeypore Portfolios of Architectural Details.*
> M. H. N. von Liechtenstein, *Holland House.*
> M. W. Porter, *What Rome Was Built With: A Description of the Stones Employed in Ancient Times for Its Building and Decoration.*
> See also the Reader's Guide entries for Homes and for Interior decoration.

Archy Moore, the White Slave; or, Memoirs of a Fugitive. R. Hildreth.

Arctic explorations: see
> H. Hendrik, *Memoirs of Hans Hendrik, The Arctic Traveler.*
> J. Jònsonn, "Jòn Jònsonn's Saga: The Genuine Autobiography of a Modern Icelander."
> E. K. Kane, *Arctic Explorations.*
> F. Nansen, *Farthest North; Being the Record of a Voyage of Exploration of the Ship "Fram" 1893–96, and of a Fifteen Months' Sleigh Journey.*
> W. L. Phelps, *Dash at the Pole.*
> E. Robins, *Magnetic North.*
> W. H. Wilson, *Rafnaland; The Strange Story of John Heath Howard.*

"Are we almost there?" (song). F. Vane.

Are You a Bromide? or, The Sulphitic Theory Expounded and Exemplified. G. Burgess.

Argonaut Edition of the Works of Bret Harte. B. Harte.

Arguments Before the Committee on Patents: see United States Congress. House Committee on Patents.

Argyll, Duke of: see H. George, *Property in Land: A Passage-at-Arms Between the Duke of Argyll and Henry George.*

"Ariadne in the Wire-Grass" (story): see L. B. Pendleton, *Bewitched: A Tale.*

Arickaree Treasure, and Other Brief Tales of Adventurous Montanians. A. G. Clarke, Jr.

Ariosto, Ludovico Giovanni: see L. Hunt, *Stories from the Italian Poets. (First Series) Dante Alighieri, With*

855

*Critical Notices of the Life and Genius of the Author;
(Second Series) Bernardo Tasso and Ludovico Giovanni
Ariosto, With Critical Notices of the Lives and Genius of
the Authors.*

Aristaenetus: see S. Propertius, *Erotica.*

Aristides: see C. M. Yonge, *Book of Worthies, Gathered
from the Old Histories and Now Written Anew.*

Aristocracy: see the Reader's Guide entries for American
social classes, for Economics and labor issues, for English social classes, and for French social classes.

Aristocracy. A Novel. J. A. Nimes.

Aristocracy of Health: A Study of Physical Culture. M. N. F.
Henderson.

Aristophanes' Apology: see R. Browning, *Balaustion's Adventures, Aristophanes' Apology.*

Aristophanes' Apology: see R. Browning, *Red Cotton Night-
Cap Country.*

Aristotle: see
  O. W. Holmes, *Autocrat of the Breakfast-Table*
    (marginalia).
  Plinius Secundus, *Natural History of Pliny* (Catalog
    entry).

Arizona: see
  J. R. Browne, *Adventures in Apache Country: A Tour
    Through Arizona and Sonora with Notes on the Silver
    Regions of Nevada.*
  C. K. Munroe, *Painted Desert; A Story of Northern
    Arizona.*
  R. Pumpelly, *Across America and Asia; Notes of a Five
    Years' Journey Around the World:* see R. Pumpelly,
    Explorations in Turkestan.
  C. Scollard, *Under Summer Skies.*

Arkansas: see
  W. Gibson, "Arkansas Fashion" (short story).
  T. B. Thorpe, "Big Bear of Arkansas" (story).

"Arkansas Fashion" (short story). W. Gibson.

Armadale; A Novel. W. W. Collins.

*Armageddon; or, The Overthrow of Romanism and Monar-
chy.* S. D. Baldwin.

Armazindy. J. W. Riley.

Arms and Armour in Antiquity and the Middle Ages. P.
Lacombe.

Armstrong, Margaret Neilson (illus.): see F. R. Stockton,
Mrs. Cliff's Yacht.

Army life (United States): see
  W. Fish, *Short Rations.*
  G. A. Forsyth, *Thrilling Days in Army Life.*
  W. Glazier, *Three Years in the Federal Cavalry.*
  R. B. Marcy, *Thirty Years of Army Life on the Border,
    Comprising Descriptions of the Indian Nomads of the
    Plains.*
  United States War Department. *Regulations for the
    Army of the United States, 1904.*
  See also the Reader's Guide entries for West Point
    Military Academy and for Warfare.

Arnold, Fr. (trans.): see A. H. Bernard. *Legends of the
Rhine.*

Arnold, Matthew: see
  H. H. Breen, *Modern English Literature: Its Blemishes
    & Defects* (Catalog entry).
  Nineteenth Century (London).

V. Streamer (comp.), *Voices of Doubt and Trust.*
  H. Van Dyke (ed.), *Little Masterpieces of English Poetry,
    by British and American Authors.*

Arnold, Thomas James (trans.): see J. W. von Goethe,
Faust; A Tragedy.

Arnold, William Thomas: see M. A. A. Ward, *William
Thomas Arnold, Journalist and Historian.*

*Around the "Pan" with Uncle Hank. His Trip Through the
Pan-American Exposition.* T. Fleming.

Around the World in a Year. G. L. Carlisle.

*Around the World with General Grant in 1877, 1878,
1879.* J. R. Young.

"Arp, Bill" (pseud.): see C. H. Smith.

Arrah-na-Pogue (play). D. Boucicault.

Arrah-na-Pogue (play): see E. H. House, *Japanese Episodes*
(Catalog entry).

Arrah-na-Poke! Or, Arrah of the Cold Pomme de Terre
(farce). C. H. Webb.

Art d'intéresser en classe; Nouveau manuel. V. F. Bernard.

"Artemus Ward" (pseud.): see C. F. Browne.

"Artemus Ward" (poem). J. Rhoades.

Artemus Ward, His Book. C. F. Browne.

Artemus Ward, His Travels. C. F. Browne.

Artemus Ward in London, and Other Papers. C. F. Browne.

Artemus Ward's Panorama. C. F. Browne.

Artful Anticks. O. Herford.

Art history and techniques: see
  American Art Review.
  Art and Letters. An Illustrated Review.
  Art Journal.
  L. Barritt, *How to Draw; A Practical Book of Instruction
    in the Art of Illustration.*
  C. Blanc, *Grammar of Painting and Engraving.*
  R. Blix, *Voile Tombe: Caricatures par Blix.*
  P. Blouet, *Woman and Artist* (novel with art as its
    theme).
  J. Cartwright, *Jean François Millet: His Life and Letters.*
  Catalogue of Oil Paintings.
  J. D. Champlin (ed.), *Cyclopedia of Painters and
    Paintings.*
  E. W. Champney, *All Around a Palette.*
  F. E. Church (Catalog entry).
  C. E. Clement, *Painters, Sculptors, Architects, Engrav-
    ers, and Their Works: A Handbook.*
  T. Cole, "Notes by T. Cole on the 'Adoration'"
    (article).
  J. B. De Forest, *Short History of Art.*
  C. S. Farrar, *History of Sculpture, Painting, and Ar-
    chitecture. Topical Lessons, with Specific References to
    Valuable Books.*
  G. Fraipont, *Art of Sketching.*
  W. P. Frith, *My Autobiography and Reminiscences.*
  A. Gilchrist, *Life of William Blake, "Pictor Ignotus."*
  P. G. Hamerton, *Life of J. M. W. Turner.*
  M. M. Heaton, *Masterpieces of Flemish Art.*
  W. D. Howells, *Little Girl Among the Old Masters.*
  A. B. M. Jameson, *Sacred and Legendary Art.*
  A. B. M. Jameson, *Sketches of Art, Literature, and
    Character.*
  F. T. Kugler, *Handbook of Painting: The German, Flem-
    ish, and Dutch Schools.*

Assommoir. É. Zola.
As Thought Is Led; Lyrics and Sonnets. A. Van Buren.
Astoria; or, Anecdotes of an Enterprise Beyond the Rocky Mountains. W. Irving.
Astronomy: see
S. A. Arrhenius, *Worlds in the Making: The Evolution of the Universe.*
S. G. Bayne, *Pith of Astronomy (Without Mathematics): The Latest Facts and Figures as Developed by the Giant Telescopes.*
D. Brewster, *Martyrs of Science; or, The Lives of Galileo, Tycho Brahe, and Kepler.*
E. F. Burr, *Ecce Coelum; or, Parish Astronomy. In Six Lectures. By a Connecticut Pastor.*
E. W. Champney, *In the Sky-Garden.*
T. Dick, *Practical Astronomer.*
Eclectic Magazine of Foreign Literature, Science, and Art.
N. C. Flammarion, *Stories of Infinity: Lumen—History of a Comet—In Infinity.*
A. V. Guillemin, *Heavens: An Illustrated Handbook of Popular Astronomy.*
A. V. Guillemin, *Sun.*
A. K. Johnston, *Home Atlas of Astronomy.*
J. N. Lockyer, *Elementary Lessons in Astronomy.*
O. J. Lodge, *Ether of Space.*
M. E. Martin, *Friendly Stars.*
S. Newcomb *Side-Lights on Astronomy and Kindred Fields of Popular Science: Essays and Addresses* (marginalia).
R. Proctor, *New Star Atlas for the Library, the School, and the Observatory, in Twelve Circular Maps.*
C. W. Saleeby, *Cycle of Life According to Modern Science* (marginalia).
C. W. Saleeby, *Evolution, the Master-Key: A Discussion of the Principle of Evolution as Illustrated in Atoms, Stars, Organic Speicies, Mind, Society and Morals.*
G. P. Serviss, *Astronomy with the Naked Eye; A New Geography of the Heavens.*
G. P. Serviss, *Curiosities of the Sky. A Popular Presentation.*
M. F. Somerville, *Personal Recollections, from Early Life to Old Age, of Mary Somerville. With Selections from Her Correspondence* (marginalia).
J. Timbs, *Things Not Generally Known, Familiarly Explained* (Catalog entry).
A. R. Wallace, *Man's Place in the Universe: A Study of the Results of Scientific Research in Relation to the Unity or Plurality of Worlds.*
A. R. Wallace, William Ramsay, *et al. Progress of the Century.*
H. G. Wells, *War of the Worlds.*
H. S. Williams, *Story of Nineteenth-Century Science.*
World of Wonders; A Record of Things Wonderful in Nature, Science, and Art.
F. Zurcher and É. Margollé, *Meteors, Aërolites, Storms, and Atmospheric Phenomena.*
Astronomy with the Naked Eye; A New Geography of the Heavens. G. P. Serviss.
As We Go. C. D. Warner.
As We Were Saying (essays). C. D. Warner.

Asylum; or, Alonzo and Melissa. I. Mitchell.
As You Like It (play). W. Shakespeare.
Atheism: see
R. Blatchford, *Merrie England* (Catalog entry).
F. P. Cobbe, *Peak in Darien, with Some Other Inquiries Touching Concerns of the Soul and the Body.*
G. P. Fisher, *Essays on the Supernatural Origin of Christianity.*
J. Froude, *Short Studies on Great Subjects* (marginalia).
T. Paine, *Age of Reason.*
H. V. M. Phelips, *Churches and Modern Thought; An Inquiry into the Grounds of Unbelief and an Appeal for Candour.*
J. M. Robertson (Catalog entry).
D. F. Strauss, *Life of Jesus, Critically Examined.*
F. M. Trollope, *Domestic Manners of the Americans* (marginalia).
Truth Seeker (magazine).
B. F. Underwood, *Essays and Lectures.*
See also the Reader's Guide entry for Agnosticism.
At Home and Abroad: A Sketch-Book of Life, Scenery, and Men. B. Taylor.
Atlantic Essays. T. W. S. Higginson.
Atlantis: The Antediluvian World. I. Donnelly.
Atlases: see
W. M. Bradley and Co., *Atlas of the World for Commercial and Library Reference.*
A. R. Colquhoun, *Greater America* (maps).
Ginn & Company's Classical Atlas, in Twenty-three Coloured Maps.
R. Proctor, *New Star Atlas for the Library, the School, and the Observatory, in Twelve Circular Maps.*
Rand, McNally & Co's General Atlas of the World.
W. C. Woodbridge, *Woodbridge and Willard's Universal Geography . . . Accompanied by Modern and Ancient Atlases.*
Atlas of the World for Commercial and Library Reference. W. M. Bradley and Co.
Atmospheric Phenomena. F. Zurcher.
At Sundown. J. G. Whittier.
Attaque du Moulin. É. Zola.
"At Teague Poteet's: A Sketch of the Hog Mountain Range" (story). J. C. Harris.
At the Back of the North Wind. G. MacDonald.
"At the Wind's Will" (poem). M. Howells.
Aucassin and Nicolette: see
A. Lang (trans.), *Aucassin and Nicolette.*
A. R. Macdonough (trans.), *Lovers of Provence: Aucassin and Nicolette.*
Auf der Höhe: see B. Auerbach, *On the Heights; A Novel.*
Augé, Claude (ed.): see P. A. Larousse, *Nouveau Larousse illustré:dictionnaire universel.*
Augustus Caesar: see A. Del Mar, *Worship of Augustus Caesar.*
"Auld lang syne" (song). R. Burns.
Aunt Jane of Kentucky (short stories). E. C. C. Obenchain.
Aunt Serena. B. W. Howard.
Aurora Leigh and Other Poems. E. B. Browning.
Ausgewählte Briefe von Friedrich von Schiller. J. C. F. von Schiller.

Authors Club: see *First Book of the Authors Club, Liber Scriptorum.*
Authors' homes: see the Reader's Guide entry for Homes.
Autobiographia; or, the Story of a Life. By Walt Whitman. Selected from His Prose Writings. W. Whitman.
Autobiographical Notes of the Life of William Bell Scott. W. B. Scott.
Autobiographies: see
  H. H. Bancroft, *Literary Industries. A Memoir.*
  P. T. Barnum, *Dollars and Sense.*
  P. T. Barnum, *Struggles and Triumphs.*
  L. Beecher, *Autobiography, Correspondence, Etc.*
  C. W. Beers, *Mind That Found Itself; An Autobiogaphy.*
  O. E. L. von Bismarck, *Bismarck, The Man and the Statesman; Being the Reflections and Reminiscences of Otto, Prince von Bismarck.*
  S. Breck, *Recollections of Samuel Breck, with Passages from His Notebooks.*
  P. H. Brown, ["Autobiography," unpublished.]
  T. Carlyle, *Reminiscences.*
  P. Cartwright, *Autobiograph y of Peter Cartwright, The Backwoods Preacher.*
  G. Casanova de Seingalt, *Mémoires de Jacques Casanova de Seingalt, Écrits par lui-même.*
  B. Cellini, *Life of Benvenuto Cellini.*
  B. Cellni, *Memoir of Benvenuto Cellini.*
  G. W. Childs, *Recollections.*
  O. Clemens, "Autobiography of a Coward" (unpublished).
  F. P. Cobbe, *Life of Frances Power Cobbe as Told by Herself.*
  W. F. Cody, *Adventures of Buffalo Bill.*
  W. F. Cody, *Life of the Hon. William F. Cody, Known as Buffalo Bill.*
  M. D. Conway, *Autobiography: Memories and Experiences of Moncure Daniel Conway.*
  B. Franklin, *Life of Benjamin Franklin, Written by Himself.*
  S. R. Franklin, *Memories of a Rear-Admiral Who Has Served for More than Half a Century in the Navy of the United States.*
  W. P. Frith, *My Autobiography and Reminiscences.*
  J. L. Gilder, *Tomboy at Work.*
  J. W. von Goethe, *Aus meinem Leben: Dichtung, und Wahrheit.*
  E. Herbert, *Autobiography.*
  A. F. F. de Frénilly, *Recollections of Baron de Frénilly, Peer of France (1768- 1828).*
  T. W. S. Higginson, *Cheerful Yesterdays. Contemporaries.*
  J. Jefferson, *Autobiography of Joseph Jefferson.*
  J. Jònsonn, "Jòn Jònsonn's Saga: The Genuine Autobiography of a Modern Icelander."
  R. Keeler, *Vagabond Adventures.*
  M. Kelly, *Reminiscences of Michael Kelly, of the King's Theatre, and Theatre Royal Drury Lane.*
  F. A. Kemble, *Records of Later Life.*
  C. Kingsley, *Charles Kingsley: His Letters and Memories of His Life.*
  A. M. L. de Lamartine. *Twenty-five Years of My Life.*
  Lutfullah, *Autobiography of Lutfullah, A*

Mohamedan Gentleman; and His Transactions with His Fellow-Creatures.
  J. McCarthy, *Reminiscences.*
  C. Mackay, *Forty Years' Recollections of Life, Literature, and Public Affairs, from 1830 to 1870.*
  M. MacLane, *Story of Mary MacLane.*
  W. C. Macready, *Macready's Reminiscences, and Selections from His Diaries and Letters.*
  J. B. A. M. de Marbot, *Mémoires du General Bon de Marbot.*
  H. Martineau, *Autobiography.*
  J. S. Mill, *Autobiography.*
  J. Miller, *Unwritten History: Life Amongst the Modocs.*
  T. Moore and W. Jerdan, *Personal Reminiscences by Moore and Jerdan.*
  S. O. Morgan, *Lady Morgan's Memoirs: Autobiography, Diaries and Correspondence.*
  J. H. Newman, *Apologia Pro Vita Sua.*
  C. É. J. G. de V. Rémusat, *Memoirs of Madame de Rémusat, 1802–1808.*
  J. J. Rousseau, *Confessions.*
  J. W. Schultz, *My Life as an Indian; The Story of a Red Woman and a White Man in the Lodges of the Blackfeet.*
  W. B. Scott, *Autobiographical Notes of the Life of William Bell Scott.*
  M. F. Somerville, *Personal Recollections, from Early Life to Old Age, of Mary Somerville. With Selections from Her Correspondence.*
  H. M. Stanley, *Autobiography of Sir Henry Morton Stanley.*
  L. Stuart, *Lady Louisa Stuart: Selections from Her Manuscripts.*
  J. G. C. Swisshelm, *Half a Century.*
  G. Ticknor, *Life, Letters, and Journals of George Ticknor.*
  E. J. Trelawny, *Adventures of a Younger Son.*
  A. Trollope, *Autobiography.*
  J. T. Trowbridge, *My Own Story, with Recollections of Noted Persons.*
  E. Văcărescu, *Kings and Queens I Have Known.*
  F. M. A. de Voltaire, *Mémoires pour servir à la vie de M. de Voltaire, écrits par lui-même.*
  E. Wakeman, *Log of an Ancient Mariner; Being the Life and Adventures of Captain Edgar Wakeman. Written by Himself and Edited by His Daughter.*
  L. Wallace, *Lew Wallace: An Autobiography* (marginalia).
  E. B. Washburne, *Recollections of a Minister to France, 1869–1877.*
  A. E. West, *Recollections, 1832 to 1886.*
  A. D. White, *Autobiography of Andrew Dickson White.*
  W. Whitman, *Autobiographia; or, the Story of a Life. By Walt Whitman. Selected from His Prose Writings.*
See also the Reader's Guide entries for Diaries, for Journals, for Memoirs, and for Personal Memoirs.
Autocrat of the Breakfast-Table. O. W. Holmes.
Autographs: see
  H. James (ed.), *Facsimiles of National Manuscripts from William the Conqueror to Queen Anne.*
  A. H. Joline, *Meditations of an Autograph Collector.*

W. T. Stead, *Portraits and Autographs: An Album for the People.*

Automobile race: see L. Barzini, Sr., *Pekin to Paris.*

Automobiles: see I. H. Gillmore, "Story That Took" (short story).

Avare: Comédie en Cinq Actes (play). J.-B. P. Molière.

Avebury, Baron: see J. Lubbock.

Aveling, Eleanor Marx (trans.): see G. Flaubert, *Madame Bovary: Provincial Manners.*

Aventures de Chevalier de Faublas. J. B. Louvet.

Aventures de Télémaque, fils d'Ulysse. F. de S. de la Mothe Fénelon.

Avery, Samuel Putnam (comp.): see H. T. Lewis, "Harp of a Thousand Strings" (burlesque sermon).

Avison, Charles: see R. Browning, *Parleyings with Certain People of Importance in Their Day* (marginalia).

Avocat Patelin: A Comedy in Three Acts (play). A. D. A. de Brueys.

Awakening of Helena Richie. M. W. C. Deland.

Awkward Age, A Novel. H. James.

Aylwin. T. Watts-Dunton.

Aztec religion: see S. E. Titcomb, *Aryan Sun-Myths: The Origin of Religions.*

Aztec Treasure-House; A Romance of Contemporaneous Antiquity. T. A. Janvier.

▌ B

"B., J." (pseud.) (illus.): see C. M. Yonge, *Lances of Lynwood.*

Babbage, Charles (inventor): see M. F. Somerville, *Personal Recollections, from Early Life to Old Age, of Mary Somerville. With Selections from Her Correspondence* (marginalia).

Babcock, Winnifred: see W. Eaton.

"Babes in the Woods" (lecture title). C. F. Browne.

"Babie Bell" (poem): see T. B. Aldrich, "Ballad of Babie Bell" (poem).

Babies: see the Reader's Guide entry for Infant care.

Babson, Joseph Edward (ed.): see L. Hunt, *Day by the Fire; and Other Papers, Hitherto Uncollected.*

Babs, The Impossible. S. Grand (pseud.).

Baby; His Care and Training. M. Wheeler.

Babylonia: see

W. S. C. Boscawen, *First of Empires, "Babylon of the Bible" in the Light of Latest Research.*

T. W. Doane, *Bible Myths and Their Parallels in Other Religions* (marginalia).

A. H. Layard, *Early Adventures in Persia, Susiana, and Babylonia.*

M. H. Potter, *Star of Babylon, A Phantasy.*

C. Rollin, *Ancient History of the Egyptians, Carthaginians, Assyrians, Babylonians, Medes and Persians, Grecians and Macedonians.*

E. S.P. Ward and H. D. Ward, *Master of the Magicians* (novel).

"Baby May" (poem). W. C. Bennett.

Baby's Opera: A Book of Old Rhymes with New Dresses. W. Crane.

Bache, René (illus.): see H. C. Lukens, *Jets and Flashes.*

Bacher, Otto H. (illus.): see S. P. M. Greene, *Vesty of the Basins; A Novel.*

Back Home. E. Wood.

Backlog Studies. C. D. Warner.

Back Numbers/Wilmans Express, Condensed. H. Wilmans.

Backsheesh! or, Life and Adventures in the Orient. T. W. Knox.

"Back to the Army Again" (poem). R. Kipling.

Bacon. R. W. Church.

Bacon Cryptograms in Shake-speare, and Other Studies. I. H. Platt.

"Bacon, Dolores M." (pseud.): see M. S. H. Bacon (ed.).

Bacon, Francis: see

D. S. Bacon, *Philosophy of the Plays of Shakspere Unfolded.*

W. S. Booth, *Some Acrostic Signatures of Francis Bacon.*

R. W. Church, *Bacon.*

S. V. Clevenger, *Fun in a Doctor's Life, Being the Adventures of an American Don Quixote* (marginalia).

L. Cornaro, *Art of Living Long* (includes a Bacon essay).

I. Donnelly, *Great Cryptogram: Francis Bacon's Cipher in the So-Called Shakespeare Plays.*

E. W. Gallup, *Bi-Literal Cypher of Sir Francis Bacon Discovered in His Works and Deciphered.*

E. W. Gallup, *Tragedy of Anne Boleyn. A Drama in Cipher Found in the Works of Sir Francis Bacon.*

G. G. Greenwood, *Shakespeare Problem Restated.*

T. B. Macaulay, *Critical and Miscellaneous Essays* (marginalia).

T. B. Macaulay, "Essay on Bacon."

T. Malory, *Morte Darthur* (Catalog entry).

J. P. W. Penzance, *Lord Penzance on the Bacon-Shakespeare Controversy. A Judicial Summing-Up.*

I. H. Platt, *Bacon Cryptograms in Shake-speare, and Other Studies.*

W. Shakespeare, *King Lear* (play) (Catalog entry).

W. Shakespeare, *Romeo and Juliet* (play) (Catalog entry).

W. Shakespeare, *Tempest* (play) (Catalog entry).

W. Shakespeare, *Works of Shakespeare* (Catalog entry).

A. C. Swinburne, *Three Plays of Shakespeare* (marginalia).

A. D. White, *History of the Warfare of Science with Theology* (marginalia).

See also the Reader's Guide entry for William Shakespeare.

Bacteria and Their Products. G. S. Woodhead.

Bad Boy's Diary. M. V. F. Victor.

Bagsby's Daughter. B. M. Van Vorst.

Bailey, James Montgomery: see H. W. Shaw, *Everybody's Friend, or Josh Billings's Encyclopedia and Proverbial Philosophy of Wit and Humor* (Catalog entry).

Bailey, Mark (co-author): see W. T. Harris, *First Reader.*

Bain, Robert Nisbet (trans.): see M. Gorky, *Tales from Gorky, Translated from the Russian.*

Baker, Henry William (hymn lyrics): see the Catalog entry for G. J. Geer.

Baker, Theodor (trans.): see M. Brée, *Groundwork of the Leschetizky Method.*

Baker, William G.: see George Washington Bates (pseud.).

Baker, William Taylor: see C. H. Baker, *Life and Character of William Taylor Baker.*

Balabodhini. M. Bahadur Rana.

Balboa, Vasco Nuñez de: see F. A. Ober, *Vasco Nuñez de Balboa.*

Balcony Stories. G. King.

Baldwin, James (ed.): see C. Nisbet, *Everybody's Writing-Desk Book.*

Bale, Edwin (pref.): see G. Fraipont, *Art of Sketching.*

Balestier, Wolcott (contr.): see R. Kipling, *Naulahka, A Story of the West and East.*

Ball, Alexander M. W.: see
E. A. C. A. Allen, "Rock Me to Sleep, Mother" (poem) (claimed authorship).
M. S. H. Bacon, *Songs Every Child Should Know: A Selection of the Best Songs of All Nations for Young People* (claimed authorship).

Ball, Robert (trans.): see R. Radau, *Wonders of Acoustics; or, The Phenomenon of Sound.*

Ball, Valentine (ed., trans.): see J. B. Tavernier, *Travels in India.*

"Ballad of Babie Bell" (poem). T. B. Aldrich.

"Ballad of the 'Bolivar'" (poem). R. Kipling.

Ballads. W. M. Thackeray.

Ballads and Other Poems. A Tennyson.

Ballads and Other Verses. J. T. Fields.

Ballet Dancer, and On Guard. M. Serao.

Ballingtons, A Novel. F. B. S. Potter.

Ballo in Maschera (opera). G. Verdi.

"Balloon Hoax" (short story). E. A. Poe.

Balloon voyages: see
N. C. Flammarion, *Wonderful Balloon Ascents; or, the Conquest of the Skies.*
W. de Fonvielle, *Thunder and Lightning.*
W. D. Howells (co-ed.), *Library of Universal Adventure by Sea and Land.*
C. P. Jones and A. L. Sykes, *Banduk jaldi banduk!: (Quick, My Rifle!).*
P. V. Mighels, *Crystal Sceptre; A Story of Adventure* (novel).
E. A. Poe, "Balloon Hoax" (short story).
J. Verne, *Five Weeks in a Balloon; or, Journeys and Discoveries in Africa, by Three Englishmen.*
J. Verne, *Mysterious Island.*
W. H. Wilson, *Rafnaland; The Strange Story of John Heath Howard.*
J. Wise, *Through the Air: A Narrative of Forty Years' Experience as an Aeronaut.*
See also the Reader's Guide entry for Entrapped vessels.

"Ballyhooly" (song). R. J. Martin.

"Balm of Gilead" (minstrel song). H. T. Bryant (arranger).

Balzac, Honoré de: see
Little French Masterpieces.
W. Shakespeare, *Works of Shakespeare* (Catalog entry).

Balzac's Contes Drolatiques; Droll Stories Collected from the Abbeys of Touraine. H. de Balzac.

Bancroft, Hubert Howe: see
T. Wright (ed.), *Early Travels in Palestine* (marginalia).
É. Zola, *Rome* (marginalia).

Banduk jaldi banduk!: (Quick, My Rifle!). C. P. Jones and A. L. Sykes.

Bangs, John Kendrick (co-author): see *Whole Family; A Novel by Twelve Authors.*

Banking: see
C. A. Conant, *Principles of Banking.*
C. A. Conant, *Principles of Money and Banking.*
Hubbard's Newspaper and Bank Directory of the World.

"Banks and braes o' Bonnie Doon" (song). R. Burns.

Banks, Isabella (Varley) (intro.): see W. Smith (ed.), *Old Yorkshire.*

"Banks of the Genesee" (poem, song): see G. W. Elliott.

Banville, Théodore de: see J. McCarthy, *Wife of Socrates* (play).

Baptist Church: see
J. D. Knowles, *Memoir of Mrs. Ann H. Judson, Late Missionary to Burmah, Including a History of the American Baptist Mission in the Burman Empire.*
J. B. Monteith, *Parson Brooks: A Plumb Powerful Hard Shell. A Story of Humble Southern Life.*

Barbara Goes to Oxford. O. H. B. Ball.

Barbara's History. A. A. B. Edwards.

Barbara's Vagaries. M. L. D. Tidball.

Barbary Sheep; A Novel. R. S. Hichens.

Barbauld, Anna Letitia: see J. A. D.-G. Ross, *Three Generations of English Women* (marginalia).

"Barber of Bagdad" (opera). P. Cornelius.

Barbié du Bocage, Jean Dennis (contr.): see J. J. Barthélemy, *Travels of Anacharis the Younger in Greece.*

Barbiere di Siviglia [The Barber of Seville] (opera). G. A. Rossini.

Barham, Richard Harris. "Look at the Clock!" (poem): see the Catalog entry for *Selected Poems, Illustrated.*

"Barine, Arvède" (pseud.): see C. Vincens.

Baring-Gould, Sabine: see L. Strachey, "Progressional" (satirical poem).

Barker, Nathan (arr.): see "Roll on, silver moon" (song).

Barnaby Rudge. C. Dickens.

Barnaby Rudge. C. Dickens: see J. Payne, "Adventure in a Forest; or, Dickens's Maypole Inn" (essay).

Barnes, Albert (Biblical scholar): see the Catalog entry for É. Zola, *Rome* (marginalia).

Barnes, Hiram Putnam (illus.): see C. Kingsley, *Song of the River.*

Barnum, Phineas Taylor: see F. T. Buckland, *Curiosities of Natural History* (Catalog entry).

"Baroness Staffe" (pseud.): see B. A. A. Soyer.

Barrack-Room Ballads and Other Verses. R. Kipling.

Barrett, Lawrence: see
W. Shakespeare, *Hamlet* (Catalog entry).
W. G. Wills, *Man o' Airlie: A Drama of the Affections* (play).
W. Winter, *Wanderers: The Poems of William Winter.*

Barrett, William Fletcher: see the Catalog entry for Society for Psychical Research.

Barrier. R. F. Beach.

Barriers Burned Away. E. P. Roe.

Barry Cornwall: see J. T. Fields, *Old Acquaintance. Barry Cornwall and Some of His Friends.*

Barry Gordon. W. F. Payson.

Barry Lyndon: see W. M. Thackeray, *Memoirs of Barry Lyndon, Esq.*

Bar Sinister. R. H. Davis.

Bartel Turaser, Drama in drei Akten (play). P. Langmann.

Bar-tending: see W. A. Schmidt, *Flowing Bowl: When and What to Drink: Full Instructions How to Prepare, Mix, and Serve Beverages.*

Barter, C. S. L. (co-trans.): see H., G. von Moltke, *Essays, Speeches and Memoirs.*

Bartlett, May (illus.): see S. E. S. Boggs, *Sandpeep.*

Bashkirtseff, Marie: see M. K. Bashkirtseva.

Basil. W. W. Collins.

Baths, Bathing, and Attractions of Aix-les-Bains, Savoy, Etc. W. Wakefield.

Battisini, Mattia (opera singer): see G. Verdi, *Ballo in Maschera* (opera).

"Battle Cry of Freedom" (song). G. F. Root.

"Battle-Field" (poem). W. C. Bryant.

"Battle hymn of the Republic" (hymn). J. W. Howe.

"Battle hymn of the Republic" (hymn): see A. Young, "There is a happy land" (hymn) (Catalog entry).

Battle Hymns of the Church. E. A. Hoffman and H. F. Sayles (comp.).

"Battle of Hohenlinden" (poem, song lyrics). T. Campbell.

Battle of Life; A Love Story. C. Dickens.

"Battle of Naseby" (poem). T. B. Macaulay.

"Battle of Prague" (music). F. Kotzwara.

Battles and Leaders of the Civil War. R. U. Johnson and C. C. Buel (eds.).

Battles of the Revolution. C. C. Coffin.

Baucis and Philemon (classical myth): see Ovid, *Art of Love, in Three Books.*

Baudelaire, Charles Pierre: see *Pastels in Prose. From the French.*

"Bay of Biscay" (song). A. Cherry.

Bayreuth: see F. S. Wilhelmina, *Memoirs of Wihelmine, Margravine of Baireuth.*

Bazar Book of Decorum. The Care of the Person, Manners, Etiquette, and Ceremonials. R. Tomes.

Beach, Emma (ed.): see *Among the Daisies. Poems Old and New.*

Beacon Lights of History. J. Lord.

Beale, Harriet Stanwood (Blaine) see (ed.) H. B. S. Blaine, *Letters of Mrs. James G. Blaine.*

Beard, Daniel Carter (illus.): see
    M. J. Crim, *Adventures of a Fair Rebel.*
    R. M. Johnston, *Billy Downs and His Likes.*
    E. J. Pullen, *Don Finimondone: Calabrian Sketches.*
    W. O. Stoddard, *Inside the White House in War Times.*
    C. F. Wong, "Wu Chih Tien, The Celestial Empress: A Chinese Historical Novel."

Beard, Frank (illus.): see F. G. Welch, *That Convention; or, Five Days a Politician.*

Bear hunts: see
    C. A. Adams, *Pete's Devils.*
    E. H. Mott, *Old Settler and His Tales of the Sugar Swamp.*
    V. Meunier (comp.), *Adventures on the Great Hunting Grounds of the World.*
    F. Nansen, *Farthest North; Being the Record of a Voyage of Exploration of the Ship "Fram" 1893–96, and of a Fifteen Months' Sleigh Journey.*
    W. O. Stoddard, *In the Open: Stories of Outdoor Life.*
    T. B. Thorpe, "Big Bear of Arkansas" (story).
    C. D. Warner, *In the Wilderness.*
    See also the Reader's Guide entry for Hunting literature.

Bear-Worshippers of Yezo; And the Island of Karafuto Saghalin. The Adventures of the Jewett Family and Their Friend Oto Nambo. E. Greey.

Beasley's Christmas Party. B. Tarkington.

Beasts of the Field. W. J. Long.

Beath, Robert Burns (intro.): see P. F. Mottelay and T. Campbell-Copeland (eds.), *Soldier in Our Civil War: A Pictorial History of the Conflict, 1861–65.*

Beaumarchais, Pierre: see G. A. Rossini, *Barbiere di Siviglia.*

Beaumont, William (trans.): see J. J. Barthélemy, *Travels of Anacharsis the Younger in Greece.*

Beau's Comedy. B. M. Dix and C. A. Harper (co-author).

Beauties of Tennyson. A. Tennyson.

"Beautiful Snow" (poem). J. W. Watson.

"Beautiful snow" (song): see F. B. Ogilvie (comp.), *Two Hundred Old-Time Songs, Containing the Words and Music of the Choicest Gems of the Old and Familiar Songs* (marginalia).

"Beautiful star in heaven" (song): see J. M. Sayles, "Star of the evening."

"Beautiful Thoughts" from Henry Drummond. H. Drummond.

Beauty and grooming advice: see
    T. Child, *Wimples and Crisping-Pins; Being Studies in the Coiffure and Ornaments of Women.*
    M. R. O. Dewing, *Beauty in Dress.*
    M. T. V. Earle, *Pot-pourri from a Surrey Garden.*
    E. A. Fletcher, *Woman Beautiful: A Practical Treatise on the Development and Preservation of Woman's Health and Beauty, and the Principles of Taste in Dress.*
    A. J. Miller, *Physical Beauty: How to Obtain and How to Preserve It.*
    S. D. Power, *Ugly-Girl Papers; or, Hints for the Toilet.*
    B. A. A. Soyer, *Lady's Dressing-Room (Le cabinet de toilette).*
    R. Tomes, *Bazar Book of Decorum. The Care of the Person, Manners, Etiquette, and Ceremonials.*

Beauty in Dress. M. R. O. Dewing.

Beauty in the Household. M. R. O. Dewing.

Beck, James M. (correspondent): see W. Shakespeare, *Works of Shakespeare* (Catalog entry).

Becket (drama). A. Tennyson.

Becket, Thomas à: see A. Tennyson, *Becket* (drama).

"Bede, Cuthbert" (pseud.): see E. Bradley.

Bede, Venerable: see J. R. Green, *Short History of the English People* (marginalia).

Bédollière, Émile de: see T. B. Aldrich, *Story of a Cat.*

"Bedott, Widow" (pseud.): see F. M. B. Whitcher.

"Bedouin Love Song" (poem). B. Taylor.

Beecher, Charles (ed.): see L. Beecher, *Autobiography, Correspondence, Etc.*

Beecher, Henry Ward: see
    Beecher Trial: A Review of the Evidence.

(ed.) *Christian Union.*
S. M. Griswold, *Sixty Years with Plymouth Church* (marginalia).
Men of the Time: A Dictionary of Contemporaries, Containing Biographical Notices of Eminent Characters of Both Sexes.
J. B. Pond (ed.), *Summer in England with Henry Ward Beecher; Giving the Addresses, Lectures, and Sermons Delivered by Him in Great Britain During The Summer of 1886.*
J. Swift, *Gulliver's Travels into Several Remote Nations of the World* (Catalog entry).
Bees: see
J. M. Baldwin, *Story of the Mind* (marginalia).
W. Busch, *Schnurrdiburr oder Die Bienen.*
N. B. De G. Doubleday, *Wild Flowers: An Aid to Knowledge of Our Wild Flowers and Their Insect Visitors.*
L. O. Howard, *Insect Book: A Popular Account of the Bees, Wasps, Ants, Grasshoppers, Flies, and Other North American Insects.*
F. Huber, *New Observations on the Natural History of Bees.*
J. Lubbock, *Ants, Bees, and Wasps: A Record of Observations on the Habits of the Social Hymenoptera.*
M. Maeterlinck, *Life of the Bee.*
J. A. Marks and J. E. Moody, *Little Busybodies; The Life of Crickets, Ants, Bees, Beetles, and Other Busybodies.*
F. S. Matthews, *Field Book of American Wild Flowers; Being a Short Description of Their Character and Habits, A Concise Definition of Their Colors, and Incidental References to the Insects Which Assist Their Fertilzation.*
M. E. J. Whitcombe, *Bygone Days in Devonshire and Cornwall, with Notes of Existing Superstitions and Customs* (marginalia).
G. White, *Natural History and Antiquities of Selborne* (Catalog entry).
See also the Reader's Guide entry for Insects.
Beethoven, Ludwig van: see L. Nohl, *Life of Beethoven.*
Beeton, Samuel Orchart (contr.): see S. Smith, *Essays Social and Political. First and Second Series.*
Beeton's Complete Letter-Writer. S. O. Beeton.
"Before" (poem). R. Browning.
Beginnings of New England; or, The Puritan Theocracy in Its Relations to Civil and Religious Liberty. J. Fiske.
"Beiden grenadiere" (song): see H. Heine, "Two grenadiers."
Being a Boy. C. D. Warner.
Belasco, David: see
J. L. Long, *Madame Butterfly.*
(trans., adaptor) C. Simon and P. F. S. Berton *Zaza, A Comedy Drama in Five Acts.*
Belden, Frank Edson (composer): see "Let each now choose" (unidentified hymn).
Belgian Congo: see the Reader's Guide entry for Congo.
Belgium: see
F. H. B. Skrine, *Fontenoy and Great Britain's Share in the War of the Austrian Succession, 1741–1748.*
R. L. Stevenson, *Inland Voyage.*

W. Wack, *Story of the Congo Free State: Social, Political, and Economic Aspects of the Belgian System of Government in Central Africa.*
Beljame, Alexandre (ed.): see J. Bellows, *Dictionary for the Pocket: French and English, English and French.*
Belknap, William Worth: see J. R. Lowell, *Letters of James Russell Lowell* (marginalia).
"Bell, Acton" (pseud.): see A. Brontë.
"Bell Buoy" (poem). R. Kipling.
Bell, Clara: see
(trans.) A. G. Barrili, *Eleventh Commandment; A Romance.*
(trans.) G. Fraipont, *Art of Sketching.*
(co-trans.) H., G. von Moltke, *Letters of Field-Marshall Count Helmuth von Moltke to His Mother and His Brothers.*
"Bell, Currer" (pseud.): see C. Brontë.
"Bell, Ellis" (pseud.): see E. Brontë.
Bell in the Fog, and Other Stories. G. F. H. Atherton.
Bell, John Graham (contr.): see J. H. Studer (ed.), *Birds of North America; One Hundred and Nineteen Artistic Colored Plates.*
Bell, Mabel Gardiner (Hubbard): see (pref.) E. P. Adams, *Story Sermons from Les Misérables.*
Bell, Nancy Regina Emily (Meugens) (trans.): see J. F. A. du P. Nadaillac, *Pre-Historic America.*
Belle Assemblée: Being a Curious Collection of Some Very Remarkable Incidents Which Happen'd to Persons of the First Quality in France. M. A.P. de Gomez.
Belle Islers; A Novel. F. K. Gifford.
"Belle Mahone" (song). J. H. McNaughton.
Belle of New York, A Musical Comedy in Two Acts (play). C. M. S. McLellan.
Belle of the Bluegrass Country. Studies in Black and White. H. D. Pittman.
"Bells" (poem). E. A. Poe.
Benares: see
A. Parker, *Hand-Book of Benares.*
C. R. Kennedy, *Servant in the House* (character in this play).
T. D. W. Talmage, *Sermons. Second Series* (Catalog entry).
"Ben Bolt; or, oh! don't you remember" (song). T. D. English.
Benedictine Order of Nuns: see
H. G. D. Liveing. *Records of Romsey Abbey: An Account of the Benedictine House of Nuns, with Notes on the Parish Church and Town (A. D. 907–1558).* H. G. D. Liveing.
Unfathomable Mystery. Benedictine Sisters of Perpetual Adoration. Clyde, Missouri.
Benefit of the Doubt. M. C. Spenser.
Benham, William (inscr.): see J. Tanswell, *History and Antiquities of Lambeth.*
Ben-Hur: A Tale of the Christ. L. Wallace.
Benjamin of Tudela: see T. Wright (ed.), *Early Travels in Palestine.*
Bennett, Charles Henry (illus.): see P. E. de Musset, *Mr. Wind and Madam Rain.*
Bensley, Martha S. (co-playwright): see C. R. Teller, "Sociological Maid. A Play in One Act."

Benson, Arthur Christopher (ed.): see Queen Victoria, *The Letters of Queen Victoria: A Selection from Her Majesty's Correspondence Between the Years 1837 and 1861.*

Bentley, George (ed.): see *Temple Bar: A London Magazine for Town and Country Readers.*

Bentzon, Thérèse: see *Revue des deux mondes* (Catalog entry).

Berard's History of United States. A. B. Berard.

"Beresford, Max" (pseud.): see A. E. Holdsworth.

Berggeist im Riesengebirge. R. Koch.

Berkeley, Henrietta, Lady: see A. A. Behn, *Love-Letters Between a Nobleman and His Sister.*

Berlin and Sans-Souci; or, Frederick the Great and His Friends. An Historical Romance. K. M. Mundt.

Bermuda: see C. Scollard, *Under Summer Skies.*

Bernard, Mrs. William Bayle (ed.): see J. Bernard, *Retrospections of America, 1797–1811.*

Bernhardt, Sarah: see

V. M. Hugo, *Angelo* (play) (Catalog entry).

J. Parton, *Life of Voltaire* (marginalia).

J. B. Racine, *Phaedra, A Tragedy in Five Acts.*

Bernheimer, Charles S. (co-author): see E. J. James, *Immigrant Jew in America.*

Berry, Agnes: see H. Martineau, *Autobiography* (marginalia).

Berry, Mary: see H. Martineau, *Autobiography* (marginalia).

Berton, Pierre François Samuel (co-author): see C. Simon, *Zaza, A Comedy Drama in Five Acts.*

Bertrand of Brittany. G. W. Deeping.

Bess of the Woods. G. W. Deeping.

Best Books: A Reader's Guide to the Choice of the Best Available Books (about 50,000) in Every Department of Science, Art, and Literature. W. S. Sonnenschein (comp.).

Bétis, Victor (co-trans.): see F. Gouin, *Art of Teaching.*

Betrothed. A. Manzoni.

Betrothed. W. Scott.

Betts, Anna Whelan (illus.): see W. J. Mills, *Caroline of Courtlandt Street* (novel).

Betty's Bright Idea. Also, Deacon Pitkin's Farm, and the First Christmas of New England. H. E. B. Stowe.

Between the Dark and the Daylight: Romances (short stories). W. D. Howells.

Between the Lines, A Story of the War (novel). C. King.

Between Two Fires. I. D. Hardy.

Beulah, A Novel. A. J. E. Wilson.

Bewick's Select Fables. Aesop.

Bewick, Thomas (illus.): see Aesop, *Bewick's Select Fables.*

Bewitched: A Tale. L. B. Pendleton.

Beyond the Great South Wall: The Secret of the Antarctic. F. M. Savile.

Beyond the Hills of Dream: see W. W. Campbell, "Love Came at Dawn" (poem).

Beyond the Mississippi: From the Great River to the Great Ocean. A. D. Richardson.

"Beyond the smiling and the weeping" (hymn). H. Bonar.

Bible: see

C. E. Beecher, *Appeal to the People in Behalf of Their Rights as Authorized Interpreters of the Bible.*

C. A. Briggs, "Criticism and Dogma" (essay).

T. W. Doane, *Bible Myths and Their Parallels in Other Religions: Being a of the Old and New Testament Myths and Miracles with Those of Heathen Nations of Antiquity.*

J. G. Frazer, *Passages of the Bible, Chosen for Their Literary Beauty and Interest.*

W. E. Griffis, *Bible Stories for Young People.*

W. E. H. Lecky, *History of the Rise and Influence of the Spirit of Rationalism in Europe* (marginalia).

J. M. Lowrie, *Adam and His Times.*

E. J. Miller, *Yoke: A Romance of the Days When the Lord Redeemed the Children of Israel from the Bondage of Egypt.*

H. Oort and I. Hooykass, *Bible for Learners.*

H. Oort and I. Hooykaas, *Bible for Young People.*

C. Reade, *Bible Characters.*

J. W. Sanborn, *Legends, Customs and Social Life of the Seneca Indians of Western New York* (Catalog entry).

W. Smith (ed.), *Concise Dictionary of the Bible, for the Use of Families and Students.*

E. C. Stanton (ed.), *Woman's Bible.*

R. L. Stevenson, *Inland Voyage* (Catalog entry).

A. D. White, *History of the Warfare of Science with Theology* (marginalia).

Women of the Bible, by Twelve Eminent Divines.

See also the Reader's Guide entries for Adam and Eve, for Bible concordances, for Bible dictionaries, for Biblical history, for Bible. New Testament, for Bible. Old Testament, for Christ, for Christianity, for Christianity and comparative religions, for Christmas, for Holy Land, for Palestine, and for Science and religion.

Bible Characters. C. Reade.

Bible concordances: see J. Eadie (ed.), *New and Complete Concordance to the Holy Scriptures.*

Bible dictionaries: see

M. G. Easton, *Illustrated Bible Dictionary.*

J. G. Frazer (comp.), *Passages of the Bible, Chosen for Their Literary Beauty and Interest.*

Bible for Learners. H. Oort.

Bible for Young People. H. Oort.

Bible Myths and Their Parallels in Other Religions: Being a Comparison of the Old and New Testament Myths and Miracles with Those of Heathen Nations of Antiquity. T. W. Doane.

Bible. New Testament: see

A. Barnes, *Notes, Explanatory and Practical, on the New Testament* (various volumes).

H. C. Greene (trans.), *Gospel of the Childhood of Our Lord Jesus Christ.*

T. Long, *Exercitation Concerning the Frequent Use of Our Lord's Prayer in the Publick Worship of God.* "Lord's Prayer."

T. B. Macaulay, *Critical and Miscellaneous Essays* (marginalia).

E. C. Mitchell, *Critical Handbook of the Greek New Testament.*

S. Phillips, *Herod: A Tragedy* (play).

A. W. Pitzer, *Ecce Deus-Homo; or, The Work and Kingdom of the Christ of Scripture.*

H. Pyle, *Rejected of Men; A Story of To-day.*

P. Schaff (ed.) *Revision of the English Version of the New Testament.*

J. R. Seeley, *Ecce Homo; A Survey of the Life and Work of Jesus Christ.*

W. B. Stevens, *Parables of the New Testment Practically Unfolded.*

R. L. Stevenson, *Prince Otto: A Romance* (Catalog entry).

Suetonius, *Lives of the Twelve Caesars* (marginalia).

W. H. Thomson, *Parables and Their Home. The Parables by the Lake.*

J. Tissot, *New Testament* [paintings].

Two—and an Indian (unidentified book).

H. Van Dyke, *Story of the Other Wise Man.*

L. Wallace, *Boyhood of Christ* (marginalia).

G. W. Warder, *Cities of the Sun.*

H. C. Watson, "Prodigal son" (sacred song).

J. Weiss, *Paul and Jesus.*

See also the Reader's Guide entries for Bible, for Christ, for Christmas, for Holy Land, and for Palestine.

Bible. Old Testament: see

T. B. Macaulay, *History of England from the Accession of James II* (Catalog entry).

J. Milton, *Milton's Paradise Lost.*

J. Silverman (Catalog entry).

R. L. Stevenson, *Prince Otto: A Romance* (Catalog entry).

G. O. Trevelyan, *Life and Letters of Lord Macaulay* (marginalia).

A. B. Warner, *Melody of the Twenty-third Psalm.*

M. M. Whiteside, *Mizpah; or, Drifting Away, by Mrs. M. McCullen Whiteside,* ("Muriel") (Catalog entry).

H. R. Woodman, *Noahs Afloat; An Historical Romance.*

T. Wright (ed.), *Early Travels in Palestine* (marginalia).

C. M. Yonge, *Book of Worthies, Gathered from the Old Histories and Now Written Anew.*

See also the Reader's Guide entries for Adam and Eve, for Bible, for Holy Land, and for Palestine.

Bible Stories for Young People. W. E. Griffis.

Biblical history: see

S. Baring-Gould, *Legends of Old Testament Characters, from the Talmud and Other Sources.*

A. Bond (ed.), *Young People's Illustrated Bible History.*

W. S. C. Boscawen, *First of Empires, "Babylon of the Bible" in the Light of Latest Research.*

J. C. Geikie, *Hours with the Bible; or, The Scriptures in the Light of Modern Discovery and Knowledge.* J. C. Geikie.

[J.] E. Renan, *Apostles. Translated from the Original French.*

E. B. Sanford (ed.), *Concise Cyclopedia of Religious Knowledge, Biblical, Theological, Historical, and Practical.*

P. N. Shuttleworth, *Consistency of Revelation with Itself and with Human Reason.*

H. Sienkiewicz. *"Quo Vadis": A Narrative of the Time of Nero* (novel).

C. E. Stowe, *Origin and History of the Books of the Bible, Both the Canonical and the Apocryphal.*

E. S. P. Ward and H. D. Ward, *Master of the Magicians* (novel).

M. Willson, *Mosaics of Bible History; The Bible Record with Illustrative Poetic and Prose Selections from Standard Literature.*

See also the Reader's Guide entries for Bible and for Bible dictionaries.

Biblical Researches in Palestine, and in the Adjacent Regions. A Journal of Travels in the Years 1838 & 1852. E. Robinson.

Biblical studies: see the Reader's Guide entry for Biblical history.

Bichard, Alphonse Adolphe (illus.): see B. Münchausen, *Adventures of Baron Munchausen.*

Bicycle of Cathay. A Novel. F. R. Stockton.

Bida, Alexandre (co-illus.): see A. R. Macdonough (trans.), *Lovers of Provence: Aucassin and Nicolette.*

Bien, J. (illus.): see J. J. Audubon, *Birds of America.*

Bierce, Ambrose: see M. D. Conway, *Autobiography: Memories and Experiences of Moncure Daniel Conway* (marginalia).

"Big Bear of Arkansas" (story). T. B. Thorpe.

Bigelow, John: see

(ed.), B. Franklin, *Life of Benjamin Franklin, Written by Himself.*

(inscr.), J. S. Gilbert, *Panama Patchwork; Poems, by James Stanley Gilbert.*

(ed.) S. J. Tilden, *Letters and Literary Memorials of Samuel J. Tilden.*

(ed.) S. J. Tilden, *Writings and Speeches of Samuel J. Tilden.*

"Bigelow, Mrs. Poultney" (pseud.): see E. E. Bigelow.

Bigelow, Poultney: see E. Crawford, "Notes from Paris" (article) (Catalog entry).

Big John Baldwin; Extracts from the Journal of an Officer of Cromwell's Army (fictional memoir). W. J. Vance.

Biglow Papers. J. R. Lowell.

Bikey the Skicycle. J. K. Bangs.

Bilderbuch ohne Bilder. H. C. Andersen.

Bilder Fibel. C. W. Sanders and J. C. Sanders.

Bi-Literal Cypher of Sir Francis Bacon. E. W. Gallup.

Billiards: see

A. Garnier, *Scientific Billiards. Garnier's Practice Shots, with Hints to Amateurs.*

Prize Essays on "Billiards as an Amusement for all Classes."

"Billings, Josh" (pseud.): see H. W. Shaw.

Bill Nye's History of the United States. E. W. Nye.

Bill Truetell, A Story of Theatrical Life. G. H. Brennan.

Billy Bellew. W. E. Norris.

Bimbi: Stories for Children. M. L. De la Ramée.

Bingen on the Rhine. C. E. S. S. Norton.

Biographical dictionaries: see

Men of the Time: A Dictionary of Contemporaries, Containing Biographical Notices of Eminent Characters of Both Sexes.

Who's Who in America: A Biographical Dictionary of Notable Living Men and

Women of the United States, 1906–1907.

Biographical Studies. W. Bagehot.

Biographies: see

J. S. C. Abbott, *History of Marie Antoinette* (and various other biographies).

A. V. G. Allen, *Life and Letters of Phillips Brooks.*

S. A. Allibone,. *Critical Dictionary of English Literature and British and American Authors*

J. Arnould, *Life of Thomas, First Lord Denman, Formerly Lord Chief Justice of England.*

W. Bagehot, *Biographical Studies.*

C. H. Baker, *Life and Character of William Taylor Baker.*

F. Bancroft, *Life of William H. Seward.*

J. Barrett, *Admiral George Dewey; A Sketch of the Man.*

W. Beattie, *Life and Letters of Thomas Campbell.*

G. W. Bethune, *Memoirs of Mrs. Joanna Bethune, by Her Son.*

J. Boswell, *Life of Samuel Johnson.*

A. Brooks, *Phillips Brooks.*

E. E. Brown, *Life of Oliver Wendell Holmes.*

J. Brown, *Marjorie Fleming, A Sketch.*

O. G. de Busbecq, *Life and Letters of Ogier Ghiselin de Busbecq.*

M. Busch, *Bismarck in the Franco-German War 1870–1871.*

M. Busch, *Unser Reichskanzler: Studien zu einem Charakterbilde.*

J. E. Cabot, *Memoir of Ralph Waldo Emerson.*

J. L. H. Campan, *Mémoires sur la Vie Privée de Marie Antoinette.*

T. Carlyle, *Life of John Sterling.*

J. Cartwright, *Jean François Millet: His Life and Letters.*

L. E. Chittenden, *Recollections of President Lincoln and His Administration.*

C. C. Coffin, *Abraham Lincoln.*

G. R. Crooks, *Life of Bishop Matthew Simpson, of the Methodist Episcopal Church.*

A. Cunningham, *Life of Robert Burns.*

M. V. Dahlgren, *Memoir of John A. Dahlgren, Rear-Admiral United States Navy, by His Widow.*

C. Darwin, *Life and Letters of Charles Darwin.*

A. Davies, *Maude Adams.*

H. Dircks, *Life, Times and Scientific Labours of the Second Marquis of Worcester.*

F. S. Drake, *Dictionary of American Biography.*

H. Dunckley, *Lord Melbourne.*

H. K. F. G. Eden, *Juliana Horatia Ewing and Her Works.*

G. Eliot, *George Eliot's Life as Related in Her Letters and Journals.*

C. H. Farnham, *Life of Francis Parkman.*

A. A. Fields, *Whittier; Notes of His Life and of His Friendships.*

J. T. Fields, *Hawthorne.*

H. W. H. Fischer, *Private Lives of William II and His Consort and Secret History of the Court of Berlin.*

P. H. Fitzgerald, *Life of George the Fourth, Including His Letters and Opinions.*

J. Forster, *Life of Jonathan Swift.*

J. A. Froude, *Thomas Carlyle: A History of His Life in London, 1834–1881.*

J. A. Froude, *Thomas Carlyle: A History of the First Forty Years of His Life, 1795–1935.*

T. Fuller, *Holy State and the Profane State.*

H. Garland, *Ulysses S. Grant, His Life and Character.*

E. C. S. Gaskell, *Life of Charlotte Brontë.*

A. Gilchrist, *Life of William Blake, "Pictor Ignotus."*

C. A. Goodrich, *Lives of the Signers to the Declaration of Independence.*

E. W. Gosse, *Thomas Gray.*

F. Greenslet, *Life of Thomas Bailey Aldrich.*

M. Hall, *Lives of the Queens of England Before the Norman Conquest.*

P. G. Hamerton, *Life of J. M. W. Turner.*

A. Hamilton, *Mémoires du Comte de Gramont.*

A. R. Hancock, *Reminiscences of Winfield Scott Hancock. By His Wife.*

A. J. C. Hare, *Memorials of a Quiet Life.*

E. F. Harkins, *Famous Authors (Men).* E. F. Harkins.

E. F. Harkins, *Little Pilgrimages Among the Men Who Have Written Famous Books.*

J. M. Haswell, *Man of His Time. . . . Napoleon III.*

J. Hawthorne, *Hawthorne and His Circle.*

J. Hawthorne, *Nathaniel Hawthorne and His Wife, A Biography.*

G. Henschel, *Personal Recollections of Johannes Brahms.*

H. Hensman, *Cecil Rhodes: A Study of a Career.*

C. F. Horne (ed.), *Great Men and Famous Women: A Series of Pen and Pencil Sketches.*

M. A. D. Howe, *American Bookmen: Sketches, Chiefly Biographical, of Certain Writers of the Nineteenth Century.*

M. A. D. Howe, *Phillips Brooks.*

W. D. Howells, *Literary Friends and Acquaintances: A Personal Retrospect of American Authorship.*

W. D. Howells, *Sketch of the Life and Character of Rutherford B. Hayes.*

A. F. Hugo, *Victor Hugo, by a Witness of His Life.*

V. M. Hugo, *Destroyer of the Second Republic.*

R. Huish, *Memoirs of George the Fourth, Descriptive of the Most Interesting Scenes of His Private and Public Life.*

A. Hullah, *Theodore Leschetizky.*

L. Hutton, *Edwin Booth.*

L. Huxley, *Life and Letters of Thomas Henry Huxley.*

T. H. Huxley, *Hume.*

A. E. N. Ireland, *Life of Jane Welsh Carlyle.*

W. Irving, *History of the Life and Voyages of Christopher Columbus.*

W. Irving, *Life of George Washington.*

W. Irving, *Life of Oliver Goldsmith.*

A. B. M. Jameson, *Memoirs of the Loves of the Poets. Biographical Sketches of Women Celebrated in Ancient and Modern Poetry.*

S. Johnson, *Lives of the Most Eminent Poets.*

T. Keightley, *Account of the Life, Opinions, and Writings of John Milton.*

M. Kremnitz, *Reminiscences of the King of Roumania.*

V. von Kubinyi, *King of Rome; A Biography.*

J. D. Knowles, *Memoir of Mrs. Ann H. Judson, Late Missionary to Burmah.*

W. H. Lamon, *Life of Abraham Lincoln.*

R. E. Lee, *Recollections and Letters of General Robert E. Lee, by His Son.*

C. E. Lester, *Life of Sam Houston (The Only Authentic Memoir of Him Ever Published)*.

G. H. Lewes, *Life of Goethe*.

G. Lippard, *Legends of the American Revolution*.

S. Longfellow (ed.), *Life of Henry Wadsworth Longfellow, with Extracts from his Journals and Correspondence*.

M. Lonsdale, *Sister Dora. A Biography*.

T. R. Lounsbury, *James Fenimore Cooper*.

J. C. Lovejoy and O. Lovejoy, *Memoir of the Rev. Elijah P. Lovejoy, Who Was Murdered in Defence of the Liberty of the Press*.

E. R. B. Lytton. *Chronicles and Characters*.

J. McCarthy, *Portraits of the Sixties*.

L. Macbean and J. Brown, *Marjorie Fleming: The Story of Pet Marjorie, Together with Her Journals and Her Letters*.

E. T. McLaren, *Dr. John Brown and His Sister Isabella*.

W. McLennan, *Spanish John; Being a Memoir, Now First Published in Complete Form, of the Early Life and Adventures of Colonel John McDonell* (novel).

G. B. Malleson, *Dupleix*.

D. Masson, *Life of John Milton, Narrated in Connexion with the Political, Ecclesiastical, and Literary History of His Time*.

W. H. Maxwell, *Life of Field-Marshal His Grace the Duke of Wellington*.

H. Mayhew, *Wonders of Science; or, Young Humphry Davy (The Cornish Apothecary's Boy, Who Taught Himself Natural Philosophy, and Eventually Became President of the Royal Society)*.

C. Meiners, *Lebensbeschreibungen berühmter Män- ner aus den Zeiten der Wiederherstellung der Wissenschaften*.

H. C. Merivale and F. T. Marzials, *Life of W. M. Thackeray*.

J. G. Millais, *Life and Letters of Sir John Everett Millais, President of the Royal Academy*.

J. Milne, *Romance of a Pro-Consul; Being the Personal Life and Memoirs of the Right Hon. Sir George Grey, K. C. B.*

J. Mitford, *Life of Milton*.

M. Mookerjee, *Onoocool Chunder Mookerjee (1829– 1871): A Memoir*.

J. Morley, *Burke*.

J. Morley, *Life of Richard Cobden*.

K. M. Mundt, *Frederick the Great and His Court. An Historical Romance*.

F. W. H. Myers, *Wordsworth*.

L. Nohl, *Life of Beethoven*.

L. Nohl, *Life of Liszt*.

L. Nohl, *Life of Wagner*.

M. O. W. Oliphant, *Memoir of the Life of Laurence Oliphant and of Alice Oliphant, His Wife*.

M. M. V. F. L. von Poschinger, *Life of the Emperor Frederick*.

B. O'Reilly, *Life of Leo XIII, from an Authentic Memoir Furnished by His Order*.

A. L. Orr, *Life and Letters of Robert Browning*.

A. B. Paine, *Th. Nast, His Period and His Pictures*.

J. Parton, *Life and Times of Aaron Burr*.

J. Parton, *Life of Voltaire*.

J. Payn, *Some Literary Recollections*.

E. L. Pierce, *Memoir and Letters of Charles Sumner*.

A. P. Primrose, *Lord Randolph Churchill*.

A. P. Primrose, *Napoleon: The Last Phase*.

C. H. Proctor, *Life of James Williams, Better Known as Professor Jim, for Half a Century Janitor of Trinity College*.

C. L. Reade and C. Reade, *Charles Reade, D. C. L., Dramatist, Novelist, and Journalist. A Memoir*.

S. J. Reid, *Lord John Russell*.

S. J. Reid, *Sketch of the Life and Times of the Rev. Sydney Smith*.

W. Reid, *William Black, Novelist: A Biography*.

A. D. Richardson, *Personal History of Ulysses S. Grant*.

M. Y. Ridenbaugh, *Biography of Ephraim McDowell, M. D., "The Father of Ovariotomy."*

F. W. Robertson, *Life, Letters, and Addresses of Fredk. W. Robertson, M.A., Incumbent of Trinity Chapel, Brighton, 1847–53*.

W. J. Rolfe, *Shakespeare the Boy, with Sketches of the Home and School Life, the Games and Sports, the Manners, Customs and Folklore of the Time*.

J. C. Ropes, *The First Napoleon. A Sketch, Political and Military*.

I. de Saint-Amand, *Jeunesse de l'Impératrice Joséphine*.

C. A. Sainte-Beuve, *Memoirs of Mme. Desbordes-Valmore*.

G. E. B. Saintsbury, *Earl of Derby*.

F. B. Sanborn (ed.), *Life and Letters of John Brown, Liberator of Kansas and Martyr of Virginia*.

C. Schurz, *Life of Henry Clay*.

J. Scott, *Partisan Life with Col. John S. Mosby*.

W. Sharp, *Life of Robert Browning*.

L. H. H. Sigourney, *Memoir of Mary Ann Hooker*.

F. H. B. Skrine, *Indian Journalist: Being the Life, Let- ters, and Correspondence of Dr. Sambhu C. Mookerjee*.

F. H. B. Skrine, *Life of Sir William Wilson Hunter*.

W. M. Sloane, *Life of Napoleon Bonaparte*.

S. Smiles, *Josiah Wedgwood, F.R.S., His Personal History*.

S. Smiles, *Life and Labor; or Characteristics of Men of Industry, Culture and Genius*.

S. Smiles, *Robert Dick, Baker of Thurso, Geologist and Botanist*.

A. G. Stedman (ed.), "Short Biographies of All Authors Represented in This Work" in *A Library of American Literature from the Earliest Settlement to the Present Time*.

A. Strickland, *Lives of the Queens of England, from the Norman Conquest; With Anecdotes of Their Courts*.

L. Stuart, *Lady Louisa Stuart: Selections from Her Manuscripts*.

C. Symmons, *Life of John Milton*.

H. Tennyson, *Alfred, Lord Tennyson; A Memoir by His Son*.

G. Ticknor, *Life of William Hickling Prescott*.

H. J. Todd, *Some Account of the Life and Writings of John Milton*.

J. Toland, *Life of John Milton*.

H. D. Traill, *Marquis of Salisbury*.

H. D. Traill, *Sterne.*

E. J. Trelawny, *Records of Shelley, Byron, and the Author.*

G. O. Trevelyan, *Life and Letters of Lord Macaulay.*

J. H. Twichell, *John Winthrop, First Governor of the Massachusetts Colony.*

R. Vallery-Radot, *Life of Pasteur.*

H. Van Dyke, *Americanism of Washington.*

M. A. A. Ward, *William Thomas Arnold, Journalist and Historian.*

A. Waugh, *Alfred, Lord Tennyson: A Study of His Life and Work.*

M. L. Weems, *Life and Memorable Actions of George Washington.*

A. H. T. Werthen, F. von, *General von Versen: ein militärisches Zeit-und Lebensbild.*

H. B. Wheatley, *Samuel Pepys and the World He Lived In.*

J. T. Wheeler, *Life and Travels of Herodotus in the Fifth Century Before Christ: An Imaginary Biography Founded on Fact.*

J. V. Widmann, *Johannes Brahms in Erinnerungen.*

O. W. Wight, *Lives and Letters of Abelard and Heloise.*

R. G. Wilberforce (co-author), *Life of the Right Reverend Samuel Wilberforce. . . . With Selections from His Diary and Correspondence.*

G. A. Wilcox, *Christian Philanthropist. A Sketch of the Life of Mr. Daniel Hand, and of His Benefaction to the American Missionary Association, for the Education of the Colored People in the Southern States of America.*

H. Wilson, *Wonderful Characters; Comprising Memoirs and Anecdotes of the Most Remarkable Persons of Every Age and Nation.*

J. H. Wilson, *Life of Charles A. Dana.*

H. E. G. de Witt, *Monsieur Guizot in Private Life, 1787–1874. By His Daughter, Madame de Witt.*

J. A. Wyeth, *Life of General Nathan Bedford Forrest.*

C. D. Yonge, *Life of Marie Antoinette, Queen of France.*

C. M. Yonge, *Book of Worthies, Gathered from the Old Histories and Now Written Anew.*

J. R. Young, *Men and Memories: Personal Reminiscences by John Russell Young.*

See also the Reader's Guide entries for Diaries, for Journals, and for Memoirs.

Biography of Ephraim McDowell, M. D., "The Father of Ovariotomy." M. Y. Ridenbaugh.

Biography of Henry Ward Beecher. W. Beecher and S. Scoville.

Biology: see

E. H. P. A. Haeckel, *Wonders of Life: A Popular Study of Biological Philosophy.*

H. S. Williams, *Story of Nineteenth-Century Science.*

Birch, Reginald Bathurst (illus.): see

E. N. Bland, *Wouldbegoods.*

F. H. Burnett, *Little Lord Fauntleroy.*

St. Nicholas: A Magazine for Boys and Girls (Catalog entry).

Bird. J. Michelet.

Bird and Bough. J. Burroughs.

"Bird at sea" (song). F. D. Hemans.

Birdcraft: A Field Book of Two Hundred Song, Game, and Water Birds. M. Wright.

Bird Homes. The Nests, Eggs, and Breeding Habits of the Land Birds. A. R. Dugmore.

Bird Neighbors. N. B. De G. Doubleday.

Birds: see

J. L. Allen, *Kentucky Cardinal; A Story.*

American Ornithology for the Home and School (periodical).

J. J. Audubon, *Birds of America, from Drawings Made in the United States and Their Territories.*

J. M. Baldwin, *Story of the Mind* (marginalia).

J. Burroughs, *Bird and Bough.*

J. Burroughs, *Birds and Bees.*

F. M. Chapman, *Handbook of Birds of Eastern North America.*

F. M. Chapman, *Warblers of North America.*

O. Davie, *Nests and Eggs of North American Birds.*

N. B. De G. Doubleday, *Bird Neighbors.*

N. B. De G. Doubleday, *Birds That Every Child Should Know.*

A. R. Dugmore, *Bird Homes. The Nests, Eggs, and Breeding Habits of the Land Birds.*

A. R. Dugmore, *Nature and the Camera. How to Photograph Live Birds and Their Nests, Animals, Wild Game.*

F. H. Eckstorm, *Woodpeckers.*

E. H. Forbush, *Useful Birds and Their Protection.*

M. K. Gregg and E. Kirby, *Stories About Birds of Land and Water.*

H. K. Job, *Among the Water-Fowl: Observation, Adventure, Photography.*

H. K. Job, *Wild Wings: Adventures of a Camera-Hunter Among the Larger Wild Birds of North America on Sea and Land.*

C. G. Leland. *Legends of the Birds.*

W. J. Long, *Fowls of the Air.*

J. Michelet, *Bird.*

H. M. Miller, *True Bird Stories from My Note-Books.*

A. Newton, *Dictionary of Birds.*

Shitakari Suzume (Japanese fairy tale).

J. H. Studer (ed.), *Birds of North America; One Hundred and Nineteen Artistic Colored Plates.*

S. K. Trimmer, *History of the Robins. In Words of One Syllable.*

H. Van Dyke, *Blue Flower* (Catalog entry).

G. White, *Natural History and Antiquities of Selborne.*

M. O. Wright, *Birdcraft: A Field Book of Two Hundred Song, Game, and Water Birds.*

M. O. Wright and E. Coues, *Citizen Bird; Scenes from Bird-Life.*

See also the Reader's Guide entry for Natural history.

Birds and Bees: Essays. J. Burroughs.

Birds and Flowers; or, Lays and Lyrics of Rural Life. M. B. Howitt.

Bird Neighbors. N. B. De G. Doubleday.

Birds of America, from Drawings Made in the United States and Their Territories. J. J. Audubon.

Birds of North America. H. J. Studer.

Birds That Every Child Should Know. N. B. De G. Doubleday.

Birney, James Gillespie: see the Catalog entry for W.

E. Channing, *Letter of William E. Channing to J. G. Birney.*

Birthday books: see

G. Eliot, *George Eliot Birthday Book.*

K. Greenaway, *Kate Greenaway's Birthday Book for Children.*

M. A. Lathbury, *Birthday Week; Pictures and Verse.*

E. S. Owen (comp.), *Whittier Birthday Book.*

E. P. Prentiss, *Susy's Six Birthdays.*

E. A. O. Somerville, *Mark Twain Birthday Book.*

Birthday Week; Pictures and Verse. M. A. Lathbury.

Bishop, Artemus (trans.): see J. Bunyan, *Pilgrim's Progress* (Hawaiian).

Bishop; Being Some Account of His Strange Adventures on the Plains. C. T. Brady.

Bishop, Henry Rowley (composer): see J. H. Payne, "Home, sweet home" (song).

Bismarck in the Franco-German War 1870–1871. M. Busch.

Bismarck, Otto Eduard Leopold von: see

M. Busch, *Bismarck in the Franco-German War 1870–1871.*

M. Busch, *Unser Reichskanzler: Studien zu einem Charakterbilde.*

Bismarck, The Man and the Statesman; Being the Reflections and Reminiscences of Otto, Prince von Bismarck. O. E. L. von Bismarck.

Bisphan, David: see R. Kipling, "Danny Deever."

Bisson, Alexandre Charles Auguste (co-author): see A. Daly (adapt.), *Lottery of Love.*

Bitter-Sweet: A Poem. J. G. Holland.

"Bivouac of the Dead" (poem). T. O'Hara.

Bjarnason, Jón (trans.): see R. B. Anderson, *Viking Tales.*

Björnson, Björnstjerne: see

W. D. Howells, "White Mr. Longfellow" (essay).

W. L. Phelps, *Essays on Modern Novelists* (marginalia).

Black Avenger of the Spanish Main. E. Z. C. Judson.

Blackbeard (pirate): see the Reader's Guide entry for Edward Teach.

Black Beauty: The Autobiography of a Horse. A. Sewell.

Blackburn, Henry (ed.): see London National Gallery, *Complete Illustrated Catalogue.*

"Black Cat" (short story). E. A. Poe.

Black Crook; An Original, Magical and Spectacular Drama in Four Acts (play). C. M. Barras.

Black Diamonds, A Novel. M. Jokai.

"Black-ey'd Susan" (poem, ballad): see J. Gay, "Sweet William's Farewell to Black-ey'd Susan" (poem, ballad).

Black Forest Village Stories. B. Auerbach.

Black Hole of Calcutta: see

J. Z. Holwell, *Genuine Narrative of the Deplorable Deaths of the English Gentlemen, and Others, Who Were Suffocated in the Black Hole in Fort William, at Calcutta.*

W. D. Howells (co-ed.), *Library of Universal Adventure by Sea and Land.*

Percy Anecdotes (Catalog entry).

Blackmore, Humphrey Purnell: see E. T. Stevens, *Flint Chips. A Guide to Pre-Historic Archaeology, as Illustrated by the Collection in the Blackmore Museum, Salisbury.*

Blackmore Museum: see E. T. Stevens, *Flint Chips. A Guide to Pre-Historic Archaeology, as Illustrated by the Collection in the Blackmore Museum, Salisbury.*

Blackmore, William Henry: see

(intro.) R. I. Dodge, *Plains of the Great West and Their Inhabitants.*

E. T. Stevens, *Flint Chips. A Guide to Pre-Historic Archaeology, as Illustrated by the Collection in the Blackmore Museum, Salisbury* (Catalog entry).

"Black, Mrs. John D." (pseud.): see M. H. Potter.

Black Phalanx; A History of the Negro Soldiers of the United States in the Wars of 1775-1812, 1861-'65. J. T. Wilson.

Black, Robert (trans.): see F. P. G. Guizot, *Popular History of France from the Earliest Times.*

Black, William: see W. Reid, *William Black, Novelist: A Biography.*

Blackstone, William: see *Blackstone's Commentaries.*

Bladen, Frank Murcott (co-ed.): see *Historical Records of New South Wales.*

Blaine, James Gillespie: see

G. Cleveland *et al. What Shall We Do With It? (Meaning the Surplus). Taxation and Revenue Discussed.*

Plutarchus, *Plutarch's Lives of Illustrious Men* (Catalog entry).

(afterword) W. T. Sherman, *Memoirs of General W. T. Sherman, Written by Himself.*

Blake, William: see

A. Gilchrist, *Life of William Blake, "Pictor Ignotus."*

J. G. Huneker, *Egoists, A Book of Supermen.*

"Blanc, Marie-Thérèse" (pseud.): see T. Bentzon.

"Blanchan, Neltje" (pseud.): see N. B. De G. Doubleday.

Blavatsky, Helena Petrovna: see

A. E. S. Smythe, *Poems, Grave and Gay* (Catalog entry).

Society for Psychical Research (Catalog entry).

Bleak House. C. Dickens.

Blennerhassett, Harman: see J. Parton, *Life and Times of Aaron Burr.*

Blessed Joan of Arc (1412–1431). A. Kerr.

Blind, Mathilde (ed.): see P. B. Shelley, *Selection from the Poems of Percy Bysshe Shelley.*

Blindness: see

Report of the Commission of 1906 to Investigate the Condition of the Blind in the State of New York.

F. H. Spearman, *Doctor Bryson, A Novel.*

Blindpits; A Story of Scottish Life (novel): see E. Taylor, *Quixstar; A Novel* (Catalog entry).

Blix, Ragnvald (illus.): see *Simplicissimus* (magazine).

Blockaders. J. Barnes.

Blondin, Charles (tightrope walker): see F. T. Buckland, *Curiosities of Natural History* (Catalog entry).

Bloss' Ancient History, for the Use of Families and Schools. C. A. B. Bloss.

Blot in the 'Scutcheon (poem): see R. Browning, *Dramas.*

Blouët, Paul: see the Catalog entry for C. J. P. Bourget, *Outre-Mer: Impressons of America.*

"Blow the man down" (song): see "Roll a man down."

Blue Book for the Year 1894: see New South Wales.

Blue Dragon, A Tale of Recent Adventure in China. C. K. Munroe.

Blue Fairy Book. Andrew Lang (ed.).

Blue Flower. H. Van Dyke.

"Blue Juniata" (song). M. D. Sullivan.

"Blush Rose" (poem). G. W. Elliott.

Boadicea (queen of the Britons): see A. E. Trumbull, *Wheel of Progress* (play).

Boat Life in Egypt and Nubia. W. C. Prime.

Boccaccio, Giovanni: see
    T. B. Macaulay, *Critical and Miscellaneous Essays* (Catalog entry).
    G. O. Trevelyan, *Life and Letters of Lord Macaulay* (marginalia).

Bôcher, Ferdinand (contr.): see D. G. de Girardin, *Joie fait pèur; comédie en un acte* (play).

Bodin, Jean: see W. E. H. Lecky, *History of the Rise and Influence of the Spirit of Rationalism in Europe* (marginalia).

Bodley Family in Town and Country. H. E. Scudder.

Bodleys Telling Stories. H. E. Scudder.

Boer War: see the Reader's Guide entry for South Africa.

Boer War Lyrics. L. Selmer.

"Boetser, Peet" (pseud.): see P. Bausch.

Bog-Myrtle and Peat: Tales. S. R. Crockett.

Bohemia: see G. P. R. James, *Heidelberg* (novel).

Bohemian Girl (opera). M. W. Balfe.

Bohemian Society. L. B. Leavitt.

Bohn, Henry George: see
    (ed.) *Chronicles of the Crusades; Contemporary Narratives.*
    (pref.) M. V. Martialis, *Epigrams of Martial Translated into English Prose.*

"Boldrewood, Rolf" (pseud.): see T. A. Browne.

Boleyn, Anne: see
    A. E. Dickinson, *Crown of Thorns, or Ann Boleyn* (play).
    W. H. Dixon, *History of Two Queens: Catherine of Aragon and Anne Boleyn.*
    E. W. Gallup, *Tragedy of Anne Boleyn. A Drama in Cipher Found in the Works of Sir Francis Bacon.*

Bombay, India: see the Reader's Guide entry for India.

Bonaparte, Napoléon François Charles Joseph: see
    J. S. C. Abbott, *History of Joseph Bonaparte, King of Naples and of Italy.*
    V. von Kubinyi, *King of Rome; A Biography.*

"Bond" (short story by [Gilbert] Emery Bemsley Pottle): see W. D. Howells and H. M. Alden (eds.), *Their Husbands' Wives.*

Bond, George Meade (ed.): see the Catalog entry for *Standards of Length.*

Bonner, Mrs. E. T.: see L. J. Velazquez.

Bonneville, Benjamin Louis Eulalie de Bonneville: see W. Irving, *Adventures of Captain Bonneville.*

"Bonnie banks of Loch Lomond" (ballad): see "Loch Lomond."

"Bonnie Charlie's Now Awa'" (poem). C. O. Nairne.

"Bonnie Doon" (song): see R. Burns, "Banks and braes o' Bonnie Doon."

"Bonny Bessy" (song). A. Ramsay.

"Bonny Eloise" (poem, song). G. W. Elliott.

Book About Doctors. J. C. Jeaffreson.

Book collecting: see
    A. Birrell, *Obiter Dicta.*
    L. Hutton, *From the Books of Laurence Hutton.*

A. H. Joline, *Diversions of a Book-Lover.*

Book dedications: see the Reader's Guide entry for Dedications to Mark Twain.

Book of American Interiors. C. W. Elliott.

Book of Clever Beasts; Studies in Unnatural History. M. Reed.

Book of Common Prayer: see the Reader's Guide entry for *Common Prayer.*

Book of Dragons. E. N. Bland.

Book of Fate: see *Napoleon's Oraculum, or, Book of Fate.*

Book of Gold, and Other Poems. J. T. Trowbridge.

Book of Joyous Children. J. W. Riley.

Book of Legends, Containing a Selection of Standard Tales from the Most Esteemed British Essayists. D. O'Sullivan (comp.).

Book of Martyrs. J. Foxe.

Book of Months. E. F. Benson.

Book of Music. R. W. Gilder.

Book of Saints and Wonders. A. Gregory.

Book of the Knife and Fork Club. Knife and Fork Club. Kansas City, Missouri.

Book of the Sonnet. L. Hunt (co-ed.).

Book of Verses. W. E. Henley.

Book of Worthies, Gathered from the Old Histories and Now Written Anew. C. M. Yonge.

Booming of Acre Hill. J. K. Bangs.

Boone, Daniel: see J. S. C. Abbott, *Daniel Boone, The Pioneer of Kentucky.*

Booth, Edwin: see
    L. Hutton, *Edwin Booth.*
    E. G. E. B. Lytton, *Richelieu; or, the Conspiracy* (play) (Catalog entry).
    W. Shakespeare, *Hamlet* (Catalog entry).
    W. Winter, *Wanderers: The Poems of William Winter.*

Booth, Mary Louise (trans.): see
    É. de Laboulaye, *Laboulaye's Fairy Book; Fairy Tales of All Nations.*
    É. de Laboulaye *Last Fairy Tales.*
    H. Martin, *Popular History of France, from the First Revolution to the Present Time.*

Booth, William Stone: see
    W. Shakespeare, *King Lear* (Catalog entry).
    W. Shakespeare, *Works of Shakespeare* (Catalog entry).

"Boots and Saddles"; or, Life in Dakota with General Custer. E. B. Custer.

Borghese Prince Scipione (intro.): see L. Barzini, Sr., *Pekin to Paris; An Account of Prince Borghese's Journey.*

Borgia, Cesare: see W. W. Astor, *Valentino, An Historical Romance of the Sixteenth Century in Italy.*

Borns, Harold W. (trans.): see
    S. A. Arrhenius, *Life of the Universe as Conceived by Man from the Earliest Ages to the Present Time.*
    S. A. Arrhenius, *Worlds in the Making: The Evolution of the Universe.*

Bosanquet, Frederick Charles Tindal (ed.): see Plinius, *Letters of Caius Plinius Caecilius Secundus.*

Bossu (play): see A. Anicet-Bourgeois.

Boston (city): see
    W. D. Howells, *Suburban Sketches* (essays).
    W. D. Howells, *Their Wedding Journey* (novel).
    W. D. Howells, *Woman's Reason* (novel).

H. James, *Bostonians* (novel).
J. B. O'Reilly (Catalog entry).
A. S. Pier, *Sentimentalists; A Novel*.
M. L. Pool, *Roweny in Boston, A Novel*.
G. Thompson, *City Crimes; or, Life in New York and Boston*.
G. Thompson, *Venus in Boston and Other Tales of Nineteenth-Century City Life*.
L. Whitney, *Burning of the Convent. A Narrative of the Destruction, by a Mob, of the Ursuline School on Mount Benedict, Charlestown, as Remembered by One of the Pupils*.
"Boston. Literary Notes" (review). L. C. Moulton.
Bostonians. H. James.
Boston *Transcript*: see E. I. Lindh.
Boswell, James: see
M. Busch, *Bismarck in the Franco-German War 1870–1871* (marginalia).
A. S. Evans, *Our Sister Republic: A Gala Trip Through Tropical Mexico in 1869- 70* (marginalia).
E. G. E. B. Lytton, *Kenelm Chillingly: His Adventures and Opinions. A Novel* (marginalia).
T. B. Macaulay, *Critical and Miscellaneous Essays* (marginalia).
Botany: see
C. Darwin, *Movements and Habits of Climbing Plants*.
C. Darwin, *Power of Movement in Plants*.
A. Gray, *Gray's School and Field Book of Botany. Consisting of "First Lessons in Botany," and Field, Forest, and Garden Botany*.
A. Gray, *How Plants Behave; How They Move, Climb, Employ Insects to Work for Them, Etc.*
A. Gray, *How Plants Grow; A Simple Introduction to Structural Botany*.
N. L. Marshall, *Mushroom Book. A Popular Guide to the Identification and Study of Our Commoner Fungi*.
Maudslay, Alfred Percival (Catalog entry).
Maudsley (unidentified author).
A. T. Slossom, *Dumb Foxglove, and Other Stories*.
S. Smiles, *Robert Dick, Baker of Thurso, Geologist and Botanist*.
E. A. Youmans, *First Book of Botany*.
See also the Reader's Guide entries for Flowers and for Gardening.
Bottle: A Drama in Two Acts. T. Taylor.
Bottom of the Sea. M. J. B. L. Sonrel.
Boucicault, Dion (co-author): see
C. Reade, *Foul Play; A Novel*.
"Wearing of the green" (song).
Bound in Shallows; A Novel. E. W. M. Brodhead.
Bounty (ship): see
D. J. Belcher, *Mutineers of the "Bounty" and Their Descendants*.
W. D. Howells (co-ed.), *Library of Universal Adventure by Sea and Land*.
Bourgeois, Louis (composer): see W. Kethe, "Old Hundred."
Bourget, Paul: see P. Blouet, "Mark Twain and Paul Bourget" (essay).
Bourget, Paul: see Charles Joseph Paul Bourget.

Boutell, Charles (trans. and intro.): see P. Lacombe, *Arms and Armour in Antiquity and the Middle Ages*.
Boutwell, George Sewall: see T. G. Allen, *Letter from an Ex-Sailor and Ex-Tramp*.
"Bowen, Marjorie" (pseud.): see G. M. V. C. Long.
Box and Cox (farce). J. M. Morton.
Box and Cox (farce). J. M. Morton: see also F. C. Burnand, *Cox and Box* (comic opera).
Boxer Rebellion: see G. Lynch, *War of the Civilisations, Being the Record of a "Foreign Devil's" Experiences with the Allies in China*.
Boxing: see
Bell's Life in London and Sporting Chronicle.
A. C. Doyle, *Rodney Stone*.
Box of Monkeys (farce). G. L. Furniss.
Boy books: see
W. T. Adams, pseud. "Oliver Optic" (Catalog entry).
L. M. Alcott, *Little Men: Life at Plumfield with Jo's Boys*.
W. L. Alden, *Adventures of Jimmy Brown, Written by Himself*.
W. L. Alden, *Jimmy Brown Trying to Find Europe, Written by Himself*.
T. B. Aldrich, *Story of a Bad Boy*.
H. Alger, Jr. (Catalog entry).
Boys on the Railroad.
P. Boyton, *Story of Paul Boyton*.
E. Busch, *Max und Moritz*.
S. Crane, *Monster and Other Stories*.
S. R. Crockett, *Cleg Kelly, Arab of the City*.
T. Day, *History of Sandford and Merton*.
A. M. Diaz, *Jimmyjohns, and Other Stories*.
E. Gellibrand, *J. Cole*.
S. Grand, *Heavenly Twins* (marginalia).
T. A. Guthrie, *Vice Versâ; or, A Lesson to Fathers*.
J. Habberton, *Worst Boy in Town*.
W. D. Howells, *Boy Life; Stories and Readings Selected from the Works of William Dean Howells*.
W. D. Howells, *Boy's Town, Described for "Harper's Young People."*
W. D. Howells, *Flight of Pony Baker; A Boy's Town Story*.
T. Hughes, *Tom Brown's School Days*.
L. Hutton, *Boy I Knew and Four Dogs*.
L. Hutton, *Boy I Knew, Four Dogs, and Some More Dogs*.
O. M. Johnson, *Eternal Boy, Being the Story of the Prodigious Hickey*.
J. O. Kaler, *Left Behind; or, Ten Days a Newsboy*.
J. O. Kaler, *Mr. Stubbs's Brother*.
J. O. Kaler, *Silent Pete; or, The Stowaways*.
J. O. Kaler, *Toby Tyler; or, Ten Weeks with a Circus*.
R. Kipling, *Stalky & Co.*
T. W. Knox, *Boy Travellers in Australasia* [and similar titles].
B. J. Lossing, *Story of the United States Navy for Boys*.
G. MacDonald, *Sir Gibbie*.
C. K. Munroe, *Campmates; A Story of the Plains* (and other titles).
W. F. Payson, *Barry Gordon*.
G. W. Peck, *Peck's Bad Boy and His Pa*.

G. W. Peck, *Peck's Fun.*

E. Phillpotts, *Human Boy Again.*

W. C. Roberts: *Boy's Account of It: A Chronicle of Foreign Travel by an Eight-Year-Old.*

H. A. Shute, *Real Diary of a Real Boy.*

C. D. Stewart, *Partners of Providence* (novel).

A. B. Stripling, *Poet in Embryo; Being the Meditations of Algernon Byron Stripling.*

W. H. Venable, *Tom Tad.*

M. V. F. Victor, *Bad Boy's Diary.*

C. D. Warner, *Being a Boy.*

C. D. Warner, "Boy the Destroyer" in *My Summer in a Garden.*

W. A. White, *Court of Boyville.*

E. Wood, *Back Home.*

Boyd, Alexander Stuart (illus.): see R. L. Stevenson, *Lowden Sabbath Morn.*

Boyesen, Hjalmar: see [J.] E. Renan, *Apostles. Translated from the Original French* (Catalog entry).

Boyhood of Christ. L. Wallace.

Boy I Knew and Four Dogs. L. Hutton.

Boy I Knew, Four Dogs, and Some More Dogs. L. Hutton.

Boylan, R. Dillon (trans.): see J. W. von Goethe, *Wilhelm Meister's Apprenticeship; A Novel.*

Boy Life; Stories and Readings Selected from the Works of William Dean Howells. W. D. Howells.

"Boy Reciter" (poem). see D. Everett, "You'd Scarce Expect One of My Age" (poem).

Boy's Account of It: A Chronicle of Foreign Travel by an Eight-Year-Old. W. C. Roberts.

Boys' and Girls' Plutarch. Being Parts of the "Lives" of Plutarch. Plutarchus.

Boy's Book of Battle-Lyrics: A Collection of Verses IllustratingSome Notable Events in the History of the United States of America. T. D. English.

"Boy's Composition on Moonlight" (comic sketch): see the Catalog entry for "Not a leaf stirred."

Boy's King Arthur. T. Malory.

Boy's Mabinogion; Being the Earliest Welsh Tales of King Arthur in the Famous Red Book of Hergest: see *Mabinogion.*

Boys of '76. C. C. Coffin.

"Boy stood on the burning deck": see F. D. Hemans, "Casabianca" (poem).

Boy's Town, Described for "Harper's Young People." W. D. Howells.

Boy Travellers in Australasia. T. W. Knox.

Boy Travellers in Central Europe. T. W. Knox.

Boy Travellers in Mexico. T. W. Knox.

Boy Travellers in Northern Europe. T. W. Knox.

Boy Travellers in South America. T. W. Knox.

Boy Travellers in the Far East. T. W. Knox.

Boy Travellers in the Russian Empire. T. W. Knox.

"Boz" (pseud.): see M. J. Sweeney (illus.).

Bracciforti, Ferdinando (co-author): see J. Millhouse, *New English and Italian Pronouncing and Explanatory Dictionary, with Many New Additions.*

Bracebridge Hall: see W. Irving, *Old Christmas and Bracebridge Hall.*

Brackett, Lyman Foster (composer): see M. B. Eddy, "Saw ye my Saviour?" (hymn).

Bradbury, William Batchelder (composer): see

E. H. Codner, "Even me" (hymn).

C. Elliott, "Just as I am" (hymn).

G. R. Root, "Battle cry of freedom" (song) (Catalog entry).

Bradford, Gamaliel (trans.): see H. von Sybel, *Founding of the German Empire by William I. Based Chiefly upon Prussian State Documents.*

Brahe, Tycho: see D. Brewster, *Martyrs of Science; or, The Lives of Galileo, Tycho Brahe, and Kepler.*

"Brahma" (poem). R. W. Emerson.

"Brahman's Son" (poem). R. H. Stoddard.

Brahms, Johannes: see

G. Henschel, *Personal Recollections of Johannes Brahms.*

J. V. Widmann, *Johannes Brahms in Erinnerungen.*

"Brains" (short story): see L. C. Moulton, *Some Women's Hearts.*

Brandon, Charles: see C. Major, *When Knighthood Was in Flower; or, The Love Story of Charles Brandon and Mary Tudor, the King's Sister* (novel).

Brangwyn, Frank (illus.) : see S. R. Crockett, *Tales of Our Coast.*

Brannan, William Penn (possible author): see H. T. Lewis, "Harp of a Thousand Strings" (burlesque sermon).

Braut von Messina: see *Schiller's Sämmtliche Werke in Zwölf Bänden.*

Bray, William (ed.): see J. Evelyn, *Diary and Correspondence of John Evelyn.*

Braybrooke, Richard Griffin, Baron (ed.): see

S. Pepys, *Diary and Correspondence of Samuel Pepys, Esq.*

S. Pepys, *Memoirs of Samuel Pepys, Esq., F.R.S. Comprising His Diary from 1659 to 1669, and a Selection from His Private Correspondence.*

"Brazen Android" (novella). W. D. O'Connor.

Brazil: see

W. E. Curtis, *Capitals of Spanish America.*

C. Darwin, *Life and Letters of Charles Darwin* (marginalia).

[Unidentified book, 1903].

M. von Versen, *Reisen in Amerika und der Südamerikanische Krieg.*

Bread Line: A Story of a Paper. A. B. Paine.

Bread Upon the Waters. D. M. M. Craik.

Bread-Winners: A Social Study. J. M. Hay.

"Break, Break, Break" (poem). A. Tennyson.

Breakfast, Luncheon and Tea. M. V. H. Terhune.

Breath of the Gods. M. M. Fenollosa.

"Breitmann, Hans" (pseud.): see C. G. Leland.

Brennan, Alfred Laurens (illus.): see *The Cid.*

Brethren. H. R. Haggard.

Brett, Harold Matthews (illus.): see M. E. W. Freeman, *By the Light of the Soul; A Novel.*

Brevities: Companion Book to "Crankisms": see L. de V. Matthewman, *Crankisms, by Lisle de Vaux Matthewman.*

Bric à Brac; Album par Carnan d'Ache. Carnan d'Ache (pseud.).

Bric-à-Brac Hunter; or, Chapters on Chinamania. H. B. Hall.

Bricks Without Straw. A Novel. A. W. Tourgée.

Bride from the Bush. E. W. Hornung.

Bride from the Bush: see *Current Literture: A Magazine of Record and Review* (marginalia).
Bride of a Day. R. B. Townshend.
Bridge (card game): see
C. Wells, *Rubáiyát of Bridge*.
See also the Reader's Guide entry for Card games.
Brief History of the Lotos Club. J. Elderkin.
Briggs, Caroline Atherton: see Caroline Atherton (Briggs) Mason.
Briggs, Charles Augustus: see
North American Review (Catalog entry).
"Sixtus" (pseud.), *Review of Professor Briggs' Inaugural Address*.
Briggs, Thomas F. (composer): see D. D. Emmett, "Jordan am a hard road to trabbel (minstrel song).
Brigham, James H. (ed.): see *American Miscellany: A Magazine of Complete Stories*.
"Bright Alfarata" (allusion to a song): see M. D. Sullivan, "Blue Juniata" (song).
Bright, Mynors (ed.): see S. Pepys, *Diary and Correspondence of Samuel Pepys, Esq.*
Bright Side of Country Life. B. Barney.
Bright Things from Everywhere: A Galaxy of Good Stories, Poems, Paragraphs, Wit, and Wisdom, Selected by Henry Abbey. H. Abbey (comp.).
"Bring my boy back again" (song). F. McGlennon.
British Letters Illustrative of Character and Social Life. E. T. Mason (ed.).
Britton, Alexander (co-ed.): see *Historical Records of New South Wales*.
Broken Road. A. E. W. Mason.
"Broken Vow" (story). C. E. S. S. Norton.
Broke of Covenden. J. C. Snaith.
Bromley, Isaac (co-author): see N. Brooks, "Punch, Brothers, Punch" (newspaper jingle).
Brontë, Anne (co-author): see E. Brontë, *Wuthering Heights and Agnes Grey*.
Brontë, Charlotte: see
(pref.) E. Brontë, *Wuthering Heights*.
A. A. B. Edwards, *Barbara's History* (Catalog entry).
E. C. S. Gaskell, *Life of Charlotte Brontë*.
Brook Book; A First Acquaintance with the Brook and Its Inhabitants Through the Changing Year. M. F. R. Miller.
Brooke, Stopford Augustus (ed.): see F. W. Robertson, *Life, Letters, and Addresses of Fredk. W. Robertson, M.A., Incumbent of Trinity Chapel, Brighton, 1847–53*.
Brook Farm: see G. W. Curtis, *Early Letters of George Wm. Curtis to John S. Dwight; Brook Farm and Concord*.
Brooklyn, New York: see T. D. W. Talmage, *Sermons. Second Series* (Catalog entry).
Brooks, Phillips: see
A. V. G. Allen, *Life and Letters of Phillips Brooks*.
A. Brooks, *Phillips Brooks*.
M. A. D. Howe, *Phillips Brooks*.
Broome, Mary Anne: see M. A. Barker.
"Brother Jacob" (short story): see G. Eliot, *Poems*.
Brotherhood with Nature: A Treasury. C. Rowley (comp.).
Brother to the Dragons, and Other Old-Time Tales. A. R. C. Troubetzkoy.
Brougham, John (co-ed.): see *Lotos Leaves*.

Brown, Alice (co-author): see *Whole Family; A Novel by Twelve Authors*.
Brown, Charles Brockden: see J. Bernard, *Retrospections of America, 1797–1811*.
Brown, John (abolitionist):
"John Brown's body" (song).
R. Keeler, "Owen Brown's Escape from Harper's Ferry" (article).
F. B. Sanborn (ed.), *Life and Letters of John Brown*.
E. C. Stedman, *Lyrics and Idylls, with Other Poems*.
Brown, (Dr.) John: see
(ed.): see C. S. Graham, *Mystifications, by Clementina Stirling Grahame*.
(co-author): see L. Macbean, *Marjorie Fleming: The Story of Pet Marjorie, Together with Her Journals and Her Letters*.
E. T. McLaren, *Dr. John Brown and His Sister Isabella*.
Brown, John, Jr. (co-ed.): see J. Brown, *Letters of Dr. John Brown*.
Brown, Kenneth (co-author): see H. B. Boone, *Redfields Succession, A Novel*.
"Brown, Mrs." (pseud.): see J. G. Austin.
Brown, Walter Francis (illus.): see
Harper's Weekly.
St. Nicholas: A Magazine for Boys and Girls (Catalog entry).
Brown, William Wells: see S. J. May, *Some Recollections of Our Antislavery Conflict*.
Browne, Charles Farrar: see
E. P. Hingston, *Genial Showman; Being Reminiscences of the Life of Artemus Ward and Pictures of a Showman's Career*.
M. A. D. Howe, *American Bookmen: Sketches, Chiefly Biographical, of Certain Writers of the Nineteenth Century*.
M. de L. Landon's *Saratoga in 1901* (marginalia).
J. Rhoades, "Artemus Ward" (poem).
World's Wit and Humor; An Encyclopedia of the Classic Wit and Humor of All Ages and Nations.
Browne, Gordon Frederick (illus.): see
D. Defoe, *Life and Surprising Adventures of Robinson Crusoe of York, Mariner*.
G. A. Henty, *St. George for England: A Tale of Cressy and Poitiers*.
Browne, Hablot Knight (illus.): see C. Dickens, *Little Dorrit*.
"Browne, Matthew" (pseud. of William Brighty Rands): see G. Eliot, *Complete Poems*.
Browning, Elizabeth: see
R. Browning, *Letters of Robert Browning and Elizabeth Barrett Browning 1845- 1846. Selected Poems, Illustrated*.
F. Thompson, *Shelley* (marginalia).
"Browning, Francis" (pseud.): see F. B. Owen.
Browning, Robert: see
M. D. Conway, *Autobiography: Memories and Experiences of Moncure Daniel Conway* (marginalia).
H. Corson, *Introduction to the Study of Robert Browning's Poetry*.
C. C. F. Greville, *Greville Memoirs; A Journal of the*

Reigns of King George IV and King William IV. (marginalia).

E. W. Howe, *Story of a Country Town* (marginalia).

W. D. W. Hyde, *Art of Optimism as Taught by Robert Browning.*

R. U. Johnson and C. C. Buel (eds.), *Battles and Leaders of the Civil War* (Catalog entry).

T. B. Macaulay, "Essay on Lord Clive" (Catalog entry).

T. B. Macaulay, "Essay on Warren Hastings" (Catalog entry).

S. MacManus, *Lad of the O'Friel's* (marginalia).

A. L. Orr, *Life and Letters of Robert Browning. Selected Poems, Illustrated.*

W. Sharp, *Life of Robert Browning.*

J. K. Stephen, *Lapsus Calami.*

F. Thompson, *Shelley* (marginalia).

L. N. Tolstoy, *Ivan the Fool; or, the Old Devil and the Three Small Devils* (Catalog entry).

H. Van Dyke (ed.), *Little Masterpieces of English Poetry, by British and American Authors.*

Brownsville Affair: see A. B. Paine, *Captain Bill McDonald, Texas Ranger. A Story of Frontier Reform.*

Brummell, Beau: see C. Knight and T. Raikes, *Personal Reminiscences by Cornelia Knight and Thomas Raikes.*

Brun, Samuel Jacques (co-ed.): see *Tableaux de la Révolution Française; An Historical Reader.*

Brünnhilde: see A. A. Chapin, *Wotan, Siegfried, and Brünnhilde.*

Bruno, Giordano: see *Pith of Astronomy (Without Mathematics): The Latest Facts and Figures as Developed by the Giant Telescopes* (marginalia).

Brushwood Boy. R. Kipling.

Bruvver Jim's Baby. P. V. Mighels.

Bryant, William Cullen: see

T. W. S. Higginson, *Cheerful Yesterdays. Contemporaries* (marginalia).

O. W. Holmes, *Autocrat of the Breakfast-Table* (Catalog entry).

(trans.) Homer, *Iliad of Homer. Translated into English Blank Verse.*

(trans.) Homer, *Odyssey of Homer. Translated into English Blank Verse.*

(contr.) *Homes of American Authors.*

(contr.) L. C. B. Robinson, *Child's Poems, from October to October, 1870–1871.*

V. Streamer (comp.), *Voices of Doubt and Trust* (marginalia).

Brydges, Samuel Egerton (ed.): see J. Milton, *Poetical Works of John Milton.*

Bub and Sis: A 20th Century New England Story. S. W. Wardwell.

Buchanan's Wife. J. M. Forman.

Buch der Lieder: see H. Heine, *Heinrich Heine's Buch der Lieder.*

"Bucket" (song). S. Woodworth.

Buckingham, Duke of: see J. Sheffield.

Buckland, Frank (ed.): see G. White, *Natural History and Antiquities of Selborne.*

Buckle, Charles Randolph (ed.): see L.-T. M. Rousselet,

India and Its Native Princes: Travels in Central India and in the Presidencies of Bombay and Bengal.

Bud; A Novel. N. Munro.

Buddhism: see

E. Arnold, *Light of Asia; or, The Great Renunciation.*

L. Hearn, *Stray Leaves from Strange Literature; Stories Reconstructed.*

É. R. Huc, *Recollections of a Journey Through Tartary, Thibet, and China, During the Years 1844, 1845, and 1846.*

A. C. Lyall, *Natural Religion in India.*

A. C. Lyall, *Verses Written in India.*

N. Notovitch, *Unknown Life of Jesus Christ.*

S. E. Titcomb, *Aryan Sun-Myths: The Origin of Religions* (marginalia).

Buel, Clarence C. (co-ed.): see R. U. Johnson, *Battles and Leaders of the Civil War.*

Buffalo Bill: see W. F. Cody, *Adventures.*

Buford, Harry T. (pseud.): see L. J. Velazquez.

Building of the Organ (poem): see H. H. Dole, *Peace and Progress, Two Symphonic Poems.*

Bull, Charles Livingston (illus.): see

J. London, *Call of the Wild.*

C. G. D. Roberts, *Kindred of the Wild; A Book of Animal Life.*

Bull-fighting: see

W. F. Cody, *Adventures of Buffalo Bill, by Col. William F. Cody (Buffalo Bill). To Which Is Appended a Short Sketch of His Life.*

S. Dill, *Roman Society in the Last Century of the Western Empire* (marginalia).

J. Hay, *Castilian Days.*

Bulgaria: see

H. Wachenhusen, *Vampyr. Novelle aus Bulgarien.*

C. Wälzel and F. F. R. Genée, *Fatinitza* (operetta).

Bulwer-Lytton, Edward George Earle Bulwer-Lytton: see E. G. E. B. Lytton.

Bulwer-Lytton, Edward Robert Bulwer-Lytton: see E. R. B. Lytton.

Bummelei. Neue Gelammelte Skizzen. E. Pötzl.

Bunker Hill: see O. W. Holmes, "Grandmother's Story of Bunker Hill Battle" (poem).

Bunn, A. (libretto): see M. W. Balfe, *Bohemian Girl.*

Bunner, Henry Cuyler (ed.): see *Puck* (magazine).

Bunnett, Fanny Elizabeth (trans.): see

B. Auerbach, *On the Heights; A Novel.*

W. Lübke, *History of Sculpture from the Earliest Ages to the Present Time.*

"Buntline, Ned" (pseud.): see E. Z. C. Judson.

Bunyan, John: see

G. Larkin, *Visions of John Bunyan, Being His Last Remains.*

W. Shakespeare, *Works of Shakespeare* (Catalog entry).

Burdette, Robert: see H. W. Shaw, *Everybody's Friend, or Josh Billings's Encyclopedia and Proverbial Philosophy of Wit and Humor* (Catalog entry).

Burial: see the Reader's Guide entries for Cremation, for Funerals, and for Premature burial.

"Burial of Sir John Moore after Corunna" (poem). C. Wolfe.

Buried Cities of Ceylon: A Guide Book. S. M. Burrows.

Buried treasure: see the Reader's Guide entry for Treasure hunts.

Burke. J. Morley.

"Burke, Barbara" (pseud.): see O. H. B. Ball.

Burke, Billie (actress): see R. De Flers, *Love Watches.*

Burke, Edmund: see J. Morley, *Burke.*

Burke, John: see *Burke's Peerage.*

Burke, John Bernard (ed.): see *Battle Abbey.*

Burke, Thomas A. (comp.): see J. B. Lamar, "Polly Peablossom's Wedding" (sketch).

Burkhardt (composer): see H. B. Smith, *Soul Kiss* (musical).

Burlin, Natalie Curtis: see Natalie Curtis.

Burma: see

    H. Fielding-Hall, *Thibaw's Queen.*

    A. Ireland, *Far Eastern Tropics: Studies in the Administration of Tropical Dependencies.*

    J. D. Knowles, *Memoir of Mrs. Ann H. Judson, Late Missionary to Burmah, Including a History of the American Baptist Mission in the Burman Empire.*

    G. E. Morrison, *Australian in China, Being the Narrative of a Quiet Journey Across China to British Burma.*

    F. Vincent, *Land of the White Elephant: Sights and Scenes in South-eastern Asia.*

Burne-Jones, Edward (illus.): see W. Morris, *Pygmalion and the Image.*

Burnett, Frances Hodgson (co-author): see A. Thomas, *Editha's Burglar* (play).

Burning of the Convent. A Narrative of the Destruction, by a Mob, of the Ursuline School on Mount Benedict, Charlestown, as Remembered by One of the Pupils. L. Whitney.

"Burns. On Receiving a Sprig of Heather in Blossom" (poem). J. G. Whittier.

Burns, Robert: see

    A. Cunningham, *Life of Robert Burns.*

    A. W. Schmidt, *Flowing Bowl: When and What to Drink.*

    Selected Poems, Illustrated.

    Suetonius, *Lives of the Twelve Caesars* (marginalia).

    J. G. Whittier, "Burns. On Receiving a Sprig of Heather in Blossom" (poem).

    W. G. Wills, *Man o' Airlie: A Drama of the Affections* (play).

Burr, Aaron: see J. Parton, *Life and Times of Aaron Burr.*

Burr, Charles Chauncey (pref.): see G. Lippard, *Legends of the American Revolution.*

Burroughs, John: see

    (intro.) N. B. De G. Doubleday, *Bird Neighbors.*

    (intro.) G. W. Peckham and E. G. Peckham, *Wasps, Social and Solitary.*

Burt, Mary Elizabeth (intro.): see J. Burroughs, *Birds and Bees.*

Burton, Richard Eugene: see

    (ed.): see N. J. Burton, *Yale Lectures on Preaching and Other Writings.*

    (intro.): see Omar Khayyám, *One Hundred Quatrains.*

Burton, William Evans (co-author): see R. J. Raymond, *Toodles* (play).

Buscapié: see M. de Cervantes Saavedra, *Exemplary Novels of Miguel de Cerantes Saavedra.*

Bush, Celeste E. (ed.): see A. B. Berard, *Berard's History of the United States.*

Bushell, Stephen Wootton (contr.): see W. T. Walters, *Oriental Ceramic Art; Illustrated by Examples from the Collection of W. T. Walters.*

Bushnell, Horace: see M. B. Cheney, *Life of Horace Bushnell.*

Business: see the Reader's Guide entries for Economics and labor issues and for Finance and business.

Butler, Arthur John (trans.): see O. E. L. von Bismarck, *Bismarck, The Man and the Statesman; Being the Reflections and Reminiscences of Otto, Prince von Bismarck.*

Butterflies: see

    N. B. De G. Doubleday, *Wild Flowers: An Aid to Knowledge of Our Wild Flowers and Their Insect Visitors.*

    W. J Holland, *Butterfly Book: A Popular Guide to a Knowledge of the Butterflies of North America.*

Butterfly Book: A Popular Guide to a Knowledge of the Butterflies of North America. W. J Holland.

Butters, Henry Augustus (financier): see New York *World* (Catalog entry).

But Yet A Woman; A Novel. A. S. Hardy.

Byerly, Thomas (ed.): see *Percy Anecdotes.*

Bygone Days in Devonshire and Cornwall, with Notes of Existing Superstitions and Customs. M. E. J. Whitcombe.

Byington, Steven Tracy (trans.): see M. Stirner, *Ego and His Own.*

By Order of the Magistrate. W. P. Ridge.

By Reef and Palm. L. Becke.

Byron, George Gordon: see

    C. C. F. Greville, *Greville Memoirs; A Journal of the Reigns of King George IV and King William IV.* (marginalia).

    H. M. Milner, *Mazeppa: A Romantic Drama in Three Acts* (play).

    New York *Tribune* (Catalog entry).

    F. T. Palgrave (comp.), *Golden Treasury of the Best Songs and Lyrical Poems in the English Language* (marginalia).

    Philadelphia *Public Ledger* (Catalog entry).

    J. A. D.-G. Ross, *Three Generations of English Women* (marginalia).

    H. E. B. Stowe, *Lady Byron Vindicated: A History of the Byron Controversy, from Its Beginning in 1816 to the Present Time.*

    E. J. Trelawny, *Records of Shelley, Byron, and the Author.*

By the Light of the Soul; A Novel. M. E. W. Freeman.

By-Ways of Europe. B. Taylor.

Byzantium: see P. S. Grant, *Search of Belisarius, A Byzantine Legend.*

▌ C

Cable, George Washington: see *Scribner's Monthly* (Catalog entry).

Cabot, John and Sebastian: see F. A. Ober, *John and Sebastian Cabot.*

Cadet Days, A Story of West Point. C. King.

Cady, Wilhelmina Wilkinson (trans.): see

    E. De Amicis, *Spain and the Spaniards.*

    E. De Amicis, *Studies of Paris.*

Caesar; A Sketch. J. A. Froude.

Caesar, Augustus: see A. Del Mar, *Worship of Augustus Caesar.*

Caesar, Julius: see
 J. S. C. Abbott, *History of Julius Caesar.*
 T. A. Dodge, *Great Captains.*
 G. Ferrero, *Greatness and Decline of Rome* (Clemens's opinion).
 J. A. Froude, *Caesar; A Sketch.*
 J. Lord, *Beacon Lights of History.*
 Napoleon the Third, *History of Julius Caesar.*
 Suetonius, *Lives of the Twelve Caesars.*
 C. M. Yonge, *Book of Worthies, Gathered from the Old Histories and Now Written Anew.*

Caesar's Column. A Story of the Twentieth Century. I. Donnelly.

Cæsar's Commentaries on the Gallic and Civil Wars. G. J. Caesar.

Cage (novel). C. R. Teller.

Caged Lion. C. M. Yonge.

Cahokia, Illinois: see N. Matson, *Pioneers of Illinois, Containing a Series of Sketches Relating to Events That Occurred Previous to 1813* (marginalia).

Caillavet, Gaston-Arman de (co-author): see R. De Flers, *Love Watches* (play).

Cairo, Illinois: see C. Dickens, *American Notes for General Circulation* (Catalog entry).

Caldecott, Randolph (illus.): see
 J. H. G. Ewing, *Daddy Darwin's Dovecot: A Country Tale.*
 J. H. G. Ewing, *Jackanapes.*
 J. H. G. Ewing, *Lob Lie-by-the-Fire; or, The Luck of Lingborough.*
 W. Irving, *Old Christmas and Bracebridge Hall.*

Calef, Robert (comp.): see S. P. Fowler (ed.), *Salem Witchcraft: Comprising More Wonders of the Invisible World, Collected by Robert Calef; and Wonders of the Invisible World, by Cotton Mather.*

Calendars: see
 R. W. Emerson, *Selections from the Writings of Ralph Waldo Emerson, Arranged Under the Days of the Year.*
 N. Hawthorne, *Selections from the Writings of Nathaniel Hawthorne, Arranged Under the Days of the Year.*
 O. Herford, (co-author): see O. Herford, *Cynic's Calendar of Revised Wisdom for 1903.*
 O. W. Holmes, *Selections from the Writings of Oliver Wendell Holmes, Arranged Under the Days of the Year.*
 H. W. Longfellow, *Selections from the Writings of Henry Wadsworth Longfellow, Arranged Under the Days of the Year.*
 J. R. Lowell, *Selections from the Writings of James Russell Lowell. Arranged Under the Days of the Year.*
 E. S. Owen (comp.), *Whittier Birthday Book.*
 K. A. Sanborn (comp.), *Indian Summer Calendar.*
 G. White, *Natural History of Selborne. With a Naturalist's Calendar and Additional Observations.*
 J. G. Whittier, *Selections from the Writings of John Greenleaf Whittier, Arranged Under the Days of the Year.*
 See also the Reader's Guide entry for Almanacs.

Calife de Bagdad (comic opera): see F. A. Boieldieu.

California: see
 M. H. Austin, *Lost Borders.*
 M. H. Austin, *Santa Lucia, A Common Story.*
 H. H. Bancroft, *Native Races of the Pacific States of North America.*
 H. S. Brooks, *Catastrophe in Bohemia, and Other Stories.*
 J. R. Browne, *Adventures in Apache Country: A Tour Through Arizona and Sonora with Notes on the Silver Regions of Nevada.*
 J. R. Browne, *Crusoe's Island: A Ramble in the Steps of Alexander Selkirk. With Sketches of Adventure in California and Washoe.*
 J. W. Bruner, *Free Prisoners: A Story of California Life.*
 A. A. Burnham, *Fostina Woodman: The Wonderful Adventurer.*
 H. Bush, *Harp of the Day; or, The Adventures and Travels of a Photographic Artist; With Other Poems.*
 T. F. Cronise, *Natural Wealth of California.*
 C. C. Harrison, *Edelweiss of the Sierras* (stories).
 B. Harte, *Drift from Two Shores* (marginalia).
 B. Harte, *In the Carquinez Woods.*
 B. Harte, *Luck of Roaring Camp, and Other Sketches.*
 B. Harte (ed.), *Outcroppings: Being Selections of California Verse.*
 B. Harte, *Tales of the Argonauts, and Other Sketches.*
 G. A. Henty, *In the Hands of the Cave-Dwellers* (novel).
 W. D. Howells (co-ed.), *Library of Universal Adventure by Sea and Land.*
 J. M. Hutchings, *Scenes of Wonder and Curiosity in California.*
 R. Keeler, *Gloverson and His Silent Partners.*
 G. A. Lawrence, *Silverland.*
 A. Mackay, *Western World; or, Travels in the United States in 1846–47: Exhibiting Them in Their Latest Development, Social, Political, and Industrial; Including a Chapter on California.*
 J. Miller, *Songs of the Sierras* (poems).
 J. Miller, *Unwritten History: Life Amongst the Modocs.*
 S. B. Morgan, *Tahoe; or, Life in California. A Romance.*
 F. Soulé (Catalog entry).
 B. Taylor, *At Home and Abroad: A Sketch-Book of Life, Scenery, and Men.*
 B. Taylor, *Eldorado; or, Adventures in the Path of Empire; Comprising a Voyage to California via Panama, Life in San Francisco and Monterey, Pictures of the Gold Region, and Experiences of Mexico Travel.*
 L. J. Velazquez, *Woman in Battle: A Narrative of the Exploits, Adventures, and Travels of Madame Loreta Janeta Velazquez, Otherwise Known as Lieutenant Harry T. Buford, Confederate States Army.*
 H. L. Wilson, *Spenders; A Tale of the Third Generation.*
 See also the Reader's Guide entries for American West, for San Francisco, and for the Sierra Nevada Mountains.

"Californian's Tale" (Twain's short story): see *First Book of the Authors Club, Liber Scriptorum.*

Caligula, Emperor: see Suetonius, *Lives of the Twelve Caesars* (Catalog entry).

Callaway, Morgan (ed.): see S. Lanier, *Select Poems of Sidney Lanier.*

"Call me pet names" (poem). F. S. L. Osgood, *Poems*.
Call of the Blood. R. S. Hichens.
Call of the Wild. J. London.
"Calm on the listening ear of night" (hymn). E. H. Sears.
Calvert, James (co-author): see T. Williams, *Fiji and the Fijians*.
Calvinism: see the Catalog entry for John Calvin.
Cambodia: see F. Vincent, *Land of the White Elephant: Sights and Scenes in South-eastern Asia*.
Cambridge, Massachusetts: see W. D. Howells, "White Mr. Longfellow" (essay).
Cambridge University: see C. A. Bristed, *Five Years in an English University*.
Camelot: see
  G. L. P. B. Du Maurier, *Legend of Camelot, Pictures and Poems, Etc.*
  J. G. Wilson, *Lyrics of Life*.
  See also the Reader's Guide entry for Arthur, King.
Cameron, James Donald: see G. Ticknor, *Life, Letters, and Journals of George Ticknor* (marginalia).
Cameos from English History. The Wars in France. C. M. Yonge.
Camille (play). A. Dumas, *fils*.
Cammarano, Salvadore (libretto): see G. Verdi, *Il Trovatore*.
Campaigning on the Oxus, and the Fall of Khiva. J. A. MacGahan.
Campbell-Copeland, T. (co-ed.): see P. F. Mottelay, *Soldier in Our Civil War: A Pictorial History of the Conflict, 1861–65*.
Campbell, George Douglas, Duke of Argyll: see H. George, *Property in Land: A Passage-at-Arms Between the Duke of Argyll and Henry George*.
Campbell, Helen (co-ed.): see H. W. Dresser, *Heart of It*.
Campbell, Lady Colin: see
  G. E. B. Campbell and M. F. Sheldon, *Everybody's Book of Correct Conduct; Being Hints for Everyday Life*.
  G. E. B. Campell (trans.), B. A. A. Soyer, *Lady's Dressing-Room (Le cabinet de toilette)*.
Campbell, Thomas: see
  W. Beattie, *Life and Letters of Thomas Campbell*. (co-author) *Book of Pleasures*.
Campbellites: see the Catalog entry for A. Campbell.
Camp Life in the Woods and the Tricks of Trapping. W. H. Gibson.
Campmates; A Story of the Plains. C. K. Munroe.
"Camptown races (Gwine to run all night)" (minstrel song). S. C. Foster.
Canada: see
  P. Blouet, *John Bull & Co.; The Great Colonial Branches of the Firm*.
  E. T. Coke, *Subaltern's Furlough: Descriptive of Scenes in Various Parts of the United States, Upper and Lower Canada, New-Brunswick, and Nova Scotia, During the Summer and Autumn of 1832*.
  F. S. Cozzens, *Acadia; or, A Month with the Blue Noses*.
  C. W. Dilke, *Greater Britain: A Record of Travel in English-Speaking Countries During 1866 and 1867*.
  L. H. Fréchette (Catalog entry).
  E. J. House, *Hunter's Camp-Fires*.

  W. Phillips (Catalog entry).
  E. T. Seton, *Wild Animals I Have Known, and 200 Drawings*.
  B. Taylor, *At Home and Abroad: A Sketch-Book of Life, Scenery, and Men*.
  H. D. Thoreau, *Yankee in Canada, with Anti-Slavery and Reform Papers*.
  H. G. Vennor (Catalog entry).
  C. D. Warner, *Studies in the South and West, with Comments on Canada*.
  C. Whitney, *On Snow-Shoes to the Barren Grounds. Twenty-Eight Hundred Miles After Musk-Oxen and Wood-Bison*.
Canadian history: see
  W. Kirby, *Golden Dog (Le chien d'or). A Romance of the Days of Louis Quinze in Quebec*.
  W. E. H. Lecky, *History of European Morals from Augustus to Charlemagne* (marginalia).
  J. Palmer, *Journal of Travels in the United States of North America, and in Lower Canada, Performed in the Year 1817*.
  F. Parkman, *Conspiracy of Pontiac and the Indian War After the Conquest of Canada*.
  F. Parkman, *Count Frontenac and New France under Louis XIV*.
  F. Parkman, *Jesuits in North America in the Seventeenth Century*.
  F. Parkman, *Montcalm and Wolfe*.
  F. Parkman, *Old Régime in Canada*.
  F. Parkman, *Pioneers of France in the New World*.
  See also the Reader's Guide entry for American history (including early Canadian history).
Canadian literature: see
  W. H. Drummond, *Habitant, and Other French-Canadian Poems*.
  L. H. Fréchette.
  C. W. Gordon (Catalog entry).
  T. C. Haliburton, *Clockmaker, or Sayings and Doings of Sam Slick*.
  B. King, *In the Garden of Charity* (and other titles)
  A. Lampman, *Among the Millet and Other Poems*.
  W. McLennan (trans.), *Songs of Old Canada*.
  B. W. Munro. *Groans and Grins of One Who Survived*.
  L. M. Montgomery, *Anne of Avonlea*.
  L. M. Montgomery, *Anne of Green Gables*.
  L. Mott, *To the Credit of the Sea* (short stories).
  G. Parker, *Northern Lights* (short stories).
  A. E. S. Smythe, *Poems, Grave and Gay*.
  A. M. Teskey, *Where the Sugar Maple Grows; Idylls of a Canadian Village*.
Candidate; A Political Romance. J. A. Altsheler.
Candide. F. M. A. de Voltaire.
Candle of Understanding, A Novel. E. Wetmore.
Canoe and Camera: A Two Hundred Mile Tour Through the Maine Forests. T. S. Steele.
Canoe trips: see
  F. W. Snekeker, *Family Canoe Trip*.
  T. S. Steele, *Canoe and Camera: A Two Hundred Mile Tour Through the Maine Forests*.
  T. S. Steele, *Paddle and Portage, from Moosehead Lake to the Aroostook River, Maine*.

R. L. Stevenson, *Inland Voyage*.
Can Telepathy Explain? Results of Psychical Research. M. J. Savage.
Canterbury, Archbishps of: see M. Fowler, *Some Notable Archbishops of Canterbury*.
Canterbury (England): see W. D. Howells, *Certain Delightful English Towns, with Glimpses of the Pleasant Country Between*.
Canterbury Tales. G. Chaucer.
Canterbury Tales: see F. Grose, *Classical Dictionary of the Vulgar Tongue* (marginalia).
Canzoni (poems). T. A. Daly.
Cape Cod Ballads, and Other Verse, by Joe Lincoln. J. C. Lincoln.
Cape Cod Folks, A Novel. S. P. M. Greene.
Capitals of Spanish America. W. B. Curtis.
Cap'n Simeon's Store. G. S. Wasson.
"Captain Ben's Choice" (short story). F. L. Pratt.
Captain Bill McDonald, Texas Ranger. A Story of Frontier Reform. A. B. Paine.
Captain Jinks, Hero. E. H. Crosby.
Captain Kydd: see "Captain Kidd" (ballad).
"Captain of my soul" (poetic phrase): see W. E. Henley, *Book of Verses*.
Captain of the Gray-Horse Troop; A Novel. H. Garland.
Captain of the Janizaries, A Story of the Times of Scanderbeg and the Fall of Constantinople. J. M. Ludlow.
Captain of the Kansas. L. Tracy.
Captain Polly. S. M. Swett.
"Captains of Industry: Henry Huttleston Rogers" (article). S. E. Moffett.
Captive of Love, Founded Upon Bakin's Japanese Romance Kumono Tayema Ama Yo No Tsuki. E. Greey.
"Captive pirate's lament" (ballad): see "Captain Kidd" (ballad).
Captives of Abb's Valley; A Legend of Frontier Life. J. M. Brown.
Captivity narratives: see
F. C. Baylor, *Juan and Juanita*.
J. M. Brown, *Captives of Abb's Valley; A Legend of Frontier Life*.
S. O. Jewett, *York Garrison—1640*.
F. W. Kelly, *Narrative of My Captivity Among the Sioux Indians*.
M. Rowlandson, *Narrative of the Captivity and the Restoration of Mrs. Mary Rowlandson*.
See also the Reader's Guide entry for Native Americans.
Captured by the Navajos. C. A. Curtis.
"Carbery, Ethna" (pseud.): see A. J. MacManus.
Card games: see
Secret Out; or, One Thousand Tricks with Cards, and Other Recreations.
See also the Reader's Guide entries for Bridge, for Poker, and for Whist.
Cardigan; A Novel. R. W. Chambers.
Cardinal's Snuff-Box (novel). H. Harland.
Carey, Henry (composer):
"God save the King" (British anthem).
S. F. Smith, "America" (anthem).

Carey, Henry Francis (trans.): see A. Dante, *Vision; or Hell*.
Caricatures: see
J. Ashton, *English Caricature and Satire on Napoleon I*.
R. Blix, *Voile Tombe: Caricatures par Blix*.
Carnan d'Ache (pseud.), *Bric à Brac; Album par Carnan d'Ache*.
Cartoons from "Punch."
J. M. Haswell, *Man of His Time. Part I, The Story of the Life of Napoleon III. And Part II, The Same Story as Told by Popular Caricaturists of the Last Thirty Years*.
Simplicissimus (magazine).
See also the Reader's Guide entry for Cartoons.
Carleton, Clifford (co-illus.): see
A. French, *Missionary Sheriff*.
W. D. Howells, *Their Wedding Journey*.
F. C. Williams, *J. Devlin—Boss: A Romance of American Politics* (novel).
Carleton, Will (intro.): see W. Smith (ed.), *Old Yorkshire*.
Carlyle, Jane Welsh: see
J. B. Carlyle, *Letters and Memorials of Jane Welsh Carlyle*.
A. E. N. Ireland, *Life of Jane Welsh Carlyle*.
Carlyle's Complete Works. T. Carlyle.
Carlyle, Thomas: see
W. Allingham, *William Allingham, A Diary*.
(ed.), J. B. W. Carlyle, *Letters and Memorials of Jane Welsh Carlyle*.
C. Fox, *Memories of Old Friends*.
J. A. Froude, *Thomas Carlyle: A History of His Life in London, 1834–1881*.
J. A. Froude, *Thomas Carlyle: A History of the First Forty Years of His Life, 1795–1835*.
Genlis, Comtesse de (Catalog entry).
(trans.), J. W. von Goethe, *Wilhelm Meister's Apprenticeship and Travels*.
A. E. N. Ireland, *Life of Jane Welsh Carlyle*.
J. McCarthy, *Portraits of the Sixties*.
G. S. Meriam, *Living Faith*.
J. Milne, *Romance of a Pro-Consul; Being the Personal Life and Memoirs of the Right Hon. Sir George Grey, K. C. B.* (marginalia).
F. S. Wilhelmina, *Memoirs of Wilhelmine, Margravine of Baireuth* (marginalia).
Carmen (opera). G. Bizet.
Carmina Sacra; or, Boston Collection of Church Music, Comprising the Most Popular Psalm and Hymn Tunes in General Use. L. Mason (comp.).
"Carminge" (contr.): see Port Louis, Mauritius *Merchants' and Planters' Gazette*.
Carnegie, Andrew: see New York *Times* (Catalog entry).
Caroline of Courtlandt Street (novel). W. J. Mills.
Carolino, Pedro (co-author): see J. da Fonseca, *New Guide of the Conversation in Portuguese and English in Two Parts*.
Carpet Bag (magazine):): see "Ensign Jehiel Stebbings" (fictional character).
Carpini, Giovanni Palamede (ed.): see B. Cellini, *Memoirs of Benvenuto Cellini*.
"Carroll, Lewis" (pseud.): see C. L. Dodgson.

Carruthers, Joseph Hector: see A. B. Paterson, *Man from Snowy River and Other Verses* (inscr.).

Cartaphilus (later known as Joseph): see M. D. Conway, *Wandering Jew* (marginalia).

Cartoons: see
 Cartoons from "Punch."
 G. L. P. B. Du Maurier, *Social Pictorial Satire; Reminiscences and Appreciations of English Illustrators of the Past Generation.*
 J. Leech, *Pictures of Life & Character. From the Collection of "Mr. Punch."*
 J. T. McCutcheon, *Mysterious Stranger and Other Cartoons.*
 See also the Reader's Guide entry for Caricatures.

Cary, Henry Francis (trans.): see Dante, *Vision; or, Hell, Purgatory and Paradise of Dante Alighieri.*

"Casabianca" (poem). F. D. Hemans.

Casa Guidi Windows. E. B. Browning.

Casanova de Seingalt: see
 F. Bernard, *Wonderful Escapes.*
 L. de R. Saint-Simon, *Memoirs of the Duke of Saint-Simon on the Reign of Louis XIV and the Regency* (marginalia).

"Case of Metaphantasmia" (short story): see W. D. Howells, *Between the Dark and the Daylight: Romances.*

"Caskoden, Edward" (pseud.): see C. Major.

"Cask of Amontillado" (short story). E. A. Poe.

Cassius Scaeva, Marcus (Roman centurion): see *Percy Anecdotes.*

Castaigne, André. (illus.): see B. Runkle, *Helmet of Navarre.*

Caste (India): see the Reader's Guide entry for Sudras (Indian caste).

Castelvecchio, L. P. de (trans.): see L. Barzini, Sr., *Pekin to Paris; Account of Prince Borghese's Journey Across Two Continents.*

Castilian Days. J. Hay.

Castle Blair: A Story of Youthful Days. F. L. Shaw.

Castle Comedy (novel). T. Buchanan.

Castle Daly: The Story of an Irish Home Thirty Years Ago. A. M. Keary.

Castor and Pollux: see B. M. Nead, *Some Hidden Sources of Fiction* (marginalia).

Cast Up by the Sea. S. W. Baker.

Casual Acquaintance: A Novel Founded on Fact. M. A. M. Hardy.

Cat and the Canary. M. Cameron.

Catastrophe in Bohemia, and Other Stories. H. S. Brooks.

Cathedral: see J. R. Lowell, *Vision of Sir Launfal. The Cathedral. Favorite Poems.*

Cathedral Days: A Tour in Southern England. A. B. Dodd.

Catherine of Aragon: see W. H. Dixon, *History of Two Queens: Catherine of Aragon and Anne Boleyn.*

Catholicism: see
 W. D. Alexander, *Review of a Pastoral Address by the Right Rev. T. N. Staley, D.D., Reformed Catholic Bishop of Honolulu.*
 S. Baring-Gould, *In Exitu Israel; An Historical Novel.*
 G. G. Coulton, *From St. Francis to Dante: Translations from the Chronicle of the Franciscan Salimbene (1221–1288).*

J. J. I. von Döllinger and J. N. Huber, *Pope and the Council.*

J. Gerard, *What Was the Gunpowder Plot? The Traditional Story Tested by Original Evidence.*

J. R. Green, *Short History of the English People* (marginalia).

É. R. Huc, *Recollections of a Journey Through Tartary, Thibet, and China, During the Years 1844, 1845, and 1846.*

R. O. Huch, *Fra Celeste und andere Erzählungen.*

J. J. Jarves, *History of the Hawaiian or Sandwich Islands* (Catalog entry).

E. G. Jordan, *May Iverson—Her Book.*

E. G. Jordan, *Tales of the Cloister.*

C. Kingsley, *Hypatia; or, New Foes with an Old Face.*

W. E. H. Lecky, *History of European Morals from Augustus to Charlemagne* (marginalia).

H. G. D. Liveing. *Records of Romsey Abbey: An Account of the Benedictine House of Nuns, with Notes on the Parish Church and Town (A. D. 907-1558).*

G. Negri, *Julian the Apostate.*

W. H. Neligan, *Rome: Its Churches, Its Charities, and Its Schools.*

J. H. Newman, *Apologia Pro Vita Sua.*

B. O'Reilly, *Life of Leo XIII, from an Authentic Memoir Furnished by His Order.*

F. Parkman, *Count Frontenac and New France Under Louis XIV* (marginalia).

F. Parkman, *Old Régime in Canada* (marginalia).

H. Pyle, *Otto of the Silver Hand* (novel).

L. von Ranke, *History of the Popes, Their Church and State, and Especially of Their Conflicts with Protestantism in the Sixteenth and Seventeenth Centuries.*

S. J. Reid, *Sketch of the Life and Times of the Rev. Sydney Smith.*

G. H. E. Slater, *Pagan at the Shrine.*

M. F. Somerville, *Personal Recollections, from Early Life to Old Age, of Mary Somerville. With Selections from Her Correspondence* (marginalia).

E. Sue, *Wandering Jew.*

Unfathomable Mystery. Benedictine Sisters of Perpetual Adoration. Clyde, Missouri.

"Veni creator spiritus" (Catholic hymn).

P. Villari, *Life and Times of Niccolò Machiavelli* (marginalia).

F. E. Wadleigh, *'Twixt Wave and Sky* (novel).

L. Whitney, *Burning of the Convent. A Narrative of the Destruction, by a Mob, of the Ursuline School on Mount Benedict, Charlestown, as Remembered by One of the Pupils.*

E. Wildman, *Aguinaldo: A Narrative of Filipino Ambitions* (Catalog entry).

N. P. S. Wiseman, *Fabiola; or, The Church of the Catacombs.*

See also the Reader's Guide entries for Christianity and for Religious persecution.

Cato, Marcus Porcius: see Plutarchus, *Plutarch's Lives of Alcibiades & Coriolanus, Aristides & Cato the Censor.*

Cats: see
 T. B. Aldrich, *Story of a Cat.*
 E. G. Allyn, *Cats' Convention.*

J. M. Baldwin, *Story of the Mind* (marginalia).

M. Cameron, *Cat and the Canary.*

Cat and Dog Stories.

P. G. Hamerton, *Chapters on Animals.*

H. M. F. H. Jackson, *Cat Stories.*

C. A. D. Janvier, *London Mews.*

Cats' Convention. E. G. Allyn.

Catskill Mountains: see C. D. Warner, *Their Pilgrimage* (novel).

Cat's-Paw. B. M. S. Croker.

Cat Stories. H. M. F. H. Jackson.

Catullus and Tibullus: see G. V. Catullus, *Works of Catullus and Tibullus.*

Causes célèbres: see

A. Fouquier, *Causes célèbres de tous les peoples.*

M. Méjan, *Recueil des causes célèbres, et des arrêts qui les ont décidées.*

Cavalier. G. W. Cable.

Cavalleria Rusticana (opera). P. Mascagni (composer).

Cavalry: see W. Glazier, *Three Years in the Federal Cavalry.*

"Cavazza, Elisabeth" (pseud.): see E. J. Pullen.

Cawnpore. G. O. Trevelyan.

Cawood, John, "Hark! what mean those holy voices" (hymn): see G. J. Geer (Catalog entry).

"Caxton, Pisistratus" (pseud.): see E. G. E. B. Lytton.

Caxton, William: see Henry VII, *Statutes of Henry VII in Exact Facsimile.*

Cecil Dreeme. T. Winthrop.

Cecil, Robert: see H. D. Traill, *Marquis of Salisbury.*

Celebrated Crimes. A. Dumas.

Cellini, Benvenuto: see

F. Bernard, *Wonderful Escapes.*

W. D. Howells (co-ed.), *Library of Universal Adventure by Sea and Land.*

C. Kingsley, *Heroes, or Greek Fairy Tales for My Children* (marginalia).

L. de R. Saint-Simon, *Memoirs of the Duke of Saint-Simon on the Reign of Louis XIV and the Regency* (Catalog entry).

Celsus (early philosopher): see T. W. Doane, *Bible Myths and Their Parallels in Other Religions* (marginalia).

'Cension. A Sketch from Paso Del Norte. M. M. Austin.

Centenary Garland; Being Pictorial Illustrations of the Novels of Sir Walter Scott, in Their Order of Publication. By George Cruikshank, and Other Artists of Eminence. C. Rogers (ed.).

Centennial and Other Poems. R. S. Pollard.

Centennial Exhibition in 1876: see

G. T. Ferris, *Gems of the Centennial Exhibition.*

O. W. Holmes, "Grandmother's Story of Bunker Hill Battle" (poem).

National Centennial Commemoration. Proceedings. Philadelphia Exhibition of 1876.

Pollard, R. S., *Centennial and Other Poems.*

B. Taylor, *National Ode.*

Centennial Ode (unidentified poem): see B. Taylor, *National Ode.*

Central Africa: Naked Truths of Naked People. C. Chaillé-Long.

Central Africa. Syme.

Central America: see

W. E. Curtis, *Capitals of Spanish America.*

J. Fiske, *Discovery of America, with Some Account of Ancient America and the Spanish Conquest.*

J. T. Goodman, *Archaic Maya Inscriptions* (Catalog entry).

J. F. A. du P. Nadaillac, *Pre-Historic America.*

See also the Reader's Guide entries for individual Central American nations.

Central Palestine and Phoenicia. W. M. Thomson.

Century Dictionary: An Encyclopedic Lexicon of the English Language. W. D. Whitney.

Century of Science and Other Essays. J. Fiske.

Ceramics: see the Reader's Guide entries for Porcelain and for Pottery.

Certain Delightful English Towns, with Glimpses of the Pleasant Country Between. W. D. Howells.

"Cervantes, Zola, Kipling & Co." (article). B. Matthews.

Ceylon: see

S. M. Burrows, *Buried Cities of Ceylon: A Guide Book.*

R. Heber, "Missionary hymn" (Catalog entry).

J. F. Hurst, *Indika. The Country and the People of India and Ceylon.*

T. W. Knox, *Boy Travellers in the Far East; Part Third, . . . in a Journey to Ceylon and India.*

Chadwick, John White (contr.): see *Women of the Bible, by Twelve Eminent Divines.*

"Chambered Nautilus" (poem). O. W. Holmes.

Chambers, William (contr.): see W. Scott, *Poetical Works of Sir Walter Scott.*

Champney, James Wells (illus.): see

E. Champney, *All Around a Palette.*

E. Champney, *In the Sky-Garden.*

E. King, *Great South: A Record of Journeys.*

Chance Acquaintance (novel). W. D. Howells.

Chandler, Zachariah: see G. Ticknor, *Life, Letters, and Journals of George Ticknor* (marginalia).

Changed Cross, and Other Religious Poems. A. D. F. Randolph (comp.)

Change of Heart (stories). M. S. Hopkins.

Channing, Grace Ellery: see

"End of the Journey" (short story) in W. D. Howells (co-ed.), *Under the Sunset.*

"The Marriage Question" (short story), in W. D. Howells (co-ed.), *Their Husbands' Wives.*

Channing, William Henry (ed.): see M. Fuller, *Memoirs of Margaret Fuller Ossoli.* Ed. William Henry Channing, Ralph Waldo Emerson, James Freeman Clarke.

Chantepie, Jules: see V. M. Hugo, *Ruy Blas.*

Chaplain of the Fleet. W. Besant.

Chaplain's Craze; Being the Mystery of Findon Friars. G. M. Fenn.

Chapman, Frank Michler (ed.): see M. O. Wright, *Four-Footed Americans and Their Kin.*

Chapman, Maria Weston (ed.): see H. Martineau, *Autobiography.*

Chappaqua, New York: see C. Cleveland. *Story of a Summer; or, Journal Leaves from Chappaqua.*

Chapters in the History of the Arts and Crafts Movement. O. L. Triggs.

Chapters on Animals. P. G. Hamerton.

Character and Logical Method of Political Economy. J. E. Cairnes.

Characteristics of Men of Industry, Culture, and Genius. S. Smiles.

Characters, or The Manners of the Age, with the Character of Theophrastus. J. de La Bruyère.

"Character Sketch: Mark Twain" (article). W. T. Stead.

Charakterbilder aus der Geschichte und Sage, für einen propädeutischen geschichtsunterricht. A. W. Grube.

Charcoal Sketches; or, Scenes in a Metropolis. J. C. Neal.

"Charge of the Light Brigade" (poem). A. Tennyson.

Chariot-Race from Ben-Hur. L. Wallace.

Charlemagne: see D. O'Sullivan (comp.), *Book of Legends, Containing a Selection of Standard Tales from the Most Esteemed British Essayists.*

Charles I: see

    J. Church, *With the King at Oxford; A Tale of the Great Rebellion.*

    M. H. Hervey, *Amyas Egerton, Cavalier* (novel).

    J. H. Shorthouse, *John Inglesant: A Romance.*

    W. M. Thackeray, *Thackeray's Lectures. The English Humorists. The Four Georges* (Catalog entry).

    W. J. Vance, *Big John Baldwin; Extracts from the Journal of an Officer of Cromwell's Army* (fictional memoir).

    W. G. Willis, *Charles the First: An Historical Tragedy. In Four Acts* (play).

    See also the Reader's Guide entry for Oliver Cromwell.

Charles I, King of Romania: see M. Kremnitz, *Reminiscences of the King of Roumania.*

Charles II: see

    H. Forneron, *Louise de Ke Louise de Keroualle, Duchess of Portsmouth, 1649–1734.*

    G. Standring, *People's History of the English Aristocracy.*

    W. M. Thackeray, *Thackeray's Lectures. The English Humorists. The Four Georges* (Catalog entry).

Charles VIII: see P. de Commynes, *Memoirs of Philip de Commines, Lord of Argenton.*

"Charles Darwin" (essay). J. Fiske.

Charles Edward, Prince: see A. MacKinnon, *Prince Charles Edward; or, The Rebellion of 1745–46.*

Charles Kingsley: His Letters and Memories. C. Kingsley.

Charles Reade, D. C. L., Dramatist, Novelist, and Journalist. A Memoir. C. L. Reade and C. Reade.

Charles the Bold: see

    P. de Commynes, *Memoirs of Philip de Commines, Lord of Argenton.*

    J. F. Kirk, *History of Charles the Bold, Duke of Burgundy.*

Charles the First: An Historical Tragedy. In Four Acts (play). W. G. Willis.

Charles William Ferdinand of Brunswick: see W. M. Thackeray, *Thackeray's Lectures. The English Humorists. The Four Georges* (Catalog entry).

Charley's Aunt (farce). B. Thomas.

"Charming May" (song): see P. Henry Hatch, "Oh, charming May!"

Chatrian, Alexandre (co-author): see

    É. Erckmann, *Madame Thérèse.*

    É. Erckmann, *Polish Jew.*

É. Erckmann, *Waterloo; A Sequel to the Conscript of 1813.*

Chatwit, The Man-Talk Bird. P. V. Mighels.

Chaucer for Children: A Golden Key. G. Chaucer.

Chaucer, Geoffrey: see

    J. R. Green, *Short History of the English People* (marginalia).

    J. A. A. J. Jusserand, *English Wayfaring Life in the Middle Ages (XIVth Century).*

    Ovid, *Art of Love, in Three Books.*

    E. Ransford, "In the Days When We Went Gypsying" (poem and song) (Catalog entry).

    W. Shakespeare, *Works of Shakespeare* (Catalog entry).

Chautauqua (entertainment): see G. Z. MacLaren (Catalog entry).

Chaytor, Henry John (trans.): see

    A. Bertholet, *Transmigration of Souls.*

    G. Ferrero, *Greatness and Decline of Rome.*

    J. Weiss, *Paul and Jesus.*

Cheerful Yesterdays. Contemporaries. T. W. S. Higginson.

"Cheiro" (pseud.): see W. J. Warner.

Cheiro's Language of the Hand. W. J. Warner.

Chemistry: see

    R. K. Duncan, *Chemistry of Commerce: A Simple Interpretation of Some New Chemistry.*

    H. Mayhew, *Wonders of Science; or, Young Humphry Davy.*

    A. R. Wallace, William Ramsay, *et al. Progress of the Century.*

    H. S. Williams, *Story of Nineteenth-Century Science.*

Chemistry of Commerce: A Simple Interpretation of Some New Chemistry. R. K. Duncan.

Chess: see

    D. W. Fiske (Catalog entry).

    A. P. Primrose, *Napoleon: The Last Phase* (marginalia).

Chesterfield, Lord: see the Catalog entry for P. D. Stanhope.

Chevalier of Pensieri-Vani. H. B. Fuller.

Cheyenne (Native American tribe): see P. H. Sheridan, *Personal Memoirs of P. H. Sheridan, General, United States Army.*

Chicago: see

    T. Dreiser, *Sister Carrie.*

    E. Field, *Culture's Garland: Being Memoranda of the Gradual Rise of Literature, Art, Music and Society in Chicago, and Other Western Ganglia.*

    W. Payne, *Jerry the Dreamer.*

    J. Ralph, *Harper's Chicago and the World's Fair.*

    E. P. Roe, *Barriers Burned Away.*

    U. B. Sinclair, *Jungle.*

    F. H. Spearman, *Doctor Bryson, A Novel.*

    C. R. Teller, *Cage* (novel).

    B. M. Van Vorst, *Bagsby's Daughter.*

    B. M. Van Vorst and M. V. Vorst, *Woman Who Toils; Being the Experiences of Two Ladies as Factory Girls.*

    C. D. Warner, *Studies in the South and West, with Comments on Canada.*

    H. L. Wilson, *Spenders; A Tale of the Third Generation.*

Chicot the Jester: see A. Dumas, *Novels.*

"Chieftain" (poem). W. Winter.

Chien d'Or. W. Kirby.

Childe Harold's Pilgrimage. G. G. Byron.

Childhood nostalgia: see

J. W. Riley, *Armazindy.*

J. W. Riley, *Book of Joyous Children.*

J. W. Riley, *Child-World.*

J. W. Riley, "Erasmus Wilson" (poem).

J. W. Riley, *"Old Swimmin'-Hole," and 'Leven More Poems.*

J. W. Riley, *Rhymes of Childhood.*

W. A. White, *Court of Boyville.*

J. G. Whittier (ed.), *Childlife: A Collection of Poems.*

J. G. Whittier (ed.), *Child Life in Prose.*

W. Willing, "Twenty years ago" (song).

E. Wood, *Back Home.*

See also the Reader's Guide entry for Boy books.

Childlife: A Collection of Poems. J. G. Whittier (ed.).

Child Life in Prose. J. G. Whittier (ed.).

"Child of sin and sorrow, filled with dismay" (hymn). T. Hastings.

Child-rearing: see the Reader's Guide entry for Parenting.

Children of the Abbey. A Tale. R. M. D. Roche.

Children of the Ghetto (novel). I. Zangwill.

Children of the Nations; A Study of Colonization and Its Problems. P. Bigelow.

Children of the New Forest. F. Marryat.

Children's and young adult literature: see

J. Abbott, *Learning to Think* (and various other children's titles).

J. H. Adams, *Harper's Machinery Book for Boys.*

L. M. Alcott, *Little Men: Life at Plumfield with Jo's Boys.*

L. M. Alcott, *Little Women; or, Meg, Jo, Beth and Amy* (novel).

I. Alden, *Pansy's Picture Book.*

Baby Days; A Selection of Songs, Stories.

J. D. D. Bacon, *Madness of Philip and Other Tales of Childhood.*

J. D. D. Bacon, *Memoirs of a Baby.*

J. D. D. Bacon, *Ten to Seventeen; A Boarding-School Diary.*

J. Baldwin, *Story of the Golden Age.*

T. K. Beecher, *In Time with the Stars; Stories for Children.*

E. N. Bland, *Wouldbegoods.*

N. Bohny, *Neues Bilderbuch.*

A. Bond (ed.), *Young People's Illustrated Bible History.*

J. Bonner, *Child's History of the United States.*

E. S. Brooks, *Chivalric Days, and the Boys and Girls Who Helped to Make Them.*

A. B. Buckley, *Fairy-Land of Science.*

A. B. Buckley, *Life and Her Children: Glimpses of Animal Life from the Amoeba to the Insects.*

F. H. Burnett, *Little Lord Fauntleroy.*

W. Busch, *Schnurrdiburr oder Die Bienen.*

F. A. C. Canfield, *Kidnapped Campers; A Story of Out-of-Doors.*

E. Champney, *All Around a Palette.*

E. W. Champney, *In the Sky-Garden.*

G. Chaucer, *Chaucer for Children: A Golden Key.*

R. S. Clarke, *Janet, A Poor Heiress.*

R. S. Clarke, *Quinnebasset Girls.*

D. M. M. Craik (various titles, especially *Studies from Life*).

W. Crane, *Baby's Opera: A Book of Old Rhymes with New Dresses.*

G. Dalziel, *Little Flower Girl, and Other Stories in Verse, by "Robin."*

C. Darwin, *What Mr. Darwin Saw in His Voyage Round the World in the Ship "Beagle."*

T. Day, *History of Sandford and Merton.*

D. Defoe, *Life and Surprising Adventures of Robinson Crusoe.*

D. Defoe, *Robinson Crusoe in Words of One Syllable.*

H. A. De Kroyft, *Story of Little Jakey.*

E. D. Deland, *Little Son of Sunshine; A Story for Boys and Girls* (and other titles).

M. L. De la Ramée, *Bimbi: Stories for Children.*

A. M. Diaz, *Jimmyjohns, and Other Stories.*

C. Dickens, *Child's History of England.*

C. L. Dodgson, *Alice in Wonderland.*

C. L. Dodgson, *Hunting of the Snark.*

C. L. Dodgson, *Through the Looking-Glass.*

W. Drysdale, *Ingulph's Chronicle of the Abbey of Croyland.*

M. Edgeworth, *Parent's Assistant; or, Stories for Children.*

E. Eggleston, *First Book in American History.*

R. Emmet, *Pretty Peggy Painting Book.*

T. D. English, *Boy's Book of Battle-Lyrics: A Collection of Verses Illustrating Some Notable Events in the History of the United States of America.*

J. H. G. Ewing, *Daddy Darwin's Dovecot: A Country Tale.*

J. H. G. Ewing, *Dolls' Wash.*

J. H. G. Ewing, *Jackanapes.*

J. H. G. Ewing, *Lob Lie-by-the-Fire; or, The Luck of Lingborough.*

Favorite Album of Fun and Fancy.

G. M. Fenn, *Chaplain's Craze; Being the Mystery of Findon Friars.*

R. H. M. Fillebrown, *Rhymes of Happy Childhood.*

M. F. Finley, *Elsie Dinsmore.*

P. W. Francis, *Remarkable Adventures of Little Boy Pip.*

M. S. Gatty, *Parables from Nature.*

E. K. C. Gibson, *Zauberlinda, The Wise Witch.*

K. Grahame, *Dream Days.*

K. Greenaway, *Kate Greenaway's Birthday Book for Children.*

W. E. Griffis, *Bible Stories for Young People.*

L. P. Hale, *Peterkin Papers.*

H. A. Hays, *Adventures of Prince Lazybones, and Other Stories.*

H. A. Hays, *Princess Idleways: A Fairy Story.*

G. A. Henty, *St. George for England: A Tale of Cressy and Poitiers.*

O. Herford, *Child's Primer of Natural History.*

J. W. Hey, *Fünfzig Fabeln für Kinder.*

T. W. S. Higginson, *Young Folks' History of the United States.*

H. Hoffmann, *Struweelpeter.*

W. Hooker, *Child's Book of Nature.*

M. B. Howitt, *Birds and Flowers; or, Lays and Lyrics of Rural Life.*
J. R. C. Hoyt, *Janet and Her Friends.*
E. Ingersoll, *Ice Queen.*
G. E. S. Jackson, *Wee Winkles & Her Friends* (and similar titles).
H. M. F. H. Jackson, *Cat Stories.*
C. A. D. Janvier, *London Mews.*
J. H. Jewett, *Easter Story.*
C. Kingsley, *Heroes, or Greek Fairy Tales for My Children.*
C. Kingsley, *Madame How and Lady Why; or, First Lessons in Earth Lore for Children.*
C. Kingsley, *Water-Babies. A Fairy Tale for a Land-Baby.*
I. C. Knox, *Little Folks' History of England.*
M. A. Lathbury, *Birthday Week; Pictures and Verse.*
M. A. Lathbury, *Twelve Times One, Illustrations of Child Life.*
E. Leslie, *American Girls' Book; or, Occupation for Play Hours.*
L. C. W. Lillie, *Household of Glen Holly.*
L. C. W. Lillie, *Story of Music and Musicians for Young Readers.*
Little Folks: A Magazine for the Young.
G. MacDonald, *At the Back of the North Wind.*
M. A. P. Mackarness, *Sunbeam Stories.*
F. Marryat, *Children of the New Forest.*
H. M. Miller, *Little Folks in Feathers and Fur, and Others in Neither.*
H. M. Miller, *Little People of Asia.*
L. M. Montgomery, *Anne of Avonlea.*
L. M. Montgomery, *Anne of Green Gables.*
L. B. Morse, *Road to Nowhere. A Story for Children.*
Mother Goose; or, The Old Nursery Rhymes.
R. K. Munkittrick, *Moon Prince, and Other Nabobs.*
R. Niedergesäss, *Kinderstubengeschichten.*
M. H. Norris (enry).
Our Stories, by the School Children.
A. B. Paine, *Little Lady—Her Book, for Girls and Boys.*
Parley's Magazine.
S. P. W. Parton, *Little Ferns for Fanny's Little Friends.*
M. E. Phillips (ed. and illus.), *Laurel Leaves for Little Folk.*
O. Pletsch, *Shnik-Shnak.*
Plutarchus, *Boys' and Girls' Plutarch.*
Plutarchus, *Children's Plutarch: Tales of the Greeks.*
B. Potter, *Tale of Peter Rabbit.*
E. P. Prentiss (various *Little Susy's* titles).
H. Pyle, *Merry Adventures of Robin Hood of Great Renown, in Nottinghamshire.*
H. Pyle, *Otto of the Silver Hand.*
H. Pyle, *Pepper & Salt; or, Seasoning for Young Folk.*
A. S. Richardson, *Pebbles and Pearls for the Young Folks.*
St. Nicholas: A Magazine for Boys and Girls.
C. W. Sanders and J. C. Sanders. *Bilder Fibel.*
C. von Schmid, *Genovefa.*
C. von Schmid, *Gute Fridolin und der böse Dietrich.*
H. E. Scudder, *Bodleys Telling Stories.*
H. E. Scudder, *Doings of the Bodley Family in Town and Country.*

S. R. Ségur, *Adventures of a Donkey.*
Simple Stories.
G. Smith, *Little Ned Happy and Flora.*
G. Smith, *Little Precious.*
G. Smith, *Loveable Tales of Janey and Josey and Joe.*
G. Smith, *Roggie and Reggie Stories.*
G. Smith, *Stories of Peter and Ellen.*
J. G. Sowerby and H. H. Emmerson, *Afternoon Tea: Rhymes for Children with Original Illustrations.*
E. Spenser, *Spenser for Children.*
H. E. B. Stowe, *Betty's Bright Idea. Also, Deacon Pitkin's Farm, and the First Christmas of New England.*
H. E. B. Stowe, *Chimney-Corner.*
H. E. B. Stowe, *Dog's Mission; or, the Story of the Old Avery House. And Other Stories.*
H. E. B. Stowe, *Little Foxes.*
H. E. B. Stowe, *Little Pussy Willow. Also, The Minister's Watermelons.*
H. E. B. Stowe, *May Flower, and Miscellaneous Writings.*
H. E. B. Stowe, *Poganuc People: Their Loves and Lives.*
H. E. B. Stowe, *Queer Little People.*
H. E. B. Stowe, *Religious Poems.*
J. Taylor and A. T. Gilbert, *Little Ann, and Other Poems.*
J. M. Thompson, *Water Wonders Every Child Should Know.*
S. K. Trimmer, *History of the Robins. In Words of One Syllable.*
E. M. S. Turner, *Seven Little Australians.*
C. T. Wheeler, *Prize Painting Book: Good Times. Pictures by Dora Wheeler.*
A. D. T. Whitney, *Summer in Leslie Goldthwaite's Life.*
K. D. S. Wiggin, *Timothy's Quest: A Story for Anybody, Young or Old, Who Cares to Read It.*
O. Wildermuth, *Für Freistunden; Erzählungen für die Jugend.*
O. Wister, *New Swiss Family Robinson: A Tale for Children of All Ages.*
S. C. Woolsey, *Nine Little Goslings.*
S. C. Woolsey, *What Katy Did: A Story.*
H. C. Wright, *Princess Liliwinkins, and Other Stories.*
J. D. Wyss, *Swiss Family Robinson. A New Translation.*
C. M. Yonge, *Child's History of France.*
C. M. Yonge, *Lances of Lynwood.*
C. M. Yonge, *Little Duke; or, Richard the Fearless* (novel).
C. M. Yonge, *Prince and the Page: A Story of the Last Crusade* (novel).
C. M. Yonge, *Young Folks' History of England.*
C. M. Yonge, *Young Folks' History of Germany.*
C. M. Yonge, *Young Folks' History of Rome.*
Young Artists, and Other Stories.
Children's Crusade. M. Schwob.
Children's Crusade; An Episode of the Thirteenth Century. G. Z. Gray.
Children's Educational Theatre. A. M. H. Heniger.
Children's Plutarch: Tales of the Greeks. Plutarchus.
Children's writings: see *Our Stories.*
Child's Book of Nature. W. Hooker.

Childs, George William: see (inscr.) F. W. Farrar, *Truths to Live By, A Companion to Everyday Christian Life.*
Child's History of England. C. Dickens.
Child's History of France. C. M. Yonge.
Child's History of the United States. J. Bonner.
Child's Poems, from October to October, 1870–1871. L. C. B. Robinson.
Child's Primer of Natural History. O. Herford.
Child-World. J. W. Riley.
Chile: see A. P. Crouch, *Señorita Montenar* (historical fiction).
Chim: His Washington Winter. M. V. Dahlgren.
Chimney-Corner. H. E. B. Stowe.
China: see the Reader's Guide entries for Porcelain and for Pottery.
China: see
   L. Barzini, Sr., *Pekin to Paris: An Account of Prince Borghese's Journey Across Two Continents in a Motor-Car.*
   A. A. A. Brassey, *Voyage in the Sunbeam, Our Home in the Ocean for Eleven Months.*
   G. L. Carlisle, *Around the World in a Year.*
   A. Carnegie, *Round the World.*
   Crisis in China.
   G. L. Dickinson, *Letters from a Chinese Official; Being an Eastern View of Western Civilization.*
   Great Religions of the World (marginalia).
   É. R. Huc, *Recollections of a Journey Through Tartary, Thibet, and China, During the Years 1844, 1845, and 1846.*
   A. Ireland, *Far Eastern Tropics: Studies in the Administration of Tropical Dependencies.*
   C. P. Jones and A. L. Sykes, *Banduk jaldi banduk!: (Quick, My Rifle!).*
   T. W. Knox, *Boy Travellers in the Far East. . . in a Journey to Japan and China.*
   T. W. Knox, *Overland Through Asia; Pictures of Siberian, Chinese, and Tartar Life. Travels and Adventures in Kamchatka, Siberia, China, Mongolia, Chinese Tartary, and European Russia, with Full Accounts of the Siberian Exiles.*
   G. Lynch, *War of the Civilisations, Being the Record of a "Foreign Devil's" Experiences with the Allies in China.*
   A. Michie, *Missionaries in China.*
   H. M. Miller, *Little People of Asia.*
   G. E. Morrison, *Australian in China, Being the Narrative of a Quiet Journey Across China to British Burma.*
   C. K. Munroe, *Blue Dragon, A Tale of Recent Adventure in China.*
   New York *Sun* (Catalog entry).
   M. C. Perry, *Narrative of the Expedition of an American Squadron to the China Seas and Japan, Performed in the Years 1852, 1853, and 1854.*
   R. Pumpelly, *Across America and Asia; Notes of a Five Years' Journey Around the World:* see R. Pumpelly, *Explorations in Turkestan.*
   J. Ralph, *Alone in China, and Other Stories.*
   S. Ransome, *Japan in Transition: A Comparative Study of the Progress, Policy, and Methods of the Japanese Since Their War with China.*
   F. von Schlegel, *Philosophy of History; in a Course of Lectures, Delivered at Vienna.*

   L. L. Seaman, *Real Triumph of Japan: The Conquest of the Silent Foe.*
   C. W. Silver, *Secular Anathema on Fakery in Business, Social and Professional Life; or, Twentieth Century Conduct.*
   A. Z. H. Y. Sīrafī, *Ancient Accounts of India and China, by Two Mohammedan Travellers.*
   F. H. Skrine and E. D. Ross, *Heart of Asia: A History of Russian Turkestan and the Central Asian Khanates from the Earliest Times.*
   W. J. Sowden, *Chips from China.*
   B. Taylor, *Visit to India, China, and Japan, in the Year 1853.*
   M. W. Townsend, *Asia and Europe: Studies* (marginalia).
   F. Vincent, *Land of the White Elephant: Sights and Scenes in South-eastern Asia.*
   J. G. Wood, *Uncivilized Races; or, Natural History of Man* (marginalia).
Chinese Americans: see the Reader's Guide entry for Racial prejudice.
"Chinese Immigration" (article). E. W. Gilliam.
Chips from China. W. J. Sowden.
Chivalric Days, and the Boys and Girls Who Helped to Make Them. E. S. Brooks.
Chivalry: see
   T. Bulfinch, *Age of Chivalry; or Legends of King Arthur.*
   J. B. Cabell, *Chivalry* (novel).
   J. B. Cabell, *Gallantry* (novel).
   J. B. Cabell, *Line of Love* (novel).
Chivalry. J. B. Cabell.
Choir Invisible. J. L. Allen.
Choses Vues: see V. M. Hugo, *Things Seen.*
Chosön, The Land of the Morning Calm: A Sketch of Korea. P. Lowell.
Choyce Drollery: Songs and Sonnets. Being a Collection of Divers Excellent Pieces of Poetry, of Several Eminent Authors. Now First Reprinted from the Edition of 1656. J. W. Ebsworth (ed.).
Christ: see
   I. Bacheller, *Vergilius; A Tale of the Coming of Christ.*
   H. W. Beecher, *Life of Jesus, The Christ.*
   M. D. Conway, *Wandering Jew* (marginalia).
   T. W. Doane, *Bible Myths and Their Parallels in Other Religions: Being a Comparison of the Old and New Testament Myths and Miracles with Those of Heathen Nations of Antiquity* (marginalia).
   M. B. Eddy, *Retrospection and Introspection* (marginalia).
   H. C. Greene (trans.), *Gospel of the Childhood of Our Lord Jesus Christ.*
   E. G. Hubbard, *Man of Sorrows. Being a Little Journey to the Home of Jesus of Nazareth.*
   J. H. Ingraham. *Prince of the House of David; or, Three Years in the Holy City.*
   J. H. Jewett, *Easter Story.*
   W. E. H. Lecky, *History of European Morals from Augustus to Charlemagne* (marginalia).
   T. B. Macaulay, *Critical and Miscellaneous Essays* (marginalia).

C. Myers, *Would Christ Belong to a Labor Union? or, Henry Fielding's Dream.*

E. P. Nesbit, *Christ, Christians, and Christianity. Book I. Jesus an Essene.*

S. Newcomb *Side-Lights on Astronomy and Kindred Fields of Popular Science: Essays and Addresses* (marginalia).

N. Notovitch, *Unknown Life of Jesus Christ.*

F. Parkman, *Old Régime in Canada* (marginalia).

A. R. Parsons, *Parsifal; The Finding of Christ Through Art: A Wagner Study.*

A. W. Pitzer, *Ecce Deus-Homo; or, The Work and Kingdom of the Christ of Scripture.*

M. Pratt, *Orthodox Preacher and Nancy; Being the Tale of the Misfortunes of a Minister who Tried to Do as Jesus Would. A Story of Ministerial Life as It Is.*

W. C. Prime, *Tent Life in the Holy Land* (marginalia).

M. J. Savage (Catalog entry).

J. R. Seeley, *Ecce Homo; A Survey of the Life and Work of Jesus Christ.*

D. F. Strauss, *Life of Jesus, Critically Examined.*

E. Sue, *Wandering Jew.*

Suetonius, *Lives of the Twelve Caesars* (marginalia).

Thomas à Kempis, *Imitation of Christ.*

W. H. Thomson, *Parables and Their Home. The Parables by the Lake.*

J. Tissot, *New Testament* [paintings].

S. E. Titcomb, *Aryan Sun-Myths: The Origin of Religions* (marginalia).

L. N. Tolstoy, *My Religion.*

L. N. Tolstoy, *Teaching of Jesus.*

H. Van Dyke, *Christ-Child in Art; A Study of Interpretation.*

H. Van Dyke, *Story of the Other Wise Man.*

L. Wallace, *Ben-Hur: A Tale of the Christ.*

L. Wallace, *Boyhood of Christ* (marginalia).

L. Wallace, *First Christmas, from "Ben-Hur"* (marginalia).

H. Walpole, *Letters of Horace Walpole, Earl of Oxford* (marginalia).

J. Weiss, *Paul and Jesus.*

See also the Reader's Guide entry for Christianity.

Christ-Child in Art; A Study of Interpretation. H. Van Dyke.

Christ, Christians, and Christianity. Book I. Jesus an Essene. E. P. Nesbit.

Christian Hymnal. A Selection of Psalms and Hymns, with Music. N. J. Burton (co- comp.)

Christianity: see

H. M. Alden, *God in His World: An Interpretation.*

W. Alexander, *Primary Convictions; Being Discussions Delivered on Subjects Connected with the Evidences of Christianity.*

W. D. Alexander, *Review of a Pastoral Address by the Right Rev. T. N. Staley, D.D., Reformed Catholic Bishop of Honolulu, Containing a Reply to Some of His Charges Against the American Protestant Mission to the Hawaiian Islands.*

T. G. Allen, *Letter from an Ex-Sailor and Ex-Tramp* (marginalia).

R. Allestree, *Whole Duty of Man.*

M. D. Babcock, *Thoughts for Every-Day Living from the Spoken and Written Words of Maltbie Davenport Babcock.*

R. Baxter, *Saints' Everlasting Rest* (Catalog entry).

C. E. Beecher, *Appeal to the People in Behalf of Their Rights as Authorized Interpreters of the Bible.*

C. E. Beecher, *Religious Training of Children in the School, the Family, and the Church.*

E. Beecher, *Conflict of the Ages; or, The Great Debate on the Moral Relations of God and Man.*

Book of Common Prayer.

C. L. Brace, *Gesta Christi; or, A History of Humane Progress Under Christianity.*

C. A. Briggs, "Criticism and Dogma" (essay).

J. Brougham, *Christian Martyrs under Constantine and Maxentius* (play).

J. Calvin (Catalog entry).

M. L. Charlesworth, *Ministering Children: A Tale Dedicated to Childhood.*

G. K. Chesterton, *Orthodoxy.*

Christian Union.

F. E. Clark, *Mossback Correspondence, Together with Mr. Mossback's Views on Certain Practical Subjects, with a Short Account of His Visit to Utopia.*

J. F. Clarke, *Selections from Sermons Preached to the Church of the Disciples.*

S. Clarke, *Mirror or Looking-Glass Both for Saints & Sinners.*

S. Clarke, *Promises of Scripture.*

S. V. Clevenger, *Evolution of Man and His Mind. A History and Discussion* (marginalia).

F. P. Cobbe, *The Peak in Darien, with Some Other Inquiries Touching Concerns of the Soul and the Body.*

Confession of Faith.

G. G. Coulton, *From St. Francis to Dante: Translations from the Chronicle of the Franciscan Salimbene (1221–1288).*

G. R. Crooks, *Life of Bishop Matthew Simpson, of the Methodist Episcopal Church.*

J. Cumming, *Great Consummation. The Millennial Rest; or, The World As It Will Be.*

A. Dante, *Vision; or, Hell, Purgatory and Paradise.*

W. J. Dawson (co-ed.), *Great English Letter-Writers* (marginalia).

S. Dill, *Roman Society in the Last Century of the Western Empire* (marginalia).

M. A. Dodge, *Stumbling-Blocks.*

R. I. Dodge, *Our Wild Indians: Thirty-Three Years' Personal Experience among the Red Men of the Great West* (marginalia).

J. J. I. von Döllinger and J. N. Huber, *Pope and the Council.*

H. Drummond, *Greatest Thing in the World. An Address* (and other titles).

J. Edwards, *Freedom of Will.*

R. C. Eucken, *Christianity and the New Idealism: A Study in the Religious Philosophy of To-day.*

F. W. Farrar, *Truths to Live By, A Companion to Every-day Christian Life.*

G. P. Fisher, *Essays on the Supernatural Origin of Christianity.*

M. Fowler, *Some Notable Archbishops of Canterbury*.

J. Foxe, *Book of Martyrs*.

E. Gibbon, *History of the Decline and Fall of the Roman Empire* (marginalia).

W. B. von Hillern, *Am Kreuz; ein Passionsroman aus Oberammergau*.

R. O. Huch, *Fra Celeste und andere Erzählungen*.

J. F. Hurst, *Short History of the Reformation*.

C. Kingsley, *Hypatia; or, New Foes with an Old Face*.

Krippen-Kalender 1899—47.

P. Lacroix, *Military and Religious Life in the Middle Ages and at the Period of the Renaissance*.

H. C. Lea, *Historical Sketch of Sacerdotal Celibacy in the Christian Church*.

H. C. Lea, *History of the Inquisition of the Middle Ages*.

W. E. H. Lecky, *History of European Morals from Augustus to Charlemagne* (marginalia).

W. E. H. Lecky, *History of the Rise and Influence of the Spirit of Rationalism in Europe* (marginalia).

A. Le Feuvre, *"Probable Sons."*

H. Keller, *World I Live In* (Catalog entry).

B. King, *In the Garden of Charity* (and other titles)

G. W. von Leibniz (Catalog entry).

C. G. Leland, *Legends of the Birds*.

A. R. B. Lindsay, *What Is Worth While?*

M. Lonsdale, *Sister Dora. A Biography*.

R. M. Manley, *Mr. Claghorn's Daughter*.

C. Mather, *Magnalia Christi Americana; or, The Ecclesiastical History of New- England*.

C. Mather, *Wonders of the Invisible World*.

J. Meikle, *Solitude Sweetened; or, Miscellaneous Meditations on Various Religious Subjects Written in Distant Parts of the World*.

G. S. Merriam, *A Living Faith*.

J. Milton, *Milton's Paradise Lost*.

Dwight Lyman Moody (Catalog entry).

L. C. Moulton, *Some Women's Hearts*.

J. O'K. Murray, *Little Lives of the Great Saints*.

C. Myers, *Would Christ Belong to a Labor Union? or, Henry Fielding's Dream*.

E. P. Nesbit, *Christ, Christians, and Christianity. Book I. Jesus an Essene*.

J. H. Newman, *Apologia Pro Vita Sua*.

Order for Daily Evening Prayer.

W. Paley, *View of the Evidences of Christianity*.

F. Parkman, *Old Régime in Canada* (marginalia).

H. V. M. Phelips, *Churches and Modern Thought; An Inquiry into the Grounds of Unbelief and an Appeal for Candour*.

W. C. Prime, *Boat Life in Egypt and Nubia* (marginalia).

A. D. F. Randolph (comp.), *Changed Cross, and Other Religious Poems*.

A. D. F. Randolph (comp.), *Shadow of the Rock, and Other Religious Poems*.

[J.] E. Renan, *L'Abesse de Jouarre* (play).

F. W. Robertson, *Life, Letters, and Addresses of Fredk. W. Robertson, M.A., Incumbent of Trinity Chapel, Brighton, 1847–53*.

H. E. Rood, *Hardwicke; A Novel*.

T. Roosevelt, *Square Deal* (marginalia).

W. H. Rule, *History of the Inquisition from Its Establishment in the Twelfth Century to Its Extinction in the Nineteenth*.

C. T. Russell, *Millennial Dawn*.

Salvation Through Grace [or] *Salvation by Grace* (unidentified book).

E. B. Sanford (ed.), *Concise Cyclopedia of Religious Knowledge, Biblical, Theological, Historical, and Practical*.

I. D. Sankey (Catalog entry).

C. von Schmid, *Genovefa*.

C. von Schmid, *Gute Fridolin und der böse Dietrich*.

M. W. Sewell, *"Our Father's Care" (A Ballad)*.

P. N. Shuttleworth, *Consistency of Revelation with Itself and with Human Reason*.

H. Sienkiewicz. *"Quo Vadis": A Narrative of the Time of Nero* (novel).

L. H. H. Sigourney, *Memoir of Mary Ann Hooker*.

"Sixtus" (pseud.), *Progressive Protestantism*.

"Sixtus" (pseud.), *Review of Professor Briggs' Inaugural Address*.

A. Smith, *Edwin of Deira* (poem).

G. Spring, *Fragments from the Study of a Pastor*.

E. T. Stephenson, *St. Olave's. A Novel*.

J. Stern, "Translation from the German" (poems).

H. E. B. Stowe, *Religious Poems*.

E. Swedenborg, *Heaven and Hell*.

T. D. W. Talmage, *Sermons. Second Series* (and other titles).

L. N. Tolstoy, *My Religion*.

L. N. Tolstoy, *Teaching of Jesus*.

S. H. Tyng, *Office and Duty of a Christian Pastor*.

T. C. Upham, *Life of Faith; in Three Parts, Embracing Some of the Scriptural Principles or Doctrines of Faith* (marginalia).

G. W. Warder, *Cities of the Sun* (Catalog entry).

J. Weiss, *Paul and Jesus*.

R. B. Westbrook, *Girard's Will and Girard College Theology* (marginalia).

A. D. White, *History of the Warfare of Science with Theology* (marginalia).

F. Wilkinson, *Strength of the Hills; A Novel*.

N. P. S. Wiseman, *Fabiola; or, The Church of the Catacombs*.

C. Zueblin, *Religion of a Democrat*.

See also the Reader's Guide entries for Afterlife, for Agnosticism, for Atheism, for Bible, for Christ, for Christianity and comparative religions, for Christmas, for Holy Land, for Inquisition, for Missionaries, for New Testament studies, for Palestine, for Prayer, for Religious persecution, for Sermons, and for individual denominations such as Catholicism or Presbyterianism.

Christianity and comparative religions: see

J. M. Baldwin, *Story of the Mind* (marginalia).

K. B. Birkeland, *Light in the Darkness; or, Christianity and Paganism*.

D. Brewster, *Martyrs of Science; or, The Lives of Galileo, Tycho Brahe, and Kepler*.

J. M. Buckley, *History of Methodism in the United States.*

J. W. Chadwick, *Old and New Unitarian Belief.*

M. D. Conway, *Sacred Anthology: A Book of Ethnical Scriptures, Collected and Edited by Moncure Daniel Conway* (marginalia).

C. Darwin, *Journal of Researches into the Natural History and Geology of the Countries Visited During the Voyage of the H.M.S. Beagle Round the World* (marginalia).

W. J. Dawson (co-ed.), *Great English Letter-Writers* (marginalia).

S. Dill, *Roman Society in the Last Century of the Western Empire* (marginalia).

T. W. Doane, *Bible Myths and Their Parallels in Other Religions* (marginalia).

R. I. Dodge, *Our Wild Indians: Thirty-Three Years' Personal Experience among the Red Men of the Great West* (marginalia).

H. Drummond, *Greatest Thing in the World. An Address.*

Great Religions of the World.

W. James, *Varieties of Religious Experience; A Study in Human Nature.*

W. H. Mallock, *New Republic; or, Culture, Faith, and Philosophy in an English Country House.*

W. H. Mallock, *Reconstruction of Religious Belief.*

G. S. Merriam, *A Living Faith.*

G. Negri, *Julian the Apostate* (marginalia).

R. K. Noyes, *Views of Religion, Collected by Rufus K. Noyes, M. D.*

F. Parkman, *Jesuits in North America in the Seventeenth Century.*

F. Parkman, *Old Régime in Canada* (marginalia).

W. M. F. Petrie, *Personal Religion in Egypt Before Christianity.*

Plutarchus, *Plutarch's Lives of Illustrious Men* (marginalia).

H. Pyle, *Rejected of Men; A Story of To-day* (marginalia).

E. Reich, *Success Among Nations.*

J. W. Sanborn, *Legends, Customs and Social Life of the Seneca Indians of Western New York* (Catalog entry).

E. B. Sanford (ed.), *Concise Cyclopedia of Religious Knowledge, Biblical, Theological, Historical, and Practical.*

N. S. Shaler, *Aspects of the Earth: A Popular Account of Some Familiar Geological Phenomena.*

E. C. Stanton (ed.), *Woman's Bible.*

W. W. Story, *Roba di Roma.*

Tacitus, *Works of Tacitus* (marginalia).

F. Thompson, *Shelley* (marginalia).

S. E. Titcomb, *Aryan Sun-Myths: The Origin of Religions* (marginalia).

M. W. Townsend, *Asia and Europe: Studies* (marginalia).

T. E. Watson, *Story of France, from the Earliest Times to the Consulate of Napoleon Bonaparte* (marginalia).

A. D. White, *History of the Warfare of Science with Theology.*

W. H. White, *Autobiography of Mark Rutherford, Dissenting Minister.*

W. H. White, *Mark Rutherford's Deliverance; Being the Second Part of His Autobiography.*

See also the Reader's Guide entries for Agnosticism, for Afterlife, for Bible, for Christ, for Christianity, for Hinduism, for Holy Land, for Islam, for New Testament studies, for Palestine, for Religious persecution, and for Science and religion.

Christianity and the New Idealism: A Study in the Religious Philosophy of To-day. R. C. Eucken.

Christian martyrs: see the Reader's Guide entries for Christianity and comparative religions, for Missionaries, and for Religious persecution.

Christian Martyrs under Constantine and Maxentius (play). J. Brougham.

Christian, Mollie Griswold (co-author): see E. Christian (co-author), *Uncooked Foods & How to Use Them.*

Christian Nurture. H. Bushnell.

Christian Philanthropist. A Sketch of the Life of Mr. Daniel Hand, and of His Benefaction to the American Missionary Association, for the Education of the Colored People in the Southern States of America. G. A. Wilcox.

Christian, Princess (trans., ed.): see F. S. Wilhelmina, *Memoirs of Frederica Sophia Wilhelmina.*

"Christian Religion" (essay). R. G. Ingersoll.

Christian Science: see

E. H. G. Clark, *Church of St. Bunco.*

M. J. Crim, *Elizabeth, Christian Scientist.*

W. De Voe, *Healing Currents from the Battery of Life.*

R. J. Ebbard, *How to Acquire and Strengthen Will-Power: Modern Psycho- Therapy.*

S. J. Hanna, *Christian Science History.*

E. R. Hardy, "Restoration" (article).

E. G. Hubbard, *Man of Sorrows. Being a Little Journey to the Home of Jesus of Nazareth* (marginalia).

R. D. Kathrens, *Side Lights on Mary Baker Eddy-Glover-Science Church Trustees Controversy. "Next Friends" Suit.*

Life Within (anonymous novel).

E. I. Lindh (article).

Literary Digest.

R. H. Newton, *Christian Science; The Truths of Spiritual Healing and Their Contribution to the Growth of Orthodoxy.*

W. A. Purrington, *Christian Science; An Exposition of Mrs. Eddy's Wonderful Discovery, including Its Legal Aspects.*

J. D. Quackenbos, *Hypnotic Therapeutics in Theory and Practice, with Numerous Illustrations of Treatment by Suggestion.*

C. E. J. G. de V. Rémusat, *Memoirs of Madame de Rémusat, 1802–1808* (Catalog entry).

O. C. Sabin, *Christology—Science of Health and Happiness; or, Metaphysical Healing Exemplified—Through Rules, Formulas and Incidents.*

J. T. Umsted, *Plea for the Priority of Domestic Missions.*

See also the Reader's Guide entries for Mary Baker Eddy and for Spiritualism and spiritual healing.

Christian Science; An Exposition of Mrs. Eddy's Wonderful Discovery, including Its Legal Aspects. W. A. Purrington.

Christian Science History. S. J. Hanna.

Christian Science; The Truths of Spiritual Healing and Their Contribution to the Growth of Orthodoxy. R. H. Newton.

Christian's Mistake. D. M. M. Craik.

Christian theosophy: see the Reader's Guide entry for Theosophy.

Christmas: see

C. F. H. Alexander, "Once in royal David's city" (Christmas carol).

C. Dickens, *Christmas Books.*

C. Dickens, *Christmas Carol in Prose.*

C. Dickens, *Master Humphrey's Clock, New Christmas Stories.*

T. W. Doane, *Bible Myths and Their Parallels in Other Religions* (marginalia).

N. Hawthorne, "Christmas Banquet" (short story).

J. H. Hopkins, Jr., "We three kings of Orient" (Christmas carol).

W. D. Howells, *Christmas Every Day and Other Stories Told for Children.*

W. D. Howells, "Christmas Spirit" (poem).

W. Irving, *Old Christmas and Bracebridge Hall.*

T. A. Janvier, *Christmas Kalends of Provence and Some Other Provençal Festivals.*

Krippen-Kalender 1899—47.

H. W. Longfellow, "Hemlock Tree" (poem).

R. E. MacAlarney, "Tim Rafferty's Romance: A Story of Christmas among 'The Finest.'"

C. C. Moore, "Night Before Christmas" (poem).

W. D. Nesbit, *Land of Make-Believe, and Other Christmas Poems.*

New York *Tribune* (Catalog entry).

A. B. Paine, "Christmas Luck" (short story).

W. Scott, *Christmas in the Olden Time.*

F. R. Stockton, *Stockton's Stories. Second Series. The Christmas Wreck and Other Stories.*

H. E. B. Stowe, *Betty's Bright Idea. Also, Deacon Pitkin's Farm, and the First Christmas of New England.*

B. Tarkington, *Beasley's Christmas Party.*

W. H. Venable, *Tom Tad.*

L. Wallace, *First Christmas, from "Ben-Hur."*

C. D. Warner, *As We Were Saying* (essays).

Weihnacht Abend.

C. Wesley, "Hark! the herald angels sing" (Christmas carol).

"Christmas Banquet" (short story). N. Hawthorne.

Christmas Books. C. Dickens.

Christmas Carol in Prose. C. Dickens.

Christmas Eve: see the Catalog entry for *Weihnacht Abend.*

Christmas Every Day and Other Stories Told for Children. W. D. Howells.

"Christmas hymn" (hymn): see E. H. Sears, "Calm on the listening ear of night."

Christmas in the Olden Time. W. Scott.

Christmas Kalends of Provence and Some Other Provençal Festivals. T. A. Janvier.

"Christmas Luck" (short story). A. B. Paine.

"Christmas Spirit" (poem). W. D. Howells.

Christology—Science of Health and Happiness; or,

Metaphysical Healing Exemplified—Through Rules, Formulas and Incidents. O. C. Sabin.

Christomanos, Constantin: see K. Chrēstomanos.

Christy, George: see *Schermerhorn's Boy.*

Christy, Howard Chandler (illus.): see

(co-illus.) W. D. Howells, *Heroines of Fiction.*

(co-illus.) E. S. Martin, *Courtship of a Careful Man, and a Few Other Courtships.*

M. Nicholson, *House of a Thousand Candles.*

F. Palmer, *Ways of the Service.*

M. A. A. Ward, *Lady Rose's Daughter, A Novel.*

Chronicle of Henry of Huntingdon. Henry of Huntingdon.

Chronicle of the Cid: see *The Cid.*

Chronicle of the Kings of England, from the Time of the Romans Government, unto the Death of King James the First. R. Baker.

Chronicles and Characters. E. R. B. Lytton.

Chronicles of Carlingford. M. O. W. Oliphant.

Chronicles of England, France, Spain, and the Adjoining Countries, from the Latter Part of the Reign of Edward II. To the Coronation of Henry IV. J. Froissart.

Chronicles of the Little Tot. E. V. Cooke.

Chrystal, Jack, & Co., and Delta Bixby; Two Stories. C. K. Munroe.

Chubb, Percival (ed.): see W. D. Howells, *Boy Life; Stories and Readings Selected from the Works of William Dean Howells.*

Chuquet, Arthur (intro.): see A. F. F. de Frénilly, *Recollections of Baron de Frénilly, Peer of France (1768- 1828).*

Church, Alfred John (trans. and ed.): see Herodotus, *Stories of the East.*

Church, Frederick Stuart (illus.): see

(co-illus.) J. C. Harris, *Uncle Remus: His Songs and His Sayings.*

(illus.) G. T. Lanigan, *Fables by G. Washington Aesop, Taken "Anywhere, Anywhere, Out of the World."*

(co-illus.) A. Tennyson, *Lady Clare.*

Churches and Modern Thought; An inquiry into the Grounds of Unbelief and an Appeal for Candour. H. V. M. Phelips.

"Church has waited long" (hymn). H. Bonar.

Churchill, Lord Randolph: see A. P. Primrose, *Lord Randolph Churchill.*

Churchill, Winston Spencer (political statesman): see

A. P. Primrose, *Lord Randolph Churchill.*

A. C. Waghorne, *Through a Peer Glass: Winnie's Adventures in Wastemonster.*

Church of England: see

G. Combe, *Notes on the United States of North America, During a Phrenological Visit in 1838–9-40* (marginalia).

H. Evans, *Our Old Nobility.*

M. Fowler, *Some Notable Archbishops of Canterbury.*

S. Grand, *Heavenly Twins* (marginalia).

M. Lonsdale, *Sister Dora. A Biography.*

F. M. Trollope, *Domestic Manners of the Americans* (marginalia).

Church of St. Bunco. G. Clark.

Chūshingura: see T. Shunsui, *Loyal Ronins: An Historical Romance, Translated from the Japanese.*

Cincinnati, Ohio: see

F. Marryat, *Second Series of a Diary in America*.

F. M. Trollope, *Domestic Manners of the Americans* (marginalia).

C. D. Warner, *Studies in the South and West, with Comments on Canada*.

"Yankee Doodle" (song) (Catalog entry).

"Circle in the Water" (story): see W. D. Howells, *Pair of Patient Lovers*.

Circumstantial Evidence, and Other Stories. F. J. Fargus.

Circus: see J. O. Kaler, *Toby Tyler; or, Ten Weeks with a Circus*.

Cities of the Sun. G. W. Warder.

Citizen Bird; Scenes from Bird-Life. M. O. Wright.

Citizen of the World. O. Goldsmith.

City and State (weekly magazine): see the Catalog entry for H. Welsh.

City-Ballads. W. Carleton.

City Boys in the Woods; or, A Trapping Venture in Maine. H. P. Wells.

City directories: see the Reader's Guide entry for Directories.

City Festivals. W. Carleton.

City of Success, and Other Poems. H. Abbey.

City of the Great King; or, Jerusalem As It Was, As It Is, and As It Is To Be. J. T. Barclay.

City That Was; A Requiem of Old San Francisco. W. H. Irwin.

"Civil Disobedience" (essay). H. Thoreau.

Civilization in the United States: First and Last Impressions of America. M. Arnold.

Civil War (American): see

J. S. C. Abbott, "Heroic Deeds of Heroic Men" (series of articles).

J. S. C. Abbott, *History of the Civil War in America*.

American Nation: A History from Original Sources by Associated Scholars. A. B. Hart (ed.).

J. Barber, *War Letters of a Disbanded Volunteer, Embracing His Experiences as Honest Old Abe's Bosom Friend and Unofficial Adviser*.

J. Barnes, *Son of Light Horse Harry*.

J. Bigelow, *Principles of Strategy, Illustrated Mainly from American Campaigns*.

W. C. Bryant (co-author), *Popular History of the United States, from the First Discovery of the Western Hemisphere by the Northmen, to the End of the Civil War*.

L. E. Chittenden, *Recollections of President Lincoln and His Administration*.

C. C. Coffin, *Drum-Beat of the Nation: The First Period of the War of the Rebellion*.

C. C. Coffin, *Marching to Victory: The Second Period of the War of Rebellion*.

C. C. Coffin, *Redeeming the Republic: The Third Period of the War of the Rebellion*.

A. W. Colton, *"Debatable Land." A Novel*.

H. Coppée, *Grant and His Campaigns: A Military Biography*.

S. W. Crawford, *Genesis of the Civil War: The Story of Sumter, 1860–1861*.

M. J. Crim, *Adventures of a Fair Rebel*.

G. Davis (Catalog entry).

H. C. Dean, *Crimes of the Civil War, and Curse of the Funding System*.

M. A. Dodge, *Skirmishes and Sketches*.

S. E. E. Edmundson, *Nurse and Spy in the Union Army*.

H. Garland, *Ulysses S. Grant, His Life and Character*.

G. H. Gordon, *War Diary of Events in the War of the Great Rebellion, 1863–1865*.

U. S. Grant, *Personal Memoirs of U. S. Grant*.

J. L. Greene, *Gen. William B. Franklin and the Operations of the Left Wing at the Battle of Fredericksburg, December 13, 1862*.

A. R. Hancock, *Reminiscences of Winfield Scott Hancock. By His Wife*.

J. C. Harris, *On the Wing of Occasions; Being the Authorized Version of Certain Curious Episodes of the Late Civil War*.

J. T. Headley, *Great Rebellion: A History of the Civil War in the United States*.

T. W. S. Higginson, *History of the United States from 986 to 1905* (marginalia).

R. Hitchcock (ed.), *Decisive Battles of America*.

J. K. Hosmer, *Outcome of the Civil War, 1863–1865*: see *American Nation: A History from Original Sources by Associated Scholars*. A. B. Hart (ed.).

W. D. Howells (co-ed.), *Library of Universal Adventure by Sea and Land*.

R. U. Johnson and C. C. Buel (eds.), *Battles and Leaders of the Civil War*.

R. H. Kellogg, *Life and Death in Rebel Prisons: Giving a Complete History of the Inhuman and Barbarous Treatment of Our Brave Soldiers by Rebel Authorities*.

C. King, *Between the Lines, A Story of the War* (novel).

C. King, *War-Time Wooing; A Story*.

R. E. Lee, *Recollections and Letters of General Robert E. Lee, by His Son*.

G. B. McClellan, *McClellan's Own Story: The War for the Union*.

G. Morris, *Aladdin O'Brien* (novel).

P. F. Mottelay and T. Campbell-Copeland (eds.), *Soldier in Our Civil War: A Pictorial History of the Conflict, 1861–65*.

L.-P.-A.-d' O. Paris, *History of the Civil War in America*.

A. Pinkerton, *Spy of the Rebellion; Being A True History of the Spy System of the United States Army During the Late Rebellion*.

J. Pope, "Second Battle of Bull Run" (article).

H. Pyle, *Yankee Doodle, An Old Friend in a New Dress* (Catalog entry).

W. Reid, *Ohio in the War: Her Statesmen, Generals, and Soldiers*.

A. D. Richardson, *Secret Service: The Field, the Dungeon, and the Escape*.

E. Robins, *Open Question; A Tale of Two Temperaments*.

F. B. Sanborn (ed.), *Life and Letters of John Brown, Liberator of Kansas and Martyr of Virginia*.

J. Scott, *Partisan Life with Col. John S. Mosby*.

P. H. Sheridan, *Personal Memoirs of P. H. Sheridan, General, United States Army*.

W. T. Sherman, *Memoirs of General William T. Sherman. By Himself.*

W. T. Sherman, *Memoirs of General W. T. Sherman, Written by Himself.*

W. O. Stoddard, *Inside the White House in War Times.*

H. E. B. Stowe, *House and home Papers.*

R. Taylor, *Destruction and Reconstruction: Personal Experiences of the Late War.*

W. J. Vance, *God's War* (novel).

W. H. Van Nortwick, *Yanks and Johnnies; or, Laugh and Grow Fat.*

L. J. Velazquez, *Woman in Battle: A Narrative of the Exploits, Adventures, and Travels of Madame Loreta Janeta Velazquez, Otherwise Known as Lieutenant Harry T. Buford, Confederate States Army.*

J. Verne, *Mysterious Island.*

W. F. Vilas (Catalog entry).

G. E. Waring, Jr., *Whip and Spur.*

J. T. Wilson, *Black Phalanx; A History of the Negro Soldiers of the United States in the Wars of 1775–1812, 1861-'65.*

J. S. Woolsey, *Hospital Days.*

J. A. Wyeth, *Life of General Nathan Bedford Forrest.*

See also the Reader's Guide entries for Civil War poems and songs and for Reconstruction in the American South.

Civil War poems and songs: see

E. L. Beers, "Picket-Guard" (poem, song), better known as "All Quiet on the Potomac Tonight."

H. H. Brownell (poet).

S. H. M. Byers, *Happy Isles, and Other Poems.*

P. S. Gilmore, "When Johnny comes marching home" (song).

"Happy land of Canaan" (song).

Harper's Pictorial History of the War with Spain (laid in sheet of notes).

B. Harte, "John Burns of Gettysbury" (poem).

"John Brown's body" (song).

J. W. Riley, *Armazindy.*

G. F. Root, Battle cry of freedom" (song, better known as "Rally round the flag").

G. F. Root, "Just before the battle, Mother" (song).

G. F. Root, "Tramp! tramp! tramp!" (song).

C. C. Sawyer, "Weeping, sad, and lonely; or, when this cruel war is over" (song).

W. G. Simms (ed.), *War Poetry of the South.*

E. C. Stedman, *Lyrics and Idylls, with Other Poems.*

R. G. White (ed.), *Poetry Lyrical, Narrative, and Satirical of the Civil War.*

H. C. Work, "Kingdom coming" (song).

H. C. Work, "Marching through Georgia" (song).

"Yankee Doodle" (song) (Catalog entry).

See also the Reader's Guide entries for Civil War (American) and for Reconstruction in the American South.

Civil War (English): see the Reader's Guide entry for Oliver Cromwell.

Clapp, Eva Katharine: see E. K. C. Gibson.

"Clare, Sister Mary Francis" (pseud.): see M. F. Cusack.

Clari; or, The Maid of Milan (operetta): see J. H. Payne, "Home, sweet home."

Clarissa; or, The History of a Young Lady (novel). S. Richardson.

Clark, Kate Upson: see the Catalog entry for A. E. Trumbull, "Mary A. Twining."

Clark, Marie Jewell (illus.): see G. E. Lewis, *Heart Echoes.*

Clark, Walter Appleton (illus.): see M W. C. Deland, *Awakening of Helena Richie.*

Clarke, James Freeman (ed.): see M. Fuller, *Memoirs of Margaret Fuller Ossoli.* Ed. William Henry Channing, Ralph Waldo Emerson, James Freeman Clarke.

Clarke, Joseph Thacher (trans.): see Munich. Pinakothek, Alte. *Catalogue of the Paintings in the Old Pinakothek, Munich.*

Clarke, Marcus Andrew Hislop (intro.): see A. L. Gordon, *Poems.*

Clarkson, Thomas: see T. W. S. Higginson, *Cheerful Yesterdays. Contemporaries* (marginalia).

Classical Dictionary, Containing an Account of the Principal Proper Names Mentioned in Ancient Authors. C. Anthon.

Classical Dictionary of the Vulgar Tongue. F. Grose.

Classic Tales. M. Edgeworth.

Class struggle: see the Reader's Guide entries for American social classes, for Economics and labor issues, for English social classes, and for French social classes.

Clay, Henry: see

D. B. Lucas and J. F. McLaughlin, *Fisher Ames-Henry Clay, Etc.*

C. Schurz, *Life of Henry Clay.*

Cleg Kelly, Arab of the City. S. R. Crockett.

Clemens, Arretinus: see Tacitus, *Works of Tacitus* (marginalia).

Clemens, Clara: see R. Grau, *Forty Years Observation of Music and the Drama by Robert Grau* (Catalog entry).

Clemens, Flavius: see Suetonius, *Lives of the Twelve Caesars* (marginalia).

Clemens, Jenny (ownership): see F. O. C. Darley, *People of America.*

Clemens, Jenny (ownership): see *Young Artists, and Other Stories.*

Clemens, Olivia (Langdon): see

T. Bulfinch, *Age of Fable; or, Beauties of Mythology* (marginalia).

M. D. Conway, *Autobiography: Memories and Experiences of Moncure Daniel Conway* (marginalia).

O. W. Holmes, *Autocrat of the Breakfast-Table* (marginalia).

G. O. Trevelyan, *Life and Letters of Lord Macaulay* (marginalia).

Clemens, Orion: see

(ed.) *Keokuk Directory.*

(ownership) J. P. Norton, *Elements of Scientific Agriculture.*

(ownership) *Galaxy. An Illustrated Magazine of Entertaining Reading.*

J. T. Umstead, *Plea for the Priority of Domestic Missions; A Discourse Delivered Before the Synod of Iowa, in Burlington, Oct. 12, 1856.*

Clemens, Samuel Langhorne: see the Reader's Guide entries for Dedications to Mark Twain and for "Twain, Mark" (pseud.).

Clemens, Susy: see
  R. Kipling, *Light That Failed* (Catalog entry).
  A. Tennyson, *Idylls of the King*.
  G. O. Trevelyan, *Life and Letters of Lord Macaulay*.
Clemens, Will Montgomery: see the Catalog entry for Charlotte (Perkins) Gilman.
Clements, Ruth Sypherd (illus.): see B. Tarkington, *Beasley's Christmas Party*.
Clemm, Maria: see (pref.) E. A. Poe, *Works of the Late Edgar Allan Poe*.
"Cleopatra" (poem). W. W. Story.
Cleopatra: see A. E. Trumbull, *Wheel of Progress* (play).
Cleveland and Stevenson: Their Lives and Record. T. Campbell-Copeland.
Cleveland, Grover: see H. W. Scott, *Distinguished Lawyers*.
"Clifford, Mrs. W. K." (pseud.): see L. L. Clifford.
Clifton, William (comp.): see F. Steers, "Last link is broken" (song).
Clinton, Emma A. (trans.): see A. M. A. Aníchkova, *Shadow of the House*.
"Clive" (poem): see R. Browning.
"Clive" (poem): see R. Browning, *Agamemnon*.
Clive, Robert: see
  T. B. Macaulay, *Critical and Miscellaneous Essays* (marginalia).
  T. B. Macaulay, "Essay on Lord Clive."
Clockmaker, or Sayings and Doings of Sam Slick. T. C. Haliburton.
Cloister and the Hearth; or, Maid, Wife, and Widow: A Matter-of-Fact Romance. C. Reade.
Clotelle; or, The Colored Heroine. W. W. Brown.
Cloth of Gold and Other Poems. T. B. Aldrich.
Clough, Arthur Hugh (ed.): see Plutarchus, *Lives of Illustrious Men*.
Club of Queer Trades. G. K. Chesterton.
Clubs and Club Life in London, with Anecdotes. J. Timbs.
Clytemestra (literary figure): see the Catalog entry for Walter Scott.
Coan, Titus Munson, M. D.: see *Galaxy. An Illustrated Magazine of Entertaining Reading*.
Coast of Bohemia. W. D. Howells.
Cobden, Richard: see J. Morley, *Life of Richard Cobden*.
Coburn, Frederick Simpson (illus.): see
  W. H. Drummond, *Great Fight. Poems and Sketches*.
  W. H. Drummond, *Habitant, and Other French-Canadian Poems*.
Cobwebs from a Library Corner. J. K. Bangs.
Cobwebs from an Empty Skull. A. Bierce.
Coca plant: see
  W. L. Herndon, *Exploration of the Valley of the Amazon*.
  W. G. Mortimer, *Peru: History of Coca, "The Divine Plant" of the Incas*.
Cochin-China (Vietnam): see F. Vincent, *Land of the White Elephant: Sights and Scenes in South-eastern Asia. A Personal Narrative of Travel and Adventure in Farther India, Embracing the Countries of Burma, Siam, Cambodia, and Cochin-China*.
Cocks, Charles (trans.): see J. Michelet, *Historical View of the French Revolution*.
Coffee and Repartee. J. K. Bangs.

Cokain, Aston: see *Dramatists of the Restoration*.
Colby, Frank Moore (co-ed.): see *New International Encyclopaedia*.
Cold Dishes for Hot Weather. Ysaguirre (pseud.) and La Marca (pseud.).
Cole, George Ralph Fitz-Roy (ed.): see J. Jònsonn, "Jòn Jònsonn's Saga: The Genuine Autobiography of a Modern Icelander."
Coleman, Alexis Irénée DuPont (trans.): see M. Maeterlinck, *Monna Vanna, A Play in Three Acts*.
Coleman, Ann Mary Butler (Crittenden) (trans.): see
  K. M. Mundt, *Berlin and Sans-Souci; or, Frederick the Great and His Friends. An Historical Romance*.
  K. M. Mundt, *Frederick the Great and His Court. An Historical Romance*.
Coleridge, Derwent (co-ed.): see S. T. Coleridge, *Poems of Samuel Taylor Coleridge*.
Coleridge, Edith (ed.): see S. C. Coleridge, *Memoir and Letters of Sara Coleridge*.
Coleridge, Edward Philip (trans., ed.): see Euripides, *Plays of Euripides*.
Coleridge, Samuel Taylor: see W. J. Dawson (co-ed.), *Great English Letter-Writers* (marginalia).
Coleridge, Sara (co-ed.): see S. T. Coleridge, *Poems of Samuel Taylor Coleridge*.
"Collaborators" (story). R. S. Hichens.
Collected Poems of Dora Sigerson Shorter. D. S. Shorter.
Collected Verse of Rudyard Kipling. R. Kipling.
Collection of Hymns, for the Use of the People Called Methodists. J. Wesley.
College Chaps. J. Weymouth.
College Series of French Plays; With English Notes. F. Bôcher (ed.).
College Tramps: A Narrative of the Adventures of a Party of Yale Students During a Summer Vacation in Europe, with Knapsack and Alpenstock, and the Incidents of a Voyage to Rotterdam and Return. F. A. Stokes.
Collier, John Payne (trans.): see J. C. F. von Schiller, *Fight with the Dragon. A Romance*.
Colonel Carter of Cartersville (novel). F. H. Smith.
Colonel Greatheart. H. C. Bailey.
Colonel's Money. L. C. W. Lillie.
Colonel's Opera Cloak. C. C. Brush.
Colonial Children. A. B. Hart (co-ed.).
Colonialism: see
  P. Bigelow, *Children of the Nations; A Study of Colonization*.
  P. Blouet, *John Bull & Co.; The Great Colonial Branches of the Firm*.
  W. F. Collier, *History of the British Empire*.
  A. R. Colquhoun, *Greater America*.
  E. H. Crosby, *Captain Jinks, Hero*.
  E. H. Crosby, *Swords and Ploughshares* (poems).
  J. A. Froude, *Oceana, or England and Her Colonies*.
  S. S. Hunter, *Imperial Gazetteer of India*.
  A. Ireland, *Far Eastern Tropics: Studies in the Administration of Tropical Dependencies*.
  J. S. Keay, "Spoliation of India" (series of articles).
  C. Kingsley, *Westward Ho!* (novel).
  R. Kipling, "Naulahka" (poem).
  R. Kipling, *Naulahka, A Story of the West and East*.

E. D. Mead, "A Righteous Setting Forth" (article).

F. M. Müller, *India: What Can It Teach Us?*

S. Newland, *Paving the Way: A Romance of the Australian Brush.*

E. Reich, *Success Among Nations.*

C. Schurz, *American Imperialism.*

C. Schurz, *For Truth, Justice and Liberty.*

J. R. Seeley, *Expansion of England; Two Courses of Lectures.*

L. Strachey, "Progressional" (satirical poem).

W. T. M. Torrens, *Empire in Asia, How We Came by It: A Book of Confessions.*

H. Welsh (Catalog entry).

H. P. Willis, *Our Philippine Problem; A Study of American Colonial Policy.*

C. E. S. Wood, *Masque of Love* (poem) (Catalog entry).

See also the Reader's Guide entries for specific countries.

Colombe's Birthday (poem): see R. Browning, *Dramas.*

Colorado: see C. W. Dilke, *Greater Britain: A Record of Travel in English-Speaking Countries During 1866 and 1867.*

Colorphobia. An Exposure of the "White Australia" Fallacy. E. W. Foxall.

Columbia University: see the Catalog entries for N. M. Butler and for B. Matthews.

Columbus, Christopher (explorer): see
 C. C. Coffin, *Story of Liberty.*
 L. De Forest (ed.), *Indian Domestic Architecture* (laid in article).
 W. Irving, *History of the Life and Voyages of Christopher Columbus.*
 F. A. Ober, *Columbus the Discoverer.*
 J. C. Van Dyke, "Lotto Portrait of Columbus" (essay).

Columbus the Discoverer. F. A. Ober.

Colvin, Sidney (ed.): see R. L. Stevenson, *Letters of Robert Louis Stevenson to His Family and Friends.*

"Come all ye young fellows" (song): see "Roll a man down" (song).

"Come Creative Spirit" (hymn): see "Veni Creator Spiritus" (hymn).

Comedy of Errors (play). W. Shakespeare.

Comedy of Human Life. H. de Balzac.

"Come, Gentle Trembler" (poem). T. B. Read.

"Come thou fount of every blessing" (hymn). R. Robinson.

"Come, ye sinners, poor and needy" (hymn). J. Hart.

Comets: see the Reader's Guide entry for Astronomy.

Coming of Billy. M. Westrup.

Coming of K—: A Set of Idyll Lays. A. A. Dowty.

Coming Race; or, the New Utopia. E. G. E. B. Lytton.

"Comin' thro' the rye" (song). R. Burns.

Commentaries. G. J. Caesar.

Commines, Philippe de: see P. de Commynes, *Memoirs of Philip de Commines, Lord of Argenton.*

Commodore Rollingpin's Humorous Illustrated Almanac. J. H. Carter.

Commodus (play): see L. Wallace, *Wooing of Malkatoon. Commodus.*

Commodus, Aelius Aurelius (Roman empire): see L. Wallace, *Wooing of Malkatoon. Commodus.*

Common Prayer: see
 Book of Common Prayer.
 Order for Daily Evening Prayer.

Common Salt: Its Use and Necessity for the Maintenance of Health and the Prevention of Disease. C. G. Gümpel.

Common Sense (pamphlet). T. Paine.

Common Sense in the Household: A Manual of Practical Housewifery. M. V. H. Terhune.

Common Shells of the Sea-shore. J. G. Wood.

Communism: see the Reader's Guide entry for Economics and labor issues.

Compendio di storia della letteratura Italiana ad uso delle scuole secondarie. F. Flamini (ed.).

Complaint; or, Night Thoughts on Life, Death, and Immortality. A. Young.

Complete Concordance to Shakespeare. M. V. C. Clarke.

Complete Exposé of Eddyism or Christian Science and the Plain Truth in Plain Terms Regarding Mary Baker G. Eddy, Founder of Christian Science. F. W. Peabody.

Complete Illustrated Catalogue: see London. National Gallery in the Catalog.

Complete Phonographer, and Reporter's Guide: An Inductive Exposition of Phonography, with Its Application to All Branches of Reporting. J. E. Munson.

Complete Poetical Works of Robert Southey, LL.D. (Late Poet Laureate.). R. Southey.

Complete Poetical Works of John Greenleaf Whittier. J. G. Whittier.

Complete Works. S. T. Coleridge.

Complete Works of John Bunyan. J. Bunyan.

Complete Works of Nathaniel Hawthorne. N. Hawthorne.

Complete Works of Samuel Taylor Coleridge. S. T. Coleridge.

Complete Works of William Shakespeare. W. Shakespeare.

Composite novels: see
 P. L. Ford (ed.), *House Party: An Account of the Stories Told at a Gathering of Famous American Authors.*
 Whole Family; A Novel by Twelve Authors.

Compositions in Outline . . . from Hawthorne's Scarlet Letter. F. O. C. Darley.

Compositions in Outline . . . from Judd's Margaret. F. O. C. Darley.

Compromises of Life, and Other Lectures and Addresses, Including Some Observations on Certain Downward Tendencies of Modern Society. H. Watterson.

Conant, Thomas Jefferson (comp.): see *A General and Analytical Index to Appletons' Annual Cyclopaedia.*

Conchology: see
 J. G. Wood, *Common Shells of the Sea-shore.*
 W. Wood, *General Conchology; or, A Description of Shells, Arranged According to the Linnean System.*

Concise Cyclopedia of Religious Knowledge, Biblical, Theological, Historical, and Practical. E. B. Sanford (ed.).

Concise Dictionary of the Bible, for the Use of Families and Students. W. Smith (ed.).

Concise History of France. F. P. G. Guizot.

Concise Review of Recent Events. A. W. Tourgée.

Concordance to Shakespeare. M. V. Clarke.

"Concord Hymn" (poem): see R. W. Emerson, "Hymn Sung at the Completion of the Concord Monument."

Concord, Massachusetts: see G. W. Curtis, *Early Letters of George Wm. Curtis to John S. Dwight; Brook Farm and Concord.*

Condensed Manual on Patented Inventions: What to Do and What Not to Do to Insure Success to the Inventor. M. L. Wynkoop.

Condensed Novels. B. Harte.

Condition of Labor. An Open Letter to Pope Leo XIII. H. George.

Confessions. J. J. Rousseau.

Confessions of a Thug. P. M. Taylor.

Confidence. H. James.

Conflict of the Ages; or, The Great Debate on the Moral Relations of God and Man. E. Beecher.

Confucianism: see
Great Religions of the World (marginalia).
Socrates (Catalog entry).

Congo: see
R. D. Casement, *Treatment of Women and Children in the Congo State.*
A. C. Doyle, *Crime of the Congo.*
Memorial Concerning Conditions in the Independent State of the Kongo. April 19, 1904.
E. D. Morel, *King Leopold's Rule in Africa.*
E. D. Morel, *Red Rubber; The Story of the Rubber Slave Trade Flourishing on the Congo in the Year of Grace 1906.*
J. Morley, *Life of Richard Cobden.*
W. M. Morrison, "Report by W. M. Morrison, American Missionary in the Congo Free State" (unidentified publication).
B. H. Nadal, "A Czar—1905" (poem).
Report of the Commission of Inquiry on the Belgian Congo.
H. L. Samuel (Catalog entry).
A. E. Scrivener, "Instances of Belgian Cruelty in Africa" (article).
W. H. Sheppard (unidentified author).
L. M. Sill, "To the Czar" (poem).
Suetonius, *Lives of the Twelve Caesars* (marginalia).
A. C. Swinburne, *Love's Cross-Currents; A Year's Letters* (Catalog entry).
H. W. Wack, *Story of the Congo Free State: Social, Political, and Economic Aspects of the Belgian System of Government in Central Africa.*
H. Ward, *My Life with Stanley's Rear Guard.*
See also the Reader's Guide entry for Leopold II, King.

Congregational Church: see
Case of C. O. Godfrey.
T. C. Upham, *Life of Faith; in Three Parts, Embracing Some of the Scriptural Principles or Doctrines of Faith* (Catalog entry).

Congreve, William: see W. M. Thackeray, *Thackeray's Lectures. The English Humourists. The Four Georges* (marginalia).

Coningsby; or, The New Generation. B. Disraeli.

Conkling, Roscoe: see A. R. Conkling, *Life and Letters of Roscoe Conkling.*

Conn, Herbert William: see *New Princeton Review* (Catalog entry).

Connecticut: see
Connecticut Magazine: An Illustrated Monthly.
A. Johnston, *Connecticut: A Study of a Commonwealth Democracy.*
W. C. Prime, *I Go A-Fishing.*
H. E. B. Stowe, *Poganuc People: Their Loves and Lives.*

"Connor, Ralph" (pseud.): see C. W. Gordon.

Conover, J. (co-author): see
On the Gridiron and Other Stories of Outdoor Sport.
On Track and Diamond.

Conquest of Canaan: A Novel. B. Tarkington.

Conquest of Rome. M. Serao.

Conquest of the Skies. F. Marion.

Consistency of Revelation with Itself and with Human Reason. P. N. Shuttleworth.

Conspiracy of Pontiac and the Indian War After the Conquest of Canada. F. Parkman.

Conspirators: see A. Dumas, *Novels.*

Conspirators, A Romance. R. W. Chambers.

Constantinople: see
I. C. S. Chandler, *Dog of Constantinople.*
J. M. Ludlow, *Captain of the Janizaries, A Story of the Times of Scanderbeg and the Fall of Constantinople.*
E. Pears, *Fall of Constantinople, Being the Story of the Fourth Crusade.*
L. Wallace, *Prince of India; or, Why Constantinople Fell.*

Constitutional History of England. H. Hallam.

Consular appointments: see L. Monti, *Adventures of a Consul Abroad.*

Consumption: see the Reader's Guide entry for Tuberculosis.

Continuous Creation; An Application of the Evolutionary Philosophy to the Christian Religion. M. Adams.

Contrasts. G. A. Kendrick.

"Contributions to the Encephalic Anatomy of the Races" (article). E. A. Spitzka.

Converse, Frank H. (co-author): see *Adventures at Sea.*

Convict; or, The Conspirator's Victim. E. Z. C. Judson.

Convict Ship. W. C. Russell.

"Conway, Hugh" (pseud.): see F. J. Fargus.

Cook, Clarence Chatham (ed.): see W. Lübke, *Outlines of the History of Art.*

Cook, William: see (contr.) J. W. von Goethe, *Faust. Eine Tragödie.*

Cook, Will Marion (composer): see J. A. Shipp, *Abyssinia* (musical comedy).

Cookbooks: see
Cassell's Dictionary of Cookery, with about 9,000 Recipes.
T. Child, *Delicate Feasting.*
E. Christian and M. G. Christian, *Uncooked Foods & How to Use Them.*
M. T. V. Earle, *Pot-pourri from a Surrey Garden.*
A. Filippini, *Handy Volume Culinary Series.*
A. Filippini, *Table: How to Buy Food, How to Cook It, and How to Serve It.*
M. V. H. Terhune, *Breakfast, Luncheon and Tea.*
M. V. H. Terhune, *Common Sense in the Household: A Manual of Practical Housewifery.*

Ysaguirre (pseud.) and La Marca (pseud.), *Cold Dishes for Hot Weather*.
See also the Reader's Guide entry for Housekeeping advice.
Cooke, George Willis (ed.): see G. W. Curtis, *Early Letters of George Wm. Curtis to John S. Dwight*.
Cooke, Rose Terry: see (contr.) *Smith College Commencement Poems, '79-'86*.
Cooking: see the Reader's Guide entry for Cookbooks.
Coolbrith, Ina Donna: see
 I. H. Gillmore (Catalog entry).
 B. Harte (ed.), *Outcroppings: Being Selections of California Verse*.
Cooley, Julia: see J. C. Altrocchi.
"Coolidge, Susan" (pseud.): see S. C. Woolsey.
Cooper, James Davis (illus.): see A. Rimmer, *Ancients Streets and Homesteads of England*.
Cooper, James Fenimore: see
 R. I. Dodge, *Our Wild Indians: Thirty-Three Years' Personal Experience among the Red Men of the Great West* (Catalog entry).
 Friendship's Offering; A Christmas, New Year, and Birthday Present (Catalog entry).
 T. W. S. Higginson, *Cheerful Yesterdays. Contemporaries* (marginalia).
 A. H. Joline, *Diversions of a Book-Lover*.
 T. R. Lounsbury, *James Fenimore Cooper*.
 B. Matthews, *Introduction to the Study of American Literature*.
 W. L. Phelps, *Essays on Modern Novelists* (marginalia).
 A. D. Richardson, *Beyond the Mississippi: From the Great River to the Great Ocean*.
 W. C. Russell, *Wreck of the "Grosvenor." An Account of the Mutiny of the Crew and the Loss of the Ship When Trying to Make the Bermudas* (Catalog entry).
 W. Winter, *Old Shrines and Ivy*.
 É. Zola, *Rome* (marginalia).
Cooper, Susan Fenimore (ed.): see J. F. Cooper, *Pages and Pictures, from the Writings of James Fenimore Cooper, with Notes*.
Cooper, Thompson (ed.): see *Men of the Time: A Dictionary of Contemporaries, Containing Biographical Notices of Eminent Characters of Both Sexes*.
Copeland, Charles (illus.): see
 W. J. Long, *Beasts of the Field*.
 W. J. Long, *Fowls of the Air*.
 W. J. Long, *School of the Woods; Some Life Studies of Animal Instincts and Animal Training*.
Copernicus, Nicolaus: see H. E. B. Stowe, *Uncle Tom's Cabin; or, Life Among the Lowly* (Catalog entry).
Coppée, Henry (ed.): see L.-P.-A.-d' O. Paris, *History of the Civil War in America*.
Copper Handbook: A Manual of the Copper Industry of the World. H. J. Stevens.
Copyright law: see
 W. Besant, *Pen and the Book*.
 A. D. A. de Brueys, *Avocat Patelin: A Comedy in Three Acts* (marginalia).
 Current Literature: A Magazine of Record and Review.
 G. B. Davis, *Elements of International Law*.
 S. J. Elder, "Duration of Copyright" (article).

T. B. Macaulay, *History of England from the Accession of James II* (Catalog entry).
E. A. Poe, *Murders of [sic] the Rue Morgue* (story) (Catalog entry).
E. A. Poe, "To Helen" (poem) (Catalog entry).
A. G. Sedgwick, "International Copyright by Judicial Decision" (article).
G. O. Trevelyan, *Life and Letters of Lord Macaulay* (marginalia).
"Copyright and Literary Property" (essay): see W. Besant, *Pen and the Book*.
Corbett, Griffith Owen: see W. Cobbett, *Year's Residence in the United States*.
Corbett, James J. (boxer): see B. W. Howard, *Guenn; A Wave on the Breton Coast* (Catalog entry).
Corbould, Edward (illus.): see G. Chaucer, *Canterbury Tales*.
Cord and Creese; A Novel. J. De Mille.
Corey, Giles: see H. W. Longfellow, *New-England Tragedies*.
Corleone; A Tale of Sicily. F. M. Crawford.
Cornhill Magazine: see G. B. Smith, "Growth of London" (article).
Cornwall: see M. E. J. Whitcombe, *Bygone Days in Devonshire and Cornwall*.
Cornwall, Barry (pseud.): see J. T. Fields.
"Coronation" (hymn): see E. Perronet, "All hail the power of Jesus' name."
Correspondence: see the Reader's Guide entry for Letters.
Correspondence of John Lothrop Motley. J. L. Motley.
Correspondence of Thomas Carlyle and Ralph Waldo Emerson. T. Carlyle.
Cortés, Hernándo: see
 J. S. C. Abbott, *History of Hernando Cortez*.
 F. A. Ober, *Hernándo Cortés*.
Cortissoz, E. M. H. (co-ed.): see E. C. Stedman (co-ed.), *Library of American Literature, from Earliest Settlement to the Present Time*.
Cory, Fanny Young (illus.): see
 J. D. D. Bacon, *Madness of Philip and Other Tales of Childhood*.
 J. D. D. Bacon, *Memoirs of a Baby*.
Coryell, John R. (co-author): see *Adventures at Sea*.
Cosimo I: see C. M. Depew, *Orations and After-Dinner Speeches of Chauncey M. Depew* (Catalog entry).
Cosmogony: see
 S. A. Arrhenius, *Life of the Universe as Conceived by Man from the Earliest Ages to the Present Time*.
 S. A. Arrhenius, *Worlds in the Making: The Evolution of the Universe*.
 S.G. Bayne, *Pith of Astronomy (Without Mathematics): The Latest Facts and Figures as Developed by the Giant Telescopes* (clipping).
 J. Timbs, *Things Not Generally Known, Familiarly Explained* (Catalog entry).
 A. R. Wallace, *Man's Place in the Universe: A Study of the Results of Scientific Research in Relation to the Unity or Plurality of Worlds*.
 G. W. Warder, *Cities of the Sun*.
 A. Winchell, *Sketches of Creation: A Popular View of*

Some of the Grand Conclusions of the Sciences in Reference to the History of Matter and of Life.

Cosmopolis. C. J. P. Bourget.

Costume historique. A. C. A. Racinet.

Cotton's Sketch-Book. Auto-Biographical Sketches of the Life, Labors and Extensive Home Travels of Rev. A. J. Cotton. A. J. Cotton.

Coues, Elliott (co-author): see M. O. Wright, *Citizen Bird; Scenes from Bird-Life.*

"Counop, Felix" (pseud.): see M. A. Geisse.

Counterfeit Presentment. Comedy (play). W. D. Howells.

Countess de Charny: see A. Dumas, *Novels.*

Count Frontenac and New France Under Louis XIV. F. Parkman.

Count of Monte Cristo. A. Dumas.

Count Robert of Paris. W. Scott.

Country Doctor. H. de Balzac.

Country of the Dwarfs. P. B. Du Chaillu.

Country Parsons: see G. Herbert.

"Country Printer" (essay). W. D. Howells.

"Country Seat" (poem): see M. B. Eddy, *Retrospection and Introspection* (marginalia).

Cours Complet de Langue Allemande. G. Cottler.

"Courting of Dinah Shadd" (short story). R. Kipling.

Court of Boyville. W. A. White.

Courtship of a Careful Man, and a Few Other Courtships. E. S. Martin.

Court trials: see

P. Deming, *Adirondack Stories.*

A. Dumas, *Celebrated Crimes.*

T. Dunphy and T. J. Cummins (comp.), *Remarkable Trials of All Countries, Particularly of the United States, Great Britain, Ireland, and France.*

F. J. Fargus, *Circumstantial Evidence, and Other Stories.*

A. Fouquier, *Causes célèbres de tous les peuples.*

H. W. Fuller, *Noted French Trials. Impostors and Adventurers.*

Gallick Reports; or, An Historical Collection of Criminal Cases.

F. Galton, *Finger Prints.*

F. T. Hill, *The Accomplice* (mystery novel).

History of the Most Remarkable Tryals in Great Britain and Ireland, in Capital Cases.

D. Jardine, *Lives and Criminal Trials of Celebrated Men.*

R. U. Johnson and C. C. Buel (eds.), *Battles and Leaders of the Civil War* (Catalog entry).

G. P. Lathrop, *Would You Kill Him? A Novel.*

E. G. E. B. Lytton, *Eugene Aram.*

G. Mackenzie, *Laws and Customes of Scotland, in Matters Criminal.*

M. Méjan, *Recueil des causes célèbres, et des arrêts qui les ont décidées.*

Memories of Westminster Hall; A Collection of Interesting Incidents, Anecdotes, and Historical Sketches Relating to Westminster Hall, Its Famous Judges and Lawyers and Its Great Trials.

S. M. Phillipps, *Famous Cases of Circumstantial Evidence.*

A. K. G. Rohlfs, *Hand and Ring.*

C. Whitehead, *Lives and Exploits of the Most Noted Highwaymen, Robbers and Murderers, of All Nations.*

G. T. Wilkinson, *Newgate Calendar Improved; Being Interesting Memoirs of Notorious Characters, Who Have Been Convicted of Offences Against the Laws of England, During the Seventeenth Century; and Continued to the Present Time.*

See also the Reader's Guide entries for Crime, for Curiosities, for Detective fiction, for Impostors, and for Law.

Cousin from India. D. M. M. Craik.

Cousin Kate (play). H. H. Davies.

"Cousin Sally Dilliard" (sketch). H. C. Jones.

"Covered Embers" (short story by E. S. Phelps): see W. D. Howells and H. M. Alden (eds.), *Their Husbands' Wives.*

Cowboy Cavalier. H. C. Morse.

Cowboys:

M. M. Austin, *'Cension. A Sketch from Paso Del Norte. Cow-Boys Ballads.*

A. H. Lewis, *Wolfville Days.*

A. H. Lewis, *Wolfville Nights.*

Cowles, Maude Alice (illus.) (alternate name): see A. B. Stripling, *Poet in Embryo; Being the Meditations of Algernon Byron Stripling.*

Cox and Box (comic opera). F. C. Burnand.

Cox and Box (comic opera). F. C. Burnand: see also S. M. Morton, *Box and Cox* (farce).

"Cox, Sunset" (pseud.): see S. S. Cox.

Cozy Corner Confidences. W. Pulitzer.

"Craddock, Charles Egbert" (pseud.): see M. N. Murfree.

"Cradle of the Deep" (poem, song). E. Willard.

Cradle of the Rose. M. Cunliffe-Owen.

"Cradle's empty, baby's gone" (song). H. Kennedy.

Craig, Hardin (co-ed.): see H. Van Dyke (ed.), *Little Masterpieces of English Poetry, by British and American Authors.*

Craig, Isa: see I. C. Knox.

Craik, Dinah Maria (Mulock): see

(ed.) J. Martin, *Legacy, Being the Life and Remains of John Martin, Schoolmaster and Poet.*

(trans.) H. E. G. Witt, *Motherless; or, A Parisian Family.*

(trans.) H. E. G. Witt, *Only Sister.*

Craik, Georgiana Marian: see G. M. C. May.

Cram, William Everett (co-author): see W. Stone (co-author), *American Animals.*

Crane, Anna Moncure: see A. M. C. Seemüller.

Crane, Theodore: see (inscr.) U. S. Grant, *Memoirs of U. S. Grant.*

Crane, Thomas Frederick (co-ed.): see *Tableaux de la Révolution Française; An Historical Reader.*

Crane, Walter (illus.): see Plutarchus, *Children's Plutarch: Tales of the Greeks.*

Cranford. E. C. S. Gaskell.

Crankisms, by Lisle de Vaux Matthewman. L. de V. Matthewman.

Crapsey, Algernon Sidney: see New York *Sun* (Catalog entry).

Crawford, Fred Erastus (co-author): see F. Parsons, *World's Best Books: A Key to the Treasures of Literature.*

Crawford, (Mrs.) G. M. (pref.): see H. Forneron, *Louise de Keroualle, Duchess of Portsmouth, 1649–1734*.
Crawford, Will (illus.): see E. P. Butler, *Pigs Is Pigs*.
"Crayon, Geoffrey" (pseud.): see W. Irving.
Cremation: see
    A. G. Cobb, "Earth-Burial and Cremation" (article).
    C. F. Gordon-Cumming, *In the Himalayas and on the Indian Plains* (marginalia).
    See also the Reader's Guide entries for Funerals and for Premature burial.
Cressy and Poitiers. G. A. Henty.
Crete: see B. Taylor, *Travels in Greece and Russia, with an Excursion to Crete*.
Crete, The Forerunner of Greece. C. H. Hawes and H. B. Hawes.
Crichton, James: see H. Wilson, *Wonderful Characters; Comprising Memoirs and Anecdotes of the Most Remarkable Persons of Every Age and Nation*.
Crim, Matt" (pseud.): see Martha Jane Crim.
Crime: see
    J. Brougham, *Lottery of Life: A Story of New York* (play).
    A. Dumas, *Celebrated Crimes*.
    F. Galton, *Finger Prints*.
    F. J. Fargus, *Circumstantial Evidence, and Other Stories*.
    R. Head and F. Kirkman, *English Rogue: Described, in the Life of Meriton Latroon, a Witty Extravagant. Being a Compleat History of the Most Eminent Cheats of Both Sexes*.
    E. W. Horning, *Shadow of the Rope* (novel).
    V. M. Hugo, *Fantine, or the Felon and the Fallen*.
    V. M. Hugo, *Misérables*.
    D. Jardine, *Lives and Criminal Trials of Celebrated Men*.
    R. U. Johnson and C. C. Buel (eds.), *Battles and Leaders of the Civil War* (Catalog entry).
    M. Leblanc, *Exploits of Arsène Lupin*.
    E. G. E. B. Lytton, *Eugene Aram*.
    W. McAdoo, *Guarding a Great City, by William McAdoo, Police Commissioner, New York City, 1904–1906*.
    R. E. MacAlarney, "Tim Rafferty's Romance: A Story of Christmas among 'The Finest.'"
    H. Martineau, *Society in America* (marginalia).
    S. M. Phillipps, *Famous Cases of Circumstantial Evidence*.
    A. G. Plympton, *Dear Daughter Dorothy*.
    M. D. Post, *Man of Last Resort; or, The Clients of Randolph Mason*.
    M. D. Post, *Strange Schemes of Randolph Mason*.
    W. P. Ridge, *By Order of the Magistrate*.
    A. K. G. Rohlfs, *Hand and Ring* (novel).
    Temple Bar: A London Magazine for Town and Country Readers (Catalog entry).
    G. Thompson, *City Crimes; or, Life in New York and Boston*.
    C. Whitehead, *Lives and Exploits of the Most Noted Highwaymen, Robbers and Murderers, of All Nations*.
    See also the Reader's Guide entries for Court trials, for Curiosities, for Detective fiction, and for Impostors.
Crimea: see

A. W. Kinglake, *Invasion of the Crimea; Its Origin, and an Account of Its Progress*.
T. W. Knox, *Backsheesh! or, Life and Adventures in the Orient*.
Crime of Sylvestre Bonnard. A. France.
Crime of the Congo. A. C. Doyle.
Crimes of the Civil War, and Curse of the Funding System. H. C. Dean.
Criminal trials: see the Reader's Guide entry for Court trials.
Crisis (pamphlet). T. Paine.
Crisp, Violet (trans.): see N. Notovich, *Unknown Life of Jesus Christ*.
Criterion; or, The Test of Talk about Familiar Things. A Series of Essays. H. T. Tuckerman.
Critical and Miscellaneous Essays. T. Carlyle.
Critical and Miscellaneous Essays. T. B. Macaulay.
Critical Dictionary of English Literature and British and American Authors. S. A. Allibone.
Critical Examination of Socialism. W. H. Mallock.
Critical Handbook of the Greek New Testament. E. C. Mitchell.
"Criticism and Dogma" (essay). C. A. Briggs.
Critique of Pure Reason. I. Kant.
Crocker, S. R. (trans.): see N. C. Flammarion, *Studies of Infinity*.
Croker, John Wilson (ed.): see
    J. Boswell, *Life of Samuel Johnson*.
    T. B. Macaulay, *Critical and Miscellaneous Essays* (marginalia).
Croker, Richard: see T. B. Macaulay, "Essay on Warren Hastings" (Catalog entry).
Cromwell, Oliver: see
    H. C. Bailey, *Colonel Greatheart*.
    T. Carlyle (ed.), *Oliver Cromwell's Letters and Speeches*.
    A. J. Church, *With the King at Oxford; A Tale of the Great Rebellion*.
    M. H. Hervey, *Amyas Egerton, Cavalier* (novel).
    T. B. Macaulay, *Speeches and Poems, with the Report and Notes on the Indian Penal Code* (marginalia).
    F. Marryat, *Children of the New Forest*.
    G. Smith, *Three English Statesmen: A Course of Lectures on the Political History of England*.
    R. H. Thorpe, "Curfew Must Not Ring To-night" (poem).
    W. J. Vance, *Big John Baldwin; Extracts from the Journal of an Officer of Cromwell's Army* (fictional memoir).
    J. G. Whittier, "Rantoul" (poem) (Catalog entry).
    See also the Reader's Guide entry for Charles I.
Cronwright-Schreiner, Samuel (co-author): see O. Schreiner, *Political Situation [in Cape Colony]*.
Crook, General George: see J. G. Bourke, *On the Border with Crook*.
Crooked Trails. F. Remington.
Cross-dressing: see
    W. Shakespeare, *As You Like It*.
    W. Shakespeare, *Cymbeline*.
    W. Shakespeare, *Merchant of Venice*.
    W. Shakespeare, *Merry Wives of Windsor*.
    W. Shakespeare, *Twelfth Night*.

W. Shakespeare, *Two Gentlemen of Verona.*

B. Thomas, *Charley's Aunt.*

L. J. Velazquez, *Woman in Battle: A Narrative of the Exploits, Adventures, and Travels of Madame Loreta Janeta Velazquez, Otherwise Known as Lieutenant Harry T. Buford, Confederate States Army.*

H. Walpole, *Letters of Horace Walpole, Earl of Oxford* (marginalia).

C. Wälzel and F. F. R. Genée, *Fatinitza* (operetta).

Cross, John Walter (ed.): see G. Eliot, *George Eliot's Life.*

Cross, Marian (Evans): see G. Eliot.

"Cross, Victoria" (pseud.): see A. S. Cory.

Crouch, Frederick Nicholls (composer): see L. M. Crawford, "Kathleen Mavourneen" (song).

Crowe, Joseph Archer (ed.): see F. T. Kugler, *Handbook of Painting: The German, Flemish, and Dutch Schools.*

"Crowfield, Christopher" (pseud.): see H. E. B. Stowe.

Crown Diamonds (opera). D. F. E. Auber.

Crowne, John: see *Dramatists of the Restoration.*

Crown of Thorns, or Ann Boleyn (play): A. E. Dickinson.

Croxall, S. (trans.): see Aesop, *Bewick's Select Fables.*

Cruden, Alexander (contr.): see J. Eadie (ed.), *New and Complete Concordance to the Holy Scriptures.*

Cruikshank, George (illus.): see

    W. H. Ainsworth, *Jack Sheppard; A Romance.*

    C. Rogers (ed.), *Centenary Garland; Being Pictorial Illustrations of the Novels of Sir Walter Scott, in Their Order of Publication. By George Cruikshank, and Other Artists of Eminence.*

Cruise of the Betsey; or, A Summer Ramble Among the Fossiliferous Deposits of the Hebrides. With Rambles of a Geologist. H. Miller.

Cruise of the Cachalot. F. T. Bullen.

Cruise of the "Ghost." W. L. Alden.

Cruise of the Midge. M. Scott.

Cruise of the Shining Light. N. Duncan.

Crusades: see

    Chronicles of the Crusades; Contemporary Narratives.

    G. Z. Gray, *Children's Crusade; An Episode of the Thirteenth Century.*

    F. Harrison, *Theophano: The Crusade of the Tenth Century; A Novel.*

    E. Pears, *Fall of Constantinople, Being the Story of the Fourth Crusade.* .

    M. Schwob, *Children's Crusade.*

    W. Scott, *Talisman.*

    T. Tasso, *Gerusalemme Liberata.*

    C. M. Yonge, *Prince and the Page: A Story of the Last Crusade.*

    See also the Reader's Guide entries for Middle Ages and for Islam.

Crusoe's Island: A Ramble in the Steps of Alexander Selkirk. J. R. Browne.

Crystal Sceptre; A Story of Adventure. P. V. Mighels.

Cuba: see

    R. A. Alger, *Spanish-American War.*

    A. R. Colquhoun, *Greater America.*

    R. H. Dana, *To Cuba and Back.*

    C. M. F. Dressel, *Cuban Spanish American War, Sketched by C. M. F. Dressel.*

    J. N. Jackson, *Winter Holiday in Summer Lands.*

    F. Matthews, *New-Born Cuba.*

    C. A. Murray, *Travels in North America During the Years 1834, 1835 & 1836, Including . . . a Visit to Cuba and the Azore Islands.*

    C. M. Pepper, *To-morrow in Cuba.*

    G. A. Sala, *Under the Sun: Essays Mainly Written in Hot Countries.*

    L. J. Velazquez, *Woman in Battle: A Narrative of the Exploits, Adventures, and Travels of Madame Loreta Janeta Velazquez, Otherwise Known as Lieutenant Harry T. Buford, Confederate States Army.*

    See also the Reader's Guide entry for Spanish American War.

Cuban Spanish American War. C. M. F. Dressel.

Cuchulain of Muirthemne: The Story of the Men of the Red Branch of Ulster. A. Gregory.

Cudjo's Cave. J. T. Trowbridge.

Culture's Garland: Being Memoranda of the Gradual Rise of Literature, Art, Music and Society in Chicago, and Other Western Ganglia. E. Field.

Cumming: see R. G. Gordon-Cumming.

Cummins, T. J. (co-author): see T. Dunphy, *Remarkable Trials.*

Cuneo, Cyrus (illus.): see R. S. Hichens, *Spirit in Prison.*

Cunningham, Peter (ed.): see H. Walpole, *Letters of Horace Walpole, Earl of Oxford.*

Cure for Anarchy. W. M. Salter.

Cureton, Elizabeth (comp.): see H. Drummond, *"Beautiful Thoughts" from Henry Drummond.*

"Curfew Must Not Ring To-night" (poem). R. H. Thorpe.

"Curing by Suggestion" (article). F. Van Eeden.

Curiosities: see

    Anecdote Library. Portraits and Views.

    E. H. Barker, *Literary Anecdotes and Contemporary Reminiscences of Professor Porson and Others. From the Manuscript Papers of the Late E. H. Barker.*

    Borrowings; A Compilation of Helpful Thoughts from Great Authors.

    E. C. Brewer, *Dictionary of Miracles: Imitative, Realistic, and Dogmatic, with Illustrations.*

    E. C. Brewer, *Dictionary of Phrase and Fable.*

    C. Buck (comp.), *Anecdotes; Religious, Moral, and Entertaining.*

    F. T. Buckland, *Curiosities of Natural History.*

    J. D. Champlin, *Young Folks' Cyclopaedia of Common Things.*

    D. M. M. Craik, *Is It True? Tales, Curious and Wonderful.*

    I. Disraeli, *Curiosities of Literature.*

    J. W. Draper, *Human Physiology, Statistical and Dynamical; or, The Conditions and Course of the Life of Man.*

    Gesta Romanorum (Catalog entry).

    J. T. Haydn, *Haydn's Dictionary of Dates and Universal Information Relating to All Ages and Nations.*

    W. D. Howells (co-ed.), *Library of Universal Adventure by Sea and Land.*

    L. Hunt, *Day by the Fire; and Other Papers, Hitherto Uncollected.*

    L. Hutton, *Curiosities of the American Stage.*

Cynic's Meditation: see W. Pulitzer, *Cozy Corner Confidences.*

Cyrus the Great: see J. S. C. Abbott, *History of Cyrus the Great.*

"Czar—1905" (poem). B. H. Nadal.

Czars: see the Reader's Guide entry for Russia.

D

Daddy Darwin's Dovecot: A Country Tale. J. H. G. Ewing.

Daddy Dave. F. W. Mason.

Dadmun, John William (arranger): see W. F. Warren, "Homeward bound" (hymn).

Daggett, Rollin Mallory (ed., intro.): see D. Kalakaua, *Legends and Myths of Hawaii: The Fables and Folk-Lore of a Strange People.*

Dahlgren, John Adolphus.: see M. V. Dahlgren, *Memoir of John A. Dahlgren, Rear- Admiral United States Navy, by His Widow.*

Daily Thoughts. T. D. W. Talmage.

Daisy Miller: A Study. H. James.

"Dale, Felix" (pseud.): see H. C. Merivale.

Dall, William Healey (ed.): see J. F. A. du P. Nadaillac, *Pre-Historic America.*

Daly, Augustin (prod.): see
J. Brougham, *Lottery of Life: A Story of New York* (play).
H. C. Bunner and E. A. Dithmar, *A Portfolio of Players.*
W. Shakespeare, *Taming of the Shrew* (play) (Catalog entry).

Damascus: see
Impressions of Damascus (unidentified book).
C. W. Stoddard, *Cruise Under the Crescent; From Suez to San Marco.*
W. M. Thomson, *Land and the Book; or, Biblical illustrations Drawn from the Manners and Customs, the Scenes and Scenery, of the Holy Land: Lebanon, Damascus and Beyond Jordan.*
C. D. Warner, *In the Levant.*

Dame aux camélias (play): see A. Dumas, *fils, Camille.*

Dame Blanche (light opera). F. A. Boieldieu.

Damien, Father: see C. W. Stoddard, *Lepers of Molokai.*

Damiens, Robert François (a would-be assassin): see G. Casanova de Seingalt, *Mémoires de Jacques Casanova de Seingalt, Écrits par lui-même.*

Damon and Pythias, A Tragedy (play). J. Banim.

Damon, Samuel Chenery: see
[*Hymns. Hawaiian.*] (inscr.).
J. J. Jarves, *History of the Hawaiian or Sandwich Islands* (Catalog entry).
(ed.): see *Temperance Advocate.*

Damrosch, Walter (composer): see R. Kipling, "Danny Deever."

Dana, Charles Anderson: see
(co-ed.) *American Cyclopaedia: A Popular Dictionary of General Knowledge.*
J. H. Wilson, *Life of Charles A. Dana.*

"Danbury News Man" (pseud.): see J. M. Bailey.

Daniel Boone, The Pioneer of Kentucky. J. S. C. Abbott.

Daniel Deronda. G. Eliot.

Daniell, Francis Henry Blackburne (co-ed.): see O. G. de Busbecq, *Life and Letters of Ogier Ghiselin de Busbecq.*

Daniels, Frank Albert (comic actor): see C. H. Hoyt, *Rag Baby* (play).

"Danny Deever" (poem). R. Kipling.

Dante, Alighieri: see
G. G. Coulton, *From St. Francis to Dante: Translations from the Chronicle of the Franciscan Salimbene (1221–1288).*
L. Hunt, *Stories from the Italian Poets. (First Series) Dante Alighieri, With Critical Notices of the Life and Genius of the Author.*
A. B. M. Jameson, *Memoirs of the Loves of the Poets. Biographical Sketches of Women Celebrated in Ancient and Modern Poetry* (marginalia).
M. O. W. Oliphant, *Makers of Florence: Dante, Giotto, Savonarola,and Their City.*
C. M. Phillimore, *Dante at Ravenna: A Study.*
D. G. Rossetti (ed. and trans.), *Dante and His Circle, with the Italian Poets Preceding Him (1100–1200- 1300). A Collection of Lyrics.*
M. F. Rossetti, *Shadow of Dante: An Essay Towards Studying Himself, His World and His Pilgrimage.*

Dante and His Circle, with the Italian Poets Preceding Him (1100–1200-1300). A Collection of Lyrics. D. G. Rossetti (ed. and trans.).

Dante at Ravenna: A Study. C. M. Phillimore.

"Dan Tucker" (song): see D. D. Emmett, "Old Dan Tucker."

Danube River: see
P. Bigelow, *Paddles and Politics Down the Danube.*
T. W. Knox, *Backsheesh! or, Life and Adventures in the Orient.*

Daphnis and Chloe: see *Greek Romances of Heliodorus, Longus, and Achilles Tatius.*

Da Ponte, Lorezno (librettist): see J. C. Mozart, *Nozze di Figaro.*

"Dare, Shirley" (pseud.): see S. D. Power.

Dargent, Yan' (illus.): see A. Assollant, *Fantastic History of the Celebrated Pierrot.*

"Darius Green and His Flying Machine" (poem): see J. T. Trowbridge, *Vagabonds, and Other Poems.*

Darius the Great: see J. S. C. Abbott, *History of Darius the Great.*

Dark o' the Moon. S. R. Crockett.

Darley, Felix Octavius Carr (illus.): see
J. M. Field, *Drama in Pokerville, The Bench and Bar of Jurytown, and Other Stories.*
H. W. Longfellow, *Longfellow's Evangeline with Illustrations by F. O. C. Darley.*
W. T. Thompson, *Major Jones's Courtship.*

Darrel of the Blessed Isles. I. Bacheller.

"D'Arve, Stéphen" (pseud.): see C. de Catelin.

Darwin, Charles: see
S. Butler, *Life and Habit.*
M. D. Conway, *Autobiography: Memories and Experiences of Moncure Daniel Conway* (marginalia).
J. Fiske, *Century of Science and Other Essays* (marginalia).
J. Fiske, "Charles Darwin" (essay).

T. W. S. Higginson, *Cheerful Yesterdays. Contemporaries* (Catalog entry).
See also the Reader's Guide entry for Evolution.
Darwin, Francis: see
(co-author): see C. Darwin, *Power of Movement in Plants.*
(ed.): see C. Darwin, *Life and Letters of Charles Darwin.*
See also the Reader's Guide entry for Evolution.
Dash at the Pole. W. L. Phelps.
Daudet, Alphonse: see *Little French Masterpieces.*
Daughter of Heth. A Novel. W. Black.
"Daughters of the Bright Brigade" (unpublished manuscript). A. V. Kelley.
D'Avenant, William: see *Dramatists of the Restoration.*
Davenport, William Henry (trans.) J. Michelet, *Bird.*
Davico, Rosalba (ed.): see E. Jarvis, "Increase of Human Life."
David Copperfield. C. Dickens.
David Copperfield. A Drama in Two Acts. J. Brougham.
David Harum: A Story of American Life. E. N. Westcott.
Davidson, Joseph: (trans.) Virgil, *Works of Virgil.*
Davie and Elisabeth. Wonderful Adventures. M. C. Dyar.
Da Vinci, Leonardo: see
T. Cole, "Notes by T. Cole on the 'Adoration.'"
D. S. Merezhkovsky, *Romance of Leonardo da Vinci, the Forerunner.*
Davis, Garrett: see the Catalog entry for F. O. Darley, *Compositions in Outline by Felix O. C. Darley, from Hawthorne's Scarlet Letter.*
Davis, G. B. (co-author): see *Adventures with Indians.*
Davis, James William (intro.): see W. Smith (ed.), *Old Yorkshire.*
Davis, Richard Harding: see
R. Kipling, "Danny Deever" (Catalog entry).
R. Kipling, "Mandalay" (Catalog entry).
Davy, Humphry: see H. Mayhew, *Wonders of Science; or, Young Humphry Davy (The Cornish Apothecary's Boy, Who Taught Himself Natural Philosophy, and Eventually Became President of the Royal Society).*
Davy, John (composer): see A. Cherry, "Bay of Biscay."
Dawley, Thomas Robinson (publisher): see *Old Abe's Jokes; Fresh from Abraham's Bosom.*
Dawn-Thought on the Reconciliation; A Volume of Pantheistic Impressions and Glimpses of Larger Religion. J. W. Lloyd.
Dawson, Catharine Amy: see C. A. Scott.
Dawson, Coningsby William (co-ed.): see
W. J. Dawson (co-ed.), *Great English Essayists.*
W. J. Dawson (co-ed.), *Great English Letter-Writers.*
Day by the Fire; and Other Papers, Hitherto Uncollected. L. Hunt.
"Day is Done" (poem). H. W. Longfellow.
"Day is past and gone" (hymn): see G. J. Geer (Catalog entry).
Day, J. Arthur (illus.): see B. T. Wilson, *Ye Mountaineer.*
Dayrolles, Solomon: see the Catalog entry for P. D. Stanhope, *Letters to His Son.*
Days Like These. E. W. Townsend.
"Days of absence" (song). J. J. Rousseau.

Days of Bruce; A Story from Scottish History (novel). G. Aguilar.
Day's Work. R. Kipling.
Dayton, Ohio: see C. Wuichet, *Sunny Side of a Busy Life.*
Deacon Pitkin's Farm. H. E. B. Stowe.
"Deacon's Masterpiece" (poem). O. W. Holmes.
"Dead Canary" (poem). G. W. Elliott.
Deane, J. C. (ed.): see *Handbook for Travellers in Ireland.*
Dear Daughter Dorothy. A. G. Plympton.
Death: see
T. Browne.
W. S. Burgess, *Eternal Laughter and Other Poems.*
A. G. Cobb, "Earth-Burial and Cremation" (article).
L. Conaro, *Art of Living Long. A New and Improved English Version of the Treatise by the Celebrated Venetian Centenarian.*
M. D. Conway, *Autobiography: Memories and Experiences of Moncure Daniel Conway* (marginalia).
T. Gray, "Elegy Written in a Country Churchyard" (poem).
M. W. Higginson, *The Drum-Beat* (short short story).
M. J. H. Holmes, *Homestead on the Hillside.*
O. W. Holmes, "Last Leaf" (poem).
O. W. Holmes, "Two Armies" (poem).
M. S. B. Hopkins, *Sixth Sense and Other Stories.*
J. Ingelow, "Divided" (poem).
R. Kipling, "They" (short story).
G. P. Lathrop, *Would You Kill Him? A Novel.*
W. E. H. Lecky, *History of European Morals from Augustus to Charlemagne* (marginalia).
J. McCarthy, *History of the Four Georges* (Catalog entry).
L. C. Moulton, *Some Women's Hearts.*
F. T. Palgrave (comp.), *Golden Treasury of the Best Songs and Lyrical Poems in the English Language* (marginalia).
Philadelphia *Public Ledger* (newspaper).
C. G. Rossetti, "Rest" (poem).
W. H. Sleeman, *Rambles and Recollections of an Indian Official.*
J. Swift, *Gulliver's Travels into Several Remote Nations of the World* (Catalog entry).
W. Tegg, *Last Act: Being the Funeral Rites of Nations and Individuals.*
W. M. Thackeray, *Thackeray's Lectures. The English Humorists. The Four Georges* (marginalia).
G. O. Trevelyan, *Life and Letters of Lord Macaulay* (marginalia).
F. Vane, "Are we almost there?" (song).
C. E. S. Wood, *Masque of Love* (poem) (Catalog entry).
H. C. Work, "Grandfather's clock" (song).
E. C. E. M. S. Wortley, *Travels in the United States, Etc., During 1849 and 1850* (marginalia).
E. Young, *Complaint; or, Night Thoughts on Life, Death, and Immortality.*
J. H. D. Zschokke, *Meditations on Death and Eternity.*
See also the Reader's Guide entries for Afterlife, for Funerals, and for Grief.
"Debatable Land": A Novel. A. W. Colton.
De Blowitz, Henri Georges: see H. G. de Blowitz.

Deborah's Diary. A Fragment (novel). A. Manning.

Decameron. G. Boccaccio.

Decameron. G. Boccaccio: see G. O. Trevelyan, *Life and Letters of Lord Macaulay.*

Décembre, Joseph (co-ed.): see J. de la Fontaine, *Fables de J. de La Fontaine.*

Decisive Battles of America. R. Hitchcock (ed.).

Decisive Battles of the Law; Narrative Studies of Eight Legal Contests Between the Years 1800 and 1886. F. T. Hill.

De Colange, Leo Auguste (ed.). *Picturesque World; or, Scenes in Many Lands.*

Decourcelle, Pierre (playwright): see C. Klein, *Two Little Vagrants* (play).

Dedications to Mark Twain (books): see

P. Bigelow, *Children of the Nations; A Study of Colonization and Its Problems.*

A. Flamma, *Dramas.*

E. Gerard, *Extermination of Love; A Fragmentary Study in Erotics.*

L. Hutton, *Boy I Knew and Four Dogs.*

F. L. Knowles (comp.), *Treasury of Humorous Poetry.*

G. M. V. C. Long, *Master of Stair.*

B. Matthews, *Historical Novel and Other Essays.*

A. B. Paine, *Ship-Dwellers: A Story of a Happy Cruise.*

E. S. Patton, *Japanese Topsyturvydom.*

E. Phillpotts, *Human Boy Again.*

G. T. Richardson and W. D. Quint, *Letters from a Son to His Self-Made Father.*

B. M. Van Vorst and M. V. Vorst, *Woman Who Toils; Being the Experiences of Two Ladies as Factory Girls.*

Deeper Harmonies and Other Poems; A Book of Verses, Essays and Selections. G. F. Viett.

Deerslayer. J. F. Cooper.

Deipnosophists; or, Banquet of the Learned, of Athenaeus. Athenaeus of Naucratis.

Deirdrè (poem). R. D. Joyce.

Delamotte, Philip Henry (illus.) see

G. White, *Natural History and Antiquities of Selborne.*

G. White, *Natural History of Selborne. With a Naturalist's Calendar and Additional Observations.*

De Lancey, William Howe: see M. De Lancey, *Week at Waterloo in 1815. Lady De Lancey's Narrative.*

De Land, Clyde Osmer (illus.): see E. V. Cooke, *Chronices of the Little Tot.*

Deland, Ellen Douglas (co-author): see *Boys on the Railroad.*

Delaware: see G. A. Townsend, *Tales of the Chesapeake.*

"Delicate Affair" (story): see G. King, *Balcony Stories.*

Delicate Feasting. T. Child.

Delina Delancey. E. M. Ros.

Delius, Nicolaus: see (ed.) W. Shakespeare, *Leopold Shakspere. The Poet's Works in Chronological Order.*

Delusions: see C. Mackay, *Memoirs of Extraordinary Popular Delusions.*

Demigod; A Novel. E. P. Jackson.

Demi-Monde (play). A. Dumas, *fils.*

Deming, Philander: see B. Harte, *Twins of Table Mountain, and Other Stories* (Catalog entry).

Democracy: see G. Ticknor, *Life, Letters, and Journals of George Ticknor* (marginalia).

Democracy, An American Novel. H. B. Adams.

Democracy in America. A. de Tocqueville.

"Demon and the Fury" (sketch). C. B. Lewis.

Demonology and Devil-Lore. M. D. Conway.

Demonology and Witchcraft: see W. Scott, *Letters on Demonology and Witchcraft.*

De Morgan, William [Frend]: see W. L. Phelps, *Essays on Modern Novelists* (marginalia).

Dempster, William Richardson (composer): see H. S. S. Blackwood, "Lament of the Irish emigrant" (song).

Denman, Thomas, Lord: see J. Arnould, *Life of Thomas, First Lord Denman, Formerly Lord Chief Justice of England.*

Denmark: see

S. S. Blicher, *Minister of Veilby.*

H. Hertz, *King René's Daughter; A Danish Lyrical Drama.*

J. G. Huneker, *Egoists, A Book of Supermen.*

J. G. Huneker, *Iconoclasts, A Book of Dramatists.*

J. P. Jacobsen, *Niels Lyhne.*

B. Taylor, *Northern Travel: Summer and Winter Pictures of Sweden, Denmark, and Lapland.*

R. Watt, "Lud og koldt Vand" (short story).

Denslow's Mother Goose. W. W. Denslow (ed., illus.).

Denslow, William Wallace (illus.): see

P. T. Barnum, *Dollars and Sense.*

L. F. Baum, *Father Goose; His Book.*

W. W. Denslow, *Denslow's Mother Goose.*

Denver, Colorado: see E. Roberts, *Shoshone and Other Western Wonders.*

Departmental Ditties. R. Kipling.

Depew, Chauncey Mitchell: see

H. W. Scott, *Distinguished American Lawyers, with Their Struggles and Triumphs in the Forum.*

W. M. Thayer, *Marvels of the New West* (Catalog entry).

G. W. Warder, *Cities of the Sun* (Catalog entry).

Depression (psychological): see

J. Brown, *Letters of Dr. John Brown, with Letters from Ruskin, Thackeray, and Others.*

W. James, *Varieties of Religious Experience; A Study in Human Nature* (marginalia).

De Profundis. O. Wilde.

"De Quille, Dan" (pseud.): see W. Wright.

De Quincey, Thomas: see W. J. Dawson (co-ed), *Great English Essayists* (inscr. about De Quincey).

Derby, G. H.: see M. de L. Landon's *Saratoga in 1901* (marginalia).

Derrick Sterling; A Story of the Mines. C. K. Munroe.

Desandré, Jules Marie (co-illus.): see J. de la Fontaine, *Fables de J. de La Fontaine.*

Desbordes-Valmore, Marceline Félicité Josèphe: see C. A. Sainte-Beuve, *Memoirs of Mme. Desbordes-Valmore.*

"Descent into the Maelstrom" (story). E. A. Poe.

Descent of Man. C. Darwin.

Deserted Village. O. Goldsmith.

Desmond Hundred. J. G. Austin.

Desoto, Hernando: see M. de Cervantes Saavedra, *Don Quixote* (Catalog entry).

Destiny of Doris; A Travel-Story of Three Continents. J. Chambers.

Destroyer of the Second Republic, Being Napoleon the Little. V. M. Hugo.

Destruction and Reconstruction: Personal Experiences of the Late War. R. Taylor.

"Destruction of Sennacherib" (poem). G. G. Byron.

Detective fiction: see

J. K. Bangs, Mrs. Raffles; Being the Adventures of an Amateur Crackswoman.

J. K. Bangs, R. Holmes & Co.; Being the Remarkable Adventures of Raffles Holmes, Esq., Detective and Amateur Cracksman by Birth.

S. E. S. Boggs, Sandpeep.

G. N. Boothby, My Strangest Case.

G. K. Chesterton, Club of Queer Trades.

A. C. Doyle, Sign of the Four.

A. C. Doyle, Study in Scarlet.

S. M. Gardenhire, Long Arm.

M. Leblanc, Exploits of Arsène Lupin.

A. Morrison, Martin Hewitt, Investigator.

A. Pinkerton, Mississippi Outlaws and the Detectives.

A. Pinkerton, Spy of the Rebellion; Being A True History of the Spy System of the United States Army During the Late Rebellion.

E. A. Poe, Murders of [sic] the Rue Morgue (story).

E. A. Poe, "Purloined Letter" (story).

M. D. Post, Man of Last Resort; or, The Clients of Randolph Mason.

M. D. Post, Strange Schemes of Randolph Mason.

A. K. G. Rohlfs, Hand and Ring (novel).

W. G. V. T. Sutphen, Gates of Chance.

See also the Reader's Guide entries for Court trials and for Crime.

Detmold: A Romance. W. H. Bishop.

Deutsche Geschichte im Zeitalter der Reformation. L. von Ranke.

Deutsche Grammatik für Amerikaner. Nach einer neuen praktischen Methode. C. Wenckebach.

Deutsche Heimat. Landschaft und Volktstum. A. Sach.

Deutsche Kultur-und Sittengeschichte. J. Scherr.

Deutscher Wortschatz oder Der passende Ausdruck. A. Schlessing.

Deux Gosses (play): see C. Klein, Two Little Vagrants (play).

Deuxième anné de grammaire. Larive et Fleury.

De Vere, Maximilian Schele: see M. S. de Vere.

Devil: see

E. C. Brewster, Dictionary of Miracles: Imitative, Realistic, and Dogmatic, with Illustrations (marginalia).

M. D. Conway, Demonology and Devil-Lore.

D. Defoe, Moll Flanders and The History of the Devil.

A. H. Layard, Nineveh and Its Remains: With an Account of a Visit to the Chaldæan Christians of Kurdistand, and the Yezidis, or Devil-Worshippers.

L. N. Tolstoy, Ivan the Fool; or, the Old Devil and the Three Small Devils.

A. D. White, History of the Warfare of Science with Theology (marginalia).

Devil's Note Book. O. Bainbridge.

Devil Tales (short stories). V. F. Boyle.

Devonshire: M. E. J. Whitcombe, Bygone Days in Devonshire and Cornwall.

Devonshire, Henriette Caroline (Vulliamy) (trans.): see R. Vallery-Radot, Life of Pasteur.

Devout Song and Poems: see J. Stern, "Translation from the German of Julius Stern."

Dewey, George: see J. Barrett, Admiral George Dewey; A Sketch of the Man.

"Dewing, Mrs T. W." (pseud.): see M. R. O. Dewing.

"Dialogue entre un philosophe et un contrôleur général des finances." F. M. A. de Voltaire.

"Dialogue entre un plaideur et un avocat." F. M. A. de Voltaire.

Dialogue of Proverbs. J. Heywood.

Dialogues of Plato. Plato.

Dialstone Lane. W. W. Jacobs.

Diamonds. W. Crookes.

Diana of the Crossways. G. Meredith.

Diana's Livery. E. W. M. Brodhead.

Diane; A Romance of the Icarian Settlement on the Mississippi River. K. H. Brown.

Diaries: see

W. Allingham, William Allingham, A Diary.

K. Chrēstomanos, Tagebuchblätter.

J. Evelyn, Diary and Correspondence of John Evelyn.

H. Gordon, War Diary of Events in the War of the Great Rebellion, 1863–1865.

W. C. Macready, Macready's Reminiscences, and Selections from His Diaries and Letters.

J. Martin, Legacy, Being the Life and Remains of John Martin, Schoolmaster and Poet.

J. A. Mitchell, Diary of Captain Josiah A. Mitchell.

S. O. Morgan, Lady Morgan's Memoirs: Autobiography, Diaries and Correspondence.

G. Morris, Diary and Letters of Gouverneur Morris.

S. Pepys, Diary and Correspondence of Samuel Pepys, Esq.

S. Pepys, Diary of Samuel Pepys, 1662–1663.

H. A. Shute. Real Diary of a Real Boy.

R. G. Wilberforce (co-author), Life of the Right Reverend Samuel Wilberforce. . . . With Selections from His Diary and Correspondence.

See also the Reader's Guide entry for Journals.

Diary and Correspondence of Samuel Pepys, Esq. S. Pepys.

Diary and Letters of Gouverneur Morris. G. Morris.

Diary in America, with Remarks on Its Institutions. F. Marryat.

Diary of an Idle Woman in Italy. F. M. Dickinson.

Diary of Jeames de la Pluche, Esq.,with His Letters. W. M. Thackeray.

Diary of Mrs. Kitty Trevylyan. E. R. Charles.

Diary of Samuel Pepys, 1662–1663. S. Pepys.

Dichtungen in Luzerner Mundart. O. Sutermeister (comp.).

Dick, Robert: see S. Smiles, Robert Dick.

Dickens, Charles: see

M. D. Conway, Autobiography: Memories and Experiences of Moncure Daniel Conway (marginalia).

T. W. Doane, Bible Myths and Their Parallels in Other Religions (marginalia).

B. Harte, Gabriel Conroy (Catalog entry).

B. Harte, *Luck of Roaring Camp, and Other Sketches* (marginalia).

B. Harte, *Twins of Table Mountain, and Other Stories* (Catalog entry).

F. G. Kitton (comp.), *Dickensiana: A Bibliography of the Literature Relating to Charles Dickens and His Writings.*

J. McCarthy, *Portraits of the Sixties.*

R. S. MacKenzie (Catalog entry).

J. Payn, *Some Literary Recollections.*

Dickensiana: A Bibliography of the Literature Relating to Charles Dickens and His Writings. F. G. Kitton (comp.).

Dickinson, Anna Elizabeth: see J. R. Lowell, *Letters of James Russell Lowell* (marginalia).

Dickinson, Emily: see

T. W. S. Higginson, "Emily Dickinson's Letters."

H. Van Dyke (ed.), *Little Masterpieces of English Poetry, by British and American Authors.*

Dictionaries: see

C. Anthon, *Classical Dictionary, Containing an Account of the Principal Proper Names Mentioned in Ancient Authors.*

J. T. Haydn, *Haydn's Dictionary of Dates and Universal Information Relating to All Ages and Nations.*

W. H. P. Phyfe, *Seven Thousand Words Often Mispronounced: A Complete Hand-Book of Difficulties in English Pronunciation.*

W. Shakespeare, *Mottoes and Aphorisms from Shakespeare. Arranged Alphabetically.*

W. Smith (ed.), *Concise Dictionary of the Bible, for the Use of Families and Students.*

Standards of Length.

See also the Reader's Guide entries for Bible dictionaries, for Cyclopedias, for Encyclopedias, for English dictionaries, for English language, for Quotations, and for individual foreign language dictionaries.

Dictionary. N. Webster.

Dictionary for the Pocket: French and English, English and French. J. Bellows.

Dictionary of American Biography. F. S. Drake.

Dictionary of biographies: see *Men of the Time: A Dictionary of Contemporaries, Containing Biographical Notices of Eminent Characters of Both Sexes.*

Dictionary of Birds. A. Newton.

Dictionary of English and American literature: see S. A. Allibone, *Critical Dictionary of English Literature and British and American Authors.*

Dictionary of Miracles: Imitative, Realistic, and Dogmatic, with Illustrations. E. C. Brewer.

Dictionary of Phrase and Fable. E. C. Brewer.

Dictionary of the English and German Languages. C. F. Grieb.

Dictionary of the English and Italian Languages. I. E. Wessely.

Dictionary of the English Language. J. E. Worcester.

Dictionary of the Hawaiian Language. L. Andrews.

Dictionnaire de la langue française. É. M. P. Littré.

Diddie, Dumps, and Tot; or, Plantation Child-Life. L. C. Pyrnelle.

Dielman, Frederick co-(illus.): see A. R. Macdonough (trans.), *Lovers of Provence: Aucassin and Nicolette.*

Different Forms of Flowers. C. Darwin.

"Difficult Case" (story). W. D. Howells.

"Difficult Case" (story): see W. D. Howells, *Pair of Patient Lovers.*

Digit of the Moon; A Hindoo Love Story. F. W. Bain.

Dilke, Charles Wentworth (contr.): see A. R. Wallace, William Ramsay, *et al. Progress of the Century.*

Dime novels: see

E. Bennett (Catalog entry).

E. Z. C. Judson, *Bloody Avenger of the Spanish Main; or, The Fiend of Blood.*

E. Z. C. Judson, *Convict; or, The Conspirator's Victim.*

E. L. Wheeler (Catalog entry).

"Dinsmore, Elsie" (literary character): see M. F. Finley, *Elsie Dinsmore.*

Diplomatic Disenchantments. E. B. Bigelow.

Diplomatic Woman. W. E. Mansfield and C. H. Mansfield.

Directories: see

C. W. E. Bardsley, *Romance of the London Directory.*

Geer's Hartford City Directory.

Hubbard's Newspaper and Bank Directory of the World.

Keokuk Directory.

G. P. Rowell, *American Newspaper Directory.*

Soard's New Orleans Directory for 1882.

Trow's Business Directory of Greater New York.

Disabilities: see

E. P. Adams, *Story Sermons from Les Misérables* (Catalog entry).

J. Brown, *Spare Hours.*

F. T. Buckland, *Curiosities of Natural History.*

D. M. M. Craik, *Little Lame Prince.*

C. Dickens, *Bleak House.*

C. Dickens, *Christmas Carol in Prose.*

C. Dickens, *Great Expectations.*

C. Dickens, *Nicholas Nickleby.*

H. Keller, *Helen Keller Souvenir No. 2 (1892–1899).*

H. Keller, *Story of My Life.*

H. Keller, *World I Live In.*

Report of the Commission of 1906 to Investigate the Condition of the Blind in the State of New York.

A. C. H. Rice, *Mr. Opp.*

B. Tarkington, *Beasley's Christmas Party.*

M. E. Waller, *Wood Carver of 'Lympus.*

T. Watts-Dunton, *Aylwin.*

M. P. Wilder, *People I've Smiled With: Recollections of a Merry Little Life.*

M. P. Wilder, *Smiling 'Round the World.*

M. P. Wilder, *Sunny Side of the Street.*

J. G. Wood, *Uncivilized Races; or, Natural History of Man* (marginalia).

S. C. Woolsey, *What Katy Did: A Story.*

Discorsi della vita sobria: see L. Cornaro, *Art of Living Long.*

Discoverie of Witchcraft, Wherein the Lewde Dealing of Witches and Witchmongers is Notablie Detected. R. Scot.

Discoveries at Ephesus, Including the Site and Remains of the Great Temple of Diana. J. T. Wood.

Discoveries in Every-day Europe; Vagrant Notes of a Rapid Journey. D. C. Seitz.

Discovery of America, with Some Account of Ancient America and the Spanish Conquest. J. Fiske.
Disputed authorship cases:
  E. A. C. A. Allen, "Rock Me to Sleep, Mother" (poem, song).
  E. L. Beers, "Picket-Guard," better known as "All Quiet on the Potomac Tonight" (poem, song).
  W. A. Butler, *Nothing to Wear: An Episode of City Life* (humorous poem).
  J. A. Joyce, *Edgar Allan Poe* (Catalog entry).
  J. W. Watson, "Beautiful Snow" (poem).
Disraeli, Benjamin: see
  W. Bagehot, *Biographical Studies.*
  (ed., contr.) I. Disraeli, *Curiosities of Literature.*
Dissertations. F. P. Dunne.
"Dissertation Upon Roast Pig" (essay). C. Lamb.
Distinguished American Lawyers, with Their Struggles and Triumphs in the Forum. H. W. Scott.
Diverse Affections: A Romance of Guernsey. H. Garland.
Diversions of a Book-Lover. A. H. Joline.
Diversions of a Diplomat in Turkey. S. S. Cox.
Diversions of a Prime Minister. B. H. Thomson.
"Divided" (poem). J. Ingelow.
Divine Comedy. A. Dante.
Divine Fire (novel). M. A. S. C. Sinclair.
Divine Tragedy. H. W. Longfellow.
Divorce (play). A. Daly.
Divorce of Catherine of Aragon. J. A. Froude.
Dix, John Adams: see M. Dix (comp.), *Memoirs of John Adams Dix.*
Dixie; or, Southern Scenes and Sketches. J. Ralph.
"Dixie's land (I wish I was in Dixie's land)" (song). D. D. Emmett.
Doane, Thomas William, *Bible Myths and Their Parallels in Other Religions*: see H. V. M. Phelips, *Churches and Modern Thought; An inquiry into the Grounds of Unbelief and an Appeal for Candour* (marginalia).
Doane, William Howard (composer): see H. Bonar, "Church has waited long" (hymn).
Dobson, [Henry] Austin: see
  (intro.) R. Herrick, *Selections.*
  (ed.) I. Walton, *Lives of John Donne, Henry Wotton, Richd Hooker, George Herbert, &c.*
Doctor Bryson, A Novel. F. H. Spearman.
Doctor Grimshawe's Secret; A Romance. N. Hawthorne.
Doctor Paley's Foolish Pigeons, and Short Sermons to Workingmen. K. Kennedy.
Doctor's Suggestions to the Community, Being a Series of Papers Upon Various Subjects from a Physician's Standpoint. D. B. S. J. Roosa.
Documentary Outline of the Philippine Case (pamphlet). L. F. Post.
Dodge, Mary Elizabeth (Mapes) (intro.): see *Baby Days; A Selection of Songs, Stories and Pictures, for Very Little Folks.*
Dodgson, Charles Lutwidge: see
  A. F. Eastman, *Flower of Puritanism (Julia Jones Beecher) 1826–1905* (Catalog entry).
  A. C. Waghorne, *Through a Peer Glass: Winnie's Adventures in Wastemonster.*
Dodo: A Detail of the Day. E. F. Benson.

"Doesticks, Q. K. Philander" (pseud.): see M. N. Thomson.
Doffed Coronet, A True Story. M. Cunliffe-Owen.
"Dogberry" (pseud.): see P. Mulford.
Dog Day; or, The Angel in the House. W. L. Emanuel.
Doggett, Allen B. (illus.): see M. E. M. Dodge, *Hans Brinker; or, the Silver Skates. A Story of Life in Holland.*
Doggett, Kate Newell (trans.): see C. Blanc, *Grammar of Painting and Engraving.*
Dog of Constantinople. I. C. S. Chandler.
Dogs: see
  J. M. Baldwin, *Story of the Mind* (marginalia).
  J. Brown, "Rab and His Friends."
  J. Brown, *Spare Hours.*
  Cat and Dog Stories.
  I. C. S. Chandler, *Dog of Constantinople.*
  M. V. Dahlgren, *Chim: His Washington Winter.*
  R. H. Davis, *Bar Sinister.*
  A. M. Downes, *Fire Fighters and their Pets.*
  W. L. Emanuel, *Dog Day; or, The Angel in the House.*
  W. L. Emanuel, *Dogs of War.*
  P. G. Hamerton, *Chapters on Animals.*
  L. Hutton, *Boy I Knew and Four Dogs.*
  L. Hutton, *Four Dogs.*
  L. Hutton, *Some More Dogs.*
  J. K. Jerome, *Three Men in a Boat (To Say Nothing of the Dog).*
  E. T. McLaren, *Dr. John Brown and His Sister Isabella.*
  K. V. Saint Maur, *Earth's Bounty.*
  H. E. B. Stowe, *Dog's Mission; or, the Story of the Old Avery House. And Other Stories.*
  H. E. B. Stowe, *Queer Little People.*
  C. Whitney, *On Snow-Shoes to the Barren Grounds. Twenty-Eight Hundred Miles After Musk-Oxen and Wood-Bison.*
  M. P. Wilder, *People I've Smiled With: Recollections of a Merry Little Life* (Catalog entry).
Dog's Mission; or, the Story of the Old Avery House. And Other Stories. H. E. B. Stowe.
Dogs of War. W. L. Emanuel.
Doings of the Bodley Family in Town and Country. H. E. Scudder.
Dolby, George: see
  F. Bôcher (ed.), *College Series of French Plays; With English Notes* (marginalia).
  M. D. Conway, *Autobiography: Memories and Experiences of Moncure Daniel Conway* (marginalia).
Dole, Helen Bennet (trans.): see V. M. Hugo. *Ninety-Three.*
Dole, Nathan Haskell: see (intro.) Omar Khayyám, *Quatrains of Omar Khayyám of Nishapur. .*
Dollars and Sense. P. T. Barnum.
Doll's House (play). H. Ibsen.
Dolls' Wash. J. H. G. Ewing.
Dombey and Son (play). J. Brougham (adapt.).
Dombey and Son. C. Dickens.
Domestic abuse: see
  C. Dickens, *David Copperfield.*
  C. F. Woolson, *Jupiter Lights; A Novel.*
Domestic Annals of Scotland from the Reformation to the Revolution. R. Chambers (comp.).

"Domestic Life" (essay). R. W. Emerson.

Domestic manuals: see the Reader's Guide entry for Housekeeping advice.

Domestic Manners of the Americans. F. M. Trollope.

Dominic, St.: see G. G. Coulton, *From St. Francis to Dante: Translations from the Chronicle of the Franciscan Salimbene (1221–1288)* (marginalia).

Donald Ross of Heimra. W. Black.

Don César de Bazan: see

  E. Fitzball, *Maritana* (opera).

  V. M. Hugo, *Ruy Blas* (play).

Don Finimondone: Calabrian Sketches. E. J. Pullen.

Don Juan. G. G. Byron.

Donkeys: see

  S. R. Ségur, *Adventures of a Donkey.*

  R. L. Stevenson, *Travels with a Donkey in the Cévennes.*

Donne, John: see I. Walton, *Lives of John Donne, Henry Wotton, Richd Hooker, George Herbert, &c.*

Don Quixote. M. de Cervantes.

Don Quixote: see

  S. V. Clevenger, *Fun in a Doctor's Life, Being the Adventures of an American Don Quixote.*

  A. B. M. Jameson, *Memoirs of the Loves of the Poets. Biographical Sketches of Women Celebrated in Ancient and Modern Poetry* (marginalia).

  W. Swinton, *Outlines of the World's History, Ancient, Medieval, and Modern* (marginalia).

"Dooley, Mr." (pseud.): see F. P. Dunne.

Doomsman. W. G. V. T. Sutphen.

"Dörchläuchting." F. Reuter.

Doré, [Paul] Gustave (illus.): see

  H. de Balzac, *Balzac's Contes Drolatiques.*

  Bible. English.

  S. T. Coleridge, *Rime of the Ancient Mariner.*

  J. Milton, *Milton's Paradise Lost.*

  B. Münchausen, *Adventures of Baron Munchausen.*

  F. Rabelais, *Works.*

  J. X. B. Saintine, *Myths of the Rhine.*

  H. A. Taine, *Tour Through the Pyrenees.*

Dorothy Forster; A Novel. W. Besant.

"Dose of Paradise" (short story). A. F. Eastman.

Double identities: see

  E. J. Bliss, *Peril of Oliver Sargent.*

  E. A. Poe, "William Wilson" (story).

  R. L. Stevenson, *Strange Case of Dr. Jekyll and Mr. Hyde* (novel).

  B. Tarkington, *Conquest of Canaan: A Novel.*

  C. W. Tayleure, *East Lynn* (play).

  G. Verdi, *Trovatore* (opera).

  See also the Reader's Guide entry for Twins.

Douglas, David (ed.): see W. Scott, *Journal of Sir Walter Scott, from the Original Manuscript at Abbotsford.*

"Douglas, Douglas, tender and true": see D. M. M. Craik, *Poems.*

"Douglas, Theo." (pseud.): see H. D. H. Everett.

Douglass, Frederick: see S. J. May, *Some Recollections of Our Antislavery Conflict.*

"Dow, Jr." (pseud.): see E. G. Paige.

"Down in Alabam'" (or "Ain't I glad I got out de wilderness") (minstrel song). J. Warner.

"Downing, Major Jack" (pseud.): see S. Smith.

"Down the Mississippi" (article). G. W. Nichols.

Down the Ravine (novel). M. N. Murfree.

"Down the River" (story). H. P. Spofford.

"Doxology" (hymn). T. Ken.

Doyle, Richard (illus.): see T. Hughes, *Scouring of the White Horse.*

Dracula. B. Stoker.

Dragon of Wantley, His Rise, His Voracity, and His Downfall: A Romance. O. Wister.

Dragons (literary motif): see

  E. N. Bland, *Book of Dragons.*

  K. Grahame, *Dream Days.*

  C. K. Munroe, *Blue Dragon, A Tale of Recent Adventure in China.*

  J. C. F. von Schiller, *Fight with the Dragon. A Romance.*

  A. R. C. Troubetzkoy, *Brother to the Dragons, and Other Old-Time Tales.*

  I. M. Van Etten, "House of the Dragons" (short story).

  O. Wister, *Dragon of Wantley, His Rise, His Voracity, and His Downfall: A Romance.*

Drake, E. L. (clipping about): see G. E. Lewis, *Heart Echoes.*

Drake, Francis (explorer): see C. Kingsley, *Westward Ho!* (novel).

Drake, Joseph Rodman: see

  F. Halleck, "On the Death of Joseph Rodman Drake" (poem).

  Ocean Scenes; or, The Perils and Beauties of the Deep.

Drama collections: see *Dramatists of the Restoration.*

Drama (history): see the Reader's Guide entry for Theatrical history.

Drama in Pokerville, The Bench and Bar of Jurytown, and Other Stories. J. M. Field.

Drama Nuevo: see W. D. Howells (adapt.), *Yorick's Love* (play).

Dramas. R. Browning.

Dramas. A. Flamma.

Dramatic Idyls: see R. Browning, *Agamemnon, La Saisiaz, Dramatic Idyls, and Jocoseria.*

Dramatic Idyls: see R. Browning, *Poetical Works of Robert Browning.*

Dramatic Lyrics, Romances, Etc. R. Browning.

Dramatic Works of Sheridan and Goldsmith. R. B. B. Sheridan.

Dramatis Personae. R. Browning.

Dr. Barnardo, the Foster-Father of "Nobody's Children." J. H. Batt.

Dr. Breen's Practice (novel). W. D. Howells.

Dream Days. K. Grahame.

Dream Life. D. G. Mitchell.

Dream of Fair Women. A. Tennyson.

Dream of Realms Beyond Us (verse drama). A. Welcker.

Dreams: see

  J. Bigelow, *Mystery of Sleep.*

  G. C. Lichtenberg (Catalog entry).

Dred: A Tale of the Great Dismal Swamp. H. E. B. Stowe.

Dreiser, Theodore: see the Catalog entry for *Success Magazine.*

Dress: see A. C. A. Racinet, *Costume historique.*

Drew, John: see W. Shakespeare, *Taming of the Shrew* (play) (Catalog entry).

Dreyfus, Alfred (French army officer): see É. Zola, *Rome* (Catalog entry).

Drift: A Sea-Shore Idyl and Other Poems. G. Arnold.

Drift from Two Shores. B. Harte.

"Drifting About"; or, What "Jeems Pipes, of Pipesville," Saw-and-Did. An Autobiography. S. C. Massett.

Driftwood. Z. J. Gray.

Drinking: see the Reader's Guide entries for Bar-tending, for Drunkenness, for Liquor, and for Temperance literature.

Dr. Jekyll and Mr. Hyde: see R. L. Stevenson, *Strange Case of Dr. Jekyll and Mr. Hyde.*

Dr. John Brown and His Sister Isabella. E. T. McLaren.

Drittes Deutsches Lesebuch. W. Gravert.

Dr. Lavendar's People. M. W. C. Deland.

"Drood, Edwin" (literary character): see C. Dickens, *Mystery of Edwin Drood.*

Dross (novel). H. S. Scott.

Dr. Rameau. G. Ohnet.

Dr. Sevier. G. W. Cable.

Drugs: see the Reader's Guide entry for Addictions.

Drum-Beat. M. W. Higginson.

Drum-Beat of the Nation: The First Period of the War of the Rebellion. C. C. Coffin.

Drummond, May Isobel (Harvey) (ed.): see W. H. Drummond, *The Great Fight. Poems and Sketches.*

Drunkenness: see

   E. T. Booth (Catalog entry).

   J. Campbell, *Lives of the Chief Justices of England* (marginalia).

   C. Dickens, *Old Curiosity Shop* (Catalog entry).

   C. Dickens, *Our Mutual Friend* (Catalog entry).

   M. A. Dodge, *Skirmishes and Sketches.*

   T. Dreiser, *Sister Carrie* (Dreiser's dubious anecdote).

   J. Edwards, *Freedom of Will* (Catalog entry).

   S. P. Fowler, *Salem Witchcraft: Comprising More Wonders of the Invisible World,* (marginalia).

   J. S. Gilbert, *Panama Patchwork; Poems, by James Stanley Gilbert* (marginalia).

   P. S. Gilmore, "When Johnny comes marching home" (song) (Catalog entry).

   F. D. Hemans, "Casabianca" (poem) (Catalog entry).

   T. W. S. Higginson, *Cheerful Yesterdays. Contemporaries* (marginalia).

   W. D. Howells, *Modern Instance* (novel).

   L. Hunt, *Town; Its Memorable Characters and Events* (Catalog entry).

   R. M. Johnston, *Dukesborough Tales* (Catalog entry).

   A. R. Le Sage, *Adventures of Gil Blas of Santillane* (novel) (Catalog entry).

   H. W. Longfellow, *Golden Legend* (marginalia).

   G. W. Moon, *Learned Men's English: The Grammarians* (marginalia).

   Omar Khayyám, *Rubáiyát of Omar Khayyám, The Astronomer-Poet of Persia, Rendered into English Verse* (Clara Clemens Samossoud's marginalia).

   E. A. Poe, "Raven" (poem) (Catalog entry).

   W. C. Prime, *Tent Life in the Holy Land* (marginalia).

A. D. Richardson, *Beyond the Mississippi: From the Great River to the Great Ocean.*

Suetonius, *Lives of the Twelve Caesars* (marginalia).

J. Vanbrugh, *Provok'd Wife. A Comedy* (Catalog entry).

S. Woodworth, "Bucket" (song) (Catalog entry).

É. Zola, *Assommoir.*

See also the Reader's Guide entries for Addictions, for Liquor, and for Temperance literature.

Dryad; A Novel. J. H. McCarthy.

Dryden, John (trans.): see Plutarchus, *Plutarch's Lives of Illustrious Men.*

Drysdale, William (co-author): see *Adventures in Field and Forest.*

Dual personalities: see the Reader's Guide entries for Double identities and for Twins.

DuBarry, Marie Jeanne Bécu: see

   C. de F. d' Hézecques, *Recollections of a Page to the Court of Louis XVI.*

   H. Walpole, *Letters of Horace Walpole, Earl of Oxford* (marginalia).

"Du bist wie eine Blume" (song, poem). H. Heine.

Dublin, New Hampshire: see T. W. S. Higginson, *Cheerful Yesterdays. Contemporaries* (Catalog entry).

Dudevant, Amandine Aurore Lucile (Dupin): see G. Sand (pseud.).

Dudley, S. J. (illus.): see K. H. Brown, *Diane.*

Duel (play). H. L. É. Lavedan.

Duffield, George (American clergyman): see A. D. White, *History of the Warfare of Science with Theology* (marginalia).

Duff-Gordon Ross, Janet Ann: see the Reader's Guide and Catalog entries for J. A. D.-G. Ross.

Dugmore, Arthur Radclyffe (photographer): see

   N. B. De G. Doubleday, *Nature's Garden: An Aid to Knowledge of Our Wild Flowers and Their Insect Visitors.*

   D. S. Jordan (co-author), *American Food and Game Fishes.*

   J. E. Rogers, *Shell Book: A Popular Guide to a Knowledge of the Families of Living Mollusks.*

   J. E. Rogers, *Tree Book: A Popular Guide to a Knowledge of the Trees of North America and to Their Uses and Cultivation.*

Duke of Gandia (play). A. C. Swinburne.

Dukesborough Tales. R. M. Johnston.

Duke's Daughter; or, The Hunchback of Paris (play): see A Anicet-Bourgeois.

Duke's Motto (play): see A. Anicet-Bourgeois.

Duke's Motto; A Melodrama. J. H. McCarthy.

Duluth, Minnesota: see M. C. Russell, *Uncle Dudley's Odd Hours; Being the Vagaries of a Country Editor.*

"Dumanoir" (Philippe-François Pinel): see

   E. Fitzball, *Maritana* (opera).

   V. M. Hugo, *Ruy Blas.*

Dumas, Alexandre: see

   H. H. Breen, *Modern English Literature: Its Blemishes & Defects* (marginalia).

   Comtesse de Genlis (Catalog entry).

Du Maurier, George (illus.): see H. James, *Washington Square.*

Dumb Foxglove, and Other Stories. A. T. Slosson.

DuMond, Frank Vincent (illus.): see
   E. W. M. Brodhead, *Earthly Paragon; A Novel.*
   A. Le Nordez, *Jeanne d'Arc, racontée par l'image d'après les sculpteurs, les graveurs et les peintres.*
   L. Wallace, *Wooing of Malkatoon. Commodus.*
Duncan, Charles C. (ship captain): see *Philanthropy Dissected: The so-Called "Act for the Further Protection of Seamen" Reviewed* (Catalog entry).
Duncan, Sara Jeannette: see S. J. D. Cotes.
Duncan, Walter Jack (illus.): see W. Gibson, "Arkansas Fashion" (short story).
Dundreary, A Four-Act Comedy. T. Taylor,
Dunn, Harvey Thomas (illus.): see R. B. Beach, *Silver Horde; A Novel.*
Dunne, Finley Peter: see
   W. Gillette, *Secret Service* (play) (Catalog entry).
   New York *Times* (Catalog entry).
"Dunning, Charlotte" (pseud.): see C. D. Wood.
Dunny, A Mountain Romance. P. V. Mighels.
Dunsmore, John Ward (illus.): see M. Wagnalls, *Palace of Danger; A Story of La Pompadour.*
Dupleix, Joseph François: see G. B. Malleson, *Dupleix.*
Durand, John (trans.): see H. A. Taine, *Ancient Régime.*
"Duration of Copyright" (article). S. J. Elder.
Dürer, Albrecht: see L. Schefer, *Artist's Married Life; Being That of Albert Dürer* (novel).
"Durst, Simon" (pseud.): see S. W. Wardwell.
Duruy, George (ed.): see P. F. J. N. Barras, *Memoirs of Barras.*
"Dusenberry" (fictional author): see E. Robinson, *Biblical Researches in Palestine, and in the Adjacent Regions. A Journal of Travels in the Years 1838 & 1852.*
Dussouchet, J. (co-author): see A. Brachet, *Petite grammaire Française.*
Duyckinck, Evert Augustus (co-ed.): see *Cyclopædia of American Literature, Embracing Personal and Critical Notices of Authors, and Selections from Their Writings.*
Duyckinck, George Long (co-ed.): see *Cyclopædia of American Literature, Embracing Personal and Critical Notices of Authors, and Selections from Their Writings.*
Dutch Republic: see the Reader's Guide entry for Holland.
Dwiggins, Clare Victor (illus.): see L. de V. Matthewman, *Crankisms, by Lisle de Vaux Matthewman.*
Dwight, John Sullivan: see G. W. Curtis, *Early Letters of George Wm. Curtis to John S. Dwight.*
Dyer, William Buckingham (illus.): see M. E. M. Sangster, *Winsome Womanhood.*
Dystopian literature: see
   E. W. M. Brodhead, *Diana's Livery.*
   J. De Mille, *Strange Manuscript Found in a Copper Cylinder.*
   I. Donnelly, *Caesar's Column. A Story of the Twentieth Century.*
   T. A. Janvier, *Women's Conquest of New York; Being an Account of the Rise and Progress of the Women's Rights Movement.*
   W. G. V. T. Sutphen, *Doomsman.*
   H. G. Wells, *When the Sleeper Wakes.*
   See also the Reader's Guide entry for Utopian literature.

Dziady (Forefathers' Eve). A. Mickiewicz.

▌ E

Eagle Badge; or, The Skokums of the Allagash. H. F. Day.
Eagle Flight: A Filipino Novel, Adapted from "Noli Me Tangere." J. Rizal.
Ealer, George (river pilot): see W. Shakespeare, *Works of Shakespeare* (Catalog entry).
Earl of Derby. G. E. B. Saintsbury.
Early Adventures in Persia, Susiana, and Babylonia. A. H. Layard.
Early French Lessons. H. Bué.
Early Letters of George Wm. Curtis to John S. Dwight; Brook Farm and Concord. G. W. Curtis.
Early reading of Samuel L. Clemens: see
   W. H. Ainsworth (Catalog entry).
   Arabian Nights.
   E. Bennett (Catalog entry).
   Bible. New Testament. English. 1859.
   R. Burns, *Works of Robert Burns.*
   G. G. Byron, "Destruction of Sennacherib" and other poems.
   G. G. Byron, *Works of Lord Byron, in Verse and Prose. Including His Letters, Journals, Etc.*
   J. L. Comstock, *Elements of Geology; Including Fossil Botany and Palæontology.*
   J. F. Cooper, *Leather-Stocking Tales.*
   J. Cundall, *Robin Hood and His Merry Foresters.*
   J. D. Dana, *Manual of Mineralogy, including Observations on Mines.*
   C. Dickens (various titles).
   J. B. Dods, *Spirit Manifestations Examined and Explained.*
   J. W. Draper, *Human Physiology, Statistical and Dynamical; or, The Conditions and Course of the Life of Man.*
   T. C. Haliburton, *Clockmaker, or Sayings and Doings of Sam Slick.*
   U. P. James, *James' River Guide.*
   E. Z. C. Judson, *Bloody Avenger of the Spanish Main; or, The Fiend of Blood.*
   S. Kirkham, *English Grammar in Familiar Lectures.*
   G. Lippard, *Legends of the American Revolution.*
   C. Lyell, *Principles of Geology.*
   J. Milton, *Poetical Works of John Milton.*
   New Testament of Our Lord and Saviour Jesus Christ (1859).
   W. Nicholson (ed.), *American Edition of the British Encyclopedia, or Dictionary of Arts and Sciences.*
   J. Olney, *Practical System of Modern Geography; or, A View of the Present State of the World, Simplified and Adapted to the Capacity of Youth.*
   Parley's Magazine.
   E. A. Poe, *Works of the Late Edgar Allan Poe.*
   W. Robertson, *Historical Disquisition Concerning the Knowledge Which the Ancients Had of India; And the Progress of Trade with That Country.*
   W. Robertson, *History of Scotland During the Reigns of Queen Mary and of King James VI Till His Accession to the Crown of England.*

W. Robertson, *History of the Discovery and Settlement of America*.

W. Scott (various titles).

W. Shakespeare, *Complete Works of William Shakespeare: Comprising His Plays and Poems, with Dr. Johnson's Preface*.

J. Swift, *Gulliver's Travels into Several Remote Nations of the World*.

F. M. A. de Voltaire, *A, B, C, ou dialogues entre A, B, C*.

F. M. A. de Voltaire, "Dialogue entre un philosophe et un contrôleur général des finances."

F. M. A. de Voltaire, "Dialogue entre un plaideur et un avocat."

H. Walpole, *Letters of Horace Walpole, Earl of Oxford* (Catalog entry).

G. S. Weaver, *Lectures on Mental Science According to the Philosophy of Phrenology*.

J. T. Wheeler, *Life and Travels of Herodotus in the Fifth Century Before Christ: An Imaginary Biography Founded on Fact*.

H. Wilson, *Wonderful Characters; Comprising Memoirs and Anecdotes of the Most Remarkable Persons of Every Age and Nation*.

Wyman's Comic Almanac for the Times, 1856.

Early Travels in Palestine, Comprising the Narratives of Arculf, Willibald, Bernard, Saewulf, Sigurd, Benjamin of Tudela, Sir John Maundeville, De La Brocquière, and Maundrell. T. Wright (ed.).

"Earth-Burial and Cremation" (article). A. G. Cobb.

Earth in Past Ages. S. B. Herrick.

"Earthlings" (novella). G. E. King.

Earthly Paradise, A Poem. W. Morris.

Earthly Paragon; A Novel. E. W. M. Brodhead.

Earth's Bounty. K. V. Saint Maur.

Easter Story. J. H. Jewett.

Eastlake, Charles Lock (ed.): see F. T. Kugler, *Handbook of Painting: The Italian Schools*.

Eastlake, Elizabeth (Rigby) (ed.): see F. T. Kugler, *Handbook of Painting: The Italian Schools*.

East Lynne (play). C. W. Tayleure.

Eastman, Charles Alexander: see "Gray Chieftain" (short story) in W. D. Howells (co-ed.), *Under the Sunset*.

Eastward. N. MacLeod.

Eastwick, Edward Backhouse (ed.): see Lutfullah, *Autobiography of Lutfullah, A Mohamedan Gentleman; and His Transactions with His Fellow-Creatures*.

Eaton, Winnifred: see W. E. Babcock.

Eben Holden. I. Bacheller.

Eben Holden's Last Day A-Fishing. I. Bacheller.

Ecce Coelum; or, Parish Astronomy. In Six Lectures. By a Connecticut Pastor. E. F. Burr.

Ecce Deus-Homo; or, The Work and Kingdom of the Christ of Scripture. A. W. Pitzer.

Ecce Femina: An Attempt to Solve the Woman Question. Being an Examination of Arguments in Favor of Female Suffrage by John Stuart Mill and Others, and a Presentation of Arguments Against the Proposed Change in the Constitution of Society. C. White.

Ecce Homo; A Survey of the Life and Work of Jesus Christ. J. R. Seeley.

Eccentricities of Genius; Memories of Famous Men and Women of the Platform and Stage. J. B. Pond.

Ecclesiastical Art in Germany During the Middle Ages. W. Lübke.

Echo (London newspaper): see the Catalog entry for H. Evans, *Our Old Nobility*.

Echoes: see

R. Radau, *Wonders of Acoustics; or, The Phenomena of Sound*.

J. Tyndall, *Sound. A Course of Eight Lectures Delivered at the Royal Institution of Great Britain*.

Eclectic Physical Geography. R. Hinman.

Eclipses: see

S. W. Baker, *Cast Up by the Sea*.

C. Columbus, *Writings of Christopher Columbus*.

J. C. Cremony, *Life Among the Apaches*.

H. R. Haggard, *King Solomon's Mines*.

J. W. Holden, *Wizard's Wanderings from China to Peru*.

Ecology, nature appreciation, and land usage:

C. C. Abbott, *In Nature's Realm*.

J. L. Allen, *Aftermath; Part Second of "A Kentucky Cardinal."*

J. L. Allen, *Kentucky Cardinal; A Story*.

J. L. Allen, *Summer in Arcady; A Tale of Nature*.

J. Burroughs, *Bird and Bough*.

J. Burroughs, *Birds and Bees. Essays*.

J. Burroughs, "Hard Fare" (essay) in *Signs and Seasons*.

J. Burroughs (ed.), *Songs of Nature*.

J. Burroughs, *Winter Sunshine*.

F. A. C. Canfield, *Kidnapped Campers; A Story of Out-of-Doors*.

F. E. Church (Catalog entry).

V. Colvin, *Adirondack Region*.

S. F. Cooper, *Rural Hours, by a Lady*.

S. A. Drake, *Heart of the White Mountains, Their Legend and Scenery*.

F. H. Eckstorm, *Penobscot Man*.

W. H. Gibson, *Camp Life in the Woods and the Tricks of Trapping*.

W. H. Gibson, *Sharp Eyes: A Rambler's Calender of Fifty-Two Weeks Among Insects, Birds, and Flowers*.

M. B. Howitt, *Birds and Flowers; or, Lays and Lyrics of Rural Life*.

E. Ingersoll, *Wild Life of Orchard and Field; Papers on American Animal Life*.

E. Ingersoll, *Wild Neighbors; Out-Door Studies in the United States*.

I. E. Jerome, *One Year's Sketch-Book*.

A. Knapp, *Upland Pastures, Being Some Out-Door Essays Dealing with the Beautiful Things That the Spring and Summer Bring*.

F. de Lanoye, *Sublime in Nature; Compiled from the Descriptions of Travellers and Celebrated Writers*.

M. McCulloch-Williams, *Field-Farings; A Vagrant Chronicle of Earth and Sky*.

M. F. R. Miller, *Brook Book; A First Acquaintance with the Brook and Its Inhabitants Through the Changing Year*.

J. H. Moore, *Universal Kinship*.

J. W. Powell, *Third Annual Report of the Bureau of*

American Ethnology to the Secretary of the Smithsonian Institution, 1879–1880.

C. G. D. Roberts, *Kindred of the Wild; A Book of Animal Life.*

C. Rowley (comp.), *Brotherhood with Nature: A Treasury.*

A. T. Slossom, *Dumb Foxglove, and Other Stories.*

W. O. Stoddard, *In the Open: Stories of Outdoor Life.*

J. M. Thompson, *Songs of Fair Weather.*

J. Thomson, *Seasons: With the Castle of Indolence* (poems).

H. D. Thoreau, *Maine Woods.*

H. D. Thoreau, *Walden; or, Life in the Woods.*

H. Van Dyke, *Blue Flower* (Catalog entry).

H. G. Vennor (Catalog entry).

C. D. Warner, *My Summer in a Garden.*

H. B. Washburn, "Shall We Hunt and Fish? Confessions of a Sentimentalist" (essay).

A. C. Wheeler, *Journey to Nature.*

A. C. Wheeler, *Making of a Country Home.*

G. White, *Natural History and Antiquities of Selborne.*

G. White, *Natural History of Selborne. With a Naturalist's Calendar and Additional Observations.*

E. Whymper, *Scrambles Amongst the Alps in the Years 1860–69.*

J. G. Wood, *Nature's Teachings; Human Invention Anticipated by Nature.*

J. G. Wood, *Our Living World; An Artistic Edition of the Rev. J. G. Wood's Natural History of Animate Creation.*

See also the Reader's Guide entries for Forest and for Natural history.

Economics and labor issues: see

D. C. Beard, *Moonblight and Six Feet of Romance.*

E. Bellamy, *Looking Backward, 2000–1887.*

J. Benton, *Truth about "Protection."*

C. M. Black, *Agitator; A Novel.*

R. Blatchford, *Merrie England.*

J. G. Brooks, *Social Unrest: Studies in Labor and Socialist Movements.*

J. E. Cairnes, *Character and Logical Method of Political Economy.*

G. Cleveland *et al. What Shall We Do With It? (Meaning the Surplus). Taxation and Revenue Discussed.*

I. Donnelly, *Caesar's Column. A Story of the Twentieth Century.*

R. T. Ely, *French and German Socialism in Modern Times.*

H. Evans, *Our Old Nobility.*

M. E. W. Freeman, *Portion of Labor.*

H. George, *Progress and Poverty: An Inquiry into the Cause of Industrial Depression and of Increase of Want with Increase of Wealth: The Remedy* (and six other titles).

S. S. Gilman, *Mothers in Council.*

E. A. G. Glasgow, *Ancient Law* (novel).

F. A. R. Goodale (ed.), *Literature of Philanthropy.*

H. Greeley, *What I Know of Farming: A Series of Brief and Plain Expositions of Practical Agriculture as an Art Based Upon Science* (Catalog entry).

J. Greenwood, *Wilds of London.*

J. Hay, *Bread-Winners: A Social Study.*

J. F. Henkle, *National Peacemaker; A Treatise on Present Conditions in the United States.*

T. H. Huxley, *Evolution and Ethics.*

A. W. Johnston, *Strikes, Labour Questions, and Other Economic Difficulties: A Short Treatise of Political Economy.*

K. Kennedy, *Doctor Paley's Foolish Pigeons, and Short Sermons to Workingmen.*

J. C. Kirwan, *Palace and Hovel; or, Phases of London Life. Being Personal Observations of an American in London.*

T. W. Lawson, *Frenzied Finance.*

E. L. Linton, *True History of Joshua Davidson, Communist.*

H. D. Lloyd, *Man, the Social Creator.*

H. D. Lloyd, *Wealth against Commonwealth.*

S. W. McAllister, *Society As I Have Found It.*

J. D. McCabe, *History of the Grange Movement; or The Farmer's War Against Monopolies.*

W. H. Mallock, *Critical Examination of Socialism.*

E. Markham, *Man with the Hoe and Other Poems.*

K. Marx (Catalog entry).

H. Mayhew, *London Labour and the London Poor.*

J. Means, *Oppressive Tariff Taxation* (pamphlet).

S. E. Moffett, *Tariff. What It Is and What It Does*: see S. E. Moffett, *Suggestions on Government.*

C. Myers, *Would Christ Belong to a Labor Union?*

S. Newcomb, *Plain Man's Talk on the Labor Question.*

M. Pratt, *Orthodox Preacher and Nancy; Being the Tale of the Misfortunes of a Minister who Tried to Do as Jesus Would. A Story of Ministerial Life as It Is.*

T. Roosevelt, *Square Deal.*

C. Rowley (comp.), *Brotherhood with Nature: A Treasury.*

W. M. Salter, *Cure for Anarchy.*

U. B. Sinclair, *Jungle.*

M. F. Somerville, *Personal Recollections, from Early Life to Old Age, of Mary Somerville. With Selections from Her Correspondence* (marginalia).

W. K. Springer, *Tariff Reform, the Paramount Issue. Speeches and Writings on the Questions Involved in the Presidential Contest of 1892.*

Standard (newspaper).

G. Standring, *People's History of the English Aristocracy.*

W. G. Sumner, *What Social Classes Owe to Each Other.*

I. M. Tarbell, *History of the Standard Oil Company.*

R. Temple, *India in 1880.*

T. Thomas, *History of Prices, and of the State of the Circulation, from 1793 to 1837.*

E. J. C. Unwin, *Hungry Forties: Life Under the Bread Tax.*

B. M. Van Vorst and M. V. Vorst, *Woman Who Toils; Being the Experiences of Two Ladies as Factory Girls.*

W. E. Walling, *Russia's Message, The True World Import of the Revolution.*

J. F. Willard, *Tramping with Tramps: Studies and Sketches of Vagabond Life.*

See also the Reader's Guide entries for American social classes, for English social classes, for Finance and business, and for French social classes.

Economy of Happiness. J. Mackaye.

Eddy, Henry Brevoort (illus.): see A. Lee, *He, She & They; Being a Faithful Record of the Woful Enjoyments and Joyful Woes of Him & Her.*

Eddy, Horatio (spiritualist): see H. S. Olcott, *People from the Other World.*

Eddy, Mary Baker: see
  W. Besant, *Pen and the Book* (marginalia).
  R. Blix, *Voile Tombe: Caricatures par Blix* (Catalog entry).
  Book of Mormon.
  E. H. G. Clark, *Church of St. Bunco.*
  T. W. Doane, *Bible Myths and Their Parallels in Other Religions* (marginalia).
  Friendship's Offering; A Christmas, New Year, and Birthday Present (Catalog entry).
  J. A. Joyce, *Edgar Allan Poe* (marginalia).
  R. D. Kathrens, *Side Lights on Mary Baker Eddy-Glover-Science Church Trustees Controversy.* "Next Friends" Suit.
  W. Kennedy, "Pirate's serenade" (song) (Catalog entry).
  W. D. McCrackan, "Mrs. Eddy's Relation to Christian Science" (article).
  F. W. Peabody, *Complete Exposé of Eddyism or Christian Science and the Plain Truth in Plain Terms Regarding Mary Baker G. Eddy, Founder of Christian Science.*
  W. A. Purrington, *Christian Science; An Exposition of Mrs. Eddy's Wonderful Discovery, including Its Legal Aspects.*
  J. D. Quackenbos, *Hypnotic Therapeutics in Theory and Practice.*
  C. É. J. G. de V. Rémusat, *Memoirs of Madame de Rémusat, 1802–1808* (Catalog entry).
  W. Shakespeare, *Works of Shakespeare* (Catalog entry).
  Suetonius, *Lives of the Twelve Caesars* (marginalia).
  G. W. Warder, *Cities of the Sun* (marginalia).
  A. D. White, *History of the Warfare of Science with Theology* (Catalog entry).
  J. H. Wiggin (Catalog entry).
  L. Wright, *How Reverend Wiggin Rewrote Mrs. Eddy's Book.*
  See also the Reader's Guide and Catalog entries for Christian Science.

Eddy, William (spiritualist): see H. S. Olcott, *People from the Other World.*

Edelweiss of the Sierras; Golden-Rod, and Other Tales. C. C. Harrison.

"Edgar Allan Poe" (essay). W. D. Howells.

Edgar Allan Poe. J. A. Joyce.

Edgcumbe, George: see H. Walpole, *Letters of Horace Walpole, Earl of Oxford* (marginalia).

Edgeworth, Richard Lovell (co-author): see M. Edgeworth, *Essay on Irish Bulls.*

Edinburgh (city): see
  C. S. Graham, *Mystifications, by Clementina Stirling Grahame.*
  C. J. Guthrie, *John Knox and John Knox's House.*
  R. L. Stevenson and L. Osbourne, *Wrecker* (novel).

"Editha" (short story): see W. D. Howells, *Between the Dark and the Daylight: Romances.*

Editha's Burglar (play). A. Thomas.

Editing: see
  M. de R.- C. Sévigné, *Letters of Madame De Sévigné to Her Daughter and Friends* (marginalia).
  Way into Print.

"Editor's Drawer" (column). C. D. Warner.

"Editor's Study" (column): see *Harper's Monthly Magazine.*

Editor: The Journal of Information for Literary Works: see the Catalog entry for *Way into Print.*

"Edmonds, S. Emma E." (pseud.): see S. E. E. Edmundson.

Edmonds, John Worth: see J. B. Dods, *Spirit Manifestations Examined and Explained.*

Edmunds, George Franklin: see G. Cleveland *et al. What Shall We Do With It? (Meaning the Surplus). Taxation and Revenue Discussed.*

Education: see the Reader's Guide entry for Teaching methods.

Edward I, King of England: see
  W. Combe, *History and Antiquities of the City of York* (marginalia).
  W. Smith, *Smaller History of England, from the Earliest Times to the Year 1862* (marginalia).
  C. M. Yonge, *Prince and the Page: A Story of the Last Crusade* (novel).

Edward III, King of England: see
  W. Combe, *History and Antiquities of the City of York* (marginalia).
  C. M. Yonge, *Lances of Lynwood.*

Edward V, King of England : see J. Timbs, *Curiosities of London, Exhibiting the Most Rare and Remarkable Objects of Interest in the Metropolis* (marginalia).

Edward VII, King of England: see
  M. D. Conway, *Autobiography: Memories and Experiences of Moncure Daniel Conway* (marginalia).
  E. Văcărescu, *Kings and Queens I Have Known.*

Edwards, E. J. (co-author): see F. E. Garrett, *Story of an African Crisis. Being the Truth About the Jameson Raid and Johannesburg Revolt of 1896.*

Edwards, George Wharton (illus.): see O. W. Holmes, *Last Leaf. Poem.*

Edwards, Harry C. (illus.): see E. D. Deland, *Alan Ransford, A Story.*

Edwards, Jonathan: see
  S. Hopkins. *Life and Character of . . . Jonathan Edwards.*
  M. W. Townsend, *Asia and Europe: Studies* (marginalia).

Edwin Booth. L. Hutton.

Edwin of Deira (poem). A. Smith.

Effects of Cross and Self -Fertilisation. C. Darwin.

Ego and His Own. M. Stirner.

Egoist: A Comedy in Narrative. G. Meredith.

Egoists, A Book of Supermen. J. G. Huneker.

"Egotism; or, The Bosom Serpent" (short story): see N. Hawthorne, "Christmas Banquet."

Egypt: see
  Athenaeus of Naucratis, *Deipnosophists; or, Banquet of the Learned, of Athenaeus.*

A. A. A. Brassey, *Voyage in the Sunbeam, Our Home in the Ocean for Eleven Months*.
G. W. Caldwell, *Oriental Rambles*.
G. L. Carlisle, *Around the World in a Year*.
A. Carnegie, *Round the World*.
J. Chambers, *Destiny of Doris; A Travel-Story of Three Continents*.
T. Child, *Wimples and Crisping-Pins; Being Studies in the Coiffure and Ornaments of Women*.
L. A. Duff-Gordon, *Letters from Egypt*.
G. M. Ebers, *Aegyptische Königstochter. Historischer Roman* (novel).
A. A. B. Edwards, *Thousand Miles Up the Nile*.
H. D. H. Everett, *Iras: A Mystery*.
C. F. Goodrich, *Report of the British Naval and Military Operations in Egypt, 1882*.
J. A. Hart, *Levantine Log-Book*.
A. W. Kinglake, *Eöthen*.
C. Kingsley, *Hypatia; or, New Foes with an Old Face*.
T. W. Knox, *Backsheesh! or, Life and Adventures in the Orient*.
F. de Lanoye, *Rameses the Great; or, Egypt 3300 Years Ago. Egypt 3300 Years Ago*.
N. MacLeod, *Eastward*.
T. Moore, *Epicurean, A Romance*.
W. M. F. Petrie, *Personal Religion in Egypt Before Christianity*.
K. J. Ploetz, *Epitome of Ancient, Mediaeval, and Modern History*.
W. C. Prime, *Boat Life in Egypt and Nubia*.
D. A. Randall, *Handwriting of God in Egypt, Sinai, and the Holy Land*.
R. Robbins, *Outlines of Ancient and Modern History on a New Plan*.
C. Rollin, *Ancient History of the Egyptians, Carthaginians, Assyrians, Babylonians, Medes and Persians, Grecians and Macedonians*.
A. Sauzay, *Wonders of Glass-Making in All Ages*.
C. Scollard, *Under Summer Skies*.
W. Shakespeare, *Antony and Cleopatra* (play).
C. W. Stoddard, *Cruise Under the Crescent; From Suez to San Marco*.
B. Stoker, *Jewel of Seven Stars* (novel).
W. W. Story, "Cleopatra" (poem).
W. Swinton, *Outlines of the World's History, Ancient, Medieval, and Modern*.
B. Taylor, *Egypt and Iceland in the Year 1874*.
B. Taylor, *Journey to Central Africa; or, Life and Landscapes from Egypt to the Negro Kingdoms of the White Nile*.
To Egypt (unidentified book).
C. D. Warner, *My Winter on the Nile, Among the Mummies and Moslems*.
M. S. Wellby, *'Twixt Sirdar and Menelik; An Account of a Year's Expedition from Zeila to Cairo Through Unknown Abyssinia*.
Einer muss heiraten! (play). A. V. Zechmeister.
Einsame Menschen. Drama. G. Hauptmann.
Elbow-Room; A Novel without a Plot. C. H. Clark.
Elderkin, John:
(co-ed.) *Lotos Leaves*.

(co-ed.) *Speeches at the Lotos Club*.
Elderly: see the Reader's Guide entry for Old age.
Eldorado; or, Adventures in the Path of Empire; Comprising a Voyage to California via Panama, Life in San Francisco and Monterey, Pictures of the Gold Region, and Experiences of Mexico Travel. B. Taylor.
Electric motors: see
R. Krause, *Starters and Regulators for Electric Motors and Generators*.
A. R. Wallace, William Ramsay, *et al. Progress of the Century*.
Elegies of Prospertius: see S. Propertius, *Erotica*.
"Elegy on Thyrza" (poem). G. G. Byron.
"Elegy Written in a Country Churchyard" (poem). T. Gray.
Elementary German: An Outline of the Grammar, with Exercises, Conversations, and Readings. C. P. Otis.
Elementary Lessons in Astronomy. J. N. Lockyer.
Elementary Spelling Book. N. Webster.
Elements of Geology; Including Fossil Botany and Palæontology. J. L. Comstock.
Elements of International Law. G. B. Davis.
Elements of Scientific Agriculture. J. P. Norton.
"Elephant" (pseud.): see "Scene on the Ohio."
Elephants: see
F. Vincent, *Land of the White Elephant: Sights and Scenes in South-eastern Asia*.
See also the Reader's Guide entry for Africa and its explorers.
Elephant's Track and Other Stories. M. E. Davis.
Elevator: Farce (play). W. D. Howells.
Eleventh Commandment; A Romance. A. G. Barrili.
Elgar, Francis (contr.): see W. Manning (comp.), *Year-Boke of the Odd Volumes*.
"Elia" (pseud.): see C. Lamb.
"Eliot, Annie" (pseud.): see A. E. Trumbull.
Eliot, George: see
L. de R. Saint-Simon, *Memoirs of the Duke of Saint-Simon on the Reign of Louis XIV and the Regency* (Catalog entry).
(trans.) D. F. Strauss, *Life of Jesus, Critically Examined*.
Elisabeth, Empress of Austria: see K. Chrēstomanos, *Tagebuchblätter*.
Elisabetta, Regina d'Inghilterra [Elizabeth, Queen of England] (opera). G. A. Rossini.
"Elizabeth" (pseud.): see M. A. B. von Arnim.
Elizabeth and Her German Garden (novel): see M. A. B. von Arnim.
Elizabeth, Christian Scientist. M. J. Crim.
Elizabeth; or, The Exiles of Siberia. A Tale, Founded upon Facts. S. Cottin.
Elizabeth, Queen (trans.): see Marguerite d'Angoulême, *Mirror of the Sinful Soul*.
Elizabeth, Queen of England: see
J. Abbott, *History of Queen Elizabeth*.
L. Aikin, *Memoirs of the Court of Queen Elizabeth*.
J. A. Froude, *History of England from the Fall of Wolsey to the Defeat of the Spanish Armada*.
P. Giacometti, *Elizabeth, Queen of England* (play).
C. Kingsley, *Westward Ho!* (novel).
G. A. Rossini, *Elisabetta, Regina d'Inghilterra* (opera).

W. Shakespeare, *Works of Shakespeare* (Catalog entry).
A. E. Trumbull, *Wheel of Progress* (play).
Elizabeth, Queen of England (play). P. Giacometti.
"Ellen Bayne" (minstrel song). S. C. Foster.
Ellen Linn. J. Abbott.
Eller, John (composer): see W. Gill and H. E. Dixey, *Adonis* (burlesque musical).
"Ellerslie" (Scottish site) see G. Aguilar, *Days of Bruce* and J. Porter, *Scottish Chiefs.*
Elliot, Frances Minto Dickinson: see the Catalog entry for F. M. Dickinson.
Ellis, William (intro.): see C. S. Stewart, *Private Journal of a Voyage to the Pacific Ocean and Residence at the Sandwich Islands.*
Ellis, William Ashton (ed., trans.): see R. Wagner, *Richard Wagner to Mathilde Wesendonck.*
Elocution: see
  G. Z. MacLaren (Catalog entry).
  See also the Reader's Guide entry for Speech improvement.
"Eloisa to Abelard" (poem). A. Pope.
Elsie Dinsmore. M. F. Finley.
Elsie Venner: A Romance of Destiny. O. W. Holmes.
Elton, C. A. (trans.): see S. Propertius, *Erotica.*
Embassy to Provence. T. A. Janvier.
"Embury, Mrs.": see S. Pindar.
Emerald and Ermine; A Tale of the Argoät. M. Cunliffe-Owen.
Emerson, Ralph Waldo: see
  J. E. Cabot, *Memoir of Ralph Waldo Emerson.*
  T. Carlyle, *Correspondence of Thomas Carlyle and Ralph Waldo Emerson.*
  Christian Science Journal (marginalia).
  M. Fuller, *Memoirs of Margaret Fuller Ossoli.* Ed. William Henry Channing, Ralph Waldo Emerson, James Freeman Clarke.
  T. W. S. Higginson, *Cheerful Yesterdays. Contemporaries* (marginalia).
  G. S. Meriam, *Living Faith.*
  (intro.): see Plutarchus, *Plutarch's Morals. Translated from the Greek by Several Hands.*
  A. C. H. Rice, *Mrs. Wiggs of the Cabbage Patch* (Catalog entry).
  (pref.): see M. Saadi, *Gulistan; or, Rose Garden, by Musle-Huddeen Sheik Saadi, of Shiraz.*
  A. K. Sartoris, *Week in a French Country-House* (Catalog entry).
  H. Van Dyke (ed.), *Little Masterpieces of English Poetry, by British and American Authors.*
Emerson's Magazine: see J. A. Dallas, "Up the Mississippi."
Emerton, James H. (illus.): see G. W. Peckham and E. G. Peckham, *Wasps, Social and Solitary.*
Emigrant's Story, and Other Poems. J. T. Trowbridge.
Emily Chester. A Novel. A. M. C. Seemüller.
"Emily Dickinson's Letters" (article). T. W. S. Higginson.
Emmerson, Henry Hetherington (co-author): see J. G. Sowerby, *Afternoon Tea: Rhymes for Children with Original Illustrations.*
Emotions: see C. Darwin, *Expression of the Emotions in Man and Animals.*

Empire in Asia, How We Came by It: A Book of Confessions. W. T. M. Torrens.
Empire State: A Compendious History of the Commonwealth of New York. B. J. Lossing.
"Encephalic Anatomy": see E. A. Spitzka, "Contributions."
Encheiridion: see Epictetus, *Selection from the Discourses of Epictetus, with the Encheiridion.*
Encyclopedias: see
  Encyclopaedia Britannica. A Dictionary of Arts, Sciences, and General Literature.
  E. Field, *Little Book of Profitable Tales* (a spoof of subscription encyclopedias).
  P. A. Larousse, *Nouveau Larousse illustré:dictionnaire universel encyclopédique.*
  New International Encyclopaedia.
  W. Nicholson (ed.), *American Edition of the British Encyclopedia, or Dictionary of Arts and Sciences.*
  See also the Reader's Guide entries for Cyclopedias and Dictionaries.
Endicott, John: see H. W. Longfellow, *New-England Tragedies.*
End of the World. E. Eggleston.
Endymion (poem). J. Keats.
Enemy Conquered. S. W. Royston.
Engel, Georg (co-author): see E. Gettke, *In Purgatory.*
England: see
  B. Dodd, *Cathedral Days: A Tour in Southern England.*
  A. Edwards, *Ought We To Visit Her? A Novel.*
  "God save the King" (British anthem).
  G. Haven, *Pilgrim's Wallet; or, Scraps of Travel Gathered in England, France, and Germany.*
  A. Hoppin, *Ups and Downs on Land and Water.*
  W. D. Howells, *Certain Delightful English Towns, with Glimpses of the Pleasant Country Between.*
  W. D. Howells, *London Films.*
  W. D. Howells, *Seven English Cities.*
  W. Irving, *Old Christmas and Bracebridge Hall.*
  J. C. Jeaffreson, *Book About Doctors.*
  L. F. W. Jewitt and S. C. Hall, *Stately Homes of England.*
  J. B. Pond, *Summer in England.*
  J. Poole, *Little Pedlington and the Pedlingtonians.*
  G. W. E. Russell, *Onlooker's Note-book.*
  H. S. Scott, *Phantom Future; A Novel.*
  J. R. Seeley, *Expansion of England; Two Courses of Lectures.*
  H. Smith (clergyman) (Catalog entry).
  J. L. Stoddard, *John L. Stoddard's Lectures.*
  H. A. Taine, *Notes on England.*
  E. Thring, *Uppingham School Songs and Borth Lyrics.*
  F. M. A. de Voltaire, *Letters Concerning the English Nation.*
  A. C. Waghorne, *Through a Peer Glass: Winnie's Adventures in Wastemonster.*
  G. E. Waring, Jr., *Whip and Spur.*
  H. G. Wells, *Wonderful Visit.*
  M. Westrup, *Coming of Billy.*
  W. Winter, *Gray Days and Gold in England and Scotland.*

See also the Reader's Guide entry for Church of
England.
English As She Is Taught. C. B. Le Row (comp.).
English dictionaries: see
    *Standard Dictionary of the English Language Upon
    Original Plans.*
    N. Webster, *American Dictionary of the English
    Language.*
    N. Webster, *Webster's Dictionary.*
    N. Webster, *Webster's International Dictionary.*
    N. Webster, *Webster's Practical Dictionary of the English
    Language.*
    W. D. Whitney, *Century Dictionary: An Encyclopedic
    Lexicon of the English Language.*
    J. E. Worcester, *Dictionary of the English Language.*
    See also the Reader's Guide entry for English language.
English drama: see
    Dramatists of the Restoration.
    B. Matthews, *Studies of the Stage.*
    W. C. Russell, *Representative Actors. A Collection of
    Criticisms, Anecdotes, Personal Descriptions, Etc., Etc.,
    Referring to Many Celebrated British Actors from the
    Sixteenth to the Present Century.*
    See also the Reader's Guide entry for Theatrical
    history.
*English Governess at the Siamese Court; Being Recollections
of Six Years in the Royal Palace at Bangkok.* A. H. E.
Leonowens.
English Grammar in Familiar Lectures. S. Kirkham.
English grammar, usage, and style: see
    C. F. Adams, Jr., "Of Some Railroad Accidents"
    (Catalog entry).
    G. Bainton (comp. and ed.), *Art of Authorship. Literary
    Reminiscences, Methods of Work, and Advice to Young
    Beginners, Personally Contributed by Leading Authors
    of the Day.*
    H. H. Breen, *Modern English Literature: Its Blemishes
    & Defects.*
    E. Buck, *Indo-Anglian Literature.*
    G. L. Craik, *Manual of English Literature and of the
    History of the English Language, with Numerous
    Specimens.*
    M. B. Eddy, *Retrospection and Introspection*
    (marginalia).
    J. da Fonesca and P. Carolino, *New Guide of the Con-
    versation in Portuguese and English in Two Parts.*
    J. T. Goodman, *Archaic Maya Inscriptions* (Catalog
    entry).
    S. Grand, *Heavenly Twins* (marginalia).
    J. R. Green, *Short History of the English People*
    (marginalia).
    T. W. S. Higginson, *Cheerful Yesterdays. Contemporaries*
    (marginalia).
    W. B. Hodgson, *Errors in the Use of English.*
    S. Horner and S. B. Horner, *Walks in Florence and Its
    Environs* (marginalia).
    F. J. Kiefer, *Legends of the Rhine from Basle to Rotter-
    dam* (Catalog entry).
    S. Kirkham, *English Grammar in Familiar Lectures.*
    C. B. Le Row (comp.), *English As She Is Taught.*
    London *Daily Chronicle.*

T. R. Lounsbury, *Standard of Usage in English.*
J. R. Lowell, *Letters of James Russell Lowell*
    (marginalia).
J. Milne, *Romance of a Pro-Consul; Being the Personal
    Life and Memoirs of the Right Hon. Sir George Grey,
    K. C. B.* (marginalia).
G. W. Moon, *Learned Men's English: The
    Grammarians.*
J. L. Motley, *Motley's Dutch Nation, Being the Rise of
    the Dutch Republic (1555-1584) Condensed* (Catalog
    entry).
Munich. Pinakothek, Alte. *Catalogue of the Paintings
    in the Old Pinakothek, Munich* (Catalog entry).
C. Nesbet, *Everybody's Writing-Desk Book.*
L. B. Pendleton. *Bewitched: A Tale* (Catalog entry).
W. H. P. Phyfe, *Seven Thousand Words Often Mispro-
    nounced: A Complete Hand-Book of Difficulties in
    English Pronunciation.*
Plutarchus, *Plutarch's Lives of Illustrious Men*
    (marginalia).
W. H. Prescott, *History of the Conquest of Peru, with
    a Preliminary View of the Civilization of the Incas*
    (Catalog entry).
A. P. Primrose, *Napoleon: The Last Phase* (marginalia).
P. M. Roget, *Thesaurus of English Words and Phrases.*
J. A. D.-G. Ross, *Three Generations of English Women*
    (marginalia).
M. A. Ross, *Delina Delaney* (marginalia).
W. Scott, *Guy Mannering; or, The Astrologer* (Catalog
    entry).
W. Sharp, *Life of Robert Browning* (marginalia).
S. O. Stedman, *Allen Bay, A Story* (marginalia).
J. Swift, *Gulliver's Travels into Several Remote Nations of
    the World* (marginalia).
W. Swinton, *Rambles Among Words; Their Poetry, His-
    tory, and Wisdom.*
Tacitus, *Works of Tacitus* (marginalia).
L. Wallace, *Ben-Hur: A Tale of the Christ* (Catalog
    entry).
L. Wallace, *Boyhood of Christ* (marginalia).
L. Wallace, *Lew Wallace: An Autobiography*
    (marginalia).
M. A. A. Ward, *Robert Elsmere* (Catalog entry).
D. Webster, *Private Correspondence of Daniel Webster*
    (Catalog entry).
J. Webster, *When Patty Went to College* (Catalog entry).
R. G. White, *Words and Their Uses, Past and Present. A
    Study of the English Language.*
F. S. Wihelmina, *Memoirs of Wilhelmine, Margravine of
    Baireuth* (marginalia).
I. Zangwill, *Master; A Novel* (Catalog entry).
See also the Reader's Guide entry for Rhetoric.
English history: see
    E. A. Abbey, *Old Songs, with Drawings by Edwin A.
    Abbey and Alfred Parsons.*
    J. Abbott, *History of Queen Elizabeth.*
    L. Aikin, *Memoirs of the Court of King James the First.*
    L. Aikin, *Memoirs of the Court of Queen Elizabeth.*
    H. C. Bailey, *Colonel Greatheart.*
    R. Baker, *Chronicle of the Kings of England, from the*

Time of the Romans Government, unto the Death of King James the First.

Battle Abbey. *The Roll of Battle Abbey, Annotated.*

T. H. Baylis, *Temple Church and Chapel of St. Ann, Etc.: An Historical Record and Guide* .

H. T. Buckle, *History of Civilization in England.*

E. G. E. Bulwer-Lytton, *Last of the Saxon Kings.*

J. Campbell, *Lives of the Chief Justices of England.*

J. Campbell, *Lives of the Lord Chancellors and Keepers of the Great Seal of England, from the Earliest Times Till the Reign of Queen Victoria.*

T. Child, *Wimples and Crisping-Pins; Being Studies in the Coiffure and Ornaments of Women.*

A. J. Church, *With the King at Oxford; A Tale of the Great Rebellion.*

W. F. Collier, *History of the British Empire.*

M. De Lancey, *Week at Waterloo in 1815. Lady De Lancey's Narrative.*

C. Dickens, *Child's History of England.*

A. E. Dickinson, *Crown of Thorns, or Ann Boleyn* (play).

W. H. Dixon, *History of Two Queens: Catherine of Aragon and Anne Boleyn.*

A. B. Dodd, *Cathedral Days: A Tour in Southern England.*

H. Dunckley, *Lord Melbourne.*

H. P. Dunster, *Historical Tales of Lancastrian Times.*

H. Evans, *Our Old Nobility.*

C. R. L. Fletcher, *Introductory History of England, from the Earliest Times to the Close of the Middle Ages.*

M. Fowler, *Some Notable Archbishops of Canterbury.*

J. Foxe, *Book of Martyrs.*

J. Froissart, *Chronicles of England, France, Spain, and the Adjoining Countries.*

J. A. Froude, *History of England from the Fall of Wolsey to the Defeat of the Spanish Armada.*

J. A. Froude, *Oceana, or England and Her Colonies.*

T. Fuller, *History of the Worthies of England*: see T. Fuller, *Holy State and the Profane State.*

J. Gerard, *What Was the Gunpowder Plot? The Traditional Story Tested by Original Evidence.*

J. R. Green, *History of the English People.*

J. R. Green, *Short History of the English People.*

M. A. E. Green, *Lives of the Princesses of England from the Norman Conquest.*

C. C. F. Greville, *Greville Memoirs; A Journal of the Reigns of King George IV and King William IV.*

M. Hall, *Lives of the Queens of England Before the Norman Conquest.*

H. Hallam, *Constitutional History of England.*

Henry VII, *Statutes of Henry VII in Exact Facsimile.*

G. A. Henty, *St. George for England: A Tale of Cressy and Poitiers* (novel).

E. Herbert, *Autobiography.*

M. H. Hervey, *Amyas Egerton, Cavalier* (novel).

C. Hindley, *Old Book Collector's Miscellany; or, a Collection of Readable Reprints of Literary Rarities.*

R. Huish, *Memoirs of George the Fourth, Descriptive of the Most Interesting Scenes of His Private and Public Life.*

D. Hume, *History of England, from the Invasion of Julius Caesar to the Revolution of 1688.*

L. Hunt, *Town; Its Memorable Characters and Events.*

Ingulf, *Ingulph's Chronicle of the Abbey of Croyland.*

J. A. A. J. Jusserand, *English Wayfaring Life in the Middle Ages (XIVth Century).*

C. Kingsley, *Westward Ho!* (novel).

C. Knight, *Popular History of England: An Illustrated History of Society and Government from the Earliest Period to Our Own Times.*

I. C. Knox, *Little Folks' History of England.*

W. E. H. Lecky, *History of England in the Eighteenth Century.*

Life and Amours of Owen Tideric, Prince of Wales, Otherwise Owen Tudor (novel).

J. Lingard, *History of England from the First Invasion by Romans.*

H. G. D. Liveing, *Records of Romsey Abbey: An Account of the Benedictine House of Nuns, with Notes on the Parish Church and Town (A. D. 907- 1558).*

T. R. Lounsbury, "Scholar of the Twelfth Century" (articles).

E. G. B. Lytton, *Harold, The Last of the Saxon Kings.*

J. McCarthy, *History of Our Own Times, from the Accession of Queen Victoria to the General Election of 1880.*

J. McCarthy, *History of Our Own Times, from the Diamond Jubilee, 1897 to the Accession of King Edward VII.*

J. McCarthy, *History of the Four Georges.*

J. McCarthy, *Portraits of the Sixties.*

J. McCarthy, *Reign of Queen Anne.*

J. McCarthy, *Reminiscences.*

T. B. Macaulay, *History of England from the Accession of James II.*

A. MacKinnon, *Prince Charles Edward; or, The Rebellion of 1745–46.*

W. H. Maxwell, *Life of Field-Marshal His Grace the Duke of Wellington.*

M. P. W. Montagu, *Letters of Lady Mary Wortley Montagu.*

G. Parker, *Ladder of Swords; A Tale of Love, Laughter and Tears* (novel).

K. J. Ploetz, *Epitome of Ancient, Mediaeval, and Modern History.*

S. Rayner, *History and Antiquities of Pudsey.*

E. Reich, *Success Among Nations.*

A. Rimmer, *Ancients Streets and Homesteads of England.*

W. J. Rolfe, *Shakespeare the Boy, with Sketches of the Home and School Life, the Games and Sports, the Manners, Customs and Folklore of the Time.*

G. E. B. Saintsbury, *Earl of Derby.*

J. H. Shorthouse, *John Inglesant: A Romance.*

F. H. B. Skrine, *Fontenoy and Great Britain's Share in the War of the Austrian Succession, 1741–1748.*

A. Smith, *Edwin of Deira* (poem).

G. Smith, *Three English Statesmen: A Course of Lectures on the Political History of England.*

W. Smith, *Morley: Ancient and Modern.*

W. Smith (ed.), *Old Yorkshire.*

W. Smith (ed.), *Registers of Topcliffe, and Morley in the*

W. R. of the County of York. Baptisms, 1654–1830. Burials, 1654–1888.

W. Smith, *Smaller History of England, from the Earliest Times to the Year 1862.*

P. H. Stanhope, *History of England, Comprising the Reign of Queen Anne until the Peace of Utrecht.*

A. P. Stanley, *Historical Memorials of Westminster Abbey.*

A. Strickland, *Lives of the Queens of England, from the Norman Conquest; With Anecdotes of Their Courts.*

J. Strutt, *Sports and Pastimes of the People of England, Including the Rural and Domestic Recreations, May Games, Mummeries, Shows, Processions, Pageants, and Pompous Spectacles.*

J. Tanswell, *History and Antiquities of Lambeth.*

A. Tennyson, *Becket* (drama).

Tewkesbury. *Official Guide to Tewkesbury.*

M. W. Townsend, *Asia and Europe: Studies Presenting the Conclusions Formed by the Author* (marginalia).

H. D. Traill, *Marquis of Salisbury.*

J. H. Trumbull (ed.), *True-Blue Laws of Connecticut and New Haven* (marginalia).

A. W. Tuer, *Follies and Fashions of Our Grandfathers.*

A. W. Tuer, *Old London Street Cries and the Cries of To-Day.*

E. J. C. Unwin, *Hungry Forties: Life Under the Bread Tax.*

A. E. West, *Recollections, 1832 to 1886.*

M. E. J. Whitcombe, *Bygone Days in Devonshire and Cornwall, with Notes of Existing Superstitions and Customs.*

G. White, *Natural History and Antiquities of Selborne.*

W. G. Willis, *Charles the First: An Historical Tragedy. In Four Acts* (play).

W. Winter, *Gray Days and Gold in England and Scotland.*

W. Winter, *Old Shrines and Ivy.*

T. Wright, *Homes of Other Days: A History of Domestic Manners and Sentiments in England, from the Earliest Known Period to Modern Times.*

C. M. Yonge, *Cameos from English History. The Wars in France.*

C. M. Yonge, *Lances of Lynwood.*

C. M. Yonge, *Little Duke; or, Richard the Fearless* (novel).

C. M. Yonge, *Parallel History of France and England; Consisting of Outlines and Dates.*

C. M. Yonge, *Young Folks' History of England.*

York Minster. Accurate Description and History of the Cathedral and Metropolitan Church of St. Peter, York, from its First Foundation.

See also the Reader's Guide entries for London, for Oliver Cromwell, and for individual kings and queens.

English humorists: see
J. Ashton, *English Caricature and Satire on Napoleon I.*
W. B. Bernand (Catalog entry).
A. Birrell, *Obiter Dicta.*
F. C. Burnand, *Happy Thoughts.*
C. Dickens, *Pickwick Papers.*
G. L. DuMaurier, *Social Pictorial Satire.*

Favorite Album of Fun and Fancy.
T. A. Guthrie, *Vice Versâ; or, A Lesson to Fathers.*
J. K. Jerome, *Three Men in a Boat (To Say Nothing of the Dog).*
C. Lamb, "Dissertation Upon Roast Pig" (essay).
J. J. Morier, *Adventures of Hajji Baba of Ispahan* (novel).
K. A. Sanborn, *Wit of Women.*
H. A. Taine, *Notes on England.*
W. M. Thackeray, *Thackeray's Lectures. The English Humourists. The Four Georges* (marginalia).
G. O. Trevelyan, *Life and Letters of Lord Macaulay* (marginalia).
See also the Reader's Guide entry for Humor collections.

English language: see
G. L. Craik, *Manual of English Literature and of the History of the English Language, with Numerous Specimens.*
C. W. Dilke, *Greater Britain: A Record of Travel in English-Speaking Countries During 1866 and 1867.*
F. Grose, *Classical Dictionary of the Vulgar Tongue.*
R. Head and F. Kirkman, *English Rogue.*
J. C. O'Connor (ed.), *Esperanto. The Student's Complete Text Book.*
R. G. White, *Words and Their Uses, Past and Present. A Study of the English Language.*
See also the Reader's Guide entry for English dictionaries.

English literature: see
G. L. Craik, *A Manual of English Literature and the History of the English Language, with Numerous Specimens.*
C. W. Dilke (ed.) ed. *Old English Plays; Being a Selection from the Early Dramatic Writers.*
W. Forsyth, *Novels and Novelists of the Eighteenth Century, in Illustration of the Manners and Morals of the Age.*
C. Fox, *Memories of Old Friends, Being Extracts from the Journals and Letters of Caroline Fox.*
W. Hazlitt, *Lectures on the Literature of the Age of Elizabeth, and Characters of Shakespear's Plays.*
C. Hindley, *Old Book Collector's Miscellany; or, a Collection of Readable Reprints of Literary Rarities.*
J. G. Huneker, *Iconoclasts, A Book of Dramatists.*
S. Lanier, *Shakespeare and His Forerunners: Studies in Elizabethan Poetry and Its Development from Early English.*
R. McWilliam, *Longmans' Handbook of English Literature. Pt. III. From Ben Jonson to Locke.*
H. A. Taine, *History of English Literature. A New Edition.*
H. B. Wheatley, *Samuel Pepys and the World He Lived In.*

Englishman's Home; A Play in Three Acts. G. L. B. Du Maurier.

Englishmen (characterized): see the Reader's Guide entry for H. B. Fearon, *Sketches of America. A Narrative of a Journey of Five Thousand Miles* (marginalia).

English Rogue: Described, in the Life of Meriton Latroon, a

Witty Extravagant. Being a Compleat History of the Most Eminent Cheats of Both Sexes. R. Head and F. Kirkman.

English social classes: see

J. H. Batt, *Dr. Barnardo, the Foster-Father of "Nobody's Children."*

Battle Abbey. *The Roll of Battle Abbey, Annotated.*

M. von Bothmer, *German Home Life* (marginalia).

A. Edwards, *Ought We To Visit Her? A Novel.*

H. Evans, *Our Old Nobility.*

S. Grand, *Heavenly Twins* (marginalia).

P. G. Hamerton, *Wenderholme. A Story of Lancashire and Yorkshire.*

H. D. Labouchère (editor of *Truth: A Weekly Journal*).

H. Martineau, *Society in America* (marginalia).

H. Mayhew, *London Labour and the London Poor* (Catalog entry).

J. A. Nimes, *Aristocracy. A Novel.*

S. J. Reid, *Sketch of the Life and Times of the Rev. Sydney Smith.*

W. P. Ridge, *Second Opportunity of Mr. Staplehurst.*

M. Roberts, *Lord Linlithgow, A Novel.*

C. Rowley (comp.), *Brotherhood with Nature: A Treasury.*

G. W. E. Russell, *Onlooker's Note-book.*

M. F. Somerville, *Personal Recollections, from Early Life to Old Age, of Mary Somerville. With Selections from Her Correspondence* (marginalia).

G. Standring, *People's History of the English Aristocracy.*

D. T. Stanley, *London Street Arabs.*

H. A. Taine, *Notes on England.*

W. M. Thackeray, *Vanity Fair, A Novel without a Hero.*

W. M. Thackeray, *Virginians; A Tale of the Last Century.*

Truth: A Weekly Journal.

A. Upward, *Slaves of Society. A Comedy in Covers: By the Man Who Heard Something.*

See also the Reader's Guide entries for American social classes, for Economics and labor issues, and for French social classes.

English Wayfaring Life in the Middle Ages (XIVth Century). J. A. A. J. Jusserand.

Engraving: see

C. Blanc, *Grammar of Painting and Engraving.*

W. O. Chapin, *Masters and Masterpieces of Engraving.*

G. Duplessis, *Wonders of Engraving.*

See also the Reader's Guide entry for Printing.

Enigma of Life; A Solution of the Great Mystery. D. W. Church.

Enoch Arden (poem). A. Tennyson.

Enquiry Concerning Human Understanding: see D. Hume, "Of Miracles" (extract).

"Enrique, Erratic" (pseud.): see H. C. Lukens.

Enslaved people: see the Reader's Guide entry for Slavery.

Entombed in Flesh. M. H. Dziewicki.

Entrapped vessels (theme): see

H. Hendrik, *Memoirs of Hans Hendrik, The Arctic Traveller* (marginalia).

W. D. Howells (co-ed.), *Library of Universal Adventure by Sea and Land.*

T. A. Janvier, *In the Sargasso Sea, A Novel.*

J. Verne, *Five Weeks in a Balloon; or, Journeys and Discoveries in Africa, by Three Englishmen* (Catalog entry).

J. G. Whittier, "Maud Miller" (poem) (Catalog entry).

J. Wise, *Through the Air: A Narrative of Forty Years' Experience as an Aeronaut* (Catalog entry).

Éon de Beaumont, Chevalier d': see H. Walpole, *Letters of Horace Walpole, Earl of Oxford* (marginalia).

Eöthen. A. W. Kinglake.

Ephesus: see

E. Falkener, *Ephesus and the Temple of Diana.*

J. T. Wood, *Discoveries at Ephesus, Including the Site and Remains of the Great Temple of Diana.*

Ephesus and the Temple of Diana. E. Falkener.

Epicurean, A Romance. T. Moore.

Epicureanism: see S. Dill, *Roman Society in the Last Century of the Western Empire* (marginalia).

Epicurus (philosopher): see W. Temple, "Upon the Gardens of Epicurus" (essay).

Epigrams of Martial Translated into English Prose. M. V. Martialis.

Epilepsy: see J. D. Quackenbos, *Hypnotic Therapeutics in Theory and Practice.*

Epithalamion: see E. Spenser, *Fairie Queene. To Which Is Added His Epithalamion.*

Epitome of Ancient, Mediaeval, and Modern History. K. J. Ploetz.

Épitres. N. Boileau-Despréaux.

Erasmus, Desiderius: see

J. Froude, *Short Studies on Great Subjects.*

C. Reade, *Cloister and the Hearth; or, Maid, Wife, and Widow: A Matter-of-Fact Romance.*

"Erasmus Wilson" (poem). J. W. Riley.

Erling the Bold. R. M. Ballantyne.

"Erlkönig" (poem, ballad). J. W. von Goethe.

Erotica: The Elegies of Propertius. S. Propertius.

Erotica: see

Arabian Nights.

H. de Balzac, *Balzac's Contes Drolatiques; Droll Stories Collected from the Abbeys of Touraine.*

G. Boccaccio, *Decameron or Ten Days' Entertainment of Boccaccio.*

R. Burns, *Merry Muses of Caledonia.*

G. Casanova de Seingalt, *Mémoires de Jacques Casanova de Seingalt, Écrits par lui-même.*

Cent Nouvelles Nouvelles.

J. Cleland, *Fanny Hill: Memoirs of a Woman of Pleasure.*

J. W. Ebsworth (ed.), *Choyce Drollery: Songs and Sonnets.*

J. W. Ebsworth (ed.), *Westminster Drolleries, Both Parts, of 1671, 1672; Being a Choice Collection of Songs and Poems, Sung at Court and Theatres.*

R. Head and F. Kirkman, *English Rogue: Described, in the Life of Meriton Latroon, a Witty Extravagant. Being a Compleat History of the Most Eminent Cheats of Both Sexes.*

J. B. Louvet de Couvrai, *Amours du chevalier de faublas.*

Marguerite d'Angoulême, *Heptameron of Margaret, Queen of Navarre.*

M. E. de Montaigne, *Works of Michael de Montaigne, Comprising His Essays, Journey into Italy, and Letters.*
Ovid, *Art of Love, in Three Books.*
Petronius Arbiter, *Satyricon*: see S. Propertius, *Erotica.*
H. V. M. Phelips, *Churches and Modern Thought; An inquiry into the Grounds of Unbelief and an Appeal for Candour* (marginalia).
S. Propertius, *Erotica: The Elegies of Propertius.*
F. Rabelais, *Works of Francis Rabelais.*
J. Swift, *Gulliver's Travels into Several Remote Nations of the World* (Catalog entry).
C. B. Wakefield (Catalog entry).
É. Zola, *Terre* (Catalog entry).
   See also the Reader's Guide entry for Sexuality.
Ernst, Louis (ed.): see T. Robertson, *Whole French Language.*
Errors in the Use of English. W. B. Hodgson.
Erstes Lesebuch. Leichte Erzählungen für ganz Kleine artige Kinder. R. Fränkel.
Erzählungen aus der alten Welt. K. F. Becker.
Escapes: see the Reader's Guide entries for Premature burial and for Prison and dungeon literature.
Escarpolette (play). G. C. Lounsbery.
Esher, Reginald Baliol Brett (ed.): see Queen Victoria, *Letters of Queen Victoria.*
Eskimos: see H. M. Miller, *Little People of Asia.*
Esperanto. The Student's Complete Text Book. J. C. O'Connor (ed.).
"Essay on Bacon." T. B. Macaulay.
Essay on Criticism (poem). A. Pope.
Essay on Irish Bulls. M. Edgeworth and R. L. Edgeworth (co-author).
"Essay on Lord Clive." T. B. Macaulay.
Essay on Man (poem). A. Pope.
Essay on Poetry. J. Sheffield.
Essay on the Genius and Writings of Pope. J. Warton.
Essay on the Warrant, Nature, and Duties of the Office of the Ruling Elder, in the Presbyterian Church. S. Miller.
"Essay on Warren Hastings." T. B. Macaulay.
Essays: see
   J. Brown, *Spare Hours.*
   J. Burroughs, *Birds and Bees. Essays.*
   T. Carlyle, *Critical and Miscellaneous Essays.*
   F. P. Cobbe, *The Peak in Darien, with Some Other Inquiries Touching Concerns of the Soul and the Body.*
   F. M. Colby, *Imaginary Obligations.*
   A. Cowley, *Essays.*
   W. J. Dawson (co-ed.), *Great English Essayists. Introductions and Notes.*
   De Quincey, T.: see W. J. Dawson (co-ed.), *Great English Essayists. Introductions and Notes* (inscr.).
   De Quincey, T., *Miscellanies: Chiefly Narrative.*
   R. W. Emerson, *Essays.*
   J. Fiske, *Century of Science and Other Essays.*
   G. B. M. Harvey, *Women, Etc. Some Leaves from an Editor's Diary.*
   W. D. Howells, *Impressions and Experiences.*
   W. D. Howells, *Suburban Sketches.*
   A. Knapp, *Upland Pastures, Being Some Out-Door Essays Dealing with the Beautiful Things That the Spring and Summer Bring.*

C. Lamb, *Essays of Elia.*
C. Lamb, *Last Essays of Elia.*
T. B. Macaulay, *Critical, Historical, and Miscellaneous Essays.*
B. Matthews, *Historical Novel and Other Essays.*
H., G. von Moltke, *Essays, Speeches and Memoirs.*
M. E. de Montaigne, *Works of Michael de Montaigne, Comprising His Essays, Journey into Italy, and Letters.*
E. J. Phelps, *Orations and Essays of Edward John Phelps, Diplomat and Statesman.*
W. L. Phelps, *Essays on Modern Novelists.*
C. A. Sainte-Beuve, *Monday-Chats, Selected and Translated from the "Causeries du Lundi."*
G. A. Sala, *Under the Sun: Essays Mainly Written in Hot Countries.*
G. Sand, *Lettres d'un Voyageur.*
A. Schopenhauer, *Essays of Arthur Schopenhauer.*
S. Smith, *Essays Social and Political. First and Second Series.*
C. W. Stoddard, *Exits and Entrances: A Book of Essays and Sketches.*
W. Temple, "Upon the Gardens of Epicurus" (essay).
H. D. Thoreau, "Civil Disobedience" (essay).
H. D. Thoreau, *Yankee in Canada, with Anti-Slavery and Reform Papers.*
H. T. Tuckerman, *Criterion; or, The Test of Talk about Familiar Things. A Series of Essays.*
B. F. Underwood, *Essays and Lectures.*
C. D. Warner, *As We Were Saying.*
C. D. Warner, *Backlog Studies.*
C. D. Warner, *My Summer in a Garden.*
C. D. Warner, *Relation of Literature to Life.*
C. D. Warner, "Simplicity" (essay).
H. Watterson, *Compromises of Life, and Other Lectures and Addresses, Including Some Observations on Certain Downward Tendencies of Modern Society.*
C. B. G. Wells, *About People.*
Essays and Lectures. B. F. Underwood.
Essays in Criticism. Second Series. M. Arnold.
Essays in Miniature. A. Repplier.
Essays of Elia: see C. Lamb, *Works of Charles Lamb.*
Essays on German Literature. H. H. Boyesen.
Essays on Modern Novelists. W. L. Phelps.
Essays on the Supernatural Origin of Christianity, with Special Reference to the Theories of Renan, Strauss, and the Tübingen School. G. P. Fisher.
Essays Social and Political. First and Second Series. S. Smith.
Essays, Speeches and Memoirs. H. G. Moltke.
Essentials of Elocution and Oratory. V. A. Pinkley.
Estelle and Other Poems. M. B. Allmond.
L'Estrange, Alfred Guy Kingam (ed.): see M. R. Mitford, *Friendships of Mary Russell Mitford as Recorded in Letters from Her Literary Correspondents.*
Eternal Boy, Being the Story of the Prodigious Hickey. O. M. Johnson.
Eternal City. T. H. H. Caine.
"Eternal Goodness" (poem). J. G. Whittier.
Eternal Laughter and Other Poems. W. S. Burgess.
"Eternal spirit, we confess" (hymn). I. Watts.
Ethel. J. J. Bell.

Ether of Space. O. J. Lodge.

Ethics: see the Reader's Guide entry for Economics and labor issues.

Ethics of Democracy: A Series of Optimistic Essays on the Natural Laws of Human Society. L. F. Post.

Ethiopia: see

W. C. Prime, *Boat Life in Egypt and Nubia.*

M. S. Wellby, *'Twixt Sirdar and Menelik: An Account of a Year's Expedition from Zeila to Cairo Through Unknown Abyssinia.*

Ethiopics; or, the Adventures of Theagenes and Chariclea: see *Greek Romances of Heliodorus, Longus, and Achilles Tatius.*

Ethnology: see J. W. Powell, *Third Annual Report of the Bureau of American Ethnology to the Secretary of the Smithsonian Institution, 1879–1880.*

Etiquette and personal conduct: see

C. S. J. Bloomfield-Moore, *Sensible Etiquette of the Best Society, Customs, Manners, Morals, and Home Culture.*

G. E. B. Campbell and M. F. Sheldon, *Everybody's Book of Correct Conduct; Being Hints for Everyday Life.*

G. M. Cooke, *Their First Formal Call.*

Habits of Good Society: A Handbook for Ladies and Gentlemen.

F. M. H. Hall, *Social Usages at Washington.*

C. B. Hartley, *Gentlemen's Book of Etiquette and Manual of Politeness.*

A. H. Jomini, *Jomini's Handbook of Military Etiquette.*

A. B. B. Longstreet, *Social Etiquette of New York.*

J. McGovern, *Golden Censer; or, the Duties of To-Day and the Hopes of the Future.*

E. Post (Catalog entry).

M. E. W. Sherwood, *Manners and Social Usages.*

M. V. H. Terhune, *Breakfast, Luncheon, and Tea.*

R. Tomes, *Bazar Book of Decorum. The Care of the Person, Manners, Etiquette, and Ceremonials.*

M. W. Townsend, *Asia and Europe: Studies* (marginalia).

G. O. Trevelyan, *Life and Letters of Lord Macaulay* (marginalia).

F. M. Trollope, *Domestic Manners of the Americans* (marginalia).

M. de Waddeville, *Monde et ses usages.*

See also the Reader's Guide entry for Moral conduct guides.

Etymology: see

W. Swinton, *Rambles Among Words; Their Poetry, History, and Wisdom.*

R. G. White, *Words and Their Uses, Past and Present. A Study of the English Language.*

Eugen, Anton Oskar (comp.): see Wilhelm II, *Kaiser's Speeches, Forming a Character Portrait of Emperor William II.*

Eugene Aram. E. G. E. B. Lytton.

Eugenics: see

E. W. Foxall, *Colorphobia. An Exposure of the "White Australia" Fallacy.*

F. Galton, *Finger Prints* (Catalog entry).

E. W. Gilliam, "Chinese Immigration" (article).

E. P. Jackson, *Demigod; A Novel.*

C. W. Saleeby, *Evolution, the Master-Key: A Discussion of the Principle of Evolution as Illustrated in Atoms, Stars, Organic Speicies, Mind, Society and Morals.* .

E. A. Spitzka, "Contributions to the Encephalic Anatomy of the Races" (article).

Euphues and His England. J. Lyly.

Euphues, The Anatomy of Wit. J. Lyly.

European history:

H. T. Buckle, *History of Civilization in England.*

C. C. Coffin, *Story of Liberty.*

E. A. Freeman, *Historical Geography of Europe.*

J. Froissart, *Chronicles of England, France, Spain, and the Adjoining Countries.*

C. A. Fyffe, *History of Modern Europe.*

S. R. Gardiner, *Thirty Years' War, 1618–1648.*

A. Gindely, *Geschichte des dreissigjährigen Krieges.*

Ginn & Company's Classical Atlas, in Twenty-three Coloured Maps.

H. Hallam, *View of the State of Europe During the Middle Ages.*

H. C. Lea, *History of the Inquisition of the Middle Ages.*

E. H. Lecky, *History of European Morals from Augustus to Charlemagne.*

W. E. H. Lecky, *History of the Rise and Influence of the Spirit of Rationalism in Europe.*

J. Lord, *Beacon Lights of History.*

E. R. B. Lytton. *Chronicles and Characters.*

D. O'Sullivan (comp.), *Book of Legends, Containing a Selection of Standard Tales from the Most Esteemed British Essayists.*

E. Reich, *Success Among Nations.*

R. Robbins, *Outlines of Ancient and Modern History on a New Plan.*

F. von Schlegel, *Philosophy of History; in a Course of Lectures, Delivered at Vienna.*

J. K. Ploetz, *Epitome of Ancient, Mediaeval, and Modern History.*

A. C. A. Racinet, *Costume historique.*

L. von Ranke, *History of the Popes, Their Church and State, and Especially of Their Conflicts with Protestantism in the Sixteenth and Seventeenth Centuries.*

W. H. Rule, *History of the Inquisition from Its Establishment in the Twelfth Century to Its Extinction in the Nineteenth.*

A. Sauzay, *Wonders of Glass-Making in All Ages.*

J. C. L. S. de Sismondi, *Historical View of the Literature of the South of Europe.*

F. H. B. Skrine, *Fontenoy and Great Britain's Share in the War of the Austrian Succession, 1741–1748.*

W. Swinton, *Outlines of the World's History, Ancient, Medieval, and Modern.*

E. Văcărescu, *Kings and Queens I Have Known.*

P. Villari, *Life and Times of Niccolò Machiavelli* (marginalia).

P. Vinogradoff, *Roman Law in Mediaeval Europe.*

C. M. Yonge, *Landmarks of History.*

See also the Reader's Guide entries for the Middle Ages and for specific nations.

Euthanasia: see L. L. Clifford, *Mrs. Keith's Crime; A Record.*

Evangeline (musical burlesque). J. C. Goodwin and E. E. Rice.

Evangeline: see *Longfellow's Evangeline with Illustrations by F. O. C. Darley.* H. W. Longfellow.

Evans, Andrew (lyricist, singer): see D. D. Emmett, "Jolly raftsman" (minstrel song).

Evans, Arthur John (pref.): see C. H. Hawes and H. B. Hawes, *Crete, The Forerunner of Greece.*

Evans, Augusta Jane: see A. J. Wilson.

Evans, Edward P.: see E. E. Evans, *Story of Kaspar Hauser from Authentic Records.*

Evans, Florence (Wilkinson): see F. Wilkinson.

Evans, Marian: see "George Eliot" (pseud.).

Evelina; or, The History of a Young Lady's Entrance into the World. F. Burney.

Evelina's Garden. M. E. W. Freeman.

"Evelyn Gladys" (pseud.): see H. Kuehn.

"Even me" (hymn). E. H. Codner.

"Even me" (hymn): see O. W. Holmes, *Autocrat of the Breakfast-Table* (marginalia).

Everaerts, Jan Nicolai: see J. Secundus (pseud.).

Everett, Edward: see M. D. Conway, *Autobiography: Memories and Experiences of Moncure Daniel Conway* (marginalia).

Evermann, Barton Warren (co-author): see D. S. Jordan (co-author), *American Food and Game Fishes: A Popular Account of All the Species Found in America North of the Equator.*

"Ever of thee I'm fondly dreaming" (song). G. Linley.

"Everpoint" (pseud.): see J. M. Field.

Evershed, Hope S. (illus.): see H. B. Moore, *Her Royal Highness Queen Bee: A Story of Fact and Fancy and Other Stories.*

Everybody's Book of Correct Conduct; Being Hints for Every-day Life. G. E. B. Campbell and M. F. Sheldon.

Everybody's Friend, or Josh Billings's Encyclopedia and Pro-verbial Philosophy of Wit and Humor. H. W. Shaw.

Everybody's Guide to Music, with Illustrated Chapters on Singing and Cultivation of the Voice. J. Booth.

Everybody's Pocket Cyclopedia of Things Worth Knowing, Things Difficult to Remember, and Tables of Reference. E. L. Sheldon.

Everybody's Writing-Desk Book. C. Nisbet.

Every Man for Himself. N. Duncan.

Every One His Own Way. E. F. Wyatt.

Evil: see V. Streamer (comp.), *Voices of Doubt and Trust* (marginalia).

Evolution: see

M. Adams, *Continuous Creation; An Application of the Evolutionary Philosophy to the Christian Religion.*

S. A. Arrhenius, *Life of the Universe as Conceived by Man from the Earliest Ages to the Present Time.*

S. A. Arrhenius, *Worlds in the Making: The Evolution of the Universe.*

R. Chambers, *Vestiges of the Natural History of Creation.*

S. V. Clevenger, *Evolution of Man and His Mind. A History and Discussion.*

E. Clodd, *Story of Creation: A Plain Account of Evolution.*

C. Darwin, *Descent of Man* [also various other titles.]

C. Darwin, *What Mr. Darwin Saw in His Voyage Round the World in the Ship "Beagle."*

H. Drummond, *Lowell Lectures on the Ascent of Man.*

T. H. Huxley, *Evolution and Ethics.*

J. H. Moore, *Universal Kinship.*

C. W. Saleeby, *Cycle of Life According to Modern Science.*

C. W. Saleeby, *Evolution, the Master-Key: A Discussion of the Principle of Evolution.*

M. J. Savage (Catalog entries).

H. Spencer (Catalog entry).

Truth Seeker (magazine).

B. F. Underwood, *Essays and Lectures.*

A. R. Wallace, William Ramsay, *et al. Progress of the Century.*

See also the Reader's Guide and Catalog entries for C. Darwin.

Evolution and Ethics. T. H. Huxley.

Evolution of Man and His Mind. A History and Discussion of the Evolution and Relation of the Mind and Body of Man and Animals. S. V. Clevenger.

Evolution, the Master-Key: A Discussion of the Principle of Evolution as Illustrated in Atoms, Stars, Organic Speicies, Mind, Society and Morals. C. W. Saleeby.

Ewing, Juliana Horatia Gatty: see H. K. F. G. Eden, *Juliana Horatia Ewing and Her Books.*

Exchanged infants: see

A. Dumas, *Man in the Iron Mask.*

E. E. G. Evans, *Story of Kaspar Hauser from Authentic Records.*

See also the Reader's Guide entries for Double identi-ties and for Twins.

Exemplary Novels of Miguel de Cerantes Saavedra. M. de Cervantes Saavedra.

Exercitation Concerning the Frequent Use of Our Lord's Prayer in the Publick Worship of God. T. Long.

Exits and Entrances: A Book of Essays and Sketches. C. W. Stoddard.

Expansion of England; Two Courses of Lectures. J. R. Seeley.

Expatriates; A Novel. L. L. Bell.

Expedition of Humphry Clinker (novel). T. G. Smollett.

Expedition of Humphry Clinker: see W. M. Thackeray, *Thackeray's Lectures. The English Humourists. The Four Georges* (marginalia).

Expedition to the Philippines. F. D. Millet.

Expert Maid-Servant. C. T. Herrick.

Exploits of Arsène Lupin. M. Leblanc.

Exploration of the Valley of the Amazon. W. L. Herndon.

Explorations in Turkestan, with an Account of The Basin of Eastern Persia and Sistan. Expedition of 1903. R. Pumpelly.

Expression of the Emotions in Man and Animals. C. Darwin.

Extermination of Love. E. Gerard.

"Eyes of Affection" (short story by George Abiah Hib-bard): see W. D. Howells and H. M. Alden (eds.), *Their Husbands' Wives.*

Eytinge, Solomon (illus.): see

C. Dickens, *Christmas Carol in Prose.*

B. Harte, *Condensed Novels.*

Ezra Jordan's Escape from the Massacre at Fort Loyall (novel). J. O. Kaler.

F

Fabeln. Drei Bücher. Nebst Abhandlungen. G. E. Lessing.
Fabiola; or, The Church of the Catacombs. N. P. S. Wiseman.
Fables: see
  Aesop, *Bewick's Select Fables.*
  T. Bulfinch, *Age of Fable; or, Beauties of Mythology.*
  J. de La Fontaine, *Fables.*
  J. de La Fontaine, *Fables de J. de La Fontaine.*
Fables by G. Washington Aesop, Taken "Anywhere, Anywhere, Out of the World." G. T. Lanigan.
Fables in Slang. G. Ade.
Fables of Aesop. Aesop.
Facsimiles of National Manuscripts from William the Conqueror to Queen Anne. H. James (ed.).
Faerie Queene. To Which Is Added His Epithalamion. E. Spenser.
Fahy, Francis Arthur (poet): see "Nora McCarty" (ballad).
Fair Barbarian. F. H. Burnett.
"Fairfax, Beatrice" (pseud.): see M. Manning.
Fairfield, A. H. (comp.): see H. E. B. Stowe, *Flowers and Fruit from the Writings of Harriet Beecher Stowe.*
Fair God; or, The Last of the 'Tzins. A Tale of the Conquest of Mexico. L. Wallace.
Fairies: see the Reader's Guide entry for Fairy tales.
Fair Lavinia, and Others. M. E. W. Freeman.
Fair Maid of Perth. W. Scott.
Fairy Book. É. de Laboulaye.
Fairy-Land of Science. A. B. Buckley.
Fairy tales: see
  H. C. Andersen, *Bilderbuch ohne Bilder.*
  H. C. Andersen, *White Swans and Other Tales.*
  A. F. von Berger, *Habsburg. Märchenspiel in drei Acten* (play).
  Blue Fairy Book (ed. Andrew Lang).
  A. von Chamisso, *Peter Schlemihl's wundersame Geschichte.*
  S. Coleridge, *Phantasmion, A Fairy Tale.*
  Elizabeth, Queen of Rumania, *Real Queen's Fairy Tales.*
  Favorite Fairy Tales: The Childhood Choice of Representative Men and Women.
  Greek Fairy Tales for My Children: see C. Kingsley, *Heroes.*
  Grimm Brothers. Jacob Grimm and Wilhelm Grimm, *Grimms' Fairy Tales.*
  Grimm's Maerchen: Brüder Grimm Kinder und Hausmaerchen. C. P. Otis (ed.).
  W. Hauff, "How the Caliph Became a Stork."
  H. A. Hays, *Princess Idleways: A Fairy Story.*
  O. Herford, *Artful Anticks.*
  E. Humperdinck, *Hänsel und Gretel* (opera).
  L. Hunt, *Day by the Fire; and Other Papers, Hitherto Uncollected.*
  R. Koch, *Berggeist im Riesengebirge.*
  É. de Laboulaye, *Laboulaye's Fairy Book; Fairy Tales of All Nations.*
  É. de Laboulaye, *Last Fairy Tales.*
  F. H. K. La Motte-Fouqué. *Undine, Eine Erzählung.*

C. G. Leland, *Hundred Riddles of the Fairy Bellaria.*
"Little Red Riding Hood."
H. W. Mabie (ed.), *Fairy Tales Every Child Should Know.*
P. E. de Musset, *Mr. Wind and Madam Rain.*
Y. T. Ozaki, *Japanese Fairy Tales.*
M. Peterson, *Prinzessin Ilse. Ein Märchen aus dem Harzgebirge.*
S. Pindar, *Legends of the Flowers.*
S. Pindar, *Midsummer Fays; or, The Holidays at Woodleigh.*
H. Pyle, *Pepper & Salt; or, Seasoning for Young Folk.*
Shitakari Suzume (Japanese fairy tale).
M. E. J. Whitcombe, *Bygone Days in Devonshire and Cornwall, with Notes of Existing Superstitions and Customs.*
G. J. Whyte-Melville, *Holmby House; A Tale of Old Northamptonshire* (novel) (Catalog entry).
E. F. Wyatt, *Every One His Own Way* (Catalog entry).
Fairy Tales Every Child Should Know. H. W. Mabie (ed.).
Fairy Tales of All Nations. É. de Laboulaye.
Faith healing: see W. De Voe, *Healing Currents from the Battery of Life.*
Fall of Constantinople, Being the Story of the Fourth Crusade. E. Pears.
Fall of Feudalism in Ireland; or, the Story of the Land League Revolution. M. Davitt.
False claimants: see the Reader's Guide entry for Impostors.
Falstaff and His Companions. Twenty-one Illustrations in Silhouette. P. Konewka.
Fame: see D. Defoe, *Moll Flanders and The History of the Devil* (marginalia).
"Familiar Letter on Art" (sketch). J. Prym.
Familiar Letters of John Adams and His Wife Abigail Adams, During the Revolution. J. Adams.
Familie Buchholz. Aus dem Leben der Hauptstadt. J. E. W. Stinde.
Famille de Jeanne d'Arc. R. B. de Molandon.
Family at Misrule. E. S. Turner.
Family Canoe Trip. F. W. Snedeker.
Family Flight. E. E. Hale.
Family Library of British Poetry from Chaucer to the Present Time (1350–1878). J. T. Fields and E. P. Whipple (eds.).
Family Library of Poetry and Song. Being Choice Selections from the Best Poets, English, Scottish, Irish, and American. W. C. Bryant (comp.).
Famous American Authors. S. K. Bolton.
Famous Authors (Men). E. F. Harkins.
Famous Cases of Circumstantial Evidence. S. M. Phillipps.
Famous Stories Every Child Should Know. H. W. Mabie (ed.).
Fancies and Facts. R. Browning.
Fanfani, Pietro (co-author): see G. Rigutini, *Vocabolario Italiano della lingua parlata.*
Fanny Hill: Memoirs of a Woman of Pleasure. J. Cleland.
Fantastic History of the Celebrated Pierrot. A. Assollant.
Fantasy of Mediterranean Travel. S. G. Bayne.
Fantine, or the Felon and the Fallen. V. M. Hugo.

Faraday, Michael: see J. Fiske, *Century of Science and Other Essays* (marginalia).

Farces:
G. L. Furniss, *A Box of Monkeys*.
W. D. Howells, *Elevator: Farce*.
W. D. Howells, *Mouse-Trap. A Farce*.
W. D. Howells, *Parlor Car. Farce*.
W. D. Howells, *Register: Farce*.
T. John, *Turn Him Out!: A Farce in One Act*.
J. Kenney, *Raising the Wind*.
C. Kraatz, *Mountain Climber*.
H. C. Merivale, *He's a Lunatic: A Farce in One Act*.
J. M. Morton, *Box and Cox*.
C. D. Taylor, "Ye Old Militia Muster."

Far Eastern Tropics: Studies in the Administration of Tropical Dependencies. A. Ireland.

"Farewell, Annie darling" (song). J. E. Stewart.

"Farewell!—But Whenever You Welcome the Hour" (poem). T. Moore.

Far-Famed Tales: see *Arabian Nights*.

Far from the Madding Crowd. T. Hardy.

Farmer's Cyclopedia of Agriculture: A Compendium of Agricultural Science and Practice. E. V. Wilcox and C. B. Smith.

Farming: see the Reader's Guide entry for Agriculture.

Farquhar, George: see W. Winter, *Old Shrines and Ivy*.

"Farquharson, Martha" (pseud.): see M. F. Finley.

Farrell, Clinton Pinckney (contr., publisher): see R. G. Ingersoll, *Works of Robert G. Ingersoll*.

Farthest North; Being the Record of a Voyage of Exploration of the Ship "Fram" 1893–96, and of a Fifteen Months' Sleigh Journey. F. Nansen.

Far West: see the Reader's Guide entry for American West.

Fashion and style: see the Reader's Guide entry for Beauty and grooming.

Fasquelle, Louis (ed.): see F. de S. de la Mothe Fénelon, *Aventures de Télémaque, fils d'Ulysse*.

Fate of Madame La Tour; A Tale of Great Salt Lake. C. Paddock.

Fate of the Children of Uisneach: see R. J. O'Duffy (ed. and trans.), *Oidhe Chloinne Uisnigh: Fate of the Children of Uisneach*.

"Father" (chapter in a composite novel). W. D. Howells.

Father Goose; His Book. L. F. Baum.

"Father in Heaven" (hymn): see "Fading, still fading."

Fatinitza (operetta). C. Wälzel and F. F. R. Genée.

Faublas: see J. B. Louvet.

Faust. J. W. von Goethe.

Faust: see H. H. Boyesen, *Goethe and Schiller: Their Lives and Works, Including a Commentary on Goethe's Faust*.

Faust von Goethe. J. W. von Goethe.

Favorite Poems, by Charles Kingsley, Owen Meredith, and Edmund Clarence Stedman. C. Kingsley.

Fawkes, Guy: see J. Gerard, *What Was the Gunpowder Plot? The Traditional Story Tested by Original Evidence*.

Fay, Gaston (co-illus.): see *Mother Goose's Melodies for Children*.

Fearful Responsibility and Other Stories. W. D. Howells.

Fearon, Henry Bradshaw: see W. Cobbett, *Year's Residence in the United States of America*.

Fechter, Charles: see A. Anicet-Bourgeois, *Le Bossu* (play).

Felicia; A Novel. F. N. D. Murfree.

Felix Holt, The Radical. G. Eliot.

Fellows, George S.: see M. D. Larrowe, *Physiological Memory; or, The Instantaneous Art of Never Forgetting* (Catalog entry).

Felon and the Fallen. V. M. Hugo.

Female Characters of Goethe. J. W. von Goethe.

Feminism: see the Reader's Guide entry for Women's rights.

Fenn, Harry (illus.): see
Niagara Book: A Complete Souvenir of Niagara Falls.
W. Scott, *Christmas in the Olden Time*.
(co-illus.) A. Tennyson, *Lady Clare*.

Fennel and Rue; A Novel. W. D. Howells.

Fenollosa, Ernest: see M. M. Fenollosa, *Breath of the Gods* (Catalog entry).

Fenwick's Career (novel). M. A. A. Ward.

Ferdinand Magellan. F. A. Ober.

Ferishtah's Fancies. R. Browning.

"Fern, Fanny" (pseud.): see S. P. Willis.

Festus: A Poem. P. J. Bailey.

Feuds: see J. W. De Forest, *Kate Beaumont* (novel).

Féval, Paul: see A. Anicet-Bourgeois, *Le Bossu* (play).

Field Book of American Wild Flowers; Being a Short Description of Their Character and Habits. F. S. Matthews.

Field, Eugene: see E. C. S. Gaskell, *Cranford* (Catalog entry).

Field-Farings; A Vagrant Chronicle of Earth and Sky. M. McCulloch-Williams.

Field, Kate: see
New York *Tribune* (Catalog entry).
L. Whiting, *After Her Death; The Story of a Summer*.

Fielding, H." (pseud.): see H. Fielding-Hall.

Fielding, Henry: see W. M. Thackeray, *Thackeray's Lectures. The English Humourists. The Four Georges* (marginalia).

Field of the Cloth of Gold (play). W. Brough. See also the Catalog entry for T. B. Aldrich, *Cloth of Gold and Other Poems*.

Fields, James Thomas: see
A. A. Fields, *Whittier; Notes of His Life and of His Friendships*.
G. R. Root, "Battle cry of freedom" (song) (Catalog entry).

Fife, Alice Maude: see the Catalog entry for A. M. F. S. Rawson.

Fifteen Years among the Mormons: Being the Narrative of Mrs. Mary Ettie V. Smith, Late of Great Salt Lake City. N. W. Green.

Fiftieth Congress of the United States: see *Memorial to the Fiftieth Congress*.

Fifine at the Fair (poem). R. Browning.

Fight at Dame Europa's School. T. Nast.

Fight with the Dragon. A Romance. J. C. F. von Schiller.

Figures and Flowers for Serious Souls. L. H. Fisher.

Fiji: see
A. L. A. Forbes, *Two Years in Fiji*.
B. C. Seemann, *Viti: An Account of a Government*

Mission to the Vitian or Fijian Islands, in the Years 1860–61. T. Williams (co-author), *Fiji and the Fijians.*

Fiji and the Fijians. T. Williams (co-author).

Fille d'Eve. H. de Balzac.

Final Memorials of Charles Lamb: see C. Lamb, *Works of Charles Lamb.*

Finance and business: see
  H. Alger (Catalog entry).
  H. Clews, *Twenty-Eight Years in Wall Street.*
  C. A. Conant, *Principles of Banking.*
  C. A. Conant, *Principles of Money and Banking.*
  R. K. Duncan, *Chemistry of Commerce: A Simple Interpretation of Some New Chemistry.*
  W. L. Fawcett, "History of the Two Pillars" (article).
  F. T. Hill, *Story of a Street; A Narrative History of Wall Street.*
  T. W. Lawson, *Frenzied Finance.*
  E. Lefevre, *Sampson Rock, of Wall Street. A Novel.*
  Letters from a Self-Made Merchant to His Son; Being the Letters Written by John Graham: see G. T. Richardson, *Letters from a Son to His Self-Made Father* (Catalog entry).
  Letters from a Son to His Self-Made Father. G. T. Richardson.
  T. Roosevelt, *Square Deal.*
  C. W. Silver, *Secular Anathema on Fakery in Business, Social and Professional Life; or, Twentieth Century Conduct.*
  S. Smiles, *Life and Labor; or Characteristics of Men of Industry, Culture and Genius.*
  M. Smith, *Plain Truths about Stock Speculation. How to Avoid Losses in Wall Street* (includes Alan Gribben's essay on Clemens as a businessman).
  H. J. Stevens, *Copper Handbook: A Manual of the Copper Industry of the World.*
  Trow's Business Directory of Greater New York.
  H. T. Tuckerman, "Old Bankers of Florence" (article).
  See also the Reader's Guide entries for Economics and labor issues and for Standard Oil Company.

Finger Prints. F. Galton.

Fink, Denman (illus.): see R. E. Beach, *Barrier.*

Finland: see
  A. Gripenberg (Catalog entry).
  B. Taylor, *Northern Travel: Summer and Winter Pictures of Sweden, Denmark, and Lapland.*

Finlay, Francis Dalzell: see
  (inscr.) *Prize Essays on "Billiards as an Amusement for All Classes."*
  (inscr.) C. Rogers (ed.), *Centenary Garland; Being Pictorial Illustrations of the Novels of Sir Walter Scott, in Their Order of Publication. By George Cruikshank, and Other Artists of Eminence.*

Finley, John H. (ed.): see R. Browning, *Complete Works of Robert Browning.*

Fiorino, Prosper (illus.): see D. C. Seitz, *Discoveries in Every-day Europe; Vagrant Notes of a Rapid Journey.*

Fire Fighters and Their Pets. A. M. Downes.

Fireman, J. C. (co-illus.): see E. Marshall, *Lizette: A Story of the Latin Quarter.*

Fireplaces: : see O. C. Gillespie (comp.), *Rumford Fireplaces and How They Are Made.*

First Biennial Report of the Nevada Historical Society, 1907–1908. Nevada State Historical Society.

First Book in American History. E. Eggleston.

First Book of Botany. E. A. Youmans.

First Christmas, from "Ben-Hur." L. Wallace.

First Christmas of New England. H. E. B. Stowe.

First Lessons in Earth Lore for Children. C. Kingsley.

First Love (novella). I. S. Turgenev.

First Napoleon. A Sketch, Political and Military. J. C. Ropes.

First of Empires, "Babylon of the Bible" in the Light of Latest Research. W. S. C. Boscawen.

"First Piano in Camp" (story): see S. P. Davis, *Short Stories.*

First Reader. W. T. Harris (co-author).

First Report of the Committee of the Society for Psychical Research: see the Catalog entry for Society for Psychical Research.

"First Snowfall" (poem). J. R. Lowell.

First Violin; A Novel. J. Fothergill.

Fischer, Henry W. H. (co-trans.): see
  H., G. von Moltke, *Letters of Field-Marshall Count Helmuth von Moltke to His Mother and His Brothers.*
  See also the Reader's Guide entry for H. W. H. Fisher.

Fischer, Kuno (lecture): see G.W. von Leibniz entry.

Fish: see D. S. Jordan (co-author), *American Food and Game Fishes: A Popular Account of All the Species Found in America North of the Equator.*

Fish, Hamilton: T. W. S. Higginson, *History of the United States from 986 to 1905.* (marginalia).

Fisher, Arabella Burton (Buckley): see A. B. Buckley.

Fisher Boy. A. Tripp.

Fisher, Henry W. H.: see
  H. W. H. Fischer, *Private Lives.*
  See also the Reader's Guide entry for H. W. H. Fischer

Fisher Ames-Henry Clay, Etc. D. B. Lucas and J. F. McLaughlin.

Fishing: see
  I. Bacheller, *Eben Holden's Last Day A-Fishing.*
  D. S. Jordan (co-author), *American Food and Game Fishes: A Popular Account of All the Species Found in America North of the Equator.*
  W. C. Prime, *I Go A-Fishing.*
  H. E. Rood, *In Camp at Bear Pond.*
  D. Sage, *Ristigouche and Its Salmon Fishing. With a Chapter on Angling Literature.*
  D. Sage, "Ten Days' Sport on Salmon Rivers."
  W. O. Stoddard, *In the Open: Stories of Outdoor Life.*
  A. Tripp, *Fisher Boy.*
  H. Van Dyke, *Blue Flower* (Catalog entry).
  C. D. Warner, *In the Wilderness.*
  H. B. Washburn, "Shall We Hunt and Fish? The Confessions of a Sentimentalist" (essay).
  G. S. Wasson, *Cap'n Simeon's Store.*
  H. P. Wells, *City Boys in the Woods; or, A Trapping Venture in Maine.*
  E. C. E. M. S. Wortley, *Travels in the United States, Etc., During 1849 and 1850* (marginalia).

Fiske, John Safford (trans.): see H. A. Taine, *Tour Through the Pyrenees*.

FitzGerald, Edward (trans.): see
  Omar Khayyám, *Rubáiyát of Omar Khayyám in English Verse*.
  Omar Khayyám, *Rubáiyát of Omar Khayyám, The Astronomer-Poet of Persia, Rendered into English Verse*.
  C. Wells, *Rubáiyát of Bridge*.

Fitzgerald, Geraldine (trans.): see M. Jokai, *Black Diamonds, A Novel*.

Five Nations. R. Kipling.

Five Weeks in a Balloon; or, Journeys and Discoveries in Africa, by Three Englishmen. J. Verne.

Five Years in an English University. C. A. Bristed.

Five Years of a Hunter's Life in the Far Interior of South Africa. R. G. Gordon-Cumming.

Flach, Pauline Bancroft (trans.): see S. O. L. Lagerlöf, *Story of Gösta Berling*.

Flagg, James Montgomery (illus.): see G. H. Brennan, *Bill Truetell, A Story of Theatrical Life*.

Flame, Electricity and the Camera; Man's Progress. G. Iles.

Flamingo Feather. C. K. Munroe.

Flaubert, Gustave: see *Little French Masterpieces*.

Flaxman, John (illus.): see Dante, *Vision; or, Hell*.

Flebbe, Beulah Marie Dix: see B. M. Dix.

Flemeng, Léopold (etcher): see G. Boccaccio, *Stories of Boccaccio*.

Fleming, A. M. K. (co-author): see A. M. Kipling, *Hand in Hand; Verses by a Mother and Daughter*.

Fleming, Marjorie: see
  J. Brown, *Marjorie Fleming, A Sketch*.
  L. Macbean and J. Brown, *Marjorie Fleming: The Story of Pet Marjorie, Together with Her Journals and Her Letters*.
  L. Macbean, *Story of Pet Marjorie (Marjory Fleming)*.

Fletcher, John (co-author): see F. Beaumont, *King and No King*.

Fletcher, R. H. (ed.): see A. D. Richardson, *Personal History of Ulysses S. Grant*.

Flight of Pony Baker; A Boy's Town Story. W. D. Howells.

Flint Chips. A Guide to Pre-Historic Archaeology, as Illustrated by the Collection in the Blackmore Museum, Salisbury. E. T. Stevens.

Flodden Field; A Tragedy. A. Austin.

Flood-tide. S. P. M. Greene.

Florence (city): see
  R. Browning (various poems).
  B. Cellini, *Memoirs of Benvenuto Cellini*.
  T. Child, *Wimples and Crisping-Pins; Being Studies in the Coiffure and Ornaments of Women*.
  H. B. Fuller, *Chevalier of Pensieri-Vani*.
  Hand-Book of Florence and Environs with Views, A Topographical Plan and the Catalogues of Galleries.
  S. Horner and J. B. Horner, *Walks in Florence and Its Environs*.
  W. D. Howells, *Tuscan Cities*.
  L. Hutton, *Literary Landmarks of Florence*.
  C. G. Leland, *Legends of Florence; Collected from the People*.
  M. O. W. Oliphant, *Makers of Florence: Dante, Giotto, Savonarola, and Their City*.

M. V. Samuels, *Florentines: A Play*.

M. F. Somerville, *Personal Recollections, from Early Life to Old Age, of Mary Somerville. With Selections from Her Correspondence* (marginalia).

T. A. Trollope, *History of the Commonwealth of Florence, from the Earliest Independence of the Commune to the Fall of the Republic in 1531*.

Florentines: A Play. M. V. Samuels.

Florida: see
  C. K. Munroe, *Flamingo Feather*.
  C. K. Munroe, *Wakulla; A Story of Adventure in Florida*.
  F. A. Ober, *Juan Ponce de Leon*.
  F. Whitmore, *Florida Farm*.

Florida Farm. F. Whitmore.

Flower and Thorn, Later Poems. T. B. Aldrich.

Flower of Puritanism (Julia Jones Beecher) 1826–1905. A. F. Eastman.

Flower O' the Vine: Romantic Ballads and Sospiri di Roma. W. Sharp.

Flowers: see
  N. B. De G. Doubleday, *Wild Flowers: An Aid to Knowledge of Our Wild Flowers and Their Insect Visitors*.
  W. H. Gibson, *Strolls by Starlight and Sunshine*.
  P. Henderson, *Practical Floriculture; A Guide to the Successful Cultivation of Florists' Plants*.
  F. S. Matthews, *Field Book of American Wild Flowers; Being a Short Description of Their Character and Habits*.
  See also the Reader's Guide entries for Botany and for Gardening.

Flowers and Fruit from the Writings of Harriet Beecher Stowe. H. E. B. Stowe.

"Flow gently, sweet Afton" (song). R. Burns.

Flowing Bowl: When and What to Drink: Full Instructions How to Prepare, Mix, and Serve Beverages. W. A. Schmidt.

Flush Times of Alabama and Mississippi. A Series of Sketches. J. G. Baldwin.

"Fly away birdling" (song). F. Abt.

"Fly away, pretty moth" (song). T. H. Bayly.

Flying: see the Reader's Guide entry for Balloon voyages.

Flying Hill Farm; A Story. S. M. Swett.

Flynn, Oscar R. (co-author): see E. J. James, *Immigrant Jew in America*.

"Flynt, Josiah" (pseud.): see Josiah Flynt Willard.

Fogarty, Thomas (illus.): see A. B. Paine, *Ship-Dwellers: A Story of a Happy Cruise*.

Folk and traditional songs: see
  "I'se gwine to de shuckin."
  "Jan and Dan."
  "Las' sack! De las' sack."
  "Old Rosin the Beau."
  "Raging Canal."
  "Roll a man down" (sea shanty).
  "Roll on, silver moon."
  "Sail away, ladies."
  "Stormy winds do blow": see "Mermaid" (sea shanty).
  "Yankee Doodle."

Folklore: see *Journal of American Folklore*.

Folk Songs. J. W. Palmer (ed.).

Follies and Fashions of Our Grandfathers. A. W. Tuer.

Folly of Eustace, and Other Stories. R. S. Hichens.

Fond Adventures: Tales of the Youth of the World. M. H. Hewlett.

Fontenoy and Great Britain's Share in the War of the Austrian Succession, 1741–1748. F. H. B. Skrine.

Foo, Wong Chin: see C. F. Wong.

Food: see the Reader's Guide entry for Cookbooks.

Fool's Errand, by One of the Fools. A. W. Tourgeé.

Foote, Mary Hallock (co-illus.): see A. R. Macdonough (trans.), *Lovers of Provence: Aucassin and Nicolette.*

Foot-Prints of the Creator. H. Miller.

Footsteps of Jeanne d'Arc; A Pilgrimage. F. Caddy.

Ford, Daniel Sharp (ed.): see *Youth's Companion; An Illustrated Weekly for Young People and the Family.*

Ford, Ford Madox: see M. D. Conway, *Autobiography: Memories and Experiences of Moncure Daniel Conway* (marginalia).

Ford, Paul Leicester: see
(ed.) C. Columbus, *Writings of Christopher Columbus, Descriptive of the Discovery and Occupation of the New World.*
(ed.) *House Party: An Account of the Stories Told at a Gathering of Famous American Authors.*

Foregone Conclusion (novel). W. D. Howells.

Foreigner. B. Gerard.

Foreign languages: see F. Gouin, *Art of Teaching and Studying Languages.*

Forester, Thomas: see
(ed., trans.) Henry of Huntingdon, *Chronicle of Henry of Huntingdon, Comprising the History of England.*
(ed., trans.) Suetonius, *Lives of the Twelve Caesars.*

Forest Folk. J. P. Kirk.

Forest Lovers, A Romance. M. H. Hewlett.

Forest Neighbors; Life Stories of Wild Animals. W. D. Hulbert.

Forest Outlaws; or, Saint Hugh and the King. E. Gilliat.

Forests: see
F. D. Hemans, *Forest Sanctuary.*
M. H. Hewlett, *Forest Lovers, A Romance.*
W. D. Hulbert, *Forest Neighbors; Life Stories of Wild Animals.*
J. P. Kirk, *Forest Folk.*
Poetry of the Woods; Passages from the Poets Descriptive of Forest Scenes, Etc.
G. H. G. Putlitz, *Was sich der Wald erzählt.*
J. Quesnay de Beaurepaire, *Woodman; A Novel.*

Forestry: see R. B. Hough, *American Woods, Exhibited by Actual Specimens and with Copious Explanatory Text.*

Forest Sanctuary. F. D. Hemans.

For Faith and Freedom. W. Besant.

Forgeries (cases): see
H. H. Breen, *Modern English Literature: Its Blemishes & Defects.*
Pioneer Mail and Indian Weekly News (Catalog entry).

Forgeries, probable forgeries, and misidentified association copies: see
R. Arnot (ed.), *Earl of Beaconsfield, K. G. Keys to the Famous Characters Delineated in His Historical Romances.*

G. W. Bacon & Co., *Bacon's "Midget" Map. Central and West London.*

A. J. B. Balfour, *Defense of Philosophic Doubt; Being an Essay on the Foundation of Belief.*

R. Baxter, *Saints' Everlasting Rest; or, A Treatise on the Blessed State of the Saints.*

G. Boccaccio, *Stories of Boccaccio (The Decameron).*

E. C. Brewer, *Guide to the Scientific Knowledge of Things Familiar.*

F. Brinkley (ed.), *Japan; Described and Illustrated by the Japanese; Written by Eminent Japanese Authorities and Scholars.*

W. H. Brown, *Historical Sketch of the Early Movement in Illinois for the Legalization of Slavery.*

R. Browning, *Rabbi Ben Ezra.*

G. Burder, *Village Sermons; or, One Hundred and One Plain and Short Discourses, on the Principal Doctrines of the Gospel.*

G. J. Caesar, *Commentarii d C. Iulio Cesare.*

A. Clarke, *Discourses on Various Subjects Relative to the Being and Attributes of God, and His Works in Creation, Providence, and Grace.*

C. W. Colton, *Colton's New Sectional Map of the State of Arkansas.*

C. W. Colton, *County & Township Map of Ohio, Indiana & Michigan.*

Marie Corelli, *Greatest Queen in the World. A Tribute to the Majesty of England. 1837–1900.*

C. H. Crandall, *Representative Sonnets by American Poets, with an Essay on the Sonnet, Its Nature and History.*

C. Crowe, *Susan Hoply; or, The Trials and Vicissitudes of a Servant Girl: A Tale of Great Interest.*

R. Cruikshank, *Cruikshank at Home: A New Family Album of Endless Entertainment.*

C. Cutter, *Anatomy and Physiology.*

J. Dalton, *Gentleman in Black, and Tales of Other Days.*

F. O. C. Darley, *Poets of the West: A Selection of Favourite American Poems with Memoirs of Their Authors.*

Doctrines and Disciplines of the Methodist Episcopal Church.

A. F. Eastman, *Flower of Puritanism (Julia Jones Beecher) 1826–1905.*

R. W. Emerson, *Miscellanies; Embracing Nature, Addresses, and Lectures.*

R. Erskine, *Gospel Sonnets; or, Spiritual Songs.*

E. Field, *Holy Cross and Other Tales.*

P. H. Fitzgerald, *Romance of the English Stage.*

J. L. Gilder, *Tomboy at Work.*

O. Goldsmith, *Goldsmith's Natural History; Abridged, for the Use of Schools.*

Harper's Monthly Magazine 76 (December 1887-May 1888).

H. R. Haweis, *Mark Twain and Bret Harte.*

G. C. Hill, *Gen. Israel Putnam. ("Old Put."): A Biography.*

K. Hofmann, *Practical Treatise on the Manufacture of Paper in All Its Branches.*

M. Holley, *Samantha at the St. Louis Exposition.*

T. P. Hunt, *Jesse Johnston and His Times.*

[Iowa.] *Statute Laws of the Territory of Iowa.*

E. Jenkins, *Ginx's Baby: His Birth and Other Misfortunes. A Satire.*

Jest Book: The Choicest Anecdotes and Sayings. M. Lemon (ed.).

Jubiläums-Feier zur Erinnerung an Die Vor 25 Jahren Durch Die Hinzunahme des "Grünen Waldes" Erfolgte Vergrösserung und Einweihung des Tivoli.

W. H. Koebel, *South America. Painted by A. S. Forrest.*

A. Lincoln, *Address Delivered Before the Springfield Washingtonian Temperance Society at the Second Presbyterian Church.*

A. H. Lincoln, *Familiar Lectures on Botany, Practical, Elementary, and Physiological.*

J. B. McClure (ed.), *Anecdotes of Abraham Lincoln and Lincoln's Stories.*

J. H. Marcet, *Conversations on Chemistry, in Which the Elements of That Science Are Familiarly Explained.*

J. H. Marcet, *Conversations on Natural Philosophy; in Which the Elements of That Science Are Familiarly Explained.*

Martyrs of Madagascar, and Other Books for Children and Youth.

Memorial to the Fiftieth Congress of the United States. Presented by the State Board of Forestry of California.

P. Millet, *Captivity Among the Oneidas in 1690–91 of Father Pierre Milet [sic] of the Society of Jesus.*

J. Milton, *Milton's Poetical Works : . . Together with the Life of the Author.*

L. Murray, *English Grammar, Adapted to the Different Classes of Learners.*

F. B. Owen, *Poems: A Holiday Book.*

Parkhurst & Wilkinson (flier).

Petits Bergers, ou Les Avantages de l'instruction. Par G. H.

Plutarchus, *Plutarch's Lives & Writings.*

R. Poole, *Marian Grantham's Child, Margaret Le Boutilier, and Rene Le Rossignol.*

T. P. Prest, *Death Grasp*: bound with C. Crowe. *Susan Hoply; or, The Trials and Vicissitudes of a Servant Girl: A Tale of Great Interest.*

L. B. Proyart, *Vie de M. D'Orléans De La Motte. Évêque d'Amiens, par M. L'Abbé Proyart.*

E. Rostand, *L'Aiglon [The Eaglet].*

J. J. É. Roy, *Hugues Capet et Son Époque.*

C. de Saint-Germain (comp. and ed.), *Practical Hypnotism: Theories and Experiments.*

W. Scott, *Roderick Dhu; or, The Lady of the Lake: Opera Libretto.*

W. Shakespeare, *Plays and Poems of Shakespeare, According to the Improved Text of Edmund Malone.*

E. S. Snell, *Gyroscope, with Experiments and Explanations.*

A. Stevens, *Sketches & Incidents; or, A Budget from the Saddle-Bags of a Superannuated Itinerant.*

R. L. Stevenson, *Prayers Written at Vailima.*

F. G. M. Stillson, *Doris: A Story of 1778.*

H. E. B. Stowe, *Uncle Tom's Cabin; A Tale of Life Among the Lowly.*

H. H. Tammen, *Objects of Interest from the Plains and Rocky Mountains.*

I. Taylor, *Fanaticism, By the Author of Natural History of Enthusiasm.*

Token and Atlantic Souvenir. A Christmas and New Year's Present. S. G. Goodrich (ed.).

A. W. Tourgeé, *Invisible Empire.*

D. B. Tower and C. Walker, *North American First Class Reader; The Fifth Book of Tower's Series.*

H. Traubel (ed.), *Camden's Compliment to Walt Whitman, May 31, 1889.*

A. Trollope, *Barchester Towers.*

D. B. Tower and C. Walker, *North American First Class Reader; The Fifth Book of Tower's Series.*

Union Pacific Railway Company (undated invitation).

T. Ware, *Sketches of the Life and Travels of Rev. Thomas Ware, Who Has Been an Itinerant Methodist Preacher for More Than Fifty Years. Written by Himself.*

W. Ware, *Probus; or, Rome in the Third Century. In Letters of Lucius M. Piso from Rome.*

W. Ware, *Zenobia; or the Fall of Palmyra: An Historical Romance. In Letters of Lucius M. Piso from Palmyra to His Friend Marcus Curtius at Rome.*

W. Ware, *Zenobia, Queen of Palmyra. A Tale of the Roman Empire in the Days of the Emperor Aurelian.*

C. A. Young, *Text-Book of General Astronomy for Colleges and Scientific Schools.*

E. Young, *Night Thoughts on Life, Death, and Immortality.*

Forget-Me-Not. Poems. L. B. Curtis.

"Forgiveness" (poem): see R. Browning, *Balaustion's Adventure, Aristophanes' Apology.*

For King or Country. A Story of the American Revolution. J. Barnes.

For Love of Country: A Story of Land and Sea in the Days of the Revolution. C. T. Brady.

"For Lud og koldt Vand" (short story). R. Watt.

Formation of Vegetable Mould. C. Darwin.

Forrest, David William (co-ed.): see J. Brown, *Letters of Dr. John Brown.*

Forrest, Edwin (actor): see

J. Banim, *Damon and Pythias, A Tragedy.*

R. M. Bird, *Gladiator.*

W. Shakespeare, Catalog entries for *Hamlet* and *Othello.*

Forrest, Nathan Bedford: see J. A. Wyeth, *Life of General Nathan Bedford Forrest.*

"Forsslund, Louise" (pseud.): see M. L. Foster.

Forster, Charles Thornton (ed.): see O. G. de Busbecq, *Life and Letters of Ogier Ghiselin de Busbecq.*

Forten, Charlotte Lottie (trans.): see É. Erckmann and A. Chatrian, *Madame Thérèse.*

For the Mikado; or A Japanese Middy in Action. C. K. Munroe.

For the Term of His Natural Life. M. A. H. Clarke.

"For to Admire" (poem). R. Kipling.

For Truth, Justice and Liberty. C. Schurz.

Fort Sumter, South Carolina: see the Reader's Guide entry for the Civil War (American).

Fortunate Island and Other Stories. C. H. Clark.

Fortune's Gate. F. B. Marshall.

Fortunes of Nigel (novel). W. Scott.

Fortune-telling: see the Reader's Guide entries for Mysticism and for Palmistry.

"Forty-Five Days' Sufferings": see *Ocean Scenes; or, The Perils and Beauties of the Deep*.

Forty-Five Guardsmen: see A. Dumas, *Novels*.

Forty Liars, and Other Lies. E. W. Nye.

Forty Modern Fables. G. Ade.

Forty-One Coloured Views of London. London.

Forty-One Years in India. From Subaltern to Commander-in-Chief. F. S. Roberts.

"Forty-Three Days in an Open Boat": see W. D. Howells (co-ed.), *Library of Universal Adventure by Sea and Land*.

Forty Years an Advertising Agent. G. P. Rowell.

Forty Years Observation of Music and the Drama. R. Grau.

Forty Years' Recollections of Life, Literature, and Public Affairs, from 1830 to 1870. C. Mackay.

Foss, Edward (intro.): *Memories of Westminster Hall; A Collection of Interesting Incidents, Anecdotes, and Historical Sketches Relating to Westminster Hall*.

Fossil Horses in America. O. C. Marsh.

Foster, Elizabeth (trans.): see L. von Ranke, *History of the Popes, Their Church and State, and Especially of Their Conflicts with Protestantism in the Sixteenth and Seventeenth Centuries*.

Foster-Father of "Nobody's Children." J. H. Batt.

Fostina Woodman: The Wonderful Adventurer. A. A. Burnham.

Foul Play; A Novel. C. Reade and D. Boucicault.

Founding of the German Empire by William I. Based Chiefly upon Prussian State Documents. H. von Sybel.

"Four Beasts in One; or, the Homo-cameleopard" (story). E. A. Poe.

Four Dogs. L. Hutton.

Four-Footed Americans and Their Kin. M. O. Wright.

Four Meetings: see H. James, *Daisy Miller: A Study*.

Fourteen Weeks in Natural Philosophy. J. D. Steele.

"Fourth Annual Message" (speech). A. Lincoln.

Fourth Crusade. E. Pears.

Four Winds of Eirinn (poems). A. J. MacManus.

Fowler, Jessie Allen: see O. S. Fowler and L. N. Fowler, *New Illustrated Self-Instructor in Phrenology and Physiology*.

Fowler, Lorenzo Niles: see
(co-author): see O. S. Fowler, *New Illustrated Self-Instructor in Phrenology and Physiology*.
(co-ed.): see *Phrenological Journal*.

Fowler, Orson Squire (co-ed.): see *Phrenological Journal and Science of Health*.

Fowls of the Air. W. J. Long.

Fox hunting: see G. E. Waring, Jr., *Whip and Spur*.

Fox sisters: see J. B. Dods, *Spirit Manifestations Examined and Explained*.

"Foxton, E." (pseud.): see S. H. Palfrey.

Fra Celeste und andere Erzählungen. R. O. Huch.

Fragments from the Study of a Pastor. G. Spring.

Fragments of Science for Unscientific People: A Series of Detached Essays, Lectures, and Reviews. J. Tyndall.

Fragonard, Jean Honoré (artist): see G. C. Lounsbery, *Escarpolette* (play).

Franc, Guillaume (composer): see W. Kethe, "Old Hundred."

Français en Amérique. P. Blouet.

France: see
T. B. Aldrich, *Queen of Sheba* (marginalia).

P. F. J. N. Barras, *Memoirs of Barras, Member of the Directorate* (marginalia).

M. E. Braddon, *Ishmaelite* (novel).

E. G. Buffum, *Sights and Sensations in France, Germany, and Switzerland*.

M. Busch, *Bismarck in the Franco-German War 1870–1871* (marginalia).

T. A. Cook, *Old Touraine: The Life and History of the Famous Chateâux of France*.

F. Coppée, *Rivals*.

E. De Amicis, *Studies of Paris*.

M. P. R. B. S. De Bury, "Spiritualization of Thought in France."

R. I. Dodge, *Our Wild Indians: Thirty-Three Years' Personal Experience among the Red Men of the Great West* (marginalia).

A. Dreyfus, *Lettres d'un Innocent; The Letters of Captain Dreyfus to His Wife*.

R. T. Ely, *French and German Socialism in Modern Times*.

H. Ford, *Gentleman of France* (play).

Gallick Reports; or, An Historical Collection of Criminal Cases.

H. Gaullieur, *Paternal State in France and Germany*.

S. Grand, *Heavenly Twins* (marginalia).

G. Haven, *Pilgrim's Wallet; or, Scraps of Travel Gathered in England, France, and Germany*.

A. Hoppin, *Ups and Downs on Land and Water*.

B. W. Howard, *Guenn; A Wave on the Breton Coast* (novel).

H. James, *Little Tour in France*.

T. A. Janvier, *Christmas Kalends of Provence and Some Other Provençal Festivals*.

T. A. Janvier, *Embassy to Provence*.

J. Kavanagh, *Nathalie; A Tale* (novel).

E. C. G. Murray, *Member for Paris: A Tale of the Second Empire*.

F. M. Peard, *Interloper; A Novel*.

A. P. Primrose, *Napoleon: The Last Phase* (marginalia).

J. A. D.-G. Ross, *Three Generations of English Women* (marginalia).

A. K. Sartoris, *Week in a French Country-House*.

D. C. Seitz, *Discoveries in Every-day Europe: Vagrant Notes of a Rapid Journey*.

M. de R.- C. Sévigné, *Letters of Madame De Sévigné to Her Daughter and Friends* (marginalia).

F. L. Shaw, *Hector: A Story*.

T. G. Smollett, *Travels through France and Italy*.

M. F. Somerville, *Personal Recollections, from Early Life to Old Age, of Mary Somerville. With Selections from Her Correspondence* (marginalia).

R. L. Stevenson, *Inland Voyage*.

H. A. Taine, *Tour Through the Pyrenees*.

M. de Waddeville, *Monde et ses usages*.

W. Wakefield, *Baths, Bathing, and Attractions of Aix-les-Bains*.

H. Walpole, *Letters of Horace Walpole, Earl of Oxford* (marginalia).

C. D. Warner, *Roundabout Journey.*

S. J. Weyman, *Under the Red Robe.*

É. Zola, *Rome* (Catalog entry).

See also the Reader's Guide entries for French history and for Napoleon Bonaparte.

France, Anatole: see

J. G. Huneker, *Egoists, A Book of Supermen.*

V. Streamer (comp.), *Voices of Doubt and Trust* (marginalia).

France and the Maid. A Drama in Three Acts. E. A. Gerrard.

France in America, 1497–1763. R. G. Thwaites.

"Frances, Mary" (pseud.): see F. W. Mason.

"Francis Furini" (poem): see R. Browning, *Parleyings with Certain People of Importance.*

Francis Joseph of Austria: see M. Cunliffe-Owen, *Keystone of Empire, Francis Joseph of Austria.*

Franconia Stories. J. Abbott.

Frankenstein; or, The Modern Prometheus (novel). M. W. G. Shelley.

Franklin, Benjamin: see

J. Bigelow, *Principles of Strategy, Illustrated Mainly from American Campaigns* (Catalog entry).

B. Hall, *Travels in North America, in the Years 1827 and 1828* (marginalia).

H. W. Shaw, *Everybody's Friend, or Josh Billings's Encyclopedia and Proverbial Philosophy of Wit and Humor* (Catalog entry).

É. Zola, *Rome* (marginalia).

Franklin, John: see E. K. Kane, *Arctic Explorations: The Second Grinnel Expedition in Search of Sir John Franklin, 1853, '54, '55.*

Franklin Square Song Collection: Two Hundred Favorite Songs and Hymns. J. P. McCaskey (comp.).

Franklin, William Buel.: see J. L. Greene, *Gen. William B. Franklin and the Operations of the Left Wing at the Battle of Fredericksburg, December 13, 1862.*

"Frank Norris" (essay). W. D. Howells.

Franz Joseph I (Emperor of Austria): see E. Văcărescu, *Kings and Queens I Have Known.*

Fraser, Horatio Nelson (co-ed.), *Speeches at the Lotos Club.*

Frau Sorge, Roman. H. Sudermann.

Freak of Freedom; or, The Republic of San Marino. J. T. Bent.

Fréchette, Louis (intro.): see W. H. Drummond, *Habitant, and Other French-Canadian Poems.*

Frederic, Harold: see S. R. Crockett, *Tales of Our Coast.*

Frederick III, German Emperor: see M. M. V. F. L. von Poschinger, *Life of the Emperor Frederick.*

Frederick V, elector Palatine of the Rhine: see G. P. R. James, *Heidelberg* (novel).

Frederick the Great: see

T. Carlyle, *History of Friedrich II.*

K. M. Mundt, *Frederick the Great and His Court. An Historical Romance.*

F. M. A. de Voltaire, *Mémoires pour servir à la vie de M. de Voltaire, écrits par lui-même.*

F. S. Wilhelmina, *Memoirs of Frederica Sophia*

Wilhelmina, Princess Royal of Prussia, Margravine of Baireuth (Catalog entry).

F. S. Wilhelmina, *Memoirs of Wilhelmine, Margravine of Baireuth* (marginalia).

Fredericks, Alfred (illus.): see

M. V. Farrington, *Tales of King Arthur and His Knights of the Round Table.*

J. K. Jerome, *Three Men in a Boat (To Say Nothing of the Dog).*

Mabinogion, Boy's Mabinogion; Being the Earliest Welsh Tales of King Arthur in the Famous Red Book of Hergest.

W. Shakespeare, *Midsummer Night's Dream* (play).

(co-illus.) A. Tennyson, *Lady Clare. Freedom of Will.* J. Edwards.

"Freedom Wheeler's Controversy with Providence: A Story of Old New England" (short story). R. T. Cooke.

"Freedom Wheeler's Controversy with Providence: A Story of Old New England" (short story): see R. T. Cooke, *Somebody's Neighbors.*

Free Joe and Other Georgian Sketches. J. C. Harris.

Freeman, M. E. W. (co-author): see *Whole Family; A Novel by Twelve Authors.*

Freeman, William Henry (co-illus.): see J. de la Fontaine, *Fables de J. de La Fontaine.*

Free Prisoners: A Story of California Life. J. W. Bruner.

French and English: A Comparison. P. G. Hamerton.

French and English Dictionary. E. Roubaud.

French and German Socialism in Modern Times. R. T. Ely.

French Authors at Home. A. E. A. Challice.

French Grammar. W. D. Whitney.

French history: see

J. S. C. Abbott, *History of Louis Philippe, King of the French.*

J. S. Abbott, *History of Napoleon Bonaparte.*

A. F. de Bacourt, *Souvenirs of a Diplomat: Private Letters from America.*

J. Berriat-Saint-Prix, *Jeanne d'Arc, ou Coup-d'oeil sur les révolutions de France au temps de Charles VI et de Charles VII.*

L. A. F. de Bourrienne, *Memoirs of Napoleon Bonaparte.*

H. T. Buckle, *History of Civilization in England.*

J. L. H. G. Campan, *Mémoires sur la Vie Privée de Marie Antoinette.*

P. de Commynes, *Memoirs of Philip de Commines, Lord of Argenton.*

T. A. Cook, *Old Touraine: The Life and History of the Famous Chateâux of France.*

G. W. Deeping, *Bertrand of Brittany* (novel).

M. H. De Lancey, *Week at Waterloo in 1815. Lady De Lancey's Narrative.*

A. Dreyfus, *Lettres d'un Innocent; The Letters of Captain Dreyfus to His Wife.*

H. Drummond, *Man of His Age.*

M. J. B. DuBarry, *Memoirs of Madame DuBarri.*

A. F. F. de Frénilly, *Recollections of Baron de Frénilly, Peer of France (1768- 1828).*

J. Froissart, *Chronicles of England, France, Spain, and the Adjoining Countries.*

G. Gualdo Priorato, *History of the Managements of*

Cardinal Julio Mazarine, Chief Minister of State of the Crown of France.

F. P. G. Guizot, *Concise History of France*.

F. P. G. Guizot, *History of France*.

F. P. G. Guizot, *Popular History of France from the Earliest Times*.

P. G. Hamerton, *French and English: A Comparison*.

A. Hamilton, *Mémoires du Comte de Gramont*.

G. A. Henty, *St. George for England: A Tale of Cressy and Poitiers* (novel).

C. de F. d' Hézecques, *Recollections of a Page to the Court of Louis XVI*.

J. O. Kaler, *Ezra Jordan's Escape from the Massacre at Fort Loyall* (novel).

S. R. Keightley, *Last Recruit of Clare's; Being Passages from the Memoirs of Anthony Dillon, Chevalier of St. Louis* (novel).

W. Kirby, *Golden Dog (Le chien d'or). A Romance of the Days of Louis Quinze in Quebec*.

J. F. Kirk, *History of Charles te Bold, Duke of Burgundy*.

W. E. H. Lecky, *History of European Morals from Augustus to Charlemagne* (Catalog entry).

Life and Amours of Owen Tideric, Prince of Wales, Otherwise Owen Tudor (novel).

E. G. E. B. Lytton, *Richelieu; or, the Conspiracy* (play).

G. B. Malleson, *Dupleix*.

J. B. A. M. de Marbot, *Mémoires du General Bon de Marbot*.

H. Martin, *Popular History of France, from the First Revolution to the Present Time*.

W. F. P. Napier, *History of the War in the Peninsula and in the South of France, from the Year 1807 to the Year 1814*.

G. Parker, *Ladder of Swords; A Tale of Love, Laughter and Tears* (novel).

F. Parkman, *Count Frontenac and New France Under Louis XIV*.

F. Parkman, *Old Régime in Canada*.

F. Parkman, *Pioneers of France in the New World*.

J. Quesnay de Beaurepaire, *Woodman; A Novel*.

C. É. J. G. de V. Rémusat, *Memoirs of Madame de Rémusat, 1802–1808*.

B. Runkle, *Helmet of Navarre*.

I. de Saint-Amand, *Jeunesse de l'Impératrice Joséphine*.

I. de Saint-Amand, *Marie Antoinette at the Tuileries, 1789–1791*.

C. A. Sainte-Beuve, *Monday-Chats, Selected and Translated from the "Causeries du Lundi."*

L. de R. Saint-Simon, *Memoirs of the Duke of Saint-Simon on the Reign of Louis XIV and the Regency*.

R. L. Stevenson, *Travels with a Donkey in the Cévennes*.

Tableaux de la Révolution Française; An Historical Reader.

H. A. Taine, *The Ancient Régime*.

R. G. Thwaites, *France in America, 1497–1763*.

F. M. A. de Voltaire, *Age of Louis XIV*.

M. Wagnalls, *Palace of Danger; A Story of La Pompadour*.

W. Warden, *Letters Written on Board His Majesty's Ship the Northumberland, and at Saint Helena; in Which the Conduct and Conversations of Napoleon Buonaparte, and His Suite, . . . Are Faithfully Described*.

E. B. Washburne, *Recollections of a Minister to France, 1869–1877*.

T. E. Watson, *Story of France, from the Earliest Times to the Consulate of Napoleon Bonaparte*.

H. E. G. de Witt, *Monsieur Guizot in Private Life, 1787–1874. By His Daughter, Madame de Witt*.

C. M. Yonge, *Cameos from English History. The Wars in France*.

C. M. Yonge, *Child's History of France*.

C. M. Yonge, *Parallel History of France and England; Consisting of Outlines and Dates*.

É. Zola, *Attaque du Moulin* (novel).

See also the Reader's Guide entries for France, for the French Revolution, for Jeanne d'Arc, for Joan of Arc, and for Napoleon Bonaparte.

French humorists: see

P. J. de Béranger (Catalog entry).

W. Besant, *French Humorists, from the Twelfth to the Nineteenth Centuries*.

P. Blouet, *Frenchman in America: Recollections of Men and Things*.

H. A. Taine, *Notes on England*.

C. M. de Talleyrand-Périgord (Catalog entry).

F. M. A. de Voltaire, *Candide*.

F. M. A. de Voltaire, "Micromégas: A Comic Romance" (short story).

See also the Reader's Guide entry for French literature.

French language: see

J. F. Ahn, *First French Course*.

K. Baedeker, *Traveller's Manual of Conversation, in Four Languages: English, French, German, Italian, with Vocabulary, Short Questions, Etc.*

J. Bellows, *Dictionary for the Pocket: French and English, English and French*.

F. Berger. *New Method of Learning the French Language*.

V. F. Bernard, *Art d'intéresser en classe; Nouveau manuel*.

A. Brachet, *Petite grammaire Française*.

J. Bunyan, [*The Pilgrim's Progress.* French and English.]

H. Bué, *Early French Lessons*.

J. J. Dussouchet, *Petite grammaire Française*.

C. Fontaine, *Livre de lecture et de conversation*.

French-English Dictionary (unidentified book).

P. G. Hamerton, *French and English: A Comparison*.

Larive et Fleury, *Deuxième anné de grammaire*.

P. A. Larousse, *Grammaire supérieure. Troisième année*.

P. A. Larousse, *Nouveau Larousse illustré:dictionnaire universel encyclopédique*.

P. A. Larousse, *Petite grammaire du premier âge*.

É. M. P. Littré, *Dictionnaire de la langue française*.

C. M. Marchand, *New Method of French Conversation*.

A. Mariot de Beauvoisin. *Summary of the French Verbs, Embracing an Entirely New System of Conjugation*.

H. G. Ollendorff, *Ollendorff's New Method of Learning to Read, Write, and Speak the French Language*.

T. Prendergast, *Mastery Series. French*.

J. A. D.-G. Ross, *Three Generations of English Women* (marginalia).

T. Robertson, *Whole French Language.*
R. S. Rosenthal, *Meisterschaft System: A Short and Practical Method of Acquiring Complete Fluency in the French Language.*
E. Roubaud, *French and English Dictionary.*
G. Vitali, *Manuel de la Conversation et du style épistolaire.*
W. D. Whitney, *French Grammar.*
French literature: see
  H. de Balzac (various titles).
  Bibliothèque Morale de La Jeunesse (juvenile fiction series).
  F. Bôcher (ed.), *College Series of French Plays; With English Notes.*
  N. Boileau-Despréaux, *Épitres.*
  M. de Bosguérard, *Scènes Enfantines.*
  A. D. A. de Brueys, *Avocat Patelin: A Comedy in Three Acts* (play).
  Cent Nouvelles Nouvelles.
  F. E. J. Coppée, *The Rivals.*
  G. Flaubert, *Madame Bovary: Provincial Manners.*
  G. Flaubert, *Salammbô.*
  J. de La Fontaine, *Fables de J. de La Fontaine.*
  A. France (three titles).
  D. G. de Girardin, *Joie fait pèur; comédie en un acte* (play).
  M. A. P. de Gomez, *Belle Assemblée: Being a Curious Collection of Some Very Remarkable Incidents Which Happen'd to Persons of the First Quality in France.*
  L. Halévy, *Abbé Constantin.*
  L. Halévy, *Parisian Points of View.*
  A. F. Hugo, *Victor Hugo, by a Witness of His Life.*
  V. M. Hugo, *Misérables.*
  J. G. Huneker, *Egoists, A Book of Supermen.*
  J. de La Bruyère, *Characters, or The Manners of the Age, with the Character of Theophrastus.*
  A. M. L. de Lamartine (two titles).
  M. Leblanc, *Exploits of Arsène Lupin.*
  J. Lemaître (Catalog entry).
  Little French Masterpieces.
  S. G. M. A. de Martel de Janville (Catalog entry).
  B. Matthews, *Studies of the Stage.*
  M. Mauris, *French Men of Letters.*
  P. Mérimée, *Prosper Mérimée's Letters to an Incognita.*
  J.-B. P. Molière, *Avare: Comédie en Cinq Actes* (play).
  M. E. de Montaigne, *Works of Michael de Montaigne, Comprising His Essays, Journey into Italy, and Letters.*
  A. de Musset (Catalog entry).
  P. E. de Musset, *Mr. Wind and Madam Rain.*
  G. Ohnet, *Dr. Rameau.*
  Pastels in Prose. From the French.
  F. Rabelais, *The Works of Francis Rabelais.*
  J. B. Racine, *Phaedra, A Tragedy in Five Acts.*
  [J.] E. Renan, *L'Abesse de Jouarre* (play).
  [J.] E. Renan, *Apostles. Translated from the Original French.*
  C. J. Rouget de Lisle, "La Marseillaise" (French national anthem).
  M. A. M. Sadlier, *Spanish Cavaliers: A Tale of the Moorish Wars in Spain.*

C. A. Sainte-Beuve, *Memoirs of Mme. Desbordes-Valmore.*
  G. Sand (two titles).
  V. Sardou (Catalog entry).
  S. R. Ségur, *Adventures of a Donkey.*
  J. C. L. S. de Sismondi, *Historical View of the Literature of the South of Europe.*
  Song of Roland.
  M. J. B. L. Sonrel, *Bottom of the Sea.*
  L. Ulbach, *Madame Gosselin* (novel).
  C. Vincens, *Alfred de Musset.*
  F. M. A. de Voltaire, *A, B, C, ou dialogues entre A, B, C.*
  F. M. A. de Voltaire, *Age of Louis XIV.*
  F. M. A. de Voltaire, *Candide.*
  F. M. A. de Voltaire, "Dialogue entre un philosphe et un contrôleur général des finances."
  F. M. A. de Voltaire, "Dialogue entre un plaideur et un avocat."
  F. M. A. de Voltaire, *Letters Concerning the English Nation.*
  F. M. A. de Voltaire, *Mémoires pour server à la vie de M. de Voltaire, écris par lui-même.*
  F. M. A. de Voltaire, "Micromégas: A Comic Romance" (short story).
  F. M. A. de Voltaire, *Zadig.*
  C. Wagner, *Âme des Choses.*
  H. E. G. Witt, *Motherless; or, A Parisian Family.*
  H. E. G. Witt, *Only Sister* (novel).
  É. Zola, *Assommoir.*
  É. Zola, *Attaque du Moulin.*
  É. Zola, *Labor: A Novel.*
  É. Zola, *Lourdes.*
  É. Zola, *Rome.*
  É. Zola, *Terre.*
  See also the Reader's Guide entries for French humorists, for French Revolution, and for *Jeanne d'Arc.*
Frenchman in America: Recollections of Men and Things. P. Blouet.
French Masterpieces: see *Little French Masterpieces.*
French Men of Letters. M. Mauris.
French Revolution. T. Carlyle.
French Revolution: see
  S. Baring-Gould, *In Exitu Israel; An Historical Novel.*
  P. F. J. N. Barras, *Memoirs of Barras, Member of the Directorate.*
  T. Carlyle, *French Revolution.*
  J. S. Clouston, *Adventures of M. D'Haricot.*
  É. Erckmann and A. Chatrian, *Madame Thérèse* (novel).
  Genlis, Comtesse de (Catalog entry).
  W. D. Howells (co-ed.), *Library of Universal Adventure by Sea and Land.*
  O. M. Johnson, *In the Name of Liberty; A Story of Terror.*
  W. E. H. Lecky, *History of England in the Eighteenth Century* (marginalia).
  H. Martineau, *Peasant and the Prince: A Story of the French Revolution.*
  J. Michelet, *Historical View of the French Revolution.*
  Moniteur.

G. Morris, *Diary and Letters of Gouverneur Morris.*
I. de Saint-Amand, *Marie Antoinette at the Tuileries, 1789–1791.*
Tableaux de la Révolution Française; An Historical Reader.
C. R. Teller, "Mirabeau: A Play in Five Acts" (play).
H. Walpole, *Letters of Horace Walpole, Earl of Oxford* (marginalia).
S. J. Weyman, *Red Cockade. A Novel.*
C. D. Yonge, *Life of Marie Antoinette, Queen of France.*
French social classes: see P. de Commynes, *Memoirs of Philip de Commines, Lord of Argenton* (marginalia).
French Spy; or, The Siege of Constantina. A Military Drama in Three Acts (play). J. T. Haines.
Frenzied Finance. T. W. Lawson.
Fridthjof's Saga; A Norse Romance. E. Tegnér.
Fridthjof the Bold: see R. B. Anderson, *Viking Tales of the North.*
Friendly Stars. M. E. Martin.
"Friend of My Youth" (essay). T. B. Aldrich.
Friendship: see V. Streamer (comp.), *In Friendship's Name.*
Friendships of Mary Russell Mitford as Recorded in Letters from Her Literary Correspondents. M. R. Mitford.
Friends in Exile. A Tale of Diplomacy, Coronets, and Hearts. L. S. Bryce.
Frikell, Wiljalba: see *Secret Out; or, One Thousand Tricks with Cards, and Other Recreations* (Catalog entry).
Frithiof's Saga; A Legend of Ancient Norway. E. Tegnér.
Frog Book: North American Toads and Frogs. M. C. Dickerson.
"Frog He Would A 'Wooing Go" (story, textile). W. Crane.
Frogs: see M. C. Dickerson, *Frog Book: North American Toads and Frogs*
"Frogs Shot Without Powder" (sketch). H. P. Leland.
Frohman, Charles (theatrical producer): see
  J. M. Barrie, *Peter Pan* (play).
  R. De Flers, *Love Watches* (play).
  N. Hawthorne, *House of the Seven Gables, A Romance* (Catalog entry).
  C. Kraatz, *Mountain Climber* (play).
  H. L. É. Lavedan, *Duel* (play).
  W. Shakespeare, *Romeo and Juliet* (play).
From a Venetian Balcony and Other Poems of Venice and the Near Lands. C. B. E. F. Lindsay.
"From Greenland's icy mountains" (hymn): see R. Heber, "Missionary hymn."
Fromme Lieder: see J. Stern, "Translation from the German of Julius Stern."
From Me to You. L. G. S. Dreyfus.
From One Generation to Another (novel). H. S. Scott.
Fromont jeune et Risler âiné. A. Daudet.
From Ponkapog to Pesth. T. B. Aldrich.
From Sea to Sea. R. Kipling.
From St. Francis to Dante: Translations from the Chronicle of the Franciscan Salimbene (1221–1288). G. G. Coulton.
From the Books of Laurence Hutton. L. Hutton.
"From the Night of Forebeing. An Ode after Easter" (poem). F. Thompson.
"From the Sea to the Desert" (article). D. Ker.

From Van Dweller to Commuter. A. B. Paine.
Frost, Arthur Burdett (illus.): see
  (co-illus.) J. K. Bangs, *Ghosts I Have Met and Some Others.*
  V. F. Boyle, *Devil Tales.*
  C. H. Clark, *Elbow-Room; A Novel without a Plot.*
  C. L. Dodgson, *Rhyme? And Reason?*
  (co-illus.) A. French, *Missionary Sheriff.*
  T. N. Page, *Pastime Stories.*
  (co-illus.) R. M. Stuart, *Second Wooing of Salina Sue, and Other Stories.*
  E. Wood, *Back Home.*
Froude, James Anthony: see
  (ed.), J. B. W. Carlyle, *Letters and Memorials of Jane Welsh Carlyle.*
  (ed.), T. Carlyle, *Reminiscences.*
Fuertes, Louis Agassiz (illus.): see
  H. M. Miller, *True Bird Stories from My Note-Books.*
  M. O. Wright and Elliott Coues, *Birdcraft: A Field Book of Two Hundred Song, Game, and Water Birds.*
  M. O. Wright, *Citizen Bird; Scenes from Bird-Life.*
Fugitive Blacksmith (novel). C. D. Stewart.
Fugitive Blacksmith; or, Events in the History of James W. C. Pennington. James W. C. Pennington.
Fuller, Frank (inscr.): see A. Laighton, *Poems by Albert Laighton.*
Fuller, Thomas: see C. Lamb, "Specimens from the Writings."
Fulton, Robert: see H. W. Shaw, *Josh Billings: His Works, Complete* (notes about Fulton laid in the book).
Funerals: see
  T. Browne.
  Philadelphia *Public Ledger.*
  W. Tegg, *Last Act: Being the Funeral Rites of Nations and Individuals.*
  J. G. Wood, *Uncivilized Races; or, Natural History of Man* (marginalia).
  See also the Reader's Guide entries for Cremation and for Premature burial.
Fünfzig Fabeln für Kinder. J. W. Hey.
Fun in a Doctor's Life, Being the Adventures of an American Don Quixote. S. V. Clevenger.
Funk, Issac Kaufman (ed.): see
  G. Croly, *Tarry Thou Till I Come; or, Salathiel, The Wandering Jew.*
  Standard Dictionary of the English Language Upon Original Plans.
Funston, Frederick: see
  E. H. Crosby, *Captain Jinks, Hero.*
  E. Wildman, *Aguinaldo: A Narrative of Filipino Ambitions* (Catalog entry).
Für Freistunden; Erzählungen für die Jugend. O. Wildermuth.
Furniture: see
  C. L. Eastlake, *Hints on Household Taste in Furniture, Upholstery, and Other Details.*
  E. Singleton, *Furniture of Our Forefathers.*
  T. Wright, *Homes of Other Days: A History of Domestic Manners and Sentiments in England, from the Earliest Known Period to Modern Times.*
Furniture of Our Forefathers. E. Singleton.

Furnivall, Frederick James (intro.): see W. Shakespeare, *Leopold Shakspere. The Poet's Works in Chronological Order.*

"Fust and His Friends: An Epilogue" (poem): see R. Browning, *Parleyings with Certain People of Importance in Their Day.*

Futtehgurh Mission: see J. J. Walsh, *Memorial of the Futtehgurh Mission and Her Martyred Missionaries, with Some Remarks on the Mutiny in India.*

Future (predictions):

H. G. Wells, *Anticipations of the Reaction of Mechanical and Scientific Progress Upon Human Life and Thought.*

H. G. Wells, *Future in America; A Search after Realities.*

Future in America; A Search after Realities. H. G. Wells.

G

Gabriel Conroy. B. Harte.

Gade, Helen R. A. (trans.): see B. Bjørnson, *Happy Boy. A Tale of Norwegian Peasant Life.*

Gadfly. E. L. B. Voynich.

Gadow, Hans Friedrich (contr.): see A. Newton, *Dictionary of Birds.*

"Gaily the troubadour" (poem, song): see T. H. Bayly.

Gainsborough, Thomas: see C. Knight and T. Raikes, *Personal Reminiscences by Cornelia Knight and Thomas Raikes.*

Gairdner, James (ed.): see *Paston Letters, 1422–1509 A. D.*

Galatea, A Pastoral Romance. M. de Cervantes Saavedra.

Galileo: see

S. G. Bayne, *Pith of Astronomy (Without Mathematics): The Latest Facts and Figures as Developed by the Giant Telescopes* (marginalia).

D. Brewster, *Martyrs of Science; or, The Lives of Galileo, Tycho Brahe, and Kepler.*

H. Dircks, *Life, Times and Scientific Labours of the Second Marquis of Worcester* (marginalia).

H. E. B. Stowe, *Uncle Tom's Cabin; or, Life Among the Lowly* (Catalog entry).

Galindo, R. E. (illus.): see I. C. Knox, *Little Folks' History of England.*

Gallantry (novel). J. B. Cabell.

Gallegher and Other Stories. R. H. Davis.

Galton, Francis (contr.): see *Prayer-Gauge Debate.*

Gambler, A Novel. K. C. Thurston.

Gambling: see

T. Wright, *Homes of Other Days: A History of Domestic Manners and Sentiments in England, from the Earliest Known Period to Modern Times.*

See also the Reader's Guide entry for Poker.

Gantillon, P. J. F. (trans.): see S. Propertius, *Erotica.*

Gardening: see

M. A. B. von Arnim, *Elizabeth and Her German Garden* (novel).

M. A. B. von Arnim, *Solitary Summer* (novel).

M. T. V. Earle, *Pot-pourri from a Surrey Garden.*

P. Henderson, *Practical Floriculture; A Guide to the Successful Cultivation of Florists' Plants.*

W. Robinson, *Wild Garden; or, Our Groves and*

Gardens Made Beautiful by the Naturalisation of Hardy Exotic Plants.

W. Temple, "Upon the Gardens of Epicurus" (essay).

C. D. Warner, *My Summer in a Garden.*

See also the Reader's Guide entries for Botany, for Flowers, and for Trees.

Garden of Allah. R. S. Hichens.

Garden of Dreams. L. C. Moulton.

Garden of Eden: see the Reader's Guide entry for Adam and Eve.

Garden of Eden. B. W. Howard.

Garfield, James: see S. Clarke, *Mirror or Looking-Glass Both for Saints & Sinners* (marginalia).

Gargantua and Pantagruel: see F. Rabelais, *Works of Francis Rabelais.*

Garnham, L. W. (trans.): see F. J. Kiefer, *Legends of the Rhine from Basle to Rotterdm.*

"Garrett, Edward" (pseud.): see I. F. Mayo.

Garrett, Edmund Henry (illus.): see

(co-illus.) W. S. Burgess, *Eternal Laughter and Other Poems.*

(co-illus.) W. Scott, *Christmas in the Olden Time.*

(co-illus.) A. Tennyson, *Lady Clare.*

(illus.) J. G. Whittier, *At Sundown.*

Garrick, David (actor): see

J. H. Jesse, *London: Its Celebrated Characters and Remarkable Places* (marginalia).

J. Vanbrugh, *Provok'd Wife. A Comedy* (play).

Garrison, Lucy McKim (co-comp.): see W. F. Allen (comp.), *Slave Songs of the United States.*

Garrison, Wendell Phillips (comp.): see C. Darwin, *What Mr. Darwin Saw in His Voyage Round the World in the Ship "Beagle."*

Garrison, William Lloyd: see S. J. May, *Some Recollections of Our Antislavery Conflict.*

Gates Ajar. E. S. Phelps.

Gates of Chance. W. G. V. T. Sutphen.

"Gath" (pseud.): see G. A. Townsend.

Gatty, Horatia Katharine Frances: see H. K. F. G. Eden.

Gatty, Juliana Horatia: see J. H. G. Ewing.

Gaul, Gilbert (illus.): see J. De Mille, *Strange Manuscript Found in a Copper Cylinder.*

Gautier, Théophile: see *Little French Masterpieces.*

Gay Lord Quex: A Comedy in Four Acts (play). A. W. Pinero.

Gay, Sydney Howard (co-author): see W. C. Bryant, *Popular History of the United States.*

Geber; A Tale of the Reign of Harun al Raschid, Khalif of Baghdad. K. A. B. Benton.

Gedichte. J. W. von Goethe.

Gedichte. H. von Olfers.

Geheimnis der Alten Mamsell. E. John.

Geier-Wally: A Tale of the Tyrol. W. von Hillern.

Gems of the Centennial Exhibition. G. T. Ferris.

Gems of the East; Sixteen Thousand Miles of Research Travel Among Wild and Tame Tribes of Enchanting Islands. A. H. S. Landor.

Gender subjects: see the Reader's Guide entries for Crossdressing, for Eroticism, for Homosexuality, for Physiology, for Prostitution, and for Sexuality.

Genee, Adeline: see H. B.Smith, *Soul Kiss* (musical).

Genée, Franz Friedrich Richard (co-author): see C. Wäl-zel, *Fatinitza* (operetta).

General Conchology; or, A Description of Shells, Arranged According to the Linnean System. W. Wood.

General von Versen: ein militärisches Zeit-und Lebensbild. A. H. T. F. von Werthen.

Genesis of the Civil War: The Story of Sumter, 1860–1861. S. W. Crawford.

Genesis of the United States. A. Brown.

Genghis Khan: see J. S. C. Abbott, *History of Genghis Khan.*

Genial Idiot, His Views and Reviews. J. K. Bangs.

Genial Showman; Being Reminiscences of the Life of Artemus Ward and Pictures of a Showman's Career. E. P. Hingston.

Genius. M. H. Potter.

Genovefa. C. von Schmid.

Genteel A. B. A. J. Dawson.

Gentleman from Indiana. B. Tarkington.

Gentleman of France (play). H. Ford.

"Gentleman of Japan and a Lady" (story): see J. L. Long, *Madame Butterfly.*

Gentleman Ragman. W. D. Nesbit.

Gentlemen's Book of Etiquette and Manual of Politeness. C. B. Hartley.

Gentle Reader. S. M. Crothers.

Genuine Narrative of the Deplorable Deaths of the English Gentlemen, and Others, Who Were Suffocated in the Black Hole in Fort William, at Calcutta. J. Z. Holwell.

Genuine Works of Josephus. F. Josephus.

Gen. William B. Franklin and the Operations of the Left Wing at the Battle of Fredericksburg, December 13, 1862. J. L. Greene.

Geoffrey de Vinsauf: see *Chronicles of the Crusades; Contemporary Narratives.*

Geography: see
   E. A. Freeman, *Historical Geography of Europe.*
   R. Hinman, *Eclectic Physical Geography.*
   F. McNally, *National Geographical Series, No. 4—An Improved System of Geography Designed for Schools, Academies, and Seminaries.*
   J. Olney, *Practical System of Modern Geography; or, A View of the Present State of the World, Simplified and Adapted to the Capacity of Youth.*
   G. R. Parkin, *Round the Empire; for the Use of Schools.*
   Rand, McNally & Co's General Atlas of the World.
   W. C. Woodbridge and E. H. Willard, *Woodbridge and Willard's Universal Geography . . . Accompanied by Modern and Ancient Atlases.*

Geology: see
   J. L. Comstock, *Elements of Geology; Including Fossil Botany and Palæontology.*
   C. Darwin, *Journal of Researches.*
   Eclectic Magazine of Foreign Literature, Science, and Art.
   J. Fiske, *Discovery of America, with Some Account of Ancient America and the Spanish Conquest.*
   E. S. Grew, *Romance of Modern Geology.*
   S. B. Herrick, *Earth in Past Ages.*
   C. Kingsley, *Madame How and Lady Why; or, First Lessons in Earth Lore for Children.*

C. Lyell, *Principles of Geology.*
H. Miller, *Cruise of the Betsey; or, A Summer Ramble Among the Fossiliferous Deposits of the Hebrides. With Rambles of a Geologist.*
H. Miller, *Foot-Prints of the Creator.*
H. Miller, *Testimony of the Rocks; or, Geology in its Bearings on the Two Theologies, Natural and Revealed.*
R. Pumpelly, *Across America and Asia; Notes of a Five Years' Journey Around the World:* see R. Pumpelly, *Explorations in Turkestan.*
C. W. Saleeby, *Cycle of Life According to Modern Science* (marginalia).
N. S. Shaler, *Aspects of the Earth: A Popular Account of Some Familiar Geological Phenomena.*
S. Smiles, *Robert Dick, Baker of Thurso, Geologist and Botanist.*
H. G. Vennor (Catalog entry).
H. S. Williams, *Story of Nineteenth-Century Science.*
A. Winchell, *Sketches of Creation: A Popular View of Some of the Grand Conclusions of the Sciences in Reference to the History of Matter and of Life.*

Geometry: see G. A. Wentworth, *Text-book of Geometry.*

George I, King of England: see
   J. McCarthy, *History of the Four Georges.*
   W. M. Thackeray, *Thackeray's Lectures. The English Humourists. The Four Georges.*

George II, King of England: see
   J. McCarthy, *History of the Four Georges.*
   W. M. Thackeray, *Thackeray's Lectures. The English Humourists. The Four Georges.*

George III, King of England: see
   J. McCarthy, *History of the Four Georges.*
   A. P. Stanley, *Historical Memorials of Westminster Abbey.*
   W. M. Thackeray, *Thackeray's Lectures. The English Humourists. The Four Georges.*

George IV, King of England: see
   P. H. Fitzgerald, *Life of George the Fourth, Including His Letters and Opinions.*
   R. Huish, *Memoirs of George the Fourth, Descriptive of the Most Interesting Scenes of His Private and Public Life.*
   J. McCarthy, *History of the Four Georges.*
   W. M. Thackeray, *Thackeray's Lectures. The English Humourists. The Four Georges.*

"George Bernard Shaw" (essay). A. Henderson.

George Eliot Birthday Book. G. Eliot.

George Eliot's Life. G. Eliot.

George, Henry: see
   K. Kennedy, *Doctor Paley's Foolish Pigeons, and Short Sermons to Workingmen.*
   L. F. Post, *Ethics of Democracy: A Series of Optimistic Essays on the Natural Laws of Human Society.*
   Standard (newspaper).

George William Curtis, An Address. J. W. Chadwick.

Georgia literature: see
   M. J. Crim, *Adventures of a Fair Rebel.*
   M. J. Crim, *Elizabeth, Christian Scientist.*
   M. J. Crim, *In Beaver Cove and Elsewhere.*
   M. A. H. Gay, *Prose and Poetry. By a Georgia Lady.*
   H. H. Hammond, *Georgians* (novel).

W. N. Harben, *Georgians; A Novel* (plus other titles).

J. C. Harris, "At Teague Poteet's: A Sketch of the Hog Mountain Range" (story).

J. C. Harris, *Free Joe and Other Georgian Sketches.*

J. C. Harris, *Nights with Uncle Remus: Myths and Legends of the Old Plantation.*

J. C. Harris, *Uncle Remus: His Songs and His Sayings.*

R. M. Johnston, *Dukesborough Tales.*

R. M. Johnston, *Mr. Absalom Billingslea, and Other Georgia Folk.*

R. M. Johnston, *Mr. Billy Downs and His Likes.*

R. M. Johnston, *Old Mark Langstan; A Tale of Duke's Creek.*

C. C. Jones, *Negro Myths from the Georgia Coast, Told in the Vernacular.*

F. A. Kemble, *Journal of a Residence on a Georgian Plantation in 1838–39.*

A. B. Longstreet, *Georgia Scenes, Characters, Incidents, &c., in the First Half Century of The Republic.*

L. B. Pendleton, *Bewitched: A Tale.*

L. B. Pendleton, *In the Wire Grass: A Novel.*

J. Sturge, *Visit to the United States in 1841.*

W. T. Thompson, *Major Jones's Courtship.*

W. T. Thompson, *Major Jones's Sketches of Travel.*

Georgians. H. H. Hammond.

Georgians; A Novel. W. N. Harben.

Georgia Scenes, Characters, Incidents, &c., in the First Half Century of The Republic. A. B. Longstreet.

Gerald of Wales: see T. R. Lounsbury, "Scholar of the Twelfth Century" (articles).

"Gerard de Lairesse" (poem): see R. Browning, *Parleyings with Certain People of Importance in Their Day.*

"Gerard, Frances" (pseud., trans.): see M. Jokai, *Black Diamonds, A Novel.*

Gerard, Henri (ed.): see *Comet* (newspaper).

Germaine massacre (1870): see R. I. Dodge, *Our Wild Indians: Thirty-Three Years' Personal Experience among the Red Men of the Great West.*

German Conversation-Grammar; A New and Practical Method of Learning the German Language. E. Otto.

German Emperor. P. Bigelow.

German history: see

    J. P. Benkard, *Geschichte der Deutschen Kaiser und Könige.*

    E. Berner, *Geschichte des Brandenburgisch-Preussischen Staates.*

    P. Bigelow, *German Emperor and His Eastern Neighbors.*

    P. Bigelow, *History of the German Struggle for Liberty.*

    P. Bigelow, *Paddles and Politics Down the Danube.*

    M. von Bothmer, *German Home Life.*

    M. Busch, *Bismarck in the Franco-German War, 1870–1871.*

    R. T. Ely, *French and German Socialism in Modern Times.*

    H. W. H. Fischer, *Private Lives of William II and His Consort and Secret History of the Court of Berlin.*

    S. R. Gardiner, *Thirty Years' War, 1618–1648.*

    A. Gindely, *Geschichte des dreissigjährigen Krieges.*

    A. W. Grube, *Charakterbilder aus der Geschichte und Sage, für einen propädeutischen geschichtsunterricht.*

W. Lübke, *Ecclesiastical Art in Germany During the Middle Ages.*

K. M. Mundt, *Frederick the Great and His Court. An Historical Romance.*

K. M. Mundt, *Berlin and Sans-Souci; or, Frederick the Great and His Friends. An Historical Romance.*

M. M. V. F. L. von Poschinger, *Life of the Emperor Frederick.*

H. Pyle, *Otto of the Silver Hand* (novel).

L. von Ranke, *Deutsche Geschichte im Zeitalter der Reformation.*

L. von Ranke, *History of the Popes, Their Church and State, and Especially of Their Conflicts with Protestantism in the Sixteenth and Seventeenth Centuries.*

E. Reich, *Success Among Nations.*

F. von Schlegel, *Philosophy of History; in a Course of Lectures, Delivered at Vienna.*

H. von Sybel, *Founding of the German Empire by William I. Based Chiefly upon Prussian State Documents.*

E. B. Washburne, *Recollections of a Minister to France, 1869–1877.*

A. H. T. Werthen, F. von, *General von Versen: ein militärisches Zeit-und Lebensbild.*

Wilhelm II, *Kaiser's Speeches, Forming a Character Portrait of Emperor William II.*

F. S. Wilhelmina, *Memoirs of Frederica Sophia Wilhelmina, Princess Royal of Prussia, Margravine of Baireuth.*

F. S. Wilhelmina, *Memoirs of Wilhelmine, Margravine of Baireuth.*

C. M. Yonge, *Young Folks' History of Germany.*

É. Zola, *Attaque du Moulin* (novel).

German Home Life. M. von Bothmer.

German language: see

    J. F. Ahn, *Ahn's First German Book, Being the First Division of Ahn's Rudiments of the German Language.*

    J. F. Ahn, *Ahn's Second German Book.*

    K. Baedeker, *Traveller's Manual of Conversation, in Four Languages: English, French, German, Italian, with Vocabulary, Short Questions, Etc.*

    N. Bohny, *Neues Bilderbuch. Anleitung zum Anschauen. Denken, Rechnen, und Sprechen fur Kinder.*

    K. A. Buchheim, *Materials for German Prose Composition; or, Selections from Modern English Writers.*

    G. Cottler, *Cours Complet de Langue Allemande.*

    R. Fränkel, *Erstes Lesebuch. Leichte Erzählungen für ganz Kleine artige Kinder.*

    First German Course, Containing Grammar, Delectus, and Exercise-Book, with Vocabularies, and Materials for German Conversation.

    German-English, English-German Dictionary.

    W. Gravert, *Drittes Deutsches Lesebuch.*

    C. F. Grieb, *Dictionary of the German and English Languages.*

    A. W. Grube, *Charakterbilder aus der Geschichte und Sage, für einen propädeutischen geschichtsunterricht.*

    G. Heness, *Leitfaden für den Unterricht in der deutschen Sprache.*

    F. Leypoldt, *New Guide to German Conversation.*

    H. Mendel, *Musikalisches Conversations-lexicon. Eine Encyklopädie.*

H. G. Ollendorff, *Ollendorff's New Method of Learning to Read, Write, and Speak the German Language.*

C. P. Otis, *Elementary German: An Outline of the Grammar, with Exercises, Conversations, and Readings.*

E. Otto, *German Conversation-Grammar; A New and Practical Method of Learning the German Language.*

T. Prendergast, *Mastery Series. German.*

P. Rosegger, *Stoansteirisch.*

R. S. Rosenthal, *Meisterschaft System: A Short and Practical Method of Acquiring Complete Fluency of Speech in the German Language.*

D. Sanders, *Wörterbuch deutscher Synonymen.*

A. Schlessing, *Deutscher Wortschatz oder Der passende Ausdruck.*

O. Sutermeister (comp.), *Dichtungen in Luzerner Mundart.*

C. Wenckebach, *Deutsche Grammatik für Amerikaner. Nach einer neuen praktischen Methode.*

W. H. Woodbury, *New Method of Learning the German Language: Embracing Both the Analytic and Synthetic Modes of Instruction.*

German literature: see

H. C. Andersen. *Bilderbuch Ohne Bilder.*

E. M. Arndt, "Lied vom Feldmarschall" (song).

B. Auerbach, *Black Forest Village Stories.*

B. Auerbach, *On the Heights; A Novel.*

A. Baskerville (ed., trans.), *Poetry of Germany.*

K. F. Becker, *Erzählungen aus der alten Welt.*

A. F. von Berger, *Habsburg. Märchenspiel in drei Acten* (play).

G. von Berlichingen (Catalog entry).

A. H. Bernard. *Legends of the Rhine.*

Bibel nach der deutschen uebersetzung von d. Martin Luthers.

"Blau blümelein" (song).

N. Bohny, *Neues Bilderbuch.*

H. H. Boyesen, *Essays on German Literature.*

H. H. Boyesen, *Goethe and Schiller: Their Lives and Works, Including a Commentary on Goethe's Faust.*

E. Bürstenbinder, *Glück auf! Roman.*

E. Bürstenbinder, *Vineta. Roman.*

W. Busch, *Max und Moritz.*

W. Busch, *Schnurrdiburr oder Die Bienen.*

A. von Chamisso, *Peter Schlemihl's wundersame Geschichte.*

G. M. Ebers, *Aegyptische Königstochter. Historischer Roman* (novel).

M. F. Ebner von Eschenbach, *Margarete.*

E. Edler, *Kampf um die Kunst. Drei Novellen.*

H. V. Felsen, *Geträumt und erlebt.*

Fliegende Blätter (magazine).

L. von François, *Letzte Reckenburgerin.*

G. Freytag, *Soll und Haben: Roman in Sechs büchern.*

J. W. von Goethe, *Faust* (and other works).

F. Halm, *Ingomar, the Barbarian* (play).

F. Halm, *Wildfeuer* (dramatic poem).

W. Hauff, "How the Caliph Became a Stork" (fairy tale).

G. Hauptmann, *Einsame Menschen. Drama.*

F. H. Hedge, *Prose Writers of Germany.*

H. Heine, "Lorelei" (and other titles).

E. von Hesse-Wartegg, *Mississippi-Fahrten: Reisebilter aus dem amerikanischen Süden (1879–1880).*

J. W. Hey, *Fünfzig Fabeln für Kinder.*

P. J. L. von Heyse, *Im Paradiese. Roman in Sieben Büchern.*

P. J. L. von Heyse, *Kinder der Welt. Roman in Sechs Büchern.*

P. J. L. von Heyse, *Novellen.*

W. B. von Hillern, *Am Kreuz; ein Passionsroman aus Oberammergau.*

H. Hoffmann, *Struweelpeter.*

R. O. Huch, *Fra Celeste und andere Erzählungen.*

E. Humperdinck, *Hänsel und Gretel* (opera).

J. G. Huneker, *Egoists, A Book of Supermen.*

J. G. Huneker, *Iconoclasts, A Book of Dramatists.*

E. John, *Geheimnis der Alten Mamsell.*

B. Kalfus, *Aus zwei Welten. Gedichte.*

G. Keller, *Leute von Seldwyla.*

J. M. Kinkel, *Hans Ibeles in London. Ein Familienbild aus dem Flüchtlingsleben.*

R. Koch, *Berggeist im Riesengebirge.*

P. Langmann, *Bartel Turaser, Drama in drei Akten* (play).

G. E. Lessing, *Fabeln. Drei Bücher. Nebst Abhandlungen.*

G. E. Lessing, *Hamburgische Briefe; Hamburgische Dramaturgie.*

G. E. Lessing, *Laokoon, oder über die Grenzen der Malerei und Poesie.*

R. Lindau (Catalog entry).

Litteratur-Institut.

C. Meiners, *Lebensbeschreibungen berühmter Männer aus den Zeiten der Wiederherstellung der Wissenschaften.*

Neue Testament unsers Herrn und Heilandes Jesu Christi.

R. Niedergesäss, *Kinderstubengeschichten.*

K. G. Nieritz, *Wunderpfeife, oder: Die Kinder von Hameln.*

H. von S. von Olfers, *Gedichte.*

M. Peterson, *Prinzessin Ilse. Ein Märchen aus dem Harzgebirge.*

O. Pletsch, *Shnik-Shnak.*

E. Pötzl, *Bummelei. Neue Gelammelte Skizzen* (and other titles).

G. H. G. Putlitz, *Was sich der Wald erzählt.*

F. Reuter, "Dörchläuchting" in *Olle Kamellen* (stories).

A. Sach, *Deutsche Heimat. Landschaft und Volktstum.*

C. W. Sanders and J. C. Sanders. *Bilder Fibel.*

L. Schefer, *Artist's Married Life; Being That of Albert Dürer* (novel).

G. Scherer, *Schönsten Deutschen Volkslieder mit ihren eigenthümlichen singweisen.*

J. Scherr, *Deutsche Kultur-und Sittengeschichte.*

L. Schick (comp.), *Schick's humoristische Bibliothek.*

J. C. F. von Schiller (various titles).

C. von Schmid, *Genovefa.*

C. von Schmid, *Gute Fridolin und der böse Dietrich.*

H. Seidel, "Tausendmarkschein" (story).

F. O. Spamer, *Männer eigner Kraft.*

F. Spielhagen, *Problematische Naturen: Roman.*

F. Spielhagen, *Reih' und Glied: Roman.*

K. Spindler, *Jude, historischer Roman.*

J. Sterne (poems).

J. E. W. Stinde, *Familie Buchholz. Aus dem Leben der Hauptstadt.*

M. Stirner, *Ego and His Own.*

H. Sudermann, *Frau Sorge, Roman.*

H. Sudermann, *Glück im Winkel; schauspiel in drei Akten von Hermann Sudermann* (play).

M. von Versen, *Reisen in Amerika und der Südamerikanische Krieg.*

A. von Wilbrandt, *Master of Palmyra. A Dramatic Poem.*

O. Wildermuth, *Für Freistunden; Erzählungen für die Jugend.*

K. Wolf, *Geschichten aus Tirol.*

J. D. Wyss, *Swiss Family Robinson. A New Translation.*

J. D. Wyss, *Swiss Family Robinson; or, The Adventures of a Shipwrecked Family on an Uninhabited Island Near New Guinea.*

A. V. Zechmeister, *Einer muss heiraten!* (play).

German politics: see

P. Bigelow, *History of the German Struggle for Liberty.*

P. Bigelow, *Paddles and Politics Down the Danube.*

R. T. Ely, *French and German Socialism.*

A. Harrison, *Pan-Germanic Doctrine; Being a Study of German Political Aims and Aspirations.*

Germany: see

J. H. Browne, *Sights and Sensations in Europe: Sketches of Travel and Adventure.*

E. G. Buffum, *Sights and Sensations in France, Germany, and Switzerland.*

M. Cunliffe-Owen, *Imperator et Rex, William II of Germany.*

H. Gaullieur, *Paternal State in France and Germany.*

G. Haven, *Pilgrim's Wallet; or, Scraps of Travel Gathered in England, France, and Germany.*

A. Hoppin, *Ups and Downs on Land and Water.*

G. P. R. James, *Heidelberg* (novel).

A. B. M. Jameson, *Sketches of Art, Literature, and Character.*

R. M. Manley, *Mr. Claghorn's Daughter* (novel).

H., G. von Moltke, *Essays, Speeches and Memoirs.*

J. Murray, *Handbook for North Germany, from the Baltic to the Black Forest, and the Rhine, from Holland to Basle.*

C. Scollard, *On Sunny Shores.*

H. von Sybel, *Founding of the German Empire by William I. Based Chiefly upon Prussian State Documents.*

B. Taylor, *At Home and Abroad: A Sketch-Book of Life, Scenery, and Men.*

See also the Reader's Guide entry for the Rhine River.

Germ Life: see H. W. Conn, *Story of Germ Life.*

Gerusalemme Liberata. T. Tasso.

Geschichte der Deutschen Kaiser und Könige. J. P. Benkard.

Geschichte des Brandenburgisch-Preussischen Staates. E. Berner.

Geschichte des dreissigjährigen Krieges. A. Gindely.

Geschichten aus Tirol. K. Wolf.

Gesta Christi; or, A History of Humane Progress Under Christianity. C. L. Brace.

"Get on board" (spiritual): see "Gospel train" (spiritual).

"Get out of the wilderness" (minstrel song): see J. Warner, "Down in Alabam'" (or "Ain't I glad I got out de wilderness").

Geträumt und erlebt. H. V. Felsen.

Gertrude of Wyoming; or, the Pennsylvanian Cottage. T. Campbell.

"Getting into Print" (Jack London): see (contr.) *Way into Print.*

"Gettysburg Address" (speech). A. Lincoln.

Ghost of Kishinefi. H. Tudor.

Ghosts: see the Reader's Guide entry for Parapsychology.

Ghosts (play). H. Ibsen.

Ghosts and Other Lectures. R. G. Ingersoll.

Ghosts I Have Met and Some Others. J. K. Bangs.

Giacomelli, Hector (illus.): see

M. B. Howitt, *Birds and Flowers; or, Lays and Lyrics of Rural Life.*

J. Michelet, *Bird.*

Gibbon, Charles (co-ed.): see A. R. Spofford (co-ed.), *Library of Choice Literature; Prose and Poetry, Selected from the Most Admired Authors.*

Gibbon, Lardner (co-author): see W. L. Herndon, *Exploration of the Valley of the Amazon.*

Gibbons, J. (co-author). *Great Religions.*

Gibraltar: see D. C. Seitz, *Discoveries in Every-day Europe: Vagrant Notes of a Rapid Journey.*

Gibson, Charles Dana (illus.): see

J. K. Bangs, *Booming of Acre Hill, and Other Reminiscences.*

R. H. Davis, *Gallegher and Other Stories.*

R. H. Davis, *Her First Appearance.*

R. H. Davis, *Soldiers of Fortune.*

Gibson, Lucy Judge (Peacock) (co-trans.): see R. C. Eucken, *Christianity and the New Idealism: A Study in the Religious Philosophy of To-day.*

Gibson, William Hamilton (illus.) see

S. A. Drake, *Heart of the White Mountains, Their Legend and Scenery.*

W. H. Gibson, *Camp Life in the Woods and the Tricks of Trapping.*

W. H. Gibson, *Highways and By-ways; or Saunterings in New England.*

W. H. Gibson, *Pastoral Days, or Memories of a New England Year.*

(co-illus.) A. R. Macdonough (trans.), *Lovers of Provence: Aucassin and Nicolette.*

Gibson, William Ralph Boyce (co-trans.): see R. C. Eucken, *Christianity and the New Idealism: A Study in the Religious Philosophy of To-day.*

Gifford, Robert Swain (illus.): see

E. De Amicis, *Holland and Its People.*

E. De Amicis, *Spain and the Spaniards*

"Gift, Theo." (pseud.): see D. H. H. Boulger.

Gilbert, Ann (Taylor) (co-author): see J. Taylor and A. T. Gilbert, *Little Ann, and Other Poems.*

Gilbert, Charles Allan (illus.): see

M. M. Kirkman, *Romance of Gilbert Holmes: An Historical Novel.*

W. Shakespeare, *Romeo and Juliet* (play).

Gilbert Neal; A Novel. W. N. Harben.

Gil Blas: see A. R. Le Sage, *Adventures of Gil Blas of Santillane.*

Giles Corey, Yeoman; A Play. M. E. W. Freeman.

Gilder, Jeanette Leonard: see C. B. Todd, *History of Redding, Connecticut.*

Gilder, Joseph: see C. B. Todd, *History of Redding, Connecticut.*

Gilder, Richard Watson: see
    R. Kipling, *Five Nations* (Catalog entry).
    New York *Times* (Catalog entry).
    A. C. H. Rice, *Mrs. Wiggs of the Cabbage Patch* (Catalog entry).
    Smith College Commencement Poems, '79–'86 (contr.).
    C. B. Todd, *History of Redding, Connecticut.*

Giles, H. A. (co-author). *Great Religions.*

Giles, John Allen (trans.): see *Chronicles of the Crusades; Contemporary Narratives.*

Gilley, John: see C. W. Eliot, *John Gilley.*

Gillmore, Parker (ed.): see L. Biart, *Adventures of a Young Naturalist.*

Gilman, Daniel Coit (co-ed.): see *New International Encyclopaedia.*

"Ginger and the Goose" (story): see F. H. Smith, "Editor's Drawer."

Ginx's Baby: His Birth and Other Misfortunes. A Satire. E. Jenkins.

Giotto: see M. O. W. Oliphant, *Makers of Florence: Dante, Giotto, Savonarola, and Their City.*

Giraldus Cambrensis: see T. R. Lounsbury, "Scholar of the Twelfth Century" (articles).

"Girardin, Mme. Émile de" (pseud.): see D. G. de Girardin.

Girard, Stephen: see R. B. Westbrook, *Girard's Will and Girard College Theology.*

Girard's Will and Girard College Theology. R. B. Westbrook.

"Give me liberty, or give me death!" (speech). P. Henry.

"Give Me Three Grains of Corn, Mother" (poem). A. B. Edwards.

"Give me three grains of corn, mother" (song): see F. B. Ogilvie (comp.), *Two Hundred Old-Time Songs, Containing the Words and Music of the Choicest Gems of the Old and Familiar Songs.*

Givers; Short Stories. M. E. W. Freeman.

"Gizen-no-Teki" (pseud.): see E. W. Foxall.

Glackens, William (illus.): see W. A. White, *In Our Town.*

Gladden, W. (co-author). *Great Religions.*

Gladiator (play). R. M. Bird.

Gladstone, William Ewart: see
    W. Bagehot, *Biographical Studies.*
    G. G. Coulton, *From St. Francis to Dante: Translations from the Chronicle of the Franciscan Salimbene (1221–1288)* (marginalia).
    J. H. Newman, *Apologia Pro Vita Sua* (Catalog entry).
    A. E. West, *Recollections, 1832 to 1886* (Catalog entry).

Gladwin, Francis (trans.): see M. Saadi, *Gulistan; or, Rose Garden, by Musle-Huddeen Sheik Saadi, of Shiraz.*

"Gladys, Evelyn" (pseud.): see H. Kuehn.

Glass-making: see A. Sauzay, *Wonders of Glass-Making in All Ages.*

Glimpses of India: A Grand Photographic History of the Land of Antiquity. J. H. Furneaux.

Glimpses of Italian Court Life; Happy Days in Italia Adorata. T. B. Batcheller.

Glimpses of the Sunny South. A. C. Artman.

"Glory" (story): see J. L. Long, *Madame Butterfly.*

"Glouvet, Jules de" (pseud.): see J. Quesnay de Beaurepaire.

Glover II, George Washington: see R. D. Kathrens, *Side Lights on Mary Baker Eddy-Glover-Science Church Trustees Controversy. "Next Friends" Suit.*

Gloverson and His Silent Partners. R. Keeler.

Glück auf! Roman. E. Bürstenbinder.

Glück im Winkel; schauspiel in drei Akten von Hermann Sudermann (play). H. Sudermann.

Godey's Lady's Book: see C. E. S. S. Norton, "Broken Vow" (story).

Godfrey, C. O.: see *Case of C. O. Godfrey* [in Hannibal, Missouri].

Godfrey of Bouillon: see T. Tasso, *Gerusalemme Liberata.*

Godfrey's Quest: A Fantastic Poem. C. B. E. F. Lindsay.

God in His World: An Interpretation. H. M. Alden.

"God is Love" (poem). J. G. Whittier.

Godiva, Lady: see H. Wilson, *Wonderful Characters; Comprising Memoirs and Anecdotes of the Most Remarkable Persons of Every Age and Nation.*

"Godolphin, Mary" (pseud.): see L. Aikin (ed.).

"Go down, Moses" (spiritual): see J. L. Hatton (ed.), *Songs of England, A Collection of English Melodies* (marginalia).

Gods and Fighting Men: The Story of the Tuatha De Danaan and of the Fianna of Ireland. A. Gregory.

"God save the Czar" (anthem): see V. A. Zhukovskiĭ, "Russian national hymn" (anthem).

God's War (novel). W. J. Vance.

"God, the all-terrible" (hymn). H. F. Chorley.

"God, the omnipotent": see H. F. Chorley, "God, the all-terrible" (hymn).

Goedeke, Karl (intro.): see *Schiller's Sämmtliche Werke in Zwölf Bänden.*

Goepp, Charles (trans.): see B. Auerbach, *Black Forest Village Stories.*

Goerz, Adolf: see F. Philippi, *As'ra* (play).

Goethe and Schiller: Their Lives and Works, Including a Commentary on Goethe's Faust.

Goethe, Johann Wolfgang von: see
    H. H. Boyesen, *Goethe and Schiller: Their Lives and Works.*
    T. Carlyle, *Wilhelm Meister.*
    G. H. Lewes, *Life of Goethe.*
    Socrates (Catalog entry).

"Go! forget me" (song). C. Wolfe.

"Gold Bug" (story). E. A. Poe.

Golden Age of Patents: A Parody of Yankee Inventiveness. W. Peck.

Golden Book of Venice: A Historical Romance of the 16th Century. F. H. L. Turnbull.

Golden Bowl. H. James.

Golden Censer; or, the Duties of To-Day and the Hopes of the Future. J. McGovern.

Golden Dog (Le chien d'or). A Romance of the Days of Louis Quinze in Quebec. W. Kirby.

Golden House. A Novel. C. D. Warner.

Golden Ladder, A Novel. M. H. Potter.

Golden Legend. H. W. Longfellow.

"Golden slippers" (song): see J. A. Bland, "Oh! Dem golden slippers" (song).

Golden Treasury of the Best Songs and Lyrical Poems in the English Language. F. T. Palgrave (comp.).

"Golden vortex in the west over the foundered sun" (line from a poem): see F. Thompson, "From the Night of Forebeing. An Ode after Easter" (poem).

Gold mining: see the Reader's Guide entry for Mining.

Goldsmith, Oliver: see
  (essay) Aesop, *Bewick's Select Fables.*
  W. Irving, *Life of Oliver Goldsmith.*
  C. Knight and T. Raikes, *Personal Reminiscences by Cornelia Knight and Thomas Raikes.*
  B. Matthews, "New Trials for Old Favorites."
  W. Shakespeare, *Works of Shakespeare* (Catalog entry).
  (co-author) R. B. B. Sheridan, *Dramatic Works of Sheridan and Goldsmith. With Goldsmith's Poems.*
  W. M. Thackeray, W. M. Thackeray, *Thackeray's Lectures. The English Humourists. The Four Georges* (marginalia).

Goldsmith's Poems: see R. B. B. Sheridan, *Dramatic Works of Sheridan and Goldsmith. With Goldsmith's Poems.*

Goldsmith, Wallace (illus.): see F. K. Gifford, *Belle Islers; A Novel.*

Goldthwaite, Vere (ed.): see R. G. Ingersoll, *Philosophy.*

Golf (sport): see W. G. V. T. Sutphen, *Golficide and Other Tales of the Fair Green.*

Golficide and Other Tales of the Fair Green. W. G. V. T. Sutphen.

Gollancz, Israel:
  (ed.) W. Shakespeare, *Temple Shakespeare.*
  (gen. ed.) I. Walton, *Lives of John Donne, Henry Wotton, Richd Hooker, George Herbert, &c.*

Gonneville, Marie de (pref.): see A. F. de Bacourt, *Souvenirs of a Diplomat: Private Letters from America.*

"Good-bye, sweetheart, good-bye" (song). R. F. Williams.

Good for the Soul. M. W. C. Deland.

Good Hunting: In Pursuit of Big Game in the West. T. Roosevelt.

Good-Natured Man (play). O. Goldsmith.

Goodrich, Samuel Griswold (ed.): see *Parley's Magazine.*

Good Stories. C. Reade.

"Good Time Going!" (poem). O. W. Holmes.

Goodwin, Philip Russell (illus.): see
  J. London, *Call of the Wild.*
  E. P. Lyle, *Lone Star.*

Goodwin, William Watson (ed.): see Plutarchus, *Plutarch's Morals. Translated from the Greek by Several Hands.*

Gordon, John Sloane (illus.): see A. M. Teskey, *Where the Sugar Maple Grows; Idylls of a Canadian Village.*

Gordon, Lady Duff: see J. A. D.-G. Ross, *Three Generations of English Women.*

Gorillas: see J. G. Wood, *Uncivilized Races; or, Natural History of Man* (marginalia).

Gospel Hymns Consolidated: see P. P. Bliss (co-ed.).

Gospel of the Childhood of Our Lord Jesus Christ. H. C. Greene (trans.).

Goss, John (illus.): see
  (co-illus.): H. C. Morse, *Cowboy Cavalier.*
  W. L. Phelps, *Dash at the Pole.*

Gosse, Edmund (trans.): see H. Ibsen, *Hedda Gabler* (play).

Götz von Berlichingen (play): see G. von Berlichingen (Catalog entry).

Götz von Berlichingen (play). J. W. von Goethe.

Goudy, Frederic William (illus.): see W. W. Denslow, *Denslow's Mother Goose.*

Gouthe-Soulard, X. (pref.): see A. Ricard, *Jeanne d'Arc, La Vénérable.*

"Go way back and sit down" (song). E. Bowman.

"Go way back and sit down" (song): see A. D. White, *History of the Warfare of Science with Theology* (marginalia).

Graduating Exercises of Peirce School: see Peirce School.

Graham, Charles (illus.): see M. P. Wilder, *Sunny Side of the Street.*

"Graham, John" (pseud.): see G. T. Richardson, *Letters from a Son to His Self-Made Father* (Catalog entry).

Grainger, James (trans.): see G. V. Catullus, *Works of Catullus and Tibullus.*

Grammaire supérieure. Troisième année. P. A. Larousse.

Grammar: see the Reader's Guide entry for English grammar, usage, and style.

Grammar of Painting and Engraving. C. Blanc.

Gramont, Philibert: see A. Hamilton, *Mémoires du Comte de Gramont.*

"Grandfather's clock" (song). H. C. Work.

Grandissimes. A Story of Creole Life. G. W. Cable.

Grandma's Attic Treasures. A Story of Old-Time Memories. M. D. Brine.

"Grandmother's Story of Bunker Hill Battle" (poem). O. W. Holmes.

Grand Theoretical and Practical Piano-School for Systematic Instruction. S. Lebert and L. Stark.

Granger crusade: see J. D. McCabe, *History of the Grange Movement; or the Farmer's War Against Monopolies.*

Grant, Allan (pseud.): see J. G. Wilson.

Grant and His Campaigns: A Military Biography. H. Coppée.

Grant in Peace. From Appomattox to Mount McGregor. A Personal Memoir. A. Badeau.

Grant's Farm [unidentified; see the Catalog entry.]

Grant, Ulysses S.: see
  Badeau, A., *Grant in Peace. From Appomattox to Mount McGregor. A Personal Memoir.*
  H. H. Breen, *Modern English Literature: Its Blemishes & Defects* (Catalog entry).
  H. Coppée, *Grant and His Campaigns: A Military Biography.*
  H. Garland, *Ulysses S. Grant, His Life and Character.*
  Grant's Farm (Catalog entry).
  T. W. S. Higginson, *Cheerful Yesterdays. Contemporaries* (Catalog entry).
  T. Malory, *Morte Darthur* (Catalog entry).
  New York *Sun* (Catalog entry).

A. D. Richardson, *Personal History of Ulysses S. Grant*.
G. Ticknor, *Life, Letters, and Journals of George Ticknor* (marginalia).
F. G. Welch, *That Convention; or, Five Days a Politician*.
J. R. Young, *Around the World with General Grant in 1877, 1878, 1879*.
"Grave of Bonaparte" (song). H. S. Washburn.
Gray Days and Gold in England and Scotland. W. Winter.
Gray Mist; A Novel. M. Cunliffe-Owen.
Gray's School and Field Book of Botany. Consisting of "First Lessons in Botany," and Field, Forest, and Garden Botany. A. Gray.
Gray, Thomas: see
  E. W. Gosse, *Thomas Gray*.
  Selected Poems, Illustrated.
"Great American Fraud: The Scavengers" (article). S. H. Adams.
"Great camp-meeting in the promised land" (spiritual): see "Walk together children" (spiritual).
Great Captains. T. A. Dodge.
Great Consummation. The Millennial Rest; or, The World As It Will Be. J. Cumming.
Great Cryptogram. I. Donnelly.
Great English Essayists. Introductions and Notes. W. J. Dawson (co-ed.) and C. W. Dawson (co-ed.).
Great English Letter-Writers, with Introductory Essays and Notes. W. J. Dawson (co-ed.) and C. W. Dawson (co-ed.).
Greater America. A. R. Colquhoun.
Greater Britain: A Record of Travel in English-Speaking Countries During 1866 and 1867. C. W. Dilke.
Greater Mischief; A Novel. M. Westrup.
Greatest Thing in the World. An Address. H. Drummond.
Great Expectations. C. Dickens.
"Great Fit" (poem). R. H. Newell.
Great Fight. Poems and Sketches. W. H. Drummond.
Great Men and Famous Women: A Series of Pen and Pencil Sketches. C. F. Horne (ed.).
Great Metropolis; A Mirror of New York. A Complete History of Metropolitan Life and Society, with Sketches of Prominent Places, Persons and Things in the City, As They Actually Exist. J. H. Browne.
Greatness and Decline of Rome. G. Ferrero.
Great Rebellion: A History of the Civil War in the United States. J. T. Headley.
Great Republic. L. H. Griffin.
Great Shadow. A. C. Doyle.
Great South: A Record of Journeys. E. King.
Greece: see
  J. R. Browne, *Yusef; or the Journey of the Frangi: A Crusade in the East*.
  C. H. Hawes and H. B. Hawes, *Crete, The Forerunner of Greece*.
  E. P. Jackson, *Demigod; A Novel*.
  T. W. Knox, *Backsheesh! or, Life and Adventures in the Orient*.
  C. Scollard, *On Sunny Shores*.
  C. W. Stoddard, *Cruise Under the Crescent; From Suez to San Marco*.

J. L. Stephens, *Incidents of Travel in Greece, Turkey, Russia, and Poland*.
B. Taylor, *Travels in Greece and Russia, with an Excursion to Crete*.
Greek history and literature: see
  C. Anthon, *Classical Dictionary, Containing an Account of the Principal Proper Names Mentioned in Ancient Authors*.
  Aristotle.
  Athenaeus of Naucratis, *Deipnosophists; or, Banquet of the Learned, of Athenaeus*.
  J.-J. Barthélemy, *Travels of Anacharsis the Younger in Greece*.
  T. Child, *Wimples and Crisping-Pins; Being Studies in the Coiffure and Ornaments of Women*.
  Epictetus, *Selection from the Discourses of Epictetus, with the Encheiridion*.
  Euripides, *Plays of Euripides*.
  E. Falkener, *Ephesus and the Temple of Diana*.
  Greek Romances of Heliodorus, Longus, and Achilles Tatius.
  C. H. Hawes, *Crete, The Forerunner of Greece*.
  Herodotus, *History of Herodotus*.
  Herodotus, *Stories of the East from Herodotus*.
  M. H. Hewlett, *Ruinous Face* (historical novel).
  Homer, *Iliad of Homer. Translated into English Blank Verse* (Catalog entry).
  Homer, *Odyssey of Homer. Translated into English Blank Verse* (Catalog entry).
  F. Josephus, *Genuine Works of Josephus*.
  C. W. C. Oman, *History of Greece from the Earliest Times to the Death of Alexander the Great*.
  Plato: see the Catalog entry for Socrates.
  Plato, *Dialogues of Plato*.
  Plutarchus, *Boys' and Girls' Plutarch. Being Parts of the "Lives" of Plutarch*.
  Plutarchus, *Children's Plutarch: Tales of the Greeks*.
  Plutarchus, *Plutarch's Lives of Alcibiades & Coriolanus, Aristides & Cato the Censor*.
  Plutarchus, *Plutarch's Lives of Illustrious Men*.
  Plutarchus, *Plutarch's Morals. Translated from the Greek by Several Hands*.
  C. Rollin, *Ancient History of the Egyptians, Carthaginians, Assyrians, Babylonians, Medes and Persians, Grecians and Macedonians*.
  F. von Schlegel, *Philosophy of History; in a Course of Lectures, Delivered at Vienna*.
  W. Smith *Smaller History of Greece, from the Earliest Times to the Roman Conquest*.
  Socrates (Catalog entry).
  J. T. Wheeler, *Life and Travels of Herodotus in the Fifth Century Before Christ: An Imaginary Biography Founded on Fact*.
  J. T. Wood, *Discoveries at Ephesus, Including the Site and Remains of the Great Temple of Diana*.
  Xeonophon.
Greek language: see A. Sidgwick, *Introduction to Greek Prose Composition, with Exercises*.
Greek mythology: see
  J. Baldwin, *Story of the Golden Age*.

K. F. Becker, *Erzählungen aus der alten Welt für die Jugend.*

T. Bulfinch, *Age of Fable; or, Beauties of Mythology.*

G. W. Cox, *Mythology of the Aryan Nations.*

A. R. Darrow, *Iphigenia: A Legend of the Iliad, and Other Poems.*

Homer, *Iliad of Homer.*

Homer, *Odyssey of Homer.*

C. Kingsley, *Heroes, or Greek Fairy Tales for My Children.*

F de S. de la Mothe Fénelon, *Aventures de Télémaque, fils d'Ulysse.*

B. M. Nead, *Some Hidden Sources of Fiction* (marginalia).

C. W. C. Oman, *History of Greece from the Earliest Times to the Death of Alexander the Great.*

Ovid, *Art of Love, in Three Books.*

H. V. Sutherland, *Idylls of Greece.*

M. W. Townsend, *Asia and Europe: Studies Presenting the Conclusions Formed by the Author* (marginalia).

Greeley, Horace: see

C. F. Browne, *Artemus Ward, His Travels.*

C. Cleveland. *Story of a Summer; or, Journal Leaves from Chappaqua* (Catalog entry).

F. G. Welch, *That Convention; or, Five Days a Politician.*

Green, Anna Katharine: see A. K. G. Rohlfs.

Green, Ashbel (intro.): see C. Buck, *Ancedotes; Religious, Moral and Entertaining.*

Green, Elizabeth Shippen (illus.): see

T. Buchanan, *Castle Comedy.*

J. B. Cabell, *Chivalry.*

R. W. Chambers, *River-Land, A Story for Children.*

A. H. Donnell, *Rebecca Mary.*

A. H. Donnell, *Very Small Person.*

R. Le Gallienne, *Old Country House.*

Greenaway, Kate (illus.): see

Mother Goose; or The Old Nursery Rhymes.

J. Taylor and A. T. Gilbert, *Little Ann, and Other Poems.*

Greene, Henry Copley (trans.): see

H. C. Greene, *Gospel of the Childhood of Our Lord Jesus Christ.*

M. Schwob, *Children's Crusade.*

"Green Hand." A "Short" Yarn. G. Cupples.

"Greenland's icy mountains" (hymn). R. Heber.

"Greeting to the Violets" (poem). R. Herrick.

Greey, Edward (trans.): see T. Shunsui, *Loyal Ronins: An Historical Romance, Translated from the Japanese.*

Grefé, W. (illus.): see J. M. Forman, *Buchanan's Wife.*

Gregory, Augusta: see W. B. Yeats, *Stories of Red Hanrahan* (Catalog entry).

"Gregory, John S." (pseud.): see I. F. Marcosson.

"Grendel, M. R." (pseud.): see G. A. Kendrick.

Greville Memoirs; A Journal of the Reigns of King George IV. and King William IV. C. C. F. Greville.

Grey, George: see J. Milne, *Romance of a Pro-Consul; Being the Personal Life and Memoirs of the Right Hon. Sir George Grey, K. C. B.*

Grey, Jane: see

J. Timbs, *Curiosities of London, Exhibiting the Most Rare and Remarkable Objects of Interest in the Metropolis* (marginalia).

A. E. Trumbull, *Masque of Culture* (play).

Grey Lady (novel). H. S. Scott.

Gribayédoff, Valerian (illus.): see

L. N. Tolstoy, *Ivan the Fool; or, the Old Devil and the Three Small Devils.*

L. N. Tolstoy, *Life is Worth Living, and Other Stories.*

Grief: see

O. W. Holmes, Voiceless" (poem).

M. S. B. Hopkins, *Sixth Sense and Other Stories.*

W. D. Howells, "Sorrow, My Sorrow" (poem).

E. Ransford, "In the Days When We Went Gypsying" (poem and song) (Catalog entry).

R. Richardson, "Requiem" (poem).

J. W. Riley, "Absence of Little Wesley" (poem). J. W. Riley.

B. F. Taylor, "Isle of the Long Ago" (poem).

A. Tennyson, "Break, Break, Break" (poem).

A. Tennyson, *In Memoriam* (poem).

A. Tennyson, *Poetical Works of Alfred Lord Tennyson, Poet Laureate* (marginalia).

F. C. F. Tiernan, "Regret" (poem).

L. Whiting, *After Her Death; The Story of a Summer.*

See also the Reader's Guide entry for Death.

Griffin, Lepel (co-author). *Great Religions.*

Griffis, William Elliot (intro.): see J. L. Motley, *Motley's Dutch Nation, Being the Rise of the Dutch Republic (1555–1584) Condensed.*

Griffith Gaunt; or, Jealousy. C. Reade.

"Grile, Dod" (pseud.): see A. Bierce.

Grimke, Charlotte Lottie Forten: see C. L. Forten (trans.), É. Erckmann and A. Chatrian, *Madame Thérèse.*

Grimm Brothers: see

Grimm Brothers. Jacob Grimm and Wilhelm Grimm, *Grimms' Fairy Tales.*

Grimm's Maerchen: Brüder Grimm Kinder und Hausmaerchen.

E. Humperdinck, *Hänsel und Gretel* (opera).

A. V. Zechmeister, *Einer muss heiraten!* (play).

Grip of Honor: A Story of Paul Jones and the American Revolution. C. T. Brady.

Griset, Ernest (illus.): see

Defoe, *Life and Surprising Adventures of Robinson Crusoe of York, Mariner.*

Favorite Album of Fun and Fancy.

Griswold, Rufus Wilmot: see (contr.) *Homes of American Authors.*

Groans and Grins of One Who Survived. B. W. Munro.

Grooming: see the Reader's Guide entry for Beauty and grooming advice.

Groundwork of the Leschetizky Method. M. Brée.

Grove, George (contr.): see S. Hensel, *Mendelssohn Family (1729–1847) from Letters and Journals.*

"Growth of London" (article). G. B. Smith.

Gruger, Frederic Rodrigo (illus.): see

G. Donworth, *Letters of Jennie Allen to Her Friend Miss Musgrove.*

B. Tarkington, *His Own People.*

W. A. White, *In Our Town.*

Guardian Angel. O. W. Holmes.

Guarding a Great City, by William McAdoo, Police Commissioner, New York City, 1904–1906. W. McAdoo.

Guenn; A Wave on the Breton Coast. B. W. Howard.

Guerre, Martin (criminal case): see
    A. Dumas, *Celebrated Crimes.*
    Gallick Reports; or, An Historical Collection of Criminal Cases.

Guerre et la Paix. Roman historique (novel). L. N. Tolstoy.

Guidebooks: see the Reader's Guide entry for Travel guidebooks.

"Guide me, O Thou great Jehovah" (hymn). J. N. Pattison.

Guides to moral conduct: see the Reader's Guide entry for Moral conduct guides.

Guide to the Collections in the Canterbury Museum, Christchurch, New Zealand. New Zealand.

Guide to Williams & Packard's System of Penmanship for Teachers and Adepts. J. D. Williams.

Guillaume Tell (William Tell) (opera). G. A. Rossini.

Guillemard, Francis Henry Hill (co-author): see A. R. Wallace, *Australasia.*

Guipon, Leon (illus.): see A. C. H. Rice, *Mr. Opp.*

Guizot, François Pierre Guillaume: see
    (contr.) E. Gibbon, *History of the Decline and Fall of the Roman Empire.*
    C. A. Sainte-Beuve, *Monday-Chats, Selected and Translated from the "Causeries du Lundi."*
    H. E. G. de Witt, *Monsieur Guizot in Private Life, 1787–1874. By His Daughter, Madame de Witt.*

Gulistan; or, Rose Garden, by Musle-Huddeen Sheik Saadi, of Shiraz. M. Saadi.

Gulliver, John Putnam (intro.). J. Bunyan, *Complete Works of John Bunyan.*

Gulliver's Travels into Several Remote Nations of the World. J. Swift.

Gum Boughs and Wattle Bloom, Gathered on Australian Hills and Plains. D. MacDonald.

"Gunga Din" (poem). R. Kipling.

Gunnar; A Tale of Norse Life. H. H. Boyesen.

Gunn's Domestic Medicine, or Poor Man's Friend, in the Hours of Affliction, Pain, and Sickness. J. C. Gunn.

Gunpowder Plot: see J. Gerard, *What Was the Gunpowder Plot? The Traditional Story Tested by Original Evidence.*

Gustaf II Adolf, King of Sweden: see T. A. Dodge, *Great Captains.*

Gute Fridolin und der böse Dietrich. C. von Schmid.

Guy Mannering; or, The Astrologer. W. Scott.

Gwendolen (character in poem): see the Catalog entry for Walter Scott.

"Gwine to run all night" (minstrel song): see S. C. Foster, "Camptown races" (minstrel song).

"Gwynne, Paul" (pseud.): see G. H. E. Slater.

Gyll, Gordon Willoughby James (trans.): see M. de Cervantes Saavedra, *Galatea, A Pastoral Romance.*

"Gyp" (pseud.): S. G. M. A. de Martel de Janville.

Gypsies: see the Reader's Guide entry for Romani people.

▌H

Habitant, and Other French-Canadian Poems. W. H. Drummond.

Habsburg. Märchenspiel in drei Acten (play). A. F. von Berger.

Haeckel, Ernst Heinrich: see W. H. Mallock, *Reconstruction of Religious Belief.*

Haggard, Henry Rider: see J. K. Stephen, *Lapsus Calami.*

"Hail, Columbia" (song). J. Hopkinson.

Hale, Edward Everett: see
    (contr.) *Homes of American Authors.*
    (contr.) E. B. Sanford (ed.), *Concise Cyclopedia of Religious Knowledge.*

Hale, Sarah Josepha (Buell): see
    (ed.) *Godey's Lady's Book.*
    (ed.) M. P. W. Montagu, *Letters of Lady Mary Wortley Montagu.*
    (ed.) M. de R.-C. Sévigné, *Letters of Madame De Sévigné to Her Daughter and Friends* (marginalia).

Hale, Susan (co-author): see E. E. Hale, *Family Flight.*

Haley, Bart (illus.): see M. P. Wilder, *Sunny Side of the Street.*

Half a Century. J. G. C. Swisshelm.

Half Hours with Insects. A. S. Packard.

Halhed, Nathaniel Brassey (trans.): See S. Propertius, *Erotica.*

Hall, Basil: see F. M. Trollope, *Domestic Manners of the Americans* (marginalia).

Hall, Charles Francis (Arctic explorer): see E. G. E. B. Lytton, *Kenelm Chillingly: His Adventures and Opinions. A Novel* (marginalia).

"Hall, Eliza Calvert" (pseud.): see E. C. C. Obenchain.

Hall, E. S. (frontispiece): see A. H. Lewis, *Wolfeville Nights.*

Hall, Foley (composer): see G. Linley, "Ever of thee I'm fondly dreaming" (song).

Hall, Govinier: see Knife and Fork Club. Kansas City, *Book of the Knife and Fork Club.*

Hall, Samuel Carter (co-author): see L. F. W. Jewitt (co-author), *Stately Homes of England.*

Hallock, Mary Anna (co-illus.): see H. W. Longfellow, *Hanging of the Crane.*

Hallowell, J. M. (co-author): see *On Track and Diamond.*

Haman: A Tragedy (blank verse play). A. E. Trumbull.

Hamburgische Briefe; Hamburgische Dramaturgie. G. E. Lessing.

Hamelin: see *Wunderpfeife, oder: Die Kinder von Hameln.*

Hamerton, Philip Gilbert (ed.). *Portfolio, An Artistic Periodical.*

Hamilton, Edward Wilbur Dean (illus.): see R. N. Stephens, *Philip Winwood; A Sketch of the Domestic History of an American Captain in the War of Independence* (novel).

"Hamilton, Gail" (pseud.): see M. A. Dodge.

Hamlet (play). W. Shakespeare.

Hamlet (play). W. Shakespeare: see
    G. Chaucer, *Canterbury Tales by Geoffrey Chaucer* (marginalia).
    F. Grose, *Classical Dictionary of the Vulgar Tongue* (marginalia).
    O. W. Holmes, *Autocrat of the Breakfast-Table* (marginalia).
    "Yankee Doodle" (song) (Catalog entry).

Hammond, Edward Payson, *Sketches of Palestine*: see J. Habberton, *Helen's Babies* (Catalog entry).

Hammond, Gertrude Demain (illus.): see W. D. Orcutt, *Spell*.

Hammond, John Hays: see N. H. Hammond, *A Woman's Part in a Revolution*.

"Hamon, Louis" (pseud.): see W. J. Warner.

"Hamong, Leigh de" (pseud.): see W. J. Warner.

Hana, A Daughter of Japan. G. Murai.

Hancock, Winfield Scott: see A. R. Hancock, *Reminiscences of Winfield Scott Hancock. By His Wife*.

Hand and Ring (novel). A. K. G. Rohlfs.

Hand and Soul. D. G. Rossetti.

Handbook for North Germany, from the Baltic to the Black Forest, and the Rhine, from Holland to Basle.

Handbook for Travellers (for various cities and nations). K. Baedeker.

Handbook for Travellers in Northern Italy. F. Palgrave.

Handbook for Travellers in Spain. J. Murray.

Handbook for Travellers in Switzerland and the Alps of Savoy and Piedmont. J. Murray.

Handbook for Travellers in Syria and Palestine. J. Murray.

Handbooks for travel: see the Reader's Guide entry for Travel guidebooks.

Hand-Book of Benares. A. Parker.

Handbook of Birds of Eastern North America. F. M. Chapman.

Handbook of English Literature. R. McWilliam.

Handbook of Marks and Monograms on Pottery and Porcelain. W. Chaffers.

Handbook of Painting: The German, Flemish, and Dutch Schools. F. T. Kugler.

Handbook of Painting: The Italian Schools. F. T. Kugler.

Hand, Daniel: see G. A. Wilcox, *Christian Philanthropist. A Sketch of the Life of Mr. Daniel Hand, and of His Benefaction to the American Missionary Association, for the Education of the Colored People in the Southern States of America*.

Hand in Hand; Verses by a Mother and Daughter. A. M. Kipling.

Hand-Made Gentleman; A Tale of the Battles of Peace. I. Bacheller.

Handwriting of God in Egypt, Sinai, and the Holy Land. D. A. Randall.

Handy Volume Culinary Series. A. Filippini.

Hanging of the Crane. H. W. Longfellow.

Hanna, Ione T. (composer): see M. A. Lee Demarest, "My ain countrie."

Hanna, Septimus James (ed.): see *Christian Science Journal*.

Hanna, Thomas King (co-illus.): see E. S. Martin, *Courtship of a Careful Man*.

Hannah. D. M. M. Craik.

Hannah Thurston: A Story of American Life. B. Taylor.

Hannibal, Missouri: see
Case of C. O. Godfrey.
M. D. Conway, *Autobiography: Memories and Experiences of Moncure Daniel Conway* (marginalia).
R. I. Holcombe, *History of Marion County, Missouri*.

Hannibal of Carthage: see T. A. Dodge, *Great Captains*.

Hans Breitmann's Party, with Other Ballads. C. G. Leland.

Hans Brinker; or, the Silver Skates. A Story of Life in Holland. M. E. M. Dodge.

Hänsel und Gretel (opera). E. Humperdinck.

Hans Ibeles in London. Ein Familienbild aus dem Flüchtlingsleben. J. M. Kinkel.

Hapgood, Isabel Florence (trans.): see M. Gorky, *Orlóff and His Wife. Tales of the Barefoot Brigade*.

Happy Boy. A Tale of Norwegian Peasant Life. B. Bjørnson.

Happy Isles, and Other Poems. S. H. M. Byers.

Happy Thoughts. F. C. Burnand.

Harben, William Nathaniel: see
W. W. Jacobs, *Salthaven* (novel) (marginalia).
W. L. Phelps, *Essays on Modern Novelists* (marginalia).

Hard Cash; A Matter-of-Fact Romance. C. Reade.

"Hard Fare" (essay): see J. Burroughs.

Harding, Charlotte (illus.): see W. D. Howells, *Fennel and Rue; A Novel*.

Hard Times. C. Dickens.

"Hard times come again no more" (song). S. C. Foster.

Hardwicke; A Novel. H. E. Rood.

Hardy Exotic Plants. W. Robinson.

Hardy, Thomas Duffus: see
M. D. Conway, *Autobiography: Memories and Experiences of Moncure Daniel Conway* (marginalia).
H. James (ed.), *Facsimiles of National Manuscripts from William the Conqueror to Queen Anne*.
W. L. Phelps, *Essays on Modern Novelists* (marginalia).

Hare, Maria Leycester: see A. J. C. Hare, *Memorials of a Quiet Life*.

"Hark! the herald angels sing" (Christmas carol). C. Wesley.

"Hark! what mean those holy voices" (hymn): see G. J. Geer (Catalog entry).

"Harland, Marion" (pseud.): see M. V. H. Terhune.

Harmsworth, Alfred Charles: see London *Daily Mail*.

Harold; A Drama. A. Tennyson.

Harold, The Last of the Saxon Kings. E. G. B. Lytton.

Harper, Carrie Anna (co-author): see B. M. Dix, *Beau's Comedy*.

Harper's Chicago and the World's Fair. J. Ralph.

Harper's Ferry: see R. Keeler, "Owen Brown's Escape from Harper's Ferry" (article).

Harper's Guide to Paris and the Exposition of 1900.

Harper's Handbook for Travelers in Europe and the East. W. P. Fetridge.

Harper's Machinery Book for Boys. J. H. Adams.

Harper's Monthly: see P. H. Coggins, "Old Sile's Clem" (story).

Harper's Popular Cyclopaedia of United States History. B. J. Lossing.

"Harp of a Thousand Strings" (burlesque sermon). H. T. Lewis.

Harp of a Thousand Strings; or, Laughter for a Lifetime. S. P. Avery (comp.): see H. T. Lewis, "Harp of a Thousand Strings" (burlesque sermon).

Harp of the Day; or, The Adventures and Travels of a Photographic Artist; With Other Poems. H. Bush.

"Harp that once through Tara's halls" (ballad). T. Moore.

Harrington, Calvin Sears (composer): see W. F. Warren, "Homeward bound" (hymn).

Harrington, John Lane (intro.): see M. S. Wellby, *'Twixt*

Sirdar and Menelik: An Account of a Year's Expedition from Zeila to Cairo Through Unknown Abyssinia.
"Harrington, Kate" (pseud.): see R. S. Pollard.
Harris, George Washington: see H. E. Taliaferro (Catalog entry).
Harris, Joel Chandler (co-ed.): see *World's Wit and Humor; An Encyclopedia of the Classic Wit and Humor of All Ages and Nations.*
Harris, Thomas Lake (spiritualist): see M. O. W. Oliphant, *Memoir of the Life of Laurence Oliphant and of Alice Oliphant, His Wife.*
Harrison and Reid: Their Lives and Record. T. Campbell-Copeland.
Harrison, Benjamin: see H. W. Scott, *Distinguished American Lawyers, with Their Struggles and Triumphs in the Forum.*
Harrison, (Mrs.) Burton: see C. C. Harrison.
Harrison, William Henry (U. S. President): see A. F. de Bacourt, *Souvenirs of a Diplomat: Private Letters from America.*
Hart, Albert Bushnell:
  (ed.) *American Nation: A History from Original Sources by Associated Scholars.*
  (co-author): see R. Hitchcock (ed.), *Decisive Battles of America.*
Hart, Mary Theresa (illus.): see
  G. E. S. Jackson, *Wee Winkles & Snowball.*
  G. E. S. Jackson, *Wee Winkles & Wideawake.*
Harte, Bret: see
  C. F. Adams, Jr., "Of Some Railroad Accidents" (Catalog entry).
  M. D. Conway, *Autobiography: Memories and Experiences of Moncure Daniel Conway* (marginalia).
  T. F. Cronise, *Natural Wealth of California* (Catalog entry).
  J. Habberton, *Jericho Road: A Story of Western Life* (marginalia).
  C. Lamb, *Works of Charles Lamb* (Catalog entry).
  W. E. H. Lecky, *History of European Morals from Augustus to Charlemagne* (Catalog entry).
  G. E. Lewis, *Heart Echoes* (laid in clipping).
  F. H. Smith, *Peter: A Novel of Which He Is Not the Hero* (marginalia).
  C. W. Stoddard, *Exits and Entrances: A Book of Essays and Sketches.*
  W. M. Thackeray, *Thackeray's Lectures. The English Humorists. The Four Georges* (Catalog entry).
  G. O. Trevelyan, *Life and Letters of Lord Macaulay* (marginalia).
Hartford City Directory: see *Geer's Hartford City Directory.*
Hartford, Connecticut: see
  E. G. Coke, *Subaltern's Furlough: Descriptive of Scenes in Various Parts of the United States.*
  G. Combe, *Notes on the United States of North America, During a Phrenological Visit in 1838-9-40.*
  J. Fiske, *Beginnings of New England; or, The Puritan Theocracy.*
  Geer's Hartford City Directory.
  T. Hamilton, *Men and Manners in America.*
  H. Howard, *Poems.*
  F. B. Terry, *Stories.*

Travelers Record (magazine, Hartford, Connecticut).
Hartford County, Connecticut: see J. H Trumbull, *Memorial History of Hartford County Connecticut 1633–1884.*
Hartley, Florence: see C. B. Hartley, *Gentlemen's Book of Etiquette and Manual of Politeness.*
Hartmann, Sadakichi (intro.): see R. Eickemeyer, *Winter.*
Harvard College: see
  H. W. Bynner, *Ode to Harvard and Other Poems.*
  G. T. Richardson, *Letters from a Son to His Self-Made Father.*
Harvey, George Brinton McClellan: see
  Harper's Weekly.
  (co-author): see *On Track and Diamond.*
Harvey, William (illus.): see
  Arabian Nights, Thousand and One Nights.
  J. Bunyan, *Pilgrim's Progress.*
Hasheesh Eater; Being Passages from the Life of a Pythagorean. F. H. Ludlow.
"Hashimura Togo" (pseud.): see W. Irwin.
Haskell, Ernest (illus.): see W. Shakespeare, *Romeo and Juliet* (play).
Hassam, Childe (illus.): see W. Scott, *Christmas in the Olden Time.*
Hastings, Warren: see
  E. Burke, *Articles of Charge of High Crimes and Misdemeanors Against Warren Hastings.*
  Junius, *Letters of Junius* (Catalog entry).
  T. B. Macaulay, "Essay on Lord Clive" (Catalog entry).
  T. B. Macaulay, "Essay on Warren Hastings."
Hatherell, William (illus.): see J. M. Forman, *Jason, A Romance.*
Hatton, John Liptrot (composer) : see R. F. Williams, "Good-bye, sweetheart, good-bye" (song).
Hauser, Kaspar: see E. E. Evans, *Story of Kaspar Hauser from Authentic Records.*
Hauvion, Andre-Casimir: see Larive et Fleury (pseud.) in the Catalog.
Havana: see G. A. Sala, *Under the Sun: Essays Mainly Written in Hot Countries.*
Haven, Alice Bradley (intro.): see F. M. B. *Widow Bedott Papers.*
Havers, Dorothea Henrietta: see D. H. H. Boulger.
Hawaii: see
  W. D. Alexander, *Review of a Pastoral Address by the Right Rev. T. N. Staley, D.D., Reformed Catholic Bishop of Honolulu, Containing a Reply to Some of His Charges Against the American Protestant Mission to the Hawaiian Islands.*
  R. Anderson, *Hawaiian Islands: Their Progress and Condition Under Missionary Labors.*
  L. Andrews, *Dictionary of the Hawaiian Language.*
  George Washington Bates (pseud.), *Sandwich Island Notes. By a Haölé.*
  A. Bishop, *Na Huaolelo a me na olelo kikeke ma ka Beritania a me ka olelo Hawaii.*
  W. R. Bliss, *Paradise in the Pacific; A Book of Travel, Adventure, and Facts in the Sandwich Islands.*
  A. A. A. Brassey, *Voyage in the Sunbeam, Our Home in the Ocean for Eleven Months.*

G. L. Carlisle, *Around the World in a Year.*

G. L. Chaney, *"Alo'ha!": A Hawaiian Salutation.*

H. T. Cheever, *Island World of the Pacific; Being the Personal Narrative and Results of Travel Through the Sandwich or Hawaiian Islands, and Other Parts of Polynesia.*

R. G. Davis, *Reports of . . . the Supreme Court of the Hawaiian Islands.*

C. Dickens, *Old Curiosity Shop; and Reprinted Pieces* (marginalia).

H. H. Gowen, *Paradise of the Pacific. Sketches of Hawaiian Scenery and Life.*

M. Hopkins, *Hawaii: The Past, Present, and Future of Its Island-Kingdom.*

J. J. Jarves, *History of the Hawaiian or Sandwich Islands.*

D. Kalakaua, *Legends and Myths of Hawaii: The Fables and Folk-Lore of a Strange People.*

W. Kennedy, "Pirate's serenade" (song).

M. H. Krout, [newspaper columns].

Lorrin, *Dictionary of the Hawaiian Language.*

Maile Quarterly.

C. S. Stewart, *Private Journal of a Voyage to the Pacific Ocean and Residence at the Sandwich Islands, in the Years 1822, 1823, 1824, and 1825.*

C. W. Stoddard, *Lepers of Molokai.*

C. W. Stoddard, *South-Sea Idyls.*

H. M. Whitney, *Tourists' Guide Through the Hawaiian Islands, Descriptive of Their Scenes and Scenery.*

J. G. Wood, *Uncivilized Races; or, Natural History of Man* (marginalia).

See also the Reader's Guide entry for South Pacific.

Hawaii and a Revolution. M. H. Krout, *Hawaiian Islands: Their Progress and Condition Under Missionary Labors.* R. Anderson.

Hawaiian language: see L. Andrews, *Dictionary of the Hawaiian Language.*

Hawaii: The Past, Present, and Future of Its Island-Kingdom. M. Hopkins.

Haweis, Mary Eliza Joy (ed., illus.): see G. Chaucer, *Chaucer for Children: A Golden Key.*

Hawes, Harriet Boyd (co-author): see C. H. Hawes, *Crete, The Forerunner of Greece.*

Hawkins, Willis Brooks ("Quills"): see the Catalog entry for L. E. Trescott.

Hawks, Francis Lister (comp.): see M. C. Perry, *Narrative of the Expedition of an American Squadron to the China Seas and Japan, Performed in the Years 1852, 1853, and 1854.*

Hawley, Joseph Roswell: see Hartford *Courant.*

Hawley, Joseph Roswell: see J. W. Watson, "Beautiful Snow" (poem).

Hawthorn and Lavender, with Other Verses. W. E. Henley.

Hawthorne. J. T. Fields.

"Hawthorne, Alice" (pseud.): see S. Winner.

Hawthorne and His Circle. J. Hawthorne.

Hawthorne, Julian: see
(intro.) W. S. Burgess, *Eternal Laughter and Other Poems.*
(intro.) E. Field, *Culture's Garland: Being Memoranda of the Gradual Rise of Literature, Art, Music and Society in Chicago, and Other Western Ganglia.*
(ed.) N. Hawthorne, *Doctor Grimshawe's Secret; A Romance.*

Hawthorne, Nathaniel: see
(pref.): D. S. Bacon *Philosophy of the Plays of Shakspere Unfolded.*
F. O. C. Darley, *Compositions in Outline by Felix O. C. Darley, from Hawthorne's Scarlet Letter.*
J. T. Fields, *Hawthorne.*
T. W. S. Higginson, *Cheerful Yesterdays. Contemporaries* (marginalia).
O. W. Holmes, *Autocrat of the Breakfast-Table.* (marginalia).
H. James, *Nathaniel Hawthorne.*
E. P. Parker (Catalog entry).

Hay, John: see
H. Greeley, *What I Know of Farming* (Catalog entry).
G. G. Greenwood, *Shakespeare Problem Restated* (marginalia).
W. D. Howells, "John Hay."

Hay, William Delisle (ed.): see W. T. Wawn, *South Sea Islanders and the Queensland Labour Trade: A Record of Voyages and Experiences in the Western Pacific, from 1875 to 1891.*

Haydn's Dictionary of Dates and Universal Information Relating to All Ages and Nations. J. T. Haydn.

Haydon, Benjamin Robert: see W. J. Dawson (co-ed.), *Great English Letter-Writers* (marginalia).

"Hayes, Henry" (pseud.): see E. W. O. Kirk.

Hayes, Rutherford Birchard: see
W. D. Howells, *Sketch of the Life and Character of Rutherford B. Hayes.*
S. J. Tilden, *Letters and Literary Memorials of Samuel J. Tilden* (Catalog entry).

Hayne, Paul Hamilton: see *Smith College Commencement Poems, '79-'86* (contr.).

Hays, William Shakespeare (composer): see C. W. Fry, "Lily of the valley" (hymn).

Haywood, Eliza (Fowler) (trans.): see M. A .P. de Gomez, *Belle Assemblée: Being a Curious Collection of Some Very Remarkable Incidents Which Happen'd to Persons of the First Quality in France.*

Hazard, Blanche Evans (co-ed.): see A. B. Hart, *Colonial Children.*

Hazard of New Fortunes (novel). W. D. Howells.

Hazelton, Isaac Brewster (illus.): see J. Weymouth, *College Chaps.*

Hazlitt, William (ed.): see M. E. de Montaigne, *Works of Michael de Montaigne, Comprising His Essays, Journey into Italy, and Letters.*

Hazlitt, William Carew (ed.): see J. Suckling, *Poems, Plays and Other Remains of Sir John Suckling. A New Edition.*

Headley, Joel Tyler (contr.): see C. D. W. Brownell, *Indian Races of North and South America.*

Head of the Family; A Novel. D. M. M. Craik.

Healey. J. Fothergill.

Healing Currents from the Battery of Life. W. De Voe.

Health and Wealth. E. G. Hubbard.

Health, fitness, and hygiene: see
Bazar Book of Health.

E. M. M. Bishop, *Seventy Years Young; or, The Unhabitual Way.*

W. Blaikie, *How to Get Strong and How to Stay So.*

F. P. Cobbe, *The Peak in Darien, with Some Other Inquiries Touching Concerns of the Soul and the Body.*

L. Conaro, *Art of Living Long. A New and Improved English Version of the Treatise by the Celebrated Venetian Centenarian.*

G. Depping, *Wonders of Bodily Strength and Skill, in All Ages and All Countries.*

W. De Voe, *Healing Currents from the Battery of Life.*

R. J. Ebbard, *How to Acquire and Strengthen Will-Power. Modern Psycho-Therapy.*

F. Forbes, *How to Be Happy Through Living.*

C. C. Haskell, *Perfect Health: How to Get It and How to Keep It.*

M. N. F. Henderson, *Aristocracy of Health: A Study of Physical Culture.*

E. G. Hubbard, *Health and Wealth.*

S. Kneipp, *My Water Cure.*

E. A. Reynolds-Ball, *Mediterranean Winter Resorts. A Practical Hand-book to the Principal Health and Pleasure Resorts on the Shores of the Mediterranean.*

O. C. Sabin, *Christology—Science of Health and Happiness; or, Metaphysical Healing Exemplified—Through Rules, Formulas and Incidents.*

W. Wakefield, *Baths, Bathing, and Attractions of Aix-les-Bains.*

J. Walker, *Anatomy, Physiology, and Hygiene: A Manual for the Use of Colleges, Schools, and General Readers.*

See also the Reader's Guide entries for Medical advice and subjects, for Mental health, and for Spiritualism and spiritual healing.

Hearing impairment: see the Reader's Guide entry for Disabilities.

Hearn, Lafcadio: see
(trans., intro.), A. France, *Crime of Sylvestre Bonnard.*
(trans., intro.), M. M. Heaton, *Masterpieces of Flemish Art.*

Heart Echoes. G. E. Lewis.

Heart of Asia: A History of Russian Turkestan and the Central Asian Khanates from the Earliest Times. F. H. Skrine and E. D. Ross.

Heart of It. A Series of Extracts from "The Power of Silence" and "The Perfect Whole." W. Dresser.

Heart of Midlothian. W. Scott.

Heart of the White Mountains, Their Legend and Scenery. S. A. Drake.

Heart Throbs in Prose and Verse Dear to the American People. J. M. Chapple (comp.).

Heath, Lyman (composer): see H. S. Washburn, "Grave of Napoleon" (song).

"Heathen Chinee" (poem): see B. Harte, *Poetical Works.*

Heaven: see the Reader's Guide entry for Afterlife.

Heaven and Hell. E. Swedenborg.

Heavenly Twins. S. Grand.

Heavens: An Illustrated Handbook of Popular Astronomy. A. V. Guillemin.

Hector: A Story. F. L. Shaw.

Hedda Gabler (play). H. Ibsen.

Heidelberg (novel). G. P. R. James.

"Heimthal, Max" (pseud.): see M. Schneckenburger.

Heinrich Heine's Buch der Lieder. H. Heine.

Heiress of Red Dog. B. Harte.

Heir of Redclyffe. C. M. Yonge.

Heke, Chief: see F. B. Maning, *Old New Zealand, A Tale of the Good Old Times.*

Helen Keller Souvenir No. 2 (1892–1899). H. Keller.

Helen of Troy: see M. H. Hewlett, *Ruinous Face* (novel).

Helen's Babies. With Some Account of Their Ways, Innocent, Crafty, Angelic, Impish, Witching and Repulsive. J. Habberton.

Helen's Babies. With Some Account of Their Ways: see
B. C. Green, *Adventures of an Old Maid. By Aunt Ruth* (Catalog entry).
E. P. Hammond, *Sketches of Palestine* (Catalog entry).

Heliodorus: see *Greek Romances of Heliodorus, Longus, and Achilles Tatius.*

Hello, Ernest: see J. G. Huneker, *Egoists, A Book of Supermen.*

Helmet of Navarre. B. Runkle.

Heloise: see
A. M. L. de Lamartine, Heloise" (story).
W. M. Thackeray, *Thackeray's Lectures. The English Humorists. The Four Georges* (marginalia).
O. W. Wight, *Lives and Letters of Abelard and Heloise.*

"Hemlock Tree" (poem). H. W. Longfellow.

Hemple, Charles Julius (trans.): see *Schiller's Complete Works.*

Henderson, William J. (co-author): see
Battle for the Pacific, and Other Adventures at Sea.
On the Gridiron and Other Stories of Outdoor Sport.

Henn, Peter (ed.): see J. F. Ahn, *Ahn's First German Book.*

Henn, Peter (ed.): see J. F. Ahn, *Ahn's Second German Book.*

Hennessy, William John (illus.): see M. D. Conway, *Necklace of Stories.*

Henry II: see A. P. Stanley, *Historical Memorials of Westminster Abbey.*

Henry III: see
W. Combe, *History and Antiquities of the City of York, from Its Origin to the Present Times* (marginalia).
A. P. Stanley, *Historical Memorials of Westminster Abbey.*

Henry IV (Parts One and Two) (plays). W. Shakespeare.

Henry IV (Parts One and Two) (plays): see F. S. Wilhelmina, *Memoirs of Wilhelmine, Margravine of Baireuth* (marginalia).

Henry IV: see J. S. C. Abbott, *History of Henry the Fourth, King of France and Navarre.*

Henry V (play). W. Shakespeare.

Henry V (play): see F. S. Wilhelmina, *Memoirs of Wilhelmine, Margravine of Baireuth* (marginalia).

Henry V: see
F. Thompson, "From the Night of Forebeing. An Ode after Easter" (Catalog entry).
C. M. Yonge, *Cameos from English History. The Wars in France* (marginalia).

Henry VII: see
D. Hume, *History of England, from the Invasion of Julius Caesar to the Revolution of 1688* (Catalog entry).
Henry VII, *Statutes of Henry VII in Exact Facsimile.*

Henry VIII (play). W. Shakespeare.
Henry VIII: see
  A. E. Dickinson, *Crown of Thorns, or Ann Boleyn* (play).
  W. H. Dixon, *History of Two Queens: Catherine of Aragon and Anne Boleyn.*
  J. A. Froude, *History of England from the Fall of Wolsey to the Defeat of the Spanish Armada.*
  E. W. Gallup, *Tragedy of Anne Boleyn. A Drama in Cipher Found in the Works of Sir Francis Bacon.*
  D. Hume, *History of England, from the Invasion of Julius Caesar to the Revolution of 1688* (Catalog entry).
  C. Major, *When Knighthood Was in Flower; or, The Love Story of Charles Brandon and Mary Tudor, the King's Sister* (novel).
  A. Manning, *Household of Sir Thos. More.*
  A. Manning, *Passages in the Life of the Faire Gospeller Mistress Anne Askew.*
  Mundt, K. M., *Henry VIII. and His Court; or, Catherine Parr. An Historical Novel.*
  J. G. Wilson (ed.), *Love in Letters; Illustrated in the Correspondence of Eminent Persons; with Biographical Sketches of the Writers.*
Henry VIII. and His Court; or, Catherine Parr. An Historical Novel. K. M. Mundt.
"Henry H. Rogers—Monopolist" (article). I. F. Marcosson.
Henry Hudson, A Brief Statement of His Aims and His Achievements. T. A. Janvier.
Henry Hudson the Navigator. The Original Documents in Which His Career Is Recorded. G. M. Asher (ed.).
Hensel, Wilhelm (illus.): see S. Hensel, *Mendelssohn Family (1729–1847) from Letters and Journals.*
Heptameron of Margaret, Queen of Navarre. Marguerite d'Angoulême.
Herbart, Johann Friedrich: see J. Adams, *Herbartian Psychology Applied to Education.*
Herbert, George: see I. Walton, *Lives of John Donne, Henry Wotton, Richd Hooker, George Herbert, &c.*
Herbert, George Robert Charles (intro.): see F. E. Maning, *Old New Zealand, A Tale of the Good Old Times.*
Herbert, Mary Elizabeth (trans.): see A. M. L. de Lamartine, *Twenty-Five Years of My Life.*
Herbert, Victor (composer): see H. B. Smith, *Little Nemo* (musical comedy).
Hereford, Charles Harold: see (ed.) W. Shakespeare, *Works of Shakespeare.*
Her First Appearance. R. H. Davis.
Herford, Oliver (illus.): see
  O. Herford, *Artful Anticks.*
  O. Herford, *Child's Primer of Natural History.*
  O. Herford, *Rubáiyát of a Persian Kitten.*
  J. J. Roche, *Her Majesty the King; A Romance of the Harem.*
  C. Wells, *Phenomenal Fauna.*
Her Majesty the King; A Romance of the Harem, Done into American from the Arabic. J. J. Roche.
Herman; or, Young Knighthood. S. H. Palfrey.
Herms, M. (co-trans.): see H., G. von Moltke, *Essays, Speeches and Memoirs.*
Hernándo Cortés. F. A. Ober.

Hero. D. M. M. Craik.
Hero and Leander. C. Marlowe.
Hero, Bread Upon the Waters, Alice Learmont. D. M. M. Craik.
Herod: A Tragedy (play). S. Phillips.
Herodotus: see
  F. E. Maning, *Old New Zealand, A Tale of the Good Old Times* (marginalia).
  J. T. Wheeler, *Life and Travels of Herodotus in the Fifth Century Before Christ: An Imaginary Biography Founded on Fact.*
Heroes and Hero Worship. T. Carlyle.
Heroes Every Child Should Know. H. W. Mabie (ed.).
Heroes of Asgard: Tales from Scandinavian Mythology. A. M. Keary and E. Keary.
Heroes, or Greek Fairy Tales for My Children. C. Kingsley.
"Heroic Deeds of Heroic Men" (series of articles). J. S. C. Abbott.
Heroines of Fiction. W. D. Howells.
Heroines That Every Child Should Know. H. W. Mabie (ed.).
Her Royal Highness Queen Bee: A Story of Fact and Fancy and Other Stories. H. B. Moore.
Her Second Love. A. C. Ogle.
Herts, Alice Minnie: see Alice Minnie (Herts) Heniger.
Herve Riel (poem). R. Browning.
Herzfeld, Marie (trans.): see J. P. Jacobsen, *Niels Lyhne.*
He's a Lunatic: A Farce in One Act. H. C. Merivale.
He, She & They; Being a Faithful Record of the Woful Enjoyments and Joyful Woes of Him & Her. A. Lee.
Hesper; A Novel. H. Garland.
Hewitt, John Hill (composer): see E. L. Beers, "Picket-Guard" (poem, song).
"H. H." (pseud.): see H. M. F. H. Jackson.
Hiawatha: see H. W. Longfellow, *Song of Hiawatha.*
Hiawatha: see H. R. Schoolcraft, *Algic Researches, Comprising Inquiries Respecting the Mental Characteristics of the North American Indians.*
Hibbard, George Abiah, "Eyes of Affection" (short story): see W. D. Howells and H. M. Alden (eds.), *Their Husbands' Wives.*
Higginson, Thomas Wentworth Storrow: see
  E. Dickinson (Catalog entry).
  (pref.): see É. Erckmann, *Madame Thérèse; or, The Volunteers of '92.*
  (co-author): see R. Hitchcock (ed.), *Decisive Battles in America.*
  J. L. Motley, *Correspondence of John Lothrop Motley* (Catalog entry).
High Alps Without Guides: Being a Narrative of Adventures in Switzerland. A. G. Girdlestone.
High Spirits: Being Certain Stories Written in Them. J. Payn.
High-Toned Sprees: A Series of Temperance Legends. Mrs. O. A. Powers.
Highways and By-ways; or Saunterings in New England. W. H. Gibson.
Highways and Byways of the Mississippi Valley. C. Johnson.
Hill, Charles Southworth (composer): see "Nora McCarty" (ballad).

History of King Philip, Sovereign Chief of the Wampanoags. J. S. C. Abbott.

History of Latin Literature from Ennius to Boethius. G. A. Simcox.

History of Louis Philippe, King of the French. J. S. C. Abbott.

History of Madame Roland. J. S. C. Abbott.

History of Margaret of Anjou. J. S. C. Abbott.

History of Marie Antoinette. J. S. C. Abbott.

History of Marion County, Missouri. R. I. Holcombe.

History of Mary, Queen of Scots. J. Abbott. See also the Catalog entry for J. Abbott, *Mary, Queen of Scots.*

History of Methodism in the United States. J. M. Buckley.

History of Modern Europe. C. A. Fyffe.

History of Napoleon Bonaparte. J. S. C. Abbott.

History of Our Own Times, from the Accession of Queen Victoria to the General Election of 1880. J. McCarthy.

History of Our Own Times, from the Diamond Jubilee, 1897 to the Accession of King Edward VII. J. McCarthy.

History of Pendennis, His Fortunes and Misfortunes, His Friends and His Greatest Enemy. W. M. Thackeray.

History of Prices, and of the State of the Circulation, from 1793 to 1837. T. Tooke.

History of Prostitution: Its Extent, Causes, and Effects Throughout the World. W. W. Sanger.

History of Pyrrhus. J. Abbott.

History of Queen Elizabeth. J. Abbott.

History of Redding, Connecticut. C. B. Todd.

History of Richard the Third. J. S. C. Abbott.

History of Romulus. J. S. C. Abbott.

History of Sandford and Merton. T. Day.

History of Scotland During the Reigns of Queen Mary and of King James VI Till His Accession to the Crown of England. W. Robertson.

History of Sculpture from the Earliest Ages to the Present Time. W. Lübke.

History of Sculpture, Painting, and Architecture. Topical Lessons, with Specific References to Valuable Books. C. S. Farrar.

History of Signboards, from the Earliest Times to the Present Day. H. D. J. van Schevichaven.

History of the American People. W. Wilson.

History of the Arts and Crafts Movement. O. L. Triggs.

History of the Big Bonanza: An Authentic Account of the Discovery, History, and Working of the World-Renowned Comstock Silver Lode of Nevada; Adventures with Mining, the Indians, and the Country. W. Wright.

History of the British Empire. W. F. Collier.

History of the Ceramic Art; A Descriptive and Philosophical Study of the Pottery of All Ages and All Nations. A. Jacquemart.

History of the Civil War in America. J. S. C. Abbott.

History of the Civil War in America. L.-P.-A.-d' O. Paris.

History of the Commonwealth of Florence, from the Earliest Independence of the Commune to the Fall of the Republic in 1531. T. A. Trollope.

History of the Conquest of Peru, with a Preliminary View of the Civilization of the Incas. W. H. Prescott.

History of the Decline and Fall of the Roman Empire. E. Gibbon.

History of the Detection, Conviction, Life and Designs of

John A. Murel, The Great Western Land Pirate. V. A. Stewart.

History of the Devil: see D. Defoe, *Moll Flanders and The History of the Devil.*

History of the Discovery and Settlement of America. W. Robertson.

History of the English People. J. R. Green.

History of the Four Georges. J. McCarthy.

History of the German Struggle for Liberty. P. Bigelow.

History of the Grange Movement; or the Farmer's War Against Monopolies. J. D. McCabe.

History of the Hawaiian or Sandwich Islands. J. J. Jarves.

History of the Hebrew Nation, and Its Literature. S. Sharpe.

History of the Inquisition from Its Establishment in the Twelfth Century to Its Extinction in the Nineteenth. W. H. Rule.

History of the Inquisition of the Middle Ages. H. C. Lea.

History of the Intellectual Development of Europe. J. W. Draper.

History of the Managements of Cardinal Julio Mazarine, Chief Minister of State of the Crown of France. G. Gualdo Priorato.

History of the Popes, Their Church and State, and Especially of Their Conflicts with Protestantism in the Sixteenth and Seventeenth Centuries. L. von Ranke.

History of the Rise and Influence of the Spirit of Rationalism in Europe. W. E. H. Lecky.

History of the Robins. In Words of One Syllable. S. Trimmer.

History of the Romans under the Empire. C. Merivale.

History of the Standard Oil Company. I. M. Tarbell.

"History of the Two Pillars" (article). W. L. Fawcett.

History of the United Netherlands from the Death of William the Silent to the Twelve Years' Truce—1609. J. L. Motley.

History of the United States: see

  C. A. Goodrich, *History of the United States.*

  T. W. S. Higginson, *History of the United States from 986 to 1905* (marginalia).

  R. Hildreth, *History of the United States of America.*

  E. W. Nye, *Bill Nye's History of the United States.*

History of the United States from 986 to 1905 (marginalia). T. W. S. Higginson.

History of the Warfare of Science with Theology. A. D. White.

History of the War in the Peninsula and in the South of France, from the Year 1807 to the Year 1814. W. F. P. Napier.

History of the Worthies of England: see T. Fuller, *Holy State and the Profane State.*

History of Two Queens: Catherine of Aragon and Anne Boleyn. W. H. Dixon.

History of Virgil A. Stewart, and His Adventure. H. R. Howard.

History of William the Conqueror. J. S. C. Abbott.

His Wisdom The Defender; A Story. S. Newcomb.

Hitchcock, Lucius Wolcott (illus.): see

  M. W. C. Deland, *Dr. Lavendar's People.*

  B. King, *Wild Olive; A Novel.*

  B. Tarkington, *Conquest of Canaan: A Novel.*

Hitherto: A Story of Yesterdays. A. D. T. Whitney.

H.M.S. Pinafore (operetta). W. S. Gilbert.
Hoch vom Kahlenberg. Heitere nd ernste Skizzen aus dem Wiener Leben. E. Pötzl.
Hocken, Elizabeth Mary Buckland (trans.): see A. J. Tasman (Catalog entry).
Hodge, Charles (American clergyman): see A. D. White, *History of the Warfare of Science with Theology* (marginalia).
Hodgson, Richard (co-ed.): see F. W. H. Myers, *Human Personality and Its Survival of Bodily Death.*
Hoey, Frances Sarah (Johnston) (trans.): see C. É. J. G. de V. Rémusat, *Memoirs of Madame de Rémusat, 1802–1808.*
Hogg, James (ed.): see R. Burns, *Works of Robert Burns.*
"Hohenlinden" (poem). T. Campbell.
Holcomb, Martha A. Lyon (trans.): see E. Tegnér, *Fridthjof's Saga; A Norse Romance.*
Holcomb, Thomas Addis Emmett (trans.): see E. Tegnér, *Fridthjof's Saga; A Norse Romance.*
Holden, Oliver (composer): see E. Perronet, "All hail the power of Jesus' name" (hymn).
Holder, Joseph B.: see J. G. Wood, *Our Living World; An Artistic Edition of the Rev. J. G. Wood's Natural History of Animate Creation.*
Holiday, Henry (illus.): see C. L. Dodgson, *Rhyme? And Reason?*
Holland: see
J. S. C. Abbott, *History of Hortense, the Daughter of Josephine, Queen of Holland.*
E. De Amicis, *Holland and Its People.*
P. Bausch (Catalog entry).
M. E. M. Dodge, *Hans Brinker; or, the Silver Skates. A Story of Life in Holland.*
J. L. Motley, *History of the United Netherlands from the Death of William the Silent to the Twelve Years' Truce—1609.*
J. L. Motley, *Motley's Dutch Nation, Being the Rise of the Dutch Republic (1555–1584) Condensed.*
C. Reade, *Cloister and the Hearth; or, Maid, Wife, and Widow: A Matter-of-Fact Romance.*
F. A. Stokes, *College Tramps: A Narrative of the Adventures of a Party of Yale Students During a Summer Vacation in Europe, with Knapsack and Alpenstock, and the Incidents of a Voyage to Rotterdam and Return.*
C. D. Warner, *Saunterings.*
Holland and Its People. E. De Amicis.
Holland House. M. H. N. von Liechtenstein.
"Holm, Saxe" (pseud.): see H. M. F. H. Jackson.
Holman, Elizabeth Alden (Curtis) (trans.): see Omar Khayyám, *One Hundred Quatrains.*
Holmby House; A Tale of Old Northamptonshire (novel). G. J. Whyte-Melville.
Holmes, Oliver Wendell: see
E. E. Brown, *Life of Oliver Wendell Holmes.*
T. W. S. Higginson, *Cheerful Yesterdays. Contemporaries* (marginalia).
New York *Tribune* (Catalog entry).
W. Shakespeare, *Hamlet* (Catalog entry).
M. F. Tupper, *Proverbial Philosophy: A Book of Thoughts and Arguments* (Catalog entry).
Waverley Magazine (Boston) (Catalog entry).

W. Winter, "Chieftain" (poem).
W. Winter, *Wanderers: The Poems of William Winter.*
Holmes, Sherlock (fictional character): see
J. K. Bangs, *R. Holmes & Co.; Being the Remarkable Adventures of Raffles Holmes, Esq., Detective and Amateur Cracksman by Birth.*
A. C. Doyle (several titles).
M. Leblanc, *Exploits of Arsène Lupin.*
Holmes, Sherwood (fictional character): see the Catalog entry for A. C. Doyle.
Holy Bible: see the Reader's Guide entry for Bible.
"Holy Ghost! With light divine" (hymn). A. Reed.
Holy Grail: see W. Crookes, *Diamonds* (Catalog entry).
Holy Land: see
J. T. Barclay, *City of the Great King; or, Jerusalem As It Was, As It Is, and As It Is To Be.*
J. R. Browne, *Yusef; or the Journey of the Frangi: A Crusade in the East.*
C. W. Elliott, *Remarkable Characters and Places of the Holy Land.*
L. M. R. Griswold, *Woman's Pilgrimage to the Holy Land; or, Pleasant Days Abroad. Being Notes of a Tour Through Europe and the East.*
E. P. Hammond, *Sketches of Palestine Descriptive of the Visit of the Rev. Edward Payson Hammond, M.A., to the Holy Land.*
Impressions of Damascus (unidentified book).
J. H. Ingraham. *Prince of the House of David; or, Three Years in the Holy City.*
Jericho and the Jordan (unidentified book).
A. M. L. de Lamartine, *Pilgrimage to the Holy Land; Comprising Recollections, Sketches, and Reflections Made During a Tour in the East, in 1832–1833.*
N. MacLeod, *Eastward.*
J. Murray, *Handbook for Travellers in Syria and Palestine.*
W. C. Prime, *Tent Life in the Holy Land.*
D. A. Randall, *Handwriting of God in Egypt, Sinai, and the Holy Land.*
E. Robinson, *Biblical Researches in Palestine, and in the Adjacent Regions. A Journal of Travels in the Years 1838 & 1852.*
C. W. Stoddard, *Cruise Under the Crescent; From Suez to San Marco.*
W. H. Thomson, *Parables and Their Home. The Parables by the Lake.*
W. M. Thomson, *Land and the Book; or, Biblical illustrations Drawn from the Manners and Customs, the Scenes and Scenery, of the Holy Land: Lebanon, Damascus and Beyond Jordan.*
E. S.P. Ward and H. D. Ward, *Master of the Magicians* (novel).
C. D. Warner, *In the Levant.*
See also the Reader's Guide entries for Jerusalem and for Palestine.
Holy State and the Profane State. T. Fuller.
"Home again" (song). M. S. Pike.
Home Atlas of Astronomy. A. K. Johnston.
Home Ballads. B. Taylor.
Home Book of Poetry. E. O. Chapman (ed.).
Home, Daniel Dunglas (spiritualist medium): see T.

W. Doane, *Bible Myths and Their Parallels in Other Religions* (marginalia).

Home decoration: see the Reader's Guide entry for Interior decoration.

Home economics: see the Reader's Guide entry for Housekeeping advice.

Home-Folks. J. W. Riley.

Home, James Archibald (ed.): see L. Stuart, *Lady Louisa Stuart: Selections from Her Manuscripts*.

Home Life, in the Light of Its Divine Idea. J. B. Brown.

Home-Maker (magazine): see A. E. Trumbull, "Mary A. Twining" (sketch).

Home Medical Library. K. Winslow (ed.).

Homer: see

J. Froude, *Short Studies on Great Subjects*.

Socrates (Catalog entry).

W. Shakespeare, *Works of Shakespeare* (Catalog entry).

J. Sheffield, *Essay on Poetry*.

Homes: see

L. F. W. Jewitt and S. C. Hall, *Stately Homes of England*.

E. S. Morse, *Japanese Homes and Their Surroundings*.

A. Rimmer, *Ancients Streets and Homesteads of England*.

T. Wright, *Homes of Other Days: A History of Domestic Manners and Sentiments in England, from the Earliest Known Period to Modern Times*.

See also the Reader's Guide entries for Architecture and for Literary landmarks.

Homes of Other Days: A History of Domestic Manners and Sentiments in England, from the Earliest Known Period to Modern Times. T. Wright.

Homestead on the Hillside. M. J. H. Holmes.

"Home, sweet home" (song). J. H. Payne.

"Homeward bound" (hymn): W. F. Warren.

Homosexuality: see

J. J. Rousseau, *Confessions* (Catalog entry).

J. A. Symonds.

O. Wilde, *De Profundis*.

"Honest Old Sam Hungerford" (poem). J. W. Riley.

Hone, William (publisher): see the Catalog entry for Bible. New Testament. Apocrypha.

Hone, William (ed.): see J. Strutt, *Sports and Pastimes of the People of England, Including the Rural and Domestic Recreations*.

Hong Kong: see A. Ireland, *Far Eastern Tropics: Studies in the Administration of Tropical Dependencies*.

Honor Ormthwaite; A Novel. H. Keddie.

Hood, Robin: see the Reader's Guide entry for Robin Hood.

Hood, Tom: see *Tom Hood's Comic Annual* (London).

Hooker, Horace: see L. H. H. Sigourney, *Memoir of Mary Ann Hooker* (Catalog entry).

Hooker, Isabella: see M. D. Conway, *Autobiography: Memories and Experiences of Moncure Daniel Conway* (marginalia).

Hooker, Mary Ann: see L. H. H. Sigourney, *Memoir of Mary Ann Hooker*.

Hooker, Richard: see I. Walton, *Lives of John Donne, Henry Wotton, Richd George Herbert, &c.*

Hooper, Charles Edward (illus.): see A. C. Wheeler, *Making of a Country Home*.

Hoosier Schoolmaster: A Story of Backwoods Life in Indiana. E. Eggleston.

Hooykaas, Isaac (co-author): see

H. Oort, *Bible for Learners*.

H. Oort, *Bible for Young People*.

"Hope, Anthony" (pseud.): see A. H. Hawkins.

Hope On! Hope Ever! Or, the Boyhood of Felix Law. M. B. Howitt.

Hopkins, Henry (intro.): see J. S. Kirtley, *Young Man and Himself; His Tasks, His Dreams, His Purposes*.

Hopkins, L. Y. Y. (illus.): see

T. B. Aldrich, *Story of a Cat*.

E. W. Nye, *Forty Liars, and Other Lies*.

Hopkirk, Edith (trans.): see Elizabeth, Queen of Rumania, *Real Queen's Fairy Tales*.

Hoppin, Augustus (illus.): see

O. W. Holmes, *Autocrat of the Breakfast-Table*.

W. D. Howells, *Their Wedding Journey*.

C. D. Warner, *Backlog Studies*.

A. D. T. Whitney, *Summer in Leslie Goldthwaite's Life*.

Horatio Plodgers; A Story of To-Day. S. H. Church.

Horner, Jack (of Belfast): see

(gift) M. A. Ross, *Delina Delaney*.

(gift) M. A. Ross, *Irene Iddesleigh*.

Horner, Joanna B. (co-author): see S. Horner, *Walks in Florence and Its Environs*.

Hornet (sinking of ship): see

W. D. Howells (co-ed.), *Library of Universal Adventure by Sea and Land*.

J. A. Mitchell, *Diary of Captain Josiah A. Mitchell*.

Hornung, Ernest William: see *Current Literture: A Magazine of Record and Review* (marginalia).

Horse Fair. J. Baldwin.

Horse-race: see R. Browning, "Muléykeh" (poem).

Horses: see

J. Abbott, *Stories of Rainbow and Lucky: Selling Lucky*.

J. M. Baldwin, *Story of the Mind* (marginalia).

"C. De Hurst," *How Women Should Ride*.

O. C. Marsh, *Fossil Horses in America*.

A. Sewell, *Black Beauty: The Autobiography of a Horse*.

A. Trollope, *Autobiography* (Catalog entry).

G. E. Waring, Jr., *Whip and Spur*.

E. N. Westcott, *David Harum: A Story of American Life*.

Hosmer, James Kendall, *Outcome of the Civil War, 1863–1865*: see A. B. Hart, *American Nation: A History from Original Sources by Associated Scholars*.

Hospital Days. J. S. Woolsey.

Hotten, John Camden: see

B. Harte, *Lectures of Bret Harte, Compiled from Various Sources*.

(co-author): see H. D. J. van Schevichaven, *History of Signboards, from the Earliest Times to the Present Day*.

Houdin, Jean Eugène Robert (magician): see W. Manning (comp.), *Year-Boke of the Odd Volumes*.

Houghton, Ellen B. (co-author): see T. Crane, *Abroad*.

Hound of the Baskervilles: see the Catalog entry for Arthur Conan Doyle.

Hour and the Man. H. Martineau.

Hour Glass Series: see D. B. Lucas and J. F. McLaughlin, *Fisher Ames-Henry Clay, Etc.*

Hour's Promise (novel). A. E. Trumbull.

"Hours there were" (song). T. Moore.

Hours with Art and Artists. G. W. Sheldon.

Hours with the Bible; or, The Scriptures in the Light of Modern Discovery and Knowledge. J. C. Geikie.

House and Home Papers. H. E. B. Stowe.

House Beautiful: Essays on Beds and Tables, Stools and Candlesticks. C. C. Cook.

House-Boat on the Styx. J. K. Bangs.

House construction: see O. C. Gillespie (comp.), *Rumford Fireplaces and How They Are Made.*

House, Edward Howard: see
  D. Boucicault, *Arrah-na-Pogue* (play).
  J. K. Newton, "Obligations of the United States to Initiate a Revision of Treaties Between the Western Powers and Japan" (Catalog entry).
  "Wearing of the green" (song).

Household of Glen Holly. L. C. W. Lillie.

Housekeeping advice: see
  Bazar Book of Health.
  C. E. Beecher and H. B. Stowe, *Principles of Domestic Science; As Applied to the Duties and Pleasures of Home.*
  J. B. Brown, *Home Life, in the Light of Its Divine Idea.*
  M. R. O. Dewing, *Beauty in the Household.*
  C. L. Eastlake, *Hints on Household Taste in Furniture, Upholstery, and Other Details.*
  C. W. Haskins, *How to Keep Household Accounts: A Manual of Family Finance.*
  C. T. Herrick, *Expert Maid-Servant.*
  R. Murray (comp.), *Modern Householder: A Manual of Domestic Economy in All Its Branches.*
  H. E. B. Stowe, *House and Home Papers.*
  H. E. B. Stowe, *We and Our Neighbors; or, the Records of an Unfashionable Street. A Novel.*
  M. V. H. Terhune, *Breakfast, Luncheon and Tea.*
  M. V. H. Terhune, *Common Sense in the Household: A Manual of Practical Housewifery.*
  M. Wheeler, *Baby; His Care and Training.*
  See also the Reader's Guide entries for Cookbooks and for Interior decoration.

Household Book of Poetry. C. A. Dana (comp.).

Household management: see the Reader's Guide entry for Housekeeping advice.

Household of Sir Thos. More. A. Manning.

House of a Thousand Candles. M. Nicholson.

House of Mirth. E. N. J. Wharton.

"House of the Dragons" (short story). I. M. Van Etten.

House of the Seven Gables, A Romance. N. Hawthorne.

House Party: An Account of the Stories Told at a Gathering of Famous American Authors. P. L. Ford (ed.).

Houston, Sam: see C. E. Lester, *Life of Sam Houston (The Only Authentic Memoir of Him Ever Published).*

Howadji in Syria. G. W. Curtis.

Howard, J. H. (illus.): see C. F. Brown, *Artemus Ward in London, and Other Papers.*

Howe, Edgar Watson: see J. Swift, *Gulliver's Travels into Several Remote Nations of the World* (Catalog entry).

Howe, Elmer P. (co-ed.): see C. S. Elliot, *Songs of Yale: A New Collection of College Songs.*

Howells, Mildred: see W. D. Howells, *Little Girl Among the Old Masters.*

Howells, William Dean: see
  C. F. Browne, *Artemus Ward, His Travels.*
  H. Garland, "Sanity in Fiction" (article).
  O. W. Holmes, *Autocrat of the Breakfast-Table* (marginalia).
  J. R. Lowell, *Letters of James Russell Lowell* (marginalia and Catalog entry).
  New York *Times* (Catalog entry).
  (contr.): see *Niagara Book: A Complete Souvenir of Niagara Falls.*
  (intro.): see *Pastels in Prose. From the French.*
  W. L. Phelps, *Essays on Modern Novelists.*
  (intro.) Plutarchus, *Children's Plutarch: Tales of the Greeks.*
  E. A. Poe, *Murders of [sic] the Rue Morgue* (story) (Catalog entry).
  Scribner's Monthly (Catalog entry).
  W. H. Thomson, *Parables and Their Home. The Parables by the Lake* (Catalog entry).
  (intro.): see L. N. Tolstoy, *Sebastopol.*
  B. O. Townsend, *Plantation Lays and Other Poems* (marginalia).
  G. O. Trevelyan, *Life and Letters of Lord Macaulay* (marginalia).
  H. C. Vedder, *American Writers of To-day.*
  (co-author): see *Whole Family; A Novel by Twelve Authors.*
  (essay): see F. S. Wilhelmina, *Memoirs of Frederica Sophia Wilhelmina, Princess Royal of Prussia, Margravine of Baireuth.*
  E. F. Wyatt, *Every One His Own Way* (Catalog entry).

How Plants Behave; How They Move, Climb, Employ Insects to Work for Them, Etc. A. Gray.

How Plants Grow; A Simple Introduction to Structural Botany. A. Gray.

"How pleasant, how divinely fair" (hymn). I. Watts.

How Reverend Wiggin Rewrote Mrs. Eddy's Book. L. Wright.

"How Sleep the Brave" (poem): see W. Collins, "Ode Written in the Beginning of the Year 1746" (poem).

Howson, John Saul (intro.): see A. Rimmer, *Ancients Streets and Homesteads of England.*

"How the Caliph Became a Stork" (fairy tale). W. Hauff.

How to Acquire and Strengthen Will-Power. Modern Psycho-Therapy. A Specific Remedy for Neurasthenia and Nervous Diseases. R. J. Ebbard.

How to Be Happy Through Living. F. Forbes.

How to Draw; A Practical Book of Instruction in the Art of Illustration. L. Barritt.

How to Get Strong and How to Stay So. W. Blaikie.

How to Keep Household Accounts: A Manual of Family Finance. C. W. Haskins.

"How to Write a Short Story" (article). R. Barr.

How Women Should Ride. "C. De Hurst" (pseud.).

"H. S." (pseud.): see *Napoleon the Third and His Court.*

Hubbard, Stephen Ashley (inscr.): see A. A. Opie, *Illustrations of Lying, in All Its Branches.*

Huber, François: see M. Maeterlinck, *Life of the Bee* (marginalia).

Huber, J. N. (co-author): see J. J. I. von Döllinger, *Pope and the Council.*

Huckleberries: see S. B. Warner, *Hills of the Shatemuc.*

Huckleberry Finn (play): see the Catalog entry for C. Dillingham (adapt.).

Hudibras. S. Butler.

Hudson, Henry: see
   G. M. Asher (ed.), *Henry Hudson the Navigator.*
   T. A. Janvier, *Henry Hudson, A Brief Statement of His Aims and His Achievements.*

Hudson, Henry Norman: see
   (ed.) W. Shakespeare, *Henry IV. Parts First and Second.*
   (ed.) W. Shakespeare, *History of King John.*
   (ed., intro.) W. Shakespeare, *King Richard the Second.*
   (ed., intro.) W. Shakespeare, *Plays of Shakespeare. Introduction and Notes Explanatory and Critical.*
   (ed.) W. Shakespeare, *Works of Shakespeare: The Text Carefully Restored.*

Hudson River Valley: see S. B. Warner, *Hills of the Shatemuc.*

Hughes, Arthur (illus.): see G. MacDonald, *At the Back of the North Wind.*

Hugh Wynne, Free Quaker, Sometime Brevet Lieutenant-Colonel on the Staff of His Excellency General Washington. S. W. Mitchell.

Hugo, Victor: see
   E. De Amicis, *Studies of Paris.*
   A. F. Hugo, *Victor Hugo, by a Witness of His Life.*
   L. Ulbach, *Madame Gosselin* (novel) (Catalog entry).

Huguenots: see
   G. Parker, *Ladder of Swords; A Tale of Love, Laughter and Tears* (novel).
   F. Parkman, *Old Régime in Canada* (marginalia).

Huldigung der Künste: see *Schiller's Sämmtliche Werke in Zwölf Bänden.*

Hull, Paul (co-author): see *On the Gridiron and Other Stories of Outdoor Sport.*

Hullah, John P. (composer), "Storm" (song).

Hulme, Thomas: see W. Cobbett, *Year's Residence in the United States of America.*

Human behavior: see the Reader's Guide entry for Moral behavior of humans.

Human body: see the Reader's Guide entry for Physiology.

Human Boy Again. E. Phillpotts.

Humane treatment of animals: see S. K. Trimmer, *History of the Robins. In Words of One Syllable.*

Human moral behavior: see the Reader's Guide entry for Moral behavior of humans.

Human nature: see the Reader's Guide entries for "Human race" and for Moral behavior of humans.

Human Personality and Its Survival of Bodily Death. F. W. H. Myers.

Human Physiology, Statistical and Dynamical; or, The Conditions and Course of the Life of Man. J. W. Draper.

"Human race": see
   S. V. Clevenger, *Evolution of Man and His Mind. A History and Discussion* (marginalia).
   G. O. Trevelyan, *Life and Letters of Lord Macaulay* (marginalia).
   A. R. Wallace, *Man's Place in the Universe: A Study*

of the Results of Scientific Research in Relation to the Unity or Plurality of Worlds (Catalog entry).
   H. G. Wells, *Wonderful Visit.*
   A. D. White, *History of the Warfare of Science with Theology* (marginalia).

Human Way. L. C. Willcox.

Humble Romance, and Other Stories. M. E. W. Freeman.

Hume, David: see
   W. J. Dawson (co-ed.), *Great English Letter-Writers* (marginalia).
   T. H. Huxley, *Hume.*

Hume. T. H. Huxley.

Humor collections: see
   J. Ashton, *English Caricature and Satire on Napoleon I.*
   W. E. Burton (comp.), *Cyclopaedia of Wit and Humor; Containing Choice and Characteristic Selections from the Writings of the Most Eminent Humorists of America, Ireland, Scotland, and England.*
   J. H. Carter, *Commodore Rollingpin's Humorous Illustrated Almanac.*
   J. H. Carter, *Log of Commodore Rollingpin: His Adventures Afloat and Ashore.*
   G. L. DuMaurier, *Social Pictorial Satire.*
   Ha! Ha! Ha!: 72 Pages of Fun by Leading Humorists.
   Hot Stuff by Famous Funny Men.
   F. L. Knowles (comp.), *Treasury of Humorous Poetry.*
   M. N. Kuka (ed., trans.), *Wit and Humour of the Persians.*
   J. Leech, *Pictures of Life & Character. From the Collection of "Mr. Punch."*
   Library of Wit and Humor by Mark Twain and Others.
   K. A. Sanborn, *Wit of Women.*
   L. Schick (comp.), *Schick's humoristische Bibliothek.*
   A. R. Spofford (co-ed.) and R. E. Shapley (co-ed.), *Library of Wit and Humor, Prose and Poetry, Selected from the Literature of All Times and Nations.*
   World's Wit and Humor; An Encyclopedia of the Classic Wit and Humor of All Ages and Nations.
   See also the Reader's Guide entries for American humorists, for English humorists, and for French humorists.

Humor studies: see
   W. Besant, *French Humorists, from the Twelfth to the Nineteenth Century.*
   H. R. Haweis, *American Humorists: Lectures Delivered at the Royal Institution.*
   K. A. Sanborn, *Wit of Women.*

Humphrey, Mabel (illus.): see A. B. Paine, *Little Lady—Her Book, for Girls and Boys.*

Humphry Clinker: see T. G. Smollett, *Expedition of Humphry Clinker* (novel).

Hundred Riddles of the Fairy Bellaria. C. G. Leland.

Hungary: see
   M. Jokai, *Black Diamonds, A Novel.*
   W. N. Lowe (trans.), *Magyar Songs. Selections from Hungarian Poets.*

Hungry Forties: Life Under the Bread Tax. E. J. C. Unwin.

"Hungry Heart" (short story). J. W. De Forest.

Hunter's Camp-Fires. E. J. House.

Hunter, William Wilson: see F. H. B. Skrine, *Life of Sir William Wilson Hunter.*

Huntingdon, Henry of: see Henry of Huntingdon.
Hunting literature: see
C. A. Adams, *Pete's Devils*.
Adventures in Field and Forest, by Frank H[amilton]. Spearman, Harold Martin, F. S. Palmer, William Drysdale, and Others.
F. G. Aflalo, *Sketch of the Natural History of Australia, with Some Notes on Sport*.
I. Bacheller, *Silas Strong, Emperor of the Woods*.
J. Beerbohm, *Wanderings in Patagonia; or, Life Among the Ostrich-Hunters*.
P. B. Du Chaillu, *Wild Life Under the Equator. Narrated for Young People*.
W. H. Gibson, *Camp Life in the Woods and the Tricks of Trapping*.
R. G. Gordon-Cumming, *Five Years of a Hunter's Life in the Far Interior of South Africa*.
E. J. House, *Hunter's Camp-Fires*.
W. D. Howells (co-ed.), *Library of Universal Adventure by Sea and Land*.
M. McCulloch-Williams, *Field-Farings; A Vagrant Chronicle of Earth and Sky*.
V. Meunier (comp.), *Adventures on the Great Hunting Grounds of the World*.
E. H. Mott, *Old Settler and His Tales of the Sugar Swamp*.
J. M. Murphy, *Sporting Adventures in the Far West*.
A. Nicols, *Wild Life and Adventure in the Australian Bush: Four Years' Personal Experience*.
H. E. Rood, *In Camp at Bear Pond*.
T. Roosevelt, *Good Hunting: In Pursuit of Big Game in the West*.
K. G. Schillings, *In Wildest Africa*.
K. G. Schillings, *With Flash-light and Rifle; Photographing by Flash-light at Night the Wild Animal World of Equatorial Africa*.
E. T. Seton, *Wild Animals I Have Known, and 200 Drawings*.
T. B. Thorpe, "Big Bear of Arkansas" (story).
G. E. Waring, Jr., *Whip and Spur*.
C. D. Warner, *In the Wilderness*.
H. B. Washburn, "Shall We Hunt and Fish? The Confessions of a Sentimentalist" (essay).
H. P. Wells, *City Boys in the Woods; or, A Trapping Venture in Maine*.
C. Whitney, *On Snow-Shoes to the Barren Grounds. Twenty-Eight Hundred Miles After Musk-Oxen and Wood-Bison*.
T. Wright, *Homes of Other Days: A History of Domestic Manners and Sentiments in England, from the Earliest Known Period to Modern Times*.
See also the Reader's Guide entry for Bear hunts.
Hunting of the Snark, and Other Poems and Verses. C. L. Dodgson.
Hunt, Leigh: see
B. Harte, *Twins of Table Mountain, and Other Stories* (marginalia).
G. O. Trevelyan, *Life and Letters of Lord Macaulay* (marginalia).
Hunt, Thomas Sterry: see A. Winchell, *Sketches of Creation: A Popular View of Some of the Grand Conclusions*

of the Sciences in Reference to the History of Matter and of Life (marginalia).
Hurd, Fayette (ed.): see J. Milton, *Treasures from the Prose Writings of John Milton*.
Hurst, Hal [Henry William Lowe] (illus.): see R. Barr, *A Woman Intervenes*.
Hutchinson Family (singing group): see T. W. S. Higginson, *Cheerful Yesterdays. Contemporaries* (marginalia).
Hutt, Henry (illus.): see G. L. Richmond, *Indifference of Juliet*.
Hutton, Eleanor (co-author): see L. Hutton, *Laurence and Eleanor Hutton*.
Hutton, Laurence (co-intro.): see J. Bernard, *Retrospections of America, 1797–1811*.
Huxley, Thomas Henry: see
R. Chambers, *Vestiges of the Natural History of Creation*.
T. W. Doane, *Bible Myths and Their Parallels in Other Religions* (marginalia).
L. Huxley, *Life and Letters of Thomas Henry Huxley*.
W. H. Mallock, *Reconstruction of Religious Belief*.
Hydrotherapy: see S. Kneipp, *My Water Cure*.
Hygiene: see the Reader's Guide entry for Health, fitness, and hygiene.
Hymn collections: see the Reader's Guide entry for Hymnals.
Hymnal: According to the Use of the Protestant Episcopal Church in the United States of America.
Hymnals: see
H. W. Beecher (comp.), *Plymouth Collection of Hymns and Tunes, for the Use of Christian Congregations*.
P. P. Bliss (co-ed.), *Gospel Hymns Consolidated*.
N. J. Burton (co-comp.), *Christian Hymnal. A Selection of Psalms and Hymns, with Music, for Use in Public Worship*.
Chrisian Science Hymnal.
Devotional Hymns. Selected from Various Authors.
E. A. Hoffman and H. F. Sayles (comp.), *Battle Hymns of the Church*.
Hymnal: According to the Use of the Protestant Episcopal Church in the United States of America.
L. Mason (comp.), *Carmina Sacra; or, Boston Collection of Church Music, Comprising the Most Popular Psalm and Hymn Tunes in General Use*.
NA HIMENI HOOLEA, HE MAU MELE MA KA UHANE, E HOOLEA AI (Hawaiian hymns).
C. S. Robinson (comp.), *Laudes Domini: A Selection of Spiritual Songs, Ancient and Modern*.
J. Wesley, *Collection of Hymns, for the Use of the People Called Methodists*.
See also the Reader's Guide entry for Hymns.
Hymns: see
S. F. Adams, "Nearer, my God, to Thee."
C. F. H. Alexander, "Once in royal David's city" (Christmas carol).
P. P. Bliss, "Only an armour-bearer."
H. Bonar, "Beyond the smiling and the weeping."
H. Bonar, "Church has waited long."
P. H. Brown, "I love to steal a while away."
H. F. Chorley, "God, the all-terrible."
E. H. Codner, "Even me."

M. A. L. Demarest, "My ain countrie."

"Doxology": see T. Ken, "Praise God, from whom all blessings flow."

M. B. Eddy, "O'er waiting harp strings of the mind" (hymn).

M. B. Eddy, "Saw ye my Saviour?" (hymn).

C. Elliott, "Just as I am, without one plea."

"Fading, still fading, the last beam is shining."

J. Fawcett, "Lord, dismiss us with Thy blessing."

C. W. Fry, "Lily of the valley."

G. J. Geer (Catalog entry).

J. Hart, "Come, ye sinners, poor and needy."

T. Hastings, "Child of sin and sorrow, filled with dismay."

R. Heber, "Missionary hymn" ("From Greenland's icy mountains").

J. H. Hopkins, Jr., "We three kings of Orient" (Christmas carol).

J. W. Howe, "Battle hymn of the Republic."

"How firm a foundation" (authorship not established).

T. Ken, "Praise God, from whom all blessings flow" ("Doxology").

W. Kethe, "Old hundred," also known as "Old hundredth."

"Let each now choose" (unidentified).

W. A. Muhlenberg, "I would not live alway."

"O refresh us": see J. Fawcett, "Lord, dismiss us with Thy blessing."

R. Palmer, "My faith looks up to Thee."

J. N. Pattison, "Guide me, O thou great Jehovah."

E. Perronet, "All hail the power of Jesus' name."

A. Reed, "Holy Ghost! With light divine."

R. Robinson, "Come thou fount of every blessing."

E. H. Sears, "Calm on the listening ear of night."

E. H. Sears, "Christmas hymn": see E. H. Sears, "Calm on the listening ear of night."

A. Steele, "O for a sweet, inspiring ray."

S. Stennett, "On Jordan's stormy banks I stand."

"Veni Creator Spiritus (Come Creative Spirit)".

W. F. Warren, "Homeward bound."

H. C. Watson, "Prodigal son."

I. Watts, "Against idleness."

I. Watts, "Against quarrelling and fighting."

I. Watts, "Alas, and did my Saviour bleed!"

I. Watts, "Am I a soldier of the cross?"

I. Watts, "Eternal spirit, we confess."

I. Watts, "How pleasant, how divinely fair."

I. Watts, "Let dogs delight to bark and bite" (better known as "Against quarrelling").

C. Wesley, "Hark! the herald angels sing" (Christmas carol).

C. Wesley, "Son of the Carpenter! receive."

E. H. Willard, "Rocked in the cradle of the deep."

A. Young, "There is a happy land."

See also the Reader's Guide entry for Hymnals.

"Hymn Sung at the Completion of the Concord Monument" (poem). R. W. Emerson.

Hypatia; or, New Foes with an Old Face. C. Kingsley.

Hyperion, A Romance. H. W. Longfellow.

Hypnotic Therapeutics in Theory and Practice, with

Numerous Illustrations of Treatment by Suggestion. J. D. Quackenbos.

Hypnotism: see

E. Bellamy, *Looking Backward, 2000–1887.*

R. J. Ebbard, *How to Acquire and Strengthen Will-Power. Modern Psycho-Therapy.*

M. B. Eddy, *Manual of the Mother Church, the First Church of Christ, Scientist, in Boston, Massachusetts* (marginalia).

F. Van Eeden, "Curing by Suggestion" (article).

W. James, *Principles of Psychology.*

W. James, *Varieties of Religious Experience; A Study in Human Nature* (marginalia).

J. D. Quackenbos, *Hypnotic Therapeutics in Theory and Practice, with Numerous Illustrations of Treatment by Suggestion.*

C. de Saint-Germain, *Practical Hypnotism: Theories and Experiments.*

See also the Reader's Guide entry for Spiritualism and spiritual healing.

I

"I am far frae my hame" (poem, hymn): see M. A. L. Demarest, "My ain countrie."

Ibsen, Henrik: see J. G. Huneker, *Egoists, A Book of Supermen.*

Iceland: see

R. B. Anderson and J. Bjarnason (trans.), *Viking Tales of the North.*

G. W. Dasent (ed., trans.), *Story of Burnt Njal; or, Life in Iceland in the Tenth Century.*

D. W. Fiske (Catalog entry).

J. Jònsonn, "Jòn Jònsonn's Saga: The Genuine Autobiography of a Modern Icelander."

B. Taylor, *Egypt and Iceland in the Year 1874.*

See also the Reader's Guide entry for Scandinavian mythology.

Ice Queen. E. Ingersoll.

"Ich wollt' meine Lieb'" (song). H. Heine.

Iconoclasts, A Book of Dramatists. J. G. Huneker.

Idaho: see E. Talbot, *My People of the Plains.*

"I don't 'low no coon to fool roun' me": see "I don't allow no coons to hurt my feelings" (minstrel song).

"I dreamt I dwelt in marble halls" (song): see M. W. Balfe, *Bohemian Girl* (opera).

Idylls of a Canadian Village. A. M. Teskey.

Idylls of Greece. H. V. Sutherland.

Idylls of the King. A. Tennyson.

Idyl of the Rhine. L. P. Myers.

"I Feel I'm Growing Auld, Gude-Wife" (poem). J. Linen.

I Go A-Fishing. W. C. Prime.

"I had an old horse whose name was Methusalem" (minstrel song). See H. T. Bryant, "Balm of Gilead."

"I hear the hoofs, or the lost child" (minstrel song).

Île des Pingouins. A. France.

Iles, George: see

(pref.): see J. N. Larned (ed.), *Literature of American History: A Bibliographical Guide.*

(inscr.) W. McLennan, *Spanish John; Being a Memoir, Now First Published in Complete Form, of the Early Life and Adventures of Colonel John McDonell.*

(inscr.) W. H. Mallock, *Reconstruction of Religious Belief*.

(inscr.) V. Streamer (comp.), *Voices of Doubt and Trust*.

Iliad: see

A. R. Darrow, *Iphigenia: A Legend of the Iliad, and Other Poems*.

J. Sheffield, *Essay on Poetry*.

Iliad of Homer. Homer.

Ilka on the Hill-top, and Other Stories. H. H. Boyesen.

Illington, Margaret: see L. M. Boutet de Monvel, *Joan of Arc* (inscr.).

Illinois: see

N. Matson, *Pioneers of Illinois, Containing a Series of Sketches Relating to Events That Occurred Previous to 1813*.

W. Payne, *Jerry the Dreamer*.

Illustrated Bible Dictionary. M. G. Easton.

Illustrations of Lying, in All Its Branches. A. A. Opie.

Illustrations to Browning's Poems. Browning Society.

Illustrations to Goethe's Faust. J. W. von Goethe.

Illustrators: see G. L. P. B. Du Maurier, *Social Pictorial Satire; Reminiscences and Appreciations of English Illustrators of the Past Generation*.

"I love to steal a while away" (hymn). P. H. Brown.

Imaginary Obligations. F. M. Colby.

Imitation of Christ. Thomas à Kempis.

Immigrant Jew in America. E. J. James.

Immigration: see

F. C. Baylor, *Juan and Juanita*.

D. M. M. Craik, *Studies from Life*.

E. W. Gilliam, "Chinese Immigration" (article).

E. J. James, *Immigrant Jew in America*.

Immortal; or, One of the "Forty." A. Daudet.

"Immortality Ode": see W. Wordsworth, "Ode."

Im Paradiese. Roman in Sieben Büchern. P. J. L. von Heyse.

Imperative Duty. A Novel. W. D. Howells.

Imperator et Rex, William II of Germany. M. Cunliffe-Owen.

Imperial Gazetteer of India. S. S. Hunter.

Imperialism: see the Reader's Guide entry for Colonialism.

"Imp of the Perverse" (short story). E. A. Poe.

Impostors: see

H. H. Breen, *Modern English Literature: Its Blemishes & Defects*.

E. C. Brewster, *Dictionary of Miracles: Imitative, Realistic, and Dogmatic, with Illustrations*.

A. Fouquier, *Causes célèbres de tous les peuples*.

B. Franklin, *Life of Benjamin Franklin, Written by Himself* (marginalia).

H. W. Fuller, *Noted French Trials. Impostors and Adventurers*.

Gallick Reports; or, An Historical Collection of Criminal Cases.

G. G. Greenwood, *Shakespeare Problem Restated* (marginalia).

Historical Sketches Relating to Westminster Hall, Its Famous Judges and Lawyers and Its Great Trials.

London *Standard* (Catalog entry).

See also the Reader's Guide entries for Court trials, for Crime, and for Disputed authorship cases.

Impressionist Sketches: see R. Blatchford, *Merrie England* (Catalog entry).

Impressions and Experiences (essays). W. D. Howells.

Impressions of Theophrastus Such. G. Eliot.

"Impromptu" (music). F. P. Schubert.

Improvement of the Mind. I. Watts.

In a Cathedral City. A Tale. B. Thomas.

In Beaver Cove and Elsewhere. M. J. Crim.

In Black and White: see R. Kipling, *Kipling in Black and White*.

Inca civilization: see

W. G. Mortimer, *Peru: History of Coca, "The Divine Plant" of the Incas*.

W. H. Prescott, *History of the Conquest of Peru, with a Preliminary View of the Civilization of the Incas*.

In Camp at Bear Pond. H. E. Rood.

Incarnation of the Snow. F. W. Bain.

Incidents in My Life. D. D. Home.

Incidents in the Life of a Slave Girl, Written by Herself. H. Jacobs.

Incidents of Travel. J. L. Stephens.

Inconnu. The Unknown. N. C. Flammarion.

"Increase of Human Life" (article). E. Jarvis.

In Darkest Africa; or, the Quest, Rescue, and Retreat of Emin, Governor of Equatoria. H. M. Stanley.

"In days of old" (song): see E. Thomas, "Warrior bold" (song).

Inderwick, Frederick Andrew (intro.): see J. P. W. Penzance, *Lord Penzance on the Bacon-Shakespeare Controversy. A Judicial Summing-Up*.

India: see

G. R. Aberigh-Mackay, *Serious Reflections and Other Contributions, Etc.*

E. Arnold, *India Revisited*.

M. Bahadur Rana, *Balabodhini*.

E. Buck, *Indo-Anglian Literature*.

H. T. Buckle, *History of Civilization in England*.

G. W. Caldwell, *Oriental Rambles*.

G. L. Carlisle, *Around the World in a Year*.

A. Carnegie, *Round the World*.

F. M. Coleman, *Typical Pictures of Indian Natives, Being Reproductions from Photographs*.

G. W. Cox, *Mythology of the Aryan Nations*.

B. M. S. Croker, *Cat's-Paw*.

B. M. S. Croker, *Mr. Jervis*.

C. F. Despard, *Rajah's Heir; A Novel*.

L. De Forest (ed.), *Indian Domestic Architecture*.

C. W. Dilke, *Greater Britain: A Record of Travel in English-Speaking Countries During 1866 and 1867*.

J. Fergusson, *History of Architecture in All Countries from the Earliest Times*.

H. W. French, *Our Boys in India: The Wanderings of Two Young Americans in Hindustan*.

J. H. Furneaux, *Glimpses of India: A Grand Photographic History of the Land of Antiquity*.

C. F. Gordon-Cumming, *In the Himalayas and on the Indian Plains*.

W. W. Hunter, *Indian Empire: Its History, People, and Products*.

J. F. Hurst, *Indika. The Country and the People of India and Ceylon.*

S. S. Jacob (ed.), *Jeypore Portfolios of Architectural Details.*

J. S. Keay, "Spoliation of India" (series of articles).

R. Kipling, *From Sea to Sea: Letters of Travel.*

R. Kipling, *Jungle Book.*

R. Kipling, *Kim.*

E. F. Knight, *Where Three Empires Meet: A Narrative of Recent Travel in Kashmir, Western Tibet, Gilgit, and the Adjoining Countries.*

W. Knighton, *Private Life of an Eastern King.*

T. W. Knox, *Boy Travellers in the Far East; Part Third, . . . in a Journey to Ceylon and India.*

Lutfullah, *Autobiography of Lutfullah, A Mohamedan Gentleman; and His Transactions with His Fellow-Creatures.*

A. C. Lyall, *Natural Religion in India.*

A. C. Lyall, *Verses Written in India.*

T. B. Macaulay, "Essay on Lord Clive" (Catalog entry).

T. B. Macaulay, "Essay on Warren Hastings" (Catalog entry).

T. B. Macaulay, *Speeches and Poems, with the Report and Notes on the Indian Penal Code.*

G. B. Malleson, *Dupleix.*

F. E. Maning, *Old New Zealand, A Tale of the Good Old Times* (marginalia).

A. E. W. Mason, *Broken Road.*

W. H. Maxwell, *Life of Field-Marshal His Grace the Duke of Wellington.*

Modi, Jivanji Jamshedji (Catalog entry).

M. Mookerjee, *Onoocool Chunder Mookerjee (1829–1871): A Memoir.*

S. C. Mukerji, *Traveller's Guide to Agra, Containing an Account of the Past History, the Antiquities, and the Principal Sights of Agra.*

F. M. Müller, *India: What Can It Teach Us?*

N. Notovitch, *Unknown Life of Jesus Christ.*

A. Parker, *Hand-Book of Benares.*

Pioneer Mail and Indian Weekly News.

C. D. Poston, *Parsees: A Lecture.*

F. S. Roberts, *Forty-One Years in India. From Subaltern to Commander-in-Chief.*

W. Robertson, *Historical Disquisition Concerning the Knowledge Which the Ancients Had of India; And the Progress of Trade with That Country.*

L.-T. M. Rousselet, *India and Its Native Princes: Travels in Central India and in the Presidencies of Bombay and Bengal.*

S. S. B. Saraswati (trans.), *Upanishad Prasada.*

F. von Schlegel, *Philosophy of History; in a Course of Lectures, Delivered at Vienna.*

J. R. Seeley, *Expansion of England; Two Courses of Lectures.*

A. Z. H. Y. Sîrafî, *Ancient Accounts of India and China, by Two Mohammedan Travellers.*

F. H. B. Skrine, *Indian Journalist: Being the Life, Letters, and Correspondence of Dr. Sambhu C. Mookerjee.*

F. H. B. Skrine, *Life of Sir William Wilson Hunter.*

W. H. Sleeman, *Journey Through the Kingdom of Oude, in 1849–1850.*

W. H. Sleeman, *Rambles and Recollections of an Indian Official.*

W. H. Sleeman, *Report on the Depredations Committed by the Thug Gangs of Upper and Central India.*

W. H. Sleeman, *Thugs or Phansigars of India; Comprising a History of the Rise and Progress of That Extraordinary Fraternity of Assassins.*

E. Sue, *Wandering Jew.*

J. B. Tavernier, *Travels in India.*

B. Taylor, *Visit to India, China, and Japan, in the Year 1853.*

R. Temple, *India in 1880.*

W. T. M. Torrens, *Empire in Asia, How We Came by It: A Book of Confessions.*

M. W. Townsend, *Asia and Europe: Studies* (marginalia).

G. O. Trevelyan, *Life and Letters of Lord Macaulay* (marginalia).

J. Verne, *Tour of the World in Eighty Days* (novel).

L. Wallace, *Prince of India; or, Why Constantinople Fell.*

W. J. Warner, *Cheiro's Language of the Hand.*

E. L. Weeks, "Recent Impressions of Anglo-Indian Life" (article).

M. Westrup, *Coming of Billy.*

See also the Reader's Guide entries for Black Hole of Calcutta, for Ceylon, for Indian mutiny of 1857, and for Taj Mahal.

India and Its Native Princes: Travels in Central India and in the Presidencies of Bombay and Bengal. L.-T. M. Rousselet.

India in 1880. R. Temple.

Indiana: see

A. J. Cotton, *Cotton's Sketch-Book. Auto-Biographical Sketches of the Life, Labors and Extensive Home Travels of Rev. A. J. Cotton.*

E. Eggleston, *Hoosier Schoolmaster: A Story of Backwoods Life in Indiana.*

B. Tarkington, *Conquest of Canaan: A Novel.*

B. Tarkington, *Gentleman from Indiana.*

B. Tarkington, *His Own People.*

J. M. Thompson (Catalog entries).

Indian Domestic Architecture. L. De Forest (ed.).

Indian Empire: Its History, People, and Products. W. W. Hunter.

Indian History for Young Folks. F. S. Drake.

Indian Journalist: Being the Life, Letters, and Correspondence of Dr. Sambhu C. Mookerjee. F. H. B. Skrine.

Indian Legends [of Minnesota Lakes]. T. M. Newson.

"Indian Music": see J. C. Fillmore, "A Study."

Indian mutiny of 1857: see

S. Birch (Catalog entry).

B. M. S. Croker, *Mr. Jervis.*

W. H. Fitchett, *Tale of the Great Mutiny.*

W. Forbes-Mitchell, *Reminiscences of the Great Mutiny, 1857–59.*

W. D. Howells (co-ed.), *Library of Universal Adventure by Sea and Land.*

J. S. T. Inglis, *Siege of Lucknow. A Diary.*

H. M. Lawrence (Catalog entry).

G. B. Malleson, *Indian Mutiny of 1857.*

F. A. W. Steel, *On the Face of the Waters; A Tale of the Mutiny.*

L. Tracy, *Red Year; A Story of the Indian Mutiny.*

G. O. Trevelyan, *Cawnpore* (marginalia).

J. J. Walsh, *Memorial of the Futtehgurh Mission and Her Martyred Missionaries, with Some Remarks on the Mutiny in India.*

See also the Reader's Guide entry for India.

Indian Mutiny of 1857. G. B. Malleson.

Indian mythology: see G. W. Cox, *Mythology of the Aryan Nations.*

Indian Races of North and South America, Comprising an Account of the Principal Aboriginal Races. C. D. W. Brownell.

Indians: see the Reader's Guide entry for Native Americans.

Indians' Book; An Offering by the American Indians of Indian Lore, Musical and Narrative. N. Curtis (ed.).

Indian Summer (novel). W. D. Howells.

Indian Summer Calendar. K. A. Sanborn (comp.).

Indian Tales and Legends: see H. R. Schoolcraft, *Algic Researches, Comprising Inquiries Respecting the Mental Characteristics of the North American Indians.*

"Indian Tribes" (unidentified book title): see G. Caitlin.

India Revisited. E. Arnold.

India: What Can It Teach Us? F. M. Müller.

Indifference of Juliet. G. L. Richmond.

Indika. The Country and the People of India and Ceylon. J. F. Hurst.

Indo-Anglian Literature. E. Buck.

In Exitu Israel; An Historical Novel. S. Baring-Gould.

Infancy and Childhood. F. F. Wood.

Infant care: see

M. T. P. Mann, *Moral Culture of Infancy, and Kindergarten Guide.*

M. Wheeler, *Baby; His Care and Training.*

F. F. Wood, *Infancy and Childhood.*

Infant damnation: see R. M. Manley, *Mr. Claghorn's Daughter.*

Infants: see

T. B. Aldrich, "Ballad of Babie Bell" (poem).

Baby Days; A Selection of Songs, Stories.

J. D. D. Bacon, *Memoirs of a Baby.*

W. C. Bennett, "Baby May" (poem).

M. D. Brine, *My Boy and I; or, On the Road to Slumberland.*

W. Crane, *Baby's Opera: A Book of Old Rhymes with New Dresses.*

C. H. Hoyt, *Rag Baby* (play).

E. Jenkins, *Ginx's Baby: His Birth and Other Misfortunes. A Satire.*

H. Kennedy, "Cradle's empty, baby's gone" (song).

C. Kingsley, *Water-Babies. A Fairy Tale for a Land-Baby.*

L. C. W. Lillie, *Phil and the Baby.*

P. V. Mighels, *Bruvver Jim's Baby.*

"Rock-a-bye baby" (nursery lullaby).

See also the Reader's Guide entry for Exchanged infants.

In Far Lochaber; A Novel. W. Black.

Influence of Sea Power Upon History, 1660–1783. A. T. Mahan (see Catalog entry for A. T. Mahan).

In Foreign Lands. D. F. Beatty.

In Friendship's Name. V. Streamer (comp.).

Ingalls, John James (intro.): see H. W. Scott *Distinguished American Lawyers, with Their Struggles and Triumphs in the Forum.*

Ingersoll, Robert Green: see

(intro.) E. C. Beall (Catalog entry).

Hartford *Courant* (Catalog entry).

R. K. Noyes, *Views of Religion, Collected by Rufus K. Noyes, M. D.* (marginalia).

Truth Seeker (magazine).

L. Wallace, *First Christmas, from "Ben-Hur"* (marginalia).

Ingomar, the Barbarian (play). F. Halm.

In Great Waters: Four Stories. T. A. Janvier.

Ingulph's Chronicle of the Abbey of Croyland. Ingulf.

Inlander. H. Robertson.

Inland Voyage. R. L. Stevenson.

In Memoriam (poem). A. Tennyson.

Inn Album (poem): see R. Browning, *Poetical Works.*

In Nature's Realm. C. C. Abbott.

Inner Shrine; A Novel of Today. B. King.

In Ole Virginia; or, Marse Chan and Other Stories. T. N. Page.

In Our Town. W. A. White.

In Purgatory (play). E. Gettke.

Inquisition: see

H. C. Lea, *History of the Inquisition of the Middle Ages.*

W. H. Rule, *History of the Inquisition from Its Establishment in the Twelfth Century to Its Extinction in the Nineteenth.*

R. Scot, *Discoverie of Witchcraft, Wherein the Lewde Dealing of Witches and Witchmongers is Notablie Detected.*

Insanity: see the Reader's Guide entries for Mental health and for Mental illness.

Insect Book: A Popular Account of the Bees, Wasps, Ants, Grasshoppers, Flies, and Other North American Insects. L. O. Howard.

Insectivorous Plants. C. Darwin.

Insects:

J. M. Baldwin, *Story of the Mind* (marginalia).

L. O. Howard, *Insect Book: A Popular Account of the Bees, Wasps, Ants, Grasshoppers, Flies, and Other North American Insects.*

L. O. Howard, *Mosquitoes: How They Live; How They Carry Disease.*

W. E. Kirby, *Insects: Foes and Friends.*

J. Lubbock, *Ants, Bees, and Wasps: A Record of Observations on the Habits of the Social Hymenoptera.*

H. C. McCook, *Ant Communities, and How They Are Governed.*

H. C. McCook, *Nature's Craftsmen: Popular Studies of Ants and Other Insects.*

J. A. Marks and J. E. Moody, *Little Busybodies; The Life of Crickets, Ants, Bees, Beetles, and Other Busybodies.*

F. S. Matthews, *Field Book of American Wild Flowers; Being a Short Description of Their Character and*

Habits, A Concise Definition of Their Colors, and Incidental References to the Insects Which Assist Their Fertilization.

M. W. Morley, *Wasps and Their Ways.*

A. S. Packard, *Half Hours with Insects.*

G. W. Peckham and E. G. Peckham, *Wasps, Social and Solitary.*

See also the Reader's Guide entry for Bees.

Inside the White House in War Times. W. O. Stoddard.

Inspirational messages: see

M. B. Howitt, *Hope On! Hope Ever! Or, the Boyhood of Felix Law.*

A. R. B. Lindsay, *What Is Worth While?*

J. W. Lloyd, *Dawn-Thought on the Reconciliation; A Volume of Pantheistic Impressions and Glimpses of Larger Religion.*

J. McGovern, *Golden Censer; or, the Duties of To-Day and the Hopes of the Future.*

G. L. Raymond, *Psychology of Inspiration; An Attempt to Distinguish Religious from Scientific Truth.*

K. A. Sanborn (comp.), *Indian Summer Calendar.*

R. Seeberg, *Revelation and Inspiration.*

F. O. Spamer, *Männer eigner Kraft.*

See also the Reader's Guide entries for Mental health, for Self-improvement, and for Spiritualism and spiritual healing.

"Instances of Belgian Cruelty in Africa" (article). A. E. Scrivener.

Instinct of Step-fatherhood. L. L. Bell.

In Sun or Shade (poems). L. M. Sill.

Intelligence of Animals, with Illustrative Anecdotes. E. Menault.

Interdict: see the Catalog entry for A. P. Stanley, *Historical Memorials of Westminster Abbey.*

Interior decoration: see

Artistic Houses; Being a Series of Interior Views of a Number of the Most Beautiful and Celebrated Homes in the United States; with a Description of the Art Treasures Contained Therein.

C. C. Cook, *House Beautiful: Essays on Beds and Tables, Stools and Candlesticks.*

M. R. O. Dewing. *Beauty in the Household.*

C. L. Eastlake, *Hints on Household Taste in Furniture, Upholstery, and Other Details.*

C. W. Elliott, *Book of American Interiors.*

L. F. W. Jewitt and S. C. Hall, *Stately Homes of England.*

See also the Reader's Guide entries for Architecture, for Furniture, and for Housekeeping advice.

Interior design: see the Reader's Guide entry for Interior decoration.

Interloper; A Novel. F. M. Peard.

"International Copyright by Judicial Decision" (article). A. G. Sedgwick.

International Episode. H. James.

International Episode: see also H. James, *Daisy Miller: A Study. An International Episode. Four Meetings.*

In the Brush; or, Old-Time Social, Political, and Religious Life in the Southwest. H. W. Pierson.

In the Carquinez Woods. B. Harte.

"In the Days When We Went Gypsying" (poem, song). E. Ransford.

In the Footprints of Charles Lamb. B. E. Martin.

In the Garden of Charity. B. King.

In the Garden of Dreams: Lyrics and Sonnets. L. C. Moulton.

In the Hands of the Cave-Dwellers. G. A. Henty.

In the Heights. R. W. Gilder.

In the Himalayas and on the Indian Plains. C. F. Gordon-Cumming.

In the Levant. C. D. Warner.

"In the Literary Market" (Albert Bigelow Paine): see (contr.) *Way into Print.*

In the Morning Glow; Short Stories. R. R. Gilson.

In the Name of Liberty; A Story of Terror. O. M. Johnson.

In the Old Herrick House, and Other Stories. E. D. Deland.

In the Open: Stories of Outdoor Life. W. O. Stoddard.

In the Potter's House. G. D. Eldridge.

In the Sargasso Sea, A Novel. T. A. Janvier.

In the Sky-Garden. E. Champney.

In the "Stranger People's" Country. M. N. Murfree.

"In the sweet by and by" (hymn). S. F. Bennett.

In the Tennessee Mountains. M. N. Murfree.

In the Wilderness. C. D. Warner.

In the Wire Grass: A Novel. L. B. Pendleton.

In Time with the Stars; Stories for Children. T. K. Beecher.

Introduction to Greek Prose Composition, with Exercises. A. Sidgwick.

Introduction to the Literature of Europe in the Fifteenth, Sixteenth, and Seventeenth Centuries. H. Hallam.

Introduction to the Study of American Literature. B. Matthews.

Introduction to the Study of Robert Browning's Poetry. H. Corson.

Introduction to the Study of Theory: A Sequel to the "Elements of Music." F. S. Peterson.

Introductory History of England, from the Earliest Times to the Close of the Middle Ages. C. R. L. Fletcher.

Intrusions of Peggy. A. H. Hawkins.

Invader; A Novel. M. L. B. Woods.

Invasion of the Crimea; Its Origin, and an Account of Its Progress. A. W. Kinglake.

Invention of Printing. T. L. De Vinne.

Inventions: see

T. L. De Vinne, *Invention of Printing.*

G. Iles, *Flame, Electricity and the Camera; Man's Progress.*

G. Iles, *Inventors at Work, with Chapters on Discovery.*

J. G. Wood, *Nature's Teachings; Human Invention Anticipated by Nature.*

M. L. Wynkoop, *Condensed Manual on Patented Inventions: What to Do and What Not to Do to Insure Success to the Inventor.*

See also the Reader's Guide entries for Patents and for Science.

Inventions of the Idiot. J. K. Bangs.

Inventors at Work, with Chapters on Discovery. G. Iles.

Investigations and Experience of M. Shawtinbach, at Saar Soong Sumatra. E. R. Smilie.

"Invictus" (poem): see W. E. Henley, *Book of Verses.*

Invisible Man. A Grotesque Romance. H. G. Wells.
Involuntary Chaperon. M. Cameron.
In Wildest Africa. K. G. Schillings.
Iolanthe (operetta). W. S. Gilbert.
Iowa: see
    [Keokuk]: *City of Keokuk in 1856. A View of the City. Keokuk Directory and Business Mirror for the Year 1857.*
    J. T. Umstead, *Plea for the Priority of Domestic Missions; A Discourse Delivered Before the Synod of Iowa, in Burlington, Oct. 12, 1856.*
Iphigenia: A Legend of the Iliad, and Other Poems. A. R. Darrow.
I promessi sposi. A. Manzoni.
Iran: see
    A. H. Layard, *Early Adventures in Persia, Susiana, and Babylonia.*
    A. H. Layard, *Nineveh and Its Remains: With an Account of a Visit to the Chaldæan Christians of Kurdistand.*
    J. J. Morier, *Adventures of Hajji Baba of Ispahan* (novel).
I Rantzu (opera). P. Mascagni (composer).
Iraq: see
    A. H. Layard, *Nineveh and Its Remains: With an Account of a Visit to the Chaldæan Christians of Kurdistand.*
    H. J. Ross, *Letters from the East by Henry James Ross, 1837–1857.*
Iras: A Mystery. H. D. H. Everett.
Ireland: see
    S. G. Bayne, *On a Jaunting-Car Through Donegal and Connemara.*
    M. F. Cusack, *Three Visits to Knock.*
    M. Davitt, *Fall of Feudalism in Ireland; or, the Story of the Land League Revolution.*
    Handbook for Travellers in Ireland.
    A. M. Keary, *Castle Daly: The Story of an Irish Home Thirty Years Ago.*
    H. Kingsley, *Ravenshoe.*
    J. MacPhilpin, *Apparitions and Miracles at Knock.*
    J. B. O'Reilly (Catalog entry).
    M. A. Ross, *Irene Iddesleigh.*
    F. L. Shaw, *Castle Blair: A Story of Youthful Days.*
    W. M. Thackeray, *Sketch Books. The Paris Sketch Book of Mr. M. A. Titmarsh. The Irish Sketch Book of a Journey from Cornhill to Grand Cairo.*
    G. F. Train (Catalog entry).
Irish American fiction: see R. E. MacAlarney, "Tim Rafferty's Romance: A Story of Christmas among 'The Finest.'"
Irish Bulls: see M. Edgeworth and R. L. Edgeworth (co-author), *Essay on Irish Bulls.*
"Irish famine" (poem, song): see A. A. B. Edwards, "Give Me Three Grains of Corn, Mother" (poem, song).
Irish history and literature: see
    R. B. Barry, *Life of Charles Stewart Parnell.*
    H. S. S. Blackwood, "Lament of the Irish emigrant" (song).
    D. Boucicault, *Arrah-na-Pogue; or, The Wicklow Wedding* (play).
    D. Boucicault, *Shaughraun* (play).

    L. M. Crawford, "Kathleen Mavourneen" (song).
    M. Davitt, *Fall of Feudalism in Ireland.*
    M. Edgeworth and R. L. Edgeworth (co-author), *Essay on Irish Bulls.*
    A. A. B. Edwards, "Give Me Three Grains of Corn, Mother." (poem, song).
    A. Gregory, *Book of Saints and Wonders.*
    A. M. Keary, *Castle Daly: The Story of an Irish Home Thirty Years Ago.*
    A. J. MacManus, *Four Winds of Eirinn* (poems).
    S. MacManus, *Lad of the O'Friel's.*
    T. Moore, "Harp that once through Tara's halls" (ballad).
    S. O. Morgan, *Lady Morgan's Memoirs: Autobiography, Diaries and Correspondence.*
    "Nora McCarty" (ballad).
    R. B. O'Brien, *Life of Charles Stewart Parnell, 1846–1891.*
    W. D. O'Brien (Catalog entry).
    J. Pilgrim, *Limerick Boy; or, Paddy's Mischief. An Original Farce, in One Act* (play).
    M. A. Ross, *Delina Delaney.*
    M. A. Ross, *Irene Iddesleigh.*
    E. A. Œ. Somerville and V. F.Martin, *Some Experiences of an Irish R. M.*
    K. C. Thurston, *Gambler, A Novel.*
    "Wearing of the green" (song).
    "Willie Reilly" (folk ballad).
    W. G. Wills, "Man o'Airlie" (song).
    W. G. Wills, *Man o' Airlie: A Drama of the Affections* (play).
    W. B. Yeats, *Stories of Red Hanrahan.*
Irish mythology: see
    A. Gregory, *Cuchulain of Muirthemne: The Story of the Men of the Red Branch of Ulster.*
    A. Gregory, *Gods and Fighting Men: The Story of the Tuatha De Danaan and of the Fianna of Ireland.*
    A. Gregory, *Poets and Dreamers: Studies & Translations from the Irish, by Lady Gregory.*
    R. D. Joyce, *Deirdrè* (poem).
    J. Macpherson, *Poems of Ossian, the Son of Fingal. Translated from the Original Gaelic.*
    R. J. O'Duffy (ed. and trans.), *Oidhe Chloinne Uisnigh: Fate of the Children of Uisneach.*
Irish Sketch Book of a Journey from Cornhill to Grand Cairo. see W. M. Thackeray, *Sketch Books. The Paris Sketch Book of Mr. M. A. Titmarsh. The Irish Sketch Book of a Journey from Cornhill to Grand Cairo.*
"Iron, Ralph" (pseud.): see O. Schreiner.
"Ironquill" (pseud.): see E. F. Ware.
Iroquois (Native American tribe): see F. Parkman, *Old Régime in Canada* (marginalia).
Irving, Henry: see
    A. W. Pinero, *Gay Lord Quex: A Comedy in Four Acts* (play) (Catalog entry).
    J. L. Toole (Catalog entry).
    W. G. Willis (adapt.), *Olivia* (play).
    W. Winter, *Wanderers: The Poems of William Winter.*
Irving, Washington: see
    D. Boucicault (adapt.), *Rip Van Winkle* (play).

T. W. S. Higginson, *Cheerful Yesterdays. Contemporaries* (marginalia).

H. B. Tree (adapt.), *Rip Van Winkle* (play).

Ishmaelite (novel). M. E. Braddon.

Is It True? Tales, Curious and Wonderful. D. M. M. Craik.

Islam: see

T. B. Aldrich, *From Ponkapog to Pesth.*

E. Arnold, *Pearls of the Faith; or, Islam's Rosary. Being the Ninety-nine Beautiful Names of Allah (Asmâ-el-husnâ).*

K. A. B. Benton, *Geber; A Tale of the Reign of Harun al Raschid, Khalif of Baghdad.*

R. F. Burton, *Personal Narrative of a Pilgrimage to El-Medinah and Meccah.*

I. C. S. Chandler, *Dog of Constantinople.*

L. De Forest (ed.), *Indian Domestic Architecture.*

T. W. Doane, *Bible Myths and Their Parallels in Other Religions: Being a Comparison of the Old and New Testament Myths and Miracles with Those of Heathen Nations of Antiquity* (marginalia).

W. Irving, *Alhambra: A Series of Tales and Sketches of the Moors and Spaniards.*

D. Ker, "From the Sea to the Desert" (article).

Koran: Commonly Called the Alkoran of Mohammed.

Lutfullah, *Autobiography of Lutfullah, A Mohamedan Gentleman; and His Transactions with His Fellow-Creatures.*

E. R. B. Lytton. *Chronicles and Characters.*

"Mohammedan's Prayer" (poem).

W. C. Prime, *Tent Life in the Holy Land* (marginalia).

F. von Schlegel, *Philosophy of History; in a Course of Lectures, Delivered at Vienna.*

A. Z. H. Y. Sîrafi, *Ancient Accounts of India and China, by Two Mohammedan Travellers.*

M. W. Townsend, *Asia and Europe: Studies* (marginalia).

C. D. Warner, *My Winter on the Nile, Among the Mummies and Moslems.*

See also the Reader's Guide entries for Crusades, for Moors, and for Spain.

Island of Enchantment. J. M. Forman.

Island of Karafuto. E. Greey.

Island World of the Pacific; Being the Personal Narrative and Results of Travel Through the Sandwich or Hawaiian Islands, and Other Parts of Polynesia. H. T. Cheever.

"Isle of the Long Ago" (poem). B. F. Taylor.

Isles of the Princes. S. S. Cox.

Israel: E. J. Miller, *Yoke: A Romance of the Days When the Lord Redeemed the Children of Israel from the Bondage of Egypt.*

Italian Grammar. C. H. Grandgent.

Italian Journeys. W. D. Howells.

Italian language: see

K. Baedeker, *Traveller's Manual of Conversation, in Four Languages: English, French, German, Italian, with Vocabulary, Short Questions, Etc.*

C. Cardelli, *Nouvelle Methode Pratique de Langue Italienne.*

F. Flamini (ed.), *Compendio di storia della letteratura Italiana ad uso delle scuole secondarie.*

C. H. Grandgent, *Italian Grammar.*

J. Millhouse and F. Bracciforti, *New English and Italian Pronouncing and Explanatory Dictionary, with Many New Additions.*

G. Rigutini and P. Fanfani, *Vocabolario Italiano della lingua parlata.*

H. Swan, *Travellers' Colloquial Italian. A Handbook for English-Speaking Travellers and Students.*

G. Vitali, *Manuel de la Conversation et du style épistolaire.*

I. E. Wessely (co-author), *New Pocket Dictionary of the English and Italian Languages.*

Italy: see

J. S. C. Abbott, *History of Joseph Bonaparte, King of Naples and of Italy.*

W. W. Astor, *Valentino, An Historical Romance of the Sixteenth Century in Italy.*

K. Baedeker, *Italy. Handbook for Travellers.*

A. G. Barrili, *Eleventh Commandment; A Romance.*

T. B. Batcheller, *Glimpses of Italian Court Life.*

W. H. Bishop, *Detmold: A Romance.*

J. H. Browne, *Sights and Sensations in Europe: Sketches of Travel and Adventure.*

J. R. Browne, *Yusef; or the Journey of the Frangi: A Crusade in the East.*

A. Carnegie, *Round the World.*

B. Cellini, *Memoirs of Benvenuto Cellini.*

J. Chambers, *Destiny of Doris; A Travel-Story of Three Continents.*

F. M. Dickinson, *Diary of an Idle Woman in Italy.*

A. A. B. Edwards, *Untrodden Peaks and Unfrequented Valleys. A Midsummer Ramble in the Dolomites.*

A. Fogazzaro, *Mistero del Poeta: Romanzo.*

H. B. Fuller, *Chevalier of Pensieri-Vani.*

E. Gifford, *Provenzano the Proud.*

R. S. Hichens, *Spirit in Prison* (novel).

A. Hoppin, *Ups and Downs on Land and Water.*

W. D. Howells, *Italian Journeys.*

W. D. Howells, *Roman Holidays and Others.*

W. D. Howells, *Tuscan Cities.*

W. D. Howells, *Venetian Life.*

W. McLennan, *Spanish John; Being a Memoir, Now First Published in Complete Form, of the Early Life and Adventures of Colonel John McDonell.*

M. Maeterlinck, *Monna Vanna, A Play in Three Acts.*

A. Manzoni, *I promessi sposi. The Betrothed.*

M. P. W. Montagu, *Letters of Lady Mary Wortley Montagu.*

F. Palgrave, *Handbook for Travellers in Northern Italy.*

Petrarch (Catalog entry).

C. M. Phillimore, *Dante at Ravenna: A Study.*

S. Phillips, *Paolo & Francesca: A Tragedy in Four Acts* (play).

E. J. Pullen, *Don Finimondone: Calabrian Sketches.*

L. von Ranke, *History of the Popes, Their Church and State, and Especially of Their Conflicts with Protestantism in the Sixteenth and Seventeenth Centuries.*

S. Rogers, "Venice," Part X, collected in *Italy, A Poem.*

J. Ruskin, *Roadside Songs of Tuscany.*

C. Scollard, *Under Summer Skies.*

D. C. Seitz, *Discoveries in Every-day Europe: Vagrant Notes of a Rapid Journey.*

M. Serao, *Conquest of Rome* (novel).
T. G. Smollett, *Travels through France and Italy*.
L. Viardot, *Wonders of Italian Art*.
P. Villari, *Life and Times of Niccolò Machiavelli* (marginalia).
E. L. B. Voynich, *Gadfly*.
C. D. Warner, *Saunterings*.
J. Webster, *Jerry Junior*.
See also the Reader's Guide entries for Florence, for Milan, for Pompeii, for Sicily, and for Venice.
Italy, A Poem: see S. Rogers, "Venice."
Itinerary of Rabbi Benjamin of Tudela. B. J. Benjamin of Tudela.
It Is Never Too Late to Mend; A Matter-of-Fact Romance. C. Reade: see C. Reade, *Foul Play; A Novel*.
"I Travelled among Unknown Men" (poem). W. Wordsworth.
Ivanhoe; A Romance. W. Scott.
"Ivàn Ivànovitch" (poem): see R. Browning, *Agamemnon*.
Ivanowski, Sigismond (illus.): see L. Wallace, *Chariot-Race from Ben-Hur*.
Ivan the Fool; or, the Old Devil and the Three Small Devils. L. N. Tolstoy.
I've Got the Blues Tonight & Other Troubles (pamphlet). J. A. Kirlicks.
Ives, George Burnham (trans.): see *Little French Masterpieces*.
"I've wandered to the village, Tom" (song): see W. Willing, "Twenty years ago" (song).
"I wish I was in Dixie's land" (song). D. D. Emmett.
"I would not live alway" (song). W. A. Muhlenberg.
"I would that my love" (song). H. Heine.

J

"Jabberwocky" (poem): see
C. L. Dodgson, *Through the Looking-Glass*."
A. F. Eastman, *Flower of Puritanism (Julia Jones Beecher) 1826–1905*.
Jaccaci, August Florian: see
(gift) H. J. Ross, *Letters from the East by Henry James Ross, 1837–1857*.
I. M. Tarbell, *History of the Standard Oil Company* (Catalog entry).
(gift) R. Vallery-Radot, *Life of Pasteur*.
Jackanapes. J. H. G. Ewing.
Jackass Gulch (California): see F. M. Trollope, *Domestic Manners of the Americans* (marginalia).
"Jack Downing in Portland": see S. Smith (Catalog entry).
Jack Hardin's Rendering of the Arabian Nights; Being a New Translation in Up-to-Date English. J. W. Scott.
Jack o' Legs: see F. Grose, *Classical Dictionary of the Vulgar Tongue* (marginalia).
Jack Sheppard; A Romance. W. H. Ainsworth.
Jackson, Abraham Reeves: see J. N. Jackson, *Winter Holiday in Summer Lands* (Catalog entry).
Jackson, Andrew:
E. T. Coke, *Subaltern's Furlough: Descriptive of Scenes in Various Parts of the United States*.
C. H. Peck, *Jacksonian Epoch*.

Jackson, Charles Thomas: see T. W. S. Higginson, *Cheerful Yesterdays. Contemporaries* (marginalia).
Jackson, Daniel (claimant to authorship): see I. Mitchell, *Asylum; or, Alonzo and Melissa*.
Jacksonian Epoch. C. H. Peck.
Jack the Giant Killer; or, Harlequin King Arthur and Ye Knights of Ye Round Table (extravaganza). H. J. Byron.
"Jacob, Bibliophile" (pseud.): see P. Lacroix.
Jacoby, Harold (intro.): see M. E. Martin, *Friendly Stars*.
Jakanapes. J. H. G. Ewing.
Jalland, G. H. (illus.): see G. J. Whyte-Melville, *Holmby House; A Tale of Old Northamptonshire* (novel).
James I, King of England : see
L. Aikin, *Memoirs of the Court of King James the First*.
R. Baker, *Chronicle of the Kings of England, from the Time of the Romans Government, unto the Death of King James the First*.
J. Gerard, *What Was the Gunpowder Plot? The Traditional Story Tested by Original Evidence*.
W. Scott, *Fortunes of Nigel* (novel).
J. H. Trumbull (ed.), *True-Blue Laws of Connecticut and New Haven*.
James I, King of Scotland: see C. M. Yonge, *Caged Lion*.
James II, King of England: see T. B. Macaulay, *History of England from the Accession of James II*.
James V, King of Scotland: see R. Barr, *Prince of Good Fellows*.
James Fenimore Cooper. T. R. Lounsbury.
James, Henry: see
(intro.): R. Kipling, *Mine Own People*.
(co-author): *Whole Family; A Novel by Twelve Authors*.
James Inwick, Ploughman and Elder. P. H. Hunter.
Jameson Raid: see the Reader's Guide entry for South Africa.
James' River Guide; Containing Descriptions of All the Cities, Towns, and Principal Objects of Interest on the Navigable Waters of the Mississippi Valley. U. P. James.
James Watt. A. Carnegie.
Jane Austen. W. L. Phelps.
Jane Eyre. C. Brontë.
Jane Field; A Novel. M. E. W. Freeman.
Janet and Her Friends. J. R. C. Hoyt.
Janet, a Poor Heiress. R. S. Clarke.
Janet's Home. A. M. Keary.
"Janus" (pseud.): see J. J. I. von Döllinger and J. N. Huber.
Janvier, Thomas Allibone: see
(contr.) *Armies of To-day; A Description of the Armies of the Leading Nations*.
(contr.) "Sage-Brush Hen" (short story) in W. D. Howells (co-ed.), *Under the Sunset*.
(intro.) W. Sharp, *Flower O' the Vine: Romantic Ballads and Sospiri di Roma*.
Japan: see
A. J. Beveridge, *Russian Advance*.
A. A. A. Brassey, *Voyage in the Sunbeam, Our Home in the Ocean for Eleven Months*.
G. W. Caldwell, *Oriental Rambles*.
G. L. Carlisle, *Around the World in a Year*.
A. Carnegie, *Round the World*.
W. Eaton, [Various titles.]

H. B. Fearon, *Sketches of America. A Narrative of a Journey of Five Thousand Miles* (marginalia).

M. M. Fenollosa, *Breath of the Gods.*

E. Greey, *Bear-Worshippers of Yezo; And the Island of Karafuto Saghalin. The Adventures of the Jewett Family and Their Friend Oto Nambo.*

E. Greey, *Captive of Love, Founded Upon Bakin's Japanese Romance Kumono Tayema Ama Yo No Tsuki.*

E. Greey, *Wonderful City of Tokio; or, Further Adventures of the Jewett Family and Their Friend Oto Nambo.*

E. Greey, *Young Americans in Japan; or, The Adventures of the Jewett Family and Their Friend Oto Nambo.*

E. H. House, *Japanese Episodes.*

T. W. Knox, *Boy Travellers in the Far East. . . in a Journey to Japan and China.*

H. M. Miller, *Little People of Asia.*

A. B. F.- Mitford, *Tales of Old Japan.*

E. S. Morse, *Japanese Homes and Their Surroundings.*

C. K. Munroe, *For the Mikado; or, A Japanese Middy in Action.*

G. Murai, *Hana, A Daughter of Japan.*

J. K. Newton, "Obligations of the United States to Initiate a Revision of Treaties Between the Western Powers and Japan."

H. Ōhashi (manuscript poems).

Y. T. Ozaki, *Japanese Fairy Tales.*

A. Parsons, *Notes in Japan.*

E. S. Patton, *Japanese Topsyturvydom.*

M. C. Perry, *Narrative of the Expedition of an American Squadron to the China Seas and Japan, Performed in the Years 1852, 1853, and 1854.*

R. Pumpelly, *Across America and Asia:* see R. Pumpelly, *Explorations in Turkestan.*

S. Ransome, *Japan in Transition: A Comparative Study of the Progress, Policy, and Methods of the Japanese Since Their War with China.*

H. Saito, *Love and Spring: Selections from the "Kokinshū."*

E. R. Scidmore, *Jinrikisha Days in Japan.*

L. L. Seaman, *Real Triumph of Japan: The Conquest of the Silent Foe.*

Shitakari Suzume (Japanese fairy tale).

T. Shunsui, *Loyal Ronins: An Historical Romance, Translated from the Japanese.*

C. W. Silver, *Secular Anathema on Fakery in Business, Social and Professional Life; or, Twentieth Century Conduct.*

B. Taylor, *Visit to India, China, and Japan, in the Year 1853.*

J. Verne, *Tour of the World in Eighty Days* (novel).

J. G. Wood, *Uncivilized Races; or, Natural History of Man* (marginalia).

Japanese Blossom. W. Eaton.

Japanese Episodes. E. H. House.

Japanese Fairy Tales. Y. T. Ozaki.

Japanese Homes and Their Surroundings. E. S. Morse.

Japanese Nightingale. W. Eaton.

Japanese Schoolboy. W. Irwin.

Japanese Topsyturvydom. E. S. Patton.

Japan in Transition: A Comparative Study of the Progress,

Policy, and Methods of the Japanese Since Their War with China. S. Ransome.

Jason, A Romance. J. M. Forman.

Jasper, Theodore (illus.): see J. H. Studer (ed.), *Birds of North America; One Hundred and Nineteen Artistic Colored Plates.*

Java: see T. W. Knox, *Travellers in the Far East; Part Second, . . . in a Journey to Siam and Java.*

Jayne's Medical Almanac and Guide to Health: see D. Jayne.

J. Cole. E. Gellibrand.

J. Devlin—Boss: A Romance of American Politics. F. C. Williams.

Jealousy. C. Reade.

Jean François Millet: His Life and Letters. J. Cartwright.

Jeanne d'Arc:

J J. Berriat-Saint-Prix, *Jeanne d'Arc, ou Coup-d'oeil sur les révolutions de France au temps de Charles VI et de Charles VII.*

F. Caddy, *Footsteps of Jeanne d'Arc; A Pilgrimage.*

C. A. de Chabannes, *Vierge Lorraine, Jeanne d'Arc.*

J. Fabre, *Procès de condamnation de Jeanne d'Arc.*

A. France, *Vie de Jeanne d'Arc.*

A. Lang, *Maid of France, Being the Story of the Life and Death of Jeanne d'Arc.*

A. Lang, *Monk of Fife: A Romance of the Days of Jeanne d'Arc.*

A. Le Nordez, *Jeanne d'Arc, racontée par l'image d'après les sculpteurs, les graveurs et les peintres.*

J. Michelet, *Jeanne d'Arc (1412–1432).*

R. B. de Molandon, *Famille de Jeanne d'Arc.*

M. Monahan, "Saint Mark" (article).

T. D. Murray *Jeanne d'Arc, Maid of Orleans, Deliverer of France; Being the Story of Her Life, Her Achievements, and Her Death.*

M. O. W. Oliphant, *Jeanne d'Arc: Her Life and Death.*

H. Parr, *Life and Death of Jeanne d'Arc, Called the Maid.*

J. É. J. Quicherat (comp.), *Procès de condamnation et de réhabilitation de Jeanne d'Arc, dite La Pucelle, publiés pour la premiere fois d'après les manuscrits de la Bibliothèque Royale.*

A. Ricard, *Jeanne d'Arc, La Vénérable, d'après les documents verses au procès de sa canonisation en cour de Rome.*

M. Sepet, *Jeanne d'Arc.*

H. A. Wallon, *Jeanne d'Arc, par H. Wallon.*

See also the Reader's Guide entry for Joan of Arc.

Jefferies, Richard (pref.): see G. White, *Natural History of Selborne. With a Naturalist's Calendar and Additional Observations.*

Jefferson, Joseph (actor): see

T. B. Aldrich, *Cloth of Gold and Other Poems* (Catalog entry).

D. Boucicault (adapt.), *Rip Van Winkle.*

M. D. Conway, *Autobiography: Memories and Experiences of Moncure Daniel Conway* (marginalia).

W. Irving, "Rip Van Winkle" (short story) (Catalog entry).

(illus.): see W. Winter, *Trip to England.*

Jefferson, Thomas: see

D. B. Lucas and J. F. McLaughlin, *Fisher Ames-Henry Clay, Etc.*

F. M. Trollope, *Domestic Manners of the Americans* (marginalia).

Jehovah's Witnesses: see C. T. Russell, *Millennial Dawn: The Plan of the Ages.*

Jephthah (Biblical figure): see G. O. Trevelyan, *Life and Letters of Lord Macaulay* (marginalia).

Jerdan, William (co-author): see T. Moore and W. Jerdan, *Personal Reminiscences by Moore and Jerdan.*

Jericho and the Jordan (unidentified author).

Jericho Road: A Story of Western Life. J. Habberton.

Jerry Junior. J. Webster.

Jerry the Dreamer. W. Payne.

"Jersey Centenarian" (sketch): see B. Harte, *Tales of the Argonauts, and Other Sketches.*

Jerusalem: see

J. T. Barclay, *City of the Great King; or, Jerusalem As It Was, As It Is, and As It Is To Be.*

W. H. Bartlett, *Walks About the City and Environs of Jerusalem.*

J. A. Hart, *Levantine Log-Book.*

N. MacLeod, *Eastward.*

C. W. Stoddard, *Cruise Under the Crescent; From Suez to San Marco.*

W. M. Thomson, *Land and the Book; or, Biblical illustrations Drawn from the Manners and Customs, the Scenes and Scenery, of the Holy Land: Lebanon, Damascus and Beyond Jordan.*

C. D. Warner, *In the Levant.*

Jess & Co. J. J. Bell.

"Jessie, the flower of Dumblane" (song): see S. Woodworth, "Bucket."

Jessup, Alexander (ed.): see *Little French Masterpieces.*

Jesuits: see

F. Parkman, *Jesuits in North America in the Seventeenth Century.*

F. Parkman, *Old Régime in Canada* (marginalia).

G. H. E. Slater, *Pagan at the Shrine.*

Jets and Flashes. H. C. Lukens.

Jeunesse de l'Impératrice Joséphine. I. de Saint-Amand.

Jewel of Seven Stars. B. Stoker.

Jewett, Clarence Frederick (ed.): see J. H Trumbull, *Memorial History of Hartford County Connecticut 1633–1884.*

Jewett, Helen (murder case): see H. Martineau, *Society in America* (marginalia).

Jewett, Sarah Orne: see A. A. Fields, *Whittier; Notes of His Life and of His Friendships.*

Jewish history and culture: see

B. J. Benjamin of Tudela, *Itinerary of Rabbi Benjamin of Tudela.*

E. C. Brewster, *Dictionary of Miracles: Imitative, Realistic, and Dogmatic, with Illustrations* (marginalia).

T. Buchanan, *Judith Triumphant* (novel).

W. Combe, *History and Antiquities of the City of York, from Its Origin to the Present Times* (marginalia).

G. Eliot, *Daniel Deronda* (novel).

É. Erckmann and A. Chatrian, *Polish Jew* (novel).

K. E. Franzos, *Jews of Barnow. Stories.*

K. E. Franzos, "Namensstudien" (essay).

G. Freytag, *Soll und Haben: Roman in Sechs büchern.*

R. W. Gilder, *In the Heights* (Catalog entry).

H. Hapgood, *Spirit of the Ghetto. Studies of the Jewish Quarter in New York.*

A. M. H. Heniger, *Children's Educational Theatre.*

T. Herzl, *Judenstaat.*

T. Herzl, *New Ghetto [Das Neue Ghetto].*

A. S. Isaacs, *Stories from the Rabbis.*

E. J. James, *Immigrant Jew in America.*

C. Kingsley, *Hypatia; or, New Foes with an Old Face.*

M. Kremnitz, *Reminiscences of the King of Roumania.*

W. E. H. Lecky, *History of the Rise and Influence of the Spirit of Rationalism in Europe* (marginalia).

New York *Times* (Catalog entry).

S. Sharpe, *History of the Hebrew Nation, and Its Literature.*

K. Spindler, *Jude, historischer Roman.*

J. Timbs, *Curiosities of London, Exhibiting the Most Rare and Remarkable Objects of Interest in the Metropolis* (marginalia).

I. Zangwill, *Children of the Ghetto* (novel).

I. Zangwill, *Master; A Novel* (Catalog entry).

Jews of Barnow (stories). K. E. Franzos.

Jeypore Portfolios of Architectural Details. S. S. Jacob (ed.).

Jibbenainosay: see R. M. Bird, *Nick of the Woods; or The Jibbenainosay.*

"Jim Bludso, of the Prairie Belle" (poem): see

G. G. Greenwood, *Shakespeare Problem Restated* (marginalia).

J. Hay, *Pike County Ballads and Other Pieces.*

Jimmieboy: see J. K. Bangs, *Bikey the Skicycle.*

Jimmy Brown Trying to Find Europe, Written by Himself. W. L. Alden.

Jimmyjohns, and Other Stories. A. M. Diaz.

Jinrikisha Days in Japan. E. R. Scidmore.

Joachim of Floris (Italian mystic): see F. Parkman, *Old Régime in Canada* (marginalia).

Joanna Traill, Spinster. A. E. Holdsworth.

Joan of Arc:

L. M. Boutet de Monvel, *Joan of Arc.*

A. E. K. S. Bray, *Joan of Arc, and the Times of Charles the Seventh, King of France.*

A. France, *Life of Joan of Arc*: see also A. France, *Vie de Jeanne d'Arc.*

T. De Quincey, "Joan of Arc" (essay).

E. A. Gerrard, *France and the Maid. A Drama in Three Acts.*

J. E. Goodman (Catalog entry).

R. S. Gower, *Joan of Arc.*

A. Kerr, *Blessed Joan of Arc (1412–1431).*

J. O'Hagan, *Joan of Arc.*

G. Porter, "Maid, A Drama in Five Acts" (typescript of a play).

J. C. F. von Schiller, *Jungfrau von Orleans.*

G. Skelton, *Joan of Arc: A Historical Drama* (play).

P. H. Stanhope, *Joan of Arc.*

C. R. Teller, "Sociological Maid. A Play in One Act."

A. E. Trumbull, *Wheel of Progress* (play).

J. Tuckey, *Joan of Arc, "The Maid."*

E. Wildman, *Aguinaldo: A Narrative of Filipino Ambitions* (Catalog entry).

H. Wilson, *Wonderful Characters; Comprising Memoirs and Anecdotes of the Most Remarkable Persons of Every Age and Nation.*

C. M. Yonge, *Cameos from English History. The Wars in France* (Catalog entry).

É. Zola, *Rome* (Catalog entry).

See also the Reader's Guide entry for Jeanne d'Arc.

Jocoseria: see R. Browning, *Agamemnon, La Saisiaz, Dramatic Idyls, and Jocoseria.*

Johann, Philipp Grot (illus.): see H. Heine, *Heinrich Heine's Buch der Lieder.*

Johannes Brahms in Erinnerungen. J. V. Widmann.

Johannesburg in Arms 1895–96, Being the Observations of a Casual Spectator. C. G. Thomas.

Johannesburg, South Africa: see the Reader's Guide entry for South Africa.

John and Sebastian Cabot. F. A. Ober.

John Bodewin's Testimony. M. H. Foote.

John Brent. T. Winthrop.

John Bull & Co.; The Great Colonial Branches of the Firm. P. Blouet.

John Bull's Other Island. G. B. Shaw.

"John Burns of Gettysbury" (poem). B. Harte.

Johnes, Thomas,: see

(trans.) *Chronicles of the Crusades; Contemporary Narratives.*

(trans.) J. Froissart, *Chronicles of England, France, Spain, and the Adjoining Countries.*

John Faa. S. R. Crockett.

John Gilley. C. W. Eliot.

John Halifax, Gentleman. A Novel. D. M. M. Craik.

"John Hay in Literature" (essay). W. D. Howells.

John Inglesant: A Romance. J. H. Shorthouse.

John, King of England: see A. P. Stanley, *Historical Memorials of Westminster Abbey.*

John Knox and John Knox's House. C. J. Guthrie.

John Leighton, Jr.; A Novel. K. N. Trask.

John L. Stoddard's Lectures. J. L. Stoddard.

"Johnny Sands" (folk ballad): see "There was a woman in our town" (folk ballad).

John Percyfield: The Anatomy of Cheerfulness. C. H. Henderson.

Johns, Al (composer): see E. Bowman, "Go way back and sit down" (song).

John Smith, Democrat: His Two Days' Canvass. A. P. Bettersworth.

Johnson, Alfred J. (illus.): see E. M. S. Turner, *Seven Little Australians.*

Johnson, Alice (co-ed.): see F. W. H. Myers, *Human Personality and Its Survival of Bodily Death.*

"Johnson, Benjamin F." (pseud.): see J. W. Riley.

Johnson, Charlotte: see C. R. Teller.

Johnson, Merle (illus.): see

P. W. Francis, *Remarkable Adventures of Little Boy Pip.*

B. Harte, *Lectures of Bret Harte, Compiled from Various Sources.*

Johnson, Reginald Brimley (ed.): see W. L. Phelps, "Introduction," *The Novels and Letters of Jane Austen.*

Johnson, Rossiter (comp.): see G. T. Lanigan, "Threnody."

Johnson, S. A. (ship captain): see *Truth: A Weekly Journal.*

Johnson, Samuel: see

J. Boswell, *Life of Samuel Johnson.*

M. Busch, *Bismarck in the Franco-German War 1870–1871* (marginalia).

A. S. Evans, *Our Sister Republic: A Gala Trip Through Tropical Mexico in 1869–70* (marginalia).

S. Grand, *Heavenly Twins* (marginalia).

C. Knight and T. Raikes, *Personal Reminiscences by Cornelia Knight and Thomas Raikes.*

E. G. E. B. Lytton, *Kenelm Chillingly: His Adventures and Opinions. A Novel* (marginalia).

(pref.): see W. Shakespeare, *Complete Works of William Shakespeare.*

W. M. Thackeray, *Thackeray's Lectures. The English Humourists. The Four Georges* (marginalia).

H. Walpole, *Letters of Horace Walpole, Earl of Oxford* (marginalia).

J. G. Wilson (ed.), *Love in Letters;, Illustrated in the Correspondence of Eminent Persons; with Biographical Sketches of the Writers.*

Johnson, William Lyman (composer): see M. B. Eddy, "O'er waiting harp strings of the mind" (hymn).

Johnson, William Martin (illus.): see

C. Kingsley, *Hypatia; or, New Foes with an Old Face.*

C. Reade, *Cloister & the Hearth; or, Maid, Wife, and Widow: A Matter-of-Fact Romance.*

L. Wallace, *Ben-Hur: A Tale of the Christ.*

L. Wallace, *First Christmas, from "Ben-Hur."*

Johnson, Willis Fletcher (co-author): see J. T. Headley, *Stanley's Adventures in the Wilds of Africa: A Graphic Account of the Several Expeditions of Henry M. Stanley.*

Johnston, Charles (co-author): see *Crisis in China.*

Johnston, Harry Hamilton (intro.): see E. D. Morel, *Red Rubber; The Story of the Rubber Slave Trade Flourishing on the Congo in the Year of Grace 1906.*

"John's Trial" (story): see P. Deming, *Adirondack Stories.*

John the Baptist: see H. Pyle, *Rejected of Men; A Story of To-day.*

John Van Buren, Politician; A Novel of To-day (unidentified author).

John Ward, Preacher. M. W. C. Deland.

John Winthrop, First Governor of the Massachusetts Colony. J. H. Twichell.

Joie fait pèur; comédie en un acte (play). D. G. Girardin.

Joinville, Jean de: see *Chronicles of the Crusades; Contemporary Narratives.*

"Jolly raftsman" (minstrel song). D. D. Emmett.

Jomini's Handbook of Military Etiquette. A. H. Jomini.

Jonas's Stories; Related to Rollo and Lucy. J. Abbott.

Jones, Alexander J. (intro.): see W. M. Springer, *Tariff Reform, the Paramount Issue. Speeches and Writings on the Questions Involved in the Presidential Contest of 1892.*

Jones, Alfred Garth (co-illus.): see Elizabeth, Queen of Rumania, *A Real Queen's Fairy Tales.*

Jones, I. (composer): "I don't allow no coons to hurt my feelings" (minstrel song).

Jones, Jeremiah (trans.): see the Catalog entry for Bible. New Testament. Apocrypha.

"Jones, Major Joseph" (pseud.): see W. T. Thompson.

Jones, Paul: see C. T. Brady, *Grip of Honor: A Story of Paul Jones and the American Revolution.*

Jones, Paul (arranger). "Get back to the wilderness" (waltz).

"Jòn Jònsonn's Saga: The Genuine Autobiography of a Modern Icelander." J. Jònsonn.

Jonson, Ben: see

F. T. Buckland, *Curiosities of Natural History* (Catalog entry).

G. G. Greenwood, *Shakespeare Problem Restated* (marginalia).

R. McWilliam, *Longmans' Handbook of English Literature. Pt. III. From Ben Jonson to Locke.*

Jordan: see W. M. Thomson, *Land and the Book; or, Biblical illustrations Drawn from the Manners and Customs, the Scenes and Scenery, of the Holy Land: Lebanon, Damascus and Beyond Jordan.*

"Jordan am a hard road to trabbel (minstrel song). D. D. Emmett.

Jordan, Elizabeth (co-author): see *Whole Family; A Novel by Twelve Authors.*

Jordan River: see T. Wright (ed.), *Early Travels in Palestine* (marginalia).

Jordan, William James (illus.): see C. Wuichet, *Sunny Side of a Busy Life.*

Joseph (earlier known as Cartaphilus): see the Catalog entry for M. D. Conway, *Wandering Jew* (marginalia).

Joseph Andrews. H. Fielding.

Josephine. E. D. Deland.

Josephine, Empress: see

I. de Saint-Amand, *Jeunesse de l'Impératrice Joséphine.*

C. É. J. G. de V. Rémusat, *Memoirs of Madame de Rémusat, 1802–1808* (Catalog entry).

Josephus, Flavius: see E. Gibbon, *History of the Decline and Fall of the Roman Empire* (Catalog entry).

Josh Billings' Farmers' Alminax for the Year 1870. H. W. Shaw.

Josh Billings: His Works, Complete. H. W. Shaw.

Joshua Davidson. E. Linton.

Josiah Allen's Wife. M. Holley.

Josiah Wedgwood, F.R.S., His Personal History. S. Smiles.

Jottings, by Edwin Ransford: see E. Ransford, "In the Days When We Went Gypsying" (poem and song).

Joubert, Joseph: see C. A. Sainte-Beuve, *Monday-Chats, Selected and Translated from the "Causeries du Lundi."*

Journalism: see

J. L. Gilder, *Tomboy at Work.*

W. R. Hearst (Catalog entry).

H. C. Lukens, *Jets and Flashes* (Catalog entry).

J. Ralph, *Making of a Journalist.*

W. Reid, "Schools of Journalism" (article).

H. White (Catalog entry).

J. H. Wilson, *Life of Charles A. Dana.*

Journal of a Residence on a Georgian Plantation in 1838–39. F. A. Kemble.

Journal of Researches. C. Darwin.

Journal of Sir Walter Scott, from the Original Manuscript at Abbotsford. W. Scott.

Journal of the Plague Year. D. Defoe.

Journal of the Society for Psychical Research: see the Catalog entry for Society for Psychical Research.

Journal of Travels in the United States of North America,

and in Lower Canada, Performed in the Year 1817. J. Palmer.

Journals:

H. F. Amiel, *Amiel's Journal: The Journal Intime of Henri-Frédéric Amiel.*

M. K. Bashkirtseva, *Marie Bashkirtseff; The Journal of a Young Artist.*

G. G. Byron, *Works of Lord Byron, in Verse and Prose. Including His Letters, Journals, Etc.*

J. B. Elgin, *Letters and Journals of James, Eighth Earl of Elgin.*

G. Eliot, *George Eliot's Life as Related in Her Letters and Journals.*

E. J. Eyre, *Journals of Expeditions of Discovery into Central Australia.*

C. Fox, *Memories of Old Friends, Being Extracts from the Journals and Letters of Caroline Fox.*

C. C. F. Greville, *Greville Memoirs; A Journal of the Reigns of King George IV. and King William IV.*

G. Grey, *Journals of Two Expeditions of Discovery in North-West and Western Australia, During the Years 1837, 38, and 39.*

G. Henschel, *Personal Recollections of Johannes Brahms.*

S. Hensel, *Mendelssohn Family (1729–1847) from Letters and Journals.*

F. A. Kemble, *Journal of a Residence on a Georgian Plantation in 1838–39.*

S. Longfellow (ed.), *Life of Henry Wadsworth Longfellow, with Extracts from his Journals and Correspondence.*

W. Scott, *Journal of Sir Walter Scott, from the Original Manuscript at Abbotsford.*

C. S. Stewart, *Private Journal of a Voyage to the Pacific Ocean and Residence at the Sandwich Islands, in the Years 1822, 1823, 1824, and 1825.*

G. Ticknor, *Life, Letters, and Journals of George Ticknor.*

See also the Reader's Guide entry for Diaries.

Journals of Expeditions of Discovery into Central Australia, and Overland from Adelaide to King George's Sound, in 1840–1, Including an Account of the Manners and Customs of the Aborigines, and the State of Their Relations with Europeans. E. J. Eyre.

Journals of Two Expeditions of Discovery in North-West and Western Australia, During the Years 1837, 38, and 39. G. Grey.

Journey through the Kingdom of Oude, in 1849–1850. W. H. Sleeman.

Journey to Central Africa; or, Life and Landscapes from Egypt to the Negro Kingdoms of the White Nile. B. Taylor.

Journey to Nature. A. C. Wheeler.

Journey to the Centre of the Earth. J. Verne.

Jowett, Benjamin (trans.): see Plato, *Dialogues of Plato.*

Juan and Juanita. F. C. Baylor.

Juan Ponce de Leon. F. A. Ober.

Jubilee Singers: see

"John Brown's body" (song).

T. Malory, *Morte Darthur* (Catalog entry).

J. B. T. Marsh, *Story of the Jubilee Singers, with Their Songs.*

"We shall walk through the valley" (song).

See also the Catalog and Reader's Guide entries for Spirituals.

Judaism: see the Reader's Guide entry for Jewish history and culture.

Judd, Edward P.: see E. P. Hammond, *Sketches of Palestine* (inscr.).

Judd, Sylvester: see F. O. C. Darley, *Compositions in Outline*.

Jude, historischer Roman. K. Spindler.

Judenstaat. T. Herzl.

Jude the Obscure. T. Hardy.

Judgment. A Novel. A. Brown.

Judgment Books. E. F. Benson.

Judgment of Eve, and Other Stories. M. A. S. C. Sinclair.

Juliana Horatia Ewing and Her Books. H. K. F. G. Eden.

Julien, F. (ed.): see É. Zola, *Attaque du Moulin*.

Judith of Bethulia, A Tragedy (play). T. B. Aldrich.

Judith of the Plains; A Novel. M. Manning.

Judith Shakespeare; Her Love Affairs and Other Adventures. W. Black.

Judith Triumphant (novel). T. Buchanan.

Judson, Ann (Hasseltine): see *Memoir of Mrs. Ann H. Judson, Late Missionary to Burmah*.

Jugs (liquor): see G. O. Trevelyan, *Life and Letters of Lord Macaulay* (marginalia).

Juif errant: see E. Sue, *Wandering Jew*.

Julian the Apostate. G. Negri.

Julianus, Flavius Claudius, Emperor of Rome: see G. Negri, *Julian the Apostate*.

Julius Caesar (play). W. Shakespeare.

Jungfrau von Orleans (play). J. C. F. von Schiller.

Jungle. U. B. Sinclair.

Jungle Book. R. Kipling.

Jupiter Lights; A Novel. C. F. Woolson.

Jupiter (planet): see

S.G. Bayne, *Pith of Astronomy (Without Mathematics): The Latest Facts and Figures as Developed by the Giant Telescopes* (clipping).

New York *Sun* (Catalog entry).

Jupiter (Roman god): see

T. W. Doane, *Bible Myths and Their Parallels in Other Religions*. (marginalia).

M. W. Townsend, *Asia and Europe: Studies* (marginalia).

"Just as I am, without one plea" (hymn). C. Elliott.

"Just before the battle, Mother" (song). G. F. Root.

Just So Stories for Little Children. R. Kipling.

Juvenile literature: see the Reader's Guide entry for Children's and young adult literature.

K

Kaffir customs: see J. G. Wood, *Uncivilized Races; or, Natural History of Man; Being a Complete Account of the Manners and Customs, and the Physical, Social, and Religious Condition and Characteristics, of the Uncivilized Races of Men, Throughout the Entire World*.

Ka hele malihini ana mai keia ao aku a hiki i kela ao: see J. Bunyan, *Pilgrim's Progress* (Hawaiian).

Kaiser's Speeches, Forming a Character Portrait of Emperor William II. Wilhelm II.

Kaloolah: Adventures of Jonathan Romer of Nantucket (novel). W. S. Mayo.

Kamp mit dem Drachen: see J. C. F. von Schiller, *Fight with the Dragon. A Romance*.

Kampf um die Kunst. Drei Novellen. K. E. Edler.

Kansas: see

E. B. Custer, *Tenting on the Plains; or, General Custer in Kansas and Texas*.

E. W. Howe, *Moonlight Boy*.

E. W. Howe, *Story of a Country Town*.

C. K. Munroe, *Campmates; A Story of the Plains*.

E. F. Ware, *Some of the Rhymes of Ironquill. (A Book of Moods)*.

W. A. White, *Court of Boyville*.

W. A. White, *In Our Town*.

Kansas City: see

Knife and Fork Club. Kansas City, Missouri. *Book of the Knife and Fork Club*.

G. W. Warder, *Cities of the Sun*.

C. D. Warner, *Studies in the South and West, with Comments on Canada*.

Kappes, Alfred (illus.): see

T. Malory, *Boy's King Arthur*.

H. S. Olcott, *People from the Other World*.

Kate Beaumont. J. W. De Forest.

Kate Greenaway's Birthday Book for Children. K. Greenaway.

"Kathleen Mavourneen" (song). L. M. Crawford.

Katrine, A Novel. E. M. Lane.

Kaulbach, Wilhelm von (illus.): see

J. W. von Goethe, *Female Characters of Goethe*.

J. W. von Goethe, *Reineke Fuchs*.

Kean, Edmund (actor): see W. Shakespeare, *Hamlet* (Catalog entry).

Keary, Eliza (co-author): see A. M. Keary, *Heroes of Asgard: Tales from Scandinavian Mythology*.

Keats, John: see

W. J. Dawson (co-ed.), *Great English Letter-Writers* (marginalia).

F. T. Palgrave (comp.), *Golden Treasury of the Best Songs and Lyrical Poems in the English Language* (marginalia).

H. Van Dyke (ed.), *Little Masterpieces of English Poetry, by British and American Authors*.

J. G. Wilson (ed.), *Love in Letters; Illustrated in the Correspondence of Eminent Persons; with Biographical Sketches of the Writers*.

Keats, John, "On First Looking into Chapman's Homer": see F. P. Cobbe, *The Peak in Darien, with Some Other Inquiries Touching Concerns of the Soul and the Body*.

Keen, Eliot (illustrator): see C. P. Jones and A. L. Sykes, *Banduk jaldi banduk!: (Quick, My Rifle!)*.

Keene, Charles (illustrator): see G. L. P. B. Du Maurier, *Social Pictorial Satire; Reminiscences and Appreciations of English Illustrators of the Past Generation*.

Keep, Virginia (illus.): see T. N. Page, *Two Prisoners*.

Kei-Sai Yei-sen (illus.): see T. Shunsui, *Loyal Ronins: An Historical Romance, Translated from the Japanese*.

Keller, Arthur Ignatius. (illus.): see

I. Bacheller, *Darrel of the Blessed Isles*.

E. N. Bland, *Red House; A Novel*.

W. Churchill, *Mr. Crewe's Career.*
S. Grand, *Babs, the Impossible.*
(co-illus.) W. D. Howells, *Heroines of Fiction.*
W. D. Howells, *Ragged Lady: A Novel.*
F. H. Smith, *Peter: A Novel of Which He Is Not the Hero.*
E. S. Van Zandt, *With Sword and Crucifix; Being an Account of the Strange Adventures of Count Louis de Sancerre, Companion of Sieur de la Salle.*
H. B. M. Watson, *Adventurers; A Tale of Treasure Trove.*
Keller, A. J. (illus.): see J. Barnes, *Loyal Traitor: A Story of the War of 1812.*
Keller, Helen: see
S. C. Woolsey, *Last Verses* (Catalog entry).
Youth's Companion; An Illustrated Weekly for Young People and the Family (Catalog entry).
Kellerhoven, Franz (illus.): see
P. Lacroix, *Arts in the Middle Ages, and at the Period of the Renaissance.*
P. Lacroix, *Manners, Customs, and Dress During the Middle Ages.*
P. Lacroix, *Military and Religious Life in the Middle Ages and at the Period of the Renaissance.*
"Kelly, Mrs. Tom" (pen name): see M. S. Kelly.
Kelly, Walter Keating: see
(trans.) G. Boccaccio, *Decameron.*
(trans.) G. Boccaccio, *Stories of Boccaccio.*
(trans.) G. V. Catullus, *Works of Catullus and Tibullus, and the Vigil of Venus.*
(trans.) M. de Cervantes Saavedra, *Exemplary Novels of Miguel de Cerantes Saavedra.*
(trans.) Marguerite d'Angoulême, *Heptameron of Margaret, Queen of Navarre.*
(ed.) S. Propertius, *Erotica.*
Kemble, Adelaide: see Adelaide (Kemble) Sartoris.
Kemble, Edward Windsor : see
(illus.) M. Crim, *In Beaver Cove and Elsewhere.*
(illus.) J. C. Lincoln, *Cape Cod Ballads, and Other Verse, by Joe Lincoln.*
(illus.) J. W. Riley, *Poems Here at Home.*
(co-illus.) F. H. Smith, *Colonel Carter of Cartersville* (novel).
(co-illus.) R. M. Stuart, *Second Wooing of Salina Sue, and Other Stories.*
Kemp, Oliver (illus.): see C. C. Abbott, *In Nature's Realm.*
Kempis, Thomas à: see Thomas à Kempis.
Kenelm Chillingly: His Adventures and Opinions. A Novel. E. G. E. B. Lytton.
Kenilworth; A Romance. W. Scott.
Kennedy, William Sloane: see W. Whitman, *Autobiographia; or, the Story of a Life. By Walt Whitman. Selected from His Prose Writings.*
Kentons (novel). W. D. Howells.
Kentucky: see
J. L. Allen, *Aftermath; Part Second of "A Kentucky Cardinal."*
J. L. Allen, *Choir Invisible.*
J. L. Allen, *Kentucky Cardinal; A Story.*
J. L. Allen, *Summer in Arcady; A Tale of Nature.*
G. Davis (Catalog entry).

H. B. Fearon, *Sketches of America. A Narrative of a Journey of Five Thousand Miles* (marginalia).
Louisville, Kentucky *Evening Post.*
E. C. C. Obenchain, *Aunt Jane of Kentucky* (short stories).
H. D. Pittman, *Belle of the Bluegrass Country. Studies in Black and White.*
A. C. H. Rice, *Mr. Opp.*
A. C. H. Rice, *Mrs. Wiggs of the Cabbage Patch.*
M. Y. Ridenbaugh, *Biography of Ephraim McDowell, M. D., "The Father of Ovariotomy."*
A. M. Roach, *Some Successful Marriages.*
G. D. Sherley (Catalog entry).
C. D. Warner, *Studies in the South and West, with Comments on Canada.*
Kentucky Cardinal; A Story. J. L. Allen.
Kepler, Johann: see D. Brewster, *Martyrs of Science; or, The Lives of Galileo, Tycho Brahe, and Kepler.*
Kerker, Gustave Adolph (composer): see C. M. S. McLellan, *Belle of New York, A Musical Comedy in Two Acts* (play).
Kern, May R. (illus.): see A. J. Miller, *Physical Beauty: How to Obtain and How to Preserve It.*
Keroualle, Louise de: see H. Forneron, *Louise de Keroualle, Duchess of Portsmouth, 1649–1734.*
"Kerr, Orpheus C." (pseud.): see R. H. Newell.
Kersands, Billy (minstrel performer): see J. E. Stewart, "Mary's gone with a Coon" (minstrel song).
Ketchum, Lewey (character): see F. H. Eckstorm, *Penobscot Man.*
Ketten, Maurice (illus.): see D. C. Seitz, *Discoveries in Every-day Europe: Vagrant Notes of a Rapid Journey.*
Keystone of Empire, Francis Joseph of Austria. M. Cunliffe-Owen.
Khiva: see J. A. MacGahan, *Campaigning on the Oxus, and the Fall of Khiva.*
Kialimark, George (composer): see
T. Moore, "Araby's daughter."
S. Woodworth, "Bucket" ("Old oaken bucket").
Kidd, William: see C. Ellms, *Pirates Own Book; or, Authentic Narratives of the Lives, Exploits, and Executions of the Most Celebrated Sea Robbers.*
Kidnapped; Being Memoirs of the Adventures of David Balfour in the Year 1751 (novel). R. L. Stevenson.
Kidnapped Campers; A Story of Out-of-Doors. F. A. C. Canfield.
"Killaloe" (song). R. J. Martin.
Kilmeny. W. Black.
Kim. R. Kipling.
Kimball, Charlotte (co-author): see E. J. James, *Immigrant Jew in America.*
Kinder der Welt. Roman in Sechs Büchern. P. J. L. von Heyse.
Kindergarten: see M. T. P. Mann, *Moral Culture of Infancy, and Kindergarten Guide.*
Kinderstubengeschichten. R. Niedergesäss.
Kindred of the Wild; A Book of Animal Life. C. G. D. Roberts.
King and No King (play). F. Beaumont and J. Fletcher.
King Arthur: see the Reader's Guide entry for Arthur, King.

King, Clarence: see B. Harte, *Drift from Two Shores* (marginalia).

King, David (intro.): see J. Eadie (ed.), *New and Complete Concordance to the Holy Scriptures.*

King, Grace: see
A. Daly, *Divorce* (play) (Catalog entry).
Revue des deux mondes (Catalog entry).

"Kingdom coming" (song). H. C. Work.

King John (play). W. Shakespeare.

King Lear (play). W. Shakespeare.

King Leopold's Rule in Africa. E. D. Morel.

"King of Denmark's Ride" (poem). C. Norton.

King of Rome; A Biography. V. von Kubinyi.

King René's Daughter; A Danish Lyrical Drama (play). H. Hertz.

Kings and Queens I Have Known, by Hélène Vacaresco. E. Văcărescu.

Kingsley, Charles: see
F. P. Cobbe, *Life of Frances Power Cobbe as Told by Herself* (marginalia).
M. D. Conway, *Autobiography: Memories and Experiences of Moncure Daniel Conway* (marginalia).

Kingsley, Frances Eliza (ed.): see C. Kingsley, *Charles Kingsley: His Letters and Memories of His Life.*

Kingsley, George (composer): see
W. A. Muhlenberg, "I would not live alway" (song).
S. Stennett, "On Jordan's stormy banks I stand" (hymn).

Kingsley, Maurice: see "Tio Juan" (short story) in W. D. Howells (co-ed.), *Under the Sunset.*

King Solomon's Mines. H. R. Haggard.

King Spruce; A Novel. H. F. Day.

Kingston, William Henry Giles (ed.): see J. D. Wyss, *Swiss Family Robinson. A New Translation.*

King Victor and King Charles: A Tragedy (poem): see R. Browning, *Dramas.*

King Victor and King Charles: A Tragedy (poem): see R. Browning, *Pauline; Paracelsus; Strafford; Sordello.*

Kinnear, M. H. (ed.): see J. P. W. Penzance, *Lord Penzance on the Bacon-Shakespeare Controversy. A Judicial Summing-Up.*

Kinney, Margaret West (illus.): see
W. Churchill, *Mr. Crewe's Career.*
(co-illus.) E. S. Martin, *Courtship of a Careful Man, and a Few Other Courtships.*

Kinney, Troy (illus.): see W. Churchill, *Mr. Crewe's Career.*

Kinzbrunner, Carl (trans.): see R. Krause, *Starters and Regulators for Electric Motors and Generators.*

Kipling, Rudyard: see
F. E. Church (Catalog entry).
London *World.*
B. Matthews, "Cervantes, Zola, Kipling & Co." (article).
J. W. Riley, *Poems Here at Home* (Catalog entry).
L. de R. Saint-Simon, *Memoirs of the Duke of Saint-Simon on the Reign of Louis XIV and the Regency* (marginalia).
J. K. Stephen, *Lapsus Calami.*
F. B. Terry, *Stories* (Catalog entry).
W. M. Thackeray, *History of Pendennis, His Fortunes*

and Misfortunes, His Friends and His Greatest Enemy (Catalog entry).

Kirby, Elizabeth (co-author): see M. K. Gregg and E. Kirby, *Stories About Birds of Land and Water.*

Kirby, Rollin G. (illus.): see W. Irwin, *Letters of a Japanese Schoolboy("Hashimura Togo).*

Kirby, William Forsell (intro.): see W. E. Kirby, *Insects: Foes and Friends.*

Kirchenhoffer, Henry: see *Napoleon's Oraculum, or, Book of Fate.*

Kirkman, Francis (co-author): see R. Head, *English Rogue.*

Kismet. G. Fleming.

Kisses of Johannes Secundus: see S. Propertius, *Erotica.*

Kiss of Glory. G. D. Boylan.

"Kitto" (story): see J. L. Long, *Madame Butterfly.*

Kitto, John, *Illustrated History of the Holy Bible*: see A. Bond (ed.), *Young People's Illustrated Bible History.*

Kitton, Frederick George (ed.): see C. Dickens, *Poems and Verses.*

Kittredge, Herman Eugene (contr.): see R. G. Ingersoll, *Works of Robert G. Ingersoll.*

Kleinere prosaische Schriften: see *Schiller's Sämmtliche Werke in Zwölf Bänden.*

Klingemann, Carl (trans.): see S. Hensel, *Mendelssohn Family (1729–1847) from Letters and Journals.*

Klinkowström, M. Alfons de (comp.): see K. W. L. F. von Metternich-Winneburg-Beilstein, *Memoirs of Prince Metternich.*

Kneass, Nelson (composer): see T. D. English, "Ben Bolt; or, oh! don't you remember" (song).

Knight, Charles (ed.): see *English Cyclopædia, Conducted by Charles Knight.*

Knight, George S. (actor): see J. C. Goodwin and E. E. Rice, *Evangeline* (musical burlesque).

Knight, Joseph Philip (composer): see
E. H. Willard, "Rocked in the cradle of the deep" (hymn).
C. Wolfe, "Go! forget me" (song).

Knights: see
T. Bulfinch, *Age of Chivalry; or, Legends of King Arthur.*
H. J. Byron, *Jack the Giant Killer; or, Harlequin King Arthur and Ye Knights of Ye Round Table* (extravaganza).
J. B. Cabell, *Chivalry* (novel).
J. B. Cabell, *Gallantry* (novel).
J. B. Cabell, *Line of Love* (novel).
M. V. Farrington, *Tales of King Arthur and His Knights of the Round Table.*
M. H. Hewlett, *Forest Lovers, A Romance* (novel).
P. Kester, *When Knighthood Was in Flower* (play).
C. Major, *When Knighthood Was in Flower; or, The Love Story of Charles Brandon and Mary Tudor, the King's Sister* (novel).
T. Malory, *Boy's King Arthur.*
T. Malory, *Morte Darthur.*
M. E. M. Sangster, *Little Knights and Ladies; Verses for Young People.*
W. Scott, *Ivanhoe; A Romance.*
A. Tennyson, *Idylls of the King.*

Knights Templar: see T. H. Baylis, *Temple Church and Chapel of St. Ann, Etc.* (marginalia).

"Knight's Toast" (poem): see W. Scott, "St. Leon's Toast" (poem).

Knott, James Proctor: see M. C. Russell, *Uncle Dudley's Odd Hours; Being the Vagaries of a Country Editor.*

Knox, John: see C. J. Guthrie, *John Knox and John Knox's House.*

Knox, John Armoy (co-author): see A. E. Sweet, *On a Mexican Mustang, through Texas, from the Gulf to the Rio Grande.*

Knox, Robert (intro.): see E. P. Hammond, *Sketches of Palestine.*

Koch, Karl: see J. Fiske, *Century of Science and Other Essays* (marginalia).

Komroff, Manuel: see A. M. H. Heniger, *Children's Educational Theatre* (Catalog entry).

Korea: see
> H. N. Allen, *Things Korean; A Collection of Sketches and Anecdotes, Missionary and Diplomatic.*
> P. Lowell, *Chosön, The Land of the Morning Calm: A Sketch of Korea.*

Kozlay, Charles Meeker (ed., inscr.): see B. Harte, *Lectures of Bret Harte, Compiled from Various Sources.*

Kravchinski, Sergei M.: see W. M. Thackeray, *Thackeray's Lectures. The English Humorists. The Four Georges* (Catalog entry).

Kuenen, Abraham (contr.): see
> H. Oort, *Bible for Learners.*
> H. Oort, *Bible for Young People.*

Kühnemann, Eugen (ed.): see J. C. F. von Schiller, *Ausgewählte Briefe von Friedrich von Schiller.*

Ku Klux Klan: see
> T. Dixon, *Leopard's Spots: A Romance of the White Man's Burden—1865–1900.*
> J. A. Wyeth, *Life of General Nathan Bedford Forrest.*

Kulóskap the Master, and Other Algonkin Poems. C. G. Leland (trans.) and J. D. Prince (co-trans.).

Kurz, Hermann (intro.): see P. Konewka, *Falstaff and His Companions. Twenty-one Illustrations in Silhouette.*

▌L

LaBarge, Joseph: see H. M. Chittenden, *History of Early Steamboat Navigation on the Missouri River: Life and Adventures of Joseph LaBarge.*

Labor: see the Reader's Guide entry for Work.

Labor: A Novel (Travail). É. Zola.

Labor issues: see the Reader's Guide entry for Economics and labor issues.

Labouchère. Henry DuPré (ed.): see *Truth: A Weekly Journal.*

Laboulaye's Fairy Book; Fairy Tales of All Nations.

Lackland, William (trans.): see
> J. Verne, *Five Weeks in a Balloon; or, Journeys and Discoveries in Africa, by Three Englishmen.*
> F. Zurcher and É. Margollé, *Meteors, Aërolites, Storms, and Atmospheric Phenomena.*

Lacy, John: see *Dramatists of the Restoration.*

Ladder of Swords; A Tale of Love, Laughter and Tears. G. Parker.

Lad of the O'Friel's. S. MacManus.

Lady Audley's Secret (novel): see M. E. Braddon, *Ishmaelite.*

Lady Byron Vindicated: A History of the Byron Controversy, from Its Beginning in 1816 to the Present Time. H. E. B. Stowe.

Lady Clare. A. Tennyson.

Lady in the White Veil. R. C. O'Neill.

Lady Louisa Stuart: Selections from Her Manuscripts. L. Stuart.

Lady Morgan's Memoirs: Autobiography, Diaries and Correspondence. S. O. Morgan.

Lady of La Garaye. C. E. S. S. Norton.

Lady of Lyons, or Love and Pride (play). E. G. E. B. Lytton.

Lady of the Aroostook (novel). W. D. Howells.

Lady of the Lake (poem). W. Scott.

Lady of the Regency. M. S. Rawson.

Lady Rose's Daughter, A Novel. M. A. A. Ward.

Lady's Dressing-Room (Le cabinet de toilette). B. A. A. Soyer.

Laffan, William Mackay (pref.): see W. T. Walters, *Oriental Ceramic Art; Illustrated by Examples from the Collection of W. T. Walters.*

La Garaye, Marie Marguerite La Motte-Picquet, Comtesse de: see C. E. S. S. Norton, *Lady of La Garaye.*

Laguillermie, Frederic Auguste (illus.): see B. Cellini, *Life of Benvenuto Cellini.*

Lalla Rookh, An Oriental Romance. T. Moore.

Lalor, John Joseph (trans.): see L. Nohl, *Life of Beethoven.*

La Marca (pseud., co-author): see Ysaguirre (pseud.), *Cold Dishes for Hot Weather.*

Lamarck, Jean Baptiste Pierre Antoine de Monet de: see J. Fiske, *Century of Science and Other Essays* (marginalia).

Lamartine, Alphone: see P. Mérimée, *Prosper Mérimée's Letters to an Incognita.*

Lamb, Charles: see
> B. E. Martin, *In the Footprints of Charles Lamb.*
> W. M. Thackeray, *Thackeray's Lectures. The English Humorists. The Four Georges* (Catalog entry).
> J. G. Wilson (ed.), *Love in Letters; Illustrated in the Correspondence of Eminent Persons; with Biographical Sketches of the Writers.*

Lamb, George (trans.): see G. V. Catullus, *Works of Catullus and Tibullus.*

Lamb, Mary Ann (co-author): see C. Lamb, *Tales from Shakespeare.*

Lamb, William: see H. Dunckley, *Lord Melbourne.*

"Lambert, Louis" (pseud.): see P. S. Gilmore.

Lambeth: see J. Tanswell, *History and Antiquities of Lambeth.*

"Lament of the Irish emigrant" (song). H. S. S. Blackwood.

Lances of Lynwood. C. M. Yonge.

Land and the Book; or, Biblical illustrations Drawn from the Manners and Customs, the Scenes and Scenery, of the Holy Land: Lebanon, Damascus and Beyond Jordan. W. M. Thomson.

Land Beyond the Forest: Facts, Figures and Fancies from Transylvania. E. Gerard.

Landlord at Lion's Head (novel). W. D. Howells.

Landmarks of History. C. M. Yonge.

Land of Make-Believe, and Other Christmas Poems. W. D. Nesbit.

Land of Riddles (Russia of To-day). H. M. Ganz.

Land of the White Elephant: Sights and Scenes in South-eastern Asia. A Personal Narrative of Travel and Adventure in Farther India, Embracing the Countries of Burma, Siam, Cambodia, and Cochin-China. F. Vincent.

Landon, Melville De Lancey: see *Library of Wit and Humor by Mark Twain and Others. With the Philosophy of Wit and Humor by Melville D. Landon, A. M. (Eli Perkins).*

Land Question, What It Involves, and How Alone It Can Be Settled. H. George.

Landsleute. Kleine Beobachtungen eines Wieners. E. Pötzl.

Lands of the Saracens. B. Taylor.

Lane, William Edward (trans., ed.): see *Arabian Nights, Thousand and One Nights.*

Lang, Andrew: see
(trans.): *Aucassin and Nicolette.*
(intro.): R. Kipling, *Courting of Dinah Shad and Other Stories.*
(contr.): A. R. Wallace, William Ramsay, *et al. Progress of the Century.*
(co-ed.): *World's Wit and Humor; An Encyclopedia of the Classic Wit and Humor of All Ages and Nations.*

Lang, Ossian Herbert: see L. E. Trescott (Catalog entry).

Langdon, Jervis: see T. K. Beecher, *Jervis Langdon, 1809–1870.*

Langen, Albert (ed.): see *Simplicissimus* (magazine).

Langhorne, John (co-trans.): see Plutarchus, *Plutarch's Lives of Alcibiades & Coriolanus, Aristides & Cato the Censor.*

Langhorne, William (co-trans.): see Plutarchus, *Plutarch's Lives of Alcibiades & Coriolanus, Aristides & Cato the Censor.*

Langland, William: see J. A. A. J. Jusserand, *English Way-faring Life in the Middle Ages (XIVth Century).*

Languages: see F. Gouin, *Art of Teaching and Studying Languages.*

Lanier, Sidney: see
T. W. S. Higginson, *Cheerful Yesterdays. Contemporaries* (marginalia).
(ed., intro.) *Mabinogion, Boy's Mabinogion; Being the Earliest Welsh Tales of King Arthur in the Famous Red Book of Hergest.*
(ed.) T. Malory, *Boy's King Arthur.*

Laodicean: A Story of To-day. T. Hardy.

Laokoon, oder über die Grenzen der Malerei und Poesie. G. E. Lessing.

Laplace, Pierre Simon de: see J. Timbs, *Things Not Generally Known, Familiarly Explained* (marginalia).

Lapsus Calami. J. K. Stephen.

"Larboard watch" (song). T. E. Williams.

Larimer, George Horace: see G. T. Richardson, *Letters from a Son to His Self-Made Father* (Catalog entry).

Larned, Joseph Nelson (ed.): see D. Gray, *Letters, Poems and Selected Prose Writings of David Gray.*

"Larwood, Jacob" (pseud.): see H. D. J. van Schevichaven.

La Salle and the Discovery of the Great West. F. Parkman.

La Salle, René-Robert Cavelier, Sieur de: see
F. Parkman, *La Salle and the Discovery of the Great West.*
E. S. Van Zile, *With Sword and Crucifix; Being an Account of the Strange Adventures of Count Louis de Sancerre, Companion of Sieur de la Salle, on the Lower Mississippi in the Year of Grace 1682.*

Last Act: Being the Funeral Rites of Nations and Individuals. W. Tegg.

"Last beam" (hymn): see "Fading, still fading, the last beam is shining" (hymn).

Last Days of Pompeii. E. G. E. B. Lytton.

Last Essays of Elia. C. Lamb.

Last Fairy Tales. É. de Laboulaye.

"Last Leaf" (poem). O. W. Holmes.

"Last link is broken" (song). F. Steers.

Last of the Barons. E. G. E. B. Lytton.

Last of the Mohicans. J. F. Cooper.

Last of the 'Tzins. L. Wallace.

Last Recruit of Clare's; Being Passages from the Memoirs of Anthony Dillon, Chevalier of St. Louis (novel). S. R. Keightley.

"Last Rose of Summer" (poem, song). T. Moore.

"Last rose of summer" (song): see F. von Flotow, *Martha, or the Market at Richmond* (opera).

La Saisiaz: see R. Browning, *Agamemnon, La Saisiaz, Dramatic Idyls, and Jocoseria.*

Last Verses. S. C. Woolsey.

Later Adventures of Wee Macgreegor. J. J. Bell.

Latham, O'Neill (illus.): see H. L. Wilson, *Spenders; A Tale of the Third Generation.*

Latin America: see the Reader's Guide entries for Central America and for South America.

Latin Grammar for Schools and Colleges. A. Harkness.

Latin language: see
A. Harkness, *Latin Grammar for Schools and Colleges.*
R. F. Leighton, *Latin Lessons Adapted to Allen and Greenough's Latin Grammar.*
J. W. Sanborn, *Method of Teaching the Elements of the Latin Language as Employed at Phillips Academy, Exeter, New Hampshire.*
G. A. Simcox, *History of Latin Literature from Ennius to Boethius.*
See also the Reader's Guide entry for Roman Empire.

Latin Lessons Adapted to Allen and Greenough's Latin Grammar. R. F. Leighton.

Latter-Day Poems. W. Cowie.

Latter-day Saints: see *Book of Mormon.*

Laudes Domini: A Selection of Spiritual Songs, Ancient and Modern. C. S. Robinson (comp.).

Laughter: see
W. S. Burgess, *Eternal Laughter and Other Poems.*
S. S. Cox, *Diversions of a Diplomat in Turkey* (Catalog entry).
C. Darwin, *Expression of the Emotions in Men and Animals.*
T. Hobbes, *Leviathan; or the Matter, Forme and Power of a Common Wealth Ecclesiastical and Civil.*
W. D. Howells, *Foregone Conclusion.*
W. D. Howells, *Mouse-Trap. A Farce.*

W. D. Howells, *Their Silver Wedding Journey* (novel).

C. Kingsley, *Charles Kingsley: His Letters and Memories of His Life*.

G. Meredith, *Diana of the Crossways*.

J. W. Riley, Old Soldier's Story" (humorous story).

W. Shakespeare, *Works of Shakespeare* (Catalog entry).

C. D. Warner, "Adirondacks Verified" (essay).

F. M. B. Whitcher, *Widow Bedott Papers* (Catalog entry).

Launen. Neue Sammlung augewählter Skizzen. E. Pötzl.

"Laureate Despair" (essay). M. D. Conway.

Laurel Leaves for Little Folk. M. E. Phillips (ed. and illus.).

Laurence and Eleanor Hutton. L. Hutton.

Lavrof, Petr Alekseevich (pref.): see S. M. Kravchinski, *Underground Russia: Revolutionary Profiles and Sketches from Life*.

Law: see

Blackstone's Commentaries.

J. Campbell, *Lives of the Chief Justices of England*.

G. B. Davis, *Elements of International Law*.

F. T. Hill, *Decisive Battles of the Law; Narrative Studies of Eight Legal Contests Between the Years 1800 and 1886*.

J. S. Jones, *People's Lawyer* (play).

H. D. Labouchère (editor of *Truth: A Weekly Journal*).

G. Mackenzie, *Laws and Customs of Scotland, in Matters Criminal*.

H. W. Scott, *Distinguished American Lawyers, with Their Struggles and Triumphs in the Forum*.

J. H. Trumbull (ed.), *True-Blue Laws of Connecticut and New Haven* (marginalia).

Truth: A Weekly Journal.

P. Vinogradoff, *Roman Law in Mediaeval Europe*.

F. M. A. de Voltaire, "Dialogue entre un plaideur et un avocat."

S. Webster, *Two Treaties of Paris and the Supreme Court*.

C. M. Yonge, *Cameos from English History. The Wars in France* (marginalia).

See also the Reader's Guide entries for Court trials and for Crime.

Lawrence, William Hurd (illus.): see J. B. Cabell, *Chivalry*.

Laws and Customs of Scotland, in Matters Criminal. G. Mackenzie.

Laws of Scientific Hand Reading; A Practical Treatise on the Art Commonly Called Palmistry. W. G. Benham.

Lawson, Sam (literary character): see

H. E. B. Stowe, *Dog's Mission; or, the Story of the Old Avery House. And Other Stories*.

H. E. B. Stowe, *Oldtown Fireside Stories*.

H. E. B. Stowe, *Oldtown Folks*.

Lawson, Thomas William: see F. P. Dunne, *Dissertations by Mr. Dooley* (Catalog entry).

Lawton, Mary (actress): see H. L. É. Lavedan, *Duel* (play).

Lay of the Last Minstrel (poem). W Scott.

Lays of Ancient Rome (poems). T. B. Macaulay.

Lea, Francis J. (British Navy physician): see *Truth: A Weekly Journal*.

Learned Men's English: The Grammarians. G. W. Moon.

Learning to Think. J. Abbott.

Leather-Stocking Tales. J. F. Cooper.

Leaves from Australian Forests (poetry): see H. C. Kendall, *Poems of Henry Clarence Kendall*.

Leaves of Grass. W. Whitman.

Leaves of Grass by Walt Whitman, Including a Fac-simile Autobiography, Variorum Readings of the Poems, and a Department of Gathered Leaves. W. Whitman.

Lebensbeschreibungen berühmter Männer aus den Zeiten der Wiederherstellung der Wissenschaften. C. Meiners.

Lecture agents: see J. B. Pond, *Eccentricities of Genius; Memories of Famous Men and Women of the Platform and Stage*.

Lectures: see

T. Carlyle, *Sartor Resartus and Lectures*.

W. K. Clifford. *Lectures and Essays by the Late William Kingdon Clifford*.

H. Greeley. *Hints Toward Reforms in Lectures, Addresses and Other Writings*.

B. Harte, *Lectures of Bret Harte, Compiled from Various Sources*.

W. Hazlitt, *Lectures on the Literature of the Age of Elizabeth, and Characters of Shakespear's Plays*.

G. Ingersoll (various entries).

W. M. Thackeray, *Thackeray's Lectures. The English Humorists. The Four Georges. Complete in One Volume*.

J. Tyndall, *Sound. A Course of Eight Lectures Delivered at the Royal Institution of Great Britain*.

B. F. Underwood, *Essays and Lectures*.

H. Watterson, *Compromises of Life, and Other Lectures and Addresses, Including Some Observations on Certain Downward Tendencies of Modern Society*.

G. S. Weaver, *Lectures on Mental Science According to the Philosophy of Phrenology*.

See also he Reader's Guide entry for Public speaking.

Lectures and Essays by the Late William Kingdon Clifford. W. K. Clifford.

Lectures on Heroes: see T. Carlyle, *Sartor Resartus and Lectures*.

Lectures on Mental Science According to the Philosophy of Phrenology. G. S. Weaver.

Lectures on the Literature of the Age of Elizabeth, and Characters of Shakespear's Plays. W. Hazlitt.

Leddy in Her Ain Richt: A Brief Romance. M. S. Kelly.

Ledyard, Addie (illus.): see G. A. Baker, *Point-Lace and Diamonds. Poems*.

Lee, Francis Lightfoot: see *Pennsylvania Magazine of History and Biography*.

Lee, Henry (ed.): see F. T. Buckland, *Curiosities of Natural History*.

Lee, J. M. (comp.): see Knife and Fork Club, *Book of the Knife and Fork Club*.

Lee, Robert Edward: see J. Barnes, *Son of Light Horse Harry*.

Lee, S. Adams (co-ed.): see L. Hunt (co-ed.), *Book of the Sonnet*.

"Lee, Vernon" (pseud.): see V. Paget.

Leech, John (illustrator): see G. L. P. B. Du Maurier, *Social Pictorial Satire; Reminiscences and Appreciations of English Illustrators of the Past Generation*.

Leedle Yawcob Strauss (poems). C. F. Adams.

Lees, George Frederic William (trans.), A. F. F. de
Frénilly, *Recollections of Baron de Frénilly, Peer of France
(1768–1828)*.
Left Behind; or, Ten Days a Newsboy. J. O. Kaler.
*Legacy, Being the Life and Remains of John Martin, School-
master and Poet*. J. Martin.
Le Gallienne, Richard: see
(intro.) J. C. Altrocchi, *Poems of a Child; Being Poems
Written Between the Ages of Six and Ten*.
(trans.) Hāfiz, *Odes from the Divan of Hafiz*.
"Legend Beautiful": see "Theologian's Tale"in *Tales of a
Wayside Inn*. H. W. Longfellow.
"Legend of Ai Kanaka" (article): see *Maile Quarterly*.
Legend of Camelot, Pictures and Poems, Etc. G. L. P. B. Du
Maurier.
Legend of Montrose (novel). W. Scott.
"Legend of Rabbi Ben Levi" (poem). H. W. Longfellow.
Legend of the Castle of Drachenfels (poem). J. M. Stewart.
Legend of the Rhine. W. M. Thackeray.
*Legends and Myths of Hawaii: The Fables and Folk-Lore of
a Strange People*. D. Kalakaua.
*Legends, Customs and Social Life of the Seneca Indians of
Western New York*. J. W. Sanborn.
Legends of Florence; Collected from the People. C. G.
Leland.
Legends of Old Testament Characters. S. Baring-Gould.
Legends of the American Revolution. G. Lippard.
Legends of the Birds. C. G. Leland.
Legends of the Flowers. S. Pindar.
Legends of the Rhine. A. H. Bernard.
Legends of the Rhine from Basle to Rotterdam. F. J. Kiefer.
Legouvé, Ernest (co-author), *Bataille de Dames* (play): see
F. Bocher (ed.), *College Series of French Plays*.
Leighton, Frederic: see
J. G. Millais, *Life and Letters of Sir John Everett Millais*.
(illus.): see A. K. Sartoris, *Week in a French
Country-House*.
Leila; or, the Siege of Granada. E. R. B. Lytton.
Leitfaden für den Unterricht in der deutschen Sprache. G.
Heness.
Leland, John (hymn lyrics): see the Catalog entry for G.
J. Geer.
Leloir, Maurice (illus.): see L. Sterne, *Sentimental Journey
Through France and Italy, by Mr. Yorick*.
"Lemon, Don" (pseud.): see C. Nisbet, *Everybody's
Writing-Desk Book*.
Lemon, Mark (ed.): see *Jest Book: The Choicest Anecdotes
and Sayings*.
Leo XIII, Pope: see
H. George, *Condition of Labor. An Open Letter to Pope
Leo XIII*.
B. O'Reilly, *Life of Leo XIII, from an Authentic Memoir
Furnished by His Order*.
*Leopard's Spots: A Romance of the White Man's Bur-
den—1865–1900*. T. Dixon.
Leopold II, King : see
R. W. Gilder, *In the Heights* (Catalog entry).
*Memorial Concerning Conditions in the Independent
State of the Kongo. April 19, 1904* (marginalia).
E. D. Morel, *King Leopold's Rule in Africa*.
W. M. Morrison, "Report by W. M. Morrison,

American Missionary in the Congo Free State"
(unidentified publication).
B. H. Nadal, "A Czar—1905" (poem).
H. L. Samuel (Catalog entry).
E. Schuyler, *Turkistan; Notes of a Journey in Russian
Turkistan, Khokand, Bukhara, and Kuldja* (note laid
in volume).
W. H. Sheppard (Catalog entry).
L. M. Sill, "To the Czar" (poem).
Suetonius, *Lives of the Twelve Caesars* (marginalia).
A. C. Swinburne, *Love's Cross-Currents; A Year's Letters*
(Catalog entry).
H. W. Wack, *Story of the Congo Free State: Social,
Political, and Economic Aspects of the Belgian System
of Government in Central Africa* (marginalia).
See also the Reader's Guide entry for Congo.
Leopold Shakspere. The Poet's Works in Chronological Order.
W. Shakespeare.
Lepers of Molokai. C. W. Stoddard.
Leprosy: see
H. H. Gowen, *Paradise of the Pacific. Sketches of Ha-
waiian Scenery and Life*.
C. W. Stoddard, *Lepers of Molokai*.
Leschetizky, Theodor: see
M. Brée, *Groundwork of the Leschetizky Method*.
F. Chopin, *Pianoforte Werke*.
A. Hullah, *Theodor Leschetizky*.
Leslie, Ernest (composer): see E. A. C. A. Allen, "Rock
Me to Sleep, Mother" (poem, song).
Leslie, John: see C. C. F. Greville, *Greville Memoirs*
(Catalog entry).
Lessons in Love. K. N. Trask.
L'Estrange, Alfred Guy Kingam (ed.): see M. R. Mitford,
*Friendships of Mary Russell Mitford as Recorded in Letters
from Her Literary Correspondents*.
"Lest we forget" (refrain of poem): see R. Kipling, "Re-
cessional" (poem).
"Let dogs delight to bark and bite" (hymn). I. Watts
(hymn better known as "Against quarrelling").
Letter from an Ex-Sailor. T. G. Allen.
"Letter from Billy Patterson Himself" (sketch). W. T.
Porter.
Letter of William E. Channing to J. G. Birney. W. E.
Channing.
Letters: see
J. Adams, *Familiar Letters of John Adams and His Wife
Abigail Adams, During the Revolution*.
E. C. Agassiz (ed.), *Louis Agassiz, His Life and
Correspondence*.
A. V. G. Allen, *Life and Letters of Phillips Brooks*.
W. Beattie, *Life and Letters of Thomas Campbell*.
L. Beecher, *Autobiography, Correspondence, Etc.*
H. B. S. Blaine, *Letters of Mrs. James G. Blaine*.
J. Brown, *Letters of Dr. John Brown, with Letters from
Ruskin, Thackeray, and Others*.
O. G. de Busbecq, *Life and Letters of Ogier Ghiselin de
Busbecq*.
G. G. Byron, *Works of Lord Byron, in Verse and Prose.
Including His Letters*.
T. Carlyle, *Correspondence of Thomas Carlyle and Ralph
Waldo Emerson*.

T. Carlyle, *Letters.*

T. Carlyle (ed.), *Oliver Cromwell's Letters and Speeches.*

M. B. Cheney, *Life and Letters of Horace Bushnell.*

S. C. Coleridge, *Memoir and Letters of Sara Coleridge.*

A. R. Conkling, *Life and Letters of Roscoe Conkling.*

G. W. Curtis, *Early Letters of George Wm. Curtis to John S. Dwight; Brook Farm and Concord.*

C. Darwin, *Life and Letters of Charles Darwin.*

W. J. Dawson (co-ed.), *Great English Letter-Writers, with Introductory Essays and Notes.*

A. Dreyfus, *Lettres d'un Innocent; The Letters of Captain Dreyfus to His Wife.*

L. A. Duff-Gordon, *Letters from Egypt.*

J. B. Elgin, *Letters and Journals of James, Eighth Earl of Elgin.*

G. Eliot, *George Eliot's Life as Related in Her Letters and Journals.*

R. W. Emerson, *Letters and Social Aims.*

J. Evelyn, *Diary and Correspondence of John Evelyn.*

P. H. Fitzgerald, *Life of George the Fourth, Including His Letters and Opinions.*

C. Fox, *Memories of Old Friends, Being Extracts from the Journals and Letters of Caroline Fox.*

G. Henschel, *Personal Recollections of Johannes Brahms.*

S. Hensel, *Mendelssohn Family (1729–1847) from Letters and Journals.*

T. Hood, *Up the Rhine.*

W. D. Howells, *Letters Home* (fictitious letters).

L. Huxley, *Life and Letters of Thomas Henry Huxley.*

S. Johnson, *Letters of Samuel Johnson, LL.D.*

C. Kingsley, *Charles Kingsley: His Letters and Memories of His Life.*

C. Lamb, *Works of Charles Lamb.*

E. Lear, *Letters of Edward Lear.*

R. E. Lee, *Recollections and Letters of General Robert E. Lee, by His Son.*

S. Longfellow (ed.), *Life of Henry Wadsworth Longfellow, with Extracts from his Journals and Correspondence.*

W. C. Macready, *Macready's Reminiscences, and Selections from His Diaries and Letters.*

E. T. Mason (ed.), *British Letters Illustrative of Character and Social Life.*

J. G. Millais, *Life and Letters of Sir John Everett Millais, President of the Royal Academy.*

M. R. Mitford, *Friendships of Mary Russell Mitford as Recorded in Letters from Her Literary Correspondents.*

H., G. von Moltke, *Letters of Field-Marshall Count Helmuth von Moltke to His Mother and His Brothers.*

M. P. W. Montagu, *Letters of Lady Mary Wortley Montagu.*

M. B. de Montaigne, *Works of Michael de Montaigne, Comprising His Essays, Journey into Italy, and Letters.*

H. More, *Letters.*

S. O. Morgan, *Lady Morgan's Memoirs: Autobiography, Diaries and Correspondence.*

G. Morris, *Diary and Letters of Gouverneur Morris.*

J. L. Motley, *Correspondence of John Lothrop Motley.*

A. L. Orr, *Life and Letters of Robert Browning.*

Paston Letters, 1422–1509 A. D.

S. Pepys, *Diary and Correspondence of Samuel Pepys, Esq.*

S. Pepys, *Memoirs of Samuel Pepys, Esq., F.R.S. Comprising His Diary from 1659 to 1669, and a Selection from His Private Correspondence.*

E. L. Pierce, *Memoir and Letters of Charles Sumner.*

Plinius Caecilius Secundus, *Letters of Caius Plinius Caecilius Secundus.*

J. S. Quesné, *Lettres de la Vallée de Montmorency.*

W. Reid, *Memoirs and Correspondence of Lyon Playfair, First Lord Playfair of St. Andrews.*

F. W. Robertson, *Life, Letters, and Addresses of Fredk. W. Robertson.*

H. J. Ross, *Letters from the East by Henry James Ross, 1837–1857.*

J. A. D.-G. Ross, *Three Generations of English Women* (marginalia).

F. B. Sanborn (ed.), *Life and Letters of John Brown, Liberator of Kansas and Martyr of Virginia.*

J. C. F. von Schiller, *Ausgewählte Briefe von Friedrich von Schiller.*

M. de R.- C. Sévigné, *Letters of Madame De Sévigné to Her Daughter and Friends.*

M. F. Somerville, *Personal Recollections, from Early Life to Old Age, of Mary Somerville. With Selections from Her Correspondence.*

R. L. Stevenson, *Letters of Robert Louis Stevenson to His Family and Friends.*

L. Stuart, *Lady Louisa Stuart: Selections from Her Manuscripts.*

G. Ticknor, *Life, Letters, and Journals of George Ticknor.*

S. J. Tilden, *Letters and Literary Memorials of Samuel J. Tilden.*

G. O. Trevelyan, *Life and Letters of Lord Macaulay.*

Victoria, Queen of Great Britain and Ireland, *The Letters of Queen Victoria: A Selection from Her Majesty's Correspondence Between the Years 1837 and 1861.*

F. M. A. de Voltaire, *Letters Concerning the English Nation.*

R. Wagner, *Richard Wagner to Mathilde Wesendonck.*

W. Warden, *Letters Written on Board His Majesty's Ship the Northumberland, and at Saint Helena; in Which the Conduct and Conversations of Napoleon Buonaparte, and His Suite, . . . Are Faithfully Described.*

D. Webster, *Private Correspondence of Daniel Webster.*

O. W. Wight, *Lives and Letters of Abelard and Heloise.*

R. G. Wilberforce (co-author), *Life of the Right Reverend Samuel Wilberforce. . . . With Selections from His Diary and Correspondence.*

See also the *Letters* entries below as well as the Reader's Guide entry for Love letters.

Letters. T. Carlyle.

Letters and Journals of James, Eighth Earl of Elgin. J. B. Elgin.

Letters and Literary Memorials of Samuel J. Tilden. S. J. Tilden.

Letters and Memorials of Jane Welsh Carlyle, Prepared for Publication by Thomas Carlyle. J. B. W. Carlyle.

Letters and Social Aims. R. W. Emerson.

Letters Concerning the English Nation. F. M. A. de Voltaire.

Letters from a Chinese Official. G. L. Dickinson.

Letters from a Self-Made Merchant to His Son; Being the Letters Written by John Graham: see G. T. Richardson, *Letters from a Son to His Self-Made Father* (Catalog entry).

Letters from a Son to His Self-Made Father. G. T. Richardson and W. D. Quint.

Letters from Egypt. L. A. Duff-Gordon.

Letters from the East by Henry James Ross, 1837–1857. H. J. Ross.

Letters Home (fictitious epistolary collection). W. D. Howells.

Letters of a Japanese Schoolboy. W. Irwin.

Letters of Caius Plinius Caecilius Secundus. Plinius Caecilius Secundus.

Letters of Dr. John Brown, with Letters from Ruskin, Thackeray, and Others. J. Brown.

Letters of Edward Lear. E. Lear.

Letters of Field-Marshall Count Helmuth von Moltke to His Mother and His Brothers. H. G. von Moltke.

Letters of Horace Walpole, Earl of Oxford. H. Walpole.

Letters of Jennie Allen to Her Friend Miss Musgrove. G. Donworth.

Letters of Junius. Junius.

Letters of Lady Wortley Montagu. M. P. W. Montagu.

Letters of Madame De Sévigné to Her Daughter and Friends. M. de R.-C. Sévigné.

Letters of Mrs. James G. Blaine. H. B. Blaine.

Letters of Queen Victoria: A Selection from Her Majesty's Correspondence Between the Years 1837 and 1861. Victoria, Queen of Great Britain and Ireland.

Letters of Robert Browning and Elizabeth Barrett Browning 1845–1846. R. Browning and E. B. Browning.

Letters of Robert Louis Stevenson to His Family and Friends. R. L. Stevenson.

Letters on Demonology and Witchcraft, Addressed to J. G. Lockhart, Esq. W. Scott.

Letters, Poems and Selected Prose Writings of David Gray. D. Gray.

Letters to His Son. P. D. Stanhope.

Letters to M. G. and H. G. J. Ruskin.

Letters Written on Board His Majesty's Ship the Northumberland, and at Saint Helena; in Which the Conduct and Conversations of Napoleon Buonaparte, and His Suite, . . . Are Faithfully Described. W. Warden.

"Letter to Hercules Langrishe on the Subject of the Roman Catholics of Ireland." E. Burke.

Letter to Ministers and Elders, on the Sin of Holding Slaves, and the Duty of Immediate Emancipation. J. G. Birney.

Letter-writing guides: see

S. O. Beeton, *Beeton's Complete Letter-Writer.*

W. J. Dawson (co-ed.), *Great English Letter-Writers.*

A. Martine, *Martine's Sensible Letter-Writer; Being a Comprehensive and Complete Guide and Assistant.*

G. Vitali, *Manuel de la Conversation et du style épistolaire.*

"*Lettre de Cachet*"*and Other Stories.* C. Hoyos.

Lettres de la Vallée de Montmorency. J. S. Quesné.

Lettres d'un Innocent; The Letters of Captain Dreyfus to His Wife. A. Dreyfus.

Lettres d'un Voyageur. G. Sand.

Lettres philosophique sur les Anglais: see F. M. A. de Voltaire, *Letters Concerning the English Nation.*

"Let Us to Billiards": see *Prize Essays on "Billiards as an Amusement for all Classes."*

Letzte Reckenburgerin. L. von François.

Leute von Seldwyla. G. Keller.

Levantine Log-Book. J. A. Hart.

Léveillé, Jean Baptiste François (illus.): see A. Le Pileur, *Wonders of the Human Body. From the French.*

Leveridge, Richard (composer): see J. Gay, "Sweet William's Farewell to Black-ey'd Susan" (poem, ballad).

Levering, Albert (illus.): see

J. K. Bangs, *Mrs. Raffles; Being the Adventures of an Amateur Crackswoman.*

J. S. Clouston, *Adventures of M. D'Haricot.*

Levi, Maurice (composer): see H. B. Smith, *Soul Kiss* (musical).

Leviathan; or the Matter, Forme and Power of a Common Wealth Ecclesiastical and Civil. T. Hobbes.

Lewes, George Henry (ed.): see J. W. von Goethe, *Female Characters of Goethe.*

Lewis, Charles Bertrand (pseud. "M. Quad"): see *Current Literture: A Magazine of Record and Review* (marginalia).

Lewis, Charlton Thomas (trans.): see O. E. L. von Bismarck, *Love Letters of Bismarck.*

Lew Wallace: An Autobiography. L. Wallace.

Leyendecker, Joseph Christian (illus.): see G. D. Boylan, *Kiss of Glory.*

Liber Scriptorum: see *First Book of the Authors Club, Liber Scriptorum.*

Liberty: see

C. C. Coffin, *Story of Liberty.*

O. M. Johnson, *In the Name of Liberty.*

Libraries (London): see *Paston Letters, 1422–1509 A. D.*

Libraries (private): see

A. H. Joline, *Diversions of a Book-Lover.*

T. B. Macaulay, *History of England from the Accession of James II* (Catalog entry).

Library of American Literature, from Earliest Settlement to the Present Time. E. C. Stedman (co-ed.) and E. M. H. Cortissoz (co-ed.).

Library of Choice Literature; Prose and Poetry, Selected from the Most Admired Authors. A. R. Spofford and C. Gibbon (co-ed.).

"Library of Literary Hogwash" (Mark Twain's collection): see Volume One (Chapter 9) of this present work.

Library of Universal Adventure by Sea and Land. W. D. Howells (co-ed.).

Library of Wit and Humor, Prose and Poetry, Selected from the Literature of All Times and Nations. A. R. Spofford (co-ed.).

"Lied vom Feldmarschall" (song). E. M. Arndt.

"Lienhardt, August" (pseud.): see B. Wirth.

Lies: see

Bible. English. [1875] (marginalia).

J. Froude, *Thomas Carlyle: A History of the First Forty Years of His Life, 1795–1835* (marginalia).

A. A. Opie, *Illustrations of Lying, in All Its Branches.*

F. Parkman, "Some of the Reasons Against Woman Suffrage" (Catalog entry).

M. Stirner, *Ego and His Own.*

A. Tennyson, *Harold; A Drama* (marginalia).

L. Wallace, *Lew Wallace: An Autobiography* (marginalia).

Life Among the Apaches. J. C. Cremony.

Life and Adventures in the Orient. T. W. Knox.

Life and Adventures of Martin Chuzzlewit. C. Dickens.

Life and Character of . . . Jonathan Edwards. S. Hopkins.

Life and Character of William Taylor Baker. C. H. Baker.

Life and Death in Rebel Prisons: Giving a Complete History of the Inhuman and Barbarous Treatment of Our Brave Soldiers by Rebel Authorities. R. H. Kellogg.

Life and Death of Jeanne d'Arc, Called the Maid. H. Parr.

Life and Habit. S. Butler.

Life and Habits of Wild Animals. D. G. Elliot.

Life and Her Children: Glimpses of Animal Life from the Amoeba to the Insects. A. B. Buckley.

Life and Labor; or Characteristics of Men of Industry, Culture and Genius. S. Smiles.

Life and Letters of Charles Darwin. C. Darwin.

Life and Letters of Charles Lamb: see C. Lamb, *Works of Charles Lamb.*

Life and Letters of Horace Bushnell. M. B. Cheney.

Life and Letters of John Brown. F. B. Sanborn (ed.).

Life and Letters of Lord Macaulay. G. O. Trevelyan.

Life and Letters of Ogier Ghiselin de Busbecq. O. G. de Busbecq.

Life and Letters of Phillips Brooks. A. V. G. Allen.

Life and Letters of Roscoe Conkling. A. R. Conkling.

Life and Letters of Sir John Everett Millais, President of the Royal Academy. J. G. Millais.

Life and Letters of Thomas Campbell. W. Beattie.

Life and Letters of Thomas Henry Huxley. L. Huxley.

Life and Memorable Actions of George Washington. M. L. Weems.

Life and Opinions of Tristram Shandy, Gentleman. L. Sterne.

Life and Strange Surprising Adventures of Robinson Crusoe. D. Defoe.

Life and Times of Aaron Burr. J. Parton.

Life and Times of Niccolò Machiavelli. P. Villari.

Life and Travels of Herodotus in the Fifth Century Before Christ: An Imaginary Biography Founded on Fact. J. T. Wheeler.

Life and Works of Charlotte Brontë and Her Sisters. Charlotte Brontë.

Life for a Life, A Novel. D. M. M. Craik.

Life in California. S. B. Morgan.

Life in Danbury. J. M. Bailey.

Life Is Worth Living, and Other Stories. L. N. Tolstoy.

Life, Letters, and Addresses of Fredk. W. Robertson, M.A., Incumbent of Trinity Chapel, Brighton, 1847–53. F. W. Robertson.

Life, Letters, and Journals of George Ticknor. G. Ticknor.

Life of Abraham Lincoln. W. H. Lamon.

Life of Abraham Lincoln, Drawn from Original Sources. I. M. Tarbell.

Life of Beethoven. L. Nohl.

Life of Benjamin Franklin, Written by Himself. B. Franklin.

Life of Benvenuto Cellini. B. Cellini.

Life of Bishop Matthew Simpson, of the Methodist Episcopal Church. G. R. Crooks.

Life of Charles A. Dana. J. H. Wilson.

Life of Charles Stewart Parnell, 1846–1891. R. B. O'Brien.

Life of Faith; in Three Parts, Embracing Some of the Scriptural Principles or Doctrines of Faith. T. C. Upham.

Life of Field-Marshal His Grace the Duke of Wellington. W. H. Maxwell.

Life of Frances Power Cobbe as Told by Herself. F. P. Cobbe.

Life of Gargantua and Pantagruel: see F. Rabelais, *Works of Francis Rabelais.*

Life of General Nathan Bedford Forrest. J. A. Wyeth.

Life of George the Fourth, Including His Letters and Opinions. P. H. Fitzgerald.

Life of George Washington. W. Irving.

Life of Goethe. G. H. Lewes.

Life of Henry Clay. C. Schurz.

Life of Henry Wadsworth Longfellow, with Extracts from his Journals and Correspondence. S. Longfellow (ed.).

Life of James Williams, Better Known as Professor Jim, for Half a Century Janitor of Trinity College. C. H. Proctor.

Life of Jane Welsh Carlyle. A. E. Ireland.

Life . . . of Jesus Christ. J. R. Seeley.

Life of Jesus, Critically Examined. D. F. Strauss.

Life of Jesus, The Christ. H. W. Beecher.

Life of J. M. W. Turner. P. G. Hamerton.

Life of John Milton. C. Symmons.

Life of John Milton. J. Toland.

Life of John Milton, Narrated in Connexion with the Political, Ecclesiastical, and Literary History of His Time. D. Masson.

Life of John Sterling. T. Carlyle.

Life of Jonathan Swift. Volume the First, 1667–1711. J. Forster.

Life of Leo XIII, from an Authentic Memoir Furnished by His Order. B. O'Reilly.

Life of Liszt. L. Nohl.

Life of Marie Antoinette, Queen of France. C. D. Yonge.

Life of Mark M. Pomeroy. M. E. P. Tucker.

Life of Michael Angelo. H. F. Grimm (co-author).

Life of Napoleon Bonaparte. W. M. Sloane.

Life of Oliver Goldsmith. W. Irving.

Life of Oliver Wendell Holmes. E. E. Brown.

Life of Pasteur. R. Vallery-Radot.

Life of Percy Bysshe Shelley. E. Dowden.

Life of Richard Cobden. J. Morley.

Life of Robert Browning. W. Sharp.

Life of Robert Burns. A. Cunningham.

Life of Sam Houston (The Only Authentic Memoir of Him Ever Published). C. E. Lester.

Life of Samuel Johnson. J. Boswell.

Life of Sir William Wilson Hunter. F. H. B. Skrine.

Life of the Bee. M. Maeterlinck.

Life of the Emperor Frederick. M. M. V. F. L. von Poschinger.

Life of the Hon. William F. Cody, Known as Buffalo Bill. W. F. Cody.

Life of the Right Reverend Samuel Wilberforce. . . . With Selections from His Diary and Correspondence. R. G. Wilberforce (co-author).

Life . . . of the Second Marquis of Worcester. H. Dircks.

Life of the Universe as Conceived by Man from the Earliest Ages to the Present Time. S. A. Arrhenius.

Life of Thomas Bailey Aldrich. F. Greenslet.

Life of Thomas, First Lord Denman, Formerly Lord Chief Justice of England. J. Arnould.

Life of Voltaire. J. Parton.

Life of Wagner. L. Nohl.

Life of William Blake, "Pictor Ignotus." A. Gilchrist.

Life of William H. Seward. F. Bancroft.

Life of W. M. Thackeray. H. C. Merivale and F. T. Marzials.

"Life on the ocean wave" (song). E. Sargent.

"Life's Accolade" (short story by Abby Meguire Roach): see W. D. Howells and H. M. Alden (eds.), *Their Husbands' Wives*.

Life's Common Way (novel). A. E. Trumbull.

Life's Handicap. R. Kipling.

Life's Shop Window. A. S. Cory.

Liffith Lank; or, Lunacy. C. H. Webb.

"Lifted Veil" (novella): see G. Eliot, *Poems*.

"Light" (poem). F. W. Bourdillon.

Lightfoot, Joseph Barber: see G. G. Coulton, *From St. Francis to Dante: Translations from the Chronicle of the Franciscan Salimbene (1221–1288)* (marginalia).

Light in Dends Wood, and Other Stories. T. Dagless.

Light in the Darkness; or, Christianity and Paganism. K. B. Birkeland.

Lightning: see

    W. de Fonvielle, *Thunder and Lightning*.

    C. B. Lewis ("M. Quad," "Demon and the Fury" (sketch).

    R. K. Noyes, *Views of Religion, Collected by Rufus K. Noyes, M. D.* (marginalia).

    J. Tyndall, *Fragments of Science for Unscientific People: A Series of Detached Essays, Lectures, and Reviews*.

    P. Villari, *Life and Times of Niccolò Machiavelli* (marginalia).

    World of Wonders; A Record of Things Wonderful in Nature, Science, and Art.

    F. Zurcher and É. Margollé, *Meteors, Aërolites, Storms, and Atmospheric Phenomena*.

Light of Asia; or, The Great Renunciation. E. Arnold.

"Light of Stars" (poem). H. W. Longfellow.

Light of the Star; A Novel. H. Garland.

Light That Failed. R. Kipling.

Lillie, John (trans.): see C. E. J. G. de V. Rémusat, *Memoirs of Madame de Rémusat, 1802–1808*.

"Lilly Dale" (minstrel song). H. S. Thompson.

"Lily of the valley" (gospel hymn). C. W. Fry.

Limerick Boy; or, Paddy's Mischief. An Original Farce, in One Act (play). J. Pilgrim.

Linche, Paul (composer): see H. B. Smith, *Soul Kiss* (musical).

Lincoln, Abraham: see

    F. Bancroft, *Life of William H. Seward*.

    N. Brooks, "Personal Reminiscences of Lincoln" (essay).

L. E. Chittenden, *Recollections of President Lincoln and His Administration*.

C. C. Coffin, *Abraham Lincoln*.

J. C. Harris, *On the Wing of Occasions; Being the Authorized Version of Certain Curious Episodes of the Late Civil War, Including the Hitherto Suppressed Narrative of the Kidnapping of President Lincoln*.

W. H. Lamon. *Life of Abraham Lincoln*.

T. Malory, *Morte Darthur* (Catalog entry).

C. Marlowe, *Hero and Leander* (Catalog entry).

Old Abe's Jokes; Fresh from Abraham's Bosom.

H. W. Scott, *Distinguished American Lawyers*.

W. T. Sherman, *Memoirs of General William T. Sherman. By Himself* (marginalia).

W. O. Stoddard, *Inside the White House in War Times*.

I. M. Tarbell, *Life of Abraham Lincoln, Drawn from Original Sources*.

W. M. Thayer, *Pioneer Boy, and How He Became President*.

W. Willing, "Twenty years ago" (song) (Catalog entry).

Lincoln, George Melville (inscr.): see T. H. H. Caine, *Eternal City*.

Line of Love (novel). J. B. Cabell.

"Lines Composed a Few Miles above Tintern Abbey" (poem). W. Wordsworth.

Lines on the Egyptian Obelisk. B. H. Cutter.

Lin McLean. O. Wister.

Linnaeus, Carolus: see J. Fiske, *Century of Science and Other Essays* (marginalia).

Lion and the Mouse (play). C. Klein.

Lion Hunter of South Africa: Five Years' Adventures in the Far Interior of South Africa, with Notices of the Native Tribes and Savage Animals: see R. G. Gordon-Cumming, *Five Years of a Hunter's Life in the Far Interior of South Africa*.

Liquor: see

    L. Beecher, *Autobiography, Correspondence, Etc.*

    J. C. Harris, "At Teague Poteet's: A Sketch of the Hog Mountain Range" (story).

    Q. H. F. Horace, *Odes* (Catalog entry).

    W. Reid, "Some Southern Reminiscences" (essay).

    F. von Schlegel, *Philosophy of History; in a Course of Lectures, Delivered at Vienna*.

    J. Timbs, *Curiosities of London, Exhibiting the Most Rare and Remarkable Objects of Interest in the Metropolis* (marginalia).

    G. O. Trevelyan, *Life and Letters of Lord Macaulay* (marginalia).

    R. B. Westbrook, *Girard's Will and Girard College Theology* (marginalia).

    S. Woodworth, "Bucket" (song) (Catalog entry).

    T. Wright, *Homes of Other Days: A History of Domestic Manners and Sentiments in England, from the Earliest Known Period to Modern Times*.

    See also the Reader's Guide entries for Addictions, for Bar-Tending, for Drunkenness, and for Temperance literature.

Liszt, Franz: see L. Nohl, *Life of Liszt*.

Literary and Social Silhouettes. H. H. Boyesen.

Literary anecdotes: see I. Disraeli, *Curiosities of Literature*.

Literary Anecdotes and Contemporary Reminisences of Professor Porson and Others. From the Manuscript Papers of the Late E. H. Barker. E. H. Barker.

Literary anthologies: see

K. A. Buchheim, *Materials for German Prose Composition; or, Selections from Modern English Writers.*

Chambers's Cyclopaedia of English Literature: A History, Critical and Biographical, of British and American Authors, with Specimens of Their Writings.

A. R. Spofford and C. Gibbon (ed.), *Library of Choice Literature; Prose and Poetry, Selected from the Most Admired Authors.*

Literary criticism: see the Reader's Guide entry for Literary guides and criticism.

Literary Friends and Acquaintances: A Personal Retrospect of American Authorship. W. D. Howells.

Literary guides and criticism: see

S. A. Allibone, *Critical Dictionary of English Literature and British and American Authors.*

W. Archer, *America To-Day: Observations and Reflections.*

M. Arnold, *Essays in Criticism.*

E. H. Barker, *Literary Anecdotes and Contemporary Reminisences of Professor Porson and Others, From the Manuscript Papers of the Late E. H. Barker.*

A. Birrell, *Obiter Dicta.*

H. H. Breen, *Modern English Literature: Its Blemishes & Defects.*

E. C. Brewer, *Reader's Handbook of Allusions, References, Plots and Stories.*

M. E. Burt, *Literary Landmarks: A Guide to Good Reading for Young People, and Teachers' Assistant.*

Chambers's Cyclopaedia of English Literature: A History, Critical and Biographical, of British and American Authors, with Specimens of Their Writings.

J. F. Clarke, *Memorial and Biographical Sketches.*

F. M. Colby, *Imaginary Obligations.*

D. M. M. Craik, *Studies from Life.*

G. L. Craik, *Manual of English Literature and of the History of the English Language, with Numerous Specimens.*

C. H. Crandall, *Representative Sonnets by American Poets, with an Essay on the Sonnet, Its Nature and History.*

S. M. Crothers, *Gentle Reader.*

Cyclopædia of American Literature, Embracing Personal and Critical Notices of Authors, and Selections from Their Writings.

I. Disraeli, *Curiosities of Literature.*

W. Forsyth, *Novels and Novelists of the Eighteenth Century, in Illustration of the Manners and Morals of the Age.*

H. Garland, "Sanity in Fiction" (article).

H. Hallam, *Introduction to the Literature of Europe in the Fifteenth, Sixteenth, and Seventeenth Centuries.*

W. Hazlitt, *Lectures on the Literature of the Age of Elizabeth, and Characters of Shakespear's Plays.*

O. W. Holmes, *Autocrat of the Breakfast-Table.*

C. F. Horne, *Technique of the Novel: The Elements of the Art, Their Evolution and Present Use.*

W. D. Howells, "American Literature" (column).

W. D. Howells, "Edgar Allan Poe" (essay).

W. D. Howells, "Frank Norris" (essay).

W. D. Howells, *Heroines of Fiction.*

W. D. Howells, "John Hay in Literature" (essay).

W. D. Howells, *Literary Friends and Acquaintances: A Personal Retrospect of American Authorship.*

W. D. Howells, *Literature and Life: Studies.*

W. D. Howells, "Mark Twain" (essay).

W. D. Howells, New Historical Romances" (essay).

W. D. Howells, "Thomas Bailey Aldrich" (essay).

W. D. Howells, "White Mr. Longfellow" (essay).

J. G. Huneker, *Egoists, A Book of Supermen.*

L. Hunt and S. A. Lee (eds.), *Book of the Sonnet.*

W. D. W. Hyde, *Art of Optimism as Taught by Robert Browning.*

H. James, *Nathaniel Hawthorne.*

S. Johnson, *Lives of the Most Eminent Poets.*

A. H. Joline, *Diversions of a Book-Lover.*

F. G. Kitton (comp.), *Dickensiana: A Bibliography of the Literature Relating to Charles Dickens and His Writings.*

S. Lanier, *Shakespeare and His Forerunners: Studies in Elizabethan Poetry and Its Development from Early English.*

J. Lemaître (Catalog entry).

T. R. Lounsbury, *James Fenimore Cooper.*

H. W. Mabie, *William Shakespeare: Poet, Dramatist, and Man.*

J. McCarthy, *Reminiscences.*

R. McWilliam, *Longmans' Handbook of English Literature. Pt. III. From Ben Jonson to Locke.*

B. Matthews, "American Fiction Again" (essay).

B. Matthews, *Aspects of Fiction and Other Ventures in Criticism.*

B. Matthews, "Cervantes, Zola, Kipling & Co." (article).

B. Matthews, "Penalty of Humor" (essay).

B. Matthews, "New Trials for Old Favorites" (article).

B. Matthews, *Parts of Speech: Essays on English.*

M. Mauris, *French Men of Letters.*

F. Parsons, *World's Best Books: A Key to the Treasures of Literature.*

J. Payn, *Some Literary Recollections.*

W. L. Phelps, *Essays on Modern Novelists.*

Reference Catalogue of Current Literature Containing the Full Titles of Books Now in Print and On Sale with the Prices.

A. Repplier, *Essays in Miniature.*

W. Shakespeare, *Mottoes and Aphorisms from Shakespeare. Arranged Alphabetically.*

W. Shakespeare, *Works of Shakespeare* (Catalog entry).

J. Sheffield, *Essay on Poetry.*

J. C. L. S. de Sismondi, *Historical View of the Literature of the South of Europe.*

W. S. Sonnenshein (comp.), *Best Books: A Reader's Guide to the Choice of the Best Available Books (about 50,000) in Every Department of Science, Art, and Literature.*

A. R. Spofford and C. Gibbon (ed.), *Library of Choice Literature; Prose and Poetry, Selected from the Most Admired Authors.*

A. G. Stedman (ed.), "Short Biographies of All Authors Represented in This Work" in *A Library of American Literature from the Earliest Settlement to the Present Time.*

E. C. Stedman (co-ed.), *Library of American Literature, from Earliest Settlement to the Present Time.*

C. W. Stoddard, *Exits and Entrances: A Book of Essays and Sketches.*

H. A. Taine, *History of English Literature. A New Edition.*

A. R. Wallace, William Ramsay, *et al. Progress of the Century.*

C. D. Warner, *Relation of Literature to Life.*

W. Wilson, *Mere Literature, and Other Essays.*

W. Winter, *Old Shrines and Ivy.*

T. Wright, *Homes of Other Days: A History of Domestic Manners and Sentiments in England, from the Earliest Known Period to Modern Times.*

See also the Reader's Guide entries for American drama, for American literature (criticism), and for Theatrical history.

Literary impostors: see the Reader's Guide entries for Disputed authorship cases and for Impostors.

Literary Industries. A Memoir. H. H. Bancroft.

Literary landmarks (American): see

T. B. Aldrich, *Cloth of Gold and Other Poems* (Catalog entry).

F. W. Halsey (ed.), *American Authors and Their Homes: Personal Descriptions & Interviews.*

E. F. Harkins, *Little Pilgrimages Among the Men Who Have Written Famous Books.*

Homes of American Authors, Comprising Anecdotal, Personal, and Descriptive Sketches, by Various Writers.

Literary landmarks (international):

L. Hutton, *Literary Landmarks of Florence.*

L. Hutton, *Literary Landmarks of Rome.*

L. Hutton, *Literary Landmarks of Venice.*

B. E. Martin, *In the Footprints of Charles Lamb.*

Literary Landmarks of Florence. L. Hutton.

Literary Landmarks of Rome. L. Hutton.

Literary Landmarks of Venice. L. Hutton.

Literary Recollections. J. Payn.

Literature and Life: Studies. W. D. Howells.

Literature of American History: A Bibliographical Guide. J. N. Larned (ed.).

Literature of Philanthropy. F. A. R. Goodale (ed.).

Litta-Visconti-Arese, Duchess Janie (trans.): see G. Negri, *Julian the Apostate.*

Little Ann, and Other Poems. J. Taylor and A. T. Gilbert.

"Little Billee" (ballad). W. M. Thackeray.

Little Book of Profitable Tales. E. Field.

Little Boy Pip. P. W. Francis.

Little Brother; and Other Genre-Pictures. F. H. Ludlow.

Little Busybodies; The Life of Crickets, Ants, Bees, Beetles, and Other Busybodies. J. A. Marks.

Littledale, Richard Frederic: see (contr.) *Prayer-Gauge Debate.*

Little Dorrit. C. Dickens.

Little Duke; or, Richard the Fearless (novel). C. M. Yonge.

Little Ferns for Fanny's Little Friends. S. P. W. Parton.

Little Flower Girl, and Other Stories in Verse, by "Robin." G. Dalziel.

Little Folks' History of England. I. C. Knox.

Little Folks in Feathers and Fur, and Others in Neither. H. M. Miller.

Little Foxes. H. E. B. Stowe.

Little Girl Among the Old Masters. W. D. Howells.

Little Knights and Ladies; Verses for Young People. M. E. M. Sangster.

Little Lady—Her Book, for Girls and Boys. A. B. Paine.

Little Lame Prince. D. M. M. Craik.

Little Lives of the Great Saints. J. O'K. Murray.

Little Lord Fauntleroy. F. H. Burnett.

Little Masterpieces of English Poetry, by British and American Authors. H. Van Dyke (ed.).

Little Men: Life at Plumfield with Jo's Boys. L. M. Alcott.

Little Minister. J. M. Barrie.

Little Ned Happy and Flora. G. Smith.

Little Nemo (musical comedy). H. B. Smith.

Little Pedlington and the Pedlingtonians. J. Poole.

Little People of Asia. H. M. Miller.

Little Pilgrimages Among the Men Who Have Written Famous Books. E. F. Harkins.

Little Precious. G. Smith.

Little Pussy Willow. Also, The Minister's Watermelons. H. E. B. Stowe.

Little Shepherd of Kingdom Come. J. Fox, Jr.

Little Sister to the Wilderness; A Novel. L. L. Bell.

Little Son of Sunshine; A Story for Boys and Girls. E. D. Deland.

Little Sunshine's Holiday. D. M. M. Craik.

Little Susy's Little Servants. E. P. Prentiss.

Little Susy's Six Birthdays. E. P. Prentiss.

Little Susy's Six Teachers. E. P. Prentiss.

Little Tour in France. H. James.

"Little Violinist" (story). T. B. Aldrich.

Little White Bird; or, Adventures in Kensington Gardens. J. M. Barrie.

Little Women; or, Meg, Jo, Beth and Amy. L. M. Alcott.

Lives and Criminal Trials of Celebrated Men. D. Jardine.

Lives and Exploits of the Most Noted Highwaymen, Robbers and Murderers, of All Nations, Drawn from the Most Authentic Sources and Brought Down to the Present Time. C. Whitehead.

Lives and Letters of Abelard and Heloise. O. W. Wight.

Lives of John Donne, Henry Wotton, Richd Hooker, George Herbert, &c. I. Walton.

Lives of the Chief Justices of England. J. Campbell.

Lives of the Lord Chancellors and Keepers of the Great Seal of England, from the Earliest Times Till the Reign of Queen Victoria. J. Campbell.

Lives of the Most Eminent English Poets. S. Johnson.

Lives of the Most Excellent Painters, Sculptors, and Architects, from Cimabue to Our Times. G. Vasari.

Lives of the Princesses of England from the Norman Conquest. M. A. E. Green.

Lives of the Queens of England Before the Norman Conquest. M. Hall.

Lives of the Queens of England, from the Norman Conquest; With Anecdotes of Their Courts. A. Strickland.

Lives of the Queens of Scotland and English Princesses

B. M. Van Vorst, *Bagsby's Daughter*.

M. A. A. Ward, *Fenwick's Career* (novel).

C. D. Warner, *Saunterings*.

A. Watson, *Savage Club: A Medley of History, Anecdote, and Reminiscence by Aaron Watson, With a Chapter by Mark Twain*.

H. G. Wells, *When the Sleeper Wakes*.

R. G. White, "London Streets" (article).

W. H. White, *Autobiography of Mark Rutherford, Dissenting Minister* (novel).

C. M. Yonge, *Cameos from English History. The Wars in France* (marginalia).

See also the Reader's Guide entry for English history.

London. C. Knight.

London. A New Edition. W. Besant.

London: A Pilgrimage. P. Doré and B. Jerrold.

London Art Journal (magazine): see *Art Journal*.

London Films. W. D. Howells.

London: Its Celebrated Characters and Remarkable Places. J. H. Jesse.

London, Jack: see (contr.) *Way into Print*.

London Labour and the London Poor. H. Mayhew.

London Lyrics. F. Locker-Lampson.

London Mews. C. A. D. Janvier.

London; or, City Life in the Last Century. W. H. Ainsworth.

London Street Arabs. D. T. Stanley.

"London Streets" (article). R. E. White.

Lone Furrow. W. A. Fraser.

Lone Star. E. P. Lyle.

"Long ago" (song). T. H. Bayly.

"Long Ago" (poem): see B. F. Taylor, "Isle of the Long Ago" (poem).

Long Arm. S. M. Gardenhire.

Long, George (trans.): see Epictetus, *Selection from the Discourses of Epictetus, with the Encheiridion*.

Long Island Farmer's Poems. B. H. Cutter.

Longfellow, Henry Wadsworth: see

(trans.), Dante Alighieri, *The Divine Comedy of Dante Alighieri*.

T. W. S. Higginson, *Cheerful Yesterdays. Contemporaries* (marginalia).

O. W. Holmes, *Autocrat of the Breakfast-Table* (Catalog entry).

W. D. Howells, "White Mr. Longfellow" (essay).

S. Longfellow (ed.), *Life of Henry Wadsworth Longfellow, with Extracts from his Journals and Correspondence*.

Selected Poems, Illustrated.

B. O. Townsend, *Plantation Lays and Other Poems* (marginalia).

H. Van Dyke (ed.), *Little Masterpieces of English Poetry, by British and American Authors*.

W. Winter, *Old Shrines and Ivy*.

W. Winter, *Wanderers: The Poems of William Winter*.

Longfellow's Evangeline with Illustrations by F. O. C. Darley. H. W. Longfellow.

"Longing" (poem). J. R. Lowell.

"Long, long ago" (song): see T. H. Bayly, "Long ago" (song).

Longmans' Handbook of English Literature. Pt. III. From Ben Jonson to Locke. R. McWilliam.

Longpré, Paul de (illus.): see M. S. Gatty, *Parables from Nature*.

Longus: see *Greek Romances of Heliodorus, Longus, and Achilles Tatius*.

Long Vacation Ramble of a London Clerk. T. Hughes.

Long, William Joseph: see *Outlook* (Catalog entry).

"Look at the Clock!" (poem): see the Catalog entry for *Selected Poems, Illustrated*.

Looking Backward, 2000–1887. E. Bellamy.

Lord Beaupré. H. James: see H. James, *Private Life*.

Lord, Chester Sanders (co-ed.), *Speeches at the Lotos Club*.

"Lord, dismiss us with Thy blessing" (hymn). J. Fawcett.

Lord, John (intro.): see J. Froissart, *Chronicles of England, France, Spain, and the Adjoining Countries*.

Lord John Russell. S. J. Reid.

Lord Linlithgow, A Novel. M. Roberts.

Lord Melbourne. H. Dunckley.

Lord Penzance on the Bacon-Shakespeare Controversy. A Judicial Summing-Up. J. P. W. Penzance.

Lord Randolph Churchill. A. P. Primrose.

Lord's Prayer: see T. Long, *Exercitation Concerning the Frequent Use of Our Lord's Prayer in the Publick Worship of God*.

"Lorelei" (song). H. Heine.

"Lorelei" (song): see F. J. Kiefer, *Legends of the Rhine from Basle to Rotterdam*.

Lorna Doone: A Romance of Exmoor. R. D. Blackmore.

Lorna Doone: A Romance of Exmoor: see W. L. Phelps, *Essays on Modern Novelists*.

Lorne, Marquis of: see J. G. Argyll, *Viscount Palmerston, K. G.*

Lost Borders. M. H. Austin.

"Lost child" (minstrel song): see "I hear the hoofs, or the lost child" (minstrel song).

Lost Love. A. C. Ogle.

Lost Opportunity: see L. N. Tolstoy, *Ivan the Fool; or, the Old Devil and the Three Small Devils*.

Lost Tasmanian Race. J. Bonwick.

Lothair. B. Disraeli.

Lothrop, George Parsons (contr.): see N. Hawthorne, *Complete Works of Nathaniel Hawthorne*.

Lotos Club: see

J. Elderkin, *Brief History of the Lotos Club*.

Lotos Leaves.

Speeches at the Lotos Club.

Lottery of Life: A Story of New York (play). J. Brougham.

Lottery of Love (play). A. Daly (adapt.).

"Lotto Portrait of Columbus" (essay). J. C. Van Dyke.

Louis IX (Saint Louis): see *Chronicles of the Crusades; Contemporary Narratives*.

Louis X: see C. M. Yonge, *Parallel History of France and England; Consisting of Outlines and Dates* (marginalia).

Louis XI: see P. de Commynes, *Memoirs of Philip de Commines, Lord of Argenton*.

Louis XIV: see

G. Gualdo Priorato, *History of the Managements of Cardinal Julio Mazarine, Chief Minister of State of the Crown of France*.

C. A. Sainte-Beuve, *Monday-Chats, Selected and Translated from the "Causeries du Lundi."*

L. de R. Saint-Simon, *Memoirs of the Duke of Saint-Simon on the Reign of Louis XIV and the Regency* (marginalia).

Louis XV: see

M. J. B. DuBarry, *Memoirs of Madame DuBarri.*

A. F. F. de Frénilly, *Recollections of Baron de Frénilly, Peer of France (1768-1828)* (marginalia).

W. Kirby, *Golden Dog (Le chien d'or). A Romance of the Days of Louis Quinze in Quebec.*

M. Wagnalls, *Palace of Danger; A Story of La Pompadour.*

Louis XVI: see

A. F. F. de Frénilly, *Recollections of Baron de Frénilly, Peer of France (1768-1828)* (marginalia).

C. de F. d' Hézecques, *Recollections of a Page to the Court of Louis XVI.*

F. M. A. de Voltaire, *Age of Louis XVI.*

C. D. Yonge, *Life of Marie Antoinette, Queen of France.*

Louis Agassiz, His Life and Correspondence. E. C. Agassiz (ed.).

Louise de Keroualle, Duchess of Portsmouth, 1649–1734. H. Forneron.

Louisiana. F. H. Burnett.

Louisiana: see

D. Boucicault, *Octoroon; or, Life in Louisiana* (play).

A. M. Buckner, *Towards the Gulf; A Romance of Louisiana.*

F. H. Burnett, *Louisiana.*

G. W. Cable, *Old Creole Days.*

G. W. Cable, *Strange True Stories of Louisiana.*

M. Reid, *Quadroon; or, A Lover's Adventures in Louisiana.*

R. M. Stuart, *Story of Babette, A Little Creole Girl.*

B. Taylor, *Visit to India, China, and Japan, in the Year 1853* (Catalog entry).

R. Taylor, *Destruction and Reconstruction: Personal Experiences of the Late War.*

C. D. Warner, *Studies in the South and West, with Comments on Canada.*

Louis Philippe: see J. S. C. Abbott, *History of Louis Philippe, King of the French.*

Lourdes. É. Zola.

"Love" (poem). W. W. Campbell.

Loveable Tales of Janey and Josey and Joe. G. Smith.

Love Affairs of an Old Maid. L. L. Bell.

Love Among the Gamins, and Other Poems. D. L. Proudfit.

Love Among the Mistletoe and Poems. J. B. Elmore.

Love and Parentage, Applied to the Improvement of Offspring, Including Important Directions and Suggestions to Lovers and the Married. O. S. Fowler.

Love and Spring: Selections from the "Kokinshū." H. Saito.

"Love Came at Dawn" (poem). W. W. Campbell.

Love Chase (play). O. S. Clemens.

Love Epistles of Aristaenetus: see S. Propertius, *Erotica.*

Love-in-a-Mist. P. Wheeler.

Love in Chief. A Novel. R. K. Weekes.

Love in Idleness: A Tale of Bar Harbor. F. M. Crawford.

Love in Letters; Illustrated in the Correspondence of Eminent Persons; with Biographical Sketches of the Writers. J. G. Wilson (ed.).

Lovejoy, Elijah Parish: see .

C. Lovejoy and O. Lovejoy, *Memoir of the Rev. Elijah P. Lovejoy, Who Was Murdered in Defence of the Liberty of the Press.*

F. Marryat, *Second Series of a Diary in America.*

Lovejoy, Owen (co-author): see J. C. Lovejoy and O. Lovejoy, *Memoir of the Rev. Elijah P. Lovejoy, Who Was Murdered in Defence of the Liberty of the Press.*

Love Letters:

A. A. Behn, *Love-Letters Between a Nobleman and His Sister* (fictional epistolary novel).

O. E. L. von Bismarck, *Love Letters of Bismarck; Being Letters to His Fiancée and Wife, 1846–1889.*

J. Hawthorne, *Nathaniel Hawthorne and His Wife, A Biography.*

D. O. Temple, *Love Letters of Dorothy Osborne to Sir William Temple.*

J. G. Wilson (ed.), *Love in Letters; Illustrated in the Correspondence of Eminent Persons; with Biographical Sketches of the Writers.*

See also the Reader's Guide entry for Letters.

Love-Letters Between a Nobleman and His Sister; With the History of Their Adventures. A. A. Behn.

Love Letters of Bismarck; Being Letters to His Fiancée and Wife, 1846–1889. O. E. L. von Bismarck.

Love Letters of Dorothy Osborne to Sir William Temple. D. O. Temple.

"Love Me Little, Love Me Long" (novel). C. Reade.

Love of Monsieur, A Novel. G. F. Gibbs.

Love of Parson Lord, and Other Stories. M. E. W. Freeman.

Lovers of Provence: Aucassin and Nicolette. A. R. Macdonough (trans.).

Love's Cross-Currents; A Year's Letters. A. C. Swinburne.

Loves of Clitopho and Leucippe: see *Greek Romances of Heliodorus, Longus, and Achilles Tatius.*

Loves of the Angels, A Poem. T. Moore.

"Love's Queen" (poem). W. Winter.

Love Watches (play). R. De Flers.

Lowden Sabbath Morn. R. L. Stevenson.

Lowell, James Russell: see

C. C. F. Greville, *Greville Memoirs* (marginalia).

T. W. S. Higginson, *Cheerful Yesterdays. Contemporaries* (marginalia).

(contr.) E. A. Poe, *Works of the Late Edgar Allan Poe.*

G. Ticknor, *Life, Letters, and Journals of George Ticknor* (Catalog entry).

H. C. Wilbur (Catalog entry).

Lowell Lectures on the Ascent of Man. H. Drummond.

Lowell, Orson Byron (illus.): see

F. R. Stockton, *Bicycle of Cathay. A Novel.*

J. Webster, *Jerry Junior.*

Lowell, Percival: see S. G. Bayne, *Pith of Astronomy (Without Mathematics)* (clipping).

Low Tide on Grand Pré. B. Carman.

Loyal Ronins: An Historical Romance, Translated from the Japanese. T. Shunsui.

Loyal Traitor: A Story of the War of 1812. J. Barnes.

Lubbock, John: see M. Maeterlinck, *Life of the Bee* (marginalia).

Lucid Intervals. E. S. Martin.

Lucile. E. R. B. Lytton.

Luck of Roaring Camp, and Other Sketches. B. Harte.

Lucretius (Roman philosophical poet): see T. Paine, *Age of Reason* (Catalog entry).

"Lud og koldt Vand" (short story). R. Watt.

Lullabies: see "Rock-a-bye baby" (nursery lullaby).

Lumley, Arthur (illus.): see M. D. L. Landon, *Saratoga in 1901. Fun, Love, Society & Satire.*

Lunatic at Large; A Novel. J. S. Clouston.

Luther, Martin: see

E. R. Charles, *Chronicles of the Schönberg-Cotta Family.*

C. C. Coffin, *Story of Liberty.*

J. Froude, *Short Studies on Great Subjects.*

J. F. Hurst, *Short History of the Reformation.*

M. Stirner, *Ego and His Own.*

A. D. White, *History of the Warfare of Science with Theology* (Catalog entry).

See also the Reader's Guide entries for Bible. German and for Protestant Reformation.

Luxilla: A Romance. G. E. Miller.

Lvov, Aleksei Fyodorovich (composer): see V. A. Zhukovskiĭy, "Russian national hymn" (anthem).

Lyde, Elsie Leslie (inscr.): see H. Pyle, *Merry Adventures of Robin Hood.*

Lyell, Charles: see J. Fiske, *Century of Science and Other Essays* (marginalia).

Lying: see the Reader's Guide entry for Lies.

Lynching: see

E. A. G. Glasgow, *The Voice of the People* (novel).

R. M. Jonas, "Timed to an African Chant" (poem).

St. Louis *Republican.*

W. T. Sherman, *Memoirs of General William T. Sherman. By Himself* (marginalia about San Francisco).

E. L. Wheeler (Catalog entry).

Lyne, Edward (co-illus.): see W. S. Burgess, *Eternal Laughter and Other Poems.*

Lyon, Isabel Van Kleek: see

C. Darwin, *Journal of Researches into the Natural History and Geology of the Countries Visited During the Voyage of the H.M.S. Beagle Round the World* (marginalia).

W. Shakespeare, *King Lear* (Catalog entry).

Lyrics. C. R. Fabbri.

Lyrics. E. J. P. Nicholson.

Lyrics and Idylls, with Other Poems. E. C. Stedman.

Lyrics and Rhymes. J. Sadler.

Lyrics of Life. J. G. Wilson.

Lyrics of New England, and Other Poems. J. H. Flagg.

Lyriska stämningar (poems). E. E. N. Lundberg.

Lyte, Eliphalet Oram (composer): see J. P. McCaskey (comp.), *Franklin Square Song Collection: Two Hundred Favorite Songs and Hymns.*

Lytton, E. R. B. (co-author): see C. Kingsley, *Favorite Poems.*

Lytton, Lady Constance (appendix): see M. T. Earle, *Pot-Pourri from a Surrey Garden.*

▌M

"Maartens, Maarten" (pseud.): see J. M. W. van der P. Schwartz.

Mabinogion: see T. Bulfinch, *Age of Chivalry; or, Legends of King Arthur.*

Macbeth (play). W. Shakespeare.

Macbeth (play): see P. C. Tacitus, *Works of Tacitus* (marginalia).

McCabe, Joseph (trans.): see E. H. P. A. Haeckel, *Wonders of Life: A Popular Study of Biological Philosophy.*

McCall, John A.: see New York *Times* (Catalog entry).

"McCall, Sidney" (pseud.): see M. M. Fenollosa.

Macaulay, Margaret: see G. O. Trevelyan, *Life and Letters of Lord Macaulay* (marginalia).

Macaulay, Thomas Babington: see

C. Fox, *Memories of Old Friends.*

T. W. S. Higginson, *Cheerful Yesterdays. Contemporaries* (marginalia).

G. O. Trevelyan, *Life and Letters of Lord Macaulay* (marginalia).

Macaulay, Zachary: see

T. W. S. Higginson, *Cheerful Yesterdays. Contemporaries* (marginalia).

H. More, *Letters* (Catalog entry).

McClellan, George Brinton: see

K. W. L. F. von Metternich-Winneburg-Beilstein, *Memoirs of Prince Metternich* (Catalog entry).

W. C. Prime, *Tent Life in the Holy Land* (Catalog entry).

McClellan's Own Story: The War for the Union. G. B. McClellan.

"McClintock, G. Ragsdale" (pseud. invented by Mark Twain): see S. W. Royston.

McClumpha, C. F. (co-trans.): see H. K. B. von Moltke, *Essays, Speeches and Memoirs.*

McCosh, Jame: see (contr.) *Prayer-Gauge Debate.*

McCulloch, John (composer): see W. Scott, *Roderick Dhu; or, The Lady of the Lake: Opera Libretto.*

McCullough, John Griffith (ed.): see E. J. Phelps, *Orations and Essays of Edward John Phelps, Diplomat and Statesman.*

McCutcheon, John Tinney (illus.): see

G. Ade, *People You Know.*

G. Ade, *Pink Marsh. A Story of the Streets and Town.*

Macdonald, George E. (editor): see *Truth Seeker* (magazine).

MacDonald, William (co-author): see T. W. S. Higginson, *History of the United States from 986 to 1905.*

McDonald, William Jesse: see A. B. Paine, *Captain Bill McDonald, Texas Ranger. A Story of Frontier Reform.*

MacDonell, John: see W. McLennan, *Spanish John; Being a Memoir, Now First Published in Complete Form, of the Early Life and Adventures of Colonel John McDonell.*

McDougall, Walter Hugh (illus.): see W. Peck, *Golden Age of Patents: A Parody of Yankee Inventiveness.*

Macdowall, M. W. (trans.): see K. E. Franzos, *Jews of Barnow.*

McDowell, Ephraim: see M. Y. Ridenbaugh, *Biography of Ephraim McDowell, M. D., "The Father of Ovariotomy."*

McDowell, Joseph: see *Biography of Ephraim McDowell, M. D., "The Father of Ovariotomy."* (Catalog entry).

McElrath, Frances (co-author): see *Adventures with Indians*.

McFall, Frances Elizabeth Clarke: see Sarah Grand (pseud.).

McGlasson, Eva Wilder: see E. W. M. Brodhead.

McGranahan, J. (co-ed.): see P. P. Bliss, *Gospel Hymns Consolidated*.

McGuffey's Eclectic Readers. W. H. McGuffey.

Mackay, Charles: see O. W. Holmes, "A Good Time Going!" (poem).

Mackay, George Robert Aberigh: see G. R. Aberigh-Mackay.

McKinley, William: see
    R. A. Alger, *Spanish-American War* (Catalog entry).
    T. G. Allen, *Letter from an Ex-Sailor and Ex-Tramp* (marginalia).
    F. M. Colby, *Imaginary Obligations* (marginalia).
    H. P. Willis, *Our Philippine Problem; A Study of American Colonial Policy* (marginalia).

Mackinnon, Hamilton Nisbet Crawford (ed.): see M. A. H. Clarke, *Austral Edition of the Selected Works of Marcus Clarke*.

McLaren, Elizabeth T. (intro.): see J. Brown, *Letters of Dr. John Brown*.

"Maclaren, Ian" (pseud.): see J. Watson.

McLaughlin, James Fairfax (co-author): see D. B. Lucas, *Fisher Ames-Henry Clay, Etc.*

Maclean, George (ed.): see Bible. English 1874, *New Illustrated Bible for the Young*.

McLean, Sarah Pratt.: see S. P. M. Greene.

Maclise, Daniel (illus.): see F. S. Mahony, *Reliques of Father Prout*.

MacManus, Seumas (ed.): see A. J. MacManus, *Four Winds of Eirinn* (poems).

MacPeever Wrangles. A. P. MacDonald.

Macready's Reminiscences, and Selections from His Diaries and Letters. W. C. Macready.

McVickar, Harry Whitney (illus.): see
    The Cid.
    H. James, *International Episode*.
    Pastels in Prose. From the French.
    C. D. Warner, *As We Were Saying* (essays).

Mabie, Hamilton Wright (ed.): see *Outlook* (Catalog entry).

"Machiavelli" (review). W. D. Howells.

Machiavelli and the Modern State: Chapters on His "Prince," His Use of History and His Idea of Morals. L. Dyer.

Machiavelli, Niccolò: see
    L. Dyer, *Machiavelli and the Modern State: Chapters on His "Prince," His Use of History and His Idea of Morals*.
    W. D. Howells, ["Machiavelli,"] (book review).
    P. Villari, *Life and Times of Niccolò Machiavelli*.

Macy, John Albert: see
    W. S. Booth, *Some Acrostic Signatures of Francis Bacon*.
    G. G. Greenwood, *Shakespeare Problem Restated*.
    (contr.) H. Keller, *Story of My Life*.

Madagascar: see
    W. Ellis, *Three Visits to Madagascar During the Years 1853–1854-1856*.

W. M. Thackeray, "Little Billee" (ballad).

Madame Bovary: Provincial Manners. G. Flaubert.

"Madame Butterfly": see J. L. Long, *Madame Butterfly*.

Madame Delphine. G. W. Cable.

Madame Gosselin (novel). L. Ulbach.

Madame How and Lady Why; or, First Lessons in Earth Lore for Children. C. Kingsley.

Madame La Tour. C. Paddock.

Madame Thérèse; or, The Volunteers of '92. É. Erckmann and A. Chatrian.

Madcap Violet. W. Black.

Madelon; A Novel. M. E. W. Freeman.

Madness of Philip and Other Tales of Childhood. J. D. D. Bacon.

Mad World (play). J. W. Bruner.

Magazines: see
    American Architect and Building News.
    American Miscellany. A Magazine of Complete Stories.
    American Publisher.
    Atlantic Monthly.
    Aurore. Littéraire, artistique, social.
    Blackwood's Magazine.
    Borderland: A Quarterly Review and Index.
    Carpet Bag (Boston): see "Ensign Jehiel Stebbings" (fictional character).
    Century Magazine.
    Christian Union.
    City and State (see the Catalog entry for H. Welsh).
    Collier's Weekly.
    Connecticut Magazine: An Illustrated Monthly.
    Cornhill Magazine.
    Cosmopolitan.
    Critic.
    Current Literature: A Magazine of Record and Review.
    Eclectic Magazine of Foreign Literature, Science, and Art.
    Editor: The Journal of Information for Literary Works (see the Catalog entry for *Way into Print*).
    Ethical World (London).
    Fliegende Blätter.
    Galaxy. An Illustrated Magazine of Entertaining Reading.
    Globe: A Magazine of Literary Record and Criticism.
    Godey's Lady's Book.
    Good Literature.
    Harper's Bazar.
    Harper's Monthly Magazine.
    Harper's Weekly.
    Home-Maker: An Illustrated Monthly Magazine.
    Independent (New York City).
    Knickerbocker; or, New York Monthly Magazine.
    Ladies' Home Journal.
    Life Magazine.
    Literary Digest.
    Literature.
    Littell's Living Age.
    Little Folks: A Magazine for the Young.
    London Art Journal.
    Lords and Commons (London).
    McClure's Magazine.
    Melbourne *Punch*.

Missionary Herald at Home and Abroad (Boston).
Missionary Review of the World.
Munsey's Magazine.
Maile Quarterly.
Nation.
New Princeton Review.
New York Christian Advocate.
Nineteenth Century (London).
North American Review.
Notes and Queries (London).
Old Guard.
Packard's Monthly: The Young Men's Magazine (New York).
Papyrus: A Magazine of Individuality.
Parley's Magazine.
Pennsylvania Magazine of History and Biography.
Pflüger's Archiv für die gesammte Physiologie des Menschen und der Thiere
Popular Science Monthly.
Presbyterian Observer.
Publishers' Weekly: see *Publishers' Trade List Annual, 1907.*
Puck (New York City).
Punch (London).
Railway Age.
Review of Reviews (London).
Revue des deux mondes.
G. P. Rowell, *Forty Years an Advertising Agent.*
St. Nicholas: A Magazine for Boys and Girls.
Sartain's Union Magazine of Literature and Art.
Saturday Review of Politics, Literature, Science and Art (London).
Scientific American.
Scribner's Magazine.
Scribner's Monthly.
Simplicissimus (Munich).
Success Magazine.
Sunday School Times.
Temple Bar: A London Magazine for Town and Country Readers.
T. P.'s Weekly (London).
Travelers Record (Hartford, Connecticut).
Truth: A Weekly Journal (London).
Truth Seeker.
Vanity Fair (New York City).
Waverley Magazine (Boston).
World's Work (New York City).
Youth and Home (New York City).
Youth's Companion; An Illustrated Weekly for Young People and the Family (Boston).
Magellan, Ferdinand: see
   F. A. Ober, *Ferdinand Magellan.*
   T. Wright (ed.), *Early Travels in Palestine* (marginalia).
Magic: see
   A. Assolant, *Fantastic History of the Celebrated Pierrot.*
   J. W. Holden, *Wizard's Wanderings from China to Peru.*
   W. Manning (comp.), *Year-Boke of the Odd Volumes.*
   Secret Out; or, One Thousand Tricks with Cards, and Other Recreations.
   T. Wright, *Narratives of Sorcery and Magic, from the Most Authentic Sources.*

"Magic of a Voice" (story): see W. D. Howells, *Pair of Patient Lovers.*
Magnalia Christi Americana; or, The Ecclesiastical History of New-England. C. Mather.
Magnetic North. E. Robins.
Magyar Songs. Selections from Hungarian Poets. W. N. Loew (trans.).
"Mahon, Lord" (pseud.): see P. H. Stanhope.
Maid. B. W. Howard.
"Maid, A Drama in Five Acts" (typescript of a play). G. Porter.
Maid Ellice. D. H. H. Boulger.
Maidment, J. (co-ed.): see *Dramatists of the Restoration.*
Maid of France, Being the Story of the Life and Death of Jeanne d'Arc. A. Lang.
Maid of Killeena. W. Black.
Maid of Orleans (play): see J. C. F. von Schiller, *Jungfrau von Orleans* (play).
Maile Wreath (magazine): see *Maile Quarterly.*
Main, Hubert Platt (composer): see M. A. L. Demarest, "My ain countrie" (poem, hymn).
Maine: see
   S. E. S. Boggs, *Sandpeep.*
   F. M. Crawford, *Love in Idleness: A Tale of Bar Harbor.*
   H. F. Day, *Eagle Badge; or, The Skokums of the Allagash.*
   H. F. Day, *King Spruce; A Novel.*
   S. A. Drake, *Heart of the White Mountains, Their Legend and Scenery.*
   F. H. Eckstorm, *Penobscot Man.*
   C. W. Eliot, *John Gilley, Maine Farmer and Fisherman.*
   F. K. Gifford, *Belle Islers; A Novel.*
   R. Herrick (Catalog entry).
   S. O. Jewett, *Queen's Twin, and Other Stories.*
   S. O. Jewett, *York Garrison—1640.*
   J. O. Kaler, *Ezra Jordan's Escape from the Massacre at Fort Loyall* (novel).
   S. Smith ("Major Jack Downing," pseud.).
   T. S. Steele, *Canoe and Camera: A Two Hundred Mile Tour Through the Maine Forests.*
   T. S. Steele, *Paddle and Portage, from Moosehead Lake to the Aroostook River, Maine.*
   H. D. Thoreau, *Maine Woods.*
   C. D. Warner, *Their Pilgrimage* (novel).
   G. S. Wasson, *Cap'n Simeon's Store.*
   H. P. Wells, *City Boys in the Woods; or, A Trapping Venture in Maine.*
Maine (ship): see
   J. Fiske, *Century of Science and Other Essays* (marginalia).
   J. Swift, *Gulliver's Travels into Several Remote Nations of the World* (Catalog entry).
Maine Woods. H. D. Thoreau.
Maitland, Caroline: see Dollie Radford (co-ed.)
Major, Charles: see P. Kester, *When Knighthood Was in Flower* (play).
Major Jones's Courtship. W. T. Thompson.
Major Jones's Sketches of Travel. W. T. Thompson.
Majors and Minors: Poems. P. L. Dunbar.
Make Believe. H. D. Lowry.
Makepeace, Emily (trans.): see P. E. de Musset, *Mr. Wind and Madam Rain.*

Maker of History. E. P. Oppenheim.

Makers of Florence: Dante, Giotto, Savonarola, and Their City. M. O. W. Oliphant.

Makers of Moons. R. W. Chambers.

Makers of Venice: Doges, Conquerors, Painters, and Men of Letters. M. O. W. Oliphant.

Making of a Country Home. A. C. Wheeler.

Making of a Journalist. J. Ralph.

Malaysia: see
  A. Ireland, *Far Eastern Tropics: Studies in the Administration of Tropical Dependencies.*
  A. R. Wallace, *Australasia.*

Malbone: An Oldport Romance. T. W. S. Higginson.

Mallarmé, Stéphane: see *Pastels in Prose. From the French.*

Malleus Maleficarum, or Hexenhammer. H. K. Institoris.

Malleville. J. Abbott.

Mallory, John Allan (ed.): see J. Campbell, *Lives of the Lord Chancellors.*

Mam' Linda; A Novel. W. N. Harben.

"Mandalay" (poem). R. Kipling.

Mandeville, (Sir) John: see
  Plinius Secundus, *Natural History of Pliny* (Catalog entry).
  T. Wright (ed.), *Early Travels in Palestine* (marginalia).

Man from America, A Sentimental Comedy. E. B. De La Pasture.

Man from Snowy River and Other Verses. A. B. Paterson.

Man in the Iron Mask: see
  A. Dumas (Catalog entries).
  World of Wonders; A Record of Things Wonderful in Nature, Science, and Art.

"Man in the moon" (song). See J. Thornton, "My sweetheart's the man in the moon" (song).

Man, Isle of: see H. Caine, *Manxman, A Novel.*

Männer eigner Kraft. F. O. Spamer.

Manners and Social Usages. M. E. W. Sherwood.

Manners, Customs, and Dress During the Middle Ages. P. Lacroix.

"Mann, Mrs. Horace" (pseud.): see M. T. P. Mann.

Manning, Marie: see "Prophetess of the Land of No-Smoke" (short story) in W. D. Howells (co-ed.), *Under the Sunset.*

"Man o'Airlie" (song). W. G. Wills (lyrics).

Man o' Airlie: A Drama of the Affections (play). W. G. Wills.

Man of His Age. H. Drummond.

Man of His Time. J. M. Haswell.

Man of Last Resort; or, The Clients of Randolph Mason. M. D. Post.

Man of Sorrows. Being a Little Journey to the Home of Jesus of Nazareth. E. G. Hubbard.

Man of the World (London newspaper): see the London *World* entry.

Mansfield Park. A Novel. J. Austen.

Man's Place in the Universe: A Study of the Results of Scientific Research in Relation to the Unity or Plurality of Worlds. A. R. Wallace.

Man's Progress. G. Iles.

Man, The Social Creator. H. D. Lloyd.

Manual of Conversations, Hawaiian and English. A. Bishop.

Manual of English Literature and of the History of the English Language, with Numerous Specimens. G. L. Craik.

Manual of Mineralogy. J. D. Dana.

Manual of Patriotism, for Use in the Public Schools of the State of New York. C. F. Skinner.

Manual of Phonography; or, Writing by Sound. I. Pitman.

Manual of the Authors Club. Authors Club.

Manual of the Mother Church. M. B. Eddy.

Manuel de la Conversation et du style épistolaire. G. Vitali.

"Man Was Made to Mourn" (poem). R. Burns.

Man Who Laughs. V. M. Hugo.

"Man without a Country" (short story). E. E. Hale.

Man with the Hoe and Other Poems. E. Markham.

Man Wonderful in the House Beautiful: An Allegory Teaching the Principles of Physiology and Hygiene, and the Effects of Stimulants and Narcotics. C. B. Allen and M. A. W. Allen.

Manxman, A Novel. H. Caine.

Many Inventions. R. Kipling.

"Maori, a Pakeha" (pseud.): see F. E. Maning.

Maple Dell of '76. Mrs. O. A. Powers.

Marble Faun, or The Romance of the Monte Beni. N. Hawthorne.

Marcel (novel). M. A. A. Ward.

Marchand, John Norval (illus.): see H. Garland, *Money Magic; A Novel.*

"Marching through Georgia" (song). H. C. Work.

Marching to Victory: The Second Period of the War of Rebellion. C. C. Coffin.

Mardi Gras (festive holiday): see
  Puck (New York City magazine) (Catalog entry).
  Punch (London magazine) (Catalog entry).

Marduk (God of ancient Babylonia): see T. W. Doane, *Bible Myths and Their Parallels in Other Religions* (marginalia).

"Mare Rubrum" (poem). O. W. Holmes.

Margaret, An Idyll. G. M. Acklom.

Margaret. A Tale of the Real and the Ideal, Blight and Bloom. S. Judd.

Margaret Maitland of Sunnyside. M. O. W. Oliphant.

Margaret of Anjou: see J. S. C. Abbott, *History of Margaret of Anjou.*

Margarete. M. F. Ebner von Eschenbach.

Margaret Vincent, A Novel. L. L. Clifford.

Marginalia (Clemens's habit): see O. W. Holmes, *Autocrat of the Breakfast-Table* (Catalog entry).

Margollé, Élie (co-author): see F. Zurcher, *Meteors, Aërolites, Storms, and Atmospheric Phenomena.*

Margravine of Bayreuth: see F. S. Wilhelmina.

Marguerte de Valois. A. Dumas, *Novels.*

"Mariana" (poem). A. Tennyson.

Maria Stuart: ein Trauerspiel (play). J. C. F. von Schiller.

Marie, Adrien (illus.): see A. J. Church, *Two Thousand Years Ago; or, The Adventures of a Roman Boy.*

Marie Antoinette: see
  J. S. C. Abbott, *History of Marie Antoinette.*
  J. L. H. Campan, *Mémoires sur la Vie Privée de Marie Antoinette.*

I. de Saint-Amand, *Marie Antoinette at the Tuileries, 1789–1791*.

C. D. Yonge, *Life of Marie Antoinette, Queen of France*.

Marie Bashkirtseff; The Journal of a Young Artist. M. K. Bashkirtseva.

Marie Celeste (ship): see London *Illustrated News*.

Marion County, Missouri: see R. I. Holcombe, *History of Marion County, Missouri*.

"Marion, Fulgence" (pseud.): see N. C. Flammarion.

Marital advice: see

J. B. Brown, *Home Life, in the Light of Its Divine Idea*.

M. A. Dodge, *Stumbling-Blocks*.

O. S. Fowler, *Love and Parentage, Applied to the Improvement of Offspring, Including Important Directions and Suggestions to Lovers and the Married*.

C. K. D. Patmore, *Angel in the House*.

W. Pulitzer, *Cozy Corner Confidences*.

A. M. Roach, *Some Successful Marriages*.

F. E. Wadleigh, *'Twixt Wave and Sky* (novel).

S. R. Wells, *Wedlock; or, the Right Relation of the Sexes; Disclosing the Laws of Conjugal Selection, and Showing Who May, and Who May Not Marry*.

Maritana (opera). E. Fitzball.

Marius; or, The Son of the Revolution. V. M. Hugo.

Marjorie. J. H. McCarthy.

Marjorie Daw and Other People. T. B. Aldrich.

Marjorie Fleming, A Sketch. J. Brown.

Marjorie Fleming: The Story of Pet Marjorie, Together with Her Journals and Her Letters. L. Macbean and J. Brown.

Market for an Impulse. A Novel. W. W. Tufts.

Markham, Richard (ed., intro.): see *The Cid*.

Mark Heffron. A Novel. A. W. Bailey.

Mark Rutherford's Deliverance; Being the Second Part of His Autobiography. W. H. White.

"Mark Twain" (pseud.): see the Reader's Guide entries for Dedications to Mark Twain, for Samuel Langhorne Clemens, and for "Twain, Mark."

"Mark Twain and His Recent Works" (essay). F. R. Stockton.

"Mark Twain (A Nocturne of the Mississippi)" (poem). C. Stern.

Mark Twain Birthday Book. E. A. O. Somerville.

"Marlitt, Eugenie" (pseud.): see E. John.

"Marlow, Sidney" (pseud.): see P. H. Coggins.

Marlowe, Christopher (playwright): see "Gettysburg Address" (Catalog entry).

Marmion, Shakerley: see *Dramatists of the Restoration*.

Marquis of Salisbury. H. D. Traill.

Marriage: see

L. M. Alcott, *Moods*.

A. M. A. Aníchkova, *Shadow of the House*.

M. H. Austin, *Santa Lucia, A Common Story*.

L. Becke, *By Reef and Palm*.

E. C. Brewster, *Dictionary of Miracles: Imitative, Realistic, and Dogmatic, with Illustrations* (marginalia).

M. D. Conway, *Autobiography: Memories and Experiences of Moncure Daniel Conway* (marginalia).

J. A. D.-G. Ross, *Three Generations of English Women* (marginalia).

A. M. C. Seemüller, *Emily Chester. A Novel*.

J. C. Snaith, *Broke of Covenden*.

E. C. Stedman, *Poetical Works of Edmund Clarence Stedman*.

F. Thompson, *Shelley* (marginalia).

L. J. Velazquez, *Woman in Battle: A Narrative of the Exploits, Adventures, and Travels of Madame Loreta Janeta Velazquez, Otherwise Known as Lieutenant Harry T. Buford, Confederate States Army*.

J. G. Wood, *Uncivilized Races; or, Natural History of Man* (marginalia).

Marriage advice: see the Reader's Guide entry for Marital advice.

Marriage of Figaro (opera): see J. C. Mozart, *Nozze di Figaro*.

Marriage of William Ashe. M. A. A. Ward.

"Marriage Question" (short story by Grace Ellery Channing): see W. D. Howells and H. M. Alden (eds.), *Their Husbands' Wives*.

Mars, Antony (co-author): see A. Daly (adapt.), *Lottery of Love*.

Mars, Ethel (illus.): see

G. Smith, *Loveable Tales of Janey and Josey and Joe*.

G. Smith, *Roggie and Reggie Stories*.

G. Smith, *Stories of Peter and Ellen*.

Mars (planet): see H. G. Wells, *War of the Worlds*.

"Marse Chan. A Tale of Old Virginia" (short story): see T. N. Page, *In Old Virginia*.

Marseillaise" (French national anthem). C. J. Rouget de Lisle.

Marsh, Henry (illus.): see C. C. Cook, *House Beautiful: Essays on Beds and Tables, Stools and Candlesticks*.

Marsh, Othniel Charles: see A. D. A. de Brueys, *Avocat Patelin: A Comedy in Three Acts* (marginalia).

Martha, or the Market at Richmond (opera). F. von Flotow.

Martial, Marcus Valerius: see M. V. Martialis.

Martian. G. L. P. B. Du Maurier.

Martin Chuzzlewit. C. Dickens.

"Martin, Edward Winslow" (pseud.): see J. D. McCabe.

Martin, Eliabeth Gilbert (trans.): see I. de Saint-Amand, *Marie Antoinette at the Tuileries, 1789–1791*.

Martin, Frederick (ed.): see *Statesman's Year-Book: Statistical and Historical Annual of the States of the World*.

Martin, Harold (co-author): see *Adventures in Field and Forest*.

Martin Hewitt, Investigator. A. Morrison.

Martin, John (co-illus.): see J. Milton, *Poetical Works of John Milton*.

Martin, Theodore (trans.): see H. Hertz, *King René's Daughter*.

Martin, Violet Florence (co-author): see E. A. Œ. Somerville and V. F. Martin, *Some Recollections of an Irish R.M.*

Martineau, Harriet: see J. Payn, *Some Literary Recollections*.

Martine's Sensible Letter-Writer; Being a Comprehensive and Complete Guide and Assistant. A. Martine.

Martyrdom of an Empress. M. Cunliffe-Owen.

Martyred Fool; A Novel. D. C. Murray.

Martyrs: see the Reader's Guide entry for Religious persecution.

Martyrs of Science; or, The Lives of Galileo, Tycho Brahe, and Kepler. D. Brewster.

"Marvel, Ik" (pseud.): see D. G. Mitchell.

Marvels of Animal Life. C. F. Holder.

Marvels of the New West: A Vivid Portrayal of the Stupendous Marvels in the Vast Wonderland West of the Missouri River. W. M. Thayer.

Marx, Karl: see
 G. Flaubert, *Madame Bovary: Provincial Manners* (Catalog entry).
 W. H. Mallock, *Critical Examination of Socialism.*

"Mary A. Twining" (sketch). A. E. Trumbull.

Mary Erskine. J. Abbott.

"'Mary Gloster'" (poem). R. Kipling.

Maryland: see
 J. R. Randall, *Maryland, My Maryland, and Other Poems.*
 G. A. Townsend, *Tales of the Chesapeake.*

Maryland, My Maryland, and Other Poems. J. R. Randall.

Mary, Queen of Scots. J. Abbott. See also the Catalog entry for J. Abbott, *History of Mary, Queen of Scots.*

"Mary's gone with a Coon" (minstrel song). J. E. Stewart.

Masked Ball (opera): see G. Verdi, *Ballo in Maschero.*

Mason, Lowell (composer): see
 S. F. Adams, "Nearer, my God, to Thee."
 R. Heber, "From Greenland's icy mountains."

Mason, Randolph (fictional character): see the Catalog entry for M. D. Post.

Mason, Robert Lindsay (illus.): see F. M. Savile, *Beyond the Great South Wall: The Secret of the Antarctic.*

Masque of Culture (play). A. E. Trumbull.

Masque of Love (poem). C. E. S. Wood.

"Masque of the Red Death" (short story). E. A. Poe.

Massachusetts: see
 G. W. Curtis, *Early Letters of George Wm. Curtis to John S. Dwight; Brook Farm and Concord.*
 S. S. Gilman, *Mothers in Council.*
 M. A. Green, *Springfield, 1636–1886; History of Town and City.*
 W. D. Howells, "White Mr. Longfellow" (essay).
 J. H. Twichell, *John Winthrop, First Governor of the Massachusetts Colony.*
 L. Whitney, *Burning of the Convent. A Narrative of the Destruction, by a Mob, of the Ursuline School on Mount Benedict, Charlestown, as Remembered by One of the Pupils.*

Massacres of the Mountains: A History of the Indian Wars of the Far West. J. P. Dunn.

"Massa's in de cold, cold ground" (minstrel song). S. C. Foster.

Massenet, Jules (composer): see V. M. Hugo, *Ruy Blas.*

Masson, Frédéric (ed.): see *Art and Letters. An Illustrated Review.*

Masson, Gustave (ed.): see F. P. G. Guizot, *Concise History of France.*

Master; A Novel. I. Zangwill.

Master Builder (play). H. Ibsen.

Masterfolk, Wherein Is Attempted the Unravelling of the Strange Affair of My Lord Wyntwarde of Cavil and Miss Betty Modeyne. H. MacFall.

Master Humphrey's Clock. C. Dickens.

Master of Palmyra. A Dramatic Poem. A. von Wilbrandt.

Master of Palmyra. A Dramatic Poem: see E. A. Poe, "Masque of the Red Death" (short story) (Catalog entry).

Master of Silence. A Romance. I. Bacheller.

Master of Stair. G. M. V. C. Long.

Master of the Magicians. E. S. Phelps and H. D. Ward.

Masterpieces of Flemish Art. M. M. Heaton.

Masters and Masterpieces of Engraving. W. O. Chapin.

Master's Violin. M. Reed.

Mastery Series. T. Prendergast.

Mate of the "Mary Ann"; A Story. S. M. Swett.

"Matet, Lucas" (pseud.): see M. S. L. K. Harrison.

Mather, Cotton: see S. P. Fowler (ed.), *Salem Witchcraft: Comprising More Wonders of the Invisible World, Collected by Robert Calef; and Wonders of the Invisible World, by Cotton Mather.*

Mathews, William (ed., trans.): see C. A. Sainte-Beuve, *Monday-Chats, Selected and Translated from the "Causeries du Lundi."*

Matter-of-Fact Girl, A Novel. D. H. H. Boulger.

Matteson, David Maydole (comp.), *Anayltic Index*: see *American Nation: A History from Original Sources by Associated Scholars.* A. B. Hart (ed.).

Matthews, Brander: see
 (co-intro.): see J. Bernard, *Retrospections of America, 1797–1811.*
 (intro.): see L. Halévy, *Parisian Points of View.*
 New Princeton Review (Catalog entry).
 (co-ed.): see *World's Wit and Humor; An Encyclopedia of the Classic Wit and Humor of All Ages and Nations.*

Matthews, Edith Virginia Brander (trans.): see L. Halévy, *Parisian Points of View.*

Mattos, Alexander Louis Teixeira de (trans.): see M. Leblanc, *Exploits of Arsène Lupin.*

Maud, and Other Poems. A. Tennyson.

"Maud Muller" (poem). J. G. Whittier.

Maude Adams. A. Davies.

Maude, Aylmer (co-trans.): see L. N. Tolstoy, *Teaching of Jesus.*

Maude, Louise (Shanks) (co-trans.): see L. N. Tolstoy, *Teaching of Jesus.*

Maupassant, Guy de: see *Little French Masterpieces.*

Mauritius: see J.-H. B. de Saint-Pierre, *Paul et Virginie.*

Maxim, Hiram Stevens (inventor): see A. D. White, *History of the Warfare of Science with Theology* (Catalog entry).

Max und Moritz. W. Busch.

Maxwell, Mary Elizabeth (Braddon): see M. E. Braddon.

Mayan civilization: see
 J. T. Goodman, *Archaic Maya Inscriptions.*
 F. M. Savile, *Beyond the Great South Wall: The Secret of the Antarctic.*

Maybrick, Michael (composer): see
 E. Thomas, "Warrior bold" (song).
 F. E. Weatherly, "Nancy Lee" (song).

Mayer, Alexander Liezen (illus.): see J. W. von Goethe, *Faust; A Tragedy.*

May Flower, and Miscellaneous Writings. H. E. B. Stowe.

May Iverson—Her Book. E. G. Jordan.

"May, Sophie" (pseud.): see R. S. Clarke.

Mazarin, Jules: see

G. Gualdo Priorato, *History of the Managements of Cardinal Julio Mazarine, Chief Minister of State of the Crown of France.*

C. A. Sainte-Beuve, *Monday-Chats, Selected and Translated from the "Causeries du Lundi."*

Mazeppa (narrative poem). G. G. Byron.

Mazeppa: A Romantic Drama in Three Acts (play). H. M. Milner.

Mazzanovich, L. (co-illus.): see B. Tarkington, *His Own People.*

Meacham, Frank White (arr.): see F. McGlennon, "Bring my boy back again" (song).

Means, John O.: see (intro.) *Prayer-Gauge Debate.*

Mears, William Ellis (illus.): see

J. Barnes. *Son of Light Horse Harry.*

E. D. Deland, *Josephine.*

E. D. Deland, *Little Son of Sunshine; A Story for Boys and Girls.*

S. M. Gardenhire, *Long Arm.*

H. Garland, *Tyranny of the Dark.*

H. E. Rood, *In Camp at Bear Pond.*

Measurements: see the Catalog entry for *Standards of Length.*

Mechanics' and Engineers' Pocket-Book of Tables, Rules, and Formulas Pertaining to Mechanics, Mathematics, and Physics. C. H. Haswell.

Medical advice and subjects: see

S. H. Adams, "Great American Fraud: The Scavengers" (article).

C. B. Allen and M. A. W. Allen, *Man Wonderful in the House Beautiful: An Allegory Teaching the Principles of Physiology and Hygiene, and the Effects of Stimulants and Narcotics.*

L. R. Andrews, *White Peril; or, How I Cured Myself of Consumption at Home.*

Bazar Book of Health.

J. J. Bell, *Jess & Co.* (Clara Clemens's note laid in about the rest-cure).

T. M. Coan, *Ounces of Prevention.*

F. P. Cobbe, *The Peak in Darien, with Some Other Inquiries Touching Concerns of the Soul and the Body.*

G. W. Deeping, *Woman's War; A Novel.*

A. C. Doyle, *Round the Red Lamp; Being Facts and Fancies of Medical Life.*

A. C. Doyle, *Stark Munro Letters; Being a Series of Twelve Letters Written by J. Stark Munro, M. B.*

R. J. Ebbard, *How to Acquire and Strengthen Will-Power. Modern Psycho-Therapy.*

J. A. Froude, *Thomas Carlyle: A History of His Life in London, 1834–1881* (marginalia).

C. G. Gümpel, *Common Salt: its Use and Necessity for the Maintenance of Health and the Prevention of Disease.*

J. C. Gunn, *Gunn's Domestic Medicine, or Poor Man's Friend, in the Hours of Affliction, Pain, and Sickness.*

C. C. Haskell, *Perfect Health: How to Get It and How to Keep It.*

T. W. S. Higginson, *Cheerful Yesterdays. Contemporaries* (marginalia).

O. W. Holmes, "Two Armies" (poem).

R. James, *Medicinal Dictionary.*

D. Jayne, *Jayne's Medical Almanac and Guide to Health.*

J. C. Jeaffreson, *Book About Doctors.*

E. A. Reynolds-Ball, *Mediterranean Winter Resorts. A Practical Hand-book to the Principal Health and Pleasure Resorts on the Shores of the Mediterranean.*

M. Y. Ridenbaugh, *Biography of Ephraim McDowell, M. D., "The Father of Ovariotomy."*

D. B. S. J. Roosa, *Doctor's Suggestions to the Community, Being a Series of Papers Upon Various Subjects from a Physician's Standpoint.*

F. H. Spearman, *Doctor Bryson, A Novel.*

C. W. Stiles (Catalog entry).

J. H. Trumbull (ed.), *True-Blue Laws of Connecticut and New Haven* (marginalia).

J. Tyndall, *Fragments of Science for Unscientific People: A Series of Detached Essays, Lectures, and Reviews.*

F. Van Eeden, "Curing by Suggestion" (article).

A. R. Wallace, William Ramsay, *et al. Progress of the Century.*

W. Warden, *Letters Written on Board His Majesty's Ship the Northumberland, and at Saint Helena* (marginalia).

F. S. Wilhelmina, *Memoirs of Wilhelmine, Margravine of Baireuth* (marginalia).

H. S. Williams, *Story of Nineteenth-Century Science.*

K. Winslow (ed.), *Home Medical Library.*

See also the Reader's Guide entry for Health, fitness, and hygiene.

Medicinal Dictionary. R. James.

Medical dictionaries: see Medical advice and subjects.

Médicin de campagne: see H. de Balzac, *Country Doctor.*

Medieval history: see the Reader's Guide entry for Middle Ages.

Medina, Louisa H. (adapt.): see R. M. Bird, *Nick of the Wood.*

Meditations of an Autograph Collector. A. H. Joline.

Meditations on Death and Eternity. J. H. D. Zschokke.

Meditations Poétiques. A. M. L. de Lamartine.

Mediterranean Coast: see

S. G. Bayne, *Fantasy of Mediterranean Travel.*

J. Chambers, *Destiny of Doris; A Travel-Story of Three Continents.*

E. A. Reynolds-Ball, *Mediterranean Winter Resorts.*

C. W. Stoddard, *Cruise Under the Crescent; From Suez to San Marco.*

C. D. Warner, *Roundabout Journey.*

Mediterranean Winter Resorts. A Practical Hand-book to the Principal Health and Pleasure Resorts on the Shores of the Mediterranean. E. A. Reynolds-Ball.

Mediums (spiritual): see the Reader's Guide entries for Parapsychology and for Spiritualism and spiritual healing.

"Mee, Huan" (pseud.): see W. E. Mansfield and C. H. Mansfield.

"Meet me by moonlight " (song). J. A. Wade.

Meg of the Scarlet Foot; A Novel. W. E. Tirebuck.

Meineke, Christopher (composer): see F. D. Hemans, "Bird at sea" (song).

Meisterschaft System: A Short and Practical Method of

Acquiring Complete Fluency in the French Language. R. S. Rosenthal.

Meister von Palmyra: see A. von Wilbrandt, *Master of Palmyra. A Dramatic Poem.*

Melancholy: see the Reader's Guide entry for Depression.

Melancholy Narrative of the Distressful Voyage and the Miraculous Recovery of Captain David Harrison of the Sloop, Peggy. D. Harrison.

Melbourne, Australia: see T. A. Browne, *Old Melbourne Memories.*

Melmoth, William (trans.): see Plinius, *Letters of Caius Plinius Caecilius Secundus.*

Melody of the Twenty-third Psalm. A. B. Warner.

Member for Paris: A Tale of the Second Empire. E. C. G. Murray.

Memoir: *Charles Reade, D. C. L., Dramatist, Novelist, and Journalist. A Memoir.* C. L. Reade and C. Reade.

Memoir and Letters of Charles Sumner. E. L. Pierce.

Memoir and Letters of Sara Coleridge. S. C. Coleridge.

Mémoires de Jacques Casanova de Seingalt, Écrits par lui-même. G. Casanova de Seingalt.

Mémoires du Comte de Gramont. A. Hamilton.

Mémoires du General Bon de Marbot. J. B. A. M. de Marbot.

Mémoires pour servir à la vie de M. de Voltaire, écrits par lui-même. F. M. A. de Voltaire.

Mémoires sur la Vie Privée de Marie Antoinette. J. L. H. Campan.

Memoir of John A. Dahlgren, Rear-Admiral United States Navy, by His Widow. M. V. Dahlgren.

Memoir of Mary Ann Hooker. L. H. H. Sigourney.

Memoir of Mrs. Ann H. Judson, Late Missionary to Burmah, Including a History of the American Baptist Mission in theBurman Empire. J. D. Knowles.

Memoir of Ralph Waldo Emerson. J. E. Cabot.

Memoir of the Life of Laurence Oliphant and of Alice Oliphant, His Wife. M. O. W. Oliphant.

Memoir of the Rev. Elijah P. Lovejoy, Who Was Murdered in Defence of the Liberty of the Press. J. C. Lovejoy and O. Lovejoy.

Memoirs:

  M. Fuller, *Memoirs of Margaret Fuller Ossoli.*

  U. S. Grant, *Personal Memoirs of U. S. Grant.*

  C. C. F. Greville, *Greville Memoirs; A Journal of the Reigns of King George IV. and King William IV.* (marginalia).

  H., G. von Moltke, *Essays, Speeches and Memoirs.*

  S. O. Morgan, *Lady Morgan's Memoirs: Autobiography, Diaries and Correspondence.*

  P. H. Sheridan, *Personal Memoirs of P. H. Sheridan, General, United States Army.*

  L. Stuart, *Lady Louisa Stuart: Selections from Her Manuscripts.*

  See also the Reader's Guide entries for Autobiographies, for Biographies, for Diaries, and for Journals.

Memoirs and Correspondence of Lyon Playfair, First Lord Playfair of St. Andrews. W. Reid.

Memoirs of a Baby. J. D. D. Bacon.

Memoirs of a Physician: see A. Dumas, *Novels.*

Memoirs of a Russian Governor. S. D. Urusov.

Memoirs of Barras, Member of the Directorate. P. F. J. N. Barras.

Memoirs of Barry Lyndon. Esq. W. M. Thackeray.

Memoirs of Benvenuto Cellini. B. Cellini.

Memoirs of Celebrated Characters. A. M. L. de Lamartine.

Memoirs of Extraordinary Popular Delusions. C. Mackay.

Memoirs of Frederica Sophia Wilhelmina, Princess Royal of Prussia, Margravine of Baireuth. F. S. Wilhelmina.

Memoirs of General William T. Sherman. By Himself. W. T. Sherman.

Memoirs of General W. T. Sherman, Written by Himself. W. T. Sherman.

Memoirs of George the Fourth, Descriptive of the Most Interesting Scenes of His Private and Public Life. R. Huish.

Memoirs of Hans Hendrik, The Arctic Traveller (marginalia). H. Hendrik.

Memoirs of John Adams Dix. M. Dix (comp.).

Memoirs of Madame de Rémusat, 1802–1808. C. É. J. G. de V. Rémusat.

Memoirs of Madame DuBarri. M. J. B. DuBarry.

Memoirs of M. de Blowitz. M. de Blowitz.

Memoirs of Mme. Desbordes-Valmore. C. A. Sainte-Beuve.

Memoirs of Mrs. Joanna Bethune. G. W. Bethune.

Memoirs of Napoleon Bonaparte: see L. A. F. de Bourrienne.

Memoirs of Philip de Commines, Lord of Argenton. P. de Commynes.

Memoirs of Prince Metternich. K. W. L. F. von Metternich-Winneburg-Beilstein.

Memoirs of Samuel Pepys, Esq., F.R.S. Comprising His Diary from 1659 to 1669, and a Selection from His Private Correspondence. S. Pepys.

Memoirs of Shelley. T. L. Peacock.

Memoirs of Sherlock Holmes: see the Catalog entry for Arthur Conan Doyle.

Memoirs of the Court of King James the First. L. Aikin.

Memoirs of the Court of Queen Elizabeth. L. Aikin.

Memoirs of the Duke of Saint-Simon on the Reign of Louis XIV and the Regency. L. de R. Saint-Simon.

Memoirs of the Loves of the Poets. Biographical Sketches of Women Celebrated in Ancient and Modern Poetry. A. B. M. Jameson.

Memoirs of Wilhelmine, Margravine of Baireuth. F. S. Wilhelmina.

"Memorabilia" (poem). R. Browning.

Memorable Days in America. W. Faux.

Memorial and Biographical Sketches. J. F. Clarke.

Memorial History of Hartford County. J. H. Trumbull.

Memorial of the Fuuehgurh Mission. J. J. Walsh.

Memorials. J. B. W. Carlyle.

Memorials of a Quiet Life. A. J. C. Hare.

Memories of a Rear-Admiral Who Has Served for More than Half a Century in the Navy of the United States. S. R. Franklin.

Memories of Old Friends, Being Extracts from the Journals and Letters of Caroline Fox. C. Fox.

Memory: see M. D. Larrowe, *Physiological Memory; or, The Instantaneous Art of Never Forgetting.*

Memphis, Tennessee: see

  E. von Hesse-Wartegg, *Mississippi-Fahrten: Reisebilter aus dem amerikanischen Süden (1879–1880).*

C. D. Stewart, *Fugitive Blacksmith* (novel).
F. M. Trollope, *Domestic Manners of the Americans* (marginalia).
C. D. Warner, *Studies in the South and West, with Comments on Canada.*
Men and Manners in America. T. Hamilton.
Men and Memories: Personal Reminiscences by John Russell Young. J. R. Young.
Men and Women (poems). R. Browning.
Menasci, Guido (libretto): see P. Mascagni, *Cavalleria Rusticana* (opera).
Mendelssohn Family (1729–1847) from Letters and Journals. S. Henschel.
Mendelssohn, Felix (composer): see
  H. Heine, "Ich wollt' meine Lieb' ergösse sich" (song).
  C. Wesley, "Hark! the herald angels sing" (Christmas carol).
Menken, Adah Isaacs (actress): see H. M. Milner, *Mazeppa: A Romantic Drama* (play).
Men of Iron. H. Pyle.
Men of the Mountain. S. R. Crockett.
Mental health: see
  M. D. Babcock, *Thoughts for Every-Day Living from the Spoken and Written Words of Maltbie Davenport Babcock.*
  O. W. Holmes, *Guardian Angel* (novel).
  W. D. W. Hyde, *Art of Optimism as Taught by Robert Browning.*
  J. Mackaye, *Economy of Happiness.*
  G. S. Meriam, *Living Faith.*
  É. Metchnikoff, *Nature of Man; Studies in Optimistic Philosophy.*
  C. W. Silver, *Secular Anathema on Fakery in Business, Social and Professional Life; or, Twentieth Century Conduct.*
  See also the Reader's Guide entries for Depression (psychological), for Health, fitness, and hygiene, for Inspirational messages, for Mental illness, and for Spiritualism and spiritual healing.
Mental illness: see
  T. B. Aldrich, *Queen of Sheba.*
  C. W. Beers, *Mind That Found Itself; An Autobiography.*
  J. S. Buckingham, *America, Historical, Statistic, and Descriptive.*
  G. Combe, *Notes on the United States of North America, During a Phrenological Visit in 1838–9-40* (Catalog entry).
  R. Kipling, *Phantom 'Rickshaw, and Other Tales.*
  G. White, *Natural History and Antiquities of Selborne* (Catalog entry).
  C. F. Woolson, *Jupiter Lights; A Novel.*
Mental Photographs: An Album for Confessions of Tastes, Habits, and Convictions. R. Saxton (ed.).
Mental telepathy: see the Reader's Guide entry for Telepathy.
Mercedes, and Later Lyrics. T. B. Aldrich.
Merchant of Venice (play). W. Shakespeare.
Merchants' and Planters' Gazette. Port Louis.
Mercury (planet): see C. W. Saleeby, *Cycle of Life According to Modern Science* (marginalia).
Mercy Philbrick's Choice. H. M. F. H. Jackson.

Meredith, George: see
  J. Barrie, *Neither Dorking nor the Abbey* (tribute to Meredith).
  (intro.) L. A. Duff-Gordon, *Letters from Egypt.*
  (intro.) D. S. Shorter *Collected Poems of Dora Sigerson Shorter.*
"Meredith, Owen" (pseud.): see E. R. B. Lytton.
Mere Literature, and Other Essays. W. Wilson.
Mérimée, Prosper: see *Little French Masterpieces.*
Merlette, Auguste Nicolas: see Larive et Fleury (pseud.) in the Catalog.
Merrie England. R. Blatchford.
Merrill, Frank Thayer. (illus.): see L. M. Alcott, *Little Women; or, Meg, Jo, Beth, and Amy.*
Merrill, Stuart (ed., trans.): see *Pastels in Prose. From the French.*
"Merriman, Charles Eustace" (pseud.): see G. T. Richardson and W. D. Quint.
"Merriman, Henry Seton" (pseud.): see H. S. Scott.
Merritt, Wesley (contr.): see *Armies of To-day; A Description of the Armies of the Leading Nations.*
Merry Adventures of Robin Hood of Great Renown, in Nottinghamshire. H. Pyle.
Merry Muses of Caledonia. R. Burns.
Merry Wives of Windsor (play). W. Shakespeare.
Message and Melody; A Book of Verse. R. E. Burton.
Meteors, Aërolites, Storms, and Atmospheric Phenomena. F. Zurcher.
Methodism: see
  J. M. Buckley, *History of Methodism in the United States.*
  P. Cartwright, *Autobiography of Peter Cartwright, the Backwoods Preacher.*
  E. R. Charles, *Diary of Mrs. Kitty Trevylyan; A Story of the Times of Whitefield and the Wesleys.*
  A. J. Cotton, *Cotton's Sketch-Book. Auto-Biographical Sketches of the Life, Labors and Extensive Home Travels of Rev. A. J. Cotton.*
  G. R. Crooks, *Life of Bishop Matthew Simpson, of the Methodist Episcopal Church.*
  J. Wesley, *Collection of Hymns, for the Use of the People Called Methodists.*
Method of Teaching the Elements of the Latin Language as Employed at Phillips Academy, Exeter, New Hampshire. J. W. Sanborn.
Metternich, Pauline: see M. de R.-C. Sévigné, *Letters of Madame De Sévigné to Her Daughter and Friends* (Catalog entry).
Metternich, Richard (ed.): see K. W. L. F. von Metternich-Winneburg-Beilstein, *Memoirs of Prince Metternich.*
Mexico: see
  M. M. Austin, *'Cension. A Sketch from Paso Del Norte.*
  F. C. Baylor, *Juan and Juanita.*
  L. Biart, *Adventures of a Young Naturalist.*
  H. S. Brooks, *Catastrophe in Bohemia, and Other Stories.*
  W. E. Curtis, *Capitals of Spanish America.*
  A. S. Evans, *Our Sister Republic: A Gala Trip Through Tropical Mexico in 1869–70.*

J. Fiske, *Discovery of America, with Some Account of Ancient America and the Spanish Conquest.*

J. T. Goodman, *Archaic Maya Inscriptions* (Catalog entry).

J. N. Jackson, *Winter Holiday in Summer Lands.*

T. A. Janvier, *Aztec Treasure-House; A Romance of Contemporaneous Antiquity.*

T. W. Knox, *Boy Travellers in Mexico.*

F. A. Ober, *Hernándo Cortés.*

W. O. Stoddard, *Red Mustang, A Story of the Mexican Border.*

B. Taylor, *Eldorado; or, Adventures in the Path of Empire; Comprising a Voyage to California via Panama, Life in San Francisco and Monterey, Pictures of the Gold Region, and Experiences of Mexico Travel.*

L. Wallace, *Fair God; or, The Last of the 'Tzins. A Tale of the Conquest of Mexico.*

Meynell, Alice (intro.): see H. C. Greene (trans.), *Gospel of the Childhood of Our Lord Jesus Christ.*

Meynell, Wilfrid (contr.): see F. Thompson, *Shelley.*

Michaelangelo: see H. F. Grimm (co-author), *Life of Michael Angelo.*

Michigan: see
   B. R. Hoover, *Pa Flickinger's Folks.*
   G. E. Lewis, *Heart Echoes.*

"Micromégas: A Comic Romance; Being a Severe Satire Upon the Philosophy, Ignorance and Self-Conceit of Mankind" (short story). F. M. A. de Voltaire.

Middle Ages: see
   C. L. Brace, *Gesta Christi; or, A History of Humane Progress Under Christianity.*
   E. S. Brooks, *Chivalric Days, and the Boys and Girls Who Helped to Make Them.*
   T. Bulfinch, *Age of Chivalry; or Legends of King Arthur.*
   J. B. Cabell, *Chivalry* (novel).
   J. B. Cabell, *Gallantry* (novel).
   J. B. Cabell, *Line of Love* (novel).
   Chronicles of the Crusades; Contemporary Narratives.
   G. G. Coulton, *From St. Francis to Dante: Translations from the Chronicle of the Franciscan Salimbene (1221–1288).*
   G. W. Deeping, *Bertrand of Brittany* (novel).
   C. R. L. Fletcher, *Introductory History of England, from the Earliest Times to the Close of the Middle Ages.*
   Gesta Romanorum.
   G. Z. Gray, *Children's Crusade; An Episode of the Thirteenth Century.*
   J. R. Green, *Short History of the English People* (marginalia).
   H. Hallam, *View of the State of Europe During the Middle Ages.*
   M. H. Hewlett, *Fond Adventures: Tales of the Youth of the World* (fiction).
   M. H. Hewlett, *Forest Lovers, A Romance* (novel).
   Ingulf, *Ingulph's Chronicle of the Abbey of Croyland.*
   J. A. A. J. Jusserand, *English Wayfaring Life in the Middle Ages (XIVth Century).*
   P. Lacombe, *Arms and Armour in Antiquity and the Middle Ages.*
   P. Lacroix, *Arts in the Middle Ages, and at the Period of the Renaissance.*

P. Lacroix, *Manners, Customs, and Dress During the Middle Ages.*

P. Lacroix, *Military and Religious Life in the Middle Ages and at the Period of the Renaissance.*

W. Langland, *Vision Concerning Piers Plowman.*

H. C. Lea, *Historical Sketch of Sacerdotal Celibacy in the Christian Church.*

H. C. Lea, *History of the Inquisition of the Middle Ages.*

H. G. D. Liveing, *Records of Romsey Abbey: An Account of the Benedictine House of Nuns, with Notes on the Parish Church and Town (A. D. 907–1558).*

T. R. Lounsbury, "Scholar of the Twelfth Century."

W. Lübke, *Ecclesiastical Art in Germany During the Middle Ages.*

J. Michelet, *Sorcière: The Witch of the Middle Ages.*

Paston Letters, 1422–1509 A. D.

H. Pyle, *Otto of the Silver Hand* (novel).

C. Reade, *Cloister and the Hearth; or, Maid, Wife, and Widow: A Matter-of-Fact Romance.*

A. Rimmer, *Ancients Streets and Homesteads of England.*

W. H. Rule, *History of the Inquisition from Its Establishment in the Twelfth Century to Its Extinction in the Nineteenth.*

M. Schwob, *Children's Crusade.*

A. Smith, *Edwin of Deira* (poem).

W. Swinton, *Outlines of the World's History, Ancient, Medieval, and Modern.*

P. Vinogradoff, *Roman Law in Mediaeval Europe.*

G. E. Waring, Jr., *Whip and Spur.*

C. M. Yonge, *Landmarks of History.*

See also the Reader's Guide entry for Crusades.

Middle East: see the Reader's Guide entries for Holy Land, for Islam, for Palestine, and for Persian literature.

Middlemarch: A Study of Provincial Life. G. Eliot.

Midge. H. C. Bunner.

Midsummer Fays; or, The Holidays at Woodleigh. S. Pindar.

Midsummer Night's Dream (play). W. Shakespeare.

Mighels, Philip Verrell: see
   (co-author) *Adventures with Indians.*
   (contr.) "Little Pioneer" (short story) in W. D. Howells (co-ed.), *Under the Sunset.*

Mikado (operetta). W. S. Gilbert.

Milan, Italy: see
   W. W. Astor, *Sforza, A Story of Milan.*
   Clari; or, The Maid of Milan (operetta): see J. H. Payne, "Home, sweet home."
   H. Harland, *Cardinal's Snuff-Box* (novel).
   G. M. V. Long, *Viper of Milan: A Romance of Lombardy.*
   M. C. Spenser, *Benefit of the Doubt.*

Miles, Nelson A. (intro.): see *Harper's Pictorial History of the War with Spain.*

Military and Religious Life in the Middle Ages and at the Period of the Renaissance. P. Lacroix.

Military etiquette: see
   A. H. Jomini, *Jomini's Handbook of Military Etiquette. Reglement für die Verheirathung der Officiers.*

Mill, John Stuart: see C. White, *Ecce Femina: An Attempt to Solve the Woman Question. Being an Examination of*

Arguments in Favor of Female Suffrage by John Stuart Mill and Others.

Millais, John Everett: see J. G. Millais, *Life and Letters of Sir John Everett Millais, President of the Royal Academy.*

Millar, Harold Robert (illus.): see E. N. Bland, *Book of Dragons.*

Millennial Dawn. C. T. Russell.

Miller, Cincinnatus Heine: see "Joaquin Miller" (pseud.).

"Miller, Edward Winslow" (pseud.): see J. D. McCabe.

Miller, Joaquin: see

M. D. Conway, *Autobiography: Memories and Experiences of Moncure Daniel Conway* (marginalia).

I. D. Hardy (Catalog entry).

L. B. Leavitt, *Bohemian Society.*

C. W. Stoddard, *Exits and Entrances: A Book of Essays and Sketches.*

A. Trollope, *Autobiography* (Catalog entry).

"Miller, Olive Thorne" (pseud.): see H. M. Miller.

Millet, Francis Davis: see

O. Khayyám, (inscr.) *Rubáiyát of Omar Khayyám in English Verse.*

G. Ticknor, *Life, Letters, and Journals of George Ticknor* (marginalia).

(trans.): see L. N. Tolstoy, *Sebastopol.*

Milliken, Elsie Leslie (Lyde) (inscr.): see H. Pyle, *Merry Adventures of Robin Hood.*

Milman, Henry Hart: see

(contr.) E. Gibbon, *History of the Decline and Fall of the Roman Empire.*

(contr.) T. B. Macaulay, *History of England from the Accession of James II.*

Mill on the Floss. G. Eliot.

Milner, Henry M. *Mazeppa: A Romantic Drama in Three Acts* (play).

Milton, John: see

J. Bunyan, *Pilgrim's Progress* (Catalog entry).

S. Johnson, *Lives of the Most Eminent Poets.*

T. Keightley, *Account of the Life, Opinions, and Writings of John Milton.*

A. Manning, *Deborah's Diary. A Fragment* (novel).

D. Masson *Life of John Milton, Narrated in Connexion with the Political, Ecclesiastical, and Literary History of His Time.*

J. Mitford, *Life of Milton.*

W. Scott, *Lay of the Last Minstrel* (poem) (Catalog entry).

W. Shakespeare, *Works of Shakespeare* (Catalog entry).

C. Symmons, *Life of John Milton.*

H. J. Todd, *Some Account of the Life and Writings of John Milton.*

J. Toland, *Life of John Milton.*

H. Van Dyke (ed.), *Little Masterpieces of English Poetry, by British and American Authors.*

Milton's Paradise Lost. J. Milton.

Mind (journal): see C. W. Silver, *Secular Anathema on Fakery in Business, Social and Professional Life; or, Twentieth Century Conduct.*

Mind cure: see the Reader's Guide entries for Hypnotism and for Spiritualism and spiritual healing.

Mind That Found Itself; An Autobiography. C. W. Beers.

Mine Own People. R. Kipling.

Mining: see

T. B. Aldrich, *Prudence Palfrey. A Novel.*

H. S. Brooks, *Catastrophe in Bohemia, and Other Stories.*

J. W. Bruner, *Free Prisoners: A Story of California Life.*

A. A. Burnham, *Fostina Woodman: The Wonderful Adventurer.*

A. G. Clarke, Jr., *Arickaree Treasure, and Other Brief Tales of Adventurous Montanians.*

T. F. Cronise, *Natural Wealth of California.*

W. Crookes, *Diamonds.*

J. D. Dana, *Manual of Mineralogy, including Observations on Mines.*

R. H. Davis, *Soldiers of Fortune.*

H. R. Haggard, *King Solomon's Mines.*

J. M. Hutchings, *Scenes of Wonder and Curiosity in California.*

R. Keeler, *Gloverson and His Silent Partners.*

Manual of Mineralogy, including Obserations on Mines.

P. V. Mighels, *Bruvver Jim's Baby.*

Mining Life in Wales.

C. K. Munroe, *Derrick Sterling; A Story of the Mines.*

F. H. Smith, *Peter: A Novel of Which He Is Not the Hero* (marginalia).

T. B. H. Stenhouse, *Rocky Mountain Saints: A Full and Complete History of the Mormons, . . . and the Development of the Great Mineral Wealth of the Territory of Utah.*

H. J. Stevens, *Copper Handbook: A Manual of the Copper Industry of the World.*

B. Taylor, *Eldorado; or, Adventures in the Path of Empire; Comprising a Voyage to California via Panama, Life in San Francisco and Monterey, Pictures of the Gold Region, and Experiences of Mexico Travel.*

W. E. Tirebuck, *Meg of the Scarlet Foot; A Novel.*

J. Tyler, *Livingstone Lost and Found; or, Africa and Its Explorers.*

L. J. Velazquez, *Woman in Battle: A Narrative of the Exploits, Adventures, and Travels of Madame Loreta Janeta Velazquez, Otherwise Known as Lieutenant Harry T. Buford, Confederate States Army.*

See also the Reader's Guide entries for California, for Sierra Nevada Mountains, and for Silver mining.

Ministering Children: A Tale Dedicated to Childhood. M. L. Charlesworth.

Minister of Veilby. S. S. Blicher.

Minister's Wooing. H. E. B. Stowe.

Minnesota: see

C. D. W. Brownell, *Indian Races of North and South America.*

E. Eggleston, *Mystery of Metropolisville.*

T. M. Newson, *Indian Legends [of Minnesota Lakes].*

M. C. Russell, *Uncle Dudley's Odd Hours; Being the Vagaries of a Country Editor.*

O. G. Wall, *Recollections of the Sioux Massacre.*

C. D. Warner, *Studies in the South and West, with Comments on Canada.*

Minstrel shows: see

Schermerhorn's Boy (minstrel farce).

A. C. H. Rice, *Mrs. Wiggs of the Cabbage Patch* (Catalog entry).

See also the Reader's Guide entry for Minstrel songs.
Minstrel songs: see
    J. A. Bland, "Oh! Dem golden slippers."
    H. T. Bryant (arranger), "Balm of Gilead."
    "Buffalo gals."
    "Down in Tennessee."
    D. D. Emmett, "Dixie's land (I wish I was in Dixie's land)."
    D. D. Emmett, "Jolly raftsman."
    D. D. Emmett, "Jordan am a hard road to trabbel."
    D. D. Emmett, "Old Dan Tucker."
    S. C. Foster, "Camptown races (Gwine to run all night)."
    S. C. Foster, "Ellen Bayne."
    S. C. Foster, "Massa's in de cold, cold ground."
    S. C. Foster, "My old Kentucky home, good night."
    S. C. Foster, "Nelly Bly."
    S. C. Foster, "Old Black Joe."
    S. C. Foster, "Old Dog Tray."
    S. C. Foster, "Old folks at home."
    "Happy land of Canaan."
    "I don't allow no coons to hurt my feelings."
    "I had an old horse whose name was Methusalem": see
        H. T. Bryant, "Balm of Gilead."
    "I hear the hoofs, or the lost child."
    "Jinny git de hoecake done."
    H. Kennedy, "Cradle's empty, baby's gone."
    "Old Joe."
    E. Sargent, "Life on the ocean wave."
    J. E. Stewart, "Farewell, Annie darling."
    J. E. Stewart, "Mary's gone with a Coon."
    M. D. Sullivan. "Blue Juniata."
    "There is a boarding-house far, far away": see
        D. H. Morrison (comp.), *Treasury of Song for the Home Circle: The Richest, Best-Loved Gems, Sacred and Secular* (marginalia).
        F. B. Ogilvie (comp.), *Two Hundred Old-Time Songs, Containing the Words and Music of the Choicest Gems of the Old and Familiar Songs* (marginalia).
        A. Young, "There is a happy land" (hymn).
    H. S. Thompson, "Lilly Dale."
    J. Warner, "Down in Alabam'" (or "Ain't I glad I got out de wilderness").
    C. White, "Old Bob Ridley."
    W. M. Whitlock (comp.), *Whitlock's Collection of Ethiopian Melodies as Sung with Great Applause by William Whitlock at the Principal Theatres in the United States.*
    T. E. Williams, "Larboard watch."
    A. Young, "There is a boarding-house, far far away" (Billy Rice's comical parody of a hymn, "There is a happy land").
    See also the Reader's Guide entry for Minstrel shows.
Minto, William (ed.): see W. B. Scott, *Autobiographical Notes of the Life of William Bell Scott.*
"Mirabeau: A Play in Five Acts" (play). C. R. Teller.
Mirabeau, Comtesse de (pref.): see A. F. de Bacourt, *Souvenirs of a Diplomat: Private Letters from America.*
Miracles: see

E. C. Brewster, *Dictionary of Miracles: Imitative, Realistic, and Dogmatic, with Illustrations.*
T. Browne (Catalog entry).
S. Clarke, *Mirror or Looking-Glass Both for Saints & Sinners* (marginalia).
G. G. Coulton, *From St. Francis to Dante: Translations from the Chronicle of the Franciscan Salimbene (1221–1288).*
W. Crookes, *Diamonds* (Catalog entry).
M. F. Cusack, *Three Visits to Knock.*
T. W. Doane, *Bible Myths and Their Parallels in Other Religions.*
D. Hume, "Of Miracles" (extract from *Enquiry Concerning Human Understanding*).
J. MacPhilpin, *Apparitions and Miracles at Knock.*
C. Mather, *Magnalia Christi Americana.*
W. H. Neligan, *Rome: Its Churches, Its Charities, and Its Schools.*
W. Paley, *View of the Evidences of Christianity.*
J. W. Sanborn, *Legends, Customs and Social Life of the Seneca Indians of Western New York* (Catalog entry).
W. W. Story, *Roba di Roma.*
D. F. Strauss, *Life of Jesus, Critically Examined.*
Suetonius, *Lives of the Twelve Caesars* (marginalia).
Tacitus, *Works of Tacitus* (marginalia).
J. Tyndall, *Fragments of Science for Unscientific People: A Series of Detached Essays, Lectures, and Reviews.*
G. E. Waring, Jr., *Whip and Spur.*
"Miraculous Pitcher" (short story). N. Hawthorne.
Mirandola, Pico della: see C. Meiners, *Lebensbeschreibungen berühmter Männer aus den Zeiten der Wiederherstellung der Wissenschaften.*
Mirror of the Sea. J. Conrad.
Mirror of the Sinful Soul. Marguerite d'Angoulême.
Mirror or Looking-Glass Both for Saints & Sinners. S. Clarke.
Miscegenation: see the Reader's Guide entry for Racial prejudice.
Miscellaneous Poems. A. Tennyson.
Miscellaneous Writings. M. B. Eddy.
Miscellanies: see the Catalog entry for P. H. Stanhope, *Joan of Arc.*
Miscellanies. W. M. Thackeray.
Misérables: see E. P. Adams, *Story Sermons from Les Misérables.*
Misérables. V. M. Hugo.
Miss Bellard's Inspiration; A Novel. W. D. Howells.
Miss Betty of New York. E. D. Deland.
Miss Brown, A Novel. V. Paget.
Missionaries: see
    W. D. Alexander, *Review of a Pastoral Address by the Right Rev. T. N. Staley, D.D., Reformed Catholic Bishop of Honolulu, Containing a Reply to Some of His Charges Against the American Protestant Mission to the Hawaiian Islands.*
    H. N. Allen, *Things Korean; A Collection of Sketches and Anecdotes, Missionary and Diplomatic.*
    American Church Missionary Register.
    R. Anderson, *Hawaiian Islands: Their Progress and Condition Under Missionary Labors.*

Bible. New Testament. Arabic. 1867. *Arabic New Testament.*

K. B. Birkeland, *Light in the Darkness; or, Christianity and Paganism.*

Reminiscences of a Journey Around the Globe.

J. Chalmers, *Pioneer Life and Work in New Guinea, 1877–1894.*

F. E. Clark, *New Way Around an Old World.*

G. L. Dickinson, *Letters from a Chinese Official; Being an Eastern View of Western Civilization* (marginalia).

Great Religions of the World (marginalia).

R. Heber, "Missionary hymn" ("From Greenland's icy mountains") (hymn).

É. R. Huc, *Recollections of a Journey Through Tartary, Thibet, and China, During the Years 1844, 1845, and 1846.*

J. J. Jarves, *History of the Hawaiian or Sandwich Islands* (Catalog entry).

J. Lubbock, *Ants, Bees, and Wasps: A Record of Observations on the Habits of the Social Hymenoptera* (Catalog entry).

G. Lynch, *War of the Civilisations, Being the Record of a "Foreign Devil's" Experiences with the Allies in China.*

J. D. Knowles, *Memoir of Mrs. Ann H. Judson, Late Missionary to Burmah, Including a History of the American Baptist Mission in the Burman Empire.*

H. Mayhew, *London Labour and the London Poor* (Catalog entry).

A. Michie, *Missionaries in China.*

G. E. Morrison, *Australian in China, Being the Narrative of a Quiet Journey Across China to British Burma.*

W. M. Morrison, "Report by W. M. Morrison, American Missionary in the Congo Free State" (unidentified publication).

New York *Sun* (Catalog entry).

Outlook (Catalog entry).

A. Parker, *Hand-Book of Benares* (Catalog entry).

F. Parkman, *Count Frontenac and New France Under Louis XIV* (marginalia).

F. Parkman, *Jesuits in North America in the Seventeenth Century* (marginalia).

F. Parkman, *Old Régime in Canada* (marginalia).

F. W. Robertson, *Life, Letters, and Addresses of Fredk. W. Robertson, M.A., Incumbent of Trinity Chapel, Brighton, 1847–53.*

M. Russell, *Polynesia; or, An Historical Account of the Principal islands of the South Sea including New Zealand.*

A. E. Scrivener, "Instances of Belgian Cruelty in Africa" (article).

W. H. Sheppard (Catalog entry).

C. W. Silver, *Secular Anathema on Fakery in Business, Social and Professional Life; or, Twentieth Century Conduct.*

E. Talbot, *My People of the Plains.*

W. M. Thomson, *Central Palestine and Phoenicia.*

Two—and an Indian (unidentified book).

J. Tyler, *Livingstone Lost and Found; or, Africa and Its Explorers.*

J. J. Walsh, *Memorial of the Futtehgurh Mission and Her Martyred Missionaries, with Some Remarks on the Mutiny in India.*

A. D. White, *History of the Warfare of Science with Theology* (marginalia).

G. A. Wilcox, *Christian Philanthropist. A Sketch of the Life of Mr. Daniel Hand, and of His Benefaction to the American Missionary Association, for the Education of the Colored People in the Southern States of America.*

F. Wilkinson, *Strength of the Hills; A Novel.*

T. Williams (co-author), *Fiji and the Fijians.*

J. G. Wood, *Uncivilized Races; or, Natural History of Man* (marginalia).

Missionaries in China. A. Michie.

"Missionary hymn." R. Heber.

Missionary Review of the World (magazine): see A. E. Scrivener, "Instances of Belgian Cruelty in Africa" (article).

Missionary Sheriff; Being Incidents in the Life of a Plain Man Who Tried to Do His Duty. A. French.

Mississippi: see

J. G. Baldwin, *Flush Times of Alabama and Mississippi.*

N. Davis, *Wallace Rhodes, A Novel.*

L. C. Pyrnelle, *Diddie, Dumps, and Tot; or, Plantation Child-Life.*

R. Taylor, *Destruction and Reconstruction: Personal Experiences of the Late War.*

F. M. Trollope, *Domestic Manners of the Americans* (marginalia).

Mississippi-Fahrten: Reisebilter aus dem amerikanischen Süden (1879–1880). E. von Hesse-Wartegg.

Mississippi Outlaws and the Detectives. A. Pinkerton.

Mississippi River: see

E. Atkinson (Catalog entry).

D. S. Bacon, *Philosophy of the Plays of Shakspere Unfolded.*

K. H. Brown, *Diane; A Romance of the Icarian Settlement on the Mississippi River.*

J. H. Carter, *Commodore Rollingpin's Humorous Illustrated Almanac.*

J. H. Carter, *Log of Commodore Rollingpin: His Adventures Afloat and Ashore.*

Z. Cramer, *Navigator.*

D. A. Curtis, *Stand Pat; or, Poker Stories from the Mississippi.*

J. A. Dallas, "Up the Mississippi" (article).

C. Dickens, *Martin Chuzzlewit.*

C. Dickens, *Notes for General Circulation.*

J. Disturnell, *Sailing on the Great Lakes and Rivers of America.*

E. Eggleston, *End of the World.*

W. L. Fawcett, "History of the Two Pillars" (article).

W. L. Fawcett, "Old-Time Oriental Trade" (article).

G. H. Gordon, *War Diary of Events in the War of the Great Rebellion, 1863–1865.*

B. Hall, *Travels in North America, in the Years 1827 and 1828* (marginalia).

T. Hamilton, *Men and Manners in America.*

J. Hay, *Pike County Ballads and Other Pieces.*

E. von Hesse-Wartegg, *Mississippi-Fahrten: Reisebilter aus dem amerikanischen Süden (1879–1880).*

A. J. Hoeffler, "Sketches on the Upper Mississippi, by the Author of 'Three Weeks in Cuba.'"

U. P. James, *James' River Guide; Containing Descriptions of All the Cities, Towns, and Principal Objects of Interest on the Navigable Waters of the Mississippi Valley.*

C. Johnson, *Highways and Byways of the Mississippi Valley.*

R. Keeler, "New Orleans," "On the Mississippi" (series of articles).

R. Keeler, *Vagabond Adventures.*

E. King, *Great South: A Record of Journeys.*

M. M. Kirkman, *Romance of Gilbert Holmes: An Historical Novel.*

F. Marryat, *Second Series of a Diary in America.*

H. Martineau, *Retrospect of Western Travel.*

G. B. Merrick, *Old Times on the Upper Mississippi; The Recollections of a Steamboat Pilot from 1854 to 1863.*

C. K. Munroe, *Campmates; A Story of the Plains.*

C. A. Murray, *Travels in North America During the Years 1834, 1835 & 1836, Including . . . a Visit to Cuba and the Azore Islands.*

G. W. Nichols, "Down the Mississippi" (article).

F. Parkman, *La Salle and the Discovery of the Great West.*

H. W. Pierson, *In the Brush; or, Old-Time Social, Political, and Religious Life in the Southwest.*

A. Pinkerton, *Mississippi Outlaws and the Detectives.*

A. C. H. Rice, *Mr. Opp* (Catalog entry).

A. D. Richardson, *Beyond the Mississippi: From the Great River to the Great Ocean.*

C. Stern, "Mark Twain (A Nocturne of the Mississippi)" (poem).

C. D. Stewart, *Fugitive Blacksmith* (novel).

C. D. Stewart, *Partners of Providence* (novel).

B. Taylor, *Visit to India, China, and Japan, in the Year 1853* (Catalog engry).

M. W. Townsend, *Asia and Europe: Studies* (marginalia).

F. M. Trollope, *Domestic Manners of the Americans* (marginalia).

E. S. Van Zandt, *With Sword and Crucifix; Being an Account of the Strange Adventures of Count Louis de Sancerre, Companion of Sieur de la Salle.*

E. C. E. M. S. Wortley, *Travels in the United States, Etc., During 1849 and 1850* (marginalia).

"Miss Malony on the Chinese Question" (sketch). M. E. M. Dodge.

Miss Moore. D. M. M. Craik.

Missouri: see

J. B. Monteith, *Parson Brooks: A Plumb Powerful Hard Shell. A Story of Humble Southern Life.*

L. P. Myers, *Idyl of the Rhine.*

E. H. Orthwein, *Songs of the Beloved.*

See also the Reader's Guide entry for Hannibal, Missouri.

Missouri River: see

H. M. Chittenden, *History of Early Steamboat Navigation on the Missouri River: Life and Adventures of Joseph LaBarge.*

C. D. Stewart, *Partners of Providence* (novel).

Miss Primrose. A Novel. R. R. Gilson.

Mistero del Poeta: Romanzo. A. Fogazzaro.

"Mistletoe Bough" (poem). T. H. Bayly.

Mistress and Maid, A Household Story. D. M. M. Craik.

Mistress of the Ranch; A Novel. F. T. Clark.

Mitchell, Peter Chalmers (trans., ed.): see É. Metchnikoff, *Nature of Man; Studies in Optimistic Philosophy.*

Mitford, Algernon Bertram Freeman-Mitford, *Tales of Old Japan*: see T. Shunsui and E. Greey, *The Loyal Ronins: An Historical Romance, Translated from the Japanese* (marginalia).

Mitford, John (contr.): see J. Swift, *Gulliver's Travels into Several Remote Nations of the World.*

"Mithridates" (poem). R. W. Emerson.

Mizner, Addison (co-author): see O. Herford, *Cynic's Calendar of Revised Wisdom for 1903.*

Mizpah; or, Drifting Away, by Mrs. M. McCullen Whiteside, ("Muriel"). M. M. Whiteside.

"Mocasson": see I. F. Marcosson.

Moccasin Ranch; A Story of Dakota. H. Garland.

Modern Alchemist, and Other Poems. L. W. Dodd.

Modern Bethesda, or The Gift of Healing Restored. A. E. Newton (ed.).

Modern Chronicle. W. Churchill.

Modern English Literature: Its Blemishes & Defects. H. H. Breen.

Modern Householder: A Manual of Domestic Economy in All Its Branches. R. Murray (comp.).

Modern Instance (novel). W. D. Howells.

Modern Novelists: see W. L. Phelps, *Essays.*

Modern Painters. J. Ruskin.

Modocs (Native American tribe): see J. Miller, *Unwritten History: Life Amongst the Modocs.*

Moeller, Henry Nicholas (illus.): see E. Furth, *Tourist; Outward and Homeward Bound.*

Molini, Guiseppe (ed.): see B. Cellini, *Memoirs of Benvenuto Cellini.*

Moll Flanders and The History of the Devil. D. Defoe.

"Monadnoc" (poem). R. W. Emerson.

Monahan, Michael (ed.): see *Papyrus: A Magazine of Individuality.*

Monarch and Other Poems. J. H. Fiagg.

Monday-Chats, Selected and Translated from the "Causeries du Lundi." C. A. Sainte-Beuve.

Monde et ses usages. M. de Waddeville.

Money Magic; A Novel. H. Garland.

Mongkut, King of Siam: see A. H. E. Leonowens, *English Governess at the Siamese Court; Being Recollections of Six Years in the Royal Palace at Bangkok.*

Mongolia: see

É. R. Huc, *Recollections of a Journey Through Tartary, Thibet, and China, During the Years 1844, 1845, and 1846.*

T. W. Knox, *Overland Through Asia; Pictures of Siberian, Chinese, and Tartar Life. Travels and Adventures in Kamchatka, Siberia, China, Mongolia, Chinese Tartary, and European Russia, with Full Accounts of the Siberian Exiles.*

Monk, Hank (stagecoach driver): see C. F. Browne, *Artemus Ward, His Travels.*

"Monkey's Paw" (short story). W. W. Jacobs.

"Monkey's Trick": see *Ocean Scenes; or, The Perils and Beauties of the Deep.*

Monk of Fife: A Romance of the Days of Jeanne d'Arc. A. Lang.

Monna Vanna, A Play in Three Acts. M. Maeterlinck.

Monologues. M. I. T. Fisk.

Monsieur Guizot in Private Life, 1787–1874. By His Daughter, Madame de Witt. H. E. G. de Witt.

Monsieur Motte. G. E. King.

Monster and Other Stories. S. Crane.

Montague, Charles Edward (co-author): see M. A. A. Ward, *William Thomas Arnold, Journalist and Historian.*

Montaigne, Michel Eyquem de: see

W. Swinton, *Outlines of the World's History, Ancient, Medieval, and Modern* (marginalia).

J. G. Wood, *Uncivilized Races; or, Natural History of Man* (marginalia).

Montalba, Clara (illus.): see C. B. E. F. Lindsay, *From a Venetian Balcony and Other Poems of Venice and the Near Lands.*

Montana (territory and state): see

A. G. Clarke, Jr., *Arickaree Treasure, and Other Brief Tales of Adventurous Montanians.*

T. J. Dimsdale, *Vigilantes of Montana; or, Popular Justice in the Rocky Mountains.*

A. D. Richardson, *Beyond the Mississippi: From the Great River to the Great Ocean.*

Mont Blanc: see

C. de Catelin, *Histoire du Mont Blanc et de la vallée de Chamonix. Ascensions catastrophes célèbres, depuis les prémieres explorations.*

A. R. Smith, *Story of Mont Blanc.*

Montcalm and Wolfe. F. Parkman.

Montmorency, La Vallée de: see J. S. Quesné, *Lettres de la Vallée de Montmorency.*

Moods (novel). L. M. Alcott.

Moods in Rhymes. E. F. Ware.

Moody, I. E. (co-author): see J. A. Marks, *Little Busybodies; The Life of Crickets, Ants, Bees, Beetles, and Other Busybodies.*

Mookerjee, Sambhu C.: see F. H. B. Skrine, *Indian Journalist: Being the Life, Letters, and Correspondence of Dr. Sambhu C. Mookerjee.*

Moon, George Washington: see J. R. Lowell, *Letters of James Russell Lowell* (marginalia).

Moonblight and Six Feet of Romance. D. C. Beard.

Moonlight Boy. E. W. Howe.

Moon Metal (science fiction novel). G. P. Serviss.

Moon Prince, and Other Nabobs. R. K. Munkittrick.

Moore, Julia Ann (Davis) (poet): see

M. A. Ross, *Irene Iddesleigh* (Catalog entry).

W. Shakespeare, *Works of Shakespeare* (Catalog entry).

Moore, Thomas: see

G. G. Byron, "To Thomas Moore" (poem).

M. B. Eddy, *Retrospection and Introspection* (marginalia).

H. B. Fearon, *Sketches of America. A Narrative of a Journey of Five Thousand Miles* (marginalia).

F. T. Palgrave (comp.), *Golden Treasury of the Best Songs and Lyrical Poems in the English Language* (marginalia).

"We'll sing the wine-cup and the lass" (song).

"Wine-cup is circling" (poem, song).

Moors: see

S. Clarke, *Mirror or Looking-Glass Both for Saints & Sinners* (marginalia).

W. Irving, *Alhambra: A Series of Tales and Sketches of the Moors and Spaniards.*

See also the Reader's Guide entries for Islam and for Spain.

Moral behavior of humans: see

L. R. Andrews, *White Peril; or, How I Cured Myself of Consumption at Home* (marginalia).

D. Defoe, *Moll Flanders and The History of the Devil* (marginalia).

L. Dyer, *Machiavelli and the Modern State: Chapters on His "Prince," His Use of History and His Idea of Morals.*

W. Forsyth, *Novels and Novelists of the Eighteenth Century, in Illustration of the Manners and Morals of the Age.*

W. E. H. Lecky, *History of European Morals from Augustus to Charlemagne.*

O. J. Lodge, *Substance of Faith Allied with Science; A Catechism for Parents and Teachers.*

C. Mackay, *Memoirs of Extraordinary Popular Delusions and Madness of Crowds.*

J. H. Moore, *Universal Kinship* (Catalog entry).

G. Negri, *Julian the Apostate* (marginalia).

F. Parkman, *Old Régime in Canada* (marginalia).

W. L. Phelps, *Essays on Modern Novelists* (marginalia).

Plutarchus, *Plutarch's Morals. Translated from the Greek by Several Hands.*

A. D. White, *History of the Warfare of Science with Theology in Christendom* (marginalia).

F. Wilkinson, *Strength of the Hills; A Novel* (Catalog entry).

Moral conduct guides: see

J. Abbott, *The Way to Do Good; or, The Christian Character Mature.*

C. B. Allen and M. A. W. Allen, *Man Wonderful in the House Beautiful: An Allegory Teaching the Principles of Physiology and Hygiene, and the Effects of Stimulants and Narcotics.*

C. S. J. Bloomfield-Moore. *Sensible Etiquette of the Best Society, Customs, Manners, Morals, and Home Culture.*

M. A. Dodge, *Stumbling-Blocks.*

B. Franklin, *Life of Benjamin Franklin, Written by Himself.*

J. McGovern, *Golden Censer; or, the Duties of To-Day and the Hopes of the Future.*

C. W. Silver, *Secular Anathema on Fakery in Business, Social and Professional Life; or, Twentieth Century Conduct.* C. W. Silver.

L. N. Tolstoy, *Life is Worth Living, and Other Stories.*

S. H. Tyng, *Office and Duty of a Christian Pastor.*

See also the Reader's Guide entry for Etiquette and personal conduct.

Moral Culture of Infancy, and Kindergarten Guide. M. T. P. Mann.

Morals of Marcus Ordeyne. A Novel. W. J. Locke.

Moran, Thomas (co-illus.): see H. W. Longfellow, *Hanging of the Crane*.

More, Hannah: see J. G. Wilson (ed.), *Love in Letters; Illustrated in the Correspondence of Eminent Persons; with Biographical Sketches of the Writers*.

More, Thomas: see A. Manning, *Household of Sir Thos. More*.

Moreau, L. G. (trans.): see A. Dreyfus, *Lettres d'un Innocent; The Letters of Captain Dreyfus to His Wife*.

More Fables. G. Ade.

Morel, Edmund Dene: see H. L. Samuel (Catalog entry).

"Morell, Sir Charles" (pseud.): see J. K. Ridley.

Morgan, Henry (pirate): see H. Pyle, *Stolen Treasure*.

Morgan, Walter Jenks (illus.): see E. Spenser, *Spenser for Children*.

Morland, Samuel (English inventor): see S. Pepys, *Diary of Samuel Pepys* (Catalog entry).

Morley: see
W. Smith, *Morley: Ancient and Modern*.
W. Smith (ed.), *Registers of Topcliffe, and Morley in the W. R. of the County of York. Baptisms, 1654–1830. Burials, 1654–1888*.

Morley: Ancient and Modern. W. Smith.

Morley, Henry: see
(intro.) R. Chambers, *Vestiges of the Natural History of Creation*.
(intro.) A. Cowley, *Essays*.
(intro.) Samuel Pepys, *Diary of Samuel Pepys, 1662–1663*.
(ed.) Plutarchus, *Plutarch's Lives of Alcibiades & Coriolanus, Aristides & Cato the Censor*.

Morley, John (ed.): see
E. W. Gosse, *Thomas Gray*.
T. H. Huxley, *Hume*.

Mormonism: see
Book of Mormon.
C. W. Dilke, *Greater Britain: A Record of Travel in English-Speaking Countries During 1866 and 1867*.
N. W. Green, *Fifteen Years among the Mormons: Being the Narrative of Mrs. Mary Ettie V. Smith, Late of Great Salt Lake City*.
J. Hyde, Jr., *Mormonism: Its Leaders and Designs*.
C. Paddock, *Fate of Madame La Tour; A Tale of Great Salt Lake*.
E. Roberts, *Shoshone and Other Western Wonders*.
T. B. H. Stenhouse, *Rocky Mountain Saints: A Full and Complete History of the Mormons, . . . and the Development of the Great Mineral Wealth of the Territory of Utah*.
E. Talbot, *My People of the Plains*.
L. J. Velazquez, *Woman in Battle: A Narrative of the Exploits, Adventures, and Travels of Madame Loreta Janeta Velazquez, Otherwise Known as Lieutenant Harry T. Buford, Confederate States Army*.
C. V. V. Waite, *Mormon Prophet and His Harem; or, an Authentic History of Brigham Young, His Numerous Wives and Children*.

Mormonism: Its Leaders and Designs. J. Hyde, Jr.

Mormon Prophet and His Harem; or, an Authentic History of Brigham Young, His Numerous Wives and Children. C. V. V. Waite.

Morocco:
T. B. Aldrich, *From Ponkapog to Pesth*.
S. Bonsal, *Morocco As It Is*.
W. F. Payson, *Barry Gordon*.
C. D. Warner, *Roundabout Journey*.

Morocco As It Is. S. Bonsal.

Morris, Charles (intro.): see S. E. Titcomb, *Aryan Sun-Myths: The Origin of Religions*.

Morris, Pete (singer): see "Raging Canal" (song).

Morse, Charlotte Dunning (Wood): see C. D. Wood.

Morse, Edna (illus.): see L. B. Morse, *Road to Nowhere. A Story for Children*.

Morse, Samuel Finley Brown (illus.): see H. C. Morse, *Cowboy Cavalier*.

Morte Darthur. T. Malory.

"Morton, Hugh" (pseud.): see C. M. S. McLellan.

Morton, Thomas (historical figure): see J. H. Trumbull (ed.), *True-Blue Laws of Connecticut and New Haven* (marginalia).

Mosaics of Bible History; The Bible Record with Illustrative Poetic and Prose Selections from Standard Literature. M. Willson.

Mosby, John Singleton: see J. Scott, *Partisan Life with Col. John S. Mosby*.

Moser, James Henry (co-illus.): see J. C. Harris, *Uncle Remus: His Songs and His Sayings*.

Moser, Koloman (illus.): see E. Pötzl, *Bummelei. Neue Gelammelte Skizzen*.

Moses (Biblical figure): see
C. F. H. Alexander, "Burial of Moses" (poem).
S. Baring-Gould, *Legends of Old Testament Characters*.
"Go down, Moses" (spiritual).
H. More, *Moses in the Bulrushes* (poem).

Moses in the Bulrushes (poem). H. More.

Mosquitoes: How They Live; How They Carry Disease. L. O. Howard.

Mossback Correspondence, Together with Mr. Mossback's Views on Certain Practical Subjects, with a Short Account of His Visit to Utopia. F. E. Clark.

Mosses from an Old Manse. N. Hawthorne.

"Mother" (poem). W. D. Howells.

Mother and the Father. Dramatic Passages. W. D. Howells.

Mother Goose: see
L. F. Baum, *Father Goose; His Book*.
W. W. Denslow (ed., illus.), *Denslow's Mother Goose*.
J. W. Elliott, *Mother Goose's Nursery Rhymes and Nursery Songs*.
Mother Goose (Catalog entry).
Mother Goose's Melodies for Children.
A. D. T. Whitney, *Mother Goose for Grown Folks*.
See also the Reader's Guide entry for Nursery rhymes and the Catalog entry for Nursery rhymes.

Mother Goose for Grown Folks. A. D. T. Whitney.

Mother Goose's Nursery Rhymes and Nursery Songs. J. W. Elliott.

Motherless; or, A Parisian Family. H. E. G. Witt.

Mother of the Man. E. Phillpotts.

Mothers in Council. S. S. Gilman.

Mothers' Club of Cambridge, Massachusetts: see S. S. Gilman, *Mothers in Council*.

Motherwell, William (ed.): see R. Burns, *Works of Robert Burns*.

Moths: N. B. De G. Doubleday, *Wild Flowers: An Aid to Knowledge of Our Wild Flowers and Their Insect Visitors*.

Motley, John Lothrop: see
O. W. Holmes, *Autocrat of the Breakfast-Table* (marginalia).
E. G. E. B. Lytton, *Kenelm Chillingly: His Adventures and Opinions. A Novel* (marginalia).
J. Swift, *Gulliver's Travels into Several Remote Nations of the World* (Catalog entry).

Motley's Dutch Nation, Being the Rise of the Dutch Republic (1555–1584) Condensed. J. L. Motley.

Motors: see R. Krause, *Starters and Regulators for Electric Motors and Generators*.

"Mott, Ed." (pseud.): see E. H. Mott.

Mottoes and Aphorisms from Shakespeare. Arranged Alphabetically. W. Shakespeare.

Moulton, Louise Chandler: see New York *Tribune* (Catalog entry).

Mountain Adventures in Various Parts of the World. Selected from the Narratives of Celebrated Travellers. J. T. Headley (ed.).

Mountain Climber (play). C. Kraatz.

Mountain climbing: see
C. de Catelin, *Histoire du Mont Blanc et de la vallée de Chamonix. Ascensions catastrophes célèbres, depuis les prémières explorations*.
A. G. Girdlestone, *High Alps Without Guides: Being a Narrative of Adventures in Switzerland*.
J. T. Headley (ed.), *Mountain Adventures in Various Parts of the World. Selected from the Narratives of Celebrated Travellers*.
T. W. Hinchliff, *Summer Months Among the Alps; With the Ascent of Monte Rosa*.
W. D. Howells (co-ed.), *Library of Universal Adventure by Sea and Land*.
C. Scollard, *Under Summer Skies* (visits the Alps).
A. R. Smith, *Story of Mont Blanc*.
E. Whymper, *Scrambles Amongst the Alps in the Years 1860–69*.

Mountaineer (poetry). B. T. Wilson.

Mountaineering in the Sierra Nevada. C. King.

Mountain Europa. J. Fox, Jr.

Mountain Meadows massacre: see C. V. V. Waite, *Mormon Prophet and His Harem; or, an Authentic History of Brigham Young, His Numerous Wives and Children*.

Mount Edgcumbe, George, Earl of: see H. Walpole, *Letters of Horace Walpole, Earl of Oxford* (marginalia).

Mourning Bride (play). W. Congreve.

"Mouse, To a" (poem). R. Burns.

Mouse-Trap. A Farce (play). W. D. Howells.

Movements and Habits of Climbing Plants. C. Darwin.

Mowatt, James Alexander: see the Catalog entry for Mowatt.

"Mowbray, J. P." (pseud.): see A. C. Wheeler.

Mr. Absalom Billingslea, and Other Georgia Folk. R. M. Johnston.

Mr. Billy Downs and His Likes. R. M. Johnston.

Mr. Claghorn's Daughter. R. M. Manley.

Mr. Crewe's Career. W. Churchill.

"Mr. Dooley" (pseud.): see F. P. Dunne.

Mr. Jervis. B. M. S. Croker.

"Mr. Lang on the Art of Mark Twain" (essay). A. Lang.

Mr. Opp. A. C. H. Rice.

Mr. Pennycook's Boy. J. J. Bell.

Mr. Stubbs's Brother. J. O. Kaler.

Mr. Wind and Madam Rain. P. E. de Musset.

Mrs. Beauchamp Brown. J. G. Austin.

Mrs. Brown Series. G. Rose.

Mrs. Cliff's Yacht. F. R. Stockton.

"Mrs. Eddy's Relation to Christian Science" (article). W. D. McCrackan.

Mrs. Farrell (novel): see W. D. Howells, *Private Theatricals* (novel).

Mrs. Keith's Crime; A Record. L. L. Clifford.

"Mrs. Partington" (literary character): see B. P. Shillaber, *Life and Sayings of Mrs. Partington and Others of the Family*.

Mrs. Raffles; Being the Adventures of an Amateur Crackswoman. J. K. Bangs.

Mrs. Skagg's Husbands, and Other Sketches. B. Harte.

Mrs. Wiggs of the Cabbage Patch. A. C. H. Rice.

Much Ado About Nothing (play). W. Shakespeare.

Mugwumps: see S. Woodworth, "Bucket" (song) (Catalog entry).

"Mühlbach, Luise" (pseud.): see K. M. Mundt.

Muir, Richard (illus.): see C. W. Saleeby, *Cycle of Life According to Modern Science*.

"Muléykeh" (poem): see R. Browning, *Agamemnon*.

Mulford, Prentice: see M. D. Conway, *Autobiography: Memories and Experiences of Moncure Daniel Conway* (marginalia).

Müller, C. E. R. (trans.): see S. Lebert and L. Stark, *Grand Theoretical and Practical Piano-School for Systematic Instruction*.

Müller, F. Max (trans.): see I. Kant, *Critique of Pure Reason*.

Mulock, Dinah Maria: see D. M. M. Craik.

Mumford, Ethel Watts (co-author): see O. Herford, *Cynic's Calendar of Revised Wisdom for 1903*.

Mummies and Moslems. C. D. Warner.

Münch-Bellinghausen, Eligius von: see F. Halm.

Mungen, William: see "Pop! goes the weasel" (children's song).

Munich: see E. C. E. M. S. Wortley, *Travels in the United States, Etc., During 1849 and 1850* (marginalia).

Munro, A. G. (trans.): see A. Assollant, *Fantastic History of the Celebrated Pierrot*.

Munroe, Kirk (co-author): see *Battle for the Pacific, and Other Adventures at Sea*.

Murders of [sic] the Rue Morgue (story). E. A. Poe.

Murel, John A.: see the Reader's Guide entry for John A. Murrell.

"Muriel" (pseud.): see M. M. Whiteside.

Murray, Lindley: see G. W. Moon, *Learned Men's English: The Grammarians*.

Murrell, John A. (land pirate): see
H. R. Howard, *History of Virgil A. Stewart, and His Adventure*.
F. Marryat, *Second Series of a Diary in America*.
V. A. Stewart, *History of the Detection, Conviction, Life*

and Designs of John A. Murel, The Great Western Land Pirate.

Murrells, James: see E. Gregory, Narrative of James Murrells' ("Jemmy Morrill") Seventeen Years' Exile among the Wild Blacks of North Queensland, and His Life and Shipwreck and Terrible Adventures among Savage Tribes.

Mushroom Book. A Popular Guide to the Identification and Study of Our Commoner Fungi. N. L. Marshall.

Music: see

  J. Booth, Everybody's Guide to Music, with Illustrated Chapters on Singing and Cultivation of the Voice.

  M. Brée, Groundwork of the Leschetizky Method.

  F. Chopin, Pianoforte Werke.

  R. W. Gilder, A Book of Music (poems on the theme of music).

  W. H. Hadow, Studies in Modern Music.

  G. Henschel, Personal Recollections of Johannes Brahms.

  R. Hughes, Żal, An International Romance.

  A. Hullah, Theodor Leschetizky.

  S. Lebert and L. Stark, Grand Theoretical and Practical Piano-School for Systematic Instruction.

  H. Mendel, Musikalisches Conversations-lexicon. Eine Encyklopädie.

  F. S. Peterson, Introduction to the Study of Theory: A Sequel to the "Elements of Music."

  R. A. Schumann, Music and Musicians. Essays and Criticisms.

  P. I. Tchaikovsky, Textbook on Harmony.

  G. P. Upton, Standard Operas: Their Plots, Their Music, and Their Composers.

  R. Wagner, Richard Wagner to Mathilde Wesendonck.

  M. A. A. Ward, Robert Elsmere (Catalog entry).

  J. V. Widmann, Johannes Brahms in Erinnerungen.

  See also the Reader's Guide entries for Musicals, for Music history, for Operas, and for Operettas.

Musical Play for Amateurs. J. K. Bangs.

Musicals: see

  J. K. Bangs, The Worsted Man; A Musical Play for Amateurs.

  W. Gill and H. E. Dixey, Adonis (burlesque musical).

  J. C. Goodwin and E. E. Rice, Evangeline (musical burlesque).

Music and Musicians. Essays and Criticisms. R. A. Schumann.

Music Hath Charms. E. V. M. Ferguson.

"Music hath charms to soothe the savage breast" (line): see W. Congreve, Mourning Bride (play).

Music history: see

  R. Grau, Forty Years Observation of Music and the Drama by Robert Grau.

  A. Hullah, Theodore Leschetizky.

  L. C. W. Lillie, Story of Music and Musicians for Young Readers.

  M. Reintzel (comp.), Musician's Year Book.

  See also the Reader's Guide entry for Music.

Musician's Year Book. M. Reintzel (comp.).

Music Master (play). C. Klein.

Musikalisches Conversations-lexicon. Eine Encyklopädie. H. Mendel.

Muslim countries: see Islam.

Musset, Alfred de: see C. Vincens, Alfred de Musset.

Mutineers of the "Bounty" and Their Descendants in Pitcairn and Norfolk Islands. D. J. Belcher.

"My ain countrie" (poem, hymn). M. A. L. Demarest.

My Autobiography and Reminiscences. W. P. Frith.

My Boy and I; or, On the Road to Slumberland. M. D. Brine.

Myers, Frederic William Henry: see

  E. Gurney, Phantasms of the Living.

  Society for Psychical Research.

"My faith looks up to Thee" (hymn). R. Palmer.

"My First Speech" (poem): see D. Everett, "You'd Scarce Expect One of My Age" (poem).

"My heart is in the highlands" (song). R. Burns.

"My Kingdom" (poem). P. Duoir.

My Lady Nobody; A Novel. J. M. W. van der P. Schwartz.

"My Last Thought" (poem): see J. Rizal, Eagle Flight: A Filipino Novel.

My Life as an Indian; The Story of a Red Woman and a White Man in the Lodges of the Blackfeet. J. W. Schultz.

My Life on the Plains. G. A. Custer.

My Life with Stanley's Rear Guard. H. Ward.

"My Novel," by Pisistratus Caxton; or, Varieties in English Life. E. G. E. B. Lytton.

"My old Kentucky home, good night" (minstrel song). S. C. Foster.

My Own Story, with Recollections of Noted Persons. J. T. Trowbridge.

My People of the Plains. E. Talbot.

Myrbach, Felicien de (illus.): see W. McLennan, Spanish John; Being a Memoir, Now First Published in Complete Form, of the Early Life and Adventures of Colonel John McDonell.

My Religion. L. N. Tolstoy.

Mysterious Island. J. Verne.

"Mysterious Stranger" (story). J. Taylor.

Mysterious Stranger and Other Cartoons. J. T. McCutcheon.

Mystery fiction: see individual book titles, plus the Reader's Guide entries for Court trials, for Crime, and for Detective fiction.

Mystery of Abel Forefinger. W. Drysdale.

Mystery of Edwin Drood. C. Dickens.

Mystery of Metropolisville. E. Eggleston.

Mystery of Sleep. J. Bigelow.

Mystery of the Sea; A Novel. B. Stoker.

Mystifications, by Clementina Stirling Grahame. C. S. Graham.

Mysticism: see

  W. W. Atkinson, Advanced Course in Yogii Philosophy and Oriental Occultism.

  J. K. Bangs, Toppleton's Client; or, A Spirit in Exile.

  A. Bertholet, Transmigration of Souls.

  F. P. Cobbe, The Peak in Darien, with Some Other Inquiries Touching Concerns of the Soul and the Body.

  H. D. H. Everett, Iras: A Mystery.

  F. J. Fargus, Circumstantial Evidence, and Other Stories.

  W. H. Helm, Studies in Style.

  E. G. E. B. Lytton, Zanoni.

  Napoleon's Oraculum, or, Book of Fate.

  C. Wagner, Âme des Choses.

  O. Wilde, Picture of Dorian Gray (novel).

F. B. Wilson, *Paths to Power.*

See also the Reader's Guide entries for Inspirational messages, for Parapsychology, and for Spiritualism and spiritual healing.

My Strangest Case. G. N. Boothby.

My Study Windows (essays). J. R. Lowell.

My Summer in a Garden. C. D. Warner.

"My sweetheart's the man in the moon" (song). J. Thornton.

Mythology: see

T. Bulfinch, *Age of Fable; or, Beauties of Mythology.*

G. W. Cox, *Mythology of the Aryan Nations.*

T. W. Doane, *Bible Myths and Their Parallels in Other Religions.*

I. Donnelly, *Atlantis: The Antediluvian World.*

G. L. P. B. Du Maurier, *Legend of Camelot, Pictures and Poems, Etc.*

A. W. Grube, *Charakterbilder aus der Geschichte und Sage, für einen propädeutischen geschichtsunterricht.*

L. Hunt, *Day by the Fire; and Other Papers, Hitherto Uncollected.*

C. C. Jones, *Negro Myths from the Georgia Coast, Told in the Vernacular.*

B. M. Nead, *Some Hidden Sources of Fiction* (marginalia).

See also the Reader's Guide entries for Greek mythology, for Roman literature, and for national literatures.

Mythology of the Aryan Nations. G. Cox.

Myths of the Rhine. J. X. B. Saintine.

My Water Cure. S. Kneipp.

My Wife and I: or, Harry Henderson's History. H. E. B. Stowe.

My Winter on the Nile, Among the Mummies and Moslems. C. D. Warner.

N

NA HIMENI HOOLEA, HE MAU MELE MA KA UHANE, E HOOLEA AI (Hawaiian hymns.)

Na Huaolelo a me na olelo kikeke ma ka Beritania a me a olelo Hawaii. A. Bishop.

"Namensstudien" (essay). K. B. Franzos.

Names: see

C. Anthon, *Classical Dictionary, Containing an Account of the Principal Proper Names Mentioned in Ancient Authors.*

C. W. E. Bardsley, *Curiosities of Puritan Nomenclature.*

C. W. E. Bardsley, *Our English Surnames: Their Sources and Significances.*

Battle Abbey. *The Roll of Battle Abbey, Annotated.*

Century Cyclopedia of Names.

"Nancy Lee" (song). F. E. Weatherly.

Nansen, Fridtjof: see M. D. Conway, *Autobiography: Memories and Experiences of Moncure Daniel Conway* (marginalia).

Napier, Robina (trans.): see K. W. L. F. von Metternich-Winneburg-Beilstein, *Memoirs of Prince Metternich.*

Napoleon Bonaparte: see

J. S. C. Abbott, *History of Napoleon Bonaparte.*

J. Ashton, *English Caricature and Satire on Napoleon I.*

L. A. F. de Bourrienne, *Memoirs of Napoleon Bonaparte.*

T. Buchanan, *Castle Comedy* (novel).

M. De Lancey, *Week at Waterloo in 1815. Lady De Lancey's Narrative.*

T. A. Dodge, *Great Captains.*

A. C. Doyle, *Great Shadow; A Novel.*

A. C. Doyle, *Rodney Stone.*

É. Erckmann and A. Chatrian, *Waterloo; A Sequel to the Conscript of 1813.*

J. B. A. M. de Marbot, *Mémoires du General Bon de Marbot.*

K. W. L. F. von Metternich-Winneburg-Beilstein, *Memoirs of Prince Metternich.*

W. F. P. Napier, *History of the War in the Peninsula and in the South of France, from the Year 1807 to the Year 1814.*

A. P. Primrose, *Napoleon: The Last Phase.*

C. É. J. G. de V. Rémusat, *Memoirs of Madame de Rémusat, 1802–1808* (Catalog entry).

J. C. Ropes, *The First Napoleon. A Sketch, Political and Military.*

I. de Saint-Amand, *Jeunesse de l'Impératrice Joséphine.*

W. M. Sloane, *Life of Napoleon Bonaparte.*

W. Swinton, *Outlines of the World's History, Ancient, Medieval, and Modern* (marginalia).

W. Warden, *Letters Written on Board His Majesty's Ship the Northumberland, and at Saint Helena; in Which the Conduct and Conversations of Napoleon Buonaparte, and His Suite, . . . Are Faithfully Described* (marginalia).

H. S. Washburn, "Grave of Bonaparte" (song).

T. E. Watson, *Story of France, from the Earliest Times to the Consulate of Napoleon Bonaparte.*

J. G. Wilson (ed.), *Love in Letters; Illustrated in the Correspondence of Eminent Persons; with Biographical Sketches of the Writers.*

World of Wonders; A Record of Things Wonderful in Nature, Science, and Art.

See also the Catalog entry for *Napoleon's Oraculum, or, Book of Fate.*

Napoleon: The Last Phase. A. P. Primrose.

Napoléon II: see the Reader's Guide entry for Bonaparte, Napoléon François Charles Joseph.

Napoleon III (Louis Napoleon): see

J. M. Haswell, *Man of His Time.*

V. M. Hugo. *Destroyer of the Second Republic.*

Napoleon the Third and His Court, by a Retired Diplomatist.

Narrative of Amos Dresser. A. Dresser.

Narrative of an Expedition into Central Australia, Performed Under the Authority of Her Majesty's Government, During the Years 1844, 5, and 6. Together with a Notice of the Province of South Australia, in 1847. C. Sturt.

Narrative of an Expedition to the Zambesi and Its Tributaries. D. Livingstone.

Narrative of Arthur Gordon Pym of Nantucket (novel). E. A. Poe.

Narrative of James Murrells' ("Jemmy Morrill") Seventeen Years' Exile among the Wild Blacks of North Queensland, and His Life and Shipwreck and Terrible Adventures among Savage Tribes. E. Gregory. *Narrative of My Captivity Among the Sioux Indians.* F. W. Kelly.

Narrative of the Expedition of an American Squadron to the China Seas and Japan, Performed in the Years 1852, 1853, and 1854. M. C. Perry.

Narratives of Sorcery and Magic, from the Most Authentic Sources. T. Wright.

"Nasby, Petroleum V." (pseud.): see D. R. Locke.

Nash, Treadway Russell (ed.): see S. Butler, *Hudibras.*

Nast's Illustrated Almanac for 1873. T. Nast.

Nast, Thomas: see
> *Harper's Weekly.*
> D. R. Locke, *Struggles (Social, Financial, and Political) of Petroleum V. Nasby.*
> A. B. Paine, *Th. Nast, His Period and His Pictures.*
> (illus.) H. W. Shaw, *Everybody's Friend, or Josh Billings's Encyclopedia and Proverbial Philosophy of Wit and Humor.*
> (illus.) H. W. Shaw, *Josh Billings: His Works, Complete.*

Natal, the Land and its Story. R. Russell.

Natchez, Mississippi: see
> New Orleans *Times-Democrat* (Catalog entry).
> F. M. Trollope, *Domestic Manners of the Americans* (marginalia).

Nathalie; A Tale. J. Kavanagh.

Nathaniel Hawthorne. H. James.

Nathaniel Hawthorne and His Wife, A Biography. J. Hawthorne.

National centennial celebration in 1876: see the Reader's Guide entry for Centennial celebration in 1876.

National Gallery (London): see London. National Gallery in the Catalog.

National Geographical Series, No. 4—An Improved System of Geography Designed for Schools, Academies, and Seminaries. F. McNally.

National Ode (poem). B. Taylor.

National Peacemaker; A Treatise on Present Conditions in the United States. J. F. Henkle.

Native Americans: see
> J. S. C. Abbott, *History of King Philip, Sovereign Chief of the Wampanoags.*
> C. A. Adams, *Pete's Devils.*
> *Adventures with Indians.*
> H. H. Bancroft, *Native Races of the Pacific States of North America.*
> F. C. Baylor, *Juan and Juanita.*
> J. G. Bourke, *On the Border with Crook.*
> J. M. Brown, *Captives of Abb's Valley; A Legend of Frontier Life.*
> C. D. W. Brownell, *Indian Races of North and South America.*
> J. S. Buckingham, *America, Historical, Statistic, and Descriptive.*
> G. Caitlin (Catalog entry).
> S. V. Clevenger, *Fun in a Doctor's Life, Being the Adventures of an American Don Quixote* (marginalia).
> C. C. Coffin, *Old Times in the Colonies.*
> C. Columbus, *Writings of Christopher Columbus, Descriptive of the Discovery and Occupation of the New World* (Catalog entry).
> J. C. Cremony, *Life Among the Apaches.*
> C. A. Curtis, *Captured by the Navajos.*
> N. Curtis (ed.), *Indians' Book; An Offering by the*

American Indians of Indian Lore, Musical and Narrative.
> E. B. Custer, *"Boots and Saddles"; or, Life in Dakota with General Custer.*
> E. B. Custer, *Tenting on the Plains; or, General Custer in Kansas and Texas.*
> G. A. Custer, *My Life on the Plains.*
> R. I. Dodge, *Our Wild Indians: Thirty-Three Years' Personal Experience among the Red Men of the Great West.*
> R. I. Dodge, *Plains of the Great West and Their Inhabitants, Being a Description of the Plains, Game, Indians, &c. of the Great North American Desert.*
> F. S. Drake, *Indian History for Young Folks.*
> S. A. Drake, *Heart of the White Mountains, Their Legend and Scenery.*
> J. P. Dunn, *Massacres of the Mountains: A History of the Indian Wars of the Far West.*
> J. O. Faversham, *The Squaw Man. A Novel.*
> H. B. Fearon, *Sketches of America. A Narrative of a Journey of Five Thousand Miles* (marginalia).
> J. C. Fillmore, "Study of Indian Music" (essay).
> J. Fiske, *Discovery of America, with Some Account of Ancient America and the Spanish Conquest.*
> W. Glazier, *Three Years in the Federal Cavalry.*
> G. B. Grinnell, *Punishment of the Stingy, and Other Indian Stories.*
> A. B. Hart, *Colonial Children.*
> B. Harte, *In the Carquinez Woods.*
> G. A. Henty, *In the Hands of the Cave-Dwellers.*
> W. D. Howells (co-ed.), *Library of Universal Adventure by Sea and Land.*
> W. Irving, *Adventures of Captain Bonneville.*
> S. O. Jewett, *York Garrison—1640.*
> J. O. Kaler, *Ezra Jordan's Escape from the Massacre at Fort Loyall* (novel).
> D. B. R. Keim, *Sheridan's Troopers on the Borders: A Winter Campaign on the Plains.*
> F. W. Kelly, *Narrative of My Captivity Among the Sioux Indians.*
> W. E. H. Lecky, *History of European Morals from Augustus to Charlemagne* (marginalia).
> W. E. H. Lecky, *History of the Rise and Influence of the Spirit of Rationalism in Europe* (marginalia).
> C. G. Leland (trans.) and J. D. Prince (co-trans.), *Kulóskap the Master, and Other Algonkin Poems; Translated Metrically.*
> "Macallum" (unidentified author).
> R. B. Marcy, *Thirty Years of Army Life on the Border, Comprising Descriptions of the Indian Nomads of the Plains.*
> N. Matson, *Pioneers of Illinois, Containing a Series of Sketches Relating to Events That Occurred Previous to 1813.*
> *Memorial Concerning Conditions in the Independent State of the Kongo. April 19, 1904* (marginalia).
> J. Miller, *Unwritten History: Life Amongst the Modocs.*
> C. K. Munroe, *Campmates; A Story of the Plains.*
> C. K. Munroe, *Flamingo Feather.*
> C. A. Murray, *Travels in North America During the Years 1834, 1835 & 1836, Including a Summer Residence with the Pawnee Tribe of Indians.*

J. F. A. du P. Nadaillac, *Pre-Historic America.*

T. M. Newson, *Indian Legends [of Minnesota Lakes].*

F. Parkman, *Conspiracy of Pontiac and the Indian War After the Conquest of Canada.*

F. Parkman, *Old Régime in Canada.*

F. Parkman, *Oregon Trail: Sketches of Prairie and Rocky-Mountain Life.*

J. W. Powell, *Third Annual Report of the Bureau of American Ethnology to the Secretary of the Smithsonian Institution, 1879–1880.*

F. Remington, *Crooked Trails.*

F. Remington, *Stories of Peace and War.*

A. D. Richardson, *Beyond the Mississippi: From the Great River to the Great Ocean.*

M. Rowlandson, *Narrative of the Captivity and the Restoration of Mrs. Mary Rowlandson.*

J. W. Sanborn, *Legends, Customs and Social Life of the Seneca Indians of Western New York.*

H. R. Schoolcraft, *Algic Researches, Comprising Inquiries Respecting the Mental Characteristics of the North American Indians.*

J. W. Schultz, *My Life as an Indian; The Story of a Red Woman and a White Man in the Lodges of the Blackfeet.*

P. H. Sheridan, *Personal Memoirs of P. H. Sheridan, General, United States Army.*

E. T. Stevens, *Flint Chips. A Guide to Pre-Historic Archaeology, as Illustrated by the Collection in the Blackmore Museum, Salisbury.*

W. O. Stoddard, *Two Arrows: A Story of Red and White.*

A. E. Sweet, *On a Mexican Mustang, through Texas, from the Gulf to the Rio Grande.*

E. Talbot, *My People of the Plains.*

R. G. Thwaites, *France in America, 1497–1763.*

R. B. Townshend, *Bride of a Day.*

J. H. Trumbull (ed.), *True-Blue Laws of Connecticut and New Haven* (marginalia).

Two—and an Indian (unidentified book).

J. Verne, *Tour of the World in Eighty Days* (novel).

O. G. Wall, *Recollections of the Sioux Massacre.*

C. Whitney, *On Snow-Shoes to the Barren Grounds. Twenty-Eight Hundred Miles After Musk-Oxen and Wood-Bison.*

H. P. Willis, *Our Philippine Problem; A Study of American Colonial Policy* (marginalia).

C. E. S. Wood, *Masque of Love* (poem) (Catalog entry).

J. G. Wood, *Uncivilized Races; or, Natural History of Man* (marginalia).

T. Wright (ed.), *Early Travels in Palestine* (marginalia).

W. Wright, *History of the Big Bonanza: An Authentic Account of the Discovery, History, and Working of the World-Renowned Comstock Silver Lode of Nevada; Adventures with Mining, the Indians, and the Country.*

W. Wright, "Washoe Rambles" (articles).

Native Races of the Pacific States of North America. H. H. Bancroft.

Natural history: see

    C. C. Abbott, *In Nature's Realm.*

    L. Biart, *Adventures of a Young Naturalist.*

F. T. Buckland, *Curiosities of Natural History.*

A. B. Buckley, *Fairy-Land of Science.*

A. B. Buckley, *Life and Her Children: Glimpses of Animal Life from the Amoeba to the Insects.*

J. Burroughs, *Winter Sunshine* (and other titles).

M. C. Dickerson, *Frog Book: North American Toads and Frogs.*

R. L. Ditmars, *Reptile Book: A Comprehensive Popularized Work.*

N. B. De G. Doubleday *Nature's Garden: An Aid to Knowledge of Our Wild Flowers and Their Insect Visitors.*

P. B. Du Chaillu, *Wild Life Under the Equator.*

A. R. Dugmore, *Nature and the Camera. How to Photograph Live Birds and Their Nests, Animals, Wild Game.*

D. G. Elliot, *Life and Habits of Wild Animals.*

R. L. Garner, *Speech of Monkeys.*

M. S. Gatty, *Parables from Nature.*

W. H. Gibson, *Camp Life in the Woods and the Tricks of Trapping.*

W. H. Gibson, *Sharp Eyes; A Rambler's Calendar of Fifty-Two Weeks Among Insects, Birds, and Flowers.*

W. H. Gibson, *Strolls by Starlight and Sunshine.*

P. G. Hamerton, *Chapters on Animals.*

O. Herford, *Child's Primer of Natural History.*

E. S. Holden, *Real Things in Nature, A Reading Book of Science for American Boys and Girls.*

C. F. Holder, *Marvels of Animal Life.*

W. Hooker, *Child's Book of Nature.*

M. B. Howitt, *Birds and Flowers; or, Lays and Lyrics of Rural Life.*

M. B. Howitt, *Our Four-Footed Friends.*

W. D. Hulbert, *Forest Neighbors; Life Stories of Wild Animals.*

E. Ingersoll, *Wild Life of Orchard and Field; Papers on American Animal Life.*

E. Ingersoll, *Wild Neighbors; Out-Door Studies in the United States.*

H. K. Job, *Among the Water-Fowl: Observation, Adventure, Photography.*

H. K. Job, *Wild Wings: Adventures of a Camera-Hunter Among the Larger Wild Birds of North America on Sea and Land.*

D. S. Jordan (co-author), *American Food and Game Fishes: A Popular Account of All the Species Found in America North of the Equator.*

W. E. Kirby, *Insects: Foes and Friends.*

A. Knapp, *Upland Pastures, Being Some Out-Door Essays.*

H. Lee, *Octopus; or, The "Devil-Fish" of Fiction and of Fact.*

W. J. Long, *Beasts of the Field.*

W. J. Long, *School of the Woods; Some Life Studies of Animal Instincts and Animal Training.*

H. W. Mabie, *Under the Trees and Elsewhere.*

M. McCulloch-Williams, *Field-Farings; A Vagrant Chronicle of Earth and Sky.*

J. A. Marks and J. E. Moody, *Little Busybodies; The Life of Crickets, Ants, Bees, Beetles, and Other Busybodies.*

E. Menault, *Intelligence of Animals, with Illustrative Anecdotes.*

J. Michelet, *Bird.*

H. M. Miller, *Little Folks in Feathers and Fur, and Others in Neither.*

M. F. R. Miller, *Brook Book; A First Acquaintance with the Brook and Its Inhabitants Through the Changing Year.*

M. W. Morley, *Wasps and Their Ways.*

A. S. Packard, *Half Hours with Insects.*

G. W. Peckham and E. G. Peckham, *Wasps, Social and Solitary* (Catalog entry).

Plinius Secundus, *Natural History of Pliny.*

C. G. D. Roberts, *Kindred of the Wild; A Book of Animal Life.*

J. E. Rogers, *Shell Book: A Popular Guide to a Knowledge of the Families of Living Mollusks.*

E. T. Seton, *Wild Animals I Have Known, and 200 Drawings.*

A. T. Slossom, *Dumb Foxglove, and Other Stories.*

M. J. B. L. Sonrel, *Bottom of the Sea.*

Spectator (London journal).

W. O. Stoddard, *In the Open: Stories of Outdoor Life.*

W. Stone (co-author), *American Animals.*

S. K. Trimmer, *History of the Robins. In Words of One Syllable.*

A. C. Wheeler, *Journey to Nature.*

G. White, *Natural History and Antiquities of Selborne.*

G. White, *Natural History of Selborne. With a Naturalist's Calendar and Additional Observations.*

J. G. Wood, *Common Shells of the Sea-shore.*

J. G. Wood, *Nature's Teachings; Human Invention Anticipated by Nature.*

J. G. Wood, *Our Living World; An Artistic Edition of the Rev. J. G. Wood's Natural History of Animate Creation.*

W. Wood, *General Conchology; or, A Description of Shells, Arranged According to the Linnean System*

World of Wonders; A Record of Things Wonderful in Nature, Science, and Art.

M. O. Wright, *Four-Footed Americans and Their Kin.*

See also the Reader's Guide entries for Bees, for Birds, for Botany, for Butterflies, for Flowers, for Gardening, for Insects, and for Moths as well as the Reader's Guide entry for Ecology, nature appreciation, and land usage.

Natural History and Antiquities of Selborne. G. White.

Natural History of Pliny. Plinius Secundus.

Natural History of Selborne. With a Naturalist's Calendar and Additional Observations. G. White.

Natural Law in the Spiritual World. H. Drummond.

Naturalism (literary movement): see

S. Crane, *Monster and Other Stories. Monster and Other Stories.*

E. W. Howe, *Story of a Country Town.*

J. P. Jacobsen, *Niels Lyhne.*

G. Moore (Catalog entry).

Natural philosophy: see

G. P. Quackenbos *Natural Philosophy, Embracing the Most Recent Discoveries in the Various Branches of*

Physics, and Exhibiting the Application of Scientific Principles in Everyday Life.

J. D. Steele, *Fourteen Weeks in Natural Philosophy.*

Natural Religion in India. A. C. Lyall.

Natural science: see the Reader's Guide entry for Natural history.

Natural Wealth of California. T. F. Cronise.

Nature: see F. de Lanoye, *Sublime in Nature; Compiled from the Descriptions of Travellers and Celebrated Writers.*

Nature and Culture. H. W. Mabie.

Nature and Life: Sermons. R. Collyer.

Nature and the Camera. How to Photograph Live Birds and Their Nests, Animals, Wild Game. A. R. Dugmore.

Nature of Man; Studies in Optimistic Philosophy. É. Metchnikoff.

Nature's Craftsmen: Popular Studies of Ants and Other Insects. H. C. McCook.

Nature's Garden: An Aid to Knowledge of Our Wild Flowers and Their Insect Visitors. N. B. De G. Doubleday.

Nature's Teachings; Human Invention Anticipated by Nature. J. G. Wood.

"Naulahka" (poem). R. Kipling.

Naulahka, A Story of the West and East. R. Kipling.

Navaho tribe: see R. B. Townshend and L. J. D. B. Townshend, *Bride of a Day.*

Navigator; or, The Traders' Useful Guide. Z. Cramer.

Navy: see the Reader's Guide entry for United States Navy.

Neal, Alice Bradley (intro.): see F. M. B. *Widow Bedott Papers.*

Neal, Max Dalhoff (adapt.): see C. Kraatz, *Mountain Climber* (farce).

"Nearer, my God, to Thee" (hymn). S. F. Adams.

'Neath Austral Skies. Poems. E. B. Loughran.

Necklace of Stories. M. D. Conway.

Needham, Alicia Adélaïde (composer): see "Nora McCarty" (ballad).

Needles and Pins; A Novel. J. H. McCarthy.

Negro Myths from the Georgia Coast, Told in the Vernacular. C. C. Jones.

Neighbor Jackwood. J. T. Trowbridge.

Neither Dorking nor the Abbey (tribute to G. Meredith). J. Barrie.

"Nelly Bly" (minstrel song). S. C. Foster.

Nelson, Harold (co-illus.): see Elizabeth, Queen of Rumania, *A Real Queen's Fairy Tales.*

Nelson, Horatio: see J. G. Wilson (ed.), *Love in Letters; Illustrated in the Correspondence of Eminent Persons; with Biographical Sketches of the Writers.*

Neptune (planet): see

S.G. Bayne, *Pith of Astronomy (Without Mathematics): The Latest Facts and Figures as Developed by the Giant Telescopes* (clipping).

New York *Herald* (Catalog entry).

M. F. Somerville, *Personal Recollections, from Early Life to Old Age, of Mary Somerville. With Selections from Her Correspondence* (Catalog entry).

Nero, Emperor: see

H. Sienkiewicz, *"Quo Vadis": A Narrative of the Time of Nero.*

Suetonius, *Lives of the Twelve Caesars* (Catalog entry).

Nesbit, Edith: see E. N. Bland.
Nests and Eggs of North American Birds. O. Davie.
Netherlands: see the Reader's Guide entry for Holland.
Nettleship, John Trivett (illus.): see A. Nicols, *Wild Life and Adventure in the Australian Bush: Four Years' Personal Experience.*
Neue Ghetto: see T. Herzl, *New Ghetto* (play).
Neue Melusine. J. W. von Goethe.
Neues Bilderbuch. Anleitung zum Anschauen. Denken, Rechnen, und Sprechen fur Kinder. N. Bohny.
Neuville, Alphonse Marie de (illus.): see
  F. P. G. Guizot, *History of France.*
  F. P. G. Guizot, *Popular History of France from the Earliest Times.*
Nevada: see
  J. R. Browne, *Adventures in Apache Country: A Tour Through Arizona and Sonora with Notes on the Silver Regions of Nevada.*
  J. R. Browne, *Crusoe's Island: A Ramble in the Steps of Alexander Selkirk. With Sketches of Adventure in California and Washoe.*
  J. R. Browne, "A Peep at Washoe" (articles).
  G. A. Lawrence, *Silverland.*
  P. V. Mighels, *Bruvver Jim's Baby.*
  P. V. Mighels, *Chatwit, The Man-Talk Bird.*
  Nevada State Historical Society. *First Biennial Report of the Nevada Historical Society, 1907–1908.*
  W. F. Stewart, *Pleasant Hours in an Eventful Life.*
  H. L. Wilson, *Spenders; A Tale of the Third Generation.*
  W. Wright, *History of the Big Bonanza: An Authentic Account of the Discovery, History, and Working of the World-Renowned Comstock Silver Lode of Nevada.*
  W. Wright, "Washoe Rambles" (articles).
New and Complete Concordance to the Holy Scriptures. J. Eadie (ed.).
New Atmosphere. M. A. Dodge.
New-Born Cuba. F. Matthews.
Newcomes; Memoirs of a Most Respectable Family. W. M. Thackeray.
New Conceptions in Science, with a Foreword on the Relationship of Science and Progress. C. Snyder.
New, Edmund Hort (illus.): see J. Wells, *Oxford and Its Colleges.*
"New Element Radium" (article). E. G. Merritt.
Newell, Peter (illus.): see
  J. K. Bangs, *Bikey the Skicylce & Other Tales of Jimmieboy.*
  (co-illus.) J. K. Bangs, *Ghosts I Have Met.*
  J. K. Bangs, *Pursuit of the House-Boat.*
  G. M. Cooke, *Their First Formal Call.*
  C. L. Dodgson, *Alice in Wonderland.*
  C. L. Dodgson, *Hunting of the Snark.*
  C. L. Dodgson, *Through the Looking-Glass.*
  Favorite Fairy Tales: The Childhood Choice of Representative Men and Women.
  M. Reed, *Book of Clever Beasts; Studies in Unnatural History.*
New England: see
  I. C. Cabell, *Seen from the Saddle.*
  C. C. Coffin, *Old Times in the Colonies.*
  C. C. Coffin, *Story of Liberty.*

  G. L. Collin, *Putnam Place* (short stories).
  A. W. Colton, *"Debatable Land." A Novel.*
  R. T. Cooke, "Freedom Wheeler's Controversy with Providence: A Story of Old New England" (short story).
  R. T. Cooke, *Somebody's Neighbors.*
  R. T. Cooke, *Steadfast: The Story of a Saint and a Sinner.*
  J. Fiske, *Beginnings of New England; or, The Puritan Theocracy.*
  J. H. Flagg, *Lyrics of New England, and Other Poems.*
  M. E. W. Freeman, *New England Nun, and Other Stories.*
  W. H. Gibson, *Highways and By-ways; or Saunterings in New England.*
  W. H. Gibson, *Pastoral Days, or Memories of a New England Year.*
  B. C. Greene, *New England Conscience.*
  S. P. M. Greene, *Cape Cod Folks, A Novel.*
  S. P. M. Greene, *Flood-tide.*
  S. P. M.. Greene, *Vesty of the Basins; A Novel.*
  M. J. H. Holmes, *Homestead on the Hillside.*
  W. D. Howells, *Landlord at Lion's Head* (novel).
  S. O. Jewett, *Tales of New England.*
  G. A. Kendrick, *Contrasts.*
  G. L. Kittredge, *Old Farmer and His Almanack; Being Some Observations on Life and Manners in New England a Hundred Years Ago.*
  J. C. Lincoln, *Cape Cod Ballads, and Other Verse, by Joe Lincoln.*
  H. W. Longfellow, *New-England Tragedies.*
  H. E. B. Stowe, *Betty's Bright Idea. Also, Deacon Pitkin's Farm, and the First Christmas of New England.*
  H. E. B. Stowe, *Dog's Mission; or, the Story of the Old Avery House. And Other Stories.*
  H. E. B. Stowe, *Minister's Wooing.*
  A. Tripp, *Fisher Boy.*
  A. E. Trumbull, *Life's Common Way* (novel).
  S. W. Wardwell, *Bub and Sis: A 20th Century New England Story.*
  G. S. Wasson, *Cap'n Simeon's Store.*
  J. G. Whittier, *Snow-Bound. A Winter Idyl.*
  See also the Reader's Guide entry for Puritans in New England.
New England Conscience. B. C. Greene.
New Englander (periodical): see T. R. Lounsbury, "Scholar of the Twelfth Century."
New England Nun, and Other Stories. M. E. W. Freeman.
New-England Tragedies. H. W. Longfellow.
New English and Italian Pronouncing and Explanatory Dictionary, with Many New Additions. J. Millhouse and F. Bracciforti.
New Foes with an Old Face. C. Kingsley.
Newgate Calendar Improved; Being Interesting Memoirs of Notorious Characters, Who Have Been Convicted of Offences Against the Laws of England, During the Seventeenth Century; and Continued to the Present Time. G. T. Wilkinson.
New Ghetto (play). T. Herzl.
New Guide of the Conversation in Portuguese and English in Two Parts. J. da Fonseca.

New Guide to German Conversation. F. Leypoldt.

New Guinea: see J. Chalmers, *Pioneer Life and Work in New Guinea, 1877–1894.*

New Hampshire: see
S. A. Drake, *Heart of the White Mountains, Their Legend and Scenery.*
W. C. Prime, *I Go A-Fishing.*
J. W. Sanborn, *Method of Teaching the Elements of the Latin Language as Employed at Phillips Academy, Exeter, New Hampshire.*

New Haven, Connecticut: see
T. Hamilton, *Men and Manners in America.*
J. H. Trumbull (ed.), *True-Blue Laws of Connecticut and New Haven.*

"New Historical Romances" (essay). W. D. Howells.

New Illustrated Bible for the Young: see Bible. English 1874.

New Illustrated Self-instructor in Phrenology and Physiology. O. S. Fowler.

New Jersey: see
W. J. Mills, *Caroline of Courtlandt Street* (novel).
Our Stories, by the School Children of the State of New Jersey, Fifteen Years of Age and Under.
C. D. Warner, *Their Pilgrimage* (novel).

New Magdalen. A Novel. W. W. Collins.

Newman, Clyde James (illus.): see G. Ade, *More Fables.*

Newman, John Henry: see W. E. H. Lecky, *History of European Morals from Augustus to Charlemagne* (marginalia).

"Newman, Richard Brinsley" (pseud.): see F. K. Gifford.

New Method of French Conversation. C. M. Marchand.

New Method of Learning the French Language. F. Berger.

New Method of Learning the German Language: Embracing Both the Analytic and Synthetic Modes of Instruction. W. H. Woodbury.

New Mexico: see R. B. Townshend, *Bride of a Day.*

New Observations on the Natural History of Bees. F. Huber.

New Orleans: see
G. W. Cable, *Old Creole Days.*
R. Keeler, "New Orleans," "On the Mississippi" (series of articles).
G. King, *Balcony Stories.*
M. M. Kirkman, *Romance of Gilbert Holmes: An Historical Novel.*
Soard's New Orleans Directory for 1882.
R. M. Stuart, *Story of Babette, A Little Creole Girl.*
F. M. Trollope, *Domestic Manners of the Americans* (marginalia).
C. D. Warner, *Studies in the South and West, with Comments on Canada.*
M. M. Whiteside, *Mizpah; or, Drifting Away, by Mrs. M. McCullen Whiteside, ("Muriel").*
E. C. E. M. S. Wortley, *Travels in the United States, Etc., During 1849 and 1850* (marginalia).

"New Orleans" (article). R. Keeler.

New Pocket Dictionary of the English and Italian Languages. I. E. Wessely (co-author).

New Republic; or, Culture, Faith, and Philosophy in an English Country House. W. H. Mallock.

"New Shakespeare Discoveries: Shakespeare as a Man among Men" (article). C. W. Wallace.

News of the World (London newspaper): see the London *World* entry.

New South Wales. D. M. Gane.

Newspaper Directory: see G. P. Rowell, *American Newspaper Directory.*

Newspapers: see
Boston *Evening Transcript.*
Boston *True Flag* (weekly).
Cleveland, Ohio *Herald.*
Comet.
Galignani's Messenger.
Hannibal *Journal.*
Hartford *Courant.*
William Randolph Hearst.
Hartford, Connecticut *Courant.*
Honolulu *Temperance Advocate & Seamen's Friend.*
Hubbard's Newspaper and Bank Directory.
Italie (Rome).
Junius, *Letters of Junius* (defense of the the press).
Littell's Living Age.
Lloyd's Weekly.
London *Daily Chronicle.*
London *Daily Mail.*
London *Daily News.*
London *Illustrated News.*
London *Man of the World* (see the Catalog entry for London *World*).
London *Morning Post.*
London *News of the World* (see the Catalog entry for London *World*).
London *Standard.*
London *Times.*
London *World.*
Louisville, Kentucky *Courier.*
Louisville, Kentucky *Evening Post.*
Melbourne *Age.*
H. Martineau, *Society in America* (marginalia). `
Münchener Tages-Anzeiger.
Naples *Observer.*
New Orleans *Times-Democrat.*
New York *American and Journal.*
New York *Evening Post.*
New York *Evening Sun.*
New York *Graphic.*
New York *Herald.*
New York *Sun.*
New York *Times.*
New York *Tribune.*
New York *Weekly.*
New York *Weekly Post.*
New York *World.*
Outlook (New York City).
Pall Mall Gazette (London).
Philadelphia *Public Ledger.*
Pioneer Mail and Indian Weekly News.
Port Louis, Mauritius *Merchants' and Planters' Gazette.*
Pressburger Zeitung, Erstes stuct.
G. P. Rowell, *American Newspaper Directory, 1888.*
G. P. Rowell, *Forty Years an Advertising Agent.*
M. C. Russell, *Uncle Dudley's Odd Hours; Being the Vagaries of a Country Editor.*

St. Louis *Republican*.

St. Paul *Pioneer Press*.

San Francisco *Herald*: see W. T. Sherman, *Memoirs of General William T. Sherman. By Himself* (marginalia).

San Francisco *Morning Call*.

Spirit of the Times: A Chronicle of the Turf, Field Sports, Literature and the Stage.

Standard (New York City).

Sydney, Australia *Bulletin*.

Unitarian Herald (Manchester, England).

Vienna *Neue Freie Presse*.

Washington *National Intelligencer*.

New Star Atlas for the Library, the School, and the Observatory, in Twelve Circular Maps. R. Proctor.

New Swiss Family Robinson: A Tale for Children of All Ages. O. Wister.

New Testament: see the Reader's Guide entry for Bible. New Testament and the Catalog entry for Bible. New Testament.

New Testament [paintings]. J. Tissot.

Newton Forster; or, The Merchant Service. F. Marryat.

Newton, James Rogers: see A. E. Newton (ed.), *Modern Bethesda, or The Gift of Healing Restored*.

"New Trials for Old Favorites" (article). B. Matthews.

New Way Around an Old World. F. E. Clark.

New Year's Bargain. S. C. Woolsey.

"New Year's Eve" (poem). T. Hardy: see W. L. Phelps, *Essays on Modern Novelists* (marginalia).

New York in Bondage. J. D. Townsend.

New York City: see

J. Brougham, *Lottery of Life: A Story of New York* (play).

J. H. Browne, *Great Metropolis; A Mirror of New York. A Complete History of Metropolitan Life and Society, with Sketches of Prominent Places, Persons and Things in the City*.

T. Dreiser, *Sister Carrie*.

H. Hapgood, *Spirit of the Ghetto. Studies of the Jewish Quarter in New York*.

C. C. Harrison, *Story of Helen of Troy*.

A. M. H. Heniger, *Children's Educational Theatre*.

W. T. Hornaday, *Popular Official Guide to the New York Zoological Park*.

E. W. Howe, *Moonlight Boy*.

H. James, *Washington Square*.

A. B. P. Longstreet, *Social Etiquette of New York*.

E. G. E. B. Lytton, *Kenelm Chillingly: His Adventures and Opinions. A Novel* (marginalia).

W. McAdoo, *Guarding a Great City, by William McAdoo, Police Commissioner, New York City, 1904–1906*.

R. E. MacAlarney, "Tim Rafferty's Romance: A Story of Christmas among 'The Finest.'"

S. W. McAllister, *Society As I Have Found It*.

C. M. S. McLellan, *Belle of New York, A Musical Comedy in Two Acts* (play).

F. A. Mathews, *Undefiled: A Novel of To-day*.

W. J. Mills, *Caroline of Courtlandt Street* (novel).

J. F. Mines, *Tour Around New York, and My Summer Acre; Being the Recreations of Mr. Felix Oldboy*.

C. Morris. *Pasteboard Crown: A Story of the New York Stage* (novel).

Old Guard (periodical).

M. E. W. Sherwood, *A Transplanted Rose; A Story of New York Society*.

W. G. V. T. Sutphen, *Doomsman*.

G. Thompson, *City Crimes; or, Life in New York and Boston*.

E. W. Townsend, *Days Like These; A Novel*.

Trow's Business Directory of Greater New York.

I. M. Van Etten, "House of the Dragons" (short story).

B. M. Van Vorst and M. V. Vorst, *Woman Who Toils; Being the Experiences of Two Ladies as Factory Girls*.

E. N. J. Wharton, *House of Mirth*.

R. G. White, "London Streets" (article).

F. Wilkinson, *Strength of the Hills; A Novel*.

See also the Reader's Guide entry for Tammany Hall politics.

New York Stage. C. Morris.

New York (state): see

I. Bacheller, *Eben Holden*.

I. Bacheller, *Eben Holden's Last Day A-Fishing*.

A. R. Conkling, *Life and Letters of Roscoe Conkling*.

S. Crane, *Monster and Other Stories*.

C. M. Depew, *Orations and After-Dinner Speeches of Chauncey M. Depew*.

M. Dix (comp.), *Memoirs of John Adams Dix*.

O. W. Holmes, *Autocrat of the Breakfast-Table* (marginalia).

W. Irving, "Rip Van Winkle" (short story).

W. Irving, *Sketch-Book of Geoffrey Crayon*.

John Van Buren, Politician; A Novel of To-day.

B. J. Lossing. *Empire State: A Compendious History of the Commonwealth of New York*.

J. F. Mines, *Tour Around New York, and My Summer Acre; Being the Recreations of Mr. Felix Oldboy*.

W. C. Prime, *I Go A-Fishing*.

Report of the Commission of 1906 to Investigate the Condition of the Blind in the State of New York.

J. W. Sanborn, *Legends, Customs and Social Life of the Seneca Indians of Western New York*.

C. F. Skinner, *Manual of Patriotism, for Use in the Public Schools of the State of New York*.

S. J. Tilden, *Letters and Literary Memorials of Samuel J. Tilden*.

S. J. Tilden, *Writings and Speeches of Samuel J. Tilden*.

A. L. Townsend, *On the Verge: A Romance of the Centennial*.

E. N. Westcott, *David Harum: A Story of American Life*.

New Zealand: see the Reader's Guide entry for Australia and New Zealand.

Next Door. C. L. R. Burnham.

Nez Perce (Native Americans): see C. E. S. Wood, *Masque of Love* (poem) (Catalog entry).

Niagara Falls: see

Niagara Book: A Complete Souvenir of Niagara Falls.

B. Taylor, *At Home and Abroad: A Sketch-Book of Life, Scenery, and Men*.

C. D. Warner, *Their Pilgrimage* (novel).

Nicholas Comenius; or Ye Pennsylvania Schoolmaster of Ye Olden Time. W. Riddle.

Nicholas Nickleby. C. Dickens.

Nicholson, John Page (ed.): see L.-P.-A.-d' O. Paris, *History of the Civil War in America.*

Nick Baba's Last Drink and Other Sketches. G. P. Goff.

Nick of the Woods; or The Jibbenainosay. R. M. Bird.

Nicolson, George (contr.): see the Catalog entry for *Spectator.*

Nicotiana; or, the Smoker's and Snuff-Taker's Companion: Containing the History of Tobacco. H. J. Meller.

Niels Lyhne. J. P. Jacobsen.

Nietzsche, Friedrich: see J. G. Huneker, *Egoists, A Book of Supermen.*

"Night Before Christmas" (poem). C. C. Moore.

"Night Has a Thousand Eyes" (poem): see F. W. Bourdillon, "Light" (poem).

Nights with Uncle Remus: Myths and Legends of the Old Plantation. J. C. Harris.

Night Thoughts: see A. Young, *Complaint; or, Night Thoughts on Life, Death, and Immortality.*

Nihilist Princess. L. M. Gagneur.

"Nikola Tesla" (article). T. C. Martin.

Nile River: see

A. A. B. Edwards, *Thousand Miles Up the Nile.*

J. A. Hart, *Levantine Log-Book.*

A. Hoppin, *On the Nile.*

T. W. Knox, *Backsheesh! or, Life and Adventures in the Orient.*

H. M. Stanley, *Through the Dark Continent; or, The Sources of the Nile.*

B. Taylor, *Journey to Central Africa; or, Life and Landscapes from Egypt to the Negro Kingdoms of the White Nile.*

Nine Little Goslings. S. C. Woolsey.

Ninety-Three. V. M. Hugo.

Nineveh and Its Remains: With an Account of a Visit to the Chaldæan Christians of Kurdistand. A. H. Layard.

Noahs Afloat; An Historical Romance. H. R. Woodman.

Noble Blood. J. Hawthorne.

Noble Life. D. M. M. Craik.

"Nobleman of the Steppe" (short story). I. S. Turgenev.

"Noblesse Oblige" (pseud.). H. Evans.

Noblesse Oblige. H. Keddie.

Noiré, Ludwig (intro.): see I. Kant, *Critique of Pure Reason.*

"*Noli Me Tangere*": see J. Rizal, *Eagle Flight: A Filipino Novel.*

"Nomadic Life in Palestine": see W. C. Prime, *Tent Life in the Holy Land.*

"No pearl ever lay in Omar's green water": see T. Moore, "Araby's daughter" (song).

Nordez, Albert-Leon-Marie Le: see A. Le Nordez.

Norma (opera). V. Bellini.

Norraikow, Adolphus (trans.): see

L. N. Tolstoy, *Ivan the Fool; or, the Old Devil and the Three Small Devils.*

L. N. Tolstoy, *Life is Worth Living, and Other Stories.*

Norris, Frank: see W. D. Howells, "Frank Norris" (essay).

Norse legends: see the Reader's Guide entries for Iceland and for Scandinavian mythology.

North American history: see the Reader's Guide entries

for American history (including early Canadian history) and for Canadian history.

North American travel writings: see

W. Archer, *America To-Day: Observations and Reflections.*

M. Arnold, *Civilization in the United States: First and Last Impressions of America.*

A. F. de Bacourt, *Souvenirs of a Diplomat: Private Letters from America.*

A. Badlam, *Wonders of Alaska.*

J. Bernard, *Retrospections of America, 1797–1811.*

P. Blouet, *Frenchman in America: Recollections of Men and Things.*

C. J. P. Bourget, *Outre-Mer: Impressons of America.*

J. S. Buckingham, *America, Historical, Statistic, and Descriptive.*

W. Cobbett, *Year's Residence in the United States of America.*

E. T. Coke, *Subaltern's Furlough: Descriptive of Scenes in Various Parts of the United States, Upper and Lower Canada, New-Brunswick, and Nova Scotia, During the Summer and Autumn of 1832.*

G. Combe, *Notes on the United States of North America, During a Phrenological Visit in 1838–9-40.*

F. S. Cozzens, *Acadia; or, A Month with the Blue Noses.*

A. E. Dickinson, *Ragged Register (Of People Places and Opinions).*

C. W. Dilke, *Greater Britain: A Record of Travel in English-Speaking Countries During 1866 and 1867.*

S. A. Drake, *Heart of the White Mountains, Their Legend and Scenery.*

W. Faux, *Memorable Days in America; Being a Journal of a Tour to the United States.*

H. B. Fearon, *Sketches of America.*

L. H. Griffin, *Great Republic.*

B. Hall, *Travels in North America, in the Years 1827 and 1828.*

T. Hamilton, *Men and Manners in America.*

F. A. Kemble, *Journal of a Residence on a Georgian Plantation in 1838–39.*

F. A. Kemble, *Records of Later Life.*

E. King, *Great South: A Record of Journeys.*

A. Mackay, *Western World; or Travels in the United States in 1846–47.*

F. Marryat, *Diary in America, with Remarks on Its Institutions.*

F. Marryat, *Second Series of a Diary in America.*

H. Martineau, *Retrospect of Western Travel.*

H. Martineau, *Society in America.*

C. A. Murray, *Travels in North America During the Years 1834, 1835 & 1836, Including a Summer Residence with the Pawnee Tribe of Indians.*

J. Palmer, *Journal of Travels in the United States of North America, and in Lower Canada, Performed in the Year 1817.*

F. Parkman, *Oregon Trail: Sketches of Prairie and Rocky-Mountain Life.*

R. Pumpelly, *Across America and Asia; Notes of a Five Years' Journey Around the World:* see R. Pumpelly, *Explorations in Turkestan.*

A. D. Richardson, *Beyond the Mississippi: From the Great River to the Great Ocean.*

E. Roberts, *Shoshone and Other Western Wonders.*

C. Schultz, *Travels on an Inland Voyage Through the States.*

J. Sturge, *Visit to the United States in 1841.*

B. Taylor, *At Home and Abroad: A Sketch-Book of Life, Scenery, and Men.*

B. Taylor, *Eldorado; or, Adventures in the Path of Empire; Comprising a Voyage to California via Panama, Life in San Francisco and Monterey, Pictures of the Gold Region, and Experiences of Mexico Travel.*

W. M. Thayer, *Marvels of the New West: A Vivid Portrayal of the Stupendous Marvels in the Vast Wonderland West of the Missouri River.*

H. D. Thoreau, *Yankee in Canada, with Anti-Slavery and Reform Papers.*

A. de Tocqueville, *Democracy in America.*

F. M. Trollope, *Domestic Manners of the Americans.*

J. Verne, *Tour of the World in Eighty Days* (novel).

C. D. Warner, *Studies in the South and West, with Comments on Canada.*

E. C. E. M. S. Wortley, *Travels in the United States, Etc., During 1849 and 1850.*

See also the Reader's Guide entries for American West and for Travel writings.

Northanger Abbey. J. Austen.

North Carolina: see

M. J. Crim, *Adventures of a Fair Rebel.*

E. M. Lane, *Katrine, A Novel.*

H. E. Taliaferro (Catalog entry).

A. W. Tourgée, *Bricks Without Straw. A Novel.*

A. W. Tourgée, *Fool's Errand, by One of the Fools.*

Northern Lights (short stories). G. Parker.

Northern Travel: Summer and Winter Pictures of Sweden, Denmark, and Lapland. B. Taylor.

North Pole: see Arctic explorations.

"North wind doth blow": see the Catalog entry for Nursery Rhymes.

Norton, Andrews: see T. Carlyle, *Correspondence of Thomas Carlyle and Ralph Waldo Emerson 1834–1872* (marginalia).

Norton, Charles Eliot: see

(ed.) T. Carlyle, *Correspondence of Thomas Carlyle and Ralph Waldo Emerson.*

(trans.) A. Dante, *Divine Comedy of Dante Alighieri.*

(ed.) J. R. Lowell, *Letters of James Russell Lowell.*

Norton, Emperor: see A. S. Evans, *Our Sister Republic: A Gala Trip Through Tropical Mexico in 1869–70* (marginalia).

Norway: see

B. Bjørnson, *Happy Boy. A Tale of Norwegian Peasant Life.*

H. H. Boyesen, *Gunnar; A Tale of Norse Life.*

H. H. Boyesen, *Ilka on the Hill-top, and Other Stories.*

H. Ibsen (various titles of plays).

T. W. Knox, *Boy Travellers in Northern Europe.*

A. Strindberg (Catalog entry).

E. Tegnér, *Frithiof's Saga; A Legend of Ancient Norway.*

See also the Reader's Guide entry for Scandinavian mythology.

Nostalgia: see the Reader's Guide entry for Childhood nostalgia.

Nostromo; A Tale of the seaboard. J. Conrad.

"Not a leaf stirred" (comic sketch): see its Catalog entry.

Not Easily Jealous. I. D. Hardy.

Noted French Trials. Impostors and Adventurers. H. W. Fuller.

"Notes by T. Cole on the 'Adoration'" (essay, engraving). T. Cole.

Notes, Explanatory and Practical, on the New Testament. A. Barnes.

"Notes from Paris" (article): see E. Crawford.

Notes in Japan. A. Parsons.

Notes on England. H. A. Taine.

Notes on Rupert's America: see W. Cobbett.

Notes on the United States of North America, During a Phrenological Visit in 1838-9-40. G. Combe.

Nothing to Wear: An Episode of City Life (humorous poem): see W. A. Butler.

Nott, G. F. (trans.): see S. Propertius, *Erotica.*

Nouveau Larousse illustré:dictionnaire universel encyclopédique. P. A. Larousse.

Nouvelle Methode Pratique de Langue Italienne. C. Cardelli.

Nova Scotia: see

E. T. Coke, *Subaltern's Furlough: Descriptive of Scenes in Various Parts of the United States, Upper and Lower Canada, New-Brunswick, and Nova Scotia, During the Summer and Autumn of 1832.*

F. S. Cozzens, *Acadia; or, A Month with the Blue Noses.*

Novellen. P. J. L. von Heyse.

Novels. A. Dumas.

Novels and Novelists of the Eighteenth Century, in Illustration of the Manners and Morals of the Age. W. Forsyth.

Novum Organum. F. Bacon.

Nozze di Figaro (opera). J. C. Mozart.

Nuggets and Dust Panned Out in California. A. Bierce.

'Nunquam' (pseud.): see R. Blatchford.

Nuremberg: see

A. B. M. Jameson, *Sketches of Art, Literature, and Character.*

A. Strong, *Toymaker of Nuremberg; A Play.*

Nuremberg (photographs). See the Catalog entry.

Nuremberg; A Poem. H. W. Longfellow.

Nurse and Spy in the Union Army: Comprising the Adventures and Experiences of a Woman in Hospitals, Camps and Battle-Fields. S. E. E. Edmundson.

Nursery Rhymes: see

L. F. Baum, *Father Goose; His Book.*

W. Crane, *Baby's Opera: A Book of Old Rhymes with New Dresses.*

"Kilkenny Cats" (nursery rhyme).

"Mary Had a Little Lamb" (nursery rhyme).

Mother Goose; or, The Old Nursery Rhymes.

"Pop! goes the weasel" (children's song).

"Rock-a-bye baby" (nursery lullaby).

"Twinkle, Twinkle, Little Star" (nursery rhyme).

"Who Killed Cock Robin" (nursery rhyme).

E. F. Wyatt, *Every One His Own Way* (Catalog entry).

See also the Reader's Guide and Catalog entries for

Mother Goose and the Catalog entry for Nursery rhymes.

Nurses:

S. E. E. Edmundson, *Nurse and Spy in the Union Army.*

J. S. Woolsey, *Hospital Days.*

Nussir-u-Deen, King: see W. Knighton, *Private Life of an Eastern King.*

"Nye, Bill" (pseud.): see E. W. Nye.

▌O

"Oak" (poem and song). G. P. Morris.

Oakleigh. E. D. Deland.

Oates, Titus (conspiracy figure): see T. B. Macaulay, *History of England from the Accession of James II* (Catalog entry).

Oberammergau Passion Plays: see J. M. von Tautphoeus, *Quits, A Novel.*

Obiter Dicta. A. Birrell.

Obituaries: see the Reader's Guide entries for Death and for Funerals.

"Obligations of the United States to Initiate a Revision of Treaties Between the Western Powers and Japan" (essay). J. K. Newton.

"Oblige, Noblesse" (pseud.): see H. Evans.

O'Brien, Fitz-James: see the Catalog entry for S. O'Brien.

Occasional Poems. J. C. Lord.

Occult subjects: see the Reader's Guide entry for Mysticism.

Occupation for Play Hours. E. Leslie.

Oceana, or England and Her Colonies. J. A. Froude.

Oceanography: M. J. B. L. Sonrel, *Bottom of the Sea.*

Oceans: see the Reader's Guide entry for Sea adventures and voyages.

O'Connell, Daniel: see D. B. Lucas and J. F. McLaughlin, *Fisher Ames-Henry Clay, Etc.*

O'Connor, Thomas Power (ed.): see *T. P.'s Weekly.*

Octopus; or, The "Devil Fish" of Fiction and Fact. H. Lee.

Octoroon; or, Life in Louisiana (play). D. Boucicault.

Odd-Volumes' Year-Book. W. Manning.

"Ode for a Social Meeting, with Slight Alterations by a Tee-totaler" (poem). O. W. Holmes.

"Ode on the Intimations of Immortality" (poem). W. Wordsworth.

"Ode to Freedom" (poem): see C. E. S. Wood, *Masque of Love* (poem) (Catalog entry).

Ode to Girlhood and Other Poems. A. A. S. James.

Ode to Harvard and Other Poems. H. W. Bynner.

Odes. Horace.

Odes from the Divan of Hafiz. Hāfiz.

"Ode Written in the Beginning of the Year 1746" (poem). W. Collins.

Odyssey of Homer. Homer.

"O'er waiting harp strings of the mind" (hymn). M. B. Eddy.

"Of all the girls that are so smart" (song): see H. Carey, "Sally in our alley."

Office and Duty of a Christian Pastor. S. H. Tyng.

Official Guide to Tewkesbury: see the Catalog entry for Tewkesbury.

Off the Skelligs: A Novel. J. Ingelow.

"Of Miracles" (extract from *Enquiry Concerning Human Understanding*): see D. Hume, "Of Miracles."

"O for a sweet, inspiring ray" (hymn). A. Steele.

"Of Some Railroad Accidents" (article). C. F. Adams, Jr.

Of the House of Chloe; A Tale of the Times. E. Marston.

"Oft in the stilly night" (song). T. Moore.

Ogilvies. A Novel. D. M. M. Craik.

"Oh, charming May!" (song). P. Henry Hatch.

Oh! Christina! J. J. Bell.

"Oh, Darkies, hab you seen Ole Massa" (song): see H. C. Work, "Kingdom coming" (song).

"Oh! Dem golden slippers" (song). J. A. Bland.

"Oh! Don't you remember" (song). T. D. English.

Ohio: see

O. W. Holmes, *Autocrat of the Breakfast-Table* (marginalia).

J. B. Naylor, *Ralph Marlowe; A Novel.*

W. Reid, *Ohio in the War: Her Statesmen, Generals, and Soldiers.*

F. M. Trollope, *Domestic Manners of the Americans* (marginalia).

C. Wuichet, *Sunny Side of a Busy Life.*

Ohio in the War: Her Statesmen, Generals, and Soldiers. W. Reid.

Ohio River: see

Z. Cramer, *Navigator.*

T. Hamilton, *Men and Manners in America.*

A. C. H. Rice, *Mr. Opp* (Catalog entry).

"Oh, refresh us": see J. Fawcett, "Lord, dismiss us with Thy blessing" (hymn).

"Oh, rise an' shine" (spiritual): see "Rise and shine."

Oidhe Chloinne Uisnigh: Fate of the Children of Uisneach. R. J. O'Duffy (ed. and trans.).

Old Acquaintance. Barry Cornwall and Some of His Friends. J. T. Fields.

Old age: see

L. L. Bell, *Love Affairs of an Old Maid.*

M. E. W. Freeman, "Old-Maid Aunt" (story).

B. C. Greene, *Adventures of an Old Maid. By Aunt Ruth.*

B. Harte, "John Burns of Gettysburg" (poem).

W. D. Howells, *Silver Wedding Journey* (novel).

R. Kipling, "Old Men" (poem).

G. L. Kittredge, *Old Farmer and His Almanack; Being Some Observations on Life and Manners in New England a Hundred Years Ago.*

J. Linen, "I Feel I'm Growing Auld, Gude-Wife" (poem).

J. R. Lowell, *Letters of James Russell Lowell* (Catalog entry).

D. G. Mitchell, *About Old Story-Tellers; Of How and When They Lived, and What Stories They Told.*

J. F. Mines, *Tour Around New York, and My Summer Acre; Being the Recreations of Mr. Felix Oldboy.*

W. Morris, "Shameful Death."

E. H. Mott, *Old Settler and His Tales of the Sugar Swamp.*

Omar Khayyám, *Rubáiyát of Omar Khayyám, the Astronomer-Poet of Persia.*

J. W. Riley, "Honest Old Sam Hungerford" (poem).

M. Saadi, *Gulistan; or, Rose Garden, by Musle-Huddeen Sheik Saadi, of Shiraz.*

K. A. Sanborn (comp.), *Indian Summer Calendar.*

Old and New Unitarian Belief. J. W. Chadwick.

"Old Bankers of Florence" (article). H. T. Tuckerman.

"Old Black Joe" (minstrel song). S. C. Foster.

"Old Bob Ridley" (minstrel song). C. White.

Old Book Collector's Miscellany; or, a Collection of Readable Reprints of Literary Rarities. C. Hindley (ed.).

"Oldboy, Felix" (pseud.): see J. F. Mines.

Old Christmas and Bracebridge Hall. W. Irving.

Old Country House. R. Le Gallienne.

Old Creole Days. G. W. Cable.

Old Curiosity Shop. C. Dickens.

"Old Dan Tucker" (song). D. D. Emmett.

"Old Dog Tray" (minstrel song). S. C. Foster.

Old English literature: see
  Beowulf.
  C. W. Dilke (ed.) *Old English Plays; Being a Selection from the Early Dramatic Writers.*

Old English Plays; Being a Selection from the Early Dramatic Writers. C. W. Dilke (ed.).

Old Farmer and His Almanack; Being Some Observations on Life and Manners in New England a Hundred Years Ago. G. L. Kittredge.

Old-Fashioned Girl. L. M. Alcott.

"Old folks at home" (minstrel song). S. C. Foster.

Old Friends. A. Lang.

Old Homestead (play). D. Thompson [assisted by G. W. Ryer].

Old House at Sandwich. A Novel. J. Hatton.

"Old hundred" (hymn). W. Kethe.

Old London Street Cries and the Cries of To-Day. A. W. Tuer.

"Old-Maid Aunt" (story). M. E. W. Freeman.

Old Mark Langstan; A Tale of Duke's Creek. R. M. Johnston.

Old Melbourne Memories. T. A. Browne.

"Old Men" (poem). R. Kipling.

"Old Militia Muster" (unpublished farce). C. D. Taylor.

Old New Zealand, A Tale of the Good Old Times. F. E. Maning.

Old Nursery Rhymes. Mother Goose.

"Old oaken bucket" (song): see S. Woodworth, "Bucket" (song).

"Old Pictures in Florence" (poem): see R. Browning, *Men and Women.*

Old Régime in Canada. F. Parkman.

"Old, old sea": see T. B. Read, "Come, Gentle Trembler" (poem).

Old Roman World: The Grandeur and Fall of Its Civilization. J. Lord.

Old Settler and His Tales of Sugar Swamp. E. H. Mott.

Old Shrines and Ivy. W. Winter.

"Old Si" (pseud.): see S. W. Small.

"Old Sile's Clem" (story). P. H. Coggins.

"Old Soldier's Story." J. W. Riley.

Old Songs, with Drawings by Edwin A. Abbey and Alfred Parsons. E. A. Abbey.

Old Southwest: see the Reader's Guide entry for Southern frontier.

Old Story-Tellers. D. G. Mitchell.

"Old Swimmin'-Hole," and 'Leven More Poems. J. W. Riley.

Old Testament: see the Reader's Guide entry for Bible and the Catalog entries for Bible. Old Testament.

"Old-Time Oriental Trade" (article). W. L. Fawcett.

Old Times in the Colonies. C. C. Coffin.

Old Times on the Upper Mississippi; The Recollections of a Steamboat Pilot from 1854 to 1863. G. B. Merrick.

Old Touraine: The Life and History of the Famous Chateâux of France. T. A. Cook.

Old Town by the Sea. T. B. Aldrich.

Oldtown Fireside Stories. H. E. B. Stowe.

Oldtown Folks. H. E. B. Stowe.

Old Wells Dug Out. T. D. W. Talmage.

Old Yorkshire. W. Smith (ed.).

Olio of Domestic Verses. E. C. Judson.

Oliphant, Laurence: see M. O. W. Oliphant, *Memoir of the Life of Laurence Oliphant and of Alice Oliphant, His Wife.*

Olive. A Novel. D. M. Mulock.

Oliver Cromwell's Letters and Speeches: With Elucidations. T. Carlyle (ed.).

Oliver, Grace A. (intro.): see M. Edgeworth, *Classic Tales.*

"Oliver Optic" (pseud.): see W. T. Adams.

Oliver Sargent. E. J. Bliss.

Oliver Twist. C. Dickens.

Olivia (play). W. G. Willis (adapt.).

Olle Kamellen (stories): see F. Reuter, "Dörchläuchting."

Ollendorff, Heinrich Gottfried: see H. Hendrik, *Memoirs of Hans Hendrik, The Arctic Traveller* (marginalia).

Ollendorff's New Method of Learning to Read, Write, and Speak the French Language. H. G. Ollendorff.

Ollendorff's New Method of Learning to Read, Write, and Speak the German Language. H. G. Ollendorff.

Olympian Nights. J. K. Bangs.

Omar Khayyám: see the Reader's Guide entry for *Rubáiyát of Omar Khayyám.*

On a Jaunting-Car Through Donegal and Connemara. S. G. Bayne.

"On a lone barren isle" (song): see H. S. Washburn, "Grave of Bonaparte" (song).

On a Mexican Mustang, through Texas, from the Gulf to the Rio Grande. A. E. Sweet.

"Once in royal David's city" (Christmas carol). C. F. H. Alexander.

One Hundred Quatrains from the Rubáiyát. Omar Khayyám.

One Summer. B. W. Howard.

One Year Abroad. B. W. Howard.

One Year's Sketch-Book. I. E. Jerome.

"On First Looking into Chapman's Homer" (poem). J. Keats. See also F. P. Cobbe, *The Peak in Darien, with Some Other Inquiries Touching Concerns of the Soul and the Body.*

"On Friday morn" (song): see "Mermaid" (sea shanty).

On Heroes, Hero-Worship, and the Heroic. T. Carlyle.

"On Jordan's stormy banks I stand" (hymn). S. Stennett.

Onlooker's Note-Book. G. W. E. Russell.

Only a Butterfly, and Other Stories. G. M. C. May.

"Only an armour-bearer" (hymn). P. P. Bliss.

"'Only Me'" (poem). C. A. B. Mason.

Only Sister. H. E. G. Witt.
Onoocool Chunder Mookerjee (1829–1871): A Memoir. M. Mookerjee.
On Peter's Island. A. R. Ropes.
On Snow-Shoes to the Barren Grounds. Twenty-Eight Hundred Miles After Musk-Oxen and Wood-Bison. C. Whitney.
On Sunny Shores. C. Scollard.
On the Border with Crook. J. G. Bourke.
On the Face of the Waters; A Tale of the Mutiny. F. A. W. Steel.
On the Heights; A Novel. B. Auerbach.
"On the Mississippi" (article). R. Keeler.
On the Nile. A. Hoppin.
On the Origin of Species. C. Darwin.
"On the Power of Sound." W. Wordsworth.
"On the Prospect of Planting Arts and Learning America" (poem). G. Berkeley.
On the Verge: A Romance of the Centennial. A. L. Townsend.
On the Wing of Occasions; Being the Authorized Version of Certain Curious Episodes of the Late Civil War. J. C. Harris.
Onward (poem): see H. H. Dole, *Peace and Progress, Two Symphonic Poems.*
"Onward, Christian Soldiers" (hymn): see
S. Baring-Gould, *In Exitu Israel; An Historical Novel.*
G L. Dickinson, *Letters from a Chinese Official.*
L. Strachey, "Progressional" (satirical poem).
Open-Eyed Conspiracy: An Idyl of Saratoga (novel). W. D. Howells.
Open Question; A Tale of Two Temperaments. E. Robins.
Operas: see
D. F. E. Auber, *Crown Diamonds [Les Diamonts de la Couronne]* (romantic comic opera).
M. W. Balfe, *Bohemian Girl* (opera).
V. Bellini, *Norma* (opera).
G. Bizet, *Carmen* (opera).
F. A. Boieldieu, *Calife de Bagdad* (comic opera).
F. A. Boieldieu, *Dame Blanche* (light opera).
F. C. Burnand, *Cox and Box* (comic opera).
A. A. Chapin, *Wotan, Siegfried, and Brünnhilde* (guide to Wagner's operas).
E. Fitzball, *Maritana* (opera).
F. von Flotow, *Martha, or the Market at Richmond* (opera).
E. Humperdinck, *Hänsel und Gretel* (opera).
B. Lumley, *Reminiscences of the Opera.*
P. Mascagni, *Cavalleria Rusticana* (opera).
P. Mascagni, *I Rantzu* (opera).
G. Puccini, *Tosca* (opera).
G. A. Rossini, *Barbiere di Siviglia [The Barber of Seville]* (opera).
G. A. Rossini, *Elisabetta, Regina d'Inghilterra [Elizabeth, Queen of England]* (opera).
G. A. Rossini, *Guillaume Tell [William Tell]* (opera).
W. Scott, *Roderick Dhu; or, The Lady of the Lake: Opera Libretto.*
G. P. Upton, *Standard Operas: Their Plots, Their Music, and Their Composers.*
G. Verdi, *Ballo in Maschera* (opera).

G. Verdi, *Rigoletto* (opera).
G. Verdi, *Siegfried* (opera).
G. Verdi, *Traviata* (opera).
G. Verdi, *Trovatore* (opera).
R. Wagner, *Lohengrin, Son of Parsifal* (opera).
R. Wagner, *Parsifal* (opera).
R. Wagner, *Siegfried* (opera).
R. Wagner, *Tannhäuser* (opera).
R. Wagner, *Tristan und Isolde* (opera).
C. D. Warner, *Roundabout Journey.*
Operettas: see
H. C. Bunner, *Three Operettas. Music by Oscar Weil.*
W. S. Gilbert, *H. M. S. Pinafore* (operetta).
W. S. Gilbert, *Iolanthe* (operetta).
W. S. Gilbert, *Mikado* (operetta).
W. S. Gilbert, *Patience; or, Bunthorne's Bride* (operetta).
W. S. Gilbert, *Yeomen of the Guard* (operetta).
J. L. Long, *Madame Butterfly* (operetta).
C. Wälzel and F. F. R. Genée, *Fatinitza* (operetta).
'Op-o'-me-Thumb (one-act play). F. Fenn and R. Pryce.
Opper, Frederick Burr (illus.): see E. W. Nye, *Bill Nye's History of the United States.*
Oppressive Tariff Taxation (pamphlet). J. Means.
"Optic, Oliver" (pseud.): see W. T. Adams.
Orations: see the Reader's Guide entry for Speeches.
Orations and Essays of Edward John Phelps, Diplomat and Statesman. E. J. Phelps.
"Orator" (poem). G. E. Woodberry.
Oratory: see the Reader's Guide entries for Speeches and for Speech improvement.
Ordway, J. P. (composer): see M. S. Pike, "Home again" (song).
"O refresh us": see J. Fawcett, "Lord, dismiss us with Thy blessing."
Oregon: see A. D. Richardson, *Beyond the Mississippi: From the Great River to the Great Ocean.*
Oregon Trail: Sketches of Prairie and Rocky-Mountain Life. F. Parkman.
"O'Rell, Max" (pseud.): see P. Blouet.
Oriental Ceramic Art; Illustrated by Examples from the Collection of W. T. Walters. W. T. Walters.
Oriental Rambles. G. W. Caldwell.
"Original, Ab." (pseud.): see J. Sadler.
Original Poems. J. A. D. Moore.
Origin and History of the Books of the Bible, Both the Canonical and the Apocryphal. C. E. Stowe.
Origin of Species. C. Darwin.
Orléans de la Motte, Louis-François-Gabriel d': see L. B. Proyart, *Vie de M. D'Orléans De La Motte. Évêque d'Amiens, par M. L'Abbé Proyart.*
Orlóff and His Wife. Tales of the Barefoot Brigade. M. Gorky.
Orme and Sons: see *Prize Essays.*
Orphans: see
L. M. Alcott, *Little Men: Life at Plumfield with Jo's Boys.*
J. H. Batt, *Dr. Barnardo, the Foster-Father of "Nobody's Children."*
S. E. S. Boggs, *Sandpeep.*
C. Dickens, *David Copperfield.*
C. Dickens, *Great Expectations.*

C. Dickens, *Oliver Twist.*
E. C. S. Gaskell, *Ruth.*
G. A. Kendrick, *Contrasts.*
A. Le Feuvre, *"Probable Sons."*
M. A. A. Ward, *History of David Grieve* (novel).
A. J. E. Wilson, *Beulah, A Novel.*
Orthodox Preacher and Nancy; Being the Tale of the Misfortunes of a Minister who Tried to Do as Jesus Would. A Story of Ministerial Life as It Is. M. Pratt.
Orthodoxy. G. K. Chesterton.
Orton, Arthur : see the Reader's Guide entry for Tichborne Claimant.
Osborne, Dorothy: see D. O. Temple.
Osbourne, Lloyd (co-author): see
   R. L. Stevenson, *Wrecker* (novel).
   R. L. Stevenson, *Wrong Box* (novel).
Ossian: see J. Macpherson, *Poems of Ossian, the Son of Fingal. Translated from the Original Gaelic.*
Ossoli, Giovanni Angelo: see M. Fuller, *Memoirs of Margaret Fuller Ossoli.*
Ostertag, Blanche Adele (illus.): see M. E. Burt (ed.), *Poems That Every Child Should Know: A Selection of the Best Poems of All Times.*
Othello (play). W. Shakespeare.
Othello (play): see H. R. F. Brown, *Studies in the History of Venice.*
Otho, Marcus Salvius (Emperor): see Tacitus, *Works of Tacitus* (marginalia).
Otis, Charles Pomeroy (ed.), *Grimm's Maerchen: Brüder Grimm Kinder und Hausmaerchen.*
"Otis, James" (pseud.): see J. O. Kaler.
"Otto, Franz" (pseud.): see F. O. Spamer.
Otto of the Silver Hand. H. Pyle.
Oudh: see *Private Life of an Eastern King.*
Ought We To Visit Her? A Novel. A. Edwards.
"Ouida" (pseud.): see M. L. De la Ramée.
Ounces of Prevention. T. M. Coan.
Our American Cousin (play): see T. Taylor, *Dundreary, A Four-Act Comedy.*
Our Best Society (play). I. Browne.
Our Boys in India: The Wanderings of Two Young Americans in Hindustan, with Their Adventures on the Sacred Rivers and Wild Mountains, Etc. H. W. French.
Our Children in the Other Life. C. Giles.
Our English Surnames: Their Sources and Significances. C. W. E. Bardsley.
"Our Father's Care" (A Ballad). M. W. Sewell.
Our Four-Footed Friends. M. B. Howitt.
Our Great West: A Study of the Present Conditions and Future Possibilities. J. Ralph.
Our Home in the Ocean for Eleven Months. A. Brassey.
Our Lady's Inn; A Novel. J. S. Clouston.
Our Living World; An Artistic Edition of the Rev. J. G. Wood's Natural History of Animate Creation. J. G. Wood.
Our Mutual Friend. C. Dickens.
Our Old Nobility. H. Evans.
Our Philippine Problem; A Study of American Colonial Policy. H. P. Willis.
Our Presidents, and How We Make Them. A Historical Survey of How Each Man Came to Hold the Office. A. K. McClure.
Our Sister Republic: A Gala Trip Through Tropical Mexico in 1869–70. A. S. Evans.
"Our Spanish Prisoners at Portsmouth" (essay). W. D. Howells.
Our Wife; or, the Rose of Amiens: A Comic Drama in Two Acts. J. M. Morton.
Our Wild Indians: Thirty-Three Years' Personal Experience among the Red Men of the Great West. R. I. Dodge.
Our Work as a Church. T. K. Beecher.
Outcome of the Civil War, 1863–1865. J. K. Hosmer: see A. B. Hart (ed.) *American Nation: A History from Original Sources by Associated Scholars.*
Outcroppings: Being Selections of California Verse. B. Harte (ed.).
Outdoor Studies. E. Ingersoll.
Outlaws: see
   J. Cundall, *Robin Hood and His Merry Foresters.*
   T. J. Dimsdale, *Vigilantes of Montana; or, Popular Justice in the Rocky Mountains.*
   E. Gilliat, *Forest Outlaws; or, Saint Hugh and the King.*
   J. W. von Goethe, *Götz von Berlichingen* (play).
   F. Grose, *Classical Dictionary of the Vulgar Tongue* (marginalia).
   T. W. S. Higginson, *Travellers and Outlaws, Episodes in American History.*
   H. R. Howard, *History of Virgil A. Stewart, and His Adventure.*
   A. Pinkerton, *Mississippi Outlaws and the Detectives.*
   H. Pyle, *Merry Adventures of Robin Hood of Great Renown, in Nottinghamshire.*
   V. A. Stewart, *History of the Detection, Conviction, Life and Designs of John A. Murel, The Great Western Land Pirate.*
   E. M. Tappan, *Robin Hood, His Book.*
   C. Whitehead, *Lives and Exploits of the Most Noted Highwaymen, Robbers and Murderers, of All Nations, Drawn from the Most Authentic Sources and Brought Down to the Present Time.*
   G. T. Wilkinson, *Newgate Calendar Improved; Being Interesting Memoirs of Notorious Characters, Who Have Been Convicted of Offences Against the Laws of England, During the Seventeenth Century; and Continued to the Present Time.*
   World of Wonders; A Record of Things Wonderful in Nature, Science, and Art.
Outlines of Ancient and Modern History on a New Plan. R. Robbins.
Outlines of the History of Art. W. Lübke.
Out of the Question: A Comedy (play). W. D. Howells.
Outre-Mer: Impressions of America. C. J. P. Bourget.
"Outward Bound" (poem): see D. M. M. Craik, *Poems.*
Overland Through Asia. T. Knox.
"Over-Soul" (essay). R. W. Emerson.
"Over the Cossack Steppes" (article). D. Ker.
Over the Plum-Pudding (short story). J. K. Bangs.
Ovid: see T. Bulfinch, *Age of Fable; or, Beauties of Mythology.*
"Owen, Ashford" (pseud.): see A. C. Ogle.

"Owen Brown's Escape from Harper's Ferry" (article). R. Keeler.

Owen, John: see T. Long, *Exercitation Concerning the Frequent Use of Our Lord's Prayer in the Publick Worship of God* (religious tract).

Owen, Will (illus.): see
W. W. Jacobs, *Sailors' Knots* (stories).
W. W. Jacobs, *Salthaven* (novel).

Owens, John Edmond: see J. S. Jones, *People's Lawyer* (play).

"O what, if we are Christ's" (hymn): see G. J. Geer (Catalog entry).

Oxford and Its Colleges. J. Wells.

Oxford (England): see W. D. Howells, *Certain Delightful English Towns, with Glimpses of the Pleasant Country Between.*

Oxford University: see
O. H. B. Ball, *Barbara Goes to Oxford.*
E. Bradley, *Adventures of Mr. Verdant Green.*
T. Hughes, *Tom Brown at Oxford.*
J. Wells, *Oxford and Its Colleges.*

Oxus River: see J. A. MacGahan, *Campaigning on the Oxus, and the Fall of Khiva.*

▌P

Pacchiarotto and How He Worked in Distemper: see R. Browning, *Red Cotton Night-Cap Country.*

Pacha of Many Tales. F. Marryat.

Pacific Ocean: see *Battle for the Pacific, and Other Adventures at Sea.*

Pacifism: see the Reader's Guide entries for Spanish-AmericanWar and for Warfare.

Packard, Silas Sadler (co-author): see J. D. Williams, *Guide to Williams & Packard's System of Penmanship for Teachers and Adepts.*

Paddle and Portage, from Moosehead Lake to the Aroostook River, Maine. T. S. Steele.

Paddles and Politics Down the Danube. P. Bigelow.

Paddock, Mrs. A. G.: see C. Paddock.

Pa Flickinger's Folks. B. R. Hoover.

Pagan at the Shrine. G. H. E. Slater.

Pages and Pictures, from the Writings of James Fenimore Cooper, with Notes. J. F. Cooper.

Page to a royal court:
C. de F. d' Hézecques, *Recollections of a Page to the Court of Louis XVI.*
C. M. Yonge, *Prince and the Page: A Story of the Last Crusade.*

Page, Walter Hines (ed.): see *World's Work* (magazine).

Paige, James W. (inventor): see
Pall Mall Gazette (London) (Catalog entry).
M. L. Wynkoop, *Condensed Manual on Patented Inventions: What to Do and What Not to Do to Insure Success to the Inventor* (Catalog entry).

Paine, Albert Bigelow: see (contr.) *Way into Print.*

Paine, Augustus Gibson, Sr.: see (inscr.) Z. Cramer, *Navigator.*

Paine, Thomas: see
O. Khayyám, *Rubáiyát of Omar Khayyám in English Verse* (marginalia).
Truth Seeker (magazine).

B. F. Underwood, *Essays and Lectures.*

H. Walpole, *Letters of Horace Walpole, Earl of Oxford* (marginalia).

Painted Desert; A Story of Northern Arizona. C. K. Munroe.

Painted Shadows. R. Le Gallienne.

Painters, Sculptors, Architects, Engravers, and Their Works: A Handbook. C. E. Clement.

Pair of Patient Lovers. W. D. Howells.

Paiutes (Native American tribe): see W. Wright, "Washoe Rambles" (articles).

"Pakeha Maori" (pseud.): see F. E. Maning.

Palace and Hovel; or, Phases of London Life. Being Personal Observations of an American in London. D. J. Kirwan.

Palace of Danger; A Story of La Pompadour. M. Wagnalls.

"Palatine" (poem). W. S. Cather.

Paleontology: see
E. S. Grew, *Romance of Modern Geology, Describing in Simple But Exact Language the Making of the Earth with Some Account of Prehistoric Animal Life.*
O. C. Marsh, *Fossil Horses in America.*
H. S. Williams, *Story of Nineteenth-Century Science.*

Palestine: see
E. P. Hammond, *Sketches of Palestine.*
J. A. Hart, *Levantine Log-Book.*
T. W. Knox, *Backsheesh! or, Life and Adventures in the Orient.*
N. MacLeod, *Eastward.*
J. Murray, *Handbook for Travellers in Syria and Palestine.*
"Nomadic Life in Palestine": see W. C. Prime, *Tent Life in the Holy Land.*
W. C. Prime, *Tent Life in the Holy Land* (Catalog entry).
E. Robinson, *Biblical Researches in Palestine, and in the Adjacent Regions. A Journal of Travels in the Years 1838 & 1852.*
C. Scollard, *Under Summer Skies.*
B. Taylor, *Lands of the Saracens; or, Pictures of Palestine, Asia Minor, Sicily, and Spain.*
W. H. Thomson, *Parables and Their Home. The Parables by the Lake.*
W. M. Thomson, *Central Palestine and Phoenicia.*
W. M. Thomson, *Land and the Book; or, Biblical illustrations Drawn from the Manners and Customs, the Scenes and Scenery, of the Holy Land: Lebanon, Damascus and Beyond Jordan.*
T. Wright (ed.), *Early Travels in Palestine, Comprising the Narratives of Arculf, Willibald, Bernard, Saewulf, Sigurd, Benjamin of Tudela, Sir John Maundeville, De La Brocquière, and Maundrell.*
See also the Reader's Guide entry for Holy Land.

Palgrave, Francis Turner:
(ed.) J. Keats, *Poetical Works of John Keats.*
(hymn lyrics): see the Catalog entry for G. J. Geer.

Palliser, Fanny (Marryat) Bury (trans.): see A. Jacquemart, *History of the Ceramic Art; A Descriptive and Philosophical Study of the Pottery of All Ages and All Nations.*

Palm Branches. S. M. Mills.

Palmer, F. S. (co-author): see *Adventures in Field and Forest.*

Palmerston, Viscount: see

J. G. Argyll, *Viscount Palmerston, K. G.*

W. Bagehot, *Biographical Studies.*

Palmistry: see

W. G. Benham, *Laws of Scientific Hand Reading; A Practical Treatise on the Art Commonly Called Palmistry.*

W. T. Stead, "Suggested Test Reading" (article).

W. T. Stead, "Test Readings of Mark Twain's Hands" (article).

M. W. Townsend, *Asia and Europe: Studies* (marginalia).

W. J. Warner, *Cheiro's Language of the Hand.*

See also the Reader's Guide entries for Mysticism and for Parapsychology.

Palm reading: see the Reader's Guide entry for Palmistry.

Pamela; or, Virtue Rewarded (novel). S. Richardson.

Panama: see

F. A. Ober, *Vasco Nuñez de Balboa.*

B. Taylor, *Eldorado; or, Adventures in the Path of Empire; Comprising a Voyage to California via Panama, Life in San Francisco and Monterey, Pictures of the Gold Region, and Experiences of Mexico Travel.*

Panama Patchwork; Poems, by James Stanley Gilbert. J. S. Gilbert.

Pan-American Exposition (1901): see T. Fleming, *Around the "Pan" with Uncle Hank. His Trip Through the Pan-American Exposition.*

Pan-Germanic Doctrine; Being a Study of German Political Aims and Aspirations. A. Harrison.

Pansy's Picture Book. I. Alden.

Pantheism: see J. W. Lloyd, *Dawn-Thought on the Reconciliation; A Volume of Pantheistic Impressions and Glimpses of Larger Religion.*

Paolo & Francesca: A Tragedy in Four Acts (play). S. Phillips.

Parables and Their Home. The Parables by the Lake. W. H. Thomson.

Parables from Nature. M. S. Gatty.

Parables of the New Testament Practically Unfolded. W. B. Stevens.

Paracelsus (poem): see R. Browning, *Dramas.*

Paracelsus (poem): see R. Browning, *Pauline; Paracelsus; Strafford; Sordello.*

Paradise in the Pacific; A Book of Travel, Adventure, and Facts in the Sandwich Islands. W. R. Bliss.

Paradise Lost. J. Milton.

Paradise Lost: see T. Keightley, *Account of the Life, Opinions, and Writings of John Milton. With an Introduction to Paradise Lost.*

Paradise of the Pacific. Sketches of Hawaiian Scenery and Life. H. H. Gowen.

Paraguayan War: see M. von Versen, *Reisen in Amerika und der Südamerikanische Krieg.*

Parallel History of France and England; Consisting of Outlines and Dates. C. M. Yonge.

Paranormal topics: see the Reader's Guide entry for Parapsychology.

Parapsychology: see

I. Bacheller, *The Master of Silence. A Romance.*

J. K. Bangs, *Ghosts I Have Met and Some Others.*

J. Bigelow, *Mystery of Sleep.*

V. F. Boyle, *Devil Tales.*

F. T. Buckland, *Curiosities of Natural History* (Catalog entry).

R. H. Davis, *Vera, The Medium.*

W. F. De Morgan, *Alice-For-Short: A Dichronism.*

T. W. Doane, *Bible Myths and Their Parallels in Other-Religions* (marginalia).

J. B. Dods, *Spirit Manifestations Examined and Explained.*

N. C. Flammarion, *Inconnu. The Unknown.*

E. A. Fletcher, *Woman Beautiful: A Practical Treatise on the Development and Preservation of Woman's Health and Beauty, and the Principles of Taste in Dress* (Catalog entry).

I. K. Funk, *Psychic Riddle.*

E. Gurney, *Phantasms of the Living.*

D. D. Home, *Incidents in My Life.*

W. D. Howells, *Between the Dark and the Daylight: Romances.*

W. D. Howells (co-ed.), *Library of Universal Adventure by Sea and Land.*

W. D. Howells, *Undiscovered Country.*

W. W. Jacobs, "Monkey's Paw" (short story).

S. O. Jewett, "Miss Tempy's Watchers" in *Tales of New England.*

R. Kipling, *Phantom 'Rickshaw, and Other Tales.*

R. Kipling, "They" (short story).

O. A. Liljencrantz, *Randvar the Songsmith; A Romance of Norumbega.*

E. G. E. B. Lytton, *Zanoni.*

B. Matthews, *Tales of Fantasy and Fact.*

F. W. H. Myers, *Human Personality and Its Survival of Bodily Death.*

A. E. S. Smythe, *Poems, Grave and Gay.*

Society for Psychical Research (London).

B. Stoker, *Dracula.*

B. Stoker, *Jewel of Seven Stars.*

B. Taylor, *At Home and Abroad: A Sketch-Book of Life, Scenery, and Men.*

F. B. Terry, *Stories.*

C. Wagner, *Âme des Choses.*

M. E. J. Whitcombe, *Bygone Days in Devonshire and Cornwall, with Notes of Existing Superstitions and Customs.*

F. B. Wilson, *Paths to Power.*

See also the Reader's Guide entries for Mysticism, for Palmistry, for Phrenology, for Society for Psychical Research, for Spiritualism and Spiritual healing, and for Telepathy.

Parenting: see

C. E. Beecher, *Religious Training of Children in the School, the Family, and the Church.*

H. Bushnell, *Christian Nurture.*

M. L. Charlesworth, *Ministering Children: A Tale Dedicated to Childhood.*

S. C. Coleridge, *Memoir and Letters of Sara Coleridge.*

O. S. Fowler, *Love and Parentage, Applied to the*

Improvement of Offspring, Including Important Directions and Suggestions to Lovers and the Married.

S. S. Gilman, *Mothers in Council.*

M. T. P. Mann, *Moral Culture of Infancy, and Kindergarten Guide.*

T. Roosevelt, *Square Deal* (marginalia).

F. F. Wood, *Infancy and Childhood.*

Parent's Assistant; or, Stories for Children. M. Edgeworth.

Paris: see

K. Baedeker, *Paris and Its Environs. Handbook for Travellers.*

L. Barzini, Sr., *Pekin to Paris: An Account of Prince Borghese's Journey Across Two Continents in aMotor-Car.* L. Barzini, Sr.

M. D. Conway, *Autobiography: Memories and Experiences of Moncure Daniel Conway* (marginalia).

E. Crawford, "Notes from Paris" (article).

E. De Amicis, *Studies of Paris.*

Galignani's New Paris Guide for 1867.

L. Halévy, *Parisian Points of View.*

A. S. Hardy, *But Yet A Woman; A Novel.*

Harper's Guide to Paris and the Exposition of 1900.

O. W. Holmes, *Autocrat of the Breakfast-Table* (marginalia).

E. Marshall, *Lizette: A Story of the Latin Quarter* (novel).

E. C. G. Murray, *Member for Paris: A Tale of the Second Empire.*

B. Runkle, *Helmet of Navarre.*

R. L. Stevenson and L. Osbourne, *Wrecker* (novel).

W. M. Thackeray, *Sketch Books. The Paris Sketch Book of Mr. M. A. Titmarsh. The Irish Sketch Book of a Journey from Cornhill to Grand Cairo.*

C. D. Warner, *Saunterings.*

A. D. White, *History of the Warfare of Science with Theology in Christendom* (marginalia).

É. Zola, *Assommoir.*

Paris and Its Environs. Handbook for Travellers. K. Baedeker.

Paris, Gustave (pref.): see A. R. Macdonough (trans.), *Lovers of Provence: Aucassin and Nicolette.*

Parisian Points of View. L. Halévy.

Paris Sketch Book of Mr. M. A. Titmarsh: see W. M. Thackeray, *Sketch Books. The Paris Sketch Book of Mr. M. A. Titmarsh. The Irish Sketch Book of a Journey from Cornhill to Grand Cairo.*

Parker, Edwin Pond: see

N. J. Burton (co-comp.), *Christian Hymnal. A Selection of Psalms and Hymns, with Music.*

(arr.) A. Reed, "Holy Ghost! With light divine" (hymn).

Parker, Gilbert: see S. R. Crockett, *Tales of Our Coast.*

"Parker, Jenny Marsh" (pseud.): see J. M. Parker.

Parker, Louis Napoleon. (trans.): see H. L. É. Lavedan, *Duel.*

Parker, Matthew: see M. Fowler, *Some Notable Archbishops of Canterbury* (marginalia).

Parker, Theodore: see J. F. Clarke, *Memorial and Biographical Sketches.*

Parkinson, William Edward (illus.): see G. MacDonald, *Rough Shaking.*

Parkman, Francis: see

J. J. I. von Döllinger and J. N. Huber, *Pope and the Council* (notes laid in).

C. H. Farnham, *Life of Francis Parkman.*

W. E. H. Lecky, *History of European Morals from Augustus to Charlemagne* (marginalia).

"Parley, Peter" (pseud.): see S. G. Goodrich.

Parleyings with Certain People of Imporance in Their Day. R. Browning.

Parlor Car. W. D. Howells.

Parnassus. R. W. Emerson (ed.).

Parnell, Charles Stewart: see

R. B. Barry, *Life of Charles Stewart Parnell.*

R. B. O'Brien, *Life of Charles Stewart Parnell, 1846–1891.*

Parr, Catharine: see K. M. Mundt, *Henry VIII. and His Court; or, Catherine Parr. An Historical Novel.*

Parr, Thomas: see H. Wilson, *Wonderful Characters; Comprising Memoirs and Anecdotes of the Most Remarkable Persons of Every Age and Nation.*

Parry, Edward Abbott (ed.): see D. O. Temple, *Love Letters of Dorothy Osborne to Sir William Temple, 1652–54.*

Parsees: see

Jivanji Jamshedji Modi (Catalog entry).

C. D. Poston, *Parsees: A Lecture.*

Parsifal (opera). R. Wagner.

Parsifal; The Finding of Christ Through Art: A Wagner Study. A. R. Parsons.

Parson Brooks: A Plumb Powerful Hard Shell. A Story of Humble Southern Life. J. B. Monteith.

Parsons, Alfred (illus.): see

E. A. Abbey, *Old Songs, with Drawings by Edwin A. Abbey and Alfred Parsons.*

H. A. Dobson (ed.), *Quiet Life. Verses by Various Hands.*

W. Robinson, *Wild Garden; or, Our Groves and Gardens Made Beautiful by the Naturalisation of Hardy Exotic Plants.*

Parsons, George Frederic (intro.): see H. de Balzac, *Comedy of Human Life.*

Parting and a Meeting (novel). W. D. Howells.

"Parting of the Ways" (poem). J. B. Gilder.

"Partington, Mrs." (literary character): see B. P. Shillaber.

Partisan Life with Col. John S. Mosby. J. Scott.

Partners of Providence (novel). C. D. Stewart.

Parton, Sara Payson (Willis): see S. P. Willis.

Parts of Speech: Essays on English. B. Matthews.

Pascal, Blaise: see C. A. Sainte-Beuve, *Monday-Chats, Selected and Translated from the "Causeries du Lundi."*

Passages in the Life of the Faire Gospeller Mistress Anne Askew. A. Manning.

Passages of the Bible, Chosen for Their Literary Beauty and Interest. J. G. Frazer (comp.).

Passport. R. Bagot.

Past and Present: see T. Carlyle, *Sartor Resartus.*

Pasteboard Crown: A Story of the New York Stage (novel). C. Morris.

Pasteur, Louis: see

J. Fiske, *Century of Science and Other Essays* (marginalia).

R. Vallery-Radot, *Life of Pasteur.*

A. D. White, *History of the Warfare of Science with Theology* (marginalia).

Pastime Stories. T. N. Page.

Pastoral Amours of Daphnis and Chloe: see *Greek Romances of Heliodorus, Longus, and Achilles Tatius*.

Pastoral Days, or Memories of a New England Year. W. H. Gibson.

Pastor's Story and Other Pieces; or, Prose and Poetry: see M. A. H. Gay, *Prose and Poetry. By a Georgia Lady*.

Pasture, Elizabeth de la: see E. B. De La Pasture.

Patents: see
United States Congress. House Committee on Patents. *Arguments Before the Committee on Patents*.
See also the Reader's Guide entry for Inventions.

Paternal State in France and Germany. H. Gaullieur.

Pathfinder. J. F. Cooper.

Paths to Power. F. B. Wilson.

Patience; or, Bunthorne's Bride. W. S. Gilbert.

Paton, Joseph Noël (illus.): see
S. T. Coleridge, *Rime of the Ancient Mariner*.
C. Kingsley, *Water-Babies. A Fairy Tale for a Land-Baby*.

Patriotism: see the Reader's Guide entry for American patriotism.

Pattison, Dorothy Wyndlow: see M. Lonsdale, *Sister Dora. A Biography*.

Patton, Charlotte Kimball (co-author): see E. J. James, *Immigrant Jew in America*.

Paul (Biblical figure): see *Life of Faith; in Three Parts, Embracing Some of the Scriptural Principles or Doctrines of Faith* (marginalia).

Paul and Jesus. J. Weiss.

Paulding, J. R. (co-author): see E. J. James, *Immigrant Jew in America*.

Paul et Virginie. J.-H. B. de Saint-Pierre.

Pauline; Paracelsus; Strafford; Sordello; Pippa Passes; King Victor and King Charles. R. Browning.

Paulinus (Roman missionary to England): see A. Smith, *Edwin of Deira* (poem).

"Paul, John" (pseud.): see C. H. Webb.

Paving the Way: A Romance of the Australian Brush. S. Newland.

Pawnee (Native American tribe): see
"Macallum" (Catalog entry).
C. A. Murray, *Travels in North America During the Years 1834, 1835 & 1836, Including a Summer Residence with the Pawnee Tribe of Indians*.

"Paxton, Philip" (pseud.): see S. A. Hammett.

Pax Vobiscum. H. Drummond.

Payn, George (co-author): see I. E. Wessely (co-author), *New Pocket Dictionary of the English and Italian Languages*.

Payne, Edward John (ed.): see E. Burke, *Select Works*.

Peabody, Frederick William: see M. B. Eddy, *Manual of the Mother Church*.

Peace and Progress, Two Symphonic Poems. N. H. Dole.

Peake, Elmore Elliott: see "Back to Indiana" (short story) in W. D. Howells (co-ed.), *Under the Sunset*.

Peak in Darien, with Some Other Inquiries Touching Concerns of the Soul and the Body. F. P. Cobbe.

Peale, Charles Wilson: see C. A. Munn, *Three Types of Washington Portraits: John Trumbull, Charles Wilson Peale, Gilbert Stuart*.

Pearl Island. A. Caster.

Pearls of the Faith; or, Islam's Rosary. Being the Ninety-nine Beautiful Names of Allah (Asmâ-el-husnâ). E. Arnold.

Pearson, Edwin (pref.): see Aesop, *Bewick's Select Fables*.

Peasant and the Prince: A Story of the French Revolution. H. Martineau.

Peattie, Elia Wilkinson: see "Madonna of the Desert" (short story) in W. D. Howells (co-ed.), *Under the Sunset*.

Pebbles and Pearls for the Young Folks. A. S. Richardson.

Peckham, Elizabeth Gifford (co-author): see G. W. Peckham and E. G. Peckham, *Wasps, Social and Solitary*.

Peck, Harry Thurston (co-ed.): see *New International Encyclopaedia*.

Peck's Bad Boy and His Pa. G. W. Peck.

Peck's Fun. G. W. Peck.

Peckster Professorship; An Episode in the History of Psychical Research. J. P. Quincy.

Peel, Robert: see
W. Bagehot, *Biographical Studies*.
C. Knight and T. Raikes, *Personal Reminiscences by Cornelia Knight and Thomas Raikes*.

"Peep at Washoe" (essay). J. R. Browne.

Peeps at People; Being Certain Papers from the Writings of Anne Warrington Witherup. J. K. Bangs.

Pegasus im Joche. J. C. F. von Schiller.

Pegram, Frederick (illus.): see E. P. Oppenheim, *Maker of History*.

Peg Woffington, Christie Johnstone, and Other Stories. C. Reade.

Pekin to Paris: An Account of Prince Borghese's Journey Across Two Continents in a Motor-Car. L. Barzini, Sr.

"Pelloquet, Théodore" (pseud.): see F. Bernard.

Pembroke; A Novel. M. E. W. Freeman.

"Penalty of Humor" (essay). B. Matthews.

Pen and the Book. W. Besant.

Penfield, Edward (illus.): see J. K. Bangs, *Peeps at People*.

Penmanship: see J. D. Williams (co-author), *Guide to Williams & Packard's System of Penmanship for Teachers and Adepts*.

Pennell, Joseph (illus.): see
E. De Amicis, *Holland and Its People*.
H. James, *Little Tour in France* (Catalog entry).

Pennsylvania: see
T. Campbell, *Gertrude of Wyoming; or, the Pennsylvanian Cottage*.
W. Riddle, *Nicholas Comenius; or Ye Pennsylvania Schoolmaster of Ye Olden Time*.

Penobscot Man. F. H. Eckstorm.

Penobscot River (Maine): see
F. H. Eckstorm, *Penobscot Man*.
T. S. Steele, *Canoe and Camera: A Two Hundred Mile Tour Through the Maine Forests*.

Penseroso. J. Milton.

People from the Other World. H. S. Olcott.

People I've Smiled With: Recollections of a Merry Little Life. M. P. Wilder.

People of America. F. O. C. Darley.

People's History of the English Aristocracy. G. Standring.

People's Lawyer (play). J. S. Jones.

People You Know. G. Ade.

Pepper & Salt; or, Seasoning for Young Folk. H. Pyle.

Pepys, Samuel: see

 M. Busch, *Bismarck in the Franco-German War 1870–1871* (marginalia).

 G. F. Pardon, *Routledge's Guide to London and Its Suburbs* (marginalia).

 L. de R. Saint-Simon, *Memoirs of the Duke of Saint-Simon on the Reign of Louis XIV and the Regency* (marginalia).

 H. B. Wheatley, *Samuel Pepys and the World He Lived In*.

 F. S. Wilhelmina, *Memoirs of Frederica Sophia Wilhelmina, Princess Royal of Prussia, Margravine of Baireuth* (marginalia).

"Percy, Florence" (pseud.): see E. A. C. A. Allen.

"Percy, Reuben" (pseud.): see *Percy Anecdotes*.

"Percy, Sholto" (pseud.): see *Percy Anecdotes*.

"Percy, Stephen" (pseud.): see J. Cundall.

Percy, William Alexander: see C. Stern, "Mark Twain (A Nocturne of the Mississippi)" (poem).

Père Goriot. H. de Balzac.

Perfect Day and Other Poems: see I. D. Coolbrith.

Perfect Health: How to Get It and How to Keep It. C. C. Haskell.

Pericles: see

 Plutarchus, *Plutarch's Lives of Illustrious Men* (marginalia).

 J. T. Wheeler, *Life and Travels of Herodotus in the Fifth Century Before Christ: An Imaginary Biography Founded on Fact*.

Peril of Oliver Sargent. E. J. Bliss.

Perilous Secret. C. Reade.

Periodicals: see the Reader's Guide entry for Magazines.

Period of Guerrilla Warfare. Philippine Information Society.

Perkins, Charles Callahan: see

 (ed.) J. D. Champlin, *Cyclopedia of Painters and Paintings*.

 (ed.) C. L. Eastlake, *Hints on Household Taste*.

Perkins, Charlotte: see the Catalog entry for Charlotte (Perkins) Gilman.

"Perkins, Eli" (pseud.): see M. D. L. Landon.

Perkins, Granville (illus.): see A. Tennyson, *Lady Clare*.

Perlycross. R. D. Blackmore.

Perplexed Philosopher, Being an Examination of Mr. Herbert Spencer's Various Utterances on the Land Question. H. George.

Perrin, Marshall Livingston (trans.): see H. von Sybel, *Founding of the German Empire by William I. Based Chiefly upon Prussian State Documents*.

Perry, Thomas Sergeant (co-ed.): see W. D. Howells (co-ed.), *Library of Universal Adventure by Sea and Land*.

Persian literature (and imitations): see

 Arabian Nights, Thousand and One Nights.

 "Arab's Farewell to His Steed" (poem). C. E. S. S. Norton.

 "Araby's daughter" (song). T. Moore.

 K. A. B. Benton, *Geber; A Tale of the Reign of Harun al Raschid, Khalif of Baghdad*.

 R. Browning, "Muléykeh" (poem).

 Hāfiz, *Odes from the Divan of Hafiz*.

 W. Hauff, "How the Caliph Became a Stork" (fairy tale).

 L. Hearn, *Stray Leaves from Strange Literature; Stories Reconstructed*.

 R. S. Hichens, *Garden of Allah* (novel).

 L. Hunt, "Abou Ben Adhem" (poem).

 M. N. Kuka (ed., trans.), *Wit and Humour of the Persians*.

 J. J. Morier, *Adventures of Hajji Baba, of Ispahan* (novel).

 Omar Khayyám, *Rubáiyát* (various translations).

 H. C. Rawlinson (Catalog entry).

 J. K. Ridley, *Tales of the Genii; or The Delightful Lessons of Horam, the Son of Asmar*.

 J. J. Roche, *Her Majesty the King; A Romance of the Harem, Done into American from the Arabic*.

 M. Saadi, *Gulistan; or, Rose Garden, by Musle-Huddeen Sheik Saadi, of Shiraz*.

 J. W. Scott, *Jack Hardin's Rendering of the Arabian Nights; Being a New Translation in Up-to-Date English*.

 A. Z. H. Y. Sīrafi, *Ancient Accounts of India and China, by Two Mohammedan Travellers*.

 B. Taylor, "Bedouin Love Song" (poem).

 H. Van Dyke, *Story of the Other Wise Man*.

Personal History of Ulysses S. Grant. A. D. Richardson.

Personal Memoirs of P. H. Sheridan, General, United States Army. P. H. Sheridan.

Personal Memoirs of U. S. Grant. U. S. Grant.

Personal Narrative of a Pilgrimage to El-Medinah and Meccah. R. F. Burton.

Personal Recollections, from Early Life to Old Age, of Mary Somerville. With Selections from Her Correspondence. M. F. Somerville.

Personal Recollections of Johannes Brahms. G. Hensel.

Personal Religion in Egypt Before Christianity. W. M. F. Petrie.

Personal Reminiscences by Cornelia Knight and Thomas Raikes. C. Knight (co-author).

Personal Reminiscences by Moore and Jerdan. T. Moore and W. Jerdan.

"Personal Reminiscences of Lincoln" (essay). N. Brooks.

Peru: see

 W. E. Curtis, *Capitals of Spanish America*.

 W. G. Mortimer, *Peru: History of Coca, "The Divine Plant" of the Incas*.

 W. H. Prescott, *History of the Conquest of Peru, with a Preliminary View of the Civilization of the Incas*.

Peter: A Novel of Which He Is Not the Hero. F. H. Smith.

Peter Ibbetson. G. L. P. B. Du Maurier.

Peterkin Papers. L. P. Hale.

Peter Pan (character): see J. M. Barrie, *Little White Bird; or, Adventures in Kensington Gardens*.

Peter Pan, or the Boy Who Wouldn't Grow Up (play). J. M. Barrie.

Peter Rabbit (literary character): see B. Potter, *Tale of Peter Rabbit*.

Peter Schlemihl's wundersame Geschichte. A. von Chamisso.

See also the Reader's Guide entries for Cuba and for the Spanish American War.

Phillips, Barnet (pref.): see K. E. Franzos, *Jews of Barnow. Stories.*

Phillips Brooks. A. Brooks.

Phillips Brooks. M. A. D. Howe.

Phillips, Edward (contr.): see R. Baker, *Chronicle of the Kings of England, from the Time of the Romans Government, unto the Death of King James the First.*

Phillips, Wendell: see

T. W. S. Higginson, *Cheerful Yesterdays. Contemporaries* (marginalia).

O. W. Holmes, *Autocrat of the Breakfast-Table* (marginalia).

Philosophe sous les toits: Journal d'un homme heureux. É. Souvestre.

Philosophy: see

Aristotle (Catalog entry).

A. W. Bailey, *Mark Heffron. A Novel.*

T. Browne (Catalog entry).

W. K. Clifford, *Lectures and Essays by the Late William Kingdon Clifford.*

J. Edwards, *Freedom of Will.*

Epictetus, *Selection from the Discourses of Epictetus, with the Encheiridion.*

T. Fowler, *Locke.*

E. H. P. A. Haeckel, *Wonders of Life: A Popular Study of Biological Philosophy.*

T. Hobbes, *Leviathan; or the Matter, Forme and Power of a Common Wealth Ecclesiastical and Civil.*

D. Hume, *Enquiry Concerning Human Understanding*: see D. Hume, "Of Miracles" (extract).

J. G. Huneker, *Egoists, A Book of Supermen.*

T. H. Huxley, *Hume.*

I. Kant, *Critique of Pure Reason.*

W. E. H. Lecky, *History of European Morals from Augustus to Charlemagne* (Catalog entry).

W. E. H. Lecky, *History of the Rise and Influence of the Spirit of Rationalism in Europe.*

G. W. von Leibniz (Catalog entry).

G. C. Lichtenberg (Catalog entry).

J. Locke (Catalog entry).

J. Mackaye, *Economy of Happiness.*

É. Metchnikoff, *Nature of Man; Studies in Optimistic Philosophy.*

J. S. Mill, *Autobiography.*

J. S. Mill, *System of Logic, Ratiocinative and Inductive; Being a Connected View of the Principles of Evidence and the Methods of Scientific Investigation.*

F. W. Nietzsche, *Thus Spake Zarathustra; A Book for All and None.*

T. Paine, *Age of Reason.*

Plato, *Dialogues of Plato.*

A. Schopenhauer, *Essays of Arthur Schopenhauer.*

B. Spinoza: see W. James, *Varieties of Religious Experience; A Study in Human Nature* (marginalia).

M. Stirner, *Ego and His Own.*

V. Streamer (comp.), *Voices of Doubt and Trust.*

E. Swedenborg, *Heaven and Hell.*

W. Temple, "Upon the Gardens of Epicurus" (essay).

A. R. Wallace, William Ramsay, *et al. Progress of the Century.*

See also the Reader's Guide entry for Natural philosophy.

Philosophy of History; in a Course of Lectures, Delivered at Vienna. F. von Schlegel.

Philosophy of Ingersoll. R. G. Ingersoll.

Philosophy of Making Love. H. E. Gorst.

Philosophy of the Plays of Shakspere Unfolded. D. S. Bacon.

Phineas Finn. A. Trollope.

Phineas Redux. A. Trollope.

Phipson, Thomas Lamb: see

(trans., ed.) W. de Fonvielle, *Thunder and Lightning.*

(trans.) A. V. Guillemin, *Sun.*

"Phiz" (pseud.): see H. K. Browne (illus.).

"Phoenix, John" (pseud.): see G. H. Derby.

Phoenixiana; or, Sketches and Burlesques. G. H. Derby.

Phonography: see the Reader's Guide entry for Shorthand.

Photographic Views of Cape Town: see Cape Town, South Africa.

Photography: see

H. Bush, *Harp of the Day; or, The Adventures and Travels of a Photographic Artist.*

F. M. Coleman, *Typical Pictures of Indian Natives, Being Reproductions from Photographs.*

A. R. Dugmore, *Nature and the Camera. How to Photograph Live Birds and Their Nests, Animals, Wild Game.*

R. Eickemeyr, Jr., *Winter, Pictured by Rudolf Eickemeyr, Jr.*

J. H. Furneaux, *Glimpses of India: A Grand Photographic History of the Land of Antiquity.*

G. Iles, *Flame, Electricity and the Camera; Man's Progress.*

H. K. Job, *Among the Water-Fowl: Observation, Adventure, Photography.*

H. K. Job, *Wild Wings: Adventures of a Camera-Hunter Among the Larger Wild Birds of North America on Sea and Land.*

D. S. Jordan (co-author), *American Food and Game Fishes.*

New South Wales. Photographs.

R. Saxton (ed.), *Mental Photographs: An Album for Confessions of Tastes, Habits, and Convictions.*

K. G. Schillings, *With Flash-light and Rifle; Photographing by Flash-light at Night the Wild Animal World of Equatorial Africa.*

T. S. Steele, *Canoe and Camera: A Two Hundred Mile Tour Through the Maine Forests.*

Phrenology: see

G. Ade, *Fables in Slang.*

E. C. Beall (Catalog entry).

G. Combe, *Notes on the United States of North America, During a Phrenological Visit in 1838–9-40.*

J. W. Draper, *Human Physiology, Statistical and Dynamical; or, The Conditions and Course of the Life of Man.*

O. S. Fowler, *Love and Parentage, Applied to the Improvement of Offspring, Including Important Directions and Suggestions to Lovers and the Married.*

O. S. Fowler, *New Illustrated Self-Instructor in Phrenology and Physiology*.

Galaxy. An Illustrated Magazine of Entertaining Reading.

S. Kirkham, *English Grammar in Familiar Lectures* (Catalog entry).

W. E. H. Lecky, *History of European Morals from Augustus to Charlemagne* (Catalog entry).

Phrenological Journal and Science of Health.

W. M. Thackeray, *Thackeray's Lectures. The English Humorists. The Four Georges* (marginalia).

A. R. Wallace, *Wonderful Century; Its Successes and Its Failures*.

G. S. Weaver, *Lectures on Mental Science According to the Philosophy of Phrenology*.

S. R. Wells, *Wedlock; or, the Right Relation of the Sexes; Disclosing the Laws of Conjugal Selection, and Showing Who May, and Who May Not Marry*.

Wyman's Comic Almanac for the Times, 1856.

Physical Beauty: How to Obtain and How to Preserve It. A. J. Miller.

Physical training: see the Reader's Guide entry for Health, fitness, and hygiene.

Physics: see

A. A. Cazin, *Phenomena and Laws of Heat*.

O. J. Lodge, *Ether of Space*.

O. J. Lodge, "What Is Life" (article).

G. P. Quackenbos, *Natural Philosophy, Embracing the Most Recent Discoveries in the Various Branches of Physics, and Exhibiting the Application of Scientific Principles in Everyday Life*.

A. R. Wallace, William Ramsay, *et al. Progress of the Century*.

H. S. Williams, *Story of Nineteenth-Century Science*.

Physiological Memory; or, The Instantaneous Art of Never Forgetting. M. D. Larrowe.

Physiology: see

E. W. R. von Brücke, *Vorlesungen über Physiologie*.

C. Cutter, *Anatomy and Physiology*.

J. W. Draper, *Human Physiology, Statistical and Dynamical; or, The Conditions and Course of the Life of Man*.

O. S. Fowler, *New Illustrated Self-Instructor in Phrenology and Physiology*.

A. Le Pileur, *Wonders of the Human Body. From the French*.

J. Marshall, *Anatomy for Artists*.

J. Walker, *Anatomy, Physiology, and Hygiene: A Manual for the Use of Colleges, Schools, and General Readers*.

See also the Reader's Guide entry for Anatomy.

Pianoforte Werke. F. Chopin.

Piave, F. M. (libretto): see G. Verdi, *La Traviata*.

Picciola. J. X. B. Saintine.

Pichaud, Marie: see (inscr.) C. Vincens, *Alfred de Musset*.

"Picket-Guard" (poem, song). E. L. Beers.

Pickwick Papers. C. Dickens.

Pictorial Field-Book of the War of 1812. B. J. Lossing.

Picture of Dorian Gray (novel). O. Wilde.

Picture of St. John. B. Taylor.

Pictures by Dora Wheeler. C. Wheeler.

Pictures from Italy and American Notes. C. Dickens.

Pictures of Life & Character. From the Collection of "Mr. Punch." J. Leech.

Picturesque America: see R. Keeler, "On the Mississippi" (magazine series).

Picturesque Sicily. W. A. Paton.

Picturesque World; or, Scenes in Many Lands. A. L. De Colange (ed.).

Pied Piper of Hamelin: see *Wunderfeife, oder: Die Kinder von Hameln*.

Pierce, Henry Niles (trans.): see K. M. Mundt, *Henry VIII. and His Court; or, Catherine Parr. An Historical Novel*.

Piers Plowman: see W. Langland, *Vision Concerning Piers Plowman*.

Pigs Is Pigs. E. P. Butler.

Pike County Ballads and Other Pieces. J. Hay.

Pike County Folks: see E. H. Mott, "Old Settler" (sketch).

Pilgrimage to the Holy Land; Comprising Recollections, Sketches, and Reflections Made During a Tour in the East, in 1832–1833. A. M. L. de Lamartine.

Pilgrim's Progress. J. Bunyan.

Pilgrim's Wallet; or, Scraps of Travel Gathered in England, France, and Germany. G. Haven.

Pillar of Light. L. Tracy.

"Pilot" (poem, song). T. H. Bayly.

Piloting: see the Reader's Guide entries for specific rivers and for River navigation.

"P. I. Man" (pseud.): see J. C. Goldsmith (Catalog entry).

Pinafore (operetta): see W. S. Gilbert, *H. M. S. Pinafore* (operetta).

Pineider, F. and J. (eds.): see *Hand-Book of Florence and Environs with Views, A Topographical Plan and the Catalogues of Galleries*.

Pinel, Philippe-François ("Dumanoir"): see

E. Fitzball, *Maritana* (opera).

V. M. Hugo, *Ruy Blas*.

Pink and White Tyranny: A Society Novel. H. E. B. Stowe.

Pink Marsh. A Story of the Streets and Town. G. Ade.

Pioneer Boy, and How He Became President. W. M. Thayer.

Pioneer Life and Work in New Guinea, 1877–1894. J. Chalmers.

Pioneers. J. F. Cooper.

Pioneers of France in the New World. F. Parkman.

Pioneers of Illinois, Containing a Series of Sketches Relating to Events That Occurred Previous to 1813. N. Matson.

"Pipes, Jeems" (pseud.): see S. C. Massett.

Pippa Passes: A Drama: see R. Browning, *Pauline; Paracelsus; Strafford; Sordello*.

Pirates: see

C. Ellms, *Pirates Own Book; or, Authentic Narratives of the Lives, Exploits, and Executions of the Most Celebrated Sea Robbers*.

H. Pyle, *Ruby of Kishmoor*.

H. Pyle, *Stolen Treasure*.

R. J. Raymond and W. E. Burton, *Toodles. A Domestic Drama in Two Acts*.

R. L. Stevenson, *Treasure Island*.

F. R. Stockton, *Mrs. Cliff's Yacht*.

B. Stoker, *Mystery of the Sea; A Novel*.

J. Verne, *Mysterious Island*.

World of Wonders; A Record of Things Wonderful in Nature, Science, and Art.

See also the Reader's Guide entry for Treasure hunts.

"Pirate's lament" (ballad): see "Captain Kidd" (ballad).

Pirates Own Book; or, Authentic Narratives of the Lives, Exploits, and Executions of the Most Celebrated Sea Robbers. C. Ellms.

"Pirate's serenade" (song). W. Kennedy.

"Piso, Lucius M." (pseud.): see W. Ware.

Pith of Astronomy (Without Mathematics): The Latest Facts and Figures as Developed by the Giant Telescopes. S. G. Bayne.

Pitt, William: see G. Smith, *Three English Statesmen: A Course of Lectures on the Political History of England.*

Plagiarism: see

H. H. Breen, *Modern English Literature: Its Blemishes & Defects.*

O. W. Holmes, *Songs in Many Keys.*

Plague Year: see D. Defoe, *Journal of the Plague Year.*

"Plain Language from Truthful James" (poem): see B. Harte, *Poetical Works.*

Plain Man's Talk on the Labor Question. S. Newcomb.

Plains of the Great West and Their Inhabitants. R. I. Dodge.

Plain Speaking. D. M. M. Craik.

Plain Tales from the Hills (short stories). R. Kipling.

Plain Talks on Familiar Subjects. J. G. Holland.

Plain Truths about Stock Speculation. How to Avoid Losses in Wall Street. M. Smith.

Plank, George Wolfe (illus.): see W. H. Howells, *Rescue of Desdemona, and Other Verse.*

Plantation Child-Life. L. Pyrnelle.

Plantation Lays and Other Poems. B. O. Townsend.

Plantation songs of enslaved African Americans: see the Reader's Guide entry for "Spirituals."

Planter; A Novel. H. Whitaker.

Play-Actress. S. R. Crockett.

Players Club (New York City): see *Players* (directory of members).

Playfair, Lyon: see W. Reid, *Memoirs and Correspondence of Lyon Playfair, First Lord Playfair of St. Andrews.*

Plays. G. B. Shaw.

Plays of Euripides. Euripides.

Plays of Shakespeare. Introduction and Notes Explanatory and Critical. W. Shakespeare.

Plea for the Priority of Domestic Missions; A Discourse Delivered Before the Synod of Iowa, in Burlington, Oct. 12, 1856. J. T. Umsted.

Pleasant Hours in an Eventful Life. W. F. Stewart.

Pleasures of Hope: see *Book of Pleasures.*

Pleasures of Hope. T. Campbell.

Pleasures of Imagination: see *Book of Pleasures.*

Pleasures of Memory: see *Book of Pleasures.*

Plinius Caecilius Secundus, Gaius: see N. S. Shaler, *Aspects of the Earth* (marginalia).

Pliny: see Plinius Secundus and Plinius Caecilius Secundus.

Plutarch: see Plutarchus.

Plutarch's Lives of Alcibiades & Coriolanus, Aristides & Cato the Censor. Plutarchus.

Plutarch's Lives of Illustrious Men. Plutarchus.

Plutarch's Morals. Translated from the Greek by Several Hands. Plutarchus.

Plymouth Church: see S. M. Griswold, *Sixty Years with Plymouth Church.*

Plymouth Collection of Hymns and Tunes, for the Use of Christian Congregations. H. W. Beecher (comp).

Plymouth Pulpit. H. W. Beecher.

Plymouth Rock: see E. De Amicis, *Holland and Its People* (tipped in note about Plymouth Rock).

Pocket R. L. S.; Being Favourite Passages from the Works of Stevenson.

Podmore, Frank (co-author): see E. Gurney, *Phantasms of the Living.*

Poe, Edgar Allan: see

F. M. Colby, *Imaginary Obligations* (marginalia).

W. D. Howells, "Edgar Allan Poe" (essay).

J. A. Joyce, *Edgar Allan Poe.*

F. W. Thomas, "'Tis Said That Absence Conquers Love" (poem, song) (Catalog entry).

H. C. Watson, "Prodigal son" (Catalog entry).

W. Winter, *Wanderers: The Poems of William Winter.*

Poems:

H. Abbey.

T. B. Aldrich.

M. Arnold.

M. I. Brown.

E. B. Browning.

F. L. Bushnell.

G. G. Byron.

S. T. Coleridge.

D. M. M. Craik.

G. Eliot.

M. A. Geisse.

A. L. Gordon.

D Gray.

T. Gray.

O. W. Holmes.

H. Howard.

J. Ingelow.

H. C. Kendall.

J. M. Kennedy.

A. Laighton.

C. Lamb.

H. W. Longfellow.

E. R. B. Lytton.

G. Meredith.

J. A. Moore.

F. S. L. Osgood.

A. A. Procter.

D. S. Shorter.

C. W. Stoddard.

R. Southey.

L. B. Van Nada.

G. H. Van Zandt.

J. G. Whittier.

W. Winter.

Poems All The Way From Pike. R. Love.

Poems and Translations. E. Thring.

Poems & Verses. E. S. Martin.

Poems and Verses of Charles Dickens. C. Dickens.

Poems by Albert Laighton. A. Laighton.

Poems from October to October. L. C. Robinson.
Poems, Grave and Gay. A. E. S. Smythe.
Poems Here at Home. J. W. Riley.
Poems of a Child; Being Poems Written Between the Ages of Six and Ten. J. C. Altrocchi.
Poems of George Harrison Van Zandt. G. H. Van Zandt.
Poems of Henry Clarence Kendall. H. C. Kendall.
Poems of Henry Wadsworth Longfellow. H. W. Longfellow.
Poems of Nature and Sentiment. W. Wordsworth.
Poems of Oliver Wendell Holmes. O. W. Holmes.
Poems of Ossian, the Son of Fingal. Translated from the Original Gaelic. J. Macpherson.
Poems of Owen Meredith. E. R. B. Lytton.
Poems of the Past and the Present. T. Hardy.
Poems of Thomas Gray. T. Gray.
Poems of William Winter. W. Winter.
Poems, Plays and Other Remains of Sir John Suckling. A New Edition. J. Suckling.
Poems, Sacred, Passionate, and Humorous. N. P. Willis.
Poems That Every Child Should Know: A Selection of the Best Poems of All Times. M. E. Burt (ed.).
Poems, Together with Brother Jacob and The Lifted Veil. G. Eliot.
Poenamo: Sketches of the Early Days of New Zealand. J. L. Campbell.
Poetic and Dramatic Works. R. Browning.
Poetical Works: see
  L. Bishop, *Poetical Works of Levi Bishop.*
  R. Browning, *Poetical Works of Robert Browning.*
  B. Harte, *Poetical Works of Bret Harte.*
  R. Heber, *Poetical Works of Reginald Heber, Late Bishop of Calcutta.*
  T. Hood, *Poetical Works of Thomas Hood.*
  J. Ingelow, *Poetical Works of Jean Ingelow, including the Shepherd Lady and Other Poems.*
  J. Keats, *Poetical Works of John Keats.*
  H. W. Longfellow, *Poetical Works of Henry Wadsworth Longfellow.*
  J. R. Lowell, *Poetical Works of James Russell Lowell.*
  J. Milton, *Poetical Works of John Milton.*
  D. G. Rossetti, *Poetical Works of Dante Gabriel Rossetti.*
  W. Scott, *Poetical Works of Sir Walter Scott.*
  P. B. Shelley, *Poetical Works of Percy Bysshe Shelley.*
  E. C. Stedman, *Poetical Works of Edmund Clarence Stedman.*
  A. Tennyson, *Poetical Works of Alfred, Lord Tennyson, Poet Laureate.*
  W. Wordsworth. *Poetical Works of Wordsworth.*
Poet in Embryo; Being the Meditations of Algernon Byron Stripling. A. B. Stripling.
"Poet Lariat" (humorous award): see L. E. Trescott.
Poetry anthologies: see the Reader's Guide entry for Poetry collections.
Poetry collections: see
  H. Abbey (comp.), *Bright Things from Everywhere: A Galaxy of Good Stories, Poems, Paragraphs, Wit, and Wisdom.*
  Among the Daisies. Poems Old and New.
  A. Baskerville (ed., trans.), *Poetry of Germany.*
  W. C. Bryant (comp.), *Family Library of Poetry and Song. Being Choice Selections from the Best Poets, English, Scottish, Irish, and American.*
  M. E. Burt (ed.), *Poems That Every Child Should Know; A Selection of the Best Poems of All Times.*
  E. O. Chapman (ed.), *Home Book of Poetry.*
  J. M. Chapple (comp.), *Heart Throbs in Prose and Verse Dear to the American People.*
  C. A. Dana (comp.), *Household Book of Poetry.*
  J. W. Ebsworth (ed.), *Choyce Drollery: Songs and Sonnets.*
  J. W. Ebsworth (ed.), *Westminster Drolleries, Both Parts, of 1671, 1672; Being a Choice Collection of Songs and Poems, Sung at Court and Theatres.*
  R. W. Emerson (ed.), *Parnassus.*
  J. T. Fields and E. P. Whipple (eds.), *Family Library of British Poetry from Chaucer to the Present Time (1350–1878).*
  Friendship's Offering; A Christmas, New Year, and Birthday Present.
  M. L. Goddard (co-comp.), *Sea and Shore: A Collection of Poems.*
  L. Hunt and S. A. Lee (eds.), *Book of the Sonnet.*
  I. E. Jerome, *One Year's Sketch-Book.*
  C. Kingsley, *Favorite Poems, by Charles Kingsley, Owen Meredith, and Edmund Clarence Stedman.*
  F. L. Knowles (comp.), *Treasury of Humorous Poetry.*
  H. W. Longfellow (ed.), *Poets and Poetry of Europe.*
  W. N. Lowe (trans.), *Magyar Songs. Selections from Hungarian Poets.*
  E. S. Owen (comp.), *Whittier Birthday Book.*
  F. T. Palgrave (comp.), *Golden Treasury of the Best Songs and Lyrical Poems in the English Language.*
  F. T. Palgrave (comp.), *Treasury of Sacred Song, Selected from the English Lyrical Poetry of Four Centuries.*
  J. W. Palmer (ed.), *Folk Songs.*
  T. Percy (ed.), *Reliques of Ancient English Poetry.*
  Poet and the Painter; or, Gems of Art and Song.
  Poetry of the Woods; Passages from the Poets Descriptive of Forest Scenes, Etc.
  A. D. F. Randolph (comp.), *Changed Cross, and Other Religious Poems.*
  A. D. F. Randolph (comp.), *Shadow of the Rock, and Other Religious Poems.*
  D. G. Rossetti (ed. and trans.), *Dante and His Circle, with the Italian Poets Preceding Him (1100–1200-1300). A Collection of Lyrics.*
  C. Rowley (comp.), *Brotherhood with Nature: A Treasury.*
  Selected Poems, Illustrated.
  W. G. Simms (ed.), *War Poetry of the South.*
  H. Van Dyke (ed.), *Little Masterpieces of English Poetry, by British and American Authors.*
  R. G. White (ed.), *Poetry Lyrical, Narrative, and Satirical of the Civil War.*
  J. G. Whittier (ed.), *Childlife: A Collection of Poems.*
  See also the Reader's Guide entry for Anthologies.
Poetry Lyrical, Narrative, and Satirical of the Civil War. R. G. White (ed.)
Poetry of Germany. A. Baskerville (ed., trans.).
Poetry of the Pacific: Selections and Original Poems from the

Poets of the Pacific States: see the Catalog entry for M. W. Newman (ed.).

Poets and Dreamers: Studies & Translations from the Irish, by Lady Gregory. A. Gregory.

Poets and Poetry of Europe. H. W. Longfellow (ed.).

Poganuc People: Their Loves and Lives. H. E. B. Stowe.

Point-Lace and Diamonds. Poems. G. A. Baker.

Poiré, Emmanuel: see Carnan d'Ache (pseud.), *Bric à Brac; Album par Carnan d'Ache*.

Poisson, Jeanne-Antoinette: see M. Wagnalls, *Palace of Danger; A Story of La Pompadour*.

Poker: see

D. A. Curtis, *Stand Pat; or, Poker Stories from the Mississippi*.

J. M. Field, *Drama in Pokerville, The Bench and Bar of Jurytown, and Other Stories*.

Bret Harte (various short stories).

See also the Reader's Guide entry for Card games.

Poland: see

G. Freytag, *Soll und Haben: Roman in Sechs büchern*.

K. E. Franzos, *Jews of Barnow. Stories*.

A. Mickiewicz, *Dziady (Forefathers' Eve)*.

J. Porter, *Thaddeus of Warsaw*.

J. L. Stephens, *Incidents of Travel in Greece, Turkey, Russia, and Poland*.

Pole Baker; A Novel. W. N. Harben.

Polikushka: see L. N. Tolstoy, *Ivan the Fool; or, the Old Devil and the Three Small Devils*.

Polish Jew. É. Erckmann and A. Chatrian.

Politianus, Angelus: see C. Meiners, *Lebensbeschreibungen berühmter Männer aus den Zeiten der Wiederherstellung der Wissenschaften*.

Political science: see

J. E. Cairnes, *Character and Logical Method of Political Economy*.

A. R. Colquhoun, *Greater America*.

L. Dyer, *Machiavelli and the Modern State: Chapters on His "Prince," His Use of History and His Idea of Morals*.

H. Gaullieur, *Paternal State in France and Germany*.

C. F. Goodrich, *Report of the British Naval and Military Operations in Egypt, 1882*.

A. Harrison, *Pan-Germanic Doctrine; Being a Study of German Political Aims and Aspirations*.

T. Hobbes, *Leviathan; or the Matter, Forme and Power of a Common Wealth Ecclesiastical and Civil*.

A. Johnston, *Connecticut: A Study of a Commonwealth Democracy*.

C. Marriott, *Uncle Sam's Business Told for Young Americans*.

S. E. Moffett, *Suggestions on Government*.

J. K. Newton, "Obligations of the United States to Initiate a Revision of Treaties Between the Western Powers and Japan."

L. F. Post, *Ethics of Democracy: A Series of Optimistic Essays on the Natural Laws of Human Society*.

E. Reich, *Success Among Nations*.

G. Smith, *Three English Statesmen: A Course of Lectures on the Political History of England*.

S. Smith, *Essays Social and Political. First and Second Series*.

M. W. Townsend, *Asia and Europe: Studies Presenting the Conclusions Formed by the Author*.

P. Villari, *Life and Times of Niccolò Machiavelli* (marginalia).

S. Webster, *Two Treaties of Paris and the Supreme Court*.

See also the Reader's Guide entries for American politics and for Economics and labor issues.

Political Situation [in Cape Colony]. O. Schreiner.

Pollock, William Frederick: see

(co-ed., intro.) W. K. Clifford, *Lectures and Essays by the Late William Kingdon Clifford*.

(ed.) W. C. Macready, *Macready's Reminiscences, and Selections from His Diaries and Letters*.

"Polly Peablossom's Wedding" (sketch). J. B. Lamar.

Polly Peablossom's Wedding, and Other Tales, T. A. Burke (comp.): see the Reader's Guide entry for J. B. Lamar.

Polygamy: see

J. Hyde, Jr., *Mormonism: Its Leaders and Designs*.

C. Paddock *Fate of Madame La Tour; A Tale of Great Salt Lake*.

T. B. H. Stenhouse, *Rocky Mountain Saints: A Full and Complete History of the Mormons, . . . and the Development of the Great Mineral Wealth of the Territory of Utah*.

C. V. V. Waite, *Mormon Prophet and His Harem; or, an Authentic History of Brigham Young, His Numerous Wives and Children*.

Polyglot Bible: see Bible. Polyglot.

Polynesia; or, An Historical Account of the Principal islands of the South Sea including New Zealand. M. Russell.

Pomeroy, Mark M.: see M. E. P. Tucker, *Life of Mark M. Pomeroy*.

Pompadour, Madame de: see M. Wagnalls, *Palace of Danger; A Story of La Pompadour*.

Pompeii: see

C. Dickens, *Pictures from Italy and American Notes*.

J. A. Hart, *Levantine Log-Book*.

W. D. Howells, *Roman Holidays and Others*.

W. Irving, "Rip Van Winkle" (short story) (Catalog entry).

E. G. E. B. Lytton, *Last Days of Pompeii*.

T. B. Macaulay, *History of England from the Accession of James II* (Catalog entry).

M. Monnier, *Wonders of Pompeii. Translated from the Original French*.

Plinius, *Letters of Caius Plinius Caecilius Secundus*.

N. S. Shaler, *Aspects of the Earth: A Popular Account of Some Familiar Geological Phenomena* (marginalia).

M. F. Somerville, *Personal Recollections, from Early Life to Old Age, of Mary Somerville. With Selections from Her Correspondence* (marginalia).

Washington *National Intelligencer*.

Ponce de Leon, Juan: see F. A. Ober, *Juan Ponce de Leon*.

Pond, James Burton: see

H. Caine, *Manxman, A Novel* (inscr.).

U. S. Grant, *Memoirs of U. S. Grant* (inscr.).

Ladies' Home Journal (Catalog entry).

Ponkapog Papers. T. B. Aldrich.

Pontiac: see F. Parkman, *Conspiracy of Pontiac and the Indian War After the Conquest of Canada*.

Pool (game): see the Reader's Guide entry for Billiards.

Pool, Maria Louise (co-author): see *Adventures at Sea.*

Poor Richard's Almanack. B. Franklin.

Pope, Alexander: see
(trans.) Homer, *Iliad of Homer.*
J. Warton, *Essay on the Genius and Writings of Pope.*
J. G. Wilson (ed.), *Love in Letters; Illustrated in the Correspondence of Eminent Persons; with Biographical Sketches of the Writers.*

Pope and the Council. J. J. I. von Döllinger.

"Pop Goes the Weasel": see the Nursery Rhymes entry in the Catalog.

Poppy Garden (novella). E. M. Morgan.

Popular History of England. F. P. G. Guizot.

Popular History of England: An Illustrated History of Society and Government from the Earliest Period to Our Own Times. C. Knight.

Popular History of France from the Earliest Times. F. P. G. Guizot.

Popular History of France, from the First Revolution to the Present Time. H. Martin.

Popular History of the United States, from the First Discovery of the Western Hemisphere by the Northmen, to the End of the Civil War. W. C. Bryant (co-author).

Popular Official Guide to the New York Zoological Park. W. T. Hornaday.

Porcelain: see
W. Chaffers, *Handbook of Marks and Monograms on Pottery and Porcelain.*
H. B. Hall, *Bric-à-Brac Hunter; or, Chapters on Chinamania.*
W. C. Prime, *Pottery and Porcelain of All Times and Nations.*
See also the Reader's Guide entry for Pottery.

Porson, Richard: see E. H. Barker, *Literary Anecdotes and Contemporary Reminisences of Professor Porson and Others, From the Manuscript Papers of the Late E. H. Barker.*

Porter, James (criminal): see C. Whitehead, *Lives and Exploits of the Most Noted Highwaymen, Robbers and Murderers, of All Nations.*

Porter, Josias Leslie (ed.): see J. Murray, *Handbook for Travellers in Syria and Palestine.*

Porter, William Trotter (ed.): see
H. C. Jones, "Cousin Sally Dilliard" (sketch).
H. P. Leland, "Frogs Shot Without Powder" (sketch).
Spirit of the Times: A Chronicle of the Turf, Field Sports, Literature and the Stage.

Portfolio of Players. H. C. Bunner and E. A. Dithmar.

Portion of Labor. M. E. W. Freeman.

Port of Missing Men. M. Nicholson.

Portrait of a Lady. H. James.

Portrait of Zelide. G. Scott.

Portraits and Autographs: An Album for the People. W. T. Stead.

Portraits of the Sixties. J. McCarthy.

Portuguese language: see *New Guide of the Conversation in Portuguese and English in Two Parts.* J. da Fonseca.

Post, Charles Johnson (illus.): see W. G. V. T. Sutphen, *Gates of Chance.*

Post, Helen (Wilmans): see H. Wilmans.

Post, Louis Freeland (intro.): see D. C. Beard, *Moonblight and Six Feet of Romance.*

Potiphar Papers. G. W. Curtis.

Potiphar Papers: see I. Browne, *Our Best Society* (play).

Pot-pourri from a Surrey Garden. M. T. V. Earle.

Pott, Constance Mary (Fearon) (ed.): see F. Bacon, *Promus of Formularies and Elegancies (Being Private Notes, Circ. 1594, Hitherto Unpublished) by Francis Bacon. Illustrated and Elucidated by Passages from Shakespeare.*

Pottery: see
W. Chaffers, *Handbook of Marks and Monograms on Pottery and Porcelain.*
A. Jacquemart, *History of the Ceramic Art; A Descriptive and Philosophical Study of the Pottery of All Ages and All Nations.*
W. C. Prime, *Pottery and Porcelain of All Times and Nations.*
S. Smiles, *Josiah Wedgwood, F.R.S., His Personal History.*
W. T. Walters, *Oriental Ceramic Art; Illustrated by Examples from the Collection of W. T. Walters.*
See also the Reader's Guide entry for Porcelain.

Pottery and Porcelain of All Times and Nations. W. C. Prime.

Pottle, Gilbert Emery Bemsley: see "Bond" (short story) in W. D. Howells and H. M. Alden (eds.), *Their Husbands' Wives.*

"Powell, Frances" (pseud.): see F. P. Case.

Power of Movement in Plants. C. Darwin.

Powers, Ada Wilmans: see H. Wilmans.

Poynter, Eleanor Frances: see D. H. H. Boulger, *Maid Ellice.*

Practical Astronomer. T. Dick.

Practical Dictionary. N. Webster.

Practical Elements of Rhetoric, with Illustrative Examples. J. F. Genung.

Practical Floriculture; A Guide to the Successful Cultivation of Florists' Plants. P. Henderson.

Practical Hypnotism: Theories and Experiments. C. de Saint-Germain.

Practical Lawn Tennis. J. Dwight.

Practical System of Modern Geography; or, A View of the Present State of the World, Simplified and Adapted to the Capacity of Youth. J. Olney.

"Praed, Mrs. Campbell" (pseud.): see R. C. M.-P. Praed.

Praetexta (Roman noblewoman): see F. Parkman, *Old Régime in Canada* (marginalia).

Prague: see F. Kotzwara, "Battle of Prague" (music).

"Praise God, from whom all blessings flow" (hymn). T. Ken.

Prang, Louis (illus.): see J. G. Wood, *Our Living World; An Artistic Edition of the Rev. J. G. Wood's Natural History of Animate Creation.*

Pratt & Whitney Company: see the Catalog entry for *Standards of Length.*

Prayer: see
Book of Common Prayer.
"Lord's Prayer."
Order for Daily Evening Prayer.
Prayer-Gauge Debate.

Predestination doctrine: see T. C. Upham, *Life of Faith;*

in Three Parts, Embracing Some of the Scriptural Principles or Doctrines of Faith (marginalia).
Pre-Historic America. J. F. A. du P. Nadaillac.
Premature burial (theme): see
T. H. Bayly, "Mistletoe Bough" (poem).
E. A. Poe, "Cask of Amontillado" (story).
Pre-Raphaelites: see
V. Paget, *Miss Brown, A Novel*.
D. G. Rossetti (ed. and trans.), *Dante and His Circle, with the Italian Poets Preceding Him (1100–1200–1300). A Collection of Lyrics*.
W. B. Scott, *Autobiographical Notes of the Life of William Bell Scott*.
Presbyterianism: see
Address to the Presbyterians of Kentucky: Proposing a Plan for the Instruction and Emancipation of Their Slaves.
J. Bunyan, *Pilgrim's Progress* (Catalog entry).
S. R. Crockett, *Play-Actress* (novel).
C. J. Guthrie, *John Knox and John Knox's House*.
R. M. Manley, *Mr. Claghorn's Daughter* (novel).
S. Miller, *Essay on the Warrant, Nature, and Duties of the Office of the Ruling Elder, in the Presbyterian Church*.
H. W. Pierson, *In the Brush; or, Old-Time Social, Political, and Religious Life in the Southwest*.
Presbyterian Magazine: see the Catalog entry for *Presbyterian Observer*.
Presbyterian Observer.
G. Spring, *Fragments from the Study of a Pastor*.
W. M. Thomson, *Central Palestine and Phoenicia*.
J. T. Umstead, *Plea for the Priority of Domestic Missions; A Discourse Delivered Before the Synod of Iowa, in Burlington, Oct. 12, 1856*.
"Prescott, E. Livingston" (pseud.): see E. K. S. Jay.
Prescott, William Hickling: see
J. J. I. von Döllinger and J. N. Huber, *Pope and the Council* (notes laid in).
G. Ticknor, *Life of William Hickling Prescott*.
L. Wallace, *Ben-Hur: A Tale of the Christ* (Catalog entry).
"Presland, John" (pseud.): see G. Skelton.
Preston, Harriet Waters.: see
(co-comp.) see: M. L. Goddard (co-comp.), *Sea and Shore: A Collection of Poems*.
(trans.) C. A. Sainte-Beuve, *Memoirs of Mme. Desbordes-Valmore*.
Preston, May Wilson (illus.): see C. Wells, *Rubáiyát of Bridge*.
Pretended Aunt: see M. de Cervantes Saavedra, *Exemplary Novels of Miguel de Cerantes Saavedra*.
Pretty Peggy Painting Book. R. Emmet.
Pretty Sister of José. F. H. Burnett.
Pride and Prejudice. J. Austen.
Priest to the Temple; or, The Country Parson. G. Herbert.
Primary Convictions; Being Discussions Delivered on Subjects Connected with the Evidences of Christianity. W. Alexander.
Prime, William Cowper: see
(ed., contr.) G. B. McClellan, *McClellan's Own Story: The War for the Union*.

L. Sterne, *Sentimental Journey Through France and Italy, by Mr. Yorick* (Catalog entry).
Primitive Man. L. Figuier.
Primrose, A. P. (pref.): see G. R. Parkin, *Round the Empire; for the Use of Schools*.
Prince and the Page: A Story of the Last Crusade. C. M. Yonge.
Prince Borghese's Journey. L. Barzini, Sr.
Prince Charles Edward. A. MacKinnon.
Prince Deukalion: A Lyrical Drama. B. Taylor.
Prince Fortunatus. W. Black.
Prince Hohenstiel-Schwangau, Saviour of Society (poem). R. Browning.
Prince, John Dyneley (co-trans.): see C. G. Leland, *Kulóskap the Master, and Other Algonkin Poems*.
Prince of Good Fellows. R. Barr.
Prince of India; or, Why Constantinople Fell. L. Wallace.
Prince of the House of David; or, Three Years in the Holy City. J. H. Ingraham.
Prince Otto: A Romance. R. L. Stevenson.
Princess. M. H. Potter.
Princess, A Medley. A. Tennyson.
Princess, A Medley. A. Tennyson: see A. D. A. de Brueys, *Avocat Patelin: A Comedy in Three Acts* (marginalia).
Princess Christian of Schleswig-Holstein (trans., ed.): see F. S. Wilhelmina, *Memoirs of Wilhelmine, Margravine of Baireuth*.
Princess Idleways: A Fairy Story. H. A. Hays.
Princess Liliwinkins, and Other Stories. H. C. Wright.
Princess Olga. E. Wardman.
Principles of Banking. C. A. Conant.
Principles of Domestic Science; As Applied to the Duties and Pleasures of Home. C. E. Beecher and H. E. B. Stowe (co-author).
Principles of Geology. C. Lyell.
Principles of Money and Banking. C. A. Conant.
Principles of Psychology. W. James.
Principles of Strategy, Illustrated Mainly from American Campaigns. J. Bigelow.
Printing: see
American Bookmaker.
W. Besant, *Pen and the Book* (marginalia).
R. Browning, *Pauline; Paracelsus; Strafford; Sordello* (marginalia).
W. O. Chapin, *Masters and Masterpieces of Engraving*.
T. L. De Vinne, *Invention of Printing*.
G. Duplessis, Georges. *Wonders of Engraving*.
W. D. Howells, "Country Printer" (essay).
W. D. Howells, *Impressions and Experiences* (essays).
See also the Reader's Guide entry for Engraving.
Prinzessin Ilse. Ein Märchen aus dem Harzgebirge. M. Peterson.
"Prior, James" (pseud.): see the Catalog entry for J. P. Kirk.
Prison and dungeon literature: see
W. Ainswworth, *The Tower of London*.
F. Bernard, *Wonderful Escapes*.
T. Carlyle, *The French Revolution*.
G. Casanova de Seingalt, *Mémoires de Jacques Casanova de Seingalt, Écrits par lui-même*.
B. Cellini, *Life*.

M. A. H. Clarke, *For the Term of His Natural Life.*

C. Dickens, *Tale of Two Cities.*

A. Dumas, *Count of Monte Cristo.*

A. Dumas, *Man in the Iron Mask.*

E. W. Hornung, *Rogue's March, A Romance.*

W. D. Howells, "Our Spanish Prisoners at Portsmouth" (essay).

R. H. Kellogg, *Life and Death in Rebel Prisons: Giving a Complete History of the Inhuman and Barbarous Treatment of Our Brave Soldiers by Rebel Authorities.*

J. S. Laurie, *Story of Australasia: Its Discovery, Colonisation, and Development.*

T. B. Macaulay, *Speeches and Poems, with the Report and Notes on the Indian Penal Code.*

W. Raleigh (Catalog entry).

A. D. Richardson, *Secret Service: The Field, the Dungeon, and the Escape.*

J. X. B. Saintine, *Picciola.*

M. Serao, *Ballet Dancer, and On Guard.*

F. von der Trenck, *Life of Baron Frederic Trenck.*

"Prisoner of Chillon" (poem). G. G. Byron.

Prisoner of Ornith Farm. F. P. Case.

Prisoners of Hope. A Tale of Colonial Virginia. M. Johnston.

Prittie, E. J. (illus.): see R. H. Fillebrown, *Rhymes.*

Private Correspondence of Daniel Webster. D. Webster.

Private Journal of a Voyage to the Pacific Ocean and Residence at the Sandwich Islands, in the Years 1822, 1823, 1824, and 1825. C. S. Stewart.

Private Life. H. James.

Private Life of an Eastern King. W. Knighton.

Private Lives of William II and His Consort and Secret History of the Court of Berlin. H. W. H. Fischer.

Private Theatricals (novel). W. D. Howells.

Prize fighting: see the Reader's Guide entry for Boxing.

Prize Painting Book: Good Times. Pictures by Dora Wheeler. C. T. Wheeler.

"*Probable Sons.*" A. Le Feuvre.

Problematische Naturen: Roman. F. Spielhagen.

Procès de condamnation de Jeanne d'Arc. J. Fabre.

Procès de condamnation et de réhabilitation de Jeanne d'Arc, dite La Pucelle, publiés pour Ia premiere fois d'après les manuscrits de la Bibliothèque Royale. J. É. J. Quicherat (comp.).

Procter, Adelaide Anne: see G. A. Stevens, "Storm" (song).

Procter, Bryan Waller: see J. T. Fields, *Old Acquaintance. Barry Cornwall and Some of His Friends.*

Proctor, Richard Anthony (ed.): see A. V. Guillemin, *Heavens: An Illustrated Handbook of Popular Astronomy.*

"Prodigal son" (sacred song). H. C. Watson.

Profanity: see

L. Hutton, *Boy I Knew and Four Dogs.*

H. Martineau, *Autobiography* (marginalia).

M. F. Tupper, *Proverbial Philosophy: A Book of Thoughts and Arguments, Originally Treated* (Catalog entry).

Professor (play). W. Gillette.

Professor at the Breakfast-Table. O. W. Holmes.

Professor Jim (nickname): see C. H. Proctor, *Life of James Williams, Better Known as Professor Jim, for Half a Century Janitor of Trinity College.*

Progress and Poverty: An Inquiry into the Cause of Industrial Depression and of Increase of Want with Increase of Wealth: The Remedy. H. George.

"Progressional" (satirical poem). L. Strachey.

Progressive Protestantism. "Sixtus" (pseud.).

Progress of the Century. W. R. Wallace, W. Ramsay, *et al.*

Promises of Scripture. S. Clarke.

Promus of Formularies and Elegancies (Being Private Notes, Circ. 1594, Hitherto Unpublished) by Francis Bacon. Illustrated and Elucidated by Passages from Shakespeare. F. Bacon.

Property in Land: A Passage-at-Arms Between the Duke of Argyll and Henry George. H. George.

Prophecies: see

S. D. Baldwin, *Armageddon; or, The Overthrow of Romanism and Monarchy.*

Napoleon's Oraculum, or, Book of Fate.

Prophet of the Great Smoky Mountains. M. N. Murfree.

Prose and Poetry. By a Georgia Lady. M. A. H. Gay.

Prose Writers of Germany. F. H. Hedge.

Prosper Mérimée's Letters to an Incognita. P. Mérimée.

Prostitution: see

W. W. Sanger, *History of Prostitution: Its Extent, Causes, and Effects Throughout the World.*

H. E. B. Stowe, *We and Our Neighbors; or, the Records of an Unfashionable Street. A Novel.*

I. M. Van Etten, "House of the Dragons" (short story).

J. W. Watson, "Beautiful Snow" (poem).

Protection or Free Trade: An Examination of the Tariff Question with Especial Regard to the Interests of Labor. H. George.

Protestant Episcopal: see *Order for Daily Evening Prayer.*

Protestant Reformation: see

R. Chambers (comp.), *Domestic Annals of Scotland from the Reformation to the Revolution.*

J. F. Hurst, *Short History of the Reformation.*

L. von Ranke, *Deutsche Geschichte im Zeitalter der Reformation.*

L. von Ranke, *History of the Popes, Their Church and State, and Especially of Their Conflicts with Protestantism in the Sixteenth and Seventeenth Centuries.*

F. von Schlegel, *Philosophy of History; in a Course of Lectures, Delivered at Vienna.*

See also the Reader's Guide entry for Martin Luther.

Proud Prince. J. H. McCarthy.

"Prout, Father" (pseud.): see F. S. Mahony.

Provenzano the Proud. E. Gifford.

Proverbial Philosophy: A Book of Thoughts and Arguments, Originally Treated. M. F. Tupper.

Proverbs: see

J. Heywood, *Dialogue of Proverbs.*

A. Hislop, *Proverbs of Scotland; with Explanatory and Illustrative Notes, and a Glossary.*

Proverbs of Scotland; with Explanatory and Illustrative Notes, and a Glossary. A. Hislop.

Providence (as a concept): see

S. Clarke, *Mirror or Looking-Glass Both for Saints & Sinners* (marginalia).

R. T. Cooke, "Freedom Wheeler's Controversy with

Providence: A Story of Old New England" (short story).

Henry of Huntingdon, *Chronicle of Henry of Hunting-don, Comprising the History of England, from the Invasion of Julius Caesar to the Accession of Henry II* (marginalia).

C. Mather, *Magnalia Christi Americana; or, The Ecclesiastical History of New-England.*

Tacitus, *Works of Tacitus* (marginalia).

Provok'd Wife. A Comedy (play). J. Vanbrugh.

Prudence Palfrey. A Novel. T. B. Aldrich.

Prue and I. G. W. Curtis.

"Prune, Nat" (pseud.): see J. Weymouth.

Prussia: see the Reader's Guide entries for Germany.

"P. S." (pseud.): see (trans.) S. R. Ségur, *Adventures of a Donkey.*

"Psalm of Life" (poem). H. W. Longfellow.

Pseudosciences: see the Reader's Guide entries for Mysticism, for Palmistry, for Parapsychology, for Phrenology, for Spiritualism and spiritual healing, and for Telepathy.

Psychical phenomena: see the Reader's Guide entry for Parapsychology.

Psychical research: see the Reader's Guide entry for Parapsychology and the Reader's Guide and Catalog entries for Society for Psychical Research.

Psychic Riddle. I. K. Funk.

Psychology: see
J. Adams, *Herbartian Psychology Applied to Education, Being a Series of Essays Applying the Psychology of Johann Friedrich Herbart.*
J. M. Baldwin, *Story of the Mind.*
S. Freud (Catalog entry).
W. James, *Principles of Psychology.*
W. James, *Varieties of Religious Experience; A Study in Human Nature.*
R. von Krafft-Ebing, *Psychopathia Sexualis, with Special Reference to Contrary Sexual Instinct: A Medico-Legal Study.*
G. L. Raymond, *Psychology of Inspiration; An Attempt to Distinguish Religious from Scientific Truth.*

Psychology of Inspiration; An Attempt to Distinguish Religious from Scientific Truth. G. L. Raymond.

Psychopathia Sexualis, with Special Reference to Contrary Sexual Instinct: A Medico-Legal Study. R. von Krafft-Ebing.

Public speaking: see
G. W. Hervey, *System of Christian Rhetoric, for the Use of Preachers and Other Speakers.*
O. W. Holmes, *Autocrat of the Breakfast-Table.* (marginalia).

Publishers:
Publishers' Trade List Annual, 1907.
Reference Catalogue of Current Literature Containing the Full Titles of Books Now in Print and On Sale.
See also the Reader's Guide entries for Editing and for Printing.

Publishers' Weekly: see *Publishers' Trade List Annual, 1907.*

Publishing: see the Reader's Guide entry for Editing and for Publishers.

Puck of Pook's Hill. R. Kipling.

Pudsey: see S. Rayner, *History and Antiquities of Pudsey.*

Pugin, Augusutus Charles (co-illus.): see London, *Forty-One Coloured Views of London.*

Pulitzer, Joseph: see New York *World* (Catalog entry).

"Pullen, Mrs. Stanley T." (pseud.): see E. J. Pullen.

Punch (London magazine): see
F. C. Burnand (ed., author).
Cartoons from "Punch."
G. L. P. B. Du Maurier, *Legend of Camelot, Pictures and Poems, Etc.*
G. L. P. B. Du Maurier, *Social Pictorial Satire; Reminiscences and Appreciations of English Illustrators of the Past Generation.*
J. Leech, *John Leech's Pictures of Life & Character. From the Collection of "Mr. Punch."*
H. A. Taine, *Notes on England.*
B. Taylor, *At Home and Abroad: A Sketch-Book of Life, Scenery, and Men.*
T. Taylor, *Bottle: A Drama in Two Acts* (Catalog entry).

"Punch, Brothers, Punch" (newspaper jingle). N. Brooks.

"Punch, Brothers, Punch" (newspaper jingle): see also *Horse-Car Poetry.*

Punishment: see the Reader's Guide entry for Torture and punishment.

Punishment of the Stingy, and Other Indian Stories. G. B. Grinnell.

Puns: see O. W. Holmes, *Soundings from the Atlantic.*

Puppenheim (play): see H. Ibsen, *Doll House* (play).

Puritan Rebellion (English): see the Reader's Guide entry for Oliver Cromwell.

Puritans in New England: see
J. G. Austin, *Standish of Standish: A Story of the Pilgrims.*
C. W. E. Bardsley, *Curiosities of Puritan Nomenclature.*
C. C. Coffin, *Old Times in the Colonies.*
E. De Amicis, *Holland and Its People* (tipped in note about Plymouth Rock).
J. Fiske, *Beginnings of New England; or, The Puritan Theocracy.*
A. B. Hart, *Colonial Children.*
S. Hopkins. *Life and Character of . . . Jonathan Edwards.*
C. Mather, *Magnalia Christi Americana; or, The Ecclesiastical History of New-England from Its First Planting in the Year 1620, unto the Year of Our Lord, 1698.*
C. Mather, *Wonders of the Invisible World.*
F. Parkman, *Count Frontenac and New France Under Louis XIV* (marginalia).
H. E. B. Stowe, *Minister's Wooing.*
J. H. Trumbull (ed.), *True-Blue Laws of Connecticut and New Haven* (marginalia).
J. H. Twichell, *John Winthrop, First Governor of the Massachusetts Colony.*
T. Wright, *Narratives of Sorcery and Magic, from the Most Authentic Sources.*
See also the Reader's Guide entry for New England.

"Purloined Letter" (story). E. A. Poe.

Purple and Homespun; A Novel. S. M. Gardenhire.

"Purple Eyes" (short story): see J. L. Long *Madame Butterfly.*

Pursuit of the House-Boat. J. K. Bangs.

"Pursuit of the Piano" (story): see W. D. Howells, *Pair of Patient Lovers.*

Putnam Place. G. L. Collin.

Putnam's Monthly: see J. A. Dallas, "Up the Mississippi" (article).

Put Yourself in His Place. A Novel. C. Reade.

Pygmalion and the Image. W. Morris.

Pyle, Howard (illus.): see
  J. Baldwin, *Island of Enchantment.*
  J. Baldwin, *Story of the Golden Age.*
  J. B. Cabell, *Chivalry.*
  J. B. Cabell, *Line of Love.*
  J. M. Forman, *Island of Enchantment.*

"Pylodet, L." (pseud.): see F. Leypoldt.

Pym, Arthur Gordon (title character): see E. A. Poe, *Narrative of Arthur Gordon Pym of Nantucket* (novel).

Pym, Horace Noble (ed.): see C. Fox, *Memories of Old Friends.*

Pym, John: see G. Smith, *Three English Statesmen: A Course of Lectures on the Political History of England.*

Pyrrhus, King of Epirus: see J. Abbott, *History of Pyrrhus.*

❙ Q

Q. Horatti Flacci Opera omnia. Horace.

"Quad, M." (pseud.): see C. B. Lewis.

Quadroon; or, A Lover's Adventures in Louisiana. M. Reid.

Quaker City controversy: see the Catalog entry for *Philanthropy Dissected: The so-Called "Act for the Further Protection of Seamen" Reviewed.*

Quality of Mercy. W. D. Howells.

Quatrains of Omar Khayyám of Nishapur, Translated from the Persian into English Verse. Omar Khayyám.

Quebec: see W. Kirby, *Golden Dog (Le chien d'or). A Romance of the Days of Louis Quinze in Quebec.*

Queechy. S. B. Warner.

Queen Bee. H. B. Moore.

Queen Mary, A Drama. A. Tennyson.

Queen of Hearts. A Dramatic Fantasia. For Private Theatricals (play). J. B. Greenough.

Queen of Sheba. T. B. Aldrich.

Queen's Necklace: see A. Dumas, *Novels.*

Queen's Twin, and Other Stories. S. O. Jewett.

Queen Titania. H. H. Boyesen.

Queer Little People. H. E. B. Stowe.

Quentin Durward. W. Scott.

Questions on Higginson's Young Folks' History: see T. W. S. Higginson, *Young Folks' History of the United States.*

Quick, Dorothy: see (inscr.) L. M. Boutet de Monvel, *Joan of Arc.*

Quiet Life. Verses by Various Hands. H. A. Dobson (ed.).

"Quill, John" (pseud.): see C. H. Clark.

Quimby, Phineas Parkhurst: see
  E. H. G. Clark, *Church of St. Bunco.*
  H. W. Dresser, *Heart of It.*

Quin, Charles William (trans., ed.): see N. C. Flammarion, *Wonders of Optics.*

Quinnebasset Girls. R. S. Clarke.

Quint, Wilder Dwight (co-author): see G. T. Richardson, *Letters from a Son to His Self-Made Father.*

Quits, A Novel. J. M. von Tautphoeus.

Quixstar; A Novel. E. Taylor.

Quotations: see
  Anecdote Library. Portraits and Views.
  E. H. Barker, *Literary Anecdotes and Contemporary Reminisences of Professor Porson and Others, From the Manuscript Papers of the Late E. H. Barker.*
  J. Barlett, *Shakespeare Phrase Book.*
  S. A. Bent, *Short Sayings of Great Men. With Historical and Explanatory Notes.*
  Borrowings: A Compilation of Helpful Thoughts from Great Authors.
  E. C. Brewer. *Reader's Handbook of Allusions, References, Plots and Stories.*
  C. Buck (comp.), *Anecdotes; Religious, Moral, and Entertaining.*
  H. Drummond, *"Beautiful Thoughts" from Henry Drummond.*
  J. W. Forney, *Anecdotes of Public Men.*
  J. Heywood, *Dialogue of Proverbs.*
  A. Hislop, *Proverbs of Scotland; with Explanatory and Illustrative Notes, and a Glossary.*
  K. A. Sanborn (comp.), *Indian Summer Calendar. Wise Sayings of the Great and Good.*

"Quo Vadis": A Narrative of the Time of Nero (novel). H. Sienkiewicz.

❙ R

"Rab and His Friends." J. Brown.

Rabbi Ben Ezra (poem). R. Browning.

Rabelais, Francis: see
  W. Besant, *French Humorists, from the Twelfth to the Nineteenth Centuries.*
  L. C. Moulton, "Boston. Literary Notes" (Catalog entry).
  W. M. Thackeray, *Thackeray's Lectures. The English Humourists. The Four Georges* (marginalia).

Racial prejudice:
  J. Abbott, *Stories of Rainbow and Lucky: Selling Lucky.*
  D. Boucicault, *Octoroon; or, Life in Louisiana* (play).
  A. M. Buckner, *Towards the Gulf; A Romance of Louisiana.*
  G. W. Cable (Catalog entries).
  C. W. Dilke, *Greater Britain: A Record of Travel in English-Speaking Countries During 1866 and 1867.*
  T. Dixon, Jr., *Leopard's Spots: A Romance of the White Man's Burden—1865–1900.*
  M. E. M. Dodge, "Miss Malony on the Chinese Question" (sketch).
  E. W. Foxall, *Colorphobia. An Exposure of the "White Australia" Fallacy.*
  E. W. Gilliam, "Chinese Immigration" (article).
  O. Goldsmith, *Citizen of the World* (Catalog entry).
  E. W. Kemble (Catalog entry).
  G. A. Lawrence, *Silverland.*
  C. Meiners, *Lebensbeschreibungen berühmter Männer aus den Zeiten der Wiederherstellung der Wissenschaften.*
  "Mulatto" (incident in an unidentified book).
  S. Newland, *Paving the Way: A Romance of the Australian Brush.*
  North American Review.

A. B. Paine, *Captain Bill McDonald, Texas Ranger. A Story of Frontier Reform.*

R. C. M.-P. Praed, *Australian Life, Black and White.*

M. Reid, *Quadroon; or, A Lover's Adventures in Louisiana.*

E. A. Spitzka, "Contributions to the Encephalic Anatomy of the Races" (article).

J. T. Trowbridge, *Cudjo's Cave.*

J. T. Trowbridge, *Neighbor Jackwood.*

A. E. Trumbull, *Hour's Promise* (novel).

C. D. Warner, *Studies in the South and West, with Comments on Canada.*

J. G. Wood, *Uncivilized Races; or, Natural History of Man* (marginalia).

C. F. Woolson, *Jupiter Lights; A Novel.*

C. Zueblin, *Religion of a Democrat.*

Rackham, Arthur (illus.): see R. Kipling, *Puck of Pook's Hill.*

Radford, Dollie (co-ed.): see W. Allingham, *William Allingham, A Diary.*

Radford, Ernest William (ed.). *Illustrations to Browning's Poems.*

Radium: see E. G. Merritt, "New Element Radium" (article).

"Radium and Radioactivity" (article). M. Curie.

Rae, John (ed., intro.): see Henry VII, *Statutes of Henry VII in Exact Facsimile.*

Rae, William Fraser (trans.): see H. A. Taine, *Notes on England.*

Raffles, Arthur J. (fictional character): see
J. K. Bangs, *Mrs. Raffles; Being the Adventures of an Amateur Cracksmoman.*
J. K. Bangs, *R. Holmes & Co.; Being the Remarkable Adventures of Raffles Holmes.*
E. W. Hornung, *Shadow of the Rope* (Catalog entry).

Rafnaland; The Strange Story of John Heath Howard. W. H. Wilson.

Rag Baby (play). C. H. Hoyt.

Ragged Lady: A Novel. W. D. Howells.

Ragged Register (Of People Places and Opinions). A. E. Dickinson.

Ragsdale, William Phileppus: see C. W. Stoddard, *Lepers of Molokai.*

Raid of the Russian Cruiser "Kaskowiski": An Old Story of Auckland. D. M. Luckie.

Raiders. S. R. Crockett.

Raikes, Thomas (co-author): see C. Knight (co-author), *Personal Reminiscences by Cornelia Knight and Thomas Raikes.*

Railroad of Love (play). A. Daly (adapt.).

Railroads: see
C. F. Adams, Jr., "Of Some Railroad Accidents" (article).
Boys on the Railroad.
J. P. Knott (Catalog entry).
Railway Age.
F. B. Terry, *Stories.*
J. F. Willard, *Tramping with Tramps: Studies and Sketches of Vagabond Life.*

Railton, Herbert (illus.): see F. W. Farrar, *Westminster Abbey.*

"Raimond, C. E." (pseud.): see E. Robins.

Raising the Wind (farce). J. Kenney.

Rajah's Heir; A Novel. C. F. Despard.

"Rally round the flag" (song): see G. R. Root, "Battle cry of freedom" (song).

Ralph, Lester (illus.): see H. C. Bailey, *Colonel Greatheart.*

Ralph Marlowe; A Novel. J. B. Naylor.

Ralston, William (illus.): see A. J. Dawson, *Genteel A. B.*

"Ramacharaka, Yogi" (pseud.): see W. W. Atkinson.

Rambler (periodical): see S. Johnson, *Letters of Samuel Johnson, LL.D.* (Catalog entry).

Rambler's Calendar. W. H. Gibson.

Rambles Among Words; Their Poetry, History, and Wisdom. W. Swinton.

Rambles and Recollections of an Indian Official. W. H. Sleeman.

"Rambouillon" (reference): see C. Flammarion, *Stories of Infinity.*

Ramée, Marie Louise de la: see M. L. De la Ramée.

Rameses the Great; or, Egypt 3300 Years Ago. F. de Lanoye.

Ramsay, William: see
(co-author): see A. R. Wallace, *Progress of the Century.*
A. Winchell, *Sketches of Creation: A Popular View of Some of the Grand Conclusions of the Sciences in Reference to the History of Matter and of Life* (marginalia).

Randall, William Brighty (intro.): see G. Eliot, *Complete Poems.*

Randolph, Anson Davies Fitz (ed.): see *Devotional Hymns.*

Randolph, John: see D. B. Lucas and J. F. McLaughlin, *Fisher Ames-Henry Clay, Etc.*

Randolph, Margaret Barker Landers (illus.): see
C. Scollard, *On Sunny Shores.*
C. Scollard, *Under Summer Skies.*

Randolph Mason: see *Strange Schemes of Randolph Mason.* M. D. Post.

Randvar the Songsmith; A Romance of Norumbega. O. A. Liljencrantz.

"Rantoul" (poem). J. G. Whittier.

Raspe, Rudolph Erich: see B. Münchausen, *Adventures of Baron Munchausen.*

Rationalism: see W. E. H. Lecky, *History of the Rise and Influence of the Spirit of Rationalism in Europe.*

"Raven" (poem). E. A. Poe.

Raven-Hill, Leonard (illus.): see E. Phillpotts, *Human Boy Again.*

Ravenshoe. H. Kingsley.

Rawlinson, George (trans. and co-ed.): see Herodotus, *History of Herodotus.*

Rawlinson, Henry Creswicke (trans. and co-ed.): see Herodotus, *History of Herodotus.*

Read, Opie: see H. E. Taliaferro (Catalog entry).

Reade, Compton (co-author): see C. L. Reade, *Charles Reade, D. C. L., Dramatist, Novelist, and Journalist. A Memoir.*

Reader's Handbook of Allusions, References, Plots and Stories. E. C. Brewer.

Reading: see
M. E. Burt, *Literary Landmarks: A Guide to Good Reading for Young People, and Teachers' Assistant.*
Reference Catalogue of Current Literature Containing

the Full Titles of Books Now in Print and On Sale with the Prices.

W. Shakespeare, *Works of Shakespeare* (Catalog entry).

W. S. Sonnenshein (comp.), *Best Books: A Reader's Guide to the Choice of the Best Available Books (about 50,000) in Every Department of Science, Art, and Literature.*

"Ready—If Needed!" (poem): see W. J. Lampton, *Yawps and Other Things.*

Real Diary of a Real Boy. H. A. Shute.

Real Queen's Fairy Tales. Elizabeth, Queen of Rumania.

Real Things in Nature, A Reading Book of Science for American Boys and Girls. E. S. Holden.

Real Triumph of Japan: The Conquest of the Silent Foe. L. L. Seaman.

Rebecca Mary. A. H. Donnell.

Rebellious Heroine: A Story. J. K. Bangs.

Reber, Franz von (intro.): see Munich. Pinakothek, Alte. *Catalogue of the Paintings in the Old Pinakothek, Munich.*

"Recent Impressions of Anglo-Indian Life" (article). E. L. Weeks.

"Recessional" (poem). R. Kipling.

Recollections. G. W. Childs.

Recollections. G. Sand.

Recollections, 1832 to 1886. A. E. West.

Recollections and Letters of General Robert E. Lee, by His Son. R. E. Lee.

Recollections of a Journey Through Tartary, Thibet, and China, During the Years 1844, 1845, and 1846. É. R. Huc.

Recollections of a Minister to France, 1869–1877. E. B. Washburne.

Recollections of a Page to the Court of Louis XVI. C. de F. d' Hézecques.

Recollections of Baron de Frénilly, Peer of France (1768–1828). A. F. F. de Frénilly.

Recollections of Geoffrey Hamlyn (novel). H. Kingsley.

Recollections of Geoffrey Hamlyn (novel): see I. Zangwill, *Master; A Novel* (Catalog entry).

Recollections of President Lincoln and His Administration. L. E. Chittenden.

Recollections of Samuel Breck, with Passages from His Notebooks. S. Breck.

Recollections of the Last Days of Shelley and Byron: see E. J. Trelawny, *Records of Shelley, Byron, and the Author.*

Recollections of the Sioux Massacre. O. G. Wall.

Reconstruction in the American South: see

C. C. Brush, *Colonel's Opera Cloak.*

A. M. Buckner, *Towards the Gulf; A Romance of Louisiana.*

H. C. Dean, *Crimes of the Civil War, and Curse of the Funding System.*

T. Dixon, *Leopard's Spots: A Romance of the White Man's Burden—1865–1900.*

E. A. G. Glasgow, *Voice of the People* (novel).

T. W. S. Higginson, *History of the United States from 986 to 1905* (marginalia).

H. D. Pittman, *Belle of the Bluegrass Country. Studies in Black and White.*

R. Taylor, *Destruction and Reconstruction: Personal Experiences of the Late War.*

A. W. Tourgée, *Bricks Without Straw. A Novel.*

A. W. Tourgée, *Fool's Errand, by One of the Fools.*

G. A. Wilcox, *Christian Philanthropist. A Sketch of the Life of Mr. Daniel Hand, and of His Benefaction to the American Missionary Association, for the Education of the Colored People in the Southern States of America.*

J. A. Wyeth, *Life of General Nathan Bedford Forrest.*

See also the Reader's Guide entry for Civil War (American).

Reconstruction of Religious Belief. W. H. Mallock.

Records of a Journey. A Prologue. D. W. Church.

Records of Later Life. F. A. Kemble.

Records of Romsey Abbey: An Account of the Benedictine House of Nuns, with Notes on the Parish Church and Town (A. D. 907–1558). H. G. D. Liveing.

Records of Shelley, Byron, and the Author. E. J. Trelawny.

Record of the Year (magazine): see *Horse-Car Poetry.*

Recueil des causes célèbres, et des arrêts qui les ont décidées. M. Méjan.

Red Axe. S. R. Crockett.

Red Cockade. A Novel. S. J. Weyman.

Red Cotton Night-Cap Country (poem). R. Browning.

Red Cotton Night-Cap Country (poem): see R. Browning, *Fifine at the Fair.*

Redding, Connecticut: see

W. E. Grumman, *Revolutionary Soldiers of Redding, Connecticut, and the Record of Their Services.*

C. B. Todd, *History of Redding, Connecticut.*

"Red Dog" (short story). R. Kipling.

Redeeming the Republic: The Third Period of the War of the Rebellion. C. C. Coffin.

Redemption of Kenneth Galt. W. N. Harben.

Redfields Succession. H. B. Boone.

Red House; A Novel. B. N. Bland.

Red Mustang, A Story of the Mexican Border. W. O. Stoddard.

Red Rubber; The Story of the Rubber Slave Trade Flourishing on the Congo in the Year of Grace 1906. E. D. Morel.

Red Year; A Story of the Indian Mutiny. L. Tracy.

Re-Echoes from Coondambo. R. Bruce.

Reed, Chester Albert (ed.): see *American Ornithology for the Home and School.*

Reeve, Henry (ed.): see C. C. F. Greville, *Greville Memoirs.*

Reformation: see the Reader's Guide entry for Protestant Reformation.

"Reformation of Uncle Billy" (short story). E. P. Butler.

Regent's Daughter: see A. Dumas, *Novels.*

Register: Farce (play). W. D. Howells.

Registers of Topcliffe, and Morley in the W. R. of the County of York. Baptisms, 1654–1830. Burials, 1654–1888. W. Smith (ed.).

"Regret" (poem). F. C. F. Tiernan.

Regulations for the Army. United States War Department.

Rehan, Ada: see W. Shakespeare, *Taming of the Shrew* (play) (Catalog entry).

"Reid, Christian" (pseud.): see F. C. F. Tiernan.

Reid, Gilbert (co-author): see *Crisis in China.*

Reid, Stuart Johnson (ed.): see J. G. Argyll, *Viscount Palmerston, K. G.*

Reid, Whitelaw: see
American Cyclopaedia: A Popular Dictionary of General Knowledge.
(contr.) *Lotos Leaves*.
J. H. Newman, *Apologia Pro Vita Sua* (Catalog entry).
New York *Tribune* (Catalog entry).
H. G. Ollendorff, *Ollendorff's New Method of Learning to Read, Write, and Speak the French Language* (Catalog entry).
J. Ruskin, *Stones of Venice* (Catalog entry).
W. Winter, *Trip to England* (Catalog entry).
W. Winter, *Wanderers: The Poems of William Winter*.

Reign of Queen Anne. J. McCarthy.

Reih' und Glied: Roman. F. Spielhagen.

Reincarnation: see the Reader's Guide entries for Spiritualism and spiritual healing.

Reinecke Fuchs. J. W. von Goethe.

Reinhart, Charles Stanley (illus.): see C. D. Warner, *Their Pilgrimage* (novel).

Reisen in Amerika und der Südamerikanische Krieg. M. von Versen.

Rejected of Men; A Story of To-day. H. Pyle.

Relation of Literature to Life. C. D. Warner.

Religio Animae, and Other Poems. A. B. Richards.

Religion and science: see the Reader's Guide entry for Science and religion.

Religion of a Democrat. C. Zueblin.

Religious intolerance: see the Reader's Guide entry for Religious persecution.

Religious persecution: see
D. Brewster, *Martyrs of Science; or, The Lives of Galileo, Tycho Brahe, and Kepler*.
J. Brougham, *Christian Martyrs under Constantine and Maxentius* (play).
J. Foxe, *Book of Martyrs*.
A. F. Heard, *Russian Church and Russian Dissent,Comprising Orthodoxy, Dissent, and Erratic Sects*.
H. C. Lea, *History of the Inquisition of the Middle Ages*.
W. E. H. Lecky, *History of European Morals from Augustus to Charlemagne* (marginalia).
H. W. Longfellow, *New-England Tragedies*.
Martyrs of Madagascar, and Other Books for Children and Youth.
G. Parker, *Ladder of Swords; A Tale of Love, Laughter and Tears* (novel).
F. Parkman, *Jesuits in North America in the Seventeenth Century*.
F. Parkman, *Old Régime in Canada* (marginalia).
W. H. Rule, *History of the Inquisition from Its Establishment in the Twelfth Century to Its Extinction in the Nineteenth*.
G. H. E. Slater, *Pagan at the Shrine*.
L. Whitney, *Burning of the Convent. A Narrative of the Destruction, by a Mob, of the Ursuline School on Mount Benedict, Charlestown, as Remembered by One of the Pupils*.
N. P. S. Wiseman, *Fabiola; or, The Church of the Catacombs*.

See also the Reader's Guide entries for Christianity and comparative religions, for Missionaries, and for Science and religion.

Religious Poems. H. E. B. Stowe.

Religious Training of Children in the School, the Family, and the Church. C. E. Beecher.

Reliques of Ancient English Poetry. T. Percy (ed.).

Reliques of Father Prout. F. S. Mahony.

Relyea, Charles M. (illus.): see J. W. Riley, *Rubáiyát of Doc Sifers*.

Remarkable Adventures of Little Boy Pip. P. W. Francis.

Remarkable Characters and Places of the Holy Land. C. W. Elliott.

Remarkable Trials of All Countries. T. Dunphy.

"Remarkable Wreck of the 'Thomas Hyke,'" (story): see F. R. Stockton, *Stockton's Stories. Second Series*.

Remington, Frederic: see
(inscr.) H. M. Chittenden, *History of Early Steamboat Navigation on the Missouri River: Life and Adventures of Joseph LaBarge*.
(frontispiece.): see A. H. Lewis, *Wolfville Days*.
(illus.) see C. Whitney, *On Snow-Shoes to the Barren Grounds. Twenty-Eight Hundred Miles After Musk-Oxen and Wood-Bison*.

Reminiscences. T. Carlyle.

Reminiscences. J. McCarthy.

Reminiscences of Michael Kelly, of the King's Theatre, and Theatre Royal Drury Lane. M. Kelly.

Reminiscences of the Great Mutiny, 1857–59, Including the Relief, Siege, and Capture of Lucknow, and the Campaigns in Rohilcund and Oude. W. Forbes-Mitchell.

Reminiscences of the King of Roumania. M. Kremnitz.

Reminiscences of the Opera. B. Lumley.

Reminiscences of Urban and Suburban Life. J. K. Bangs.

Reminiscences of Walt Whitman with Extracts from His Letters and Remarks on His Writings. W. S. Kennedy: see
W. Whitman, *Autobiographia; or, the Story of a Life. By Walt Whitman. Selected from His Prose Writings*.

Reminiscences of Winfield Scott Hancock. By His Wife. A. R. Hancock.

Rémusat, Paul de (ed.): see C. É. J. G. de V. Rémusat, *Memoirs of Madame de Rémusat, 1802–1808*.

Renaissance:
P. Lacroix, *Arts in the Middle Ages, and at the Period of the Renaissance*.
P. Lacroix, *Military and Religious Life in the Middle Ages and at the Period of the Renaissance*.

Renan, Ernest: see G. P. Fisher, *Essays on the Supernatural Origin of Christianity*.

Renshaw, Lucy (travel companion): see A. A. B. Edwards, *Untrodden Peaks and Unfrequented Valleys*.

"Report by W. M. Morrison, American Missionary in the Congo Free State" (unidentified publication). W. M. Morrison.

"Report of a Journey." A. E. Scrivener.

Report of the British Naval and Military Operations in Egypt, 1882. C. F. Goodrich.

Report on the Depredations Committed by the Thug Gangs of Upper and Central India. W. H. Sleeman.

Reports . . . by the Supreme Court of the Hawaiian Islands. R. G. Davis.

Representative Actors. A Collection of Criticisms, Anecdotes, Personal Descriptions, Etc., Etc., Referring to Many Celebrated British Actors from the Sixteenth to the Present Century. W. C. Russell.

Reptile Book: A Comprehensive Popularized Work. R. L. Ditmars.

"Requiem" (poem). R. Richardson.

Rescue of Desdemona, and Other Verse. W. H. Howells.

Residences: see the Reader's Guide entry for Homes.

"Rest" (poem). C. G. Rossetti.

"Restoration" (article). E. R. Hardy.

Restoration dramatists: see *Dramatists of the Restoration*.

Resurrection of the Gods: see D. S. Merezhkovsky, *Romance of Leonardo da Vinci, the Forerunner*.

Retrospection and Introspection. M. B. Eddy.

Retrospections of America, 1797–1811. J. Bernard.

Retrospect of Western Travel. H. Martineau.

Return of the Druses (poem): see R. Browning, *Dramas*.

"Return of the Soul" (story). R. S. Hichens.

Retzsch, [Friedrich August] Moritz (illus.): see
  J. W. von Goethe, *Illustrations to Goethe's Faust.*
  J. C. F. von Schiller, *Fight with the Dragon. A Romance.*
  J. C. F. von Schiller, *Schiller's Pegasus im Joche.*

Revelation and Inspiration. R. Seeberg.

Revelation. Notes on New Testament. A. Barnes.

Reverie and Other Poems. R. A. Chesebrough.

Reveries of a Bachelor; or, a Book of the Heart. D. G. Mitchell.

Review of a Pastoral Address by the Right Rev. T. N. Staley, D.D., Reformed Catholic Bishop of Honolulu, Containing a Reply to Some of His Charges Against the American Protestant Mission to the Hawaiian Islands.

Review of Professor Brigg's Inaugural Address. "Sixtus" (pseud.).

Revision of the English Version of the New Testament. P. Schaff (ed.).

Revolutionary Soldiers of Redding, Connecticut, and the Record of Their Services. W. E. Grumman.

Reynolds, Joshua (painter): see C. Knight and T. Raikes, *Personal Reminiscences by Cornelia Knight and Thomas Raikes.*

Rhetoric: see
  J. F. Genung, *Practical Elements of Rhetoric, with Illustrative Examples.*
  G. W. Hervey, *System of Christian Rhetoric, for the Use of Preachers and Other Speakers.*

Rhine from Rotterdam to Constance. Handbook for Travellers. K. Baedeker.

Rhine River: see
  K. Baedeker, *Rhine from Rotterdam to Constance. Handbook for Travellers.*
  A. H. Bernard, *Legends of the Rhine.*
  T. Hood, *Up the Rhine.*
  F. J. Kiefer, *Legends of the Rhine from Basle to Rotterdam.*
  L. P. Myers, *Idyl of the Rhine.*
  J. X. B. Saintine, *Myths of the Rhine.*
  M. Schneckenburger, "Wacht am Rhein" (poem, song).
  W. M. Thackeray. *Legend of the Rhine.*

Rhode Island: see S. W. Wardwell, *Bub and Sis: A 20th Century New England Story.*

Rhodes, Cecil: see H. Hensman, *Cecil Rhodes: A Study of a Career.*

R. Holmes & Co.; Being the Remarkable Adventures of Raffles Holmes, Esq., Detective and Amateur Cracksman by Birth. J. K. Bangs.

Rhyme? And Reason? (poems). C. L. Dodgson.

Rhymes and Jingles. M. E. M. Dodge.

Rhymes of Childhood. J. W. Riley.

Rhymes of Happy Childhood. R. H. M. Fillebrown.

Rhys, Ernest (General ed., Camelot Series): see G. White, *Natural History of Selborne. With a Naturalist's Calendar and Additional Observations.*

"Rice, Billy" (pseud. of William H. Pearl): see A. Young, "There is a happy land" (comical parody).

Rice, Clarence C.: see *Christian Science Journal* (marginalia).

Rice, Edward (composer): see W. Gill and H. E. Dixey, *Adonis* (burlesque musical).

Rice, James *(*co-author): see
  W. Besant, *Chaplain of the Fleet.*
  W. Besant, *Seamy Side, A Story.*

Rich, Elihu: see
  (trans., ed.) A. A. Cazin, *Phenomena and Laws of Heat.*
  (trans., ed.) M. J. B. L. Sonrel, *Bottom of the Sea.*

Richard Carvel. W. Churchill.

Richard I: see
  Chronicles of the Crusades; Contemporary Narratives.
  W. Scott, *Ivanhoe; A Romance.*
  C. M. Yonge, *Little Duke; or, Richard the Fearless* (novel).

Richard II (play). W. Shakespeare.

Richard II: see A. P. Stanley, *Historical Memorials of Westminster Abbey.*

Richard the Second of England. J. Abbott.

Richard III (play). W. Shakespeare.

Richard III: see
  J. S. C. Abbott, *History of Richard the Third.*
  W. Smith, *Smaller History of England, from the Earliest Times to the Year 1862* (marginalia).
  J. Timbs, *Curiosities of London, Exhibiting the Most Rare and Remarkable Objects of Interest in the Metropolis* (marginalia).

Richard of Devizes: see *Chronicles of the Crusades; Contemporary Narratives.*

Richards, Frank (illus.): see S. R. Crockett, *Red Axe.*

Richards, Frederick Thompson (co-illus.): see J. K. Bangs, *Ghosts I Have Met.*

Richardson, H. T. (co-author): see F. Parsons, *World's Best Books: A Key to the Treasures of Literature.*

Richardson, V. W. (compiler): see G. W. Peck, *Peck's Fun.*

Richard Wagner to Mathilde Wesendonck. R. Wagner.

Richelieu; or, the Conspiracy (play). E. G. E. B. Lytton.

Rickoff, Andrew J. (co-author): see W. T. Harris, *First Reader.*

Riddle of the Universe: see E. H. P. A. Haeckel, *Wonders of Life: A Popular Study of Biological Philosophy.*

Rienzi, the Last of the Roman Tribunes. E. G. E. B. Lytton.

Riese, Friedrich Wilhelm (libretto): see F. von Flotow, *Martha, or the Market at Richmond* (opera).

Riggs, Mrs. George Christopher: see K. D. Wiggin.
"Righteous Setting Forth" (article). E. D. Mead.
Rigoletto (opera). G. Verdi.
Rigutini, Giuseppi (co-author): see I. E. Wessely (co-author), *New Pocket Dictionary of the English and Italian Languages.*
Riley, Henry Thomas (trans.): see
  M. J. B. DuBarry, *Memoirs of Madame DuBarri.*
  Ingulf, *Ingulph's Chronicle of the Abbey of Croyland.*
Riley, James Whitcomb: see J. B. Pond, *Eccentricities of Genius; Memories of Famous Men and Women of the Platform and Stage* (marginalia).
Riley, John Henry: see W. Crookes, *Diamonds.*
Rime of the Ancient Mariner (poem). S. T. Coleridge.
Rime of the Ancient Mariner: see H. Van Dyke (ed.), *Little Masterpieces of English Poetry, by British and American Authors* (marginalia).
Ring and the Book (poem). R. Browning.
Rink, Henry (trans.): see H. Hendrik, *Memoirs of Hans Hendrik, The Arctic Traveler.*
Ripley, George (co-ed.): see *American Cyclopaedia: A Popular Dictionary of General Knowledge.*
Ripley, M. M. (trans.): see F. P. G. Guizot, *Popular History of England.*
"Rip Van Winkle" (story). W. Irving.
"Rip Van Winkle" (story): see F. J. Kiefer, *Legends of the Rhine from Basle to Rotterdam* (Catalog entry).
Rip Van Winkle (play): see
  D. Boucicault (adapt.).
  H. B. Tree (adapt.).
Rise and Fall of the Mustache and Other "Hawk-Eyetems." R. J. Burdette.
Rise of Silas Lapham. W. D. Howells.
Rising, Franklin Samuel: see *American Church Missionary Register.*
Ristigouche and Its Salmon Fishing. With a Chapter on Angling Literature. D. Sage.
Ritchie, Anna Cora (Ogden) Mowatt: see the Catalog entry for Mowatt.
Ritchie, Anne Thackeray (pref.): see A. K. Sartoris, *Week in a French Country-House.*
Ritter, Fanny Raymond (trans.; ed.): see R. A. Schumann, *Music and Musicians. Essays and Criticisms.*
Rivals. F. Coppée.
Rivals (play). R. B. B. Sheridan.
River; A Novel. E. Phillpotts.
River-Land, A Story for Children. R. W. Chambers.
River-piloting: see the Reader's Guide entry for River navigation.
River navigation: see
  P. Boyton, *Story of Paul Boyton. Voyages on All the Great Rivers of the World.*
  Z. Cramer, *Navigator; or The Traders' Useful Guide.*
  J. Disturnell, *Sailing on the Great Lakes and Rivers of America.*
  U. P. James, *James' River Guide; Containing Descriptions of All the Cities, Towns, and Principal Objects of Interest on the Navigable Waters of the Mississippi Valley.*
  E. King, *Great South: A Record of Journeys.*

See also the Reader's Guide entries for the Mississippi River and for other specific rivers.
"Rivers, Pearl" (pseud.): see E. J. P. Nicholson.
"Rives, Amélie" (pseud.): see A. R. C. Troubetzkoy.
Roach, Abby Meguire, "Life's Accolade" (short story): see W. D. Howells and H. M. Alden (eds.), *Their Husbands' Wives.*
Roadside Songs of Tuscany. J. Ruskin.
Road to Nowhere. A Story for Children. L. B. Morse.
Roba di Roma. W. W. Story.
Robers, Arthur (ed.): see H. More, *Letters* (Catalog entry).
Robert Dick, Baker of Thurso, Geologist and Botanist. S. Smiles.
Robert Elsmere (novel). M. A. A. Ward.
Robert Falconer. G. MacDonald.
Robert Merry's Museum for Boys and Girls: see *Parley's Magazine.*
"Roberts, Bobs" (pseud.): see W. C. Roberts.
Roberts, Earl (intro.): see F. H. B. Skrine, *Fontenoy and Great Britain's Share in the War of the Austrian Succession 1741–48.*
Robertson, Joseph Clinton (co-ed.): see *Percy Anecdotes.*
Robertson, Thomas William (ed.): see C. F. Browne, *Artemus Ward's Panorama.*
Robert the Bruce: see G. Aguilar, *Days of Bruce; A Story from Scottish History* (novel).
Robeson, George Maxwell: see G. Ticknor, *Life, Letters, and Journals of George Ticknor* (marginalia).
"Robin" (pseud.): see G. Dalziel.
"Robin Adair" (song). C. Keppel.
Robin Hood: see
  J. Cundall, *Robin Hood and His Merry Foresters.*
  E. Gilliat, *Forest Outlaws; or, Saint Hugh and the King.*
  F. Grose, *Classical Dictionary of the Vulgar Tongue* (marginalia).
  H. Pyle, *Merry Adventures of Robin Hood of Great Renown, in Nottinghamshire.*
  W. Scott, *Ivanhoe; A Romance* (Catalog entry).
  E. M. Tappan, *Robin Hood, His Book.*
Robin Hood and His Merry Foresters. J. Cundall.
Robin Hood, His Book. E. M. Tappan.
Robinson, Charles (illus.): see H. D. Lowry, *Make Believe.*
Robinson Crusoe. D. Defoe.
Robinson Crusoe: see
  J. R. Browne, *Crusoe's Island: A Ramble in the Steps of Alexander Selkirk.*
  W. Cowper, "Verses Supposed to be Written by Alexander Selkirk."
  B. Matthews, *Americanisms and Briticisms, with Other Essays on Other Isms.*
  J. D. Wyss, *Swiss Family Robinson. A New Translation.*
Robinson Crusoe in Words of One Syllable. D. Defoe.
Robinson, Edward: see W. C. Prime, *Tent Life in the Holy Land* (marginalia).
Robinson, Rachel (or Rachael) (illus.): see
  E. D. Deland, *Miss Betty.*
  G. E. S. Jackson, *Wee Winkles & Her Friends.*
  G. E. S. Jackson, *Wee Winkles at the Mountains.*

Robinson, Tracy (intro.): see J. S. Gilbert, *Panama Patchwork; Poems, by James Stanley Gilbert.*

Rob Roy (novel). W. Scott.

Rob Roy (novel): see W. D. Howells, *April Hopes* (Catalog entry).

Roche, Charles Émile. (trans.): see P. F. J. N. Barras, *Memoirs of Barras.*

"Rocked in the cradle of the deep" (hymn). E. H. Willard.

"Rocked in the cradle of the deep" (hymn): see J. L. Hatton (ed.), *Songs of England, A Collection of English Melodies*

Rockefeller, John Davison: see S. Dill, *Roman Society in the Last Century of the Western Empire* (marginalia).

"Rock Me to Sleep, Mother" (poem, song). E. A. C. A. Allen.

"Rock Me to Sleep, Mother" (poem, song): see also S. G. Bayne, *Pith of Astronomy* (marginalia).

Rocky Mountains: see

    F. T. Clark, *Mistress of the Ranch; A Novel.*

    T. J. Dimsdale, *Vigilantes of Montana; or, Popular Justice in the Rocky Mountains.*

    W. Irving, *Astoria; or, Anecdotes of an Enterprise Beyond the Rocky Mountains.*

    E. Roberts, *Shoshone and Other Western Wonders.*

    T. B. H. Stenhouse, *Rocky Mountain Saints: A Full and Complete History of the Mormons.*

    See also the Reader's Guide entry for the American West.

Rocky Mountain Saints: A Full and Complete History of the Mormons, . . . and the Development of the Great Mineral Wealth of the Territory of Utah. T. B. H. Stenhouse.

Roderick Dhu; or, The Lady of the Lake: Opera Libretto: see W. Scott.

Roderick Random: see T. G. Smollett, *Adventures of Roderick Random* (novel).

Rodney Stone. A. C. Doyle.

Rodolphus. J. Abbott.

Rogers, Alex (co-author): see J. A. Shipp, *Abyssinia* (musical comedy).

Rogers, Henry Huttleston (subject): see

    F. P. Dunne, *Dissertations by Mr. Dooley* (Catalog entry).

    T. W. Lawson, *Frenzied Finance.*

    I. F. Marcosson, "Henry H. Rogers—Monopolist."

    S. E. Moffett, "Captains of Industry" (article).

Rogers, Samuel (author): see *Book of Pleasures.*

Rogers, William Allen (illus.): see J. O. Kaler, *Mr. Stubbs's Brother.*

Roget, John Lewis (ed.): see P. M. Roget, *Thesaurus of English Words and Phrases.*

Roggie and Reggie Stories. G. Smith.

Rogue's March, A Romance. E. W. Hornung.

Roland and Hildegarde, A Legend of the Castle of Drachenfels, in Humorous Verse. J. M. Stewart.

Rolfe, William James: see

    W. Shakespeare, *Two Gentlemen of Verona* (play) (Catalog entry).

    (ed.) W. Shakespeare, *Works of Shakespeare.*

Rollingpin, Commodore (pseud.): see J. H. Carter.

Rollo Books. J. Abbot.

Roll of Battle Abbey. Battle Abbey.

"Roll on, silver moon" (song): see E. C. E. M. S. Wortley, *Travels in the United States, Etc., During 1849 and 1850* (marginalia).

Rollo's Tour in Europe. J. Abbot.

Romance of a Pro-Consul; Being the Personal Life and Memoirs of the Right Hon. Sir George Grey, K. C. B. J. Milne.

Romance of Gilbert Holmes: An Historical Novel. M. M. Kirkman.

Romance of Leonardo da Vinci, the Forerunner. D. S. Merezhkovsky.

Romance of Modern Geology, Describing in Simple But Exact Language the Making of the Earth with Some Account of Prehistoric Animal Life. E. S. Grew.

Romance of Summer Seas; A Novel. V. A. J. Davis.

Romance of the London Directory. C. W. E. Bardsley.

Roman empire: see

    Athenaeus of Naucratis, *Deipnosophists; or, Banquet of the Learned, of Athenaeus.*

    J. B. Bury, *Student's Roman Empire. A History of the Roman Empire from Its Foundation to the Death of Marcus Aurelius (27 B.C.-180 A.D.).*

    G. J. Caesar, *Cæsar's Commentaries on the Gallic and Civil Wars.*

    T. Child, *Wimples and Crisping-Pins; Being Studies in the Coiffure and Ornaments of Women.*

    A. J. Church, *Two Thousand Years Ago; or, The Adventures of a Roman Boy.*

    A. Del Mar, *Worship of Augustus Caesar.*

    S. Dill, *Roman Society from Nero to Marcus Aurelius.*

    S. Dill, *Roman Society in the Last Century of the Western Empire.*

    E. Falkener, *Ephesus and the Temple of Diana.*

    G. Ferrero, *Greatness and Decline of Rome.*

    J. A. Froude, *Caesar; A Sketch.*

    E. Gibbon, *History of the Decline and Fall of the Roman Empire.*

    A. W. Grube, *Charakterbilder aus der Geschichte und Sage, für einen propädeutischen geschichtsunterricht.*

    W. E. H. Lecky, *History of European Morals from Augustus to Charlemagne.*

    J. Lord, *Old Roman World: The Grandeur and Fall of Its Civilization.*

    E. G. E. B. Lytton, *Last Days of Pompeii.*

    E. G. E. B. Lytton, *Rienzi, the Last of the Roman Tribunes.*

    C. Merivale, *History of the Romans under the Empire.*

    M. Monnier, *Wonders of Pompeii. Translated from the Original French.*

    G. Negri, *Julian the Apostate.*

    Napoleon the Third, *History of Julius Caesar.*

    K. J. Ploetz, *Epitome of Ancient, Mediaeval, and Modern History.*

    M. W. Porter, *What Rome Was Built With: A Description of the Stones Employed in Ancient Times for Its Building and Decoration.*

    A. Sauzay, *Wonders of Glass-Making in All Ages.*

    F. von Schlegel, *Philosophy of History; in a Course of Lectures, Delivered at Vienna.*

H. Sienkiewicz, *"Quo Vadis": A Narrative of the Time of Nero*.

W. Smith, *Smaller History of Greece, from the Earliest Times to the Roman Conquest*.

W. W. Story, *Roba di Roma*.

Suetonius, *Lives of the Twelve Caesars*.

W. Swinton, *Outlines of the World's History, Ancient, Medieval, and Modern*.

P. C. Tacitus, *Works of Tacitus*.

M. W. Townsend, *Asia and Europe: Studies* (marginalia).

P. Vinogradoff, *Roman Law in Mediaeval Europe*.

L. Wallace, *Wooing of Malkatoon. Commodus*.

J. T. Wood, *Discoveries at Ephesus, Including the Site and Remains of the Great Temple of Diana*.

C. M. Yonge, *Young Folks' History of Rome*.

See also the Reader's Guide entries for Augustus Caesar, for Julius Caesar, for Latin language, and for Roman literature.

Roman Holidays and Others. W. D. Howells.

Romani, F. (libretto): see V. Bellini, *Norma*.

Romania: see M. Kremnitz, *Reminiscences of the King of Roumania*.

Romani people: see

S. R. Crockett, *Raiders; Being Some Passages in the Life of John Faa, Lord and Earl of Little Egypt*.

G. Eliot, *Spanish Gypsy. A Poem*.

E. Gerard, *Land Beyond the Forest: Facts, Figures and Fancies from Transylvania*.

J. A. D.-G. Ross, *Three Generations of English Women* (marginalia).

H. Wachenhusen, *Vampyr. Novelle aus Bulgarien*.

T. Watts-Dunton, *Aylwin*.

Roman Law in Mediaeval Europe. P. Vinogradoff.

Roman literature: see

C. Anthon, *Classical Dictionary, Containing an Account of the Principal Proper Names Mentioned in Ancient Authors*.

T. Bulfinch, *Age of Fable; or, Beauties of Mythology*.

G. J. Caesar, *Cæsar's Commentaries on the Gallic and Civil Wars*.

G. V. Catullus, *Works of Catullus and Tibullus, and the Vigil of Venus*.

M. T. Cicero, *Select Orations*.

T. W. Doane, *Bible Myths and Their Parallels in Other Religions*. (marginalia).

Horace, *Odes*.

Horace, *Q. Horatii Flacci Opera omnia*.

L. Hutton, *Literary Landmarks of Rome*.

F. Josephus, *Genuine Works of Josephus*.

Lucretius: see T. Paine, *Age of Reason* (Catalog entry).

M. V. Martialis, *Epigrams of Martial Translated into English Prose*.

B. M. Nead, *Some Hidden Sources of Fiction* (marginalia).

Ovid, *Art of Love, in Three Books*.

Petronius Arbiter, *Satyricon*: see S. Propertius, *Erotica*.

Plinius, *Letters of Caius Plinius Caecilius Secundus*.

Plinius Secundus, *Natural History of Pliny*.

Plutarchus, *Boys' and Girls' Plutarch*.

Plutarchus, *Children's Plutarch: Tales of the Greeks*.

Plutarchus, *Plutarch's Lives of Alcibiades & Coriolanus, Aristides & Cato the Censor*.

Plutarchus, *Plutarch's Lives of Illustrious Men*.

S. Propertius, *Erotica*.

G. A. Simcox, *History of Latin Literature from Ennius to Boethius*.

Suetonius, *Lives of the Twelve Caesars*.

P. C. Tacitus, *Works of Tacitus*.

Virgil, *Works of Virgil*.

See also the Reader's Guide entries for Latin language and for Roman Empire.

Roman mythology: see the Reader's Guide entry for Roman literature.

Roman Singer. F. M. Crawford.

Roman Society from Nero to Marcus Aurelius. S. Dill.

Roman Society in the Last Century of the Western Empire. S. Dill.

Rome: see

T. H. H. Caine, *Eternal City*.

A. J. C. Hare, *Walks in Rome*.

W. D. Howells, *Roman Holidays and Others*.

L. Hutton, *Literary Landmarks of Rome*.

W. H. Neligan, *Rome: Its Churches, Its Charities, and Its Schools*.

M. Serao, *Conquest of Rome* (novel).

W. Sharp, *Flower O' the Vine: Romantic Ballads and Sospiri di Roma*.

W. W. Story, *Roba di Roma*.

A. C. Swinburne, *Duke of Gandia* (play).

C. D. Warner, *Saunterings*.

Rome. É. Zola.

Romeo and Juliet (play). W. Shakespeare.

Rome: Its Churches, Its Charities, and Its Schools. W. H. Neligan.

Romola. G. Eliot.

Romsey Abbey: see H. G. D. Liveing, *Records of Romsey Abbey*.

Romulus: see J. S. C. Abbott, *History of Romulus*.

Roosevelt, Theodore: see

W. Allingham, *William Allingham, A Diary* (marginalia).

G. G. Coulton, *From St. Francis to Dante: Translations from the Chronicle of the Franciscan Salimbene (1221–1288)* (marginalia).

(intro.) H. K. Job, *Wild Wings: Adventures of a Camera-Hunter Among the Larger Wild Birds of North America on Sea and Land*.

New York *Herald* (Catalog entry).

New York *World* (Catalog entry).

(intro.) A. B. Paine, *Captain Bill McDonald, Texas Ranger. A Story of Frontier Reform*.

Suetonius, *Lives of the Twelve Caesars* (Catalog entry).

G. O. Trevelyan, *Life and Letters of Lord Macaulay* (marginalia).

H. Watterson, *Compromises of Life, and Other Lectures and Addresses, Including Some Observations on Certain Downward Tendencies of Modern Society* (Catalog entry).

Root, Edward K. (reference): see *Fliegende Blätter*.

Ropes, Mary Emily (co-author): see A. R. Ropes, *On Peter's Island*.

"Ros, Emanda M'Kittrick" (pseud.): see M. A. Ross.

Rosa, H. (illus.): see B. J. Lossing, *Empire State: A Compendious History of the Commonwealth of New York.*

Rosamund Gray, Essays, Letters, and Poems: see C. Lamb, *Works of Charles Lamb.*

Roscoe, Thomas: see
> (trans.) B. Cellini, *Memoirs of Benvenuto Cellini, A Florentine Artist.*
> (trans., contr.) J. C. L. S. de Sismondi, *Historical View of the Literature of the South of Europe.*

Roscoe, William (ed.): see A. Pope, *Works of Alexander Pope, Esq., with Notes and Illustrations, by Himself and Others.*

Rosebery, Earl of (pref.): see G. R. Parkin, *Round the Empire.*

Rosebery, Lord: see A. P. Primrose.

Rosemary and Rue. E. W. Champney.

Rosenthal, Herman (trans., ed.): see
> H. M. Ganz, *Land of Riddles (Russia of To-day).*
> S. D. Urusov, *Memoirs of a Russian Governor.*

Rosetta Stone: see the Catalog entry for H. C. Rawlinson.

"Rosin the Bow" (song): see "Old Rosin the Beau."

"Ross, Adrian" (pseud.): see A. R. Ropes and M. E. Ropes, *On Peter's Island* (novel).

Ross, Edward Denison (co-author): see F. H. Skrine, *Heart of Asia: A History of Russian Turkestan and the Central Asian Khanates from the Earliest Times.*

Ross, James (ed.): see M. Saadi, *Gulistan; or, Rose Garden, by Musle-Huddeen Sheik Saadi, of Shiraz.*

Ross, Janet Ann (Duff-Gordon): see
> (ed.) L. A. Duff-Gordon, *Letters from Egypt.*
> (ed.) H. J. Ross, *Letters from the East by Henry James Ross, 1837–1857.*

"Ross, Martin" (pseud.) of Violet Florence Martin: see E. A. Œ. Somerville and V. F. Martin, *Some Experiences of an Irish R. M.*

Rossetti, Dante Gabriel: see W. Allingham, *William Allingham, A Diary.*

Rossetti, William Michael (ed. and pref.): see D. G. Rossetti, *Poetical Works of Dante Gabriel Rossetti.*

Roth, Henry (illus.): see D. A. Curtis, *Stand Pat; or, Poker Stories from the Mississippi.*

Roughing It in the Bush. S. S. Moodie. *Rough Shaking.* G. MacDonald.

Roundabout Journey. C. D. Warner.

Round-Robin Series (anonymous novels): see
> *Desmond Hundred.*
> *Georgians.* H. H. Hammond.
> *Homoselle.*
> *Lesson in Love.*
> *Madame Lucas.*
> *Rosemary and Rue.* E. W. Champney.
> *Tallahassee Girl.* J. M. Thompson.

Round the Empire; for the Use of Schools. G. R. Parkin.

Round the Galley Fire. W. C. Russell.

Round the Horn Before the Mast. A. B. Lubbock.

Round the Red Lamp. A. C. Doyle.

Round the World. A. Carnegie.

Rousseau, Jean Jacques: see C. A. Sainte-Beuve, *Monday-Chats, Selected and Translated from the "Causeries du Lundi."*

Routledge's Guide to London and Its Suburbs. G. F. Pardon.

Rowan, Frederica McLean (trans.): see J. H. D. Zschokke, *Meditations on Death and Eternity.*

Rowe, George Stringer (ed.): see T. Thomas (co-author), *Fiji and the Fijians.*

Roweny in Boston, A Novel. M. L. Pool.

Rowlandson, Thomas (co-illus.): see London, *Forty-One Coloured Views of London.*

Roxana, or the Fortunate Mistress. D. Defoe.

Roxburghe Ballads. Collection of Ancient Songs and Ballads. C. Hindley (ed.).

Royal Truths. H. W. Beecher.

Roye, Jean de: see P. de Commynes, *Memoirs of Philip de Commines, Lord of Argenton.*

Royle, Edwin Milton: see J. O. Faversham, *The Squaw Man. A Novel.*

Royston, Samuel Watson: see
> Homer, *Odyssey of Homer, Translated into English Blank Verse* (Catalog entry).
> W. Shakespeare, *Othello* (play) (Catalog entry).
> W. Shakespeare, *Works of Shakespeare* (Catalog entry).

Rubáiyát of a Persian Kitten. O. Herford.

Rubáiyát of Bridge. C. Wells.

Rubáiyát of Doc Sifers. J. W. Riley.

Rubáiyát of Omar Khayyám. Omar Khayyám.

Rubáiyát of Omar Khayyám: see also
> G. D. Eldridge, *In the Potter's House.*
> O. Herford, *Rubáiyát of a Persian Kitten.*
> T. Paine, *Age of Reason* (Catalog entry).
> J. W. Riley, *Rubáiyát of Doc Sifers.*
> M. Saadi, *Gulistan; or, Rose Garden, by Musle-Huddeen Sheik Saadi, of Shiraz* (Catalog entry).
> M. A. A. Ward, *Fenwick's Career* (novel) (marginalia).
> C. Wells, *Rubáiyát of Bridge.*

Rubicon River: see Suetonius, *Lives of the Twelve Caesars* (Catalog entry).

Ruby of Kishmoor. H. Pyle.

Rudder Grange. F. R. Stockton.

Ruinous Face. M. H. Hewlett.

Rulers of Kings; A Novel. G. F. H. Atherton.

Rumford Fireplaces and How They Are Made. G. C. Gillespie (comp.).

Rural Hours, by a Lady. S. F. Cooper.

Ruskin, John: see
> J. Brown, *Letters of Dr. John Brown, with Letters from Ruskin, Thackeray, and Others.*
> T. W. S. Higginson, *Atlantic Essays* (marginalia).

Russell, Charles (trans.): see G. Depping, *Wonders of Bodily Strength and Skill, in All Ages and All Countries.*

Russell, Henry (composer): see
> G. P. Morris, "Oak" (song).
> E. Sargent, "Life on the ocean wave" (song).

Russell, John: see S. J. Reid, *Lord John Russell.*

Russell, Lillian: see
> F. P. Dunne, *Dissertations by Mr. Dooley* (Catalog entry).
> G. Z. MacLaren (Catalog entry).

Russell, Mary Annette, Countess Russell: see M. A. B. von Arnim.

Russell, May Dow Russell Young (ed.): see J. R. Young,

Men and Memories: Personal Reminiscences by John Russell Young.
Russell, William Clark: see S. R. Crockett, *Tales of Our Coast.*
Russia: see
M. K. Bashkirtseva, *Marie Bashkirtseff; The Journal of a Young Artist.*
A. J. Beveridge, *Russian Advance.*
F. E. Clark, *New Way Around an Old World.*
S. Cottin, *Elizabeth; or, The Exiles of Siberia. A Tale, Founded upon Facts.*
Free Russia: The Organ of the English Society of Friends of Russian Freedom.
L. M. Gagneur, *Nihilist Princess* (novel).
H. M. Ganz, *Land of Riddles (Russia of To-day).*
R. W. Gilder, *In the Heights* (Catalog entry).
M. Gorky, *Orlóff and His Wife. Tales of the Barefoot Brigade.*
M. Gorky, *Tales from Gorky, Translated from the Russian.*
A. F. Heard, *Russian Church and Russian Dissent, Comprising Orthodoxy, Dissent, and Erratic Sects.*
J. G. Huneker, *Iconoclasts, A Book of Dramatists.*
G. Kennan, *Siberia and the Exile System.*
G. Kennan, *Tent Life in Siberia, and Adventures Among the Koraks and Other Tribes in Kamtchatka and Northern Asia.*
D. Ker, "Over the Cossack Steppes" (article).
T. W. Knox, *Boy Travellers in the Russian Empire.*
T. W. Knox, *Overland Through Asia; Pictures of Siberian, Chinese, and Tartar Life. Travels and Adventures in Kamchatka, Siberia, China, Mongolia, Chinese Tartary, and European Russia, with Full Accounts of the Siberian Exiles.*
S. M. Kravchinski, *Russia Under the Tsars.*
S. M. Kravchinski, *Underground Russia: Revolutionary Profiles and Sketches from Life.*
D. M. Luckie, *Raid of the Russian Cruiser "Kaskowiski": An Old Story of Auckland.*
J. A. MacGahan, *Campaigning on the Oxus, and the Fall of Khiva.*
C. T. Marvin, *Russians at the Gates of Herat.*
V. Meunier (comp.), *Adventures on the Great Hunting Grounds of the World.*
B. H. Nadal, "A Czar—1905" (poem).
New York *Sun* (Catalog entry).
A. P. Primrose, *Napoleon: The Last Phase* (marginalia).
R. Pumpelly, *Across America and Asia; Notes of a Five Years' Journey Around the World:* see R. Pumpelly, *Explorations in Turkestan.*
A. R. Ropes and M. E. Ropes, *On Peter's Island* (novel).
E. Schuyler, *Turkistan; Notes of a Journey in Russian Turkistan, Khokand, Bukhara, and Kuldja.*
L. L. Seaman, *Real Triumph of Japan: The Conquest of the Silent Foe.*
L. M. Sill, "To the Czar" (poem).
C. W. Silver, *Secular Anathema on Fakery in Business, Social and Professional Life; or, Twentieth Century Conduct.*

F. H. Skrine and E. D. Ross, *Heart of Asia: A History of Russian Turkestan and the Central Asian Khanates from the Earliest Times.*
W. T. Stead, "Character Sketch: Mark Twain" (Catalog entry).
J. L. Stephens, *Incidents of Travel in Greece, Turkey, Russia, and Poland.*
A. C. Swinburne, *Love's Cross-Currents; A Year's Letters* (Catalog entry).
B. Taylor, *Travels in Greece and Russia, with an Excursion to Crete.*
C. R. Teller, *Cage* (novel) (Catalog entry).
L. N. Tolstoy, *Anna Karénine* (novel).
L. N. Tolstoy, *Guerre et la Paix* (novel).
L. N. Tolstoy, *Ivan the Fool; or, the Old Devil and the Three Small Devils.*
L. N. Tolstoy, *Life is Worth Living, and Other Stories.*
L. N. Tolstoy, *My Religion.*
L. N. Tolstoy, *Sebastopol.*
I. S. Turgenev, *First Love* (novella).
I. S. Turgenev, "Nobleman of the Steppe" (short story).
I. S. Turgenev, *Smoke* (novel).
I. S. Turgenev, *Torrents of Spring* (novel).
I. S. Turgenev, "Visions, A Phantasy."
S. D. Urusov, *Memoirs of a Russian Governor.*
W. E. Walling, *Russia's Message, The True World Import of the Revolution.*
V. A. Zhukovskiĭy, "Russian national hymn" (anthem).
K. Zilliacus, *Russian Revolutionary Movement.*
Russian Advance. A. J. Beveridge.
Russian Church and Russian Dissent, Comprising Orthodoxy, Dissent, and Erratic Sects. A. F. Heard.
"Russian national hymn" (anthem). V. A. Zhukovskiĭy.
Russian Revolutionary Movement. K. Zilliacus.
Russians at the Gates of Herat. C. T. Marvin.
Russia's Message, The True World Import of the Revolution. W. E. Walling.
Russia Under the Tsars. S. M. Kravchinski.
Ruth (novel). E. C. S. Gaskell.
"Rutherford, Mark" (pseud.): see W. H. White.
Ruy Blas (play). V. Hugo.
Ryer, George W. (contr.): see D. Thompson, *Old Homestead.*

S

Sacred and Legendary Art. A. B. M. Jameson.
Sacred Anthology. M. D. Conway (ed.).
"Sadlier, Mrs. James" (pseud.): see M. A. M. Sadlier.
Sagas of Thornstein: see R. B. Anderson, *Viking Tales of the North.*
Sage, Dean: see H. D. Thoreau, *Maine Woods* (Catalog entry).
Sahara desert: see
R. S. Hichens, *Garden of Allah.*
D. Ker, "From the Sea to the Desert" (article).
Sailing on the Great Lakes and Rivers of America. J. Disturnell.
"Sailor-boy's dream, an admired ballad" (song). T. V. D. Wiesenthal.

"Sailor's hymn": see E. H. Willard, "Rocked in the cradle of the deep" (hymn).

Sailors' Knots. W. W. Jacobs.

Sailors' Language: A Collection of Sea-Terms and Their Definitions. W. C. Russell.

Sailor's Sweetheart. An Account of the Wreck of the Sailing Ship "Waldershare." W. C. Russell.

Saints: see

    E. Gilliat, *Forest Outlaws; or, Saint Hugh and the King.*

    A. Gregory, *Book of Saints and Wonders.*

    J. O'K. Murray, *Little Lives of the Great Saints.*

    G. E. Waring, Jr., *Whip and Spur.*

    See also the Reader's Guide entries for individual saints.

"St. Aubyn, Alan" (pseud.): see F. B. Marshall.

St. Chad: see G. E. Waring, Jr., *Whip and Spur.*

St. Francis: see G. G.Coulton, *From St. Francis to Dante.*

St. George for England: A Tale of Cressy and Poitiers. G. A. Henty.

St. John, Bayle (trans.): see L. de R. Saint-Simon, *Memoirs of the Duke of Saint-Simon on the Reign of Louis XIV and the Regency.*

St. John's Wooing, A Story. M. G. McClelland.

"St. Leon's Toast" (poem). W. Scott.

"St. Louis" (article): see R. Keeler, "New Orleans" (article).

St. Louis, Missouri: see

    H. B. Fearon, *Sketches of America. A Narrative of a Journey of Five Thousand Miles* (marginalia).

    R. Keeler, "New Orleans," "On the Mississippi" (series of articles).

    C. A. Murray, *Travels in North America During the Years 1834, 1835 & 1836, Including . . . a Visit to Cuba and the Azore Islands.*

    L. P. Myers, *Idyl of the Rhine.*

    C. D. Warner, *Studies in the South and West, with Comments on Canada.*

St. Mark: see "Mary Had a Little Lamb" (Catalog entry).

"Saint Mark" (article). M. Monahan.

St. Nicholas Hotel: see M. D. Conway, *Autobiography: Memories and Experiences of Moncure Daniel Conway* (marginalia).

St. Olave's. A Novel. E. T. Stephenson.

St. Paul, Minnesota: see St. Paul *Pioneer Press.*

St. Sebastian: see *Percy Anecdotes.*

St. Sebastian: see N. P. S. Wiseman, *Fabiola; or, The Church of the Catacombs.*

Saints' Everlasting Rest. R. Baxter (Catalog entry).

Saint-Simon, L. de R.: see

    W. Shakespeare, *Works of Shakespeare* (Catalog entry).

    G. Standring, *People's History of the English Aristocracy* (Catalog entry).

    F. S. Wilhelmina, *Memoirs of Wilhelmine, Margravine of Baireuth* (marginalia).

St. Thomas of Canterbury: see T. H. Baylis, *Temple Church and Chapel of St. Ann, Etc.* (marginalia).

St. Xavier, Francis: see A. D. White, *History of the Warfare of Science with Theology* (Catalog entry).

Saisiaz: see R. Browning, *Agamemnon.*

Saito, Shiuichiro (trans.): see T. Shunsui, *Loyal Ronins: An Historical Romance, Translated from the Japanese.*

Salammbô. G. Flaubert.

Sale, George (trans.): see *Koran: Commonly Called the Alkoran of Mohammed.*

Salem Witchcraft: Comprising More Wonders of the Invisible World, Collected by Robert Calef; and Wonders of the Invisible World, by Cotton Mather. S. P. Fowler (ed.)

Salimbene, Fra.: see G. G. Coulton, *From St. Francis to Dante: Translations from the Chronicle of the Franciscan Salimbene (1221–1288).*

Salisbury: see E. T. Stevens, *Flint Chips. A Guide to Pre-Historic Archaeology, as Illustrated by the Collection in the Blackmore Museum, Salisbury.*

"Sally in our alley" (song). H. Carey.

"Sally in our alley" (song): see

    E. A. Abbey, *Old Songs, with Drawings by Edwin A. Abbey and Alfred Parsons.*

    J. L. Hatton (ed.), *Songs of England, A Collection of English Melodies.*

Salmon fishing: see

    D. Sage, *Ristigouche and Its Salmon Fishing. With a Chapter on Angling Literature.*

    H. Van Dyke, *Blue Flower* (Catalog entry).

Salthaven. W. W. Jacobs.

Salt Lake City: see E. Roberts, *Shoshone and Other Western Wonders.*

Salvation by Grace: see *Salvation Through Grace.*

Salvianus (priest): see S. Dill, *Roman Society in the Last Century of the Western Empire* (marginalia).

Salvini, Tommaso (actor): see W. Shakespeare, *Othello* (Catalog entry).

Samoa: see the Reader's Guide entry for South Pacific.

"Sampleton, Samuel" (pseud.): see L. Monti.

Sampson Rock, of Wall Street. A Novel. E. Lefevre.

Sand, George: see

    P. Mérimée, *Prosper Mérimée's Letters to an Incognita.*

    C. Vincens, *Alfred de Musset.*

Sanders, William Basevi (trans.): see H. James (ed.), *Facsimiles of National Manuscripts from William the Conqueror to Queen Anne.*

Sandford and Merton: see T. Day, *History of Sandford and Merton.*

Sandham, Henry (illus.): see F. C. Baylor, *Juan and Juanita.*

Sandpeep. S. E. S. Boggs.

Sandwich Island Notes. By a Haölé. G. W. Bates (pseud.).

Sandwich Islands: see the Reader's Guide entry for Hawaii.

San Francisco: see

    H. Bush, *Harp of the Day; or, The Adventures and Travels of a Photographic Artist; With Other Poems.*

    T. F. Cronise, *Natural Wealth of California.*

    C. W. Dilke, *Greater Britain: A Record of Travel in English-Speaking Countries During 1866 and 1867.*

    J. M. Hutchings, *Scenes of Wonder and Curiosity in California.*

    W. H. Irwin, *City That Was; A Requiem of Old San Francisco.*

    W. A. Kendall, *Voice My Soul Heard.*

    M. W. Newman (Catalog entry).

    T. Roosevelt, *Square Deal* (Catalog entry).

W. T. Sherman, *Memoirs of General William T. Sherman. By Himself* (marginalia).

F. Soulé (Catalog entry).

R. L. Stevenson and L. Osbourne, *Wrecker* (novel).

W. F. Stewart, *Pleasant Hours in an Eventful Life.*

B. Taylor, *At Home and Abroad: A Sketch-Book of Life, Scenery, and Men.*

B. Taylor, *Eldorado; or, Adventures in the Path of Empire; Comprising a Voyage to California via Panama, Life in San Francisco and Monterey, Pictures of the Gold Region, and Experiences of Mexico Travel.*

A. L. Townsend, *On the Verge: A Romance of the Centennial.*

San Francisco *Herald*: see W. T. Sherman, *Memoirs of General William T. Sherman. By Himself* (marginalia).

"Sanity in Fiction" (article). H. Garland.

Sankey, Ira David: see
(co-ed.) P. P. Bliss, *Gospel Hymns Consolidated.*
(arranger) C. W. Fry, "Lily of the valley" (hymn).

Santa Lucia, A Common Story. M. H. Austin.

Sarah, Frances (trans.): see C. de Rémusat. *Memoirs.*

Saratoga in 1901. Fun, Love, Society & Satire. M. D. L. Landon.

Saratoga, New York: see
M. D. L. Landon, *Saratoga in 1901. Fun, Love, Society & Satire.*
C. D. Warner, *Their Pilgrimage* (novel).

Sartor Resartus. T. Carlyle.

Satan: see
M. Curie, "Radium and Radioactivity."
J. W. von Goethe, *Faust: A Tragedy.*
H. W. Longfellow, *Golden Legend* (marginalia).
E. G. Merritt, "New Element Radium."
J. Milton, *Paradise Lost.*
See also the Reader's Guide entry for Devil.

Satyricon of Petronius Arbiter: see S. Propertius, *Erotica.*

Saunders, Thomas Bailey (trans.): see A. Schopenhauer, *Essays of Arthur Schopenhauer.*

Saunterings. C. D. Warner.

Savage Club: A Medley of History, Anecdote, and Reminiscence by Aaron Watson, With a Chapter by Mark Twain. A. Watson.

Savage Club (London): see
M. D. Conway, *Autobiography: Memories and Experiences of Moncure Daniel Conway* (marginalia).
A. Watson, *Savage Club: A Medley of History, Anecdote, and Reminiscence by Aaron Watson, With a Chapter by Mark Twain.*

Savage, Minot Judson: see V. Streamer (comp.), *Voices of Doubt and Trust.*

Savonarola, Girolamo: see
G. Eliot, *Romola.*
M. O. W. Oliphant, *Makers of Florence: Dante, Giotto, Savonarola, and Their City.*

Saw Up and Saw Down; or, The Fruits of Industry and Self-Reliance. H. C. Knight.

"Saw ye my Saviour?" (hymn). M. B. Eddy.

"Say, Darkies, hab you seen Ole Massa" (song): see H. C. Work, "Kingdom coming" (song).

Saxe Holm's Stories. H. M. F. H. Jackson.

"Say, Wilt Thou Think of Me When I'm Away" (poem). H. Alford.

Scandals: see
Beecher Trial: A Review of the Evidence.
A. A. Behn, *Love-Letters Between a Nobleman and His Sister; With the History of Their Adventures.*
A. Dreyfus, *Lettres d'un Innocent; The Letters of Captain Dreyfus to His Wife.*
J. L. Greene, *Gen. William B. Franklin and the Operations of the Left Wing at the Battle of Fredericksburg, December 13, 1862.*
S. M. Griswold, *Sixty Years with Plymouth Church* (marginalia).
Select Poetical Works of Lord Byron.
See also the Reader's Guide entry for the Tichborne claimant.

Scanderbeg: see J. M. Ludlow, *Captain of the Janizaries, A Story of the Times of Scanderbeg and the Fall of Constantinople.*

Scandinavia: see S. S. Blicher, *Minister of Veilby.*

Scandinavian mythology: see
R. B. Anderson, *Viking Tales of the North.*
R. M. Ballantyne, *Erling the Bold; A Tale of the Norse Sea-Kings.*
H. H. Boyesen, *Gunnar; A Tale of Norse Life.*
T. Bulfinch, *Age of Fable; or, Beauties of Mythology.*
G. W. Cox, *Mythology of the Aryan Nations.*
G. W. Dasent (ed., trans.), *Story of Burnt Njal; or, Life in Iceland in the Tenth Century.*
A. M. Keary and E. Keary, *Heroes of Asgard: Tales from Scandinavian Mythology.*
O. A. Liljencrantz, *Randvar the Songsmith; A Romance of Norumbega.*
W. Morris, *Story of Sigurd the Volsung and the Fall of the Niblungs.*
E. Tegnér, *Frithiof's Saga; A Legend of Ancient Norway.*
E. Tegnér, *Fridthjof's Saga; A Norse Romance.*
W. H. Wilson, *Rafnaland; The Strange Story of John Heath Howard.*
See also the Reader's Guide entries for the literatures of individual Scandinavian countries.

Scarlet Letter, A Romance. N. Hawthorne.

Scènes Enfantines. M. de Bosguérard.

Schell, Frederic B. (illus.): see
A. Tennyson, *Beauties of Tennyson.*
(co-illus.) A. Tennyson, *Lady Clare.*

Schenck, Robert Cumming: see J. Swift, *Gulliver's Travels into Several Remote Nations of the World* (Catalog entry).

Scherezade: see *Arabian Nights.*

Schick's humoristische Bibliothek. L. Schick (comp.).

Schierbrand, Wolf von (trans., ed.): see Wilhelm II, *Kaiser's Speeches, Forming a Character Portrait of Emperor William II.*

Schiller, J. C. F. von: see
H. H. Boyesen, *Goethe and Schiller: Their Lives and Works.*
A. W. Schmidt, *Flowing Bowl: When and What to Drink: Full Instructions How to Prepare, Mix, and Serve Beverages.*

Schiller's Sämmtliche Werke in Zwölf Bänden. J. C. F. von
Schiller.
Schlemihl, Peter: see A. von Chamisso, *Shadowless Man.*
Schmidt, Johann Kaspar: see "Max Stirner" (pseud.).
Schmidt, Kaspar: see Max Stirner (pseud.) in J. G.
Huneker, *Egoists, A Book of Supermen.*
Schnurrdiburr oder Die Bienen. W. Busch.
Schönberg-Cotta Family. E. R. Charles.
*Schönsten Deutschen Volkslieder mit ihren eigenthümlichen
singweisen.* G. Scherer.
School Days at Rugby. T. Hughes.
*School of the Woods; Some Life Studies of Animal Instincts
and Animal Training.* W. J. Long.
School-Room Guide. E. V. De Graff.
"Schools of Journalism" (article). W. Reid.
School textbooks: see
S. Kirkham, *English Grammar in Familiar Lectures.*
McGuffey's Eclectic Readers.
J. Olney, *Practical System of Modern Geography; or, A
View of the Present State of the World, Simplified and
Adapted to the Capacity of Youth.*
See also the Reader's Guide entries for Early reading of
Samuel L. Clemens and for Teaching methods.
Schröer, F. (trans.): see A. von Chamisso, *Peter Schlemihl's
wundersame Geschichte.*
Schröer, Karl Julius (ed.), J. W. von Goethe, *Faust von
Goethe.*
Schumann, Robert Alexander (composer): see H. Heine,
"Two grenadiers" (song).
Schwabe, Carlos (illus.): see H. C. Greene (trans.), *Gospel
of the Childhood of Our Lord Jesus Christ.*
Science: see
M. Curie, "Radium and Radioactivity" (article).
J. Fiske, *Century of Science and Other Essays.*
H. Mayhew, *Wonders of Science; or, Young Humphry
Davy (The Cornish Apothecary's Boy, Who Taught
Himself Natural Philosophy, and Eventually Became
President of the Royal Society).*
E. G. Merritt, "New Element Radium" (article).
S. Newcomb *Side-Lights on Astronomy and Kindred
Fields of Popular Science: Essays and Addresses.*
Popular Science Monthly.
R. Radau, *Wonders of Acoustics; or, The Phenomena of
Sound.*
C. W. Saleeby, *Cycle of Life According to Modern
Science.*
C. W. Saleeby, *Evolution, the Master-Key: A Discussion
of the Principle of Evolution.*
C. Snyder, *New Conceptions in Science, with a Foreword
on the Relationship of Science and Progress.*
J. Tyndall, *Fragments of Science for Unscientific People:
A Series of Detached Essays, Lectures, and Reviews.*
J. Tyndall, *Sound. A Course of Eight Lectures Delivered
at the Royal Institution of Great Britain.*
R. Vallery-Radot, *Life of Pasteur.*
A. R. Wallace, *Man's Place in the Universe: A Study
of the Results of Scientific Research in Relation to the
Unity or Plurality of Worlds.*
A. R. Wallace, William Ramsay, *et al. Progress of the
Century.*

A. R. Wallace, *Wonderful Century; Its Successes and Its
Failures.*
H. G. Wells, *Anticipations of the Reaction of Mechani-
cal and Scientific Progress Upon Human Life and
Thought.*
H. S. Williams, *Story of Nineteenth-Century Science.*
G. S. Woodhead, *Bacteria and Their Products.*
*World of Wonders; A Record of Things Wonderful in
Nature, Science, and Art.*
See also the Reader's Guide entries for Chemistry, for
Inventions, for Physics, and for other fields related
to science.
Science and Health; A Key to the Scriptures. M. B. Eddy.
Science and religion: see
M. Adams, *Continuous Creation; An Application of the
Evolutionary Philosophy to the Christian Religion.*
D. Brewster, *Martyrs of Science; or, The Lives of Galileo,
Tycho Brahe, and Kepler.*
R. Chambers, *Vestiges of the Natural History of
Creation.*
W. K. Clifford, *Lectures and Essays by the Late William
Kingdon Clifford.*
E. Clodd, *Story of Creation: A Plain Account of
Evolution.*
G. G. Coulton, *From St. Francis to Dante: Transla-
tions from the Chronicle of the Franciscan Salimbene
(1221–1288)* (marginalia).
H. Drummond, *Greatest Thing in the World. An
Address.*
O. J. Lodge, *Substance of Faith Allied with Science; A
Catechism for Parents and Teachers.*
W. H. Mallock, *Reconstruction of Religious Belief.*
H. Miller, *Foot-Prints of the Creator.*
H. Miller, *Testimony of the Rocks; or, Geology in its
Bearings on the Two Theologies, Natural and Revealed.*
R. K. Noyes, *Views of Religion, Collected by Rufus K.
Noyes, M. D.* (marginalia).
H. V. M. Phelips, *Churches and Modern Thought; An
inquiry into the Grounds of Unbelief and an Appeal
for Candour.*
G. L. Raymond, *Psychology of Inspiration; An Attempt
to Distinguish Religious from Scientific Truth.*
J.M. Robertson (Catalog entry).
H. E. Rood, *Hardwicke; A Novel.*
A. R. Wallace, *Man's Place in the Universe: A Study
of the Results of Scientific Research in Relation to the
Unity or Plurality of Worlds.*
A. R. Wallace, William Ramsay, *et al. Progress of the
Century.*
A. D. White, *History of the Warfare of Science with
Theology* (marginalia).
A. Winchell, *Sketches of Creation: A Popular View of
Some of the Grand Conclusions of the Sciences in Refer-
ence to the History of Matter and of Life.*
See also the Reader's Guide entries for Christian-
ity and comparative religions and for Religious
persecution.
Science fiction: see
E. F. Benson, *Judgment Books.*
R. D. Blackmore, *Lorna Doone: A Romance of Exmoor.*
E. J. Bliss, *Peril of Oliver Sargent.*

T. H. H. Caine, *Eternal City*.

R. W. Chambers (Catalog entries).

A. von Chamisso, *Peter Schlemihl's wundersame Geschichte*.

C. H. Clark, *Fortunate Island and Other Stories*.

I. Donnelly, *Atlantis: The Antediluvian World*.

I. Donnelly, *Caesar's Column. A Story of the Twentieth Century*.

M. C. Dyar, *Davie and Elisabeth, Wonderful Adventures*.

R. S. Hichens, *Folly of Eustace, and Other Stories*.

E. P. Jackson, *Demigod; A Novel*.

E. G. E. B. Lytton, *Coming Race; or, the New Utopia*.

P. V. Mighels, *Crystal Sceptre; A Story of Adventure*.

S. Newcomb, *His Wisdom the Defender; A Story*.

F.-J. O'Brien (Catalog entry).

W. D. O'Connor, "Brazen Android" (novella).

J. Payn, *High Spirits: Being Certain Stories Written in Them*.

F. M. Savile, *Beyond the Great South Wall: The Secret of the Antarctic*.

G. P. Serviss, *Moon Metal* (science fiction novel).

M. W. G. Shelley, *Frankenstein; or, The Modern Prometheus* (novel).

E. R. Smilie, *Investigations and Experience of M. Shawtinbach, at Saar Soong Sumatra. A Set or Sequel to "The Manatitlans."*

B. Stoker, *Mystery of the Sea; A Novel*.

W. G. V. T. Sutphen, *Doomsman*.

F. M. A. de Voltaire, "Micromégas: A Comic Romance" (short story).

H. Wachenhusen, *Vampyr. Novelle aus Bulgarien*.

H. G. Wells, *Invisible Man. A Grotesque Romance*.

H. G. Wells, *Time Machine*.

H. G. Wells, *War of the Worlds*.

H. G. Wells, *When the Sleeper Wakes*.

H. G. Wells, *Wonderful Visit*.

W. H. Wilson, *Rafnaland; The Strange Story of John Heath Howard*.

M. L. B. Woods, *Invader; A Novel*.

Science (history): see

D. Brewster, *Martyrs of Science; or, The Lives of Galileo, Tycho Brahe, and Kepler*.

A. D. White, *History of the Warfare of Science with Theology*.

Scientific Billiards. Garnier's Practice Shots, with Hints to Amateurs. A. Garnier.

Scoble, Andrew Richard (ed.): see P. de Commynes, *Memoirs of Philip de Commines, Lord of Argenton*.

Scotch (liquor): see G. O. Trevelyan, *Life and Letters of Lord Macaulay* (marginalia).

Scotland: see

H. T. Buckle, *History of Civilization in England*.

R. Chambers (comp.), *Domestic Annals of Scotland from the Reformation to the Revolution*.

C. C. Coffin, *Story of Liberty*.

C. S. Graham, *Mystifications, by Clementina Stirling Grahame*.

A. Hislop, *Proverbs of Scotland; with Explanatory and Illustrative Notes, and a Glossary*.

W. E. H. Lecky, *History of England in the Eighteenth Century* (marginalia).

W. E. H. Lecky, *History of the Rise and Influence of the Spirit of Rationalism in Europe* (marginalia).

G. Mackenzie, *Laws and Customes of Scotland, in Matters Criminal*.

A. MacKinnon, *Prince Charles Edward; or, The Rebellion of 1745–46*.

H. Miller, *Cruise of the Betsey; or, A Summer Ramble Among the Fossiliferous Deposits of the Hebrides*.

W. Robertson, *History of Scotland During the Reigns of Queen Mary and of King James VI Till His Accession to the Crown of England*.

W. Scott, *Letters on Demonology and Witchcraft*.

W. Scott, *Tales of a Grandfather: History of Scotland*.

J. L. Stoddard, *John L. Stoddard's Lectures*.

A. Strickland, *Lives of the Queens of Scotland and English Princesses Connected with the Regal Succession of Great Britain*.

W. G. Wills, *Man o' Airlie: A Drama of the Affections* (play).

W. Winter, *Gray Days and Gold in England and Scotland*.

C. M. Yonge, *Story of James I of Scotland*.

See also the Reader's Guide entry for Scottish literature.

"Scots wha hae' wi' Wallace bled" (song). R. Burns.

Scottish and American Poems of James Kennedy. J. M. Kennedy.

Scottish Chiefs (novel). J. Porter.

Scottish literature: see

G. Aguilar, *Days of Bruce; A Story from Scottish History* (novel).

"Annie Laurie" (song).

J. Brown, *Marjorie Fleming, A Sketch*.

R. Burns, "Auld lang syne" (poem, song), plus other titles.

G. Combe, *Notes on the United States of North America, During a Phrenological Visit in 1838–9-40*.

S. R. Crockett, *Bog-Myrtle and Peat: Tales, Chiefly of Galloway*.

S. R. Crockett, *Cleg Kelly, Arab of the City* (plus other titles).

J. Cumming, *Great Consummation. The Millennial Rest; or, The World As It Will Be*.

M. A. L. Demarest, "My ain countrie" (poem, hymn).

H. Drummond, *Natural Law in the Spiritual World* (and other titles).

C. S. Graham, *Mystifications, by Clementina Stirling Grahame*.

T. Hamilton, *Men and Manners in America*.

T. N. Hepburn, *Sunshine and Haar; Some Further Glimpses of Life at Barncraig*.

P. H. Hunter, *James Inwick, Ploughman and Elder*.

H. Keddie, *Honor Ormthwaite; A Novel*.

H. Keddie, *Noblesse Oblige*.

M. S. Kelly, *Leddy in Her Ain Richt: A Brief Romance*.

J. M. Kennedy, *Scottish and American Poems of James Kennedy*.

C. Keppel, "Robin Adair" (song).

J. Linen, "I Feel I'm Growing Auld, Gude-Wife" (poem).

"Loch Lomond" ("Bonnie banks of Loch Lomond") (ballad).

G. M. V. C. Long, *Master of Stair.*

T. B. Macaulay, *History of England from the Accession of James II* (Catalog entry).

L. Macbean and J. Brown, *Marjorie Fleming: The Story of Pet Marjorie, Together with Her Journals and Her Letters.*

A. P. MacDonald, *MacPeever Wrangles.*

G. MacDonald, *Sir Gibbie* (and also other titles).

J. Macpherson, *Poems of Ossian, the Son of Fingal. Translated from the Original Gaelic.*

I. F. Mayo (Catalog entry).

J. Meikle, *Solitude Sweetened; or, Miscellaneous Meditations on Various Religious Subjects Written in Distant Parts of the World.*

C. O. Nairne, "Bonnie Charlie's Now Awa'" (poem).

One Hundred Songs of Scotland. Words and Music.

J. Porter, *Scottish Chiefs* (novel).

A. Ramsay, "Bonny Bessy" (song).

W. Scott, *Rob Roy* (plus other titles).

R. L. Stevenson, *Kidnapped; Being Memoirs of the Adventures of David Balfour in the Year 1751* (novel).

R. L. Stevenson, *Lowden Sabbath Morn* (poem).

E. Taylor, *Quixstar; A Novel.*

M. G. Todd, *Windyhaugh; A Novel* (Catalog entry).

J. Watson (Catalog entry).

See also the Reader's Guide entry for Scotland.

Scottish National Church: see J. Cumming, *Great Consummation. The Millennial Rest; or, The World As It Will Be.*

Scott, Walter: see

(trans.): see G. von Berlichingen (Catalog entry).

W. D. Howells, *April Hopes* (Catalog entry).

R. S. MacKenzie (Catalog entry).

W. L. Phelps, *Essays on Modern Novelists* (marginalia).

C. Rogers (ed.), *Centenary Garland; Being Pictorial Illustrations of the Novels of Sir Walter Scott, in Their Order of Publication. By George Cruikshank, and Other Artists of Eminence.*

H. E. B. Stowe, *Queer Little People.*

L. Stuart, *Lady Louisa Stuart: Selections from Her Manuscripts.*

W. M. Thackeray, *Thackeray's Lectures. The English Humorists. The Four Georges* (Catalog entry).

J. G. Wilson (ed.), *Love in Letters; Illustrated in the Correspondence of Eminent Persons; with Biographical Sketches of the Writers.*

Scouring of the White Horse. T. Hughes.

Scoville, S., Jr. (co-author): see

On the Gridiron and Other Stories of Outdoor Sport. On Track and Diamond.

"Scow Life in Egypt": see W. C. Prime, *Boat Life in Egypt.*

Scrambles Amongst the Alps in the Years 1860–69. E. Whymper.

Scribe, Eugène (co-author), *Bataille de Dames* (play): see F. Bocher (ed.), *College Series of French Plays.*

Scudder, Horace Elisha (ed.): see S. Breck, *Recollections of Samuel Breck, with Passages from His Notebooks.*

Sculpture: see

C. S. Farrar, *History of Sculpture, Painting, and Architecture.*

W. Lübke, *History of Sculpture from the Earliest Ages to the Present Time.*

A. Saint-Gaudens (Catalog entry).

Sea adventures and voyages: see

Adventures at Sea, by F[rank]. H. Converse, John R. Coryell, Rear-Admiral T. H. Stevens, Maria Louise Pool, and Others.

W. L. Alden, *Cruise of the "Ghost."*

S. W. Baker, *Cast Up by the Sea.*

Battle for the Pacific, and Other Adventures at Sea.

D. J. Belcher, *Mutineers of the "Bounty" and Their Descendants in Pitcairn and Norfolk Islands.*

W. Black, *White Wings; A Yachting Novel.*

Brassey, A. A. A., *Voyage in the Sunbeam, Our Home in the Ocean for Eleven Months.*

F. T. Bullen, *Cruise of the Cachalot Round the World after Sperm Whales.*

F. T. Bullen, *Log of a Sea-Waif: Being Recollections of the First Four Years of My Sea Life.*

H. T. Cheever, *Island World of the Pacific; Being the Personal Narrative and Results of Travel Through the Sandwich or Hawaiian Islands, and Other Parts of Polynesia.*

S. R. Crockett, *Tales of Our Coast.*

S. M. Crothers, *Gentle Reader.*

A. Cunningham, "A Wet Sheet and a Flowing Sea" (poem, British sea song).

G. Cupples, *"Green Hand." A "Short" Yarn.*

R. H. Dana, *To Cuba and Back. A Vacation Voyage.*

R. H. Dana, *Two Years Before the Mast: A Personal Narrative.*

C. Darwin, *What Mr. Darwin Saw in His Voyage Round the World in the Ship "Beagle."*

V. A. J. Davis, *Romance of Summer Seas; A Novel.*

J. De Mille, *Cord and Creese; A Novel.*

J. De Mille, *Strange Manuscript Found in a Copper Cylinder.*

N. Duncan, *Cruise of the Shining Light.*

N. Duncan, *Every Man for Himself.*

G. F. Gibbs, *Love of Monsieur, A Novel.*

M. L. Goddard (co-comp.), *Sea and Shore: A Collection of Poems.*

S. Grand, *Heavenly Twins* (marginalia about sea voyages).

S. P. M. Greene, *Flood-tide.*

E. Gregory, *Narrative of James Murrells' ("Jemmy Morrill") Seventeen Years' Exile among the Wild Blacks of North Queensland, and His Life and Shipwreck and Terrible Adventures among Savage Tribes.*

S. A. Hammett, *Wonderful Adventures of Captain Priest: A Tale of But Few Incidents and No Plot in Particular, with Other Legends.*

D. Harrison, *Melancholy Narrative of the Distressful Voyage and the Miraculous Recovery of Captain David Harrison of the Sloop, Peggy.*

W. D. Howells and T. S. Perry (eds.), *Library of Universal Adventure by Sea and Land.*

W. D. Howells, *Woman's Reason; A Novel.*

W. Irving, *History of the Life and Voyages of Christopher Columbus.*

W. W. Jacobs, *Dialstone Lane* (novel).

W. W. Jacobs, *Sailors' Knots* (short stories).

W. W. Jacobs, *Salthaven* (novel).

T. A. Janvier, *In Great Waters: Four Stories.*

T. A. Janvier, *In the Sargasso Sea, A Novel.*

J. D. J. Kelley, *Ship's Company and Other Sea People.*

C. Kingsley, *Westward Ho!* (novel).

R. Kipling, Ballad of the 'Bolivar'" (poem).

R. Kipling, "'Mary Gloster'" (poem).

R. Kipling, *Seven Seas.*

J. B. P. Lee, *Uncle William, The Man Who Was Shif'less.*

London *Illustrated News.*

A. B. Lubbock, *Round the Horn Before the Mast.*

F. McGlennon, "Bring my boy back again" (song).

A. T. Mahan (Catalog entry).

F. Marryat, *Newton Forster; or, The Merchant Service.*

W. S. Mayo, *Kaloolah: Adventures of Jonathan Romer of Nantucket* (novel)

H. Melville (Catalog entry).

"Mermaid" (sea shanty).

H. Miller, *Cruise of the Betsey; or, A Summer Ramble Among the Fossiliferous Deposits of the Hebrides.*

J. A. Mitchell, *Diary of Captain Josiah A. Mitchell.*

L. Mott, *To the Credit of the Sea* (short stories).

F. Nansen, *Farthest North; Being the Record of a Voyage of Exploration of the Ship "Fram" 1893–96, and of a Fifteen Months' Sleigh Journey.*

M. Nicholson, *Port of Missing Men.*

F. A. Ober, *Amerigo Vespucci.*

F. A. Ober, *Columbus the Discoverer.*

F. A. Ober, *Ferdinand Magellan.*

F. A. Ober, *John and Sebastian Cabot.*

F. A. Ober, *Juan Ponce de Leon.*

F. A. Ober, *Vasco Nuñez de Balboa.*

Ocean Scenes; or, The Perils and Beauties of the Deep (compilation).

A. B. Paine, *Ship-Dwellers: A Story of a Happy Cruise.*

M. C. Perry, *Narrative of the Expedition of an American Squadron to the China Seas and Japan, Performed in the Years 1852, 1853, and 1854.*

Philanthropy Dissected: The so-Called "Act for the Further Protection of Seamen" Reviewed.

M. S. Pike, "Home again" (song).

E. A. Poe, *Narrative of Arthur Gordon Pym of Nantucket* (novel).

M. Robertson, *Spun-Yarn; Sea Stories.*

"Roll a man down" (sea shanty).

W. C. Russell, *Alone on a Wide Wide Sea: A Novel.*

W. C. Russell, *Convict Ship.*

W. C. Russell, *Round the Galley Fire.*

W. C. Russell, *Sailors' Language: A Collection of Sea-Terms and Their Definitions.*

W. C. Russell, *Sailor's Sweetheart. An Account of the Wreck of the Sailing Ship "Waldershare."*

W. C. Russell, *Wreck of the "Grosvenor." An Account of the Mutiny of the Crew and the Loss of the Ship When Trying to Make the Bermudas.*

E. Sargent, "Life on the ocean wave" (song).

H. S. Scott, *Phantom Future; A Novel.*

M. Scott, *Cruise of the Midge.*

M. Scott, *Tom Cringle's Log.*

W. T. Sherman, *Memoirs of General William T. Sherman. By Himself* (marginalia).

J. Slocum, *Voyage of the Liberdade.*

M. J. B. L. Sonrel, *Bottom of the Sea.*

R. L. Stevenson and L. Osbourne, *Wrecker* (novel).

C. S. Stewart, *Private Journal of a Voyage to the Pacific Ocean and Residence at the Sandwich Islands, in the Years 1822, 1823, 1824, and 1825.*

F. R. Stockton, *Mrs. Cliff's Yacht.*

F. R. Stockton, "Remarkable Wreck of the 'Thomas Hyke'" (short story, collected in *Stockton's Stories. Second Series*).

F. R. Stockton, *Stockton's Stories. Second Series. The Christmas Wreck and Other Stories.*

C. W. Stoddard, *Cruise Under the Crescent; From Suez to San Marco.*

C. W. Stoddard, *South-Sea Idyls.*

B. Stoker, *Mystery of the Sea; A Novel.*

S. M. Swett, *Captain Polly.*

S. M. Swett, *Mate of the "Mary Ann"; A Story.*

J. Swift, *Gulliver's Travels into Several Remote Nations of the World.*

L. Tracy, *Captain of the Kansas.*

J. Verne, *Tour of the World in Eighty Days* (novel).

J. Verne, *Twenty Thousand Leagues Under the Sea* (novel).

E. Wakeman, *Log of an Ancient Mariner; Being the Life and Adventures of Captain Edgar Wakeman. Written by Himself and Edited by His Daughter.*

G. S. Wasson, *Cap'n Simeon's Store.*

H. B. M. Watson, *Adventurers; A Tale of Treasure Trove.*

W. T. Wawn, *South Sea Islanders and the Queensland Labour Trade: A Record of Voyages and Experiences in the Western Pacific, from 1875 to 1891.*

T. V. D. Wiesenthal, "Sailor-boy's dream, an admired ballad" (song).

E. H. Willard, "Rocked in the cradle of the deep" (hymn).

T. E. Williams, "Larboard watch" (song).

J. D. Wyss, *Swiss Family Robinson. A New Translation.*

J. D. Wyss, *Swiss Family Robinson; or, The Adventures of a Shipwrecked Family on an Uninhabited Island Near New Guinea.*

See also the Reader's Guide entries for Travel writings and for United States Navy.

Sea and Shore: A Collection of Poems. M. L. Goddard (co-comp.).

Seamen's Friend: see *Temperance Advocate.*

Seamy Side, A Story. W. Besant.

Search of Belisarius, A Byzantine Legend. P. S. Grant.

Sears, Barnas (ed.): see P. M. Roget, *Thesaurus of English Words and Phrases.*

Seasoning for Young Folk. H. Pyle.

Seasons: With the Castle of Indolence (poems). J. Thomson.

Sea terminology: see W. C. Russell, *Sailors' Language: A Collection of Sea-Terms and Their Definitions.*

Seawell, Molly Elliot (co-author): see *Boys on the Railroad.*

Sebastopol. L. N. Tolstoy.

"Second Battle of Bull Run" (article). J. Pope.

"Second Inaugural Address" (speech). A. Lincoln.

Second Opportunity of Mr. Staplehurst. W. P. Ridge.

Second Wooing of Salina Sue, and Other Stories. R. M. Stuart.

Secret Agent; A Simple Tale. J. Conrad.

Secretary to Bayne, M. P. W. P. Ridge.

Secret History of the Court of Berlin: see H. W. Fischer, *Private Lives of William II and His Consort.*

Secret Mission. E. Gerard.

Secret of the Old Mamsell: see E. John, *Geheimnis der Alten Mamsell.*

Secret Service (play). W. Gillette.

Secret Service: The Field, the Dungeon, and the Escape. A. D. Richardson.

Secular Anathema on Fakery in Business, Social and Professional Life; or, Twentieth Century Conduct. C. W. Silver.

Secundus, Johannes: see S. A. Propertius, *Elegies of Propertius, . . . and the Kisses of Johannes Secundus.*

Seelye, Sarah Emma: see S. E. E. Edmundson.

Seen from the Saddle. I. C. Cabell.

Selborne: see

G. White, *Natural History and Antiquities of Selborne.*

G. White, *Natural History of Selborne. With a Naturalist's Calendar and Additional Observations.*

Selected Poems, by Walt Whitman. W. Whitman.

Selected Prose Writings. D. Gray.

Selection from the Discourses of Epictetus, with the Encheiridion. Epictetus.

Selection from the Poems of Percy Bysshe Shelley. P. B. Shelley.

Selections from Coleridge. S. T. Coleridge.

Selections from Sermons Preached to the Church of the Disciples. J. F. Clarke.

Selections from the Poetry of Robert Herrick. R. Herrick.

Selections from the Writings of Ralph Waldo Emerson, Arranged Under the Days of the Year. R. W. Emerson.

Selections from the Writings of Nathaniel Hawthorne, Arranged Under the Days of the Year. N. Hawthorne.

Selections from the Writings of Oliver Wendell Holmes, Arranged Under the Days of the Year. O. W. Holmes.

Selections from the Writings of Henry Wadsworth Longfellow, Arranged Under the Days of the Year. H. W. Longfellow.

Selections from the Writings of James Russell Lowell. Arranged Under the Days of the Year. J. R. Lowell.

Selections from the Writings of John Greenleaf Whittier, Arranged Under the Days of the Year. J. G. Whittier.

Selections from the Writings of Lord Macaulay. T. B. Macaulay.

Select Orations. Cicero.

Select Poems of Sidney Lanier. S. Lanier.

Select Poetical Works of Felicia Hemans. F. D. Hemans.

Select Poetical Works of Lord Byron. G. G. Byron.

Select Works. E. Burke.

Seléné (poem). A. R. C. Troubetzkoy.

Self-improvement: see

H. Alger (Catalog entry).

E. A. Fletcher, *Woman Beautiful: A Practical Treatise on the Development and Preservation of Woman's Health and Beauty, and the Principles of Taste in Dress.*

O. S. Fowler and L. N. Fowler, *New Illustrated Self-Instructor in Phrenology and Physiology.*

C. C. Haskell, *Perfect Health: How to Get It and How to Keep It.*

H. C. Knight, *Saw Up and Saw Down; or, The Fruits of Industry and Self-Reliance.*

M. D. Larrowe, *Physiological Memory; or, The Instantaneous Art of Never Forgetting.*

Letters from a Self-Made Merchant to His Son. G. T. Richardson.

Letters from a Son to His Self-Made Father. G. T. Richardson.

A. J. Miller, *Physical Beauty: How to Obtain and How to Preserve It.*

M. E. M. Sangster, *Winsome Womanhood.*

See also the Reader's Guide entries for Beauty and grooming advice and for Inspirational messages.

Selkirk, Alexander: see

J. R. Browne, *Crusoe's Island: A Ramble in the Steps of Alexander Selkirk.*

W. Cowper, "Verses Supposed to be Written by Alexander Selkirk."

Seminoles (Native Americans): see C. K. Munroe, *Campmates; A Story of the Plains.*

Sempers, Charles T.: see F. W. Haley (ed.), *American Authors and Their Homes* (Catalog entry).

"Sence little Wesley went" (line from poem): see J. W. Riley, "Absence of Little Wesley" (poem).

Seneca Indians: J. W. Sanborn, *Legends, Customs and Social Life of the Seneca Indians of Western New York.*

Señorita Montenar. A. P. Crouch.

Sense and Sensibility. J. Austen.

Sensible Etiquette of the Best Society, Customs, Manners, Morals, and Home Culture. C. S. J. Bloomfield-Moore.

Sentimentalists; A Novel. A. S. Pier.

Sentimental Journey Through France and Italy, by Mr. Yorick. L. Sterne.

Sentimental Song Book. J. A. D. Moore.

Sepoy Mutiny: see the Reader's Guide entry for Indian mutiny of 1857.

Seraphica; A Romance. J. H. McCarthy.

Seraphita: see H. de Balzac, *Comedy of Human Life.*

Serena, A Novel. V. F. Boyle.

Serious Reflections and Other Contributions, Etc. G. R. Aberigh-Mackay.

Sermons:

E. P. Adams, *Story Sermons from Les Misérables.*

J. F. Clark, *Selections from Sermons Preached to the Church of the Disciples.*

R. Collyer, *Nature and Life: Sermons.*

W. J. Dawson (co-ed.), *Great English Letter-Writers* (marginalia).

O. Goldsmith, *Deserted Village* (Catalog entry).

F. W. Robertson, *Life, Letters, and Addresses of Fredk. W. Robertson, M.A., Incumbent of Trinity Chapel, Brighton, 1847–53.*

F. W. Robertson, *Sermons.*

M. J. Savage (unidentified sermon).

G. Spring, *Fragments from the Study of a Pastor.*

T. D. W. Talmage, *Sermons. Second Series.*

J. Timbs, *Curiosities of London, Exhibiting the Most*

Rare and Remarkable Objects of Interest in the Metropolis (marginalia).
S. H. Tyng, *Office and Duty of a Christian Pastor.*
Unfathomable Mystery. Benedictine Sisters of Perpetual Adoration. Clyde, Missouri.
Serpent: see M. de Cervantes Saavedra, *Exemplary Novels of Miguel de Cerantes Saavedra.*
Serrano, Mary Jane (trans.): see M. K. Bashkirtseva, *Marie Bashkirtseff; The Journal.*
Servant in the House (play). C. R. Kennedy.
Sesame and Lilies: Three Lectures. J. Ruskin.
Setchell, Dan (actor): see J. Brougham (adapt.), *Dombey and Son.*
Seth, F. (illus.): see F. G. Aflalo, *Sketch of the Natural History of Australia, with Some Notes on Sport.*
Seton, Ernest Thompson (illus.): see M. O. Wright, *Four-Footed Americans and Their Kin.*
"Setoun, Gabriel" (pseud.): see T. N. Hepburn.
Seven Churches. T. K. Beecher.
Seven Dreamers. A. T. Slosson.
Seven English Cities. W. D. Howells.
Seven Little Australians. E. M. S. Turner.
Seven Seas. R. Kipling.
Seven Thousand Words Often Mispronounced: A Complete Hand-Book of Difficulties in English Pronunciation. W. H. P. Phyfe.
Seventy Years Young; or, The Unhabitual Way. E. M. M. Bishop.
Several Orations of Demosthenes, Exciting the Athenians to Oppose the Exorbitant Power of Philip King of Macedon. Demosthenes.
Sévigné, Marie de Rabutin-Chantal, Marquise de: see J. G. Wilson (ed.), *Love in Letters; Illustrated in the Correspondence of Eminent Persons; with Biographical Sketches of the Writers.*
Seward, William Henry: see
F. Bancroft, *Life of William H. Seward.*
A. S. Evans, *Our Sister Republic: A Gala Trip Through Tropical Mexico in 1869–70* (marginalia).
Sex in Education; or, A Fair Chance for Girls. E. H. Clarke.
Sexuality: see
E. H. Clarke, *Sex in Education; or, A Fair Chance for Girls.*
R. von Krafft-Ebing, *Psychopathia Sexualis, with Special Reference to Contrary Sexual Instinct: A Medico-Legal Study.*
J. Marshall, *Anatomy for Artists.*
See also the Reader's Guide entries for Cross-dressing, for Erotica, for Homosexuality, for Physiology, and for Prostitution.
Sexual violence: see
R. I. Dodge, *Our Wild Indians: Thirty-Three Years' Personal Experience among the Red Men of the Great West* (marginalia).
R. I. Dodge, *Plains of the Great West and Their Inhabitants, Being a Description of the Plains, Game, Indians, &c. of the Great North American Desert.*
J. P. Dunn, *Massacres of the Mountains: A History of the Indian Wars of the Far West.*
Sforza, A Story of Milan. W. W. Astor.

"S., H." (pseud.): see *Napoleon the Third and His Court.*
Shackford, Charles Chauncy (trans.): see P. Konewka, *Falstaff and His Companions. Twenty-one Illustrations in Silhouette.*
Shadowless Man. A. von Chamisso.
Shadow of a Dream. W. D. Howells.
Shadow of Dante: An Essay Towards Studying Himself, His World and His Pilgrimage. M. F. Rossetti.
Shadow of the House. A. M. A. Aníchkova.
Shadow of the Rock, and Other Religious Poems, A. D. F. Randolph (comp.).
Shadow of the Rope. E. W. Hornung.
Shadows (poems): M. A. D. Howe.
Shadow World. H. Garland.
Shakers: see
E. W. M. Brodhead, *Diana's Livery.*
J. S. Buckingham, *America, Historical, Statistic, and Descriptive.*
W. D. Howells, "Shaker Village."
W. D. Howells, *Undiscovered Country.*
"Shaker Village." W. D. Howells.
Shakespeare and His Forerunners: Studies in Elizabethan Poetry and Its Development from Early English. S. Lanier.
Shakespeare Phrase Book. J. Bartlett.
Shakespeare Problem Restated. G. G. Greenwood.
Shakespeare's England. W. Winter.
Shakespeare the Boy, with Sketches of the Home and School Life, the Games and Sports, the Manners, Customs and Folklore of the Time. W. J. Rolfe.
Shakespeare, William: see
D. S. Bacon, *Philosophy of the Plays of Shakspere Unfolded.*
F. Bacon, *Promus of Formularies and Elegancies (Being Private Notes, Circ. 1594, Hitherto Unpublished) by Francis Bacon. Illustrated and Elucidated by Passages from Shakespeare.*
J. Bartlett, *Shakespeare Phrase Book.*
W. Black, *Judith Shakespeare; Her Love Affairs and Other Adventures.*
W. S. Booth, *Some Acrostic Signatures of Francis Bacon.*
H. H. Breen, *Modern English Literature: Its Blemishes & Defects* (marginalia).
J. Bunyan, *Pilgrim's Progress* (Catalog entry).
M. de Cervantes Saavedra, *Don Quixote* (Catalog entry).
M. V. C. Clarke, *Complete Concordance to Shakespeare.*
S. V. Clevenger, *Fun in a Doctor's Life, Being the Adventures of an American Don Quixote* (marginalia).
L. C. Davis (ed.), *Story of the Memorial Fountain to Shakespeare at Stratford-upon-Avon.*
W. J. Dawson (co-ed.), *Great English Letter-Writers* (marginalia).
I. Donnelly, *Great Cryptogram: Francis Bacon's Cipher in the So-Called Shakespeare Plays.*
E. Dowden, *Shakspere: A Critical Study of His Mind and Art.*
H. W. H. Fischer, *Private Lives of William II and His Consort and Secret History of the Court of Berlin* (marginalia).
E. W. Gallup, *Bi-Literal Cypher of Sir Francis Bacon Discovered in His Works and Deciphered.*

G. G. Greenwood, *Shakespeare Problem Restated.*

W. Hazlitt, *Lectures on the Literature of the Age of Elizabeth, and Characters of Shakespear's Plays.*

C. Knight, *Studies of Shakspere; Forming a Companion
to Every Edition of the Text.*

P. Konewka, *Falstaff and His Companions. Twenty-one
Illustrations in Silhouette.*

C. Lamb and M. A. Lamb, *Tales from Shakespeare.*

S. Lanier, *Shakespeare and His Forerunners: Studies in
Elizabethan Poetry and Its Development from Early
English.*

S. Lee (Catalog entry).

H. W. Mabie, *William Shakespeare: Poet, Dramatist,
and Man.*

T. B. Macaulay, *Critical and Miscellaneous Essays*
(marginalia).

F. T. Palgrave (comp.), *Golden Treasury of the Best
Songs and Lyrical Poems in the English Language*
(marginalia).

J. P. W. Penzance, *Lord Penzance on the Bacon-Shakespeare Controversy. A Judicial Summing-Up.*

S. Pepys, *Diary of Samuel Pepys* (Catalog entry).

I. H. Platt, *Bacon Cryptograms in Shake-speare, and
Other Studies.*

J. W. Riley, *"Old Swimmin'-Hole," and 'Leven More
Poems* (Catalog entry).

W. J. Rolfe, *Shakespeare the Boy, with Sketches of the
Home and School Life, the Games and Sports, the
Manners, Customs and Folklore of the Time.*

A. W. Schmidt, *Flowing Bowl: When and What to
Drink.*

A. C. Swinburne, *Age of Shakespeare.*

A. C. Swinburne, *Three Plays of Shakespeare.*

S. A. Tannenbaum, *Was William Shakespeare a Gentleman? Some Questions in Shakespeare's Biography
Determined.*

W. M. Thackeray, *Thackeray's Lectures. The English
Humourists. The Four Georges* (marginalia).

H. Van Dyke (ed.), *Little Masterpieces of English Poetry,
by British and American Authors.*

C. W. Wallace, "New Shakespeare Discoveries: Shakespeare as a Man among Men" (article).

A. D. White, *History of the Warfare of Science with
Theology* (marginalia).

F. S. Wilhelmina, *Memoirs of Wilhelmine, Margravine
of Baireuth* (marginalia).

W. Winter, *Old Shrines and Ivy.*

W. Winter, *Shakespeare's England.*

See also the Reader's Guide entries for Francis Bacon
and for individual plays by Shakespeare, e.g.,
Hamlet.

Shaler, Nathaniel Southgate: see

(contr.) *Niagara Book: A Complete Souvenir of Niagara
Falls.*

Plinius, *Letters of Caius Plinius Caecilius Secundus*
(Catalog entry).

L. de R. Saint-Simon, *Memoirs of the Duke of Saint-
Simon on the Reign of Louis XIV and the Regency*
(marginalia).

"Shall We Hunt and Fish? Confessions of a Sentimentalist" (essay). H. B. Washburn.

"Shameful Death" (poem). W. Morris.

"Shapcott, Reuben" (pseud. editor): see W. H. White.

Shapley, Rufus Edmonds (co-ed.): see A. R. Spofford
(co-ed.), *Library of Wit and Humor, Prose and Poetry,
Selected from the Literature of All Times and Nations.*

"Sharon waves": see E. H. Sears, "Calm on the listening
ears of night" (hymn).

*Sharp Eyes: A Rambler's Calender of Fifty-Two Weeks
Among Insects, Birds, and Flowers.* W. H. Gibson.

Shaughraun (play). D. Boucicault.

Shaw, George Bernard: see A. Henderson, "George Bernard Shaw" (essay).

Shaw, Henry Wheeler ("Josh Billings"): see

Homer, *Iliad of Homer. Translated into English Blank
Verse* (Catalog entry).

M. de L. Landon, *Saratoga in 1901* (marginalia).

J. H. Trumbull (ed.), *True-Blue Laws of Connecticut
and New Haven* (marginalia).

She: A History of Adventure. H. R. Haggard.

"Shed not a tear" (song). T. H. Bayly.

"She Dwelt among the Untrodden Ways" (poem). W.
Wordsworth.

Sheffield, John: see Homer, *Odyssey of Homer. Translated
into English Blank Verse by William Cullen Bryant*
(Catalog entry).

Sheldon, Eli Lemon (co-author): see C. Nisbet, *Everybody's Writing-Desk Book.*

Sheldon, George William (ed.), *Artistic Houses; Being a
Series of Interior Views of a Number of the Most Beautiful
and Celebrated Homes in the United States.*

Sheldon, Mary (co-author): see G. E. B. Campbell and
M. F. Sheldon, *Everybody's Book of Correct Conduct;
Being Hints for Everyday Life.* .

*Shell Book: A Popular Guide to a Knowledge of the Families
of Living Mollusks.* J. E. Rogers.

Shelley. F. Thompson.

"Shelley. By One Who Knew Him." T. L. Hunt.

Shelley, Harriet: see T. L. Peacock, *Memoirs of Shelley.*

Shelley, Percy Bysshe: see

R. Browning, *Pauline; Paracelsus; Strafford; Sordello*
(marginalia).

E. Dowden, *Life of Percy Bysshe Shelley.*

T. L. Hunt, "Shelley. By One Who Knew Him."

F. T. Palgrave (comp.), *Golden Treasury of the Best
Songs and Lyrical Poems in the English Language*
(marginalia).

T. L. Peacock, *Memoirs of Shelley.*

Selected Poems, Illustrated.

F. Thompson, *Shelley.*

E. J. Trelawny, *Records of Shelley, Byron, and the Author.*

H. Van Dyke (ed.), *Little Masterpieces of English Poetry,
by British and American Authors.*

"Shepard, William" (pseud.): see W. S. Walsh.

"Shepherd, Ettrick" (pseud. of James Hogg) (ed.): see R.
Burns, *Works of Robert Burns.*

Shepherd, Jack (British criminal): see C. Whitehead,
*Lives and Exploits of the Most Noted Highwaymen, Rob-
bers and Murderers, of All Nations.*

Shepherd of Salisbury Plain (tract). H. More.

Sheppard, William Ludwell (illus.): see H. W. Pierson, *In*

the Brush; or, Old-Time Social, Political, and Religious Life in the Southwest.

Sheridan, Helen Selina: see H. S. S. Blackwood.

Sheridan, Philip Henry: see D. B. R. Keim, *Sheridan's Troopers on the Borders: A Winter Campaign on the Plains.*

Sheridan, Richard Brinsley: see
(trans.): see S. Propertius, *Erotica.*
W. Winter, *Old Shrines and Ivy.*

Sheridan's Troopers on the Borders: A Winter Campaign on the Plains. D. B. R. Keim.

Sherman, Lucius Adelno (trans.): see E. Tegnér, *Frithiof's Saga; A Legend of Ancient Norway.*

Sherman, William Tecumseh (intro.): see R. I. Dodge, *Our Wild Indians: Thirty-Three Years' Personal Experience among the Red Men of the Great West.*

Sherwood, Mary Neal (trans.): see A. Daudet, *Sidonie.*

Sherwood, Rosina Emmet: see R. Emmet.

She Stoops to Conquer (play). O. Goldsmith.

"She wore a wreath of roses" (song). T. H. Bayly.

Shinn, Florence Scovel (illus.): see
A. Caster, *Pearl Island.*
J. L. Gilder, *Tomboy.*

Ship-Dwellers: A Story of a Happy Cruise. A. B. Paine.

Ship of Dreams. M. L. Foster.

Ships: see F. T. Jane, *All the World's Fighting Ships.*

Ships and Havens. H. Van Dyke.

Ship's Company and Other Sea People. J. D. J. Kelley.

Ships That Pass in the Night. B. Harraden.

Shirley. C. Brontë.

"Shirley, Philip" (pseud.): see A. L. Townsend.

Shnik-Shnak. O. Pletsch.

Shore, Thomas Teignmouth (intro.): see Münchausen, *Adventures of Baron Munchausen.*

"Short Biographies of All Authors Represented in This Work." A. G. Stedman (ed.).

Shorthand: see
E. B. Burnz, *Burnz' Phonic Shorthand.*
J. E. Munson, *Complete Phonographer, and Reporter's Guide: An Inductive Exposition of Phonography, with Its Application to All Branches of Reporting.*
Peirce School, Philadelphia. *Annual Graduating Exercises of Peirce School of Business and Shorthand . . . 1882 to 1892.*
I. Pitman, *Manual of Phonography; or, Writing by Sound.*

Short History of Art. J. B. De Forest.

Short History of the English People. J. R. Green.

Short History of the Reformation. J. F. Hurst.

Short Rations. W. Fish.

Short Sayings of Great Men. With Historical and Explanatory Notes. S. A. Bent.

Short Stories. S. P. Davis.

Short Studies on Great Subjects. J. A. Froude.

Shoshone and Other Western Wonders. E. Roberts.

Shoshone (Native American tribe): see E. Talbot, *My People of the Plains.*

Shoulders of Atlas; A Novel. M. E. W. Freeman.

Shrader, Edwin Roscoe (illus.): see H. F. Day, *King Spruce; A Novel.*

Shropshire Lad. A. E. Housman.

Shucking song: see "I'se gwine to de shuckin" (song).

Shunshō, Tamenaga: see T. Shunsui.

Siam: see
T. W. Knox, *Boy Travellers in the Far East; Part Second, . . . in a Journey to Siam and Java.*
A. H. E. Leonowens, *English Governess at the Siamese Court; Being Recollections of Six Years in the Royal Palace at Bangkok.*
H. M. Miller, *Little People of Asia.*
F. Vincent, *Land of the White Elephant: Sights and Scenes in South-eastern Asia.*

Siberia: see
F. E. Clark, *New Way Around an Old World.*
S. Cottin, *Elizabeth; or, The Exiles of Siberia. A Tale, Founded upon Facts.*
G. Kennan, *Siberia and the Exile System.*
G. Kennan, *Tent Life in Siberia, and Adventures Among the Koraks and Other Tribes in Kamtchatka and Northern Asia.*
H. M. Miller, *Little People of Asia.*

Siberia and the Exile System. G. Kennan.

Sicily: see
F. M. Crawford, *Corleone; A Tale of Sicily.*
R. S. Hichens, *Call of the Blood* (novel).
W. A. Paton, *Picturesque Sicily.*
N. S. Shaler, *Aspects of the Earth: A Popular Account of Some Familiar Geological Phenomena* (clipping).
B. Taylor, *Lands of the Saracens; or, Pictures of Palestine, Asia Minor, Sicily, and Spain.*

Siddhartha: see E. Arnold, *Light of Asia; or, The Great Renunciation.*

Side-Lights on Astronomy and Kindred Fields of Popular Science: Essays and Addresses. S. Newcomb.

Side Lights on Mary Baker Eddy-Glover-Science Church Trustees Controversy. "Next Friends" Suit. R. D. Kathrens.

Sidney, Philip: see W. M. Thackeray, *Thackeray's Lectures. The English Humourists. The Four Georges* (marginalia).

Sidonie. A. Daudet.

Sidonius Apollinaris: see the Reader's Guide entry for Apollinaris Sidonius.

Siège de Berlin, et d'autres contes, par Alphonse Daudet. A. Daudet.

Siege of Calais and Other Poems. A. L. Frisbie.

Siege of Granada. E. G. E. B. Lytton.

Siege of Lucknow. A Diary. J. S. T. Inglis.

Siegfried: see A. A. Chapin, *Wotan, Siegfried, and Brünnhilde.*

Siegfried (opera). R. Wagner.

Sienkiewicz, Henryk: see W. L. Phelps, *Essays on Modern Novelists* (marginalia).

Sierra Leone: see T. M. Winterbottom, *Account of the Native Africans in the Neighbourhood of Sierra Leone.*

Sierra Nevada Mountains (California): see
J. W. Bruner, *Free Prisoners: A Story of California Life.*
A. A. Burnham, *Fostina Woodman: The Wonderful Adventurer.*
C. C. Harrison, *Edelweiss of the Sierras; Golden-Rod and Other Tales* (stories).
B. Harte, *Luck of Roaring Camp, and Other Sketches.*
B. Harte, *Tales of the Argonauts, and Other Sketches.*

W. D. Howells (co-ed.), *Library of Universal Adventure by Sea and Land.*

J. M. Hutchings, *Scenes of Wonder and Curiosity in California.*

R. Keeler, *Gloverson and His Silent Partners.*

C. King, *Mountaineering in the Sierra Nevada.*

P. V. Mighels, *Dunny, A Mountain Romance.*

J. Miller, *Songs of the Sierras* (poems).

S. B. Morgan, *Tahoe; or, Life in California. A Romance.*

C. K. Munroe, *Campmates; A Story of the Plains.*

B. Taylor, *At Home and Abroad: A Sketch-Book of Life, Scenery, and Men.*

H. L. Wilson, *Spenders; A Tale of the Third Generation.*

See also the Reader's Guide entries for the American West, for California, and for Mining.

Sights and Sensations in Europe: Sketches of Travel and Adventure. J. H. Browne.

Sights and Sensations in France, Germany and Switzerland. E. G. Buffum.

Sign of the Four. A. C. Doyle.

Signs and Seasons: see J. Burroughs, "Hard Fare" (essay).

Silas Lapham: see W. D. Howells, *Rise of Silas Lapham.*

Silas Strong, Emperor of the Woods. I. Bacheller.

Silcher, Friedrich (composer): see H. Heine, "Lorelei" (song).

Silence of Mrs. Harrold. S. M. Gardenhire.

Silent Door. F. Wilkinson.

Silent Pete; or, The Stowaways. J. O. Kaler.

Silver Horde; A Novel. R. E. Beach.

Silverland. G. A. Lawrence.

Silverman, Joseph (Rabbi): see New York *Times* (Catalog entry).

Silver mining: see

T. B. Aldrich, "Little Violinist" (story) (Catalog entry).

J. R. Browne, *Adventures in Apache Country: A Tour Through Arizona and Sonora with Notes on the Silver Regions of Nevada.*

G. A. Lawrence, *Silverland.*

H. L. Wilson, *Spenders; A Tale of the Third Generation.*

W. Wright, *History of the Big Bonanza: An Authentic Account of the Discovery, History, and Working of the World-Renowned Comstock Silver Lode of Nevada.*

See also the Reader's Guide entry for Mining.

Silver Skates. M. M. Dodge.

Simmons, Edward Everett (artist): see

B. W. Howard, *Guenn; A Wave on the Breton Coast* (Catalog entry).

A. Lincoln, "Gettysburg Address" (Catalog entry).

Simms, William Gilmore: see

(ed.) W. Shakespeare, *Complete Works of William Shakespeare: Comprising His Plays and Poems.*

V. Streamer (comp.), *Voices of Doubt and Trust* (marginalia).

Simons, Michael Laird (co-ed.), *Cyclopædia of American Literature, Embracing Personal and Critical Notices of Authors, and Selections from Their Writings.*

Simpleton: see C. Reade, *Griffith Gaunt; or, Jealousy.*

"Simplicity" (essay). C. D. Warner.

Simpson, Friench (trans.): see Omar Khayyám, *Paraphrase of the Philosophical Quatrains of Omar Khayyám.*

Simpson, Mary Charlotte Mair (Senior) (trans.): see

H. E. G. de Witt, *Monsieur Guizot in Private Life, 1787–1874.*

Simpson, Matthew: see G. R. Crooks, *Life of Bishop Matthew Simpson, of the Methodist Episcopal Church.*

Simpson, Mrs. John (trans.): see J. Quesnay de Beaurepaire, *Woodman; A Novel.*

Sims, George Robert (trans.): see H. de Balzac, *Balzac's Contes Drolatiques.*

Sinful Peck; A Novel. M. Robertson.

"Sinner, please don't let this harvest pass" (spiritual): see "I know that my Redeemer lives."

Sintram and His Companions: see F. H. K. La Motte-Fouqué, *Undine: A Romance.*

Sioux (Native American tribe): see

C. D. W. Brownell, *Indian Races of North and South America.*

F. W. Kelly, *Narrative of My Captivity Among the Sioux Indians.*

J. Verne, *Tour of the World in Eighty Days* (novel).

O. G. Wall, *Recollections of the Sioux Massacre.*

Sir Gibbie. G. MacDonald.

"Sir Guy of the Dolorous Blast" (poem): see W. Morris, "Shameful Death."

Sir Mortimer. A Novel. M. Johnston.

Sir Richard Escombe; A Romance. M. Pemberton.

Sister Dora. A Biography. M. Lonsdale.

Sister's Bye-Hours. J. Ingelow.

Sisters of Perpetual Adoration: see the Catalog entry for *Unfathomable Mystery.*

Sisters' Tragedy, with Other Poems, Lyrical and Dramatic. T. B. Aldrich.

Sixteen Poems by William Allingham. W. Allingham.

Sixth Sense and Other Stories. M. S. B. Hopkins.

Six Trees; Short Stories. M. E. W. Freeman.

Sixty Years with Plymouth Church. S. M. Griswold.

Skelton, Joseph Ratcliffe (illus.): see M. H. Hervey, *Amyas Egerton, Cavalier.*

Skepticism: see the Reader's Guide entry for Agnosticism.

Sketch-Book. A. J. Cotton.

Sketch-Book of Geoffrey Crayon, Gent. W. Irving.

Sketch Books. The Paris Sketch Book of Mr. M. A. Titmarsh. The Irish Sketch Book of a Journey from Cornhill to Grand Cairo. W. M. Thackeray.

Sketches. L. H. H. Sigourney.

Sketches by Boz. C. Dickens.

Sketches of America. A Narrative of a Journey of Five Thousand Miles Through the Eastern and Western States of America. H. B. Fearon.

Sketches of Art, Literature, and Character. A. B. M. Jameson.

Sketches of Creation: A Popular View of Some of the Grand Conclusions of the Sciences in Reference to the History of Matter and of Life. A. Winchell.

Sketches of Palestine. E. P. Hammond.

"Sketches on the Upper Mississippi, by the Author of 'Three Weeks in Cuba.'" A. J. Hoeffler.

"Sketchley, Arthur" (pseud.): see G. Rose.

Sketch of the Life and Character of Rutherford B. Hayes. W. D. Howells.

Sketch of the Life and Times of the Rev. Sydney Smith. S. J. Reid.

Sketch of the Natural History of Australia, with Some Notes on Sport. F. G. Aflalo.

Skirmishes and Sketches. M. A. Dodge.

Skrine, Francis Henry Bennett: see W. Bagehot, *Biographical Studies.*

Slade, Joseph Alfred: see T. J. Dimsdale, *Vigilantes of Montana; or, Popular Justice in the Rocky Mountains.*

Slanderers. G. W. Deeping.

Slang: see the Reader's Guide entry for English language.

Slavery: see

J. Abbott, *Stories of Raninbow and Lucky: Selling Lucky.*

Address to the Presbyterians of Kentucky: Proposing a Plan for the Instruction and Emancipation of Their Slaves.

W. F. Allen (comp.), *Slave Songs of the United States.*

Am. Col. N. E. Society, Dec. 22, 1886.

American Nation: A History from Original Sources by Associated Scholars. A. B. Hart (ed.).

S. W. Baker, *Cast Up by the Sea* (novel).

C. Ball, *Slavery in the United States: A Narrative of the Life and Adventures of Charles Ball, A Black Man.*

J. G. Birney, *Letter to Ministers and Elders, on the Sin of Holding Slaves, and the Duty of Immediate Emancipation.*

W. W. Brown, *Clotelle; or, The Colored Heroine.*

J. S. Buckingham, *America, Historical, Statistic, and Descriptive.*

W. E. Channing, *Letter of William E. Channing to J. G. Birney* [bound with other pamphlets].

L. M. Child, *Anti-Slavery Catechism.*

J. F. Clarke, *Memorial and Biographical Sketches.*

C. C. Coffin, *Old Times in the Colonies.*

Declaration of Sentiments and Constitution of the Anti-Slavery Society.

C. W. Dilke, *Greater Britain: A Record of Travel in English-Speaking Countries During 1866 and 1867.*

F. Douglass (Catalog entry).

"Down in Tennessee" (minstrel song).

A. Dresser, *Narrative of Amos Dresser.*

W. Faux, *Memorable Days in America; Being a Journal of a Tour to the United States.*

H. B. Fearon, *Sketches of America. A Narrative of a Journey of Five Thousand Miles* (marginalia).

S. M. Griswold, *Sixty Years with Plymouth Church* (marginalia).

B. Hall, *Travels in North America, in the Years 1827 and 1828* (marginalia).

T. Hamilton, *Men and Manners in America.*

J. C. Harris, *Free Joe and Other Georgian Sketches.*

J. C. Harris, *Nights with Uncle Remus: Myths and Legends of the Old Plantation.*

J. C. Harris, *Uncle Remus: His Songs and His Sayings.*

D. Harrison, *Melancholy Narrative of the Distressful Voyage and the Miraculous Recovery of Captain David Harrison of the Sloop, Peggy.*

A. B. Hart, *Slavery and Abolition, 1831–1841*: see A. B. Hart (ed.) *American Nation: A History from Original Sources by Associated Scholars.*

L. Hearn, *Youma, Story of a West Indian Slave.*

T. W. S. Higginson, *History of the United States from 986 to 1905* (marginalia).

T. W. S. Higginson, *Travellers and Outlaws, Episodes in American History.*

R. Hildreth, *Archy Moore, the White Slave; or, Memoirs of a Fugitive.*

J. K. Hosmer, *Outcome of the Civil War, 1863–1865*: see *American Nation: A History from Original Sources by Associated Scholars.* A. B. Hart (ed.).

W. D. Howells (co-ed.), *Library of Universal Adventure by Sea and Land.*

H. Jacobs, *Incidents in the Life of a Slave Girl, Written by Herself.*

H. H. Johnston, *History of a Slave* (enslaved Africans in Western Sudan).

Jubilee Singers (see the Reader's Guide entry for Jubilee Singers).

F. A. Kemble, *Journal of a Residence on a Georgian Plantation in 1838–39.*

W. E. H. Lecky, *History of European Morals from Augustus to Charlemagne* (marginalia).

W. E. H. Lecky, *History of the Rise and Influence of the Spirit of Rationalism in Europe* (marginalia).

J. C. Lovejoy and O. Lovejoy, *Memoir of the Rev. Elijah P. Lovejoy, Who Was Murdered in Defence of the Liberty of the Press.*

J. Lubbock, *Ants, Bees, and Wasps: A Record of Observations on the Habits of the Social Hymenoptera* (Catalog entry).

F. Marryat, *Second Series of a Diary in America.*

H. Martineau, *Retrospect of Western Travel* (marginalia).

H. Martineau, *Society in America* (marginalia).

F. W. Mason, *Daddy Dave.*

S. J. May, *Some Recollections of Our Anti-Slavery Conflict.*

W. S. Mayo, *Kaloolah: Adventures of Jonathan Romer of Nantucket* (novel).

"Mulatto" (incident in an unidentified book).

S. Northup, *Twelve Years a Slave.*

R. K. Noyes, *Views of Religion, Collected by Rufus K. Noyes, M. D.* (marginalia).

Old Guard (periodical).

T. N. Page, *In Ole Virginia; or, Marse Chan and Other Stories.*

S. H. Palfrey, *Herman; or, Young Knighthood.*

J. W. C. Pennington *Fugitive Blacksmith; or, Events in the History of James W. C. Pennington.*

Plato, *Dialogues of Plato* (Catalog entry).

C. H. Proctor, *Life of James Williams, Better Known as Professor Jim, for Half a Century Janitor of Trinity College.*

L. C. Pyrnelle, *Diddie, Dumps, and Tot; or, Plantation Child-Life.*

M. Reid, *Quadroon; or, A Lover's Adventures in Louisiana.*

E. Robins, *Open Question; A Tale of Two Temperaments.*

D. Ruggles. *Abrogation of the Seventh Commandment by the American Churches.*

J. Ruskin, *Modern Painters* (Catalog entry).

F. B. Sanborn (ed.), *Life and Letters of John Brown, Liberator of Kansas and Martyr of Virginia.*

W. T. Sherman, *Memoirs of General William T. Sherman. By Himself* (marginalia).

Spirituals (see the Catalog and Reader's Guide entries).

H. P. Spofford, "Down the River" (story).

H. M. Stanley, *Slavery and the Slave Trade in Africa*.

W. Still, *Underground Rail Road. A Record of Facts, Authentic Narratives, Letters, &c., Narrating the Hardships, Hair-breadth Escapes, and Death Struggles of the Slaves in Their Efforts for Freedom*.

H. B. E. Stowe, *Dred: A Tale of the Great Dismal Swamp*.

H. E. E. Stowe, *Uncle Tom's Cabin; or, Life Among the Lowly*.

J. Sturge, *Visit to the United States in 1841*.

W. T. Thompson, *Major Jones's Sketches of Travel*.

H. D. Thoreau, *Yankee in Canada, with Anti-Slavery and Reform Papers*.

A. de Tocqueville, *Democracy in America*.

F. M. Trollope, *Domestic Manners of the Americans* (marginalia).

J. T. Trowbridge, *Cudjo's Cave*.

J. T. Trowbridge, *Neighbor Jackwood*.

J. Tyler, *Livingstone Lost and Found; or, Africa and Its Explorers*.

T. C. Upham, *Life of Faith; in Three Parts, Embracing Some of the Scriptural Principles or Doctrines of Faith* (Catalog entry).

J. G. Whittier, "Rantoul" (poem) (Catalog entry).

J. T. Wilson, *Black Phalanx; A History of the Negro Soldiers of the United States in the Wars of 1775–1812, 1861-'65*.

C. M. Yonge, *Cameos from English History. The Wars in France* (marginalia).

See also the Reader's Guide entries for African Americans, Ku Klux Klan, Racial prejudice, and Reconstruction in the American South.

Slavery and Abolition, 1831–1841. A. B. Hart.

Slavery and the Slave Trade in Africa. H. M. Stanley.

Slavery in the United States: A Narrative of the Life and Adventures of Charles Ball, A Black Man. C. Ball.

"Slave Ship" (painting): see J. Ruskin, *Modern Painters* (Catalog entry).

Slaves of Society. A Comedy in Covers: By the Man Who Heard Something. A. Upward.

Slave Songs of the United States. W. F. Allen (comp.).

Sledd, William Greenough Thayer (ed.): see S. T. Coleridge, *Complete Works of Samuel Taylor Coleridge*.

Sleep: see J. Bigelow, *Mystery of Sleep*.

"Slick, Sam" (pseud.): see T. C. Haliburton.

Sloan, John French (illus.): see T. A. Daly, *Canzoni*.

Sloane, George (illus.): see A. Fuller, *Venetian June*.

Sloman, Jane (composer): see "Roll on, silver moon" (song).

Slovenly Peter. see H. Hoffmann, *Struweelpeter*.

Smaller History of England, from the Earliest Times to the Year 1862. W. Smith.

Smaller History of Greece, from the Earliest Times to the Roman Conquest. W. Smith.

Smallpox: see J. W. C. Pennington, *Fugitive Blacksmith; or, Events in the History of James W. C. Pennington* (Catalog entry).

Smedley, William Thomas (illus.): see J. K. Bangs, *Rebellious Heroine: A Story*.

A. Brown, *Judgment, A Novel*.

E. E. Hale, *Susan's Escort, and Others*.

C. D. Warner, *Golden House*.

"Smile, R. Elton" (pseud.): see E. R. Smilie.

Smiling 'Round the World. M. P. Wilder.

Smith, Benjamin Eli: see
(ed.) *Century Cyclopedia*.
(ed. and trans.) Epictetus, *Epictetus: Selections from His Discourses as Reported by Arrian*.

Smith, Clarence B. (co-author): see E. V. Wilcox, *Farmer's Cyclopedia of Agriculture: A Compendium of Agricultural Science and Practice*.

Smith College Commencement Poems: see E. S. Phelps.

Smith, Eli (co-author): see E. Robinson, *Biblical Researches in Palestine, and in the Adjacent Regions. A Journal of Travels in the Years 1838 & 1852*.

Smith, Francis Hopkinson: see
(co-illus.) O. W. Holmes, *Last Leaf. Poem*.
E. Post (Catalog entry).
F. H. Smith, "Editor's Drawer: Ginger and the Goose" (story).

Smith, John Mohr (illus.): see C. Lamb and M. A. Lamb, *Tales from Shakespeare*.

Smith, Joseph: see *Book of Mormon*.

Smith, Lucy Toulmin (trans.): see J. A. A. J. Jusserand, *English Wayfaring Life in the Middle Ages (XIVth Century)*.

Smith, Philip (contr.): see W. Smith, *Smaller History of England, from the Earliest Times to the Year 1862*.

Smith, Rowland (ed., trans.): see *Greek Romances of Heliodorus, Longus, and Achilles Tatius*.

Smith, Sydney: see S. J. Reid, *Sketch of the Life and Times of the Rev. Sydney Smith*.

Smith, Vincent Arthur (ed.): see W. H. Sleeman, *Rambles and Recollections of an Indian Official*.

Smith, William: see (contr.) E. Gibbon, *History of the Decline and Fall of the Roman Empire*.

Smith, William: see (ed.) S. Rayner, *History and Antiquities of Pudsey*.

Smoke (novel). I. S. Turgenev.

Smoking: see the Reader's Guide entry for Tobacco.

"Smoking Song" (poem). F. M. Finch.

Smollett, Tobias George: see
(trans.) A. R. Le Sage, *Adventures of Gil Blas of Santillane*.
W. M. Thackeray, *Thackeray's Lectures. The English Humourists. The Four Georges* (marginalia).

Smyth, George B. (co-author): see *Crisis in China*.

Smythe, Carlyle (lecture agent): see (inscr.) D. G. Rossetti, *Poetical Works of Dante Gabriel Rossetti*.

Snakes: see R. L. Ditmars, *Reptile Book: A Comprehensive Popularized Work*.

Snorri Sturluson: see R. M. Ballantyne, *Erling, The Bold, A Tale of the Norse Sea-Kings*.

Snowball. J. E. Jackson.

Snow-Bound. A Winter Idyl. J. G. Whittier.

Snow-Shoes and Sledges. C. K. Munroe.

Social classes: see the Reader's Guide entries for American social classes, for Economics and labor issues, for English social classes, and for French social classes.

Social etiquette: see the Reader's Guide entry for Etiquette and personal conduct.

Social Etiquette of New York. A. B. Longstreet.

Socialism: see the Reader's Guide entry for Economics and labor issues.

Social ostracism: see A. Edwards, *Ought We To Visit Her? A Novel.*

Social Pictorial Satire; Reminiscences and Appreciations of English Illustrators of the Past Generation. G. L. P. B. Du Maurier.

Social Problems. H. George.

Social Unrest: Studies in Labor and Socialist Movements. J. G. Brooks.

Social Usages at Washington. F. M. H. Hall.

Society as I Have Found It. S. W. McAllister.

Society for Psychical Research (London): see

F. W. H. Myers, *Human Personality and Its Survival of Bodily Death.*

J. P. Quincy, *Peckster Professorship; An Episode in the History of Psychical Research.*

F. B. Wilson, *Paths to Power.*

See also the Reader's Guide entries for Mysticism, for Parapsychology, and for Telepathy.

Society in America. H. Martineau.

"Sociological Maid. A Play in One Act." C. R. Teller and Martha S. Bensley.

Socrates: see

J. R. Green, *Short History of the English People* (marginalia).

J. Lord, *Beacon Lights of History.*

Plato, *Dialogues of Plato* (Catalog entry).

A. E. Trumbull, *Masque of Culture* (play).

Solar eclipses: see the Reader's Guide entry for Eclipses.

"Soldier an' Sailor Too" (poem). R. Kipling.

Soldier in Our Civil War: A Pictorial History of the Conflict, 1861–65. P. F. Mottelay and T. Campbell-Copeland (eds.).

Soldiers of Fortune. R. H. Davis.

Soldier Stories. R. Kipling.

Soll und Haben: Roman in Sechs büchern. G. Freytag.

Solitary Summer (novel). M. A. B. von Arnim.

"Solitude" (poem). E. W. Wheeler: see J. A. Joyce, *Edgar Allan Poe* (Catalog entry).

Solitude Sweetened; or, Miscellaneous Meditations on Various Religious Subjects Written in Distant Parts of the World. J. Meikle.

Solon Shingle (play). J. S. Jones.

Some Account of the Life and Writings of John Milton. H. J. Todd.

Some Acrostic Signatures of Francis Bacon. W. S. Booth.

Some Adventures of Captain Simon Suggs, Late of the Tallapoosa Volunteers. J. J. Hooper.

Somebody's Neighbors. R. T. Cooke.

Some Experiences of an Irish R. M. E. A. Œ. Somerville and V. F. Martin.

Some Hidden Sources of Fiction. B. M. Nead.

Some Literary Recollections. J. Payn.

Some More Dogs. L. Hutton.

Some Notable Archbishops of Canterbury. M. Fowler.

"Some of the Reasons Against Woman Suffrage" (essay). F. Parkman.

Some of the Rhymes of Ironquill. (A Book of Moods). E. F. Ware.

Some Recollections of Our Antislavery Conflict. S. J. May.

Somerset, Edward: see H. Dircks, *Life, Times and Scientific Labours.*

Somerville, Martha (ed.): see M. F. Somerville, *Personal Recollections, from Early Life to Old Age, of Mary Somerville. With Selections from Her Correspondence.*

"Some Southern Reminiscences" (essay). W. Reid.

Some Successful Marriages. A. M. Roach.

Some Women's Hearts. L. C. Moulton.

Song collections: see

E. A. Abbey, *Old Songs, with Drawings by Edwin A. Abbey and Alfred Parsons.*

M. S. H. Bacon (ed.), *Songs Every Child Should Know: A Selection of the Best Songs of All Nations for Young People.*

W. C. Bryant (comp.), *Family Library of Poetry and Song. Being Choice Selections from the Best Poets, English, Scottish, Irish, and American.*

Cow-Boys Ballads.

D. M. M. Craik, *Songs of Our Youth.*

N. Curtis (ed.), *Indians' Book; An Offering by the American Indians of Indian Lore, Musical and Narrative.*

C. S. Elliot (ed.), *Songs of Yale: A New Collection of College Songs.*

J. L. Hatton (ed.), *Songs of England, A Collection of English Melodies.*

R. Head and F. Kirkman, *English Rogue: Described, in the Life of Meriton Latroon, a Witty Extravagant. Being a Compleat History of the Most Eminent Cheats of Both Sexes.*

C. Hindley (ed.), *Roxburghe Ballads. Collection of Ancient Songs and Ballads.*

J. P. McCaskey (comp.), *Franklin Square Song Collection: Two Hundred Favorite Songs and Hymns.*

D. H. Morrison (comp.), *Treasury of Song for the Home Circle: The Richest, Best-Loved Gems, Sacred and Secular.*

F. B. Ogilvie (comp.), *Two Hundred Old-Time Songs, Containing the Words and Music of the Choicest Gems of the Old and Familiar Songs.*

One Hundred Songs of Scotland. Words and Music.

Our Children's Songs.

T. Percy (ed.), *Reliques of Ancient English Poetry.*

G. Scherer, *Schönsten Deutschen Volkslieder mit ihren eigenthümlichen singweisen.*

E. Thring, *Uppingham School Songs and Borth Lyrics.*

W. M. Whitlock (comp.), *Whitlock's Collection of Ethiopian Melodies as Sung with Great Applause by William Whitlock at the Principal Theatres in the United States.*

Song of Autumn, and Other Poems. H. M. Bland.

Songs Every Child Should Know: A Selection of the Best Songs of All Nations for Young People. M. S. H. Bacon (ed.).

Songs from the Golden Gate: see I. D. Coolbrith.

Song of Hiawatha. H. W. Longfellow.

"Song of Nature" (poem). R. W. Emerson.

"Song of the Camp" (poem). B. Taylor.

"Song of the Fieldmarshal" (song): see the Catalog entry
for "Feldmarschall."
Song of the River. C. Kingsley.
Songs: see the Reader's Guide entries for Civil War
(American), for Folk and traditional songs, for Hym-
nals, for Hymns, for Minstrel songs, and for Song
collections.
Songs in Many Keys. O. W. Holmes.
Songs of England, A Collection of English Melodies. J. L.
Hatton (ed.).
Songs of Fair Weather. J. M. Thompson.
Songs of Nature. J. Burroughs.
Songs of Old Canada. W. McLennan (trans.).
Songs of Our Youth. D. M. M. Craik.
Songs of Sorrow and Miscellaneous Poems. A. L. Frisbie.
Songs of the Beloved. E. H. Orthwein.
Songs of the Sierras (poems). J. Miller.
Songs of Two Centuries. W. Carleton.
Songs of Yale: A New Collection of College Songs. C. S.
Elliot (ed.).
Sonnet: see
C. H. Crandall, *Representative Sonnets by American
Poets, with an Essay on the Sonnet, Its Nature and
History.*
L. Hunt and S. A. Lee (eds.), *Book of the Sonnet.*
"Sonnet 144" (poem). W. Shakespeare.
Sonnets. B. Michaelangelo.
Sonnets and Poems. W. E. Leonard.
Sonnets and Songs. H. H. Whitney.
Sonnini, M. (trans.): see *Napoleon's Oraculum, or, Book
of Fate.*
Son of Light Horse Harry. J. Barnes.
Son of Royal Langbrith, A Novel. W. D. Howells.
"Son of the Carpenter! receive" (hymn). C. Wesley.
"Sons of the Bright Brigade" (unpublished manuscript).
A. V. Kelley.
Soper, James Hamlin Gardner (illus.): see W. Churchill,
Modern Chronicle.
"Sophie May" (pseud.): see R. S. Clarke.
Sophy of Kravonia; A Novel. A. H. Hawkins.
Sorcery: see T. Wright, *Narratives of Sorcery and Magic,
from the Most Authentic Sources.*
Sorcière: The Witch of the Middle Ages. J. Michelet.
Sordello (poem). R. Browning.
Sordello (poem): see R. Browning, *Men and Women.*
Sordello (poem): see R. Browning, *Pauline; Paracelsus;
Strafford; Sordello.*
Sorrow: see the Reader's Guide entry for Grief.
"Sorrow, My Sorrow" (poem). W. D. Howells.
Sothern, Edward A. (actor): see T. Taylor, *Dundreary, A
Four-Act Comedy.*
Sothern, Edward H. (actor): see T. Taylor, *Dundreary, A
Four-Act Comedy.*
Soul Kiss (musical). H. B. Smith.
Soul's Tragedy (poem): see R. Browning, *Dramas.*
Sound: see the Reader's Guide entry for Acoustics.
Soundings from the Atlantic. O. W. Holmes.
Source Readers in American History: see A. B. Hart and B.
E. Hazard.
South Africa: see

P. Blouet, *John Bull & Co.; The Great Colonial Branches
of the Firm.*
Cape Town, South Africa. *Photographic Views of Cape
Town, South Africa.*
W. Crookes, *Diamonds.*
A. C. Doyle, *War in South Africa: Its Cause and
Conduct.*
F. E. Garrett and E. J. Edwards, *Story of an African
Crisis. Being the Truth About the Jameson Raid and
Johannesburg Revolt of 1896.*
R. G. Gordon-Cumming, *Five Years of a Hunter's Life
in the Far Interior of South Africa.*
N. H. Hammond, *A Woman's Part in a Revolution.*
H. Hensman, *Cecil Rhodes: A Study of a Career.*
B. Mitford (Catalog entry).
R. Russell, *Natal, The Land and its Story.*
O. Schreiner, *Political Situation [in Cape Colony].*
O. Schreiner, *Story of an African Farm. A Novel.*
L. Selmer, *Boer War Lyrics.*
F. R. Statham, *South Africa as It Is.*
G. M. Theal, *South Africa: The Cape Colony, Natal,
Orange Free State, South African Republic, and All
Other Territories South of the Zambesi.*
C. G. Thomas, *Johannesburg in Arms 1895–96, Being
the Observations of a Casual Spectator.*
J. Tyler, *Livingstone Lost and Found; or, Africa and Its
Explorers.*
See also the Reader's Guide entry for Africa and its
explorers.
South Africa as It Is. F. R. Statham.
*South Africa: The Cape Colony, Natal, Orange Free State,
South African Republic, and All Other Territories South
of the Zambesi.* G. M. Theal.
South America: see
J. Beerbohm, *Wanderings in Patagonia; or, Life Among
the Ostrich-Hunters.*
A. A. A. Brassey, *Voyage in the Sunbeam, Our Home in
the Ocean for Eleven Months.*
C. D. W. Brownell, *Indian Races of North and South
America.*
W. E. Curtis, *Capitals of Spanish America.*
J. Fiske, *Discovery of America, with Some Account of
Ancient America and the Spanish Conquest.*
W. L. Herndon, *Exploration of the Valley of the
Amazon.*
T. W. Knox, *Boy Travellers in South America.*
V. Meunier (comp.), *Adventures on the Great Hunting
Grounds of the World.*
M. von Versen, *Reisen in Amerika und der Südameri-
kanische Krieg.*
See also the Reader's Guide entries for individual
South American nations.
South Carolina: see
J. W. De Forest, *Kate Beaumont* (novel).
B. O. Townsend, *Plantation Lays and Other Poems.*
Southern fiction: see the Reader's Guide entry for Ameri-
can South.
Southern frontier (the Old Southwest): see the Reader's
Guide entry for American South.
Southern literature: see the Reader's Guide entry for
American South.

Southern region of the United States: see the Reader's Guide entry for American South.

Southey, Robert: see
  (ed.) J. Bunyan, *Pilgrim's Progress*.
  (trans.) *The Cid*.
  W. J. Dawson (co-ed.), *Great English Letter-Writers* (marginalia).

South Pacific: see
  M. M. Ballou, *Under the Southern Cross; or, Travels in Australia, Tasmania, New Zealand, Samoa, and Other Pacific Islands*.
  Battle for the Pacific, and Other Adventures at Sea.
  L. Becke, *By Reef and Palm*.
  D. J. Belcher, *Mutineers of the "Bounty" and Their Descendants in Pitcairn and Norfolk Islands*.
  H. T. Cheever, *Island World of the Pacific; Being the Personal Narrative and Results of Travel Through the Sandwich or Hawaiian Islands, and Other Parts of Polynesia*.
  C. Dickens, *Old Curiosity Shop; and Reprinted Pieces* (marginalia).
  C. W. Dilke, *Greater Britain: A Record of Travel in English-Speaking Countries During 1866 and 1867*.
  A. L. A. Forbes, *Two Years in Fiji*.
  F. H. H. Guillemard, *Malaysia and the Pacific Archipelagoes*: see A. R. Wallace, *Australasia*.
  J. D. J. Kelley, *Ship's Company and Other Sea People*.
  M. Russell, *Polynesia; or, An Historical Account of the Principal islands of the South Sea including New Zealand*.
  B. C. Seemann, *Viti: An Account of a Government Mission to the Vitian or Fijian Islands, in the Years 1860–61*.
  C. S. Stewart, *Private Journal of a Voyage of a Voyage to the Pacific Ocean*.
  C. W. Stoddard, *South-Sea Idyls*.
  T. Thomas (co-author), *Fiji and the Fijians*.
  B. H. Thomson, *Diversions of a Prime Minister*.
  A. R. Wallace, *Australasia*.
  W. T. Wawn, *South Sea Islanders and the Queensland Labour Trade: A Record of Voyages and Experiences in the Western Pacific, from 1875 to 1891*.
  J. D. Wyss, *Swiss Family Robinson. A New Translation*.
  J. D. Wyss, *Swiss Family Robinson; or, The Adventures of a Shipwrecked Family on an Uninhabited Island Near New Guinea*.
  See also the Reader's Guide entry for Hawaii.

South Pole: see Antarctic.

South-Sea Idyls. C. W. Stoddard.

South Sea Islanders and the Queensland Labour Trade: A Record of Voyages and Experiences in the Western Pacific, from 1875 to 1891. W. T. Wawn.

Souvenirs of a Diplomat: Private Letters from America. A. F. de Bacourt.

Sowers; A Novel. H. S. Scott.

Spain: see
  H. T. Buckle, *History of Civilization in England*.
  [Cid.] *The Chronicle of the Cid*.
  E. De Amicis, *Spain and the Spaniards*.
  S. Dill, *Roman Society in the Last Century of the Western Empire* (marginalia).
  W. H. Dixon, *History of Two Queens: Catherine of Aragon and Anne Boleyn*.
  J. Fiske, *Discovery of America, with Some Account of Ancient America and the Spanish Conquest*.
  J. Froissart, *Chronicles of England, France, Spain, and the Adjoining Countries*.
  J. Hay, *Castilian Days*.
  W. D. Howells, *Roman Holidays and Others*.
  W. Irving, *Alhambra: A Series of Tales and Sketches of the Moors and Spaniards*.
  E. R. B. Lytton, *Leila; or, the Siege of Granada*.
  W. McLennan, *Spanish John; Being a Memoir, Now First Published in Complete Form, of the Early Life and Adventures of Colonel John McDonell*.
  J. Murray, *Handbook for Travellers in Spain*.
  W. F. P. Napier, *History of the War in the Peninsula and in the South of France, from the Year 1807 to the Year 1814*.
  New York *Tribune* (Catalog entry).
  M. A. M. Sadlier, *Spanish Cavaliers: A Tale of the Moorish Wars in Spain*.
  G. H. E. Slater, *Pagan at the Shrine*.
  H. A. Taine, *Tour Through the Pyrenees*.
  B. Taylor, *Lands of the Saracens; or, Pictures of Palestine, Asia Minor, Sicily, and Spain*.
  G. Ticknor, *Life of William Hickling Prescott* (Catalog entry).
  C. D. Warner, *Roundabout Journey*.
  See also the Reader's Guide entry for Spanish-American War.

Spain and the Spaniards. E. De Amicis.

Spanish-American War. R. A. Alger.

Spanish-American War: see
  R. A. Alger, *Spanish-American War*.
  T. G. Allen, *Letter from an Ex-Sailor and Ex-Tramp* (marginalia).
  C. M. F. Dressel, *Cuban Spanish American War, Sketched by C. M. F. Dressel*.
  J. Fiske, *Century of Science and Other Essays* (marginalia).
  C. C. F. Greville, *Greville Memoirs; A Journal of the Reigns of King George IV. and King William IV.* (marginalia).
  Harper's Pictorial History of the War with Spain.
  W. D. Howells, "Editha" (short story) in *Between the Dark and the Daylight: Romances*.
  W. D. Howells, "Our Spanish Prisoners at Portsmouth" (essay).
  H. C. Lodge, *War with Spain*.
  F. Matthews, *New-Born Cuba*.
  C. M. Pepper, *To-morrow in Cuba*.
  L. F. Post, *Documentary Outline of the Philippine Case* (marginalia).
  See also the Reader's Guide entries for Cuba and for the Philippines.

Spanish Cavaliers: A Tale of the Moorish Wars in Spain. M. A. M. Sadlier.

Spanish Gypsy. A Poem. G. Eliot.

Spanish John; Being a Memoir, Now First Published in Complete Form, of the Early Life and Adventures of Colonel John McDonell. W. McLennan.

Spare Hours. J. Brown.

"Spare Hours" [*sic*]: see W. F. Stewart, *Pleasant Hours in an Eventful Life* (poems).

"Sparkling and Bright" (poem). C. F. Hoffman.

Sparrowgrass Papers; or, Living in the Country. F. S. Cozzens.

Spearman, Frank Hamilton (co-author): see
    Adventures in Field and Forest.
    Battle for the Pacific, and Other Adventures at Sea.

Specimens of the English Dramatic Poets: see C. Lamb, *Works of Charles Lamb*.

Speckter, Otto (illus.): see J. W. Hey, *Fünfzig Fabeln für Kinder*.

Spectator: see J. Addison.

"Spectator": see *Prayer-Gauge Debate*.

Speech: see the Reader's Guide entry for Speech improvement.

Speeches: see
    T. Carlyle (ed.), *Oliver Cromwell's Letters and Speeches*.
    M. T. Cicero, *Select Orations*.
    H. Clay, *Speeches*.
    H. C. Dean, *Crimes of the Civil War, and Curse of the Funding System* (Catalog entry).
    Demosthenes, *Several Orations of Demosthenes, Exciting the Athenians to Oppose the Exorbitant Power of Philip King of Macedon*.
    C. M. Depew, *Orations and After-Dinner Speeches of Chauncey M. Depew*.
    H. Greeley, *Hints Toward Reforms in Lectures, Addresses and Other Writings*.
    J. P. Knott (Catalog entry).
    T. B. Macaulay, *Speeches and Poems, with the Report and Notes on the Indian Penal Code*.
    H. G. von Moltke, *Essays, Speeches and Memoirs*.
    E. J. Phelps, *Orations and Essays of Edward John Phelps, Diplomat and Statesman*.
    W. Phillips (Catalog entry).
    F. W. Robertson, *Life, Letters, and Addresses of Fredk. W. Robertson, M.A., Incumbent of Trinity Chapel, Brighton, 1847–53*.
    Speeches at the Lotos Club.
    S. J. Tilden, *Writings and Speeches of Samuel J. Tilden*.
    Wilhelm II, *Kaiser's Speeches, Forming a Character Portrait of Emperor William II*.

Speech improvement: see
    E. D. D. Jones, *Techniques of Speech*.
    W. H. P. Phyfe, *Seven Thousand Words Often Mispronounced: A Complete Hand-Book of Difficulties in English Pronunciation*.
    V. A. Pinkley, *Essentials of Elocution and Oratory*.

"Speech of Hon. John F. Shafroth, of Colorado, in the House of Representatives, Tuesday, December 17, 1901." J. F. Shafroth.

Speech of Monkeys. R. L. Garner.

Speech therapy: see J. D. Quackenbos, *Hypnotic Therapeutics in Theory and Practice, with Numerous Illustrations of Treatment by Suggestion*.

Spell. W. D. Orcutt.

Spelling: see
    G. Donworth, *Letters of Jennie Allen to Her Friend Miss Musgrove*.

N. Webster, *Elementary Spelling Book*.

Spencer, Herbert: see
    J. Fiske, *Century of Science and Other Essays* (marginalia).
    H. George, *Perplexed Philosopher, Being an Examination of Mr. Herbert Spencer's Various Utterances on the Land Question*.
    W. H. Mallock, *Reconstruction of Religious Belief*.
    V. Streamer (comp.), *Voices of Doubt and Trust*.
    Unitarian Herald (Manchester, England).

Spenders; A Tale of the Third Generation. H. L. Wilson.

Spenser, Edmund: W. Shakespeare, *Works of Shakespeare* (Catalog entry).

Spenser for Children. E. Spenser.

Sphinx: see W. C. Prime, *Boat Life in Egypt and Nubia* (Catalog entry).

Spiders: see G. W. Peckham and E. G. Peckham, *Wasps, Social and Solitary*.

Spies: see the Reader's Guide entry for Spy literature.

Spinoza, Baruch (philosopher): see W. James, *Varieties of Religious Experience; A Study in Human Nature* (marginalia).

Spirit in Prison. R. S. Hichens.

Spirit Manifestations Examined and Explained. J. B. Dods.

Spirit of Rationalism in Europe: see W. E. H. Lecky, *History of the Rise and Influence*.

Spirit of the Ghetto. Studies of the Jewish Quarter in New York. H. Hapgood.

Spirit of the Times (periodical): see
    H. C. Jones, "Cousin Sally Dilliard" (sketch).
    H. P. Leland, "Frogs Shot Without Powder" (sketch).

Spiritualism and spiritual healing: see
    W. W. Atkinson, *Advanced Course in Yogii Philosophy and Oriental Occultism*.
    J. K. Bangs, *Toppleton's Client; or, A Spirit in Exile*.
    A. Bertholet, *Transmigration of Souls*.
    R. H. Davis, *Vera, the Medium*.
    W. De Voe, *Healing Currents from the Battery of Life*.
    T. W. Doane, *Bible Myths and Their Parallels in Other Religions: Being a Comparison of the Old and New Testament Myths and Miracles with Those of Heathen Nations of Antiquity* (marginalia).
    J. B. Dods, *Spirit Manifestations Examined and Explained*.
    H. W. Dresser, *Heart of It. A Series of Extracts from "The Power of Silence" and "The Perfect Whole."*
    H. Drummond, *Natural Law in the Spiritual World*.
    R. J. Ebbard, *How to Acquire and Strengthen Will-Power. Modern Pyscho-Therapy*.
    M. B. Eddy, *Science and Health; A Key to the Scriptures* (Catalog entry).
    I. K. Funk, *Psychic Riddle*.
    H. Garland, *Tyranny of the Dark*.
    C. Giles, *Our Children in the Other Life*.
    D. D. Home, *Incidents in My Life*.
    P. Mulford (Catalog entry).
    F. W. H. Myers, *Human Personality and Its Survival of Bodily Death*.
    A. E. Newton (ed.), *Modern Bethesda, or The Gift of Healing Restored*.
    R. H. Newton, *Christian Science; The Truths of*

Spiritual Healing and Their Contribution to the Growth of Orthodoxy.

H. S. Olcott, *People from the Other World.*

J. P. Quincy, *Peckster Professorship; An Episode in the History of Psychical Research.*

O. C. Sabin, *Christology—Science of Health and Happiness; or, Metaphysical Healing Exemplified—Through Rules, Formulas and Incidents.*

V. Sardou (Catalog entry).

M. J. Savage, *Can Telepathy Explain? Results of Psychical Research* (Catalog entry).

R. Seeberg, *Revelation and Inspiration.*

C. W. Silver, *Secular Anathema on Fakery in Business, Social and Professional Life; or, Twentieth Century Conduct.*

D. T. Stanley, *London Street Arabs* (Catalog entry).

B. Taylor, *At Home and Abroad: A Sketch-Book of Life, Scenery, and Men.*

B. Taylor, *Hannah Thurston: A Story of American Life.*

S. E. Titcomb, *Aryan Sun-Myths: The Origin of Religions* (Catalog entry).

A. E. Trumbull, *Wheel of Progress* (play).

J. Tyndall, *Fragments of Science for Unscientific People: A Series of Detached Essays, Lectures, and Reviews.*

B. F. Underwood, *Essays and Lectures.*

T. Watts-Dunton, *Aylwin.*

L. Whiting, *After Her Death; The Story of a Summer.*

L. Whiting, *World Beautiful. Second Series.*

F. S. Wilhelmina, *Memoirs of Wilhelmine, Margravine of Baireuth* (marginalia).

H. Wilmans, *Back Numbers/Wilmans Express, Condensed.*

F. B. Wilson, *Paths to Power.*

See also the Reader's Guide entries for Christian Science, for Inspirational messages, for Mary Baker Eddy, for Mental health, for Mysticism, and for Parapsychology.

"Spiritualization of Thought in France" (essay). M. P. R. B. S. De Bury.

Spirituals: see

W. F. Allen (comp.), *Slave Songs of the United States.*
"Go, chain the lion down."
"Go down, Moses."
"Gospel train."
"I know that my Redeemer lives."
"It causes me to tremble."
J. B. T. Marsh, *Story of the Jubilee Singers, with Their Songs.*
"Ol' ark's a moverin'."
"Rise and shine."
"Roll, Jordan, roll."
"Sail away, ladies" (traditional folk song).
"Sinner, please don't let this harvest pass": see " I know that my Redeemer lives."
"Steal away to Jesus."
"Swing low, sweet chariot."
"There's a meeting here to-night."
"Walk together children."
"We shall walk through the valley."
"You'll be an angel by and by" (invented spiritual): see "Sail away, ladies."

See also the Reader's Guide entry for Jubilee Singers and the Catalog entry for Spirituals.

Spofford, Ainsworth Rand: see T. Thomas, *History of Prices, and of the State of the Circulation, from 1793 to 1837* (Catalog entry).

"Spoliation of India" (series of articles). J. S. Keay.

Sporting Adventures in the Far West. J. M. Murphy.

Sports and Pastimes of the People of England, Including the Rural and Domestic Recreations, May Games, Mummeries, Shows, Processions, Pageants, and Pompous Spectacles. J. Strutt.

Sports literature: see
On the Gridiron and Other Stories of Outdoor Sport.
On Track and Diamond.
See also the Reader's Guide entry for Boxing.

Sprenger, Jakob (co-author): see H. K. Institoris, *Malleus Maleficarum, or Hexenhammer.*

Springfield, 1636–1886; History of Town and City. M. A. Green.

Spun-Yarn; Sea Stories. M. Robertson.

Spy: A Tale of the Neutral Ground. J. F. Cooper.

Spy literature:
S. E. E. Edmundson, *Nurse and Spy in the Union Army.*
J. T. Haines, *French Spy; or, The Siege of Constantina. A Military Drama in Three Acts* (play).
W. E. Mansfield and C. H. Mansfield, *Diplomatic Woman.*
E. P. Oppenheim, *Maker of History.*
A. Pinkerton, *Spy of the Rebellion; Being A True History of the Spy System of the United States Army During the Late Rebellion.*

Spyk, Peter (play character): see J. R. Planché, *Loan of a Lover: A Vaudeville in One Act* (play).

Square Deal. T. Roosevelt.

Squaw Man. A Novel. J. O. Faversham.

"Squire, Francis" (pseud.): see F. B. S. Potter.

Squire, Maud Hunt: (illus.): see
G. Smith, *Loveable Tales of Janey and Josey and Joe.*
G. Smith, *Roggie and Reggie Stories.*
G. Smith, *Stories of Peter and Ellen.*

Sri Lanka: see the Reader's Guide entry for Ceylon.

Stadler, Joseph Constantine (co-illus.): see London. *Forty-one Coloured Views of London.*

Stadtmenschen. Ein Wiener Skizzenbuch. E. Pötzl.

"Staffe, Baroness" (pseud.): see B. A. A. Soyer.

Staley, Thomas Nettleship: see
W. D. Alexander, *Review of a Pastoral Address by the Right Rev. T. N. Staley, D.D., Reformed Catholic Bishop of Honolulu, Containing a Reply to Some of His Charges Against the American Protestant Mission to the Hawaiian Islands.*
H. Mayhew, *London Labour and the London Poor* (Catalog entry).

Stalky & Co.: see R. Kipling, *Writings in Prose and Verse.*

Stallbaum, Johann Gottfried (ed.): see Horace, *Q. Horatii Flacci Opera omnia.*

Stammering: see J. D. Quackenbos, *Hypnotic Therapeutics in Theory and Practice, with Numerous Illustrations of Treatment by Suggestion.*

Standard of Usage in English. T. R. Lounsbury.

Standard Oil Company: see
 T. W. Lawson, *Frenzied Finance.*
 H. D. Lloyd, *Wealth against Commonwealth.*
 I. F. Marcosson, "Henry H. Rogers—Monopolist."
 S. E. Moffett, "Captains of Industry: Henry Hut-
  tleston Rogers" (article).
 I. M. Tarbell, *History of the Standard Oil Company.*
*Standard Operas: Their Plots, Their Music, and Their Com-
 posers.* G. P. Upton.
Stand Fast, Craig-Royston! W. Black.
Standish of Standish: A Story of the Pilgrims. J. G. Austin.
Stand Pat; or, Poker Stories from the Mississippi. D. A.
 Curtis.
Stanhope, Philip Dormer: see B. Hall, *Travels in North
 America, in the Years 1827 and 1828* (marginalia).
Stanley, Arthur Penrhy (pref.): see J. B. Elgin, *Letters and
 Journals.*
Stanley, Dorothy (ed.): see H. M. Stanley, *Autobiography
 of Sir Henry Morton Stanley.*
Stanley, Edward George Geoffrey Smith: see
 (trans.): see Homer, *Iliad of Homer.*
 G. E. B. Saintsbury, *Earl of Derby.*
Stanley, Henry Morton: see
 M. D. Conway, *Autobiography: Memories and Experi-
  ences of Moncure Daniel Conway* (marginalia).
 M. D. Conway, *Wandering Jew* (marginalia).
 J. T. Headley, *Stanley's Adventures in the Wilds of Africa:
  A Graphic Account of the Several Expeditions of Henry
  M. Stanley.*
 J. Tyler, *Livingstone Lost and Found; or, Africa and Its
  Explorers.*
 H. Ward, *My Life with Stanley's Rear Guard.*
*Stanley's Adventures in the Wilds of Africa: A Graphic Ac-
 count of the Several Expeditions of Henry M. Stanley.* J.
 T. Headley.
Stanton, Edwin McMasters: see W. C. Prime, *Tent Life in
 the Holy Land* (Catalog entry).
Stanwood, Avis A. B.: see A. A. Burham.
Stark, Louis (co-author): see S. Lebert, *Grand Theoretical
 and Practical Piano-School for Systematic Instruction.*
Stark Munro Letters. A. C. Doyle.
Star of Babylon, A Phantasy. M. H. Potter.
"Star of the evening" (song). J. M. Sayles.
"Star-spangled banner" (anthem). F. S. Key.
"Star-spangled banner" (anthem): see D. B. Lucas and J.
 F. McLaughlin, *Fisher Ames-Henry Clay, Etc.*
Starters and Regulators for Electric Motors and Generators.
 R. Krause.
State Board of Forestry of California: see *Memorial to the
 Fiftieth Congress.*
Stately Homes of England. L. F. W. Jewitt and S. C. Hall.
Station Amusements in New Zealand. M. A. Barker.
Station Life in New Zealand. M. A. Barker.
Statutes of Henry VII in Exact Facsimile. Henry VII.
Stead, William Thomas (ed.): see *Review of Reviews.*
Steadfast: The Story of a Saint and a Sinner. R. T. Cooke.
Steam-engine (invention): see H. Dircks, *Life, Times and
 Scientific Labours of the Second Marquis of Worcester.*
Stebbins, George Coles (co-ed.): see P. P. Bliss, *Gospel
 Hymns Consolidated.*
Stedman, Arthur [Griffin]: see

(gen. ed.) I. Bacheller, *Master of Silence. A Romance.*
(ed.) *First Book of the Authors Club, Liber Scriptorum.*
(gen. ed.) E. J. Pullen, *Don Finimondone: Calabrian
 Sketches.*
(gen. ed.) A. Repplier, *Essays in Miniature.*
(contr.) E. C. Stedman (co-ed.), *Library of American
 Literature, from Earliest Settlement to the Present
 Time.*
(gen. ed.) W. Whitman, *Autobiographia; or, the Story
 of a Life.*
(general ed.) W. Whitman, *Selected Poems, by Walt
 Whitman.*
Stedman, Edmund Clarence: see
 (co-author) C. Kingsley, *Favorite Poems.*
 (intro.) A. R. Macdonough (trans.), *Lovers of Provence:
  Aucassin and Nicolette.*
Steele, Frederic Dorr (illus.): see R. H. Davis, *Vera, The
 Medium.*
Steele, Richard: see
 W. M. Thackeray, *Thackeray's Lectures. The English
  Humorists. The Four Georges* (marginalia).
 See also the Catalog and Reader's Guide entries for J.
  Addison.
Stenography: see the Reader's Guide entry for
 Phonography.
Stephen, King of England: see Henry of Huntingdon,
 *Chronicle of Henry of Huntingdon, Comprising the His-
 tory of England, from the Invasion of Julius Caesar to the
 Accession of Henry II. Also, The Acts of Stephen, King of
 England and Duke of Normandy.*
Stephen, Leslie (ed.): see W. K. Clifford, *Lectures and
 Essays by the Late William Kingdon Clifford.*
Stephens, Alice Barber (illus.): see
 M. W. C. Deland, *Where the Laborers Are Few.*
 A. M. Roach, *Some Successful Marriages.*
Stephens, George: see
 (trans.) R. B. Anderson, *Viking Tales of the North.*
 (ed.) H. Hendrik, *Memoirs of Hans Hendrik, The Arctic
  Traveler.*
Stephens, Henry (co-illus.): see *Mother Goose's Melodies
 for Children.*
"Stepniak, Sergius" (pseud.): see S. M. Kravchinski.
Sterling, John: see T. Carlyle, *Life of John Sterling.*
Sterne. H. D. Traill.
Sterne, Laurence: see
 W. M. Thackeray, *Thackeray's Lectures. The English
  Humourists. The Four Georges* (marginalia).
 H. D. Traill, *Sterne.*
Sterner, Albert (illus.): see
 M. A. A. Ward, *Fenwick's Career* (novel).
 M. A. A. Ward, *Marriage of William Ashe* (novel).
Stevens, Rowan (co-author): see *Battle for the Pacific, and
 Other Adventures at Sea.*
Stevens, T. H. (co-author): see *Adventures at Sea.*
Stevens, William Dodge (illus.): see M. Cameron, *Cat
 and the Canary.*
Stevenson, John Andrew (arranger): see T. Moore, "Oft
 in the stilly night" (song).
Stevenson, Robert Louis: see
 W. J. Dawson (co-ed.), *Great English Letter-Writers*
  (marginalia).

A. H. Joline, *Diversions of a Book-Lover* (Catalog entry).

W. L. Phelps, *Essays on Modern Novelists* (marginalia).

C. W. Stoddard, *Exits and Entrances: A Book of Essays and Sketches.*

Stewardson, John (illus.): see O. Wister, *Dragon of Wantley, His Rise, His Voracity, and His Downfall: A Romance.*

Stewart, John Wolcott (contr.): see E. J. Phelps, *Orations and Essays of Edward John Phelps, Diplomat and Statesman.*

Stewart, Virgil A.: see H. R. Howard, *History of Virgil A. Stewart, and His Adventure.*

Stewart, William Morris: see W. T. Sherman, *Memoirs of General William T. Sherman. By Himself* (marginalia).

Stickit Minister. S. R. Crockett.

Stillwater Tragedy. T. B. Aldrich.

Stirner, Max: see J. G. Huneker, *Egoists, A Book of Supermen.*

Stoansteirisch. P. Rosegger.

Stock speculation: see the Reader's Guide entry for Finance and business.

Stockton's Stories. Second Series. The Christmas Wreck and Other Stories. F. R. Stockton.

Stodart, Jemima Henrietta (Brown), "Mrs. John Riddle" (trans.): see L. Schefer, *Artist's Married Life; Being That of Albert Dürer.*

Stoddard, Charles Warren: see

M. D. Conway, *Autobiography: Memories and Experiences of Moncure Daniel Conway* (marginalia).

T. F. Cronise, *Natural Wealth of California* (Catalog entry).

B. Harte (ed.), *Outcroppings: Being Selections of California Verse.*

Stoddard, Richard Henry (ed.): see

C. C. F. Greville, *Greville Memoirs; A Journal of the Reigns of King George IV. and King William IV.* (marginalia).

L. Hearn, *Stray Leaves from Strange Literature; Stories Reconstructed* (Catalog entry).

C. Knight and T. Raikes, *Personal Reminiscences by Cornelia Knight and Thomas Raikes.*

P. Mérimée, *Prosper Mérimée's Letters.*

T. Moore and W. Jerdan, *Personal Reminiscences by Moore and Jerdan.*

New Princeton Review (Catalog entry).

Stoddard, William Osborn (co-author): see *Adventures with Indians.*

Stolen Treasure. H. Pyle.

Stone, Asa A.: see A. Dresser, *Narrative of Amos Dresser.*

Stonehenge: see D. M. M. Craik, *Studies from Life.*

Stone of Destiny. K. D. Mackay.

Stones of Venice. J. Ruskin.

"Stoney Lonesome" (story): see F. B. Terry, *Stories.*

Stories. F. B. Terry.

Stories About Birds of Land and Water. M. K. Gregg and E. Kirby.

Stories for Children.

T. K. Beecher.

M. Edgeworth.

Stories from Four Languages Retold in English. W. Brooks.

Stories from the Italian Poets. L. Hunt.

Stories from the Rabbis. A. S. Isaacs.

Stories of Adventure. J. Verne.

Stories of Infinity: Lumen—History of a Comet—In Infinity. C. Flammarion.

Stories of Outdoor Life. W. O. Stoddard.

Stories of Peace and War. F. Remington.

Stories of Peter and Ellen. G. Smith.

Stories of Red Hanrahan. W. B. Yeats.

Stories of the East from Herodotus. Herodotus.

"Storm" (song). G. A. Stevens.

"Storm at sea" (song): see G. A. Stevens, "Storm" (song).

"Stormy winds do blow": see "Mermaid" (sea shanty).

Story and Song of Black Roderick. D. S. Shorter.

Story of a Bad Boy. T. B. Aldrich.

Story of a Cat. T. B. Aldrich.

Story of a Country Town. E. W. Howe. See also the Catalog entry for E. Eggleston, *Mystery of Metropolisville.*

"Story of Adam and Eve." J. H. Friswell.

Story of an African Crisis. Being the Truth About the Jameson Raid and Johannesburg Revolt of 1896. F. E. Garrett and E. J. Edwards.

Story of an African Farm. A Novel. O. Schreiner.

Story of a Story, and Other Stories. B. Matthews.

Story of a Street; A Narrative History of Wall Street. F. T. Hill.

Story of a Summer; or, Journal Leaves from Chappaqua. C. Cleveland.

Story of Australasia: Its Discovery, Colonisation, and Development. J. S. Laurie.

Story of Babette, A Little Creole Girl. R. M. Stuart.

Story of Burnt Njal; or, Life in Iceland at the End of the Tenth Century. G. W. Dasent (ed., trans.)

Story of Creation: A Plain Account of Evolution. E. Clodd.

Story of France, from the Earliest Times to the Consulate of Napoleon Bonaparte. T. E. Watson.

Story of Germ Life. H. W. Conn.

Story of Gösta Berling. S. O. L. Lagerlöf.

Story of Helen of Troy. C. C. Harrison.

Story of James I of Scotland. C. M. Yonge.

Story of Kaspar Hauser from Authentic Records. E. E. G. Evans.

Story of Land and Sea. C. T. Brady.

Story of Liberty. C. C. Coffin.

Story of Little Jakey. H. A. De Kroyft.

Story of Margaret Kent. E. W. O. Kirk.

Story of Mary MacLane. M. MacLane.

Story of Mont Blanc. A. R. Smith.

Story of Music and Musicians for Young Readers. L. C. W. Lillie.

Story of My Life. H. Keller.

Story of Nineteenth-Century Science. H. S. Williams.

Story of Paul Boyton. P. Boyton.

Story of Pet Marjorie (Marjory Fleming). L. Macbean.

Story of Sigurd the Volsung and the Fall of the Niblungs. W. Morris.

Story of the Candlesticks. V. M. Hugo.

Story of the Congo Free State: Social, Political, and Economic Aspects of the Belgian System of Government in Central Africa. H. W. Wack.

Story of the Gadsbys: see R. Kipling, *Writings in Prose and Verse.*

Story of the Golden Age. J. Baldwin.

Story of the Jubilee Singers, with Their Songs. J. B. T. Marsh.

Story of the Life of Napoleon III. J. M. Haswell.

Story of the Memorial Fountain to Shakespeare at Stratford-upon-Avon. L. C. Davis (ed.).

Story of the Mind. J. M. Baldwin.

Story of the Other Wise Man. H. Van Dyke.

Story of the United States Navy for Boys. B. J. Lossing.

Story of West Africa. M. H. Kingsley.

Story Sermons from Les Misérables. E. P. Adams.

"*Story That Took*" (short story). I. H. Gillmore.

Story, William Wetmore: see M. E. Phillips (ed. and illus.), *Laurel Leaves for Little Folk* (Catalog entry).

Stotts, William E. (owner): see *Maps and Views to Accompany a Message from the President of the United States.*

Stowe, Harriet Elizabeth (Beecher): see
  (co-author) C. E. Beecher, *Principles of Domestic Science; As Applied to the Duties and Pleasures of Home.*
  T. W. S. Higginson, *Cheerful Yesterdays. Contemporaries* (marginalia).
  J. A. D.-G. Ross, *Three Generations of English Women* (marginalia).
  M. F. Somerville, *Personal Recollections, from Early Life to Old Age, of Mary Somerville. With Selections from Her Correspondence* (marginalia).
  G. O. Trevelyan, *Life and Letters of Lord Macaulay* (marginalia).
  T. C. Upham, *Life of Faith; in Three Parts, Embracing Some of the Scriptural Principles or Doctrines of Faith* (Catalog entry).
  É. Zola, *Rome* (marginalia).

Strachey, Edward (ed.): see T. Malory, *Morte Darthur.*

Strachey, Lady (Constance [Braham] Strachie (ed.): see E. Lear, *Letters of Edward Lear.*

Strachey, Lionel. "Progressional" (satirical poem): see G. L. Dickinson, *Letters from a Chinese Official* (newspaper clipping).

Strachey, Lionel (co-ed.): see *World's Wit and Humor; An Encyclopedia of the Classic Wit and Humor of All Ages and Nations.*

Strafford: A Tragedy. R. Browning.

Strafford: A Tragedy: see R. Browning, *Pauline; Paracelsus; Strafford; Sordello.*

Strange Adventures of a House-Boat. W. Black.

Strange Case of Dr. Jekyll and Mr. Hyde (novel). R. L. Stevenson.

Strange Case of Dr. Jekyll and Mr. Hyde: see E. J. Bliss, *Peril of Oliver Sargent.*

Strange Manuscript Found in a Copper Cylinder. J. De Mille.

"*Stranger People's*" *Country.* M. N. Murfree.

Stranger Than Fiction: see H. Welsh.

Strange Schemes of Randolph Mason. M. D. Post.

Strange Tales. E. C. G. Murray.

Strange True Stories of Louisiana. G. W. Cable.

"*Strannik, Ivan*" (pseud.): see A. M. Aníchkova.

Strauss, David Friedrich: see G. P. Fisher, *Essays on the Supernatural Origin of Christianity.*

"Strauss, Yawcob": see C. F. Adams, *Leedle Yawcob Strauss.*

Stray Leaves from Strange Literature; Stories Reconstructed. L. Hearn.

Strength of the Hills; A Novel. F. Wilkinson.

Strickland, Elizabeth (co-author): see
  A. Strickland, *Lives of the Queens of England, from the Norman Conquest; With Anecdotes of Their Courts.*
  A. Strickland, *Lives of the Queens of Scotland and English Princesses Connected with the Regal Succession of Great Britain.*

Strickland, William Peter (ed.): see P. Cartwright, *Autobiography of Peter Cartwright.*

Strikes, Labour Questions, and Other Economic Difficulties: A Short Treatise of Political Economy. A. W. Johnston.

Strindberg, August: see H. Ibsen, *Hedda Gabler* (Catalog entry).

Strolls by Starlight and Sunshine. W. H. Gibson.

Struggles and Triumphs. P. T. Barnum.

Struggles (Social, Financial, and Political) of Petroleum V. Nasby. D. R. Locke.

Struwwelpeter. H. Hoffmann.

Strype, John (ed.): see J. Stow, *Survey of London.*

Stuart and Bamboo; A Novel. S. P. M. Greene.

Stuart, Gilbert: see C. A. Munn, *Three Types of Washington Portraits: John Trumbull, Charles Wilson Peale, Gilbert Stuart.*

Student's Roman Empire. A History of the Roman Empire from Its Foundation to the Death of Marcus Aurelius (27 B.C.-180 A.D.). J. B. Bury.

Studies from Life. D. M. M. Craik.

Studies in Modern Music. W. H. Hadow.

Studies in Style. W. H. Helm.

Studies in the History of Venice. H. R. F. Brown.

Studies in the South and West, with Comments on Canada. C. D. Warner.

Studies in Unnatural History. M. Reed.

Studies of Paris. E. De Amicis.

Studies of Shakspere; Forming a Companion to Every Edition of the Text. C. Knight.

Studies of the Stage. B. Matthews.

Study in Scarlet. A. C. Doyle.

"*Study of Indian Music*" (essay). J. C. Fillmore.

Stumbling Block. J. M. Forman.

Stumbling Blocks. M. A. Dodge.

Sturgis, Russell (contr.): see E. Singleton, *Furniture of Our Forefathers.*

Sturluson, Snorri: see R. M. Ballantyne, *Erling the Bold, A Tale of the Norse Sea-Kings.*

Sturm, Julius Karl Reinhold: see "J. Stern" (pseud.).

Stuyvesant. J. Abbott.

Style: see the Reader's Guide entry for English grammar, usage, and style.

Subaltern's Furlough: Descriptive of Scenes in Various Parts of the United States, Upper and Lower Canada, New-Brunswick, and Nova Scotia, During the Summer and Autumn of 1832. E. T. Coke.

Sublime in Nature; Compiled from the Descriptions of Travellers and Celebrated Writers. F. de Lanoye.

Substance of Faith Allied with Science; A Catechism for Parents and Teachers. O. J. Lodge.

Substitute. W. N. Harben.

Suburban Sketches (essays). W. D. Howells.

Success Among Nations. E. Reich.

Sudermann, Hermann: see W. L. Phelps, *Essays on Modern Novelists* (marginalia).

Sudras (Indian caste): see H. T. Buckle, *History of Civilization in England.*

Sue, Marie Joseph: see E. Sue, *Wandering Jew.*

Suetonius: see S. Pepys, *Diary of Samuel Pepys* (Catalog entry).

Suffering Millions (novel). R. O. Cross.

Suffragettes: see the Reader's Guide entry for Women's rights.

"Suggested Test Reading" (article). W. T. Stead.

Suggestions on Government. S. E. Moffett.

Suggs, Simon (literary character): see J. J. Hooper, *Some Adventures of Captain Simon Suggs, Late of the Tallapoosa Volunteers.*

Suicide: see
  W. Allingham, *William Allingham, A Diary* (marginalia).
  G. P. Lathrop, *Would You Kill Him? A Novel.*
  W. E. H. Lecky, *History of European Morals from Augustus to Charlemagne* (marginalia).
  J. R. Lowell, *Letters of James Russell Lowell* (marginalia).
  T. B. Macaulay, *Critical and Miscellaneous Essays* (marginalia).
  A. P. Primrose, *Napoleon: The Last Phase* (marginalia).
  M. Reed, *Book of Clever Beasts; Studies in Unnatural History.*

Sulaymān, Al-tājr (co-author): see A. Z. H. Y. Sīrafī, *Ancient Accounts of India and China, by Two Mohammedan Travellers.*

Sulli, Giorgio M. (vocal teacher): see G. Verdi, *Ballo in Maschera.*

Sullivan, Arthur Seymour (composer): see
  S. Baring-Gould, *In Exitu Israel; An Historical Novel* (Catalog entry).
  G. L. Dickinson, *Letters from a Chinese Official.*
  W. S. Gilbert, *H. M. S. Pinafore* (operetta).
  W. S. Gilbert, *Iolanthe* (operetta).
  W. S. Gilbert, *Mikado* (operetta).
  W. S. Gilbert, *Patience; or, Bunthorne's Bride* (operetta).
  W. S. Gilbert, *Yeomen of the Guard* (operetta).
  L. Strachey, "Progressional" (satirical poem).

Sullivan, Edmund Joseph (illus.): see R. Barr, *Prince of Good Fellows.*

Sumatra: see E. R. Smilie, *Investigations and Experience of M. Shawtinbach, at Saar Soong Sumatra.*

Sumichrast, Frederick C. de (ed.): see L. Halévy, *Abbé Constantin.*

Summary of the French Verbs, Embracing an Entirely New System of Conjugation. A. Mariot de Beauvoisin.

Summer in Africa (unidentified book title).

Summer in Arcady; A Tale of Nature. J. L. Allen.

Summer in Leslie Goldthwaite's Life. A. D. T. Whitney.

Summer in England with Henry Ward Beecher; Giving the Addresses, Lectures, and Sermons Delivered by Him in Great Britain During The Summer of 1886. J. B. Pond (ed.).

Summer Months Among the Alps; With the Ascent of Monte Rosa. T. W. Hinchliff.

"Summer on Horseback" (mistaken title): see I. C. Cabell, *Seen from the Saddle.*

Summer Sketches (unidentified book title).

Sumner, Charles: see
  (intro.) D. R. Locke, *Struggles (Social, Financial, and Political) of Petroleum V. Nasby.*
  E. L. Pierce, *Memoir and Letters of Charles Sumner.*

Sumner, Heywood (illus.): see F. H. K. La Motte-Fouqué, *Undine: A Romance, and Sintram and His Companions.*

Sun. A. V. Guillemin.

Sun (solar star): see S.G. Bayne, *Pith of Astronomy (Without Mathematics): The Latest Facts and Figures as Developed by the Giant Telescopes* (Catalog entry).

Sunbeam Stories. M. A. P. Mackarness.

Sunnyfield, The Adventures of Podsy and June. L. M. Sill.

Sunny Side of a Busy Life. C. Wuichet.

Sunny Side of the Street. M. P. Wilder.

Sunshine and Haar; Some Further Glimpses of Life at Barncraig. T. N. Hepburn.

Supernatural events: see the Reader's Guide entry for Parapsychology.

Supernatural fiction: see the Reader's Guide entry for Science fiction.

Suphayalat, Queen of Burma: see H. Fielding-Hall, *Thibaw's Queen.*

Suppé, Franz von (composer): see C. Wälzel, *Fatinitza* (operetta).

Supreme Surrender: A Novel. A. M. Low.

Surprises du divorce (play): see A. Daly, *Lottery.*

"Surprise Party to Mark Twain." W. D. Howells.

Survey of London. J. Stow.

Susan's Escort, and Others. E. E. Hale.

Susy. B. Harte.

Susy's Six Birthdays. E. P. Prentiss.

Susy's Six Teachers. E. P. Prentiss.

Sutherland, Alexander (ed.): see H. C. Kendall, *Poems of Henry Clarence Kendall.*

Sut Lovingood: Yarns Spun by a "Nat'ral Born Durn'd Fool." G. W. Harris.

Sutphen, William Gilbert Van Tassel (co-author): see *On Track and Diamond.*

Sutro, Alfred (trans.): see M. Maeterlinck, *Life of the Bee.*

Sutro, Esther Stella Isaacs (comp.): see M. Maeterlinck, *Thoughts from Maeterlinck, Chosen and Arranged by E. S. S.*

Svensk-Engelsk hand-ordbok. V. E. Öman.

Swain, Joseph (illus.): see N. MacLeod, *Eastward.*

Swallow Barn; or, A Sojourn in the Old Dominion. J. P. Kennedy.

Swan, Howard (co-trans.): see F. Gouin, *Art of Teaching.*

"Swanee River" (minstrel song): see S. C. Foster, "Old folks at home."

Sweden: see
  English and Swedish Dictionary (unidentified book).
  S. O. L. Lagerlöf, *Story of Gösta Berling.*
  E. E. N. Lundberg, *Lyriska stämningar* (poems).
  V. E. Öman, *Svensk-Engelsk hand-ordbok.*
  A. Strindberg (Catalog entry).

B. Taylor, *Northern Travel: Summer and Winter Pictures of Sweden, Denmark, and Lapland.*

E. Tegnér, *Frithiof's Saga; A Legend of Ancient Norway.* See also the Reader's Guide entry for Scandinavian mythology.

Swedenborg, Emanuel: see C. Giles, *Our Children in the Other Life.*

Swedish language: see *English and Swedish Dictionary.*

Sweeney, Morgan J. (illus.): see C. F. Adams, *Leedle Yawcob Strauss.*

"Sweet by and by" (hymn). S. F. Bennett.

"Sweet Ellen Bayne" (minstrel song): see S. C. Foster, "Ellen Bayne."

Sweet Singer of Michigan": Later Poems. J. A. D. Moore.

"Sweet William's Farewell to Black-ey'd Susan" (poem, ballad). J. Gay.

Swete, Charles (ed.): see S. K. Trimmer, *History of the Robins. In Words of One Syllable.*

Swift, Jonathan: see

J. Forster, *Life of Jonathan Swift. Volume the First, 1667–1711.*

O. W. Holmes, *Autocrat of the Breakfast-Table* (marginalia).

J. McCarthy, *History of the Four Georges* (Catalog entry).

W. M. Thackeray, *Thackeray's Lectures. The English Humourists. The Four Georges* (marginalia).

F. M. Trollope, *Domestic Manners of the Americans* (marginalia).

Swinburne, Algernon Charles: see J. R. Lowell, *Letters of James Russell Lowell* (marginalia).

Swiss Family Robinson. A New Translation. J. D. Wyss.

Swiss Family Robinson; or, The Adventures of a Shipwrecked Family on an Uninhabited Island Near New Guinea. J. D. Wyss.

Swiss Family Robinson: see O. Wister, *New Swiss Family Robinson: A Tale for Children of All Ages.*

Switzerland: see

K. Baedeker, *Switzerland and the Adjacent Portions of Italy, Savoy, and the Tyrol. Handbook for Travellers.*

E. G. Buffum, *Sights and Sensations in France, Germany, and Switzerland.*

A. Hoppin, *Ups and Downs on Land and Water.*

J. Murray, *Handbook for Travellers in Switzerland and the Alps of Savoy and Piedmont.*

D. C. Seitz, *Discoveries in Every-day Europe: Vagrant Notes of a Rapid Journey.*

B. Taylor, *At Home and Abroad: A Sketch-Book of Life, Scenery, and Men.*

C. D. Warner, *Saunterings.*

See also the Reader's Guide entry for Mountain climbing.

Switzerland and the Adjacent Portions of Italy, Savoy, and the Tyrol. Handbook for Travellers. K. Baedeker.

Swords and Ploughshares. E. H. Crosby.

Sykes, A. L. (co-author): see C. P. Jones, *Banduk jaldi banduk!: (Quick, My Rifle!).*

"Sylva, Carmen" (pseud.): see Elizabeth, Queen of Rumania.

Symonds, John Addington (trans.): see

B. Cellini, *Life of Benvenuto Cellini.*

C. Kingsley, *Heroes, or Greek Fairy Tales for My Children* (marginalia).

Symonds, William Samuel (ed.): see H. Miller, *Cruise of the Betsey; or, A Summer Ramble Among the Fossiliferous Deposits of the Hebrides.*

"Symphony in B minor" ("Unfinished symphony"). F. P. Schubert.

Syria: see

G. W. Curtis, *Howadji in Syria.*

T. W. Knox, *Backsheesh! or, Life and Adventures in the Orient.*

A. H. Layard, *Nineveh and Its Remains: With an Account of a Visit to the Chaldæan Christians of Kurdistand.*

H. M. Miller, *Little People of Asia.*

J. Murray, *Handbook for Travellers in Syria and Palestine.*

C. Scollard, *On Sunny Shores.*

W. H. Thomson, *Parables and Their Home. The Parables by the Lake.*

System of Christian Rhetoric, for the Use of Preachers and Other Speakers. G. W. Hervey.

System of Logic, Ratiocinative and Inductive; Being a Connected View of the Principles of Evidence and the Methods of Scientific Investigation. J. S. Mill.

Szold, Henrietta (co-author): see E. J. James, *Immigrant Jew in America.*

T

Table: How to Buy Food, How to Cook It, and How to Serve It. A. Filippini.

Tacitus, Publius Cornelius: see W. Shakespeare, *Macbeth* (play) (Catalog entry).

Taft, William Howard: see Suetonius, *Lives of the Twelve Caesars* (Catalog entry).

Tagebuchblätter. K: Chrëstomanos.

Tahiti: see

A. A. A. Brassey, *Voyage in the Sunbeam, Our Home in the Ocean for Eleven Months.*

C. W. Stoddard, *South-Sea Idyls.*

Tahoe; or, Life in California. A Romance. S. B. Morgan.

"Tah-rah-rah-boom-de-aye!" (song): see J. H. Sayers, "Ta-ra-ra-boom-de-ay!" (song).

Taine, Hippolyte Adolphe: see W. James, *Varieties of Religious Experience; A Study in Human Nature* (marginalia).

Taj Mahal: see

W. W. Hunter, *Indian Empire: Its History, People, and Products.*

Omar Khayyám, *One Hundred Quatrains* (Catalog entry).

B. Taylor, *Visit to India, China, and Japan, in the Year 1853* (Catalog engry).

R. Vallery-Radot, *Life of Pasteur* (marginalia).

J. S. Woolsey, *Hospital Days* (Catalog entry).

Taking the Bastille. A. Dumas.

Tale of Peter Rabbit. B. Potter.

Tale of the Great Mutiny. W. H. Fitchett.

Tale of True Love, and Other Poems. A. Austin.

Tale of Two Cities. C. Dickens.

Tales from Gorky, Translated from the Russian. M. Gorky.

Tales from Shakespeare. C. Lamb and M. A. Lamb.
Tales of a Grandfather: History of Scotland. W. Scott.
Tales of a Time and Place. G. E. King.
Tales of a Wayside Inn. H. W. Longfellow.
Tales of a Wayside Inn: see also "Legend of Rabbi Ben Levin" (poem).
Tales of Fantasy and Fact (stories). B. Matthews.
Tales of Janey, Josey, and Joe. G. Smith.
Tales of King Arthur and His Knights of the Round Table. M. V. Farrington.
Tales of New England. S. O. Jewett.
Tales of Old Japan. A. B. F.- Mitford.
Tales of Our Coast. S. R. Crockett.
Tales of the Argonauts, and Other Sketches. B. Harte.
Tales of the Chesapeake. G. A. Townsend.
Tales of the Cloister. E. G. Jordan.
Tales of the Genii; or, The Delightful Lessons of Horam, the Son of Asmar. J. K. Ridley.
Talfourd, Thomas Noon (ed.): see C. Lamb, *Works of Charles Lamb*.
Talisman. W. Scott.
Talking Woman (Monologues). M. I. T. Fisk.
Tallahassee Girl. J. M. Thompson.
Talleyrand-Périgord, C. M.: see
 T. B. Aldrich, *Cloth of Gold and Other Poems* (Catalog entry).
 G. O. Trevelyan, *Life and Letters of Lord Macaulay* (marginalia).
Tallis, Thomas (composer): see A. Steele, "O for a sweet, inspiring ray."
Tall tales: see E. H. Mott, *Old Settler and His Tales of Sugar Swamp*.
Talmage, Thomas De Witt: see
 F. M. Trollope, *Domestic Manners of the Americans* (marginalia).
 C. Wesley, "Son of the Carpenter! receive" (hymn) (Catalog entry).
Talmud: see S. Baring-Gould, *Legends of Old Testament Characters*.
Tamayo y Baus, Manuel: see W. D. Howells (adapt.), *Yorick's Love* (play).
Taming of the Shrew (play). W. Shakespeare.
Tammany Hall politics: see
 T. A. Janvier, *Women's Conquest of New York; Being an Account of the Rise and Progress of the Women's Rights Movement*.
 John Van Buren, Politician; A Novel of To-day.
 Omar Khayyám, *One Hundred Quatrains* (Catalog entry).
 A. B. Paine, *Th. Nast, His Period and His Pictures*.
 J. D. Townsend, *New York in Bondage*.
 W. Shakespeare, *Richard III* (play) (Catalog entry).
 See also the Reader's Guide entry for New York City.
"Tam O'Shanter's Ride" (poem). R. Burns.
Tancred; or, The New Crusade. B. Disraeli.
Tankerville, Ford Grey, First earl of: see A. A. Behn, *Love-Letters Between a Nobleman and His Sister*.
Tannhäuser (opera). R. Wagner.
Taper Lights. E. B. Sherman.
"Ta-ra-ra-boom-de-ay!" (song). H. J. Sayers.

Tarbell, Ida Minerva: see C. B. Todd, *History of Redding, Connecticut*.
Targioni-Tozzetti, Giovanni (libretto): see P. Mascagni, *Cavalleria Rusticana* (opera).
Tariff Reform, the Paramount Issue. Speeches and Writings on the Questions Involved in the Presidential Contest of 1892. W. M. Springer.
Tariffs: see the Reader's Guide entry for Economics and labor issues.
Tarry Thou Till I Come; or, Salathiel, The Wandering Jew. G. Croly.
Tasistro, Louis Fitzgerald (trans.): see L.-P.-A.-d' O. Paris, *History of the Civil War in America*.
Tasmania: see
 J. Bonwick, *Lost Tasmanian Race*.
 R. B. Smyth, *Aborigines of Victoria: With Notes Relating to the Habits of the Natives of OtherParts of Australia and Tasmania*.
Tasso, Bernardo: see L. Hunt, *Stories from the Italian Poets. (First Series) Dante Alighieri, With Critical Notices of the Life and Genius of the Author; (Second Series) Bernardo Tasso and Ludovico Giovanni Ariosto, With Critical Notices of the Lives and Genius of the Authors*.
Tatham, John: see *Dramatists of the Restoration*.
Tatius (Achilles): see *Greek Romances of Heliodorus, Longus, and Achilles Tatius*.
"Tausendmarkschein" (story). H. Seidel.
Tavern Club: see M. A. D. Howe, *Shadows* (Catalog entry).
Taylor, Ann (co-author): see J. Taylor, *Little Ann*.
Taylor, Bayard: see
 (trans.) J. W. von Goethe, *Faust*.
 (trans.) J. W. von Goethe, *Illustrations to Goethe's Faust*.
 E. C. E. M. S. Wortley, *Travels in the United States, Etc., During 1849 and 1850* (marginalia).
Taylor, Charles Jay: see
 (co-illus.) H. C. Bunner, *Three Operettas*.
 (illus.) W. Fish, *Short Rations*.
 (illus.) C. D. Stewart, *Partners of Providence* (novel).
Taylor, Frank Walter (illus.): see A. R. C. Troubetzkoy, *Trix and Over-the-Moon*.
Taylor, James B. (composer): see C. F. Hoffman, "Sparkling and Bright."
Taylor, Susannah: see J. A. D.-G. Ross, *Three Generations of English Women*.
Taylor, William Cooke (contr.): see J. Swift, *Gulliver's Travels into Several Remote Nations of the World*.
Teach, Edmund (pirate): see C. Ellms, *Pirates Own Book; or, Authentic Narratives of the Lives, Exploits, and Executions of the Most Celebrated Sea Robbers*.
Teaching methods: see
 J. Adams, *Herbartian Psychology Applied to Education, Being a Series of Essays Applying the Psychology of Johann Friedrich Herbart*.
 C. E. Beecher, *Religious Training of Children in the School, the Family, and the Church*.
 C. A. Bristed, *Five Years in an English University*.
 M. E. Burt, *Literary Landmarks: A Guide to Good Reading for Young People, and Teachers' Assistant*.
 S. C. Coleridge, *Memoir and Letters of Sara Coleridge* (Catalog entry).

E. V. De Graff, *School-Room Guide*.

E. Eggleston, *Hoosier Schoolmaster: A Story of Back-woods Life in Indiana*.

F. Gouin, *Art of Teaching and Studying Languages*.

W. T. Harris, *First Reader*.

W. Irving, *Sketch-Book of Geoffrey Crayon, Gent*.

C. B. Le Row, *"Young Idea"; or, Common School Culture*.

M. T. P. Mann, *Moral Culture of Infancy, and Kinder-garten Guide*.

W. Riddle, *Nicholas Comenius; or Ye Pennsylvania Schoolmaster of Ye Olden Time*.

J. W. Sanborn, *Method of Teaching the Elements of the Latin Language as Employed at Phillips Academy, Exeter, New Hampshire*.

T. Wright, *Homes of Other Days: A History of Domestic Manners and Sentiments in England, from the Earliest Known Period to Modern Times*.

See also the Reader's Guide entry for School textbooks.

Teaching of Jesus. L. N. Tolstoy.

Technique of Speech. E. D. D. Jones.

Technique of the Novel: The Elements of the Art, Their Evolution and Present Use. C. F. Horne.

Tegnér, Esaias: see R. B. Anderson, *Viking Tales of the North*.

Telepathy: see

L. M. Alcott, *Moods* (novel).

I. Bacheller, *The Master of Silence. A Romance*.

N. C. Flammarion, *Inconnu. The Unknown*.

M. J. Savage, *Can Telepathy Explain? Results of Psychical Research*.

A. M. C. Seemüller, *Emily Chester. A Novel*.

See also the Reader's Guide entries for Mysticism and for Parapsychology.

Telescopes: see

N. C. Flammarion, *Wonders of Optics*.

See also the Reader's Guide entry for Astronomy.

Tell, William: see

J. S. Knowles, *William Tell* (play).

G. A. Rossini, *Guillaume Tell* (opera).

J. C. F. von Schiller, *Wilhelm Tell, Schauspiel*.

"Temblor Muy Terrible" (poem): see W. F. Stewart, *Pleasant Hours in an Eventful Life*.

Temperaments (psychological classifications): see

E. C. Beall (Catalog entry).

T. M. Coan, *Ounces of Prevention*.

Galaxy. An Illustrated Magazine of Entertaining Reading.

W. James, *Varieties of Religious Experience; A Study in Human Nature* (marginalia).

W. L. Phelps, *Essays on Modern Novelists* (marginalia).

E. Robins, *Open Question; A Tale of Two Temperaments*.

G. S. Weaver, *Lectures on Mental Science According to the Philosophy of Phrenology*.

Temperance literature: see

S. H. Adams, "Great American Fraud: The Scavengers" (article).

T. S. Arthur (Catalog entry).

E. J. Bliss, *Peril of Oliver Sargent*.

R. O. Cross, *Suffering Millions* (novel).

G. W. Deeping, *Woman's War; A Novel*.

M. A. Dodge, *Skirmishes and Sketches*.

G. P. Goff, *Nick Baba's Last Drink and Other Sketches*.

O. W. Holmes, "Ode for a Social Meeting, with Slight Alterations by a Tee-totaler" (poem).

Mrs. O. A. Powers, *High-Toned Sprees: A Series of Temperance Legends*.

Mrs. O. A. Powers, *Maple Dell of '76*.

L. H. H. Sigourney, *Sketches*.

J. G. C. Swisshelm, *Half a Century* (Catalog entry).

C. Tacitus, *Works of Tacitus* (Catalog entry).

T. Taylor, *Bottle: A Drama in Two Acts*.

Temperance Advocate.

M. M. Whiteside, *Mizpah; or, Drifting Away, by Mrs. M. McCullen Whiteside, ("Muriel")*.

C. F. Woolson, *Jupiter Lights; A Novel*.

See also the Reader's Guide entries for Drunkenness and for Liquor.

Tempest (play). W. Shakespeare.

"Tempest Rages" (song): see G. A. Stevens, "Storm" (song).

Temple Church and Chapel of St. Ann, Etc.: An Historical Record and Guide. T. H. Baylis.

Temple Shakespeare. W. Shakespeare.

Temple, William: see

L. Cornaro, *Art of Living Long* (includes a Temple essay).

D. O. Temple, *Love Letters of Dorothy Osborne to Sir William Temple, 1652–54*.

"Templeton" (pseud.): see G. H. Munroe.

Ten Boys from History. K. D. Swettser.

Ten Days a Newsboy. J. O. Kaler.

"Ten Days' Sport on Salmon Rivers" (essay). D. Sage.

Ten Months A Captive among Filipinos; Being a Narrative of Adventure and Observation During Imprisonment on the Island of Luzon, P. I. A. Sonnichsen.

Tennessee: see

Laws of Tennessee.

M. N. Murfree, *Down the Ravine*.

M. N. Murfree, *In the Tennessee Mountains*.

M. N. Murfee, *Prophet of the Great Smoky Mountains*.

M. N. Murfree, *"Stranger People's" Country*.

C. D. Stewart, *Fugitive Blacksmith* (novel).

"Tennessee's Partner" (short story). B. Harte.

Tenniel, John (illus.): see C. L. Dodgson, *Through the Looking-Glass, and What She Found There*.

Ten Nights in a Bar-Room, and What I Saw There: see T. S. Arthur (Catalog entry).

Tennis: see J. Dwight, *Practical Lawn Tennis*.

Tennyson, Alfred Lord: see

W. Allingham, *William Allingham, A Diary*.

M. D. Conway, *Autobiography: Memories and Experiences of Moncure Daniel Conway* (Catalog entry).

M. D. Conway, "Laureate Despair, A Discourse."

J. McCarthy, *Portraits of the Sixties*.

T. Malory, *Morte Darthur* (Catalog entry).

W. Scott, *Lay of the Last Minstrel* (poem) (Catalog entry).

Selected Poems, Illustrated.

W. Shakespeare, *Works of Shakespeare* (Catalog entry).

H. Tennyson, *Alfred, Lord Tennyson; A Memoir by His Son.*

H. Van Dyke (ed.), *Little Masterpieces of English Poetry, by British and American Authors.*

A. Waugh, *Alfred, Lord Tennyson: A Study of His Life and Work.*

Tennyson's Suppressed Poems, Now for the First Time Collected. A. Tennyson.

Tent Dwellers. A. B. Paine.

Ten Thousand Wonderful Things; Comprising the Marvelous and Rare, Odd, Curious, Quaint, Eccentric, and Extraordinary in All Ages and Nations. E. F. King (ed.).

Ten Times One Is Ten, and Other Stories. E. E. Hale.

Tenting on the Plains; or, General Custer in Kansas and Texas. E. B. Custer.

Tent Life in Siberia, and Adventures Among the Koraks and Other Tribes in Kamtchatka and Northern Asia. G. Kennan.

Tent Life in the Holy Land. W. C. Prime.

Ten to Seventeen; A Boarding-School Diary. J. D. D. Bacon.

Terhune, Mary Virginia (Hawes) (ed.): see A. E. Trumbull, "Mary A. Twining."

Terre. É. Zola.

Terrible Temptation: see C. Reade, *Peg Woffington, Christie Johnstone, and Other Stories.*

"Terrifiante histoire de mes dents" (story). M. Schwob.

Tesla, Nikola: see T. C. Martin, "Nikola Tesla" (article).

Testimony of the Rocks; or, Geology in its Bearings on the Two Theologies, Natural and Revealed. H. Miller.

"Test Readings of Mark Twain's Hands" (article). W. T. Stead.

Teuffel, Blanche Willis (Howard), Baroness von: see the Catalog entries for B. W. Howard.

Tewkesbury, England: see the Catalog entry for Tewkesbury. *Official Guide to Tewkesbury.*

Texas: see

E. B. Custer, *Tenting on the Plains; or, General Custer in Kansas and Texas.*

C. E. Lester, *Life of Sam Houston (The Only Authentic Memoir of Him Ever Published).*

A. H. Lewis, *Wolfville Days.*

A. H. Lewis, *Wolfville Nights.*

E. P. Lyle, *Lone Star.*

H. C. Morse, *Cowboy Cavalier.*

A. B. Paine, *Captain Bill McDonald, Texas Ranger. A Story of Frontier Reform.*

A. E. Sweet, *On a Mexican Mustang, through Texas, from the Gulf to the Rio Grande.*

C. B. Wakefield (Catalog entry).

Text-book of Geometry. G. A. Wentworth.

Textbook on Harmony. P. I. Tchaikovsky.

Thackeray, William Makepeace: see

J. Brown, *Letters of Dr. John Brown, with Letters from Ruskin, Thackeray, and Others.*

C. Lamb, *Works of Charles Lamb* (Catalog entry).

H. C. Merivale and F. T. Marzials, *Life of W. M. Thackeray.*

J. Payn, *Some Literary Recollections.*

F. H. Smith, *Peter: A Novel of Which He Is Not the Hero* (Catalog entry).

T. G. Smollett, *Expedition of Humphry Clinker* (novel) (Catalog entry).

W. Temple, "Upon the Gardens of Epicurus" (essay) (Catalog entry).

J. Swift, *Gulliver's Travels into Several Remote Nations of the World* (Catalog entry).

Thackeray's Complete Works. W. M. Thackeray.

Thackeray's Lectures. The English Humorists. The Four Georges. Complete in One Volume. W. M. Thackeray.

Thaddeus of Warsaw. J. Porter.

Thailand: see the Reader's Guide entry for Siam.

"Thanatopsis" (poem). W. C. Bryant.

"Thanatopsis" (poem): see V. Streamer (comp.), *Voices of Doubt and Trust.*

"Thanet, Octave" (pseud.): see A. French.

Thankful Blossom (short story). B. Harte.

That Affair in Philadelphia. S. Darby.

That Artful Vicar: The Story of What a Clergyman Tried to Do for Others and Did for Himself. E. C. G. Murray.

That Beautiful Wretch; A Brighton Story. W. Black.

That Convention; or, Five Days a Politician. F. G. Welch.

That Lass O'Lowrie's. F. H. Burnett.

Theater: see the Reader's Guide entry for Theatrical history.

Theatrical history: see

F. Coppée, *Rivals.*

C. W. Dilke (ed.) *Old English Plays; Being a Selection from the Early Dramatic Writers.*

R. Grau, *Forty Years Observation of Music and the Drama by Robert Grau.*

M. Kelly, *Reminiscences of Michael Kelly, of the King's Theatre, and Theatre Royal Drury Lane.*

W. C. Macready, *Macready's Reminiscences, and Selections from His Diaries and Letters.*

B. Matthews, *Studies of the Stage.*

W. C. Russell, *Representative Actors. A Collection of Criticisms, Anecdotes, Personal Descriptions, Etc., Etc., Referring to Many Celebrated British Actors from the Sixteenth to the Present Century.*

See also the Reader's Guide entries for American drama and for English drama.

Theatrical Journey—Work and Anecdotical Recollections of Sol Smith. S. F. Smith.

Their First Formal Call. G. M. Cooke.

Their Husbands' Wives. W. D. Howells (co-ed.).

Their Pilgrimage (novel). C. D. Warner.

Their Silver Wedding Journey (novel). W. D. Howells.

Their Wedding Journey (novel). W. D. Howells.

"Theologian's Tale": see "Legend Beautiful" in *Tales of a Wayside Inn.* H. W. Longfellow.

Theology and science: see Science and religion

Theophano: The Crusade of the Tenth Century; A Novel. F. Harrison.

Theophrastus (character): see J. de La Bruyère, *Characters, or The Manners of the Age, with the Character of Theophrastus.*

Theory of the Modern Scientific Game of Whist. W. Pole.

Theosophy: see

R. Blatchford, *Merrie England* (Catalog entry).

H. S. Olcott, *People from the Other World.*

R. Seeberg, *Revelation and Inspiration.*

A. E. S. Smythe, *Poems, Grave and Gay.*
"There is a boarding-house far, far away' (adapted song):
see
    D. H. Morrison (comp.), *Treasury of Song for the
    Home Circle: The Richest, Best-Loved Gems, Sacred
    and Secular* (marginalia).
    F. B. Ogilvie (comp.), *Two Hundred Old-Time Songs,
    Containing the Words and Music of the Choicest Gems
    of the Old and Familiar Songs* (marginalia).
    A. Young, "There is a happy land" (hymn).
"There is a happy land" (hymn). A. Young.
"There was a row in Silver Street": see R. Kipling, *Depart-
    mental Ditties, Barrack-Room Ballads.*
Thesaurus of English Words and Phrases. P. M. Roget.
"They" (short story). R. Kipling.
"They stole, they stole my child away": see "I hear the
    hoofs, or the lost child" (minstrel song).
Thibaw's Queen. H. Fielding-Hall.
*Things Korean; A Collection of Sketches and Anecdotes, Mis-
    sionary and Diplomatic.* H. N. Allen.
Things Not Generally Known, Familiarly Explained. J.
    Timbs.
Things Seen. V. Hugo.
*Third Annual Report of the Bureau of American Ethnology
    to the Secretary of the Smithsonian Institution, 1879–
    1880.* J. W. Powell.
*Thirty Years of Army Life on the Border, Comprising
    Descriptions of the Indian Nomads of the Plains.* R. B.
    Marcy.
Thirty Years' War: see
    S. R. Gardiner, *Thirty Years' War, 1618–1648.*
    A. Gindely, *Geschichte des dreissigjährigen Krieges.*
"This Spray of Western Pine." L. B. P. Lardner.
"This World Is All a Fleeting Show" (poem). T. Moore.
Th. Nast, His Period and His Pictures. A. B. Paine.
"Thomas Atkins" (poem): see R. Kipling, "Tommy."
"Thomas Bailey Aldrich" (biographical sketch). W. D.
    Howells.
*Thomas Carlyle: A History of His Life in London, 1834–
    1881.* J. A. Froude.
*Thomas Carlyle: A History of the First Forty Years of His
    Life, 1795–1835.* J. A. Froude.
Thomas, E. (composer): see F. W. Thomas, "'Tis Said
    That Absence Conquers Love" (poem, song).
Thomas Gray. E. W. Gosse.
Thomas Wingfold, Curate. G. MacDonald.
Thompson, Eben Francis (trans.): see Omar Khayyám,
    Quatrains of Omar Khayyám of Nishapur.
Thomson, Alexander (trans.): see Suetonius, *Lives of the
    Twelve Caesars* (marginalia).
Thomson, Hugh (illus.): see J. L. Allen, *Aftermath; Part
    Second of "A Kentucky Cardinal."*
Thomson, John (composer): see W. Kennedy, "Pirate's
    serenade" (song).
Thomson, Joseph Charles (ed.): see A. Tennyson, *Tenny-
    son's Suppressed Poems, Now for the First Time Collected.*
Thoreau, Henry David: see D. Sage, "Ten Days' Sport on
    Salmon Rivers" (Catalog entry).
"Thorne, Olive" (pseud.): see H. M. Miller.
"Those Evening Bells" (poem, parody). T. Hood.
"Those Evening Bells" (poem). T. Moore.

*Thoughts for Every-Day Living from the Spoken and Written
    Words of Maltbie Davenport Babcock.* M. D. Babcock.
*Thoughts from Maeterlinck, Chosen and Arranged by E. S.
    S. M. Maeterlinck.*
Thoughts in Verse. I. M. Freeland.
Thoughts of a Fool. H. Kuehn.
"Thou hast wounded the spirit that loved thee" (song). E.
    A. Porter.
"Thou say'st 'Take up thy cross'" (hymn): see G. J. Geer
    (Catalog entry).
Thousand and One Nights: see *Arabian Nights.*
Thousand Miles Up the Nile. A. A. B. Edwards.
*Three English Statesmen: A Course of Lectures on the Politi-
    cal History of England.* G. Smith.
Three Generations of English Women. J. A. D.-G. Ross.
Three Kings of Orient. J. H. Hopkins.
Three Men in a Boat (To Say Nothing of the Dog). J. K.
    Jerome.
Three Musketeers: see A. Dumas, *Novels.*
"Three Musketeers" (short story). R. Kipling: see R.
    Kipling, *Plain Tales from the Hills.*
Three Operettas. H. C. Bunner.
Three Plays of Shakespeare. A. C. Swinburne.
*Three Types of Washington Portraits: John Trumbull, Charles
    Wilson Peale, Gilbert Stuart.* C. A. Munn.
Three Visits to Knock. M. F. Cusack.
*Three Visits to Madagascar During the Years 1853–1854-
    1856.* W. Ellis.
Three Weeks (novel). E. S. Glyn.
Three Years in the Federal Cavalry. W. Glazier.
"Threnody" (poem). G. T. Lanigan.
Thrift. S. Smiles.
Thrilling Days in Army Life. G. A. Forsyth.
Thring, George Herbert (contributor): see W. Besant, *Pen
    and the Book.*
Thring, Sarah Eliza (ed., intro.): see
    E. Thring, *Addresses.*
    E. Thring, *Poems and Translations.*
    E. Thring, *Uppingham School Songs and Borth Lyrics.*
Through a Peer Glass: Winnie's Adventures in Wastemonster.
    A. C. Waghorne.
*Through the Air: A Narrative of Forty Years' Experience as
    an Aeronaut.* J. Wise.
*Through the Dark Continent; or, The Sources of the Nile,
    Around the Great Lakes of Equatorial Africa, and Down
    the Livingstone River to the Atlantic Ocean.* H. M.
    Stanley.
Through the Eye of the Needle: A Romance. W. D. Howells.
Through the Looking-Glass. C. L. Dodgson.
Thuggee (India): see
    T. B. Macaulay, "Essay on Warren Hastings" (Catalog
    entry).
    W. H. Sleeman, *Report on the Depredations Committed
    by the Thug Gangs of Upper and Central India.*
    W. H. Sleeman, *Thugs or Phansigars of India; Compris-
    ing a History of the Rise and Progress of That Extraor-
    dinary Fraternity of Assassins.*
    E. Sue, *Wandering Jew.*
*Thugs or Phansigars of India; Comprising a History of the
    Rise and Progress of That Extraordinary Fraternity of As-
    sassins.* W. H. Sleeman.

Thulstrup, Bror Thure de (illus.): see G. Croly, *Tarry Thou Till I Come; or, Salathiel, The Wandering Jew.*

Thunder storms: see the Reader's Guide entry for Lightning.

Thunder and Lightning. W. de Fonvielle.

Thus Spake Zarathustra. F. W. Nietzsche.

"Thy corn-fields green, and sunny vines" (poem line): see T. B. Macaulay, *Lays of Ancient Rome.*

Tia Finginda: see M. de Cervantes Saavedra, *Exemplary Novels of Miguel de Cerantes Saavedra.*

Tibbitts, Mabel (illus.): see E. K. Gibson, *Zauberlinda, the Wise Witch.*

Tibullus, Albius: see the Catalog entry for G. V. Catullus, *Works of Catullus and Tibullus.*

Tibet: see

   É. R. Huc, *Recollections of a Journey Through Tartary, Thibet, and China, During the Years 1844, 1845, and 1846.*

   C. P. Jones and A. L. Sykes, *Banduk jaldi banduk!: (Quick, My Rifle!).*

   E. F. Knight, *Where Three Empires Meet: A Narrative of Recent Travel in Kashmir, Western Tibet, Gilgit, and the Adjoining Countries.*

   H. M. Miller, *Little People of Asia.*

Tichborne claimant: see

   B. Franklin, *Life of Benjamin Franklin, Written by Himself* (marginalia).

   G. G. Greenwood, *Shakespeare Problem Restated* (marginalia).

   London *Standard* (London).

   Memories of Westminster Hall; A Collection of Interesting Incidents, Anecdotes, and Historical Sketches Relating to Westminster Hall.

Tideric, Owen: see *Life and Amours of Owen Tideric, Prince of Wales, Otherwise Owen Tudor* (novel).

Tiffany, Louis C. & Co.: see (designer) M. D. Brine, *My Boy and I; or, On the Road to Slumberland.*

Tille, Alexander (trans.): see F. W. Nietzsche, *Thus Spake Zarathustra; A Book for All and None.*

Tillinghast, William Hopkins (trans.): see K. J. Ploetz, *Epitome of Ancient, Mediaeval, and Modern History.*

Tilton, Caroline (trans.): see E. De Amicis, *Holland and Its People.*

Tilton, Elizabeth: see

   Beecher Trial: A Review of the Evidence.

   J. Swift, *Gulliver's Travels into Several Remote Nations of the World* (Catalog entry).

Timber (notes and reflections). B. Jonson.

Timbs, John (pref.): see *Percy Anecdotes.*

"Timed to an African Chant" (poem). R. M. Jonas.

Time Machine. H. G. Wells.

Timothy's Quest: A Story for Anybody, Young or Old, Who Cares to Read It. K. D. S. Wiggin.

"Tim Rafferty's Romance: A Story of Christmas among 'The Finest'" (short story). R. E. MacAlarney.

Tinkletop's Crime, and Other Stories. G. R. Sims.

Tintoretto: see W. Lübke, *Outlines of the History of Art* (marginalia).

Tischendorf, Constantin von: see C. E. Stowe, *Origin and History of the Books of the Bible, Both the Canonical and the Apocryphal* (Catalog entry).

"'Tis Only My Husband" (sketch): see J. C. Neal, *Charcoal Sketches; or, Scenes in a Metropolis.*

"'Tis Said That Absence Conquers Love" (poem). F. W. Thomas.

"'Tis the last rose of summer" (song). T. Moore.

"Titcomb, Timothy" (pseud.): see J. G. Holland.

"Titmarsh, M. A." (pseud.): see W. M. Thackeray.

Titus Andronicus (play). W. Shakspeare.

Toads: see M. C. Dickerson, *Frog Book: North American Toads and Frogs.*

"To a Mouse" (poem). R. Burns.

"To an Absent One" (poem). W. Mungen. See also the Catalog entry for "Pop! goes the weasel" (children's song).

"To Annette" (poem). R. Richardson.

Tobacco: see

   L. Beecher, *Autobiography, Correspondence, Etc.*

   E. L. Beers, "Picket-Guard" (poem, song).

   F. M. Finch, "Smoking Song" (poem).

   R. Herrick (Catalog entry).

   C. F. Hoffman, "Sparkling and Bright" (poem, song).

   H. J. Meller, *Nicotiana; or, the Smoker's and Snuff-Taker's Companion: Containing the History of Tobacco.*

   W. Raleigh (Catalog entry).

   J. H. Trumbull (ed.), *True-Blue Laws of Connecticut and New Haven* (marginalia).

   P. Villari, *Life and Times of Niccolò Machiavelli* (marginalia).

   World of Wonders; A Record of Things Wonderful in Nature, Science, and Art.

   E. C. E. M. S. Wortley, *Travels in the United States, Etc., During 1849 and 1850* (marginalia).

Toby Tyler; or, Ten Weeks with a Circus. J. O. Kaler.

Tocci, Giacomo and Giovanni (conjoined twins): see *Scientific American.*

To Cuba and Back. R. H. Dana.

Togo, Hashimura (pseud.): see W. Irwin.

"To Helen" (poem). E. A. Poe.

Toilers of the Sea. V. Hugo.

Tokyo (city): see E. Greey, *Wonderful City of Tokio; or, Further Adventures of the Jewett Family and Their Friend Oto Nambo.*

Tomalyn's Quest, A Novel. G. B. Burgin.

"To Mark Twain" (poem). L. J. Bridgman.

"To Mark Twain" (poem). J. A. Kirlicks.

"To Mark Twain,/'First Missourian,'/of Hannibal" (poem): see R. Love, *Poems All the Way from Pike.*

"To Mark Twain" (poem): see J. Sadler, *Lyrics and Rhymes.*

Tomboy at Work. J. L. Gilder.

Tom Brown at Oxford. T. Hughes.

Tom Brown's School Days. T. Hughes.

Tom Cringle's Log. M. Scott.

Tom Jones. H. Fielding.

To-morrow in Cuba. C. M. Pepper.

"Tommy" (poem). R. Kipling.

Tom Tad. W. H. Venable.

Tonga: see B. H. Thomson, *Diversions of a Prime Minister.*

Tongue-Cut Sparrow: see *Shitakiri Suzume.*

Tony, the Maid; A Novelette.

Toodles. A Domestic Drama in Two Acts. R. J. Raymond and W. E. Burton.

Toodles (play): see T. W. S. Higginson, *Cheerful Yesterdays. Contemporaries* (marginalia).

"Too Late" (poem): see D. M. M. Craik, *Poems*.

Topcliffe: see W. Smith (ed.), *Registers of Topcliffe, and Morley in the W. R. of the County of York. Baptisms, 1654–1830. Burials, 1654–1888.*

Toppleton's Client; or, A Spirit in Exile. J. K. Bangs.

"To R. K." (poem): see J. K. Stephen, *Lapsus Calami*.

Torrents of Spring (novel). I. S. Turgenev.

Torture and punishment: see

G. Casanova de Seingalt, *Mémoires de Jacques Casanova de Seingalt, Écrits par lui-même*.

R. I. Dodge, *Our Wild Indians: Thirty-Three Years' Personal Experience among the Red Men of the Great West*.

R. I. Dodge, *Plains of the Great West and Their Inhabitants, Being a Description of the Plains, Game, Indians, &c. of the Great North American Desert*.

J. P. Dunne, *Massacres of the Mountains: A History of the Indian Wars of the Far West*.

H. D. Labouchère (editor of *Truth: A Weekly Journal*).

A. Manning, *Passages in the Life of the Faire Gospeller Mistress Anne Askew*.

New York *Tribune* (Catalog entry).

M. W. Townsend, *Asia and Europe: Studies* (marginalia).

J. H. Trumbull (ed.), *True-Blue Laws of Connecticut and New Haven* (marginalia).

Truth: A Weekly Journal.

T. Wright, *Homes of Other Days: A History of Domestic Manners and Sentiments in England, from the Earliest Known Period to Modern Times*.

See also the Reader's Guide entries for Prison and dungeon literature and for Witchcraft.

Tory's Guest (play). V. Mapes.

Tosca (opera). G. Puccini.

"Total Depravity of Inaninate Things" (sketch). K. K. C. Walker.

To the Credit of the Sea (short stories). L. Mott.

"To the Czar." L. M. Sill.

To the Front; A Sequel to Cadet Days. C. King.

"To Thomas Atkins" (poem): see R. Kipling, "Tommy."

"To Thomas Moore" (poem). G. G. Byron.

Tour Around New York, and My Summer Acre; Being the Recreations of Mr. Felix Oldboy. J. F. Miles.

Tourist; Outward and Homeward Bound. E. Furth.

Tourists' Guide Through the Hawaiian Islands, Descriptive of Their Scenes and Scenery. H. M. Whitney.

Tournaments: see the Reader's Guide entry for Knights.

Tour of the World in Eighty Days (novel). J. Verne.

Tour Through the Pyrenees. H. A. Taine.

Towards the Gulf; A Romance of Louisiana. A. M. Buckner.

Towle, George M. (trans.): see J. Verne, *Tour of the World in Eighty Days* (novel).

Town; Its Memorable Characters and Events. L. Hunt.

Townsend, Frederick Henry (illus.): see S. J. D. Cotes, *American Girl in London*.

Townsend, Harry (illus.): see W. F. Payson, *Barry Gordon*.

Townshend, Dorothea (Baker) (co-author): see R. B. Townshend, *Bride of a Day*.

Towry, M. H. (ed.): see E. Spenser, *Spenser for Children*.

Toymaker of Nuremberg; A Play. A. Strong.

Traffics and Discoveries. R. Kipling.

Tragedy of Anne Boleyn. A Drama in Cipher Found in the Works of Sir Francis Bacon. E. W. Gallup.

Tragedy of a Nose. E. Gerard.

Tragedy of Julius Caesar (play): W. Shakespeare.

Tragic octoroon (theme): see

D. Boucicault, *Octoroon; or, Life in Louisiana* (play).

M. Reid, *Quadroon; or, A Lover's Adventures in Louisiana*.

J. T. Trowbridge, *Neighbor Jackwood*.

Trail of the Lonesome Pine. J. Fox, Jr.

Trail of the Serpent. M. E. Braddon.

Tramping with Tramps: Studies and Sketches of Vagabond Life. J. F. Willard.

Tramps: see the Reader's Guide entry for Vagrancy.

"Tramp! Tramp! Tramp!" (song). G. F. Root.

"Translation from the German" (poems). J. Sterne.

Transmigration of Souls. A. Bertholet.

Transplanted Rose; A Story of New York Society. M. E. Sherwood.

Trapping: see the Reader's Guide entry for Hunting literature.

Travail. É. Zola.

Traveler from Altruria. W. D. Howells.

Traveler's Manual. K. Baedeker.

Travelers Record (periodical): see F. Morgan.

Travel guidebooks: see

K. Baedeker, *Austria, Including Hungary, Transylvania, Dalmatia, and Bosnia*.

K. Baedeker, *Italy. Handbook for Travellers*.

K. Baedeker, *London and Its Environs. Handbook for Travellers*.

K. Baedeker, *Paris and Its Environs. Handbook for Travellers*.

K. Baedeker, *Rhine from Rotterdam to Constance. Handbook for Travellers*.

K. Baedeker, *Switzerland and the Adjacent Portions of Italy, Savoy, and the Tyrol. Handbook for Travellers*.

K. Baedeker, *Traveller's Manual of Conversation, in Four Languages: English, French, German, Italian*.

T. H. Baylis, *Temple Church and Chapel of St. Ann, Etc.: An Historical Record and Guide*.

S. M. Burrows, *Buried Cities of Ceylon: A Guide Book*.

S. A. Drake, *Heart of the White Mountains, Their Legend and Scenery*.

Galignani's New Paris Guide for 1867.

Handbook for Travellers in Ireland.

Hand-Book of Florence and Environs with Views, A Topographical Plan and the Catalogues of Galleries.

A. J. C. Hare, *Walks in London*.

A. J. C. Hare, *Walks in Rome*.

Harper's Chicago and the World's Fair. J. Ralph.

Harper's Handbook for Travelers in Europe and the East. W. P. Fetridge.

S. Horner and S. B. Horner, *Walks in Florence and Its Environs*.

S. C. Mukerji, *Traveller's Guide to Agra, Containing an*

Account of the Past History, the Antiquities, and the Principal Sights of Agra.

J. Murray, *Handbook for North Germany, from the Baltic to the Black Forest, and the Rhine, from Holland to Basle.*

J. Murray, *Handbook for Travellers in Spain.*

J. Murray, *Handbook for Travellers in Switzerland and the Alps of Savoy and Piedmont.*

J. Murray, *Handbook for Travellers in Syria and Palestine.*

F. Palgrave, *Handbook for Travellers in Northern Italy.*

G. F. Pardon, *Routledge's Guide to London and Its Suburbs.*

A. Parker, *Hand-Book of Benares.*

Tewkesbury. *Official Guide to Tewkesbury.*

W. Wakefield, *Baths, Bathing, and Attractions of Aix-les-Bains, Savoy.*

See also the Reader's Guide entry for Travel writings.

Travel handbooks: see the Reader's Guide entry for Travel guidebooks.

Traveling Thirds. G. F. H. Atherton.

Traveller from Altruria (novel). W. D. Howells.

Travellers and Outlaws, Episodes in American History. T. W. S. Higginson.

Travellers' Colloquial Italian. A Handbook for English-Speaking Travellers and Students. H. Swan.

Traveller's Guide to Agra, Containing an Account of the Past History, the Antiquities, and the Principal Sights of Agra. S. C. Mukerji.

Travellers in Northern Italy. F. Palgrave.

Traveller's Manual of Conversation, in Four Languages: English, French, German, Italian. K. Baedeker.

Travels in Greece and Russia. B. Taylor.

Travels in India. J. B. Tavernier.

Travels in North America During the Years 1834, 1835 & 1836. C. A. Murray.

Travels in North America, in the Years 1827 and 1828. B. Hall.

Travels in the United States, Etc., During 1849 and 1850. E. C. E. M. S. Wortley.

Travels of a Lady's Maid. By "A. B." C. P. Stokes.

Travels of Anacharsis the Younger in Greece. J. J. Barthélemy.

Travels of Two Mohamedans Through India and China in the Ninth Century: see A. Z. H. Y. Sîrafi and Al-tājr Sulaymān , *Ancient Accounts of India and China, by Two Mohammedan Travellers.*

Travels on an Inland Voyage [United States]. C. Schultz.

Travels through France and Italy. T. G. Smollett.

Travels with a Donkey in the Cévenees. R. L. Stevenson.

Travel writings: see

Adventures of Famous Travellers in Many Lands, with Descriptions of Manners, Customs, and Places. Thrilling Adventures on Land and Sea.

T. B. Aldrich, *From Ponkapog to Pesth.*

M. M. Ballou, *Under the Southern Cross; or, Travels in Australia, Tasmania, New Zealand, Samoa, and Other Pacific Islands.*

J. T. Barclay, *City of the Great King; or, Jerusalem As It Was, As It Is, and As It Is To Be.*

M. A. Barker, *Station Amusements in New Zealand.*

J. J. Barthélemy, *Travels of Anacharsis the Younger in Greece.*

T. B. Batcheller, *Glimpses of Italian Court Life; Happy Days in Italia Adorata.*

S. G. Bayne, *Fantasy of Mediterranean Travel.*

S. G. Bayne, *On a Jaunting-Car Through Donegal and Connemara.*

J. Beerbohm, *Wanderings in Patagonia; or, Life Among the Ostrich-Hunters.*

B. J. Benjamin of Tudela, *Itinerary of Rabbi Benjamin of Tudela.*

L. Biart, *Adventures of a Young Naturalist.*

W. R. Bliss, *Paradise in the Pacific; A Book of Travel, Adventure, and Facts in the Sandwich Islands.*

S. Bonsal, *Morocco As It Is.*

P. Boyton, *Story of Paul Boyton. Voyages on All the Great Rivers of the World.*

J. H. Browne, *Sights and Sensations in Europe: Sketches of Travel and Adventure.*

J. R. Browne, *Crusoe's Island: A Ramble in the Steps of Alexander Selkirk. With Sketches of Adventure in California and Washoe.*

J. R. Browne, *Yusef; or the Journey of the Frangi: A Crusade in the East.*

E. G. Buffum, *Sights and Sensations in France, Germany, and Switzerland.*

R. F. Burton, *Personal Narrative of a Pilgrimage to El-Medinah and Meccah.*

H. Bush, *Harp of the Day; or, The Adventures and Travels of a Photographic Artist; With Other Poems.*

G. L. Carlisle, *Around the World in a Year.*

A. Carnegie, *Round the World.*

J. Chambers, *Destiny of Doris; A Travel-Story of Three Continents.*

T. A. Cook, *Old Touraine: The Life and History of the Famous Chateâux of France.*

S. S. Cox, *Diversions of a Diplomat in Turkey.*

S. S. Cox, *Isles of the Princes; or, The Pleasures of Prinkipo.*

G. W. Curtis, *Howadji in Syria.*

W. E. Curtis, *Capitals of Spanish America.*

C. Darwin, *What Mr. Darwin Saw in His Voyage Round the World in the Ship "Beagle."*

C. Dickens, *Pictures from Italy.*

C. Dickens, *Uncommercial Traveller.*

F. M. Dickinson, *Diary of an Idle Woman in Italy.*

C. W. Dilke, *Greater Britain: A Record of Travel in English-Speaking Countries During 1866 and 1867.*

A. B. Dodd, *Cathedral Days: A Tour in Southern England.*

P. Doré and B. Jerrold, *London: A Pilgrimage.*

A. A. B. Edwards, *Thousand Miles Up the Nile.*

A. A. B. Edwards, *Untrodden Peaks and Unfrequented Valleys. A Midsummer Ramble in the Dolomites.*

W. Ellis, *Three Visits to Madagascar During the Years 1853–1854-1856.*

E. J. Eyre, *Journals of Expeditions of Discovery into Central Australia.*

E. Falkener, *Ephesus and the Temple of Diana.*

W. P. Fetridge, *Harper's Handbook for Travelers in Europe and the East.*

A. L. A. Forbes, *Two Years in Fiji.*

H. W. French, *Our Boys in India: The Wanderings of Two Young Americans in Hindustan.*

E. Furth, *Tourist; Outward and Homeward Bound.*

W. H. Gibson, *Highways and By-ways; or Saunterings in New England.*

E. Gregory, *Narrative of James Murrells' ("Jemmy Morrill") Seventeen Years' Exile among the Wild Blacks of North Queensland, and His Life and Shipwreck and Terrible Adventures among Savage Tribes.*

L. M. R. Griswold, *Woman's Pilgrimage to the Holy Land; or, Pleasant Days Abroad. Being Notes of a Tour Through Europe and the East.*

J. A. Hart, *Levantine Log-Book.*

G. Haven, *Pilgrim's Wallet; or, Scraps of Travel Gathered in England, France, and Germany.*

J. T. Headley (ed.), *Mountain Adventures in Various Parts of the World. Selected from the Narratives of Celebrated Travellers.*

Herodotus, *Stories of the East from Herodotus.*

T. Hood, *Up the Rhine.*

A. Hoppin, *On the Nile.*

A. Hoppin, *Ups and Downs on Land and Water.*

W. D. Howells, *Certain Delightful English Towns, with Glimpses of the Pleasant Country Between.*

W. D. Howells, *Italian Journeys.*

W. D. Howells, *London Films.*

W. D. Howells, *Roman Holidays and Others.*

W. D. Howells, *Seven English Cities.*

W. D. Howells, *Tuscan Cities.*

W. D. Howells, *Venetian Life.*

É. R. Huc, *Recollections of a Journey Through Tartary, Thibet, and China, During the Years 1844, 1845, and 1846.*

J. N. Jackson, *Winter Holiday in Summer Lands.*

H. James, *Little Tour in France.*

A. B. M. Jameson, *Sketches of Art, Literature, and Character.*

T. A. Janvier, *Christmas Kalends of Provence and Some Other Provençal Festivals.*

T. A. Janvier, *Embassy to Provence.*

J. Jefferson, *Autobiography of Joseph Jefferson.*

R. M. Johnston, *Two Gray Tourists: From Papers of Mr. Philemon Perch.*

R. Keeler, *Vagabond Adventures.*

J. D. J. Kelley, *Ship's Company and Other Sea People.*

D. Ker, "From the Sea to the Desert" (article).

D. Ker, "Over the Cossack Steppes" (article).

A. W. Kinglake, *Eōthen.*

R. Kipling, *From Sea to Sea: Letters of Travel.*

E. F. Knight, *Where Three Empires Meet: A Narrative of Recent Travel in Kashmir, Western Tibet, Gilgit, and the Adjoining Countries.*

T. W. Knox, *Backsheesh! or, Life and Adventures in the Orient.*

T. W. Knox, *Boy Travellers in Australasia* [and similar titles].

T. W. Knox. *Overland Through Asia.*

A. M. L. de Lamartine, *Pilgrimage to the Holy Land; Comprising Recollections, Sketches, and Reflections Made During a Tour in the East, in 1832–1833.*

A. H. S. Landor, *Gems of the East; Sixteen Thousand Miles of Research Travel Among Wild and Tame Tribes of Enchanting Islands.*

F. de Lanoye, *Sublime in Nature; Compiled from the Descriptions of Travellers and Celebrated Writers.*

G. A. Lawrence, *Silverland.*

A. H. Layard, *Early Adventures in Persia, Susiana, and Babylonia.*

A. H. Layard, *Nineveh and Its Remains: With an Account of a Visit to the Chaldæan Christians of Kurdistan.*

D. Livingstone and C. Livingstone, *Narrative of an Expedition to the Zambesi and Its Tributaries.*

P. Lowell, *Chosön, The Land of the Morning Calm: A Sketch of Korea.*

A. Mackay, *Western World; or Travels in the United States in 1846–47.*

N. MacLeod, *Eastward.*

J. Mandeville (Catalog entry).

C. T. Marvin, *Russians at the Gates of Herat.*

J. J. Morier, *Adventures of Hajji Baba of Ispahan* (novel).

S. C. Mukerji, *Traveller's Guide to Agra, Containing an Account of the Past History, the Antiquities, and the Principal Sights of Agra.*

E. P. Parker (Catalog entry).

A. Parsons, *Notes in Japan.*

W. A. Paton, *Picturesque Sicily.*

M. C. Perry, *Narrative of the Expedition of an American Squadron to the China Seas and Japan, Performed in the Years 1852, 1853, and 1854.*

W. C. Prime, *Boat Life in Egypt and Nubia.*

W. C. Prime, *Tent Life in the Holy Land.*

E. J. Pullen, *Don Finimondone: Calabrian Sketches.*

R. Pumpelly, *Explorations in Turkestan, with an Account of The Basin of Eastern Persia and Sistan. Expedition of 1903.*

E. A. Reynolds-Ball, *Mediterranean Winter Resorts. A Practical Hand-book to the Principal Health and Pleasure Resorts on the Shores of the Mediterranean.*

H. J. Ross, *Letters from the East by Henry James Ross, 1837–1857.*

L.-T. M. Rousselet, *India and Its Native Princes: Travels in Central India and in the Presidencies of Bombay and Bengal.*

G. A. Sala, *Under the Sun: Essays Mainly Written in Hot Countries.*

G. Sand, *Lettres d'un Voyageur.*

E. Schuyler, *Turkistan; Notes of a Journey in Russian Turkistan, Khokand, Bukhara, and Kuldja.*

C. Scollard, *On Sunny Shores.*

C. Scollard, *Under Summer Skies.*

B. C. Seemann, *Viti: An Account of a Government Mission to the Vitian or Fijian Islands, in the Years 1860–61.*

D. C. Seitz, *Discoveries in Every-day Europe: Vagrant Notes of a Rapid Journey.*

A. Z. H. Y. Sîrafî, *Ancient Accounts of India and China, by Two Mohammedan Travellers.*

W. H. Sleeman, *Journey Through the Kingdom of Oude, in 1849–1850.*

W. H. Sleeman, *Rambles and Recollections of an Indian Official.*

T. G. Smollett, *Travels through France and Italy.*

W. J. Sowden, *Chips from China.*

J. L. Stephens, *Incidents of Travel in Greece, Turkey, Russia, and Poland.*

R. L. Stevenson, *Inland Voyage.*

R. L. Stevenson, *Travels with a Donkey in the Cévenees.*

C. S. Stewart, *Private Journal of a Voyage to the Pacific Ocean and Residence at the Sandwich Islands.*

C. W. Stoddard, *Cruise Under the Crescent; From Suez to San Marco.*

C. W. Stoddard, *South-Sea Idyls.*

J. L. Stoddard, *John L. Stoddard's Lectures.*

C. P. Stokes, *Travels of a Lady's Maid. By "A. B."*

F. A. Stokes, *College Tramps: A Narrative of the Adventures of a Party of Yale Students During a Summer Vacation in Europe, with Knapsack and Alpenstock, and the Incidents of a Voyage to Rotterdam and Return.*

C. Sturt, *Narrative of an Expedition into Central Australia, Performed Under the Authority of Her Majesty's Government, During the Years 1844, 5, and 6. Together with a Notice of the Province of South Australia, in 1847.*

H. A. Taine, *Notes on England.*

H. A. Taine, *Tour Through the Pyrenees.*

J. B. Tavernier, *Travels in India.*

B. Taylor, *At Home and Abroad: A Sketch-Book of Life, Scenery, and Men.*

B. Taylor, *By-Ways of Europe.*

B. Taylor, *Egypt and Iceland in the Year 1874.*

B. Taylor, *Eldorado; or, Adventures in the Path of Empire; Comprising a Voyage to California via Panama, Life in San Francisco and Monterey, Pictures of the Gold Region, and Experiences of Mexico Travel.*

B. Taylor, *Journey to Central Africa; or, Life and Landscapes from Egypt to the Negro Kingdoms of the White Nile.*

B. Taylor, *Lands of the Saracens; or, Pictures of Palestine, Asia Minor, Sicily, and Spain.*

B. Taylor, *Northern Travel: Summer and Winter Pictures of Sweden, Denmark, and Lapland.*

B. Taylor, *Travels in Greece and Russia, with an Excursion to Crete.*

B. Taylor, *Views A-Foot; or, Europe Seen with Knapsack and Staff.*

B. Taylor, *Visit to India, China, and Japan, in the Year 1853.*

B. H. Thomson, *Diversions of a Prime Minister.*

W. M. Thomson, *Central Palestine and Phoenicia.*

W. M. Thomson, *Land and the Book; or, Biblical illustrations Drawn from the Manners and Customs, the Scenes and Scenery, of the Holy Land: Lebanon, Damascus and Beyond Jordan.*

M. von Versen, *Reisen in Amerika und der Südamerikanische krieg.*

F. Vincent, *Land of the White Elephant: Sights and Scenes in South-eastern Asia. A Personal Narrative of Travel and Adventure.*

C. D. Warner, *In the Levant.*

C. D. Warner, *My Winter on the Nile, Among the Mummies and Moslems.*

C. D. Warner, *Roundabout Journey.*

C. D. Warner, *Saunterings.*

C. D. Warner, *Their Pilgrimage* (novel).

M. S. Wellby, *'Twixt Sirdar and Menelik; An Account of a Year's Expedition from Zeila to Cairo Through Unknown Abyssinia.*

C. Whitney, *On Snow-Shoes to the Barren Grounds. Twenty-Eight Hundred Miles After Musk-Oxen and Wood-Bison.*

H. M. Whitney, *Tourists' Guide Through the Hawaiian Islands, Descriptive of Their Scenes and Scenery.*

J. F. Willard, *Tramping with Tramps: Studies and Sketches of Vagabond Life.*

W. Winter, *Gray Days and Gold in England and Scotland.*

W. Winter, *Old Shrines and Ivy.*

W. Winter, *Trip to England.*

T. Wright (ed.), *Early Travels in Palestine, Comprising the Narratives of Arculf, Willibald, Bernard, Saewulf, Sigurd, Benjamin of Tudela, Sir John Maundeville, De La Brocquière, and Maundrell.*

See also the Reader's Guide entries for North American travel writings, for Sea adventures and voyages, for Travel guidebooks, and for individual countries.

"Travers, Graham" (pseud.): see M. G. Todd.

Traviata (opera). G. Verdi.

Treasure hunts:

A. G. Clarke, Jr., *Arickaree Treasure, and Other Brief Tales of Adventurous Montanians.*

W. W. Jacobs, *Dialstone Lane.*

E. A. Poe, "Gold Bug" (story).

H. Pyle, *Stolen Treasure.*

R. L. Stevenson, *Treasure Island* (novel).

B. Stoker, *Mystery of the Sea; A Novel.*

H. B. M. Watson, *Adventurers; A Tale of Treasure Trove.*

See also the Reader's Guide entry for Pirates.

Treasure Island (novel). R. L. Stevenson.

Treasures from the Prose Writings of John Milton. J. Milton.

Treasury of Humorous Poetry. F. L. Knowles (comp.).

Treasury of Sacred Song, Selected from the English Lyrical Poetry of Four Centuries. F. T. Palgrave (comp.)

Treasury of Song for the Home Circle: The Richest, Best-Loved Gems, Sacred and Secular. D. H. Morrison (comp).

Treatment of Women and Children in the Congo State. R. D. Casement.

Tree Book: A Popular Guide to a Knowledge of the Trees of North America and to Their Uses and Cultivation. J. E. Rogers.

Trees: see

J. S. Brisbin, *Trees and Tree-Planting.*

R. B. Hough. *American Woods, Exhibited by Actual Specimens and with Copious Explanatory Text.*

J. E. Rogers, *Tree Book: A Popular Guide to a Knowledge of the Trees of North America and to Their Uses and Cultivation.*

See also the Reader's Guide entry for Gardening.

Trees and Tree-Planting. J. S. Brisbin.

Trench, [Frederick] Herbert (trans.): see D. S.

Merezhkovsky, *Romance of Leonardo da Vinci, the Forerunner.*

Trenck, Baron Friedrich von der : see

F. Bernard, *Wonderful Escapes.*

W. D. Howells (co-ed.), *Library of Universal Adventure by Sea and Land.*

H. Wilson, *Wonderful Characters; Comprising Memoirs and Anecdotes of the Most Remarkable Persons of Every Age and Nation.*

"Trent, Hilary" (pseud.): see R. M. Manley.

Trent (ship): see J. Fiske, *Century of Science and Other Essays* (marginalia).

"Treu und herzinniglich" (German song): see C. Keppel, "Robin Adair" (English version).

Trevelyan, George Otto (ed.): see L. Macaulay, *Selections from the Writings of Lord Macaulay.*

Trevelyan, Hannah More Macaulay (ed.): see T. B. Macaulay, *History of England from the Accession of James II.*

Trials: see Reader's Guide entry for Court trials.

Triangular Society. Leaves from the Life of a Portland Family. E. A. C. A. Allen.

Tribulations of a Princess. M. Cunliffe-Owen.

Trident and the Net; A Novel. M. Cunliffe-Owen.

Trilby. G. L. P. B. Du Maurier.

Trinity College, Hartford, Connecticut: see C. H. Proctor, *Life of James Williams, Better Known as Professor Jim, for Half a Century Janitor of Trinity College.*

Trip to England. W. Winter.

Trist, Sidney G. (anti-vivisection activist): see E. W. R. von Brücke, *Vorlesungen über Physiologie.*

Tristan und Isolde (opera). R. Wagner.

Tristram Shandy: see L. Sterne, *Life and Opinions of Tristram Shandy, Gentleman.*

"Triton, Willie" (pseud.): see A. Tripp.

Triumphant Democracy. A. Carnegie.

Triumph of Life; A Novel. W. F. Payson.

Triumph of Music: see O. S. Clemens, *Love Chase.*

Trix and Over-the-Moon. A. R. C. Troubetzkoy.

Trixy. E. S. Phelps.

"Trois-Étoiles" (pseud.): see E. C. G. Murray.

Trois Mousquetaires. A. Dumas.

Trojan War: see the Reader's Guide entries for Greek history and literature and also for Helen of Troy.

Troll Garden. W. S. Cather.

Trollope, Anthony: see M. D. Conway, *Autobiography: Memories and Experiences of Moncure Daniel Conway* (marginalia).

Trollope, Frances see B. Hall, *Travels in North America, in the Years 1827 and 1828.*

Troth, Henry (photographer): see N. B. De G. Doubleday, *Nature's Garden: An Aid to Knowledge of Our Wild Flowers and Their Insect Visitors.*

Troubador (opera): see G. Verdi, *Trovatore.*

Trovatore (opera). G. Verdi.

"Troyes, Jean de" (pseud.): see P. de Commynes.

True and the Beautiful in Nature, Art, Morals, and Religion. J. Ruskin.

True Bills. G. Ade.

True Bird Stories from My Note-Books. H. M. Miller.

True-Blue Laws of Connecticut and New Haven. J. H. Trumbull (ed.).

True History of Joshua Davidson, Communist. E. L. Linton.

Trumbull, James Hammond: see

W. C. Prime, *Tent Life in the Holy Land* (Catalog entry).

H. W. Shaw, *Everybody's Friend, or Josh Billings's Encyclopedia and Proverbial Philosophy of Wit and Humor* (Catalog entry).

Trumbull, John: see C. A. Munn, *Three Types of Washington Portraits: John Trumbull, Charles Wilson Peale, Gilbert Stuart.*

Truth: see the Reader's Guide entry for Lies.

Truth about "Protection." J. Benton.

Truth: A Weekly Journal: see H. D. Labouchère (Catalog entry).

Truth Seeker (magazine): see B. F. Underwood, *Essays and Lectures.* (Catalog entry).

Truths to Live By, A Companion to Everyday Christian Life. F. W. Farrar.

Tuberculosis: see L. R. Andrews, *White Peril; or, How I Cured Myself of Consumption at Home.*

Tübingen School: see G. P. Fisher, *Essays on the Supernatural Origin of Christianity.*

Tucker, Henry (composer): see

C. C. Sawyer, "Weeping, sad, and lonely; or, when this cruel war is over" (song).

J. M. Sayles, "Star of the evening."

Tudor, Mary: see C. Major, *When Knighthood Was in Flower; or, The Love Story of Charles Brandon and Mary Tudor, the King's Sister* (novel).

Tudor, Owen: see *Life and Amours of Owen Tideric, Prince of Wales, Otherwise Owen Tudor* (novel).

Tufts, F. N. (comp.): see Knife and Fork Club, *Book of the Knife and Fork Club.*

Tupper, Martin Farquhar: see *Lady's Gift; or, Souvenir of Friendship* (Catalog entry).

Turkey: see

J. R. Browne, *Yusef; or the Journey of the Frangi: A Crusade in the East.*

S. S. Cox, *Diversions of a Diplomat in Turkey.*

S. S. Cox, *Isles of the Princes; or, The Pleasures of Prinkipo.*

J. A. Hart, *Levantine Log-Book.*

T. W. Knox, *Backsheesh! or, Life and Adventures in the Orient.*

A. H. Layard, *Nineveh and Its Remains: With an Account of a Visit to the Chaldæan Christians of Kurdistand.*

H. M. Miller, *Little People of Asia.*

M. P. W. Montagu, *Letters of Lady Mary Wortley Montagu.*

H. J. Ross, *Letters from the East by Henry James Ross, 1837–1857.*

J. L. Stephens, *Incidents of Travel in Greece, Turkey, Russia, and Poland.*

M. W. Townsend, *Asia and Europe: Studies* (marginalia).

Turkistan; Notes of a Journey in Russian Turkistan, Khokand, Bukhara, and Kuldja. E. Schuyler.

Turner, Joseph Mallard William: see

P. G. Hamerton, *Life of J. M. W. Turner.*

(co-illus.) J. Milton, *Poetical Works of John Milton*.
J. Ruskin, *Modern Painters* (Catalog entry).

Turner, Nat: T. W. Higginson, *Travellers and Outlaws, Episodes in American History*.

Turn Him Out!: A Farce in One Act (play). T. John.

Turtles: see R. L. Ditmars, *Reptile Book: A Comprehensive Popularized Work*.

Tuscan Cities. W. D. Howells.

Tuthill, Louisa Caroline (contr.): see J. Ruskin, *True and the Beautiful in Nature, Art, Morals, and Religion*.

"Twain, Mark" (pseud.): see
(contr.) G. Bainton (comp. and ed.), *Art of Authorship. Literary Reminiscences, Methods of Work, and Advice to Young Beginners*.
T. Bentzon (Catalog entry about her translation of Mark Twain's story).
P. Blouet, "Mark Twain and Paul Bourget" (essay).
Book for an Hour.
L. J. Bridgman, "To Mark Twain" (poem).
W. M. Clemens, *Mark Twain, His Life and Work: A Biographical Sketch*.
H. K. F. G. Eden, *Juliana Horatia Ewing and Her Books*.
First Book of the Authors Club, Liber Scriptorum (contains Mark Twain's short story "Californian's Tale").
(intro.) J. da Fonesca and P. Carolino, *New Guide of the Conversation in Portuguese and English in Two Parts*.
F. W. Halsey (ed.), *American Authors and Their Homes: Personal Descriptions & Interviews* (Catalog entry).
M. Hapgood (Catalog entry).
E. F. Harkins, *Famous Authors (Men)*. E. F. Harkins.
E. F. Harkins, *Little Pilgrimages Among the Men Who Have Written Famous Books*.
W. D. Howells, "Mark Twain" (essay).
W. D. Howells, "Mark Twain: An Inquiry" (essay).
W. D. Howells, "Surprise Party to Mark Twain."
(contr.) W. D. Howells (co-ed.), *Library of Universal Adventure by Sea and Land*.
J. A. Kirlicks, "To Mark Twain" (poem).
A. Lang, "Mr. Lang on the Art of Mark Twain."
R. Love, "To Mark Twain,/'First Missourian,'/of Hannibal" (poem): see R. Love, *Poems All the Way from Pike*.
A. Matthews, "Mark Twain—His Work" (essay).
Men of the Time: A Dictionary of Contemporaries, Containing Biographical Notices of Eminent Characters of Both Sexes.
M. Monahan, "Saint Mark" (article).
(contr.) *Niagara Book: A Complete Souvenir of Niagara Falls*.
W. Nicholson, *Twelve Portraits. Second Series*.
W. L. Phelps, *Essays on Modern Novelists* (marginalia).
W. L. Phelps, "Introduction," *Novels and Letters of Jane Austen*.
J. Sadler, "To Mark Twain" (poem): see J. Sadler, *Lyrics and Rhymes*.
E. A. O. Somerville, *Mark Twain Birthday Book*.
(contr.) *Speeches at the Lotos Club*.
W. T. Stead, "Character Sketch: Mark Twain."
W. T. Stead, "Suggested Test Reading" (article).

W. T. Stead, "Test Readings of Mark Twain's Hands" (article).
A. G. Stedman (ed.), "Short Biographies of All Authors Represented in This Work."
C. Stern, "Mark Twain (A Nocturne of the Mississippi)" (poem).
F. R. Stockton, "Mark Twain and His Recent Works" (essay).
A. E. Trumbull, "Mary A. Twining" (sketch) (Catalog entry).
W. W. Tufts, *Market for an Impulse. A Novel*.
H. Van Dyke, *Blue Flower* (inscribed with a poetic tribute to Mark Twain).
Vanity Fair (magazine) (possible origin of Mark Twain's pen name).
H. C. Vedder, *American Writers of To-day*.
W. S. Walsh, *Authors and Authorship*.
(contr.) A. Watson, *Savage Club: A Medley of History, Anecdote, and Reminiscence by Aaron Watson, With a Chapter by Mark Twain*. A. Watson.
R. Watt, "For Lud og koldt Vand" (translation of a Mark Twain story).
Who's Who in America: A Biographical Dictionary of Notable Living Men and Women of the United States, 1906–1907.
World's Wit and Humor; An Encyclopedia of the Classic Wit and Humor of All Ages and Nations.
(intro.) W. Wright, *History of the Big Bonanza: An Authentic Account of the Discovery, History, and Working of the World-Renowned Comstock Silver Lode of Nevada*.
J. R. Young, *Men and Memories: Personal Reminiscences by John Russell Young*.
See also the Reader's Guide entry for Dedications to Mark Twain.

Tweed, William Marcy (New York City politician): see
A. B. Paine, *Th. Nast, His Period and His Pictures*.
J. D. Townsend, *New York in Bondage*.

Twelfth Night (play). W. Shakespeare.

Twelve Times One, Illustrations of Child Life. M. A. Lathbury.

Twelve Portraits. Second Series. W. Nicholson.

Twelve Years a Slave. S. Northup.

Twenty-Eight Years in Wall Street. H. Clews.

Twenty-Five Years of My Life. A. M. L. de Lamartine.

Twenty Thousand Leagues Under the Sea. J. Verne.

Twenty Years After: see A. Dumas, *Novels*.

"Twenty years ago" (song). W. Willing.

Twenty Years Ago. From the Journal of a Girl in Her Teens. D. M. M. Craik.

Twichell, Joseph Hopkins: see
(co-comp.) N. J. Burton, *Christian Hymnal. A Selection of Psalms and Hymns, with Music*.
(contr.): N. J. Burton, *Yale Lectures on Preaching and Other Writings*.

Twins: see
A. M. Diaz, *Jimmyjohns, and Other Stories*.
B. Harte, *Twins of Table Mountain, and Other Stories*.
(conjoined): see *Scientific American*.
See also the Reader's Guide entry for Double identities.

Twins of Table Mountain, and Other Stories. B. Harte.

'Twixt Sirdar and Menelik; An Account of a Year's Expedition from Zeila to Cairo Through Unknown Abyssinia. M. S. Wellby.

'Twixt Wave and Sky (novel). F. E. Wadleigh.

"Two Armies" (poem). O. W. Holmes.

Two Arrows: A Story of Red and White. W. O. Stoddard.

Two Destinies; A Novel. W. W. Collins.

Two Foscari: An Historical Tragedy. G. G. Byron.

Two Gentlemen of Verona (play). W. Shakespeare.

Two Gray Tourists: From Papers of Mr. Philemon Perch. R. M. Johnston.

"Two grenadiers" (song). H. Heine.

Two Hundred Old-Time Songs, Containing the Words and Music of the Choicest Gems of the Old and Familiar Songs. F. B. Ogilvie (comp.).

Two Little Vagrants (play). C. Klein.

Two Men of Sandy Bar (play). B. Harte.

Two Prisoners. T. N. Page.

Two Thousand Years Ago; or, The Adventures of a Roman Boy. A. J. Church.

Two Treaties of Paris and the Supreme Court. S. Webster.

Two Years Ago. C. Kingsley.

Two Years Before the Mast: A Personal Narrative. R. H. Dana.

Two Years in Fiji. A. L. A. Forbes.

Two Years in the French West Indies. L. Hearn.

Tyler, John (U. S. President): see A. F. de Bacourt, *Souvenirs of a Diplomat: Private Letters from America*.

Tyler, Wat: see C. M. Yonge, *Cameos from English History. The Wars in France* (marginalia).

Tyndall, John (contr.): see *Prayer-Gauge Debate*.

Tyner, James Noble: see G. Ticknor, *Life, Letters, and Journals of George Ticknor* (marginalia).

Typical Pictures of Indian Natives. F. M. Coleman.

Tyrolean stories: see K. Wolf, *Geschichten aus Tirol*.

Tyranny of the Dark. H. Garland.

Tyrwhitt, Thomas (ed.): G. Chaucer, *Canterbury Tales*.

"Tytler, Sarah" (pseud.): see H. Keddie.

▌U

"Über alien Gipfeln ist Ruh'" (poem). J. W. von Goethe.

Udvalgte Skitzer. J. F. Ahn (trans.).

Ugly-Girl Papers; or Hints for the Toilet. S. D. Power.

Uisneach: see A. Gregory, *Fate*.

Ulysses S. Grant, His Life and Character. H. Garland.

Uncivilized Races; or, Natural History of Man; Being a Complete Account of the Manners and Customs, and the Physical, Social, and Religious Condition and Characteristics, of the Uncivilized Races of Men, Throughout the Entire World. J. G. Wood.

Uncle Dudley's Odd Hours; Being the Vagaries of a Country Editor. M. C. Russell.

"Uncle Joshua Downing in Boston" (sketch): see S. Smith (Catalog entry).

Uncle Remus: His Songs and His Sayings. J. C. Harris.

Uncle Sam's Business Told for Young Americans. C. Marriott.

Uncle Tom's Cabin; or, Life Among the Lowly (play). G. L. Aiken.

Uncle Tom's Cabin; or, Life Among the Lowly. H. E. B. Stowe.

Uncle William, The Man Who Was Shif'less. J. B. P. Lee.

Uncommercial Traveller. C. Dickens.

Uncooked Foods & How to Use Them. E. Christian and M. G. Christian.

Undefiled: A Novel of To-day. F. A. Mathews.

Under Bow Bells; A City Book for All Readers (stories and sketches). J. Hollingshead.

Underground Rail Road. A Record of Facts, Authentic Narratives, Letters, &c., Narrating the Hardships, Hairbreadth Escapes, and Death Struggles of the Slaves in Their Efforts for Freedom. W. Still.

Underground Russia: Revolutionary Profiles and Sketches from Life. S. M. Kravchinski.

Underhill, Zoe Dana: see "Inn of San Jacinto" (short story) in W. D. Howells (co-ed.), *Under the Sunset*.

Under Summer Skies. C. Scollard.

Under the Deodars (short stories): see R. Kipling, *Writings in Prose and Verse*.

Under the Greenwood Tree; or, The Mellstock Quire—A Rural Painting of the Dutch School. T. Hardy.

Under the Red Robe. S. J. Weyman.

Under the Southern Cross; or, Travels in Australia, Tasmania, New Zealand, Samoa, and Other Pacific Islands. M. M. Ballou.

Under the Sun: Essays Mainly Written in Hot Countries. G. A. Sala.

Under the Sunset. W. D. Howells (co-ed.).

Under the Trees and Elsewhere. H. W. Mabie.

Under Two Flags. M. L. De la Ramée.

Underwood, Clarence Frederick (illus.): see M. Nicholson, *Port of Missing Men*.

Underwood, Sarah A. Francis: see B. F. Underwood, *Essays and Lectures* (Catalog entry).

Undine, A Romance. F. H. K. La Motte-Fouqué.

Undine: A Romance, and Sintram and His Companions. F. H. K. La Motte-Fouqué.

Undine, Eine Erzählung. F. H. K. La Motte-Fouqué.

Undiscovered Country. W. D. Howells.

Unequal Match. A Comedy in Three Acts. T. Taylor.

"Unfinished symphony": see F. P. Schubert, "Symphony in B minor."

Unger, Gladys (adapt.): see R. De Flers, *Love Watches* (play).

Unitarianism: see

   J. W. Chadwick, *George William Curtis, An Address*.

   J. W. Chadwick, *Old and New Unitarian Belief*.

   J. F. Clarke, *Memorial and Biographical Sketches* (Catalog entry).

   J. F. Clarke, *Selections from Sermons Preached to the Church of the Disciples*.

   R. Collyer, *Nature and Life: Sermons*.

   T. Parker (Catalog entry).

   M. J. Savage (unidentified sermon).

Unitarian Herald (Manchester, England.

United States history: see the Reader's Guide entry for American history (including early Canadian history).

United States Navy: see

   J. Barrett, *Admiral George Dewey; A Sketch of the Man*.

M. V. Dahlgren, *Memoir of John A. Dahlgren, Rear-Admiral United States Navy, by His Widow.*

S. R. Franklin, *Memories of a Rear-Admiral Who Has Served for More than Half a Century in the Navy of the United States.*

F. T. Jane, *All the World's Fighting Ships.*

B. J. Lossing, *Story of the United States Navy for Boys.*

A. R. Wallace, William Ramsay, *et al. Progress of the Century.*

R. F. Zogbaum, *"All Hands"; Pictures of Life in the United States Navy.*

Universal Geography. W. C. Woodbridge.

Universal Kinship. J. H. Moore.

Unknown Life of Jesus Christ. N. Notovich.

"Unparalleled Adventure of One Hans Pfaall" (short story). E. A. Poe.

"Unpleasant book": see [Unidentified book, 1907].

Unser Reichskanzler: Studien zu einem Charakterbilde. M. Busch.

Untrodden Peaks and Unfrequented Valleys. A Midsummer Ramble in the Dolomites. A. A. B. Edwards.

Unwin, Jane Cobden: see J. Morley, *Life of Richard Cobden* (inscr.).

Unwritten History: Life Amongst the Modocs. J. Miller.

Upanishad Prasada: see S. S. B. Saraswati (trans.).

"Up at a Villa—Down in the City" (poem). R. Browning.

Upland Pastures, Being Some Out-Door Essays. A. Knapp.

Upon a Cast. C. D. Wood.

"Upon the Gardens of Epicurus" (essay). W. Temple.

Uppingham School Songs and Borth Lyrics. E. Thring.

Ups and Downs on Land and Water. A. Hoppin.

"Up the Mississippi" (article). J. A. Dallas.

Up the Rhine. T. Hood.

Up the River. F. W. Shelton.

Upton, George Putnam (trans.): see
L. Nohl, *Life of Liszt.*
L. Nohl, *Life of Wagner.*

Urban and Suburban Life. J. K. Bangs.

Ursula: see H. de Balzac, *Comedy of Human Life.*

"Ursula, Countess von Eppinghoven" (pseud.): see H. W. H. Fischer.

Useful Birds and Their Protection. E. H. Forbush.

Utah: see
C. Paddock, *Fate of Madame La Tour; A Tale of Great Salt Lake.*
E. Roberts, *Shoshone and Other Western Wonders.*
T. B. H. Stenhouse, *Rocky Mountain Saints: A Full and Complete History of the Mormons, . . . and the Development of the Great Mineral Wealth of the Territory of Utah.*
See also the Reader's Guide entry for Mormons.

Utopian literature: see
E. Bellamy, *Looking Backward, 2000–1887.*
K. H. Brown, *Diane; A Romance of the Icarian Settlement on the Mississippi River.*
F. E. Clark, *Mossback Correspondence, Together with Mr. Mossback's Views on Certain Practical Subjects, with a Short Account of His Visit to Utopia.*
W. D. Howells, *Through the Eye of the Needle: A Romance.*
W. D. Howells, *Traveller from Altruria.*

M. H. M. Kinkaid, *Walda; A Novel.*

E. G. E. B. Lytton, *Coming Race; or, the New Utopia.*

W. H. Mallock, *New Republic; or, Culture, Faith, and Philosophy in an English Country House.*

S. Newcomb, *His Wisdom the Defender; A Story.*

J. Payn, *High Spirits: Being Certain Stories Written in Them.*

See also the Reader's Guide entry for Dystopian literature.

Uzbekistan: see J. A. MacGahan, *Campaigning on the Oxus, and the Fall of Khiva.*

▌V

"V" (pseud.): see E. V. M. Ferguson.

Vagabond Adventures. R. Keeler.

Vagabonds, and Other Poems. J. T. Trowbridge.

Vagrancy: see
J. J. McCook (Catalog entry).
J. H. Trumbull (ed.), *True-Blue Laws of Connecticut and New Haven* (marginalia).
J. F. Willard, *Tramping with Tramps: Studies and Sketches of Vagabond Life.*

Vagrant Chronicle of Earth and Sky. M. M. Williams.

Valentino, An Historical Romance of the Sixteenth Century in Italy. W. W. Astor.

Vampires: see
B. Stoker, *Dracula.*
H. Wachenhusen, *Vampyr. Novelle aus Bulgarien.*

Vampyr. Novelle aus Bulgarien. H. Wachenhusen.

Van Buren, Martin (U. S. President): see A. F. de Bacourt, *Souvenirs of a Diplomat: Private Letters from America.*

Vanderbilt, Cornelius ("Commodore"): see
Packard's Monthly: The Young Men's Magazine (Catalog entry).
J. G. Wood, *Uncivilized Races; or, Natural History of Man* (marginalia).

Van Dyke, Henry: see
"Some Remarks on Gulls, with a Foot-note on a Fish" (essay): see H. B. Washburn, "Shall We Hunt and Fish? Confessions of a Sentimentalist" (essay).
(contr.) *Whole Family; A Novel by Twelve Authors.*
(contr.) *Women of the Bible, by Twelve Eminent Divines.*

Van Eeden, Frederick: see *World's Work* (magazine).

Vane, Harry: see J. Fiske, *Century of Science.*

Vanity Fair, A Novel without a Hero. W. M. Thackeray.

Van Laun, Henri (trans.): see H. A. Taine, *History of English Literature. A New Edition.*

Van Vorst, Marie : see
(inscr.) A. B. Dodd, *Cathedral Days: A Tour in Southern England.*
(inscr.) G. Meredith, *Works of George Meredith.*
(co-author): B. M. Van Vorst, *Bagsby's Daughter.*
(co-author): B. M. Van Vorst, *Woman Who Toils; Being the Experiences of Two Ladies as Factory Girls.*

Variation of Animals and Plants Under Domestication. C. Darwin.

Varieties of Religious Experience; A Study in Human Nature. W. James.

Various Contrivances by Which Orchids Are Fertilized. C. Darwin.

Vasco Nuñez de Balboa. F. A. Ober.

Vaughn, Robert (ed., intro.): see J. Milton, *Milton's Paradise Lost.*

Vawter, Will (illus.): see J. W. Riley, *Book of Joyous Children.*

Vegetarianism: see E. Christian and M. G. Christian, *Uncooked Foods & How to Use Them.*

Veilby: see S. S. Blicher, *Minister of Veilby.*

Venetian June. A. Fuller.

Venetian Life. W. D. Howells.

Venetians; A Novel. M. E. Braddon.

Venice: see

M. E. Braddon, *Venetians; A Novel.*

H. R. F. Brown, *Studies in the History of Venice.*

T. Child, *Wimples and Crisping-Pins; Being Studies in the Coiffure and Ornaments of Women.*

A. Fuller, *Venetian June.*

W. D. Howells, *Fearful Responsibility and Other Stories.*

W. D. Howells, *Foregone Conclusion.*

W. D. Howells, *Venetian Life.*

L. Hutton, *Literary Landmarks of Venice.*

R. U. Johnson and C. C. Buel (eds.), *Battles and Leaders of the Civil War* (Catalog entry).

C. B. E. F. Lindsay, *From a Venetian Balcony and Other Poems of Venice and the Near Lands.*

M. O. W. Oliphant, *Makers of Venice: Doges, Conquerors, Painters, and Men of Letters.*

E. P. Parker (Catalog entry).

S. Rogers, "Venice" (poem).

J. Ruskin, *Stones of Venice.*

C. W. Stoddard, *Cruise Under the Crescent; From Suez to San Marco.*

F. H. L. Turnbull, *Golden Book of Venice: A Historical Romance of the 16th Century.*

"Venice" (poem). S. Rogers.

Venus and Adonis (poem). W. Shakespeare.

Venus in Boston and Other Tales of Nineteenth-Century City Life. G. Thompson.

Vera, The Medium. R. H. Davis.

"Verbrecher aüs verbrener Ehne" (story). J. C. F. von Schiller.

Vere, Maximilian Schele de (trans.): see J. X. B. Saintine. *Myths of the Rhine.*

Verga, Giovanni (writer): see P. Mascagni, *Cavalleria Rusticana* (opera).

Vergil: see Virgil in the Catalog.

Vergilius; A Tale of the Coming of Christ. I. Bacheller.

Vermont: see M. E. Waller, *Wood Carver of 'Lympus.*

Verrall, Arthur Woollgar (co-trans.): see A. Daudet, *Immortal; or, One of the "Forty."*

Verrall, Margaret de Gaudrion Merrifield (co-trans.): see A. Daudet, *Immortal; or, One of the "Forty."*

Versen, General M. von: see A. H. T. Werthen, F. von, *General von Versen: ein militärisches Zeit-und Lebensbild.*

Verses. By H. H. H. M. F. H. Jackson.

"Verses Supposed to be Written by Alexander Selkirk" (poem). W. Cowper.

Verses Written in India. A. C. Lyall.

Very Small Person. A. H. Donnell.

Vespucci, Amerigo: see F. A. Ober, *Amerigo Vespucci.*

Vestiges of the Natural History of Creation. R. Chambers.

Vesty of the Basins; A Novel. S. P. M. Greene.

Vesuvius (volcano): see the Reader's Guide entry for Pompeii.

Vicar of Wakefield. O. Goldsmith.

Vicar of Wakefield: see W. G. Willis (adapt.), *Olivia* (play).

Vice Versâ; or, A Lesson to Fathers. T. A. Guthrie.

Vicomte of Bragelonne. A. Dumas.

Victor Emmanuel II: see E. Văcărescu, *Kings and Queens I Have Known.*

Victor Hugo, by a Witness of His Life. A. F. Hugo.

Victoria, Helena Augusta, Princess Christian of Schleswig-Holstein (trans., ed.): see F. S. Wihelmina, *Memoirs of Wilhelmine, Margravine of Baireuth.*

Victoria, Queen: see

J. G. Argyll, *Viscount Palmerston, K. G.*

M. von Bothmer, *German Home Life* (marginalia).

H. Dunckley, *Lord Melbourne.*

A. S. Evans, *Our Sister Republic: A Gala Trip Through Tropical Mexico in 1869–70* (marginalia).

E. Văcărescu, *Kings and Queens I Have Known.*

Vie de Jeanne d'Arc. A. France.

Vie de M. D'Orléans De La Motte. Évêque d'Amiens, par M. L'Abbé Proyart. L. B. Proyart.

Vienna: see

W. D. Howells, *Fearful Responsibility and Other Stories.*

Litteratur-Institut.

E. Pötzl, *Hoch vom Kahlenberg. Heitere nd ernste Skizzen aus dem Wiener Leben.*

E. Pötzl, *Landsleute. Kleine Beobachtungen eines Wieners.*

E. Pötzl, *Stadtmenschen. Ein Wiener Skizzenbuch.*

Vienna *Neue Freie Presse.*

Vierge Lorraine, Jeanne d'Arc. C. A. de Chabannes.

View of the Evidences of Christianity. W. Paley.

View of the State of Europe During the Middle Ages. H. Hallam.

Views A-Foot; or, Europe Seen with Knapsack and Staff. B. Taylor.

Views of Religion, Collected by Rufus K. Noyes, M. D. R. K. Noyes.

Vigil of Venus: see G. V. Catullus, *Works of Catullus and Tibullus, and the Vigil of Venus.*

Vigilantes of Montana; or, Popular Justice in the Rocky Mountains. T. J. Dimsdale.

Vignettes in Rhyme and Vers de Société (Now First Collected). H. A. Dobson.

Vikings: see the Reader's Guide entry for Scandinavian mythology.

Viking Tales of the North. R. B. Anderson and J. Bjarnason (trans.).

"Village Blacksmith" (poem). H. W. Longfellow.

"Village Green" (comic sketch): see C. F. Browne, *Artemus Ward, His Travels.*

Villari, Linda (White) Mazini (trans.): see P. Villari, *Life and Times of Niccolò Machiavelli.*

Villari, Pasquale (intro.): see G. Negri, *Julian the Apostate.*

Villette. C. Brontë.

Villon, Francois (French poet): see J. H. McCarthy, *Needles and Pins; A Novel.*

Vincent, Benjamin (ed.): see J. T. Haydn, *Haydn's Dictionary of Dates and Universal Information Relating to All Ages and Nations.*

Vinci, Leonardo da: see L. Da Vinci.

Vineta. Roman. E. Bürstenbinder.

Vineyard, J. J. (comp.): see Knife and Fork Club, *Book of the Knife and Fork Club.*

Viper of Milan: A Romance of Lombardy. G. M. V. Long.

Virgil: see T. Bulfinch, *Age of Fable; or, Beauties of Mythology.*

Virginia: see

J. M. Brown, *Captives of Abb's Valley; A Legend of Frontier Life.*

C. W. Dilke, *Greater Britain: A Record of Travel in English-Speaking Countries During 1866 and 1867.*

E. A. G. Glasgow, *Voice of the People* (novel).

M. Johnston, *Prisoners of Hope. A Tale of Colonial Virginia.*

M. Johnston, *Sir Mortimer. A Novel.*

J. P. Kennedy, *Swallow Barn; or, A Sojourn in the Old Dominion.*

T. N. Page, *In Ole Virginia; or, Marse Chan and Other Stories.*

F. B. Sanborn (ed.), *Life and Letters of John Brown, Liberator of Kansas and Martyr of Virginia.*

J. Scott, *Partisan Life with Col. John S. Mosby.*

F. H. Smith, *Colonel Carter of Cartersville* (novel).

S. O. Stedman, *Allen Bay, A Story.*

J. Sturge, *Visit to the United States in 1841.*

W. M. Thackeray, *Virginians; A Tale of the Last Century.*

A. R. C. Troubetzkoy, *Virginia of Virginia.*

J. H. Trumbull (ed.), *True-Blue Laws of Connecticut and New Haven* (marginalia).

W. J. Vance, *Big John Baldwin; Extracts from the Journal of an Officer of Cromwell's Army* (fictional memoir).

Virginians; A Tale of the Last Century. W. M. Thackeray.

Virginia of Virginia. A. R. C. Troubetzkoy.

Viscount Palmerson, K. G. J. G. Argyll.

Vision Concerning Piers Plowman. W. Langland.

"Vision of Judgment" (poem). G. G. Byron.

Vision of Sir Launfal (poem). J. R. Lowell.

Vision of Sir Launfal. The Cathedral. Favorite Poems. J. R. Lowell.

Vision; or, Hell. A. Dante.

"Visions, A Phantasy" (story). I. S. Turgenev.

Visions of John Bunyan, Being His Last Remains. G. Larkin.

"Visit from St. Nicholas" (poem). C. C. Moore.

Visits. H. James: see H. James, *Private Life.*

Visit to India, China, and Japan, in the Year 1853. B. Taylor.

"Visit to the Asylum for Aged and Decayed Punsters" (story): see O. W. Holmes, *Soundings.*

Visit to the United States in 1841. J. Sturge.

Viti: An Account of a Government Mission to the Vitian or Fijian Islands, in the Years 1860–61. B. C. Seemann.

"Vivian, Philip" (pseud.): see H. V. M. Phelips.

Vivisection: see

E. W. R. von Brücke, *Vorlesungen über Physiologie.*

F. P. Cobbe, *Peak in Darien, with Some Other Inquiries Touching Concerns of the Soul and the Body. An Octave of Essays.*

E. Marson, *Of the House of Chloe; A Tale of the Times.*

Pflüger's Archiv für die gesammte Physiologie des Menschen und der Thiere (journal).

E. S. Phelps, *Trixy.*

Viewpoints Against Vivisection from Some Great Minds.

Vix (horse): see G. E. Waring, Jr., *Whip and Spur.*

Vizetelly, Ernest Alfred (trans.): see É. Zola, *Rome.*

Vocabolario Italiano della lingua parlata. G. Rigutini and P. Fanfani.

"Voiceless" (poem). O. W. Holmes.

Voice instruction: see the Reader's Guide entry for Music.

Voice My Soul Heard (poetry). W. A. Kendall.

Voice of the People (novel). E. A. G. Glasgow.

Voices of Doubt and Trust. V. Streamer (comp.).

Voile Tombe: Caricatures par Blix. R. Blix.

Volcanoes: see

World of Wonders; A Record of Things Wonderful in Nature, Science, and Art.

See also the Reader's Guide entries for Aetna and for Pompeii.

Voltaire, Francois Marie Arouet de: see

H. W. H. Fischer, *Private Lives of William II and His Consort and Secret History of the Court of Berlin.*

Gesta Romanorum (Catalog entry).

J. Parton, *Life of Voltaire.*

Vorlesungen über Physiologie. E. W. R. von Brücke.

Vorse, Mary Heaton (co-author): see *Whole Family; A Novel by Twelve Authors.*

Voyage in the Sunbeam, Our Home in the Ocean for Eleven Months. A. A. A. Brassey.

Voyage of the Liberdade. J. Slocum.

Voyage to the Fortunate Isles, Etc. S. M. B. Piatt.

W

"W., F. G." (pseud.): see F. G. Welch.

Waagan, Gustav Friedrich (ed.): see F. Kugler, *Handbook of Painting: The German, Flemish, and Dutch Schools.*

"Wacht am Rhein" (poem, song). M. Schneckenburger.

Wade, Joseph Augustine (composer): see T. Moore, "Hours there were."

Wages of Sin. M. S. L. K. Harrison.

Wagner, Richard: see

A. A. Chapin, *Wotan, Siegried, and Brünnhilde.*

W. H. Hadow, *Studies in Modern Music* (Clara's marginalia).

L. Nohl, *Life of Wagner.*

E. W. Nye, *Forty Liars, and Other Lies* (Catalog entry).

A. R. Parsons, *Parsifal; The Finding of Christ Through Art: A Wagner Study.*

T. Uhlig (Catalog entry).

C. D. Warner, *Roundabout Journey.*

F. S. Wilhelmina, *Memoirs of Frederica Sophia Wilhelmina, Princess Royal of Prussia, Margravine of Baireuth* (Catalog entry).

F. S. Wilhelmina, *Memoirs of Wilhelmine, Margravine of Baireuth* (Catalog entry).

Wagoner of the Alleghanies. A Poem of the Days of Seventy-Six (poem). T. B. Read.

Wake, William (trans.): see the Catalog entry for Bible. New Testament. Apocrypha.

Wakeman-Curtis, Minnie (ed.): see E. Wakeman, *Log of an Ancient Mariner; Being the Life and Adventures of Captain Edgar Wakeman. Written by Himself and Edited by His Daughter.*

Wakulla; A Story of Adventure in Florida. C. K. Munroe.

Walda; A Novel. M. H. M. Kinkaid.

Walden; or, Life in the Woods. H. D. Thoreau.

Wales (history): see
T. R. Lounsbury, "Scholar of the Twelfth Century" (articles).
Mabinogion, Boy's Mabinogion; Being the Earliest Welsh Tales of King Arthur in the Famous Red Book of Hergest.
Mining Life in Wales.

Walker, Frederick (illus.): see W. M. Thackeray, *Adventures of Philip on His Way Through the World.*

Walker, James L. (pref.): see M. Stirner, *Ego and His Own.*

"Walker, Mrs. Edward Ashley" (pseud.): see K. K. C. Walker.

Walker, William Henry (illus.): see C. L. Dodgson, *Alice's Adventures in Wonderland.*

Walks About the City and Environs of Jerusalem. W. H. Bartlett.

Walks and Talks about London. J. Timbs.

Walks in Florence and Its Environs. S. Horner and J. B. Horner.

Walks in London. A. J. C. Hare.

Walks in Rome. A. J. C. Hare.

Wallace; A Franconia Story. J. Abbott.

Wallace, Alfred Russel: see
J. Fiske, *Century of Science and Other Essays* (marginalia).
J. Fiske, "Charles Darwin" (essay).

Wallace, Lewis: see
(contr.) G. Croly, *Tarry Thou Till I Come; or, Salathiel, The Wandering Jew.*
W. H. Prescott, *History of the Conquest of Peru, with a Preliminary View of the Civilization of the Incas* (Catalog entry).
G. H. Van Zandt, *Poems of George Harrison Van Zandt* (Catalog entry).

Wallace Rhodes, A Novel. N. Davis.

Wallace, William: see J. Porter, *Scottish Chiefs* (novel).

Wallace, William Vincent (composer): see
E. Fitzball, *Maritana* (opera).
V. M. Hugo, *Ruy Blas.*

Wallenstein, Albrecht von (Austrian general): see T. B. Macaulay, *Critical and Miscellaneous Essay* (marginalia).

Wall Street: see the Reader's Guide entry for Finance and business.

Walpole, Horace: see
J. H. Jesse, *London: Its Celebrated Characters and Remarkable Places* (marginalia).
J. McCarthy, *History of the Four Georges.*

Walrond, Theodore (ed.): see J. B. Elgin, *Letters and Journals.*

Walsh, G. E (co-author): see *Battle for the Pacific, and Other Adventures at Sea.*

"Walton, Augustus Q." (pseud.): see V. A. Stewart.

Walton, J. A. (illus.): see H. Drummond, *Man of His Age.*

Wanamaker, John: see *Sunday School Times* (periodical).

"Wanderer" (song): see F. P. Schubert, "Wandern."

Wanderers: The Poems of William Winter. W. Winter.

Wandering Heir: see C. Reade, *Griffith Gaunt; or, Jealousy.*

Wandering Jew: see
M. D. Conway, *Wandering Jew.*
G. Croly, *Tarry Thou Till I Come; or, Salathiel, The Wandering Jew.*
E. Sue, *Wandering Jew.*

Wanderings in Patagonia; or, Life Among the Ostrich-Hunters. J. Beerbohm.

"Wandern" (song). F. P. Schubert.

War and Peace (novel): see L. N. Tolstoy, *Guerre et la Paix. Roman historique.*

Warblers of North America. F. M. Chapman.

War Diary of Events in the War of the Great Rebellion, 1863–1865. G. H. Gordon.

"Ward, Artemus" (pseud.): see C. F. Browne.

Ward, Bernard Rowland (ed.): see M. De Lancey, *Week at Waterloo in 1815. Lady De Lancey's Narrative.*

Ward, Elizabeth Stuart (Phelps): see E. S. Phelps.

Ward, Herbert Dickinson (co-author): see E. S. Phelps, *The Master of the Magicians.*

"Ward, Mrs. Harrietta Oxnard " (pseud.): see C. S. J. Bloomfield-Moore.

Ward, Mrs. Humphry: see M. A. A. Ward.

Ward, Mary Augusta (Arnold): see
(trans., intro., ed.) H. F. Amiel, *Amiel's Journal: The Journal Intime of Henri-Frédéric Amiel.*
W. L. Phelps, *Essays on Modern Novelists.*

Ward, William Hayes (co-ed.): see *World's Wit and Humor; An Encyclopedia of the Classic Wit and Humor of All Ages and Nations.*

Warder, George Woodward: see *Standard Dictionary of the English Language Upon Original Plans* (Catalog entry).

Wardle, Thomas: see (inscr.) I. Walton, *Lives of John Donne, Henry Wotton, Richd Hooker, George Herbert, &c.*

Ware, Charles Pickard (co-comp.): see W. F. Allen (comp.), *Slave Songs of the United States.*

"Ware, Martin L." (pseud.): see M. L. Wynkoop.

Warfare: see
Armies of To-day; A Description of the Armies of the Leading Nations.
J. Bigelow, *Principles of Strategy, Illustrated Mainly from American Campaigns.*
D. M. M. Craik, *Studies from Life.*
Dailey. *War Pictures* (unidentified book).
T. A. Dodge, *Great Captains.*
T. D. English, *Boy's Book of Battle-Lyrics: A Collection of Verses Illustrating Some Notable Events in the History of the United States of America.*
J. Fiske, *Century of Science and Other Essays* (marginalia).
R. Hitchcock (ed.), *Decisive Battles of America.*
W. D. Howells, "Editha" (short story) in *Between the Dark and the Daylight: Romances.*
F. T. Jane, *All the World's Fighting Ships.*

A. H. Jomini, *Jomini's Handbook of Military Etiquette*.
A. H. Jomini, *Précis de l'Art de la Guerre*.
P. Lacombe, *Arms and Armour in Antiquity and the Middle Ages; Also a Descriptive Note of Modern Weapons*.
P. Lacroix, *Military and Religious Life in the Middle Ages and at the Period of the Renaissance*.
H. C. Lodge, *War with Spain*.
J. R. Lowell, *Letters of James Russell Lowell* (marginalia).
A. T. Mahan (Catalog entry).
H. K. B. von Moltke, *Essays, Speeches and Memoirs*.
W. F. P. Napier, *History of the War in the Peninsula and in the South of France, from the Year 1807 to the Year 1814*.
F. Palmer, *Ways of the Service*.
Philippine Information Society. *A Period of Guerrilla Warfare, November 1899, to September 1900* (pamphlet).
J. C. Ropes, *The First Napoleon. A Sketch, Political and Military*.
F. H. B. Skrine, *Fontenoy and Great Britain's Share in the War of the Austrian Succession 1741–48*.
E. C. Stedman, *Lyrics and Idylls, with Other Poems*.
United States War Department. *Regulations for the Army of the United States, 1904*.
A. R. Wallace, William Ramsay, *et al. Progress of the Century*.
H. G. Wells, *War of the Worlds*.
E. Wildman, *Aguinaldo: A Narrative of Filipino Ambitions* (marginalia).
J. G. Wood, *Uncivilized Races; or, Natural History of Man* (marginalia).
See also the Reader's Guide entries for Army life (United States), for Military etiquette, and for wars with specific names.
Warfield, David (actor): see C. Klein, *Music Master* (play).
War in South Africa: Its Cause and Conduct. A. C. Doyle.
War Letters of a Disbanded Volunteer, Embracing His Experiences as Honest Old Abe's Bosom Friend and Unofficial Adviser. J. Barber.
"Warm summer sun" (line from poem): see R. Richardson, "Annette" (poem).
Warner, Charles Dudley: see
  H. H. Bancroft, *Literary Industries. A Memoir* (Catalog entry).
  H. H. Bancroft, *Native Races of the Pacific States of North America* (Catalog entry).
  (intro.) I. C. Cabell, *Seen from the Saddle*.
  A. A. Fields, *Charles Dudley Warner*.
  U. S. Grant, *Memoirs of U. S. Grant* (inscr.).
  F. B. Sanborn (ed.), *Life and Letters of John Brown, Liberator of Kansas and Martyr of Virginia* (Catalog entry).
  World's Wit and Humor; An Encyclopedia of the Classic Wit and Humor of All Ages and Nations.
"Warner, Hannah" (pseud.): see J. H. Jewett.
"Warner, Leigh de" (pseud.): see W. J. Warner.
War of 1812: see
  J. Barnes, *Loyal Traitor: A Story of the War of 1812*.

B. J. Lossing, *Pictorial Field-Book of the War of 1812*.
J. T. Wilson, *Black Phalanx; A History of the Negro Soldiers of the United States in the Wars of 1775–1812, 1861–'65*.
War of the Civilisations, Being the Record of a "Foreign Devil's Experiences with the Allies in China. G. Lynch.
War of the Worlds. H. G. Wells.
War Pictures: see Dailey.
War Poetry of the South. W. G. Simms (ed.).
"Warren Hastings" (essay). T. B. Macaulay.
"Warrior bold" (song). E. Thomas.
Wartegg, Ernst Von Hesse-: See the Catalog entry for E. von Hesse-Wartegg.
War-Time Wooing; A Story. C. King.
Warwick, Rhode Island: see J. G. Wood, *Uncivilized Races; or, Natural History of Man* (marginalia).
War with Spain. H. C. Lodge.
Washington: A Drama, in Five Acts. M. F. Tupper.
Washington, District of Columbia: see H. B. Adams, *Democracy, An American Novel*.
Washington, George: see
  W. Irving, *Life of George Washington*.
  G. Lippard, *Legends of the American Revolution*.
  V. Mapes, *Tory's Guest* (play).
  S. W. Mitchell, *Hugh Wynne, Free Quaker, Sometime Brevet Lieutenant-Colonel on the Staff of His Excellency General Washington*.
  C. A. Munn, *Three Types of Washington Portraits: John Trumbull, Charles Wilson Peale, Gilbert Stuart*.
  T. Roosevelt, *Square Deal* (Catalog entry).
  W. Shakespeare, *Works of Shakespeare* (Catalog entry).
  W. M. Thackeray, *Virginians; A Tale of the Last Century*.
  M. F. Tupper, *Washington: A Drama, in Five Acts*.
  H. Van Dyke, *Americanism of Washington*.
  M. L. Weems, *Life and Memorable Actions of George Washington*.
  E. Wildman, *Aguinaldo: A Narrative of Filipino Ambitions* (Catalog entry).
Washington Square. H. James.
"Washoe Rambles" (articles). W. Wright.
Wasps: see the Reader's Guide entry for Insects.
Wasps and Their Ways. M. W. Morley.
Wasps, Social and Solitary. G. W. Peckham and E. G. Peckham.
Was sich der Wald erzählt. G. H. G. Putlitz.
Was William Shakespeare a Gentleman? Some Questions in Shakespeare's Biography Determined. S. A. Tannenbaum.
"Watanna, Onoto" (pseud.): see W. Eaton.
Watch Tower Society: see C. T. Russell, *Millennial Dawn: The Plan of the Ages*.
Water-Babies. A Fairy Tale for a Land-Baby. C. Kingsley.
Water cure: see S. Kneipp, *My Water Cure*.
Waterloo: see M. De Lancey, *Week at Waterloo in 1815. Lady De Lancey's Narrative*.
Waterloo; A Sequel to the Conscript of 1813. É. Erckmann and A. Chatrian.
Waters, Clara Erskine (Clement): see C. E. Clement.
Waters of Hercules. E. Gerard.
Water Wonders Every Child Should Know. J. M. Thompson.

Watson, Hy. (illus.): see A. B. Paine, *Tent Dwellers*.
Watt, James: see
A. Carnegie, *James Watt*.
H. Dircks, *Life, Times and Scientific Labours of the Second Marquis of Worcester*.
W. Shakespeare, *Works of Shakespeare* (Catalog entry).
Watterson, Henry: see G. Cleveland *et al. What Shall We Do With It? (Meaning the Surplus). Taxation and Revenue Discussed*.
Watts, William Henry: see (gift) Tewkesbury. *Official Guide to Tewkesbury*.
Waud, Alfred Rudolph (illus.): see R. Keeler, "New Orleans," "On the Mississippi" (series of articles).
Waverley Novels. W. Scott.
Waverley; or, 'Tis Sixty Years Since. W. Scott.
"Way down in Tennessee" (song): see the Catalog entry for "Down in Tennessee" (minstrel song).
Ways of the Service. F. Palmer.
Way to Do Good; or, The Christian Character Mature. J. Abbott.
Wealth against Commonwealth. H. D. Lloyd.
We and Our Neighbors; or, the Records of an Unfashionable Street. A Novel. H. E. B. Stowe.
"We are far from home on the stormy main" (song): see F. McGlennon, "Bring my boy back again" (song).
Weather: see
W. de Fonvielle, *Thunder and Lightning*.
E. W. Hornung, *Bride from the Bush* (Twain quotes a passage in the Appendix to *The American Claimant*).
C. B. Lewis ("M. Quad," "Demon and the Fury" (Twain quotes a passage in the Appendix to *The American Claimant*).
F. N. D. Murfree, *Felicia; A Novel* (Twain quotes a passage in the Appendix to *The American Claimant*).
M. N. Murfree, *In the "Stranger People's" Country: A Novel* (Twain quotes a passage in the Appendix to *The American Claimant*).
W. D. O'Connor, "Brazen Android" (Twain quotes a passage in the Appendix to Twain's *The American Claimant*).
C. Scollard, *Under Summer Skies* (Twain quotes a passage in the Appendix to Twain's *The American Claimant*).
F. Zurcher and É. Margollé, *Meteors, Aërolites, Storms, and Atmospheric Phenomena*.
See also the Reader's Guide entry for Lightning.
Webb, Charles Henry: see B. Harte (ed.), *Outcroppings: Being Selections of California Verse*.
Webster, Charles Luther: see M. D. Conway, *Autobiography: Memories and Experiences of Moncure Daniel Conway* (marginalia).
Webster, Charles L. & Co.: *Illustrated Catalogue of Charles L. Webster Co.'s Publications*.
Webster, Daniel: see W. T. Sherman, *Memoirs of General William T. Sherman. By Himself* (marginalia).
Webster, [Daniel] Fletcher (ed.): see D. Webster, *Private Correspondence of Daniel Webster*.
Webster, Joseph Philbrick (composer): see S. F. Bennett, "Sweet by and by" (hymn).
Webster's Dictionary. N. Webster.
Webster's International Dictionary. N. Webster.

Webster's Practical Dictionary of the English Language. N. Webster.
Wedgwood, Josiah: see S. Smiles, *Josiah Wedgwood, F.R.S., His Personal History*.
Wedlock; or, the Right Relation of the Sexes; Disclosing the Laws of Conjugal Selection, and Showing Who May, and Who May Not Marry. S. R. Wells.
Week at Waterloo in 1815. Lady De Lancey's Narrative. M. De Lancey.
Week in a French Country-House. A. K. Sartoris.
Week in a French Country-House. A. K. Sartoris: see A. C. H. Rice, *Mrs. Wiggs of the Cabbage Patch* (Catalog entry).
Week in Hepsidam; Being the First and Only True Account of the Mountains, Men, Manners and Morals Thereof. G. W. Bagby.
"Wee Willie Winkie" (short story): see R. Kipling, *Writings in Prose and Verse*.
Wee Winkles & Her Friends. G. E. S. Jackson.
Wee Winkles & Snowball. G. E. S. Jackson.
Wee Winkles & Wideawake. G. E. S. Jackson.
Wee Winkles at the Mountains. G. E. S. Jackson.
"Weeping, sad, and lonely; or, when this cruel war is over" (song). C. C. Sawyer.
We Four and Two More. I. Clark
Weguelin, John Reinhard (illus.): see L. Wallace, *Wooing of Malkatoon. Commodus*.
Weight-lifting: see the Reader's Guide entry for Health, fitness, and hygiene.
Weil, Francis (composer): see F. S. Lock Osgood, *Poems* (Catalog entry).
Weil, Oscar (composer): see H. C. Bunner, *Three Operetta. Music by Oscar Weil*.
Weir, Harrison (illus.): see S. K. Trimmer, *History of the Robins. In Words of One Syllable*.
Weldon, Charles Dater (illus.): see
(co-illus.) H. C. Bunner, *Three Operettas*.
(illus.) J. Ralph, *Alone in China, and Other Stories*.
Well at the World's End (fantasy novel). W. Morris.
Wellington, Arthur Wellesley, Duke of: see
C. Knight and T. Raikes, *Personal Reminiscences by Cornelia Knight and Thomas Raikes*.
W. H. Maxwell, *Life of Field-Marshal His Grace the Duke of Wellington*.
Wells, Amos Russel: see (contr.) *Way into Print*.
Wells, Horace: see T. W. S. Higginson, *Cheerful Yesterdays. Contemporaries* (marginalia).
Wells, Samuel Roberts (ed.): see *Phrenological Journal and Science of Health*.
Wells, W. L. (illus.): see E. W. Howe, *Story of a Country Town*.
Wenderholme. A Story of Lancashire and Yorkshire. P. G. Hamerton.
"Wentworth, May" (pseud.): see M. W. Newman.
Wenzell, Albert Beck (illus.): see E. N. J. Wharton, *House of Mirth*.
Werewolf: see O. A. Liljencrantz, *Randvar the Songsmith; A Romance of Norumbega*.
Werke. J. W. von Goethe.
"Werner, E." (pseud.): see E. Bürstenbinder.

Wescoatt, Vivien (inscr. by Clara Clemens Samossoud): see J. J. Bell, *Jess & Co.*

Wesendonck, Mathilde: see R. Wagner, *Richard Wagner to Mathilde Wesendonck.*

Wesley, Charles: see E. R. Charles, *Diary of Mrs.Kitty Trevylyan; A Story of the Times of Whitefield and the Wesleys.*

Wesley, John: see E. R. Charles, *Diary of Mrs. Kitty Trevylyan; A Story of the Times of Whitefield and the Wesleys.*

West: see the Reader's Guide entry for American West.

West African Mail (newspaper): see H. L. Samuel (Catalog entry).

Westall, William (trans.): see S. M. Kravchinski, *Russia Under the Tsars.*

Westendorf, Katharine (co-ed.): see H. W. Dresser, *Heart of It.*

Western United States: see the Reader's Guide entry for American West.

Western World; or Travels in the United States in 1846–47. A. Mackay.

West Indies: see
L. Hearn, *Two Years in the French West Indies.*
L. Hearn, *Youma, Story of a West Indian Slave.*

Westminster Abbey. F. W. Farrar.

Westminster Abbey: see A. P. Stanley, *Historical Memorials of Westminster Abbey.*

Westminster Confession: see R. M. Manley, *Mr. Claghorn's Daughter.*

Westminster Drolleries, Both Parts, of 1671, 1672; Being a Choice Collection of Songs and Poems, Sung at Court and Theatres. J. W. Ebsworth (ed.)

Westminster Hall: see *Memories of Westminster Hall; A Collection of Interesting Incidents, Anecdotes, and Historical Sketches Relating to Westminster Hall.*

West, N. (trans.): see R. Krause, *Starters and Regulators for Electric Motors and Generators.*

West Point Military Academy: see
F. M. Colby, *Imaginary Obligations* (marginalia).
C. King, *Cadet Days; A Story of West Point.*
C. King, *To the Front; A Sequel to Cadet Days.*
J. R. Lowell, *Letters of James Russell Lowell* (marginalia).
E. A. Poe, *Murders of [sic] the Rue Morgue and Other Tales* (Catalog entry).
C. E. S. Wood, *Masque of Love* (poem) (Catalog entry).

Westward Ho! (novel). C. Kingsley.

"We three kings of Orient" (Christmas carol). J. H. Hopkins, Jr.

"Wet Sheet and a Flowing Sea" (poem, song). A. Cunningham.

"We Too" (poem): see J. Ingelow, "Divided" (poem).

"We won't go home till morning" (song). S. C. Foster.

Wey, Francis (pref.): see C. de Catelin, *Histoire du Mont Blanc et de la vallée de Chamonix.*

Whaling: see F. T. Bullen, *Cruise of the Cachalot Round the World after Sperm Whales.*

"What I Did, Gail Hamilton" (poem). J. M. Parker.

What I Know of Farming: A Series of Brief and Plain Expositions of Practical Agriculture as an Art Based Upon Science. H. Greeley.

"What is home without a mother?" (song). S. Winner.

"What is Life" (article). O. J. Lodge.

What Is Worth While? A. R. Lindsay.

What Katy Did: A Story. S. C. Woolsey.

What Mr. Darwin Saw in His Voyage Round the World in the Ship "Beagle." C. Darwin.

What Rome Was Built With: A Description of the Stones Employed in Ancient Times for Its Building and Decoration. M. W. Porter.

What Shall We Do With It? (Meaning the Surplus). Taxation and Revenue Discussed. G. Cleveland *et al.*

What Social Classes Owe to Each Other. W. G. Sumner.

What Was the Gunpowder Plot? The Traditional Story Tested by Original Evidence. J. Gerard.

What Will He Do With It? E. G. E. B. Lytton.

Wheatley, Leonard Abercromby (trans.): see W. Lübke, *Ecclesiastical Art in Germany During the Middle Ages.*

Wheeler, Candace (contr.): see C. T. Wheeler, *Prize Painting Book: Good Times. Pictures by Dora Wheeler.*

Wheeler, Doris (illus.): see M. D. Brine, *My Boy and I; or, On the Road to Slumberland.*

Wheeler, William Almon.: see W. D. Howells, *Sketch of the Life of Rutherford B. Hayes. Also a Biographical Sketch of William A. Wheeler.*

Wheel of Progress (play). A. E. Trumbull.

"When I am far away" (song). M. P. Eayrs.

"When I am gone" (song). T. H. Bayly.

"When Johnny comes marching home" (song). P. S. Gilmore.

When Knighthood Was in Flower (play). P. Kester.

When Knighthood Was in Flower; or, The Love Story of Charles Brandon and Mary Tudor (novel). C. Major.

When Love is Young. A Novel. R. R. Gilson.

When Patty Went to College. J. Webster.

When the Sleeper Wakes. H. G. Wells.

"When this cruel war is over": see C. C. Sawyer, "Weeping, sad, and lonely; or, when this cruel war is over" (song).

Where the Laborers Are Few. M. W. C. Deland.

Where the Sugar Maple Grows; Idylls of a Canadian Village. A. M. Teskey.

Where Three Empires Meet: A Narrative of Recent Travel in Kashmir, Western Tibet, Gilgit, and the Adjoining Countries. E. F. Knight.

Whip and Spur. G. E. Waring, Jr.

Whist: see
W. Pole, *Theory of the Modern Scientific Game of Whist.*
E. F. Ware, *Some of the Rhymes of Ironquill. (A Book of Moods).*
See also the Reader's Guide entry for Card games.

"Whist" (poem): see E. F. Ware, *Some of the Rhymes of Ironquill. (A Book of Moods).*

Whistler, James Abbott McNeill: see F. M. Colby, *Imaginary Obligations* (marginalia).

Whiston, William (trans.): see F. Josephus, *Genuine Works of Josephus.*

Whitaker, Samuel F. G. (trans.): see A. D. A. de Brueys, *Avocat Patelin: A Comedy in Three Acts* (play).

Whitcombe, Mrs. Henry Pennel: see M. E. J. Whitcombe.

White, Andrew Dickson: see

(intro.) *Tableaux de la Révolution Française; An Historical Reader.*

(pref.) J. F. Willard, *Tramping with Tramps: Studies and Sketches of Vagabond Life.*

White Birches. A Novel. A. E. Trumbull.

White elephants: see

F. Vincent, *Land of the White Elephant: Sights and Scenes in South-eastern Asia.*

World of Wonders; A Record of Things Wonderful in Nature, Science, and Art. White Fawn; or, The Loves of Prince Buttercup and the Princess Daisy (play). J. Mortimer.

White, Horatio Stevens (ed.): see C. P. Otis, *Elementary German: An Outline of the Grammar, with Exercises, Conversations, and Readings.*

White, John Stuart (ed.): see Plutarchus, *Boys' and Girls' Plutarch. Being Parts of the "Lives" of Plutarch.*

White Mountains: see S. A. Drake, *Heart of the White Mountains, Their Legends and Scenery.*

White Swans and Other Tales. H. C. Andersen.

Whitefield, George: see

E. R. Charles, *Diary of Mrs. Kitty Trevylyan; A Story of the Times of Whitefield and the Wesleys.*

(adapt.) C. Wesley, "Hark! the herald angels sing" (Christmas carol).

Whiteing, Richard (trans. and ed.): see F. Bernard, *Wonderful Escapes.*

Whiteing, Richard (inscr.): see W. S. Sonnenschein (comp.), *Best Books: A Reader's Guide to the Choice of the Best Available Books.*

White Lies. C. Reade.

"White Mr. Longfellow" (essay). W. D. Howells.

White Peril; or, How I Cured Myself of Consumption at Home. L. R. Andrews.

White Wings; A Yachting Novel. W. Black.

Whitlock's Collection of Ethiopian Melodies as Sung with Great Applause by William Whitlock at the Principal Theatres in the United States. W. M. Whitlock (comp.).

Whitman, Sidney: see

(ed. and intro.) M. Kremnitz, *Reminiscences of the King of Roumania.*

(ed. and intro.): see M. M. V. F. L. von Poschinger, *Life of the Emperor Frederick.*

Whitman, Walt: see

J. McCarthy, *Reminiscences.*

J. Swift, *Gulliver's Travels into Several Remote Nations of the World* (Catalog entry).

C. Zueblin, *Religion of a Democrat.*

Whitmore, Franklin G.: see (inscr. by Clemens) U. S. Grant, *Memoirs of U. S. Grant.*

Whitmore, Frederic (trans.): see T. Tasso, *Amyntas, A Sylvan Fable.*

Whitmore, William R. (illus.): see

T. Tasso, *Amyntas, A Sylvan Fable.*

F. Whitmore, *Florida Farm.*

Whitney, William Dwight: see (ed.) J. W. von Goethe, *Faust. Eine Tragödie.*

Whittier Birthday Book. E. S. Owen (comp.).

Whittier Birthday Dinner (1877): see W. H. Bishop, *Detmold: A Romance.*

Whittier, John Greenleaf: see

(inscr. by Clemens) R. Burns, *Works of Robert Burns.*

(inscr. by Clemens) A. Cunningham, *Life of Robert Burns.*

A. A. Fields, *Whittier; Notes of His Life and of His Friendships.*

T. W. S. Higginson, *Cheerful Yesterdays. Contemporaries* (marginalia).

S. J. May, *Some Recollections of Our Antislavery Conflict.*

J. Sturge, *Visit to the United States in 1841.*

Whittier; Notes of His Life and of His Friendships. A. A. Fields.

"Who Killed Cock Robin": see Catalog entry for Nursery Rhymes.

Whole Duty of Man. R. Allestree.

Whole French Language. T. Robertson.

Whymper, Edward (engraver): see D. G. Elliot, *Life and Habits of Wild Animals.*

Whymper, Josiah Wood (engraver): see D. G. Elliot, *Life and Habits of Wild Animals.*

Whyte, Frederic (trans.): see K. G. Schillings, *In Wildest Africa.*

Wicksteed, Philip Henry (trans.): see

H. Oort, *Bible for Learners.*

H. Oort, *Bible for Young People.*

"Widow Bedott" (pseud.): see F. M. B. Whitcher.

Widow Bedott Papers. F. M. B. Whitcher.

Wife of Socrates (play). J. H. McCarthy.

Wiggin, James Henry: see L. Wright, *How Reverend Wiggin Rewrote Mrs. Eddy's Book.*

Wight, Orlando Williams (ed.): see M. E. de Montaigne, *Works of Michael de Montaigne, Comprising His Essays, Journey into Italy, and Letters.*

Wikkey: A Scrap, by Yam. H. Vaders.

Wilberforce, [Albert] Basil Orme: see W. Crookes, *Diamonds.*

Wilberforce, Basil: see T. Malory, *Morte Darthur* (Catalog entry).

Wilberforce, Samuel: see R. G. Wilberforce (co-author), *Life of the Right Reverend Samuel Wilberforce. . . . with Selections from His Diary and Correspondence.*

Wilberforce, William: see

T. W. S. Higginson, *Cheerful Yesterdays. Contemporaries* (marginalia).

A. D. White, *History of the Warfare of Science with Theology* (marginalia).

Wilbour, Charles Edwin (trans.): see

A. F. Hugo, *Victor Hugo, by a Witness of His Life.*

V. Hugo, *Marius; or, The Son of the Revolution.*

Wilbur, Homer C.: see *Sartain's Union Magazine of Literature and Art.*

"Wilbur, Parson Homer" (pseud. of J. R. Lowell): see H. C. Homer (Catalog entry).

Wilcox, Ella (Wheeler): see

L. R. Andrews, *White Peril; or, How I Cured Myself of Consumption at Home* (marginalia).

J. A. Joyce, *Edgar Allan Poe* (Catalog entry).

Wilcox, Marrion (ed.): see *Harper's History of the War in the Philippines.*

Wild Animals I Have Known, and 200 Drawings. E. T. Seton.

Wild Eelin: Her Escapades. W. Black.

Wildfeuer (dramatic poem). F. Halm.

Wild Flowers: An Aid to Knowledge of Our Wild Flowers and Their Insect Visitors. N. B. De G. Doubleday.

Wild Garden; or, Our Groves and Gardens Made Beautiful by the Naturalisation of Hardy Exotic Plants. W. Robinson.

Wild Life and Adventure in the Australian Bush: Four Years' Personal Experience. A. Nicols.

Wild Life of Orchard and Field; Papers on American Animal Life. E. Ingersoll.

Wild Life Under the Equator. P. B. Du Chaillu.

Wild Neighbors; Out-Door Studies in the United States. E. Ingersoll.

Wild Olive; A Novel. B. King.

Wilds of London. J. Greenwood.

Wild Wings: Adventures of a Camera-Hunter Among the Larger Wild Birds of North America on Sea and Land. H. K. Job.

Wilhelm II, Emperor of Germany and King of Prussia: see

M. Cunliffe-Owen, *Imperator et Rex, William II of Germany*.

H. W. H. Fischer, *Private Lives*.

Wilhelm, Karl (composer): see M. Schneckenburger, "Wacht am Rhein" (song).

Wilhelm Meister's Apprenticeship and Travels. J. W. von Goethe.

Wilhelm Meister's Apprenticeship; A Novel. J. W. von Goethe.

Wilhelm Tell, Schauspiel (play). J. C. F. von Schiller.

"Wilhelmi, Alexander Victor" (pseud.): see A. V. Zechmeister.

Wilhelmina, Queen of the Netherlands: see E. Văcărescu, *Kings and Queens I Have Known*.

Wilkins, Mary Eleanor: see M. E. W. Freeman.

Wilkinson, John Gardner (trans. and co-ed.): see Herodotus, *History of Herodotus*.

Willard, Emma Hart (co-author): see W. C. Woodbridge, *Woodbridge and Willard's Universal Geography . . . Accompanied by Modern and Ancient Atlases*.

Willard, Josiah Flynt: see "Jamie the Kid" (short story) in W. D. Howells (co-ed.), *Under the Sunset*.

William I: see H. von Sybel, *Founding of the German Empire by William I*.

William II, Emperor of Germany and King of Prussia: see the Reader's Guide entries for Wilhelm II, Emperor of Germany and King of Prussia.

William Allingham, A Diary. W. Allingham.

William Black, Novelist: A Biography. W. Reid.

William Shakespeare: Poet, Dramatist, and Man. H. W. Mabie.

William Taylor Baker. C. H. Baker.

William Tell (play). J. S. Knowles.

William Tell (play): see J. C. F. von Schiller, *Wilhelm Tell*.

William the Conqueror: see J. S. C. Abbott, *History of William the Conqueror*.

William Thomas Arnold, Journalist and Historian. M. A. A. Ward.

Williams, Bert A. (composer): see J. A. Shipp, *Abyssinia* (musical comedy).

Williams, Charles David (illus.): see

T. Dixon, *Leopard's Spots: A Romance of the White Man's Burden—1865–1900*.

E. Marshall, *Lizette: A Story of the Latin Quarter*.

B. Tarkington, *Monsieur Beaucaire*.

J. Webster, *When Patty Went to College*.

Williams, James: see C. H. Proctor, *Life of James Williams, Better Known as Professor Jim, for Half a Century Janitor of Trinity College*.

Williams, Jesse L. (co-author): see *On the Gridiron*.

Williams, Martha McCulloch: see M. McCulloch-Williams.

Williams, Peter (trans.): see J. N. Pattison, "Guide me, O Thou great Jehovah" (hymn).

Williams, True W. (co-illus.): see H. S. Olcott, *People from the Other World*.

Williams, William, "Guide me, O Thou great Jehovah" (hymn): see J. N. Pattison, arranger.

"William Wilson" (story). E. A. Poe.

"Willie we have missed you" (song). S. C. Foster.

Willis, Nathaniel Parker (contr.): see E. A. Poe, *Works of the Late Edgar Allan Poe*.

Willow and Wattle: Poems: see R. Richardson, "Annette" (poem).

Wilson, David (illus.): see A. C. Waghorne, *Through a Peer Glass: Winnie's Adventures in Wastemonster*.

Wilson, Francis (actor): see C. Kraatz, *Mountain Climber* (play).

"Wilson, Mrs. H. L." (pseud.): see R. C. O'Neill.

Wilson, John: see *Dramatists of the Restoration*.

Wilson, L. J. (illus.): see J. S. Clouston, *Lunatic at Large; A Novel*.

Wimples and Crisping-Pins; Being Studies in the Coiffure and Ornaments of Women. T. Child.

Window in Thrums. J. M. Barrie.

Windyhaugh; A Novel. M. G. Todd.

Wings of the Morning. L. Tracy.

Winslow Plain. S. P. M. Greene.

Winsome Womanhood. M. E. M. Sangster.

Winter. R. Eickemeyer.

Winterfeast. C. R. Kennedy.

Winter Holiday in Summer Lands. J. N. Jackson.

Winter Sunshine. J. Burroughs.

Winter, William (ed. and intro.): see G. Arnold, *Drift: A Sea-Shore Idyl and Other Poems*.

Winthrop, John: see J. H. Twichell, *John Winthrop, First Governor of the Massachusetts Colony*.

Wisconsin: see G. W. Peck, *Peck's Fun: Being Extracts from the "LaCrosse Sun," and "Peck's Sun," Milwaukee. The Cream of Mr. Peck's Writings of the Past Ten Years*.

Wister, Owen: see É. Zola, *Terre* (Catalog entry).

Wit and Humour of the Persians. M. N. Kuka.

Witchcraft: see

H. de Balzac, *Balzac's Contes Drolatiques; Droll Stories Collected from the Abbeys of Touraine*.

S. Clarke, *Mirror or Looking-Glass Both for Saints & Sinners*.

C. C. Coffin, *Old Times in the Colonies*.

M. D. Conway, *Demonology*.

S. P. Fowler (ed.), *Salem Witchcraft: Comprising More Wonders of the Invisible World, Collected by Robert*

Calef; and Wonders of the Invisible World, by Cotton Mather.

H. K. Institorius and J. Sprenger, *Malleus Maleficarum, or Hexenhammer.*

W. E. H. Lecky, *History of England in the Eighteenth Century* (marginalia).

W. E. H. Lecky, *History of the Rise and Influence of the Spirit of Rationalism in Europe* (marginalia).

M. Luther (Catalog entry).

C. Mackay, *Memoirs of Extraordinary Popular Delusions.*

G. Mackenzie, *Laws and Customs of Scotland, in Matters Criminal.*

C. Mather, *Wonders of the Invisible World.*

J. Michelet, *Sorcière: The Witch of the Middle Ages.*

R. Scot, *Discoverie of Witchcraft, Wherein the Lewde Dealing of Witches and Witchmongers is Notablie Detected.*

W. Scott, *Letters on Demonology and Witchcraft, Addressed to J. G. Lockhart, Esq.*

W. Shakespeare, *Works of Shakespeare* (Catalog entry).

M. E. J. Whitcombe, *Bygone Days in Devonshire and Cornwall, with Notes of Existing Superstitions and Customs.*

T. Wright, *Narratives of Sorcery and Magic, from the Most Authentic Sources.*

Witching Hour. A. Thomas.

"With Bernard de Mandeville" (poem): see R. Browning, *Parleyings with Certain People of Importance in Their Day.*

"With Daniel Bartoli" (poem): see R. Browning, *Parleyings with Certain People of Importance in Their Day.*

With Edged Tools; A Novel. H. S. Scott.

"Witherup, Anne Warrington" (pseud.): see J. K. Bangs.

With Flash-light and Rifle; Photographing by Flash-light at Night the Wild Animal World of Equatorial Africa. K. G. Schillings.

With Sword and Crucifix; Being an Account of the Strange Adventures of Count Louis de Sancerre, Companion of Sieur de la Salle. E. S. Van Zile.

With the King at Oxford; A Tale of the Great Rebellion. A. J. Church.

Witness of the Sun. A. Rives.

Wit of Women. K. A. Sanborn.

Witt, Henriette Elizabeth (Guizot) de: see (contr.) F. P. G. Guizot, *Popular History of England from the Earliest Times to the Reign of Queen Victoria.*

Wizard's Wanderings from China to Peru. J. W. Holden.

Woermann, Karl (co-author): see A. F. G. A. Woltmann, *History of Ancient, Early Christian, and Mediaeval Painting.*

Wolf, Joseph (illus.): see D. G. Elliot, *Life and Habits of Wild Animals.*

Wolfe, James: see F. Parkman, *Montcalm and Wolfe.*

Wolfville Days. A. H. Lewis.

Wolfville Nights. A. H. Lewis.

Wolseley, Garnet: see (contr.) *Armies of To-day; A Description of the Armies of the Leading Nations.*

Woman and Artist. P. Blouet.

Woman Beautiful: A Practical Treatise on the Development and Preservation of Woman's Health and Beauty, and the Principles of Taste in Dress. E. A. Fletcher.

Woman-Hater. A Novel. C. Reade.

Woman in Battle: A Narrative of the Exploits, Adventures, and Travels of Madame Loreta Janeta Velazquez, Otherwise Known as Lieutenant Harry T. Buford, Confederate States Army. L. J. Velazquez.

Woman Intervenes; or, the Mistress of the Mine. R. Barr.

Woman's Bible. E. C. Stanton (ed.).

Woman's Part in a Revolution. N. H. Hammond.

Woman's Pilgrimage to the Holy Land; or, Pleasant Days Abroad. Being Notes of a Tour Through Europe and the East. L. M. R. Griswold.

Woman's Reason; A Novel. W. D. Howells.

Woman's Thoughts about Women. D. M. M. Craik.

Woman's War; A Novel. G. W. Deeping.

Woman Who Toils; Being the Experiences of Two Ladies as Factory Girls. B. M. Van Vorst.

Women Beware Women (play by T. Middleton): see C. W. Dilke (ed.) *Old English Plays; Being a Selection from the Early Dramatic Writers.*

Women, Etc. Some Leaves from an Editor's Diary. G. B. M. Harvey.

Women's Conquest of New York; Being an Account of the Rise and Progress of the Women's Rights Movement. T. A. Janvier.

Women's rights: see

A. M. A. Aníchkova, *Shadow of the House.*

M. A. B. von Arnim, *Solitary Summer* (novel).

M. H. Austin, *Santa Lucia, A Common Story.*

M. K. Bashkirtseva, *Marie Bashkirtseff; The Journal of a Young Artist.*

E. F. Benson, *Dodo: A Detail of the Day.*

C. M. Black, *Agitator; A Novel.*

D. H. H. Boulger, *Matter-of-Fact Girl.*

H. H. Boyesen, *Queen Titania* (Catalog entry).

E. W. M. Brodhead, *Diana's Livery.*

A. M. Buckner, *Towards the Gulf; A Romance of Louisiana.*

E. B. Burnz, *Burnz' Phonic Shorthand for Schools, Business Writing and Reporting* (Catalog entry).

F. A. C. Canfield, *Kidnapped Campers; A Story of Out-of-Doors* (Catalog entry).

K. Chopin (speculative entry).

S. H. Church, *Horatio Plodgers; A Story of To-Day.*

J. F. Clarke, *Memorial and Biographical Sketches* (Catalog entry).

L. L. Clifford, *Margaret Vincent, A Novel* (Catalog entry).

F. P. Cobbe, *The Peak in Darien, with Some Other Inquiries Touching Concerns of the Soul and the Body.*

A. S. Cory, *Life's Shop Window.*

D. M. M. Craik, *Woman's Thoughts about Women.*

D. Defoe, *Moll Flanders and The History of the Devil.*

M. W. C. Deland, *Awakening of Helena Richie.*

M. W. C. Deland, *John Ward, Preacher.*

E. B. De La Pasture, *Peter's Mother.*

M. A. Dodge, *New Atmosphere.*

A. F. Eastman, "Dose of Paradise" (short story).

S. E. E. Edmundson, *Nurse and Spy in the Union Army.*

I. M. Freeland, *Thoughts in Verse.*

A. French, *Missionary Sheriff; Being Incidents in the Life of a Plain Man Who Tried to Do His Duty.*

M. Fuller, *Memoirs of Margaret Fuller Ossoli.*

J. L. Gilder, *Tomboy at Work.*

C. P. Gilman (Catalog entry).

E. A. G. Glasgow, *Voice of the People* (novel).

E. S. Glyn, *Three Weeks* (novel).

F. A. R. Goodale (ed.), *Literature of Philanthropy.*

S. Grand, *Heavenly Twins* (marginalia).

B. C. Greene, *Adventures of an Old Maid. By Aunt Ruth.*

H. R. Haggard, *She: A History of Adventure.*

M. S. L. K. Harrison. *Wages of Sin.*

G. B. M. Harvey, *Women, Etc. Some Leaves from an Editor's Diary.*

A. E. Holdsworth, *Joanna Traill, Spinster.*

W. D. Howells, *Dr. Breen's Practice* (novel).

W. D. Howells, *Heroines of Fiction.*

W. D. Howells, *Mouse-Trap. A Farce* (play).

W. D. Howells (co-ed.), *Under the Sunset.*

R. O. Huch, *Fra Celeste und andere Erzählungen.*

T. A. Janvier, *Women's Conquest of New York; Being an Account of the Rise and Progress of the Women's Rights Movement.*

M. Johnston, *Prisoners of Hope. A Tale of Colonial Virginia* (Catalog entry).

J. M. Jonas, "Timed to an African Chant" (poem).

F. A. Kemble, *Journal of a Residence on a Georgian Plantation in 1838–39.*

K. Kennedy, *Doctor Paley's Foolish Pigeons, and Short Sermons to Workingmen.*

C. Kingsley, *Hypatia; or, New Foes with an Old Face.*

M. H. M. Kinkaid, *Walda; A Novel.*

J. P. Kirk, *Forest Folk.*

H. C. Knight, *Saw Up and Saw Down; or, The Fruits of Industry and Self-Reliance.*

I. C. Knox, *Little Folks' History of England.*

A. H. E. Leonowens, *English Governess at the Siamese Court; Being Recollections of Six Years in the Royal Palace at Bangkok.*

Olive Logan (Catalog entry).

H. Martineau, *Autobiography.*

C. A. B. Mason, "'Only Me'" (poem).

I. F. Mayo (Catalog entry).

M. McCulloch-Williams, *Field-Farings; A Vagrant Chronicle of Earth and Sky* (Catalog entry).

A. J. Miller, *Physical Beauty: How to Obtain and How to Preserve It.*

C. E. S. S. Norton (Catalog entry).

E. C. C. Obenchain, *Aunt Jane of Kentucky* (short stories).

F. Parkman, "Some of the Reasons Against Woman Suffrage" (essay).

E. S. Phelps, *Trixy* (Catalog entry).

K. A. Sanborn, *Wit of Women.*

M. E. M. Sangster, *Winsome Womanhood.*

F. L. Shaw (roving journalist).

E. B. Sherman, *Taper Lights.*

M. F. Somerville, *Personal Recollections, from Early Life to Old Age, of Mary Somerville. With Selections from Her Correspondence.*

E. C. Stanton (ed.), *Woman's Bible.*

H. E. B. Stowe, *Lady Byron Vindicated: A History of the Byron Controversy, from Its Beginning in 1816 to the Present Time.*

H. E. B. Stowe, *We and Our Neighbors; or, the Records of an Unfashionable Street. A Novel.*

J. G. C. Swisshelm, *Half a Century* (Catalog entry).

C. R. Teller, *Cage* (novel).

M. V. H. Terhune, *Common Sense in the Household: A Manual of Practical Housewifery* (Catalog entry).

R. H. Thorpe, "Curfew Must Not Ring To-night" (Catalog entry).

M. G. Todd, *Windyhaugh; A Novel* (Catalog entry).

F. M. Trollope, *Domestic Manners of the Americans* (marginalia).

A. E. Trumbull, *Life's Common Way* (novel).

Truth Seeker (magazine).

B. F. Underwood, *Essays and Lectures.*

I. M. Van Etten, "House of the Dragons" (short story).

C. B. G. Wells, *About People.*

C. White, *Ecce Femina: An Attempt to Solve the Woman Question. Being an Examination of Arguments in Favor of Female Suffrage by John Stuart Mill and Others, and a Presentation of Arguments Against the Proposed Change in the Constitution of Society.*

A. D. T. Whitney, *Hitherto: A Story of Yesterdays.*

A. D. T. Whitney, *Summer in Leslie Goldthwaite's Life.*

L. C. Willcox, *Human Way* (Catalog entry).

S. P. Willis (pseud. "Fanny Fern") (Catalog entry).

H. Wilmans, *Back Numbers/Wilmans Express, Condensed.*

Women of the Bible, by Twelve Eminent Divines.

J. G. Wood, *Uncivilized Races; or, Natural History of Man* (marginalia).

C. F. Woolson, *What Katy Did: A Story.*

Wonderful Adventures of Captain Priest: A Tale of But Few Incidents and No Plot in Particular, with Other Legends. S. A. Hammett.

Wonderful Balloon Ascents; or, the Conquest of the Skies. N. C. Flammarion.

Wonderful Century; Its Successes and Its Failures. W. R. Wallace.

Wonderful Characters; Comprising Memoirs and Anecdotes of the Most Remarkable Persons of Every Age and Nation. Collected from the Most Authentic Sources. H. Wilson.

Wonderful City of Tokio; or, Further Adventures of the Jewett Family and Their Friend Oto Nambo. E. Greey.

Wonderful Escapes. F. Bernard.

Wonderful Visit. H. G. Wells.

Wonderful Wizard of Oz (fantasy novel by L. Frank Baum): see E. K. C. Gibson, *Zauberlinda, The Wise Witch.*

Wonders of Acoustics; or, The Phenomenon of Sound. R. Radau.

Wonders of Alaska. A. Badlam.

Wonders of Bodily Strength and Skill, in All Ages and All Countries. G. Depping.

Wonders of Engraving. G. Duplessis.

Wonders of Glass-Making in All Ages. A. Sauzay.
Wonders of Italian Art. L. Viardot.
Wonders of Life: A Popular Study of Biological Philosophy. E. H. P. A. Haeckel. *Wonders of Optics.* N. C. Flammarion.
Wonders of Pompeii. Translated from the Original French. M. Monnier.
Wonders of Science; or, Young Humphry Davy (The Cornish Apothecary's Boy, Who Taught Himself Natural Philosophy, and Eventually Became President of the Royal Society). H. Mayhew.
Wonders of the Human Body. From the French. A. Le Pileur.
Wonders of the Invisible World. C. Mather.
Wonders of the Invisible World: see also S. P. Fowler (ed.), *Salem Witchcraft: Comprising More Wonders of the Invisible World, Collected by Robert Calef; and Wonders of the Invisible World, by Cotton Mather.*
Woodall, Henry (contr.): see the Catalog entry for *Spectator.*
Woodbridge and Willard's Universal Geography . . . Accompanied by Modern and Ancient Atlases. W. C. Woodbridge.
Wood Carver of 'Lympus. M. E. Waller.
Wood, Ellen (Price): see C. W. Tayleure, *East Lynne* (play).
Wood, Mary Ellen (comp.): see L. Hutton and E. Hutton, *Laurence and Eleanor Hutton.*
"Wood, Mrs. Henry" (pseud.): see C. W. Tayleure, *East Lynne* (play).
Woodman; A Novel. J. Quesnay de Beaurepaire.
"Woodman, Spare That Tree" (poem and song). G. P. Morris.
Woodpeckers. F. H. Eckstorm.
Woodville, Richard Caton (illus.): see P. Bigelow, *History of the German Struggle for Liberty.*
Woodward (composer): see H. B. Smith, *Soul Kiss* (musical).
Wooing of Malkatoon. Commodus. L. Wallace.
Wooing of Wistaria. W. Eaton.
Wooing o' T; A Novel. A. F. Hector.
Worcester, Second Marquis of: see H. Dircks, *Life, Times and Scientific Labours of the Second Marquis of Worcester.*
Words and Their Uses, Past and Present. A Study of the English Language. R. G. White.
Wordsworth, William: see
G. H. Calvert, *Wordsworth: A Biographical Aesthetic Study.*
F. W. H. Myers, *Wordsworth.*
H. Van Dyke (ed.), *Little Masterpieces of English Poetry, by British and American Authors.*
Work (its pleasure): see O. W. Holmes, *Autocrat of the Breakfast-Table* (marginalia).
Works of
H. de Balzac.
C. Brontë.
R. Burns.
G. G. Byron.
Catullus and Tibullus.
T. Chalmers.

S. T. Coleridge.
T. de Quincey.
C. Dickens.
R. G. Ingersoll.
W. Irving.
R. Kipling.
C. Lamb.
M. E. de Montaigne.
F. Parkman.
E. A. Poe.
A. Pope.
F. Rabelais.
W. Shakespeare.
P. C. Tacitus.
A. Tibullus: see *Works of Catullus and Tibullus.*
Virgil.
World Beautiful. Second Series. L. Whiting.
World history: see
K. J. Ploetz, *Epitome of Ancient, Mediaeval, and Modern History.*
C. Rollin, *Ancient History of the Egyptians, Carthaginians, Assyrians, Babylonians, Medes and Persians, Grecians and Macedonians.*
W. Swinton, *Outlines of the World's History, Ancient, Medieval, and Modern.*
World I Live In. H. Keller.
"World is all a fleeting show" (poem). T. Moore.
World's Best Books: A Key to the Treasures of Literature. F. Parsons.
World's Fair of 1893: see J. Ralph, *Harper's Chicago and the World's Fair.*
Worlds in the Making; The Evolution of the Universe. S. A. Arrhenius.
World's Work (journal): see I. F. Marcosson, "Henry H. Rogers—Monopolist" (article).
Wormeley, Katherine Prescott (trans.): see
H. de Balzac, *Comedy of Human Life.*
H. de Balzac, *Country Doctor.*
Worship of Augustus Caesar. A. Del Mar.
Worst Boy in Town. J. Habberton.
Worsted Man; A Musical Play. J. K. Bangs.
Wörterbuch deutscher Synonymen. D. Sanders.
Wotan, Siegfried, and Brünnhilde. A. A. Chapin.
Wotton, Henry: see I. Walton, *Lives of John Donne, Henry Wotton, Richd Hooker, George Herbert, &c.*
Wouldbegoods. E. N. Bland.
Would Christ Belong to a Labor Union? or, Henry Fielding's Dream. C. Myers.
Would You Kill Him? A Novel. G. P. Lathrop.
Wraxall, Lascelles (trans.): see V. Hugo, *Marius; or, The Son of the Revolution.*
Wreath of Remembrance. M. Y. W.
Wrecker. R. L. Stevenson and L. Osbourne.
Wreck of the "Grosvenor." An Account of the Mutiny of the Crew and the Loss of the Ship When Trying to Make the Bermudas. W. C. Russell.
Wright, George Hand (illus.): see the Catalog entry for K. D. S. Wiggin.
Writing advice: see G. Bainton (comp. and ed.), *Art of Authorship. Literary Reminiscences, Methods of Work,*

and Advice to Young Beginners, Personally Contributed by Leading Authors of the Day.

Writings and Speeches of Samuel J. Tilden. S. J. Tilden.

Writings in Prose and Verse *of Rudyard Kipling.* R. Kipling.

Writings of Christopher Columbus. C. Colombus.

"Written after Swimming from Sestos to Abydos" (poem). G. G. Byron.

Wrong Box (novel). R. L. Stevenson and L. Osbourne.

"Wu Chih Tien, The Celestial Empress: A Chinese Historical Novel." C. F. Wong.

Wunderpfeife, oder: Die Kinder von Hameln. K. G. Nieritz.

Wuthering Heights. E. Brontë.

Wyatt, Edith (co-author): see *Whole Family; A Novel by Twelve Authors.*

Wycliffe, John: see
J. Foxe, *Book of Martyrs.*
J. R. Green, *Short History of the English People* (marginalia).

Wyndham, George: see
(pref.) J. Ruskin, *Letters to M. G. and H. G.*
(intro.) F. Thompson, *Shelley.*

Wyndham Towers. T. B. Aldrich.

Wyoming: see
F. W. Kelly, *Narrative of My Captivity Among the Sioux Indians.*
M. Manning, *Judith of the Plains; A Novel.*
E. Roberts, *Shoshone and Other Western Wonders.*
E. Talbot, *My People of the Plains.*

▌X

Xavier, St. Francis: see A. D. White, *History of the Warfare of Science with Theology* (Catalog entry).

▌Y

Yale College: see C. S. Elliot and E. P. Howe, *Songs of Yale: A New Collection of College Songs.*

Yale Lectures on Preaching and Other Writings. N. J. Burton.

"Yam" (pseud.): see H. Vaders.

Yankee Doodle, An Old Friend in a New Dress. H. Pyle.

Yankee in Canada, with Anti-Slavery and Reform Papers. H. D. Thoreau.

Yanks and Johnnies; or, Laugh and Grow Fat. W. H. Van Nortwick.

Yawps and Other Things. W. J. Lampton.

Year-Boke of the Odd Volumes. W. Manning (comp.).

Year's Residence in the United States. W. Cobbett.

Yeats, William Butler: see
(ed.) W. Allingham, *Sixteen Poems by William Allingham.*
(pref.) A. Gregory, *Cuchulain of Muirthemne: The Story of the Men of the Red Branch of Ulster.*
(pref.) A. Gregory, *Gods and Fighting Men: The Story of the Tuatha De Danaan and of the Fianna of Ireland.*

Yei-Sen, Kei-Sai (illus.): see T. Shunsui, *The Loyal Ronins: An Historical Romance, Translated from the Japanese.*

Yellowstone: see E. Roberts, *Shoshone and Other Western Wonders.*

"Ye Mariners of England" (poem). T. Campbell.

Ye Mountaineer. B. T. Wilson.

"Ye Old Militia Muster" (unpublished farce). C. D. Taylor.

Yeomen of the Guard. W. S. Gilbert.

Yesterday, To-day, and Forever (poem). E. H. Bickerstetk.

Yeto, Genjiro (illus.): see W. Eaton, *Japanese Nightingale.*

Yohn, Frederick Coffay (illus.): see
J. Fox, Jr., *Little Shepherd of Kingdom Come.*
J. Fox, Jr., *Trail of the Lonesome Pine.*

Yoke: A Romance of the Days When the Lord Redeemed the Children of Israel from the Bondage of Egypt. E. J. Miller.

Yolande. A Novel. W. Black.

Yonge, Charles Duke: see
(trans.) Athenaeus of Naucratis, *Deipnosophists; or, Banquet of the Learned, of Athenaeus.*
(trans.) Cicero, *Select Orations.*
(ed.) H. Walpole, *Letters of Horace Walpole, Selected and Edited by Charles Duke Yonge.*

Yonge, Charlotte Mary (trans.): see C. de F. d' Hézecques, *Recollections of a Page to the Court of Louis XVI.*

Yorick's Love (play). W. D. Howells (adapt.).

York, England: see
W. Combe, *History and Antiquities of the City of York.*
W. D. Howells, *Seven English Cities.*
W. Smith (ed.), *Registers of Topcliffe, and Morley in the W. R. of the County of York. Baptisms, 1654–1830. Burials, 1654–1888.*

York, Maine: see the Catalog entry for Robert Herrick.

York Minster, *Accurate Description and History of the Cathedral and Metropolitan Church of St. Peter, York, from its First Foundation.*

York Garrison—1640. S. O. Jewett.

"Yorke, Oliver" (pseud.): see F. S. Mahony.

Yorkshire: see W. Smith (ed.), *Old Yorkshire.*

"You'd Scarce Expect One of My Age" (poem). D. Everett.

"You'll be an angel by and by": see the Catalog entry for "Sail away, ladies" (folk song).

Youma, Story of a West Indian Slave. L. Hearn.

Young adult literature: see the Reader's Guide entry for Children's and young adult literature.

Young Alaskans. E. Hough.

Young Americans in Japan; or, The Adventures of the Jewett Family and Their Friend Oto Nambo. E. Greey.

Young, Brigham: see C. V. V. Waite, *Mormon Prophet and His Harem; or, an Authentic History of Brigham Young, His Numerous Wives and Children.*

Young Folks' Cyclopaedia of Common Things. J. D. Champlin.

Young Folks' Cyclopaedia of Persons and Places. J. D. Champlin.

Young Folks' History of England. C. M. Yonge.

Young Folks' History of Germany. C. M. Yonge.

Young Folks' History of Rome. C. M. Yonge.

Young Folks' History of the United States. T. W. S. Higginson.

"Young Idea"; or, Common School Culture. C. B. Le Row.

Young Lucretia, and Other Stories. M. E. W. Freeman.

Young Man and Himself; His Tasks, His Dreams, His Purposes. J. S. Kirtley.

Young Man in a Hurry (short stories). R. W. Chambers.

Young, May Dow Russell (ed.): see J. R. Young, *Men and Memoirs*.

Young People's Illustrated Bible History. A. Bond (ed.).

Young, William (trans.): see V. Hugo, *Man Who Laughs*.

Yukon Territory: see E. Robins, *Magnetic North*.

Z

Zadig. F. M. A. de Voltaire.

Žal, An International Romance. R. Hughes.

Zamenhof, Ludwik Lejzer (contr.): see J. C. O'Connor (ed.), *Esperanto. The Student's Complete Text Book*.

Zanoni. E. G. E. B. Lytton.

Zauberlinda, The Wise Witch. E. K. C. Gibson.

Zaza, A Comedy Drama in Five Acts (play). C. Simon and P. F. S. Berton.

Zenobia: see A. E. Trumbull, *Masque of Culture* (play).

Zick, Henry (trans.): see K. G. Schillings, *With Flash-light and Rifle; Photographing by Flash-light at Night the Wild Animal World of Equatorial Africa*.

Ziegfield, Florenz (producer): see H. B. Smith, *Soul Kiss* (musical).

Ziegler, Lee Woodward (illus.): see W. Eaton, *Japanese Blossom*.

Zimmern, Alfred Eckhard (trans.): see G. Ferrero, *Greatness and Decline of Rome*.

Zogbaum, Rufus Fairchild (illus.): see G. A. Forsyth, *Thrilling Days in Army Life*.

Zola, Émile: see

E. De Amicis, *Studies of Paris*.

B. Matthews, "Cervantes, Zola, Kipling & Co." (article).

Zoos: see W. T. Hornaday, *Popular Official Guide to the New York Zoological Park*.

Marginalia in Belton Townsend, Plantation Lays.

Supplement to the Critical Bibliography
in Volume One

BOOKS AND ARTICLES RELATED TO SAMUEL L. CLEMENS'S READING

CHAMPAGNE, MILDRED. "Mark Twain at Bermuda," *Human Life* 11 (May 1910): 15, 40. Reprinted in the *Mark Twain Journal* 38.1 (Spring 2000): 10-12 and in *Mark Twain: The Complete Interviews*, ed. Gary Scharnhorst (Tuscaloosa: University of Alabama Press, 2006), pp. 694-699.

When a determined twenty-five-year-old reporter disregarded Clemens's wishes to be left alone in his final illness, she gained what is believed to be the final interview he ever granted. The picture she drew of him revealed that reading remained a crucial diversion for him even as his health deteriorated. "I . . . paused in astonishment before a glass door. Through it I peered into the room. A white iron bed stood within three feet of the door, and upon it, full length and face downward, lay a familiar figure in a white linen suit, with a band of black crepe around his arm. A number of books were spread out before him on the bed, and he was poring into them, bearing his weight on his elbows and resting his shaggy white head in his hands. It was Mark Twain" (p. 15). Mildred Champagne (she continued to use this name, though she married Leslie Moore in 1907) was born on March 13, 1885, but her obituary continues to elude researchers. She had definitely passed away by 2 January 1947, when the Boston *Post* alluded to "the late Mildred Champagne." Her career after this feat of bearding Mark Twain in his sickroom was trailblazing at the time. For decades she wrote a highly popular love advice column for the Boston *Post*, edited a magazine devoted to love and sentiment, and published several books describing the various forms that human love can take. But she also became a playwright, staging her productions in Boston theaters, as well as composing "Love makes the world go 'round" (1908), "Say, do you love me, dear?" (1908), "My heart is longing for its mate" (1911), and other songs.

COARD, ROBERT L. "Tom Sawyer, Sturdy Centenarian," *Midwest Quarterly* 17 (July 1976): 329-349.

In the course of paying tribute to Mark Twain's enduring novel, Coard examined a number of the boy books that emanated from Thomas Hughes' *Tom Brown's School Days*.

GELLER, EVELYN. "Tom Sawyer, Tom Bailey, and the Bad-Boy Genre," *Wilson Library Bulletin* 51.3 (November 1976): 245-250.

Boy books have much in common, but they also vary in degrees of "social conscience." Geller focused especially on the examples developed by Twain and Thomas Bailey Aldrich.

GRIBBEN, ALAN. "Living in Mark Twain's Mind: A Fifty-Year Puzzle," in *Critical Insights: Patriotism*, ed. Robert C. Evans.

Ipswich, Massachussetts: Salem Press, 2021, pp. 144-159.

Gribben provides his most candid account of the half-century project to inventory Twain's reading.

———."Reading," in *Mark Twain in Context*, ed. John Bird. Cambridge, England: Cambridge University Press, 2020, pp. 14-23.

This is the only essay in which Gribben employed his research findings to appraise the unexpected strengths and various odd subjects that showed up in Clemens's library collection.

KLEVAY, ROBERT. "Mark Twain's Reading in Classical Literature: An Overview," *Mark Twain Journal: The Author and His Era* 57.1 (Spring 2019): 112-132.

Examining an advance copy of Alan Gribben's *Mark Twain's Literary Resources: A Reconstruction of His Library and Reading*, Robert Klevay described Clemens's surprisingly wide familiarity with ancient Greek and Roman works of history and literature. Klevay took note of the English translations furnished by the industrious editor and publisher Henry G. Bohn, surveyed the historical accounts of the Roman Empire that Clemens owned, and categorized the classical writings in Clemens's personal library.

KRAUTH, LELAND. *Mark Twain & Company: Six Literary Relations*. Athens: University of Georgia Press, 2003.

Krauth took a fresh look at Twain's interactions with half a dozen of his prominent contemporaries: Matthew Arnold, Bret Harte, William Dean Howells, Rudyard Kipling, Robert Louis Stevenson, and Harriet Beecher Stowe. This study complicated many usual assumptions in startling and revealing ways. In the case of Stowe, for example, Krauth perceived her as an invisible but powerful influence: "Like a ghost . . . she haunted his creative work."

MAC DONNELL, KEVIN. "How Samuel Clemens Found 'Mark Twain' in Carson City," *Mark Twain Journal* 50.1-2 (Spring/Fall 2012): 8-47.

The eminent Mark Twain collector and expert Kevin Mac Donnell set forth a compelling argument that in Carson City in 1863 Samuel L. Clemens very likely (and crucially) noticed the use of the name "Mark Twain" in the 26 January 1861 issue of *Vanity Fair*, a humor magazine edited by Charles Godfrey Leland and Charles Farrar Browne in New York City.

———. "Mark Twain at Ten Paces: Facts Versus Fictions in the Origin of 'Mark Twain' as a Nom de Plume," *Mark Twain Journal: The Author and His Era* 57.1 (Spring 2019): 77-111.

In the event that not everyone concurred with his contention that Samuel L. Clemens got the inspiration for his famous pen name from a so-named character in a burlesque piece titled "The North Star" that appeared in the 26 January 1861 issue of *Vanity Fair*, Kevin Mac Donnell returned here with additional evidence, some of it photographic, to support his case. A newsstand that no doubt carried copies of the popular periodical *Vanity Fair* was located only yards away from where Sam and Orion Clemens stepped out of their stagecoach in August 1861, and in addition Clemens soon gained access to newspaper offices that kept exchange files of back issues of various publications. Mac Donnell devoted half a dozen pages to disputing and dismissing the "ridiculous" notion that the "Mark Twain" pseudonym had its origins in a "bar tab story."

————. "Mark Twain Did Read *Vanity Fair*—in Nevada," *Mark Twain Journal: The Author and His Era* 58.1 (Spring 2020): 146-156.

Mac Donnell determinedly countered Gary Scharnhorst's reasoning about the bar-tab theory as an explanation for Mark Twain's legendary nom de plume (see the entry below for Scharnhorst, 2019), analyzing in particular a letter Scharnhorst had cited that Clemens wrote on 18 July 1899.

Mark Twain and Fairhaven. Fairhaven, Massachusetts: Millicent Library, [1913].

Clemens's supportive gestures toward the Millicent Library, named after the daughter of Clemens's financial savior Henry H. Rogers, are recounted here.

A New Orleans Author in Mark Twain's Court: Letters from Grace King's New England Sojourns, ed. Miki Pfeffer. Foreword by Steve Courtney. Baton Rouge: Louisiana State University Press, 2019.

Pfeffer collected and annotated the warm and extensive correspondence exchanged between Grace King and the Clemenses that developed after her lengthy initial visit to New England in 1887. Many of these letters had not been examined previously and they opened up new insights into the Clemens family's dynamics as well as the activities of a Southern author who has often been critically underrated.

OBER, K. PATRICK. *Mark Twain and Medicine: "Any Mummery Will Cure."* Columbia: University of Missouri Press, 2003.

In the course of tracing the medical therapies available in Mark Twain's lifetime and the uses he made of dubious cures in his literature, Dr. Ober alluded to a number of books on the subject with which Twain was seemingly acquainted.

PRCHAL, TIM. "The Bad Boys and the New Man: The Role of Tom Sawyer and Similar Characters in the Reconstruction of Masculinity," *American Literary Realism* 36.3 (Spring 2004): 187-205.

Prchal reviewed representative books in the Bad Boy stream of fictionalized autobiography, drawing parallels to what would occur to adult males. "These realistic stories of boyhood helped to shape shared conceptions of real boyhood, and these conceptions then became part of a matrix upon which to culturally redefine masculinity" (p. 203).

SANBORN, MARGARET. *Mark Twain, The Bachelor Years: A Biography.* New York: Doubleday, 1990.

Sanborn was careful to mention the books that made an impact on Clemens in his younger years, and her summary of his earliest reading (pp. 57-58) remains especially commendable.

SCHARNHORST, GARY. *The Life of Mark Twain.* 3 vols. Columbia: University of Missouri Press, 2018-2022.

In the most comprehensive study of Clemens's life undertaken since Albert Bigelow Paine's *Mark Twain: A Biography* (1912), Scharnhorst had the space to touch at least passingly on many literary friendships and mutual influences that earlier biographies often had to skip over.

————. "Mark Twain's *Nom de Plume* Redux: A Reply to Kevin Mac Donnell," *Mark Twain Journal: The Author and His Era* 57.2 (Fall 2019): 21-27.

Mark Twain biographer Scharnhorst vigorously disputed the theory advanced by Kevin Mac Donnell that Clemens found his pen name in an issue of *Vanity Fair*. Among other points, Scharnhorst cited as evidence a letter Clemens wrote in 1899 that Scharnhorst interpreted as corroborating the bar-tab explanation for the nickname "Mark Twain."

SLOANE, DAVID E. E. "Literary Comedians," in *Mark Twain in Context*, ed. John Bird. Cambridge, England: Cambridge University Press, 2020, pp. 58-67.

Sloane concisely reviewed certain effects that Artemus Ward, Joseph C. Neal, B. P. Shillaber, Mortimer Thomson, and other writers labeled "Literary Comedians" had on Mark Twain.

————. "Mark Twain's Comedy: The 1870s," *Studies in American Humor* 2.3 (January 1976): 146-156.

This early essay deftly illustrated what distinguished Mark Twain from his predecessors and contemporaries in the field of American humor.

WALKER, FRANKLIN. *Irreverent Pilgrims: Melville, Browne, and Mark Twain in the Holy Land.* Seattle: University of Washington Press, 1974.

Walker's book reminded us that Mark Twain was not the first literary American to tour and describe Palestine memorably, though Twain's accounts became the most famous.

WONHAM, HENRY B. "Southwestern Humor," in *Mark Twain in Context*, ed. John Bird. Cambridge, England: Cambridge University Press, 2020, pp. 49-57.

Southern frontier sketches by Johnson J. Hooper, John Pendleton Kennedy, A. B. Longstreet, and others had identifiable counterparts in Mark Twain's fiction.

CORRECTIONS AND ADDITIONS TO VOLUME ONE

Page 11, right-hand column, line 12: 1886 >>>> 1887

Page 100, right-hand column, line 28: *Geoffry Hamlyn* >>>> *Geoffrey Hamlyn*

Page 100, right-hand column, line 34: Geoffry Hamlin >>>> Geoffrey Hamlin

Page 103, right-hand column, line 1: (d. 1855). >>>> (1815–1879).

Page 120, right-hand column, line 22: the dean of women at >>>> a French literature instructor and college dean at

Page 250, left-hand column, line 38: 87 (April 1929) >>>> 87.4 (April 1929)

FIVE DECADES OF RESEARCH AND TRAVEL —
From top, left to right: Alan Gribben and Polly Peck inspect
The Rime of the Ancient Mariner *at the Mark Twain*
House, Hartford, Connecticut, 1977; Alan Gribben and
family with Anne Cushman, former librarian of the Mark
Twain Library, Redding, Connecticut, and Bigelow Paine
Cushman, grandson of Twain biographer Albert Bigelow
Paine, Deer Isle, Maine, 1987; Alan Gribben and Irene
Wong, Clemens Conference, Hannibal, Missouri, 2019;
Conducting research at the Mark Twain Library, Redding,
Connecticut, 2019; Irene Wong at The Mysterious Stranger
Conference, Elmira College, Elmira, New York, 2008.
Photographs in Volumes One and Two of books and places
not otherwise credited were mostly taken by Irene Wong.

CPSIA information can be obtained
at www.ICGtesting.com
Printed in the USA
BVHW010308060622
638866BV00001BA/1